THE
MOTION PICTURE
GUIDE

THE MOTION PICTURE GUIDE™

INDEX
K-Z

Jay Robert Nash
Stanley Ralph Ross

CINEBOOKS, INC.
Chicago, 1987
Publishers of THE COMPLETE FILM RESOURCE CENTER

Publishers: Jay Robert Nash, Stanley Ralph Ross; **Editor-in-Chief:** Jay Robert Nash; **Executive Editor:** Stanley Ralph Ross; **Associate Publisher:** Kenneth H. Petchenik; **Editor in Chief:** Jim McCormick; **Production Director:** William Leahy; **Senior Editor:** David Tardy; **Senior Staff Writer:** James J. Mulay; **Staff Writers:** Daniel Curran, Michael Theobald, Arnie Bernstein, Phil Pantone; **Associate Editors:** Oksana Lydia Creighton, Jeffrey H. Wallenfeldt, Michaela Tuohy, Jeannette Hori; **Chief Researcher:** William C. Clogston; **Research Assistant:** Shelby Payne.

Editorial and Sales Offices: CINEBOOKS, 990 Grove, Evanston, Illinois 60201.

Library of Congress Catalog Number: 85-71145
ISBN: 0-933997-00-0 THE MOTION PICTURE GUIDE (10 Vols.)
       0-933997-11-6 THE MOTION PICTURE GUIDE (2 Vols.)
       0-933997-13-2 THE MOTION PICTURE GUIDE (Vol. XII-Index)

Printed in the United States
First Edition

2 3 4 5 6 7 8 9 10

K

K.C.
SUPERFLY(1972)

Lo K.M.
SECRET, THE(1979, Hong Kong), p

Patricia Ka
PICK A STAR(1937)

Lau Ka-chun
1984
AH YING(1984, Hong Kong)

Cheung Ka-yan
1984
AH YING(1984, Hong Kong)

Dayton Ka'Ne
HURRICANE(1979); BEYOND THE REEF(1981)

Wi Kuki Kaa
1984
BOUNTY, THE(1984); UTU(1984, New Zealand)

Fred Kaad
WALK INTO HELL(1957, Aus.)

Francis Kaai
HURRICANE, THE(1937)

Ravi Kaant
KENNER(1969)

Hanna Kaapa
WEIRD WOMAN(1944)

Suzanne Kaaren
BOTTOMS UP(1934); SLEEPERS EAST(1934); WILD GOLD(1934); STRANGERS ALL(1935); WOMEN MUST DRESS(1935); GREAT ZIEGFELD, THE(1936); WHITE LEGION, THE(1936); ANGEL(1937); HERE'S FLASH CASEY(1937); RHYTHM IN THE CLOUDS(1937); SING WHILE YOU'RE ABLE(1937); WHEN'S YOUR BIRTHDAY?(1937); WILDCATTER, THE(1937); BLONDES AT WORK(1938); MILLION TO ONE, A(1938); PHANTOM RANGER(1938); SWEETHEARTS(1938); TRADE WINDS(1938); MIRACLES FOR SALE(1939); DEVIL BAT, THE(1941); RAGS TO RICHES(1941); ROAR OF THE PRESS(1941); I MARRIED AN ANGEL(1942); RATIONING(1944)

Liana Kaarina
PRELUDE TO ECSTASY(1963, Fin.)

Preben Kaas
OPERATION CAMEL(1961, Den.), a, w

Walter Kaasa
PARALLELS(1980, Can.)

Barna Kabay
1984
REVOLT OF JOB, THE(1984, Hung./Ger.), d, w

Jacquie Kabelis
SHOCK WAVES(1977), cos

Henry Kaberske
Misc. Silents
DAUGHTER OF THE DON, THE(1917), d

Ish Kabibble
THAT'S RIGHT–YOU'RE WRONG(1939); YOU'LL FIND OUT(1940); PLAYMATES(1941); MY FAVORITE SPY(1942); AROUND THE WORLD(1943); RIDING HIGH(1950)

Ish Kabibble [M.A. Bogue]
SWING FEVER(1943)

Henry Kabierske
Misc. Silents
ARGONAUTS OF CALIFORNIA(1916), d

Gyula Kabos
HIPPOLYT, THE LACKEY(1932, Hung.); MISS PRESIDENT(1935, Hung.)

Ilona Kabos
HANDS OF ORLAC, THE(1964, Brit./Fr.), md

Josef Kabrt
FANTASTIC PLANET(1973, Fr./Czech.), anim

Hajime Kaburagi
MAN FROM THE EAST, THE(1961, Jap.), m; EAST CHINA SEA(1969, Jap.), m; SECRETS OF A WOMAN'S TEMPLE(1969, Jap.), m

Mayasa Kaburagi
NUTCRACKER FANTASY(1979), set d

Jan Kacer
DEATH IS CALLED ENGELCHEN(1963, Czech.)

Vasili Kachalov
Misc. Silents
WHITE EAGLE, THE(1928, USSR)

M. Kachalova
SUMMER TO REMEMBER, A(1961, USSR), w

Philip Kachaturian
GONE IN 60 SECONDS(1974), m

E. Kachaturyan
MY NAME IS IVAN(1963, USSR), md; SANDU FOLLOWS THE SUN(1965, USSR), md

Bunny Kacher
CITY THAT NEVER SLEEPS(1953)

Lou Kachivas
MIGHTY MOUSE IN THE GREAT SPACE CHASE(1983), d

Andre Morgan Robert Kachler
MEGAFORCE(1982), w

Nancy Coan Kaclik
GOIN' SOUTH(1978)

S.A. Kacyzna
DYBBUK THE(1938, Pol.), w

George Kaczender
DON'T LET THE ANGELS FALL(1969, Can.), d, w; U-TURN(1973, Can.), p&d, ed; IN PRAISE OF OLDER WOMEN(1978, Can.), d, ed; AGENCY(1981, Can.), d; CHANEL SOLITAIRE(1981), d
Misc. Talkies
GIRL IN BLUE, THE(1974), d

Chester Kaczenski
RETURN, THE(1980), art d; PINK MOTEL(1983), art d; WACKO(1983), art d
1984
ROADHOUSE 66(1984), prod d

Jane Kaczmarek
UNCOMMON VALOR(1983)
1984
DOOR TO DOOR(1984); FALLING IN LOVE(1984)

Jerzy Kaczmarek
JOAN OF THE ANGELS(1962, Pol.)

Kazmierz Kaczor
MAN OF MARBLE(1979, Pol.)

Yuko Kada
TROUT, THE(1982, Fr.)

Kada-Abd-el-Kader
Silents
MARE NOSTRUM(1926)

Fred Kadane
COMMON LAW WIFE(1963), p

Otis Kadani
PLAY MISTY FOR ME(1971)

Jan Kadar
DEATH IS CALLED ENGELCHEN(1963, Czech.), d; SHOP ON MAIN STREET, THE(1966, Czech.), d, w; ANGEL LEVINE, THE(1970), d; ADRIFT(1971, Czech.), d, w; LIES MY FATHER TOLD ME(1975, Can.), d

Gustav Kadelburg
WHITE HORSE INN, THE(1959, Ger.), w

Karlton Kadell
NIGHT OF EVIL(1962)

Ben Kadish
INDIAN FIGHTER, THE(1955), w; JOHN AND MARY(1969), p

Ellis Kadison
DON'T GIVE UP THE SHIP(1959), w; GIT!(1965), p&d, w; CAT, THE(1966), p&d; GNOME-MOBILE, THE(1967), w; THEATRE OF DEATH(1967, Brit.), w; YOU'VE GOT TO BE SMART(1967), d&w

Harry Kadison
SEEDS OF FREEDOM(1943, USSR); KISS OF DEATH(1947)

Louis Kadison
VILNA LEGEND, A(1949, U.S./Pol.)

Kadja
Silents
KING OF KINGS, THE(1927)

Karen Kadler
FRANCIS JOINS THE WACS(1954); KISS OF FIRE(1955); IT CONQUERED THE WORLD(1956); BEATNIKS, THE(1960); DEVIL'S MESSENGER, THE(1962 U.S./Swed.)

D. Kadnikov
TRAIN GOES TO KIEV, THE(1961, USSR)

Pavel Kadochnikov
IVAN THE TERRIBLE(Part I, 1947, USSR); SECRET MISSION(1949, USSR) .

Peter Kadochnikov
TIGER GIRL(1955, USSR)

Larisa Kadochnikova
RESURRECTION(1963, USSR); SHADOWS OF FORGOTTEN ANCESTORS(1967, USSR)

Haruki Kadokawa
VIRUS(1980, Jap.), p; TIME SLIP(1981, Jap.), p

Esther Kadosh
DREAMER, THE(1970, Israel)

L. Kadrov
DUEL, THE(1964, USSR); THERE WAS AN OLD COUPLE(1967, USSR)

Adriana Kaegi
1984
AGAINST ALL ODDS(1984)

Jim Kaehner
LAST GANGSTER, THE(1937)

Katharine Kaelred
Misc. Silents
GIRL WITH THE GREEN EYES, THE(1916); ENLIGHTEN THY DAUGHTER(1917)

Katherine Kaelred
Misc. Silents
YOUR GIRL AND MINE(1914); WINGED IDOL, THE(1915); MAMA'S AFFAIR(1921)

Bert Kaempfert
TERROR AFTER MIDNIGHT(1965, Ger.), m; MAN COULD GET KILLED, A(1966), m; ELEPHANT CALLED SLOWLY, AN(1970, Brit.), m; YOU CAN'T WIN 'EM ALL(1970, Brit.), m

Waldemar Kaempfert
NUDE IN HIS POCKET(1962, Fr.), w

Chichinou Kaeppler
MOONRAKER(1979, Brit.)

Morton Kaer
Silents
COLLEGE(1927)

Norimasa Kaeriyama
Misc. Silents
GLOW OF LIFE, THE(1918, Jap.), d; LASCIVIOUSNESS OF THE VIPER, THE(1920, Jap.), d

Domenica Kaesdorf
LEFT-HANDED WOMAN, THE(1980, Ger.), cos

Erich Kaestner
PARADISE FOR THREE(1938), w

Paul Kaethler
SUPERMAN III(1983)
Hannes Kaetner
MARRIAGE OF MARIA BRAUN, THE(1979, Ger.); COUSINS IN LOVE(1982)
1984
LOVE IN GERMANY, A(1984, Fr./Ger.)
Helmut Kaeutner
CAPTAIN FROM KOEPENICK, THE(1956, Ger.), d, w
Eddie Kafafian
WALK THE DARK STREET(1956); CRIME OF PASSION(1957); FLESH AND THE SPUR(1957); MOTORCYCLE GANG(1957); SHAKE, RATTLE, AND ROCK!(1957)
Lee Kafafian
EVERY LITTLE CROOK AND NANNY(1972)
David Kaff
1984
THIS IS SPINAL TAP(1984)
Franz Kafka
TRIAL, THE(1963, Fr./Ital./Ger.), d&w; CASTLE, THE(1969, Ger.), w
Hans Kafka
CROSSROADS(1938, Fr.), d; DEAD MAN'S SHOES(1939, Brit.), w
John H. Kafka
JOHNNY DOESN'T LIVE HERE ANY MORE(1944), w
John Kafka
THEY MET IN BOMBAY(1941), w; CROSSROADS(1942), w; DESTINATION UNKNOWN(1942), w; WOMAN WHO CAME BACK(1945), w; MAN ON A STRING(1960), w
Michael David Kafka
YOUNG GIANTS(1983)
Tamara Kafka
VERONIKA VOSS(1982, Ger.)
George Kafkaris
PRIVATE RIGHT, THE(1967, Brit.); MAGUS, THE(1968, Brit.)
Ric Kafoed
1984
CONSTANCE(1984, New Zealand), art d
Ezra Kafry
1984
SAHARA(1984)
Edward Kag
STRANGER FROM PECOS, THE(1943), md
Mariko Kaga
PLEASURES OF THE FLESH, THE(1965); TWILIGHT PATH(1965, Jap.); SNOW COUNTRY(1969, Jap.); CREATURE CALLED MAN, THE(1970, Jap.); SILENCE HAS NO WINGS(1971, Jap.); MUDDY RIVER(1982, Jap.)
Jeremy Paul Kagan
HEROES(1977), d; SCOTT JOPLIN(1977), d; BIG FIX, THE(1978), d; CHOSEN, THE(1982), d; STING II, THE(1983), d
Marilyn Kagan
FOXES(1980)
1984
INITIATION, THE(1984)
Ai Kagawa
1984
WARRIORS OF THE WIND(1984, Jap.), anim
Kyoko Kagawa
SECRET SCROLLS(PART I)**1/2 (1968, Jap.); WOMEN IN PRISON(1957, Jap.); DEATH ON THE MOUNTAIN(1961, Jap.); LOWER DEPTHS, THE(1962, Jap.); MOTHRA(1962, Jap.); TILL TOMORROW COMES(1962, Jap.); HIGH AND LOW(1963, Jap.); PRODIGAL SON, THE(1964, Jap.); RED BEARD(1966, Jap.); DAREDEVIL IN THE CASTLE(1969, Jap.); MAN IN THE STORM, THE(1969, Jap.); SANSHO THE BAILIFF(1969, Jap.); TOKYO STORY(1972, Jap.)
Ryosuke Kagawa
UGETSU(1954, Jap.); TATSU(1962, Jap.); SANSHO THE BAILIFF(1969, Jap.)
Yukie Kagawa
EAST CHINA SEA(1969, Jap.)
Ivar Kage
WALPURGIS NIGHT(1941, Swed.)
Jack Kagel
STOOLIE, THE(1972)
James Kagel
PARASITE(1982), spec eff
Isamu Kageyama
FOX WITH NINE TAILS, THE(1969, Jap.), art d
Lloyd Kagin
PUTNEY SWOPE(1969)
Marcia Kagno
HOLE IN THE WALL(1929)
Irving Kahal
FOOTLIGHT PARADE(1933), art d
Roger Kahan
BIZARRE BIZARRE(1939, Fr.), ph
Saul Kahan
SCHLOCK(1973); KENTUCKY FRIED MOVIE, THE(1977)
Stephen Kahan
SUPERMAN(1978)
Steve Kahan
INSIDE MOVES(1980); TOY, THE(1982)
Kahana
CASTAWAY COWBOY, THE(1974)
Misc. Talkies
BROTHER, CRY FOR ME(1970)
Kim Kahana
1984
EXTERMINATOR 2(1984)
Duke Kahanamoko
MISTER ROBERTS(1955)
Duke Kahanamoku
GIRL OF THE PORT(1930); ISLE OF ESCAPE(1930); WAKE OF THE RED WITCH(1949)

Silents
ADVENTURE(1925); LORD JIM(1925); OLD IRONSIDES(1926); WOMAN WISE(1928); RESCUE, THE(1929); WHERE EAST IS EAST(1929)
B. B. Kahane
THERE'S THAT WOMAN AGAIN(1938), p; THOSE HIGH GREY WALLS(1939), p; LADY IN QUESTION, THE(1940), p; HER FIRST BEAU(1941), p
Jackie Kahane
80 STEPS TO JONAH(1969)
Roger Kahane
MADLY(1970, Fr.), d, w
Amnon Kahanovitsh
THEY WERE TEN(1961, Israel)
Natsuko Kahara
MOMENT OF TERROR(1969, Jap.); NIGHT OF THE SEAGULL, THE(1970, Jap.)
Milt Kahl
THREE CABALLEROS, THE(1944), anim; MAKE MINE MUSIC(1946), anim; SONG OF THE SOUTH(1946), anim; SO DEAR TO MY HEART(1949), anim; ALICE IN WONDERLAND(1951), anim d; PETER PAN(1953), anim; LADY AND THE TRAMP(1955), anim d; ONE HUNDRED AND ONE DALMATIANS(1961), anim; SWORD IN THE STONE, THE(1963), anim; MARY POPPINS(1964), anim; JUNGLE BOOK, THE(1967), anim d; ROBIN HOOD(1973), anim d; RESCUERS, THE(1977), anim d
Milton Kahl
SNOW WHITE AND THE SEVEN DWARFS(1937), anim; PINOCCHIO(1940), anim d; BAMBI(1942), anim; ARISTOCATS, THE(1970), anim d
Hugo Werner Kahle
MOSCOW SHANGHAI(1936, Ger.)
Charles Kahlenberg
COAL MINER'S DAUGHTER(1980); SIX PACK(1982)
1984
FLASH OF GREEN, A(1984)
Hugh Kahler
Silents
RESCUE, THE(1917), w
Wolf Kahler
BARRY LYNDON(1975, Brit.); MARCH OR DIE(1977, Brit.); BOYS FROM BRAZIL, THE(1978); LADY VANISHES, THE(1980, Brit.); ROUGH CUT(1980, Brit.); PRIEST OF LOVE(1981, Brit.); RAIDERS OF THE LOST ARK(1981, Brit.); SEA WOLVES, THE(1981, Brit.); FIREFOX(1982); REMEMBRANCE(1982, Brit.); HIGH ROAD TO CHINA(1983); KEEP, THE(1983)
1984
RIDDLE OF THE SANDS, THE(1984, Brit.)
Kahlil
MAIDSTONE(1970)
Al Kahn
1984
TERMINATOR, THE(1984)
Allen Kahn
WIZARD OF GORE, THE(1970), w; YEAR OF THE YAHOO(1971), w
Barra Kahn
TRADING PLACES(1983)
Bernie Kahn
BAREFOOT EXECUTIVE, THE(1971), w
Brigitte Kahn
EMPIRE STRIKES BACK, THE(1980); PRIVATES ON PARADE(1982)
1984
PRIVATES ON PARADE(1984, Brit.)
David Kahn
ULTIMATE THRILL, THE(1974)
E.J. Kahn, Jr.
THREE STRIPES IN THE SUN(1955), w
Edward L. Kahn
HOMICIDE SQUAD(1931), d; RESURRECTION(1931), ed
Enrique Kahn
SUNBURN(1979)
Florence Kahn
SECRET AGENT, THE(1936, Brit.)
Frances Kahn
BLOOD OF FU MANCHU, THE(1968, Brit.)
George Kahn
BOY OF THE STREETS(1937), p
Gilbert Lawrence Kahn
FADE TO BLACK(1980)
Gordon Kahn
X MARKS THE SPOT(1931), w; DEATH KISS, THE(1933), w; CROSBY CASE, THE(1934), w; GIGOLETTE(1935), w; PEOPLE'S ENEMY, THE(1935), w; NAVY BLUES(1937), w; I STAND ACCUSED(1938), w; MAMA RUNS WILD(1938), w; TENTH AVENUE KID(1938), w; EX-CHAMP(1939), w; MICKEY, THE KID(1939), w; NEWSBOY'S HOME(1939), w; S.O.S. TIDAL WAVE(1939), w; WOLF OF NEW YORK(1940), w; BUY ME THAT TOWN(1941), w; WORLD PREMIERE(1941), w; NORTHWEST RANGERS(1942), w; YANK ON THE BURMA ROAD, A(1942), w; COWBOY AND THE SENORITA(1944), w; LIGHTS OF OLD SANTA FE(1944), w; SONG OF NEVADA(1944), w; BLONDE ALIBI(1946), w; HER KIND OF MAN(1946), w; RUTHLESS(1948), w; WHIPLASH(1948), w; STREETS OF SAN FRANCISCO(1949), w
Grace Kahn
I'LL SEE YOU IN MY DREAMS(1951), w
Gus Kahn
WHOOPEE(1930), w; DAY AT THE RACES, A(1937), m; BRIDAL SUITE(1939), m; ONCE UPON A TIME(1944), m/1
Ivan Kahn
STAR DUST(1940), w
Jonathan Kahn
SAILOR WHO FELL FROM GRACE WITH THE SEA, THE(1976, Brit.)
Karen Kahn
INCHON(1981)
Lili Kahn
FLEMISH FARM, THE(1943, Brit.)

Lilly Kahn
DAY TO REMEMBER, A(1953, Brit.); CAT GIRL(1957); NOWHERE TO GO(1959, Brit.)
Lily Kahn
NOW BARABBAS WAS A ROBBER(1949, Brit.); TALE OF FIVE WOMEN, A(1951, Brit.); HOUSE OF THE SEVEN HAWKS, THE(1959)
Madeline Kahn
WHAT'S UP, DOC?(1972); FROM THE MIXED-UP FILES OF MRS. BASIL E. FRANKWEILER(1973); PAPER MOON(1973); BLAZING SADDLES(1974); YOUNG FRANKENSTEIN(1974); ADVENTURES OF SHERLOCK HOLMES' SMARTER BROTHER, THE(1975, Brit.); AT LONG LAST LOVE(1975); WON TON TON, THE DOG WHO SAVED HOLLYWOOD(1976); HIGH ANXIETY(1977); CHEAP DETECTIVE, THE(1978); MUPPET MOVIE, THE(1979); FIRST FAMILY(1980); HAPPY BIRTHDAY, GEMINI(1980); SIMON(1980); WHOLLY MOSES(1980); HISTORY OF THE WORLD, PART 1(1981); YELLOWBEARD(1983)
1984
CITY HEAT(1984); SLAPSTICK OF ANOTHER KIND(1984)
Mary Kahn
VIXENS, THE(1969)
Michael Kahn
RAGE(1972), ed; TROUBLE MAN(1972), ed; BLACK JACK(1973), ed; SPOOK WHO SAT BY THE DOOR, THE(1973), ed; BLACK BELT JONES(1974), ed; GOLDEN NEEDLES(1974), ed; SAVAGE IS LOOSE, THE(1974), ed; TRUCK TURNER(1974), ed; DEVIL'S RAIN, THE(1975, U.S./Mex.), ed; ULTIMATE WARRIOR, THE(1975), ed; RETURN OF A MAN CALLED HORSE, THE(1976), ed; CLOSE ENCOUNTERS OF THE THIRD KIND(1977), ed; EYES OF LAURA MARS(1978), ed; ICE CASTLES(1978), ed; 1941(1979), ed; USED CARS(1980), ed; RAIDERS OF THE LOST ARK(1981), ed; POLTERGEIST(1982), ed; TABLE FOR FIVE(1983), ed; TWILIGHT ZONE–THE MOVIE(1983), ed
1984
FALLING IN LOVE(1984), ed; INDIANA JONES AND THE TEMPLE OF DOOM(1984), ed
Milt Kahn
HOLLYWOOD BOULEVARD(1976)
Milton Kahn
HOUSE OF ROTHSCHILD, THE(1934); WEDDING PRESENT(1936)
Philip Kahn
YOU'RE TELLING ME(1942), ed
Richard Kahn
BRONZE BUCKAROO, THE(1939), p,d&w
Richard C. Kahn
SECRET MENACE(1931), d, w; BAD BOY(1939), w; HARLEM RIDES THE RANGE(1939), p&d; SON OF INGAGI(1940), p&d
Misc. Talkies
TWO-GUN MAN FROM HARLEM(1938), d; BUZZY RIDES THE RANGE(1940), d; BUZZY AND THE PHANTOM PINTO(1941), d
Rick Kahn
SQUEEZE PLAY(1981)
Robert Kahn
ENDLESS LOVE(1981)
Ronald Kahn
PRUDENCE AND THE PILL(1968, Brit.), bp
Ronald J. Kahn
SEASIDE SWINGERS(1965, Brit.), p; MUMSY, NANNY, SONNY, AND GIRLY(1970, Brit.), p
Ronnie Kahn
TOYS ARE NOT FOR CHILDREN(1972)
Sajid Kahn
MAYA(1966)
Sheldon Kahn
ONE FLEW OVER THE CUCKOO'S NEST(1975), ed; GREAT SCOUT AND CATHOUSE THURSDAY, THE(1976), ed; MIKEY AND NICKY(1976), ed; ENEMY OF THE PEOPLE, AN(1978), ed; SAME TIME, NEXT YEAR(1978), ed; ELECTRIC HORSEMAN, THE(1979), ed; PRIVATE BENJAMIN(1980), ed; ABSENCE OF MALICE(1981), ed; KISS ME GOODBYE(1982), ed
1984
GHOSTBUSTERS(1984), ed; UNFAITHFULLY YOURS(1984), ed
Shelly Kahn
BLOODBROTHERS(1978), ed
William Kahn
NIGHT EDITOR(1946); ONE TOO MANY(1950); GIRL ON THE BRIDGE, THE(1951); EDGE OF HELL(1956)
Mohammad Kahnemout
CARAVANS(1978, U.S./Iranian)
Alexis Kahner
AMOROUS ADVENTURES OF MOLL FLANDERS, THE(1965)
Paul Kahnert
DEADLY EYES(1982), p
Jara Kahout
COMEBACK TRAIL, THE(1982)
Vijay Kahsyap
GANDHI(1982)
Rongo Tupatea Kahu
1984
SILENT ONE, THE(1984, New Zealand)
Chang Kai
Misc. Silents
BLUE EXPRESS(1929, USSR)
Hisataka Kai
FINAL WAR, THE(1960, Jap.), w
Johannes Kai
SEVEN DARING GIRLS(1962, Ger.), w; ISLE OF SIN(1963, Ger.), d&w
Jung Kai
GENERAL DIED AT DAWN, THE(1936)
Lani Kai
BLUE HAWAII(1961)
Aleksandr Kaidanovsky
STALKER(1982, USSR)

Alexandr Kaidanovsky
TEST OF PILOT PIRX, THE(1978, Pol./USSR)
Helen E. Kaider
CHRISTMAS STORY, A(1983)
Hideo Kaijo
H-MAN, THE(1959, Jap.), w
Pam Kail
MAYTIME IN MAYFAIR(1952, Brit.)
Liis Kailey
STAR 80(1983)
Zehava Kailos
1984
AMBASSADOR, THE(1984)
Jim Kain
MALOU(1983)
Kusune Kainosho
UGETSU(1954, Jap.), cos
Maurice E. Kains
Silents
DOWN TO THE SEA IN SHIPS(1923), ph; TELL IT TO THE MARINES(1926)
Nick Kairis
SMALL CIRCLE OF FRIENDS, A(1980)
Hugh Kairs [Shepherd]
MUSIC MAKER, THE(1936, Brit.), d
Valerie Kairys
VANISHING POINT(1971)
Ardyth Kaiser
RAGGEDY ANN AND ANDY(1977)
Burt Kaiser
FEMALE JUNGLE, THE(1955), a, p, w
Ervin Kaiser
Misc. Silents
RASPUTIN(1930)
Erwin Kaiser
ADDRESS UNKNOWN(1944); HEAVENLY DAYS(1944); ONCE UPON A TIME(1944); GIRL IN WHITE, THE(1952)
George Kaiser
GHOST COMES HOME, THE(1940), w
Helen Kaiser
DANCE HALL(1929); RIO RITA(1929)
Henry Kaiser
HISTORY OF THE WORLD, PART 1(1981); TO BE OR NOT TO BE(1983)
Kurt Kaiser
WAY OUT(1966), m
May Kaiser
Silents
SILVER WINGS(1922)
Norman Kaiser [Norman Kerry]
Silents
MANHATTAN MADNESS(1916)
Norman F. Kaiser
LAST HOUSE ON DEAD END STREET(1977), p
Roland Kaiser
AFFAIRS OF JULIE, THE(1958, Ger.); ROSES FOR THE PROSECUTOR(1961, Ger.); GIRL AND THE LEGEND, THE(1966, Ger.)
Sid Kaiser
INVASION OF THE BEE GIRLS(1973); BLACK BELT JONES(1974)
Sissi Kaiser
BREAD OF LOVE, THE(1954, Swed.); BRINK OF LIFE(1960, Swed.)
Willy Kaiser
Silents
PASSION(1920, Ger.)
Skil Kaiser-Passini
FIVE DAYS ONE SUMMER(1982)
Maui Kaito
Silents
WHITE FLOWER, THE(1923)
Anita Kajlichova
MAN FROM THE FIRST CENTURY, THE(1961, Czech.)
Asakazu Kakai
STRAY DOG(1963, Jap.), ph
Kostas Kakavas
LISA, TOSCA OF ATHENS(1961, Gr.)
A. Kalaberdin
TRAIN GOES TO KIEV, THE(1961, USSR)
Vera Kalabova
FIFTH HORSEMAN IS FEAR, THE(1968, Czech.), w
Mohamed Kalach
CIRCLE OF DECEIT(1982, Fr./Ger.)
Ya'acov Kalach
MY MARGO(1969, Israel), ph
Robert Kalaf
1984
NATURAL, THE(1984)
Kalaho
MILESTONES(1975)
Kalantan
SON OF SINBAD(1955)
Kalapu
RETURN TO PARADISE(1953)
Aft Kalapu
PACIFIC DESTINY(1956, Brit.)
Stavros Kalarogiou
MATCHMAKING OF ANNA, THE(1972, Gr.)
Julius Kalas
EMPEROR AND THE GOLEM, THE(1955, Czech.), m
Leonid Kalashnikov
RED TENT, THE(1971, Ital./USSR), ph

Kalassu
Misc. Talkies
BOARDING HOUSE(1984)
Mikhail Kalatozov
WINGS OF VICTORY(1941, USSR), d; CRANES ARE FLYING, THE(1960, USSR),
p&d; LETTER THAT WAS NEVER SENT, THE(1962, USSR), d
Mikhail K. Kalatozov
RED TENT, THE(1971, Ital./USSR), d
Horali Kalayji
TARGET: HARRY(1980)
Dale Kalberg
DON'T ANSWER THE PHONE(1980)
Terri Kalbus
KENNY AND CO.(1976)
Terrie Kalbus
PHANTASM(1979)
Lee Kalcheim
IS THIS TRIP REALLY NECESSARY?(1970), w
Krysztof Kalczynski
PORTRAIT OF LENIN(1967, Pol./USSR)
Richard E. Kald
NEW YEAR'S EVIL(1980)
Kendal Kaldwell
LONELY LADY, THE(1983)
Christa Kale
NIGHT THEY ROBBED BIG BERTHA'S, THE(1975)
Daniel Kaleikini, Jr.
HAWAIIANS, THE(1970)
Charle Kaleina
KING OF COMEDY, THE(1983)
Charlene Kaleina
SUBWAY RIDERS(1981)
Bonita Kalem
Misc. Talkies
FIVE ANGRY WOMEN(1975)
Gordon Kalem
Silents
LITTLE WILD GIRL, THE(1928), t
Toni Kalem
WANDERERS, THE(1979); PRIVATE BENJAMIN(1980); PATERNITY(1981); I'M
DANCING AS FAST AS I CAN(1982); LOVE(1982, Can.); SILENT RAGE(1982); TWO OF
A KIND(1983)
1984
RECKLESS(1984)
Harry Kalenberg
BEFORE WINTER COMES(1969, Brit.)
Mieczyslaw Kalenik
KNIGHTS OF THE TEUTONIC ORDER, THE(1962, Pol.)
Berwick Kaler
BLOODTHIRSTY BUTCHERS(1970); MAN WITH TWO HEADS, THE(1972); RATS
ARE COMING! THE WEREWOLVES ARE HERE!, THE(1972)
James Otis Kaler
TOBY TYLER(1960), w
Edd Kaleroff
SIDELONG GLANCES OF A PIGEON KICKER, THE(1970), m
Charles Kaley
LORD BYRON OF BROADWAY(1930); SINGING BUCKAROO, THE(1937)
Vi Kaley
ROYAL DEMAND, A(1933, Brit.); VIRGINIA'S HUSBAND(1934, Brit.); CHILDREN
OF THE FOG(1935, Brit.); MAN WITHOUT A FACE, THE(1935, Brit.); GAY OLD
DOG(1936, Brit.); LIVE AGAIN(1936, Brit.); LOVE AT SEA(1936, Brit.); MEN OF
YESTERDAY(1936, Brit.); TALKING FEET(1937, Brit.); ON VELVET(1938, Brit.);
SECOND MR. BUSH, THE(1940, Brit.); FACING THE MUSIC(1941, Brit.); FRONT
LINE KIDS(1942, Brit.); DUMMY TALKS, THE(1943, Brit.); OLD MOTHER RILEY,
DETECTIVE(1943, Brit.); GIVE ME THE STARS(1944, Brit.); KISS THE BRIDE
GOODBYE(1944, Brit.); TROJAN BROTHERS, THE(1946); FOOL AND THE PRIN-
CESS, THE(1948, Brit.); VICE VERSA(1948, Brit.); MY BROTHER JONATHAN(1949,
Brit.); WEAKER SEX, THE(1949, Brit.); MUDLARK, THE(1950, Brit.); NO ROOM AT
THE INN(1950, Brit.); OLD MOTHER RILEY, HEADMISTRESS(1950, Brit.); SILK
NOOSE, THE(1950, Brit.); SOMETHING IN THE CITY(1950, Brit.); SCARLET
THREAD(1951, Brit.); MY WIFE'S LODGER(1952, Brit.); PAUL TEMPLE RE-
TURNS(1952, Brit.)
Misc. Talkies
BEHIND THE HEADLINES(1953)
John Kalfas
SONG OF THE LOON(1970)
Jean Pierre Kalfon
BIRDS COME TO DIE IN PERU(1968, Fr.)
Jean-Pierre Kalfon
NIGHT OF LUST(1965, Fr.); TO BE A CROOK(1967, Fr.); WEEKEND(1968, Fr./Ital.);
LES GAULOISES BLEUES(1969, Fr.); ZIG-ZAG(1975, Fr/Ital.); DOGS OF WAR,
THE(1980, Brit.); CONDORMAN(1981); CONFIDENTIALLY YOURS(1983, Fr.)
1984
DOG DAY(1984, Fr.); LOVE ON THE GROUND(1984,Fr.)
Pierre Kalfon
SWEET AND SOUR(1964, Fr./Ital.), p; TASTE FOR WOMEN, A(1966, Fr./Ital.), p;
FINO A FARTI MALE(1969, Fr./Ital.), p; SINGAPORE, SINGAPORE(1969, Fr./Ital.),
p, w
1984
TO CATCH A COP(1984, Fr.), p
Frederick Kalgren
Misc. Silents
LUXURY(1921)
Eric Kalhurst
VIRTUOUS SIN, THE(1930)
Bob Kaliban
WHAT'S SO BAD ABOUT FEELING GOOD?(1968); IF EVER I SEE YOU
AGAIN(1978); SOMETHING SHORT OF PARADISE(1979)

Bertha Kalich
Silents
AMBITION(1916)
Misc. Silents
MARTA OF THE LOWLANDS(1914); SLANDER(1916)
Jacob Kalich
YIDDLE WITH HIS FIDDLE(1937, Pol.), art d; FIDDLER ON THE ROOF(1971)
Misc. Silents
MAZEL TOV(1924)
Lillian Kalich
Misc. Silents
MARTA OF THE LOWLANDS(1914)
Janusz Kalicinski
MAN OF IRON(1981, Pol.), ph
Isabella Kaliff
Misc. Talkies
AWOL(1973)
Makhail Kalik
LULLABY(1961, USSR), ed
Mikhail Kalik
LULLABY(1961, USSR), d
Mosei Kalik
SANDU FOLLOWS THE SUN(1965, USSR), d, w
Maxine Kalil
SUDDEN TERROR(1970, Brit.)
Mailoa Kalili
FAIR WIND TO JAVA(1953)
Maiola Kalili
HURRICANE SMITH(1952)
Manuella Kalili
EBB TIDE(1937)
Bill Kaliloa
PAGAN LOVE SONG(1950)
Radovan Kalina
FIFTH HORSEMAN IS FEAR, THE(1968, Czech.), w
Valdimir Kalina
MATTER OF DAYS, A(1969, Fr./Czech.), w
Maria Kalinciska
MAN OF MARBLE(1979, Pol.), ed
M. P. Kalinin
MYSTERIOUS ISLAND(1941, USSR), w
S. Kalinin
GROWN-UP CHILDREN(1963, USSR), makeup; OPTIMISTIC TRAGEDY, THE(1964,
USSR), makeup
Sergei Kalinin
SYMPHONY OF LIFE(1949, USSR)
Sergey Kalinin
RESURRECTION(1963, USSR); HOUSE WITH AN ATTIC, THE(1964, USSR)
Ernst Kalinke
LAST TOMAHAWK, THE(1965, Ger./Ital./Span.), ph
Ernst W. Kalinke
BEGGAR STUDENT, THE(1958, Ger.), ph; PHONY AMERICAN, THE(1964, Ger.),
ph; APACHE GOLD(1965, Ger.), ph; DESPERADO TRAIL, THE(1965, Ger./Yugo.), ph;
INVISIBLE DR. MABUSE, THE(1965, Ger.), ph; TREASURE OF SILVER LAKE(1965,
Fr./Ger./Yugo.), ph; LAST OF THE RENEGADES(1966, Fr./Ital./Yugo.), ph;
BLOOD DEMON(1967, Ger.), ph; U-47 LT. COMMANDER PRIEN(1967, Ger.), ph;
MARK OF THE DEVIL(1970, Ger./Brit.), ph
Marc Kalinoski
ADOLESCENTS, THE(1967, Can.)
Vanda Kalinova
END OF AUGUST AT THE HOTEL OZONE, THE(1967, Czech.)
Tadeusz Kalinowski
BOXER(1971, Pol.)
Waldemar Kalinowski
HEAVEN'S GATE(1980); BREATHLESS(1983)
1984
RED DAWN(1984)
Waldimar Kalinowski
TESTAMENT(1983), set d
Edward Kalinski
FRIGHTMARE(1974, Brit.)
Ruth Kalinsky
Silents
MEG(1926, Brit.)
Joan Kalionzes
COP HATER(1958)
Stefan Kalipha
CUBA(1979); FOR YOUR EYES ONLY(1981); SUPERMAN III(1983)
Stephan Kaliphi
BABYLON(1980, Brit.)
Armand Kalis
ALGIERS(1938)
Jan Kalis
VOYAGE TO THE END OF THE UNIVERSE(1963, Czech.), ph; FIFTH HORSEMAN
IS FEAR, THE(1968, Czech.), w, ph; SIGN OF THE VIRGIN(1969, Czech.), ph
Jen Kalis
VOYAGE TO THE END OF THE UNIVERSE(1963, Czech.), spec eff
Bernhard Kalisch
PINOCCHIO(1969, E. Ger.), makeup
Bertha Kalish
Misc. Silents
LOVE AND HATE(1916)
Mel Kalish
ALEXANDER'S RAGTIME BAND(1938)
Ron Kalish
TAKE THE MONEY AND RUN(1969), ed; BANANAS(1971), ed; LOVE AND
DEATH(1975), ed; SLEEPAWAY CAMP(1983), ed
1984
ACT, THE(1984), ed

Mechild Kalisky
LEFT-HANDED WOMAN, THE(1980, Ger.)
Mike Kalist
DELIRIUM(1979)
Adrian Kalitka
SOPHIE'S CHOICE(1982)
Armand Kaliz
NOAH'S ARK(1928); AVIATOR, THE(1929); GOLD DIGGERS OF BROADWAY(1929); MARRIAGE PLAYGROUND, THE(1929); TWIN BEDS(1929); L'ENIGMATIQUE MONSIEUR PARKES(1930); HONEYMOON LANE(1931); LITTLE CAESAR(1931); MEN OF THE SKY(1931); THIS MODERN AGE(1931); THREE WISE GIRLS(1932); DESIGN FOR LIVING(1933); FLYING DOWN TO RIO(1933); SECRET SINNERS(1933); GEORGE WHITE'S SCANDALS(1934); UPPER WORLD(1934); DIAMOND JIM(1935); HERE'S TO ROMANCE(1935); RUGGLES OF RED GAP(1935); DESIRE(1936); KING AND THE CHORUS GIRL, THE(1937); ARTISTS AND MODELS ABROAD(1938); GOLD DIGGERS IN PARIS(1938); I'LL GIVE A MILLION(1938); JOSETTE(1938); LETTER OF INTRODUCTION(1938); TRIP TO PARIS, A(1938); VACATION FROM LOVE(1938); FOR LOVE OR MONEY(1939); MIDNIGHT(1939); MIRACLES FOR SALE(1939); NINOTCHKA(1939); OFF THE RECORD(1939); TOPPER TAKES A TRIP(1939); DOWN ARGENTINE WAY(1940); SKYLARK(1941); ZIEGFELD GIRL(1941)
Silents
INNOCENT(1918); TEMPTRESS, THE(1926); YELLOW FINGERS(1926); STOLEN BRIDE, THE(1927); WANDERING GIRLS(1927); LINGERIE(1928)
Misc. Silents
YELLOW TICKET, THE(1918); BELLE OF BROADWAY, THE(1926); BETTER WAY, THE(1926); FAST AND FURIOUS(1927); SAY IT WITH DIAMONDS(1927); TEMPTATIONS OF A SHOP GIRL(1927); DEVIL'S CAGE, THE(1928); WIFE'S RELATIONS, THE(1928); WOMAN'S WAY, A(1928)
Armond Kaliz
Silents
JOSSELYN'S WIFE(1926)
Richard Kalk
NEW CENTURIONS, THE(1972)
Richard E. Kalk
SHAMPOO(1975)
Eric Kalkhurst
UNFAITHFUL(1931)
Ferenc Kallai
WITNESS, THE(1982, Hung.)
D. Kallas
ELECTRA(1962, Gr.)
Sandor Kallay
MADAME BUTTERFLY(1932)
Jackie Kallen
TOUGH ENOUGH(1983)
Kitty Kallen
SECOND GREATEST SEX, THE(1955)
Marlain Kallevig
MARLOWE(1969)
Helena Kallianiotes
BABY MAKER, THE(1970); FIVE EASY PIECES(1970); KANSAS CITY BOMBER(1972); SHANKS(1974); DROWNING POOL, THE(1975); PASSOVER PLOT, THE(1976, Israel); STAY HUNGRY(1976)
Helena Kallianiotis
EUREKA(1983, Brit.)
Liz Kallimeyer
SOMEBODY KILLED HER HUSBAND(1978)
Anna Kallina
Misc. Silents
PRINCE AND THE DANCER(1929, Ger.)
Eskil Kalling
SILENCE, THE(1964, Swed.)
Ismo Kallio
MAKE LIKE A THIEF(1966, Fin.)
Jan Kallis
ROCKET TO NOWHERE(1962, Czech.), ph, spec eff; NIGHTS OF PRAGUE, THE(1968, Czech.), ph
Stanley Kallis
HOT ANGEL, THE(1958), p, w; OPERATION DAMES(1959), p, w; ROADRACERS, THE(1959), p, w
Dick Kallman
HELL CANYON OUTLAWS(1957); BORN TO BE LOVED(1959); VERBOTEN!(1959); BACK STREET(1961); DREAM MAKER, THE(1963, Brit.); DOCTOR, YOU'VE GOT TO BE KIDDING(1967)
Helena Kalloaniotes
RENALDO AND CLARA(1978)
Kalloch
AWFUL TRUTH, THE(1937), cos; GIRLS CAN PLAY(1937), cos; IT'S ALL YOURS(1937), cos; GOLDEN BOY(1939), cos; GOOD GIRLS GO TO PARIS(1939), cos; LONE WOLF SPY HUNT, THE(1939), cos; MR. SMITH GOES TO WASHINGTON(1939), cos; MUSIC IN MY HEART(1940), cos; BABES ON BROADWAY(1941), cos; H.M. PULHAM, ESQ.(1941), cos; LIFE BEGINS FOR ANDY HARDY(1941), cos; CAIRO(1942), cos; CROSSROADS(1942), cos; FOR ME AND MY GAL(1942), cos; I MARRIED AN ANGEL(1942), cos; MRS. MINIVER(1942), cos; PANAMA HATTIE(1942), cos
Fred Kalloch
I AM THE LAW(1938), cos
Robert Kalloch
THAT'S MY BOY(1932), cos; BITTER TEA OF GENERAL YEN, THE(1933), cos; LADY FOR A DAY(1933), cos; WRECKER, THE(1933), cos; MOST PRECIOUS THING IN LIFE(1934), cos; ONE NIGHT OF LOVE(1934), cos; SISTERS UNDER THE SKIN(1934), cos; MURDER IN GREENWICH VILLAGE(1937), cos; PAID TO DANCE(1937), cos; RACKETEERS IN EXILE(1937), cos; SHADOW, THE(1937), cos; VENUS MAKES TROUBLE(1937), cos; WOMAN IN DISTRESS(1937), cos; WOMEN OF GLAMOUR(1937), cos; HOLIDAY(1938), cos; NO TIME TO MARRY(1938), cos; SQUADRON OF HONOR(1938), cos; START CHEERING(1938), cos; THERE'S ALWAYS A WOMAN(1938), cos; WHO KILLED GAIL PRESTON?(1938), cos; WOMEN IN PRISON(1938), cos; HIS GIRL FRIDAY(1940), cos; ISLAND OF DOOMED MEN(1940), cos; LADY IN QUESTION, THE(1940), cos; HONKY TONK(1941), cos;

RINGSIDE MAISIE(1941), cos; VANISHING VIRGINIAN, THE(1941), cos; YOU'LL NEVER GET RICH(1941), cos; JOHNNY EAGER(1942), cos; JOURNEY FOR MARGARET(1942), cos; PACIFIC RENDEZVOUS(1942), cos; RIO RITA(1942), cos; SHIP AHOY(1942), cos; SOMEWHERE I'LL FIND YOU(1942), cos; TORTILLA FLAT(1942), cos; WE WERE DANCING(1942), cos; WHITE CARGO(1942), cos; SUSPENSE(1946), cos; MR. BLANDINGS BUILDS HIS DREAM HOUSE(1948), cos
Robert Kallock
IT HAPPENED ONE NIGHT(1934), cos; ONLY ANGELS HAVE WINGS(1939), cos
Irene Kallosch
HE STAYED FOR BREAKFAST(1940), cos
Raymond Kallund
TEMPTATION(1936)
Max Kalmanowicz
CHILDREN, THE(1980), p, d
Michael Kalmansohn
DEATH GAME(1977)
Bert Kalmar
CUCKOOS, THE(1930), w; TOP SPEED(1930), w; BROADMINDED(1931), w; HORSE FEATHERS(1932), w; KID FROM SPAIN, THE(1932), w; DUCK SOUP(1933), w; HIPS, HIPS, HOORAY(1934), w; BRIGHT LIGHTS(1935), w; KENTUCKY KERNELS(1935), w; NIGHT AT THE OPERA, A(1935), w; WALKING ON AIR(1936), w; LIFE OF THE PARTY, THE(1937), w; SHIP AHOY(1942), w; LOOK FOR THE SILVER LINING(1949), w; THREE LITTLE WORDS(1950), w
Bert Kalmar, Jr.
GREAT GUY(1936)
Burt Kalmar
CIRCUS CLOWN(1934), w
Laszlo Kalmar
SUN SHINES, THE(1939, Hung.), d
Nadine Kalmes
DR. JEKYLL'S DUNGEON OF DEATH(1982)
Bea Kalmus
DISC JOCKEY(1951)
Natalie Kalmus
HER JUNGLE LOVE(1938), art d; HOLLYWOOD CAVALCADE(1939), cons; MARYLAND(1940), ph
Florian Kalo
DIALOGUE(1967, Hung.)
Savos Kalogeras
WHY ROCK THE BOAT?(1974, Can.), ph
Jerry Kalogeratos
MOONLIGHTING WIVES(1966), ph; FRENCH QUARTER(1978), ph
Xenie Kalogeropoulos
LISA, TOSCA OF ATHENS(1961, Gr.); MIDWIFE, THE(1961, Greece)
Spyros Kalogyrou
STEFANIA(1968, Gr.)
A. Kalsati
CAPTAIN GRANT'S CHILDREN(1939, USSR), ph
Erwin Kalser
ESCAPE TO GLORY(1940); DRESSED TO KILL(1941); UNDERGROUND(1941); BERLIN CORRESPONDENT(1942); KING'S ROW(1942); MISSION TO MOSCOW(1943); WATCH ON THE RHINE(1943); PURPLE HEART, THE(1944); STRANGE AFFAIR(1944); THEY LIVE IN FEAR(1944); U-BOAT PRISONER(1944); HOTEL BERLIN(1945); TWO SMART PEOPLE(1946); STALAG 17(1953)
Fred Kalsey
MEXICAN SPITFIRE OUT WEST(1940)
H. V. Kaltenborn
MR. SMITH GOES TO WASHINGTON(1939); BABE RUTH STORY, THE(1948); DAY THE EARTH STOOD STILL, THE(1951)
Abraham Kaluna
FORBIDDEN ISLAND(1959)
George Kaluna
REAL GLORY, THE(1939)
Witold Kaluski
YOUNG GIRLS OF WILKO, THE(1979, Pol./Fr.)
E. Kaluzhski
1812(1944, USSR)
William Kalvino
WINNING TEAM, THE(1952)
Kaly
VERY HAPPY ALEXANDER(1969, Fr.)
Arcady Kalzaty
LAST HILL, THE(1945, USSR), ph
Galen Kam
HAWAIIANS, THE(1970)
Lam Chi Kam
Misc. Talkies
KUNG FU HALLOWEEN(1981), d
Mara Kam
TWO HUNDRED MOTELS(1971, Brit.), anim
Ng Kam-wah
1984
AH YING(1984, Hong Kong), ed
Kyoko Kama
TOKYO JOE(1949)
Frank Kamagi
SABRE JET(1953)
A. Kamagorova
OPTIMISTIC TRAGEDY, THE(1964, USSR), ed
Kamahl
NED KELLY(1970, Brit.)
Kolimau Kamai
WHITE HEAT(1934)
Indra Kamajozo
Misc. Talkies
ASSIGNMENT ABROAD(1955)
Jon Rashad Kamal
STAR TREK: THE MOTION PICTURE(1979)

Kamalakant
TIGER AND THE FLAME, THE(1955, India)
Steven W. Kaman
SQUEEZE PLAY(1981)
Lu Kamante
STRANGER'S GUNDOWN, THE(1974, Ital.)
Joe Kamaryst
PARIS CALLING(1941)
Joe Kamaryt
CRACK-UP(1946); FLAME OF ARABY(1951)
Joseph Kamaryt
HE STAYED FOR BREAKFAST(1940); ONCE UPON A HONEYMOON(1942); MISSION TO MOSCOW(1943); EXILE, THE(1947)
Hosei Kamatsu
DOUBLE SUICIDE(1970, Jap.)
James Kamau
LIVING FREE(1972, Brit.)
Karl Kamb
MAIN STREET AFTER DARK(1944), w; PARDON MY PAST(1945), w; CARNEGIE HALL(1947), w; LULU BELLE(1948), w; PITFALL(1948), w; WHISPERING SMITH(1948), w; KID FROM TEXAS, THE(1950), w; CAPTIVE CITY(1952), w
Stan Kamber
YOUNG LIONS, THE(1958); WARLOCK(1959); CACTUS IN THE SNOW(1972); BAD CHARLESTON CHARLIE(1973), w; PENITENTIARY II(1982)
Misc. Talkies
WELCOME HOME, BROTHER CHARLES(1975)
Yuka Kamebuchi
MARCO(1973)
Mitsuyo Kamei
SONG FROM MY HEART, THE(1970, Jap.)
George Kamel
WINGS OVER THE PACIFIC(1943)
Joe Kamel
GIDGET GOES TO ROME(1963); MINNESOTA CLAY(1966, Ital./Fr./Span.)
Stanley Kamel
CORVETTE SUMMER(1978); IN SEARCH OF HISTORIC JESUS(1980); MAKING LOVE(1982); STAR 80(1983)
Jackie Kamen
LOVE NOW...PAY LATER(1966, Ital.)
Jay Kamen
NORTH DALLAS FORTY(1979), ed; SPLIT IMAGE(1982), ed
Michael Kamen
NEXT MAN, THE(1976), m; BETWEEN THE LINES(1977), m; STUNTS(1977), m; POLYESTER(1981), m; VENOM(1982, Brit.), m; DEAD ZONE, THE(1983), m
Milt Kamen
ME, NATALIE(1969); OUT OF TOWNERS, THE(1970); BELIEVE IN ME(1971); THIS IS A HIJACK(1973); MOTHER, JUGS & SPEED(1976); W.C. FIELDS AND ME(1976)
Misc. Talkies
GROUP MARRIAGE(1972)
Robert Mark Kamen
TAPS(1981), w; SPLIT IMAGE(1982), w
1984
KARATE KID, THE(1984), w
Yu. Kamenetskiy
DAY THE WAR ENDED, THE(1961, USSR), lyrics
Theoderos Kamenidis
ISLAND OF LOVE(1963)
Alexandre Kamenka
Silents
ITALIAN STRAW HAT, AN(1927, Fr.), art d
Catherine Kamenka
IS PARIS BURNING?(1966, U.S./Fr.)
Pete Kameron
YOU BETTER WATCH OUT(1980), p
Katherine Kamhi
SLEEPAWAY CAMP(1983)
Ken Kamholz
1984
NATURAL, THE(1984)
Virginia Kami
LOVE CAPTIVE, THE(1934)
Takeshi Kamikubo
THREE STRIPES IN THE SUN(1955)
Susan Kamini
MARY, MARY, BLOODY MARY(1975, U.S./Mex.)
Didier Kaminka
NADA GANG, THE(1974, Fr./Ital.); BANZAI(1983, Fr.), a, w
1984
HERE COMES SANTA CLAUS(1984), w; MY NEW PARTNER(1984, Fr.), w
Bernie Kamins
FORTY THIEVES(1944), w
Susan Kamins
HOMETOWN U.S.A.(1979)
Esther Rokhl Kaminska
Misc. Silents
MIRELE EFROS(1912, USSR); SLAUGHTER, THE(1913, USSR)
Ida Kaminska
WITHOUT A HOME(1939, Pol.); SHOP ON MAIN STREET, THE(1966, Czech.); ANGEL LEVINE, THE(1970)
Misc. Silents
MIRELE EFROS(1912, USSR)
Regina Kaminska
Misc. Silents
MIRELE EFROS(1912, USSR); CANTOR'S DAUGHTER, THE(1913, USSR); FATALNA KLATWA(1913, USSR); STRANGER, THE(1913, USSR)
S. Kaminska
WALKOVER(1969, Pol.)

Zbigniew Kaminski
YOUNG GIRLS OF WILKO, THE(1979, Pol./Fr.), w
Alfons Kaminsky
FOURTEEN, THE(1973, Brit.)
Avrom Yitskhok Kaminsky
Misc. Silents
FORGOTTEN, THE(1912, USSR), d; CANTOR'S DAUGHTER, THE(1913, USSR), d; FATALNA KLATWA(1913, USSR), d; HIS WIFE'S HUSBAND(1913, Pol.), d; SLAUGHTER, THE(1913, USSR), d; STEPMOTHER, THE(1914, USSR), d
Dana Kaminsky
1984
IRRECONCILABLE DIFFERENCES(1984)
Eda Kaminsky
VILNA LEGEND, A(1949, U.S./Pol.)
Howard Kaminsky
HOMEBODIES(1974), w
Mike Kaminsky
NORSEMAN, THE(1978)
Stuart Kaminsky
1984
ONCE UPON A TIME IN AMERICA(1984), w
Ahmed Kamis
GLASS SPHINX, THE(1968, Egypt/Ital./Span.)
Shigeru Kamiyama
ZATOICHI MEETS YOJIMBO(1970, Jap.)
Sojin Kamiyama
SAMURAI(1955, Jap.); SEVEN SAMURAI, THE(1956, Jap.)
Silents
BAT, THE(1926)
Gordon Kamka
POLYESTER(1981)
Piotr Kamler
CHRONOPOLIS(1982, Fr.), p,d,w,ph,&prod d, anim
Hickey Kamm
GIRL RUSH, THE(1955)
Franz Kammauf
MONEY ON THE STREET(1930, Aust.)
Klaus Kammer
COURT MARTIAL(1962, Ger.)
Nancy-Elizabeth Kammer
LIANNA(1983)
Siegbert Kammerer
SLAVERS(1977, Ger.), cos
Kyoko Kamo
NAVY WIFE(1956)
Matsukichi Kamo
NAVY WIFE(1956)
Michiyo Kamo
NAVY WIFE(1956)
Kip Kamoi
WHITE HUNTRESS(1957, Brit.)
Samir Kamoun
CANNONBALL RUN, THE(1981)
Samir Kamour
MEGAFORCE(1982)
Irene Kamp
LOVE IN A GOLDFISH BOWL(1961), w; PARIS BLUES(1961), w; LION, THE(1962, Brit.), w; SANDPIPER, THE(1965), w; MR. QUILP(1975, Brit.), w
Louis Kamp
LION, THE(1962, Brit.), w; SANDPIPER, THE(1965), w; MR. QUILP(1975, Brit.), w
Paul Kamp
Silents
BIG TOWN IDEAS(1921); GET YOUR MAN(1921)
Misc. Silents
TOMBOY, THE(1921)
Gustav Kampendonk
FREDDY UNTER FREMDEN STERNEN(1962, Ger.), w
Fritz Kampers
CASE VAN GELDERN(1932, Ger.)
Misc. Silents
STONE RIDER, THE(1923, Ger.); BERLIN AFTER DARK(1929, Ger.)
V. Fritz Kampers
MANULESCU(1933, Ger.)
Rudolf Kampf
LAST CHANCE, THE(1945, Switz.)
Peter Kamph
CIRCLE OF DECEIT(1982, Fr./Ger.)
Ralph Kamplen
BOBBIKINS(1959, Brit.), ed; ROMAN SPRING OF MRS. STONE, THE(1961, U.S./Brit.), ed
Steve Kampmann
TOWING(1978)
Judith Kaham Kampmann
TWICE UPON A TIME(1983)
Winnetou Kampmann
MALOU(1983)
Tony Kamreither
CHANGE OF MIND(1969)
V. Kamskiy
DUEL, THE(1964, USSR), art d; WELCOME KOSTYA!(1965, USSR), art d
Kamtong
YANK IN INDO-CHINA, A(1952)
Richie Kamuca
KINGS GO FORTH(1958)
Shunshin Kan
TATTOO(1981)
Akika Kana
ONIMASA(1983, Jap.)

Henry Kana
1984
LAST NIGHT AT THE ALAMO(1984)
Yoshinori Kanada
1984
WARRIORS OF THE WIND(1984, Jap.), anim
Mary Kanae
ROAD TO BALI(1952)
Cara Kanak
HONEYSUCKLE ROSE(1980)
Anna Kanakis
NEW BARBARIANS, THE(1983, Ital.)
1984
AFTER THE FALL OF NEW YORK(1984, Ital./Fr.); WARRIORS OF THE WASTE-
LAND(1984, Ital.)
Toni Kanal
LONG DUEL, THE(1967, Brit.)
Siv Kanalv
PASSION OF ANNA, THE(1970, Swed.), ed; RITUAL, THE(1970, Swed.), ed
Siv Kanalv-Lundgren
TOUCH, THE(1971, U.S./Swed.), ed
Steve Kanaly
LIFE AND TIMES OF JUDGE ROY BEAN, THE(1972); DILLINGER(1973); ACT OF
VENGEANCE(1974); MY NAME IS NOBODY(1974, Ital./Fr./Ger.); SUGARLAND
EXPRESS, THE(1974); TERMINAL MAN, THE(1974); WIND AND THE LION,
THE(1975); MIDWAY(1976)
1984
FLESHBURN(1984)
Ross Kananga
LIVE AND LET DIE(1973, Brit.), stunts
Ross Kananza
Misc. Talkies
DEVIL RIDER(1971)
Kiri Te Kanawa
DON GIOVANNI(1979, Fr./Ital./Ger.)
Richard Kanayan
SHOOT THE PIANO PLAYER(1962, Fr.)
A. Kanayeva
DREAM OF A COSSACK(1982, USSR)
K. Kanayeva
BRIDE WITH A DOWRY(1954, USSR)
Nancy Kandal
Misc. Talkies
HEROWORK(1977)
Asmat Kandaurishvili
STEPCHILDREN(1962, USSR)
Aben Kandel
HIGH PRESSURE(1932), w; SING AND LIKE IT(1934), w; MANHATTAN
MOON(1935), w; SHE GETS HER MAN(1935), w; COME CLOSER, FOLKS(1936), w;
HOT MONEY(1936), w; MORE THAN A SECRETARY(1936), w; THEY WON'T FOR-
GET(1937), w; THUNDER IN THE CITY(1937, Brit.), w; RIO(1939), w; CITY, FOR
CONQUEST(1941), w; IRON MAJOR, THE(1943), w; THREE RUSSIAN GIRLS(1943),
w; WHAT'S BUZZIN COUSIN?(1943), w; BIG CITY(1948), w; FIGHTER, THE(1952),
w; KID MONK BARONI(1952), w; SINGING IN THE DARK(1956), w; TIMETA-
BLE(1956), w; HORRORS OF THE BLACK MUSEUM(1959, U.S./Brit.), w; KON-
GA(1961, Brit.), w; BERSERK(1967), w; TROG(1970, Brit.), w; CRAZE(1974, Brit.), w
Stephen Kandel
MAGNIFICENT ROUGHNECKS(1956), w; SINGING IN THE DARK(1956), w;
FRONTIER GUN(1958), w; BATTLE OF THE CORAL SEA(1959), w; CHAMBER OF
HORRORS(1966), w; CANNON FOR CORDOBA(1970), w
Vladimir Kandell
Z.P.G.(1972)
John Kander
SOMETHING FOR EVERYONE(1970), m; STILL OF THE NIGHT(1982), m; BLUE
SKIES AGAIN(1983), m
1984
PLACES IN THE HEART(1984), m
Milos Kandic
HOROSCOPE(1950, Yugo.)
Sheila Kandlbinder
WHY WOULD I LIE(1980)
Vera Kandy
FORTY THOUSAND HORSEMEN(1941, Aus.)
Alex Kandyba
WE LIVE AGAIN(1934)
Alan Kane
UP WITH THE LARK(1943, Brit.); NUREMBERG(1961), p
Alice J. Kane
UNMARRIED WOMAN, AN(1978)
Arite Kane
EYES OF LAURA MARS(1978), m
Arthur S. Kane
Silents
REAL ADVENTURE, THE(1922), p
Artie Kane
BAT PEOPLE, THE(1974), m; LOOKING FOR MR. GOODBAR(1977), m; NIGHT OF
THE JUGGLER(1980), m; WRONG IS RIGHT(1982), m
Babe Kane
SLIGHTLY HONORABLE(1940)
Beatrice Kane
DICK BARTON–SPECIAL AGENT(1948, Brit.); DICK BARTON AT BAY(1950, Brit.);
FAKE, THE(1953, Brit.)
Bill Kane
MORO WITCH DOCTOR(1964, U.S./Phil.)
Bradley Kane
1984
FLAMINGO KID, THE(1984)

Byron Kane
LADY FROM SHANGHAI, THE(1948); WITHOUT WARNING(1952); BIG HEAT,
THE(1953); EASY TO LOVE(1953); GOG(1954); JOHNNY DARK(1954); MA AND PA
KETTLE AT WAIKIKI(1955); RACK, THE(1956); TEA AND SYMPATHY(1956); MON-
STER THAT CHALLENGED THE WORLD, THE(1957); FOR THOSE WHO THINK
YOUNG(1964); PATSY, THE(1964); LADY SINGS THE BLUES(1972); PINK PANTHER
STRIKES AGAIN, THE(1976, Brit.); S.O.B.(1981)
Candy Kane
MR. PATMAN(1980, Can.)
Carol Kane
CARNAL KNOWLEDGE(1971); DESPERATE CHARACTERS(1971); WEDDING IN
WHITE(1972, Can.); LAST DETAIL, THE(1973); DOG DAY AFTERNOON(1975);
HESTER STREET(1975); HARRY AND WALTER GO TO NEW YORK(1976); ANNIE
HALL(1977); VALENTINO(1977, Brit.); WORLD'S GREATEST LOVER, THE(1977);
MAFU CAGE, THE(1978); MUPPET MOVIE, THE(1979); SABINA, THE(1979, Span./
Swed.); WHEN A STRANGER CALLS(1979); NORMAN LOVES ROSE(1982, Aus.);
PANDEMONIUM(1982)
1984
OVER THE BROOKLYN BRIDGE(1984); RACING WITH THE MOON(1984); SECRET
DIARY OF SIGMUND FREUD, THE(1984)
Misc. Talkies
BLOOD OF THE IRON MAIDEN(1969); KEEPING ON(1981)
Carole Kane
IS THIS TRIP REALLY NECESSARY?(1970)
Dennis Kane
FRENCH QUARTER(1978), p&d, w
Diana Kane
Silents
MISS BLUEBEARD(1925); NEW COMMANDMENT, THE(1925); BLUEBEARD'S
SEVEN WIVES(1926)
Misc. Silents
BROWN DERBY, THE(1926); PERFECT SAP, THE(1927)
Ed Kane
COHENS AND KELLYS IN AFRICA, THE(1930); CASTLE ON THE HUDSON(1940);
MEET JOHN DOE(1941); SING ANOTHER CHORUS(1941); ZIS BOOM BAH(1941)
Eddie Kane
ILLUSION(1929); KIBITZER, THE(1929); STREET GIRL(1929); TIMES SQUA-
RE(1929); WHY BRING THAT UP?(1929); DOORWAY TO HELL(1930); FRA-
MED(1930); LET'S GO PLACES(1930); PUTTIN' ON THE RITZ(1930); SQUEALER,
THE(1930); EX-BAD BOY(1931); GOLDIE(1931); PUBLIC ENEMY, THE(1931); SMART
MONEY(1931); JEWEL ROBBERY(1932); MUMMY, THE(1932); ONCE IN A LIFE-
TIME(1932); WESTERN LIMITED(1932); BACHELOR MOTHER(1933); DON'T BET
ON LOVE(1933); SECRET SINNERS(1933); THRILL HUNTER, THE(1933); BORN TO
BE BAD(1934); DAMES(1934); HUMAN SIDE, THE(1934); IT HAPPENED ONE
NIGHT(1934); TWENTY MILLION SWEETHEARTS(1934); WONDER BAR(1934);
HOORAY FOR LOVE(1935); MILLION DOLLAR BABY(1935); OLD HOMESTEAD,
THE(1935); SWEET MUSIC(1935); TWO FOR TONIGHT(1935); LOVE ON A BET(1936);
SMALL TOWN GIRL(1936); TWO IN A CROWD(1936); ALL OVER TOWN(1937);
MANHATTAN MERRY-GO-ROUND(1937); MELODY FOR TWO(1937); PICK A
STAR(1937); SMALL TOWN BOY(1937); SOMETHING TO SING ABOUT(1937); STAR
IS BORN, A(1937); TIME OUT FOR ROMANCE(1937); WESTLAND CASE, THE(1937);
GIVE ME A SAILOR(1938); GLADIATOR, THE(1938); HOLLYWOOD ROUN-
DUP(1938); MR. BOGGS STEPS OUT(1938); SWISS MISS(1938); THREE LOVES HAS
NANCY(1938); YOU CAN'T TAKE IT WITH YOU(1938); ICE FOLLIES OF 1939(1939);
MISSING DAUGHTERS(1939); MR. SMITH GOES TO WASHINGTON(1939); ROVIN'
TUMBLEWEEDS(1939); STAR REPORTER(1939); SWEEPSTAKES WINNER(1939);
MUSIC IN MY HEART(1940); CONFESSIONS OF BOSTON BLACKIE(1941); DUDE
COWBOY(1941); GREAT AMERICAN BROADCAST, THE(1941); LAS VEGAS
NIGHTS(1941); SIGN OF THE WOLF(1941); TWO LATINS FROM MANHAT-
TAN(1941); COLLEGE SWEETHEARTS(1942); LUCKY LEGS(1942); MAN'S WORLD,
A(1942); TRAMP, TRAMP, TRAMP(1942); FLESH AND FANTASY(1943); IS EVERY-
BODY HAPPY?(1943); LAUGH YOUR BLUES AWAY(1943); MISSION TO MOS-
COW(1943); PASSPORT TO SUEZ(1943); REVEILLE WITH BEVERLY(1943);
SECRETS OF THE UNDERGROUND(1943); SHE HAS WHAT IT TAKES(1943); DARK
MOUNTAIN(1944); JAM SESSION(1944); LAKE PLACID SERENADE(1944);
LOUISIANA HAYRIDE(1944); MINSTREL MAN(1944); TWO GIRLS AND A SAI-
LOR(1944); UP IN ARMS(1944); DANCING IN MANHATTAN(1945); MAN FROM
OKLAHOMA, THE(1945); SWING OUT, SISTER(1945); WONDER MAN(1945); DEAD-
LINE FOR MURDER(1946); DEVIL BAT'S DAUGHTER, THE(1946); JOLSON STORY,
THE(1946); NIGHT AND DAY(1946); MY WILD IRISH ROSE(1947); MEXICAN
HAYRIDE(1948)
Edward Kane
COUNTY FAIR, THE(1932); FORGOTTEN WOMEN(1932); LOVE IS A RACK-
ET(1932); MIDNIGHT PATROL, THE(1932); GAMBLING LADY(1934); TAKE THE
STAND(1934); TWO HEADS ON A PILLOW(1934); CURTAIN FALLS, THE(1935);
SCHOOL FOR GIRLS(1935); MORTAL STORM, THE(1940), m; DOUBLE TROU-
BLE(1941); SUN VALLEY SERENADE(1941)
Frank Kane
KEY WITNESS(1960), w
Frank Gruber Kane
IN OLD SACRAMENTO(1946), w
Fred W. Kane
ENEMY OF WOMEN(1944), p
Gail Kane
Silents
WISE HUSBANDS(; DAN(1914); JUNGLE, THE(1914); MEN SHE MARRIED,
THE(1916); BRIDE'S SILENCE, THE(1917); FALSE FRIEND, THE(1917); IDLE
HANDS(1921); WHITE SISTER, THE(1923); CONVOY(1927)
Misc. Silents
ARIZONA(1913); HER GREAT MATCH(1915); LABYRINTH, THE(1915); PIT,
THE(1915); VIA WIRELESS(1915); HEART OF A HERO(1916); PAYING THE
PRICE(1916); SCARLET OATH, THE(1916); VELVET PAW, THE(1916); AS MAN
MADE HER(1917); GAME OF WITS, A(1917); ON DANGEROUS GROUND(1917); RED
WOMAN, THE(1917); SERPENT'S TOOTH, THE(1917); SOULS IN PAWN(1917);
SOUTHERN PRIDE(1917); UPPER CRUST, THE(1917); WHOSE WIFE?(1917);
DAREDEVIL, THE(1918); LOVE'S LAW(1918); SOMEONE MUST PAY(1919); EMPTY
ARMS(1920); IDLE HANDS(1920)

Gasil Kane
Misc. Silents
GREAT DIAMOND ROBBERY, THE(1914)
George Kane
LONE STAR RANGER(1942), w
Hanry Kane
COP HATER(1958), w
Helen Kane
GREAT GABBO, THE(1929); NOTHING BUT THE TRUTH(1929); SWEETIE(1929); DANGEROUS NAN McGREW(1930); HEADS UP(1930); POINTED HEELS(1930); THREE LITTLE WORDS(1950)
Henry Kane
MUGGER, THE(1958), w
Irene Kane
KILLER'S KISS(1955)
J. I. Kane
Silents
BUCKING THE TRUTH(1926), w
J. K. Kane
CEILNG ZERO(1935)
Jack Kane
Misc. Silents
VIRTUOUS VAMP, A(1919); WILD, WILD SUSAN(1925)
Jackson Kane
SHOWDOWN(1973)
Jackson D. Kane
THOMASINE AND BUSHROD(1974); MAN WHO FELL TO EARTH, THE(1976, Brit.)
Janice Kane
23 PACES TO BAKER STREET(1956)
Jason Kane
GUMSHOE(1972, Brit.)
Jayson William Kane
SKYJACKED(1972)
Jeremy Kane
PROUD RIDER, THE(1971, Can.)
Jim Kane
JULIA(1977)
Jimmy Kane
CHALLENGE TO BE FREE(1976)
Misc. Talkies
BEYOND THE LAW(1930)
Misc. Silents
MYSTERY VALLEY(1928)
Joe Kane
HER MAN(1930), ed; SUICIDE FLEET(1931), ed, md; SWEEPSTAKES(1931), ed; PRESTIGE(1932), ed; ARSON GANG BUSTERS(1938), d; BORN TO BE WILD(1938), d; HELL'S OUTPOST(1955), d; MAVERICK QUEEN, THE(1956), d; GUNFIRE AT INDIAN GAP(1957), d; LAST STAGECOACH WEST, THE(1957), d; LAWLESS EIGHTIES, THE(1957), d; SPOILERS OF THE FOREST(1957), d; CROOKED CIRCLE, THE(1958), d; MAN WHO DIED TWICE, THE(1958), d; NOTORIOUS MR. MONKS, THE(1958), d; COUNTRY BOY(1966), a, d; TRACK OF THUNDER(1967), d
Misc. Talkies
ARSON RACKET SQUAD(1938), d
Joel Kane
TIN STAR, THE(1957), w
Inspector John Kane, San Francisco Police Department
LINEUP, THE(1958), tech adv
Johnny Kane
MAN WITH MY FACE, THE(1951)
Joseph Kane
OVERLAND BOUND(1929), w; BIG MONEY(1930), ed; NIGHT WORK(1930), ed; BIG GAMBLE, THE(1931), ed; LONELY WIVES(1931), ed; IS MY FACE RED?(1932), ed; YOUNG BRIDE(1932), ed; SONG OF THE EAGLE(1933), ed; STRICTLY PERSONAL(1933), ed; NO MORE WOMEN(1934), ed; LITTLE MEN(1935), ed; MC FADDEN'S FLATS(1935), ed; MELODY TRAIL(1935), d; SAGEBRUSH TROUBADOR(1935), d; TUMBLING TUMBLEWEEDS(1935), d; DARKEST AFRICA(1936), d; GUNS AND GUITARS(1936), d; KING OF THE PECOS(1936), d; LAWLESS NINETIES, THE(1936), d; LONELY TRAIL, THE(1936), d; RIDE, RANGER, RIDE(1936), d; COME ON, COWBOYS(1937), d; GHOST TOWN GOLD(1937), d; GIT ALONG, LITTLE DOGIES(1937), d; GUNSMOKE RANCH(1937), d; HEART OF THE ROCKIES(1937), d; OH, SUSANNA(1937), d; OLD CORRAL, THE(1937), d; PARADISE EXPRESS(1937), d; PUBLIC COWBOY NO. 1(1937), d; ROUNDUP TIME IN TEXAS(1937), d; SPRINGTIME IN THE ROCKIES(1937), d; YODELIN' KID FROM PINE RIDGE(1937), d; BILLY THE KID RETURNS(1938), d; GOLD MINE IN THE SKY(1938), d; MAN FROM MUSIC MOUNTAIN(1938), d; OLD BARN DANCE, THE(1938), d; SHINE ON, HARVEST MOON(1938), d; UNDER WESTERN STARS(1938), d; ARIZONA KID, THE(1939), p&d; COME ON RANGERS(1939), d; DAYS OF JESSE JAMES(1939), p&d; FRONTIER PONY EXPRESS(1939), p&d; IN OLD CALIENTE(1939), p&d; IN OLD MONTEREY(1939), d; ROUGH RIDERS' ROUNDUP(1939), p&d; SAGA OF DEATH VALLEY(1939), p&d; SOUTHWARD HO!(1939), p&d; WALL STREET COWBOY(1939), p&d; BORDER LEGION, THE(1940), p&d; CARSON CITY KID(1940), p&d, w; COLORADO(1940), p&d; RANGER AND THE LADY, THE(1940), p&d; YOUNG BILL HICKOK(1940), p&d; YOUNG BUFFALO BILL(1940), p&d; BAD MAN OF DEADWOOD(1941), p&d; GREAT TRAIN ROBBERY, THE(1941), p&d; IN OLD CHEYENNE(1941), p&d; JESSE JAMES AT BAY(1941), p&d; NEVADA CITY(1941), p&d; RAGS TO RICHES(1941), p&d; RED RIVER VALLEY(1941), p&d; ROBIN HOOD OF THE PECOS(1941), p&d; SHERIFF OF TOMBSTONE(1941), p&d; HEART OF THE GOLDEN WEST(1942), p&d; MAN FROM CHEYENNE(1942), p&d; RIDIN' DOWN THE CANYON(1942), p&d; SONS OF THE PIONEERS(1942), p&d; SOUTH OF SANTA FE(1942), p&d; SUNSET ON THE DESERT(1942), p&d; SUNSET SERENADE(1942), p&d; HANDS ACROSS THE BORDER(1943), d; IDAHO(1943), p&d; KING OF THE COWBOYS(1943), d; MAN FROM MUSIC MOUNTAIN(1943), d; SILVER SPURS(1943), d; SONG OF TEXAS(1943), d; COWBOY AND THE SENORITA(1944), d; SONG OF NEVADA(1944), d; YELLOW ROSE OF TEXAS, THE(1944), d; CHEATERS, THE(1945), p&d; DAKOTA(1945), p&d; FLAME OF THE BARBARY COAST(1945), p&d; IN OLD SACRAMENTO(1946), p&d; PLAINSMAN AND THE LADY(1946), p&d; WYOMING(1947), p&d; GALLANT LEGION, THE(1948), p&d; OLD LOS ANGELES(1948), p&d; PLUNDERERS, THE(1948), p&d; BRIMSTONE(1949), p&d; LAST BANDIT, THE(1949), p&d; CALIFORNIA PASSAGE(1950), p&d; ROCK ISLAND TRAIL(1950), d; SAVAGE HORDE, THE(1950), p&d; FIGHTING

COAST GUARD(1951), p&d; OH! SUSANNA(1951), p&d; SEA HORNET, THE(1951), p&d; HOODLUM EMPIRE(1952), d; RIDE THE MAN DOWN(1952), p&d; WOMAN OF THE NORTH COUNTRY(1952), p&d; FAIR WIND TO JAVA(1953), p&d; SAN ANTONE(1953), p&d; SEA OF LOST SHIPS(1953), p&d; ROAD TO DENVER, THE(1955), d; TIMBERJACK(1955), d; VANISHING AMERICAN, THE(1955), d; ACCUSED OF MURDER(1956), p&d; THUNDER OVER ARIZONA(1956), p&d; DUEL AT APACHE WELLS(1957), p&d; SMOKE IN THE WIND(1975), d
Misc. Talkies
IN OLD LOS ANGELES(1948), d; SEARCH FOR THE EVIL ONE(1967), d
Joseph Inman Kane
JUBILEE TRAIL(1954), d
Joseph P. Kane
ROMANCE ON THE RANGE(1942), p&d
Katherine "Sugar" Kane
LOVE ON TOAST(1937)
Kathryn Kane
SWING, SISTER, SWING(1938); SPIRIT OF CULVER, THE(1939); THAT HAGEN GIRL(1947)
Kristi Kane
SKATETOWN, U.S.A.(1979)
Lida Kane
FOLLOW THE LEADER(1930)
Linda Kane
HOTHEAD(1963)
Lionel Kane
BEST OF EVERYTHING, THE(1959)
Lou Kane
PUBLIC AFFAIR, A(1962); MAD ROOM, THE(1969); WHAT EVER HAPPENED TO AUNT ALICE?(1969)
Louise Kane
WYOMING(1947); HE WALKED BY NIGHT(1948); EMERGENCY WEDDING(1950); OH! SUSANNA(1951)
M.J. Kane
SWINGING BARMAIDS, THE(1976)
Margo Kane
RUNNING BRAVE(1983, Can.)
Marjorie Kane
BORDER ROMANCE(1930); GREAT DIVIDE, THE(1930); LADIES IN LOVE(1930); MERRILY WE LIVE(1938); MAN FROM FRISCO(1944); MILDRED PIERCE(1945)
Marjorie "Babe" Kane
BE YOURSELF(1930); NIGHT WORK(1930); SUNNY SKIES(1930); SWEETHEARTS(1938); LITTLE ACCIDENT(1939); DESIGN FOR SCANDAL(1941); GIRL TROUBLE(1942); SLIGHTLY DANGEROUS(1943)
Marvin Kane
PRIZE OF GOLD, A(1955); PORTRAIT IN SMOKE(1957, Brit.)
Mary Kane
Misc. Silents
MARY OF THE MOVIES(1923)
Michael Kane
SUCCESSFUL FAILURE, A(1934), w; LONELY ARE THE BRAVE(1962); BEDFORD INCIDENT, THE(1965, Brit.); PROMISE HER ANYTHING(1966, Brit.); LOVE IN A FOUR LETTER WORLD(1970, Can.); THREE DAYS OF THE CONDOR(1975); HOT STUFF(1979), w; KIDNAPPING OF THE PRESIDENT, THE(1980, Can.); MIDDLE AGE CRAZY(1980, Can.); SMOKEY AND THE BANDIT II(1980), w; XANADU(1980), w; HARD COUNTRY(1981), w; LEGEND OF THE LONE RANGER, THE(1981), w; SOUTHERN COMFORT(1981), w; ALL THE RIGHT MOVES(1983), w; CROSS COUNTRY(1983, Can.)
1984
BEAR, THE(1984), w; UTU(1984, New Zealand), cos
Mike Kane
FOOLIN' AROUND(1980), w
Pat Kane
FATHER WAS A FULLBACK(1949)
Patsy Kane
HOLLYWOOD HOTEL(1937)
Patsy "Babe" Kane
SINGING MARINE, THE(1937)
Patti Kane
GIDGET(1959)
"Red" Kane
"IMP"PROBABLE MR. WEE GEE, THE(1966)
Richard Kane
1984
GIVE MY REGARDS TO BROAD STREET(1984, Brit.)
Robert Kane
SYNCOPATION(1929), p; HE WALKED BY NIGHT(1948), p
Robert G. Kane
KISSES FOR MY PRESIDENT(1964), w; VILLAIN, THE(1979), w
Robert T. Kane
MOTHER'S BOY(1929), p; DARING YOUNG MAN, THE(1935), p; DRESSED TO THRILL(1935), p; ORCHIDS TO YOU(1935), p; SPRING TONIC(1935), p; UNDER PRESSURE(1935), p; DINNER AT THE RITZ(1937, Brit.), p; UNDER THE RED ROBE(1937, Brit.), p; WINGS OF THE MORNING(1937, Brit.), p; SMILING ALONG(1938, Brit.), p; INSPECTOR HORNLEIGH(1939, Brit.), p; SHIPYARD SALLY(1940, Brit.), p; SO THIS IS LONDON(1940, Brit.), p; VERY YOUNG LADY, A(1941), p; GREEN COCKATOO, THE(1947, Brit.), p
Sandra Kane
MUTINY ON THE BLACKHAWK(1939); TEENAGE GANG DEBS(1966)
Sandy Lee Kane
STING OF DEATH(1966)
Shirley Kane
FOOLIN' AROUND(1980)
Sid Kane
TRAPPED(1949); YOUNG MAN WITH A HORN(1950); NORTH BY NORTHWEST(1959); TWELVE HOURS TO KILL(1960); FRONTIER UPRISING(1961); INVASION OF THE STAR CREATURES(1962)
Sugar Kane
SUNSET MURDER CASE(1941)

Teri Kane
1984
OLD ENOUGH(1984), cos
Vincent Kane
MOUSE AND THE WOMAN, THE(1981, Brit.), w
Walter Kane
NIGHT PARADE(1929, Brit.)
Whitford Kane
HIDE-OUT(1934); GHOST AND MRS. MUIR, THE(1942); ADVENTURES OF MARK TWAIN, THE(1944); MY DOG RUSTY(1948); WALLS OF JERICHO(1948); WHO KILLED "DOC" ROBBIN?(1948); JUDGE STEPS OUT, THE(1949)
Ryunosuke Kaneda
MERRY CHRISTMAS MR. LAWRENCE(1983, Jap./Brit.)
Toshio Kaneda
TIME SLIP(1981, Jap.), w
Antonia Kaneem
TORCH, THE(1950)
Ginny Kaneen
LIVE A LITTLE, LOVE A LITTLE(1968)
Victor Kanefsky
GANJA AND HESS(1973), ed; NIGHT OF THE ZOMBIES(1981), ed; BLOODSUCK- ING FREAKS(1982), ed
Kazue Kaneko
MY GEISHA(1962)
Masakatsu Kaneko
EARLY AUTUMN(1962, Jap.), p; SCHOOL FOR SEX(1966, Jap.), p; THIN LINE, THE(1967, Jap.), p; TWO IN THE SHADOW(1968, Jap.), p
Miyoshi Kaneko
FIGHT FOR THE GLORY(1970, Jap.)
Nobuo Kaneko
IKIRU(1960, Jap.); SOLDIER'S PRAYER, A(1970, Jap.)
Seitan Kaneko
WALL-EYED NIPPON(1963, Jap.), p
Yuki Kaneko
STOPOVER TOKYO(1957)
Yuso Kaneko
GAMERA VERSUS VIRAS(1968, Jap), spec eff
Yuzo Kaneko
GAMERA VERSUS GAOS(1967, Jap.), spec eff
Ruth Kaner
BLAST OF SILENCE(1961)
Jeff Kanew
WICKED DIE SLOW, THE(1968), a, w; BLACK RODEO(1972), p,d&ed; NATURAL ENEMIES(1979), d&w, ed; ORDINARY PEOPLE(1980), ed; EDDIE MACON'S RUN(1983), d&w, ed
1984
REVENGE OF THE NERDS(1984), d
Hsuing Kang
FLYING GUILLOTINE, THE(1975, Chi.)
Moon Kang
YONGKARI MONSTER FROM THE DEEP(1967 S.K.)
John Kangan
BRITISH INTELLIGENCE(1940), w
Said Kangarani
CYCLE, THE(1979, Iran)
John Kani
WILD GEESE, THE(1978, Brit.); MARIGOLDS IN AUGUST(1980, South Africa); GRASS IS SINGING, THE(1982, Brit./Swed.)
1984
KILLING HEAT(1984); MARIGOLDS IN AUGUST(1984, S. Africa)
Cynthia Kania
TABLE FOR FIVE(1983)
Keizo Kanie
MUDDY RIVER(1982, Jap.)
Marek Kanievska
1984
ANOTHER COUNTRY(1984, Brit.), d
Maria Kaniewska
EVE WANTS TO SLEEP(1961, Pol.)
Fay Kanin
BLONDIE FOR VICTORY(1942), w; SUNDAY PUNCH(1942), w; DOUBLE LIFE, A(1947), w; GOODBYE, MY FANCY(1951), w; MY PAL GUS(1952), w; RHAPSODY(1954), w; OPPOSITE SEX, THE(1956), w; TEACHER'S PET(1958), w; RIGHT APPROACH, THE(1961), w; SWORDSMAN OF SIENA, THE(1962, Fr./Ital.), w; OUTRAGE, THE(1964), w; RICH AND FAMOUS(1981)
Garson Kanin
MAN TO REMEMBER, A(1938), d; NEXT TIME I MARRY(1938), d; BACHELOR MOTHER(1939), d; GREAT MAN VOTES, THE(1939), d; MY FAVORITE WIFE(1940), d; THEY KNEW WHAT THEY WANTED(1940), d; TOM, DICK AND HARRY(1941), d; LADY TAKES A CHANCE, A(1943), w; MORE THE MERRIER, THE(1943), w; FROM THIS DAY FORWARD(1946), w; DOUBLE LIFE, A(1947), w; ADAM'S RIB(1949), w; BORN YESTERDAY(1951), w; MARRYING KIND, THE(1952), w; PAT AND MI- KE(1952), w; IT SHOULD HAPPEN TO YOU(1954), w; HIGH TIME(1960), w; RAT RACE, THE(1960), w; RIGHT APPROACH, THE(1961), w; SOME KIND OF A NUT(1969), d&w; WHERE IT'S AT(1969), d&w
Gary Kanin
SECOND THOUGHTS(1983)
Michael Kanin
PANAMA LADY(1939), w; THEY MADE HER A SPY(1939), w; ANNE OF WINDY POPLARS(1940), w; SUNDAY PUNCH(1942), w; WOMAN OF THE YEAR(1942), w; CROSS OF LORRAINE, THE(1943), w; CENTENNIAL SUMMER(1946), w; DOUBLE LIFE, A(1947), p; HONEYMOON(1947), w; WHEN I GROW UP(1951), d&w; MY PAL GUS(1952), w; RHAPSODY(1954), w; OPPOSITE SEX, THE(1956), w; TEACHER'S PET(1958), w; RIGHT APPROACH, THE(1961), w; SWORDSMAN OF SIENA, THE(1962, Fr./Ital.), w; OUTRAGE, THE(1964), w, w; HOW TO COMMIT MAR- RIAGE(1969), w
Taaichi Kankura
YOG-MONSTER FROM SPACE(1970, Jap.), ph

Taiichi Kankura
WALL-EYED NIPPON(1963, Jap.), ph; NIGHT IN BANGKOK(1966, Jap.), ph; THREE DOLLS FROM HONG KONG(1966, Jap.), ph; DESTROY ALL MON- STERS(1969, Jap.), ph; LATITUDE ZERO(1969, U.S./Jap.), ph; SPACE AMOEBA, THE(1970, Jap.), ph
A. Kanmeyer
Silents
TARGET, THE(1916)
George E. Kann
ROSE OF THE RIO GRANDE(1938), p
Lillie Kann
I WAS A MALE WAR BRIDE(1949)
Lilly Kann
ESCAPE TO DANGER(1943, Brit.); WOMAN TO WOMAN(1946, Brit.); FLESH AND BLOOD(1951, Brit.); BETRAYED(1954); EIGHT O'CLOCK WALK(1954, Brit.); WHIRL- POOL(1959, Brit.); LONG SHADOW, THE(1961, Brit.); NO TREE IN THE STREET(1964, Brit.)
Lily Kann
FRENZY(1946, Brit.); BAD SISTER(1947, Brit.); WOMAN IN THE HALL, THE(1949, Brit.); CLOUDED YELLOW, THE(1950, Brit.); MRS. FITZHERBERT(1950, Brit.); BACKGROUND(1953, Brit.); TWICE UPON A TIME(1953, Brit.); KID FOR TWO FARTHINGS, A(1956, Brit.)
Gretchen Kanne
PSYCHOPATH, THE(1973)
Misc. Talkies
EYE FOR AN EYE, AN(1975)
Phil Kanneally
DEADHEAD MILES(1982)
Alexis Kanner
REACH FOR GLORY(1963, Brit.); CROSSPLOT(1969, Brit.); GOODBYE GEMI- NI(1970, Brit.); CONNECTING ROOMS(1971, Brit.)
1984
KINGS AND DESPERATE MEN(1984, Brit.), a, p&d w
Jackie Kannon
DIARY OF A BACHELOR(1964)
Jim Kannon
GETAWAY, THE(1972)
Mike Kannon
WILD GUITAR(1962); RAT PFINK AND BOO BOO(1966)
John Kannowin
YELLOW CANARY, THE(1944, Brit.)
Junko Kano
ODD OBSESSION(1961, Jap.); BUDDHA(1965, Jap.); GREAT WALL, THE(1965, Jap.)
Takeshi Kano
HAPPINESS OF US ALONE(1962, Jap.), art d
Ryohei Kanokogi
GOODBYE GIRL, THE(1977)
Ryokei Kanokogi
NEXT MAN, THE(1976)
Lyle Kanouse
MY TUTOR(1983)
Enrico Kant
Silents
NERO(1922, U.S./Ital.)
Aram Kantarian
NIGHT TIDE(1963), p
Vicki Kantenwine
MERMAIDS OF TIBURON, THE(1962)
Bob Kanter
TWO AND TWO MAKE SIX(1962, Brit.); WAR LOVER, THE(1962, U.S./Brit.); THIN RED LINE, THE(1964); WINTER A GO-GO(1965), a, w
Hal Kanter
MY FAVORITE SPY(1951), w; TWO TICKETS TO BROADWAY(1951), w; ROAD TO BALI(1952), w; HERE COME THE GIRLS(1953), w; MONEY FROM HOME(1953), w; OFF LIMITS(1953), w; ABOUT MRS. LESLIE(1954), w; CASANOVA'S BIG NIGHT(1954), w; ARTISTS AND MODELS(1955), w; ROSE TATTOO, THE(1955), w; LOVING YOU(1957), d, w; I MARRIED A WOMAN(1958), d; MARDI GRAS(1958), w; ONCE UPON A HORSE(1958), p,d&w; LET'S MAKE LOVE(1960), w; BACHELOR IN PARADISE(1961), w; BLUE HAWAII(1961), w; POCKETFUL OF MIRACLES(1961), w; MOVE OVER, DARLING(1963), w; DEAR BRIGETTE(1965), w
Igo Kanter
KINGDOM OF THE SPIDERS(1977), p
Jay Kanter
VILLAIN(1971, Brit.), p; X Y & ZEE(1972, Brit.), p; FEAR IS THE KEY(1973), p
Joseph Kanter
STUDENT BODY, THE(1976)
Marianne Kanter
PAWNBROKER, THE(1965); HALLUCINATION GENERATION(1966); DEVIL'S AN- GELS(1967)
Marin Kanter
ENDANGERED SPECIES(1982); LADIES AND GENTLEMEN, THE FABULOUS STAINS(1982); LOVELESS, THE(1982)
Richard Kanter
WILD RIDERS(1971), d&w
Misc. Talkies
AFFAIRS OF ROBIN HOOD, THE(1981), d
Rick Kanter
WILD PARTY, THE(1975)
Nancy Kantner
LOVELESS, THE(1982), ed
Bernard R. Kantor
FRATERNITY ROW(1977)
Herman Kantor
STORY OF SEABISCUIT, THE(1949)
Igo Kantor
MOTOR PSYCHO(1965), m; BUBBLE, THE(1967), ed; GOOD MORNING... AND GOODBYE(1967), m; HILLBILLYS IN A HAUNTED HOUSE(1967), md; FINDERS KEEPERS, LOVERS WEEPERS(1968), m; PROJECTIONIST, THE(1970), m; JUD(1971), p; PICKUP ON 101(1972), md; SCORCHY(1976), m; KENTUCKY FRIED MOVIE, THE(1977), md; KINGDOM OF THE SPIDERS(1977), ed; HARDLY WORK-

ING(1981), p; KILL AND KILL AGAIN(1981), p; COMEBACK TRAIL, THE(1982), m
1984
NIGHT SHADOWS(1984), p

Igor Kantor
JAIL BAIT(1954), ed

Lenard Kantor
TIGHT SPOT(1955), w

Leonard Kantor
JAMBOREE(1957), w; HONEYBABY, HONEYBABY(1974), w

Lisa Deborah Kantor
JUD(1971)

Mackinlay Kantor
VOICE OF BUGLE ANN(1936), w; MOUNTAIN MUSIC(1937), w; MAN FROM DAKOTA, THE(1940), w; HAPPY LAND(1943), w; GENTLE ANNIE(1944), w; BEST YEARS OF OUR LIVES, THE(1946), w; ROMANCE OF ROSY RIDGE, THE(1947), w; HANNAH LEE(1953), w; WIND ACROSS THE EVERGLADES(1958)

MacKinley Kantor
FOLLOW ME, BOYS!(1966), w

Mark Kantor
INTERNS, THE(1962)

McKinlay Kantor
GUN CRAZY(1949), w

Norman Kantor
NINE MILES TO NOON(1963), p

Richard Kantor
BABY, IT'S YOU(1983)

Julius Kantorez
Silents
ADVENTUROUS YOUTH(1928, Brit.)

Ivar Kants
PLUMBER, THE(1980, Aus.)
1984
BROTHERS(1984, Aus.)

Otto Kanturek
FREEDOM OF THE SEAS(1934, Brit.), ph; MISTER CINDERS(1934, Brit.), ph; THOSE WERE THE DAYS(1934, Brit.), ph; ABDUL THE DAMNED(1935, Brit.), ph; CLOWN MUST LAUGH, A(1936, Brit.), ph; LOVE IN EXILE(1936, Brit.), ph; STUDENT'S ROMANCE, THE(1936, Brit.), d, ed; APRIL BLOSSOMS(1937, Brit.), ph; LET'S MAKE A NIGHT OF IT(1937, Brit.), ph; OVER SHE GOES(1937, Brit.), ph; PLEASE TEACHER(1937, Brit.), ph; HOLD MY HAND(1938, Brit.), ph; HOUSEMASTER(1938, Brit.), ph; PRISONER OF CORBAL(1939, Brit.), ph; NIGHT TRAIN(1940, Brit.), ph; ONE NIGHT IN PARIS(1940, Brit.), ph; SHIPYARD SALLY(1940, Brit.), ph; SO THIS IS LONDON(1940, Brit.), ph; GIRL IN THE NEWS, THE(1941, Brit.), ph; MISSING TEN DAYS(1941, Brit.), ph; PIRATES OF THE SEVEN SEAS(1941, Brit.), ph
Silents
WOMAN ON THE MOON, THE(1929, Ger.), ph

Ivar Kantz
DAWN(1979, Aus.)

Mitsuji Kanu
TUNNEL TO THE SUN(1968, Jap.), ph

Pocho Kanuha
KONA COAST(1968)

Red Kanuha
KONA COAST(1968)

Steve Kanyon
PEOPLE NEXT DOOR, THE(1970)

Gabor Kanz
ASSISTANT, THE(1982, Czech.)

Hideo Kanze
KUROENKO(1968, Jap); LOST SEX(1968, Jap.); SUMMER SOLDIERS(1972, Jap.)

Noelle Kao
HUSBANDS(1970)

Kaoudoune
OLIVE TREES OF JUSTICE, THE(1967, Fr.)

M. Cher Kaoui
LAWRENCE OF ARABIA(1962, Brit.)

Hussein Kaouk
CIRCLE OF DECEIT(1982, Fr./Ger.)

Amnon Kapeliouk
HANNAH K.(1983, Fr.)

Jeffrey Kapelman
SEIZURE(1974), p

John Kapelos
THIEF(1981); CLASS(1983); DOCTOR DETROIT(1983)
1984
SIXTEEN CANDLES(1984)

Broinslau Kaper
COMRADE X(1940), m; DULCY(1940), m; I TAKE THIS WOMAN(1940), m; WE WHO ARE YOUNG(1940), m; BLONDE INSPIRATION(1941), m; DR. KILDARE'S WEDDING DAY(1941), m; H.M. PULHAM, ESQ.(1941), m; RAGE IN HEAVEN(1941), m; TWO-FACED WOMAN(1941), m; WHEN LADIES MEET(1941), m; WOMAN'S FACE(1941), m; AFFAIRS OF MARTHA, THE(1942), m; CROSSROADS(1942), m; FINGERS AT THE WINDOW(1942), m; JOHNNY EAGER(1942), m; KEEPER OF THE FLAME(1942), m; SOMEWHERE I'LL FIND YOU(1942), m; WE WERE DANCING(1942), m; WHITE CARGO(1942), m; ABOVE SUSPICION(1943), m; BATAAN(1943), m; CROSS OF LORRAINE, THE(1943), m; HEAVENLY BODY, THE(1943), m; SLIGHTLY DANGEROUS(1943), m; GASLIGHT(1944), m; MARRIAGE IS A PRIVATE AFFAIR(1944), m; MRS. PARKINGTON(1944), m; BEWITCHED(1945), m; WITHOUT LOVE(1945), m; SECRET HEART, THE(1946), m; STRANGER THE(1946), m; THREE WISE FOOLS(1946), m; CYNTHIA(1947), m; GREEN DOLPHIN STREET(1947), m; HIGH WALL, THE(1947), m; SONG OF LOVE(1947), md; B. F.'S DAUGHTER(1948), m; HOMECOMING(1948), m; ACT OF VIOLENCE(1949), m; GREAT SINNER, THE(1949), m; SECRET GARDEN, THE(1949), m; THAT FORSYTE WOMAN(1949), m; GROUNDS FOR MARRIAGE(1950), m; KEY TO THE CITY(1950), m; LIFE OF HER OWN, A(1950), m; MALAYA(1950), m; SKIPPER SURPRISED HIS WIFE, THE(1950), m; TO PLEASE A LADY(1950), m; IT'S A BIG COUNTRY(1951), m; MR. IMPERIUM(1951), m; RED BADGE OF COURAGE, THE(1951), m; SHADOW IN THE SKY(1951), m; THREE GUYS NAMED MIKE(1951), m; INVITATION(1952), m; WILD NORTH, THE(1952), m; ACTRESS, THE(1953), md; LILI(1953), m; NAKED SPUR, THE(1953), m; RIDE, VAQUERO!(1953), m; SAA-

DIA(1953), m; HER TWELVE MEN(1954), m; RHAPSODY(1954), m; THEM!(1954), m; GLASS SLIPPER, THE(1955), m; PRODIGAL, THE(1955), m; QUENTIN DURWARD(1955), m; FOREVER DARLING(1956), m; POWER AND THE PRIZE, THE(1956), m; SOMEBODY UP THERE LIKES ME(1956), m; SWAN, THE(1956), m; BARRETTS OF WIMPOLE STREET, THE(1957), m; JET PILOT(1957), m; AUNTIE MAME(1958), m; BROTHERS KARAMAZOV, THE(1958), m; GREEN MANSIONS(1959), m; SCAPEGOAT, THE(1959, Brit.), m; BUTTERFIELD 8(1960), m; HOME FROM THE HILL(1960), m; ADA(1961), m; TWO LOVES(1961), m; MUTINY ON THE BOUNTY(1962), m; KISSES FOR MY PRESIDENT(1964), m; LORD JIM(1965, Brit.), m; TOBRUK(1966), m; WAY WEST, THE(1967), m; DON'T GO NEAR THE WATER(1975), m

Bronislav Kaper
QUENTIN DURWARD(1955), md

Bronislaw Kaper
DAUGHTER OF EVIL(1930, Ger.), m; MAN STOLEN(1934, Fr.), m; ESCAPADE(1935), m; DAY AT THE RACES, A(1937), m; OUR VINES HAVE TENDER GRAPES(1945), m; COUNTERPOINT(1967), m; FLEA IN HER EAR, A(1968, Fr.), m

Propislau Kaper
ANGEL WORE RED, THE(1960), m

Waldemar Kapezyk
EMIL AND THE DETECTIVE(1931, Ger.)

D. Kapka
NIGHT BEFORE CHRISTMAS, A(1963, USSR)

Bill Kaplan
NAKED ANGELS(1969), ph

Brenda Kaplan
SQUEEZE PLAY(1981)

Chad Kaplan
MARTYR, THE(1976, Ger./Israel)

Elliot Kaplan
FINNEGANS WAKE(1965), m; PLAYGROUND, THE(1965), m; CRY BLOOD, APACHE(1970), m; FOOD OF THE GODS, THE(1976), m

Elliott Kaplan
SQUARE ROOT OF ZERO, THE(1964), m, md

Gabe Kaplan
NOBODY'S PERFEKT(1981); TULIPS(1981, Can), w

Gabriel Kaplan
FAST BREAK(1979)

Henry Kaplan
GIRL ON THE BOAT, THE(1962, Brit.), d

Hoissaye Kaplan
BALTIC DEPUTY(1937, USSR), ph

I. Kaplan
LADY WITH THE DOG, THE(1962, USSR), art d; OVERCOAT, THE(1965, USSR), art d

J.S. Kaplan
ASSAULT ON PRECINCT 13(1976), p

Jacques Kaplan
ROUND TRIP(1967)

Jeanne Kaplan
MADE FOR EACH OTHER(1971)

Jeremy Kaplan
CIRCLE OF IRON(1979, Brit.)
Misc. Talkies
PHANTOM KID, THE(1983)

Jo Ann Kaplan
XTRO(1983, Brit.), w, ed

Jonathan Kaplan
SLAMS, THE(1973), d; STUDENT TEACHERS, THE(1973), d; NIGHT CALL NURSES(1974), d; TRUCK TURNER(1974), d; WHITE LINE FEVER(1975, Can.), d, w; CANNONBALL(1976, U.S./Hong Kong); HOLLYWOOD BOULEVARD(1976); MR. BILLION(1977), d, w; OVER THE EDGE(1979), d; HEART LIKE A WHEEL(1983), d

Lazarus Kaplan
SAGA OF DRACULA, THE(1975, Span.), w

M. Kaplan
SON OF MONGOLIA(1936, USSR), ph

Mady Kaplan
DEER HUNTER, THE(1978); HEAVEN'S GATE(1980); TOUCHED(1983)

Marc Kaplan
FAST BREAK(1979), w

Mark Kaplan
1984
FLAMINGO KID, THE(1984)

Marvin Kaplan
ADAM'S RIB(1949); FRANCIS(1949); KEY TO THE CITY(1950); REFORMER AND THE REDHEAD, THE(1950); ANGELS IN THE OUTFIELD(1951); BEHAVE YOURSELF(1951); CRIMINAL LAWYER(1951); FAT MAN, THE(1951); I CAN GET IT FOR YOU WHOLESALE(1951); FABULOUS SENORITA, THE(1952); WAKE ME WHEN IT'S OVER(1960); IT'S A MAD, MAD, MAD, MAD WORLD(1963); NEW KIND OF LOVE, A(1963); NUTTY PROFESSOR, THE(1963); GREAT RACE, THE(1965); OPERATION DELILAH(1966, U.S./Span.); FREAKY FRIDAY(1976)
Misc. Talkies
CRAWLING ARM, THE(1973); SEVERED ARM(1973); FANGS(1974)

Michael Kaplan
HEROES OF THE SEA(1941), ph; THANK GOD IT'S FRIDAY(1978), cos; BLADE RUNNER(1982), cos; FLASHDANCE(1983), cos
1984
AGAINST ALL ODDS(1984), cos; AMERICAN DREAMER(1984), cos; THIEF OF HEARTS(1984), cos

Mike Kaplan
BUFFALO BILL AND THE INDIANS, OR SITTING BULL'S HISTORY LESSON(1976); WELCOME TO L.A.(1976)

Mike E. Kaplan
1984
CHOOSE ME(1984)

Nelly Kaplan
VERY CURIOUS GIRL, A(1970, Fr.), d, w, ed; CHARLES AND LUCIE(1982, Fr.), d, ed

Robert J. Kaplan
SCARECROW IN A GARDEN OF CUCUMBERS(1972), p, d
Misc. Talkies
GUMS(1976), d
Russ Kaplan
DAKOTA(1945); SWORD IN THE DESERT(1949); JOE PALOOKA MEETS HUMPHREY(1950)
Russell Kaplan
COPPER CANYON(1950)
Shelley Kaplan
P.O.W., THE(1973)
Sol Kaplan
APACHE TRAIL(1942), m; TALES OF MANHATTAN(1942), m; HOLLOW TRIUMPH(1948), m; BLACK BOOK, THE(1949), m; PORT OF NEW YORK(1949), m; TRAPPED(1949), m; MISTER 880(1950), m; 711 OCEAN DRIVE(1950), m; HALLS OF MONTEZUMA(1951), m; HOUSE ON TELEGRAPH HILL(1951), m; I CAN GET IT FOR YOU WHOLESALE(1951), m; I'D CLIMB THE HIGHEST MOUNTAIN(1951), m; RAWHIDE(1951), m; SECRET OF CONVICT LAKE, THE(1951), m; DEADLINE– U.S.A.(1952), m; DIPLOMATIC COURIER(1952), m; KANGAROO(1952), m; RED SKIES OF MONTANA(1952), m; RETURN OF THE TEXAN(1952), m; SOMETHING FOR THE BIRDS(1952), m; WAY OF A GAUCHO(1952), m; DESTINATION GOBI(1953), m; NIAGARA(1953), m; TITANIC(1953), m; TREASURE OF THE GOLDEN CONDOR(1953), m; SALT OF THE EARTH(1954), m; BURGLAR, THE(1956), m; HAPPY ANNIVERSARY(1959), m; GIRL OF THE NIGHT(1960), m; VICTORS, THE(1963), m; YOUNG LOVERS, THE(1964), m&md; JUDITH(1965), m; SPY WHO CAME IN FROM THE COLD, THE(1965, Brit.), m; EXPLOSION(1969, Can.), m; LIVING FREE(1972, Brit.), m, md; LIES MY FATHER TOLD ME(1975, Can.), m; OVER THE EDGE(1979), m
Shlomit Kaplansky
THEY WERE TEN(1961, Israel)
Alexi Kapler
BLUE BIRD, THE(1976), w
Boris D. Kaplin
LET NO MAN WRITE MY EPITAPH(1960), p
Herb Kaplow
Misc. Talkies
FORBIDDEN UNDER THE CENSORSHIP OF THE KING(1973)
Herb Kaplowitz
GALAXINA(1980)
Matt Kaplowitz
NIGHT OF THE ZOMBIES(1981), m
Nancy Kapner
WORM EATERS, THE(1981), w
Sharon Kapner
DR. COPPELIUS(1968, U.S./Span.)
Arnold Kapnick
BANG THE DRUM SLOWLY(1973)
Joe Kapo
FRISCO KID, THE(1979)
Jennifer Kapoor
SHAKESPEARE WALLAH(1966, India)
Jennifer Kapoor [M. Kendal]
1984
HOME AND THE WORLD, THE(1984, India)
Kunai Kapoor
SIDDHARTHA(1972)
Pincho Kapoor
HOUSEHOLDER, THE(1963, US/India); SHAKESPEARE WALLAH(1966, India); GURU, THE(1969, U.S./India); BOMBAY TALKIE(1970, India)
Pinchoo Kapoor
SIDDHARTHA(1972)
S. P. Kapoor
LOOK BACK IN ANGER(1959)
Shashi Kapoor
HOUSEHOLDER, THE(1963, US/India); SHAKESPEARE WALLAH(1966, India); MATTER OF INNOCENCE, A(1968, Brit.); BOMBAY TALKIE(1970, India); SIDDHARTHA(1972); HEAT AND DUST(1983, Brit.)
Petros Kapoularis
RED LANTERNS(1965, Gr.), art d
George Kapp
KING OF COMEDY, THE(1983)
Joe Kapp
WORLD'S GREATEST ATHLETE, THE(1973); LONGEST YARD, THE(1974); TWO-MINUTE WARNING(1976); CHOIRBOYS, THE(1977); SEMI-TOUGH(1977)
Peter Kapp
MY NAME IS PECOS(1966, Ital.)
Rebacca Kapp
ELECTRA GLIDE IN BLUE(1973)
Karl G. Kappel
STREET FIGHTER(1959), p
Alfred Kappeler
Misc. Silents
NYMPH OF THE FOOTHILLS, A(1918)
Alfred Kappler
Silents
AMERICAN WIDOW, AN(1917)
Kendall Kapps
DAUGHTER OF ROSIE O'GRADY, THE(1950)
Walter Kapps
PRICE OF FLESH, THE(1962, Fr.), d
Bo Kaprall
TUNNELVISION(1976); FM(1978); HOMETOWN U.S.A.(1979)
Valerie Kaprisky
BREATHLESS(1983)
Dana Kaproff
EMPIRE OF THE ANTS(1977), m; WHEN A STRANGER CALLS(1979), m; DEATH VALLEY(1982), m; PANDEMONIUM(1982), m; GOLDEN SEAL, THE(1983), m

D. Kapsakis
YOU CAME TOO LATE(1962, Gr.), d
Sokrates Kapsaskis
LISA, TOSCA OF ATHENS(1961, Gr.), d; HOT MONTH OF AUGUST, THE(1969, Gr.), p,d&w
Sam Kapu, Jr.
KONA COAST(1968)
Venco Kapural
1984
MEMED MY HAWK(1984, Brit.)
Vjenceslav Kapural
1984
NADIA(1984, U.S./Yugo.)
Frank Kaquitts
BUFFALO BILL AND THE INDIANS, OR SITTING BULL'S HISTORY LESSON(1976)
Edmund Kara
MOONSHINE WAR, THE(1970), cos
Zoia Karabanova
MISSION TO MOSCOW(1943); SONG TO REMEMBER, A(1945)
Zola Karabanova
NORTHWEST OUTPOST(1947)
Zoya Karabanova
Misc. Silents
WOMAN WITH A DAGGER(1916, USSR); EVA(1918, USSR); LOVE - HATE - DEATH(1918, USSR)
Ron Karabatsos
PRINCE OF THE CITY(1981); FLASHDANCE(1983)
1984
COTTON CLUB, THE(1984)
Tolis Karachalios
STATUE, THE(1971, Brit.)
Michaela Karacic
SOPHIE'S CHOICE(1982)
Evie Karafotias
LITTLE LAURA AND BIG JOHN(1973)
Hermine Karaghuez
GUNS(1980, Fr.)
Galya Karakulova
DAY THE WAR ENDED, THE(1961, USSR)
Kokta Karalashvili
Misc. Silents
ELISO(1928, USSR)
Chris Karallis
1984
KIPPERBANG(1984, Brit.)
Eddie Karam
TULIPS(1981, Can), m
Elena Karam
AMERICA, AMERICA(1963); LADYBUG, LADYBUG(1963); LOVE WITH THE PROPER STRANGER(1963); UP THE DOWN STAIRCASE(1967); DESPERATE CHARACTERS(1971); F.I.S.T.(1978)
Mia Karam
MURDER CAN BE DEADLY(1963, Brit.); SHADOW OF FEAR(1963, Brit.); 20,000 POUNDS KISS, THE(1964, Brit.)
S. Karamash
KIEV COMEDY, A(1963, USSR); MOTHER AND DAUGHTER(1965, USSR)
Vassili Karamesinis
FIVE GIANTS FROM TEXAS(1966, Ital./Span.)
Vassili Karamis
CENTURION, THE(1962, Fr./Ital.)
Nizwar Karanj
1984
INDIANA JONES AND THE TEMPLE OF DOOM(1984)
Srdjan Karanovic
FRAGRANCE OF WILD FLOWERS, THE(1979, Yugo.), d, w
Rashid Karapiet
1984
PASSAGE TO INDIA, A(1984, Brit.)
Mikis Karapiperis
1984
LITTLE DRUMMER GIRL, THE(1984), art d
Anton Karas
COME DANCE WITH ME(1950, Brit.); THIRD MAN, THE(1950, Brit.), m
Nico Karaski
ASTRO-ZOMBIES, THE(1969), m
Effie Karath
LOOKIN' TO GET OUT(1982)
Frances Karath
BECAUSE OF YOU(1952); BECAUSE THEY'RE YOUNG(1960)
Francie Karath
GYPSY(1962)
Jimmy Karath
TAKE ME TO TOWN(1953)
Kym Karath
SPENCER'S MOUNTAIN(1963); THRILL OF IT ALL, THE(1963); GOOD NEIGHBOR SAM(1964); SOUND OF MUSIC, THE(1965)
O. Karavaychuk
SHE-WOLF, THE(1963, USSR), m
Theodoros A. Karavidas
POSTMAN ALWAYS RINGS TWICE, THE(1981)
Selan Karay
ZOMBIE CREEPING FLESH(1981, Ital./Span.); NIGHT OF THE ZOMBIES(1983, Span./Ital.)
Kara Karayev
DON QUIXOTE(1961, USSR), m
Ivana Karbanova
DAISIES(1967, Czech.); MARTYRS OF LOVE(1968, Czech.)

Bruce Karcher
GAS-S-S-S!(1970)
Karchow
M(1933, Ger.)
Alexander Kardan
WE'LL SMILE AGAIN(1942, Brit.)
Lili Kardell
LOOKING FOR DANGER(1957); SWINGIN' SUMMER, A(1965)
Karin Kardian
NIGHTBEAST(1982)
Larry Kardish
SLOW RUN(1968), p,d,w&ph, ed
Alexander Kardo
Misc. Silents
PRINCE AND THE PAUPER, THE(1929, Aust./Czech.), d
L. Kardonskiy
DIMKA(1964, USSR)
Istvan Kardos
FATHER(1967, Hung.)
Leslie Kardos
DARK STREETS OF CAIRO(1940), d; NO LEAVE, NO LOVE(1946), w; STRIP, THE(1951), d; SMALL TOWN GIRL(1953), d; DANCE WITH ME, HENRY(1956), w; MAN WHO TURNED TO STONE, THE(1957), d; TIJUANA STORY, THE(1957), d
Kare
MARGIN, THE,(1969, Braz.)
Irena Karel
SIGNALS-AN ADVENTURE IN SPACE(1970, E. Ger./Pol.)
Ann Karell
ONE-TRICK PONY(1980)
Annette Karell
BEYOND THE CURTAIN(1960, Brit.)
Danuta Karell
NIGHT TO REMEMBER, A(1958, Brit.)
Y. Karelov
LAST GAME, THE(1964, USSR), d
Harvey Karels
KID FROM BOOKLYN, THE(1946)
Silents
MERRY WIDOW, THE(1925)
Fred Kareman
LET'S ROCK(1958); LOVESICK(1983)
Anna Karen
WRONG MAN, THE(1956); SKI BUM, THE(1971); ON THE BUSES(1972, Brit.)
Bedrich Karen
MERRY WIVES, THE(1940, Czech.); SKELETON ON HORSEBACK(1940, Czech.); DEVIL'S TRAP, THE(1964, Czech.)
Debbie Karen
BLACKOUT(1978, Fr./Can.), ed
Debra Karen
MEATBALLS(1979, Can.), ed; YESTERDAY(1980, Can.), ed; HAPPY BIRTHDAY TO ME(1981), ed
James Karen
FRANKENSTEIN MEETS THE SPACE MONSTER(1965); HERCULES IN NEW YORK(1970); I NEVER SANG FOR MY FATHER(1970); RIVALS(1972); OPENING NIGHT(1977); F.I.S.T.(1978); CHINA SYNDROME, THE(1979); JAZZ SINGER, THE(1980); TAKE THIS JOB AND SHOVE IT(1981); FRANCES(1982); POLTERGEIST(1982); TIME WALKER(1982)
1984
SAM'S SON(1984)
Jim Karen
AMAZING GRACE(1974)
Kames Karen
ALL THE PRESIDENT'S MEN(1976)
Kenny Karen
IF EVER I SEE YOU AGAIN(1978)
Leo Karen
STEPPENWOLF(1974), art d
Margo Karen
CONFIDENCE GIRL(1952)
Nicole Karen
WHAT'S NEW, PUSSYCAT?(1965, U.S./Fr.); BEAUTIFUL SWINDLERS, THE(1967, Fr./Ital./Jap./Neth.)
Suzanne Karen
UNDERCOVER MAN(1936)
Diane Karene
Misc. Silents
RASPUTIN(1930)
Peter Kares
NIGHT THEY ROBBED BIG BERTHA'S, THE(1975), p&d
Nikolay Karetnikov
PEACE TO HIM WHO ENTERS(1963, USSR), m
Emil Karewicz
EIGHTH DAY OF THE WEEK, THE(1959, Pol./Ger.); KNIGHTS OF THE TEUTONIC ORDER, THE(1962, Pol.)
Emil Karewiez
KANAL(1961, Pol.)
Jenny Karezi
RED LANTERNS(1965, Gr.)
Tzeni Karezi
AUNT FROM CHICAGO(1960, Gr.)
Robin Karfo
ECHOES(1983)
Fred Karger
FROM HERE TO ETERNITY(1953), m/l; DON'T KNOCK THE ROCK(1956), md; HE LAUGHED LAST(1956), md; ROCK AROUND THE CLOCK(1956), md; JUKE BOX RHYTHM(1959), m; DON'T KNOCK THE TWIST(1962), m; HOOTENANNY HOOT(1963), md; GET YOURSELF A COLLEGE GIRL(1964), m; YOUR CHEATIN' HEART(1964), m&md; HARUM SCARUM(1965), m; WHEN THE BOYS MEET THE GIRLS(1965), m, md; FRANKIE AND JOHNNY(1966), m&md; HOLD ON(1966), m; FASTEST GUITAR ALIVE, THE(1967), m; HOT RODS TO HELL(1967), m, md;

LOVE-INS, THE(1967), m, md; RIOT ON SUNSET STRIP(1967), m; FOR SINGLES ONLY(1968), m; TIME TO SING, A(1968), m; YOUNG RUNAWAYS, THE(1968), m; ANGEL, ANGEL, DOWN WE GO(1969), m; MOONSHINE WAR, THE(1970), m; LONERS, THE(1972), m; NECROMANCY(1972), m
Freddy Karger
SOUND OFF(1952), m
Maxwell Karger
Silents
ALIAS MRS. JESSOP(1917), sup; AMERICAN WIDOW, AN(1917), sup; OUTWITTED(1917), sup; ALIAS JIMMY VALENTINE(1920), sup; FINE FEATHERS(1921), sup; IDLE RICH, THE(1921), d; MAN WHO, THE(1921), d; GOLDEN GIFT, THE(1922), d; KISSES(1922), d
Misc. Silents
HOLE IN THE WALL, THE(1921), d; MESSAGE FROM MARS, A(1921), d; TRIP TO PARADISE, A(1921), d
Lucky Kargo
GIRL SMUGGLERS(1967); PROJECTIONIST, THE(1970)
Misc. Talkies
DEATH ON CREDIT(1976)
Aristedes Karides-Fuchs
NAKED BRIGADE, THE(1965, U.S./Gr.), ph
Dick Karie
ELECTRA GLIDE IN BLUE(1973)
Richard Karie
VAN, THE(1977); THIEF(1981)
Walter Karig
ZOTZ!(1962), w
Patricia Karim
HEAT OF THE SUMMER(1961, Fr.)
Karin
TRUNK TO CAIRO(1966, Israel/Ger.)
Debbie Karin
FINAL ASSIGNMENT(1980, Can.), ed
Ella Karin
UGLY ONES, THE(1968, Ital./Span.)
Margot Karin
NEVER SAY GOODBYE(1956)
Rita Karin
GANG THAT COULDN'T SHOOT STRAIGHT, THE(1971); UP THE SANDBOX(1972); BIG FIX, THE(1978); SOPHIE'S CHOICE(1982)
Vladimir Karin
Misc. Silents
UPRISING(1918, USSR), d; MOTHER(1920, USSR); FIGHT FOR THE 'ULTIMATUM' FACTORY(1923, USSR)
Karina
Silents
DAWN(1917, Brit.)
Anna Karina
CLEO FROM 5 TO 7(1961, Fr.); WOMAN IS A WOMAN, A(1961, Fr./Ital.); MAID FOR MURDER(1963, Brit.); MY LIFE TO LIVE(1963, Fr.); THREE FABLES OF LOVE(1963, Fr./Ital./Span.); SWEET AND SOUR(1964, Fr./Ital.); ALPHAVILLE, A STRANGE CASE OF LEMMY CAUTION(1965, Fr.); CIRCLE OF LOVE(1965, Fr.); LE PETIT SOLDAT(1965, Fr.); SCHEHERAZADE(1965, Fr./Ital./Span.); BAND OF OUTSIDERS(1966, Fr.); MADE IN U.S.A.(1966, Fr.); STRANGER, THE(1967, Algeria/Fr./Ital.); DE L'AMOUR(1968, Fr./Ital.); MAGUS, THE(1968, Brit.); OLDEST PROFESSION, THE(1968, Fr./Ital./Ger.); PIERROT LE FOU(1968, Fr.); BEFORE WINTER COMES(1969, Brit.); JUSTINE(1969); NUN, THE(1971, Fr.); SALZBURG CONNECTION, THE(1972); CHINESE ROULETTE(1977, Ger.); BREAD AND CHOCOLATE(1978, Ital.)
1984
AVE MARIA(1984, Fr.)
Sandra Karina
PORT OF MISSING GIRLS(1938)
Karinska
JOAN OF ARC(1948), cos; MIDSUMMER NIGHT'S DREAM, A(1966), cos
Barbara Karinska
PIRATE, THE(1948), cos
Mme. Barbara Karinska
UNCONQUERED(1947), cos
Mme. Karinska
HANS CHRISTIAN ANDERSEN(1952), cos
Vic Karis
ARENA, THE(1973)
Toyomi Karita
MYSTERIOUS SATELLITE, THE(1956, Jap.)
Debbie Karjala
HOUSE BY THE LAKE, THE(1977, Can.), ed
Raymond Kark
COLD TURKEY(1971); YOUR THREE MINUTES ARE UP(1973); RUBY(1977); SKATEBOARD(1978)
Krystyna Karkowska
SOPHIE'S CHOICE(1982)
Steve Karkus
EASY RIDER(1969), spec eff; SILENT SCREAM(1980), spec eff
Dick Karl
THEY WERE EXPENDABLE(1945)
Robert Karl
MY SIX LOVES(1963)
Roger Karl
GOLEM, THE(1937, Czech./Fr.); LUCREZIA BORGIA(1937, Fr.); BETRAYAL(1939, Fr.); DOLL, THE(1962, Fr.); TIGHT SKIRTS, LOOSE PLEASURES(1966, Fr.)
Misc. Silents
L'HOMME DU LARGE(1920, Fr.); LA FEMME DE NULLE PART(1922, Fr.)
Serge Freddy Karl
ROAD IS FINE, THE(1930, Fr.)
John Karlan
Misc. Talkies
KILLER'S DELIGHT(1978)

Richard Karlan
SNOW DOG(1950); UNION STATION(1950); BRIGHT VICTORY(1951); RACKET, THE(1951); RHUBARB(1951); SAILOR BEWARE(1951); SIERRA PASSAGE(1951); UNKNOWN MAN, THE(1951); DREAMBOAT(1952); LOVE IS BETTER THAN EVER(1952); O. HENRY'S FULL HOUSE(1952); WAIT 'TIL THE SUN SHINES, NELLIE(1952); BLOWING WILD(1953); TANGIER INCIDENT(1953); CAPTAIN KIDD AND THE SLAVE GIRL(1954); ABBOTT AND COSTELLO MEET THE MUMMY(1955); TOUGHEST MAN ALIVE(1955); ACCUSED OF MURDER(1956); HOLLYWOOD OR BUST(1956); STEEL JUNGLE, THE(1956); ROCK ALL NIGHT(1957); CROOKED CIRCLE, THE(1958); MAN WHO DIED TWICE, THE(1958); INSIDE THE MAFIA(1959); STAR!(1968)

Nicholas Karlash
COSSACKS IN EXILE(1939, Ukrainian)

Olga Karlatos
WIFEMISTRESS(1979, Ital.); ZOMBIE(1980, Ital.)
1984
ONCE UPON A TIME IN AMERICA(1984); PURPLE RAIN(1984)

Ursula Karlband
WITNESS OUT OF HELL(1967, Ger./Yugo.), ed

Marianne Karlbeck
JUST ONCE MORE(1963, Swed.); PASSION OF ANNA, THE(1970, Swed.); FANNY AND ALEXANDER(1983, Swed./Fr./Ger.)

Jonathan Karle
WILD GUITAR(1962)

John Karlen
DAUGHTERS OF DARKNESS(1971, Bel./ Fr./ Ger./ Ital.); NIGHT OF DARK SHADOWS(1971); SMALL TOWN IN TEXAS, A(1976); PENNIES FROM HEAVEN(1981)
1984
GIMME AN 'F'(1984); IMPULSE(1984); RACING WITH THE MOON(1984)

Karlice
TOWN WENT WILD, THE(1945), cos; WILD WEST(1946), cos

Bo Peep Karlin
HAPPY DAYS(1930); SOMETHING TO SING ABOUT(1937); BYE BYE BIRDIE(1963)

Fred Karlin
UP THE DOWN STAIRCASE(1967), m; YOURS, MINE AND OURS(1968), m&md; STALKING MOON(1969), m; STERILE CUCKOO, THE(1969), m; BABY MAKER, THE(1970), m; COVER ME BABE(1970), m; LOVERS AND OTHER STRANGERS(1970), m; BELIEVE IN ME(1971), m; MARRIAGE OF A YOUNG STOCKBROKER, THE(1971), m; EVERY LITTLE CROOK AND NANNY(1972), m; LITTLE ARK, THE(1972), m; WESTWORLD(1973), m; CHOSEN SURVIVORS(1974 U.S.-Mex.), m; GRAVY TRAIN, THE(1974), m; MIXED COMPANY(1974), m; SPIKES GANG, THE(1974), m; TAKE, THE(1974), m; BABY BLUE MARINE(1976), m; FUTUREWORLD(1976), m; JOE PANTHER(1976), m; LEADBELLY(1976), m; GREASED LIGHTNING(1977), m; MEAN DOG BLUES(1978), m; CALIFORNIA DREAMING(1979), m; RAVAGERS, THE(1979), m; CLOUD DANCER(1980), m; LOVING COUPLES(1980), m

Miriam Karlin
DOWN AMONG THE Z MEN(1952, Brit.); DEEP BLUE SEA, THE(1955, Brit.); WOMAN FOR JOE, THE(1955, Brit.); FUN AT ST. FANNY'S(1956, Brit.); TOUCH OF THE SUN, A(1956, Brit.); ROOM AT THE TOP(1959, Brit.); CROSSROADS TO CRIME(1960, Brit.); ENTERTAINER, THE(1960, Brit.); HAND IN HAND(1960, Brit.); MILLIONAIRESS, THE(1960, Brit.); FOURTH SQUARE, THE(1961, Brit.); WATCH IT, SAILOR!(1961, Brit.); I THANK A FOOL(1962, Brit.); PHANTOM OF THE OPERA, THE(1962, Brit.); HEAVENS ABOVE!(1963, Brit.); SMALL WORLD OF SAMMY LEE, THE(1963, Brit.); BARGEE, THE(1964, Brit.); LADIES WHO DO(1964, Brit.); OPERATION SNAFU(1965, Brit.); JUST LIKE A WOMAN(1967, Brit.); CLOCKWORK ORANGE, A(1971, Brit.); MAHLER(1974, Brit.)

The Karlins
DIAMONDS FOR BREAKFAST(1968, Brit.)

Boris Karloff
BEHIND THAT CURTAIN(1929); UNHOLY NIGHT, THE(1929); BAD ONE, THE(1930); MOTHERS CRY(1930); SEA BAT, THE(1930); UTAH KID, THE(1930); CRACKED NUTS(1931); CRIMINAL CODE(1931); FIVE STAR FINAL(1931); FRANKENSTEIN(1931); GRAFT(1931); GUILTY GENERATION, THE(1931); I LIKE YOUR NERVE(1931); MAD GENIUS, THE(1931); PARDON US(1931); PUBLIC DEFENDER, THE(1931); SMART MONEY(1931); TONIGHT OR NEVER(1931); YELLOW TICKET, THE(1931); YOUNG DONOVAN'S KID(1931); ALIAS THE DOCTOR(1932); BEHIND THE MASK(1932); BUSINESS AND PLEASURE(1932); MASK OF FU MANCHU, THE(1932); MIRACLE MAN, THE(1932); MUMMY, THE(1932); NIGHT WORLD(1932); OLD DARK HOUSE, THE(1932); SCARFACE(1932); BLACK CAT, THE(1934); GHOUL, THE(1934, Brit.); GIFT OF GAB(1934); HOUSE OF ROTHSCHILD, THE(1934); LOST PATROL, THE(1934); BLACK ROOM(1935); RAVEN, THE(1935); CHARLIE CHAN AT THE OPERA(1936); MAN WHO LIVED AGAIN, THE(1936, Brit.); THE INVISIBLE RAY(1936); WALKING DEAD, THE(1936); JUGGERNAUT(1937, Brit.); NIGHT KEY(1937); WEST OF SHANGHAI(1937); INVISIBLE MENACE, THE(1938); MR. WONG, DETECTIVE(1938); MAN THEY COULD NOT HANG, THE(1939); MR. WONG IN CHINATOWN(1939); MYSTERY OF MR. WONG, THE(1939); SON OF FRANKENSTEIN(1939); TOWER OF LONDON(1939); APE, THE(1940); BEFORE I HANG(1940); BLACK FRIDAY(1940); BRITISH INTELLIGENCE(1940); DEVIL'S ISLAND(1940); DOOMED TO DIE(1940); FATAL HOUR, THE(1940); MAN WITH NINE LIVES, THE(1940); YOU'LL FIND OUT(1940); DEVIL COMMANDS, THE(1941); BOOGIE MAN WILL GET YOU, THE(1942); CLIMAX, THE(1944); HOUSE OF FRANKENSTEIN(1944); BODY SNATCHER, THE(1945); ISLE OF THE DEAD(1945); BEDLAM(1946); DICK TRACY MEETS GRUESOME(1947); LURED(1947); SECRET LIFE OF WALTER MITTY, THE(1947); UNCONQUERED(1947); TAP ROOTS(1948); ABBOTT AND COSTELLO MEET THE KILLER, BORIS KARLOFF(1949); STRANGE DOOR, THE(1951); BLACK CASTLE, THE(1952); COLONEL MARCH INVESTIGATES(1952,Brit.); HINDU, THE(1953, Brit.); MONSTER OF THE ISLAND(1953, Ital.); ABBOTT AND COSTELLO MEET DR. JEKYLL AND MR. HYDE(1954); VOODOO ISLAND(1957); FRANKENSTEIN 1970(1958); HAUNTED STRANGLER, THE(1958, Brit.); CORRIDORS OF BLOOD(1962, Brit.); RAVEN, THE(1963); TERROR, THE(1963); COMEDY OF TERRORS, THE(1964); DIE, MONSTER DIE(1965, Brit.); DAYDREAMER, THE(1966); GHOST IN THE INVISIBLE BIKINI(1966); MAD MONSTER PARTY(1967); SORCERERS, THE(1967, Brit.); VENETIAN AFFAIR, THE(1967); FEAR CHAMBER, THE(1968, US/Mex.); HOUSE OF EVIL(1968, U.S./Mex.); SNAKE PEOPLE, THE(1968, Mex./U.S.); TARGETS(1968); CRIMSON CULT, THE(1970, Brit.); CAULDRON OF BLOOD(1971, Span.); INCREDIBLE INVASION, THE(1971, Mex./U.S.)

Silents
DUMB GIRL OF PORTICI(1916); HIS MAJESTY THE AMERICAN(1919); LAST OF THE MOHICANS, THE(1920); CHEATED HEARTS(1921); ALTAR STAIRS, THE(1922); PRISONER, THE(1923); DYNAMITE DAN(1924); LADY ROBINHOOD(1925); PRAIRIE WIFE, THE(1925); OLD IRONSIDES(1926); PRINCESS FROM HOBOKEN, THE(1927); SOFT CUSHIONS(1927); LITTLE WILD GIRL, THE(1928); ANNE AGAINST THE WORLD(1929); DEVIL'S CHAPLAIN(1929); PHANTOM OF THE NORTH(1929)
Misc. Silents
INFIDEL, THE(1922); MAN FROM DOWNING STREET, THE(1922); FORBIDDEN CARGO(1925); BELLS, THE(1926); FLAMING FURY(1926); PHANTOM BUSTER, THE(1927); BURNING THE WIND(1929)

Sonia Karlov
LUCKY IN LOVE(1929)

Katie Karlovitz
CREEPSHOW(1982)

Elma Karlowa
BEGGAR STUDENT, THE(1958, Ger.); BIMBO THE GREAT(1961, Ger.); KING, QUEEN, KNAVE(1972, Ger./U.S.); CRIME AND PASSION(1976, U.S., Ger.); FOX AND HIS FRIENDS(1976, Ger.); FEDORA(1978, Ger./Fr.)

Robert Karlowsky
THE CRAZIES(1973)

John Karlsen
NAKED MAJA, THE(1959, Ital./U.S.); IT HAPPENED IN ATHENS(1962); CLEOPATRA(1963); WITCH'S CURSE, THE(1963, Ital.); BAMBOLE!(1965, Ital.); CRACK IN THE WORLD(1965); CHRISMAS THAT ALMOST WASN'T. THE(1966, Ital.); EL GRECO(1966, Ital., Fr.); MODESTY BLAISE(1966, Brit.); SHE BEAST, THE(1966, Brit./Ital./Yugo.); MISSION STARDUST(1968, Ital./Span./Ger.)

Phil Karlson
SHANGHAI COBRA, THE(1945), d; BEHIND THE MASK(1946), d; BOWERY BOMBSHELL(1946), d; DARK ALIBI(1946), d; LIVE WIRES(1946), d; MISSING LADY, THE(1946), d; SWING PARADE OF 1946(1946), d; WIFE WANTED(1946), d; BLACK GOLD(1947), d; KILROY WAS HERE(1947), d; LOUISIANA(1947), d; ADVENTURES IN SILVERADO(1948), d; LADIES OF THE CHORUS(1948), d; THUNDERHOOF(1948), d; BIG CAT, THE(1949), d; DOWN MEMORY LANE(1949), d; IROQUOIS TRAIL, THE(1950), d; LORNA DOONE(1951), d; MASK OF THE AVENGER(1951), d; TEXAS RANGERS, THE(1951), d; BRIGAND, THE(1952), d; KANSAS CITY CONFIDENTIAL(1952), d; SCANDAL SHEET(1952), d; 99 RIVER STREET(1953), d; THEY RODE WEST(1954), d; FIVE AGAINST THE HOUSE(1955), d; HELL'S ISLAND(1955), d; PHENIX CITY STORY, THE(1955), d; TIGHT SPOT(1955), d; BROTHERS RICO, THE(1957), d; GUNMAN'S WALK(1958), d; HELL TO ETERNITY(1960), d; KEY WITNESS(1960), d; SECRET WAYS, THE(1961), d; YOUNG DOCTORS, THE(1961), d; KID GALAHAD(1962), d; SCARFACE MOB, THE(1962), d; RAMPAGE(1963), d; SILENCERS, THE(1966), d; TIME FOR KILLING, A(1967), d; WRECKING CREW, THE(1968), d; HORNET'S NEST(1970), d; BEN(1972), d; WALKING TALL(1973), d; FRAMED(1975), d

John Karlssen
FRANCIS OF ASSISI(1961)

Liesl Karlstadt
ARENT WE WONDERFUL?(1959, Ger.)

Phil Karlstein [Karlson]
WAVE, A WAC AND A MARINE, A(1944), d; G.I. HONEYMOON(1945), d; THERE GOES KELLY(1945), d

Oscar Karlweis
ST. BENNY THE DIP(1951); FIVE FINGERS(1952); JUGGLER, THE(1953); TONIGHT WE SING(1953); MEET ME IN LAS VEGAS(1956)

Oskar Karlweis
DIE MANNER UM LUCIE(1931)

Oscar Karlweiss
DOLLY GETS AHEAD(1931, Ger.); ANYTHING CAN HAPPEN(1952)

Cydra Karlyn
FIST OF FEAR, TOUCH OF DEATH(1980)

Michael Karm
ANNIE HALL(1977)

Henning Karmack
VENOM(1968, Den.), p

Annette Karman
SPESSART INN, THE(1961, Ger.)

Janice Karman
SWITCHBLADE SISTERS(1975)

Sam Karmann
LA BALANCE(1983, Fr.)

David Karmansky
BEAST WITH A MILLION EYES, THE(1956), p&d

Alex Karmel
SOMETHING WILD(1961), w

Steve Karmen
CANDIDATE, THE(1964), m; TEENAGE GANG DEBS(1966), m; TEENAGE MOTHER(1967), m

Andrasne Karmento
FORBIDDEN RELATIONS(1983, Hung.), ed

Eva Karmento
ANGI VERA(1980, Hung.), ed
1984
BRADY'S ESCAPE(1984, U.S./Hung.), ed; DIARY FOR MY CHILDREN(1984, Hung.), ed

Marin Karmitz
1984
LE BON PLAISIR(1984, Fr.), p

Mario Karmolinska
JOVITA(1970, Pol.), cos

Steve Karmon
JUKE BOX RACKET(1960)

Bill Karn
GANG BUSTERS(1955), d, w; MA BARKER'S KILLER BROOD(1960), d; FIVE MINUTES TO LIVE(1961), d

William Karn
CASEY'S SHADOW(1978)

Victoria Karnafel
DEER HUNTER, THE(1978)
Lt.J.G. Thomas Karnahan
TOWERING INFERNO, THE(1974)
Leila Karnelly
GOLDIE(1931)
Lelia Karnelly
COCK-EYED WORLD, THE(1929); MARRIED IN HOLLYWOOD(1929)
Lola Karnelly
HER MAN(1930)
Robert Karner
RODEO(1952)
Bob Karnes
TRAPPED(1949)
Joe Karnes
PHFFFT!(1954); OPPOSITE SEX, THE(1956)
Robert Karnes
CAPTAIN FROM CASTILE(1947); DAISY KENYON(1947); KISS OF DEATH(1947);
MIRACLE ON 34TH STREET, THE(1947); NIGHTMARE ALLEY(1947); CALL
NORTHSIDE 777(1948); CRY OF THE CITY(1948); LUCK OF THE IRISH(1948); ROAD
HOUSE(1948); SCUDDA-HOO! SCUDDA-HAY!(1948); STREET WITH NO NAME,
THE(1948); WHEN MY BABY SMILES AT ME(1948); HILLS OF OKLAHOMA(1950);
KISS TOMORROW GOODBYE(1950); THREE HUSBANDS(1950); CASA MANA-
NA(1951); HE RAN ALL THE WAY(1951); STARLIFT(1951); UTAH WAGON
TRAIN(1951); LURE OF THE WILDERNESS(1952); STEEL TOWN(1952); STORM
OVER TIBET(1952); WILD BLUE YONDER, THE(1952); FROM HERE TO ETER-
NITY(1953); PROJECT MOONBASE(1953); SEMINOLE(1953); RIDERS TO THE
STARS(1954); HALF HUMAN(1955, Jap.); STAGECOACH TO FURY(1956); SPOILERS
OF THE FOREST(1957); FEAR NO MORE(1961); FIVE GUNS TO TOMBSTONE(1961);
ONE SPY TOO MANY(1966); CHARRO(1969); GLASS HOUSES(1972); EXECUTIVE
ACTION(1973); GABLE AND LOMBARD(1976)
Shirley Karnes
PAN-AMERICANA(1945)
Todd Karnes
BATTLE ZONE(1952); MUTINY(1952)
Joseph Karney
NAKED CITY, THE(1948)
Maria Karnilova
UNSINKABLE MOLLY BROWN, THE(1964)
Fred Karno
DON'T RUSH ME(1936, Brit.), p, w; JAILBIRDS(1939, Brit.), w; MONSIEUR VER-
DOUX(1947)
Misc. Silents
EARLY BIRDS(1923, Brit.)
Fred Karno, Jr.
Silents
GOLD RUSH, THE(1925)
Mitsukai Karno
ONIMASA(1983, Jap.), m
S. Karnovich-Valua
GARNET BRACELET, THE(1966, USSR)
Thomas Karnowski
SWORD AND THE SORCERER, THE(1982), w
Roscoe Karns
JAZZ SINGER, THE(1927); BEGGARS OF LIFE(1928); SHOPWORN ANGEL,
THE(1928); NEW YORK NIGHTS(1929); THIS THING CALLED LOVE(1929); COSTEL-
LO CASE, THE(1930); LITTLE ACCIDENT(1930); MAN TROUBLE(1930); SAFETY IN
NUMBERS(1930); TROOPERS THREE(1930); DIRIGIBLE(1931); GORILLA,
THE(1931); LAUGHING SINNERS(1931); LEFTOVER LADIES(1931); MANY A
SLIP(1931); CROOKED CIRCLE(1932); IF I HAD A MILLION(1932); NIGHT AFTER
NIGHT(1932); ONE WAY PASSAGE(1932); ROADHOUSE MURDER, THE(1932);
STOWAWAY(1932); TWO AGAINST THE WORLD(1932); UNDER-COVER MAN(1932);
ALICE IN WONDERLAND(1933); GAMBLING SHIP(1933); GRAND SLAM(1933);
LADY'S PROFESSION, A(1933); LAWYER MAN(1933); ONE SUNDAY AFTER-
NOON(1933); PLEASURE(1933); TODAY WE LIVE(1933); COME ON, MARINES(1934);
ELMER AND ELSIE(1934); I SELL ANYTHING(1934); IT HAPPENED ONE
NIGHT(1934); SEARCH FOR BEAUTY(1934); SHOOT THE WORKS(1934); TWEN-
TIETH CENTURY(1934); WOMEN IN HIS LIFE, THE(1934); ALIBI IKE(1935); FOUR
HOURS TO KILL(1935); FRONT PAGE WOMAN(1935); RED HOT TIRES(1935); TWO
FISTED(1935); WINGS IN THE DARK(1935); BORDER FLIGHT(1936); CAIN AND
MABEL(1936); THREE CHEERS FOR LOVE(1936); THREE MARRIED MEN(1936);
WOMAN TRAP(1936); CLARENCE(1937); MURDER GOES TO COLLEGE(1937);
NIGHT OF MYSTERY(1937); ON SUCH A NIGHT(1937); PARTNERS IN CRIME(1937);
DANGEROUS TO KNOW(1938); SCANDAL STREET(1938); THANKS FOR THE
MEMORY(1938); TIP-OFF GIRLS(1938); YOU AND ME(1938); DANCING CO-ED(1939);
EVERYTHING'S ON ICE(1939); KING OF CHINATOWN(1939); THAT'S RIGHT-
YOU'RE WRONG(1939); DOUBLE ALIBI(1940); HIS GIRL FRIDAY(1940); LADIES
MUST LIVE(1940); MEET THE MISSUS(1940); SATURDAY'S CHILDREN(1940);
THEY DRIVE BY NIGHT(1940); FOOTSTEPS IN THE DARK(1941); GAY VAGA-
BOND, THE(1941); PETTICOAT POLITICS(1941); ROAD TO HAPPINESS(1942);
TRAGEDY AT MIDNIGHT, A(1942); WOMAN OF THE YEAR(1942); YOKEL
BOY(1942); YOU CAN'T ESCAPE FOREVER(1942); HIS BUTLER'S SISTER(1943); MY
SON, THE HERO(1943); OLD ACQUAINTANCE(1943); RIDING HIGH(1943); STAGE
DOOR CANTEEN(1943); HI, GOOD-LOOKIN'(1944); MINSTREL MAN(1944); NAVY
WAY, THE(1944); AVALANCHE(1946); I RING DOORBELLS(1946); ONE WAY TO
LOVE(1946); THAT'S MY MAN(1947); VIGILANTES OF BOOMTOWN(1947); DEVIL'S
CARGO, THE(1948); INSIDE STORY, THE(1948); TEXAS, BROOKLYN AND HEAV-
EN(1948); ONIONHEAD(1958); MAN'S FAVORITE SPORT[?](1964)
Silents
POOR RELATIONS(1919); AFRAID TO FIGHT(1922); BLUFF(1924); MIDNIGHT
EXPRESS, THE(1924); OVERLAND LIMITED, THE(1925); WINGS(1927); JAZZ
MAD(1928); WARMING UP(1928); OBJECT-ALIMONY(1929)
Misc. Silents
FAMILY HONOR, THE(1920); LIFE OF THE PARTY, THE(1920); TOO MUCH
MARRIED(1921); MORAN OF THE MARINES(1928); WIN THAT GIRL(1928)
Roscue Karns
SPEED TO SPARE(1948)

Tod Karns
MY FOOLISH HEART(1949)
Todd Karns
ANDY HARDY'S PRIVATE SECRETARY(1941); COURTSHIP OF ANDY HARDY,
THE(1942); EAGLE SQUADRON(1942); IT'S A WONDERFUL LIFE(1946); GOOD
SAM(1948); IT'S A SMALL WORLD(1950); MAGNIFICENT YANKEE, THE(1950);
FLAT TOP(1952); JET JOB(1952); MY SON, JOHN(1952); CHINA VENTURE(1953);
CLIPPED WINGS(1953); MISSION OVER KOREA(1953); CAINE MUTINY, THE(1954)
Virginia Karns
BABES IN TOYLAND(1934)
Paul Karo
DEMONSTRATOR(1971, Aus.)
Jimmy Karoubi
WOMAN FOR JOE, THE(1955, Brit.); PIERROT LE FOU(1968, Fr./Ital.)
Theo Karousos
YOU CAME TOO LATE(1962, Gr.); THANOS AND DESPINA(1970, Fr./Gr.)
Giorgos Karoussos
PHAEDRA(1962, U.S./Gr./Fr.)
Beverly Karp
MY DINNER WITH ANDRE(1981), p
David Karp
SOL MADRID(1968), w; CHE!(1969), w; YOUNG REBEL, THE(1969, Fr./Ital./Span.),
w
Ivan Karp
UNMARRIED WOMAN, AN(1978)
Lynn Karp
FANTASIA(1940), anim; PINOCCHIO(1940), anim
Soni Karp
DELTA FACTOR, THE(1970), cos
Jan Karpas
MIDSUMMERS NIGHT'S DREAM, A(1961, Czech), anim
Curtis Karpe
PUBLIC WEDDING(1937)
Gaby Karpeles
TRUNKS OF MR. O.F., THE(1932, Ger.)
I. Karpenko
MOTHER AND DAUGHTER(1965, USSR), ed
Eleri Karpeta
ELECTRA(1962, Gr.)
Elinor Karpf
ADAM AT 6 A.M.(1970), w
Eve Karpf
TOUCH OF CLASS, A(1973, Brit.)
Stephen Karpf
ADAM AT 6 A.M.(1970), w
Milan Karpisek
DIVINE EMMA, THE(1983, Czech,)
A. Karpov
GORDEYEV FAMILY, THE(1961, U.S.S.R.)
Craig Karpf
YOUNG LIONS, THE(1958)
Darwin Karr
Silents
MR. BARNES OF NEW YORK(1914); TANGLE, THE(1914)
Misc. Silents
FIGHT FOR MILLIONS, THE(1913); CALL OF THE SEA, THE(1915); HEARTS AND
THE HIGHWAY(1915); VILLAGE HOMESTEAD, THE(1915); BRITTON OF THE
SEVENTH(1916)
David Karr
MONEY TRAP, THE(1966), p; WELCOME TO HARD TIMES(1967), p
Gary Karr
1984
DELIVERY BOYS(1984), ed
Harriet Karr
DREAMER, THE(1970, Israel)
Hilliard Karr
Silents
OH, WHAT A NIGHT!(1926)
Mabel Karr
COLOSSUS OF RHODES, THE(1961, Ital., Fr., Span.); DIABOLICAL DR. Z, THE(1966
Span./Fr.)
Michael Karr
TRIAL OF BILLY JACK, THE(1974), ed
Tom Karr
DEATHDREAM(1972, Can.), p&d
Tom Karr [Bob Clark]
DERANGED(1974, Can.), p
Alex Karras
PAPER LION(1968); BLAZING SADDLES(1974); WIN, PLACE, OR STEAL(1975);
FM(1978); JACOB TWO-TWO MEETS THE HOODED FANG(1979, Can.); WHEN TIME
RAN OUT(1980); NOBODY'S PERFEKT(1981); PORKY'S(1982); VICTOR/VIC-
TORIA(1982)
1984
AGAINST ALL ODDS(1984)
Misc. Talkies
GREAT LESTER BOGGS, THE(1975)
Athan Karras
DARK ODYSSEY(1961)
Stralis Karras
RECONSTRUCTION OF A CRIME(1970, Ger.), w
Jacques Karre
FRENCHMAN'S CREEK(1944); LADY IN THE DARK(1944)
Richard Karron
FUN WITH DICK AND JANE(1977); WORLD'S GREATEST LOVER, THE(1977);
ONE AND ONLY, THE(1978); FATSO(1980); HISTORY OF THE WORLD, PART 1(1981)
Michael Kars
REBEL ROUSERS(1970), w

Chico Kasinoir
1984
MUPPETS TAKE MANHATTAN, THE(1984)
Harold Kasket
MADE IN HEAVEN(1952, Brit.); MOULIN ROUGE(1952); HOUSE OF THE ARROW, THE(1953, Brit.); SAADIA(1953); BEAU BRUMMELL(1954); UP TO HIS NECK(1954, Brit.); DOCTOR AT SEA(1955, Brit.); MAN OF THE MOMENT(1955, Brit.); ONE GOOD TURN(1955, Brit.); WARRIORS, THE(1955); MAN WHO KNEW TOO MUCH, THE(1956); KEY MAN, THE(1957, Brit.); OUT OF THE CLOUDS(1957, Brit.); PICKUP ALLEY(1957, Brit.); STOWAWAY GIRL(1957, Brit.); NAKED EARTH, THE(1958, Brit.); SEVENTH VOYAGE OF SINBAD, THE(1958); WONDERFUL THINGS!(1958, Brit.); HEART OF A MAN, THE(1959, Brit.); LADY IS A SQUARE, THE(1959, Brit.); NAVY LARK, THE(1959, Brit.); WHIRLPOOL(1959, Brit.); BOY WHO STOLE A MILLION, THE(1960, Brit.); SANDS OF THE DESERT(1960, Brit.); S.O.S. PACIFIC(1960, Brit.); TOMMY THE TOREADOR(1960, Brit.); FOURTH SQUARE, THE(1961, Brit.); GREEN HELMET, THE(1961, Brit.); LOSS OF INNOCENCE(1961, Brit.); ROMAN SPRING OF MRS. STONE, THE(1961, U.S./Brit.); WEEKEND WITH LULU, A(1961, Brit.); LIFE IS A CIRCUS(1962, Brit.); VILLAGE OF DAUGHTERS(1962, Brit.); NINE HOURS TO RAMA(1963, U.S./Brit.); RETURN OF MR. MOTO, THE(1965, Brit.); ARABE-SQUE(1966); WHERE'S JACK?(1969, Brit.); TRAIL OF THE PINK PANTHER, THE(1982); CURSE OF THE PINK PANTHER(1983)
Harold Kaskett
HOTEL SAHARA(1951, Brit.)
Laurin Kaski
RUNNERS(1983, Brit.)
Kasmin
1984
BIGGER SPLASH, A(1984)
Elfriede Kaspar
LONE CLIMBER, THE(1950, Brit./Aust.)
T. Kasparova
SUN SHINES FOR ALL, THE(1961, USSR), cos; PEACE TO HIM WHO EN-TERS(1963, USSR), cos
Holger Kasper
LEGEND OF COUGAR CANYON(1974)
Misc. Talkies
SECRET OF NAVAJO CAVE(1976)
Macky Kasper
$100 A NIGHT(1968, Ger.)
Sina Kasper
1984
MOSCOW ON THE HUDSON(1984)
Jerome Kass
BLACK STALLION RETURNS, THE(1983), w
Katyana Kass
OPTIMISTS, THE(1973, Brit.)
Lee Kass
IN THE NAVY(1941); WINDOW, THE(1949)
Nance Kass
1984
OLD ENOUGH(1984)
Peter Kass
TIME OF THE HEATHEN(1962), d&w, ed
Ronald S. Kass
STUD, THE(1979, Brit.), p
Kassagi
PICKPOCKET(1963, Fr.)
Lillian Kassan
NIGHTFALL(1956)
Mohammed Kassas
1984
LITTLE DRUMMER GIRL, THE(1984)
M. Kassatskaya
Misc. Silents
LOVE OF A STATE COUNCILLOR(1915, USSR)
Art Kassel
JANIE GETS MARRIED(1946); NIGHT AND DAY(1946)
Mohamed Ben Kassen
BATTLE OF ALGIERS, THE(1967, Ital./Alger.)
Jack Kassewitz
1984
HARRY AND SON(1984)
Helen Kassler
Silents
GOLD RUSH, THE(1925)
Peter A. Kassler
I CAN'T ESCAPE(1934), p
Marie Kassova
FOUR GIRLS IN TOWN(1956)
Peter Kassowitz
MY LIFE TO LIVE(1963, Fr.)
Art Kassul
10(1979); LOVING COUPLES(1980)
Pierre Kast
RED CLOAK, THE(1961, Ital./Fr.), w; NUDE IN HIS POCKET(1962, Fr.), d; SEASON FOR LOVE, THE(1963, Fr.), d, w
Thrasos Kastanakes
GIRL CAN'T STOP, THE(1966, Fr./Gr.), w
Bruno Kaster
Misc. Silents
CARNIVAL OF CRIME(1929, Ger.)
Herbert Kastle
CROSS COUNTRY(1983, Can.), w
Leonard Kastle
HONEYMOON KILLERS, THE(1969), d&w
Bruno Kastner
Misc. Silents
HILDE WARREN AND DEATH(1916, Ger.); THOU SHALT NOT STEAL(1929, Ger.)

Elliot Kastner
HARPER(1966), p; COUNT YOUR BULLETS(1972), p; 11 HARROWHOUSE(1974, Brit.), p; BIG SLEEP, THE½(1978, Brit.), p; DEATH VALLEY(1982), p; MAN, WOM-AN AND CHILD(1983), p
Elliott Kastner
BUS RILEY'S BACK IN TOWN(1965), p; KALEIDOSCOPE(1966, Brit.), p; BOBO, THE(1967, Brit.), p; SWEET NOVEMBER(1968), p; WHERE EAGLES DARE(1968, Brit.), p; WHEN EIGHT BELLS TOLL(1971, Brit.), p; COPS AND ROBBERS(1973), p; RANCHO DELUXE(1975), p; MISSOURI BREAKS, THE(1976), p; "EQUUS"(1977), p; BLACK JOY(1977, Brit.), p; LITTLE NIGHT MUSIC, A(1977, Aust./U.S./Ger.), p; FFOLKES(1980, Brit.), p; ABSOLUTION(1981, Brit.), p
1984
GARBO TALKS(1984), p; OXFORD BLUES(1984), p
Erich Kastner
EMIL AND THE DETECTIVE(1931, Ger.), w; EMIL(1938, Brit.), w; TWICE UPON A TIME(1953), w; PARENT TRAP, THE(1961), d&w; EMIL AND THE DETEC-TIVES(1964), w
John Kastner
DON'T LET THE ANGELS FALL(1969, Can.)
Peter Kastner
NOBODY WAVED GOODBYE(1965, Can.); YOU'RE A BIG BOY NOW(1966); B.S. I LOVE YOU(1971); FRIGHTMARE(1983)
Vladimir Kasyanov
Misc. Silents
DEATH OF THE GODS(1917, USSR), d
L. Kasyanova
DON QUIXOTE(1961, USSR)
Kurt Kasznar
LIGHT TOUCH, THE(1951); ANYTHING CAN HAPPEN(1952); GLORY AL-LEY(1952); HAPPY TIME, THE(1952); LOVELY TO LOOK AT(1952); TALK ABOUT A STRANGER(1952); ALL THE BROTHERS WERE VALIANT(1953); GIVE A GIRL A BREAK(1953); GREAT DIAMOND ROBBERY(1953); KISS ME KATE(1953); LI-LI(1953); RIDE, VAQUERO!(1953); SOMBRERO(1953); LAST TIME I SAW PARIS, THE(1954); VALLEY OF THE KINGS(1954); FLAME OF THE ISLANDS(1955); JUMP INTO HELL(1955); MY SISTER EILEEN(1955); ANYTHING GOES(1956); LEGEND OF THE LOST(1957, U.S./Panama/Ital.); FOR THE FIRST TIME(1959, U.S./Ger./Ital.); JOURNEY, THE(1959, U.S./Aust.); ARMS AND THE MAN(1962, Ger.); 55 DAYS AT PEKING(1963); AMBUSHERS, THE(1967); CASINO ROYALE(1967, Brit.); KING'S PIRATE(1967); PERILS OF PAULINE, THE(1967)
C. Kasznia
JOVITA(1970, Pol.)
Lucjan Kaszycki
PARTINGS(1962, Pol.), m
Elizabeth Kata
NIGHT WALKER, THE(1964), w; PATCH OF BLUE, A(1965), d&w
Piotr Kataev
THREE TALES OF CHEKHOV(1961, USSR), ph
Tsuneo Katagiri
SEVEN SAMURAI, THE(1956, Jap.)
Julia Katayama
NAVY WIFE(1956)
P. Katayev
HOME FOR TANYA, A(1961, USSR), ph
Valentin Katayev
SON OF THE REGIMENT(1948, USSR), w
Kazuhiko Katch
ALL RIGHT, MY FRIEND(1983, Japan), md
Kuit Katch
GIRL IN THE KREMLIN, THE(1957)
Kurt Katch
MAN AT LARGE(1941); WOLF MAN, THE(1941); BERLIN CORRESPONDENT(1942); COUNTER-ESPIONAGE(1942); DESPERATE JOURNEY(1942); QUIET PLEASE, MURDER(1942); SECRET AGENT OF JAPAN(1942); WIFE TAKES A FLYER, THE(1942); BACKGROUND TO DANGER(1943); EDGE OF DARKNESS(1943); MIS-SION TO MOSCOW(1943); PURPLE V, THE(1943); STRANGE DEATH OF ADOLF HITLER, THE(1943); THEY CAME TO BLOW UP AMERICA(1943); WATCH ON THE RHINE(1943); ALI BABA AND THE FORTY THIEVES(1944); CONSPIRATORS, THE(1944); MAKE YOUR OWN BED(1944); MASK OF DIMITRIOS, THE(1944); MUMMY'S CURSE, THE(1944); PURPLE HEART, THE(1944); SEVENTH CROSS, THE(1944); SALOME, WHERE SHE DANCED(1945); ANGEL ON MY SHOUL-DER(1946); RENDEZVOUS 24(1946); STRANGE JOURNEY(1946); SONG OF LO-VE(1947); ADVENTURES OF HAJJI BABA(1954); SECRET OF THE INCAS(1954); ABBOTT AND COSTELLO MEET THE MUMMY(1955); HOT CARS(1956); NEVER SAY GOODBYE(1956); PHARAOH'S CURSE(1957); BEAST OF BUDAPEST, THE(1958); YOUNG LIONS, THE(1958)
Vahe Katcha
HOOK, THE(1962), w; GALIA(1966, Fr./Ital.), w; TWO WEEKS IN SEPTEM-BER(1967, Fr./Brit.), w; FEMMINA(1968 Fr./Ital./Ger.), w; SABRA(1970, Fr./Ital./Israel), w; BURGLARS, THE(1972, Fr./Ital.), w
Pete G. Katchenaro
ROAD TO MOROCCO(1942)
Pete Katchenaro
PURPLE HEART, THE(1944); SONG OF OLD WYOMING(1945); SONG OF THE SARONG(1945)
Aram Katcher
SPY HUNT(1950); LIGHT TOUCH, THE(1951); BACK AT THE FRONT(1952); INVA-SION U.S.A.(1952); DREAM WIFE(1953); EAST OF SUMATRA(1953); KING OF THE KHYBER RIFLES(1953); PARIS MODEL(1953); THUNDER IN THE EAST(1953); FLIGHT TO HONG KONG(1956); GIRL IN THE KREMLIN, THE(1957); FEMALE ANIMAL, THE(1958); RIGHT HAND OF THE DEVIL, THE(1963), a, p&d, w, ed, makeup; DO NOT DISTURB(1965); PERILS OF PAULINE, THE(1967)
Leo Katcher
BETWEEN MIDNIGHT AND DAWN(1950), w; M(1951), w; THEY RODE WEST(1954), w; NAKED STREET, THE(1955), w; EDDY DUCHIN STORY, THE(1956), w; HARD MAN, THE(1957), w; PARTY GIRL(1958), w; KING OF THE ROARING TWENTIES–THE STORY OF ARNOLD ROTHSTEIN(1961), w; ISLAND OF LO-VE(1963), w

Robert Katcher
  BEHIND THE RISING SUN(1943); JACK LONDON(1943)
Edward Kate
  DRAGNET(1974), md
Kateb
  L'ETOILE DU NORD(1983, Fr.)
Sam Kateman
  CODE OF THE CACTUS(1939), p
Katerinaki
  SIGNS OF LIFE(1981, Ger.)
Bernard Kates
  YOU'RE IN THE NAVY NOW(1951); TWELVE HOURS TO KILL(1960); JUDGMENT AT NUREMBERG(1961); SUPER COPS, THE(1974)
Katharine Kath
  CIRCUS WORLD(1964)
Katherine Kath
  MOULIN ROUGE(1952); ANASTASIA(1956); PERIL FOR THE GUY(1956, Brit.); TOUCH OF THE SUN, A(1956, Brit.); LET'S BE HAPPY(1957, Brit.); DANGEROUS YOUTH(1958, Brit.); MAN WHO WOULDN'T TALK, THE(1958, Brit.); BEASTS OF MARSEILLES, THE(1959, Brit.); SUBWAY IN THE SKY(1959, Brit.); GIGOT(1962); FURY AT SMUGGLERS BAY(1963, Brit.); MC GUIRE, GO HOME!(1966, Brit.); ASSASSINATION BUREAU, THE(1969, Brit.); MARY, QUEEN OF SCOTS(1971, Brit.)
Pam Kath
  ELECTRA GLIDE IN BLUE(1973)
Terry Kath
  ELECTRA GLIDE IN BLUE(1973)
Katharyna
  CIRCUS WORLD(1964)
Katherine Dunham and Her Troupe
  STORMY WEATHER(1943)
Katherine Dunham Dance Troupe with Eartha Kitt
  CASBAH(1948)
Katherine Dunham Dancers
  PARDON MY SARONG(1942)
Rupe Kathner
  GLENROWAN AFFAIR, THE(1951, Aus.), a, d&w
David Katims
  FRIDAY THE 13TH PART III(1982)
Diana Katis
  PRIVILEGED(1982, Brit.)
Norman Katkov
  IT HAPPENED TO JANE(1959), w; ONCE YOU KISS A STRANGER(1969), w; VIVA KNIEVEL!(1977), w
Cha Kato
  HOTSPRINGS HOLIDAY(1970, Jap.)
Daisuke Kato
  SAMURAI(PART II)** (1967, Jap.); RASHOMON(1951, Jap.); SAMURAI(1955, Jap.); SEVEN SAMURAI, THE(1956, Jap.); IKIRU(1960, Jap.); I BOMBED PEARL HARBOR(1961, Jap.); NIGHT IN HONG KONG, A(1961, Jap.); YOJIMBO(1961, Jap.); EARLY AUTUMN(1962, Jap.); STAR OF HONG KONG(1962, Jap.); WISER AGE(1962, Jap.); LONELY LANE(1963, Jap.); SNOW IN THE SOUTH SEAS(1963, Jap.), a, w; WHEN A WOMAN ASCENDS THE STAIRS(1963, Jap.); LIFE OF OHARU(1964, Jap.); NAKED GENERAL, THE(1964, Jap.); JUDO SAGA(1965, Jap.); TWILIGHT PATH(1965, Jap.); GAMBLING SAMURAI, THE(1966, Jap.); RISE AGAINST THE SWORD(1966, Jap.); WE WILL REMEMBER(1966, Jap.); DAPHNE, THE(1967); THIN LINE, THE(1967, Jap.); EMPEROR AND A GENERAL, THE(1968, Jap.); ONCE A RAINY DAY(1968, Jap.); TWO IN THE SHADOW(1968, Jap.); MOMENT OF TERROR(1969, Jap.); OUR SILENT LOVE(1969, Jap.)
Go Kato
  SCARLET CAMELLIA, THE(1965, Jap.); REBELLION(1967, Jap.)
Haruko Kato
  EAST CHINA SEA(1969, Jap.); GIRL I ABANDONED, THE(1970, Jap.)
Haruya Kato
  MOTHRA(1962, Jap.)
Kazuo Kato
  I LIVE IN FEAR(1967, Jap.); GOKE, BODYSNATCHER FROM HELL(1968, Jap.)
Miki Kato
  PRIVATE LIVES OF ADAM AND EVE, THE(1961)
Takeshi Kato
  HAPPINESS OF US ALONE(1962, Jap.); HIGH AND LOW(1963, Jap.); NONE BUT THE BRAVE(1965, U.S./Jap.); REBELLION(1967, Jap.); EMPEROR AND A GENERAL, THE(1968, Jap.); GIRL I ABANDONED, THE(1970, Jap.); SUMMER SOLDIERS(1972, Jap.)
Yasuhide Kato
  NAKED GENERAL, THE(1964, Jap.), art d; PRODIGAL SON, THE(1964, Jap.), art d; MAN IN THE STORM, THE(1969, Jap.), art d
Yoshi Kato
  SCARLET CAMELLIA, THE(1965, Jap.); HIKEN YABURI(1969, Jap.); DOUBLE SUICIDE(1970, Jap.); KURAGEJIMA–LEGENDS FROM A SOUTHERN ISLAND(1970, Jap.)
Lenore Katon
  AGE OF CONSENT(1969, Austral.)
Rosanne Katon
  CHESTY ANDERSON, U.S. NAVY(1976); MOTEL HELL(1980); LUNCH WAGON(1981); ZAPPED!(1982)
1984
  CITY GIRL, THE(1984)
Misc. Talkies
  MUTHERS, THE(1976); EBONY, IVORY AND JADE(1977)
Piroska Katona
  DIALOGUE(1967, Hung.), cos
Victor Katona
  MRS. PYM OF SCOTLAND YARD(1939, Brit.), p; ROOM FOR TWO(1940, Brit.), p; TURNERS OF PROSPECT ROAD, THE(1947, Brit.), p, w; ONCE UPON A DREAM(1949, Brit.), w; TWENTY QUESTIONS MURDER MYSTERY, THE(1950, Brit.), p, w; DON'T BLAME THE STORK(1954, Brit.), p, w
Usha Katrak
  GURU, THE(1969, U.S./India)

Manos Katrakis
  ANTIGONE(1962 Gr.); ELECTRA(1962, Gr.); RED LANTERNS(1965, Gr.); DREAM OF PASSION, A(1978, Gr.)
Sister Katrina
  AND NOW MIGUEL(1966)
Andonia Katsaros
  LOOT(1971, Brit.); TIME AFTER TIME(1979, Brit.)
Antonia Katsaros
  AGE OF CONSENT(1969, Austral.)
Robert Katscher
  WONDER BAR(1934), w
Rudolf Katscher
  TRAPEZE(1932, Ger.), w; INVISIBLE OPPONENT(1933, Ger.), d
Rudolp Katscher
  COPPER, THE(1930, Brit.), w
Rudolph Katscher
  SHOT AT DAWN, A(1934, Ger.), w
Milton Katselas
  WHEN YOU COMIN' BACK, RED RYDER?(1979), d; BUTTERFLIES ARE FREE(1972), d; FORTY CARATS(1973), d; REPORT TO THE COMMISSIONER(1975), d
Aleka Katselli
  ELECTRA(1962, Gr.)
Nico Katsiotes
  BAREFOOT BATTALION, THE(1954, Gr.), w
Katsou the Dog
  LADIES OF THE PARK(1964, Fr.)
Dinos Katsourdis
  ANTIGONE(1962 Gr.), ph
Dinos Katsourides
  MATCHMAKING OF ANNA, THE(1972, Gr.), p
Dinos Katsouridis
  WE HAVE ONLY ONE LIFE(1963, Gr.), ph
Shintara Katsu
  DEVIL'S TEMPLE(1969, Jap.)
Shintari Katsu
  ZATOICHI MEETS YOJIMBO(1970, Jap.)
Shintaro Katsu
  BUDDHA(1965, Jap.); GREAT WALL, THE(1965, Jap.); SHOWDOWN FOR ZATOICHI(1968, Jap.); ZATOICHI(1968, Jap.); MAGOICHI SAGA, THE(1970, Jap.); TENCHU!(1970, Jap.); ZATOICHI CHALLENGED(1970, Jap.); ZATOICHI'S CONSPIRACY(1974, Jap.), a, p
K. Katsumoto
  BRIDGE ON THE RIVER KWAI, THE(1957)
Kokan Katsura
  FRIENDLY KILLER, THE(1970, Jap.)
Kokinji Katsura
  MAN FROM THE EAST, THE(1961, Jap.)
Kokinjo Katsura
  ROAD TO ETERNITY(1962, Jap.)
Maki Katsura
  JUDO SHOWDOWN(1966, Jap.)
Yoko Katsuragi
  SCANDAL(1964, Jap.)
Bill [William] Katt
  LATE LIZ, THE(1971)
Geraldine Katt
  FOUR IN A JEEP(1951, Switz.)
Nick Katt
1984
  GREMLINS(1984)
William Katt
  CARRIE(1976); FIRST LOVE(1977); BIG WEDNESDAY(1978); BUTCH AND SUNDANCE: THE EARLY DAYS(1979)
Monte Katterjohn
  BROADWAY BABIES(1929), w; PARADISE ISLAND(1930), w; PARTY GIRL(1930), w; DAUGHTER OF THE DRAGON(1931), w
Silents
  WALKING BACK(1928), w
Monte J. Katterjohn
Silents
  CAPTIVE GOD, THE(1916), w
Monte M. Katterjohn
Silents
  APOSTLE OF VENGEANCE, THE(1916), w; JUNGLE CHILD, THE(1916), w; PATRIOT, THE(1916), w; FEMALE OF THE SPECIES(1917), w; ALIEN ENEMY, AN(1918), w; CARMEN OF THE KLONDIKE(1918), w; INSIDE THE LINES(1918), w; LORD LOVES THE IRISH, THE(1919), w; SHEIK, THE(1921), w; IMPOSSIBLE MRS. BELLEW, THE(1922), w; MORAN OF THE LADY LETTY(1922), w; ETERNAL STRUGGLE, THE(1923), w; MY AMERICAN WIFE(1923), w; SOCIAL CELEBRITY, A(1926), w
Nick Katurich
  BAMBOO SAUCER, THE(1968); MRS. POLLIFAX-SPY(1971)
Masaru Katutani
1984
  ANTARCTICA(1984, Jap.), p
Alan Katz
  HAPPY BIRTHDAY TO ME(1981)
Allan Katz
Misc. Talkies
  HARD FEELINGS(1981)
Bernard Katz
  STREET CORNER(1948), m
Brent Katz
  AMITYVILLE II: THE POSSESSION(1982)
Clifford Katz
  MOUNTAIN FAMILY ROBINSON(1979), ed

Eric Katz
HI, MOM!(1970), m

Erica Katz
AMITYVILLE II: THE POSSESSION(1982)

Fred Katz
BUCKET OF BLOOD, A(1959), m; WASP WOMAN, THE(1959), m; SKI TROOP ATTACK(1960), m; CREATURE FROM THE HAUNTED SEA(1961), m; LITTLE SHOP OF HORRORS(1961), m

Gloria Katz
AMERICAN GRAFFITI(1973), w; DEAD PEOPLE(1974), p, w; LUCKY LADY(1975), w; FRENCH POSTCARDS(1979), a, p, w; MORE AMERICAN GRAFFITI(1979), w
1984
BEST DEFENSE(1984), p, w; INDIANA JONES AND THE TEMPLE OF DOOM(1984), w

Lee Katz
HEART OF THE NORTH(1938), w; BLACKWELL'S ISLAND(1939), w; CODE OF THE SECRET SERVICE(1939), w; I AM NOT AFRAID(1939), w; KID NIGHTIN-GALE(1939), w; MAN WHO DARED, THE(1939), w; NO PLACE TO GO(1939), w; RETURN OF DR. X, THE(1939), w; WATERFRONT(1939), w; WOMEN IN THE WIND(1939), w; BRITISH INTELLIGENCE(1940), w

Max Katz
Misc. Talkies
JIM THE MAN(1967), d

Patty Katz
POPEYE(1980)

Peter Katz
DON'T LOOK NOW(1973, Brit./Ital.), p

Pitzy Katz
DOUGH BOYS(1930)

Robert Katz
MASSACRE IN ROME(1973, Ital.), w; CASSANDRA CROSSING, THE(1977), w; KAMIKAZE '89(1983, Ger.), w; SALAMANDER, THE(1983, U.S./Ital./Brit.), w

Saul Katz
WHY RUSSIANS ARE REVOLTING(1970)

Sid Katz
HEY, LET'S TWIST!(1961), ed; PASSION HOLIDAY(1963); WHO SAYS I CAN'T RIDE A RAINBOW!(1971), ed; RANCHO DELUXE(1975), ed

Sidney Katz
STRANGE ONE, THE(1957), ed; ER LOVE A STRANGER(1958), ed; PUSHER, THE(1960), p, ed; ROUND TRIP(1967), ed; LOVELY WAY TO DIE, A(1968), ed; PAPER LION(1968), ed; SWIMMER, THE(1968), ed; LAST SUMMER(1969), ed; DIARY OF A MAD HOUSEWIFE(1970), ed; HOUSE OF DARK SHADOWS(1970), ed; LOVERS AND OTHER STRANGERS(1970), ed; DEALING: OR THE BERKELEY-TO-BOSTON FORTY-BRICK LOST-BAG BLUES(1971), ed; HAPPINESS CAGE, THE(1972), ed; PLAY IT AS IT LAYS(1972), ed; LIFE STUDY(1973), ed; SUMMER WISHES, WINTER DREAMS(1973), ed; MAN ON A SWING(1974), ed; CHILD IS A WILD THING, A(1976), ed; PREMONITION, THE(1976), ed

Stephen Katz
DEAD PEOPLE(1974), ph; BITTERSWEET LOVE(1976), ph; LAS VEGAS LA-DY(1976), ph; OUR WINNING SEASON(1978), ph; LITTLE DRAGONS, THE(1980), ph

Stephen M. Katz
YOUR THREE MINUTES ARE UP(1973), ph; BEST FRIENDS(1975), ph; POM POM GIRLS, THE(1976), ph; JOYRIDE(1977), ph; KENTUCKY FRIED MOVIE, THE(1977), ph; BLUES BROTHERS, THE(1980), ph

Steve Katz
ANGELS HARD AS THEY COME(1971), ph; HEX(1973), w

Steven Katz
STUDENT TEACHERS, THE(1973), ph

Wilbur Katz
BLACKWELL'S ISLAND(1939), w

Z. Katz
DYBBUK THE(1938, Pol.)

Gabriel Katza
KELLY'S HEROES(1970, U.S./Yugo.), p

Chuck Katzaian
DEATH MACHINES(1976)

Sandra Katzel
1984
REVENGE OF THE NERDS(1984)

Dorothea Katzer
1984
CLASS ENEMY(1984, Ger.), cos

Lee H. Katzin
HEAVEN WITH A GUN(1969), d; WHAT EVER HAPPENED TO AUNT ALI-CE?(1969), d; PHYNX, THE(1970), d; LE MANS(1971), d; SALZBURG CONNECTION, THE(1972), d

Gabriel Katzka
TAKING OF PELHAM ONE, TWO, THREE, THE(1974), p; MARLOWE(1969), p; SOLDIER BLUE(1970), p; WHO'LL STOP THE RAIN?(1978), p; BUTCH AND SUN-DANCE: THE EARLY DAYS(1979), p; BEAST WITHIN, THE(1982), p; LORDS OF DISCIPLINE, THE(1983), p

Alfred Katzman
NIGHTMARE IN BLOOD(1978), ed

Bruce Katzman
HANGAR 18(1980)

Jerome F. Katzman
ANGEL, ANGEL, DOWN WE GO(1969), p

Jerry Katzman
LONERS, THE(1972), p

Leonard Katzman
SPACE MONSTER(1965), d&w

Lon Katzman
PROPHECY(1979)

Sam Katzman
DANGER AHEAD(1935), p; FACE IN THE FOG, A(1936), p; KELLY OF THE SECRET SERVICE(1936), p; PUT ON THE SPOT(1936), p; RIO GRANDE ROMAN-CE(1936), p; RIP ROARIN' BUCKAROO(1936), p; AMATEUR CROOK(1937), p&d; CHEYENNE RIDES AGAIN(1937), p; LOST RANCH(1937), p&d; MYSTERY RAN-GE(1937), p; TWO MINUTES TO PLAY(1937), p; $1,000,000 RACKET(1937), p; BROTHERS OF THE WEST(1938), p&d; FEUD OF THE TRAIL(1938), p; ORPHAN OF THE PECOS(1938), p&d; PHANTOM OF THE RANGE, THE(1938), p; FIGHTING RENEGADE(1939), p; OUTLAW'S PARADISE(1939), p; TEXAS WILDCATS(1939), p; TRIGGER FINGERS ½(1939), p; BOYS OF THE CITY(1940), p; EAST SIDE KIDS(1940), p; STRAIGHT SHOOTER(1940), p; THAT GANG OF MINE(1940), p; BOWERY BLITZKRIEG(1941), p; FLYING WILD(1941), p; INVISIBLE GHOST, THE(1941), p; PRIDE OF THE BOWERY(1941), p; SPOOKS RUN WILD(1941), p; ZIS BOOM BAH(1941), p; BLACK DRAGONS(1942), p; BOWERY AT MIDNIGHT(1942), p; COLLEGE SWEETHEARTS(1942), p; CORPSE VANISHES, THE(1942), p; LET'S GET TOUGH(1942), p; MR. WISE GUY(1942), p; 'NEATH BROOKLYN BRIDGE(1942), p; SMART ALECKS(1942), p; APE MAN, THE(1943), p; CLANCY STREET BOYS(1943), p; GHOSTS ON THE LOOSE(1943), p; KID DYNAMITE(1943), p; MR. MUGGS STEPS OUT(1943), p; SPOTLIGHT SCANDALS(1943), p; BLOCK BUSTERS(1944), p; BOW-ERY CHAMPS(1944), p; CRAZY KNIGHTS(1944), p; FOLLOW THE LEADER(1944), p; MILLION DOLLAR KID(1944), p; RETURN OF THE APE MAN(1944), p; VOODOO MAN(1944), p; COME OUT FIGHTING(1945), p; DOCKS OF NEW YORK(1945), p; MR. MUGGS RIDES AGAIN(1945), p; BETTY CO-ED(1946), p; FREDDIE STEPS OUT(1946), p; HIGH SCHOOL HERO(1946), p; JUNIOR PROM(1946), p; GLAMOUR GIRL(1947), p; LAST OF THE REDMEN(1947), p; LITTLE MISS BROADWAY(1947), p; TWO BLONDES AND A REDHEAD(1947), p; VACATION DAYS(1947), p; I SUR-RENDER DEAR(1948), p; JUNGLE JIM(1948), p; MANHATTAN ANGEL(1948), p; MARY LOU(1948), p; PRINCE OF THIEVES, THE(1948), p; RACING LUCK(1948), p; TRIPLE THREAT(1948), p; BARBARY PIRATE(1949), p; CHINATOWN AT MID-NIGHT(1949), p; LOST TRIBE, THE(1949), p; MUTINEERS, THE(1949), p; CAPTIVE GIRL(1950), p; CHAIN GANG(1950), p; LAST OF THE BUCCANEERS(1950), p; MARK OF THE GORILLA(1950), p; PYGMY ISLAND(1950), p; REVENUE AGENT(1950), p; STATE PENITENTIARY(1950), p; TYRANT OF THE SEA(1950), p; FURY OF THE CONGO(1951), p; HURRICANE ISLAND(1951), p; JUNGLE MAN-HUNT(1951), p; MAGIC CARPET, THE(1951), p; PURPLE HEART DIARY(1951), p; WHEN THE REDSKINS RODE(1951), p; YANK IN KOREA, A(1951), p; BRAVE WARRIOR(1952), p; CALIFORNIA CONQUEST(1952), p; GOLDEN HAWK, THE(1952), p; JUNGLE JIM IN THE FORBIDDEN LAND(1952), p; LAST TRAIN FROM BOMBAY(1952), p; PATHFINDER, THE(1952), p; THIEF OF DAMAS-CUS(1952), p; VOODOO TIGER(1952), p; YANK IN INDO-CHINA, A(1952), p; CHARGE OF THE LANCERS(1953), p; CONQUEST OF COCHISE(1953), p; FLAME OF CALCUTTA(1953), p; FORT TI(1953), p; FORTY-NINTH MAN, THE(1953), p; JACK MCCALL, DESPERADO(1953), p; KILLER APE(1953), p; PRINCE OF PI-RATES(1953), p; PRISONERS OF THE CASBAH(1953), p; SAVAGE MUTINY(1953), p; SERPENT OF THE NILE(1953), p; SIREN OF BAGDAD(1953), p; SKY COMMAN-DO(1953), p; SLAVES OF BABYLON(1953), p; VALLEY OF THE HEADHUN-TERS(1953), p; BATTLE OF ROGUE RIVER(1954), p; CANNIBAL ATTACK(1954), p; DRUMS OF TAHITI(1954), p; IRON GLOVE, THE(1954), p; JESSE JAMES VERSUS THE DALTONS(1954), p; JUNGLE MAN-EATERS(1954), p; LAW VS. BILLY THE KID, THE(1954), p; MASTERSON OF KANSAS(1954), p; MIAMI STORY, THE(1954), p; SARACEN BLADE, THE(1954), p; CREATURE WITH THE ATOM BRAIN(1955), p; DEVIL GODDESS(1955), p; GUN THAT WON THE WEST, THE(1955), p; INSIDE DETROIT(1955), p; JUNGLE MOON MEN(1955), p; NEW ORLEANS UNCEN-SORED(1955), p; PIRATES OF TRIPOLI(1955), p; SEMINOLE UPRISING(1955), p; TEEN-AGE CRIME WAVE(1955), p; BLACKJACK KETCHUM, DESPERADO(1956), p; CHA-CHA-CHA BOOM(1956), p; DON'T KNOCK THE ROCK(1956), p; HOUSTON STORY, THE(1956), p; MIAMI EXPOSE(1956), p; ROCK AROUND THE CLOCK(1956), p; RUMBLE ON THE DOCKS(1956), p; URANIUM BOOM(1956), p; WEREWOLF, THE(1956), p; CALYPSO HEAT WAVE(1957), p; ESCAPE FROM SAN QUEN-TIN(1957), p; GIANT CLAW, THE(1957), p; MAN WHO TURNED TO STONE, THE(1957), p; NIGHT THE WORLD EXPLODED, THE(1957), p; TIJUANA STORY, THE(1957), p; UTAH BLAINE(1957), p; ZOMBIES OF MORA TAU(1957), p; CRASH LANDING(1958), p; GOING STEADY(1958), p; LAST BLITZKRIEG, THE(1958), p; LIFE BEGINS AT 17(1958), p; WORLD WAS HIS JURY, THE(1958), p; FLYING FONTAINES, THE(1959), p; JUKE BOX RHYTHM(1959), p; ENEMY GENERAL, THE(1960), p; WIZARD OF BAGHDAD, THE(1960), p; PIRATES OF TORTUGA(1961), p; TWIST AROUND THE CLOCK(1961), p; DON'T KNOCK THE TWIST(1962), p; WILD WESTERNERS, THE(1962), p; HOOTENANNY HOOT(1963), p; GET YOUR-SELF A COLLEGE GIRL(1964), p; KISSIN' COUSINS(1964), p; YOUR CHEATIN' HEART(1964), p; HARUM SCARUM(1965), p; WHEN THE BOYS MEET THE GIRLS(1965), p; HOLD ON(1966), p; FASTEST GUITAR ALIVE, THE(1967), p; HOT RODS TO HELL(1967), p; LOVE-INS, THE(1967), p; RIOT ON SUNSET STRIP(1967), p; FOR SINGLES ONLY(1968), p; TIME TO SING, A(1968), p; YOUNG RUNAWAYS, THE(1968), p

Sherril Lynn Katzman
BUTCH AND SUNDANCE: THE EARLY DAYS(1979)

Marvin Katzoff
H.O.T.S.(1979)
1984
HARDBODIES(1984)

Iftah Katzur
1984
AMBASSADOR, THE(1984)

Gene Kauer
MA BARKER'S KILLER BROOD(1960), m; FIVE MINUTES TO LIVE(1961), m; SILENT WITNESS, THE(1962), m; AGENT FOR H.A.R.M.(1966), m; MOTHER GOOSE A GO-GO(1966), m; WARKILL(1968, U.S./Phil.), m; PROUD AND THE DAMNED, THE(1972), m; ADVENTURES OF THE WILDERNESS FAMILY, THE(1975), m; ACROSS THE GREAT DIVIDE(1976), m
1984
SACRED GROUND(1984), m

Guenther Kauer
ASTOUNDING SHE-MONSTER, THE(1958), m

Walther Kauer
BLACK SPIDER, THE(1983, Swit.), w

Jim Kauf
CLASS(1983), w

M. James Kauf, Jr.
WACKO(1983), w

Joe Kaufenberg
LONE WOLF McQUADE(1983)

Susan Kaufenberg
LONE WOLF McQUADE(1983)

Jonathan Kaufer
SOUP FOR ONE(1982), d&w
Cristen Kauffman
1984
JOY OF SEX(1984)
Daniel Kauffman
Misc. Talkies
ALICE GOODBODY(1974); GOSH(1974)
John Kauffman
CINDERELLA LIBERTY(1973)
Misc. Talkies
DIDN'T YOU HEAR(1983)
Maurice Kauffman
MAN WITHOUT A BODY, THE(1957, Brit.); GORGO(1961, Brit.)
Paula Kauffman
GLORY BOY(1971)
Reginald Wright Kauffman
SCHOOL FOR GIRLS(1935), w
Shirley Kauffman
Misc. Talkies
ARNOLD'S WRECKING CO.(1973)
Tamara Lynn Kauffman
ROARIN' LEAD(1937)
Boris Kauffmann
CINDERELLA(1937, Fr.), ph
Jerry Kaufherr
FINNEY(1969)
Al Kaufman
Silents
AFRAID TO FIGHT(1922); WHITE HANDS(1922); MARRY IN HASTE(1924); NEW CHAMPION(1925)
Misc. Silents
GOD'S GOLD(1921); TIGER TRUE(1921)
Albert A. Kaufman
Silents
COURAGE(1921), p
Allan Kaufman
HELL CANYON OUTLAWS(1957), w
Andy Kaufman
GOD TOLD ME TO(1976); IN GOD WE TRUST(1980); HEARTBEEPS(1981); MY BREAKFAST WITH BLASSIE(1983)
Anthony Kaufman
DOCTOR FAUSTUS(1967, Brit.)
Bel Kaufman
UP THE DOWN STAIRCASE(1967), w
Bob Kaufman
FLOWER THIEF, THE(1962); GETTING STRAIGHT(1970), w
Boris Kaufman
L'ATALANTE(1947, Fr.), ph; GARDEN OF EDEN(1954), ph; ON THE WATERFRONT(1954), ph; BABY DOLL(1956), ph; CROWDED PARADISE(1956), ph; PATTERNS(1956), ph; SINGING IN THE DARK(1956), ph; 12 ANGRY MEN(1957), ph; THAT KIND OF WOMAN(1959), ph; FUGITIVE KIND, THE(1960), ph; SPLENDOR IN THE GRASS(1961), ph; LONG DAY'S JOURNEY INTO NIGHT(1962), ph; ALL THE WAY HOME(1963), ph; GONE ARE THE DAYS(1963), ph; WORLD OF HENRY ORIENT, THE(1964), ph; PAWNBROKER, THE(1965), ph; GROUP, THE(1966), ph; BROTHERHOOD, THE(1968), ph; BYE BYE BRAVERMAN(1968), ph; UPTIGHT(1968), ph; TELL ME THAT YOU LOVE ME, JUNIE MOON(1970), ph
Brett Kaufman
ELECTRA GLIDE IN BLUE(1973)
Charles Kaufman
BREAKFAST FOR TWO(1937), w; SATURDAY'S HEROES(1937), w; BLOND CHEAT(1938), w; EXPOSED(1938), w; SAINT IN NEW YORK, THE(1938), w; MODEL WIFE(1941), w; CYNTHIA(1947), w; RETURN TO PARADISE(1953), w; RACERS, THE(1955), w; STORY OF ESTHER COSTELLO, THE(1957, Brit.), w; BRIDGE TO THE SUN(1961), w; FREUD(1962), w; MOTHER'S DAY(1980), d, w; SQUEEZE PLAY(1981), w; WAITRESS(1982), w
Silents
CIVILIZATION(1916), ph; JOYOUS LIAR, THE(1919), ph; FLIRT, THE(1922), ph; STEP ON IT!(1922), ph; MERRY-GO-ROUND(1923), ph; WHAT WIVES WANT(1923), ph; GIRL ON THE STAIRS, THE(1924), ph; LAW FORBIDS, THE(1924), ph
Charles S. Kaufman
PARIS CALLING(1941), w
Christine Kaufman
SWORDSMAN OF SIENA, THE(1962, Fr./Ital.)
Chuck Kaufman
GREAT WHITE, THE(1982, Ital.)
Curt Kaufman
UP IN SMOKE(1978)
David Kaufman
HOT SUMMER WEEK(1973, Can.), w
David M. Kaufman
WEREWOLVES ON WHEELS(1971), w
Edward Kaufman
MAKING THE GRADE(1929), w; AGGIE APPLEBY, MAKER OF MEN(1933), w; COCKEYED CAVALIERS(1934), w; GAY DIVORCEE, THE(1934), w; HIPS, HIPS, HOORAY(1934), w; GOING HIGHBROW(1935), w; MC FADDEN'S FLATS(1935), w; ROMANCE IN MANHATTAN(1935), w; STAR OF MIDNIGHT(1935), w; EX-MRS. BRADFORD, THE(1936), p; LADY CONSENTS, THE(1936), p; SMARTEST GIRL IN TOWN(1936), p; WALKING ON AIR(1936), p; WE'RE ONLY HUMAN(1936), p; BREAKFAST FOR TWO(1937), p; LIFE OF THE PARTY, THE(1937), p; WISE GIRL(1937), p; RADIO CITY REVELS(1938), p; NEWS IS MADE AT NIGHT(1939), p; AFFECTIONATELY YOURS(1941), w; THEY ALL KISSED THE BRIDE(1942), p; SONG OF SCHEHERAZADE(1947), p
Ernie Kaufman
STAKEOUT ON DOPE STREET(1958)
Ethel Kaufman
Misc. Silents
CHILDREN OF THE GHETTO, THE(1915); WORMWOOD(1915)

Evelyn Kaufman
THUNDER ISLAND(1963)
Frank Kaufman
BATTLE OF LOVE'S RETURN, THE(1971), m
George Kaufman
NOT SO DUMB(1930), w; STAR SPANGLED RHYTHM(1942), w
George S. Kaufman
COCOANUTS, THE(1929), w; ANIMAL CRACKERS(1930), w; ROYAL FAMILY OF BROADWAY, THE(1930), w; JUNE MOON(1931), w; EXPERT, THE(1932), w; MAKE ME A STAR(1932), w; ONCE IN A LIFETIME(1932), w; TENDERFOOT, THE(1932), w; DINNER AT EIGHT(1933), w; ROMAN SCANDALS(1933), w; ELMER AND ELSIE(1934), w; MAN WITH TWO FACES, THE(1934), w; HELLO SWEETHEART(1935, Brit.), w; NIGHT AT THE OPERA, A(1935), w; BLONDE TROUBLE(1937), w; DANCE, CHARLIE, DANCE(1937), w; FIRST LADY(1937), w; STAGE DOOR(1937), w; YOU CAN'T TAKE IT WITH YOU(1938), w; NO PLACE TO GO(1939), w; ANGEL FROM TEXAS, AN(1940), w; DULCY(1940), w; GEORGE WASHINGTON SLEPT HERE(1942), w; MAN WHO CAME TO DINNER, THE(1942), w; DARK TOWER, THE(1943, Brit.), w; GOOD FELLOWS, THE(1943), w; LATE GEORGE APLEY, THE(1947), w; MERTON OF THE MOVIES(1947), d; DANCING IN THE DARK(1949), w; THREE SAILORS AND A GIRL(1953), w; SOLID GOLD CADILLAC, THE(1956), w; SILK STOCKINGS(1957), w
Silents
DULCY(1923), w; MERTON OF THE MOVIES(1924), w; BEGGAR ON HORSEBACK(1925), w
Henry Kaufman
MYSTERY SUBMARINE(1963, Brit.)
Herbert Kaufman
GUNSMOKE IN TUCSON(1958), p
Irwin Kaufman
SARGE GOES TO COLLEGE(1947)
Joe Kaufman
BEHIND THE MASK(1946), p; MISSING LADY, THE(1946), p; SHADOW RETURNS, THE(1946), p; BABE RUTH STORY, THE(1948), p
Joseph Kaufman
SENSATION HUNTERS(1945), p; LUCKY NICK CAIN(1951), p; PANDORA AND THE FLYING DUTCHMAN(1951, Brit.), p; SUDDEN FEAR(1952), p; LONG JOHN SILVER(1954, Aus.), p; ANOTHER TIME, ANOTHER PLACE(1958), p; BLACK TIGHTS(1962, Fr.), p; JOHNNY GOT HIS GUN(1971)
Misc. Talkies
HEAVY TRAFFIC(1974)
Silents
HOUSE NEXT DOOR, THE(1914); ASHES OF EMBERS(1916), d; NANETTE OF THE WILDS(1916), d; AMAZONS, THE(1917), d; ARMS AND THE GIRL(1917), d; GREAT EXPECTATIONS(1917), d
Misc. Silents
DARKNESS BEFORE DAWN, THE(1915); HEARTACHES(1915), d; DOLLARS AND THE WOMAN(1916), d; SORROWS OF HAPPINESS(1916), d; TRAVELING SALESMAN, THE(1916), d; WORLD'S GREAT SNARE, THE(1916), d; BROADWAY JONES(1917), d; LAND OF PROMISE, THE(1917), d; SHIRLEY KAYE(1917), d; SONG OF SONGS, THE(1918), d
Karen Kaufman
CROOKS IN CLOISTERS(1964, Brit.); RATTLE OF A SIMPLE MAN(1964, Brit.)
Ken Kaufman
1984
VAMPING(1984), m
L. Kaufman
WAITRESS(1982), ph
Leonard Kaufman
BIRDS DO IT(1966), w
Leonard B. Kaufman
CLARENCE, THE CROSS-EYED LION(1965), p
Lloyd Kaufman
BATTLE OF LOVE'S RETURN, THE(1971), a, p, d,w&ed; ROCKY(1976); FINAL COUNTDOWN, THE(1980); SQUEEZE PLAY(1981), p, ph; WAITRESS(1982), p; STUCK ON YOU(1983), p, w, ph
1984
FIRST TURN-ON!, THE(1984), p, w, ph; STUCK ON YOU(1984), p, w
M. Kaufman
CASH ON DELIVERY(1956, Brit.)
Maurice Kaufman
IT'S A WONDERFUL WORLD(1956, Brit.); SHOT IN THE DARK, A(1964); ABOMINABLE DR. PHIBES, THE(1971, Brit.); BLOOMFIELD(1971, Brit./Israel); FRIGHT(1971, Brit.)
Michael Kaufman
STARTING OVER(1979)
Mikhail Kaufman
Misc. Silents
MOSCOW(1927, USSR), d
Millard Kaufman
GUN CRAZY(1949), w; UNKNOWN WORLD(1951), w; ALADDIN AND HIS LAMP(1952), w; TAKE THE HIGH GROUND(1953), w; BAD DAY AT BLACK ROCK(1955), w; RAINTREE COUNTY(1957), w; NEVER SO FEW(1959), w; CONVICTS FOUR(1962), d&w; WAR LORD, THE(1965), w; LIVING FREE(1972, Brit.), w; KLANSMAN, THE(1974), w
Monica Kaufman
SHARKY'S MACHINE(1982)
P. Kaufman
WANDERERS, THE(1979), w
Paul Kaufman
NIGHT SHIFT(1982)
Phil Kaufman
FEARLESS FRANK(1967), p,d&w; OUTLAW JOSEY WALES, THE(1976), w
Philip Clarke Kaufman
HOWZER(1973), p
Philip Kaufman
GOLDSTEIN(1964), d&w; GREAT NORTHFIELD, MINNESOTA RAID, THE(1972), d, w; WHITE DAWN, THE(1974), d; INVASION OF THE BODY SNATCHERS(1978), d; WANDERERS, THE(1979), d; RAIDERS OF THE LOST ARK(1981), w; RIGHT STUFF, THE(1983), d&w

Reginald Wright Kaufman
Silents
MIDNIGHT LIFE(1928), w
Rita Kaufman
HAT CHECK GIRL(1932), cos; ME AND MY GAL(1932), cos; SHERLOCK HOL-MES(1932), cos; MR. SKITCH(1933), cos; POWER AND THE GLORY, THE(1933), cos; STATE FAIR(1933), cos; WORST WOMAN IN PARIS(1933), cos; CHANGE OF HEART(1934), cos; NOW I'LL TELL(1934), cos; SPRINGTIME FOR HENRY(1934), cos; WORLD MOVES ON, THE(1934), cos
Robert Kaufman
DR. GOLDFOOT AND THE BIKINI MACHINE(1965), w; SKI PARTY(1965), w; DR. GOLDFOOT AND THE GIRL BOMBS(1966, Ital.), w; EXILES, THE(1966), ph; COOL ONES THE(1967), w; DIVORCE AMERICAN STYLE(1967), w; I LOVE MY WI-FE(1970), a, w; FREEBIE AND THE BEAN(1974), w; HARRY AND WALTER GO TO NEW YORK(1976), w; HAPPY HOOKER GOES TO WASHINGTON, THE(1977), w; LOVE AT FIRST BITE(1979), w; HOW TO BEAT THE HIGH COST OF LIVING(1980), p, w; NOTHING PERSONAL(1980, Can.), w; SPLIT IMAGE(1982), w
Rose Kaufman
WANDERERS, THE(1979), w
S. Jay Kaufman
Silents
WANTED FOR MURDER(1919), w; GREATER THAN FAME(1920), w
Sam Kaufman
MONKEY'S PAW, THE(1933), makeup
Silents
KISMET(1920); RAGS TO RICHES(1922)
Seth Kaufman
1984
BODY ROCK(1984); HIGHWAY TO HELL(1984); RUNNING HOT(1984)
Stanley Kaufman
BATTLE OF LOVE'S RETURN, THE(1971)
Sue Kaufman
DIARY OF A MAD HOUSEWIFE(1970), w
Susan Kaufman
HE KNOWS YOU'RE ALONE(1980), art d
Will Kaufman
NURSE EDITH CAVELL(1939); MYSTERY SEA RAIDER(1940); THOUSANDS CHEER(1943); STORM OVER LISBON(1944); WHERE DO WE GO FROM HERE?(1945)
William Kaufman
MAN I MARRIED, THE(1940)
Willie Kaufman
BEASTS OF BERLIN(1939)
Willy Kaufman
CONFESSIONS OF A NAZI SPY(1939); BRITISH INTELLIGENCE(1940); UNDER-GROUND(1941); HITLER(1962)
Wolfe Kaufman
LONE WOLF MEETS A LADY, THE(1940), w; SUED FOR LIBEL(1940), w
Christine Kaufmann
EMBEZZLED HEAVEN(1959,Ger.); TOWN WITHOUT PITY(1961, Ger./Switz./U.S.); CONSTANTINE AND THE CROSS(1962, Ital.); ESCAPE FROM EAST BERLIN(1962); TARAS BULBA(1962); PHONY AMERICAN, THE(1964, Ger.); RED LIPS(1964, Fr./Ital.); WILD AND WONDERFUL(1964); MAEDCHEN IN UNIFORM(1965, Ger./Fr.); TERROR AFTER MIDNIGHT(1965, Ger.); MURDERS IN THE RUE MORGUE(1971); EGON SCHIELE–EXCESS AND PUNISHMENT(1981, Ger.); LILI MARLEEN(1981, Ger.); LOLA(1982, Ger.)
Cristine Kaufmann
LAST DAYS OF POMPEII, THE(1960, Ital.)
Gunter Kaufmann
IN A YEAR OF THIRTEEN MOONS(1980, Ger.)
Gunther Kaufmann
MARRIAGE OF MARIA BRAUN, THE(1979, Ger.); LOLA(1982, Ger.); VERONIKA VOSS(1982, Ger.); KAMIKAZE '89(1983, Ger.); QUERELLE(1983, Ger./Fr.); WAR AND PEACE(1983, Ger.)
Joseph Kaufmann
JUD(1971); PRIVATE DUTY NURSES(1972)
Misc. Talkies
BRUTE CORPS(1972)
Maurice Kaufmann
COMPANIONS IN CRIME(1954, Brit.); HANDCUFFS, LONDON(1955, Brit.); LOVE MATCH, THE(1955, Brit.); SECRET VENTURE(1955, Brit.); THREE CASES OF MURDER(1955, Brit.); FIND THE LADY(1956, Brit.); GIRL IN THE PICTURE, THE(1956, Brit.); THE CREEPING UNKNOWN(1956, Brit.); DATE WITH DISAS-TER(1957, Brit.); FIRE DOWN BELOW(1957, U.S./Brit.); ZOO BABY(1957, Brit.); BEHEMOTH, THE SEA MONSTER(1959, Brit.); LIFE IN EMERGENCY WARD 10(1959, Brit.); TOP FLOOR GIRL(1959, Brit.); HOUSE OF MYSTERY(1961, Brit.); TARNISHED HEROES(1961, Brit.); ON THE BEAT(1962, Brit.); PLAY IT COOL(1963, Brit.); WE SHALL SEE(1964, Brit.); DIE, DIE, MY DARLING(1965, Brit.); PSYCHO-CIRCUS(1967, Brit.); CRY WOLF(1968, Brit.); MAN OF VIOLENCE(1970, Brit.)
Karl Kauger
GERMANY, YEAR ZERO(1949, Ger.)
Mary Kauila
1984
BOUNTY, THE(1984)
Alan Kaul
CHINA SYNDROME, THE(1979)
Bernard Kaum
MARKED WOMAN(1937), m
Bernhard [Bernard] Kaun
SOULS AT SEA(1937), m
Bernard Kaun
CHINA CLIPPER(1936), m; BRAVADOS, THE(1958), md
Bernhard Kaun
BIG CITY BLUES(1932), m; FAREWELL TO ARMS, A(1932), m; 20,000 YEARS IN SING SING(1933), m; CASE OF THE CURIOUS BRIDE, THE(1935), m; DAN-GEROUS(1936), m; PETRIFIED FOREST, THE(1936), m; BLACK LEGION, THE(1937), m; RETURN OF DR. X, THE(1939), m; SPECIAL DELIVERY(1955, Ger.), m, md

Darrlynn Kaun
FRATERNITY ROW(1977)
Gina Kaus
LUXURY LINER(1933), w; AFFAIR LAFONT, THE(1939, Fr.), w; CHARLIE CHAN IN THE CITY OF DARKNESS(1939), w; CONFLICT(1939, Fr.), w; PRISON WITHOUT BARS(1939, Brit.), w; ISLE OF MISSING MEN(1942), w; NIGHT BEFORE THE DIVORCE, THE(1942), w; THEY ALL KISSED THE BRIDE(1942), w; WIFE TAKES A FLYER, THE(1942), w; HER SISTER'S SECRET(1946), w; JULIA MIS-BEHAVES(1948), w; RED DANUBE, THE(1949), w; THREE SECRETS(1950), w; WE'RE NOT MARRIED(1952), w; ALL I DESIRE(1953), w; ROBE, THE(1953), w. Philip Dunne; DEVIL IN SILK(1968, Ger.), w
Helmut Kautner
FILM WITHOUT A NAME(1950, Ger.), w; DEVIL'S GENERAL, THE(1957, Ger.), d, w; LAST BRIDGE, THE(1957, Aust.), d, w; AFFAIRS OF JULIE, THE(1958, Ger.), d, w; RESTLESS YEARS, THE(1958), d; STRANGER IN MY ARMS(1959), d; REST IS SILENCE, THE(1960, Ger.), p,d&w; DIE GANS VON SEDAN(1962, Fr./Ger.), d, w; GLASS OF WATER, A(1962, Cgr.), d, w
Jozsef Kautzky
ROUND UP, THE(1969, Hung.)
Al Kauwe
TIKO AND THE SHARK(1966, U.S./Ital./Fr.)
Caroline Kava
HEAVEN'S GATE(1980)
Tasso Kavadia
STEFANIA(1968, Gr.)
Tashin Kavalcioglu
L'IMMORTELLE(1969, Fr./Ital./Turkey), m
Betty Kavanagh
ROMEO AND JULIET(1966, Brit.)
Brian Kavanagh
LONG WEEKEND(1978, Aus.), ed; ODD ANGRY SHOT, THE(1979, Aus.), ed
Denis Kavanagh
NIGHT COMES TOO SOON(1948, Brit.), d; FLIGHT FROM VIENNA(1956, Brit.), d&w; FIGHTING MAD(1957, Brit.), d
H.T. Kavanagh
DARBY O'GILL AND THE LITTLE PEOPLE(1959), w
Jake Kavanagh
STAIRCASE(1969 U.S./Brit./Fr.)
John Kavanagh
MC KENZIE BREAK, THE(1970); PADDY(1970, Irish)
1984
CAL(1984, Ireland)
Kevin Kavanagh
PRIZE OF ARMS, A(1962, Brit.), w; SANDERS(1963, Brit.), w
Kevon Kavanagh
MILLION EYES OF SU-MURU, THE(1967, Brit.), w
Pat Kavanagh
MINSTREL BOY, THE(1937, Brit.); OLD MOTHER RILEY, DETECTIVE(1943, Brit.)
Seamus Kavanagh
PROFESSOR TIM(1957, Ireland)
Ted Kavanagh
IT'S THAT MAN AGAIN(1943, Brit.), w; TIME FLIES(1944, Brit.), w; GEORGE IN CIVVY STREET(1946, Brit.), w
Brian Kavanaugh
DEVIL'S PLAYGROUND, THE(1976, Aus.), ed; CHANT OF JIMMIE BLACKSMITH, THE(1980, Aus.), ed
Denis Kavanaugh
ROCK YOU SINNERS(1957, Brit.), d
Dorrie Kavanaugh
HESTER STREET(1975)
Frances Kavanaugh
DRIFTIN' KID, THE(1941), w; DYNAMITE CANYON(1941), w; ARIZONA ROUND-UP(1942), w; LONE STAR LAW MEN(1942), w; TRAIL RIDERS(1942), w; WESTERN MAIL(1942), w; BLAZING GUNS(1943), w; LAW RIDES AGAIN, THE(1943), w; ARIZONA WHIRLWIND(1944), w; DEATH VALLEY RANGERS(1944), w; OUTLAW TRAIL(1944), w; SONORA STAGECOACH(1944), w; WESTWARD BOUND(1944), w; SONG OF OLD WYOMING(1945), w; WILDFIRE(1945), w; CARAVAN TRAIL, THE(1946), w; COLORADO SERENADE(1946), w; DRIFTIN' RIVER(1946), w; GOD'S COUNTRY(1946), w; ROMANCE OF THE WEST(1946), w; STARS OVER TEX-AS(1946), w; TUMBLEWEED TRAIL(1946), w; WILD WEST(1946), w; WHITE STAL-LION(1947), w; ENCHANTED VALLEY, THE(1948), w; PRAIRIE OUTLAWS(1948), w; DARING CABALLERO, THE(1949), w; FIGHTING STALLION, THE(1950), w; FORBIDDEN JUNGLE(1950), w; CATTLE QUEEN(1951), w
Francis Kavanaugh
RIDING THE SUNSET TRAIL(1941), w; WILD HORSE STAMPEDE(1943), w
Katharine Kavanaugh
EVERY SATURDAY NIGHT(1936), w; HOT WATER(1937), w; DOWN ON THE FARM(1938), w; HIS EXCITING NIGHT(1938), w; QUICK MILLIONS(1939), w; YOUNG AS YOU FEEL(1940), w
Silents
FAR CRY, THE(1926), w
Katherine Kavanaugh
EDUCATING FATHER(1936), w; OFF TO THE RACES(1937), w; SAFETY IN NUM-BERS(1938), w; TRIP TO PARIS, A(1938), w; EVERYBODY'S BABY(1939), w; JONES FAMILY IN HOLLYWOOD, THE(1939), w; ON THEIR OWN(1940), w
Leonard Kavanaugh
THAT LUCKY TOUCH(1975, Brit.)
Mags Kavanaugh
HONKY TONK FREEWAY(1981)
Michael Kavanaugh
1984
BAY BOY(1984, Can.), spec eff
Patrick Kavanaugh
NAKED BRIGADE, THE(1965, U.S./Gr.)
Darryl Kavann
CARRY ON CABBIE(1963, Brit.)
Jean Kave
MAEVA(1961)

Fred Kavens
Silents
SWORD OF VALOR, THE(1924)
Y. Kaverina
Misc. Silents
ELDER VASILI GRYAZNOV(1924, USSR)
Karin Kavli
ALL THESE WOMEN(1964, Swed.)
Steve Kavner
HOMETOWN U.S.A.(1979)
Nikos Kavoudikis
RAPE, THE(1965, Gr.), ph; STEFANIA(1968, Gr.), ph
Nicos Kavoukides
MATCHMAKING OF ANNA, THE(1972, Gr.), ph
N. Kavoukidis
CANNON AND THE NIGHTINGALE, THE(1969, Gr.), ph
Takis Kavouras
ASSAULT ON AGATHON(1976, Brit./Gr.)
N. Kavunovskiy
SANDU FOLLOWS THE SUN(1965, USSR)
Fuad Kavur
1984
MEMED MY HAWK(1984, Brit.), p
Bob Kawa
TAKE DOWN(1979)
Mori Kawa
HEARSE, THE(1980), ph
Yasunari Kawabata
TWIN SISTERS OF KYOTO(1964, Jap.), w; SNOW COUNTRY(1969, Jap.), w; THOU-SAND CRANES(1969, Jap.), w; THROUGH DAYS AND MONTHS(1969 Jap.), w; LAKE, THE(1970, Jap.), w
Clifford Kawada
SUICIDE BATTALION(1958); VARAN THE UNBELIEVABLE(1962, U.S./Jap.)
Anwar Kawadri
NUTCRACKER(1982, Brit.), d
Hiroshi Kawaguchi
BUDDHA(1965, Jap.); GREAT WALL, THE(1965, Jap.); FLOATING WEEDS(1970, Jap.)
Matsutaro Kawaguchi
UGETSU(1954, Jap.), w; NIGHT OF THE SEAGULL, THE(1970, Jap.), w; GEISHA, A(1978, Jap.), w
Matsutaru Kawaguchi
GOLDEN DEMON(1956, Jap.), w
Motozo Kawahara
NO GREATER LOVE THAN THIS(1969, Jap.), art d
Takashi Kawahara
1984
PERILS OF GWENDOLINE, THE(1984, Fr.)
Yoshio Kawahara
1984
ADERYN PAPUR(1984, Brit.)
June Kawai
OPERATION BOTTLENECK(1961); WALK, DON'T RUN(1966)
Shigayaoshi Kawai
KARATE, THE HAND OF DEATH(1961)
Kenchiro Kawaji
FRANKENSTEIN CONQUERS THE WORLD(1964, Jap./US)
Tamio Kawaji
WEIRD LOVE MAKERS, THE(1963, Jap.); WHIRLPOOL OF WOMAN(1966, Jap.); GAPPA THE TRIFIBIAN MONSTER(1967, Jap.); GANGSTER VIP, THE(1968, Jap.)
Jerzy Kawalerowicz
JOAN OF THE ANGELS(1962, Pol.), d, w
Ko Kawamata
NAKED YOUTH(1961, Jap.), ph; INHERITANCE, THE(1964, Jap.), ph; SCARLET CAMELLIA, THE(1965, Jap.), ph
Toru Kawane
MONSTERS FROM THE UNKNOWN PLANET(1975, Jap.)
Choichiro Kawarazaki
GIRL I ABANDONED, THE(1970, Jap.); KURAGEJIMA–LEGENDS FROM A SOUTHERN ISLAND(1970, Jap.)
Shizue Kawarazaki
DOUBLE SUICIDE(1970, Jap.)
Anwar Kawardi
Misc. Talkies
NUTCRACKER(1984), d
Keizo Kawasaki
MYSTERIOUS SATELLITE, THE(1956, Jap.)
Kiezo Kawasaki
BUDDHA(1965, Jap.)
Shintaro Kawasaki
TRAITORS(1957, Jap.), ph
Hiroyuki Kawase
GODZILLA VERSUS THE SMOG MONSTER(1972, Jap.); GODZILLA VS. MEGA-LON(1976, Jap.)
Akimasa Kawashima
1984
FAMILY GAME, THE(1984, Jap.), ed
Taizo Kawashima
TORA! TORA! TORA!(1970, U.S./Jap.), art d
Yuzo Kawashima
DANGEROUS KISS, THE(1961, Jap.), d; THIS MADDING CROWD(1964, Jap.), d
Keizo Kawaski
BUDDHA(1965, Jap.)
Mokuami Kawatake
SCANDALOUS ADVENTURES OF BURAIKAN, THE(1970, Jap.), w
Dionysos Kawathas
SISTERS, OR THE BALANCE OF HAPPINESS(1982, Ger.)

Yarunori Kawauchi
MAN IN THE MOONLIGHT MASK, THE(1958, Jap.), w
Janice Kawaye
1984
NIGHT OF THE COMET(1984)
Seizaburo Kawazu
DANGEROUS KISS, THE(1961, Jap.); ETERNITY OF LOVE(1961, Jap.); SECRET OF THE TELEGIAN, THE(1961, Jap.); YOJIMBO(1961, Jap.); MOTHRA(1962, Jap.); INSECT WOMAN, THE(1964, Jap.); SAGA OF THE VAGABONDS(1964, Jap.); JUDO SHOWDOWN(1966, Jap.); DAREDEVIL IN THE CASTLE(1969, Jap.); EAST CHINA SEA(1969, Jap.)
Yasuke Kawazu
NAKED YOUTH(1961, Jap.)
Yusuke Kawazu
ROAD TO ETERNITY(1962, Jap.); INHERITANCE, THE(1964, Jap.); PASSION(1968, Jap.); PLAY IT COOL(1970, Jap.); SOLDIER'S PRAYER, A(1970, Jap.); VIXEN(1970, Jap.)
Seizaburo Kawazy
GEISHA, A(1978, Jap.)
Mohindra Nath Kawlra
LOVESICK(1983)
Holger Kax
VALLEY OF EAGLES(1952, Brit.)
Andrew Kay
CRY, THE BELOVED COUNTRY(1952, Brit.); JOE(1970), cos
Andy Kay
BATTLE OF LOVE'S RETURN, THE(1971)
Anita Kay
CONFESSIONS OF A POP PERFORMER(1975, Brit.)
Misc. Silents
PRINCE AND BETTY, THE(1919)
Anne Kay
GOLDEN BOY(1939)
Arthur Kay
FOX MOVIETONE FOLLIES(1929), a, md; SUNNY SIDE UP(1929), md; WORDS AND MUSIC(1929), md; ARE YOU THERE?(1930), md; BIG TRAIL, THE(1930), m; CITY GIRL(1930), m; FOX MOVIETONE FOLLIES OF 1930(1930), md; JUST IMAG-INE(1930), md; OH, FOR A MAN!(1930), md; PRINCESS AND THE PLUMBER, THE(1930), md; HARMONY LANE(1935), md; ONE FRIGHTENED NIGHT(1935), md; DANIEL BOONE(1936), md; HOUSE OF A THOUSAND CANDLES, THE(1936), md; I CONQUER THE SEA(1936), md; GIRL SAID NO, THE(1937), a, md; RIDERS OF THE WHISTLING SKULL(1937), m
Silents
EXALTED FLAPPER, THE(1929), m
Barry Kay
DON QUIXOTE(1973, Aus.), cos
Beatrice Kay
DIAMOND HORSESHOE(1945); UNDERWORLD U.S.A.(1961); TIME FOR DYING, A(1971)
Bernard Kay
DOCTOR ZHIVAGO(1965); THEY CAME FROM BEYOND SPACE(1967, Brit.); CONQUEROR WORM, THE(1968, Brit.); INTERLUDE(1968, Brit.); SHUTTERED ROOM, THE(1968, Brit.); TORTURE GARDEN(1968, Brit.); DARLING LILI(1970); TROG(1970, Brit.); LADY CAROLINE LAMB(1972, Brit./Ital.); HUNTING PARTY, THE(1977, Brit.); SINBAD AND THE EYE OF THE TIGER(1977, U.S./Brit.); SWEENEY(1977, Brit.)
Bernice Kay
WIDE OPEN TOWN(1941); GIRLS' TOWN(1942)
Billy Kay
LONG JOHN SILVER(1954, Aus.)
Bobby Kay
THREE RING CIRCUS(1954)
Bruce Kay
DREAMER(1979), set d; HOLLYWOOD KNIGHTS, THE(1980), set d
Carol Kay
INCREDIBLY STRANGE CREATURES WHO STOPPED LIVING AND BECAME CRAZY MIXED-UP ZOMBIES, THE(1965)
Charles Kay
BACHELOR OF HEARTS(1958, Brit.); PICCADILLY THIRD STOP(1960, Brit.); YOUNG AND WILLING(1964, Brit.); DEADLY AFFAIR, THE(1967, Brit.); NIJIN-SKY(1980, Brit.)
1984
AMADEUS(1984)
Christian Kay
BLUE HAWAII(1961); NEW KIND OF LOVE, A(1963)
David Kay
DUFFY(1968, Brit.), spec eff
Denise Kay
FAMILY HONEYMOON(1948)
Dianne Kay
1941(1979)
Dina Kay
IT'S A DEAL(1930)
Eddie Kay
WITH LOVE AND KISSES(1937), md; SONG OF THE DRIFTER(1948), md
Edward Kay
STREETS OF NEW YORK(1939), md; APE, THE(1940), m; ARIZONA BOUND(1941), m; GUN MAN FROM BODIE, THE(1941), md; KING OF THE ZOMBIES(1941), md; LET'S GO COLLEGIATE(1941), md; NO GREATER SIN(1941), md; ROAR OF THE PRESS(1941), md; SIGN OF THE WOLF(1941), md; FOREIGN AGENT(1942), md; GHOST TOWN LAW(1942), m; ISLE OF MISSING MEN(1942), md; KLONDIKE FURY(1942), md; MAN FROM HEADQUARTERS(1942), md; MEET THE MOB(1942), md; 'NEATH BROOKLYN BRIDGE(1942), md; ROAD TO HAPPINESS(1942), md; SMART ALECKS(1942), md; CAMPUS RHYTHM(1943), m; GHOSTS ON THE LOOSE(1943), md; KID DYNAMITE(1943), md; MELODY PARADE(1943), m, md; MR. MUGGS STEPS OUT(1943), md; NEARLY EIGHTEEN(1943), md; RHYTHM PARADE(1943), md; SARONG GIRL(1943), md; SILVER SKATES(1943), md; SIX GUN GOSPEL(1943), md; SMART GUY(1943), md; SPOTLIGHT SCANDALS(1943), md; ALASKA(1944), md; DETECTIVE KITTY O'DAY(1944), md; FOLLOW THE LEADER(1944), md; GHOST GUNS(1944), md; HOT RHYTHM(1944), md; LADY,

LET'S DANCE(1944), md; LAND OF THE OUTLAWS(1944), md; LAW MEN(1944), md; LAW OF THE VALLEY(1944), m, md; MILLION DOLLAR KID(1944), md; OH, WHAT A NIGHT(1944), md; PARTNERS OF THE TRAIL(1944), md; RAIDERS OF THE BORDER(1944), md; RANGE LAW(1944), md; COME OUT FIGHTING(1945), md; DOCKS OF NEW YORK(1945), md; MR. MUGGS RIDES AGAIN(1945), md; SCARLET CLUE, THE(1945), md; BRINGING UP FATHER(1946), m; DRIFTING ALONG(1946), md; FACE OF MARBLE, THE(1946), md; GENTLEMAN FROM TEXAS(1946), md; HIGH SCHOOL HERO(1946), m; IN FAST COMPANY(1946), md; SHADOW RETURNS, THE(1946), md; BOWERY BUCKAROOS(1947), md; LAND OF THE LAWLESS(1947), md; NEWS HOUNDS(1947), md; RIDIN' DOWN THE TRAIL(1947), md; SARGE GOES TO COLLEGE(1947), md; SONG OF THE WASTELAND(1947), md; COURTIN' TROUBLE(1948), md; FEATHERED SERPENT, THE(1948), md; FRENCH LEAVE(1948), md; FRONTIER AGENT(1948), md; GUN TALK(1948), md; GUNNING FOR JUSTICE(1948), md; MUSIC MAN(1948), md; OUTLAW BRAND(1948), md; RANGERS RIDE, THE(1948), md; SHANGHAI CHEST, THE(1948), md; SILVER TRAILS(1948), md; SMART POLITICS(1948), md; ACROSS THE RIO GRANDE(1949), md; ANGELS IN DISGUISE(1949), md; BOMBA ON PANTHER ISLAND(1949), md; FIGHTING FOOLS(1949), md; GUN LAW JUSTICE(1949), md; GUN RUNNER(1949), m; HIDDEN DANGER(1949), md; HOLD THAT BABY!(1949), md; JOE PALOOKA IN THE BIG FIGHT(1949), md; LAW OF THE WEST(1949), m; LAWLESS CODE(1949), md; RANGE JUSTICE(1949), md; RANGE LAND(1949), m; ROARING WESTWARD(1949), md; SHADOWS OF THE WEST(1949), m; SKY DRAGON(1949), md; STAMPEDE(1949), m; TRAIL'S END(1949), md; BLONDE DYNAMITE(1950), m; FATHER MAKES GOOD(1950), md; FATHER'S WILD GAME(1950), md; FENCE RIDERS(1950), md; GUNSLINGERS(1950), m; JIGGS AND MAGGIE OUT WEST(1950), md; LAW OF THE PANHANDLE(1950), md; OUTLAW GOLD(1950), md; OUTLAWS OF TEXAS(1950), md; OVER THE BORDER(1950), md; SIDESHOW(1950), md; SILVER RAIDERS(1950), md; SNOW DOG(1950), md; SQUARE DANCE KATY(1950), md; TRIPLE TROUBLE(1950), md; ABILENE TRAIL(1951), md; BOWERY BATTALION(1951), md; CRAZY OVER HORSES(1951), md; LET'S GO NAVY(1951), md; MONTANA DESPERADO(1951), md; FEUDIN' FOOLS(1952), md; HERE COME THE MARINES(1952), m; THUNDER PASS(1954), m

Edward J. Kay
WOLF CALL(1939), m; WHERE ARE YOUR CHILDREN?(1943), md; WINGS OVER THE PACIFIC(1943), md; VOODOO MAN(1944), md; WHAT A MAN!(1944), md; DIVORCE(1945), m, md; FASHION MODEL(1945), md; SOUTH OF THE RIO GRANDE(1945), md; SUNBONNET SUE(1945), m, md; THERE GOES KELLY(1945), md; BLACK MARKET BABIES(1946), md; DANGEROUS MONEY(1946), md; DECOY(1946), m; DON'T GAMBLE WITH STRANGERS(1946), md; JOE PALOOKA, CHAMP(1946), md; LIVE WIRES(1946), md; MR. HEX(1946), md; SPOOK BUSTERS(1946), md; SWEETHEART OF SIGMA CHI(1946), md; SWING PARADE OF 1946(1946), md; UNDER ARIZONA SKIES(1946), md; WIFE WANTED(1946), md; BLACK GOLD(1947), md; FALL GUY(1947), md; FLASHING GUNS(1947), md; GINGER(1947), md; HARD BOILED MAHONEY(1947), md; KILROY WAS HERE(1947), md; SONG OF MY HEART(1947), md; TRAP, THE(1947), md; VACATION DAYS(1947), md; VIOLENCE(1947), m, md; ANGELS ALLEY(1948), m; BUNGALOW 13(1948), md; CHECKERED COAT, THE(1948), md; CROSSED TRAILS(1948), m; DOCKS OF NEW ORLEANS(1948), m; FIGHTING MAD(1948), md; HUNTED, THE(1948), m; I WOULDN'T BE IN YOUR SHOES(1948), m, md; INCIDENT(1948), md; JIGGS AND MAGGIE IN SOCIETY(1948), md; JINX MONEY(1948), m; JOE PALOOKA IN WINNER TAKE ALL(1948), m; KIDNAPPED(1948), m, md; KING OF THE BANDITS(1948), md; MYSTERY OF THE GOLDEN EYE, THE(1948), md; OKLAHOMA BLUES(1948), md; PARTNERS OF THE SUNSET(1948), md; RANGE RENEGADES(1948), md; ROCKY(1948), md; SMUGGLERS' COVE(1948), md; STAGE STRUCK(1948), md; TROUBLE MAKERS(1948), md; BLACK MIDNIGHT(1949), md; FORGOTTEN WOMEN(1949), md; I CHEATED THE LAW(1949), md; JOE PALOOKA IN THE COUNTERPUNCH(1949), m; LAWTON STORY, THE(1949), md; LEAVE IT TO HENRY(1949), md; MASTER MINDS(1949), m, md; TRAIL OF THE YUKON(1949), md; TUNA CLIPPER(1949), m, md; WEST OF EL DORADO(1949), md; WESTERN RENEGADES(1949), m; WOLF HUNTERS, THE(1949), m&md; ADMIRAL WAS A LADY, THE(1950), ph; BIG TIMBER(1950), m; BLUES BUSTERS(1950), m; GREAT PLANE ROBBERY(1950), m; HOT ROD(1950), m; HUMPHREY TAKES A CHANCE(1950), md; JOE PALOOKA MEETS HUMPHREY(1950), m; KILLER SHARK(1950), md; LUCKY LOSERS(1950), md; SHORT GRASS(1950), m; WEST OF WYOMING(1950), md; I WAS AN AMERICAN SPY(1951), m; RHYTHM INN(1951), md; SIERRA PASSAGE(1951), m, md; YELLOW FIN(1951), md; DESERT PURSUIT(1952), md; HOLD THAT LINE(1952), md; JET JOB(1952), m, md; NO HOLDS BARRED(1952), md; SEA TIGER(1952), m; STEEL FIST, THE(1952), m; COW COUNTRY(1953), m; MEXICAN MANHUNT(1953), md; MURDER WITHOUT TEARS(1953), m; HIGHWAY DRAGNET(1954), m; RACING BLOOD(1954), m; BETRAYED WOMEN(1955), m; BIG TIP OFF, THE(1955), m; LAS VEGAS SHAKEDOWN(1955), m; NIGHT FREIGHT(1955), m&md; PORT OF HELL(1955), m; TOUGHEST MAN ALIVE(1955), m; TREASURE OF RUBY HILLS(1955), m, md; YAQUI DRUMS(1956), m, md; JOHNNY ROCCO(1958), m, md; CREATION OF THE HUMANOIDS(1962), p; MODERN MARRIAGE, A(1962), m, md

Fiona Kay
1984
VIGIL(1984, New Zealand)

Geraldine Kay
CRIME OF DR. CRESPI, THE(1936)

Gilbert Kay
Misc. Talkies
WHITE COMANCHE(1967), d

Gilbert L. Kay
THREE BAD SISTERS(1956), d; SECRET DOOR, THE(1964), d

Gordon Kay
BANDITS OF DARK CANYON(1947), p; WILD FRONTIER, THE(1947), p; BOLD FRONTIERSMAN, THE(1948), p; CARSON CITY RAIDERS(1948), p; DENVER KID, THE(1948), p; DESPERADOES OF DODGE CITY(1948), p; MARSHAL OF AMARILLO(1948), p; OKLAHOMA BADLANDS(1948), p; RENEGADES OF SONORA(1948), p; BANDIT KING OF TEXAS(1949), p; DEATH VALLEY GUNFIGHTER(1949), p; FRONTIER INVESTIGATOR(1949), p; NAVAJO TRAIL RAIDERS(1949), p; POWDER RIVER RUSTLERS(1949), p; SHERIFF OF WICHITA(1949), p; WYOMING BANDIT, THE(1949), p; CODE OF THE SILVER SAGE(1950), p; COVERED WAGON RAID(1950), p; FRISCO TORNADO(1950), p; GUNMEN OF ABILENE(1950), p; RUSTLERS ON HORSEBACK(1950), p; SALT LAKE RAIDERS(1950), p; VIGILANTE HIDEOUT(1950), p; NIGHT RIDERS OF MONTANA(1951), p; ROUGH RIDERS OF DURANGO(1951), p; WELLS FARGO GUNMASTER(1951), p; UNGUARDED MOMENT, THE(1956), p; MAN AFRAID(1957), p; QUANTEZ(1957), p; DAY OF THE BAD MAN(1958), p; SAGA OF HEMP BROWN, THE(1958), p; TWILIGHT FOR THE GODS(1958), p; VOICE IN THE MIRROR(1958), p; HELL BENT FOR LEATHER(1960), p; SEVEN WAYS FROM SUNDOWN(1960), p; POSSE FROM HELL(1961), p; SIX BLACK HORSES(1962), p; SHOWDOWN(1963), p; BULLET FOR A BADMAN(1964), p; HE RIDES TALL(1964), p; TAGGART(1964), p; FLUFFY(1965), p; GUNPOINT(1966), p; YOUNG WARRIORS, THE(1967), p; JOANNA(1968, Brit.), makeup

Hadley Kay
MEATBALLS(1979, Can.); SUPERMAN II(1980); HEAD ON(1981, Can.)

Harold Kay
THUNDER IN THE BLOOD(1962, Fr.)

Henriette Kay
OF MICE AND MEN(1939)

Henry Kay
TRIAL AND ERROR(1962, Brit.); OLIVER!(1968, Brit.)

Hershy Kay
GREAT ST. LOUIS BANK ROBBERY, THE(1959), md

Janet Kay
MARK OF CAIN, THE(1948, Brit.)

Jerry Kay
JACKTOWN(1962), art d; EASY RIDER(1969), art d

Jim Kay
SEEDS OF EVIL(1981), d&w

Jody Kay
Misc. Talkies
ONE ARMED EXECUTIONER(1980); DEATH SCREAMS(1982)

Joel Kay
GAMBLING DAUGHTERS(1941), w

John Paul Kay
GOSPEL ROAD, THE(1973)

Joyce Kay
PRISONER OF SHARK ISLAND, THE(1936); PUT ON THE SPOT(1936); RIO GRANDE ROMANCE(1936); LIFE BEGINS WITH LOVE(1937); MERRY-GO-ROUND OF 1938(1937)

Karol Kay
SECOND HAND WIFE(1933); SHE WAS A LADY(1934)

Kathleen Kay
MONEY TALKS(1933, Brit.), cos
Silents
KID, THE(1921)

Katie Kay
CAN YOU HEAR ME MOTHER?(1935, Brit.)

Kwesi Kay
1984
PIGS(1984, Ireland)

Lillian Kay
STAKEOUT ON DOPE STREET(1958)

Lonnie Kay
MIDNIGHT MAN, THE(1974)

Louise Kay
NO BLADE OF GRASS(1970, Brit.)

Marilyn Kay
MOONLIGHT IN HAVANA(1942); HI, BUDDY(1943)

Marjorie Kay
Misc. Silents
SHERLOCK HOLMES(1916)

Marnie Kay
SUBSTITUTION(1970)

Mary Allen Kay
BORDER SADDLEMATES(1952)

Mary Ellen Kay
GIRLS' SCHOOL(1950); STREETS OF GHOST TOWN(1950); TARZAN AND THE SLAVE GIRL(1950); DESERT OF LOST MEN(1951); FORT DODGE STAMPEDE(1951); RODEO KING AND THE SENORITA(1951); SILVER CITY BONANZA(1951); THUNDER IN GOD'S COUNTRY(1951); WELL, THE(1951); WELLS FARGO GUNMASTER(1951); COLORADO SUNDOWN(1952); LAST MUSKETEER, THE(1952); VICE SQUAD(1953); VIGILANTE TERROR(1953); LONG WAIT, THE(1954); THUNDER PASS(1954); YUKON VENGEANCE(1954); BUFFALO GUN(1961)
Misc. Talkies
LAST MUSKETEER, THE(1952)

Melanie Kay
1984
ALLEY CAT(1984), makeup

Pamela G. Kay
1984
WEEKEND PASS(1984)

Pat Kay
GRAND ESCAPADE, THE(1946, Brit.)

Patricia Kay
TROCADERO(1944)

Philip Kay
LOYAL HEART(1946, Brit.)
Misc. Silents
MYSTERY OF THE DIAMOND BELT(1914, Brit.)

Phylis Kay
SMITHEREENS(1982)

Richard Kay
WILD WEED(1949), p; UNTAMED WOMEN(1952), p; GOLDEN MISTRESS, THE(1954), p; CURUCU, BEAST OF THE AMAZON(1956), p; GIRLS ON THE LOOSE(1958), p; LIVE FAST, DIE YOUNG(1958), p; THREE SISTERS(1974, Brit.)

Robert Kay
LITTLE FRIEND(1934, Brit.)

Roger Kay
CABINET OF CALIGARI, THE(1962), p&d; SHOOT OUT AT BIG SAG(1962), d, w

Sibylla Kay
JOANNA(1968, Brit.); NIGHT DIGGER, THE(1971, Brit.); VAMPIRE CIRCUS(1972, Brit.)

Steven Kay
GIANT(1956)

Suzan Kay
KAMOURASKA(1973, Can./Fr.), ed
Suzie Kay
WEST SIDE STORY(1961)
Sydney John Kay
YOUNG AND THE GUILTY, THE(1958, Brit.), m
Sylvia Kay
THAT KIND OF GIRL(1963, Brit.); LEATHER BOYS, THE(1965, Brit.); RAP-TURE(1965); OUTBACK(1971, Aus.); WHO IS KILLING THE GREAT CHEFS OF EUROPE?(1978, US/Ger.)
Una Kay
RABID(1976, Can.)
Wanda Kay
OUR NEIGHBORS–THE CARTERS(1939)
Kay, Katya and Kay
VARIETY HOUR(1937, Brit.)
Kay Kyser and His Band
STAGE DOOR CANTEEN(1943)
Kay Kyser and His Orchestra
THOUSANDS CHEER(1943)
Kay Kyser's Band
THAT'S RIGHT–YOU'RE WRONG(1939); YOU'LL FIND OUT(1940); MY FAVORITE SPY(1942); AROUND THE WORLD(1943); CAROLINA BLUES(1944)
Kay Kyser's Orchestra
PLAYMATES(1941); SWING FEVER(1943)
Kay Thompson Ensemble
MANHATTAN MERRY-GO-ROUND(1937)
Olga Kaya
CLAMBAKE(1967); EXPLOSION(1969, Can.)
Shigeru Kayama
GODZILLA, RING OF THE MONSTERS(1956, Jap.), w; MYSTERIANS, THE(1959, Jap.), w
Yoshiko Kayama
HOTSPRINGS HOLIDAY(1970, Jap.)
Yuzo Kayama
MAN AGAINST MAN(1961, Jap.); MAN FROM THE EAST, THE(1961, Jap.); WESTWARD DESPERADO(1961, Jap.); DIFFERENT SONS(1962, Jap.); HAPPINESS OF US ALONE(1962, Jap.); SANJURO(1962, Jap.); CHUSHINGURA(1963, Jap.); HONOLULU-TOKYO-HONG KONG(1963, Hong Kong/Jap.); OPERATION X(1963, Jap.); WARRING CLANS(1963, Jap.); YEARNING(1964, Jap.); JUDO SAGA(1965, Jap.); IT STARTED IN THE ALPS(1966, Jap.); NIGHT IN BANGKOK(1966, Jap.); RED BEARD(1966, Jap.); WE WILL REMEMBER(1966, Jap.); LET'S GO, YOUNG GUY!(1967, Jap.); SWORD OF DOOM, THE(1967, Jap.); EMPEROR AND A GENERAL, THE(1968, Jap.); GOODBYE, MOSCOW(1968, Jap.); SIEGE OF FORT BISMARK(1968, Jap.); TWO IN THE SHADOW(1968, Jap.); SUN ABOVE, DEATH BELOW(1969, Jap.); YOUNG GUY GRADUATES(1969, Jap.); YOUNG GUY ON MT. COOK(1969, Jap.); CREATURE CALLED MAN, THE(1970, Jap.); DUEL AT EZO(1970, Jap.)
George Kayara
4D MAN(1959)
Arthur Kaye
LOVE ME FOREVER(1935); RENFREW OF THE ROYAL MOUNTED(1937), md; WALLABY JIM OF THE ISLANDS(1937), md
Barry Kaye
JAMBOREE(1957)
Benjamin M. Kaye
SHE COULDN'T SAY NO(1930), w; SHE COULDN'T SAY NO(1941), w
Beryl Kaye
GOOD COMPANIONS, THE(1957, Brit.)
Buddy Kaye
GREAT RUPERT, THE(1950), m; WHERE THE HOT WIND BLOWS(1960, Fr., Ital.), m/1; KILL A DRAGON(1967), m
Caren Kaye
CHECKMATE(1973); CUBA CROSSING(1980); SOME KIND OF HERO(1982); MY TUTOR(1983)
Celia Kaye
ISLAND OF THE BLUE DOLPHINS(1964); FLUFFY(1965); WILD SEED(1965); FINAL COMEDOWN, THE(1972); RATTLERS(1976)
Chip Kaye
STROKER ACE(1983)
Clarissa Kaye
AGE OF CONSENT(1969, Austral.); NED KELLY(1970, Brit.); ADAM'S WO-MAN(1972, Austral.)
Claude Kaye
BROADWAY TO HOLLYWOOD(1933)
Claudell Kaye
DOUGHNUTS AND SOCIETY(1936)
Claudelle Kaye
MANHATTAN MELODRAMA(1934); FLAME WITHIN, THE(1935); SPEED(1936)
Danny Kaye
UP IN ARMS(1944); WONDER MAN(1945); KID FROM BOOKLYN, THE(1946); SECRET LIFE OF WALTER MITTY, THE(1947); SONG IS BORN, A(1948); INSPEC-TOR GENERAL, THE(1949); IT'S A GREAT FEELING(1949); ON THE RIVERA(1951); HANS CHRISTIAN ANDERSEN(1952); KNOCK ON WOOD(1954); WHITE CHRIST-MAS(1954); COURT JESTER, THE(1956); ME AND THE COLONEL(1958); MERRY ANDREW(1958); FIVE PENNIES, THE(1959); ON THE DOUBLE(1961); MAN FROM THE DINERS' CLUB, THE(1963); MADWOMAN OF CHAILLOT, THE(1969)
Darwood Kaye
HEROES OF THE SADDLE(1940); BEST FOOT FORWARD(1943); MY REPUTA-TION(1946)
Davey Kaye
BIGGEST BUNDLE OF THEM ALL, THE(1968)
David Kaye
WRONG ARM OF THE LAW, THE(1963, Brit.)
Davy Kaye
EVERYTHING IS RHYTHM(1940, Brit.); FUN AT ST. FANNY'S(1956, Brit.); MIL-LIONAIRESS, THE(1960, Brit.); POT CARRIERS, THE(1962, Brit.); CROOKS IN CLOISTERS(1964, Brit.); PUSSYCAT ALLEY(1965, Brit.); THOSE MAGNIFICENT MEN IN THEIR FLYING MACHINES; OR HOW I FLEWFROM LONDON TO PARIS IN 25 HOURS AND 11 MINUTES(1965, Brit.); CARRY ON COWBOY(1966, Brit.); CHITTY CHITTY BANG BANG(1968, Brit.)

Misc. Talkies
SATAN'S HARVEST(1970)
Del Kaye
WITCHMAKER, THE(1969)
Dennis Kaye
LILLIAN RUSSELL(1940)
Donna Kaye
KENTUCKY JUBILEE(1951)
Doug Kaye
LINCOLN CONSPIRACY, THE(1977)
Eddie Kaye
HEADLINE CRASHER(1937); PAROLED FROM THE BIG HOUSE(1938); LURE OF THE ISLANDS(1942), md
Edna Kaye
THIRD TIME LUCKY(1950, Brit.)
Edward Kaye
WOLVES OF THE SEA(1938); FAHRENHEIT 451(1966, Brit.)
Edward E. Kaye
YANKS ARE COMING, THE(1942), w
Edward L. Kaye
SING WHILE YOU'RE ABLE(1937), md
Elaine Kaye
PATTERNS(1956); STRANGE LOVERS(1963)
Ethel Kaye
Silents
NEW MOON, THE(1919)
Frances Kaye
Silents
LITTLE MISS HOOVER(1918)
Misc. Silents
(
Gail Kaye
JANE EYRE(1935)
Gertrude Kaye
GIVE US THE MOON(1944, Brit.)
Gordon Kaye
JABBERWOCKY(1977, Brit.); LITTLEST HORSE THIEVES, THE(1977)
Greg Kaye
1984
THEY'RE PLAYING WITH FIRE(1984)
Henrietta Kaye
DISPUTED PASSAGE(1939)
Ian Kaye
SUMMER HOLIDAY(1963, Brit.)
Janet Kaye
RELUCTANT WIDOW, THE(1951, Brit.)
Joan Kaye
GLASS HOUSES(1972); CLAUDINE(1974); THIEVES(1977)
Joey Kaye
KES(1970, Brit.)
John Kaye
RAFFERTY AND THE GOLD DUST TWINS(1975), w; AMERICAN HOT WAX(1978), w; WHERE THE BUFFALO ROAM(1980), w
Judy Kaye
JUST TELL ME WHAT YOU WANT(1980)
Kaplan Kaye
NIGHT TRAIN FOR INVERNESS(1960, Brit.); WHISPERERS, THE(1967, Brit.)
Karen Kaye
LORDS OF FLATBUSH, THE(1974)
Laura Kaye
KING, MURRAY(1969); WORLD ACCORDING TO GARP, The(1982)
Leo Kaye
NEWS HOUNDS(1947); SONG OF MY HEART(1947); ON OUR MERRY WAY(1948); OPEN SECRET(1948)
Lila Kaye
SEE NO EVIL(1971, Brit.); AMERICAN WEREWOLF IN LONDON, AN(1981)
Lora Kaye
HELLO DOWN THERE(1969)
Louis S. Kaye
OPENED BY MISTAKE(1940), w; TOO MANY BLONDES(1941), w; DUDES ARE PRETTY PEOPLE(1942), w; FLYING WITH MUSIC(1942), w
Lucie Kaye
JIM HANVEY, DETECTIVE(1937); PORTIA ON TRIAL(1937)
Marilyn Kaye
MY REPUTATION(1946)
Mary Ellen Kaye
FRANCIS IN THE HAUNTED HOUSE(1956); RUNAWAY DAUGHTERS(1957); VOODOO WOMAN(1957)
Melody Kaye
HOTEL PARADISO(1966, U.S./Brit.)
Moira Kaye
TASTE OF HONEY, A(1962, Brit.)
Nancy Kaye
SCREWBALLS(1983), cos
Nora Kaye
GOODBYE MR. CHIPS(1969, U.S./Brit.), ch; NIJINSKY(1980, Brit.), p; PENNIES FROM HEAVEN(1981), p
Norman Kaye
DIAMONDS FOR BREAKFAST(1968, Brit.), m; ILLUMINATIONS(1976, Aus.), m; INSIDE LOOKING OUT(1977, Aus.), a, m; BUDDIES(1983, Aus.); LONELY HEARTS(1983, Aus.), a, m
1984
MAN OF FLOWERS(1984, Aus.)
Nowell Kaye
Silents
PRESUMPTION OF STANLEY HAY, MP, THE(1925, Brit.), w
Paul Kaye
EASY TO LOVE(1934); HI, NELLIE!(1934); ROMANCE IN THE RAIN(1934); SIDE STREETS(1934); NIGHT LIFE OF THE GODS(1935)

Sparky Kaye
OCEAN'S ELEVEN(1960)

Stanton Kaye
GEORG(1964), a, p,d&w, ed
Misc. Talkies
BRANDY IN THE WILDERNESS(1969), d

Stubby Kaye
YOU CAN'T RUN AWAY FROM IT(1956); TAXI(1953); GUYS AND DOLLS(1955); LI'L ABNER(1959); FORTY POUNDS OF TROUBLE(1962); COOL MIKADO, THE(1963, Brit.); SEX AND THE SINGLE GIRL(1964); CAT BALLOU(1965); WAY WEST, THE(1967); MONITORS, THE(1969); SWEET CHARITY(1969); COCKEYED COWBOYS OF CALICO COUNTY, THE(1970); COOL IT, CAROL!(1970, Brit.); SIX PACK ANNIE(1975)
Misc. Talkies
CAN HIERONYMUS MERKIN EVER FORGET MERCY HUMPPE AND FIND TRUE HAPPINESS?(1969); DIRTIEST GIRL I EVER MET, THE(1973)

Susie Kaye
TAMMY AND THE DOCTOR(1963)

Suzi Kaye
ANGRY BREED, THE(1969)

Suzie Kaye
WILD, WILD WINTER(1966); WOMEN OF THE PREHISTORIC PLANET(1966); CLAMBAKE(1967); C'MON, LET'S LIVE A LITTLE(1967); IT'S A BIKINI WORLD(1967)

Toni Kaye
PENNIES FROM HEAVEN(1981)

Virginia Kaye
STAGE DOOR CANTEEN(1943)

Sheila Kaye-Smith
LOVES OF JOANNA GODDEN, THE(1947, Brit.), w

Barbara Kayen
WRONG MAN, THE(1956)

Ken Kayer
YOU HAVE TO RUN FAST(1961)

Kyosti Kayhko
MAKE LIKE A THIEF(1966, Fin.)

Howard Kaylan
GET CRAZY(1983)

Vi Kayley
HANGMAN WAITS, THE(1947, Brit.)

Sammy Kaylin
DANTE'S INFERNO(1935), m, md; PADDY O'DAY(1935), md; HUMAN CARGO(1936), md

Samuel Kaylin
CHARLIE CHAN'S GREATEST CASE(1933), md; DR. BULL(1933), m; MAD GAME, THE(1933), md; PILGRIMAGE(1933), md; SHANGHAI MADNESS(1933), md; BABY, TAKE A BOW(1934), md; CHARLIE CHAN IN LONDON(1934), md; CHARLIE CHAN'S COURAGE(1934), md; EVER SINCE EVE(1934), md; JUDGE PRIEST(1934), md; MURDER IN TRINIDAD(1934), md; PURSUED(1934), md; SHE LEARNED ABOUT SAILORS(1934), md; SLEEPERS EAST(1934), m; THREE ON A HONEYMOON(1934), md; 365 NIGHTS IN HOLLYWOOD(1934), md; BACHELOR OF ARTS(1935), md; BLACK SHEEP(1935), md; CHARLIE CHAN IN EGYPT(1935), md; CHARLIE CHAN IN PARIS(1935), md; CHARLIE CHAN IN SHANGHAI(1935), md; GINGER(1935), md; GREAT HOTEL MURDER(1935), m; LIFE BEGINS AT 40(1935), md; MUSIC IS MAGIC(1935), md; MYSTERY WOMAN(1935), m; SILK HAT KID(1935), m; STEAMBOAT ROUND THE BEND(1935), md; THUNDER IN THE NIGHT(1935), m; YOUR UNCLE DUDLEY(1935), md; $10 RAISE(1935), md; BACK TO NATURE(1936), m; CAREER WOMAN(1936), m; CHAMPAGNE CHARLIE(1936), m; CHARLIE CHAN AT THE CIRCUS(1936), md; CHARLIE CHAN AT THE OPERA(1936), md; CHARLIE CHAN AT THE RACE TRACK(1936), md; CHARLIE CHAN'S SECRET(1936), md; CRIME OF DR. FORBES(1936), md; EDUCATING FATHER(1936), md; EVERY SATURDAY NIGHT(1936), md; GENTLE JULIA(1936), md; HIGH TENSION(1936), md; LITTLE MISS NOBODY(1936), md; MY MARRIAGE(1936), md; PEPPER(1936), md; SONG AND DANCE MAN, THE(1936), m; STAR FOR A NIGHT(1936), md; THANK YOU, JEEVES(1936), md; THIRTY SIX HOURS TO KILL(1936), md; ANGEL'S HOLIDAY(1937), md; BIG BUSINESS(1937), md; BIG TOWN GIRL(1937), md; BORN RECKLESS(1937), md; BORROWING TROUBLE(1937), md; CHARLIE CHAN AT MONTE CARLO(1937), m; CHARLIE CHAN AT THE OLYMPICS(1937), md; CHARLIE CHAN ON BROADWAY(1937), md; CHECKERS(1937), md; CRACK-UP, THE(1937), m; DANGEROUSLY YOURS(1937), md; FAIR WARNING(1937), md; GREAT HOSPITAL MYSTERY, THE(1937), md; HOLY TERROR, THE(1937), md; HOT WATER(1937), md; LADY ESCAPES, THE(1937), md; LAUGHING AT TROUBLE(1937), md; MIDNIGHT TAXI(1937), md; OFF TO THE RACES(1937), md; ONE MILE FROM HEAVEN(1937), md; SHE HAD TO EAT(1937), md; SING AND BE HAPPY(1937), md; STEP LIVELY, JEEVES(1937), md; THANK YOU, MR. MOTO(1937), md; THAT I MAY LIVE(1937), md; THINK FAST, MR. MOTO(1937), m, md; TIME OUT FOR ROMANCE(1937), md; WILD AND WOOLLY(1937), md; 45 FATHERS(1937), md; ALWAYS IN TROUBLE(1938), m; CHANGE OF HEART(1938), md; CHARLIE CHAN IN HONOLULU(1938), md; CITY GIRL(1938), md; DOWN ON THE FARM(1938), m, md; FIVE OF A KIND(1938), m; INTERNATIONAL SETTLEMENT(1938), md; ISLAND IN THE SKY(1938), md; KEEP SMILING(1938), md; LOVE ON A BUDGET(1938), m, md; MEET THE GIRLS(1938), md; MR. MOTO TAKES A CHANCE(1938), md; MR. MOTO TAKES A VACATION(1938), md; MR. MOTO'S GAMBLE(1938), md; MYSTERIOUS MR. MOTO(1938), m, md; ONE WILD NIGHT(1938), m, md; PASSPORT HUSBAND(1938), md; RASCALS(1938), md; ROAD DEMON(1938), md; SAFETY IN NUMBERS(1938), md; SHARPSHOOTERS(1938), md; SPEED TO BURN(1938), md; TIME OUT FOR MURDER(1938), md; TRIP TO PARIS, A(1938), md; UP THE RIVER(1938), md; WALKING DOWN BROADWAY(1938), md; WHILE NEW YORK SLEEPS(1938), md; BOY FRIEND(1939), md; CHARLIE CHAN AT TREASURE ISLAND(1939), md; CHARLIE CHAN IN RENO(1939), md; CHARLIE CHAN IN THE CITY OF DARKNESS(1939), md; CHASING DANGER(1939), md; CHICKEN WAGON FAMILY(1939), md; ESCAPE, THE(1939), m; FRONTIER MARSHAL(1939), md; HEAVEN WITH A BARBED WIRE FENCE(1939), m; HONEYMOON'S OVER, THE(1939), md; INSIDE STORY(1939), md; IT COULD HAPPEN TO YOU(1939), md; JONES FAMILY IN HOLLYWOOD, THE(1939), md; MR. MOTO IN DANGER ISLAND(1939), md; MR. MOTO'S LAST WARNING(1939), md; NEWS IS MADE AT NIGHT(1939), md; PACK UP YOUR TROUBLES(1939), md; PARDON OUR NERVE(1939), md; QUICK MILLIONS(1939), md; STOP, LOOK, AND LOVE(1939), md; TOO BUSY TO WORK(1939), md; WINNER TAKE ALL(1939), md; 20,000 MEN A YEAR(1939), md; CHARLIE

CHAN IN PANAMA(1940), md; CHARLIE CHAN'S MURDER CRUISE(1940), md; CITY OF CHANCE(1940), md; FREE, BLONDE AND 21(1940), md; HIGH SCHOOL(1940), md; MAN WHO WOULDN'T TALK, THE(1940), md; ON THEIR OWN(1940), md; SAILOR'S LADY(1940), md; SHOOTING HIGH(1940), md; VIVA CISCO KID(1940), md; YOUNG AS YOU FEEL(1940), md; LEATHER BURNERS, THE(1943), m

Samuel Kaylon
EVERYBODY'S BABY(1939), md

Miriam Kaylor
UNTAMED WOMEN(1952)

Robert Kaylor
CARNY(1980), d, w

Jan Kayne
MY DREAM IS YOURS(1949); RADAR SECRET SERVICE(1950); FBI GIRL(1951); GHOST CHASERS(1951); I CAN GET IT FOR YOU WHOLESALE(1951); PEOPLE AGAINST O'HARA, THE(1951); ROAD TO BALI(1952)

Rosanne Kayon
COACH(1978)

Lauryl Kays
INDEPENDENCE DAY(1983)

Margaret Kays
KEEP YOUR POWDER DRY(1945)

Roderick Kays
CARRY ON COWBOY(1966, Brit.), ed

Beau Kayser
TAXI DRIVER(1976)

Carl Kayser
RUGGED O'RIORDANS, THE(1949, Aus.), ph; JEDDA, THE UNCIVILIZED(1956, Aus.), ph; WALK INTO HELL(1957, Aus.), ph; NO MAN IS AN ISLAND(1962), ph

Karen Kaysing
GRAND THEFT AUTO(1977)

Frederich Kayssler
CAPTAIN FROM KOEPENICK(1933, Ger.)

Friedrich Kayssler
CASE VAN GELDERN(1932, Ger.); GOLD(1934, Ger.); GIRL FROM THE MARSH CROFT, THE(1935, Ger.)
Misc. Silents
MODERN DU BARRY, A(1928, Ger.), d

S. Kayukov
UNIVERSITY OF LIFE(1941, USSR); MAGIC VOYAGE OF SINBAD, THE(1962, USSR); DREAM OF A COSSACK(1982, USSR)

Kay Wright
MIGHTY MOUSE IN THE GREAT SPACE CHASE(1983), d

Eric Kaz
THEY ALL LAUGHED(1981)

Fred Kaz
MONITORS, THE(1969), a, m; LITTLE MURDERS(1971), m

Elizabeth Kaza
PAUL AND MICHELLE(1974, Fr./Brit.); BEAST, THE(1975, Fr.)

Zitto Kazaan
BEYOND EVIL(1980)

Costa Kazakos
IPHIGENIA(1977, Gr.)

Ye. Kazakov
MEET ME IN MOSCOW(1966, USSR)

Ken Kazama
THAT MAN BOLT(1973)

Chris Kazan
VISITORS, THE(1972), p, w

Elia Kazan
BLUES IN THE NIGHT(1941); CITY, FOR CONQUEST(1941); TREE GROWS IN BROOKLYN, A(1945), d; BOOMERANG(1947), d; GENTLEMAN'S AGREEMENT(1947), d; SEA OF GRASS, THE(1947), d; PINKY(1949), d; PANIC IN THE STREETS(1950), d; STREETCAR NAMED DESIRE, A(1951), d; VIVA ZAPATA!(1952), d; MAN ON A TIGHTROPE(1953), d; ON THE WATERFRONT(1954), d; EAST OF EDEN(1955), p&d; BABY DOLL(1956), p&d; FACE IN THE CROWD, A(1957), p&d; WILD RIVER(1960), p&d; SPLENDOR IN THE GRASS(1961), p&d; AMERICA, AMERICA(1963), p,d&w; ARRANGEMENT, THE(1969), p,d&w; VISITORS, THE(1972), d; LAST TYCOON, THE(1976), d

Joe Kazan
BOOMERANG(1947)

Lainie Kazan
DAYTON'S DEVILS(1968); LADY IN CEMENT(1968); ROMANCE OF A HORSE THIEF(1971); MY FAVORITE YEAR(1982); ONE FROM THE HEART(1982)

Maria Kazan
SEANCE ON A WET AFTERNOON(1964 Brit.); WRONG BOX, THE(1966, Brit.)

Nicholas Kazan
FRANCES(1982), w

Sandra Kazan
DOG DAY AFTERNOON(1975)

Vangelis Kazan
SISTERS, THE(1969, Gr.)

Zitto Kazan
LEPKE(1975, U.S./Israel)

"Kazan"
FEROCIOUS PAL(1934)

Kazan the Dog
JAWS OF JUSTICE(1933)

Howard Kazanjian
MORE AMERICAN GRAFFITI(1979), p; RETURN OF THE JEDI(1983), p

T. Kazankova
WAR AND PEACE(1968, USSR)

Zitto Kazann
GIRL FROM PETROVKA, THE(1974); SWINGING BARMAIDS, THE(1976); TRACKDOWN(1976)
1984
RED DAWN(1984)

V. Kazanskiy
THERE WAS AN OLD COUPLE(1967, USSR)
Alexander Kazantsev
STORM PLANET(1962, USSR), w
Nikos Kazantzakis
ZORBA THE GREEK(1964, U.S./Gr.), w
Ben Kazaskow
FRENCH CONNECTION, THE(1971), art d
N. Kazbegi
FATHER OF A SOLDIER(1966, USSR), art d
Ladislav Kazda
DEVIL'S TRAP, THE(1964, Czech.); SWEET LIGHT IN A DARK ROOM(1966, Czech.)
Yelena Kazelkova
RED AND THE WHITE, THE(1969, Hung./USSR)
Shoko Kazemi
TORA-SAN PART 2(1970, Jap.)
Morteza Kazerouni
POPPY IS ALSO A FLOWER, THE(1966)
John Kazian
GREAT WALDO PEPPER, THE(1975), stunts
Nikos Kazis
GIRL OF THE MOUNTAINS(1958, Gr.); ANTIGONE(1962 Gr.)
Tim Kazurinsky
MY BODYGUARD(1980); NEIGHBORS(1981)
Iau Kea
THREE STOOGES GO AROUND THE WORLD IN A DAZE, THE(1963)
Robert Keable
Silents
RECOMPENSE(1925), w
James Keach
CANNONBALL(1976, U.S./Hong Kong); DEATH PLAY(1976); COMES A HORSE-MAN(1978); FM(1978); HURRICANE(1979); LONG RIDERS, THE(1980); LOVE LETTERS(1983); NATIONAL LAMPOON'S VACATION(1983)
1984
RAZOR'S EDGE, THE(1984)
Misc. Talkies
SUNBURST(1975); GOD BLESS DR. SHAGETZ(1977); SMOKEY AND THE HOT-WIRE GANG(1980)
Kalen Keach
LONG RIDERS, THE(1980)
Stacy Keach
UP IN SMOKE(1978); SECRET ENEMIES(1942); ISLAND OF LOVE(1963); BREWST-ER McCLOUD(1970); TRAVELING EXECUTIONER, THE(1970); DOC(1971); FAT CITY(1972); LIFE AND TIMES OF JUDGE ROY BEAN, THE(1972); NEW CENTU-RIONS, THE(1972); GRAVY TRAIN, THE(1974); LUTHER(1974); WATCHED(1974); CONDUCT UNBECOMING(1975, Brit.); KILLER INSIDE ME, THE(1976); STREET PEOPLE(1976, U.S./Ital.); SQUEEZE, THE(1977, Brit.); GRAY LADY DOWN(1978); TWO SOLITUDES(1978, Can.); SLAVE OF THE CANNIBAL GOD(1979, Ital.); LONG RIDERS, THE(1980), a, w; NINTH CONFIGURATION, THE(1980); CHEECH AND CHONG'S NICE DREAMS(1981); ROAD GAMES(1981, Aus.); BUTTERFLY(1982); THAT CHAMPIONSHIP SEASON(1982)
Misc. Talkies
PRISONER OF THE CANNIBAL GOD(1978, Ital.)
Stacy Keach, Jr.
HEART IS A LONELY HUNTER, THE(1968)
Stacy Keach, Sr.
PARALLAX VIEW, THE(1974); SATURDAY THE 14TH(1981)
1984
LIES(1984, Brit.)
John Keaka
RAMPAGE(1963)
Tom Kealiinohomoku
Misc. Talkies
APOCALYPSE 3:16(1964)
Kenneth Kealing
Misc. Silents
SHADOWS OF SUSPICION(1919)
Pua Kealoha
RAINBOW ISLAND(1944)
Geraldine Keams
OUTLAW JOSEY WALES, THE(1976)
Betty Kean
MOONLIGHT MASQUERADE(1942); GALS, INCORPORATED(1943); SING A JIN-GLE(1943); HI, GOOD-LOOKIN'(1944); MURDER IN THE BLUE ROOM(1944); MY GAL LOVES MUSIC(1944); SLIGHTLY TERRIFIC(1944); SEDUCTION, THE(1982)
1984
DREAMSCAPE(1984)
Charles Kean
LONE COWBOY(1934)
E. Arthur Kean
MURPH THE SURF(1974), w
Edward Kean
SING A JINGLE(1943)
Georgina Kean
Misc. Talkies
KILLER'S MOON(1978)
Jane Kean
SAILORS ON LEAVE(1941); MR. MAGOO'S HOLIDAY FESTIVAL(1970)
Misc. Talkies
CHATTERBOX(1977)
Jean Kean
PETE'S DRAGON(1977)
Joshua Kean
Silents
EMERALD OF THE EAST(1928, Brit.)
Julia Kean
Misc. Silents
ONE ARABIAN NIGHT(1923, Brit.)

Julie Kean
Silents
ALL ROADS LEAD TO CALVARY(1921, Brit.); NOT FOR SALE(1924, Brit.)
Maire Kean
BROTH OF A BOY(1959, Brit.)
Marie Kean
JACQUELINE(1956, Brit.); ROONEY(1958, Brit.); POACHER'S DAUGHTER, THE(1960, Brit.); QUARE FELLOW, THE(1962, Brit.); GIRL WITH GREEN EYES(1964, Brit.); STORK TALK(1964, Brit.); CUL-DE-SAC(1966, Brit.); FIGHTING PRINCE OF DONEGAL, THE(1966, Brit.); TIME LOST AND TIME REMEMBERED(1966, Brit.); GREAT CATHERINE(1968, Brit.); RYAN'S DAUGHTER(1970, Brit.); BARRY LYN-DON(1975, Brit.)
Mary Kean
BIG GAMBLE, THE(1961)
Richard Kean
SOMEWHERE I'LL FIND YOU(1942); BEAUTIFUL BLONDE FROM BASHFUL BEND, THE(1949); STORM OVER WYOMING(1950); STORY OF WILL ROGERS, THE(1952); COURT JESTER, THE(1956)
Robert Emmett Kean
DEVIL AND DANIEL WEBSTER, THE(1941)
Adam Keane
SWORD OF SHERWOOD FOREST(1961, Brit.)
Basil Keane
HARDER THEY COME, THE(1973, Jamaica); COUNTRYMAN(1982, Jamaica)
Charles Keane
UNTAMED FURY(1947); LES MISERABLES(1952); DESERT RATS, THE(1953); HANNAH LEE(1953); LOOSE IN LONDON(1953); PROJECT MOONBASE(1953); TITANIC(1953); YOUNG BESS(1953); HOT CARS(1956); HOT ROD GIRL(1956); RE-VOLT OF MAMIE STOVER, THE(1956); 23 PACES TO BAKER STREET(1956); SEVEN GUNS TO MESA(1958); UNDERWATER WARRIOR(1958); YELLOW CANARY, THE(1963)
Charles R. Keane
INTERRUPTED MELODY(1955); SCARLET COAT, THE(1955)
Charles Robert Keane
CAREER GIRL(1960)
Christopher Keane
HUNTER, THE(1980), w
Constance Keane [Veronica Lake]
DANCING CO-ED(1939); SORORITY HOUSE(1939); FORTY LITTLE MO-THERS(1940); YOUNG AS YOU FEEL(1940)
Desmond Keane
ANOTHER SHORE(1948, Brit.)
Dick Keane
FEAR IN THE NIGHT(1947)
Doris Keane
Misc. Silents
ROMANCE(1920)
Eamonn Keane
BROTHERLY LOVE(1970, Brit.); UNDERGROUND(1970, Brit.)
Ed Keane
MERRY FRINKS, THE(1934); G-MEN(1935); NAUGHTY MARIETTA(1935); SHIP-MATES FOREVER(1935); MAN WHO LIVED TWICE(1936); ONCE A DOCTOR(1937); VICE RACKET(1937); I AM THE LAW(1938); NANCY DREW-DETECTIVE(1938); TORCHY GETS HER MAN(1938); ROARING TWENTIES, THE(1939); WINGS OF THE NAVY(1939); FUGITIVE FROM JUSTICE, A(1940); HIDDEN ENEMY(1940); MONEY AND THE WOMAN(1940); 'TIL WE MEET AGAIN(1940); VIRGINIA CITY(1940); SERGEANT YORK(1941); THEY DIED WITH THEIR BOOTS ON(1942); WILD-CAT(1942); YANKEE DOODLE DANDY(1942); WOMAN OF DISTINCTION, A(1950)
Edward Keane
HIS WOMAN(1931); SECRETS OF A SECRETARY(1931); STOLEN HEAVEN(1931); ANN CARVER'S PROFESSION(1933); BORN TO BE BAD(1934); DESIRABLE(1934); GAMBLING LADY(1934); GIRL IN DANGER(1934); GREEN EYES(1934); I AM SUZANNE(1934); JEALOUSY(1934); KANSAS CITY PRINCESS(1934); LOST LADY, A(1934); ONE NIGHT OF LOVE(1934); STAMBOUL QUEST(1934); WONDER BAR(1934); BEHIND THE EVIDENCE(1935); BORDER BRIGANDS(1935); FRISCO KID(1935); FRONT PAGE WOMAN(1935); IRISH IN US, THE(1935); MILLS OF THE GODS(1935); NIGHT AT THE OPERA, A(1935); ONE EXCITING ADVENTURE(1935); PAGE MISS GLORY(1935); PUBLIC OPINION(1935); SHOW THEM NO MERCY(1935); STRANDED(1935); WHISPERING SMITH SPEAKS(1935); WOMAN IN RED, THE(1935); COLLEEN(1936); DANGEROUS(1936); DOWN THE STRETCH(1936); GOLDEN ARROW, THE(1936); IT HAD TO HAPPEN(1936); PAROLE(1936); PRIN-CESS COMES ACROSS, THE(1936); SINGING KID, THE(1936); ALCATRAZ IS-LAND(1937); CALIFORNIA MAIL, THE(1937); CALIFORNIAN, THE(1937); CHARLIE CHAN AT THE OLYMPICS(1937); CONFESSION(1937); FIREFLY, THE(1937); HIGH, WIDE AND HANDSOME(1937); I PROMISE TO PAY(1937); SEVENTH HEA-VEN(1937); WESTBOUND MAIL(1937); WHEN YOU'RE IN LOVE(1937); ALEXAND-ER'S RAGTIME BAND(1938); BORDER G-MAN(1938); HOLLYWOOD ROUNDUP(1938); I DEMAND PAYMENT(1938); MARIE ANTOINETTE(1938); SER-GEANT MURPHY(1938); SHADOWS OVER SHANGHAI(1938); SHOPWORN AN-GEL(1938); SLANDER HOUSE(1938); TOY WIFE, THE(1938); YOU CAN'T TAKE IT WITH YOU(1938); CONFESSIONS OF A NAZI SPY(1939); FRONTIER PONY EX-PRESS(1939); HEROES IN BLUE(1939); MY WIFE'S RELATIVES(1939); STAND UP AND FIGHT(1939); CHARLIE CHAN IN PANAMA(1940); DEVIL'S ISLAND(1940); I TAKE THIS WOMAN(1940); MIDNIGHT LIMITED(1940); SAILOR'S LADY(1940); SON OF MONTE CRISTO(1940); DOUBLE CROSS(1941); MEET JOHN DOE(1941); RIDE, KELLY, RIDE(1941); ICE-CAPADES REVUE(1942); MAN WITH TWO LIVES, THE(1942); TRAITOR WITHIN, THE(1942); WHO DONE IT?(1942); WHO IS HOPE SCHUYLER?(1942); DEATH VALLEY MANHUNT(1943); GOVERNMENT GIRL(1943); I ESCAPED FROM THE GESTAPO(1943); MISSION TO MOSCOW(1943); SOMEONE TO REMEMBER(1943); SONG OF BERNADETTE, THE(1943); TRUCK BUSTERS(1943); CALIFORNIA JOE(1944); LADY AND THE MONSTER, THE(1944); SOUTH OF DIXIE(1944); WHEN STRANGERS MARRY(1944); COLONEL EFFING-HAM'S RAID(1945); FASHION MODEL(1945); NOB HILL(1945); ROGUES GAL-LERY(1945); SCARLET STREET(1945); ANGEL ON MY SHOULDER(1946); IF I'M LUCKY(1946); IT'S A WONDERFUL LIFE(1946); JOLSON STORY, THE(1946); NIGHT EDITOR(1946); OUT CALIFORNIA WAY(1946); ROLL ON TEXAS MOON(1946); DESIRE ME(1947); INVISIBLE WALL, THE(1947); ROSES ARE RED(1947); SADDLE PALS(1947); TRAIL TO SAN ANTONE(1947); CHICKEN EVERY SUNDAY(1949); HELLFIRE(1949); IT HAPPENS EVERY SPRING(1949); MADAME BOVARY(1949); STORY OF SEABISCUIT, THE(1949); BARON OF ARIZONA, THE(1950); TWILIGHT

IN THE SIERRAS(1950); SHOW BOAT(1951); DEADLINE–U.S.A.(1952); COURT-MARTIAL OF BILLY MITCHELL, THE(1955); MODERN MARRIAGE, A(1962)
Misc. Talkies
DRAGNET, THE(1936)
Glen Keane
FOX AND THE HOUND, THE(1981), anim
Hamilton Keane
MY BROTHER'S KEEPER(1949, Brit.)
James Keane
THREE DAYS OF THE CONDOR(1975); ROSE, THE(1979); BRUBAKER(1980); CANNERY ROW(1982); 48 HOURS(1982); 10 TO MIDNIGHT(1983)
1984
ADVENTURES OF BUCKAROO BANZAI: ACROSS THE 8TH DIMENSION, THE(1984)
Misc. Silents
MONEY(1915), d; SPREADING EVIL, THE(1919), d; WHISPERING WOMEN(1921), d
Jo Anna Keane
OFFICER AND A GENTLEMAN, AN(1982)
Kerrie Keane
INCUBUS, THE(1982, Can.); SPASMS(1983, Can.)
Laurence Keane
1984
BIG MEAT EATER(1984, Can.), p
Lawrence Keane
1984
BIG MEAT EATER(1984, Can.), w, ed
Lewis Keane
VOYAGE TO THE PREHISTORIC PLANET(1965)
Maire Keane
PROFESSOR TIM(1957, Ireland); HOME IS THE HERO(1959, Ireland)
Mary Keane
Misc. Silents
CIPHER KEY, THE(1915)
R.E. Keane
DARING YOUNG MAN, THE(1942)
R. Emmett Keane
HOT MONEY(1936)
Raymond Keane
MARRIAGE BY CONTRACT(1928); LOOSE ANKLES(1930)
Misc. Talkies
VANISHING MEN(1932)
Silents
APRIL FOOL(1926); LONE EAGLE, THE(1927)
Misc. Silents
MIDNIGHT SUN, THE(1926); MAGIC GARDEN, THE(1927); HOW TO HANDLE WOMEN(1928)
Richard Keane
MY FAVORITE BRUNETTE(1947)
Robert Keane
BOYS TOWN(1938)
Robert E. Keane
CAPTAIN THUNDER(1931); WHISTLER, THE(1944); RED DRAGON, THE(1946); DOUBLE LIFE, A(1947); HENRY, THE RAINMAKER(1949); ATOMIC KID, THE(1954)
Robert Emmet Keane
GRAND JURY(1936); MEN OF BOYS TOWN(1941); GENTLEMAN FROM NO-WHERE, THE(1948)
Robert Emmett Keane
LAUGH AND GET RICH(1931); MEN CALL IT LOVE(1931); ENLIGHTEN THY DAUGHTER(1934); MAD LOVE(1935); BIG NOISE, THE(1936); DOWN THE STRETCH(1936); JAILBREAK(1936); JIM HANVEY, DETECTIVE(1937); LIVE, LOVE AND LEARN(1937); MAN OF THE PEOPLE(1937); SARATOGA(1937); UNDER SUSPI-CION(1937); ARSENE LUPIN RETURNS(1938); BILLY THE KID RETURNS(1938); BORN TO BE WILD(1938); CHASER, THE(1938); LAST EXPRESS, THE(1938); STRANGE FACES(1938); THERE'S ALWAYS A WOMAN(1938); TOO HOT TO HAN-DLE(1938); CAFE SOCIETY(1939); CONFESSIONS OF A NAZI SPY(1939); FIFTH AVENUE GIRL(1939); HAWAIIAN NIGHTS(1939); ONE HOUR TO LIVE(1939); OUTSIDE THESE WALLS(1939); PACK UP YOUR TROUBLES(1939); ROOKIE COP, THE(1939); SPELLBINDER, THE(1939); STREETS OF NEW YORK(1939); THESE GLAMOUR GIRLS(1939); 6000 ENEMIES(1939); BORDER LEGION, THE(1940); DOU-BLE ALIBI(1940); LILLIAN RUSSELL(1940); LONE WOLF MEETS A LADY, THE(1940); MICHAEL SHAYNE, PRIVATE DETECTIVE(1940); SAINT TAKES OVER, THE(1940); SLIGHTLY TEMPTED(1940); TIN PAN ALLEY(1940); COWBOY AND THE BLONDE, THE(1941); DESIGN FOR SCANDAL(1941); DEVIL AND MISS JONES, THE(1941); HELLO SUCKER(1941); HIGH SIERRA(1941); IN THE NAVY(1941); MIDNIGHT ANGEL(1941); MR. AND MRS. SMITH(1941); WILD GEESE CAL-LING(1941); A-HAUNTING WE WILL GO(1942); GIVE OUT, SISTERS(1942); LADY IN A JAM(1942); LADY IS WILLING, THE(1942); MAN WHO WOULDN'T DIE, THE(1942); MY FAVORITE BLONDE(1942); REMEMBER PEARL HARBOR(1942); SABOTAGE SQUAD(1942); THIS TIME FOR KEEPS(1942); DANCING MASTERS, THE(1943); HE HIRED THE BOSS(1943); JITTERBUGS(1943); SALUTE FOR THREE(1943); HI, GOOD-LOOKIN'(1944); IMPATIENT YEARS, THE(1944); KANSAS CITY KITTY(1944); SWEET AND LOWDOWN(1944); HER LUCKY NIGHT(1945); OVER 21(1945); PATRICK THE GREAT(1945); SCARED STIFF(1945); STRANGE MR. GREGORY, THE(1945); WHY GIRLS LEAVE HOME(1945); YOU CAME ALONG(1945); FOOL'S GOLD(1946); HOODLUM SAINT, THE(1946); LIVE WIRES(1946); NIGHT EDITOR(1946); RAINBOW OVER TEXAS(1946); SHADOW RETURNS, THE(1946); FEAR IN THE NIGHT(1947); HER HUSBAND'S AFFAIRS(1947); I WONDER WHO'S KISSING HER NOW(1947); MILLIE'S DAUGHTER(1947); NEWS HOUNDS(1947); ANGELS ALLEY(1948); I SURRENDER DEAR(1948); INCIDENT(1948); OUT OF THE STORM(1948); RETURN OF THE WHISTLER, THE(1948); TIMBER TRAIL, THE(1948); WHEN MY BABY SMILES AT ME(1948); EVERYBODY DOES IT(1949); FOLLOW ME QUIETLY(1949); FRONTIER INVESTIGATOR(1949); JOLSON SINGS AGAIN(1949); MARY RYAN, DETECTIVE(1949); NAVAJO TRAIL RAIDERS(1949); SUSANNA PASS(1949); THERE'S A GIRL IN MY HEART(1949); YOU'RE MY EVERYTHING(1949); BLONDIE'S HERO(1950); FATHER MAKES GOOD(1950); HILLS OF OKLAHOMA(1950); LIFE OF HER OWN, A(1950); WHEN GANGLAND STRIKES(1956)

Shannon Keane
1984
BIG MEAT EATER(1984, Can.)
Teri Keane
TRIBUTE(1980, Can.)
Tom Keane
BATTLE OF GREED(1934)
Charles R. Keans
CALYPSO JOE(1957)
Tommy Kearins
HIGH AND DRY(1954, Brit.)
Robert J. Kearn
ANNA KARENINA(1935), ed
Carolyn Kearney
HOT ROD GIRL(1956); DAMN CITIZEN(1958); THING THAT COULDN'T DIE, THE(1958); YOUNG AND WILD(1958)
Charles Kearney
WICKER MAN, THE(1974, Brit.); LOCAL HERO(1983, Brit.)
1984
COMFORT AND JOY(1984, Brit.)
Cheryal Kearney
CLEOPATRA JONES(1973), set d; BAD NEWS BEARS, THE(1976), set d; SOUNDER, PART 2(1976), set d; SPARKLE(1976), set d; HERO AIN'T NOTHIN' BUT A SAND-WICH, A(1977), set d; SEMI-TOUGH(1977), set d; MANITOU, THE(1978), set d
Cheryl Kearney
MOTHER, JUGS & SPEED(1976), set d
Conal Kearney
OUTSIDER, THE(1980)
Gene Kearney
GAMES(1967), w; MAN CALLED GANNON, A(1969), w
Gene R. Kearney
NIGHT OF THE LEPUS(1972), w
Jill Kearney
ONE FROM THE HEART(1982)
John Kearney
HONOR AMONG LOVERS(1931); DR. JEKYLL'S DUNGEON OF DEATH(1982); GIRO CITY(1982, Brit.)
Misc. Silents
EIGHT BELLS(1916)
John Twist Patrick Kearney
HIS FAMILY TREE(1936), w
Michael Kearney
ALL THE WAY HOME(1963); SWIMMER, THE(1968); EFFECT OF GAMMA RAYS ON MAN-IN-THE-MOON MARIGOLDS, THE(1972)
Muriel Kearney
POLO JOE(1936)
Pat Kearney
IT HAPPENED HERE(1966, Brit.)
Patrick Kearney
DARKENED ROOMS(1929), w,Patrick Konesky; FAST COMPANY(1929), w; DOOMED BATTALION, THE(1932), w; PLACE IN THE SUN, A(1951), w
Silents
MAN'S MAN, A(1929), w
Philip Kearney
PRIVATE PARTS(1972), w
Sheryl Kearney
SPOOK WHO SAT BY THE DOOR, THE(1973), set d
Kearney & Browning
SAY IT WITH FLOWERS(1934, Brit.)
Allen Kearns
TANNED LEGS(1929); VERY IDEA, THE(1929); LOVIN' THE LADIES(1930)
Bernard Kearns
SLEEPING DOGS(1977, New Zealand)
Bill Kearns
BED AND BOARD(1971, Fr.); DESTRUCTORS, THE(1974, Brit.)
Billy Kearns
PURPLE NOON(1961, Fr./Ital.); DAY AND THE HOUR, THE(1963, Fr./ Ital.); FIVE MILES TO MIDNIGHT(1963, U.S./Fr./Ital.); NO TIME FOR ECSTASY(1963, Fr.); UP FROM THE BEACH(1965); COUNTERFEIT CONSTABLE, THE(1966, Fr.); IS PARIS BURNING?(1966, U.S./Fr.); PLAYTIME(1973, Fr.); MARATHON MAN(1976)
1984
JUST THE WAY YOU ARE(1984)
Brantley F. Kearns
MC CABE AND MRS. MILLER(1971)
Elizabeth Kearns
DOWN AMONG THE Z MEN(1952, Brit.)
Geraldine Kearns
CAR, THE(1977)
Jack Kearns
MADISON SQUARE GARDEN(1932)
Joe Kearns
OUR MISS BROOKS(1956)
Joseph Kearns
ALICE IN WONDERLAND(1951); HARD, FAST, AND BEAUTIFUL(1951); DADDY LONG LEGS(1955); STORM CENTER(1956); GIRL MOST LIKELY, THE(1957); GIFT OF LOVE, THE(1958); ANATOMY OF A MURDER(1959)
Michael Kearns
1984
BODY DOUBLE(1984)
Nan Kearns
MR. H. C. ANDERSEN(1950, Brit.)
Phil Kearns
DEAD MEN DON'T WEAR PLAID(1982)
William Kearns
TRIAL, THE(1963, Fr./Ital./Ger.)
Natividad Rios Kearsley
SEEMS LIKE OLD TIMES(1980)

Maurice Keary
SAINTS AND SINNERS(1949, Brit.)
F. Brent Keast
FRATERNITY ROW(1977)
Paul Keast
COMBAT SQUAD(1953); HANNAH LEE(1953); ONE DESIRE(1955); FIRST TRAVELING SALESLADY, THE(1956); HIGH SOCIETY(1956); I WAS A TEENAGE FRANKENSTEIN(1958); PARTY GIRL(1958); SNOWFIRE(1958); SPIRAL ROAD, THE(1962)
Harry Keatan
SINISTER URGE, THE(1961)
Gwen Keate
HAPPY DAYS(1930)
Candi Keath
Misc. Talkies
JOEY(1977)
Alice Keating
I FOUND STELLA PARISH(1935); GREAT ZIEGFELD, THE(1936); YOU CAN'T TAKE IT WITH YOU(1938); ZAZA(1939); THIRD FINGER, LEFT HAND(1940); NEW YORK TOWN(1941); SHE KNEW ALL THE ANSWERS(1941); JOHNNY EAGER(1942); MAJOR AND THE MINOR, THE(1942); MY FAVORITE BLONDE(1942); YOUNGEST PROFESSION, THE(1943)
Arthur Keating
1984
ANNE DEVLIN(1984, Ireland), ed
Charles Keating
FUNNY MONEY(1983, Brit.)
Elizabeth Keating
UP THE RIVER(1930); MAD PARADE, THE(1931)
F. Serrano Keating
Misc. Silents
RED LOVE(1925); BIG SHOW, THE(1926)
Fred Keating
CAPTAIN HATES THE SEA, THE(1934); I LIVE MY LIFE(1935); NITWITS, THE(1935); SHANGHAI(1935); TO BEAT THE BAND(1935); DEVIL ON HORSEBACK, THE(1936); THIRTEEN HOURS BY AIR(1936); MELODY FOR TWO(1937); WHEN'S YOUR BIRTHDAY?(1937); DR. RHYTHM(1938); PRISON TRAIN(1938); ETERNALLY YOURS(1939); SOCIETY SMUGGLERS(1939); TIN PAN ALLEY(1940)
Graham Keating
NED KELLY(1970, Brit.)
Helen Keating
UP THE RIVER(1930); MAD PARADE, THE(1931)
Henry Keating
HOME IS THE HERO(1959, Ireland), w
John Keating
INNOCENT BYSTANDERS(1973, Brit.), m, md
Johnny Keating
HOTEL(1967), m; ROBBERY(1967, Brit.), m
Keavin Keating
WATCHED(1974), ph
Larry Keating
SONG OF THE SARONG(1945); DANCING IN THE DARK(1949); TULSA(1949); WHIRLPOOL(1949); I WAS A SHOPLIFTER(1950); MISTER 880(1950); MOTHER DIDN'T TELL ME(1950); MY BLUE HEAVEN(1950); RIGHT CROSS(1950); STELLA(1950); THREE SECRETS(1950); WHEN WILLIE COMES MARCHING HOME(1950); BANNERLINE(1951); BRIGHT VICTORY(1951); COME FILL THE CUP(1951); FOLLOW THE SUN(1951); FRANCIS GOES TO THE RACES(1951); LIGHT TOUCH, THE(1951); MATING SEASON, THE(1951); TOO YOUNG TO KISS(1951); WHEN WORLDS COLLIDE(1951); ABOUT FACE(1952); CARSON CITY(1952); MONKEY BUSINESS(1952); SOMETHING FOR THE BIRDS(1952); ABOVE AND BEYOND(1953); GIVE A GIRL A BREAK(1953); INFERNO(1953); LION IS IN THE STREETS, A(1953); SHE'S BACK ON BROADWAY(1953); GYPSY COLT(1954); DADDY LONG LEGS(1955); BEST THINGS IN LIFE ARE FREE, THE(1956); EDDY DUCHIN STORY, THE(1956); BUSTER KEATON STORY, THE(1957); STOPOVER TOKYO(1957); WAYWARD BUS, THE(1957); WHO WAS THAT LADY?(1960); BOYS' NIGHT OUT(1962); INCREDIBLE MR. LIMPET, THE(1964); I EAT YOUR SKIN(1971), ed
Laverne Keating
FRANKENSTEIN MEETS THE SPACE MONSTER(1965), ed
Michael Keating
JULIUS CAESAR(1970, Brit.)
Mimi Julia Keating
HOT STUFF(1979)
Monica Keating
ONE OF OUR SPIES IS MISSING(1966)
Paul Keating
Silents
TIE THAT BINDS, THE(1923), w
William J. Keating
SLAUGHTER ON TENTH AVENUE(1957), w
Buster Keaton
DOUGH BOYS(1930); FREE AND EASY(1930); PARLOR, BEDROOM AND BATH(1931); SIDEWALKS OF NEW YORK(1931); PASSIONATE PLUMBER(1932); SPEAK EASILY(1932); WHAT! NO BEER?(1933); OLD SPANISH CUSTOM, AN(1936, Brit.); HOLLYWOOD CAVALCADE(1939); JONES FAMILY IN HOLLYWOOD, THE(1939), w; QUICK MILLIONS(1939), w; LI'L ABNER(1940); NEW MOON(1940); VILLAIN STILL PURSUED HER, THE(1940); FOREVER AND A DAY(1943); SAN DIEGO, I LOVE YOU(1944); TWO GIRLS AND A SAILOR(1944); SHE WENT TO THE RACES(1945); THAT NIGHT WITH YOU(1945); THAT'S THE SPIRIT(1945); GOD'S COUNTRY(1946); IN THE GOOD OLD SUMMERTIME(1949); LOVABLE CHEAT, THE(1949); YOU'RE MY EVERYTHING(1949); SUNSET BOULEVARD(1950); LIMELIGHT(1952); AROUND THE WORLD IN 80 DAYS(1956); ADVENTURES OF HUCKLEBERRY FINN, THE(1960); IT'S A MAD, MAD, MAD, MAD WORLD(1963); PAJAMA PARTY(1964); BEACH BLANKET BINGO(1965); HOW TO STUFF A WILD BIKINI(1965); SERGEANT DEADHEAD(1965); FUNNY THING HAPPENED ON THE WAY TO THE FORUM, A(1966); WAR ITALIAN STYLE(1967, Ital.)
Silents
SAPHEAD, THE(1921); OUR HOSPITALITY(1923), a, d; THREE AGES, THE(1923), a, d; NAVIGATOR, THE(1924), a, d; SHERLOCK, JR.(1924), a, d; GO WEST(1925), a, d&w; SEVEN CHANCES(1925), a, d; BATTLING BUTLER(1926), a, d; COLLEGE(1927); GENERAL, THE(1927), a, d, w; CAMERAMAN, THE(1928); STEAM-

BOAT BILL, JR.(1928); SPITE MARRIAGE(1929)
Buster Keaton, Jr.
Silents
OUR HOSPITALITY(1923)
Camille Keaton
I SPIT ON YOUR GRAVE(1983)
Diane Keaton
LOVERS AND OTHER STRANGERS(1970); GODFATHER, THE(1972); PLAY IT AGAIN, SAM(1972); SLEEPER(1973); GODFATHER, THE, PART II(1974); LOVE AND DEATH(1975); HARRY AND WALTER GO TO NEW YORK(1976); I WILL ...I WILL ...FOR NOW(1976); ANNIE HALL(1977); LOOKING FOR MR. GOODBAR(1977); INTERIORS(1978); MANHATTAN(1979); REDS(1981); SHOOT THE MOON(1982)
1984
LITTLE DRUMMER GIRL, THE(1984); MRS. SOFFEL(1984)
Harry Keaton
DESERT MESA(1935)
Joe Keaton
Silents
GENERAL, THE(1927); STEAMBOAT BILL, JR.(1928)
Joseph Keaton
Silents
OUR HOSPITALITY(1923); SHERLOCK, JR.(1924)
Michael Keaton
NIGHT SHIFT(1982); MR. MOM(1983)
1984
JOHNNY DANGEROUSLY(1984)
Dolores Keator
DR. NO(1962, Brit.)
Mark Keats
PUNISHMENT PARK(1971)
Mildred Keats
Misc. Silents
QUEEN OF THE SEA(1918)
Norman Keats
TIGHT SPOT(1955)
Robert Keats
TALK OF THE TOWN(1942)
Steven Keats
FRIENDS OF EDDIE COYLE, THE(1973); DEATH WISH(1974); GAMBLER, THE(1974); HESTER STREET(1975); GUMBALL RALLY, THE(1976); SKY RIDERS(1976, U.S./Gr.); BLACK SUNDAY(1977); AMERICAN SUCCESS COMPANY, THE(1980); HANGAR 18(1980); SILENT RAGE(1982)
Viola Keats
ENEMY OF THE POLICE(1933, Brit.); HIS GRACE GIVES NOTICE(1933, Brit.); MATINEE IDOL(1933, Brit.); TOO MANY WIVES(1933, Brit.); NIGHT OF THE PARTY, THE(1934, Brit.); POINTING FINGER, THE(1934, Brit.); TOO MANY MILLIONS(1934, Brit.); HER LAST AFFAIRE(1935, Brit.); MISTER HOBO(1936, Brit.); TWO WHO DARED(1937, Brit.); ROMAN SPRING OF MRS. STONE, THE(1961, U.S./Brit.); TWO WIVES AT ONE WEDDING(1961, Brit.); SHE DIDN'T SAY NO!(1962, Brit.); TAMAHINE(1964, Brit.); WITCHCRAFT(1964, Brit.); OPERATION SNAFU(1965, Brit.); DEVIL'S OWN, THE(1967, Brit.)
William Keaulani
DEVIL AT FOUR O'CLOCK, THE(1961)
Vernon Keays
STRICTLY IN THE GROOVE(1942), d; ARIZONA TRAIL(1943), d; MARSHAL OF GUNSMOKE(1944), d; TRAIL TO GUNSIGHT(1944), d; DANGEROUS INTRUDER(1945), d; ROCKIN' IN THE ROCKIES(1945), d; LANDRUSH(1946), d; LAWLESS EMPIRE(1946), d; WHIRLWIND RAIDERS(1948), d
Misc. Talkies
BLAZING THE WESTERN TRAIL(1945), d; RHYTHM ROUND-UP(1945), d; SING ME A SONG OF TEXAS(1945), d
Hugh Keays-Byrne
STONE(1974, Aus.); MAN FROM HONG KONG(1975); BLUE FIN(1978, Aus.); MAD MAX(1979, Aus.); CHAIN REACTION(1980, Aus.); DAY AFTER HALLOWEEN, THE(1981, Aus.)
1984
STRIKEBOUND(1984, Aus.)
Syed Kechico
FIRECRACKER(1981), p
Carlo Kechler
GHOST, THE(1965, Ital.); PRIMITIVE LOVE(1966, Ital.); OPIATE '67(1967, Fr./Ital.); WILD, WILD PLANET, THE(1967, Ital.)
Chuck Kechne
RETURN FROM WITCH MOUNTAIN(1978), cos
Baby Jane Keckley
ROARIN' LEAD(1937)
Jane Keckley
GODLESS GIRL, THE(1929); DYNAMITE(1930); HIDE-OUT, THE(1930); ONE YEAR LATER(1933); STRANGE PEOPLE(1933); MURDER ON THE CAMPUS(1934); NOTORIOUS BUT NICE(1934); QUITTERS, THE(1934); STOLEN SWEETS(1934); PADDY O'DAY(1935); SHOT IN THE DARK, A(1935); WORLD ACCUSES, THE(1935); DEATH FROM A DISTANCE(1936); GIRL OF THE OZARKS(1936); NEXT TIME WE LOVE(1936); SHOW BOAT(1936); THEODORA GOES WILD(1936); GUNSMOKE RANCH(1937); PLAINSMAN, THE(1937); SOULS AT SEA(1937); IN OLD MONTANA(1939); UNION PACIFIC(1939); DOCTOR TAKES A WIFE(1940); NORTHWEST MOUNTED POLICE(1940); STRANGER ON THE THIRD FLOOR(1940); BUY ME THAT TOWN(1941)
Silents
PARSON OF PANAMINT, THE(1916); MOLLY ENTANGLED(1917); HUCK AND TOM(1918); SOUL OF YOUTH, THE(1920); RAGS TO RICHES(1922); ARE YOU A FAILURE?(1923); JUST LIKE A WOMAN(1923); ONLY 38(1923); AFLAME IN THE SKY(1927); ANGEL OF BROADWAY, THE(1927); KING OF KINGS, THE(1927); CRAIG'S WIFE(1928); HAROLD TEEN(1928); MASKED ANGEL(1928); ON TO RENO(1928); ROAD HOUSE(1928); WALKING BACK(1928); OBJECT-ALIMONY(1929)
Misc. Silents
VIRGINIA COURTSHIP, A(1921); DEADWOOD COACH, THE(1924); MILE-A-MINUTE MAN, THE(1926)

Wee Willie Keeler
CHEYENNE WILDCAT(1944)
Engene Keeley
RETURN FROM THE ASHES(1965, U.S./Brit.)
Maura Keeley
BROTHERLY LOVE(1970, Brit.); UNDERGROUND(1970, Brit.)
Kim Keelin
Misc. Talkies
DEATH MAY BE YOUR SANTA CLAUS(1969)
Kenneth Keeling
DEVIL'S PLOT, THE(1948, Brit.)
Lucille Keeling
GOLD DIGGERS OF 1937(1936)
Robert Lee Keeling
Silents
COUNTERFEIT(1919); RECKLESS YOUTH(1922); SUCCESS(1923)
Misc. Silents
LA BELLE RUSSE(1919); PRINCESS JONES(1921)
Chuck D. Keen
JONIKO AND THE KUSH TA KA(1969), p, w&ph
Diane Keen
HERE WE GO ROUND THE MULBERRY BUSH(1968, Brit.); POPDOWN(1968, Brit.); SWEENEY(1977, Brit.); SHILLINGBURY BLOWERS, THE(1980, Brit.); SILVER DREAM RACER(1982, Brit.)
Earl Keen
ON STAGE EVERYBODY(1945); WHITE TIE AND TAILS(1946); IT SHOULD HAPPEN TO YOU(1954)
Geoffrey Keen
ODD MAN OUT(1947, Brit.); FALLEN IDOL, THE(1949, Brit.); HOUR OF GLORY(1949, Brit.); CHANCE OF A LIFETIME(1950, Brit.); CLOUDED YELLOW, THE(1950, Brit.); IT'S HARD TO BE GOOD(1950, Brit.); SEVEN DAYS TO NOON(1950, Brit.); THIRD MAN, THE(1950, Brit.); TREASURE ISLAND(1950, Brit.); CHEER THE BRAVE(1951, Brit.); GREEN GROW THE RUSHES(1951, Brit.); HIGH TREASON(1951, Brit.); CRY, THE BELOVED COUNTRY(1952, Brit.); HIS EXCELLENCY(1952, Brit.); SCOTLAND YARD INSPECTOR(1952, Brit.); STRANGER IN BETWEEN, THE(1952, Brit.); GENEVIEVE(1953, Brit.); LONG MEMORY, THE(1953, Brit.); MEET MR. LUCIFER(1953, Brit.); ANGELS ONE FIVE(1954, Brit.); BLACK GLOVE(1954, Brit.); COURT MARTIAL(1954, Brit.); DOCTOR IN THE HOUSE(1954, Brit.); HIGH AND DRY(1954, Brit.); ROB ROY, THE HIGHLAND ROGUE(1954, Brit.); TURN THE KEY SOFTLY(1954, Brit.); DIVIDED HEART, THE(1955, Brit.); DOCTOR AT SEA(1955, Brit.); GLASS TOMB, THE(1955, Brit.); PASSAGE HOME(1955, Brit.); STORM OVER THE NILE(1955, Brit.); BLONDE SINNER(1956, Brit.); LOSER TAKES ALL(1956, Brit.); MAN WHO NEVER WAS, THE(1956, Brit.); POSTMARK FOR DANGER(1956, Brit.); BIRTHDAY PRESENT, THE(1957, Brit.); DOCTOR AT LARGE(1957, Brit.); PANIC IN THE PARLOUR(1957, Brit.); SHE PLAYED WITH FIRE(1957, Brit.); SPANISH GARDENER, THE(1957, Span.); THIRD KEY, THE(1957, Brit.); TOWN ON TRIAL(1957, Brit.); TRIPLE DECEPTION(1957, Brit.); SECRET PLACE, THE(1958, Brit.); TOWN LIKE ALICE, A(1958, Brit.); BEYOND THIS PLACE(1959, Brit.); BOY AND THE BRIDGE, THE(1959, Brit.); DEADLY RECORD(1959, Brit.); DEVIL'S BAIT(1959, Brit.); HORRORS OF THE BLACK MUSEUM(1959, U.S./Brit.); NOWHERE TO GO(1959, Brit.); SCAPEGOAT, THE(1959, Brit.); STRANGE AFFECTION(1959, Brit.); ANGRY SILENCE, THE(1960, Brit.); SINK THE BISMARCK!(1960, Brit.); NO LOVE FOR JOHNNIE(1961, Brit.); SPARE THE ROD(1961, Brit.); LISA(1962, Brit.); LIVE NOW–PAY LATER(1962, Brit.); MATTER OF WHO, A(1962, Brit.); ROOM-MATES(1962, Brit.); SPIRAL ROAD, THE(1962); CRACKSMAN, THE(1963, Brit.); MIND BENDERS, THE(1963, Brit.); RETURN TO SENDER(1963, Brit.); TORPEDO BAY(1964, Ital./Fr.); DOCTOR ZHIVAGO(1965); HEROES OF TELEMARK, THE(1965, Brit.); BORN FREE(1966); BERSERK(1967); MALPAS MYSTERY, THE(1967, Brit.); THUNDERBIRD 6(1968, Brit.); CROMWELL(1970, Brit.); TASTE THE BLOOD OF DRACULA(1970, Brit.); SACCO AND VANZETTI(1971, Ital./Fr.); DOOMWATCH(1972, Brit.); LIVING FREE(1972, Brit.); DR. SYN, ALIAS THE SCARECROW(1975); SPY WHO LOVED ME, THE(1977, Brit.); MOONRAKER(1979, Brit.); FOR YOUR EYES ONLY(1981); AMIN–THE RISE AND FALL(1982, Kenya); OCTOPUSSY(1983, Brit.)
Misc. Talkies
LICENSED TO LOVE AND KILL(1979, Brit.)
George Keen
Misc. Silents
DUNGEON OF DEATH, THE(1915, Brit.)
Kit Keen
REUNION(1932, Brit.)
Madelyn Keen
CAT ATE THE PARAKEET, THE(1972)
Misc. Talkies
POT! PARENTS! POLICE!(1975)
Malcolm Keen
WOLVES(1930, Brit.); HOUSE OF UNREST, THE(1931, Brit.); JEALOUSY(1931, Brit.); 77 PARK LANE(1931, Brit.); DANGEROUS GROUND(1934, Brit.); NIGHT OF THE PARTY, THE(1934, Brit.); WHISPERING TONGUES(1934, Brit.); SCOTLAND YARD COMMANDS(1937, Brit.); SIXTY GLORIOUS YEARS(1938, Brit.); MYSTERY OF ROOM 13(1941, Brit.); GREAT MR. HANDEL, THE(1942, Brit.); LADY AND THE BANDIT, THE(1951); LORNA DOONE(1951); MATING SEASON, THE(1951); ROB ROY, THE HIGHLAND ROGUE(1954, Brit.); SHE PLAYED WITH FIRE(1957, Brit.); I ACCUSE(1958, Brit.); OPERATION AMSTERDAM(1960, Brit.); FRANCIS OF ASSISI(1961); TWO AND TWO MAKE SIX(1962, Brit.); MACBETH(1963); WALK IN THE SHADOW(1966, Brit.)
Silents
JIMMY(1916, Brit.); LOST CHORD, THE(1917, Brit.); FEAR O' GOD(1926, Brit./Ger.); LODGER, THE(1926, Brit.); MANXMAN, THE(1929, Brit.)
Misc. Silents
MASTER OF MEN, A(1917, Brit.); BILL FOR DIVORCEMENT, A(1922); FEAR O'GOD(1926, Brit.)
Noah Keen
BIG HAND FOR THE LITTLE LADY, A(1966); CAPER OF THE GOLDEN BULLS, THE(1967); BATTLE FOR THE PLANET OF THE APES(1973); TOM SAWYER(1973); GABLE AND LOMBARD(1976)
Misc. Talkies
BLACK STARLET(1974)

Pat Keen
KIND OF LOVING, A(1962, Brit.); MEMOIRS OF A SURVIVOR(1981, Brit.)
Richard Keen
HIGH SOCIETY(1956)
Sam Keen
SLEEPING CAR(1933, Brit.)
William Keen
TOO SOON TO LOVE(1960)
Christy Keenan
1984
BLIND DATE(1984)
Edgar Keenan
LAST GUNFIGHTER, THE(1961, Can.), set d
Edward Keenan
Silents
EMBARRASSMENT OF RICHES, THE(1918)
Frank Keenan
Silents
DESPOILER, THE(1915); JIM GRIMSBY'S BOY(1916); BRIDE OF HATE, THE(1917); CRAB, THE(1917); MORE TROUBLE(1918); SCARS OF JEALOUSY(1923); GILDED BUTTERFLY, THE(1926); LORNA DOONE(1927)
Misc. Silents
COWARD, THE(1915); LONG CHANCE, THE(1915); HONOR THY NAME(1916); PHANTOM, THE(1916); SIN YE DO, THE(1916); STEPPING STONE, THE(1916); THOROUGHBRED, THE(1916); PUBLIC DEFENDER(1917); BELLS, THE(1918); LOADED DICE(1918); RULER OF THE ROAD(1918); BROTHERS DIVIDED(1919), a, d; FALSE CODE, THE(1919); GATES OF BRASS(1919); MASTER MAN, THE(1919); MIDNIGHT STAGE, THE(1919); SILVER GIRL, THE(1919), a, d; TODD OF THE TIMES(1919); WORLD AFLAME, THE(1919); DOLLAR FOR DOLLAR(1920), a, d; SMOULDERING EMBERS(1920), a, d; HEARTS AFLAME(1923); WAR'S WOMEN(1923); WOMEN WHO GIVE(1924); DIXIE HANDICAP, THE(1925); EAST LYNNE(1925); MY LADY'S LIPS(1925)
Gabrielle Keenan
LIGHT YEARS AWAY(1982, Fr./Switz.)
Harry Keenan
Silents
MAN WHO COULD NOT LOSE, THE(1914)
Misc. Silents
TOAST OF DEATH, THE(1915); WINGED IDOL, THE(1915); HIGHEST BID, THE(1916); LAST ACT, THE(1916); MAN WHO WOULD NOT DIE, THE(1916); SOUL MATES(1916); STRENGTH OF DONALD MCKENZIE, THE(1916); TORCH BEARER, THE(1916)
Haydn Keenan
27A(1974, Aus.), a, p
Lee Keenan
GREAT MUPPET CAPER, THE(1981)
Paul Keenan
HONKY TONK FREEWAY(1981)
Sheila Keenan
RISKY BUSINESS(1983)
William J. Keenan
KING KONG ESCAPES(1968, Jap.), w
Carolyn Keene
NANCY DREW–DETECTIVE(1938), w; NANCY DREW AND THE HIDDEN STAIRCASE(1939), w
Day Keene
TROUBLE WITH GIRLS(AND HOW TO GET INTO IT), THE*1/2 (1969), w; JOY HOUSE(1964, Fr.), w
Dick Keene
JOAN OF OZARK(1942); THEY GOT ME COVERED(1943); VARIETY GIRL(1947); ISN'T IT ROMANTIC?(1948); CHICAGO DEADLINE(1949); NO MAN OF HER OWN(1950); WHITE CHRISTMAS(1954)
Ed Keene
HARD ROCK HARRIGAN(1935)
Edward Keene
ONE YEAR LATER(1933); MAN OF IRON(1935); FOR THE SERVICE(1936); RIDERS OF THE TIMBERLINE(1941)
George Keene
Silents
SOLDIER AND A MAN, A(1916, Brit.)
Misc. Silents
(; LIFE OF AN ACTRESS, THE(1915, Brit.); NON-CONFORMIST PARSON, A(1919, Brit.); SWEET AND TWENTY(1919, Brit.); BLACK SHEEP, THE(1920, Brit.); NOTHING ELSE MATTERS(1920, Brit.); SCARLET WOOING, THE(1920, Brit.); WOMAN OF THE IRON BRACELETS, THE(1920, Brit.)
Hamilton Keene
MIDDLE WATCH, THE(1930, Brit.); SUSPENSE(1930, Brit.); ILLEGAL(1932, Brit.); NEW HOTEL, THE(1932, Brit.); BLUE SQUADRON, THE(1934, Brit.); LEAVE IT TO BLANCHE(1934, Brit.); LITTLE STRANGER(1934, Brit.); MOUNTAINS O'MOURNE(1938, Brit.); ROSE OF TRALEE(1938, Ireland); MUTINY OF THE ELSINORE, THE(1939, Brit.); I'LL TURN TO YOU(1946, Brit.); TRIAL OF MADAM X, THE(1948, Brit.); IT'S NOT CRICKET(1949, Brit.); SECOND MATE, THE(1950, Brit.); WHILE THE SUN SHINES(1950, Brit.); PAUL TEMPLE'S TRIUMPH(1951, Brit.); TREAD SOFTLY(1952, Brit.); DEVIL'S JEST, THE(1954, Brit.); ROB ROY, THE HIGHLAND ROGUE(1954, Brit.); INNOCENTS IN PARIS(1955, Brit.); SEE HOW THEY RUN(1955, Brit.)
Silents
LOST PATROL, THE(1929, Brit.)
Madora Keene
TRUE TO LIFE(1943)
Michael Keene
VIOLATED(1953); ROOGIE'S BUMP(1954)
Mike Keene
WRONG MAN, THE(1956); SATAN IN HIGH HEELS(1962); PSYCHOMANIA(1964)
Milford Keene
I AM THE CHEESE(1983)
Norman Keene
POLICE CALL(1933), w

Ralph Keene
BOY, A GIRL AND A BIKE, A(1949 Brit.), p, w; DOUBLE CONFESSION(1953, Brit.), w

Raymond Keene
HELLO SISTER(1930)

Richard Keene
WHY LEAVE HOME?(1929); WORDS AND MUSIC(1929); BIG PARTY, THE(1930); GOLDEN CALF, THE(1930); HAPPY DAYS(1930); UP THE RIVER(1930); WILD COMPANY(1930); MOONLIGHT AND PRETZELS(1933); SHE MARRIED A COP(1939); CHARLIE CHAN'S MURDER CRUISE(1940); ROAD TO SINGAPORE(1940); ROAD TO ZANZIBAR(1941); MURDER IS MY BUSINESS(1946); ROAD TO BALI(1952); COUNTRY GIRL, THE(1954); THAT CERTAIN FEELING(1956)

Rogers Keene
Silents
SILENT COMMAND, THE(1923)

Tom Keene
SUICIDE FLEET(1931); BEYOND THE ROCKIES(1932); COME ON DANGER!(1932); FREIGHTERS OF DESTINY(1932); GHOST VALLEY(1932); PARTNERS(1932); RENEGADES OF THE WEST(1932); SADDLE BUSTER, THE(1932); CHEYENNE KID, THE(1933); CROSSFIRE(1933); SCARLET RIVER(1933); SON OF THE BORDER(1933); SUNSET PASS(1933); OUR DAILY BREAD(1934); DESERT GOLD(1936); DRIFT FENCE(1936); TIMOTHY'S QUEST(1936); DRUMS OF DESTINY(1937); GLORY TRAIL, THE(1937); GOD'S COUNTRY AND THE MAN(1937); UNDER STRANGE FLAGS(1937); WHERE TRAILS DIVIDE(1937); LAW COMMANDS, THE(1938); OLD LOUISIANA(1938); PAINTED TRAIL, THE(1938); REBELLION(1938); ROMANCE OF THE ROCKIES(1938); DRIFTIN' KID, THE(1941); DYNAMITE CANYON(1941); RIDING THE SUNSET TRAIL(1941); WANDERERS OF THE WEST(1941); ARIZONA ROUNDUP(1942); LONE STAR LAW MEN(1942); WESTERN MAIL(1942); BERLIN EXPRESS(1948); IF YOU KNEW SUSIE(1948); RACE STREET(1948); TRAIL OF ROBIN HOOD(1950); FAT MAN, THE(1951); ONCE UPON A HORSE(1958); PLAN 9 FROM OUTER SPACE(1959)
Misc. Talkies
REBELLION(1936); WHERE TRAILS END(1942)

Valley Keene
SON OF THE RENEGADE(1953); SPARTACUS(1960)

Tom Keene [George Duryea/Richard Powers]
SUNDOWN TRAIL(1931); HONG KONG NIGHTS(1935); RAW TIMBER(1937); BROTHERS IN THE SADDLE(1949); MILKMAN, THE(1950)

Eliott Keener
1984
TIGHTROPE(1984)

Hazel Keener
I LOVE YOU AGAIN(1940); THAT GANG OF MINE(1940); UNTAMED(1940); MURDER BY INVITATION(1941); SO PROUDLY WE HAIL(1943); STORY OF DR. WASSELL, THE(1944); UNDERCURRENT(1946); DOUBLE LIFE, A(1947); JOAN OF ARC(1948); CAGED(1950); MILKMAN, THE(1950); RACKET, THE(1951)
Silents
EMPTY HANDS(1924); GALLOPING GALLAGHER(1924); NORTH OF NEVADA(1924); FRESHMAN, THE(1925); PORTS OF CALL(1925); VANISHING HOOFS(1926); ONE HOUR OF LOVE(1927)
Misc. Silents
DANGEROUS COWARD, THE(1924); FIGHTING SAP, THE(1924); HARD HITTIN' HAMILTON(1924); HIS FORGOTTEN WIFE(1924); MASK OF LOPEZ, THE(1924); SILENT STRANGER, THE(1924); TEN DAYS(1925); GINGHAM GIRL, THE(1927)

Ken Keener
DELIVERANCE(1972)

Susan Keener
ULTIMATE WARRIOR, THE(1975)

Suzanne Keener
LOVE AT FIRST SIGHT(1930)

Maj. Gen. Keeney, USAF/Res. Ret.
COURT-MARTIAL OF BILLY MITCHELL, THE(1955), tech adv

Dennis Keep
1984
ALLEY CAT(1984)

Michael Keep
WAY WEST, THE(1967); 40 GUNS TO APACHE PASS(1967); STACEY!(1973)

Stephen Keep
LOVE AND MONEY(1982)

Harry Keepers
Silents
RIP-TIDE, THE(1923), ph

Harry L. Keepers
Silents
JOHNNY RING AND THE CAPTAIN'S SWORD(1921), ph; JUST A SONG AT TWILIGHT(1922), ph

Dave Keesan
WOLVES(1930, Brit.), ph

Dick Keese
BIG TOWN AFTER DARK(1947)

Oscar Keesee
TERROR IS A MAN(1959, U.S./Phil.); CRY OF BATTLE(1963); RAIDERS OF LEYTE GULF(1963 U.S./Phil.)

Peyton Keesee
TERROR IS A MAN(1959, U.S./Phil.)

Oscar Keesee, Jr.
STEEL CLAW, THE(1961)

Norm Keesing
SCARECROW, THE(1982, New Zealand)

Allen Keesling
BABY MAKER, THE(1970)

Thomas Keeswald
Misc. Silents
LOVE'S PILGRIMAGE TO AMERICA(1916)

Worth Keeter
WOLFMAN(1979), d&w, makeup; LADY GREY(1980), d; LIVING LEGEND(1980), d

Worth Keeter III
1984
ROTWEILER: DOGS OF HELL(1984), d

Katherine Keeton
EXPRESSO BONGO(1959, Brit.); TOO HOT TO HANDLE(1961, Brit.); SPY WHO CAME IN FROM THE COLD, THE(1965, Brit.)

Viola Keets
NO TIME FOR TEARS(1957, Brit.)

Sen. Estes Kefauver
CAPTIVE CITY(1952); MAD AT THE WORLD(1955)

John Keffer
BIRCH INTERVAL(1976)

Robert Kegerreis
Silents
BALLET GIRL, THE(1916)
Misc. Silents
MESSAGE TO GARCIA, A(1916); MISS DECEPTION(1917)

Al Kegerris
LAWLESS, THE(1950), set d

Alfred Kegerris
WHISTLE STOP(1946), set d; BIG TOWN AFTER DARK(1947), set d; WATERFRONT AT MIDNIGHT(1948), set d

Alfred E. Kegerris
CLAUDELLE INGLISH(1961), set d

Alfred Keggeris
BIG TOWN SCANDAL(1948), set d; MANHANDLED(1949), set d

Peter Keglevic
BELLA DONNA(1983, Ger.), d&w

Kermit Kegley
NAKED CITY, THE(1948); DOUBLE DYNAMITE(1951)

Jack Kehler
STRANGE INVADERS(1983)

Charles Kehoe
FLAMING FRONTIER(1958, Can.)

Chuck Kehoe
WOLF DOG(1958, Can.)

Jack Kehoe
GANG THAT COULDN'T SHOOT STRAIGHT, THE(1971); FRIENDS OF EDDIE COYLE, THE(1973); SERPICO(1973); STING, THE(1973); LAW AND DISORDER(1974); CARWASH(1976); FISH THAT SAVED PITTSBURGH, THE(1979); MELVIN AND HOWARD(1980); ON THE NICKEL(1980); REDS(1981); STAR CHAMBER, THE(1983); TWO OF A KIND(1983)
1984
KILLERS, THE(1984); POPE OF GREENWICH VILLAGE, THE(1984); WILD LIFE, THE(1984)

Don Kehr
BABY, IT'S YOU(1983)

Kathie Kei
CHARLIE CHAN AND THE CURSE OF THE DRAGON QUEEN(1981)

Hans-Jurgen Keibach
FORMULA, THE(1980), art d

Dvora Keidar
DREAMER, THE(1970, Israel)

Avi Keiddar
1984
LITTLE DRUMMER GIRL, THE(1984)

Brian Keifer
Z.P.G.(1972)

Kurt Keifer
SKY RIDERS(1976, U.S./Gr.)

Phillip Keiffer
JOAN OF ARC(1948)

Vivian Keiffer
KID MILLIONS(1934)

Leonard Keigel
LEVIATHAN(1961, Fr.), d, w

William Keighley
RESURRECTION(1931); FOOTLIGHT PARADE(1933), d; LADIES THEY TALK ABOUT(1933), a, d; BABBITT(1934), d; BIG HEARTED HERBERT(1934), d; DOCTOR MONICA(1934), d; EASY TO LOVE(1934), d; JOURNAL OF A CRIME(1934), d; KANSAS CITY PRINCESS(1934), d; G-MEN(1935), d; MARY JANE'S PA(1935), d; RIGHT TO LIVE, THE(1935), d; SPECIAL AGENT(1935), d; STARS OVER BROADWAY(1935), d; BULLETS OR BALLOTS(1936), d; GREEN PASTURES(1936), d; SINGING KID, THE(1936), d; GOD'S COUNTRY AND THE WOMAN(1937), d; PRINCE AND THE PAUPER, THE(1937), d; VARSITY SHOW(1937), d; ADVENTURES OF ROBIN HOOD, THE(1938), d; BROTHER RAT(1938), d; SECRETS OF AN ACTRESS(1938), d; VALLEY OF THE GIANTS(1938), d; EACH DAWN I DIE(1939), d; YES, MY DARLING DAUGHTER(1939), d; FIGHTING 69TH, THE(1940), d; NO TIME FOR COMEDY(1940), d; TORRID ZONE(1940), d; BRIDE CAME C.O.D., THE(1941), d; FOUR MOTHERS(1941), d; GEORGE WASHINGTON SLEPT HERE(1942), d; MAN WHO CAME TO DINNER, THE(1942), d; HONEYMOON(1947), d; STREET WITH NO NAME, THE(1948), d; ROCKY MOUNTAIN(1950), d; CLOSE TO MY HEART(1951), d; MASTER OF BALLANTRAE, THE(1953, U.S./Brit.), d

Cyril Keightley
Silents
SPENDTHRIFT, THE(1915)

Keiko
CONFESSIONS OF AN OPIUM EATER(1962)

Kishi Keiko
YAKUZA, THE(1975, U.S./Jap.)

Bill Keil
ONE HUNDRED AND ONE DALMATIANS(1961), anim; MAN CALLED FLINTSTONE, THE(1966), anim

Margaret-Rose Keil
THAT KIND OF GIRL(1963, Brit.)

Virginia Keiley
KING ARTHUR WAS A GENTLEMAN(1942, Brit.); MISS LONDON LTD.(1943, Brit.); CAESAR AND CLEOPATRA(1946, Brit.); LOCKET, THE(1946); NOCTURNE(1946); IF WINTER COMES(1947); HOMECOMING(1948); MAN OF EVIL(1948, Brit.); OPERATION MURDER(1957, Brit.)

Alice Keillor
RACE FOR YOUR LIFE, CHARLIE BROWN(1977), ed

Warren Keillor
STARSHIP INVASIONS(1978, Can.), spec eff

Virginia Keily
ROSE OF TRALEE(1942, Brit.); STRANGE CASE OF DR. MANNING, THE(1958, Brit.)

Betty Lou Keim
TEENAGE REBEL(1956); THESE WILDER YEARS(1956); WAYWARD BUS, THE(1957); SOME CAME RUNNING(1959)

Nili Keinan
EVERY BASTARD A KING(1968, Israel)

Eberhard Keindorff
MRS. WARREN'S PROFESSION(1960, Ger.), w; ARMS AND THE MAN(1962, Ger.), w; END OF MRS. CHENEY(1963, Ger.), w; I, TOO, AM ONLY A WOMAN(1963, Ger.), w; FRONTIER HELLCAT(1966, Fr./Ital./Ger./Yugo.), w; ONLY A WOMAN(1966, Ger.), w; 24 HOURS IN A WOMAN'S LIFE(1968, Fr./Ger.), w

Kurt Keintel
EMBEZZLED HEAVEN(1959,Ger.)

Andrew Keir
LADY CRAVED EXCITEMENT, THE(1950, Brit.); BRAVE DON'T CRY, THE(1952, Brit.); HIGH AND DRY(1954, Brit.); SCOTCH ON THE ROCKS(1954, Brit.); HIGH FLIGHT(1957, Brit.); SUSPENDED ALIBI(1957, Brit.); HEART OF A CHILD(1958, Brit.); NIGHT TO REMEMBER, A(1958, Brit.); TREAD SOFTLY STRANGER(1959, Brit.); DAY THEY ROBBED THE BANK OF ENGLAND, THE(1960, Brit.); PIRATES OF BLOOD RIVER, THE(1962, Brit.); CLEOPATRA(1963); DEVIL-SHIP PIRATES, THE(1964, Brit.); FALL OF THE ROMAN EMPIRE, THE(1964); TORPEDO BAY(1964, Ital./Fr.); LORD JIM(1965, Brit.); DALEKS–INVASION EARTH 2155 A.D.(1966, Brit.); DRACULA–PRINCE OF DARKNESS(1966, Brit.); FIGHTING PRINCE OF DONEGAL, THE(1966, Brit.); LONG DUEL, THE(1967, Brit.); VIKING QUEEN, THE(1967, Brit.); ATTACK ON THE IRON COAST(1968, U.S./Brit.); FIVE MILLION YEARS TO EARTH(1968, Brit.); ROYAL HUNT OF THE SUN, THE(1969, Brit.); LAST GRENADE, THE(1970, Brit.); NIGHT VISITOR, THE(1970, Swed./U.S.); MARY, QUEEN OF SCOTS(1971, Brit.); ZEPPELIN(1971, Brit.); ADAM'S WOMAN(1972, Austral.); BLOOD FROM THE MUMMY'S TOMB(1972, Brit.); THIRTY NINE STEPS, THE(1978, Brit.); LION OF THE DESERT(1981, Libya/Brit.)

Christine Keir
MEN OF THE SEA(1951, Brit.)

David Keir
FIND THE LADY(1936, Brit.); GHOST GOES WEST, THE(1936); HEARTS OF HUMANITY(1936, Brit.); HOWARD CASE, THE(1936, Brit.); TALKING FEET(1937, Brit.); SKY RAIDERS, THE(1938, Brit.); GIRL WHO FORGOT, THE(1939, Brit.); THIS MAN IS NEWS(1939, Brit.); TWO FOR DANGER(1940, Brit.); ATLANTIC FERRY(1941, Brit.); THIS ENGLAND(1941, Brit.); FRONT LINE KIDS(1942, Brit.); LET THE PEOPLE SING(1942, Brit.); SALUTE JOHN CITIZEN(1942, Brit.); AT DAWN WE DIE(1943, Brit.); LAMP STILL BURNS, THE(1943, Brit.); SHIPBUILDERS, THE(1943, Brit.); GIVE ME THE STARS(1944, Brit.); IT HAPPENED ONE SUNDAY(1944, Brit.); MEET SEXTON BLAKE(1944, Brit.); MY AIN FOLK(1944, Brit.); HONEYMOON HOTEL(1946, Brit.); I'LL TURN TO YOU(1946, Brit.); WALTZ TIME(1946, Brit.); TAWNY PIPIT(1947, Brit.); CAPTIVE HEART, THE(1948, Brit.); HATTER'S CASTLE(1948, Brit.); NIGHT COMES TOO SOON(1948, Brit.); HER MAN GILBEY(1949, Brit.); WARNING TO WANTONS, A(1949, Brit.); PINK STRING AND SEALING WAX(1950, Brit.); WHILE THE SUN SHINES(1950, Brit.); HER PANELLED DOOR(1951, Brit.); HONEYMOON DEFERRED(1951, Brit.); PORTRAIT OF CLARE(1951, Brit.); GAMBLER AND THE LADY, THE(1952, Brit.); MR. LORD SAYS NO(1952, Brit.); ROB ROY, THE HIGHLAND ROGUE(1954, Brit.)

Dennis Keir
EDUCATION OF SONNY CARSON, THE(1974)

Sean Keir
GREYFRIARS BOBBY(1961, Brit.)

Ursula Keir
VINTAGE, THE(1957), w

Judy Keirn
DEADLY AFFAIR, THE(1967, Brit.)

William Keirnan
RIO LOBO(1970), set d

Howard Keiser
NIGHT SONG(1947); I REMEMBER MAMA(1948); LOUISA(1950)

Zelda Keiser
SKY PIRATE, THE(1970)

Keisha
RENEGADE GIRLS(1974)

Jan Keisser
1984
RIVER RAT, THE(1984), ph

Harvey Keitel
WHO'S THAT KNOCKING AT MY DOOR?(1968); MEAN STREETS(1973); ALICE DOESN'T LIVE HERE ANYMORE(1975); THAT'S THE WAY OF THE WORLD(1975); BUFFALO BILL AND THE INDIANS, OR SITTING BULL'S HISTORY LESSON(1976); MOTHER, JUGS & SPEED(1976); TAXI DRIVER(1976); WELCOME TO L.A.(1976); DUELLISTS, THE(1977, Brit.); BLUE COLLAR(1978); FINGERS(1978); EAGLE'S WING(1979, Brit.); DEATHWATCH(1980, Fr./Ger.); SATURN 3(1980); BORDER, THE(1982); EXPOSED(1983); LA NUIT DE VARENNES(1983, Fr./Ital.)
1984
CORRUPT(1984, Ital.); DREAM ONE(1984, Brit./Fr.); FALLING IN LOVE(1984)
Misc. Talkies
COP KILLERS(1984)

Agnes Newton Keith
THREE CAME HOME(1950), w

Alan Keith
YESTERDAY'S ENEMY(1959, Brit.); SUICIDE SQUADRON(1942, Brit.); GIVE US THE MOON(1944, Brit.); WORLD OWES ME A LIVING, THE(1944, Brit.); LONG KNIFE, THE(1958, Brit.)

Anthony Keith
Misc. Silents
REDEEMED(1915, Brit.); ISLAND OF WISDOM, THE(1920, Brit.), a, d

Bill Keith
BALLAD OF A GUNFIGHTER(1964), ed

Bonnie Keith
D.C. CAB(1983)

Brian Keith
ARROWHEAD(1953); ALASKA SEAS(1954); JIVARO(1954); BAMBOO PRISON, THE(1955); FIVE AGAINST THE HOUSE(1955); TIGHT SPOT(1955); VIOLENT MEN, THE(1955); NIGHTFALL(1956); STORM CENTER(1956); CHICAGO CONFIDENTIAL(1957); DINO(1957); HELL CANYON OUTLAWS(1957); RUN OF THE ARROW(1957); APPOINTMENT WITH A SHADOW(1958); DESERT HELL(1958); FORT DOBBS(1958); SIERRA BARON(1958); VILLA!(1958); VIOLENT ROAD(1958); YOUNG PHILADELPHIANS, THE(1959); TEN WHO DARED(1960); DEADLY COMPANIONS, THE(1961); PARENT TRAP, THE(1961); MOON PILOT(1962); SAVAGE SAM(1963); PLEASURE SEEKERS, THE(1964); RAIDERS, THE(1964); THOSE CALLOWAYS(1964); TIGER WALKS, A(1964); HALLELUJAH TRAIL, THE(1965); NEVADA SMITH(1966); RARE BREED, THE(1966); RUSSIANS ARE COMING, THE RUSSIANS ARE COMING, THE(1966); WAY...WAY OUT(1966); REFLECTIONS IN A GOLDEN EYE(1967); WITH SIX YOU GET EGGROLL(1968); GAILY, GAILY(1969); KRAKATOA, EAST OF JAVA(1969); MC KENZIE BREAK, THE(1970); SUPPOSE THEY GAVE A WAR AND NOBODY CAME?(1970); SCANDALOUS JOHN(1971); SOMETHING BIG(1971); WIND AND THE LION, THE(1975); YAKUZA, THE(1975, U.S./Jap.); JOE PANTHER(1976); NICKELODEON(1976); HOOPER(1978); METEOR(1979); MOONRAKER(1979, Brit.); MOUNTAIN MEN, THE(1980); CHARLIE CHAN AND THE CURSE OF THE DRAGON QUEEN(1981); SHARKY'S MACHINE(1982)
Misc. Talkies
APPOINTMENT WITH A SHADOW(1957)

Byron Keith
STRANGER THE(1946); DALLAS(1950); JOURNEY INTO LIGHT(1951); QUEEN FOR A DAY(1951); BLACK LASH, THE(1952); ABBOTT AND COSTELLO MEET THE KEYSTONE KOPS(1955); GREAT BANK ROBBERY, THE(1969)

Carlos Keith
BODY SNATCHER, THE(1945), w; BEDLAM(1946), w

David Keith
SEVENTH DAWN, THE(1964); GREAT SANTINI, THE(1979); ROSE, THE(1979); BRUBAKER(1980); BACK ROADS(1981); TAKE THIS JOB AND SHOVE IT(1981); OFFICER AND A GENTLEMAN, AN(1982); INDEPENDENCE DAY(1983); LORDS OF DISCIPLINE, THE(1983)
1984
FIRESTARTER(1984)

Debbra Keith
LET'S FACE IT(1943)

Desmond Keith
STOP PRESS GIRL(1949, Brit.)

Donald Keith
LONE WOLF'S DAUGHTER, THE(1929); SHOULD A GIRL MARRY?(1929); BRANDED MEN(1931); FIRST AID(1931); ARM OF THE LAW(1932); MIDNIGHT LADY(1932); SPEED MADNESS(1932); BIG BLUFF, THE(1933); OUTLAW JUSTICE(1933); GUILTY PARENTS(1934)
Misc. Talkies
TWISTED RAILS(1935)
Silents
PLASTIC AGE, THE(1925); DANCING MOTHERS(1926); SPECIAL DELIVERY(1927); WAY OF ALL FLESH, THE(1927); JUST OFF BROADWAY(1929); PHANTOM OF THE NORTH(1929)
Misc. Silents
BAREE, SON OF KAZAN(1925); BOOMERANG, THE(1925); MY LADY OF WHIMS(1925); PARISIAN LOVE(1925); WITH THIS RING(1925); COLLEGIATE(1926); BROADWAY MADNESS(1927); CRUISE OF THE HELLION, THE(1927); WHIRLPOOL OF YOUTH, THE(1927); WILD GEESE(1927); BARE KNEES(1928); COMRADES(1928); DEVIL'S CAGE, THE(1928); TOP SERGEANT MULLIGAN(1928)

Frank Keith
BIG CARNIVAL, THE(1951)

Hardy Keith
ZAPPED!(1982)

Herbert Keith
Silents
BROKEN MELODY, THE(1929, Brit.), w

Ian Keith
LIGHT FINGERS(1929); PRISONERS(1929); ABRAHAM LINCOLN(1930); BOUDOIR DIPLOMAT(1930); GREAT DIVIDE, THE(1930); PRINCE OF DIAMONDS(1930); DECEIVER, THE(1931); PHANTOM OF PARIS, THE(1931); SIN SHIP(1931); SUSAN LENOX–HER FALL AND RISE(1931); TAILOR MADE MAN, A(1931); SIGN OF THE CROSS, THE(1932); QUEEN CHRISTINA(1933); CLEOPATRA(1934); CRUSADES, THE(1935); DANGEROUS CORNER(1935); THREE MUSKETEERS, THE(1935); DON'T GAMBLE WITH LOVE(1936); MARY OF SCOTLAND(1936); PREVIEW MURDER MYSTERY(1936); WHITE LEGION, THE(1936); BUCCANEER, THE(1938); COMET OVER BROADWAY(1938); ALL THIS AND HEAVEN TOO(1940); SEA HAWK, THE(1940); REMEMBER PEARL HARBOR(1942); SUNDOWN KID, THE(1942); BORDERTOWN GUNFIGHTERS(1943); CORREGIDOR(1943); FIVE GRAVES TO CAIRO(1943); HERE COMES KELLY(1943); I ESCAPED FROM THE GESTAPO(1943); MAN FROM THUNDER RIVER, THE(1943); PAYOFF, THE(1943); THAT NAZTY NUISANCE(1943); WILD HORSE STAMPEDE(1943); ARIZONA WHIRLWIND(1944); BOWERY CHAMPS(1944); CASANOVA IN BURLESQUE(1944); CHINESE CAT, THE(1944); COWBOY FROM LONESOME RIVER(1944); CAPTAIN KIDD(1945); FOG ISLAND(1945); IDENTITY UNKNOWN(1945); NORTHWEST TRAIL(1945); PHANTOM OF THE PLAINS(1945); SHE GETS HER MAN(1945); SONG OF OLD WYOMING(1945); SPANISH MAIN, THE(1945); UNDER WESTERN SKIES(1945); DICK TRACY VS. CUEBALL(1946); MR. HEX(1946); STRANGE WOMAN, THE(1946); VALLEY OF THE ZOMBIES(1946); BORDER FEUD(1947); DICK TRACY'S DILEMMA(1947); FOREVER AMBER(1947); NIGHTMARE ALLEY(1947); BLACK SHIELD OF FALWORTH, THE(1954); DUEL ON THE MISSISSIPPI(1955); IT CAME FROM BENEATH THE SEA(1955); NEW YORK CONFIDENTIAL(1955); PRINCE OF PLAYERS(1955); TEN COMMANDMENTS, THE(1956)
Misc. Talkies
DIVINE LADY, THE(1929)
Silents
LOVE'S WILDERNESS(1924); MY SON(1925); TOWER OF LIES, THE(1925); CONVOY(1927); WHAT EVERY GIRL SHOULD KNOW(1927)
Misc. Silents
CHRISTINE OF THE HUNGRY HEART(1924); HER LOVE STORY(1924); MANHANDLED(1924); ENTICEMENT(1925); TALKER, THE(1925); GREATER GLORY,

THE(1926); LILY, THE(1926); PRINCE OF TEMPTERS, THE(1926); TRUTHFUL SEX, THE(1926); MAN'S PAST, A(1927); LOOK OUT GIRL, THE(1928); STREET OF ILLUSION, THE(1928)

Isabelle Keith
BARNUM WAS RIGHT(1929)
Silents
FOUR HORSEMEN OF THE APOCALYPSE, THE(1921); DESERT FLOWER, THE(1925); KING OF KINGS, THE(1927); ANNE AGAINST THE WORLD(1929)

Jane Keith
SEA WOLF, THE(1930); SECRET CALL, THE(1931)

Jennifer Keith
WINTER KILLS(1979)

June Keith
Misc. Silents
BUNCH OF KEYS, A(1915); MAN TRAIL, THE(1915)

Max Keith
JUST FOR YOU(1952)

Michael Keith
KING KONG VERSUS GODZILLA(1963, Jap.)

Nils Keith
Misc. Silents
BURNING GOLD(1927)

Patti Jean Keith
SPEEDWAY(1968)

Paul Keith
LAST AMERICAN VIRGIN, THE(1982)

Penelope Keith
TAKE A GIRL LIKE YOU(1970, Brit,); THINK DIRTY(1970, Brit.); HOUND OF THE BASKERVILLES, THE(1980, Brit.); PRIEST OF LOVE(1981, Brit.)

Richard Keith
ZERO HOUR!(1957); CRASH LANDING(1958); FUN WITH DICK AND JANE(1977)

Robert Keith
JUST IMAGINE(1930); BAD COMPANY(1931); WHITE SHOULDERS(1931); DESTRY RIDES AGAIN(1932), w; SCANDAL FOR SALE(1932), w; UNEXPECTED FATHER(1932), w; SPIRIT OF CULVER, THE(1939); BOOMERANG(1947); MY FOOLISH HEART(1949); EDGE OF DOOM(1950); REFORMER AND THE REDHEAD, THE(1950); WOMAN ON THE RUN(1950); BRANDED(1951); FOURTEEN HOURS(1951); HERE COMES THE GROOM(1951); I WANT YOU(1951); JUST ACROSS THE STREET(1952); SOMEBODY LOVES ME(1952); BATTLE CIRCUS(1953); DEVIL'S CANYON(1953); SMALL TOWN GIRL(1953); WILD ONE, THE(1953); DRUM BEAT(1954); GUYS AND DOLLS(1955); LOVE ME OR LEAVE ME(1955); UNDERWATER!(1955); YOUNG AT HEART(1955); BETWEEN HEAVEN AND HELL(1956); RANSOM(1956); WRITTEN ON THE WIND(1956); MEN IN WAR(1957); MY MAN GODFREY(1957); LINEUP, THE(1958); TEMPEST(1958, Ital./Yugo./Fr.); THEY CAME TO CORDURA(1959); CIMARRON(1960); POSSE FROM HELL(1961); DUEL OF CHAMPIONS(1964 Ital./Span.)
Silents
OTHER KIND OF LOVE, THE(1924)

Roberta Keith
PUFNSTUF(1970)

Ron Keith
GURU, THE MAD MONK(1971)

Ronald Keith
HIGH SOCIETY(1955)

Rosalind Keith
ANNAPOLIS FAREWELL(1935); GLASS KEY, THE(1935); IT'S A GREAT LIFE(1936); KING OF THE ROYAL MOUNTED(1936); POPPY(1936); THEODORA GOES WILD(1936); CRIMINALS OF THE AIR(1937); DANGEROUS ADVENTURE, A(1937); FIGHT TO THE FINISH, A(1937); FIND THE WITNESS(1937); MOTOR MADNESS(1937); PAROLE RACKET(1937); UNDER SUSPICION(1937); WESTBOUND MAIL(1937); ARSON GANG BUSTERS(1938); CLIPPED WINGS(1938); BAD BOY(1939); MANHATTAN SHAKEDOWN(1939); TROUBLE IN SUNDOWN(1939); LADIES OF WASHINGTON(1944)
Misc. Talkies
ARSON RACKET SQUAD(1938)

Sheila Keith
FRIGHTMARE(1974, Brit.); HOUSE OF WHIPCORD(1974, Brit.); CONFESSIONAL, THE(1977, Brit.); COMEBACK, THE(1982, Brit.); HOUSE OF LONG SHADOWS, THE(1983, Brit.); RETURN OF THE SOLDIER, THE(1983, Brit.)

Sherwood Keith
SILENT CALL, THE(1961); CASE OF PATTY SMITH, THE(1962); TERRIFIED!(1963); BEST MAN, THE(1964)

Shiela Keith
GET CHARLIE TULLY(1976, Brit.)

Sidney Keith
IT'S THAT MAN AGAIN(1943, Brit.)

Sydney Keith
ORDERS IS ORDERS(1934, Brit.); WISE GUYS(1937, Brit.); BATTLE OF THE SEXES, THE(1960, Brit.)

"Tex" Keith
Misc. Silents
THREE BUCKAROOS, THE(1922)

William H. Keith
Silents
DOWN TO EARTH(1917)

Colin Keith-Johnson
OPEN ALL NIGHT(1934, Brit.); PRICE OF FOLLY, THE(1937, Brit.)
Silents
SOMEHOW GOOD(1927, Brit.)

Colin Keith-Johnston
LUCKY IN LOVE(1929); BERKELEY SQUARE(1933); EXILE, THE(1947); ENCHANTMENT(1948); JOAN OF ARC(1948); KISS THE BLOOD OFF MY HANDS(1948); FANCY PANTS(1950); LEFT-HANDED GUN, THE(1958)

Jane Keithley
WHOOPEE!(1930)

Jane Keithly
FLORODORA GIRL, THE(1930)

G. Kekisheva
SLEEPING BEAUTY, THE(1966, USSR)

Anne Kelagh
ROAD TO FORTUNE, THE(1930, Brit.)

A. Kelber
RASPUTIN(1939, Fr.), ph

Catherine Kelber
OUTSIDER, THE(1980), ed

Cathy Kelber
LOVE IS A BALL(1963), ed

M. Kelber
HEART OF PARIS(1939, Fr.), ph

Michael Kelber
BAL TABARIN(1952), ph; AMBASSADOR'S DAUGHTER, THE(1956), ph; STORY OF A THREE DAY PASS, THE(1968, Fr.), ph

Michel Kelber
UN CARNET DE BAL(1938, Fr.), ph; DEVIL IN THE FLESH, THE(1949, Fr.), ph; LES PARENTS TERRIBLES(1950, Fr.), ph; NAKED WOMAN, THE(1950, Fr.), ph; BEAUTY AND THE DEVIL(1952, Fr./Ital.), ph; LOVERS OF TOLEDO, THE(1954, Fr./Span./Ital.), ph; RED AND THE BLACK, THE(1954, Fr./Ital.), ph; FRENCH CANCAN(1956, Fr.), ph; MAIN STREET(1956, Span.), ph; HUNCHBACK OF NOTRE DAME, THE(1957, Fr.), ph; JOHN PAUL JONES(1959), ph; LULU(1962, Aus.), ph; VIEW FROM THE BRIDGE, A(1962, Fr./Ital.), ph; EMPIRE OF NIGHT, THE(1963, Fr.), ph; IN THE FRENCH STYLE(1963, U.S./Fr.), ph; MAGNIFICENT SINNER(1963, Fr.), ph; HOW NOT TO ROB A DEPARTMENT STORE(1965, Fr./Ital.), ph; MATA HARI(1965, Fr./Ital.), ph; JOHNNY BANCO(1969, Fr./Ital./Ger.), ph

A. Kelberer
OTHELLO(1960, U.S.S.R.)

Voinquel Michael Kelbes
RUY BLAS(1948, Fr.), ph

Herbert Kelcey
Misc. Silents
AFTER THE BALL(1914); SPHINX, THE(1916)

Kele
TRAIN ROBBERY CONFIDENTIAL(1965, Braz.)

Peter Keleghan
SCREWBALLS(1983)

Virginia Keley
THREE CAME HOME(1950)

Pamela Kelier
LAST PICTURE SHOW, THE(1971)

W.P. Kelino
Misc. Silents
FORDINGTON TWINS, THE(1920, Brit.), d

Jack Kelk
SOMEBODY UP THERE LIKES ME(1956)

Jackie Kelk
BORN TO BE BAD(1934); PAJAMA GAME, THE(1957)

Ed Sherman Kell
Silents
GUN RUNNER, THE(1928), ed

J. S. Kell
Silents
COLLEGE(1927), ed

Jayne Kell
1984
EXTERMINATOR 2(1984)

Michael Kell
VERY NATURAL THING, A(1974); ZELIG(1983)

Sherman Kell
Silents
GENERAL, THE(1927), ed; STEAMBOAT BILL, JR.(1928), ed

Wayne Kell
LITTLE SEX, A(1982)

Clarence Buddington Kelland
SPEAK EASILY(1932), w; CAT'S PAW, THE(1934), w; THIRTY-DAY PRINCESS(1934), w; FLORIDA SPECIAL(1936), w; MR. DEEDS GOES TO TOWN(1936), w; STRIKE ME PINK(1936), w; MR. DODD TAKES THE AIR(1937), w; STAND-IN(1937), w; MR. BOGGS STEPS OUT(1938), w; ARIZONA(1940), w; FOR BEAUTY'S SAKE(1941), w; SCATTERGOOD BAINES(1941), w; SCATTERGOOD MEETS BROADWAY(1941), w; SCATTERGOOD PULLS THE STRINGS(1941), w; CINDERELLA SWINGS IT(1942), w; HIGHWAYS BY NIGHT(1942), w; SCATTERGOOD RIDES HIGH(1942), w; SCATTERGOOD SURVIVES A MURDER(1942), w; VALLEY OF THE SUN(1942), w; SUGARFOOT(1951), w
Silents
EFFICIENCY EDGAR'S COURTSHIP(1917), w; CONFLICT, THE(1921), w; ACROSS THE DEAD-LINE(1922), w; STEADFAST HEART, THE(1923), w; HEARTS AND FISTS(1926), w

John Kelland
FAREWELL PERFORMANCE(1963, Brit.); ATTACK ON THE IRON COAST(1968, U.S./Brit.); SUMARINE X-1(1969, Brit.); BEAST IN THE CELLAR, THE(1971, Brit.); NOTHING BUT THE NIGHT(1975, Brit.)

Edgar Kellar
Silents
JESSE JAMES AS THE OUTLAW(1921), set d; JESSE JAMES UNDER THE BLACK FLAG(1921), set d

Leon Kellar
Silents
WEST POINT(1928)

Bob Kellard
MY SISTER EILEEN(1942)

Ralph Kellard
WOMEN EVERYWHERE(1930)
Silents
COST, THE(1920); MASTER MIND, THE(1920)
Misc. Silents
HER MOTHER'S SECRET(1915); PRECIOUS PACKET, THE(1916); HILLCREST MYSTERY, THE(1918); SCREAM IN THE NIGHT, A(1919); RESTLESS SEX, THE(1920); VEILED MARRIAGE, THE(1920); LOVE, HATE AND A WOMAN(1921); VIRTUOUS LIARS(1924)

Robert Kellard

CORPSE CAME C.O.D., THE(; SECOND HONEYMOON(1937); ALWAYS IN TROUBLE(1938); BATTLE OF BROADWAY(1938); ISLAND IN THE SKY(1938); JOSETTE(1938); MY LUCKY STAR(1938); TIME OUT FOR MURDER(1938); WALKING DOWN BROADWAY(1938); WHILE NEW YORK SLEEPS(1938); BOY FRIEND(1939); HERE I AM A STRANGER(1939); STOP, LOOK, AND LOVE(1939); WIFE, HUSBAND AND FRIEND(1939); DOWN IN SAN DIEGO(1941); GENTLEMAN FROM DIXIE(1941); PRAIRIE PIONEERS(1941); SHADOW OF THE THIN MAN(1941); MAN FROM HEADQUARTERS(1942); DRUMS OF FU MANCHU(1943); GILDA(1946); ARGYLE SECRETS, THE(1948); CANON CITY(1948); RED, HOT AND BLUE(1949); TOO LATE FOR TEARS(1949)

Thomas Kellard

LIFE BEGINS IN COLLEGE(1937)

Alec Kellaway

BROKEN MELODY(1938, Aus.); DAD AND DAVE COME TO TOWN(1938, Aus.); LOVERS AND LUGGERS(1938, Aus.); GONE TO THE DOGS(1939, Aus.); ANTS IN HIS PANTS(1940, Aus.); VENGEANCE OF THE DEEP(1940, Aus.); SMITHY(1946, Aus.); PACIFIC ADVENTURE(1947, Aus.); KANGAROO KID, THE(1950, Aus./U.S.); SQUEEZE A FLOWER(1970, Aus.)

Misc. Talkies

LET GEORGE DO IT(1938, Aus.)

Cecil Kellaway

IT ISN'T DONE(1937, Aus.), a, w; BLOND CHEAT(1938); DOUBLE DANGER(1938); EVERYBODY'S DOING IT(1938); MAID'S NIGHT OUT(1938); NIGHT SPOT(1938); TARNISHED ANGEL(1938); THIS MARRIAGE BUSINESS(1938); GUNGA DIN(1939); INTERMEZZO: A LOVE STORY(1939); MEXICAN SPITFIRE(1939); MR. CHEDWORTH STEPS OUT(1939, Aus.); SUN NEVER SETS, THE(1939); WE ARE NOT ALONE(1939); WUTHERING HEIGHTS(1939); ADVENTURE IN DIAMONDS(1940); BROTHER ORCHID(1940); DIAMOND FRONTIER(1940); HOUSE OF THE SEVEN GABLES, THE(1940); INVISIBLE MAN RETURNS, THE(1940); LADY WITH RED HAIR(1940); LETTER, THE(1940); MEXICAN SPITFIRE OUT WEST(1940); MUMMY'S HAND, THE(1940); PHANTOM RAIDERS(1940); SOUTH OF SUEZ(1940); APPOINTMENT FOR LOVE(1941); BAHAMA PASSAGE(1941); BIRTH OF THE BLUES(1941); BURMA CONVOY(1941); NEW YORK TOWN(1941); NIGHT OF JANUARY 16TH(1941); SMALL TOWN DEB(1941); VERY YOUNG LADY, A(1941); WEST POINT WIDOW(1941); ARE HUSBANDS NECESSARY?(1942); I MARRIED A WITCH(1942); LADY HAS PLANS, THE(1942); MY HEART BELONGS TO DADDY(1942); NIGHT IN NEW ORLEANS, A(1942); STAR SPANGLED RHYTHM(1942); TAKE A LETTER, DARLING(1942); CRYSTAL BALL, THE(1943); FOREVER AND A DAY(1943); GOOD FELLOWS, THE(1943); IT AIN'T HAY(1943); AND NOW TOMORROW(1944); FRENCHMAN'S CREEK(1944); MRS. PARKINGTON(1944); PRACTICALLY YOURS(1944); KITTY(1945); LOVE LETTERS(1945); COCKEYED MIRACLE, THE(1946); EASY TO WED(1946); MONSIEUR BEAUCAIRE(1946); POSTMAN ALWAYS RINGS TWICE, THE(1946); ALWAYS TOGETHER(1947); UNCONQUERED(1947); VARIETY GIRL(1947); DECISION OF CHRISTOPHER BLAKE, THE(1948); JOAN OF ARC(1948); LUCK OF THE IRISH(1948); DOWN TO THE SEA IN SHIPS(1949); PORTRAIT OF JENNIE(1949); HARVEY(1950); KIM(1950); REFORMER AND THE REDHEAD, THE(1950); FRANCIS GOES TO THE RACES(1951); HALF ANGEL(1951); HIGHWAYMAN, THE(1951); KATIE DID IT(1951); JUST ACROSS THE STREET(1952); MY WIFE'S BEST FRIEND(1952); BEAST FROM 20,000 FATHOMS, THE(1953); CRUISIN' DOWN THE RIVER(1953); PARIS MODEL(1953); THUNDER IN THE EAST(1953); YOUNG BESS(1953); FEMALE ON THE BEACH(1955); INTERRUPTED MELODY(1955); PRODIGAL, THE(1955); TOY TIGER(1956); JOHNNY TROUBLE(1957); PROUD REBEL, THE(1958); SHAGGY DOG, THE(1959); FRANCIS OF ASSISI(1961); PRIVATE LIVES OF ADAM AND EVE, THE(1961); TAMMY, TELL ME TRUE(1961); ZOTZ!(1962); CARDINAL, THE(1963); HUSH... HUSH, SWEET CHARLOTTE(1964); QUICK, LET'S GET MARRIED(1965); SPINOUT(1966); ADVENTURES OF BULLWHIP GRIFFIN, THE(1967); FITZWILLY(1967); GUESS WHO'S COMING TO DINNER(1967); GETTING STRAIGHT(1970)

Roger Kellaway

PAPER LION(1968), m; WHO FEARS THE DEVIL(1972), m; LEGACY(1976), m; STAR IS BORN, A(1976), m; MOUSE AND HIS CHILD, THE(1977), m; MAFU CAGE, THE(1978), m; DARK, THE(1979), m; JAWS OF SATAN(1980), m; SILENT SCREAM(1980), m; EVILSPEAK(1982), m; SATAN'S MISTRESS(1982), m

Sylvia Kellaway

IT ISN'T DONE(1937, Aus.); ORPHAN OF THE WILDERNESS(1937, Aus.)

The Kellaways

HE FOUND A STAR(1941, Brit.)

Sylvia Kellawy

WILD INNOCENCE(1937, Aus.)

Ed Kelleher

INVASION OF THE BLOOD FARMERS(1972), w; SHRIEK OF THE MUTILATED(1974), w

John V. Kelleher

FINNEGANS WAKE(1965)

Randy Kelleher

TAKING TIGER MOUNTAIN(1983, U.S./Welsh), m

Jane Kellem

THING WITH TWO HEADS, THE(1972)

Jane Kellen

Misc. Talkies

IF YOU DON'T STOP IT, YOU'LL GO BLIND(1977)

Mike Kellen

PHYNX, THE(1970)

Pascale Kellen

MAMMA DRACULA(1980, Bel./Fr.), makeup

Edward Febo Kelleng

DANGER: DIABOLIK(1968, Ital./Fr.)

Keller

LETTERS FROM MY WINDMILL(1955, Fr.)

Alfred Keller

DAYS OF BUFFALO BILL(1946), ph; G.I. WAR BRIDES(1946), ph; LAST CROOKED MILE, THE(1946), ph; MYSTERIOUS MR. VALENTINE, THE(1946), ph; RIO GRANDE RAIDERS(1946), ph; HOMESTEADERS OF PARADISE VALLEY(1947), ph; OREGON TRAIL SCOUTS(1947), ph; OTHER LOVE, THE(1947), ph; SPOILERS OF THE NORTH(1947), ph; VIGILANTES OF BOOMTOWN(1947), ph; WESTERN HERITAGE(1948), ph

Alfred S. Keller

ALONG THE OREGON TRAIL(1947), ph; UNDER COLORADO SKIES(1947), ph; WEB OF DANGER, THE(1947), ph; WILD FRONTIER, THE(1947), ph

Allen Keller

HEAVEN'S GATE(1980); LOOKIN' TO GET OUT(1982)

Bill Keller

TWO-LANE BLACKTOP(1971)

Brooklyn Keller

Silents

FIRES OF CONSCIENCE(1916)

Misc. Silents

LEOPARD'S BRIDE, THE(1916); VENGEANCE IS MINE!(1916); PRICE OF HER SOUL, THE(1917)

Christa Keller

SINS OF ROSE BERND, THE(1959, Ger.)

Clara Keller

Misc. Talkies

SINFUL DWARF, THE(1973)

Daniel Keller

HORNET'S NEST(1970)

Derek Keller

NO BLADE OF GRASS(1970, Brit.)

Dorothy Keller

SINGLE ROOM FURNISHED(1968)

Edgar Keller

Misc. Silents

CLOUDED NAME, THE(1919)

Ernest Keller

THAT TENNESSEE BEAT(1966)

Frank Keller

BONNIE PARKER STORY, THE(1958), ed; GHOST OF DRAGSTRIP HOLLOW(1959), ed; JONATHAN LIVINGSTON SEAGULL(1973), ed; FOR PETE'S SAKE(1977), ed

Frank P Keller

COME BLOW YOUR HORN(1963), ed

Frank P. Keller

FIVE PENNIES, THE(1959), ed; POCKETFUL OF MIRACLES(1961), ed; SAFE AT HOME(1962), ed; PAPA'S DELICATE CONDITION(1963), ed; FOR THOSE WHO THINK YOUNG(1964), ed; CYBORG 2087(1966), ed; TARZAN AND THE VALLEY OF GOLD(1966 U.S./Switz.), ed; BEACH RED(1967), ed; BULLITT(1968), ed; JOHN AND MARY(1969), ed; MURPHY'S WAR(1971, Brit.), ed; HOT ROCK, THE(1972), ed; ROLLING THUNDER(1977), ed

Fred A. Keller

1984

VAMPING(1984)

Misc. Talkies

TUCK EVERLASTING(1981)

Frederick King Keller

EYES OF THE AMARYLLIS, THE(1982), d

1984

VAMPING(1984), d, w

Misc. Talkies

TUCK EVERLASTING(1981), d

Georges Keller

SIX IN PARIS(1968, Fr.), w

Gertrude Keller

Silents

IMMIGRANT, THE(1915); SECRET ORCHARD(1915)

Misc. Silents

CLUE, THE(1915)

Grace Keller

Silents

KID, THE(1921)

Greta Keller

REUNION IN FRANCE(1942)

Harold Keller

CHRISTIAN LICORICE STORE, THE(1971)

Harry Keller

INSIDE INFORMATION(1939), ed; MYSTERY OF THE WHITE ROOM(1939), ed; WITNESS VANISHES, THE(1939), ed; BLACK HILLS EXPRESS(1943), ed; CANYON CITY(1943), ed; DAYS OF OLD CHEYENNE(1943), ed; DEATH VALLEY MANHUNT(1943), ed; KING OF THE COWBOYS(1943), ed; MAN FROM THUNDER RIVER, THE(1943), ed; RAIDERS OF SUNSET PASS(1943), ed; CALIFORNIA JOE(1944), ed; CODE OF THE PRAIRIE(1944), ed; FIREBRANDS OF ARIZONA(1944), ed; LARAMIE TRAIL, THE(1944), ed; MOJAVE FIREBRAND(1944), ed; SHERIFF OF SUNDOWN(1944), ed; STAGECOACH TO MONTEREY(1944), ed; TUCSON RAIDERS(1944), ed; GRISSLY'S MILLIONS(1945), ed; SONG OF MEXICO(1945), ed; STEPPIN' IN SOCIETY(1945), ed; UTAH(1945), ed; GUY COULD CHANGE, A(1946), ed; MY PAL TRIGGER(1946), ed; PASSKEY TO DANGER(1946), ed; SPECTER OF THE ROSE(1946), ed; SUN VALLEY CYCLONE(1946), ed; THE CATMAN OF PARIS(1946), ed; ANGEL AND THE BADMAN(1947), ed; NORTHWEST OUTPOST(1947), ed; ROBIN OF TEXAS(1947), ed; RUSTLERS OF DEVIL'S CANYON(1947), ed; SADDLE PALS(1947), ed; TWILIGHT ON THE RIO GRANDE(1947), ed; HOMICIDE FOR THREE(1948), ed; MADONNA OF THE DESERT(1948), ed; MOONRISE(1948), ed; SON OF GOD'S COUNTRY(1948), ed; RED MENACE, THE(1949), ed; RED PONY, THE(1949), ed; ROSE OF THE YUKON(1949), ed; STREETS OF SAN FRANCISCO(1949), ed; TOO LATE FOR TEARS(1949), ed; ARIZONA COWBOY, THE(1950), ed; BLONDE BANDIT, THE(1950), d; BORDERLINE(1950), ed; COVERED WAGON RAID(1950), ed; HIT PARADE OF 1951(1950), ed; LONELY HEARTS BANDITS(1950), ed; SHOWDOWN, THE(1950), ed; TARNISHED(1950), d; BELLE LE GRAND(1951), ed; DAKOTA KID, THE(1951), ed; DESERT OF LOST MEN(1951), p&d; FORT DODGE STAMPEDE(1951), p&d; BLACK HILLS AMBUSH(1952), p&d; CAPTIVE OF BILLY THE KID(1952), p; LEADVILLE GUNSLINGER(1952), p&d; ROSE OF CIMARRON(1952), d; THUNDERING CARAVANS(1952), d; BANDITS OF THE WEST(1953), d; EL PASO STAMPEDE(1953), d; MARSHAL OF CEDAR ROCK(1953), d; RED RIVER SHORE(1953), d; SAVAGE FRONTIER(1953), d; PHANTOM STALLION, THE(1954), d; UNGUARDED MOMENT, THE(1956), d; MAN AFRAID(1957), d; QUANTEZ(1957), d; DAY OF THE BAD MAN(1958), d; FEMALE ANIMAL, THE(1958), d; SEVEN DOWN TO TERROR(1958), d; TOUCH OF EVIL(1958), d; VOICE IN THE MIRROR(1958), d; SEVEN WAYS FROM SUNDOWN(1960), d; TAMMY, TELL ME TRUE(1961), d; SIX

BLACK HORSES(1962), d; TAMMY AND THE DOCTOR(1963), d; BRASS BOTTLE, THE(1964), d; KITTEN WITH A WHIP(1964), p; SEND ME NO FLOWERS(1964), p; MIRAGE(1965), p; THAT FUNNY FEELING(1965), p; TEXAS ACROSS THE RIVER(1966), p; IN ENEMY COUNTRY(1968), p&d; SKIN GAME(1971), p; STIR CRAZY(1980), ed; STRIPES(1981), ed; HANKY-PANKY(1982), ed; MAN WHO WASN'T THERE, THE(1983), ed
Misc. Talkies
COMMANDO CODY(1953), d
Helen Keller
MIRACLE WORKER, THE(1962), w
Hiram Keller
FELLINI SATYRICON(1969, Fr./Ital.); ROME WANTS ANOTHER CAESAR(1974, Ital.); LIFESPAN(1975, U.S./Brit./Neth.); COUNTRYMAN(1982, Jamaica)
J.H. Keller
Misc. Silents
STRIPPED FOR A MILLION(1919)
Jason Keller
HONKY TONK FREEWAY(1981)
Jerry Keller
YOU LIGHT UP MY LIFE(1977); IF EVER I SEE YOU AGAIN(1978)
Joan Keller
SPIDER BABY(1968)
Kathleen Keller
KRAMER VS. KRAMER(1979)
Lew Keller
1001 ARABIAN NIGHTS(1959), w
Lon Keller
FOUR POSTER, THE(1952), anim
Louise Keller
Silents
PLUNDERER, THE(1915), w
Marthe Keller
FUNERAL IN BERLIN(1966, Brit.); DEVIL BY THE TAIL, THE(1969, Fr./Ital.); GIVE HER THE MOON(1970, Fr./Ital.); AND NOW MY LOVE(1975, Fr.); DOWN THE ANCIENT STAIRCASE(1975, Ital.); MARATHON MAN(1976); BLACK SUNDAY(1977); BOBBY DEERFIELD(1977); FEDORA(1978, Ger./Fr.); FORMULA, THE(1980); AMATEUR, THE(1982); WAGNER(1983, Brit./Hung./Aust.)
Martin Keller
DIVIDED HEART, THE(1955, Brit.)
Max Keller
DEADLY BLESSING(1981), p
Mel Keller
REBELS AGAINST THE LIGHT(1964), m; SANDS OF BEERSHEBA(1966, U.S./Israel), m
Michael Keller
LIVE A LITTLE, LOVE A LITTLE(1968); STAY AWAY, JOE(1968)
Micheline Keller
DEADLY BLESSING(1981), p
Nell Clark Keller
Silents
OUT OF A CLEAR SKY(1918)
Nell Clarke Keller
Misc. Silents
TEN NIGHTS IN A BAR ROOM(1921)
Nell Keller
ONCE UPON A TIME(1944)
Ora Keller
SILENT WITNESS, THE(1962)
Ravenell Keller III
BEING THERE(1979)
Sam Keller
JESSE JAMES' WOMEN(1954)
Sarah Keller
TERROR(1979, Brit.)
Misc. Talkies
SEVEN DOORS OF DEATH(1983)
Shane Keller
HONKY TONK FREEWAY(1981)
Sheldon Keller
BUONA SERA, MRS. CAMPBELL(1968, Ital.), w; CLEOPATRA JONES(1973), w; MOVIE MOVIE(1978), w
Susan Keller
CLOWN MURDERS, THE(1976, Can.)
Teddy Keller
SILENT WITNESS, THE(1962)
W.E. Keller
FALCON'S ADVENTURE, THE(1946), art d
Walter E. Keller
SCOUNDREL, THE(1935), art d; FALCON'S BROTHER, THE(1942), art d; GREAT GILDERSLEEVE, THE(1942), art d; PIRATES OF THE PRAIRIE(1942), art d; FALCON IN DANGER, THE(1943), art d; FALCON STRIKES BACK, THE(1943), art d; FIGHTING FRONTIER(1943), art d; GHOST SHIP, THE(1943), art d; LEOPARD MAN, THE(1943), art d; MEXICAN SPITFIRE'S BLESSED EVENT(1943), art d; PETTICOAT LARCENY(1943), art d; SEVENTH VICTIM, THE(1943), art d; THIS LAND IS MINE(1943), art d; MADEMOISELLE FIFI(1944), art d; MARINE RAIDERS(1944), art d; THOSE ENDEARING YOUNG CHARMS(1945), art d; ZOMBIES ON BROADWAY(1945), art d; STEP BY STEP(1946), art d; TRUTH ABOUT MURDER, THE(1946), art d; DESPERATE(1947), art d; RIFFRAFF(1947), art d; WOMAN ON THE BEACH, THE(1947), art d; FIGHTING FATHER DUNNE(1948), art d; RACE STREET(1948), art d; RACHEL AND THE STRANGER(1948), art d; FOLLOW ME QUIETLY(1949), art d; WINDOW, THE(1949), art d; HUNT THE MAN DOWN(1950), art d; NEVER A DULL MOMENT(1950), art d; RIDER FROM TUCSON(1950), art d; WOMAN ON PIER 13, THE(1950), art d; ON THE LOOSE(1951), art d; ROADBLOCK(1951), art d; PACE THAT THRILLS, THE(1952), art d; HITCH-HIKER, THE(1953), art d; SON OF SINBAD(1955), art d; I MARRIED A WOMAN(1958), art d
Silents
OLD HOME WEEK(1925), art d; NEW KLONDIKE, THE(1926), art d

Walter F. Keller
DYNAMITE PASS(1950), art d
Walter Keller
POWDER TOWN(1942), art d; I WALKED WITH A ZOMBIE(1943), art d; GIRL RUSH(1944), art d; BODY SNATCHER, THE(1945), art d; FIRST YANK INTO TOKYO(1945), art d; ISLE OF THE DEAD(1945), art d; RADIO STARS ON PARADE(1945), art d; BEDLAM(1946), art d; DICK TRACY MEETS GRUESOME(1947), art d; GIRL IN EVERY PORT, A(1952), art d; TARZAN'S SAVAGE FURY(1952), art d; DANGEROUS MISSION(1954), art d; PRIVATE HELL 36(1954), art d; I COVER THE UNDERWORLD(1955), art d; MAN ALONE, A(1955), art d; NO MAN'S WOMAN(1955), art d; RAGE AT DAWN(1955), art d; ROAD TO DENVER, THE(1955), art d; VANISHING AMERICAN, THE(1955), art d; MAN IS ARMED, THE(1956), art d; MAVERICK QUEEN, THE(1956), art d; TERROR AT MIDNIGHT(1956), art d; THUNDER OVER ARIZONA(1956), art d; WHEN GANGLAND STRIKES(1956), art d; PERSUADER, THE(1957), art d; GIRL IN THE WOODS(1958), art d
William Keller
INVASION OF THE BEE GIRLS(1973)
John E. Kellerd
Misc. Silents
FIGHT, THE(1915)
Annette Kellerman
Misc. Silents
QUEEN OF THE SEA(1918); WHAT WOMEN LOVE(1920); VENUS OF THE SOUTH SEAS(1924)
Barbara Kellerman
SATAN'S SLAVE(1976, Brit.); QUATERMASS CONCLUSION(1980, Brit.); MONSTER CLUB, THE(1981, Brit.)
Maurice Kellerman
VIKING, THE(1931), ph
Sally Kellerman
REFORM SCHOOL GIRL(1957); HANDS OF A STRANGER(1962); THIRD DAY, THE(1965); THE BOSTON STRANGLER, THE(1968); APRIL FOOLS, THE(1969); BREWSTER McCLOUD(1970); M(1970); LAST OF THE RED HOT LOVERS(1972); LOST HORIZON(1973); REFLECTION OF FEAR, A(1973); SLITHER(1973); RAFFERTY AND THE GOLD DUST TWINS(1975); BIG BUS, THE(1976); WELCOME TO L.A.(1976); MOUSE AND HIS CHILD, THE(1977); LITTLE ROMANCE, A(1979, U.S./Fr.); FOXES(1980); LOVING COUPLES(1980); SERIAL(1980); HEAD ON(1981, Can.)
Susan Kellerman
OH, HEAVENLY DOG!(1980)
Annette Kellermann
Silents
NEPTUNE'S DAUGHTER(1914)
Misc. Silents
DAUGHTER OF THE GODS, A(1916)
Barbara Kellermann
SEA WOLVES, THE(1981, Brit.)
H. Kellermann
TRANSATLANTIC TUNNEL(1935, Brit.), w
Susan Kellermann
WHERE THE BUFFALO ROAM(1980)
Kiki Kellet
JOAN OF ARC(1948)
Pete Kellet
PRISONER OF ZENDA, THE(1979)
Bob Kellett
SAN FERRY ANN(1965, Brit.), p, w; GIRL STROKE BOY(1971, Brit.), d; UP POMPEII(1971, Brit.), d; UP THE CHASTITY BELT(1971, Brit.), d; OUR MISS FRED(1972, Brit.), d; UP THE FRONT(1972, Brit.), d; DON'T JUST LIE THERE, SAY SOMETHING!(1973, Brit.), d; SPANISH FLY(1975, Brit.), d
Misc. Talkies
ALF GARNETT SAGA, THE(1972), d; ARE YOU BEING SERVED?(1977), d
Pete Kellett
ENFORCER, THE(1951); JALOPY(1953); BETRAYED WOMEN(1955); BIG TIP OFF, THE(1955); HOUSTON STORY, THE(1956); REPRISAL(1956)
Robert Kellett
JUST LIKE A WOMAN(1967, Brit.), p
Misc. Talkies
TIGHTROPE TO TERROR(1977, Brit.), d
Al Kelley
NAKED CITY, THE(1948)
Silents
DESERTED AT THE ALTAR(1922), d
Albert Kelley
WOMAN RACKET, THE(1930), d; DOUBLE CROSS(1941), d; SUBMARINE BASE(1943), d; SLIPPY MCGEE(1948), d; STREET CORNER(1948), d, w
Silents
HOME STUFF(1921), d
Misc. Silents
DANCING DAYS(1926), d; HIS NEW YORK WIFE(1926), d; SHAMEFUL BEHAVIOR?(1926), d
Alice Kelley
DATE WITH JUDY, A(1948); JUNE BRIDE(1948); BUCKAROO SHERIFF OF TEXAS(1951); AGAINST ALL FLAGS(1952); FRANCIS GOES TO WEST POINT(1952); SON OF ALI BABA(1952); GOLDEN BLADE, THE(1953); MA AND PA KETTLE ON VACATION(1953); TAKE ME TO TOWN(1953); MA AND PA KETTLE AT HOME(1954)
Barbara Kelley
FLYING FONTAINES, THE(1959); X-15(1961)
Barry Kelley
BOOMERANG(1947); FORCE OF EVIL(1948); FIGHTING MAN OF THE PLAINS(1949); JOHNNY STOOL PIGEON(1949); KNOCK ON ANY DOOR(1949); MA AND PA KETTLE(1949); MR. BELVEDERE GOES TO COLLEGE(1949); RED, HOT AND BLUE(1949); TOO LATE FOR TEARS(1949); UNDERCOVER MAN, THE(1949); ASPHALT JUNGLE, THE(1950); BLACK HAND, THE(1950); CAPTURE, THE(1950); GREAT MISSOURI RAID, THE(1950); KILLER THAT STALKED NEW YORK, THE(1950); LOVE THAT BRUTE(1950); RIGHT CROSS(1950); SINGING GUNS(1950); SOUTHSIDE 1-1000(1950); WABASH AVENUE(1950); 711 OCEAN DRIVE(1950); FRANCIS GOES TO THE RACES(1951); WELL, THE(1951); BACK AT THE FRONT(1952); CARRIE(1952); WOMAN OF THE NORTH COUNTRY(1952); CHAMP FOR A DAY(1953); LAW AND ORDER(1953); REMAINS TO BE SEEN(1953); SOUTH

SEA WOMAN(1953); VICE SQUAD(1953); LONG WAIT, THE(1954); SHANGHAI STORY, THE(1954); NEW YORK CONFIDENTIAL(1955); TRIAL(1955); WOMEN'S PRISON(1955); ACCUSED OF MURDER(1956); JOKER IS WILD, THE(1957); MONKEY ON MY BACK(1957); TALL STRANGER, THE(1957); WINGS OF EAGLES, THE(1957); BUCCANEER, THE(1958); BUCHANAN RIDES ALONE(1958); ICE PALACE(1960); CLOWN AND THE KID, THE(1961); POLICE DOG STORY, THE(1961); SECRET OF DEEP HARBOR(1961); JACK THE GIANT KILLER(1962); MANCHURIAN CANDIDATE, THE(1962); RIO CONCHOS(1964); ROBIN AND THE SEVEN HOODS(1964); LOVE BUG, THE(1968)

Bob Kelley
TRIPLE THREAT(1948); CRAZYLEGS, ALL AMERICAN(1953); FUZZY PINK NIGHTGOWN, THE(1957)

Buddy Kelley
TWO-GUN TROUBADOR(1939)

Burt Kelley
BLONDIE'S BIG MOMENT(1947), p

De Forest Kelley
FEAR IN THE NIGHT(1947); TAXI(1953); HOUSE OF BAMBOO(1955); VIEW FROM POMPEY'S HEAD, THE(1955); WARLOCK(1959); BLACK SPURS(1965); WACO(1966)

De Forrest Kelley
VARIETY GIRL(1947); ILLEGAL(1955)

DeForest Kelley
CANON CITY(1948); DUKE OF CHICAGO(1949); MALAYA(1950); RAINTREE COUNTY(1957); LAW AND JAKE WADE, THE(1958); GUNFIGHT AT COMANCHE CREEK(1964); WHERE LOVE HAS GONE(1964); MARRIAGE ON THE ROCKS(1965); TOWN TAMER(1965); APACHE UPRISING(1966); NIGHT OF THE LEPUS(1972); STAR TREK: THE MOTION PICTURE(1979); STAR TREK II: THE WRATH OF KHAN(1982)
1984
STAR TREK III: THE SEARCH FOR SPOCK(1984)

DeForrest Kelley
MAN IN THE GREY FLANNEL SUIT, THE(1956); TENSION AT TABLE ROCK(1956); GUNFIGHT AT THE O.K. CORRAL(1957)

Eva P. Kelley
RED RUNS THE RIVER(1963)

George Kelley
CAROLINA BLUES(1944), ph; OUTLAWS OF THE ROCKIES(1945), ph

George F. Kelley
COWBOY BLUES(1946), ph; LAST DAYS OF BOOT HILL(1947), ph; LONE HAND TEXAN, THE(1947), ph; BUCKAROO FROM POWDER RIVER(1948), ph; PHANTOM VALLEY(1948), ph; SIX-GUN LAW(1948), ph

Jack Kelley
PEGGY(1950)

John B. Kelley
STARHOPS(1978), p

John Kelley
MIRACLE WOMAN, THE(1931); TIMOTHY'S QUEST(1936); EXPOSED(1938); YOU CAN'T BEAT THE IRISH(1952, Brit.)

J. Winthrop Kelley
Misc. Silents
GIRL OF THE SEA(1920), d

John T. Kelley
RAGE TO LIVE, A(1965), w; REDEEMER, THE(1965, Span.), w; ZIGZAG(1970), w

Kitty Kelley
LEMON DROP KID, THE(1934)

Lew Kelley
STATE TROOPER(1933); DIAMOND JIM(1935); NITWITS, THE(1935)

Martin Kelley
SAM'S SONG(1971)

Martin J. Kelley
Misc. Talkies
SOUTH OF HELL MOUNTAIN(1971)

Mary Kelley
IT'S A DATE(1940); LOVE THY NEIGHBOR(1940)

P.J. Kelley
SPOOKS RUN WILD(1941)

Renee Kelley
Silents
ALL FOR A GIRL(1915)

Richard Kelley
TOP OF THE HEAP(1972), ph

Richard A. Kelley
BISCUIT EATER, THE(1972), ph

Robert Kelley
Misc. Silents
HER SECRET(1917)

Robert P. Kelley
TENDER MERCIES(1982)

Russ Kelley
EARTH VS. THE FLYING SAUCERS(1956), spec eff

Sharon Ann Kelley
ROSE BOWL STORY, THE(1952)

Virginia Kelley
CARNIVAL(1946, Brit.); COME TO THE STABLE(1949)

W.A. Kelley
WINSLOW BOY, THE(1950)

W. Wallace Kelley
STORY OF DR. WASSELL, THE(1944), spec eff; UNCONQUERED(1947), spec eff; ERRAND BOY, THE(1961), ph; LADIES MAN, THE(1961), ph; IT'S ONLY MONEY(1962), ph; NUTTY PROFESSOR, THE(1963), ph; WHO'S MINDING THE STORE?(1963), ph; DISORDERLY ORDERLY, THE(1964), ph; PATSY, THE(1964), ph; STAGE TO THUNDER ROCK(1964), ph; FAMILY JEWELS, THE(1965), ph; TOWN TAMER(1965), ph; APACHE UPRISING(1966), ph; PARADISE, HAWAIIAN STYLE(1966), ph; THREE ON A COUCH(1966), ph; BIG MOUTH, THE(1967), ph; FASTEST GUITAR ALIVE, THE(1967), ph; RED TOMAHAWK(1967), ph; BUCKSKIN(1968), ph; COMIC, THE(1969), ph; HOOK, LINE AND SINKER(1969), ph; WATERMELON MAN(1970), ph; WHICH WAY TO THE FRONT?(1970), ph

Wallace Kelley
SANGAREE(1953), ph; BRIDGES AT TOKO-RI, THE(1954), ph; YOUNG CAPTIVES, THE(1959), ph

Walter Kelley
WHEN WORLDS COLLIDE(1951); COME BACK LITTLE SHEBA(1952); MARTY(1955); MEN IN WAR(1957); LASSIE'S GREAT ADVENTURE(1963); NIGHT OF THE LEPUS(1972); PAT GARRETT AND BILLY THE KID(1973); KILLER ELITE, THE(1975); CONVOY(1978); OSTERMAN WEEKEND, THE(1983)

William P. Kelley
WILD REBELS, THE(1967); SAVAGES FROM HELL(1968); HOOKED GENERATION, THE(1969), set d

Winthrop Kelley
Misc. Silents
SUBMARINE EYE, THE(1917), d

Dennis Kelli
1984
RUNAWAY(1984)

Mike Kellin
AT WAR WITH THE ARMY(1950); HURRICANE SMITH(1952); LONELYHEARTS(1958); WONDERFUL COUNTRY, THE(1959); GREAT IMPOSTOR, THE(1960); MOUNTAIN ROAD, THE(1960); WACKIEST SHIP IN THE ARMY, THE(1961); HELL IS FOR HEROES(1962); INVITATION TO A GUNFIGHTER(1964); BANNING(1967); INCIDENT, THE(1967); THE BOSTON STRANGLER(1968); MALTESE BIPPY, THE(1969); RIOT(1969); COVER ME BABE(1970); PEOPLE NEXT DOOR, THE(1970); FOOLS' PARADE(1971); FREEBIE AND THE BEAN(1974); LAST PORNO FLICK, THE(1974); GOD TOLD ME TO(1976); NEXT STOP, GREENWICH VILLAGE(1976); GIRLFRIENDS(1978); MIDNIGHT EXPRESS(1978, Brit.); ON THE YARD(1978); JUST BEFORE DAWN(1980); PATERNITY(1981); SO FINE(1981); ECHOES(1983); SLEEPAWAY CAMP(1983)

Roy Kelline
CONVOY(1940), ph

Frank Kelling
GULLIVER'S TRAVELS(1939), anim d

Jack Kelling
LAST BLITZKRIEG, THE(1958)

Thom Kelling
HUNTED IN HOLLAND(1961, Brit.)

Blanche Kellino
Silents
PRIDE OF THE NORTH, THE(1920, Brit.)

P. Kellino
I MET A MURDERER(1939, Brit.), w

Pam Kellino
I MET A MURDERER(1939, Brit.), p

Pamela Kellino
I MET A MURDERER(1939, Brit.); THEY WERE SISTERS(1945, Brit.); UPTURNED GLASS, THE(1947, Brit.), a, w; PANDORA AND THE FLYING DUTCHMAN(1951, Brit.); LADY POSSESSED(1952), a, w

R. Kellino
I MET A MURDERER(1939, Brit.), d, ph

Roy Kellino
FOREIGN AFFAIRES(1935, Brit.), ph; PHANTOM LIGHT, THE(1935, Brit.), ph; POT LUCK(1936, Brit.), ph; RHYTHM IN THE AIR(1936, Brit.), ph; TROUBLED WATERS(1936, Brit.), ph; WRATH OF JEALOUSY(1936, Brit.), ph; AREN'T MEN BEASTS?(1937, Brit.), ph; CATCH AS CATCH CAN(1937, Brit.), d; CONCERNING MR. MARTIN(1937, Brit.), d; LAST ADVENTURERS, THE(1937, Brit.), d, ph; YOU'RE IN THE ARMY NOW(1937, Brit.), ph; KATE PLUS TEN(1938, Brit.), ph; I MET A MURDERER(1939, Brit.), p; PROUD VALLEY, THE(1941, Brit.), ph; SHIPS WITH WINGS(1942, Brit.), ph; NINE MEN(1943, Brit.), ph; UNDERGROUND GUERRILLAS(1944, Brit.), spec eff; 48 HOURS(1944, Brit.), spec eff; JOHNNY FRENCHMAN(1946, Brit.), ph; GUILT IS MY SHADOW(1950, Brit.), d, w; LADY POSSESSED(1952), d; CHARADE(1953), d; SILKEN AFFAIR, THE(1957, Brit.), d
Silents
ROB ROY(1922, Brit.)

W. P. Kellino
ALF'S CARPET(1929, Brit.), d; ALF'S BUTTON(1930, Brit.), d; POISONED DIAMOND, THE(1934, Brit.), d&w; SOMETIMES GOOD(1934, Brit.), d; LEND ME YOUR WIFE(1935, Brit.), d, w; HOT NEWS(1936, Brit.), d; PAY BOX ADVENTURE(1936, Brit.), d
Silents
ANGEL ESQUIRE(1919, Brit.), d; AUTUMN OF PRIDE, THE(1921, Brit.), d; ROB ROY(1922, Brit.), d; MATING OF MARCUS, THE(1924, Brit.), d; NOT FOR SALE(1924, Brit.), d; FURTHER ADVENTURES OF THE FLAG LIEUTENANT(1927, Brit.), d; SMASHING THROUGH(1928, Brit.), d
Misc. Silents
BILLY'S SPANISH LOVE SPASM(1915, Brit.), d; MAN IN POSSESSION, THE(1915, Brit.), d; ONLY MAN, THE(1915, Brit.), d; PERILS OF PORK PIE(1916, Brit.), d; TALE OF A SHIRT(1916, Brit.), d; GREEN TERROR, THE(1919, Brit.), d; FALL OF A SAINT, THE(1920, Brit.), d; SAVED FROM THE SEA(1920, Brit.), d; CLASS AND NO CLASS(1921, Brit.), d; FORTUNE OF CHRISTINA MCNAB, THE(1921, Brit.), d; SOUL'S AWAKENING, A(1922, Brit.), d; YOUNG LOCHINVAR(1923, Brit.), d; HIS GRACE GIVES NOTICE(1924, Brit.), d; LOVES OF COLLEEN BAWN, THE(1924, Brit.), d; CONFESSIONS(1925, Brit.), d; GOLD CURE, THE(1925), d; WE WOMEN(1925, Brit.), d; SAILORS DON'T CARE(1928, Brit.), d

Will Kellino
REGAL CAVALCADE(1935, Brit.), d

Kelljan
RETURN OF COUNT YORGA, THE(1971), w

Bob Kelljan
COUNT YORGA, VAMPIRE(1970), d&w; RETURN OF COUNT YORGA, THE(1971), d; SCREAM BLACULA SCREAM(1973), d; BLACK OAK CONSPIRACY(1977), d

Robert Kelljan
GLASS CAGE, THE(1964); HELL'S ANGELS ON WHEELS(1967); PSYCH-OUT(1968); ACT OF VENGEANCE(1974), d

Ben Kellman
STUCK ON YOU(1983)
1984
STUCK ON YOU(1984)

Louis W. Kellman
BURGLAR, THE(1956), p
Morris Kellman
PAPER LION(1968), ph
William Kellner
QUEEN OF SPADES(1948, Brit.), art d; KIND HEARTS AND CORONETS(1949, Brit.), art d; SARABAND(1949, Brit.), art d; RUN FOR YOUR MONEY, A(1950, Brit.), art d; LAVENDER HILL MOB, THE(1951, Brit.), art d; WOODEN HORSE, THE(1951), prod d; SECRET PEOPLE(1952, Brit.), art d; TWILIGHT WOMEN(1953, Brit.), art d; I AM A CAMERA(1955, Brit.), art d; TECKMAN MYSTERY, THE(1955, Brit), prod d; SUDDENLY, LAST SUMMER(1959, Brit.), art d; SIEGE OF SIDNEY STREET, THE(1960, Brit.), art d; KITCHEN, THE(1961, Brit.), art d; SHE DIDN'T SAY NO!(1962, Brit.), prod d; COME FLY WITH ME(1963), art d; V.I.P.s, THE(1963, Brit.), art d; OTHELLO(1965, Brit.), art d; YELLOW ROLLS-ROYCE, THE(1965, Brit.), art d
Harold Kellock
HOUDINI(1953), w
Michael Kelloff
FIRE AND ICE(1983)
Cornelia Kellog
Silents
LINGERIE(1928)
John Kellog
JOHNNY O'CLOCK(1947)
Ray Kellog
WITH A SONG IN MY HEART(1952), spec eff; GENTLEMEN PREFER BLONDES(1953), spec eff; HOUSE OF BAMBOO(1955), spec eff; RAINS OF RANCHIPUR, THE(1955), spec eff; COURT JESTER, THE(1956); CHANDLER(1971)
Alva Kellogg
THREE COMRADES(1938)
Bruce Kellogg
DEERSLAYER(1943); BARBARY COAST GENT(1944); MARRIAGE IS A PRIVATE AFFAIR(1944); THEY WERE EXPENDABLE(1945); THIS MAN'S NAVY(1945); SHADOWS OVER CHINATOWN(1946); MYSTERY OF THE GOLDEN EYE, THE(1948); EVERYBODY DOES IT(1949); UNKNOWN WORLD(1951)
Cecil Kellogg
STORMY(1935); TEXAS RANGERS, THE(1936); THUNDER TRAIL(1937); RAWHIDE(1938); GERONIMO(1939); CHIP OF THE FLYING U(1940); OUTLAW, THE(1943)
D.A. Kellogg
BITTERSWEET LOVE(1976), w
Dorothe Kellogg
GARMENT JUNGLE, THE(1957)
Dorothy Kellogg
PURSUIT TO ALGIERS(1945)
Frances Kellogg
LAWLESS LAND(1937); MY LIFE WITH CAROLINE(1941)
Gayle Kellogg
TOUGH ASSIGNMENT(1949); OPERATION PACIFIC(1951); OPERATION SECRET(1952); WILD BLUE YONDER, THE(1952); THUNDER OVER THE PLAINS(1953); CRIME WAVE(1954); THEM!(1954); SATAN'S SATELLITES(1958)
John Kellogg
WITHOUT RESERVATIONS(1946); HIGH SCHOOL(1940); SAILOR'S LADY(1940); YOUNG TOM EDISON(1940); KNOCKOUT(1941); MOB TOWN(1941); PRIDE OF THE YANKEES, THE(1942); TO BE OR NOT TO BE(1942); THIRTY SECONDS OVER TOKYO(1944); WING AND A PRAYER(1944); CRIMSON CANARY(1945); THIS MAN'S NAVY(1945); WALK IN THE SUN, A(1945); MR. DISTRICT ATTORNEY(1946); SOMEWHERE IN THE NIGHT(1946); STRANGE LOVE OF MARTHA IVERS, THE(1946); GANGSTER, THE(1947); KING OF THE WILD HORSES(1947); OUT OF THE PAST(1947); ROBIN OF TEXAS(1947); SUDDENLY IT'S SPRING(1947); 13TH HOUR, THE(1947); BORROWED TROUBLE(1948); FIGHTING BACK(1948); SECRET SERVICE INVESTIGATOR(1948); SINISTER JOURNEY(1948); STATION WEST(1948); BAD MEN OF TOMBSTONE(1949); HOLD THAT BABY!(1949); HOUSE OF STRANGERS(1949); PORT OF NEW YORK(1949); SAMSON AND DELILAH(1949); TWELVE O'CLOCK HIGH(1949); BUNCO SQUAD(1950); HUNT THE MAN DOWN(1950); KANSAS RAIDERS(1950); COME FILL THE CUP(1951); ELEPHANT STAMPEDE(1951); ENFORCER, THE(1951); TOMORROW IS ANOTHER DAY(1951); GREATEST SHOW ON EARTH, THE(1952); JET JOB(1952); RAIDERS, THE(1952); RANCHO NOTORIOUS(1952); FIGHTING LAWMAN, THE(1953); SILVER WHIP, THE(1953); THOSE REDHEADS FROM SEATTLE(1953); AFRICAN MANHUNT(1955); EDGE OF THE CITY(1957); GO NAKED IN THE WORLD(1961); CONVICTS FOUR(1962)
Misc. Talkies
KNIFE FOR THE LADIES, A(1973)
John G. Kellogg
GORILLA AT LARGE(1954)
Lynn Kellogg
CHARRO(1969)
Marjorie Kellogg
TELL ME THAT YOU LOVE ME, JUNIE MOON(1970), w; ROSEBUD(1975), w; BELL JAR, THE(1979), w
Norman Kellogg
Silents
GIRL FROM RIO, THE(1927), w
Ray Kellogg
BEHIND THE EIGHT BALL(1942); SLATTERY'S HURRICANE(1949), spec eff; DESERT FOX, THE(1951), spec eff; I'LL SEE YOU IN MY DREAMS(1951); YOU'RE IN THE NAVY NOW(1951), spec eff; DEADLINE–U.S.A.(1952), spec eff; DIPLOMATIC COURIER(1952), spec eff; DREAMBOAT(1952), spec eff; MONKEY BUSINESS(1952), spec eff; MY COUSIN RACHEL(1952), spec eff; PHONE CALL FROM A STRANGER(1952), spec eff; PONY SOLDIER(1952), spec eff; BENEATH THE 12-MILE REEF(1953), spec eff; DESERT RATS, THE(1953), spec eff; NIAGARA(1953), spec eff; PICKUP ON SOUTH STREET(1953), spec eff; PRESIDENT'S LADY, THE(1953), spec eff; ROBE, THE(1953), spec eff; SO THIS IS LOVE(1953); TITANIC(1953), spec eff; VICKI(1953), spec eff; WHITE WITCH DOCTOR(1953), spec eff; DEMETRIUS AND THE GLADIATORS(1954), spec eff; GARDEN OF EVIL(1954), spec eff; HELL AND HIGH WATER(1954), spec eff; PRINCE VALIANT(1954), spec eff; RIVER OF NO RETURN(1954), spec eff; THERE'S NO BUSINESS LIKE SHOW BUSINESS(1954), spec eff; GOOD MORNING, MISS DOVE(1955), spec eff; LEFT HAND OF GOD, THE(1955), spec eff; MAN CALLED PETER, THE(1955), spec eff; RACERS, THE(1955), spec eff; SEVEN CITIES OF GOLD(1955), spec eff; SEVEN YEAR ITCH, THE(1955),

spec eff; SOLDIER OF FORTUNE(1955), spec eff; TALL MEN, THE(1955), spec eff; UNTAMED(1955), spec eff; D-DAY, THE SIXTH OF JUNE(1956), spec eff; LOVE ME TENDER(1956), spec eff; ON THE THRESHOLD OF SPACE(1956), spec eff; 23 PACES TO BAKER STREET(1956), spec eff; APACHE WARRIOR(1957); BOY ON A DOLPHIN(1957), spec eff; DESK SET(1957), spec eff; OH, MEN! OH, WOMEN!(1957), spec eff; THREE BRAVE MEN(1957), spec eff; WAY TO THE GOLD, THE(1957), spec eff; GIANT GILA MONSTER, THE(1959), d, w; KILLER SHREWS, THE(1959), d; I PASSED FOR WHITE(1960); MY DOG, BUDDY(1960), d&w; RAYMIE(1960); MUSIC MAN, THE(1962); I'D RATHER BE RICH(1964); ROUSTABOUT(1964); HOLD ON(1966); GREEN BERETS, THE(1968), d
Roy Kellogg
EXPERIMENT IN TERROR(1962)
Sharon Kellogg
HUMAN FACTOR, THE(1975)
Virginia Kellogg
ROAD TO RENO(1931), w; MARY STEVENS, M.D.(1933), w; STOLEN HOLIDAY(1937), w; T-MEN(1947), w; WHITE HEAT(1949), w; CAGED(1950), w; SCREAMING EAGLES(1956), w
William Kellogg
ONE MAN'S LAW(1940); RETURN OF WILD BILL, THE(1940); TRAILING DOUBLE TROUBLE(1940); YOUNG BUFFALO BILL(1940); KANSAS CYCLONE(1941); CITY OF SILENT MEN(1942); HOME IN WYOMIN'(1942); THEY RAID BY NIGHT(1942)
William A. Kellogg
WEST OF ABILENE(1940)
Jane Kells
HALF A SIXPENCE(1967, Brit.); SONG OF NORWAY(1970)
Janie Kells
MACBETH(1971, Brit.); ELEPHANT MAN, THE(1980, Brit.)
Kelly
ON THE TOWN(1949), ch
Kelly the Dog
KELLY AND ME(1957)
Adele Kelly
Misc. Silents
WHAT HAPPENED TO FATHER(1915)
Al Kelly
SINGING IN THE DARK(1956)
Albert Kelly
JUNGLE BRIDE(1933), d
Silents
STAGE KISSES(1927), d; CAMPUS KNIGHTS(1929), d, w
Misc. Silents
CHARGE OF THE GAUCHOS, THE(1928), d; CONFESSIONS OF A WIFE(1928), d
Alice Kelly
GLASS WEB, THE(1953)
Ann Kelly
NATCHEZ TRACE(1960)
Misc. Talkies
FRONTIER WOMAN(1956)
Anthony Kelly
Silents
BAR SINISTER, THE(1917), w; IMPOSTER, THE(1918), w
Anthony P. Kelly
Silents
GREAT LEAP, THE(1914), w; LIGHT AT DUSK, THE(1916), w
Anthony Paul Kelly
THREE FACES EAST(1930), w; BRITISH INTELLIGENCE(1940), w
Silents
WAY DOWN EAST(1920), w; LOVE'S REDEMPTION(1921), w; PLAYTHINGS OF DESTINY(1921), w; STARDUST(1921), w; SILENT COMMAND, THE(1923), w
B.J. Kelly
EARL OF CHICAGO, THE(1940)
Barbara Kelly
DESERT HAWK, THE(1950); TALE OF FIVE WOMEN, A(1951, Brit.); CASTLE IN THE AIR(1952, Brit.); GLAD TIDINGS(1953, Brit.); LOVE IN PAWN(1953, Brit.); JET STORM(1961, Brit.)
Misc. Talkies
THIRTEENTH GREEN(1954, Brit.)
Barry Kelly
FILE ON THELMA JORDAN, THE(1950); FLYING LEATHERNECKS(1951); GUNFIRE AT INDIAN GAP(1957); ELMER GANTRY(1960); EXTRAORDINARY SEAMAN, THE(1969)
Bebe Kelly
Misc. Talkies
FANGS(1974)
Bill Kelly
BRIDGE TO THE SUN(1961), ph; CHANGES(1969); DAREDEVIL, THE(1971)
Bill E. Kelly
MISSION MARS(1968); CHANGES(1969), w
Bob Kelly
1984
CORRUPT(1984, Ital.)
Silents
GOLD RUSH, THE(1925)
Brendan Kelly
WAY WE WERE, THE(1973); ANGELS HARD AS THEY COME(1971); MELVIN AND HOWARD(1980)
Brian Kelly
THUNDER ISLAND(1963); FLIPPER'S NEW ADVENTURE(1964); AROUND THE WORLD UNDER THE SEA(1966); COMPANY OF KILLERS(1970)
Buddy Kelly
IN OLD MONTANA(1939)
Burt Kelly
BETWEEN FIGHTING MEN(1932), p; DYNAMITE RANCH(1932), p; COME ON TARZAN(1933), p; DRUM TAPS(1933), p; FARGO EXPRESS(1933), p; PHANTOM THUNDERBOLT(1933), p; STUDY IN SCARLET, A(1933), p; WOMAN IN THE DARK(1934), p; GIGOLETTE(1935), p; PEOPLE'S ENEMY, THE(1935), p; NAVY BLUES(1937), p; SECRETS OF A NURSE(1938), p; STRANGE FACES(1938), p; SWING, SISTER, SWING(1938), p, w; CODE OF THE STREETS(1939), p; EX-CHAMP(1939), p; I STOLE A MILLION(1939), p; RISKY BUSINESS(1939), p; SPIRIT

OF CULVER, THE(1939), p; TWO BRIGHT BOYS(1939), p; BLACK FRIDAY(1940), p; HOUSE OF THE SEVEN GABLES, THE(1940), p; PRIVATE AFFAIRS(1940), p; SANDY GETS HER MAN(1940), p; SANDY IS A LADY(1940), p; BACHELOR DADDY(1941), p; BLACK CAT, THE(1941), p; INVISIBLE WOMAN, THE(1941), p; MIDNIGHT ANGEL(1941), p; NINE GIRLS(1944), p; STRANGE AFFAIR(1944), p; LEAVE IT TO BLONDIE(1945), p; BLONDIE KNOWS BEST(1946), p; BLONDIE'S LUCKY DAY(1946), p; LIFE WITH BLONDIE(1946), p; MEET ME ON BROADWAY(1946), p; ONE WAY TO LOVE(1946), p; BLONDIE'S HOLIDAY(1947), p; SWORDSMAN, THE(1947), p

Carol Kelly
CRUEL TOWER, THE(1956); DESPERADOES ARE IN TOWN, THE(1956); TOWARD THE UNKNOWN(1956); DANIEL BOONE, TRAIL BLAZER(1957); TERROR IN A TEXAS TOWN(1958)

Carole Kelly
THOMAS CROWN AFFAIR, THE(1968)

Carolee Kelly
GIRL IN THE RED VELVET SWING, THE(1955)

Carrie Kelly
OTHER SIDE OF MIDNIGHT, THE(1977)

Charles Kelly
CRY FREEDOM(1961, Phil.)

Chris Kelly
EDDIE AND THE CRUISERS(1983), set d
1984
EVERY PICTURE TELLS A STORY(1984, Brit.), ed; GOODBYE PEOPLE, THE(1984), set d

Christian Kelly
FOURTEEN, THE(1973, Brit.)

Christine Kelly
SCRATCH HARRY(1969)

Christopher Kelly
1984
ULTIMATE SOLUTION OF GRACE QUIGLEY, THE(1984), set d

Claire Kelly
SCANDAL INCORPORATED(1956); BADLANDERS, THE(1958); PARTY GIRL(1958); SNOWFIRE(1958); UNDERWATER WARRIOR(1958); ASK ANY GIRL(1959); LOVED ONE, THE(1965); GUIDE FOR THE MARRIED MAN, A(1967); INADMISSIBLE EVIDENCE(1968, Brit.); CHILDISH THINGS(1969); WHAT EVER HAPPENED TO AUNT ALICE?(1969); UP YOUR TEDDY BEAR(1970); STRAIGHT ON TILL MORNING(1974, Brit.)

Clare Kelly
HARD DAY'S NIGHT, A(1964, Brit.); GEORGY GIRL(1966, Brit.); WHISPERERS, THE(1967, Brit.); ALL NEAT IN BLACK STOCKINGS(1969, Brit.); AND SOON THE DARKNESS(1970, Brit.); RECKONING, THE(1971, Brit.)

Clyde Kelly
DEAD ONE, THE(1961)

Colleen Kelly
BUCK ROGERS IN THE 25TH CENTURY(1979)

Craig Kelly
PROJECT X(1949); FURIES, THE(1950); EDGE OF FURY(1958); SATAN'S SATELLITES(1958); SILENCE(1974)

Craig G. Kelly
DIRTY HARRY(1971)

Daniel Kelly
Misc. Silents
SUPREME PASSION, THE(1921)

Dave Kelly
WRONG MAN, THE(1956); GIRL WITH GREEN EYES(1964, Brit.); ULYSSES(1967, U.S./Brit.); ITALIAN JOB, THE(1969, Brit.); MC KENZIE BREAK, THE(1970); STRAIGHT TIME(1978)

David Kelly
QUACKSER FORTUNE HAS A COUSIN IN THE BRONX(1970); RED MONARCH(1983, Brit.)
1984
JIGSAW MAN, THE(1984, Brit.)

David Blake Kelly
HAND, THE(1960, Brit.)

David Patrick Kelly
WARRIORS, THE(1979); HAMMETT(1982); 48 HOURS(1982)
1984
DREAMSCAPE(1984)

Dawn Carver Kelly
DR. JEKYLL'S DUNGEON OF DEATH(1982)

Debrah Kelly
LUNCH WAGON(1981)

Dee Kelly
GOODBYE PORK PIE(1981, New Zealand)

Dermot Kelly
ANOTHER SHORE(1948, Brit.); DUBLIN NIGHTMARE(1958, Brit.); BROTH OF A BOY(1959, Brit.); DEVIL'S BAIT(1959, Brit.); HOME IS THE HERO(1959, Ireland); POACHER'S DAUGHTER, THE(1960, Brit.); QUARE FELLOW, THE(1962, Brit.); WRONG ARM OF THE LAW, THE(1963, Brit.); CUP FEVER(1965, Brit.); YELLOW ROLLS-ROYCE, THE(1965, Brit.); PANIC(1966, Brit.); PLANK, THE(1967, Brit.); HEADLINE HUNTERS(1968, Brit.); MRS. BROWN, YOU'VE GOT A LOVELY DAUGHTER(1968, Brit.); STAIRCASE(1969 U.S./Brit./Fr.); SUBTERFUGE(1969, US/Brit.)

Des Kelly
SCARECROW, THE(1982, New Zealand)

Desmond Kelly
SMASH PALACE(1982, New Zealand)

Diarmuid Kelly
TREASURE ISLAND(1950, Brit.)

Don Kelly
STRANGER ON THE THIRD FLOOR(1940); BIG LAND, THE(1957); BOMBERS B-52(1957); CROOKED CIRCLE, THE(1958); NOTORIOUS MR. MONKS, THE(1958); TANK BATTALION(1958)

Dorothy Kelly
YANKEE DOODLE DANDY(1942); FALCON AND THE CO-EDS, THE(1943); SKY'S THE LIMIT, THE(1943)

Silents
WHEELS OF JUSTICE(1915); ARTIE, THE MILLIONAIRE KID(1916); AWAKENING, THE(1917)
Misc. Silents
PAWNS OF MARS(1915); LAW DECIDES, THE(1916); SALVATION JOAN(1916); SUPREME TEMPTATION, THE(1916); MAELSTROM, THE(1917); MONEY MILL, THE(1917)

Duke Kelly
Misc. Talkies
MY NAME IS LEGEND(1975), a, d

Eammon Kelly
EXCALIBUR(1981)

Eamon Kelly
Misc. Talkies
PHILADELPHIA HERE I COME(1975)

Ed Kelly
RAILROADED(1947)
Misc. Talkies
DANDY(1973)

Eddie Kelly
NIGHT AND DAY(1946)

Edward Kelly
BUNKER BEAN(1936), d; WITHIN THESE WALLS(1945); SONG OF SCHEHERAZADE(1947)

Edward Kelly, Jr.
SOMEWHERE IN THE NIGHT(1946)

Eleanor Mercein Kelly
Silents
KILDARE OF STORM(1918), w

Emmett Kelly
FAT MAN, THE(1951); GREATEST SHOW ON EARTH, THE(1952); WIND ACROSS THE EVERGLADES(1958); CLOWN AND THE KIDS, THE(1968, U.S./Bulgaria)

Ernest Kelly
INSPECTOR CLOUSEAU(1968, Brit.), makeup

Errol Kelly
1984
INDIANA JONES AND THE TEMPLE OF DOOM(1984), art d

Evelyn Kelly
MURDER AT THE VANITIES(1934)

Frank Kelly
ESCAPE FROM HONG KONG(1942)

Fred Kelly
THIS IS THE ARMY(1943); DEEP IN MY HEART(1954)

Garrie Kelly
WHERE THE BUFFALO ROAM(1980); HARD COUNTRY(1981)

Gene Kelly
FOR ME AND MY GAL(1942), a, ch; CROSS OF LORRAINE, THE(1943); DU BARRY WAS A LADY(1943); PILOT NO. 5(1943); THOUSANDS CHEER(1943); CHRISTMAS HOLIDAY(1944); COVER GIRL(1944), a, ch; ANCHORS AWEIGH(1945), a, ch; ZIEGFELD FOLLIES(1945); LIVING IN A BIG WAY(1947), a, ch; PIRATE, THE(1948), a, ch; THREE MUSKETEERS, THE(1948); ON THE TOWN(1949), a, d; TAKE ME OUT TO THE BALL GAME(1949), a, w, ch; BLACK HAND, THE(1950); SUMMER STOCK(1950), a, ch; AMERICAN IN PARIS, AN(1951); IT'S A BIG COUNTRY(1951); DEVIL MAKES THREE, THE(1952); LOVE IS BETTER THAN EVER(1952); SINGIN' IN THE RAIN(1952), a, d; BRIGADOON(1954), a, ch; CREST OF THE WAVE(1954, Brit.); DEEP IN MY HEART(1954); IT'S ALWAYS FAIR WEATHER(1955), a, d, ch; INVITATION TO THE DANCE(1956), a, d&w, ch; HAPPY ROAD, THE(1957), a, p&d; LES GIRLS(1957); MARJORIE MORNINGSTAR(1958); TUNNEL OF LOVE, THE(1958), d; INHERIT THE WIND(1960); LET'S MAKE LOVE(1960); GIGOT(1962), d; WHAT A WAY TO GO(1964), a, ch; GUIDE FOR THE MARRIED MAN, A(1967), d; YOUNG GIRLS OF ROCHEFORT, THE(1968, Fr.); HELLO, DOLLY!(1969), d; CHEYENNE SOCIAL CLUB, THE(1970), p&d; FORTY CARATS(1973); VIVA KNIEVEL!(1977); XANADU(1980)

George Edward Kelly
Silents
CRAIG'S WIFE(1928), w

George [Joe] Kelly
POLITICAL ASYLUM(1975, Mex./Guatemalan)

George Kelly
MEN ARE LIKE THAT(1930), w; SHOW-OFF, THE(1934), w; DOUBTING THOMAS(1935), w; THANKS A MILLION(1935); CRAIG'S WIFE(1936), w; OLD HUTCH(1936), w; TOO BUSY TO WORK(1939), w; SHOW-OFF, THE(1946), w; HARRIET CRAIG(1950), w
1984
MOSCOW ON THE HUDSON(1984)
Silents
GOING THE LIMIT(1925)
Misc. Silents
FAGASA(1928)

Gerald Kelly
1984
BLIND DATE(1984)

Gladys Kelly
Misc. Silents
ALL FOR A HUSBAND(1917)

Grace Kelly
FOURTEEN HOURS(1951); HIGH NOON(1952); MOGAMBO(1953); BRIDGES AT TOKO-RI, THE(1954); COUNTRY GIRL, THE(1954); DIAL M FOR MURDER(1954); REAR WINDOW(1954); GREEN FIRE(1955); TO CATCH A THIEF(1955); HIGH SOCIETY(1956); SWAN, THE(1956); POPPY IS ALSO A FLOWER, THE(1966)

Graham Kelly
CALLING BULLDOG DRUMMOND(1951, Brit.), ph

Greg Kelly
FATTY FINN(1980, Aus.)

Gregory Kelly
Silents
MANHATTAN(1924)
Misc. Silents
SHOW OFF, THE(1926)

Hal Kelly
TO HAVE AND HAVE NOT(1944)
Harry Kelly
NED KELLY(1970, Brit.)
Helen Kelly
Silents
M'LISS(1918)
Hilary Kelly
1984
MAN OF FLOWERS(1984, Aus.)
Hobart Kelly
Silents
SALVAGE(1921)
Hubert Kelly
GOODBYE GIRL, THE(1977); VOICES(1979)
Hugh Kelly
BONNIE PRINCE CHARLIE(1948, Brit.); FIGHTING PIMPERNEL, THE(1950, Brit.); BROKEN HORSESHOE, THE(1953, Brit.)
Irene Kelly
DIRTY DINGUS MAGEE(1970)
Misc. Talkies
DISCIPLES OF DEATH(1975); ENTER THE DEVIL(1975)
Jack Kelly
STORY OF ALEXANDER GRAHAM BELL, THE(1939); YOUNG MR. LINCOLN(1939); WEST POINT STORY, THE(1950); WHERE DANGER LIVES(1950); NEW MEXICO(1951); PEOPLE WILL TALK(1951); SUBMARINE COMMAND(1951); NO ROOM FOR THE GROOM(1952); RED BALL EXPRESS(1952); SALLY AND SAINT ANNE(1952); WILD BLUE YONDER, THE(1952); COLUMN SOUTH(1953); GLASS WEB, THE(1953); GUNSMOKE(1953); LAW AND ORDER(1953); REDHEAD FROM WYOMING, THE(1953); STAND AT APACHE RIVER, THE(1953); DRIVE A CROOKED ROAD(1954); MAGNIFICENT OBSESSION(1954); THEY RODE WEST(1954); BAMBOO PRISON, THE(1955); BLACK TUESDAY(1955); CULT OF THE COBRA(1955); DOUBLE JEOPARDY(1955); NIGHT HOLDS TERROR, THE(1955); TO HELL AND BACK(1955); VIOLENT MEN, THE(1955); FORBIDDEN PLANET(1956); JULIE(1956); SHE DEVIL(1957); TAMING SUTTON'S GAL(1957); HONG KONG AFFAIR(1958); FEVER IN THE BLOOD, A(1961); FBI CODE 98(1964); LOVE AND KISSES(1965); YOUNG BILLY YOUNG(1969)
1984
OH GOD! YOU DEVIL(1984)
Silents
BULLET MARK, THE(1928), t; FREE LIPS(1928), w; SOULS AFLAME(1928), t
Capt. Jack Kelly
Silents
JACK, SAM AND PETE(1919, Brit.)
James Kelly
DR. BLOOD'S COFFIN(1961), w; THREE ON A SPREE(1961, Brit.), w; MAN IN THE DARK(1963, Brit.), w; TOMORROW AT TEN(1964, Brit.), w; LOVED ONE, THE(1965), cos; BEAST IN THE CELLAR, THE(1971, Brit.), d&w; NIGHT HAIR CHILD(1971, Brit.), d; W(1974), w; SUDDEN FURY(1975, Can.), ph; LINE, THE(1982)
Misc. Silents
RARIN' TO GO(1924)
James A. Kelly
12 ANGRY MEN(1957)
James B. Kelly
OUTRAGEOUS!(1977, Can.), ph; HAPPY BIRTHDAY, GEMINI(1980), ph
James "Buddy" Kelly
CODE OF THE FEARLESS(1939)
James L. Kelly
FULLER BRUSH GIRL, THE(1950)
James L. "Tiny" Kelly
MILLION DOLLAR MERMAID(1952)
Janet Kelly
GREAT CATHERINE(1968, Brit.); LAST SHOT YOU HEAR, THE(1969, Brit.)
Janice Kelly
FOR LOVE AND MONEY(1967)
Jeane Kelly
Misc. Talkies
OBEAH(1935)
Jeanette Kelly
FOREST, THE(1983)
Jeanne Kelly [Jean Brooks]
CRIME OF DR. CRESPI, THE(1936); DEVIL'S PIPELINE, THE(1940); INVISIBLE KILLER, THE(1940); MIRACLE ON MAIN STREET, A(1940); SON OF ROARING DAN(1940); BUCK PRIVATES(1941); DANGEROUS GAME, A(1941); MAN FROM MONTANA(1941); MEET THE CHUMP(1941); TOO MANY BLONDES(1941); FIGHTING BILL FARGO(1942)
Jim Kelly
MELINDA(1972); ENTER THE DRAGON(1973); BLACK BELT JONES(1974); GOLDEN NEEDLES(1974); THREE THE HARD WAY(1974); TAKE A HARD RIDE(1975, U.S./Ital.); HOT POTATO(1976); ONE DOWN TWO TO GO(1982)
Misc. Talkies
BLACK BELT JONES(1974); BLACK SAMURAI(1977); FREEZE BOMB(1980)
Jimmie Kelly
HARBOR OF MISSING MEN(1950)
Jimmy Kelly
KID FROM BOOKLYN, THE(1946); SHAMUS(1973); IF EVER I SEE YOU AGAIN(1978)
Jo Ann Kelly
VIOLENT WOMEN(1960)
Joe Kelly
NATIONAL BARN DANCE(1944)
John Kelly
FROM HEADQUARTERS(1929); MAN HUNTER, THE(1930); SUBWAY EXPRESS(1931); SUICIDE FLEET(1931); DEVIL IS DRIVING, THE(1932); HELL DIVERS(1932); TWO SECONDS(1932); WINNER TAKE ALL(1932); BOWERY, THE(1933); LITTLE GIANT, THE(1933); GOODBYE LOVE(1934); KID MILLIONS(1934); LITTLE MISS MARKER(1934); MANY HAPPY RETURNS(1934); MEN OF THE NIGHT(1934); DR. SOCRATES(1935); MOTIVE FOR REVENGE(1935); PUBLIC HERO NO. 1(1935); SPECIAL AGENT(1935); STOLEN HARMONY(1935); STRANDED(1935); WE'RE IN THE MONEY(1935); AFTER THE THIN MAN(1936); EASY MONEY(1936); GENTLE-

MAN FROM LOUISIANA(1936); IT HAD TO HAPPEN(1936); LADY LUCK(1936); NAVY WIFE(1936); OUR RELATIONS(1936); POLO JOE(1936); POOR LITTLE RICH GIRL(1936); SAN FRANCISCO(1936); TIMOTHY'S QUEST(1936); WHIPSAW(1936); ANGEL'S HOLIDAY(1937); ARMORED CAR(1937); EXCLUSIVE(1937); FUGITIVE IN THE SKY(1937); LAST GANGSTER, THE(1937); LIVE, LOVE AND LEARN(1937); MERRY-GO-ROUND OF 1938(1937); PORTIA ON TRIAL(1937); WINGS OVER HONOLULU(1937); YOU CAN'T BUY LUCK(1937); 23 ½ HOURS LEAVE(1937); BRINGING UP BABY(1938); CONVICTS AT LARGE(1938); FEMALE FUGITIVE(1938); ANOTHER THIN MAN(1939); MEET DR. CHRISTIAN(1939); SERGEANT MADDEN(1939); SUDDEN MONEY(1939); THESE GLAMOUR GIRLS(1939); THEY SHALL HAVE MUSIC(1939); WOLF CALL(1939); BLACK FRIDAY(1940); BOWERY BOY(1940); I WANT A DIVORCE(1940); MY LITTLE CHICKADEE(1940); ROAD TO SINGAPORE(1940); MANPOWER(1941); PITTSBURGH KID, THE(1941); SHADOW OF THE THIN MAN(1941); THREE SONS O'GUNS(1941); DR. BROADWAY(1942); GIRL TROUBLE(1942); JAIL HOUSE BLUES(1942); LARCENY, INC.(1942); MOONTIDE(1942); MY GAL SAL(1942); TALES OF MANHATTAN(1942); JACK LONDON(1943); NO TIME FOR LOVE(1943); ONCE UPON A TIME(1944); SEE HERE, PRIVATE HARGROVE(1944); SUMMER STORM(1944); WING AND A PRAYER(1944); BLONDE FROM BROOKLYN(1945); I'LL TELL THE WORLD(1945); TIGER WOMAN, THE(1945); TRAIL TO VENGEANCE(1945); WONDER MAN(1945); CROSS MY HEART(1946); DARK CORNER, THE(1946); SOFIA(1948); SOMEONE AT THE DOOR(1950, Brit.); FLESH AND BLOOD(1951, Brit.); DEATH OF AN ANGEL(1952, Brit.); I'M A STRANGER(1952, Brit.); PICKWICK PAPERS, THE(1952, Brit.); TREASURE HUNT(1952, Brit.); BLACK KNIGHT, THE(1954); MAN WITH A MILLION(1954, Brit.); TIM DRISCOLL'S DONKEY(1955, Brit.); STRANGER'S MEETING(1957, Brit.); JET OVER THE ATLANTIC(1960); LAST REBEL, THE(1961, Mex.); I'VE GOTTA HORSE(1965, Brit.); TARZAN AND THE VALLEY OF GOLD(1966 U.S./Switz.); WHERE'S JACK?(1969, Brit.); BROTHERLY LOVE(1970, Brit.); QUACKSER FORTUNE HAS A COUSIN IN THE BRONX(1970); TWO MULES FOR SISTER SARA(1970); SOMETHING BIG(1971); BUCK AND THE PREACHER(1972); JORY(1972); REVENGERS, THE(1972, U.S./Mex.); MIDDLE AGE CRAZY(1980, Can.), ed; STRANGE BREW(1983); UTILITIES(1983, Can.), ed
John T. Kelly
Silents
ARTIE, THE MILLIONAIRE KID(1916)
Joseph Kelly
THAT CHAMPIONSHIP SEASON(1982)
J. Patrick Kelly III
SHEBA BABY(1975), prod d
Judith Kelly
MARRIAGE IS A PRIVATE AFFAIR(1944), w
Judy Kelly
CRIME ON THE HILL(1933, Brit.); HAWLEY'S OF HIGH STREET(1933, Brit.); LOVE NEST, THE(1933, Brit.); MANNEQUIN(1933, Brit.); MONEY TALKS(1933, Brit.); PRIVATE LIFE OF HENRY VIII, THE(1933); THEIR NIGHT OUT(1933, Brit.); BLACK ABBOT, THE(1934, Brit.); FOUR MASKED MEN(1934, Brit.); THINGS ARE LOOKING UP(1934, Brit.); ANYTHING MIGHT HAPPEN(1935, Brit.); CAPTAIN BILL(1935, Brit.); CHARING CROSS ROAD(1935, Brit.); IT'S A BET(1935, Brit.); MARRY THE GIRL(1935, Brit.); REGAL CAVALCADE(1935, Brit.); FIRST OFFENCE(1936, Brit.); LIMPING MAN, THE(1936, Brit.); STAR FELL FROM HEAVEN, A(1936, Brit.); UNDER PROOF(1936, Brit.); AREN'T MEN BEASTS?(1937, Brit.); BOYS WILL BE GIRLS(1937, Brit.); LAST CHANCE, THE(1937, Brit.); MAKE-UP(1937, Brit.); OVER SHE GOES(1937, Brit.); PRICE OF FOLLY, THE(1937, Brit.); JANE STEPS OUT(1938, Brit.); DEAD MAN'S SHOES(1939, Brit.); NORTH SEA PATROL(1939, Brit.); GEORGE AND MARGARET(1940, Brit.); MIDAS TOUCH, THE(1940, Brit.); ONE NIGHT IN PARIS(1940, Brit.); HOUSE OF MYSTERY(1941, Brit.); PIRATES OF THE SEVEN SEAS(1941, Brit.); AT DAWN WE DIE(1943, Brit.); BUTLER'S DILEMMA, THE(1943, Brit.); IT HAPPENED ONE SUNDAY(1944, Brit.); DEAD OF NIGHT(1946, Brit.); DANCING WITH CRIME(1947, Brit.); WARNING TO WANTONS, A(1949, Brit.)
Silents
HONEYMOON AHEAD(1927, Brit.)
Karen Kelly
1984
GIMME AN 'F'(1984)
Karen Lee Kelly
1984
HARDBODIES(1984)
Karolee Kelly
OTHER WOMAN, THE(1954); GIRL RUSH, THE(1955); I DIED A THOUSAND TIMES(1955); COME ON, THE(1956)
Kathleen Kelly
DANGEROUS GROUND(1934, Brit.); DESIGNING WOMEN(1934, Brit.); WHAT HAPPENED TO HARKNESS(1934, Brit.); DEPUTY DRUMMER, THE(1935, Brit.); FOREIGN AFFAIRES(1935, Brit.); LEND ME YOUR WIFE(1935, Brit.); OH, WHAT A NIGHT(1935); AVENGING HAND, THE(1936, Brit.); DON'T RUSH ME(1936, Brit.); MYSTERIOUS MR. DAVIS, THE(1936, Brit.); SCARAB MURDER CASE, THE(1936, Brit.); STRANGE CARGO(1936, Brit.); DOMINANT SEX, THE(1937, Brit.); HEART'S DESIRE(1937, Brit.); LITTLE MISS SOMEBODY(1937, Brit.); LIVE WIRE, THE(1937, Brit.); WHO KILLED JOHN SAVAGE?(1937, Brit.); BAD BOY(1938, Brit.); MUTINY OF THE ELSINORE, THE(1939, Brit.)
Kay K. Kelly
LOVE IS A CAROUSEL(1970)
Kelitta Kelly
1984
REPO MAN(1984)
Kevin Kelly
AMAZING TRANSPARENT MAN, THE(1960)
Kitty Kelly
NIGHT IS OURS(1930, Fr.); BACHELOR APARTMENT(1931); BEHIND OFFICE DOORS(1931); WHITE SHOULDERS(1931); GIRL CRAZY(1932); LADIES OF THE JURY(1932); MEN OF CHANCE(1932); GIRL IN 419(1933); TOO MUCH HARMONY(1933); ALL OF ME(1934); FARMER TAKES A WIFE, THE(1935); DIZZY DAMES(1936); MAN BEHIND THE MASK, THE(1936, Brit.); RHYTHM IN THE AIR(1936, Brit.); BLOSSOMS ON BROADWAY(1937); MEN WITH WINGS(1938); GERONIMO(1939); ROAD TO SINGAPORE(1940); THOSE WERE THE DAYS(1940); WOMEN WITHOUT NAMES(1940); MAD DOCTOR, THE(1941); LADY IS WILLING, THE(1942); LARCENY, INC.(1942); LUCKY JORDAN(1942); THEY ALL KISSED THE BRIDE(1942); SO PROUDLY WE HAIL(1943); PRACTICALLY YOURS(1944); LOST MISSILE, THE(1958, U.S./Can.); TWELVE HOURS TO KILL(1960)

Misc. Talkies
WOMAN'S MAN, A(1934)
Silents
KISS IN THE DARK, A(1925)

Kiva Kelly
C. C. AND COMPANY(1971)

Lacy Kelly
COMMON LAW WIFE(1963)

Lew Kelly
BARNUM WAS RIGHT(1929); WOMAN RACKET, THE(1930); HEAVEN ON EARTH(1931); I TAKE THIS WOMAN(1931); AIR MAIL(1932); DEVIL PAYS, THE(1932); I AM A FUGITIVE FROM A CHAIN GANG(1932); IF I HAD A MILLION(1932); LADY AND GENT(1932); MILLION DOLLAR LEGS(1932); MIRACLE MAN, THE(1932); PACK UP YOUR TROUBLES(1932); SCANDAL FOR SALE(1932); TOM BROWN OF CULVER(1932); HARD TO HANDLE(1933); LAUGHTER IN HELL(1933); MAN OF THE FOREST(1933); STRANGE PEOPLE(1933); TILLIE AND GUS(1933); FIFTEEN WIVES(1934); HUMAN SIDE, THE(1934); KEY, THE(1934); OLD-FASHIONED WAY, THE(1934); SIX OF A KIND(1934); TAKE THE STAND(1934); WHAT'S YOUR RACKET?(1934); GOIN' TO TOWN(1935); IN PERSON(1935); MAN ON THE FLYING TRAPEZE, THE(1935); MISSISSIPPI(1935); PORT OF LOST DREAMS(1935); PUBLIC OPINION(1935); SOCIETY FEVER(1935); TWO FISTED(1935); DEATH FROM A DISTANCE(1936); IT HAD TO HAPPEN(1936); LADY LUCK(1936); LONE WOLF RETURNS, THE(1936); MAN I MARRY, THE(1936); MURDER AT GLEN ATHOL(1936); RAINBOW ON THE RIVER(1936); THREE OF A KIND(1936); TIMOTHY'S QUEST(1936); WILD BRIAN KENT(1936); WINDS OF THE WASTELAND(1936); ALL OVER TOWN(1937); FORLORN RIVER(1937); HIGH, WIDE AND HANDSOME(1937); MOUNTAIN MUSIC(1937); PARADISE EXPRESS(1937); SOME BLONDES ARE DANGEROUS(1937); WESTERN GOLD(1937); BORN TO BE WILD(1938); FLIRTING WITH FATE(1938); GOLD MINE IN THE SKY(1938); LAWLESS VALLEY(1938); MAN FROM MUSIC MOUNTAIN(1938); PAINTED DESERT, THE(1938); PANAMA PATROL(1939); SAGA OF DEATH VALLEY(1939); THREE TEXAS STEERS(1939); TOUGH KID(1939); TWENTY MULE TEAM(1940); WESTERNER, THE(1940); CYCLONE ON HORSEBACK(1941); GAY FALCON, THE(1941); GREAT TRAIN ROBBERY, THE(1941); HONKY TONK(1941); LAST OF THE DUANES(1941); LITTLE FOXES, THE(1941); LUCKY DEVILS(1941); ROAD AGENT(1941); BEHIND THE EIGHT BALL(1942); MAGNIFICENT AMBERSONS, THE(1942); SHUT MY BIG MOUTH(1942); KEEP 'EM SLUGGING(1943); LADY OF BURLESQUE(1943); MAD GHOUL, THE(1943); SO'S YOUR UNCLE(1943)

Lou Kelly
OVERLAND EXPRESS, THE(1938)

Louis H. Kelly
ST. IVES(1976); CHEAP DETECTIVE, THE(1978)

M.G. Kelly
STAR IS BORN, A(1976); BUDDY HOLLY STORY, THE(1978); ROLLER BOOGIE(1979)

Mabel Kelly
Misc. Talkies
THIRTY YEARS LATER(1938)
Misc. Silents
MIDNIGHT ACE, THE(1928); THIRTY YEARS LATER(1928)

Maisie Kelly
CRY, THE BELOVED COUNTRY(1952, Brit.), cos

Margaret Kelly
LOST IN A HAREM(1944); COWBOYS, THE(1972); PUBERTY BLUES(1983, Aus.), p, w

Margot Kelly
Silents
ARTISTIC TEMPERAMENT, THE(1919, Brit.)

Marianne Candace Kelly
LIEUTENANT WORE SKIRTS, THE(1956)

Mark Kelly
ONE IN A MILLION(1936), w; PIGSKIN PARADE(1936), w; MR. DOODLE KICKS OFF(1938), w; LITTLE MEN(1940), w; MAN FROM DOWN UNDER, THE(1943), w

Marlene Kelly
YOUNG SINNER, THE(1965)

Martin J. Kelly
FINNEGANS WAKE(1965)

Martine Kelly
LADY IN THE CAR WITH GLASSES AND A GUN, THE(1970, U.S./Fr.); DESTRUCTORS, THE(1974, Brit.)
1984
LIFE IS A BED OF ROSES(1984, Fr.)

Mary Kelly
MELODY AND ROMANCE(1937, Brit.); MARGIE(1940); MOB TOWN(1941); MODEL WIFE(1941)

Maura Kelly
MC KENZIE BREAK, THE(1970)

Maurice Kelly
YOU WILL REMEMBER(1941, Brit.); TILL THE CLOUDS ROLL BY(1946); YOU WERE MEANT FOR ME(1948); GIRL MOST LIKELY, THE(1957); MY SIX LOVES(1963); FAMILY JEWELS, THE(1965)

Mia Kelly
1984
NO SMALL AFFAIR(1984)

Michael Kelly
FOLLY TO BE WISE(1953); RECOIL(1953); DELAYED ACTION(1954, Brit.); PARATROOPER(1954, Brit.); YOU LUCKY PEOPLE(1955, Brit.); LINKS OF JUSTICE(1958); ORDERS TO KILL(1958, Brit.); HONKYTONK MAN(1982), ed

Mickey Kelly
HEART BEAT(1979)

Mike Kelly
Misc. Talkies
HEROES THREE(1984)

Monika Kelly
CORPSE GRINDERS, THE(1972)

Monty Kelly
FLIGHT TO HONG KONG(1956), m

Myra Kelly
Silents
LITTLE MISS SMILES(1922), w

Nancy Kelly
GIRL ON THE BARGE, THE(1929); CONVENTION GIRL(1935); SUBMARINE PATROL(1938); FRONTIER MARSHAL(1939); JESSE JAMES(1939); STANLEY AND LIVINGSTONE(1939); TAIL SPIN(1939); HE MARRIED HIS WIFE(1940); ONE NIGHT IN THE TROPICS(1940); PRIVATE AFFAIRS(1940); SAILOR'S LADY(1940); PARACHUTE BATTALION(1941); SCOTLAND YARD(1941); VERY YOUNG LADY, A(1941); FLY BY NIGHT(1942); FRIENDLY ENEMIES(1942); TO THE SHORES OF TRIPOLI(1942); TARZAN'S DESERT MYSTERY(1943); TORNADO(1943); WOMEN IN BONDAGE(1943); DOUBLE EXPOSURE(1944); GAMBLER'S CHOICE(1944); SHOW BUSINESS(1944); BETRAYAL FROM THE EAST(1945); FOLLOW THAT WOMAN(1945); SONG OF THE SARONG(1945); WOMAN WHO CAME BACK(1945); MURDER IN THE MUSIC HALL(1946); BAD SEED, THE(1956); CROWDED PARADISE(1956)
1984
GHOSTBUSTERS(1984)

Ned Kelly
20TH CENTURY OZ(1977, Aus.)

Norman Kelly
INVASION OF THE BLOOD FARMERS(1972)

P. J. Kelly
BELOVED ENEMY(1936); SECRET SEVEN, THE(1940); EVER SINCE VENUS(1944); THAT'S MY BABY(1944); TONIGHT AND EVERY NIGHT(1945); DEVOTION(1946)

Pat Kelly
GUNMAN'S CODE(1946), ed; PAPER MOON(1973), cos

Patrick J. Kelly
ADVENTURE'S END(1937); MISSING GUEST, THE(1938)

Patrick Kelly
BULLDOG DRUMMOND ESCAPES(1937); WILD BEAUTY(1946), ed

Patsy Kelly
GOING HOLLYWOOD(1933); COUNTESS OF MONTE CRISTO, THE(1934); GIRL FROM MISSOURI, THE(1934); PARTY'S OVER, THE(1934); EVERY NIGHT AT EIGHT(1935); GO INTO YOUR DANCE(1935); PAGE MISS GLORY(1935); THANKS A MILLION(1935); KELLY THE SECOND(1936); PIGSKIN PARADE(1936); PRIVATE NUMBER(1936); SING, BABY, SING(1936); EVER SINCE EVE(1937); NOBODY'S BABY(1937); PICK A STAR(1937); WAKE UP AND LIVE(1937); COWBOY AND THE LADY, THE(1938); MERRILY WE LIVE(1938); THERE GOES MY HEART(1938); GORILLA, THE(1939); HIT PARADE OF 1941(1940); BROADWAY LIMITED(1941); PLAYMATES(1941); ROAD SHOW(1941); TOPPER RETURNS(1941); IN OLD CALIFORNIA(1942); SING YOUR WORRIES AWAY(1942); DANGER! WOMEN AT WORK(1943); LADIES' DAY(1943); MY SON, THE HERO(1943); CROWDED SKY, THE(1960); PLEASE DON'T EAT THE DAISIES(1960); NAKED KISS, THE(1964); GHOST IN THE INVISIBLE BIKINI(1966); C'MON, LET'S LIVE A LITTLE(1967); ROSEMARY'S BABY(1968); PHYNX, THE(1970); FREAKY FRIDAY(1976); NORTH AVENUE IRREGULARS, THE(1979)

Paul Kelly
GIRL FROM CALGARY(1932); BROADWAY THROUGH A KEYHOLE(1933); LONE AVENGER, THE(1933), p; BLIND DATE(1934); DEATH OF THE DIAMOND(1934); LOVE CAPTIVE, THE(1934); PRESIDENT VANISHES, THE(1934); SIDE STREETS(1934); PUBLIC HERO NO. 1(1935); SCHOOL FOR GIRLS(1935); SILK HAT KID(1935); SPEED DEVILS(1935); STAR OF MIDNIGHT(1935); WHEN A MAN'S A MAN(1935); ACCUSING FINGER, THE(1936); COUNTRY BEYOND, THE(1936); HERE COMES TROUBLE(1936); IT'S A GREAT LIFE(1936); MURDER WITH PICTURES(1936); MY MARRIAGE(1936); SONG AND DANCE MAN, THE(1936); WOMEN ARE TROUBLE(1936); FIT FOR A KING(1937); FRAME-UP, THE(1937); IT HAPPENED OUT WEST(1937); JOIN THE MARINES(1937); NAVY BLUE AND GOLD(1937); PAROLE RACKET(1937); ADVENTURE IN SAHARA(1938); DEVIL'S PARTY, THE(1938); ISLAND IN THE SKY(1938); JUVENILE COURT(1938); MISSING GUEST, THE(1938); NURSE FROM BROOKLYN(1938); TORCHY BLANE IN PANAMA(1938); FLYING IRISHMAN, THE(1939); FORGED PASSPORT(1939); ROARING TWENTIES, THE(1939); WITHIN THE LAW(1939); 6000 ENEMIES(1939); FLIGHT COMMAND(1940); GIRLS UNDER TWENTY-ONE(1940); HOWARDS OF VIRGINIA, THE(1940); INVISIBLE STRIPES(1940); QUEEN OF THE MOB(1940); WYOMING(1940); I'LL WAIT FOR YOU(1941); MR. AND MRS. NORTH(1941); MYSTERY SHIP(1941); PARACHUTE BATTALION(1941); ZIEGFELD GIRL(1941); CALL OUT THE MARINES(1942); FLYING TIGERS(1942); TARZAN'S NEW YORK ADVENTURE(1942); TOUGH AS THEY COME(1942); MAN FROM MUSIC MOUNTAIN(1943); DEAD MAN'S EYES(1944); FACES IN THE FOG(1944); STORY OF DR. WASSELL, THE(1944); ALLOTMENT WIVES, INC.(1945); CHINA'S LITTLE DEVILS(1945); GRISSLY'S MILLIONS(1945); SAN ANTONIO(1945); CAT CREEPS, THE(1946); DEADLINE FOR MURDER(1946); GLASS ALIBI, THE(1946); STRANGE JOURNEY(1946); ADVENTURE ISLAND(1947); CROSSFIRE(1947); FEAR IN THE NIGHT(1947); SPOILERS OF THE NORTH(1947); FILE ON THELMA JORDAN, THE(1950); FRENCHIE(1950); GUILTY OF TREASON(1950); SECRET FURY, THE(1950); SIDE STREET(1950); PAINTED HILLS, THE(1951); SPRINGFIELD RIFLE(1952); GUNSMOKE(1953); SPLIT SECOND(1953); DUFFY OF SAN QUENTIN(1954); HIGH AND THE MIGHTY, THE(1954); JOHNNY DARK(1954); STEEL CAGE, THE(1954); SQUARE JUNGLE, THE(1955); STORM CENTER(1956); BAILOUT AT 43,000(1957); CURFEW BREAKERS(1957)
Misc. Talkies
NOT A LADIES MAN(1942); CAMERONS, THE(1974)
Silents
NEW KLONDIKE, THE(1926); SLIDE, KELLY, SLIDE(1927); SPECIAL DELIVERY(1927)
Misc. Silents
KNIGHTS OF THE SQUARE TABLE(1917); OLD OAKEN BUCKET, THE(1921)

Paula Kelly
SUN VALLEY SERENADE(1941); WALKING MY BABY BACK HOME(1953); SWEET CHARITY(1969); ANDROMEDA STRAIN, THE(1971); COOL BREEZE(1972); TOP OF THE HEAP(1972); TROUBLE MAN(1972); SOYLENT GREEN(1973); SPOOK WHO SAT BY THE DOOR, THE(1973); LOST IN THE STARS(1974), a, ch; THREE TOUGH GUYS(1974, U.S./Ital.); UPTOWN SATURDAY NIGHT(1974); DRUM(1976)

Peggy Kelly
Silents
IN BORROWED PLUMES(1926); JOY GIRL, THE(1927)
Misc. Silents
GREATER THAN MARRIAGE(1924); LILLIES OF THE STREETS(1925); SCHOOL FOR WIVES(1925); UNKNOWN LOVER, THE(1925)

Peter Kelly
VIRGIN SOLDIERS, THE(1970, Brit.)
Rachel Kelly
1984
SCREAM FOR HELP(1984)
Raymond Kelly
LUCKY NIGHT(1939)
Renee Kelly
SCARLET THREAD(1951, Brit.)
Silents
ALL SORTS AND CONDITIONS OF MEN(1921, Brit.); LIKENESS OF THE NIGHT, THE(1921, Brit.)
Misc. Silents
BETTER MAN, THE(1915); WESTWARD HO!(1919, Brit.); FOUL PLAY(1920, Brit.)
Robert Kelly
KID FROM LEFT FIELD, THE(1953)
Misc. Silents
RANGER AND THE LAW, THE(1921), d; BLUE BLAZES(1922), d
Ron Kelly
WAITING FOR CAROLINE(1969, Can.), d, w; KING OF THE GRIZZLIES(1970) d
Roy Kelly
EXORCIST II: THE HERETIC(1977), spec eff
Roz Kelly
OWL AND THE PUSSYCAT, THE(1970); OKAY BILL(1971); YOU'VE GOT TO WALK IT LIKE YOU TALK IT OR YOU'LL LOSE THAT BEAT(1971); FEMALE RESPONSE, THE(1972); NEW YEAR'S EVIL(1980); AMERICAN POP(1981); FULL MOON HIGH(1982)
Scotch Kelly
RETURN OF THE RAT, THE(1929, Brit.)
Scott Kelly
Misc. Talkies
MY NAME IS LEGEND(1975)
Seamus Kelly
MOBY DICK(1956, Brit.)
Misc. Talkies
JOHNSTOWN MONSTER, THE(1971)
Sean Kelly
HIGH FLIGHT(1957, Brit.); BITTER VICTORY(1958, Fr.); MAN INSIDE, THE(1958, Brit.); TANK FORCE(1958, Brit.); BANDIT OF ZHOBE, THE(1959); IDOL ON PARADE(1959, Brit.); GREEN HELMET, THE(1961, Brit.); GANG WAR(1962, Brit.); WAR LOVER, THE(1962, U.S./Brit.); FOLLOW THE BOYS(1963); MYSTERY SUBMARINE(1963, Brit.); VICTORS, THE(1963); WEST 11(1963, Brit.); FIRST MEN IN THE MOON(1964, Brit.); SQUADRON 633(1964, U.S./Brit.); 633 SQUADRON(1964); COWBOYS, THE(1972)
Sharon Kelly
HUSTLE(1975)
Misc. Talkies
ALICE GOODBODY(1974); GOSH(1974); CARNAL MADNESS(1975)
Sheets Kelly
PUPPET ON A CHAIN(1971, Brit.), ph
Skeets Kelly
EDGE OF THE WORLD, THE(1937, Brit.), ph; TARZAN'S GREATEST ADVENTURE(1959, Brit.), ph; BLUE MAX, THE(1966) ph
Susan Kelly
DONDI(1961); WILD HARVEST(1962); CANDIDATE, THE(1964)
T. Howard Kelly
Silents
LOVER'S ISLAND(1925), w
Ted Kelly
NOTORIOUS(1946)
Terence Kelly
MC CABE AND MRS. MILLER(1971); STAR 80(1983)
Misc. Talkies
ACCIDENT(1983)
Teresa Kelly
BILLY JACK(1971)
Terrence Kelly
GOLDEN SEAL, THE(1983)
Terry Kelly
CHRISTINA(1974, Can.); BEAR ISLAND(1980, Brit.-Can.)
Thomas F. Kelly
CHINA DOLL(1958), w
Tim Kelly
CRY OF THE BANSHEE(1970, Brit.), w; SUGAR HILL(1974), w
Tiny Jimmie Kelly
MOONRISE(1948)
"Tiny" Jimmie Kelly
PEOPLE AGAINST O'HARA, THE(1951); PAT AND MIKE(1952)
Tom Kelly
HE WALKED BY NIGHT(1948); WEDNESDAY CHILDREN, THE(1973)
1984
AGAINST ALL ODDS(1984)
Tommy Kelly
ADVENTURES OF TOM SAWYER, THE(1938); PECK'S BAD BOY WITH THE CIRCUS(1938); GONE WITH THE WIND(1939); THEY SHALL HAVE MUSIC(1939); CURTAIN CALL(1940); GALLANT SONS(1940); IRENE(1940); MILITARY ACADEMY(1940); DOUBLE DATE(1941); LIFE BEGINS FOR ANDY HARDY(1941); NICE GIRL?(1941); MUG TOWN(1943); FABULOUS TEXAN, THE(1947); MAGNIFICENT YANKEE, THE(1950)
Tracey Kelly
CLINIC, THE(1983, Aus.)
Trigg Kelly
GAY DECEIVERS, THE(1969)
Valerie Kelly
METEOR(1979)
Vince Kelly
DRACULA(THE DIRTY OLD MAN) (1969)

Virginia Kelly
FANCY PANTS(1950)
W. A. Kelly
ANOTHER SHORE(1948, Brit.); WOMAN HATER(1949, Brit.)
W. Wallace Kelly
LOOK IN ANY WINDOW(1961), ph; DAY OF THE EVIL GUN(1968), ph
Wallace Kelly
DR. CYCLOPS(1940), spec eff; GREATEST SHOW ON EARTH, THE(1952), ph; WAR OF THE WORLDS, THE(1953), spec eff; TEN COMMANDMENTS, THE(1956), ph; VERTIGO(1958), ph
Walt Kelly
FANTASIA(1940), anim; DUMBO(1941), anim; RELUCTANT DRAGON, THE(1941), anim
Walter Kelly
FATHER OF THE BRIDE(1950); WELL, THE(1951); FEMALE ANIMAL, THE(1958); LOST COMMAND, THE(1966)
Walter C. Kelly
SEAS BENEATH, THE(1931); MC FADDEN'S FLATS(1935); VIRGINIA JUDGE, THE(1935), a, w; LAUGHING IRISH EYES(1936)
Misc. Talkies
TUGBOAT PRINCESS(1936)
William Kelly
SEEDS OF FREEDOM(1943, USSR), ph; TROUBLE IN THE GLEN(1954, Brit.)
William B. Kelly
COUNTRY MUSIC HOLIDAY(1958), ph
William J. Kelly
BELOW THE SEA(1933); WOMAN ACCUSED(1933); SIX OF A KIND(1934)
Silents
PROUD FLESH(1925)
Misc. Silents
SECRET STRINGS(1918); WHEN MY SHIP COMES IN(1919); PARISIAN NIGHTS(1925)
Paul Kelman
GAS(1981, Can.); MY BLOODY VALENTINE(1981, Can.)
Rick Kelman
MAN CALLED PETER, THE(1955); RESTLESS ONES, THE(1965); FIRST TIME, THE(1969)
Rickey Kelman
KATHY O'(1958); STEP DOWN TO TERROR(1958); FOLLOW ME, BOYS!(1966)
Ricky Kelman
KETTLES ON OLD MACDONALD'S FARM, THE(1957); ONCE UPON A HORSE(1958); CRITIC'S CHOICE(1963)
Ricky William Kelman
LAST TRAIN FROM GUN HILL(1959)
Ronnie Kelman
EXPLOSIVE GENERATION, THE(1961)
Terry Kelman
BUS STOP(1956); BIG CAPER, THE(1957); YOUNG STRANGER, THE(1957); KATHY O'(1958)
Hi Kelos
OPERATION THUNDERBOLT(1978, ISRAEL)
Moultrie Kelsall
LAST HOLIDAY(1950, Brit.); FRANCHISE AFFAIR, THE(1952, Brit.); HOUR OF THIRTEEN, THE(1952); YOU'RE ONLY YOUNG TWICE(1952, Brit.); ALBERT, R.N.(1953, Brit.); JOHNNY ON THE RUN(1953, Brit.); LANDFALL(1953, Brit.); MASTER OF BALLANTRAE, THE(1953, U.S./Brit.); HIGH AND DRY(1954, Brit.); TROUBLE IN THE GLEN(1954, Brit.); QUENTIN DURWARD(1955); SEA SHALL NOT HAVE THEM, THE(1955, Brit.); WARRIORS, THE(1955); MAN WHO NEVER WAS, THE(1956, Brit.); NOW AND FOREVER(1956, Brit.); ABANDON SHIP(1957, Brit.); BARRETTS OF WIMPOLE STREET, THE(1957); INN OF THE SIXTH HAPPINESS, THE(1958); LAW AND DISORDER(1958, Brit.); VIOLENT PLAYGROUND(1958, Brit.); YOUR PAST IS SHOWING(1958, Brit.); BEYOND THIS PLACE(1959, Brit.); LEFT, RIGHT AND CENTRE(1959); BATTLE OF THE SEXES, THE(1960, Brit.); FLAME OVER INDIA(1960, Brit.); GREYFRIARS BOBBY(1961, Brit.); LIGHT IN THE PIAZZA(1962); BIRTHDAY PARTY, THE(1968, Brit.); ONE MORE TIME(1970, Brit.)
Moultrie R. Kelsall
CAPTAIN HORATIO HORNBLOWER(1951, Brit.)
Moutrie Kelsall
LAVENDER HILL MOB, THE(1951, Brit.)
Richalene Kelsay
CHICKEN CHRONICLES, THE(1977), cos
Ross Kelsay
THEY RAN FOR THEIR LIVES(1968), ph; SKATEBOARD(1978), ph
Ken Kelsch
DRILLER KILLER(1979), ph; DON'T GO IN THE HOUSE(1980)
Dick Kelsey
FANTASIA(1940), art d; PINOCCHIO(1940), art d; DUMBO(1941), art d; MAKE MINE MUSIC(1946), w; ALICE IN WONDERLAND(1951), w
Franklin Kelsey
KNIGHT WITHOUT ARMOR(1937, Brit.)
Franklyn Kelsey
JOSSER ON THE FARM(1934, Brit.); ONCE IN A NEW MOON(1935, Brit.); LITTLE MISS MOLLY(1940)
Fred Kelsey
ON TRIAL(1928); TENDERLOIN(1928); DONOVAN AFFAIR, THE(1929); FALL OF EVE, THE(1929); LAST WARNING, THE(1929); SMILING IRISH EYES(1929); GOT WHAT SHE WANTED(1930); MEN WITHOUT LAW(1930); MURDER ON THE ROOF(1930); ONLY SAPS WORK(1930); ROAD TO PARADISE(1930); SCARLET PAGES(1930); SHE GOT WHAT SHE WANTED(1930); WIDE OPEN(1930); GOING WILD(1931); SUBWAY EXPRESS(1931); YOUNG DONOVAN'S KID(1931); DISCARDED LOVERS(1932); GUILTY AS HELL(1932); IF I HAD A MILLION(1932); RED-HAIRED ALIBI, THE(1932); TRIAL OF VIVIENNE WARE, THE(1932); BOWERY, THE(1933); FOOTLIGHT PARADE(1933); GIRL MISSING(1933); GOLD DIGGERS OF 1933(1933); BELOVED(1934); CRIME DOCTOR, THE(1934); MOTH, THE(1934); SHADOWS OF SING SING(1934); TWENTIETH CENTURY(1934); YOUNG AND BEAUTIFUL(1934); CARNIVAL(1935); DANGER AHEAD(1935); DEATH FLIES EAST(1935); DIAMOND JIM(1935); LIGHTNING STRIKES TWICE(1935); ONE FRIGHTENED NIGHT(1935); PUBLIC MENACE(1935); SAGEBRUSH TROUBADOR(1935); SCHOOL FOR GIRLS(1935); CHARLIE CHAN AT THE OPERA(1936); DARK HOUR, THE(1936); PRIVATE NUMBER(1936); ALL OVER TOWN(1937); DAMSEL IN DISTRESS, A(1937);

LOVE AND HISSES(1937); LOVE IS NEWS(1937); SECOND HONEYMOON(1937); SUPER SLEUTH(1937); THAT I MAY LIVE(1937); TIME OUT FOR ROMANCE(1937); YOU CAN'T BEAT LOVE(1937); JOSETTE(1938); MR. MOTO'S GAMBLE(1938); MY LUCKY STAR(1938); ROUGH RIDERS' ROUNDUP(1939); TELL NO TALES(1939); LITTLE BIT OF HEAVEN, A(1940); LONE WOLF KEEPS A DATE, THE(1940); INVISIBLE GHOST, THE(1941); LONE WOLF TAKES A CHANCE, THE(1941); ONE FOOT IN HEAVEN(1941); SECRETS OF THE LONE WOLF(1941); COUNTER-ESPION-AGE(1942); GENTLEMAN JIM(1942); IN THIS OUR LIFE(1942); JUKE GIRL(1942); KING'S ROW(1942); LADY GANGSTER(1942); LARCENY, INC.(1942); MAN WHO CAME TO DINNER, THE(1942); MURDER IN THE BIG HOUSE(1942); MY FAVORITE BLONDE(1942); THEY DIED WITH THEIR BOOTS ON(1942); X MARKS THE SPOT(1942); YANKEE DOODLE DANDY(1942); MURDER ON THE WATER-FRONT(1943); NORTHERN PURSUIT(1943); ONE DANGEROUS NIGHT(1943); THANK YOUR LUCKY STARS(1943); CRIME BY NIGHT(1944); DOUGHGIRLS, THE(1944); CHRISTMAS IN CONNECTICUT(1945); COME OUT FIGHTING(1945); INCENDIARY BLONDE(1945); STRANGE MR. GREGORY, THE(1945); BRINGING UP FATHER(1946); HOW DO YOU DO?(1946); MY REPUTATION(1946); NOBODY LIVES FOREVER(1946); NORA PRENTISS(1947); STALLION ROAD(1947); NOOSE HANGS HIGH, THE(1948); SILVER RIVER(1948); FLAXY MARTIN(1949); FOUN-TAINHEAD, THE(1949); DALLAS(1950); ONCE A THIEF(1950); HANS CHRISTIAN ANDERSEN(1952); MY SIX CONVICTS(1952); O. HENRY'S FULL HOUSE(1952); MURDER WITHOUT TEARS(1953); RACING BLOOD(1954); MESA OF LOST WOM-EN, THE(1956)
Misc. Talkies
HOT OFF THE PRESS(1935); MARSHALS IN DISGUISE(1954)
Silents
LIGHT OF VICTORY(1919); DESERTED AT THE ALTAR(1922); ONE CLEAR CALL(1922); SONG OF LIFE, THE(1922); SOUTH OF SUVA(1922); ELEVENTH HOUR, THE(1923); SOULS FOR SALE(1923); LAWFUL CHEATERS(1925); PATHS TO PARA-DISE(1925); ATTA BOY!(1926); DOUBLING WITH DANGER(1926); SOCIAL HIGH-WAYMAN, THE(1926); THAT'S MY BABY(1926); THIRD DEGREE, THE(1926); HELD BY THE LAW(1927); SOFT CUSHIONS(1927); HAROLD TEEN(1928); NAUGHTY BABY(1929)
Misc. Silents
SOCIETY SENSATION, A(1918); WHEN THE DESERT SMILES(1919); ONE-WAY TRAIL, THE(1920), d; PUPPETS OF FATE(1921); SMOOTH AS SATIN(1925); GORIL-LA, THE(1927); THIRTEENTH HOUR, THE(1927)
Fred A. Kelsey
TRUE TO LIFE(1943); LONE WOLF MEETS A LADY, THE(1940); LONE WOLF STRIKES, THE(1940); RIDING HIGH(1943)
Misc. Silents
FIGHTING GRINGO, THE(1917), d
Gerald Kelsey
GOLDEN RABBIT, THE(1962, Brit.), w
Harry Kelsey
Silents
ABRAHAM LINCOLN(1924)
James Kelsey
SCANDAL SHEET(1931)
Linda Kelsey
MIDNIGHT MAN, THE(1974)
Tom Kelsey
PURPLE HAZE(1982), w
Bobby Kelso
Silents
JACK KNIFE MAN, THE(1920)
Ed Kelso
UP IN THE AIR(1940), w; YOU'RE OUT OF LUCK(1941), w
Edmond Kelso
TEX RIDES WITH THE BOY SCOUTS(1937), w; OVERLAND STAGE RAI-DERS(1938), w; ROLL, WAGONS, ROLL(1939), w; GANG'S ALL HERE(1941), w; LET'S GO COLLEGIATE(1941), w; RIDING THE CHEROKEE TRAIL(1941), w; SIGN OF THE WOLF(1941), w; TOP SERGEANT MULLIGAN(1941), w; FRECKLES COMES HOME(1942), w; LURE OF THE ISLANDS(1942), w; MEET THE MOB(1942), w; THERE GOES KELLY(1945), w
Edmund Kelso
MYSTERY OF THE HOODED HORSEMEN, THE(1937), w; OUTLAWS OF SONO-RA(1938), w; PANAMINT'S BAD MAN(1938), w; ROLLIN' PLAINS(1938), w; UTAH TRAIL(1938), w; SUNDOWN ON THE PRAIRIE(1939), w; KING OF THE ZOM-BIES(1941), w; POLICE BULLETS(1942), w; PRIVATE BUCKAROO(1942), w; RE-VENGE OF THE ZOMBIES(1943), w; SWING PARADE OF 1946(1946), w
Harry Kelso
OF HUMAN BONDAGE(1946), art d
James Kelso
TEXANS, THE(1938); OUR LEADING CITIZEN(1939)
Jim Kelso
MILLION DOLLAR LEGS(1939)
Ken Kelso
MANGANINNIE(1982, Aus.), w
Maude P. Kelso
Silents
WASTED LIVES(1925), w
Maym Kelso
Silents
JOHNNY GET YOUR GUN(1919); MALE AND FEMALE(1919); KICK IN(1922); WOMAN WHO WALKED ALONE, THE(1922)
Misc. Silents
GLASS HOUSES(1922); DOLLAR DOWN(1925)
Mayme Kelso
Silents
SAMSON(1914); ONE MILLION DOLLARS(1915); REBECCA OF SUNNYBROOK FARM(1917); SECRET GAME, THE(1917); THOSE WITHOUT SIN(1917); OLD WIVES FOR NEW(1918); IN FOR THIRTY DAYS(1919); HELP WANTED–MALE!(1920); JACK STRAW(1920); DUCKS AND DRAKES(1921); ONE WILD WEEK(1921); PEN-ROD(1922); SLANDER THE WOMAN(1923); NELLIE, THE BEAUTIFUL CLOAK MODEL(1924); FLAMING WATERS(1925); UNCHASTENED WOMAN(1925); LIGHT-NING REPORTER(1926); DROPKICK, THE(1927); VANITY(1927)
Misc. Silents
ONE MILLION DOLLARS(1915); WARNING, THE(1915); SLANDER(1916); CAS-TLES FOR TWO(1917); HONOR OF HIS HOUSE, THE(1918); THINGS WE LOVE,

THE(1918); WIDOW'S MIGHT, THE(1918); WHY SMITH LEFT HOME(1919); YOU NEVER SAID SUCH A GIRL(1919); CONRAD IN QUEST OF HIS YOUTH(1920); HER STURDY OAK(1921); MARCH HARE, THE(1921); MARRIAGE MARKET, THE(1923); MODERN MATRIMONY(1923); GIRLS MEN FORGET(1924)
Vernon Kelso
ONCE IN A NEW MOON(1935, Brit.); MRS. PYM OF SCOTLAND YARD(1939, Brit.); GIRL WHO COULDN'T QUITE, THE(1949, Brit.); DELAVINE AFFAIR, THE(1954, Brit.); EIGHT O'CLOCK WALK(1954, Brit.); SQUARE RING, THE(1955, Brit.)
Anna Kelson
Misc. Silents
FLAMES OF WRATH(1923)
George Kelson
Misc. Silents
TENTH CASE, THE(1917), d; PURPLE LILY, THE(1918), d; STOLEN OR-DERS(1918), d; STRONG WAY, THE(1918), d; WAY OUT, THE(1918), d
Stuart Kelson
Silents
JUST SUPPOSE(1926), ph
Herbert Kelt
MARGIE(1946)
John Kelt
BUCKET OF BLOOD(1934, Brit.)
Silents
BRIDAL CHAIR, THE(1919, Brit.); ADVENTURES OF MR. PICKWICK, THE(1921, Brit.); MASTER OF CRAFT, A(1922, Brit.)
Misc. Silents
MAN WHO WON, THE(1918, Brit.)
Jerie Kelter
SLAYER, THE(1982), set d
1984
BREAKIN' 2: ELECTRIC BOOGALOO(1984), set d; CHATTANOOGA CHOO CHOO(1984), set d
Ken Keltner
KID FROM CLEVELAND, THE(1949)
Dorrit Kelton
ROSE TATTOO, THE(1955)
Gael Kelton
Silents
SOULS AFLAME(1928)
Misc. Silents
FAGASA(1928)
Jane Kelton
Misc. Talkies
BLONDE GODDESS(1982)
Pert Kelton
SALLY(1929); HOT CURVES(1930); BED OF ROSES(1933); BOWERY, THE(1933); BACHELOR BAIT(1934); MEANEST GAL IN TOWN, THE(1934); PURSUED(1934); SING AND LIKE IT(1934); ANNIE OAKLEY(1935); HOORAY FOR LOVE(1935); LIGHTNING STRIKES TWICE(1935); MARY BURNS, FUGITIVE(1935); CAIN AND MABEL(1936); KELLY THE SECOND(1936); SITTING ON THE MOON(1936); HIT PARADE, THE(1937); LAUGHING AT TROUBLE(1937); MEET THE BOY FRIEND(1937); WOMEN OF GLAMOUR(1937); RHYTHM OF THE SADDLE(1938); SLANDER HOUSE(1938); YOU CAN'T TAKE IT WITH YOU(1938); WHISPERING ENEMIES(1939); MUSIC MAN, THE(1962); LOVE AND KISSES(1965); COMIC, THE(1969)
Richard Kelton
MARGIE(1946); MC Q(1974); SILENCE(1974); ULTIMATE WARRIOR, THE(1975)
Keltoum
HASSAN, TERRORIST(1968, Algerian)
Yashar Kemal
1984
MEMED MY HAWK(1984, Brit.), d&w
Muza Kemanai
WALL-EYED NIPPON(1963, Jap.)
Colin Kemball
RAINBOW JACKET, THE(1954, Brit.)
Stella Kemball
IT HAPPENED HERE(1966, Brit.); RICHARD'S THINGS(1981, Brit.)
Paul Kember
GREAT TRAIN ROBBERY, THE(1979, Brit.); AMERICAN WEREWOLF IN LON-DON, AN(1981); MC VICAR(1982, Brit.)
Harry Kemble
SOMEWHERE IN ENGLAND(1940, Brit.)
Lillian Kemble
Misc. Silents
HOUSE OF MIRRORS, THE(1916); MY HUSBAND'S FRIEND(1918); SHATTERED FAITH(1923)
Stella Kemble
HERE WE GO ROUND THE MULBERRY BUSH(1968, Brit.)
Vivian Kemble
MAN IN THE DARK(1963, Brit.), w
Anthony Kemble-Cooper
ROMEO AND JULIET(1936)
Lilian Kemble-Cooper
RAGE IN HEAVEN(1941); WOMAN'S FACE(1941)
Lillian Kemble-Cooper
WHITE ANGEL, THE(1936); WOMAN REBELS, A(1936); WE ARE NOT ALO-NE(1939)
Lily Kemble-Cooper
MY FAIR LADY(1964)
Violet Kemble-Cooper
OUR BETTERS(1933); CARDINAL RICHELIEU(1935); DAVID COPPER-FIELD(1935); VANESSA, HER LOVE STORY(1935); ROMEO AND JULIET(1936)
John Kemeny
DRYLANDERS(1963, Can.), ed; APPRENTICESHIP OF DUDDY KRAVITZ, THE(1974, Can.), p; WHITE LINE FEVER(1975, Can.), p; SHADOW OF THE HAWK(1976, Can.), p; ICE CASTLES(1978), p; QUEST FOR FIRE(1982, Fr./Can.), p
1984
BAY BOY(1984, Can.), p; LOUISIANE(1984, Fr./Can.), p

Harry Kemer
ARNELO AFFAIR, THE(1947), ed

Rodney Kemerer
1984
THIS IS SPINAL TAP(1984)

Steve Kemis
LIONS LOVE(1969)

Ralph Kemlem
MURDER ON THE SET(1936, Brit.), ed

Harry Kemm
MURDER BY DEATH(1976), art d

Harry R. Kemm
NEW YORK, NEW YORK(1977), art d

Jean Kemm
Misc. Silents
LES DEUX MARQUISES(1916, Fr.), d; HONNEUR D'ARTISTE(1917, Fr.), d; LE DEDALE(1917, Fr.), d; ANDRE CORNELIS(1918, Fr.), d; LE DELAI(1918, Fr.), d; L'OBSTACLE(1918, Fr.), d; L'ENIGME(1919, Fr.), d; LE DESTIN EST MAITRE(1920, Fr.), d; MICHELINE(1920, Fr.), d; MISS ROVEL(1920, Fr.), d; HANTISE(1922, Fr.), d; L'ABSOLUTION(1922, Fr.), d; LE FERME DU CHOQUART(1922, Fr.), d; CE PAUVRE CHERI(1923, Fr.), d; ANDRE CORNELIS(1927, Fr.), d

Ed Kemmer
BEHIND THE HIGH WALL(1956); SIERRA STRANGER(1957); EARTH VS. THE SPIDER(1958); SPIDER, THE(1958); MARA OF THE WILDERNESS(1966); EXECUTIVE ACTION(1973)

Edward Kemmer
CALYPSO JOE(1957); PANAMA SAL(1957); GIANT FROM THE UNKNOWN(1958); HONG KONG CONFIDENTIAL(1958); HOT ANGEL, THE(1958); TOO MUCH, TOO SOON(1958); CROWDED SKY, THE(1960)

Warren Kemmerling
CONVICTS FOUR(1962); GUN STREET(1962); INCIDENT IN AN ALLEY(1962); TRAUMA(1962); LOVED ONE, THE(1965); NAVAJO RUN(1966); LAWYER, THE(1969); CHEYENNE SOCIAL CLUB, THE(1970); HIT(1973); FRAMED(1975); 92 IN THE SHADE(1975, U.S./Brit.); EAT MY DUST!(1976); CLOSE ENCOUNTERS OF THE THIRD KIND(1977); DARK, THE(1979)
Misc. Talkies
SHOCK HILL(1966)

Warren J. Kemmerling
BROTHER JOHN(1971); FAMILY PLOT(1976)

Bill Kemmill
GROOVE TUBE, THE(1974)

Amanda Kemp
FUNNY MONEY(1983, Brit.)

Anthony Kemp
BOYS OF PAUL STREET, THE(1969, Hung./US); CROMWELL(1970, Brit.); LOLA(1971, Brit./Ital.)
Misc. Talkies
LIONHEART(1970)

Antony Kemp
CRY WOLF(1968, Brit.)

Bill Kemp
BREAKING POINT(1976)

Brandis Kemp
1984
SURF II(1984)

Bruce Kemp
HARD TRAIL(1969); MIGHTY GORGA, THE(1969); SCAVENGERS, THE(1969)

Carroll Kemp
CRY BLOOD, APACHE(1970)

Dan Kemp
RUN, ANGEL, RUN(1969); CRY BLOOD, APACHE(1970); HELL'S BLOODY DEVILS(1970); CAHILL, UNITED STATES MARSHAL(1973)

Daniel Kemp
LOSERS, THE(1970)

David Kemp
ISLAND WOMEN(1958)

Edward Kemp
FRAGMENT OF FEAR(1971, Brit.); TOUCH OF CLASS, A(1973, Brit.)
Misc. Talkies
BLINKER'S SPY-SPOTTER(1971)

Elisabeth Kemp
KILLING HOUR, THE(1982)

Elizabeth Kemp
HE KNOWS YOU'RE ALONE(1980)

Ellison Kemp
TO SIR, WITH LOVE(1967, Brit.)

Eric Kemp
MR. H. C. ANDERSEN(1950, Brit.)

Gypsy Kemp
TOUCH OF THE OTHER, A(1970, Brit.)

Jack Kemp
GREEN FIELDS(1937), ed; BOY! WHAT A GIRL(1947), ed; SEPIA CINDERELLA(1947), ed; MIRACLE IN HARLEM(1948), d

James Kemp
27A(1974, Aus.)

Jan Kemp
NIKKI, WILD DOG OF THE NORTH(1961, U.S./Can.), cos

Jeremy Kemp
FACE OF A STRANGER(1964, Brit.); DR. TERROR'S HOUSE OF HORRORS(1965, Brit.); OPERATION CROSSBOW(1965, U.S./Ital.); BLUE MAX, THE(1966); CAST A GIANT SHADOW(1966); ASSIGNMENT K(1968, Brit.); STRANGE AFFAIR, THE(1968, Brit.); TWIST OF SAND, A(1968, Brit.); DARLING LILI(1970); GAMES, THE(1970); SUDDEN TERROR(1970, Brit.); POPE JOAN(1972, Brit.); BLOCKHOUSE, THE(1974, Brit.); BELSTONE FOX, THE(1976, 1976); EAST OF ELEPHANT ROCK(1976, Brit.); SEVEN-PER-CENT SOLUTION, THE(1977, Brit.); CARAVANS(1978, U.S./Iranian); LEOPARD IN THE SNOW(1979, Brit./Can.); PRISONER OF ZENDA, THE(1979); RETURN OF THE SOLDIER, THE(1983, Brit.); UNCOMMON VALOR(1983)
1984
TOP SECRET!(1984)

Misc. Talkies
JAMAICAN GOLD(1971)

Joan Kemp
JOURNEY FOR MARGARET(1942)

Johnny Kemp
ISLAND WOMEN(1958)

Katia Borg Valli Kemp
GREAT MUPPET CAPER, THE(1981)

Ken Kemp
1984
FOOTLOOSE(1984)

Kenner C. Kemp
PEPE(1960)

Kenner G. Kemp
PROFESSOR BEWARE(1938); SO BIG(1953)

Lindsay Kemp
SAVAGE MESSIAH(1972, Brit.); WICKER MAN, THE(1974, Brit.); VALENTINO(1977, Brit.)
1984
MIDSUMMER NIGHT'S DREAM, A(1984, Brit./Span.), a, prod d

Lindsey Kemp
1984
MIDSUMMER NIGHT'S DREAM, A(1984, Brit./Span.), cos

Lynda Kemp
RUNNING(1979, Can.), cos; NOTHING PERSONAL(1980, Can.), cos; TICKET TO HEAVEN(1981), cos

Mae Kemp
Misc. Silents
CALL OF HIS PEOPLE, THE(1922)

Margaret Kemp
Silents
SHERLOCK HOLMES(1922)

Matty Kemp
MILLION DOLLAR COLLAR, THE(1929); COMMON CLAY(1930); CITY STREETS(1931); AIR EAGLES(1932); DOWN TO EARTH(1932); PHANTOM OF CRESTWOOD, THE(1932); PROBATION(1932); TESS OF THE STORM COUNTRY(1932); THRILL OF YOUTH(1932); JUSTICE TAKES A HOLIDAY(1933); CITY PARK(1934); CROSS STREETS(1934); WINE, WOMEN, AND SONG(1934); TANGO(1936); CRIMINALS OF THE AIR(1937); HERE'S FLASH CASEY(1937); HOUSE OF SECRETS, THE(1937); RED LIGHTS AHEAD(1937); CAMPUS CONFESSIONS(1938); I DEMAND PAYMENT(1938); LAW OF THE TEXAN(1938); MILLION DOLLAR LEGS(1939); LOOK WHO'S LAUGHING(1941); CHATTERBOX(1943); LINDA BE GOOD(1947), p; MILLION DOLLAR WEEKEND(1948), p, w; FRENCH LINE, THE(1954), w
Silents
RUSTLER'S RANCH(1926); GOOD-BYE KISS, THE(1928); MAGNIFICENT FLIRT, THE(1928)

Paul Kemp
BLONDE NIGHTINGALE(1931, Ger.); DOLLY GETS AHEAD(1931, Ger.); THREEPENNY OPERA, THE(1931, Ger./U.S.); INVISIBLE OPPONENT(1933, Ger.); M(1933, Ger.); BOCCACCIO(1936, Ger.)

Ramiro Gomez Kemp
DEVIL'S SISTERS, THE(1966)

Roger Kemp
DAY AND THE HOUR, THE(1963, Fr./ Ital.); AWAKENING, THE(1980); SUPERMAN II(1980); DRAGONSLAYER(1981)

Ted Kemp
FAR COUNTRY, THE(1955)

Tom Kemp
FLAMING FRONTIER(1958, Can.), art d; WOLF DOG(1958, Can.), art d; PUNISHMENT PARK(1971)

Valli Kemp
DOCTOR PHIBES RISES AGAIN(1972, Brit.)

Joan Kemp-Walsh
ALL IN(1936, Brit.)

Jean Kemp-Welch
BUSMAN'S HONEYMOON(1940, Brit.)

Joan Kemp-Welch
ONCE A THIEF(1935, Brit.); GIRL IN THE TAXI(1937, Brit.); GIRLS IN THE STREET(1937, Brit.); CITADEL, THE(1938); GIRL IN THE STREET(1938, Brit.); GIRL IN DISTRESS(1941, Brit.); HARD STEEL(1941, Brit.); PIMPERNEL SMITH(1942, Brit.); TALK ABOUT JACQUELINE(1942, Brit.); WINGS AND THE WOMAN(1942, Brit.); RHYTHM SERENADE(1943, Brit.)

Joan Kemp-Welsh
SCHOOL FOR HUSBANDS(1939, Brit.)

Arthur Kempel
WACKO(1983), m
1984
FLESHBURN(1984), m; NINJA III–THE DOMINATION(1984), m

Leo Kempenski
WHITE ZOMBIE(1932), m

Al Kemper
SMALL CIRCLE OF FRIENDS, A(1980), set d

Brenda Kemper
ELEPHANT MAN, THE(1980, Brit.)

Charles Kemper
ANGEL COMES TO BROOKLYN, AN(1945); SOUTHERNER, THE(1945); GALLANT JOURNEY(1946); SISTER KENNY(1946); BELLE STARR'S DAUGHTER(1947); GUNFIGHTERS, THE(1947); KING OF THE WILD HORSES(1947); SHOCKING MISS PILGRIM, THE(1947); THAT HAGEN GIRL(1947); FIGHTING FATHER DUNNE(1948); FURY AT FURNACE CREEK(1948); YELLOW SKY(1948); ADVENTURE IN BALTIMORE(1949); DOOLINS OF OKLAHOMA, THE(1949); INTRUDER IN THE DUST(1949); CALIFORNIA PASSAGE(1950); MR. MUSIC(1950); NEVADAN, THE(1950); STARS IN MY CROWN(1950); TICKET TO TOMAHAWK(1950); WAGONMASTER(1950); WHERE DANGER LIVES(1950); ON DANGEROUS GROUND(1951)

Dennis Kemper
MY BROTHER'S WEDDING(1983)

Doris Kemper
VOICE OF THE TURTLE, THE(1947); EASTER PARADE(1948); SMART WO-MAN(1948); TUNA CLIPPER(1949); CAGED(1950); FATHER'S WILD GAME(1950); NO WAY OUT(1950); ELOPEMENT(1951); GHOST CHASERS(1951); I CAN GET IT FOR YOU WHOLESALE(1951); ROOM FOR ONE MORE(1952); TALL MEN, THE(1955); CRASHING LAS VEGAS(1956); OKLAHOMAN, THE(1957); YOUNG AND DANGER-OUS(1957)

M. Kemper
Misc. Silents
TSAR NIKOLAI II(1917, USSR)

Ray Kemper
NAVY BOUND(1951)

Rozene Kemper
PASSION(1954)

Victor Kemper
HUSBANDS(1970), ph; MAGIC GARDEN OF STANLEY SWEETHART, THE(1970), ph; LAST TYCOON, THE(1976), ph; OH, GOD!(1977), ph; SLAP SHOT(1977), ph

Victor J. Kemper
HOSPITAL, THE(1971), ph; THEY MIGHT BE GIANTS(1971), ph; WHO IS HARRY KELLERMAN AND WHY IS HE SAYING THOSE TERRIBLE THINGS ABOUT ME?(1971), ph; CANDIDATE, THE(1972), ph; LAST OF THE RED HOT LO-VERS(1972), ph; FRIENDS OF EDDIE COYLE, THE(1973), ph; FROM THE MIXED-UP FILES OF MRS. BASIL E. FRANKWEILER(1973), ph; GORDON'S WAR(1973), ph; SHAMUS(1973), ph; GAMBLER, THE(1974), ph; DOG DAY AFTERNOON(1975), ph; REINCARNATION OF PETER PROUD, THE(1975), ph; MIKEY AND NICKY(1976), ph; STAY HUNGRY(1976), ph; AUDREY ROSE(1977), ph; COMA(1978), ph; EYES OF LAURA MARS(1978), ph; MAGIC(1978), ph; ONE AND ONLY, THE(1978), ph; ...AND JUSTICE FOR ALL(1979), ph; JERK, THE(1979), ph; FINAL COUNTDOWN, THE(1980), ph; NIGHT OF THE JUGGLER(1980), ph; XANADU(1980), ph; CHU CHU AND THE PHILLY FLASH(1981), ph; FOUR SEASONS, THE(1981), ph; AUTHOR! AUTHOR!(1982), ph; PARTNERS(1982), ph; MR. MOM(1983), ph; NATIONAL LAM-POON'S VACATION(1983), ph
1984
CLOAK AND DAGGER(1984), ph; LONELY GUY, THE(1984), ph

Charles Kemperer
SCARLET STREET(1945)

Ruth Kempf
LIVE AND LET DIE(1973, Brit.)

Gerald Kempinski
CAESAR AND CLEOPATRA(1946, Brit.); SPRINGTIME(1948, Brit.)

Gerard Kempinski
WOMAN TO WOMAN(1946, Brit.); GHOSTS OF BERKELEY SQUARE(1947, Brit.); HIGH FURY(1947, Brit.)

Gerchardt Kempinski
WE'LL SMILE AGAIN(1942, Brit.)

Gerhard Kempinski
HOME SWEET HOME(1945, Brit.)

Gerhardt Kempinski
TALK ABOUT JACQUELINE(1942, Brit.); THURSDAY'S CHILD(1943, Brit.); FRENZY(1946, Brit.); WANTED FOR MURDER(1946, Brit.); SHOWTIME(1948, Brit.)

Thomas Kempinski
THESE ARE THE DAMNED(1965, Brit.)

Tom Kempinski
OTHELLO(1965, Brit.); COP-OUT(1967, Brit.); WHISPERERS, THE(1967, Brit.); COM-MITTEE, THE(1968, Brit.); MRS. BROWN, YOU'VE GOT A LOVELY DAUGHT-ER(1968, Brit.); DOCTOR IN TROUBLE(1970, Brit.); MC KENZIE BREAK, THE(1970); MOON ZERO TWO(1970, Brit.); PRAISE MARX AND PASS THE AMMUNITION(1970, Brit.); RECKONING, THE(1971, Brit.); GUMSHOE(1972, Brit.)

Gerhard Kempinsky
LADY FROM LISBON(1942, Brit.)

Helga Kempke
FOX AND HIS FRIENDS(1976, Ger.), cos

Lillian Kemple-Cooper
LETTER, THE(1940)

Ralph Kemplen
SAINT MEETS THE TIGER, THE(1943, Brit.), ed; YOUNG MAN'S FANCY(1943, Brit.), ed; MR. PERRIN AND MR. TRAILL(1948, Brit.), ed; GAY LADY, THE(1949, Brit.), ed; AFRICAN QUEEN, THE(1951, U.S./Brit.), ed; NAUGHTY ARLETTE(1951, Brit.), ed; PANDORA AND THE FLYING DUTCHMAN(1951, Brit.), ed; THEY WERE NOT DIVIDED(1951, Brit.), ed; TWILIGHT WOMEN(1953, Brit.), ed; COURT MAR-TIAL(1954, Brit.), ed; GOOD DIE YOUNG, THE(1954, Brit.), ed; STORY OF ESTHER COSTELLO, THE(1957, Brit.), ed; SPANIARD'S CURSE, THE(1958, Brit.), d; THREE MEN IN A BOAT(1958, Brit.), ed; ROOM AT THE TOP(1959, Brit.), ed; SAVAGE INNOCENTS, THE(1960, Brit.), ed; FREUD(1962), ed; CEREMONY, THE(1963, U.S./Span.), ed; MACBETH(1963), ed; NIGHT OF THE IGUANA, THE(1964), ed; MAN FOR ALL SEASONS, A(1966, Brit.), ed; KISS THE GIRLS AND MAKE THEM DIE(1967, U.S./Ital.), ed; OLIVER!(1968, Brit.), ed; GOODBYE MR. CHIPS(1969, U.S./Brit.), ed; TO KILL A CLOWN(1972), ed; DAY OF THE JACKAL, THE(1973, Brit./Fr.), ed; ODESSA FILE, THE(1974, Brit./Ger.), ed; GOLDEN RENDEZVOUS(1977), ed; ES-CAPE TO ATHENA(1979, Brit.), ed; NO SEX PLEASE-WE'RE BRITISH(1979, Brit.), ed; GREAT MUPPET CAPER, THE(1981), ed; DARK CRYSTAL, THE(1982, Brit.), ed

Willy Kemplen
DUFFY(1968, Brit.), ed; BEFORE WINTER COMES(1969, Brit.), ed; BROTHERLY LOVE(1970, Brit.), ed; LOOKING GLASS WAR, THE(1970, Brit.), ed; DAD'S AR-MY(1971, Brit.), ed; EMBASSY(1972, Brit.), ed; SIDDHARTHA(1972), ed; UNDER MILK WOOD(1973, Brit.), ed; DESTRUCTORS, THE(1974, Brit.), ed; PHASE IV(1974), ed; CLEOPATRA JONES AND THE CASINO OF GOLD(1975 U. S. Hong Kong), ed; DIRTY KNIGHT'S WORK(1976, Brit.), ed

Kurt Kempler
BIG STAMPEDE, THE(1932), w; RIDING TORNADO, THE(1932), w; TWO-FISTED LAW(1932), w; ELEVENTH COMMANDMENT(1933), w; SHRIEK IN THE NIGHT, A(1933), w; TELEGRAPH TRAIL, THE(1933), w

Ralph Kempler
ALEXANDER THE GREAT(1956), ed

R. Kemplin
SAINT'S VACATION, THE(1941, Brit.), ed

Ralph Kemplin
MY HEART IS CALLING(1935, Brit.), ed; MOULIN ROUGE(1952), ed; BEAT THE DEVIL(1953), ed

Brenda Kempner
PERSECUTION AND ASSASSINATION OF JEAN-PAUL MARAT AS PERFORMED BY THE INMATES OF THE ASYLUM OF CHARENTON UNDER THE DIRECTION OF THE MARQUIS DE SADE, THE(1967, Brit.); SMASHING TIME(1967 Brit.); ALF 'N' FAMILY(1968, Brit.); JOANNA(1968, Brit.); NEVER SAY NEVER AGAIN(1983)

Teddy Kempner
YENTL(1983)

Rachel Kempson
GIRL IN DISTRESS(1941, Brit.); WOMAN'S VENGEANCE, A(1947); CAPTIVE HEART, THE(1948, Brit.); SEA SHALL NOT HAVE THEM, THE(1955, Brit.); TOM JONES(1963, Brit.); THIRD SECRET, THE(1964, Brit.); CURSE OF THE FLY(1965, Brit.); GEORGY GIRL(1966, Brit.); GRAND PRIX(1966); JOKERS, THE(1967, Brit.); CHARGE OF THE LIGHT BRIGADE, THE(1968, Brit.); THANK YOU ALL VERY MUCH(1969, Brit.); TWO GENTLEMEN SHARING(1969, Brit.); VIRGIN SOLDIERS, THE(1970, Brit.); JANE EYRE(1971, Brit.)

John Kempt
SCARECROW, THE(1982, New Zealand)

Josef Kemr
MARKETA LAZAROVA(1968, Czech.); NINTH HEART, THE(1980, Czech.); DIVINE EMMA, THE(1983, Czech,)

Takakura Ken
YAKUZA, THE(1975, U.S./Jap.)

Ken Collyer Band
WEST 11(1963, Brit.)

Ken Darby and The Kings's Men
HONOLULU(1939)

The Ken Darby Chorus
MAKE MINE MUSIC(1946)

Ken Johnson's West Indian Band
TORSO MURDER MYSTERY, THE(1940, Brit.)

Dolores Kenan
LOCAL COLOR(1978)

Bob Kenaston
PROUD AND THE PROFANE, THE(1956); TIN STAR, THE(1957); SPRING BREAK(1983), stunts
1984
LAST STARFIGHTER, THE(1984)

Rita Kenaston
DAYS OF WINE AND ROSES(1962); MANCHURIAN CANDIDATE, THE(1962)

Kendal
YOL(1982, Turkey), m

Canna Kendal
YELLOW HAT, THE(1966, Brit.)

Felicity Kendal
VALENTINO(1977, Brit.)

Geoffrey Kendal
SHAKESPEARE WALLAH(1966, India)

Jennifer Kendal
BOMBAY TALKIE(1970, India); HEAT AND DUST(1983, Brit.)

Tony Kendal [Luciano Stella]
FANTASTIC THREE, THE(1967, Ital./Ger./Fr./Yugo.)

Victor Kendal
LAW OF THE JUNGLE(1942)

Bernard Kendall
QUEST FOR FIRE(1982, Fr./Can.)

Betty Kendall
CHILD OF MANHATTAN(1933)

Campbell Kendall
Misc. Silents
TILLY OF BLOOMSBURY(1921, Brit.)

Cavan Kendall
HERE WE GO ROUND THE MULBERRY BUSH(1968, Brit.); EUREKA(1983, Brit.)

Cy Kendall
WITHOUT RESERVATIONS(1946); BULLDOG EDITION(1936); DANCING PIRA-TE(1936); HOT MONEY(1936); KING OF THE PECOS(1936); LONELY TRAIL, THE(1936); MAN HUNT(1936); SAN FRANCISCO(1936); SEA SPOILERS, THE(1936); SWORN ENEMY(1936); WOMEN ARE TROUBLE(1936); ANGEL'S HOLIDAY(1937); BORROWING TROUBLE(1937); LAND BEYOND THE LAW(1937); LAST GANGSTER, THE(1937); MEET THE BOY FRIEND(1937); ONCE A DOCTOR(1937); PUBLIC WEDDING(1937); THEY WON'T FORGET(1937); WHITE BONDAGE(1937); CRIME SCHOOL(1938); GIRL OF THE GOLDEN WEST, THE(1938); GOLD IS WHERE YOU FIND IT(1938); HAWAII CALLS(1938); INVISIBLE MENACE, THE(1938); LITTLE MISS THOROUGHBRED(1938); NEXT TIME I MARRY(1938); NIGHT HAWK, THE(1938); RAWHIDE(1938); VALLEY OF THE GIANTS(1938); ANGELS WASH THEIR FACES(1939); CALLING ALL MARINES(1939); FUGITIVE AT LARGE(1939); STAND UP AND FIGHT(1939); ANDY HARDY MEETS DEBUTANTE(1940); HOUSE ACROSS THE BAY, THE(1940); HULLABALOO(1940); MEN WITHOUT SOULS(1940); MY FAVORITE WIFE(1940); YOUTH WILL BE SERVED(1940); BILLY THE KID(1941); HONKY TONK(1941); MIDNIGHT ANGEL(1941); MYSTERY SHIP(1941); RIDE, KELLY, RIDE(1941); ROBIN HOOD OF THE PECOS(1941); ALIAS BOSTON BLACKIE(1942); FLY BY NIGHT(1942); JOHNNY EAGER(1942); NIGHT TO REMEM-BER, A(1942); ROAD TO MOROCCO(1942); SILVER QUEEN(1942); WIFE TAKES A FLYER, THE(1942); AFTER MIDNIGHT WITH BOSTON BLACKIE(1943); CHANCE OF A LIFETIME, THE(1943); GENTLE GANGSTER, A(1943); LADY TAKES A CHANCE, A(1943); WHISPERING FOOTSTEPS(1943); CHINESE CAT, THE(1944); CRIME BY NIGHT(1944); GIRL RUSH(1944); KISMET(1944); LADY IN THE DEATH HOUSE(1944); LAST RIDE, THE(1944); OUTLAW TRAIL(1944); ROGER TOUHY, GANGSTER!(1944); TALL IN THE SADDLE(1944); WAVE, A WAC AND A MARINE, A(1944); WHISTLER, THE(1944); WILSON(1944); CISCO KID RETURNS, THE(1945); CORNERED(1945); DANCING IN MANHATTAN(1945); POWER OF THE WHISTLER, THE(1945); SHADOW OF TERROR(1945); SHE GETS HER MAN(1945); TAHITI NIGHTS(1945); THOUSAND AND ONE NIGHTS, A(1945); TIGER WOMAN, THE(1945); BLONDE FOR A DAY(1946); GLASS ALIBI, THE(1946); INVISIBLE INFORMER(1946); FARMER'S DAUGHTER, THE(1947); LADY IN THE LAKE(1947); SINBAD THE SAILOR(1947); CALL NORTHSIDE 777(1948); FIGHTING MAD(1948); IN THIS CORNER(1948); PERILOUS WATERS(1948); RACE STREET(1948); SWORD OF THE AVENGER(1948)

Cyrus Kendall
DOCKS OF NEW YORK(1945)
Cyrus [Cy] Kendall
SKY MURDER(1940)
Cyrus W. Kendall
PACIFIC LINER(1939); TWELVE CROWDED HOURS(1939); SAINT TAKES OVER, THE(1940); FARGO KID, THE(1941); TARZAN'S NEW YORK ADVENTURE(1942); SCARLET STREET(1945)
Cyrus W. "Cy" Kendall
TROUBLE IN SUNDOWN(1939); PRAIRIE LAW(1940)
David Kendall
LUGGAGE OF THE GODS(1983), d&w
1984
STRIKEBOUND(1984, Aus.)
Dick Kendall
WATCHER IN THE WOODS, THE(1980, Brit.), spec eff
Felicity Kendall
SHAKESPEARE WALLAH(1966, India)
Harry Kendall
Silents
WITHOUT HOPE(1914); JAMESTOWN(1923)
Henry Kendall
FLYING FOOL, THE(1931, Brit.); FRENCH LEAVE(1931, Brit.); HOUSE OPPOSITE, THE(1931, Brit.); RICH AND STRANGE(1932, Brit.); WATCH BEVERLY(1932, Brit.); WHY SAPS LEAVE HOME(1932, Brit.); COUNSEL'S OPINION(1933, Brit.); FLAW, THE(1933, Brit.); GHOST CAMERA, THE(1933, Brit.); GREAT STUFF(1933, Brit.); IRON STAIR, THE(1933, Brit.); KING OF THE RITZ(1933, Brit.); MAN OUTSIDE, THE(1933, Brit.); MAN WHO WON, THE(1933, Brit.); THIS WEEK OF GRACE(1933, Brit.); TIMBUCTOO(1933, Brit.); CRAZY PEOPLE(1934, Brit.); DEATH AT A BROAD-CAST(1934, Brit.); GIRL IN POSSESSION(1934, Brit.); GUEST OF HONOR(1934, Brit.); LEAVE IT TO BLANCHE(1934, Brit.); MAN I WANT, THE(1934, Brit.); SOMETIMES GOOD(1934, Brit.); WITHOUT YOU(1934, Brit.); LEND ME YOUR WIFE(1935, Brit.); THREE WITNESSES(1935, Brit.); WIFE OR TWO, A(1935, Brit.); MURDER ON THE SET(1936, Brit.); MYSTERIOUS MR. DAVIS, THE(1936, Brit.); SHADOW, THE(1936, Brit.); TWELVE GOOD MEN(1936, Brit.); COMPULSORY WIFE, THE(1937, Brit.); IT'S NOT CRICKET(1937, Brit.), a, w; ROMANCE AND RICHES(1937, Brit.); SIDE STREET ANGEL(1937, Brit.); TAKE A CHANCE(1937, Brit.); SCHOOL FOR HUS-BANDS(1939, Brit.); BUTLER'S DILEMMA, THE(1943, Brit.); FACTS OF LOVE(1949, Brit.); HELTER SKELTER(1949, Brit.); MURDER WILL OUT(1953, Brit.); ALLIGATOR NAMED DAISY, AN(1957, Brit.); NOTHING BARRED(1961, Brit.); SHADOW OF THE CAT, THE(1961, Brit.)
Jackie Kendall
WILD SCENE, THE(1970)
Jo Kendall
SCUM(1979, Brit.)
Kay Kendall
CHAMPAGNE CHARLIE(1944, Brit.); DREAMING(1944, Brit.); FIDDLERS THREE(1944, Brit.); CAESAR AND CLEOPATRA(1946, Brit.); WALTZ TIME(1946, Brit.); DANCE HALL(1950, Brit.); NIGHT AND THE CITY(1950, Brit.); HAPPY GO LOVELY(1951, Brit.); CURTAIN UP(1952, Brit.); DEAD ON COURSE(1952, Brit.); IT STARTED IN PARADISE(1952, Brit.); GENEVIEVE(1953, Brit.); MEET MR. LUCI-FER(1953, Brit.); MY HEART GOES CRAZY(1953, Brit.); SHADOW MAN(1953, Brit.); WOMAN IN HIDING(1953, Brit.); DOCTOR IN THE HOUSE(1954, Brit.); FAST AND LOOSE(1954, Brit.); CONSTANT HUSBAND, THE(1955, Brit.); LADY GODIVA RIDES AGAIN(1955, Brit.); QUENTIN DURWARD(1955, Brit.); SQUARE RING, THE(1955, Brit.); ABDULLAH'S HAREM(1956, Brit./Egypt.); SIMON AND LAURA(1956, Brit.); LES GIRLS(1957); RELUCTANT DEBUTANTE, THE(1958); ONCE MORE, WITH FEEL-ING(1960)
Kenneth Kendall
RECKLESS MOMENTS, THE(1949); BRAIN, THE(1965, Ger./Brit.); THEY CAME FROM BEYOND SPACE(1967, Brit.)
Lee Kendall
YOUNG JESSE JAMES(1960)
Marie Kendall
SAY IT WITH FLOWERS(1934, Brit.); HAPPY DAYS ARE HERE AGAIN(1936, Brit.)
Merelina Kendall
THAT LUCKY TOUCH(1975, Brit.)
1984
1984(1984, Brit.)
Nick Kendall
FERRY TO HONG KONG(1959, Brit.)
Preston Kendall
Misc. Silents
HEADS WIN(1919), d
Richard Kendall
VENGEANCE(1964), ph; VOICES(1979)
Robert Kendall
SONG OF SCHEHERAZADE(1947); CASBAH(1948); WOMEN OF PITCAIRN IS-LAND, THE(1957); MA BARKER'S KILLER BROOD(1960)
Sarah Kendall
SLAYER, THE(1982)
Sury Kendall
CRAZE(1974, Brit.)
Suzy Kendall
UP JUMPED A SWAGMAN(1965, Brit.); LIQUIDATOR, THE(1966, Brit.); SAND-WICH MAN, THE(1966, Brit.); PENTHOUSE, THE(1967, Brit.); PSYCHO-CIRCUS(1967, Brit.); TO SIR, WITH LOVE(1967, Brit.); UP THE JUNCTION(1968, Brit.); 30 IS A DANGEROUS AGE, CYNTHIA(1968, Brit.); FRAULEIN DOKTOR(1969, Ital./Yugo.); GAMBLERS, THE(1969); BIRD WITH THE CRYSTAL PLUMAGE, THE(1970, Ital./Ger.); DARKER THAN AMBER(1970); ASSAULT(1971, Brit.); DIARY OF A CLOIS-TERED NUN(1973, Ital./Fr./Ger.); FEAR IS THE KEY(1973); TALES THAT WITNESS MADNESS(1973, Brit.); TORSO(1974, Ital.)
Misc. Talkies
SPASMO(1976)
Tony Kendall
MACHINE GUN McCAIN(1970, Ital.); PEOPLE WHO OWN THE DARK(1975, Span.); YETI(1977, Ital.)
Misc. Talkies
ISLAND OF LOST GIRLS(1975); OIL(1977, Ital.)

Tony Kendall [L. Stella]
WHAT!(1965, Fr./Brit./Ital.)
Tony Kendall [Luciano Stella]
SERENADE FOR TWO SPIES(1966, Ital./Ger.)
Victor Kendall
ATLANTIC(1929 Brit.), w; FLYING SCOTSMAN, THE(1929, Brit.), w; HIGH SEAS(1929, Brit.), w; LADY FROM THE SEA, THE(1929, Brit.), w; NOT SO QUIET ON THE WESTERN FRONT(1930, Brit.), w; YOUNG WOODLEY(1930, Brit.), w; FASCI-NATION(1931, Brit.), w; GABLES MYSTERY, THE(1931, Brit.), w; LOVE STORM, THE(1931, Brit.), w; NIGHT BIRDS(1931, Brit.), w; MAID OF THE MOUNTAINS, THE(1932, Brit.), w; MONEY FOR NOTHING(1932, Brit.), w; CHARMING DECEIV-ER, THE(1933, Brit.), w; DICK TURPIN(1933, Brit.), w; SLEEPLESS NIGHTS(1933, Brit.), w; GABLES MYSTERY, THE(1938, Brit.), w; MEET MR. PENNY(1938, Brit.), w; NIGHT ALONE(1938, Brit.), w; SAVE A LITTLE SUNSHINE(1938, Brit.), w; DEAD MEN ARE DANGEROUS(1939, Brit.), w; CHUMP AT OXFORD, A(1940); MY SON, MY SON!(1940); NEW MOON(1940); MYSTERY OF ROOM 13(1941, Brit.), w; RAGE IN HEAVEN(1941)
Silents
WEEKEND WIVES(1928, Brit.), w
William Kendall
KING'S CUP, THE(1933, Brit.); THAT'S A GOOD GIRL(1933, Brit.); DOCTOR'S ORDERS(1934, Brit.); DEBT OF HONOR(1936, Brit.); SKY'S THE LIMIT, THE(1937, Brit.); SWEET DEVIL(1937, Brit.); THIS'LL MAKE YOU WHISTLE(1938, Brit.); BLIND FOLLY(1939, Brit.); DANCE LITTLE LADY(1954, Brit.); ONE WAY TICKET TO HELL(1955); JUMPING FOR JOY(1956, Brit.); IDOL ON PARADE(1959, Brit.); LEFT, RIGHT AND CENTRE(1959); STRICTLY CONFIDENTIAL(1959, Brit.); MAN WITH THE GREEN CARNATION, THE(1960, Brit.); SANDS OF THE DESERT(1960, Brit.); TOUCH OF LARCENY, A(1960, Brit.); HOUSE OF FRIGHT(1961); LIVE NOW–PAY LATER(1962, Brit.); GREAT ST. TRINIAN'S TRAIN ROBBERY, THE(1966, Brit.); JOKERS, THE(1967, Brit.); ASSASSINATION BUREAU, THE(1969, Brit.)
Patricia Kendall-John
GREEK TYCOON, THE(1978)
Janos Kende
WINTER WIND(1970, Fr./Hung.), ph; ROME WANTS ANOTHER CAESAR(1974, Ital.), ph; FORBIDDEN RELATIONS(1983, Hung.), ph
Lt. Col. Edward R. Kendel, USAF
ETERNAL SEA, THE(1955), tech adv
Joy Kendell
MORE THAN A SECRETARY(1936)
Victor Kendell
MISS V FROM MOSCOW(1942)
William Kendell
MAGIC NIGHT(1932, Brit.)
Tibor Kenderesi
1984
BRADY'S ESCAPE(1984, U.S./Hung.)
Betty Kendig
IN LOVE WITH LIFE(1934)
J. D. Kendis
JAWS OF THE JUNGLE(1936), p; CRUSADE AGAINST RACKETS(1937), p; PAROLED FROM THE BIG HOUSE(1938), p; WOLVES OF THE SEA(1938), p; SECRETS OF A MODEL(1940), p; YOUTH AFLAME(1945), p
William Kendis
UNDERSEA GIRL(1957)
Bayard Kendrick
LAST EXPRESS, THE(1938), w; BRIGHT VICTORY(1951), w
Baynard Kendrick
EYES IN THE NIGHT(1942), w
Bertie Kendrick
RIDING HIGH(1937, Brit.)
Henry Kendrick
DEVIL'S ANGELS(1967); HELL'S BELLES(1969); HAWMPS!(1976); PURSUIT OF D.B. COOPER, THE(1981)
Henry M. Kendrick
1984
REVENGE OF THE NERDS(1984)
Jack Kendrick
VICTORY(1981)
Lola Kendrick
TWO TICKETS TO BROADWAY(1951); NIGHT RUNNER, THE(1957); WIL-LARD(1971)
Richard Kendrick
SLEEPING CITY, THE(1950); MAN ON A STRING(1960)
Ruby Kendrick
Silents
BLIND HUSBANDS(1919)
Eddie Kendrix
BUS IS COMING, THE(1971)
Mel Keneally
CROWD ROARS, THE(1932)
Thomas Keneally
LIBIDO(1973, Aus.), w; DEVIL'S PLAYGROUND, THE(1976, Aus.); CHANT OF JIMMIE BLACKSMITH, THE(1980, Aus.), a, w
Alexander Kenedi
LIKELY STORY, A(1947), w
Alexander G. Kenedi
MARRY THE BOSS' DAUGHTER(1941), w
Kitty Kenehan
MR. H. C. ANDERSEN(1950, Brit.)
Errett LeRoy Kenepp
Misc. Silents
MAN NOBODY KNOWS, THE(1925), d
Seow Teow Keng
SAINT JACK(1979)
Alexa Kenin
LITTLE DARLINGS(1980); HONKYTONK MAN(1982)
Maya Kenin
PURSUIT OF HAPPINESS, THE(1971)

Geoffrey Kenion
DEVILS OF DARKNESS, THE(1965, Brit.); DR. JEKYLL AND SISTER HYDE(1971, Brit.)
Don Kenito
CAESAR AND CLEOPATRA(1946, Brit.)
Sahara Kenji
MAN FROM THE EAST, THE(1961, Jap.)
Jacqueline Kenley
IT'S A BIG COUNTRY(1951)
Thelma Kenley
Misc. Silents
SKY-EYE(1920)
John Kenlo [Julius Weinstein]
MODERN MARRIAGE, A(1962), p, w
Robert Kenly
1984
SECRET PLACES(1984, Brit.)
William Kenn
SACCO AND VANZETTI(1971, Ital./Fr.)
Conover Kennard
1984
SCANDALOUS(1984)
John B. Kennard
WHITE HUNTER(1965), ph
Max Kennard
GOODBYE PORK PIE(1981, New Zealand)
Victor Kennard
Silents
IRON RING, THE(1917); JOURNEY'S END(1918)
Misc. Silents
BURGLAR, THE(1917); SOUL OF BUDDHA, THE(1918); VOLUNTEER, THE(1918)
James Kennaway
VIOLENT PLAYGROUND(1958, Brit.), w; TUNES OF GLORY(1960, Brit.), w; MIND BENDERS, THE(1963, Brit.), w; SHOES OF THE FISHERMAN, THE(1968), w; BATTLE OF BRITAIN, THE(1969, Brit.), w; BROTHERLY LOVE(1970, Brit.), w
Bob Kenneally
TWO RODE TOGETHER(1961)
Pam Kenneally
SKATEBOARD(1978)
Phil Kenneally
PRETTY BOY FLOYD(1960); TOMB OF THE UNDEAD(1972), ph; LITTLE CIGARS(1973); HARRY AND WALTER GO TO NEW YORK(1976)
Philip Kenneally
MAN ON A TIGHTROPE(1953); SPELL OF THE HYPNOTIST(1956); DEAD TO THE WORLD(1961); LITTLE BIG MAN(1970); OUTFIT, THE(1973); MAC ARTHUR(1977)
Robert Kenneally
RIDE THE WILD SURF(1964); THREE NUTS IN SEARCH OF A BOLT(1964)
Adam Kennedy
UNTIL THEY SAIL(1957); COURT-MARTIAL OF BILLY MITCHELL, THE(1955); BAILOUT AT 43,000(1957); MEN IN WAR(1957); TALL STRANGER, THE(1957); DOVE, THE(1974, Brit.), w; DOMINO PRINCIPLE, THE(1977), w; RAISE THE TITANIC(1980, Brit.), w
Alfred C. Kennedy
PAINTED WOMAN(1932), w
Alita Kennedy
1984
SCANDALOUS(1984)
Ann Kennedy
Misc. Silents
SCAR OF SHAME, THE(1927)
Arthur Kennedy
BAD MEN OF MISSOURI(1941); CITY, FOR CONQUEST(1941); HIGH SIERRA(1941); HIGHWAY WEST(1941); KNOCKOUT(1941); STRANGE ALIBI(1941); DESPERATE JOURNEY(1942); THEY DIED WITH THEIR BOOTS ON(1942); AIR FORCE(1943); DEVOTION(1946); BOOMERANG(1947); CHEYENNE(1947); CHAMPION(1949); CHICAGO DEADLINE(1949); TOO LATE FOR TEARS(1949); WALKING HILLS, THE(1949); WINDOW, THE(1949); GLASS MENAGERIE, THE(1950); BRIGHT VICTORY(1951); RED MOUNTAIN(1951); BEND OF THE RIVER(1952); GIRL IN WHITE, THE(1952); LUSTY MEN, THE(1952); RANCHO NOTORIOUS(1952); CRASH-OUT(1955); DESPERATE HOURS, THE(1955); IMPULSE(1955, Brit.); MAN FROM LARAMIE, THE(1955); NAKED DAWN, THE(1955); TRIAL(1955); RAWHIDE YEARS, THE(1956); PEYTON PLACE(1957); TWILIGHT FOR THE GODS(1958); HOME IS THE HERO(1959, Ireland); SOME CAME RUNNING(1959); SUMMER PLACE, A(1959); ELMER GANTRY(1960); CLAUDELLE INGLISH(1961); MURDER SHE SAID(1961, Brit.); ADVENTURES OF A YOUNG MAN(1962); BARABBAS(1962, Ital.); LAWRENCE OF ARABIA(1962, Brit.); CHEYENNE AUTUMN(1964); ITALIANO BRAVA GENTE(1965, Ital./USSR); JOY IN THE MORNING(1965); MURIETA(1965, Span.); FANTASTIC VOYAGE(1966); NEVADA SMITH(1966); MONDAY'S CHILD(1967, U.S./Arg.); ANZIO(1968, Ital.); DAY OF THE EVIL GUN(1968); MINUTE TO PRAY, A SECOND TO DIE, A(1968, Ital.); HAIL, HERO!(1969); SHARK(1970, U.S./Mex.); GLORY BOY(1971); DON'T OPEN THE WINDOW(1974, Ital.); SENTINEL, THE(1977); TEMPTER, THE(1978, Ital.); CAULDRON OF DEATH, THE(1979, Ital.); HUMANOID, THE(1979, Ital.); COVERT ACTION(1980, Ital.)
Misc. Talkies
FAMILY KILLER(1975); BRUTAL JUSTICE(1978)
Silents
PRUNELLA(1918)
Aubrey Kennedy
FACE ON THE BARROOM FLOOR, THE(1932), p, w
Aubrey M. Kennedy
Misc. Silents
LIQUID GOLD(1919), d; SKY-EYE(1920), d
Bert Kennedy
PUBLIC ENEMY'S WIFE(1936); ESCAPE TO GLORY(1940); SEALED CARGO(1951)
Betty Kennedy
CHEECH AND CHONG'S NEXT MOVIE(1980)
Bill Kennedy
BUSSES ROAR(1942); MISSION TO MOSCOW(1943); MURDER ON THE WATERFRONT(1943); NORTHERN PURSUIT(1943); PRINCESS O'ROURKE(1943); TRUCK BUSTERS(1943); CRIME BY NIGHT(1944); DESTINATION TOKYO(1944); HOLLY-

WOOD CANTEEN(1944); MR. SKEFFINGTON(1944); ESCAPE IN THE DESERT(1945); RHAPSODY IN BLUE(1945); BACHELOR'S DAUGHTERS, THE(1946); DON'T GAMBLE WITH STRANGERS(1946); THAT BRENNAN GIRL(1946); GANGSTER, THE(1947); NEWS HOUNDS(1947); WEB OF DANGER, THE(1947); I WOULDN'T BE IN YOUR SHOES(1948); IN THIS CORNER(1948); JOAN OF ARC(1948); SOUTHERN YANKEE, A(1948); FORGOTTEN WOMEN(1949); LAW OF THE WEST(1949); SHADOWS OF THE WEST(1949); TRAIL OF THE YUKON(1949); BORDER OUTLAWS(1950); BORDER RANGERS(1950); GUNSLINGERS(1950); PEGGY(1950); STORM OVER WYOMING(1950); TRAIN TO TOMBSTONE(1950); TWO LOST WORLDS(1950); ABILENE TRAIL(1951); CANYON RAIDERS(1951); NEVADA BADMEN(1951); SILVER CITY BONANZA(1951); RED PLANET MARS(1952); I DIED A THOUSAND TIMES(1955); UNCHAINED(1955); MALE AND FEMALE SINCE ADAM AND EVE(1961, Arg.); FUN ON A WEEKEND(1979)
Misc. Talkies
OVERLAND TRAILS(1948); SHERIFF OF MEDICINE BOW, THE(1948); TRIGGERMAN(1948)
Billy Kennedy
I SHOT BILLY THE KID(1950)
Bob Kennedy
KID FROM CLEVELAND, THE(1949)
Burt Kennedy
MAN IN THE VAULT(1956), w; SEVEN MEN FROM NOW(1956), w; GUN THE MAN DOWN(1957), w; TALL T, THE(1957), w; FORT DOBBS(1958), w; RIDE LONESOME(1959), w; YELLOWSTONE KELLY(1959), w; COMANCHE STATION(1960), w; CANADIANS, THE(1961, Brit.), d&w; SIX BLACK HORSES(1962), w; MAIL ORDER BRIDE(1964), d&w; ROUNDERS, THE(1965), d, w; MONEY TRAP, THE(1966), d; RETURN OF THE SEVEN(1966, Span.); WAR WAGON, THE(1967), d; WELCOME TO HARD TIMES(1967), d, w; STAY AWAY, JOE(1968), w; GOOD GUYS AND THE BAD GUYS, THE(1969), d; SUPPORT YOUR LOCAL SHERIFF(1969), d; YOUNG BILLY YOUNG(1969), d, w; DIRTY DINGUS MAGEE(1970), p&d; DESERTER, THE(1971 Ital./Yugo.), d; HANNIE CALDER(1971, Brit.), d; SUPPORT YOUR LOCAL GUNFIGHTER(1971), d; TRAIN ROBBERS(1973), d&w; KILLER INSIDE ME, THE(1976), d; LITTLEST HORSE THIEVES, THE(1977), w
Misc. Talkies
WOLF LAKE(1979), d
Byron Kennedy
MAD MAX(1979, Aus.), p, w; ROAD WARRIOR, THE(1982, Aus.), p
C. Warren Kennedy
FOUR FOR THE MORGUE(1962)
Charles Kennedy
CRIME WITHOUT PASSION(1934)
Cheryl Kennedy
GET CHARLIE TULLY(1976, Brit.)
Clara Genevieve Kennedy
Silents
EYES OF THE HEART(1920), w
Dan Kennedy
FRIENDLY PERSUASION(1956)
Daun Kennedy
FALCON AND THE CO-EDS, THE(1943); HIGHER AND HIGHER(1943); FALCON OUT WEST, THE(1944); MADEMOISELLE FIFI(1944); SEVEN DAYS ASHORE(1944); SHOW BUSINESS(1944); SALOME, WHERE SHE DANCED(1945); THIS LOVE OF OURS(1945); THRILL OF BRAZIL, THE(1946)
David Kennedy
VORTEX(1982)
Dawn Kennedy
BOWERY BOMBSHELL(1946)
Deborah Kennedy
TIM(1981, Aus.)
Dick Kennedy
PASSION HOLIDAY(1963)
Don Kennedy
ANNAPOLIS STORY, AN(1955); HELL'S OUTPOST(1955); TO HELL AND BACK(1955); UNCHAINED(1955); INVISIBLE INVADERS(1959); SPRING AFFAIR(1960); WALK LIKE A DRAGON(1960); STUNT MAN, THE(1980)
Dorothy Kennedy
STARLIFT(1951); ROOM FOR ONE MORE(1952); DREAM WIFE(1953); JACK SLADE(1953); CRY VENGEANCE(1954); WIRETAPPERS(1956)
Doug Kennedy
ALLIGATOR PEOPLE, THE(1959)
Douglas Kennedy
ARISE, MY LOVE(1940); GHOST BREAKERS, THE(1940); NORTHWEST MOUNTED POLICE(1940); THOSE WERE THE DAYS(1940); WAY OF ALL FLESH, THE(1940); WOMEN WITHOUT NAMES(1940); GREAT MR. NOBODY, THE(1941); MAD DOCTOR, THE(1941); ROUNDUP, THE(1941); ALWAYS TOGETHER(1947); DARK PASSAGE(1947); LIFE WITH FATHER(1947); NORA PRENTISS(1947); POSSESSED(1947); STALLION ROAD(1947); THAT HAGEN GIRL(1947); UNFAITHFUL, THE(1947); UNSUSPECTED, THE(1947); VOICE OF THE TURTLE, THE(1947); DECISION OF CHRISTOPHER BLAKE, THE(1948); EMBRACEABLE YOU(1948); JOHNNY BELINDA(1948); ONE SUNDAY AFTERNOON(1948); ROMANCE ON THE HIGH SEAS(1948); TO THE VICTOR(1948); WHIPLASH(1948); ADVENTURES OF DON JUAN(1949); EAST SIDE, WEST SIDE(1949); FIGHTING MAN OF THE PLAINS(1949); FLAXY MARTIN(1949); FOUNTAINHEAD, THE(1949); JOHN LOVES MARY(1949); LOOK FOR THE SILVER LINING(1949); ONE LAST FLING(1949); RANGER OF CHEROKEE STRIP(1949); SOUTH OF RIO(1949); SOUTH OF ST. LOUIS(1949); CARIBOO TRAIL, THE(1950); CHAIN GANG(1950); CONVICTED(1950); MONTANA(1950); REVENUE AGENT(1950); CALLAWAY WENT THATAWAY(1951); CHINA CORSAIR(1951); I WAS AN AMERICAN SPY(1951); INDIAN UPRISING(1951); LION HUNTERS, THE(1951); OH! SUSANNA(1951); TEXAS RANGERS, THE(1951); FOR MEN ONLY(1952); FORT OSAGE(1952); HOODLUM EMPIRE(1952); RIDE THE MAN DOWN(1952); ALL-AMERICAN, THE(1953); GUN BELT(1953); JACK MCCALL, DESPERADO(1953); MEXICAN MANHUNT(1953); SAFARI DRUMS(1953); SAN ANTONE(1953); SEA OF LOST SHIPS(1953); TORPEDO ALLEY(1953); WAR PAINT(1953); BIG CHASE, THE(1954); CRY VENGEANCE(1954); LONE GUN, THE(1954); MASSACRE CANYON(1954); RAILS INTO LARAMIE(1954); SITTING BULL(1954); ETERNAL SEA, THE(1955); STRANGE LADY IN TOWN(1955); WYOMING RENEGADES(1955); LAST WAGON, THE(1956); STRANGE INTRUDER(1956); WIRETAPPERS(1956); CHICAGO CONFIDENTIAL(1957); HELL'S CROSSROADS(1957); LAST OF THE BADMEN(1957); ROCKABILLY BABY(1957); BONNIE PARKER STORY, THE(1958); LONE RANGER AND THE LOST CITY OF

GOLD, THE(1958); LONE TEXAN(1959); AMAZING TRANSPARENT MAN, THE(1960); FLIGHT OF THE LOST BALLOON(1961); FASTEST GUITAR ALIVE, THE(1967); VALLEY OF MYSTERY(1967); DESTRUCTORS, THE(1968)

Douglas R. Kennedy
LAST TRAIN FROM BOMBAY(1952); LAND UNKNOWN, THE(1957)

Duan Kennedy
GIRL RUSH(1944); NIGHT IN PARADISE, A(1946)

E. J. Kennedy
MACUSHLA(1937, Brit.); RIVER OF UNREST(1937, Brit.); SCRUFFY(1938, Brit.); GENTLE GUNMAN, THE(1952, Brit.); YOU CAN'T BEAT THE IRISH(1952, Brit.)

Earl Kennedy
PROJECT X(1949), w

Ed Kennedy
Silents
RACING FOR LIFE(1924); BETTER 'OLE, THE(1926); GAY OLD BIRD, THE(1927)
Misc. Silents
GOING CROOKED(1926)

Edgar Kennedy
THEY HAD TO SEE PARIS(1929); WELCOME DANGER(1929); BAD COMPANY(1931); QUICK MILLIONS(1931); CARNIVAL BOAT(1932); HOLD'EM JAIL(1932); LITTLE ORPHAN ANNIE(1932); PENGUIN POOL MURDER, THE(1932); ROCKABYE(1932); WESTWARD PASSAGE(1932); CROSSFIRE(1933); DUCK SOUP(1933); PROFESSIONAL SWEETHEART(1933); SCARLET RIVER(1933); SON OF THE BORDER(1933); TILLIE AND GUS(1933); ALL OF ME(1934); HEAT LIGHTNING(1934); KID MILLIONS(1934); KING KELLY OF THE U.S.A(1934); MONEY MEANS NOTHING(1934); MURDER ON THE BLACKBOARD(1934); TWENTIETH CENTURY(1934); WE'RE RICH AGAIN(1934); COWBOY MILLIONAIRE(1935); FLIRTING WITH DANGER(1935); GRIDIRON FLASH(1935); LITTLE BIG SHOT(1935); LIVING ON VELVET(1935); MARINES ARE COMING, THE(1935); RENDEZVOUS AT MIDNIGHT(1935); SILVER STREAK, THE(1935); WOMAN WANTED(1935); $1,000 A MINUTE(1935); BRIDE COMES HOME(1936); FATAL LADY(1936); MAD HOLIDAY(1936); RETURN OF JIMMY VALENTINE, THE(1936); ROBIN HOOD OF EL DORADO(1936); SAN FRANCISCO(1936); SMALL TOWN GIRL(1936); THREE MEN ON A HORSE(1936); YOURS FOR THE ASKING(1936); DOUBLE WEDDING(1937); HOLLYWOOD HOTEL(1937); STAR IS BORN, A(1937); SUPER SLEUTH(1937); TRUE CONFESSION(1937); WHEN'S YOUR BIRTHDAY?(1937); BLACK DOLL, THE(1938); HEY! HEY! U.S.A.(1938, Brit.); PECK'S BAD BOY WITH THE CIRCUS(1938); SCANDAL STREET(1938); CHARLIE MC CARTHY, DETECTIVE(1939); EVERYTHING'S ON ICE(1939); IT'S A WONDERFUL WORLD(1939); LAUGH IT OFF(1939); LITTLE ACCIDENT(1939); BRIDE WORE CRUTCHES, THE(1940); DR. CHRISTIAN MEETS THE WOMEN(1940); LI'L ABNER(1940); MARGIE(1940); QUARTERBACK, THE(1940); SANDY GETS HER MAN(1940); SANDY IS A LADY(1940); WHO KILLED AUNT MAGGIE?(1940); BLONDIE IN SOCIETY(1941); PUBLIC ENEMIES(1941); REMEDY FOR RICHES(1941); HILLBILLY BLITZKRIEG(1942); IN OLD CALIFORNIA(1942); PARDON MY STRIPES(1942); SNUFFY SMITH, YARD BIRD(1942); THERE'S ONE BORN EVERY MINUTE(1942); AIR RAID WARDENS(1943); CRAZY HOUSE(1943); FALCON STRIKES BACK, THE(1943); GIRL FROM MONTEREY, THE(1943); HITLER'S MADMAN(1943); IT HAPPENED TOMORROW(1944); ANCHORS AWEIGH(1945); CAPTAIN TUGBOAT ANNIE(1945); HEAVEN ONLY KNOWS(1947); UNFAITHFULLY YOURS(1948); MY DREAM IS YOURS(1949); MAD WEDNESDAY(1950)
Misc. Talkies
COSMO JONES, CRIME SMASHER(1943)
Silents
TILLIE'S PUNCTURED ROMANCE(1914); SUBMARINE PIRATE, A(1915); ACROSS THE PACIFIC(1926); OH, WHAT A NURSE!(1926); WEDDING BILL$(1927)
Misc. Silents
WRONG MR. WRIGHT, THE(1927)

Edith Kennedy
Silents
MOLLY ENTANGLED(1917), w; BRAVEST WAY, THE(1918), w; JANE GOES A' WOOING(1919), w; ROMANCE AND ARABELLA(1919), w; CROOKED STREETS(1920), w; FOOD FOR SCANDAL(1920), w; OH, LADY, LADY(1920), w; DON'T CALL ME LITTLE GIRL(1921), w; SEEING'S BELIEVING(1922), w; YOUTH TO YOUTH(1922), w

Edith M. Kennedy
Silents
PAIR OF SILK STOCKINGS, A(1918), w

Edmund Kennedy
CASTLE SINISTER(1932, Brit.)

Edward Kennedy
LANDSLIDE(1937, Brit.); PANIC IN THE STREETS(1950)

Evelyn Kennedy
FREAKY FRIDAY(1976), cos

Fiona Kennedy
WICKER MAN, THE(1974, Brit.)

Flo Kennedy
BORN IN FLAMES(1983)

Florence Kennedy
WHO SAYS I CAN'T RIDE A RAINBOW!(1971)
Misc. Talkies
BUSH PILOT(1947)

Florynce Kennedy
LANDLORD, THE(1970)

Francine Kennedy
DOWN TO EARTH(1947)

Frank Kennedy
HELL'S BELLES(1969); RIO LOBO(1970); NIGHT OF THE LEPUS(1972)

Fred Kennedy
SHE WORE A YELLOW RIBBON(1949); RIO GRANDE(1950); CHARGE AT FEATHER RIVER, THE(1953); SEARCHERS, THE(1956); HORSE SOLDIERS, THE(1959)

Gayle Kennedy
1984
TAIL OF THE TIGER(1984, Aus.)

George Kennedy
CONCORDE, THE–AIRPORT '79(; LITTLE SHEPHERD OF KINGDOM COME(1961); LONELY ARE THE BRAVE(1962); SILENT WITNESS, THE(1962); CHARADE(1963); MAN FROM THE DINERS' CLUB, THE(1963); HUSH... HUSH, SWEET CHARLOTTE(1964); ISLAND OF THE BLUE DOLPHINS(1964); MC HALE'S NAVY(1964); STRAIT-JACKET(1964); FLIGHT OF THE PHOENIX, THE(1965); IN HARM'S WAY(1965); MIRAGE(1965); SHENANDOAH(1965); SONS OF KATIE ELDER, THE(1965); COOL HAND LUKE(1967); DIRTY DOZEN, THE(1967, Brit.); HURRY SUNDOWN(1967); BALLAD OF JOSIE(1968); BANDOLERO!(1968); LEGEND OF LYLAH CLARE, THE(1968); PINK JUNGLE, THE(1968); THE BOSTON STRANGLER, THE(1968); GAILY, GAILY(1969); GOOD GUYS AND THE BAD GUYS, THE(1969); GUNS OF THE MAGNIFICENT SEVEN(1969); AIRPORT(1970); DIRTY DINGUS MAGEE(1970); ...TICK...TICK...TICK...(1970); ZIGZAG(1970); FOOLS' PARADE(1971); CAHILL, UNITED STATES MARSHAL(1973); LOST HORIZON(1973); AIRPORT 1975(1974); EARTHQUAKE(1974); THUNDERBOLT AND LIGHTFOOT(1974); EIGER SANCTION, THE(1975); HUMAN FACTOR, THE(1975); AIRPORT '77(1977); BRASS TARGET(1978); DEATH ON THE NILE(1978, Brit.); MEAN DOG BLUES(1978); THE DOUBLE McGUFFIN(1979); DEATH SHIP(1980, Can.); JUST BEFORE DAWN(1980); STEEL(1980); VIRUS(1980, Jap.); MODERN ROMANCE(1981); SEARCH AND DESTROY(1981); WACKO(1983)
1984
BOLERO(1984); CHATTANOOGA CHOO CHOO(1984); RARE BREED(1984); SAVAGE DAWN(1984)
Misc. Talkies
HOTWIRE(1980); STRIKING BACK(1981); JUPITER MENACE, THE(1982)

Gerald Kennedy
MANGO TREE, THE(1981, Aus.)

Gerard Kennedy
ELIZA FRASER(1976, Aus.); RAW DEAL(1977, Aus.); IRISHMAN, THE(1978, Aus.); NEWSFRONT(1979, Aus.); FATTY FINN(1980, Aus.); LAST OF THE KNUCKLEMEN, THE(1981, Aus.)
Misc. Talkies
MAMA'S GONE A-HUNTING(1976); PLAINS OF HEAVEN, THE(1982)

Grace Kennedy
APPLE, THE(1980 U.S./Ger.)

Graham Kennedy
THEY'RE A WEIRD MOB(1966, Aus.); DON'S PARTY(1976, Aus.); ODD ANGRY SHOT, THE(1979, Aus.); CLUB, THE(1980, Aus.); RETURN OF CAPTAIN INVINCIBLE, THE(1983, Aus./U.S.)
1984
KILLING FIELDS, THE(1984, Brit.)

Harold Kennedy
HANNAH LEE(1953); SECURITY RISK(1954); RUN FOR COVER(1955); EVERYTHING'S DUCKY(1961)

Harold J. Kennedy
CHAIN OF CIRCUMSTANCE(1951); CAPTIVE CITY(1952); IT SHOULD HAPPEN TO YOU(1954); RIOT IN CELL BLOCK 11(1954); IF HE HOLLERS, LET HIM GO(1968)

Hazel Kennedy
Silents
SNOB, THE(1924)

Heather Kennedy
Misc. Talkies
GETTING IT ON(1983)

Iris Kennedy
FORTY THOUSAND HORSEMEN(1941, Aus.)

J. P. Kennedy
BLOCKADE(1928, Brit.)

J.Z. Kennedy
GLADIATORS, THE(1970, Swed.)

Jack Kennedy
SKYLINE(1931); LAST MILE, THE(1932); LOVE AFFAIR(1932); PAINTED WOMAN(1932); WOMAN FROM MONTE CARLO, THE(1932); SKYWAY(1933); HE COULDN'T TAKE IT(1934); KID MILLIONS(1934); PERSONALITY KID, THE(1934); SIXTEEN FATHOMS DEEP(1934); TWO HEADS ON A PILLOW(1934); HIS NIGHT OUT(1935); MARY JANE'S PA(1935); SCHOOL FOR GIRLS(1935); SHE GETS HER MAN(1935); NEVADA(1936); RED RIVER VALLEY(1936); SAN FRANCISCO(1936); BORN TO THE WEST(1937); CAPTAINS COURAGEOUS(1937); GANGSTER'S BOY(1938); ROMANCE OF THE LIMBERLOST(1938); I AM A CRIMINAL(1939); APE, THE(1940); EMERGENCY SQUAD(1940); FATAL HOUR, THE(1940); PUBLIC ENEMIES(1941); STRANGE CASE OF DR. RX, THE(1942); UNDERDOG, THE(1943)

James Kennedy
MY HEART GOES CRAZY(1953, Brit.); LOCAL HERO(1983, Brit.)

Jay Richard Kennedy
TO THE ENDS OF THE EARTH(1948), w; I'LL CRY TOMORROW(1955), w; CHAIRMAN, THE(1969), w

Jayne Kennedy
BODY AND SOUL(1981)
Misc. Talkies
MUTHERS, THE(1976); BIG TIME(1977); DEATH FORCE(1978)

Jim Kennedy
NIGHT VISITOR, THE(1970, Swed./U.S.)

Jimmy Kennedy
AROUND THE TOWN(1938, Brit.)

Jo Kennedy
STARSTRUCK(1982, Aus.)

Joe Kennedy
SAINTS AND SINNERS(1949, Brit.)

John Kennedy
PAROLE(1936); RED SKIES OF MONTANA(1952); WINNING TEAM, THE(1952); SLEEPING BEAUTY(1959), anim; BUCK AND THE PREACHER(1972); DEADLY TRACKERS(1973); CONRACK(1974)

John William Kennedy
HAPPY BIRTHDAY, GEMINI(1980)

Joseph P. Kennedy
TRESPASSER, THE(1929), p; WHAT A WIDOW(1930), p
Silents
QUEEN KELLY(1929), p

Joyce Kennedy
BRACELETS(1931, Brit.); MAN FROM CHICAGO, THE(1931, Brit.); SAY IT WITH MUSIC(1932, Brit.); DANGEROUS GROUND(1934, Brit.); RETURN OF BULLDOG DRUMMOND, THE(1934, Brit.); BLACK MASK(1935, Brit.); DEBT OF HONOR(1936, Brit.); DOMMED CARGO(1936, Brit.); HAIL AND FAREWELL(1936, Brit.); TWELVE GOOD MEN(1936, Brit.); BIG FELLA(1937, Brit.); NURSEMAID WHO DISAPPEARED, THE(1939, Brit.)

June Kennedy
EARTH VS. THE SPIDER(1958)
Kathleen Kennedy
E.T. THE EXTRA-TERRESTRIAL(1982), p
Kathy Lee Kennedy
1984
INITIATION, THE(1984)
Ken Kennedy
SILENT WITNESS, THE(1962), p&d; IRON ANGEL(1964), d&w; VELVET TRAP, THE(1966), d&w
Misc. Talkies
KINO, THE PADRE ON HORSEBACK(1977), d
Kenn Kennedy
CRUEL SEA, THE(1953)
Kevin Kennedy
PINOCCHIO IN OUTER SPACE(1965, U.S./Bel.)
King Kennedy
ON PROBATION(1935); SEVEN DAYS LEAVE(1942); HIGHER AND HIGHER(1943)
L.F. Kennedy
SAVAGE GOLD(1933), ed
Larry Kennedy
PLEDGEMASTERS, THE(1971)
Laura Kennedy
OFFENDERS, THE(1980)
Laurie Kennedy
WEDDING PARTY, THE(1969)
Lem F. Kennedy
Silents
DOWN UPON THE SUWANNEE RIVER(1925), d
Misc. Silents
POWER WITHIN, THE(1921), d
Leo Kennedy
Silents
CAPRICE OF THE MOUNTAINS(1916)
Leon Isaac Kennedy
PENITENTIARY(1979); BODY AND SOUL(1981), a, w; PENITENTIARY II(1982); LONE WOLF McQUADE(1983)
Lyn Crost Kennedy
RAIDERS, THE(1952), w
Lyn Kennedy
TEENAGE GANG DEBS(1966)
Ludovic Kennedy
HEAVENS ABOVE!(1963, Brit.); 10 RILLINGTON PLACE(1971, Brit.), w
Madge Kennedy
MARRYING KIND, THE(1952); MAIN STREET TO BROADWAY(1953); RAINS OF RANCHIPUR, THE(1955); CATERED AFFAIR, THE(1956); LUST FOR LIFE(1956); THREE BAD SISTERS(1956); HOUSEBOAT(1958); NICE LITTLE BANK THAT SHOULD BE ROBBED, A(1958); NORTH BY NORTHWEST(1959); PLUNDERERS OF PAINTED FLATS(1959); LET'S MAKE LOVE(1960); THEY SHOOT HORSES, DON'T THEY?(1969); BABY MAKER, THE(1970); DAY OF THE LOCUST, THE(1975); MARATHON MAN(1976)
Silents
BABY MINE(1917); FAIR PRETENDER, THE(1918); OUR LITTLE WIFE(1918); PERFECT LADY, A(1918); DAUGHTER OF MINE(1919); DOLLARS AND SENSE(1920); TRUTH, THE(1920)
Misc. Silents
NEARLY MARRIED(1917); DANGER GAME, THE(1918); FRIEND HUSBAND(1918); KINGDOM OF YOUTH, THE(1918); SERVICE STAR, THE(1918); DAY DREAMS(1919); LEAVE IT TO SUSAN(1919); STRICTLY CONFIDENTIAL(1919); THROUGH THE WRONG DOOR(1919); BLOOMING ANGEL, THE(1920); GIRL WITH A JAZZ HEART, THE(1920); GIRL WITH THE JAZZ HEART, THE(1920); HELP YOURSELF(1920); HIGHEST BIDDER, THE(1921); OH MARY BE CAREFUL(1921); PURPLE HIGHWAY, THE(1923); THREE MILES OUT(1924); BAD COMPANY(1925); LYING WIVES(1925); SCANDAL STREET(1925); OH, BABY!(1926)
Margaret Kennedy
CONSTANT NYMPH, THE(1933, Brit.), w; ESCAPE ME NEVER(1935, Brit.), w; OLD CURIOSITY SHOP, THE(1935, Brit.), w; DREAMING LIPS(1937, Brit.), w; PRISON WITHOUT BARS(1939, Brit.), w; STOLEN LIFE(1939, Brit.), w; MIDAS TOUCH, THE(1940, Brit.), w; MOZART(1940, Brit.), w; RETURN TO YESTERDAY(1940, Brit.), w; CONSTANT NYMPH, THE(1943), w; MAN IN GREY, THE(1943, Brit.), w; RHYTHM SERENADE(1943, Brit.), w; YOU CAN'T DO WITHOUT LOVE(1946, Brit.), w; ESCAPE ME NEVER(1947), w; TAKE MY LIFE(1948, Brit.), w; IF THIS BE SIN(1950, Brit.), w
Marma Kennedy
WONDER BAR(1934)
Mary Jo Kennedy
WILD RACERS, THE(1968); PADDY(1970, Irish)
Mattie Kennedy
ISN'T IT ROMANTIC?(1948)
Maxwell Kennedy
I KNOW WHERE I'M GOING(1947, Brit.)
Merna Kennedy
BARNUM WAS RIGHT(1929); BROADWAY(1929); SKINNER STEPS OUT(1929); EMBARRASSING MOMENTS(1930); RAMPANT AGE, THE(1930); WORLDLY GOODS(1930); MIDNIGHT SPECIAL(1931); ALL-AMERICAN, THE(1932); GAY BUCKAROO, THE(1932); GHOST VALLEY(1932); LADY WITH A PAST(1932); RED-HAIRED ALIBI, THE(1932); ARIZONA TO BROADWAY(1933); BIG CHANCE, THE(1933); DON'T BET ON LOVE(1933); EASY MILLIONS(1933); EMERGENCY CALL(1933); LAUGHTER IN HELL(1933); POLICE CALL(1933); SON OF A SAILOR(1933); I LIKE IT THAT WAY(1934); JIMMY THE GENT(1934)
Silents
CIRCUS, THE(1928)
Myrna Kennedy
COME ON TARZAN(1933)
Neal Kennedy
ANOTHER DAWN(1937)
Neil Kennedy
POPE JOAN(1972, Brit.); RULING CLASS, THE(1972, Brit.); TALES THAT WITNESS MADNESS(1973, Brit.); JUBILEE(1978, Brit.)

Noel Kennedy
PRINCE AND THE PAUPER, THE(1937)
Pat Kennedy
MY BRILLIANT CAREER(1980, Aus.)
Patricia Kennedy
OFFICE PICNIC, THE(1974, Aus.); GETTING OF WISDOM, THE(1977, Aus.)
Patrick Kennedy
MONITORS, THE(1969), ed; TRIBES(1970), ed; WELCOME HOME, SOLDIER BOYS(1972), ed; CINDERELLA LIBERTY(1973), ed; HEROES(1977), ed; SCOTT JOPLIN(1977), ed; BIG FIX, THE(1978), ed; AIRPLANE!(1980), ed; SAVAGE HARVEST(1981), ed; MR. MOM(1983), ed
Phyllis Kennedy
STAGE DOOR(1937); ARTISTS AND MODELS ABROAD(1938); JOY OF LIVING(1938); MOTHER CAREY'S CHICKENS(1938); VIVACIOUS LADY(1938); EAST SIDE OF HEAVEN(1939); LOVE AFFAIR(1939); DR. CHRISTIAN MEETS THE WOMEN(1940); RHYTHM ON THE RIVER(1940); CAUGHT IN THE DRAFT(1941); UNFINISHED BUSINESS(1941); LADY IN A JAM(1942); TIME TO KILL(1942); YANKEE DOODLE DANDY(1942); CONEY ISLAND(1943); HEAVENLY BODY, THE(1943); IS EVERYBODY HAPPY?(1943); LAUGH YOUR BLUES AWAY(1943); ONCE UPON A TIME(1944); PARTNERS IN TIME(1946); LIVING IN A BIG WAY(1947); WHERE THERE'S LIFE(1947); SMART WOMAN(1948); CHICAGO DEADLINE(1949); ONCE MORE, MY DARLING(1949); YOU'RE MY EVERYTHING(1949); THREE LITTLE WORDS(1950); WAC FROM WALLA WALLA, THE(1952); MY FAIR LADY(1964)
Richard Kennedy
J.W. COOP(1971); LIMIT, THE(1972); CALIFORNIA SPLIT(1974); FAREWELL, MY LOVELY(1975); SIX PACK ANNIE(1975); TOM HORN(1980)
Misc. Talkies
CAPTURE OF BIGFOOT, THE(1979)
Rick Kennedy
1984
RAZORBACK(1984, Aus.)
Rigg Kennedy
DAYTON'S DEVILS(1968); JESSIE'S GIRLS(1976); SLUMBER PARTY MASSACRE, THE(1982)
Riggs Kennedy
HOT SUMMER WEEK(1973, Can.)
Robert Kennedy
ON THE RUN(1969, Brit.); LEO THE LAST(1970, Brit.)
Ron Kennedy
MOONLIGHTER, THE(1953); KILLERS FROM SPACE(1954); HIDDEN GUNS(1956); TEA AND SYMPATHY(1956); BATTLE OF BLOOD ISLAND(1960); SPRING AFFAIR(1960); GIRLS ON THE BEACH(1965); HARLOW(1965)
Rowan Kennedy
COMING OF AGE(1938, Brit.), w
Ryan Kennedy
SLUMBER PARTY MASSACRE, THE(1982)
S. K. Kennedy
DUEL IN THE JUNGLE(1954, Brit.), w
Sarah Kennedy
WORKING GIRLS, THE(1973)
Misc. Talkies
TELEPHONE BOOK, THE(1971); SAMMY SOMEBODY(1976)
Sean Kennedy
JOURNEY TO SHILOH(1968); MADIGAN(1968)
Sheila Kennedy
SPRING BREAK(1983)
1984
ELLIE(1984); FIRST TURN-ON!, THE(1984)
Suella Kennedy
TWICE UPON A TIME(1983), w
Suzanne Kennedy
1984
THEY'RE PLAYING WITH FIRE(1984)
Thomas Kennedy
Silents
KISMET(1920)
Tiny Kennedy
FIREBALL JUNGLE(1968)
Tom Kennedy
TRUE TO LIFE(1943); BIG NEWS(1929); COHENS AND KELLYS IN ATLANTIC CITY, THE(1929); GLAD RAG DOLL, THE(1929); SHANNONS OF BROADWAY, THE(1929); SEE AMERICA THIRST(1930); CAUGHT(1931); GANG BUSTER, THE(1931); IRON MAN, THE(1931); IT PAYS TO ADVERTISE(1931); MONKEY BUSINESS(1931); DEVIL IS DRIVING, THE(1932); IF I HAD A MILLION(1932); LADY AND GENT(1932); MADISON SQUARE GARDEN(1932); NIGHT AFTER NIGHT(1932); PACK UP YOUR TROUBLES(1932); BLONDIE JOHNSON(1933); LAWYER MAN(1933); MAN OF THE FOREST(1933); SHE DONE HIM WRONG(1933); 42ND STREET(1933); DOWN TO THEIR LAST YACHT(1934); HOLLYWOOD PARTY(1934); STRICTLY DYNAMITE(1934); SHE COULDN'T TAKE IT(1935); HOLLYWOOD BOULEVARD(1936); POPPY(1936); RETURN OF SOPHIE LANG, THE(1936); ADVENTUROUS BLONDE(1937); ARMORED CAR(1937); BEHIND THE HEADLINES(1937); BIG SHOT, THE(1937); CASE OF THE STUTTERING BISHOP, THE(1937); CRASHING HOLLYWOOD(1937); FLY-AWAY BABY(1937); FORTY NAUGHTY GIRLS(1937); LIVING ON LOVE(1937); MARRIED BEFORE BREAKFAST(1937); MARRY THE GIRL(1937); SHE HAD TO EAT(1937); SLAVE SHIP(1937); SMART BLONDE(1937); SWING IT SAILOR(1937); WISE GIRL(1937); BLONDES AT WORK(1938); CRIME RING(1938); GO CHASE YOURSELF(1938); HE COULDN'T SAY NO(1938); MAKING THE HEADLINES(1938); TORCHY BLANE IN CHINATOWN(1938); TORCHY BLANE IN PANAMA(1938); TORCHY GETS HER MAN(1938); COVERED TRAILER, THE(1939); DAY THE BOOKIES WEPT, THE(1939); LONG SHOT, THE(1939); PARDON OUR NERVE(1939); SOCIETY LAWYER(1939); THESE GLAMOUR GIRLS(1939); TORCHY PLAYS WITH DYNAMITE(1939); TORCHY RUNS FOR MAYOR(1939); ANGEL FROM TEXAS, AN(1940); CURTAIN CALL(1940); FLOWING GOLD(1940); MEXICAN SPITFIRE OUT WEST(1940); MILLIONAIRE PLAYBOY(1940); POP ALWAYS PAYS(1940); REMEMBER THE NIGHT(1940); SPORTING BLOOD(1940); ANGELS WITH BROKEN WINGS(1941); GREAT SWINDLE, THE(1941); MEXICAN SPITFIRE'S BABY(1941); OFFICER AND THE LADY, THE(1941); SAILORS ON LEAVE(1941); THIEVES FALL OUT(1941); BROADWAY(1942); MEXICAN SPITFIRE'S ELEPHANT(1942); PARDON MY STRIPES(1942); WILDCAT(1942); DIX-

IE(1943); HERE COMES ELMER(1943); HIT PARADE OF 1943(1943); IS EVERYBODY HAPPY?(1943); LADIES' DAY(1943); O, MY DARLING CLEMENTINE(1943); PETTICOAT LARCENY(1943); RIDING HIGH(1943); SO'S YOUR UNCLE(1943); STAGE DOOR CANTEEN(1943); AND THE ANGELS SING(1944); MOONLIGHT AND CACTUS(1944); ONCE UPON A TIME(1944); PRACTICALLY YOURS(1944); PRINCESS AND THE PIRATE, THE(1944); ROSIE THE RIVETER(1944); MAN WHO WALKED ALONE, THE(1945); SPANISH MAIN, THE(1945); VOICE OF THE WHISTLER(1945); BRINGING UP FATHER(1946); MIGHTY MCGURK, THE(1946); BURNING CROSS, THE(1947); DANGEROUS YEARS(1947); PRETENDER, THE(1947); DEVIL'S CARGO, THE(1948); JINX MONEY(1948); PALEFACE, THE(1948); FIGHTING FOOLS(1949); MUTINEERS, THE(1949); SQUARE DANCE JUBILEE(1949); THEY LIVE BY NIGHT(1949); THUNDER IN THE PINES(1949); BORDER RANGERS(1950); TRIPLE TROUBLE(1950); HAVANA ROSE(1951); LET'S GO NAVY(1951); GOLD FEVER(1952); HOLD THAT LINE(1952); INVASION U.S.A.(1952); ROAD AGENT(1952); SOME LIKE IT HOT(1959); IT'S A MAD, MAD, MAD, MAD WORLD(1963); BOUNTY KILLER, THE(1965); TIME WALKER(1982), d
Silents
ISLAND OF INTRIGUE, THE(1919); MICKEY(1919); AFRAID TO FIGHT(1922); FLIRT, THE(1922); IF YOU BELIEVE IT, IT'S SO(1922); OUR LEADING CITIZEN(1922); SCARAMOUCHE(1923); AS MAN DESIRES(1925); FEARLESS LOVER, THE(1925); HIGH AND HANDSOME(1925); BEHIND THE FRONT(1926); BETTER 'OLE, THE(1926); YANKEE SENOR, THE(1926); FIREMAN, SAVE MY CHILD(1927); SILVER VALLEY(1927); ALIAS THE DEACON(1928); HOLD 'EM YALE!(1928); MARKED MONEY(1928); NONE BUT THE BRAVE(1928); TILLIE'S PUNCTURED ROMANCE(1928); WIFE SAVERS(1928)
Misc. Silents
WITH NAKED FISTS(1923); SIR LUMBERJACK(1926); WE'RE IN THE NAVY NOW(1926); LOVE OVER NIGHT(1928)
William Kennedy
MAKE YOUR OWN BED(1944)
1984
COTTON CLUB, THE(1984), w; FEAR CITY(1984)
Alastair Kenneil
HERO(1982, Brit.)
Caroline Kenneil
HERO(1982, Brit.)
John Kennell
RIDE THE WILD SURF(1964)
Sheila Kennelly
NO. 96(1974, Aus.)
Elly Kenner
1984
BLACK ROOM, THE(1984), d
Warren Kenner
SOUNDER, PART 2(1976)
Rosalind Kennerdale
BROKEN MELODY(1938, Aus.)
Norman Kenneson
LET'S SCARE JESSICA TO DEATH(1971), set d
Harry Kenneth
Misc. Silents
EAGLE'S NEST(1915)
Keith Kenneth
LIMEHOUSE BLUES(1934); CARDINAL RICHELIEU(1935); CLIVE OF INDIA(1935); DANIEL BOONE(1936); I COVER THE WAR(1937); LITTLE PRINCESS, THE(1939); PARIS HONEYMOON(1939); WE ARE NOT ALONE(1939); BOMBAY CLIPPER(1942)
George Kennett
PRIVATE LIVES OF ADAM AND EVE, THE(1961), w; BOY, DID I GET A WRONG NUMBER!(1966), w
John Kennett
PERIL FOR THE GUY(1956, Brit.), w
Bill Kenney
PARDON MY SARONG(1942); DIAMONDS ARE FOREVER(1971, Brit.), art d; DRIVE, HE SAID(1971); BAKER'S HAWK(1976), prod d; DANDY, THE ALL AMERICAN GIRL(1976), art d; DRUM(1976), art d; CHOIRBOYS, THE(1977), art d; UNCLE JOE SHANNON(1978), prod d; CHANGE OF SEASONS, A(1980), set d; MOUNTAIN MEN, THE(1980), prod d; EDDIE MACON'S RUN(1983), prod d; TOUGH ENOUGH(1983), prod d
1984
TANK(1984), prod d; WINDY CITY(1984), prod d
Clyde Kenney
LONELY TRAIL, THE(1936)
Colin Kenney
CLUE OF THE NEW PIN, THE(1929, Brit.)
Silents
HONEYMOON AHEAD(1927, Brit.)
Don Kenney
PLAYGIRLS AND THE BELLBOY, THE(1962,Ger.); TONIGHT FOR SURE(1962)
Douglas Kenney
BETWEEN THE LINES(1977); NATIONAL LAMPOON'S ANIMAL HOUSE(1978), a, w; CADDY SHACK(1980), p, w
Elena Kenney
STRANGE BREW(1983), set d
Horace Kenney
LOVE, LIFE AND LAUGHTER(1934, Brit.); ROAD HOUSE(1934, Brit.); COCK O' THE NORTH(1935, Brit.); LET THE PEOPLE SING(1942, Brit.); WE'LL SMILE AGAIN(1942, Brit.); THEATRE ROYAL(1943, Brit.); HERE COMES THE SUN(1945, Brit.); COUNTER BLAST(1948, Brit.); DEVIL'S PLOT, THE(1948, Brit.); SOMETHING IN THE CITY(1950, Brit.)
Jack Kenney
JEALOUSY(1934); PERFECT SPECIMEN, THE(1937); RECKLESS LIVING(1938); HELL'S KITCHEN(1939); LAUGH IT OFF(1939); WYOMING OUTLAW(1939); GANG'S ALL HERE(1941); LARCENY, INC.(1942); SLEEPY LAGOON(1943); SUSPENSE(1946); CATTLE TOWN(1952); HOUSE OF WAX(1953); SHE'S BACK ON BROADWAY(1953); SOUTH SEA WOMAN(1953); COUNTRY GIRL, THE(1954); CRIME WAVE(1954); CHICAGO CONFIDENTIAL(1957); TIN STAR, THE(1957); INSIDE THE MAFIA(1959); INVISIBLE INVADERS(1959); VICE RAID(1959); CAGE OF EVIL(1960); THREE CAME TO KILL(1960); WALKING TARGET, THE(1960)

Silents
NORTHERN CODE(1925); BEAUTY AND BULLETS(1928)
Misc. Silents
HIDDEN LOOT(1925)
James Kenney
YOUNG MR. PITT, THE(1942, Brit.); CIRCUS BOY(1947, Brit.); VICE VERSA(1948, Brit.); OUTSIDER, THE(1949, Brit.); TRAPPED BY THE TERROR(1949, Brit.); CAPTAIN HORATIO HORNBLOWER(1951, Brit.); GENTLE GUNMAN, THE(1952, Brit.); MAGIC BOX, THE(1952, Brit.); OUTCAST OF THE ISLANDS(1952, Brit.); SLASHER, THE(1953, Brit.); GOOD DIE YOUNG, THE(1954, Brit.); RED DRESS, THE(1954, Brit.); DOCTOR AT SEA(1955, Brit.); LOVE MATCH, THE(1955, Brit.); SEA SHALL NOT HAVE THEM, THE(1955, Brit.); ABOVE US THE WAVES(1956, Brit.); BATTLE HELL(1956, Brit.); DYNAMITERS, THE(1956, Brit.); SON OF A STRANGER(1957, Brit.); BEASTS OF MARSEILLES, THE(1959, Brit.); HIDDEN HOMICIDE(1959, Brit.); NO SAFETY AHEAD(1959, Brit.); AMBUSH IN LEOPARD STREET(1962, Brit.)
Jan Kenney
NOT QUITE DECENT(1929)
Joan Kenney
BACHELOR IN PARIS(1953, Brit.)
Joel P. Kenney
MIDNIGHT MADNESS(1980)
June Kenney
CITY STORY(1954); SAGA OF THE VIKING WOMEN AND THEIR VOYAGE TO THE WATERS OF THE GREAT SEA SERPENT, THE(1957); SORORITY GIRL(1957); TEENAGE DOLL(1957); HOT CAR GIRL(1958); BLOODLUST(1959); CAT BURGLAR, THE(1961)
Ron Kenney
WILD RIDERS(1971), makeup
Sean Kenney
MACHISMO-40 GRAVES FOR 40 GUNS(1970); CORPSE GRINDERS, THE(1972)
Misc. Talkies
MANSON MASSACRE, THE(1976)
Sean David Kenney
TERMINAL ISLAND(1973)
Edith Kennick
Silents
WESTERN LUCK(1924)
Alan Kennington
TERROR HOUSE(1942, Brit.), w; YOU CAN'T ESCAPE(1955, Brit.), w
Ann Kennington
KISS THE BRIDE GOODBYE(1944, Brit.)
Jill Kennington
BLOW-UP(1966, Brit.)
Lyn Kennington
WHERE EAGLES DARE(1968, Brit.)
Capt. Kenny
CANON CITY(1948)
Clyde Kenny
ENTER ARSENE LUPIN(1944)
Colin Kenny
GRUMPY(1930); LIMEHOUSE BLUES(1934); LOST LADY, A(1934); MYSTERY OF MR. X, THE(1934); PAINTED VEIL, THE(1934); CAPTAIN BLOOD(1935); DARK ANGEL, THE(1935); MAN WHO RECLAIMED HIS HEAD, THE(1935); THANK YOU, JEEVES(1936); TILL WE MEET AGAIN(1936); BULLDOG DRUMMOND COMES BACK(1937); FIREFLY, THE(1937); MAID OF SALEM(1937); ADVENTURES OF ROBIN HOOD, THE(1938); BOOLOO(1938); LIGHT THAT FAILED, THE(1939); MURDER IS NEWS(1939); RAFFLES(1939); TOWER OF LONDON(1939); WE ARE NOT ALONE(1939); EARL OF CHICAGO, THE(1940); FOREIGN CORRESPONDENT(1940); HOUSE OF THE SEVEN GABLES, THE(1940); SEA HAWK, THE(1940); RAGE IN HEAVEN(1941); JOURNEY FOR MARGARET(1942); MRS. MINIVER(1942); TWO TICKETS TO LONDON(1943); LODGER, THE(1944); NONE BUT THE LONELY HEART(1944); PEARL OF DEATH, THE(1944); PRINCESS AND THE PIRATE, THE(1944); KITTY(1945); MINISTRY OF FEAR(1945); LOCKET, THE(1946); NIGHT AND DAY(1946); THREE STRANGERS(1946); CALCUTTA(1947); EXILE, THE(1947); MOSS ROSE(1947); MOURNING BECOMES ELECTRA(1947); KISS THE BLOOD OFF MY HANDS(1948); JOHNNY STOOL PIGEON(1949); THAT FORSYTE WOMAN(1949); STORY OF THREE LOVES, THE(1953); DESIREE(1954); MY FAIR LADY(1964); WHERE LOVE HAS GONE(1964)
Silents
ROMANCE OF TARZAN, THE(1918); TARZAN OF THE APES(1918); LAST STRAW, THE(1920); BLACK BEAUTY(1921); LITTLE LORD FAUNTLEROY(1921); SEEING'S BELIEVING(1922); WATCH HIM STEP(1922)
Misc. Silents
UNEXPECTED PLACES(1918); SILENT PAL(1925)
Elizabeth Kenny
SISTER KENNY(1946), w
Jack Kenny
MANHATTAN MELODRAMA(1934); WE LIVE AGAIN(1934); TOAST OF NEW YORK, THE(1937); YOU CAN'T CHEAT AN HONEST MAN(1939); STRIKE UP THE BAND(1940); MISSION TO MOSCOW(1943); ATLANTIC CITY(1944); DEADLINE AT DAWN(1946); MY DREAM IS YOURS(1949); THESE WILDER YEARS(1956); HONG KONG CONFIDENTIAL(1958); TOUGHEST GUN IN TOMBSTONE(1958); GAMBLER WORE A GUN, THE(1961); GUN FIGHT(1961); WHEN THE CLOCK STRIKES(1961); YOU HAVE TO RUN FAST(1961); MAN WHO SHOT LIBERTY VALANCE, THE(1962)
James Kenny
GLORY AT SEA(1952, Brit.); BIG HAND FOR THE LITTLE LADY, A(1966)
Joan Kenny
YOU CAN'T BEAT THE IRISH(1952, Brit.)
June Kenny
ATTACK OF THE PUPPET PEOPLE(1958); SPIDER, THE(1958)
Ken Kenny
ONE FLEW OVER THE CUCKOO'S NEST(1975)
Paul Kenny
EXTERMINATORS, THE(1965 Fr.), w
Sean Kenny
I THANK A FOOL(1962, Brit.), prod d, md; STOP THE WORLD-I WANT TO GET OFF(1966, Brit.), prod d
Misc. Talkies
RUNNING WITH THE DEVIL(1973)

Thomas D. Kenny
YOUNG GIRLS OF ROCHEFORT, THE(1968, Fr.)
William Kenny
CARRIE(1976), art d
Kenny Baker's Dozen
BLACK GLOVE(1954, Brit.)
Kenny Ball and His Jazzmen
RING-A-DING RHYTHM(1962, Brit. 73m Amicus/COL bw (G.B: IT'S TRAD, DAD!);
SING AND SWING(1964, Brit.)
Harry Kenoi
BLACK BIRD, THE(1975)
Larry Kenoras
1984
SACRED GROUND(1984)
Tony Kenrick
NOBODY'S PERFEKT(1981), w
Robert Kensinger
OSTERMAN WEEKEND, THE(1983)
Patsy Kensit
GREAT GATSBY, THE(1974); BLUE BIRD, THE(1976); HANOVER STREET(1979,
Brit.)
Mr. Kent
STUCK ON YOU(1983)
1984
STUCK ON YOU(1984)
Mrs Kent
Silents
FOOLISH WIVES(1920)
Allegra Kent
MIDSUMMER NIGHT'S DREAM, A(1966)
April Kent
I'VE LIVED BEFORE(1956); ROCK, PRETTY BABY(1956); INCREDIBLE SHRINK-
ING MAN, THE(1957); TAMMY AND THE BACHELOR(1957)
Arnold Kent
MEXICAN SPITFIRE'S ELEPHANT(1942); SAN ANTONIO(1945)
Silents
WOMAN ON TRIAL, THE(1927); EASY COME, EASY GO(1928)
Misc. Silents
HULA(1927); WORLD AT HER FEET, THE(1927); WOMAN DISPUTED, THE(1928)
Arthur Kent
CLASS OF 1984(1982, Can.), p
Barbara Kent
LONESOME(1928); SHAKEDOWN, THE(1929); WELCOME DANGER(1929); DUMB-
BELLS IN ERMINE(1930); FEET FIRST(1930); NIGHT RIDE(1930); WHAT MEN
WANT(1930); CHINATOWN AFTER DARK(1931); GRIEF STREET(1931); INDIS-
CREET(1931); BEAUTY PARLOR(1932); EMMA(1932); EXPOSED(1932); FREIGHT-
ERS OF DESTINY(1932); NO LIVING WITNESS(1932); PRIDE OF THE LEGION,
THE(1932); VANITY FAIR(1932); BIG PAYOFF, THE(1933); HER FORGOTTEN
PAST(1933); MY MOTHER(1933); OLIVER TWIST(1933); MARRIAGE ON APPROV-
AL(1934); GUARD THAT GIRL(1935); OLD MAN RHYTHM(1935); SWELL-
HEAD(1935); UNDER AGE(1941)
Misc. Talkies
SELF DEFENSE(1933)
Silents
FLESH AND THE DEVIL(1926); PROWLERS OF THE NIGHT(1926); DROPKICK,
THE(1927); LONE EAGLE, THE(1927); NO MAN'S LAW(1927); STOP THAT
MAN(1928)
Misc. Silents
SMALL BACHELOR, THE(1927); MODERN MOTHERS(1928); THAT'S MY DAD-
DY(1928)
Bertha Kent
Silents
JANE EYRE(1921)
Burton Kent
HUMAN TARGETS(1932), p
Carl Kent
THEY WON'T BELIEVE ME(1947); FALCON IN HOLLYWOOD, THE(1944); MUSIC
IN MANHATTAN(1944); MY PAL, WOLF(1944); FALCON IN SAN FRANCISCO,
THE(1945); JOHNNY ANGEL(1945); TWO O'CLOCK COURAGE(1945); DE-
SPERATE(1947); SOUND OF FURY, THE(1950)
Cecil Kent
NORSEMAN, THE(1978)
Charles Kent
Silents
CHRISTIAN, THE(1914); FLORIDA ENCHANTMENT, A(1914); MR. BARNES OF
NEW YORK(1914); SYLVIA GRAY(1914); BATTLE CRY OF PEACE, THE(1915); ON
HER WEDDING NIGHT(1915); PRICE FOR FOLLY, A(1915); KENNEDY SQUA-
RE(1916); COUNTERFEIT(1919); MISS DULCIE FROM DIXIE(1919); MAN AND HIS
WOMAN(1920); RAINBOW(1921); SINGLE TRACK, THE(1921); RAGGED EDGE,
THE(1923)
Misc. Silents
MILLION BID, A(1914); HEIGHTS OF HAZARDS, THE(1915); PAWNS OF
MARS(1915); BLUE ENVELOPE MYSTERY, THE(1916); BRITTON OF THE SEV-
ENTH(1916); CHATTEL, THE(1916); ENEMY, THE(1916); ISLAND OF SURPRISE,
THE(1916); ROSE OF THE SOUTH(1916); SUPREME TEMPTATION, THE(1916);
VITAL QUESTION, THE(1916); WHOM THE GODS DESTROY(1916); DUPLICITY OF
HARGRAVES, THE(1917); KITTY MACKAY(1917); MARRIAGE SPECULATION,
THE(1917); QUESTION, THE(1917); SOLDIERS OF CHANCE(1917); GAMBLERS,
THE(1919); PAINTED WORLD, THE(1919); THIN ICE(1919); FORBIDDEN VAL-
LEY(1920); CHARMING DECEIVER, THE(1921); LEOPARDESS, THE(1923)
Christopher Kent
GYPSY FURY(1950, Fr.)
Christopher Kent [Alf Kjellin]
MADAME BOVARY(1949)
Colin Kent
SONG OF THE FORGE(1937, Brit.)
Crauford Kent
SHOW FOLKS(1928); CHARLATAN, THE(1929); COME ACROSS(1929); WOLF OF
WALL STREET, THE(1929); DEVIL TO PAY, THE(1930); GIRL OF THE PORT(1930);
IN THE NEXT ROOM(1930); LADIES LOVE BRUTES(1930); SECOND FLOOR MYS-

TERY, THE(1930); SEVEN KEYS TO BALDPATE(1930); SWEETHEARTS AND
WIVES(1930); THREE FACES EAST(1930); UNHOLY THREE, THE(1930); GRIEF
STREET(1931); TRANSATLANTIC(1931); WOMEN MEN MARRY(1931); FIGHTING
GENTLEMAN, THE(1932); FILE 113(1932); MENACE, THE(1932); PURCHASE PRICE,
THE(1932); SALLY OF THE SUBWAY(1932); SINISTER HANDS(1932); THIRTEENTH
GUEST, THE(1932); WESTERN LIMITED(1932); EAGLE AND THE HAWK,
THE(1933); HER RESALE VALUE(1933); HUMANITY(1933); ONLY YESTER-
DAY(1933); SAILOR BE GOOD(1933); EVELYN PRENTICE(1934); LITTLE MISS
MARKER(1934); WE LIVE AGAIN(1934); I FOUND STELLA PARISH(1935); MAG-
NIFICENT OBSESSION(1935); MAN WHO RECLAIMED HIS HEAD, THE(1935);
MUTINY ON THE BOUNTY(1935); VANESSA, HER LOVE STORY(1935); CHARGE
OF THE LIGHT BRIGADE, THE(1936); DANIEL BOONE(1936); DOWN THE
STRETCH(1936); HITCH HIKE TO HEAVEN(1936); IT COULDN'T HAVE HAP-
PENED–BUT IT DID(1936); O'MALLEY OF THE MOUNTED(1936); NAVY SPY(1937);
TOAST OF NEW YORK, THE(1937); LETTER OF INTRODUCTION(1938); LOVE,
HONOR AND BEHAVE(1938); SERVICE DE LUXE(1938); ROVIN' TUM-
BLEWEEDS(1939); WE ARE NOT ALONE(1939); EARL OF CHICAGO, THE(1940);
FOREIGN CORRESPONDENT(1940); SEA HAWK, THE(1940); INTERNATIONAL
SQUADRON(1941); PARIS CALLING(1941); SHINING VICTORY(1941); YANK IN
THE R.A.F., A(1941); FLIGHT LIEUTENANT(1942); JOURNEY FOR MAR-
GARET(1942); KEEPER OF THE FLAME(1942); CONSTANT NYMPH, THE(1943);
MYSTERIOUS DOCTOR, THE(1943); FOUR JILLS IN A JEEP(1944); LODGER,
THE(1944); DOLLY SISTERS, THE(1945); FATAL WITNESS, THE(1945); KITTY(1945);
DEVOTION(1946); IMPERFECT LADY, THE(1947); SAMSON AND DELILAH(1949);
TEA FOR TWO(1950); PAINTING THE CLOUDS WITH SUNSHINE(1951); PAT AND
MIKE(1952)
Silents
LITTLE MISS BROWN(1915); SIMON THE JESTER(1915); LOVE'S TOLL(1916);
ANTICS OF ANN, THE(1917); DANGER MARK, THE(1918); KILDARE OF
STORM(1918); KNIFE, THE(1918); LOVE FLOWER, THE(1920); JANE EYRE(1921);
SHADOWS OF THE SEA(1922); SHIRLEY OF THE CIRCUS(1922); ABYSMAL BRUTE,
THE(1923); EAGLE'S FEATHER, THE(1923); MOTHERS-IN-LAW(1923); FLOWING
GOLD(1924); LOVER'S LANE(1924); PAINTED FLAPPER, THE(1924); EASY MO-
NEY(1925); MAN AND MAID(1925); PRIDE OF THE FORCE, THE(1925); COLLEGE
DAYS(1926); OUTSIDER, THE(1926); PIRATES OF THE SKY(1927); INTO NO MAN'S
LAND(1928); MANHATTAN KNIGHTS(1928); OLYMPIC HERO, THE(1928); OUT
WITH THE TIDE(1928)
Misc. Silents
NEDRA(1915); PRETENDERS, THE(1915); DOLLARS AND THE WOMAN(1916);
EVIL THEREOF, THE(1916); HER BLEEDING HEART(1916); SORROWS OF HAPPI-
NESS(1916); BROADWAY JONES(1917); DOUBLE CROSSED(1917); THAIS(1917);
BETTER HALF, THE(1918); ORDEAL OF ROSETTA, THE(1918); SONG OF SONGS,
THE(1918); TRAP, THE(1918); CAREER OF KATHERINE BUSH, THE(1919); GOOD
GRACIOUS ANNABELLE(1919); CLOTHES(1920); OTHER MEN'S SHOES(1920);
YOUTHFUL FOLLY(1920); PLAYTHING OF BROADWAY, THE(1921); HIDDEN
WOMAN, THE(1922); OTHER WOMEN'S CLOTHES(1922); SELF-MADE WIFE,
THE(1923); DADDIES(1924); GUILTY ONE, THE(1924); TURNED UP(1924); VIRTUE'S
REVOLT(1924); SEVEN KEYS TO BALDPATE(1925); HIS DOG(1927); MISSING LINK,
THE(1927); MOTHER(1927); BITTER SWEETS(1928); FOREIGN LEGION, THE(1928)
Craufurd Kent
SOUTH OF SUEZ(1940)
Misc. Silents
SILAS MARNER(1922)
Crawford Kent
BODY AND SOUL(1931); ADVENTURES OF ROBIN HOOD, THE(1938)
Misc. Silents
DOLLARS AND THE WOMAN(1920)
Daisy Kent
Silents
WEST OF THE RAINBOW'S END(1926), w
David Kent
TWO RODE TOGETHER(1961); UNDERWORLD U.S.A.(1961); HUD(1963); NORSE-
MAN, THE(1978)
Don Kent
HARD, FAST, AND BEAUTIFUL(1951)
Dorothea Kent
AUGUST WEEK-END(1936, Brit.); FLYING HOSTESS(1936); MORE THAN A
SECRETARY(1936); AS GOOD AS MARRIED(1937); CARNIVAL QUEEN(1937); GIRL
WITH IDEAS, A(1937); PRESCRIPTION FOR ROMANCE(1937); SOME BLONDES
ARE DANGEROUS(1937); GOODBYE BROADWAY(1938); HAVING WONDERFUL
TIME(1938); LAST EXPRESS, THE(1938); STRANGE FACES(1938); YOUNG FUGI-
TIVES(1938); YOUTH TAKES A FLING(1938); MILLION DOLLAR LEGS(1939);
RISKY BUSINESS(1939); SHE MARRIED A COP(1939); CROSS COUNTRY RO-
MANCE(1940); DANGER AHEAD(1940); FLIGHT ANGELS(1940); NO, NO NANET-
TE(1940); IT STARTED WITH EVE(1941); CALL OF THE CANYON(1942); KING OF
THE COWBOYS(1943); STAGE DOOR CANTEEN(1943); ARMY WIVES(1944);
CAROLINA BLUES(1944); PIN UP GIRL(1944); TEN CENTS A DANCE(1945); BE-
HIND THE MASK(1946); MISSING LADY, THE(1946); IT HAPPENED ON 5TH
AVENUE(1947)
Earl Kent
GUY NAMED JOE, A(1943)
Elizabeth Kent
DON'T RUSH ME(1936, Brit.); FATHER STEPS OUT(1937, Brit.); NIGHT RIDE(1937,
Brit.); RACING ROMANCE(1937, Brit.); WHY PICK ON ME?(1937, Brit.); DANCE OF
DEATH, THE(1938, Brit.)
Ellie Kent
GARMENT JUNGLE, THE(1957); PAL JOEY(1957); SHADOW ON THE WINDOW,
THE(1957); EVERYTHING'S DUCKY(1961); TWENTY PLUS TWO(1961)
Enid Kent
SOME KIND OF HERO(1982)
Faith Kent
PUMPKIN EATER, THE(1964, Brit.); DR. TERROR'S HOUSE OF HORRORS(1965,
Brit.); OUR MOTHER'S HOUSE(1967, Brit.); CARRY ON AGAIN, DOCTOR(1969, Brit.);
DARWIN ADVENTURE, THE(1972, Brit.)
Gary Kent
BATTLE CRY(1959); RUN HOME SLOW(1965); THRILL KILLERS, THE(1965); MAN
CALLED DAGGER, A(1967), spec eff; HELL'S CHOSEN FEW(1968); PSYCH-
OUT(1968), a, spec eff; SAVAGE SEVEN, THE(1968); TARGETS(1968); SATAN'S
SADISTS(1969); HARD ROAD, THE(1970); HELL'S BLOODY DEVILS(1970); MACHIS-
MO–40 GRAVES FOR 40 GUNS(1970); INSIDE AMY(1975)

George Kent
Misc. Talkies
DEVIL WOLF OF SHADOW MOUNTAIN, THE(1964), d; BODY FEVER(1981)
George Kent
COCKLESHELL HEROES, THE(1955), w
Gerald Kent
LITTLE FRIEND(1934, Brit.); TROUBLE IN THE AIR(1948, Brit.); NO HIGHWAY IN THE SKY(1951, Brit.)
Gia Kent
PRIDE AND PREJUDICE(1940)
Humphrey Kent
WORLD OWES ME A LIVING, THE(1944, Brit.); DICK BARTON STRIKES BACK(1949, Brit.); HORROR OF DRACULA, THE(1958, Brit.); HALF A SIXPENCE(1967, Brit.)
Irene Kent
ONE PLUS ONE(1961, Can.), makeup
J. Crauford Kent
MURDER AT DAWN(1932); LOST JUNGLE, THE(1934)
Jan Kent
THEM NICE AMERICANS(1958, Brit.); SATIN MUSHROOM, THE(1969)
Jane Kent
Silents
TIDES OF FATE(1917)
Janice Kent
1984
CRIMES OF PASSION(1984)
Jean Kent
WHO'S YOUR FATHER?(1935, Brit.); IT'S THAT MAN AGAIN(1943, Brit.); MISS LONDON LTD.(1943, Brit.); WARN THAT MAN(1943, Brit.); BEES IN PARADISE(1944, Brit.); CHAMPAGNE CHARLIE(1944, Brit.); SOLDIER, SAILOR(1944, Brit.); 2,000 WOMEN(1944, Brit.); MADONNA OF THE SEVEN MOONS(1945, Brit.); NOTORIOUS GENTLEMAN(1945, Brit.); CARAVAN(1946, Brit.); CARNIVAL(1946, Brit.); WICKED LADY, THE(1946, Brit.); LOVES OF JOANNA GODDEN, THE(1947, Brit.); MAGIC BOW, THE(1947, Brit.); BOND STREET(1948, Brit.); MAN OF EVIL(1948, Brit.); SMUGGLERS, THE(1948, Brit.); GAY LADY, THE(1949, Brit.); SLEEPING CAR TO TRIESTE(1949, Brit.); WATERLOO ROAD(1949, Brit.); FIVE ANGLES ON MURDER(1950, Brit.); GOOD TIME GIRL(1950, Brit.); TAMING OF DOROTHY, THE(1950, Brit.); BROWNING VERSION, THE(1951, Brit.); RELUCTANT WIDOW, THE(1951, Brit.); BIG FRAME, THE(1953, Brit.); SHADOW OF FEAR(1956, Brit.); PRINCE AND THE SHOWGIRL, THE(1957, Brit.); BONJOUR TRISTESSE(1958); HAUNTED STRANGLER, THE(1958, Brit.); BEYOND THIS PLACE(1959, Brit.); BLUEBEARD'S TEN HONEYMOONS(1960, Brit.); PLEASE TURN OVER(1960, Brit.); SHOUT AT THE DEVIL(1976, Brit.)
Misc. Talkies
MISSION OF THE SEA HAWK(1962, Brit.)
Jeanne Kent
BANK RAIDERS, THE(1958, Brit.)
Jim Kent
HILLBILLYS IN A HAUNTED HOUSE(1967)
John Kent
Misc. Talkies
LOW BLOW, THE(1970)
Jose Kent
TUNNELVISION(1976)
Julia Kent
RAMPARTS WE WATCH, THE(1940)
Karl Kent
LAST BLITZKRIEG, THE(1958)
Keneth Kent
PIRATES OF THE SEVEN SEAS(1941, Brit.); SUICIDE SQUADRON(1942, Brit.); TIME TO KILL, A(1955, Brit.)
Kenneth Kent
NORTH SEA PATROL(1939, Brit.); CASTLE OF CRIMES(1940, Brit.); NIGHT TRAIN(1940, Brit.); HOUSE OF MYSTERY(1941, Brit.); IDOL OF PARIS(1948, Brit.)
Lanita Kent
PASSION HOLIDAY(1963)
Larry Kent
HAUNTED HOUSE, THE(1928); MIDSTREAM(1929); SEAS BENEATH, THE(1931); WOMEN WON'T TELL(1933); GOLDEN ARROW, THE(1936); MAN HUNT(1936); UNFINISHED BUSINESS(1941); DADDY LONG LEGS(1955); MAN CALLED PETER, THE(1955); SWEET SUBSTITUTE(1964, Can.), p,d&w; HIGH(1968, Can.), p,d&w; ONE MAN(1979, Can.); YESTERDAY(1980, Can.), d
Silents
EYES RIGHT(1926); LOVELORN, THE(1927); SEA TIGER, THE(1927); HEAD MAN, THE(1928); HEART OF A FOLLIES GIRL, THE(1928); DEVIL'S APPLE TREE(1929)
Misc. Silents
OBEY THE LAW(1926); HER WILD OAT(1927); MCFADDEN FLATS(1927); WOMEN'S WARES(1927); HANGMAN'S HOUSE(1928); HAUNTED HOUSE, THE(1928); MAD HOUR(1928); SPIRIT OF YOUTH, THE(1929)
Laurence Kent
WHEN TOMORROW DIES(1966, Can.), d, w
Laurence L. Kent
Misc. Talkies
CARESSED(1965), d
Lee Kent
RAGGEDY ANN AND ANDY(1977), ed
Lenny Kent
DISC JOCKEY(1951); THIRTY FOOT BRIDE OF CANDY ROCK, THE(1959); TWIST AROUND THE CLOCK(1961); THRILL OF IT ALL, THE(1963); WHAT A WAY TO GO(1964); HOW SWEET IT IS(1968)
Leon Kent
HUMAN TARGETS(1932)
Misc. Silents
HORSE SENSE(1924); PALS(1925)
Leon D. Kent
Silents
BY RIGHT OF POSSESSION(1917)
Misc. Silents
RED VIRGIN, THE(1915), d

Lois Kent
FOUR HOURS TO KILL(1935); GIRL OF THE OZARKS(1936); HOLLYWOOD BOULEVARD(1936); TOO MANY PARENTS(1936); SCANDAL STREET(1938)
Marjorie Kent
BLONDIE KNOWS BEST(1946); BLONDIE'S LUCKY DAY(1946); LIFE WITH BLONDIE(1946); BLONDIE IN THE DOUGH(1947); BLONDIE'S ANNIVERSARY(1947); BLONDIE'S BIG MOMENT(1947); BLONDIE'S HOLIDAY(1947); BLONDIE'S REWARD(1948); BLONDIE'S SECRET(1948); BLONDIE HITS THE JACKPOT(1949); BLONDIE'S BIG DEAL(1949); BEWARE OF BLONDIE(1950); BLONDIE'S HERO(1950)
Marshall Kent
TEENAGE THUNDER(1957); DECKS RAN RED, THE(1958); LAST VOYAGE, THE(1960); RING OF FIRE(1961)
Martin Kent
1984
NIGHTMARE ON ELM STREET, A(1984), m/1
Mary Kent
RACE STREET(1948); CANADIAN PACIFIC(1949); CARIBOO TRAIL, THE(1950); PLACE IN THE SUN, A(1951)
Michael Kent
SONG OF THE ROAD(1937, Brit.), d&w; DESPERATE ADVENTURE, A(1938); DULCIMER STREET(1948, Brit.); JULIA MISBEHAVES(1948); MANIACS ON WHEELS(1951, Brit.); STONE(1974, Aus.)
Natalie Kent
LARGE ROPE, THE(1953, Brit.)
Norman Kent
WINCHESTER '73(1950); JUBILEE TRAIL(1954)
Paul Kent
RUBY(1977); STAR TREK II: THE WRATH OF KHAN(1982)
Richard Kent
GETTING OF WISDOM, THE(1977, Aus.), art d; HIGH ANXIETY(1977), set d; NIGHTWING(1979), set d
Robert Kent
CAR 99(1935); FOUR HOURS TO KILL(1935); ONE HOUR LATE(1935); TWO FOR TONIGHT(1935); COUNTRY BEYOND, THE(1936); CRIME OF DR. FORBES(1936); DIMPLES(1936); KING OF THE ROYAL MOUNTED(1936); LOVE BEFORE BREAKFAST(1936); REUNION(1936); ANGEL'S HOLIDAY(1937); BORN RECKLESS(1937); CHARLIE CHAN AT MONTE CARLO(1937); NANCY STEELE IS MISSING(1937); STEP LIVELY, JEEVES(1937); THAT I MAY LIVE(1937); GANG BULLETS(1938); GLADIATOR, THE(1938); LITTLE ORPHAN ANNIE(1938); MR. MOTO TAKES A CHANCE(1938); WANTED BY THE POLICE(1938); ALMOST A GENTLEMAN(1939); ANDY HARDY GETS SPRING FEVER(1939); CALLING ALL MARINES(1939); CONVICT'S CODE(1939); EAST SIDE OF HEAVEN(1939); FOR LOVE OR MONEY(1939); SECRET OF DR. KILDARE, THE(1939); ONE MILLION B.C.(1940); BLONDE COMET(1941); SUNSET IN WYOMING(1941); TWILIGHT ON THE TRAIL(1941); FOREST RANGERS, THE(1942); STAGECOACH EXPRESS(1942); FIND THE BLACKMAILER(1943); GUNG HO!(1943); NORTHERN PURSUIT(1943); YANKS AHOY(1943); HOT RHYTHM(1944); WHAT A MAN!(1944); FALCON IN SAN FRANCISCO, THE(1945), w; WHAT NEXT, CORPORAL HARGROVE?(1945); JOE PALOOKA, CHAMP(1946); IT'S A JOKE, SON!(1947), w; FEDERAL AGENT AT LARGE(1950); FOR HEAVEN'S SAKE(1950); RADAR SECRET SERVICE(1950); WILD BLUE YONDER, THE(1952); COUNTRY GIRL, THE(1954); CARNY(1980)
Robert E. Kent
ALL-AMERICAN SWEETHEART(1937), w; PAID TO DANCE(1937), w; HIGHWAY PATROL(1938), w; JUVENILE COURT(1938), w; WHO KILLED GAIL PRESTON?(1938), w; CHARLIE CHAN IN RENO(1939), w; ALWAYS A BRIDE(1940), w; CALLING ALL HUSBANDS(1940), w; FATHER IS A PRINCE(1940), w; GAMBLING ON THE HIGH SEAS(1940), w; KING OF THE LUMBERJACKS(1940), w; LADIES MUST LIVE(1940), w; BAD MEN OF MISSOURI(1941), w; CASE OF THE BLACK PARROT, THE(1941), w; BULLET SCARS(1942), w; CITY OF SILENT MEN(1942), w; I WAS FRAMED(1942), w; SPY SHIP(1942), w; ADVENTURES IN IRAQ(1943), w; FIND THE BLACKMAILER(1943), w; GILDERSLEEVE ON BROADWAY(1943), w; MURDER ON THE WATERFRONT(1943), w; TRUCK BUSTERS(1943), w; GILDERSLEEVE'S GHOST(1944), w; GIRL RUSH(1944), w; RADIO STARS ON PARADE(1945), w; TWO O'CLOCK COURAGE(1945), w; DICK TRACY VS. CUEBALL(1946), w; FALCON'S ADVENTURE, THE(1946), w; GENIUS AT WORK(1946), w; DICK TRACY MEETS GRUESOME(1947), w; GAS HOUSE KIDS GO WEST(1947), w; GAS HOUSE KIDS IN HOLLYWOOD(1947), w; PHILO VANCE RETURNS(1947), w; RED STALLION, THE(1947), w; ASSIGNED TO DANGER(1948), w; RECKLESS MOMENTS, THE(1949), w; LAST OF THE BUCCANEERS(1950), w; WHEN THE REDSKINS RODE(1951), w; BRAVE WARRIOR(1952), w; CALIFORNIA CONQUEST(1952), w; GOLDEN HAWK, THE(1952), w; PATHFINDER, THE(1952), w; THIEF OF DAMASCUS(1952), w; CHARGE OF THE LANCERS(1953), w; FLAME OF CALCUTTA(1953), w; FORT TI(1953), w; SERPENT OF THE NILE(1953), w; SIREN OF BAGDAD(1953), w; DRUMS OF TAHITI(1954), w; IRON GLOVE, THE(1954), w; JESSE JAMES VERSUS THE DALTONS(1954), w; MIAMI STORY, THE(1954), w; INSIDE DETROIT(1955), w; SEMINOLE UPRISING(1955), w; DON'T KNOCK THE ROCK(1956), w; ROCK AROUND THE CLOCK(1956), w; WEREWOLF, THE(1956), w; CHICAGO CONFIDENTIAL(1957), p; GUN DUEL IN DURANGO(1957), p; UTAH BLAINE(1957), w; BADMAN'S COUNTRY(1958), p; CURSE OF THE FACELESS MAN(1958), p; GUNS, GIRLS AND GANGSTERS(1958), p&w; HONG KONG CONFIDENTIAL(1958), p; IT! THE TERROR FROM BEYOND SPACE(1958), p; TOUGHEST GUN IN TOMBSTONE(1958), p; FOUR SKULLS OF JONATHAN DRAKE, THE(1959), p; INSIDE THE MAFIA(1959), p; INVISIBLE INVADERS(1959), p; PIER 5, HAVANA(1959), p; RIOT IN JUVENILE PRISON(1959), p; VICE RAID(1959), p; CAGE OF EVIL(1960), p; DOG'S BEST FRIEND, A(1960), p; GUNFIGHTERS OF ABILENE(1960), p; MUSIC BOX KID, THE(1960), p; NOOSE FOR A GUNMAN(1960), p; OKLAHOMA TERRITORY(1960), p; THREE CAME TO KILL(1960), p; WALKING TARGET, THE(1960), p; BOY WHO CAUGHT A CROOK(1961), p; CLOWN AND THE KID, THE(1961), p; FIVE GUNS TO TOMBSTONE(1961), p; FLIGHT THAT DISAPPEARED, THE(1961), p; FRONTIER UPRISING(1961), p; GAMBLER WORE A GUN, THE(1961), p; GUN FIGHT(1961), p; MARY HAD A LITTLE(1961, Brit.), w; OPERATION BOTTLENECK(1961), p; POLICE DOG STORY, THE(1961), p; SECRET OF DEEP HARBOR(1961), p; WHEN THE CLOCK STRIKES(1961), p; YOU HAVE TO RUN FAST(1961), p; DEADLY DUO(1962), p; GUN STREET(1962), p; INCIDENT IN AN ALLEY(1962), p; SAINTLY SINNERS(1962), p; BEAUTY AND THE BEAST(1963), p; DIARY OF A MADMAN(1963), p, w; TWICE TOLD TALES(1963), p; BLOOD ON THE ARROW(1964), w; GET YOURSELF A COLLEGE GIRL(1964), w; QUICK GUN, THE(1964), w; WHEN THE BOYS MEET THE GIRLS(1965), w; FASTEST GUITAR ALIVE, THE(1967), w; HOT RODS TO HELL(1967), w; TIME TO SING, A(1968), w;

CHRISTINE JORGENSEN STORY, THE(1970), w
Robert F. Kent
TWICE TOLD TALES(1963), w
Roberta Kent
TUNNELVISION(1976)
Sharon Kent
TURN ON TO LOVE(1969)
Misc. Talkies
BEWARE THE BLACK WIDOW(1968)
Stapleton Kent
MAGNIFICENT YANKEE, THE(1950); SHAKEDOWN(1950); LADY AND THE BANDIT, THE(1951); MATING SEASON, THE(1951); SON OF DR. JEKYLL, THE(1951); INVITATION(1952); DONOVAN'S BRAIN(1953); GUYS AND DOLLS(1955)
Suzanne Kent
CHEECH AND CHONG'S NICE DREAMS(1981); HISTORY OF THE WORLD, PART 1(1981); TAKE THIS JOB AND SHOVE IT(1981); PANDEMONIUM(1982)
1984
MASS APPEAL(1984)
Ted Kent
DRAKE CASE, THE(1929), ed; IT CAN BE DONE(1929), ed; FREE LOVE(1930), ed; UP FOR MURDER(1931), ed; THEY JUST HAD TO GET MARRIED(1933), ed; GLAMOUR(1934), ed; LOVE CAPTIVE, THE(1934), ed; ATLANTIC ADVENTURE(1935), ed; BRIDE OF FRANKENSTEIN, THE(1935), ed; NIGHT LIFE OF THE GODS(1935), ed; STRAIGHT FROM THE HEART(1935), ed; MY MAN GODFREY(1936), ed; NEXT TIME WE LOVE(1936), ed; SHOW BOAT(1936), ed; MERRY-GO-ROUND OF 1938(1937), ed; ROAD BACK,THE(1937), ed; LADY IN THE MORGUE(1938), ed; LETTER OF INTRODUCTION(1938), ed; MISSING EVIDENCE(1939), ed; PIRATES OF THE SKIES(1939), ed; SON OF FRANKENSTEIN(1939), ed; SUN NEVER SETS, THE(1939), ed; UNEXPECTED FATHER(1939), ed; DOUBLE ALIBI(1940), ed; ENEMY AGENT(1940), ed; LA CONGA NIGHTS(1940), ed; LOVE, HONOR AND OH, BABY(1940), ed; MARGIE(1940), ed; SEVEN SINNERS(1940), ed; APPOINTMENT FOR LOVE(1941), ed; BACK STREET(1941), ed; BLACK CAT, THE(1941), ed; BURMA CONVOY(1941), ed; MR. DYNAMITE(1941), ed; WOLF MAN, THE(1941), ed; BROADWAY(1942), ed; GHOST OF FRANKENSTEIN, THE(1942), ed; NORTH TO THE KLONDIKE(1942), ed; AMAZING MRS. HOLLIDAY(1943), ed; HERS TO HOLD(1943), ed; HIS BUTLER'S SISTER(1943), ed; CHRISTMAS HOLIDAY(1944), ed; LADY ON A TRAIN(1945), ed; BECAUSE OF HIM(1946), ed; BONZO GOES TO COLLEGE(1952), ed; GUNSMOKE(1953), ed; MAN OF A THOUSAND FACES(1957), ed; RABBIT TRAP, THE(1959), ed
Ted J. Kent
BAD SISTER(1931), ed; SEED(1931), ed; KISS BEFORE THE MIRROR, THE(1933), ed; REMEMBER LAST NIGHT(1935), ed; MAGNIFICENT BRUTE, THE(1936), ed; THREE SMART GIRLS(1937), ed; SERVICE DE LUXE(1938), ed; THREE SMART GIRLS GROW UP(1939), ed; GREEN HELL(1940), ed; SWING IT SOLDIER(1941), ed; MADAME SPY(1942), ed; CAN'T HELP SINGING(1944), ed; PATRICK THE GREAT(1945), ed; MAGNIFICENT DOLL(1946), ed; RUNAROUND, THE(1946), ed; SO GOES MY LOVE(1946), ed; EXILE, THE(1947), ed; TIME OUT OF MIND(1947), ed; FOR THE LOVE OF MARY(1948), ed; LETTER FROM AN UNKNOWN WOMAN(1948), ed; CITY ACROSS THE RIVER(1949), ed; CRISS CROSS(1949), ed; JOHNNY STOOL PIGEON(1949), ed; YES SIR, THAT'S MY BABY(1949), ed; FRENCHIE(1950), ed; SIERRA(1950), ed; SOUTH SEA SINNER(1950), ed; SPY HUNT(1950), ed; BEDTIME FOR BONZO(1951), ed; FLAME OF ARABY(1951), ed; RAGING TIDE, THE(1951), ed; SMUGGLER'S ISLAND(1951), ed; THUNDER ON THE HILL(1951), ed; BATTLE AT APACHE PASS, THE(1952), ed; HORIZONS WEST(1952), ed; MA AND PA KETTLE AT THE FAIR(1952), ed; SCARLET ANGEL(1952), ed; STEEL TOWN(1952), ed; GLASS WEB, THE(1953), ed; GOLDEN BLADE, THE(1953), ed; LAW AND ORDER(1953), ed; WALKING MY BABY BACK HOME(1953), ed; BLACK SHIELD OF FALWORTH, THE(1954), ed; CREATURE FROM THE BLACK LAGOON(1954), ed; DESTRY(1954), ed; FRANCIS JOINS THE WACS(1954), ed; RAILS INTO LARAMIE(1954), ed; FOXFIRE(1955), ed; PRIVATE WAR OF MAJOR BENSON, THE(1955), ed; PURPLE MASK, THE(1955), ed; AWAY ALL BOATS(1956), ed; BEHIND THE HIGH WALL(1956), ed; KELLY AND ME(1957), ed; MAN AFRAID(1957), ed; MIDNIGHT STORY, THE(1957), ed; TAMMY AND THE BACHELOR(1957), ed; FLOOD TIDE(1958), ed; MONSTER ON THE CAMPUS(1958), ed; TIME TO LOVE AND A TIME TO DIE, A(1958), ed; OPERATION PETTICOAT(1959), ed; THIS EARTH IS MINE(1959), ed; THAT TOUCH OF MINK(1962), ed; UGLY AMERICAN, THE(1963), ed; BRASS BOTTLE, THE(1964), ed; FATHER GOOSE(1964), ed; ISLAND OF THE BLUE DOLPHINS(1964), ed; MIRAGE(1965), ed; APPALOOSA, THE(1966), ed; BLINDFOLD(1966), ed; ROUGH NIGHT IN JERICHO(1967), ed
Tony Kent
FIXED BAYONETS(1951); POINT OF TERROR(1971)
Walter Kent
SONG OF THE OPEN ROAD(1944), m; THUNDERING JETS(1958); BLOOD(1974, Brit.), p; SHE DANCES ALONE(1981, Aust./U.S.)
Willard Kent
PRISON SHADOWS(1936); DEATH IN THE SKY(1937)
William Kent
SCARLET LETTER, THE(1934); WHISTLE AT EATON FALLS(1951)
Silents
WHEN KNIGHTHOOD WAS IN FLOWER(1922)
William "Billy" Kent
SATURDAY'S MILLIONS(1933)
William C. Kent
REG'LAR FELLERS(1941), w
Willis Kent
HURRICANE HORSEMAN(1931), p; LAW OF THE TONG(1931), p; BATTLING BUCKAROO(1932), p; CHEYENNE CYCLONE, THE(1932), p; DRIFTER, THE(1932), p; SCARLET WEEKEND, A(1932), w; SINISTER HANDS(1932), p; RACING STRAIN, THE(1933), p, w; SUCKER MONEY(1933), p, w; MAN FROM HELL, THE(1934), p; ROAD TO RUIN(1934), p; ARIZONA BADMAN(1935), p; CHEYENNE TORNADO(1935), p; CIRCLE OF DEATH(1935), p; MAD YOUTH(1940), p,d&w
Silents
LINDA(1929), ed
Calvin Kentfield
CRAZY QUILT, THE(1966)
Douglas Kentish
ENTERTAINING MR. SLOANE(1970, Brit.), p

Elizabeth Kentish
YOU CAN'T ESCAPE(1955, Brit.); IT'S GREAT TO BE YOUNG(1956, Brit.)
Robert Kentman
Silents
FALSE BRANDS(1922)
Sandor Kentner
BOYS OF PAUL STREET, THE(1969, Hung./US)
Earle Kenton
Misc. Silents
LOVE, HONOR AND BEHAVE(1920), d
Eric C. Kenton
LEFTOVER LADIES(1931), d; NAVAL ACADEMY(1941), d; ALWAYS A BRIDESMAID(1943), d; CRAZY HOUSE(1943), p
Eric Kenton
GUILTY AS HELL(1932), d
Erle C. Kenton
FATHER AND SON(1929), d; MEXICALI ROSE(1929), d; SONG OF LOVE, THE(1929), d; ROYAL ROMANCE, A(1930), d; LAST PARADE, THE(1931), d; LOVER COME BACK(1931), d; X MARKS THE SPOT(1931), d; STRANGER IN TOWN(1932), d; BIG EXECUTIVE(1933), d; DISGRACED(1933), d; ISLAND OF LOST SOULS(1933), d; YOU'RE TELLING ME(1934), d; PARTY WIRE(1935), d; PUBLIC MENACE(1935), d; COUNTERFEIT(1936), d; DEVIL'S SQUADRON(1936), d; END OF THE TRAIL(1936), a, d; DEVIL'S PLAYGROUND(1937), d; RACKETEERS IN EXILE(1937), d; SHE ASKED FOR IT(1937), d; LADY OBJECTS, THE(1938), d; LITTLE TOUGH GUYS IN SOCIETY(1938), d; ESCAPE TO PARADISE(1939), d; EVERYTHING'S ON ICE(1939), d; FLYING CADETS(1941), d; MELODY FOR THREE(1941), d; PETTICOAT POLITICS(1941), d; REMEDY FOR RICHES(1941), d; THEY MEET AGAIN(1941), d; FRISCO LILL(1942), d; GHOST OF FRANKENSTEIN, THE(1942), d; NORTH TO THE KLONDIKE(1942), d; PARDON MY SARONG(1942), d; WHO DONE IT?(1942), d; HOW'S ABOUT IT?(1943), d; IT AIN'T HAY(1943), d; HOUSE OF FRANKENSTEIN(1944), d; HOUSE OF DRACULA(1945), d; SHE GETS HER MAN(1945), d; CAT CREEPS, THE(1946), d; LITTLE MISS BIG(1946), d; ONE TOO MANY(1950), d
Silents
LOVE TOY, THE(1926), d; NAME THE WOMAN(1928), d&w; NOTHING TO WEAR(1928), d
Misc. Silents
DOWN ON THE FARM(1920), d; MARRIED LIFE(1920), d; TEA-WITH A KICK(1923), d; DANGER SIGNAL, THE(1925), d; FOOL AND HIS MONEY, A(1925), d; RED HOT TIRES(1925), d; OTHER WOMEN'S HUSBANDS(1926), d; REJUVINATION OF AUNT MARY, THE(1927), d; BARE KNEES(1928), d; COMPANIONATE MARRIAGE, THE(1928), d; GOLF WIDOWS(1928), d; SIDESHOW, THE(1928), d; SPORTING AGE, THE(1928), d; STREET OF ILLUSION, THE(1928), d; TRAIL MARRIAGE(1929), d
Erle Kenton
FROM HELL TO HEAVEN(1933), d; SEARCH FOR BEAUTY(1934), d; BEST MAN WINS, THE(1935), d; GRAND EXIT(1935), d
Silents
SMALL TOWN IDOL, A(1921), d; WEDDING BILL$(1927), d
Misc. Silents
PALM BEACH GIRL, THE(1926), d; SAP, THE(1926), d; GIRL IN THE PULLMAN, THE(1927), d
Hal Kenton
WILD GUITAR(1962)
J. B. Kenton
LAW BEYOND THE RANGE(1935); LIFE BEGINS AT 40(1935)
James B. "Pop" Kenton
WAGON WHEELS(1934); YOU'RE TELLING ME(1934); SHE COULDN'T TAKE IT(1935)
Pop Kenton
BIG EXECUTIVE(1933); SEARCH FOR BEAUTY(1934)
William Kenton
Misc. Silents
BISHOP OF THE OZARKS, THE(1923)
The Kentones
6.5 SPECIAL(1958, Brit.)
Kentucky Mountain Boys
JUMP(1971)
Allan Kenward
SUBMARINE D-1(1937)
Allen Kenward
TWO SMART PEOPLE(1946), w
Allen R. Kenward
CRY HAVOC(1943), w
John Kenworthy
TRON(1982)
Katherine Kenworthy
CAPTAINS COURAGEOUS(1937); WYOMING OUTLAW(1939); TWENTY MULE TEAM(1940)
Caro Kenyatta
TRADER HORN(1973); YOUNG NURSES, THE(1973); CLEOPATRA JONES AND THE CASINO OF GOLD(1975 U. S. Hong Kong)
A. G. Kenyon
Silents
GIRL IN THE DARK, THE(1918), w; NOBODY'S WIFE(1918)
Alan Kenyon
PACIFIC ADVENTURE(1947, Aus.), art d
Albert Kenyon
Silents
NOBODY'S BRIDE(1923), w; SHOOTIN' FOR LOVE(1923), w; MONSTER, THE(1925), w
Charles Kenyon
SHOW BOAT(1929), w; LOST ZEPPELIN(1930), w; OFFICE WIFE, THE(1930), w; RECAPTURED LOVE(1930), w; BOUGHT(1931), w; MILLIE(1931), w; MY PAST(1931), w; NIGHT NURSE(1931), w; PARTY HUSBAND(1931), w; RIVER'S END(1931), w; ALIAS THE DOCTOR(1932), w; CROONER(1932), w; MAN WANTED(1932), w; STREET OF WOMEN(1932), w; UNDER EIGHTEEN(1932), w; I LOVED A WOMAN(1933), w; WORKING MAN, THE(1933), w; DOCTOR MONICA(1934), w; FIREBIRD, THE(1934), w; JOURNAL OF A CRIME(1934), w; MANDALAY(1934), w; GIRL FROM TENTH AVENUE, THE(1935), w; GOOSE AND THE

GANDER, THE(1935), w; MIDSUMMER'S NIGHT'S DREAM, A(1935), w; GOLDEN ARROW, THE(1936), w; PETRIFIED FOREST, THE(1936), w; CRACK-UP, THE(1937), w; ROAD BACK,THE(1937), w; 100 MEN AND A GIRL(1937), w; LADY OBJECTS, THE(1938), w; ROAD TO RENO, THE(1938), w; LADY WITH RED HAIR(1940), w; HIGHWAY WEST(1941), w; IT COMES UP LOVE(1943), w; MAN IN HALF-MOON STREET, THE(1944), w; UNWRITTEN CODE, THE(1944), w; PHANTOM OF THE PLAINS(1945), w; STRANGE JOURNEY(1946), w

Silents

NOBODY'S WIFE(1918), w; JOYOUS TROUBLEMAKERS, THE(1920), w; PENALTY, THE(1920), w; STOP THIEF(1920), w; BEATING THE GAME(1921), w; BUNTY PULLS THE STRINGS(1921), w; INVISIBLE POWER, THE(1921), w; RAILROADED(1923), w; SECOND HAND LOVE(1923), w; HEARTS OF OAK(1924), w; IRON HORSE, THE(1924), w; ROUGHNECK, THE(1924), w; ARIZONA ROMEO, THE(1925), w; DICK TURPIN(1925), w; OLD SOAK, THE(1926), w; ALIAS THE DEACON(1928), w

Charles A. Kenyon

Silents

KINDLING(1915), w; ROUGH LOVER, THE(1918), w

Curtis Kenyon

LLOYDS OF LONDON(1936), w; LOVE AND HISSES(1937), w; WAKE UP AND LIVE(1937), w; THANKS FOR EVERYTHING(1938), w; SHE KNEW ALL THE ANSWERS(1941), w; SEVEN DAYS LEAVE(1942), w; TWIN BEDS(1942), w; SALUTE FOR THREE(1943), w; PRINCESS AND THE PIRATE, THE(1944), w; FABULOUS DORSEYS, THE(1947), w; TULSA(1949), w; TWO FLAGS WEST(1950), w; PERSUADER, THE(1957), w

Doris Kenyon

HOME TOWNERS, THE(1928); INTERFERENCE(1928); BEAU BANDIT(1930); ALEXANDER HAMILTON(1931); BARGAIN, THE(1931); ROAD TO SINGAPORE(1931); RULING VOICE, THE(1931); MAN CALLED BACK, THE(1932); YOUNG AMERICA(1932); COUNSELLOR-AT-LAW(1933); NO MARRIAGE TIES(1933); VOLTAIRE(1933); HUMAN SIDE, THE(1934); WHOM THE GODS DESTROY(1934); ALONG CAME LOVE(1937); GIRLS' SCHOOL(1938); MAN IN THE IRON MASK, THE(1939)

Silents

GIRL'S FOLLY, A(1917); MAN WHO FORGOT, THE(1917); ON TRIAL(1917); WILD HONEY(1919); RULING PASSION, THE(1922); SHADOWS OF THE SEA(1922); SURE FIRE FLINT(1922); LEND ME YOUR HUSBAND(1924); MONSIEUR BEAUCAIRE(1924); IF I MARRY AGAIN(1925); UNGUARDED HOUR, THE(1925); LADIES AT PLAY(1926)

Misc. Silents

(; MAN WHO STOOD STILL, THE(1916); OCEAN WAIF, THE(1916); PAWN OF FATE, THE(1916); TRAVELING SALESMAN, THE(1916); EMPRESS, THE(1917); GREAT WHITE TRAIL, THE(1917); STREET OF SEVEN STARS, THE(1918); BANDBOX, THE(1919); TWILIGHT(1919); HARVEST MOON, THE(1920); GET-RICH-QUICK WALLINGFORD(1921); BRIGHT LIGHTS OF BROADWAY(1923); LAST MOMENT, THE(1923); YOU ARE GUILTY(1923); BORN RICH(1924); IDLE TONGUES(1924); LOVE BANDIT, THE(1924); NEW SCHOOL TEACHER, THE(1924); RESTLESS WIVES(1924); HALF-WAY GIRL, THE(1925); I WANT MY MAN(1925); THIEF IN PARADISE, A(1925); BLONDE SAINT, THE(1926); MEN OF STEEL(1926); MISMATES(1926); VALLEY OF THE GIANTS, THE(1927); BURNING DAYLIGHT(1928); HAWK'S NEST, THE(1928)

Ethel Kenyon

BRANDED(1931); GOOD SPORT(1931); BY WHOSE HAND?(1932); RICH ARE ALWAYS WITH US, THE(1932)

Gwen Kenyon

DAUGHTER OF SHANGHAI(1937); HOLD'EM NAVY!(1937); THRILL OF A LIFETIME(1937); ARTISTS AND MODELS ABROAD(1938); COCOANUT GROVE(1938); SAY IT IN FRENCH(1938); TROPIC HOLIDAY(1938); YOU AND ME(1938); CAFE SOCIETY(1939); FREE, BLONDE AND 21(1940); CONFESSIONS OF BOSTON BLACKIE(1941); UNDER AGE(1941); YOU'LL NEVER GET RICH(1941); CORPSE VANISHES, THE(1942); LAWLESS PLAINSMEN(1942); MAN FROM HEADQUARTERS(1942); MEET THE MOB(1942); RIDING HIGH(1943); SARONG GIRL(1943); TORNADO(1943); CHARLIE CHAN IN THE SECRET SERVICE(1944); GREAT MIKE, THE(1944); IN OLD NEW MEXICO(1945)

Ian Kenyon

UNCENSORED(1944, Brit.)

Joan Kenyon

STOLEN HEAVEN(1931)

Joey Kenyon

GUMSHOE(1972, Brit.)

Mary Kenyon

EARL OF PUDDLESTONE(1940); SAN FERNANDO VALLEY(1944); SING, NEIGHBOR, SING(1944); COLORADO SERENADE(1946); SECRETS OF A SORORITY GIRL(1946)

Nancy Kenyon

Silents

AFTER MANY YEARS(1930, Brit.)

Neil Kenyon

GREAT GAME, THE(1930); LOVES OF ROBERT BURNS, THE(1930, Brit.); GIRL THIEF, THE(1938)

Pat Kenyon

CONSTANT HUSBAND, THE(1955, Brit.)

Robert Kenyon

Misc. Silents

HIDDEN LAW, THE(1916); STEALERS, THE(1920); POWER WITHIN, THE(1921); SILAS MARNER(1922)

Sandy Kenyon

AL CAPONE(1959); NEVADA SMITH(1966); EASY COME, EASY GO(1967); AROUSERS, THE(1973); BREEZY(1973); TOM SAWYER(1973); RANCHO DELUXE(1975); MAC ARTHUR(1977); WHEN TIME RAN OUT(1980)

1984

BLAME IT ON THE NIGHT(1984)

Misc. Talkies

LOCH NESS HORROR, THE(1983)

Taldo Kenyon

MAGIC SWORD, THE(1962)

Ken Kenzle

SASQUATCH(1978)

Barbara Keogh

NICE GIRL LIKE ME, A(1969, Brit.); VIRGIN SOLDIERS, THE(1970, Brit.); ABOMINABLE DR. PHIBES, THE(1971, Brit.)

Des Keogh

ULYSSES(1967, U.S./Brit.); MC KENZIE BREAK, THE(1970); RYAN'S DAUGHTER(1970, Brit.); FLIGHT OF THE DOVES(1971)

Doreen Keogh

ZOO BABY(1957, Brit.); CHRISTMAS TREE, THE(1966, Brit.); TWO A PENNY(1968, Brit.); DARLING LILI(1970)

Finola Keogh

1984

SCRUBBERS(1984, Brit.)

Garrett Keogh

CRIMINAL CONVERSATION(1980, Ireland); EXCALIBUR(1981)

Pat Keogh

SKY RAIDERS, THE(1938, Brit.); OLD MOTHER RILEY, DETECTIVE(1943, Brit.); SECOND MATE, THE(1950, Brit.)

Tom Keogh

PIRATE, THE(1948), cos

John Keonig

THIS IS THE ARMY(1943), art d

Eric Keown

GHOST GOES WEST, THE(1936), w

John Kephart

ON THE YARD(1978)

Kepich

M(1933, Ger.)

Shell Kepler

HOMEWORK(1982)

Virginia Kepler

WONDER MAN(1945)

Violet Keppel

Silents

GREAT LOVE, THE(1918)

Keppel and Betty

ON THE AIR(1934, Brit.)

Charles Keppen

JEALOUSY(1934)

Charley Keppen

SWORN ENEMY(1936)

Alfred Keppler

Silents

PRODIGAL WIFE, THE(1918)

Carol Diane Keppler

PICTURE OF DORIAN GRAY, THE(1945)

Edward Keppler

Misc. Silents

BANDBOX, THE(1919)

Werner Keppler

STAR TREK II: THE WRATH OF KHAN(1982), makeup

Wolfgang Keppler

MOSCOW SHANGHAI(1936, Ger.)

Nicholas Kepros

1984

AMADEUS(1984)

Donald I. Ker

WAKAMBA!(1955), ph

Evelyn Ker

PLAYTIME(1963, Fr.)

Evelyne Ker

1984

A NOS AMOURS(1984, Fr.)

Karine Ker

MICHELLE(1970, Fr.)

Lilian Ker

DEATHSTALKER(1983, Arg./U.S.)

Lilliam Ker

1984

DEATHSTALKER, THE(1984)

Harry Keramidas

MEMORY OF US(1974), ed; MASSACRE AT CENTRAL HIGH(1976), ed; TOUCHED(1983), ed

1984

CHILDREN OF THE CORN(1984), ed

Annie Kerani

AND NOW MY LOVE(1975, Fr.)

Jean Keraudy

NIGHT WATCH, THE(1964, Fr./Ital.)

Michele Kerbash

BATTLE OF ALGIERS, THE(1967, Ital./Alger.)

Samia Kerbash

BATTLE OF ALGIERS, THE(1967, Ital./Alger.)

Alice Kerbert

I REMEMBER MAMA(1948)

Peggy Kerbert

I REMEMBER MAMA(1948)

Elsie Kerbinhathorn

PRIME TIME, THE(1960), ed

Eva Kerbler

TWO IN A SLEEPING BAG(1964, Ger.)

Michiel Kerbosch

LIFT, THE(1983, Neth.)

Yves Kerboul

JE T'AIME, JE T'AIME(1972, Fr./Swed.)

Adrian Kerbrat

CROSSROADS(1942)

Bill Kerby

GRAVY TRAIN, THE(1974), w; HOOPER(1978), w

Marian Kerby
TUMBLEDOWN RANCH IN ARIZONA(1941)
Marion Kerby
FOR YOU I DIE(1947)
Paul Kerby
SWEETHEARTS(1938)
William Kerby
ROSE, THE(1979), w
Ken Kercheval
PRETTY POISON(1968); COVER ME BABE(1970); RABBIT, RUN(1970); SEVEN UPS, THE(1973); NETWORK(1976); LINCOLN CONSPIRACY, THE(1977); F.I.S.T.(1978)
George Kerebel
ARTISTS AND MODELS ABROAD(1938)
Gabriel Kerekes
RAMPARTS WE WATCH, THE(1940)
Duci Kerekjarto
ANGEL(1937)
Oleg Kerensky
REDS(1981)
Zoltan Kerenyi
DIALOGUE(1967, Hung.), ed
Archil Kereselidze
STEPCHILDREN(1962, USSR), m
Sonja Kereskenji
1984
NADIA(1984, U.S./Yugo.)
Richard Kereszi
PAGAN ISLAND(1961), makeup
Hans E. Kerhnert
MAN ON A TIGHTROPE(1953), art d
Jean-Pierre Kerien
PALACE OF NUDES(1961, Fr./Ital.); MURIEL(1963, Fr./Ital.)
M. Jean Pierre Kerien
SEPTEMBER STORM(1960)
Wanda Kerien
MURIEL(1963, Fr./Ital.)
Kerima
OUTCAST OF THE ISLANDS(1952, Brit.); FATAL DESIRE(1953); LAND OF THE PHARAOHS(1955); QUIET AMERICAN, THE(1958); JESSICA(1962, U.S./Ital./Fr.); SHIP OF CONDEMNED WOMEN, THE(1963, ITAL.)
Jackie Kerin
NEXT OF KIN(1983, Aus.)
Germaine Kerjean
IT HAPPENED AT THE INN(1945, Fr.); AFFAIRS OF MESSALINA, THE(1954, Ital.); DEADLIER THAN THE MALE(1957, Fr.); NANA(1957, Fr./Ital.); DEVIL AND THE TEN COMMANDMENTS, THE(1962, Fr.)
Charles Kerk
DOUBLE HARNESS(1933), art d
Nikki Kerkes
NIGHT IN PARADISE, A(1946)
Max Kerlow
FOXTROT(1977, Mex./Swiss)
David Kerman
OUTSIDE OF PARADISE(1938); SWEETHEARTS(1938); MYSTIC CIRCLE MURDER(1939); WOMEN IN THE WIND(1939); MURDER, INC.(1960); EDUCATION OF SONNY CARSON, THE(1974)
Jill Kerman
DECLINE AND FALL... OF A BIRD WATCHER(1969, Brit.)
Robert Kerman
GOODBYE GIRL, THE(1977)
Misc. Talkies
MISSION HILL(1982)
David Kermen
NAKED CITY, THE(1948)
Norberto Kermer
TANK COMMANDOS(1959)
Harry Kermidas
DRACULA'S DOG(1978), ed
Barbara Kermode
1984
FINDERS KEEPERS(1984)
Andrea Kermot
Misc. Talkies
FOLLOW ME(1969)
Robert J. Kerms
WOMEN, THE(1939), ed
Cecil Kern
Silents
RAINBOW(1921)
Daniel Kern
ROCKET ATTACK, U.S.A.(1961)
David Kern
AMERICANA(1981), ed
1984
BLACK ROOM, THE(1984), ed
Donald Kern
FACE OF MARBLE, THE(1946)
Erich Kern
UNWILLING AGENT(1968, Ger.), w
George Kern
Misc. Silents
UNFOLDMENT, THE(1922), d
Grace Kern
HONOR AMONG LOVERS(1931); MAID OF SALEM(1937); ROARIN' LEAD(1937)
Hal Kern
ALIBI(1929), ed; LOCKED DOOR, THE(1929), ed; NEW YORK NIGHTS(1929), ed; PUTTIN' ON THE RITZ(1930), ed; CORSAIR(1931), ed; REBECCA(1940), ed; STAGE DOOR CANTEEN(1943), ed; TARZAN TRIUMPHS(1943), ed

Hal C. Kern
INDISCREET(1931), ed; REACHING FOR THE MOON(1931), ed; HELL BELOW(1933), ed; NIGHT FLIGHT(1933), ed; GARDEN OF ALLAH, THE(1936), ed; PRISONER OF ZENDA, THE(1937), ed; YOUNG IN HEART, THE(1938), ed; GONE WITH THE WIND(1939), ed; INTERMEZZO: A LOVE STORY(1939), ed; MADE FOR EACH OTHER(1939), ed; SINCE YOU WENT AWAY(1944), ed; SPELLBOUND(1945), ed; DUEL IN THE SUN(1946), ed; PARADINE CASE, THE(1947), ed
Silents
EAGLE, THE(1925), ed
Harold Kern
LITTLE LORD FAUNTLEROY(1936), ed
Jake Kern
MELODY LANE(1929)
James Kern
SHINE ON, HARVEST MOON(1944), w; LUM AND ABNER ABROAD(1956), p&d, w
James V. Kern
THANKS A MILLION(1935); THAT'S RIGHT-YOU'RE WRONG(1939), w; IF I HAD MY WAY(1940), w; YOU'LL FIND OUT(1940), w; LOOK WHO'S LAUGHING(1941), w; PLAYMATES(1941), w; THANK YOUR LUCKY STARS(1943), w; DOUGHGIRLS, THE(1944), d, w; HORN BLOWS AT MIDNIGHT, THE(1945), w; HER KIND OF MAN(1946), w; NEVER SAY GOODBYE(1946), d, w; STALLION ROAD(1947), d; APRIL SHOWERS(1948), d; SECOND WOMAN, THE(1951), d; TWO TICKETS TO BROADWAY(1951), d
Jerome Kern
SALLY(1929), w; SUNNY(1930), w, m; MEN OF THE SKY(1931), w; CAT AND THE FIDDLE(1934), w; MUSIC IN THE AIR(1934), w; FLAME WITHIN, THE(1935), m; ROBERTA(1935), w, m; SWEET ADELINE(1935), w; SHOW BOAT(1936), w, m; SWING TIME(1936), m; HIGH, WIDE AND HANDSOME(1937), m; JOY OF LIVING(1938), m; SUNNY(1941), m; YOU WERE NEVER LOVELIER(1942), m; BROADWAY RHYTHM(1944), w; CENTENNIAL SUMMER(1946), m; SHOW BOAT(1951), m, w; LOVELY TO LOOK AT(1952), w
Johnny Kern
FIGHTING FOOLS(1949)
Madeline Kern
PORKY'S II: THE NEXT DAY(1983)
Peter Kern
FOX AND HIS FRIENDS(1976, Ger.); MOTHER KUSTERS GOES TO HEAVEN(1976, Ger.); WILD DUCK, THE(1977, Ger./Aust.); DESPAIR(1978, Ger.); OUR HITLER, A FILM FROM GERMANY(1980, Ger.)
Robert Kern
NEW ORLEANS(1929), ed; THREE LIVE GHOSTS(1929), ed; MR. ROBINSON CRUSOE(1932), ed; WHEN LADIES MEET(1941), ed
Silents
HUSBANDS AND LOVERS(1924), ed; GRAIN OF DUST, THE(1928), ed
Robert H. Kern
ROBIN HOOD OF EL DORADO(1936), ed
Robert J. Kern
BE YOURSELF(1930), ed; LOTTERY BRIDE, THE(1930), ed; PENTHOUSE(1933), ed; PRIZEFIGHTER AND THE LADY, THE(1933), ed; CHAINED(1934), ed; THIN MAN, THE(1934), ed; VIVA VILLA!(1934), ed; DAVID COPPERFIELD(1935), ed; AFTER THE THIN MAN(1936), ed; LONGEST NIGHT, THE(1936), ed; TROUBLE FOR TWO(1936), ed; FIREFLY, THE(1937), ed; NAVY BLUE AND GOLD(1937), ed; NIGHT MUST FALL(1937), ed; MARIE ANTOINETTE(1938), ed; SWEETHEARTS(1938), ed; CALLING DR. KILDARE(1939), ed; IDIOT'S DELIGHT(1939), ed; FLIGHT COMMAND(1940), ed; PRIDE AND PREJUDICE(1940), ed; STRANGE CARGO(1940), ed; WYOMING(1940), ed; BILLY THE KID(1941), ed; SHADOW OF THE THIN MAN(1941), ed; BORN TO SING(1942), ed; HER CARDBOARD LOVER(1942), ed; TENNESSEE JOHNSON(1942), ed; TISH(1942), ed; I DOOD IT(1943), ed; NATIONAL VELVET(1944), ed; WHITE CLIFFS OF DOVER, THE(1944), ed; WEEKEND AT THE WALDORF(1945), ed; GREEN YEARS, THE(1946), ed; SEA OF GRASS, THE(1947), ed; SONG OF LOVE(1947), ed; LUXURY LINER(1948), ed; THREE MUSKETEERS, THE(1948), ed; INTRUDER IN THE DUST(1949), ed; SCENE OF THE CRIME(1949), ed; SECRET GARDEN, THE(1949), ed; CRISIS(1950), ed; OUTRIDERS, THE(1950), ed; TO PLEASE A LADY(1950), ed; ANGELS IN THE OUTFIELD(1951), ed; SOLDIERS THREE(1951), ed; PLYMOUTH ADVENTURE(1952), ed; WHEN IN ROME(1952), ed
Silents
ETERNAL STRUGGLE, THE(1923), ed; ELLA CINDERS(1926), ed; BACHELOR'S PARADISE(1928), ed; TOILERS, THE(1928), ed; TRAGEDY OF YOUTH, THE(1928), ed
Robert J. Kern, Jr.
TWO WEEKS IN ANOTHER TOWN(1962), ed; HOOK, THE(1962), ed; NIGHT SHIFT(1982), ed
Ronni Kern
CHANGE OF SEASONS, A(1980), w; AMERICAN POP(1981), w
Russell S. Kern
Misc. Talkies
SPITTIN' IMAGE(1983), d
Hans Gustl Kernamyr
VIENNA WALTZES(1961, Aust.), w
David Kernan
CAPTAINS COURAGEOUS(1937); GAOLBREAK(1962, Brit.); MIX ME A PERSON(1962, Brit.); FAREWELL PERFORMANCE(1963, Brit.); ZULU(1964, Brit.); FRANKENSTEIN MEETS THE SPACE MONSTER(1965); OTLEY(1969, Brit.)
Reginald Kernan
ARTURO'S ISLAND(1963, Ital.); NAKED AUTUMN(1963, Fr.); GREED IN THE SUN(1965, Fr./ Ital.)
Sarah Kernan
Silents
KID, THE(1921)
Harry Kernell
HOORAY FOR LOVE(1935)
William Kernell
AIR CIRCUS, THE(1928), w
Silents
DON'T MARRY(1928), t; HOMESICK(1928), t; NEW YEAR'S EVE(1929), t; SIN SISTER, THE(1929), t

Sarah Kernen
Silents
HEARTS OF MEN(1919)
Ben Kerner
BLOODY BROOD, THE(1959, Can.), w
Bruce Kerner
EXPLOSIVE GENERATION, THE(1961)
Bruce M. Kerner
1984
TERMINATOR, THE(1984)
Gus Kerner
HONEYMOON IN BALI(1939)
Guy Kerner
WICKED GO TO HELL, THE(1961, Fr.)
Hazel Kerner
KILLER AT LARGE(1947)
Norberto Kerner
I OUGHT TO BE IN PICTURES(1982)
Misc. Talkies
LOSING GROUND(1982)
Donna Kerness
UNSTRAP ME(1968)
Francoise Embry Kernevez
RETURN OF MARTIN GUERRE, THE(1983, Fr.), makeup
Karin Kernke
HEAD, THE(1961, Ger.); LOVE FEAST, THE(1966, Ger.)
Peter Kernohan
DERELICT, THE(1937, Brit.)
Herb Kerns
LONG GOODBYE, THE(1973)
Hubert Kerns
TAKE ME OUT TO THE BALL GAME(1949); THEM!(1954); YOUNG LIONS, THE(1958)
Hubie Kerns
JIM THORPE–ALL AMERICAN(1951); I DIED A THOUSAND TIMES(1955); FOUR GIRLS IN TOWN(1956); BABY FACE NELSON(1957); SKATEBOARD(1978); SWORD AND THE SORCERER, THE(1982)
Ira Kerns
NASHVILLE REBEL(1966), w
Joanna Kerns
COMA(1978)
John Kerns
HERE COMES MR. JORDAN(1941)
Linda Kerns
1984
MOSCOW ON THE HUDSON(1984); OVER THE BROOKLYN BRIDGE(1984)
Sandra Kerns
HOUSE CALLS(1978); GREEN ICE(1981, Brit.)
Jack Kerouac
SUBTERRANEANS, THE(1960), w
Nina V. Kerova
LIQUID SKY(1982), a, w
Zora Kerova
GRIM REAPER, THE(1981, Ital.)
Zora Kerowa
1984
WARRIORS OF THE WASTELAND(1984, Ital.)
Theodore Kerpez
1984
REVENGE OF THE NERDS(1984)
Klara Kerpin
HIDING PLACE, THE(1975), cos; NO LONGER ALONE(1978), cos
Alvah Milton Kerr
Silents
BY RIGHT OF POSSESSION(1917), w
Anita Kerr
LIMBO(1972), m
Annette Kerr
PRICE OF SILENCE, THE(1960, Brit.); MURDER MOST FOUL(1964, Brit.); PRUDENCE AND THE PILL(1968, Brit.); PRIVATE LIFE OF SHERLOCK HOLMES, THE(1970, Brit.)
Arthur Kerr
SECRET PATROL(1936); STAMPEDE(1936); FURY AND THE WOMAN(1937); WHAT PRICE VENGEANCE?(1937); DEATH GOES NORTH(1939)
Barry R. Kerr
Misc. Talkies
FORBIDDEN UNDER THE CENSORSHIP OF THE KING(1973), d
Bill Kerr
PENNY POINTS TO PARADISE(1951, Brit.); MY DEATH IS A MOCKERY(1952, Brit.); APPOINTMENT IN LONDON(1953, Brit.); YOU KNOW WHAT SAILORS ARE(1954, Brit.); DAM BUSTERS, THE(1955, Brit.); NIGHT MY NUMBER CAME UP, THE(1955, Brit.); PORT OF ESCAPE(1955, Brit.); CAPTAIN'S TABLE, THE(1960, Brit.); DOCTOR IN DISTRESS(1963, Brit.); PAIR OF BRIEFS, A(1963, Brit.); WRONG ARM OF THE LAW, THE(1963, Brit.); FUNNY THING HAPPENED ON THE WAY TO THE FORUM, A(1966); CARNABY, M.D.(1967, Brit.); CONFESSIONAL, THE(1977, Brit.); GALLIPOLI(1981, Aus.); PIRATE MOVIE, THE(1982, Aus.); YEAR OF LIVING DANGEROUSLY, THE(1982, Aus.)
1984
RAZORBACK(1984, Aus.); VIGIL(1984, New Zealand)
Bob Kerr
THEY HAD TO SEE PARIS(1929); ISLAND OF LOST SOULS(1933)
Bruce Kerr
BRAIN THAT WOULDN'T DIE, THE(1959); MAN FROM SNOWY RIVER, THE(1983, Aus.)
Cecil Kerr
Silents
EXPERIMENT, THE(1922, Brit.)

Charles Kerr
LI'L ABNER(1940), w; VACATION IN RENO(1946), w
Charlotte Kerr
HELDINNEN(1962, Ger.), w; NEW LIFE STYLE, THE(1970, Ger.)
1984
SWANN IN LOVE(1984, Fr.Ger.)
David Kerr
ADVENTURE FOR TWO(1945, Brit.)
Deborah Kerr
COURAGEOUS MR. PENN, THE(1941, Brit.); MAJOR BARBARA(1941, Brit.); AVENGERS, THE(1942, Brit.); COLONEL BLIMP(1945, Brit.); LOVE ON THE DOLE(1945, Brit.); VACATION FROM MARRIAGE(1945, Brit.); ADVENTURESS, THE(1946, Brit.); BLACK NARCISSUS(1947, Brit.); HUCKSTERS, THE(1947); IF WINTER COMES(1947); HATTER'S CASTLE(1948, Brit.); EDWARD, MY SON(1949, U.S./Brit.); KING SOLOMON'S MINES(1950); PLEASE BELIEVE ME(1950); QUO VADIS(1951); PRISONER OF ZENDA, THE(1952); DREAM WIFE(1953); FROM HERE TO ETERNITY(1953); JULIUS CAESAR(1953); THUNDER IN THE EAST(1953); YOUNG BESS(1953); END OF THE AFFAIR, THE(1955, Brit.); KING AND I, THE(1956); PROUD AND THE PROFANE, THE(1956); TEA AND SYMPATHY(1956); AFFAIR TO REMEMBER, AN(1957); HEAVEN KNOWS, MR. ALLISON(1957); BONJOUR TRISTESSE(1958); SEPARATE TABLES(1958); BELOVED INFIDEL(1959); COUNT YOUR BLESSINGS(1959); JOURNEY, THE(1959, U.S./Aust.); GRASS IS GREENER, THE(1960); SUNDOWNERS, THE(1960); INNOCENTS, THE(1961, U.S./Brit.); NAKED EDGE, THE(1961); CHALK GARDEN, THE(1964, Brit.); NIGHT OF THE IGUANA, THE(1964); MARRIAGE ON THE ROCKS(1965); CASINO ROYALE(1967, Brit.); EYE OF THE DEVIL(1967, Brit.); PRUDENCE AND THE PILL(1968, Brit.); ARRANGEMENT, THE(1969); GYPSY MOTHS, THE(1969)
Dick Kerr
FRISCO KID(1935)
Don Kerr
TRUE TO LIFE(1943); STRANGER ON THE THIRD FLOOR(1940); MEXICAN SPITFIRE'S BABY(1941); LADIES' DAY(1943); LET'S FACE IT(1943); MURDER, MY SWEET(1945); THERE GOES KELLY(1945); NOTORIOUS(1946); DESPERATE(1947); OH, YOU BEAUTIFUL DOLL(1949); STRIP, THE(1951)
Don Thaddeus Kerr
ROARING TWENTIES, THE(1939)
Donald Kerr
TIME OF YOUR LIFE, THE(1948); CARNIVAL LADY(1933); FROM HELL TO HEAVEN(1933); PICTURE SNATCHER(1933); MURDER IN THE MUSEUM(1934); GEORGE WHITE'S 1935 SCANDALS(1935); HOT TIP(1935); MAGNIFICENT OBSESSION(1935); MILLIONS IN THE AIR(1935); SHE COULDN'T TAKE IT(1935); SPANISH CAPE MYSTERY(1935); LOVE ON THE RUN(1936); ROSE BOWL(1936); SWING TIME(1936); CIRCUS GIRL(1937); DON'T TELL THE WIFE(1937); HIDEAWAY GIRL(1937); SWING HIGH, SWING LOW(1937); TAMING THE WILD(1937); ANGELS WITH DIRTY FACES(1938); BORN TO FIGHT(1938); FOUR DAUGHTERS(1938); GANG BULLETS(1938); GO CHASE YOURSELF(1938); LADY IN THE MORGUE(1938); SKY GIANT(1938); TEST PILOT(1938); KING OF THE TURF(1939); LUCKY NIGHT(1939); MR. SMITH GOES TO WASHINGTON(1939); SUDDEN MONEY(1939); CHASING TROUBLE(1940); FRAMED(1940); HOUSE ACROSS THE BAY, THE(1940); MAD YOUTH(1940); SAINT'S DOUBLE TROUBLE, THE(1940); WEST OF CARSON CITY(1940); DEVIL BAT, THE(1941); LOOK WHO'S LAUGHING(1941); ROAR OF THE PRESS(1941); ROLLIN' HOME TO TEXAS(1941); MAYOR OF 44TH STREET, THE(1942); SOMEWHERE I'LL FIND YOU(1942); TRUE TO THE ARMY(1942); DIXIE(1943); HAPPY GO LUCKY(1943); IS EVERYBODY HAPPY?(1943); SO'S YOUR UNCLE(1943); THEY GOT ME COVERED(1943); AND THE ANGELS SING(1944); ATLANTIC CITY(1944); HAT CHECK HONEY(1944); MOON OVER LAS VEGAS(1944); PRACTICALLY YOURS(1944); SOUTH OF DIXIE(1944); WEEKEND PASS(1944); HER LUCKY NIGHT(1945); HOLLYWOOD AND VINE(1945); IT'S A PLEASURE(1945); MAN WHO WALKED ALONE, THE(1945); NAUGHTY NINETIES, THE(1945); ON STAGE EVERYBODY(1945); UNDER WESTERN SKIES(1945); WOMAN IN THE WINDOW, THE(1945); DECOY(1946); KID FROM BROOKLYN, THE(1946); LITTLE GIANT(1946); MURDER IS MY BUSINESS(1946); NIGHT EDITOR(1946); NOCTURNE(1946); RIDE THE PINK HORSE(1947); ROAD TO RIO(1947); SONG OF THE THIN MAN(1947); CANON CITY(1948); HE WALKED BY NIGHT(1948); I WOULDN'T BE IN YOUR SHOES(1948); IF YOU KNEW SUSIE(1948); SECRET BEYOND THE DOOR, THE(1948); WHIPLASH(1948); KNOCK ON ANY DOOR(1949); SET-UP, THE(1949); SHADOWS OF THE WEST(1949); MILKMAN, THE(1950); PEGGY(1950); PERFECT STRANGERS(1950); SHAKEDOWN(1950); SIDESHOW(1950); SQUARE DANCE KATY(1950); THREE LITTLE WORDS(1950); WOMAN OF DISTINCTION, A(1950); DETECTIVE STORY(1951); FLAMING FEATHER(1951); LULLABY OF BROADWAY, THE(1951); PAINTING THE CLOUDS WITH SUNSHINE(1951); PRIDE OF MARYLAND(1951); RHUBARB(1951); CARRIE(1952); LOST IN ALASKA(1952); MEET ME AT THE FAIR(1952); SHE'S WORKING HER WAY THROUGH COLLEGE(1952); SNIPER, THE(1952); CLOWN, THE(1953); FARMER TAKES A WIFE, THE(1953); GLASS WEB, THE(1953); ABBOTT AND COSTELLO MEET DR. JEKYLL AND MR. HYDE(1954); FOUR GUNS TO THE BORDER(1954); REDHEAD FROM MANHATTAN(1954); THERE'S NO BUSINESS LIKE SHOW BUSINESS(1954); THREE RING CIRCUS(1954); ABBOTT AND COSTELLO MEET THE KEYSTONE KOPS(1955); ABBOTT AND COSTELLO MEET THE MUMMY(1955); ONE DESIRE(1955); FRIENDLY PERSUASION(1956); YAQUI DRUMS(1956); JAILHOUSE ROCK(1957); SOME CAME RUNNING(1959); TWELVE HOURS TO KILL(1960)
Misc. Talkies
DRAGNET, THE(1936)
Donnie Kerr
GREAT McGINTY, THE(1940)
E. Katherine Kerr
TATTOO(1981); LOVESICK(1983); REUBEN, REUBEN(1983); SILKWOOD(1983)
Ed Kerr
O.S.S.(1946)
Ede Kerr
ISABEL(1968, Can.)
Elizabeth Kerr
YELLOW STOCKINGS(1930, Brit.); MESSENGER OF PEACE(1950); SIX BRIDGES TO CROSS(1955); DOGS(1976); ONE MAN JURY(1978); WHY WOULD I LIE(1980); GOING BERSERK(1983)
Fred Kerr
MIDSHIPMAID GOB(1932, Brit.); LORD OF THE MANOR(1933, Brit.); MAN FROM TORONTO, THE(1933, Brit.)

Silents
12-10(1919, Brit.)
Frederick Kerr
WATERLOO BRIDGE(1931); DEVIL TO PAY, THE(1930); LADY OF SCANDAL, THE(1930); RAFFLES(1930); ALWAYS GOODBYE(1931); BORN TO LOVE(1931); FRANKENSTEIN(1931); FRIENDS AND LOVERS(1931); HONOR OF THE FAMILY(1931); BEAUTY AND THE BOSS(1932); BUT THE FLESH IS WEAK(1932); LOVERS COURAGEOUS(1932)
Gene Kerr
GIRLS' TOWN(1942), w
Geoffrey Kerr
ONCE A LADY(1931); RUNAROUND, THE(1931); WOMEN LOVE ONCE(1931); GHOST GOES WEST, THE(1936), w; LIVING DANGEROUSLY(1936, Brit.), w; STAR FELL FROM HEAVEN, A(1936, Brit.), w; SWEET DEVIL(1937, Brit.), w; TENTH MAN, THE(1937, Brit.), w; WEEKEND MILLIONAIRE(1937, Brit.), w; BREAK THE NEWS(1938, Brit.), w; UNDER YOUR HAT(1940, Brit.), w; BOMBSIGHT STOLEN(1941, Brit.), w; CALENDAR, THE(1948, Brit.), w; JASSY(1948, Brit.), w; FOOLS RUSH IN(1949, Brit.), w
Silents
PROFLIGATE, THE(1917, Brit.); 12-10(1919, Brit.); MIRAGE, THE(1920, Brit.); JUST SUPPOSE(1926)
Misc. Silents
USURPER, THE(1919, Brit.); TORN SAILS(1920, Brit.); MAN FROM HOME, THE(1922)
Harry Kerr
MOONSHINE MOUNTAIN(1964)
Harry D. Kerr
Silents
CHEATERS(1927), w
Herbert Kerr
PUTNEY SWOPE(1969); DEALING: OR THE BERKELEY-TO-BOSTON FORTY-BRICK LOST-BAG BLUES(1971)
Ingrid Kerr
MY THIRD WIFE GEORGE(1968)
Jacqueline Kerr
ROCK, ROCK, ROCK!(1956)
Jane Kerr
PAINTED VEIL, THE(1934); LES MISERABLES(1935); SHE GETS HER MAN(1935); GARDEN OF ALLAH, THE(1936); YOU CAN'T HAVE EVERYTHING(1937)
Jay Kerr
HARD COUNTRY(1981)
Jean Kerr
THAT CERTAIN FEELING(1956), w; PLEASE DON'T EAT THE DAISIES(1960), w; MARY, MARY(1963), w
Joe Kerr
NAKED CITY, THE(1948); MILKMAN, THE(1950); RIOT IN CELL BLOCK 11(1954)
John Kerr
TREASURE ISLAND(1934); STRATTON STORY, THE(1949); COBWEB, THE(1955); GABY(1956); TEA AND SYMPATHY(1956); MEN OF SHERWOOD FOREST(1957, Brit.); VINTAGE, THE(1957); SOUTH PACIFIC(1958); CROWDED SKY, THE(1960); GIRL OF THE NIGHT(1960); PIT AND THE PENDULUM, THE(1961); SEVEN WOMEN FROM HELL(1961); SILENT PARTNER, THE(1979, Can.)
Joseph Kerr
ALL MY SONS(1948); PERFECT STRANGERS(1950); THAT CERTAIN FEELING(1956)
Judy Kerr
FIRST LOVE(1977); CANNERY ROW(1982)
Kendra Kerr
HOT ROD HULLABALOO(1966)
Larry Kerr
BEST THINGS IN LIFE ARE FREE, THE(1956); WILL SUCCESS SPOIL ROCK HUNTER?(1957); LOST MISSILE, THE(1958, U.S./Can.)
Laura Kerr
BRAZIL(1944), w; FARMER'S DAUGHTER, THE(1947), w; MY DREAM IS YOURS(1949), w; GROUNDS FOR MARRIAGE(1950), w; BATTLE CIRCUS(1953), w
Marcia Kerr
1984
SAVAGE STREETS(1984)
Mary Kerr
DOUBLE NEGATIVE(1980, Can.), art d; NOTHING PERSONAL(1980, Can.), art d
Richard Kerr
FRAGMENT OF FEAR(1971, Brit.)
Robert Kerr
LIFE BEGINS AT 40(1935)
Robert P. Kerr
Misc. Silents
TRIP TO CHINATOWN, A(1926), d; 30 BELOW ZERO(1926), d
Sondra Kerr
STRIPPER, THE(1963)
Sophie Kerr
WOMAN ACCUSED(1933), w; BIG HEARTED HERBERT(1934), w; PEOPLE WILL TALK(1935), w
Silents
FICKLE WOMEN(1920), w
Suzanne Kerr
KISS THE BLOOD OFF MY HANDS(1948)
Eddie Kerrant
SECOND CHANCE(1953)
Zito Kerras
PEOPLE MEET AND SWEET MUSIC FILLS THE HEART(1969, Den./Swed.)
Linda Kerridge
FADE TO BLACK(1980)
1984
MIXED BLOOD(1984); STRANGERS KISS(1984); SURF II(1984)
Mary Kerridge
ANNA KARENINA(1948, Brit.); RICHARD III(1956, Brit.); DUKE WORE JEANS, THE(1958, Brit.); LAW AND DISORDER(1958, Brit.); NAVY HEROES(1959, Brit.); CURSE OF THE VOODOO(1965, Brit.); NO LONGER ALONE(1978)

Roy Kerridge
MIX ME A PERSON(1962, Brit.), w
Jean-Pierre Kerrien
TRAPEZE(1956)
Bill Kerrigan
1984
MEMOIRS(1984, Can.), ph
Bobby Kerrigan
LONDON MELODY(1930, Brit.)
J. M. Kerrigan
LUCKY IN LOVE(1929); LIGHTNIN'(1930); BLACK CAMEL, THE(1931); DON'T BET ON WOMEN(1931); MERELY MARY ANN(1931); UNDER SUSPICION(1931); CARELESS LADY(1932); FIGHTING CARAVANS(1932); MONKEY'S PAW(1932); FOUNTAIN, THE(1934); LONE COWBOY(1934); LOST PATROL, THE(1934); FARMER TAKES A WIFE, THE(1935); COLLEEN(1936); GENERAL DIED AT DAWN, THE(1936); LLOYDS OF LONDON(1936); LONDON BY NIGHT(1937); MOTOR MADNESS(1937); SHALL WE DANCE(1937); VACATION FROM LOVE(1938); SABOTAGE(1939); TWO THOROUGHBREDS(1939); UNDERCOVER AGENT(1939); 6000 ENEMIES(1939); CONGO MAISIE(1940); CURTAIN CALL(1940); LONG VOYAGE HOME, THE(1940); THREE CHEERS FOR THE IRISH(1940); ADVENTURE IN WASHINGTON(1941); VANISHING VIRGINIAN, THE(1941); CAPTAINS OF THE CLOUDS(1942); MR. LUCKY(1943); FIGHTING SEABEES, THE(1944); CRIME DOCTOR'S WARNING(1945); ABIE'S IRISH ROSE(1946); LUCK OF THE IRISH(1948); TWO OF A KIND(1951); SILVER WHIP, THE(1953); MEET ME IN LAS VEGAS(1956)
J. Warren Kerrigan
Silents
SAMSON(1914); MEASURE OF A MAN, THE(1916); PRISONER OF THE PINES(1918); END OF THE GAME, THE(1919); JOYOUS LIAR, THE(1919); LORD LOVES THE IRISH, THE(1919); GREEN FLAME, THE(1920); NIGHT LIFE IN HOLLYWOOD(1922); COVERED WAGON, THE(1923); GIRL OF THE GOLDEN WEST, THE(1923)
Misc. Silents
BECKONING TRAIL, THE(1916); GAY LORD WARING, THE(1916); LANDON'S LEGACY(1916); POOL OF FLAME, THE(1916); SILENT BATTLE, THE(1916); SOCIAL BUCCANEER, THE(1916); SON OF THE IMMORTALS, A(1916); MAN'S MAN, A(1917); THREE X GORDON(1918); TURN OF THE CARD, THE(1918); BEST MAN, THE(1919); COME AGAIN SMITH(1919); DRIFTERS, THE(1919); COAST OF OPPORTUNITY, THE(1920); DREAM CHEATER, THE(1920); HOUSE OF WHISPERS, THE(1920); LIVE SPARKS(1920); NO.99(1920); $30,000(1920); MAN FROM BRODNEY'S, THE(1923); THUNDERING DAWN(1923); CAPTAIN BLOOD(1924)
Joseph M. Kerrigan
FOX MOVIETONE FOLLIES OF 1930(1930); SONG O' MY HEART(1930); RAINBOW TRAIL(1932); AIR HOSTESS(1933); STUDY IN SCARLET, A(1933); HAPPINESS AHEAD(1934); KEY, THE(1934); MODERN HERO, A(1934); TREASURE ISLAND(1934); BARBARY COAST(1935); FEATHER IN HER HAT, A(1935); HOT TIP(1935); INFORMER, THE(1935); WEREWOLF OF LONDON, THE(1935); HEARTS IN BONDAGE(1936); LAUGHING IRISH EYES(1936); PLOUGH AND THE STARS, THE(1936); PRISONER OF SHARK ISLAND, THE(1936); SPECIAL INVESTIGATOR(1936); SPENDTHRIFT(1936); TIMOTHY'S QUEST(1936); BARRIER, THE(1937); LET'S MAKE A MILLION(1937); LITTLE ORPHAN ANNIE(1938); RIDE A CROOKED MILE(1938); FLYING IRISHMAN, THE(1939); GONE WITH THE WIND(1939); GREAT MAN VOTES, THE(1939); KID FROM TEXAS, THE(1939); SORORITY HOUSE(1939); TWO BRIGHT BOYS(1939); UNION PACIFIC(1939); WITNESS VANISHES, THE(1939); ZERO HOUR, THE(1939); NO TIME FOR COMEDY(1940); ONE CROWDED NIGHT(1940); SEA HAWK, THE(1940); UNTAMED(1940); YOUNG TOM EDISON(1940); APPOINTMENT FOR LOVE(1941); WOLF MAN, THE(1941); ACTION IN THE NORTH ATLANTIC(1943); BIG BONANZA, THE(1944); WILSON(1944); GREAT JOHN L. THE(1945); SHE WENT TO THE RACES(1945); SPANISH MAIN, THE(1945); TARZAN AND THE AMAZONS(1945); BLACK BEAUTY(1946); FIGHTING O'FLYNN, THE(1949); MRS. MIKE(1949); SEALED CARGO(1951); MY COUSIN RACHEL(1952); PARK ROW(1952); WILD NORTH, THE(1952); 20,000 LEAGUES UNDER THE SEA(1954); BAR SINISTER, THE(1955); FASTEST GUN ALIVE(1956)
Misc. Silents
LITTLE OLD NEW YORK(1923)

Katherine Kerrigan
SKINNER STEPS OUT(1929)
Kathleen Kerrigan
WICKED(1931)
Silents
SAMSON(1914)
Misc. Silents
UPLIFTERS, THE(1919); WORLD AFLAME, THE(1919)
Keith Kerrigan
REDHEAD FROM WYOMING, THE(1953); SON OF SINBAD(1955)
T.J. Kerrigan
Misc. Silents
PEGGY, THE WILL O' THE WISP(1917)
Hershel Kerrona
RETURN OF SABATA(1972, Ital./Fr./Ger.)
Jessie Douglas Kerruish
UNDYING MONSTER, THE(1942), w
Anita Kerry
CASE OF THE LUCKY LEGS, THE(1935); MISS PACIFIC FLEET(1935); PAYOFF, THE(1935); WE'RE IN THE MONEY(1935); FRESHMAN LOVE(1936); MAN HUNT(1936); MURDER OF DR. HARRIGAN, THE(1936)
Anne Kerry
LOVESICK(1983)
Dan Kerry
UNDERCURRENT(1946)
Daniel Kerry
STRANGE VOYAGE(1945)
Donald Kerry
LOVE FROM A STRANGER(1947)
Evelyn Kerry
LADYKILLERS, THE(1956, Brit.)

John Kerry
TRACKDOWN(1976); SUMMER SCHOOL TEACHERS(1977); NORTH AVENUE IRREGULARS, THE(1979)
Misc. Talkies
BAD GEORGIA ROAD(1977)
Margaret Kerry
CANON CITY(1948); IF YOU KNEW SUSIE(1948)
Norman Kerry
PHANTOM OF THE OPERA, THE(1929); BACHELOR APARTMENT(1931); EXFLAME(1931); AIR EAGLES(1932); PHANTOM OF SANTA FE(1937); TANKS A MILLION(1941)
Silents
AMARILLY OF CLOTHESLINE ALLEY(1918); GOOD NIGHT, PAUL(1918); GETTING MARY MARRIED(1919); BURIED TREASURE(1921); WILD GOOSE, THE(1921); ACQUITTAL, THE(1923); HUNCHBACK OF NOTRE DAME, THE(1923); IS MONEY EVERYTHING?(1923); MERRY-GO-ROUND(1923); CYTHEREA(1924); DARING YOUTH(1924); PHANTOM OF THE OPERA, THE(1925); BARRIER, THE(1926); ANNIE LAURIE(1927); IRRESISTIBLE LOVER, THE(1927); UNKNOWN, THE(1927); LOVE ME AND THE WORLD IS MINE(1928)
Misc. Silents
LITTLE PRINCESS, THE(1917); ROSE O' PARADISE(1918); UP THE ROAD WITH SALLIE(1918); DARK STAR, THE(1919); SOLDIERS OF FORTUNE(1919); TOTON(1919); VIRTOUS SINNERS(1919); PASSION'S PLAYGROUND(1920); SPLENDID HAZARD, A(1920); GET-RICH-QUICK WALLINGFORD(1921); LITTLE ITALY(1921); PROXIES(1921); BROTHERS UNDER THE SKIN(1922); MAN FROM HOME, THE(1922); THREE LIVE GHOSTS(1922, Brit.); SATIN GIRL, THE(1923); BETWEEN FRIENDS(1924); BUTTERFLY(1924); SHADOW OF THE EAST, THE(1924); FIFTH AVENUE MODELS(1925); LORRAINE OF THE LIONS(1925); PRICE OF PLEASURE, THE(1925); LOVE THIEF, THE(1926); MADEMOISELLE MODISTE(1926); UNDER WESTERN SKIES(1926); BODY AND SOUL(1927); CLAW, THE(1927); FOREIGN LEGION, THE(1928); WOMAN FROM MOSCOW, THE(1928); BONDMAN, THE(1929, Brit.); MAN, WOMAN AND WIFE(1929); PRINCE OF HEARTS, THE(1929); TRAIL MARRIAGE(1929); WOMAN I LOVE, THE(1929)
Pat X. Kerry
BULLDOG DRUMMOND'S PERIL(1938)
Glenn Kerschner
MAD PARADE, THE(1931), ph
William Kersen
TEN GENTLEMEN FROM WEST POINT(1942)
Bill Kersh
HAREM BUNCH; OR WAR AND PIECE, THE(1969)
Gerald Kersh
NINE MEN(1943, Brit.), w; NIGHT AND THE CITY(1950, Brit.), w; SCENT OF MYSTERY(1960), w
Kathy Kersh
AMERICANIZATION OF EMILY, THE(1964)
Clifford Kershaw
ALL THINGS BRIGHT AND BEAUTIFUL(1979, Brit.)
Doug Kershaw
ZACHARIAH(1971); DAYS OF HEAVEN(1978)
John Kershaw
LONELY LADY, THE(1983), w
1984
YELLOW HAIR AND THE FORTRESS OF GOLD(1984), w
Wilette Kershaw
Silents
VORTEX, THE(1927, Brit.)
Willette Kershaw
Misc. Silents
CECILIA OF THE PINK ROSES(1918)
Glen Kershner
MEET THE WIFE(1931), ph
Glenn Kershner
ISLAND CAPTIVES(1937), d
Silents
STRONG MAN, THE(1926), ph; LONG PANTS(1927), ph
Irvin Kershner
STAKEOUT ON DOPE STREET(1958), d, w; YOUNG CAPTIVES, THE(1959), d; HOODLUM PRIEST, THE(1961), d; FACE IN THE RAIN, A(1963), d; LUCK OF GINGER COFFEY, THE(1964, U.S./Can.), d; FINE MADNESS, A(1966), d; FLIMFLAM MAN, THE(1967), d; LOVING(1970), d; UP THE SANDBOX(1972), d; S(1974), d; RETURN OF A MAN CALLED HORSE, THE(1976), d; EYES OF LAURA MARS(1978), d; EMPIRE STRIKES BACK, THE(1980), d; NEVER SAY NEVER AGAIN(1983), d
Kerss
MADHOUSE(1974, Brit.), spec eff
Alexander Kerst
48 HOURS TO ACAPULCO(1968, Ger.)
Hyman Kerstein
RIDE THE HIGH WIND(1967, South Africa), p
Alice Kersten
WONDER MAN(1945)
Corinne Kersten
MURMUR OF THE HEART(1971, Fr./Ital./Ger.)
Katja Kersten
RADIO ON(1980, Brit./Ger.)
Larry Kert
LASSIE, COME HOME(1943); SYNANON(1965)
Michael Kertes
Misc. Silents
MRS. DANE'S CONFESSION(1922, Brit.), d
Csaba Kertesz
JOY(1983, Fr./Can.), art d
David C. Kertesz
UNSUSPECTED, THE(1947), spec eff
Harry Kerua
ADVENTURES OF MARCO POLO, THE(1938)

Genevieve Kervine
PLEASURES AND VICES(1962, Fr.)
Brian Kerwin
HOMETOWN U.S.A.(1979)
Misc. Talkies
GETTING WASTED(1980)
David Kerwin
ARIZONA KID, THE(1939); KNOCKOUT(1941)
Harry Kerwin
STING OF DEATH(1966), makeup; FLESH FEAST(1970), prod d; BARRACUDA(1978), p&w
Harry E. Kerwin
MY THIRD WIFE GEORGE(1968), p&d, ed
Misc. Talkies
GOD'S BLOODY ACRE(1975), d; CHEERING SECTION(1977), d; TOMCATS(1977), d
Lance Kerwin
Misc. Talkies
MYSTERIOUS STRANGER(1982)
Maureen Kerwin
DESTRUCTORS, THE(1974, Brit.)
1984
MISUNDERSTOOD(1984)
Rooney Kerwin
ABSENCE OF MALICE(1981); PORKY'S II: THE NEXT DAY(1983)
Shane Kerwin
1984
RACING WITH THE MOON(1984)
William Kerwin
LIVING VENUS(1961); HOOKED GENERATION, THE(1969); BARRACUDA(1978), a, d
Caro Keryatta
CLEOPATRA JONES(1973)
Leo Kerz
GUILTY BYSTANDER(1950), prod d&art d; TERESA(1951), art d; ER LOVE A STRANGER(1958), art d; ODDS AGAINST TOMORROW(1959), art d
Ken Kesey
SOMETIMES A GREAT NOTION(1971), w; ONE FLEW OVER THE CUCKOO'S NEST(1975), w
Mohammad Ali Keshavarz
CARAVANS(1978, U.S./Iranian)
Suna Keskin
YOU CAN'T WIN 'EM ALL(1970, Brit.)
Eero Keskitalo
TIME OF ROSES(1970, Fin.)
Henry Kesler
THREE RUSSIAN GIRLS(1943), d
Henry S. Kesler
IN A LONELY PLACE(1950), p; FIVE STEPS TO DANGER(1957), p,d&w
A. Kesmatov
VOW, THE(1947, USSR.), ph
Jillian Kesner
STUDENT BODY, THE(1976); STARHOPS(1978); FIRECRACKER(1981); TRICK OR TREATS(1982)
Dave Kessan
ONE EMBARRASSING NIGHT(1930, Brit.), ph
George Kessel
PARIS AFTER DARK(1943), w
Georges Kessel
JOAN OF PARIS(1942), w
Joseph Kessel
MAYERLING(1937, Fr.), w; WOMAN I LOVE, THE(1937), w; THEY ARE NOT ANGELS(1948, Fr.), w; SIROCCO(1951), w; LOVER'S NET(1957, Fr.), w; LION, THE(1962, Brit.), w; NIGHT OF THE GENERALS, THE(1967, Brit./Fr.), w; BELLE DE JOUR(1968, Fr.), w; MAYERLING(1968, Brit./Fr.), w; L'ARMEE DES OMBRES(1969, Fr./Ital.), w; HORSEMEN, THE(1971), w
Joseph Kesselring
ARSENIC AND OLD LACE(1944), w
Joseph O. Kesserling
AGGIE APPLEBY, MAKER OF MEN(1933), w
Norman Kessing
NATE AND HAYES(1983, U.S./New Zealand)
Alice Kessler
BEGGAR STUDENT, THE(1958, Ger.); LOVE AND THE FRENCHWOMAN(1961, Fr.); SODOM AND GOMORRAH(1962, U.S./Fr./Ital.); DOUBLE DECEPTION(1963, Fr.); ERIK THE CONQUEROR(1963, Fr./Ital.); CORPSE OF BEVERLY HILLS, THE(1965, Ger.)
Beatrice Kessler
BLACK SPIDER, THE(1983, Swit.)
Bodo Kessler
GERMANY IN AUTUMN(1978, Ger.), ph
Bruce Kessler
ANGELS FROM HELL(1968), d; KILLERS THREE(1968), d; GAY DECEIVERS, THE(1969), d; SIMON, KING OF THE WITCHES(1971), d
Catherine Kessler
MURDER BY DECREE(1979, Brit.)
Edith Kessler
Silents
WHAT DO MEN WANT?(1921)
Misc. Silents
TO PLEASE ONE WOMAN(1920)
Ellen Kessler
BEGGAR STUDENT, THE(1958, Ger.); LOVE AND THE FRENCHWOMAN(1961, Fr.); SODOM AND GOMORRAH(1962, U.S./Fr./Ital.); DOUBLE DECEPTION(1963, Fr.); ERIK THE CONQUEROR(1963, Fr./Ital.); CORPSE OF BEVERLY HILLS, THE(1965, Ger.)
Eva Kessler
PARSIFAL(1983, Fr.)

Francine Kessler
TRACK OF THE MOONBEAST(1976)
Irene Kessler
LUCKY STAR, THE(1980, Can.)
Kathy Kessler
MUSCLE BEACH PARTY(1964)
Lori Kessler
1984
SPLASH(1984)
Lyle Kessler
LOVE IN A TAXI(1980); TOUCHED(1983), a, w
Quinn Kessler
Misc. Talkies
SHE(1983)
Robert Kessler
1984
BODY ROCK(1984)
Todd Kessler
1984
PREPPIES(1984), w
Walter Kessler
LADY SURRENDERS, A(1930), set d
Wulf Kessler
BLOODLINE(1979)
Zale Kessler
PRODUCERS, THE(1967); CHEAP DETECTIVE, THE(1978); CLONUS HORROR, THE(1979); HISTORY OF THE WORLD, PART 1(1981); PRIVATE SCHOOL(1983); TO BE OR NOT TO BE(1983)
Jillian Kessner
RAW FORCE(1982)
Julian Kessner
Misc. Talkies
TRICK OR TREATS(1983)
Frank Kessock
CAVALIER OF THE WEST(1931), ph
Dave Kesson
SPLINTERS(1929, Brit.), ph; LOVES OF ROBERT BURNS, THE(1930, Brit.), ph
David Kesson
Silents
DINTY(1920), ph; BOB HAMPTON OF PLACER(1921), ph; PENROD(1922), ph; STRANGER'S BANQUET(1922), ph; ETERNAL THREE, THE(1923), ph; RENDEZ-VOUS, THE(1923), ph; TESS OF THE D'URBERVILLES(1924), ph; UNHOLY THREE, THE(1925), ph; MIKE(1926), ph; SKYROCKET, THE(1926), ph; WILD OATS LA-NE(1926), ph; MY BEST GIRL(1927), ph
Frank Kesson
LAND OF THE SILVER FOX(1928), ph; MIDNIGHT TAXI, THE(1928), ph; MY MAN(1928), ph; WOMEN THEY TALK ABOUT(1928), ph; NO DEFENSE(1929), ph; ONE STOLEN NIGHT(1929), ph; COLLEGE LOVERS(1930), ph
Silents
CAVEMAN, THE(1926), ph; SEA BEAST, THE(1926), ph; HILLS OF KENTUCK-Y(1927), ph; MATINEE LADIES(1927), ph; SAILOR IZZY MURPHY(1927), ph; SAIL-OR'S SWEETHEART, A(1927), ph; SILVER SLAVE, THE(1927), ph; POWDER MY BACK(1928), ph
Jessie Kesson
ANOTHER TIME, ANOTHER PLACE(1983, Brit.), d&w
1984
ANOTHER TIME, ANOTHER PLACE(1984, Brit.), d&w
Magnus Kesster
WOMAN'S FACE, A(1939, Swed.); ONLY ONE NIGHT(1942, Swed.)
Sara Kestelman
ZARDOZ(1974, Brit.); LISZTOMANIA(1975, Brit.); BREAK OF DAY(1977, Aus.)
Bob Kesten
SKIN GAME, THE(1965, Brit.), w
Michele Kesten
TIGER MAKES OUT, THE(1967)
Stephen F. Kesten
AMITYVILLE 3-D(1983), p
Jim Kester
POM POM GIRLS, THE(1976); VAN, THE(1977); MALIBU BEACH(1978); VAN NUYS BLVD.(1979); MY TUTOR(1983)
Karen Kester
BARON OF ARIZONA, THE(1950); ENFORCER, THE(1951)
Max Kester
WEEKEND MILLIONAIRE(1937, Brit.), w; CROOKS TOUR(1940, Brit.), w; GEORGE IN CIVVY STREET(1946, Brit.), w; TICKET TO PARADISE(1961, Brit.), w
Paul Kester
Silents
FOOD FOR SCANDAL(1920), w
George Kesterson [Victor Adamson, Denver Dixon, Art Mix]
Misc. Silents
RIDERS OF BORDER BAY(1925); ROPED BY RADIO(1925); MAN FROM THE RIO GRANDE, THE(1926); PATHS OF FLAME(1926); SALT LAKE TRAIL(1926); SHADOW RANGER(1926)
Erich Kestin
TEMPORARY WIDOW, THE(1930, Ger./Brit.); BLONDE NIGHTINGALE(1931, Ger.)
Lea Kestin
JESUS CHRIST, SUPERSTAR(1973)
John Keston
MAN OF VIOLENCE(1970, Brit.)
Steve Ketcher
REVENGE OF THE NINJA(1983)
Cliff Ketchum
PORK CHOP HILL(1959); YOUNG LAND, THE(1959)
Dave Ketchum
GOOD NEIGHBOR SAM(1964); BLESS THE BEASTS AND CHILDREN(1971); MAIN EVENT, THE(1979); NORTH AVENUE IRREGULARS, THE(1979)
David Ketchum
YOUR THREE MINUTES ARE UP(1973); HAZING, THE(1978), w; LOVE AT FIRST BITE(1979)

Harriet Ketchum
PAPER MOON(1973)
Philip Ketchum
DEVIL'S TRAIL, THE(1942), w
Minajlo Jan Ketic
HOROSCOPE(1950, Yugo.)
Fulvia Ketoff
KREMLIN LETTER, THE(1970)
Eric Kettelhut
Silents
KRIEMHILD'S REVENGE(1924, Ger.), art d; SIEGFRIED(1924, Ger.), art d
Erich Kettelhut
BOMBARDMENT OF MONTE CARLO, THE(1931, Ger.), art d; F.P. 1 DOESN'T ANSWER(1933, Ger.), art d; FINAL CHORD, THE(1936, Ger.), set d; THOUSAND EYES OF DR. MABUSE, THE(1960, Fr./Ital./Ger.), art d; U-47 LT. COMMANDER PRIEN(1967, Ger.), art d
Sepp Ketterer
APRIL 1, 2000(1953, Aust.), ph; YOU ARE THE WORLD FOR ME(1964, Aust.), ph
The Kettering Triplets
ETERNALLY YOURS(1939)
Diane Ketterling
1984
EXTERMINATOR 2(1984)
Anne Kettle
GUTTER GIRLS(1964, Brit.)
Charles Kettle
Silents
ADVENTURES OF CAPTAIN KETTLE, THE(1922, Brit.)
Erich Kettlehut
Silents
METROPOLIS(1927, Ger.), art d
Gary Kettler
OPERATION SECRET(1952)
Ruth Kettlewell
ROOM AT THE TOP(1959, Brit.); SONS AND LOVERS(1960, Brit.); CLUE OF THE NEW PIN, THE(1961, Brit.); GUTTER GIRLS(1964, Brit.); OH! WHAT A LOVELY WAR(1969, Brit.); NO BLADE OF GRASS(1970, Brit.); ZEPPELIN(1971, Brit.)
Hans-Joachim Ketzlin
THAT WOMAN(1968, Ger.)
Andrea Keuer
LOLA(1982, Ger.)
William L. Keuhl
SOUTH SEA WOMAN(1953), set d
Sylvia Keuler
RAIDERS OF THE LOST ARK(1981), anim
Margot Keune
SPETTERS(1983, Holland)
Tsui Siu Keung
SECRET, THE(1979, Hong Kong)
Mark Keuning
DARK CITY(1950); THREE CAME HOME(1950)
Derek Keurvorst
1984
MRS. SOFFEL(1984)
Jack Kevan
LAND UNKNOWN, THE(1957), spec eff; MAN OF A THOUSAND FACES(1957), makeup; MONSTER OF PIEDRAS BLANCAS, THE(1959), a, p; 7TH COMMAND-MENT, THE(1961), w; STREET IS MY BEAT, THE(1966), w
John Kevan
EXPERT'S OPINION(1935, Brit.); LOVE UP THE POLE(1936, Brit.); SECRET VOICE, THE(1936, Brit.); 13 MEN AND A GUN(1938, Brit.); GARRISON FOLLIES(1940, Brit.)
James Kevin
YOUNG AND WILD(1958)
Jeff Kevin
NO. 96(1974, Aus.)
Sandy Kevin
PALM SPRINGS WEEKEND(1963); CINCINNATI KID, THE(1965); KELLY'S HEROES(1970, U.S./Yugo.); PATTON(1970); MAN WHO LOVED CAT DANCING, THE(1973); WILD McCULLOCHS, THE(1975)
Kevin & Gary
POPDOWN(1968, Brit.)
E.M. Kevke
INCREDIBLY STRANGE CREATURES WHO STOPPED LIVING AND BECAME CRAZY MIXED-UP ZOMBIES, THE(1965), w
Alexander Key
ESCAPE TO WITCH MOUNTAIN(1975), w; RETURN FROM WITCH MOUN-TAIN(1978), w
Alice Key
ACTORS AND SIN(1952)
Alison Key
BLACK PANTHER, THE(1977, Brit.)
Mrs. E. J. Key
Silents
DAUGHTER OF LOVE, A(1925, Brit.), w
Eugene Key
SOLDIER, THE(1982)
Janet Key
CHAIRMAN, THE(1969); VAMPIRE LOVERS, THE(1970, Brit.); PERCY(1971, Brit.); DRACULA A.D. 1972(1972, Brit.); LADY CAROLINE LAMB(1972, Brit./Ital.); AND NOW THE SCREAMING STARTS(1973, Brit.); DEVIL WITHIN HER, THE(1976, Brit.)
1984
1984(1984, Brit.)
Kathleen Key
KLONDIKE ANNIE(1936)
Silents
FOUR HORSEMEN OF THE APOCALYPSE, THE(1921); ROOKIE'S RETURN, THE(1921); BEAUTIFUL AND DAMNED, THE(1922); WEST OF CHICAGO(1922); NORTH OF HUDSON BAY(1923); RENDEZVOUS, THE(1923); RENO(1923); REVELA-TION(1924); BEN-HUR(1925); LOVER'S OATH, A(1925); COLLEGE DAYS(1926); DES-ERT'S TOLL, THE(1926); HEY! HEY! COWBOY(1927); IRISH HEARTS(1927);

PHANTOM OF THE NORTH(1929)
Misc. Silents
TROUBLE SHOOTER, THE(1924)
Lotis M. Key
BLACK MAMA, WHITE MAMA(1973)
Peter Key
CRAWLING EYE, THE(1958, Brit.), w
Ted Key
$1,000,000 DUCK(1971), w; DIGBY, THE BIGGEST DOG IN THE WORLD(1974, Brit.), w; GUS(1976), w; CAT FROM OUTER SPACE, THE(1978), w
Sandro Key-Aberg
VIBRATION(1969, Swed.), w
Dr. John Keye
WINGS OF EAGLES, THE(1957), tech adv
Basil N. Keyes
CROSS MY HEART(1937, Brit.), w
Bob Keyes
FEUDIN' FOOLS(1952)
Burt Keyes
HUGO THE HIPPO(1976, Hung./U.S.), m
Clay Keyes
CHARING CROSS ROAD(1935, Brit.), w
Daniel Keyes
CHARLY(1968), w; ME, NATALIE(1969); I NEVER SANG FOR MY FATHER(1970); 1776(1972)
Don Keyes
MY DOG, BUDDY(1960)
Donald Keyes
CYCLONE RANGER(1935), ph
Silents
WILD OATS LANE(1926), ph
Donald Biddle Keyes
Silents
TEN COMMANDMENTS, THE(1923), ph
Earl Keyes
RETURN TO CAMPUS(1975)
Evelyn Keyes
ARTISTS AND MODELS ABROAD(1938); BUCCANEER, THE(1938); MEN WITH WINGS(1938); SONS OF THE LEGION(1938); GONE WITH THE WIND(1939); SUDDEN MONEY(1939); UNION PACIFIC(1939); BEFORE I HANG(1940); LADY IN QUESTION, THE(1940); SLIGHTLY HONORABLE(1940); BEYOND THE SACRAMENTO(1941); FACE BEHIND THE MASK, THE(1941); HERE COMES MR. JORDAN(1941); LADIES IN RETIREMENT(1941); ADVENTURES OF MARTIN EDEN, THE(1942); FLIGHT LIEUTENANT(1942); DANGEROUS BLONDES(1943); DESPERADOES, THE(1943); THERE'S SOMETHING ABOUT A SOLDIER(1943); NINE GIRLS(1944); STRANGE AFFAIR(1944); THOUSAND AND ONE NIGHTS, A(1945); JOLSON STORY, THE(1946); RENEGADES(1946); THRILL OF BRAZIL, THE(1946); JOHNNY O'CLOCK(1947); ENCHANTMENT(1948); MATING OF MILLIE, THE(1948); MR. SOFT TOUCH(1949); MRS. MIKE(1949); KILLER THAT STALKED NEW YORK, THE(1950); IRON MAN, THE(1951); PROWLER, THE(1951); SMUGGLER'S ISLAND(1951); ONE BIG AFFAIR(1952); IT HAPPENED IN PARIS(1953, Fr.); SHOOT FIRST(1953, Brit.); 99 RIVER STREET(1953); HELL'S HALF ACRE(1954); SEVEN YEAR ITCH, THE(1955); TOP OF THE WORLD(1955); AROUND THE WORLD IN 80 DAYS(1956)
Evohn Keyes
Misc. Talkies
RIO GRANDE(1949)
George Keyes
ONLY WAY HOME, THE(1972)
Geraldine Keyes
SCHOOL FOR SECRETS(1946, Brit.)
Gladys Keyes
CHARING CROSS ROAD(1935, Brit.), w
Herwood Keyes
HOODLUM SAINT, THE(1946), cos
Irwin Keyes
NOCTURNA(1979); PRIZE FIGHTER, THE(1979); WARRIORS, THE(1979); PRIVATE EYES, THE(1980); ZAPPED!(1982)
1984
EXTERMINATOR 2(1984)
Joe Keyes
1984
SONGWRITER(1984)
Joe Keyes, Jr.
WHERE'S POPPA?(1970); WILLIE DYNAMITE(1973), w
John Keyes
RACKETY RAX(1932)
Lilian Keyes
BOOTS! BOOTS!(1934, Brit.)
Marion Keyes
KEEP YOUR POWDER DRY(1945), cos
Marion Herwood Keyes
HER HIGHNESS AND THE BELLBOY(1945), cos; WITHOUT LOVE(1945), cos. Irene; POSTMAN ALWAYS RINGS TWICE, THE(1946), cos; BODY AND SOUL(1947), cos
Peggy Keyes
RIDERS OF THE DAWN(1937); FLIGHT ANGELS(1940)
Robert Keyes
CRIME AGAINST JOE(1956)
Roger Keyes
SCHOOL FOR SECRETS(1946, Brit.)
Stephen Keyes
LAND OF THE OUTLAWS(1944); OKLAHOMA RAIDERS(1944); DEADLINE(1948)
Stephen [Steve] Keyes
DEAD MAN'S GOLD(1948)
Steve Keyes
MUSTANG(1959)

Steven Keyes
Misc. Talkies
SUNSET CARSON RIDES AGAIN(1948)
Vernon Keyes
Misc. Talkies
TRIGGER LAW(1944), d; UTAH KID, THE(1944), d
Maj. Donald E. Keyhoe
EARTH VS. THE FLYING SAUCERS(1956), w
Mark Keyloun
THOSE LIPS, THOSE EYES(1980); FORTY DEUCE(1982); SUDDEN IMPACT(1983)
1984
GIMME AN 'F'(1984); MIKE'S MURDER(1984)
George Keymas
BORDER RANGERS(1950); ACTORS AND SIN(1952); FLAME OF CALCUTTA(1953); KING OF THE KHYBER RIFLES(1953); ROBE, THE(1953); SALOME(1953); SIREN OF BAGDAD(1953); BAIT(1954); BLACK DAKOTAS, THE(1954); DRUMS OF TAHITI(1954); THEY RODE WEST(1954); APACHE AMBUSH(1955); BAMBOO PRISON, THE(1955); SANTA FE PASSAGE(1955); VANISHING AMERICAN, THE(1955); WYOMING RENEGADES(1955); FURY AT GUNSIGHT PASS(1956); KENTUCKY RIFLE(1956); MAVERICK QUEEN, THE(1956); THUNDER OVER ARIZONA(1956); WHITE SQUAW, THE(1956); APACHE WARRIOR(1957); GUNFIRE AT INDIAN GAP(1957); PLUNDER ROAD(1957); STORM RIDER, THE(1957); UTAH BLAINE(1957); COLE YOUNGER, GUNFIGHTER(1958); GUNSMOKE IN TUCSON(1958); STUDS LONIGAN(1960); ARIZONA RAIDERS(1965); BEAU GESTE(1966); OTHER SIDE OF MIDNIGHT, THE(1977)
The Keynotes
MELODY IN THE DARK(1948, Brit.)
Anthony Nelson Keys
PIRATES OF BLOOD RIVER, THE(1962, Brit.), p; CRIMSON BLADE, THE(1964, Brit.), p; DEVIL-SHIP PIRATES, THE(1964, Brit.), p; GORGON, THE(1964, Brit.), p; BRIGAND OF KANDAHAR, THE(1965, Brit.), p; FRANKENSTEIN CREATED WOMAN(1965, Brit.), p; SECRET OF BLOOD ISLAND, THE(1965, Brit.), p; PLAGUE OF THE ZOMBIES, THE(1966, Brit.), p; RASPUTIN-THE MAD MONK(1966, Brit.), p; REPTILE, THE(1966, Brit.), p; DEVIL'S OWN, THE(1967, Brit.), p; MUMMY'S SHROUD, THE(1967, Brit.), p; DEVIL'S BRIDE, THE(1968, Brit.), p; FRANKENSTEIN MUST BE DESTROYED!(1969, Brit.), p, w
Bob Keys
KANSAS PACIFIC(1953)
Jimi Keys
Misc. Talkies
BLOODRAGE(1979)
Nelson Keys
SPLINTERS(1929, Brit.); ALMOST A DIVORCE(1931, Brit.); DREAMS COME TRUE(1936, Brit.); ELIZA COMES TO STAY(1936, Brit.); IN THE SOUP(1936, Brit.); LAST JOURNEY, THE(1936, Brit.); KNIGHTS FOR A DAY(1937, Brit.); WAKE UP FAMOUS(1937, Brit.)
Silents
ONCE UPON A TIME(1918, Brit.); MADAME POMPADOUR(1927, Brit.); MUMSIE(1927, Brit.)
Misc. Silents
JUDGED BY APPEARANCES(1916, Brit.); CASTLES IN THE AIR(1923, Brit.); TIPTOES(1927, Brit.); SCARLET DAREDEVIL, THE(1928, Brit.); WHEN KNIGHTS WERE BOLD(1929, Brit.)
Peggy Keys
CONFESSION(1937); RAW TIMBER(1937)
Robert Keys
UNTIL THEY SAIL(1957); BIG JIM McLAIN(1952); ISLAND IN THE SKY(1953); SON OF BELLE STARR(1953); TROUBLE ALONG THE WAY(1953); BAD FOR EACH OTHER(1954); BOUNTY HUNTER, THE(1954); HIGH AND THE MIGHTY, THE(1954); EMERGENCY HOSPITAL(1956); MAN IN THE VAULT(1956); REVOLT AT FORT LARAMIE(1957); STREET OF DARKNESS(1958), a, p; OPERATION PETTICOAT(1959)
Misc. Talkies
STREET OF DARKNESS(1958)
Rod Keys
BIG JOB, THE(1965, Brit.), ed; CARRY ON SCREAMING(1966, Brit.), ed; DON'T LOSE YOUR HEAD(1967, Brit.), ed; ISLAND OF THE BURNING DAMNED(1971, Brit.), ed
Steven Keys
WEST OF THE ALAMO(1946)
William Keys
WILD SCENE, THE(1970), w
Hugh Keys-Byrne
TRESPASSERS, THE(1976, Aus.)
Chuck Keyser
THEM NICE AMERICANS(1958, Brit.); FIRST MAN INTO SPACE(1959, Brit.); SUBWAY IN THE SKY(1959, Brit.)
Stephanie Keyser
BABY, IT'S YOU(1983)
Keystone Cops
DOWN MEMORY LANE(1949)
Alice Keywan
SILENCE OF THE NORTH(1981, Can.), art d
Bob Keyworth
C. C. AND COMPANY(1971)
George Kezas
WOMAN OF THE YEAR(1942)
Gyorgy Kezdi
FATHER(1967, Hung.); WITNESS, THE(1982, Hung.)
Zsolt Kezdi-Kovacs
FORBIDDEN RELATIONS(1983, Hung.), d&w
Glen Kezer
NO WAY TO TREAT A LADY(1968)
Glenn Kezer
WEREWOLF OF WASHINGTON(1973)
Tullio Kezich
SOUND OF TRUMPETS, THE(1963, Ital.); MAN WHO CAME FOR COFFEE, THE(1970, Ital.), w

M. Khablenko
SHE-WOLF, THE(1963, USSR), art d
A. Khachanian
Misc. Silents
NAMUS(1926, USSR)
Olya Khachapuridze
MAGIC WEAVER, THE(1965, USSR)
Aram Khachaturian
IRON CURTAIN, THE(1948), m; OTHELLO(1960, U.S.S.R.), m
Aram Khachaturyan
JOVITA(1970, Pol.), m
E. Khachaturyan
VIOLIN AND ROLLER(1962, USSR), md
Micholas Khadarik
LOST MOMENT, THE(1947)
B. Khaidarov
CITY OF YOUTH(1938, USSR)
Mary Khal
BLOW-UP(1966, Brit.)
Josette Khalil
CIRCLE OF DECEIT(1982, Fr./Ger.)
Persis Khambatta
CONDUCT UNBECOMING(1975, Brit.); WILBY CONSPIRACY, THE(1975, Brit.); STAR TREK: THE MOTION PICTURE(1979); NIGHTHAWKS(1981); MEGAFORCE(1982)
Abas Khan
TARZAN GOES TO INDIA(1962, U.S./Brit./Switz.)
Ali Akbar Khan
GODDESS, THE(1962, India), m
Amjad Khan
1984
MOHAN JOSHI HAAZIR HO(1984, India)
Amzad Khan
CHESS PLAYERS, THE(1978, India)
Bismilla Khan
MUSIC ROOM, THE(1963, India)
Feroz Khan
TARZAN GOES TO INDIA(1962, U.S./Brit./Switz.)
George Khan
OUT OF THE DEPTHS(1946)
Gordon Khan
SHEIK STEPS OUT, THE(1937), w
Iska Khan
BELLE DE JOUR(1968, Fr.); FIENDISH PLOT OF DR. FU MANCHU, THE(1980)
Lilly Khan "Kann"
THIRD MAN, THE(1950, Brit.)
Naseem Khan
LONG DUEL, THE(1967, Brit.)
Pasha Khan
CONQUEST(1937); FLIGHT FROM GLORY(1937)
Rashid Khan
GUIDE, THE(1965, U.S./India)
Sajik Khan
HEAT AND DUST(1983, Brit.)
Salamat Khan
MUSIC ROOM, THE(1963, India)
Shari Khan
TOO HOT TO HANDLE(1961, Brit.)
Ustad Ali Akbar Khan
HOUSEHOLDER, THE(1963, US/India), m
Ustad Imrat Khan
1984
MAJDHAR(1984, Brit.), m
Ustad Vilayat Khan
MUSIC ROOM, THE(1963, India), md
Ustad Vilayet Khan
GURU, THE(1969, U.S./India), m
Ustad Waheed Khan
MUSIC ROOM, THE(1963, India)
Yassan Khan
1984
AMERICAN DREAMER(1984)
Z.H. Khan
1984
PASSAGE TO INDIA, A(1984, Brit.)
Yevgeniya Khanayeva
MOSCOW DOES NOT BELIEVE IN TEARS(1980, USSR)
Julie Khaner
VIDEODROME(1983, Can.)
A. Khanov
GENERAL SUVOROV(1941, USSR)
Alexander Khanzhonkov
Misc. Silents
DEFENCE OF SEVASTOPOL(1911, USSR), d
T. Kharchenko
JACK FROST(1966, USSR)
Ye. Kharchenko
SONG OF THE FOREST(1963, USSR)
Leo Kharibian
DON'T RAISE THE BRIDGE, LOWER THE RIVER(1968, Brit.), ch
S. Kharitonova
CRANES ARE FLYING, THE(1960, USSR)
H. Kharkov
Silents
ARSENAL(1929, USSR)
Alexei Kharlamov
Misc. Silents
DEATH BAY(1926, USSR)

A. Kharyakov
TRAIN GOES TO KIEV, THE(1961, USSR)
Yu. Khaso
SANDU FOLLOWS THE SUN(1965, USSR)
M. Khatuntseva
GROWN-UP CHILDREN(1963, USSR)
B. Khaykin
SLEEPING BEAUTY, THE(1966, USSR), md
Hassan Khayyam
RAZOR'S EDGE, THE(1946); CALCUTTA(1947); WHEN WORLDS COLLIDE(1951); KING OF THE KHYBER RIFLES(1953); BON VOYAGE(1962)
Hassan Khayyan
INTRIGUE(1947)
Hassen Khayyan
CASBAH(1948)
Malak Khazai
MEETINGS WITH REMARKABLE MEN(1979, Brit.), set d
Z. Khazrevin
SON OF MONGOLIA(1936, USSR), w
A. Khbilya
VOW, THE(1947, USSR.)
Franklin Khedouri
SATURDAY NIGHT AT THE BATHS(1975), w
Ivan Kheil
LOVES OF A BLONDE(1966, Czech.)
Chrisanf Kheronsky
MUMU(1961, USSR), w
A. Kheruvimov
Misc. Silents
FLOOD(1915, USSR)
Iosif Kheyfits
LADY WITH THE DOG, THE(1962, USSR), d&w
Gudrun Mardou Khiess
ROMA(1972, Ital./Fr.)
E. Khil
SONG OVER MOSCOW(1964, USSR)
Stanislav Khitrov
PEACE TO HIM WHO ENTERS(1963, USSR)
L. Khityayeva
NIGHT BEFORE CHRISTMAS, A(1963, USSR)
Lyudmila Khityayeva
AND QUIET FLOWS THE DON(1960 USSR)
S. Khizhnyak
MUMU(1961, USSR), spec eff
N. Khlibko
THERE WAS AN OLD COUPLE(1967, USSR)
Grigori Khmara
Misc. Silents
QUEEN OF THE SCREEN(1916, USSR); THOUGHT(1916, USSR); DON'T BUILD YOUR HAPPINESS ON YOUR WIFE AND CHILD(1917, USSR); BRUISED BY THE STORMS OF LIFE(1918, USSR)
Ilia Khmara
NORTH STAR, THE(1943); ARCH OF TRIUMPH(1948)
V. Khmara
MUMU(1961, USSR)
Nikolai Khmelyov
Misc. Silents
DOMESTIC-AGITATOR(1920, USSR)
Shirak Khojayan
EVICTORS, THE(1979), ed
A. Khokhlov
ADMIRAL NAKHIMOV(1948, USSR)
Konstantin Khokhlov
Misc. Silents
GREEN SPIDER, THE(1916, USSR); STRONG MAN, THE(1917, USSR)
Khokhlova
Misc. Silents
DEATH RAY, THE(1925, USSR)
Alexandra Khokhlova
Misc. Silents
BY THE LAW(1926, USSR); YOUR ACQUAINTANCE(1927, USSR)
Georgiy Kholnyy
HUNTING IN SIBERIA(1962, USSR), ph
Vera Kholodnaya
Misc. Silents
SONG OF TRIUMPHANT LOVE(1915, USSR); LIFE FOR A LIFE, A(1916, USSR); WOMAN WHO INVENTED LOVE, THE(1918, USSR)
Vera Kholodnya
Misc. Silents
LIVING CORPSE, A(1918, USSR)
Roman Khomyatov
RED AND THE WHITE, THE(1969, Hung./USSR)
Anton Khorava
LAST HILL, THE(1945, USSR)
Philippe Khorsand
1984
EDITH AND MARCEL(1984, Fr.); LES COMPERES(1984, Fr.)
Lucas Khosa
PENNYWHISTLE BLUES, THE(1952, South Africa)
Durga Khote
HOUSEHOLDER, THE(1963, US/India)
M. Khotuntseva
SONG OVER MOSCOW(1964, USSR)
Shakib Khouri
24 HOURS TO KILL(1966, Brit.)
George Khoury
KIM(1950); MALAYA(1950); TEN TALL MEN(1951); HAREM GIRL(1952); KING OF THE KHYBER RIFLES(1953); SALOME(1953); ABBOTT AND COSTELLO MEET THE MUMMY(1955); LOOKING FOR DANGER(1957); SABU AND THE MAGIC RING(1957); 20 MILLION MILES TO EARTH(1957)

Nejib Khoury
MOHAMMAD, MESSENGER OF GOD(1976, Lebanon/Brit.), art d

Ron Khoury
DETROIT 9000(1973)

V. Khovanskaya
ITALIANO BRAVA GENTE(1965, Ital./USSR), ph

Ye. Khovanskaya
WAR AND PEACE(1968, USSR)

R. Khozak
SONS AND MOTHERS(1967, USSR), m

Mikhail Khrabrov
WAR AND PEACE(1968, USSR)

Daniil Khrabrovitskiy
CLEAR SKIES(1963, USSR), w; NINE DAYS OF ONE YEAR(1964, USSR), w

Tikhon Khrenikov
SIX P.M.(1946, USSR), m

B. Khrennikov
TAXI TO HEAVEN(1944, USSR), spec eff

T. Khrennikov
DREAM OF A COSSACK(1982, USSR), m

Tikhon Khrennikov
TRAIN GOES EAST, THE(1949, USSR), m; BALLAD OF A HUSSAR(1963, USSR), m

N. Khryashchikov
CLEAR SKIES(1963, USSR); OPTIMISTIC TRAGEDY, THE(1964, USSR); WAR AND PEACE(1968, USSR)

I. Khudoleyev
Misc. Silents
WOMAN WHO INVENTED LOVE, THE(1918, USSR); LOCKSMITH AND CHANCELLOR(1923, USSR)

K. Khudyakov
GROWN-UP CHILDREN(1963, USSR)

Kakhi Khutsishvili
STEPCHILDREN(1962, USSR), art d

A. Khvilla
HEROES ARE MADE(1944, USSR)

A. Khvilya
SECRET BRIGADE, THE(1951 USSR)

Aleksandr Khvylya
TRAIN GOES TO KIEV, THE(1961, USSR); NIGHT BEFORE CHRISTMAS, A(1963, USSR); RESURRECTION(1963, USSR); DUEL, THE(1964, USSR); MAGIC WEAVER, THE(1965, USSR); JACK FROST(1966, USSR)

T. Khyarm
DEAD MOUNTAINEER HOTEL, THE(1979, USSR)

Hassan Khyyam
DREAM WIFE(1953)

Johnnie Kiado
MARRYING KIND, THE(1952)

Omar Kiam
KID MILLIONS(1934), cos; WE LIVE AGAIN(1934), cos; CLIVE OF INDIA(1935), cos; DARK ANGEL, THE(1935), cos; FOLIES DERGERE(1935), cos; SPLENDOR(1935), cos; WEDDING NIGHT, THE(1935), cos; COME AND GET IT(1936), cos; DODSWORTH(1936), cos; ONE RAINY AFTERNOON(1936), cos; STRIKE ME PINK(1936), cos; THESE THREE(1936), cos; DEAD END(1937), cos; HURRICANE, THE(1937), cos; STAR IS BORN, A(1937), cos; STELLA DALLAS(1937), cos; WOMAN CHASES MAN(1937), cos; ADVENTURES OF MARCO POLO, THE(1938), cos; ALGIERS(1938), cos; COWBOY AND THE LADY, THE(1938), cos; GOLDWYN FOLLIES, THE(1938), cos; WUTHERING HEIGHTS(1939), cos; ZENOBIA(1939), cos

Elene Kiamos
PATTERNS(1956)

Eleni Kiamos
DIARY OF A BACHELOR(1964)

Walter Kiaulehn
LOLA MONTES(1955, Fr./Ger.)

Yurgent Kibach
MAGICIAN OF LUBLIN, THE(1979, Israel/Ger.), art d

Margerita Kibalchich
Misc. Silents
SHACKLED BY FILM(1918, USSR)

Vera Kibardina
NEW HORIZONS(1939, USSR)

Guy B. Kibbee
WONDER BAR(1934)

Guy Kibbee
BLONDE CRAZY(1931); CITY STREETS(1931); FLYING HIGH(1931); LAUGHING SINNERS(1931); MAN OF THE WORLD(1931); NEW ADVENTURES OF GET-RICH-QUICK WALLINGFORD, THE(1931); SIDE SHOW(1931); STOLEN HEAVEN(1931); BIG CITY BLUES(1932); CENTRAL PARK(1932); CONQUERORS, THE(1932); CROONER(1932); CROWD ROARS, THE(1932); DARK HORSE, THE(1932); FIREMAN, SAVE MY CHILD(1932); HIGH PRESSURE(1932); MAN WANTED(1932); MOUTHPIECE, THE(1932); PLAY GIRL(1932); RAIN(1932); SCARLET DAWN(1932); SO BIG(1932); STRANGE LOVE OF MOLLY LOUVAIN, THE(1932); TAXI!(1932); TWO SECONDS(1932); UNION DEPOT(1932); WINNER TAKE ALL(1932); CONVENTION CITY(1933); FOOTLIGHT PARADE(1933); GIRL MISSING(1933); GOLD DIGGERS OF 1933(1933); HAVANA WIDOWS(1933); LADY FOR A DAY(1933); LIFE OF JIMMY DOLAN, THE(1933); LILLY TURNER(1933); SILK EXPRESS, THE(1933); WORLD CHANGES, THE(1933); 42ND STREET(1933); BABBITT(1934); BIG HEARTED HERBERT(1934); DAMES(1934); EASY TO LOVE(1934); HAROLD TEEN(1934); MERRY FRINKS, THE(1934); MERRY WIVES OF RENO, THE(1934); CAPTAIN BLOOD(1935); CAPTAIN JANUARY(1935); DON'T BET ON BLONDES(1935); GOING HIGH-BROW(1935); I LIVE FOR LOVE(1935); MARY JANE'S PA(1935); WHILE THE PATIENT SLEPT(1935); BIG NOISE, THE(1936); EARTHWORM TRACTORS(1936); I MARRIED A DOCTOR(1936); LITTLE LORD FAUNTLEROY(1936); M'LISS(1936); THREE MEN ON A HORSE(1936); BIG SHOT, THE(1937); CAPTAIN'S KID, THE(1937); DON'T TELL THE WIFE(1937); JIM HANVEY, DETECTIVE(1937); MAMA STEPS OUT(1937); MOUNTAIN JUSTICE(1937); RIDING ON AIR(1937); BAD MAN OF BRIMSTONE(1938); JOY OF LIVING(1938); OF HUMAN HEARTS(1938); RICH MAN, POOR GIRL(1938); THREE COMRADES(1938); THREE LOVES HAS NANCY(1938); BABES IN ARMS(1939); BAD LITTLE ANGEL(1939); HENRY GOES ARIZONA(1939); IT'S A WONDERFUL WORLD(1939); LET FREEDOM RING(1939); MR. SMITH GOES TO WASHINGTON(1939); CHAD HANNA(1940); OUR

TOWN(1940); STREET OF MEMORIES(1940); DESIGN FOR SCANDAL(1941); IT STARTED WITH EVE(1941); SCATTERGOOD BAINES(1941); SCATTERGOOD MEETS BROADWAY(1941); SCATTERGOOD PULLS THE STRINGS(1941); CINDERELLA SWINGS IT(1942); MISS ANNIE ROONEY(1942); SCATTERGOOD RIDES HIGH(1942); SCATTERGOOD SURVIVES A MURDER(1942); SUNDAY PUNCH(1942); THERE'S ONE BORN EVERY MINUTE(1942); THIS TIME FOR KEEPS(1942); TISH(1942); WHISTLING IN DIXIE(1942); GIRL CRAZY(1943); POWER OF THE PRESS(1943); DIXIE JAMBOREE(1945); HORN BLOWS AT MIDNIGHT, THE(1945); COWBOY BLUES(1946); RED STALLION, THE(1947); ROMANCE OF ROSY RIDGE, THE(1947); FORT APACHE(1948); THREE GODFATHERS, THE(1948)

Misc. Talkies
LONE STAR MOONLIGHT(1946); SINGING ON THE TRAIL(1946); OVER THE SANTA FE TRAIL(1947)

Jeff Kibbee
VALDEZ IS COMING(1971)

Linc Kibbee
VALDEZ IS COMING(1971), a, spec eff

Lois Kibbee
CADDY SHACK(1980)

Milt Kibbee
SWEET MUSIC(1935); LAW IN HER HANDS, THE(1936); LOVE BEGINS AT TWENTY(1936); MAN HUNT(1936); TREACHERY RIDES THE RANGE(1936); WALKING DEAD, THE(1936); DEVIL'S SADDLE LEGION, THE(1937); WHITE BONDAGE(1937); OVERLAND STAGE RAIDERS(1938); BLONDIE TAKES A VACATION(1939); ACROSS THE SIERRAS(1941); KANSAS CYCLONE(1941); ONE FOOT IN HEAVEN(1941); IN OLD CALIFORNIA(1942); LONE RIDER AND THE BANDIT, THE(1942); LONE RIDER IN CHEYENNE, THE(1942); MAJOR AND THE MINOR, THE(1942); RAIDERS OF THE WEST(1942); DIXIE DUGAN(1943); SHE HAS WHAT IT TAKES(1943); BLAZING FRONTIER(1944); THREE LITTLE SISTERS(1944); WHEN STRANGERS MARRY(1944); SCARLET CLUE, THE(1945); FREDDIE STEPS OUT(1946); HIGH SCHOOL HERO(1946); JUNIOR PROM(1946); SOMEWHERE IN THE NIGHT(1946); DESPERATE(1947); VACATION DAYS(1947)

Milton Kibbee
HEROES FOR SALE(1933); KENNEL MURDER CASE, THE(1933); PICTURE SNATCHER(1933); 42ND STREET(1933); GAMBLING LADY(1934); I SELL ANYTHING(1934); IT HAPPENED ONE NIGHT(1934); I'VE GOT YOUR NUMBER(1934); JIMMY THE GENT(1934); MAN WITH TWO FACES, THE(1934); ST. LOUIS KID, THE(1934); TWENTY MILLION SWEETHEARTS(1934); UPPER WORLD(1934); ALIBI IKE(1935); CASE OF THE CURIOUS BRIDE, THE(1935); CASINO MURDER CASE, THE(1935); DON'T BET ON BLONDES(1935); DR. SOCRATES(1935); FRISCO KID(1935); GOING HIGHBROW(1935); GOOSE AND THE GANDER, THE(1935); I FOUND STELLA PARISH(1935); IN CALIENTE(1935); SECRET BRIDE, THE(1935); SPECIAL AGENT(1935); STRANDED(1935); SWEET ADELINE(1935); TRAVELING SALESLADY, THE(1935); BULLETS OR BALLOTS(1936); CASE OF THE BLACK CAT, THE(1936); CHINA CLIPPER(1936); DANGEROUS(1936); I MARRIED A DOCTOR(1936); MOONLIGHT ON THE PRAIRIE(1936); MURDER BY AN ARISTOCRAT(1936); POLO JOE(1936); PUBLIC ENEMY'S WIFE(1936); SONS O' GUNS(1936); TRAILIN' WEST(1936); BLAZING SIXES(1937); CALIFORNIA MAIL, THE(1937); CHEROKEE STRIP(1937); EMPTY HOLSTERS(1937); GREEN LIGHT(1937); GUNS OF THE PECOS(1937); KID GALAHAD(1937); LAND BEYOND THE LAW(1937); LIVE, LOVE AND LEARN(1937); MARKED WOMAN(1937); PUBLIC WEDDING(1937); READY, WILLING AND ABLE(1937); SMART BLONDE(1937); ACCIDENTS WILL HAPPEN(1938); ANNABEL TAKES A TOUR(1938); CITY GIRL(1938); GOLD IS WHERE YOU FIND IT(1938); ANOTHER THIN MAN(1939); CAT AND THE CANARY, THE(1939); DODGE CITY(1939); HOUSE OF FEAR, THE(1939); LITTLE ACCIDENT(1939); MR. SMITH GOES TO WASHINGTON(1939); ROARING TWENTIES, THE(1939); SERGEANT MADDEN(1939); THUNDER AFLOAT(1939); WOMEN IN THE WIND(1939); CAPTAIN IS A LADY, THE(1940); DANCE, GIRL, DANCE(1940); EDISON, THE MAN(1940); GIVE US WINGS(1940); REMEMBER THE NIGHT(1940); RETURN OF FRANK JAMES, THE(1940); STRIKE UP THE BAND(1940); THAT GANG OF MINE(1940); THIRD FINGER, LEFT HAND(1940); BARNACLE BILL(1941); BILLY THE KID'S RANGE WAR(1941); DESIGN FOR SCANDAL(1941); NEW YORK TOWN(1941); THEY MEET AGAIN(1941); TRIAL OF MARY DUGAN, THE(1941); TWO GUN SHERIFF(1941); UNHOLY PARTNERS(1941); BILLY THE KID TRAPPED(1942); GENTLEMAN JIM(1942); HEART OF THE RIO GRANDE(1942); JUKE GIRL(1942); JUNGLE SIREN(1942); MAD DOCTOR OF MARKET STREET, THE(1942); MY GAL SAL(1942); MY HEART BELONGS TO DADDY(1942); QUEEN OF BROADWAY(1942); SABOTEUR(1942); STREET OF CHANCE(1942); TARZAN'S NEW YORK ADVENTURE(1942); WESTWARD HO(1942); AIR RAID WARDENS(1943); DR. GILLESPIE'S CRIMINAL CASE(1943); HAPPY LAND(1943); IRON MAJOR, THE(1943); KEEP 'EM SLUGGING(1943); NEVER A DULL MOMENT(1943); NORTHERN PURSUIT(1943); SEVENTH VICTIM, THE(1943); WESTERN CYCLONE(1943); CONTENDER, THE(1944); EVE OF ST. MARK, THE(1944); IN THE MEANTIME, DARLING(1944); JOHNNY DOESN'T LIVE HERE ANY MORE(1944); MY BUDDY(1944); RATIONING(1944); STORY OF DR. WASSELL, THE(1944); TOGETHER AGAIN(1944); ANCHORS AWEIGH(1945); COME OUT FIGHTING(1945); MISS SUSIE SLAGLE'S(1945); MR. MUGGS RIDES AGAIN(1945); OUT OF THIS WORLD(1945); ROGUES GALLERY(1945); SCARLET STREET(1945); STRANGE HOLIDAY(1945); WHITE PONGO(1945); BLUE DAHLIA, THE(1946); BRIDE WORE BOOTS, THE(1946); CONQUEST OF CHEYENNE(1946); CROSS MY HEART(1946); EASY TO WED(1946); FLYING SERPENT, THE(1946); FROM THIS DAY FORWARD(1946); LARCENY IN HER HEART(1946); TOMORROW IS FOREVER(1946); UNDERCURRENT(1946); WAKE UP AND DREAM(1946); BODY AND SOUL(1947); DESERT FURY(1947); HIGH BARBAREE(1947); HIGH WALL, THE(1947); HOMESTEADERS OF PARADISE VALLEY(1947); LITTLE MISS BROADWAY(1947); WELCOME STRANGER(1947); FORCE OF EVIL(1948); LADY FROM SHANGHAI, THE(1948); OLD-FASHIONED GIRL, AN(1948); RIVER LADY(1948); DAUGHTER OF THE WEST(1949); STATE DEPARTMENT–FILE 649(1949); COUNTY FAIR(1950); DESERT HAWK, THE(1950); BLUE BLOOD(1951); THREE DESPERATE MEN(1951); BOOTS MALONE(1952); GREATEST SHOW ON EARTH, THE(1952); HERE COME THE NELSONS(1952); LAS VEGAS STORY, THE(1952); NARROW MARGIN, THE(1952); RODEO(1952); BORN TO THE SADDLE(1953)

Milton [B.] Kibbee
WHEN THE REDSKINS RODE(1951)

Roland Kibbee
ANGEL ON MY SHOULDER(1946), w; NIGHT IN CASABLANCA, A(1946), w; TELL IT TO THE JUDGE(1949), w; PAINTING THE CLOUDS WITH SUNSHINE(1951), w; PARDON MY FRENCH(1951, U.S./Fr.), w; TEN TALL MEN(1951), w; CRIMSON PIRATE, THE(1952), w; DESERT SONG, THE(1953), w; THREE SAILORS AND A GIRL(1953), w; VERA CRUZ(1954), w; TOP SECRET AFFAIR(1957), w; DEVIL'S

DISCIPLE, THE(1959), w; AMOROUS ADVENTURES OF MOLL FLANDERS, THE(1965), w; APPALOOSA, THE(1966), w; VALDEZ IS COMING(1971), w; MIDNIGHT MAN, THE(1974), p&d, w

Lawrence Kibble
BEAT THE BAND(1947), w

Estelle Kibby
Silents
EAGLE'S MATE, THE(1914)

Seth Kibel
1984
DREAM ONE(1984, Brit./Fr.)

sung by Yevgeniy Kibkalo
QUEEN OF SPADES(1961, USSR)

Yevgeniy Kibkalo
TSAR'S BRIDE, THE(1966, USSR)

Belva Kibler
MEDIUM, THE(1951)

Leonard Kibrick
KID MILLIONS(1934); LOVE IS NEWS(1937); FISHERMAN'S WHARF(1939); IT'S A WONDERFUL WORLD(1939); JESSE JAMES(1939); ROSE OF WASHINGTON SQUARE(1939); ROXIE HART(1942)

Sidney Kibrick
FLIGHT LIEUTENANT(1942)

Jake Kickley
DANCE MALL HOSTESS(1933)

Chuck Kicks
SPLIT, THE(1968)

Kid
Silents
HELP WANTED–MALE!(1920)

Jim Kid
Silents
JORDAN IS A HARD ROAD(1915)

Texas Kid
Silents
ON THIN ICE(1925)

Tomoko Kida
LAST UNICORN, THE(1982), ed
1984
WARRIORS OF THE WIND(1984, Jap.), ed

Marvin Kidas
IT'S A DEAL(1930), set d

Bert Kidd
HAPPY DAYS ARE HERE AGAIN(1936, Brit.)

Billy Kidd
BENJAMIN(1973, Ger.)

David Kidd
SIX PACK ANNIE(1975), w

Delena Kidd
ROOM AT THE TOP(1959, Brit.)

Eddie Kidd
HANOVER STREET(1979, Brit.)

John Kidd
BEGGAR'S OPERA, THE(1953); PLUNDERERS OF PAINTED FLATS(1959); THERE WAS A CROOKED MAN(1962, Brit.); JOKERS, THE(1967, Brit.); CONQUEROR WORM, THE(1968, Brit.)

Jonathan Kidd
MACABRE(1958); WINK OF AN EYE(1958); SEVEN THIEVES(1960); 7TH COMMANDMENT, THE(1961); ONE AND ONLY GENUINE ORIGINAL FAMILY BAND, THE(1968); DAY OF THE LOCUST, THE(1975)

Lenetta Kidd
STING II, THE(1983)

Michael Kidd
HAPPY DAYS ARE HERE AGAIN(1936, Brit.); WHERE'S CHARLEY?(1952, Brit.), ch; BAND WAGON, THE(1953), ch; KNOCK ON WOOD(1954), ch; SEVEN BRIDES FOR SEVEN BROTHERS(1954), ch; GUYS AND DOLLS(1955), ch; IT'S ALWAYS FAIR WEATHER(1955); MERRY ANDREW(1958), d, ch; LI'L ABNER(1959), ch; STAR!(1968), ch; HELLO, DOLLY!(1969), ch; SMILE(1975); MOVIE MOVIE(1978), a, ch

Rae Kidd
UNASHAMED(1938)

Robert Kidd
WELCOME TO THE CLUB(1971)

Sam Kidd
BATTLE HELL(1956, Brit.)

Annie Kidder
EUREKA(1983, Brit.)

Hugh Kidder
HIS PRIVATE SECRETARY(1933)

Margot Kidder
GAILY, GAILY(1969); QUACKSER FORTUNE HAS A COUSIN IN THE BRONX(1970); SISTERS(1973); BLACK CHRISTMAS(1974, Can.); GRAVY TRAIN, THE(1974); QUIET DAY IN BELFAST, A(1974, Can.); GREAT WALDO PEPPER, THE(1975); REINCARNATION OF PETER PROUD, THE(1975); 92 IN THE SHADE(1975, U.S./Brit.); SUPERMAN(1978); AMITYVILLE HORROR, THE(1979); SUPERMAN II(1980); WILLIE AND PHIL(1980); HEARTACHES(1981, Can.); SOME KIND OF HERO(1982); SUPERMAN III(1983); TRENCHCOAT(1983)
1984
LOUISIANE(1984, Fr./Can.)
Misc. Talkies
SHOOT THE SUN DOWN(1981)

Nor Kiddie
DON'T RUSH ME(1936, Brit.)

Meglin Kiddies
SHIPMATES FOREVER(1935)

Nicole Kidman
BMX BANDITS(1983); BUSH CHRISTMAS(1983, Aus.)

James Kidnie
CURTAINS(1983, Can.)

Caroline Kido
CONFESSIONS OF AN OPIUM EATER(1962); NUN AND THE SERGEANT, THE(1962)

Shino Kido
SCARLET CAMELLIA, THE(1965, Jap.), p

Hideo Kidokoro
ROAD TO ETERNITY(1962, Jap.)

The Kidoodlers
BARNYARD FOLLIES(1940); MELODY AND MOONLIGHT(1940); VILLAGE BARN DANCE(1940)

Hans Jurgen Kiebach
MAD EXECUTIONERS, THE(1965, Ger.), art d; MONSTER OF LONDON CITY, THE(1967, Ger.), art d; PHANTOM OF SOHO, THE(1967, Ger.), art d

Hans-Juergen Kiebach
CORRUPT ONES, THE(1967, Ger.), art d

Hans-Jurgen Kiebach
RETURN OF DR. MABUSE, THE(1961, Ger./Fr./Ital.), art d

Jurgen Kiebach
DEAD RUN(1961, Fr./Ital./Ger.), art d; DEFECTOR, THE(1966, Ger./Fr.), art d; FROZEN ALIVE(1966, Brit./Ger.), art d; HANNIBAL BROOKS(1969, Brit.), art d; CABARET(1972), art d; APPLE, THE(1980 U.S./Ger.), prod d

Max Kiebach
DE SADE(1969)

Kevin Kieberly
ENCOUNTER WITH THE UNKNOWN(1973)

Helen Kiedy
YOUTH AFLAME(1945), w

Russell Kiefel
SINGER AND THE DANCER, THE(1977, Aus.); BREAKER MORANT(1980, Aus.)

Douglas Kiefer
PROLOGUE(1970, Can.), ph; ONE MAN(1979, Can.), ph

Philip Kiefer
SIXTEEN FATHOMS DEEP(1934)

Warren Kiefer
CASTLE OF THE LIVING DEAD(1964, Ital./Fr.), w; BEYOND THE LAW(1967, Ital.), w; LAST REBEL, THE(1971), w

Lucy Kieffer
LA MARSEILLAISE(1938, Fr.)

Major Kieffer
IT HAPPENED ON 5TH AVENUE(1947)

Philip Kieffer
FORT APACHE(1948); PILLARS OF THE SKY(1956)

Maj. Philip Kieffer
PLACE IN THE SUN, A(1951); LONG GRAY LINE, THE(1955)

Donald W. Kiehl
1984
PRODIGAL, THE(1984)

William Kiehl
DIARY OF A MAD HOUSEWIFE(1970)

Richard Kiel
PHANTOM PLANET, THE(1961); EEGAH!(1962); MAGIC SWORD, THE(1962); HOUSE OF THE DAMNED(1963); LASSIE'S GREAT ADVENTURE(1963); ROUSTABOUT(1964); HUMAN DUPLICATORS, THE(1965); LAS VEGAS HILLBILLYS(1966); MAN CALLED DAGGER, A(1967); SKIDOO(1968); LONGEST YARD, THE(1974); FLASH AND THE FIRECAT(1976); SILVER STREAK(1976); SPY WHO LOVED ME, THE(1977, Brit.); FORCE 10 FROM NAVARONE(1978, Brit.); THEY WENT THAT-A-WAY AND THAT-A-WAY(1978); HUMANOID, THE(1979, Ital.); MOONRAKER(1979, Brit.); SO FINE(1981); HYSTERICAL(1983); WAR OF THE WIZARDS(1983, Taiwan)
1984
CANNONBALL RUN II(1984)

Sue Kiel
1984
REPO MAN(1984)

Zdzislaw Kielanowski
WALKOVER(1969, Pol.), art d; JOVITA(1970, Pol.), set d

Carl Kielblock
PLAINSONG(1982)

Barbie Kielian
STUCK ON YOU(1983)

Wolfgang Kieling
$(DOLLARS)**1/2 (1971); DAS LETZTE GEHEIMNIS(1959, Ger.); DEAD RUN(1961, Fr./Ital./Ger.); END OF MRS. CHENEY(1963, Ger.); TORN CURTAIN(1966); HOUSE OF 1,000 DOLLS(1967, Ger./Span./Brit.); AMSTERDAM AFFAIR, THE(1968 Brit.); VENGEANCE OF FU MANCHU, THE(1968, Brit./Ger./Hong Kong/Ireland); SIGNALS-AN ADVENTURE IN SPACE(1970, E. Ger./Pol.)

Barbie Kiellan
1984
STUCK ON YOU(1984)

Shelley K. Kielsen
TERMS OF ENDEARMENT(1983)

Helen Kiely
SEVEN DOORS TO DEATH(1944), d&w

Bill Kiem
BREAKHEART PASS(1976)

Shih Kien
ENTER THE DRAGON(1973)

Petra Kiener
GERMANY IN AUTUMN(1978, Ger.)

Jan Kiepura
FAREWELL TO LOVE(1931, Brit.); BE MINE TONIGHT(1933, Brit.); MY HEART IS CALLING(1935, Brit.); MY SONG FOR YOU(1935, Brit.); GIVE US THIS NIGHT(1936)

Andrew Kier
ABSOLUTION(1981, Brit.)

David Kier
WISE GUYS(1937, Brit.)

SIN' AND A-FIGHTIN'(1948); YOU GOTTA STAY HAPPY(1948); YOU WERE MEANT FOR ME(1948); FREE FOR ALL(1949); MA AND PA KETTLE(1949); MR. SOFT TOUCH(1949); SUN COMES UP, THE(1949); MA AND PA KETTLE GO TO TOWN(1950); RIDING HIGH(1950); MA AND PA KETTLE BACK ON THE FARM(1951); MA AND PA KETTLE AT THE FAIR(1952); MA AND PA KETTLE ON VACATION(1953); MA AND PA KETTLE AT HOME(1954); MA AND PA KETTLE AT WAIKIKI(1955)
Richard Kilbride
PLAYGROUND, THE(1965)
Charles Kilburn
THAT CERTAIN SOMETHING(1941, Aus.)
Doris Hume Kilburn
DARK PURPOSE(1964), w
Martin Kilburn
WILD BLUE YONDER, THE(1952)
Melanie Kilburn
1984
LITTLE DRUMMER GIRL, THE(1984)
Terence Kilburn
FIEND WITHOUT A FACE(1958); LOLITA(1962)
Misc. Talkies
BULLDOG DRUMMOND AT BAY(1947); BULLDOG DRUMMOND STRIKES BACK(1947)
Terrance Kilburn
SLAVES OF BABYLON(1953)
Terry Kilburn
CHRISTMAS CAROL, A(1938); LORD JEFF(1938); SWEETHEARTS(1938); ADVENTURES OF SHERLOCK HOLMES, THE(1939); ANDY HARDY GETS SPRING FEVER(1939); GOODBYE MR. CHIPS(1939, Brit.); THEY SHALL HAVE MUSIC(1939); FOREIGN CORRESPONDENT(1940); SWISS FAMILY ROBINSON(1940); MERCY ISLAND(1941); RANDOM HARVEST(1942); YANK AT ETON, A(1942); KEYS OF THE KINGDOM, THE(1944); NATIONAL VELVET(1944); BLACK BEAUTY(1946); SONG OF SCHEHERAZADE(1947); CHALLENGE, THE(1948); THIRTEEN LEAD SOLDIERS(1948); FAN, THE(1949); FORTUNES OF CAPTAIN BLOOD(1950); TYRANT OF THE SEA(1950); ONLY THE VALIANT(1951)
Carole Lee Kilby
WOMEN, THE(1939)
Sheryl Kilby
SHARKY'S MACHINE(1982)
Robert Kilcullen
FINNEY(1969)
Marion Kildany
PAJAMA PARTY(1964)
Dorothy Kildare
NATION AFLAME(1937)
Nora Kildare
GODLESS GIRL, THE(1929)
Silents
KING OF KINGS, THE(1927)
Edward Kilenyi
DELUGE(1933), m; OVERLAND EXPRESS, THE(1938), m, md; KILLERS OF THE WILD(1940), m
Dr. Edward Kilenyi
BELLE STARR'S DAUGHTER(1947), m; TENDER YEARS, THE(1947), m, md
Jed Kiley
HELL'S HIGHWAY(1932)
Jim Kiley
LUM AND ABNER ABROAD(1956)
John Kiley
PICTURES(1982, New Zealand), ed
Richard Kiley
MOB, THE(1951); EIGHT IRON MEN(1952); SNIPER, THE(1952); PICKUP ON SOUTH STREET(1953); BLACKBOARD JUNGLE, THE(1955); PHENIX CITY STORY, THE(1955); SPANISH AFFAIR(1958, Span.); PENDULUM(1969); LITTLE PRINCE, THE(1974, Brit.); LOOKING FOR MR. GOODBAR(1977); ENDLESS LOVE(1981)
Misc. Talkies
HOMEWARD BORNE(1957)
Dr. Edward Kileyni
INTERNATIONAL CRIME(1938), md
Katherine Kilfoyle
Misc. Silents
EARLY BIRDS(1923, Brit.)
Paul Kilfoyle
YOUR NUMBER'S UP(1931)
Kilgallen
SINNER TAKE ALL(1936)
James Kilgannon
CAPTAINS COURAGEOUS(1937); STAND UP AND FIGHT(1939)
Jimmie Kilgannon
TEXANS, THE(1938); ESCAPE TO GLORY(1940)
Jim Kilganon
OUR RELATIONS(1936)
Michael Kilgarriff
DARK CRYSTAL, THE(1982, Brit.)
Nancy Kilgas
ATHENA(1954); SEVEN BRIDES FOR SEVEN BROTHERS(1954); FUNNY FACE(1957); SHAKE, RATTLE, AND ROCK!(1957); HIGH SCHOOL HELLCATS(1958); SPIDER, THE(1958)
P. Kilgas
HAMLET(1966, USSR)
George Kilgen
FIGHTING 69TH, THE(1940)
Col. Kilgore
COUNTERSPY MEETS SCOTLAND YARD(1950)
Al Kilgore
WORLD OF HANS CHRISTIAN ANDERSEN, THE(1971, Jap.), d&w
Jim Kilgore
HARLOW(1965), ph

Judy Kilgore
GAMBLING DAUGHTERS(1941)
Merle Kilgore
SECOND FIDDLE TO A STEEL GUITAR(1965); NASHVILLE(1975); COAL MINER'S DAUGHTER(1980); ROADIE(1980)
Joseph Kilgour
Silents
BATTLE CRY OF PEACE, THE(1915); LYING LIPS(1921); JANICE MEREDITH(1924); ON PROBATION(1924); TORMENT(1924); ONE YEAR TO LIVE(1925); LET'S GET MARRIED(1926)
Misc. Silents
THOU ART THE MAN(1915); TURN OF THE ROAD, THE(1915); WHO KILLED JOE MERRION?(1915); THOU ART THE MAN(1916); WRITING ON THE WALL, THE(1916); EASIEST WAY, THE(1917); HER EXCELLENCY, THE GOVERNOR(1917); RUNAWAY ROMANY(1917); HEART OF ROMANCE, THE(1918); HOUSE OF GOLD, THE(1918); HOUSE OF MIRTH, THE(1918); SHELL GAME, THE(1918); SILENT WOMAN, THE(1918); SOCIAL HYPOCRITES(1918); BLIND MAN'S EYES(1919); FAVOR TO A FRIEND, A(1919); LION'S DEN, THE(1919); ONE-THING-AT-A-TIME O'DAY(1919); BROKEN GATE, THE(1920); LOVE(1920); YELLOW TAIFUN, THE(1920); YELLOW TYPHOON, THE(1920); I AM GUILTY(1921); MOTHER O' MINE(1921); MIDNIGHT ALARM, THE(1923); PONJOLA(1923); TORRENT, THE(1924); TRY AND GET IT(1924); PERCY(1925); TOP OF THE WORLD, THE(1925)
Pitseolala Kili
WHITE DAWN, THE(1974)
Astrid Kilian
MARK OF THE DEVIL II(1975, Ger./Brit.)
Mike Kilian
FOUR JILLS IN A JEEP(1944); MARINE RAIDERS(1944); STORY OF DR. WASSELL, THE(1944); WING AND A PRAYER(1944); PERILOUS WATERS(1948); STREET WITH NO NAME, THE(1948); THAT WONDERFUL URGE(1948)
Victor Kilian
WISER SEX, THE(1932); AFTER THE DANCE(1935); AIR HAWKS(1935); BAD BOY(1935); GIRL FRIEND, THE(1935); PUBLIC MENACE(1935); BANJO ON MY KNEE(1936); LADY FROM NOWHERE(1936); MUSIC GOES ROUND, THE(1936); RAMONA(1936); RIFF-RAFF(1936); ROAD TO GLORY, THE(1936); FAIR WARNING(1937); IT HAPPENED IN HOLLYWOOD(1937); IT'S ALL YOURS(1937); LEAGUE OF FRIGHTENED MEN(1937); SEVENTH HEAVEN(1937); TOVARICH(1937); ADVENTURES OF TOM SAWYER, THE(1938); GOLD DIGGERS IN PARIS(1938); MARIE ANTOINETTE(1938); PRISON BREAK(1938); BLACKMAIL(1939); CONVICT'S CODE(1939); FIGHTING THOROUGHBREDS(1939); HUCKLEBERRY FINN(1939); NEVER SAY DIE(1939); ORPHANS OF THE STREET(1939); PARIS HONEYMOON(1939); RETURN OF THE CISCO KID(1939); ST. LOUIS BLUES(1939); ALL THIS AND HEAVEN TOO(1940); BARNYARD FOLLIES(1940); CHAD HANNA(1940); DR. CYCLOPS(1940); INVISIBLE STRIPES(1940); KING OF THE LUMBERJACKS(1940); LITTLE OLD NEW YORK(1940); MARK OF ZORRO, THE(1940); OUT WEST WITH THE PEPPERS(1940); RETURN OF FRANK JAMES, THE(1940); SANTA FE TRAIL(1940); THEY KNEW WHAT THEY WANTED(1940); 'TIL WE MEET AGAIN(1940); TORRID ZONE(1940); TUGBOAT ANNIE SAILS AGAIN(1940); VIRGINIA CITY(1940); YOUNG TOM EDISON(1940); BLOOD AND SAND(1941); DATE WITH THE FALCON, A(1941); I WAS A PRISONER ON DEVIL'S ISLAND(1941); MOB TOWN(1941); SECRETS OF THE LONE WOLF(1941); SERGEANT YORK(1941); WESTERN UNION(1941); ATLANTIC CONVOY(1942); REAP THE WILD WIND(1942); THIS GUN FOR HIRE(1942); HITLER'S MADMAN(1943); IRON MAJOR, THE(1943); JOHNNY COME LATELY(1943); OX-BOW INCIDENT, THE(1943); BARBARY COAST GENT(1944); BELLE OF THE YUKON(1944); DANGEROUS PASSAGE(1944); MEET ME IN ST. LOUIS(1944); UNCERTAIN GLORY(1944); BEHIND CITY LIGHTS(1945); FIGHTING GUARDSMAN(1945); SPANISH MAIN, THE(1945); SPELLBOUND(1945); DUEL IN THE SUN(1946); LITTLE GIANT(1946); SMOKY(1946); YEARLING, THE(1946); NORTHWEST STAMPEDE(1948); YELLOW SKY(1948); COLORADO TERRITORY(1949); I SHOT JESSE JAMES(1949); MADAME BOVARY(1949); RIMFIRE(1949); WYOMING BANDIT, THE(1949); BANDIT QUEEN(1950); FLAME AND THE ARROW, THE(1950); OLD FRONTIER, THE(1950); ONE TOO MANY(1950); RETURN OF JESSE JAMES, THE(1950); SHOWDOWN, THE(1950); TALL TARGET, THE(1951); UNKNOWN WORLD(1951)
Victor Kilian, Jr.
GOLD RUSH MAISIE(1940); SO PROUDLY WE HAIL(1943)
Victor Kilian, Sr.
NO WAY OUT(1950)
S. Kiligin
GENERAL SUVOROV(1941, USSR)
Paul B. Kililman
WHAT'S UP, DOC?(1972)
Frank Kiliman
ANATOMY OF A PSYCHO(1961)
Herbert Kilitz
WOODEN HORSE, THE(1951)
Viscountess Kilkerry
UNFAITHFUL(1931)
Victor Killan
GENTLEMAN'S AGREEMENT(1947)
Michael Killanin
QUIET MAN, THE(1952), p; RISING OF THE MOON, THE(1957, Ireland), p; GIDEON OF SCOTLAND YARD(1959, Brit.), p
Madelyn Killeen
TOYS ARE NOT FOR CHILDREN(1972)
John O. Killens
ODDS AGAINST TOMORROW(1959), w; SLAVES(1969), w
The Killer
Silents
BLACK CYCLONE(1925)
Misc. Silents
DEVIL HORSE, THE(1926)
Jack Killeser
BEAST WITH A MILLION EYES, THE(1956), ed
Mike Killian
MADE FOR EACH OTHER(1939); UNCONQUERED(1947)

Robert Killian
DAY THE FISH CAME OUT, THE(1967. Brit./Gr.)
Victor Killian
ADVENTURE IN MANHATTAN(1936); SHAKEDOWN(1936); BOYS TOWN(1938); DUST BE MY DESTINY(1939); ONLY ANGELS HAVE WINGS(1939); BOMBER'S MOON(1943); KISMET(1944)
Frank Killibrew
MAN IN THE MIDDLE(1964, U.S./Brit.)
Alan Killick
CATLOW(1971, Span.), ed
Jack Killifer
LIGHTS OF NEW YORK(1928), ed; TERROR, THE(1928), ed; CONQUEST(1929), ed; ON WITH THE SHOW(1929), ed; SO LONG LETTY(1929), ed; TIME, THE PLACE AND THE GIRL, THE(1929), ed; LOCAL BOY MAKES GOOD(1931), ed; SMART MONEY(1931), ed; SOLDIER'S PLAYTHING, A(1931), ed; IT'S TOUGH TO BE FAMOUS(1932), ed; MATCH KING, THE(1932), ed; UNION DEPOT(1932), ed; FEMALE(1933), ed; GRAND SLAM(1933), ed; MAYOR OF HELL, THE(1933), ed; BABBITT(1934), ed; FASHIONS OF 1934(1934), ed; MIDNIGHT ALIBI(1934), ed; REGISTERED NURSE(1934), ed; SMARTY(1934), ed; BROADWAY HOSTESS(1935), ed; G-MEN(1935), ed; LITTLE BIG SHOT(1935), ed; NIGHT AT THE RITZ, A(1935), ed; RIGHT TO LIVE, THE(1935), ed; BULLETS OR BALLOTS(1936), ed; ROAD GANG(1936), ed; TIMES SQUARE PLAYBOY(1936), ed; DRAEGERMAN COURAGE(1937), ed; GOD'S COUNTRY AND THE WOMAN(1937), ed; MARKED WOMAN(1937), ed; THAT CERTAIN WOMAN(1937), ed; MEN ARE SUCH FOOLS(1938), ed; SWING YOUR LADY(1938), ed; VALLEY OF THE GIANTS(1938), ed; KID FROM KOKOMO, THE(1939), ed; ROARING TWENTIES, THE(1939), ed; THEY MADE ME A CRIMINAL(1939), ed; GRANNY GET YOUR GUN(1940), ed; TORRID ZONE(1940), ed; HIGH SIERRA(1941), ed; HIGHWAY WEST(1941), ed; SMILING GHOST, THE(1941), ed; BIG SHOT, THE(1942), ed; GENTLEMAN JIM(1942), ed; MAN WHO CAME TO DINNER, THE(1942), ed; BACKGROUND TO DANGER(1943), ed; NORTHERN PURSUIT(1943), ed; HOODLUM, THE(1951), ed
Anna Killina
AFFAIRS OF MAUPASSANT(1938, Aust.)
Tim Killinback
GREAT PONY RAID, THE(1968, Brit.)
Helen Killinger
RETURN TO CAMPUS(1975)
Jack Killiter
CHILD IS BORN, A(1940), ed
Frank Killmond
TAKE A GIANT STEP(1959); PSYCHO(1960); HUD(1963); THAT FUNNY FEELING(1965)
Joseph Killorin
YOUNG DON'T CRY, THE(1957)
Edward Killy
FRECKLES(1935), d; SEVEN KEYS TO BALDPATE(1935), d; MURDER ON A BRIDLE PATH(1936), d; SECOND WIFE(1936), d; WANTED: JANE TURNER(1936), d; BIG SHOT, THE(1937), d; CHINA PASSAGE(1937), d; SATURDAY'S HEROES(1937), d; QUICK MONEY(1938), d; STAGE TO CHINO(1940), d; WAGON TRAIN(1940), d; BANDIT TRAIL, THE(1941), d; CYCLONE ON HORSEBACK(1941), d; FARGO KID, THE(1941), d; LAND OF THE OPEN RANGE(1941), d; ROBBERS OF THE RANGE(1941), d; COME ON DANGER(1942), d; RIDING THE WIND(1942), d; NEVADA(1944), d; WANDERER OF THE WASTELAND(1945), d; WEST OF THE PECOS(1945), d
Jean-Claude Killy
SNOW JOB(1972)
Allan Kilman
ROMANTIC COMEDY(1983)
Peter Kilman
OLLY, OLLY, OXEN FREE(1978); WINTER KILLS(1979)
Sam Kilman
RETURN TO MACON COUNTY(1975); FINAL EXAM(1981)
Bill Kilmer
LAST TIME I SAW ARCHIE, THE(1961)
Val Kilmer
1984
TOP SECRET!(1984)
Ruta Kilmonis [Lee]
SEVEN BRIDES FOR SEVEN BROTHERS(1954)
Barbara Kilner
NIGHT BIRDS(1931, Brit.); HOT NEWS(1936, Brit.)
Kilongalonga
SANDERS OF THE RIVER(1935, Brit.)
Bennett Kilpack
WAY BACK HOME(1932)
Lincoln Kilpartick
UPTOWN SATURDAY NIGHT(1974)
Eric Kilpatrick
O'HARA'S WIFE(1983)
Florence Kilpatrick
VIRGINIA'S HUSBAND(1934, Brit.), w
Silents
VIRGINIA'S HUSBAND(1928, Brit.), w
Herbert Kilpatrick
MOTIVE FOR REVENGE(1935), ph
Ilsa Kilpatrick
CASTLE SINISTER(1932, Brit.)
Lincoln Kilpatrick
COP HATER(1958); LOVELY WAY TO DIE, A(1968); MADIGAN(1968); WHAT'S SO BAD ABOUT FEELING GOOD?(1968); CURIOUS FEMALE, THE(1969); GENERATION(1969); LOST MAN, THE(1969); STILETTO(1969); RED, WHITE AND BLACK, THE(1970); BROTHER JOHN(1971); HONKY(1971); OMEGA MAN, THE(1971); COOL BREEZE(1972); SOYLENT GREEN(1973); CHOSEN SURVIVORS(1974 U.S.-Mex.); TOGETHER BROTHERS(1974); MASTER GUNFIGHTER, THE(1975); DEADLY FORCE(1983)
Reid Kilpatrick
GIRLS ON PROBATION(1938); SWEETHEARTS(1938); HELL'S KITCHEN(1939); INDIANAPOLIS SPEEDWAY(1939); KID FROM KOKOMO, THE(1939); SWEEPSTAKES WINNER(1939); LEATHER-PUSHERS, THE(1940); MURDER IN THE AIR(1940); BRIDE CAME C.O.D., THE(1941); IN THIS OUR LIFE(1942); MADAME

SPY(1942); DIVORCE(1945); SCARLET CLUE, THE(1945); FIGHTING MAD(1948)
Shirley Kilpatrick
ASTOUNDING SHE-MONSTER, THE(1958)
Tom Kilpatrick
TRAPPED BY G-MEN(1937), w; WHISPERING ENEMIES(1939), w; DR. CYCLOPS(1940), w; MAN BETRAYED, A(1941), w; ADVENTURES IN SILVERADO(1948), w; PALOMINO, THE(1950), w
Silents
ACQUITTAL, THE(1923), w
Ed Kilroy
RATIONING(1944)
Edward Kilroy
MIRACLES FOR SALE(1939); EYES IN THE NIGHT(1942)
Gene Kilroy
GREATEST, THE(1977, U.S./Brit.)
Mathias Kilroy
LEGACY, THE(1979, Brit.); FFOLKES(1980, Brit.)
Thomas Kilshaw
LADY IN A JAM(1942)
Anthony Kilshawe
SCOTCH ON THE ROCKS(1954, Brit.)
Tony Kilshawe
END OF THE ROAD, THE(1954, Brit.)
Gene Kilty
1984
UP THE CREEK(1984)
Lilly Kilvert
SCENIC ROUTE, THE(1978), art d; ROCKERS(1980), art d; DEEP IN THE HEART(1983), prod d
Lily Kilvert
ALAMBRISTA!(1977), art d
Nick Kilvertus
HAPPY BIRTHDAY TO ME(1981)
C.G. Kim
NIGHT OF THE IGUANA, THE(1964)
Christal Kim
1984
RHINESTONE(1984)
Clarence Kim
DIAMOND HEAD(1962)
Claudia Kim
1984
JOHNNY DANGEROUSLY(1984)
Evan Kim
BABY BLUE MARINE(1976); KENTUCKY FRIED MOVIE, THE(1977); GO TELL THE SPARTANS(1978); CAVEMAN(1981); MEGAFORCE(1982)
Haekyung Kim
MONSTER WANGMAGWI(1967, S. K.)
Hikap Kim
MONSTER WANGMAGWI(1967, S. K.)
Joseph Kim
KEYS OF THE KINGDOM, THE(1944); PURPLE HEART, THE(1944); BLOOD ON THE SUN(1945); FIRST YANK INTO TOKYO(1945); SAMURAI(1945); DEVIL SHIP(1947); FRANCIS(1949); NO ESCAPE(1953); DRAGON'S GOLD(1954); LOVE IS A MANY-SPLENDORED THING(1955); OPERATION PETTICOAT(1959); LEPKE(1975, U.S./Israel)
Joy Kim
HIGH AND THE MIGHTY, THE(1954); BLOOD ALLEY(1955)
Judith Kim
1984
STARMAN(1984)
June Kim
CONFESSIONS OF AN OPIUM EATER(1962)
June Y. Kim
DONOVAN'S REEF(1963)
Kiduck Kim
YONGKARI MONSTER FROM THE DEEP(1967 S.K.), d
Lai Mon Kim
Misc. Silents
FOR THE FREEDOM OF THE EAST(1918)
Lei Kim
WALK, DON'T RUN(1966)
Leigh Kim
SOME KIND OF HERO(1982)
Mac Kim
BIGAMIST,THE(1953)
Randy Kim
HAWAIIANS, THE(1970)
Sam Kim
Silents
DAWN OF THE EAST(1921)
Sang Kim
FAME(1980)
Stephen Kim
1984
HOT AND DEADLY(1984), ph
Stephen B. Kim
GETTING OVER(1981), ph&ed
Suzanna Kim
CRUSADE AGAINST RACKETS(1937); GOOD EARTH, THE(1937)
Suzanne Kim
SINGING MARINE, THE(1937)
Whamok Kim
HUNTERS, THE(1958)
The Kim Loo Sisters
MEET MISS BOBBY SOCKS(1944)
Ann Kimball
I WAS A COMMUNIST FOR THE F.B.I.(1951); ON MOONLIGHT BAY(1951); TWO TICKETS TO BROADWAY(1951)

Anne Kimball
PORT SINISTER(1953)
Misc. Talkies
OUTLAW'S SON(1954)
Bruce Kimball
CAIN'S WAY(1969); WILD WHEELS(1969); HARD ROAD, THE(1970); THING WITH TWO HEADS, THE(1972); PSYCHOPATH, THE(1973); PIPE DREAMS(1976); MOON-SHINE COUNTY EXPRESS(1977); SUPER VAN(1977); MALIBU BEACH(1978)
Buddy Kimball
THIRTEEN WOMEN(1932), ed
C.K. Kimball
HALF-NAKED TRUTH, THE(1932), ed
Charles Kimball
LADIES OF THE JURY(1932), ed; STATE'S ATTORNEY(1932), ed; SHE-DEVIL ISLAND(1936, Mex.), p; NO MAN'S LAND(1964), ed; LIVING COFFIN, THE(1965, Mex.), ed
Charles L. Kimball
MONKEY'S PAW, THE(1933), ed; PAST OF MARY HOLMES, THE(1933), ed; SOFIA(1948), ed; TORCH, THE(1950), ed; STRONGHOLD(1952, Mex.), ed; COMAN-CHE(1956), ed; BIG BOODLE, THE(1957), ed
Doug Kimball
MEDIUM COOL(1969)
E.M. Kimball
Misc. Silents
MAN WHO FOUND HIMSELF, THE(1915); FEAST OF LIFE, THE(1916)
Edward Kimball
MODERN TIMES(1936)
Silents
CHRISTIAN, THE(1914); TANGLED FATES(1916)
Misc. Silents
MAGDA(1917); MODERN OTHELLO, A(1917); CLAW, THE(1918); HOUSE OF GLASS, THE(1918); SAVAGE WOMAN, THE(1918); SILK HUSBANDS AND CALICO WIVES(1920); I'LL SHOW YOU THE TOWN(1925)
Edward M. Kimball
Silents
LITTLE MISS BROWN(1915); COMMON LAW, THE(1916); HIDDEN SCAR, THE(1916); CHARGE IT(1921)
Misc. Silents
DEEP PURPLE, THE(1915); WITHOUT A SOUL(1916); WOMAN ALONE, A(1917); BETTER WIFE, THE(1919); MIDCHANNEL(1920); MASQUERADER, THE(1922); YANKEE DOODLE, JR.(1922)
Fenn Kimball
HONG KONG NIGHTS(1935), p; I COVER CHINATOWN(1938), p
Frederic Kimball
AUTHOR! AUTHOR!(1982)
Helen Kimball
KID FROM BOOKLYN, THE(1946)
John Kimball
RAGGEDY ANN AND ANDY(1977), anim
Lee Kimball
ENDLESS LOVE(1981)
Louis Kimball
Silents
SHOULD A WIFE WORK?(1922)
Misc. Silents
THROUGH THE STORM(1922)
Pauline Kimball
Misc. Silents
FEAST OF LIFE, THE(1916)
Robert Kimball
JOHNNY STOOL PIGEON(1949)
Russell Kimball
CYCLONE KID, THE(1942), art d; FLYING TIGERS(1942), art d; GIRL FROM ALASKA(1942), art d; HEART OF THE GOLDEN WEST(1942), art d; HI, NEIGH-BOR(1942), art d; HOME IN WYOMIN'(1942), art d; ICE-CAPADES REVUE(1942), art d; IN OLD CALIFORNIA(1942), art d; JOAN OF OZARK(1942), art d; LONDON BLACKOUT MURDERS(1942), art d; MOONLIGHT MASQUERADE(1942), art d; OLD HOMESTEAD, THE(1942), art d; OUTLAWS OF PINE RIDGE(1942), art d; PHAN-TOM PLAINSMEN, THE(1942), art d; REMEMBER PEARL HARBOR(1942), art d; RIDIN' DOWN THE CANYON(1942), art d; ROMANCE ON THE RANGE(1942), art d; SHADOWS ON THE SAGE(1942), art d; SHEPHERD OF THE OZARKS(1942), art d; SLEEPYTIME GAL(1942), art d; SOMBRERO KID, THE(1942), art d; SONS OF THE PIONEERS(1942), art d; SUNDOWN KID, THE(1942), art d; SUNSET SERENA-DE(1942), art d; TRAITOR WITHIN, THE(1942), art d; VALLEY OF HUNTED MEN(1942), art d; WESTWARD HO(1942), art d; X MARKS THE SPOT(1942), art d; CHATTERBOX(1943), art d; DAYS OF OLD CHEYENNE(1943), art d; DEAD MAN'S GULCH(1943), art d; DEATH VALLEY MANHUNT(1943), art d; FALSE FACES(1943), art d; FUGITIVE FROM SONORA(1943), art d; HEADIN' FOR GOD'S COUN-TRY(1943), art d; HERE COMES ELMER(1943), art d; HIT PARADE OF 1943(1943), art d; HOOSIER HOLIDAY(1943), art d; IDAHO(1943), art d; IN OLD OK-LAHOMA(1943), art d; JOHNNY DOUGHBOY(1943), art d; MAN FROM MUSIC MOUNTAIN(1943), art d; MAN FROM THE RIO GRANDE, THE(1943), art d; MAN FROM THUNDER RIVER, THE(1943), art d; MANTRAP, THE(1943), art d; MYS-TERY BROADCAST(1943), art d; NOBODY'S DARLING(1943), art d; O, MY DAR-LING CLEMENTINE(1943), art d; PURPLE V, THE(1943), art d; RAIDERS OF SUNSET PASS(1943), art d; SANTA FE SCOUTS(1943), art d; SECRETS OF THE UNDERGROUND(1943), art d; SHANTYTOWN(1943), art d; SILVER SPURS(1943), art d; SLEEPY LAGOON(1943), art d; SONG OF TEXAS(1943), art d; SWING YOUR PARTNER(1943), art d; TAHITI HONEY(1943), art d; THUMBS UP(1943), art d; THUNDERING TRAILS(1943), art d; WAGON TRACKS WEST(1943), art d; WEST SIDE KID(1943), art d; WHISPERING FOOTSTEPS(1943), art d; YOUTH ON PARADE(1943), art d; JAMBOREE(1944), art d; LADY AND THE MONSTER, THE(1944), art d; LAKE PLACID SERENADE(1944), art d; MAN FROM FRIS-CO(1944), art d; MY BEST GAL(1944), art d; PORT OF 40 THIEVES, THE(1944), art d; ROSIE THE RIVETER(1944), art d; SILENT PARTNER(1944), art d; STORM OVER LISBON(1944), art d; DAKOTA(1945), art d; EARL CARROLL'S VANITIES(1945), art d; LONE TEXAS RANGER(1945), art d; LOVE, HONOR AND GOODBYE(1945), art d; MEXICANA(1945), art d; PHANTOM SPEAKS, THE(1945), art d; SPORTING CHANCE, A(1945), art d; SWINGIN' ON A RAINBOW(1945), art d; THREE'S A CROWD(1945), art d; VAMPIRE'S GHOST, THE(1945), art d; MURDER IN THE

MUSIC HALL(1946), art d; MC HALE'S NAVY(1964), art d; MC HALE'S NAVY JOINS THE AIR FORCE(1965), art d; SULLIVAN'S EMPIRE(1967), art d; VALLEY OF MYSTERY(1967), art d; THREE GUNS FOR TEXAS(1968), art d; THIS SAVAGE LAND(1969), art d
Shirley Kimball
TWO TICKETS TO BROADWAY(1951)
Ward Kimball
SNOW WHITE AND THE SEVEN DWARFS(1937), anim; FANTASIA(1940), anim; PINOCCHIO(1940), anim d; DUMBO(1941), anim d; RELUCTANT DRAGON, THE(1941), a, anim; THREE CABALLEROS, THE(1944), anim; MAKE MINE MU-SIC(1946), anim; FUN AND FANCY FREE(1947), anim d; ALICE IN WONDER-LAND(1951), anim d; PETER PAN(1953), anim; BABES IN TOYLAND(1961), w; MARY POPPINS(1964), anim; BEDKNOBS AND BROOMSTICKS(1971), anim d
Ann Kimbell
JUNE BRIDE(1948); FORT OSAGE(1952)
Anne Kimbell
FEUDIN' FOOLS(1952); MERRY WIDOW, THE(1952); WAGONS WEST(1952); CLIPPED WINGS(1953); GOLDEN IDOL, THE(1954); MONSTER FROM THE OCEAN FLOOR, THE(1954); GIRLS AT SEA(1958, Brit.)
Bruce Kimbell
ROLLERCOASTER(1977)
Helen Kimbell
SHOW BOAT(1951)
Stuart Kimbell
1984
STREETS OF FIRE(1984)
Peggy Kimber
LOST BOUNDARIES(1949)
Tim Kimber
HEART LIKE A WHEEL(1983)
John Kimberley
SKULLDUGGERY(1970)
Maggie Kimberley
WHERE THE BULLETS FLY(1966, Brit.); MUMMY'S SHROUD, THE(1967, Brit.); CONQUEROR WORM, THE(1968, Brit.)
Marguerite Kimberley
1984
LOVELINES(1984)
Kimberley and Page
LADY IN DISTRESS(1942, Brit.)
Eve Kimberly
DANTE'S INFERNO(1935)
Kay Kimberly
WATERMELON MAN(1970)
Maria Kimberly
TRAFFIC(1972, Fr.)
Sharron Kimberly
PARTY, THE(1968)
Lawrence Kimble
ALL-AMERICAN CHUMP(1936), w; SUBMARINE D-1(1937), w; BELOVED BRAT(1938), w; LOVE, HONOR AND BEHAVE(1938), w; ADVENTURES OF JANE ARDEN(1939), w; NO PLACE TO GO(1939), w; OFF THE RECORD(1939), w; IT ALL CAME TRUE(1940), w; BUGLE SOUNDS, THE(1941), w; DEVIL PAYS OFF, THE(1941), w; PUBLIC ENEMIES(1941), w; PARDON MY STRIPES(1942), w; PIERRE OF THE PLAINS(1942), w; JOHNNY DOUGHBOY(1943), w; TAHITI HONEY(1943), w; MUSIC IN MANHATTAN(1944), w; SEVEN DAYS ASHORE(1944), w; PAN-AMERICANA(1945), w; ZOMBIES ON BROADWAY(1945), w; BAMBOO BLONDE, THE(1946), w; CRIMINAL COURT(1946), w; SAN QUENTIN(1946), w; TRUTH ABOUT MURDER, THE(1946), w; ANGEL ON THE AMAZON(1948), w; FLAME, THE(1948), w; I, JANE DOE(1948), w; MYSTERY IN MEXICO(1948), w; COVER-UP(1949), w; AVENGERS, THE(1950), w; HIT PARADE OF 1951(1950), w; ONE WAY STREET(1950), w; TWO OF A KIND(1951), w
Robert Kimble
FUZZ(1972), ed
Robert L. Kimble
SIDECAR RACERS(1975, Aus.), ed; BATTLESTAR GALACTICA(1979), ed
Billy Kimbley
SHEP COMES HOME(1949); RAIDERS OF TOMAHAWK CREEK(1950); SILVER CITY BONANZA(1951)
Marketa Kimbrel
REACHING OUT(1983)
Barbara Kimbrell
PAT AND MIKE(1952)
Lois Kimbrell
LATIN LOVERS(1953); EDDY DUCHIN STORY, THE(1956); RACK, THE(1956); THESE WILDER YEARS(1956)
1984
RED DAWN(1984)
Marketa Kimbrell
PAWNBROKER, THE(1965)
Art Kimbro
1984
BEVERLY HILLS COP(1984)
Clinton Kimbro
YOUNG NURSES, THE(1973), d
Charles Kimbrough
FRONT, THE(1976); SEDUCTION OF JOE TYNAN, THE(1979); STARTING OVER(1979); IT'S MY TURN(1980)
Clinet Kimbrough
CRAZY MAMA(1975)
Clint Kimbrough
HOT SPELL(1958); BLOODY MAMA(1970); VON RICHTHOFEN AND BROWN(1970); LAST MOVIE, THE(1971); NIGHT CALL NURSES(1974)
Emily Kimbrough
OUR HEARTS WERE YOUNG AND GAY(1944), w
John Kimbrough
LONE STAR RANGER(1942); SUNDOWN JIM(1942)

Matthew Kimbrough
EDDIE MACON'S RUN(1983)
Phillip Kimbrough
LOVELESS, THE(1982)
Jeffrey Kime
QUARTET(1981, Brit./Fr.); JOY(1983, Fr./Can.); STATE OF THINGS, THE(1983)
Monica Kimick
THREE WEIRD SISTERS, THE(1948, Brit.), ed; UNEASY TERMS(1948, Brit.), ed;
MAN ON THE RUN(1949, Brit.), ed; LAST HOLIDAY(1950, Brit.), ed; NO PLACE FOR
JENNIFER(1950, Brit.), ed; ACCURSED, THE(1958, Brit.), ed
Kay Kimler
ROCK 'N' ROLL HIGH SCHOOL(1979); CHARLIE CHAN AND THE CURSE OF THE
DRAGON QUEEN(1981)
Newell P. Kimlin
DIAL 1119(1950), ed; INSIDE STRAIGHT(1951), ed; MAN WITH A CLOAK,
THE(1951), ed; TALL TARGET, THE(1951), ed; APACHE WAR SMOKE(1952), ed;
CARBINE WILLIAMS(1952), ed; TALK ABOUT A STRANGER(1952), ed; YOU FOR
ME(1952), ed; HALF A HERO(1953), ed; JEOPARDY(1953), ed; BAD DAY AT BLACK
ROCK(1955), ed; LOVE AND KISSES(1965), ed
Rose Kimman
Silents
WHEN SECONDS COUNT(1927)
Adam Kimmel
WANDERERS, THE(1979)
Ann Kimmel
1984
NOT FOR PUBLICATION(1984), p
Anne Kimmel
EATING RAOUL(1982), p
Bruce Kimmel
FIRST NUDIE MUSICAL, THE(1976), a, d, w, m, md; RACQUET(1979); CREA-
TURE WASN'T NICE,THE(1981), a, d&w
Dana Kimmel
FRIDAY THE 13TH PART III(1982)
Kathryn Kimmel
FIRST NUDIE MUSICAL, THE(1976)
Leslie Kimmel
VANQUISHED, THE(1953)
Lester Kimmel
FLAMINGO ROAD(1949)
Dana Kimmell
LONE WOLF McQUADE(1983); SWEET SIXTEEN(1983)
1984
FRIDAY THE 13TH–THE FINAL CHAPTER(1984)
Donald Kimmell
TAPS(1981)
Leslie Kimmell
LADY TAKES A SAILOR, THE(1949); HOUSE BY THE RIVER(1950); TALL TAR-
GET, THE(1951); OUTLAW'S SON(1957)
M. W. Kimmich
MOSCOW SHANGHAI(1936, Ger.), w
Max Kimmich
SECRET AGENT(1933, Brit.), w
Monica Kimmick
DEAD MAN'S SHOES(1939, Brit.), ed
Anthony Kimmins
GOLDEN CAGE, THE(1933, Brit.); BYPASS TO HAPPINESS(1934, Brit.), d&w;
DIPLOMATIC LOVER, THE(1934, Brit.), d; NIGHT CLUB QUEEN(1934, Brit.), w;
WHITE ENSIGN(1934, Brit.); ALL AT SEA(1935, Brit.), d; HIS MAJESTY AND
CO(1935, Brit.), d; ONCE IN A NEW MOON(1935, Brit.), d&w; WHILE PARENTS
SLEEP(1935, Brit.), w; KEEP YOUR SEATS PLEASE(1936, Brit.), w; LABURNUM
GROVE(1936, Brit.), w; QUEEN OF HEARTS(1936, Brit.), w; FEATHER YOUR
NEST(1937, Brit.), w; KEEP FIT(1937, Brit.), d, w; SCOTLAND YARD COM-
MANDS(1937, Brit.), w; SHOW GOES ON, THE(1937, Brit.), w; TALK OF THE
DEVIL(1937, Brit.), w; WHERE THERE'S A WILL(1937, Brit.), w; WHO'S YOUR
LADY FRIEND?(1937, Brit.), w; I SEE ICE(1938), d, w; COME ON GEORGE(1939,
Brit.), d, w; TROUBLE BREWING(1939, Brit.), d, w; IT'S IN THE AIR(1940, Brit.),
d&w; UNDER YOUR HAT(1940, Brit.), w; BONNIE PRINCE CHARLIE(1948, Brit.), d;
MINE OWN EXECUTIONER(1948, Brit.), p, d; FLESH AND BLOOD(1951, Brit.), d;
MEN OF THE SEA(1951, Brit.), w; PASSIONATE SENTRY, THE(1952, Brit.), p&d;
MR. DENNING DRIVES NORTH(1953, Brit.), p, d; TOP OF THE FORM(1953, Brit.),
w; AUNT CLARA(1954, Brit.), p&d; SMILEY(1957, Brit.), p&d, w; SMILEY GETS A
GUN(1959, Brit.), p&d, w; AMOROUS MR. PRAWN, THE(1965, Brit.), d, w
Ken Kimmins
THIEVES(1977)
Kenneth Kimmins
NETWORK(1976); SHOOT THE MOON(1982)
Verena Kimmins
SMILEY GETS A GUN(1959, Brit.)
Anthony Kimmons
CAPTAIN'S PARADISE, THE(1953, Brit.), p&d
Brad Kimp
RIDERS OF THE TIMBERLINE(1941)
Lawrence Kimple
BELLS OF CAPISTRANO(1942), w
Daisaka Kimura
TIDAL WAVE(1975, U.S./Jap.), ph
Daisaku Kimura
VIRUS(1980, Jap.), ph
Isao Kimura
SNOW COUNTRY(1969, Jap.)
Ko Kimura
IKIRU(1960, Jap.); HIGH AND LOW(1963, Jap.); STRAY DOG(1963, Jap.)
Ko "Isao" Kimura
SEVEN SAMURAI, THE(1956, Jap.)
Mitsuko Kimura
THREE STRIPES IN THE SUN(1955)

Motoyasu Kimura
MUDDY RIVER(1982, Jap.), p
Saburo Kimura
FFOLKES(1980, Brit.)
Takeo Kimura
GANGSTER VIP, THE(1968, Jap.), art d; FRIENDLY KILLER, THE(1970, Jap.), art
d
Takeshi Kimura
SECRET SCROLLS(PART I)**1/2 (1968, Jap.), w, w; RODAN(1958, Jap.), w; H-MAN,
THE(1959, Jap.), w; MYSTERIANS, THE(1959, Jap.), w; FINAL WAR, THE(1960,
Jap.), w; LAST WAR, THE(1962, Jap.), w; ATTACK OF THE MUSHROOM PEO-
PLE(1964, Jap.), w; HUMAN VAPOR, THE(1964, Jap.), w; YOUNG SWORD-
SMAN(1964, Jap.), w; LOST WORLD OF SINBAD, THE(1965, Jap.), w;
WHIRLWIND(1968, Jap.), w
Toshie Kimura
GODZILLA VERSUS THE SMOG MONSTER(1972, Jap.)
Takeshi Kimuri
GORATH(1964, Jap.), w
Kimursi
KING SOLOMON'S MINES(1950)
A. Kin
WAR AND PEACE(1968, USSR)
Jesse Kinaru
VISIT TO A CHIEF'S SON(1974)
Russell Kinball
MOUNTAIN RHYTHM(1942), art d
Jud Kinberg
MOONFLEET(1955), p; REACH FOR GLORY(1963, Brit.), p, w; SIEGE OF THE
SAXONS(1963, Brit.), p, w; EAST OF SUDAN(1964, Brit.), w; COLLECTOR,
THE(1965), p; HAPPENING, THE(1967), p; MAGUS, THE(1968, Brit.), p
Judson Kinberg
VAMPIRE CIRCUS(1972, Brit.), w; SELL OUT, THE(1976), w
Billy Kinbley
PREJUDICE(1949)
Aron Kincaid
BEACH BALL(1965); DR. GOLDFOOT AND THE BIKINI MACHINE(1965); GIRLS
ON THE BEACH(1965); SKI PARTY(1965); GHOST IN THE INVISIBLE BIKINI(1966);
HAPPIEST MILLIONAIRE, THE(1967); PROUD AND THE DAMNED, THE(1972);
CANNONBALL(1976, U.S./Hong Kong)
Misc. Talkies
CREATURE OF DESTRUCTION(1967); CREATURES OF DARKNESS(1969)
Gary Kincaid
PALM SPRINGS WEEKEND(1963)
Jason Kincaid
KILLING OF A CHINESE BOOKIE, THE(1976)
Knox Kincaid
Silents
SILVER WINGS(1922)
Perle Kincaid
ISN'T IT ROMANTIC?(1948)
Robert Kincaid
1984
MIKE'S MURDER(1984)
Tim Kincaid
FEMALE RESPONSE, THE(1972), d, w; QUADROON(1972); YOUNG NURSES,
THE(1973), prod d
Myra Kinch
LIVES OF A BENGAL LANCER(1935)
Felice Kinchelow
SOLOMON KING(1974)
Roslyn Kind
Misc. Talkies
I'M GOING TO BE FAMOUS(1981)
Sophie Kind
AMIN–THE RISE AND FALL(1982, Kenya); GIRO CITY(1982, Brit.)
Jullan Kindahl
WILD STRAWBERRIES(1959, Swed.)
Cy Kindall
DANCING IN MANHATTAN(1945)
Ann N. Kindberg
TOOLBOX MURDERS, THE(1978), w
Malcolm Kindell
FABIAN OF THE YARD(1954, Brit.)
Harold Kinder
STROKER ACE(1983)
Joseph Kinder
INVASION OF THE STAR CREATURES(1962), makeup
S. P. Kinder
Silents
IVANHOE(1913), ph
Stuart Kinder
Silents
IF(1916, Brit.), d
Misc. Silents
FORGOTTEN(1914, Brit.), d
Kristen Kinderman
1984
REVENGE OF THE NERDS(1984)
Elmo Kindermann
TRAIN, THE(1965, Fr./Ital./U.S.)
Helmo Kindermann
I AIM AT THE STARS(1960); MAGIC FOUNTAIN, THE(1961); QUESTION 7(1961,
U.S./Ger.); NO TIME FOR ECSTASY(1963, Fr.); SECRET INVASION, THE(1964)
Ludek Kindermann
ROCKET TO NOWHERE(1962, Czech.)
Tom Kindle
SUPER VAN(1977); BUDDY BUDDY(1981)

Carol King
MAKING LOVE(1982)
Carole King
BIONIC BOY, THE(1977, Hong Kong/Phil.)
Casey King
MAKING IT(1971)
Misc. Talkies
BONE(1972)
Charles King
BROADWAY MELODY, THE(1929); CHASING RAINBOWS(1930); OH! SAILOR, BEHAVE!(1930); REMOTE CONTROL(1930); ALIAS THE BAD MAN(1931); BRANDED MEN(1931); RANGE LAW(1931); TWO GUN MAN, THE(1931); CORNERED(1932); GAY BUCKAROO, THE(1932); GHOST CITY(1932); HONOR OF THE MOUNTED(1932); MAN'S LAND, A(1932); POCATELLO KID(1932); YOUNG BLOOD(1932); CRASHING BROADWAY(1933); DUDE BANDIT, THE(1933); FIGHTING CHAMP(1933); FIGHTING PARSON, THE(1933); LONE AVENGER, THE(1933); OUTLAW JUSTICE(1933); PICTURE SNATCHER(1933); SON OF THE BORDER(1933); STRAWBERRY ROAN(1933); INSIDE INFORMATION(1934); JEALOUSY(1934); LADY BY CHOICE(1934); FIGHTING TROOPER, THE(1935); HIS FIGHTING BLOOD(1935); IVORY-HANDLED GUN(1935); NORTHERN FRONTIER(1935); OUTLAWED GUNS(1935); RED BLOOD OF COURAGE(1935); SINGING VAGABOND, THE(1935); TRAIL OF TERROR(1935); TUMBLING TUMBLEWEEDS(1935); WHOLE TOWN'S TALKING, THE(1935); CROOKED TRAIL, THE(1936); FAST BULLETS(1936); GUNS AND GUITARS(1936); KID RANGER, THE(1936); LAST OF THE WARRENS, THE(1936); LAW RIDES, THE(1936); LAWLESS NINETIES, THE(1936); LIBELED LADY(1936); LUCKY TERROR(1936); MEN OF THE PLAINS(1936); O'MALLEY OF THE MOUNTED(1936); PRESCOTT KID, THE(1936); RED RIVER VALLEY(1936); RIP ROARIN' BUCKAROO(1936); SUNSET OF POWER(1936); VALLEY OF THE LAWLESS(1936); BLACK ACES(1937); DOOMED AT SUNDOWN(1937); FIGHTING DEPUTY, THE(1937); HEADIN' FOR THE RIO GRANDE(1937); HEADLINE CRASHER(1937); HITTIN' THE TRAIL(1937); IDAHO KID, THE(1937); ISLAND CAPTIVES(1937); LAWMAN IS BORN, A(1937); LOVE IS NEWS(1937); MYSTERY OF THE HOODED HORSEMEN, THE(1937); RED ROPE, THE(1937); RIDERS OF THE ROCKIES(1937); RIDIN' THE LONE TRAIL(1937); ROOTIN' TOOTIN' RHYTHM(1937); SANTA FE BOUND(1937); SING, COWBOY, SING(1937); SMOKE TREE RANGE(1937); SUNDOWN SAUNDERS(1937); TEX RIDES WITH THE BOY SCOUTS(1937); TROUBLE IN TEXAS(1937); DANGER VALLEY(1938); FRONTIER TOWN(1938); GOLD MINE IN THE SKY(1938); GUN PACKER(1938); IN EARLY ARIZONA(1938); MAN'S COUNTRY(1938); ON THE GREAT WHITE TRAIL(1938); PHANTOM OF THE RANGE, THE(1938); PHANTOM RANGER(1938); ROLLIN' PLAINS(1938); SANTA FE STAMPEDE(1938); SONGS AND BULLETS(1938); THUNDER IN THE DESERT(1938); UTAH TRAIL(1938); COWBOYS FROM TEXAS(1939); DOWN THE WYOMING TRAIL(1939); FEUD OF THE RANGE(1939); FRONTIER PONY EXPRESS(1939); FRONTIERS OF '49(1939); LAW COMES TO TEXAS, THE(1939); LONE STAR PIONEERS(1939); MAN FROM TEXAS, THE(1939); MESQUITE BUCKAROO(1939); MUTINY IN THE BIG HOUSE(1939); OKLAHOMA FRONTIER(1939); RIDERS OF THE FRONTIER(1939); ROLL, WAGONS, ROLL(1939); ROLLIN' WESTWARD(1939); SONG OF THE BUCKAROO(1939); SOUTH OF THE BORDER(1939); SUNDOWN ON THE PRAIRIE(1939); TAMING OF THE WEST, THE(1939); WILD HORSE CANYON(1939); BILLY THE KID IN TEXAS(1940); CHEYENNE KID, THE(1940); DEATH RIDES THE RANGE(1940); LAW AND ORDER(1940); LIGHTNING STRIKES WEST(1940); ONE MAN'S LAW(1940); PONY POST(1940); RIDERS FROM NOWHERE(1940); SON OF THE NAVY(1940); WEST OF CARSON CITY(1940); BILLY THE KID WANTED(1941); BILLY THE KID'S FIGHTING PALS(1941); BILLY THE KID'S ROUNDUP(1941); BURY ME NOT ON THE LONE PRAIRIE(1941); DESERT BANDIT(1941); FORBIDDEN TRAILS(1941); GUN MAN FROM BODIE, THE(1941); LAW OF THE RANGE(1941); LONE RIDER AMBUSHED, THE(1941); LONE RIDER CROSSES THE RIO, THE(1941); LONE RIDER FIGHTS BACK, THE(1941); LONE RIDER IN GHOST TOWN, THE(1941); OUTLAWS OF THE RIO GRANDE(1941); ROAR OF THE PRESS(1941); TEXAS MARSHAL, THE(1941); ARIZONA STAGECOACH(1942); BELOW THE BORDER(1942); GHOST TOWN LAW(1942); LAW AND ORDER(1942); LONE STAR LAW MEN(1942); OVERLAND STAGECOACH(1942); PIRATES OF THE PRAIRIE(1942); PRAIRIE PALS(1942); RAIDERS OF THE WEST(1942); RANGERS TAKE OVER, THE(1942); RIDERS OF THE WEST(1942); SHERIFF OF SAGE VALLEY(1942); TRAIL RIDERS(1942); BAD MEN OF THUNDER GAP(1943); BORDER BUCKAROOS(1943); CALLING WILD BILL ELLIOTT(1943); CATTLE STAMPEDE(1943); DANGER! WOMEN AT WORK(1943); DESPERADOES, THE(1943); FIGHTING VALLEY(1943); HAUNTED RANCH, THE(1943); KID RIDES AGAIN, THE(1943); KING OF THE COWBOYS(1943); LAND OF HUNTED MEN(1943); MAN FROM THUNDER RIVER, THE(1943); OUTLAWS OF STAMPEDE PASS(1943); RETURN OF THE RANGERS, THE(1943); RIDERS OF THE RIO GRANDE(1943); STRANGER FROM PECOS, THE(1943); TWO FISTED JUSTICE(1943); WESTERN CYCLONE(1943); ARIZONA WHIRLWIND(1944); BRAND OF THE DEVIL(1944); CALIFORNIA JOE(1944); CODE OF THE PRAIRIE(1944); DEAD OR ALIVE(1944); DEATH VALLEY RANGERS(1944); DEVIL RIDERS(1944); FOLLOW THE BOYS(1944); FRONTIER OUTLAWS(1944); FUZZY SETTLES DOWN(1944); LAND OF THE OUTLAWS(1944); LAW OF THE VALLEY(1944); MARSHAL OF RENO(1944); OUTLAW TRAIL(1944); PINTO BANDIT, THE(1944); RAIDERS OF RED GAP(1944); RUSTLER'S HIDEOUT(1944); SONORA STAGECOACH(1944); TEXAS KID, THE(1944); THUNDERING GUN SLINGERS(1944); VALLEY OF VENGEANCE(1944); BORDER BADMEN(1945); ENEMY OF THE LAW(1945); FIGHTING BILL CARSON(1945); FLAMING BULLETS(1945); FRONTIER FUGITIVES(1945); HIS BROTHER'S GHOST(1945); MARKED FOR MURDER(1945); NAVAJO TRAIL, THE(1945); SHADOWS OF DEATH(1945); THREE IN THE SADDLE(1945); AMBUSH TRAIL(1946); CARAVAN TRAIL, THE(1946); COLORADO SERENADE(1946); GHOST OF HIDDEN VALLEY(1946); LAWLESS BREED, THE(1946); PRAIRIE BADMEN(1946); QUEEN OF BURLESQUE(1946); THUNDER TOWN(1946); KILLER AT LARGE(1947); LAW OF THE LASH(1947); RIDIN' DOWN THE TRAIL(1947); WHITE STALLION(1947); WISTFUL WIDOW OF WAGON GAP, THE(1947); WYOMING(1947); HAWK OF POWDER RIVER, THE(1948); OKLAHOMA BLUES(1948)
Misc. Talkies
MAN FROM ARIZONA, THE(1932); MYSTERY RANCH(1934); SILVER BULLET, THE(1935); SONGS AND SADDLES(1938); BILLY THE KID'S GUN JUSTICE(1940); WILD HORSE RANGE(1940); ALONG THE SUNDOWN TRAIL(1942); OUTLAWS OF BOULDER PASS(1942); WHERE TRAILS END(1942); OATH OF VENGEANCE(1944); GANGSTER'S DEN(1945)
Capt. Charles King
Silents
UNDER FIRE(1926), w

Charles King III
GUY NAMED JOE, A(1943)
Charles Croker King
CHARGE OF THE LIGHT BRIGADE, THE(1936); LIBELED LADY(1936); PIGSKIN PARADE(1936); STAGE STRUCK(1936)
Charles E. King
CURFEW BREAKERS(1957), p
Charles King, Jr.
GOD'S COUNTRY AND THE MAN(1937); LUCK OF ROARING CAMP, THE(1937); STARLIGHT OVER TEXAS(1938); WHERE THE BUFFALO ROAM(1938); KEEP 'EM FLYING(1941); EAGLE SQUADRON(1942); COWBOY IN THE CLOUDS(1943); BOSS OF THE RAWHIDE(1944); GANGSTERS OF THE FRONTIER(1944); SPOOK TOWN(1944); NAVAJO KID, THE(1946); OUTLAW OF THE PLAINS(1946)
Charles King, Sr.
THREE ON A TICKET(1947)
Charles L. King
OKLAHOMA CYCLONE(1930); DAWN TRAIL, THE(1931); FIGHTING THRU(1931); MISSISSIPPI(1935)
Misc. Talkies
BEYOND THE LAW(1930)
Silents
SINGING RIVER(1921); MERRY-GO-ROUND(1923); SLIM FINGERS(1929)
Misc. Silents
PRICE OF YOUTH, THE(1922); HEARTS OF THE WEST(1925)
Charlie King
DESERT PHANTOM(1937); GAMBLING TERROR, THE(1937); LIGHTNIN' CRANDALL(1937); TRUSTED OUTLAW, THE(1937); GREAT MIKE, THE(1944)
Charmion King
NOBODY WAVED GOODBYE(1965, Can.); DON'T LET THE ANGELS FALL(1969, Can.); WHO HAS SEEN THE WIND(1980, Can.)
Cheryl King
LOVE CHILD(1982)
Christopher King
TRUE TO LIFE(1943); STAR SPANGLED RHYTHM(1942); CRYSTAL BALL, THE(1943); FOR WHOM THE BELL TOLLS(1943); SALUTE FOR THREE(1943); LADY IN THE DARK(1944)
Claude King
BEHIND THAT CURTAIN(1929); BLACK WATCH, THE(1929); MADAME X(1929); MYSTERIOUS DR. FU MANCHU, THE(1929); STRANGE CARGO(1929); FOLLOW THRU(1930); IN GAY MADRID(1930); LOVE AMONG THE MILLIONAIRES(1930); PRINCE OF DIAMONDS(1930); SECOND FLOOR MYSTERY, THE(1930); SON OF THE GODS(1930); ARROWSMITH(1931); DEVOTION(1931); HEARTBREAK(1931); ONCE A LADY(1931); RANGO(1931); RECKLESS HOUR, THE(1931); TRANSATLANTIC(1931); WOMEN LOVE ONCE(1931); BEHIND THE MASK(1932); FORBIDDEN(1932); MC KENNA OF THE MOUNTED(1932); SHANGHAI EXPRESS(1932); SHERLOCK HOLMES(1932); CHARLIE CHAN'S GREATEST CASE(1933); HE LEARNED ABOUT WOMEN(1933); HELLO SISTER!(1933); WHITE WOMAN(1933); CHARLIE CHAN IN LONDON(1934); CITY PARK(1934); LONG LOST FATHER(1934); MOONSTONE, THE(1934); MURDER IN TRINIDAD(1934); MYSTERY OF MR. X, THE(1934); NOW I'LL TELL(1934); STOLEN SWEETS(1934); TWO HEADS ON A PILLOW(1934); WORLD MOVES ON, THE(1934); DARK ANGEL, THE(1935); GILDED LILY, THE(1935); GREAT IMPERSONATION, THE(1935); LAST OUTPOST, THE(1935); LIVES OF A BENGAL LANCER(1935); RIGHT TO LIVE, THE(1935); SMART GIRL(1935); $1,000 A MINUTE(1935); BELOVED ENEMY(1936); IT COULDN'T HAVE HAPPENED–BUT IT DID(1936); LEATHERNECKS HAVE LANDED, THE(1936); THREE ON THE TRAIL(1936); HAPPY-GO-LUCKY(1937); LANCER SPY(1937); LOVE UNDER FIRE(1937); MAYTIME(1937); STAR IS BORN, A(1937); BOOLOO(1938); FOUR MEN AND A PRAYER(1938); MAN-PROOF(1938); MARIE ANTOINETTE(1938); WITHIN THE LAW(1939); NEW MOON(1940); PHILADELPHIA STORY, THE(1940); SPORTING BLOOD(1940); SUSAN AND GOD(1940); YEAR OF THE YAHOO(1971)
Silents
JUDY OF ROGUES' HARBOUR(1920); SCARAB RING, THE(1921); SIX DAYS(1923); KNOCKOUT, THE(1925); UNGUARDED HOUR, THE(1925); PARADISE(1926); SILENT LOVER, THE(1926); LONDON AFTER MIDNIGHT(1927); MR. WU(1927); SINGED(1927); LOVE AND LEARN(1928); NIGHT OF MYSTERY, A(1928); OH, KAY(1928); OUTCAST(1928); RED HAIR(1928); SPORTING GOODS(1928); WARMING UP(1928)
Misc. Silents
IRISH LUCK(1925)
Clydie King
STAR IS BORN, A(1976)
Cy King
ON STAGE EVERYBODY(1945)
D. King
JUST BEFORE DAWN(1980), ph
Damu King
GUESS WHAT HAPPENED TO COUNT DRACULA(1970); SHAFT(1971); SWEET JESUS, PREACHER MAN(1973)
Misc. Talkies
BLACK GODFATHER, THE(1974); BLACK STARLET(1974); BLACKJACK(1978)
Daniel King
MY BROTHER JONATHAN(1949, Brit.)
Dave King
GO TO BLAZES(1962, Brit.); ROAD TO HONG KONG, THE(1962, U.S./Brit.); UP THE CHASTITY BELT(1971, Brit.); RITZ, THE(1976); CUBA(1979); REDS(1981); LONG GOOD FRIDAY, THE(1982, Brit.)
David King
PIRATES OF TORTUGA(1961); STRANGE BEDFELLOWS(1965); GOLDEN LADY, THE(1979, Brit.)
Della King
Silents
ORPHAN OF THE SAGE(1928), ed
Della M. King
Silents
AIR HAWK, THE(1924), ed; AVENGING RIDER, THE(1928), ed; BANTAM COWBOY, THE(1928), ed; BREED OF THE SUNSETS(1928), ed; DOG LAW(1928), ed; MAN IN THE ROUGH(1928), ed; AMAZING VAGABOND(1929), ed

Denis King
SWEENEY(1977, Brit.), m; PRIVATES ON PARADE(1982), m
Dennis King
VAGABOND KING, THE(1930); DEVIL'S BROTHER, THE(1933); BETWEEN TWO WORLDS(1944); MIRACLE, THE(1959); SOME KIND OF A NUT(1969)
1984
PRIVATES ON PARADE(1984, Brit.), m
Dennis King, Jr.
SCARLET COAT, THE(1955); RESTLESS BREED, THE(1957); LET'S MAKE LOVE(1960)
Diana King
ONCE A CROOK(1941, Brit.); MAN IN GREY, THE(1943, Brit.); GIRL RUSH(1944); SPELL OF AMY NUGENT, THE(1945, Brit.); FAREWELL TO ARMS, A(1957); MAN WHO WOULDN'T TALK, THE(1958, Brit.); TEENAGE BAD GIRL(1959, Brit.); OFFBEAT(1961, Brit.); DIE, DIE, MY DARLING(1965, Brit.); THEY CAME FROM BEYOND SPACE(1967, Brit.); SCHIZO(1977, Brit.)
Misc. Talkies
BLACK CARRION(1984)
Don King
LAST FIGHT, THE(1983)
Donald King
WIZ, THE(1978); WHO KILLED "DOC" ROBBIN?(1948)
1984
MOSCOW ON THE HUDSON(1984)
Dorothy King
SING ALONG WITH ME(1952, Brit.)
Drew King
SIEGE(1983, Can.), m
Duane King
MUSCLE BEACH PARTY(1964)
Edith King
BELLE STARR'S DAUGHTER(1947); BLAZE OF NOON(1947); CALCUTTA(1947); GALLANT BLADE, THE(1948); GIRL ON THE RUN(1961)
Edward King
THIN RED LINE, THE(1964)
Eleanor King
BIRTH OF A BABY(1938)
Eleanore King
PRIVATE WORLDS(1935)
Emmett King
SHOPWORN ANGEL, THE(1928); RENO(1930); WESTWARD PASSAGE(1932); PRESIDENT VANISHES, THE(1934); PRISONER OF ZENDA, THE(1937); MAN IN THE IRON MASK, THE(1939)
Silents
FAIR PRETENDER, THE(1918); LITTLE LORD FAUNTLEROY(1921); SILVER CAR, THE(1921); BEAUTIFUL AND DAMNED, THE(1922); KENTUCKY DERBY, THE(1922); ACQUITTAL, THE(1923); NEAR LADY, THE(1923); AIR HAWK, THE(1924); CAPTAIN JANUARY(1924); DARK STAIRWAYS(1924); FIGHTING AMERICAN, THE(1924); OVERLAND LIMITED, THE(1925); ARIZONA SWEEPSTAKES(1926); LAUGH, CLOWN, LAUGH(1928); MIDNIGHT MADNESS(1928)
Misc. Silents
OUT OF THE NIGHT(1918); FEAR WOMAN, THE(1919); FOOLS AND THEIR MONEY(1919); NO.99(1920); EDEN AND RETURN(1921); THREE SEVENS(1921); DON QUICKSHOT OF THE RIO GRANDE(1923); BARBARA FRIETCHIE(1924); GOD OF MANKIND(1928)
Emmett C. King
Silents
KISMET(1920); LYING LIPS(1921); MISTRESS OF SHENSTONE, THE(1921); DEVIL'S CARGO, THE(1925)
Misc. Silents
LAFAYETTE, WE COME!(1918); IN HIS BROTHER'S PLACE(1919)
Emmett O. King
CLIVE OF INDIA(1935)
Enid King
Silents
IF FOUR WALLS TOLD(1922, Brit.)
Ernest King
RADIO LOVER(1936, Brit.), p
Evelyn King
CHECKERED FLAG, THE(1963); GUIDE FOR THE MARRIED MAN, A(1967); CAPTAIN MILKSHAKE(1970)
Everett King
PEACE FOR A GUNFIGHTER(1967)
Frances King
STEP LIVELY(1944)
Frank King
SUSPENSE(1946), p; GANGSTER, THE(1947), p; DUDE GOES WEST, THE(1948), p; GUN CRAZY(1949), p; SOUTHSIDE 1-1000(1950), p; DRUMS IN THE DEEP SOUTH(1951), p; DEATH OF AN ANGEL(1952, Brit.), w; MUTINY(1952), p; RING, THE(1952), p; CARNIVAL STORY(1954), p; BRAVE ONE, THE(1956), p; WHAT A CARVE UP!(1962, Brit.), w; CAPTAIN SINDBAD(1963), p; MAYA(1966), p; HEAVEN WITH A GUN(1969), p
Dr. Frank King
GHOUL, THE(1934, Brit.), w
Frank O. King
CORKY OF GASOLINE ALLEY(1951), w; GASOLINE ALLEY(1951), d&w
Franklin King
WHEN STRANGERS MARRY(1944), p; DILLINGER(1945), p
Fred King
Misc. Talkies
GUNSMOKE(1947), d
Freeman King
BUDDY HOLLY STORY, THE(1978); UNDER THE RAINBOW(1981)
1984
FLETCH(1984); MIKE'S MURDER(1984)
G.W. King
DANCE OF THE DWARFS(1983, U.S., Phil.), w

Gaby King
$100 A NIGHT(1968, Ger.)
Geoffrey King
WISHBONE, THE(1933, Brit.)
George King
DEADLOCK(1931, Brit.), p&d; MEN OF STEEL(1932, Brit.), d; SELF-MADE LADY(1932, Brit.), p; ENEMY OF THE POLICE(1933, Brit.), d; HER IMAGINARY LOVER(1933, Brit.), d; HIGH FINANCE(1933, Brit.), d; I ADORE YOU(1933, Brit.), d; MATINEE IDOL(1933, Brit.), d; MAYFAIR GIRL(1933, Brit.), d; SMITHY(1933, Brit.), d; TOO MANY WIVES(1933, Brit.), d; ADVENTURE LIMITED(1934, Brit.), d; BLUE SQUADRON, THE(1934, Brit.), d; GET YOUR MAN(1934, Brit.), p&d; GUEST OF HONOR(1934, Brit.), d; LITTLE STRANGER(1934, Brit.), p,d&w; MURDER AT THE INN(1934, Brit.), d; NINE FORTY-FIVE(1934, Brit.), d; OH NO DOCTOR!(1934, Brit.), p,d&w; SILVER SPOON, THE(1934, Brit.), d; TO BE A LADY(1934, Brit.), p&d; FULL CIRCLE(1935, Brit.), d; HANDLE WITH CARE(1935, Brit.), p; LEND ME YOUR HUSBAND(1935, Brit.), p; MAN WITHOUT A FACE, THE(1935, Brit.), p, d; WINDFALL(1935, Brit.), p, d; CRIMES OF STEPHEN HAWKE, THE(1936, Brit.), p&d; GAY OLD DOG(1936, Brit.), p, d; REASONABLE DOUBT(1936, Brit.), d; DOUBLE EXPOSURES(1937, Brit.), p; ELDER BROTHER, THE(1937, Brit.), p; IT'S NEVER TOO LATE TO MEND(1937, Brit.), p&d; MERRY COMES TO STAY(1937, Brit.), p&d; RIDING HIGH(1937, Brit.), p; TICKET OF LEAVE MAN, THE(1937, Brit.), p&d; UNDER A CLOUD(1937, Brit.), p&d; WANTED(1937, Brit.), p&d; JOHN HALIFAX–GENTLEMAN(1938, Brit.), p&d; SEXTON BLAKE AND THE HOODED TERROR(1938, Brit.), p&d; SILVER TOP(1938, Brit.), p&d; DANCING CO-ED(1939, Brit.), ch; DEMON BARBER OF FLEET STREET, THE(1939, Brit.), p&d; FACE AT THE WINDOW, THE(1939, Brit.), p&d; IDIOT'S DELIGHT(1939, Brit.), ch; CASE OF THE FRIGHTENED LADY, THE(1940. Brit.), d; CHINESE DEN, THE(1940, Brit.), p&d; CRIMES AT THE DARK HOUSE(1940, Brit.), p&d; GEORGE AND MARGARET(1940, Brit.), d; TWO FOR DANGER(1940, Brit.), d; ZIS BOOM BAH(1941), ch; AT DAWN WE DIE(1943, Brit.), d; SPITFIRE(1943, Brit.), p; CANDLELIGHT IN ALGERIA(1944, Brit.), p&d; CODE OF SCOTLAND YARD(1948), p&d; SHOWTIME(1948, Brit.), p, d; FORBIDDEN(1949, Brit.), p&d; EIGHT O'CLOCK WALK(1954, Brit.), p
Dr. George S. King
SLAVE SHIP(1937), w
Gerald King
TIME, THE PLACE AND THE GIRL, THE(1929)
Gillian King
TOMMY(1975, Brit.)
Gloria King
THIS STUFF'LL KILL YA!(1971)
Hal King
THREE CABALLEROS, THE(1944), anim; MAKE MINE MUSIC(1946), anim; SONG OF THE SOUTH(1946), anim; FUN AND FANCY FREE(1947), anim; MELODY TIME(1948), animators; SO DEAR TO MY HEART(1949), anim; SQUARE DANCE JUBILEE(1949); CINDERELLA(1950), anim; ALICE IN WONDERLAND(1951), anim; PETER PAN(1953), anim; LADY AND THE TRAMP(1955), anim d; SLEEPING BEAUTY(1959), anim; ONE HUNDRED AND ONE DALMATIANS(1961), anim; SWORD IN THE STONE, THE(1963), anim; ARISTOCATS, THE(1970), anim; ROBIN HOOD(1973), anim
Hanna King
IN-LAWS, THE(1979)
Harry King
IN OLD CHICAGO(1938), d
Henry King
SHE GOES TO WAR(1929), d; EYES OF THE WORLD, THE(1930), d; HELL HARBOR(1930), d; LIGHTNIN'(1930), d; MERELY MARY ANN(1931), d; OVER THE HILL(1931), d; WOMAN IN ROOM 13, THE(1932), d; I LOVED YOU WEDNESDAY(1933), d; STATE FAIR(1933), d; CAROLINA(1934), d; MARIE GALANTE(1934), d; ONE MORE SPRING(1935), d; WAY DOWN EAST(1935), d; COUNTRY DOCTOR, THE(1936), d; LLOYDS OF LONDON(1936), d; RAMONA(1936), d; SEVENTH HEAVEN(1937), d; ALEXANDER'S RAGTIME BAND(1938), d; JESSE JAMES(1939), d; STANLEY AND LIVINGSTONE(1939), d; CHAD HANNA(1940), d; LITTLE OLD NEW YORK(1940), d; MARYLAND(1940), d; REMEMBER THE DAY(1941), d; YANK IN THE R.A.F., A(1941), d; BLACK SWAN, THE(1942), d; MRS. MINIVER(1942); YANKS ARE COMING, THE(1942); SONG OF BERNADETTE, THE(1943), d; SPOTLIGHT SCANDALS(1943); WILSON(1944), d; BELL FOR ADANO, A(1945), d; OUT OF THIS WORLD(1945); MARGIE(1946), d; DEEP WATERS(1948), d; PRINCE OF FOXES(1949), d; TWELVE O'CLOCK HIGH(1949), d; GUNFIGHTER, THE(1950), d; DAVID AND BATHSHEBA(1951), d; I'D CLIMB THE HIGHEST MOUNTAIN(1951), d; O. HENRY'S FULL HOUSE(1952), d; WAIT 'TIL THE SUN SHINES, NELLIE(1952), d; KING OF THE KHYBER RIFLES(1953), d; LOVE IS A MANY-SPLENDORED THING(1955), d; UNTAMED(1955), d; CAROUSEL(1956), d; SUN ALSO RISES, THE(1957), d; BRAVADOS, THE(1958), d; BELOVED INFIDEL(1959), d; THIS EARTH IS MINE(1959), d; TENDER IS THE NIGHT(1961), d
Silents
SHOULD A WIFE FORGIVE?(1915); JOY AND THE DRAGON(1916), a, d; BRIDE'S SILENCE, THE(1917), d; ALL THE WORLD TO NOTHING(1919), d; THIS HERO STUFF(1919), d; HELP WANTED–MALE!(1920), a, d; MISTRESS OF SHENSTONE, THE(1921), d; SALVAGE(1921), d; STING OF THE LASH(1921); TOL'ABLE DAVID(1921), d, w; SEVENTH DAY, THE(1922), d; SONNY(1922), p&d, w; WHITE SISTER, THE(1923), d; ANY WOMAN(1925), d; ROMOLA(1925), d; STELLA DALLAS(1925), d; PARTNERS AGAIN(1926), d; WINNING OF BARBARA WORTH, THE(1926), d
Misc. Silents
LITTLE MARY SUNSHINE(1916), a, d; PAY DIRT(1916), a, d; POWER OF EVIL, THE(1916); SHADOWS AND SUNSHINE(1916), a, d; CLIMBER, THE(1917), a, d; DEVIL'S BAIT, THE(1917); GAME OF WITS, A(1917), a, d; MAINSPRING, THE(1917), a, d; MATE OF THE SALLY ANN, THE(1917); SOULS IN PAWN(1917), d; SOUTHERN PRIDE(1917), d; SUNSHINE AND GOLD(1917), a, d; TOLD AT THE TWILIGHT(1917), a, d; TWIN KIDDIES(1917), a, d; VENGEANCE OF THE DEAD(1917), d; BEAUTY AND THE ROGUE(1918), d; HEARTS OR DIAMONDS?(1918), d; HOBBS IN A HURRY(1918), d; LOCKED HEART, THE(1918), a, d; POWERS THAT PREY(1918), d; SOCIAL BRIARS(1918), d; UP ROMANCE ROAD(1918), d; BRASS BUTTONS(1919), d; FUGITIVE FROM MATRIMONY(1919), d; SIX FEET FOUR(1919), d; SOME LIAR(1919), d; SPORTING CHANCE, A(1919), d; WHEN A MAN RIDES ALONE(1919), d; WHERE THE WEST BEGINS(1919), d; 23 ½ HOURS ON LEAVE(1919), d; DICE OF DESTINY(1920), d; HAUNTING SHADOWS(1920), d; LIVE WIRE HICK, A(1920), d; ONE HOUR BEFORE DAWN(1920), d; UNCHARTED CHANNELS(1920), d; WHITE DOVE, THE(1920), d; WHEN WE WERE TWENTY-ONE(1921), d; BOND BOY, THE(1922), d; FURY(1922), d; SACKCLOTH

AND SCARLET(1925), d; MAGIC FLAME, THE(1927), d; WOMAN DISPUTED, THE(1928), d

Herman King
I SELL ANYTHING(1934); RING, THE(1952), p; CAPTAIN SINDBAD(1963), p

Hetty King
LET'S MAKE UP(1955, Brit.)

Honey King
SON OF SINBAD(1955)

Hugh King
STORM, THE(1938), w; FLIGHT AT MIDNIGHT(1939), w; THREAT, THE(1949), p, w; DIAL 1119(1950), w; UNDERWATER!(1955), w

Humphrey King
WESTWARD PASSAGE(1932), w

Hyman King
BAD MEN OF TOMBSTONE(1949), p

Irene King
GARMENT JUNGLE, THE(1957)

Ivan King
SILVER DARLINGS, THE(1947, Brit.), art d; DAUGHTER OF DARKNESS(1948, Brit.), art d; THIS WAS A WOMAN(1949, Brit.), art d; THIRD TIME LUCKY(1950, Brit.), art d; LAUGHTER IN PARADISE(1951, Brit.), art d; SHOOT FIRST(1953, Brit.), art d; VILLAGE, THE(1953, Brit./Switz.), art d; TONIGHT'S THE NIGHT(1954, Brit.), art d; YOUR PAST IS SHOWING(1958, Brit.), art d; TWO-HEADED SPY, THE(1959, Brit.), art d; HAND IN HAND(1960, Brit.), art d; VILLAGE OF THE DAMNED(1960, Brit.), art d; FIVE GOLDEN HOURS(1961, Brit.), art d; OPERATION SNATCH(1962, Brit.), art d; WHAT A CARVE UP!(1962, Brit.), art d; FRIENDS AND NEIGHBORS(1963, Brit.), art d; CROSSPLOT(1969, Brit.), art d; ALL THE WAY UP(1970, Brit.), prod d

Ivy King
Silents
MYSTERY OF MR. BERNARD BROWN(1921, Brit.)

J. King
JUST BEFORE DAWN(1980), ph

Jack King
MADAME SATAN(1930); MAID HAPPY(1933, Brit.), w; MEN OF THE NIGHT(1934); FUGITIVE SHERIFF, THE(1936); HEROES OF THE RANGE(1936); LAWLESS RIDERS(1936); CODE OF THE CACTUS(1939); GUN MAN FROM BODIE, THE(1941); MONSTER OF HIGHGATE PONDS, THE(1961, Brit.), ed

Jackie King
1984
SONGWRITER(1984)

James King
ZIEGFELD FOLLIES(1945)

James B. King
Silents
FANGS OF JUSTICE(1926), ph

Janel King
PSYCHO FROM TEXAS(1982)

Janet King
YOU WERE MEANT FOR ME(1948)

Janice King
MELVIN AND HOWARD(1980)

Jean King
NIGHT HAS A THOUSAND EYES(1948)

Jean Paul King
DARK AT THE TOP OF THE STAIRS, THE(1960); SEND ME NO FLOWERS(1964)

Jeff King
SUNNYSIDE(1979), w

Jeffrey Bryan King
SMOKEY AND THE BANDIT II(1980)

Jennifer King
SOYLENT GREEN(1973)

Jim King
TRICK BABY(1973)

Joe King
BATTLE OF PARIS, THE(1929); LAUGHING LADY, THE(1930); ROADHOUSE NIGHTS(1930); TRIAL OF VIVIENNE WARE, THE(1932); STRANDED(1935); ROAD GANG(1936); ARMORED CAR(1937); ALEXANDER'S RAGTIME BAND(1938); IN OLD CHICAGO(1938); STRANGE FACES(1938); DESTRY RIDES AGAIN(1939); EAST SIDE OF HEAVEN(1939); MR. SMITH GOES TO WASHINGTON(1939); OFF THE RECORD(1939); SMASHING THE MONEY RING(1939); YOU CAN'T CHEAT AN HONEST MAN(1939); BLACK FRIDAY(1940); CHARLIE CHAN AT THE WAX MUSEUM(1940); DANGER ON WHEELS(1940); IT'S A DATE(1940); THREE CHEERS FOR THE IRISH(1940); YOU'RE NOT SO TOUGH(1940); STRANGE ALIBI(1941); BUTCH MINDS THE BABY(1942); FALLEN SPARROW, THE(1943); IRON MAJOR, THE(1943); KEEP 'EM SLUGGING(1943); SHE HAS WHAT IT TAKES(1943); SWEET ROSIE O'GRADY(1943); BEAUTIFUL BUT BROKE(1944); MAGNIFICENT DOLL(1946); RANCHO NOTORIOUS(1952), cos; MOONLIGHTER, THE(1953), cos; MAN WITH THE GOLDEN ARM, THE(1955), cos; NOT AS A STRANGER(1955), cos; PRIDE AND THE PASSION, THE(1957), cos; DEFIANT ONES, THE(1958), cos; ON THE BEACH(1959), cos; EXODUS(1960), cos; INHERIT THE WIND(1960), cos; JUDGMENT AT NUREMBERG(1961), cos; GUESS WHO'S COMING TO DINNER(1967), cos; SECRET OF SANTA VITTORIA, THE(1969), cos; CREEPSHOW(1982)
Silents
ANSWER, THE(1918); FALSE EVIDENCE(1919); NORTH WIND'S MALICE, THE(1920); ANNE OF LITTLE SMOKY(1921); IDOL OF THE NORTH, THE(1921); MORAL FIBRE(1921); SCARAB RING, THE(1921); SISTERS(1922); TIN GODS(1926)
Misc. Silents
HER BITTER CUP(1916), d; BETTY AND THE BUCCANEERS(1917); SEA MASTER, THE(1917); WILD WINSHIP'S WIDOW(1917); EVERYWOMAN'S HUSBAND(1918); HAND AT THE WINDOW, THE(1918); HEIRESS FOR A DAY(1918); IRISH EYES(1918); LAST REBEL, THE(1918); PRICE OF APPLAUSE, THE(1918); SHIFTING SANDS(1918); UNTIL THEY GET ME(1918); LOVE'S PRISONER(1919); WAY OF THE STRONG, THE(1919); CHILDREN NOT WANTED(1920); GIRL WITH A JAZZ HEART, THE(1920); GIRL WITH THE JAZZ HEART, THE(1920); MAN AND WOMAN(1920); WOMAN GOD SENT, THE(1920); MAN AND WOMAN(1921); BIG BROTHER(1923); COUNTERFEIT LOVE(1923); TWENTY-ONE(1923); MASKED DANCER, THE(1924)

Joel King
FRIGHTMARE(1983), ph

John King
STOLEN HARMONY(1935); CRASH DONOVAN(1936); LOVE BEFORE BREAKFAST(1936); NEXT TIME WE LOVE(1936); MERRY-GO-ROUND OF 1938(1937); ROAD BACK, THE(1937); THREE SMART GIRLS(1937); BREAKING THE ICE(1938); CHARLIE CHAN IN HONOLULU(1938); CRIME OF DR. HALLET(1938); MR. MOTO TAKES A VACATION(1938); SHARPSHOOTERS(1938); STATE POLICE(1938); HARDYS RIDE HIGH, THE(1939); INSIDE STORY(1939); THREE MUSKETEERS, THE(1939); GENTLEMAN FROM ARIZONA, THE(1940); HALF A SINNER(1940); MIDNIGHT LIMITED(1940); RANGE BUSTERS, THE(1940); TRAILING DOUBLE TROUBLE(1940); WEST OF PINTO BASIN(1940); FUGITIVE VALLEY(1941); KID'S LAST RIDE, THE(1941); SADDLE MOUNTAIN ROUNDUP(1941); TONTO BASIN OUTLAWS(1941); TRAIL OF THE SILVER SPURS(1941); TUMBLEDOWN RANCH IN ARIZONA(1941); UNDERGROUND RUSTLERS(1941); WRANGLER'S ROOST(1941); ARIZONA STAGECOACH(1942); LAW OF THE JUNGLE(1942); ROCK RIVER RENEGADES(1942); TEXAS TO BATAAN(1942); THUNDER RIVER FEUD(1942); TRAIL RIDERS(1942); HAUNTED RANCH, THE(1943); TWO FISTED JUSTICE(1943); RENEGADE GIRL(1946); HISTORY OF THE WORLD, PART 1(1981); LOVELESS, THE(1982)
Misc. Talkies
OUTLAWS' HIGHWAY(1934); BOOT HILL BANDITS(1942); TEXAS TROUBLE SHOOTERS(1942); ALIEN ZONE(1978)
Silents
GOLD RUSH, THE(1925)

John King III
GUESS WHAT HAPPENED TO COUNT DRACULA(1970); PSYCHO FROM TEXAS(1982)

Joleen King
SUDDENLY IT'S SPRING(1947); UNSUSPECTED, THE(1947); PERFECT STRANGERS(1950)

Jolene King
DISPUTED PASSAGE(1939)

Jonna King
1984
MEATBALLS PART II(1984)

Joseph King
ALIBI IKE(1935); BROADWAY HOSTESS(1935); FRISCO KID(1935); FRONT PAGE WOMAN(1935); LET 'EM HAVE IT(1935); MAN OF IRON(1935); SHIPMATES FOREVER(1935); SPECIAL AGENT(1935); WE'RE IN THE MONEY(1935); BULLETS OR BALLOTS(1936); CASE OF THE VELVET CLAWS, THE(1936); CHINA CLIPPER(1936); JAILBREAK(1936); MOONLIGHT ON THE PRAIRIE(1936); POLO JOE(1936); PUBLIC ENEMY'S WIFE(1936); SATAN MET A LADY(1936); SINGING KID, THE(1936); SNOWED UNDER(1936); SONS O' GUNS(1936); WALKING DEAD, THE(1936); FLY-AWAY BABY(1937); GOD'S COUNTRY AND THE WOMAN(1937); HOT WATER(1937); LAND BEYOND THE LAW(1937); SAN QUENTIN(1937); SECOND HONEYMOON(1937); SLIM(1937); THAT MAN'S HERE AGAIN(1937); WHITE BONDAGE(1937); ARSENE LUPIN RETURNS(1938); CITY STREETS(1938); HEART OF THE NORTH(1938); CODE OF THE SECRET SERVICE(1939); MY SON IS A CRIMINAL(1939); YOU CAN'T GET AWAY WITH MURDER(1939); ALWAYS A BRIDE(1940); BLONDIE GOES LATIN(1941); BULLETS FOR O'HARA(1941); BIG SHOT, THE(1942); GLASS KEY, THE(1942); THEY DIED WITH THEIR BOOTS ON(1942); BOMBARDIER(1943); WITNESS FOR THE PROSECUTION(1957), cos
Silents
RIGHT TO LIE, THE(1919); SALVATION NELL(1921); VALLEY OF SILENT MEN, THE(1922)
Misc. Silents
SELFISH WOMAN, THE(1916); SWEET KITTY BELLAIRS(1916); HELL HATH NO FURY(1917); VORTEX, THE(1918); BROADWAY BUBBLE, THE(1920)

Joseph King, Sr.
ONCE A DOCTOR(1937)

Judith King
IF I WERE KING(1938); SAY IT IN FRENCH(1938); HOTEL IMPERIAL(1939); MIDNIGHT(1939); OUR NEIGHBORS–THE CARTERS(1939)

Judy King
CAFE SOCIETY(1939); $1,000 A TOUCHDOWN(1939)
Silents
SEVEN CHANCES(1925); GAY RETREAT, THE(1927)
Misc. Silents
BONANZA BUCKAROO, THE(1926); EL RELICARIO(1926); SPEEDING THROUGH(1926)

Juliet King
TOMMY(1975, Brit.)

Kang Pak King
NIGHT IN HONG KONG, A(1961, Jap.)

Karen King
LUSTY MEN, THE(1952)

Katherine King
1984
AMERICAN TABOO(1984)

Kathleen King
SSSSSSSS(1973)

Ken King
POLYESTER(1981)

Kenneth King
ILLIAC PASSION, THE(1968)

Kevin King
TERROR EYES(1981)

Kewpie King
Misc. Silents
BATTLING BUDDY(; (1924)

Kip King
TEA AND SYMPATHY(1956); DINO(1957); JOHNNY TROUBLE(1957); KISS THEM FOR ME(1957); PEYTON PLACE(1957); PROPER TIME, THE(1959); THUNDER ALLEY(1967); WESTWORLD(1973); MURPH THE SURF(1974)

L. H. King
Silents
WATCH YOUR STEP(1922)

Larry King
1984
GHOSTBUSTERS(1984)
Larry L. King
BEST LITTLE WHOREHOUSE IN TEXAS, THE(1982), w
Leila King
Silents
LIEUTENANT DARING RN AND THE WATER RATS(1924, Brit.)
Leslie King
Misc. Talkies
ALICE IN WONDERLAND(1931); GAS PUMP GIRLS(1979)
Silents
ORPHANS OF THE STORM(1922); STREETS OF NEW YORK, THE(1922)
Lew King
IT'S A SMALL WORLD(1935)
Lewis King
Silents
PEACEFUL PETERS(1922), d
Misc. Silents
DEVIL'S DOORYARD, THE(1923), d; LAW RUSTLERS, THE(1923), d; SUN DOG TRAILS(1923), d
Lily King
KING OF CHINATOWN(1939)
Lloyd King
OUTLAWS IS COMING, THE(1965)
Loretta King
BRIDE OF THE MONSTER(1955)
Lou King
YOU CAN'T TAKE IT WITH YOU(1938)
Louis King
MEXICALI ROSE(1929); LONE RIDER, THE(1930), d; MEN WITHOUT LAW(1930), d; SHADOW RANCH(1930), d; WAY OF ALL MEN, THE(1930); BORDER LAW(1931), d; DECEIVER, THE(1931), d; DESERT VENGEANCE(1931), d; FIGHTING SHERIFF, THE(1931), d; ARM OF THE LAW(1932), d; COUNTY FAIR, THE(1932), d; FAME STREET(1932), d; LIFE IN THE RAW(1933), d; ROBBERS' ROOST(1933), d; MURDER IN TRINIDAD(1934), d; PURSUED(1934), d; BACHELOR OF ARTS(1935), d; CHARLIE CHAN IN EGYPT(1935), d; WAY DOWN EAST(1935), d; BENGAL TIGER(1936), d; ROAD GANG(1936), d; SONG OF THE SADDLE(1936), d; SPECIAL INVESTIGATOR(1936), d; BULLDOG DRUMMOND COMES BACK(1937), d; BULLDOG DRUMMOND'S REVENGE(1937), d; DRAEGERMAN COURAGE(1937), d; MELODY FOR TWO(1937), d; THAT MAN'S HERE AGAIN(1937), d; WILD MONEY(1937), d; WINE, WOMEN AND HORSES(1937), d; BULLDOG DRUMMOND IN AFRICA(1938), d; HUNTED MEN(1938), d; ILLEGAL TRAFFIC(1938), d; PRISON FARM(1938), d; TIP-OFF GIRLS(1938), d; FIFTH AVENUE GIRL(1939); PERSONS IN HIDING(1939), d; TOM SAWYER, DETECTIVE(1939), d; UNDERCOVER DOCTOR(1939), d; MOON OVER BURMA(1940), d; SEVENTEEN(1940), d; TYPHOON(1940), d; WAY OF ALL FLESH, THE(1940), d; YOUNG AMERICA(1942), d; CHETNIKS(1943), d; LADIES OF WASHINGTON(1944), d; THUNDERHEAD-SON OF FLICKA(1945), d; SMOKY(1946), d; GREEN GRASS OF WYOMING(1948), d; MRS. MIKE(1949), d; SAND(1949), d; FRENCHIE(1950), d; LION AND THE HORSE, THE(1952), d; POWDER RIVER(1953), d; SABRE JET(1953), d; DANGEROUS MISSION(1954), d; MASSACRE(1956), d
Misc. Talkies
CROOKED ROAD(1932), d; DRIFTING SOULS(1932), d
Silents
SINGING RIVER(1921); DEVIL'S CARGO, THE(1925); BOY RIDER, THE(1927), d; IS YOUR DAUGHTER SAFE?(1927), d; BANTAM COWBOY, THE(1928), d; ORPHAN OF THE SAGE(1928), d; YOUNG WHIRLWIND(1928), d; FRECKLED RASCAL, THE(1929), d; LITTLE SAVAGE, THE(1929), d; PALS OF THE PRAIRIE(1929), d
Misc. Silents
PRINTER'S DEVIL, THE(1923); SLINGSHOT KID, THE(1927), d; FIGHTIN' REDHEAD, THE(1928), d; LITTLE BUCKAROO, THE(1928), d; PINTO KID, THE(1928), d; ROUGH RIDIN' RED(1928), d; TERROR(1928), d; TERROR MOUNTAIN(1928), d; VAGABOND CUB, THE(1929), d
Louise King
OCTOPUSSY(1983, Brit.)
Luana King
Misc. Talkies
KAHUNA!(1981)
Lulu King
COP HATER(1958)
Lulu B. King
ACT ONE(1964)
Lynda King
BRIDAL PATH, THE(1959, Brit.)
Mabel King
WIZ, THE(1978); GANJA AND HESS(1973); BINGO LONG TRAVELING ALL-STARS AND MOTOR KINGS, THE(1976); SCOTT JOPLIN(1977); JERK, THE(1979); GONG SHOW MOVIE, THE(1980); GETTING OVER(1981)
Misc. Talkies
BLOOD COUPLE(1974)
Maclyn King
Silents
EVERY WOMAN'S PROBLEM(1921)
Maggie King
CACTUS IN THE SNOW(1972)
Malcolm King
DON GIOVANNI(1979, Fr./Ital./Ger.)
Manuel King
DARKEST AFRICA(1936)
Marjorie King
GREAT GABBO, THE(1929); SUSAN LENOX–HER FALL AND RISE(1931); MY WEAKNESS(1933)
Silents
MAN IN THE ROUGH(1928)
Mark King
CAVEMAN(1981)

Martin King
POOR COW(1968, Brit.)
Mary King
LITTLE OF WHAT YOU FANCY, A(1968, Brit.)
Matty King
GOLD DIGGERS OF 1935(1935); SWING, SISTER, SWING(1938), ch; AFFECTIONATELY YOURS(1941), ch; WILD BILL HICKOK RIDES(1942), ch; MURDER ON THE WATERFRONT(1943), ch; BLUES BUSTERS(1950)
Maurice King
I KILLED THAT MAN(1942), p; KLONDIKE FURY(1942), p; RUBBER RACKETEERS(1942), p; I ESCAPED FROM THE GESTAPO(1943), p; UNKNOWN GUEST, THE(1943), p; JOHNNY DOESN'T LIVE HERE ANY MORE(1944), p; DILLINGER(1945), p; SUSPENSE(1946), p; DUDE GOES WEST, THE(1948), p; GUN CRAZY(1949), p; SOUTHSIDE 1-1000(1950), p; DRUMS IN THE DEEP SOUTH(1951), p; MUTINY(1952), p; RING, THE(1952), p; CARNIVAL STORY(1954), p; BRAVE ONE, THE(1956), p; MAYA(1966), p; HEAVEN WITH A GUN(1969), p
Max King
FOREIGN AGENT(1942), p; SPY TRAIN(1943), p
Max M. King
MEN OF SAN QUENTIN(1942), p; NORTHWEST TRAIL(1945), p; KILLER DILL(1947), p
Meegan King
CAT MURKIL AND THE SILKS(1976); HUMANOIDS FROM THE DEEP(1980)
Misc. Talkies
SWEATER GIRLS(1978); MONEY TO BURN(1981)
Michael King
DAN'S MOTEL(1982); POWERFORCE(1983), d
Michelle King
BREAKDOWN(1953)
Mike King
CONFESSIONS OF A POP PERFORMER(1975, Brit.)
Mollie King
Silents
ALL MAN(1916); KICK IN(1917)
Misc. Silents
FATE'S BOOMERANG(1916); SUMMER GIRL, THE(1916); WOMAN'S POWER, A(1916); BLIND MAN'S LUCK(1917); ON-THE-SQUARE GIRL, THE(1917); SUSPENCE(1919); WOMEN MEN FORGET(1920); SUSPICIOUS WIVES(1921); HER MAJESTY(1922)
Morgana King
GODFATHER, THE(1972); GODFATHER, THE, PART II(1974); NUNZIO(1978)
Muriel King
SYLVIA SCARLETT(1936), cos; STAGE DOOR(1937), cos; CASANOVA BROWN(1944), cos; WOMAN IN THE WINDOW, THE(1945), cos
Murray J. King
LIPSTICK(1965, Fr./Ital.), p
Murray Ramsey King
KING, MURRAY(1969)
Nancy Louise King
TRAILING DOUBLE TROUBLE(1940)
Nel King
ALL NIGHT LONG(1961, Brit.), w
Nellie King
Silents
WILD HONEY(1919)
Nelson King
MOTHER IS A FRESHMAN(1949)
Nicholas King
JOY RIDE(1958); LONG, HOT SUMMER, THE(1958); YOUNG LIONS, THE(1958); THREAT, THE(1960)
Nicola King
LORDS OF DISCIPLINE, THE(1983)
Noel King
THEY ALL LAUGHED(1981)
Oamu King
TOP OF THE HEAP(1972)
Olive King
KIMBERLEY JIM(1965, South Africa)
Owen King
CHINA CLIPPER(1936); MR. DODD TAKES THE AIR(1937); SUBMARINE D-1(1937); COMET OVER BROADWAY(1938); PATIENT IN ROOM 18, THE(1938); CHILD IS BORN, A(1940); MURDER IN THE AIR(1940); DIVE BOMBER(1941)
Patricia King
GREAT RACE, THE(1965)
Patty King
LONG NIGHT, THE(1947); KISS THE BLOOD OFF MY HANDS(1948); HENRY, THE RAINMAKER(1949); RED PONY, THE(1949)
Paul King
STRANGER AT MY DOOR(1950, Brit.), p; DEVIL'S JEST, THE(1954, Brit.), p; WILD HERITAGE(1958), w; OPERATION PETTICOAT(1959), w; THIS EARTH IS MINE(1959)
Pee Wee King
LAST PICTURE SHOW, THE(1971), m
Peggy King
BAD AND THE BEAUTIFUL, THE(1952); TORCH SONG(1953); ABBOTT AND COSTELLO MEET THE MUMMY(1955); ZERO HOUR!(1957)
Perry King
POSSESSION OF JOEL DELANEY, THE(1972); SLAUGHTERHOUSE-FIVE(1972); LORDS OF FLATBUSH, THE(1974); MANDINGO(1975); WILD PARTY, THE(1975); LIPSTICK(1976); CHOIRBOYS, THE(1977); DIFFERENT STORY, A(1978); SEARCH AND DESTROY(1981); CLASS OF 1984(1982, Can.); KILLING HOUR, THE(1982)
Misc. Talkies
STRIKING BACK(1981)
Pete King
FAMILY JEWELS, THE(1965), m; LAST OF THE SECRET AGENTS?, THE(1966), m
Peter King
SAY HELLO TO YESTERDAY(1971, Brit.), w; STONE(1974, Aus.)

Petra King
KRAMER VS. KRAMER(1979)
Philip King
TWENTY QUESTIONS MURDER MYSTERY, THE(1950, Brit.); CURTAIN UP(1952, Brit.), w; EIGHT O'CLOCK WALK(1954, Brit.); SEE HOW THEY RUN(1955, Brit.), w; PANIC IN THE PARLOUR(1957, Brit.), w; WATCH IT, SAILOR!(1961, Brit.), w; IMMORAL CHARGE(1962, Brit.), w; TUSK(1980, Fr.), art d
Polly King
Misc. Talkies
TOMCATS(1977)
Raleigh King
Silents
CREATION(1922, Brit.)
Misc. Silents
ISLAND OF ROMANCE, THE(1922, Brit.)
Ramsay King
BEAST WITHIN, THE(1982)
Raymond King
GETAWAY, THE(1972)
[Raymond] Sherwood King
LADY FROM SHANGHAI, THE(1948), w
Reba King
LOUISIANA HAYRIDE(1944)
Rex King
BIG SHOW, THE(1937); GREASER'S PALACE(1972)
Rey King
RAW FORCE(1982)
Reymond King
FIRECRACKER(1981)
Rich King
OFF THE WALL(1977), d, w
Richard King
1984
FIRST TURN-ON!, THE(1984), ed
Rick King
1984
HARD CHOICES(1984), d&w
Robb Wilson King
FRIDAY THE 13TH PART III(1982), art d; SWAMP THING(1982), prod d, art d; LOSIN' IT(1983), prod d; OSTERMAN WEEKEND, THE(1983), art d
Robert King
SILVER DARLINGS, THE(1947, Brit.), md; OUT OF TOWNERS, THE(1970); PROJECTIONIST, THE(1970); GET CARTER(1971, Brit.), art d; HAIL(1973); IN PRAISE OF OLDER WOMEN(1978, Can.)
Robert L. King
NOW YOU SEE HIM, NOW YOU DON'T(1972), w; WOLFEN(1981)
Robert Louis King
1984
EXTERMINATOR 2(1984)
Roger King
GOT IT MADE(1974, Brit.), set d; MUSIC MACHINE, THE(1979, Brit.), art d
Rose King
SINGING MARINE, THE(1937)
Rufus King
MURDER BY THE CLOCK(1931), w; MURDER AT THE VANITIES(1934), w; NOTORIOUS GENTLEMAN, A(1935), w; LOVE LETTERS OF A STAR(1936), w; HIDDEN HAND, THE(1942), w; WHITE TIE AND TAILS(1946), w; SECRET BEYOND THE DOOR, THE(1948), w
Silents
SILENT COMMAND, THE(1923), w
Ruth King
Silents
DEVIL'S PASSKEY, THE(1920); CHEATER REFORMED, THE(1921); FIFTY CANDLES(1921); HE WHO GETS SLAPPED(1924); LADY FROM HELL, THE(1926)
Misc. Silents
LAND OF LONG SHADOWS(1917); MEN OF THE DESERT(1917); OPEN PLACES(1917); RANGE BOSS, THE(1917); WINNING GRANDMA(1918); BEGGAR IN PURPLE, A(1920); DRIFTIN' THRU(1926)
Sandra King
DANGER ON WHEELS(1940)
Saxon King
Misc. Silents
INDESTRUCTIBLE WIFE, THE(1919)
Seth King
MR. BILLION(1977), cos
Sidney King
SHERLOCK HOLMES' FATAL HOUR(1931, Brit.); MAD HATTERS, THE(1935, Brit.); GABLES MYSTERY, THE(1938, Brit.); QUIET WEDDING(1941, Brit.); GLASS MOUNTAIN, THE(1950, Brit)
Silver King
Silents
SUNSET LEGION, THE(1928)
Simon King
POOR COW(1968, Brit.)
Sonny King
SERGEANTS 3(1962); ROBIN AND THE SEVEN HOODS(1964)
Stacey King
MONEY TRAP, THE(1966)
Stacy King
SKIDOO(1968); SWEET RIDE, THE(1968)
Stanley King
LIVING ON VELVET(1935); IT COULD HAPPEN TO YOU(1937); IF I WERE KING(1938); TIP-OFF GIRLS(1938); SOMEWHERE IN ENGLAND(1940, Brit.)
Stanley E. King
SHOW THEM NO MERCY(1935)
Stephanie King
STEEL TRAP, THE(1952); MAD DOG COLL(1961)

Stephen King
CARRIE(1976), w; SHINING, THE(1980), w; CREEPSHOW(1982), a, w; CHRISTINE(1983), w; CUJO(1983), w; DEAD ZONE, THE(1983), w
1984
CHILDREN OF THE CORN(1984), w; FIRESTARTER(1984), w
Steven King
KNIGHTRIDERS(1981)
Stevie King
POOR COW(1968, Brit.)
Sydney King
KING'S CUP, THE(1933, Brit.); FLYING FORTRESS(1942, Brit.); THOSE KIDS FROM TOWN(1942, Brit.); CALENDAR, THE(1948, Brit.); SILENT ENEMY, THE(1959, Brit.)
Tara King
DRIVER, THE(1978); STARTING OVER(1979); WANDERERS, THE(1979); 48 HOURS(1982)
Ted King
C. C. AND COMPANY(1971)
Tedd King
NAKED ANGELS(1969); SKI BUM, THE(1971)
Thomas King
SMASH PALACE(1982, New Zealand)
Tony King
MY BODY HUNGERS(1967); SHAFT(1971); KING OF MARVIN GARDENS, THE(1972); GORDON'S WAR(1973); HELL UP IN HARLEM(1973); BUCKTOWN(1975); REPORT TO THE COMMISSIONER(1975); SUPER SPOOK(1975), a, w; SPARKLE(1976); CANNIBALS IN THE STREETS(1982, Ital./Span.); SHARKY'S MACHINE(1982); TOY, THE(1982); BIG SCORE, THE(1983)
1984
LAST HUNTER, THE(1984, Ital.)
Tracy Ann King
HAMMER(1972)
Vaughn King
NATIVE LAND(1942)
W. Geoffrey King
LONG NIGHT, THE(1976)
Walter King
GINGER(1935); LOTTERY LOVER(1935); SPRING TONIC(1935); HOUSEHOLDER, THE(1963, US/India)
Walter Wolf [Woolf] King
TODAY I HANG(1942)
Walter Woolf King
NIGHT AT THE OPERA, A(1935); ONE MORE SPRING(1935); CALL IT A DAY(1937); SWISS MISS(1938); WALKING DOWN BROADWAY(1938); BALALAIKA(1939); BIG TOWN CZAR(1939); HOUSE OF FEAR, THE(1939); SOCIETY SMUGGLERS(1939); GO WEST(1940); MELODY FOR THREE(1941); SMART ALECKS(1942); YANK IN LIBYA, A(1942); YANKS AHOY(1943); STARS AND STRIPES FOREVER(1952); CALL ME MADAM(1953); CITY THAT NEVER SLEEPS(1953); TAXI(1953); TONIGHT WE SING(1953); BOTTOM OF THE BOTTLE, THE(1956); TEN COMMANDMENTS, THE(1956); JOKER IS WILD, THE(1957); HONG KONG CONFIDENTIAL(1958); KATHY O'(1958); HELEN MORGAN STORY, THE(1959); OUTSIDER, THE(1962); ROSIE!(1967)
Wayne King
DOMINO PRINCIPLE, THE(1977)
White King
SINGING BUCKAROO, THE(1937)
"White King"
FIGHTING DEPUTY, THE(1937)
William King
TERESA(1951)
Woodie King
TOGETHER FOR DAYS(1972); SERPICO(1973)
Woodie King, Jr.
LONG NIGHT, THE(1976), p, d, w
Wright King
STREETCAR NAMED DESIRE, A(1951); BOLD AND THE BRAVE, THE(1956); STAGECOACH TO FURY(1956); YOUNG GUNS, THE(1956); HOT ROD RUMBLE(1957); CAST A LONG SHADOW(1959); GUNFIGHT AT DODGE CITY, THE(1959); DANGEROUS CHARTER(1962); KING RAT(1965); FINIAN'S RAINBOW(1968); PLANET OF THE APES(1968); JOURNEY THROUGH ROSEBUD(1972); INVASION OF THE BEE GIRLS(1973)
Yolanda King
HOPSCOTCH(1980)
Zalman King
SKI BUM, THE(1971); YOU'VE GOT TO WALK IT LIKE YOU TALK IT OR YOU'LL LOSE THAT BEAT(1971); NEITHER BY DAY NOR BY NIGHT(1972, U.S./Israel); SOME CALL IT LOVING(1973); PASSOVER PLOT, THE(1976, Israel); BLUE SUNSHINE(1978); ROADIE(1980), w; TELL ME A RIDDLE(1980); GALAXY OF TERROR(1981)
Misc. Talkies
TRIP WITH THE TEACHER(1975); SAMMY SOMEBODY(1976)
King and Tillie the dogs
YOU NEVER CAN TELL(1951)
The King Brothers
6.5 SPECIAL(1958, Brit.)
King Cole Trio
STARS ON PARADE(1944)
The King Cole Trio
HERE COMES ELMER(1943); PISTOL PACKIN' MAMA(1943); SEE MY LAWYER(1945); MAKE BELIEVE BALLROOM(1949)
King Cotton the Horse
VIVA MAX!(1969)
King Sisters
LARCENY WITH MUSIC(1943); ON STAGE EVERYBODY(1945)
The King Sisters
FOLLOW THE BAND(1943); MEET THE PEOPLE(1944); CUBAN PETE(1946)
King Sisters Quartette
SECOND FIDDLE(1939)

King Solomon III
TRADER HORN(1973)
King the Horse
GOLD FEVER(1952)
King Tut
Silents
SPEEDY(1928)
King Tut the Dog
THUNDERBOLT(1929)
Silents
ONE MINUTE TO PLAY(1926)
Magdalen King-Hall
WICKED LADY, THE(1946, Brit.), w; WICKED LADY, THE(1983, Brit.), w
Stephen King-Hall
MIDDLE WATCH, THE(1930, Brit.), w; MIDSHIPMAID GOB(1932, Brit.), w; ADMIRALS ALL(1935, Brit.), w; TROPICAL TROUBLE(1936, Brit.), w; MIDDLE WATCH, THE(1939, Brit.), w; CARRY ON ADMIRAL(1957, Brit.), w; GIRLS AT SEA(1958, Brit.), w
John King-Kelly
GHOST SHIP(1953, Brit.); CASE OF THE RED MONKEY(1955, Brit.)
Dave King-Wood
JAMBOREE(1957)
David King-Wood
NO HAUNT FOR A GENTLEMAN(1952, Brit.); UNHOLY FOUR, THE(1954, Brit.); PRIVATE'S PROGRESS(1956, Brit.); BREAK IN THE CIRCLE, THE(1957, Brit.); MEN OF SHERWOOD FOREST(1957, Brit.); STOLEN AIRLINER, THE(1962, Brit.)
The King's Men
LET'S GO NATIVE(1930); LAW OF THE PAMPAS(1939); RENEGADE TRAIL(1939); ST. LOUIS BLUES(1939); KNIGHTS OF THE RANGE(1940); SHOWDOWN, THE(1940); STAGECOACH WAR(1940); MAN FROM MONTANA(1941); ROUNDUP, THE(1941); CALL OUT THE MARINES(1942); JUKE BOX JENNY(1942); FOLLOW THE BAND(1943); HI, BUDDY(1943); YOU'RE A LUCKY FELLOW, MR. SMITH(1943); HEAVENLY DAYS(1944); MAKE MINE MUSIC(1946); FUN AND FANCY FREE(1947)
Edith Kingden
SHE COULDN'T TAKE IT(1935)
Edith Kingdom
THE CRASH(1932); IT'S A GIFT(1934); AFTER THE THIN MAN(1936)
Lewis Kingdom
DESERT JUSTICE(1936), w
Dorothy Kingdon
Silents
GOVERNOR'S BOSS, THE(1915); IRON MAN, THE(1925)
Edith Kingdon
ONCE A LADY(1931); TREASURE ISLAND(1934); LIVE, LOVE AND LEARN(1937)
Frank Kingdon
Silents
PARTNERS OF THE NIGHT(1920)
Julie Kingdon
STAGE DOOR(1937)
Barbara Kinghorn
MY WAY(1974, South Africa)
Sally Kinghorn
MONTY PYTHON AND THE HOLY GRAIL(1975, Brit.)
Sally Kinghorne
1984
PASSAGE TO INDIA, A(1984, Brit.)
Henry Kingi
TRUCK TURNER(1974); LET'S DO IT AGAIN(1975), stunts; SMOKE IN THE WIND(1975); ULTIMATE WARRIOR, THE(1975); CARWASH(1976); PIECE OF THE ACTION, A(1977), stunts; STIR CRAZY(1980)
John Kingley
GOLD(1974, Brit.)
Terry Kingley
FIVE DAYS ONE SUMMER(1982)
1984
SCANDALOUS(1984)
Dong Kingman
55 DAYS AT PEKING(1963)
Tarka Kings
SECRETS(1971)
the Kings Men
SING A JINGLE(1943)
Kings Men Quartet
ALEXANDER'S RAGTIME BAND(1938)
Kings of The Caribbean Steel Band
HEART WITHIN, THE(1957, Brit.)
Jacob Kingsberry
Misc. Silents
VOLCANO, THE(1919)
John Kingsbridge
SHARK(1970, U.S./Mex.), w
Craig Kingsbury
JAWS(1975)
Jacob Kingsbury
Misc. Silents
WHISPER MARKET, THE(1920)
Jan Kingsbury
LET THE BALLOON GO(1977, Aus.)
Michael Kingsbury
RICHARD'S THINGS(1981, Brit.)
Sandra Kingsbury
GOOD DISSONANCE LIKE A MAN, A(1977)
Guy Kingsford
DRACULA'S DAUGHTER(1936); POLO JOE(1936); SWORN ENEMY(1936); HAPPY-GO-LUCKY(1937); DOUBLE TROUBLE(1941); GET-AWAY, THE(1941); LUCKY DEVILS(1941); RAGE IN HEAVEN(1941); THAT HAMILTON WOMAN(1941); YANK IN THE R.A.F., A(1941); HOUSE OF ERRORS(1942); LAW OF THE JUNGLE(1942); SHERLOCK HOLMES AND THE SECRET WEAPON(1942); STAGECOACH EXPRESS(1942); TEXAS TO BATAAN(1942); FIRST COMES COURAGE(1943); IMMORTAL SERGEANT, THE(1943); NORTHERN PURSUIT(1943); PARIS AFTER

DARK(1943); SAHARA(1943); GREEN DOLPHIN STREET(1947); LONE WOLF IN LONDON(1947); SECOND CHANCE(1947); WHERE THERE'S LIFE(1947); FIGHTER SQUADRON(1948); NIGHT WIND(1948); SCENE OF THE CRIME(1949); CUSTOMS AGENT(1950); ELEPHANT STAMPEDE(1951); SON OF DR. JEKYLL, THE(1951); FORT VENGEANCE(1953); SALOME(1953); KILLER LEOPARD(1954); INSIDE DETROIT(1955); MOONFLEET(1955); SCARLET COAT, THE(1955); TEEN-AGE CRIME WAVE(1955); DECKS RAN RED, THE(1958)
Walter Kingsford
OUTWARD BOUND(1930); PRESIDENT VANISHES, THE(1934); PURSUIT OF HAPPINESS, THE(1934); I FOUND STELLA PARISH(1935); MELODY LINGERS ON, THE(1935); MYSTERY OF EDWIN DROOD, THE(1935); NAUGHTY MARIETTA(1935); SHANGHAI(1935); TALE OF TWO CITIES, A(1935); WHITE COCKATOO(1935); FRANKIE AND JOHNNY(1936); HEARTS DIVIDED(1936); LITTLE LORD FAUNTLEROY(1936); MAD HOLIDAY(1936); MEET NERO WOLFE(1936); MUSIC GOES ROUND, THE(1936); PROFESSIONAL SOLDIER(1936); SPEED(1936); STORY OF LOUIS PASTEUR, THE(1936); THE INVISIBLE RAY(1936); TROUBLE FOR TWO(1936); BULLDOG DRUMMOND ESCAPES(1937); CAPTAINS COURAGEOUS(1937); DEVIL IS DRIVING, THE(1937); DOUBLE OR NOTHING(1937); I'LL TAKE ROMANCE(1937); IT COULD HAPPEN TO YOU(1937); LEAGUE OF FRIGHTENED MEN(1937); LIFE OF EMILE ZOLA, THE(1937); MAYTIME(1937); MY DEAR MISS ALDRICH(1937); STOLEN HOLIDAY(1937); ALGIERS(1938); CAREFREE(1938); IF I WERE KING(1938); LONE WOLF IN PARIS, THE(1938); LORD JEFF(1938); PARADISE FOR THREE(1938); SAY IT IN FRENCH(1938); THERE'S ALWAYS A WOMAN(1938); TOY WIFE, THE(1938); YANK AT OXFORD, A(1938); YOUNG DR. KILDARE(1938); YOUNG IN HEART, THE(1938); CALLING DR. KILDARE(1939); DANCING CO-ED(1939); JUAREZ(1939); MAN IN THE IRON MASK, THE(1939); MIRACLES FOR SALE(1939); SECRET OF DR. KILDARE, THE(1939); SMASHING THE SPY RING(1939); WITNESS VANISHES, THE(1939); ADVENTURE IN DIAMONDS(1940); DISPATCH FROM REUTERS, A(1940); DR. KILDARE GOES HOME(1940); DR. KILDARE'S CRISIS(1940); DR. KILDARE'S STRANGE CASE(1940); KITTY FOYLE(1940); LUCKY PARTNERS(1940); STAR DUST(1940); CORSICAN BROTHERS, THE(1941); DEVIL AND MISS JONES, THE(1941); DR. KILDARE'S VICTORY(1941); DR. KILDARE'S WEDDING DAY(1941); ELLERY QUEEN AND THE PERFECT CRIME(1941); HIT THE ROAD(1941); H.M. PULHAM, ESQ.(1941); LONE WOLF TAKES A CHANCE, THE(1941); PEOPLE VS. DR. KILDARE(1941); UNHOLY PARTNERS(1941); CALLING DR. GILLESPIE(1942); DR. GILLESPIE'S NEW ASSISTANT(1942); FINGERS AT THE WINDOW(1942); FLY BY NIGHT(1942); LOVES OF EDGAR ALLAN POE, THE(1942); MY FAVORITE BLONDE(1942); BOMBER'S MOON(1943); DR. GILLESPIE'S CRIMINAL CASE(1943); FLIGHT FOR FREEDOM(1943); FOREVER AND A DAY(1943); HI DIDDLE DIDDLE(1943); MR. LUCKY(1943); BETWEEN TWO WOMEN(1944); GHOST CATCHERS(1944); HITLER GANG, THE(1944); MR. SKEFFINGTON(1944); SECRETS OF SCOTLAND YARD(1944); THREE MEN IN WHITE(1944); VELVET TOUCH, THE(1948); SLATTERY'S HURRICANE(1949); EXPERIMENT ALCATRAZ(1950); KIM(1950); DESERT FOX, THE(1951); MY FORBIDDEN PAST(1951); SOLDIERS THREE(1951); TARZAN'S PERIL(1951); TWO DOLLAR BETTOR(1951); BRIGAND, THE(1952); CONFIDENCE GIRL(1952); PATHFINDER, THE(1952); LOOSE IN LONDON(1953); WALKING MY BABY BACK HOME(1953); SEARCH FOR BRIDEY MURPHY, THE(1956); MERRY ANDREW(1958)
Albert Kingsley
CONDEMNED(1929)
Arthur Kingsley
BOOTS! BOOTS!(1934, Brit.)
Ben Kingsley
FEAR IS THE KEY(1973); GANDHI(1982); BETRAYAL(1983, Brit.)
Carol Kingsley
MAN OUTSIDE, THE(1968, Brit.)
Charles Kingsley
WATER BABIES, THE(1979, Brit.), w
Christine Kingsley
1,000 SHAPES OF A FEMALE(1963)
Dorothy Kingsley
LOOK WHO'S LAUGHING(1941), w; GIRL CRAZY(1943), w; BATHING BEAUTY(1944), w; BROADWAY RHYTHM(1944), w; EASY TO WED(1946), w; DATE WITH JUDY, A(1948), w; ON AN ISLAND WITH YOU(1948), w; NEPTUNE'S DAUGHTER(1949), w; SKIPPER SURPRISED HIS WIFE, THE(1950), w; TWO WEEKS WITH LOVE(1950), w; ANGELS IN THE OUTFIELD(1951), w; IT'S A BIG COUNTRY(1951), w; TEXAS CARNIVAL(1951), w; WHEN IN ROME(1952), w; DANGEROUS WHEN WET(1953), w; KISS ME KATE(1953), w; SMALL TOWN GIRL(1953), w; SEVEN BRIDES FOR SEVEN BROTHERS(1954), w; JUPITER'S DARLING(1955), w; PAL JOEY(1957), w; GREEN MANSIONS(1959), w; CAN-CAN(1960), w; PEPE(1960), w; VALLEY OF THE DOLLS(1967), w
Dorthy Kingsley
DON'T GO NEAR THE WATER(1975), w
Edward Kingsley
LIFE BEGINS TOMORROW(1952, Fr.), p; SPICE OF LIFE(1954, Fr.), p
Edward L. Kingsley
FILM WITHOUT A NAME(1950, Ger.), titles
Evelyn Kingsley
TOYS ARE NOT FOR CHILDREN(1972)
Florence Morse Kingsley
Silents
ENVY(1917), w
Florida Kingsley
Silents
GREATER THAN FAME(1920); ANNABEL LEE(1921); CLAY DOLLARS(1921)
Misc. Silents
TURMOIL, THE(1916); BOY GIRL, THE(1917); HIDDEN FIRES(1918); THOU SHALT NOT(1919)
Frank Kingsley
Silents
ONE WILD WEEK(1921); FIGHTING AMERICAN, THE(1924)
Misc. Silents
BISHOP'S EMERALDS, THE(1919); BOY CRAZY(1922); MARRIED FLAPPER, THE(1922)
Gershon Kingsley
DREAMER, THE(1970, Israel), m; SAM'S SONG(1971), m

Ian Kingsley
BLUE MAX, THE(1966)
James Kingsley
SCREAM BLACULA SCREAM(1973)
Kathryn Kingsley
Silents
INNER MAN, THE(1922)
Laura Kingsley
1984
RHINESTONE(1984)
Martin Kingsley
GUNSLINGER(1956); OKLAHOMA WOMAN, THE(1956)
Michael Kingsley
NO HIGHWAY IN THE SKY(1951, Brit.)
Mona Kingsley
Silents
OAKDALE AFFAIR, THE(1919); DUST FLOWER, THE(1922)
Misc. Silents
LIVING LIES(1922)
Nigel Kingsley
OLIVER!(1968, Brit.); MELODY(1971, Brit.)
Pierce Kingsley
Silents
SILVER THREADS AMONG THE GOLD(1915), d; DESERTED AT THE AL-
TAR(1922), w
Misc. Silents
AFTER THE BALL(1914), d
Sidney Kingsley
MEN IN WHITE(1934), w; HOMECOMING(1948), w; DETECTIVE STORY(1951), w
Susan Kingsley
COAL MINER'S DAUGHTER(1980); POPEYE(1980)
1984
OLD ENOUGH(1984); RECKLESS(1984)
William L. Kingsley
SMOKEY AND THE BANDIT–PART 3(1983)
Terry Kingsley-Smith
MOLLY AND LAWLESS JOHN(1972), a, w
Kingsmen
HOW TO STUFF A WILD BIKINI(1965)
Walter Kingson
MIRACLE IN THE RAIN(1956)
Bobby Kingston
NIGHT MAYOR, THE(1932)
Claude Kingston
CURSE OF FRANKENSTEIN, THE(1957, Brit.); COUNT FIVE AND DIE(1958, Brit.);
KILL ME TOMORROW(1958, Brit.); WOMAN'S TEMPTATION, A(1959, Brit.)
Earl Kingston
Misc. Talkies
DAMIEN'S ISLAND(1976)
Edith Kingston
JANE EYRE(1935)
Gladys Kingston
PROBLEM GIRLS(1953)
Harry Kingston
DOUBLE DYNAMITE(1951); VIVA ZAPATA!(1952)
Jerome Kingston
CAUGHT IN THE FOG(1928), w; FANCY BAGGAGE(1929), w; STARK MAD(1929),
w; HELP YOURSELF(1932, Brit.), w
Silents
POWDER MY BACK(1928), w
Kiwi Kingston
EVIL OF FRANKENSTEIN, THE(1964, Brit.); HYSTERIA(1965, Brit.)
Lenore Kingston
YOUNG CAPTIVES, THE(1959)
Mark Kingston
LOVE IS A SPLENDID ILLUSION(1970, Brit.); HITLER: THE LAST TEN DAYS(1973,
Brit./Ital.); SAINT JACK(1979)
1984
GIVE MY REGARDS TO BROAD STREET(1984, Brit.)
Muriel Kingston
Misc. Silents
DAWN OF REVENGE(1922); NEW MINISTER(1922); WHITE HELL(1922); VALLEY
OF LOST SOULS, THE(1923); TWIN FLAPPERS(1927); MASKED LOVER, THE(1928)
Natalie Kingston
STREET ANGEL(1928); RIVER OF ROMANCE(1929); HER WEDDING NIGHT(1930);
SWELLHEAD, THE(1930); UNDER TEXAS SKIES(1931); FORGOTTEN(1933); HIS
PRIVATE SECRETARY(1933)
Silents
KID BOOTS(1926); SILENT LOVER, THE(1926); WET PAINT(1926); LOVE MAKES
'EM WILD(1927); NIGHT OF LOVE, THE(1927); GIRL IN EVERY PORT, A(1928)
Misc. Silents
LOST AT SEA(1926); FRAMED(1927); HARVESTER, THE(1927); HIS FIRST FLA-
ME(1927); LOST AT THE FRONT(1927); PAINTED POST(1928); PORT OF MISSING
GIRLS, THE(1928)
Thomas Kingston
JAM SESSION(1944); FATHER IS A BACHELOR(1950)
Tom Kingston
ADVENTURE(1945); MAN WHO DARED, THE(1946); MISS GRANT TAKES RICH-
MOND(1949); SCANDAL SHEET(1952); PHFFFT!(1954)
Wally Kingston
MAN IN GREY, THE(1943, Brit.)
Winifred Kingston
SQUAW MAN, THE(1931); BOY AND THE BRIDGE, THE(1959, Brit.)
Silents
BREWSTER'S MILLIONS(1914); CALL OF THE NORTH, THE(1914); SQUAW MAN,
THE(1914); VIRGINIAN, THE(1914); WHERE THE TRAIL DIVIDES(1914); CAPTAIN
COURTESY(1915); PARSON OF PANAMINT, THE(1916); BEYOND(1921); TRAIL OF
THE AXE, THE(1922)

Misc. Silents
CALL OF THE CUMBERLANDS, THE(1915); GENTLEMAN FROM INDIANA,
A(1915); LOVE ROUTE, THE(1915); SEVENTH NOON, THE(1915); BEN BLAIR(1916);
DAVID GARRICK(1916); DAVY CROCKETT(1916); SON OF ERIN, A(1916); DURAND
OF THE BAD LANDS(1917); NORTH OF FIFTY-THREE(1917); SCARLET PIMPER-
NEL, THE(1917); SPY, THE(1917); LIGHT OF WESTERN STARS, THE(1918); CORSI-
CAN BROTHERS, THE(1920)
Teinosuke Kinguasa
Misc. Silents
CRAZY PAGE, A(1926, Jap.), d
Teinosuke Kingugasa
Misc. Silents
CROSSWAYS(1928, Jap.), d
Henry Kinji
MR. BILLION(1977)
Mimi Kinkade
1984
BODY ROCK(1984)
Lisa Kinkaid
OMOO OMOO, THE SHARK GOD(1949)
Cleves Kinkead
COMMON CLAY(1930), w; PRIVATE NUMBER(1936), w
Randal Kinkead
DIVIDED HEART, THE(1955, Brit.)
Debra Kinlaw
DOZENS, THE(1981)
Kathleen Kinmont
1984
HARDBODIES(1984)
Tony Kinna
YOU ONLY LIVE ONCE(1969, Fr.)
Cora Kinnaird
FRENCH LIEUTENANT'S WOMAN, THE(1981)
Roy Kinnear
BOYS, THE(1962, Brit.); TIARA TAHITI(1962, Brit.); HEAVENS ABOVE!(1963, Brit.);
SMALL WORLD OF SAMMY LEE, THE(1963, Brit.); SPARROWS CAN'T SING(1963,
Brit.); FRENCH DRESSING(1964, Brit.); PLACE TO GO, A(1964, Brit.); HELP!(1965,
Brit.); HILL, THE(1965, Brit.); UNDERWORLD INFORMERS(1965, Brit.); FUNNY
THING HAPPENED ON THE WAY TO THE FORUM, A(1966); DEADLY AFFAIR,
THE(1967, Brit.); HOW I WON THE WAR(1967, Brit.); MINI-AFFAIR, THE(1968, Brit.);
BED SITTING ROOM, THE(1969, Brit.); LOCK UP YOUR DAUGHTERS(1969, Brit.);
EGGHEAD'S ROBOT(1970, Brit.); FIRECHASERS, THE(1970, Brit.); ON A CLEAR
DAY YOU CAN SEE FOREVER(1970); SCROOGE(1970, Brit.); TASTE THE BLOOD OF
DRACULA(1970, Brit.); MELODY(1971, Brit.); WILLY WONKA AND THE CHOCO-
LATE FACTORY(1971); PIED PIPER, THE(1972, Brit.); RENTADICK(1972, Brit.);
JUGGERNAUT(1974, Brit.); THREE MUSKETEERS, THE(1974, Panama); ADVEN-
TURES OF SHERLOCK HOLMES' SMARTER BROTHER, THE(1975, Brit.); BARRY
MC KENZIE HOLDS HIS OWN(1975, Aus.); FOUR MUSKETEERS, THE(1975); ONE
OF OUR DINOSAURS IS MISSING(1975, Brit.); ROYAL FLASH(1975, Brit.); HERBIE
GOES TO MONTE CARLO(1977); LAST REMAKE OF BEAU GESTE, THE(1977);
WATERSHIP DOWN(1978, Brit.); HAWK THE SLAYER(1980, Brit.); HOUND OF THE
BASKERVILLES, THE(1980, Brit.); HAMMETT(1982)
Murray Kinnel
PURCHASE PRICE, THE(1932)
Murray Kinnell
OLD ENGLISH(1930); PRINCESS AND THE PLUMBER, THE(1930); BLACK CAM-
EL, THE(1931); DECEIVER, THE(1931); HONOR OF THE FAMILY(1931); PUBLIC
ENEMY, THE(1931); RECKLESS LIVING(1931); SECRET SIX, THE(1931); ARE YOU
LISTENING?(1932); GRAND HOTEL(1932); MAN WHO PLAYED GOD, THE(1932);
MATCH KING, THE(1932); MENACE, THE(1932); MOUTHPIECE, THE(1932); PAINT-
ED WOMAN(1932); SECRETS OF THE FRENCH POLICE(1932); SUCCESSFUL
CALAMITY, A(1932); UNDER EIGHTEEN(1932); I LOVED A WOMAN(1933); VOL-
TAIRE(1933); ZOO IN BUDAPEST(1933); AFFAIRS OF A GENTLEMAN(1934); ANNE
OF GREEN GABLES(1934); CHARLIE CHAN IN LONDON(1934); CHARLIE CHAN'S
COURAGE(1934); HAT, COAT AND GLOVE(1934); HOUSE OF ROTHSCHILD,
THE(1934); I AM SUZANNE(1934); MURDER IN TRINIDAD(1934); SUCH WOMEN
ARE DANGEROUS(1934); CAPTAIN BLOOD(1935); CARDINAL RICHELIEU(1935);
CHARLIE CHAN IN PARIS(1935); GREAT IMPERSONATION, THE(1935); KIND
LADY(1935); RENDEZVOUS(1935); SILVER STREAK, THE(1935); THREE MUS-
KETEERS, THE(1935); BIG GAME, THE(1936); FOUR DAYS WONDER(1936);
LLOYDS OF LONDON(1936); MAKE WAY FOR A LADY(1936); MARY OF SCOT-
LAND(1936); ONE RAINY AFTERNOON(1936); WITNESS CHAIR, THE(1936); DA-
MAGED LIVES(1937); OUTCAST(1937); PRINCE AND THE PAUPER, THE(1937);
THINK FAST, MR. MOTO(1937)
Murry Kinnell
CAPTAINS COURAGEOUS(1937)
Clyde Kinney
FLAMING GUNS(1933); FOURTH HORSEMAN, THE(1933); TEXAS TRAIL(1937);
I'M FROM THE CITY(1938)
Dawn Kinney
MADAME BOVARY(1949)
Dick Kinney
MAKE MINE MUSIC(1946), w; 1001 ARABIAN NIGHTS(1959), w
Harold Kinney
SEA WOLF, THE(1930); BODY AND SOUL(1931); SECRET SERVICE(1931)
Jack Kinney
PINOCCHIO(1940), d; DUMBO(1941), d; BILLY THE KID TRAPPED(1942); PRAI-
RIE PALS(1942); THREE CABALLEROS, THE(1944), d; MAKE MINE MUSIC(1946),
d; FUN AND FANCY FREE(1947), d; MELODY TIME(1948), d; ADVENTURES OF
ICHABOD AND MR. TOAD(1949), d; 1001 ARABIAN NIGHTS(1959), d; SONG OF
NORWAY(1970), anim
Jim Kinney
FOURTH HORSEMAN, THE(1933)
Martin Kinney
Silents
INNER MAN, THE(1922)
Ray Kinney
WAIKIKI WEDDING(1937); SAVAGE DRUMS(1951)

Ron Kinney
TRADER HORNEE(1970), makeup
Sharon Kinney
POPEYE(1980), a, ch
Tiffany Kinney
EXORCIST II: THE HERETIC(1977)
William Kinney
OPERATION PETTICOAT(1959)
Ronald Kinnoch
LONG DARK HALL, THE(1951, Brit.), set d; PRIVATE INFORMATION(1952, Brit.), p, w; BURNT EVIDENCE(1954, Brit.), p; SECRET MAN, THE(1958, Brit.), p&d; VILLAGE OF THE DAMNED(1960, Brit.), p; INVASION QUARTET(1961, Brit.), p; POSTMAN'S KNOCK(1962, Brit.), p; CAIRO(1963), p; INADMISSIBLE EVIDENCE(1968, Brit.), p
Bob Kino
WALK, DON'T RUN(1966)
Goro Kino
Silents
HAUNTED PAJAMAS(1917); BRAVEST WAY, THE(1918); MIDNIGHT PATROL, THE(1918); PURPLE CIPHER, THE(1920); TALE OF TWO WORLDS, A(1921); WHERE LIGHTS ARE LOW(1921)
Misc. Silents
HONORABLE FRIEND, THE(1916); LITTLE RED DECIDES(1918); TOKIO SIREN, A(1920); FIRST BORN, THE(1921); FIVE DAYS TO LIVE(1922)
Lloyd Kino
BATTLE AT BLOODY BEACH(1961); SEVEN WOMEN FROM HELL(1961); HORIZONTAL LIEUTENANT, THE(1962); WOMAN HUNT(1962); SURF PARTY(1964); MARINE BATTLEGROUND(1966, U.S/S.K.); DID YOU HEAR THE ONE ABOUT THE TRAVELING SALESLADY?(1968); GLASS HOUSES(1972); TASTE OF HELL, A(1973); LAST TYCOON, THE(1976); MIDWAY(1976); FORCED VENGEANCE(1982); HAMMETT(1982)
Robert Kino
SOUTH SEA WOMAN(1953); SNOW CREATURE, THE,(1954); HOUSE OF BAMBOO(1955); CRIMSON KIMONO, THE(1959); CRY FOR HAPPY(1961); FLOWER DRUM SONG(1961); THREE STOOGES GO AROUND THE WORLD IN A DAZE, THE(1963); MORITURI(1965); UGLY DACHSHUND, THE(1966)
1984
SWORDKILL(1984)
Teinosuke Kinogasa
Misc. Silents
SLUMS OF TOKYO(1930, Jap.), d
Bob Kinoshita
GUN FEVER(1958), art d; PHANTOM PLANET, THE(1961), art d; NUN AND THE SERGEANT, THE(1962), art d; PRIVATE NAVY OF SGT. O'FARRELL, THE(1968), art d
Chuji Kinoshita
HUMAN CONDITION, THE(1959, Jap.), m; PANDA AND THE MAGIC SERPENT(1961, Jap.), m; ROAD TO ETERNITY(1962, Jap.), m; EYES, THE SEA AND A BALL(1968 Jap.), m; FAREWELL, MY BELOVED(1969, Jap.), m; SOLDIER'S PRAYER, A(1970, Jap.), m
Keisuke Kinoshita
BALLAD OF NARAYAMA(1961, Jap.), d&w; EYES, THE SEA AND A BALL(1968 Jap.), d&w; ONCE A RAINY DAY(1968, Jap.), w
Robert K. Kinoshita
1984
LOVELINES(1984), art d
Robert Kinoshita
CARNIVAL ROCK(1957), set d; SAGA OF THE VIKING WOMEN AND THEIR VOYAGE TO THE WATERS OF THE GREAT SEA SERPENT, THE(1957), art d; TEENAGE DOLL(1957), art d; MACABRE(1958), art d; RABBIT TEST(1978), art d; MAN WITH BOGART'S FACE, THE(1980), prod d; GOING APE!(1981), art d
Ryo Kinoshita
SCHOOL FOR SEX(1966, Jap.), d
Kinou the Dog
TWO OF US, THE(1968, Fr.)
Ernest Kinoy
BROTHER JOHN(1971), w; BUCK AND THE PREACHER(1972), w; LEADBELLY(1976), w
Charles Kinp
BILLY THE KID IN SANTA FE(1941)
Charles Kinross
BARTLEBY(1970, Brit.)
E. P. Kinsella
Silents
ALLEY OF GOLDEN HEARTS, THE(1924, Brit.), w
Patrick Kinsella
BANANA RIDGE(1941, Brit.)
Walter Kinsella
TATTOOED STRANGER, THE(1950)
Patrick Kinser-Lau
SAMMY STOPS THE WORLD zero(1978)
Gayne Kinsey
GIRL TROUBLE(1942)
Ham Kinsey
PACK UP YOUR TROUBLES(1932); OUR RELATIONS(1936); SWISS MISS(1938)
Lance Kinsey
THINGS ARE TOUGH ALL OVER(1982)
Linace Kinsey
DOCTOR DETROIT(1983)
Leonid Kinskey
BIG BROADCAST, THE(1932); TROUBLE IN PARADISE(1932); DUCK SOUP(1933); GIRL WITHOUT A ROOM(1933); STORM AT DAYBREAK(1933); THREE-CORNERED MOON(1933); CHANGE OF HEART(1934); HOLLYWOOD PARTY(1934); MANHATTAN MELODRAMA(1934); MERRY WIDOW, THE(1934); WE LIVE AGAIN(1934); GILDED LILY, THE(1935); GOIN' TO TOWN(1935); LES MISERABLES(1935); LIVES OF A BENGAL LANCER(1935); GARDEN OF ALLAH, THE(1936); GENERAL DIED AT DAWN, THE(1936); NEXT TIME WE LOVE(1936); RHYTHM ON THE RANGE(1936); ROAD TO GLORY, THE(1936); CAFE METROPOLE(1937); ESPIONAGE(1937); MAKE A WISH(1937); MARRIED BEFORE BREAKFAST(1937); MAYTIME(1937); MEET THE BOY FRIEND(1937); MY DEAR MISS ALDRICH(1937);

SHEIK STEPS OUT, THE(1937); WE'RE ON THE JURY(1937); 100 MEN AND A GIRL(1937); FLIRTING WITH FATE(1938); GREAT WALTZ, THE(1938); OUTSIDE OF PARADISE(1938); PROFESSOR BEWARE(1938); THREE BLIND MICE(1938); TRIP TO PARIS, A(1938); DAY-TIME WIFE(1939); EVERYTHING HAPPENS AT NIGHT(1939); EXILE EXPRESS(1939); ON YOUR TOES(1939); SPELLBINDER, THE(1939); STORY OF VERNON AND IRENE CASTLE, THE(1939); DOWN ARGENTINE WAY(1940); HE STAYED FOR BREAKFAST(1940); BROADWAY LIMITED(1941); LADY FOR A NIGHT(1941); SO ENDS OUR NIGHT(1941); THAT NIGHT IN RIO(1941); WEEKEND IN HAVANA(1941); BROOKLYN ORCHID(1942); CASABLANCA(1942); CINDERELLA SWINGS IT(1942); I MARRIED AN ANGEL(1942); SOMEWHERE I'LL FIND YOU(1942); TALK OF THE TOWN(1942); GILDERSLEEVE ON BROADWAY(1943); PRESENTING LILY MARS(1943); CAN'T HELP SINGING(1944); FIGHTING SEABEES, THE(1944); THAT'S MY BABY(1944); MONSIEUR BEAUCAIRE(1946); ALIMONY(1949); GREAT SINNER, THE(1949); NANCY GOES TO RIO(1950); HONEYCHILE(1951); GOBS AND GALS(1952); GLORY(1955); MAN WITH THE GOLDEN ARM, THE(1955)
Klaus Kinski
DECISION BEFORE DAWN(1951); TIME TO LOVE AND A TIME TO DIE, A(1958); DARK EYES OF LONDON(1961); COUNTERFEIT TRAITOR, THE(1962); DOCTOR ZHIVAGO(1965); BANG, BANG, YOU'RE DEAD(1966); LAST OF THE RENEGADES(1966, Fr./Ital./Ger./Yugo.); PLEASURE GIRLS, THE(1966, Brit.); THAT MAN IN ISTANBUL(1966, Fr./Ital./Span.); TRAITOR'S GATE(1966, Brit./Ger.); BULLET FOR THE GENERAL, A(1967, Ital.); FIVE GOLDEN DRAGONS(1967, Brit.); FOR A FEW DOLLARS MORE(1967, Ital./Ger./Span.); MILLION EYES OF SU-MURU, THE(1967, Brit.); PSYCHO-CIRCUS(1967, Brit.); GRAND SLAM(1968, Ital., Span., Ger.); JUSTINE(1969, Ital./Span.); RUTHLESS FOUR, THE(1969, Ital./Ger.); FIVE GOLDEN DRAGONS(1967, Brit.); SONS OF SATAN(1969, Ital./Fr./Ger.); VENUS IN FURS(1970, Ital./Brit./Ger.); COUNT DRACULA(1971, Sp., Ital., Ger., Brit.); CREATURE WITH THE BLUE HAND(1971, Ger.); SLAUGHTER HOTEL(1971, Ital.); WEB OF THE SPIDER(1972, Ital./Fr.); TO KILL OR TO DIE(1973, Ital.); LIFESPAN(1975, U.S./Brit./Neth.); MAIN THING IS TO LOVE, THE(1975, Ital./Fr.); GENIUS, THE(1976, Ital./Fr./Ger.); AGUIRRE, THE WRATH OF GOD(1977, W. Ger.); OPERATION THUNDERBOLT(1978, ISRAEL); NOSFERATU, THE VAMPIRE(1979, Fr./Ger.); SCHIZOID(1980); BUDDY BUDDY(1981); ANDROID(1982); FITZCARRALDO(1982); LOVE AND MONEY(1982); SOLDIER, THE(1982); VENOM(1982, Brit.)
1984
LITTLE DRUMMER GIRL, THE(1984); SECRET DIARY OF SIGMUND FREUD, THE(1984)
Misc. Talkies
SALT IN THE WOUND(1972); DEATH SMILES ON A MURDER(1974)
Klaus Kinski [Claus Guenther Nakszynski]
SCOTLAND YARD HUNTS DR. MABUSE(1963, Ger.)
Nastassia Kinski
TESS(1980, Fr./Brit.); CAT PEOPLE(1982); ONE FROM THE HEART(1982); EXPOSED(1983); MOON IN THE GUTTER, THE(1983, Fr./Ital.)
Nastassja Kinski
TO THE DEVIL A DAUGHTER(1976, Brit./Ger.)
1984
HOTEL NEW HAMPSHIRE, THE(1984); PARIS, TEXAS(1984, Ger./Fr.); UNFAITHFULLY YOURS(1984)
Leonard Kinsky
LOVE ON THE RUN(1936)
Leonid Kinsky
ALGIERS(1938); BALL OF FIRE(1941)
Jonathan Kinsler
1984
CHINESE BOXES(1984, Ger./Brit.); FLIGHT TO BERLIN(1984, Ger./Brit.)
Howard Kinsley
1984
BIRDY(1984)
Marilyn Kinsley
PERFECT SNOB, THE(1941); VERY YOUNG LADY, A(1941); HOODLUM SAINT, THE(1946); SHOW BOAT(1951)
Peter Kinsley
THIS, THAT AND THE OTHER(1970, Brit.)
Lee Kinsolving
ALL THE YOUNG MEN(1960); DARK AT THE TOP OF THE STAIRS, THE(1960); EXPLOSIVE GENERATION, THE(1961)
William Kinsolving
FAN'S NOTES, A(1972, Can.), w
Edwin Kinter
BUSTIN' LOOSE(1981)
Vivian Kintisch
PARSIFAL(1983, Fr.)
Teinosuke Kinugasa
GATE OF HELL(1954, Jap.), d&w; ACTOR'S REVENGE, AN(1963, Jap.), w
Franciska Kinz
COW AND I, THE(1961, Fr., Ital., Ger.)
Franziska Kinz
RASPUTIN(1932, Ger.)
Sharyn Kinzie
HELLCATS, THE(1968)
Siegfried Kiok
GOOSE GIRL, THE(1967, Ger.), art d
John Kiouses
HIDE IN PLAIN SIGHT(1980)
Manart Kipen
LIFE BEGINS FOR ANDY HARDY(1941)
Herbert Kiper
DANCING HEART, THE(1959, Ger.)
Kipkoske
LAST SAFARI, THE(1967, Brit.)
Kiplagat
TOTO AND THE POACHERS(1958, Brit.)
Dick Kipling
HIDE-OUT(1934); TOAST OF NEW YORK, THE(1937); MILDRED PIERCE(1945); PERFECT STRANGERS(1950)

Edward Kipling
Silents
BREAKING POINT, THE(1924)
Richard Kipling
ROSE BOWL(1936); GIRLS CAN PLAY(1937); SWING HIGH, SWING LOW(1937); WOMEN OF GLAMOUR(1937); ACCIDENTS WILL HAPPEN(1938); TEST PILOT(1938); CALLING PHILO VANCE(1940); MY LOVE CAME BACK(1940); SANTA FE TRAIL(1940); LOVE CRAZY(1941); MEET JOHN DOE(1941); OUT OF THE FOG(1941); JOHNNY EAGER(1942); MISS V FROM MOSCOW(1942); THEY ALL KISSED THE BRIDE(1942); BEHIND PRISON WALLS(1943); EDGE OF DARKNESS(1943); GIRL CRAZY(1943); DANNY BOY(1946); SMASH-UP, THE STORY OF A WOMAN(1947); UP IN CENTRAL PARK(1948); FURIES, THE(1950); CARRIE(1952); VOODOO TIGER(1952); ALASKA SEAS(1954); GIRL RUSH, THE(1955)
Rudyard Kipling
CAPTAINS COURAGEOUS(1937), w; ELEPHANT BOY(1937, Brit.), w; WEE WILLIE WINKIE(1937), w; GUNGA DIN(1939), w; LIGHT THAT FAILED, THE(1939), w; JUNGLE BOOK(1942), w; KIM(1950), w; SOLDIERS THREE(1951), w; JUNGLE BOOK, THE(1967), w; MAN WHO WOULD BE KING, THE(1975, Brit.), w
Silents
FOOL THERE WAS, A(1915), w; NAULAHKA, THE(1918), w
Claude Kipnis
CRY DR. CHICAGO(1971)
Leonard Kipnis
OEDIPUS REX(1957, Can.), p
Kelle Kipp
DINER(1982)
Ronn Kipp
1984
KILLPOINT(1984)
Manart Kippen
CORSICAN BROTHERS, THE(1941); WOMAN'S FACE(1941); JUNGLE SIREN(1942); KEEPER OF THE FLAME(1942); ONCE UPON A HONEYMOON(1942); WIFE TAKES A FLYER, THE(1942); BACKGROUND TO DANGER(1943); MISSION TO MOSCOW(1943); SONG OF BERNADETTE, THE(1943); THREE RUSSIAN GIRLS(1943); FLAME OF THE BARBARY COAST(1945); ROUGHLY SPEAKING(1945)
Manart Kipper
HILLBILLY BLITZKRIEG(1942)
Manart Kippin
MILDRED PIERCE(1945)
Dezso Kiraly
ADRIFT(1971, Czech.)
Erno Kiraly
LAKE PLACID SERENADE(1944); JOAN OF ARC(1948)
Rosie Kiraly
BLUE IDOL, THE(1931, Hung.)
John Kiras
SWIMMER, THE(1968), makeup
Richard Kirbel
DING DONG WILLIAMS(1946)
Alice Kirby
TRUE TO LIFE(1943); STAR SPANGLED RHYTHM(1942); CRYSTAL BALL, THE(1943); FOR WHOM THE BELL TOLLS(1943); SALUTE FOR THREE(1943); LADY IN THE DARK(1944); LUSTY MEN, THE(1952)
B. Kirby, Jr.
YOUNG GRADUATES, THE(1971); HARRAD EXPERIMENT, THE(1973); GODFATHER, THE, PART II(1974); SUPERDAD(1974)
Ben Kirby
DRAUGHTSMAN'S CONTRACT, THE(1983, Brit.)
Bill Kirby
TWO-HEADED SPY, THE(1959, Brit.), p
Bruce Kirby
CATCH-22(1970); HOW TO FRAME A FIGG(1971); J.W. COOP(1971); COMMITMENT, THE(1976)
Misc. Talkies
FYRE(1979)
Bruce Kirby, Jr.
CINDERELLA LIBERTY(1973); BABY BLUE MARINE(1976)
Bruno Kirby
BETWEEN THE LINES(1977); ALMOST SUMMER(1978); BORDERLINE(1980); WHERE THE BUFFALO ROAM(1980); MODERN ROMANCE(1981)
1984
BIRDY(1984); THIS IS SPINAL TAP(1984)
Misc. Talkies
KISS MY GRITS(1982)
Dave Kirby
Silents
MAILMAN, THE(1923); KING OF THE TURF, THE(1926); NIGHT OWL, THE(1926)
Misc. Silents
SPIRIT OF THE U.S.A., THE(1924); BURNING BRIDGES(1928)
David Kirby
Silents
POPPY GIRL'S HUSBAND, THE(1919); LIGHTNING ROMANCE(1924); NELLIE, THE BEAUTIFUL CLOAK MODEL(1924); EASY MONEY(1925); LAST EDITION, THE(1925); LAWFUL CHEATERS(1925); RIDIN' THE WIND(1925); FIGHTING EDGE(1926); SHIELD OF HONOR, THE(1927); SUNSET DERBY, THE(1927)
Misc. Silents
BLINDFOLDED(1918); VIRTOUS SINNERS(1919); DANGER AHEAD(1923); MAN WHO PLAYED SQUARE, THE(1924); MASK OF LOPEZ, THE(1924); SNOB BUSTER, THE(1925); DANGER QUEST(1926); FIGHTING EDGE, THE(1926); ROYAL AMERICAN, THE(1927); SILENT AVENGER, THE(1927)
Derek Kirby
LOVE MATCH, THE(1955, Brit.)
Fred Kirby
KENTUCKY JUBILEE(1951)
Silents
OLIVER TWIST, JR.(1921); ON TIME(1924)
Misc. Silents
HEARTS OF YOUTH(1921)

Frederick Kirby
Silents
CHILDREN OF THE NIGHT(1921)
Gene Kirby
1984
NATURAL, THE(1984), tech adv
George Kirby
CYNARA(1932); BARRETTS OF WIMPOLE STREET, THE(1934); HUMAN SIDE, THE(1934); WHITE ANGEL, THE(1936); WHO KILLED JOHN SAVAGE?(1937, Brit.); DAWN PATROL, THE(1938); HARD TO GET(1938); MARIE ANTOINETTE(1938); ISLAND OF LOST MEN(1939); RAFFLES(1939); INVISIBLE MAN RETURNS, THE(1940); GREAT LIE, THE(1941); MAN WITH TWO LIVES, THE(1942); RANDOM HARVEST(1942); APE MAN, THE(1943); GUY NAMED JOE, A(1943); NORTHERN PURSUIT(1943); FRENCHMAN'S CREEK(1944); JANE EYRE(1944); MAKE YOUR OWN BED(1944); NATIONAL VELVET(1944); SCARLET CLAW, THE(1944); SHAKE HANDS WITH MURDER(1944); UNINVITED, THE(1944); WHITE CLIFFS OF DOVER, THE(1944); ROGUES GALLERY(1945); TONIGHT AND EVERY NIGHT(1945); CLUNY BROWN(1946); NIGHT AND DAY(1946); CALCUTTA(1947); OH DAD, POOR DAD, MAMA'S HUNG YOU IN THE CLOSET AND I'M FEELIN' SO SAD(1967); SHAGGY D.A., THE(1976)
Jay Kirby
UNDERCOVER MAN(1942); BORDER PATROL(1943); COLT COMRADES(1943); HOPPY SERVES A WRIT(1943); LEATHER BURNERS, THE(1943); LOST CANYON(1943); MARSHAL OF RENO(1944); SHERIFF OF LAS VEGAS(1944); ROCKIN' IN THE ROCKIES(1945); DAYS OF BUFFALO BILL(1946); OKLAHOMA BADLANDS(1948); OUTLAW BRAND(1948); PARTNERS OF THE SUNSET(1948); SON OF GOD'S COUNTRY(1948); SUNDOWN RIDERS(1948); WAGON WHEELS WESTWARD(1956)
Jessie Kirby
DON'T LOOK IN THE BASEMENT(1973)
John Kirby
AIR STRIKE(1955); ANNAPOLIS STORY, AN(1955); COMMITMENT, THE(1976); FIRST NUDIE MUSICAL, THE(1976)
John Mason Kirby
SAVAGE WEEKEND(1983), p
Joyce Kirby
MIDSHIPMAID GOB(1932, Brit.); BRITANNIA OF BILLINGSGATE(1933, Brit.); FIRE RAISERS, THE(1933, Brit.); THIRTEENTH CANDLE, THE(1933, Brit.); WALTZ TIME(1933, Brit.); ARE YOU A MASON?(1934, Brit.); IT'S A BOY(1934, Brit.); HAIL AND FAREWELL(1936, Brit.); COMPULSORY WIFE, THE(1937, Brit.); MAYFAIR MELODY(1937, Brit.)
June Kirby
GUYS AND DOLLS(1955); GARMENT JUNGLE, THE(1957)
Kay Kirby
CONQUEST OF CHEYENNE(1946)
Lisa Kirby
B. F.'S DAUGHTER(1948)
Madge Kirby
Misc. Silents
FLASH OF FATE, THE(1918)
Malcolm Kirby
SOAPBOX DERBY(1958, Brit.)
Marion Kirby
HER FIRST ROMANCE(1940)
Max Kirby
THERE GOES THE BRIDE(1933, Brit.); TICKET OF LEAVE(1936, Brit.); GREAT MR. HANDEL, THE(1942, Brit.); COURTNEY AFFAIR, THE(1947, Brit.); MAYTIME IN MAYFAIR(1952, Brit.); TAMAHINE(1964, Brit.); SPACEFLIGHT IC-1(1965, Brit.)
Michael Kirby
KEEP YOUR POWDER DRY(1945); THEY WERE EXPENDABLE(1945); WEEKEND AT THE WALDORF(1945); COUNTESS OF MONTE CRISTO, THE(1948); HOMECOMING(1948); SUMMER HOLIDAY(1948); BUGSY MALONE(1976, Brit.); HOUSE BY THE LAKE, THE(1977, Can.); IN PRAISE OF OLDER WOMEN(1978, Can.); MEATBALLS(1979, Can.); SILENT PARTNER, THE(1979, Can.); MR. PATMAN(1980, Can.); AGENCY(1981, Can.); DIRTY TRICKS(1981, Can.)
Misc. Talkies
GIRL IN BLUE, THE(1974)
Newt Kirby
ROARIN' LEAD(1937); ROUGH RIDIN' RHYTHM(1937); WILDCAT OF TUCSON(1941)
Olive Kirby
I'LL TURN TO YOU(1946, Brit.); TROJAN BROTHERS, THE(1946); DELAYED ACTION(1954, Brit.); EMBEZZLER, THE(1954, Brit.); CONSTANT HUSBAND, THE(1955, Brit.); MURDER ON APPROVAL(1956, Brit.); HONOURABLE MURDER, AN(1959, Brit.); TOP FLOOR GIRL(1959, Brit.)
Misc. Silents
MODERN YOUTH(1926)
Ollie Kirby
Misc. Silents
APACHE DANCER, THE(1923); GENTLEMAN UNAFRAID(1923); MYSTERIOUS GOODS(1923); TANGO CAVALIER(1923); MIDNIGHT SECRETS(1924); NEVER TOO LATE(1925)
Paul Kirby
HIGH(1968, Can.)
Misc. Talkies
CYNTHIA'S SISTER(1975)
Peter Kirby
SMOKY MOUNTAIN MELODY(1949)
Ralph Kirby
COWBOY SERENADE(1942)
Randy Kirby
FIREBALL JUNGLE(1968)
"Red" Kirby
Silents
SHAME(1921); IS THAT NICE?(1926)
Rhet Kirby
UNCLE TOM'S CABIN(1969, Fr./Ital./Ger./Yugo.)

Roger Kirby
TEN GENTLEMEN FROM WEST POINT(1942)
Stanley Kirby
JIMMY BOY(1935, Brit.); HEARTS OF HUMANITY(1936, Brit.); MEN OF YESTER-DAY(1936, Brit.)
Steve Kirby
IT!(1967, Brit.); PRIVILEGE(1967, Brit.); SUMARINE X-1(1969, Brit.)
Stoddard Kirby
DARK AT THE TOP OF THE STAIRS, THE(1960)
T. Kirby
POT LUCK(1936, Brit.)
Terence Kirby
1984
CHILDREN OF THE CORN(1984), p
William Kirby
OSCAR WILDE(1960, Brit.), p; LIFE AT THE TOP(1965, Brit.), p
William C. Kirby
CALL OF THE CIRCUS(1930)
Lothar Kirchem
DEAD PIGEON ON BEETHOVEN STREET(1972, Ger.), art d
Sdenka Kirchen
WAR AND PEACE(1956, Ital./U.S.)
Helmut Kircher
BATTLE OF BRITAIN, THE(1969, Brit.)
Jean Kircher
MARY OF SCOTLAND(1936)
Judith Kircher
MARY OF SCOTLAND(1936)
Herbert Kirchhoff
GLASS OF WATER, A(1962, Cgr.), art d; CITY OF SECRETS(1963, Ger.), art d; DER FREISCHUTZ(1970, Ger.), art d
Hugo Kirchhoffer
RHAPSODY IN BLUE(1945)
Basil Kirchin
ASSIGNMENT K(1968, Brit.), m; NEGATIVES(1968, Brit.), m; SHUTTERED ROOM, THE(1968, Brit.), m; STRANGE AFFAIR, THE(1968, Brit.), m; I START COUN-TING(1970, Brit.), m; ABOMINABLE DR. PHIBES, THE(1971, Brit.), m; MUTATIONS, THE(1974, Brit.), m
Dieter Kirchlechner
HAMLET(1962, Ger.); I DEAL IN DANGER(1966)
1984
LOVE IN GERMANY, A(1984, Fr./Ger.)
Hartmut Kirchner
NOT RECONCILED, OR "ONLY VIOLENCE HELPS WHERE IT RULES"(1969, Ger.)
Hedi Kirchner
EIGHT GIRLS IN A BOAT(1932, Ger.)
Jean Kirchner
THREE GODFATHERS(1936)
Kendra Kirchner
ANDROID(1982)
Rainer Kirchner
CHRONICLE OF ANNA MAGDALENA BACH(1968, Ital., Ger.)
Stephen Kirchner
MAJOR AND THE MINOR, THE(1942); MOTHER WORE TIGHTS(1947)
Herbert Kirchoff
CAPTAIN FROM KOEPENICK, THE(1956, Ger.), set d
Milos Kirek
WARM DECEMBER, A(1973, Brit.); FINAL CONFLICT, THE(1981)
Milow Kirek
NEVER SAY NEVER AGAIN(1983)
Yu. Kireyev
NINE DAYS OF ONE YEAR(1964, USSR); OPTIMISTIC TRAGEDY, THE(1964, USSR)
Kirgiz State Opera Corps de Ballet
MORNING STAR(1962, USSR)
George Kirgo
BEST MAN, THE(1964); RED LINE 7000(1965), w; SPINOUT(1966), w; DON'T MAKE WAVES(1967), w; VOICES(1973, Brit.), w
Vladimiros Kiriakos
SUMMER LOVERS(1982)
Zinaida Kirienko
AND QUIET FLOWS THE DON(1960 USSR)
Arsene Kirilloff
GREEN FINGERS(1947)
Kirillov
Misc. Silents
MIRACLE-MAKER(1922, USSR)
Andrei Kirillov
MOSCOW-CASSIOPEIA(1974, USSR), ph; TEENAGERS IN SPACE(1975, USSR), ph
Mikahil Kirillov
DIMKA(1964, USSR), ph
P. Kirillov
MEN OF THE SEA(1938, USSR); GREAT CITIZEN, THE(1939, USSR)
Misc. Silents
INFINITE SORROW(1922, USSR)
Irone Kiriloff
SOMEWHERE IN FRANCE(1943, Brit.)
P. Kirilov
SKI BATTALION(1938, USSR)
Nadao Kirino
DESTROY ALL MONSTERS(1969, Jap.)
Harumi Kiritachi
GAMERA THE INVINCIBLE(1966, Jap.)
Eva Kiritta
SAVAGE HARVEST(1981)
Zoya Kiriyenko
DESTINY OF A MAN(1961, USSR)

Al Kirk
SHAFT(1971)
Charles Kirk
JEALOUSY(1929), set d; HONOR AMONG LOVERS(1931), art d; BED OF RO-SES(1933), art d; MORNING GLORY(1933), art d; INFORMER, THE(1935), art d; JALNA(1935), art d; ROMANCE IN MANHATTAN(1935), art d; STAR OF MID-NIGHT(1935), art d
Silents
SORROWS OF SATAN(1926), art d
Charles M. Kirk
Silents
DREAM STREET(1921), set d; ONE EXCITING NIGHT(1922), set d; ORPHANS OF THE STORM(1922), art d; WHITE ROSE, THE(1923), set d; AMERICA(1924), art d; "THAT ROYLE GIRL"(1925), art d; SALLY OF THE SAWDUST(1925), art d; ALOMA OF THE SOUTH SEAS(1926), art d
David Kirk
DATELINE DIAMONDS(1966, Brit.); HURRY UP OR I'LL BE 30(1973)
David Kirk, Sr.
PUTNEY SWOPE(1969)
Donald Kirk
BORDER FLIGHT(1936); SUNSET OF POWER(1936); VENUS MAKES TROU-BLE(1937); SHOWDOWN, THE(1940)
Elsie Kirk
PRODUCERS, THE(1967)
Evans Kirk
Misc. Silents
WHITE LIES(1920)
Gary Kirk
1984
IMPULSE(1984)
Jack Kirk
FIGHTING THRU(1931); CHEYENNE CYCLONE, THE(1932); GOLD(1932); TOMB-STONE CANYON(1932); GUN LAW(1933); KING OF THE ARENA(1933); WHEN A MAN RIDES ALONE(1933); DUDE RANGER, THE(1934); HONOR OF THE RAN-GE(1934); THUNDER OVER TEXAS(1934); TRAIL DRIVE, THE(1934); COWBOY AND THE BANDIT, THE(1935); IN OLD SANTA FE(1935); LAWLESS RANGE(1935); NEW FRONTIER, THE(1935); STORMY(1935); CATTLE THIEF, THE(1936); GUNS AND GUITARS(1936); KING OF THE PECOS(1936); LAWLESS NINETIES, THE(1936); LONELY TRAIL, THE(1936); MOONLIGHT ON THE PRAIRIE(1936); SINGING COWBOY, THE(1936); SONG OF THE GRINGO(1936); THUNDERBOLT(1936); TOO MUCH BEEF(1936); COME ON, COWBOYS(1937); DOOMED AT SUNDOWN(1937); GIT ALONG, LITTLE DOGIES(1937); GUN LORDS OF STIRRUP BASIN(1937); GUN RANGER, THE(1937); GUNS OF THE PECOS(1937); GUNSMOKE RANCH(1937); HIT THE SADDLE(1937); OH, SUSANNA(1937); RANGE DEFENDERS(1937); RIDERS OF THE WHISTLING SKULL(1937); RIDIN' THE LONE TRAIL(1937); ROUNDUP TIME IN TEXAS(1937); SINGING OUTLAW(1937); SPRINGTIME IN THE ROCKIES(1937); SUNDOWN SAUNDERS(1937); TRAIL OF VENGEANCE(1937); YODELIN' KID FROM PINE RIDGE(1937); GHOST TOWN RIDERS(1938); GUILTY TRAILS(1938); HEROES OF THE HILLS(1938); LAST STAND, THE(1938); OUTLAW EXPRESS(1938); OUTLAWS OF SONORA(1938); OUTLAWS OF THE PRAIRIE(1938); OVERLAND STAGE RAIDERS(1938); PALS OF THE SADDLE(1938); PRAIRIE JUSTICE(1938); PRAIRIE MOON(1938); RHYTHM OF THE SADDLE(1938); UNDER WESTERN STARS(1938); WILD HORSE RODEO(1938); COLORADO SUNSET(1939); COME ON RANGERS(1939); COWBOYS FROM TEXAS(1939); FRONTIER PONY EX-PRESS(1939); HONOR OF THE WEST(1939); NIGHT RIDERS, THE(1939); PHANTOM STAGE, THE(1939); ROUGH RIDERS' ROUNDUP(1939); ROVIN' TUM-BLEWEEDS(1939); WYOMING OUTLAW(1939); CARSON CITY KID(1940); GAUCHO SERENADE(1940); LONE STAR RAIDERS(1940); MELODY RANCH(1940); ONE MAN'S LAW(1940); PIONEERS OF THE FRONTIER(1940); PIONEERS OF THE WEST(1940); ROCKY MOUNTAIN RANGERS(1940); TEXAS TERRORS(1940); TULSA KID, THE(1940); UNDER TEXAS SKIES(1940); YOUNG BILL HICKOK(1940); BAD MAN OF DEADWOOD(1941); DEATH VALLEY OUTLAWS(1941); GANGS OF SONO-RA(1941); IN OLD CHEYENNE(1941); JESSE JAMES AT BAY(1941); KANSAS CYCLONE(1941); NEVADA CITY(1941); PALS OF THE PECOS(1941); PRAIRIE PIONEERS(1941); SHERIFF OF TOMBSTONE(1941); SIERRA SUE(1941); SINGING HILL, THE(1941); UNDER FIESTA STARS(1941); HOME IN WYOMIN'(1942); IN OLD CALIFORNIA(1942); JESSE JAMES, JR.(1942); LONE PRAIRIE, THE(1942); MAN FROM CHEYENNE(1942); PARDON MY GUN(1942); PHANTOM PLAINSMEN, THE(1942); ROMANCE ON THE RANGE(1942); SHERIFF OF SAGE VALLEY(1942); SOUTH OF SANTA FE(1942); SUNSET SERENADE(1942); VALLEY OF HUNTED MEN(1942); WEST OF TOMBSTONE(1942); WESTWARD HO(1942); CANYON CI-TY(1943); CARSON CITY CYCLONE(1943); DEATH VALLEY MANHUNT(1943); HAIL TO THE RANGERS(1943); KING OF THE COWBOYS(1943); MAN FROM THE RIO GRANDE, THE(1943); OVERLAND MAIL ROBBERY(1943); RAIDERS OF SUNSET PASS(1943); SANTA FE SCOUTS(1943); SILVER SPURS(1943); BENEATH WESTERN SKIES(1944); CHEYENNE WILDCAT(1944); CODE OF THE PRAIRIE(1944); COWBOY AND THE SENORITA(1944); FIREBRANDS OF ARIZONA(1944); HIDDEN VALLEY OUTLAWS(1944); LADY AND THE MONSTER, THE(1944); MAN FROM FRIS-CO(1944); MARSHAL OF RENO(1944); MOJAVE FIREBRAND(1944); OUTLAWS OF SANTA FE(1944); PRIDE OF THE PLAINS(1944); SAN ANTONIO KID, THE(1944); SHERIFF OF LAS VEGAS(1944); SHERIFF OF SUNDOWN(1944); SILVER CITY KID(1944); STAGECOACH TO MONTEREY(1944); STORM OVER LISBON(1944); TUCSON RAIDERS(1944); COLORADO PIONEERS(1945); CORPUS CHRISTI BAN-DITS(1945); LONE TEXAS RANGER(1945); PHANTOM OF THE PLAINS(1945); SHERIFF OF CIMARRON(1945); SUNSET IN EL DORADO(1945); TOPEKA TERROR, THE(1945); TRAIL OF KIT CARSON(1945); CONQUEST OF CHEYENNE(1946); DESERT HORSEMAN, THE(1946); HER ADVENTUROUS NIGHT(1946); HOME ON THE RANGE(1946); SUN VALLEY CYCLONE(1946); TERRORS ON HORSEBACK(1946); HOMESTEADERS OF PARADISE VALLEY(1947); OREGON TRAIL SCOUTS(1947); BOLD FRONTIERSMAN, THE(1948); GALLANT LEGION, THE(1948); OKLAHOMA BADLANDS(1948); WAGON WHEELS WESTWARD(1956)
Misc. Talkies
SUNDOWN TRAIL, THE(1975)
Jack-Lee Kirk
KANGAROO(1952), art d
Jeremy Kirk
MADISON AVENUE(1962), w

Joann Kirk
DARK, THE(1979)
Joe Kirk
SPOOKS RUN WILD(1941); MR. WISE GUY(1942); PARDON MY SARONG(1942); SMART ALECKS(1942); WHO DONE IT?(1942); GYPSY WILDCAT(1944); BLONDE RANSOM(1945); HERE COME THE CO-EDS(1945); NAUGHTY NINETIES, THE(1945); INSIDE JOB(1946); LITTLE GIANT(1946); WEB, THE(1947); ABBOTT AND COSTELLO MEET FRANKENSTEIN(1948); MEXICAN HAYRIDE(1948); MY DEAR SECRETARY(1948); NOOSE HANGS HIGH, THE(1948); IMPACT(1949); COMIN' ROUND THE MOUNTAIN(1951); JACK AND THE BEANSTALK(1952); ABBOTT AND COSTELLO GO TO MARS(1953); FORT ALGIERS(1953); NIGHT FREIGHT(1955); BEYOND A REASONABLE DOUBT(1956); HOT SHOTS(1956)
Joseph Kirk
X MARKS THE SPOT(1942); MARGIN FOR ERROR(1943); SWEETHEARTS OF THE U.S.A.(1944); LOST IN ALASKA(1952)
Kenneth Kirk
DOWNHILL RACER(1969)
Laurence Kirk
STAND BY FOR ACTION(1942), w
Linda Kirk
DESTRUCTORS, THE(1968)
Lorena Kirk
CHANGE OF HABIT(1969)
Mark Lee Kirk
DRUMS ALONG THE MOHAWK(1939), art d; WIFE, HUSBAND AND FRIEND(1939), art d; TOM, DICK AND HARRY(1941), art d; FALLEN SPARROW, THE(1943), art d; ROYAL SCANDAL, A(1945), art d; GENTLEMAN'S AGREEMENT(1947), art d; CALL NORTHSIDE 777(1948), art d; IRON CURTAIN, THE(1948), art d; PRINCE OF FOXES(1949), art d; MY WIFE'S BEST FRIEND(1952), art d; REVOLT OF MAMIE STOVER, THE(1956), art d; GIFT OF LOVE, THE(1958), art d
Mark-Lee Kirk
EVERYBODY'S OLD MAN(1936), art d; SING, BABY, SING(1936), art d; TO MARY-WITH LOVE(1936), art d; LOVE AND HISSES(1937), art d; ON THE AVENUE(1937), art d; WAKE UP AND LIVE(1937), art d; THANKS FOR EVERYTHING(1938), art d; YOUNG MR. LINCOLN(1939), art d; GRAPES OF WRATH(1940), art d; KITTY FOYLE(1940), art d; MY FAVORITE WIFE(1940), art d; JOURNEY INTO FEAR(1942), art d; MAGNIFICENT AMBERSONS, THE(1942), art d; MR. LUCKY(1943), art d; I'LL BE SEEING YOU(1944), art d; SINCE YOU WENT AWAY(1944), set d; JUNIOR MISS(1945), art d; MOSS ROSE(1947), art d; STELLA(1950), art d; WAY OF A GAUCHO(1952), art d; WHITE WITCH DOCTOR(1953), art d; PRINCE VALIANT(1954), art d; GOOD MORNING, MISS DOVE(1955), art d; PRINCE OF PLAYERS(1955), art d; TALL MEN, THE(1955), art d; SUN ALSO RISES, THE(1957), art d; THREE BRAVE MEN(1957), art d; REMARKABLE MR. PENNYPACKER, THE(1959), art d
Marklee Kirk
THIN ICE(1937), art d
Michael Kirk
DANGER! WOMEN AT WORK(1943); FOLLOW THE BOYS(1944)
Phyllis Kirk
LIFE OF HER OWN, A(1950); MRS. O'MALLEY AND MR. MALONE(1950); OUR VERY OWN(1950); TWO WEEKS WITH LOVE(1950); THREE GUYS NAMED MIKE(1951); ABOUT FACE(1952); IRON MISTRESS, THE(1952); STOP, YOU'RE KILLING ME(1952); HOUSE OF WAX(1953); THUNDER OVER THE PLAINS(1953); CRIME WAVE(1954); RIVER BEAT(1954); CANYON CROSSROADS(1955); BACK FROM ETERNITY(1956); JOHNNY CONCHO(1956); CITY AFTER MIDNIGHT(1957, Brit.); SAD SACK, THE(1957)
Ralph G. Kirk
Silents
SCRAPPER, THE(1922), w
Robert Wellington Kirk
SAVAGE WILD, THE(1970)
Sharon Kirk
CHRISTINA(1974, Can.)
Stanley Kirk
UP FOR THE CUP(1931, Brit.)
Tom J. Kirk
DOWNHILL RACER(1969)
Tom Kirk
MOTHER GOOSE A GO-GO(1966); TRACK OF THUNDER(1967)
Misc. Talkies
UNKISSED BRIDE(1966); MY NAME IS LEGEND(1975)
Tommy Kirk
OLD YELLER(1957); SHAGGY DOG, THE(1959); SNOW QUEEN, THE(1959, USSR); SWISS FAMILY ROBINSON(1960); ABSENT-MINDED PROFESSOR, THE(1961); BABES IN TOYLAND(1961); BON VOYAGE(1962); MOON PILOT(1962); SAVAGE SAM(1963); SON OF FLUBBER(1963); MISADVENTURES OF MERLIN JONES, THE(1964); PAJAMA PARTY(1964); MONKEY'S UNCLE, THE(1965); VILLAGE OF THE GIANTS(1965); GHOST IN THE INVISIBLE BIKINI(1966); MARS NEEDS WOMEN(1966); CATALINA CAPER, THE(1967); IT'S A BIKINI WORLD(1967); IT'S ALIVE(1968)
Ronald Kirkbride
GIRL NAMED TAMIRO, A(1962), w
Elisabeth Kirkby
NO. 96(1974, Aus.)
Stanley Kirkby
SMALL MAN, THE(1935, Brit.); FATHER O'FLYNN(1938, Irish)
The Kirkby Sisters
GREAT GAY ROAD, THE(1931, Brit.)
Bill Kirkchenbaurer
SKATETOWN, U.S.A.(1979)
Donald Kirke
FOLLOW THE LEADER(1930); BLONDIE JOHNSON(1933); FOURTH HORSEMAN, THE(1933); HIDDEN GOLD(1933); WOMEN WON'T TELL(1933); GHOST WALKS, THE(1935); LET 'EM HAVE IT(1935); IN HIS STEPS(1936); BIG SHOT, THE(1937); COUNTRY GENTLEMEN(1937); EMPEROR'S CANDLESTICKS, THE(1937); MANNEQUIN(1937); MIDNIGHT MADONNA(1937); OH, SUSANNA(1937); PARADISE EXPRESS(1937); RANGE DEFENDERS(1937); SHADOW, THE(1937); SMOKE TREE RANGE(1937); HAWAII CALLS(1938); I DEMAND PAYMENT(1938); ZIEGFELD GIRL(1941); NIGHT FOR CRIME, A(1942); OUTLAWS OF PINE RIDGE(1942); HOP-

PY'S HOLIDAY(1947); SCANDAL INCORPORATED(1956); GARMENT JUNGLE, THE(1957)
Donald Kirke, Jr.
RIDE 'EM COWBOY(1936)
Shirley Kirkes
PENNIES FROM HEAVEN(1981)
Correan Kirkham
Misc. Silents
BLACK SHADOWS(1920); BARE KNUCKLES(1921)
Katherine Kirkham
Misc. Silents
SOCIAL AMBITION(1918)
Kathleen Kirkham
Silents
MODERN MUSKETEER, A(1917); ARIZONA(1918); ROMANCE OF TARZAN, THE(1918); TARZAN OF THE APES(1918); HER FIVE-FOOT HIGHNESS(1920); LITTLE 'FRAID LADY, THE(1920); BEAU REVEL(1921); NOBODY'S KID(1921); SKY PILOT, THE(1921); HOMESPUN VAMP, A(1922); LONELY ROAD, THE(1923); REGULAR FELLOW, A(1925); ISLE OF RETRIBUTION, THE(1926); KING OF THE TURF, THE(1926)
Misc. Silents
HOUSE OF LIES, THE(1916); CLEAN GUN, THE(1917); DEVIL'S ASSISTANT, THE(1917); EYES OF THE WORLD, THE(1917); HIS SWEETHEART(1917); MASKED HEART, THE(1917); PHANTOM SHOTGUN, THE(1917); DIPLOMATIC MISSION, A(1918); FOR HUSBANDS ONLY(1918); IN SEARCH OF ARCADY(1919); JOSSELYN'S WIFE(1919); MASTER MAN, THE(1919); THIRD KISS, THE(1919); BEAUTY MARKET, THE(1920); DOLLAR FOR DOLLAR(1920); FRIVOLOUS WIVES(1920); PARLOR, BEDROOM AND BATH(1920); WHEN DAWN CAME(1920); FOOLISH MATRONS, THE(1921); PILGRIMS OF THE NIGHT(1921); BACK TO YELLOW JACKET(1922); ONE EIGHTH APACHE(1922); OTHER MEN'S DAUGHTERS(1923)
Corinne Kirkin
WIZARD OF GORE, THE(1970)
Alex Kirkland
PASSPORT TO HELL(1932)
Alexander Kirkland
TARNISHED LADY(1931); SURRENDER(1931); ALMOST MARRIED(1932); CHARLIE CHAN'S CHANCE(1932); DEVIL'S LOTTERY(1932); STRANGE INTERLUDE(1932); BLACK BEAUTY(1933); BONDAGE(1933); HUMANITY(1933); SOCIAL REGISTER(1934); 13 RUE MADELEINE(1946); FACE IN THE CROWD, A(1957)
David Kirkland
RIDERS OF THE CACTUS(1931), p, d&w; MAYOR OF 44TH STREET, THE(1942)
Silents
IN SEARCH OF A SINNER(1920), d; NOTHING BUT THE TRUTH(1920), d, w; ROWDY, THE(1921), d; HANDS ACROSS THE BORDER(1926), d; REGULAR SCOUT, A(1926), d&w
Misc. Silents
CRIPPLED HAND, THE(1916), d; TEMPERAMENTAL WIFE, A(1919), d; VIRTUOUS VAMP, A(1919), d; LOVE EXPERT, THE(1920), d; PERFECT WOMAN, THE(1920), d; BAREFOOT BOY, THE(1923), d; FOR ANOTHER WOMAN(1924), d; TOMBOY, THE(1924), d; ALL AROUND FRYING PAN(1925), d; WHO CARES(1925), d; TOUGH GUY, THE(1926), d; TWO-GUN MAN, THE(1926), d; GINGHAM GIRL, THE(1927), d; UNEASY PAYMENTS(1927), d; YOURS TO COMMAND(1927), d; CANDY KID, THE(1928), d; SOUL OF MEXICO(1932, Mex.), d
Erik Kirkland
SKIDOO(1968), w
Geoffrey Kirkland
MIDNIGHT EXPRESS(1978, Brit.), prod d; FAME(1980), prod d; SHOOT THE MOON(1982), prod d; RIGHT STUFF, THE(1983), prod d
1984
BIRDY(1984), prod d
Hardee Kirkland
Silents
LOST BRIDEGROOM, THE(1916); EYE FOR EYE(1918); HER GREAT CHANCE(1918); LES MISERABLES(1918); JOHNNY-ON-THE-SPOT(1919); ACE OF HEARTS, THE(1921); FROM THE GROUND UP(1921); PERFECT CRIME, A(1921); SHERLOCK BROWN(1921); YOUTH TO YOUTH(1922); ARE YOU A FAILURE?(1923); MAILMAN, THE(1923); ARIZONA ROMEO, THE(1925)
Misc. Silents
WHEN FALSE TONGUES SPEAK(1917); FACE BETWEEN, THE(1922); HONOR FIRST(1922); THEY LIKE 'EM ROUGH(1922); WHILE PARIS SLEEPS(1923)
Jack Kirkland
WALL STREET(1929), w; FAST AND LOOSE(1930), w; HEADS UP(1930), w; NOW AND FOREVER(1934), w; WINGS IN THE DARK(1935), w; ADVENTURE IN MANHATTAN(1936), w; FRANKIE AND JOHNNY(1936), w; SUTTER'S GOLD(1936), w; TOBACCO ROAD(1941), w; AMAZING MONSIEUR FABRE, THE(1952, Fr.), w; GOLDEN COACH, THE(1953, Fr./Ital.), w; MANDINGO(1975), w
John Kirkland
ZOO IN BUDAPEST(1933), w
Misc. Talkies
CURSE OF THE HEADLESS HORSEMAN(1972), d
John S. Kirkland
MILLS OF THE GODS(1935), w
Muriel Kirkland
COCKTAIL HOUR(1933); FAST WORKERS(1933); HOLD YOUR MAN(1933); SECRET OF THE BLUE ROOM(1933); TO THE LAST MAN(1933); LITTLE MAN, WHAT NOW?(1934); NANA(1934); WHITE PARADE, THE(1934)
Sally Kirkland
WAY WE WERE, THE(1973); GOING HOME(1971); CINDERELLA LIBERTY(1973); STING, THE(1973); YOUNG NURSES, THE(1973); BIG BAD MAMA(1974); BITE THE BULLET(1975); CRAZY MAMA(1975); PIPE DREAMS(1976); STAR IS BORN, A(1976); HOMETOWN U.S.A.(1979); PRIVATE BENJAMIN(1980); HUMAN HIGHWAY(1982); LOVE LETTERS(1983)
Misc. Talkies
COMING APART(1969); BRAND X(1970); FATAL GAMES(1983); KILLING TOUCH, THE(1983)
John Kirkley
OPERATOR 13(1934)

Darrell Kirkman
FAME(1980)
Amy Kirkpatric
ENTITY, THE(1982)
John Kirkpatric
Misc. Talkies
SCREAM IN THE STREETS, A(1972)
Ches Kirkpatrick
WORDS AND MUSIC(1929)
David Kirkpatrick
GREAT TEXAS DYNAMITE CHASE, THE(1976), w
George Kirkpatrick
SNOWBALL EXPRESS(1972)
H. Kirkpatrick
THROWBACK, THE(1935), ph; SILVER SPURS(1936), ph; EMPTY SADDLES(1937), ph
H. J. Kirkpatrick
SECOND HONEYMOON(1931), ph
Helen Kirkpatrick
GREEN SLIME, THE(1969)
Herbert Kirkpatrick
PHANTOM IN THE HOUSE, THE(1929), ph; FOURTH ALARM, THE(1930), ph; WORLDLY GOODS(1930), ph; IVORY-HANDLED GUN(1935), ph; MUTINY AHEAD(1935), ph; PERFECT CLUE, THE(1935), ph; WESTERN COURAGE(1935), ph; WESTERN FRONTIER(1935), ph; BOSS RIDER OF GUN CREEK(1936), ph; CATTLE THIEF, THE(1936), ph; COWBOY AND THE KID,THE(1936), ph; FOR THE SERVICE(1936), ph; HEIR TO TROUBLE(1936), ph; LAWLESS RIDERS(1936), ph; RIDE 'EM COWBOY(1936), ph; SUNSET OF POWER(1936), ph; SANDFLOW(1937), ph; SPLIT IMAGE(1982)
Silents
OH, WHAT A NIGHT!(1926), ph; PRETTY CLOTHES(1927), ph; STRANDED(1927), ph; THUMBS DOWN(1927), ph; MARRY THE GIRL(1928), ph; MILLION FOR LOVE, A(1928), ph; HUNTED MEN(1930), ph; OKLAHOMA SHERIFF, THE(1930), ph
Herbert J. Kirkpatrick
RAMPANT AGE, THE(1930), ph
Jess Kirkpatrick
SET-UP, THE(1949); D.O.A.(1950); MOB, THE(1951); WELL, THE(1951); CAPTIVE CITY(1952); FAST COMPANY(1953); NO ESCAPE(1953); MIRACLE IN THE RAIN(1956); UNDERSEA GIRL(1957); LONG, HOT SUMMER, THE(1958); 10 NORTH FREDERICK(1958); ALASKA PASSAGE(1959); TOMBOY AND THE CHAMP(1961); INCIDENT IN AN ALLEY(1962)
Jesse Kirkpatrick
JUDGE, THE(1949); ON THE LOOSE(1951); CLOWN, THE(1953); SQUARE JUNGLE, THE(1955); STAR IN THE DUST(1956); SPACE MASTER X-7(1958); THESE THOUSAND HILLS(1959)
Jesse B. Kirkpatrick
STOP THAT CAB(1951); OUTSIDE THE LAW(1956)
Joan Kirkpatrick
NAUGHTY ARLETTE(1951, Brit.)
John Kirkpatrick
MAMA STEPS OUT(1937), w
Katherine Kirkpatrick
DR. HECKYL AND MR. HYPE(1980)
Maggie Kirkpatrick
GETTING OF WISDOM, THE(1977, Aus.); NIGHT OF THE PROWLER, THE(1979, Aus.); PIRATE MOVIE, THE(1982, Aus.)
Patti Kirkpatrick
1984
MEATBALLS PART II(1984)
Peggy Kirkpatrick
LONG NIGHT, THE(1976)
Robert Kirkpatrick
GEEK MAGGOT BINGO(1983), w
Bill Kirksey
WAITRESS(1982)
Dianne Kirksey
RICH KIDS(1979)
Kirk Kirksey
UPTIGHT(1968); SWEET CHARITY(1969); HI, MOM!(1970)
Van Kirksey
UPTIGHT(1968); COTTON COMES TO HARLEM(1970); LANDLORD, THE(1970); KING OF MARVIN GARDENS, THE(1972); SCREAM BLACULA SCREAM(1973)
William Kirksey
SQUEEZE PLAY(1981)
1984
FIRST TURN-ON!, THE(1984)
Ski Kirkwell
EVEL KNIEVEL(1971)
Catherine Kirkwood
Misc. Silents
SOUL FOR SALE, A(1918)
Gene Kirkwood
HOT RODS TO HELL(1967); RIOT ON SUNSET STRIP(1967); COMES A HORSEMAN(1978), p; IDOLMAKER, THE(1980), p; GORKY PARK(1983), p; KEEP, THE(1983), p; NIGHT IN HEAVEN, A(1983), p
1984
POPE OF GREENWICH VILLAGE, THE(1984), p
Jack Kirkwood
CHICKEN EVERY SUNDAY(1948); FANCY PANTS(1950); FATHER MAKES GOOD(1950); HUMPHREY TAKES A CHANCE(1950); NEVER A DULL MOMENT(1950)
James Kirkwood
BLACK WATERS(1929); DEVIL'S HOLIDAY, THE(1930); SPOILERS, THE(1930); WORLDLY GOODS(1930); HOLY TERROR, A(1931); OVER THE HILL(1931); YOUNG SINNERS(1931); CARELESS LADY(1932); CHARLIE CHAN'S CHANCE(1932); CHEATERS AT PLAY(1932); LENA RIVERS(1932); MY PAL, THE KING(1932); RAINBOW TRAIL(1932); SHE WANTED A MILLIONAIRE(1932); HIRED WIFE(1934); LADY FROM CHEYENNE(1941); NO HANDS ON THE CLOCK(1941); GOVERNMENT GIRL(1943); MADAME CURIE(1943); DRIFTWOOD(1947); JOAN OF ARC(1948); UNTAMED BREED, THE(1948); DOOLINS OF OKLAHOMA, THE(1949); INTRUDER IN

THE DUST(1949); ROSEANNA McCOY(1949); NEVADAN, THE(1950); STAGE TO TUCSON(1950); MAN IN THE SADDLE(1951); SANTA FE(1951); I DREAM OF JEANIE(1952); LAST POSSE, THE(1953); SUN SHINES BRIGHT, THE(1953); WINNING OF THE WEST(1953); WOMAN THEY ALMOST LYNCHED, THE(1953); PASSION(1954); SEARCH FOR BRIDEY MURPHY, THE(1956); MOMMIE DEAREST(1981); SOME KIND OF HERO(1982), w
Silents
CLASSMATES(1914), d; EAGLE'S MATE, THE(1914), a, d; FLOOR ABOVE, THE(1914), d; HOME SWEET HOME(1914); MOUNTAIN RAT, THE(1914), a, d; CINDERELLA(1915), d; DAWN OF A TOMORROW, THE(1915), d; ESMERALDA(1915), d; FANCHON THE CRICKET(1915), d; LITTLE PAL(1915), a, d; MASQUERADERS, THE(1915), d; MISTRESS NELL(1915), d; RAGS(1915), d; LOST BRIDEGROOM, THE(1916), d; EVE'S DAUGHTER(1918), d; I WANT TO FORGET(1918), d&w; BRANDING IRON, THE(1920); BOB HAMPTON OF PLACER(1921); WISE FOOL, A(1921); EBB TIDE(1922); EAGLE'S FEATHER, THE(1923); ANOTHER MAN'S WIFE(1924); PAINTED FLAPPER, THE(1924); "THAT ROYLE GIRL"(1925); LOVER'S ISLAND(1925); POLICE PATROL, THE(1925); RECKLESS LADY, THE(1926)
Misc. Silents
BEHIND THE SCENES(1914), a, d; LORD CHUMLEY(1914), d; GAMBLER'S ADVOCATE(1915); HEART OF JENNIFER, THE(1915), a, d; DREAM OR TWO AGO, A(1916), d; DULCIE'S ADVENTURE(1916), d; FAITH(1916), d; OLD HOMESTEAD, THE(1916), d; SAINTS AND SINNERS(1916), d; SUSIE SNOWFLAKE(1916), d; ANNIE-FOR-SPITE(1917), d; GENTLE INTRUDER, THE(1917), d; INNOCENCE OF LIZETTE, THE(1917), d; MELISSA OF THE HILLS(1917), d; OVER THERE(1917), d; PERIWINKLE(1917), d; OUT OF THE NIGHT(1918), d; ROMANCE OF THE UNDERWORLD, A(1918), d; STRUGGLE EVERLASTING, THE(1918), d; BILL APPERSON'S BOY(1919), d; IN WRONG(1919), d; FORBIDDEN THING, THE(1920); IN THE HEART OF A FOOL(1920); LOVE(1920); LUCK OF THE IRISH, THE(1920); SCOFFER, THE(1920); GREAT IMPERSONATION, THE(1921); MAN–WOMAN–MARRIAGE(1921); MAN FROM HOME, THE(1922); PINK GODS(1922); SIN FLOOD, THE(1922); UNDER TWO FLAGS(1922); HUMAN WRECKAGE(1923); PONJOLA(1923); YOU ARE GUILTY(1923); BROKEN BARRIERS(1924); CIRCE THE ENCHANTRESS(1924); DISCONTENTED HUSBANDS(1924); GERALD CRANSTON'S LADY(1924); LOVE'S WHIRLPOOL(1924); WANDERING HUSBANDS(1924); SECRETS OF THE NIGHT(1925); TOP OF THE WORLD, THE(1925); BUTTERFLIES IN THE RAIN(1926); WISE GUY, THE(1926); MILLION DOLLAR MYSTERY(1927)
James R. Kirkwood
HEARTS IN EXILE(1929); TIME, THE PLACE AND THE GIRL, THE(1929)
Joe Kirkwood
FIGHTING MAD(1948); HUMPHREY TAKES A CHANCE(1950)
Misc. Talkies
JOE PALOOKA IN THE KNOCKOUT(1947)
Joe Kirkwood, Jr.
JOE PALOOKA, CHAMP(1946); NIGHT AND DAY(1946); JOE PALOOKA IN WINNER TAKE ALL(1948); JOE PALOOKA IN THE BIG FIGHT(1949); JOE PALOOKA IN THE COUNTERPUNCH(1949); JOE PALOOKA IN THE SQUARED CIRCLE(1950); JOE PALOOKA MEETS HUMPHREY(1950); JOE PALOOKA IN TRIPLE CROSS(1951); MARRIAGE-GO-ROUND, THE(1960)
Katherine Kirkwood
Misc. Silents
PAYMENT, THE(1916); VAGABOND PRINCE, THE(1916)
Pat Kirkwood
SAVE A LITTLE SUNSHINE(1938, Brit.); COME ON GEORGE(1939, Brit.); ME AND MY PAL(1939, Brit.); BAND WAGGON(1940, Brit.); FLIGHT FROM FOLLY(1945, Brit.); NO LEAVE, NO LOVE(1946); ONCE A SINNER(1952, Brit.); STARS IN YOUR EYES(1956, Brit.); AFTER THE BALL(1957, Brit.); INCREDIBLY STRANGE CREATURES WHO STOPPED LIVING AND BECAME CRAZY MIXED-UP ZOMBIES, THE(1965), art d
Ray Kirkwood
CYCLONE RANGER(1935), p; LAWLESS BORDER(1935), p; SCREAM IN THE NIGHT(1943), p
Madame E. Kirkwood-Hackett
LAST HOLIDAY(1950, Brit.)
Jack Kirland
GILDED LILY, THE(1935), w
Leonard Kirman
CARNIVAL OF BLOOD(1976), p,d&w
C.L. Kirmse
GIRL FROM THE MARSH CROFT, THE(1935, Ger.), set d
Michael Kirner
BIG GAME, THE(1972)
Ivan Kirov
SPECTER OF THE ROSE(1946)
Kirov State Academic Theatre Corps de Ballet
SLEEPING BEAUTY, THE(1966, USSR)
V. Kirpalov
QUEEN OF SPADES(1961, USSR)
Dimitri Kirsanoff
TONIGHT THE SKIRTS FLY(1956, Fr.), d
Misc. Silents
L'IRONIE DU DESTIN(1924, Fr.), d; MENILMONTANT(1926, Fr.), d; DESTIN(1927, Fr.), d; SABLES(1928, Fr.), d
Monique Kirsanoff
MANON(1950, Fr.), ed; TONIGHT THE SKIRTS FLY(1956, Fr.), ed; TENDER SCOUNDREL(1967, Fr./Ital.), ed
Bunny Kirsch
HILDUR AND THE MAGICIAN(1969)
Nancy Kirsch
1984
MUPPETS TAKE MANHATTAN, THE(1984)
Oona Kirsch
1984
FOREVER YOUNG(1984, Brit.)
Liselotte Kirschbaum
DECISION BEFORE DAWN(1951)
Debra Kirschenbaum
VISITING HOURS(1982, Can.)

Patricia Kirschner
FOXHOLE IN CAIRO(1960, Brit.), ch
William Kirschner
DIARY OF ANNE FRANK, THE(1959); QUICK AND THE DEAD, THE(1963); CORPSE GRINDERS, THE(1972)
Rudiger Kirschstein
COUP DE GRACE(1978, Ger./Fr.)
John Kirsh
JESUS(1979), d
Misc. Talkies
FRIEND OR FOE(1982, Brit.), d
Oona Kirsh
1984
SACRED HEARTS(1984, Brit.)
Mori Kirshida
ZATOICHI MEETS YOJIMBO(1970, Jap.)
Don Kirshner
TOOMORROW(1970, Brit.), p
Jack Kirshner
EVIL, THE(1978), ed
Steve Kirshoff
FRIDAY THE 13TH PART II(1981), spec eff
Iris Kirskey
NATIONAL VELVET(1944)
Jacques Kirsner
GIRL FROM LORRAINE, A(1982, Fr./Switz.), w; LA PASSANTE(1983, Fr./Ger.), w
Monique Kirsonoff
COUNT OF MONTE-CRISTO(1955, Fr., Ital.), ed
Hans Helmut Kirst
NIGHT OF THE GENERALS, THE(1967, Brit./Fr.), w
Alix Kirsta
YOUNG GIRLS OF ROCHEFORT, THE(1968, Fr.)
Carrie Kirstein
INTERNECINE PROJECT, THE(1974, Brit.)
Rosemarie Kirstein
ORDERED TO LOVE(1963, Ger.)
Alice Kirsten
SUSPENSE(1946)
Daphne Kirsten
HIGH(1968, Can.)
Dorothy Kirsten
MR. MUSIC(1950); GREAT CARUSO, THE(1951)
Sue Kirsten
HIGH(1968, Can.)
Kris Kirstofferson
VIGILANTE FORCE(1976)
Louise Kirtland
ROSELAND(1977)
Mike Kirton
SPRING BREAK(1983), stunts
Harvey Kirtzman
MAD MONSTER PARTY(1967), w
Kitty Kirwan
EDGE OF THE WORLD, THE(1937, Brit.); MACUSHLA(1937, Brit.); VICAR OF BRAY, THE(1937, Brit.); WHO GOES NEXT?(1938, Brit.); I KNOW WHERE I'M GOING(1947, Brit.); ODD MAN OUT(1947, Brit.); FLOODTIDE(1949, Brit.)
Patric Kirwan
DRUMS(1938, Brit.), w
Patrick Kirwan
BULLDOG DRUMMOND AT BAY(1937, Brit.), w; TROOPSHIP(1938, Brit.), w; CHALLENGE, THE(1939, Brit.), w; CONVOY(1940), w; FUGITIVE, THE(1940, Brit.), w; HUMAN MONSTER, THE(1940, Brit.), w; PIRATES OF THE SEVEN SEAS(1941, Brit.), w; AVENGERS, THE(1942, Brit.), w; SHIPS WITH WINGS(1942, Brit.), w; UNPUBLISHED STORY(1942, Brit.), w; ESCAPE TO DANGER(1943, Brit.), w; RANDOLPH FAMILY, THE(1945, Brit.), w; TURNERS OF PROSPECT ROAD, THE(1947, Brit.), w; CAPTIVE HEART, THE(1948, Brit.), w; ONCE UPON A DREAM(1949, Brit.), w; TWENTY QUESTIONS MURDER MYSTERY, THE(1950, Brit.), w; HOTEL SAHARA(1951, Brit.), w; DESPERATE MOMENT(1953, Brit.), w; FAKE, THE(1953, Brit.), w; TOP OF THE FORM(1953, Brit.), w; UP TO HIS NECK(1953, Brit.), w; JACQUELINE(1956, Brit.), w; DANGEROUS EXILE(1958, Brit.), w; ROONEY(1958, Brit.), w; BROTH OF A BOY(1959, Brit.), w; THIS OTHER EDEN(1959, Brit.), w; TOMMY THE TOREADOR(1960, Brit.), w; HELLIONS, THE(1962, Brit.), w; JOHNNY NOBODY(1965, Brit.), w
Cornelia Kirwin
THRILL OF BRAZIL, THE(1946)
Patrick Kirwin
TALE OF FIVE WOMEN, A(1951, Brit.), w; POACHER'S DAUGHTER, THE(1960, Brit.), w
William Kirwin
DECOY FOR TERROR(1970, Can.)
James Kirwood
Misc. Silents
ENVIRONMENT(1917), d
V. Kiryanov
MARRIAGE OF BALZAMINOV, THE(1966, USSR)
P. Kiryutin
DREAM OF A COSSACK(1982, USSR)
P. Kiryutkin
HOME FOR TANYA, A(1961, USSR); SUMMER TO REMEMBER, A(1961, USSR); CLEAR SKIES(1963, USSR); WAR AND PEACE(1968, USSR)
Milan Kis
ASSISTANT, THE(1982, Czech.)
Kanta Kisaragi
SAMURAI(1955, Jap.)
Joe Kisch
DUEL AT SILVER CREEK, THE(1952), set d
Ryalton Kisch
FOLLY TO BE WISE(1953), md

V. Kiselev
GREAT CITIZEN, THE(1939, USSR)
P. Kiselyov
GIRL AND THE BUGLER, THE(1967, USSR), art d
V. Kiselyova
SOUND OF LIFE, THE(1962, USSR), cos; NINE DAYS OF ONE YEAR(1964, USSR), cos
Terry Kiser
RACHEL, RACHEL(1968); FAST CHARLIE... THE MOONBEAM RIDER(1979); RICH KIDS(1979); SEVEN(1979); STEEL(1980); ALL NIGHT LONG(1981); LOOKER(1981); MAKING LOVE(1982); SIX PACK(1982)
1984
SURF II(1984)
Virginia Kiser
ME AND MY BROTHER(1969); WHO SAYS I CAN'T RIDE A RAINBOW!(1971); DEATH PLAY(1976); 10(1979); MOMMIE DEAREST(1981); POLTERGEIST(1982); THIS IS ELVIS(1982); SPACE RAIDERS(1983)
1984
MICKI AND MAUDE(1984)
Joe Kish
FORT APACHE(1948), set d; THREE GODFATHERS, THE(1948), set d; SHE WORE A YELLOW RIBBON(1949), set d; KISS TOMORROW GOODBYE(1950), set d; WAGONMASTER(1950), set d; HORIZONS WEST(1952), set d; FRIENDLY PERSUASION(1956), set d; DEFIANT ONES, THE(1958), set d; PHANTOM PLANET, THE(1961), set d; TWENTY PLUS TWO(1961), set d; CONFESSIONS OF AN OPIUM EATER(1962), set d; LIVELY SET, THE(1964), set d
Joseph Kish
HEAT'S ON, THE(1943), set d; REVEILLE WITH BEVERLY(1943), set d; WHAT'S BUZZIN COUSIN?(1943), set d; HEY, ROOKIE(1944), set d; ESCAPE IN THE FOG(1945), art d; KISS AND TELL(1945), set d; NIGHT SONG(1947), set d; JOAN OF ARC(1948), set d; CROOKED WAY, THE(1949), set d; RED CANYON(1949), set d; CRY DANGER(1951), set d; LADY FROM TEXAS, THE(1951), md; REDHEAD FROM WYOMING, THE(1953), set d; SEMINOLE(1953), set d; WAR ARROW(1953), set d; APACHE(1954), set d; HIGH SOCIETY(1955), set d; JAIL BUSTERS(1955), set d; CRASHING LAS VEGAS(1956), set d; FIGHTING TROUBLE(1956), set d; HOT SHOTS(1956), set d; INVASION OF THE BODY SNATCHERS(1956), prod d; SPY CHASERS(1956), set d; BABY FACE NELSON(1957), set d; HOLD THAT HYPNOTIST(1957), set d; UP IN SMOKE(1957), set d; IN THE MONEY(1958), set d; JOURNEY TO THE CENTER OF THE EARTH(1959), set d; RETURN OF THE FLY(1959), set d; LOST WORLD, THE(1960), set d; WILD RIVER(1960), set d; GEORGE RAFT STORY, THE(1961), set d; KING OF THE ROARING TWENTIES–THE STORY OF ARNOLD ROTHSTEIN(1961), set d; LITTLE SHEPHERD OF KINGDOM COME(1961), set d; CONVICTS FOUR(1962), set d; IT'S A MAD, MAD, MAD, MAD WORLD(1963), set d; LADY IN A CAGE(1964), set d; SHIP OF FOOLS(1965), set d; SLENDER THREAD, THE(1965), set d
Sally Kishbaugh
1984
BEVERLY HILLS COP(1984)
Keiko Kishi
RIFIFI IN TOKYO(1963, Fr./Ital.); INHERITANCE, THE(1964, Jap.); LOVE UNDER THE CRUCIFIX(1965, Jap.); UNINHIBITED, THE(1968, Fr./Ital./Span.); MASTERMIND(1977)
Teruko Kishi
INSECT WOMAN, THE(1964, Jap.); GIRL I ABANDONED, THE(1970, Jap.)
Yoshio Kishi
FINNEGANS WAKE(1965), ed
Kuichiro Kishida
GODZILLA, RING OF THE MONSTERS(1956, Jap.), spec eff; GODZILLA VS. THE THING(1964, Jap.), spec eff
Kyoko Kishida
DIPLOMAT'S MANSION, THE(1961, Jap.); WOMAN IN THE DUNES(1964, Jap.); SCHOOL FOR SEX(1966, Jap.); FACE OF ANOTHER, THE(1967, Jap.); PASSION(1968, Jap.); SOLDIER'S PRAYER, A(1970, Jap.); VIXEN(1970, Jap.)
Mori Kishida
LAKE OF DRACULA(1973, Jap.); GODZILLA VERSUS THE COSMIC MONSTER(1974, Jap.)
Shin Kishida
SHOGUN ASSASSIN(1980, Jap.)
Fujii Kishii
Silents
PEACOCK FAN(1929)
Gin-ichi Kishimoto
SAMURAI FROM NOWHERE(1964, Jap.), p
Masayoshi Kishimoto
FOX WITH NINE TAILS, THE(1969, Jap.), ph
Hideo Kisho
ROAD TO ETERNITY(1962, Jap.)
Ephraim Kishon
SALLAH(1965, Israel), d&w
Billie Kishonti
MEATBALLS(1979, Can.)
Ildiko Kishonti
CONFIDENCE(1980, Hung.); MEPHISTO(1981, Ger.)
Anil Kishore
TIGER AND THE FLAME, THE(1955, India)
Stefan Kisielewski
GUESTS ARE COMING(1965, Pol.), m
Kirk I. Kiskella
DEATH VALLEY(1982)
Ivana Kislinger
NAKED MAJA, THE(1959, Ital./U.S.); WHAT DID YOU DO IN THE WAR, DADDY?(1966)
Kismet
PASSION HOLIDAY(1963)
Esther Kiss
MEN OF TOMORROW(1935, Brit.); BALL AT SAVOY(1936, Brit.); SILENT PLAYGROUND, THE(1964, Brit.), p

Manya Kiss
SUN SHINES, THE(1939, Hung.)
Manyi Kiss
DIALOGUE(1967, Hung.)
Ruth Kissane
BOY NAMED CHARLIE BROWN, A(1969), anim
Michael Kissaun
TRENCHCOAT(1983)
David I. Kissel
1984
BROADWAY DANNY ROSE(1984)
Charles Kissinger
ABBY(1974); SHEBA BABY(1975); GRIZZLY(1976)
Misc. Talkies
ASYLUM OF SATAN(1972); THREE ON A MEATHOOK(1973); ZEBRA KILLER, THE(1974)
Miriam Kissinger
DANGEROUS MONEY(1946), w; TRAP, THE(1947), w
Van Kissling [Vaclav Kyzlink]
FABULOUS WORLD OF JULES VERNE, THE(1961, Czech.)
Lee Kissman
CHAMELEON(1978)
Henri Kistemaeckers
KING OF THE RITZ(1933, Brit.), w
Henry Kistemaeckers
Silents
EYE FOR EYE(1918), w
Henry Kistemaeker
NIGHT IS OURS(1930, Fr.), w
Akemi Kita
DANGEROUS KISS, THE(1961, Jap.); MAN AGAINST MAN(1961, Jap.); ATRAGON(1965, Jap.); FIGHT FOR THE GLORY(1970, Jap.)
Masatake Kita
MAGIC BOY(1960, Jap.), anim
Ryuji Kita
EMPEROR AND A GENERAL, THE(1968, Jap.)
Ryusuke Kita
HOTSPRINGS HOLIDAY(1970, Jap.); PERFORMERS, THE(1970, Jap.)
Takeo Kita
SECRET SCROLLS(PART I) (1968, Jap.), art d, art d; GIGANTIS(1959, Jap./U.S.), art d; H-MAN, THE(1959, Jap.), art d; MOTHRA(1962, Jap.), art d; FRANKENSTEIN CONQUERS THE WORLD(1964, Jap./US), art d; GHIDRAH, THE THREE-HEADED MONSTER(1965, Jap.), art d; KING KONG ESCAPES(1968, Jap.), art d; DESTROY ALL MONSTERS(1969, Jap.), art d; LATITUDE ZERO(1969, U.S./Jap.), set d; MONSTER ZERO(1970, Jap.), art d; YOG-MONSTER FROM SPACE(1970, Jap.), art d
Tatsuo Kita
RODAN(1958, Jap.), art d
Sanae Kitabayashi
SONG FROM MY HEART, THE(1970, Jap.)
Tanie Kitabayashi
ENJO(1959, Jap.); ODD OBSESSION(1961, Jap.); INSECT WOMAN, THE(1964, Jap.)
Taniye Kitabayashi
HARP OF BURMA(1967, Jap.)
Yangi Kitadani
WALK, DON'T RUN(1966)
Tawny Kitaen
1984
PERILS OF GWENDOLINE, THE(1984, Fr.)
Yataro Kitagami
PERFORMERS, THE(1970, Jap.)
T. Kitagawa
ANATAHAN(1953, Jap.)
Fumie Kitahara
GIRL I ABANDONED, THE(1970, Jap.)
Yoshio Kitahara
GAMERA VERSUS GAOS(1967, Jap.)
Yoshiro Kitahara
BUDDHA(1965, Jap.); GAMERA THE INVINCIBLE(1966, Jap.)
Sei Kitaizumi
FRIENDLY KILLER, THE(1970, Jap.), ph
Eizo Kitamura
GOKE, BODYSNATCHER FROM HELL(1968, Jap.)
Kazuo Kitamura
INSECT WOMAN, THE(1964, Jap.); YEARNING(1964, Jap.); KURAGEJIMA-LEGENDS FROM A SOUTHERN ISLAND(1970, Jap.); TORA! TORA! TORA!(1970, U.S./Jap.); SUMMER SOLDIERS(1972, Jap.)
Tanie Kitamura
TUNNEL TO THE SUN(1968, Jap.)
Kinya Kitaoji
RIVER OF FOREVER(1967, Jap.); OUR SILENT LOVE(1969, Jap.); GLOWING AUTUMN(1981, Jap.)
Kinya Kitaoli
BAND OF ASSASSINS(1971, Jap.)
Joanna Kitau
WEST OF ZANZIBAR(1954, Brit.)
Johanna Kitau
IVORY HUNTER(1952, Brit.)
Akiyoshi Kitaura
HOTSPRINGS HOLIDAY(1970, Jap.)
Akira Kitazaki
GAMERA VERSUS VIRAS(1968, Jap), ph; GAMERA VERSUS GUIRON(1969, Jap.), ph; GAMERA VERSUS MONSTER K(1970, Jap.), ph
George Kitchel
IT SHOULD HAPPEN TO YOU(1954)
Cathy Kitchen
ANGELO MY LOVE(1983)
Dorothy Kitchen
Silents
BRONCHO TWISTER(1927); WAY OF ALL FLESH, THE(1927); BANTAM COWBOY, THE(1928); BREED OF THE SUNSETS(1928); FANGS OF THE WILD(1928)

Misc. Silents
RIDING RENEGADE, THE(1928)
Fred Kitchen
WILD BOY(1934, Brit.); MY BROTHER JONATHAN(1949, Brit.)
Fred Kitchen, Jr.
OLD MOTHER RILEY OVERSEAS(1943, Brit.); DEMOBBED(1944, Brit.); TAKE A POWDER(1953, Brit.); ONE GOOD TURN(1955, Brit.)
Jack Kitchen
NIGHT PARADE(1929, Brit.), ed; LAUGH AND GET RICH(1931), ed; PERFECT ALIBI, THE(1931, Brit.), ed; MELODY CRUISE(1933), ed; COCKEYED CAVALIERS(1934), ed
Silents
CAPTAIN CARELESS(1928), ed; ORPHAN OF THE SAGE(1928), ed; GUN LAW(1929), ed
Jan Kitchen
ANGELO MY LOVE(1983)
Kathy Kitchen
MUTATIONS, THE(1974, Brit.)
Lawrence Kitchen
PIMPERNEL SMITH(1942, Brit.); BAD LORD BYRON, THE(1949, Brit.), w
Michael Kitchen
UNMAN, WITTERING AND ZIGO(1971, Brit.); DRACULA A.D. 1972(1972, Brit.)
Mark Howard Kitchens, Jr.
CARNY(1980)
H. Milner Kitchin
Silents
WARNING, THE(1927), w
Jack Kitchin
FRAMED(1930), ed; PEACH O' RENO(1931), ed; AGE OF CONSENT(1932), ed; PENGUIN POOL MURDER, THE(1932), ed; ROADHOUSE MURDER, THE(1932), ed; WHAT PRICE HOLLYWOOD?(1932), ed; FLYING DOWN TO RIO(1933), ed; LITTLE WOMEN(1933), ed; LUCKY DEVILS(1933), ed; OUR BETTERS(1933), ed; PENNY PARADISE(1938, Brit.), p; COME ON GEORGE(1939, Brit.), p; TROUBLE BREWING(1939, Brit.), p; MINE OWN EXECUTIONER(1948, Brit.), p
John Kitchin
SECRET SERVICE(1931), ed
Laurence Kitchin
NORTH SEA PATROL(1939, Brit.); SALOON BAR(1940, Brit.)
Lawrence Kitchin
POISON PEN(1941, Brit.)
Milner Kitchin
ESCAPE(1930, Brit.), ed
Kithnou
CAREERS(1929)
Mlle. Kithnou
Silents
MARE NOSTRUM(1926)
Judy Kitky
CREMATORS, THE(1972), w
Cole Kitosch
AVENGER, THE(1966, Ital.)
Cole Kitosh [Alberto Dell'Acqua]
UP THE MACGREGORS(1967, Ital./Span.)
Martin Kitrosser
FRIDAY THE 13TH PART III(1982), w
1984
MEATBALLS PART II(1984), w
Ken Kitson
LITTLEST HORSE THIEVES, THE(1977)
May Kitson
Misc. Silents
BURNING QUESTION, THE(1919); FIRING LINE, THE(1919); FATHER TOM(1921); OTHER WOMEN'S CLOTHES(1922)
Eartha Kitt
NEW FACES(1954); ANNA LUCASTA(1958); MARK OF THE HAWK, THE(1958); ST. LOUIS BLUES(1958); SYNANON(1965); UNCLE TOM'S CABIN(1969, Fr./Ital./Ger./Yugo.); UP THE CHASTITY BELT(1971, Brit.); FRIDAY FOSTER(1975)
Bert Kittel
NEIGHBORS(1981)
Gerhard Kittler
DECISION BEFORE DAWN(1951); LOVE FEAST, THE(1966, Ger.)
Billy Kittridge
WORDS AND MUSIC(1929)
John Kitzmiller
VARIETY LIGHTS(1965, Ital.)
John Kitzmiller
TO LIVE IN PEACE(1947, Ital.); WITHOUT PITY(1949, Ital.); NAKED EARTH, THE(1958, Brit.); LOST SOULS(1961, Ital.); DR. NO(1962, Brit.); SERGEANT JIM(1962, Yugo.); REVOLT OF THE MERCENARIES(1964, Ital./Span.); SON OF CAPTAIN BLOOD, THE(1964, U.S./Ital./Span.); TIGER OF THE SEVEN SEAS(1964, Fr./Ital.); CAVE OF THE LIVING DEAD(1966, Yugo./Ger.); UNCLE TOM'S CABIN(1969, Fr./Ital./Ger./Yugo.)
Lois Kiuchi
WALK, DON'T RUN(1966)
Kivalina
Misc. Silents
KIVALINA OF THE ICE LANDS(1925)
Nancy Kivan
Misc. Talkies
DEADLY AND THE BEAUTIFUL(1974)
C.K. Kivari
STEEL FIST, THE(1952), w
Barry Kivel
1984
NATURAL, THE(1984)
Lilly Kivert
LOVELESS, THE(1982), prod d

Eve Kivi
DAY THE EARTH FROZE, THE(1959, Fin./USSR)
David Kivlin
CHARRIOTS OF FIRE(1981, Brit.)
Til Kiwe
LONGEST DAY, THE(1962); GREAT ESCAPE, THE(1963); HANNIBAL BROOKS(1969, Brit.); ODESSA FILE, THE(1974, Brit./Ger.)
Tile Kiwe
ONE, TWO, THREE(1961)
Kiwi
AMONG HUMAN WOLVES(1940 Brit.)
Blasio Kiyaga
NAKED EARTH, THE(1958, Brit.)
Nijiko Kiyokawa
TEAHOUSE OF THE AUGUST MOON, THE(1956); LOWER DEPTHS, THE(1962, Jap.); SNOW COUNTRY(1969, Jap.); VENGEANCE IS MINE(1980, Jap.)
1984
BALLAD OF NARAYAMA, THE(1984, Jap.)
Soji Kiyokawa
TATSU(1962, Jap.)
Tamae Kiyokawa
MY GEISHA(1962)
Bob Kizer
BATTLE BEYOND THE STARS(1980), ed
R.J. Kizer
TIMERIDER(1983), ed
Robert Kizer
GALAXY EXPRESS(1982, Jap.), ed
Robert J. Kizer
GALAXY OF TERROR(1981), ed; SPACE RAIDERS(1983), ed
1984
HAMBONE AND HILLIE(1984), ed
Seiichi Kizuka
ANGRY ISLAND(1960, Jap.), ph; BRIDGE TO THE SUN(1961), ph
Diana Kjaer
GEORGIA, GEORGIA(1972)
Helge Kjaerulff-Schmidt
LURE OF THE JUNGLE, THE(1970, Den.)
Morten Kjaerulff-Schmidt
WEEKEND(1964, Den.)
Palle Kjaerulff-Schmidt
WEEKEND(1964, Den.), d
Tine Kjaerulff-Schmidt
WEEKEND(1964, Den.)
Ingeborg Kjeldsen
WHEN THE GIRLS TAKE OVER(1962); SMOKEY AND THE BANDIT(1977)
Jim Kjelgaard
BIG RED(1962), w
Alf Kjellin
NIGHT IN JUNE, A(1940, Swed.); APPASSIONATA(1946, Swed.); TORMENT(1947, Swed.); AFFAIRS OF A MODEL(1952, Swed.); IRON MISTRESS, THE(1952); MY SIX CONVICTS(1952); JUGGLER, THE(1953); ILLICIT INTERLUDE(1954, Swed.); VICTORS, THE(1963); TWO LIVING, ONE DEAD(1964, Brit./Swed.); SHIP OF FOOLS(1965); ASSAULT ON A QUEEN(1966); ICE STATION ZEBRA(1968); MIDAS RUN(1969), d; MC MASTERS, THE(1970), d; ZANDY'S BRIDE(1974)
Lilli Kjellin
TRUE AND THE FALSE, THE(1955, Swed.)
Wic Kjellin
MY FATHER'S MISTRESS(1970, Swed.), ed; RAVEN'S END(1970, Swed.), ed
Wicl Kjellin
GIRLS, THE(1972, Swed.), ed
Ingvar Kjellson
SHAME(1968, Swed.); SHORT IS THE SUMMER(1968, Swed.); FLIGHT OF THE EAGLE(1983, Swed.)
Don Kjestrup
1984
CONSTANCE(1984, New Zealand)
Sidney Klaber
JOHNNY YUMA(1967, Ital.), ed
Jack Klaff
STAR WARS(1977); FOR YOUR EYES ONLY(1981)
Roy Klaffki
Silents
HER FIVE-FOOT HIGHNESS(1920), ph; HUMAN STUFF(1920), ph; INFAMOUS MISS REVELL, THE(1921), ph; ADORABLE DECEIVER, THE(1926), ph; QUEEN O' DIAMONDS(1926), w; WEDDING MARCH, THE(1927), ph
Eugen Klagemann
MARRIAGE IN THE SHADOWS(1948, Ger.), ph; MURDERERS AMONG US(1948, Ger.), ph; MERRY WIVES OF WINDSOR, THE(1952, Ger.), ph
Robert Klager
CLOSE-UP(1948), ed
William M. Klages
RECORD CITY(1978), ph
Thomas Klameth
HEIDI(1954, Switz.); HEIDI AND PETER(1955, Switz.)
Robert Klane
WHERE'S POPPA?(1970), w; EVERY LITTLE CROOK AND NANNY(1972), w; FIRE SALE(1977), w; THANK GOD IT'S FRIDAY(1978), d
1984
UNFAITHFULLY YOURS(1984), w
Francois Klanfer
CHICAGO 70(1970)
P. I. Klansky
MYSTERIOUS ISLAND(1941, USSR)
Alex Klapp
CURIOUS DR. HUMPP(1967, Arg.)
Barvara Klar
OFFENDERS, THE(1980)

Gary Klar
HERO AT LARGE(1980); TRADING PLACES(1983)
Norman Klar
HITCHHIKERS, THE(1972)
Hans Klardie
WOLFPEN PRINCIPLE, THE(1974, Can.), ph
Madelyn Klare
Silents
ALL WOMAN(1918)
G. Klaren
MANULESCU(1933, Ger.), w
Georg Klaren
WOZZECK(1962, E. Ger.), d&w
Dr. Georg C. Klaren
PILLARS OF SOCIETY(1936, Ger.), w
Gary Klarr
GLORIA(1980)
Eleonore Klarwein
PEPPERMINT SODA(1979, Fr.)
Phillip Klass
ILLIAC PASSION, THE(1968)
Tom Klassen
1984
OASIS, THE(1984), w
R. Klatchkin
MY FATHER'S HOUSE(1947, Palestine)
Rafael Klatchkin
TWO KOUNEY LEMELS(1966, Israel)
Raphael Klatchkin
TEL AVIV TAXI(1957, Israel)
Seymour Klate
RIVER NIGER, THE(1976), prod d; SOMEWHERE IN TIME(1980), prod d
Raphel Klatschkin
FLYING MATCHMAKER, THE(1970, Israel)
Leon Klatzken
LONESOME TRAIL, THE(1955), m; SILVER STAR, THE(1955), m
David Klatzkin
KING SOLOMON OF BROADWAY(1935), md
Leon Klatzkin
TALES OF ROBIN HOOD(1951), m; MR. WALKIE TALKIE(1952), m; TWO-GUN LADY(1956), m; FIEND WHO WALKED THE WEST, THE(1958), m; GO, JOHNNY, GO!(1959), m
Geitan Klauber
GREAT ARMORED CAR SWINDLE, THE(1964)
Gertan Klauber
DON'T PANIC CHAPS!(1959, Brit.); KITCHEN, THE(1961, Brit.); THREE ON A SPREE(1961, Brit.); CARRY ON CLEO(1964, Brit.); CARRY ON SPYING(1964, Brit.); DATELINE DIAMONDS(1966, Brit.); DEADLY AFFAIR, THE(1967, Brit.); BEFORE WINTER COMES(1969, Brit.); CARRY ON HENRY VIII(1970, Brit.); CRY OF THE BANSHEE(1970, Brit.); WUTHERING HEIGHTS(1970, Brit.); PIED PIPER, THE(1972, Brit.); OPERATION DAYBREAK(1976, U.S./Brit./Czech.); SEVEN-PER-CENT SOLUTION, THE(1977, Brit.); OCTOPUSSY(1983, Brit.)
1984
TOP SECRET!(1984)
Gerten Klauber
FOLLOW THAT CAMEL(1967, Brit.)
Marcel Klauber
I'M FROM ARKANSAS(1944), w; GAY BLADES(1946), w; RED BALL EXPRESS(1952), w; CODE TWO(1953), w; CARNIVAL STORY(1954), w; CIRCUS OF LOVE(1958, Ger.), w; GIRL IN THE WOODS(1958), w
Marcy Klauber
JUNGLE BRIDE(1933), m; WOMAN IN THE DARK(1934), w; GIGOLETTE(1935), m; FOLLIES GIRL(1943), w
Georg Klaup
SOMEWHERE IN BERLIN(1949, E. Ger.), p
Henry Klaus
Silents
FOUR HORSEMEN OF THE APOCALYPSE, THE(1921)
Jack Klaus
HANS CHRISTIAN ANDERSEN(1952)
Steffen Klaus
NAKED AMONG THE WOLVES(1967, Ger.)
Eric Klauss
HUNS, THE(1962, Fr./Ital.), w
Walter Klaven
SPELL OF THE HYPNOTIST(1956)
Walter Klavun
MOB, THE(1951); IT SHOULD HAPPEN TO YOU(1954); OKEFENOKEE(1960); LISETTE(1961); SILENT NIGHT, BLOODY NIGHT(1974); BRINK'S JOB, THE(1978); SEDUCTION OF JOE TYNAN, THE(1979)
Goldie Kleban
MY FAIR LADY(1964)
A. Klebanova
GORDEYEV FAMILY, THE(1961, U.S.S.R.), ed
Damon Klebroyd
HORROR OF PARTY BEACH, THE(1964)
Joe Klecko
SMOKEY AND THE BANDIT II(1980); CANNONBALL RUN, THE(1981)
Helmut Klee
SLAVERS(1977, Ger.), spec eff
Lawrence L. Klee
LINEUP, THE(1958), w
Richard Klee
SCREAM OF FEAR(1961, Brit.); IMPACT(1963, Brit.)
Theresa Klee
QUEEN HIGH(1930)
Walter Klee
CONFESSIONS OF A ROGUE(1948, Fr.), titles; SAVAGE BRIGADE(1948, Fr.), ed; RING AROUND THE CLOCK(1953, Ital.), ed

Helen Kleeb
MAGNIFICENT OBSESSION(1954); WITNESS TO MURDER(1954); DAY OF FURY, A(1956); FRIENDLY PERSUASION(1956); THERE'S ALWAYS TOMORROW(1956); CURSE OF THE UNDEAD(1959); CAGE OF EVIL(1960); YOUNG SAVAGES, THE(1961); MANCHURIAN CANDIDATE, THE(1962); HUSH... HUSH, SWEET CHARLOTTE(1964); SEVEN DAYS IN MAY(1964); SEX AND THE SINGLE GIRL(1964); HALLELUJAH TRAIL, THE(1965); FORTUNE COOKIE, THE(1966); FITZWILLY(1967); HALLS OF ANGER(1970); STAR SPANGLED GIRL(1971)

Gunter Kleeman
I SPIT ON YOUR GRAVE(1983)

Nicole Kleeman
1984
PLOUGHMAN'S LUNCH, THE(1984, Brit.)

Danny Klega
PRIZE, THE(1963); 36 HOURS(1965); RUSSIANS ARE COMING, THE RUSSIANS ARE COMING, THE(1966)

Darine Klega
GREAT MUPPET CAPER, THE(1981)

Tony Kleiboer
DR. FRANKENSTEIN ON CAMPUS(1970, Can.)

Karen Kleiman
DRIVER, THE(1978)

Gay Kleimenhapen
DIFFERENT STORY, A(1978)

Adelaide Klein
NAKED CITY, THE(1948); C-MAN(1949); ENFORCER, THE(1951); TROUBLEMAKER, THE(1964)

Al Klein
ONE YEAR LATER(1933); 365 NIGHTS IN HOLLYWOOD(1934); OH, YOU BEAUTIFUL DOLL(1949)

Aladar Klein
NORSEMAN, THE(1978), ed

Alan Klein
WHAT A CRAZY WORLD(1963, Brit.), a, w

Alexander Klein
COUNTERFEIT TRAITOR, THE(1962), d&w

Allen Klein
WITHOUT EACH OTHER(1962), p; MRS. BROWN, YOU'VE GOT A LOVELY DAUGHTER(1968, Brit.), p; HOLY MOUNTAIN, THE(1973, U.S./Mex.), p; GREEK TYCOON, THE(1978), p

Anne Klein
HAPPY MOTHER'S DAY... LOVE, GEORGE(1973), cos

Arthur Klein
LOVESICK(1983)

Bernard Klein
ZITA(1968, Fr.)

Bob Klein
Silents
LIVE WIRES(1921); DO AND DARE(1922); ALIAS THE NIGHT WIND(1923)

Calvin Klein
PLAYERS(1979), cos

Charles Klein
LION AND THE MOUSE, THE(1928), w; GAMBLERS, THE(1929), w; PLEASURE CRAZED(1929), d
Silents
DAUGHTERS OF MEN(1914), w; THIRD DEGREE, THE(1926), w; AUCTIONEER, THE(1927), w; SIN SISTER, THE(1929), d
Misc. Silents
BLINDFOLD(1928), d

Curly Klein
SEX AND THE SINGLE GIRL(1964)

Danny Klein
MIKEY AND NICKY(1976)

David Klein
POLYESTER(1981)

Deborah Ann Klein
MELVIN AND HOWARD(1980)

Dick Klein
LIFE BEGINS IN COLLEGE(1937)

Elinor Klein
STILL OF THE NIGHT(1982)

Elizabeth Klein
1984
VAMPING(1984)

Erik S. Klein
NAKED AMONG THE WOLVES(1967, Ger.)

Fred Klein
HARLOW(1965)

Gerald Klein
ZELIG(1983)

Gerard Klein
LA PASSANTE(1983, Fr./Ger.)

Hal Klein
CONVICT STAGE(1965), p; FORT COURAGEOUS(1965), p; WAR PARTY(1965), p; AMBUSH BAY(1966), p; KILL A DRAGON(1967), p; MORE DEAD THAN ALIVE(1968), p; IMPASSE(1969), p; ANGEL UNCHAINED(1970), p; BARQUERO(1970), p

Herbert Klein
LOVE IS A HEADACHE(1938), w

I. W. Klein
FRONT, THE(1976); MAGIC(1978); ON THE RIGHT TRACK(1981)

Irwin Klein
BIG GAME, THE(1936)

Jacques Klein
PRICE OF FLESH, THE(1962, Fr.), ph

Jaime Klein
PANDEMONIUM(1982), w

Janine Klein
MISTER FREEDOM(1970, Fr.), cos

Jean-Pierre Klein
LAST METRO, THE(1981, Fr.); NORTH STAR, THE(1982, Fr.); L'ETOILE DU NORD(1983, Fr.)

John Klein
TAKING OFF(1971), w

Jordan Klein
HELLO DOWN THERE(1969), ph

Jordon Klein
JOE PANTHER(1976), ph

Julius Klein
WANTED: JANE TURNER(1936), w
Misc. Silents
CITY OF TEMPTATION(1929, Brit.)

Karl-Heinz Klein
CHRONICLE OF ANNA MAGDALENA BACH(1968, Ital., Ger.)

Kathleen Jean Klein
1984
WINDY CITY(1984)

Larry Klein
INVITATION TO A GUNFIGHTER(1964), w
Misc. Talkies
ADVERSARY, THE(1970), d

Luce Klein
YO YO(1967, Fr.)

Marcus G. Klein
NOBODY'S PERFECT(1968), tech adv

Nita Klein
MURIEL(1963, Fr./Ital.)

Patsy Klein
LILITH(1964)

Paul Klein
Silents
NIGHT CRY, THE(1926), w

Philip Klein
RIVER, THE(1928), w; STREET ANGEL(1928), w; OH, FOR A MAN!(1930), w; BLACK CAMEL, THE(1931), w; CHARLIE CHAN CARRIES ON(1931), w; HUSH MONEY(1931), w; RIDERS OF THE PURPLE SAGE(1931), w; SPIDER, THE(1931), w; BACHELOR'S AFFAIRS(1932), w; GAY CABALLERO, THE(1932), w; HAT CHECK GIRL(1932), w; RAINBOW TRAIL(1932), w; TOO BUSY TO WORK(1932), w; TRIAL OF VIVIENNE WARE, THE(1932), w; HOT PEPPER(1933), w; PILGRIMAGE(1933), w; BABY, TAKE A BOW(1934), w; STAND UP AND CHEER(1934 80m FOX bw), w; DANTE'S INFERNO(1935), w; ELINOR NORTON(1935), w; PIER 13(1940), w
Silents
SOCIAL HIGHWAYMAN, THE(1926), w; ANKLES PREFERRED(1927), w; IS ZAT SO?(1927), w; DON'T MARRY(1928), w; FOUR SONS(1928), w

Phillip Klein
CHANDU THE MAGICIAN(1932), w; CHARLIE CHAN'S CHANCE(1932), w; I LOVED YOU WEDNESDAY(1933), w

Ray Klein
1984
OH GOD! YOU DEVIL(1984), spec eff

Rita Klein
ROVER, THE(1967, Ital.)

Robert Klein
THIRTEENTH GUEST, THE(1932); LANDLORD, THE(1970); OWL AND THE PUSSYCAT, THE(1970); PURSUIT OF HAPPINESS, THE(1971); RIVALS(1972); HOOPER(1978); BELL JAR, THE(1979); NOBODY'S PERFEKT(1981); STRIPES(1981); LAST UNICORN, THE(1982)
Silents
BRIDE'S SILENCE, THE(1917); ANN'S FINISH(1918); BLUSHING BRIDE, THE(1921); DANTE'S INFERNO(1924); ANCIENT MARINER, THE(1925)
Misc. Silents
SOULS IN PAWN(1917); SOUTHERN PRIDE(1917); MARRIED IN HASTE(1919); LADY FROM LONGACRE, THE(1921)

Sally Klein
1984
EYES OF FIRE(1984)

Stewart Klein
DEATHTRAP(1982)

Tim Klein
SOLDIER, THE(1982)

Wally Klein
HARD TO GET(1938), w; INDIANAPOLIS SPEEDWAY(1939), w; OKLAHOMA KID, THE(1939), w; THEY DIED WITH THEIR BOOTS ON(1942), w

William Klein
PEOPLE WILL TALK(1951); PURPLE HEART DIARY(1951); MISTER FREEDOM(1970, Fr.), d&w

William R. Klein
VOODOO TIGER(1952); FORTY-NINTH MAN, THE(1953); SKY COMMANDO(1953)

Wolfgang Klein
AMERICAN SUCCESS COMPANY, THE(1980)

Robert Klein-Lork
BLUE ANGEL, THE(1930, Ger.)

Rudolf Klein-Rogge
WORLD WITHOUT A MASK, THE(1934, Ger.); TESTAMENT OF DR. MABUSE, THE(1943, Ger.)
Silents
METROPOLIS(1927, Ger.); SPIES(1929, Ger.)
Misc. Silents
MOVING IMAGE, THE(1920, Ger.); FOUR AROUND THE WOMAN(1921, Ger.); DR. MABUSE, THE GAMBLER(1922, Ger.); STONE RIDER, THE(1923, Ger.)

Rudolph Klein-Rogge
INTERMEZZO(1937, Ger.)
Silents
CABINET OF DR. CALIGARI, THE(1921, Ger.); KRIEMHILD'S REVENGE(1924, Ger.)

Misc. Silents
DESTINY(1921, Ger.)
Willy A. Kleinau
CAPTAIN FROM KOEPENICK, THE(1956, Ger.)
Henry Kleinbach
BIG BROWN EYES(1936)
Henry Kleinbach [Brandon]
SIGN OF THE CROSS, THE(1932); BABES IN TOYLAND(1934); PREVIEW MURDER MYSTERY(1936)
Avi Kleinberger
1984
AMBASSADOR, THE(1984); MISSING IN ACTION(1984)
David Kleinberger
WACKY WORLD OF DR. MORGUS, THE(1962)
Eberhard Kleindorff
AMONG VULTURES(1964, Ger./Ital./Fr./Yugo.), w
George Kleine
Silents
DANGER SIGNAL, THE(1915), d; KEEP MOVING(1915), d
Misc. Silents
JULIUS CAESAR(1914, Ital.), d; NAIDRA, THE DREAM WOMAN(1914, Ger.), d; DUBARRY(1915), d
Burt Kleiner
YOU BETTER WATCH OUT(1980), p
Harry Kleiner
FALLEN ANGEL(1945), w; STREET WITH NO NAME, THE(1948), w; KANGAROO(1952), w; RED SKIES OF MONTANA(1952), w; MISS SADIE THOMPSON(1953), w; SALOME(1953), w; CARMEN JONES(1954), w; HOUSE OF BAMBOO(1955), w; VIOLENT MEN, THE(1955), w; GARMENT JUNGLE, THE(1957), p, w; CRY TOUGH(1959), p, w; RABBIT TRAP, THE(1959), p; ICE PALACE(1960), w; FEVER IN THE BLOOD, A(1961), w; FANTASTIC VOYAGE(1966), w; BULLITT(1968), w; MADIGAN(1968), w; LE MANS(1971), w
Sergio Kleiner
INCREDIBLE INVASION, THE(1971, Mex./U.S.)
Towje Kleiner
ODESSA FILE, THE(1974, Brit./Ger.)
Mary Ellen Kleinhall
PUNISHMENT PARK(1971)
Nick Kleinholtz
MY BROTHER HAS BAD DREAMS(1977)
Nick Kleinholtz III
SIGN OF AQUARIUS(1970)
Nick Kleinholz III
SCREAM BLOODY MURDER(1972)
A. Kleinman
FORCED ENTRY(1975), ph
Dan Kleinman
RAGE(1972), w
Manny Kleinmuntz
TO BE OR NOT TO BE(1983)
Peter Kleinow
SPACEHUNTER: ADVENTURES IN THE FORBIDDEN ZONE(1983), spec eff
1984
TERMINATOR, THE(1984), spec eff
Frank E. Kleinschmidt
Misc. Silents
PRIMITIVE LOVE(1927), d
Carl Kleinschmitt
MIDDLE AGE CRAZY(1980, Can.), w
Randal Kleiser
GREASE(1978), d; BLUE LAGOON, THE(1980), p&d; RICH AND FAMOUS(1981); SUMMER LOVERS(1982), d&w
1984
GRANDVIEW, U.S.A.(1984), d
Randall Kleiser
STREET PEOPLE(1976, U.S./Ital.), w
Renie Kleivdal
1984
KAMILLA(1984, Norway)
Harry Klekas
MAN OR GUN(1958)
Maggie Klekas
1984
FLASH OF GREEN, A(1984)
M. Klemens
TWO ARE GUILTY(1964, Fr.)
Otto Klement
ROMANCE AND RICHES(1937, Brit.), p; TWO WHO DARED(1937, Brit.), p; FANTASTIC VOYAGE(1966), w
Catharina Klemm
PARSIFAL(1983, Fr.)
Judith Klemm
PARSIFAL(1983, Fr.)
Werner Klemperer
WRONG MAN, THE(1956)
Werner Klemperer
DEATH OF A SCOUNDREL(1956); FLIGHT TO HONG KONG(1956); FIVE STEPS TO DANGER(1957); ISTANBUL(1957); KISS THEM FOR ME(1957); GODDESS, THE(1958); HIGH COST OF LOVING, THE(1958); HOUSEBOAT(1958); JUDGMENT AT NUREMBERG(1961); OPERATION EICHMANN(1961); ESCAPE FROM EAST BERLIN(1962); YOUNGBLOOD HAWKE(1964); SHIP OF FOOLS(1965); WICKED DREAMS OF PAULA SCHULTZ, THE(1968)
John Klempner
GIVE MY REGARDS TO BROADWAY(1948), w; LETTER TO THREE WIVES, A(1948), w; THREE FOR JAMIE DAWN(1956), w
Margaret Klenck
1984
HARD CHOICES(1984)

Walter Klenhard
1984
SCARRED(1984)
Norman Klenman
NOW THAT APRIL'S HERE(1958, Can.), p, w; SWISS CONSPIRACY, THE(1976, U.S./Ger.), w
Jaroslav Klenot
LEMONADE JOE(1966, Czech.)
Hermine Klepac
DOUBLE DOOR(1934), w
V. Klepatskaya
TSAR'S BRIDE, THE(1966, USSR)
Gerald Kleppel
SWEET LOVE, BITTER(1967), ed
G. Klering
RAINBOW, THE(1944, USSR)
Rose Marie Klespitz
STARDUST(1974, Brit.)
Michael Kless
PANDEMONIUM(1982)
Karen Klett
RED SKY AT MORNING(1971)
Elisabeth Klettenhauer
TONIO KROGER(1968, Fr./Ger.)
Max Kletter
Misc. Talkies
SONG OF SONGS(1935)
Richard Kletter
BLACK STALLION RETURNS, THE(1983), w; NEVER CRY WOLF(1983), w
Benson Kleve
Silents
NETS OF DESTINY(1924, Brit.)
Joan Kleven
HARD TIMES(1975)
Max Kleven
BILLY THE KID VS. DRACULA(1966); PERILS OF PAULINE, THE(1967), a, stunts; COTTON COMES TO HARLEM(1970), stunts; DILLINGER(1973), stunts; 99 AND 44/100% DEAD(1974); HARD TIMES(1975), a, stunts; SILENT MOVIE(1976), stunts; RUCKUS(1981), d&w
1984
HOT DOG...THE MOVIE(1984), stunts; PROTOCOL(1984), stunts
Max Klevin
THREE TOUGH GUYS(1974, U.S./Ital.)
Dorothy Klewer
FILE ON THELMA JORDAN, THE(1950)
Marian Kley
ETERNAL SUMMER(1961), ed
Jerzy Kleyn
CONDUCTOR, THE(1981, Pol.)
Ronald Kleyweg
SKATETOWN, U.S.A.(1979)
Paul Klib
TWICE A MAN(1964)
Roland Klick
JIMMY ORPHEUS(1966, Ger.), d&w, m&ed
Rudolph Klicks
FOUR COMPANIONS, THE(1938, Ger.)
E. H. Klienert
I'M FROM ARKANSAS(1944), p
Erwin Klietsch
GIRL FROM THE MARSH CROFT, THE(1935, Ger.)
Gary Kliger
NORMAN LOVES ROSE(1982, Aus.)
Ann Kligge
AMERICAN SUCCESS COMPANY, THE(1980)
Paul Kligman
WILLIE MCBEAN AND HIS MAGIC MACHINE(1965, U.S./Jap.)
Benjamin Klime
PRESCOTT KID, THE(1936), ph
A. Klimenko
CLEAR SKIES(1963, USSR), spec eff; OPTIMISTIC TRAGEDY, THE(1964, USSR), spec eff
Alexandre Klimenko
MATTER OF DAYS, A(1969, Fr./Czech.)
Susan Klimist
BACKLASH(1947)
Arkady Klimov
STORM PLANET(1962, USSR), ph
E. Klimov
WELCOME KOSTYA!(1965, USSR), d
P. Klimov
SANDU FOLLOWS THE SUN(1965, USSR), makeup
Natalya Klimova
HYPERBOLOID OF ENGINEER GARIN, THE(1965, USSR)
Leon Klimovsky
DESERT WARRIOR(1961 Ital./Span.), d; DR. JEKYLL AND THE WOLFMAN(1971, Span.), d; VAMPIRE'S NIGHT ORGY, THE(1973, Span./Ital.), d; I HATE MY BODY(1975, Span./Switz.), d, w; SAGA OF DRACULA, THE(1975, Span.), d
Leon Klimovsky [Leon Klim]
WEREWOLF VS. THE VAMPIRE WOMAN, THE(1970, Span./Ger.), d
Michael Klinbell
SHAPE OF THINGS TO COME, THE(1979, Can.)
A. A. Kline
RACKETEER, THE(1929), w; RICH PEOPLE(1929), w; WHAT A MAN(1930), w
Barbara Kline
Misc. Talkies
HENRY'S NIGHT IN(1969)

Ben Kline

LAST OF THE LONE WOLF(1930), ph; RANGE FEUD, THE(1931), ph; CALIFORNIA TRAIL, THE(1933), ph; KING OF THE WILD HORSES, THE(1934), ph; COLORADO TRAIL(1938), ph; CYCLONE PRAIRIE RANGERS(1944), d; ARSON SQUAD(1945), ph; DON RICARDO RETURNS(1946), ph; JUDGE, THE(1949), ph

Misc. Talkies

SADDLE LEATHER LAW(1944), d

Silents

RED LANE, THE(1920), ph; NIGHT HORSEMAN, THE(1921), ph; CHASING THE MOON(1922), ph; SKY HIGH(1922), ph; PURE GRIT(1923), ph; OUTLAW'S DAUGHTER, THE(1925), ph; SENSATION SEEKERS(1927), ph

Benjamin Kline

PAINTED FACES(1929), ph; WOMAN TO WOMAN(1929), ph; JOURNEY'S END(1930), ph; PEACOCK ALLEY(1930), ph; TROOPERS THREE(1930), ph; BRANDED(1931), ph; DARING DANGER(1932), ph; END OF THE TRAIL(1932), ph; FIGHTING FOOL, THE(1932), ph; FIGHTING MARSHAL, THE(1932), ph; FINAL EDITION(1932), ph; HELLO TROUBLE(1932), ph; LAST MAN(1932), ph; MC KENNA OF THE MOUNTED(1932), ph; RIDIN' FOR JUSTICE(1932), ph; RIDING TORNADO, THE(1932), ph; SHOTGUN PASS(1932), ph; SOUTH OF THE RIO GRANDE(1932), ph; TEXAS CYCLONE(1932), ph; TWO-FISTED LAW(1932), ph; WAR CORRESPONDENT(1932), ph; EAST OF FIFTH AVE.(1933), ph; HOLD THE PRESS(1933), ph; MY WOMAN(1933), ph; PAROLE GIRL(1933), ph; POLICE CAR 17(1933), ph; STATE TROOPER(1933), ph; WHEN STRANGERS MARRY(1933), ph; WOMAN I STOLE, THE(1933), ph; WRECKER, THE(1933), ph; FOG(1934), ph; HELL BENT FOR LOVE(1934), ph; HELL CAT, THE(1934), ph; I'LL FIX IT(1934), ph; LET'S FALL IN LOVE(1934), ph; LINEUP, THE(1934), ph; NINTH GUEST, THE(1934), ph; PARTY'S OVER, THE(1934), ph; SHADOWS OF SING SING(1934), ph; WHIRLPOOL(1934), ph; WHOM THE GODS DESTROY(1934), ph; AWAKENING OF JIM BURKE(1935), ph; GALLANT DEFENDER(1935), ph; GUARD THAT GIRL(1935), ph; IN SPITE OF DANGER(1935), ph; LAW BEYOND THE RANGE(1935), ph; MEN OF THE HOUR(1935), ph; SUPERSPEED(1935), ph; WHITE LIES(1935), ph; PRIDE OF THE MARINES(1936), ph; ALL-AMERICAN SWEETHEART(1937), ph; DANGEROUS ADVENTURE, A(1937), ph; FRAME-UP THE(1937), ph; GAME THAT KILLS, THE(1937), ph; SPEED TO SPARE(1937), ph; CALL OF THE ROCKIES(1938), ph; EXTORTION(1938), ph; JUVENILE COURT(1938), ph; LAW OF THE PLAINS(1938), ph; LITTLE MISS ROUGHNECK(1938), ph; SOUTH OF ARIZONA(1938), ph; WEST OF CHEYENNE(1938), ph; WOMEN IN PRISON(1938), ph; HOMICIDE BUREAU(1939), ph; KONGA, THE WILD STALLION(1939), ph; MAN FROM SUNDOWN, THE(1939), ph; MAN THEY COULD NOT HANG, THE(1939), ph; WOMAN IS THE JUDGE, A(1939), ph; BABIES FOR SALE(1940), ph; BEFORE I HANG(1940), ph; CAFE HOSTESS(1940), ph; CONVICTED WOMAN(1940), ph; FIVE LITTLE PEPPERS IN TROUBLE(1940), ph; ISLAND OF DOOMED MEN(1940), ph; MAN WITH NINE LIVES, THE(1940), ph; MEN WITHOUT SOULS(1940), ph; MY SON IS GUILTY(1940), ph; NOBODY'S CHILDREN(1940), ph; OUT WEST WITH THE PEPPERS(1940), ph; SCANDAL SHEET(1940), ph; BIG BOSS, THE(1941), ph; KING OF DODGE CITY(1941), ph; MEDICO OF PAINTED SPRINGS, THE(1941), ph; NORTH FROM LONE STAR(1941), ph; PRAIRIE STRANGER(1941), ph; RIDERS OF THE BADLANDS(1941), ph; THUNDER OVER THE PRAIRIE(1941), ph; BAD MEN OF THE HILLS(1942), ph; LAWLESS PLAINSMEN(1942), ph; LONE STAR VIGILANTES, THE(1942), ph; RIDERS OF THE NORTHLAND(1942), ph; FIGHTING BUCKAROO, THE(1943), ph; HAIL TO THE RANGERS(1943), ph; LAW OF THE NORTHWEST(1943), ph; RIDERS OF THE NORTHWEST MOUNTED(1943), ph; ROBIN HOOD OF THE RANGE(1943), ph; SILVER CITY RAIDERS(1943), ph; EVER SINCE VENUS(1944), ph; RIDING WEST(1944), ph; SHE'S A SOLDIER TOO(1944), ph; SHE'S A SWEETHEART(1944), ph; SUNDOWN VALLEY(1944), d; LET'S GO STEADY(1945), ph; TAHITI NIGHTS(1945), ph; TEN CENTS A DANCE(1945), ph; DANGEROUS MILLIONS(1946), ph; DEADLINE FOR MURDER(1946), ph; JOE PALOOKA, CHAMP(1946), ph; STRANGE JOURNEY(1946), ph; BACKLASH(1947), ph; CRIMSON KEY, THE(1947), ph; DANGEROUS YEARS(1947), ph; INVISIBLE WALL, THE(1947), ph; JEWELS OF BRANDENBURG(1947), ph; ROSES ARE RED(1947), ph; SECOND CHANCE(1947), ph; SHOOT TO KILL(1947), ph; ARTHUR TAKES OVER(1948), ph; FIGHTING BACK(1948), ph; HALF PAST MIDNIGHT(1948), ph; LAST OF THE WILD HORSES(1948), ph; NIGHT WIND(1948), ph; APACHE CHIEF(1949), ph; MISS MINK OF 1949(1949), ph; OMOO OMOO, THE SHARK GOD(1949), ph; TREASURE OF MONTE CRISTO(1949), ph; TROUBLE PREFERRED(1949), ph; TUCSON(1949), ph; EVERYBODY'S DANCIN'(1950), ph; HOLIDAY RHYTHM(1950), ph; OPERATION HAYLIFT(1950), ph; BLADES OF THE MUSKETEERS(1953), ph; NO ESCAPE(1953), ph

Misc. Talkies

SAGEBRUSH HEROES(1945), d

Silents

WOLF LAW(1922), ph

Benjamin H. Kline

SON OF DAVY CROCKETT, THE(1941), ph; DETOUR(1945), ph; HOW DO YOU DO?(1946), ph; I RING DOORBELLS(1946), ph; DANGER STREET(1947), ph; CHA-CHA-CHA BOOM(1956), w; DON'T KNOCK THE ROCK(1956), ph; MIAMI EXPOSE(1956), ph; ROCK AROUND THE CLOCK(1956), ph; RUMBLE ON THE DOCKS(1956), ph; SECRET OF TREASURE MOUNTAIN(1956), ph; CALYPSO HEAT WAVE(1957), ph; ESCAPE FROM SAN QUENTIN(1957), ph; GIANT CLAW, THE(1957), ph; MAN WHO TURNED TO STONE, THE(1957), ph; NIGHT THE WORLD EXPLODED, THE(1957), ph; TIJUANA STORY, THE(1957), ph; UTAH BLAINE(1957), ph; ZOMBIES OF MORA TAU(1957), ph; BADMAN'S COUNTRY(1958), ph; CRASH LANDING(1958), ph; GOING STEADY(1958), ph; WORLD WAS HIS JURY, THE(1958), ph; MUNSTER, GO HOME(1966), ph

Benjamin N. Kline

CLUB HAVANA(1946), ph

Benjamine Kline

MAN TRAILER, THE(1934), ph; WESTBOUND MAIL(1937), ph

Bob Kline

FACE ON THE BARROOM FLOOR, THE(1932), ph; PLUNDERERS OF PAINTED FLATS(1959)

Brady Kline

PAINTED DESERT, THE(1931); BLONDE VENUS(1932); PHANTOM EXPRESS, THE(1932)

Brenda Kline

SECRET EVIDENCE(1941), w

Dick Kline

ENTER MADAME(1935)

Edward F. Kline

CRAZY HOUSE(1943), d

Elmer L. Kline

HAMMETT(1982)

Gerald Kline

EYES OF LAURA MARS(1978)

Gerald M. Kline

1984

FALLING IN LOVE(1984)

Herbert Kline

YOUTH RUNS WILD(1944), w; BOY, A GIRL, AND A DOG, A(1946), d, w; MY FATHER'S HOUSE(1947, Palestine), p, d; ILLEGAL ENTRY(1949), w; KID FROM CLEVELAND, THE(1949), d, w; FIGHTER, THE(1952), d, w; PRINCE OF PIRATES(1953), w

Issy Kline

GOLDEN GLOVES STORY, THE(1950)

Jack Kline

INVASION(1965, Brit.), spec eff

James Kline

COMES A HORSEMAN(1978); ELECTRIC HORSEMAN, THE(1979); TOM HORN(1980)

Jim Kline

DESTRUCTORS, THE(1968); PANIC IN THE CITY(1968)

John Kline

YOUNG DYNAMITE(1937), ph

Kevin Kline

SOPHIE'S CHOICE(1982); BIG CHILL, THE(1983); PIRATES OF PENZANCE, THE(1983)

Penjamin Kline

RENDEZVOUS 24(1946), ph

Richard Kline

CHAMBER OF HORRORS(1966), ph; HANG'EM HIGH(1968), ph; GAILY, GAILY(1969), ph; KOTCH(1971), ph; MECHANIC, THE(1972), ph; HARRAD SUMMER, THE(1974), ph; FIREPOWER(1979, Brit.), ph; TILT(1979), ph

Richard H. Kline

CAMELOT(1967), ph; THE BOSTON STRANGLER, THE(1968), ph; BACKTRACK(1969), ph; DREAM OF KINGS, A(1969), ph; MOONSHINE WAR, THE(1970), ph; ANDROMEDA STRAIN, THE(1971), ph; BLACK GUNN(1972), ph; HAMMERSMITH IS OUT(1972), ph; WHEN THE LEGENDS DIE(1972), ph; BATTLE FOR THE PLANET OF THE APES(1973), ph; DON IS DEAD, THE(1973), ph; HARRAD EXPERIMENT, THE(1973), ph; SOYLENT GREEN(1973), ph; MR. MAJESTYK(1974), ph; TERMINAL MAN, THE(1974), ph; MANDINGO(1975), ph; KING KONG(1976), ph; WON TON TON, THE DOG WHO SAVED HOLLYWOOD(1976), ph; FURY, THE(1978), ph; WHO'LL STOP THE RAIN?(1978), ph; STAR TREK: THE MOTION PICTURE(1979), ph; COMPETITION, THE(1980), ph; TOUCHED BY LOVE(1980), ph; BODY HEAT(1981), ph; DEATH WISH II(1982), ph; BREATHLESS(1983), ph; DEAL OF THE CENTURY(1983), ph; MAN, WOMAN AND CHILD(1983), ph

1984

ALL OF ME(1984), ph; HARD TO HOLD(1984), ph

Robert Kline

MELODY OF THE PLAINS(1937), ph; PRIDE OF THE ARMY(1942), ph; LITTLEST HOBO, THE(1958)

1984

NIGHT PATROL(1984)

Steve Kline

BORDERLINE(1980), w

Val Kline

BEACH GIRLS(1982)

Wally Kline

SKIPALONG ROSENBLOOM(1951), p

William Kline

COVER GIRL(1944); IT HAPPENED ON 5TH AVENUE(1947)

Alex Kliner

MAN, A WOMAN, AND A BANK, A(1979, Can.); FIRST BLOOD(1982)

Leland Klinetop

RED RUNS THE RIVER(1963)

Buddy Kling

GREAT TEXAS DYNAMITE CHASE, THE(1976)

Howard Kling

1984

VAMPING(1984), p, prod d

Sazon Kling

Misc. Silents

MOHICAN'S DAUGHTER, THE(1922)

Valery Kling

BROKEN ENGLISH(1981)

Dawn Klingberg

LONELY HEARTS(1983, Aus.)

1984

MAN OF FLOWERS(1984, Aus.)

Ray Klinge

JUNIOR MISS(1945); THAT HAGEN GIRL(1947)

Heinz Klingenberg

MAGIC FIRE(1956)

Brendan Klinger

SOMETHING WICKED THIS WAY COMES(1983)

Judson Klinger

ENDANGERED SPECIES(1982), w

Kurt Klinger

ROMAN HOLIDAY(1953)

Michael Klinger

BLACK TORMENT, THE(1965, Brit.), p; CUL-DE-SAC(1966, Brit.), p; BABY LOVE(1969, Brit.), w; GET CARTER(1971, Brit.), p; PULP(1972, Brit.), p; SOMETHING TO HIDE(1972, Brit.), p; GOLD(1974, Brit.), p; SHOUT AT THE DEVIL(1976, Brit.), p; TOMORROW NEVER COMES(1978, Brit./Can.), p

Paul Klinger

MARRIAGE IN THE SHADOWS(1948, Ger.); RED-DRAGON(1967, Ital./Ger./US)

Ruth Klinger
LORDS OF FLATBUSH, THE(1974)
Warner Klinger
JOURNEY'S END(1930)
Werner Klinger
TERROR OF DR. MABUSE, THE(1965, Ger.), d
Michael Klingher
JEKYLL AND HYDE...TOGETHER AGAIN(1982)
Werner Klingler
ORDERED TO LOVE(1963, Ger.), d
Lawrence Klingman
HIS MAJESTY O'KEEFE(1953), w
Lynzee Klingman
ONE FLEW OVER THE CUCKOO'S NEST(1975), ed; YOU LIGHT UP MY LI-
FE(1977), ed; ALMOST SUMMER(1978), ed; HAIR(1979), ed; TRUE CONFES-
SIONS(1981), ed
Al Klink
SUN VALLEY SERENADE(1941)
Zeno Klinker
LOOK WHO'S LAUGHING(1941), w
Fritz Klippel
JAZZBAND FIVE, THE(1932, Ger,)
Evelyn Klippian
HIGH RISK(1981)
Steve Klisanin
WILD WOMEN OF WONGO, THE(1959)
Jean Klissak
NIGHT OF THE FOLLOWING DAY, THE(1969, Brit.), ph
Stu Klitsner
TIME AFTER TIME(1979, Brit.)
Stuart P. Klitsner
FOOLS(1970); DIRTY HARRY(1971)
Vassili Kliucharev
DAYS AND NIGHTS(1946, USSR)
Dr. Horst-Dieter Klock
MARRIAGE OF MARIA BRAUN, THE(1979, Ger.)
Till Klockow
DANTON(1931, Ger.)
Eugen Kloepfer
TALES OF THE UNCANNY(1932, Ger.); PRIVATE LIFE OF LOUIS XIV(1936, Ger.)
Eugene Kloepfer
1914(1932, Ger.)
Klondike
Misc. Silents
LAW'S LASH, THE(1928); MARLIE THE KILLER(1928)
Helmuth Klonka
EIGHT GIRLS IN A BOAT(1932, Ger.)
Darren Kloomok
STUCK ON YOU(1983), ed
1984
STUCK ON YOU(1984), ed; VAMPING(1984), ed
Eugen Klopfer
Misc. Silents
NEW YEAR'S EVE(1923, Ger.); STREET, THE(1927, Ger.)
Arseniy Klopotovskiy
MAGIC WEAVER, THE(1965, USSR), spec eff; JACK FROST(1966, USSR), art d
Julia Klopp
SQUIRM(1976)
Jutta Kloppel
1984
LOVE IN GERMANY, A(1984, Fr./Ger.)
Georg Kloren
SECRET AGENT(1933, Brit.), w
John Klorer
GUEST WIFE(1945), w; THIS LOVE OF OURS(1945), w; GOOD SAM(1948), w;
TENSION(1949), w; PRETTY BABY(1950), w; STARLIFT(1951), w; NEVER SAY
GOODBYE(1956), w
John D. Klorer
ON SUCH A NIGHT(1937), w; SEVEN MILES FROM ALCATRAZ(1942), w; HERS
TO HOLD(1943), w; TOP OF THE WORLD(1955), w
Elmar Klos
DEATH IS CALLED ENGELCHEN(1963, Czech.), d; SHOP ON MAIN STREET,
THE(1966, Czech.), d, w; ADRIFT(1971, Czech.), w
Juergen Klose
1984
CLASS ENEMY(1984, Ger.), w
Edward Klosinski
MAN OF MARBLE(1979, Pol.), ph; YOUNG GIRLS OF WILKO, THE(1979, Pol./Fr.),
ph; MAN OF IRON(1981, Pol.), ph; BELLA DONNA(1983, Ger.), ph
J. Klosinski
GREAT BIG WORLD AND LITTLE CHILDREN, THE(1962, Pol.)
Janusz Klosinski
WALKOVER(1969, Pol.); SARAGOSSA MANUSCRIPT, THE(1972, Pol.)
Roman Klosowski
EVE WANTS TO SLEEP(1961, Pol.); EROICA(1966, Pol.)
Pierre Klossowski
AU HASARD, BALTHAZAR(1970, Fr.)
Barbara Kloth
GERMAN SISTERS, THE(1982, Ger.), art d
Claude Klotz
DRACULA AND SON(1976, Fr.), w
Florence Klotz
SOMETHING FOR EVERYONE(1970), cos; LITTLE NIGHT MUSIC, A(1977, Aust./
U.S./Ger.), cos
George Klotz
SPECIAL DELIVERY(1955, Ger.), ed; WIND ACROSS THE EVERGLADES(1958),
ed; AND NOW MY LOVE(1975, Fr.), ed; DREAM OF PASSION, A(1978, Gr.), ed

Georges Klotz
QUESTION 7(1961, U.S./Ger.), ed; GIRL WITH THE GOLDEN EYES, THE(1962,
Fr.), ed; WANDERER, THE(1969, Fr.), ed; ANOTHER MAN, ANOTHER CHAN-
CE(1977 Fr/US), ed; CHANEL SOLITAIRE(1981), ed
1984
JUST THE WAY YOU ARE(1984), ed
Isabelle Kloucowsky
MURMUR OF THE HEART(1971, Fr./Ital./Ger.)
Jane Klove
ISLAND OF THE BLUE DOLPHINS(1964), w; AND NOW MIGUEL(1966), w; MY
SIDE OF THE MOUNTAIN(1969), w
Steven Kloves
1984
RACING WITH THE MOON(1984), w
Henryk Kluba
WALKOVER(1969, Pol.)
Alexander Kluge
GERMANY IN AUTUMN(1978, Ger.), d; WAR AND PEACE(1983, Ger.), d&w
Emma Kluge
Misc. Silents
PRIMITIVE WOMAN, THE(1918)
George Kluge
CITIZEN SAINT(1947)
Herbert Kluge
Misc. Silents
PORI(1930, Ger.)
P. F. Kluge
DOG DAY AFTERNOON(1975), w; EDDIE AND THE CRUISERS(1983), w
Garry Kluger
SKATETOWN, U.S.A.(1979)
Adam Klugman
1984
FLAMINGO KID, THE(1984)
Caren Klugman
TAKING OFF(1971)
Jack Klugman
TIMETABLE(1956); 12 ANGRY MEN(1957); CRY TERROR(1958); DAYS OF WINE
AND ROSES(1962); I COULD GO ON SINGING(1963); YELLOW CANARY, THE(1963);
ACT ONE(1964); HAIL MAFIA(1965, Fr./Ital.); DETECTIVE, THE(1968); SPLIT,
THE(1968); GOODBYE COLUMBUS(1969); WHO SAYS I CAN'T RIDE A RAIN-
BOW!(1971); TWO-MINUTE WARNING(1976)
Kate Klugman
WARRIORS, THE(1979)
Lynn Klugman
NETWORK(1976)
Robert Klugston
Misc. Silents
FOR THE FREEDOM OF IRELAND(1920)
Helen Klumph
Silents
LOVE'S WILDERNESS(1924), w
Raymond A. Klune
HELL AND HIGH WATER(1954), p
Tom Klunis
DAY THE FISH CAME OUT, THE(1967. Brit./Gr.); NEXT MAN, THE(1976);
TAPS(1981)
Jan Klusak
END OF AUGUST AT THE HOTEL OZONE, THE(1967, Czech.), m; MARTYRS OF
LOVE(1968, Czech.), a, m; NIGHTS OF PRAGUE, THE(1968, Czech.); REPORT ON
THE PARTY AND THE GUESTS, A(1968, Czech.); END OF A PRIEST(1970, Czech.), m
Pavel Klushantsev
STORM PLANET(1962, USSR), d, w
Walter Klusner
YOU'VE GOT TO WALK IT LIKE YOU TALK IT OR YOU'LL LOSE THAT
BEAT(1971)
Gena Klyachkovskiy
VIOLIN AND ROLLER(1962, USSR)
Ksenia Klyaro
Misc. Silents
TRANSPORT OF FIRE(1931, USSR)
I. Klyucharyov
SONG OF THE FOREST(1963, USSR), md
V. Klyukin
DIMKA(1964, USSR)
I. Klyukvin
Misc. Silents
WINGS OF A SERF(1926, USSR)
Boris Kmelnizki
RED TENT, THE(1971, Ital./USSR)
L. Kmit
DIARY OF A NAZI(1943, USSR)
Leonid Kmit
MUMU(1961, USSR)
Franz Knaak
Misc. Silents
PEST IN FLORENZ(1919, Ger.)
Jacoba Knaapan
HOG WILD(1980, Can.)
Skelton Knaggs
STRANGERS ON A HONEYMOON(1937, Brit.); SOUTH RIDING(1938, Brit.); TOR-
TURE SHIP(1939); U-BOAT 29(1939, Brit.); GHOST SHIP, THE(1943); HEADIN' FOR
GOD'S COUNTRY(1943); INVISIBLE MAN'S REVENGE(1944); LODGER, THE(1944);
NONE BUT THE LONELY HEART(1944); HOUSE OF DRACULA(1945); ISLE OF THE
DEAD(1945); DICK TRACY VS. CUEBALL(1946); SCANDAL IN PARIS, A(1946);
TERROR BY NIGHT(1946); DICK TRACY MEETS GRUESOME(1947); FOREVER
AMBER(1947); PALEFACE, THE(1948); MASTER MINDS(1949); BLACKBEARD THE
PIRATE(1952); ROGUE'S MARCH(1952); MOONFLEET(1955)

Judy Knaiz
HELLO, DOLLY!(1969)
Jan Knakal
LEMONADE JOE(1966, Czech.), art d
Stanley Knap
LIQUID SKY(1982)
Bob Knapp
THY NEIGHBOR'S WIFE(1953)
Bud Knapp
NEVER TAKE CANDY FROM A STRANGER(1961, Brit.); INVITATION TO MUR-
DER(1962, Brit.); CHILD UNDER A LEAF(1975, Can.)
Budd Knapp
WHY ROCK THE BOAT?(1974, Can.); IN PRAISE OF OLDER WOMEN(1978, Can.)
1984
KINGS AND DESPERATE MEN(1984, Brit.)
Charles Knapp
GENTLE PEOPLE AND THE QUIET LAND, THE(1972); CHINATOWN(1974); DARK-
TOWN STRUTTERS(1975); SPECIALIST, THE(1975); MOTHER, JUGS &
SPEED(1976); WORLD'S GREATEST LOVER, THE(1977); BUTCH AND SUNDANCE:
THE EARLY DAYS(1979); BLADE RUNNER(1982); TWILIGHT ZONE–THE MO-
VIE(1983)
Charles W. Knapp
J.W. COOP(1971)
Daniel Knapp
MOUNTAIN MEN, THE(1980)
David Knapp
PARRISH(1961); PLEDGEMASTERS, THE(1971)
Deborah Knapp
GREAT WALDO PEPPER, THE(1975)
Dorothy Knapp
WHOOPEE(1930)
Douglas Knapp
DARK STAR(1975), ph; ASSAULT ON PRECINCT 13(1976), ph
Douglas H. Knapp
FIRST NUDIE MUSICAL, THE(1976), ph
Evalyn Knapp
MOTHERS CRY(1930); SINNER'S HOLIDAY(1930); BARGAIN, THE(1931); MIL-
LIONAIRE, THE(1931); SIDE SHOW(1931); SMART MONEY(1931); BIG CITY
BLUES(1932); FIREMAN, SAVE MY CHILD(1932); HIGH PRESSURE(1932);
MADAME RACKETEER(1932); NIGHT MAYOR, THE(1932); STRANGE LOVE OF
MOLLY LOUVAIN, THE(1932); SUCCESSFUL CALAMITY, A(1932); TAXI!(1932);
THIS SPORTING AGE(1932); VANISHING FRONTIER, THE(1932); AIR HOS-
TESS(1933); BACHELOR MOTHER(1933); CORRUPTION(1933); DANCE, GIRL,
DANCE(1933); HIS PRIVATE SECRETARY(1933); POLICE CAR 17(1933); SLIGHTLY
MARRIED(1933); STATE TROOPER(1933); MAN'S GAME, A(1934); SPEED
WINGS(1934); CONFIDENTIAL(1935); FIRETRAP, THE(1935); IN OLD SANTA
FE(1935); LADIES CRAVE EXCITEMENT(1935); ONE FRIGHTENED NIGHT(1935);
BULLDOG EDITION(1936); LAUGHING IRISH EYES(1936); THREE OF A
KIND(1936); HAWAIIAN BUCKAROO(1938); RAWHIDE(1938); WANTED BY THE
POLICE(1938); LONE WOLF TAKES A CHANCE, THE(1941); ROAR OF THE
PRESS(1941); TWO WEEKS TO LIVE(1943)
Evelyn Knapp
RIVER'S END(1931); IDIOT'S DELIGHT(1939); MR. SMITH GOES TO WASHING-
TON(1939)
Fred Knapp
DIRTYMOUTH(1970)
Geraldine Knapp
MY FAVORITE SPY(1951)
Gordon Knapp
Silents
STORMY SEAS(1923)
Gregory Knapp
VIRUS(1980, Jap.), w
Harry Knapp
MANHUNT IN THE JUNGLE(1958); DAUGHTER OF THE SUN GOD(1962); TIME
FOR DYING, A(1971), ed
Harry V. Knapp
FASTEST GUN ALIVE(1956), ed
Jack Knapp
MARINES ARE HERE, THE(1938), w
Silents
KING OF THE RODEO(1929)
Marion Knapp
Silents
SPREADING DAWN, THE(1917)
Robert Knapp
STRANGE FASCINATION(1952); SILENT RAIDERS(1954); MESA OF LOST WOM-
EN, THE(1956); SCANDAL INCORPORATED(1956); OUTLAW'S SON(1957); REVOLT
AT FORT LARAMIE(1957); TOMAHAWK TRAIL(1957); HOT CAR GIRL(1958); RAW-
HIDE TRAIL, THE(1958); GUNMEN FROM LAREDO(1959); THREAT, THE(1960);
STOOLIE, THE(1972)
Simone Knapp
VIVA MARIA(1965, Fr./Ital.), makeup; SAILOR FROM GIBRALTAR, THE(1967,
Brit.), makeup; VOYAGE OF SILENCE(1968, Fr.), makeup
Stanley Knapp
MOTHER'S DAY(1980)
Terence Knapp
URGE TO KILL(1960, Brit.); OTHELLO(1965, Brit.)
Wilfred Knapp
JOHNNY CONCHO(1956)
Wilfrid Knapp
GIRL HE LEFT BEHIND, THE(1956); GREAT AMERICAN PASTIME, THE(1956)
Nina Knapskog
1984
KAMILLA(1984, Norway)
M.J. Knatchbull
STORIES FROM A FLYING TRUNK(1979, Brit.), ed

Charles Knatt
Misc. Talkies
MELON AFFAIR, THE(1979)
Nikita Knatz
RUSSIANS ARE COMING, THE RUSSIANS ARE COMING, THE(1966); IN THE
HEAT OF THE NIGHT(1967); HOW SWEET IT IS(1968); THOMAS CROWN AFFAIR,
THE(1968); GAILY, GAILY(1969); I LOVE MY WIFE(1970); LE MANS(1971), art d;
DEVIL'S RAIN, THE(1975, U.S./Mex.), prod d
Jim Knaub
MAN WHO LOVED WOMEN, THE(1983)
Gustav A. Knauer
JOHNNY STEALS EUROPE(1932, Ger.), set d
E. Knausmyuller
DAY THE WAR ENDED, THE(1961, USSR); PEACE TO HIM WHO ENTERS(1963,
USSR); FORTY-NINE DAYS(1964, USSR); LAST GAME, THE(1964, USSR); ITALIANO
BRAVA GENTE(1965, Ital./USSR); WAR AND PEACE(1968, USSR)
Nigel Kneale
THE CREEPING UNKNOWN(1956, Brit.), w; ABOMINABLE SNOWMAN OF THE
HIMALAYAS, THE(1957, Brit.), w; ENEMY FROM SPACE(1957, Brit.), w; LOOK
BACK IN ANGER(1959), w; ENTERTAINER, THE(1960, Brit.), w; DAMN THE DEFI-
ANT!(1962, Brit.), w; FIRST MEN IN THE MOON(1964, Brit.), w; DEVIL'S OWN,
THE(1967, Brit.), w; FIVE MILLION YEARS TO EARTH(1968, Brit.), w; QUATER-
MASS CONCLUSION(1980, Brit.), w
Ambrose Knebel
1984
COUNTRY(1984)
Emil Knebel
WILD IS MY LOVE(1963), ph
Fletcher Knebel
SEVEN DAYS IN MAY(1964), w
Levi L. Knebel
1984
COUNTRY(1984)
Peter Knecht
SEVEN(1979)
Rene Knecht
NIGHT GAMES(1980)
Alvin Knechtel
CARELESS AGE(1929), spec eff; GREAT DIVIDE, THE(1930), ph
Silents
LEECH, THE(1921), ph; IS MONEY EVERYTHING?(1923), ph; DROPKICK,
THE(1927), ph
Lloyd Knechtel
MONKEY'S PAW, THE(1933), spec eff; WILD YOUTH(1961), ph
Alvin Knechter
HOT STUFF(1929), ph
Tom Kneebone
LUCK OF GINGER COFFEY, THE(1964, U.S./Can.)
Jo Anna Kneeland
DR. COPPELIUS(1968, U.S./Span.), ch; MYSTERIOUS HOUSE OF DR. C.,
THE(1976), w, ch
Ted Kneeland
DR. COPPELIUS(1968, U.S./Span.), d&w; PSYCHOUT FOR MURDER(1971, Arg./
Ital.), d; MYSTERIOUS HOUSE OF DR. C., THE(1976), p&d, w
Wayne Kneeland
CLASS(1983)
Wayne C. Kneeland
RISKY BUSINESS(1983)
Hildegard Knef
LULU(1962, Aus.); HYPNOSIS(1966, Ger./Sp./Ital.); FEDORA(1978, Ger./Fr.)
Hildegard Knef [Hildegarde Neff]
MURDERERS AMONG US(1948, Ger.); LOST CONTINENT, THE(1968, Brit.)
Karl Kneidinger
STORM IN A WATER GLASS(1931, Aust.)
Peter Kneip
NOT RECONCILED, OR "ONLY VIOLENCE HELPS WHERE IT RULES"(1969, Ger.)
Seymour Kneitel
GULLIVER'S TRAVELS(1939), anim d
Catalaine Knell
DR. HECKYL AND MR. HYPE(1980)
David Knell
DEVIL AND MAX DEVLIN, THE(1981); MAKING LOVE(1982)
1984
SPLASH(1984)
Gael Knepfer
HILDUR AND THE MAGICIAN(1969)
Paul Knepler
LOVES OF MADAME DUBARRY, THE(1938, Brit.), w; HEAVEN IS ROUND THE
CORNER(1944, Brit.), w
Tony Kneppers
TRAFFIC(1972, Fr.)
Tony Knesich
GLORIA(1980)
Lloyd Knetchel
RIO RITA(1929), ph
Charles Knetchke
SOMEWHERE IN BERLIN(1949, E. Ger.)
Robert Knettles
HELL AND HIGH WATER(1933)
John Kneubuhl
SCREAMING SKULL, THE(1958), p, w; TWO ON A GUILLOTINE(1965), w
John H. Kneubuhl
TRUE STORY OF LYNN STUART, THE(1958), w
L. Kniazev
ADMIRAL NAKHIMOV(1948, USSR)
Darryl Knibb
COME BACK CIHARLESTON BLUE(1972)

Henry H. Knibbs
MOUNTED STRANGER, THE(1930), w
Henry Herbert Knibbs
Silents
OVERLAND RED(1920), w; TONY RUNS WILD(1926), w
Richard Knibbs
MY WAY(1974, South Africa)
Paine Knickerbocher
TEACHER'S PET(1958)
Will Knickerbocker
NOBODY'S PERFEKT(1981); PORKY'S(1982); JAWS 3-D(1983); NIGHT IN HEAVEN, A(1983); PORKY'S II: THE NEXT DAY(1983); SMOKEY AND THE BANDIT–PART 3(1983)
1984
HARRY AND SON(1984)
The Knickerbockers
OUT OF SIGHT(1966)
Barbara Knieger
TIME AFTER TIME(1979, Brit.), set d
Jurgen Knieper
AMERICAN FRIEND, THE(1977, Ger.), m; STATE OF THINGS, THE(1983), m
1984
GERMANY PALE MOTHER(1984, Ger.), m
Evel Knievel
VIVA KNIEVEL!(1977)
Al Knight
ROUNDUP TIME IN TEXAS(1937)
Albert Knight
MURDER IN THE MUSEUM(1934)
Andrew Knight
HUCKLEBERRY FINN(1974)
Andy Knight
BATTLE FOR THE PLANET OF THE APES(1973)
Arthur Knight
PLAY IT AS IT LAYS(1972)
Ashley Knight
CATCH ME A SPY(1971, Brit./Fr.); MELODY(1971, Brit.); WARLORDS OF ATLAN-TIS(1978, Brit.)
Baker Knight
SWAMP COUNTRY(1966)
Barry Knight
SECRET OF THE FOREST, THE(1955, Brit.)
Bill Knight
HOMEWORK(1982)
Captain C.W.R. Knight
I KNOW WHERE I'M GOING(1947, Brit.)
Castleton Knight
FLYING SCOTSMAN, THE(1929, Brit.), d; LADY FROM THE SEA, THE(1929, Brit.), d; PLAYTHING, THE(1929, Brit.), d; KISSING CUP'S RACE(1930, Brit.), p&d, w; FOR FREEDOM(1940, Brit.), p
Charles Knight
PALS OF THE SADDLE(1938); LODGER, THE(1944); PEARL OF DEATH, THE(1944); EASY TO WED(1946); RENDEZVOUS 24(1946); TERROR BY NIGHT(1946); EXILE, THE(1947); IVY(1947); KILLER DILL(1947)
Charlott Knight
20 MILLION MILES TO EARTH(1957), w
Charlotte Knight
VALLEY OF THE DOLLS(1967)
Christopher Knight
STUDS LONIGAN(1960); IF A MAN ANSWERS(1962); JUST YOU AND ME, KID(1979)
Cunitia Knight
NICE GIRL LIKE ME, A(1969, Brit.)
Damien Knight
REDEEMER, THE(1978)
David Knight
CHANCE MEETING(1954, Brit.); EYEWITNESS(1956, Brit.); ACROSS THE BRID-GE(1957, Brit.); OUT OF THE CLOUDS(1957, Brit.); TEARS FOR SIMON(1957, Brit.); MISSILE FROM HELL(1960, Brit.); STORY OF DAVID, A(1960, Brit.); DEVIL'S AGENT, THE(1962, Brit.); NIGHTMARE(1963, Brit.); CLUE OF THE TWISTED CANDLE(1968, Brit.)
Davidson Knight
BUGSY MALONE(1976, Brit.)
Don Knight
KILL A DRAGON(1967); HELL WITH HEROES, THE(1968); HAWAIIANS, THE(1970); TOO LATE THE HERO(1970); SOMETHING BIG(1971); TRADER HORN(1973); APPLE DUMPLING GANG, THE(1975); TREASURE OF MATECUM-BE(1976); TUNNELVISION(1976), ph; SWAMP THING(1982)
Dudley Knight
CANDIDATE, THE(1972); ONE IS A LONELY NUMBER(1972); FIRST FAMI-LY(1980); FIRST MONDAY IN OCTOBER(1981)
Eddie Knight
MURDER SHE SAID(1961, Brit.), makeup; MURDER AT THE GALLOP(1963, Brit.), makeup; LADIES WHO DO(1964, Brit.), makeup; MRS. BROWN, YOU'VE GOT A LOVELY DAUGHTER(1968, Brit.), makeup; FRANKENSTEIN MUST BE DE-STROYED!(1969, Brit.), makeup; SOME GIRLS DO(1969, Brit.), makeup; WHO SLEW AUNTIE ROO?(1971, U.S./Brit.), makeup; NOTHING BUT THE NIGHT(1975, Brit.), makeup
Edmond Knight
HAMLET(1948, Brit.); HELEN OF TROY(1956, Ital)
Edmund Knight
SINK THE BISMARCK!(1960, Brit.)
Edward Knight
PERCY(1971, Brit.), makeup; SMILE ORANGE(1976, Jamaican), p
Elisabeth Knight
MC CABE AND MRS. MILLER(1971)
Elizabeth Knight
OLIVER!(1968, Brit.); VILLAIN(1971, Brit.)

Eric Knight
THIS ABOVE ALL(1942), w; LASSIE, COME HOME(1943), w; SON OF LAS-SIE(1945), w; PACK, THE(1977)
Ernest Knight
1984
BLESS THEIR LITTLE HEARTS(1984)
Esmond Knight
DEADLOCK(1931, Brit.); ROMANY LOVE(1931, Brit.); 77 PARK LANE(1931, Brit.); RINGER, THE(1932, Brit.); BERMONDSEY KID, THE(1933, Brit.); BLUE SQUADRON, THE(1934, Brit.); FATHER AND SON(1934, Brit.); GIRLS WILL BE BOYS(1934, Brit.); LEST WE FORGET(1934, Brit.); STRAUSS' GREAT WALTZ(1934, Brit.); WOMAN-HOOD(1934, Brit.); CRIME UNLIMITED(1935, Brit.); DANDY DICK(1935, Brit.); SOME DAY(1935, Brit.); BLACK ROSES(1936, Ger.); CLOWN MUST LAUGH, A(1936, Brit.); VICAR OF BRAY, THE(1937, Brit.); WEDDINGS ARE WONDERFUL(1938, Brit.); ARSENAL STADIUM MYSTERY, THE(1939, Brit.); BLACKOUT(1940, Brit.); FIN-GERS(1940, Brit.); THIS ENGLAND(1941, Brit.); CANTERBURY TALE, A(1944, Brit.); HALF-WAY HOUSE, THE(1945, Brit.); SILVER FLEET, THE(1945, Brit.); HENRY V(1946, Brit.); BLACK NARCISSUS(1947, Brit.); END OF THE RIVER, THE(1947, Brit.); HOLIDAY CAMP(1947, Brit.); RED SHOES, THE(1948, Brit.); INHERITANCE, THE(1951, Brit.); RIVER, THE(1951); GIRDLE OF GOLD(1952, Brit.); WILD HEART, THE(1952, Brit.); STEEL KEY, THE(1953, Brit.); RICHARD III(1956, Brit.); PRINCE AND THE SHOWGIRL, THE(1957, Brit.); MISSILE FROM HELL(1960, Brit.); PEEP-ING TOM(1960, Brit.); SPY WHO CAME IN FROM THE COLD, THE(1965, Brit.); WINTER'S TALE, THE(1968, Brit.); ANNE OF THE THOUSAND DAYS(1969, Brit.); WHERE'S JACK?(1969, Brit.); BOY WHO TURNED YELLOW, THE(1972, Brit.); ROBIN AND MARIAN(1976, Brit.)
1984
ELEMENT OF CRIME, THE(1984, Den.)
Felix Knight
BABES IN TOYLAND(1934); PICK A STAR(1937)
Frank Knight
FLOOD, THE(1963, Brit.)
Frederick Knight
DULCIMER STREET(1948, Brit.); MANIACS ON WHEELS(1951, Brit.)
Fuzzy Knight
ADVENTURES OF GALLANT BESS(1948); HELL'S HIGHWAY(1932); HER BODY-GUARD(1933); SHE DONE HIM WRONG(1933); SITTING PRETTY(1933); SUNSET PASS(1933); THIS DAY AND AGE(1933); TO THE LAST MAN(1933); UNDER THE TONTO RIM(1933); BELLE OF THE NINETIES(1934); CAT'S PAW, THE(1934); COME ON, MARINES(1934); GAY BRIDE, THE(1934); GIRL FROM MISSOURI(1934); LAST ROUND-UP, THE(1934); MOULIN ROUGE(1934); MUSIC IN THE AIR(1934); OPERATOR 13(1934); SHE HAD TO CHOOSE(1934); BEHOLD MY WIFE(1935); DANGER AHEAD(1935); GEORGE WHITE'S 1935 SCANDALS(1935); HOME ON THE RANGE(1935); MARY BURNS, FUGITIVE(1935); MURDER MAN(1935); NIGHT ALARM(1935); OLD HOMESTEAD, THE(1935); TRAILS OF THE WILD(1935); VAGA-BOND LADY(1935); WANDERER OF THE WASTELAND(1935); AND SUDDEN DEATH(1936); BARS OF HATE(1936); DIZZY DAMES(1936); KELLY OF THE SECRET SERVICE(1936); PUT ON THE SPOT(1936); RIO GRANDE ROMANCE(1936); SEA SPOILERS(1936); SONG OF THE GRINGO(1936); SONG OF THE TRAIL(1936); TRAIL OF THE LONESOME PINE, THE(1936); WILDCAT TROOPER(1936); AMA-TEUR CROOK(1937); COUNTY FAIR(1937); COURAGE OF THE WEST(1937); GOLD RACKET, THE(1937); MOUNTAIN JUSTICE(1937); MOUNTAIN MUSIC(1937); PLAINSMAN, THE(1937); SINGING OUTLAW(1937); WITH LOVE AND KIS-SES(1937); BORDER WOLVES(1938); COWBOY AND THE LADY, THE(1938); FLYING FISTS, THE(1938); JOY OF LIVING(1938); LAST STAND, THE(1938); QUICK MO-NEY(1938); SPAWN OF THE NORTH(1938); WHERE THE WEST BEGINS(1938); DESPERATE TRAILS(1939); OKLAHOMA FRONTIER(1939); UNION PACIFIC(1939); BAD MAN FROM RED BUTTE(1940); BRIGHAM YOUNG–FRONTIERSMAN(1940); CHIP OF THE FLYING U(1940); JOHNNY APOLLO(1940); LAW AND ORDER(1940); MY LITTLE CHICKADEE(1940); PONY POST(1940); RAGTIME COWBOY JOE(1940); REMEMBER THE NIGHT(1940); RIDERS OF PASCO BASIN(1940); SON OF ROAR-ING DAN(1940); WEST OF CARSON CITY(1940); ARIZONA CYCLONE(1941); BAD-LANDS OF DAKOTA(1941); BOSS OF BULLION CITY(1941); BURY ME NOT ON THE LONE PRAIRIE(1941); COWBOY AND THE BLONDE, THE(1941); HORROR IS-LAND(1941); LAW OF THE RANGE(1941); MAN FROM MONTANA(1941); MASKED RIDER, THE(1941); NEW YORK TOWN(1941); RAWHIDE RANGERS(1941); SHE-PHERD OF THE HILLS, THE(1941); APACHE TRAIL(1942); BOSS OF HANGTOWN MESA(1942); BUTCH MINDS THE BABY(1942); DEEP IN THE HEART OF TEX-AS(1942); FIGHTING BILL FARGO(1942); JUKE GIRL(1942); LADY IN A JAM(1942); LITTLE JOE, THE WRANGLER(1942); SILVER BULLET, THE(1942); STAGECOACH BUCKAROO(1942); ALLERGIC TO LOVE(1943); ARIZONA TRAIL(1943); CHEYENNE ROUNDUP(1943); CORVETTE K-225(1943); FRONTIER LAW(1943); HE'S MY GUY(1943); LONE STAR TRAIL, THE(1943); OLD CHISHOLM TRAIL(1943); RAID-ERS OF SAN JOAQUIN(1943); TENTING TONIGHT ON THE OLD CAMP GROUND(1943); COWBOY AND THE SENORITA(1944); HI, GOOD-LOOKIN'(1944); MARSHAL OF GUNSMOKE(1944); OKLAHOMA RAIDERS(1944); OLD TEXAS TRAIL, THE(1944); RIDERS OF THE SANTA FE(1944); SINGING SHERIFF, THE(1944); TAKE IT BIG(1944); TRAIL TO GUNSIGHT(1944); TRIGGER TRAIL(1944); BAD MEN OF THE BORDER(1945); BEYOND THE PECOS(1945); CODE OF THE LAWLESS(1945); FRISCO SAL(1945); FRONTIER GAL(1945); RENEGADES OF THE RIO GRANDE(1945); SENORITA FROM THE WEST(1945); SONG OF THE SA-RONG(1945); SWING OUT, SISTER(1945); TRAIL TO VENGEANCE(1945); GIRL ON THE SPOT(1946); GUN TOWN(1946); GUNMAN'S CODE(1946); HER ADVENTUROUS NIGHT(1946); LAWLESS BREED, THE(1946); RUSTLER'S ROUNDUP(1946); EGG AND I, THE(1947); APACHE CHIEF(1949); DOWN TO THE SEA IN SHIPS(1949); RIMFIRE(1949); COLORADO RANGER(1950); CROOKED RIVER(1950); FAST ON THE DRAW(1950); HILLS OF OKLAHOMA(1950); HOSTILE COUNTRY(1950); MAR-SHAL OF HELDORADO(1950); WEST OF THE BRAZOS(1950); CANYON RAI-DERS(1951); HONEYCHILE(1951); NEVADA BADMEN(1951); SHOW BOAT(1951); SKIPALONG ROSENBLOOM(1951); STAGE TO BLUE RIVER(1951); FARGO(1952); FEUDIN' FOOLS(1952); KANSAS TERRITORY(1952); LAWLESS COWBOYS(1952); NIGHT RAIDERS(1952); OKLAHOMA ANNIE(1952); RANCHO NOTORIOUS(1952); RODEO(1952); TOPEKA(1953); VIGILANTE TERROR(1953); NAKED HILLS, THE(1956); NOTORIOUS MR. MONKS, THE(1958); THESE THOUSAND HILLS(1959); BOUNTY KILLER, THE(1965); WACO(1966); HOSTILE GUNS(1967)
Misc. Talkies
I HATE WOMEN(1934); HOT OFF THE PRESS(1935); SILKS AND SADDLES(1938); BOSS OF BOOMTOWN(1944); FEUDIN' RHYTHM(1949); STAGECOACH DRI-VER(1951); WANTED DEAD OR ALIVE(1951); GOLD RAIDERS, THE(1952); GUN-MAN, THE(1952)

Gladys Knight
PIPE DREAMS(1976)
Glen Knight
THEY WON'T BELIEVE ME(1947); MEN WITHOUT WOMEN(1930), m; DESPER-ATE(1947)
Hank Knight
Silents
SPEEDY(1928)
Harlan Knight
FIGHTING SHERIFF, THE(1931); HEAVEN ON EARTH(1931); TO THE LAST MAN(1933); LAUGHING BOY(1934)
Silents
JANE EYRE(1921); CRITICAL AGE, THE(1923); STEADFAST HEART, THE(1923); JANICE MEREDITH(1924); WARRENS OF VIRGINIA, THE(1924); KNOCKOUT, THE(1925)
Misc. Silents
COUNTRY FLAPPER, THE(1922); LITTLE RED SCHOOLHOUSE, THE(1923); MAN FROM GLENGARRY, THE(1923); HIS BUDDY'S WIFE(1925); WIVES OF THE PROPHET, THE(1926)
Harlan E. Knight
TOL'ABLE DAVID(1930); WHISTLIN' DAN(1932); STORY OF TEMPLE DRAKE, THE(1933)
Henry Knight
GAMBLING SEX(1932), d; TROUBLE IN TEXAS(1937)
Harry S. Knight
CRIME PATROL, THE(1936), p
Horace Knight
Misc. Silents
POLLY OF THE FOLLIES(1922)
Howard Knight
LIFE IN EMERGENCY WARD 10(1959, Brit.); SHADOW OF THE CAT, THE(1961, Brit.); TO SIR, WITH LOVE(1967, Brit.)
Humphrey Knight
LOVE IN PAWN(1953, Brit.), w
J.P. Knight
CAMPUS HONEYMOON(1948), m
Jack Knight
KEY TO HARMONY(1935, Brit.); LOVE TEST, THE(1935, Brit.); LONG GOODBYE, THE(1973); WICKED, WICKED(1973)
James Knight
KISSING CUP'S RACE(1930, Brit.); SAFE AFFAIR, A(1931, Brit.); THIRD STRING, THE(1932, Brit.); OVERNIGHT(1933, Brit.); LOST IN THE LEGION(1934, Brit.); SEXTON BLAKE AND THE BEARDED DOCTOR(1935, Brit.); GIRL IN DIS-TRESS(1941, Brit.); COLONEL BLIMP(1945, Brit.); GIRL IN A MILLION, A(1946, Brit.); JOHNNY FRENCHMAN(1946, Brit.); LOYAL HEART(1946, Brit.); SAN DEMETRIO, LONDON(1947, Brit.); MY SISTER AND I(1948, Brit.)
Silents
KNAVE OF HEARTS, THE(1919, Brit.); POWER OF RIGHT, THE(1919, Brit.); BRENDA OF THE BARGE(1920, Brit.); EDUCATION OF NICKY, THE(1921, Brit.); BEAUTIFUL KITTY(1923, Brit.); MR. NOBODY(1927, Brit.); POWER OVER MEN(1929, Brit.)
Misc. Silents
HAPPY WARRIOR, THE(1917, Brit.); BIG MONEY(1918, Brit.); DECEPTION(1918, Brit.); NATURE'S GENTLEMAN(1918, Brit.); RILKA(1918, Brit.); SPLENDID COW-ARD, THE(1918, Brit.); GATES OF DUTY(1919, Brit.); MAN WHO FORGOT, THE(1919, Brit.); SILVER GREYHOUND, THE(1919, Brit.); LOVE IN THE WELSH HILLS(1921, Brit.); ONE MOMENT'S TEMPTATION(1922, Brit.); HORNET'S NEST(1923, Brit.); LADY OWNER, THE(1923, Brit.); MEN WHO FORGET(1923, Brit.); WHAT PRICE LOVING CUP?(1923, Brit.); GREAT TURF MYSTERY, THE(1924, Brit.); TRAINER AND THE TEMPTRESS(1925, Brit.); BALL OF FORTUNE, THE(1926, Brit.); MARIA MAR-TEN(1928, Brit.)
Jimmy Knight
SOLDIER, SAILOR(1944, Brit.)
John Knight
MAIN CHANCE, THE(1966, Brit.), d
June Knight
LADIES MUST LOVE(1933); TAKE A CHANCE(1933); CROSS COUNTRY CRUI-SE(1934); GIFT OF GAB(1934); WAKE UP AND DREAM(1934); BROADWAY MELODY OF 1936(1935); BREAK THE NEWS(1938, Brit.); VACATION FROM LOVE(1938); HOUSE ACROSS THE BAY, THE(1940); LILAC DOMINO, THE(1940, Brit.)
Karen Knight
UP IN ARMS(1944)
Kathy Knight
Misc. Talkies
LOVE AND KISSES(?)
Keith Knight
MEATBALLS(1979, Can.); HOG WILD(1980, Can.); GAS(1981, Can.); MY BLOODY VALENTINE(1981, Can.); CLASS OF 1984(1982, Can.); OF UNKNOWN ORIGIN(1983, Can.)
Larry Knight
JOKER IS WILD, THE(1957)
Lillian Knight
Silents
STAGE MADNESS(1927)
Lynda Knight
OCTOPUSSY(1983, Brit.)
Malcolm Knight
DEVIL ON HORSEBACK(1954, Brit.); WOMAN'S ANGLE, THE(1954, Brit.); WIT-NESS, THE(1959, Brit.); TOO YOUNG TO LOVE(1960, Brit.); LIVE NOW-PAY LATER(1962, Brit.); RESCUE SQUAD, THE(1963, Brit.)
Silents
REDHEADS PREFERRED(1926), ed
Marcia Knight
SKYDIVERS, THE(1963); HOW DO I LOVE THEE?(1970)
Marcie Knight
STOOLIE, THE(1972); STANLEY(1973); IMPULSE(1975); MAKO: THE JAWS OF DEATH(1976)

Marcy Knight
DARKER THAN AMBER(1970)
Maurice Elvey Knight
FOR FREEDOM(1940, Brit.), d
Michael Knight
PASSPORT TO PIMLICO(1949, Brit.); ITALIAN JOB, THE(1969, Brit.), art d; MUSIC LOVERS, THE(1971, Brit.), art d; BABY, IT'S YOU(1983)
Nina Knight
ATTACK OF THE MAYAN MUMMY(1963, U.S./Mex.)
Norma Knight
NEW HOUSE ON THE LEFT, THE(1978, Brit.)
Misc. Talkies
LAST STOP ON THE NIGHT TRAIN(1976)
Patricia Knight
FABULOUS TEXAN, THE(1947); ROSES ARE RED(1947); SHOCKPROOF(1949); SECOND FACE, THE(1950); MAGIC FACE, THE(1951, Aust.)
Paul Knight
GARMENT JUNGLE, THE(1957)
Percy Knight
Silents
SHERLOCK HOLMES(1922)
Pete Knight
BLACK RODEO(1972)
Peter Knight
CRIMSON CULT, THE(1970, Brit.), m; SUNSTRUCK(1973, Aus.), m; CHOICE OF ARMS(1983, Fr.), md
Red Knight
BLONDE COMET(1941); DUKE OF THE NAVY(1942)
Ronald Knight
GALAXINA(1980)
Rosalind Knight
BLUE MURDER AT ST. TRINIAN'S(1958, Brit.); CARRY ON NURSE(1959, Brit.); KITCHEN, THE(1961, Brit.); CARRY ON TEACHER(1962, Brit.); THERE WAS A CROOKED MAN(1962, Brit.); TOM JONES(1963, Brit.); START THE REVOLUTION WITHOUT ME(1970); MR. QUILP(1975, Brit.); LADY VANISHES, THE(1980, Brit.)
Russ Knight
DUSTY AND SWEETS McGEE(1971)
Sandra Knight
FRANKENSTEIN'S DAUGHTER(1958); THUNDER ROAD(1958); TERROR AT BLACK FALLS(1962); TOWER OF LONDON(1962); TERROR, THE(1963); BLOOD BATH(1966)
Shirley Knight
FIVE GATES TO HELL(1959); DARK AT THE TOP OF THE STAIRS, THE(1960); ICE PALACE(1960); COUCH, THE(1962); HOUSE OF WOMEN(1962); SWEET BIRD OF YOUTH(1962); FLIGHT FROM ASHIYA(1964, U.S./Jap.); DUTCHMAN(1966, Brit.); GROUP, THE(1966); COUNTERFEIT KILLER, THE(1968); PETULIA(1968, U.S./Brit.); RAIN PEOPLE, THE(1969); JUGGERNAUT(1974, Brit.); BEYOND THE POSEIDON ADVENTURE(1979); ENDLESS LOVE(1981); SENDER, THE(1982, Brit.)
Stephen Knight
1984
BLACK ROOM, THE(1984)
Misc. Talkies
BLACK ROOM, THE(1983)
Steve Knight
LITTLE BIG SHOT(1952, Brit.)
Sunny Knight
FLAMINGO ROAD(1949)
Ted Knight
CAGE OF EVIL(1960); PSYCHO(1960); THIRTEEN FIGHTING MEN(1960); TWELVE HOURS TO KILL(1960); CRY FOR HAPPY(1961); TWO RODE TOGETHER(1961); HITLER(1962); SWINGIN' ALONG(1962); THIRTEEN WEST STREET(1962); CANDI-DATE, THE(1964); YOUNG DILLINGER(1965); COUNTDOWN(1968); M(1970); CAD-DY SHACK(1980)
Terence Knight
VIRGIN AND THE GYPSY, THE(1970, Brit.), prod d
Terry Knight
INCIDENT, THE(1967), m; ALF 'N' FAMILY(1968, Brit.), prod d; DAD'S ARMY(1971, Brit.), art d
Tom Knight
BLACK ANGEL(1946), p
Tracy Knight
DARKEST AFRICA(1936), w
Vick Knight
MURDER ON THE YUKON(1940), m; IT HAPPENED ON 5TH AVENUE(1947), w; LOUISIANA(1947), w
Victor Knight
PROLOGUE(1970, Can.); TERROR TRAIN(1980, Can.); HAPPY BIRTHDAY TO ME(1981)
Vivienne Knight
FLOODS OF FEAR(1958, Brit.), w; LAW AND DISORDER(1958, Brit.), w; GO TO BLAZES(1962, Brit.), w; MODEL MURDER CASE, THE(1964, Brit.), w
William Knight
LADY IN QUESTION, THE(1940), makeup
Wyatt Knight
PORKY'S(1982); PORKY'S II: THE NEXT DAY(1983)
Michael Knightingale
INTERNECINE PROJECT, THE(1974, Brit.)
Tim Knightley
1984
SCRUBBERS(1984, Brit.)
Reggie Knighton
AMERICATHON(1979), m
Rosemary Knighton
TWO TICKETS TO BROADWAY(1951)
Herbert Knippenberg
WHERE THE HOT WIND BLOWS(1960, Fr., Ital.); FANNY HILL: MEMOIRS OF A WOMAN OF PLEASURE zero(1965)

Jos Knipscheer
LITTLE ARK, THE(1972)
Krzysztof Knittel
CAMERA BUFF(1983, Pol.), m
Francesca Knittel-Bowyer
DAN'S MOTEL(1982)
Audry Kniveton
CHRISTINA(1974, Can.)
Knize
BREATH OF SCANDAL, A(1960), cos
James Knobeloch
HEAVEN'S GATE(1980)
William Knoblauch
GERTRUD(1966, Den.)
Edward Knoblock
SPEAKEASY(1929), w; KISMET(1930), w; KNOWING MEN(1930, Brit.), w; LOVE COMES ALONG(1930), w; SIN OF MADELON CLAUDET, THE(1931), w; MEN OF STEEL(1932, Brit.), w; CHU CHIN CHOW(1934, Brit.), w; EVENSONG(1934, Brit.), w; AMATEUR GENTLEMAN(1936, Brit.), w; RED WAGON(1936), w; MOONLIGHT SONATA(1938, Brit.), w; MAD MEN OF EUROPE(1940, Brit.), w; KISMET(1944), w; KISMET(1955), w
Silents
KISMET(1920), w; APPEARANCES(1921), w, w; THREE MUSKETEERS, THE(1921), w; ROSITA(1923), w; MUMSIE(1927, Brit.), w
Lucille Knoch
BAD AND THE BEAUTIFUL, THE(1952); CLOWN, THE(1953); SABRE JET(1953); EXECUTIVE SUITE(1954)
Lucy Knoch
BLUE DAHLIA, THE(1946); TO EACH HIS OWN(1946); TWO TICKETS TO BROADWAY(1951); JOKER IS WILD, THE(1957)
Jack Knoche
DANGEROUS TO KNOW(1938); KING OF ALCATRAZ(1938); DISBARRED(1939); HOTEL IMPERIAL(1939); INVITATION TO HAPPINESS(1939)
Charles Knode
JABBERWOCKY(1977, Brit.), cos; MONTY PYTHON'S LIFE OF BRIAN(1979, Brit.), a, cos; HOUND OF THE BASKERVILLES, THE(1980, Brit.), cos; BLADE RUNNER(1982), cos; NEVER SAY NEVER AGAIN(1983), cos
Karen Knoght
RECKLESS AGE(1944)
Harley Knoles
Silents
GILDED CAGE, THE(1916), d; ADVENTURES OF CAROL, THE(1917), d; CABARET, THE(1918), d; COST, THE(1920), d; GREAT SHADOW, THE(1920), d; GUILTY OF LOVE(1920), d; LAND OF HOPE AND GLORY(1927, Brit.), d
Misc. Silents
ANTIQUE DEALER, THE(1915), d; GREATER WILL, THE(1915), d; BOUGHT AND PAID FOR(1916), d; DEVIL'S TOY, THE(1916), d; HIS BROTHER'S WIFE(1916), d; MISS PETTICOATS(1916), d; SUPREME SACRIFICE, THE(1916), d; BURGLAR, THE(1917), d; LITTLE DUCHESS, THE(1917), d; PAGE MYSTERY, THE(1917), d; SOCIAL LEPER, THE(1917), d; SOULS ADRIFT(1917), d; SQUARE DEAL, A(1917), d; STOLEN PARADISE, THE(1917), d; GATES OF GLADNESS(1918), d; STOLEN ORDERS(1918), d; VOLUNTEER, THE(1918), d; WANTED - A MOTHER(1918), d; BOLSHEVISM ON TRIAL(1919), d; LITTLE WOMEN(1919), d; HALF AN HOUR(1920), d; ROMANTIC ADVENTURESS, A(1920), d; CARNIVAL(1921, Brit.), d; BOHEMIAN GIRL, THE(1922, Brit.), d; LEW TYLER'S WIVES(1926), d; OH, BABY!(1926), d; RISING GENERATION, THE(1928, Brit.), d; WHITE SHEIK, THE(1928, Brit.), d
Harry Knoles
Silents
OLDEST LAW, THE(1918), d
Harvey Knoles
Misc. Silents
PRICE OF PRIDE, THE(1917), d
Jurgen Knop
NEW LIFE STYLE, THE(1970, Ger.), a, w
Patricia Knop
PASSOVER PLOT, THE(1976, Israel), w
Patricia Louisiana Knop
LADY OSCAR(1979, Fr./Jap.), w; SILENCE OF THE NORTH(1981, Can.), w
Christopher Knopf
KING'S THIEF, THE(1955), w; TALL STRANGER, THE(1957), w; 20 MILLION MILES TO EARTH(1957), w; JOY RIDE(1958), w; HELL BENT FOR LEATHER(1960), w; EMPEROR OF THE NORTH POLE(1973), w; POSSE(1975), w; CHOIRBOYS, THE(1977), w; SCOTT JOPLIN(1977), w
Edwin A. Knopf
BORDER LEGION, THE(1930), d
Edwin C. Knopf
EDWARD, MY SON(1949, U.S./Brit.), p
Edwin H. Knopf
LIGHT OF WESTERN STARS, THE(1930), d; ONLY SAPS WORK(1930), d; SANTA FE TRAIL, THE(1930), d; SLIGHTLY SCARLET(1930), D; EAST OF BORNEO(1931), w; NICE WOMAN(1932), d, w; REBEL, THE(1933, Ger.), d&w; S.O.S. ICEBERG(1933), w; WEDDING NIGHT, THE(1935), w; TRIAL OF MARY DUGAN, THE(1941), p; VALLEY OF DECISION, THE(1945), p; SAILOR TAKES A WIFE, THE(1946), p; SECRET HEART, THE(1946), p; CYNTHIA(1947), p; B. F.'S DAUGHTER(1948), p; MALAYA(1950), p; LAW AND THE LADY, THE(1951), p&d; MR. IMPERIUM(1951), p, w; NIGHT INTO MORNING(1951), p; FEARLESS FAGAN(1952), p; GREAT DIAMOND ROBBERY(1953), p; LILI(1953), p; SCANDAL AT SCOURIE(1953), p; DIANE(1955), p; GLASS SLIPPER, THE(1955), p; KING'S THIEF, THE(1955), p; GABY(1956), p; TIP ON A DEAD JOCKEY(1957), p
Marty Knopf
GETTING TOGETHER(1976), ph
Edwin Knopf
FREE LOVE(1930), w; BAD SISTER(1931), w; PICCADILLY JIM(1936), w; I'LL WAIT FOR YOU(1941), p; VANISHING VIRGINIAN, THE(1941), p; CROSSROADS(1942), p; CROSS OF LORRAINE, THE(1943), p; CRY HAVOC(1943), p
Verna Knopf
SINCE YOU WENT AWAY(1944)

Mark Knopfler
LOCAL HERO(1983, Brit.), m
1984
CAL(1984, Ireland), m; COMFORT AND JOY(1984, Brit.), m
Greg Knoph
Misc. Talkies
ILSA, SHE WOLF OF THE SS(1975)
Marty Knoph
NO PLACE TO HIDE(1975), ph
Magda Knopke
BECKET(1964, Brit.)
Freda Knorr
HAUNTING, THE(1963)
P. Knorr
Misc. Silents
1812(1912, USSR); TERRIBLE REVENGE, A(1913, USSR); VOLGA AND SIBERIA(1914, USSR)
Fedor Knorre
DARK IS THE NIGHT(1946, USSR), w; ROAD HOME, THE(1947, USSR), w
Hansi Knoteck
GIRL FROM THE MARSH CROFT, THE(1935, Ger.); MAN WHO WAS SHERLOCK HOLMES, THE(1937, Ger.)
Hansi Knotecks
GREH(1962, Ger./Yugo.)
Fred Knoth
DEADLY MANTIS, THE(1957), spec eff; LAND UNKNOWN, THE(1957), spec eff; HELLFIGHTERS(1968), spec eff
A. Charles Knott
DON'T EVER LEAVE ME(1949, Brit.), ed; QUARTET(1949, Brit.), ed
Albert Knott
Silents
LAMPLIGHTER, THE(1921)
Alfred Knott
Silents
ROLLING HOME(1926)
Charles Knott
PLACE OF ONE'S OWN, A(1945, Brit.), ed; THEY WERE SISTERS(1945, Brit.), ed; CARAVAN(1946, Brit.), ed; ROOT OF ALL EVIL, THE(1947, Brit.), ed; JASSY(1948, Brit.), ed; SNOWBOUND(1949, Brit.), ed
Clara Knott
Misc. Silents
OLD LADY 31(1920)
Ethelbert Knott
Silents
BRAT, THE(1919)
Frederick Knott
MAN BAIT(1952, Brit.), w; DIAL M FOR MURDER(1954), w; WAIT UNTIL DARK(1967), w
Grenville Knott
THUNDERBIRDS ARE GO(1968, Brit.), art d
James Knott
TAHITIAN, THE(1956), p, d, w, ph
Lydia Knott
OVERLAND BOUND(1929); GUILTY?(1930); MEN WITHOUT LAW(1930); IF I HAD A MILLION(1932); ROCKY RHODES(1934); FAIR WARNING(1937)
Silents
AS YE SOW(1914); COMMON LAW, THE(1916); CRIME AND PUNISHMENT(1917); DARK ROAD, THE(1917); SHOULD A WOMAN TELL?(1920); BEATING THE GAME(1921); BREAKING POINT, THE(1921); INFAMOUS MISS REVELL, THE(1921); LURE OF YOUTH, THE(1921); ACROSS THE DEAD-LINE(1922); AFRAID TO FIGHT(1922); FLIRT, THE(1922); SUPER-SEX, THE(1922); DOLLAR DEVILS(1923); GARRISON'S FINISH(1923); HELD TO ANSWER(1923); ST. ELMO(1923); WOMAN OF PARIS, A(1923); RACING FOR LIFE(1924); FEARLESS LOVER, THE(1925); HIGH AND HANDSOME(1925); ROSE OF THE WORLD(1925); KENTUCKY HANDICAP(1926); KING OF KINGS, THE(1927); PRETTY CLOTHES(1927)
Misc. Silents
COURT-MARTIALED(1915); PAYING THE PRICE(1916); CLODHOPPER, THE(1917); SUDDEN JIM(1917); DANGER, GO SLOW(1918); BACHELOR'S WIFE, A(1919); LITTLE DIPLOMAT, THE(1919); POINTING FINGER, THE(1919); PEACEFUL VALLEY(1920); SCRAP IRON(1921); ISLE OF LOVE, THE(1922); CHALK MARKS(1924); PERFECT FLAPPER, THE(1924); WOMEN FIRST(1924); LIFE OF AN ACTRESS(1927)
Robbie Knott
BUDDY HOLLY STORY, THE(1978), spec eff
Robby Knott
1984
REPO MAN(1984), spec eff
Knott Limited
UP IN SMOKE(1978), art d; FRIGHTMARE(1983), art d
Don Knotts
NO TIME FOR SERGEANTS(1958); WAKE ME WHEN IT'S OVER(1960); LAST TIME I SAW ARCHIE, THE(1961); IT'S A MAD, MAD, MAD, MAD WORLD(1963); MOVE OVER, DARLING(1963); INCREDIBLE MR. LIMPET, THE(1964); GHOST AND MR. CHICKEN, THE(1966); RELUCTANT ASTRONAUT, THE(1967), a, w; SHAKIEST GUN IN THE WEST, THE(1968); LOVE GOD?, THE(1969); HOW TO FRAME A FIGG(1971), a, w; APPLE DUMPLING GANG, THE(1975); GUS(1976); NO DEPOSIT, NO RETURN(1976); HERBIE GOES TO MONTE CARLO(1977); HOT LEAD AND COLD FEET(1978); APPLE DUMPLING GANG RIDES AGAIN, THE(1979); PRIZE FIGHTER, THE(1979); PRIVATE EYES, THE(1980)
1984
CANNONBALL RUN II(1984)
Matthew Know
ONE PLUS ONE(1969, Brit.)
Alice Knowland
Silents
MARTHA'S VINDICATION(1916); FAIR ENOUGH(1918); GIRLS DON'T GAMBLE(1921); ON THE HIGH SEAS(1922); KING OF KINGS, THE(1927); ADORABLE CHEAT, THE(1928)

Misc. Silents
STRONGER LOVE, THE(1916); INNOCENT'S PROGRESS(1918); FULL OF PEP(1919); SATAN JUNIOR(1919); ARCTIC ADVENTURE(1922)

Grace Knowland
COMMON LAW WIFE(1963), w

Joseph Knowland
ESCAPE FROM ALCATRAZ(1979); LITTLE MISS MARKER(1980)

Nic Knowland
SECRETS(1971), ph

Marilyn Knowlden
HUSBAND'S HOLIDAY(1931); WOMEN LOVE ONCE(1931); CONQUERORS, THE(1932); IMITATION OF LIFE(1934); DAVID COPPERFIELD(1935); LES MISERABLES(1935); ANTHONY ADVERSE(1936); RAINBOW ON THE RIVER(1936); SHOW BOAT(1936); WOMAN REBELS, A(1936); SLAVE SHIP(1937); ANGELS WITH DIRTY FACES(1938); BAREFOOT BOY(1938); JUST AROUND THE CORNER(1938); MARIE ANTOINETTE(1938); MEN WITH WINGS(1938); HIDDEN POWER(1939); WAY OF ALL FLESH, THE(1940); SON OF FURY(1942)

Marilynn Knowlden
CISCO KID(1931)

Marilyn Knowldon
EASY TO TAKE(1936)

Marjorie Knowler
CHRISTINA(1974, Can.)

Arthur Knowles
GIRL IN DISTRESS(1941, Brit.), ph

Bernard Knowles
AULD LANG SYNE(1929, Brit.), ph; CANARIES SOMETIMES SING(1930, Brit.), ph; FRENCH LEAVE(1931, Brit.), ph; HOUND OF THE BASKERVILLES(1932, Brit.), ph; FALLING FOR YOU(1933, Brit.), ph; GOOD COMPANIONS(1933, Brit.), ph; WHITE FACE(1933, Brit.), ph; POWER(1934, Brit.), ph; BORN FOR GLORY(1935, Brit.), ph; JACK AHOY!(1935, Brit.), ph; EAST MEETS WEST(1936, Brit.), ph; KING OF THE DAMNED(1936, Brit.), ph; RHODES(1936, Brit.), ph; SECRET AGENT, THE(1936, Brit.), ph; KING SOLOMON'S MINES(1937, Brit.), ph; SABOTAGE(1937, Brit.), ph; TAKE MY TIP(1937, Brit.), ph; YOUNG AND INNOCENT(1938, Brit.), ph; FRENCH WITHOUT TEARS(1939, Brit.), ph; JAMAICA INN(1939, Brit.), ph; MIKADO, THE(1939, Brit.), ph; GASLIGHT(1940), ph; GIRL IN DISTRESS(1941, Brit.), ph; QUIET WEDDING(1941, Brit.), ph; SAINT'S VACATION, THE(1941, Brit.), ph; VOICE IN THE NIGHT, A(1941, Brit.), ph; TALK ABOUT JACQUELINE(1942, Brit.), ph; UNPUBLISHED STORY(1942, Brit.), ph; SECRET MISSION(1944, Brit.), ph; ADVENTURE FOR TWO(1945, Brit.), ph; PLACE OF ONE'S OWN, A(1945, Brit.), d; BAD SISTER(1947, Brit.), d; LADY SURRENDERS, A(1947, Brit.), ph; MAGIC BOW, THE(1947, Brit.), d; EASY MONEY(1948, Brit.), d; JASSY(1948, Brit.), d; SMUGGLERS, THE(1948, Brit.), d; HER MAN GILBEY(1949, Brit.), ph; LOST PEOPLE, THE(1950, Brit.), d; PERFECT WOMAN, THE(1950, Brit.), d, w; RELUCTANT WIDOW, THE(1951, Brit.), d; NORMAN CONQUEST(1953, Brit.), d, w; DEATH OF MICHAEL TURBIN, THE(1954, Brit.), d; FOREVER MY HEART(1954, Brit.), d; HANDCUFFS, LONDON(1955, Brit.), d; MURDER ON APPROVAL(1956, Brit.), d; SPACEFLIGHT IC-1(1965, Brit.), d; FROZEN ALIVE(1966, Brit./Ger.), d; HELL IS EMPTY(1967, Brit./Ital), d, w

C.J. Knowles
ILLEGAL(1932, Brit.), ph

Carl Knowles
ACROSS THE SIERRAS(1941); WING AND A PRAYER(1944); HERE COME THE CO-EDS(1945); JOAN OF ARC(1948)

Cyril Knowles
AVENGERS, THE(1942, Brit.), ph; TALK ABOUT JACQUELINE(1942, Brit.), ph; UNPUBLISHED STORY(1942, Brit.), ph; SECRET MISSION(1944, Brit.), ph; ZARAK(1956, Brit.), ph; BANDIT OF ZHOBE, THE(1959, Brit.), ph; SODOM AND GOMORRAH(1962, U.S./Fr./Ital.), ph

Cyril J. Knowles
CALENDAR, THE(1948, Brit.), ph

Elizabeth Knowles
RED SKY AT MORNING(1971); WILD RIDERS(1971)

Harley Knowles
Misc. Silents
CLEOPATRA(1913)

J. H. Knowles
Silents
KINKAID, GAMBLER(1916)

John Knowles
SEPARATE PEACE, A(1972), w

Patric Knowles
GIRL IN THE CROWD, THE(1934, Brit.); NORAH O'NEALE(1934, Brit.); POISONED DIAMOND, THE(1934, Brit.); ABDUL THE DAMNED(1935, Brit.); HONOURS EASY(1935, Brit.); MEN OF TOMORROW(1935, Brit.); REGAL CAVALCADE(1935, Brit.); BROWN WALLET, THE(1936, Brit.); CHARGE OF THE LIGHT BRIGADE, THE(1936); CROWN VS STEVENS(1936); FAIR EXCHANGE(1936, Brit.); GIVE ME YOUR HEART(1936); IRISH FOR LUCK(1936, Brit.); MISTER HOBO(1936, Brit.); STUDENT'S ROMANCE, THE(1936, Brit.); WRATH OF JEALOUSY(1936, Brit.); EXPENSIVE HUSBANDS(1937); IT'S LOVE I'M AFTER(1937); ADVENTURES OF ROBIN HOOD, THE(1938); FOUR'S A CROWD(1938); HEART OF THE NORTH(1938); PATIENT IN ROOM 18, THE(1938); SISTERS, THE(1938); STORM OVER BENGAL(1938); TORCHY BLANE IN CHINATOWN(1938); ANOTHER THIN MAN(1939); BEAUTY FOR THE ASKING(1939); FIVE CAME BACK(1939); HONEYMOON'S OVER, THE(1939); SPELLBINDER, THE(1939); TWO'S COMPANY(1939, Brit.); ANNE OF WINDY POPLARS(1940); BILL OF DIVORCEMENT(1940); MARRIED AND IN LOVE(1940); WOMEN IN WAR(1940); HOW GREEN WAS MY VALLEY(1941); WOLF MAN, THE(1941); LADY IN A JAM(1942); MYSTERY OF MARIE ROGET, THE(1942); SIN TOWN(1942); STRANGE CASE OF DR. RX, THE(1942); WHO DONE IT?(1942); ALL BY MYSELF(1943); ALWAYS A BRIDESMAID(1943); CRAZY HOUSE(1943); FOREVER AND A DAY(1943); FRANKENSTEIN MEETS THE WOLF MAN(1943); HIT THE ICE(1943); CHIP OFF THE OLD BLOCK(1944); PARDON MY RHYTHM(1944); THIS IS THE LIFE(1944); KITTY(1945); MASQUERADE IN MEXICO(1945); BRIDE WORE BOOTS, THE(1946); MONSIEUR BEAUCAIRE(1946); OF HUMAN BONDAGE(1946); O.S.S.(1946); DREAM GIRL(1947); IVY(1947); VARIETY GIRL(1947); ISN'T IT ROMANTIC?(1948); BIG STEAL, THE(1949); THREE CAME HOME(1950); QUEBEC(1951); MUTINY(1952); TARZAN'S SAVAGE FURY(1952); FLAME OF CALCUTTA(1953); JAMAICA RUN(1953); KHYBER PATROL(1954); WORLD FOR RANSOM(1954); NO MAN'S WOMAN(1955); BAND OF ANGELS(1957); AUNTIE MAME(1958); FROM THE EARTH TO THE MOON(1958); WAY WEST, THE(1967);

DEVIL'S BRIGADE, THE(1968); IN ENEMY COUNTRY(1968); MAN, THE(1972); ARNOLD(1973); TERROR IN THE WAX MUSEUM(1973)

Paula Knowles
1984
INITIATION, THE(1984)

Julia Knowlton
SAND CASTLE, THE(1961), ed

Vianna Knowlton
Silents
AFTER THE SHOW(1921), w

Kim Knowton
RAIDERS OF THE LOST ARK(1981), anim

Alexander Knox
CHEER BOYS CHEER(1939, Brit.); PHANTOM STRIKES, THE(1939, Brit.); SEA WOLF, THE(1941); COMMANDOS STRIKE AT DAWN, THE(1942); THIS ABOVE ALL(1942); NONE SHALL ESCAPE(1944); WILSON(1944); OVER 21(1945); SISTER KENNY(1946), a, w; SIGN OF THE RAM, THE(1948); JUDGE STEPS OUT, THE(1949), a, w; TOKYO JOE(1949); I'D CLIMB THE HIGHEST MOUNTAIN(1951); MAN IN THE SADDLE(1951); SATURDAY'S HERO(1951); SON OF DR. JEKYLL, THE(1951); TWO OF A KIND(1951); PAULA(1952); GREATEST LOVE, THE(1954, Ital.); SLEEPING TIGER, THE(1954, Brit.); DIVIDED HEART, THE(1955, Brit.); NIGHT MY NUMBER CAME UP, THE(1955, Brit.); ONE JUST MAN(1955, Brit.); ALIAS JOHN PRESTON(1956); HIDDEN FEAR(1957); HIGH TIDE AT NOON(1957, Brit.); REACH FOR THE SKY(1957, Brit.); CHASE A CROOKED SHADOW(1958, Brit.); DAVY(1958, Brit.); INTENT TO KILL(1958, Brit.); VIKINGS, THE(1958); PASSIONATE SUMMER(1959, Brit.); TWO-HEADED SPY, THE(1959, Brit.); WRECK OF THE MARY DEAR, THE(1959); CRACK IN THE MIRROR(1960); OPERATION AMSTERDAM(1960, Brit.); OSCAR WILDE(1960, Brit.); LONGEST DAY, THE(1962); IN THE COOL OF THE DAY(1963); MAN IN THE MIDDLE(1964, U.S./Brit.); WOMAN OF STRAW(1964, Brit.); CRACK IN THE WORLD(1965); MISTER MOSES(1965); THESE ARE THE DAMNED(1965, Brit.); KHARTOUM(1966, Brit.); MODESTY BLAISE(1966, Brit.); PSYCHOPATH, THE(1966, Brit.); SHARE OUT, THE(1966, Brit.); ACCIDENT(1967, Brit.); HOW I WON THE WAR(1967, Brit.); YOU ONLY LIVE TWICE(1967, Brit.); 25TH HOUR, THE(1967, Fr./Ital./Yugo.); SHALAKO(1968, Brit.); VILLA RIDES(1968); FRAULEIN DOKTOR(1969, Ital./Yugo.); SKULLDUGGERY(1970); NICHOLAS AND ALEXANDRA(1971, Brit.); PUPPET ON A CHAIN(1971, Brit.); CHOSEN, THE(1978, Brit./Ital.); GORKY PARK(1983)
Misc. Talkies
BIKINI PARADISE(1967)

Ann Knox
ONLY THING YOU KNOW, THE(1971, Can.)

Buddy Knox
JAMBOREE(1957)
Misc. Talkies
SWEET COUNTRY ROAD(1981)

David Knox
IT ALWAYS RAINS ON SUNDAY(1949, Brit.); HUE AND CRY(1950, Brit.)

Doris Knox
SERVANT, THE(1964, Brit.)

Elyse Knox
WAKE UP AND LIVE(1937); FREE, BLONDE AND 21(1940); GIRL FROM AVENUE A(1940); GIRL IN 313(1940); LILLIAN RUSSELL(1940); STAR DUST(1940); YOUTH WILL BE SERVED(1940); FOOTLIGHT FEVER(1941); SHERIFF OF TOMBSTONE(1941); TANKS A MILLION(1941); ARABIAN NIGHTS(1942); HAY FOOT(1942); MUMMY'S TOMB, THE(1942); TOP SERGEANT(1942); HI' YA, SAILOR(1943); HIT THE ICE(1943); KEEP 'EM SLUGGING(1943); MR. BIG(1943); SO'S YOUR UNCLE(1943); ARMY WIVES(1944); FOLLOW THE BOYS(1944); MOONLIGHT AND CACTUS(1944); WAVE, A WAC AND A MARINE, A(1944); JOE PALOOKA, CHAMP(1946); SWEETHEART OF SIGMA CHI(1946); BLACK GOLD(1947); LINDA BE GOOD(1947); FIGHTING MAD(1948); I WOULDN'T BE IN YOUR SHOES(1948); JOE PALOOKA IN WINNER TAKE ALL(1948); FORGOTTEN WOMEN(1949); JOE PALOOKA IN THE COUNTERPUNCH(1949); THERE'S A GIRL IN MY HEART(1949)
Misc. Talkies
JOE PALOOKA IN THE KNOCKOUT(1947)

Foster Knox
Silents
SQUAW MAN, THE(1914)

Harold E. Knox
GANG WAR(1958), p; SHOWDOWN AT BOOT HILL(1958), p

Herman Knox
ANGELS FROM HELL(1968), ph

Ken Knox
GIANT GILA MONSTER, THE(1959); BEYOND THE TIME BARRIER(1960); MY DOG, BUDDY(1960)

Louella Knox
Misc. Silents
SOCIETY WOLVES(1916)

Lucille Knox
BUS STOP(1956)

Matt Knox
RATTLERS(1976)

Matthew Knox
PRIVATE ENTERPRISE, A(1975, Brit.), art d

Mickey Knox
KILLER McCOY(1947); I WALK ALONE(1948); JUNGLE PATROL(1948); ACCUSED, THE(1949); ANGELS IN DISGUISE(1949); ANY NUMBER CAN PLAY(1949); CITY ACROSS THE RIVER(1949); KNOCK ON ANY DOOR(1949); WHITE HEAT(1949); DESTINATION BIG HOUSE(1950); OUTSIDE THE WALL(1950); WESTERN PACIFIC AGENT(1950); CRIMINAL LAWYER(1951); SATURDAY'S HERO(1951); UP FRONT(1951); GARDEN OF EDEN(1954); SINGING IN THE DARK(1956); VIEW FROM THE BRIDGE, A(1962, Fr./Ital.); VICTORS, THE(1963); TENTH VICTIM, THE(1965, Fr./Ital.); BEYOND THE LAW(1968); BIGGEST BUNDLE OF THEM ALL, THE(1968); WILD 90(1968); DON'T TURN THE OTHER CHEEK(1974, Ital./Ger./Span.), p; BOBBY DEERFIELD(1977); INCHON(1981); LONELY LADY, THE(1983)
1984
BOLERO(1984)

Mona Knox
PETTY GIRL, THE(1950); TARZAN AND THE SLAVE GIRL(1950); TWO TICKETS TO BROADWAY(1951); ARMY BOUND(1952); GREATEST SHOW ON EARTH, THE(1952); HOLD THAT LINE(1952); KID MONK BARONI(1952); LAS VEGAS

STORY, THE(1952); THUNDERING CARAVANS(1952); GIRL NEXT DOOR, THE(1953); JALOPY(1953); HOLD BACK TOMORROW(1955); ESCAPE FROM TERROR(1960); ROSEMARY'S BABY(1968)

Norman Knox
FOREVER YOUNG, FOREVER FREE(1976, South Afr.)

Pat Knox
SILENT PARTNER(1944)

Patricia Knox
CITY OF MISSING GIRLS(1941); LADY FOR A NIGHT(1941); SING FOR YOUR SUPPER(1941); SECRETS OF A CO-ED(1942); GIRLS IN CHAINS(1943); O, MY DARLING CLEMENTINE(1943); CASANOVA IN BURLESQUE(1944); MAN FROM FRISCO(1944); PORT OF 40 THIEVES, THE(1944); TRAIL OF TERROR(1944); FLAMING BULLETS(1945); I ACCUSE MY PARENTS(1945); GENTLEMEN WITH GUNS(1946); PRAIRIE BADMEN(1946); EXPOSED(1947); POST OFFICE INVESTIGATOR(1949); INSURANCE INVESTIGATOR(1951)
Misc. Talkies
BORDER ROUNDUP(1942); SINGING SPURS(1948)

Robert Knox
Misc. Talkies
SCREAM BLOODY MURDER(1973)

Stephen Knox
AMERICAN GRAFFITI(1973)

Stuart Knox
Silents
LILAC TIME(1928)

Teddy Knox
IT'S IN THE BAG(1936, Brit.); SKYLARKS(1936, Brit.); OKAY FOR SOUND(1937, Brit.), a, w; ALF'S BUTTON AFLOAT(1938, Brit.); GASBAGS(1940, Brit.); LIFE IS A CIRCUS(1962, Brit.)

Terence Knox
HEART LIKE A WHEEL(1983)
1984
LIES(1984, Brit.)
Misc. Talkies
LIES(1983)

Teresa Knox
STACY'S KNIGHTS(1983)

Walter Knox
SUNDOWN(1941)

Paul Knuckles
SLAUGHTER(1972), stunts; SMALL TOWN IN TEXAS, A(1976), stunts

Barbara Knudsen
MEET DANNY WILSON(1952)

Bill Knudsen
INVITATION TO HAPPINESS(1939)

Clyde Knudsen
HIGH YELLOW(1965), p

David Knudsen
Misc. Silents
SYV DAGER FOR ELISABETH(1927, Swed.)

Elsebet Knudsen
WEEKEND(1964, Den.)

Kolbjorn Knudsen
WINTER LIGHT, THE(1963, Swed.)

Lillemor Knudsen
WILL ANY GENTLEMAN?(1955, Brit.); KEEP IT CLEAN(1956, Brit.)

Mette Knudsen
1984
ZAPPA(1984, Den.)

Nancy Knudsen
OUTBACK(1971, Aus.)

Peggy Knudsen
BIG SLEEP, THE(1946); HUMORESQUE(1946); NEVER SAY GOODBYE(1946); SHADOW OF A WOMAN(1946); STOLEN LIFE, A(1946); MY WILD IRISH ROSE(1947); ROSES ARE RED(1947); STALLION ROAD(1947); UNFAITHFUL, THE(1947); HALF PAST MIDNIGHT(1948); PERILOUS WATERS(1948); TROUBLE PREFERRED(1949); COPPER CANYON(1950); BETRAYED WOMEN(1955); GOOD MORNING, MISS DOVE(1955); UNCHAINED(1955); BOTTOM OF THE BOTTLE, THE(1956); HILDA CRANE(1956)

Pete Knudsen
CHILDREN OF GOD'S EARTH(1983, Norwegian), m

Poul Knudsen
DAY OF WRATH(1948, Den.), w

Barbara Knudson
UNION STATION(1950); LADY FROM TEXAS, THE(1951); SON OF ALI BABA(1952); ONE DESIRE(1955); CRY BABY KILLER, THE(1958)

Barbara Ann Knudson
IRON MAN, THE(1951)

Frederic Knudson
PRAIRIE LAW(1940), ed; ALONG THE RIO GRANDE(1941), ed; BACHELOR AND THE BOBBY-SOXER, THE(1947), ed; BORN TO BE BAD(1950), ed

Frederick Knudson
ROOKIE COP, THE(1939), ed

Harlan Knudson
DUCHESS AND THE DIRTWATER FOX, THE(1976)

Kurt Knudson
1984
COLD FEET(1984)

Peggy Knudson
ISTANBUL(1957)
Misc. Talkies
IN SELF DEFENSE(1947)

Thurston Knudson
CALL OF THE SOUTH SEAS(1944), m

Floyd Knudston
COLOSSUS OF NEW YORK, THE(1958), ed

Frederic Knudston
SATURDAY'S HEROES(1937), ed; BORDER G-MAN(1938), ed; COME ON DANGER(1942), ed

William Knudston
BRIDE FOR SALE(1949), ed

Fred Knudtsen
RUN FOR THE SUN(1956), ed

Frederick Knudtsen
CROSSFIRE(1933), ed

Floyd Knudtson
LEATHER SAINT, THE(1956), ed; SEARCH FOR BRIDEY MURPHY, THE(1956), ed; BEAU JAMES(1957), ed; DEVIL'S HAIRPIN, THE(1957), ed

Fred Knudtson
HEADLINE SHOOTER(1933), ed; SCARLET RIVER(1933), ed; I CAN'T ESCAPE(1934), ed; RIDING THE WIND(1942), ed; GUNFIRE AT INDIAN GAP(1957), ed; MAN WHO DIED TWICE, THE(1958), ed; NOTORIOUS MR. MONKS, THE(1958), ed; MINNIE AND MOSKOWITZ(1971), ed

Frederic Knudtson
SON OF THE BORDER(1933), ed; BIG GAME, THE(1936), ed; TWO IN REVOLT(1936), ed; MEET THE MISSUS(1937), ed; SOLDIER AND THE LADY, THE(1937), ed; PAINTED DESERT, THE(1938), ed; RENEGADE RANGER(1938), ed; SHE'S GOT EVERYTHING(1938), ed; ARIZONA LEGION(1939), ed; FIGHTING GRINGO, THE(1939), ed; RACKETEERS OF THE RANGE(1939), ed; TIMBER STAMPEDE(1939), ed; BULLET CODE(1940), ed; LEGION OF THE LAWLESS(1940), ed; MARINES FLY HIGH, THE(1940), ed; STAGE TO CHINO(1940), ed; TRIPLE JUSTICE(1940), ed; WAGON TRAIN(1940), ed; BANDIT TRAIL, THE(1941), ed; LAND OF THE OPEN RANGE(1941), ed; SIX GUN GOLD(1941), ed; THUNDERING HOOFS(1941), ed; THIS LAND IS MINE(1943), ed; STATION WEST(1948), ed; DANGEROUS PROFESSION, A(1949), ed; EASY LIVING(1949), ed; STRANGE BARGAIN(1949), ed; WINDOW, THE(1949), ed; WALK SOFTLY, STRANGER(1950), ed; HIS KIND OF WOMAN(1951), ed; ANGEL FACE(1953), ed; SON OF SINBAD(1955), ed; PRIDE AND THE PASSION, THE(1957), ed; CROOKED CIRCLE, THE(1958), ed; DEFIANT ONES, THE(1958), ed; CRY TOUGH(1959), ed; ON THE BEACH(1959), ed; GREAT IMPOSTOR, THE(1960), ed; JUDGMENT AT NUREMBERG(1961), ed; POSSE FROM HELL(1961), ed; PRESSURE POINT(1962), ed; THIRD OF A MAN(1962), ed; IT'S A MAD, MAD, MAD, MAD WORLD(1963), ed

Frederich Knudtson
LAWLESS VALLEY(1938), ed

Frederick Knudtson
GUN LAW(1938), ed; MARSHAL OF MESA CITY, THE(1939), ed; TROUBLE IN SUNDOWN(1939), ed; CYCLONE ON HORSEBACK(1941), ed; FARGO KID, THE(1941), ed; ROBBERS OF THE RANGE(1941), ed; CRACK-UP(1946), ed; NOT AS A STRANGER(1955), ed

Fredric Knudtson
DUDE COWBOY(1941), ed; INHERIT THE WIND(1960), ed

Gustav Knuth
TROMBA, THE TIGER MAN(1952, Ger.); RATS, THE(1955, Ger.); BEGGAR STUDENT, THE(1958, Ger.); DAY WILL COME, A(1960, Ger.); HIPPODROME(1961, Aust./Ger.); HOUSE OF THE THREE GIRLS, THE(1961, Aust.); FOREVER MY LOVE(1962); FREDDY UNTER FREMDEN STERNEN(1962, Ger.); GIRL AND THE LEGEND, THE(1966, Ger.); HEIDI(1968, Aust.)

Klaus Knuth
FOREVER MY LOVE(1962)

Linda Knutson
SUMMER AND SMOKE(1961)

Lars Knutzon
GERTRUD(1966, Den.)

L. Knyazev
CLEAR SKIES(1963, USSR); OPTIMISTIC TRAGEDY, THE(1964, USSR)

Aleksandr Knyazhinsky
STALKER(1982, USSR), ph

Ko
LITTLE ARK, THE(1972)

Chin Ko
VERMILION DOOR(1969, Hong Kong), w

Hideo Ko
GOKE, BODYSNATCHER FROM HELL(1968, Jap.)

Keisuke Ko
TOPSY-TURVY JOURNEY(1970, Jap.)

Ko-Hal
SHARK WOMAN, THE(1941)

Harry Koady
OLD MOTHER RILEY'S CIRCUS(1941, Brit.)

Guenter Kob
DOCTOR OF ST. PAUL, THE(1969, Ger.), set d

G. Kobakhidze
FATHER OF A SOLDIER(1966, USSR)

Georges Kobakhidze
INNOCENTS IN PARIS(1955, Brit.)

Ruth Kobart
PETULIA(1968, U.S./Brit.); DIRTY HARRY(1971); HINDENBURG, THE(1975); HOW TO SUCCEED IN BUSINESS WITHOUT REALLY TRYING(1976)

Frank Kobata
THREE CAME HOME(1950)

Akira Kobayashi
FRIENDLY KILLER, THE(1970, Jap.)

Katsuhiko Kobayashi
BUDDHA(1965, Jap.)

Kazuyuki Kobayashi
1984
WARRIORS OF THE WIND(1984, Jap.), anim

Keiji Kobayashi
TIDAL WAVE(1975, U.S./Jap.)

Keiju Kobayashi
ETERNITY OF LOVE(1961, Jap.); EARLY AUTUMN(1962, Jap.); HAPPINESS OF US ALONE(1962, Jap.); SANJURO(1962, Jap.); WISER AGE(1962, Jap.); CHUSHINGURA(1963, Jap.); MY HOBO(1963, Jap.); NAKED GENERAL, THE(1964, Jap.); PRESSURE OF GUILT(1964, Jap.); SAMURAI ASSASSIN(1965, Jap.); WE WILL REMEMBER(1966, Jap.); DAPHNE, THE(1967); THIN LINE, THE(1967, Jap.); EMPEROR AND A GENERAL, THE(1968, Jap.); OUR SILENT LOVE(1969, Jap.); BAND OF ASSASSINS(1971, Jap.)

Kenju Kobayashi
PROPHECIES OF NOSTRADAMUS(1974, Jap.)
Kyuzo Kobayashi
GOKE, BODYSNATCHER FROM HELL(1968, Jap.), w
Masaki Kobayashi
HUMAN CONDITION, THE(1959, Jap.), d, w; ROAD TO ETERNITY(1962, Jap.), d, w; HAHAKIRI(1963, Jap.), d; INHERITANCE, THE(1964, Jap.), d; KWAIDAN(1965, Jap.), d; REBELLION(1967, Jap.), d; SOLDIER'S PRAYER, A(1970, Jap.), p, d, w; GLOWING AUTUMN(1981, Jap.), d
Mieko Kobayashi
1984
SWORDKILL(1984)
Naomi Kobayashi
SECRETS OF A WOMAN'S TEMPLE(1969, Jap.)
Setsuo Kobayashi
FIRES ON THE PLAIN(1962, Jap.), ph; ACTOR'S REVENGE, AN(1963, Jap.), ph; PASSION(1968, Jap.), ph; THOUSAND CRANES(1969, Jap.), ph; PLAY IT COOL(1970, Jap.), ph; VIXEN(1970, Jap.), ph
Shigeo Kobayashi
HELL IN THE PACIFIC(1968), makeup; KUROENKO(1968, Jap), makeup
Shoji Kobayashi
HAHAKIRI(1963, Jap.); PLEASURES OF THE FLESH, THE(1965); SHOGUN ASSAS-SIN(1980, Jap.)
Shun'ichi Kobayashi
TORA-SAN PART 2(1970, Jap.), w
Tadashi Kobayashi
TEMPTRESS AND THE MONK, THE(1963, Jap.)
Taisuke Kobayashi
HOTSPRINGS HOLIDAY(1970, Jap.)
Tetsuko Kobayashi
ATRAGON(1965, Jap.)
Toshie Kobayashi
GIRL I ABANDONED, THE(1970, Jap.)
Toshiko Kobayashi
NAKED YOUTH(1961, Jap.); SUMMER SOLDIERS(1972, Jap.)
Tsuneo Kobayashi
MAN IN THE MOONLIGHT MASK, THE(1958, Jap.), d
Tsuruko Kobayashi
CRY FOR HAPPY(1961); MAJORITY OF ONE, A(1961); VARAN THE UNBELIEVA-BLE(1962, U.S./Jap.); TARZAN'S THREE CHALLENGES(1963)
Yukihiko Kobayashi
SPACE AMOEBA, THE(1970, Jap.)
Yukiko Kobayashi
DESTROY ALL MONSTERS(1969, Jap.); YOG-MONSTER FROM SPACE(1970, Jap.)
Mieko Kobayshi
LAST MARRIED COUPLE IN AMERICA, THE(1980)
Pamela V. Kobbe
WRONG IS RIGHT(1982)
Arthuro Kobe
CONDEMNED(1929)
Gail Kobe
TEN COMMANDMENTS, THE(1956); GUNSMOKE IN TUCSON(1958)
Arthur Kober
IT PAYS TO ADVERTISE(1931), w; SECRET CALL, THE(1931), w; UP POPS THE DEVIL(1931), w; FALSE MADONNA(1932), w; GUILTY AS HELL(1932), w; MAKE ME A STAR(1932), w; ME AND MY GAL(1932), w; BONDAGE(1933), w; BROADWAY BAD(1933), w; HEADLINE SHOOTER(1933), w; INFERNAL MACHINE(1933), w; IT'S GREAT TO BE ALIVE(1933), w; MAMA LOVES PAPA(1933), w; MEET THE BARON(1933), w; HOLLYWOOD PARTY(1934), w; PALOOKA(1934), w; CALM YOURSELF(1935), w; GINGER(1935), w; GREAT HOTEL MURDER(1935), w; BIG BROADCAST OF 1937, THE(1936), w; EARLY TO BED(1936), w; HAVING WONDER-FUL TIME(1938), w; LITTLE FOXES, THE(1941), w; WINTERTIME(1943), w; IN THE MEANTIME, DARLING(1944), w; DON JUAN QUILLIGAN(1945), w; MY OWN TRUE LOVE(1948), w
Marta Kober
FRIDAY THE 13TH PART II(1981); BABY, IT'S YOU(1983)
1984
FRIDAY THE 13TH-THE FINAL CHAPTER(1984)
Otar Koberidze
STEPCHILDREN(1962, USSR); DREAM COME TRUE, A(1963, USSR), a, d; ITALIA-NO BRAVA GENTE(1965, Ital./USSR); TSAR'S BRIDE, THE(1966, USSR); RED TENT, THE(1971, Ital./USSR)
Alexander Kobes
THERESE AND ISABELLE(1968, U.S./Ger.)
Michi Kobi
TOKYO AFTER DARK(1959); HELL TO ETERNITY(1960); TWELVE TO THE MOON(1960); CRY FOR HAPPY(1961)
Bogumil Kobiela
ASHES AND DIAMONDS(1961, Pol.); YELLOW SLIPPERS, THE(1965, Pol.); EROI-CA(1966, Pol.); SARAGOSSA MANUSCRIPT, THE(1972, Pol.)
Koblenzova
ROMANCE OF SEVILLE, A(1929, Brit.)
Erich Kobler
SNOW WHITE(1965, Ger.), d; SNOW WHITE AND ROSE RED(1966, Ger.), d; SHOEMAKER AND THE ELVES, THE(1967, Ger.), d
John Kobler
FORGOTTEN WOMAN, THE(1939), w
Nicholas Kobliansky
STRANGE WIVES(1935); NORTHWEST OUTPOST(1947)
Nick Kobliansky
SWING HIGH, SWING LOW(1937); EVERYTHING HAPPENS AT NIGHT(1939); MISSION TO MOSCOW(1943); DOUGHGIRLS, THE(1944)
Josef Koblizek
DIAMONDS OF THE NIGHT(1968, Czech.)
Akio Kobori
RODAN(1958, Jap.); MAN IN THE STORM, THE(1969, Jap.)
Jerry Kobrin
FRASIER, THE SENSUOUS LION(1973), a, w

Richard Kobritz
CHRISTINE(1983), p
Dorothy Kobs
FRIDAY THE 13TH(1980)
Makoto Koburi
IKIRU(1960, Jap.)
Nicholas Kobyliansky
Silents
LAST COMMAND, THE(1928)
Bogdan Koca
1984
SHIVERS(1984, Pol.)
Angelika Koch
CABARET(1972)
Betty Koch
NIGHTFALL(1956); GARMENT JUNGLE, THE(1957)
C.J. Koch
YEAR OF LIVING DANGEROUSLY, THE(1982, Aus.), w
Carl Koch
LA MARSEILLAISE(1938, Fr.), w; RULES OF THE GAME, THE(1939, Fr.), w; NIGHT OF THE FULL MOON, THE(1954, Brit.), w
Carlo Koch
UNA SIGNORA DELL'OVEST(1942, Ital), d, w
Edward Koch
HELL'S ISLAND(1955)
Mayor Edward I. Koch
1984
MUPPETS TAKE MANHATTAN, THE(1984)
Eileen Koch
FINNEGANS WAKE(1965)
Elaine Koch
BIG POND, THE(1930)
Franz Koch
SERGEANT BERRY(1938, Ger.), ph; WATER FOR CANITOGA(1939, Ger.), ph; LONG IS THE ROAD(1948, Ger.), ph
Freddy Koch
OPERATION LOVEBIRDS(1968, Den.)
Georg August Koch
F.P. 1 DOESN'T ANSWER(1933, Ger.)
Silents
KRIEMHILD'S REVENGE(1924, Ger.)
Howard Koch
LETTER, THE(1940), w; SEA HAWK, THE(1940), w; VIRGINIA CITY(1940), w; SHINING VICTORY(1941), w; CASABLANCA(1942), w; IN THIS OUR LIFE(1942), w; MISSION TO MOSCOW(1943), w; IN OUR TIME(1944), w; RHAPSODY IN BLUE(1945), w; THREE STRANGERS(1946), w; LETTER FROM AN UNKNOWN WOMAN(1948), w; NO SAD SONGS FOR ME(1950), w; THIRTEENTH LETTER, THE(1951), w; BLACK SLEEP, THE(1956), w; LOSS OF INNOCENCE(1961, Brit.), w; WAR LOVER, THE(1962, U.S./Brit.), w; SQUADRON 633(1964, U.S./Brit.), w; 633 SQUADRON(1964), w; FOX, THE(1967), w; AIRPLANE II: THE SEQUEL(1982), p
Howard Koch [Peter Howard]
FINGER OF GUILT(1956, Brit.), w
Howard W. Koch
WAR PAINT(1953), p; BEACHHEAD(1954), p; SHIELD FOR MURDER(1954), d; YELLOW TOMAHAWK, THE(1954), p; BIG HOUSE, U.S.A.(1955), d; DESERT SANDS(1955), p; FORT YUMA(1955), p; BROKEN STAR, THE(1956), p; CRIME AGAINST JOE(1956), p; EMERGENCY HOSPITAL(1956), p; HOT CARS(1956), p; QUINCANNON, FRONTIER SCOUT(1956), p; REBEL IN TOWN(1956), p; THREE BAD SISTERS(1956), p; BOP GIRL GOES CALYPSO(1957), d; DALTON GIRLS, THE(1957), p; GIRL IN BLACK STOCKINGS(1957), d; HELL BOUND(1957), p; JUN-GLE HEAT(1957), d; PHARAOH'S CURSE(1957), p; REVOLT AT FORT LARA-MIE(1957), p; TOMAHAWK TRAIL(1957), p; UNTAMED YOUTH(1957), d; VOODOO ISLAND(1957), p; WAR DRUMS(1957), p; ANDY HARDY COMES HOME(1958), d; FORT BOWIE(1958), p; FRANKENSTEIN 1970(1958), d; VIOLENT ROAD(1958), p; BORN RECKLESS(1959), d; LAST MILE, THE(1959), d; ODD COUPLE, THE(1968), p; ON A CLEAR DAY YOU CAN SEE FOREVER(1970), p; PLAZA SUITE(1971), p; STAR SPANGLED GIRL(1971), p; LAST OF THE RED HOT LOVERS(1972), p; BADGE 373(1973), p&d; ONCE IS NOT ENOUGH(1975), p; SOME KIND OF HERO(1982), p
Howard W. Koch, Jr.
IDOLMAKER, THE(1980), p; HONKY TONK FREEWAY(1981), p; GORKY PARK(1983), p; KEEP, THE(1983), p; NIGHT IN HEAVEN, A(1983), p
Hugh B. Koch
Silents
ANTON THE TERRIBLE(1916)
Lotte Koch
CITY OF TORMENT(1950, Ger.)
Marianna Koch
FISTFUL OF DOLLARS, A(1964, Ital./Ger./Span.)
Marianne Koch
AFFAIRS OF DR. HOLL(1954, Ger.); NIGHT PEOPLE(1954); DEVIL'S AGENT, THE(1962, Brit.); HELDINNEN(1962, Ger.); SANDERS(1963, Brit.); DIE FLEDER-MAUS(1964, Aust.); COAST OF SKELETONS(1965, Brit.); FROZEN ALIVE(1966, Brit./Ger.); PLACE CALLED GLORY, A(1966, Span./Ger.); SUNSCORCHED(1966, Span./Ger.); TRUNK TO CAIRO(1966, Israel/Ger.); MONSTER OF LONDON CITY, THE(1967, Ger.); SANDY THE SEAL(1969, Brit.)
Marrianne Koch
DEVIL'S GENERAL, THE(1957, Ger.)
Norma Koch
ROSE OF CIMARRON(1952), cos; SLIGHTLY SCARLET(1956), cos; SAYONA-RA(1957), cos; CRY FOR HAPPY(1961), cos; LAST SUNSET, THE(1961), cos; WHA-TEVER HAPPENED TO BABY JANE?(1962), cos; FOUR FOR TEXAS(1963), cos; KINGS OF THE SUN(1963), cos; HUSH... HUSH, SWEET CHARLOTTE(1964), cos; FLIGHT OF THE PHOENIX, THE(1965), cos; WAY WEST, THE(1967), cos; MACKEN-NA'S GOLD(1969), cos; GRISSOM GANG, THE(1971), cos; LADY SINGS THE BLUES(1972), cos
Norman Koch
TARAS BULBA(1962), cos

Randi Koch
CHILDREN OF GOD'S EARTH(1983, Norwegian)
Uwe-Karsten Koch
1984
LOOSE CONNECTIONS(1984, Brit.)
Vladimir Koch
NINTH CIRCLE, THE(1961, Yugo.), w
Walter Koch
WHITE HORSE INN, THE(1959, Ger.)
Wolfgang Koch
YOUNG GO WILD, THE(1962, Ger.)
Afanasi Kochetkov
MUMU(1961, USSR)
Edda Kochi
ALICE IN THE CITIES(1974, W. Ger.)
Momoko Kochi
HALF HUMAN(1955, Jap.); GODZILLA, RING OF THE MONSTERS(1956, Jap.); MYSTERIANS, THE(1959, Jap.)
Premyal Koci
NINTH HEART, THE(1980, Czech.)
Anneliese Kocialek
TINDER BOX, THE(1968, E. Ger.), w
Marian Kociniak
DANTON(1983)
Frank Kock
HOUSE OF LIFE(1953, Ger.), ph
Suzana Kocurikova
MAN WHO LIES, THE(1970, Czech./Fr.)
Dara Kocy
XICA(1982, Braz.)
Hulya Kocyigit [Julie Kotch]
DRY SUMMER(1967, Turkey)
Wanda Koczewska
GUESTS ARE COMING(1965, Pol.)
Zoltan Kodaly
SUN SHINES, THE(1939, Hung.), m
Fumio Kodama
1984
REVENGE OF THE NERDS(1984)
Jiro Kodama
KARATE, THE HAND OF DEATH(1961)
Kiyoshi Kodama
DEATH ON THE MOUNTAIN(1961, Jap.); ETERNITY OF LOVE(1961, Jap.); WE WILL REMEMBER(1966, Jap.)
Rene Kodehoff
BLOOD IN THE STREETS(1975, Ital./Fr.)
Kinshichi Kodera
UGETSU(1954, Jap.), ch
Jiri Kodet
SWEET LIGHT IN A DARK ROOM(1966, Czech.)
Nikolay Kodin
WAR AND PEACE(1968, USSR)
Sosie Kodjian
TEARS OF HAPPINESS(1974)
James Kodl
FEMALE JUNGLE, THE(1955)
Jim Kodl
T.R. BASKIN(1971)
Kokuten Kodo
IDIOT, THE(1963, Jap.)
Kunihori Kodo
SEVEN SAMURAI, THE(1956, Jap.)
Kuninori Kodo
SAMURAI(PART II)** (1967, Jap.); SCANDAL(1964, Jap.)
Eisei Koe
HOUSE OF STRANGE LOVES, THE(1969, Jap.), p
Rainer Koechermann
DANCING HEART, THE(1959, Ger.)
Kai Koed
REPTILICUS(1962, U.S./Den.), set d
Johan Koegelenberg
WILD SEASON(1968, South Africa)
Bonnie Koehler
LULU(1978, ed; STACY'S KNIGHTS(1983), ed
Dave Koehler
FORT APACHE(1948), spec eff; TARGET EARTH(1954), spec eff
David Koehler
CHINA DOLL(1958), spec eff; SHE DEMONS(1958), spec eff; ESCORT WEST(1959), spec eff; DEADLY COMPANIONS, THE(1961), spec eff; NOTORIOUS LANDLADY, THE(1962), spec eff; CHASE, THE(1966), spec eff
Frederick Koehler
MR. MOM(1983)
Jean Koehler
WITHOUT RESERVATIONS(1946)
Ted Koehler
CURLY TOP(1935), m; STORMY WEATHER(1943), w
William R. Koehler
INCREDIBLE JOURNEY, THE(1963), animal sup; UGLY DACHSHUND, THE(1966), animal t.
Maurits Koek
LITTLE ARK, THE(1972)
Michael Koen
SEVENTH DAWN, THE(1964), w
Fred J. Koenekamp
GREAT BANK ROBBERY, THE(1969), ph; FLAP(1970), ph; UPTOWN SATURDAY NIGHT(1974), ph; POSSE(1975), ph; BAD NEWS BEARS IN BREAKING TRAINING, THE(1977), ph; ISLANDS IN THE STREAM(1977), ph; OTHER SIDE OF MIDNIGHT, THE(1977), ph; SWARM, THE(1978), ph; AMITYVILLE HORROR, THE(1979), ph; CHAMP, THE(1979), ph; FIRST FAMILY(1980), ph; HUNTER, THE(1980), ph; WHEN TIME RAN OUT(1980), ph; FIRST MONDAY IN OCTOBER(1981), ph; WRONG IS

RIGHT(1982), ph; YES, GIORGIO(1982), ph
1984
ADVENTURES OF BUCKAROO BANZAI: ACROSS THE 8TH DIMENSION, THE(1984), ph
Fred Koenekamp
ONE OF OUR SPIES IS MISSING(1966), ph; ONE SPY TOO MANY(1966), ph; SPY IN THE GREEN HAT, THE(1966), ph; SPY WITH MY FACE, THE(1966), ph; DOCTOR, YOU'VE GOT TO BE KIDDING(1967), ph; KARATE KILLERS, THE(1967), ph; LIVE A LITTLE, LOVE A LITTLE(1968), ph; SOL MADRID(1968), ph; STAY AWAY, JOE(1968), ph; HEAVEN WITH A GUN(1969), ph; PATTON(1970), ph; BILLY JACK(1971), ph; HAPPY BIRTHDAY, WANDA JUNE(1971), ph; SKIN GAME(1971), ph; KANSAS CITY BOMBER(1972), ph; MAGNIFICENT SEVEN RIDE, THE(1972), ph; RAGE(1972), ph; STAND UP AND BE COUNTED(1972), ph; HARRY IN YOUR POCKET(1973), ph; PAPILLON(1973), ph; TOWERING INFERNO, THE(1974), ph; DOC SAVAGE... THE MAN OF BRONZE(1975), ph; WHITE LINE FEVER(1975, Can.), ph; WILD McCULLOCHS, THE(1975), ph; EMBRYO(1976), ph; DOMINO PRINCIPLE, THE(1977), ph; FUN WITH DICK AND JANE(1977), ph; LOVE AND BULLETS(1979, Brit.), ph; TWO OF A KIND(1983), ph
H.D. Koenekamp
SANTA FE TRAIL(1940), spe eff; JUNE BRIDE(1948), spec eff
H. E. Koenekamp
MIDSUMMER'S NIGHT'S DREAM, A(1935), spec eff
H. F. Koenekamp
CHARGE OF THE LIGHT BRIGADE, THE(1936), spec eff; ISLE OF FURY(1936), spec eff; BLACK LEGION, THE(1937), spec eff; GREAT O'MALLEY, THE(1937), spec eff; GREEN LIGHT(1937), spec eff; SAN QUENTIN(1937), spec eff; SUBMARINE D-1(1937), spec eff; PRIVATE LIVES OF ELIZABETH AND ESSEX, THE(1939), spec eff; WE ARE NOT ALONE(1939), spec eff; SEA HAWK, THE(1940), spec eff; THEY DRIVE BY NIGHT(1940), spec eff; TORRID ZONE(1940), spec eff; VIRGINIA CITY(1940), spec eff; HIGH SIERRA(1941), spec eff; MANPOWER(1941), spec eff; SEA WOLF, THE(1941), spec eff; WAGONS ROLL AT NIGHT, THE(1941), spec eff; WINGS FOR THE EAGLE(1942), spec eff; AIR FORCE(1943), spec eff; THANK YOUR LUCKY STARS(1943), spec eff; DARK PASSAGE(1947), spec eff; THAT WAY WITH WOMEN(1947), spec eff; FIGHTER SQUADRON(1948), spec eff; TREASURE OF THE SIERRA MADRE, THE(1948), spec eff; WINTER MEETING(1948), spec eff; FOUNTAINHEAD, THE(1949), spec eff; IT'S A GREAT FEELING(1949), spec eff; LADY TAKES A SAILOR, THE(1949), spec eff; WHITE HEAT(1949), spec eff; STRANGERS ON A TRAIN(1951), spec eff; MARA MARU(1952), spec eff; WINNING TEAM, THE(1952), spec eff; SOUTH SEA WOMAN(1953), spec eff; DRUM BEAT(1954), spec eff; STAR IS BORN, A(1954), spec eff; COURT-MARTIAL OF BILLY MITCHELL, THE(1955), spec eff; YOUNG AT HEART(1955), spec eff; SPIRIT OF ST. LOUIS, THE(1957), spec eff
Silents
WIZARD OF OZ, THE(1925), ph; IT MUST BE LOVE(1926), ph; SPUDS(1927), ph
Hans Koenekamp
ROUGHLY SPEAKING(1945), spec eff
Fred Koenekarnp
CARBON COPY(1981), ph
Ben Koenig
TROUBLE AT MIDNIGHT(1937), p; WESTBOUND LIMITED(1937), p
Charles Koenig
MAGIC FACE, THE(1951, Aust.)
Heino Koenig
IDEAL LODGER, THE(1957, Ger.), ph
Klaus Koenig
PEDESTRIAN, THE(1974, Ger.), ph; END OF THE GAME(1976, Ger./Ital.), ph
Laird Koenig
CAT, THE(1966), w; RED SUN(1972, Fr./Ital./Span.), w; LITTLE GIRL WHO LIVES DOWN THE LANE, THE(1977, Can.), w; ATTENTION, THE KIDS ARE WATCHING(1978, Fr.), w; BLOODLINE(1979), w; INCHON(1981), w
Mabelle Koenig
FIGHTING KENTUCKIAN, THE(1949)
Mark Koenig
PRIDE OF THE YANKEES, THE(1942); BABE RUTH STORY, THE(1948)
Mende Koenig
COME OUT FIGHTING(1945); DOCKS OF NEW YORK(1945); MR. MUGGS RIDES AGAIN(1945)
Mendy Koenig
RIVER GANG(1945)
Raymond Koenig
BLACULA(1972), w; SCREAM BLACULA SCREAM(1973), w
Walter Koenig
STRANGE LOVERS(1963); STAR TREK: THE MOTION PICTURE(1979); STAR TREK II: THE WRATH OF KHAN(1982)
1984
STAR TREK III: THE SEARCH FOR SPOCK(1984)
Wilhelm Koenig
"W" PLAN, THE(1931, Brit.)
Rene Koening
PARADISE POUR TOUS(1982, Fr.), m
Corinne Koeningswarter
TEN DAYS' WONDER(1972, Fr.)
Olive Koenitz
MAVERICK QUEEN, THE(1956), cos; GATHERING OF EAGLES, A(1963), cos
John Koensgen
DEAD ZONE, THE(1983)
Wolfgang Koeppen
GLASS TOWER, THE(1959, Ger.), w
Diana Koerner
BARRY LYNDON(1975, Brit.)
Ernest Koerner
MISTRESS OF ATLANTIS, THE(1932, Ger.), ph
Jacques Koerpel
WAR IS A RACKET(1934), a, p&d
Jacques A. Koerpel
ECSTASY(1940, Czech.), w
Nicolai Koesberg
Silents
JANICE MEREDITH(1924)

Wallace Koessler
MANY A SLIP(1931), art d

Walter Koessler
TARZAN AND THE AMAZONS(1945), art d; INVISIBLE WALL, THE(1947), art d; ROSES ARE RED(1947), art d; SHED NO TEARS(1948), art d; THIRTEEN LEAD SOLDIERS(1948), art d; RED STALLION IN THE ROCKIES(1949), art d

Jan Koester
HEIDI(1968, Aust.)

John Koester
SQUARES(1972), ph

Graeme Koestveld
FIRE IN THE STONE, THE(1983, Aus.), w

Erika Koeth
LIFE AND LOVES OF MOZART, THE(1959, Ger.)

Herbert Kofer
NAKED AMONG THE WOLVES(1967, Ger.)

Charles Koff
MAN FROM PLANET X, THE(1951), m; CAPTIVE WOMEN(1952), m; SWORD OF VENUS(1953), m

Karl Kofler
SHE DANCES ALONE(1981, Aust./U.S.), ph

Rick Kofoed
NATE AND HAYES(1983, U.S./New Zealand), art d
1984
UTU(1984, New Zealand), art d

Helen Koford
SINCE YOU WENT AWAY(1944); SHADOWED(1946)

Helen Koford [Terry Moore]
MARYLAND(1940); SON OF LASSIE(1945)

Jim Koford
RESCUERS, THE(1977), ed; FOX AND THE HOUND, THE(1981), ed

Dagmar Kofronova
DEVIL'S TRAP, THE(1964, Czech.); DO YOU KEEP A LION AT HOME?(1966, Czech.)

Yasushi Koga
YOSAKOI JOURNEY(1970, Jap.)

Edward Kogan
ROSELAND(1977)

Ephraim Kogan
FACES IN THE DARK(1960, Brit.), w

Leonide Kogan
MY NIGHT AT MAUD'S(1970, Fr.)

Milt Kogan
DARKTOWN STRUTTERS(1975); SUNSHINE BOYS, THE(1975); DR. BLACK AND MR. HYDE(1976); SWINGING BARMAIDS, THE(1976); PROTECTORS, BOOK 1, THE(1981); E.T. THE EXTRA-TERRESTRIAL(1982); WAVELENGTH(1983)
1984
WOMAN IN RED, THE(1984)
Misc. Talkies
HEROWORK(1977); ANGEL OF H.E.A.T.(1982)

Milt [Lewis] Kogan
LUCKY LADY(1975)

Nathan Kogan
DREAMER, THE(1970, Israel)

Sergio Kogan
DOCTOR CRIMEN(1953, Mex.), p

Kogar the Swinging Pipe
RAT PFINK AND BOO BOO(1966)

Arnie Kogen
BIRDS DO IT(1966), w

Peter Kogeones
DREAM OF KINGS, A(1969)

Josef Koggel
DIAMONDS OF THE NIGHT(1968, Czech.)

Michiyo Kogure
SAMURAI(PART II)** (1967, Jap.); DRUNKEN ANGEL(1948, Jap.); WOMEN IN PRISON(1957, Jap.); NIGHT IN HONG KONG, A(1961, Jap.); TEA AND RICE(1964, Jap.); HOTSPRINGS HOLIDAY(1970, Jap.); GEISHA, A(1978, Jap.)

R. William Koh
SEVENTH DAWN, THE(1964)

Glenn Kohan
BLUE LAGOON, THE(1980)

Lisa Kohane
POSSESSION OF JOEL DELANEY, THE(1972)

Julius Kohanyi
SUMMER'S CHILDREN(1979, Can.), p, d

Stanford S. Kohlberg
BLOOD FEAST(1963), p

Dennis Kohler
THAT NIGHT(1957); PORTRAIT IN BLACK(1960)

Don Kohler
ROAD HOUSE(1948); STREET WITH NO NAME, THE(1948); THAT WONDERFUL URGE(1948); YOU GOTTA STAY HAPPY(1948); MISS MINK OF 1949(1949); KILLER THAT STALKED NEW YORK, THE(1950); NO WAY OUT(1950); HOUSE ON TELEGRAPH HILL(1951); MEET ME AFTER THE SHOW(1951); MR. BELVEDERE RINGS THE BELL(1951); AFFAIR IN TRINIDAD(1952); ASSIGNMENT–PARIS(1952); DREAMBOAT(1952); GIRL NEXT DOOR, THE(1953); WAR OF THE WORLDS, THE(1953); HARDER THEY FALL, THE(1956)

Fred Kohler
BROADWAY BABIES(1929); DUMMY, THE(1929); LEATHERNECK, THE(1929); SAY IT WITH SONGS(1929); SPIELER, THE(1929); HELL'S HEROES(1930); LASH, THE(1930); LIGHT OF WESTERN STARS, THE(1930); ROADHOUSE NIGHTS(1930); UNDER A TEXAS MOON(1930); CORSAIR(1931); FIGHTING CARAVANS(1931); RIGHT OF WAY, THE(1931); X MARKS THE SPOT(1931); 99 WOUNDS(1931); CARNIVAL BOAT(1932); TEXAS BAD MAN(1932); DELUGE(1933); FOURTH HORSEMAN, THE(1933); QUEEN CHRISTINA(1933); SHIP OF WANTED MEN(1933); FIDDLIN' BUCKAROO, THE(1934); HONOR OF THE RANGE(1934); LAST ROUND-UP, THE(1934); LITTLE MAN, WHAT NOW?(1934); MAN FROM HELL, THE(1934); BORDER BRIGANDS(1935); FRISCO KID(1935); HARD ROCK HARRIGAN(1935); TIMES SQUARE LADY(1935); WEST OF THE PECOS(1935); ACCUSING FINGER, THE(1936); DANGEROUS INTRIGUE(1936); FOR THE SERVICE(1936); DAUGHTER

OF SHANGHAI(1937); HEART OF THE WEST(1937); PLAINSMAN, THE(1937); BLOCKADE(1938); BUCCANEER, THE(1938); GANGS OF NEW YORK(1938); GALLANT LEGION, THE(1948); RUBY(1977)
Misc. Talkies
LIGHTNING TRIGGERS(1935); MEN OF ACTION(1935); TRAIL'S END(1935)
Silents
POLLY OF THE STORM COUNTRY(1920); PARTNERS OF THE TIDE(1921); SCRAPPER, THE(1922); SON OF THE WOLF, THE(1922); ANNA CHRISTIE(1923); ELEVENTH HOUR, THE(1923); NORTH OF HUDSON BAY(1923); ABRAHAM LINCOLN(1924); IRON HORSE, THE(1924); DICK TURPIN(1925); RIDERS OF THE PURPLE SAGE(1925); ICE FLOOD, THE(1926); OLD IRONSIDES(1926); CITY GONE WILD, THE(1927); DEVIL'S MASTERPIECE, THE(1927); ROUGH RIDERS, THE(1927); SHOOTIN' IRONS(1927); UNDERWORLD(1927); WAY OF ALL FLESH, THE(1927); DRAGNET, THE(1928); STAIRS OF SAND(1929)
Misc. Silents
CYCLONE BLISS(1921); DAUGHTER OF THE LAW, A(1921); TRIMMED(1922); RED WARNING, THE(1923); SHADOWS OF THE NORTH(1923); THREE WHO PAID(1923); FIGHTING FURY(1924); GAY DEFENDER, THE(1927); OPEN RANGE(1927); CHINATOWN CHARLIE(1928); SHOWDOWN, THE(1928); VANISHING PIONEER, THE(1928); QUITTER, THE(1929)

Fred Kohler, Jr.
RENEGADES(1930); MOVIE CRAZY(1932); GRAND OLD GIRL(1935); HOOSIER SCHOOLMASTER(1935); PARIS IN SPRING(1935); RED SALUTE(1935); STEAMBOAT ROUND THE BEND(1935); FLASH GORDON(1936); PIGSKIN PARADE(1936); PRISONER OF SHARK ISLAND, THE(1936); SINS OF MAN(1936); STRIKE ME PINK(1936); TOLL OF THE DESERT(1936); HOLY TERROR, THE(1937); LIFE BEGINS IN COLLEGE(1937); ROARING TIMBER(1937); HOLD THAT CO-ED(1938); LAWLESS VALLEY(1938); PRISON NURSE(1938); RIDE A CROOKED MILE(1938); TEXAS STAMPEDE(1939); YOUNG MR. LINCOLN(1939); HALF A SINNER(1940); BAHAMA PASSAGE(1941); NEVADA CITY(1941); TWO GUN SHERIFF(1941); BOSS OF HANGTOWN MESA(1942); LONE STAR RANGER(1942); LUCKY JORDAN(1942); RAIDERS OF THE RANGE(1942); WESTERN MAIL(1942); CALLING WILD BILL ELLIOTT(1943); IRON MAJOR, THE(1943); NO TIME FOR LOVE(1943); BIG BONANZA, THE(1944); FRENCHMAN'S CREEK(1944); MR. WINKLE GOES TO WAR(1944); SEE HERE, PRIVATE HARGROVE(1944); STORY OF DR. WASSELL, THE(1944); UP IN MABEL'S ROOM(1944); WHY GIRLS LEAVE HOME(1945); O.S.S.(1946); UNCONQUERED(1947); FEUDIN', FUSSIN' AND A-FIGHTIN'(1948); LOADED PISTOLS(1948); GAY AMIGO, THE(1949); RANGE JUSTICE(1949); SAMSON AND DELILAH(1949); TOUGH ASSIGNMENT(1949); TWILIGHT IN THE SIERRAS(1950); TWO LOST WORLDS(1950); RED BADGE OF COURAGE, THE(1951); SPOILERS OF THE PLAINS(1951); GREATEST SHOW ON EARTH, THE(1952); HOODLUM EMPIRE(1952); BORN TO THE SADDLE(1953); RACING BLOOD(1954); TEN COMMANDMENTS, THE(1956); DANIEL BOONE, TRAIL BLAZER(1957); JOURNEY TO FREEDOM(1957); TERROR IN A TEXAS TOWN(1958); THIRTEEN FIGHTING MEN(1960)
Misc. Talkies
PECOS KID, THE(1935); SIX-GUN DECISION(1953)

Fred Kohler, Sr.
RIVER OF ROMANCE(1929); SAL OF SINGAPORE(1929); THUNDERBOLT(1929); OTHER MEN'S WOMEN(1931); SOLDIER'S PLAYTHING, A(1931); WOMAN HUNGRY(1931); RIDER OF DEATH VALLEY(1932); WILD HORSE MESA(1932); UNDER THE TONTO RIM(1933); GOIN' TO TOWN(1935); MISSISSIPPI(1935); STORMY(1935); WILDERNESS MAIL(1935); ARIZONA MAHONEY(1936); TEXAS RANGERS, THE(1936); BILLY THE KID RETURNS(1938); FORBIDDEN VALLEY(1938); LAWLESS VALLEY(1938); PAINTED DESERT, THE(1938)

Henry Kohler
FEET FIRST(1930), ph; YOUR NUMBER'S UP(1931), ph
Silents
GIRL SHY(1924), ph; FRESHMAN, THE(1925), ph

Henry L. Kohler
WELCOME DANGER(1929), ph

Henry N. Kohler
Silents
FOR HEAVEN'S SAKE(1926), ph

Manfred R. Kohler
BLOOD DEMON(1967, Ger.), w; LAST MERCENARY, THE(1969, Ital./Span./Ger.), w

Marga Kohler
Silents
PASSION(1920, Ger.)

Walter Kohler
AFFAIR IN TRINIDAD(1952); WRONG MAN, THE(1956); HITLER(1962)

W. Kohlhaase
FIRST SPACESHIP ON VENUS(1960, Ger./Pol.), w

Christof Kohlhofer
VORTEX(1982)

Alphonse Kohlmar
SCARLET DAWN(1932)

Fred Kohlmar
BLIND ALLEY(1939), p; COAST GUARD(1939), p; LADY AND THE MOB, THE(1939), p; LONE WOLF STRIKES, THE(1940), p; TALL, DARK AND HANDSOME(1941), p; THAT NIGHT IN RIO(1941), p; ARE HUSBANDS NECESSARY?(1942), p; GHOST AND MRS. MUIR, THE(1942), p; GLASS KEY, THE(1942), p; LADY HAS PLANS, THE(1942), p; LUCKY JORDAN(1942), p; TAKE A LETTER, DARLING(1942), p; LET'S FACE IT(1943), p; NO TIME FOR LOVE(1943), p; RIDING HIGH(1943), p; AND NOW TOMORROW(1944), p; DARK CORNER, THE(1946), p; WELL-GROOMED BRIDE, THE(1946), p; KISS OF DEATH(1947), p; LATE GEORGE APLEY, THE(1947), p; FURY AT FURNACE CREEK(1948), p; LUCK OF THE IRISH(1948), p; THAT WONDERFUL URGE(1948), p; YOU WERE MEANT FOR ME(1948), p; FATHER WAS A FULLBACK(1949), p; LOVE THAT BRUTE(1950), p; MOTHER DIDN'T TELL ME(1950), p; WHEN WILLIE COMES MARCHING HOME(1950), p; CALL ME MISTER(1951), p; ELOPEMENT(1951), p; YOU'RE IN THE NAVY NOW(1951), p; LES MISERABLES(1952), p; DOWN AMONG THE SHELTERING PALMS(1953), p; IT SHOULD HAPPEN TO YOU(1954), p; PHFFFT!(1954), p; MY SISTER EILEEN(1955), p; PICNIC(1955), p; THREE STRIPES IN THE SUN(1955), p; FULL OF LIFE(1956), p; SOLID GOLD CADILLAC, THE(1956), p; PAL JOEY(1957), p; GUNMAN'S WALK(1958), p; LAST ANGRY MAN, THE(1959), p; DEVIL AT FOUR O'CLOCK, THE(1961), p; WACKIEST SHIP IN THE ARMY, THE(1961), p; NOTORIOUS LANDLADY, THE(1962), p; BYE BYE BIRDIE(1963), p; HOW TO STEAL A MILLION(1966), p; FLEA IN HER EAR, A(1968, Fr.), p; ONLY GAME IN TOWN,

THE(1970), p

Lee D. Kohlmar
PERSONALITY(1930)

Lee Kohlmar
KIBITZER, THE(1929); CAUGHT SHORT(1930); CHILDREN OF PLEASURE(1930); MELODY MAN(1930); SINS OF THE CHILDREN(1930); JEWEL ROBBERY(1932); SCARLET DAWN(1932); SILVER DOLLAR(1932); STRANGE CASE OF CLARA DEANE, THE(1932); TENDERFOOT, THE(1932); FORGOTTEN(1933); I LOVE THAT MAN(1933); ROMAN SCANDALS(1933); SHE DONE HIM WRONG(1933); SON OF KONG(1933); HOUSE OF ROTHSCHILD, THE(1934); MUSIC IN THE AIR(1934); SHOOT THE WORKS(1934); TWENTIETH CENTURY(1934); WHEN STRANGERS MEET(1934); BREAK OF HEARTS(1935); FARMER TAKES A WIFE, THE(1935); FOUR HOURS TO KILL(1935); GIRL FRIEND, THE(1935); HERE COMES COOKIE(1935); LOVE IN BLOOM(1935); MC FADDEN'S FLATS(1935); ONE MORE SPRING(1935); RENDEZVOUS(1935); RUGGLES OF RED GAP(1935); DEATH FROM A DISTANCE(1936); SON COMES HOME, A(1936); KING AND THE CHORUS GIRL, THE(1937)
Silents
HIGH HEELS(1921), d; ORPHANS OF THE STORM(1922)
Misc. Silents
SECRET GIFT, THE(1920); BREAKING HOME TIES(1922)

Christian Kohlund
PEDESTRIAN, THE(1974, Ger.); DISORDER AND EARLY TORMENT(1977, Ger.)

Aaron M. Kohn
DAMN CITIZEN(1958)

Ben G. Kohn
BEST MAN WINS, THE(1935), w; STORMY(1935), w; LADY FROM NOWHERE(1936), w; ADVENTURE'S END(1937), w; ONCE A DOCTOR(1937), w; PIRATES OF THE SKIES(1939), w

Ben Grauman Kohn
CHINATOWN NIGHTS(1929), w; MANHATTAN MOON(1935), w; HE COULDN'T SAY NO(1938), w; YOUNG FUGITIVES(1938), w; HEAVEN WITH A BARBED WIRE FENCE(1939), w; GOLDEN HOOFS(1941), w; AMERICAN EMPIRE(1942), w
Silents
LINGERIE(1928), t; STAIRS OF SAND(1929), t

Gabriel Kohn
WEDDINGS AND BABIES(1960)

Howard Kohn
ROLLOVER(1981), w

John Kohn
REACH FOR GLORY(1963, Brit.), p, w; SIEGE OF THE SAXONS(1963, Brit.), w; COLLECTOR, THE(1965), w; FATHOM(1967), p; MAGUS, THE(1968, Brit.), p; FIGURES IN A LANDSCAPE(1970, Brit.), p; STRANGE VENEGEANCE OF ROSALIE, THE(1972), p, w; THEATRE OF BLOOD(1973, Brit.), p; GOLDENGIRL(1979), w
1984
RACING WITH THE MOON(1984), p

Jose Kohn
REBELLION OF THE HANGED, THE(1954, Mex.), p

Lola Kohn
HEAT OF THE SUMMER(1961, Fr.), p; HOT HOURS(1963, Fr.), p

Martin Kohn
SENSATION HUNTERS(1945), ed

Melanie Kohn
RACE FOR YOUR LIFE, CHARLIE BROWN(1977)

Nate Kohn
ZULU DAWN(1980, Brit.), p

Nathaniel Kohn
SLAVERS(1977, Ger.), w

Robin Kohn
SNOOPY, COME HOME(1972)

Rose Simon Kohn
PILLOW TO POST(1945), w; TRIAL WITHOUT JURY(1950), w

Howard E. Kohn II
HIDDEN FEAR(1957), p

Frederick Kohner
SINS OF MAN(1936), w; MAD ABOUT MUSIC(1938), w; MEN IN HER LIFE, THE(1941), w; JOHNNY DOUGHBOY(1943), w; LADY AND THE MONSTER, THE(1944), w; LAKE PLACID SERENADE(1944), w; PAN-AMERICANA(1945), w; THREE DARING DAUGHTERS(1948), w; NANCY GOES TO RIO(1950), w; HOLLYWOOD STORY(1951), w; NEVER WAVE AT A WAC(1952), w; TOY TIGER(1956), w; GIDGET(1959), w; GIDGET GOES HAWAIIAN(1961), w; GIDGET GOES TO ROME(1963), w

Fredrick Kohner
IT'S A DATE(1940), w; TAHITI HONEY(1943), w

Pancho Kohner
MR. SYCAMORE(1975), p&d, w; ST. IVES(1976), p; WHITE BUFFALO, THE(1977), p; LOVE AND BULLETS(1979, Brit.), p; WHY WOULD I LIE(1980), p; 10 TO MIDNIGHT(1983), p
1984
EVIL THAT MEN DO, THE(1984), p
Misc. Talkies
BRIDGE IN THE JUNGLE, THE(1971), d

Paul Kohner
HOUSE DIVIDED, A(1932), p; EAST OF JAVA(1935), p; PRODIGAL SON, THE(1935), p; NEXT TIME WE LOVE(1936), p
Silents
LOVE ME AND THE WORLD IS MINE(1928), w

Susan Kohner
TO HELL AND BACK(1955); LAST WAGON, THE(1956); DINO(1957); TROOPER HOOK(1957); BIG FISHERMAN, THE(1959); GENE KRUPA STORY, THE(1959); IMITATION OF LIFE(1959); ALL THE FINE YOUNG CANNIBALS(1960); BY LOVE POSSESSED(1961); FREUD(1962)

Col. Nichola Kohopleff
ROMAN HOLIDAY(1953)

Eduard Kohout
BOHEMIAN RAPTURE(1948, Czech); DISTANT JOURNEY(1950, Czech.)

Jan Kohout
EMPEROR AND THE GOLEM, THE(1955, Czech.), ed

Jara Kohout
WHAT'S SO BAD ABOUT FEELING GOOD?(1968); PROJECTIONIST, THE(1970)

Walter Kohut
PEDESTRIAN, THE(1974, Ger.)

Jean-Pierre Kohut [Svelko]
SUCH A GORGEOUS KID LIKE ME(1973, Fr.), art d; STORY OF ADELE H., THE(1975, Fr.), art d; ZIG-ZAG(1975, Fr/Ital.), art d; SMALL CHANGE(1976, Fr.), art d; FRENCH POSTCARDS(1979), art d; LOVE ON THE RUN(1980, Fr.), art d; LAST METRO, THE(1981, Fr.), art d; WOMAN NEXT DOOR, THE(1981, Fr.), art d; CHOICE OF ARMS(1983, Fr.), art d & cos; CONFIDENTIALLY YOURS(1983, Fr.)

Hideo Koi
GAPPA THE TRIFIBIAN MONSTER(1967, Jap.), p

Takashi Koide
IDIOT, THE(1963, Jap.), p; SCANDAL(1964, Jap.), p

Asao Koike
ETERNITY OF LOVE(1961, Jap.); INSECT WOMAN, THE(1964, Jap.)

Kazumi Koike
GEISHA, A(1978, Jap.), art d

Kazuo Koike
SHOGUN ASSASSIN(1980, Jap.), w

Tomoo Koike
FRIENDLY KILLER, THE(1970, Jap.); ZATOICHI CHALLENGED(1970, Jap.)

Thomas Koil
Misc. Silents
GODS OF FATE, THE(1916)

Hiroshi Koisumi
GODZILLA VS. THE THING(1964, Jap.)

Aarre Koivisto
PRELUDE TO ECSTASY(1963, Fin.), art d; MOONWOLF(1966, Fin./Ger.), art d

Hajime Koizimi
KING KONG VERSUS GODZILLA(1963, Jap.), ph

Fukuso Koizumi
OPERATION ENEMY FORT(1964, Jap.), ph

Fukuzo Koizumi
SANJURO(1962, Jap.), ph; CHALLENGE TO LIVE(1964, Jap.), ph; SIEGE OF FORT BISMARK(1968, Jap.), ph

Hajime Koizumi
H-MAN, THE(1959, Jap.), ph; BATTLE IN OUTER SPACE(1960), ph; MOTHRA(1962, Jap.), ph; VARAN THE UNBELIEVABLE(1962, U.S./Jap.), w, ph; ATTACK OF THE MUSHROOM PEOPLE(1964, Jap.), ph; DAGORA THE SPACE MONSTER(1964, Jap.), ph; FRANKENSTEIN CONQUERS THE WORLD(1964, Jap./US), ph; GODZILLA VS. THE THING(1964, Jap.), ph; HUMAN VAPOR, THE(1964, Jap.), ph; ATRAGON(1965, Jap.), ph; GHIDRAH, THE THREE-HEADED MONSTER(1965, Jap.), ph; KING KONG ESCAPES(1968, Jap.), ph; MONSTER ZERO(1970, Jap.), ph; WAR OF THE GARGANTUAS, THE(1970, Jap.), ph

Hiroshi Koizumi
GIGANTIS(1959, Jap./U.S.); I BOMBED PEARL HARBOR(1961, Jap.); NIGHT IN HONG KONG, A(1961, Jap.); DIFFERENT SONS(1962, Jap.); MOTHRA(1962, Jap.); STAR OF HONG KONG(1962, Jap.); ATTACK OF THE MUSHROOM PEOPLE(1964, Jap.); DAGORA THE SPACE MONSTER(1964, Jap.); ATRAGON(1965, Jap.); GHIDRAH, THE THREE-HEADED MONSTER(1965, Jap.); DAPHNE, THE(1967); GODZILLA VERSUS THE COSMIC MONSTER(1974, Jap.)

Hajime Koizumil
GORATH(1964, Jap.), ph

Ugljesa Kojadinovic
KAYA, I'LL KILL YOU!(1969, Yugo./Fr.)

Shirak Kojayan
NORSEMAN, THE(1978), ed

Goseki Kojima
SHOGUN ASSASSIN(1980, Jap.), w

Jun Kojima
SONG FROM MY HEART, THE(1970, Jap.)

Motoji Kojima
GOYOKIN(1969, Jap.), art d; DUEL AT EZO(1970, Jap.), art d

Kim Chiu Kok
WE OF THE NEVER NEVER(1983, Aus.)

Nevena Kokanova
DETOUR, THE(1968, Bulgarian); PEACH THIEF, THE(1969, Bulgaria)

Gyula Kokas
LOVE IN THE AFTERNOON(1957)

Michel Kokas
LOVE IN THE AFTERNOON(1957)

Peggy Kokernot
RACE WITH THE DEVIL(1975)

Kauko Kokkonen
MAKE LIKE A THIEF(1966, Fin.)

Koko
HILLS OF OKLAHOMA(1950); BORDER SADDLEMATES(1952); COLORADO SUNDOWN(1952); FOR YOUR EYES ONLY(1981)

"Koko"
SILVER CITY BONANZA(1951)

Koko the Horse
REDWOOD FOREST TRAIL(1950); UNDER MEXICALI STARS(1950); RODEO KING AND THE SENORITA(1951); THUNDER IN GOD'S COUNTRY(1951); UTAH WAGON TRAIN(1951); LAST MUSKETEER, THE(1952); OLD OKLAHOMA PLAINS(1952); SOUTH PACIFIC TRAIL(1952); OLD OVERLAND TRAIL(1953); RED RIVER SHORE(1953); SHADOWS OF TOMBSTONE(1953); PHANTOM STALLION, THE(1954)

Koko the Miracle Horse
IRON MOUNTAIN TRAIL(1953)

Henry Kokojan
UNDER AGE(1964), ph

Yumiko Kokonoe
JUDO SAGA(1965, Jap.)

Irene Kokonova
GALILEO(1968, Ital./Bul.)

Seryozha Kokorev
WELCOME KOSTYA!(1965, USSR)

Yannis Kokos
SHOCK TREATMENT(1973, Fr.), art d
I. Kokrashvili
FATHER OF A SOLDIER(1966, USSR)
Victor Kokriakov
IN THE NAME OF LIFE(1947, USSR)
Christina Kokubo
YAKUZA, THE(1975, U.S./Jap.); MIDWAY(1976)
Issac Kol
1984
AMBASSADOR, THE(1984), p
Gheorghi Kolaiancey
GALILEO(1968, Ital./Bul.)
Boris Kolar
Misc. Talkies
RETURN TO THE LAND OF OZ(1971, U.S./Yugo.), d
Erik Kolar
DISTANT JOURNEY(1950, Czech.), w
Phil Kolar
HAPPY DAYS(1930)
Dimo Kolarov
CLOWN AND THE KIDS, THE(1968, U.S./Bulgaria), ph
Henry Kolarz
GREAT BRITISH TRAIN ROBBERY, THE(1967, Ger.), w
Lisa Kolasa
1984
REVENGE OF THE NERDS(1984)
C. William Kolb
Misc. Silents
BLUFF(1916); LONESOME TOWN(1916); MILLION FOR MARY, A(1916); PECK O'
PICKLES(1916)
C. William Kolb [Clarence Kolb]
Misc. Silents
GLORY(1917)
Clarence Kolb
TRUE TO LIFE(1943); AFTER THE THIN MAN(1936); FURY(1936); MAID OF
SALEM(1937); PORTIA ON TRIAL(1937); TOAST OF NEW YORK, THE(1937); WELLS
FARGO(1937); CAREFREE(1938); GIVE ME A SAILOR(1938); GOLD IS WHERE YOU
FIND IT(1938); LAW WEST OF TOMBSTONE, THE(1938); MERRILY WE LIVE(1938);
AMAZING MR. WILLIAMS(1939); BEWARE SPOOKS(1939); FIVE LITTLE PEPPERS
AND HOW THEY GREW(1939); GOOD GIRLS GO TO PARIS(1939); HONOLU-
LU(1939); I WAS A CONVICT(1939); IT COULD HAPPEN TO YOU(1939); OUR
LEADING CITIZEN(1939); SOCIETY LAWYER(1939); FIVE LITTLE PEPPERS AT
HOME(1940); HIS GIRL FRIDAY(1940); MAN WHO TALKED TOO MUCH(1940);
MICHAEL SHAYNE, PRIVATE DETECTIVE(1940); NO TIME FOR COMEDY(1940);
TUGBOAT ANNIE SAILS AGAIN(1940); CAUGHT IN THE DRAFT(1941); HELL-
ZAPOPPIN'(1941); NIGHT OF JANUARY 16TH(1941); NOTHING BUT THE
TRUTH(1941); YOU'RE IN THE ARMY NOW(1941); BEDTIME STORY(1942); TRUE
TO THE ARMY(1942); FALCON IN DANGER, THE(1943); SKY'S THE LIMIT,
THE(1943); IRISH EYES ARE SMILING(1944); SOMETHING FOR THE BOYS(1944);
STANDING ROOM ONLY(1944); 3 IS A FAMILY(1944); ROAD TO ALCATRAZ(1945);
WHAT A BLONDE(1945); KID FROM BOOKLYN, THE(1946); WHITE TIE AND
TAILS(1946); BLONDIE IN THE DOUGH(1947); CHRISTMAS EVE(1947); LOST
HONEYMOON(1947); PILGRIM LADY, THE(1947); ADAM'S RIB(1949); ROSE BOWL
STORY, THE(1952); MAN OF A THOUSAND FACES(1957); SHAKE, RATTLE, AND
ROCK!(1957); FUN ON A WEEKEND(1979)
Misc. Talkies
FABULOUS JOE, THE(1946)
Clarence William Kolb
Misc. Silents
THREE PALS(1916); BELOVED ROGUES(1917)
Gideon Kolb
GOLD(1974, Brit.)
Jean Kolb
CALL, THE(1938, Fr.)
John Kolb
Silents
THREE'S A CROWD(1927)
Misc. Silents
LOST AT THE FRONT(1927)
John Philip Kolb
Silents
KNOCKOUT, THE(1925); TWINKLETOES(1926)
Josef Kolb
LOVES OF A BLONDE(1966, Czech.); FIREMAN'S BALL, THE(1968, Czech.); MOST
BEAUTIFUL AGE, THE(1970, Czech.)
Ken Kolb
GETTING STRAIGHT(1970), w; SNOW JOB(1972), w
Kenneth Kolb
SEVENTH VOYAGE OF SINBAD, THE(1958), w
Mina Kolb
WHAT'S SO BAD ABOUT FEELING GOOD?(1968); LOVING(1970); EVERY LITTLE
CROOK AND NANNY(1972); BOOGEYMAN II(1983)
Therese Kolb
Misc. Silents
BLANCHETTE(1921, Fr.); APPASSIONATA(1929, Fr.)
Wallace Kolb
Misc. Silents
IF WINTER COMES(1923)
Kolb & Dill
Silents
TWO FLAMING YOUTHS(1927)
Michael Kolba
KING OF COMEDY, THE(1983)
Lynne Kolber
TICKET TO HEAVEN(1981)
Susanne Kolber
BRAINWASHED(1961, Ger.)

Christopher Kolberg
Misc. Talkies
NINJA MISSION(1984)
Victor Kolberg
LANCER SPY(1937)
W. J. Kolberg
LIFE BEGINS AT 40(1935)
Krzysztof Kolberger
CONTRACT, THE(1982, Pol.)
Rene Koldehoff
REVENGERS, THE(1972, U.S./Mex.); MASTER TOUCH, THE(1974, Ital./Ger.); SOL-
DIER OF ORANGE(1979, Dutch)
Scott Kolden
CHARLEY AND THE ANGEL(1973); WHALE OF A TALE, A(1977); DAY TIME
ENDED, THE(1980, Span.)
Gottfried Kolditz
SIGNALS-AN ADVENTURE IN SPACE(1970, E. Ger./Pol.), d, w
George Kole
NORTH STAR, THE(1943)
Nicholas Koleff
1984
NATURAL, THE(1984)
G. Kolganov
NINE DAYS OF ONE YEAR(1964, USSR), art d
K. A. Kolhatker
MEN AGAINST THE SUN(1953, Brit.)
Kristof Kolhofer
OFFENDERS, THE(1980)
Reinhardt Kolidehoff
BORSALINO AND CO.(1974, Fr.)
Rene Kolidehoff
JUST A GIGOLO(1979, Ger.)
Lee Kolima
DIMENSION 5(1966)
1984
CANNONBALL RUN II(1984)
I. Kolin
LULLABY(1961, USSR)
Jiri Kolin
WISHING MACHINE(1971, Czech.), ph
Nikelai Kolin
Misc. Silents
SECRETS OF THE ORIENT(1932, Ger.)
Nikolai Kolin
Misc. Silents
KEAN(1924, Fr.)
Richard Kolin
LAS RATAS NO DUERMEN DE NOCHE(1974, Span./Fr.)
Nicolas Koline
SHOW GOES ON, THE(1938, Brit.)
Silents
NAPOLEON(1927, Fr.)
Misc. Silents
LE CHANT DE L'AMOUR TRIOMPHANT(1923, Fr.); LE CHIFFONNIER DE PA-
RIS(1924, Fr.); AME D'ARTISTE(1925, Fr.); LE PRINCE CHARMANT(1925, Fr.)
Marge Kolitsky
THIEF(1981)
Zvi Kolitz
HILL 24 DOESN'T ANSWER(1955, Israel), w
Scott Kolk
HOLD YOUR MAN(1929); MARIANNE(1929); ALL QUIET ON THE WESTERN
FRONT(1930); DYNAMITE(1930); FOR THE DEFENSE(1930); MY SIN(1931)
Henry Kolker
COQUETTE(1929); PLEASURE CRAZED(1929); VALIANT, THE(1929); BAD ONE,
THE(1930); DU BARRY, WOMAN OF PASSION(1930); EAST IS WEST(1930); GOOD
INTENTIONS(1930); WAY OF ALL MEN, THE(1930); DON'T BET ON WOMEN(1931);
I LIKE YOUR NERVE(1931); INDISCREET(1931); ONE HEAVENLY NIGHT(1931);
QUICK MILLIONS(1931); UNHOLY GARDEN, THE(1931); DEVIL AND THE
DEEP(1932); DOWN TO EARTH(1932); FAITHLESS(1932); FIRST YEAR, THE(1932);
JEWEL ROBBERY(1932); RASPUTIN AND THE EMPRESS(1932); THE CRASH(1932);
WASHINGTON MASQUERADE(1932); BABY FACE(1933); BEDTIME STORY,
A(1933); BUREAU OF MISSING PERSONS(1933); GIGOLETTES OF PARIS(1933);
GOLDEN HARVEST(1933); HELL BELOW(1933); HELLO SISTER!(1933); I LOVED A
WOMAN(1933); KEYHOLE, THE(1933); LOVE, HONOR, AND OH BABY!(1933); MEET
THE BARON(1933); NARROW CORNER, THE(1933); POWER AND THE GLORY,
THE(1933); GIRL FROM MISSOURI, THE(1934); HELL CAT, THE(1934); IMITATION
OF LIFE(1934); I'VE GOT YOUR NUMBER(1934); JOURNAL OF A CRIME(1934); KID
MILLIONS(1934); LADY BY CHOICE(1934); LET'S TRY AGAIN(1934); LOST LADY,
A(1934); LOVE TIME(1934); MILLION DOLLAR RANSOM(1934); NAME THE WOM-
AN(1934); NOTORIOUS BUT NICE(1934); NOW AND FOREVER(1934); SHE LOVES
ME NOT(1934); SISTERS UNDER THE SKIN(1934); SUCCESS AT ANY PRICE(1934);
WHOM THE GODS DESTROY(1934); WONDER BAR(1934); BLACK ROOM,
THE(1935); CASE OF THE CURIOUS BRIDE, THE(1935); CHARLIE CHAN IN
PARIS(1935); DIAMOND JIM(1935); FLORENTINE DAGGER, THE(1935); FRISCO
WATERFRONT(1935); GHOST WALKS, THE(1935); LADIES LOVE DANGER(1935);
LAST DAYS OF POMPEII, THE(1935); MAD LOVE(1935); MYSTERY MAN,
THE(1935); ONE EXCITING ADVENTURE(1935); ONE NEW YORK NIGHT(1935);
RECKLESS(1935); RED HOT TIRES(1935); RED SALUTE(1935); SHIPMATES FOREV-
ER(1935); SING SING NIGHTS(1935); SOCIETY DOCTOR(1935); THREE KIDS AND A
QUEEN(1935); TIMES SQUARE LADY(1935); BULLETS OR BALLOTS(1936); COL-
LEGIATE(1936); GREAT GUY(1936); HONEYMOON LIMITED(1936); IN HIS
STEPS(1936); MAN WHO LIVED TWICE(1936); MY MARRIAGE(1936); ROMEO AND
JULIET(1936); SITTING ON THE MOON(1936); THEODORA GOES WILD(1936);
CONQUEST(1937); DEVIL IS DRIVING, THE(1937); GREEN LIGHT(1937); LET THEM
LIVE(1937); MAID OF SALEM(1937); ONCE A DOCTOR(1937); THEY WANTED TO
MARRY(1937); THOROUGHBREDS DON'T CRY(1937); UNDER COVER OF
NIGHT(1937); COWBOY AND THE LADY, THE(1938); HOLIDAY(1938); INVISIBLE
MENACE, THE(1938); LOVE IS A HEADACHE(1938); MARIE ANTOINETTE(1938);
SAFETY IN NUMBERS(1938); TOO HOT TO HANDLE(1938); HERE I AM A STRAN-
GER(1939); HIDDEN POWER(1939); LET US LIVE(1939); MAIN STREET LA-

WYER(1939); PARENTS ON TRIAL(1939); REAL GLORY, THE(1939); SHOULD HUSBANDS WORK?(1939); THESE GLAMOUR GIRLS(1939); UNION PACIFIC(1939); GRAND OLE OPRY(1940); MONEY AND THE WOMAN(1940); GREAT SWINDLE, THE(1941); LAS VEGAS NIGHTS(1941); MAN WHO LOST HIMSELF, THE(1941); PARSON OF PANAMINT, THE(1941); SING FOR YOUR SUPPER(1941); WOMAN'S FACE(1941); REUNION IN FRANCE(1942); SARONG GIRL(1943); BLUE-BEARD(1944); SECRET LIFE OF WALTER MITTY, THE(1947)
Silents
HOW MOLLY MADE GOOD(1915); BRAT, THE(1919); FIGHTER, THE(1921), d; ANY WOMAN(1925); WET PAINT(1926); ROUGH HOUSE ROSIE(1927); DON'T MARRY(1928)
Misc. Silents
BETTER MAN, THE(1915); WARNING, THE(1915); HOUSE OF MIRTH, THE(1918); SHELL GAME, THE(1918); SOCIAL HYPOCRITES(1918); BLACKIE'S REDEMPTION(1919); JEANNE OF THE GUTTER(1919); MAN'S COUNTRY, A(1919), d; PARISIAN TIGRESS, THE(1919); WOMAN MICHAEL MARRIED, THE(1919), d; BRIGHT SKIES(1920), d; GREATEST LOVE, THE(1920), d; HEART OF TWENTY, THE(1920), d; PALACE OF THE DARKENED WINDOWS, THE(1920), d; THIRD GENERATION, THE(1920), d; BUCKING THE TIGER(1921), d; DISRAELI(1921), d; WHO AM I?(1921), d; LEOPARDESS, THE(1923), d; PURPLE HIGHWAY, THE(1923), d; SNOW BRIDE, THE(1923), d; SWORDS AND THE WOMAN(1923, Brit.), d; NEGLECTED WOMEN(1924, Brit.), d; HELL'S 400(1926); PALACE OF PLEASURE, THE(1926); WINNING THE FUTURITY(1926); KISS IN A TAXI, A(1927); MIDNIGHT ROSE(1928)
Don Koll
WAY WE WERE, THE(1973); NO WAY TO TREAT A LADY(1968); VALACHI PAPERS, THE(1972, Ital./Fr.); JULIA(1977)
Rene Kolldehof
ROMANTIC ENGLISHWOMAN, THE(1975, Brit./Fr.)
Heinhard Kolldehoff
CONFESS DR. CORDA(1960, Ger.)
Reinhard Kolldehoff
CAPTAIN FROM KOEPENICK, THE(1956, Ger.); THOUSAND EYES OF DR. MABUSE, THE(1960, Fr./Ital./Ger.); SECRET WAYS, THE(1961); WILLY(1963, U.S./Ger.)
Reinhard "Rene" Kolldehoff
COUNTERFEIT TRAITOR, THE(1962)
Reinhardt Kolldehoff
OPERATION DAYBREAK(1976, U.S./Brit./Czech.)
Rene Kolldehoff
ALL THE WAY, BOYS(1973, Ital.); SHOUT AT THE DEVIL(1976, Brit.)
1984
LITTLE DRUMMER GIRL, THE(1984)
Amos Kollek
WORLDS APART(1980, U.S., Israel), a, p, w
Peter Kollek
IN A YEAR OF THIRTEEN MOONS(1980, Ger.)
N. Kollen
DAY THE EARTH FROZE, THE(1959, Fin./USSR); WAR AND PEACE(1968, USSR)
Dagmar Koller
LITTLE NIGHT MUSIC, A(1977, Aust./U.S./Ger.)
Hilde Koller
DREAM OF SCHONBRUNN(1933, Aus.)
Lawrence Koller
THIS IS ELVIS(1982)
Fred Kollhanck
LAST BRIDGE, THE(1957, Aust.), ph
Nikki Kollins
DON'T GO IN THE HOUSE(1980)
Erich Kollmar
SHADOWS(1960), ph; BLAST OF SILENCE(1961), a, ph
Kerry Kollmar
PAJAMA PARTY(1964)
Richard Kollmar
CLOSE-UP(1948)
Richard Kollmar, Jr.
WEDDING PARTY, THE(1969)
H.F. Kollner
SCHLAGER-PARADE(1953), w; HIPPODROME(1961, Aust./Ger.), w
Richard Kollorsz
SCARLET EMPRESS, THE(1934), art d
H.W. Kolm-Veltee
DON JUAN(1956, Aust.), d, w
Ron Kolman
HARRAD EXPERIMENT, THE(1973)
Nina Kolment
TEMPEST(1982)
Fred Kolo
I'M DANCING AS FAST AS I CAN(1982), art d
Ronald Kolodgie
WILD PARTY, THE(1975), cos
V. Kolokoltsev
FATHER OF A SOLDIER(1966, USSR)
Walter Kolomoku
Silents
IDOL DANCER, THE(1920)
G. Kolosov
OVERCOAT, THE(1965, USSR)
Vova Kolotygin
LAST GAME, THE(1964, USSR)
V. Kolpakov
DON QUIXOTE(1961, USSR); HAMLET(1966, USSR); THERE WAS AN OLD COUPLE(1967, USSR)
Max Kolpe
DANCING ON A DIME(1940), w; HEARTBEAT(1946), w
Max Kolpet
GERMANY, YEAR ZERO(1949, Ger.), w
Jess Kolpin
VENOM(1968, Den.)

Henki Kolstad
PASSIONATE DEMONS, THE(1962, Norway); HUNGER(1968, Den./Norway/Swed.)
Lasse Kolstad
ISLAND AT THE TOP OF THE WORLD, THE(1974)
Charles Kolster
Silents
DOG OF THE REGIMENT(1927), ed
Clarence Kolster
HOT CURVES(1930), ed; PEACOCK ALLEY(1930), ed; SUNNY SKIES(1930), ed; THOROUGHBRED, THE(1930), ed; TROOPERS THREE(1930), ed; WINGS OF ADVENTURE(1930), ed; FRANKENSTEIN(1931), ed; PAINTED DESERT, THE(1931), ed; DOOMED BATTALION, THE(1932), ed; IMPATIENT MAIDEN(1932), ed; OLD DARK HOUSE, THE(1932), ed; HAVANA WIDOWS(1933), ed; UNKNOWN VALLEY(1933), ed; CIRCUS CLOWN(1934), ed; FIGHTING CODE, THE(1934), ed; I'VE GOT YOUR NUMBER(1934), ed; KING OF THE WILD HORSES, THE(1934), ed; ST. LOUIS KID, THE(1934), ed; TWENTY MILLION SWEETHEARTS(1934), ed; MARY JANE'S PA(1935), ed; MISS PACIFIC FLEET(1935), ed; SPECIAL AGENT(1935), ed; WHITE COCKATOO(1935), ed; HOT MONEY(1936), ed; LAW IN HER HANDS, THE(1936), ed; POLO JOE(1936), ed; BACK IN CIRCULATION(1937), ed; EMPTY HOLSTERS(1937), ed; HER HUSBAND'S SECRETARY(1937), ed; ONCE A DOCTOR(1937), ed; SH! THE OCTOPUS(1937), ed; FOUR'S A CROWD(1938), ed; GOLD IS WHERE YOU FIND IT(1938), ed; GOING PLACES(1939), ed; HELL'S KITCHEN(1939), ed; ON YOUR TOES(1939), ed; ANGEL FROM TEXAS, AN(1940), ed; BROTHER RAT AND A BABY(1940), ed; RIVER'S END(1940), ed; SOUTH OF SUEZ(1940), ed; BAD MEN OF MISSOURI(1941), ed; THIEVES FALL OUT(1941), ed; MEN OF TEXAS(1942), ed; SPOILERS, THE(1942), ed; WILD BILL HICKOK RIDES(1942), ed; ADVENTURES IN IRAQ(1943), ed; MYSTERIOUS DOCTOR, THE(1943), ed; TRUCK BUSTERS(1943), ed; MAKE YOUR OWN BED(1944), ed; OF HUMAN BONDAGE(1946), ed; ESCAPE ME NEVER(1947), ed; SMART GIRLS DON'T TALK(1948), ed; WOMAN IN WHITE, THE(1948), ed; ALWAYS LEAVE THEM LAUGHING(1949), ed; SOUTH OF ST. LOUIS(1949), ed; BARRICADE(1950), ed; DALLAS(1950), ed; STORM WARNING(1950), ed; CLOSE TO MY HEART(1951), ed; FORT WORTH(1951), ed; SUGARFOOT(1951), ed; BIG TREES, THE(1952), ed; OPERATION SECRET(1952), ed; SHE'S WORKING HER WAY THROUGH COLLEGE(1952), ed; SOUTH SEA WOMAN(1953), ed; SYSTEM, THE(1953), ed; BOUNTY HUNTER, THE(1954), ed; DRUM BEAT(1954), ed; I DIED A THOUSAND TIMES(1955), ed; LONE RANGER, THE(1955), ed; TARGET ZERO(1955), ed; BURNING HILLS, THE(1956), ed; SHOOT-OUT AT MEDICINE BEND(1957), ed; FORT DOBBS(1958), ed
Silents
RAGS TO RICHES(1922), ed; COUNTRY KID, THE(1923), ed; ON THIN ICE(1925), ed; BROKEN HEARTS OF HOLLYWOOD(1926), ed; FIGHTING EDGE(1926), ed; HIS JAZZ BRIDE(1926), ed; LITTLE IRISH GIRL, THE(1926), ed; NIGHT CRY, THE(1926), ed; THIRD DEGREE, THE(1926), ed; GINSBERG THE GREAT(1927), ed; HUSBANDS FOR RENT(1927), ed
Gyula Koltai
FATHER(1967, Hung.)
Janos Koltai
ROUND UP, THE(1969, Hung.)
Lajos Koltai
ANGI VERA(1980, Hung.), ph; CONFIDENCE(1980, Hung.), ph; MEPHISTO(1981, Ger.), ph
Sonja Kolthoff
TOPAZ(1969, Brit.)
A. Koltsaty
TRAIN GOES EAST, THE(1949, USSR), ph
Arkadiy Koltsatyy
FORTY-NINE DAYS(1964, USSR), ph
Mira Koltsava
SPRINGTIME ON THE VOLGA(1961, USSR)
Viktor Koltsov
SUN SHINES FOR ALL, THE(1961, USSR); PEACE TO HIM WHO ENTERS(1963, USSR)
Grigoriy Koltunov
LETTER THAT WAS NEVER SENT, THE(1962, USSR), w
Gitte Kolvig
1984
ZAPPA(1984, Den.), cos
Natou Koly
BLACK AND WHITE IN COLOR(1976, Fr.)
Hajime Kolzumi
MYSTERIANS, THE(1959, Jap.), ph
Jimmie Komack
DAMN YANKEES(1958); SENIOR PROM(1958)
Jimmy Komack
HOLE IN THE HEAD, A(1959)
Tetsu Komai
BULLDOG DRUMMOND(1929); CHINATOWN NIGHTS(1929); WELCOME DANGER(1929); EAST IS WEST(1930); RETURN OF DR. FU MANCHU, THE(1930); DAUGHTER OF THE DRAGON(1931); SHE WANTED A MILLIONAIRE(1932); WAR CORRESPONDENT(1932); ISLAND OF LOST SOULS(1933); STUDY IN SCARLET, A(1933); FOUR FRIGHTENED PEOPLE(1934); NOW AND FOREVER(1934); HONG KONG NIGHTS(1935); OIL FOR THE LAMPS OF CHINA(1935); WITHOUT REGRET(1935); ISLE OF FURY(1936); KLONDIKE ANNIE(1936); PRINCESS COMES ACROSS, THE(1936); ROAMING LADY(1936); CHINA PASSAGE(1937); SINGING MARINE, THE(1937); THAT MAN'S HERE AGAIN(1937); WEST OF SHANGHAI(1937); REAL GLORY, THE(1939); LETTER, THE(1940); SUNDOWN(1941); GREEN DOLPHIN STREET(1947); TASK FORCE(1949); TOKYO JOE(1949); JAPANESE WAR BRIDE(1952); TANK BATTALION(1958); NIGHT WALKER, THE(1964)
Silents
OLD IRONSIDES(1926)
Tetsui Komai
SECRETS OF WU SIN(1932)
Carolyn Komant
HOUSE OF WOMEN(1962)
Chris Komar
HAIR(1979)

Dora Komar
OPERETTA(1949, Ger.)
Sergei Komarov
Misc. Silents
DEATH RAY, THE(1925, USSR); BY THE LAW(1926, USSR)
Sergey Komarov
SPACE SHIP, THE(1935, USSR)
E. Komarova
Misc. Silents
ENGINEER PRITE'S PROJECT(1918, USSR)
N. Komarovskaya
Misc. Silents
THOUGHT(1916, USSR)
Katamasa Komatsu
SILENCE HAS NO WINGS(1971, Jap.)
Naramasa Komatsu
PLEASURES OF THE FLESH, THE(1965)
Sakyo Komatsu
TIDAL WAVE(1975, U.S./Jap.), w; VIRUS(1980, Jap.), w
Kazuo Komatsubara
GALAXY EXPRESS(1982, Jap.), anim d
1984
WARRIORS OF THE WIND(1984, Jap.), d
Komeda
CUL-DE-SAC(1966, Brit.), m
Christopher Komeda
FEARLESS VAMPIRE KILLERS, OR PARDON ME BUT YOUR TEETH ARE IN MY NECK, THE(1967), m; RIOT(1969), m
Krysztof Komeda
BEAUTIFUL SWINDLERS, THE(1967, Fr./Ital./Jap./Neth.), m
Kryzystof Komeda
KNIFE IN THE WATER(1963, Pol.), m
Krzysztof Komeda
BARRIER(1966, Pol.), m; EPILOGUE(1967, Den.), m; HUNGER(1968, Den./Norway/Swed.), m; ROSEMARY'S BABY(1968), m; PEOPLE MEET AND SWEET MUSIC FILLS THE HEART(1969, Den./Swed.), m
Harry Komer
ADVENTURES OF GALLANT BESS(1948), ed; MAIN STREET AFTER DARK(1944), ed; BEWITCHED(1945), ed; GALLANT BESS(1946), ed
Theodor Komisarjevsky
YELLOW STOCKINGS(1930, Brit.), d
Misc. Silents
YELLOW STOCKINGS(1928, Brit.), d
A. Komissarov
WAR AND PEACE(1968, USSR)
N. Komissarov
DIARY OF A NAZI(1943, USSR)
N.V. Komissarov
HEROES OF THE SEA(1941)
P. Komissarov
DREAM OF A COSSACK(1982, USSR)
Mitsue Komiya
MAN IN THE MOONLIGHT MASK, THE(1958, Jap.)
Kiyoshi Komiyama
ANGRY ISLAND(1960, Jap.)
Istvan Komlos
MEPHISTO(1981, Ger.)
Charly Kommer
48 HOURS TO ACAPULCO(1968, Ger.)
M. V. Kommisarov
MYSTERIOUS ISLAND(1941, USSR)
Hideaki Komori
SONG FROM MY HEART, THE(1970, Jap.)
Maja Komorowska
YOUNG GIRLS OF WILKO, THE(1979, Pol./Fr.); CONTRACT, THE(1982, Pol.)
Lea Kompaniejec
Misc. Silents
CANTOR'S DAUGHTER, THE(1913, USSR); STEPMOTHER, THE(1914, USSR)
Manuel Komroff
SCARLET EMPRESS, THE(1934), w; SMALL TOWN BOY(1937), d&w; MAGIC BOW, THE(1947, Brit.), w
Tom Komuro
NAVY WIFE(1956)
B. Komyakov
HOUSE WITH AN ATTIC, THE(1964, USSR), art d
H. Kon
DYBBUK THE(1938, Pol.), m
Toko Kon
LOVE UNDER THE CRUCIFIX(1965, Jap.), w
Yasutaro Kon
PLEASURES OF THE FLESH, THE(1965), art d
Albert Konan-Koffi
CHARLES AND LUCIE(1982, Fr.)
C. Konarski
CHRISTMAS CAROL, A(1951, Brit.)
Andrei Konchalovskiy
VIOLIN AND ROLLER(1962, USSR), w
A. Konchalovsky
MY NAME IS IVAN(1963, USSR)
Karen Kondazian
YES, GIORGIO(1982)
Isami Kondo
BAND OF ASSASSINS(1971, Jap.)
Mieko Kondo
BUDDHA(1965, Jap.)
H. Kondoh
ANATAHAN(1953, Jap.)

Aphrodite Kondos
ROAD GAMES(1981, Aus.), cos; PIRATE MOVIE, THE(1982, Aus.), cos; ESCAPE 2000(1983, Aus.), cos
1984
TREASURE OF THE YANKEE ZEPHYR(1984), cos
Marek Kondrad
YELLOW SLIPPERS, THE(1965, Pol.)
Marek Kondrat
MAN OF IRON(1981, Pol.); DANTON(1983)
1984
SHIVERS(1984, Pol.)
Tadeusz Kondrat
WALKOVER(1969, Pol.)
N. Kondratyev
SOUND OF LIFE, THE(1962, USSR); OPTIMISTIC TRAGEDY, THE(1964, USSR); MAGIC WEAVER, THE(1965, USSR)
I. Kondratyeva
SECRET BRIGADE, THE(1951 USSR)
Robert Kondyra
ROCKY II(1979)
Kim Kondziola
SMOKEY AND THE BANDIT–PART 3(1983)
Ansa Konen
TELEFON(1977)
Jackie Kong
BEING, THE(1983), d&w
1984
NIGHT PATROL(1984), p, d, w, ed
King Kong
PURPLE HEART, THE(1944)
Patricia Kong
HAMMETT(1982)
Shirlee Kong
CHAMP, THE(1979)
Tsang Kong
ONE NIGHT STAND(1976, Fr.)
Lynn Kongkham
DEER HUNTER, THE(1978)
Reiko Kongo
SANSHO THE BAILIFF(1969, Jap.)
Josef Konicek
LEMONADE JOE(1966, Czech.), ch; LADY ON THE TRACKS, THE(1968, Czech.), ch
Stepan Konicek
DESERTER AND THE NOMADS, THE(1969, Czech./Ital.), m
Michel Koniencny
L'ETOILE DU NORD(1983, Fr.)
Joel Konig
DAVID(1979, Ger.), w
Klaus Konig
SUMMER RUN(1974), ph
Lia Konig
WORLDS APART(1980, U.S., Israel)
Frank Konigsberg
1984
JOY OF SEX(1984), p
E.L. Konigsburg
FROM THE MIXED-UP FILES OF MRS. BASIL E. FRANKWEILER(1973), w
Hans Koningsberger
WALK WITH LOVE AND DEATH, A(1969), w; REVOLUTIONARY, THE(1970, Brit.), w
Horin Konishi
Silents
ISOBEL(1920)
Lee Konitz
DESPERATE CHARACTERS(1971), m
Tatyana Koniukhova
MOSCOW DOES NOT BELIEVE IN TEARS(1980, USSR)
Fahro Konjhodzic
EVENT, AN(1970, Yugo.); MEETINGS WITH REMARKABLE MEN(1979, Brit.)
1984
MEMED MY HAWK(1984, Brit.)
Sam Konnella
Silents
WHITE YOUTH(1920)
Shuji Konno
MAGIC BOY(1960, Jap.), anim
Akitake Kono
TEMPTRESS AND THE MONK, THE(1963, Jap.); SANSHO THE BAILIFF(1969, Jap.)
Yoshimi Kono
LIFE OF OHARU(1964, Jap.), ph
Jushiro Konoe
ZATOICHI CHALLENGED(1970, Jap.)
Toshiaki Konoe
LIFE OF OHARU(1964, Jap.)
Wieslawa Konopelska
MAN OF MARBLE(1979, Pol.), cos
Kenneth Konopka
HOUSE ON 92ND STREET, THE(1945)
Magda Konopka
HELL BOATS(1970, Brit.); WHEN DINOSAURS RULED THE EARTH(1971, Brit.); BLINDMAN(1972, Ital.); RE: LUCKY LUCIANO(1974, Fr./Ital.)
Robert K. Konoshita
GONG SHOW MOVIE, THE(1980), art d
N. Konovalov
VOW, THE(1947, USSR.)
Nikolai Konovalov
SPRING(1948, USSR)

S. Konovalova
WAR AND PEACE(1968, USSR)
P. Konoykhin
OPTIMISTIC TRAGEDY, THE(1964, USSR)
Dorothy Konrad
SWEET BIRD OF YOUTH(1962); TICKLE ME(1965); FUTUREWORLD(1976); RACQUET(1979)
Father Joseph Konrad
DOGS OF WAR, THE(1980, Brit.)
Jozsef Konrad
ROUND UP, THE(1969, Hung.); WINTER WIND(1970, Fr./Hung.)
Kazimierz Konrad
YELLOW SLIPPERS, THE(1965, Pol.), ph
Inge Konrads
STOLEN IDENTITY(1953)
G. Konskiy
RESURRECTION(1963, USSR)
A. Konsovskiy
RESURRECTION(1963, USSR)
A. Konsovsky
CONCENTRATION CAMP(1939, USSR)
Alexei Konsovsky
FATHERS AND SONS(1960, USSR)
Anna Konstam
THEY DRIVE BY NIGHT(1938, Brit.); YOUNG AND INNOCENT(1938, Brit.); TOO DANGEROUS TO LIVE(1939, Brit.); MIDAS TOUCH, THE(1940, Brit.); SALOON BAR(1940, Brit.); WATERLOO ROAD(1949, Brit.)
Phillis Konstam
COMPROMISED!(1931, Brit.)
Phyllis Konstam
ESCAPE(1930, Brit.); MURDER(1930, Brit.); GENTLEMAN OF PARIS, A(1931); SKIN GAME, THE(1931, Brit.); TILLY OF BLOOMSBURY(1931, Brit.); VOICE OF THE HURRICANE(1964)
Anna Konstant
STREET SCENE(1931)
Ernst Konstantin
JOURNEY, THE(1959, U.S./Aust.)
Mme. Konstantin
NOTORIOUS(1946)
Gilad Konstantiner
JUDITH(1965)
Dimitri Konstantinov
WAR AND PEACE(1956, Ital./U.S.)
L. Konstantinova
THREE SISTERS, THE(1969, USSR)
Panos Kontellis
SISTERS, THE(1969, Gr.), w
Maro Kontou
ANTIGONE(1962 Gr.)
Nada Konvalinkova
ADELE HASN'T HAD HER SUPPER YET(1978, Czech.)
Jeffrey Konvitz
SILENT NIGHT, BLOODY NIGHT(1974), p, w; SENTINEL, THE(1977), p, w; GORP(1980), p, w
Tadeusz Konwicki
JOAN OF THE ANGELS(1962, Pol.), w; SALTO(1966, Pol.), d&w; JOVITA(1970, Pol.), w
Charles Konya
WHERE THE BUFFALO ROAM(1980)
Toshio Konya
ONIBABA(1965, Jap.), p
A. Konyashin
MARRIAGE OF BALZAMINOV, THE(1966, USSR)
Vitaliy Konyayev
CLEAR SKIES(1963, USSR); RED AND THE WHITE, THE(1969, Hung./USSR)
Tatyana Konyukhova
SUN SHINES FOR ALL, THE(1961, USSR); MARRIAGE OF BALZAMINOV, THE(1966, USSR); RED AND THE WHITE, THE(1969, Hung./USSR)
Jack Konzal
CYCLE SAVAGES(1969)
Joseph Koo
DEADLY CHINA DOLL(1973, Hong Kong), m
Regina Koo
MY THIRD WIFE GEORGE(1968)
Guich Koock
SUGARLAND EXPRESS, THE(1974); MACKINTOSH & T.J.(1975); PIRANHA(1978); NORTH DALLAS FORTY(1979); SEVEN(1979)
Arthur J. Kookan
DEVIL DOGS OF THE AIR(1935), art d
Asit Koomar
OBJECTIVE, BURMA!(1945)
Frank Koomen
THIN RED LINE, THE(1964); GREEN BERETS, THE(1968)
Francis Koon
THUNDER ROAD(1958)
Gavin Koon
FOLLOW THAT DREAM(1962)
Robin Koon
FOLLOW THAT DREAM(1962)
Nam Koong-woon
LAST WOMAN OF SHANG, THE(1964, Hong Kong)
Edmond Koons
HEALTH(1980), ph
Edmond L. Koons
PERFECT COUPLE, A(1979), ph
Edmund Koons
MODERN PROBLEMS(1981), ph

Bill Koontz
CANYON AMBUSH(1952); GUN FIGHT(1961)
Dean R. Koontz
DEMON SEED(1977), w
Mel Koontz
ESCAPE TO BURMA(1955), animal t
Al Kooper
LANDLORD, THE(1970), m
Toto Koopman
PRIVATE LIFE OF DON JUAN, THE(1934, Brit.)
Willie Koopman
DON'T JUST STAND THERE(1968)
Richard Kooris
MONGREL(1982), ph
Cecelia Kootenay
LITTLE BIG MAN(1970)
Pete Kooy
TAKE ME OUT TO THE BALL GAME(1949); ESCAPE TO BURMA(1955); DEATH IN SMALL DOSES(1957)
Peter Kooy
OBJECTIVE, BURMA!(1945); PARIS UNDERGROUND(1945)
Mike Kopach
GOOD TIMES(1967)
Thomas Kopache
STRANGE INVADERS(1983); WITHOUT A TRACE(1983)
Tom Kopache
1984
HOME FREE ALL(1984)
Zep Kopal
FABULOUS WORLD OF JULES VERNE, THE(1961, Czech.), art d
Ilya Kopalin
Misc. Silents
MOSCOW(1927, USSR), d
Steve Kopanke
STACY'S KNIGHTS(1983)
Richard Kopans
GUNS(1980, Fr.), ph
Simonie Kopapik
WHITE DAWN, THE(1974)
Mike Kopcha
SIMON, KING OF THE WITCHES(1971)
Kopecky
GOLEM, THE(1937, Czech./Fr.), set d
Milos Kopecky
MAN FROM THE FIRST CENTURY, THE(1961, Czech.); BARON MUNCHAUSEN(1962, Czech.); LEMONADE JOE(1966, Czech.); NIGHTS OF PRAGUE, THE(1968, Czech.); SIR, YOU ARE A WIDOWER(1971, Czech.); ADELE HASN'T HAD HER SUPPER YET(1978, Czech.); DIVINE EMMA, THE(1983, Czech,)
Gisela Kopel
ADVENTURERS, THE(1970)
Bernie Kopell
GOOD NEIGHBOR SAM(1964); LOVED ONE, THE(1965); BLACK JACK(1973)
Fritzi Kopell
LIFE STUDY(1973)
Arnold Kopelson
FOOLIN' AROUND(1980), p
Macit Koper
1984
HORSE, THE(1984, Turk.)
Sam Koperwas
DEAR MR. WONDERFUL(1983, Ger.), w
N. Koperzhinskaya
KIEV COMEDY, A(1963, USSR)
Father Stephen Kopestonsky
DEER HUNTER, THE(1978)
Gunther Kopf
HEIDI(1968, Aust.), ph
Jean-Pierre Kopf
1984
SWANN IN LOVE(1984, Fr.Ger.)
Fred Kopietz
SLEEPING BEAUTY(1959), anim
Arthur Kopit
BUFFALO BILL AND THE INDIANS, OR SITTING BULL'S HISTORY LESSON(1976), w
Arthur L. Kopit
OH DAD, POOR DAD, MAMA'S HUNG YOU IN THE CLOSET AND I'M FEELIN' SO SAD(1967), w
Joe Kopmar
DANIEL(1983)
Beate Kopp
ALL-AROUND REDUCED PERSONALITY-OUTTAKES, THE(1978, Ger.)
Dan Kopp
WEREWOLVES ON WHEELS(1971)
Rudolph Kopp
SIGN OF THE CROSS, THE(1932), m; CLEOPATRA(1934), m; CRUSADES, THE(1935), m; VOICE OF BUGLE ANN(1936), m
Rudolph G. Kopp
GALLANT BESS(1946), m; MY BROTHER TALKS TO HORSES(1946), m; BRIDE GOES WILD, THE(1948), m, m; TENTH AVENUE ANGEL(1948), m; DOCTOR AND THE GIRL, THE(1949), md; MYSTERY STREET(1950), m; BANNERLINE(1951), m; CALLING BULLDOG DRUMMOND(1951, Brit.), m; IT'S A BIG COUNTRY(1951), m; VENGEANCE VALLEY(1951), m; DESPERATE SEARCH(1952), md; DEVIL MAKES THREE, THE(1952), m; CRY OF THE HUNTED(1953), m; GREAT DIAMOND ROBBERY(1953), md; GYPSY COLT(1954), m
Deborah Koppel
SEDUCTION, THE(1982); DOCTOR DETROIT(1983)

Herman D. Koppel
LURE OF THE JUNGLE, THE(1970, Den.), m
Maria Koppenhoefer
TALES OF THE UNCANNY(1932, Ger.)
Maria Koppenhofer
FINAL CHORD, THE(1936, Ger.)
Helga Kopperl
GETTING TOGETHER(1976)
Barbara Kopple
Misc. Talkies
KEEPING ON(1981), d
Charles Koppleman
VIVA MAX!(1969), md
Frank Koppola
MAN, WOMAN AND CHILD(1983)
1984
HOT DOG...THE MOVIE(1984)
Petr Kopriva
MARTYRS OF LOVE(1968, Czech.)
Dana Koproff
BIG RED ONE, THE(1980), m
Mike Kopscha
GAY DECEIVERS, THE(1969)
Joseph Kopta
PICKUP(1951), w
M. Korabelnikova
JACK FROST(1966, USSR)
Pierre Korainik
CANNABIS(1970, Fr.), d, w
S. Koralkow
THREE DAYS OF VIKTOR TSCHERNIKOFF(1968, USSR)
Arthur Korb
FEELIN' GOOD(1966), m
Liliane Korb
STORY OF A THREE DAY PASS, THE(1968, Fr.), ed
Michael Korb
TWO THOUSAND MANIACS!(1964)
Otomar Korbelar
DAY THAT SHOOK THE WORLD, THE(1977, Yugo./Czech.)
Hilde Korber
GIRL OF THE MOORS, THE(1961, Ger.); DEVIL IN SILK(1968, Ger.)
Serge Korber
1984
DOG DAY(1984, Fr.), w
Joyce R. Korbin
1984
MOSCOW ON THE HUDSON(1984)
Peter Korbuly
WITNESS, THE(1982, Hung.)
William Korbut
1984
ISAAC LITTLEFEATHERS(1984, Can.)
Jacik Korcelli
GREAT BIG WORLD AND LITTLE CHILDREN, THE(1962, Pol.), ph
Korchagina-Alexandrovskaya
HOUSE OF GREED(1934, USSR)
Konstantin Korchmarev
MILITARY SECRET(1945, USSR), m
Alexander Korda
HER PRIVATE LIFE(1929), d; SQUALL, THE(1929), d; LILIES OF THE FIELD(1930), d; PRINCESS AND THE PLUMBER, THE(1930), d; WOMEN EVERYWHERE(1930), d; DIE MANNER UM LUCIE(1931), p&d; RESERVED FOR LADIES(1932, Brit.), p&d; WEDDING REHEARSAL(1932, Brit.), p&d; COUNSEL'S OPINION(1933, Brit.), d; MARIUS(1933, Fr.), d; OVERNIGHT(1933, Brit.), p; PRIVATE LIFE OF HENRY VIII, THE(1933), p, d; STRANGE EVIDENCE(1933, Brit.), d; CATHERINE THE GREAT(1934, Brit.), p; FOR LOVE OR MONEY(1934, Brit.), p; PRIVATE LIFE OF DON JUAN, THE(1934, Brit.), p&d; MEN OF TOMORROW(1935, Brit.), p; SANDERS OF THE RIVER(1935, Brit.), p; SCARLET PIMPERNEL, THE(1935, Brit.), p, d; GHOST GOES WEST, THE(1936), p; GIRL FROM MAXIM'S, THE(1936, Brit.), p, d; I STAND CONDEMNED(1936, Brit.), p; REMBRANDT(1936, Brit.), p&d; THINGS TO COME(1936, Brit.), p; DARK JOURNEY(1937, Brit.), p; ELEPHANT BOY(1937, Brit.), p; FOREVER YOURS(1937, Brit.), p; KNIGHT WITHOUT ARMOR(1937, Brit.), p; MAN WHO COULD WORK MIRACLES, THE(1937, Brit.), p; MEN ARE NOT GODS(1937, Brit.), p; MURDER ON DIAMOND ROW(1937, Brit.), p; DIVORCE OF LADY X. THE(1938, Brit.), p; DRUMS(1938, Brit.), p; RETURN OF THE SCARLET PIMPERNEL(1938, Brit.), p; CLOUDS OVER EUROPE(1939, Brit.), p; FOUR FEATHERS, THE(1939, Brit.), p; CONQUEST OF THE AIR(1940), p; LION HAS WINGS, THE(1940, Brit.), p; OLD BILL AND SON(1940, Brit.), p; OVER THE MOON(1940, Brit.), p; THIEF OF BAGHDAD, THE(1940, Brit.), p, d; TWENTY-ONE DAYS TOGETHER(1940, Brit.), p; LYDIA(1941), p; THAT HAMILTON WOMAN(1941), p&d; JUNGLE BOOK(1942), p; VACATION FROM MARRIAGE(1945, Brit.), p&d; ANNA KARENINA(1948, Brit.), p; IDEAL HUSBAND, AN(1948, Brit.), p&d; FIGHTING PIMPERNEL, THE(1950, Brit.), p; THIRD MAN, THE(1950, Brit.), p; DEEP BLUE SEA, THE(1955, Brit.), p
Silents
STOLEN BRIDE, THE(1927), d; NIGHT WATCH, THE(1928), d
Misc. Silents
SAMSON AND DELILAH(1922, Aust.), d; MADAME WANTS NO CHILDREN(1927, Ger.), d; PRIVATE LIFE OF HELEN OF TROY, THE(1927), d; YELLOW LILY, THE(1928), d; LOVE AND THE DEVIL(1929), d
David Korda
MAN FRIDAY(1975, Brit.), p; GREAT SCOUT AND CATHOUSE THURSDAY, THE(1976), p; LOOPHOLE(1981, Brit.), p
Kay Korda
STOP THE WORLD-I WANT TO GET OFF(1966, Brit.)
Maria Korda
FASTEST GUITAR ALIVE, THE(1967); FOR SINGLES ONLY(1968)

Michael Korda
TENDER IS THE NIGHT(1961)
Nino Korda
24-HOUR LOVER(1970, Ger.); LOLA(1982, Ger.)
Susanne Korda
ESCAPE TO BERLIN(1962, U.S./Switz./Ger.); THAT WOMAN(1968, Ger.)
Vincent Korda
WEDDING REHEARSAL(1932, Brit.), art d; MARIUS(1933, Fr.), prod d; PRIVATE LIFE OF HENRY VIII, THE(1933), art d; CATHERINE THE GREAT(1934, Brit.), prod d; PRIVATE LIFE OF DON JUAN, THE(1934, Brit.), prod d; MEN OF TOMORROW(1935, Brit.), set d; SANDERS OF THE RIVER(1935, Brit.), prod d; SCARLET PIMPERNEL, THE(1935, Brit.), prod d; GHOST GOES WEST, THE(1936), prod d; GIRL FROM MAXIM'S, THE(1936, Brit.), set d; I STAND CONDEMNED(1936, Brit.), set d; REMBRANDT(1936, Brit.), prod d; THINGS TO COME(1936, Brit.), prod d; ACTION FOR SLANDER(1937, Brit.), art d; ELEPHANT BOY(1937, Brit.), prod d; MAN WHO COULD WORK MIRACLES, THE(1937, Brit.), prod d; MEN ARE NOT GODS(1937, Brit.), prod d; MURDER ON DIAMOND ROW(1937, Brit.), prod d; DRUMS(1938, Brit.), prod d; FOUR FEATHERS, THE(1939, Brit.), prod d; PRISON WITHOUT BARS(1939, Brit.), art d; U-BOAT 29(1939, Brit.), prod d; LION HAS WINGS, THE(1940, Brit.), prod d; OLD BILL AND SON(1940, Brit.), prod d; OVER THE MOON(1940, Brit.), prod d; THIEF OF BAGHDAD, THE(1940, Brit.), prod d; TWENTY-ONE DAYS TOGETHER(1940, Brit.), art d; LYDIA(1941, Brit.), prod d; MAJOR BARBARA(1941, Brit.), prod d; THAT HAMILTON WOMAN(1941), prod d; JUNGLE BOOK(1942), prod d; TO BE OR NOT TO BE(1942), prod d; VACATION FROM MARRIAGE(1945, Brit.), prod d; BONNIE PRINCE CHARLIE(1948, Brit.), prod d; IDEAL HUSBAND, AN(1948, Brit.), set d; FALLEN IDOL, THE(1949, Brit.), prod d; THIRD MAN, THE(1950, Brit.), prod d; BREAKING THE SOUND BARRIER(1952), set d; OUTCAST OF THE ISLANDS(1952, Brit.), prod d; GREAT GILBERT AND SULLIVAN, THE(1953, Brit.), w; MURDER ON MONDAY(1953, Brit.), prod d; FIRE OVER AFRICA(1954, Brit.), art d; HOLLY AND THE IVY, THE(1954, Brit.), set d; DEEP BLUE SEA, THE(1955, Brit.), prod d; SUMMERTIME(1955), art d; SCENT OF MYSTERY(1960), prod d, art d; LONGEST DAY, THE(1962), art d; YELLOW ROLLS-ROYCE, THE(1965, Brit.), art d
Zoltan Korda
WOMEN EVERYWHERE(1930), w; FOR LOVE OR MONEY(1934, Brit.), d; MEN OF TOMORROW(1935, Brit.), d; SANDERS OF THE RIVER(1935, Brit.), d; ELEPHANT BOY(1937, Brit.), d; FOREVER YOURS(1937, Brit.), d; DRUMS(1938, Brit.), d; FOUR FEATHERS, THE(1939, Brit.), d; CONQUEST OF THE AIR(1940), d; THIEF OF BAGHDAD, THE(1940, Brit.), d; JUNGLE BOOK(1942), d; SAHARA(1943), d, w; COUNTER-ATTACK(1945), p&d; MACOMBER AFFAIR, THE(1947), d; WOMAN'S VENGEANCE, A(1947), p&d; CRY, THE BELOVED COUNTRY(1952, Brit.), p, d; STORM OVER THE NILE(1955, Brit.), p, d
Marija Kordic
FRAULEIN DOKTOR(1969, Ital./Yugo.), makeup
Bernardo Kordon
ALIAS BIG SHOT(1962, Argen.), w
Marie Kordus
ROCK 'N' ROLL HIGH SCHOOL(1979), art d
Walter Koremin
TOP BANANA(1954)
Koren
ROMEO AND JULIET(1955, USSR)
Sergey Koren
MAGIC VOYAGE OF SINBAD, THE(1962, USSR), ch
Vera Korene
SECOND BUREAU(1936, Fr.); CAFE DE PARIS(1938, Fr.); DOUBLE CRIME IN THE MAGINOT LINE(1939, Fr.); SAVAGE BRIGADE(1948, Fr.)
S. Korenev
SUN SHINES FOR ALL, THE(1961, USSR); HOUSE ON THE FRONT LINE, THE(1963, USSR)
Lydia Koreneva
Misc. Silents
LIFE FOR A LIFE, A(1916, USSR)
V. Koretskiy
KIEV COMEDY, A(1963, USSR)
Alexandra Korey
PIRATES OF PENZANCE, THE(1983)
Arnold Korff
DOUGH BOYS(1930); MEN OF THE NORTH(1930); ROYAL FAMILY OF BROADWAY, THE(1930); AMBASSADOR BILL(1931); AMERICAN TRAGEDY, AN(1931); UNHOLY GARDEN, THE(1931); YELLOW TICKET, THE(1931); EVENINGS FOR SALE(1932); SCARLET DAWN(1932); SECRETS OF THE FRENCH POLICE(1932); BLACK MOON(1934); ALL THE KING'S HORSES(1935); MAGNIFICENT OBSESSION(1935); PARIS IN SPRING(1935); SHANGHAI(1935); WINGS IN THE DARK(1935)
Misc. Silents
HAUNTED CASTLE, THE(1921, Ger.)
K. Korieniev
AMPHIBIOUS MAN, THE(1961, USSR)
Anni Korin
YOU ARE THE WORLD FOR ME(1964, Aust.)
Ana Korita
LOSERS, THE(1970)
P. Korizno
Misc. Silents
TRAITOR(1926, USSR)
Miliza Korjus
GREAT WALTZ, THE(1938)
Jon Korkes
OUT OF TOWNERS, THE(1970); LITTLE MURDERS(1971); CINDERELLA LIBERTY(1973); DAY OF THE DOLPHIN, THE(1973); OUTSIDE MAN, THE(1973, U.S./FR.); FRONT PAGE, THE(1974); TWO-MINUTE WARNING(1976); BETWEEN THE LINES(1977); JAWS OF SATAN(1980)
Jonathon Korkes
CATCH-22(1970)
Boris Korlin
Misc. Silents
COVE OF MISSING MEN(1918)

Cynthia Korman
TELL ME THAT YOU LOVE ME, JUNIE MOON(1970)
Gene Korman
SLAMS, THE(1973), p
Harvey Korman
LIVING VENUS(1961); GYPSY(1962); SON OF FLUBBER(1963); LAST OF THE SECRET AGENTS?, THE(1966); LORD LOVE A DUCK(1966); MAN CALLED FLINT-STONE, THE(1966); THREE BITES OF THE APPLE(1967); DON'T JUST STAND THERE(1968); APRIL FOOLS, THE(1969); BLAZING SADDLES(1974); HUCKLEBER-RY FINN(1974); HIGH ANXIETY(1977); AMERICATHON(1979); FIRST FAMI-LY(1980); HERBIE GOES BANANAS(1980); HISTORY OF THE WORLD, PART 1(1981); TRAIL OF THE PINK PANTHER, THE(1982); CURSE OF THE PINK PANTHER(1983)
Verna Korman
GAL WHO TOOK THE WEST, THE(1949); KETTLES ON OLD MACDONALD'S FARM, THE(1957)
Audrey Korn
UP IN ARMS(1944); DUFFY'S TAVERN(1945); BLUE DAHLIA, THE(1946)
David Korn
CAPTAIN MILKSHAKE(1970), a, ed
Iris Korn
WHITE LIGHTNING(1973)
1984
DADDY'S DEADLY DARLING(1984)
Nikolai Korn
ONCE THERE WAS A GIRL(1945, USSR)
Ken Kornbluh
LIMBO(1972)
Laura Kornbluh
LIMBO(1972)
Bruce Kornbluth
GOING HOME(1971); JENNIFER ON MY MIND(1971); SHOOT IT: BLACK, SHOOT IT: BLUE(1974); DISTANCE(1975)
Helena Kornel
LAST YEAR AT MARIENBAD(1962, Fr./Ital.)
Irma Kornelia
Silents
CAMPUS FLIRT, THE(1926)
Diana Korner
CREATURE WITH THE BLUE HAND(1971, Ger.)
Herbert Korner
MOONWOLF(1966, Fin./Ger.), ph
Ingeborg Korner
TOXI(1952, Ger.)
V. Korneyev
DAY THE WAR ENDED, THE(1961, USSR)
I. Korneyeva
SLEEPING BEAUTY, THE(1966, USSR)
Gail Kornfeld
AMATEUR DADDY(1932)
Eric Wolfgang Korngold
ADVENTURES OF ROBIN HOOD, THE(1938), m
Erich Wolfgang Korngold
CAPTAIN BLOOD(1935), m; MIDSUMMER'S NIGHT'S DREAM, A(1935), md; AN-THONY ADVERSE(1936), m; ANOTHER DAWN(1937), m; PRINCE AND THE PAUP-ER, THE(1937), m; JUAREZ(1939), m; PRIVATE LIVES OF ELIZABETH AND ESSEX, THE(1939), m; SEA HAWK, THE(1940), m; SEA WOLF, THE(1941), m; KING'S ROW(1942), m; CONSTANT NYMPH, THE(1943), m; DECEPTION(1946), m; DEVOTION(1946), m; OF HUMAN BONDAGE(1946), m; ESCAPE ME NEVER(1947), m; MAGIC FIRE(1956), m
Mark Korngute
NEW YEAR'S EVIL(1980)
Natasha Korniloff
HAMLET(1976, Brit.), cos
Mary Kornman
ARE THESE OUR CHILDREN?(1931); COLLEGE HUMOR(1933); FLYING DOWN TO RIO(1933); NEIGHBORS' WIVES(1933); MADAME DU BARRY(1934); PICTURE BRIDES(1934); QUITTERS, THE(1934); STRICTLY DYNAMITE(1934); DESERT TRAIL(1935); ROARING ROADS(1935); SMOKEY SMITH(1935); DAN MAT-THEWS(1936); SWING IT, PROFESSOR(1937); YOUTH ON PAROLE(1937); KING OF THE NEWSBOYS(1938); I AM A CRIMINAL(1939); ON THE SPOT(1940)
Misc. Talkies
ADVENTUROUS KNIGHTS(1935); CALLING OF DAN MATTHEWS, THE(1936)
Tony Kornman
Silents
HUNCHBACK OF NOTRE DAME, THE(1923), ph
Verna Kornman
CASANOVA BROWN(1944); MA AND PA KETTLE GO TO TOWN(1950)
Ted Kornowicz
RUMPELSTILTSKIN(1965, Ger.), ph; PUSS 'N' BOOTS(1967, Ger.), ph
Malka Kornstein
COUNSELLOR-AT-LAW(1933)
Korobei
Silents
BATTLESHIP POTEMKIN, THE(1925, USSR)
Len Korobkin
MAD MONSTER PARTY(1967), w
Agnes Korolenko
Silents
GHOST TRAIN, THE(1927, Brit.)
Vladimir Korolenko
SOUND OF LIFE, THE(1962, USSR), w
V. Korolkevich
TIGER GIRL(1955, USSR)
M. Korolyov
DON QUIXOTE(1961, USSR)
L. Korolyova
MUMU(1961, USSR); NIGHT BEFORE CHRISTMAS, A(1963, USSR)

Ye. Korolyova
WHEN THE TREES WERE TALL(1965, USSR)
V. Korotkov
MARRIAGE OF BALZAMINOV, THE(1966, USSR)
Igor Korovikov
VIOLIN AND ROLLER(1962, USSR)
Harry Korris
SOMEWHERE IN ENGLAND(1940, Brit.); SOMEWHERE IN CAMP(1942, Brit.); SOMEWHERE ON LEAVE(1942, Brit.); HAPPIDROME(1943, Brit.), a, w
Ilse Korseck
TRUNKS OF MR. O.F., THE(1932, Ger.)
Korsh
Misc. Silents
WINGS OF A SERF(1926, USSR)
V. Korsh-Sablin
SECRET BRIGADE, THE(1951 USSR), d
Harry Korshak
HIT(1973), p; SHEILA LEVINE IS DEAD AND LIVING IN NEW YORK(1975), p; GABLE AND LOMBARD(1976), p
Dennis Kort
BIG BUS, THE(1976); MODERN ROMANCE(1981)
1984
ANGEL(1984)
Danny Kortchmar
1984
THIS IS SPINAL TAP(1984)
Michael Kortchmar
LOVE IN A TAXI(1980), w
Oldrich Korte
INTIMATE LIGHTING(1969, Czech.), m
D. Kortesz
Misc. Silents
RICHTOFEN(1932, Ger.), d
Dick Korthaze
SWEET CHARITY(1969)
M. Kortkin
TAXI TO HEAVEN(1944, USSR), spec eff
Bob Kortman
VIRGINIAN, THE(1929); BRANDED(1931); CIMARRON(1931); CITY STREETS(1931); SUBWAY EXPRESS(1931); CORNERED(1932); FIGHTING FOOL, THE(1932); GOLD(1932); NIGHT RIDER, THE(1932); WHITE EAGLE(1932); WORLD AND THE FLESH, THE(1932); KING OF THE ARENA(1933); PHANTOM THUNDER-BOLT, THE(1933); SUNSET PASS(1933); BULLDOG DRUMMOND STRIKES BACK(1934); FIDDLIN' BUCKAROO, THE(1934); FIGHTING CODE, THE(1934); KID MILLIONS(1934); MAN'S GAME, A(1934); SMOKING GUNS(1934); SPITFIRE(1934); TRAIL DRIVE, THE(1934); WHEN A MAN SEES RED(1934); CRIMSON TRAIL, THE(1935); LONELY TRAIL, THE(1936); ROMANCE RIDES THE RANGE(1936); SONG OF THE SADDLE(1936); SWIFTY(1936); TRAIL OF THE LONESOME PINE, THE(1936); WINDS OF THE WASTELAND(1936); GHOST TOWN GOLD(1937); LAW FOR TOMBSTONE(1937); LUCK OF ROARING CAMP, THE(1937); RANGER COUR-AGE(1937); RANGERS STEP IN, THE(1937); SANDFLOW(1937); SMOKE TREE RANGE(1937); LAW OF THE TEXAN(1938); LAW WEST OF TOMBSTONE, THE(1938); MYSTERIOUS RIDER, THE(1938); PAINTED TRAIL, THE(1938); RENEGADE RANG-ER(1938); STAGECOACH DAYS(1938); WEST OF RAINBOW'S END(1938); OK-LAHOMA KID, THE(1939); RENEGADE TRAIL(1939); TIMBER STAMPEDE(1939); HIDDEN GOLD(1940); LAW AND ORDER(1940); STAGECOACH WAR(1940); BOSS OF BULLION CITY(1941); BURY ME NOT ON THE LONE PRAIRIE(1941); DEATH VALLEY OUTLAWS(1941); FUGITIVE VALLEY(1941); LAW OF THE RANGE(1941); RAWHIDE RANGERS(1941); SHEPHERD OF THE HILLS, THE(1941); THUNDER-ING HOOFS(1941); TWILIGHT ON THE TRAIL(1941); WIDE OPEN TOWN(1941); BANDIT RANGER(1942); FIGHTING BILL FARGO(1942); FOREST RANGERS, THE(1942); JESSE JAMES, JR.(1942); SUNDOWN KID, THE(1942); AVENGING RIDER, THE(1943); BLACK HILLS EXPRESS(1943); FORTY THIEVES(1944); OUT-LAWS OF SANTA FE(1944); WHISPERING SKULL, THE(1944); ALONG CAME JONES(1945); UNCONQUERED(1947); WILD HARVEST(1947); PALEFACE, THE(1948); WHISPERING SMITH(1948); SAMSON AND DELILAH(1949); SORROW-FUL JONES(1949); STREETS OF LAREDO(1949); COPPER CANYON(1950); FANCY PANTS(1950); BIG CARNIVAL, THE(1951); FLAMING FEATHER(1951); MATING SEASON, THE(1951)
Raymond Kortman
BLACK ACES(1937)
Robert Kortman
CONQUERING HORDE, THE(1931); PARDON US(1931); 24 HOURS(1931); FUGI-TIVE, THE(1933); ISLAND OF LOST SOULS(1933); RAINBOW RANCH(1933); TER-ROR TRAIL(1933); SIXTEEN FATHOMS DEEP(1934); IVORY-HANDLED GUN(1935); WILD MUSTANG(1935); FEUD OF THE WEST(1936); HEROES OF THE RAN-GE(1936); TEXAS TRAIL(1937); YOU CAN'T TAKE IT WITH YOU(1938); HOTEL IMPERIAL(1939); OKLAHOMA FRONTIER(1939); DAYS OF OLD CHEYENNE(1943); CALIFORNIA JOE(1944); GUNS OF THE LAW(1944); PINTO BANDIT, THE(1944); MARKED FOR MURDER(1945); STAGECOACH OUTLAWS(1945); LANDRUSH(1946)
Misc. Talkies
SADDLE LEATHER LAW(1944); GUNNING FOR VENGEANCE(1946)
Silents
CAPTIVE GOD, THE(1916); HELL'S HINGES(1916); LIEUT. DANNY, U.S.A.(1916); ANOTHER MAN'S BOOTS(1922); ARABIAN LOVE(1922); TRAVELIN' ON(1922); WOLF PACK(1922); ALL THE BROTHERS WERE VALIANT(1923); SUNRISE–A SONG OF TWO HUMANS(1927)
Misc. Silents
NO-GOOD GUY, THE(1916); WAIFS, THE(1916); NARROW TRAIL, THE(1917); MONTANA BILL(1921); GUN SHY(1922); WHITE SHEEP, THE(1924); BLOOD WILL TELL(1927); FLEETWING(1928)
Robert F. Kortman
TWO YEARS BEFORE THE MAST(1946)
Fritz Kortner
DANTON(1931, Ger.); KARAMAZOV(1931, Ger.); CHU CHIN CHOW(1934, Brit.); EVENSONG(1934, Brit.); ABDUL THE DAMNED(1935, Brit.); CROUCHING BEAST, THE(1936, U. S./Brit.); BOMBS OVER LONDON(1937, Brit.); DREYFUS CASE, THE(1940, Brit.); PURPLE V(1943); STRANGE DEATH OF ADOLF HITLER, THE(1943), a, w; HITLER GANG, THE(1944); RAZOR'S EDGE, THE(1946); SOME-WHERE IN THE NIGHT(1946); WIFE OF MONTE CRISTO, THE(1946); BRASHER

DOUBLOON, THE(1947); BERLIN EXPRESS(1948); CITY OF SECRETS(1963, Ger.), d, w

Misc. Talkies
ALI BABA NIGHTS(1953)

Silents
PANDORA'S BOX(1929, Ger.)

Misc. Silents
OTHER SELF, THE(1918, Aust.); BACKSTAIRS(1921, Ger.); WARNING SHADOWS(1924, Ger.); HANDS OF ORLAC, THE(1925, Aust.); SHIP OF LOST MEN, THE(1929, Ger.); SPY OF MME. POMPADOUR(1929, Ger.); THREE LOVES(1931, Ger.)

Fritz UA Kortner
VICIOUS CIRCLE, THE(1948)

Peter Kortner
THERE'S A GIRL IN MY SOUP(1970, Brit.), w

Peter Kortos
Silents
UNHOLY THREE, THE(1925)

Bob Kortrnan
COME ON TARZAN(1933)

Doug Korty
CRAZY QUILT, THE(1966)

John Korty
CRAZY QUILT, THE(1966), p,d,w&ph, ed; FUNNYMAN(1967), d, w, ph, anim; RIVERRUN(1968), d, w, ph; CANDIDATE, THE(1972), ph; SILENCE(1974), d; ALEX AND THE GYPSY(1976), d; OLIVER'S STORY(1978), d, w; TWICE UPON A TIME(1983), d, w

Charles Korvin
ENTER ARSENE LUPIN(1944); THIS LOVE OF OURS(1945); TEMPTATION(1946); BERLIN EXPRESS(1948); KILLER THAT STALKED NEW YORK, THE(1950); LYDIA BAILEY(1952); TARZAN'S SAVAGE FURY(1952); SANGAREE(1953); THUNDERSTORM(1956); SHIP OF FOOLS(1965); MAN WHO HAD POWER OVER WOMEN, THE(1970, Brit.); INSIDE OUT(1975, Brit.)

Y. Korvin-Krukovsky
Misc. Silents
PALACE AND FORTRESS(1924, USSR)

Lydia Korwin
Misc. Silents
LIFE OF GENEVIEVE, THE(1922)

David Kory
DONDI(1961)

Annie Korzen
RENT CONTROL(1981); TOOTSIE(1982)

Benni Korzen
FOREPLAY(1975), p; RENT CONTROL(1981), p

Andrzej Korzynski
MAN OF MARBLE(1979, Pol.), m; MAN OF IRON(1981, Pol.), m; POSSESSION(1981, Fr./Ger.), m

Jennie C. Kos
1984
CHEECH AND CHONG'S THE CORSICAN BROTHERS(1984)

Emil Kosa
LOST WORLD, THE(1960), spec eff

Emil Kosa, Jr.
JOURNEY TO THE CENTER OF THE EARTH(1959), spec eff; NORTH TO ALASKA(1960), spec eff; WIZARD OF BAGHDAD, THE(1960), spec eff; SNOW WHITE AND THE THREE STOOGES(1961), spec eff; TENDER IS THE NIGHT(1961), spec eff; CLEOPATRA(1963), spec eff; MOVE OVER, DARLING(1963), spec eff; TAKE HER, SHE'S MINE(1963), spec eff; FATE IS THE HUNTER(1964), spec eff; GOODBYE CHARLIE(1964), spec eff; JOHN GOLDFARB, PLEASE COME HOME(1964), spec eff; SHOCK TREATMENT(1964), spec eff; WHAT A WAY TO GO(1964), spec eff; AGONY AND THE ECSTASY, THE(1965), spec eff; DEAR BRIGETTE(1965), spec eff; DO NOT DISTURB(1965), spec eff; MORITURI(1965), spec eff; REWARD, THE(1965), spec eff; SOUND OF MUSIC, THE(1965), spec eff; VON RYAN'S EXPRESS(1965), spec eff; FANTASTIC VOYAGE(1966), spec eff; STAGECOACH(1966), spec eff; WAY...WAY OUT(1966), spec eff; DOCTOR DOLITTLE(1967), spec eff; FLIM-FLAM MAN, THE(1967), spec eff; GUIDE FOR THE MARRIED MAN, A(1967), spec eff; IN LIKE FLINT(1967), spec eff; ST. VALENTINE'S DAY MASSACRE, THE(1967), spec eff; VALLEY OF THE DOLLS(1967), spec eff; PLANET OF THE APES(1968), spec eff; STAR!(1968), spec eff; HELLO, DOLLY!(1969), spec eff

Kazuya Kosaka
YOUTH IN FURY(1961, Jap.)

Kyoko Kosaka
MADE IN U.S.A.(1966, Fr.)

Shutaro Kosaka
1984
WARRIORS OF THE WIND(1984, Jap.), anim

George Kosana
NIGHT OF THE LIVING DEAD(1968); THERE'S ALWAYS VANILLA(1972)

V. Kosarev
QUEEN OF SPADES(1961, USSR)

V. Kosarikhin
WAR AND PEACE(1968, USSR)

Chris Kosburg
SUBWAY RIDERS(1981)

Nina Koschetz
SUMMER STORM(1944)

Julia Koschka
ALRAUNE(1952, Ger.)

Maria Koscialkowska
PASSENGER, THE(1970, Pol.)

Silva Koscina
MICHAEL STROGOFF(1960, Fr./Ital./Yugo.)

Sylva Koscina
TOTO IN THE MOON(1957, Ital./Span.); YOUNG HUSBANDS(1958, Ital./Fr.); HERCULES(1959, Ital.); HERCULES' PILLS(1960, Ital.); HERCULES UNCHAINED(1960, Ital./Fr.); MIGHTY CRUSADERS, THE(1961, Ital.); JESSICA(1962, U.S./Ital./Fr.); SIEGE OF SYRACUSE(1962, Fr./Ital.); SWORDSMAN OF SIENA, THE(1962, Fr./Ital.); THREE FABLES OF LOVE(1963, Fr./Ital./Span.); LET'S TALK ABOUT WOMEN(1964, Fr./Ital.); LOVE ON THE RIVIERA(1964, Fr./Ital.); LOVE, THE ITALIAN WAY(1964, Ital.); DOUBLE BED, THE(1965, Fr./Ital.); JULIET OF THE SPIRITS(1965, Fr./Ital./

W.Ger.); LITTLE NUNS, THE(1965, Ital.); LOVE IN 4 DIMENSIONS(1965 Fr./Ital.); RAILROAD MAN, THE(1965, Ital.); JUDEX(1966, Fr./Ital.); LOVE AND MARRIAGE(1966, Ital.); THAT MAN IN ISTANBUL(1966, Fr./Ital./Span.); DEADLIER THAN THE MALE(1967, Brit.); MADE IN ITALY(1967, Fr./Ital.); THREE BITES OF THE APPLE(1967); GIRL GAME(1968, Braz./Fr./Ital.); LOVELY WAY TO DIE, A(1968); SECRET WAR OF HARRY FRIGG, THE(1968); FIGHT FOR ROME(1969, Ger./Rum.); JOHNNY BANCO(1969, Fr./Ital./Ger.); JUSTINE(1969, Ital./Span.); SHE AND HE(1969, Ital.); HORNET'S NEST(1970); BATTLE OF THE NERETVA(1971, Yugo./Ital./Ger.); ITALIAN CONNECTION, THE(1973, U.S./Ital./Ger.); SLASHER, THE(1975); HOUSE OF EXORCISM, THE(1976, Ital.); SOME LIKE IT COOL(1979, Ger./Aust./Ital./Fr.); SUNDAY LOVERS(1980, Ital./Fr.)

Misc. Talkies
MANIPULATOR, THE(1972)

Sylvia Koscina
AGENT 8 3/4(1963, Brit.)

Ken Kosek
THEY ALL LAUGHED(1981)

Yuji Koseki
MOTHRA(1962, Jap.), m; LONELY LANE(1963, Jap.), m

Fritz Koselka
FORBIDDEN MUSIC(1936, Brit.), w; LITTLE MELODY FROM VIENNA(1948, Aust.), w

H. Koser
Silents
AMERICA(1924)

H. E. Koser
Silents
GOOD-BYE, BILL(1919)

John J. Koshel
IN GOD WE TRUST(1980)

Peter Koshel
WINTER KILLS(1979); IN GOD WE TRUST(1980)

G. Koshelyov
WAR AND PEACE(1968, USSR), set d

Marina Koshetz
HOLIDAY IN MEXICO(1946); NO LEAVE, NO LOVE(1946); LUXURY LINER(1948); GREAT CARUSO, THE(1951); ON THE RIVERA(1951); DESIREE(1954); PLEASE DON'T EAT THE DAISIES(1960); SINGING NUN, THE(1966); BUSYBODY, THE(1967)

Mme. Nina Koshetz
ALGIERS(1938)

Nina Koshetz
ENTER MADAME(1935); OUR HEARTS WERE YOUNG AND GAY(1944); CHASE, THE(1946); IT'S A SMALL WORLD(1950); CAPTAIN PIRATE(1952); HOT BLOOD(1956)

N. Kosheverova
TIGER GIRL(1955, USSR), d

Kanji Koshiba
SANSHO THE BAILIFF(1969, Jap.)

Mikio Koshiba
GEISHA, A(1978, Jap.)

Fubuki Koshiji
DON'T CALL ME A CON MAN(1966, Jap.)

Hideko Koshikawa
ESCAPADE IN JAPAN(1957)

Jonathan Koshner
GAMBLER, THE(1974)

Jerzy Kosinski
BEING THERE(1979), w; REDS(1981)

George Koskas
DOLL, THE(1962, Fr.), art d

Bill Koski
RECOMMENDATION FOR MERCY(1975, Can.)

George Koski
KING, MURRAY(1969)

Maria Koski
SAGA OF DRACULA, THE(1975, Span.)

Erol Koskin
YOU CAN'T WIN 'EM ALL(1970, Brit.)

David Kosky
MURDER IN THE CATHEDRAL(1952, Brit.), ph

Martin Kosleck
DAUGHTER OF EVIL(1930, Ger.); FASHIONS OF 1934(1934); CONFESSIONS OF A NAZI SPY(1939); NICK CARTER, MASTER DETECTIVE(1939); NURSE EDITH CAVELL(1939); CALLING PHILO VANCE(1940); FOREIGN CORRESPONDENT(1940); DEVIL PAYS OFF, THE(1941); INTERNATIONAL LADY(1941); MAD DOCTOR, THE(1941); UNDERGROUND(1941); ALL THROUGH THE NIGHT(1942); BERLIN CORRESPONDENT(1942); FLY BY NIGHT(1942); MANILA CALLING(1942); NAZI AGENT(1942); BOMBER'S MOON(1943); CHETNIKS(1943); NORTH STAR, THE(1943); HITLER GANG, THE(1944); MUMMY'S CURSE, THE(1944); SECRETS OF SCOTLAND YARD(1944); FROZEN GHOST, THE(1945); GANGS OF THE WATERFRONT(1945); PURSUIT TO ALGIERS(1945); SPIDER, THE(1945); STRANGE HOLIDAY(1945); CRIME OF THE CENTURY(1946); HOUSE OF HORRORS(1946); JUST BEFORE DAWN(1946); SHE-WOLF OF LONDON(1946); WIFE OF MONTE CRISTO, THE(1946); ASSIGNED TO DANGER(1948); HALF PAST MIDNIGHT(1948); SMUGGLERS' COVE(1948); SOMETHING WILD(1961); HITLER(1962); FLESH EATERS, THE(1964); MORITURI(1965); 36 HOURS(1965); AGENT FOR H.A.R.M.(1966); WHICH WAY TO THE FRONT?(1970); MAN WITH BOGART'S FACE, THE(1980)

Al Koslik
INBREAKER, THE(1974, Can.)

Paul Koslo
LOSERS, THE(1970); OMEGA MAN, THE(1971); SCANDALOUS JOHN(1971); VANISHING POINT(1971); JOE KIDD(1972); WELCOME HOME, SOLDIER BOYS(1972); CLEOPATRA JONES(1973); LAUGHING POLICEMAN, THE(1973); LOLLY-MADONNA XXX(1973); STONE KILLER, THE(1973); BOOTLEGGERS(1974); FREEBIE AND THE BEAN(1974); MR. MAJESTYK(1974); DROWNING POOL, THE(1975); ROOSTER COGBURN(1975); VOYAGE OF THE DAMNED(1976, Brit.); MANIAC!(1977); TOMORROW NEVER COMES(1978, Brit./Can.); LOVE AND BULLETS(1979, Brit.); HEAVEN'S GATE(1980)

1984
HAMBONE AND HILLIE(1984)
Alexis Kosloff
Silents
DANCER'S PERIL, THE(1917)
Maurice Kosloff
HOODLUM, THE(1951), p; MOVIE STUNTMEN(1953), p
Theodore Kosloff
MADAME SATAN(1930); SUNNY(1930), ch; RAVEN, THE(1935), ch; STAGE
DOOR(1937); SAMSON AND DELILAH(1949), ch
Silents
SOMETHING TO THINK ABOUT(1920); AFFAIRS OF ANATOL, THE(1921); DICTA-
TOR, THE(1922); TO HAVE AND TO HOLD(1922); ADAM'S RIB(1923); LAW OF THE
LAWLESS, THE(1923); BEGGAR ON HORSEBACK(1925); NEW LIVES FOR
OLD(1925); VOLGA BOATMAN, THE(1926); KING OF KINGS, THE(1927); WOMAN
WISE(1928)
Misc. Silents
CITY OF MASKS, THE(1920); PRINCE CHAP, THE(1920); WHY CHANGE YOUR
WIFE?(1920); FOOL'S PARADISE(1921); GREEN TEMPTATION, THE(1922); LANE
THAT HAD NO TURNING, THE(1922); CHILDREN OF JAZZ(1923); DON'T CALL IT
LOVE(1924); LITTLE ADVENTURESS, THE(1927)
I. C. Koslov
MYSTERIOUS ISLAND(1941, USSR)
Lidia Koslovich
1984
BASILEUS QUARTET(1984, Ital.)
S. V. Koslovski
Silents
STORM OVER ASIA(1929, USSR), set d
Ron Koslow
LIFEGUARD(1976), w
1984
FIRSTBORN(1984), p, w
Jon Koslowsky
SEED OF INNOCENCE(1980), ed
1984
HOSPITAL MASSACRE(1984), ed
Kosma
LA MARSEILLAISE(1938, Fr.), m
Joseph Kosma
GRAND ILLUSION(1938, Fr.), m; LA BETE HUMAINE(1938, Fr.), m; RULES OF
THE GAME, THE(1939, Fr.), md; CHILDREN OF PARADISE(1945, Fr.), m; GATES OF
THE NIGHT(1950, Fr.), m; WAYS OF LOVE(1950, Ital./Fr.), m; CROSSROADS OF
PASSION(1951, Fr.), m; LA MARIE DU PORT(1951, Fr.), m; LOVERS OF VERONA,
THE(1951, Fr.), m; PASSION FOR LIFE(1951, Fr.), m; GREEN GLOVE, THE(1952), m;
PERFECTIONIST, THE(1952, Fr.), m; INNOCENTS IN PARIS(1955, Brit.), m, md;
MAIN STREET(1956, Span.), m; PARIS DOES STRANGE THINGS(1957, Fr./Ital.), m;
CASE OF DR. LAURENT(1958, Fr.), m; DEMONIAQUE(1958, Fr.), m; DOCTOR'S
DILEMMA, THE(1958, Brit.), m; LADY CHATTERLEY'S LOVER(1959, Fr.), m; PIC-
NIC ON THE GRASS(1960, Fr.), m; LOVE AND THE FRENCHWOMAN(1961, Fr.), m;
DOLL, THE(1962, Fr.), m; ELUSIVE CORPORAL, THE(1963, Fr.), m; IN THE
FRENCH STYLE(1963, U.S./Fr.), m; MAGNIFICENT SINNER(1963, Fr.), m; THANK
HEAVEN FOR SMALL FAVORS(1965, Fr.), m; LE PETIT THEATRE DE JEAN
RENOIR(1974, Fr.), m
Vladimir Kosma
TALL BLOND MAN WITH ONE BLACK SHOE, THE(1973, Fr.), m
Wieslawa Kosmalska
MAN OF IRON(1981, Pol.)
Nick Kosonic
VIDEODROME(1983, Can.), art d
Yoko Kosono
SANSHO THE BAILIFF(1969, Jap.)
Danny Kosow
RUBY(1971)
Alan Koss
FRIENDS OF EDDIE COYLE, THE(1973); FIRE AND ICE(1983); WAVE-
LENGTH(1983)
Bobby Kosser
HARDCORE(1979); HARDLY WORKING(1981)
Kristina Kossi
1984
FLAMINGO KID, THE(1984)
Jack Kosslyn
AMAZING COLOSSAL MAN, THE(1957); DEVIL'S HAIRPIN, THE(1957); ATTACK
OF THE PUPPET PEOPLE(1958); MARACAIBO(1958); SPIDER, THE(1958); WAR OF
THE COLOSSAL BEAST(1958); MAGIC SWORD, THE(1962); PLAY MISTY FOR
ME(1971); BREEZY(1973); HIGH PLAINS DRIFTER(1973); EIGER SANCTION,
THE(1975); EMPIRE OF THE ANTS(1977)
Monika Kossmann
PRIZE OF GOLD, A(1955)
David Kossoff
GOOD BEGINNING, THE(1953, Brit.); CHANCE MEETING(1954, Brit.); I AM A
CAMERA(1955, Brit.); SVENGALI(1955, Brit.); WOMAN FOR JOE, THE(1955, Brit.);
IRON PETTICOAT, THE(1956, Brit.); KID FOR TWO FARTHINGS, A(1956, Brit.); NOW
AND FOREVER(1956, Brit.); WHO DONE IT?(1956, Brit.); 1984(1956, Brit.); PORTRAIT
IN SMOKE(1957, Brit.); TRIPLE DECEPTION(1957, Brit.); COUNT FIVE AND
DIE(1958, Brit.); INDISCREET(1958); INNOCENT SINNERS(1958, Brit.); HOUSE OF
THE SEVEN HAWKS, THE(1959); JOURNEY, THE(1959, U.S./Aust.); MOUSE THAT
ROARED, THE(1959, Brit.); CONSPIRACY OF HEARTS(1960, Brit.); INN FOR TROU-
BLE(1960, Brit.); HOUSE OF FRIGHT(1961); JET STORM(1961, Brit.); FREUD(1962);
MOUSE ON THE MOON, THE(1963, Brit.); SUMMER HOLIDAY(1963, Brit.); RING OF
SPIES(1964, Brit.)
Bobbie-Ellyne Kosstrin
ABSENCE OF MALICE(1981)
Don Kost
THOSE LIPS, THOSE EYES(1980)
Fred Kost
PASSION HOLIDAY(1963)

Anton Kosta
T-MEN(1947); WOMAN FROM TANGIER, THE(1948)
Sonja Kosta
DECISION BEFORE DAWN(1951)
Irwin Kostal
MARY POPPINS(1964), m; SOUND OF MUSIC, THE(1965), md; CHITTY CHITTY
BANG BANG(1968, Brit.), md; CHARLOTTE'S WEB(1973), md; BLUE BIRD,
THE(1976), m; PETE'S DRAGON(1977), m, md
Andre Kostalanetz
I DREAM TOO MUCH(1935), md
Maria Kostandarou
THANOS AND DESPINA(1970, Fr./Gr.)
Spyros Kostantopoulos
CANNON AND THE NIGHTINGALE, THE(1969, Gr.)
Jozef Kostecki
EROICA(1966, Pol.)
Andre Kostelanetz
THAT GIRL FROM PARIS(1937), m, md
Leigh Kostelanetz
SMASHING TIME(1967 Brit.)
Dorothy Koster
WONDER MAN(1945)
Henry Koster [Herman Kosterlitz]
JAZZBAND FIVE, THE(1932, Ger.), w; THERE GOES THE BRIDE(1933, Brit.), w;
THREE SMART GIRLS(1937), d; 100 MEN AND A GIRL(1937), d; AFFAIRS OF
MAUPASSANT(1938, Aust.), d; RAGE OF PARIS, THE(1938), d; FIRST LOVE(1939),
d; THREE SMART GIRLS GROW UP(1939), d; SPRING PARADE(1940), d; IT START-
ED WITH EVE(1941), p, d; BETWEEN US GIRLS(1942), p&d; MUSIC FOR MIL-
LIONS(1944), d; TWO SISTERS FROM BOSTON(1946), d; BISHOP'S WIFE,
THE(1947), d; UNFINISHED DANCE,THE(1947), d; LUCK OF THE IRISH(1948), d;
COME TO THE STABLE(1949), d; INSPECTOR GENERAL, THE(1949), d; HAR-
VEY(1950), d; MY BLUE HEAVEN(1950), d; WABASH AVENUE(1950), d; ELOPE-
MENT(1951), d; MR. BELVEDERE RINGS THE BELL(1951), d; NO HIGHWAY IN
THE SKY(1951, Brit.), d; MY COUSIN RACHEL(1952), d; O. HENRY'S FULL
HOUSE(1952), d; STARS AND STRIPES FOREVER(1952), d; ROBE, THE(1953), d;
DESIREE(1954), d; GOOD MORNING, MISS DOVE(1955), d; MAN CALLED PETER,
THE(1955), d; VIRGIN QUEEN, THE(1955), d; D-DAY, THE SIXTH OF JUNE(1956),
d; POWER AND THE PRIZE, THE(1956), d; MY MAN GODFREY(1957), d; FRAU-
LEIN(1958), d; NAKED MAJA, THE(1959, Ital./U.S.), d; STORY OF RUTH, THE(1960),
d; FLOWER DRUM SONG(1961), d; MR. HOBBS TAKES A VACATION(1962), d;
TAKE HER, SHE'S MINE(1963), p&d; DEAR BRIGETTE(1965), p&d; SINGING NUN,
THE(1966), d
Jonna Koster
SPETTERS(1983, Holland)
Liselotte Koster
FINAL CHORD, THE(1936, Ger.)
Nicholas Koster
MY COUSIN RACHEL(1952); STARS AND STRIPES FOREVER(1952); ROBE,
THE(1953)
Nicolas Koster
DESIREE(1954)
Tom Koster
ONE FROM THE HEART(1982)
Aleksandar Kostic
LOVE AFFAIR; OR THE CASE OF THE MISSING SWITCHBOARD OPERA-
TOR(1968, Yugo.)
Mihajilo Kostic
NINTH CIRCLE, THE(1961, Yugo.)
E. Kostin
STALKER(1982, USSR)
V. Kostina
RESURRECTION(1963, USSR)
Peter Kostka
WHAT WOULD YOU SAY TO SOME SPINACH(1976, Czech.)
Kostrichkin
ENEMIES OF PROGRESS(1934, USSR)
Andrei Kostrichkin
Misc. Silents
CLOAK, THE(1926, USSR)
Michael Kostrick
THEY WERE EXPENDABLE(1945); TILL THE END OF TIME(1946); LOVE ME OR
LEAVE ME(1955); JUMBO(1962)
N. Kostromsky
Misc. Silents
DOMESTIC-AGITATOR(1920, USSR)
V. Kostyrenko
KIEV COMEDY, A(1963, USSR)
Jim Kosub
STACY'S KNIGHTS(1983)
Tadeusz Kosudarski
KNIGHTS OF THE TEUTONIC ORDER, THE(1962, Pol.); LOTNA(1966, Pol.)
Isamu Kosugi
NEW EARTH, THE(1937, Jap./Ger.)
Misc. Silents
METROPOLITAN SYMPHONY(1929, Jap.)
Kane Kosugi
REVENGE OF THE NINJA(1983)
Masao Kosugi
YOUTH IN FURY(1961, Jap.), ph; FIGHT FOR THE GLORY(1970, Jap.), ph; HOT-
SPRINGS HOLIDAY(1970, Jap.), ph
Sho Kosugi
ENTER THE NINJA(1982); REVENGE OF THE NINJA(1983), a, ch
1984
NINJA III–THE DOMINATION(1984), a, ch
Yoshio Kosugi
MADAME BUTTERFLY(1955 Ital./Jap.); SAMURAI(1955, Jap.); SEVEN SAMURAI,
THE(1956, Jap.); MYSTERIANS, THE(1959, Jap.); MOTHRA(1962, Jap.); TATSU(1962,
Jap.); GODZILLA VS. THE THING(1964, Jap.); EMPEROR AND A GENERAL,
THE(1968, Jap.)

I. Kosykh
FATHER OF A SOLDIER(1966, USSR)

Vitya Kosykh
WELCOME KOSTYA!(1965, USSR); FATHER OF A SOLDIER(1966, USSR); GIRL AND THE BUGLER, THE(1967, USSR)

Irvin Koszewski
THINGS ARE TOUGH ALL OVER(1982)

Balazs Kosztolanyi
WINTER WIND(1970, Fr./Hung.)

Johann Iwan Kot
1984
NEVERENDING STORY, THE(1984, Ger.), art d

Eddie Kotal
EASY LIVING(1949)

Henry Kotani
Silents
TYPHOON, THE(1914); WRATH OF THE GODS, THE or THE DESTRUCTION OF SAKURA JIMA(1914); JOHNNY GET YOUR GUN(1919), ph

Tom Kotani
BUSHIDO BLADE, THE(1982 Brit./U.S.), d

Kura Kotanio
Silents
SABLE LORCHA, THE(1915)

Howard W. Kotch
GHOST TOWN(1956), p

Hugo B. Kotch
Silents
JOAN THE WOMAN(1916)

Ted Kotcheff
LIFE AT THE TOP(1965, Brit.), d; TWO GENTLEMEN SHARING(1969, Brit.), d; OUTBACK(1971, Aus.), d; BILLY TWO HATS(1973, Brit.), d; APPRENTICESHIP OF DUDDY KRAVITZ, THE(1974, Can.), d; FUN WITH DICK AND JANE(1977), d; WHO IS KILLING THE GREAT CHEFS OF EUROPE?(1978, US/Ger.), d; NORTH DALLAS FORTY(1979), d, w; FIRST BLOOD(1982), d; SPLIT IMAGE(1982), p&d; UNCOMMON VALOR(1983), d

William T. Kotcheff
TIARA TAHITI(1962, Brit.), d

Pete Kotehernaro
LETTER, THE(1940)

Apollonia Kotero
1984
PURPLE RAIN(1984)

Jerbanu Kothawala
Silents
EMERALD OF THE EAST(1928, Brit.), w

Epp Kotkas
Misc. Talkies
WHAT MAISIE KNEW(1976)

Carrie Kotkin
TAKING OFF(1971)

Clarisse Kotkin
NEW YEAR'S EVIL(1980)

Edward Kotkin
NEIGHBORS(1981)

Bill Kotler
HEY THERE, IT'S YOGI BEAR(1964), ph; MAN CALLED FLINTSTONE, THE(1966), ph

Oded Kotler
SANDS OF BEERSHEBA(1966, U.S./Israel); EVERY BASTARD A KING(1968, Israel); NOT MINE TO LOVE(1969, Israel); SIMCHON FAMILY, THE(1969, Israel); HANNAH K.(1983, Fr.)

Marge Kotlisky
1984
SIXTEEN CANDLES(1984)

V. Kotochnev
SWORD AND THE DRAGON, THE(1960, USSR), w

Jorga Kotrbova
90 DEGREES IN THE SHADE(1966, Czech./Brit.)

Markos Kotsikos
GONE IN 60 SECONDS(1974)

George Kotsonaros
BEGGARS OF LIFE(1928); SHAKEDOWN, THE(1929); DANGEROUS PARADISE(1930); HONEYMOON LANE(1931)
Silents
CATCH AS CATCH CAN(1927); TENDER HOUR, THE(1927); FIFTY-FIFTY GIRL, THE(1928); STREET OF SIN, THE(1928)
Misc. Silents
BODY PUNCH, THE(1929)

Jacqueline Kott
SCOBIE MALONE(1975, Aus.)
1984
CAREFUL, HE MIGHT HEAR YOU(1984, Aus.)

Carol Kottenbrook
SLAYER, THE(1982)

Eva Kotthaus
FAREWELL TO ARMS, A(1957); NUN'S STORY, THE(1959)

Otto Kottka
Silents
KING OF KINGS, THE(1927)

Joe Kottler
B.S. I LOVE YOU(1971)

Claud Kottmann
MARRIAGE OF MARIA BRAUN, THE(1979, Ger.), art d

Natascha Kotto
LIMIT, THE(1972)

Yaphet Kotto
NOTHING BUT A MAN(1964); FIVE CARD STUD(1968); THOMAS CROWN AFFAIR, THE(1968); LIBERATION OF L.B. JONES, THE(1970); ACROSS 110TH STREET(1972); LIMIT, THE(1972), a, p&d, w; MAN AND BOY(1972); LIVE AND LET DIE(1973, Brit.); TRUCK TURNER(1974); FRIDAY FOSTER(1975); REPORT TO THE COMMISSIONER(1975); SHARK'S TREASURE(1975); DRUM(1976); MONKEY HUSTLE, THE(1976); BLUE COLLAR(1978); ALIEN(1979); BRUBAKER(1980); DEATH VENGEANCE(1982); STAR CHAMBER, THE(1983)
Misc. Talkies
BONE(1972)

Marge Kotusky
MY BODYGUARD(1980)

Jan Kotva
SIGN OF THE VIRGIN(1969, Czech.)

Vaclav Kotva
NIGHTS OF PRAGUE, THE(1968, Czech.)

John Kotze
MILLION EYES OF SU-MURU, THE(1967, Brit.), ph

Tanoh Kouao
BLACK AND WHITE IN COLOR(1976, Fr.)

Charly Koubesserian
MAGNIFICENT ONE, THE(1974, Fr./Ital.)

Alexandre Koubitzky
Silents
NAPOLEON(1927, Fr.)

Lydia Koubkova
Misc. Silents
BREAK-UP, THE(1930, USSR)

Colette Kouchner
NAKED HEARTS(1970, Fr.), ed

Jim Kouf
1984
AMERICAN DREAMER(1984), w; UP THE CREEK(1984), w

M. James Kouf, Jr.
PINK MOTEL(1983), p, w; UTILITIES(1983, Can.), w

Mohamed Kouka
PLAY DIRTY(1969, Brit.)

Princess Kouka
DARK SANDS(1938, Brit.)

Nader Kouklani
SIAVASH IN PERSEPOLIS(1966, Iran)

Pierre Koulak
BIRDS COME TO DIE IN PERU(1968, Fr.); BORSALINO(1970, Fr.); DESTRUCTORS, THE(1974, Brit.)

Art Koulias
SILENCERS, THE(1966)

Vasco Koulolia
TOUCH OF THE OTHER, A(1970, Brit.)

Georges Koulouris
CONFIDENTIALLY YOURS(1983, Fr.)

Maya Koumani
FIRE MAIDENS FROM OUTER SPACE(1956, Brit.); IT'S A WONDERFUL WORLD(1956, Brit.); LAST MAN TO HANG, THE(1956, Brit.); FIGHTING WILDCATS, THE(1957, Brit.); FIRE DOWN BELOW(1957, U.S./Brit.); UNDERCOVER GIRL(1957, Brit.); DIPLOMATIC CORPSE, THE(1958, Brit.); BANDIT OF ZHOBE, THE(1959); HIDDEN HOMICIDE(1959, Brit.); HORRORS OF THE BLACK MUSEUM(1959, U.S./Brit.); SON OF ROBIN HOOD(1959, Brit.); STRICTLY CONFIDENTIAL(1959, Brit.); PRICE OF SILENCE, THE(1960, Brit.)

Menis Koumantareas
MATCHMAKING OF ANNA, THE(1972, Gr.), w

Irene Koumarianou
IPHIGENIA(1977, Gr.)

Arghyris Kounadis
ANTIGONE(1962 Gr.), m

Liza Koundouri
ELECTRA(1962, Gr.)

Nikos Koundouros
YOUNG APHRODITES(1966, Gr.), p, d

Miranda Kounelaki
ATLAS(1960)

Deborah Kounnas
CADDIE(1976, Aus.)

Elsa Kourani
SUDDENLY, A WOMAN!(1967, Den.)

Thali Kouri
NINE HOURS TO RAMA(1963, U.S./Brit.)

Nikos Kourkoulos
SPOILED ROTTEN(1968, Gr.)
Misc. Talkies
BANDITS IN ROME(1967, Ital.)

Sergei Kournakoff
1812(1944, USSR)

Kostas Kourtis
RED LANTERNS(1965, Gr.)

Vienneula Koussefhane
FANTASIES(1981)

Ari Koutay
TWO KOUNEY LEMELS(1966, Israel)

Ken Koutnik
SLAUGHTER TRAIL(1951)

Annita Koutsouveli
SONG AND THE SILENCE, THE(1969)

Jon Kouzouyan
TEARS OF HAPPINESS(1974)

Amelia Kova
FORCE OF ARMS(1951)

Irene Kova [Irena Kasikova]
VOYAGE TO THE END OF THE UNIVERSE(1963, Czech.)

Betty Kovac
BLAST OF SILENCE(1961)

Roland Kovac
48 HOURS TO ACAPULCO(1968, Ger.), m

Rudolf Kovac
SEVENTH CONTINENT, THE(1968, Czech./Yugo.), art d
Jozo Kovacevic
TREASURE OF SILVER LAKE(1965, Fr./Ger./Yugo.)
Kornell Kovach
MONTENEGRO(1981, Brit./Swed.), m
Oleg Kovachev
CLOWN AND THE KIDS, THE(1968, U.S./Bulgaria)
Andre Kovachevitch
TONI(1968, Fr.)
Nancy Kovack
STRANGERS WHEN WE MEET(1960); CRY FOR HAPPY(1961); WILD WESTERN-ERS, THE(1962); DIARY OF A MADMAN(1963); JASON AND THE AR-GONAUTS(1963, Brit.); GREAT SIOUX MASSACRE, THE(1965); OUTLAWS IS COMING, THE(1965); SYLVIA(1965); FRANKIE AND JOHNNY(1966); SILENCERS, THE(1966); TARZAN AND THE VALLEY OF GOLD(1966 U.S./Switz.); ENTER LAUGHING(1967); MAROONED(1969)
Sandy Kovack
IMPROPER CHANNELS(1981, Can.)
Bela Kovacs
PARK ROW(1952); DESERT SANDS(1955); TO CATCH A THIEF(1955)
Ernie Kovacs
OPERATION MAD BALL(1957); BELL, BOOK AND CANDLE(1958); IT HAPPENED TO JANE(1959); NORTH TO ALASKA(1960); OUR MAN IN HAVANA(1960, Brit.); PEPE(1960); STRANGERS WHEN WE MEET(1960); WAKE ME WHEN IT'S OVER(1960); FIVE GOLDEN HOURS(1961, Brit.); SAIL A CROOKED SHIP(1961)
Eva Kovacs
PURSUIT(1975)
Geza Kovacs
MEPHISTO(1981, Ger.); DEAD ZONE, THE(1983)
Istvan Kovacs
FORTRESS, THE(1979, Hung.)
Laszlo [Leslie] Kovacs
NASTY RABBIT, THE(1964); BLOOD OF DRACULA'S CASTLE(1967), ph; HELL'S ANGELS ON WHEELS(1967), ph; MAN CALLED DAGGER, A(1967), ph; MANTIS IN LACE(1968), ph; PSYCH-OUT(1968), ph; SAVAGE SEVEN, THE(1968), ph; SINGLE ROOM FURNISHED(1968), ph; TARGETS(1968), ph; EASY RIDER(1969), ph; THAT COLD DAY IN THE PARK(1969, U.S./Can.), ph; ALEX IN WONDERLAND(1970), ph; FIVE EASY PIECES(1970), ph; GETTING STRAIGHT(1970), ph; HELL'S BLOODY DEVILS(1970), ph; REBEL ROUSERS(1970), ph; LAST MOVIE, THE(1971), ph; MAR-RIAGE OF A YOUNG STOCKBROKER, THE(1971), ph; KING OF MARVIN GAR-DENS, THE(1972), ph; POCKET MONEY(1972), ph; WHAT'S UP, DOC?(1972), ph; PAPER MOON(1973), ph; REFLECTION OF FEAR, A(1973), ph; SLITHER(1973), ph; STEELYARD BLUES(1973), ph; FREEBIE AND THE BEAN(1974), ph; HUCKLEBER-RY FINN(1974), ph; AT LONG LAST LOVE(1975), ph; SHAMPOO(1975), ph; BABY BLUE MARINE(1976), ph; HARRY AND WALTER GO TO NEW YORK(1976), ph; NICKELODEON(1976), ph; CLOSE ENCOUNTERS OF THE THIRD KIND(1977), ph; FOR PETE'S SAKE(1977), ph; NEW YORK, NEW YORK(1977), ph; F.I.S.T.(1978), ph; PARADISE ALLEY(1978), ph; BUTCH AND SUNDANCE: THE EARLY DAYS(1979), ph; HEART BEAT(1979), ph; THE RUNNER STUMBLES(1979), ph; INSIDE MO-VES(1980), ph; LEGEND OF THE LONE RANGER, THE(1981), ph; FRANCES(1982), ph
1984
CRACKERS(1984), ph; GHOSTBUSTERS(1984), ph
Mary Kovacs
SEX AND THE SINGLE GIRL(1964)
Mia Kovacs
ON THE AIR LIVE WITH CAPTAIN MIDNIGHT(1979)
Roland Kovacs
JONATHAN(1973, Ger.), m
Thomas C. Kovacs
HOG WILD(1980, Can.)
Tom Kovacs
MY BLOODY VALENTINE(1981, Can.)
Zoltan Kovacs
WINTER WIND(1970, Fr./Hung.)
Ota Koval
FIFTH HORSEMAN IS FEAR, THE(1968, Czech.), w
Valentin A. Koval
WATERLOO(1970, Ital./USSR)
Ivan Koval-Samborski
DAUGHTER OF EVIL(1930, Ger.)
Ivan Koval-Samborskiy
HUNTING IN SIBERIA(1962, USSR)
I. Koval-Samborsky
CONCENTRATION CAMP(1939, USSR)
Ivan Koval-Samborsky
Misc. Silents
MOTHER(1926, USSR); FORTY-FIRST, THE(1927, USSR); GIRL WITH THE HAT-BOX(1927, USSR)
Ye. Kovalenko
FAREWELL, DOVES(1962, USSR)
Faith Kovaleski
BOY NAMED CHARLIE BROWN, A(1969), anim
Mark Kovalyov
STAR INSPECTOR, THE(1980, USSR), d, w
L. Kovalyova
SLEEPING BEAUTY, THE(1966, USSR)
Natalie Kovanko
Misc. Silents
LES CONTES LES MILLES ET UNE NUITS(1922, Fr.); LE CHANT DE L'AMOUR TRIOMPHANT(1923, Fr.); LE PRINCE CHARMANT(1925, Fr.)
Rudolf Kovar
DOCTOR DETROIT(1983)
Emanuel Kovarik
TRANSPORT FROM PARADISE(1967, Czech.)
Frantisek Kovarik
DEVIL'S TRAP, THE(1964, Czech.)

Vasek Kovarik
DESERTER AND THE NOMADS, THE(1969, Czech./Ital.)
Georg Kovary
SECRET WAYS, THE(1961)
Edna Kove
MURDER REPORTED(1958, Brit.)
John Kove
FASCINATION(1931, Brit.)
Kenneth Kove
GREAT GAME, THE(1930); MURDER(1930, Brit.); ALMOST A DIVORCE(1931, Brit.); CHANCE OF A NIGHT-TIME, THE(1931, Brit); DOWN RIVER(1931, Brit.); FASCINA-TION(1931, Brit.); GABLES MYSTERY, THE(1931, Brit.); M'BLIMEY(1931, Brit.); MISCHIEF(1931, Brit.); OUT OF THE BLUE(1931, Brit.); HELP YOURSELF(1932, Brit.); HER FIRST AFFAIRE(1932, Brit.); COUNTY FAIR(1933, Brit.); CRIME ON THE HILL(1933, Brit.); MAN FROM TORONTO, THE(1933, Brit.); WIVES BEWARE(1933, Brit.); CRAZY PEOPLE(1934, Brit.); CRIM-SON CANDLE, THE(1934, Brit.); LEAVE IT TO BLANCHE(1934, Brit.); LIFE OF THE PARTY(1934, Brit.); YOUTHFUL FOLLY(1934, Brit.); LOOK UP AND LAUGH(1935, Brit.); MARRY THE GIRL(1935, Brit.); RADIO PIRATES(1935, Brit.); SCARLET PIMPERNEL, THE(1935, Brit.); BANK MESSENGER MYSTERY, THE(1936, Brit.); CHEER UP!(1936, Brit.); TALKING FEET(1937, Brit.); ASKING FOR TROUBLE(1942, Brit.); THEY KNEW MR. KNIGHT(1945, Brit.); TREASURE HUNT(1952, Brit.); INNOCENTS IN PARIS(1955, Brit.); ORGANIZER, THE(1964, Fr./Ital./Yugo.); DR. TERROR'S HOUSE OF HORRORS(1965, Brit.)
Martin Kove
SAVAGES(1972); DEATH RACE 2000(1975); WHITE LINE FEVER(1975, Can.); WILD PARTY, THE(1975); FOUR DEUCES, THE(1976); MR. BILLION(1977); WHITE BUF-FALO, THE(1977); SEVEN(1979); BLOOD TIDE(1982)
1984
KARATE KID, THE(1984)
V. Kovel
DON QUIXOTE(1961, USSR)
Hilde Koveloff
PRISON WITHOUT BARS(1939, Brit.), w
J.K. Kovenberg
Misc. Silents
SIMPLE TAILOR, THE(1934, USSR)
Nataline Kovenko
Misc. Silents
MICHEL STROGOFF(1926, Fr.)
Ed Kovens
GAMBLER, THE(1974); Q(1982)
Edward Kovens
PURSUIT OF HAPPINESS, THE(1971)
Eddie Kover
FOLLOW THE BOYS(1944); HERE COME THE WAVES(1944)
Edward Kover
RAZOR'S EDGE, THE(1946)
Frederic Kovert
Misc. Silents
FIRST NIGHT, THE(1927)
Dmitri Shoshta Kovich
GREAT CITIZEN, THE(1939, USSR), m
Ed Kovins
IF EVER I SEE YOU AGAIN(1978)
Randy Kovitz
KNIGHTRIDERS(1981)
V. Kovrigin
SPACE SHIP, THE(1935, USSR); ADMIRAL NAKHIMOV(1948, USSR)
Vasili Kovrigin
DESERTER(1934, USSR)
Misc. Silents
SPECTRE HAUNTS EUROPE, A(1923, USSR)
G. Kovrov
GENERAL SUVOROV(1941, USSR)
John Kowal
PORTRAIT OF A MOBSTER(1961)
Jon Kowal
SPLIT, THE(1968); WRECKING CREW, THE(1968)
Mitchel Kowal
BIG BLUFF, THE(1955)
Mitchell Kowal
VIOLATED(1953); RIVER OF NO RETURN(1954); ABBOTT AND COSTELLO MEET THE MUMMY(1955); JUPITER'S DARLING(1955); JOHN PAUL JONES(1959); 55 DAYS AT PEKING(1963); GUESTS ARE COMING(1965, Pol.), titles
Sergei M. Kowalchik
FINAL COUNTDOWN, THE(1980)
Billy Kowalchuk
BLOODY BROOD, THE(1959, Can.)
August Kowalczyk
SARAGOSSA MANUSCRIPT, THE(1972, Pol.)
Maurice Kowaleski
DEATH HUNT(1981)
Maurice Kowalewski
HARD TIMES(1975); RAISE THE TITANIC(1980, Brit.)
Mitchell Kowall
CASS TIMBERLANE(1947); DEEP IN MY HEART(1954); ROGUE COP(1954)
Bernard Kowalski
ATTACK OF THE GIANT LEECHES(1959), d; STILETTO(1969), d
Bernard L. Kowalski
HOT CAR GIRL(1958), d; NIGHT OF THE BLOOD BEAST(1958), d; BLOOD AND STEEL(1959), d; KRAKATOA, EAST OF JAVA(1969), d; MACHO CALLAHAN(1970), p, d; SSSSSSSS(1973), d
Dean Kowalski
KOTCH(1971)
Donald Kowalski
KOTCH(1971)

Frank Kowalski
MAN CALLED SLEDGE, A(1971, Ital.), w; SSSSSSSS(1973); BRING ME THE HEAD OF ALFREDO GARCIA(1974), w
Peter Kowalski
KRAKATOA, EAST OF JAVA(1969)
Raymond Kowalski
1984
PHILADELPHIA EXPERIMENT, THE(1984)
Waclaw Kowalski
EVE WANTS TO SLEEP(1961, Pol.)
Wladyslaw Kowalski
LOVE AT TWENTY(1963, Fr./Ital./Jap./Pol./Ger.)
1984
SHIVERS(1984, Pol.)
Barbara Kowan [Shelley]
WOMAN IN HIDING(1953, Brit.)
Peter Kowitz
STIR(1980, Aus.)
Hesam Kowsar
1984
MISSION, THE(1984), w
Genki Koyama
BEACH RED(1967)
Shigeru Koyama
REBELLION(1967, Jap.); GOODBYE, MOSCOW(1968, Jap.); KILL(1968, Jap.); CREATURE CALLED MAN, THE(1970, Jap.); RED LION(1971, Jap.)
Tadashi Koyama
WORLD OF HANS CHRISTIAN ANDERSEN, THE(1971, Jap.), art d, anim
Toru Koyanagi
YOUTH AND HIS AMULET, THE(1963, Jap.)
Mikhaylo Mikhaylovich Koysyubinskiy
SHADOWS OF FORGOTTEN ANCESTORS(1967, USSR), w
Shigeru Koyuma
1984
ANTARCTICA(1984, Jap.)
Jeff Koz
1984
LAST HORROR FILM, THE(1984), m
Bill Koza
MY BODYGUARD(1980)
William Koza
MICKEY ONE(1965)
Andras Kozak
FATHER(1967, Hung.); RED AND THE WHITE, THE(1969, Hung./USSR); ROUND UP, THE(1969, Hung.); WINTER WIND(1970, Fr./Hung.)
Harley Kozak
HOUSE ON SORORITY ROW, THE(1983)
Jolanta Kozak
CONTRACT, THE(1982, Pol.)
Josef Kozak
SWEET LIGHT IN A DARK ROOM(1966, Czech.)
J. Kozak-Sutowicz
YOUNG GIRLS OF WILKO, THE(1979, Pol./Fr.)
Mikhail Kozakov
NINE DAYS OF ONE YEAR(1964, USSR); RED AND THE WHITE, THE(1969, Hung./USSR)
Kolya Kozarev
VIOLIN AND ROLLER(1962, USSR)
Bonnie Kozek
BOXOFFICE(1982), ed
Nishioica Kozen
ZATOICHI'S CONSPIRACY(1974, Jap.), p
G. Kozhakina
BRIDE WITH A DOWRY(1954, USSR); LETTER THAT WAS NEVER SENT, THE(1962, USSR)
Boris Kozhukhov
ITALIANO BRAVA GENTE(1965, Ital./USSR)
Joan Kozian
Misc. Talkies
NURSES FOR SALE(1977)
Zdsilaw Kozien
MAN OF MARBLE(1979, Pol.)
Marijan Kozina
SERGEANT JIM(1962, Yugo.), m
Mladen Kozina
ISLE OF SIN(1963, Ger.)
N. Kozinin
SOUND OF LIFE, THE(1962, USSR)
Frank Kozinsky
PAPER BULLETS(1941), p
Maurice Kozinsky
PAPER BULLETS(1941), p
Gregory Kozintsev
NEW HORIZONS(1939, USSR), d&w
Grigori Kozintsev
Misc. Silents
CLOAK, THE(1926, USSR), d; DEVIL'S WHEEL, THE(1926, USSR), d; CLUB OF THE BIG DEED, THE(1927, USSR), d; NEW BABYLON, THE(1929, USSR), d
Grigoriy Kozintsev
DON QUIXOTE(1961, USSR), d; HAMLET(1966, USSR), d&w
Grigori Kozintzen
Misc. Silents
ADVENTURES OF AN OCTOBERITE, THE(1924, USSR), d
Gene Koziol
WORLD'S GREATEST SINNER, THE(1962)
William Kozlenka
RAW EDGE(1956), w

William Kozlenko
STRANGER IN TOWN, A(1943), w; HOLIDAY IN MEXICO(1946), w; DANCE WITH ME, HENRY(1956), w
K. Kozlenkova
LULLABY(1961, USSR); JACK FROST(1966, USSR)
Al Kozlik
1984
MRS. SOFFEL(1984)
Chick Kozloff
YOU'VE GOT TO WALK IT LIKE YOU TALK IT OR YOU'LL LOSE THAT BEAT(1971)
B.A. Kozlov
DIARY OF A REVOLUTIONIST(1932, USSR), ph
Kolya Kozlov
LAST GAME, THE(1964, USSR)
Yura Kozlov
SUMMER TO REMEMBER, A(1961, USSR)
I. Kozlovsky
BORIS GODUNOV(1959, USSR)
Sergei Kozlovsky
DESERTER(1934, USSR), prod d
Myron Kozman
DELIRIUM(1979)
Okazaki Kozo
YAKUZA, THE(1975, U.S./Jap.), ph
Tokkan Kozo
Misc. Silents
I WAS BORN, BUT...(1932, Jap.)
Roger Kozol
WITHOUT A TRACE(1983)
Michael Kozoll
FIRST BLOOD(1982), w
Mr. Kozowski
SERENITY(1962)
G. Kozshoun
NO GREATER LOVE(1944, USSR)
Yoshiyuki Kozu
DEATH ON THE MOUNTAIN(1961, Jap.), m; THREE DOLLS FROM HONG KONG(1966, Jap.), m
Ernst Kozub
DER FREISCHUTZ(1970, Ger.)
Michal Kozuch
MARKETA LAZAROVA(1968, Czech.)
Aleksander Kozyr
SKY CALLS, THE(1959, USSR), d
Alexander Kozyr
BATTLE BEYOND THE SUN(1963), d
K. Kozyreva
SONG OVER MOSCOW(1964, USSR), ed
Tom Kraa
ETERNAL MASK, THE(1937, Swiss)
Elise Kraal
MAN'S FAVORITE SPORT[?](1964)
Jeroen Krabbe
LITTLE ARK, THE(1972); SOLDIER OF ORANGE(1979, Dutch); SPETTERS(1983, Holland)
1984
FOURTH MAN, THE(1984, Neth.)
Assemblyman Walter Krabien
CANDIDATE, THE(1972)
Sammuel Krachmalnick
DIE LAUGHING(1980)
Benjamin Kradolfer
BLACK SPIDER, THE(1983, Swit.)
Scott Kradolfer
1984
BOSTONIANS, THE(1984)
Jurgen Kraeft
NOT RECONCILED, OR "ONLY VIOLENCE HELPS WHERE IT RULES"(1969, Ger.)
Volkert Kraeft
SERPENT'S EGG, THE(1977, Ger./U.S.)
F.W. Kraemer
DREYFUS CASE, THE(1931, Brit.), p, d; FLYING SQUAD, THE(1932, Brit.), d; DAUGHTERS OF TODAY(1933, Brit.), p&d
Hans Kraemmer
BARBER OF SEVILLE, THE(1973, Ger./Fr.)
Barbara Krafft
ASHES AND DIAMONDS(1961, Pol.); TONIGHT A TOWN DIES(1961, Pol.)
John Krafft
SHOW FOLKS(1928), w; NOISY NEIGHBORS(1929), w; UNWRITTEN LAW, THE(1932), w; MYSTERY MAN, THE(1935), w; ARIZONA RAIDERS, THE(1936), w; LADY LUCK(1936), w; HERE'S FLASH CASEY(1937), w; THIRTEENTH MAN, THE(1937), w; TELEPHONE OPERATOR(1938), w; I AM A CRIMINAL(1939), w; SWEEPSTAKES WINNER(1939), w; LAUGHING AT DANGER(1940), w; IN OLD CHEYENNE(1941), w; MOUNTAIN MOONLIGHT(1941), w; FOREIGN AGENT(1942), w; MAN FROM HEADQUARTERS(1942), w; TELL IT TO A STAR(1945), w
Silents
PACE THAT THRILLS, THE(1925), t, ed; UNGUARDED HOUR, THE(1925), t; CORPORAL KATE(1926), t; VANITY(1927), t; WHITE GOLD(1927), t; ANNAPOLIS(1928), t; CHICAGO(1928), t; HOLD 'EM YALE(1928), t; LET 'ER GO GALLEGHER(1928), t; MARKED MONEY(1928), t; ON TO RENO(1928), t; STAND AND DELIVER(1928), t
John W. Krafft
MILLION DOLLAR BABY(1935), w; DEATH FROM A DISTANCE(1936), w; MISSING GIRLS(1936), w; MURDER AT GLEN ATHOL(1936), w; HOUSE OF SECRETS, THE(1937), w; REBELLIOUS DAUGHTERS(1938), w; SLANDER HOUSE(1938), w; CONVICT'S CODE(1939), w; DEERSLAYER(1943), w; SMART GUY(1943), w
Silents
LADY FROM HELL, THE(1926), t&ed

Barbara Krafftowna
SARAGOSSA MANUSCRIPT, THE(1972, Pol.)
Beatrice Kraft
KISMET(1944); RAINS OF RANCHIPUR, THE(1955)
Charles Kraft
BREACH OF PROMISE(1942, Brit.), ed
Evelyne Kraft
KISMET(1944); MADDEST CAR IN THE WORLD, THE(1974, Ger.); GOLIATHON(1979, Hong Kong)
H.S. Kraft
SMARTEST GIRL IN TOWN(1936), w; STORMY WEATHER(1943), w
Henry Kraft
STORY OF DR. WASSELL, THE(1944)
Hy Kraft
TOP BANANA(1954), w
Jill Kraft
THREE HUSBANDS(1950); TAKE CARE OF MY LITTLE GIRL(1951)
John Kraft
SQUARE SHOULDERS(1929), titles
Silents
ANGEL OF BROADWAY, THE(1927), t; DRESS PARADE(1927), t
Marion Kraft
LAST SUMMER(1969), ed
Richard Kraft
GAMERA THE INVINCIBLE(1966, Jap.), w
Virginia Kraft
Misc. Silents
ROSEMARY(1915); VALIANTS OF VIRGINIA, THE(1916)
William Kraft
PSYCHIC KILLER(1975), m; AVALANCHE(1978), m; FIRE AND ICE(1983), m
Kraftwerk
RADIO ON(1980, Brit./Ger.), m
Fred Krager
KISSIN' COUSINS(1964), md
Marc Krah
DEVIL SHIP(1947); INTRIGUE(1947); RIFFRAFF(1947); ALIAS A GENTLEMAN(1948); TRAIN TO ALCATRAZ(1948); CRISS CROSS(1949); SORROWFUL JONES(1949); CALL OF THE KLONDIKE(1950); MACAO(1952); STRANGE FASCINATION(1952); BENEATH THE 12-MILE REEF(1953); I'LL CRY TOMORROW(1955); LOVE IS A MANY-SPLENDORED THING(1955)
Mark Krah
SKY HIGH(1952)
Hilde Krahl
ONE APRIL 2000(1952, Aust.); APRIL 1, 2000(1953, Aust.); ETERNAL WALTZ, THE(1959, Ger.); GLASS OF WATER, A(1962, Cgr.); TERROR AFTER MIDNIGHT(1965, Ger.)
Maria Krahn
PILLARS OF SOCIETY(1936, Ger.); PRIVATE LIFE OF LOUIS XIV(1936, Ger.)
Michael Kraike
RENEGADES(1946), p; LADY GAMBLES, THE(1949), p; DAY OF THE NIGHTMARE(1965), exec p; WILD SCENE, THE(1970), w; OCTAMAN(1971), p; AMAZING DOBERMANS, THE(1976), w
Michel Kraike
CALL A MESSENGER(1939), w; NIGHT PLANE FROM CHUNGKING(1942), p; HENRY ALDRICH HAUNTS A HOUSE(1943), p; HENRY ALDRICH, BOY SCOUT(1944), p; YOU CAN'T RATION LOVE(1944), p; BOSTON BLACKIE BOOKED ON SUSPICION(1945), p; EADIE WAS A LADY(1945), p; FIGHTING GUARDSMAN, THE(1945), p; I LOVE A BANDLEADER(1945), p; TEN CENTS A DANCE(1945), p; TALK ABOUT A LADY(1946), p; BEAT THE BAND(1947), p; DESPERATE(1947), p; CRISS CROSS(1949), p; JUDGE STEPS OUT, THE(1949), p; WOMAN IN HIDING(1949), p; FRENCHIE(1950), p; SIERRA(1950), p; SOUTH SEA SINNER(1950), p; BEDTIME FOR BONZO(1951), p; THUNDER ON THE HILL(1951), p
Carl Kraines
PARTNERS(1982); SLAYER, THE(1982)
Krake
TUSK(1980, Fr.)
Marcello Krakoff
TRENCHCOAT(1983); UNCOMMON VALOR(1983)
Rocky Krakoff
TESTAMENT(1983)
Jane Krakowski
NATIONAL LAMPOON'S VACATION(1983)
Ivan Kral
FOREIGNER, THE(1978), m, md; DINER(1982), m
Boris Kralj
SERGEANT JIM(1962, Yugo.)
Mirko Kraljev
HOROSCOPE(1950, Yugo.)
Peter Krall
ADOPTION, THE(1978, Fr.), w
Erika Krallk
LEFT-HANDED WOMAN, THE(1980, Ger.)
Leonid Kralnekov
BALLAD OF A HUSSAR(1963, USSR), ph
Rolf Kralowitz
UNWILLING AGENT(1968, Ger.)
Hans Kraly
PATRIOT, THE(1928), w; DEVIL MAY CARE(1929), w; LAST OF MRS. CHEYNEY, THE(1929), w; LADY OF SCANDAL, THE(1930), w; LADY'S MORALS, A(1930), w; JUST A GIGOLO(1931), w; PRIVATE LIVES(1931), w; MY LIPS BETRAY(1933), w; BY CANDLELIGHT(1934), w; BROADWAY GONDOLIER(1935), w; 100 MEN AND A GIRL(1937), w; BROADWAY SERENADE(1939), w; IT STARTED WITH EVE(1941), w; WEST POINT WIDOW(1941), w; MAD GHOUL, THE(1943), w
Silents
PASSION(1920, Ger.), w; ONE ARABIAN NIGHT(1921, Ger.), w; ROSITA(1923), w; FORBIDDEN PARADISE(1924), w; EAGLE, THE(1925), w; KISS ME AGAIN(1925), w; KIKI(1926), w; SO THIS IS PARIS(1926), w; QUALITY STREET(1927), w; ETERNAL LOVE(1929), w; KISS, THE(1929), w; WILD ORCHIDS(1929), w

Arthur Kram
WHERE LOVE HAS GONE(1964), set d
Alojz Kramar
SHOP ON MAIN STREET, THE(1966, Czech.)
K. Kramarchuk
LULLABY(1961, USSR); SANDU FOLLOWS THE SUN(1965, USSR)
L. Kramareskiy
WAR AND PEACE(1968, USSR)
L. Kramarevskiy
MORNING STAR(1962, USSR), w
Andrei Kramarevsky
1984
MOSCOW ON THE HUDSON(1984)
Ludmila Kramarevsky
1984
MOSCOW ON THE HUDSON(1984)
S. Kramarov
FAREWELL, DOVES(1962, USSR); HOUSE ON THE FRONT LINE, THE(1963, USSR)
Savely Kramarov
1984
MOSCOW ON THE HUDSON(1984); 2010(1984)
David Kramarsky
CRY BABY KILLER, THE(1958), p
Kramer
FANTASTIC THREE, THE(1967, Ital./Ger./Fr./Yugo.), w
Al Kramer
OKLAHOMAN, THE(1957)
Allan Kramer
DEMETRIUS AND THE GLADIATORS(1954)
Allen Kramer
STAR IS BORN, A(1954); STAKEOUT ON DOPE STREET(1958); YOUNG CAPTIVES, THE(1959)
Ann Kramer
TWO TICKETS TO BROADWAY(1951)
Arthur Kramer
KISS OF DEATH(1947)
Benjamin Kramer
1984
LOOSE CONNECTIONS(1984, Brit.)
Bert Kramer
LADY SINGS THE BLUES(1972); MISTER BROWN(1972); MOMENT BY MOMENT(1978)
Bob Kramer
BLESS THE BEASTS AND CHILDREN(1971)
Burton Kramer
THUNDER OVER THE PRAIRIE(1941), ed; RIDERS OF THE NORTHLAND(1942), ed; EL DORADO PASS(1949), ed
Casey Kramer
THE RUNNER STUMBLES(1979)
Cecile Kramer
TWILIGHT ON THE TRAIL(1941), w; SILVER QUEEN(1942), w; BUFFALO BILL(1944), w; HOPPY'S HOLIDAY(1947), w; RAMROD(1947), w
David Kramer
HANDS OF A STRANGER(1962)
Don Kramer
MEXICAN SPITFIRE'S BLESSED EVENT(1943); FOLLOW THE BOYS(1944); HERE COME THE WAVES(1944); SHINE ON, HARVEST MOON(1944)
Frank Kramer [GianFranco Parolini]
SNAFU(1945), set d; BANDIT OF SHERWOOD FOREST, THE(1946), set d; NOTORIOUS LONE WOLF, THE(1946), p; QUICK ON THE TRIGGER(1949), set d; FANTASTIC THREE, THE(1967, Ital./Ger./Fr./Yugo.), d; SABATA(1969, Ital.), d, w; BOUNTY HUNTERS, THE(1970, Ital.), d; ADIOS SABATA(1971, Ital./Span.), d; RETURN OF SABATA(1972, Ital./Fr./Ger.), d; GOD'S GUN(1977), d; YETI(1977, Ital.), d, w
F.W. Kramer
TIN GODS(1932, Brit.), p&d
George Kramer
FIVE BOLD WOMEN(1960)
Glen Kramer
FRANCIS IN THE HAUNTED HOUSE(1956); PILLARS OF THE SKY(1956); ROCK, PRETTY BABY(1956); MISTER CORY(1957)
Hope Kramer
FLYING SERPENT, THE(1946); I WAS A COMMUNIST FOR THE F.B.I.(1951)
Ida Kramer
ABIE'S IRISH ROSE(1928)
Jack Kramer
ENEMY BELOW, THE(1957)
Jack N. Kramer
HELL SQUAD(1958)
Jane Kramer
IN THE COUNTRY(1967)
Jeffrey Kramer
HOLLYWOOD BOULEVARD(1976); YOU LIGHT UP MY LIFE(1977); JAWS II(1978); HALLOWEEN II(1981); HEARTBEEPS(1981)
Jeffrey C. Kramer
JAWS(1975)
Joani Kramer
SHE-DEVILS ON WHEELS(1968)
John Kramer
WINDFLOWERS(1968); STUDENT TEACHERS, THE(1973); TRUCK TURNER(1974); EAT MY DUST!(1976); HOLLYWOOD BOULEVARD(1976); ONE MAN(1979, Can.), ed
Misc. Talkies
COVER GIRL MODELS(1975)
Jonathan Kramer
MIDNIGHT COWBOY(1969)
Katharine Kramer
THE RUNNER STUMBLES(1979)

Larry Kramer
WOMEN IN LOVE(1969, Brit.), p, w; LOST HORIZON(1973), w
Leopold Kramer
MONEY ON THE STREET(1930, Aust.); ECSTASY(1940, Czech.)
Louis Kramer
Misc. Talkies
LOVE AND SACRIFICE(1936)
Marc Kramer
POLO JOE(1936)
Margaret Kramer
SKY PIRATE, THE(1970)
Michael Kramer
OVER THE EDGE(1979)
Noel Kramer
BOYS IN COMPANY C, THE(1978, U.S./Hong Kong)
Paul Kramer
LIFE OF HER OWN, A(1950)
Peggy Kramer
Misc. Talkies
HOT CHILD(1974); NYMPH(1974)
Phil Kramer
HANDS ACROSS THE TABLE(1935)
Remi Kramer
HIGH VELOCITY(1977), d, w
Richard Kramer
AMERICAN TRAGEDY, AN(1931); CASTLE OF BLOOD(1964, Fr./Ital.), ph
Robert Kramer
IN THE COUNTRY(1967), p, ed, d, w; EDGE, THE(1968), a, p, d&w; ICE(1970), a, d&w; MILESTONES(1975), d,w&ed, ph; GUNS(1980, Fr.), a, d&w; STATE OF THINGS, THE(1983), a, w
Searle Kramer
MR. UNIVERSE(1951), w; TWO GALS AND A GUY(1951), w
Seymour Kramer
PENTHOUSE RHYTHM(1945), m
Stanley Kramer
SO THIS IS NEW YORK(1948), p; CHAMPION(1949), p; HOME OF THE BRAVE(1949), p; CYRANO DE BERGERAC(1950), p; MEN, THE(1950), p; DEATH OF A SALESMAN(1952), p; EIGHT IRON MEN(1952), p; FOUR POSTER, THE(1952), p; HAPPY TIME, THE(1952), p; HIGH NOON(1952), p; MEMBER OF THE WEDDING, THE(1952), p; MY SIX CONVICTS(1952), p; SNIPER, THE(1952), p; JUGGLER, THE(1953), p; WILD ONE, THE(1953), p; 5,000 FINGERS OF DR. T. THE(1953), p; CAINE MUTINY, THE(1954), p; NOT AS A STRANGER(1955), p&d; PRIDE AND THE PASSION, THE(1957), p&d; DEFIANT ONES, THE(1958), p&d; ON THE BEACH(1959), p&d; INHERIT THE WIND(1960), p&d; JUDGMENT AT NUREMBERG(1961), p&d; PRESSURE POINT(1962), p; CHILD IS WAITING, A(1963), p; IT'S A MAD, MAD, MAD, MAD WORLD(1963), p&d; SHIP OF FOOLS(1965), p&d; GUESS WHO'S COMING TO DINNER(1967), p&d; SECRET OF SANTA VITTORIA, THE(1969), p&d; R.P.M.(1970), p&d; BLESS THE BEASTS AND CHILDREN(1971), p&d; OKLAHOMA CRUDE(1973), p&d; DOMINO PRINCIPLE, THE(1977), p&d; THE RUNNER STUMBLES(1979), p&d
Stephanie Kramer
MAN WITH TWO BRAINS, THE(1983)
Sy Kramer
MAN IN THE GLASS BOOTH, THE(1975); CHEECH AND CHONG'S NEXT MOVIE(1980)
Wright Kramer
GLADIATOR, THE(1938); PROFESSOR BEWARE(1938); GOOD GIRLS GO TO PARIS(1939); NO PLACE TO GO(1939); ANNE OF WINDY POPLARS(1940); BEFORE I HANG(1940); DARK STREETS OF CAIRO(1940); SHOWDOWN, THE(1940); SCOTLAND YARD(1941)
Edythe Kramera
UNDER A TEXAS MOON(1930)
Albert Kraml
DAS BOOT(1982)
Francis Kramm
FABULOUS WORLD OF JULES VERNE, THE(1961, Czech.), anim
Hans Kramm
POLYESTER(1981)
Joseph Kramm
SHRIKE, THE(1955), w
Richard Krammer
HAPPINESS C.O.D.(1935)
Glen Kramner
WRITTEN ON THE WIND(1956)
G. Krampf
EVERYTHING IS THUNDER(1936, Brit.), ph
Guenther Krampf
DAUGHTER OF EVIL(1930, Ger.), ph
Gunthar Krampf
OUTSIDER, THE(1940, Brit.), ph
Gunther Krampf
BELLS, THE(1931, Brit.), ph; LUCKY NUMBER, THE(1933, Brit.), ph; OUTSIDER, THE(1933, Brit.), ph; ROME EXPRESS(1933, Brit.), ph; DEATH AT A BROADCAST(1934, Brit.), ph; GHOUL, THE(1934, Brit.), ph; LITTLE FRIEND(1934, Brit.), ph; LITTLE STRANGER(1934, Brit.), ph; POWER(1934, Brit.), ph; TRANSATLANTIC TUNNEL(1935, Brit.), ph; AMATEUR GENTLEMAN(1936, Brit.), ph; MAN OF AFFAIRS(1937, Brit.), ph; GAIETY GIRLS, THE(1938, Brit.), ph; MARIGOLD(1938, Brit.), ph; BLACK EYES(1939, Brit.), ph; DEAD MAN'S SHOES(1939, Brit.), ph; CONVOY(1940), ph; FUGITIVE, THE(1940, Brit.), ph; THREE COCKEYED SAILORS(1940, Brit.), ph; BLACK SHEEP OF WHITEHALL, THE(1941 Brit.), ph; FALSE RAPTURE(1941), ph; SABOTAGE AT SEA(1942, Brit.), ph; TERROR HOUSE(1942, Brit.), ph; WOMEN AREN'T ANGELS(1942, Brit.), ph; SUSPECTED PERSON(1943, Brit.), ph; WARN THAT MAN(1943, Brit.), ph; FAME IS THE SPUR(1947, Brit.), ph; MEET ME AT DAWN(1947, Brit.), ph; THIS WAS A WOMAN(1949, Brit.), ph; TINKER(1949, Brit.), ph; PORTRAIT OF CLARE(1951, Brit.), ph
Silents
STUDENT OF PRAGUE, THE(1927, Ger.), ph; PANDORA'S BOX(1929, Ger.), ph

Gunther Krampff
FRANCHISE AFFAIR, THE(1952, Brit.), ph
Gunther Kramph
FRENZY(1946, Brit.), ph
Jiri Krampol
OPERATION DAYBREAK(1976, U.S./Brit./Czech.)
Anthony Kramreither
HUMONGOUS(1982, Can.), p
Arthur Krams
BRIDE GOES WILD, THE(1948), set d, set d; LUXURY LINER(1948), set d; PIRATE, THE(1948), set d; SOUTHERN YANKEE, A(1948), set d; THREE DARING DAUGHTERS(1948), set d; EAST SIDE, WEST SIDE(1949), set d; NEPTUNE'S DAUGHTER(1949), set d; KIM(1950), set d; MAN WITH A CLOAK, THE(1951), set d; MERRY WIDOW, THE(1952), set d; ROGUE'S MARCH(1952), set d; LILI(1953), set d; TO CATCH A THIEF(1955), set d; MAN WHO KNEW TOO MUCH, THE(1956), set d; RAINMAKER, THE(1956), set d; HIGH SCHOOL CONFIDENTIAL(1958), set d; CAREER(1959), set d; VISIT TO A SMALL PLANET(1960), set d; SUMMER AND SMOKE(1961), set d; GIRL NAMED TAMIRO, A(1962), set d; WHO'S BEEN SLEEPING IN MY BED?(1963), set d; WIVES AND LOVERS(1963), set d; CARPETBAGGERS, THE(1964), set d; MARRIAGE ON THE ROCKS(1965), set d; SYLVIA(1965), set d; TICKLE ME(1965), set d; SWINGER, THE(1966), set d; EASY COME, EASY GO(1967), set d; PRESIDENT'S ANALYST, THE(1967), set d; HANG'EM HIGH(1968), set d; HOW SWEET IT IS(1968), set d
Hanz Kramsky
DIAMONDS(1975, U.S./Israel), spec eff
Andrew Krance
LAST SUMMER(1969)
Binton Krancer
LYDIA(1964, Can.), w, ed
Burt Krancer
LIFT, THE(1965, Brit./Can.), d&w
Ed Kranepool
ODD COUPLE, THE(1968)
Jon Kranhouse
BRAINWAVES(1983), ph; TASTE OF SIN, A(1983), ph
1984
HAMBONE AND HILLIE(1984), ph
Ana Kranjcec
APACHE GOLD(1965, Ger.)
Raoul Kranshaar
COLORADO SUNSET(1939), m
Debbie Krant
1984
SLOW MOVES(1984)
Bob Krantz, Jr.
PASSION HOLIDAY(1963)
Gosta Krantz
SWEDISH WEDDING NIGHT(1965, Swed.)
Lasse Krantz
MY FATHER'S MISTRESS(1970, Swed.)
Robert Krantz
1984
WOMAN IN RED, THE(1984)
Steve Krantz
COOLEY HIGH(1975), p; RUBY(1977), w; WHICH WAY IS UP?(1977), p; JENNIFER(1978), p, w; SWAP MEET(1979), p, w
Jack Kranz
KID GALAHAD(1937)
Mario Kranz
HIPPODROME(1961, Aust./Ger.)
Hillary Jane Kranze
ZORRO, THE GAY BLADE(1981), ed
Evelyn Krape
DIMBOOLA(1979, Aus.); CLINIC, THE(1983, Aus.)
Sid Krasey
NEXT OF KIN(1983, Aus.)
G. Krasheninnikov
FORTY-NINE DAYS(1964, USSR); THERE WAS AN OLD COUPLE(1967, USSR)
Andrzej Krasicki
PASSENGER, THE(1970, Pol.)
Mary Ann Krasiniski
CONDUCTOR, THE(1981, Pol.)
Bob Krasker
SAINT MEETS THE TIGER, THE(1943, Brit.), ph
Robert Krasker
DRUMS(1938, Brit.), ph; OVER THE MOON(1940, Brit.), ph; ROSE OF TRALEE(1942, Brit.), ph; GENTLE SEX, THE(1943, Brit.), ph; BRIEF ENCOUNTER(1945, Brit.), ph; CAESAR AND CLEOPATRA(1946, Brit.), ph; HENRY V(1946, Brit.), ph; ODD MAN OUT(1947, Brit.), ph; BONNIE PRINCE CHARLIE(1948, Brit.), ph; ANGEL WITH THE TRUMPET, THE(1950, Brit.), ph; THIRD MAN, THE(1950, Brit.), ph; GREAT MANHUNT, THE(1951, Brit.), ph; INHERITANCE, THE(1951, Brit.), ph; WONDER BOY(1951, Brit./Aust.), ph; ANOTHER MAN'S POISON(1952, Brit.), ph; CRY, THE BELOVED COUNTRY(1952, Brit.), ph; NEVER LET ME GO(1953, U.S./Brit.), ph; MALTA STORY(1954, Brit.), ph; ROMEO AND JULIET(1954, Brit.), ph; THAT LADY(1955, Brit.), ph; ALEXANDER THE GREAT(1956), ph; TRAPEZE(1956), ph; RISING OF THE MOON, THE(1957, Ireland), ph; STORY OF ESTHER COSTELLO, THE(1957, Brit.), ph; BEHIND THE MASK(1958, Brit.), ph; DOCTOR'S DILEMMA, THE(1958, Brit.), ph; QUIET AMERICAN, THE(1958), ph; LIBEL(1959, Brit.), ph; EL CID(1961, U.S./Ital.), ph; ROMANOFF AND JULIET(1961), ph; BILLY BUDD(1962), ph; CONCRETE JUNGLE, THE(1962, Brit.), ph; GUNS OF DARKNESS(1962, Brit.), ph; RUNNING MAN, THE(1963, Brit.), ph; FALL OF THE ROMAN EMPIRE, THE(1964), ph; HEROES OF TELEMARK(1965, Brit.), ph; TRAP, THE(1967, Can./Brit.), ph; SENSO(1968, Ital.), ph
Harold Krasket
MOUSE THAT ROARED, THE(1959, Brit.)
Maria Krasna
CONFESS DR. CORDA(1960, Ger.)

x

Norman Krasna

HOLLYWOOD SPEAKS(1932), w; THAT'S MY BOY(1932), w; LOVE, HONOR, AND OH BABY!(1933), w; MEET THE BARON(1933), w; PAROLE GIRL(1933), w; SO THIS IS AFRICA(1933), w; RICHEST GIRL IN THE WORLD, THE(1934), w; FOUR HOURS TO KILL(1935), w; HANDS ACROSS THE TABLE(1935), w; ROMANCE IN MANHATTAN(1935), w; FURY(1936), w; WIFE VERSUS SECRETARY(1936), w; AS GOOD AS MARRIED(1937), w; BIG CITY(1937), p, w; KING AND THE CHORUS GIRL, THE(1937), w; FIRST 100 YEARS, THE(1938), p, w; THREE LOVES HAS NANCY(1938), p; YOU AND ME(1938), w; BACHELOR MOTHER(1939), w; IT'S A DATE(1940), w; DEVIL AND MISS JONES, THE(1941), p, w; FLAME OF NEW ORLEANS, THE(1941), w; IT STARTED WITH EVE(1941), w; MR. AND MRS. SMITH(1941), w; PRINCESS O'ROURKE(1943), d&w; BRIDE BY MISTAKE(1944), w; PRACTICALLY YOURS(1944), w; DEAR RUTH(1947), w; DEAR WIFE(1949), w; JOHN LOVES MARY(1949), w; BIG HANGOVER, THE(1950), p,d&w; BEHAVE YOURSELF(1951), p; BLUE VEIL, THE(1951), p; TWO TICKETS TO BROADWAY(1951), p; LUSTY MEN, THE(1952), p; WHITE CHRISTMAS(1954), w; AMBASSADOR'S DAUGHTER, THE(1956), p,d&w; BUNDLE OF JOY(1956), w; INDISCREET(1958), w; LET'S MAKE LOVE(1960), w; WHO WAS THAT LADY?(1960), p, w; MY GEISHA(1962), w; SUNDAY IN NEW YORK(1963), w; I'D RATHER BE RICH(1964), w

Philip N. Krasna

CRASHING THRU(1939), p

A. S. Krasnapolski

MYSTERIOUS ISLAND(1941, USSR)

Phil Krasne

TRIGGER PALS(1939), p

Philip Krasne

SOME MAY LIVE(1967, Brit.), p

Philip N. Krasne

MURDER ON THE YUKON(1940), p; SARONG GIRL(1943), p; CALL OF THE JUNGLE(1944), p; CHARLIE CHAN IN BLACK MAGIC(1944), p; CHARLIE CHAN IN THE SECRET SERVICE(1944), p; CHINESE CAT, THE(1944), p; CISCO KID RETURNS, THE(1945), p; IN OLD NEW MEXICO(1945), p; SOUTH OF THE RIO GRANDE(1945), p; DEVIL'S CARGO, THE(1948), p; VALIANT HOMBRE, THE(1948), p; DARING CABALLERO, THE(1949), p; GAY AMIGO, THE(1949), p; SATAN'S CRADLE(1949), p; GIRL FROM SAN LORENZO, THE(1950), p; DESTINATION 60,-000(1957), p; PAWNEE(1957), p; DRUMS OF AFRICA(1963), p; BOY CRIED MURDER, THE(1966, Ger./Brit./Yugo.), p; WEDDING NIGHT(1970, Ireland), p; 1,000 CONVICTS AND A WOMAN(1971, Brit.), p

Philip S. Krasne

SULTAN'S DAUGHTER, THE(1943), p

Phillip Krasne

FIGHTING MAD(1939), p

Milton Krasner

WITHOUT RESERVATIONS(1946), ph; TWO WEEKS IN ANOTHER TOWN(1962), ph; GOLDEN HARVEST(1933), ph; I LOVE THAT MAN(1933), ph; SITTING PRETTY(1933), ph; STRICTLY PERSONAL(1933), ph; DEATH OF THE DIAMOND(1934), ph; GREAT FLIRTATION, THE(1934), ph; PARIS INTERLUDE(1934), ph; PRIVATE SCANDAL(1934), ph; SHE MADE HER BED(1934), ph; GREAT GOD GOLD(1935), ph; GREAT IMPERSONATION, THE(1935), ph; MAKE A MILLION(1935), ph; MURDER IN THE FLEET(1935), ph; VIRGINIA JUDGE, THE(1935), ph; WOMEN MUST DRESS(1935), ph; CHEERS OF THE CROWD(1936), ph; FORBIDDEN HEAVEN(1936), ph; GIRL ON THE FRONT PAGE, THE(1936), ph; HONEYMOON LIMITED(1936), ph; LAUGHING IRISH EYES(1936), ph; LOVE LETTERS OF A STAR(1936), ph; MISTER CINDERELLA(1936), ph; YELLOWSTONE(1936), ph; GIRL WITH IDEAS, A(1937), ph; LADY FIGHTS BACK(1937), ph; LOVE IN A BUNGALOW(1937), ph; MYSTERIOUS CROSSING(1937), ph; OH DOCTOR(1937), ph; PRESCRIPTION FOR ROMANCE(1937), ph; SHE'S DANGEROUS(1937), ph; THERE GOES THE GROOM(1937), ph; WE HAVE OUR MOMENTS(1937), ph; CRIME OF DR. HALLET(1938), ph; DEVIL'S PARTY, THE(1938), ph; JURY'S SECRET, THE(1938), ph; MIDNIGHT INTRUDER(1938), ph; MISSING GUEST, THE(1938), ph; NURSE FROM BROOKLYN(1938), ph; STORM, THE(1938), ph; FAMILY NEXT DOOR, THE(1939), ph; HOUSE OF FEAR, THE(1939), ph; I STOLE A MILLION(1939), ph; LITTLE ACCIDENT(1939), ph; MISSING EVIDENCE(1939), ph; NEWSBOY'S HOME(1939), ph; YOU CAN'T CHEAT AN HONEST MAN(1939), ph; BANK DICK, THE(1940), ph; DIAMOND FRONTIER(1940), ph; HIRED WIFE(1940), ph; HOUSE OF THE SEVEN GABLES, THE(1940), ph; INVISIBLE MAN RETURNS, THE(1940), ph; MAN FROM MONTREAL, THE(1940), ph; OH JOHNNY, HOW YOU CAN LOVE!(1940), ph; PRIVATE AFFAIRS(1940), ph; SANDY IS A LADY(1940), ph; SKI PATROL(1940), ph; TRAIL OF THE VIGILANTES(1940), ph; ZANZIBAR(1940), ph; BACHELOR DADDY(1941), ph; BUCK PRIVATES(1941), ph; LADY FROM CHEYENNE(1941), ph; PARIS CALLING(1941), ph; THIS WOMAN IS MINE(1941), ph; TOO MANY BLONDES(1941), ph; ARABIAN NIGHTS(1942), ph; GENTLEMAN AFTER DARK, A(1942), ph; GHOST OF FRANKENSTEIN, THE(1942), ph; MEN OF TEXAS(1942), ph; PARDON MY SARONG(1942), ph; SPOILERS, THE(1942), ph; GUNG HO!(1943), ph; MAD GHOUL, THE(1943), ph; SO'S YOUR UNCLE(1943), ph; TWO TICKETS TO LONDON(1943), ph; WE'VE NEVER BEEN LICKED(1943), ph; HAT CHECK HONEY(1944), ph; INVISIBLE MAN'S REVENGE(1944), ph; ALONG CAME JONES(1945), ph; DELIGHTFULLY DANGEROUS(1945), ph; SCARLET STREET(1945), ph; WOMAN IN THE WINDOW, THE(1945), ph; DARK MIRROR, THE(1946), ph; DOUBLE LIFE, A(1947), ph; EGG AND I, THE(1947), ph; FARMER'S DAUGHTER, THE(1947), ph; SOMETHING IN THE WIND(1947), ph; SAXON CHARM, THE(1948), ph; UP IN CENTRAL PARK(1948), ph; ACCUSED, THE(1949), ph; HOLIDAY AFFAIR(1949), ph; HOUSE OF STRANGERS(1949), ph; SET-UP, THE(1949), ph; ALL ABOUT EVE(1950), ph; NO WAY OUT(1950), ph; THREE CAME HOME(1950), ph; HALF ANGEL(1951), ph; I CAN GET IT FOR YOU WHOLESALE(1951), ph; MODEL AND THE MARRIAGE BROKER, THE(1951), ph; PEOPLE WILL TALK(1951), ph; RAWHIDE(1951), ph; DEADLINE–U.S.A.(1952), ph; DREAMBOAT(1952), ph; MONKEY BUSINESS(1952), ph; O. HENRY'S FULL HOUSE(1952), ph; PHONE CALL FROM A STRANGER(1952), ph; DREAM WIFE(1953), ph; TAXI(1953), ph; VICKI(1953), ph; DEMETRIUS AND THE GLADIATORS(1954), ph; DESIREE(1954), ph; GARDEN OF EVIL(1954), ph; THREE COINS IN THE FOUNTAIN(1954), ph; GIRL IN THE RED VELVET SWING, THE(1955), ph; HOW TO BE VERY, VERY, POPULAR(1955), ph; RAINS OF RANCHIPUR, THE(1955), ph; SEVEN YEAR ITCH, THE(1955), ph; BUS STOP(1956), ph; 23 PACES TO BAKER STREET(1956), ph; AFFAIR TO REMEMBER, AN(1957), ph; BOY ON A DOLPHIN(1957), ph; KISS THEM FOR ME(1957), ph; CERTAIN SMILE, A(1958), ph; GIFT OF LOVE, THE(1958), ph; COUNT YOUR BLESSINGS(1959), ph; MAN WHO UNDERSTOOD WOMEN, THE(1959), ph; REMARKABLE MR. PENNYPACKER, THE(1959), ph; BELLS ARE RINGING(1960), ph; HOME FROM THE HILL(1960), ph; GO NAKED

IN THE WORLD(1961), ph; KING OF KINGS(1961), ph; FOUR HORSEMEN OF THE APOCALYPSE, THE(1962), ph; HOW THE WEST WAS WON(1962), ph; SWEET BIRD OF YOUTH(1962), ph; COURTSHIP OF EDDY'S FATHER, THE(1963), ph; LOVE WITH THE PROPER STRANGER(1963), ph; TICKLISH AFFAIR, A(1963), ph; ADVANCE TO THE REAR(1964), ph; FATE IS THE HUNTER(1964), ph; GOODBYE CHARLIE(1964), ph; LOOKING FOR LOVE(1964), ph; RED LINE 7000(1965), ph; SANDPIPER, THE(1965), ph; MADE IN PARIS(1966), ph; SINGING NUN, THE(1966), ph; HURRY SUNDOWN(1967), ph; ST. VALENTINE'S DAY MASSACRE, THE(1967), ph; VENETIAN AFFAIR, THE(1967), ph; BALLAD OF JOSIE(1968), ph; DON'T JUST STAND THERE(1968), ph; STERILE CUCKOO, THE(1969), ph; BENEATH THE PLANET OF THE APES(1970), ph

Milton R. Krasner

CRASH DONOVAN(1936), ph

N. Krasnoshchyokov

LULLABY(1961, USSR)

M. Krasnostavsky

DESERTER(1934, USSR), w

V. Krasnovetsky

DIARY OF A NAZI(1943, USSR)

V. Krasnovitsky

HEROES ARE MADE(1944, USSR)

F. Krasny

FORTY-NINE DAYS(1964, USSR), spec eff

Paul Krasny

CHRISTINA(1974, Can.), d; JOE PANTHER(1976), d

Katja Krassin

WHILE THE SUN SHINES(1950$c Brit.), cos

Olga Krassina

QUEEN OF SPADES(1961, USSR)

Josef Krastel

CARDINAL, THE(1963); MIRACLE OF THE WHITE STALLIONS(1963)

G. Krasulya

KATERINA IZMAILOVA(1969, USSR)

Dick Kratina

LOVE STORY(1970), ph; PURSUIT OF HAPPINESS, THE(1971), ph; SAFE PLACE, A(1971), ph; COME BACK CHARLESTON BLUE(1972), ph; SUPER COPS, THE(1974), ph; HAPPY HOOKER, THE(1975), ph; SENTINEL, THE(1977), ph; FIREPOWER(1979, Brit.), ph

Richard Kratina

BORN TO WIN(1971), ph; AARON LOVES ANGELA(1975), ph

Richard Kratine

ANGEL LEVINE, THE(1970), ph

Dick Kratins

BELIEVE IN ME(1971), ph

Paul Kratka

FRIDAY THE 13TH PART III(1982)

Milos V. Kratochvil

DEVIL'S TRAP, THE(1964, Czech.), w

Radovan Kraty

STOLEN DIRIGIBLE, THE(1966, Czech.), w

Charles Krauf

Silents

SEVEN SISTERS, THE(1915)

Major Fred A. Kraus

FIRST TO FIGHT(1967), tech adv

Georg Kraus

MAN ON A TIGHTROPE(1953), ph; DEVIL STRIKES AT NIGHT, THE(1959, Ger.), ph; ENCOUNTERS IN SALZBURG(1964, Ger.), ph

Hans Kraus

DISORDER AND EARLY TORMENT(1977, Ger.)

Karin Kraus

NOT RECONCILED, OR "ONLY VIOLENCE HELPS WHERE IT RULES"(1969, Ger.)

Shmulik Kraus

1984

AMBASSADOR, THE(1984)

Walter Kraus

EIGER SANCTION, THE(1975)

Bernard Krause

LAST DAYS OF MAN ON EARTH, THE(1975, Brit.), m

Billy Krause

LIVELY SET, THE(1964)

Dieter Krause

MAN BETWEEN, THE(1953, Brit.)

Georg Krause

HEAD, THE(1961, Ger.), ph; COURT MARTIAL(1962, Ger.), ph; ESCAPE FROM EAST BERLIN(1962), ph; IT'S HOT IN PARADISE(1962, Ger./Yugo.), ph; SEVEN DARING GIRLS(1962, Ger.), ph; ISLE OF SIN(1963, Ger.), ph

George Krause

PATHS OF GLORY(1957), ph

Gertie Krause

MOTHERS OF TODAY(1939)

Gertrude Krause

MOTEL, THE OPERATOR(1940)

Klaus Krause

DECISION BEFORE DAWN(1951)

Nathalie Krause

Misc. Silents

HVEM ER HUN?(1914, Den.)

Richard Krause

TEX(1982)

Tom Krause

DER FREISCHUTZ(1970, Ger.); MARRIAGE OF FIGARO, THE(1970, Ger.)

Willy Krause

LAST TEN DAYS, THE(1956, Ger.); TRAPEZE(1956)

Kenneth Krausgill

WORLD OF HENRY ORIENT, THE(1964), set d

Ralph Kraushaar

COWBOY AND THE PRIZEFIGHTER(1950), m

Raoul Kraushaar
ROVIN' TUMBLEWEEDS(1939), md; CAROLINA MOON(1940), md; MELODY RANCH(1940), md; RIDE, TENDERFOOT, RIDE(1940), md; BACK IN THE SADDLE(1941), m; DOWN MEXICO WAY(1941), md; RIDIN' ON A RAINBOW(1941), md; SUNSET IN WYOMING(1941), m; COWBOY SERENADE(1942), md; HEART OF THE RIO GRANDE(1942), md; HOME IN WYOMIN'(1942), md; EL PASO KID, THE(1946), md; STORK BITES MAN(1947), m, md; SKY LINER(1949), m, md; ZAMBA(1949), m; PREHISTORIC WOMEN(1950), m; SECOND FACE, THE(1950), m; BASKETBALL FIX, THE(1951), m; BRIDE OF THE GORILLA(1951), m; LONGHORN, THE(1951), md; STAGE TO BLUE RIVER(1951), md; SWORD OF MONTE CRISTO, THE(1951), m; ABBOTT AND COSTELLO MEET CAPTAIN KIDD(1952), m; AFRICAN TREASURE(1952), md; FARGO(1952), m; KANSAS TERRITORY(1952), m; MAN FROM BLACK HILLS, THE(1952), m; MAVERICK, THE(1952), m; NIGHT RAIDERS(1952), md; ROSE OF CIMARRON(1952), m; TEXAS CITY(1952), md; UNTAMED WOMEN(1952), m; WACO(1952), m; BLUE GARDENIA, THE(1953), m; FIGHTING LAWMAN, THE(1953), m; FORT ALGIERS(1953), md; HOMESTEADERS, THE(1953), m; INVADERS FROM MARS(1953), m; MARKSMAN, THE(1953), m; MARRY ME AGAIN(1953), m; REBEL CITY(1953), m; STAR OF TEXAS(1953), m; TEXAS BAD MAN(1953), m; TOPEKA(1953), m; VIGILANTE TERROR(1953), m; BITTER CREEK(1954), m; FORTYNINERS, THE(1954), m; GOLDEN MISTRESS, THE(1954), m; OUTLAW'S DAUGHTER, THE(1954), m; TWO GUNS AND A BADGE(1954), m; MAGNIFICENT MATADOR, THE(1955), m, md; BLACK WHIP, THE(1956), m; CURUCU, BEAST OF THE AMAZON(1956), m; MOHAWK(1956), m; BACK FROM THE DEAD(1957), m; COPPER SKY(1957), m; RESTLESS BREED, THE(1957), md; RIDE A VIOLENT MILE(1957), m, md; UNKNOWN TERROR, THE(1957), m, md; BLOOD ARROW(1958), m; COOL AND THE CRAZY, THE(1958), m; DESERT HELL(1958), m; ISLAND OF LOST WOMEN(1959), m; MUSTANG(1959), m; THIRTY FOOT BRIDE OF CANDY ROCK, THE(1959), m, md; SEPTEMBER STORM(1960), m; BILLY THE KID VS. DRACULA(1966), m; EYE FOR AN EYE, AN(1966), m; JESSE JAMES MEETS FRANKENSTEIN'S DAUGHTER(1966), m; DELTA FACTOR, THE(1970), m; DIRTY O'NEIL(1974), m; SIX PACK ANNIE(1975), m

Raul Kraushaar
SUNSET IN WYOMING(1941), md

Carola Krauskopf
SLEEPING BEAUTY(1965, Ger.), ch

Charles Krauss
Silents
ONE OF OUR GIRLS(1914)

Gerd Krauss
MERRY WIVES OF WINDSOR, THE(1966, Aust.), set d

German Krauss
Misc. Talkies
HOUSE OF SHADOWS(1977, Arg.)

Henry Krauss
LES MISERABLES(1936, Fr.)
Silents
ENCHANTMENT(1920, Brit.); NAPOLEON(1927, Fr.)
Misc. Silents
PAPA HULIN(1916, Fr.), d; LE CHEMINEAU(1917, Fr.), d; MARION DE LORME(1918, Fr.), d; FROMONT JEUNNE ET RISLER AINE(1921, Fr.), d; LES TROIS MASQUES(1921, Fr.), d; LES OMBRES QUI PASSANT(1924, Fr.); LA CALVAIRE DE DONA PISA(1925, Fr.), d; POIL DE CAROTTE(1926, Fr.)

Jacque Krauss
PEPE LE MOKO(1937, Fr.), prod d

Jacques Krauss
THEY WERE FIVE(1938, Fr.), art d; LOVE STORY(1949, Fr.), prod d

Sam Krauss
ROYAL HUNT OF THE SUN, THE(1969, Brit.)

Werner Krauss
BURG THEATRE(1936, Ger.)
Silents
CABINET OF DR. CALIGARI, THE(1921, Ger.); DECAMERON NIGHTS(1924, Brit.); STUDENT OF PRAGUE, THE(1927, Ger.); TARTUFFE(1927, Ger.)
Misc. Silents
ALL FOR A WOMAN(1921, Ger.); OTHELLO(1922, Ger.); WAXWORKS(1924, Ger.); SECRETS OF A SOUL(1925, Ger.); NANA(1926, Fr.); MIDSUMMER NIGHT'S DREAM, A(1928, Ger.); ROYAL SCANDAL(1929, Ger.); CROWN OF THORNS(1934, Ger.)

Kay Krausse
PRIVATE DETECTIVE(1939), w

Arthur Kraussneck
Misc. Silents
CHRONICLES OF THE GRAY HOUSE, THE(1923, Ger.)

Karl Krautgartner
DO YOU KEEP A LION AT HOME?(1966, Czech.)

Barbara Krauthamer
SQUARE ROOT OF ZERO, THE(1964)

L. Krauzova
SPRINGTIME ON THE VOLGA(1961, USSR)

Donald Kravanth
GATES TO PARADISE(1968, Brit./Ger.), w

Calina Kravchenko
ISLAND OF DOOM(1933, USSR)

G. Kravchenko
WAR AND PEACE(1968, USSR)

Victor Kravchenko
ELEPHANT MAN, THE(1980, Brit.)

Haskell Kraver
SILKWOOD(1983)

Rochelle Kravit
TWO OF A KIND(1983)

Rochelle L. Kravit
1984
UNFAITHFULLY YOURS(1984)

Joel Gordon Kravitz
MIDNIGHT MAN, THE(1974)

Michael Kravitz
MOTHER'S DAY(1980), p

Steven Kravitz
SUDDEN IMPACT(1983)
1984
WOMAN IN RED, THE(1984)

Jadwiga Krawczyk
SARAGOSSA MANUSCRIPT, THE(1972, Pol.)

Antoinette Kray
HUSBANDS(1970)

Michael Kray
DAY OF THE NIGHTMARE(1965)

Walter Kray
FORT MASSACRE(1958); PIER 5, HAVANA(1959); MACHISMO--40 GRAVES FOR 40 GUNS(1970)

Leonid Kraynenkov
GARNET BRACELET, THE(1966, USSR), ph

Milton Krear
MAN CALLED FLINTSTONE, THE(1966), ed

Helmut Krebs
YOUNG LORD, THE(1970, Ger.)

Nita Krebs
TERROR OF TINY TOWN, THE(1938)

Roger Krebs
CAGE OF NIGHTINGALES, A(1947, Fr.)

Warren Krech
Misc. Silents
TOWN THAT FORGOT GOD, THE(1922)

Irwin Krechaf
HAVE A NICE WEEKEND(1975), ed

Jan Kreczmar
PASSENGER, THE(1970, Pol.)

Angela Krefeld
HIDEOUT, THE(1956, Brit.); THREE MEN IN A BOAT(1958, Brit.)

Alex Kregar
LAST HOUSE ON DEAD END STREET(1977)

Krehan
M(1933, Ger.)

Paul Kreibich
MY OWN TRUE LOVE(1948); KNOCK ON ANY DOOR(1949)

Martin Kreidt
RAIDERS OF THE LOST ARK(1981)

Karlheinz Kreienbaum
RESTLESS NIGHT, THE(1964, Ger.)

Frank Kreig
HOUSE ON 92ND STREET, THE(1945); ALL MY SONS(1948); NO MINOR VICES(1948); OH, YOU BEAUTIFUL DOLL(1949); THIEVES' HIGHWAY(1949); DALLAS(1950); LONELY HEARTS BANDITS(1950); SNIPER, THE(1952); ALL ASHORE(1953); WAR OF THE WORLDS, THE(1953); NAKED STREET, THE(1955); JAILHOUSE ROCK(1957); RAINTREE COUNTY(1957); COUNT YOUR BLESSINGS(1959); SEVEN FACES OF DR. LAO(1964); THREE NUTS IN SEARCH OF A BOLT(1964); VERY SPECIAL FAVOR, A(1965); GUNN(1967)

Barbara Kreiger
ANNIE HALL(1977), set d; IDOLMAKER, THE(1980), set d

Barbara Paula Kreiger
1984
SONGWRITER(1984), set d

Lee Kreiger
CONVICTS FOUR(1962); CLAMBAKE(1967)

Nick Kreiger
OBSESSION(1976)

H. Krein
FIDDLER ON THE ROOF(1971)

Werner Krein
LA BOHEME(1965, Ital.), ph

Mitch Kreindel
BEING THERE(1979); MODERN PROBLEMS(1981)

Werner Kreindl
FORMULA, THE(1980)

Anne Kreis
SUCH A GORGEOUS KID LIKE ME(1973, Fr.)

George Kreisl
LADY AND THE TRAMP(1955), anim; HEY THERE, IT'S YOGI BEAR(1964), anim; MAN CALLED FLINTSTONE, THE(1966), anim

Fritz Kreisler
KING STEPS OUT, THE(1936), m

Otto Kreisler
SMALL TOWN STORY(1953, Brit.), p

Gusti Kreissl
FEAR EATS THE SOUL(1974, Ger.)

Howard B. Kreitsek
MISTER ROCK AND ROLL(1957), p; COUNTRY MUSIC HOLIDAY(1958), p; TEENAGE MILLIONAIRE(1961), p; ILLUSTRATED MAN, THE(1969), p, w; RABBIT, RUN(1970), p, w; BREAKOUT(1975), w; WALKING TALL, PART II(1975), w; FINAL CHAPTER-WALKING TALL zero(1977), w

Jules Kreitzer
CAYMAN TRIANGLE, THE(1977)

Otomar Krejca
DISTANT JOURNEY(1950, Czech.); MAN FROM THE FIRST CENTURY, THE(1961, Czech.)

Jiri Krejcik
DIVINE EMMA, THE(1983, Czech,), d, w

Kim Krejus
MOUTH TO MOUTH(1978, Aus.)

Lotti Krekel
CATAMOUNT KILLING, THE(1975, Ger.)

Erwin Kreker
HELP I'M INVISIBLE(1952, Ger.), w

Miroslawa Krelik
BEADS OF ONE ROSARY, THE(1982, Pol.), art d

Eddie Krell
DELIRIUM(1979), w

S.S. Krellberg
ENEMIES OF THE LAW(1931), p

Samuel S. Krellberg
THUNDERBOLT(1936), p

Jirinka Krelsova
BOHEMIAN RAPTURE(1948, Czech)

Felix Krembs
Silents
HEART OF MARYLAND, THE(1921)

Theodore Kremer
Silents
BERTHA, THE SEWING MACHINE GIRL(1927), w

Kris Kremo
LOOKIN' TO GET OUT(1982)

Fritz Krenn
ISLAND RESCUE(1952, Brit.)

Jan Krenz
KANAL(1961, Pol.), m; KNIGHTS OF THE TEUTONIC ORDER, THE(1962, Pol.), md; EROICA(1966, Pol.), m

M. Krepkogorskaya
BOUNTIFUL SUMMER(1951, USSR)

David Kreps
1984
SPLASH(1984)

Vera Kresadlova
INTIMATE LIGHTING(1969, Czech.); MOST BEAUTIFUL AGE, THE(1970, Czech.)

Lee Kresel
BLACK MAGIC(1949); ALAKAZAM THE GREAT!(1961, Jap.), w; GUNS OF THE BLACK WITCH(1961, Fr./Ital.), d; TRAPP FAMILY, THE(1961, Ger.), w; MOTHRA(1962, Jap.), d; PRISONER OF THE IRON MASK(1962, Fr./Ital.), d; SERAFINO(1970, Fr./Ital.), d

Connie Kreski
OUTSIDE MAN, THE(1973, U.S./FR.); BLACK BIRD, THE(1975)
Misc. Talkies
CAN HIERONYMUS MERKIN EVER FORGET MERCY HUMPPE AND FIND TRUE HAPPINESS?(1969)

Carl Kress
LIBERATION OF L.B. JONES, THE(1970), ed; WATERMELON MAN(1970), ed; DOCTORS' WIVES(1971), ed; ACT OF VENGEANCE(1974), ed; SUGAR HILL(1974), ed; TOWERING INFERNO, THE(1974), ed; DRUM(1976), ed; AUDREY ROSE(1977), ed; MAN, A WOMAN, AND A BANK, A(1979, Can.), ed; METEOR(1979), ed; HOPSCOTCH(1980), ed; LOOKER(1981), ed; STROKER ACE(1983), ed
1984
CANNONBALL RUN II(1984), ed

Earl Kress
FOX AND THE HOUND, THE(1981), w

Harold Kress
APACHE WAR SMOKE(1952), d; HORSEMEN, THE(1971), ed; STAND UP AND BE COUNTED(1972), ed; ICEMAN COMETH, THE(1973), ed

Harold F. Kress
UNTIL THEY SAIL(1957), ed; BROADWAY SERENADE(1939), ed; IT'S A WONDERFUL WORLD(1939), ed; REMEMBER?(1939), ed; THESE GLAMOUR GIRLS(1939), ed; ANDY HARDY MEETS DEBUTANTE(1940), ed; BITTER SWEET(1940), ed; COMRADE X(1940), ed; NEW MOON(1940), ed; H.M. PULHAM, ESQ.(1941), ed; RAGE IN HEAVEN(1941), ed; UNHOLY PARTNERS(1941), ed; MRS. MINIVER(1942), ed; RANDOM HARVEST(1942), ed; CABIN IN THE SKY(1943), ed; MADAME CURIE(1943), ed; DRAGON SEED(1944), ed; YEARLING, THE(1946), ed; COMMAND DECISION(1948), ed; DATE WITH JUDY, A(1948), ed; EAST SIDE, WEST SIDE(1949), ed; GREAT SINNER, THE(1949), ed; MINIVER STORY, THE(1950, Brit./U.S.), ed; NO QUESTIONS ASKED(1951), d; PAINTED HILLS, THE(1951), d; RIDE, VAQUERO!(1953), ed; SAADIA(1953), ed; ROSE MARIE(1954), ed; VALLEY OF THE KINGS(1954), ed; COBWEB, THE(1955), ed; GREEN FIRE(1955), ed; I'LL CRY TOMORROW(1955), ed; PRODIGAL, THE(1955), ed; RACK, THE(1956), ed; TEAHOUSE OF THE AUGUST MOON, THE(1956), ed; SILK STOCKINGS(1957), ed; IMITATION GENERAL(1958), ed; MERRY ANDREW(1958), ed; COUNT YOUR BLESSINGS(1959), ed; WORLD, THE FLESH, AND THE DEVIL, THE(1959), ed; HOME FROM THE HILL(1960), ed; KING OF KINGS(1961), ed; HOW THE WEST WAS WON(1962), ed; GREATEST STORY EVER TOLD, THE(1965), ed; ALVAREZ KELLY(1966), ed; AMBUSHERS, THE(1967), ed; LUV(1967), ed; POSEIDON ADVENTURE, THE(1972), ed; TOWERING INFERNO, THE(1974), ed; 99 AND 44/100% DEAD(1974), ed; GATOR(1976), ed; OTHER SIDE OF MIDNIGHT, THE(1977), ed; VIVA KNIEVEL!(1977), ed; SWARM, THE(1978), ed

Lee Kressel
LOVERS AND LIARS(1981, Ital.), d

Harry Kressing
SOMETHING FOR EVERYONE(1970), w

Patricia Krest
STRAIT-JACKET(1964)

Krestinksy
Misc. Silents
KIRA KIRALINA(1927, USSR)

V. Krestyaninov
LITTLE HUMPBACKED HORSE, THE(1962, USSR), anim

Robert Kretschmann
HEROES(1977)

Dieto Kretzchmar
GAS(1981, Can.)

Herbert Kretzmer
TOO HOT TO HANDLE(1961, Brit.), w; THINK DIRTY(1970, Brit.), w

Peter Kreuder
SCHLAGER-PARADE(1953)

Knud Kreuger
INTERNATIONAL SQUADRON(1941)

Kurt Kreuger
YANK IN THE R.A.F., A(1941); EDGE OF DARKNESS(1943); PURPLE V, THE(1943); SAHARA(1943); STRANGE DEATH OF ADOLF HITLER, THE(1943); MADEMOISELLE FIFI(1944); NONE SHALL ESCAPE(1944); ESCAPE IN THE DESERT(1945); PARIS UNDERGROUND(1945); SPIDER, THE(1945); DARK CORNER, THE(1946);

SENTIMENTAL JOURNEY(1946); UNFAITHFULLY YOURS(1948); SPY HUNT(1950); FEAR(1956, Ger.); ENEMY BELOW, THE(1957); WHAT DID YOU DO IN THE WAR, DADDY?(1966); ST. VALENTINE'S DAY MASSACRE, THE(1967)

Paul Kreuger
MIDNIGHT TAXI, THE(1928)

Stubby Kreuger
CAPTAINS COURAGEOUS(1937)

Peter Kreunder
CONFESSION(1937), m

Vicki Joy Kreutzer
SCANDAL AT SCOURIE(1953)

Elisabeth Kreuzer
ALICE IN THE CITIES(1974, W. Ger.)

Lisa Kreuzer
KINGS OF THE ROAD(1976, Ger.); AMERICAN FRIEND, THE(1977, Ger.); RADIO ON(1980, Brit./Ger.)
1984
BASILEUS QUARTET(1984, Ital.); FLIGHT TO BERLIN(1984, Ger./Brit.)

Frantisek Kreuzman
MERRY WIVES, THE(1940, Czech.)

A. Krevalid
HAMLET(1966, USSR)

Marika Krevata
POLICEMAN OF THE 16TH PRECINCT, THE(1963, Gr.)

Rose Kreves
BATTLING MARSHAL(1950), w

Eva Krewskan
Misc. Talkies
ATOMIC WAR BRIDE(1966)

Steven Krey
WORLD ACCORDING TO GARP, The(1982)

I. Kriauzaite
DEAD MOUNTAINEER HOTEL, THE(1979, USSR)

Alice Kriby
LUCKY JORDAN(1942)

Vasili Krichevsky
Silents
EARTH(1930, USSR), art d

Karen Krick
PARSIFAL(1983, Fr.)

Jaroslav Kricka
MERRY WIVES, THE(1940, Czech.), m

Ursula Krieg
FREDDY UNTER FREMDEN STERNEN(1962, Ger.)

Barbara Krieger
DEMON SEED(1977), set d; METEOR(1979), set d; WHERE THE BUFFALO ROAM(1980), set d

Lee Krieger
ONE WAY WAHINI(1965)

Nicholous R. Krieger
NIGHT OF BLOODY HORROR zero(1969)

Nick Krieger
1984
TIGHTROPE(1984)

Robin Krieger
1984
PHILADELPHIA EXPERIMENT, THE(1984)

Roger Krieger
PLASTIC DOME OF NORMA JEAN, THE(1966)

Stu Krieger
GOODBYE FRANKLIN HIGH(1978), w
1984
WHERE THE BOYS ARE '84(1984), w

Stuart Krieger
SEED OF INNOCENCE(1980), w

Vickie Kriegler
COMPETITION, THE(1980)

Anneline Kriel
KILL AND KILL AGAIN(1981)

Werner Krien
SOMEWHERE IN BERLIN(1949, E. Ger.), ph; TROMBA, THE TIGER MAN(1952, Ger.), ph; TRAPP FAMILY, THE(1961, Ger.), ph; HELDINNEN(1962, Ger.), ph; ADORABLE JULIA(1964, Fr./Aust.), ph; MAEDCHEN IN UNIFORM(1965, Ger./Fr.), ph

Lucien Krier
IF IT'S TUESDAY, THIS MUST BE BELGIUM(1969)

Christopher Kriesa
1984
KARATE KID, THE(1984)

Anneliese Krigar
PUSS 'N' BOOTS(1967, Ger.), ed

Carolyn Krigbaum
HOSPITAL, THE(1971); NETWORK(1976)

Alice Krige
CHARRIOTS OF FIRE(1981, Brit.); GHOST STORY(1981)

Tai Krige
KILL AND KILL AGAIN(1981), ph

Freda Krigh
DOLL'S HOUSE, A(1973, Brit.)

Jack Krik
RIDE, TENDERFOOT, RIDE(1940)

S. Krilov
CITY OF YOUTH(1938, USSR)

Sergei Krilov
THIRTEEN, THE(1937, USSR)

Viju Krim
BLOODSUCKING FREAKS(1982)

Harry Krimer
HEART OF A NATION, THE(1943, Fr.)

Nika Krimnus
SANDU FOLLOWS THE SUN(1965, USSR)
Michael Krims
PHONY AMERICAN, THE(1964, Ger.), w
Mildred Krims
CRIMSON ROMANCE(1934), w
Milton Krims
UNMASKED(1929); DUDE RANCH(1931), w; RANGE FEUD, THE(1931), w; SOUTH
OF THE RIO GRANDE(1932), w; AFFAIRS OF A GENTLEMAN(1934), w; I GIVE MY
LOVE(1934), w; YOUNG AND BEAUTIFUL(1934), w; GRAND OLD GIRL(1935), w;
HARMONY LANE(1935), w; STRANGERS ALL(1935), w; WEST OF THE PE-
COS(1935), w; FORBIDDEN TRAIL(1936), w; SPEED(1936), w; GREAT O'MALLEY,
THE(1937), w; GREEN LIGHT(1937), w; SECRETS OF AN ACTRESS(1938), w; SIS-
TERS, THE(1938), w; CONFESSIONS OF A NAZI SPY(1939), w; WE ARE NOT
ALONE(1939), w; DISPATCH FROM REUTERS, A(1940), w; LADY WITH RED
HAIR(1940), w; IRON CURTAIN, THE(1948), w; PRINCE OF FOXES(1949), w; ONE
MINUTE TO ZERO(1952), w; CROSSED SWORDS(1954), d&w; TENNESSEE'S PART-
NER(1955), w; MOHAWK(1956), w; COMMANDO(1962, Ital., Span., Bel., Ger.), w;
SECRET MARK OF D'ARTAGNAN, THE(1963, Fr./Ital.), w
Misc. Talkies
UNMASKED(1929)
Misc. Silents
UNMASKED(1929)
C. L. Krimse
LONG IS THE ROAD(1948, Ger.), art d
John Krimsky
EMPEROR JONES, THE(1933), p
Smoke Kring
PARIS PLAYBOYS(1954), cos
Margarita Krinitsyna
KIEV COMEDY, A(1963, USSR)
Robert D. Krintzman
STARHOPS(1978), p
Jayut Kripilani
HEAT AND DUST(1983, Brit.)
David Krippner
WOMEN AND BLOODY TERROR(1970)
Kernan Kripps
WITH LOVE AND KISSES(1937)
Henry Krips
PACIFIC ADVENTURE(1947, Aus.), ed
Gregori F. Kris
NUN AND THE SERGEANT, THE(1962)
Hilda Kriseman
FIDDLER ON THE ROOF(1971)
John Krish
WOMAN IN THE HALL, THE(1949, Brit.), ed; COMPANIONS IN CRIME(1954,
Brit.), d; SALVAGE GANG, THE(1958, Brit.), d, w; UNEARTHLY STRANGER,
THE(1964, Brit.), d; WILD AFFAIR, THE(1966, Brit.), d&w; DECLINE AND FALL...
OF A BIRD WATCHER(1969, Brit.), d; MAN WHO HAD POWER OVER WOMEN,
THE(1970, Brit.), d
Richard Krisher
ST. VALENTINE'S DAY MASSACRE, THE(1967); TONY ROME(1967); DETECTIVE,
THE(1968)
H.S. Krishnamurthy
1984
PASSAGE TO INDIA, A(1984, Brit.)
P.B. Krishnan
JUNGLE, THE(1952), art d
Krishnanbose
ADVERSARY, THE(1973, Ind.)
Nino Krisman
VERY HANDY MAN, A(1966, Fr./Ital.), p; VIOLENT FOUR, THE(1968, Ital.)
Nino E. Krisman
CRAZY JOE(1974), p
Peter Kriss
LONELINESS OF THE LONG DISTANCE RUNNER, THE(1962, Brit.); MIX ME A
PERSON(1962, Brit.); SQUADRON 633(1964, U.S./Brit.); 633 SQUADRON(1964)
Sylvia Kristel
CONCORDE, THE–AIRPORT '79(; ALICE, OR THE LAST ESCAPADE(1977, Fr.);
BEHIND THE IRON MASK(1977); MYSTERIES(1979, Neth.); GOODBYE EM-
MANUELLE(1980, Fr.); NUDE BOMB, THE(1980); LADY CHATTERLEY'S LO-
VER(1981, Fr./Brit.); PRIVATE LESSONS(1981); PRIVATE SCHOOL(1983)
Ilene Kristen
PREACHERMAN(1971); WHY WOULD I LIE(1980)
Jon Kristen
CHARGE OF THE LIGHT BRIGADE, THE(1936)
Lidia Kristen
YOUNG FRANKENSTEIN(1974); PROMISES IN THE DARK(1979); BLACK MAR-
BLE, THE(1980)
Marta Kristen
SAVAGE SAM(1963); BEACH BLANKET BINGO(1965); TERMINAL ISLAND(1973);
ONCE(1974); BATTLE BEYOND THE STARS(1980)
Dorothy Krister
HAPPY DAYS(1930)
Ted Kristian
ICE STATION ZEBRA(1968)
Cay Kristiansen
ORDET(1957, Den.)
Erik Kristiansen
EDVARD MUNCH(1976, Norway/Swed.)
Henning Kristiansen
EPILOGUE(1967, Den.), ph; HUNGER(1968, Den./Norway/Swed.), ph; PEOPLE
MEET AND SWEET MUSIC FILLS THE HEART(1969, Den./Swed.), ph; NIGHT
VISITOR, THE(1970, Swed./U.S.), ph; ONLY WAY, THE(1970, Panama/Den./U.S.),
ph; KING LEAR(1971, Brit./Den.), ph
Terje Kristiansen
1984
KAMILLA(1984, Norway), p, w

Stanley Kristien
YOUNG SAVAGES, THE(1961)
Kris Kristofferson
CISCO PIKE(1971), a, m; LAST MOVIE, THE(1971), a, m; BLUME IN LOVE(1973);
PAT GARRETT AND BILLY THE KID(1973); BRING ME THE HEAD OF ALFREDO
GARCIA(1974); ALICE DOESN'T LIVE HERE ANYMORE(1975); SAILOR WHO FELL
FROM GRACE WITH THE SEA, THE(1976, Brit.); STAR IS BORN, A(1976); SEMI-
TOUGH(1977); CONVOY(1978); HEAVEN'S GATE(1980); ROLLOVER(1981)
1984
FLASHPOINT(1984); SONGWRITER(1984)
Carol Kristy
YOUR THREE MINUTES ARE UP(1973)
Anthony Kristye
TOMB OF TORTURE(1966, Ital.), w
Anthony Kristye [Antonio Boccacci]
TOMB OF TORTURE(1966, Ital.), d
Karl Kritel
HIPPODROME(1961, Aust./Ger.)
Yu. Kritenko
MOTHER AND DAUGHTER(1965, USSR)
Eleni Kriti
CANNON AND THE NIGHTINGALE, THE(1969, Gr.)
Alkis Kritikos
FOR YOUR EYES ONLY(1981)
N. Kriuchkov
CITY OF YOUTH(1938, USSR); SKI BATTALION(1938, USSR)
Nikolai Kriuchkov
THIRTEEN, THE(1937, USSR)
V. Kriuger
MEN OF THE SEA(1938, USSR)
Nikolai Kriukov
LAD FROM OUR TOWN(1941, USSR), m; SYMPHONY OF LIFE(1949, USSR), m
V.I. Kriukov
HOUSE OF DEATH(1932, USSR), m
A. Krivchenva
BORIS GODUNOV(1959, USSR)
Jonathan Krivine
SISTER-IN-LAW, THE(1975), p
M. Krivova
MARRIAGE OF BALZAMINOV, THE(1966, USSR)
M. Kriz
MOST BEAUTIFUL AGE, THE(1970, Czech.)
Serge Krizman
SONG OF MY HEART(1947); GLASS WALL, THE(1953), art d; CRIME IN THE
STREETS(1956), art d; FLIGHT TO HONG KONG(1956), art d; RIDE THE HIGH
IRON(1956), art d; FUZZY PINK NIGHTGOWN, THE(1957), art d; TIME LIMIT(1957),
art d; LONELYHEARTS(1958), art d; GUNFIGHT AT DODGE CITY, THE(1959), art
d; PORGY AND BESS(1959), art d; CAGE OF EVIL(1960), art d; FIVE GUNS TO
TOMBSTONE(1960), art d; FRONTIER UPRISING(1961), art d; GAMBLER WORE A
GUN, THE(1961), art d; GUN FIGHT(1961), art d; POLICE DOG STORY, THE(1961),
art d; PROMISES, PROMISES(1963), art d; BIG BOUNCE, THE(1969), art d; LOVE AT
FIRST BITE(1979), prod d
Les Krizsan
SIEGE(1983, Can.), ph
Joseph A. Kroculick
EVERY SPARROW MUST FALL(1964), m
Michael Kroecher
EVERY MAN FOR HIMSELF AND GOD AGAINST ALL(1975, Ger.)
Barry Kroeger
ACT OF MURDER, AN(1948); GUILTY OF TREASON(1950); BLOOD ALLEY(1955)
Berry Kroeger
TOM, DICK AND HARRY(1941); CRY OF THE CITY(1948); DARK PAST, THE(1948);
IRON CURTAIN, THE(1948); ACT OF VIOLENCE(1949); BLACK MAGIC(1949);
CHICAGO DEADLINE(1949); DOWN TO THE SEA IN SHIPS(1949); FIGHTING MAN
OF THE PLAINS(1949); GUN CRAZY(1949); SWORD OF MONTE CRISTO, THE(1951);
BATTLES OF CHIEF PONTIAC(1952); YELLOWNECK(1955); MAN IN THE
VAULT(1956); SEVEN THIEVES(1960); STORY OF RUTH, THE(1960); WALKING
TARGET, THE(1960); ATLANTIS, THE LOST CONTINENT(1961); HITLER(1962);
WOMAN HUNT(1962); YOUNGBLOOD HAWKE(1964); CHAMBER OF HOR-
RORS(1966); NIGHTMARE IN WAX(1969); WILD SCENE, THE(1970); INCREDIBLE
TWO-HEADED TRANSPLANT, THE(1971); MEPHISTO WALTZ, THE(1971); SEVEN
MINUTES, THE(1971); PETS(1974); DEMON SEED(1977)
Wolf Kroeger
UNCANNY, THE(1977, Brit./Can.), prod d; IN PRAISE OF OLDER WOMEN(1978,
Can.), art d; QUINTET(1979), art d; POPEYE(1980), prod d; FIRST BLOOD(1982), prod
d; SPLIT IMAGE(1982), prod d; STREAMERS(1983), prod d
1984
BAY BOY(1984, Can.), prod d
Erich Kroehnke
BIMBO THE GREAT(1961, Ger.), w
Carl Kroenke
CALL NORTHSIDE 777(1948)
Chris Kroesen
MAGIC CHRISTMAS TREE(1964), a, p
Franz-Xaver Kroetz
JAIL BAIT(1977, Ger.), w
Helge Krog
ON THE SUNNYSIDE(1936, Swed.), w
Tim Krog
BOOGEY MAN, THE(1980), m; BOOGEYMAN II(1983), m
Elke Kroger
GENGHIS KHAN(U.S./Brit./Ger./Yugo)
Dan Krogh
WIZARD OF GORE, THE(1970), ph
Daniel P. Krogh
THIS STUFF'LL KILL YA!(1971), ph
Odo Krohmann
GLASS TOWER, THE(1959, Ger.), w; KING IN SHADOW(1961, Ger.), w

Charles Krohn
SUGAR HILL(1974)
Maurice Krohner
OVERTURE TO GLORY(1940)
Misc. Talkies
JEWISH KING LEAR(1935)
Sara Krohner
GOLDBERGS, THE(1950)
Sarah Krohner
Misc. Talkies
MIRELE EFROS(1939)
Erich Krohnke
JUSTINE(1969, Ital./Span.), w; TEN LITTLE INDIANS(1975, Ital./Fr./Span./Ger.), w
Roman Kroiter
NOBODY WAVED GOODBYE(1965, Can.), p
V. Krokhin
FORTY-NINE DAYS(1964, USSR)
Anatoly Kroll
1984
JAZZMAN(1984, USSR), m
Don Kroll
HOW TO SUCCEED IN BUSINESS WITHOUT REALLY TRYING(1976)
Eva Kroll
THEY WERE SO YOUNG(1955), ed; PATHS OF GLORY(1957), ed; RESTLESS NIGHT, THE(1964, Ger.), ed
Harry Harrison Kroll
CABIN IN THE COTTON(1932), w
Natasha Kroll
MUSIC LOVERS, THE(1971, Brit.), prod d; HIRELING, THE(1973, Brit.), prod d; ABSOLUTION(1981, Brit.), prod d
Stan Kroll
VERY PRIVATE AFFAIR, A(1962, Fr./Ital.)
John Krollers
GIRL ON THE RUN(1961)
Ann Kroman
Misc. Silents
MEDICINE MAN, THE(1917); MIDNIGHT MAN(1917); HER DECISION(1918); HONEST MAN, AN(1918)
Ann Kroman [Ann Forrest]
Silents
TAR HEEL WARRIOR, THE(1917)
Misc. Silents
BIRTH OF PATRIOTISM, THE(1917)
Grigori Kromarov
DEAD MOUNTAINEER HOTEL, THE(1979, USSR), d
Kromberg
THREE STEPS NORTH(1951), set d
E. Kromberg
HANNIBAL(1960, Ital.), art d
Ernesto Kromberg
QUEEN OF THE PIRATES(1961, Ital./Ger.), art d; RAGE OF THE BUCCANEERS(1963, Ital.), art d; SECRET MARK OF D'ARTAGNAN, THE(1963, Fr./Ital.), set d; TIGER OF THE SEVEN SEAS(1964, Fr./Ital.), art d; MYSTERY OF THUG ISLAND, THE(1966, Ital./Ger.), art d; LION OF ST. MARK(1967, Ital.), art d
Margaret Kromgols
SPOOK WHO SAT BY THE DOOR, THE(1973)
Penny Krompier
PUFNSTUF(1970)
Annika Kronberg
PASSION OF ANNA, THE(1970, Swed.)
Fred Krone
STEEL FIST, THE(1952); HOUSTON STORY, THE(1956); APACHE TERRITORY(1958); FIREBRAND, THE(1962); HAND OF DEATH(1962); YOUNG GUNS OF TEXAS(1963); ARIZONA RAIDERS(1965); CONVICT STAGE(1965); FORT COURAGEOUS(1965); WAR PARTY(1965); YOUNG FURY(1965); LOVE BUG, THE(1968); GREAT BANK ROBBERY, THE(1969); HELL'S BELLES(1969); LIFE AND TIMES OF JUDGE ROY BEAN, THE(1972); LIMIT, THE(1972)
Kurt Kronefeld
DAMNED, THE(1948, Fr.)
Ben Kronen
VICE SQUAD(1982); DOCTOR DETROIT(1983)
1984
DREAMSCAPE(1984); FEAR CITY(1984)
Adrienne Kronenberg
FLASH GORDON(1980)
Bruce Kronenberg
NESTING, THE(1981)
Josef Kroner
MAN WHO LIES, THE(1970, Czech./Fr.); ADRIFT(1971, Czech.)
Jozef Kroner
SHOP ON MAIN STREET, THE(1966, Czech.)
Maurice Kroner
MOTEL, THE OPERATOR(1940)
Max Kronert
Silents
ONE ARABIAN NIGHT(1921, Ger.)
Harry Kronman
BOWERY BOY(1940), w
Richard Kronold
FORBIDDEN JOURNEY(1950, Can.)
Kronos
DAVID AND GOLIATH(1961, Ital.)
Steven Kronovet
1984
NATURAL, THE(1984)
Jeremy Joe Kronsberg
EVERY WHICH WAY BUT LOOSE(1978), w; ANY WHICH WAY YOU CAN(1980), w; GOING APE!(1981), d&w

Henning Kronstam
BLACK TIGHTS(1962, Fr.)
Members of the Kroo Tribes
SANDERS OF THE RIVER(1935, Brit.)
Margareta Krook
BRINK OF LIFE(1960, Swed.); SWEDISH WEDDING NIGHT(1965, Swed.); PERSONA(1967, Swed.)
Margaretha Krook
ADVENTURES OF PICASSO, THE(1980, Swed.)
Peter Kroonenburg
HEARTACHES(1981, Can.), p
Pieter Kroonenburg
CROSS COUNTRY(1983, Can.), p
Sandy Kroopf
1984
BIRDY(1984), w
Jan Kropacedk
DAY THAT SHOOK THE WORLD, THE(1977, Yugo./Czech.), cos
G. Kropachyov
HAMLET(1966, USSR), art d
Kaare Kroppan
TERRORISTS, THE(1975, Brit.)
Bernard Krosinksy
WIRE SERVICE(1942), art d
Lee Kross
GET OUTTA TOWN(1960)
Krotkin
MORNING STAR(1962, USSR), spec eff
M. Krotkin
QUEEN OF SPADES(1961, USSR), spec eff; SONG OVER MOSCOW(1964, USSR), spec eff; SLEEPING BEAUTY, THE(1966, USSR), spec eff
Yuri Krotkov
RED MONARCH(1983, Brit.), w
Daniel P. Krough
YEAR OF THE YAHOO(1971), ph
B.S. Kroul
FLY NOW, PAY LATER(1969)
Tom Kroutil
ONLY WAY HOME, THE(1972)
Richard Krown
WHAT'S UP, TIGER LILY?(1966), ed
Stavros Krozos
BAREFOOT BATTALION, THE(1954, Gr.)
Karol Krska
SEVENTH CONTINENT, THE(1968, Czech./Yugo.), ph
Vaclav Krska
BOHEMIAN RAPTURE(1948, Czech.), d&w; GIRL WITH THREE CAMELS, THE(1968, Czech.), d, w
Vlado Krstulovic
APACHE GOLD(1965, Ger.)
Kru
Silents
CHANG(1927)
Ernst Krubowski
YOUNG LORD, THE(1970, Ger.)
Jack Kruchen
JUST ACROSS THE STREET(1952)
O. Kruchinina
OTHELLO(1960, U.S.S.R.), cos; MAGIC VOYAGE OF SINBAD, THE(1962, USSR), cos
Nikolai Kruchkov
BALLAD OF A SOLDIER(1960, USSR)
Leon Kruczkowski
TONIGHT A TOWN DIES(1961, Pol.), w; KNIGHTS OF THE TEUTONIC ORDER, THE(1962, Pol.), w
Peter Krueder
BURG THEATRE(1936, Ger.), m
Vladimir Kruegar
ISLAND OF DOOM(1933, USSR)
Bum Krueger
EIGHTH DAY OF THE WEEK, THE(1959, Pol./Ger.)
Carl Krueger
GOLDEN GLOVES STORY, THE(1950), p; SABRE JET(1953), p, w; COMANCHE(1956), p, w
Christiane Krueger
48 HOURS TO ACAPULCO(1968, Ger.)
Harold Krueger
MADAME BOVARY(1949)
Jack Krueger
NOCTURNA(1979), art d
Kurt Krueger
MAN HUNT(1941); BACKGROUND TO DANGER(1943); MOON IS DOWN, THE(1943); HOTEL BERLIN(1945); LEGION OF THE DOOMED(1958)
Misc. Talkies
TO DIE IN PARIS(1968)
Larraine Krueger
UNHOLY PARTNERS(1941)
Lorraine Krueger
NEW FACES OF 1937(1937); EVERYBODY'S DOING IT(1938); EXPOSED(1938); I'M FROM THE CITY(1938); IDIOT'S DELIGHT(1939); DANCE, GIRL, DANCE(1940); FARMER'S DAUGHTER, THE(1940); GOLDEN GLOVES(1940); ADVENTURES OF A ROOKIE(1943); HE'S MY GUY(1943); HI, BUDDY(1943); SARONG GIRL(1943); CAREER GIRL(1944); SLIGHTLY TERRIFIC(1944); OUT OF THIS WORLD(1945); ONE EXCITING WEEK(1946)
Otto Krueger
COVER GIRL(1944)
Paul Krueger
POSTMAN ALWAYS RINGS TWICE, THE(1946); SOUTHERN YANKEE, A(1948)

Paul W. Krueger
DREAMER, THE(1936, Ger.)
Karen Kruer
HARDCORE(1979)
Amy Krug
EYES OF A STRANGER(1980); HARDLY WORKING(1981)
Lee Krug
NOBODY'S PERFEKT(1981); PIRANHA II: THE SPAWNING(1981, Neth.)
U. Krug
Misc. Silents
INFINITE SORROW(1922, USSR)
Alma Kruger
CRAIG'S WIFE(1936); LOVE LETTERS OF A STAR(1936); THESE THREE(1936); BREEZING HOME(1937); MAN IN BLUE, THE(1937); MIGHTY TREVE, THE(1937); VOGUES OF 1938(1937); 100 MEN AND A GIRL(1937); GREAT WALTZ, THE(1938); MARIE ANTOINETTE(1938); MOTHER CAREY'S CHICKENS(1938); TARNISHED ANGEL(1938); TOY WIFE, THE(1938); BALALAIKA(1939); CALLING DR. KILDARE(1939); MADE FOR EACH OTHER(1939); SECRET OF DR. KILDARE, THE(1939); ANNE OF WINDY POPLARS(1940); DR. KILDARE GOES HOME(1940); DR. KILDARE'S CRISIS(1940); DR. KILDARE'S STRANGE CASE(1940); HIS GIRL FRIDAY(1940); YOU'LL FIND OUT(1940); BLONDE INSPIRATION(1941); DR. KILDARE'S VICTORY(1941); DR. KILDARE'S WEDDING DAY(1941); PEOPLE VS. DR. KILDARE, THE(1941); PUDDIN' HEAD(1941); TRIAL OF MARY DUGAN, THE(1941); CALLING DR. GILLESPIE(1942); DR. GILLESPIE'S NEW ASSISTANT(1942); SABOTEUR(1942); THAT OTHER WOMAN(1942); DR. GILLESPIE'S CRIMINAL CASE(1943); BABES ON SWING STREET(1944); BETWEEN TWO WOMEN(1944); MRS. PARKINGTON(1944); OUR HEARTS WERE YOUNG AND GAY(1944); THREE MEN IN WHITE(1944); COLONEL EFFINGHAM'S RAID(1945); CRIME DOCTOR'S WARNING(1945); DO YOU LOVE ME?(1946); SCANDAL IN PARIS, A(1946); DARK DELUSION(1947); FOREVER AMBER(1947); FUN ON A WEEKEND(1979)
Bum Kruger
DEVIL MAKES THREE, THE(1952); YOUNG GO WILD, THE(1962, Ger.)
Christiane Kruger
DE SADE(1969); LITTLE MOTHER(1973, U.S./Yugo./Ger.); INTERNECINE PROJECT, THE(1974, Brit.)
1984
LE DERNIER COMBAT(1984, Fr.)
Misc. Talkies
STAR MAIDENS(1976, Brit.)
David Kruger
CLAUDINE(1974)
Faith Kruger
LIFE WITH FATHER(1947); UNSUSPECTED, THE(1947); FIVE FINGERS(1952); CRIME WAVE(1954)
Franz Kruger
GERMANY, YEAR ZERO(1949, Ger.)
Fred Kruger
GIRLS ON THE LOOSE(1958)
G.J. Kruger
GOLGOTHA(1937, Fr.), ph
Hans-Helmut Kruger
NAKED AMONG THE WOLVES(1967, Ger.)
Hardy Kruger
MOON IS BLUE, THE(1953); AS LONG AS YOU'RE NEAR ME(1956, Ger.); BACHELOR OF HEARTS(1958, Brit.); ONE THAT GOT AWAY, THE(1958, Brit.); CHANCE MEETING(1960, Brit.); CONFESS DR. CORDA(1960, Ger.); REST IS SILENCE, THE(1960, Ger.); DIE GANS VON SEDAN(1962, Fr/Ger.); HATARI!(1962); SUNDAYS AND CYBELE(1962, Fr.); FLIGHT OF THE PHOENIX, THE(1965); TAXI FOR TOBRUK(1965, Fr./Span./Ger.); DEFECTOR, THE(1966, Ger./Fr.); FEMMINA(1968 Fr./Ital./Ger.); UNINHIBITED, THE(1968, Fr./Ital./Span.); SECRET OF SANTA VITTORIA, THE(1969); LADY OF MONZA, THE(1970, Ital.); BATTLE OF THE NERETVA(1971, Yugo./Ital./Ger.); NIGHT HAIR CHILD(1971, Brit.); RED TENT, THE(1971, Ital./USSR); BARRY LYNDON(1975, Brit.); PAPER TIGER(1975, Brit.); BRIDGE TOO FAR, A(1977, Brit.); BLUE FIN(1978, Aus.); WILD GEESE, THE(1978, Brit.); WRONG IS RIGHT(1982)
Misc. Talkies
DEATH OF A STRANGER(1976)
Harold Kruger
MY FAVORITE SPY(1942)
Harold S. Kruger
NEPTUNE'S DAUGHTER(1949)
Harold "Stubby" Kruger
TALK OF THE TOWN(1942); DEVIL'S CANYON(1953)
Henry Kruger
CASTLE OF BLOOD(1964, Fr./Ital.)
J. Kruger
PEARLS OF THE CROWN(1938, Fr.), ph
Jack Kruger
Misc. Silents
UNKNOWN RIDER, THE(1929)
Jacqueline Kruger
LOOK IN ANY WINDOW(1961)
James Durkin Kruger
SECRET OF THE BLUE ROOM(1933)
Jeffrey Kruger
ROCK YOU SINNERS(1957, Brit.), p, m
Jeffrey S. Kruger
SWEET BEAT(1962, Brit.), p
Jules Kruger
END OF THE WORLD, THE(1930, Fr.), ph; LES MISERABLES(1936, Fr.), ph; PEPE LE MOKO(1937, Fr.), ph; THE BEACHCOMBER(1938, Brit.), ph; THEY WERE FIVE(1938, Fr.), ph; ESCAPE FROM YESTERDAY(1939, Fr.), ph; SIDEWALKS OF LONDON(1940, Brit.), ph; HEART OF A NATION, THE(1943, Fr.), ph; STRANGERS IN THE HOUSE(1949, Fr.), ph
Silents
NAPOLEON(1927, Fr.), ph
Lori Kruger
1984
NO SMALL AFFAIR(1984)

Lorraine Kruger
MODEL WIFE(1941)
Lutz Kruger
PINOCCHIO(1969, E. Ger.)
M. Kruger
JUST A BIG, SIMPLE GIRL(1949, Fr.), ph
Michael Kruger
NOT RECONCILED, OR "ONLY VIOLENCE HELPS WHERE IT RULES"(1969, Ger.)
Otto Kruger
BEAUTY FOR SALE(1933); EVER IN MY HEART(1933); PRIZEFIGHTER AND THE LADY, THE(1933); TURN BACK THE CLOCK(1933); CHAINED(1934); CRIME DOCTOR, THE(1934); GALLANT LADY(1934); MEN IN WHITE(1934); PARIS INTERLUDE(1934); SPRINGTIME FOR HENRY(1934); TREASURE ISLAND(1934); WOMEN IN HIS LIFE, THE(1934); TWO SINNERS(1935); VANESSA, HER LOVE STORY(1935); DRACULA'S DAUGHTER(1936); LADY OF SECRETS(1936); LIVING DANGEROUSLY(1936, Brit.); BARRIER, THE(1937); COUNSEL FOR CRIME(1937); GLAMOROUS NIGHT(1937, Brit.); THEY WON'T FORGET(1937); EXPOSED(1938); HOUSEMASTER(1938, Brit.); I AM THE LAW(1938); THANKS FOR THE MEMORY(1938); ANOTHER THIN MAN(1939); BLACK EYES(1939, Brit.); DISBARRED(1939); WOMAN IS THE JUDGE, A(1939); ZERO HOUR, THE(1939); DISPATCH FROM REUTERS, A(1940); DR. EHRLICH'S MAGIC BULLET(1940); HIDDEN MENACE, THE(1940, Brit.); MAN I MARRIED, THE(1940); SCANDAL SHEET(1940); SEVENTEEN(1940); BIG BOSS, THE(1941); FALSE RAPTURE(1941); MEN IN HER LIFE, THE(1941); MERCY ISLAND(1941); FRIENDLY ENEMIES(1942); HITLER'S CHILDREN(1942); NIGHT PLANE FROM CHUNGKING(1942); SABOTEUR(1942); SECRETS OF A CO-ED(1942); AMAZING MR. FORREST, THE(1943, Brit.); CORREGIDOR(1943); POWER OF THE PRESS(1943); STAGE DOOR CANTEEN(1943); TARZAN'S DESERT MYSTERY(1943); KNICKERBOCKER HOLIDAY(1944); STORM OVER LISBON(1944); THEY LIVE IN FEAR(1944); EXPOSED(1938); HOUSEMASTER(1938, Brit.); ALLOTMENT WIVES, INC.(1945); CHICAGO KID, THE(1945); EARL CARROLL'S VANITIES(1945); ESCAPE IN THE FOG(1945); GREAT JOHN L. THE(1945); JUNGLE CAPTIVE(1945); MURDER, MY SWEET(1945); ON STAGE EVERYBODY(1945); WOMAN WHO CAME BACK(1945); WONDER MAN(1945); DUEL IN THE SUN(1946); FABULOUS SUZANNE, THE(1946); LOVE AND LEARN(1947); LULU BELLE(1948); SMART WOMAN(1948); 711 OCEAN DRIVE(1950); PAYMENT ON DEMAND(1951); VALENTINO(1951); HIGH NOON(1952); BLACK WIDOW(1954); MAGNIFICENT OBSESSION(1954); LAST COMMAND, THE(1955); COLOSSUS OF NEW YORK, THE(1958); YOUNG PHILADELPHIANS, THE(1959); CASH McCALL(1960); WONDERFUL WORLD OF THE BROTHERS ERIMM, THE(1962); SEX AND THE SINGLE GIRL(1964)
Silents
UNDER THE RED ROBE(1923)
Paul Kruger
IDLE RICH, THE(1929); HELLO, EVERYBODY(1933); PURSUIT OF HAPPINESS, THE(1934); FOLIES DERGERE(1935); KLONDIKE ANNIE(1936); PRINCESS COMES ACROSS, THE(1936); ROSE BOWL(1936); HIGH, WIDE AND HANDSOME(1937); MOUNTAIN MUSIC(1937); MEN WITH WINGS(1938); SHOPWORN ANGEL(1938); HOTEL IMPERIAL(1939); OUR LEADING CITIZEN(1939); TEXAS RANGERS RIDE AGAIN(1940); WOMEN WITHOUT NAMES(1940); CASTLE IN THE DESERT(1942); THEY DIED WITH THEIR BOOTS ON(1942); TAMPICO(1944); COLONEL EFFINGHAM'S RAID(1945); THEY WERE EXPENDABLE(1945); RENDEZVOUS 24(1946); SUSPENSE(1946); TWO SMART PEOPLE(1946); HIGH BARBAREE(1947); HIGH WALL(1947); CANON CITY(1948); MALAYA(1950); UNKNOWN MAN, THE(1951); DREAMBOAT(1952); FARMER TAKES A WIFE, THE(1953); MISSISSIPPI GAMBLER, THE(1953); VICKI(1953); BROKEN LANCE(1954); DEMETRIUS AND THE GLADIATORS(1954); GIANT(1956)
Silents
FORTUNE HUNTER, THE(1927)
Richard Kruger
SNOW WHITE AND ROSE RED(1966, Ger.)
Stubby Kruger
BROADWAY BIG SHOT(1942); DUKE OF THE NAVY(1942); THEY WERE EXPENDABLE(1945); TILL THE END OF TIME(1946); MISTER ROBERTS(1955); SPARTACUS(1960)
Werner Kruger
RUMPELSTILTSKIN(1965, Ger.)
Wilhelm P. Kruger
FOUR COMPANIONS, THE(1938, Ger.)
Kruger and Fossard
ANNE-MARIE(1936, Fr.), ph
Kruger-Ulrich
PILLARS OF SOCIETY(1936, Ger.), p
Lou Krugg
MANCHURIAN CANDIDATE, THE(1962)
Lea Krugher
BLOOD AND BLACK LACE(1965, Ital.)
L. Kruglyy
LULLABY(1961, USSR); SANDU FOLLOWS THE SUN(1965, USSR)
Lou Krugman
TO THE ENDS OF THE EARTH(1948); WHERE THE SIDEWALK ENDS(1950); HINDU, THE(1953, Brit.); RAINS OF RANCHIPUR, THE(1955); MAN WHO KNEW TOO MUCH, THE(1956); HONG KONG CONFIDENTIAL(1958); I WANT TO LIVE!(1958); PURPLE GANG, THE(1960); IRMA LA DOUCE(1963); ISLAND OF LOVE(1963); MIGHTY JUNGLE, THE(1965, U.S./Mex.)
Saul Krugman
CRAZY MAMA(1975); CANNONBALL(1976, U.S./Hong Kong); FAST CHARLIE... THE MOONBEAM RIDER(1979), p
Saul J. Krugman
ALL-AMERICAN BOY, THE(1973), p
Nikolai Kruichkov
LAD FROM OUR TOWN(1941, USSR); LAST HILL, THE(1945, USSR)
John C. Kruize
1984
NIGHT SHADOWS(1984), w
Nichola Krujac
TERROR IN THE JUNGLE(1968)
E. Kruk
BORDER STREET(1950, Pol.)

Reiko Kruk
NOSFERATU, THE VAMPIRE(1979, Fr./Ger.), makeup
1984
PERILS OF GWENDOLINE, THE(1984, Fr.), makeup
Hans Krull
RESTLESS NIGHT, THE(1964, Ger.)
Ester Krumbachova
DAISIES(1967, Czech.), w; DIAMONDS OF THE NIGHT(1968, Czech.), cos; FIFTH HORSEMAN IS FEAR, THE(1968, Czech.), w; MARTYRS OF LOVE(1968, Czech.), w; REPORT ON THE PARTY AND THE GUESTS, A(1968, Czech.), w, cos
Sergio Krumbel
ANTONY AND CLEOPATRA(1973, Brit.)
Eugene Krumenacker
TAPS(1981)
Joseph Krumgold
BLACKMAILER(1936), w; LADY FROM NOWHERE(1936), w; LONE WOLF RE-TURNS, THE(1936), w; JIM HANVEY, DETECTIVE(1937), w; JOIN THE MARI-NES(1937), w; LADY BEHAVE(1937), w; MAIN STREET LAWYER(1939), w; CROOKED ROAD, THE(1940), w; PHANTOM SUBMARINE, THE(1941), w; SEVEN MILES FROM ALCATRAZ(1942), w; MAGIC TOWN(1947), w; DREAM NO MO-RE(1950, Palestine), p, d&w; AND NOW MIGUEL(1966), w
Sigmund Krumgold
FIGHTING CARAVANS(1931), m; OUR NEIGHBORS–THE CARTERS(1939), md; UNION PACIFIC(1939), m; GOLDEN GLOVES(1940), md; LADY EVE, THE(1941), md; MONSTER AND THE GIRL, THE(1941), m; ONE NIGHT IN LISBON(1941), md; SULLIVAN'S TRAVELS(1941), md; HAIL THE CONQUERING HERO(1944), md
Paul Albert Krumm
JONATHAN(1973, Ger.)
Walter Krumm
BLACK SPIDER, THE(1983, Swit.)
Herman Krumpfel
FINGER POINTS, THE(1931)
Eberhard Krumschmidt
NOTORIOUS(1946)
Mara Krup
FOR A FEW DOLLARS MORE(1967, Ital./Ger./Span.)
Gene Krupa
SOME LIKE IT HOT(1939); SYNCOPATION(1942); GLAMOUR GIRL(1947); MAKE BELIEVE BALLROOM(1949); GLENN MILLER STORY, THE(1953); BENNY GOOD-MAN STORY, THE(1956)
Peter Krupenin
FACE TO FACE(1976, Swed.), set d
Eliska Krupka
PENNIES FROM HEAVEN(1981)
Jack Krupnick
KILLING OF A CHINESE BOOKIE, THE(1976); HOW TO BEAT THE HIGH COST OF LIVING(1980)
Eric Krupnik
PUTNEY SWOPE(1969)
Erick Krupnik
YOU'VE GOT TO WALK IT LIKE YOU TALK IT OR YOU'LL LOSE THAT BEAT(1971)
S. Krupnik
DREAM COME TRUE, A(1963, USSR)
Mitsuko Krusabue
THIN LINE, THE(1967, Jap.)
Carl Krusada
BAR L RANCH(1930), w; FIREBRAND JORDAN(1930), w; PHANTOM OF THE DESERT(1930), w; RIDIN' LAW(1930), w; WESTWARD BOUND(1931), w; FIGHTING HERO(1934), w; COYOTE TRAILS(1935), w; FAST BULLETS(1936), w; SANTA FE BOUND(1937), w; SKULL AND CROWN(1938), w; EL DIABLO RIDES(1939), w; FEUD OF THE RANGE(1939), w; PAL FROM TEXAS, THE(1939), w; KID FROM SANTA FE, THE(1940), w; PINTO CANYON(1940), w; RIDERS FROM NO-WHERE(1940), w; WILD HORSE VALLEY(1940), w
Silents
KING OF THE SADDLE(1926), w; VALLEY OF BRAVERY, THE(1926), w; BEAUTY AND BULLETS(1928), w; GATE CRASHER, THE(1928), w; EYES OF THE UNDER-WORLD(1929), w; PHANTOM OF THE NORTH(1929), w
Jack Kruschen
RED, HOT AND BLUE(1949); GAMBLING HOUSE(1950); NO WAY OUT(1950); WHERE DANGER LIVES(1950); WOMAN FROM HEADQUARTERS(1950); YOUNG MAN WITH A HORN(1950); COMIN' ROUND THE MOUNTAIN(1951); CUBAN FIREBALL(1951); PEOPLE AGAINST O'HARA, THE(1951); CONFIDENCE GIRL(1952); MEET DANNY WILSON(1952); TROPICAL HEAT WAVE(1952); ABBOTT AND COSTELLO GO TO MARS(1953); BLUEPRINT FOR MURDER, A(1953); FAST COMPANY(1953); MA AND PA KETTLE ON VACATION(1953); MONEY FROM HOME(1953); WAR OF THE WORLDS, THE(1953); IT SHOULD HAPPEN TO YOU(1954); LONG, LONG TRAILER, THE(1954); TENNESSEE CHAMP(1954); UN-TAMED HEIRESS(1954); CAROLINA CANNONBALL(1955); DIAL RED O(1955); NIGHT HOLDS TERROR, THE(1955); SOLDIER OF FORTUNE(1955); JULIE(1956); OUTSIDE THE LAW(1956); STEEL JUNGLE, THE(1956); BADLANDS OF MON-TANA(1957); REFORM SCHOOL GIRL(1957); CRY TERROR(1958); DECKS RAN RED, THE(1958); FRAULEIN(1958); ANGRY RED PLANET, THE(1960); APARTMENT, THE(1960); LAST VOYAGE, THE(1960); SEVEN WAYS FROM SUNDOWN(1960); STUDS LONIGAN(1960); LADIES MAN, THE(1961); LOVER COME BACK(1961); CAPE FEAR(1962); CONVICTS FOUR(1962); FOLLOW THAT DREAM(1962); MC LINTOCK!(1963); UNSINKABLE MOLLY BROWN, THE(1964); DEAR BRIGET-TE(1965); HARLOW(1965); CAPRICE(1967); HAPPENING, THE(1967); $1,000,000 DUCK(1971); FREEBIE AND THE BEAN(1974); GUARDIAN OF THE WILDER-NESS(1977); SATAN'S CHEERLEADERS(1977); SUNBURN(1979); UNDER THE RAINBOW(1981)
Misc. Talkies
LEGEND OF THE WILD(1981); MONEY TO BURN(1981)
Dick Kruse
SILENT WITNESS, THE(1962)
Hans Kruse
RETURN TO PARADISE(1953); PACIFIC DESTINY(1956, Brit.)

J. Henry Kruse
FIGHTING HERO(1934), ph
John Kruse
HELL DRIVERS(1958, Brit.), w; SEA FURY(1959, Brit.), w; OCTOBER MOTH(1960, Brit.), d&w; ECHO OF BARBARA(1961, Brit.), w; CROSSPLOT(1969, Brit.), w; AS-SAULT(1971, Brit.), w; TERROR FROM UNDER THE HOUSE(1971, Brit.), w
Lottie Kruse [Cruze]
Misc. Silents
GIRL ALASKA, THE(1919)
R. Wayne Kruse
ESCAPE ARTIST, THE(1982)
Robert Kruse
92 IN THE SHADE(1975, U.S./Brit.)
Olive Krushat
G.I. JANE(1951)
N. Krychitov
IMMORTAL GARRISON, THE(1957, USSR)
Barbara Kryczmonik
WALKOVER(1969, Pol.), ed
Johnny Krykamp
LUCKY STAR, THE(1980, Can.)
Alik Krylov
CLEAR SKIES(1963, USSR)
S. Krylov
MY NAME IS IVAN(1963, USSR); PEACE TO HIM WHO ENTERS(1963, USSR); RESURRECTION(1963, USSR)
Pyotr Krymov
LADY WITH THE DOG, THE(1962, USSR)
Maria Kryshanovskia
Misc. Silents
CRIME AND PUNISHMENT(1929, Ger.)
N. Kryuchkov
BOUNTIFUL SUMMER(1951, USSR); MAGIC VOYAGE OF SINBAD, THE(1962, USSR)
Nikolay Kryuchkov
MARRIAGE OF BALZAMINOV, THE(1966, USSR); THERE WAS AN OLD COU-PLE(1967, USSR)
Yu. Kryuchkov
WAR AND PEACE(1968, USSR)
Igor Kryukov
WELCOME KOSTYA!(1965, USSR)
Nikolai Kryukov
DAYS AND NIGHTS(1946, USSR), m
Nikolay Kryukov
LETTER THAT WAS NEVER SENT, THE(1962, USSR), m
Eva Krzyzewska
ASHES AND DIAMONDS(1961, Pol.)
Eva Krzyzewski
RAT(1960, Yugo.)
Peter Ksiezopolski
LORD OF THE FLIES(1963, Brit.)
Anatoli Ktorov
Misc. Silents
BROKEN CHAINS(1925, USSR)
Anatoliy Ktorov
WAR AND PEACE(1968, USSR)
Pong-su Ku
MARINE BATTLEGROUND(1966, U.S/S.K.)
Li Kuan
VERMILION DOOR(1969, Hong Kong)
Polly Shang Kuan
Misc. Talkies
RETURN OF 18 BRONZEMEN(1984)
I. Kuang
TRIPLE IRONS(1973, Hong Kong), w; FLYING GUILLOTINE, THE(1975, Chi.), w
Chiang Kuang-chao
LAST WOMAN OF SHANG, THE(1964, Hong Kong); LOVE ETERNE, THE(1964, Hong Kong); LADY GENERAL, THE(1965, Hong Kong); SHEPHERD GIRL, THE(1965, Hong Kong); FEMALE PRINCE, THE(1966, Hong Kong); MERMAID, THE(1966, Hong Kong); VERMILION DOOR(1969, Hong Kong)
Reiko Kuba
SAYONARA(1957)
August Kuban
DESERTER AND THE NOMADS, THE(1969, Czech./Ital.)
Ilse Kubaschewski
DAS LETZTE GEHEIMNIS(1959, Ger.), p
Josef Kubat
DIAMONDS OF THE NIGHT(1968, Czech.)
Anatoliy Kubatskiy
NIGHT BEFORE CHRISTMAS, A(1963, USSR); MAGIC WEAVER, THE(1965, USSR); JACK FROST(1966, USSR)
Karen Kubeck
SATAN'S MISTRESS(1982), spec eff, makeup
Peggy Kubena
TABLE FOR FIVE(1983)
Hana Kuberova
FIREMAN'S BALL, THE(1968, Czech.)
Cheryl Kubert
PAL JOEY(1957)
Hans-Karl Kubiak
RED-DRAGON(1967, Ital./Ger./US), w
Thomas Kubiak
COLD RIVER(1982)
Tom Kubiak
1984
LONELY GUY, THE(1984)
Alex Kubik
SECOND THOUGHTS(1983)

Gail Kubik
C-MAN(1949), m; TWO GALS AND A GUY(1951), m; DESPERATE HOURS, THE(1955), m

Lawrence Kubik
ZACHARIAH(1971), a, p

Kubin
DREAM TOWN(1973, Ger.), d&w

Yvonne Kubis
CHOIRBOYS, THE(1977), cos; COMA(1978), cos; TIME AFTER TIME(1979, Brit.), cos

Marta Kubisova
MARTYRS OF LOVE(1968, Czech.)

S. Kubitzky
ESCAPE TO BERLIN(1962, U.S./Switz./Ger.)

Tom Kubjak
ROMANTIC COMEDY(1983)

Ursula Kubler
VERY PRIVATE AFFAIR, A(1962, Fr./Ital.); LOVE ON A PILLOW(1963, Fr./Ital.); FIRE WITHIN, THE(1964, Fr./Ital.); LES CREATURES(1969, Fr./Swed.)

Akira Kubo
THRONE OF BLOOD(1961, Jap.); WESTWARD DESPERADO(1961, Jap.); SANJURO(1962, Jap.); ATTACK OF THE MUSHROOM PEOPLE(1964, Jap.); THREE DOLLS FROM HONG KONG(1966, Jap.); SON OF GODZILLA(1967, Jap.); KILL(1968, Jap.); DESTROY ALL MONSTERS(1969, Jap.); MONSTER ZERO(1970, Jap.); SPACE AMOEBA, THE(1970, Jap.); YOG-MONSTER FROM SPACE(1970, Jap.)

Akiyo Kubo
SPOILS OF THE NIGHT(1969, Jap.)

Guy Kubo
LAST UNICORN, THE(1982), anim

Keinosuke Kubo
LAKE, THE(1970, Jap.), p

Ikuro Kubokawa
ZATOICHI(1968, Jap.), p

Elizabeth Kubota
1984
BEST DEFENSE(1984)

Reiji Kubota
GANGSTER VIP, THE(1968, Jap.), w

Takayuki Kubota
MECHANIC, THE(1972)

Ruth Sobotka Kubrick
KILLING, THE(1956), art d

Stanley Kubrick
FEAR AND DESIRE(1953), p&d, w, ph, ed; KILLER'S KISS(1955), p, d, w, ph, ed; KILLING, THE(1956), d, w; PATHS OF GLORY(1957), d, w; SPARTACUS(1960), d; LOLITA(1962), d; DR. STRANGELOVE: OR HOW I LEARNED TO STOP WORRYING AND LOVE THE BOMB(1964), p&d, w; 2001: A SPACE ODYSSEY(1968, U.S./Brit.), p&d, w, spec eff; CLOCKWORK ORANGE, A(1971, Brit.), p,d&w; BARRY LYNDON(1975, Brit.), p, d, w; SHINING, THE(1980), p&d, w

Vivian Kubrick
2001: A SPACE ODYSSEY(1968, U.S./Brit.)

Bernard Kuby
1984
IMPULSE(1984); KARATE KID, THE(1984)
Misc. Talkies
DEATH JOURNEY(1976)

Bernie Kuby
NEW YORK, NEW YORK(1977); FURY, THE(1978); HOUSE CALLS(1978); SAME TIME, NEXT YEAR(1978); PROMISES IN THE DARK(1979)

Erich Kuby
ROSEMARY(1960, Ger.), w

Jaroslav Kuccra
ADELE HASN'T HAD HER SUPPER YET(1978, Czech.), ph

Jaroslav Kucera
DAISIES(1967, Czech.), ph; DIAMONDS OF THE NIGHT(1968, Czech.), ph

George Kuchar
UNSTRAP ME(1968), d&w
Misc. Talkies
CORRUPTION OF THE DAMNED(1965), d

Jarmila Kucharova
FIREMAN'S BALL, THE(1968, Czech.)

V. Kuchinsky
MOSCOW DOES NOT BELIEVE IN TEARS(1980, USSR), p

Erich Kuchler
LOVE FEAST, THE(1966, Ger.), ph

M. Kuchynsky
Silents
ARSENAL(1929, USSR)

Wolfgang Kuck
NOT RECONCILED, OR "ONLY VIOLENCE HELPS WHERE IT RULES"(1969, Ger.)

Gertrude Kuckelman
HOUSE OF LIFE(1953, Ger.)

Gertrud Kuckelmann
GOLDEN PLAGUE, THE(1963, Ger.)

Sabine Kuckelmann
PARSIFAL(1983, Fr.)

Z. Kucowna
GREAT BIG WORLD AND LITTLE CHILDREN, THE(1962, Pol.)

Peter Kuczka
WINDOWS OF TIME, THE(1969, Hung.), w

Jay M. Kude
FLESH MERCHANT, THE(1956), w

Naboro Kudisahi
KARATE, THE HAND OF DEATH(1961)

I. Kudriatsev
CONCENTRATION CAMP(1939, USSR)

I. Kudriavtsev
ON HIS OWN(1939, USSR)

Ye. Kudryashov
DAY THE WAR ENDED, THE(1961, USSR); DESTINY OF A MAN(1961, USSR); SUMMER TO REMEMBER, A(1961, USSR)

Gertrud Kueckelmann
DANCING HEART, THE(1959, Ger.)

Bill Kuehl
BEN HUR(1959)

Will L. Kuehl
DRUM BEAT(1954), set d

William Kuehl
DARK PASSAGE(1947), set d; VOICE OF THE TURTLE, THE(1947), set d; FOUNTAINHEAD, THE(1949), set d; GIRL FROM JONES BEACH, THE(1949), set d; JOHN LOVES MARY(1949), set d; ENFORCER, THE(1951), set d; WINNING TEAM, THE(1952), set d; COURT-MARTIAL OF BILLY MITCHELL, THE(1955), set d; PAJAMA GAME, THE(1957), set d; LEFT-HANDED GUN, THE(1958), set d; MRS. POLLIFAX-SPY(1971), set d; STEAGLE, THE(1971), set d

William H. Kuehl
LAD: A DOG(1962), set d; CHAMBER OF HORRORS(1966), set d

William L. Kuehl
DAMNED DON'T CRY, THE(1950), set d; COME FILL THE CUP(1951), set d; ROOM FOR ONE MORE(1952), set d; I DIED A THOUSAND TIMES(1955), set d; MISTER ROBERTS(1955), set d; WRONG MAN, THE(1956), art d; SPIRIT OF ST. LOUIS, THE(1957), set d; NAKED AND THE DEAD, THE(1958), set d; PARRISH(1961), set d; SUSAN SLADE(1961), set d; COUCH, THE(1962), set d; CRITIC'S CHOICE(1963), set d; INCREDIBLE MR. LIMPET, THE(1964), set d; MAN FROM GALVESTON, THE(1964), set d; MARRIAGE ON THE ROCKS(1965), set d; FINIAN'S RAINBOW(1968), set d; FIRECREEK(1968), set d; MORE DEAD THAN ALIVE(1968), set d; GREAT BANK ROBBERY, THE(1969), set d; OMEGA MAN, THE(1971), set d

William T. Kuehl
OPERATION SECRET(1952), set d

Andrew J. Kuehn
Misc. Talkies
FLUSH(1981, Brit.), d

Jurgen Kuehn
ZELIG(1983)

Jan Kuehnemund
1984
HARDBODIES(1984)

Paul Kuek
CLINIC, THE(1983, Aus.)

Gertrud Kuekelmann
LIFE AND LOVES OF MOZART, THE(1959, Ger.)

Eduard Kuenecke
RENDEZ-VOUS(1932, Ger.), m

Dan Kuenster
SECRET OF NIMH, THE(1982), anim

Charles Kuenstle
DEATH OF A GUNFIGHTER(1969)

Frank Kuenstler
GUNS OF THE TREES(1964)

Yoshiko Kuga
SECRET SCROLLS(PART I)**1/2 (1968, Jap.); WOMEN IN PRISON(1957, Jap.); NAKED YOUTH(1961, Jap.); OHAYO(1962, Jap.); IDIOT, THE(1963, Jap.); WHIRLWIND(1968, Jap.); DAREDEVIL IN THE CASTLE(1969, Jap.); THROUGH DAYS AND MONTHS(1969 Jap.)

J. Alvin Kugelmass
TWO-HEADED SPY, THE(1959, Brit.), w

Anton Kuh
ROBBER SYMPHONY, THE(1937, Brit.), w

James Randolph Kuhl
HAPPENING, THE(1967)

Johnny Kuhl
Misc. Talkies
RED ROSES OF PASSION(1967)

William Kuhl
WE'VE NEVER BEEN LICKED(1943)

Walter Kuhle
Silents
METROPOLIS(1927, Ger.)

Brigitte Kuhlenthal
OUR HITLER, A FILM FROM GERMANY(1980, Ger.), cos

Fred Kuhler, Jr.
BARON OF ARIZONA, THE(1950)

Ron Kuhlman
TO BE OR NOT TO BE(1983)
1984
SPLASH(1984)

Wolfgang Kuhlman
$(DOLLARS)**1/2 (1971)

Carl Kuhlmann
LA HABANERA(1937, Ger.)

Harald Kuhlmann
LOST HONOR OF KATHARINA BLUM, THE(1975, Ger.)

Allan Dale Kuhn
MURPH THE SURF(1974), w

Andre Kuhn
I HATE MY BODY(1975, Span./Switz.), p

David W. Kuhn
1984
BIRDY(1984)

George Kuhn
DELINQUENTS, THE(1957); MARRIAGE OF MARIA BRAUN, THE(1979, Ger.), cos

Gil Kuhn
ROSE BOWL(1936)

Grace Kuhn
THREE STOOGES GO AROUND THE WORLD IN A DAZE, THE(1963), cos; ONE MAN'S WAY(1964), cos

Gus Kuhn
BRITANNIA OF BILLINGSGATE(1933, Brit.)
Hans Kuhn
DIVIDED HEART, THE(1955, Brit.)
Henri Kuhn
UP FROM THE BEACH(1965)
Irene Kuhn
MASK OF FU MANCHU, THE(1932), w
James A. Kuhn
TOM SAWYER(1973)
Kevin P. Kuhn
1984
BIRDY(1984)
Michael Kuhn
ON THE LOOSE(1951); HOUSE ON SORORITY ROW, THE(1983)
Mickey Kuhn
GONE WITH THE WIND(1939); JUAREZ(1939); S.O.S. TIDAL WAVE(1939); WHEN TOMORROW COMES(1939); I WANT A DIVORCE(1940); ROUGHLY SPEAKING(1945); THIS LOVE OF OURS(1945); TREE GROWS IN BROOKLYN, A(1945); SEARCHING WIND, THE(1946); STRANGE LOVE OF MARTHA IVERS, THE(1946); HIGH CONQUEST(1947); MAGIC TOWN(1947); RED RIVER(1948); SCENE OF THE CRIME(1949); STREETCAR NAMED DESIRE, A(1951); LAST FRONTIER, THE(1955)
Micky Kuhn
DICK TRACY(1945); BROKEN ARROW(1950)
Richard Kuhn
MC LINTOCK!(1963), prod d
Erik Kuhnau
WEEKEND(1964, Den.)
David Kuhne
DIABOLICAL DR. Z, THE(1966 Span./Fr.), w
Friedrich Kuhne
Misc. Silents
HOUND OF THE BASKERVILLES, THE(1914, Ger.); DARK CASTLE, THE(1915)
Stacey Kuhne
MAKING LOVE(1982)
Wolfgang Kuhne
WOZZECK(1962, E. Ger.)
Wolfgang Kuhnemann
DECISION BEFORE DAWN(1951)
John Kuhner
Misc. Talkies
BARBARA(1970)
Hanns Kuhnert
NIGHT PEOPLE(1954), art d; HELDINNEN(1962, Ger.), art d; WORLD IN MY POCKET, THE(1962, Fr./Ital./Ger.), art d
Leopold Kuhnert
MIRACLE OF THE WHITE STALLIONS(1963), makeup
Wolfgang Kuhnlenz
LAST OF THE RENEGADES(1966, Fr./Ital./Ger./Yugo.), p; BLOOD DEMON(1967, Ger.), p
Kukhie Kuhns
ROAD TO BALI(1952)
Gerd Kuhr
1984
SWANN IN LOVE(1984, Fr.Ger.), m
Peter Kuiper
WILLY(1963, U.S./Ger.); SECRET OF SANTA VITTORIA, THE(1969)
John Kuipers
SOMETHING'S ROTTEN(1979, Can.), m
F N. Kuirkhin
COUNTRY BRIDE(1938, USSR)
Asami Kuji
STAR OF HONG KONG(1962, Jap.)
Eiko Kujo
YOUTH IN FURY(1961, Jap.)
Sasha Kukareko
GORDEYEV FAMILY, THE(1961, U.S.S.R.)
Radovan Kukavsky
GIRL WITH THREE CAMELS, THE(1968, Czech.)
Kh. Kukels
TSAR'S BRIDE, THE(1966, USSR), ph
Lev Kuklin
THEY CALL ME ROBERT(1967, USSR), w
Bernie Kukoff
1984
JOHNNY DANGEROUSLY(1984), w
Michale Kukulewich
RIP-OFF(1971, Can.)
George Kukura
DIVINE EMMA, THE(1983, Czech,)
Juraj Kukura
NINTH HEART, THE(1980, Czech.)
Sergey Kulagin
UNCOMMON THIEF, AN(1967, USSR)
Derek Kulai
DAY THE FISH CAME OUT, THE(1967. Brit./Gr.)
V. Kulakov
CITY OF YOUTH(1938, USSR); RESURRECTION(1963, USSR)
Vassily Kulakov
THIRTEEN, THE(1937, USSR)
Chester Kulas, Jr.
DEADLY BLESSING(1981)
Peter Kulas
LOOKIN' TO GET OUT(1982)
Karl Georg Kulb
LONG IS THE ROAD(1948, Ger.), w
Andrew Kulberg
CARDIAC ARREST(1980), m

Nikolai Kulchitsky
SKY CALLS, THE(1959, USSR), ph
Michael Kulcsar
MEGAFORCE(1982)
Mike Kulcsar
HERBIE GOES TO MONTE CARLO(1977); RAISE THE TITANIC(1980, Brit.)
Boris Kuleshov
Misc. Silents
ENGINEER PRITE'S PROJECT(1918, USSR)
Lev Kuleshov
Misc. Silents
ENGINEER PRITE'S PROJECT(1918, USSR), d; EXTRAORDINARY ADVENTURES OF MR. WEST IN THE LAND OF THE BOLSHEVIKS(1924, USSR), d; DEATH RAY, THE(1925, USSR), d; BY THE LAW(1926, USSR), d; YOUR ACQUAINTANCE(1927, USSR), d
Ernest Kulganin
Misc. Silents
ENGINEER PRITE'S PROJECT(1918, USSR)
Stefan Kulhanek
DIE FLEDERMAUS(1964, Aust.), makeup
Bob Kulic
OPERATION DAYBREAK(1976, U.S./Brit./Czech.), art d
Bohuslav Kulic
90 DEGREES IN THE SHADE(1966, Czech./Brit.), art d; DEATH OF TARZAN, THE(1968, Czech), art d
Eleanore Kulicek
LONE CLIMBER, THE(1950, Brit./Aust.)
Barry Kulick
SITTING TARGET(1972, Brit.), p
J. Barry Kulick
TWO GENTLEMEN SHARING(1969, Brit.), p
Lev Kulidzhanov
HOME FOR TANYA, A(1961, USSR), d; WHEN THE TREES WERE TALL(1965, USSR), p&d
Andrei Kuliev
THIRTEEN, THE(1937, USSR)
Lev Kulijanov
CRIME AND PUNISHMENT(1975, USSR), d&w
Buzz Kulik
EXPLOSIVE GENERATION, THE(1961), d; YELLOW CANARY, THE(1963), d; READY FOR THE PEOPLE(1964), d; WARNING SHOT(1967), p, d; SERGEANT RYKER(1968), d; VILLA RIDES(1968), d; RIOT(1969), d; TO FIND A MAN(1972), d; SHAMUS(1973), d; HUNTER, THE(1980), d
Jeni Kulik
BAT PEOPLE, THE(1974)
V. Kulik
QUEEN OF SPADES(1961, USSR); TRAIN GOES TO KIEV, THE(1961, USSR); DUEL, THE(1964, USSR); SANDU FOLLOWS THE SUN(1965, USSR); FATHER OF A SOLDIER(1966, USSR); GARNET BRACELET, THE(1966, USSR)
G. Kulikov
CLEAR SKIES(1963, USSR)
Marton Kulinyi
WINTER WIND(1970, Fr./Hung.)
Juni Kulis
NIGHT OF THE ZOMBIES(1981)
Henry "Bomber Kulkavich" Kulky
ALIAS THE CHAMP(1949); MIGHTY JOE YOUNG(1949); JIGGS AND MAGGIE OUT WEST(1950); SIERRA STRANGER(1957)
Henry Kulky
LIKELY STORY, A(1947); NORTHWEST OUTPOST(1947); CALL NORTHSIDE 777(1948); RED DANUBE, THE(1949); TAKE ME OUT TO THE BALL GAME(1949); TARZAN'S MAGIC FOUNTAIN(1949); BODYHOLD(1950); SOUTH SEA SINNER(1950); WABASH AVENUE(1950); BANDITS OF EL DORADO(1951); FIXED BAYONETS(1951); FORCE OF ARMS(1951); GUY WHO CAME BACK, THE(1951); KID FROM AMARILLO, THE(1951); LOVE NEST(1951); YOU NEVER CAN TELL(1951); GOBS AND GALS(1952); MY WIFE'S BEST FRIEND(1952); NO HOLDS BARRED(1952); RED SKIES OF MONTANA(1952); TARGET HONG KONG(1952); WHAT PRICE GLORY?(1952); WORLD IN HIS ARMS, THE(1952); CHARGE AT FEATHER RIVER, THE(1953); CLIPPED WINGS(1953); DOWN AMONG THE SHELTERING PALMS(1953); GLORY BRIGADE, THE(1953); LION IS IN THE STREETS, A(1953); POWDER RIVER(1953); 5,000 FINGERS OF DR. T. THE(1953); FIREMAN SAVE MY CHILD(1954); HELL AND HIGH WATER(1954); PHANTOM OF THE RUE MORGUE(1954); STAR IS BORN, A(1954); STEEL CAGE, THE(1954); TOBOR THE GREAT(1954); YUKON VENGEANCE(1954); ABBOTT AND COSTELLO MEET THE KEYSTONE KOPS(1955); GIRL IN THE RED VELVET SWING, THE(1955); I'LL CRY TOMORROW(1955); ILLEGAL(1955); JAIL BUSTERS(1955); LOVE ME OR LEAVE ME(1955); NEW YORK CONFIDENTIAL(1955); PRINCE OF PLAYERS(1955); TO HELL AND BACK(1955); GUNFIGHT AT DODGE CITY, THE(1959); UP PERISCOPE(1959); GUNS OF THE TIMBERLAND(1960); ALL FALL DOWN(1962); GLOBAL AFFAIR, A(1964)
Adolph Edward Kull
WIFE OF MONTE CRISTO, THE(1946), ph
Ed Kull
FEROCIOUS PAL(1934), ph
Eddie Kull
EL DIABLO RIDES(1939), ph; RODEO RHYTHM(1941), ph
Edmund Kull
PORT OF HATE(1939), ph
Edward Kull
CYCLONE KID(1931), ph; HEADIN' FOR TROUBLE(1931), ph; FIGHTING GENTLEMAN, THE(1932), ph; FORTY-NINERS, THE(1932), ph; HUMAN TARGETS(1932), ph; MAN FROM NEW MEXICO, THE(1932), ph; SCARLET BRAND(1932), ph; SO IT'S SUNDAY(1932), ph; CARNIVAL LADY(1933), ph; DEADWOOD PASS(1933), ph; HIGH GEAR(1933), ph; PENAL CODE, THE(1933), ph; WAR OF THE RANGE(1933), ph; WHEN A MAN RIDES ALONE(1933), ph; MARRIAGE ON APPROVAL(1934), ph; NEW ADVENTURES OF TARZAN(1935), d, ph; TUNDRA(1936), ph; TARZAN AND THE GREEN GODDESS(1938), d, ph; MESQUITE BUCKAROO(1939), ph; SMOKY TRAILS(1939), ph; CHEYENNE KID, THE(1940), ph; COVERED WAGON TRAILS(1940), ph; BLACK MARKET RUSTLERS(1943), ph; COWBOY COMMANDOS(1943), ph; ARIZONA WHIRLWIND(1944), ph; DEATH

VALLEY RANGERS(1944), ph; GUNS OF THE LAW(1944), ph; OUTLAW TRAIL(1944), ph; PINTO BANDIT, THE(1944), ph; SONORA STAGECOACH(1944), ph; WHISPERING SKULL, THE(1944), ph; MARKED FOR MURDER(1945), ph; WHITE STALLION(1947), ph; ARCTIC FURY(1949), ph
Misc. Talkies
MAN'S BEST FRIEND(1935), d
Silents
BULLDOG COURAGE(1922), d; MAKING THE VARSITY(1928), ph; MANHATTAN KNIGHTS(1928), ph
Misc. Silents
POINTING FINGER, THE(1919), d; MAN TRACKERS, THE(1921), d; BARRIERS OF FOLLY(1922), d
Edward A. Kull
KID FROM SANTA FE, THE(1940), ph; LAND OF THE SIX GUNS(1940), ph; PIONEER DAYS(1940), ph; RIDERS FROM NOWHERE(1940), ph
Silents
APACHE RAIDER, THE(1928), ph
Edward S. Kull
MURDER AT DAWN(1932), ph; OUT OF SINGAPORE(1932), ph; SAVAGE GIRL, THE(1932), ph
Jacob Kull
TUNDRA(1936), ph
Eivor Kullberg
SHAME(1968, Swed.)
Jari Kulle
SMILES OF A SUMMER NIGHT(1957, Swed.); DEVIL'S EYE, THE(1960, Swed.); SECRETS OF WOMEN(1961, Swed.); ALL THESE WOMEN(1964, Swed.); SWEDISH WEDDING NIGHT(1965, Swed.); DEAR JOHN(1966, Swed.); LOVE MATES(1967, Swed.); SHORT IS THE SUMMER(1968, Swed.); FANNY AND ALEXANDER(1983, Swed./Fr./Ger.)
Sid Kuller
ARGENTINE NIGHTS(1940), w; HIT PARADE OF 1941(1940), w; BIG STORE, THE(1941), w; SLAUGHTER TRAIL(1951), w
Sidney Kuller
LIFE BEGINS IN COLLEGE(1937), w
John Kullers
KISS OF DEATH(1947); TAXI(1953); HUSBANDS(1970)
John Red Kullers
KILLING OF A CHINESE BOOKIE, THE(1976)
John "Red" Kullers
HOUSE OF STRANGERS(1949); GOLDEN GLOVES STORY, THE(1950)
Charles Kullman
BOMBARDMENT OF MONTE CARLO, THE(1931, Ger.); SONG OF SCHEHERA-ZADE(1947)
Charles Kullmann
GOLDWYN FOLLIES, THE(1938)
Bernardo Kullock
TERRACE, THE(1964, Arg.)
Nancy Kulp
MODEL AND THE MARRIAGE BROKER, THE(1951); MARRYING KIND, THE(1952); STEEL TOWN(1952); HERE COME THE GIRLS(1953); SHANE(1953); SABRINA(1954); COUNT THREE AND PRAY(1955); FOREVER DARLING(1956); GOD IS MY PARTNER(1957); KISS THEM FOR ME(1957); SHOOT-OUT AT MEDICINE BEND(1957); THREE FACES OF EVE, THE(1957); FIVE GATES TO HELL(1959); LAST TIME I SAW ARCHIE, THE(1961); TWO LITTLE BEARS, THE(1961); MOON PILOT(1962); WHO'S MINDING THE STORE?(1963); PATSY, THE(1964); STRANGE BEDFELLOWS(1965); NIGHT OF THE GRIZZLY, THE(1966); ARISTOCATS, THE(1970)
Ethel Kulsar
FANTASIA(1940), art d
Will Kuluva
ABANDONED(1949); VIVA ZAPATA!(1952); OPERATION MANHUNT(1954); SHRIKE, THE(1955); CRIME IN THE STREETS(1956); ODDS AGAINST TOMORROW(1959); GO NAKED IN THE WORLD(1961); SPIRAL ROAD, THE(1962); SPY IN THE GREEN HAT, THE(1966); TO TRAP A SPY(1966); CHRISTINE JORGENSEN STORY, THE(1970)
Kristopher Kum
1984
PERILS OF GWENDOLINE, THE(1984, Fr.)
Kuma the Dog
SHE AND HE(1967, Jap.)
Ben Kumagai
PENNY SERENADE(1941)
Denice Kumagai
GO TELL THE SPARTANS(1978)
Frank Kumagai
TOKYO JOE(1949); CROSSWINDS(1951); HALLS OF MONTEZUMA(1951); SOUTH SEA WOMAN(1953); HUNTERS, THE(1958); TOKYO AFTER DARK(1959); FLOWER DRUM SONG(1961); WALK, DON'T RUN(1966)
Jiro Kumagai
SEVEN SAMURAI, THE(1956, Jap.)
Takeshi Kumagai
BARBARIAN AND THE GEISHA, THE(1958)
Frank Kumagi
PICKUP ON SOUTH STREET(1953)
Masao Kumagi
TOPSY-TURVY JOURNEY(1970, Jap.), art d; YOSAKOI JOURNEY(1970, Jap.), art d
Kei Kumai
TUNNEL TO THE SUN(1968, Jap.), d, w
Ndaniso Kumala
RHODES(1936, Brit.)
Alfred Kumalo
ELEPHANT GUN(1959, Brit.)
Y. Kumankov
MAGIC VOYAGE OF SINBAD, THE(1962, USSR), art d
Ananda Kumar
SANDOKAN THE GREAT(1964, Fr./Ital./Span.)

Asis Kumar
MUSIC ROOM, THE(1963, India), m
Hemanta Kumar
SIDDHARTHA(1972), m
Milena Kumar
CARMEN, BABY(1967, Yugo./Ger.), cos
Sanjeev Kumar
CHESS PLAYERS, THE(1978, India)
Sudarshan Kumar
KENNER(1969), ch
Roshan Kumari
MUSIC ROOM, THE(1963, India)
Kumatzaikuma
STRANGE WORLD(1952)
Antonin Kumbera
DIAMONDS OF THE NIGHT(1968, Czech.)
Harry Kumel
DAUGHTERS OF DARKNESS(1971, Bel./ Fr./ Ger./ Ital.), d, w; MALPERTIUS(1972, Bel./Fr.), d
L. Kumicheva
BRIDE WITH A DOWRY(1954, USSR)
John Kummel
DEATHCHEATERS(1976, Aus.)
Claire Kummer
HARMONY AT HOME(1930), w
Clare Kummer
PLEASURE CRAZED(1929), w; ANNABELLE'S AFFAIRS(1931), w; SUCCESSFUL CALAMITY, A(1932), w; HER MASTER'S VOICE(1936), w
Frederic Arnold Kummer
Silents
IVORY SNUFF BOX, THE(1915), w; TOWN SCANDAL, THE(1923), w
Frederick Arnold Kummer
Silents
SPITFIRE, THE(1924), w
Luitpold Kummer
DECISION BEFORE DAWN(1951)
Dave Kummins
PATTERNS(1956), ed
David Kummins
LOST BOUNDARIES(1949), ed; JOE LOUIS STORY, THE(1953), ed
Kumok
GOLEM, THE(1937, Czech./Fr.), m
Juhani Kumpulinen
MAKE LIKE A THIEF(1966, Fin.)
Toshie Kumura
SILENCE HAS NO WINGS(1971, Jap.)
Rudy Kumze
1984
DEATHSTALKER, THE(1984)
Li Kun
LOVE ETERNE, THE(1964, Hong Kong); LADY GENERAL, THE(1965, Hong Kong)
Lin Huang Kun
REVENGE OF THE SHOGUN WOMEN(1982, Taiwan), w
Magda Kun
DANCE BAND(1935, Brit.); OLD MOTHER RILEY IN PARIS(1938, Brit.); ROOM FOR TWO(1940, Brit.); OLD MOTHER RILEY OVERSEAS(1943, Brit.); HEAVEN IS ROUND THE CORNER(1944, Brit.); MEET SEXTON BLAKE(1944, Brit.); DEAD OF NIGHT(1946, Brit.)
Vilmos Kun
MEPHISTO(1981, Ger.)
Penny Kunard
PRIME TIME, THE(1960)
Al Kunde
MISSION TO MOSCOW(1943); ROSEANNA McCOY(1949); SANTA FE(1951); SOMETHING TO LIVE FOR(1952)
Ann Kunde
WOMAN'S WORLD(1954); FIRST TRAVELING SALESLADY, THE(1956); JUBAL(1956)
Anne Kunde
MADAME BOVARY(1949); FATHER OF THE BRIDE(1950); SCARLET COAT, THE(1955)
Anne M. Kunde
SOMETHING TO LIVE FOR(1952)
Al Kundee
GANGWAY FOR TOMORROW(1943)
Anne Kundee
GANGWAY FOR TOMORROW(1943)
Anne Kundi
HOLLYWOOD BARN DANCE(1947)
Frederic Kundtson
FIGHTING FATHER DUNNE(1948), ed
James Simon Kunen
STRAWBERRY STATEMENT, THE(1970), a, w
Dina Kunewa
KONA COAST(1968)
Eva Lee Kuney
PENNY SERENADE(1941); Hl BEAUTIFUL(1944)
Scott Kuney
KRAMER VS. KRAMER(1979)
Nan Kunghsun
DEADLY CHINA DOLL(1973, Hong Kong)
Keiko Kuni
YOUTH IN FURY(1961, Jap.)
Satoko Kuni
MY GEISHA(1962)
Takeo Kunihiro
I BOMBED PEARL HARBOR(1961, Jap.), w

Carl Kuniholm
DARK STAR(1975)
Howard Kunin
MAJOR DUNDEE(1965), ed; ROLLER BOOGIE(1979), ed; FADE TO BLACK(1980),
ed; CLASS OF 1984(1982, Can.), ed
Mash Kunitomi
NAVY WIFE(1956)
George Kunkel
Silents
BY THE WORLD FORGOT(1918); WHERE MEN ARE MEN(1921)
Misc. Silents
MAGNIFICENT MEDDLER, THE(1917); CHANGING WOMAN, THE(1918)
Robert Kunkel
Misc. Silents
BRAND, THE(1919)
Russ Kunkel
1984
THIS IS SPINAL TAP(1984)
Ilse Kunkele
CASTLE, THE(1969, Ger.); JONATHAN(1973, Ger.)
Zeliko Kunkera
TALL WOMEN, THE(1967, Aust./Ital./Span.), p
Evelyn Kunncki
FOX AND HIS FRIENDS(1976, Ger.)
Evelyn Kunneke
JUST A GIGOLO(1979, Ger.)
Narla Kunogh
JEDDA, THE UNCIVILIZED(1956, Aus.)
Doris Kunstmann
HITLER: THE LAST TEN DAYS(1973, Brit./Ital.)
Vera Kunstmann
FIRST SPACESHIP ON VENUS(1960, Ger./Pol.), spec eff
Jackie Kuntarich
JAWS 3-D(1983)
Carl Kuntze
RAIDERS OF LEYTE GULF(1963 U.S./Phil.), w
R. Kuntze
TREMENDOUSLY RICH MAN, A(1932, Ger.), ph
Reimar Kuntze
TRUNKS OF MR. O.F., THE(1932, Ger.), ph; PRIVATE LIFE OF LOUIS XIV(1936,
Ger.), ph; CARMEN(1949, Span.), ph
Reimer Kuntze
JAZZBAND FIVE, THE(1932, Ger,), ph
Reinhardt Kuntze
MY SONG GOES ROUND THE WORLD(1934, Brit.), ph
Erich Kunz
LIFE AND LOVES OF MOZART, THE(1959, Ger.); HOUSE OF THE THREE GIRLS,
THE(1961, Aust.)
Peter Kunz
NIGHT OF THE ZOMBIES(1981), spec eff; ECHOES(1983), spec eff
Eleonore Kunze
5 SINNERS(1961, Ger.), ed
Christoph Kunzer
FEDORA(1978, Ger./Fr.)
Norbert Kunzie
LAST BRIDGE, THE(1957, Aust.), w
Joseph Kuo
Misc. Talkies
RETURN OF 18 BRONZEMEN(1984), d
Li Kuo-hua
ENCHANTING SHADOW, THE(1965, Hong Kong)
Irina Kupchenko
UNCLE VANYA(1972, USSR)
Irving Kupcinet
ANATOMY OF A MURDER(1959)
Karyn Kupcinet
LADIES MAN, THE(1961)
Linda Kupecek
MC CABE AND MRS. MILLER(1971); MARIE-ANN(1978, Can.)
Robert J. Kuper
THIEF(1981)
Howard Kuperman
PRINCE AND THE PAUPER, THE(1969), ed; LITTLE MURDERS(1971), ed; LE-
GEND OF NIGGER CHARLEY, THE(1972), ed; SOUL OF NIGGER CHARLEY,
THE(1973), ed; NIGHT THE LIGHTS WENT OUT IN GEORGIA, THE(1981), p
Kurt Kupfer
CITIZEN SAINT(1947)
Margarete Kupfer
TREMENDOUSLY RICH MAN, A(1932, Ger.)
Silents
ONE ARABIAN NIGHT(1921, Ger.); WOMAN ON THE MOON, THE(1929, Ger.)
Margrete Kupfer
RENDEZ-VOUS(1932, Ger.)
Robert Kupferberg
MR. KLEIN(1976, Fr.), p
Meter Kupferman
BLACK LIKE ME(1964), m
Meyer Kupferman
BLAST OF SILENCE(1961), m; HALLELUJAH THE HILLS(1963), m; GOLD-
STEIN(1964), m; DOUBLE-BARRELLED DETECTIVE STORY, THE(1965), m; FEAR-
LESS FRANK(1967), m; TRUMAN CAPOTE'S TRILOGY(1969), m
Edward A. Kuplerski
Misc. Talkies
CURSE OF KILIMANJARO(1978), d
Jack Kupp
SKYDIVERS, THE(1963), a, ph
Joel Kupperman
CHIP OFF THE OLD BLOCK(1944)

Aleksandr Kuprin
GARNET BRACELET, THE(1966, USSR), w
G. Kupriyanov
MARRIAGE OF BALZAMINOV, THE(1966, USSR), ph
Anita Kupsch
ESCAPE FROM EAST BERLIN(1962)
Bohuslav Kupsovsky
MOST BEAUTIFUL AGE, THE(1970, Czech.)
Ninjin Kurabu
SCANDALOUS ADVENTURES OF BURAIKAN, THE(1970, Jap.), p
V. Kurach
SONG OF THE FOREST(1963, USSR), spec eff
Koreyoshi Kurahara
LONGING FOR LOVE(1966, Jap.), d, w
1984
ANTARCTICA(1984, Jap.), p, d, w
Koreyoshi Kurakara
WEIRD LOVE MAKERS, THE(1963, Jap.), d
Marina Kurakova
SOUND OF LIFE, THE(1962, USSR)
Peter Kuran
DAY TIME ENDED, THE(1980, Span.), David Allen; Q(1982), spec eff
1984
DREAMSCAPE(1984), spec eff
Willy Kurant
MASCULINE FEMININE(1966, Fr./Swed.), ph; TRANS-EUROP-EXPRESS(1968,
Fr.), ph; IMMORTAL STORY, THE(1969, Fr.), ph; LES CREATURES(1969, Fr./Swed.),
ph; CANNABIS(1970, Fr.), ph; HARPER VALLEY, P.T.A.(1978), ph; MAMMA
DRACULA(1980, Bel./Fr.), ph; T.A.G.: THE ASSASSINATION GAME(1982), ph
Shintaro Kuraoka
JUDO SHOWDOWN(1966, Jap.)
Lennard Kuras
WHO'S THAT KNOCKING AT MY DOOR?(1968)
Leonard Kuras
TOP OF THE HEAP(1972)
Seiji Kurasaki
1984
BALLAD OF NARAYAMA, THE(1984, Jap.)
Katharine Kurasch
YOUNG MAN WITH A HORN(1950)
Lev Kuravlev
WHEN THE TREES WERE TALL(1965, USSR)
Mazarov Kuravlyov
LAST GAME, THE(1964, USSR)
A. Kurc
DYBBUK THE(1938, Pol.)
Jan Kurcik
ROCKET TO NOWHERE(1962, Czech.)
Robert Kurcz
RISKY BUSINESS(1983)
L. Kurdyumova
SOUND OF LIFE, THE(1962, USSR)
A. Kure
YIDDLE WITH HIS FIDDLE(1937, Pol.)
Chitose Kurenai
LONGING FOR LOVE(1966, Jap.)
Erkki Kurenniemi
TIME OF ROSES(1970, Fin.), spec eff
Vilma Kurer
WALK EAST ON BEACON(1952)
Kevin Kurgis
1984
GIRLS NIGHT OUT(1984), w
Adolph Kuri
WILD HORSE MESA(1947), set d; WESTERN HERITAGE(1948), set d
Chiharu Kuri
YOSAKOI JOURNEY(1970, Jap.)
Emil Kuri
DUEL IN THE SUN(1946), set d; I REMEMBER MAMA(1948), set d
Emile Kuri
I'LL BE SEEING YOU(1944), set d; IT'S A WONDERFUL LIFE(1946), set d; SCAN-
DAL IN PARIS, A(1946), set d; PARADINE CASE, THE(1947), set d; ROPE(1948), set
d; STATE OF THE UNION(1948), set d; HEIRESS, THE(1949), set d; TOP O' THE
MORNING(1949), set d; DARK CITY(1950), set d; RIDING HIGH(1950), set d; DETEC-
TIVE STORY(1951), set d; HERE COMES THE GROOM(1951), set d; PLACE IN THE
SUN, A(1951), set d; ACTRESS, THE(1953), set d; SHANE(1953), set d; WAR OF THE
WORLDS, THE(1953), set d; EXECUTIVE SUITE(1954), set d; 20,000 LEAGUES
UNDER THE SEA(1954), set d; DAVY CROCKETT AND THE RIVER PIRATES(1956),
set d; GREAT LOCOMOTIVE CHASE, THE(1956), set d; WESTWARD HO THE
WAGONS!(1956), set d; JOHNNY TREMAIN(1957), set d; OLD YELLER(1957), set d;
LIGHT IN THE FOREST, THE(1958), set d; TONKA(1958), set d; DARBY O'GILL AND
THE LITTLE PEOPLE(1959), set d; SHAGGY DOG, THE(1959), set d; POLLYAN-
NA(1960), set d; SIGN OF ZORRO, THE(1960), set d; TEN WHO DARED(1960), set d;
TOBY TYLER(1960), set d; PARENT TRAP, THE(1961), set d; BON VOYAGE(1962),
set d; INCREDIBLE JOURNEY, THE(1963), set d; SAVAGE SAM(1963), set d; SON OF
FLUBBER(1963), set d; SUMMER MAGIC(1963), set d; MARY POPPINS(1964), set d;
MISADVENTURES OF MERLIN JONES, THE(1964), set d; THOSE CAL-
LOWAYS(1964), set d; TIGER WALKS, A(1964), set d; MONKEY'S UNCLE,
THE(1965), set d; THAT DARN CAT(1965), set d; FOLLOW ME, BOYS!(1966), set d;
LT. ROBIN CRUSOE, U.S.N.(1966), set d; UGLY DACHSHUND, THE(1966), set d;
GNOME-MOBILE, THE(1967), set d; HAPPIEST MILLIONAIRE, THE(1967), set d;
MONKEYS, GO HOME!(1967), set d; HORSE IN THE GRAY FLANNEL SUIT,
THE(1968), set d; LOVE BUG, THE(1968), set d; NEVER A DULL MOMENT(1968), set
d; ONE AND ONLY GENUINE ORIGINAL FAMILY BAND, THE(1968), set d;
RASCAL(1969), set d; SMITH(1969), set d; BOATNIKS, THE(1970), set d; COMPUTER
WORE TENNIS SHOES, THE(1970), set d; SCANDALOUS JOHN(1971), set d; WILD
COUNTRY, THE(1971), set d; $1,000,000 DUCK(1971), set d; NAPOLEON AND
SAMANTHA(1972), set d; SNOWBALL EXPRESS(1972), set d

Emilie Kuri
MOON PILOT(1962), set d
John Kuri
REPORT TO THE COMMISSIONER(1975), set d; LEADBELLY(1976), set d
Komaki Kurihara
MAGOICHI SAGA, THE(1970, Jap.)
Thomas Kurihara
Misc. Silents
DEVIL'S DOUBLE, THE(1916); CURSE OF IKU, THE(1918); HER AMERICAN HUSBAND(1918); HOPPER, THE(1918)
Tom Kurihara
Silents
BRAVEST WAY, THE(1918)
Jude Kuring
JOURNEY AMONG WOMEN(1977, Aus.); SINGER AND THE DANCER, THE(1977, Aus.)
Jerry Kurinsky
1984
REVENGE OF THE NERDS(1984)
Sumiko Kurishima
Misc. Silents
YOUNG MISS(1930, Jap.)
Asahi Kurizuka
HARBOR LIGHT YOKOHAMA(1970, Jap.)
John Kurkjian
TEARS OF HAPPINESS(1974), p
Emile Kurl
NOW YOU SEE HIM, NOW YOU DON'T(1972), set d
David Kurlan
JOE LOUIS STORY, THE(1953)
Dave Kurland
PRINCE OF FOXES(1949)
Gilbert Kurland
HALF A SINNER(1934), ed
Harriet Kurland
1984
CORRUPT(1984, Ital.)
Jeffrey Kurland
FAN, THE(1981), cos
1984
BROADWAY DANNY ROSE(1984), cos
Daniel Kurlick
BLACK ZOO(1963)
Adia Kurnetzoff
LANCER SPY(1937)
Harry Kurnitz
FAST COMPANY(1938), w; FAST AND FURIOUS(1939), w; FAST AND LOOSE(1939), w; I LOVE YOU AGAIN(1940), w; SHADOW OF THE THIN MAN(1941), w; PACIFIC RENDEZVOUS(1942), w; SHIP AHOY(1942), w; HEAVENLY BODY, THE(1943), w; THEY GOT ME COVERED(1943), w; SEE HERE, PRIVATE HARGROVE(1944), w; THIN MAN GOES HOME, THE(1944), w; WHAT NEXT, CORPORAL HARGROVE?(1945), w; SOMETHING IN THE WIND(1947), w; WEB, THE(1947), w; ONE TOUCH OF VENUS(1948), w; ADVENTURES OF DON JUAN(1949), w; INSPECTOR GENERAL, THE(1949), w; KISS IN THE DARK, A(1949), p, w; LADY TAKES A SAILOR, THE(1949), p; MY DREAM IS YOURS(1949), w; PRETTY BABY(1950), p; MAN BETWEEN, THE(1953, Brit.), w; MELBA(1953, Brit.), w; TONIGHT WE SING(1953), w; LOVE LOTTERY, THE(1954, Brit.), w; LAND OF THE PHARAOHS(1955), w; HAPPY ROAD, THE(1957), w; SILK STOCKINGS(1957), w; WITNESS FOR THE PROSECUTION(1957), w; ONCE MORE, WITH FEELING(1960), w; SURPRISE PACKAGE(1960), w; HATARI!(1962), w; GOODBYE CHARLIE(1964), w; SHOT IN THE DARK, A(1964), w
Susumu Kurobe
NONE BUT THE BRAVE(1965, U.S./Jap.); WHAT'S UP, TIGER LILY?(1966); SON OF GODZILLA(1967, Jap.); DESTROY ALL MONSTERS(1969, Jap.)
Nikolai Kurochkin
BRIDE WITH A DOWRY(1954, USSR)
Junko Kuroda
GIRL I ABANDONED, THE(1970, Jap.)
Kimiyoshi Kuroda
MAJIN(1968, Jap.), spec eff
Kiyomi Kuroda
ONIBABA(1965, Jap.), ph; KUROENKO(1968, Jap), ph; LOST SEX(1968, Jap.), ph
Kiyoshi Kuroda
ISLAND, THE(1962, Jap.), ph
Tokuzo Kuroda
DEATH ON THE MOUNTAIN(1961, Jap.), ph; SNOW IN THE SOUTH SEAS(1963, Jap.), ph
Yoshio Kuroda
GULLIVER'S TRAVELS BEYOND THE MOON(1966, Jap.), d
Yoshitami Kuroiwa
KILL(1968, Jap.), ed; GODZILLA VERSUS THE SMOG MONSTER(1972, Jap.), ed
Yataro Kurokawa
GATE OF HELL(1954, Jap.)
Hikaru Kuroki
LATITUDE ZERO(1969, U.S./Jap.)
Kazuo Kuroki
SILENCE HAS NO WINGS(1971, Jap.), d, w
Ken Kuroki
HARBOR LIGHT YOKOHAMA(1970, Jap.)
T. Kuronuma
VARAN THE UNBELIEVABLE(1962, U.S./Jap.), w
Takashi Kuronuma
RODAN(1958, Jap.), w
Ken Kurosa
THREE CAME HOME(1950)
Akira Kurosawa
DRUNKEN ANGEL(1948, Jap.), w; RASHOMON(1951, Jap.), d, w; SEVEN SAMURAI, THE(1956, Jap.), d, w, ed; HIDDEN FORTRESS, THE(1959, Jap.), d, w; IKIRU(1960, Jap.), d, w; THRONE OF BLOOD(1961, Jap.), p, d, w, ed; YOJIMBO(1961, Jap.), d, w; LOWER DEPTHS, THE(1962, Jap.), p, d; SANJURO(1962, Jap.), d, w, ed;

HIGH AND LOW(1963, Jap.), d, w; IDIOT, THE(1963, Jap.), d, w; STRAY DOG(1963, Jap.), d, w; FISTFUL OF DOLLARS, A(1964, Ital./Ger./Span.), w; OUTRAGE, THE(1964), w; SAGA OF THE VAGABONDS(1964, Jap.), w; SCANDAL(1964, Jap.), d, w; JUDO SAGA(1965, Jap.), w; RED BEARD(1966, Jap.), d, w; I LIVE IN FEAR(1967, Jap.), d, w; DODESKA-DEN(1970, Jap.), d, w; DERSU UZALA(1976, Jap./USSR), d, w; KAGEMUSHA(1980, Jap.), p, d, w
Haruyasu Kurosawa
HOUSE OF STRANGE LOVES, THE(1969, Jap.), art d
Toshio Kurosawa
EMPEROR AND A GENERAL, THE(1968, Jap.); GOODBYE, MOSCOW(1968, Jap.); MOMENT OF TERROR(1969, Jap.); DUEL AT EZO(1970, Jap.); PROPHECIES OF NOSTRADAMUS(1974, Jap.)
Willi Kurout
NIGHT OF THE FOLLOWING DAY, THE(1969, Brit.), ph
G. Kurovskiy
LADY WITH THE DOG, THE(1962, USSR); WAR AND PEACE(1968, USSR)
Bozena Kurowska
LOTNA(1966, Pol.)
Ron Kurowski
CREATURE WASN'T NICE,THE(1981)
Tetsuko Kuroyanagi
SUMMER SOLDIERS(1972, Jap.)
Bob Kurrie
EXPERT, THE(1932), ph
Robert Kurrie
DANCING SWEETIES(1930), ph; GOD'S GIFT TO WOMEN(1931), ph; ILLICIT(1931), ph; CROOKED CIRCLE(1932), ph
Robert B. Kurrie
RESURRECTION(1931), ph
Robert B. Kurris
Silents
EASY TO MAKE MONEY(1919), ph
R.B. Kurrle
EVANGELINE(1929), ph
Robert Kurrle
RIO RITA(1929), ph; FURIES, THE(1930), ph; HIT THE DECK(1930), ph; MAYBE IT'S LOVE(1930), ph; MOBY DICK(1930), ph; HER MAJESTY LOVE(1931), ph; RIVER'S END(1931), ph; ROAD TO SINGAPORE(1931), ph; SMART MONEY(1931), ph; CROONER(1932), ph; HIGH PRESSURE(1932), ph; JEWEL ROBBERY(1932), ph; MATCH KING, THE(1932), ph; ONE WAY PASSAGE(1932), ph; STRANGE LOVE OF MOLLY LOUVAIN, THE(1932), ph; WINNER TAKE ALL(1932), ph; LAWYER MAN(1933), ph
Silents
LURE OF YOUTH, THE(1921), ph; PLAYTHINGS OF DESTINY(1921), ph; SILVER WINGS(1922), ph; ALL THE BROTHERS WERE VALIANT(1923), ph; ABRAHAM LINCOLN(1924), ph; WINGS OF THE STORM(1926), ph; STOLEN BRIDE, THE(1927), ph; TENDER HOUR, THE(1927), ph; SADIE THOMPSON(1928), ph; FOUR FEATHERS(1929), ph
Robert B. Kurrle
Silents
ISOBEL(1920), ph; HER MAD BARGAIN(1921), ph; INVISIBLE FEAR, THE(1921), ph; QUESTION OF HONOR, A(1922), ph; JOANNA(1925), ph; RAMONA(1928), ph; EVANGELINE(1929), ph
Dieter Kursawe
1984
LOVE IN GERMANY, A(1984, Fr./Ger.)
Henry Kurse
ON PROBATION(1935), ph
Raymond Kurshals
HAIR(1979)
Jane Kurson
DON'T GO IN THE HOUSE(1980), ed; NEIGHBORS(1981), ed
Akira Kursosawa
LOWER DEPTHS, THE(1962, Jap.), w
Hans Kurt
HIPPODROME(1961, Aust./Ger.)
Lisbet Kurt
OPERATION CAMEL(1961, Den.)
Kurt Edelhagen Orchestra
DIE FLEDERMAUS(1964, Aust.)
Paul Kurta
1984
PERFECT STRANGERS(1984), p; SPECIAL EFFECTS(1984), p
Kurth
M(1933, Ger.)
Ralf Kurth
NOT RECONCILED, OR "ONLY VIOLENCE HELPS WHERE IT RULES"(1969, Ger.)
Joseph Kurthy
SUN SHINES, THE(1939, Hung.)
L.T. Kurtmann
TURN ON TO LOVE(1969), p
Peggy Kurton
Misc. Silents
DADDY(1917, Brit.)
Alwyn Kurts
EARTHLING, THE(1980); TIM(1981, Aus.)
Misc. Talkies
NEWMAN SHAME, THE(1977)
Hella Kurty
CANDLELIGHT IN ALGERIA(1944, Brit.); HOTEL RESERVE(1946, Brit.)
Billy Kurtz
DOUBLE STOP(1968)
Efrem Kurtz
MACBETH(1948), md
Emelie Kurtz
Silents
LAST LAUGH, THE(1924, Ger.)

Gary Kurtz
HOSTAGE, THE(1966), ed; AMERICAN GRAFFITI(1973), p; STAR WARS(1977), p; EMPIRE STRIKES BACK, THE(1980), p; DARK CRYSTAL, THE(1982, Brit.), p
Marcia Jean Kurtz
BELIEVE IN ME(1971); BORN TO WIN(1971); PANIC IN NEEDLE PARK(1971); STOOLIE, THE(1972); DOG DAY AFTERNOON(1975); PLEASANTVILLE(1976); NOMADIC LIVES(1977)
1984
COLD FEET(1984); ONCE UPON A TIME IN AMERICA(1984)
Philip Kurtz, Jr.
GENTLE PEOPLE AND THE QUIET LAND, THE(1972)
Swoosie Kurtz
FIRST LOVE(1977); SLAP SHOT(1977); OLIVER'S STORY(1978); WORLD ACCORDING TO GARP, The(1982)
1984
AGAINST ALL ODDS(1984)
Walter Kurtz
TALE OF FIVE WOMEN, A(1951, Brit.), art d; INTRUDER, THE(1962)
Laszlo Kurucsai
FATHER(1967, Hung.)
Janos Kurucz
DIAMONDS ARE FOREVER(1971, Brit.)
1984
TOP SECRET!(1984)
Kim Kurumada
1984
MIKE'S MURDER(1984), p
Stephen Kurumada
SOME KIND OF HERO(1982)
Dharmasdasa Kuruppu
1984
INDIANA JONES AND THE TEMPLE OF DOOM(1984)
Diane Kurys
PEPPERMINT SODA(1979, Fr.), d&w; COCKTAIL MOLOTOV(1980, Fr.), d, w; ENTRE NOUS(1983, Fr.), d&w
Ron Kurz
FRIDAY THE 13TH PART II(1981), w; FRIDAY THE 13TH PART III(1982), w; OFF THE WALL(1983), w
David Kurzon
HELL WITH HEROES, THE(1968)
Mitsuko Kusabue
DANGEROUS KISS, THE(1961, Jap.); NIGHT IN HONG KONG, A(1961, Jap.); HAPPINESS OF US ALONE(1962, Jap.); STAR OF HONG KONG(1962, Jap.); WISER AGE(1962, Jap.); HONOLULU-TOKYO-HONG KONG(1963, Hong Kong/Jap.); LONELY LANE(1963, Jap.); YEARNING(1964, Jap.); LOST WORLD OF SINBAD, THE(1965, Jap.); TWO IN THE SHADOW(1968, Jap.)
Takeshi Kusaka
SILENCE HAS NO WINGS(1971, Jap.)
1984
ANTARCTICA(1984, Jap.)
Goro Kusakaba
1984
BALLAD OF NARAYAMA, THE(1984, Jap.), p
Masao Kusakari
HINOTORI(1980, Jap.); VIRUS(1980, Jap.)
Naoya Kusakawa
TWO IN THE SHADOW(1968, Jap.); DESTROY ALL MONSTERS(1969, Jap.)
Daigo Kusano
PLEASURES OF THE FLESH, THE(1965)
Clyde Kusatsu
MIDWAY(1976); BLACK SUNDAY(1977); FRISCO KID, THE(1979); METEOR(1979); CHALLENGE, THE(1982)
Clyde Kusatu
CHOIRBOYS, THE(1977)
Dale Kusch
1984
WOMAN IN RED, THE(1984)
Daniel Kusel
SHOWDOWN, THE(1940), w
Harold Kusel
SHOWDOWN, THE(1940), w
Daniel Kusell
LOVE ISLAND(1952), w
Harold Kusell
FIGHT FOR YOUR LADY(1937), w; NEW FACES OF 1937(1937), w
Maurice Kusell
GREAT GABBO, THE(1929), ch; PATRICIA GETS HER MAN(1937, Brit.), w
Misc. Silents
LOVE NEVER DIES(1916)
Maurice L. Kusell
BROADWAY(1929), ch; FOX MOVIETONE FOLLIES OF 1930(1930), ch; PUTTIN' ON THE RITZ(1930), ch
Peter Kushabsky
GIRL FROM POLTAVA(1937)
Beverly Kushida
MANITOU, THE(1978)
Donald Kushner
TRON(1982), p
A. Kushnirenko
KIEV COMEDY, A(1963, USSR)
Ilona Kusmierska
PORTRAIT OF LENIN(1967, Pol./USSR)
Yuko Kusonoki
UNHOLY DESIRE(1964, Jap.)
Richard Kuss
THUNDER IN DIXIE(1965); DEER HUNTER, THE(1978)
Daniel Kussell
PARTY'S OVER, THE(1934), w

Harold Kussell
THERE GOES THE GROOM(1937), w
Susan Kussman
STEAGLE, THE(1971)
Anne-Marie Kuster
DEEP END(1970 Ger./U.S.)
Renate Kuster
ORDERED TO LOVE(1963, Ger.)
Michael Kustow
TELL ME LIES(1968, Brit.), w
Daikichiro Kusube
MAGIC BOY(1960, Jap.), anim
Hiroyuki Kusuda
BALLAD OF NARAYAMA(1961, Jap.), ph; EYES, THE SEA AND A BALL(1968 Jap.), ph
Eiji Kusuhara
ELEPHANT MAN, THE(1980, Brit.); FFOLKES(1980, Brit.)
Toshie Kusunoki
YOSAKOI JOURNEY(1970, Jap.)
Tuko Kusunoki
LONGING FOR LOVE(1966, Jap.)
Yuko Kusunoki
GOKE, BODYSNATCHER FROM HELL(1968, Jap.)
Hedda Kuszewski
Silents
LIGHT AT DUSK, THE(1916)
Jaroslaw Kuszewski
JOAN OF THE ANGELS(1962, Pol.)
W. Dee Kutach
GETAWAY, THE(1972)
Ari Kutai
CLEAR ALL WIRES(1933); FLYING MATCHMAKER, THE(1970, Israel)
M. Kutakhova
SPRINGTIME ON THE VOLGA(1961, USSR)
Josef Kutalek
FIREMAN'S BALL, THE(1968, Czech.)
Jeff Kutash
SIGN OF AQUARIUS(1970), ch
Ahmet Kutbay
MEETINGS WITH REMARKABLE MEN(1979, Brit.)
I. Kutchenkov
Misc. Silents
REVOLT IN THE DESERT(1932, USSR)
Todd Kutches
ENTITY, THE(1982)
Kutee
CHICKEN CHRONICLES, THE(1977)
Kay E. Kuter
TIME FOR KILLING, A(1967); WATERMELON MAN(1970)
1984
LAST STARFIGHTER, THE(1984)
Kay Kuter
DESIREE(1954); SABRINA(1954); CITY OF SHADOWS(1955); GUYS AND DOLLS(1955); MOLE PEOPLE, THE(1956); STEEL JUNGLE, THE(1956); UNDER FIRE(1957); BIG NIGHT, THE(1960)
Leo E. Kuter
LAST RIDE, THE(1944), art d; THAT WAY WITH WOMEN(1947), art d; TOWARD THE UNKNOWN(1956), spec eff
Silents
HURRICANE KID, THE(1925), art d; WHAT HAPPENED TO JONES(1926), art d; CAPTAIN SALVATION(1927), art d
Leo F. Kuter
COME FILL THE CUP(1951), art d
Leo K. Kuter
NORTHERN PURSUIT(1943), art d; THANK YOUR LUCKY STARS(1943), art d; DESTINATION TOKYO(1944), art d; ALWAYS TOGETHER(1947), art d; KEY LARGO(1948), art d; TO THE VICTOR(1948), art d; FLAMINGO ROAD(1949), art d; SOUTH OF ST. LOUIS(1949), art d; TASK FORCE(1949), art d; CHAIN LIGHTNING(1950), art d; HIGHWAY 301(1950), art d; STORM WARNING(1950), art d; CLOSE TO MY HEART(1951), art d; I WAS A COMMUNIST FOR THE F.B.I.(1951), art d; OPERATION PACIFIC(1951), art d; TANKS ARE COMING, THE(1951), art d; THIS WOMAN IS DANGEROUS(1952), art d; THREE SAILORS AND A GIRL(1953), art d; TROUBLE ALONG THE WAY(1953), art d; DRUM BEAT(1954), art d; TARGET ZERO(1955), a, art d; MIRACLE IN THE RAIN(1956), art d; OUR MISS BROOKS(1956), art d; STEEL JUNGLE, THE(1956), art d; ONIONHEAD(1958), art d; RIO BRAVO(1959), art d; SUMMER PLACE, A(1959), art d; DARK AT THE TOP OF THE STAIRS, THE(1960), art d; SINS OF RACHEL CADE, THE(1960), art d; PARRISH(1961), art d; SUSAN SLADE(1961), art d; HOUSE OF WOMEN(1962), art d; ROME ADVENTURE(1962), art d; PT 109(1963), art d; ENSIGN PULVER(1964), art d; YOUNGBLOOD HAWKE(1964), art d; THREE ON A COUCH(1966), art d
Leo Kuter
HOLLYWOOD CANTEEN(1944), art d; VERY THOUGHT OF YOU, THE(1944), art d; CONFIDENTIAL AGENT(1945), art d; PILLOW TO POST(1945), art d; PRIDE OF THE MARINES(1945), art d; UNFAITHFUL, THE(1947), art d
Zdenek Kutil
DEVIL'S TRAP, THE(1964, Czech.)
Jane Kutler
SCARECROW IN A GARDEN OF CUCUMBERS(1972)
Leo E. Kutler
Silents
SKINNER'S DRESS SUIT(1926), art d
F. Kutlik
SUBWAY RIDERS(1981)
Jerry Kutner
IN MACARTHUR PARK(1977), ed
Nanette Kutner
BIG CITY(1948), w

Richard Kutner
SALLY'S HOUNDS(1968)
Rima Kutner
BLACK KLANSMAN, THE(1966)
Ray Kutos
1984
MIRRORS(1984), art d
Rolf Kutschera
DIE FLEDERMAUS(1964, Aust.); $100 A NIGHT(1968, Ger.)
Viktor Kutschera
Misc. Silents
PAREMA, CRERATURE FROM THE STARWORLD(1922, Aust.)
Imano Kutt
FLY NOW, PAY LATER(1969)
Michael Kutter
PARSIFAL(1983, Fr.)
Kazimierz Kutz
BEADS OF ONE ROSARY, THE(1982, Pol.), d&w
Walter Kutz
MAEDCHEN IN UNIFORM(1965, Ger./Fr.), set d
Aida Kutzenoff
SPAWN OF THE NORTH(1938)
Ernst Kutzinski
NOT RECONCILED, OR "ONLY VIOLENCE HELPS WHERE IT RULES"(1969, Ger.)
Hans Kutzner
ROSES FOR THE PROSECUTOR(1961, Ger.), art d
Kuumba
MANDINGO(1975); SOUNDER, PART 2(1976)
Luigi Kuveiller
WE STILL KILL THE OLD WAY(1967, Ital.), ph; FRAULEIN DOKTOR(1969, Ital./Yugo.), ph; INVESTIGATION OF A CITIZEN ABOVE SUSPICION(1970, Ital.), ph; LADY OF MONZA, THE(1970, Ital.), ph; QUIET PLACE IN THE COUNTRY, A(1970, Ital./Fr.), ph; MAN CALLED SLEDGE, A(1971, Ital.), ph; AVANTI!(1972), ph; DEEP RED(1976, Ital.), ph
George Kuwa
Silents
MIDSUMMER MADNESS(1920); ROUND UP, THE(1920); INVISIBLE FEAR, THE(1921); NOBODY'S FOOL(1921); SHERLOCK BROWN(1921); BEAUTIFUL AND DAMNED, THE(1922); ENTER MADAME(1922); MORAN OF THE LADY LETTY(1922); DADDY(1923); ETERNAL STRUGGLE, THE(1923); MAN FROM WYOMING, THE(1924); OH, DOCTOR(1924); STORM DAUGHTER, THE(1924); ENCHANTED HILL, THE(1926); NUT-CRACKER, THE(1926); NIGHT BRIDE, THE(1927); WHITE PANTS WILLIE(1927); AFTER THE STORM(1928); SECRET HOUR, THE(1928)
Misc. Silents
BOTTLE IMP, THE(1917)
Miyuki Kuwano
NAKED YOUTH(1961, Jap.); RED BEARD(1966, Jap.)
Ryotaro Kuwata
TWIN SISTERS OF KYOTO(1964, Jap.), p; SNOW COUNTRY(1969, Jap.), prod d
Shoichi Kuwayama
INSECT WOMAN, THE(1964, Jap.); EAST CHINA SEA(1969, Jap.)
William Kux
CALIFORNIA SUITE(1978)
Sandy Kuykendall
1984
UP THE CREEK(1984)
Adia Kuynetzoff
FRANKENSTEIN MEETS THE WOLF MAN(1943)
Ruth Kuzab
STRANGERS IN THE CITY(1962)
I. Kuzbetsov
HOME FOR TANYA, A(1961, USSR)
Ryu Kuze
SANJURO(1962, Jap.), tech adv
Dudley Kuzello
THANK YOUR LUCKY STARS(1943)
Gleb Kuzentsov
Misc. Silents
TRANSPORT OF FIRE(1931, USSR)
N. Kuzmin
OVERCOAT, THE(1965, USSR); HAMLET(1966, USSR)
Helen Kuzmina
THIRTEEN, THE(1937, USSR)
N. Kuzmina
CLEAR SKIES(1963, USSR)
Ye. Kuzmina
DUEL, THE(1964, USSR)
Yelena Kuzmina
Misc. Silents
NEW BABYLON, THE(1929, USSR)
A. Kuznetsov
NEW HORIZONS(1939, USSR); DESTINY OF A MAN(1961, USSR); DUEL, THE(1964, USSR)
Anatoliy Kuznetsov
SUN SHINES FOR ALL, THE(1961, USSR), ph; PEACE TO HIM WHO ENTERS(1963, USSR), ph; WELCOME KOSTYA!(1965, USSR), ph
I. Kuznetsov
CITY OF YOUTH(1938, USSR); SILENCE OF DR. EVANS, THE(1973, USSR)
Isai Kuznetsov
LULLABY(1961, USSR), w; MOSCOW–CASSIOPEIA(1974, USSR), w; TEENAGERS IN SPACE(1975, USSR), w
Ivan Kuznetsov
DARK IS THE NIGHT(1946, USSR)
M. Kuznetsov
BOUNTIFUL SUMMER(1951, USSR)
Mikhail Kuznetsov
IVAN THE TERRIBLE(Part I, 1947, USSR); IN THE NAME OF LIFE(1947, USSR); MAGIC WEAVER, THE(1965, USSR)

Mikhall Kuznetsov
ADVENTURE IN ODESSA(1954, USSR)
N. Kuznetsov
MAGIC WEAVER, THE(1965, USSR)
Olya Kuznetsov
THIRTEEN, THE(1937, USSR)
S. Kuznetsov
SLEEPING BEAUTY, THE(1966, USSR)
Misc. Silents
BEILIS CASE, THE(1917, USSR)
Shura Kuznetsov
LULLABY(1961, USSR)
V. Kuznetsova
YOLANTA(1964, USSR), makeup
Vera Kuznetsova
HOME FOR TANYA, A(1961, USSR); LULLABY(1961, USSR); THERE WAS AN OLD COUPLE(1967, USSR)
Ada Kuznetzoff
BULLDOG DRUMMOND'S BRIDE(1939)
Adi Kuznetzoff
LOVE ON THE RUN(1936)
Adia Kuznetzoff
EASY LIVING(1937); I'LL TAKE ROMANCE(1937); MADAME X(1937); MAYTIME(1937); EVERYBODY SING(1938); SWISS MISS(1938); LET FREEDOM RING(1939); PACIFIC LINER(1939); TORTURE SHIP(1939); TROPIC FURY(1939); DEVIL'S ISLAND(1940); SECOND CHORUS(1940); ARABIAN NIGHTS(1942); FOR WHOM THE BELL TOLLS(1943); HELLO, FRISCO, HELLO(1943); MISSION TO MOSCOW(1943); SEVENTH VICTIM, THE(1943); LOST IN A HAREM(1944); PRINCESS AND THE PIRATE, THE(1944); RAINBOW ISLAND(1944)
Aida Kuznetzoff
THAT'S MY BABY(1944)
G.P. Kuznetzov
HOUSE OF DEATH(1932, USSR)
Gleb Kuznetzov
Misc. Silents
RIVALS(1933, USSR)
I. Kuznetzov
SEVEN BRAVE MEN(1936, USSR)
Mikhail Kuznetzov
TAXI TO HEAVEN(1944, USSR)
I. Kuznovich
TRAIN GOES TO KIEV, THE(1961, USSR)
Alena Kvetova
FIREMAN'S BALL, THE(1968, Czech.)
B. Kvin
LAST GAME, THE(1964, USSR)
I. Kvitayshvili
FATHER OF A SOLDIER(1966, USSR)
V. Kvitka
SONG OF THE FOREST(1963, USSR)
Denisa Kvorakova
MARTYRS OF LOVE(1968, Czech.)
Pero Kvrgic
STEPPE, THE(1963, Fr./Ital.)
Shang Kwah-wu
Misc. Silents
SONG OF CHINA(1936, Chi.)
Danny Kwan
IN-LAWS, THE(1979); CHEECH AND CHONG'S NICE DREAMS(1981); SO FINE(1981)
Mary Kwan
YOU LIGHT UP MY LIFE(1977)
Moon Kwan
Silents
BROKEN BLOSSOMS(1919)
Nancy Kwan
WORLD OF SUZIE WONG, THE(1960); FLOWER DRUM SONG(1961); MAIN ATTRACTION, THE(1962, Brit.); FATE IS THE HUNTER(1964); HONEYMOON HOTEL(1964); TAMAHINE(1964, Brit.); ARRIVEDERCI, BABY!(1966, Brit.); LT. ROBIN CRUSOE, U.S.N.(1966); WILD AFFAIR, THE(1966, Brit.); CORRUPT ONES, THE(1967, Ger.); NOBODY'S PERFECT(1968); WRECKING CREW, THE(1968); GIRL WHO KNEW TOO MUCH, THE(1969); MC MASTERS, THE(1970); WONDER WOMEN(1973, Phil.); PROJECT: KILL(1976); NIGHT CREATURE(1979)
Misc. Talkies
SUPERCOCK(1975); FORTRESS IN THE SUN(1978); STREETS OF HONG KONG(1979)
Frank Kwanaga
HOUSE OF BAMBOO(1955)
Lee Kwan-Young
FIENDISH PLOT OF DR. FU MANCHU, THE(1980)
Wlodzimiers Kwaskowski
YELLOW SLIPPERS, THE(1965, Pol.)
Cyril Kwaza
CRY, THE BELOVED COUNTRY(1952, Brit.)
Atlim Kweli
SHARKY'S MACHINE(1982)
Halina Kwiatkoska
ASHES AND DIAMONDS(1961, Pol.)
Tadeusz Kwiatkowski
SARAGOSSA MANUSCRIPT, THE(1972, Pol.), w
Leonard Kwit
NIGHTMARE IN WAX(1969), ed
Beulah Kwoh
LOVE IS A MANY-SPLENDORED THING(1955)
Hyukjin Kwon
MONSTER WANGMAGWI(1967, S. K.), p
Joseph Kwong
1984
BAD MANNERS(1984), w

Laura Kwong
RIVERRUN(1968)
Mabel Kwong
1984
NIGHTSONGS(1984)
Ny Cheuk Kwong
OUTPOST IN MALAYA(1952, Brit.)
Peter Kwong
STRAIGHT TIME(1978)
1984
SLAPSTICK OF ANOTHER KIND(1984)
Bert Kwouk
GOLDFINGER(1964, Brit.); CURSE OF THE FLY(1965, Brit.); VENGEANCE OF FU MANCHU, THE(1968, Brit./Ger./Hong Kong/Ireland); DEEP END(1970 Ger./U.S.)
Burk Kwouk
REVENGE OF THE PINK PANTHER(1978)
Burt Kwouk
INN OF THE SIXTH HAPPINESS, THE(1958); PASSPORT TO CHINA(1961, Brit.); TERROR OF THE TONGS, THE(1961, Brit.); SATAN NEVER SLEEPS(1962); SHOT IN THE DARK, A(1964); SINISTER MAN, THE(1965, Brit.); BANG, BANG, YOU'RE DEAD(1966); LOST COMMAND, THE(1966); YOU ONLY LIVE TWICE(1967, Brit.); HIGH COMMISSIONER, THE(1968, U.S./Brit.); SHOES OF THE FISHERMAN, THE(1968); CHAIRMAN, THE(1969); RETURN OF THE PINK PANTHER, THE(1975, Brit.); ROLLERBALL(1975); PINK PANTHER STRIKES AGAIN, THE(1976, Brit.); LAST REMAKE OF BEAU GESTE, THE(1977); FIENDISH PLOT OF DR. FU MANCHU, THE(1980); TRAIL OF THE PINK PANTHER, THE(1982)
Ky-Duyen
SHANGHAI DRAMA, THE(1945, Fr.)
Robert Kya-Hill
SLAVES(1969); RIVALS(1972); SHAFT'S BIG SCORE(1972); DEATH WISH(1974)
Ronald Kyaing
INN OF THE SIXTH HAPPINESS, THE(1958)
Lydia Kyasht
Misc. Silents
BLACK SPIDER, THE(1920, Brit.)
Sandra Kybartas
SCREWBALLS(1983), art d
Jonathon Kydd
SWINGIN' MAIDEN, THE(1963, Brit.)
Sam Kydd
HELL, HEAVEN OR HOBOKEN(1958, Brit.); THEY CAME BY NIGHT(1940, Brit.); FLY AWAY PETER(1948, Brit.); GIRL IN THE PAINTING, THE(1948, Brit.); LOVE IN WAITING(1948, Brit.); SONG FOR TOMORROW, A(1948, Brit.); TROUBLE IN THE AIR(1948, Brit.); VENGEANCE IS MINE(1948, Brit.); FLOODTIDE(1949, Brit.); GAY LADY, THE(1949, Brit.); HOUR OF GLORY(1949, Brit.); MADNESS OF THE HEART(1949, Brit.); PASSPORT TO PIMLICO(1949, Brit.); POET'S PUB(1949, Brit.); SAINTS AND SINNERS(1949, Brit.); SCOTT OF THE ANTARCTIC(1949, Brit.); STOP PRESS GIRL(1949, Brit.); CLOUDED YELLOW, THE(1950, Brit.); CURE FOR LOVE, THE(1950, Brit.); MAGNET, THE(1950, Brit.); SECOND MATE, THE(1950, Brit.); TREASURE ISLAND(1950, Brit.); CHEER THE BRAVE(1951, Brit.); DARK MAN, THE(1951, Brit.); GALLOPING MAJOR, THE(1951, Brit.); HIGH TREASON(1951, Brit.); PENNY POINTS TO PARADISE(1951, Brit.); POOL OF LONDON(1951, Brit.); FOUR AGAINST FATE(1952, Brit.); HOT ICE(1952, Brit.); HOUR OF THIRTEEN, THE(1952); SECRET PEOPLE(1952, Brit.); SING ALONG WITH ME(1952, Brit.); CRUEL SEA, THE(1953); DEATM GOES TO SCHOOL(1953, Brit.); MURDER WILL OUT(1953, Brit.); SAILOR OF THE KING(1953, Brit.); STEEL KEY, THE(1953, Brit.); TERROR ON A TRAIN(1953); TRENT'S LAST CASE(1953, Brit.); DETECTIVE, THE(1954, Qit.); DEVIL ON HORSEBACK(1954, Brit.); EMBEZZLER, THE(1954, Brit.); END OF THE ROAD, THE(1954, Brit.); FINAL APPOINTMENT(1954, Brit.); RADIO CAB MURDER(1954, Brit.); RAINBOW JACKET, THE(1954, Brit.); RUNAWAY BUS, THE(1954, Brit.); THEY WHO DARE(1954, Brit.); CONSTANT HUSBAND, THE(1955, Brit.); JOSEPHINE AND MEN(1955, Brit.); PASSAGE HOME(1955, Brit.); STORM OVER THE NILE(1955, Brit.); WARRIORS, THE(1955); WHERE THERE'S A WILL(1955, Brit.); YOU CAN'T ESCAPE(1955, Brit.); HIDEOUT, THE(1956, Brit.); HOME AND AWAY(1956, Brit.); IT'S A WONDERFUL WORLD(1956, Brit.); JACQUELINE(1956, Brit.); KID FOR TWO FARTHINGS, A(1956, Brit.); LADYKILLERS, THE(1956, Brit.); RAMSBOTTOM RIDES AGAIN(1956, Brit.); SPIN A DARK WEB(1956, Brit.); TIGER IN THE SMOKE(1956, Brit.); CARRY ON ADMIRAL(1957, Brit.); JUST MY LUCK(1957, Brit.); RAISING A RIOT(1957, Brit.); REACH FOR THE SKY(1957, Brit.); SMALLEST SHOW ON EARTH, THE(1957, Brit.); THIRD KEY, THE(1957, Brit.); ALL AT SEA(1958, Brit.); DANGEROUS EXILE(1958, Brit.); FURTHER UP THE CREEK!(1958, Brit.); HAPPY IS THE BRIDE(1958, Brit.); LAW AND DISORDER(1958, Brit.); ORDERS TO KILL(1958, Brit.); SAFECRACKER, THE(1958, Brit.); UP THE CREEK(1958, Brit.); HOUND OF THE BASKERVILLES(1959, Brit.); I'M ALL RIGHT, JACK(1959, Brit.); STRANGE AFFECTION(1959, Brit.); DEAD LUCKY(1960, Brit.); FOLLOW THAT HORSE!(1960, Brit.); HOUSE IN MARSH ROAD, THE(1960, Brit.); MAN IN A COCKED HAT(1960, Bri.); PRICE OF SILENCE, THE(1960, Brit.); THIRTY NINE STEPS, THE(1960, Brit.); CLUE OF THE SILVER KEY, THE(1961, Brit.); RISK, THE(1961, Brit.); SECRET OF MONTE CRISTO, THE(1961, Brit.); CIRCUS FRIENDS(1962, Brit.); LIFE IS A CIRCUS(1962, Brit.); THERE WAS A CROOKED MAN(1962, Brit.); SWINGIN' MAIDEN, THE(1963, Brit.); SMOKESCREEN(1964, Brit.); ISLAND OF TERROR(1967, Brit.); PROJECTED MAN, THE(1967, Brit.); SMASHING TIME(1967 Brit.); ALF 'N' FAMILY(1968, Brit.); MOON ZERO TWO(1970, Brit.); TOO LATE THE HERO(1970); 10 RILLINGTON PLACE(1971, Brit.); CONFESSIONS OF A WINDOW CLEANER(1974, Brit.); YESTERDAY'S HERO(1979, Brit.); SHILLINGBURY BLOWERS, THE(1980, Brit.); EYE OF THE NEEDLE(1981)
Misc. Talkies
YOUNG DETECTIVE, THE(1964, Brit.)
Louise Kyes
ASSAULT ON PRECINCT 13(1976), cos
Nancy Kyes
HALLOWEEN III: SEASON OF THE WITCH(1982)
David Kyle
CAT MURKIL AND THE SILKS(1976); HALLOWEEN(1978)
George Kyle
ENDLESS LOVE(1981)
1984
ALPHABET CITY(1984)

Gordon Kyle
WHO KILLED VAN LOON?(1984, Brit.), p, d
Helen Ray Kyle
Silents
WARRENS OF VIRGINIA, THE(1924)
Howard Kyle
Silents
WILD HONEY(1919)
John Kyle
WHISPERING SMITH VERSUS SCOTLAND YARD(1952, Brit.)
Ragna Kyle
DESPERATE WOMEN, THE(?)
Ray Kyle
SHE'S BACK ON BROADWAY(1953)
Dwania Kyles
1984
BROTHER FROM ANOTHER PLANET, THE(1984)
Milan Kymlicka
LAST ACT OF MARTIN WESTON, THE(1970, Can./Czech.), m; REINCARNATE, THE(1971, Can.), m; WEDDING IN WHITE(1972, Can.), m
Peter B. Kyne
HELL'S HEROES(1930), w; NEVER THE TWAIN SHALL MEET(1931), w; WILD HORSE(1931), w; LOCAL BAD MAN(1932), w; PRIDE OF THE LEGION, THE(1932), w; STOKER, THE(1932), w; FLAMING GUNS(1933), w; MY MOTHER(1933), w; CAPPY RICKS RETURNS(1935), w; DANGER AHEAD(1935), w; GALLANT DEFENDER(1935), w; $10 RAISE(1935), w; BARS OF HATE(1936), w; FACE IN THE FOG, A(1936), w; KELLY OF THE SECRET SERVICE(1936), w; MYSTERIOUS AVENGER, THE(1936), w; PUT ON THE SPOT(1936), w; RIO GRANDE ROMANCE(1936), w; SECRET PATROL(1936), w; STAMPEDE(1936), w; THREE GODFATHERS(1936), w; WITHOUT ORDERS(1936), w; AFFAIRS OF CAPPY RICKS(1937), w; ANYTHING FOR A THRILL(1937), w; CODE OF THE RANGE(1937), w; GO-GETTER, THE(1937), w; HEADLINE CRASHER(1937), w; ONE MAN JUSTICE(1937), p; TAMING THE WILD(1937), w; TOUGH TO HANDLE(1937), w; YOUNG DYNAMITE(1937), w; BORN TO FIGHT(1938), w; RACING BLOOD(1938), w; VALLEY OF THE GIANTS(1938), w; PARSON OF PANAMINT, THE(1941), w; RIDE, KELLY, RIDE(1941), w; HE HIRED THE BOSS(1943), w; THREE GODFATHERS, THE(1948), w; BELLE LE GRAND(1951), w; BLUE BLOOD(1951), w; BRONCO BUSTER(1952), w
Silents
JUDGE NOT OR THE WOMAN OF MONA DIGGINGS(1915), w; PARSON OF PANAMINT, THE(1916), w; BEAUTIFUL GAMBLER, THE(1921), w; CAPPY RICKS(1921), w; NEVER THE TWAIN SHALL MEET(1925), w, t; WAR PAINT(1926), w; CALIFORNIA(1927), w; FREEDOM OF THE PRESS(1928), w; RAWHIDE KID, THE(1928), w
Peter Bernard Kyne
Silents
TEN DOLLAR RAISE, THE(1921), w; KINDRED OF THE DUST(1922), w; LONG CHANCE, THE(1922), w; MAKING A MAN(1922), w; PRIDE OF PALOMAR, THE(1922), w; WHILE SATAN SLEEPS(1922), w; TIE THAT BINDS, THE(1923), w; ENCHANTED HILL, THE(1926), w; FOREIGN DEVILS(1927), w; JIM THE CONQUEROR(1927), w; MAN IN HOBBLES, THE(1928), w
Peter Kyne
BIG PAYOFF, THE(1933), w
Machiko Kyo
RASHOMON(1951, Jap.); GATE OF HELL(1954, Jap.); UGETSU(1954, Jap.); TEAHOUSE OF THE AUGUST MOON, THE(1956); ODD OBSESSION(1961, Jap.); BUDDHA(1965, Jap.); GREAT WALL, THE(1965, Jap.); DAPHNE, THE(1967); FACE OF ANOTHER, THE(1967, Jap.); THOUSAND CRANES(1969, Jap.); FLOATING WEEDS(1970, Jap.)
Utako Kyo
TOPSY-TURVY JOURNEY(1970, Jap.)
Tamae Kyokawa
MY GEISHA(1962)
Ekkehard Kyrath
THEY WERE SO YOUNG(1955), ph
Ero Kyriakaki
RED LANTERNS(1965, Gr.)
Anna Kyriakou
ZORBA THE GREEK(1964, U.S./Gr.)
William Kyriakys
DARK ODYSSEY(1961), p&d, w, ed
Paul Kyriazi
DEATH MACHINES(1976), d
George Kyritsis
DAYS OF 36(1972, Gr.)
Tzvyan Kyrla
ROAD TO LIFE(1932, USSR)
H. Kyser
INVISIBLE OPPONENT(1933, Ger.)
Hans Kyser
Silents
FAUST(1926, Ger.), w
Kay Kyser
THAT'S RIGHT–YOU'RE WRONG(1939); YOU'LL FIND OUT(1940); PLAYMATES(1941); MY FAVORITE SPY(1942); AROUND THE WORLD(1943); SWING FEVER(1943); CAROLINA BLUES(1944)
Charles H. Kyson
Misc. Silents
BRUTE MASTER, THE(1920), d
Charles Kyson
WEST OF NEVADA(1936), w

L

L.A.P.D.
DRAGNET(1954), tech adv
L.C. Dubin
BEWARE OF LADIES(1937), w
Paul L'Amoreaux
DESERT RAVEN, THE(1965)
Louis L'Amour
EAST OF SUMATRA(1953), w; HONDO(1953), w; FOUR GUNS TO THE BORDER(1954), w; TREASURE OF RUBY HILLS(1955), w; BLACKJACK KETCHUM, DESPERADO(1956), w; BURNING HILLS, THE(1956), w; TALL STRANGER, THE(1957), w; UTAH BLAINE(1957), w; GUNS OF THE TIMBERLAND(1960), w; HELLER IN PINK TIGHTS(1960), w; TAGGART(1964), w; KID RODELO(1966, U.S./Span.), w; CATLOW(1971, Span.), w; CANCEL MY RESERVATION(1972), w; MAN CALLED NOON, THE(1973, Brit.), w
Paul L'Anglais
WHISPERING CITY(1947, Can.), p
L'Atalier
SYMPHONIE FANTASTIQUE(1947, Fr.), p
Guy L'Ecuyer
JACOB TWO-TWO MEETS THE HOODED FANG(1979, Can.); LUCKY STAR, THE(1980, Can.)
Dick L'Estrange
KILLERS OF THE WILD(1940), p
Silents
BLAZING DAYS(1927); ONE GLORIOUS SCRAP(1927); ARIZONA CYCLONE(1928)
Jill L'Estrange
KILLERS OF THE WILD(1940)
Misc. Talkies
TOPA TOPA(1938)
Julien L'Estrange
Silents
SOLD(1915); QUEST OF LIFE, THE(1916)
Misc. Silents
BELLA DONNA(1915); GIRL WITH THE GREEN EYES, THE(1916); DAYBREAK(1918)
Marcel L'Herbier
SACRIFICE OF HONOR(1938, Fr.), d, w; ENTENTE CORDIALE(1939, Fr.), d; RASPUTIN(1939, Fr.), d; LIVING CORPSE, THE(1940, Fr.), d, w; FOOLISH HUSBANDS(1948, Fr.), d; SAVAGE BRIGADE(1948, Fr.), d
Misc. Silents
ROSE FRANCE(1919, Fr.), d; LE CARNIVAL DES VERITES(1920, Fr.), d; L'HOMME DU LARGE(1920, Fr.), d; ELDORADO(1921, Fr.), d; VILLA DESTIN(1921, Fr.), d; DON JUAN ET FAUST(1923, Fr.), d; L'INHUMAINE(1923, Fr.), d; LE VERTIGE(1926, Fr.), d; LE DIABLE AU COEUR(1928, Fr.), d
Judith L'Heureux
FAME(1980)
Pierre L'Homme
KING OF HEARTS(1967, Fr./Ital.), ph; MOTHER AND THE WHORE, THE(1973, Fr.), ph
Jean L'Hote
MY UNCLE(1958, Fr.), w; DIE GANS VON SEDAN(1962, Fr/Ger.), w
Tina L'Hotsky
LOVELESS, THE(1982)
Rouget de l'Isle
LA MARSEILLAISE(1938, Fr.), m
Geoffrey L'Oise
PHANTOM OF THE OPERA, THE(1962, Brit.); SING AND SWING(1964, Brit.)
Bert L'Orle
STARS OVER BROADWAY(1935), ed
Oliver La Baddie
Misc. Silents
FIRST WOMAN, THE(1922)
Fidel La Barba
SUSANNAH OF THE MOUNTIES(1939), w
Joe La Barba
FALCON'S ALIBI, THE(1946)
Donna La Barr
FOOTLIGHT PARADE(1933); LADY GAMBLES, THE(1949)
Arthur La Bern
IT ALWAYS RAINS ON SUNDAY(1949, Brit.), w; PAPER ORCHID(1949, Brit.), w; GOOD TIME GIRL(1950, Brit.), w; DEAD MAN'S EVIDENCE(1962, Brit.), w; FREEDOM TO DIE(1962, Brit.), w; VERDICT, THE(1964, Brit.), w; INCIDENT AT MIDNIGHT(1966, Brit.), w
Louis La Bey
I MET HIM IN PARIS(1937)
Emile La Bigne
WEST SIDE STORY(1961), makeup
La Bionda
SUPER FUZZ(1981), m
Erin La Bissonier
IN THE MONEY(1934)
Erin La Bissoniere
PLAYBOY OF PARIS(1930); STORM, THE(1930); RIP TIDE(1934)
Silents
EAGER LIPS(1927); LIGHT IN THE WINDOW, THE(1927); GYPSY OF THE NORTH(1928)
Misc. Silents
MILLION DOLLAR MYSTERY(1927)
Ethel La Blance
HEADIN' EAST(1937), w
Ethel La Blanche
FLIRTING WITH FATE(1938), w; MAN HUNTERS OF THE CARIBBEAN(1938), w; PIRATES ON HORSEBACK(1941), w

Elina La Bourdette
AMAZING MONSIEUR FABRE, THE(1952, Fr.)
Katie La Bourdette
1984
JOHNNY DANGEROUSLY(1984)
Myrna La Bow
YOUR THREE MINUTES ARE UP(1973)
Angie La Bozzetta
ROAD GAMES(1981, Aus.)
Simone La Brousse
CORNERED(1945); THIS LOVE OF OURS(1945)
Raffack La Capria
DRIVER'S SEAT, THE(1975, Ital.), w
Raffaele La Capria
MOMENT OF TRUTH, THE(1965, Ital./Span.), w; MORE THAN A MIRACLE(1967, Ital./Fr.), w; EBOLI(1980, Ital.), w
Gregory La Cava
SATURDAY'S CHILDREN(1929), d; SMART WOMAN(1931), d; AGE OF CONSENT(1932), d; SYMPHONY OF SIX MILLION(1932), d; AFFAIRS OF CELLINI, THE(1934), d; GALLANT LADY(1934), d; PRIVATE WORLDS(1935), d, w; MY MAN GODFREY(1936), d, w; STAGE DOOR(1937), d, w; FIFTH AVENUE GIRL(1939), p&d; UNFINISHED BUSINESS(1941), p&d; LADY IN A JAM(1942), p&d; LIVING IN A BIG WAY(1947), d, w
Silents
WOMANHANDLED(1925), d; LET'S GET MARRIED(1926), d; SO'S YOUR OLD MAN(1926), p&d; HALF A BRIDE(1928), d
Misc. Silents
HIS NIBS(1921), d; NEW SCHOOL TEACHER, THE(1924), d; RESTLESS WIVES(1924), d; SAY IT AGAIN(1926), d; GAY DEFENDER, THE(1927), d; PARADISE FOR TWO(1927), d; RUNNING WILD(1927), d; FEEL MY PULSE(1928), d
Joe La Cava
TENDER IS THE NIGHT(1961)
Joseph La Cava
MONSTER OF PIEDRAS BLANCAS, THE(1959)
Louis La Cava
HOUSE OF WOMEN(1962), makeup; TALES OF TERROR(1962), makeup; MARA OF THE WILDERNESS(1966), makeup
Peg La Centra
CRIME OF PASSION(1957)
Joseph La Chelle
COME TO THE STABLE(1949), ph
Peter La Corte
GODFATHER, THE, PART II(1974)
Henry La Cossit
NIGHT RIDE(1930), w
Henry La Cossitt
HOMICIDE SQUAD(1931), w
Father Paul la Couline
I CONFESS(1953), tech adv
Joe La Creta
SMALL CIRCLE OF FRIENDS, A(1980)
Arda La Croix
Misc. Silents
DAUGHTER OF MACGREGOR, A(1916)
Emile La Croix
Silents
POOR LITTLE RICH GIRL, A(1917); WOMAN'S MAN(1920)
Misc. Silents
BROADWAY SAINT, A(1919); FOOL AND HIS MONEY, A(1920)
Joe La Due
TRACKDOWN(1976)
Lyzanne La Due
IN LIKE FLINT(1967)
Oliver La Farge
LAUGHING BOY(1934), w
Jean La Fayette
DANCE, GIRL, DANCE(1940)
Art La Fleur
1984
CITY HEAT(1984)
Virginia La Fonde
Silents
GATEWAY OF THE MOON, THE(1928)
Bert La Fortesa
WARKILL(1968, U.S./Phil.)
Lorraine La Fosse
LONDON MELODY(1930, Brit.); MELODY OF MY HEART(1936, Brit.)
George La Fountaine
TWO-MINUTE WARNING(1976), w
1984
FLASHPOINT(1984), w
Zaira La Fratta
LITTLE MARTYR, THE(1947, Ital.)
Ian La Frenais
JOKERS, THE(1967, Brit.), w; HANNIBAL BROOKS(1969, Brit.), w; ATCH ME A SPY(1971, Brit./Fr.), w; VILLAIN(1971, Brit.), w; LIKELY LADS, THE(1976, Brit.), w; DOING TIME(1979, Brit.), p, w; PRISONER OF ZENDA, THE(1979), w; BULLSHOT(1983), p
Celine La Freniere
CITY ON FIRE(1979 Can.), w
Ian La Fresnais
VIRGIN SOLDIERS, THE(1970, Brit.), w
Lina La Galla
SEDUCED AND ABANDONED(1964, Fr./Ital.)
Henri La Garde
Silents
MARRIAGE CLAUSE, THE(1926)
Misc. Silents
WAGES OF CONSCIENCE(1927)

Jocelyne La Garde
HAWAII(1966)
Jerome La Grasse
Silents
GREY DEVIL, THE(1926); WHEN SECONDS COUNT(1927)
Misc. Silents
GENTLEMAN PREFFERED, A(1928)
Ernesto La Guardia
MISSION BATANGAS(1968)
Fiorello La Guardia
CRAZY HOUSE(1943)
Bernard La Jarrige
MAN ABOUT TOWN(1947, Fr.); MADAME ROSA(1977, Fr.)
Roger La Joie
HOW COME NOBODY'S ON OUR SIDE?(1975)
Chris La Kome
WEDDING, A(1978)
Jack La Lanne
LADIES MAN, THE(1961)
Charles M. La Loggia
FEAR NO EVIL(1981), p
Danica La Loggia
FELLINI SATYRICON(1969, Fr./Ital.)
Danika La Loggia
ALFREDO, ALFREDO(1973, Ital.)
F. La Loggia
FEAR NO EVIL(1981), m
Frank La Loggia
FEAR NO EVIL(1981), p, d&w
Bobbie La Mache
HOUSE OF ROTHSCHILD, THE(1934)
Isabel La Mai
NO MORE LADIES(1935)
Elsier La Maie
Misc. Silents
UNFORTUNATE SEX, THE(1920), d
Isabel La Mal
DESIRE(1936); TOAST OF NEW YORK, THE(1937); WINGS OVER HONOLU-
LU(1937); CASANOVA BROWN(1944); MEN ON HER MIND(1944)
Isabelle La Mal
FUGITIVE LADY(1934); YOU'RE TELLING ME(1934); RUGGLES OF RED
GAP(1935); MEET JOHN DOE(1941); MURDER BY INVITATION(1941); OBLIGING
YOUNG LADY(1941); SECRETS OF A CO-ED(1942)
Donna La Manna
1984
SUBURBIA(1984)
Marie La Manna
Misc. Silents
SLAVEY STUDENT, THE(1915)
Piero La Mantia
NEST OF VIPERS(1979, Ital.), p
Laurence La Mar
SUNDOWN(1941)
Barbara La Marr
Silents
NUT, THE(1921); THREE MUSKETEERS, THE(1921); ARABIAN LOVE(1922); PRIS-
ONER OF ZENDA, THE(1922); ETERNAL STRUGGLE, THE(1923); HERO, THE(1923);
POOR MEN'S WIVES(1923); SOULS FOR SALE(1923); ST. ELMO(1923); STRANGERS
OF THE NIGHT(1923); MY HUSBAND'S WIVES(1924), w
Misc. Silents
DOMESTIC RELATIONS(1922); QUINCY ADAMS SAWYER(1922); TRIFLING
WOMEN(1922); ETERNAL CITY, THE(1923); SANDRA(1924); SHOOTING OF DAN
MCGREW, THE(1924); THY NAME IS WOMAN(1924); WHITE MOTH, THE(1924);
HEART OF A SIREN(1925); WHITE MONKEY, THE(1925); GIRL FROM MONTMAR-
TRE, THE(1926)
Margaret La Marr
HAPPY DAYS(1930); JUST IMAGINE(1930); KID FROM SPAIN, THE(1932); 42ND
STREET(1933)
Silents
RED WINE(1928)
Richard La Marr
ONE NIGHT OF LOVE(1934); ALL MY SONS(1948)
Ruth La Marr
Misc. Silents
WHITE HELL(1922)
Alfonso P. La Mastra
CHROME AND HOT LEATHER(1971), ed
Isobel La Mel
MY SON, THE HERO(1943)
William La Messena
ALL THAT JAZZ(1979)
Alice La Mont
SATAN MET A LADY(1936)
Connie La Mont
Misc. Silents
SCARLET YOUTH(1928)
Frank La Mont
FOX MOVIETONE FOLLIES(1929)
Harry La Mont
Silents
BLOOD AND SAND(1922); PEACEFUL PETERS(1922)
Julian La Mothe
Silents
WINDING STAIR, THE(1925), w
Dick La Motte
RETURN OF A MAN CALLED HORSE, THE(1976), cos
Jean La Motte
Misc. Silents
FOLLY OF VANITY, THE(1924)

Marguerite De La Motte
Silents
JUST LIKE A WOMAN(1923); GIRL WHO WOULDN'T WORK, THE(1925)
Richard La Motte
ISLAND OF DR. MOREAU, THE(1977), cos
Dea St. La Mount
HUNTER, THE(1980)
Pierre La Mure
MOULIN ROUGE(1952), w
Ed La Niece
Silents
RANGE RIDERS, THE(1927); WESTERN COURAGE(1927)
Misc. Silents
DOUBLE O, THE(1921); RIDERS OF THE WEST(1927); THUNDERING THOMP-
SON(1929)
Dee La Nore
PALEFACE, THE(1948)
Nick La Padula
THAT'S THE WAY OF THE WORLD(1975)
Vittorio La Paglia
HIGH INFIDELITY(1965, Fr./Ital.); HAWKS AND THE SPARROWS, THE(1967, Ital.)
James La Para
Misc. Silents
MOTHER MACHREE(1922)
Harry La Pearl
Silents
STILL WATERS(1915)
Arturo La Pegna
1984
BASILEUS QUARTET(1984, Ital.), p
Anthony La Penna
PAISAN(1948, Ital.)
J. Anthony la Penna
ROOM TO LET(1949, Brit.)
Georganne La Piere
JENNIFER(1978)
La Pillina
PANDORA AND THE FLYING DUTCHMAN(1951, Brit.)
Louise La Planche
LOUISIANA PURCHASE(1941); ZIEGFELD GIRL(1941); ROAD TO MOROC-
CO(1942); STAR SPANGLED RHYTHM(1942); THIS GUN FOR HIRE(1942); FOR
WHOM THE BELL TOLLS(1943); LADY OF BURLESQUE(1943); RIDING HIGH(1943);
SALUTE FOR THREE(1943); AND THE ANGELS SING(1944); PRACTICALLY
YOURS(1944); RAINBOW ISLAND(1944)
Rosemary La Planche
100 MEN AND A GIRL(1937); IRENE(1940); AROUND THE WORLD(1943); FALCON
OUT WEST, THE(1944); HEAVENLY DAYS(1944); MADEMOISELLE FIFI(1944);
NONE BUT THE LONELY HEART(1944); STEP LIVELY(1944); YOUTH RUNS
WILD(1944); PAN-AMERICANA(1945); STRANGLER OF THE SWAMP(1945); DEVIL
BAT'S DAUGHTER, THE(1946); OLD-FASHIONED GIRL, AN(1948)
Misc. Talkies
GOLDEN HANDS OF KURIGAL, THE(1949)
Beatrice La Plante
Misc. Silents
ROSE OF THE WEST(1919); BEGGAR PRINCE, THE(1920); FIXED BY GEOR-
GE(1920)
Laura La Plante
HOLD YOUR MAN(1929); LAST WARNING, THE(1929); LOVE TRAP, THE(1929);
SCANDAL(1929); SHOW BOAT(1929); CAPTAIN OF THE GUARD(1930); GOD'S GIFT
TO WOMEN(1931); LONELY WIVES(1931); MEN ARE LIKE THAT(1931); SEA
GHOST, THE(1931); HER IMAGINARY LOVER(1933, Brit.); CHURCH MOUSE,
THE(1934, Brit.); GIRL IN POSSESSION(1934, Brit.); WIDOW'S MIGHT(1934, Brit.);
MAN OF THE MOMENT(1935, Brit.); LITTLE MISTER JIM(1946)
Silents
BIG TOWN IDEAS(1921); OLD SWIMMIN' HOLE, THE(1921); WALL FLOWER,
THE(1922); CROOKED ALLEY(1923); OUT OF LUCK(1923); SHOOTIN' FOR LO-
VE(1923); EXCITEMENT(1924); RIDE FOR YOUR LIFE(1924); BEAUTIFUL CHEAT,
THE(1926); SKINNER'S DRESS SUIT(1926); CAT AND THE CANARY, THE(1927);
THANKS FOR THE BUGGY RIDE(1928)
Misc. Silents
"813"(1920); PLAY SQUARE(1921); BURNING WORDS(1923); CROOKED AL-
LEY(1923); DEAD GAME(1923); RAMBLIN' KID, THE(1923); BUTTERFLY(1924);
DANGEROUS BLONDE, THE(1924); FAST WORKER, THE(1924); FATAL PLUNGE,
THE(1924); SPORTING YOUTH(1924); YOUNG IDEAS(1924); DANGEROUS INNO-
CENCE(1925); SMOULDERING FIRES(1925); BUTTERFLIES IN THE RAIN(1926);
HER BIG NIGHT(1926); MIDNIGHT SUN, THE(1926); POKER FACES(1926);
BEWARE OF WINDOWS(1927); LOVE THRILL, THE(1927); SILK STOCKINGS(1927);
FINDERS KEEPERS(1928); HOME JAMES(1928)
Violet La Plante
Silents
WALLOPING WALLACE(1924); HURRICANE KID, THE(1925); MY HOME
TOWN(1928)
Misc. Silents
BATTLING BUDDY(; (1924); HIS MAJESTY THE OUTLAW(1924); RAMBLIN'
GALOOT, THE(1926)
Richard La Pore
MANCHURIAN CANDIDATE, THE(1962)
Arturo La Porta
LA TRAVIATA(1968, Ital.)
Fred La Porta
HIDEOUS SUN DEMON, THE(1959)
Elizza La Porte
Silents
STUDENT OF PRAGUE, THE(1927, Ger.)
Philippe La Prelle
ME AND MY BROTHER(1969)
Robert La Presle
MR. SATAN(1938, Brit.), ph

Antonio La Raina
SCANDAL IN SORRENTO(1957, Ital./Fr.)
Arthur La Ral
ENEMY BELOW, THE(1957)
Barbara La Rene
WONDER MAN(1945)
Baby La Reno
Silents
BREWSTER'S MILLIONS(1914)
Dick La Reno
Silents
BREWSTER'S MILLIONS(1914); MAN FROM HOME, THE(1914); READY MO-
NEY(1914); ROSE OF THE RANCHO(1914); SQUAW MAN, THE(1914); VIRGINIAN,
THE(1914); WARRENS OF VIRGINIA, THE(1915); TARGET, THE(1916); ISO-
BEL(1920); OUT OF THE SILENT NORTH(1922); PLAYING IT WILD(1923); OH, YOU
TONY!(1924); RIDIN' MAD(1924); SEA HORSES(1926); APACHE RAIDER, THE(1928)
Misc. Silents
RECLAMATION, THE(1916); MR. LOGAN, USA(1918); GO GET 'EM GARRIN-
GER(1919); HELL SHIP, THE(1920); SPIRIT OF GOOD, THE(1920); CRASHIN'
THROUGH(1924); THREE DAYS TO LIVE(1924); WATERFRONT WOLVES(1924);
GOLD FROM WEEPAH(1927)
Dick La Reno, Jr.
Misc. Silents
BLUE BLAZES(1926)
Jack La Reno
Silents
BLUSHING BRIDE, THE(1921)
Miss La Reno
DANCE OF LIFE, THE(1929)
Richard La Reno
Silents
SPINDLE OF LIFE, THE(1917); KINGDOM OF LOVE, THE(1918)
Misc. Silents
BLACK ORCHIDS(1917); REWARD OF THE FAITHLESS, THE(1917)
Utahna La Reno
Silents
SQUAW MAN, THE(1914)
Mary La Roche
LINEUP, THE(1958)
Pierre La Roche
GOIN' DOWN THE ROAD(1970, Can.)
William La Roche
Silents
BUCKING THE TRUTH(1926)
Norman La Rochelle
SEDUCTION OF JOE TYNAN, THE(1979)
Pierre Drieu La Rochelle
FIRE WITHIN, THE(1964, Fr./Ital.), w; WOMAN AT HER WINDOW, A(1978,
Fr./Ital./Ger.), w
Rodney La Rock
Silents
EFFICIENCY EDGAR'S COURTSHIP(1917)
Rod La Rocque
DELIGHTFUL ROGUE(1929); LOCKED DOOR, THE(1929); LET US BE GAY(1930);
ONE ROMANTIC NIGHT(1930); S.O.S. ICEBERG(1933); HI GAUCHO!(1936);
CLOTHES AND THE WOMAN(1937, Brit.); SHADOW STRIKES, THE(1937); TAMING
THE WILD(1937); INTERNATIONAL CRIME(1938)
Silents
PERFECT LADY, A(1918); MISS CRUSOE(1919); NOTORIETY(1922); SLIM SHOUL-
DERS(1922); FRENCH DOLL, THE(1923); JAZZMANIA(1923); TEN COMMAND-
MENTS, THE(1923); CODE OF THE SEA(1924); FORBIDDEN PARADISE(1924);
SOCIETY SCANDAL, A(1924); COMING OF AMOS, THE(1925); NIGHT LIFE OF NEW
YORK(1925); RED DICE(1926); HOLD 'EM YALE!(1928); SHOW PEOPLE(1928);
STAND AND DELIVER(1928); OUR MODERN MAIDENS(1929)
Misc. Silents
DREAM DOLL, THE(1917); HIDDEN FIRES(1918); LET'S GET A DIVORCE(1918);
MONEY MAD(1918); PERFECT 36, A(1918); VENUS MODEL, THE(1918); TRAP,
THE(1919); COMMON SIN, THE(1920); DISCARDED WOMAN, THE(1920); GARTER
GIRL, THE(1920); STOLEN KISS, THE(1920); PAYING THE PIPER(1921); CHAL-
LENGE, THE(1922); WHAT'S WRONG WITH THE WOMEN?(1922); FEET OF
CLAY(1924); PHANTOM JUSTICE(1924); TRIUMPH(1924); BRAVEHEART(1925);
GOLDEN BED, THE(1925); WILD, WILD SUSAN(1925); BACHELOR BRIDES(1926);
CRUISE OF THE JASPER B, THE(1926); GIGOLO(1926); FIGHTING EAGLE,
THE(1927); RESURRECTION(1927); CAPTAIN SWAGGER(1928); LOVE OVER
NIGHT(1928); ONE WOMAN IDEA, THE(1929)
Roderick La Rocque
Misc. Silents
FILLING HIS OWN SHOES(1917)
Julius La Rosa
LET'S ROCK(1958)
Poupee La Rose
PARIS OOH-LA-LA!(1963, U.S./Fr.)
Rose La Rose
QUEEN OF BURLESQUE(1946)
Carmen La Roux
SON OF OKLAHOMA(1932); CHEYENNE RIDES AGAIN(1937)
Rita La Roy
SERGEANT YORK(; DELIGHTFUL ROGUE(1929); AMOS 'N' ANDY(1930); CON-
SPIRACY(1930); LILIES OF THE FIELD(1930); LOVIN' THE LADIES(1930); HOLY
TERROR, A(1931); TRAVELING HUSBANDS(1931); BACHELOR'S AFFAIRS(1932);
BLONDE VENUS(1932); HONOR OF THE PRESS(1932); HOT SATURDAY(1932);
SINNERS IN THE SUN(1932); WHILE PARIS SLEEPS(1932); NAME THE WO-
MAN(1934); ONE IS GUILTY(1934); WHIRLPOOL(1934); HOLLYWOOD BOULE-
VARD(1936); MANDARIN MYSTERY, THE(1937); BORDER G-MAN(1938);
CONDEMNED WOMEN(1938); DANGEROUS TO KNOW(1938)
Marga la Rubia
Silents
ARSENE LUPIN(1916, Brit.)

Misc. Silents
BETTA THE GYPSY(1918, Brit.)
Danny La Rue
OUR MISS FRED(1972, Brit.)
Emily La Rue
ZAZA(1939); WHAT DID YOU DO IN THE WAR, DADDY?(1966); STRAIGHT
TIME(1978)
Fontaine La Rue
Silents
SINS OF ROZANNE(1920); EXIT THE VAMP(1921); FAITH HEALER, THE(1921);
BLIND BARGAIN, A(1922); LOVE LETTER, THE(1923); DAUGHTERS OF TO-
DAY(1924)
Misc. Silents
BOOTS(1919); WOMAN UNDER COVER, THE(1919); LOST ROMANCE, THE(1921);
UNSEEN HANDS(1924); HIS NEW YORK WIFE(1926)
Jack La Rue, Jr.
YOUNG NURSES, THE(1973)
Jane La Rue
Misc. Silents
TRACY THE OUTLAW(1928)
Jerry La Rue
LIAR'S DICE(1980)
John La Rue
Misc. Silents
RECKLESS MONEY(1926)
Adrienne La Russa
PSYCHOUT FOR MURDER(1971, Arg./Ital.)
Ed La Saint
HIGH SPEED(1932)
Bobbie La Salle
1984
RHINESTONE(1984)
Bobby La Salle
FIRST YANK INTO TOKYO(1945); MISFITS, THE(1961)
Dick La Salle
TANK BATTALION(1958), m
Katherine La Salle
Misc. Silents
BANKER'S DAUGHTER, THE(1914); FIGHT, THE(1915)
Pierre La Salle
OF FLESH AND BLOOD(1964, Fr./Ital.), w
Richard La Salle
BOY WHO CAUGHT A CROOK(1961), m; SECRET OF DEEP HARBOR(1961), m;
SNIPER'S RIDGE(1961), m; WHEN THE CLOCK STRIKES(1961), m; WILD
YOUTH(1961), m; YOU HAVE TO RUN FAST(1961), m; FIREBRAND, THE(1962), m;
INCIDENT IN AN ALLEY(1962), m; MERMAIDS OF TIBURON, THE(1962), m;
CALIFORNIA(1963), m; DAY MARS INVADED EARTH, THE(1963), m; TWICE TOLD
TALES(1963), m; BLOOD ON THE ARROW(1964), m; DESERT RAVEN, THE(1965),
m; AMBUSH BAY(1966), m; BOY, DID I GET A WRONG NUMBER!(1966), m
Jo Jo La Savio
LAW OF THE PAMPAS(1939)
Joe La Shelle
Silents
WHISPERING SMITH(1926), ph
Joseph La Shelle
HAPPY LAND(1943), ph; BERMUDA MYSTERY(1944), ph; EVE OF ST. MARK,
THE(1944), ph; LAURA(1944), ph; BELL FOR ADANO, A(1945), ph; DOLL FA-
CE(1945), ph; HANGOVER SQUARE(1945), ph; CLUNY BROWN(1946), ph; FOXES
OF HARROW, THE(1947), ph; LATE GEORGE APLEY, THE(1947), ph; DEEP WA-
TERS(1948), ph; LUCK OF THE IRISH(1948), ph; ROAD HOUSE(1948), ph; EVERY-
BODY DOES IT(1949), ph; FAN, THE(1949), ph; MOTHER DIDN'T TELL
ME(1950), ph; WHERE THE SIDEWALK ENDS(1950), ph; ELOPEMENT(1951), ph;
GUY WHO CAME BACK, THE(1951), ph; LES MISERABLES(1952), ph; MY COUSIN
RACHEL(1952), ph; OUTCASTS OF POKER FLAT, THE(1952), ph; SOMETHING FOR
THE BIRDS(1952), ph; DANGEROUS CROSSING(1953), ph; MR. SCOUTMAS-
TER(1953), ph; RIVER OF NO RETURN(1954), ph; MARTY(1955), ph; RUN FOR THE
SUN(1956), ph; STORM FEAR(1956), ph; ABDUCTORS, THE(1957), ph; BACHELOR
PARTY, THE(1957), ph; I WAS A TEENAGE WEREWOLF(1957), ph; NO DOWN
PAYMENT(1957), ph; LONG, HOT SUMMER, THE(1958), ph; CAREER(1959), ph;
IRMA LA DOUCE(1963), ph; CHASE, THE(1966), ph; SEVEN WOMEN(1966), ph; 80
STEPS TO JONAH(1969), ph
Kirk La Shelle
VIRGINIAN, THE(1929), w; VIRGINIAN, THE(1946), w
Silents
VIRGINIAN, THE(1914), w; VIRGINIAN, THE(1923), w
Dick La Strange
Silents
SQUAW MAN, THE(1914); GIRL OF THE GOLDEN WEST, THE(1915); WARRENS
OF VIRGINIA, THE(1915)
Natalie La Supervia
Misc. Silents
FUGITIVE, THE(1925)
Charles La Torre
CASABLANCA(1942); LIFE BEGINS AT 8:30(1942); MY SISTER EILEEN(1942);
BACKGROUND TO DANGER(1943); DIXIE(1943); MISSION TO MOSCOW(1943);
SONG OF BERNADETTE, THE(1943); THREE HEARTS FOR JULIA(1943); HAIRY
APE, THE(1944); JAM SESSION(1944); KISMET(1944); PASSAGE TO MARSEIL-
LE(1944); UNCERTAIN GLORY(1944); BELL FOR ADANO, A(1945); YOLANDA AND
THE THIEF(1945); YOU CAME ALONG(1945); TROUBLE MAKERS(1948); WHEN MY
BABY SMILES AT ME(1948); BOMBA AND THE HIDDEN CITY(1950); 711 OCEAN
DRIVE(1950); DIPLOMATIC COURIER(1952); TALK ABOUT A STRANGER(1952);
THREE COINS IN THE FOUNTAIN(1954); OMAR KHAYYAM(1957); LAST OF THE
SECRET AGENTS?, THE(1966)
Giuseppe La Torre
FEDORA(1946), ph; VERGINITA(1953, Ital.), ph; SULEIMAN THE CONQUER-
OR(1963, Ital.), ph
Phil La Toska
WAY DOWN EAST(1935)

Donna La Tour
HOUSE OF STRANGERS(1949)
Robert La Tourneaux
BOYS IN THE BAND, THE(1970)
Peter La Trobe
ORDERS TO KILL(1958, Brit.)
Mike La Valley
FORBIDDEN WORLD(1982), spec eff
William La Valley
THIEF(1981)
Laura La Varnie
DEVIL'S HOLIDAY, THE(1930)
Silents
MICKEY(1919)
Misc. Silents
UNPAINTED WOMAN, THE(1919); UP IN THE AIR ABOUT MARY(1922)
Marie La Varre
Silents
CRIMSON DOVE, THE(1917)
Myrtland La Varre
Silents
KNOCKOUT REILLY(1927)
Jean La Vell
JOAN OF ARC(1948)
Barbara La Velle
HAPPY DAYS(1930)
Kay La Velle
TWO DOLLAR BETTOR(1951)
Pear La Velle
HAPPY DAYS(1930)
June La Vere
Silents
MAID OF THE WEST(1921)
Misc. Silents
DANGER(1923)
Jane La Verne
MELODY LANE(1929); SHOW BOAT(1929)
Silents
NEW YEAR'S EVE(1929)
Larry La Verne
Silents
RACING FOR LIFE(1924)
Lucile La Verne
Silents
AMERICA(1924)
Lucille La Verne
ABRAHAM LINCOLN(1930); SINNER'S HOLIDAY(1930); AMERICAN TRAGEDY, AN(1931); GREAT, MEADOW, THE(1931); LITTLE CAESAR(1931); 24 HOURS(1931); ALIAS THE DOCTOR(1932); WHILE PARIS SLEEPS(1932); PILGRIMAGE(1933); BELOVED(1934); MIGHTY BARNUM, THE(1934); SCHOOL FOR GIRLS(1935); TALE OF TWO CITIES, A(1935)
Silents
POLLY OF THE CIRCUS(1917); PRAISE AGENT, THE(1919); ORPHANS OF THE STORM(1922); WHITE ROSE, THE(1923); HIS DARKER SELF(1924)
Misc. Silents
ZAZA(1923); SUN-UP(1925); LAST MOMENT, THE(1928)
Anton La Vey
DEVIL'S RAIN, THE(1975, U.S./Mex.)
Diane La Vey
DEVIL'S RAIN, THE(1975, U.S./Mex.)
Emile La Vigne
SWORD IN THE DESERT(1949), makeup; FRIENDLY PERSUASION(1956), makeup; 20,000 EYES(1961), makeup; KINGS OF THE SUN(1963), makeup; LOVED ONE, THE(1965), makeup; WHERE IT'S AT(1969), makeup; MONTE WALSH(1970), makeup; PRIME CUT(1972), makeup
Gracille La Vinder
ADAM'S RIB(1949)
Juliet La Violette
Silents
REJECTED WOMAN, THE(1924)
Juliette La Violette
Silents
WHITE SISTER, THE(1923)
Wesley La Violette
Misc. Talkies
BODY IS A SHELL, THE(1957)
Raoul La Vista
BEAST OF HOLLOW MOUNTAIN, THE(1956), m
Raul La Vista
FOR THE LOVE OF MIKE(1960), m
La'ili
RETURN TO PARADISE(1953)
Jean La'Ple
Silents
LADIES AT EASE(1927), t
Barbara Laage
B. F.'S DAUGHTER(1948); ACT OF LOVE(1953); GUILTY?(1956, Brit.); HAPPY ROAD, THE(1957); PARIS BLUES(1961); SOFT SKIN ON BLACK SILK(1964, Fr./Span.); THERESE AND ISABELLE(1968, U.S./Ger.); BED AND BOARD(1971, Fr.)
Florence LaBadie
Misc. Silents
CARDINAL RICHELIEU'S WARD(1914); GOD'S WITNESS(1915); M. LECOQ(1915); PRICE OF HER SILENCE, THE(1915); DIVORCE AND THE DAUGHTER(1916); FIVE FAULTS OF FLO, THE(1916); FUGITIVE, THE(1916); MASTER SHAKESPEARE, STROLLING PLAYER(1916); PILLORY, THE(1916); SAINT, DEVIL AND WOMAN(1916); HER LIFE AND HIS(1917); MAN WITHOUT A COUNTRY, THE(1917); WAR AND THE WOMAN(1917); WHEN LOVE WAS BLIND(1917); WOMAN IN WHITE, THE(1917)

Bob Labansat
BEAST OF YUCCA FLATS, THE(1961); SKATETOWN, U.S.A.(1979), cos
Adele Labanset
RAINS CAME, THE(1939)
Fidel LaBarba
FOOTLIGHT SERENADE(1942), w
Joe LaBarba
WHIPLASH(1948)
Marta Labarr
BALL AT SAVOY(1936, Brit.); SECOND BUREAU(1937, Brit.); BREAK THE NEWS(1938, Brit.); SINGING COP, THE(1938, Brit.); TORSO MURDER MYSTERY, THE(1940, Brit.); IT HAPPENED TO ONE MAN(1941, Brit.); MAXWELL ARCHER, DETECTIVE(1942, Brit.); CONSPIRACY IN TEHERAN(1948, Brit.)
Andre Labarthe
LIFE BEGINS TOMORROW(1952, Fr.)
Andre S. Labarthe
MY LIFE TO LIVE(1963, Fr.)
Robert LaBassiere
BOY FRIEND, THE(1971, Brit.); REVENGE OF THE PINK PANTHER(1978)
Vincent LaBauve
SWEET JESUS, PREACHER MAN(1973)
Anne-Marie Labaye
LE CIEL EST A VOUS(1957, Fr.)
Leon Label
PASSION HOLIDAY(1963)
Gene Labell
DEAD MEN DON'T WEAR PLAID(1982)
Vincenzo Labella
FRANCIS OF ASSISI(1961), tech adv; AND THERE CAME A MAN(1968, Ital.), w; MOSES(1976, Brit./Ital.), p
Gene LaBelle
CHILDISH THINGS(1969)
Michel Labelle
FANTASTICA(1980, Can./Fr.)
Michel Rene LaBelle
HAPPY BIRTHDAY TO ME(1981)
Patti LaBelle
1984
SOLDIER'S STORY, A(1984)
Benoit Laberge
1984
HOTEL NEW HAMPSHIRE, THE(1984)
Arthur LaBern
TIME TO REMEMBER(1962, Brit.), w; ACCIDENTAL DEATH(1963, Brit.), w; FRENZY(1972, Brit.), w
Jose Maria Labernie
EVERY DAY IS A HOLIDAY(1966, Span.)
Alla Labetskaya
GORDEYEV FAMILY, THE(1961, U.S.S.R.)
Louis LaBey
SUEZ(1938)
Elisabeth Labi
LEAP INTO THE VOID(1982, Ital.)
Eugene Labiche
Silents
ITALIAN STRAW HAT, AN(1927, Fr.), w
Lloyd Labie
AND NOW THE SCREAMING STARTS(1973, Brit.)
Labina
LAST SAFARI, THE(1967, Brit.)
I. Labina
WAR AND PEACE(1968, USSR)
David Labisoa
ENTITY, THE(1982)
Erin LaBissoniere
GOOD DAME(1934)
Gelles LaBlanc
GOSPEL ROAD, THE(1973)
Ethel LaBlanche
HOLLYWOOD ROUNDUP(1938), w; EXILE EXPRESS(1939), w
Fib LaBlanque
GHASTLY ONES, THE(1968)
DeVaughn LaBon
RED, WHITE AND BLACK, THE(1970)
Halina Labonarska
MAN OF IRON(1981, Pol.)
Terry Labonte
STROKER ACE(1983)
Sam Laborador
GENERAL DIED AT DAWN, THE(1936)
Nicolas Laborczy
SMALL CIRCLE OF FRIENDS, A(1980), set d
Jean Laborde
DON'T TEMPT THE DEVIL(1964, Fr./Ital.), w
C. Laboreur
MARIE OF THE ISLES(1960, Fr.), ed
Ella Laboriel
UNDER FIRE(1983)
Juan Jose Laboriel
SLAUGHTER(1972)
Prof. Henri Laborit
MON ONCLE D'AMERIQUE(1980, Fr.), a, w
Matthew Laborteaux
WOMAN UNDER THE INFLUENCE, A(1974); KING OF THE GYPSIES(1978)
Elina Labourdette
SHANGHAI DRAMA, THE(1945, Fr.); EDWARD AND CAROLINE(1952, Fr.); TO PARIS WITH LOVE(1955, Brit.); PARIS DOES STRANGE THINGS(1957, Fr./Ital.); TRUTH ABOUT WOMEN, THE(1958, Brit.); LOLA(1961, Fr./Ital.); TALES OF PARIS(1962, Fr./Ital.); FIVE MILES TO MIDNIGHT(1963, U.S./Fr./Ital.); LADIES OF THE PARK(1964, Fr.); TWO ARE GUILTY(1964, Fr.)

Dominique Labourier
IT ONLY HAPPENS TO OTHERS(1971, Fr./Ital.); CELINE AND JULIE GO BOAT-ING(1974, Fr.), a, w; LE PETIT THEATRE DE JEAN RENOIR(1974, Fr.); JONAH-WHO WILL BE 25 IN THE YEAR 2000(1976, Switz.); CITY OF WOMEN(1980, Ital./Fr.); LA PASSANTE(1983, Fr./Ger.)

Hilary Labow
ROCKY HORROR PICTURE SHOW, THE(1975, Brit.)

John Labow
WINTER KEPT US WARM(1968, Can.)

Armond Labowitz
1984
SPECIAL EFFECTS(1984), ed

Jean-Pierre Labrande
MR. KLEIN(1976, Fr.), p

Jean-Claude Labrecque
TAKE IT ALL(1966, Can.), ph; CAT IN THE SACK, THE(1967, Can.), ph; GREAT BIG THING, A(1968, U.S./Can.), ph

Jacques Labreque
SOHO CONSPIRACY(1951, Brit.); ACTION STATIONS(1959, Brit.)

Coral Labrie
L'AMOUR(1973)

Ginger LaBrie
1984
AGAINST ALL ODDS(1984)

Maurice Labro
DEADLY DECOYS, THE(1962, Fr.), d, w

Philippe Labro
MADE IN U.S.A.(1966, Fr.); WITHOUT APPARENT MOTIVE(1972, Fr.), d, w

Michel Labry
DON'T PLAY WITH MARTIANS(1967, Fr.), w

Pierre Labry
MAN STOLEN(1934, Fr.); ANNE-MARIE(1936, Fr.); CARNIVAL IN FLAND-ERS(1936, Fr.); STORY OF A CHEAT, THE(1938, Fr.); ENTENTE CORDIALE(1939, Fr.); IT HAPPENED AT THE INN(1945, Fr.); BELLMAN, THE(1947, Fr.); DEVIL'S ENVOYS, THE(1947, Fr.)

Vladimir Labsky
ADELE HASN'T HAD HER SUPPER YET(1978, Czech.), set d; NINTH HEART, THE(1980, Czech.), set d

Nick Labuschagne
DEMON, THE(1981, S. Africa), m

Andre Labussiere
TOPKAPI(1964), set d

Henri Labussiere
WAR OF THE BUTTONS(1963 Fr.)

Jose Lacaba
JAGUAR(1980, Phil.), w

Daniel Lacambre
WILD RACERS, THE(1968), ph; EROTIQUE(1969, Fr.), ph; PADDY(1970, Irish), ph; VELVET VAMPIRE, THE(1971), ph; TERMINAL ISLAND(1973), ph; MACON COUN-TY LINE(1974), ph; SIX PACK ANNIE(1975), ph; LADY IN RED, THE(1979), ph; BATTLE BEYOND THE STARS(1980), ph; HUMANOIDS FROM THE DEEP(1980), ph; SATURDAY THE 14TH(1981), ph

Peter Lacangelo
HANKY-PANKY(1982)

Dominique Lacarriere
JULES AND JIM(1962, Fr.); SOFT SKIN, THE(1964, Fr.)

Francis Lacassin
JUDEX(1966, Fr./Ital.), w; JE T'AIME, JE T'AIME(1972, Fr./Swed.)

George LaCava
LAUGH AND GET RICH(1931), w

Gregory LaCava
BIG NEWS(1929), d; HIS FIRST COMMAND(1929), d, w; LAUGH AND GET RICH(1931), d; HALF-NAKED TRUTH, THE(1932), d, w; BED OF ROSES(1933), d; GABRIEL OVER THE WHITE HOUSE(1933), d; WHAT EVERY WOMAN KNOWS(1934), d; SHE MARRIED HER BOSS(1935), d; PRIMROSE PATH(1940), p&d, w

Joe LaCava
HOLD THAT GHOST(1941)

Leo LaCava
YOU GOTTA STAY HAPPY(1948), makeup

Lou Lacava
PAY OR DIE(1960), spec eff

Louis LaCava
PREMATURE BURIAL, THE(1962), makeup

Yolanda Lacca
LAURA(1944); STORY OF G.I. JOE, THE(1945); CHASE, THE(1946)

Ann Lace
SECRET HEART, THE(1946)

Lentia Lace
FEDERAL AGENT(1936)

Rita Lacedo
STRONGHOLD(1952, Mex.)

Peg LaCentra
COWBOY BLUES(1946); HUMORESQUE(1946); MAN I LOVE, THE(1946); SMASH-UP, THE STORY OF A WOMAN(1947); EMERGENCY HOSPITAL(1956); DARK AT THE TOP OF THE STAIRS, THE(1960)

Jose Carlos Lacerda
BYE-BYE BRASIL(1980, Braz.)

Jacques Lacerte
LOVE ME DEADLY(1972), d&w

Adele Lacey
KID FROM SPAIN, THE(1932); WHEN A MAN RIDES ALONE(1933)

Bruce Lacey
RING-A-DING RHYTHM(1962, Brit. 73m Amicus/COL bw (G.B: IT'S TRAD, DAD!); MOUSE ON THE MOON, THE(1963, Brit.); HELP!(1965, Brit.); KNACK ... AND HOW TO GET IT, THE(1965, Brit.); SMASHING TIME(1967 Brit.)

Carl Lacey
LOYAL HEART(1946, Brit.)

Catharine Lacey
LADY VANISHES, THE(1938, Brit.)

Catherine Lacey
CASTLE OF CRIMES(1940, Brit.); BOMBSIGHT STOLEN(1941, Brit.); POISON PEN(1941, Brit.); CARNIVAL(1946, Brit.); BAD SISTER(1947, Brit.); I KNOW WHERE I'M GOING(1947, Brit.); WHEN THE BOUGH BREAKS(1947, Brit.); OCTOBER MAN, THE(1948, Brit.); TIGHT LITTLE ISLAND(1949, Brit.); PINK STRING AND SEALING WAX(1950, Brit.); DECISION AGAINST TIME(1957, Brit.); INNOCENT SIN-NERS(1958, Brit.); MAD LITTLE ISLAND(1958, Brit.); SOLITARY CHILD, THE(1958, Brit.); ANOTHER SKY(1960 Brit.); SHADOW OF THE CAT, THE(1961, Brit.); SERV-ANT, THE(1964, Brit.); MUMMY'S SHROUD, THE(1967, Brit.); SORCERERS, THE(1967, Brit.); PRIVATE LIFE OF SHERLOCK HOLMES, THE(1970, Brit.)

Cathryn Lacey
MARDI GRAS MASSACRE(1978)

Clay Lacey
LAST CHASE, THE(1981), ph

Enrique Lacey
UNDER THE PAMPAS MOON(1935)

Frank Lacey
PATH OF GLORY, THE(1934, Brit.)

Franklin Lacey
MUSIC MAN, THE(1962), w

Franklyn Lacey
RAIN FOR A DUSTY SUMMER(1971, U.S./Span.), w

Squadron Ldr. Ginger Lacey
BATTLE OF BRITAIN, THE(1969, Brit.), tech adv

Jacqueline Lacey
ACCIDENTAL DEATH(1963, Brit.)

Laura Lacey
I LOVE MY WIFE(1970)

Margaret Lacey
ROTTEN TO THE CORE(1956, Brit.); HAPPY IS THE BRIDE(1958, Brit.); I'M ALL RIGHT, JACK(1959, Brit.); RISK, THE(1961, Brit.); SEANCE ON A WET AFTER-NOON(1964 Brit.); FAMILY WAY, THE(1966, Brit.); DEADLY AFFAIR, THE(1967, Brit.); FAR FROM THE MADDING CROWD(1967, Brit.); THERE'S A GIRL IN MY SOUP(1970, Brit.); BLACK BEAUTY(1971, Brit./Ger./Span.); DIAMONDS ARE FOREVER(1971, Brit.); CRY OF THE PENGUINS(1972, Brit.); RULING CLASS, THE(1972, Brit.); RICHARD'S THINGS(1981, Brit.)
1984
SECRET PLACES(1984, Brit.)

Patti Lacey
FOUR JACKS AND A JILL(1941)

Petra Lacey
NUN AT THE CROSSROADS, A(1970, Ital./Span.)

Rebecca Lacey
Misc. Talkies
TIGHTROPE TO TERROR(1977, Brit.)

Ronald Lacey
BOYS, THE(1962, Brit.); OF HUMAN BONDAGE(1964, Brit.); HAVING A WILD WEEKEND(1965, Brit.); FEARLESS VAMPIRE KILLERS, OR PARDON ME BUT YOUR TEETH ARE IN MY NECK, THE(1967); HOW I WON THE WAR(1967, Brit.); OTLEY(1969, Brit.); TAKE A GIRL LIKE YOU(1970, Brit,); SAY HELLO TO YESTER-DAY(1971, Brit.); GAWAIN AND THE GREEN KNIGHT(1973, Brit.); LAST DAYS OF MAN ON EARTH, THE(1975, Brit.); MR. QUILP(1975, Brit.); NIJINSKY(1980, Brit.); ZULU DAWN(1980, Brit.); RAIDERS OF THE LOST ARK(1981); FIREFOX(1982); TRENCHCOAT(1983); YELLOWBEARD(1983)
1984
ADVENTURES OF BUCKAROO BANZAI: ACROSS THE 8TH DIMENSION, THE(1984); MAKING THE GRADE(1984); SAHARA(1984); SWORD OF THE VAL-IANT(1984, Brit.)

Vivienne Lacey
WEB OF SUSPICION(1959, Brit.); LINDA(1960, Brit.); MISSING NOTE, THE(1961, Brit.)

Andree Lachapelle
DON'T LET THE ANGELS FALL(1969, Can.)

Lucien Lacharmoise
LUCRECE BORGIA(1953, Ital./Fr.), ed

Catherine Lachens
1984
SWANN IN LOVE(1984, Fr.Ger.)

Taylor Lacher
SANTEE(1973); DEVIL TIMES FIVE(1974); MR. MAJESTYK(1974); BAKER'S HAWK(1976); FINAL CHAPTER–WALKING TALL zero(1977); FORCE OF ONE, A(1979); RUCKUS(1981)

Charles Lachman
MORE(1969, Luxembourg), p

Donna Blue Lachman
1984
WHAT YOU TAKE FOR GRANTED(1984)

Edward Lachman
LORDS OF FLATBUSH, THE(1974), ph; UNION CITY(1980), ph

Edward Lachman, Jr.
SCALPEL(1976), ph

Harry Lachman
COMPULSORY HUSBAND, THE(1930, Brit.), d; GREENWOOD TREE, THE ze-ro(1930, Brit.), d; SONG OF SOHO(1930, Brit.), d, w; UNDER THE GREENWOOD TREE(1930, Brit.), d, w; YELLOW MASK, THE(1930, Brit.), d; LOVE HABIT, THE(1931, Brit.), d; ARENT WE ALL?(1932, Brit.), d; DOWN OUR STREET(1932, Brit.), d&w; INSULT(1932, Brit.), d; FACE IN THE SKY(1933), d; OUTSIDER, THE(1933, Brit.), d, w; PADDY, THE NEXT BEST THING(1933), d; BABY, TAKE A BOW(1934); GEORGE WHITE'S SCANDALS(1934), d; I LIKE IT THAT WAY(1934), d; NADA MAS QUE UNA MUJER(1934), d; DANTE'S INFERNO(1935), d; DRESSED TO THRILL(1935), d; CHARLIE CHAN AT THE CIRCUS(1936), d; MAN WHO LIVED TWICE(1936), d; OUR RELATIONS(1936), d; DEVIL IS DRIVING, THE(1937), d; IT HAPPENED IN HOLLYWOOD(1937), d; NO TIME TO MARRY(1938), d; MURDER OVER NEW YORK(1940), d; THEY CAME BY NIGHT(1940, Brit.), d; CHARLIE CHAN IN RIO(1941), d; DEAD MEN TELL(1941), d; CASTLE IN THE DESERT(1942), d; DR. RENAULT'S SECRET(1942), d; LOVES OF EDGAR ALLAN POE, THE(1942), d

Silents
WEEKEND WIVES(1928, Brit.), d
Mort Lachman
YOURS, MINE AND OURS(1968), w; MIXED COMPANY(1974), w
Stanley Lachman
AMAZING COLOSSAL MAN, THE(1957)
Marc Lachmann
HOORAY FOR LOVE(1935), w
A. Lloyd Lack
Misc. Silents
THINK IT OVER(1917)
C. Lack
LA BABY SITTER(1975, Fr./Ital./Gen.), ed
Christiane Lack
MAIN THING IS TO LOVE, THE(1975, Ital./Fr.), ed
George Lack
WHERE THE BULLETS FLY(1966, Brit.), art d; SOME MAY LIVE(1967, Brit.), prod d; BLISS OF MRS. BLOSSOM, THE(1968, Brit.), art d; MY SIDE OF THE MOUNTAIN(1969), art d; SAVAGE MESSIAH(1972, Brit.), art d
Otto Lack [Otto Lackovic]
VOYAGE TO THE END OF THE UNIVERSE(1963, Czech.)
Simon Lack
GOODBYE MR. CHIPS(1939, Brit.); JUST WILLIAM(1939, Brit.); SONS OF THE SEA(1939, Brit.); PROUD VALLEY, THE(1941, Brit.); SILVER DARLINGS, THE(1947, Brit.); BONNIE PRINCE CHARLIE(1948, Brit.); PORT OF ESCAPE(1955, Brit.); COURT MARTIAL OF MAJOR KELLER, THE(1961, Brit.); TROUBLE IN THE SKY(1961, Brit.); DURANT AFFAIR, THE(1962, Brit.); LONGEST DAY, THE(1962); MACBETH(1963); OPERATION SNAFU(1965, Brit.); CLUE OF THE TWISTED CANDLE(1968, Brit.); ALL AT SEA(1970, Brit.); BUSHBABY, THE(1970); TROG(1970, Brit.)
Stephen Lack
HEAD ON(1981, Can.); SCANNERS(1981, Can.)
1984
PERFECT STRANGERS(1984)
Steve Lack
RUBBER GUN, THE(1977, Can.), a, w
Susanna Lack
PURPLE HAZE(1982)
Helen Lackaye
Silents
KNIFE, THE(1918)
James Lackaye
Silents
CHRISTIAN, THE(1914); BATTLE CRY OF PEACE, THE(1915)
Misc. Silents
YORK STATE FOLKS(1915); UPSTART, THE(1916); PALS FIRST(1918)
Ruth Lackaye
Misc. Silents
BAB THE FIXER(1917); TWIN KIDDIES(1917); MIDNIGHT BURGLAR, THE(1918); MISS MISCHIEF MAKER(1918)
Wilton Lackaye
Silents
TRILBY(1915)
Misc. Silents
CHILDREN OF THE GHETTO, THE(1915); MAN OF SHAME, THE(1915); PIT, THE(1915); GOD'S CRUCIBLE(1921); WHAT'S WRONG WITH THE WOMEN?(1922); FOR WOMAN'S FAVOR(1924); LONE WOLF, THE(1924)
Wilton Lackaye, Jr.
REGISTERED NURSE(1934), w
Brad Lackey
Misc. Talkies
ONE CHANCE TO WIN(1976)
Douglas Lackey
SILENT WITNESS, THE(1962), m; AGENT FOR H.A.R.M.(1966), m; MOTHER GOOSE A GO-GO(1966), m; WARKILL(1968, U.S./Phil.), m; PROUD AND THE DAMNED, THE(1972), m; ADVENTURES OF THE WILDERNESS FAMILY, THE(1975), m; ACROSS THE GREAT DIVIDE(1976), m; FURTHER ADVENTURES OF THE WILDERNESS FAMILY–PART TWO(1978), m
Edward Lackey
Silents
KING OF KINGS, THE(1927); SOULS AFLAME(1928)
John Lackey
CREEPING TERROR, THE(1964), art d, spec eff
Michael Lackey
LONG RIDERS, THE(1980)
W.T. Lackey
PHANTOM BROADCAST, THE(1933), p; LOST IN THE STRATOSPHERE(1935), p
Misc. Silents
ROARING FIRES(1927), d
William Lackey
NAVY SECRETS(1939), p; DESTINATION BIG HOUSE(1950), p; INSURANCE INVESTIGATOR(1951), p; PRIDE OF MARYLAND(1951), p; SECRETS OF MONTE CARLO(1951), p; STREET BANDITS(1951), p
William T. Lackey
KLONDIKE(1932), p; CITY LIMITS(1934), p; GIRL O' MY DREAMS(1935), p; NUT FARM, THE(1935), p; GANGSTER'S BOY(1938), p; STREETS OF NEW YORK(1939), p; FATAL HOUR, THE(1940), p; HAUNTED HOUSE, THE(1940), p; TOMBOY(1940), p; HERE COMES KELLY(1943), p
Ben Lackland
BOOMERANG(1947)
Frank Lackteen
UNDER TWO FLAGS(1936); CRACKED NUTS(1931); LAW OF THE TONG(1931); COME ON DANGER!(1932); LAND OF WANTED MEN(1932); TEXAS PIONEERS(1932); NAGANA(1933); RUSTLERS' ROUNDUP(1933); TARZAN THE FEARLESS(1933); BRITISH AGENT(1934); ESCAPE FROM DEVIL'S ISLAND(1935); RENDEZVOUS(1935); CHARGE OF THE LIGHT BRIGADE, THE(1936); COMIN' ROUND THE MOUNTAIN(1936); ISLE OF FURY(1936); MUMMY'S BOYS(1936); I COVER THE WAR(1937); LEFT-HANDED LAW(1937); FOUR MEN AND A PRAYER(1938); SUEZ(1938); GIRL AND THE GAMBLER, THE(1939); JUAREZ(1939); KANSAS TERRORS, THE(1939); RAINS CAME, THE(1939); 6000 ENEMIES(1939); CAPTAIN CAUTION(1940); DR. EHRLICH'S MAGIC BULLET(1940); GIRL FROM

HAVANA(1940); LUCKY CISCO KID(1940); MOON OVER BURMA(1940); MUMMY'S HAND, THE(1940); SEA HAWK, THE(1940); STAGECOACH WAR(1940); STRANGE CARGO(1940); SEA WOLF, THE(1941); SOUTH OF TAHITI(1941); ARABIAN NIGHTS(1942); BOMBS OVER BURMA(1942); CAPTAINS OF THE CLOUDS(1942); HALF WAY TO SHANGHAI(1942); REAP THE WILD WIND(1942); ABOVE SUSPICION(1943); CHETNIKS(1943); FOR WHOM THE BELL TOLLS(1943); FRONTIER BADMEN(1943); PASSPORT TO SUEZ(1943); SAHARA(1943); SONG OF BERNADETTE, THE(1943); MASK OF DIMITRIOS, THE(1944); MOONLIGHT AND CACTUS(1944); STORY OF DR. WASSELL, THE(1944); FRONTIER GAL(1945); THOUSAND AND ONE NIGHTS, A(1945); UNDER WESTERN SKIES(1945); SINGIN' IN THE CORN(1946); OREGON TRAIL SCOUTS(1947); MAN-EATER OF KUMAON(1948); COWBOY AND THE INDIANS, THE(1949); DAUGHTER OF THE JUNGLE(1949); MYSTERIOUS DESPERADO, THE(1949); SON OF A BADMAN(1949); DAKOTA LIL(1950); DESERT HAWK, THE(1950); INDIAN TERRITORY(1950); KIM(1950); FLAMING FEATHER(1951); PRINCE WHO WAS A THIEF, THE(1951); BIG SKY, THE(1952); DESERT PURSUIT(1952); KING OF THE KHYBER RIFLES(1953); NORTHERN PATROL(1953); PHANTOM OF THE RUE MORGUE(1954); DEVIL GODDESS(1955); TEN COMMANDMENTS, THE(1956); FLESH AND THE SPUR(1957); THREE CAME TO KILL(1960); REQUIEM FOR A GUNFIGHTER(1965)
Misc. Talkies
TREASON(1933)
Silents
PONY EXPRESS, THE(1925); UNKNOWN CAVALIER, THE(1926); WARNING, THE(1927)
Misc. Silents
VIRGIN, THE(1924)
Charles Lackworthy
PHANTOM SHIP(1937, Brit.), w
Jerry Lacoe, Jr.
MRS. O'MALLEY AND MR. MALONE(1950)
Andre Lacombe
THAT OBSCURE OBJECT OF DESIRE(1977, Fr./Span.)
Georges Lacombe
ROOM UPSTAIRS, THE(1948, Fr.), d; SEVEN DEADLY SINS, THE(1953, Fr./Ital.), d; LIGHT ACROSSS THE STREET, THE(1957, Fr.), d
Silents
ITALIAN STRAW HAT, AN(1927, Fr.), art d
Gilles Lacombe
1984
AVE MARIA(1984, Fr.), art d; DREAM ONE(1984, Brit./Fr.), prod d,, spec eff,
Francis Lacombrade
THIS SPECIAL FRIENDSHIP(1967, Fr.)
Daniel Lacombre
AROUSERS, THE(1973), ph
Cathy Lacommare
1984
SPLATTER UNIVERSITY(1984)
Bob Laconi
NIGHT OF THE ZOMBIES(1981)
Henry Lacossitt
SEE AMERICA THIRST(1930), w
Edmond Lacoste
GIRL IN TROUBLE(1963), ed
Roland LaCoste
1984
UNTIL SEPTEMBER(1984)
Jose-Andre Lacour
DEATH IN THE GARDEN(1977, Fr./Mex.), w
Rene Lacourt
MR. HULOT'S HOLIDAY(1954, Fr.)
Daniel Lacourtois
DOCTEUR POPAUL(1972, Fr.)
Denis LaCroix
RABID(1976, Can.); DEATH HUNT(1981); RUNNING BRAVE(1983, Can.)
Georges Lacroix
Misc. Silents
DANS LA RAFALE(1916, Fr.), d; L'HEURE TRAGIQUE(1916, Fr.), d; BEAUTE QUI MEURT(1917, Fr.), d; LES ECRITS RESTENT(1917, Fr.), d; HAINE(1918, Fr.), d; SON DESTIN(1919, Fr.), d; LA VENGEANCE DE MALLET(1920, Fr.), d; PASSIONNEMENT(1921, Fr.), d
Jason LaCurto
BIG TOWN(1932)
Adele Lacy
42ND STREET(1933)
Misc. Talkies
VANISHING MEN(1932)
Alva Lacy
JACK MCCALL, DESPERADO(1953)
Alva Marie Lacy
FANCY PANTS(1950)
Beatriz Lacy
GRAVEYARD OF HORROR(1971, Span.)
Catherine Lacy
CRACK IN THE MIRROR(1960); ABDUCTION(1975)
Chuck Lacy
SNOW WHITE AND THE THREE STOOGES(1961)
Frank Lacy
WOMEN WHO PLAY(1932, Brit.)
George Lacy
MY OLD DUCHESS(1933, Brit.)
Jean Lacy
GUILTY PARENTS(1934)
Jerry Lacy
HOUSE OF DARK SHADOWS(1970); PLAY IT AGAIN, SAM(1972)
Joe Lacy
FLAME OVER VIETNAM(1967, Span./Ger.), d, w; TREASURE OF MAKUBA, THE(1967, U.S./Span.), d; WITCH WITHOUT A BROOM, A(1967, U.S./Span.), d

Margo Lacy
COLD RIVER(1982)
Paul Lacy
LADY LUCK(1946)
Ronald Lacy
HOUND OF THE BASKERVILLES, THE(1983, Brit.)
Tom Lacy
BELIEVE IN ME(1971); GANG THAT COULDN'T SHOOT STRAIGHT, THE(1971);
LADY LIBERTY(1972, Ital./Fr.); SWASHBUCKLER(1976); FIRST LOVE(1977)
1984
BUDDY SYSTEM, THE(1984)
Vivienne Lacy
BREATH OF LIFE(1962, Brit.)
Laura Lacz
CONTRACT, THE(1982, Pol.)
Lad the Dog
LAD: A DOG(1962)
Ladah
Silents
CHANG(1927)
Andy Ladas
Misc. Talkies
OUTLAW QUEEN(1957)
Alan Ladd
ONCE IN A LIFETIME(1932); TOM BROWN OF CULVER(1932); ISLAND OF LOST
SOULS(1933); SATURDAY'S MILLIONS(1933); PIGSKIN PARADE(1936); BORN TO
THE WEST(1937); LAST TRAIN FROM MADRID, THE(1937); SOULS AT SEA(1937);
COME ON, LEATHERNECKS(1938); FRESHMAN YEAR(1938); GOLDWYN FOLLIES,
THE(1938); BEASTS OF BERLIN(1939); RULERS OF THE SEA(1939); BROTHER RAT
AND A BABY(1940); CAPTAIN CAUTION(1940); GANGS OF CHICAGO(1940); HER
FIRST ROMANCE(1940); HOWARDS OF VIRGINIA, THE(1940); IN OLD MIS-
SOURI(1940); LIGHT OF WESTERN STARS, THE(1940); MEET THE MISSUS(1940);
THOSE WERE THE DAYS(1940); BLACK CAT, THE(1941); CITIZEN KANE(1941);
GREAT GUNS(1941); PAPER BULLETS(1941); PETTICOAT POLITICS(1941); RELUC-
TANT DRAGON, THE(1941); THEY MET IN BOMBAY(1941); GLASS KEY, THE(1942);
JOAN OF PARIS(1942); LUCKY JORDAN(1942); STAR SPANGLED RHYTHM(1942);
THIS GUN FOR HIRE(1942); CHINA(1943); AND NOW TOMORROW(1944); DUFFY'S
TAVERN(1945); SALTY O'ROURKE(1945); BLUE DAHLIA, THE(1946); O.S.S.(1946);
TWO YEARS BEFORE THE MAST(1946); CALCUTTA(1947); MY FAVORITE BRU-
NETTE(1947); VARIETY GIRL(1947); WILD HARVEST(1947); BEYOND GLO-
RY(1948); SAIGON(1948); WHISPERING SMITH(1948); CHICAGO DEADLINE(1949);
GREAT GATSBY, THE(1949); CAPTAIN CAREY, U.S.A(1950); APPOINTMENT WITH
DANGER(1951); BRANDED(1951); RED MOUNTAIN(1951); IRON MISTRESS,
THE(1952); BOTANY BAY(1953); DESERT LEGION(1953); SHANE(1953); THUNDER
IN THE EAST(1953); BLACK KNIGHT, THE(1954); DRUM BEAT(1954), a, p; HELL
BELOW ZERO(1954, Brit.); PARATROOPER(1954, Brit.); SASKATCHEWAN(1954); MC
CONNELL STORY, THE(1955); HELL ON FRISCO BAY(1956); SANTIAGO(1956); BIG
LAND, THE(1957); BOY ON A DOLPHIN(1957); BADLANDERS, THE(1958); DEEP
SIX, THE(1958); PROUD REBEL, THE(1958); MAN IN THE NET(1959); ALL THE
YOUNG MEN(1960); GUNS OF THE TIMBERLAND(1960); ONE FOOT IN HELL(1960);
THIRTEEN WEST STREET(1962); CARPETBAGGERS, THE(1964); DUEL OF CHAM-
PIONS(1964 Ital./Span.)
Alan Ladd, Jr.
WALKING STICK, THE(1970, Brit.), p; SEVERED HEAD, A(1971, Brit.), p; VIL-
LAIN(1971, Brit.), p; DEVIL'S WIDOW, THE(1972, Brit.), p; X Y & ZEE(1972, Brit.), p;
FEAR IS THE KEY(1973), p
Alana Ladd
GUNS OF THE TIMBERLAND(1960); YOUNG GUNS OF TEXAS(1963); DUEL OF
CHAMPIONS(1964 Ital./Span.)
Carol Lee Ladd
DEEP SIX, THE(1958)
Cheryl Ladd
NOW AND FOREVER(1983, Aus.)
1984
PURPLE HEARTS(1984)
David Ladd
BIG LAND, THE(1957); PROUD REBEL, THE(1958); DOG OF FLANDERS, A(1959);
SAD HORSE, THE(1959); RAYMIE(1960); MISTY(1961); R.P.M.(1970); CATLOW(1971,
Span.); DEATHLINE(1973, Brit.); JONATHAN LIVINGSTON SEAGULL(1973);
KLANSMAN, THE(1974); DAY OF THE LOCUST, THE(1975); TREASURE OF JAMAI-
CA REEF, THE(1976); WILD GEESE, THE(1978, Brit.)
Misc. Talkies
CAPTIVE(1980); BEYOND THE UNIVERSE(1981)
Diane Ladd
SOMETHING WILD(1961); REIVERS, THE(1969); MACHO CALLAHAN(1970); RE-
BEL ROUSERS(1970); STEAGLE, THE(1971); WHITE LIGHTNING(1973); CHINA-
TOWN(1974); ALICE DOESN'T LIVE HERE ANYMORE(1975); EMBRYO(1976); ALL
NIGHT LONG(1981); SOMETHING WICKED THIS WAY COMES(1983)
Dianne Ladd
WILD ANGELS, THE(1966)
Fred Ladd
PINOCCHIO IN OUTER SPACE(1965, U.S./Bel.), p; JOURNEY TO THE BEGIN-
NING OF TIME(1966, Czech.), w; JOURNEY BACK TO OZ(1974), w
Hank Ladd
LAS VEGAS NIGHTS(1941); ERRAND BOY, THE(1961)
Margaret Ladd
FRIENDS OF EDDIE COYLE, THE(1973); WEDDING, A(1978); ESCAPE ARTIST,
THE(1982); I'M DANCING AS FAST AS I CAN(1982)
Marian Ladd
RECKLESS(1935)
Marion Ladd
DANTE'S INFERNO(1935); MILLIONS IN THE AIR(1935)
Schuyler Ladd
Silents
DIMPLES(1916)
Misc. Silents
LAND OF HOPE, THE(1921)

Tom Ladd
MEN IN HER LIFE, THE(1941); HOLIDAY RHYTHM(1950)
Tommy Ladd
GIRL MOST LIKELY, THE(1957)
Highland Laddie
Silents
CALL FROM THE WILD, THE(1921)
Laddie the Dog
OUTWARD BOUND(1930); SON OF LASSIE(1945)
Ladi Ladebo
COUNTDOWN AT KUSINI(1976, Nigerian), p, w
the LaDell Sisters
COUNTRY MUSIC HOLIDAY(1958)
Bob Laden
TO FIND A MAN(1972), makeup; SENTINEL, THE(1977), makeup
Robert Laden
HUSBANDS(1970), makeup; GANG THAT COULDN'T SHOOT STRAIGHT,
THE(1971), makeup; PURSUIT OF HAPPINESS, THE(1971), makeup;
THIEVES(1977), makeup
Walter Ladengast
DECISION BEFORE DAWN(1951); EVERY MAN FOR HIMSELF AND GOD
AGAINST ALL(1975, Ger.); NOSFERATU, THE VAMPIRE(1979, Fr./Ger.)
Fred Laderman
PINOCCHIO IN OUTER SPACE(1965, U.S./Bel.), w
Janice Ladik
THINGS ARE TOUGH ALL OVER(1982)
Alexander Ladikou
RED LANTERNS(1965, Gr.)
Mikulas Ladizinsky
SHOP ON MAIN STREET, THE(1966, Czech.)
Stefan Ladizinsky
DESERTER AND THE NOMADS, THE(1969, Czech./Ital.)
Nicole Ladmiral
DIARY OF A COUNTRY PRIEST(1954, Fr.)
Gerhard Ladner
INDECENT(1962, Ger.), set d
Aldo Lado
HUMANOID, THE(1979, Ital.), w
Jose Lado
MAN'S HOPE(1947, Span.)
Marta Lado
CONFORMIST, THE(1971, Ital., Fr)
Erzsi Lados
FATHER(1967, Hung.)
Maria Fernanda Ladron de Guevara
NUN AT THE CROSSROADS, A(1970, Ital./Span.)
Jeanne LaDuke
GREEN PROMISE, THE(1949)
Leroy O. Ladwig
Silents
BACKSTAGE(1927), ed
Lady
Silents
BLACK CYCLONE(1925)
Misc. Silents
DEVIL HORSE, THE(1926)
"Lady"
KING OF THE WILD HORSES, THE(1934)
Kentucky Lady
LADY'S FROM KENTUCKY, THE(1939)
Lady Carlisle
ONE FAMILY(1930, Brit.)
Lady Keble
ONE FAMILY(1930, Brit.)
The Lady Killer's Quartet
IT ALL CAME TRUE(1940)
Lady Lavery
ONE FAMILY(1930, Brit.)
Lady Ravensdale
ONE FAMILY(1930, Brit.)
Lady Rowlands
OPENING NIGHT(1977)
M. Ladygin
OVERCOAT, THE(1965, USSR)
Maria Ladynina
COUNTRY BRIDE(1938, USSR)
Marina Ladynina
SIX P.M.(1946, USSR)
N. Ladynina
DEVOTION(1955, USSR)
Ye. Ladyzhenskaya
NINE DAYS OF ONE YEAR(1964, USSR), ed
Beth Laemmle
Silents
GATE CRASHER, THE(1928)
Carl Laemmle
MISSISSIPPI GAMBLER(1929), p; PHANTOM OF THE OPERA, THE(1929), p;
SHOW BOAT(1929), a, p; HELL'S HEROES(1930), p; LITTLE ACCIDENT(1930), p;
S.O.S. ICEBERG(1933), p; IMITATION OF LIFE(1934), p; LITTLE MAN, WHAT
NOW?(1934), p
Silents
IRRESISTIBLE LOVER, THE(1927), sup
Carl Laemmle, Jr.
WATERLOO BRIDGE(1931), p; LONESOME(1928), p; BROADWAY(1929), p; COL-
LEGE LOVE(1929), p; ALL QUIET ON THE WESTERN FRONT(1930), p; CAT
CREEPS, THE(1930), p; LADY SURRENDERS, A(1930), p; BAD SISTER(1931), p;
DRACULA(1931), p; EAST OF BORNEO(1931), p; FRANKENSTEIN(1931), p; IRON
MAN, THE(1931), p; MANY A SLIP(1931), p; SPIRIT OF NOTRE DAME, THE(1931),
p; STRICTLY DISHONORABLE(1931), p; AIR MAIL(1932), p; COHENS, AND KEL-
LYS IN HOLLYWOOD, THE(1932), p; IMPATIENT MAIDEN(1932), p; MUMMY,

THE(1932), p; MURDERS IN THE RUE MORGUE(1932), p; MY PAL, THE KING(1932), p; NIGHT WORLD(1932), p; OLD DARK HOUSE, THE(1932), p; ONCE IN A LIFETIME(1932), p; RIDER OF DEATH VALLEY(1932), p; SCANDAL FOR SALE(1932), p; TEXAS BAD MAN(1932), p; TOM BROWN OF CULVER(1932), p; COUNSELLOR-AT-LAW(1933), p; HIDDEN GOLD(1933), p; INVISIBLE MAN, THE(1933), p; KISS BEFORE THE MIRROR, THE(1933), p; SATURDAY'S MILLIONS(1933), p; BELOVED(1934), p; BLACK CAT, THE(1934), p; GIFT OF GAB(1934), p; LOVE BIRDS(1934), p; BRIDE OF FRANKENSTEIN, THE(1935), p; NIGHT LIFE OF THE GODS(1935), p; REMEMBER LAST NIGHT(1935), p; SHOW BOAT(1936), p

Edward Laemmle
DRAKE CASE, THE(1929), d; LASCA OF THE RIO GRANDE(1931), d; TEXAS BAD MAN(1932), d; EMBARRASSING MOMENTS(1934), d; NOTORIOUS GENTLEMAN, A(1935), d
Silents
SPOOK RANCH(1925), d; CHEATING CHEATERS(1927), d; HELD BY THE LAW(1927), d
Misc. Silents
TOP O' THE MORNING, THE(1922), d; VICTOR, THE(1923), d; MAN IN BLUE, THE(1925), d; WOMAN'S FAITH, A(1925), d; STILL ALARM, THE(1926), d; WHOLE TOWN'S TALKING, THE(1926), d; THIRTEENTH JUROR, THE(1927), d; MAN, WOMAN AND WIFE(1929), d

Ernest Laemmle
Misc. Silents
RANGE COURAGE(1927), d

Ernst Laemmle
PHANTOM OF THE OPERA, THE(1929), d; WHAT MEN WANT(1930), d
Silents
PROWLERS OF THE NIGHT(1926), d, w; PHYLLIS OF THE FOLLIES(1928), d
Misc. Silents
SUNSET TRAIL, THE(1924), d; BRONCHO BUSTER, THE(1927), d; HANDS OFF(1927), d; ONE MAN GAME, A(1927), d; RED CLAY(1927), d; GRIP OF THE YUKON, THE(1928), d

Max Laemmle
LIONS LOVE(1969)

Olle Laensberg
RAILROAD WORKERS(1948, Swed.), w

Luigi Laezza
TEMPEST(1982)

Francois Lafarge
AU HASARD, BALTHAZAR(1970, Fr.); LIKE A TURTLE ON ITS BACK(1981, Fr.)

Patrick Lafarge
VERY CURIOUS GIRL, A(1970, Fr.), art d

Gabriele Lafari
1984
WOMAN IN FLAMES, A(1984, Ger.)

Marie LaFavre
Silents
DIVORCE GAME, THE(1917)

Yves Lafaye
LA VIE CONTINUE(1982, Fr.), ph

Andree Lafayette
Misc. Silents
TRILBY(1923); SURVIVAL(1930, Ger.)

Cristiana Lafayette
ERNESTO(1979, Ital.), cos

Gregory LaFayette
UNDER FIRE(1957)

Jean LaFayette
HOMECOMING(1948)

Jeanne Lafayette
EVERYTHING HAPPENS AT NIGHT(1939); SEPTEMBER AFFAIR(1950); HANS CHRISTIAN ANDERSEN(1952); SOMETHING TO LIVE FOR(1952); TO CATCH A THIEF(1955)

John Lafayette
GOOD LUCK, MISS WYCKOFF(1979)

Nanette Lafayette
PARIS IN SPRING(1935); LOVE ON THE RUN(1936)

Nannette Lafayette
BOY MEETS GIRL(1938)

Nenette Lafayette
PRINCESS COMES ACROSS, THE(1936)

Ruby Lafayette
MARRIAGE BY CONTRACT(1928); NOT SO DUMB(1930)
Silents
MIRACLE MAN, THE(1919); POLLY OF THE STORM COUNTRY(1920); COMING OF AMOS, THE(1925); WEDDING SONG, THE(1925)
Misc. Silents
MAN TRAP, THE(1917); MOTHER O'MINE(1917); BEAUTY IN CHAINS(1918); SUE OF THE SOUTH(1919); POWER OF A LIE, THE(1922)

Robert Lafevre
COURRIER SUD(1937, Fr.), ph

Kevin Laffan
IT'S A 2"6" ABOVE THE GROUND WORLD(1972, Brit.), w

Patricia Laffan
NOTORIOUS GENTLEMAN(1945, Brit.); CARAVAN(1946, Brit.); HANGMAN'S WHARF(1950, Brit.); QUO VADIS(1951); I'LL GET YOU(1953, Brit.); SHOOT FIRST(1953, Brit.); DEVIL GIRL FROM MARS(1954, Brit.); DON'T BLAME THE STORK(1954, Brit.); 23 PACES TO BAKER STREET(1956); HIDDEN HOMICIDE(1959, Brit.); CROOKS IN CLOISTERS(1964, Brit.); WHO KILLED VAN LOON?(1984, Brit.)

Patrick Laffan
GIRL WITH GREEN EYES(1964, Brit.); WEDDING NIGHT(1970, Ireland); BARRY LYNDON(1975, Brit.)

Marcy Lafferty
STAR TREK: THE MOTION PICTURE(1979); DAY TIME ENDED, THE(1980, Span.)

James Laffey
Silents
ETERNAL TEMPTRESS, THE(1917); JIM THE PENMAN(1921); POLICE PATROL, THE(1925)

Yolande Laffon
LIFE AND LOVES OF BEETHOVEN, THE(1937, Fr.); ANGELS OF THE STREETS(1950, Fr.)

Colette Laffont
Misc. Talkies
GOLD DIGGERS, THE(1984, Brit.)

Patrice Laffont
GENDARME OF ST. TROPEZ, THE(1966, Fr./Ital.)

Robert Laffont
BITTER VICTORY(1958, Fr.), p

Doug Laffoon
IN MACARTHUR PARK(1977)

Rene-Louis Lafforgue
LOVERS OF TERUEL, THE(1962, Fr.), a, w; JULIE THE REDHEAD(1963, Fr.), a, m

Yolande Laffron
MAYERLING(1937, Fr.)

Reggie Lafining
CASANOVA IN BURLESQUE(1944), ph

Jean Lafitte
LOVE IN MOROCCO(1933, Fr.), art d

Paul Lafitte
MISTER HOBO(1936, Brit.), w; ROTHSCHILD(1938, Fr.), w

Art LaFleur
CANNERY ROW(1982); I OUGHT TO BE IN PICTURES(1982); JEKYLL AND HYDE...TOGETHER AGAIN(1982); WARGAMES(1983)
1984
UNFAITHFULLY YOURS(1984)

Jean LaFleur
RABID(1976, Can.), ed; HOUSE BY THE LAKE, THE(1977, Can.), ed; MY BLOODY VALENTINE(1981, Can.), ed; SPACEHUNTER: ADVENTURES IN THE FORBIDDEN ZONE(1983), w

Joy LaFleur
WHISPERING CITY(1947, Can.); SINS OF THE FATHERS(1948, Can.)

Thomas LaFleur
TAKING OF PELHAM ONE, TWO, THREE, THE(1974)

C.D. LaFleure
Misc. Talkies
ALICE GOODBODY(1974)

George LaFollette-Zabriskie
SUMMERDOG(1977), w

Sherry LaFollette-Zabriskie
SUMMERDOG(1977), w

Bernadette Lafont
LE BEAU SERGE(1959, Fr.); WEB OF PASSION(1961, Fr.); GAME FOR SIX LOVERS, A(1962, Fr.); ARMY GAME, THE(1963, Fr.); MALE HUNT(1965, Fr./Ital.); SLEEPING CAR MURDER THE(1966, Fr.); THIEF OF PARIS, THE(1967, Fr./Ital.); SOPHIE'S WAYS(1970, Fr.); VERY CURIOUS GIRL, A(1970, Fr.); ATCH ME A SPY(1971, Brit./Fr.); MOTHER AND THE WHORE, THE(1973, Fr.); SUCH A GORGEOUS KID LIKE ME(1973, Fr.); ZIG-ZAG(1975, Fr/Ital.); VIOLETTE(1978, Fr.); WE'LL GROW THIN TOGETHER(1979, Fr.); LIKE A TURTLE ON ITS BACK(1981, Fr.); CLARETTA AND BEN(1983, Ital., Fr.)
1984
DOG DAY(1984, Fr.); PERILS OF GWENDOLINE, THE(1984, Fr.)

Duffy LaFont
EASY RIDER(1969)

Jean-Philippe Lafont
1984
BIZET'S CARMEN(1984, Fr./Ital.)

Pauline Lafont
1984
BAY BOY(1984, Can.)

Marie Laforet
LEVIATHAN(1961, Fr.); PURPLE NOON(1961, Fr./Ital.); GIRL WITH THE GOLDEN EYES, THE(1962, Fr.); HOW NOT TO ROB A DEPARTMENT STORE(1965, Fr./Ital.); MALE HUNT(1965, Fr./Ital.); JACK OF DIAMONDS(1967, U.S./Ger.)

Bert LaForteza
NO MAN IS AN ISLAND(1962)

Gina Laforteza
DAUGHTERS OF SATAN(1972)

Tony LaFortezza
VERDICT, THE(1982)

Ian LaFrenais
IT'S NOT THE SIZE THAT COUNTS(1979, Brit.), w

Daniel Lagache
LIFE BEGINS TOMORROW(1952, Fr.)

Lina Lagalla
CLIMAX, THE(1967, Fr., Ital.)

Ellen LaGamba
ONLY WHEN I LAUGH(1981)

James Lagan
IVY(1947)

Giuseppe Lagana
ALLEGRO NON TROPPO(1977, Ital.), anim

James Lagano
FOXES OF HARROW, THE(1947)

Jimmy Lagano
FOREVER AMBER(1947)

Jean-Jacques Lagarde
MURIEL(1963, Fr./Ital.)

Ovila Lagare
OPERATION MANHUNT(1954)

John LaGatta
ARTISTS AND MODELS(1937)

Limbo Lagdameo
AMBUSH BAY(1966)

Theo Lageard
MIDNIGHT EPISODE(1951, Brit.), p; MEET MR. MALCOLM(1954, Brit.), p

Martin Lager
OFFERING, THE(1966, Can.), w; SHAPE OF THINGS TO COME, THE(1979, Can.), w; KLONDIKE FEVER(1980), w
Gustav Lagerberg
DOLLAR(1938, Swed.)
Karl Lagerfeld
TEN DAYS' WONDER(1972, Fr.), cos; L'AMOUR(1973)
Ake Lagergren
JUST ONCE MORE(1963, Swed.); FANNY AND ALEXANDER(1983, Swed./Fr./Ger.)
Elin Lagergren
Misc. Silents
EROTIKON(1920, Swed.)
Par Lagerkvist
BARABBAS(1962, Ital.), w
Lovisa Lagerlof
Silents
TOWER OF LIES, THE(1925), w
Selma Lagerlof
GIRL FROM THE MARSH CROFT, THE(1935, Ger.), w; GIRL OF THE MOORS, THE(1961, Ger.), w
Sture Lagerwall
WALPURGIS NIGHT(1941, Swed.); DEVIL'S EYE, THE(1960, Swed.)
John Lageu
NO LONGER ALONE(1978), prod d
Jorge Lago
WIDOWS' NEST(1977, U.S./Span.)
Mario Lago
EARTH ENTRANCED(1970, Braz.)
Peter Lago
LAW AND DISORDER(1974)
Salvadore Lago
ONE STEP TO HELL(1969, U.S./Ital./Span.)
Oscar Lagomarsino
SUMMERSKIN(1962, Arg.), set d; HAND IN THE TRAP, THE(1963, Arg./Span.), art d; TERRACE, THE(1964, Arg.), art d; THE EAVESDROPPER(1966, U.S./Arg.), art d
Georges Lagonelli
UP TO HIS EARS(1966, Fr./Ital.), spec eff
Shreeram Lagoo
GANDHI(1982)
Alexander Lagorio
HELL ON EARTH(1934, Ger.), ph
Paul Lagos
CAPTAIN MILKSHAKE(1970)
Poppy Lagos
I WANNA HOLD YOUR HAND(1978); PERFECT COUPLE, A(1979); HUNTER, THE(1980); GOING APE!(1981)
Vicki Lagos
SON OF THE RED CORSAIR(1963, Ital.)
Vicky Lagos
GIRL FROM VALLADOLIO(1958, Span.)
Jacques Lagrange
MR. HULOT'S HOLIDAY(1954, Fr.), w; MY UNCLE(1958, Fr.), w; TRAFFIC(1972, Fr.), w; PLAYTIME(1973, Fr.), w
Louise Lagrange
Silents
SAINTED DEVIL, A(1924); SIDESHOW OF LIFE, THE(1924)
Misc. Silents
LA DANSEUSE ORCHIDEE(1928, Fr.); MODEL FROM MONTMARTE, THE(1928, Fr.); LA MARCHE NUPTIALE(1929, Fr.)
Jimmy Laine [Abel Ferrara]
MS. 45(1981)
Valerie Lagrange
GREEN MARE, THE(1961, Fr./Ital.); LOVE AND THE FRENCHWOMAN(1961, Fr.); MORGAN THE PIRATE(1961, Fr./Ital.); SWEET AND SOUR(1964, Fr./Ital.); CIRCLE OF LOVE(1965, Fr.); MALE COMPANION(1965, Fr./Ital.); MAN AND A WOMAN, A(1966, Fr.); UP TO HIS EARS(1966, Fr./Ital.); WEEKEND(1968, Fr./Ital.)
A. Lagranskiy
WELCOME KOSTYA!(1965, USSR)
Maurice Lagrenee
DEVIL IN THE FLESH, THE(1949, Fr.)
Michael LaGuardia
PRIZE FIGHTER, THE(1979); SO FINE(1981)
Edward Laguna
FROM HERE TO ETERNITY(1953)
Laguna Festival of Art Players
SILVER CHALICE, THE(1954)
I.I. Lagutin
ALEXANDER NEVSKY(1939)
Joaquin LaHabana
FORT APACHE, THE BRONX(1981)
Tulsi Lahari
MUSIC ROOM, THE(1963, India)
Zvi Lahat
RABBI AND THE SHIKSE, THE(1976, Israel)
Sally Lahee
VENOM(1982, Brit.)
Kirsten Lahman
$(DOLLARS)**1/2 (1971)
Ilse Lahn
MURDER IS MY BEAT(1955), p
Lori Lahner
SUMMER STORM(1944)
Bert Lahr
FLYING HIGH(1931); LOVE AND HISSES(1937); MERRY-GO-ROUND OF 1938(1937); JOSETTE(1938); JUST AROUND THE CORNER(1938); WIZARD OF OZ, THE(1939); ZAZA(1939); SHIP AHOY(1942); SING YOUR WORRIES AWAY(1942); MEET THE PEOPLE(1944); ALWAYS LEAVE THEM LAUGHING(1949); MR. UNIVERSE(1951); ROSE MARIE(1954); SECOND GREATEST SEX, THE(1955); NIGHT THEY RAIDED MINSKY'S, THE(1968)

Henry Lahrman
BULLDOG DRUMMOND STRIKES BACK(1934), w
Itto Bent Lahsen
DAUGHTER OF THE SANDS(1952, Fr.)
Christine Lahti
...AND JUSTICE FOR ALL(1979); WHOSE LIFE IS IT ANYWAY?(1981); LADIES AND GENTLEMEN, THE FABULOUS STAINS(1982)
1984
SWING SHIFT(1984)
Elmer Lahti
PRELUDE TO ECSTASY(1963, Fin.), ed
Gary Lahti
KNIGHTRIDERS(1981)
Jim Lahti
1984
RENO AND THE DOC(1984, Can.), ed
Al Lai
REVENGE OF THE NINJA(1983)
Francis Lai
MAN AND A WOMAN, A(1966, Fr.), m; MASCULINE FEMININE(1966, Fr./Swed.), m; BOBO, THE(1967, Brit.), m; I'LL NEVER FORGET WHAT'S 'IS NAME(1967, Brit.), m; LIVE FOR LIFE(1967, Fr./Ital.), m; MAYERLING(1968, Brit./Fr.), m; HANNIBAL BROOKS(1969, Brit.), m; HOUSE OF CARDS(1969), m; LEATHER AND NYLON(1969, Fr./Ital.), m; LIFE LOVE DEATH(1969, Fr./Ital.), m; THREE INTO TWO WON'T GO(1969, Brit.), m; GAMES, THE(1970), m; HELLO—GOODBYE(1970), m; LOVE IS A FUNNY THING(1970, Fr./Ital.), m; LOVE STORY(1970), m; MADLY(1970, Fr.), m; RIDER ON THE RAIN(1970, Fr./Ital.), m; CROOK, THE(1971, Fr.), m; LEGEND OF FRENCHIE KING, THE(1971, Fr./Ital./Span./Brit.), m; AND HOPE TO DIE(1972 Fr/US), m; VISIT TO A CHIEF'S SON(1974), m; AND NOW MY LOVE(1975, Fr.), m; CHILD UNDER A LEAF(1975, Can.), m; LA BABY SITTER(1975, Fr./Ital./Gen.), m; ANOTHER MAN, ANOTHER CHANCE(1977 Fr/US), m; WIDOWS' NEST(1977, U.S./Span.), m; CAT AND MOUSE(1978, Fr.), m; INTERNATIONAL VELVET(1978, Brit.), m; BEYOND THE REEF(1981), m; BOLERO(1982, Fr.), m
1984
DOG DAY(1984, Fr.), m; EDITH AND MARCEL(1984, Fr.); HERE COMES SANTA CLAUS(1984), m; MY NEW PARTNER(1984, Fr.), m
Judith Lai
INN OF THE SIXTH HAPPINESS, THE(1958)
Me Me Lai
REVENGE OF THE PINK PANTHER(1978)
Angelo Laiacona
YOUNG DOCTORS, THE(1961), art d
Michael T. Laide
1984
MOSCOW ON THE HUDSON(1984)
Betty Laidlaw
ENLIGHTEN THY DAUGHTER(1934), w; INSIDE INFORMATION(1934), w; GIRL SAID NO, THE(1937), w; RHYTHM RACKETEER(1937, Brit.), w; PERSONAL SECRETARY(1938), w
Ethan Laidlaw
BRIDE OF THE DESERT(1929); DANGEROUS CURVES(1929); VIRGINIAN, THE(1929); PARDON MY GUN(1930); CITY STREETS(1931); DISHONORED(1931); FIGHTING MARSHAL, THE(1932); OUT OF SINGAPORE(1932); KING KONG(1933); JEALOUSY(1934); FIGHTING SHADOWS(1935); POWDERSMOKE RANGE(1935); SEA SPOILERS, THE(1936); SILLY BILLIES(1936); SONG OF THE GRINGO(1936); SPECIAL INVESTIGATOR(1936); TWO IN REVOLT(1936); YELLOW DUST(1936); GAME THAT KILLS, THE(1937); NIGHT KEY(1937); ONE MAN JUSTICE(1937); PAID TO DANCE(1937); THIS IS MY AFFAIR(1937); TOAST OF NEW YORK, THE(1937); TWO-FISTED SHERIFF(1937); BORDER G-MAN(1938); GUN LAW(1938); I'M FROM THE CITY(1938); JUVENILE COURT(1938); KING OF THE NEWSBOYS(1938); PENITENTIARY(1938); RACKET BUSTERS(1938); RHYTHM OF THE SADDLE(1938); TIP-OFF GIRLS(1938); COLORADO SUNSET(1939); COWBOYS FROM TEXAS(1939); FRONTIER MARSHAL(1939); HOME ON THE PRAIRIE(1939); HOTEL IMPERIAL(1939); JESSE JAMES(1939); NIGHT OF NIGHTS, THE(1939); NIGHT RIDERS, THE(1939); SPOILERS OF THE RANGE(1939); THEY SHALL HAVE MUSIC(1939); THREE TEXAS STEERS(1939); WESTERN CARAVANS(1939); INVISIBLE STRIPES(1940); LAW AND ORDER(1940); MARINES FLY HIGH, THE(1940); NORTHWEST MOUNTED POLICE(1940); QUEEN OF THE MOB(1940); SON OF ROARING DAN(1940); STAGE TO CHINO(1940); TULSA KID, THE(1940); TWO-FISTED RANGERS(1940); WAGON TRAIN(1940); BURY ME NOT ON THE LONE PRAIRIE(1941); LAST OF THE DUANES(1941); LAW OF THE RANGE(1941); RIDERS OF THE BADLANDS(1941); SEA WOLF, THE(1941); TEXAS(1941); WYOMING WILDCAT(1941); COWBOY SERENADE(1942); FOREST RANGERS(1942); LITTLE JOE, THE WRANGLER(1942); LONE STAR VIGILANTES, THE(1942); LUCKY LEGS(1942); SABOTAGE SQUAD(1942); STAGECOACH EXPRESS(1942); VALLEY OF THE SUN(1942); BORDER BUCKAROOS(1943); DESPERADOES, THE(1943); FUGITIVE FROM SONORA(1943); LONE STAR TRAIL, THE(1943); OUTLAW, THE(1943); JAM SESSION(1944); MARSHAL OF GUNSMOKE(1944); OKLAHOMA RAIDERS(1944); DALTONS RIDE AGAIN(1945); RENEGADES OF THE RIO GRANDE(1945); ROAD TO UTOPIA(1945); WEST OF THE PECOS(1945); CALIFORNIA(1946); KILLERS, THE(1946); LAWLESS EMPIRE(1946); MAGNIFICENT DOLL(1946); RUSTLER'S ROUNDUP(1946); SINGIN' IN THE CORN(1946); TWO YEARS BEFORE THE MAST(1946); CHEYENNE(1947); FABULOUS TEXAN, THE(1947); SECRET LIFE OF WALTER MITTY, THE(1947); SENATOR WAS INDISCREET, THE(1947); WEB, THE(1947); WISTFUL WIDOW OF WAGON GAP, THE(1947); BUCKAROO FROM POWDER RIVER(1948); JOAN OF ARC(1948); PALEFACE, THE(1948); RELENTLESS(1948); SIX-GUN LAW(1948); STATION WEST(1948); LARAMIE(1949); ROSEANNA McCOY(1949); COPPER CANYON(1950); GREAT MISSOURI RAID, THE(1950); TRAVELING SALESWOMAN(1950); WHERE DANGER LIVES(1950); WINCHESTER '73(1950); FLAMING FEATHER(1951); IRON MAN, THE(1951); RIDIN' THE OUTLAW TRAIL(1951); CARRIE(1952); GREATEST SHOW ON EARTH, THE(1952); HURRICANE SMITH(1952); LAWLESS BREED, THE(1952); MONTANA TERRITORY(1952); LAW AND ORDER(1953); POWDER RIVER(1953); SCARLET COAT, THE(1955); VIOLENT MEN, THE(1955); HOT BLOOD(1956); GUNFIGHT AT THE O.K. CORRAL(1957)
Silents
IS THAT NICE?(1926); OUT OF THE WEST(1926); RACING ROMANCE(1926); SONORA KID, THE(1927); WOLF'S CLOTHING(1927); LITTLE SAVAGE, THE(1929); OUTLAWED(1929)

Misc. Silents
WYOMING WILDCAT, THE(1925); MASQUERADE BANDIT, THE(1926); WILD TO GO(1926); BREED OF COURAGE(1927); SILENT RIDER, THE(1927); WHEN DANGER CALLS(1927)

Kosmo Laidlaw
BABYLON(1980, Brit.)

Roy Laidlaw
Silents
DESPOILER, THE(1915); PATRIOT, THE(1916); FEMALE OF THE SPECIES(1917); ALIEN ENEMY, AN(1918); ARE YOU LEGALLY MARRIED?(1919); ACE OF HEARTS, THE(1921); POVERTY OF RICHES, THE(1921); HUNCHBACK OF NOTRE DAME, THE(1923); SNOB, THE(1924); SPLENDID ROAD, THE(1925); IS THAT NICE?(1926)
Misc. Silents
VAGABOND PRINCE, THE(1916); GUNFIGHTER, THE(1917); SWEETHEART OF THE DOOMED(1917); DEADLIER SEX, THE(1920); RIDIN' STREAK, THE(1925); WHERE ROMANCE RIDES(1925); NOT FOR PUBLICATION(1927)

William R. Laidlaw
COMMAND DECISION(1948), w

Alice Laidley
Silents
"THAT ROYLE GIRL"(1925)

Betty Laidlow
DANGER ON THE AIR(1938), w

Ralph Laidlow
Misc. Silents
BACK TO GOD'S COUNTRY(1919 US/Can.)

Ray Laidlow
Silents
HIS ROBE OF HONOR(1918)

Roy Laidlow
Misc. Silents
LIVE SPARKS(1920)

Virginia Laight
CURTAINS(1983, Can.)

Veikko Laihanen
MAKE LIKE A THIEF(1966, Fin.), p

Charles Laiken
RENT CONTROL(1981)

Charlie Laiken
ROLLOVER(1981)
1984
LONELY GUY, THE(1984)

Jewell Lain
CRASH LANDING(1958)

Sue Lain
LINE, THE(1982)

Clare Laine
1984
LAUGHTER HOUSE(1984, Brit.)

Cleo Laine
6.5 SPECIAL(1958, Brit.); ROMAN SPRING OF MRS. STONE, THE(1961, U.S./Brit.); THIRD ALIBI, THE(1961, Brit.)

Corrine Laine
UNDERSEA GIRL(1957)

Frankie Laine
MAKE BELIEVE BALLROOM(1949); WHEN YOU'RE SMILING(1950); SUNNY SIDE OF THE STREET(1951); RAINBOW 'ROUND MY SHOULDER(1952); BRING YOUR SMILE ALONG(1955); HE LAUGHED LAST(1956); MEET ME IN LAS VEGAS(1956); LAST PICTURE SHOW, THE(1971), m

Jeff Laine
Misc. Talkies
CHEERING SECTION(1977)

Jennifer Laine
1984
CAGED FURY(1984, Phil.)

Jimmy Laine
DRILLER KILLER(1979)

Lillian Laine
BULLET FOR STEFANO(1950, Ital.)

Pascal Laine
LACEMAKER, THE(1977, Fr.), w; COUSINS IN LOVE(1982), w

Ray Laine
THERE'S ALWAYS VANILLA(1972); HUNGRY WIVES(1973)

Bob Laing
ON HER MAJESTY'S SECRET SERVICE(1969, Brit.), art d; FRENZY(1972, Brit.), art d; SHOUT AT THE DEVIL(1976, Brit.), art d; SORCERER(1977), set d; GANDHI(1982), art d

Brent E. Laing
1984
PHILADELPHIA EXPERIMENT, THE(1984)

Eleanor Laing
KID FROM CANADA, THE(1957, Brit.)

Frederick Laing
ODD OBSESSION(1961, Jap.), titles

Hugh Laing
BRIGADOON(1954)

John Laing
IN NAME ONLY(1939); RUBBER GUN, THE(1977, Can.), ed; BEYOND REASONABLE DOUBT(1980, New Zeal.), d
1984
TREASURE OF THE YANKEE ZEPHYR(1984), ed

Martin Laing
1984
DARK ENEMY(1984, Brit.)

Robert Laing
PERFECT FRIDAY(1970, Brit.), art d; GOLD(1974, Brit.), art d; ROLLERBALL(1975), art d; LITTLEST HORSE THIEVES, THE(1977), art d; NIGHT GAMES(1980), prod d; HIGH ROAD TO CHINA(1983), prod d

Robert W. Laing
TRAVELS WITH MY AUNT(1972, Brit.), art d

Effie Lairch
TRIPLE TROUBLE(1950)

Benjamin Laird
VILLA!(1958), ed; DOG OF FLANDERS, A(1959), ed; BIG SHOW, THE(1961), ed

Bob Laird
VICE SQUAD(1982)

Cecily Browne Laird
LONELY LADY, THE(1983)

Connie Laird
GUEST IN THE HOUSE(1944)

Doug Laird
VICE SQUAD(1982)

Effie Laird
BENEATH WESTERN SKIES(1944); MAN FROM FRISCO(1944); GEORGE WHITE'S SCANDALS(1945); GOOD SAM(1948); HOUSE BY THE RIVER(1950); WAGONS WEST(1952)

Jack Laird
DARK INTRUDER(1965), p

Jennifer Laird
SCARECROW IN A GARDEN OF CUCUMBERS(1972)

Jenny Laird
AULD LANG SYNE(1937, Brit.); LAST CHANCE, THE(1937, Brit.); PASSENGER TO LONDON(1937, Brit.); WHAT A MAN!(1937, Brit.); LILY OF LAGUNA(1938, Brit.); JUST WILLIAM(1939, Brit.); LAMP STILL BURNS, THE(1943, Brit.); WANTED FOR MURDER(1946, Brit.); BLACK NARCISSUS(1947, Brit.); GIRL ON THE CANAL, THE(1947, Brit.); EYE WITNESS(1950, Brit.); LIFE IN HER HANDS(1951, Brit.); LONG DARK HALL, THE(1951, Brit.); MENACE IN THE NIGHT(1958, Brit.); CONSPIRACY OF HEARTS(1960, Brit.); VILLAGE OF THE DAMNED(1960, Brit.)

Joan Laird
SALT OF THE EARTH(1954), ed

John Laird
NIGHT AT EARL CARROLL'S, A(1940); NORTHWEST MOUNTED POLICE(1940); THOSE WERE THE DAYS(1940)

Julie Laird
HIS BROTHER'S WIFE(1936)

Kenneth Laird
JOURNEY AMONG WOMEN(1977, Aus.)

Landon Laird
RODEO RHYTHM(1941)

Peggy Adams Laird
SANDPIPER, THE(1965)

Stephanie Laird
DR. FRANKENSTEIN ON CAMPUS(1970, Can.)

Trevor Laird
QUADROPHENIA(1979, Brit.); BABYLON(1980, Brit.); BURNING AN ILLUSION(1982, Brit.)

Judson Laire
NAKED CITY, THE(1948); UGLY AMERICAN, THE(1963); SHOCK TREATMENT(1964)

George Lait
STORY OF G.I. JOE, THE(1945)

Jack Lait
BAD COMPANY(1931), w; MADISON SQUARE GARDEN(1932); GIRL WITHOUT A ROOM(1933), w; NEW YORK CONFIDENTIAL(1955), w; CHICAGO CONFIDENTIAL(1957), w

Jack Lait, Jr.
KENTUCKY MOONSHINE(1938), w; MARSHAL OF MESA CITY, THE(1939), w; DEATH VALLEY OUTLAWS(1941), w; SAN ANTONIO ROSE(1941), w; MISSOURI OUTLAW, A(1942), w; TEXAS MASQUERADE(1944), w

Charles Laite
Misc. Silents
AFFAIR OF THREE NATIONS, AN(1915)

Bernard Lajarrige
LES BELLES-DE-NUIT(1952, Fr.); SIMPLE CASE OF MONEY, A(1952, Fr.); FOUR BAGS FULL(1957, Fr./Ital.); BERNADETTE OF LOURDES(1962, Fr.); MAGNIFICENT TRAMP, THE(1962, Fr./Ital.); SHERLOCK HOLMES AND THE DEADLY NECKLACE(1962, Ger.); LADIES OF THE PARK(1964, Fr.); MISTRESS FOR THE SUMMER, A(1964, Fr./Ital.); MURDER AT 45 R.P.M.(1965, Fr.); COUNTERFEIT CONSTABLE, THE(1966, Fr.); MAYERLING(1968, Brit./Fr.); LES CREATURES(1969, Fr./Swed.); VIOLETTE(1978, Fr.)
1984
LE CRABE TAMBOUR(1984, Fr.)

Isabelle Lajeunesse
RABID(1976, Can.)

Laszlo Lajtha
MURDER IN THE CATHEDRAL(1952, Brit.), m

Alan Lake
HAVING A WILD WEEKEND(1965, Brit.); GYPSY GIRL(1966, Brit.); CHARLIE BUBBLES(1968, Brit.); FLAME(1975, Brit.); YESTERDAY'S HERO(1979, Brit.); BMX BANDITS(1983), ed; ESCAPE 2000(1983, Aus.), ed
1984
DON'T OPEN TILL CHRISTMAS(1984, Brit.)

Alice Lake
FROZEN JUSTICE(1929); TWIN BEDS(1929); YOUNG DESIRE(1930); WICKED(1931); SKYWAY(1933); GIRL FROM MISSOURI, THE(1934); GLAMOUR(1934); MIGHTY BARNUM, THE(1934); WHARF ANGEL(1934); FRISCO KID(1935)
Silents
SHOULD A WOMAN TELL?(1920); INFAMOUS MISS REVELL, THE(1921); ENVIRONMENT(1922); GOLDEN GIFT, THE(1922); KISSES(1922); NOBODY'S BRIDE(1923); RED LIGHTS(1923); SOULS FOR SALE(1923); SPIDER AND THE ROSE, THE(1923); OVERLAND LIMITED, THE(1925); HURRICANE, THE(1926); ANGEL OF BROADWAY, THE(1927); SPIDER WEBS(1927); OBEY YOUR HUSBAND(1928); RUNAWAY GIRLS(1928)
Misc. Silents
COME THROUGH(1917); BLACKIE'S REDEMPTION(1919); FULL OF PEP(1919); LION'S DEN, THE(1919); LOMBARDI, LTD.(1919); BODY AND SOUL(1920); MISFIT WIFE, THE(1920); SHORE ACRES(1920); GREATER CLAIM, THE(1921); HOLE IN THE WALL, THE(1921); OVER THE WIRE(1921); UNCHARTED SEAS(1921); HA-

TE(1922); I AM THE LAW(1922); BROKEN HEARTS OF BROADWAY, THE(1923); MODERN MATRIMONY(1923); UNKNOWN PURPLE, THE(1923); DANCING CHEAT, THE(1924); LAW AND THE LADY, THE(1924); LOST CHORD, THE(1925); PRICE OF SUCCESS, THE(1925); BROKEN HOMES(1926); WIVES OF THE PROPHET, THE(1926); ROARING FIRES(1927); WOMEN MEN LIKE(1928); CIRCUMSTANTIAL EVIDENCE(1929)

Arthur Lake
 AIR CIRCUS, THE(1928); DANCE HALL(1929); ON WITH THE SHOW(1929); TANNED LEGS(1929); CHEER UP AND SMILE(1930); SHE'S MY WEAKNESS(1930); INDISCREET(1931); MIDSHIPMAN JACK(1933); GIRL O' MY DREAMS(1935); ORCHIDS TO YOU(1935); SILVER STREAK, THE(1935); WOMEN MUST DRESS(1935); IT'S A GREAT LIFE(1936), w; ANNAPOLIS SALUTE(1937); EXILED TO SHANGHAI(1937); TOPPER(1937); 23 ½ HOURS LEAVE(1937); BLONDIE(1938); DOUBLE DANGER(1938); EVERYBODY'S DOING IT(1938); I COVER CHINATOWN(1938); THERE GOES MY HEART(1938); BLONDIE BRINGS UP BABY(1939); BLONDIE MEETS THE BOSS(1939); BLONDIE TAKES A VACATION(1939); BLONDIE HAS SERVANT TROUBLE(1940); BLONDIE ON A BUDGET(1940); BLONDIE PLAYS CUPID(1940); BLONDIE GOES LATIN(1941); BLONDIE IN SOCIETY(1941); BLONDIE FOR VICTORY(1942); BLONDIE GOES TO COLLEGE(1942); BLONDIE'S BLESSED EVENT(1942); DARING YOUNG MAN, THE(1942); FOOTLIGHT GLAMOUR(1943); IT'S A GREAT LIFE(1943); GHOST THAT WALKS ALONE, THE(1944); SAILOR'S HOLIDAY(1944); 3 IS A FAMILY(1944); BIG SHOW-OFF, THE(1945); LEAVE IT TO BLONDIE(1945); BLONDIE KNOWS BEST(1946); BLONDIE'S LUCKY DAY(1946); LIFE WITH BLONDIE(1946); BLONDIE IN THE DOUGH(1947); BLONDIE'S ANNIVERSARY(1947); BLONDIE'S BIG MOMENT(1947); BLONDIE'S HOLIDAY(1947); BLONDIE'S REWARD(1948); BLONDIE'S SECRET(1948); SIXTEEN FATHOMS DEEP(1948); BLONDIE HITS THE JACKPOT(1949); BLONDIE'S BIG DEAL(1949); BEWARE OF BLONDIE(1950); BLONDIE'S HERO(1950)
Silents
 SKINNER'S DRESS SUIT(1926); IRRESISTIBLE LOVER, THE(1927); HAROLD TEEN(1928); STOP THAT MAN(1928)

Bill Lake
 SHAPE OF THINGS TO COME, THE(1979, Can.)

Dawn Lake
 OUTBACK(1971, Aus.); SUNSTRUCK(1973, Aus.)

Diana Lake
 WHILE I LIVE(1947, Brit.)

Don Lake
 LOOKIN' TO GET OUT(1982)
1984
 POLICE ACADEMY(1984)

Florence Lake
 THRU DIFFERENT EYES(1929); ROGUE SONG, THE(1930); ROMANCE(1930); DRUMS OF JEOPARDY(1931); SECRET SERVICE(1931); LADIES OF THE JURY(1932); NIGHT WORLD(1932); WESTWARD PASSAGE(1932); MIDSHIPMAN JACK(1933); SWEETHEART OF SIGMA CHI(1933); TWO FISTED(1935); TO MARY-WITH LOVE(1936); LOVE IN A BUNGALOW(1937); QUALITY STREET(1937); CONDEMNED WOMEN(1938); CONVICTS AT LARGE(1938); DRAMATIC SCHOOL(1938); HAVING WONDERFUL TIME(1938); I MET MY LOVE AGAIN(1938); NEXT TIME I MARRY(1938); STAGECOACH(1939); UNION PACIFIC(1939); WHEN TOMORROW COMES(1939); FOUR JACKS AND A JILL(1941); SCATTERGOOD SURVIVES A MURDER(1942); CRASH DIVE(1943); HI' YA, SAILOR(1943); CASANOVA BROWN(1944); GOIN' TO TOWN(1944); HI BEAUTIFUL(1944); SAN DIEGO, I LOVE YOU(1944); GEORGE WHITE'S SCANDALS(1945); LITTLE GIANT(1946); STRATTON STORY, THE(1949); FARGO(1952); MAN FROM BLACK HILLS, THE(1952); MAVERICK, THE(1952); BITTER CREEK(1954); DESPERADO, THE(1954); SHE COULDN'T SAY NO(1954); FRASIER, THE SENSUOUS LION(1973); DAY OF THE LOCUST, THE(1975)
Silents
 NEW YEAR'S EVE(1929)

Fred Lake
 THUNDER OVER TANGIER(1957, Brit.)

Gladys B. Lake
 PEOPLE VS. DR. KILDARE, THE(1941)

James Lake
 SNOWBALL(1960, Brit.), w

Janet Lake
 TWO WEEKS IN ANOTHER TOWN(1962); OPPOSITE SEX, THE(1956); THESE WILDER YEARS(1956); RAINTREE COUNTY(1957); WINGS OF EAGLES, THE(1957)

Kaye Lake
 APARTMENT FOR PEGGY(1948)

Lew Lake
 SPLINTERS(1929, Brit.); GREAT GAME, THE(1930); SPLINTERS IN THE NAVY(1931, Brit.); SPLINTERS IN THE AIR(1937, Brit.)

Stuart N. Lake
 FRONTIER MARSHAL(1934), w; WELLS FARGO(1937), w; FRONTIER MARSHAL(1939), w; WESTERNER, THE(1940), w; MY DARLING CLEMENTINE(1946), w; WINCHESTER '73(1950), w; POWDER RIVER(1953), w; WICHITA(1955), tech adv

Tom Lake
 PETERSEN(1974, Aus.)

Vernoica Lake
 FLESH FEAST(1970), p

Veronica Lake
 HOLD BACK THE DAWN(1941); I WANTED WINGS(1941); SULLIVAN'S TRAVELS(1941); GLASS KEY, THE(1942); I MARRIED A WITCH(1942); STAR SPANGLED RHYTHM(1942); THIS GUN FOR HIRE(1942); SO PROUDLY WE HAIL(1943); HOUR BEFORE THE DAWN, THE(1944); BRING ON THE GIRLS(1945); DUFFY'S TAVERN(1945); HOLD THAT BLONDE(1945); MISS SUSIE SLAGLE'S(1945); OUT OF THIS WORLD(1945); BLUE DAHLIA, THE(1946); RAMROD(1947); VARIETY GIRL(1947); ISN'T IT ROMANTIC?(1948); SAIGON(1948); SAINTED SISTERS, THE(1948); SLATTERY'S HURRICANE(1949); STRONGHOLD(1952, Mex.); FLESH FEAST(1970)

Wesley Lake
 FOUR DEVILS(1929)

Samuel G. Laken
1984
 POPE OF GREENWICH VILLAGE, THE(1984)

Jim Laker
 FINAL TEST, THE(1953, Brit.)

Paule Lakis
 WOMAN HUNT(1962)

Arthur Lakner
 KIND STEPMOTHER(1936, Hung.), w

Jane Lako
 THREES, MENAGE A TROIS(1968)

Lucile Laks
 IN SEARCH OF GREGORY(1970, Brit./Ital.), w

Lila Lakshmanan
 CONTEMPT(1963, Fr./Ital.), prod d; LES CARABINIERS(1968, Fr./Ital.), ed

Ed Lakso
 OPERATION DAMES(1959)

Edward J. Lakso
 WOMAN HUNT(1962), w; GENTLE GIANT(1967), w

Edward Lakso
 HEAD ON(1971), d&w

Reginald Lal Singh
 BEN HUR(1959)

Joe Lala
 SGT. PEPPER'S LONELY HEARTS CLUB BAND(1978)

Lalande
 LA MARSEILLAISE(1938, Fr.), m

Arlette Lalande
 GATES OF PARIS(1958, Fr./Ital.), ed

Francois Lalande
 QUESTION, THE(1977, Fr.); FRENCH POSTCARDS(1979)

Francoise Lalande
 HERBIE GOES TO MONTE CARLO(1977)

Steve Lalande
1984
 BAD MANNERS(1984)

Sultan Lalani
 THAT LUCKY TOUCH(1975, Brit.)

Louis Lalanne
 ZAZIE(1961, Fr.)

Cedric Lalara
 LAST WAVE, THE(1978, Aus.)

Morris Lalara
 LAST WAVE, THE(1978, Aus.)

Jean-Francois Lalet
 TWO FOR THE ROAD(1967, Brit.)

Lohn Lalette
 REUNION(1932, Brit.)

Suzanne Lalique
 WOULD-BE GENTLEMAN, THE(1960, Fr.), cos&set d; MARRIAGE OF FIGARO, THE(1963, Fr.), set d&cos

Dari Lallou
 PUSSYCAT, PUSSYCAT, I LOVE YOU(1970)

Bill Lally
 I'LL TAKE ROMANCE(1937); PAID TO DANCE(1937); ANGELS OVER BROADWAY(1940); WE WHO ARE YOUNG(1940); CONFESSIONS OF BOSTON BLACKIE(1941); LOVE CRAZY(1941); MY FAVORITE BLONDE(1942); SABOTAGE SQUAD(1942); TALK OF THE TOWN(1942); ONE DANGEROUS NIGHT(1943); THREE HEARTS FOR JULIA(1943)

Billy Lally
 WHO KILLED GAIL PRESTON?(1938); FACE BEHIND THE MASK, THE(1941)

Chip Lally
 UNCOMMON VALOR(1983)

Harold Lally
 MAD GAME, THE(1933)

Howard Lally
 DR. BULL(1933); SLEEPERS EAST(1934); THREE ON A HONEYMOON(1934); ROBERTA(1935)

Michael Lally
 MISTER 880(1950); COURT-MARTIAL OF BILLY MITCHELL, THE(1955); HOW TO BE VERY, VERY, POPULAR(1955); PEYTON PLACE(1957); LAST RITES(1980)

Michael David Lally
 NESTING, THE(1981)

Mike Lally
 FUGITIVE LADY(1934); CEILNG ZERO(1935); SHE COULDN'T TAKE IT(1935); SUBMARINE D-1(1937); THAT CERTAIN WOMAN(1937); I STOLE A MILLION(1939); CASTLE ON THE HUDSON(1940); INVISIBLE STRIPES(1940); MURDER IN THE AIR(1940); THEY DRIVE BY NIGHT(1940); MAYOR OF 44TH STREET, THE(1942); MY FAVORITE BLONDE(1942); FALLEN SPARROW, THE(1943); GHOST SHIP, THE(1943); IRON MAJOR, THE(1943); PRACTICALLY YOURS(1944); STORY OF DR. WASSELL, THE(1944); ANGEL ON MY SHOULDER(1946); FALCON'S ALIBI, THE(1946); JOLSON STORY, THE(1946); NIGHT AND DAY(1946); TWO YEARS BEFORE THE MAST(1946); DESERT FURY(1947); GANGSTER, THE(1947); LIKELY STORY, A(1947); NIGHTMARE ALLEY(1947); OUT OF THE PAST(1947); WILD HARVEST(1947); MR. BLANDINGS BUILDS HIS DREAM HOUSE(1948); RACE STREET(1948); WHIPLASH(1948); WINTER MEETING(1948); SET-UP, THE(1949); STREETS OF LAREDO(1949); EMERGENCY WEDDING(1950); IN A LONELY PLACE(1950); PERFECT STRANGERS(1950); WHERE DANGER LIVES(1950); DOUBLE DYNAMITE(1951); ENFORCER, THE(1951); HIS KIND OF WOMAN(1951); LET'S GO NAVY(1951); ON DANGEROUS GROUND(1951); RACKET, THE(1951); TWO TICKETS TO BROADWAY(1951); KANSAS CITY CONFIDENTIAL(1952); NARROW MARGIN, THE(1952); SNIPER, THE(1952); DANGEROUS MISSION(1954); EXECUTIVE SUITE(1954); SHE COULDN'T SAY NO(1954); JET PILOT(1957); WOMAN OBSESSED(1959)

Teri Lally
1984
 COMFORT AND JOY(1984, Brit.)

William Lally
 YOU CAN'T TAKE IT WITH YOU(1938); PICKUP ON 101(1972)

William J. Lally
 RED MENACE, THE(1949)

Robbi LaLonde
SNOW WHITE AND THE THREE STOOGES(1961)
Jean Laloni
OLGA'S GIRLS(1964)
Frank Lalor
Silents
IN AGAIN-OUT AGAIN(1917); RED HOT ROMANCE(1922); CLOTHES MAKE THE PIRATE(1925)
Leslie Lalor
CRIMINAL CONVERSATION(1980, Ireland)
Daniel Laloux
SWEET AND SOUR(1964, Fr./Ital.)
Rene Laloux
FANTASTIC PLANET(1973, Fr./Czech.), d, w; LES MAITRES DU TEMPS(1982, Fr./Switz./Ger.), d, w
Chan Yiu Lam
MAN WITH THE GOLDEN GUN, THE(1974, Brit.)
Kwan Shan Lam
FERRY TO HONG KONG(1959, Brit.)
Violet Lam
SECRET, THE(1979, Hong Kong), m
1984
AH YING(1984, Hong Kong), m
David Lama
LOS AUTOMATAS DE LA MUERTE(1960, Mex.); NEUTRON EL ENMASCARADO NEGRO(1962, Mex.)
Margarito Lama
ONE WAY STREET(1950)
Karel Lamac
SCHWEIK'S NEW ADVENTURES(1943, Brit.), d, w; IT HAPPENED ONE SUN-DAY(1944, Brit.), d; THEY MET IN THE DARK(1945, Brit.), d
Allan Lamaire [Hugo Del Carril]
FIRE IN THE FLESH(1964, Fr.)
Ken Lamaire
NOTHING PERSONAL(1980, Can.)
Elizabeth LaMal
ARIZONA GANGBUSTERS(1940)
Isabel Lamal
GUILTY PARENTS(1934); MR. BOGGS STEPS OUT(1938); LADY IN A JAM(1942); PHANTOM KILLER(1942); QUEEN OF BROADWAY(1942); STORY OF DR. WAS-SELL, THE(1944)
Isabelle Lamal
SHE GETS HER MAN(1935); SHE MARRIED HER BOSS(1935); PRINCESS COMES ACROSS, THE(1936); THEODORA GOES WILD(1936); WHEN YOU'RE IN LO-VE(1937); UNFINISHED BUSINESS(1941); FLIGHT FOR FREEDOM(1943); MAD GHOUL, THE(1943); SO'S YOUR UNCLE(1943)
Isabell LaMalle
GANG BULLETS(1938)
Bobbie LaManche
KID MILLIONS(1934)
Jean-Louis Lamande
SHAMELESS OLD LADY, THE(1966, Fr.)
Joel Lamangan
YEAR OF LIVING DANGEROUSLY, THE(1982, Aus.)
Viva Lamano
FLY NOW, PAY LATER(1969), set d
Amanda LaMar
1984
LAST NIGHT AT THE ALAMO(1984)
Billy Lamar
Silents
WEST OF THE RAINBOW'S END(1926)
Misc. Silents
HI-JACKING RUSTLERS(1926); THUNDERBOLT'S TRACKS(1927)
Lucille Lamar
MAGNIFICENT OBSESSION(1954)
Marguerite Lamar
WHERE THE BUFFALO ROAM(1980)
Mary Lamar
TEACHER AND THE MIRACLE, THE(1961, Ital./Span.)
Paul Lamaraux
PRIME TIME, THE(1960)
Hedy Lamarr
ALGIERS(1938); LADY OF THE TROPICS(1939); BOOM TOWN(1940); COMRADE X(1940); I TAKE THIS WOMAN(1940); COME LIVE WITH ME(1941); H.M. PULHAM, ESQ.(1941); ZIEGFELD GIRL(1941); CROSSROADS(1942); TORTILLA FLAT(1942); WHITE CARGO(1942); HEAVENLY BODY, THE(1943); CONSPIRATORS, THE(1944); EXPERIMENT PERILOUS(1944); HER HIGHNESS AND THE BELLBOY(1945); STRANGE WOMAN, THE(1946); DISHONORED LADY(1947); LET'S LIVE A LITT-LE(1948); SAMSON AND DELILAH(1949); COPPER CANYON(1950); LADY WITH-OUT PASSPORT, A(1950); MY FAVORITE SPY(1951); LOVES OF THREE QUEENS, THE(1954, Ital./Fr.); STORY OF MANKIND, THE(1957); FEMALE ANIMAL, THE(1958)
Lawrence LaMarr
LIVING BETWEEN TWO WORLDS(1963)
Lucille LaMarr
OLD ACQUAINTANCE(1943); THANK YOUR LUCKY STARS(1943); PETTY GIRL, THE(1950); ROYAL WEDDING(1951); NO ROOM FOR THE GROOM(1952); ABBOTT AND COSTELLO MEET DR. JEKYLL AND MR. HYDE(1954)
Margaret LaMarr
LITTLE GIANT, THE(1933)
Moses LaMarr
PORGY AND BESS(1959)
Richard LaMarr
EMERGENCY WEDDING(1950)
Sam LaMarr
UNDERCOVER MAN, THE(1949)

Sammy LaMarr
FIGHTING FOOLS(1949)
Margot Lamarre
PAPERBACK HERO(1973, Can.)
Leonie Lamartine
PACK UP YOUR TROUBLES(1940, Brit.); SO EVIL MY LOVE(1948, Brit.)
Carlo Lamas
UNFAITHFULS, THE(1960, Ital.)
Fernando Lamas
AVENGERS, THE(1950); LAW AND THE LADY, THE(1951); RICH, YOUNG AND PRETTY(1951); MERRY WIDOW, THE(1952); DANGEROUS WHEN WET(1953); DIA-MOND QUEEN, THE(1953); GIRL WHO HAD EVERYTHING, THE(1953); SAN-GAREE(1953); JIVARO(1954); ROSE MARIE(1954); GIRL RUSH, THE(1955); LOST WORLD, THE(1960); PLACE CALLED GLORY, A(1966, Span./Ger.), w; KILL A DRAGON(1967); VALLEY OF MYSTERY(1967); VIOLENT ONES, THE(1967), a, d; BACKTRACK(1969); 100 RIFLES(1969); WON TON TON, THE DOG WHO SAVED HOLLYWOOD(1976); CHEAP DETECTIVE, THE(1978)
Lorenzo Lamas
GREASE(1978); TAKE DOWN(1979)
1984
BODY ROCK(1984)
Ande Lamb
WAR DOGS(1942), w; FOLLOW THE LEADER(1944), w; RIDERS OF THE SANTA FE(1944), w; RENEGADES OF THE RIO GRANDE(1945), w; UNEXPECTED GUEST(1946), w; HOPPY'S HOLIDAY(1947), w
Andre Lamb
POLICE BULLETS(1942), w; HARVEST MELODY(1943), w; TEXAN MEETS CALAMITY JANE, THE(1950), p,d&w
Anthony Lamb
AFFAIRS OF ADELAIDE(1949, U. S./Brit)
Betty Lamb *
Silents
MAN FROM MONTANA, THE(1917)
Celia Lamb
MAN IN GREY, THE(1943, Brit.)
Charles Lamb
ONCE A CROOK(1941, Brit.); GALLOPING MAJOR, THE(1951, Brit.); LAVENDER HILL MOB, THE(1951, Brit.); COME BACK PETER(1952, Brit.); CURTAIN UP(1952, Brit.); ISLAND RESCUE(1952, Brit.); DELAYED ACTION(1954, Brit.); SOLUTION BY PHONE(1954, Brit.); INTRUDER, THE(1955, Brit.); ONE JUMP AHEAD(1955, Brit.); LIGHT FINGERS(1957, Brit.); LUCKY JIM(1957, Brit.); RAISING A RIOT(1957, Brit.); ROCK AROUND THE WORLD(1957, Brit.); NUN'S STORY, THE(1959); WRECK OF THE MARY DEAR, THE(1959); MODEL FOR MURDER(1960, Brit.); SCHOOL FOR SCOUNDRELS(1960, Brit.); SHAKEDOWN, THE(1960, Brit.); CURSE OF THE WERE-WOLF, THE(1961, Brit.); OLD MAC(1961, Brit.); SWORD OF SHERWOOD FOREST(1961, Brit.); CONCRETE JUNGLE, THE(1962, Brit.); HANDS OF ORLAC, THE(1964, Brit./Fr.); HIDE AND SEEK(1964, Brit.); LIFE AT THE TOP(1965, Brit.); CHARLIE BUBBLES(1968, Brit.); FIVE MILLION YEARS TO EARTH(1968, Brit.); SOUTHERN STAR, THE(1969, Fr./Brit.); SUBTERFUGE(1969, US/Brit.); HANDS OF THE RIP-PER(1971, Brit.)
Darwin Lamb
PROFESSIONALS, THE(1966)
Derek Lamb
GOLDEN APPLES OF THE SUN(1971, Can.)
Eleanor Lamb
WHERE THE RED FERN GROWS(1974), w; AGAINST A CROOKED SKY(1975), w; SEVEN ALONE(1975), w
Gil Lamb
FLEET'S IN, THE(1942); STAR SPANGLED RHYTHM(1942); RIDING HIGH(1943); PRACTICALLY YOURS(1944); RAINBOW ISLAND(1944); HIT PARADE OF 1947(1947); HUMPHREY TAKES A CHANCE(1950); BOSS, THE(1956); TERROR IN A TEXAS TOWN(1958); GOOD NEIGHBOR SAM(1964); UGLY DACHSHUND, THE(1966); ADVENTURES OF BULLWHIP GRIFFIN, THE(1967); GNOME-MOBILE, THE(1967); LOVE BUG, THE(1968); BOATNIKS, THE(1970); NORWOOD(1970); DAY OF THE ANIMALS(1977)
Harold Lamb
CRUSADES, THE(1935), w; PLAINSMAN, THE(1937), w; BUCCANEER, THE(1938), w; SAMSON AND DELILAH(1949), w; GOLDEN HORDE, THE(1951), w; BUCCA-NEER, THE(1958), w
Irene Lamb
EAGLE HAS LANDED, THE(1976, Brit.), ed
Jane Lamb
GREEN SCARF, THE(1954, Brit.)
Jil Lamb
FLASH GORDON(1980)
John Lamb
MERMAIDS OF TIBURON, THE(1962), p,d&w, ph
Karl Lamb
LUXURY LINER(1948), w; STARLIFT(1951), w; TARZAN AND THE SHE-DE-VIL(1953), w
Larry Lamb
SUPERMAN(1978); SUPERMAN III(1983)
1984
FLIGHT TO BERLIN(1984, Ger./Brit.)
Max Lamb
APACHE UPRISING(1966), w; WACO(1966), w
Paedar Lamb
1984
REFLECTIONS(1984, Brit.)
Peadar Lamb
SECRET OF MY SUCCESS, THE(1965, Brit.); VON RICHTHOFEN AND BROWN(1970)
Peter Lamb
DEVIL'S AGENT, THE(1962, Brit.); NEVER PUT IT IN WRITING(1964)
Victor Lamb
YOUNG GRADUATES, THE(1971)
Boguslaw Lambach
TONIGHT A TOWN DIES(1961, Pol.), ph

Harry Lambart
Silents
TANGLE, THE(1914), d
Misc. Silents
HEIGHTS OF HAZARDS, THE(1915), d; CRUCIBLE OF LIFE, THE(1918), d; DOWN UNDER DONOVAN(1922, Brit.), d

Michael Lambart
HIGH COMMAND(1938, Brit.)

Lambeg Folk Dance Society
DEVIL'S ROCK(1938, Brit.)

Vivian Lambelet
GLASS MOUNTAIN, THE(1950, Brit), m

G. Lamberger
DYBBUK THE(1938, Pol.)

Ameda Lambert
STORY OF DR. WASSELL, THE(1944)

Ann Lambert
1984
TANK(1984), cos

Anne Lambert
PICNIC AT HANGING ROCK(1975, Aus.)

Anne Louise Lambert
DRAUGHTSMAN'S CONTRACT, THE(1983, Brit.)

Art Lambert
ROLLOVER(1981)

Billy Lambert
HIS AND HERS(1961, Brit.)

C. Lambert
Silents
GANGSTERS OF NEW YORK, THE(1914)

Charlotte Lambert
Misc. Silents
NOTHING TO BE DONE(1914)

Christopher Lambert
1984
GREYSTOKE: THE LEGEND OF TARZAN, LORD OF THE APES(1984)

Cindy Lambert
1984
THIEF OF HEARTS(1984)

Clara Lambert
Silents
LOVE'S TOLL(1916)

Clay Lambert
OUT OF TOWNERS, THE(1970), makeup

Constant Lambert
ANNA KARENINA(1948, Brit.), m

Dennis Lambert
TUNNELVISION(1976), m

Derek Lambert
ROUGH CUT(1980, Brit.), w

Diana Lambert
THEY CAN'T HANG ME(1955, Brit.); CIRCLE, THE(1959, Brit.); NUN'S STORY, THE(1959); SEANCE ON A WET AFTERNOON(1964 Brit.)

Diane Lambert
PRETTY MAIDS ALL IN A ROW(1971)

Douglas Lambert
SUNDAY BLOODY SUNDAY(1971, Brit.); GOT IT MADE(1974, Brit.); MOONRAKER(1979, Brit.); SATURN 3(1980); HUNGER, THE(1983)

Eddie Lambert
BIG HOUSE, THE(1930); WOMEN GO ON FOREVER(1931); HIGH GEAR(1933)

Edward P. Lambert
OTHER LOVE, THE(1947), cos

Elizabeth Lambert
SPRING BREAK(1983), makeup

Eugene Lambert
ULYSSES(1967, U.S./Brit.)

Fred Lambert
VIOLATED(1953)

Gavin Lambert
BITTER VICTORY(1958, Fr.), w; ANOTHER SKY(1960 Brit.), d&w; SONS AND LOVERS(1960, Brit.), w; ROMAN SPRING OF MRS. STONE, THE(1961, U.S./Brit.), w; INSIDE DAISY CLOVER(1965), w; WHO SLEW AUNTIE ROO?(1971, U.S./Brit.), w; I WANT WHAT I WANT(1972, Brit.), w; INTERVAL(1973, Mex./U.S.), w; I NEVER PROMISED YOU A ROSE GARDEN(1977), w; RICH AND FAMOUS(1981)

Georges Lambert
THERE'S A GIRL IN MY SOUP(1970, Brit.)

Glen Lambert
Misc. Silents
HEARTBOUND(1925), d

Harry Lambert
Silents
TODAY(1917)
Misc. Silents
SILENT WITNESS, THE(1917), d

Henri Lambert
TOMORROW IS MY TURN(1962, Fr./Ital./Ger.); TRANS-EUROP-EXPRESS(1968, Fr.)

Hugh Lambert
FINDERS KEEPERS(1966, Brit.), ch

Ida Lambert
Silents
ONLY A MILL GIRL(1919, Brit.)
Misc. Silents
CORNER MAN, THE(1921, Brit.)

Irene Lambert
Silents
SALLY OF THE SCANDALS(1928)

Jack Lambert
FOOTSTEPS IN THE NIGHT(1932, Brit.); GHOST GOES WEST, THE(1936); HOUSE BROKEN(1936, Brit.); MARIGOLD(1938, Brit.); THISTLEDOWN(1938, Brit.); OUTSIDER, THE(1940, Brit.); SPIDER, THE(1940, Brit.); CROSS OF LORRAINE, THE(1943); NINE MEN(1943, Brit.); SEEDS OF FREEDOM(1943, USSR); LOST ANGEL(1944); DUFFY'S TAVERN(1945); HIDDEN EYE, THE(1945); ABILENE TOWN(1946); HARVEY GIRLS, THE(1946); KILLERS, THE(1946); O.S.S.(1946); PLAINSMAN AND THE LADY(1946); BELLE STARR'S DAUGHTER(1947); DICK TRACY'S DILEMMA(1947); UNSUSPECTED(1947); VIGILANTES RETURN, THE(1947); DISASTER(1948); RIVER LADY(1948); BIG JACK(1949); BRIMSTONE(1949); FLOODTIDE(1949, Brit.); GREAT GATSBY, THE(1949); MASSACRE HILL(1949, Brit.); DAKOTA LIL(1950); HUE AND CRY(1950, Brit.); NORTH OF THE GREAT DIVIDE(1950); STARS IN MY CROWN(1950); ENFORCER, THE(1951); SECRET OF CONVICT LAKE, THE(1951); BEND OF THE RIVER(1952); BLACKBEARD THE PIRATE(1952); MONTANA BELLE(1952); BIG FRAME, THE(1953, Brit.); GREAT GAME, THE(1953, Brit.); SCARED STIFF(1953); TWICE UPON A TIME(1953, Brit.); 99 RIVER STREET(1953); COMPANIONS IN CRIME(1954, Brit.); VERA CRUZ(1954); AT GUNPOINT(1955); CROSS CHANNEL(1955, Brit.); KISS ME DEADLY(1955); RUN FOR COVER(1955); SEA SHALL NOT HAVE THEM, THE(1955, Brit.); STORM OVER THE NILE(1955, Brit.); THREE CASES OF MURDER(1955, Brit.); WARRIORS, THE(1955); CANYON RIVER(1956); JUMPING FOR JOY(1956, Brit.); LAST MAN TO HANG, THE(1956, Brit.); TRACK THE MAN DOWN(1956, Brit.); CHICAGO CONFIDENTIAL(1957); LITTLE HUT, THE(1957); OUT OF THE CLOUDS(1957, Brit.); TEARS FOR SIMON(1957, Brit.); HOT CAR GIRL(1958); MACHINE GUN KELLY(1958); PARTY GIRL(1958); BRIDAL PATH, THE(1959, Brit.); DAY OF THE OUTLAW(1959); SON OF ROBIN HOOD(1959, Brit.); FRECKLES(1960); SHAKEDOWN, THE(1960, Brit.); BOMB IN THE HIGH STREET(1961, Brit.); FRANCIS OF ASSISI(1961); GEORGE RAFT STORY, THE(1961); GREYFRIARS BOBBY(1961, Brit.); HOW THE WEST WAS WON(1962); FOUR FOR TEXAS(1963); CUCKOO PATROL(1965, Brit.); OPERATION SNAFU(1965, Brit.); DRACULA–PRINCE OF DARKNESS(1966, Brit.); THEY CAME FROM BEYOND SPACE(1967, Brit.); NEITHER THE SEA NOR THE SAND(1974, Brit.)

Jane Lambert
HARRAD SUMMER, THE(1974); FURY, THE(1978)

Janet Lambert
ABROAD WITH TWO YANKS(1944); UP IN MABEL'S ROOM(1944)

Jeffrey Lambert
TWILIGHT ZONE–THE MOVIE(1983)

Kathe Lambert
HOUSE OF LIFE(1953, Ger.), w

Keith E. Lambert
SCOBIE MALONE(1975, Aus.), ph

Ken Lambert
FOXY LADY(1971, Can.), ph

Lee J. Lambert
SIMON, KING OF THE WITCHES(1971)

Louise Lambert
PULP(1972, Brit.)

Lucille Lambert
LONE PRAIRIE, THE(1942)

Madeleine Lambert
BRIDE IS MUCH TOO BEAUTIFUL, THE(1958, Fr.); YOU ONLY LIVE ONCE(1969, Fr.)

Marc Lambert
SIERRA BARON(1958); GINA(1961, Fr./Mex.)

Margaret Lambert
CAGED(1950)

Mark Lambert
1984
CHAMPIONS(1984)

Martine Lambert
LOVE AND THE FRENCHWOMAN(1961, Fr.)

Maud Lambert
GIRLS ON PROBATION(1938)

Maude Lambert
DEAD END(1937)

Mel Lambert
J.W. COOP(1971); ONE FLEW OVER THE CUCKOO'S NEST(1975)

Michael Lambert
GAY INTRUDERS, THE(1946, Brit.); RECOMMENDATION FOR MERCY(1975, Can.)

Nigel Lambert
WHERE EAGLES DARE(1968, Brit.); SCREAM AND SCREAM AGAIN(1970, Brit.); FUNNY MONEY(1983, Brit.)

Patrick Lambert
LE BEAU MARIAGE(1982, Fr.)

Paul Lambert
GIRLS ON THE LOOSE(1958); SPARTACUS(1960); HOUSE OF WOMEN(1962); BIG MOUTH, THE(1967); PLANET OF THE APES(1968); GUNFIGHT, A(1971); WINDSPLITTER, THE(1971); PLAY IT AS IT LAYS(1972); WHERE DOES IT HURT?(1972); ALL THE PRESIDENT'S MEN(1976); SPARKLE(1976); DEATH WISH II(1982); WRONG IS RIGHT(1982)

Peter Lambert
BREAKING POINT, THE(1961, Brit.), p&w; GREAT ARMORED CAR SWINDLE, THE(1964), p, w

Reita Lambert
CARELESS LADY(1932), w

Rita Lambert
HELLO SISTER(1930), w

Robert K. Lambert
SORCERER(1977), ed; BRINK'S JOB, THE(1978), ed; DRIVER, THE(1978), ed; FINAL COUNTDOWN, THE(1980), ed; BORDER, THE(1982), ed
1984
HOTEL NEW HAMPSHIRE, THE(1984), ed

Steve Lambert
1984
NINJA III–THE DOMINATION(1984), stunts

Steven Lambert
REVENGE OF THE NINJA(1983)
1984
NINJA III–THE DOMINATION(1984); RACING WITH THE MOON(1984), a, stunts

Ted Lambert
FAME(1980)
Will Lambert
Silents
HURRICANE KID, THE(1925), w
William Lambert
SAILOR'S LUCK(1933), cos; IN OLD KENTUCKY(1935), cos; THANKS A MILLION(1935), ed; WAY DOWN EAST(1935), cos; WELCOME HOME(1935), cos; SONG AND DANCE MAN, THE(1936), cos; WELCOME HOME, SOLDIER BOYS(1972), cos
Professor Lamberti
TONIGHT AND EVERY NIGHT(1945); LINDA BE GOOD(1947)
William Lamberto
UNDER PRESSURE(1935), cos
Heath Lamberts
GREAT BIG THING, A(1968, U.S./Can.); TO KILL A CLOWN(1972)
Donna Lambertson
3 IS A FAMILY(1944)
Elissa Lambertson
3 IS A FAMILY(1944)
Ellie Lambetti
WASTREL, THE(1963, Ital.)
Joe Lambie
NIGHTMARES(1983)
1984
PROTOCOL(1984)
Penny Lambirth
SING AND SWING(1964, Brit.)
Jack Lamble
ATLANTIC FLIGHT(1937)
Lloyd Lamble
CURTAIN UP(1952, Brit.); ISLAND OF DESIRE(1952, Brit.); SCOTLAND YARD INSPECTOR(1952, Brit.); BOTH SIDES OF THE LAW(1953, Brit.); GREAT GILBERT AND SULLIVAN, THE(1953, Brit.); WHITE FIRE(1953, Brit.); WOMAN IN HIDING(1953, Brit.); BELLES OF ST. TRINIAN'S, THE(1954, Brit.); GREEN BUDDHA, THE(1954, Brit.); PROFILE(1954, Brit.); DYNAMITERS, THE(1956, Brit.); GIRL IN THE PICTURE, THE(1956, Brit.); MAN WHO KNEW TOO MUCH, THE(1956); MAN WHO NEVER WAS, THE(1956, Brit.); PRIVATE'S PROGRESS(1956, Brit.); TRACK THE MAN DOWN(1956, Brit.); ENEMY FROM SPACE(1957, Brit.); GOOD COMPANIONS, THE(1957, Brit.); SEA WIFE(1957, Brit.); SUSPENDED ALIBI(1957, Brit.); THERE'S ALWAYS A THURSDAY(1957, Brit.); ALL AT SEA(1958, Brit.); BANK RAIDERS, THE(1958, Brit.); BLUE MURDER AT ST. TRINIAN'S(1958, Brit.); CURSE OF THE DEMON(1958); DANGEROUS YOUTH(1958, Brit.); DUNKIRK(1958, Brit.); MAN WHO WOULDN'T TALK, THE(1958, Brit.); IT TAKES A THIEF(1960, Brit.); MAN WITH THE GREEN CARNATION, THE(1960, Brit.); PURE HELL OF ST. TRINIAN'S, THE(1961, Brit.); TERM OF TRIAL(1962, Brit.); NO TREE IN THE STREET(1964, Brit.); JOEY BOY(1965, Brit.)
John Lambon
KILLER FORCE(1975, Switz./Ireland), cos
Maureen Lambray
PRETTY BABY(1978), spec eff
Frederic Lambre
SEASON FOR LOVE, THE(1963, Fr.)
Mihalis Lambrinos
FOR THE LOVE OF BENJI(1977)
Vassili Lambrinos
ISLAND OF LOVE(1963); UNSINKABLE MOLLY BROWN, THE(1964); UP THE SANDBOX(1972); THAT MAN BOLT(1973)
Vassily Lambrinos
THEY ALL LAUGHED(1981)
Philip Lambro
GIT!(1965), m&md; AND NOW MIGUEL(1966), m
Phillip Lambro
MURPH THE SURF(1974), m
Derek Lamden
BABY LOVE(1969, Brit.)
Lea Lamedico
FORCE OF ARMS(1951)
Leonard Lamensdorf
CORNBREAD, EARL AND ME(1975), w
Tommy Lamey
PSYCHO FROM TEXAS(1982)
Ken Lamkin
SCAVENGER HUNT(1979), ph
Karen Lamm
THUNDERBOLT AND LIGHTFOOT(1974); TRACKDOWN(1976); UNSEEN, THE(1981)
Mario Lamm
SALOME(1953)
Haji Lamme
BIG FOOT(1973)
Kelly Lammers
PLANET OF DINOSAURS(1978), m
Mike Lammers
YOUNG GIANTS(1983), w
Isabel Lamon
Misc. Silents
LITTLE WOMEN(1919)
Bill Lamond
YESTERDAY(1980, Can.), w
Carole Lamond
LEARNING TREE, THE(1969)
Don Lamond
SPACE MASTER X-7(1958); HAVE ROCRET, WILL TRAVEL(1959); THREE STOOGES IN ORBIT, THE(1962); THREE STOOGES MEET HERCULES, THE(1962); THREE STOOGES GO AROUND THE WORLD IN A DAZE, THE(1963); OUTLAWS IS COMING, THE(1965); CROSS AND THE SWITCHBLADE, THE(1970); LATE LIZ, THE(1971)

George LaMond
CLOSE TO MY HEART(1951)
Angelo Lamonea
NEW YORK, NEW YORK(1977); AVALANCHE(1978); DRIVER, THE(1978)
Adele Lamont
BRAIN THAT WOULDN'T DIE, THE(1959)
B. Wayne Lamont
SECRET MENACE(1931), w; CROSS-EXAMINATION(1932); MIDNIGHT LADY(1932)
Misc. Silents
SHINING ADVENTURE, THE(1925); SPEED DEMON, THE(1925)
Bernie Lamont
LADIES IN LOVE(1930)
Charles Lamont
CIRCUMSTANTIAL EVIDENCE(1935), d; CURTAIN FALLS, THE(1935), d; FALSE PRETENSES(1935), d; GIGOLETTE(1935), d; HAPPINESS C.O.D.(1935), d; LADY IN SCARLET, THE(1935), d; SHOT IN THE DARK, A(1935), d; SONS OF STEEL(1935), d; TOMORROW'S YOUTH(1935), d; WORLD ACCUSES, THE(1935), d; AUGUST WEEKEND(1936, Brit.), d; BELOW THE DEADLINE(1936), d; BULLDOG EDITION(1936), d; DARK HOUR, THE(1936), d; LADY LUCK(1936), d; LITTLE RED SCHOOLHOUSE(1936), d; RING AROUND THE MOON(1936), d; WALLABY JIM OF THE ISLANDS(1937), d; CIPHER BUREAU(1938), d; INTERNATIONAL CRIME(1938), d; SHADOWS OVER SHANGHAI(1938), d; SLANDER HOUSE(1938), d; INSIDE INFORMATION(1939), d; LITTLE ACCIDENT(1939), p&d; LONG SHOT, THE(1939), d; PANAMA PATROL(1939), p&d; PRIDE OF THE NAVY(1939), d; UNEXPECTED FATHER(1939), d; GIVE US WINGS(1940), d; LOVE, HONOR AND OH, BABY(1940), d; OH JOHNNY, HOW YOU CAN LOVE!(1940), d; SANDY IS A LADY(1940), d; DON'T GET PERSONAL(1941), d; MELODY LANE(1941), d; MOONLIGHT IN HAWAII(1941), d; ROAD AGENT(1941), d; SAN ANTONIO ROSE(1941), d; SING ANOTHER CHORUS(1941), d; ALMOST MARRIED(1942), d; GET HEP TO LOVE(1942), d; HI, NEIGHBOR(1942), d; YOU'RE TELLING ME(1942), d; FIRED WIFE(1943), d; HIT THE ICE(1943), d; IT COMES UP LOVE(1943), d; MR. BIG(1943), d; TOP MAN(1943), d; WHEN JOHNNY COMES MARCHING HOME(1943), d; BOWERY TO BROADWAY(1944), d; HER PRIMITIVE MAN(1944), d; MERRY MONAHANS, THE(1944), d; FRONTIER GAL(1945), d; SALOME, WHERE SHE DANCED(1945), d; THAT'S THE SPIRIT(1945), d; RUNAROUND, THE(1946), d; SHE WROTE THE BOOK(1946), d; SLAVE GIRL(1947), d; UNTAMED BREED, THE(1948), d; BAGDAD(1949), d; MA AND PA KETTLE(1949), d; ABBOTT AND COSTELLO IN THE FOREIGN LEGION(1950), d; CURTAIN CALL AT CACTUS CREEK(1950), d; I WAS A SHOPLIFTER(1950), d; MA AND PA KETTLE GO TO TOWN(1950), d; ABBOTT AND COSTELLO MEET THE INVISIBLE MAN(1951), d; COMIN' ROUND THE MOUNTAIN(1951), d; FLAME OF ARABY(1951), d; ABBOTT AND COSTELLO MEET CAPTAIN KIDD(1952), d; ABBOTT AND COSTELLO GO TO MARS(1953), d; MA AND PA KETTLE ON VACATION(1953), d; ABBOTT AND COSTELLO MEET DR. JEKYLL AND MR. HYDE(1954), d; MA AND PA KETTLE AT HOME(1954), d; RICOCHET ROMANCE(1954), d; UNTAMED HEIRESS(1954), d; ABBOTT AND COSTELLO MEET THE KEYSTONE KOPS(1955), d; ABBOTT AND COSTELLO MEET THE MUMMY(1955), d; CAROLINA CANNONBALL(1955), d; LAY THAT RIFLE DOWN(1955), d; FRANCIS IN THE HAUNTED HOUSE(1956), d; KETTLES IN THE OZARKS, THE(1956), d
Charles W. Lamont
CHIP OFF THE OLD BLOCK(1944), d
Chas. Lamont
GIRL WHO CAME BACK, THE(1935), d
Connie LaMont
CHEYENNE CYCLONE, THE(1932); MERRY WIDOW, THE(1934); SYLVIA SCARLETT(1936)
Dixie Lamont
Silents
WESTERN MUSKETEER, THE(1922)
Misc. Silents
ALIAS PHIL KENNEDY(1922); WOLF'S TRAIL(1927)
Duncan Lamont
HELL, HEAVEN OR HOBOKEN(1958, Brit.); FIVE ANGLES ON MURDER(1950, Brit.); SHE SHALL HAVE MURDER(1950, Brit.); GALLOPING MAJOR, THE(1951, Brit.); MAN IN THE WHITE SUIT, THE(1952); NIGHT WON'T TALK, THE(1952, Brit.); WATERFRONT WOMEN(1952, Brit.); BIG FRAME, THE(1953, Brit.); GOLDEN COACH, THE(1953, Fr./Ital.); BURNT EVIDENCE(1954, Brit.); END OF THE ROAD, THE(1954, Brit.); MEET MR. MALCOLM(1954, Brit.); PASSING STRANGER, THE(1954, Brit.); INTRUDER, THE(1955, Brit.); PASSAGE HOME(1955, Brit.); QUENTIN DURWARD(1955); TECKMAN MYSTERY, THE(1955, Brit); BABY AND THE BATTLESHIP, THE(1957, Brit.); HIGH FLIGHT(1957, Brit.); TIME IS MY ENEMY(1957, Brit.); TALE OF TWO CITIES, A(1958, Brit.); BEN HUR(1959); THIRTY NINE STEPS, THE(1960, Brit.); TOUCH OF LARCENY, A(1960, Brit.); CIRCLE OF DECEPTION(1961, Brit.); MUTINY ON THE BOUNTY(1962); MURDER AT THE GALLOP(1963, Brit.); CRIMSON BLADE, THE(1964, Brit.); DEVIL-SHIP PIRATES, THE(1964, Brit.); EVIL OF FRANKENSTEIN, THE(1964, Brit.); BRIGAND OF KANDAHAR, THE(1965, Brit.); FRANKENSTEIN CREATED WOMAN(1965, Brit.); ARABESQUE(1966); MURDER GAME, THE(1966, Brit.); PANIC(1966, Brit.); DEVIL'S OWN, THE(1967, Brit.); FIVE MILLION YEARS TO EARTH(1968, Brit.); BATTLE OF BRITAIN, THE(1969, Brit.); DECLINE AND FALL... OF A BIRD WATCHER(1969, Brit.); POPE JOAN(1972, Brit.); NOTHING BUT THE NIGHT(1975, Brit.); LITTLEST HORSE THIEVES, THE(1977)
Frank LaMont
O'SHAUGHNESSY'S BOY(1935)
Fred Lamont
JALOPY(1953)
George Lamont
THRU DIFFERENT EYES(1929)
Harry LaMont
DIAMOND TRAIL(1933); ARTISTS AND MODELS ABROAD(1938); VALLEY OF THE SUN(1942); HOUSE OF DRACULA(1945); PURSUED(1947); SLAVE GIRL(1947)
Silents
ARE ALL MEN ALIKE?(1920); RED LANE, THE(1920)
Jack Lamont
GOLDEN RABBIT, THE(1962, Brit.), p; STRANGLEHOLD(1962, Brit.), p
Jack O. Lamont
LONG SHADOW, THE(1961, Brit.), p; BLAZE OF GLORY(1963, Brit.), p; KID RODELO(1966, U.S./Span.), p

John Lamont
MONSTER(1979)
Marie Lamont
TOUCH OF HER FLESH, THE(1967)
Marten Lamont
MURDER WITH PICTURES(1936); HIDEAWAY GIRL(1937); FOREIGN CORRE-
SPONDENT(1940); MELODY AND MOONLIGHT(1940); MUSIC IN MY HEART(1940);
PRIDE AND PREJUDICE(1940); HOW GREEN WAS MY VALLEY(1941); INTERNA-
TIONAL LADY(1941); INTERNATIONAL SQUADRON(1941); HIGHWAYS BY
NIGHT(1942); MAYOR OF 44TH STREET, THE(1942); MEXICAN SPITFIRE AT
SEA(1942); MEXICAN SPITFIRE SEES A GHOST(1942); MEXICAN SPITFIRE'S
ELEPHANT(1942); NAVY COMES THROUGH, THE(1942); POWDER TOWN(1942);
SON OF FURY(1942); FIRST COMES COURAGE(1943); LADY IN THE DARK(1944);
WATERFRONT(1944); OF HUMAN BONDAGE(1946); CHECKERED COAT,
THE(1948); MY DEAR SECRETARY(1948); SWORD IN THE DESERT(1949); RED-
WOOD FOREST TRAIL(1950)
Michael Lamont
1984
TOP SECRET!(1984), art d
Molly Lamont
DR. JOSSER KC(1931, Brit.); HOUSE OPPOSITE, THE(1931, Brit.); OLD SOLDIERS
NEVER DIE(1931, Brit.); SHADOWS(1931, Brit.); UNEASY VIRTUE(1931, Brit.);
WHAT A NIGHT!(1931, Brit.); BROTHER ALFRED(1932, Brit.); HIS WIFE'S MO-
THER(1932, Brit.); JOSSER ON THE RIVER(1932, Brit.); LAST COUPON, THE(1932,
Brit.); LORD CAMBER'S LADIES(1932, Brit.); LUCKY GIRL(1932, Brit.); MY WIFE'S
FAMILY(1932, Brit.); LEAVE IT TO ME(1933, Brit.); LETTING IN THE SUN-
SHINE(1933, Brit.); PARIS PLANE(1933, Brit.); NO ESCAPE(1934, Brit.); NORAH
O'NEALE(1934, Brit.); THIRD CLUE, THE(1934, Brit.); WHITE ENSIGN(1934, Brit.);
ALIBI INN(1935, Brit.); ANOTHER FACE(1935); HANDLE WITH CARE(1935, Brit.);
JALNA(1935); MURDER AT MONTE CARLO(1935, Brit.); OH, WHAT A NIGHT!(1935);
ROLLING HOME(1935, Brit.); JUNGLE PRINCESS, THE(1936); MARY OF SCOT-
LAND(1936); MUSS 'EM UP(1936); WOMAN REBELS, A(1936); AWFUL TRUTH,
THE(1937); DOCTOR'S DIARY, A(1937); FURY AND THE WOMAN(1937); MOON AND
SIXPENCE, THE(1942); SOMEWHERE I'LL FIND YOU(1942); GENTLE GANGSTER,
A(1943); THUMBS UP(1943); FOLLOW THE BOYS(1944); MINSTREL MAN(1944); MR.
SKEFFINGTON(1944); SUSPECT, THE(1944); WHITE CLIFFS OF DOVER, THE(1944);
DARK CORNER, THE(1946); DEVIL BAT'S DAUGHTER(1946); SO GOES MY
LOVE(1946); CHRISTMAS EVE(1947); IVY(1947); SCARED TO DEATH(1947); SOUTH
SEA SINNER(1950); FIRST LEGION, THE(1951)
Peter Lamont
WATCH YOUR STERN(1961, Brit.), set d; THIS SPORTING LIFE(1963, Brit.), set d;
ON HER MAJESTY'S SECRET SERVICE(1969, Brit.), set d; DIAMONDS ARE
FOREVER(1971, Brit.), set d; FIDDLER ON THE ROOF(1971), set d; WHEN EIGHT
BELLS TOLL(1971, Brit.), set d; SLEUTH(1972, Brit.), art d; DOVE, THE(1974, Brit.),
art d; MAN WITH THE GOLDEN GUN, THE(1974, Brit.), art d; INSIDE OUT(1975,
Brit.), art d; SEVEN-PER-CENT SOLUTION, THE(1977, Brit.), art d; SPY WHO
LOVED ME, THE(1977, Brit.), art d; FOR YOUR EYES ONLY(1981), prod d;
SPHINX(1981), art d; OCTOPUSSY(1983, Brit.), prod d
1984
TOP SECRET!(1984), prod d
Robin Lamont
GODSPELL(1973); HE KNOWS YOU'RE ALONE(1980)
Sly Lamont
LOST COMMAND, THE(1966)
Sonny Lamont
OLD MAN RHYTHM(1935); TO BEAT THE BAND(1935); STORY OF VERNON AND
IRENE CASTLE, THE(1939)
Misc. Talkies
ADVENTURES OF THE MASKED PHANTOM, THE(1939)
Syl Lamont
WORLD IN HIS ARMS, THE(1952); PORK CHOP HILL(1959); FORTY POUNDS OF
TROUBLE(1962); TARAS BULBA(1962); CAPTAIN NEWMAN, M.D.(1963); MIRA-
GE(1965); COOGAN'S BLUFF(1968)
Sylvester Lamont
VALACHI PAPERS, THE(1972, Ital./Fr.)
Ward Lamont
Misc. Silents
MIDNIGHT MAN(1917)
Franco Lamonte
GUNS OF THE BLACK WITCH(1961, Fr./Ital.)
Johnny Lamonte
MR. QUILP(1975, Brit.)
Suma Lamonte
MR. QUILP(1975, Brit.)
Lamontier
CONFLICT(1939, Fr.)
Isabelle Lamore
MADAME CURIE(1943); RAZOR'S EDGE, THE(1946)
Marsh Lamore
MIGHTY MOUSE IN THE GREAT SPACE CHASE(1983), d
Albert Lamorisse
STOWAWAY IN THE SKY(1962, Fr.), d&w, ph
Pascal Lamorisse
STOWAWAY IN THE SKY(1962, Fr.)
Gene LaMoth
Misc. Silents
MARY MORELAND(1917)
Elisa Lamothe
PLEASURES AND VICES(1962, Fr.)
Francois de Lamothe
COMEDIANS, THE(1967), art d
Francois Ide Lamothe
HOTEL PARADISO(1966, U.S./Brit.), prod d
Julian L. Lamothe
Silents
HIS ROBE OF HONOR(1918), w
Jake LaMotta
HUSTLER, THE(1961); REBELLION IN CUBA(1961); RAGING BULL(1980), w

John LaMotta
REVENGE OF THE NINJA(1983)
1984
BREAKIN' 2: ELECTRIC BOOGALOO(1984); NINJA III–THE DOMINATION(1984)
Martin LaMotte
1984
ONE DEADLY SUMMER(1984, Fr.)
Richard E. LaMotte
WIND AND THE LION, THE(1975), cos
Guilherme Lamounier
WILD PACK, THE(1972)
Cherie Lamour
SPLIT, THE(1968); WHERE ANGELS GO...TROUBLE FOLLOWS(1968)
Dorothy Lamour
JUNGLE PRINCESS, THE(1936); BIG BROADCAST OF 1938, THE(1937); HIGH,
WIDE AND HANDSOME(1937); HURRICANE, THE(1937); LAST TRAIN FROM
MADRID, THE(1937); SWING HIGH, SWING LOW(1937); THRILL OF A LIFETI-
ME(1937); HER JUNGLE LOVE(1938); SPAWN OF THE NORTH(1938); TROPIC
HOLIDAY(1938); DISPUTED PASSAGE(1939); MAN ABOUT TOWN(1939); ST. LOUIS
BLUES(1939); CHAD HANNA(1940); JOHNNY APOLLO(1940); MOON OVER BUR-
MA(1940); ROAD TO SINGAPORE(1940); TYPHOON(1940); ALOMA OF THE SOUTH
SEAS(1941); CAUGHT IN THE DRAFT(1941); ROAD TO ZANZIBAR(1941); BEYOND
THE BLUE HORIZON(1942); FLEET'S IN, THE(1942); ROAD TO MOROCCO(1942);
STAR SPANGLED RHYTHM(1942); DIXIE(1943); RIDING HIGH(1943); THEY GOT
ME COVERED(1943); AND THE ANGELS SING(1944); RAINBOW ISLAND(1944);
DUFFY'S TAVERN(1945); MASQUERADE IN MEXICO(1945); MEDAL FOR BENNY,
A(1945); ROAD TO UTOPIA(1945); MY FAVORITE BRUNETTE(1947); ROAD TO
RIO(1947); VARIETY GIRL(1947); WILD HARVEST(1947); GIRL FROM MANHAT-
TAN(1948); LULU BELLE(1948); ON OUR MERRY WAY(1948); LUCKY STIFF,
THE(1949); MANHANDLED(1949); SLIGHTLY FRENCH(1949); HERE COMES THE
GROOM(1951); GREATEST SHOW ON EARTH, THE(1952); ROAD TO BALI(1952);
ROAD TO HONG KONG, THE(1962, U.S./Brit.); DONOVAN'S REEF(1963); PAJAMA
PARTY(1964); EXTRAORDINARY SEAMAN, THE(1969); PHYNX, THE(1970); WON
TON TON, THE DOG WHO SAVED HOLLYWOOD(1976)
Robert Lamoureaux
IF PARIS WERE TOLD TO US(1956, Fr.)
Robert Lamouret
HELTER SKELTER(1949, Brit.)
Robert Lamoureux
ADVENTURES OF ARSENE LUPIN(1956, Fr./Ital.); LOVE AND THE FRENCH-
WOMAN(1961, Fr.); SECRET OF MAGIC ISLAND, THE(1964, Fr./Ital.)
Perry Lamp
1941(1979)
Friedrich Lampe
ROMAN HOLIDAY(1953)
Georgia Lampe
WONDER MAN(1945)
Jutta Lampe
GERMAN SISTERS, THE(1982, Ger.); SISTERS, OR THE BALANCE OF HAPPI-
NESS(1982, Ger.)
Karl-Heinz Lampe
CHRONICLE OF ANNA MAGDALENA BACH(1968, Ital., Ger.)
Marie Lampe
NO WAY OUT(1950)
William Lampe
Silents
SHOULD A WIFE FORGIVE?(1915)
Misc. Silents
PAINTED MADONNA, THE(1917)
Millard Lampell
SATURDAY'S HERO(1951), w; CHANCE MEETING(1960, Brit.), w; ESCAPE FROM
EAST BERLIN(1962), w; IDOL, THE(1966, Brit.), w; EAGLE IN A CAGE(1971, U.S./
Yugo.), p, w
Albert Lampert
TO SIR, WITH LOVE(1967, Brit.)
Jeffrey Lampert
KISS ME GOODBYE(1982)
Peter Lampert
OPENING NIGHT(1977)
Zohra Lampert
ODDS AGAINST TOMORROW(1959); PAY OR DIE(1960); HEY, LET'S TWIST!(1961);
POSSE FROM HELL(1961); SPLENDOR IN THE GRASS(1961); FINE MADNESS,
A(1966); BYE BYE BRAVERMAN(1968); SOME KIND OF A NUT(1969); LET'S SCARE
JESSICA TO DEATH(1971); OPENING NIGHT(1977)
1984
ALPHABET CITY(1984); TEACHERS(1984)
John Lamphear
HOW TO COMMIT MARRIAGE(1969), set d; MAGNUM FORCE(1973), set d
G. Lampin
SLIPPER EPISODE, THE(1938, Fr), w
Georges Lampin
IDIOT, THE(1948, Fr.), d; MATHIAS SANDORF(1963, Fr.), d, w
Silents
NAPOLEON(1927, Fr.)
Charles Lampkin
TOYS IN THE ATTIC(1963); FIVE(1951); RIDER ON A DEAD HORSE(1962); ONE
MAN'S WAY(1964); RARE BREED, THE(1966); JOURNEY TO SHILOH(1968);
THOMAS CROWN AFFAIR, THE(1968); WATERMELON MAN(1970); HAM-
MER(1972); MAN, THE(1972); CORNBREAD, EARL AND ME(1975); SPECIAL DELIV-
ERY(1976); ISLANDS IN THE STREAM(1977); FIRST MONDAY IN OCTOBER(1981);
S.O.B.(1981); SECOND THOUGHTS(1983)
1984
SWORDKILL(1984)
Ron Lampkin
SEABO(1978)
Misc. Talkies
DARK SUNDAY(1978)

William Lampley
DARK, THE(1979)
Louis Lamplugh
ROCKETS IN THE DUNES(1960, Brit.), w
Alexander Lampone
E.T. THE EXTRA-TERRESTRIAL(1982)
Di Ann Lampone
E.T. THE EXTRA-TERRESTRIAL(1982)
Diane Lamport
Misc. Talkies
COME ONE, COME ALL(1970)
Chus Lampreabe
NOT ON YOUR LIFE(1965, Ital./Span.)
Chus Lampreave
1984
IT'S NEVER TOO LATE(1984, Span.)
Gerhard Lamprecht
EMIL AND THE DETECTIVE(1931, Ger.), d; BARCAROLE(1935, Ger.), d; SOME-
WHERE IN BERLIN(1949, E. Ger.), d&w
Gunter Lamprecht
MARRIAGE OF MARIA BRAUN, THE(1979, Ger.); DAS BOOT(1982)
David Lampson
RETURN OF COUNT YORGA, THE(1971)
Jacquetta Lampson
ECHOES OF SILENCE(1966)
David Lamson
WE WHO ARE ABOUT TO DIE(1937), w
Harold Lamson
STARTING OVER(1979)
Mark LaMura
Misc. Talkies
ON THE LAM(1972)
Conchita Lamus
THREE DARING DAUGHTERS(1948)
Charles Lamy
Misc. Silents
MADEMOISELLE DE LA SEIGLIERE(1921, Fr.); FALL OF THE HOUSE OF USHER,
THE(1928, Fr.)
Germaine Lamy
LANCELOT OF THE LAKE(1975, Fr.), ed
Maurice Lamy
1984
LE DERNIER COMBAT(1984, Fr.); PERILS OF GWENDOLINE, THE(1984, Fr.)
Pierre Lamy
DISCREET CHARM OF THE BOURGEOISIE, THE(1972, Fr.); WHO HAS SEEN THE
WIND(1980, Can.), p; FOND MEMORIES(1982, Can.), p
Raymond Lamy
FANNY(1948, Fr.), ed; NAPOLEON(1955, Fr.), ed; MAN ESCAPED, A(1957, Fr.), ed;
ROYAL AFFAIRS IN VERSAILLES(1957, Fr.), ed; CRIME DOES NOT PAY(1962,
Fr.), ed; PICKPOCKET(1963, Fr.), ed; AU HASARD, BALTHAZAR(1970, Fr.), ed;
MOUCHETTE(1970, Fr.), ed; GENTLE CREATURE, A(1971, Fr.), ed
Phi Lan
HOA-BINH(1971, Fr.)
Rosine Lan
1984
DOG DAY(1984, Fr.), cos
Wang Lan
LADY GENERAL, THE(1965, Hong Kong)
Chou Lan-ping
LOVE ETERNE, THE(1964, Hong Kong), m
Ho Lan-shan
LAST WOMAN OF SHANG, THE(1964, Hong Kong), ph; LOVE ETERNE, THE(1964,
Hong Kong), ph
Kitty Lanahan
YOU CAN'T TAKE IT WITH YOU(1938)
Ann Lancaster
JUDGMENT DEFERRED(1952, Brit.); MAGIC BOX, THE(1952, Brit.); SECRET
PEOPLE(1952, Brit.); DURANT AFFAIR, THE(1962, Brit.); LAMP IN ASSASSIN
MEWS, THE(1962, Brit.); I'VE GOTTA HORSE(1965, Brit.); SECRET OF MY SUCCESS,
THE(1965, Brit.); FATHOM(1967); THREE BITES OF THE APPLE(1967); ALF 'N'
FAMILY(1968, Brit.); HOT MILLIONS(1968, Brit.); INADMISSIBLE EVIDENCE(1968,
Brit.); CARRY ON AGAIN, DOCTOR(1969, Brit.); DECLINE AND FALL... OF A BIRD
WATCHER(1969, Brit.); NICE GIRL LIKE ME, A(1969, Brit.); RAILWAY CHILDREN,
THE(1971, Brit.)
B. Lancaster
Silents
ALTAR STAIRS, THE(1922), w
Bill Lancaster
BAD NEWS BEARS, THE(1976), w; BAD NEWS BEARS GO TO JAPAN, THE(1978),
w; THING, THE(1982), w
Burt Lancaster
KILLERS, THE(1946); BRUTE FORCE(1947); DESERT FURY(1947); VARIETY
GIRL(1947); ALL MY SONS(1948); I WALK ALONE(1948); KISS THE BLOOD OFF MY
HANDS(1948); SORRY, WRONG NUMBER(1948); CRISS CROSS(1949); ROPE OF
SAND(1949); FLAME AND THE ARROW, THE(1950); MISTER 880(1950); JIM
THORPE–ALL AMERICAN(1951); TEN TALL MEN(1951); VENGEANCE VAL-
LEY(1951); COME BACK LITTLE SHEBA(1952); CRIMSON PIRATE, THE(1952);
FROM HERE TO ETERNITY(1953); HIS MAJESTY O'KEEFE(1953); SOUTH SEA
WOMAN(1953); THREE SAILORS AND A GIRL(1953); APACHE(1954); VERA
CRUZ(1954); KENTUCKIAN, THE(1955), a, d; ROSE TATTOO, THE(1955); RAIN-
MAKER, THE(1956); TRAPEZE(1956); GUNFIGHT AT THE O.K. CORRAL(1957);
SWEET SMELL OF SUCCESS(1957); RUN SILENT, RUN DEEP(1958); SEPARATE
TABLES(1958); DEVIL'S DISCIPLE, THE(1959); ELMER GANTRY(1960); UNFORGIV-
EN, THE(1960); JUDGMENT AT NUREMBERG(1961); YOUNG SAVAGES, THE(1961);
BIRDMAN OF ALCATRAZ(1962); CHILD IS WAITING, A(1963); LEOPARD,
THE(1963, Ital.); LIST OF ADRIAN MESSENGER, THE(1963); SEVEN DAYS IN
MAY(1964); HALLELUJAH TRAIL, THE(1965); TRAIN, THE(1965, Fr./Ital./U.S.);
PROFESSIONALS, THE(1966); SCALPHUNTERS, THE(1968); SWIMMER, THE(1968);
CASTLE KEEP(1969); GYPSY MOTHS, THE(1969); AIRPORT(1970); LAWMAN(1971);
VALDEZ IS COMING(1971); ULZANA'S RAID(1972); EXECUTIVE ACTION(1973);

SCORPIO(1973); MIDNIGHT MAN, THE(1974), a, p&d, w; BUFFALO BILL AND THE
INDIANS, OR SITTING BULL'S HISTORY LESSON(1976); CONVERSATION PIE-
CE(1976, Ital., Fr.); MOSES(1976, Brit./Ital.); 1900(1976, Ital.); CASSANDRA CROSS-
ING, THE(1977); ISLAND OF DR. MOREAU, THE(1977); TWILIGHT'S LAST
GLEAMING(1977, U.S./Ger.); GO TELL THE SPARTANS(1978); ZULU DAWN(1980,
Brit.); ATLANTIC CITY(1981, U.S./Can.); CATTLE ANNIE AND LITTLE BRITCH-
ES(1981); LOCAL HERO(1983, Brit.); OSTERMAN WEEKEND, THE(1983)
C. D. Lancaster
Silents
LITTLE IRISH GIRL, THE(1926), w
Catherine Lancaster
COSMIC MONSTERS(1958, Brit.); GREAT CATHERINE(1968, Brit.)
Cliff Lancaster
GOLD FEVER(1952), w
Fred Lancaster
Silents
SOUTH SEA LOVE(1923)
Frederick Lancaster
Silents
KISMET(1920)
G. B. Lancaster
Silents
ETERNAL STRUGGLE, THE(1923), w
Iris Lancaster
TRAIL BEYOND, THE(1934); RAINBOW ISLAND(1944); 'TILL WE MEET
AGAIN(1944)
Misc. Talkies
RIDIN' THE TRAIL(1940)
Leland Lancaster
Silents
DR. JIM(1921), ph; SHARK MASTER, THE(1921), ph; ACROSS THE DEAD-LI-
NE(1922), ph; TRACKED TO EARTH(1922), ph
Lucie Lancaster
VAGABOND KING, THE(1956); 23 PACES TO BAKER STREET(1956); SENTINEL,
THE(1977)
Osbert Lancaster
THOSE MAGNIFICENT MEN IN THEIR FLYING MACHINES; OR HOW I FLEW-
FROM LONDON TO PARIS IN 25 HOURS AND 11 MINUTES(1965, Brit.), cos
R. Lancaster
HOUSE OF SECRETS, THE(1937)
Richard Lancaster
MYSTERY OF MR. X, THE(1934); LOVE ON THE RUN(1936); HELD FOR RAN-
SOM(1938)
Rita Lancaster
CAESAR AND CLEOPATRA(1946, Brit.)
Stu Lancaster
ROPE OF FLESH(1965)
Stuart Lancaster
BORN LOSERS(1967); GOOD MORNING... AND GOODBYE(1967); MANTIS IN
LACE(1968); PRECIOUS JEWELS(1969); SATIN MUSHROOM, THE(1969); CAPTAIN
MILKSHAKE(1970); SEVEN MINUTES, THE(1971); GOODBYE, NORMA JEAN(1976)
Vickey Lancaster
NO PLACE TO HIDE(1975)
William Lancaster
MIDNIGHT MAN, THE(1974); MOSES(1976, Brit./Ital.)
Astride Lance
OPEN THE DOOR AND SEE ALL THE PEOPLE(1964)
J. J. Lance
Silents
JUDITH OF BETHULIA(1914)
Leo Lance
MANHATTAN MELODRAMA(1934)
Lia Lance
OPERATOR 13(1934)
Lila Lance
CLIVE OF INDIA(1935)
Richard Lance
NIGHT TRAIN TO MUNDO FINE(1966)
Vic Lance
MANTIS IN LACE(1968); ASTRO-ZOMBIES, THE(1969); SATIN MUSHROOM,
THE(1969); NOTORIOUS CLEOPATRA, THE(1970), m
Misc. Talkies
WEEKEND LOVER(1969)
Ariene Lancel
PALACE OF NUDES(1961, Fr./Ital.)
Patrick Lancelot
CONFESSION, THE(1970, Fr.)
Sir Lancelot
I WALKED WITH A ZOMBIE(1943); CURSE OF THE CAT PEOPLE, THE(1944); TO
HAVE AND HAVE NOT(1944); ZOMBIES ON BROADWAY(1945); BRUTE FOR-
CE(1947); LINDA BE GOOD(1947); UNKNOWN TERROR, THE(1957); BUCCANEER,
THE(1958)
George Lancer
Misc. Talkies
TEASERS, THE(1977), d
Martin Lancer
NAKED DAWN, THE(1955), art d; FEARMAKERS, THE(1958), p
Alison Lances
SMITHEREENS(1982), cos
Pino Lancetti
THREE BITES OF THE APPLE(1967), cos
John Lanchberry
COLONEL MARCH INVESTIGATES(1952, Brit.), m; PETER RABBIT AND TALES
OF BEATRIX POTTER(1971, Brit.), md
John Lanchbery
ROMEO AND JULIET(1966, Brit.), md; SWAN LAKE, THE(1967), md; DON QUIX-
OTE(1973, Aus.), md; TURNING POINT, THE(1977), md; NIJINSKY(1980, Brit.), m

Karl Lanchbury
WEBSTER BOY, THE(1962, Brit.); WHAT'S GOOD FOR THE GOOSE(1969, Brit.); HOUSE THAT VANISHED, THE(1974, Brit.); VAMPYRES, DAUGHTERS OF DRACULA(1977, Brit.)

Liz Lanchbury
NEVER PUT IT IN WRITING(1964)

Elsa Lanchester
HER STRANGE DESIRE(1931, Brit.); LOVE HABIT, THE(1931, Brit.); OFFICER'S MESS, THE(1931, Brit.); STRONGER SEX, THE(1931, Brit.); PRIVATE LIFE OF HENRY VIII, THE(1933); PRIVATE LIFE OF DON JUAN, THE(1934, Brit.); DAVID COPPERFIELD(1935); NAUGHTY MARIETTA(1935); GHOST GOES WEST, THE(1936); REMBRANDT(1936, Brit.); THE BEACHCOMBER(1938, Brit.); LADIES IN RETIREMENT(1941); SON OF FURY(1942); TALES OF MANHATTAN(1942); FOREVER AND A DAY(1943); LASSIE, COME HOME(1943); THUMBS UP(1943); PASSPORT TO DESTINY(1944); RAZOR'S EDGE, THE(1946); SPIRAL STAIRCASE, THE(1946); BISHOP'S WIFE, THE(1947); NORTHWEST OUTPOST(1947); BIG CLOCK, THE(1948); COME TO THE STABLE(1949); INSPECTOR GENERAL, THE(1949); SECRET GARDEN, THE(1949); BUCCANEER'S GIRL(1950); FRENCHIE(1950); MYSTERY STREET(1950); PETTY GIRL, THE(1950); ANDROCLES AND THE LION(1952); DREAMBOAT(1952); LES MISERABLES(1952); GIRLS OF PLEASURE ISLAND, THE(1953); HELL'S HALF ACRE(1954); THREE RING CIRCUS(1954); GLASS SLIPPER, THE(1955); WITNESS FOR THE PROSECUTION(1957); BELL, BOOK AND CANDLE(1958); HONEYMOON HOTEL(1964); MARY POPPINS(1964); PAJAMA PARTY(1964); THAT DARN CAT(1965); EASY COME, EASY GO(1967); BLACKBEARD'S GHOST(1968); ME, NATALIE(1969); RASCAL(1969); WILLARD(1971); ARNOLD(1973); TERROR IN THE WAX MUSEUM(1973); MURDER BY DEATH(1976); DIE LAUGHING(1980)
Silents
ONE OF THE BEST(1927, Brit.)

Beppe Lanci
LEAP INTO THE VOID(1982, Ital.), ph

Giuseppe Lanci
EYES, THE MOUTH, THE(1982, Ital./Fr.), ph
1984
NOSTALGHIA(1984, USSR/Ital.), ph

Cesare Lancia
GUNS OF THE BLACK WITCH(1961, Fr./Ital.)

Mauro Lanciani
WAR AND PEACE(1956, Ital./U.S.)

Louie Lanciloti
1984
WINDY CITY(1984)

Charles Lancing
WHO GOES NEXT?(1938, Brit.)

Bernard Lancret
CARNIVAL IN FLANDERS(1936, Fr.); DEVIL IS AN EMPRESS, THE(1939, Fr.); ENTENTE CORDIALE(1939, Fr.); ULTIMATUM(1940, Fr.); FOOLISH HUSBANDS(1948, Fr.); JULIETTA(1957, Fr.)

Micheline Lanctot
APPRENTICESHIP OF DUDDY KRAVITZ, THE(1974, Can.); CHILD UNDER A LEAF(1975, Can.); TI-CUL TOUGAS(1977, Can.); BLOOD AND GUTS(1978, Can.); BLOOD RELATIVES(1978, Fr./Can.)

Lucy Lancy
LADIES OF THE PARK(1964, Fr.)

Barbara Land
MANPOWER(1941)

Charles Land, Jr.
ADVENTURE IN DIAMONDS(1940), ph

Charles Land
BUCHANAN RIDES ALONE(1958), w; TESS OF THE STORM COUNTRY(1961), w

Charles E. Land
BOB AND CAROL AND TED AND ALICE(1969), ph

Deborah Leah Land
DON'T ANSWER THE PHONE(1980)

Doreen Land
NORTH BY NORTHWEST(1959)

Gail Land
FEAR STRIKES OUT(1957); SHORT CUT TO HELL(1957)

Geoffrey Land
AGAINST A CROOKED SKY(1975); JESSIE'S GIRLS(1976); NURSE SHERRI(1978)
Misc. Talkies
BLACK HEAT(1976); REDNECK MILLER(1977)

Harold Land
WEST 11(1963, Brit.); THEY SHOOT HORSES, DON'T THEY?(1969)

Jeoffrey Land
FEMALE BUNCH, THE(1969)

Mary Land
KILL OR BE KILLED(1967, Ital.); TWISTED NERVE(1969, Brit.)
Silents
QUESTION OF HONOR, A(1922); MY AMERICAN WIFE(1923)
Misc. Silents
FLYING FOOL(1925)

Paul Land
IDOLMAKER, THE(1980); SPRING BREAK(1983)

Richard Land
WONDER MAN(1945)

Robert Land
Misc. Silents
ART OF LOVE, THE(1928, Ger.), d

Sherrie Land
HAREM BUNCH; OR WAR AND PIECE, THE(1969)

Alfredo Landa
TWELVE-HANDED MEN OF MARS, THE(1964, Ital./Span.); NOT ON YOUR LIFE(1965, Ital./Span.)
1984
HOLY INNOCENTS, THE(1984, Span.)

Margot Landa
NIGHT ALONE(1938, Brit.)

Misc. Silents
RINGING THE CHANGES(1929, Brit.)

Maria Landa
TAKING OF PELHAM ONE, TWO, THREE, THE(1974); UP THE DOWN STAIRCASE(1967)

Mary Landa
THANK YOUR LUCKY STARS(1943); DESTINATION TOKYO(1944); IN OUR TIME(1944); IMPACT(1949)

May Landa
MASK OF DIMITRIOS, THE(1944)

Miguel Landa
TO TRAP A SPY(1966)

Rodolfo Landa
LOS AUTOMATAS DE LA MUERTE(1960, Mex.); CRIMINAL LIFE OF ARCHIBALDO DE LA CRUZ, THE(1962, Mex.); NEUTRON CONTRA EL DR. CARONTE(1962, Mex.)

Richard Landan
FOUR RODE OUT(1969, US/Span.), p

Arthur Landau
HARLOW(1965), w

Cecil Landau
ONCE IN A NEW MOON(1935, Brit.)

David Landau
ARROWSMITH(1931); I TAKE THIS WOMAN(1931); STREET SCENE(1931); AIR MAIL(1932); AMATEUR DADDY(1932); FALSE FACES(1932); HORSE FEATHERS(1932); I AM A FUGITIVE FROM A CHAIN GANG(1932); IT'S TOUGH TO BE FAMOUS(1932); POLLY OF THE CIRCUS(1932); PURCHASE PRICE, THE(1932); ROADHOUSE MURDER, THE(1932); TAXI!(1932); THIS RECKLESS AGE(1932); UNDER-COVER MAN(1932); UNION DEPOT(1932); 70,000 WITNESSES(1932); CRIME OF THE CENTURY, THE(1933); GABRIEL OVER THE WHITE HOUSE(1933); HERITAGE OF THE DESERT(1933); LAWYER MAN(1933); NO MARRIAGE TIES(1933); NUISANCE, THE(1933); ONE MAN'S JOURNEY(1933); SHE DONE HIM WRONG(1933); THEY JUST HAD TO GET MARRIED(1933); AS THE EARTH TURNS(1934); BEDSIDE(1934); DEATH OF THE DIAMOND(1934); JUDGE PRIEST(1934); MAN WITH TWO FACES, THE(1934); WHARF ANGEL(1934)

Mrs. David Landau
Silents
WAY DOWN EAST(1920)

Edie Landau
HOPSCOTCH(1980), p; CHOSEN, THE(1982), p

Ely Landau
LONG DAY'S JOURNEY INTO NIGHT(1962), p; MADWOMAN OF CHAILLOT, THE(1969), p; DELICATE BALANCE, A(1973), p; HOMECOMING, THE(1973), p; ICEMAN COMETH, THE(1973), p; BUTLEY(1974, Brit.), p; LOST IN THE STARS(1974), p; LUTHER(1974), p; RHINOCEROS(1974), p; GALILEO(1975, Brit.), p; IN CELEBRATION(1975, Brit.), p; MAN IN THE GLASS BOOTH, THE(1975), p; THREE SISTERS, THE(1977), p; GREEK TYCOON, THE(1978), p; HOPSCOTCH(1980), p; CHOSEN, THE(1982), p

Leslie Landau
DARK WORLD(1935, Brit.), p, w; RIVERSIDE MURDER, THE(1935, Brit.), w; WRATH OF JEALOUSY(1936, Brit.), p; LADY ESCAPES, THE(1937), p; MY BROTHER JONATHAN(1949, Brit.), w; PORTRAIT OF CLARE(1951, Brit.), p, w

Lucy Landau
THRILL OF IT ALL, THE(1963); STRANGE BEDFELLOWS(1965)

Manolo Landau
MAN IN THE WILDERNESS(1971, U.S./Span.)

Martin Landau
GAZEBO, THE(1959); NORTH BY NORTHWEST(1959); PORK CHOP HILL(1959); STAGECOACH TO DANCER'S PARK(1962); CLEOPATRA(1963); GREATEST STORY EVER TOLD, THE(1965); HALLELUJAH TRAIL, THE(1965); NEVADA SMITH(1966); THEY CALL ME MISTER TIBBS(1970); TOWN CALLED HELL, A(1971, Span./Brit.); BLACK GUNN(1972); STRANGE SHADOWS IN AN EMPTY ROOM(1977, Can./Ital.); LAST WORD, THE(1979); METEOR(1979); FALL OF THE HOUSE OF USHER, THE(1980); RETURN, THE(1980); WITHOUT WARNING(1980); ALONE IN THE DARK(1982); BEING, THE(1983)
Misc. Talkies
BLAZING MAGNUM(1976); OPERATION SNAFU(1970, Ital./Yugo.); UNDER THE SIGN OF CAPRICORN(1971); ALIEN'S RETURN, THE(1980); ACCESS CODE(1984)

Mrs. Phillip Landau
Silents
LOVE'S PENALTY(1921)

Richard H. Landau
SECRET OF THE WHISTLER(1946), w; CHRISTMAS EVE(1947), w; CROOKED WAY, THE(1949), w; LOST CONTINENT(1951), w

Richard Landau
GREAT JASPER, THE(1933), w; BACK TO BATAAN(1945), w; LITTLE IODINE(1946), w; JOHNNY ONE-EYE(1950), w; FBI GIRL(1951), w; ROADBLOCK(1951), w; STOLEN FACE(1952, Brit.), w; BAD BLONDE(1953, Brit.), w; GREAT JESSE JAMES RAID, THE(1953), w; SINS OF JEZEBEL(1953), w; SPACEWAYS(1953, Brit.), w; BLACKOUT(1954, Brit.), w; GLASS TOMB, THE(1955, Brit.), w; PEARL OF THE SOUTH PACIFIC(1955), w; RACE FOR LIFE, A(1955, Brit.), w; BLONDE BAIT(1956, U.S./Brit.), w; HOT CARS(1956), w; MAN IS ARMED, THE(1956), w; THE CREEPING UNKNOWN(1956, Brit.), w; HELL BOUND(1957), w; PHARAOH'S CURSE(1957), w; VOODOO ISLAND(1957), w; FRANKENSTEIN 1970(1958), w; VIOLENT ROAD(1958), w; BORN RECKLESS(1959), w; UP PERISCOPE(1959), w; FORT COURAGEOUS(1965), w; BLACK HOLE, THE(1979), Gerry Day

Rolf Landau
UNDERGROUND(1941)

S. Landau
YIDDLE WITH HIS FIDDLE(1937, Pol.); DYBBUK THE(1938, Pol.)

Shmuel Landau
Misc. Silents
CANTOR'S DAUGHTER, THE(1913, USSR); SLAUGHTER, THE(1913, USSR); STEPMOTHER, THE(1914, USSR)

Vivien Landau
THEY ALL LAUGHED(1981)

Landauer
STREET SINGER, THE(1937, Brit.), m
David Landbury
FFOLKES(1980, Brit.)
Roberto Lande
STATUE, THE(1971, Brit.)
Cecil Landeau
Misc. Silents
LILY OF KILLARNEY(1929, Brit.)
Gerald Landeau
NO TRACE(1950, Brit.), ed; MURDER WILL OUT(1953, Brit.), w
Michael Landeau
BAY OF SAINT MICHEL, THE(1963, Brit.)
William Landeau
THAT TOUCH OF MINK(1962)
Ben Landeck
Silents
JACK TAR(1915, Brit.), w; SOLDIER AND A MAN, A(1916, Brit.), w
Donn Landee
1984
WILD LIFE, THE(1984), m
Violetta Landek
THEY ALL LAUGHED(1981)
Dindsdale Landen
WE JOINED THE NAVY(1962, Brit.)
Dinsdale Landen
OPERATION SNATCH(1962, Brit.); PLAYBACK(1962, Brit.); VALIANT, THE(1962, Brit./Ital.); JOLLY BAD FELLOW, A(1964, Brit.); MOSQUITO SQUADRON(1970, Brit.); THINK DIRTY(1970, Brit.); YOUNG WINSTON(1972, Brit.); INTERNATIONAL VELVET(1978, Brit.)
Alan Lander
THEY'RE A WEIRD MOB(1966, Aus.)
David Lander
SPANISH GARDENER, THE(1957, Span.); TRIPLE DECEPTION(1957, Brit.); WOMAN OF MYSTERY, A(1957, Brit.); STRANGE CASE OF DR. MANNING, THE(1958, Brit.); INVASION QUARTET(1961, Brit.); TELL-TALE HEART, THE(1962, Brit.); BE MY GUEST(1965, Brit.); TWELVE CHAIRS, THE(1970); CRACKING UP(1977); 1941(1979)
David L. Lander
USED CARS(1980); WHOLLY MOSES(1980); PANDEMONIUM(1982)
Eric Lander
TRACK THE MAN DOWN(1956, Brit.)
Harald Lander
TURNING POINT, THE(1977), ch
Kurt Lander
36 HOURS(1965)
Ned Lander
STARSTRUCK(1982, Aus.); CLINIC, THE(1983, Aus.); PUBERTY BLUES(1983, Aus.)
Rosalyn Lander
AMAZING MR. BLUNDEN, THE(1973, Brit.)
Toni Lander
DANCING HEART, THE(1959, Ger.)
Federico Landeras
MARY, MARY, BLOODY MARY(1975, U.S./Mex.), ed
Frederic Landeros
HOLY MOUNTAIN, THE(1973, U.S./Mex.), ed
Frederico Landeros
EL TOPO(1971, Mex.), ed
Alan Landers
TREE, THE(1969); STACEY!(1973); ANNIE HALL(1977)
Ann Landers
PENELOPE(1966), cos; THIS PROPERTY IS CONDEMNED(1966), cos
Audrey Landers
1941(1979)
Davis Landers
WILD RACERS, THE(1968)
Hal Landers
GYPSY MOTHS, THE(1969), p; LIONS LOVE(1969); MONTE WALSH(1970), p; HOT ROCK, THE(1972), p; BANK SHOT(1974), p; DEATH WISH(1974), p
Harry Landers
C-MAN(1949); GUILTY BYSTANDER(1950); UNDERCOVER GIRL(1950); MR. UNIVERSE(1951); JACK SLADE(1953); PHANTOM FROM SPACE(1953); WILD ONE, THE(1953); DRIVE A CROOKED ROAD(1954); REAR WINDOW(1954); INDIAN FIGHTER, THE(1955); BLACK WHIP, THE(1956); MISTER CORY(1957); GALLANT HOURS, THE(1960); IN ENEMY COUNTRY(1968); CHARRO(1969)
Judy Landers
SKATETOWN, U.S.A.(1979); BLACK MARBLE, THE(1980)
Misc. Talkies
YUM-YUM GIRLS(1976)
Lew Landers
ADVENTURES OF GALLANT BESS(1948), d; NIGHT WAITRESS(1936), d; WITHOUT ORDERS(1936), d; BORDER CAFE(1937), d; CRASHING HOLLYWOOD(1937), d; DANGER PATROL(1937), d; LIVING ON LOVE(1937), d; MAN WHO FOUND HIMSELF, THE(1937), d; YOU CAN'T BUY LUCK(1937), d; ANNABEL TAKES A TOUR(1938), d; BLIND ALIBI(1938), d; CONDEMNED WOMEN(1938), d; DOUBLE DANGER(1938), d; LAW OF THE UNDERWORLD(1938), d; SKY GIANT(1938), d; SMASHING THE RACKETS(1938), d; BAD LANDS(1939), d; CONSPIRACY(1939), d; FIXER DUGAN(1939), d; GIRL AND THE GAMBLER, THE(1939), d; PACIFIC LINER(1939), d; TWELVE CROWDED HOURS(1939), d; ENEMY AGENT(1940), d; GIRL FROM HAVANA(1940), d; HONEYMOON DEFERRED(1940), d; LA CONGA NIGHTS(1940), d; SING, DANCE, PLENTY HOT(1940), d; SKI PATROL(1940), d; SLIGHTLY TEMPTED(1940), d; WAGONS WESTWARD(1940), d; BACK IN THE SADDLE(1941), d; I WAS A PRISONER ON DEVIL'S ISLAND(1941), d; LUCKY DEVILS(1941), d; MYSTERY SHIP(1941), d; RIDIN' ON A RAINBOW(1941), d; SINGING HILL, THE(1941), d; STORK PAYS OFF, THE(1941), d; ALIAS BOSTON BLACKIE(1942), d; ATLANTIC CONVOY(1942), d; BOOGIE MAN WILL GET YOU, THE(1942), d; CANAL ZONE(1942), d; HARVARD, HERE I COME(1942), d; MAN WHO RETURNED TO LIFE, THE(1942), d; SABOTAGE SQUAD(1942), d; SUBMARINE RAIDER(1942), d; AFTER MIDNIGHT WITH BOSTON BLACKIE(1943), d; DEERSLAYER(1943), d; DOUGHBOYS IN IRELAND(1943), d; JUNIOR ARMY(1943), d; MURDER IN TIMES SQUARE(1943), d; POWER OF THE PRESS(1943), d; BLACK PARACHUTE, THE(1944), d; COWBOY CANTEEN(1944), d; GHOST THAT WALKS ALONE, THE(1944), d; I'M FROM ARKANSAS(1944), d; RETURN OF THE VAMPIRE, THE(1944), d; STARS ON PARADE(1944), d; SWING IN THE SADDLE(1944), d; TWO-MAN SUBMARINE(1944), d; U-BOAT PRISONER(1944), d; ARSON SQUAD(1945), d; CRIME, INC.(1945), d; ENCHANTED FOREST, THE(1945), d; FOLLOW THAT WOMAN(1945), d; POWER OF THE WHISTLER, THE(1945), d; SHADOW OF TERROR(1945), d; TOKYO ROSE(1945), d; CLOSE CALL FOR BOSTON BLACKIE, A(1946), d; DEATH VALLEY(1946), d; HOT CARGO(1946), d; MASK OF DIIJON, THE(1946), d; SECRETS OF A SORORITY GIRL(1946), d; TRUTH ABOUT MURDER, THE(1946), d; DANGER STREET(1947), d; DEVIL SHIP(1947), d; SEVEN KEYS TO BALDPATE(1947), d; THUNDER MOUNTAIN(1947), d; UNDER THE TONTO RIM(1947), d; INNER SANCTUM(1948), d; MY DOG RUSTY(1948), d; AIR HOSTESS(1949), d; BARBARY PIRATE(1949), d; LAW OF THE BARBARY COAST(1949), d; STAGECOACH KID(1949), d; BEAUTY ON PARADE(1950), d; CHAIN GANG(1950), d; DAVY CROCKETT, INDIAN SCOUT(1950), d; DYNAMITE PASS(1950), d; GIRLS' SCHOOL(1950), d; LAST OF THE BUCCANEERS(1950), d; REVENUE AGENT(1950), d; STATE PENITENTIARY(1950), d; TYRANT OF THE SEA(1950), d; BIG GUSHER, THE(1951), d; BLUE BLOOD(1951), d; HURRICANE ISLAND(1951), d; JUNGLE MANHUNT(1951), d; MAGIC CARPET, THE(1951), d; WHEN THE REDSKINS RODE(1951), d; YANK IN KOREA, A(1951), d; ALADDIN AND HIS LAMP(1952), d; ARCTIC FLIGHT(1952), d; CALIFORNIA CONQUEST(1952), d; JUNGLE JIM IN THE FORBIDDEN LAND(1952), d; CAPTAIN JOHN SMITH AND POCAHONTAS(1953), d; MAN IN THE DARK(1953), d; RUN FOR THE HILLS(1953), d; TANGIER INCIDENT(1953), d; TORPEDO ALLEY(1953), d; CAPTAIN KIDD AND THE SLAVE GIRL(1954), d; REDHEAD FROM MANHATTAN(1954), d; CRUEL TOWER, THE(1956), d; HOT ROD GANG(1958), d; TERRIFIED!(1963), d
Misc. Talkies
CADETS ON PARADE(1942), d; NOT A LADIES MAN(1942), d; STAND BY ALL NETWORKS(1942), d; TROUBLE CHASERS(1945), d; SON OF RUSTY, THE(1947), d
Lew Landers [Louis Friedlander]
FLIGHT FROM GLORY(1937), d; THEY WANTED TO MARRY(1937), d
Marion Landers
CAPE FEAR(1962)
Matt Landers
48 HOURS(1982)
Muriel Landers
BELA LUGOSI MEETS A BROOKLYN GORILLA(1952); PONY SOLDIER(1952); PILLOW TALK(1959); MOON PILOT(1962); DOCTOR DOLITTLE(1967); WHAT AM I BID?(1967)
Paul Landers
DARK STREETS OF CAIRO(1940), ed; JUKE BOX JENNY(1942), ed
Perc Landers
BEDTIME FOR BONZO(1951)
Peter Landers
LADY LIBERTY(1972, Ital./Fr.)
Sam Landers
Silents
IT'S A BEAR(1919), ph; WHAT NO MAN KNOWS(1921), ph; SIGN OF THE ROSE, THE(1922), ph
Scott Landers
HOUSE OF STRANGERS(1949)
Tibbi Landers
MAN, A WOMAN, AND A BANK, A(1979, Can.)
Michael S. Landes
BIG SCORE, THE(1983), p
Eva Landesberg
SEARCH, THE(1948), tech adv
Steve Landesberg
YOU'VE GOT TO WALK IT LIKE YOU TALK IT OR YOU'LL LOSE THAT BEAT(1971); BLADE(1973); LOOSE SHOES(1980)
Knight Landesman
CINDERELLA LIBERTY(1973)
Clayton Landey
NORMA RAE(1979)
Dave Landfield
ERRAND BOY, THE(1961)
David Landfield
BELLBOY, THE(1960); OCEAN'S ELEVEN(1960); PEPE(1960); PLATINUM HIGH SCHOOL(1960); DON'T KNOCK THE TWIST(1962); BEACH PARTY(1963); CAPTAIN NEWMAN, M.D.(1963); NUTTY PROFESSOR, THE(1963); OPERATION BIKINI(1963)
Jerome Landfield
RISKY BUSINESS(1983)
Janet Landgard
SWIMMER, THE(1968); LAND RAIDERS(1969); MOONCHILD(1972)
Dan Landgre
LOVING COUPLES(1966, Swed.)
Inga Landgre
RAILROAD WORKERS(1948, Swed.); SEVENTH SEAL, THE(1958, Swed.); BRINK OF LIFE(1960, Swed.); DREAMS(1960, Swed.); LOVING COUPLES(1966, Swed.)
Gudrun Landgrebe
1984
WOMAN IN FLAMES, A(1984, Ger.)
Inge Landgut
EMIL AND THE DETECTIVE(1931, Ger.); M(1933, Ger.); OUR DAILY BREAD(1950, Ger.); HELP I'M INVISIBLE(1952, Ger.)
Sonny Landham
WARRIORS, THE(1979); SOUTHERN COMFORT(1981); POLTERGEIST(1982); 48 HOURS(1982)
1984
FLESHBURN(1984); ULTIMATE SOLUTION OF GRACE QUIGLEY, THE(1984)
Lennart Landheim
BREAD OF LOVE, THE(1954, Swed.), ed
Aldo Bufi Landi
GREAT HOPE, THE(1954, Ital.); NEOPOLITAN CAROUSEL(1961, Ital.); LAST OF THE VIKINGS, THE(1962, Fr./Ital.); LOVE AND LARCENY(1963, Fr./Ital.); SAMSON AND THE SLAVE QUEEN(1963, Ital.); BIGGEST BUNDLE OF THEM ALL, THE(1968)

Aldo Landi
DEAD WOMAN'S KISS, A(1951, Ital.)

Elissa Landi
CHILDREN OF CHANCE(1930, Brit.); KNOWING MEN(1930, Brit.); PRICE OF THINGS, THE(1930, Brit.); ALWAYS GOODBYE(1931); BODY AND SOUL(1931); PARISIAN, THE(1931, Fr.); WICKED(1931); YELLOW TICKET, THE(1931); DEVIL'S LOTTERY(1932); PASSPORT TO HELL(1932); SIGN OF THE CROSS, THE(1932); WOMAN IN ROOM 13, THE(1932); I LOVED YOU WEDNESDAY(1933); MASQUERADER, THE(1933); WARRIOR'S HUSBAND, THE(1933); BY CANDLELIGHT(1934); COUNT OF MONTE CRISTO, THE(1934); GREAT FLIRTATION, THE(1934); MAN OF TWO WORLDS(1934); SISTERS UNDER THE SKIN(1934); ENTER MADAME(1935); KOENIGSMARK(1935, Fr.); WITHOUT REGRET(1935); AFTER THE THIN MAN(1936); AMATEUR GENTLEMAN(1936, Brit.); MAD HOLIDAY(1936); THIRTEENTH CHAIR, THE(1937); CORREGIDOR(1943)
Silents
LONDON(1926, Brit.); BOLIBAR(1928, Brit.); INSEPARABLES, THE(1929, Brit.)
Misc. Silents
UNDERGROUND(1928, Brit.); BETRAYAL, THE(1929)

Frank Landi
SYNCOPATION(1929), ph

Gino Landi
TENTH VICTIM, THE(1965, Fr./Ital.), ch; LA TRAVIATA(1968, Ital.), ch; WATERLOO(1970, Ital./USSR), ch; STATUE, THE(1971, Brit.), ch; ROMA(1972, Ital./Fr.), ch; TEMPEST(1982), ch

Jean-Claude Landi
VERY CURIOUS GIRL, A(1970, Fr.), art d

Lilia Landi
WHITE SHEIK, THE(1956, Ital.)

Linda Landi
THOUSANDS CHEER(1943)
Misc. Silents
SHIP COMES IN, A(1928)

Marla Landi
HORNET'S NEST, THE(1955, Brit.); ACROSS THE BRIDGE(1957, Brit.); DUBLIN NIGHTMARE(1958, Brit.); FIRST MAN INTO SPACE(1959, Brit.); HOUND OF THE BASKERVILLES, THE(1959, Brit.); PIRATES OF BLOOD RIVER, THE(1962, Brit.); MURDER GAME, THE(1966, Brit.)

Michel Landi
VERY CURIOUS GIRL, A(1970, Fr.), art d

Sal Landi
1984
SAVAGE STREETS(1984)

Olga Landiak
SECRET PEOPLE(1952, Brit.)

Josiane Landic
PICNIC ON THE GRASS(1960, Fr.), cos

Domingo Landicho
YEAR OF LIVING DANGEROUSLY, THE(1982, Aus.)

Hope Landin
UNFINISHED BUSINESS(1941); DIXIE(1943); GANGWAY FOR TOMORROW(1943); SWEET AND LOWDOWN(1944); GEORGE WHITE'S SCANDALS(1945); GREAT JOHN L. THE(1945); WEEKEND AT THE WALDORF(1945); WHERE DO WE GO FROM HERE?(1945); DARK CORNER, THE(1946); GAS HOUSE KIDS(1946); HOODLUM SAINT, THE(1946); MASK OF DIIJON, THE(1946); I REMEMBER MAMA(1948); WALLS OF JERICHO(1948); SUN COMES UP, THE(1949); SUGARFOOT(1951); SCARAMOUCHE(1952); HOW TO MARRY A MILLIONAIRE(1953); SHE COULDN'T SAY NO(1954); NEW YORK CONFIDENTIAL(1955)

Joi Landing
TAKE ME OUT TO THE BALL GAME(1949)

Marina Landinina
SYMPHONY OF LIFE(1949, USSR)

Adrian Landis
EVERYTHING'S ON ICE(1939), w

Bill Landis
VORTEX(1982)

Carol Landis
FOUR'S A CROWD(1938)

Carole Landis
EMPEROR'S CANDLESTICKS, THE(1937); HOLLYWOOD HOTEL(1937); STAR IS BORN, A(1937); BLONDES AT WORK(1938); BOY MEETS GIRL(1938); MEN ARE SUCH FOOLS(1938); COWBOYS FROM TEXAS(1939); RENO(1939); THREE TEXAS STEERS(1939); MYSTERY SEA RAIDER(1940); ONE MILLION B.C.(1940); TURNABOUT(1940); CADET GIRL(1941); DANCE HALL(1941); MOON OVER MIAMI(1941); ROAD SHOW(1941); TOPPER RETURNS(1941); GENTLEMAN AT HEART, A(1942); I WAKE UP SCREAMING(1942); IT HAPPENED IN FLATBUSH(1942); MANILA CALLING(1942); MY GAL SAL(1942); ORCHESTRA WIVES(1942); POWERS GIRL, THE(1942); WINTERTIME(1943); FOUR JILLS IN A JEEP(1944); SECRET COMMAND(1944); HAVING WONDERFUL CRIME(1945); BEHIND GREEN LIGHTS(1946); IT SHOULDN'T HAPPEN TO A DOG(1946); SCANDAL IN PARIS, A(1946); OUT OF THE BLUE(1947); SILK NOOSE, THE(1950, Brit.); LUCKY MASCOT, THE(1951, Brit.)

Cullen Landis
LIGHTS OF NEW YORK(1928); CONVICT'S CODE(1930)
Silents
JOY AND THE DRAGON(1916); ALMOST A HUSBAND(1919); OUTCASTS OF POKER FLAT, THE(1919); BUNTY PULLS THE STRINGS(1921); INFAMOUS MISS REVELL, THE(1921); SNOWBLIND(1921); GAY AND DEVILISH(1922); WATCH YOUR STEP(1922); YOUTH TO YOUTH(1922); CRASHIN' THRU(1923); DOLLAR DEVILS(1923); FOG, THE(1923); SOUL OF THE BEAST(1923); FIGHTING COWARD, THE(1924); ONE LAW FOR THE WOMAN(1924); EASY MONEY(1925); ENEMY OF MEN, AN(1925); WASTED LIVES(1925); DIXIE FLYER, THE(1926); JACK O'HEARTS(1926); PERILS OF THE COAST GUARD(1926); FINNEGAN'S BALL(1927); WE'RE ALL GAMBLERS(1927); LITTLE WILD GIRL, THE(1928); ON TO RENO(1928); OUT WITH THE TIDE(1928)
Misc. Silents
SUNNY JANE(1917); GIRL FROM THE OUTSIDE, THE(1919); JINX(1919); UPSTAIRS(1919); GOING SOME(1920); IT'S A GREAT LIFE(1920); PINTO(1920); NIGHT ROSE, THE(1921); FORSAKING ALL OTHERS(1922); LOVE IN THE DARK(1922); MAN WITH TWO MOTHERS, THE(1922); REMEMBRANCE(1922); WHERE IS MY WANDERING BOY TONIGHT?(1922); FAMOUS MRS. FAIR, THE(1923); MAN LIFE

PASSED BY, THE(1923); MASTERS OF MEN(1923); MIDNIGHT ALARM, THE(1923); PIONEER TRAILS(1923); BORN RICH(1924); CHEAP KISSES(1924); MIDNIGHT FLYER, THE(1925); PAMPERED YOUTH(1925); PEACOCK FEATHERS(1925); SEALED LIPS(1925); BUFFALO BILL ON THE U.P. TRAIL(1926); CHRISTINE OF THE BIG TOPS(1926); DAVY CROCKETT AT THE FALL OF THE ALAMO(1926); FIGHTING FAILURE, THE(1926); FRENZIED FLAMES(1926); MY OLD DUTCH(1926); SMOKE EATERS, THE(1926); SWEET ROSIE O'GRADY(1926); THEN CAME THE WOMAN(1926); WINNING THE FUTURITY(1926); BROADWAY AFTER MIDNIGHT(1927); HEROES OF THE NIGHT(1927); WE'RE ALL GAMBLERS(1927); BROKEN MASK, THE(1928); MIDNIGHT ADVENTURE, THE(1928)

Harry Landis
HELL IN KOREA(1956, Brit.); BITTER VICTORY(1958, Fr.); DUNKIRK(1958, Brit.); OPERATION BULLSHINE(1963, Brit.); PRIVATE POTTER(1963, Brit.); TERRORISTS, THE(1975, Brit.)

J. Cullen Landis
Misc. Silents
WHERE THE WEST BEGINS(1919)

James Landis
UNDER FIRE(1957), w; YOUNG AND DANGEROUS(1957), w; THUNDERING JETS(1958), w; LONE TEXAN(1959), w; AIRBORNE(1962), d&w; MAGIC VOYAGE OF SINBAD, THE(1962, USSR), d; STAKEOUT!(1962), d&w; SADIST, THE(1963), d&w; NASTY RABBIT, THE(1964), d; DEADWOOD'76(1965), d; RAT FINK(1965), d&w
Misc. Talkies
JENNIE, WIFE/CHILD(1968), d

Jeanette Landis
DOCTOR IN DISTRESS(1963, Brit.); PERSECUTION AND ASSASSINATION OF JEAN-PAUL MARAT AS PERFORMED BY THE INMATES OF THE ASYLUM OF CHARENTON UNDER THE DIRECTION OF THE MARQUIS DE SADE, THE(1967, Brit.)

Jessie Royce Landis
DERELICT(1930); IT HAPPENS EVERY SPRING(1949); MR. BELVEDERE GOES TO COLLEGE(1949); MY FOOLISH HEART(1949); MOTHER DIDN'T TELL ME(1950); TONIGHT AT 8:30(1953, Brit.); TO CATCH A THIEF(1955); GIRL HE LEFT BEHIND, THE(1956); SWAN, THE(1956); MY MAN GODFREY(1957); I MARRIED A WOMAN(1958); NORTH BY NORTHWEST(1959); PRIVATE'S AFFAIR, A(1959); GOODBYE AGAIN(1961); BON VOYAGE(1962); BOYS' NIGHT OUT(1962); CRITIC'S CHOICE(1963); GIDGET GOES TO ROME(1963); AIRPORT(1970)

John Landis
BATTLE FOR THE PLANET OF THE APES(1973); SCHLOCK(1973), a, d&w; KENTUCKY FRIED MOVIE, THE(1977), d; NATIONAL LAMPOON'S ANIMAL HOUSE(1978), d; 1941(1979); BLUES BROTHERS, THE(1980), d, w; AMERICAN WEREWOLF IN LONDON, AN(1981), d&w; TRADING PLACES(1983), d; TWILIGHT ZONE-THE MOVIE(1983), d, w
1984
MUPPETS TAKE MANHATTAN, THE(1984)

Margaret Landis
Silents
AMARILLY OF CLOTHESLINE ALLEY(1918); MR. FIX-IT(1918); ALICE ADAMS(1923); WHAT WIVES WANT(1923); FIGHTER'S PARADISE(1924); HER MAN(1924); LATEST FROM PARIS, THE(1928)
Misc. Silents
BEST MAN, THE(1917); FEET OF CLAY(1917); INSPIRATIONS OF HARRY LARRABEE(1917); MARTINACHE MARRIAGE, THE(1917); PARTED CURTAINS(1921); ASHES(1922); LADDER JINX, THE(1922); ROSE O' THE SEA(1922); LOVE BRAND, THE(1923); MIRACLE BABY, THE(1923); FIGHTING HEART, A(1924); MY MAN(1924); TRIGGER FINGER(1924); WESTERN WALLOP, THE(1924); YOUTH AND ADVENTURE(1925)

Monte Landis
YOUNG FRANKENSTEIN(1974); YELLOWBEARD(1983)
1984
BODY DOUBLE(1984)

Monty Landis
MOUSE THAT ROARED, THE(1959, Brit.); SCHOOL FOR SCOUNDRELS(1960, Brit.); PURE HELL OF ST. TRINIAN'S, THE(1961, Brit.); LIVE NOW-PAY LATER(1962, Brit.); ON THE BEAT(1962, Brit.); VILLAGE OF DAUGHTERS(1962, Brit.); PLAY IT COOL(1963, Brit.); WHAT A CRAZY WORLD(1963, Brit.); OPERATION SNAFU(1965, Brit.); DOUBLE TROUBLE(1967); VULTURE, THE(1967, U.S./Brit./Can.); TARGETS(1968)

Nina Landis
Misc. Talkies
STAGEFRIGHT(1983)

Rev. Bee Landis
OTHER SIDE OF THE MOUNTAIN-PART 2, THE(1978)

Roberta Landis
Misc. Talkies
COME ONE, COME ALL(1970)

Robin Landis
STACY'S KNIGHTS(1983)

Winifred Landis
Silents
DANTE'S INFERNO(1924); GEARED TO GO(1924)
Misc. Silents
BANDIT BUSTER, THE(1926)

Jean Landlier
MOULIN ROUGE(1952)

Hannie Landman
BILLY THE KID VS. DRACULA(1966)

Francois Landoit
1984
LE CRABE TAMBOUR(1984, Fr.)

Avice Landon
NOTHING BUT THE BEST(1964, Brit.); LEATHER BOYS, THE(1965, Brit.); TWO GENTLEMEN SHARING(1969, Brit.); BLOOD ON SATAN'S CLAW, THE(1970, Brit.); ADVENTURES OF BARRY McKENZIE(1972, Austral.)

Christopher Landon
DESERT ATTACK(1958, Brit.), w

Dinsdale Landon
DIGBY, THE BIGGEST DOG IN THE WORLD(1974, Brit.)

Gale Landon
Silents
LOVE LIAR, THE(1916)

Hal Landon
IT'S A WONDERFUL LIFE(1946); SPRINGTIME IN THE SIERRAS(1947); CARSON CITY RAIDERS(1948); GALLANT LEGION, THE(1948); NAVAJO TRAIL RAIDERS(1949)

Hal Landon, Jr.
SCAVENGER HUNT(1979)

Harold Landon
SUSAN AND GOD(1940); ROLLIN' HOME TO TEXAS(1941); EAGLE SQUADRON(1942); SPIRIT OF STANFORD, THE(1942); GILDERSLEEVE'S BAD DAY(1943); GUNG HO!(1943); IRON MAJOR, THE(1943); CLAY PIGEON, THE(1949); ROADBLOCK(1951)

Harold S. Landon
GUY NAMED JOE, A(1943)

John Landon
GUESS WHAT HAPPENED TO COUNT DRACULA(1970); RATTLERS(1976), makeup

Joseph Landon
HIGH FLIGHT(1957, Brit.), w; RISE AND FALL OF LEGS DIAMOND, THE(1960), w; EXPLOSIVE GENERATION, THE(1961), w; HOODLUM PRIEST, THE(1961), w; JOHNNY COOL(1963), w; WALL OF NOISE(1963), p, w; RIO CONCHOS(1964), w; VON RYAN'S EXPRESS(1965), w; STAGECOACH(1966), w; FINIAN'S RAINBOW(1968), p

Judith Landon
ROAD TO BALI(1952)

Judy Landon
PREHISTORIC WOMEN(1950); SHOW BOAT(1951); SINGIN' IN THE RAIN(1952); BAND WAGON, THE(1953); SECOND CHANCE(1953)

Laurence Landon
...ALL THE MARBLES(1981); I, THE JURY(1982)

Laurene Landon
1984
HUNDRA(1984, Ital.); YELLOW HAIR AND THE FORTRESS OF GOLD(1984)

Lois Landon
ZIS BOOM BAH(1941); GIRL TROUBLE(1942); MAN WITH TWO LIVES, THE(1942)

Margaret Landon
ANNA AND THE KING OF SIAM(1946), w; KING AND I, THE(1956), w

Michael Landon
THESE WILDER YEARS(1956); I WAS A TEENAGE WEREWOLF(1957); GOD'S LITTLE ACRE(1958); HIGH SCHOOL CONFIDENTIAL(1958); MARACAIBO(1958); LEGEND OF TOM DOOLEY, THE(1959); ERRAND BOY, THE(1961)
1984
SAM'S SON(1984), a, d&w

Patricia Landon
KISS OF THE TARANTULA(1975)

Richard Landon
GIRL IN BLACK STOCKINGS(1957), w

Ross Landon
WHO KILLED JOHN SAVAGE?(1937, Brit.); DARK STAIRWAY, THE(1938, Brit.); GLAMOUR GIRL(1938, Brit.); CHAMBER OF HORRORS(1941, Brit.)

Ruth Landon
PRICE OF FOLLY, THE(1937, Brit.), w

Ted D. Landon
BEARS AND I, THE(1974), ph

Avice Landone
MY BROTHER JONATHAN(1949, Brit.); GUILT IS MY SHADOW(1950, Brit.); FRANCHISE AFFAIR, THE(1952, Brit.); WHITE CORRIDORS(1952, Brit.); LOVE IN PAWN(1953, Brit.); OPERATION DIPLOMAT(1953, Brit.); EMBEZZLER, THE(1954, Brit.); ESCAPE BY NIGHT(1954, Brit.); WINDFALL(1955 Brit.); EYEWITNESS(1956, Brit.); ALLIGATOR NAMED DAISY, AN(1957, Brit.); REACH FOR THE SKY(1957, Brit.); TRUE AS A TURTLE(1957, Brit.); CARVE HER NAME WITH PRIDE(1958, Brit.); RX MURDER(1958, Brit.); WIND CANNOT READ, THE(1958, Brit.); CRY FROM THE STREET, A(1959, Brit.); TEENAGE BAD GIRL(1959, Brit.); OPERATION CUPID(1960, Brit.); FIVE GOLDEN HOURS(1961, Brit.); GAOLBREAK(1962, Brit.); THIS IS MY STREET(1964, Brit.)

Edna Landor
FINGER OF GUILT(1956, Brit.)

Enda Landor
GENTLE TOUCH, THE(1956, Brit.)

Jenifer Landor
1984
SUPERGIRL(1984)

Jennifer Landor
MOONLIGHTING(1982, Brit.)

Joan Landor
THREE IN ONE(1956, Aus.)

Ray Landor
DEVIL DOLL(1964, Brit.)

Rosalyn Landor
DEVIL'S BRIDE, THE(1968, Brit.); JANE EYRE(1971, Brit.)

Pavel Landovsky
Misc. Talkies
UPPERCRUST, THE(1982)

Max Landow
ETERNAL SUMMER(1961), ph

Yona Landowska
Misc. Silents
FROM A BROADWAY TO A THRONE(1916); BILLY AND THE BIG STICK(1917)

Marcel Landowski
PALACE OF NUDES(1961, Fr./Ital.), m

Lou Landre
GIRL WITH THE RED HAIR, THE(1983, Neth.)

Jean-Pierre Landreau
TEMPTATION(1962, Fr.), m

Danny B. Landres
CATTLE DRIVE(1951), ed; TOMAHAWK(1951), ed; EARTH VS. THE FLYING SAUCERS(1956), ed; HAVE ROCRET, WILL TRAVEL(1959), ed; PLAINSMAN, THE(1966), ed

Paul Landres
LADY FIGHTS BACK(1937), ed; MAN IN BLUE, THE(1937), ed; PRESCRIPTION FOR ROMANCE(1937), ed; REPORTED MISSING(1937), ed; NURSE FROM BROOKLYN(1938), ed; ROAD TO RENO, THE(1938), ed; BAD MAN FROM RED BUTTE(1940), ed; I'M NOBODY'S SWEETHEART NOW(1940), ed; PONY POST(1940), ed; RAGTIME COWBOY JOE(1940), ed; SON OF ROARING DAN(1940), ed; ARIZONA CYCLONE(1941), ed; BACHELOR DADDY(1941), ed; GIVE OUT, SISTERS(1942), ed; PITTSBURGH(1942), ed; IT COMES UP LOVE(1943), ed; LARCENY WITH MUSIC(1943), ed; NEVER A DULL MOMENT(1943), ed; RHYTHM OF THE ISLANDS(1943), ed; SHE'S FOR ME(1943), ed; SO'S YOUR UNCLE(1943), ed; TOP MAN(1943), ed; DESTINY(1944), ed; IMPOSTER, THE(1944), ed; SCARLET CLAW, THE(1944), ed; SOUTH OF DIXIE(1944), ed; CRIMSON CANARY(1945), ed; DALTONS RIDE AGAIN, THE(1945), ed; HER LUCKY NIGHT(1945), ed; MEN IN HER DIARY(1945), ed; SEE MY LAWYER(1945), ed; SENORITA FROM THE WEST(1945), ed; SHE GETS HER MAN(1945), ed; DARK HORSE, THE(1946), ed; SHE-WOLF OF LONDON(1946), ed; BLONDE SAVAGE(1947), ed; MICHIGAN KID, THE(1947), ed; VIGILANTES RETURN, THE(1947), ed; CHECKERED COAT, THE(1948), ed; LAST OF THE WILD HORSES(1948), ed; RETURN OF WILDFIRE, THE(1948), ed; GRAND CANYON(1949), d&ed; I SHOT JESSE JAMES(1949), ed; SQUARE DANCE JUBILEE(1949), d; NAVY BOUND(1951), d; RHYTHM INN(1951), d; ARMY BOUND(1952), d; CHAIN OF EVIDENCE(1957), d; HELL CANYON OUTLAWS(1957), d; LAST OF THE BADMEN(1957), d; VAMPIRE, THE(1957), d; FLAME BARRIER, THE(1958), d; FRONTIER GUN(1958), d; JOHNNY ROCCO(1958), d; MAN FROM GOD'S COUNTRY(1958), d; OREGON PASSAGE(1958), d; RETURN OF DRACULA, THE(1958), d; GO, JOHNNY, GO!(1959), d; LONE TEXAN(1959), d; MIRACLE OF THE HILLS, THE(1959), d; MODERN MARRIAGE, A(1962), d; SON OF A GUNFIGHTER(1966, U.S./Span.), d; DRAGNET(1974), ed
Misc. Talkies
EYES OF THE JUNGLE(1953), d; NEW DAY AT SUNDOWN(1957), d

Simm Landres
RACHEL, RACHEL(1968); ALICE'S RESTAURANT(1969)

Paul Landress
FIRED WIFE(1943), ed

Budd Landreth
MONEY TRAP, THE(1966)

Carol Landrie
RUN FOR YOUR WIFE(1966, Fr./Ital.)

Maria Landrock
DECISION BEFORE DAWN(1951)

Teri Landrum
PANDEMONIUM(1982)

Aude Landry
BLOOD RELATIVES(1978, Fr./Can.); JUDGE AND THE ASSASSIN, THE(1979, Fr.)

Bob Landry
STORY OF G.I. JOE, THE(1945)

Clarence Landry
I'LL SEE YOU IN MY DREAMS(1951); VIRGIN SACRIFICE(1959)

Cy Landry
RIDING HIGH(1943)

Dennis Landry
MR. MOM(1983)

Dick Landry
EXECUTIVE SUITE(1954)

Gerald Landry
TRINITY IS STILL MY NAME(1971, Ital.)

Gerard Landry
LA BETE HUMAINE(1938, Fr.); NIGHT WITHOUT STARS(1953, Brit.); LOVERS OF TOLEDO, THE(1954, Fr./Span./Ital.); TRAPEZE(1956); DAY THE SKY EXPLODED, THE(1958, Fr./Ital.); ENEMY GENERAL, THE(1960); FIVE BRANDED WOMEN(1960); PIRATE OF THE BLACK HAWK, THE(1961, Fr./Ital.)

Jenny Landry
HELP!(1965, Brit.)

John Francois Landry
CONFESSIONS OF A POP PERFORMER(1975, Brit.)

John Landry
MOSQUITO SQUADRON(1970, Brit.); PRESSURE(1976, Brit.)

Karen Landry
PERSONALS, THE(1982)

Margaret L. Landry
IRON MAJOR, THE(1943)

Margaret Landry
ADVENTURES OF A ROOKIE(1943); FALCON AND THE CO-EDS, THE(1943); FALLEN SPARROW, THE(1943); GILDERSLEEVE ON BROADWAY(1943); GOVERNMENT GIRL(1943); LEOPARD MAN, THE(1943); MEXICAN SPITFIRE'S BLESSED EVENT(1943); MADEMOISELLE FIFI(1944); YOUTH RUNS WILD(1944)

Martin Landry
Silents
INTOLERANCE(1916)

Richard Landry
TAKE ME OUT TO THE BALL GAME(1949); PEOPLE AGAINST O'HARA, THE(1951)

David Landsberg
JERK, THE(1979); SKATETOWN, U.S.A.(1979); SHOOT THE MOON(1982)

Valerie Landsburg
THANK GOD IT'S FRIDAY(1978)

Angela Landsbury
HARVEY GIRLS, THE(1946)

Ruth Landshoff
Silents
NOSFERATU, THE VAMPIRE(1922, Ger.)

Charles Landstone
BEHIND YOUR BACK(1937, Brit.), w

Eivor Landstrom
JUST ONCE MORE(1963, Swed.)

Maria Landt
GOLDEN LINK, THE(1954, Brit.)
Etherine Landucci
SWISS MISS(1938)
George Landy
SIDEWALKS OF NEW YORK(1931), w
Hanna Landy
EXPLOSIVE GENERATION, THE(1961); OPERATION EICHMANN(1961); CONVICT STAGE(1965); FORT COURAGEOUS(1965); HARLOW(1965); IN LIKE FLINT(1967); ROSEMARY'S BABY(1968)
Hannah Landy
GIT!(1965)
Ludwig Landy
OVERTURE TO GLORY(1940), p
Michael Landy
NO BLADE OF GRASS(1970, Brit.)
Andre Landzaat
1984
BREAKIN'(1984)
A.B. Lane
TEMPLE TOWER(1930); TREASURE ISLAND(1934)
Abbe Lane
WINGS OF THE HAWK(1953); RIDE CLEAR OF DIABLO(1954); AMERICANO, THE(1955); CHICAGO SYNDICATE(1955); DONATELLA(1956, Ital.); MARACAIBO(1958); LADY DOCTOR, THE(1963, Fr./Ital./Span.); TWILIGHT ZONE–THE MOVIE(1983)
Misc. Talkies
CRICKET OF THE HEARTH, THE(1968)
Al Lane
WAY OF THE WEST, THE(1934), w; LURE OF THE WASTELAND(1939), p
Misc. Talkies
GALLOPING KID, THE(1932)
Alice Lane
LUCKY LOSER(1934, Brit.)
Allan Lane [Rocky Lane]
FORWARD PASS, THE(1929); NOT QUITE DECENT(1929); LOVE IN THE ROUGH(1930); MADAME SATAN(1930); EXPENSIVE WOMEN(1931); HONOR OF THE FAMILY(1931); NIGHT NURSE(1931); SMART MONEY(1931); STAR WITNESS(1931); MISS PINKERTON(1932); ONE WAY PASSAGE(1932); TENDERFOOT, THE(1932); WINNER TAKE ALL(1932); STOWAWAY(1936); BIG BUSINESS(1937); CHARLIE CHAN AT THE OLYMPICS(1937); DUKE COMES BACK, THE(1937); FIFTY ROADS TO TOWN(1937); LAUGHING AT TROUBLE(1937); SING AND BE HAPPY(1937); CRIME RING(1938); FUGITIVES FOR A NIGHT(1938); HAVING WONDERFUL TIME(1938); LAW WEST OF TOMBSTONE, THE(1938); MAID'S NIGHT OUT(1938); NIGHT SPOT(1938); THIS MARRIAGE BUSINESS(1938); CONSPIRACY(1939); PACIFIC LINER(1939); PANAMA LADY(1939); SPELLBINDER, THE(1939); GRAND OLE OPRY(1940); ALL-AMERICAN CO-ED(1941); DANCING MASTERS, THE(1943); CALL OF THE SOUTH SEAS(1944); SHERIFF OF SUNDOWN(1944); SILVER CITY KID(1944); STAGECOACH TO MONTEREY(1944); BELLS OF ROSARITA(1945); CORPUS CHRISTI BANDITS(1945); TOPEKA TERROR, THE(1945); TRAIL OF KIT CARSON(1945); GAY BLADES(1946); GUY COULD CHANGE, A(1946); NIGHT TRAIN TO MEMPHIS(1946); OUT CALIFORNIA WAY(1946); SANTA FE UPRISING(1946); STAGECOACH TO DENVER(1946); BANDITS OF DARK CANYON(1947); HOMESTEADERS OF PARADISE VALLEY(1947); MARSHAL OF CRIPPLE CREEK, THE(1947); OREGON TRAIL SCOUTS(1947); RUSTLERS OF DEVIL'S CANYON(1947); VIGILANTES OF BOOMTOWN(1947); WILD FRONTIER, THE(1947); BOLD FRONTIERSMAN, THE(1948); CARSON CITY RAIDERS(1948); DENVER KID, THE(1948); DESPERADOES OF DODGE CITY(1948); MARSHAL OF AMARILLO(1948); OKLAHOMA BADLANDS(1948); RENEGADES OF SONORA(1948); SUNDOWN IN SANTA FE(1948); BANDIT KING OF TEXAS(1949); DEATH VALLEY GUNFIGHTER(1949); FRONTIER INVESTIGATOR(1949); NAVAJO TRAIL RAIDERS(1949); POWDER RIVER RUSTLERS(1949); SHERIFF OF WICHITA(1949); WYOMING BANDIT, THE(1949); CODE OF THE SILVER SAGE(1950); COVERED WAGON RAID(1950); FRISCO TORNADO(1950); GUNMEN OF ABILENE(1950); RUSTLERS ON HORSEBACK(1950); SALT LAKE RAIDERS(1950); TRAIL OF ROBIN HOOD(1950); VIGILANTE HIDEOUT(1950); DESERT OF LOST MEN(1951); FORT DODGE STAMPEDE(1951); NIGHT RIDERS OF MONTANA(1951); ROUGH RIDERS OF DURANGO(1951); WELLS FARGO GUNMASTER(1951); BLACK HILLS AMBUSH(1952); CAPTIVE OF BILLY THE KID(1952); DESPERADOES OUTPOST(1952); LEADVILLE GUNSLINGER(1952); THUNDERING CARAVANS(1952); BANDITS OF THE WEST(1953); EL PASO STAMPEDE(1953); MARSHAL OF CEDAR ROCK(1953); SAVAGE FRONTIER(1953); SAGA OF HEMP BROWN, THE(1958); HELL BENT FOR LEATHER(1960); POSSE FROM HELL(1961)
Allen Lane
THEY MADE HER A SPY(1939); TWELVE CROWDED HOURS(1939)
Amanda Lane
SING WHILE YOU DANCE(1946)
Andrea Lane
PANIC IN YEAR ZERO!(1962); SILENT WITNESS, THE(1962)
Andrew Lane
VALLEY GIRL(1983), p, w
1984
NIGHT OF THE COMET(1984), p
Arthur Lane
DIAMOND CITY(1949, Brit.); INTERRUPTED JOURNEY, THE(1949, Brit.); DEAD ON COURSE(1952, Brit.); IT STARTED IN PARADISE(1952, Brit.); BLACK GLOVE(1954, Brit.); SECRET VENTURE(1955, Brit.); TRACK THE MAN DOWN(1956, Brit.); DOG AND THE DIAMONDS, THE(1962, Brit.)
Arthur A. Lane
SUNSET BOULEVARD(1950)
Barbara Lane
FIRE DOWN BELOW(1957, U.S./Brit.); HEAT AND DUST(1983, Brit.), cos
1984
LASSITER(1984), cos
Barry Lane
ONE MAN(1979, Can.)
Ben Lane
KIM(1950), makeup; MAN WITH THE GOLDEN ARM, THE(1955), makeup; PAL JOEY(1957), makeup; MOUNTAIN ROAD, THE(1960), makeup; PEPE(1960), makeup; STRANGERS WHEN WE MEET(1960), makeup; WHO WAS THAT LADY?(1960),

makeup; DEVIL AT FOUR O'CLOCK, THE(1961), makeup; GIDGET GOES HAWAIIAN(1961), makeup; MR. SARDONICUS(1961), makeup; RAISIN IN THE SUN, A(1961), makeup; TWO RODE TOGETHER(1961), makeup; UNDERWORLD U.S.A.(1961), makeup; VALLEY OF THE DRAGONS(1961), makeup; EXPERIMENT IN TERROR(1962), makeup; INTERNS, THE(1962), makeup; NOTORIOUS LANDLADY, THE(1962), makeup; THIRTEEN WEST STREET(1962), makeup; UNDERWATER CITY, THE(1962), makeup; MAN FROM THE DINERS' CLUB, THE(1963), makeup; THIRTEEN FRIGHTENED GIRLS(1963), makeup; GOOD NEIGHBOR SAM(1964), makeup; NEW INTERNS, THE(1964), makeup; ONE MAN'S WAY(1964), makeup; QUICK GUN, THE(1964), makeup; RIDE THE WILD SURF(1964), makeup; STRAIT-JACKET(1964), makeup; KING RAT(1965), makeup; LOVE HAS MANY FACES(1965), makeup; SHIP OF FOOLS(1965), makeup; SYNANON(1965), makeup; SILENCERS, THE(1966), makeup; THREE ON A COUCH(1966), makeup; TROUBLE WITH ANGELS, THE(1966), makeup; WALK, DON'T RUN(1966), makeup; GUESS WHO'S COMING TO DINNER(1967), makeup; LUV(1967), makeup; TIME FOR KILLING, A(1967), makeup; WHO'S MINDING THE MINT?(1967), makeup; WHERE ANGELS GO...TROUBLE FOLLOWS(1968), makeup; WRECKING CREW, THE(1968), makeup; COMIC, THE(1969), makeup; MAD ROOM, THE(1969), makeup; MODEL SHOP, THE(1969), makeup; GETTING STRAIGHT(1970), makeup; LIBERATION OF L.B. JONES, THE(1970), makeup; WATERMELON MAN(1970), makeup; HAPPY BIRTHDAY, WANDA JUNE(1971), makeup
Betty J. Lane
ANGEL BABY(1961), ed
Betty Lane
WONDER MAN(1945); SCREAMING SKULL, THE(1958), ed
Bill Lane
DIRTY HARRY(1971)
Billie Lane
JOAN OF OZARK(1942)
Brenda Lane
Silents
ALONG CAME RUTH(1924); NEW KLONDIKE, THE(1926)
Misc. Silents
RIP ROARIN' ROBERTS(1924)
Bruce Lane
SILVER SPURS(1936); TWO-FISTED SHERIFF(1937); HEAD(1968), spec eff
Burton Lane
BABES ON BROADWAY(1941), w; AFFAIR IN HAVANA(1957), w; FINIAN'S RAINBOW(1968), m; ON A CLEAR DAY YOU CAN SEE FOREVER(1970), w, m
Cam Lane
MAN, A WOMAN, AND A BANK, A(1979, Can.)
Campbell Lane
1984
FINDERS KEEPERS(1984)
Carol Lane
Silents
ARIZONA KID, THE(1929)
Misc. Silents
LIGHTNIN' SHOT(1928); MYSTERY VALLEY(1928); BULLETS AND JUSTICE(1929)
Charles Lane
CANARY MURDER CASE, THE(1929); SATURDAY'S CHILDREN(1929); BLONDE CRAZY(1931); SMART MONEY(1931); MOUTHPIECE, THE(1932); BOWERY, THE(1933); GOLD DIGGERS OF 1933(1933); PRIVATE DETECTIVE 62(1933); 42ND STREET(1933); TWENTIETH CENTURY(1934); TWENTY MILLION SWEETHEARTS(1934); CRIME OF DR. FORBES(1936); MILKY WAY, THE(1936); THIRTY SIX HOURS TO KILL(1936); THREE MEN ON A HORSE(1936); TICKET TO PARADISE(1936); ALI BABA GOES TO TOWN(1937); DANGER–LOVE AT WORK(1937); TRAPPED BY G-MEN(1937); VENUS MAKES TROUBLE(1937); WE'RE ON THE JURY(1937); ALWAYS IN TROUBLE(1938); BOY SLAVES(1938); CITY GIRL(1938); COCOANUT GROVE(1938); IN OLD CHICAGO(1938); JOY OF LIVING(1938); KENTUCKY(1938); PROFESSOR BEWARE(1938); THANKS FOR EVERYTHING(1938); THREE LOVES HAS NANCY(1938); YOU CAN'T TAKE IT WITH YOU(1938); CAT AND THE CANARY, THE(1939); FIFTH AVENUE GIRL(1939); GOLDEN BOY(1939); INSIDE STORY(1939); LUCKY NIGHT(1939); MIRACLES FOR SALE(1939); MR. SMITH GOES TO WASHINGTON(1939); NEWS IS MADE AT NIGHT(1939); ROSE OF WASHINGTON SQUARE(1939); SECOND FIDDLE(1939); THEY ALL COME OUT(1939); THUNDER AFLOAT(1939); BUCK BENNY RIDES AGAIN(1940); CROOKED ROAD, THE(1940); DANCING ON A DIME(1940); DOCTOR TAKES A WIFE(1940); EDISON, THE MAN(1940); ELLERY QUEEN. MASTER DETECTIVE(1940); GREAT PROFILE, THE(1940); IT'S A DATE(1940); JOHNNY APOLLO(1940); LEATHER-PUSHERS, THE(1940); ON THEIR OWN(1940); PRIMROSE PATH(1940); QUEEN OF THE MOB(1940); RHYTHM ON THE RIVER(1940); TEXAS RANGERS RIDE AGAIN(1940); WE WHO ARE YOUNG(1940); YOU CAN'T FOOL YOUR WIFE(1940); BALL OF FIRE(1941); BARNACLE BILL(1941); CITY, FOR CONQUEST(1941); ELLERY QUEEN AND THE PERFECT CRIME(1941); ELLERY QUEEN'S PENTHOUSE MYSTERY(1941); INVISIBLE WOMAN, THE(1941); LOOK WHO'S LAUGHING(1941); NEVER GIVE A SUCKER AN EVEN BREAK(1941); OBLIGING YOUNG LADY(1941); REPENT AT LEISURE(1941); SEALED LIPS(1941); SING ANOTHER CHORUS(1941); SIS HOPKINS(1941); THREE GIRLS ABOUT TOWN(1941); YOU'RE THE ONE(1941); ABOUT FACE(1942); ARE HUSBANDS NECESSARY?(1942); FLYING TIGERS(1942); FRIENDLY ENEMIES(1942); GENTLEMAN AT HEART, A(1942); GREAT MAN'S LADY, THE(1942); HOME IN WYOMIN'(1942); I WAKE UP SCREAMING(1942); LADY IN A JAM(1942); LADY IS WILLING, THE(1942); MAD MARTINDALES, THE(1942); PARDON MY SARONG(1942); RIDE 'EM COWBOY(1942); TARZAN'S NEW YORK ADVENTURE(1942); THEY ALL KISSED THE BRIDE(1942); THRU DIFFERENT EYES(1942); YOKEL BOY(1942); MR. LUCKY(1943); ARSENIC AND OLD LACE(1944); CLOSE CALL FOR BOSTON BLACKIE, A(1946); INVISIBLE INFORMER(1946); JUST BEFORE DAWN(1946); MYSTERIOUS INTRUDER(1946); SHOW-OFF, THE(1946); SWELL GUY(1946); FARMER'S DAUGHTER, THE(1947); INTRIGUE(1947); IT HAPPENED ON 5TH AVENUE(1947); LOUISIANA(1947); ROSES ARE RED(1947); APARTMENT FOR PEGGY(1948); CALL NORTHSIDE 777(1948); GENTLEMAN FROM NOWHERE, THE(1948); MOONRISE(1948); OUT OF THE STORM(1948); RACE STREET(1948); SMART WOMAN(1948); STATE OF THE UNION(1948); MISS GRANT TAKES RICHMOND(1949); MOTHER IS A FRESHMAN(1949); YOU'RE MY EVERYTHING(1949); BORDERLINE(1950); FOR HEAVEN'S SAKE(1950); LOVE THAT BRUTE(1950); RIDING HIGH(1950); CRIMINAL LAWYER(1951); HERE COMES THE GROOM(1951); I CAN GET IT FOR YOU WHOLESALE(1951); SNIPER, THE(1952); AFFAIRS OF DOBIE GILLIS, THE(1953); JUGGLER, THE(1953); REMAINS TO BE

SEEN(1953); GOD IS MY PARTNER(1957); TOP SECRET AFFAIR(1957); TEACHER'S PET(1958); BUT NOT FOR ME(1959); MATING GAME, THE(1959); THIRTY FOOT BRIDE OF CANDY ROCK, THE(1959); MUSIC MAN, THE(1962); IT'S A MAD, MAD, MAD, MAD WORLD(1963); PAPA'S DELICATE CONDITION(1963); CARPETBAG-GERS, THE(1964); GOOD NEIGHBOR SAM(1964); JOHN GOLDFARB, PLEASE COME HOME(1964); LOOKING FOR LOVE(1964); NEW INTERNS, THE(1964); BIL-LIE(1965); BIRDS AND THE BEES, THE(1965); GHOST AND MR. CHICKEN, THE(1966); UGLY DACHSHUND, THE(1966); GNOME-MOBILE, THE(1967); DID YOU HEAR THE ONE ABOUT THE TRAVELING SALESLADY(1968); WHAT'S SO BAD ABOUT FEELING GOOD?(1968); ARISTOCATS, THE(1970); GET TO KNOW YOUR RABBIT(1972); MOVIE MOVIE(1978); LITTLE DRAGONS, THE(1980); DEAD KIDS(1981 Aus./New Zealand); STRANGE INVADERS(1983)
Silents
MRS. BLACK IS BACK(1914); AWAY GOES PRUDENCE(1920); BRANDED WOM-AN, THE(1920); DR. JEKYLL AND MR. HYDE(1920); GUILTY OF LOVE(1920); IF WOMEN ONLY KNEW(1921); LOVE'S PENALTY(1921); WITHOUT LIMIT(1921); WHITE SISTER, THE(1923); SECOND YOUTH(1924); DARK ANGEL, THE(1925); ROMOLA(1925); BLIND GODDESS, THE(1926); 'MARRIAGE LICENSE?'(1926); OUT-SIDER, THE(1926); WINNING OF BARBARA WORTH, THE(1926); BARBED WI-RE(1927); MARRIED ALIVE(1927); SADIE THOMPSON(1928)
Misc. Silents
WANTED - A HUSBAND(1919); RESTLESS SEX, THE(1920); FASCINATION(1922); MYSTERY CLUB, THE(1926); SERVICE FOR LADIES(1927)
Charles L. Lane
TELEVISION SPY(1939)
Charles Levison Lane
IT HAD TO HAPPEN(1936); MR. DEEDS GOES TO TOWN(1936); INTERNES CAN'T TAKE MONEY(1937)
Charles W. Lane
Misc. Silents
BROADWAY PEACOCK, THE(1922), d
Charlie Lane
IT'S A WONDERFUL LIFE(1946)
Chick Lane
SKIMPY IN THE NAVY(1949, Brit.)
Cynthia Lane
FUZZ(1972)
David Lane
THUNDERBIRD 6(1968, Brit.), d; THUNDERBIRDS ARE GO(1968, Brit.), d; BRASS TARGET(1978), ed
Misc. Talkies
THUNDERBIRDS 6(1968), d
Desmond Lane
6.5 SPECIAL(1958, Brit.)
Diane Lane
LITTLE ROMANCE, A(1979, U.S./Fr.); TOUCHED BY LOVE(1980); CATTLE ANNIE AND LITTLE BRITCHES(1981); LADIES AND GENTLEMEN, THE FABULOUS STAINS(1982); SIX PACK(1982); OUTSIDERS, THE(1983); RUMBLE FISH(1983)
1984
COTTON CLUB, THE(1984); STREETS OF FIRE(1984)
Dick Lane
DEAR BRIGETTE(1965); KANSAS CITY BOMBER(1972); SHAGGY D.A., THE(1976)
Don Lane
1984
RAZORBACK(1984, Aus.)
Ed Lane
ZELIG(1983)
Elizabeth Lane
GETTING STRAIGHT(1970)
1984
RIVER, THE(1984)
Eric Lane
LOLITA(1962); FIRST TIME, THE(1969)
Francis Lane
TWO COLONELS, THE(1963, Ital.)
Fred Lane
ESTHER WATERS(1948, Brit.)
Garrison Lane
ROLLOVER(1981)
George Lane
FIND THE LADY(1936, Brit.); FURY AT FURNACE CREEK(1948), makeup; EX-ODUS(1960), makeup; SEVEN WOMEN FROM HELL(1961), makeup; PRESSURE POINT(1962), makeup; IT'S A MAD, MAD, MAD, MAD WORLD(1963), makeup; RHINO(1964); KIMBERLEY JIM(1965, South Africa)
Silents
ENVY(1917), ph; KATHLEEN MAVOURNEEN(1919), ph; SACRED SILENCE(1919), ph; WHILE NEW YORK SLEEPS(1920), ph
George W. Lane
Silents
SILENT COMMAND, THE(1923), ph; IT IS THE LAW(1924), ph
Georgia Lane
SECRET LIFE OF WALTER MITTY, THE(1947)
Gladys Lane
DIRTYMOUTH(1970)
Grace Lane
FEATHER, THE(1929, Brit.); TAXI FOR TWO(1929, Brit.); MAD HATTERS, THE(1935, Brit.)
Silents
OWD BOB(1924, Brit.)
Harry J. Lane
Silents
SHADOWS OF THE SEA(1922)
Harry Lane
STRANGE CARGO(1936, Brit.); JAMAICA INN(1939, Brit.); APPOINTMENT WITH CRIME(1945, Brit.); CAESAR AND CLEOPATRA(1946, Brit.); DON'T SAY DIE(1950, Brit.); OLD MOTHER RILEY'S JUNGLE TREASURE(1951, Brit.); OPERATION X(1951, Brit.); FIRE OVER AFRICA(1954, Brit.); TOO HOT TO HANDLE(1961, Brit.); MAKE MINE A DOUBLE(1962, Brit.)

Iva Lane
10 TO MIDNIGHT(1983)
Jackie Lane
FOR BETTER FOR WORSE(1954, Brit.); GAMMA PEOPLE, THE(1956); MEN OF SHERWOOD FOREST(1957, Brit.); DANGEROUS YOUTH(1958, Brit.); TRUTH ABOUT WOMEN, THE(1958, Brit.); WONDERFUL THINGS!(1958, Brit.); ANGRY HILLS, THE(1959, Brit.); GOODBYE AGAIN(1961); JET STORM(1961, Brit.); OPERA-TION SNATCH(1962, Brit.); TWO AND TWO MAKE SIX(1962, Brit.)
Jerry Lane
MY FAVORITE SPY(1951)
Jewel Lane
DEATH OF A SCOUNDREL(1956)
Jocelyn Lane
SWORD OF ALI BABA, THE(1965); TICKLE ME(1965); INCIDENT AT PHANTOM HILL(1966); POPPY IS ALSO A FLOWER, THE(1966); HOW TO SEDUCE A PLAY-BOY(1968, Aust./Fr./Ital.); HELL'S BELLES(1969); LAND RAIDERS(1969); BULLET FOR PRETTY BOY, A(1970)
John Francis Lane
LA DOLCE VITA(1961, Ital./Fr.); WITCH'S CURSE, THE(1963, Ital.); EL GRE-CO(1966, Ital., Fr.); QUIET PLACE IN THE COUNTRY, A(1970, Ital./Fr.); ROMA(1972, Ital./Fr.)
John Lane
ROVER, THE(1967, Ital.)
Kent Lane
CHANGES(1969); WILD PACK, THE(1972)
Lari Lane
ARSON FOR HIRE(1959)
Larry H. Lane
HELL'S BELLES(1969)
Larry Odell Lane
STRIPES(1981)
Lauri Lupino Lane
CARRY ON LOVING(1970, Brit.); GREAT WALTZ, THE(1972)
Laurie Lane
ARTISTS AND MODELS ABROAD(1938); HUNTED MEN(1938); TEXANS, THE(1938); TIP-OFF GIRLS(1938)
Lenita Lane
MURDER BY THE CLOCK(1931); IMITATION OF LIFE(1934); WE'RE RICH AGAIN(1934); GAY DECEPTION, THE(1935); WOMEN MUST DRESS(1935); GIRLS ON PROBATION(1938); MANHATTAN HEARTBEAT(1940); DEAD MEN TELL(1941); FOR BEAUTY'S SAKE(1941); CASTLE IN THE DESERT(1942); I WAS A COMMUNIST FOR THE F.B.I.(1951); MAD MAGICIAN, THE(1954); BAT, THE(1959)
Leona Lane
WOLF SONG(1929); DANTE'S INFERNO(1935)
Leone Lane
SATURDAY NIGHT KID, THE(1929)
Lillian Lane
CIMARRON(1931)
Linda Lane
CROSSTALK(1982, Aus.), w
Linnard Lane
STEAGLE, THE(1971)
Lloyd Lane
SERGEANT MURPHY(1938)
Lola Lane
FOX MOVIETONE FOLLIES(1929); GIRL FROM HAVANA, THE(1929); SPEAK-EASY(1929); COSTELLO CASE, THE(1930); GOOD NEWS(1930); LET'S GO PLA-CES(1930); EX-BAD BOY(1931); HELL BOUND(1931); TICKET TO CRIME(1934); ALIAS MARY DOW(1935); HIS NIGHT OUT(1935); MURDER ON A HONEY-MOON(1935); PORT OF LOST DREAMS(1935); PUBLIC STENOGRAPHER(1935); HOLLYWOOD HOTEL(1937); MARKED WOMAN(1937); SHEIK STEPS OUT, THE(1937); FOUR DAUGHTERS(1938); MR. CHUMP(1938); TORCHY BLANE IN PANAMA(1938); WHEN WERE YOU BORN?(1938); DAUGHTERS COURA-GEOUS(1939); FOUR WIVES(1939); CONVICTED WOMAN(1940); GANGS OF CHICA-GO(1940); GIRLS OF THE ROAD(1940); ZANZIBAR(1940); FOUR MOTHERS(1941); MYSTERY SHIP(1941); MISS V FROM MOSCOW(1942); LOST CANYON(1943); IDEN-TITY UNKNOWN(1945); STEPPIN' IN SOCIETY(1945); WHY GIRLS LEAVE HO-ME(1945); DEADLINE AT DAWN(1946); THEY MADE ME A KILLER(1946)
Misc. Talkies
BIG FIGHT, THE(1930); WOMAN CONDEMNED(1934); IN PARIS, A.W.O.L.(1936)
Louis Lane
NAME OF THE GAME IS KILL, THE(1968), makeup; CYCLE SAVAGES(1969), makeup; BIG FOOT(1973), makeup; WILD PARTY, THE(1975), makeup; SUPER-MAN(1978), makeup
Louise Lane
WHERE THE SIDEWALK ENDS(1950); WOMAN ON PIER 13, THE(1950); PLACE IN THE SUN, A(1951); SON OF PALEFACE(1952); REBEL WITHOUT A CAUSE(1955); DEAR BRIGETTE(1965)
Lovey Lane
TAKE MY LIFE(1942)
Lupino Lane
LOVE PARADE, THE(1929); BRIDE OF THE REGIMENT(1930); GOLDEN DAWN(1930); YELLOW MASK, THE(1930, Brit.); LOVE LIES(1931, Brit.), d; LOVE RACE, THE(1931, Brit.), d; NEVER TROUBLE TROUBLE(1931, Brit.), a, p&d; NO LADY(1931, Brit.), a, d, w; MAID OF THE MOUNTAINS(1932, Brit.), d, w; OLD SPANISH CUSTOMERS(1932, Brit.), d; WHY SAPS LEAVE HOME(1932, Brit.), p&d, w; LETTING IN THE SUNSHINE(1933, Brit.), d; MY OLD DUCHESS(1933, Brit.), d; SOUTHERN MAID, A(1933, Brit.); DEPUTY DRUMMER, THE(1935, Brit.); TRUST THE NAVY(1935, Brit.); WHO'S YOUR FATHER?(1935, Brit.), a, p, w; HOT NEWS(1936, Brit.); LAMBETH WALK, THE(1940, Brit.)
Silents
FRIENDLY HUSBAND, A(1923); ISN'T LIFE WONDERFUL(1924)
Misc. Silents
MAN IN POSSESSION, THE(1915, Brit.)
Magda Lane
Misc. Silents
LOCKED LIPS(1920)

Manda Lane
FIFTH AVENUE GIRL(1939)

Mara Lane
IT STARTED IN PARADISE(1952, Brit.); SOMETHING MONEY CAN'T BUY(1952, Brit.); TREASURE HUNT(1952, Brit.); AFFAIR IN MONTE CARLO(1953, Brit.); DECAMERON NIGHTS(1953, Brit.); SUSAN SLEPT HERE(1954); ANGELA(1955, Ital.); INNOCENTS IN PARIS(1955, Brit.)

Marc Lane [Marcello Masciocchi]
MURDER CLINIC, THE(1967, Ital./Fr.), ph

Mark Lane
EXECUTIVE ACTION(1973), w

Martin Lane
LOVE IN WAITING(1948, Brit.), w; TROUBLE IN THE AIR(1948, Brit.), w; SHE PLAYED WITH FIRE(1957, Brit.)

Maryon Lane
DANCE LITTLE LADY(1954, Brit.)

Maureen Lane
CLEOPATRA(1963); STATUE, THE(1971, Brit.)

Maurice Lane
GENTLEMEN MARRY BRUNETTES(1955); TECKMAN MYSTERY, THE(1955, Brit); NEXT TO NO TIME(1960, Brit.); PIRATES OF PENZANCE, THE(1983)

Michael Lane
WHO WAS THAT LADY?(1960); VALLEY OF THE DRAGONS(1961); HERO OF BABYLON(1963, Ital.); WAY WEST, THE(1967); STAY AWAY, JOE(1968); NEW CENTURIONS, THE(1972); MASTER GUNFIGHTER, THE(1975); STRYKER(1983, Phil.)

Mike Lane
HARDER THEY FALL, THE(1956); HELL CANYON OUTLAWS(1957); FRANKEN-STEIN 1970(1958); NAME FOR EVIL, A(1970)
Misc. Talkies
ZEBRA FORCE(1977)

Morgan Lane
GUNFIGHT AT THE O.K. CORRAL(1957); JOURNEY TO FREEDOM(1957)

Nellie Lane
Silents
CIRCUS DAYS(1923)

Nora Lane
COHENS AND KELLYS IN ATLANTIC CITY, THE(1929); SALLY(1929); MAN HUNTER, THE(1930); NIGHT WORK(1930); ONE HYSTERICAL NIGHT(1930); RAIN OR SHINE(1930); CISCO KID(1931); YOUNG SINNERS(1931); AFTER TOMOR-ROW(1932); CARELESS LADY(1932); DISORDERLY CONDUCT(1932); THIS SPORT-ING AGE(1932); TRIAL OF VIVIENNE WARE, THE(1932); JIMMY THE GENT(1934); OUTLAW DEPUTY, THE(1935); WESTERN FRONTIER(1935); SMALL TOWN GIRL(1936); BORDERLAND(1937); HOPALONG RIDES AGAIN(1937); CASSIDY OF BAR 20(1938); CITY OF CHANCE(1940); GENTLEMAN FROM ARIZONA, THE(1940); LIFE BEGINS FOR ANDY HARDY(1941); PUDDIN' HEAD(1941); SMALL TOWN DEB(1941); HEART OF THE RIO GRANDE(1942); JOAN OF OZARK(1942); UNDER-COVER MAN(1942); CHATTERBOX(1943); SECRETS OF THE UNDER-GROUND(1943); YOUNGEST PROFESSION, THE(1943); LAKE PLACID SERENADE(1944)
Misc. Talkies
WESTERN CODE(1932); SIX-GUN TRAIL(1938); TEXAS RENEGADES(1940)
Silents
JESSE JAMES(1927); GUN RUNNER, THE(1928); KIT CARSON(1928); NIGHT OF MYSTERY, A(1928); PIONEER SCOUT, THE(1928); LAWLESS LEGION, THE(1929); MASKED EMOTIONS(1929); SUNSET PASS(1929)
Misc. Silents
ARIZONA NIGHTS(1927); FLYING U RANCH, THE(1927); TEXAS TORNADO, THE(1928); MARQUIS PREFERRED(1929); SUNSET PASS(1929); LUCKY LAR-KIN(1930)

Pacho Lane
1984
RED DAWN(1984)

Pat Lane
MY SISTER EILEEN(1942); SABOTAGE SQUAD(1942); WIFE TAKES A FLYER, THE(1942); ONE DANGEROUS NIGHT(1943); THEY GOT ME COVERED(1943); SHE'S A SWEETHEART(1944); JOLSON STORY, THE(1946); SHE WROTE THE BOOK(1946); THRILL OF BRAZIL, THE(1946); DEAD RECKONING(1947); GUILT OF JANET AMES, THE(1947); JOHNNY O'CLOCK(1947); WILD HARVEST(1947); AP-POINTMENT WITH MURDER(1948); JOAN OF ARC(1948); CHICAGO DEAD-LINE(1949); SORROWFUL JONES(1949); UNDERCOVER MAN, THE(1949); DESERT LEGION(1953)

Paul Lane
1984
STREETS OF FIRE(1984)
Silents
IDLE HANDS(1921)

Paula Lane
LADIES MAN, THE(1961); MOVIE STAR, AMERICAN STYLE, OR, LSD I HATE YOU!(1966)

Priscilla Lane
VARSITY SHOW(1937); BROTHER RAT(1938); COWBOY FROM BROOKLYN(1938); FOUR DAUGHTERS(1938); LOVE, HONOR AND BEHAVE(1938); MEN ARE SUCH FOOLS(1938); DAUGHTERS COURAGEOUS(1939); DUST BE MY DESTINY(1939); FOUR WIVES(1939); ROARING TWENTIES, THE(1939); YES, MY DARLING DAUGHTER(1939); BROTHER RAT AND A BABY(1940); THREE CHEERS FOR THE IRISH(1940); BLUES IN THE NIGHT(1941); FOUR MOTHERS(1941); MILLION DOLLAR BABY(1941); SABOTEUR(1942); SILVER QUEEN(1942); MEANEST MAN IN THE WORLD, THE(1943); ARSENIC AND OLD LACE(1944); BODYGUARD(1948); FUN ON A WEEKEND(1979)

Richard Lane
CRASHING HOLLYWOOD(1937); DANGER PATROL(1937); FLIGHT FROM GLO-RY(1937); LIFE OF THE PARTY, THE(1937); NEW FACES OF 1937(1937); SATUR-DAY'S HEROES(1937); SUPER SLEUTH(1937); THERE GOES MY GIRL(1937); WISE GIRL(1937); YOU CAN'T BUY LUCK(1937); BLIND ALIBI(1938); BRINGING UP BABY(1938); CHARLIE CHAN IN HONOLULU(1938); EVERYBODY'S DOING IT(1938); EXPOSED(1938); GO CHASE YOURSELF(1938); HIS EXCITING NIGHT(1938); I'M FROM THE CITY(1938); LAST WARNING, THE(1938); MR. DOO-DLE KICKS OFF(1938); RADIO CITY REVELS(1938); THIS MARRIAGE BUSI-NESS(1938); DAY THE BOOKIES WEPT, THE(1939); ESCAPE, THE(1939); FOR LOVE OR MONEY(1939); HERO FOR A DAY(1939); IT COULD HAPPEN TO YOU(1939); MAIN STREET LAWYER(1939); MR. MOTO IN DANGER ISLAND(1939); MUTINY ON THE BLACKHAWK(1939); NEWS IS MADE AT NIGHT(1939); NICK CARTER, MASTER DETECTIVE(1939); STRONGER THAN DESIRE(1939); UNEXPECTED FA-THER(1939); UNION PACIFIC(1939); BISCUIT EATER, THE(1940); BOOM TOWN(1940); BRIDE WORE CRUTCHES, THE(1940); BROTHER ORCHID(1940); CITY OF CHANCE(1940); FREE, BLONDE AND 21(1940); HIRED WIFE(1940); MAR-GIE(1940); SANDY IS A LADY(1940); SUED FOR LIBEL(1940); TWO GIRLS ON BROADWAY(1940); YESTERDAY'S HEROES(1940); YOUTH WILL BE SER-VED(1940); CONFESSIONS OF BOSTON BLACKIE(1941); COWBOY AND THE BLONDE, THE(1941); FOR BEAUTY'S SAKE(1941); GIRL, A GUY AND A GOB, A(1941); HELLZAPOPPIN'(1941); I WANTED WINGS(1941); MAN AT LARGE(1941); MEET BOSTON BLACKIE(1941); MEET THE CHUMP(1941); NAVY BLUES(1941); PENALTY, THE(1941); RIDE, KELLY, RIDE(1941); RIDERS OF THE PURPLE SAGE(1941); ROMANCE OF THE RIO GRANDE(1941); SAN ANTONIO ROSE(1941); SUNNY(1941); TIGHT SHOES(1941); TIME OUT FOR RHYTHM(1941); A-HAUNTING WE WILL GO(1942); ALIAS BOSTON BLACKIE(1942); ARABIAN NIGHTS(1942); BOSTON BLACKIE GOES HOLLYWOOD(1942); BUTCH MINDS THE BABY(1942); DR. BROADWAY(1942); DRUMS OF THE CONGO(1942); RIDE 'EM COWBOY(1942); TIME TO KILL(1942); TO THE SHORES OF TRIPOLI(1942); AFTER MIDNIGHT WITH BOSTON BLACKIE(1943); CHANCE OF A LIFETIME, THE(1943); CORVETTE K-225(1943); CRAZY HOUSE(1943); FIRED WIFE(1943); GUNG HO!(1943); IT AIN'T HAY(1943); SWING YOUR PARTNER(1943); THANK YOUR LUCKY STARS(1943); BERMUDA MYSTERY(1944); BOWERY TO BROADWAY(1944); BRAZIL(1944); LOUISIANA HAYRIDE(1944); MR. WINKLE GOES TO WAR(1944); ONE MYSTERI-OUS NIGHT(1944); SECRET COMMAND(1944); SLIGHTLY TERRIFIC(1944); TAKE IT BIG(1944); WAVE, A WAC AND A MARINE, A(1944); BOSTON BLACKIE BOOKED ON SUSPICION(1945); BOSTON BLACKIE'S RENDEZVOUS(1945); BULLFIGHTERS, THE(1945); HERE COME THE CO-EDS(1945); TWO O'CLOCK COURAGE(1945); WHAT A BLONDE(1945); BOSTON BLACKIE AND THE LAW(1946); CLOSE CALL FOR BOSTON BLACKIE, A(1946); GIRL ON THE SPOT(1946); PHANTOM THIEF, THE(1946); SIOUX CITY SUE(1946); TALK ABOUT A LADY(1946); DEVIL SHIP(1947); HIT PARADE OF 1947(1947); OUT OF THE BLUE(1947); SONG OF SCHEHERAZA-DE(1947); BABE RUTH STORY, THE(1948); CREEPER, THE(1948); RETURN OF THE WHISTLER, THE(1948); TENTH AVENUE ANGEL(1948); TRAPPED BY BOSTON BLACKIE(1948); BIG WHEEL, THE(1949); BOSTON BLACKIE'S CHINESE VEN-TURE(1949); MISS MINK OF 1949(1949); TAKE ME OUT TO THE BALL GAME(1949); THERE'S A GIRL IN MY HEART(1949); ADMIRAL WAS A LADY, THE(1950); EVERYBODY'S DANCIN'(1950); JACKIE ROBINSON STORY, THE(1950); I CAN GET IT FOR YOU WHOLESALE(1951); YOU CAN'T SEE 'ROUND CORNERS(1969, Aus.), w; ...ALL THE MARBLES(1981), ed

Richrd Lane
OUTCASTS OF POKER FLAT, THE(1937)

Roger Lane
JUD(1971)

Rosemary Lane
HOLLYWOOD HOTEL(1937); VARSITY SHOW(1937); FOUR DAUGHTERS(1938); GOLD DIGGERS IN PARIS(1938); BLACKWELL'S ISLAND(1939); DAUGHTERS COURAGEOUS(1939); FOUR WIVES(1939); OKLAHOMA KID, THE(1939); RETURN OF DR. X, THE(1939); ALWAYS A BRIDE(1940); ANGEL FROM TEXAS, AN(1940); BOYS FROM SYRACUSE(1940); LADIES MUST LIVE(1940); FOUR MOTHERS(1941); TIME OUT FOR RHYTHM(1941); ALL BY MYSELF(1943); CHATTERBOX(1943); HARVEST MELODY(1943); TROCADERO(1944)
Misc. Talkies
SING ME A SONG OF TEXAS(1945)

Ruby Lane
GENE KRUPA STORY, THE(1959)

Rusdi Lane
DAMIEN–OMEN II(1978)

Russell Lane
TRIAL OF BILLY JACK, THE(1974)

Rusty Lane
HOUSE ON 92ND STREET, THE(1945); BEYOND A REASONABLE DOUBT(1956); BIGGER THAN LIFE(1956); HARDER THEY FALL, THE(1956); FURY AT SHOW-DOWN(1957); JOHNNY TREMAIN(1957); PORTLAND EXPOSE(1957); SHADOW ON THE WINDOW, THE(1957); DAMN CITIZEN(1958); I WANT TO LIVE!(1958); PARTY GIRL(1958); RAWHIDE TRAIL, THE(1958); FATE IS THE HUNTER(1964); NEW INTERNS, THE(1964); YOUNGBLOOD HAWKE(1964)
Misc. Talkies
RAWHIDE TRAIL, THE(1950)

Sarah Lane
I SAW WHAT YOU DID(1965)

Scott Lane
SAFE AT HOME(1962); PHANTOM OF THE PARADISE(1974)

Scott E. Lane
KLANSMAN, THE(1974)

Scott Edmund Lane
SEED OF INNOCENCE(1980)

Serpa Lane
BEAST, THE(1975, Fr.)

Steve Lane
HOW TO SAVE A MARRIAGE–AND RUIN YOUR LIFE(1968), make up

Stewart Lane
PUPPET ON A CHAIN(1971, Brit.)

Teddy Lane
MAYTIME IN MAYFAIR(1952, Brit.)

Tim E. Lane
SOD SISTERS(1969)

Tom Lane
MIRACULOUS JOURNEY(1948); COTTON COMES TO HARLEM(1970)

Tommy Lane
SHAFT(1971); GANJA AND HESS(1973); LIVE AND LET DIE(1973, Brit.); SHA-MUS(1973); BLUE SKIES AGAIN(1983); EUREKA(1983, Brit.)

Tracey Lane
SERGEANT MURPHY(1938)

Tracy Lane
MAN FROM HELL, THE(1934); MELODY TRAIL(1935); COMIN' ROUND THE MOUNTAIN(1936); LAWLESS NINETIES, THE(1936)

Trudy Lane
CHINA SYNDROME, THE(1979)
Vicky Lane
CISCO KID RETURNS, THE(1945); JUNGLE CAPTIVE(1945)
Violet Lane
GOOD COMPANIONS(1933, Brit.)
Wade Lane
PLUNDERERS OF PAINTED FLATS(1959)
Ward Lane
LAST OUTPOST, THE(1935); MAID OF SALEM(1937)
Yancie Lane
Misc. Talkies
HAWK, THE(1935); TRAIL OF THE HAWK(1935)
Willa Mae Lane
POCOMANIA(1939)
Lane-Balliff
SQUATTER'S DAUGHTER(1933, Aus.)
John Lanenz
TARZAN AND THE MERMAIDS(1948)
Eric Laneuville
OMEGA MAN, THE(1971); BLACK BELT JONES(1974); SHOOT IT: BLACK, SHOOT IT: BLUE(1974); FORCE OF ONE, A(1979); BALTIMORE BULLET, THE(1980); BACK ROADS(1981)
Ruth Laney
AMERICAN WIFE, AN(1965, Ital.); RUN FOR YOUR WIFE(1966, Fr./Ital.)
Sidney Lanfield
BIG TIME(1929), w; CHEER UP AND SMILE(1930), d; HAPPY DAYS(1930), w; HUSH MONEY(1931), d, w; THREE GIRLS LOST(1931), d; DANCE TEAM(1932), d; HAT CHECK GIRL(1932), d; SOCIETY GIRL(1932), d; BROADWAY BAD(1933), d; LAST GENTLEMAN, THE(1934), d; MOULIN ROUGE(1934), d; HOLD'EM YALE(1935), d; RED SALUTE(1935), d; HALF ANGEL(1936), d; KING OF BURLESQUE(1936), d; ONE IN A MILLION(1936), d; SING, BABY, SING(1936), d; LOVE AND HISSES(1937), d; THIN ICE(1937), d; WAKE UP AND LIVE(1937), d; ALWAYS GOODBYE(1938), d; HOUND OF THE BASKERVILLES, THE(1939), d; SECOND FIDDLE(1939), d; SWANEE RIVER(1939), d; YOU'LL NEVER GET RICH(1941), d; LADY HAS PLANS, THE(1942), d; MY FAVORITE BLONDE(1942), d; LET'S FACE IT(1943), d; MEANEST MAN IN THE WORLD, THE(1943), d; STANDING ROOM ONLY(1944), d; BRING ON THE GIRLS(1945), d; WELL-GROOMED BRIDE, THE(1946), d; TROUBLE WITH WOMEN, THE(1947), d; WHERE THERE'S LIFE(1947), d; STATION WEST(1948), d; SORROWFUL JONES(1949), d; FOLLOW THE SUN(1951), d; LEMON DROP KID, THE(1951), d; SKIRTS AHOY!(1952), d
Silents
DON'T MARRY(1928), w
Damien Lanfranchi
DAY FOR NIGHT(1973, Fr.), art d
Mario Lanfranchi
LUCIANO(1963, Ital.), p; EMPTY CANVAS, THE(1964, Fr./Ital.); DEATH SENTENCE(1967, Ital.), p,d&w; NAVAJO JOE(1967, Ital./Span.); LA TRAVIATA(1968, Ital.), d&w
Tony Lanfranchi
GRAND PRIX(1966)
Al Lang
GOLDEN BOY(1939)
Albert Lang
Misc. Silents
YELLOW TRAFFIC, THE(1914)
Andre Lang
END OF THE WORLD, THE(1930, Fr.), w; LES MISERABLES(1936, Fr.), w
Anthony Lang
SARABAND(1949, Brit.); TONY DRAWS A HORSE(1951, Brit.); SKID KIDS(1953, Brit.)
Archie Lang
GOING BERSERK(1983)
Barbara Lang
HOUSE OF NUMBERS(1957); PARTY GIRL(1958)
Caroline Lang
1984
L'ARGENT(1984, Fr./Switz.)
Charles Lang
TRUE TO LIFE(1943), ph; SHOPWORN ANGEL, THE(1928), ph; INNOCENTS OF PARIS(1929), ph; ANYBODY'S WOMAN(1930), ph; BEHIND THE MAKEUP(1930), ph; FOR THE DEFENSE(1930), ph; LIGHT OF WESTERN STARS, THE(1930), ph; SARAH AND SON(1930), ph; SEVEN DAYS LEAVE(1930), ph; SHADOW OF THE LAW(1930), ph; STREET OF CHANCE(1930), ph; TOM SAWYER(1930), ph; CAUGHT(1931), ph; MAGNIFICENT LIE(1931), ph; NEWLY RICH(1931), ph; ONCE A LADY(1931), ph; RIGHT TO LOVE, THE(1931), ph; UNFAITHFUL(1931), ph; VICE SQUAD, THE(1931), ph; DEVIL AND THE DEEP(1932), ph; FAREWELL TO ARMS, A(1932), ph; NO ONE MAN(1932), ph; THUNDER BELOW(1932), ph; TOMORROW AND TOMORROW(1932), ph; BEDTIME STORY, A(1933), ph; CRADLE SONG(1933), ph; GAMBLING SHIP(1933), ph; SHE DONE HIM WRONG(1933), ph; WAY TO LOVE, THE(1933), ph; DEATH TAKES A HOLIDAY(1934), ph; MRS. WIGGS OF THE CABBAGE PATCH(1934), ph; SHE LOVES ME NOT(1934), ph; WE'RE NOT DRESSING(1934), ph; LIVES OF A BENGAL LANCER(1935), ph; MISSISSIPPI(1935), ph; PETER IBBETSON(1935), ph; DESIRE(1936), ph; ANGEL(1937), ph; TOVARICH(1937), ph; DR. RHYTHM(1938), ph; CAT AND THE CANARY, THE(1939), ph; GRACIE ALLEN MURDER CASE(1939), ph; MIDNIGHT(1939), ph; ARISE, MY LOVE(1940), ph; BUCK BENNY RIDES AGAIN(1940), ph; GHOST BREAKERS, THE(1940), ph; ONE CROWDED NIGHT(1940); WILDCAT BUS(1940); WOMEN WITHOUT NAMES(1940), ph; HIT THE ROAD(1941); KEEP 'EM FLYING(1941); NEVER GIVE A SUCKER AN EVEN BREAK(1941); NOTHING BUT THE TRUTH(1941), ph; SAN ANTONIO ROSE(1941); SIX LESSONS FROM MADAME LA ZONGA(1941); SKYLARK(1941), ph; SUNDOWN(1941), ph; WHERE DID YOU GET THAT GIRL?(1941), ph; ARE HUSBANDS NECESSARY?(1942), ph; BOMBAY CLIPPER(1942); FOREST RANGERS, THE(1942), ph; GHOST AND MRS. MUIR, THE(1942), ph; LADY HAS PLANS, THE(1942), ph; SECRET ENEMIES(1942); STRICTLY IN THE GROOVE(1942); GUADALCANAL DIARY(1943); SO PROUDLY WE HAIL(1943), ph; TRUCK BUSTERS(1943); CRIME BY NIGHT(1944); HERE COME THE WAVES(1944), ph; I LOVE A SOLDIER(1944); LAST RIDE, THE(1944); ROGER TOUHY, GANGSTER!(1944), ph; STANDING ROOM ONLY(1944), ph; TAMPICO(1944); UNINVITED, THE(1944), ph; WING AND A PRAYER(1944), ph; DESERT FURY(1947), ph; HE

WALKED BY NIGHT(1948); NIGHT WIND(1948); EASY LIVING(1949); WOLF HUNTERS, THE(1949); CALL OF THE KLONDIKE(1950), w; KILLER SHARK(1950), a, w; SOLDIERS THREE(1951); BIG HEAT, THE(1953), ph; BLADES OF THE MUSKETEERS(1953); SALOME(1953), ph; IT SHOULD HAPPEN TO YOU(1954), ph; PHFFFT!(1954), ph; FEMALE ON THE BEACH(1955), ph; MAGNIFICENT MATADOR, THE(1955), w; MAN FROM LARAMIE, THE(1955), ph; AUTUMN LEAVES(1956), ph; SOLID GOLD CADILLAC, THE(1956), ph; MATCHMAKER, THE(1958), ph; DESIRE IN THE DUST(1960), w; LOUISIANA HUSSY(1960), w; CRITIC'S CHOICE(1963), ph; WHEELER DEALERS, THE(1963), ph; SEX AND THE SINGLE GIRL(1964), ph; INSIDE DAISY CLOVER(1965), ph; HOW TO STEAL A MILLION(1966), ph; NOT WITH MY WIFE, YOU DON'T!(1966), ph; FLIM-FLAM MAN, THE(1967), ph; HOTEL(1967), ph; WAIT UNTIL DARK(1967), ph; FLEA IN HER EAR, A(1968, Fr.), ph; CACTUS FLOWER(1969), ph; HOW TO COMMIT MARRIAGE(1969), ph; STALKING MOON, THE(1969), ph; WAR OF THE WIZARDS(1983, Taiwan)
Silents
NIGHT PATROL, THE(1926), ph
Charles Lang, Jr.
SOULS AT SEA(1937), ph; SPAWN OF THE NORTH(1938), ph; YOU AND ME(1938), ph; ZAZA(1939), ph; DANCING ON A DIME(1940), ph; SHEPHERD OF THE HILLS, THE(1941), ph; NO TIME FOR LOVE(1943), ph; PRACTICALLY YOURS(1944), ph; MISS SUSIE SLAGLE'S(1945), ph; STORK CLUB, THE(1945), ph; BLUE SKIES(1946), ph; CROSS MY HEART(1946), ph; SUDDEN FEAR(1952), ph; SABRINA(1954), ph; QUEEN BEE(1955), ph; RAINMAKER, THE(1956), ph; DECISION AT SUNDOWN(1957), w; GUNFIGHT AT THE O.K. CORRAL(1957), ph; LOVING YOU(1957), ph; SEPARATE TABLES(1958), ph; SOME LIKE IT HOT(1959), ph; FACTS OF LIFE, THE(1960), ph; MAGNIFICENT SEVEN, THE(1960), ph; STRANGERS WHEN WE MEET(1960), ph; BLUE HAWAII(1961), ph; ONE-EYED JACKS(1961), ph; SUMMER AND SMOKE(1961), ph; GIRL NAMED TAMIRO, A(1962), ph; HOW THE WEST WAS WON(1962), ph; CHARADE(1963), ph; FATHER GOOSE(1964), ph; PARIS WHEN IT SIZZLES(1964), ph
Charles B. Lang
SEPTEMBER AFFAIR(1950), ph; BIG CARNIVAL, THE(1951), ph; DOCTORS' WIVES(1971), ph; LOVE MACHINE, THE,(1971), ph; BUTTERFLIES ARE FREE(1972), ph; FORTY CARATS(1973), ph
Charles B. Lang, Jr.
WHERE THERE'S LIFE(1947), ph; FOREIGN AFFAIR, A(1948), ph; MISS TATLOCK'S MILLIONS(1948), ph; MY OWN TRUE LOVE(1948), ph; GREAT LOVER, THE(1949), ph; ROPE OF SAND(1949), ph; COPPER CANYON(1950), ph; FANCY PANTS(1950), ph; BRANDED(1951), ph; MATING SEASON, THE(1951), ph; PEKING EXPRESS(1951), ph; RED MOUNTAIN(1951), ph; AARON SLICK FROM PUNKIN CRICK(1952), ph; ATOMIC CITY, THE(1952), ph; WILD IS THE WIND(1957), ph; LAST TRAIN FROM GUN HILL(1959), ph
Christa Lang
UPPER HAND, THE(1967, Fr./Ital./Ger.); CHAMPAGNE MURDERS, THE(1968, Fr.); CHARRO(1969); DEAD PIGEON ON BEETHOVEN STREET(1972, Ger.); WHAT'S UP, DOC?(1972); NICKELODEON(1976); WHITE DOG(1982)
Christiane Lang
CHRONICLE OF ANNA MAGDALENA BACH(1968, Ital., Ger.)
Cindy Lang
CHEAP DETECTIVE, THE(1978)
Cora Lang
TOY WIFE, THE(1938)
David Lang
NORTHWEST RANGERS(1942), w; YANK ON THE BURMA ROAD, A(1942), w; ONE EXCITING NIGHT(1945), w; PEOPLE ARE FUNNY(1945), w; TRAFFIC IN CRIME(1946), w; JUNGLE FLIGHT(1947), w; WEB OF DANGER, THE(1947), w; FLAXY MARTIN(1949), w; CHAIN OF CIRCUMSTANCE(1951), w; AMBUSH AT TOMAHAWK GAP(1953), w; NEBRASKAN, THE(1953), w; BLACK HORSE CANYON(1954), w; MASSACRE CANYON(1954), w; OUTLAW STALLION, THE(1954), w; APACHE AMBUSH(1955), w; WYOMING RENEGADES(1955), w; FURY AT GUNSIGHT PASS(1956), w; SCREAMING EAGLES(1956), w; SECRET OF TREASURE MOUNTAIN(1956), w; BUCKSKIN LADY, THE(1957), w; HELLCATS OF THE NAVY(1957), w; HIRED GUN, THE(1957), w; PHANTOM STAGECOACH, THE(1957), w; KLUTE(1971), p
David A. Lang
QUEEN OF BURLESQUE(1946), w
Don Lang
6.5 SPECIAL(1958, Brit.)
Doreen Lang
WRONG MAN, THE(1956); WILD IN THE COUNTRY(1961); CABINET OF CALIGARI, THE(1962); GROUP, THE(1966)
Evelyn Lang [Marilyn Chambers]
OWL AND THE PUSSYCAT, THE(1970)
Fiesta Mei Lang
STAND UP VIRGIN SOLDIERS(1977, Brit.)
Freddie Lang
SILENCE OF THE NORTH(1981, Can.)
Frederick Lang
SEVEN SAMURAI, THE(1956, Jap.), titles
Freeman Lang
HONG KONG NIGHTS(1935)
Fritz Lang
M(1933, Ger.), d, w; LILIOM(1935, Fr.), d, w; FURY(1936), d, w; YOU ONLY LIVE ONCE(1937), d; YOU AND ME(1938), p&d; RETURN OF FRANK JAMES, THE(1940), d; MAN HUNT(1941), d; WESTERN UNION(1941), d; MOONTIDE(1942), d; HANGMEN ALSO DIE(1943), d, w; TESTAMENT OF DR. MABUSE(1943, Ger.), p&d, w; MINISTRY OF FEAR(1945), d; SCARLET STREET(1945), p&d; WOMAN IN THE WINDOW, THE(1945), d; CLOAK AND DAGGER(1946), d; SECRET BEYOND THE DOOR, THE(1948), p&d; AMERICAN GUERRILLA IN THE PHILIPPINES, AN(1950), d; HOUSE BY THE RIVER(1950), d; M(1951), w; CLASH BY NIGHT(1952), d; RANCHO NOTORIOUS(1952), d; BIG HEAT, THE(1953), d; BLUE GARDENIA, THE(1953), d; HUMAN DESIRE(1954), d; MOONFLEET(1955), d; BEYOND A REASONABLE DOUBT(1956), d; WHILE THE CITY SLEEPS(1956), d; JOURNEY TO THE LOST CITY(1960, Ger./Fr./Ital.), d, w; THOUSAND EYES OF DR. MABUSE, THE(1960, Fr./Ital./Ger.), p&d, w; CONTEMPT(1963, Fr./Ital.)
Silents
KRIEMHILD'S REVENGE(1924, Ger.), d; SIEGFRIED(1924, Ger.), d; METROPOLIS(1927, Ger.), d, w; SPIES(1929, Ger.), p&d, w; WOMAN ON THE MOON, THE(1929, Ger.), p&d

Misc. Silents
HILDE WARREN AND DEATH(1916, Ger.); GOLDEN SEA, THE(1919, Ger.), d; HALFBREED(1919, Ger.), d; HARAKIRI(1919, Ger.), d; MASTER OF LOVE, THE(1919, Ger.), d; MOVING IMAGE, THE(1920, Ger.), d; DESTINY(1921, Ger.), d; FOUR AROUND THE WOMAN(1921, Ger.), d

Gordon Lang
BOYS IN BROWN(1949, Brit.), ph; IT'S NOT CRICKET(1949, Brit.), ph; MY BROTHER'S KEEPER(1949, Brit.), ph; HA' PENNY BREEZE(1950, Brit.), ph; TALE OF FIVE WOMEN, A(1951, Brit.), ph; ARMCHAIR DETECTIVE, THE(1952, Brit.), ph; DISTANT TRUMPET(1952, Brit.), ph; I'M A STRANGER(1952, Brit.), ph; INNOCENTS IN PARIS(1955, Brit.), ph; DOG AND THE DIAMONDS, THE(1962, Brit.), ph

Harold Lang
CAIRO ROAD(1950, Brit.); CALLING BULLDOG DRUMMOND(1951, Brit.); CLOUDBURST(1952, Brit.); DEAD ON COURSE(1952, Brit.); FRANCHISE AFFAIR, THE(1952, Brit.); IT STARTED IN PARADISE(1952, Brit.); SPIDER AND THE FLY, THE(1952, Brit.); DAY TO REMEMBER, A(1953, Brit.); FOLLY TO BE WISE(1953, Brit.); GREAT GILBERT AND SULLIVAN, THE(1953, Brit.); LONG MEMORY, THE(1953, Brit.); SO LITTLE TIME(1953, Brit.); TERROR STREET(1953); ADVENTURE IN THE HOPFIELDS(1954, Brit.); BLACKOUT(1954, Brit.); DANCE LITTLE LADY(1954, Brit.); LAUGHING ANNE(1954, Brit./U.S.); PASSING STRANGER, THE(1954, Brit.); SAINT'S GIRL FRIDAY, THE(1954, Brit.); STAR OF MY NIGHT(1954, Brit.); INTRUDER, THE(1955, Brit.); IT'S A WONDERFUL WORLD(1956, Brit.); THE CREEPING UNKNOWN(1956, Brit.); FLESH IS WEAK, THE(1957, Brit.); MEN OF SHERWOOD FOREST(1957, Brit.); BETRAYAL, THE(1958, Brit.); CARVE HER NAME WITH PRIDE(1958, Brit.); CHAIN OF EVENTS(1958, Brit.); LINKS OF JUSTICE(1958); MAN WITH A GUN(1958, Brit.); PARANOIAC(1963, Brit.); DR. TERROR'S HOUSE OF HORRORS(1965, Brit.); PSYCHOPATH, THE(1966, Brit.); TWO GENTLEMEN SHARING(1969, Brit.)

Harry Lang
BAD BOY(1939); SING FOR YOUR SUPPER(1941); CAPTAIN TUGBOAT ANNIE(1945); ABBOTT AND COSTELLO GO TO MARS(1953); GOLDEN BLADE, THE(1953)

Helen Lang
REVENGE OF THE CHEERLEADERS(1976)

Howard H. Lang
Misc. Talkies
JUDGMENT BOOK, THE(1935)

Howard Lang
THIS DAY AND AGE(1933); BORN TO BE BAD(1934); HOUSE OF DANGER(1934); WITCHING HOUR, THE(1934); MYSTERY WOMAN(1935); UNDERCOVER AGENT(1935, Brit.); CALL OF THE PRAIRIE(1936); HERE'S FLASH CASEY(1937); NAVY SPY(1937); PRISONER OF ZENDA, THE(1937); MARIE ANTOINETTE(1938); MORTAL STORM, THE(1940); THIRD FINGER, LEFT HAND(1940); FLOATING DUTCHMAN, THE(1953, Brit.); DEVIL'S HARBOR(1954, Brit.); BLONDE BLACKMAILER(1955, Brit.); HIDEOUT, THE(1956, Brit.); 23 PACES TO BAKER STREET(1956); BEN HUR(1959); INNOCENT MEETING(1959, Brit.); MAN ACCUSED(1959); WOMAN'S TEMPTATION, A(1959, Brit.); DATE AT MIDNIGHT(1960, Brit.); NIGHT TRAIN FOR INVERNESS(1960, Brit.); GORGO(1961, Brit.); CORRIDORS OF BLOOD(1962, Brit.); OPERATION SNATCH(1962, Brit.); HAUNTING, THE(1963); NOTHING BUT THE BEST(1964, Brit.); RUNAWAY, THE(1964, Brit.); HE WHO RIDES A TIGER(1966, Brit.); PERFECT FRIDAY(1970, Brit.); MACBETH(1971, Brit.); 10 RILLINGTON PLACE(1971, Brit.)
Silents
PEACOCK ALLEY(1922)
Misc. Silents
CALL OF THE SEA, THE(1915); VILLAGE HOMESTEAD, THE(1915); ROMANTIC ADVENTURESS, A(1920)

Iris Lang
MISS LONDON LTD.(1943, Brit.); GIVE US THE MOON(1944, Brit.); TIME FLIES(1944, Brit.)

Israel Lang
WHERE'S POPPA?(1970)

Jeffries Lang
ALONE AGAINST ROME(1963, Ital.)

Jennings Lang
CONCORDE, THE–AIRPORT '79(, p, w; GREAT NORTHFIELD, MINNESOTA RAID, THE(1972), p; SWASHBUCKLER(1976), p; ROLLERCOASTER(1977), p; NUNZIO(1978), p; REAL LIFE(1979); LITTLE MISS MARKER(1980), p; NUDE BOMB, THE(1980), p; STING II, THE(1983), p

Jo-Anne Lang
SHAPE OF THINGS TO COME, THE(1979, Can.)

John Lang
WEE GEORDIE(1956, Brit.)

John Stevenson Lang
HIGH TIDE AT NOON(1957, Brit.); MAD LITTLE ISLAND(1958, Brit.)

Johnny Lang
I KILLED THAT MAN(1942), md

Judith Lang
COUNT YORGA, VAMPIRE(1970)
1984
SECRET PLACES(1984, Brit.), art d

Judy Lang
STRANGERS WHEN WE MEET(1960); TRIP, THE(1967)

Julia Lang
RED SHOES, THE(1948, Brit.); DR. MORELLE–THE CASE OF THE MISSING HEIRESS(1949, Brit.); STOP PRESS GIRL(1949, Brit.); UNDER CAPRICORN(1949)

June Lang
MUSIC IN THE AIR(1934); NOW I'LL TELL(1934); BONNIE SCOTLAND(1935); CAPTAIN JANUARY(1935); COUNTRY DOCTOR, THE(1936); EVERY SATURDAY NIGHT(1936); ROAD TO GLORY, THE(1936); WHITE HUNTER(1936); ALI BABA GOES TO TOWN(1937); NANCY STEELE IS MISSING(1937); WEE WILLIE WINKIE(1937); INTERNATIONAL SETTLEMENT(1938); MEET THE GIRLS(1938); ONE WILD NIGHT(1938); CAPTAIN FURY(1939); FOR LOVE OR MONEY(1939); FORGED PASSPORT(1939); INSIDE INFORMATION(1939); ZENOBIA(1939); CONVICTED WOMAN(1940); ISLE OF DESTINY(1940); DEADLY GAME, THE(1941); REDHEAD(1941); CITY OF SILENT MEN(1942); FOOTLIGHT SERENADE(1942); TOO MANY WOMEN(1942); FLESH AND FANTASY(1943); STAGE DOOR CANTEEN(1943); UP IN ARMS(1944); LIGHTHOUSE(1947)

Misc. Talkies
THREE OF A KIND(1944)

Karin Lang
OH, WHAT A NIGHT(1944); HOLLYWOOD AND VINE(1945)

Katherine Lang
MR. BELVEDERE GOES TO COLLEGE(1949)

Kathryn Lang
FLAME OF YOUTH(1949)

Kelly Lang
SKATETOWN, U.S.A.(1979)

Kenneth Lang
PRINCE OF FOXES(1949)

Lavinia Lang
PRIME OF MISS JEAN BRODIE, THE(1969, Brit.)

Lester Lang
HOUSE OF SECRETS(1929), ph

Lew Lang
Silents
AIR MAIL PILOT, THE(1928), ph

Lotte Lang
EMBEZZLED HEAVEN(1959,Ger.); HOUSE OF THE THREE GIRLS, THE(1961, Aust.); VIENNA WALTZES(1961, Aust.)

Matheson Lang
CHINESE BUNGALOW, THE(1930, Brit.); CARNIVAL(1931, Brit.), a, w; CHANNEL CROSSING(1934, Brit.); GREAT DEFENDER, THE(1934, Brit.); LITTLE FRIEND(1934, Brit.); DRAKE THE PIRATE(1935, Brit.); REGAL CAVALCADE(1935, Brit.); CARDINAL, THE(1936, Brit.)
Silents
MERCHANT OF VENICE, THE(1916, Brit.); WARE CASE, THE(1917, Brit.); MR. WU(1919, Brit.); SLAVES OF DESTINY(1924, Brit.); QUALIFIED ADVENTURER, THE(1925, Brit.); CHINESE BUNGALOW, THE(1926, Brit.)
Misc. Silents
HOUSE OPPOSITE, THE(1917, Brit.); VICTORY AND PEACE(1918, Brit.); CARNIVAL(1921, Brit.); DICK TURPIN'S RIDE TO YORK(1922, Brit.); ROMANCE OF OLD BAGDAD, A(1922, Brit.); GUY FAWKES(1923, Brit.); HELL SHIP, THE(1923, Swed.); WANDERING JEW, THE(1923, Brit.); HENRY, KING OF NAVARRE(1924, Brit.); PORT OF LOST SOULS(1924, Brit.); BEYOND THE VEIL(1925, Brit.); CHINESE BUNGALOW, THE(1926, Brit.); ISLAND OF DESPAIR, THE(1926, Brit.); KING'S HIGHWAY, THE(1927, Brit.); BLUE PETER, THE(1928, Brit.); SCARLET DAREDEVIL, THE(1928, Brit.)

Melvin Lang
DOOMED TO DIE(1940); DURANGO KID, THE(1940); QUEEN OF THE YUKON(1940); BOSS OF BULLION CITY(1941); MEET JOHN DOE(1941)

Michel Lang
GIFT, THE(1983, Fr./Ital.), d&w

Michl Lang
AREN'T WE WONDERFUL?(1959, Ger.)

Otto Lang
HELL'S ISLAND(1930); CALL NORTHSIDE 777(1948), p; FIVE FINGERS(1952), p; WHITE WITCH DOCTOR(1953), p
Silents
SECOND FIDDLE(1923)

Pat Lang
WAY WE LIVE, THE(1946, Brit.)

Paul Lang
ONLY THING YOU KNOW, THE(1971, Can.), ph

Perry Lang
ALLIGATOR(1980); BIG RED ONE, THE(1980); HEARSE, THE(1980); BODY AND SOUL(1981); CATTLE ANNIE AND LITTLE BRITCHES(1981); T.A.G.: THE ASSASSINATION GAME(1982); O'HARA'S WIFE(1983); SPRING BREAK(1983)
1984
SAHARA(1984)
Misc. Talkies
GREAT RIDE, THE(1978); GIRLS NEXT DOOR, THE(1979)

Peter Lang
DIAMOND SAFARI(1958), ph
Silents
PRIDE OF JENNICO, THE(1914); CLIMBERS, THE(1915); AUCTION BLOCK, THE(1917)
Misc. Silents
PORT OF DOOM, THE(1913); DISTRICT ATTORNEY, THE(1915); DAWN OF LOVE, THE(1916)

Philip J. Lang
NIGHT THEY RAIDED MINSKY'S, THE(1968), md

Richard Lang
CHANGE OF SEASONS, A(1980), d; MOUNTAIN MEN, THE(1980), d
Misc. Silents
CODE OF THE NORTHWEST(1926)

Robert Lang
SCHOOL FOR SECRETS(1946, Brit.); DARK MAN, THE(1951, Brit.); HAVING A WILD WEEKEND(1965, Brit.); OTHELLO(1965, Brit.); INTERLUDE(1968, Brit.); WALK WITH LOVE AND DEATH, A(1969); DANCE OF DEATH, THE(1971, Brit.); HOUSE THAT DRIPPED BLOOD, THE(1971, Brit.); SAVAGE MESSIAH(1972, Brit.); MACKINTOSH MAN, THE(1973, Brit.); NIGHT WATCH(1973, Brit.); SHOUT AT THE DEVIL(1976, Brit.); UNCLE VANYA(1977, Brit.); MEDUSA TOUCH, THE(1978, Brit.); GREAT TRAIN ROBBERY, THE(1979, Brit.); RUNNERS(1983, Brit.)

Rosemary Lang
SARABAND(1949, Brit.)

Rupert Lang
OPERATION BULLSHINE(1963, Brit.), w

Sandy Lang
SILENT RAGE(1982)

Stefy Lang
SAUL AND DAVID(1968, Ital./Span.)

Stephen Lang
WAR AND PEACE(1956, Ital./U.S.)

Stevenson Lang
ROB ROY, THE HIGHLAND ROGUE(1954, Brit.); TROUBLE IN THE GLEN(1954, Brit.); BEN HUR(1959); SNAKE WOMAN, THE(1961, Brit.)

Susan Lang
SHE MARRIED HER BOSS(1935)
Valentina Lang
8 ½(1963, Ital.)
Veronica Lang
TOMCAT, THE(1968, Brit.); DON'S PARTY(1976, Aus.); CLINIC, THE(1983, Aus.)
Walter Lang
BROTHERS(1930), d; COCK O' THE WALK(1930), d; COSTELLO CASE, THE(1930), d; HELLO SISTER(1930), d; COMMAND PERFORMANCE(1931), d; HELL BOUND(1931), d; WOMEN GO ON FOREVER(1931), d; MEET THE BARON(1933), d; NO MORE ORCHIDS(1933), d; RACETRACK(1933), w; WARRIOR'S HUSBAND, THE(1933), d, w; MIGHTY BARNUM, THE(1934), d; PARTY'S OVER, THE(1934), d; WHOM THE GODS DESTROY(1934), d; CARNIVAL(1935), d; HOORAY FOR LOVE(1935), d; LADY TUBBS(1935); LOVE BEFORE BREAKFAST(1936), d; SECOND HONEYMOON(1937), d; WIFE, DOCTOR AND NURSE(1937), d; BARONESS AND THE BUTLER, THE(1938), d; I'LL GIVE A MILLION(1938), d; LITTLE PRINCESS, THE(1939), d; BLUE BIRD, THE(1940), d; GREAT PROFILE, THE(1940), d; STAR DUST(1940), d; TIN PAN ALLEY(1940), d; MOON OVER MIAMI(1941), d; WEEKEND IN HAVANA(1941), d; MAGNIFICENT DOPE, THE(1942), d; SONG OF THE ISLANDS(1942), d; CONEY ISLAND(1943), d; GREENWICH VILLAGE(1944), d; STATE FAIR(1945), d; CLAUDIA AND DAVID(1946), d; SENTIMENTAL JOURNEY(1946), d; MOTHER WORE TIGHTS(1947), d; SITTING PRETTY(1948), d; WHEN MY BABY SMILES AT ME(1948), d; YOU'RE MY EVERYTHING(1949), d; CHEAPER BY THE DOZEN(1950), d; JACKPOT, THE(1950), d; PAID IN FULL(1950), m; ON THE RIVERA(1951), d; WITH A SONG IN MY HEART(1952), d; CALL ME MADAM(1953), d; THERE'S NO BUSINESS LIKE SHOW BUSINESS(1954), d; KING AND I, THE(1956), d; DESK SET(1957), d; BUT NOT FOR ME(1959), d; CAN-CAN(1960), d; MARRIAGE-GO-ROUND, THE(1960), d; SNOW WHITE AND THE THREE STOOGES(1961), d
Misc. Talkies
BIG FIGHT, THE(1930), d
Silents
RED KIMONO(1925), d; LADYBIRD, THE(1927), d; SALLY IN OUR ALLEY(1927), d; NIGHT FLYER, THE(1928), d
Misc. Silents
EARTH WOMAN, THE(1926), d; GOLDEN WEB, THE(1926), d; MONEY TO BURN(1926), d; COLLEGE HERO, THE(1927), d; SATIN WOMAN, THE(1927), d; ALICE THROUGH A LOOKING GLASS(1928), d; DESERT BRIDE, THE(1928), d; SPIRIT OF YOUTH, THE(1929), d
Woo Lang
Silents
AFTER MIDNIGHT(1921)
Suzanne Lang-Willar
VERY CURIOUS GIRL, A(1970, Fr.), ed; POSSESSION(1981, Fr./Ger.), ed
1984
FIRST NAME: CARMEN(1984, Fr.), ed
Alladdin Langa
HULLABALOO OVER GEORGIE AND BONNIE'S PICTURES(1979, Brit.)
Elaine Langan
JOHNNY COMES FLYING HOME(1946); SOMEWHERE IN THE NIGHT(1946)
Glenn Langan
ESPIONAGE AGENT(1939); RETURN OF DR. X, THE(1939); RIDING HIGH(1943); FOUR JILLS IN A JEEP(1944); IN THE MEANTIME, DARLING(1944); SOMETHING FOR THE BOYS(1944); WING AND A PRAYER(1944); BELL FOR ADANO, A(1945); HANGOVER SQUARE(1945); DRAGONWYCH(1946); MARGIE(1946); SENTIMENTAL JOURNEY(1946); FOREVER AMBER(1947); HOMESTRETCH, THE(1947); FURY AT FURNACE CREEK(1948); SNAKE PIT, THE(1948); TREASURE OF MONTE CRISTO(1949); IROQUOIS TRAIL, THE(1950); RAPTURE(1950, Ital.); HANGMAN'S KNOT(1952); 99 RIVER STREET(1953); BIG CHASE, THE(1954); OUTLAW TREASURE(1955); AMAZING COLOSSAL MAN, THE(1957); JUNGLE HEAT(1957); MUTINY IN OUTER SPACE(1965); CHISUM(1970)
James M. Langan
THAT CHAMPIONSHIP SEASON(1982)
John Langan
NANCY DREW-DETECTIVE(1938), d; NANCY DREW-REPORTER(1939), d
Marius Langan
HAPPY DAYS(1930)
Mary Langan
FRENCH LINE, THE(1954); SON OF SINBAD(1955)
William Langan
SWING HIGH(1930)
Barbara Langbein
HEIDI(1968, Aust.), cos
Ebbe Langberg
OPERATION CAMEL(1961, Den.)
Anthony Langdon
SAILOR'S RETURN, THE(1978, Brit.); FRENCH LIEUTENANT'S WOMAN, THE(1981)
Donald Langdon
BLOOD TIDE(1982), p, w
Fred Langdon
HANGMAN WAITS, THE(1947, Brit.), ph
Harry Langdon
SEE AMERICA THIRST(1930); SOLDIER'S PLAYTHING, A(1931); HALLELUJAH, I'M A BUM(1933); MY WEAKNESS(1933); ATLANTIC ADVENTURE(1935); WISE GUYS(1937, Brit.), d; HE LOVED AN ACTRESS(1938, Brit.); THERE GOES MY HEART(1938); FLYING DEUCES(1939), w; ZENOBIA(1939); CHUMP AT OXFORD, A(1940), w; SAPS AT SEA(1940), w; ALL-AMERICAN CO-ED(1941); DOUBLE TROUBLE(1941); MISBEHAVING HUSBANDS(1941); ROAD SHOW(1941), w; HOUSE OF ERRORS(1942), a, w; SPOTLIGHT SCANDALS(1943); BLOCK BUSTERS(1944); HOT RHYTHM(1944); SWINGIN' ON A RAINBOW(1945)
Silents
ELLA CINDERS(1926); STRONG MAN, THE(1926); TRAMP, TRAMP, TRAMP(1926); LONG PANTS(1927); THREE'S A CROWD(1927), a, d; CHASER, THE(1928), a, d; HEART TROUBLE(1928), a, d
Misc. Silents
HIS FIRST FLAME(1927)
James Langdon
Silents
THREE'S A CROWD(1927), w

Lillian Langdon
Silents
GREYHOUND, THE(1914); KINDLING(1915); LAMB, THE(1915); FLIRTING WITH FATE(1916); INTOLERANCE(1916); MARTHA'S VINDICATION(1916); REGGIE MIXES IN(1916); AMERICANO, THE(1917); I LOVE YOU(1918); DADDY LONG LEGS(1919); FOLLIES GIRL, THE(1919); HIS MAJESTY THE AMERICAN(1919); OH, LADY, LADY(1920); SWAMP, THE(1921); WHAT'S A WIFE WORTH?(1921); FOOLS OF FORTUNE(1922); KISSED(1922); LIGHTS OF THE DESERT(1922); STRANGER'S BANQUET(1922); NOBODY'S BRIDE(1923); PRISONER, THE(1923); WANTERS, THE(1923); DARING YOUTH(1924); AFTER BUSINESS HOURS(1925); COBRA(1925); JOANNA(1925); RAFFLES, THE AMATEUR CRACKSMAN(1925); PLEASURES OF THE RICH(1926); WHAT EVERY GIRL SHOULD KNOW(1927)
Misc. Silents
DIANA OF THE FOLLIES(1916); WHARF RAT, THE(1916); MIGHT AND THE MAN(1917); CROWN JEWELS(1918); EVERYWOMAN'S HUSBAND(1918); LAST REBEL, THE(1918); GOING SOME(1920); TOO MUCH WIFE(1922); CROSSED WIRES(1923); FOOTLIGHT RANGER, THE(1923); WALL STREET WHIZ, THE(1925)
Mae Clarke Langdon
UNKNOWN MAN, THE(1951)
Rose Langdon
OUR RELATIONS(1936); NATIONAL VELVET(1944); SEA OF GRASS, THE(1947)
Silents
ROAD TO MANDALAY, THE(1926)
Roy Langdon
Misc. Silents
RIDERS OF THE RANGE(1923)
Ruth Langdon
Misc. Silents
FIREBRAND, THE(1922)
Shep Langdon
THUNDER IN CAROLINA(1960)
Sue Anne Langdon
GREAT IMPOSTOR, THE(1960); STRANGERS WHEN WE MEET(1960); NEW INTERNS, THE(1964); ROUSTABOUT(1964); ROUNDERS, THE(1965); WHEN THE BOYS MEET THE GIRLS(1965); FINE MADNESS, A(1966); FRANKIE AND JOHNNY(1966); HOLD ON(1966); GUIDE FOR THE MARRIED MAN, A(1967); MAN CALLED DAGGER, A(1967); CHEYENNE SOCIAL CLUB, THE(1970); EVICTORS, THE(1979); WITHOUT WARNING(1980); ZAPPED!(1982)
Tracy-Marie Langdon
HAPPY BIRTHDAY TO ME(1981)
Victor Langdon
STROKER ACE(1983)
Ann Lange
LITTLE SEX, A(1982)
Arthur Lange
MYSTERIOUS ISLAND(1929), m; SO THIS IS COLLEGE(1929), md; FREE AND EASY(1930), m; BAD COMPANY(1931), md; BIG GAMBLE, THE(1931), md; SUICIDE FLEET(1931), md; TIP-OFF, THE(1931), md; CARNIVAL BOAT(1932), md; FREIGHTERS OF DESTINY(1932), md; HAT CHECK GIRL(1932), m; PAINTED WOMAN(1932), m; SADDLE BUSTER, THE(1932), md; LIFE IN THE RAW(1933), m; LAST TRAIL, THE(1934), m; MARIE GALANTE(1934), md; NOW I'LL TELL(1934), m, md; SERVANTS' ENTRANCE(1934), md; STAND UP AND CHEER(1934 80m FOX bw), md; WORLD MOVES ON, THE(1934), md; BAD BOY(1935), md; DOUBTING THOMAS(1935), m; IN OLD KENTUCKY(1935), md; IT'S A SMALL WORLD(1935), m; LITTLE COLONEL, THE(1935), md; ONE MORE SPRING(1935), m; ORCHIDS TO YOU(1935), md; SPRING TONIC(1935), md; THANKS A MILLION(1935), md; UNDER THE PAMPAS MOON(1935), md; BANJO ON MY KNEE(1936), md; GIRLS' DORMITORY(1936), m, md; GREAT ZIEGFELD, THE(1936), md; IT HAD TO HAPPEN(1936), md; UNDER YOUR SPELL(1936), md; WHITE FANG(1936), md; WHITE HUNTER(1936), m&md; LANCER SPY(1937), md; LOVE UNDER FIRE(1937), md; ON THE AVENUE(1937), md; THIS IS MY AFFAIR(1937), md; WESTERN GOLD(1937), md; WIFE, DOCTOR AND NURSE(1937), md; GATEWAY(1938), md; HOLD THAT CO-ED(1938), md; KIDNAPPED(1938), m, md; REBECCA OF SUNNYBROOK FARM(1938), md; SALLY, IRENE AND MARY(1938), md; SUBMARINE PATROL(1938), md; THREE BLIND MICE(1938), md; LET FREEDOM RING(1939), md; MARRIED AND IN LOVE(1940), m; DANCING MASTERS, THE(1943), m; DIXIE DUGAN(1943), m; LADY OF BURLESQUE(1943), m; BELLE OF THE YUKON(1944), m; BERMUDA MYSTERY(1944), m; CASANOVA BROWN(1944), m; ALONG CAME JONES(1945), m; IT'S A PLEASURE(1945), m, md; WOMAN IN THE WINDOW, THE(1945), m; FABULOUS SUZANNE, THE(1946), m; JUNGLE PATROL(1948), m; GOLDEN GLOVES STORY, THE(1950), m; VICIOUS YEARS, THE(1950), m; WOMAN ON THE RUN(1950), m; GROOM WORE SPURS, THE(1951), m; JAPANESE WAR BRIDE(1952), m; PRIDE OF ST. LOUIS, THE(1952), m; STEEL LADY, THE(1953), m; 99 RIVER STREET(1953), m; BEACHHEAD(1954), m; MAD MAGICIAN, THE(1954), m; RING OF FEAR(1954), m
Bernadette Lange
KNOCK(1955, Fr.)
Bill Lange
MASSACRE AT CENTRAL HIGH(1976), p
Burt Lange
CONVICTS FOUR(1962)
Carl Lange
DEVIL STRIKES AT NIGHT, THE(1959, Ger.); DESPERADO TRAIL, THE(1965, Ger./Yugo.); LAST TOMAHAWK, THE(1965, Ger./Ital./Span.); GIRL FROM HONG KONG(1966, Ger.); BLOOD DEMON(1967, Ger.)
Charles Lange
HE LEARNED ABOUT WOMEN(1933), ph
Christina Lange
1984
CRIMES OF PASSION(1984)
Claudie Lange
BIBLE...IN THE BEGINNING, THE(1966); MADE IN ITALY(1967, Fr./Ital.); MAIDEN FOR A PRINCE, A(1967, Fr./Ital.); CROSSPLOT(1969, Brit.)
David Lange
CAGED FURY(1948), w; I AM THE CHEESE(1983), a, p, w
Elaine Lange
MAN FROM OKLAHOMA, THE(1945); DANGEROUS MONEY(1946); IN OLD SACRAMENTO(1946); THE CATMAN OF PARIS(1946); UNDERCOVER WOMAN, THE(1946); WIFE WANTED(1946); LIFE WITH FATHER(1947); STALLION ROAD(1947)

Erwin Lange
TREASURE OF SILVER LAKE(1965, Fr./Ger./Yugo.), spec eff; I DEAL IN DAN-GER(1966), spec eff; RAMPAGE AT APACHE WELLS(1966, Ger./Yugo.), spec eff; FLAMING FRONTIER(1968, Ger./Yugo.), spec eff; HANNIBAL BROOKS(1969, Brit.), spec eff

Harry Lange
2001: A SPACE ODYSSEY(1968, U.S./Brit.), prod d; Z.P.G.(1972), art d; EMPIRE STRIKES BACK, THE(1980), art d; GREAT MUPPET CAPER, THE(1981), prod d; DARK CRYSTAL, THE(1982, Brit.), prod d; MONTY PYTHON'S THE MEANING OF LIFE(1983, Brit.), prod d; RETURN OF THE JEDI(1983), set d

Helmut Lange
ORDERED TO LOVE(1963, Ger.); SERENADE FOR TWO SPIES(1966, Ital./Ger.); OUR HITLER, A FILM FROM GERMANY(1980, Ger.)

Hope Lange
BUS STOP(1956); PEYTON PLACE(1957); TRUE STORY OF JESSE JAMES, THE(1957); IN LOVE AND WAR(1958); YOUNG LIONS, THE(1958); BEST OF EVERYTHING, THE(1959); POCKETFUL OF MIRACLES(1961); WILD IN THE COUNTRY(1961); LOVE IS A BALL(1963); JIGSAW(1968); DEATH WISH(1974); I AM THE CHEESE(1983)
1984
PRODIGAL, THE(1984)

Jean Lange
ERASERHEAD(1978)

Jeanne Lange
BLADE(1973); NICKEL RIDE, THE(1974); GOODBYE GIRL, THE(1977)

Jeanne M. Lange
JOE(1970)

Jessica Lange
KING KONG(1976); ALL THAT JAZZ(1979); HOW TO BEAT THE HIGH COST OF LIVING(1980); POSTMAN ALWAYS RINGS TWICE, THE(1981); FRANCES(1982); TOOTSIE(1982)
1984
COUNTRY(1984), a, p

Jim Lange
SHOOT THE MOON(1982)

Johnny Lange
EAST SIDE KIDS(1940), m; MURDER ON THE YUKON(1940), m; BILLY THE KID IN SANTA FE(1941), md; FLYING WILD(1941), m; LONE RIDER CROSSES THE RIO, THE(1941), m; PAPER BULLETS(1941), md; PRIDE OF THE BOWERY(1941), md; SPOOKS RUN WILD(1941), md; ZIS BOOM BAH(1941), md; BILLY THE KID TRAPPED(1942), m; LET'S GET TOUGH(1942), md; LONE RIDER IN CHEYENNE, THE(1942), m; MR. WISE GUY(1942), md; PRAIRIE PALS(1942), m; ROLLING DOWN THE GREAT DIVIDE(1942), m; SHERIFF OF SAGE VALLEY(1942), m; TEXAS MAN HUNT(1942), m

Kelly Lange
CHOSEN SURVIVORS(1974 U.S.-Mex.); ONCE IS NOT ENOUGH(1975); HONKY TONK FREEWAY(1981)
1984
IRRECONCILABLE DIFFERENCES(1984)

Mary Lange
MOONLIGHT AND PRETZELS(1933); ROMAN SCANDALS(1933); KID MIL-LIONS(1934)

Monique Lange
LA PRISONNIERE(1969, Fr./Ital.), w; GOODBYE EMMANUELLE(1980, Fr.), w; TROUT, THE(1982, Fr.), w

Samuel Lange
MR. DEEDS GOES TO TOWN(1936), cos; PRIDE OF THE MARINES(1936), cos; YOU MAY BE NEXT(1936), cos; LOVE FROM A STRANGER(1937, Brit.), cos; TOP-PER(1937), cos

Ted Lange
BLADE(1973); TRICK BABY(1973); FRIDAY FOSTER(1975); PASSING THROUGH(1977), w; RECORD CITY(1978)

V. Lange
LAST GAME, THE(1964, USSR)

Bruce Langehorne
IDAHO TRANSFER(1975), m; STAY HUNGRY(1976), m

George Langelaan
FLY, THE(1958), w; RETURN OF THE FLY(1959), d&w

Frank Langella
DIARY OF A MAD HOUSEWIFE(1970); TWELVE CHAIRS, THE(1970); DEADLY TRAP, THE(1972, Fr./Ital.); WRATH OF GOD, THE(1972); DRACULA(1979); THOSE LIPS, THOSE EYES(1980); SPHINX(1981)

Inge Langen
VOR SONNENUNTERGANG(1961, Ger); 24-HOUR LOVER(1970, Ger.)
Misc. Talkies
APE CREATURE(1968, Ger.)

Fred Langenfeld
LIFE BEGINS TOMORROW(1952, Fr.), ph

Sarah Langenfeld
1984
ACT, THE(1984)

Heather Langenkamp
1984
NIGHTMARE ON ELM STREET, A(1984)

Joelle Langeois
RISE OF LOUIS XIV, THE(1970, Fr.)

Fritz Langer
LONE CLIMBER, THE(1950, Brit./Aust.)

Gilda Langer
Misc. Silents
HALFBREED(1919, Ger.); MASTER OF LOVE, THE(1919, Ger.)

Irene Langer
YOUNG GRADUATES, THE(1971), cos

Stanislav Langer
SWEET LIGHT IN A DARK ROOM(1966, Czech.)

Chris Langevin
HIGH-BALLIN'(1978); THREE CARD MONTE(1978, Can.)

Sam Langevin
Misc. Talkies
ROCK 'N' RULE(1983)

Samantha Langevin
GREY FOX, THE(1983, Can.)

Bonney Langfitt
NORSEMAN, THE(1978), cos

Bonnie Langfliff
TOWN THAT DREADED SUNDOWN, THE(1977), cos

Barry Langford
SATURDAY NIGHT OUT(1964, Brit.)
1984
SAHARA(1984)

Basil Langford
Misc. Silents
LADY TETLEY'S DEGREE(1920, Brit.)

Bonita Langford
BUGSY MALONE(1976, Brit.)

Bonnie Langford
WOMBLING FREE(1977, Brit.)

Edward Langford
Silents
IRON RING, THE(1917); GUILTY OF LOVE(1920); SALVATION NELL(1921); WIFE AGAINST WIFE(1921)
Misc. Silents
LIBERTINE, THE(1916); AS MAN MADE HER(1917); DORMANT POWER, THE(1917); HUNGRY HEART, A(1917); STOLEN PARADISE, THE(1917); YANKEE PLUCK(1917); VOLCANO, THE(1919); SHADOW OF ROSALIE BYRNES, THE(1920); WOMEN MEN FORGET(1920); CRIMSON CROSS, THE(1921); PEGGY PUTS IT OVER(1921); LEOPARDESS, THE(1923)

Edward T. Langford
Misc. Silents
DARK SILENCE, THE(1916); WOMAN ALONE, A(1917)

Faith Langford
HURRY UP OR I'LL BE 30(1973)

Frances Langford
BROADWAY MELODY OF 1936(1935); EVERY NIGHT AT EIGHT(1935); BORN TO DANCE(1936); COLLEGIATE(1936); PALM SPRINGS(1936); HIT PARADE, THE(1937); HOLLYWOOD HOTEL(1937); DREAMING OUT LOUD(1940); HIT PARADE OF 1941(1940); TOO MANY GIRLS(1940); ALL-AMERICAN CO-ED(1941); SWING IT SOLDIER(1941); MISSISSIPPI GAMBLER(1942); YANKEE DOODLE DANDY(1942); COWBOY IN MANHATTAN(1943); FOLLOW THE BAND(1943); NEVER A DULL MOMENT(1943); THIS IS THE ARMY(1943); CAREER GIRL(1944); GIRL RUSH(1944); DIXIE JAMBOREE(1945); PEOPLE ARE FUNNY(1945); RADIO STARS ON PARA-DE(1945); BAMBOO BLONDE, THE(1946); BEAT THE BAND(1947); MELODY TI-ME(1948); DEPUTY MARSHAL(1949); PURPLE HEART DIARY(1951), a, w; GLENN MILLER STORY, THE(1953)

Gail Langford
JULIA MISBEHAVES(1948)

Georges Langford
TI-CUL TOUGAS(1977, Can.), m

Ralph Langford
ARMY WIVES(1944)

Robin Langford
COMEDIANS, THE(1967); PRIVATES ON PARADE(1982); RETURN OF THE SOL-DIER, THE(1983, Brit.)
1984
PRIVATES ON PARADE(1984, Brit.)

William Langford
TRUE AND THE FALSE, THE(1955, Swed.)

Chris Langham
MONTY PYTHON'S LIFE OF BRIAN(1979, Brit.)

James R. Langham
NIGHT IN NEW ORLEANS, A(1942), w

John Langham
MAKE MINE A DOUBLE(1962, Brit.)

Rainer Langhans
DIE HAMBURGER KRANKHEIT(1979, Ger./Fr.)

Janet Langhart
MEDIUM COOL(1969)

Otel Langhel
CASTLE OF BLOOD(1964, Fr./Ital.), ed

Hannelore Langhoff
NOT RECONCILED, OR "ONLY VIOLENCE HELPS WHERE IT RULES"(1969, Ger.)

Bruce Langhorne
HIRED HAND, THE(1971), m; FIGHTING MAD(1976), m; MELVIN AND HO-WARD(1980), m

Jose Maria Langlais
VIOLATED LOVE(1966, Arg.)

Paula Langlen
FOX MOVIETONE FOLLIES(1929); WORDS AND MUSIC(1929)

Amanda Langlet
PAULINE AT THE BEACH(1983, Fr.)

Daniel Langlet
COUP DE TORCHON(1981, Fr.)
1984
ONE DEADLY SUMMER(1984, Fr.)

Adria Locke Langley
LION IS IN THE STREETS, A(1953), w

B. Langley
1984(1956, Brit.), spec eff

Bruce Langley
YOUTH ON PARADE(1943); RED RIVER RENEGADES(1946); TOY, THE(1982)

Bryan Langley
NO EXIT(1930, Brit.), ph; LAST COUPON, THE(1932, Brit.), ph; LUCKY GIRL(1932, Brit.), ph; NUMBER SEVENTEEN(1932, Brit.), ph; FACING THE MUSIC(1933, Brit.), ph; LETTING IN THE SUNSHINE(1933, Brit.), ph; DOCTOR'S ORDERS(1934, Brit.), ph; HAPPY(1934, Brit.), ph; DANCE BAND(1935, Brit.), ph; HONOURS EASY(1935, Brit.), ph; REGAL CAVALCADE(1935, Brit.), ph; LIMPING MAN, THE(1936, Brit.), ph; LIVING DANGEROUSLY(1936, Brit.), ph; NO ESCAPE(1936, Brit.), ph; ROYAL

D. Langley- continued

EAGLE(1936, Brit.), ph; SOMEONE AT THE DOOR(1936, Brit.), ph; STUDENT'S ROMANCE, THE(1936, Brit.), ph; APRIL BLOSSOMS(1937, Brit.), ph; FRENCH LEAVE(1937, Brit.), ph; RIVER OF UNREST(1937, Brit.), ph; ALMOST A HONEYMOON(1938, Brit.), ph; KATHLEEN(1938, Ireland), ph; LASSIE FROM LANCASHIRE(1938, Brit.), ph; MEET MR. PENNY(1938, Brit.), ph; NIGHT ALONE(1938, Brit.), ph; DEAD MEN TELL NO TALES(1939, Brit.), ph; DISCOVERIES(1939, Brit.), ph; MRS. PYM OF SCOTLAND YARD(1939, Brit.), ph; MUTINY OF THE ELSINORE, THE(1939, Brit.), ph; WANTED BY SCOTLAND YARD(1939, Brit.), ph; HUMAN MONSTER, THE(1940, Brit.), ph; LILAC DOMINO, THE(1940, Brit.), ph; ROOM FOR TWO(1940, Brit.), ph; SPARE A COPPER(1940, Brit.), ph; SPIES OF THE AIR(1940, Brit.), ph; WHO IS GUILTY?(1940, Brit.), ph; TOWER OF TERROR, THE(1942, Brit.), ph; WHEN THE BOUGH BREAKS(1947, Brit.), ph; BOND STREET(1948, Brit.), ph; MONKEY'S PAW, THE(1948, Brit.), ph; PICCADILLY INCIDENT(1948, Brit.), ph

D. Langley
NO FUNNY BUSINESS(1934, Brit.), ph

Dorothy Langley
LAST DAYS OF DOLWYN, THE(1949, Brit.)

Edward Langley
Silents
MARK OF ZORRO(1920), art d

Edward M. Langley
Silents
THREE MUSKETEERS, THE(1921), art d; ROBIN HOOD(1922), art d; DON Q, SON OF ZORRO(1925), art d

Faith Langley
DONOVAN'S BRAIN(1953)

Herbert Langley
NUMBER SEVENTEEN(1932, Brit.); LETTING IN THE SUNSHINE(1933, Brit.); PUBLIC LIFE OF HENRY THE NINTH, THE(1934, Brit.); RUNAWAY QUEEN, THE(1935, Brit.)
Silents
FLAMES OF PASSION(1922, Brit.); WOMAN'S SECRET, A(1924, Brit.)
Misc. Silents
CHU CHIN CHOW(1923, Brit.); CUPID IN CLOVER(1929, Brit.)

Lee Langley
FLYING SAUCER, THE(1950); INTERLUDE(1968, Brit.), w

Noel Langley
SECRET OF STAMBOUL, THE(1936, Brit.), w; MAYTIME(1937), w; WIZARD OF OZ, THE(1939), w; FLORIAN(1940), w; PIRATES OF THE SEVEN SEAS(1941, Brit.), w; UNEXPECTED UNCLE(1941), w; I BECAME A CRIMINAL(1947), w; CARDBOARD CAVALIER, THE(1949, Brit.), w; EDWARD, MY SON(1949, U.S./Brit.), w; ADAM AND EVELYNE(1950, Brit.), w; TAMING OF DOROTHY, THE(1950, Brit.), w; TRIO(1950, Brit.), w; CHRISTMAS CAROL, A(1951, Brit.), w; TOM BROWN'S SCHOOL-DAYS(1951, Brit.), w; FATHER'S DOING FINE(1952, Brit.), w; IVANHOE(1952, Brit.), w; PICKWICK PAPERS, THE(1952, Brit.), p, d&w; PRISONER OF ZENDA, THE(1952), w; KNIGHTS OF THE ROUND TABLE(1953), w; ADVENTURES OF SADIE, THE(1955, Brit.), d, w; SVENGALI(1955, Brit.), d&w; SEARCH FOR BRIDEY MURPHY, THE(1956), d&w; VAGABOND KING, THE(1956), w; SNOW WHITE AND THE THREE STOOGES(1961), w

Norman Langley
MAN OF VIOLENCE(1970, Brit.), ph; HOUSE OF LONG SHADOWS, THE(1983, Brit.), ph
1984
FOREVER YOUNG(1984, Brit.), ph; WHERE IS PARSIFAL?(1984, Brit.), ph

Peter Langley
SHOOT(1976, Can.)

Robert Langley
OLIVER!(1968, Brit.)

Victor Langley
SEA WOLVES, THE(1981, Brit.)

Eric Langlois
1984
GREYSTOKE: THE LEGEND OF TARZAN, LORD OF THE APES(1984)

Lisa Langlois
BLOOD RELATIVES(1978, Fr./Can.); VIOLETTE(1978, Fr.); KLONDIKE FEVER(1980); PHOBIA(1980, Can.); HAPPY BIRTHDAY TO ME(1981); CLASS OF 1984(1982, Can.); DEADLY EYES(1982); MAN WHO WASN'T THERE, THE(1983)
1984
JOY OF SEX(1984)

Suzanne Langlois
ACT OF THE HEART(1970, Can.)

Yves Langlois
RED(1970, Can.), ed; ANGELA(1977, Can.), ed; LITTLE GIRL WHO LIVES DOWN THE LANE, THE(1977, Can.), ed; BLOOD RELATIVES(1978, Fr./Can.), ed; LUCKY STAR, THE(1980, Can.), ed; QUEST FOR FIRE(1982, Fr./Can.), ed

Arlette Langmann
ME(1970, Fr.), w,Maurice Pialat; LOULOU(1980, Fr.), w
1984
A NOS AMOURS(1984, Fr.), w

Andras Langmar
WAGNER(1983, Brit./Hung./Aust.), art d

Lawrence Langner
PURSUIT OF HAPPINESS, THE(1934), w

Marilyn Langner
SWIMMER, THE(1968)

Marina Langner
I HATE BLONDES(1981, Ital.)
Misc. Talkies
ANDREA(1979)

Philip Langner
PAWNBROKER, THE(1965), p; SLAVES(1969), p; BORN TO WIN(1971), p

Sylvia Langova
WOMAN'S ANGLE, THE(1954, Brit.); CASE OF THE RED MONKEY(1955, Brit.); INCIDENT AT MIDNIGHT(1966, Brit.); LOOKING GLASS WAR, THE(1970, Brit.); AVALANCHE EXPRESS(1979)

Caroline Langrishe
WHO IS KILLING THE GREAT CHEFS OF EUROPE?(1978, US/Ger.); EAGLE'S WING(1979, Brit.); DEATHWATCH(1980, Fr./Ger.)

Jan Langsadl
GIRL WITH THREE CAMELS, THE(1968, Czech.)

Clara Langsaner
PERSONAL MAID(1931)

Brian Langslow
GANG WAR(1962, Brit.), p

Clara Langsner
LUMMOX(1930); COUNSELLOR-AT-LAW(1933)

Joy Langstaff
SON OF SINBAD(1955)

Billie Langston
THUNDER IN CAROLINA(1960)

Jean Langston
BELLES OF ST. TRINIAN'S, THE(1954, Brit.)

Murray Langston
SKATETOWN, U.S.A.(1979); GONG SHOW MOVIE, THE(1980)
1984
NIGHT PATROL(1984), a, w

Rick Langston
MOONSHINE COUNTY EXPRESS(1977)

Ruth Langston
Misc. Silents
BROTHERS DIVIDED(1919)

Gerome Langstrome
DAY THE EARTH FROZE, THE(1959, Fin./USSR), spec eff

Basil Langton
SHADOW OF MIKE EMERALD, THE(1935, Brit.); BELLES OF ST. CLEMENTS, THE(1936, Brit.); HEIRLOOM MYSTERY, THE(1936, Brit.); ONE GOOD TURN(1936, Brit.); DOUBLE EXPOSURES(1937, Brit.); ELDER BROTHER, THE(1937, Brit.); FATHER STEPS OUT(1937, Brit.); MERRY COMES TO STAY(1937, Brit.); MINSTREL BOY, THE(1937, Brit.); MR. SMITH CARRIES ON(1937, Brit.); ALMOST A GENTLEMAN(1938, Brit.)

David Langton
SHIP THAT DIED OF SHAME, THE(1956, Brit.); ABANDON SHIP(1957, Brit.); SAINT JOAN(1957); HARD DAY'S NIGHT, A(1964, Brit.); LIQUIDATOR, THE(1966, Brit.); INCREDIBLE SARAH, THE(1976, Brit.); QUINTET(1979)

Diane Langton
CONFESSIONS OF A POP PERFORMER(1975, Brit.); CARRY ON ENGLAND(1976, Brit.); DIRTY KNIGHT'S WORK(1976, Brit.)

Hazel Langton
STELLA DALLAS(1937); WINGS OVER HONOLULU(1937)

Paul Langton
FIRST COMES COURAGE(1943); WE'VE NEVER BEEN LICKED(1943); DESTINATION TOKYO(1944); GENTLE ANNIE(1944); THIN MAN GOES HOME, THE(1944); THIRTY SECONDS OVER TOKYO(1944); HIDDEN EYE, THE(1945); THEY WERE EXPENDABLE(1945); WHAT NEXT, CORPORAL HARGROVE?(1945); HOODLUM SAINT, THE(1946); MY BROTHER TALKS TO HORSES(1946); TILL THE CLOUDS ROLL BY(1946); FOR YOU I DIE(1947); ROMANCE OF ROSY RIDGE, THE(1947); FIGHTING BACK(1948); SONG IS BORN, A(1948); TROUBLE PREFERRED(1949); BIG LEAGUER(1953); JACK SLADE(1953); RETURN FROM THE SEA(1954); SNOW CREATURE, THE,(1954); BIG KNIFE, THE(1955); MURDER IS MY BEAT(1955); TO HELL AND BACK(1955); CALYPSO HEAT WAVE(1957); CHICAGO CONFIDENTIAL(1957); INCREDIBLE SHRINKING MAN, THE(1957); UTAH BLAINE(1957); GIRL IN THE WOODS(1958); IT! THE TERROR FROM BEYOND SPACE(1958); COSMIC MAN, THE(1959); INVISIBLE INVADERS(1959); BIG NIGHT, THE(1960); THREE CAME TO KILL(1960); DIME WITH A HALO(1963); FOUR FOR TEXAS(1963); TWILIGHT OF HONOR(1963); ADVANCE TO THE REAR(1964); MAN'S FAVORITE SPORT[?](1964)

Simon Langton
COUNTERSPY MEETS SCOTLAND YARD(1950)

Hugh "Slim" Langtry
QUICK, BEFORE IT MELTS(1964)

Kenneth Langtry
HOW TO MAKE A MONSTER(1958), w; I WAS A TEENAGE FRANKENSTEIN(1958), w; HEADLESS GHOST, THE(1959, Brit.), w

Walter Lanh
Silents
BY WHOSE HAND?(1927), d

Edward Lanham
IF I'M LUCKY(1946), w

Edwin Lanham
IT SHOULDN'T HAPPEN TO A DOG(1946), w; SENATOR WAS INDISCREET, THE(1947), w

Gene Lanham
JUDGE, THE(1949), m

Miss Lani
JUMBO(1962)

Naidi Lani
REVOLT OF MAMIE STOVER, THE(1956)

Prince Lei Lani
BIRD OF PARADISE(1951)

Pua Lani
HAWAII CALLS(1938); FISHERMAN'S WHARF(1939)

Leo Lania
THREEPENNY OPERA, THE(1931, Ger./U.S.), w; TRUNKS OF MR. O.F., THE(1932, Ger.), w; TWO WHO DARED(1937, Brit.), w; ULTIMATUM(1940, Fr.), w

Billy Lanier
RED RUNS THE RIVER(1963)

Jean Lanier
CHILDREN OF PARADISE(1945, Fr.); MODIGLIANI OF MONTPARNASSE(1961, Fr./Ital.); LAST YEAR AT MARIENBAD(1962, Fr./Ital.); LAFAYETTE(1963, Fr.); SOFT SKIN, THE(1964, Fr.)

Margie Lanier
Misc. Talkies
FUGITIVE GIRLS(1975)

Phillip Lanier
Misc. Talkies
DARK SUNDAY(1978)

Sidney Lanier
WHICH WAY IS UP?(1977); WINTER KILLS(1979)
Susan Lanier
HILLS HAVE EYES, THE(1978)
Willie Lanier
BLACK SIX, THE(1974)
Caro Laniesti
SUPERZAN AND THE SPACE BOY(1972, Mex.)
Thomas Lanigan
GOLDEN HOOFS(1941), w
Robert Laning
HOSTAGE, THE(1966), w
Leo Laniz
SHANGHAI DRAMA, THE(1945, Fr.), w
Marc Lanjean
APRES L'AMOUR(1948, Fr.), m; GATES OF PARIS(1958, Fr./Ital.), md; NUDE IN HIS POCKET(1962, Fr.), m
Kim Lankeford
HARRY AND WALTER GO TO NEW YORK(1976)
Robert Lankesheer
DAVID COPPERFIELD(1970, Brit.); YOUNG WINSTON(1972, Brit.)
Ray Lankester
Silents
REPENTANCE(1922, Brit.)
Kim Lankford
MALIBU BEACH(1978); OCTAGON, THE(1980)
Jeanine Lankshear
RAPTURE(1965), makeup
Hope Lanlon
WHERE DID YOU GET THAT GIRL?(1941)
Jack Lannan
THUNDER ROAD(1958), spec eff
R.J. Lannan
TRAPEZE(1956), spec eff
Herbert Lannard
50,000 B.C.(BEFORE CLOTHING)* (1963), p
Margarete Lanner
Silents
METROPOLIS(1927, Ger.)
Susi Lanner
MOSCOW SHANGHAI(1936, Ger.)
George Lannes
MASK OF KOREA(1950, Fr.)
Georges Lannes
NOUS IRONS A PARIS(1949, Fr.); MOULIN ROUGE(1952); LUCRECE BORGIA(1953, Ital./Fr.); CASE OF DR. LAURENT(1958, Fr.)
Horace Lannes
NO EXIT(1962, U.S./Arg.), cos
Lannier
DOCTEUR LAENNEC(1949, Fr.)
Dennis Lanning
WHAT'S GOOD FOR THE GOOSE(1969, Brit.), ed; Z.P.G.(1972), ed
Don Lanning
MARINES COME THROUGH, THE(1943)
Frank Lanning
ROUGH ROMANCE(1930); WHOOPEE(1930)
Silents
JOHN NEEDHAM'S DOUBLE(1916); KENTUCKY CINDERELLA, A(1917); LITTLE PATRIOT, A(1917); HUCK AND TOM(1918); HUCKLEBERRY FINN(1920); ANOTHER MAN'S BOOTS(1922); EAST IS WEST(1922); OUT OF THE SILENT NORTH(1922); STEP ON IT!(1922); STORM, THE(1922); KID BROTHER, THE(1927); UNKNOWN, THE(1927); STAND AND DELIVER(1928)
Misc. Silents
THREE GODFATHERS, THE(1916); BARE-FISTED GALLAGHER(1919); BLUE BANDANNA, THE(1919); THAT GIRL MONTANA(1921); REMITTANCE WOMAN, THE(1923); UNKNOWN RIDER, THE(1929)
Howard Lanning
WHERE HAS POOR MICKEY GONE?(1964, Brit.), ed; CONQUEROR WORM, THE(1968, Brit.), ed; CRIMSON CULT, THE(1970, Brit.), ed
Reggie Lanning
HARVESTER, THE(1936), ph; LAUGHING IRISH EYES(1936), ph; HEROES OF THE HILLS(1938), ph; PALS OF THE SADDLE(1938), ph; SANTA FE STAM-PEDE(1938), ph; DAYS OF JESSE JAMES(1939), ph; FRONTIER VENGEAN-CE(1939), ph; HOME ON THE PRAIRIE(1939), ph; NEW FRONTIER(1939), ph; SABOTAGE(1939), ph; WYOMING OUTLAW(1939), ph; GAUCHO SERENADE(1940), ph; GRANDPA GOES TO TOWN(1940), ph; OKLAHOMA RENEGADES(1940), ph; ONE MAN'S LAW(1940), ph; RANGER AND THE LADY, THE(1940), ph; WHO KILLED AUNT MAGGIE?(1940), ph; WOLF OF NEW YORK(1940), ph; GAUCHOS OF EL DORADO(1941), ph; GREAT TRAIN ROBBERY, THE(1941), ph; MERCY IS-LAND(1941), ph; MR. DISTRICT ATTORNEY(1941), ph; PALS OF THE PECOS(1941), ph; PHANTOM COWBOY, THE(1941), ph; PITTSBURGH KID, THE(1941), ph; SUN-SET IN WYOMING(1941), ph; BELLS OF CAPISTRANO(1942), ph; CALL OF THE CANYON(1942), ph; CODE OF THE OUTLAW(1942), ph; MAN FROM CHEYEN-NE(1942), ph; SUNSET ON THE DESERT(1942), ph; WESTWARD HO(1942), ph; DAYS OF OLD CHEYENNE(1943), ph; HANDS ACROSS THE BORDER(1943), ph; HOOSIER HOLIDAY(1943), ph; IDAHO(1943), ph; KING OF THE COWBOYS(1943), ph; PISTOL PACKIN' MAMA(1943), ph; SANTA FE SCOUTS(1943), ph; SCREAM IN THE DARK, A(1943), ph; SILVER SPURS(1943), ph; SONG OF TEXAS(1943), ph; THUNDERING TRAILS(1943), ph; WAGON TRACKS WEST(1943), ph; BIG BONAN-ZA, THE(1944), ph; COWBOY AND THE SENORITA(1944), ph; FACES IN THE FOG(1944), ph; HIDDEN VALLEY OUTLAWS(1944), ph; LIGHTS OF OLD SANTA FE(1944), ph; MARSHAL OF RENO(1944), ph; MY BUDDY(1944), ph; ROSIE THE RIVETER(1944), ph; SILVER CITY KID(1944), ph; SING, NEIGHBOR, SING(1944), ph; STRANGERS IN THE NIGHT(1944), ph; THREE LITTLE SISTERS(1944), ph; TUCSON RAIDERS(1944), ph; CHEATERS, THE(1945), ph; CHEROKEE FLASH, THE(1945), ph; STEPPIN' IN SOCIETY(1945), ph; CRIME OF THE CENTURY(1946), ph; INNER CIRCLE, THE(1946), ph; PLAINSMAN AND THE LADY(1946), ph; RAIN-BOW OVER TEXAS(1946), ph; RENDEZVOUS WITH ANNIE(1946), ph; SHERIFF OF REDWOOD VALLEY(1946), ph; SIOUX CITY SUE(1946), ph; SONG OF ARIZO-NA(1946), ph; THE CATMAN OF PARIS(1946), ph; VALLEY OF THE ZOMBIES(1946),

ph; BLACKMAIL(1947), ph; CALENDAR GIRL(1947), ph; FABULOUS TEXAN, THE(1947), ph; NORTHWEST OUTPOST(1947), ph; PILGRIM LADY, THE(1947), ph; ANGEL IN EXILE(1948), ph; ANGEL ON THE AMAZON(1948), ph; CALIFORNIA FIREBRAND(1948), ph; FLAME, THE(1948), ph; GRAND CANYON TRAIL(1948), ph; I, JANE DOE(1948), ph; INSIDE STORY, THE(1948), ph; TIMBER TRAIL, THE(1948), ph; TRAIN TO ALCATRAZ(1948), ph; DOWN DAKOTA WAY(1949), ph; SANDS OF IWO JIMA(1949), ph; SUSANNA PASS(1949), ph; WAKE OF THE RED WITCH(1949), ph; HIT PARADE OF 1951(1950), ph; SAVAGE HORDE, THE(1950), ph; SHOW-DOWN, THE(1950), ph; SINGING GUNS(1950), ph; SURRENDER(1950), ph; BELLE LE GRAND(1951), ph; CUBAN FIREBALL(1951), ph; FIGHTING COAST GUARD(1951), ph; HEART OF THE ROCKIES(1951), ph; BAL TABARIN(1952), ph; HOODLUM EMPIRE(1952), ph; I DREAM OF JEANIE(1952), ph; THUNDER-BIRDS(1952), ph; TOUGHEST MAN IN ARIZONA(1952), ph; WILD BLUE YONDER, THE(1952), ph; FLIGHT NURSE(1953), ph; LADY WANTS MINK, THE(1953), ph; SEA OF LOST SHIPS(1953), ph; SWEETHEARTS ON PARADE(1953), ph; WOMAN THEY ALMOST LYNCHED(1953), ph; OUTCAST, THE(1954), ph; UNTAMED HEIRESS(1954), ph; ABBOTT AND COSTELLO MEET THE KEYSTONE KOPS(1955), ph; CAROLINA CANNONBALL(1955), ph; CITY OF SHADOWS(1955), ph; I COVER THE UNDERWORLD(1955), ph; ROAD TO DENVER, THE(1955), ph
Silents
CAMERAMAN, THE(1928), ph; SPITE MARRIAGE(1929), ph
Les Lannom
PRIME CUT(1972); FRAMED(1975); STINGRAY(1978); SOUTHERN COM-FORT(1981); SILKWOOD(1983)
Merrilee Lannon
BALL OF FIRE(1941)
Raymond Lanny
FRENCH, THEY ARE A FUNNY RACE, THE(1956, Fr.), ed
Jimmie Lano
RAINBOW ISLAND(1944)
G. Jiguel Lanoe
Silents
JUDITH OF BETHULIA(1914)
Hanri Lanoe
1984
LOUISIANE(1984, Fr./Can.), ed
Henri Lanoe
MIDNIGHT MEETING(1962, Fr.), ed; MALE COMPANION(1965, Fr./Ital.), w; DON'T PLAY WITH MARTIANS(1967, Fr.), d, w, m; THAT MAN GEORGE!(1967, Fr./Ital./Span.), w; THIEF OF PARIS, THE(1967, Fr./Ital.), ed; YO YO(1967, Fr.), ed; GIVE HER THE MOON(1970, Fr./Ital.), ed; OUTSIDE MAN, THE(1973, U.S./FR.), ed; BORSALINO AND CO.(1974, Fr.), ed; MAGNIFICENT ONE, THE(1974, Fr./Ital.), ed; MR. KLEIN(1976, Fr.), ed; BUTTERFLY ON THE SHOULDER, A(1978, Fr.), ed; MALEVIL(1981, Fr./Ger.), ed; AFRICAN, THE(1983, Fr.), m
J. J. Lanoe
Silents
RAGE OF PARIS, THE(1921); ALTAR STAIRS, THE(1922)
Jacques Lanoe
Silents
FOUR HORSEMEN OF THE APOCALYPSE, THE(1921)
Jiquel Lanoe
Silents
ETERNAL CITY, THE(1915)
Misc. Silents
TIGER'S COAT, THE(1920)
Daniel Lanois
1984
DUNE(1984), m; SURROGATE, THE(1984, Can.), m
Victor Lanoux
SHAMELESS OLD LADY, THE(1966, Fr.); YOU ONLY LIVE ONCE(1969, Fr.); TWO MEN IN TOWN(1973, Fr.); COUSIN, COUSINE(1976, Fr.); WOMAN AT HER WIN-DOW, A(1978, Fr./Ital./Ger.)
1984
DOG DAY(1984, Fr.); LOUISIANE(1984, Fr./Can.)
V. Lanovaya
RESURRECTION(1963, USSR)
Vasiliy Lanovoi
WAR AND PEACE(1968, USSR)
Andre Lanoy
Silents
NEVER SAY DIE(1924); NO OTHER WOMAN(1928)
D.A. Lanpher
SECRET OF NIMH, THE(1982), spec eff
Dorse A. Lanpher
PETE'S DRAGON(1977), anim
Fay Lanphier
Silents
AMERICAN VENUS, THE(1926)
James F. Lanphier
OPERATION PETTICOAT(1959)
James Lanphier
PERFECT FURLOUGH, THE(1958); FLIGHT OF THE LOST BALLOON(1961); EXPERIMENT IN TERROR(1962); PINK PANTHER, THE(1964); WHAT DID YOU DO IN THE WAR, DADDY?(1966); LEGEND OF LYLAH CLARE, THE(1968); PARTY, THE(1968)
Mary-Madeleine Lanphier
LOVERS AND LOLLIPOPS(1956), w; WEDDINGS AND BABIES(1960), w
Olle Lansberg
PORT OF CALL(1963, Swed.), w; DEAR JOHN(1966, Swed.), w
Janet Lansburgh
MYSTERY LAKE(1953), w
Larry Lansburgh
MYSTERY LAKE(1953), p&d; LITTLEST OUTLAW, THE(1955), p, w; HORSE IN THE GRAY FLANNEL SUIT, THE(1968), d; HANG YOUR HAT ON THE WIND(1969), p&d, w
Angela Lansbury
GASLIGHT(1944); NATIONAL VELVET(1944); PICTURE OF DORIAN GRAY, THE(1945); HOODLUM SAINT, THE(1946); TILL THE CLOUDS ROLL BY(1946); IF WINTER COMES(1947); PRIVATE AFFAIRS OF BEL AMI, THE(1947); STATE OF THE UNION(1948); TENTH AVENUE ANGEL(1948); THREE MUSKETEERS,

Bruce Lansbury- (continued)
THE(1948); RED DANUBE, THE(1949); SAMSON AND DELILAH(1949); KIND LA-DY(1951); MUTINY(1952); REMAINS TO BE SEEN(1953); LAWLESS STREET, A(1955); PURPLE MASK, THE(1955); COURT JESTER, THE(1956); PLEASE MURDER ME(1956); LONG, HOT SUMMER, THE(1958); RELUCTANT DEBUTANTE, THE(1958); BREATH OF SCANDAL, A(1960); DARK AT THE TOP OF THE STAIRS, THE(1960); BLUE HAWAII(1961); SEASON OF PASSION(1961, Aus./Brit.); ALL FALL DOWN(1962); MANCHURIAN CANDIDATE, THE(1962); IN THE COOL OF THE DAY(1963); DEAR HEART(1964); WORLD OF HENRY ORIENT, THE(1964); AMOR-OUS ADVENTURES OF MOLL FLANDERS, THE(1965); GREATEST STORY EVER TOLD, THE(1965); HARLOW(1965); MISTER BUDDWING(1966); SOMETHING FOR EVERYONE(1970); BEDKNOBS AND BROOMSTICKS(1971); DEATH ON THE NI-LE(1978, Brit.); LADY VANISHES, THE(1980, Brit.); MIRROR CRACK'D, THE(1980, Brit.); LAST UNICORN, THE(1982); PIRATES OF PENZANCE, THE(1983)

Bruce Lansbury
STORY OF THREE LOVES, THE(1953)

Edgar Lansbury
KIM(1950); WAR HUNT(1962), art d; SUBJECT WAS ROSES, THE(1968), p; DES-PERATE CHARACTERS(1971), art d; GODSPELL(1973), p

James Lansdale
KING AND COUNTRY(1964, Brit.), w

Roy Lansford
MURDER BY DECREE(1979, Brit.)

William Douglas Lansford
VILLA RIDES(1968), w; BIG CUBE, THE(1969), w

Derek Lansiaux
RANDOLPH FAMILY, THE(1945, Brit.)

Ernest Lansing
COLONEL EFFINGHAM'S RAID(1945), set d; WITHIN THESE WALLS(1945), set d; LEAVE HER TO HEAVEN(1946), set d; SOMEWHERE IN THE NIGHT(1946), set d; MIRACLE ON 34TH STREET, THE(1947), set d; CRY OF THE CITY(1948), set d; SITTING PRETTY(1948), set d; SNAKE PIT, THE(1948), set d; YELLOW SKY(1948), set d; SAND(1949), set d; YOU'RE MY EVERYTHING(1949), set d

Frances Lansing
GIRL RUSH, THE(1955); VAGABOND KING, THE(1956)

Jill Lansing
MALIBU HIGH(1979)

John Lansing
MORE AMERICAN GRAFFITI(1979); SUNNYSIDE(1979)

Joi Lansing
EASTER PARADE(1948); JULIA MISBEHAVES(1948); GIRL FROM JONES BEACH, THE(1949); NEPTUNE'S DAUGHTER(1949); ON THE RIVERA(1951); PIER 23(1951); TWO TICKETS TO BROADWAY(1951); MERRY WIDOW, THE(1952); SINGIN' IN THE RAIN(1952); FRENCH LINE, THE(1954); SON OF SINBAD(1955); BRAVE ONE, THE(1956); HOT CARS(1956); HOT SHOTS(1956); TOUCH OF EVIL(1958); HOLE IN THE HEAD, A(1959); ATOMIC SUBMARINE, THE(1960); WHO WAS THAT LA-DY?(1960); MARRIAGE ON THE ROCKS(1965); HILLBILLYS IN A HAUNTED HOUSE(1967); BIG FOOT(1973)

Joyce Lansing
COUNTERFEITERS, THE(1948)

Mary Lansing
HAPPY DAYS(1930); JUST IMAGINE(1930)

Michael Lansing
MOVIE MOVIE(1978); CHEECH AND CHONG'S NICE DREAMS(1981)

Robert Lansing
4D MAN(1959); PUSHER, THE(1960); GATHERING OF EAGLES, A(1963); UNDER THE YUM-YUM TREE(1963); EYE FOR AN EYE, AN(1966); NAMU, THE KILLER WHALE(1966); IT TAKES ALL KINDS(1969, U.S./Aus.); GRISSOM GANG, THE(1971); BLACK JACK(1973); BITTERSWEET LOVE(1976); SCALPEL(1976); EMPIRE OF THE ANTS(1977); ACAPULCO GOLD(1978); ISLAND CLAWS(1981)

Sherry Lansing
LOVING(1970); RIO LOBO(1970)

Freddie Lansit
Silents
GOLD RUSH, THE(1925)

Pat Lanski
THREE MEN IN A BOAT(1958, Brit.); ROOM AT THE TOP(1959, Brit.)

Jiri Lansky
LEMONADE JOE(1966, Czech.)

Lieb Lansky
JENNIFER ON MY MIND(1971)

Diana Lante
STORY OF A WOMAN(1970, U.S./Ital.)

Diane Lante
ROMAN HOLIDAY(1953)

William Lanteau
LI'L ABNER(1959); FACTS OF LIFE, THE(1960); HONEYMOON MACHINE, THE(1961); SEX AND THE SINGLE GIRL(1964); HOTEL(1967); FROM NOON TO THREE(1976); ON GOLDEN POND(1981)

Mieke Lanter
ZAPPED!(1982)

Philip Lanthrop
TOGETHER BROTHERS(1974), ph

Al Lanti
SWEET CHARITY(1969)

Albert Lantieri
AT LONG LAST LOVE(1975), a, ch

Franco Lantieri
MY SON, THE HERO(1963, Ital./Fr.); MINUTE TO PRAY, A SECOND TO DIE, A(1968, Ital.); CRAZY JOE(1974)

Michael Lantieri
1984
THIEF OF HEARTS(1984), spec eff

Eric Lantis
MY TUTOR(1983)

Thais Lanton
Silents
BATTLE CRY OF PEACE, THE(1915)

Robert Lantos
IN PRAISE OF OLDER WOMEN(1978, Can.), p; SUZANNE(1980, Can.), p; AGEN-CY(1981, Can.), p; PARADISE(1982), p
1984
BEDROOM EYES(1984, Can.), p

Danny Lantrip
HUCKLEBERRY FINN(1974)

Anni Lantuch
MIDDLE AGE CRAZY(1980, Can.)

A. Lantz
ELISABETH OF AUSTRIA(1931, Ger.), w

Adolph Lantz
RASPUTIN(1932, Ger.), w

James Lantz
DELINQUENTS, THE(1957)

Jim Lantz
IN COLD BLOOD(1967); ADAM AT 6 A.M.(1970)

Jorgen Lantz
HAGBARD AND SIGNE(1968, Den./Iceland/Swed.)

Lewis Lantz
VIOLENCE(1947), w

Louis Lantz
CRIME DOCTOR(1943), w; YOU'RE A LUCKY FELLOW, MR. SMITH(1943), w; MEET THE PEOPLE(1944), w; FORT DEFIANCE(1951), w; ROGUE RIVER(1951), w; LURE OF THE WILDERNESS(1952), w; RIVER OF NO RETURN(1954), w

Lynette Lantz
ASTRO-ZOMBIES, THE(1969)

Walter Lantz
DESTINATION MOON(1950), anim

Walter Lantzch
INHERITANCE IN PRETORIA(1936, Ger.)

Claudio Lanuza
SUPERZAN AND THE SPACE BOY(1972, Mex.)

Giovanni Lanuza
SUPERZAN AND THE SPACE BOY(1972, Mex.)

Rafael Lanuza
SUPERZAN AND THE SPACE BOY(1972, Mex.), d&w

Lanvin
GIRL ON A MOTORCYCLE, THE(1968, Fr./Brit.), cos

Gerard Lanvin
CHOICE OF ARMS(1983, Fr.)

Jeanne Lanvin
Silents
NAPOLEON(1927, Fr.), cos

Katiushka Lanvin
ADVENTURERS, THE(1970)

Lisette Lanvin
SAVAGE BRIGADE(1948, Fr.)

Lanvin-Castille
NEW KIND OF LOVE, A(1963), cos

Germaine Lany
DEVIL PROBABLY, THE(1977, FR.), ed

Lanz
THIRTEEN FRIGHTENED GIRLS(1963), cos

Anthony M. Lanza
WILD GUITAR(1962), ed; SADIST, THE(1963), ed; NASTY RABBIT, THE(1964), ed; WHAT'S UP FRONT(1964), p, ed; DEADWOOD'76(1965), ed; GLORY STOMPERS, THE(1967), d; INCREDIBLE TWO-HEADED TRANSPLANT, THE(1971), d, ed

Joe Lanza
VIRGIN SACRIFICE(1959)

Laura Lanza
INCREDIBLE TWO-HEADED TRANSPLANT, THE(1971)

Mario Lanza
THAT MIDNIGHT KISS(1949); TOAST OF NEW ORLEANS, THE(1950); GREAT CARUSO, THE(1951); BECAUSE YOU'RE MINE(1952); SERENADE(1956); SEVEN HILLS OF ROME, THE(1958); FOR THE FIRST TIME(1959, U.S./Ger./Ital.)

Rocco Lanza
GAS HOUSE KIDS(1946)

Amberto Lanzano
LITTLE MISS DEVIL(1951, Egypt), ph

Richard Lanzano
1984
BROADWAY DANNY ROSE(1984)

Tony Lanzelo
COLD JOURNEY(1975, Can.), ph

Pepi Lanzi
ROSE MARIE(1954)

Martina Lanzinger
PARSIFAL(1983, Fr.)

Jacques Lanzmann
WITHOUT APPARENT MOTIVE(1972, Fr.), w

Rocco Lanzo
RIVER GANG(1945)

Alvaro Lanzone
DRUMMER OF VENGEANCE(1974, Brit.), ph

Nick Lapadula
JENNIFER ON MY MIND(1971); ONLY WHEN I LAUGH(1981)

Leo Lapaire
ETERNAL MASK, THE(1937, Swiss), w

Celia Lapan
Silents
KING OF KINGS, THE(1927)

Richard Lapan
GODLESS GIRL, THE(1929)
Silents
DEVIL TO PAY, THE(1920); LITTLE MISS SMILES(1922)

Augie Lapara
WOMEN AND BLOODY TERROR(1970)

Leon Lapara
CONFESSIONS OF A ROGUE(1948, Fr.)
Basta Laparola
FLY NOW, PAY LATER(1969), w
Ernesto Lapena
SEPTEMBER STORM(1960)
Villis Lapenicks
FALLGUY(1962), ph
Vilis Lapenieks
CAPTURE THAT CAPSULE(1961), ph; MAGIC SPECTACLES(1961), ph; V.D.(1961), ph; WALK THE ANGRY BEACH(1961), ph; THIRD OF A MAN(1962), ph; NIGHT TIDE(1963), ph; SHELL SHOCK(1964), ph; VOYAGE TO THE PREHISTORIC PLANET(1965), ph; DEATHWATCH(1966), ph; MOTHER GOOSE A GO-GO(1966), ph; IF IT'S TUESDAY, THIS MUST BE BELGIUM(1969), ph; I LOVE MY WIFE(1970), ph; CISCO PIKE(1971), ph; NEWMAN'S LAW(1974), ph; CAPONE(1975), ph; TWO(1975), ph
Vilis Lapenieks, Jr.
HIDEOUS SUN DEMON, THE(1959), ph
Villis Lapenieks
QUEEN OF BLOOD(1966), ph
Vilos Lapenieks
EEGAH!(1962), ph
Sal LaPera
NUNZIO(1978)
Ralph LaPere
YOU'RE NOT SO TOUGH(1940)
Guillaume Laperrousaz
HU-MAN(1975, Fr.), w
Jerome Laperrousaz
HU-MAN(1975, Fr.), d, w
Pascal Laperrousaz
LIZA(1976, Fr./Ital.)
Brune Lapeyre
1984
L'ARGENT(1984, Fr./Switz.)
Numa Lapeyre
SO THIS IS PARIS(1954); DADDY LONG LEGS(1955)
O. Lapiado
GARNET BRACELET, THE(1966, USSR)
Marcel LaPicard
SWINGIN' ON A RAINBOW(1945), ph
Andrezej Lapicki
TONIGHT A TOWN DIES(1961, Pol.)
Andrzej Lapicki
SALTO(1966, Pol.); YOUNG GIRLS OF WILKO, THE(1979, Pol./Fr.)
Esther Lapidus
HUNGRY WIVES(1973)
Lily Lapidus
HOME SWEET HOME(1945, Brit.); HONEYMOON HOTEL(1946, Brit.); ESCAPE DANGEROUS(1947, Brit.); WHEN YOU COME HOME(1947, Brit.); DRAGON OF PENDRAGON CASTLE, THE(1950, Brit.); MAN WHO LIKED FUNERALS, THE(1959, Brit.)
Georganne LaPiere
1984
PROTOCOL(1984)
Claude Lapierre
TIKI TIKI(1971, Can.), ph
Ivan Lapikov
ANDREI ROUBLOV(1973, USSR)
B. Lapin
SON OF MONGOLIA(1936, USSR), w
V. Lapin
WAR AND PEACE(1968, USSR)
Laurie Lapinski
Misc. Talkies
PRANKS(1982)
Laurine Lapinski
DORM THAT DRIPPED BLOOD, THE(1983)
Marfa Lapkina
Misc. Silents
OLD AND NEW(1930, USSR)
Alison LaPlaca
1984
FLETCH(1984)
Louise LaPlanche
STRIKE UP THE BAND(1940); FLEET'S IN, THE(1942); YOUNG AND WILLING(1943); LADY IN THE DARK(1944)
Rosemary LaPlanche
FALCON AND THE CO-EDS, THE(1943); MEXICAN SPITFIRE'S BLESSED EVENT(1943); SWING YOUR PARTNER(1943); TWO WEEKS TO LIVE(1943); GIRL RUSH(1944); JOHNNY ANGEL(1945); BETTY CO-ED(1946); ANGELS ALLEY(1948)
Yves Laplanche
TRIAL, THE(1963, Fr./Ital./Ger.), p; SUCKER, THE(1966, Fr./Ital.), p
Harold Lapland
MASTER GUNFIGHTER, THE(1975), w
Deby LaPlante
PERSONAL BEST(1982)
Laura LaPlante
MEET THE WIFE(1931); SPRING REUNION(1957)
Rene Laplat
MOULIN ROUGE(1952)
Ted Laplat
KIRLIAN WITNESS, THE(1978)
Martin LaPlatney
DOUBLES(1978)
Boby Lapointe
SHOOT THE PIANO PLAYER(1962, Fr.); THINGS OF LIFE, THE(1970, Fr./Ital./Switz.)

Ian Lapointe
ANGELA(1977, Can.)
Jean Lapointe
ORDERS, THE(1977, Can.); ONE MAN(1979, Can.)
Paul-Marie Lapointe
CAT IN THE SACK, THE(1967, Can.)
Rene Laporte
YANK IN VIET-NAM, A(1964)
Jane Lapotaire
ASPHYX, THE(1972, Brit.); CRESCENDO(1972, Brit.); ANTONY AND CLEOPATRA(1973, Brit.); EUREKA(1983, Brit.)
Lapouri
ROMEO AND JULIET(1955, USSR)
Richard Lapp
DUEL AT DIABLO(1966); BARQUERO(1970); TIME FOR DYING, A(1971)
A. Lappas
THANOS AND DESPINA(1970, Fr./Gr.), p
Anthony Lappas
IT'S A BIG COUNTRY(1951)
Robert Laprell
Silents
FIGHTING EDGE(1926), ph
Bob Lapresle
MYSTERY JUNCTION(1951, Brit.), ph; CROW HOLLOW(1952, Brit.), ph
Robert Lapresle
WINDMILL, THE(1937, Brit.), ph; SIMPLY TERRIFIC(1938, Brit.), ph
N. Lapshina
KIEV COMEDY, A(1963, USSR)
Esther Laquin
BRAVE BULLS, THE(1951)
Catherine Lara
NO TIME FOR BREAKFAST(1978, Fr.), m; MEN PREFER FAT GIRLS(1981, Fr.), m
Michael Lara
SPRING FEVER(1983, Can.)
Odete Lara
PRETTY BUT WICKED(1965, Braz.); ANTONIO DAS MORTES(1970, Braz.)
Vicente Lara
SANTO Y BLUE DEMON CONTRA LOS MONSTRUOS(1968, Mex.)
Louise Larabee
TAKING OF PELHAM ONE, TWO, THREE, THE(1974); EVERY NIGHT AT EIGHT(1935); ACT ONE(1964); FAIL SAFE(1964)
Nelson Larabee
Silents
OH, WHAT A NURSE!(1926), ph
Nelson Laraby
MILLION DOLLAR COLLAR, THE(1929), ph
Grant Laramy
ADIOS GRINGO(1967, Ital./Fr./Span.); MURDER CLINIC, THE(1967, Ital./Fr.)
L. Lararev
ANDREI ROUBLOV(1973, USSR), ed
Kabi Laratei
FACE TO FACE(1976, Swed.)
Bob Larbey
MAGNIFICENT SEVEN DEADLY SINS, THE(1971, Brit.), w; PLEASE SIR(1971, Brit.), w
Doghmi Larbi
MAN WHO WOULD BE KING, THE(1975, Brit.); BLACK STALLION, THE(1979); BLACK STALLION RETURNS, THE(1983)
Bob Larca
VIRGIN SACRIFICE(1959)
Robert Larcebeau
MADEMOISELLE(1966, Fr./Brit.)
John Larch
BITTER CREEK(1954); PHENIX CITY STORY, THE(1955); TIGHT SPOT(1955); BEHIND THE HIGH WALL(1956); KILLER IS LOOSE, THE(1956); MAN FROM DEL RIO(1956); SEVEN MEN FROM NOW(1956); WRITTEN ON THE WIND(1956); CARELESS YEARS, THE(1957); GUN FOR A COWARD(1957); MAN IN THE SHADOW(1957); QUANTEZ(1957); FROM HELL TO TEXAS(1958); SAGA OF HEMP BROWN, THE(1958); HELL TO ETERNITY(1960); HOW THE WEST WAS WON(1962); MIRACLE OF THE WHITE STALLIONS(1963); WRECKING CREW, THE(1968); GREAT BANK ROBBERY, THE(1969); HAIL, HERO!(1969); CANNON FOR CORDOBA(1970); MOVE(1970); DIRTY HARRY(1971); PLAY MISTY FOR ME(1971); SANTEE(1973); FRAMED(1975); AMITYVILLE HORROR, THE(1979); AIRPLANE II: THE SEQUEL(1982)
Geoffrey Larcher
1984
SUGAR CANE ALLEY(1984, Fr.), set d
Dennis Larden
PHYNX, THE(1970)
Geoffrey Larder
HISTORY OF THE WORLD, PART 1(1981); DRAUGHTSMAN'S CONTRACT, THE(1983, Brit.)
John Lardner
FINGER MAN(1955), w
Ring Lardner
FAST COMPANY(1929), w; GLORIFYING THE AMERICAN GIRL(1930); JUNE MOON(1931), w; ELMER THE GREAT(1933), w; ALIBI IKE(1935), w; BLONDE TROUBLE(1937), w; COWBOY QUARTERBACK(1939), w; SO THIS IS NEW YORK(1948), w; CHAMPION(1949), w
Silents
NEW KLONDIKE, THE(1926), w
Ring Lardner, Jr.
NOTHING SACRED(1937), w; STAR IS BORN, A(1937), w; MEET DR. CHRISTIAN(1939), w; COURAGEOUS DR. CHRISTIAN, THE(1940), w; ARKANSAS JUDGE(1941), w; WOMAN OF THE YEAR(1942), w; CROSS OF LORRAINE, THE(1943), w; LAURA(1944), w; TOMORROW THE WORLD(1944), w; CLOAK AND DAGGER(1946), w; FOREVER AMBER(1947), w; AFFAIRS OF ADELAIDE(1949, U.S./Brit.), w; CINCINNATI KID, THE(1965), w; M(1970), w; LADY LIBERTY(1972, Ital./Fr.), w; GREATEST, THE(1977, U.S./Brit.), w

Gabriel Lared
MALEVIL(1981, Fr./Ger.), m
Peter Laregh
CORPSE OF BEVERLY HILLS, THE(1965, Ger.), w
Michael Laren
MANITOU, THE(1978)
Sid Larence
ARENA, THE(1973)
Dean Larents
Misc. Talkies
BEWARE THE BLACK WIDOW(1968)
Kabi Laretei
FANNY AND ALEXANDER(1983, Swed./Fr./Ger.)
Ray Largay
LILIES OF THE FIELD(1930); GRIEF STREET(1931); HIDDEN EYE, THE(1945); LAWTON STORY, THE(1949); TONIGHT WE SING(1953)
Raymond Largay
SOLDIERS AND WOMEN(1930); DARK HORSE, THE(1946); SHE WROTE THE BOOK(1946); IT HAPPENED IN BROOKLYN(1947); LOUISIANA(1947); SHOCKING MISS PILGRIM, THE(1947); VARIETY GIRL(1947); ARE YOU WITH IT?(1948); FORCE OF EVIL(1948); FOUR FACES WEST(1948); GIRL FROM MANHATTAN(1948); SLIPPY MCGEE(1948); RUSTY'S BIRTHDAY(1949); EXPERIMENT ALCATRAZ(1950); JOHNNY ONE-EYE(1950); PETTY GIRL, THE(1950); KATIE DID IT(1951); SECOND WOMAN, THE(1951); SCANDAL SHEET(1952); APRIL IN PARIS(1953); JESSE JAMES VERSUS THE DALTONS(1954)
Bernard Largemains
JULES AND JIM(1962, Fr.)
Armand Largo
TENDER IS THE NIGHT(1961)
Gonzalo Largo
THIN RED LINE, THE(1964)
LaRiana
JUKE BOX JENNY(1942)
Bernard Larimer
1984
COUNTRY(1984)
Linda Larimer
PHANTOM OF THE PARADISE(1974); DRIVE-IN(1976)
Helen Larimore
1984
WHAT YOU TAKE FOR GRANTED(1984)
N. Larin
Misc. Silents
TERCENTENARY OF THE ROMANOV DYNASTY'S ACCESSION TO THE THRONE(1913, USSR), d
Nikolai Larin
Misc. Silents
RASPUTIN(1929, USSR), d
Alexander Larinov
ONCE THERE WAS A GIRL(1945, USSR)
Al Larionov
MARRIAGE OF BALZAMINOV, THE(1966, USSR)
Vladimir Larionov
SILVER DUST(1953, USSR)
Alla Larionova
FATHERS AND SONS(1960, USSR); MAGIC VOYAGE OF SINBAD, THE(1962, USSR); THREE SISTERS, THE(1969, USSR)
Anna Larionova
TWELFTH NIGHT(1956, USSR)
Larive
LOWER DEPTHS, THE(1937, Fr.)
Jesse LaRive
URBAN COWBOY(1980)
Leon Larive
LA BETE HUMAINE(1938, Fr.); LA MARSEILLAISE(1938, Fr.); RULES OF THE GAME, THE(1939, Fr.); CHILDREN OF PARADISE(1945, Fr.); PARIS DOES STRANGE THINGS(1957, Fr./Ital.)
Kinsley Lark
NEW HOTEL, THE(1932, Brit.)
Richard Larke
MAXIME(1962, Fr.); MAYERLING(1968, Brit./Fr.)
Wynne Larke
BACKLASH(1947)
Caren Larae Larkey
1984
SOLE SURVIVOR(1984)
Art Larkin
EL CONDOR(1970)
Arthur Larkin
WIND AND THE LION, THE(1975)
Bob Larkin
STATE FAIR(1962)
1984
UNFAITHFULLY YOURS(1984)
Christopher Larkin
VERY NATURAL THING, A(1974), p&d, w
Dolly Larkin
Misc. Silents
LABYRINTH, THE(1915)
Eddie Larkin
TWO GIRLS ON BROADWAY(1940), ch
George Alan Larkin
Misc. Silents
PRIMITIVE CALL, THE(1917)
George Larkin
Silents
DEVIL'S TRAIL, THE(1919); BULLDOG COURAGE(1922); PELL STREET MYSTERY, THE(1924), a, w

Misc. Silents
ALMA, WHERE DO YOU LIVE?(1917); NATURAL LAW, THE(1917); BORDER RAIDERS, THE(1918); FRINGE OF SOCIETY, THE(1918); UNFORTUNATE SEX, THE(1920); MAN TRACKERS, THE(1921); BARRIERS OF FOLLY(1922); BOOMERANG JUSTICE(1922); SAVED BY RADIO(1922); APACHE DANCER, THE(1923); FLAMES OF PASSION(1923); FLASH, THE(1923); GENTLEMAN UNAFRAID(1923); MYSTERIOUS GOODS(1923); TANGO CAVALIER(1923); WAY OF THE TRANSGRESSOR, THE(1923); DEEDS OF DARING(1924); MIDNIGHT SECRETS(1924); STOP AT NOTHING(1924); YANKEE MADNESS(1924); GETTING 'EM RIGHT(1925); QUICK CHANGE(1925); RIGHT MAN, THE(1925); ROUGH STUFF(1925); SILVER FINGERS(1926)
Jerry Larkin
THESE THREE(1936); WE HAVE OUR MOMENTS(1937)
Joan Larkin
PETTY GIRL, THE(1950)
John Larkin
ALEXANDER HAMILTON(1931); PRODIGAL, THE(1931); SMART MONEY(1931); SPORTING BLOOD(1931); STRANGER IN TOWN(1932); TENDERFOOT, THE(1932); WET PARADE, THE(1932); DAY OF RECKONING(1933); LAZY RIVER(1934); OPERATOR 13(1934); THIN MAN, THE(1934); WITCHING HOUR, THE(1934); MISSISSIPPI(1935); NOTORIOUS GENTLEMAN, A(1935); SECRET BRIDE, THE(1935); FRANKIE AND JOHNNY(1936); GREAT ZIEGFELD, THE(1936); HEARTS DIVIDED(1936); TRAIL OF THE LONESOME PINE, THE(1936); CHARLIE CHAN AT TREASURE ISLAND(1939), w; NEWS IS MADE AT NIGHT(1939), w; ROSE OF WASHINGTON SQUARE(1939); CHARLIE CHAN AT THE WAX MUSEUM(1940), w; CHARLIE CHAN IN PANAMA(1940), w; CITY OF CHANCE(1940), w; GAY CABALLERO, THE(1940), w; LONE WOLF MEETS A LADY, THE(1940), w; ACCENT ON LOVE(1941), w; DEAD MEN TELL(1941), w; MAN AT LARGE(1941), w; MURDER AMONG FRIENDS(1941), w; CASTLE IN THE DESERT(1942), w; MAN IN THE TRUNK, THE(1942), w; MANILA CALLING(1942), w; QUIET PLEASE, MURDER(1942), d&w; SECRET AGENT OF JAPAN(1942), w; ALLERGIC TO LOVE(1943), w; BERMUDA MYSTERY(1944), w; CIRCUMSTANTIAL EVIDENCE(1945), d; DOLLY SISTERS, THE(1945), w; CLOAK AND DAGGER(1946), w; CARNIVAL IN COSTA RICA(1947), w; TWO WEEKS WITH LOVE(1950), w; HANDCUFFS, LONDON(1955, Brit.), p; SEVEN DAYS IN MAY(1964); THOSE CALLOWAYS(1964); SATAN BUG, THE(1965)
John F. Larkin
LADIES MUST LOVE(1933), w; MANDARIN MYSTERY, THE(1937), w
John Francis Larkin
FRISCO JENNY(1933), w; PARACHUTE JUMPER(1933), w; SHE HAD TO SAY YES(1933), w; MIND YOUR OWN BUSINESS(1937), w
John Larkin, Jr.
SOCIETY GIRL(1932), w
Kirsten Larkin
WHEN A STRANGER CALLS(1979)
Mary Larkin
GUNS IN THE HEATHER(1968, Brit.); BROTHERLY LOVE(1970, Brit.); MC KENZIE BREAK, THE(1970); PADDY(1970, Irish); X Y & ZEE(1972, Brit.); INTERNECINE PROJECT, THE(1974, Brit.); PSYCHOMANIA(1974, Brit.); GALILEO(1975, Brit.)
1984
RAZOR'S EDGE, THE(1984)
Peter Larkin
NEIGHBORS(1981), prod d; NIGHTHAWKS(1981), prod d; TOOTSIE(1982), prod d; REUBEN, REUBEN(1983), prod d
Red Larkin
SWAMP WATER(1941)
John Larking
1984
SQUIZZY TAYLOR(1984, Aus.)
Johnny Larkins
MAN TO MAN(1931)
Anna Larlonova
ANNA CROSS, THE(1954, USSR)
James Larmore
FOREIGN AFFAIR, A(1948)
Richard Larned
Silents
ISOBEL(1920)
Elizabeth Larner
SONG OF NORWAY(1970)
Jeremy Larner
DRIVE, HE SAID(1971), w; CANDIDATE, THE(1972), w
Stefan Larner
LIONS LOVE(1969), ph
Stevan Larner
STUDENT NURSES, THE(1970), ph; STEELYARD BLUES(1973), ph; ALMOST SUMMER(1978), ph; GOLDENGIRL(1979), ph; CADDY SHACK(1980), ph
Steve Larner
BADLANDS(1974), ph; PIPE DREAMS(1976), ph
Steven Larner
BURNT OFFERINGS(1976), ph; BUDDY HOLLY STORY, THE(1978), ph; GRAY LADY DOWN(1978), ph; TWILIGHT ZONE–THE MOVIE(1983), ph
Biacio LaRocca
DUCK, YOU SUCKER!(1972, Ital.)
Charles LaRocca
WHO'S GOT THE ACTION?(1962)
Sonny LaRocca
KING OF THE MOUNTAIN(1981)
Guy Laroche
FIVE MILES TO MIDNIGHT(1963, U.S./Fr./Ital.), a, cos; TAMAHINE(1964, Brit.), cos
Mary LaRoche
CATSKILL HONEYMOON(1950); OPERATION MAD BALL(1957); RUN SILENT, RUN DEEP(1958); GIDGET(1959); LADIES MAN, THE(1961); BYE BYE BIRDIE(1963); SWINGER, THE(1966)
Melba LaRose, Jr.
Misc. Talkies
BARBARA(1970)

Pierre Laroche
LUMIERE D'ETE(1943, Fr.), w; DEVIL'S ENVOYS, THE(1947, Fr.), w; SEVENTH JUROR, THE(1964, Fr.), w; WOMEN AND WAR(1965, Fr.), w

Rod LaRocque
MAN AND THE MOMENT, THE(1929); OUR MODERN MAIDENS(1929); BEAU BANDIT(1930); FRISCO WATERFRONT(1935); MYSTERY WOMAN(1935); TILL WE MEET AGAIN(1936); BEYOND TOMORROW(1940); DARK STREETS OF CAIRO(1940); DR. CHRISTIAN MEETS THE WOMEN(1940); MEET JOHN DOE(1941)
Misc. Talkies
DRAGNET, THE(1936)
Misc. Silents
LOVE AND THE WOMAN(1919)

Rodney LaRocque
Silents
EASY TO GET(1920)

Roderick LaRoque
Silents
ALSTER CASE, THE(1915)

Carmen LaRoux
CAVALIER OF THE WEST(1931); DEMON FOR TROUBLE, A(1934); DESERT TRAIL(1935); ISLAND CAPTIVES(1937); STARLIGHT OVER TEXAS(1938)
Misc. Talkies
TWO GUN CABALLERO(1931)

Rita LaRoy
MIDNIGHT MYSTERY(1930); SIN TAKES A HOLIDAY(1930); GAY DIPLOMAT, THE(1931); LEFTOVER LADIES(1931); SECRET WITNESS, THE(1931); YELLOW TICKET, THE(1931); AMATEUR DADDY(1932); SO BIG(1932); FROM HELL TO HEAVEN(1933); I'VE GOT YOUR NUMBER(1934); LADY FROM NOWHERE(1936); FIND THE WITNESS(1937); FLIGHT FROM GLORY(1937); MOUNTAIN MUSIC(1937); FIXER DUGAN(1939); HOLD THAT WOMAN(1940)
Misc. Talkies
PLAYTHINGS OF HOLLYWOOD(1931)

Sonia Laroze
1984
LES COMPERES(1984, Fr.)

Paul K. Larpae
WARNING SHOT(1967), spec eff

Pierre Larquay
PORTRAIT OF INNOCENCE(1948, Fr.); IF PARIS WERE TOLD TO US(1956, Fr.)

Larquey
DR. KNOCK(1936, Fr.); RECORD 413(1936, Fr.); BLUE VEIL, THE(1947, Fr.)

Pierre Larquey
SECOND BUREAU(1936, Fr.); TWO WOMEN(1940, Fr.); MOULIN ROUGE(1944, Fr.); CARNIVAL OF SINNERS(1947, Fr.); MURDERER LIVES AT NUMBER 21, THE(1947, Fr.); JENNY LAMOUR(1948, Fr.); RAVEN, THE(1948, Fr.); SYLVIA AND THE PHANTOM(1950, Fr.); SIMPLE CASE OF MONEY, A(1952, Fr.); DIABOLIQUE(1955, Fr.); ROYAL AFFAIRS IN VERSAILLES(1957, Fr.)

Michael Larrain
BUCKSKIN(1968)

Les Larraine
NIGHTMARE(1981), spec eff

Less Lar Larraine
1984
FIRST TURN-ON!, THE(1984), spec eff

Carlos Larranga
PRIDE AND THE PASSION, THE(1957)

Fernando Larranga
TERROR IN THE JUNGLE(1968); SURVIVE!(1977, Mex.)

Aurelio Gutierrez Larraya
SANDOKAN THE GREAT(1964, Fr./Ital./Span.), ph

Federico G. Larraya
PLACE CALLED GLORY, A(1966, Span./Ger.), ph

Federico Gutierrez Larraya
RUN LIKE A THIEF(1968, Span.), ph

Jose Larraz
GOLDEN LADY, THE(1979, Brit.), d

Joseph Jose Larraz
VAMPYRES, DAUGHTERS OF DRACULA(1977, Brit.), d

Joseph Larraz
HOUSE THAT VANISHED, THE(1974, Brit.), d; SYMPTOMS(1976, Brit.), d, w

Henry Larrecq
TAMMY AND THE MILLIONAIRE(1967), art d; COUNTERFEIT KILLER, THE(1968), art d; SHAKIEST GUN IN THE WEST, THE(1968), art d; THING, THE(1982), art d

Antonio Larreta
1984
HOLY INNOCENTS, THE(1984, Span.), w

August Larreta
DEATHSTALKER(1983, Arg./U.S.)
1984
DEATHSTALKER, THE(1984)

Sebastian Larreta
1984
DEATHSTALKER, THE(1984)

Vianey Larriaga
VAMPIRES, THE(1969, Mex.)

Fernand A. Larrieu, Jr.
GREATEST, THE(1977, U.S./Brit.)

Earle Larrimore
Silents
KICK-OFF, THE(1926)
Misc. Silents
INSPIRATION(1928)

Francine Larrimore
JOHN MEADE'S WOMAN(1937)
Misc. Silents
ROYAL PAUPER, THE(1917)

Rosalie Larrimore
Misc. Talkies
BEALE STREET MAMA(1946)

Mario Larrinaga
KING KONG(1933), spec eff; SON OF KONG(1933), spec eff

Rudy Larriva
SONG OF THE SOUTH(1946), anim; MELODY TIME(1948), animators; 1001 ARABIAN NIGHTS(1959), d

Tito Larriva
1984
REPO MAN(1984), m

John Larroquette
HEART BEAT(1979); GREEN ICE(1981, Brit.); STRIPES(1981); CAT PEOPLE(1982); HYSTERICAL(1983); TWILIGHT ZONE-THE MOVIE(1983)
1984
CHOOSE ME(1984); MEATBALLS PART II(1984); STAR TREK III: THE SEARCH FOR SPOCK(1984)

Christine Larroude
HUNTING PARTY, THE(1977, Brit.)

Jean Larrouquette
LA GUERRE EST FINIE(1967, Fr./Swed.)

Atle Larsen
SUICIDE MISSION(1956, Brit.)

Bob Larsen
GRIM REAPER, THE(1981, Ital.)

Bobby Larsen
QUIET PLEASE, MURDER(1942)

Buster Larsen
HIDDEN FEAR(1957); EPILOGUE(1967, Den.)

Carolyn Larsen
ROLLOVER(1981)

Elsebeth Larsen
CRAZY PARADISE(1965, Den.)

Eric Larsen
Misc. Talkies
TRAP ON COUGAR MOUNTAIN(1972)

Fred Larsen
BUFFALO BILL AND THE INDIANS, OR SITTING BULL'S HISTORY LESSON(1976)

Gerd Larsen
ROMEO AND JULIET(1966, Brit.); STORIES FROM A FLYING TRUNK(1979, Brit.)

Gerda Larsen
MAN WHO COULD CHEAT DEATH, THE(1959, Brit.); SUBWAY IN THE SKY(1959, Brit.)

Ham Larsen
ADVENTURES OF THE WILDERNESS FAMILY, THE(1975); ENEMY OF THE PEOPLE, AN(1978); FURTHER ADVENTURES OF THE WILDERNESS FAMILY-PART TWO(1978); MOUNTAIN FAMILY ROBINSON(1979)

Jack Larsen
MAN CRAZY(1953)

Johannes Larsen
CIRCLE OF IRON(1979, Brit.), set d

Keith Larsen
OPERATION PACIFIC(1951); FLAT TOP(1952); HIAWATHA(1952); PAULA(1952); ROSE BOWL STORY, THE(1952); FORT VENGEANCE(1953); SON OF BELLE STARR(1953); WAR PAINT(1953); ARROW IN THE DUST(1954); SECURITY RISK(1954); CHIEF CRAZY HORSE(1955); DESERT SANDS(1955); DIAL RED O(1955); NIGHT FREIGHT(1955); WICHITA(1955); APACHE WARRIOR(1957); BADLANDS OF MONTANA(1957); LAST OF THE BADMEN(1957); WOMEN OF THE PREHISTORIC PLANET(1966); MISSION BATANGAS(1968), a, p&d, w
Misc. Talkies
CAXAMBU(1968); OMEGANS, THE(1968); TRAP ON COUGAR MOUNTAIN(1972), d

L.H. Larsen
STALLION CANYON(1949)

Linda Lee Larsen
1984
FLASH OF GREEN, A(1984)

Neils West Larsen
BOY WHO STOLE A MILLION, THE(1960, Brit.), w

Robert W. Larsen
NARCOTICS STORY, THE(1958), p&d

Samuel James Larsen
PRODIGAL, THE(1955), w

Tambi Larsen
SECRET OF THE INCAS(1954), art d; ROSE TATTOO, THE(1955), art d; SCARLET HOUR, THE(1956), art d; WILD IS THE WIND(1957), art d; GEISHA BOY, THE(1958), art d; HOT SPELL(1958), art d; PARTY CRASHERS, THE(1958), art d; ROCK-A-BYE BABY(1958), art d; SPANISH AFFAIR(1958, Span.), art d; FIVE PENNIES, THE(1959), art d; RAT RACE, THE(1960), art d; PLEASURE OF HIS COMPANY, THE(1961), art d; IT'S ONLY MONEY(1962), art d; TOO LATE BLUES(1962), art d; HUD(1963), art d; DISORDERLY ORDERLY, THE(1964), art d; MAN'S FAVORITE SPORT [?](1964), art d; OUTRAGE, THE(1964), art d; SPY WHO CAME IN FROM THE COLD, THE(1965, Brit.), prod d; NEVADA SMITH(1966), art d; BROTHERHOOD, THE(1968), art d; GRASSHOPPER, THE(1970), art d; MOLLY MAGUIRES, THE(1970), art d; GUNFIGHT, A(1971), prod d; LIFE AND TIMES OF JUDGE ROY BEAN, THE(1972), art d; POCKET MONEY(1972), art d; OUTFIT, THE(1973), art d; THUNDERBOLT AND LIGHTFOOT(1974), art d; MOHAMMAD, MESSENGER OF GOD(1976, Lebanon/Brit.), prod d; OUTLAW JOSEY WALES, THE(1976), prod d; WHITE BUFFALO, THE(1977), prod d; HEAVEN'S GATE(1980), art d

Ted Larsen
RAW DEAL(1948), makeup; MAD WEDNESDAY(1950), makeup; M(1951), makeup; MEXICAN MANHUNT(1953), makeup; LOOPHOLE(1954), makeup

Terry Larsen
F.J. HOLDEN, THE(1977, Aus.), w

Trygve Larsen
DARK EYES OF LONDON(1961, Ger.), w

Virginia Larsen
ZAZA(1939)

William Larsen
FIVE DAYS FROM HOME(1978); HEAVEN CAN WAIT(1978)

Anne Larson
TELL ME THAT YOU LOVE ME, JUNIE MOON(1970)

Bob Larson
REDWOOD FOREST TRAIL(1950); CONTINENTAL DIVIDE(1981), p
1984
RIVER RAT, THE(1984), p

Bobby Larson
BANK DICK, THE(1940); COURAGEOUS DR. CHRISTIAN, THE(1940); FIVE LITTLE PEPPERS AT HOME(1940); FIVE LITTLE PEPPERS IN TROUBLE(1940); OUT WEST WITH THE PEPPERS(1940); BACHELOR DADDY(1941); DESIGN FOR SCANDAL(1941); HERE COMES MR. JORDAN(1941); JACKASS MAIL(1942); RIDERS OF THE NORTHLAND(1942); SHIP AHOY(1942); GOOD LUCK, MR. YATES(1943); IRON MAJOR, THE(1943); LEATHER BURNERS, THE(1943); SMART GUY(1943); UNDERDOG, THE(1943); MY PAL, WOLF(1944); UNWRITTEN CODE, THE(1944); ADVENTURES OF RUSTY(1945); BLONDIE'S LUCKY DAY(1946); CROSS MY HEART(1946); LIFE WITH BLONDIE(1946); PERSONALITY KID(1946); BLONDIE'S HOLIDAY(1947)

Bret Larson
LOOSE ENDS(1975)

Cathy Larson
LITTLE DARLINGS(1980)

Charles Larson
ANGEL IN EXILE(1948), w

Christian Larson
Misc. Talkies
BRANCHES(1971)

Christine Larson
FIGHTING RANGER, THE(1948); OUTLAW BRAND(1948); PARTNERS OF THE SUNSET(1948); SILVER TRAILS(1948); CRASHING THRU(1949); HIDDEN DANGER(1949); TRIAL WITHOUT JURY(1950); VALLEY OF FIRE(1951); WELL, THE(1951); BRAVE WARRIOR(1952); LAST TRAIN FROM BOMBAY(1952); VALLEY OF THE HEADHUNTERS(1953)

Craig Larson
SEVEN ALONE(1975)

Darrell Larson
STUDENT NURSES, THE(1970); KOTCH(1971); MAGNIFICENT SEVEN RIDE, THE(1972); OUTSIDE IN(1972); FUTUREWORLD(1976); CHINA SYNDROME, THE(1979); WHEN TIME RAN OUT(1980); FRANCES(1982); PARTNERS(1982); SIX WEEKS(1982)
1984
MIKE'S MURDER(1984)

David Larson
Misc. Talkies
CRUISIN' 57(1975)

Elsie Larson
MAN WHO DARED, THE(1933); WILD GOLD(1934)

Eric Larson
SNOW WHITE AND THE SEVEN DWARFS(1937), anim; FANTASIA(1940), anim; PINOCCHIO(1940), anim d; BAMBI(1942), anim; THREE CABALLEROS, THE(1944), anim; MAKE MINE MUSIC(1946), anim; SO DEAR TO MY HEART(1949), anim; ALICE IN WONDERLAND(1951), anim d; PETER PAN(1953), anim; LADY AND THE TRAMP(1955), anim d; SLEEPING BEAUTY(1959), d; ONE HUNDRED AND ONE DALMATIANS(1961), anim; SWORD IN THE STONE, THE(1963), anim; MARY POPPINS(1964), anim; ARISTOCATS, THE(1970), anim; ROBIN HOOD(1973), anim

Erick Larson
SONG OF THE SOUTH(1946), anim

Evelyn Larson
MAIDSTONE(1970)

George Larson
Silents
RIP VAN WINKLE(1921), ph

Glen A. Larson
BATTLESTAR GALACTICA(1979), w; MISSION GALACTICA: THE CYLON ATTACK(1979), w; CONQUEST OF THE EARTH(1980), w

Glen Larson
BUCK ROGERS IN THE 25TH CENTURY(1979), w

Howard Larson
EVEL KNIEVEL(1971)

Jack Larson
FIGHTER SQUADRON(1948); REDWOOD FOREST TRAIL(1950); ON THE LOOSE(1951); STARLIFT(1951); BATTLE ZONE(1952); KID MONK BARONI(1952); STAR OF TEXAS(1953); THREE SAILORS AND A GIRL(1953); JOHNNY TROUBLE(1957); TEENAGE MILLIONAIRE(1961); YOUNG SWINGERS, THE(1963)
1984
MIKE'S MURDER(1984), p

James A. Larson
SO LONG, BLUE BOY(1973), ph

Jay B. Larson
SUNSET COVE(1978)

John Larson
FM(1978)

Keith Larson
TORPEDO ALLEY(1953)

Kenneth Larson
ONE FROM THE HEART(1982)

Lance Larson
PSYCHOPATH, THE(1973)
Misc. Talkies
EYE FOR AN EYE, AN(1975)

Larry Larson
JEANNE EAGELS(1957); HOPSCOTCH(1980)

Leif Larson
SUICIDE MISSION(1956, Brit.)

Nancy Larson
COACH(1978), w

Patricia Larson
FRANCES(1982)

Paul Larson
DETECTIVE, THE(1968); PRETTY POISON(1968); LAST OF THE RED HOT LOVERS(1972); CHINA SYNDROME, THE(1979)

Philip Larson
HOUSE OF DARK SHADOWS(1970); PURSUIT OF HAPPINESS, THE(1971)

Rod Larson
ONE WAY WAHINI(1965), w

Scott Larson
DREAMER(1979)

Seth Larson
STRANGE MR. GREGORY, THE(1945), ed; MR. HEX(1946), ed

William Larson
GOING IN STYLE(1979)

Barbro Larsson
TIME OF DESIRE, THE(1957, Swed.)

Britta Larsson
NIGHT IN JUNE, A(1940, Swed.)

Katerina Larsson
LE VIOL(1968, Fr./Swed.)

Lars-Erik Larsson
GREAT ADVENTURE, THE(1955, Swed.), md; MAKE WAY FOR LILA(1962, Swed./Ger.), m

Lotta Larsson
FLIGHT OF THE EAGLE(1983, Swed.)

Rolf Larsson
HUGS AND KISSES(1968, Swed.); SEA GULL, THE(1968), set d

Stefan Larsson
WINTER LIGHT, THE(1963, Swed.)

Stig Larsson
1984
ELEMENT OF CRIME, THE(1984, Den.)

William Larsson
Misc. Silents
GIVE US THIS DAY(1913, Swed.)

Ariane Larteguy
MEN PREFER FAT GIRLS(1981, Fr.)

Jean Larteguy
LOST COMMAND, THE(1966), w

Charmain Larthe
TWICE UPON A TIME(1953, Brit.)

Yolande Larthe
TWICE UPON A TIME(1953, Brit.)

Lartigau
MONTE CARLO STORY, THE(1957, Ital.)

Gerard Lartigau
ARIZONA COLT(1965, It./Fr./Span.); LA GUERRE EST FINIE(1967, Fr./Swed.); THINGS OF LIFE, THE(1970, Fr./Ital./Switz.)

Martin Lartique
WAR OF THE BUTTONS(1963 Fr.)

Beverly LaRue
NIGHT OF THE WITCHES(1970)

Carmen LaRue
DAUGHTER OF SHANGHAI(1937)

Claude Larue
SLEEPING CAR TO TRIESTE(1949, Brit.)

D.C. LaRue
SGT. PEPPER'S LONELY HEARTS CLUB BAND(1978)

Emily LaRue
IT COULDN'T HAVE HAPPENED–BUT IT DID(1936); ALOMA OF THE SOUTH SEAS(1941); NEW KIND OF LOVE, A(1963)

Fontaine LaRue
WEST OF THE ROCKIES(1929)
Silents
BEYOND(1921)

Frank H. LaRue
STRANGE PEOPLE(1933)

Frank LaRue
SIDEWALKS OF NEW YORK(1931); LAW OF THE SEA(1932); ONCE IN A LIFETIME(1932); RADIO PATROL(1932); CHRISTOPHER STRONG(1933); FLYING DEVILS(1933); GAMBLING SHIP(1933); SITTING PRETTY(1933); SUNDOWN RIDER, THE(1933); THRILL HUNTER, THE(1933); FIGHTING RANGER, THE(1934); HERE COMES THE NAVY(1934); WHEN A MAN SEES RED(1934); AFTER THE DANCE(1935); GIRL WHO CAME BACK, THE(1935); HIGH SCHOOL GIRL(1935); HIS FIGHTING BLOOD(1935); MOTIVE FOR REVENGE(1935); NO RANSOM(1935); SHE COULDN'T TAKE IT(1935); SINGING VAGABOND, THE(1935); SPECIAL AGENT(1935); STRANDED(1935); THROWBACK, THE(1935); DEATH FROM A DISTANCE(1936); FORBIDDEN TRAIL(1936); HEIR TO TROUBLE(1936); RED RIVER VALLEY(1936); BOOTHILL BRIGADE(1937); CAPTAINS COURAGEOUS(1937); DANGEROUS HOLIDAY(1937); FIGHTING DEPUTY, THE(1937); FIGHTING TEXAN(1937); GUN LORDS OF STIRRUP BASIN(1937); IT HAPPENED OUT WEST(1937); LAWMAN IS BORN, A(1937); LEFT-HANDED LAW(1937); LIGHTNIN' CRANDALL(1937); MOONLIGHT ON THE RANGE(1937); PUBLIC COWBOY NO. 1(1937); THAT I MAY LIVE(1937); TRAIL OF VENGEANCE(1937); TRAPPED BY G-MEN(1937); CODE OF THE RANGERS(1938); COLORADO KID(1938); DANGER VALLEY(1938); MEXICALI KID, THE(1938); OUTLAWS OF SONORA(1938); OVERLAND STAGE RAIDERS(1938); SONGS AND BULLETS(1938); WEST OF RAINBOW'S END(1938); BIG TOWN CZAR(1939); CODE OF THE FEARLESS(1939); DOWN THE WYOMING TRAIL(1939); FEUD OF THE RANGE(1939); IN OLD MONTANA(1939); KNIGHT OF THE PLAINS(1939); LAW COMES TO TEXAS, THE(1939); LONE STAR PIONEERS(1939); MESQUITE BUCKAROO(1939); PORT OF HATE(1939); ROLL, WAGONS, ROLL(1939); SMOKY TRAILS(1939); SONG OF THE BUCKAROO(1939); SUNDOWN ON THE PRAIRIE(1939); TRIGGER PALS(1939); ARIZONA FRONTIER(1940); BILLY THE KID IN TEXAS(1940); BRIGHAM YOUNG–FRONTIERSMAN(1940); CHARLIE CHAN IN PANAMA(1940); COURAGEOUS DR. CHRISTIAN, THE(1940); DURANGO KID, THE(1940); FUGITIVE FROM A PRISON CAMP(1940); LAND OF THE SIX GUNS(1940); MURDER IN THE NIGHT(1940, Brit.); RANGE BUSTERS, THE(1940); RETURN OF WILD BILL, THE(1940); RIDERS OF PASCO BASIN(1940); SEA HAWK, THE(1940); WESTBOUND STAGE(1940); BEYOND THE

SACRAMENTO(1941); GUN MAN FROM BODIE, THE(1941); PRAIRIE STRANGER(1941); RIDERS OF BLACK MOUNTAIN(1941); ROBBERS OF THE RANGE(1941); SON OF DAVY CROCKETT, THE(1941); AMERICAN EMPIRE(1942); CYCLONE KID, THE(1942); LAWLESS PLAINSMEN(1942); MISSOURI OUTLAW, A(1942); STARDUST ON THE SAGE(1942); TRAIL RIDERS(1942); FRONTIER LAW(1943); MORE THE MERRIER, THE(1943); PAYOFF, THE(1943); ROBIN HOOD OF THE RANGE(1943); SMART GUY(1943); DEVIL RIDERS(1944); FOLLOW THE BOYS(1944); GHOST GUNS(1944); LAST HORSEMAN, THE(1944); LAURA(1944); LEAVE IT TO THE IRISH(1944); MACHINE GUN MAMA(1944); CORNERED(1945); FRONTIER FEUD(1945); LOST TRAIL, THE(1945); BORDER BANDITS(1946); GENTLEMAN FROM TEXAS(1946); UNDER ARIZONA SKIES(1946); FLASHING GUNS(1947); PRAIRIE EXPRESS(1947); RAIDERS OF THE SOUTH(1947); SECRET LIFE OF WALTER MITTY, THE(1947); COURTIN' TROUBLE(1948); CROSSED TRAILS(1948); FRONTIER AGENT(1948); GUN TALK(1948); NO ORCHIDS FOR MISS BLANDISH(1948, Brit.); OKLAHOMA BLUES(1948); RANGE RENEGADES(1948); SONG OF THE DRIFTER(1948); MISFITS, THE(1961), makeup; JOHNNY COOL(1963), makeup; SPY IN THE GREEN HAT, THE(1966); REFLECTIONS IN A GOLDEN EYE(1967), makeup; TAMING OF THE SHREW, THE(1967, U.S./Ital.), makeup; ONLY GAME IN TOWN, THE(1970), makeup

Grace LaRue
SHE DONE HIM WRONG(1933); IF I HAD MY WAY(1940)

Jack LaRue
FOLLOW THE LEADER(1930); ALL-AMERICAN, THE(1932); FAREWELL TO ARMS, A(1932); I AM A FUGITIVE FROM A CHAIN GANG(1932); MAN AGAINST WOMAN(1932); MOUTHPIECE, THE(1932); THREE ON A MATCH(1932); VIRTUE(1932); WHILE PARIS SLEEPS(1932); GIRL IN 419(1933); HEADLINE SHOOTER(1933); KENNEL MURDER CASE, THE(1933); LAWYER MAN(1933); STORY OF TEMPLE DRAKE, THE(1933); TERROR ABOARD(1933); TO THE LAST MAN(1933); WOMAN ACCUSED(1933); 42ND STREET(1933); FIGHTING ROOKIE, THE(1934); GOOD DAME(1934); MISS FANE'S BABY IS STOLEN(1934); STRAIGHT IS THE WAY(1934); TAKE THE STAND(1934); DARING YOUNG MAN, THE(1935); HEADLINE WOMAN, THE(1935); HIS NIGHT OUT(1935); LITTLE BIG SHOT(1935); MEN OF THE HOUR(1935); REMEMBER LAST NIGHT(1935); SECRET OF THE CHATEAU(1935); SPANISH CAPE MYSTERY(1935); TIMES SQUARE LADY(1935); UNDER THE PAMPAS MOON(1935); WATERFRONT LADY(1935); BRIDGE OF SIGHS(1936); DANCING PIRATE(1936); GO WEST, YOUNG MAN(1936); IT COULDN'T HAVE HAPPENED–BUT IT DID(1936); STRIKE ME PINK(1936); YELLOW CARGO(1936); HER HUSBAND LIES(1937); MIND YOUR OWN BUSINESS(1937); TENDERFOOT GOES WEST, A(1937); ARSON GANG BUSTERS(1938); BORN TO FIGHT(1938); I DEMAND PAYMENT(1938); UNDER THE BIG TOP(1938); VALLEY OF THE GIANTS(1938); IN OLD CALIENTE(1939); EAST OF THE RIVER(1940); ENEMY AGENT(1940); FORGOTTEN GIRLS(1940); FUGITIVE FROM A PRISON CAMP(1940); FOOTSTEPS IN THE DARK(1941); GENTLEMAN FROM DIXIE(1941); HARD GUY(1941); PAPER BULLETS(1941); RINGSIDE MAISIE(1941); SWAMP WOMAN(1941); DESPERATE CHANCE FOR ELLERY QUEEN, A(1942); HIGHWAYS BY NIGHT(1942); PARDON MY SARONG(1942); X MARKS THE SPOT(1942); AMAZING MR. FORREST, THE(1943, Brit.); DESERT SONG, THE(1943); GENTLE GANGSTER, A(1943); GIRL FROM MONTEREY, THE(1943); LAW RIDES AGAIN, THE(1943); NEVER A DULL MOMENT(1943); PISTOL PACKIN' MAMA(1943); SCREAM IN THE DARK, A(1943); SULTAN'S DAUGHTER, THE(1943); DANGEROUS PASSAGE(1944); FOLLOW THE LEADER(1944); LAST RIDE, THE(1944); DAKOTA(1945); ROAD TO UTOPIA(1945); SPANISH MAIN, THE(1945); STEPPIN' IN SOCIETY(1945); IN OLD SACRAMENTO(1946); MURDER IN THE MUSIC HALL(1946); SANTA FE UPRISING(1946); MY FAVORITE BRUNETTE(1947); FOR HEAVEN'S SAKE(1950); RIDE THE MAN DOWN(1952); FORTY POUNDS OF TROUBLE(1962); FOR THOSE WHO THINK YOUNG(1964); ROBIN AND THE SEVEN HOODS(1964); WON TON TON, THE DOG WHO SAVED HOLLYWOOD(1976)
Misc. Talkies
CALLING ALL CARS(1935); HOT OFF THE PRESS(1935); ELLIS ISLAND(1936); ARSON RACKET SQUAD(1938); BUSH PILOT(1947); ROBIN HOOD OF MONTEREY(1947)

James LaRue
FIREBALL JUNGLE(1968)

Janet LaRue
1984
RECKLESS(1984)

Toni LaRue
LOST IN A HAREM(1944); OUT OF THIS WORLD(1945)

Walt LaRue
NEW FRONTIER(1939); EDGE OF DARKNESS(1943); COW TOWN(1950); NORTH AVENUE IRREGULARS, THE(1979)

Adrienne Larussa
MAN WHO FELL TO EARTH, THE(1976, Brit.)

Louis LaRusso II
BEYOND THE REEF(1981), w

Yann Larvor
COLOSSUS OF RHODES, THE(1961, Ital., Fr., Span.)

Pierre Lary
MILKY WAY, THE(1969, Fr./Ital.)

Xavier Lasa
1984
ESCAPE FROM SEGOVIA(1984, Span.), m

Dick LaSalle
SPEED CRAZY(1959), m; WHY MUST I DIE?(1960), m

John LaSalle
MANTIS IN LACE(1968)

Martin LaSalle
DR. TARR'S TORTURE DUNGEON(1972, Mex.); DOGS OF WAR, THE(1980, Brit.); MISSING(1982); SORCERESS(1983); UNDER FIRE(1983)

Richard Lasalle
BIG NIGHT, THE(1960), m; FLIGHT THAT DISAPPEARED, THE(1961), m; PURPLE HILLS, THE(1961), m; BROKEN LAND, THE(1962), m; DEADLY DUO(1962), m; GUN STREET(1962), m; HANDS OF A STRANGER(1962), m; SAINTLY SINNERS(1962), m; DIARY OF A MADMAN(1963), m; POLICE NURSE(1963), m, md; QUICK GUN, THE(1964), m; TIME TRAVELERS, THE(1964), m; YANK IN VIETNAM, A(1964), m, md; ARIZONA RAIDERS(1965), m; CONVICT STAGE(1965), m; FORT COURAGEOUS(1965), m, md; WAR PARTY(1965), m; RUNAWAY GIRL(1966), m; 40 GUNS TO APACHE PASS(1967), m; DAUGHTERS OF SATAN(1972), m, md; SUPERBEAST(1972), m, md; DOCTOR DEATH: SEEKER OF SOULS(1973), ph; ALICE DOESN'T LIVE HERE ANYMORE(1975), m

Walter Lasally
PRIVATE SCHOOL(1983), ph

Luciano Lasam
SAMAR(1962)

Carolyn Lasater
DIARY OF A BACHELOR(1964)

Jerry Lasater
Misc. Talkies
MISSION TO DEATH(1966)

Jo Jo LaSavio
CROSSROADS(1942)

Judy LaScala
LENNY(1974)

Andrea Lascelle
HOUSE OF 1,000 DOLLS(1967, Ger./Span./Brit.)

Ward Lascelle
Silents
RIP VAN WINKLE(1921), p&d; MIND OVER MOTOR(1923), p&d
Misc. Silents
AFFINITIES(1922), d

Andrea Lascelles
FICKLE FINGER OF FATE, THE(1967, Span./U.S.)

Henry Lascoe
MAN WITH MY FACE, THE(1951)

Jerry Lascoe, Jr.
HOODLUM SAINT, THE(1946)

Vincent Lascoumes
EXPOSED(1983)

Gary Lasdun
THIN RED LINE, THE(1964); CRACK IN THE WORLD(1965); SILENCERS, THE(1966); GUNN(1967)

John Lasell
SUPPOSE THEY GAVE A WAR AND NOBODY CAME?(1970); HONKY(1971); ORGANIZATION, THE(1971); DEATHMASTER, THE(1972)

Dieter Laser
LOST HONOR OF KATHARINA BLUM, THE(1975, Ger.); OPERATION GANYMED(1977, Ger.); GERMANY IN AUTUMN(1978, Ger.)

Miriam Laserson
MY FATHER'S HOUSE(1947, Palestine)

Cees Laseur
THEY CAME BY NIGHT(1940, Brit.)

Harry Lash
LIBELED LADY(1936); HEADIN' EAST(1937); LIVE, LOVE AND LEARN(1937); I LOVE YOU AGAIN(1940); STRIKE UP THE BAND(1940); TWO GIRLS ON BROADWAY(1940)

Peggy Lashbrook
HUSBANDS(1970)

I. Lashchinilina
Misc. Silents
LIFE IN DEATH(1914, USSR)

Joe LaShelle
IN THIS CORNER(1948), ph

Joseph LaShelle
TAKE IT OR LEAVE IT(1944), ph; FALLEN ANGEL(1945), ph; MISTER 880(1950), ph; UNDER MY SKIN(1950), ph; MR. BELVEDERE RINGS THE BELL(1951), ph; THIRTEENTH LETTER, THE(1951), ph; CONQUEROR, THE(1956), ph; OUR MISS BROOKS(1956), ph; CRIME OF PASSION(1957), ph; FURY AT SHOWDOWN(1957), ph; FUZZY PINK NIGHTGOWN, THE(1957), ph; NAKED AND THE DEAD, THE(1958), ph; APARTMENT, THE(1960), ph; ALL IN A NIGHT'S WORK(1961), ph; HONEYMOON MACHINE, THE(1961), ph; HOW THE WEST WAS WON(1962), ph; OUTSIDER, THE(1962), ph; CHILD IS WAITING, A(1963), ph; KISS ME, STUPID(1964), ph; WILD AND WONDERFUL(1964), ph; FORTUNE COOKIE, THE(1966), ph; BAREFOOT IN THE PARK(1967), ph; KONA COAST(1968), ph

Estelle Lasheur
Misc. Silents
PHANTOM HUSBAND, A(1917)

Donald Lashey
Silents
PRICE OF A PARTY, THE(1924)

Ella Mae Lashley
TALES OF MANHATTAN(1942)

James Lashly
CANNONBALL(1976, U.S./Hong Kong)

Ray Laska
Misc. Talkies
MAN WHO SAW TOMORROW, THE(1981)

Zoe Laskari
SPOILED ROTTEN(1968, Gr.); STEFANIA(1968, Gr.)

Harris Laskawy
KING OF THE GYPSIES(1978); FORTY DEUCE(1982); WORLD ACCORDING TO GARP, The(1982)
1984
ULTIMATE SOLUTION OF GRACE QUIGLEY, THE(1984)

Jason Laskay
SMALL CIRCLE OF FRIENDS, A(1980)

Jay Laskay
HELLO DOWN THERE(1969); GRASSHOPPER, THE(1970)

Alex Lasker
FIREFOX(1982), w

Lawrence Lasker
WARGAMES(1983), w

Betty Laskey
THIS IS NOT A TEST(1962), w

Marghanita Laski
IT STARTED IN PARADISE(1952, Brit.), w; LITTLE BOY LOST(1953), w

Serge Laski
1984
PERILS OF GWENDOLINE, THE(1984, Fr.), p

Michael Laskin
PERSONALS, THE(1982)
Diane Lasko
PHOBIA(1980, Can.)
Ed Lasko
OPERATION DAMES(1959), w; ROADRACERS, THE(1959), w; BROKEN LAND, THE(1962), w
Gene Lasko
WHEN THE LEGENDS DIE(1972), p; FOUR FRIENDS(1981), p, p
Harold Lasko
WOMEN OF DESIRE(1968)
Henry Lasko
TATTOOED STRANGER, THE(1950)
J. Lasko
Misc. Talkies
BOOTS TURNER(1973), d
Andrew Laskos
COMMITMENT, THE(1976), w
Orestis Laskos
GIRL OF THE MOUNTAINS(1958, Gr.), d&w
Irena Laskowska
SALTO(1966, Pol.); MAN OF MARBLE(1979, Pol.)
Jan Laskowski
BARRIER(1966, Pol.), ph; PORTRAIT OF LENIN(1967, Pol./USSR), ph; JOVITA(1970, Pol.), ph
Jacek Laskus
1984
FAR FROM POLAND(1984), ph
Art Lasky
DUKE COMES BACK, THE(1937); NOTHING SACRED(1937); WESTERN GOLD(1937); SAN FRANCISCO DOCKS(1941), ph
Charles Lasky
LOUISIANA PURCHASE(1941)
Gil Lasky
SPIDER BABY(1968), p; GAY DECEIVERS, THE(1969), w; BLOOD AND LACE(1971), p, w; NIGHT GOD SCREAMED, THE(1975), p, w
Hal Lasky
MAN WHO WOULD NOT DIE, THE(1975)
Jay Lasky
BIRDS DO IT(1966)
Jesse L. Lasky
WITHOUT RESERVATIONS(1946), p; BERKELEY SQUARE(1933), p; POWER AND THE GLORY, THE(1933), p; WORST WOMAN IN PARIS(1933), p; ZOO IN BUDAPEST(1933), p; I AM SUZANNE(1934), p; SPRINGTIME FOR HENRY(1934), p; WHITE PARADE, THE(1934), p, w; GAY DECEPTION, THE(1935), p; HELL-DORADO(1935), p; HERE'S TO ROMANCE(1935), p; REDHEADS ON PARADE(1935), p; GAY DESPERADO, THE(1936), p; HITTING A NEW HIGH(1937), p; MUSIC FOR MADAME(1937), p; ADVENTURES OF MARK TWAIN, THE(1944), p; RHAPSODY IN BLUE(1945), p; MIRACLE OF THE BELLS, THE(1948), p
Silents
BREWSTER'S MILLIONS(1914), p; BREWSTER'S MILLIONS(1921), p
Jesse Lasky
INNOCENTS OF PARIS(1929), p; WARRIOR'S HUSBAND, THE(1933), p; AS HUSBANDS GO(1934), p; COMING OUT PARTY(1934), p; GRAND CANARY(1934), p; ONE RAINY AFTERNOON(1936), p
Silents
ARMSTRONG'S WIFE(1915), p; ALIEN SOULS(1916), p; ANTON THE TERRIBLE(1916), p
Jesse Lasky, Jr.
COMING OUT PARTY(1934), w; RED HEAD(1934), w; WHITE PARADE, THE(1934), w; MUSIC IS MAGIC(1935), w; SECRET AGENT, THE(1936, Brit.), w; UNION PACIFIC(1939), w; NORTHWEST MOUNTED POLICE(1940), w; BACK IN THE SADDLE(1941), w; SINGING HILL, THE(1941), w; STEEL AGAINST THE SKY(1941), w; OMAHA TRAIL, THE(1942), w; REAP THE WILD WIND(1942), w; UNCONQUERED(1947), w; SAMSON AND DELILAH(1949), w; LORNA DOONE(1951), w; MASK OF THE AVENGER(1951), w; NEVER TRUST A GAMBLER(1951), w; BRIGAND, THE(1952), w; THIEF OF VENICE, THE(1952), w; MISSION OVER KOREA(1953), w; SALOME(1953), w; SILVER WHIP, THE(1953), w; HELL AND HIGH WATER(1954), w; IRON GLOVE, THE(1954), w; PEARL OF THE SOUTH PACIFIC(1955), w; HOT BLOOD(1956), w; TEN COMMANDMENTS, THE(1956), w; BUCCANEER, THE(1958), w; JOHN PAUL JONES(1959), w; WIZARD OF BAGHDAD, THE(1960), w; PIRATES OF TORTUGA(1961), w; SEVEN WOMEN FROM HELL(1961), w; LAND RAIDERS(1969), w; CRIME AND PASSION(1976, U.S., Ger.), w
Leon Lasky
FOOLS FOR SCANDAL(1938)
Patricia Lasky
SILENT WITNESS, THE(1962)
Zane Lasky
NETWORK(1976); SENTINEL, THE(1977)
Mara Laso
AWFUL DR. ORLOFF, THE(1964, Span./Fr.)
Tommy LaSorda
AMERICATHON(1979)
Carol Lasowski
DEMON LOVER, THE(1977)
Jacques Lasry
HEAD, THE(1961, Ger.), m
Pierre Lasry
DRIFTER, THE(1966), p
Barbara Lass
EVE WANTS TO SLEEP(1961, Pol.); WEREWOLF IN A GIRL'S DORMITORY(1961, Ital./Aust.); LOVE AT TWENTY(1963, Fr./Ital./Jap./Pol./Ger.); RIFIFI IN TOKYO(1963, Fr./Ital.); SERENADE FOR TWO SPIES(1966, Ital./Ger.); JOVITA(1970, Pol.); PRIEST OF ST. PAULI, THE(1970, Ger.); EFFI BRIEST(1974, Ger.)
Darrel Lass
DEATHCHEATERS(1976, Aus.), art d

Darrell Lass
PULP(1972, Brit.), art d; NORMAN LOVES ROSE(1982, Aus.), prod d; WILD DUCK, THE(1983, Aus.), prod d
1984
FANTASY MAN(1984, Aus.), p, prod d
Debora Lass
THEY ALL LAUGHED(1981)
Gloria Lass
STATE OF SIEGE(1973, Fr./U.S./Ital./Ger.)
Jeanne Lass
PULP(1972, Brit.)
Henri Lassa
COUP DE TORCHON(1981, Fr.), p
Martin Lassalle
PICKPOCKET(1963, Fr.)
Walter Lassally
PASSING STRANGER, THE(1954, Brit.), ph; TOGETHER(1956, Brit.), ph; ELECTRA(1962, Gr.), ph; LONELINESS OF THE LONG DISTANCE RUNNER, THE(1962, Brit.), ph; TASTE OF HONEY, A(1962, Brit.), ph; TOM JONES(1963, Brit.), ph; PSYCHE 59(1964, Brit.), ph; ZORBA THE GREEK(1964, U.S./Gr.), ph; MADALENA(1965, Gr.), ph; DAY THE FISH CAME OUT, THE(1967. Brit./Gr.), ph; JOANNA(1968, Brit.), ph; OEDIPUS THE KING(1968, Brit.), ph; ADDING MACHINE, THE(1969), ph; THREE INTO TWO WON'T GO(1969, Brit.), ph; SOMETHING FOR EVERYONE(1970), ph; LOLA(1971, Brit./Ital.), ph; SAVAGES(1972), ph; TO KILL A CLOWN(1972), ph; HAPPY MOTHER'S DAY... LOVE, GEORGE(1973), ph; MALACHI'S COVE(1973, Brit.), ph; WILD PARTY, THE(1975), ph; PLEASANTVILLE(1976), ph; GREAT BANK HOAX, THE(1977), ph; HULLABALOO OVER GEORGIE AND BONNIE'S PICTURES(1979, Brit.), ph; PILOT, THE(1979), ph; SOMETHING SHORT OF PARADISE(1979), ph; MEMOIRS OF A SURVIVOR(1981, Brit.), ph; HEAT AND DUST(1983, Brit.), ph
1984
BOSTONIANS, THE(1984), ph
Dagmar Lassander
HATCHET FOR A HONEYMOON(1969, Span./Ital.); LEGEND OF THE WOLF WOMAN, THE(1977, Span.)
1984
BLACK CAT, THE(1984, Ital./Brit.); HOUSE BY THE CEMETERY, THE(1984, Ital.)
Finn Lassen
LURE OF THE JUNGLE, THE(1970, Den.)
Louise Lasser
WHAT'S NEW, PUSSYCAT?(1965, U.S./Fr.); WHAT'S UP, TIGER LILY?(1966), a, w; BANANAS(1971); SUCH GOOD FRIENDS(1971); EVERYTHING YOU ALWAYS WANTED TO KNOW ABOUT SEX, BUT WE'RE AFRAID TO ASK(1972); SLITHER(1973); IN GOD WE TRUST(1980)
Sid Lassick
BONNIE PARKER STORY, THE(1958); PARATROOP COMMAND(1959)
Sydney Lassick
ONE FLEW OVER THE CUCKOO'S NEST(1975); CARRIE(1976); BILLION DOLLAR HOBO, THE(1977); HOT STUFF(1979); SKATETOWN, U.S.A.(1979); HISTORY OF THE WORLD, PART 1(1981); UNSEEN, THE(1981); FAST-WALKING(1982); PANDEMONIUM(1982)
1984
NIGHT PATROL(1984); SILENT MADNESS(1984)
Misc. Talkies
NIGHTKILLERS(1983)
Lassie
BLUE SIERRA(1946); HILLS OF HOME(1948); CHALLENGE TO LASSIE(1949); SUN COMES UP, THE(1949); PAINTED HILLS, THE(1951); MAGIC OF LASSIE, THE(1978)
Misc. Talkies
NEEKA(1968)
Lassie the Dog
SON OF LASSIE(1945); LASSIE'S GREAT ADVENTURE(1963)
Misc. Talkies
LASSIE, THE VOYAGER(1966)
Silents
TOL'ABLE DAVID(1921)
Lynn D. Lasswell, Jr.
1984
PLACES IN THE HEART(1984)
Melinda Lasson
ROUND TRIP(1967)
Stuart Lasswell
WOMEN OF THE PREHISTORIC PLANET(1966)
Todd Lasswell
STREET IS MY BEAT, THE(1966)
Tom Lasswell
DON'T ANSWER THE PHONE(1980)
Brenda Last
PETER RABBIT AND TALES OF BEATRIX POTTER(1971, Brit.)
Ruth Last
ENDLESS LOVE(1981); FORT APACHE, THE BRONX(1981)
Roland LaStarza
POINT BLANK(1967); OUTFIT, THE(1973)
Gwendolyn Laster
WELL, THE(1951)
Carlo Lasticati
ANNA OF BROOKLYN(1958, Ital.), d
Adolfo Lastretti
VENUS IN FURS(1970, Ital./Brit./Ger.); CONFESSIONS OF A POLICE CAPTAIN(1971, Ital.); DEAF SMITH AND JOHNNY EARS(1973, Ital.); SHAFT IN AFRICA(1973); LION OF THE DESERT(1981, Libya/Brit.)
Carlo Lastricati
LITTLE ROMANCE, A(1979, U.S./Fr.)
Jo Lastry
LA MARSEILLAISE(1938, Fr.)
Roger Laswell
MILLION DOLLAR LEGS(1939); HALF ANGEL(1951)

Aladar Laszlo
TOP HAT(1935), w; GANGWAY FOR TOMORROW(1943), w; GIRL RUSH(1944), w

Alexander Laszlo
DOUBLE EXPOSURE(1944), m; FOLLOW THAT WOMAN(1945), m; GREAT FLAMARION, THE(1945), m; HIGH POWERED(1945), m; ONE EXCITING NIGHT(1945), m; ACCOMPLICE(1946), m; FRENCH KEY, THE(1946), m; GLASS ALIBI, THE(1946), md; JOE PALOOKA, CHAMP(1946); STRANGE IMPERSONATION(1946), md; THEY MADE ME A KILLER(1946), m; BANJO(1947), m; UNTAMED FURY(1947), m, md; YANKEE FAKIR(1947), md; SPIRITUALIST, THE(1948), m; PAROLE, INC.(1949), m; GHOST OF THE CHINA SEA(1958), m, md; NARCOTICS STORY, THE(1958), m; NIGHT OF THE BLOOD BEAST(1958), m; FORBIDDEN ISLAND(1959), m; SUBMARINE SEAHAWK(1959), m; ATOMIC SUBMARINE, THE(1960), m

Andrew Laszlo
ONE POTATO, TWO POTATO(1964), ph; YOU'RE A BIG BOY NOW(1966), ph; NIGHT THEY RAIDED MINSKY'S, THE(1968), ph; POPI(1969), ph; LOVERS AND OTHER STRANGERS(1970), ph; OUT OF TOWNERS, THE(1970), ph; OWL AND THE PUSSYCAT, THE(1970), ph; JENNIFER ON MY MIND(1971), ph; CLASS OF '44(1973), ph; COUNTDOWN AT KUSINI(1976, Nigerian), ph; SOMEBODY KILLED HER HUSBAND(1978), ph; WARRIORS, THE(1979), ph; FUNHOUSE, THE(1981), ph; SOUTHERN COMFORT(1981), ph; FIRST BLOOD(1982), ph; I, THE JURY(1982), ph
1984
STREETS OF FIRE(1984), ph; THIEF OF HEARTS(1984), ph

Ernest Laszlo
HITLER GANG, THE(1944), ph; TWO YEARS BEFORE THE MAST(1946), ph; DEAR RUTH(1947), ph; ROAD TO RIO(1947), ph; GIRL FROM MANHATTAN(1948), ph; LET'S LIVE A LITTLE(1948), ph; LULU BELLE(1948), ph; ON OUR MERRY WAY(1948), ph; BIG WHEEL, THE(1949), ph; COVER-UP(1949), ph; LUCKY STIFF, THE(1949), ph; MANHANDLED(1949), ph; D.O.A.(1950), ph; JACKIE ROBINSON STORY, THE(1950), ph; RIDING HIGH(1950), ph; M(1951), ph; WELL, THE(1951), ph; WHEN I GROW UP(1951), ph; FIRST TIME, THE(1952), ph; LADY IN THE IRON MASK(1952), ph; STEEL TRAP, THE(1952), ph; THREE FOR BEDROOM C(1952), ph; HOUDINI(1953), ph; MOON IS BLUE, THE(1953), ph; NAKED JUNGLE, THE(1953), ph; STALAG 17(1953), ph; STAR, THE(1953), ph; ABOUT MRS. LESLIE(1954), ph; APACHE(1954), ph; VERA CRUZ(1954), ph; BIG KNIFE, THE(1955), ph; KENTUCKIAN, THE(1955), ph; KISS ME DEADLY(1955), ph; BANDIDO(1956), ph; WHILE THE CITY SLEEPS(1956), ph; GUNSIGHT RIDGE(1957), ph; OMAR KHAYYAM(1957), ph; VALERIE(1957), ph; ATTACK OF THE PUPPET PEOPLE(1958), ph; RESTLESS YEARS, THE(1958), ph; SPACE CHILDREN, THE(1958), ph; TEN SECONDS TO HELL(1959), ph; INHERIT THE WIND(1960), ph; TORMENTED(1960), ph; JUDGMENT AT NUREMBERG(1961), ph; LAST SUNSET, THE(1961), ph; FOUR FOR TEXAS(1963), ph; IT'S A MAD, MAD, MAD, MAD WORLD(1963), ph; ONE MAN'S WAY(1964), ph; SHIP OF FOOLS(1965), ph; FANTASTIC VOYAGE(1966), ph; LUV(1967), ph; STAR!(1968), ph; DADDY'S GONE A-HUNTING(1969), ph; FIRST TIME, THE(1969), ph; AIRPORT(1970), ph; SHOWDOWN(1973), ph; LOGAN'S RUN(1976), ph; DOMINO PRINCIPLE, THE(1977), ph
Silents
LINDA(1929), ph

Miklos Laszlo
BIG CITY(1948), w; IN THE GOOD OLD SUMMERTIME(1949), w

Nikolaus Laszlo
SHOP AROUND THE CORNER, THE(1940), w

Stanislav Latal
MIDSUMMERS NIGHT'S DREAM, A(1961, Czech), anim

Pep Latanzi
RUMBLE ON THE DOCKS(1956), m/l Jimmy DeKnight

Albert Latasha
PRINCE OF FOXES(1949)

Jason Late
1984
SPLASH(1984)

Barbara Latell
WACO(1966)

Lyle Latell
FEDERAL FUGITIVES(1941); IN THE NAVY(1941); SHADOW OF THE THIN MAN(1941); TEXAS(1941); FLEET'S IN, THE(1942); FOREIGN AGENT(1942); LUCKY JORDAN(1942); THEY ALL KISSED THE BRIDE(1942); WIFE TAKES A FLYER, THE(1942); HAPPY GO LUCKY(1943); THEY GOT ME COVERED(1943); MEN ON HER MIND(1944); ONE MYSTERIOUS NIGHT(1944); THAT'S MY BABY(1944); DICK TRACY(1945); GEORGE WHITE'S SCANDALS(1945); HOLD THAT BLONDE(1945); DICK TRACY VS. CUEBALL(1946); MYSTERIOUS MR. VALENTINE, THE(1946); PERFECT MARRIAGE, THE(1946); SHADOWS OVER CHINATOWN(1946); DICK TRACY MEETS GRUESOME(1947); DICK TRACY'S DILEMMA(1947); GAS HOUSE KIDS IN HOLLYWOOD(1947); RIDE THE PINK HORSE(1947); SONG OF THE THIN MAN(1947); T-MEN(1947); BUNGALOW 13(1948); COBRA STRIKES, THE(1948); HE WALKED BY NIGHT(1948); NIGHT HAS A THOUSAND EYES(1948); NOOSE HANGS HIGH, THE(1948); STREET WITH NO NAME, THE(1948); SKY DRAGON(1949); TAKE ONE FALSE STEP(1949); DAMNED DON'T CRY, THE(1950); STREETCAR NAMED DESIRE, A(1951); HOUDINI(1953); HOUSE OF WAX(1953); CRIME WAVE(1954); AT GUNPOINT(1955); GIRL RUSH, THE(1955); STEEL JUNGLE, THE(1956); KELLY AND ME(1957)

Don Laterre
INVITATION TO HAPPINESS(1939)

Giovanni Laterza
BULLET FOR STEFANO(1950, Ital.), p

Eddie Lateste
1984
SMURFS AND THE MAGIC FLUTE, THE(1984, Fr./Belg.), anim

Aaron Latham
URBAN COWBOY(1980), w

Aileen Latham
PUBLIC LIFE OF HENRY THE NINTH, THE(1934, Brit.)

Ann Latham
THIEVES LIKE US(1974)

Anne Latham
Misc. Talkies
BRAIN MACHINE, THE(1972)

Billy Ray Latham
FARMER'S OTHER DAUGHTER, THE(1965)

Dwight Latham
BADLANDS OF DAKOTA(1941)

Eileen Latham
EVERYTHING OKAY(1936, Brit.)

Heather Latham
AFFAIRS OF ADELAIDE(1949, U. S./Brit)

Jack Latham
SHOW BOAT(1936); PORT OF SEVEN SEAS(1938); SOLID GOLD CADILLAC, THE(1956); DEVIL'S HAIRPIN, THE(1957); LOVING YOU(1957); WILD IN THE STREETS(1968)

Jeff Latham
FANDANGO(1970); MACHISMO-40 GRAVES FOR 40 GUNS(1970)

Larry Latham
Misc. Talkies
AFTERMATH, THE(1980)

Louise Latham
MARNIE(1964); FIRECREEK(1968); HAIL, HERO!(1969); ADAM AT 6 A.M.(1970); MAKING IT(1971); WHITE LIGHTNING(1973); SUGARLAND EXPRESS, THE(1974); 92 IN THE SHADE(1975, U.S./Brit.)
1984
MASS APPEAL(1984); PHILADELPHIA EXPERIMENT, THE(1984)

Lynn Latham
XANADU(1980); GREAT MUPPET CAPER, THE(1981)

Maxton Latham
WINDFLOWERS(1968)

Patrica Latham
ALL AT SEA(1970, Brit.), w

Patricia Latham
LONE CLIMBER, THE(1950, Brit./Aust.), w; JOHNNY ON THE RUN(1953, Brit.), w; COMPANIONS IN CRIME(1954, Brit.), w; TIM DRISCOLL'S DONKEY(1955, Brit.), w; DOG AND THE DIAMONDS, THE(1962, Brit.), w

Philip Latham
RIVALS, THE(1963, Brit.); DEVIL-SHIP PIRATES, THE(1964, Brit.); RING OF SPIES(1964, Brit.); SECRET OF BLOOD ISLAND, THE(1965, Brit.); DRACULA-PRINCE OF DARKNESS(1966, Brit.); LAST GRENADE, THE(1970, Brit.)

Red Latham
DOUGHBOYS IN IRELAND(1943)

Stuart Latham
BLACKOUT(1940, Brit.); GHOST TRAIN, THE(1941, Brit.); TAWNY PIPIT(1947, Brit.); ONE NIGHT WITH YOU(1948, Brit.); MADE IN HEAVEN(1952, Brit.); MAN IN THE WHITE SUIT, THE(1952); ONCE A SINNER(1952, Brit.); SEE HOW THEY RUN(1955, Brit.)

Squadron Leader Stuart Latham
JOURNEY TOGETHER(1946, Brit.)

Timothy Latham
MANGANINNIE(1982, Aus.)

Tony Latham
WARRIORS, THE(1979); WOLFEN(1981)

Stan Lathan
AMAZING GRACE(1974), d
1984
BEAT STREET(1984), d; GO TELL IT ON THE MOUNTAIN(1984), d

Stanley Lathburg
TEMPORARY WIDOW, THE(1930, Ger./Brit.)

Stanley Lathbury
SCHOOL FOR SCANDAL, THE(1930, Brit.); SPECKLED BAND, THE(1931, Brit.); COUNSEL'S OPINION(1933, Brit.); RAT, THE(1938, Brit.); TERROR, THE(1941, Brit.)

Stuart Lathom
NEUTRAL PORT(1941, Brit.)

Nick Lathouris
MAD MAX(1979, Aus.)

Elizabeth Lathram
WITHOUT A TRACE(1983)

Jack Lathrop
SUN VALLEY SERENADE(1941)

Larry Lathrop
SEA OF GRASS, THE(1947)

Lawrence Lathrop
NEWSBOY'S HOME(1939); ONCE UPON A TIME(1944); WOMAN IN THE WINDOW, THE(1945)

Phil Lathrop
PRIVATE LIVES OF ADAM AND EVE, THE(1961), ph; DAYS OF WINE AND ROSES(1962), ph; NEVER TOO LATE(1965), ph; MAME(1974), ph; BLACK BIRD, THE(1975), ph; KILLER ELITE, THE(1975), ph; NATIONAL LAMPOON'S CLASS REUNION(1982), ph

Philip H. Lathrop
CONCORDE, THE-AIRPORT '79(, ph; GIRLS ON THE LOOSE(1958), ph; LIVE FAST, DIE YOUNG(1958), ph; MONEY, WOMEN AND GUNS(1958), ph; PERFECT FURLOUGH, THE(1958), ph; SAGA OF HEMP BROWN, THE(1958), ph; WILD HERITAGE(1958), ph; CRY TOUGH(1959), ph; MONSTER OF PIEDRAS BLANCAS, THE(1959), ph; EXPERIMENT IN TERROR(1962), ph; LONELY ARE THE BRAVE(1962), ph; DIME WITH A HALO(1963), ph; SOLDIER IN THE RAIN(1963), ph; TWILIGHT OF HONOR(1963), ph; AMERICANIZATION OF EMILY, THE(1964), ph; PINK PANTHER, THE(1964), ph; CINCINNATI KID, THE(1965), ph; GIRL HAPPY(1965), ph; 36 HOURS(1965), ph; WHAT DID YOU DO IN THE WAR, DADDY?(1966), ph; DON'T MAKE WAVES(1967), ph; GUNN(1967), ph; HAPPENING, THE(1967), ph; POINT BLANK(1967), ph; FINIAN'S RAINBOW(1968), ph; I LOVE YOU, ALICE B. TOKLAS!(1968), ph; GYPSY MOTHS, THE(1969), ph; ILLUSTRATED MAN, THE(1969), ph; THEY SHOOT HORSES, DON'T THEY?(1969), ph; HAWAIIANS, THE(1970), ph; RABBIT, RUN(1970), ph; TRAVELING EXECUTIONER, THE(1970), ph; WILD ROVERS(1971), ph; EVERY LITTLE CROOK AND NANNY(1972), ph; PORTNOY'S COMPLAINT(1972), ph; ALL-AMERICAN BOY, THE(1973), ph; LOLLY-MADONNA XXX(1973), ph; THIEF WHO CAME TO DINNER, THE(1973), ph; AIRPORT 1975(1974), ph; EARTHQUAKE(1974), ph; HARD TIMES(1975), ph; PRISONER OF SECOND AVENUE, THE(1975), ph; SWASHBUCKLER(1976), ph; AIRPORT '77(1977), ph; DIFFERENT STORY, A(1978), ph; DRIVER, THE(1978), ph; MOMENT BY MOMENT(1978), ph; CHANGE OF SEASONS, A(1980), ph; FOOLIN' AROUND(1980), ph; LITTLE MISS MARKER(1980), ph; LOVING COU-

PLES(1980), ph; ALL NIGHT LONG(1981), ph; HAMMETT(1982), ph; JEKYLL AND HYDE...TOGETHER AGAIN(1982), ph

Robert Lathrop
ORGY OF THE DEAD(1965), art d

William Addison Lathrop
Silents
INNOCENCE OF RUTH, THE(1916), w; AMERICAN LIVE WIRE, AN(1918), w

The Lathrops
MANHATTAN MERRY-GO-ROUND(1937)

Lyle Latill
I WAS A COMMUNIST FOR THE F.B.I.(1951)

Billy Latimer
SPIELER, THE(1929)

Carl Rocky Latimer
JOE LOUIS STORY, THE(1953)

Carlo Latimer
TERROR OF THE BLACK MASK(1967, Fr./Ital.)

Cherie Latimer
RUN FOR YOUR WIFE(1966, Fr./Ital.); ANGELS HARD AS THEY COME(1971); AROUSERS, THE(1973); SHAMPOO(1975); FOUR DEUCES, THE(1976); SKY RIDERS(1976, U.S./Gr.); ROSE, THE(1979)

Denis Latimer
MC KENZIE BREAK, THE(1970)

Edyth Latimer
Silents
IMPOSTER, THE(1918)

Florence Latimer
Silents
PILGRIM, THE(1923)

Harry Latimer
Silents
FATAL FINGERS(1916. Brit.)

Henry Latimer
THIRD TIME LUCKY(1931, Brit.); STEPPING TOES(1938, Brit.)
Silents
UNDER SUSPICION(1919, Brit.); MOTORING(1927, Brit.)

Herb Latimer
STARLIFT(1951)

Hugh Latimer
UNDERCOVER AGENT(1935, Brit.); CORRIDOR OF MIRRORS(1948, Brit.); ADVENTURES OF PC 49, THE(1949, Brit.); SOMEONE AT THE DOOR(1950, Brit.); GHOST SHIP(1953, Brit.); MAN WITH A MILLION(1954, Brit.); TIM DRISCOLL'S DONKEY(1955, Brit.); LAST MAN TO HANG, THE(1956, Brit.); NARROWING CIRCLE, THE(1956, Brit.); ROGUE'S YARN(1956, Brit.); COSMIC MONSTERS(1958, Brit.); GENTLE TRAP, THE(1960, Brit.); MODEL MURDER CASE, THE(1964, Brit.); NIGHT TRAIN TO PARIS(1964, Brit.); SCHOOL FOR SEX(1969, Brit.); JANE EYRE(1971, Brit.)
Misc. Talkies
CRAWLING TERROR, THE(1958, Brit.)

Hurb Latimer
SNIPER, THE(1952)

Jonathan Latimer
THEY WON'T BELIEVE ME(1947), w; WESTLAND CASE, THE(1937), w; LADY IN THE MORGUE(1938), w; LAST WARNING, THE(1938), w; LONE WOLF SPY HUNT, THE(1939), w; PHANTOM RAIDERS(1940), w; TOPPER RETURNS(1941), w; GLASS KEY, THE(1942), w; NIGHT IN NEW ORLEANS, A(1942), w; NOCTURNE(1946), w; BEYOND GLORY(1948), w; BIG CLOCK, THE(1948), w; NIGHT HAS A THOUSAND EYES(1948), w; SEALED VERDICT(1948), w; ALIAS NICK BEAL(1949), w; COPPER CANYON(1950), w; REDHEAD AND THE COWBOY, THE(1950), w; SUBMARINE COMMAND(1951), w; BOTANY BAY(1953), w; PLUNDER OF THE SUN(1953), w; BACK FROM ETERNITY(1956), w; UNHOLY WIFE, THE(1957), w; WHOLE TRUTH, THE(1958, Brit.), w

Louise Latimer
BUNKER BEAN(1936); DON'T TURN'EM LOOSE(1936); GRAND JURY(1936); MURDER ON A BRIDLE PATH(1936); PLOT THICKENS, THE(1936); TWO IN REVOLT(1936); CALIFORNIA STRAIGHT AHEAD(1937); WE'RE ON THE JURY(1937); WINGS OVER HONOLULU(1937)

Max Latimer
DIAMONDS ARE FOREVER(1971, Brit.)

Michael Latimer
MAN FOR ALL SEASONS, A(1966, Brit.); PREHISTORIC WOMEN(1967, Brit.); MAN OF VIOLENCE(1970, Brit.); MOSQUITO SQUADRON(1970, Brit.); GOT IT MADE(1974, Brit.)

Ross Latimer
THREE DESPERATE MEN(1951)

Sheila Latimer
1984
GREYSTOKE: THE LEGEND OF TARZAN, LORD OF THE APES(1984)

Frank Latimore
IN THE MEANTIME, DARLING(1944); DOLLY SISTERS, THE(1945); RAZOR'S EDGE, THE(1946); SHOCK(1946); THREE LITTLE GIRLS IN BLUE(1946); 13 RUE MADELEINE(1946); BLACK MAGIC(1949); MATA HARI'S DAUGHTER(1954, Fr./Ital); JOHN PAUL JONES(1959); PURPLE NOON(1961, Fr./Ital.); THEN THERE WERE THREE(1961); HONEY POT, THE(1967, Brit.); SERGEANT, THE(1968); PATTON(1970); ALL THE PRESIDENT'S MEN(1976)

Latin Bob Stars
$100 A NIGHT(1968, Ger.)

Manfred Lating
MORITURI(1965); BEDKNOBS AND BROOMSTICKS(1971)

Franco Latini
JOHNNY HAMLET(1972, Ital.)

Massimo Latini
1984
BASILEUS QUARTET(1984, Ital.), ed

Nino Latino
SLAUGHTER HOTEL(1971, Ital.), w

Zoltan Latinovits
ROUND UP, THE(1969, Hung.)

N. Latinskiy
GARNET BRACELET, THE(1966, USSR)

John Latito
FRENCHMAN'S CREEK(1944)

George Latka
MATILDA(1978)

N. Latonia
HOUSE OF GREED(1934, USSR)

Jill Lator
CHAPPAQUA(1967)

Charles Latorella
NAKED CITY, THE(1948)

Maureen Latorella
NAKED CITY, THE(1948)

Charles LaTorre
LOUISIANA PURCHASE(1941); ENTER ARSENE LUPIN(1944); SONG TO REMEMBER, A(1945); THOUSAND AND ONE NIGHTS, A(1945); WALLS CAME TUMBLING DOWN, THE(1946); DOUBLE LIFE, A(1947); ANGEL ON THE AMAZON(1948); FRENCH LEAVE(1948); PANHANDLE(1948); HARBOR OF MISSING MEN(1950); SEPTEMBER AFFAIR(1950); SUNSET IN THE WEST(1950); SECRETS OF MONTE CARLO(1951)

Don Latorre
BOY OF THE STREETS(1937); JUVENILE COURT(1938); RANGE WAR(1939)

John Latouche
CABIN IN THE SKY(1943), w; DREAMS THAT MONEY CAN BUY(1948), m

Charles Latour
PURPLE MASK, THE(1955), w

Joelle Latour
SCHEHERAZADE(1965, Fr./Ital./Span.); IS PARIS BURNING?(1966, U.S./Fr.); DIANE'S BODY(1969, Fr./Czech.)

Maria Latour
MADMAN OF LAB 4, THE(1967, Fr.); VISCOUNT, THE(1967, Fr./Span./Ital./Ger.); BELLE DE JOUR(1968, Fr.)

Tammy Latour
MY BODY HUNGERS(1967)

Bob Latourneaux
PILGRIMAGE(1972)

Robert Latourneaux
VON RICHTHOFEN AND BROWN(1970)

Larry Latrae
Misc. Talkies
HORSE(1965)

Louise Latraverse
GREAT BIG THING, A(1968, U.S./Can.)

De Latraz
LOVE CONTRACT, THE(1932, Brit.), w

Fred Latremouille
MAN, A WOMAN, AND A BANK, A(1979, Can.)

Candy Latson
SYNANON(1965); LIFE STUDY(1973)

Dorothy Latta
ROLL, THUNDER, ROLL(1949); NAUGHTY ARLETTE(1951, Brit.)

James Latta
Silents
MAKING THE VARSITY(1928)

Matt Lattanzi
RICH AND FAMOUS(1981); GREASE 2(1982); MY TUTOR(1983)

Tina Lattanzi
ANNA(1951, Ital.); LOVE SPECIALIST, THE(1959, Ital.); UNFAITHFULS, THE(1960, Ital.); MINOTAUR, THE(1961, Ital.); LEOPARD, THE(1963, Ital.)

Lily Latte
LILIOM(1935, Fr.)

Irene Latter
1984
SUBURBIA(1984)

M. Lattes
LUCREZIA BORGIA(1937, Fr.), m

Marcel Lattes
FROM TOP TO BOTTOM(1933, Fr.), m

Frank Lattimore
CAST A GIANT SHADOW(1966); IF IT'S TUESDAY, THIS MUST BE BELGIUM(1969)

Alberto Lattuada
BANDIT, THE(1949, Ital.), d; WITHOUT PITY(1949, Ital.), d; ANNA(1951, Ital.), d; TEMPEST(1958, Ital./Yugo./Fr.), d, w; MAFIOSO(1962, Ital.), d; RITA(1963, Fr./Ital.), d, w; STEPPE, THE(1963, Fr./Ital.), d, w; VARIETY LIGHTS(1965, Ital.), a, p&d; w; MANDRAGOLA(1966 Fr./Ital.), d, w; MATCHLESS(1967, Ital.), d, w; FRAULEIN DOKTOR(1969, Ital./Yugo.), d, w; MAN WHO CAME FOR COFFEE, THE(1970, Ital.), d, w; WHITE SISTER(1973, Ital./Span./Fr.), d, w

Annarosa Lattuada
8 ½(1963, Ital.)

Felice Lattuada
VARIETY LIGHTS(1965, Ital.), m

Klaus-Hagen Latwesen
PRIEST OF ST. PAULI, THE(1970, Ger.)

Alice Lau [Lau Nga Lai]
UNCOMMON VALOR(1983)

Audrey Lau
DRAGON'S GOLD(1954)

Charley Lau
MAX DUGAN RETURNS(1983)

Wesley Lau
I WANT TO LIVE!(1958); ALAMO, THE(1960); VENETIAN AFFAIR, THE(1967); JOURNEY TO SHILOH(1968); PANIC IN THE CITY(1968); SKYJACKED(1972); HOMEBODIES(1974); LEPKE(1975, U.S./Israel), a, w

Marc Laub
GODFATHER, THE(1972), ed; HONEYSUCKLE ROSE(1980), ed; FOUR FRIENDS(1981), ed, ed; HAMMETT(1982), ed

1984
MISUNDERSTOOD(1984), ed
Tamara Laub
NORTH STAR, THE(1943)
William B. Laub
Silents
HER STORY(1920, Brit.), w; FALSE BRANDS(1922), w; OUTLAWS OF THE SEA(1923), t; IS LOVE EVERYTHING?(1924), t, ed; PLAYTHINGS OF DESIRE(1924), w; DAUGHTERS WHO PAY(1925), w; MAD DANCER(1925), w, ed
Mildred Laube
WORDS AND MUSIC(1929)
Kan Lauber
CHICKEN CHRONICLES, THE(1977), m
Ken Lauber
WORLD OF HENRY ORIENT, THE(1964), m; DRIFTER, THE(1966), m; SCRATCH HARRY(1969), m; HEARTS OF THE WEST(1975), m; WANDA NEVADA(1979), m; LITTLE DRAGONS, THE(1980), m; CHILLY SCENES OF WINTER(1982), m
Paula Lauc
WHAT A WAY TO GO(1964)
Agnes Lauchian
OH, MR. PORTER!(1937, Brit.)
Agnes Lauchlan
U-BOAT 29(1939, Brit.); THIS MAN IS MINE(1946 Brit.); ONCE UPON A DREAM(1949, Brit.); TIME IS MY ENEMY(1957, Brit.); WHOLE TRUTH, THE(1958, Brit.)
Charles Lauck
BASHFUL BACHELOR, THE(1942), w
Chester Lauck
DREAMING OUT LOUD(1940); BASHFUL BACHELOR, THE(1942); SO THIS IS WASHINGTON(1943); TWO WEEKS TO LIVE(1943); GOIN' TO TOWN(1944); PARTNERS IN TIME(1946); LUM AND ABNER ABROAD(1956)
Kenneth Laud
ACT OF MURDER(1965, Brit.)
Evelina Laudani
PIRATE AND THE SLAVE GIRL, THE(1961, Fr./Ital.)
Fasco Laudati
DIFFICULT YEARS(1950, Ital.), p
Philippe Laudenbach
MURIEL(1963, Fr./Ital.); MON ONCLE D'AMERIQUE(1980, Fr.); CONFIDENTIAL-LY YOURS(1983, Fr.)
Roland Laudenbach
VOYAGE TO AMERICA(1952, Fr.), w; OBSESSION(1954, Fr./Ital.), w; SECRETS D'ALCOVE(1954, Fr./Ital.), w; END OF DESIRE(1962 Fr./Ital.), w; LOVERS ON A TIGHTROPE(1962, Fr.), w
Jim Laudenslager
LADY GREY(1980), ed
Harry Lauder
AULD LANG SYNE(1929, Brit.); HAPPY DAYS(1930); END OF THE ROAD, THE(1936, Brit.)
Sir Harry Lauder
Silents
HUNTINGTOWER(1927, Brit.)
Sam Lauder
Misc. Silents
PENNY OF TOP HILL TRAIL(1921)
Tilly Lauenstein
I, TOO, AM ONLY A WOMAN(1963, Ger.); ONLY A WOMAN(1966, Ger.); OLDEST PROFESSION, THE(1968, Fr./Ital./Ger.)
Andrew Lauer
1984
BLAME IT ON THE NIGHT(1984)
William Lauer
TO ALL A GOODNIGHT(1980)
Beryl Lauerick
CONSTANT NYMPH, THE(1933, Brit.)
Hans Ulrich Laufer
MEPHISTO(1981, Ger.)
Jacob Laufer
FAN, THE(1981)
Josef Laufer
OPERATION DAYBREAK(1976, U.S./Brit./Czech.)
Richard Lauffen
JOURNEY TO THE LOST CITY(1960, Ger./Fr./Ital.)
Charles Laug
WALK IN THE SPRING RAIN, A(1970), ph
John Laughinghouse
OPERATION CIA(1965)
Agnes Laughlan
COMPULSORY WIFE, THE(1937, Brit.); WINDMILL, THE(1937, Brit.); ME AND MY PAL(1939, Brit.); YOUNG MR. PITT, THE(1942, Brit.)
Agnes Laughlin
ALF'S BUTTON AFLOAT(1938, Brit.)
Anna Laughlin
Silents
GREYHOUND, THE(1914); ORDEAL, THE(1914)
Misc. Silents
CROOKY(1915); WHAT HAPPENED TO FATHER(1915)
Frank [Tom] Laughlin
TRIAL OF BILLY JACK, THE(1974), d, w; MASTER GUNFIGHTER, THE(1975), d
Gloria Laughlin
SON OF SINBAD(1955)
John Laughlin
OFFICER AND A GENTLEMAN, AN(1982)
1984
CRIMES OF PASSION(1984); FOOTLOOSE(1984)
Michael Laughlin
DEAD KIDS(1981 Aus./New Zealand), d, w; STRANGE INVADERS(1983), d, w

Michael S. Laughlin
WHISPERERS, THE(1967, Brit.), p; JOANNA(1968, Brit.), p; CHANDLER(1971), p; CHRISTIAN LICORICE STORE, THE(1971), p; DUSTY AND SWEETS McGEE(1971), p; TWO-LANE BLACKTOP(1971), p
Mickey Laughlin
I'LL BE SEEING YOU(1944)
Sharon Laughlin
300 YEAR WEEKEND(1971); HAPPY HOOKER, THE(1975)
T.C. Laughlin II
1984
BREAKIN'(1984)
T.C. Frank [Tom Laughlin]
BILLY JACK GOES TO WASHINGTON(1977), w
Teresa Christina Laughlin
TRIAL OF BILLY JACK, THE(1974), w
Teresa Laughlin
TRIAL OF BILLY JACK, THE(1974); BILLY JACK GOES TO WASHINGTON(1977)
Tom Laughlin
TEA AND SYMPATHY(1956); THESE WILDER YEARS(1956); DELINQUENTS, THE(1957); LAFAYETTE ESCADRILLE(1958); SENIOR PROM(1958); SOUTH PACIFIC(1958); BATTLE OF THE CORAL SEA(1959); GIDGET(1959); PROPER TIME, THE(1959), a, p,d&w; TALL STORY(1960); LIKE FATHER LIKE SON(1961), a, p,d&w; YOUNG SINNER, THE(1965), a, p,d&w; BORN LOSERS(1967), a, p; BILLY JACK(1971); TRIAL OF BILLY JACK, THE(1974); MASTER GUNFIGHTER, THE(1975); BILLY JACK GOES TO WASHINGTON(1977); LEGEND OF THE LONE RANGER, THE(1981)
Rol Laughner
BOY FROM INDIANA(1950)
Charles Laughton
WOLVES(1930, Brit.); DOWN RIVER(1931, Brit.); DEVIL AND THE DEEP(1932); IF I HAD A MILLION(1932); OLD DARK HOUSE, THE(1932); PAYMENT DEFERRED(1932); PICCADILLY(1932, Brit.); SIGN OF THE CROSS, THE(1932); ISLAND OF LOST SOULS(1933); PRIVATE LIFE OF HENRY VIII, THE(1933); WHITE WOMAN(1933); BARRETTS OF WIMPOLE STREET, THE(1934); LES MISERABLES(1935); MUTINY ON THE BOUNTY(1935); RUGGLES OF RED GAP(1935); REMBRANDT(1936, Brit.); THE BEACHCOMBER(1938, Brit.); HUNCHBACK OF NOTRE DAME, THE(1939); JAMAICA INN(1939, Brit.), a, p; SIDEWALKS OF LONDON(1940, Brit.); THEY KNEW WHAT THEY WANTED(1940); IT STARTED WITH EVE(1941); STAND BY FOR ACTION(1942); TALES OF MANHATTAN(1942); TUTTLES OF TAHITI(1942); FOREVER AND A DAY(1943); MAN FROM DOWN UNDER, THE(1943); THIS LAND IS MINE(1943); CANTERVILLE GHOST, THE(1944); SUSPECT, THE(1944); CAPTAIN KIDD(1945); BECAUSE OF HIM(1946); PARADINE CASE, THE(1947); ARCH OF TRIUMPH(1948); BIG CLOCK, THE(1948); GIRL FROM MANHATTAN(1948); BRIBE, THE(1949); MAN ON THE EIFFEL TOWER, THE(1949); BLUE VEIL, THE(1951); STRANGE DOOR, THE(1951); ABBOTT AND COSTELLO MEET CAPTAIN KIDD(1952); O. HENRY'S FULL HOUSE(1952); SALOME(1953); YOUNG BESS(1953); HOBSON'S CHOICE(1954, Brit.); NIGHT OF THE HUNTER, THE(1955), d; WITNESS FOR THE PROSECUTION(1957); SPARTACUS(1960); UNDER TEN FLAGS(1960, U.S./Ital.); ADVISE AND CONSENT(1962)
Dixie Laughton
THIN MAN, THE(1934)
Eddie Laughton
ONE MAN JUSTICE(1937); VICE RACKET(1937); CONVICTED(1938); HIGHWAY PATROL(1938); LET US LIVE(1939); LONE WOLF SPY HUNT, THE(1939); MY SON IS A CRIMINAL(1939); SPECIAL INSPECTOR(1939); BLAZING SIX SHOOTERS(1940); BLONDIE HAS SERVANT TROUBLE(1940); BULLETS FOR RUSTLERS(1940); FIVE LITTLE PEPPERS IN TROUBLE(1940); GIRLS OF THE ROAD(1940); ISLAND OF DOOMED MEN(1940); LADY IN QUESTION, THE(1940); LONE WOLF KEEPS A DATE, THE(1940); MAN FROM TUMBLEWEEDS, THE(1940); MEN WITHOUT SOULS(1940); OUT WEST WITH THE PEPPERS(1940); SCANDAL SHEET(1940); TEXAS STAGECOACH(1940); WEST OF ABILENE(1940); ACROSS THE SIERRAS(1941); CONFESSIONS OF BOSTON BLACKIE(1941); I WAS A PRISONER ON DEVIL'S ISLAND(1941); MEET BOSTON BLACKIE(1941); MYSTERY SHIP(1941); OUTLAWS OF THE PANHANDLE(1941); PENNY SERENADE(1941); PHANTOM SUBMARINE, THE(1941); THREE GIRLS ABOUT TOWN(1941); YOU'LL NEVER GET RICH(1941); ATLANTIC CONVOY(1942); BOOGIE MAN WILL GET YOU, THE(1942); CANAL ZONE(1942); LAWLESS PLAINSMEN(1942); PARACHUTE NURSE(1942); SABOTAGE SQUAD(1942); SPIRIT OF STANFORD, THE(1942); SUBMARINE RAIDER(1942); TALK OF THE TOWN(1942); TRAMP, TRAMP, TRAMP(1942); WEST OF TOMBSTONE(1942); HAIL TO THE RANGERS(1943); IS EVERYBODY HAPPY?(1943); LAUGH YOUR BLUES AWAY(1943); ONE DANGEROUS NIGHT(1943); TWO SENORITAS FROM CHICAGO(1943); JAM SESSION(1944); SUNDOWN VALLEY(1944); LOST WEEKEND, THE(1945); MASQUERADE IN MEXICO(1945); WELL-GROOMED BRIDE, THE(1946); CHICKEN EVERY SUNDAY(1948)
Edward Laughton
SHOCKING MISS PILGRIM, THE(1947)
Hazel Laughton
MILKY WAY, THE(1936); PARADISE FOR THREE(1938)
Bob Lauher
WHICH WAY TO THE FRONT?(1970)
Maurice Laumain
TRAFFIC(1972, Fr.), ed
Keith Laumer
MONITORS, THE(1969), w; PEEPER(1975), w
Jean Launay
YOUNG TORLESS(1968, Fr./Ger.)
Frank Launder
CHILDREN OF CHANCE(1930, Brit.), w; HARMONY HEAVEN(1930, Brit.), w; MIDDLE WATCH, THE(1930, Brit.), w; SONG OF SOHO(1930, Brit.), w; UNDER THE GREENWOOD TREE(1930, Brit.), w; "W" PLAN, THE(1931, Brit.), w; HOBSON'S CHOICE(1931, Brit.), w; KEEPERS OF YOUTH(1931, Brit.), w; AFTER OFFICE HOURS(1932, Brit.), w; JOSSER IN THE ARMY(1932, Brit.), w; LAST COUPON, THE(1932, Brit.), w; WOMAN DECIDES, THE(1932, Brit.), d&w; FACING THE MUSIC(1933, Brit.), w; FOR THE LOVE OF MIKE(1933, Brit.), w; HAWLEY'S OF HIGH STREET(1933, Brit.), w; HAPPY(1934, Brit.), w; THOSE WERE THE DAYS(1934, Brit.), w; YOU MADE ME LOVE YOU(1934, Brit.), w; BLACK MASK(1935, Brit.), w; GET OFF MY FOOT(1935, Brit.), w; MR. WHAT'S-HIS-NAME(1935, Brit.), w; ROLLING HOME(1935, Brit.), w; SO YOU WON'T TALK?(1935, Brit.), w; DOMMED CARGO(1936, Brit.), w; EDUCATED EVANS(1936, Brit.), w; TWELVE GOOD MEN(1936, Brit.), w; WHERE'S SALLY?(1936, Brit.), w; DON'T GET ME WRONG(1937, Brit.), w;

OH, MR. PORTER!(1937, Brit.), w; EMIL(1938, Brit.), w; LADY VANISHES, THE(1938, Brit.), w; LOVES OF MADAME DUBARRY, THE(1938, Brit.), w; INSPECTOR HORNLEIGH ON HOLIDAY(1939, Brit.), w; NIGHT TRAIN(1940, Brit.), w; THEY CAME BY NIGHT(1940, Brit.), w; GIRL MUST LIVE, A(1941, Brit.), w; MAIL TRAIN(1941, Brit.), w; REMARKABLE MR. KIPPS(1942, Brit.), w; YOUNG MR. PITT, THE(1942, Brit.), w; MILLIONS LIKE US(1943, Brit.), d&w; WE DIVE AT DAWN(1943, Brit.), w; SOLDIER, SAILOR(1944, Brit.), w; 2,000 WOMEN(1944, Brit.), d, w; NOTORIOUS GENTLEMAN(1945, Brit.), p, w; ADVENTURESS, THE(1946, Brit.), d, w; GREEN FOR DANGER(1946, Brit.), p; CAPTAIN BOYCOTT(1947, Brit.), p, d, w; DULCIMER STREET(1948, Brit.), p; BLUE LAGOON, THE(1949, Brit.), p, d, w; HAPPIEST DAYS OF YOUR LIFE(1950, Brit.), p, d, w; GREAT MANHUNT, THE(1951, Brit.), p; FOLLY TO BE WISE(1953), p, d, w; GREAT GILBERT AND SULLIVAN, THE(1953, Brit.), p; BELLES OF ST. TRINIAN'S, THE(1954, Brit.), p, d, w; CONSTANT HUSBAND, THE(1955, Brit.), p; LADY GODIVA RIDES AGAIN(1955, Brit.), p, d, w; WEE GEORDIE(1956, Brit.), p, d, w; GREEN MAN, THE(1957, Brit.), p, w; SHE PLAYED WITH FIRE(1957, Brit.), p, w; SMALLEST SHOW ON EARTH, THE(1957, Brit.), p; BLUE MURDER AT ST. TRINIAN'S(1958, Brit.), p, d, w; BRIDAL PATH, THE(1959, Brit.), p, d, w; LEFT, RIGHT AND CENTRE(1959), p; PURE HELL OF ST. TRINIAN'S, THE(1961, Brit.), p, d, w; RING OF SPIES(1964, Brit.), w; JOEY BOY(1965, Brit.), p, d, w; GREAT ST. TRINIAN'S TRAIN ROBBERY, THE(1966, Brit.), p&d, w; WILDCATS OF ST. TRINIAN'S, THE(1980, Brit.), d&w

Perc Launders
THEY WON'T BELIEVE ME(1947); SING FOR YOUR SUPPER(1941); SULLIVAN'S TRAVELS(1941); FOREST RANGERS, THE(1942); FALCON AND THE CO-EDS, THE(1943); IS EVERYBODY HAPPY?(1943); SWEET ROSIE O'GRADY(1943); AND THE ANGELS SING(1944); DESTINY(1944); EXPERIMENT PERILOUS(1944); FALCON IN HOLLYWOOD, THE(1944); FALCON OUT WEST, THE(1944); TWILIGHT ON THE PRAIRIE(1944); WEEKEND PASS(1944); HER LUCKY NIGHT(1945); JOHNNY ANGEL(1945); MASQUERADE IN MEXICO(1945); SHE GETS HER MAN(1945); STORK CLUB, THE(1945); UNDER WESTERN SKIES(1945); WEST OF THE PECOS(1945); BLUE DAHLIA, THE(1946); KILLERS, THE(1946); LOVER COME BACK(1946); DESPERATE(1947); EASY COME, EASY GO(1947); EXILE, THE(1947); KISS OF DEATH(1947); SUDDENLY IT'S SPRING(1947); NAKED CITY, THE(1948); RIVER LADY(1948); SAINTED SISTERS, THE(1948); WESTERN HERITAGE(1948); YOU WERE MEANT FOR ME(1948); ABANDONED(1949); FOR HEAVEN'S SAKE(1950); MILKMAN, THE(1950); ABBOTT AND COSTELLO MEET THE INVISIBLE MAN(1951); CRAZY OVER HORSES(1951); ENFORCER, THE(1951); MEET ME AFTER THE SHOW(1951); IT GROWS ON TREES(1952); ROSE BOWL STORY, THE(1952)

S. John Launer
CREATURE WITH THE ATOM BRAIN(1955); URANIUM BOOM(1956); WEREWOLF, THE(1956); CRIME OF PASSION(1957); I WAS A TEENAGE WEREWOLF(1957); JAILHOUSE ROCK(1957); I WANT TO LIVE!(1958); MARNIE(1964); PENDULUM(1969); GABLE AND LOMBARD(1976); MOMMIE DEAREST(1981)

Georges Launter
FEMMINA(1968 Fr./Ital./Ger.), p&d

Max Laur
NO TIME FOR LOVE(1943)

Anan Laura
CHILDREN OF RAGE(1975, Brit.-Israeli), w

Esther Williams Laura
RAW WIND IN EDEN(1958)

Lister Laurance
MR. SMITH CARRIES ON(1937, Brit.), d; GLASS MOUNTAIN, THE(1950, Brit), ed

Matthew Laurance
PRINCE OF THE CITY(1981); EDDIE AND THE CRUISERS(1983)
1984
BEST DEFENSE(1984); STREETS OF FIRE(1984)

Salvatore Laurani
BULLET FOR THE GENERAL, A(1967, Ital.), w; CONFESSIONS OF A POLICE CAPTAIN(1971, Ital.), w

Bonnie Laurant
MY THIRD WIFE GEORGE(1968)

Carol Laure
GET OUT YOUR HANDKERCHIEFS(1978, Fr.)

Carole Laure
STRANGE SHADOWS IN AN EMPTY ROOM(1977, Can./Ital.); FANTASTICA(1980, Can./Fr.); VICTORY(1981)
1984
HEARTBREAKERS(1984); SURROGATE, THE(1984, Can.)
Misc. Talkies
BLAZING MAGNUM(1976)

Frank Laure
LONELYHEARTS(1958), makeup

Judson Laure
JOHN PAUL JONES(1959)

Odette Laure
HOLIDAY FOR HENRIETTA(1955, Fr.)

Allen Laurel
HORROR OF PARTY BEACH, THE(1964)

Emily Laurel
HORROR OF PARTY BEACH, THE(1964)

Stan Laurel
ROGUE SONG, THE(1930); PARDON US(1931); PACK UP YOUR TROUBLES(1932); DEVIL'S BROTHER, THE(1933); SONS OF THE DESERT(1933); BABES IN TOYLAND(1934); HOLLYWOOD PARTY(1934); BONNIE SCOTLAND(1935); BOHEMIAN GIRL, THE(1936); OUR RELATIONS(1936), a, p; PICK A STAR(1937); WAY OUT WEST(1937), a, p; BLOCKHEADS(1938); SWISS MISS(1938), a, w; FLYING DEUCES, THE(1939); KNIGHT OF THE PLAINS(1939), p; CHUMP AT OXFORD, A(1940); SAPS AT SEA(1940); GREAT GUNS(1941); A-HAUNTING WE WILL GO(1942); AIR RAID WARDENS(1943); JITTERBUGS(1943); BIG NOISE, THE(1944); NOTHING BUT TROUBLE(1944); UTOPIA(1952, Fr./Ital.)

Laurel and Hardy
BULLFIGHTERS, THE(1945)

Kay Laurell
Misc. Silents
BRAND, THE(1919); LONELY HEART(1921)

Peter Laurelli
EASY MONEY(1983)

Anthony Lauren
LEAP OF FAITH(1931, Brit.)

Dixie Lauren
10 VIOLENT WOMEN(1982)

Jeanne Lauren
CHU CHU AND THE PHILLY FLASH(1981)

Joan Lauren
THEY ALL LAUGHED(1981)

Odessa Lauren
FOLLOW THE BOYS(1944)

Ralph Lauren
WILD PARTY, THE(1975), cos; ANNIE HALL(1977), cos; MANHATTAN(1979), cos

Rod Lauren
BLACK ZOO(1963); CRAWLING HAND, THE(1963); GUN HAWK, THE(1963); TERRIFIED!(1963); YOUNG SWINGERS, THE(1963); LAW OF THE LAWLESS(1964); ONCE BEFORE I DIE(1967, U.S./Phil.); CHILDISH THINGS(1969)

S.K. Lauren
CHRISTINA(1929), w; BLONDE VENUS(1932), w; EVENINGS FOR SALE(1932), w; THOSE WE LOVE(1932), w; JENNIE GERHARDT(1933), w; MEN MUST FIGHT(1933), w; PICK-UP(1933), w; THREE-CORNERED MOON(1933), w; ONE NIGHT OF LOVE(1934), w; PARTY'S OVER, THE(1934), w; SISTERS UNDER THE SKIN(1934), w; CRIME AND PUNISHMENT(1935), w; DAMSEL IN DISTRESS, A(1937), w; THERE GOES THE GROOM(1937), w; MOTHER CAREY'S CHICKENS(1938), w; OUR NEIGHBORS–THE CARTERS(1939), w; MARRIED AND IN LOVE(1940), w; MR. AND MRS. NORTH(1941), w; WHEN LADIES MEET(1941), w; FLIGHT FOR FREEDOM(1943), w; RUTHLESS(1948), w; MY BLUE HEAVEN(1950), w

Tammy Lauren
LAST FLIGHT OF NOAH'S ARK, THE(1980)

Andre Laurence
THAT SPLENDID NOVEMBER(1971, Ital./Fr.)

Andrew Laurence
CURSE OF THE WRAYDONS, THE(1946, Brit.); MYSTERIOUS MR. NICHOLSON, THE(1947, Brit.); ROB ROY, THE HIGHLAND ROGUE(1954, Brit.); LIFE AT THE TOP(1965, Brit.); MACBETH(1971, Brit.)

Charles Laurence
CROSS CHANNEL(1955, Brit.); HELL IN KOREA(1956, Brit.); MAGNIFICENT TWO, THE(1967, Brit.)

Claudie Laurence
ROAD TO SHAME, THE(1962, Fr.)

David Laurence
RUNNING(1979, Can.)

Douglas Laurence
QUICK, BEFORE IT MELTS(1964), p; MISTER BUDDWING(1966), p; DOCTOR, YOU'VE GOT TO BE KIDDING(1967), p; LIVE A LITTLE, LOVE A LITTLE(1968), p; SPEEDWAY(1968), p; STAY AWAY, JOE(1968), p

Eddie Laurence
WILD PARTY, THE(1975)

Edwin Laurence
DOOMED CARGO(1936, Brit.)

John Laurence
MANCHURIAN CANDIDATE, THE(1962)

Ken Laurence
HOWZER(1973), d&w

Larry Laurence
LAST REBEL, THE(1971)

Lister Laurence
IN A MONASTERY GARDEN(1935), ed; CAPTAIN MOONLIGHT(1940, Brit.), ed; MAD MEN OF EUROPE(1940, Brit.), ed; LILLI MARLENE(1951, Brit.), ed

Lynley Laurence
STAR!(1968); LAST SHOT YOU HEAR, THE(1969, Brit.)

Mady Laurence
SLEEPYTIME GAL(1942)

Margaret Laurence
REUNION IN FRANCE(1942); RACHEL, RACHEL(1968), w
1984
BROTHERS(1984, Aus.)

Mary Laurence
LADY SAYS NO, THE(1951)

Michael Laurence
PICCADILLY INCIDENT(1948, Brit.); ELIZABETH OF LADYMEAD(1949, Brit.); FOR THEM THAT TRESPASS(1949, Brit.); SQUEEZE A FLOWER(1970, Aus.)

Oswald Laurence
THREE MEN IN A BOAT(1958, Brit.); HORROR OF IT ALL, THE(1964, Brit.)

Paul Laurence
METEOR(1979)

Peter Laurence
ANGEL UNCHAINED(1970)

Peter Lee Laurence
BLACK BEAUTY(1971, Brit./Ger./Span.)

Ted Laurence
COURIER OF LYONS(1938, Fr.), m; MARA MARU(1952)

Toba Laurence
STRANGE AFFAIR, THE(1968, Brit.)

W.E. Laurence
BLACK ACES(1937)

Lydia Laurens
SO FINE(1981)

James Laurenson
WOMEN IN LOVE(1969, Brit.); ASSAULT(1971, Brit.); MONSTER CLUB, THE(1981, Brit.); PINK FLOYD–THE WALL(1982, Brit.)
1984
HEARTBREAKERS(1984)
Misc. Talkies
TWO FACES OF EVIL, THE(1981, Brit.)

Phil Laurenson
WIZARD OF GORE, THE(1970)
Laurent
BOUDU SAVED FROM DROWNING(1967, Fr.), set d
A. Laurent
MY SEVEN LITTLE SINS(1956, Fr./Ital.), ed
Agnes Laurent
FRENCH MISTRESS(1960, Brit.); MARY HAD A LITTLE(1961, Brit.); NUDE IN HIS POCKET(1962, Fr.); SOFT SKIN ON BLACK SILK(1964, Fr./Span.); SELLERS OF GIRLS(1967, Fr.)
Anne Laurent
LOVE IN THE AFTERNOON(1957)
Colette Laurent
LUXURY GIRLS(1953, Ital.)
Hubert Laurent
1984
LE CRABE TAMBOUR(1984, Fr.)
Jacqueline Laurent
JUDGE HARDY'S CHILDREN(1938); DAYBREAK(1940, Fr.); COUP DE TORCHON(1981, Fr.), cos
Jacques Laurent
DANGER IS A WOMAN(1952, Fr.), w
Jean-Pierre Laurent
MOON IN THE GUTTER, THE(1983, Fr./Ital.)
Jeanne-Marie Laurent
Misc. Silents
THERESE RAQUIN(1928, Fr./Ger.)
Marc Laurent
STRANGER, THE(1967, Algeria/Fr./Ital.)
Marie Laurent
CURSE OF THE STONE HAND(1965, Mex/Chile), w
Patrick Laurent
1984
LES COMPERES(1984, Fr.)
Remi Laurent
LA CAGE AUX FOLLES(1979, Fr./Ital.); GIFT, THE(1983, Fr./Ital.)
Robert Laurent
RAZOR'S EDGE, THE(1946)
Steve Laurent
LAFAYETTE(1963, Fr.), m
Tony Laurent
BATTLE OF THE RAILS(1949, Fr.); ON THE RIVERA(1951)
Yves Saint Laurent
MOMENT TO MOMENT(1966), cos
Giuliano Laurenti
GRAND PRIX(1966), makeup; HARD CONTRACT(1969), makeup; DESERTER, THE(1971 Ital./Yugo.), makeup; HORSEMEN, THE(1971), makeup; MAN CALLED SLEDGE, A(1971, Ital.), makeup
Mario Laurentino
OPIATE '67(1967, Fr./Ital.)
Arthur Laurents
WAY WE WERE, THE(1973), w; ROPE(1948), w; ANNA LUCASTA(1949), w; CAUGHT(1949), w; HOME OF THE BRAVE(1949), w; SUMMERTIME(1955), w; ANASTASIA(1956), w; BONJOUR TRISTESSE(1958), w; WEST SIDE STORY(1961), w; GYPSY(1962), w; TURNING POINT, THE(1977), p, w
Nancy Laurents
BANDIT QUEEN(1950)
John Laurenz
WHERE ARE YOUR CHILDREN?(1943); IN OLD NEW MEXICO(1945); SUNSET PASS(1946); THRILL OF BRAZIL, THE(1946); APACHE ROSE(1947); CAPTAIN FROM CASTILE(1947); CODE OF THE WEST(1947); ARCH OF TRIUMPH(1948); BORDER OUTLAWS(1950); FEDERAL MAN(1950)
Joy Laurey
JOY(1983, Fr./Can.), w
Marius Laurey
MILKY WAY, THE(1969, Fr./Ital.)
John Lauri
DARK SANDS(1938, Brit.)
Dan Lauria
WITHOUT A TRACE(1983)
Lew Lauria
REG'LAR FELLERS(1941)
Mary Dean Lauria
HEY, GOOD LOOKIN'(1982)
Misc. Talkies
HEAVY TRAFFIC(1974)
John Lauricella
SOME OF MY BEST FRIENDS ARE...(1971), p
Pippo Lauricella
SECRET OF SANTA VITTORIA, THE(1969)
Al Laurie
DIARY OF A HIGH SCHOOL BRIDE(1959)
Edward Laurie
JAWS 3-D(1983)
Eugene Laurie
LIMELIGHT(1952), art d
Jane Laurie
RETURN OF THE SOLDIER, THE(1983, Brit.)
Joe Laurie
UNION DEPOT(1932), w
Joe Laurie, Jr.
APRIL SHOWERS(1948), w
John Laurie
JUNO AND THE PAYCOCK(1930, Brit.); HER LAST AFFAIRE(1935, Brit.); 39 STEPS, THE(1935, Brit.); AS YOU LIKE IT(1936, Brit.); EAST MEETS WEST(1936, Brit.); LADY JANE GREY(1936, Brit.); BORN THAT WAY(1937, Brit.); EDGE OF THE WORLD, THE(1937, Brit.); THERE WAS A YOUNG MAN(1937, Brit.); WINDMILL, THE(1937, Brit.); CLAYDON TREASURE MYSTERY, THE(1938, Brit.); ROYAL DIVORCE, A(1938, Brit.); TROOPSHIP(1938, Brit.); CLOUDS OVER EUROPE(1939, Brit.); FOUR FEATHERS, THE(1939, Brit.); WARE CASE, THE(1939, Brit.); CONVOY(1940);

LAUGH IT OFF(1940, Brit.); THREE COCKEYED SAILORS(1940, Brit.); GHOST OF ST. MICHAEL'S. THE(1941, Brit.); OLD MOTHER RILEY'S GHOSTS(1941, Brit.); SHIPS WITH WINGS(1942, Brit.); SUICIDE SQUADRON(1942, Brit.); GENTLE SEX, THE(1943, Brit.); LAMP STILL BURNS, THE(1943, Brit.); WORLD OWES ME A LIVING, THE(1944, Brit.); ADVENTURE FOR TWO(1945, Brit.); COLONEL BLIMP(1945, Brit.); GREAT DAY(1945, Brit.); WAY AHEAD, THE(1945, Brit.); CAESAR AND CLEOPATRA(1946, Brit.); GAY INTRUDERS(1946, Brit.); HENRY V(1946, Brit.); SCHOOL FOR SECRETS(1946, Brit.); I KNOW WHERE I'M GOING(1947, Brit.); BONNIE PRINCE CHARLIE(1948, Brit.); BROTHERS, THE(1948, Brit.); HAMLET(1948, Brit.); JASSY(1948, Brit.); MAN OF EVIL(1948, Brit.); MINE OWN EXECUTIONER(1948, Brit.); SHOWTIME(1948, Brit.); AGITATOR, THE(1949); FLOODTIDE(1949, Brit.); MADELEINE(1950, Brit.); NO TRACE(1950, Brit.); TREASURE ISLAND(1950, Brit.); TRIO(1950, Brit.); ENCORE(1951, Brit.); HAPPY GO LOVELY(1951, Brit.); INHERITANCE, THE(1951, Brit.); LAUGHTER IN PARADISE(1951, Brit.); PANDORA AND THE FLYING DUTCHMAN(1951, Brit.); TREAD SOFTLY(1952, Brit.); FAKE, THE(1953, Brit.); GREAT GAME, THE(1953, Brit.); LOVE IN PAWN(1953, Brit.); BLACK KNIGHT, THE(1954); DESTINATION MILAN(1954, Brit.); DEVIL GIRL FROM MARS(1954, Brit.); HOBSON'S CHOICE(1954, Brit.); RICHARD III(1956, Brit.); CAMPBELL'S KINGDOM(1957, Brit.); MAD LITTLE ISLAND(1958, Brit.); MURDER REPORTED(1958, Brit.); KIDNAPPED(1960); NEXT TO NO TIME(1960, Brit.); SIEGE OF THE SAXONS(1963, Brit.); LADIES WHO DO(1964, Brit.); WHY BOTHER TO KNOCK(1964, Brit.); REPTILE, THE(1966, Brit.); MISTER TEN PERCENT(1967, Brit.); DAD'S ARMY(1971, Brit.); PURE S(1976, Aus.); PRISONER OF ZENDA, THE(1979)
Piper Laurie
UNTIL THEY SAIL(1957); LOUISA(1950); MILKMAN, THE(1950); FRANCIS GOES TO THE RACES(1951); PRINCE WHO WAS A THIEF, THE(1951); HAS ANYBODY SEEN MY GAL?(1952); NO ROOM FOR THE GROOM(1952); SON OF ALI BABA(1952); GOLDEN BLADE, THE(1953); MISSISSIPPI GAMBLER, THE(1953); DANGEROUS MISSION(1954); DAWN AT SOCORRO(1954); JOHNNY DARK(1954); AIN'T MISBEHAVIN'(1955); SMOKE SIGNAL(1955); KELLY AND ME(1957); HUSTLER, THE(1961); CARRIE(1976); RUBY(1977); TIM(1981, Aus.)
Tim Laurie
STERILE CUCKOO, THE(1969)
Jay Laurier
HOBSON'S CHOICE(1931, Brit.); I'LL STICK TO YOU(1933, Brit.); WALTZ TIME(1933, Brit.); BLACK TULIP, THE(1937, Brit.); OH BOY!(1938, Brit.)
Leslie Laurier
DIRTY WORK(1934, Brit.); SAILING ALONG(1938, Brit.)
Richard Laurier
THIS REBEL BREED(1960)
Jon Laurimore
VIOLENT ENEMY, THE(1969, Brit.)
Odessa Laurin
JIVE JUNCTION(1944)
Gunnar Lauring
WHILE THE ATTORNEY IS ASLEEP(1945, Den.); CASE OF THE 44'S, THE(1964 Brit./Den.)
George Lauris
SASQUATCH(1978)
Misc. Talkies
BUFFALO RIDER(1978), d
Patricia Lauris
Misc. Talkies
BUFFALO RIDER(1978)
Priscilla Lauris
NATIONAL LAMPOON'S ANIMAL HOUSE(1978)
J. Lauriston
ILLEGAL(1932, Brit.)
Dana Laurita
DEMON SEED(1977); GOODBYE GIRL, THE(1977)
Marisa Laurito
CAFE EXPRESS(1980, Ital.)
Jonreed Lauritzen
KISS OF FIRE(1955), w
L. Laurmaa
DAY THE EARTH FROZE, THE(1959, Fin./USSR)
Agnes Laury
SNOWS OF KILIMANJARO, THE(1952); RACERS, THE(1955)
A. Lauter
HAMLET(1966, USSR)
Ed Lauter
BAD COMPANY(1972); DIRTY LITTLE BILLY(1972); HICKEY AND BOGGS(1972); MAGNIFICENT SEVEN RIDE, THE(1972); NEW CENTURIONS, THE(1972); RAGE(1972); EXECUTIVE ACTION(1973); LAST AMERICAN HERO, THE(1973); LOLLYMADONNA XXX(1973); LONGEST YARD, THE(1974); MIDNIGHT MAN, THE(1974); BREAKHEART PASS(1976); FAMILY PLOT(1976); KING KONG(1976); CHICKEN CHRONICLES, THE(1977); WHITE BUFFALO, THE(1977); MAGIC(1978); LOOSE SHOES(1980); DEATH HUNT(1981); AMATEUR, THE(1982); BIG SCORE, THE(1983); CUJO(1983); EUREKA(1983, Brit.); TIMERIDER(1983)
1984
FINDERS KEEPERS(1984); LASSITER(1984)
Harry Lauter
GAY INTRUDERS, THE(1948); INCIDENT(1948); JUNGLE PATROL(1948); MOONRISE(1948); ALIMONY(1949); BANDIT KING OF TEXAS(1949); FRONTIER INVESTIGATOR(1949); GREAT DAN PATCH, THE(1949); I WAS A MALE WAR BRIDE(1949); PRINCE OF THE PLAINS(1949); SLATTERY'S HURRICANE(1949); TUCSON(1949); TWELVE O'CLOCK HIGH(1949); WHITE HEAT(1949); WITHOUT HONOR(1949); ZAMBA(1949); EXPERIMENT ALCATRAZ(1950); I'LL GET BY(1950); NO WAY OUT(1950); ACCORDING TO MRS. HOYLE(1951); DAY THE EARTH STOOD STILL, THE(1951); FLYING LEATHERNECKS(1951); HILLS OF UTAH(1951); I WANT YOU(1951); KID FROM AMARILLO, THE(1951); LET'S GO NAVY(1951); LORNA DOONE(1951); MOB, THE(1951); RACKET, THE(1951); ROADBLOCK(1951); SILVER CITY BONANZA(1951); THUNDER IN GOD'S COUNTRY(1951); VALLEY OF FIRE(1951); WHIRLWIND(1951); APACHE COUNTRY(1952); BUGLES IN THE AFTERNOON(1952); NIGHT STAGE TO GALVESTON(1952); SEA TIGER(1952); STEEL FIST, THE(1952); TALK ABOUT A STRANGER(1952); THIS WOMAN IS DANGEROUS(1952); YUKON GOLD(1952); BIG HEAT, THE(1953); DRAGONFLY SQUADRON(1953); FIGHTER ATTACK(1953); FIGHTING LAWMAN, THE(1953); FORBIDDEN(1953); MARSHAL'S DAUGHTER, THE(1953); PACK TRAIN(1953);

PRINCE OF PIRATES(1953); TOPEKA(1953); CRIME WAVE(1954); FORTYNINERS, THE(1954); RETURN TO TREASURE ISLAND(1954); YANKEE PASHA(1954); APACHE AMBUSH(1955); AT GUNPOINT(1955); CREATURE WITH THE ATOM BRAIN(1955); CROOKED WEB, THE(1955); IT CAME FROM BENEATH THE SEA(1955); LORD OF THE JUNGLE(1955); OUTLAW TREASURE(1955); DIG THAT URANIUM(1956); EARTH VS. THE FLYING SAUCERS(1956); MAN IN THE GREY FLANNEL SUIT, THE(1956); MIAMI EXPOSE(1956); WEREWOLF, THE(1956); BADGE OF MARSHAL BRENNAN, THE(1957); DEATH IN SMALL DOSES(1957); HELLCATS OF THE NAVY(1957); JET PILOT(1957); OKLAHOMAN, THE(1957); RAIDERS OF OLD CALIFORNIA(1957); SHOOT-OUT AT MEDICINE BEND(1957); WOMEN OF PITCAIRN ISLAND, THE(1957); CRY BABY KILLER, THE(1958); GOOD DAY FOR A HANGING(1958); LAST HURRAH, THE(1958); RETURN TO WARBOW(1958); TARZAN'S FIGHT FOR LIFE(1958); TOUGHEST GUN IN TOMBSTONE(1958); DATE WITH DEATH, A(1959); GUNFIGHT AT DODGE CITY, THE(1959); LOUISIANA HUSSY(1960); BUFFALO GUN(1961); POSSE FROM HELL(1961); WILD WESTERNERS, THE(1962); IT'S A MAD, MAD, MAD, MAD WORLD(1963); CONVICT STAGE(1965); FORT COURAGEOUS(1965); SATAN BUG, THE(1965); AMBUSH BAY(1966); FOR PETE'S SAKE!(1966); FORT UTAH(1967); BARQUERO(1970); TARZAN'S JUNGLE REBELLION(1970); ESCAPE FROM THE PLANET OF THE APES(1971); TODD KILLINGS, THE(1971); SUPERBEAST(1972)
Misc. Talkies
WHIRLWIND(1951)
Helene Lauterbock
STORY OF VICKIE, THE(1958, Aust.); FOREVER MY LOVE(1962)
Maggie Lauterer
WOLFMAN(1979)
Annie Lautner
NOT RECONCILED, OR "ONLY VIOLENCE HELPS WHERE IT RULES"(1969, Ger.)
George Lautner
ROAD TO SALINA(1971, Fr./Ital.), d, w
Georges Lautner
SEVENTH JUROR, THE(1964, Fr.), d; WOMEN AND WAR(1965, Fr.), p&d, w; GALIA(1966, Fr./Ital.), d, w; GREAT SPY CHASE, THE(1966, Fr.), p&d
Alma Lauton
UNTIL THEY SAIL(1957)
Linda Lautrec
MY BREAKFAST WITH BLASSIE(1983), w,p&d, ed
Margarita Lauvergeon [Ochoa]
OPERATION DELILAH(1966, U.S./Span.), ed
Jazzmine Lauzane
TULIPS(1981, Can)
Bruno Lauzi
BETTER A WIDOW(1969, Ital.)
Bill Lava
BUGS BUNNY'S THIRD MOVIE–1001 RABBIT TALES(1982), m
William Lava
YODELIN' KID FROM PINE RIDGE(1937, m/1; RED RIVER RANGE(1938), m; SANTA FE STAMPEDE(1938), m; COWBOYS FROM TEXAS(1939), md; KANSAS TERRORS, THE(1939), m; NEW FRONTIER(1939), m; NIGHT RIDERS, THE(1939), m; THREE TEXAS STEERS(1939), m; WYOMING OUTLAW(1939), m; SHE-WOLF OF LONDON(1946), md; BIG PUNCH, THE(1948), m; EMBRACEABLE YOU(1948), m; MOONRISE(1948), m; FLAXY MARTIN(1949), m; HOMICIDE(1949), m; HOUSE ACROSS THE STREET, THE(1949), m; YOUNGER BROTHERS, THE(1949), m; BREAKTHROUGH(1950), m; COLT .45(1950), m; GREAT JEWEL ROBBER, THE(1950), m; HIGHWAY 301(1950), m; THIS SIDE OF THE LAW(1950), m; INSIDE THE WALLS OF FOLSOM PRISON(1951), m; TANKS ARE COMING, THE(1951), m; CATTLE TOWN(1952), m; MYSTERY LAKE(1953), m; PHANTOM FROM SPACE(1953), m; LITTLEST OUTLAW, THE(1955), m; FLOOD TIDE(1958), m; HELL BENT FOR LEATHER(1960), m; SEVEN WAYS FROM SUNDOWN(1960), m; SIGN OF ZORRO, THE(1960), m; PT 109(1963), m; WALL OF NOISE(1963), m; CHAMBER OF HORRORS(1966), m; ASSIGNMENT TO KILL(1968), m; CHUBASCO(1968), m; IN ENEMY COUNTRY(1968), m; GOOD GUYS AND THE BAD GUYS, THE(1969), m
John Lavachielli
LORDS OF DISCIPLINE, THE(1983)
Gino Lavagetto
ROME WANTS ANOTHER CAESAR(1974, Ital.)
Angelo Francesco Lavaginno
NAKED MAJA, THE(1959, Ital./U.S.), m
Angela Lavagna
VERY HANDY MAN, A(1966, Fr./Ital.)
Angelo Francesco Lavagnino
WOMAN OF THE RIVER(1954, Fr./Ital.), m; MAMBO(1955, Ital.), m; OTHELLO(1955, U.S./Fr./Ital.), m; LEGEND OF THE LOST(1957, U.S./Panama/Ital.), m, md; MILLER'S WIFE, THE(1957, Ital.), m; AWAKENING, THE(1958, Ital.), m; WIND CANNOT READ, THE(1958, Brit.), m; CALYPSO(1959, Fr./It.), m; PASSIONATE SUMMER(1959, Brit.), m; SIGN OF THE GLADIATOR(1959, Fr./Ger./Ital.), m, md; CONSPIRACY OF HEARTS(1960, Brit.), m; ESTHER AND THE KING(1960, U.S./Ital.), m; FIVE BRANDED WOMEN(1960), m; LAST DAYS OF POMPEII, THE(1960, Ital.), m; SAVAGE INNOCENTS, THE(1960, Brit.), m; COLOSSUS OF RHODES, THE(1961, Ital., Fr., Span.), m; GORGO(1961, Brit.), m; REVOLT OF THE SLAVES, THE(1961, Ital./Span./Ger.), m; WARRIOR EMPRESS, THE(1961, Ital.), m; WONDERS OF ALADDIN, THE(1961, Fr./Ital.), m; COMMANDO(1962, Ital., Span., Bel., Ger.), m; DAMON AND PYTHIAS(1962), m; MARCO POLO(1962, Fr./Ital.), m; NIGHT THEY KILLED RASPUTIN, THE(1962, Fr./Ital.), m; NUDE ODYSSEY(1962, Fr./Ital.), m, md; SIEGE OF SYRACUSE(1962, Fr./Ital.), m; IMPERIAL VENUS(1963, Ital./Fr.), m; MADAME(1963, Fr./Ital./Span.), m; RICE GIRL(1963, Fr./Ital.), m; SAMSON AND THE SLAVE QUEEN(1963, Ital.), m, md; WASTREL, THE(1963, Ital.), m; DARK PURPOSE(1964), m; DUEL OF CHAMPIONS(1964 Ital./Span.), m; GOLIATH AND THE VAMPIRES(1964, Ital.), m; HERCULES, SAMSON & ULYSSES(1964, Ital.), m; SON OF CAPTAIN BLOOD, THE(1964, U.S./Ital./Span.), m; GUNMEN OF THE RIO GRANDE(1965, Fr./Ital./Span.), m & md; SNOW DEVILS, THE(1965, Ital.), m; HYPNOSIS(1966, Ger./Sp./Ital.), m; MC GUIRE, GO HOME!(1966, Brit.), m; TRAMPLERS, THE(1966, Ital.), m; CHIMES AT MIDNIGHT(1967, Span.,Switz.), m; MISSION BLOODY MARY(1967, Fr./Ital./Span.), m, md; PONTIUS PILATE(1967, Fr./Ital.), m; WILD, WILD PLANET, THE(1967, Ital.), m; WAR BETWEEN THE PLANETS(1971, Ital.), m
Jean-Daniel Laval
LA BALANCE(1983, Fr.)

Lorraine LaVal
RIDERS OF THE CACTUS(1931)
Bernard Lavalette
LA BELLE AMERICAINE(1961, Fr.); TALES OF PARIS(1962, Fr./Ital.); THANK HEAVEN FOR SMALL FAVORS(1965, Fr.)
David Lavalle
GRAY LADY DOWN(1978), w
Jack LaValle
RETURN OF THE SECAUCUS SEVEN(1980)
Dominique Lavanant
LITTLE ROMANCE, A(1979, U.S./Fr.); HORSE OF PRIDE(1980, Fr.); MEN PREFER FAT GIRLS(1981, Fr.); ENTRE NOUS(1983, Fr.); LA BOUM(1983, Fr.)
Denis Lavant
ENTRE NOUS(1983, Fr.)
Bob LaVarre
FORBIDDEN ISLAND(1959)
Marie Lavarre
CAPTAIN'S ORDERS(1937, Brit.)
Pamela LaVarre
LOOSE ENDS(1975)
Joel Lavau
1984
DOG DAY(1984, Fr.), makeup
Anna Lavelle
BEACH BALL(1965); SILENCERS, THE(1966); WILD, WILD WINTER(1966)
Bradley Lavelle
1984
SUPERGIRL(1984)
Harold LaVelle
MAN IN THE NET, THE(1959), ed
Kay Lavelle
DOUBLE LIFE, A(1947); PEOPLE WILL TALK(1951)
Miriam Lavelle
GANG'S ALL HERE, THE(1943); COVER GIRL(1944); MEET THE PEOPLE(1944); SEVEN DAYS ASHORE(1944)
Albin Laven
Misc. Silents
KISS OF DEATH(1916, Swed.)
Arnold Laven
WITHOUT WARNING(1952), d; VICE SQUAD(1953), d; RACK, THE(1956), d; MONSTER THAT CHALLENGED THE WORLD, THE(1957), d; SLAUGHTER ON TENTH AVENUE(1957), d; VAMPIRE, THE(1957), p; ANNA LUCASTA(1958), d; GERONIMO(1962), p&d, w; GLORY GUYS, THE(1965), p, d; CLAMBAKE(1967), p; ROUGH NIGHT IN JERICHO(1967), d; SCALPHUNTERS, THE(1968), p; SAM WHISKEY(1969), p, d; MC KENZIE BREAK, THE(1970), p; UNDERGROUND(1970, Brit.), p
Arthur Laven
DOWN THREE DARK STREETS(1954), d
Pinchus Lavenda
Misc. Talkies
LIVE AND LAUGH(1933)
Barry Lavendar
ROWDYMAN, THE(1973, Can.), set d
Bobby Lavender
MIDNIGHT EXPRESS(1978, Brit.), cos
Ian Lavender
DAD'S ARMY(1971, Brit.); CONFESSIONS OF A POP PERFORMER(1975, Brit.)
Peter Lavender
GROUNDSTAR CONSPIRACY, THE(1972, Can.)
Lavendor
Silents
SUDS(1920)
Martha LaVenture
FLYING DOWN TO RIO(1933)
James Laver
WARNING TO WANTONS, A(1949, Brit.), w
Julio Lavera
HEAT(1970, Arg.), ph
German Laverde
YOUNG GIANTS(1983)
June Lavere
JOAN OF ARC(1948)
Didier Lavergne
RETURN OF MARTIN GUERRE, THE(1983, Fr.), makeup
Beryl Laverick
MAN OF EVIL(1948, Brit.); HER MAN GILBEY(1949, Brit.); UNFINISHED SYMPHONY, THE(1953, Aust./Brit.)
June Laverick
DUKE WORE JEANS, THE(1958, Brit.); GYPSY AND THE GENTLEMAN, THE(1958, Brit.); FOLLOW A STAR(1959, Brit.); IT HAPPENED IN ROME(1959, Ital.); SON OF ROBIN HOOD(1959, Brit.); MANIA(1961, Brit.)
Jane LaVerne
PERFECT CRIME, THE(1928)
Jean-Pierre Laverne
TWO OR THREE THINGS I KNOW ABOUT HER(1970, Fr.)
Lucille LaVerne
UNHOLY GARDEN, THE(1931); HEARTS OF HUMANITY(1932); SHE WANTED A MILLIONAIRE(1932); STRANGE ADVENTURE(1932); WILD HORSE MESA(1932); LAST TRAIL, THE(1933); KENTUCKY KERNELS(1935); SNOW WHITE AND THE SEVEN DWARFS(1937)
Marie "Fifi" Laverne
Misc. Talkies
WRESTLING QUEEN, THE(1975)
Morton Laverre
BEYOND THE LAW(1934)
Pascale Laverriere
LES ABYSSES(1964, Fr.), ed

Loretta Laversee
OTHER, THE(1972)

Jean Laverty
GREAT DIVIDE, THE(1930)
Silents
BACHELOR'S PARADISE(1928); GOOD-BYE KISS, THE(1928); SO THIS IS LO-VE(1928); CAMPUS KNIGHTS(1929); CAPTAIN LASH(1929); FUGITIVES(1929)
Misc. Silents
DOMESTIC TROUBLES(1928)

Johnny Laverty
NEW FACES(1954)

Andre Lavery
SMOKEY AND THE BANDIT–PART 3(1983), cos

Emmet Lavery
ARMY SURGEON(1942), w; GUILTY OF TREASON(1950), w; MAGNIFICENT YAN-KEE, THE(1950), w; COURT-MARTIAL OF BILLY MITCHELL, THE(1955), w

Emmett Lavery
HITLER'S CHILDREN(1942), w; FOREVER AND A DAY(1943), w; NIGHT IN PARADISE, A(1946), w; FIRST LEGION, THE(1951), w; BRIGHT ROAD(1953), w

Emmett Lavery, Sr.
BEHIND THE RISING SUN(1943), w

Mrs. John Lavery
Silents
GREAT LOVE, THE(1918)

Charles Laveton, Jr.
COWBOY(1958), ph

Arich Lavi
HILL 24 DOESN'T ANSWER(1955, Israel)

Arik Lavi
MY MARGO(1969, Israel); OPERATION THUNDERBOLT(1978, ISRAEL)

Dahlia Lavi
TWO WEEKS IN ANOTHER TOWN(1962); CANDIDE(1962, Fr.)

Daliah Lavi
RETURN OF DR. MABUSE, THE(1961, Ger./Fr./Ital.); NO TIME FOR EC-STASY(1963, Fr.); AND SO TO BED(1965, Ger.); LORD JIM(1965, Brit.); TEN LITTLE INDIANS(1965, Brit.); WHAT?(1965, Fr./Brit./Ital.); SILENCERS, THE(1966); SPY WITH A COLD NOSE, THE(1966, Brit.); CASINO ROYALE(1967, Brit.); THOSE FANTASTIC FLYING FOOLS(1967, Brit); HIGH COMMISSIONER, THE(1968, U.S./Brit.); OLD SHATTERHAND(1968, Ger./Yugo./Fr./Ital.); SOME GIRLS DO(1969, Brit.); CATLOW(1971, Span.)

Gabriele Lavia
TEMPTER, THE(1974, Ital./Brit.); BEYOND THE DOOR(1975, Ital./U.S.); DEVIL IS A WOMAN, THE(1975, Brit./Ital.); DEEP RED(1976, Ital.)

Charles Lavialle
SEVENTH JUROR, THE(1964, Fr.); SOFT SKIN, THE(1964, Fr.); MADEMOISEL-LE(1966, Fr./Brit.)

Efrat Lavie
KAZABLAN(1974, Israel)

Jacqueline Lavielle
MAYERLING(1968, Brit./Fr.)

Frank Lavier
THESE THOUSAND HILLS(1959)

Bob Lavigne
Misc. Talkies
FORBIDDEN UNDER THE CENSORSHIP OF THE KING(1973)

Emil Lavigne
MANHANDLED(1949), makeup

Emile LaVigne
TAKE ONE FALSE STEP(1949), makeup; JAIL BUSTERS(1955), makeup; LAND OF THE PHARAOHS(1955), makeup; LOOKING FOR DANGER(1957), makeup; SPOOK CHASERS(1957), makeup; IN THE MONEY(1958), makeup; QUEEN OF OUTER SPACE(1958), makeup; MAGNIFICENT SEVEN, THE(1960), makeup; GREAT ES-CAPE, THE(1963), makeup; IRMA LA DOUCE(1963), makeup; KISS ME, STU-PID(1964), makeup; SATAN BUG, THE(1965), makeup; WATERHOLE NO. 3(1967), makeup; WITH SIX YOU GET EGGROLL(1968), makeup; REIVERS, THE(1969), makeup; LE MANS(1971), makeup; SPORTING CLUB, THE(1971), make-up; REFLECTION OF FEAR, A(1973), makeup

Richard Lavigne
SECRET OF MAGIC ISLAND, THE(1964, Fr./Ital.), w

Steve Lavigne
WALK THE WALK(1970)

Denny Lavil
CREATURE WASN'T NICE,THE(1981), ph

Bernard Lavilliers
SNOW(1983, Fr.), m

Linda Lavin
1984
MUPPETS TAKE MANHATTAN, THE(1984)

Nora Lavin
ADVENTURE IN THE HOPFIELDS(1954, Brit.), w

Tom Lavin
OUT OF THE BLUE(1982), m

Gracille LaVinder
THAT HAGEN GIRL(1947); MADAME BOVARY(1949); CAGED(1950)

Charles Lavine
KING OF MARVIN GARDENS, THE(1972)

Jack Lavine
Silents
SPARROWS(1926)

Morris Lavine
DAY OF RECKONING(1933), w

Ronald LaVine
1984
INITIATION, THE(1984), ed

Sydney LaVine
MARACAIBO(1958), cos

Margaret LaVino
CONFESSION(1937), w

Arthur Lavis
BARBER OF STAMFORD HILL, THE(1963, Brit.), ph; PRIVATE POTTER(1963, Brit.), ph; HORROR OF IT ALL, THE(1964, Brit.), ph; NIGHT TRAIN TO PARIS(1964, Brit.), ph; RING OF SPIES(1964, Brit.), ph; WITCHCRAFT(1964, Brit.), ph; JOEY BOY(1965, Brit.), ph; WOMAN WHO WOULDN'T DIE, THE(1965, Brit.), ph; PENT-HOUSE, THE(1967, Brit.), ph; UP THE JUNCTION(1968, Brit.), ph

Janet Lavis
TOO MANY GIRLS(1940); WONDER MAN(1945); MAN WITH A CLOAK, THE(1951); ROYAL WEDDING(1951)

Paul Lavista
LITTLE SAVAGE, THE(1959), m

Raul Lavista
SOFIA(1948), md; WOMEN IN THE NIGHT(1948), m; BRUTE, THE(1952, Mex.), m; VERA CRUZ(1954), ed; LIFE IN THE BALANCE, A(1955), m, md; BIG BOODLE, THE(1957), m; DANIEL BOONE, TRAIL BLAZER(1957), m; ENCHANTED IS-LAND(1958), m; IMPORTANT MAN, THE(1961, Mex.), m; LA CUCARACHA(1961, Mex.), m; LITTLE ANGEL(1961, Mex.), m; MACARIO(1961, Mex.), m; LITTLE RED RIDING HOOD AND THE MONSTERS(1965, Mex.), m; EXTERMINATING ANGEL, THE(1967, Mex.), md; TOM THUMB(1967, Mex.), m; RUN FOR THE ROSES(1978), m

Karen LaVoie
1984
HARDBODIES(1984)

Louis LaVoie
MAGNIFICENT OBSESSION(1935); SHE MARRIED HER BOSS(1935)

Robert Lavoie
QUEST FOR FIRE(1982, Fr./Can.)

Arthur Lavon
Silents
MASK, THE(1921), w

Gail Lavon
KILL, THE(1968)

Henri Lavorel
VOYAGE TO AMERICA(1952, Fr.), d, w; IT HAPPENED IN PARIS(1953, Fr.), d

L. Lavosky
ROMEO AND JULIET(1955, USSR), d&w

Dora Lavrencic
DIVIDED HEART, THE(1955, Brit.)

S. Lavrentyev
Misc. Silents
THREE FRIENDS AND AN INVENTION(1928, USSR)

Franco Lavriano
VOYAGE, THE(1974, Ital.)

Yuri Lavrof
DEFENSE OF VOLOTCHAYEVSK, THE(1938, USSR)

German Lavrov
NINE DAYS OF ONE YEAR(1964, USSR), ph

Tatyana Lavrova
NINE DAYS OF ONE YEAR(1964, USSR)

Maria Lavryk
GIRL FROM POLTAVA(1937)

Phyllis Lavsky
BRIGHTY OF THE GRAND CANYON(1967), m

Richard Lavsky
BRIGHTY OF THE GRAND CANYON(1967), m

Martin Lavut
MASK, THE(1961, Can.); HEAVY METAL(1981, Can.)

Albert Law
FIRST YANK INTO TOKYO(1945)

Barbara Law
1984
BEDROOM EYES(1984, Can.); SURROGATE, THE(1984, Can.)

Burton Law
Silents
EYES OF THE HEART(1920)

Christopher Law
NIGHT CALL NURSES(1974)

Evelyn Law
SWEEPSTAKE ANNIE(1935), w

Harold Law
NOBODY'S BABY(1937), w
Misc. Talkies
NEIGHBORHOOD HOUSE(1936), d

Jack Law
PAINTING THE CLOUDS WITH SUNSHINE(1951)

John Law
SPIRIT OF NOTRE DAME, THE(1931); CASINO ROYALE(1967, Brit.), w

John Phillip Law
HIGH INFIDELITY(1965, Fr./Ital.); RUSSIANS ARE COMING, THE RUSSIANS ARE COMING, THE(1966); HURRY SUNDOWN(1967); BARBARELLA(1968, Fr./Ital.); DANGER: DIABOLIK(1968, Ital./Fr.); SERGEANT, THE(1968); SKIDOO(1968); DEATH RIDES A HORSE(1969, Ital.); THREE NIGHTS OF LOVE(1969, Ital.); CER-TAIN, VERY CERTAIN, AS A MATTER OF FACT... PROBABLE(1970, Ital.); HAWAII-ANS, THE(1970); VON RICHTHOFEN AND BROWN(1970); LAST MOVIE, THE(1971); LOVE MACHINE, THE(1971); GOLDEN VOYAGE OF SINBAD, THE(1974, Brit.); OPEN SEASON(1974, U.S./Span.); SPIRAL STAIRCASE, THE(1975, Brit.); CASSAN-DRA CROSSING, THE(1977); TARZAN, THE APE MAN(1981); TIN MAN(1983)
Misc. Talkies
TARGET OF AN ASSASSIN(1978, S. Africa)

Kenneth Law
ON THIN ICE(1933, Brit.); NO ESCAPE(1936, Brit.)

Maria Law
Misc. Silents
GREAT ALONE, THE(1922)

Marv Law
CARRY ON CONSTABLE(1960, Brit.)

Mary Law
FOR BETTER FOR WORSE(1954, Brit.)

Michael Law
SIX MEN, THE(1951, Brit.), d, w
Mildred Law
TOO MANY GIRLS(1940); EASY TO LOOK AT(1945); TONIGHT AND EVERY NIGHT(1945); LAWLESS EMPIRE(1946)
Pamela Law
DEVIL DOLL(1964, Brit.)
Phyllida Law
OTLEY(1969, Brit.); HITLER: THE LAST TEN DAYS(1973, Brit./Ital.)
Red Law
FIGHTING PIMPERNEL, THE(1950, Brit.), ed
Reska Law
PARIS UNDERGROUND(1945)
Robert Law
JUNGLE PRINCESS, THE(1936)
Rod Law
RED, WHITE AND BLACK, THE(1970)
Rodman Law
Misc. Silents
FIGHTING DEATH(1914)
Sallyanne Law
LORDS OF DISCIPLINE, THE(1983); PARTY PARTY(1983, Brit.)
Tom Law
SKIDOO(1968)
Vernon Law
ODD COUPLE, THE(1968)
Walter Law
WHOOPEE(1930); BETWEEN FIGHTING MEN(1932)
Silents
CLIMBERS, THE(1915); ROMEO AND JULIET(1916); DARLING OF PARIS, THE(1917); PERFECT LADY, A(1918); JANICE MEREDITH(1924); CLOTHES MAKE THE PIRATE(1925)
Misc. Silents
ONLY WAY OUT, THE(1915); HER DOUBLE LIFE(1916); UNWELCOME MOTHER, THE(1916); WAR BRIDE'S SECRET, THE(1916); CAMILLE(1917); HEART AND SOUL(1917); HER GREATEST LOVE(1917); SISTER AGAINST SISTER(1917); FORBIDDEN PATH, THE(1918); STOLEN HONOR(1918); IF I WERE KING(1920); GREAT ALONE, THE(1922)
William Law
AFTER THE THIN MAN(1936); GOOD EARTH, THE(1937)
Joan Lawes
UP THE RIVER(1930)
Lewis E. Lawes
OVER THE WALL(1938), w; CASTLE ON THE HUDSON(1940), w
Warden Lewis E. Lawes
20,000 YEARS IN SING SING(1933), w; YOU CAN'T GET AWAY WITH MURDER(1939), w; INVISIBLE STRIPES(1940), w
Betty Lawford
GENTLEMEN OF THE PRESS(1929); LUCKY IN LOVE(1929); OLD ENGLISH(1930); SECRETS OF A SECRETARY(1931); BERKELEY SQUARE(1933); MONKEY'S PAW, THE(1933); GALLANT LADY(1934); HUMAN SIDE, THE(1934); LET'S BE RITZY(1934); LOVE BEFORE BREAKFAST(1936); RETURN OF SHERLOCK HOLMES(1936); CRIMINAL LAWYER(1937); STOLEN HOLIDAY(1937); STAGE DOOR CANTEEN(1943); DEVIL THUMBS A RIDE, THE(1947)
Ernest Lawford
PERSONAL MAID(1931)
Silents
FIGHTER, THE(1921)
Lady May Lawford
HONG KONG(1951)
Peter Lawford
GENTLEMAN OF PARIS, A(1931); POOR OLD BILL(1931, Brit.); LORD JEFF(1938); EAGLE SQUADRON(1942); MRS. MINIVER(1942); RANDOM HARVEST(1942); THUNDER BIRDS(1942); YANK AT ETON, A(1942); CORVETTE K-225(1943); FLESH AND FANTASY(1943); GIRL CRAZY(1943); IMMORTAL SERGEANT, THE(1943); JUNIOR ARMY(1943); PILOT NO. 5(1943); PURPLE V, THE(1943); SHERLOCK HOLMES FACES DEATH(1943); SKY'S THE LIMIT, THE(1943); SOMEONE TO REMEMBER(1943); WEST SIDE KID(1943); CANTERVILLE GHOST, THE(1944); WHITE CLIFFS OF DOVER, THE(1944); PICTURE OF DORIAN GRAY, THE(1945); SON OF LASSIE(1945); ZIEGFELD FOLLIES(1945); CLUNY BROWN(1946); MY BROTHER TALKS TO HORSES(1946); TWO SISTERS FROM BOSTON(1946); GOOD NEWS(1947); IT HAPPENED IN BROOKLYN(1947); EASTER PARADE(1948); JULIA MISBEHAVES(1948); ON AN ISLAND WITH YOU(1948); LITTLE WOMEN(1949); RED DANUBE, THE(1949); PLEASE BELIEVE ME(1950); ROYAL WEDDING(1951); HOUR OF THIRTEEN, THE(1952); JUST THIS ONCE(1952); KANGAROO(1952); ROGUE'S MARCH(1952); YOU FOR ME(1952); IT SHOULD HAPPEN TO YOU(1954); NEVER SO FEW(1959); EXODUS(1960); OCEAN'S ELEVEN(1960); PEPE(1960); DEAD RUN(1961, Fr./Ital./Ger.); ADVISE AND CONSENT(1962); LONGEST DAY, THE(1962); SERGEANTS 3(1962); DEAD RINGER(1964); HARLOW(1965); SYLVIA(1965); MAN CALLED ADAM, A(1966); OSCAR, THE(1966); BUONA SERA, MRS. CAMPBELL(1968, Ital.); SALT & PEPPER(1968, Brit.); SKIDOO(1968); APRIL FOOLS, THE(1969); HOOK, LINE AND SINKER(1969); ONE MORE TIME(1970, Brit.); CLAY PIGEON(1971); THEY ONLY KILL THEIR MASTERS(1972); ROSEBUD(1975); WON TON TON, THE DOG WHO SAVED HOLLYWOOD(1976); ANGELS BRIGADE(1980); BODY AND SOUL(1981)
1984
WHERE IS PARSIFAL?(1984, Brit.)
Misc. Talkies
TOGETHERNESS(1970)
Mark Lawhead
THX 1138(1971); HOLLYWOOD HIGH(1977)
Ludwig Lawinski
COLDITZ STORY, THE(1955, Brit.); PRIVATE'S PROGRESS(1956, Brit.)
Anderson Lawler
RIVER OF ROMANCE(1929); LADY TO LOVE, A(1930); ONLY SAPS WORK(1930); GIRLS ABOUT TOWN(1931); AMERICAN MADNESS(1932); SINNERS IN THE SUN(1932); CHEYENNE KID, THE(1933); BELOVED(1934); LET'S TALK IT OVER(1934); RIP TIDE(1934); MAN WHO RECLAIMED HIS HEAD, THE(1935); RETURN OF SOPHIE LANG, THE(1936); EVER SINCE EVE(1937); FLY-AWAY BABY(1937); MR. DODD TAKES THE AIR(1937); HEART OF THE NORTH(1938);

SOMEWHERE IN THE NIGHT(1946), p
Bill Lawler
NORSEMAN, THE(1978)
Bud Lawler
JANE EYRE(1944)
Florence Lawler
MEET JOHN DOE(1941)
Iris Lawler
QUARE FELLOW, THE(1962, Brit.)
James Lawler
DAWN OVER IRELAND(1938, Irish), ph
Janet Lawler
DEEP IN THE HEART(1983), cos
Judith E. Lawler
YOUNG GIRLS OF ROCHEFORT, THE(1968, Fr.)
Margaretha Lawler
TIME OF DESIRE, THE(1957, Swed.)
Patti Lawler
INVASION OF THE SAUCER MEN(1957)
Ray Lawler
SEASON OF PASSION(1961, Aus./Brit.), w
Robert Lawler
Misc. Silents
LITTLE MEENA'S ROMANCE(1916)
Sean Lawler
URBAN COWBOY(1980)
Sylvia Lawler
LAST AMERICAN VIRGIN, THE(1982)
Treva Lawler
MISS PINKERTON(1932); MARY BURNS, FUGITIVE(1935)
Brenda Lawless
GIRL IN THE CROWD, THE(1934, Brit.)
Doc Lawless
KING OF COMEDY, THE(1983)
Eddie Lawless
Silents
IN THE DAYS OF SAINT PATRICK(1920, Brit.)
James Lawless
Misc. Talkies
JACKPOT(1982)
John Lawless
PREMONITION, THE(1976), art d
1984
OVER THE BROOKLYN BRIDGE(1984), art d
Kevin Lawless
QUIET MAN, THE(1952)
Louis Lawless
PLANET OF DINOSAURS(1978)
Pat Lawless
DRUM BEAT(1954); ABDUCTORS, THE(1957); FIREBRAND, THE(1962)
Peter Lawless
GALLIPOLI(1981, Aus.)
George Lawley
DESTINATION MOON(1950), set d
Yvonne Lawley
SCARECROW, THE(1982, New Zealand)
Joe Lawliss
RIDERS OF THE CACTUS(1931)
Misc. Talkies
FLYING LARIATS(1931)
Anderson Lawlor
HALF-MARRIAGE(1929); HOLLYWOOD SPEAKS(1932); ACE OF ACES(1933); ADVENTUROUS BLONDE(1937); CONFESSION(1937); EMPTY HOLSTERS(1937); ACCIDENTS WILL HAPPEN(1938); DAREDEVIL DRIVERS(1938); INVISIBLE MENACE, THE(1938); MYSTERY HOUSE(1938); TORCHY BLANE IN CHINATOWN(1938)
Hoey Lawlor
Silents
SCHOOL DAYS(1921), t; CAMPUS KNIGHTS(1929), t
John Lawlor
JACKSON COUNTY JAIL(1976); S.O.B.(1981)
Mary Lawlor
GOOD NEWS(1930); SHOOTING STRAIGHT(1930)
Niall Lawlor
MY SISTER AND I(1948, Brit.)
Nigel Lawlor
LOOK BEFORE YOU LOVE(1948, Brit.)
Ray Lawlor
MASK, THE(1961, Can.)
Stephanie Lawlor
Misc. Talkies
CHERRY HILL HIGH(1977); HOT T-SHIRTS(1980)
T. Jerome Lawlor
Misc. Silents
DEBT, THE(1917)
Thomas Lawlor
MIKADO, THE(1967, Brit.)
Frederick Lawluwi
1984
WHITE ELEPHANT(1984, Brit.)
Joe Lawman
THAT CERTAIN SOMETHING(1941, Aus.)
Jennifer Lawn
SOPHIE'S CHOICE(1982)
Mordecai Lawner
CLAUDINE(1974); ANNIE HALL(1977); SOUP FOR ONE(1982)
Vee Lawnhurst
CALL OF THE PRAIRIE(1936), m

Brian Lawrance
SING AS YOU SWING(1937, Brit.)
Clem Lawrance
QUIET PLEASE(1938, Brit.)
Jody Lawrance
FAMILY SECRET, THE(1951); MASK OF THE AVENGER(1951); TEN TALL MEN(1951); ALL ASHORE(1953); HOT SPELL(1958); PURPLE GANG, THE(1960)
John Lawrance
LONERS, THE(1972), w
Adam Lawrence
DRIVE-IN MASSACRE(1976)
Alfred Lawrence
FLYING DOCTOR, THE(1936, Aus.), m
Alice Lawrence
Silents
CORNER IN COLLEENS, A(1916)
Alison Lawrence
CURTAINS(1983, Can.)
Amy Lawrence
TOOTSIE(1982)
Andre Lawrence
PLEASURE SEEKERS, THE(1964); LOVE IN A FOUR LETTER WORLD(1970, Can.); AND HOPE TO DIE(1972 Fr/US)
Andrea Lawrence
COUNTESS DRACULA(1972, Brit.)
Ann Lawrence
ROUGHLY SPEAKING(1945); SENORITA FROM THE WEST(1945); CUBAN PETE(1946); HUMORESQUE(1946); UNDERCURRENT(1946); LADY IN THE LAKE(1947); GOOD SAM(1948); DALLAS(1950)
Anthony Lawrence
ROUSTABOUT(1964), w; PARADISE, HAWAIIAN STYLE(1966), w; EASY COME, EASY GO(1967), w
Arthur Lawrence
AGAINST THE WIND(1948, Brit.); LILLI MARLENE(1951, Brit.); INN FOR TROUBLE(1960, Brit.); PEEPING TOM(1960, Brit.), art d
B. Lawrence
Silents
DECAMERON NIGHTS(1924, Brit.), w
Babe Lawrence
FRONTIER TOWN(1938)
Barbara Lawrence
MARGIE(1946); CAPTAIN FROM CASTILE(1947); GIVE MY REGARDS TO BROADWAY(1948); LETTER TO THREE WIVES, A(1948); STREET WITH NO NAME, THE(1948); UNFAITHFULLY YOURS(1948); YOU WERE MEANT FOR ME(1948); MOTHER IS A FRESHMAN(1949); PEGGY(1950); TWO TICKETS TO BROADWAY(1951); HERE COME THE NELSONS(1952); ARENA(1953); PARIS MODEL(1953); STAR, THE(1953); HER TWELVE MEN(1954); JESSE JAMES VERSUS THE DALTONS(1954); MAN WITH THE GUN(1955); OKLAHOMA(1955); JOE DAKOTA(1957); KRONOS(1957); MAN IN THE SHADOW(1957)
Bert Lawrence
TIME OUT FOR RHYTHM(1941), w; ANGELS IN DISGUISE(1949), w; FIGHTING FOOLS(1949), w; MASTER MINDS(1949), w; BLUES BUSTERS(1950), w; LUCKY LOSERS(1950), w; TRIPLE TROUBLE(1950), w; GHOST CHASERS(1951), w; LET'S GO NAVY(1951), w; FEUDIN' FOOLS(1952), w; HOLD THAT LINE(1952), w; NO HOLDS BARRED(1952), w; JALOPY(1953), w; HIGH SOCIETY(1955), w; DIG THAT URANIUM(1956), w; SPY CHASERS(1956), w; UP IN SMOKE(1957), w; IN THE MONEY(1958), w; ALIAS JESSE JAMES(1959), w; PUTNEY SWOPE(1969)
Beverly Lawrence
ALL WOMAN(1967)
Bill Lawrence
MR. WISE GUY(1942); EIGHT ON THE LAM(1967), p; HOW TO COMMIT MARRIAGE(1969), p
Billy Lawrence
VILLAGE OF THE DAMNED(1960, Brit.)
Bob Lawrence
ROMAN SPRING OF MRS. STONE, THE(1961, U.S./Brit.), makeup; SECRET PARTNER, THE(1961, Brit.), makeup; MACBETH(1963), makeup; THIS SPORTING LIFE(1963, Brit.), makeup; GIRL WITH GREEN EYES(1964, Brit.), makeup; SERVANT, THE(1964, Brit.), makeup; KALEIDOSCOPE(1966, Brit.), makeup; PROMISE HER ANYTHING(1966, Brit.), makeup; LONG DAY'S DYING, THE(1968, Brit.), makeup; SEBASTIAN(1968, Brit.), makeup; THANK YOU ALL VERY MUCH(1969, Brit.), makeup; RECKONING, THE(1971, Brit.), makeup; GUMSHOE(1972, Brit.), makeup; PIED PIPER, THE(1972, Brit.), makeup; THREE SISTERS(1974, Brit.), makeup
Bobby Lawrence
QUIET PLEASE(1938, Brit.)
Brian Lawrence
FAME(1936, Brit.); LAST HOUSE ON DEAD END STREET(1977), w
Bruno Lawrence
BEYOND REASONABLE DOUBT(1980, New Zeal.); GOODBYE PORK PIE(1981, New Zealand); BATTLETRUCK(1982); SMASH PALACE(1982, New Zealand), a, w
1984
HEART OF THE STAG(1984, New Zealand), a, w; PALLET ON THE FLOOR(1984, New Zealand), m; TREASURE OF THE YANKEE ZEPHYR(1984, New Zealand); UTU(1984, New Zealand); WILD HORSES(1984, New Zealand)
Bryan Lawrence
SHE SHALL HAVE MUSIC(1935, Brit.)
Carl Lawrence
SCARLET STREET(1945), set d; TERROR BY NIGHT(1946), set d
Carol Lawrence
NEW FACES(1954); VIEW FROM THE BRIDGE, A(1962, Fr./Ital.); I'D RATHER BE RICH(1964)
Charles Lawrence
HIGH WIND IN JAMAICA, A(1965)
Charlotte Lawrence
PHFFFT!(1954); THREE FOR THE SHOW(1955); TRIAL(1955)
Chris Lawrence
SECRET DOOR, THE(1964)

Christopher Lawrence
HOUSE ON SORORITY ROW, THE(1983)
Christy Lawrence
NO RESTING PLACE(1952, Brit.)
Clem Lawrence
TAKE IT FROM ME(1937, Brit.); IT'S IN THE BLOOD(1938, Brit.)
Copeland Lawrence
EXPRESSO BONGO(1959, Brit.)
Craig Lawrence
LAKE PLACID SERENADE(1944); DARK PASSAGE(1947)
Misc. Talkies
GUNSMOKE(1947)
D.H. Lawrence
ROCKING HORSE WINNER, THE(1950, Brit.), w; LADY CHATTERLEY'S LOVER(1959, Fr.), d&w; SONS AND LOVERS(1960, Brit.), w; FOX, THE(1967), w; WOMEN IN LOVE(1969, Brit.), w; VIRGIN AND THE GYPSY, THE(1970, Brit.), w; LADY CHATTERLEY'S LOVER(1981, Fr./Brit.), w; PRIEST OF LOVE(1981, Brit.), w
Daphne Lawrence
YOUNG CYCLE GIRLS, THE(1979)
David Lawrence
ESCAPE 2000(1983, Aus.), w
De Forrest Lawrence
ADAM'S RIB(1949); WHITE HEAT(1949)
Dean Lawrence
LORDS OF DISCIPLINE, THE(1983)
Debra Lawrence
NEXT OF KIN(1983, Aus.)
Del Lawrence
BALL OF FIRE(1941); PIONEERS, THE(1941)
Delphi Lawrence
BLOOD ORANGE(1953, Brit.); DUEL IN THE JUNGLE(1954, Brit.); MEET MR. CALLAGHAN(1954, Brit.); GOLD EXPRESS, THE(1955, Brit.); DOUBLE CROSS(1956, Brit.); GENTLE TOUCH, THE(1956, Brit.); MURDER ON APPROVAL(1956, Brit.); JUST MY LUCK(1957, Brit.); STRANGER'S MEETING(1957, Brit.); BLIND SPOT(1958, Brit.); IT'S NEVER TOO LATE(1958, Brit.); MAN WHO COULD CHEAT DEATH, THE(1959, Brit.); SON OF ROBIN HOOD(1959, Brit.); TOO MANY CROOKS(1959, Brit.); FOURTH SQUARE, THE(1961, Brit.); TROUBLE IN THE SKY(1961, Brit.); SEVEN KEYS(1962, Brit.); FAREWELL PERFORMANCE(1963, Brit.); LIST OF ADRIAN MESSENGER, THE(1963); BUNNY LAKE IS MISSING(1965); FROZEN ALIVE(1966, Brit./Ger.); LAST CHALLENGE, THE(1967); ON THE RUN(1967, Brit.)
Dick Lawrence
FROM NOON TO THREE(1976), art d; STRAIGHT TIME(1978), art d
Doreen Lawrence
GREEN FINGERS(1947); WOMAN HATER(1949, Brit.)
Dorothy Lawrence
CLIMAX, THE(1944); TANGIER(1946)
Douglas C. Lawrence
MELINDA(1972)
Dov Lawrence
SAFE PLACE, A(1971)
Dwight Lawrence
FINNEY(1969)
E. Lawrence
INCREDIBLE SHRINKING MAN, THE(1957), m
Eddie Lawrence
NIGHT THEY RAIDED MINSKY'S, THE(1968); BLADE(1973); SOMEBODY KILLED HER HUSBAND(1978)
Edmund Lawrence
HOUSE OF SECRETS(1929), d
Silents
RANSOM, THE(1916), d; LOVE AUCTION, THE(1919), d, w
Misc. Silents
WARNING, THE(1915), d; PRICE OF HAPPINESS, THE(1916), d; MARRIED IN NAME ONLY(1917), d; DAUGHTER OF FRANCE, A(1918), d; FIREBRAND, THE(1918), d; HER PRICE(1918), d; LIAR, THE(1918), d; LIFE OR HONOR?(1918), d; QUEEN OF HEARTS, THE(1918), d; CHEATING HERSELF(1919), d; LOST MONEY(1919), d; LURE OF AMBITION(1919), d; MERRY-GO ROUND, THE(1919), d; WHAT WOULD YOU DO?(1920), d
Edna Lawrence
DRUMS OF DESTINY(1937); RANCHO GRANDE(1940)
Edward Lawrence
Silents
PRICE OF A PARTY, THE(1924); KNOCKOUT, THE(1925)
Misc. Silents
SCARLET WOMAN, THE(1916), d; ONE TOUCH OF NATURE(1917)
Edwin Lawrence
MIDSHIPMAID GOB(1932, Brit.); ORDERS IS ORDERS(1934, Brit.)
Elizabeth Lawrence
LILITH(1964); FOUR FRIENDS(1981)
Elliot Lawrence
VIOLATORS, THE(1957), m, md; THUNDER IN DIXIE(1965), m, md; HOT ROD HULLABALOO(1966), m, md; NETWORK(1976), m
Eric Lawrence
BUCK ROGERS IN THE 25TH CENTURY(1979)
Fanya Foss Lawrence
WHY GIRLS LEAVE HOME(1945), w
Fanya Lawrence
NIGHTMARE IN THE SUN(1964), w
Florence Lawrence
ONE RAINY AFTERNOON(1936)
Silents
ELUSIVE ISABEL(1916); GAMBLING WIVES(1924)
Misc. Silents
UNFOLDMENT, THE(1922)
Frank Lawrence
BULLDOG DRUMMOND(1929), ed; HELL'S ANGELS(1930), ed; NANA(1934), ed
Silents
ISLE OF LOST SHIPS, THE(1923), ed; SLANDER THE WOMAN(1923), ed; TORMENT(1924), ed; TEXAS STEER, A(1927), ed

Fred Lawrence
TRAILIN' WEST(1936); CAPTAIN'S KID, THE(1937); TALENT SCOUT(1937); VOGUES OF 1938(1937); DAREDEVIL DRIVERS(1938); JEZEBEL(1938); PENROD AND HIS TWIN BROTHER(1938)

Gail Lawrence
BYE BYE MONKEY(1978, Ital/Fr.); MANIAC(1980); SO FINE(1981)

Gerald Lawrence
IRON DUKE, THE(1935, Brit.)
Silents
GLORIOUS ADVENTURE, THE(1922, U.S./Brit.)
Misc. Silents
ENOCH ARDEN(1914, Brit.); HARBOUR LIGHTS, THE(1914, Brit.); ROMANY RYE, THE(1915, Brit.); BUNCH OF VIOLETS, A(1916, Brit.); GRAND BABYLON HOTEL, THE(1916, Brit.); CARROTS(1917, Brit.); FALL OF A SAINT, THE(1920, Brit.)

Gertrude Lawrence
BATTLE OF PARIS, THE(1929); ARENT WE ALL?(1932, Brit.); LORD CAMBER'S LADIES(1932, Brit.); NO FUNNY BUSINESS(1934, Brit.); MIMI(1935, Brit.); REMBRANDT(1936, Brit.); MEN ARE NOT GODS(1937, Brit.); STAGE DOOR CANTEEN(1943); GLASS MENAGERIE, THE(1950)

Glen Lawrence
FUNHOUSE, THE(1981)

Hap Lawrence
HOT LEAD AND COLD FEET(1978); COAST TO COAST(1980); LOVING COUPLES(1980); WHOLLY MOSES(1980)
1984
UP THE CREEK(1984)

Harry Lawrence
SQUEEZE A FLOWER(1970, Aus.); OUTBACK(1971, Aus.); ADAM'S WOMAN(1972, Austral.); STONE(1974, Aus.)

Henry Lawrence
SO FINE(1981)

Henry Lionel Lawrence
THESE ARE THE DAMNED(1965, Brit.), w

Hilda Lawrence
CAESAR AND CLEOPATRA(1946, Brit.)

Honor Lawrence
WALK THE WALK(1970)

Howard Lawrence
Misc. Talkies
ADVERSARY, THE(1970)

Hugh Lawrence
SHORT CUT TO HELL(1957); TOP SECRET AFFAIR(1957); FLOOD TIDE(1958); JUVENILE JUNGLE(1958); PERFECT FURLOUGH, THE(1958)

Irene Lawrence
BEHIND LOCKED DOORS(1976, S. Africa)
Misc. Talkies
ANY BODY...ANY WAY(1968)

Jack Lawrence
FRONTIER VENGEANCE(1939); OF MICE AND MEN(1939); QUARTERBACK, THE(1940), m; GANGS OF SONORA(1941)

Jacqueline Lawrence
MAN WITH TWO HEADS, THE(1972)

James C. Lawrence
FINAL COUNTDOWN, THE(1980)

James Lawrence
TABLE FOR FIVE(1983)

Jane Lawrence
SAILOR'S HOLIDAY(1944)

Jay Lawrence
MAN FROM TUMBLEWEEDS, THE(1940); KING OF DODGE CITY(1941); STALAG 17(1953); BIG CHASE, THE(1954); RIDING SHOTGUN(1954); LAWLESS STREET, A(1955); WALK THE DARK STREET(1956); HALLIDAY BRAND, THE(1957); TRAIN RIDE TO HOLLYWOOD(1975); DARK, THE(1979)

Jay O. Lawrence
SWINGIN' AFFAIR, A(1963), d

Jeanne Lawrence
MEN OF THE NIGHT(1934)

Jeff Lawrence
PATERNITY(1981); TWO OF A KIND(1983)

Jeremy Lawrence
NIGHT SHIFT(1982)
1984
BODY DOUBLE(1984)

Jerome Lawrence
AUNTIE MAME(1958), w; INHERIT THE WIND(1960), w; FIRST MONDAY IN OCTOBER(1981), w

Jerry Lawrence
HITCH-HIKER, THE(1953); X-15(1961)

Jim Lawrence
CHICAGO 70(1970); RUBBER GUN, THE(1977, Can.), ph; HIGH COUNTRY, THE(1981, Can.)

Joan Lawrence
VOICE OF THE TURTLE, THE(1947)

Jody Lawrence
SON OF DR. JEKYLL, THE(1951); BRIGAND, THE(1952); CAPTAIN JOHN SMITH AND POCAHONTAS(1953); LEATHER SAINT, THE(1956); SCARLET HOUR, THE(1956); STAGECOACH TO DANCER'S PARK(1962)

Joel David Lawrence
FORCE: FIVE(1981), prod d; RIGHT STUFF, THE(1983), set d

Joel Lawrence
ROADRACERS, THE(1959); WELCOME HOME, SOLDIER BOYS(1972)

Johanna Lawrence
THERE'S ALWAYS VANILLA(1972)

John Lawrence
IN OLD NEW MEXICO(1945); IVORY HUNTER(1952, Brit.); WHITE HUNTRESS(1957, Brit.), ph; GODDESS, THE(1958); ROCKETS IN THE DUNES(1960, Brit.); GREAT ARMORED CAR SWINDLE, THE(1964); SHOCK TREATMENT(1964); FAMILY JEWELS, THE(1965); TALES OF A SALESMAN(1965), p, w; NEVADA SMITH(1966); OUT OF SIGHT(1966); SECONDS(1966); GLORY STOMPERS, THE(1967), p, w; DESTRUCTORS, THE(1968); FREE GRASS(1969), p, w; INCREDI-

BLE TWO-HEADED TRANSPLANT, THE(1971), p, w; SEVEN MINUTES, THE(1971); ASPHYX, THE(1972, Brit.); BUSTING(1974); SAVAGE ABDUCTION(1975), p,d&w; POM POM GIRLS, THE(1976)

John S. Lawrence
Misc. Silents
SCARLET TRAIL, THE(1919), d; FOR HIS SAKE(1922), d

Jordan Lawrence
LOVE ON THE DOLE(1945, Brit.); BUT NOT IN VAIN(1948, Brit.); LOOK BACK IN ANGER(1959)

Josephine Lawrence
MAKE WAY FOR TOMORROW(1937), w

Joshua Lawrence
CANNERY ROW(1982)

Juli Lawrence
1984
HARDBODIES(1984)

Katie Lawrence
SPRING FEVER(1983, Can.)

Keith Lawrence
TO HAVE AND HAVE NOT(1944)

Kelly Lawrence
1984
LOVE STREAMS(1984)

Ken Lawrence
JACKSON COUNTY JAIL(1976)

Kenny Lawrence
FAST TIMES AT RIDGEMONT HIGH(1982)

Kiva Lawrence
SWAMP COUNTRY(1966); TO THE SHORES OF HELL(1966); SCHIZOID(1980); WRONG IS RIGHT(1982)

Larry Lawrence
FORLORN RIVER(1937); SPOOK WHO SAT BY THE DOOR, THE(1973)

Laurie Lawrence
SPLINTERS IN THE NAVY(1931, Brit.)

Lee Lawrence
GEORGE WHITE'S SCANDALS(1934)

Lilian Lawrence
Silents
THREE AGES, THE(1923)

Lillian Lawrence
PAINTED VEIL, THE(1934); TEXAS STAGECOACH(1940)
Silents
MAKING THE GRADE(1921); EAST IS WEST(1922); COMMON LAW, THE(1923); CRINOLINE AND ROMANCE(1923); STELLA MARIS(1925); SENSATION SEEKERS(1927)
Misc. Silents
FALLEN IDOL, A(1919); SOCIAL PIRATE, THE(1919); BLACK IS WHITE(1920); RISKY BUSINESS(1920); PARISIAN SCANDAL, A(1921); GIRL'S DESIRE, A(1922); WHITE SHOULDERS(1922)

Linda Lawrence
Misc. Talkies
GAS PUMP GIRLS(1979)

M. Lawrence
NIGHTMARE IN THE SUN(1964), w

Mady Lawrence
WEEKEND FOR THREE(1941); HEART OF THE RIO GRANDE(1942); YOKEL BOY(1942); PINTO BANDIT, THE(1944); SPOOK TOWN(1944); LIGHTNING RAIDERS(1945)
Misc. Talkies
OATH OF VENGEANCE(1944)

Maggie Lawrence
TANK COMMANDOS(1959)

Marc Lawrence
UNDER TWO FLAGS(1936); IF I HAD A MILLION(1932); WHITE WOMAN(1933); DON'T BET ON BLONDES(1935); DR. SOCRATES(1935); G-MEN(1935); LITTLE BIG SHOT(1935); MEN OF THE HOUR(1935); COUNTERFEIT(1936); COWBOY STAR, THE(1936); DESIRE(1936); FINAL HOUR, THE(1936); LOVE ON A BET(1936); NIGHT WAITRESS(1936); ROAD GANG(1936); TRAPPED BY TELEVISION(1936); CHARLIE CHAN ON BROADWAY(1937); COUNSEL FOR CRIME(1937); CRIMINALS OF THE AIR(1937); DANGEROUS ADVENTURE, A(1937); I PROMISE TO PAY(1937); MOTOR MADNESS(1937); MURDER IN GREENWICH VILLAGE(1937); RACKETEERS IN EXILE(1937); SAN QUENTIN(1937); SHADOW, THE(1937); WHAT PRICE VENGEANCE?(1937); ADVENTURE IN SAHARA(1938); CHARLIE CHAN IN HONOLULU(1938); CONVICTED(1938); I AM THE LAW(1938); PENITENTIARY(1938); SQUADRON OF HONOR(1938); THERE'S THAT WOMAN AGAIN(1938); WHILE NEW YORK SLEEPS(1938); WHO KILLED GAIL PRESTON?(1938); BEWARE SPOOKS(1939); BLIND ALLEY(1939); CODE OF THE STREETS(1939); DUST BE MY DESTINY(1939); EX-CHAMP(1939); HOMICIDE BUREAU(1939); HOUSEKEEPER'S DAUGHTER(1939); LONE WOLF SPY HUNT, THE(1939); ROMANCE OF THE REDWOODS(1939); SERGEANT MADDEN(1939); S.O.S. TIDAL WAVE(1939); BRIGHAM YOUNG–FRONTIERSMAN(1940); CHARLIE CHAN AT THE WAX MUSEUM(1940); GOLDEN FLEECING, THE(1940); GREAT PROFILE, THE(1940); INVISIBLE STRIPES(1940); JOHNNY APOLLO(1940); LOVE, HONOR AND OH, BABY(1940); MAN WHO TALKED TOO MUCH, THE(1940); BLOSSOMS IN THE DUST(1941); DANGEROUS GAME, A(1941); HOLD THAT GHOST(1941); LADY SCARFACE(1941); MAN WHO LOST HIMSELF, THE(1941); MONSTER AND THE GIRL, THE(1941); PUBLIC ENEMIES(1941); SUNDOWN(1941); TALL, DARK AND HANDSOME(1941); CALL OF THE CANYON(1942); NAZI AGENT(1942); 'NEATH BROOKLYN BRIDGE(1942); THIS GUN FOR HIRE(1942); YOKEL BOY(1942); EYES OF THE UNDERWORLD(1943); HIT THE ICE(1943); OX-BOW INCIDENT, THE(1943); SUBMARINE ALERT(1943); PRINCESS AND THE PIRATE, THE(1944); RAINBOW ISLAND(1944); TAMPICO(1944); DILLINGER(1945); DON'T FENCE ME IN(1945); FLAME OF THE BARBARY COAST(1945); CLOAK AND DAGGER(1946); CLUB HAVANA(1946); LIFE WITH BLONDIE(1946); VIRGINIAN, THE(1946); CAPTAIN FROM CASTILE(1947); UNCONQUERED(1947); YANKEE FAKIR(1947); I WALK ALONE(1948); KEY LARGO(1948); OUT OF THE STORM(1948); CALAMITY JANE AND SAM BASS(1949); JIGSAW(1949); TOUGH ASSIGNMENT(1949); ABBOTT AND COSTELLO IN THE FOREIGN LEGION(1950); ASPHALT JUNGLE, THE(1950); BLACK HAND, THE(1950); DESERT HAWK, THE(1950); HURRICANE ISLAND(1951); MY FAVORITE SPY(1951); HELEN OF TROY(1956, Ital); KILL HER

GENTLY(1958, Brit.); JOHNNY COOL(1963); NIGHTMARE IN THE SUN(1964), p, d; JOHNNY TIGER(1966); SAVAGE PAMPAS(1967, Span./Arg.); CUSTER OF THE WEST(1968, U.S., Span.); KRAKATOA, EAST OF JAVA(1969); FIVE MAN ARMY, THE(1970, Ital.); KREMLIN LETTER, THE(1970); DIAMONDS ARE FOREVER(1971, Brit.); FRASIER, THE SENSUOUS LION(1973); MAN WITH THE GOLDEN GUN, THE(1974, Brit.); MARATHON MAN(1976); PIECE OF THE ACTION, A(1977); FOUL PLAY(1978); GOIN' COCONUTS(1978); HOT STUFF(1979); SUPER FUZZ(1981)
1984
DADDY'S DEADLY DARLING(1984), a, p&d
Misc. Talkies
CATACLYSM(1980); DREAM NO EVIL(1984)

Marco Lawrence
SHEPHERD OF THE HILLS, THE(1941)

Margery Lawrence
DANGEROUS WOMAN(1929), w; MADONNA OF THE SEVEN MOONS(1945, Brit.), w

Marjie Lawrence
ON THE BEAT(1962, Brit.); HEAVENS ABOVE!(1963, Brit.); SPARROWS CAN'T SING(1963, Brit.); EARLY BIRD, THE(1965, Brit.); COP-OUT(1967, Brit.); INSPECTOR CLOUSEAU(1968, Brit.); TELL ME LIES(1968, Brit.); CARRY ON HENRY VIII(1970, Brit.); REMEMBRANCE(1982, Brit.)

Marjorie Lawrence
INTERRUPTED MELODY(1955), w; ONLY TWO CAN PLAY(1962, Brit.); PLACE TO GO, A(1964, Brit.); HANDS OF THE RIPPER(1971, Brit.)

Marjory Lawrence
Silents
ANTHING ONCE(1917)

Mark Lawrence
DAVID AND LISA(1962), m

Martin Lawrence
PAID TO KILL(1954, Brit.); HAND IN HAND(1960, Brit.)

Mary Lawrence
OBLIGING YOUNG LADY(1941); STRATTON STORY, THE(1949); TASK FORCE(1949); NO MAN OF HER OWN(1950); SOUND OF FURY, THE(1950); NIGHT INTO MORNING(1951); DREAM WIFE(1953); CRY IN THE NIGHT, A(1956); THESE WILDER YEARS(1956); BACK STREET(1961); BEST MAN, THE(1964)

Maurice Lawrence
BARRIER, THE(1937), m

Max Lawrence
KILL BABY KILL(1966, Ital.)

Melissa Lawrence
GOODBYE PORK PIE(1981, New Zealand)

Michael Lawrence
OTHELLO(1955, U.S./Fr./Ital.); LOVE MERCHANT, THE(1966); TASTE OF FLESH, A(1967); COLOR ME DEAD(1969, Aus.)

Mike Lawrence
JUBAL(1956)
1984
BUDDY SYSTEM, THE(1984)

Mitchell Lawrence
DESTRY(1954); RIVER OF NO RETURN(1954)

Mittie Lawrence
FUNNY GIRL(1968); NEW CENTURIONS, THE(1972); NIGHT CALL NURSES(1974)

Muriel Lawrence
BELLE LE GRAND(1951); BAL TABARIN(1952); I DREAM OF JEANIE(1952)

Patricia Lawrence
BLUE MURDER AT ST. TRINIAN'S(1958, Brit.); FERRY ACROSS THE MERSEY(1964, Brit.); HIRELING, THE(1973, Brit.); O LUCKY MAN!(1973, Brit.)

Paula Lawrence
EYES OF LAURA MARS(1978); FIREPOWER(1979, Brit.)

Peter Lawrence
BURNING, THE(1981), w

Peter Lee Lawrence
FEW BULLETS MORE, A(1968, Ital./Span.)
Misc. Talkies
HELL IN NORMANDY(1968, Brit.)

Quentin Lawrence
CRAWLING EYE, THE(1958, Brit.), d; CASH ON DEMAND(1962, Brit.), d; PLAYBACK(1962, Brit.), d; WE SHALL SEE(1964, Brit.), d; SECRET OF BLOOD ISLAND, THE(1965, Brit.), d; MAN WHO FINALLY DIED, THE(1967, Brit.), d

Ray Lawrence
1984
SUBURBIA(1984)

Raymond Lawrence
INTERFERENCE(1928); CARELESS AGE(1929); MYSTERY OF MR. X, THE(1934); SECRETS OF CHINATOWN(1935); ALIBI FOR MURDER(1936); YOUNG BESS(1953); DRUMS OF TAHITI(1954)
Misc. Silents
QUEEN O' TURF(1922)

Reginald Lawrence
MEN MUST FIGHT(1933), w

Richard J. Lawrence
RIGHT STUFF, THE(1983), art d

Richard James Lawrence
SOMETHING WICKED THIS WAY COMES(1983), art d
1984
AGAINST ALL ODDS(1984), art d

Richard Lawrence
MAGIC(1978), art d; MIDNIGHT MADNESS(1980), art d; FORCE: FIVE(1981), art d

Robert Lawrence
CITY OF FEAR(1959), ed; DAY OF THE OUTLAW(1959), ed; TOKYO AFTER DARK(1959), ed; SPARTACUS(1960), ed; EL CID(1961, U.S./Ital.), ed; 55 DAYS AT PEKING(1963), ed; FALL OF THE ROMAN EMPIRE, THE(1964), ed; IS PARIS BURNING?(1966, U.S./Fr.), ed; UPTIGHT(1968), ed; LOVING(1970), ed; PROMISE AT DAWN(1970, U.S./Fr.), ed; FIDDLER ON THE ROOF(1971), ed; GOLDEN APPLES OF THE SUN(1971, Can.), p; UP THE SANDBOX(1972), ed; WHIFFS(1975), ed; I WILL ...I WILL ...FOR NOW(1976), ed; FINGERS(1978), ed; EXPOSED(1983), ed; NEVER SAY NEVER AGAIN(1983), ed

Silents
ALL FOR A GIRL(1915)
Misc. Silents
TIGER MAN, THE(1918); FOLKS FROM WAY DOWN EAST(1924)

Robert L. Lawrence
HARVEY MIDDLEMAN, FIREMAN(1965), p

Robert Web Lawrence
Misc. Silents
BATTLE OF BALLOTS, THE(1915)

Rosina Lawrence
MUSIC IS MAGIC(1935); WELCOME HOME(1935); YOUR UNCLE DUDLEY(1935); $10 RAISE(1935); CHARLIE CHAN'S SECRET(1936); GREAT ZIEGFELD, THE(1936); MISTER CINDERELLA(1936); GENERAL SPANKY(1937); NOBODY'S BABY(1937); PICK A STAR(1937); WAY OUT WEST(1937)
Misc. Talkies
NEIGHBORHOOD HOUSE(1936)

Scott Lawrence
Misc. Talkies
GOD'S BLOODY ACRE(1975); TOMCATS(1977)

Sheldon Lawrence
CROOKED SKY, THE(1957, Brit.); FIGHTING WILDCATS, THE(1957, Brit.); MAN WITHOUT A BODY, THE(1957, Brit.); LONG KNIFE, THE(1958, Brit.); MARK OF THE PHOENIX(1958, Brit.); SHERIFF OF FRACTURED JAW, THE(1958, Brit.); STORMY CROSSING(1958, Brit.); THEM NICE AMERICANS(1958, Brit.); BLUEBEARD'S TEN HONEYMOONS(1960, Brit.); GIRLS OF LATIN QUARTER(1960, Brit.); IDENTITY UNKNOWN(1960, Brit.); PURSUERS, THE(1961, Brit.); TOO HOT TO HANDLE(1961, Brit.); TRANSATLANTIC(1961, Brit.); HOT MONEY GIRL(1962, Brit./Ger.); SWEET BEAT(1962, Brit.); TRAITORS, THE(1963, Brit.)

Shirley Lawrence
GENTLE TOUCH, THE(1956, Brit.); SATELLITE IN THE SKY(1956); DEVIL'S BAIT(1959, Brit.); UPSTAIRS AND DOWNSTAIRS(1961, Brit.); SECRET DOOR, THE(1964); WILLARD(1971)

Sid Lawrence
ROAD HUSTLERS, THE(1968); HELL'S BLOODY DEVILS(1970); REBEL ROUSERS(1970)

Stanley Lawrence
LITTLE MISS MARKER(1980); FIRST MONDAY IN OCTOBER(1981)

Stephanie Lawrence
O LUCKY MAN!(1973, Brit.)

Stephen Lawrence
BANG THE DRUM SLOWLY(1973), m; ONE SUMMER LOVE(1976), m; ALICE, SWEET ALICE(1978), m
1984
MIRRORS(1984), m

Stephen J. Lawrence
JENNIFER ON MY MIND(1971), m

Steve Lawrence
STAND UP AND BE COUNTED(1972); BLUES BROTHERS, THE(1980)
1984
LONELY GUY, THE(1984)

Susan Lawrence
LEO AND LOREE(1980)

Suzanne Remey Lawrence
1984
DELIVERY BOYS(1984)

T.E. Lawrence
LAWRENCE OF ARABIA(1962, Brit.), w

Ted Lawrence
OPERATION SECRET(1952)

Tedd Lawrence
ROOGIE'S BUMP(1954)

Terry Lawrence
TROOPER HOOK(1957)

Tom Lawrence
FUZZ(1972); MITCHELL(1975); HARRY AND WALTER GO TO NEW YORK(1976); WARGAMES(1983)

Toni Lawrence
1984
DADDY'S DEADLY DARLING(1984)

Veronica Lawrence
SOLO(1978, New Zealand/Aus.)

Vi Lawrence
PAGAN LADY(1931), ed

Vincent Lawrence
CRAZY THAT WAY(1930), w; LOVE IN THE ROUGH(1930), w; MONTE CARLO(1930), w; PLAYBOY OF PARIS(1930), w; I TAKE THIS WOMAN(1931), w; JUNE MOON(1931), w; MAGNIFICENT LIE(1931), w; MEN CALL IT LOVE(1931), w; SCANDAL SHEET(1931), w; MOVIE CRAZY(1932), w; NIGHT AFTER NIGHT(1932), w; SINNERS IN THE SUN(1932), w; CLEOPATRA(1934), w; GOOD DAME(1934), w; LET'S TRY AGAIN(1934), w; NOW AND FOREVER(1934), w; BEHOLD MY WIFE(1935), w; HANDS ACROSS THE TABLE(1935), w; ONE-WAY TICKET(1935), w; PETER IBBETSON(1935), w; JOHN MEADE'S WOMAN(1937), w; MANPROOF(1938), w; TEST PILOT(1938), w; LUCKY NIGHT(1939), w; MOON OVER MIAMI(1941), w; GENTLEMAN JIM(1942), w; ADVENTURE(1945), w; SEA OF GRASS, THE(1947), w

Viola Lawrence
THIS IS HEAVEN(1929), ed; WHAT A WIDOW(1930), ed; MAN'S CASTLE, A(1933), ed; SAILOR BE GOOD(1933), ed; LADY BY CHOICE(1934), ed; NO GREATER GLORY(1934), ed; PARTY'S OVER, THE(1934), ed; WHOM THE GODS DESTROY(1934), ed; FEATHER IN HER HAT, A(1935), ed; LOVE ME FOREVER(1935), ed; PARTY WIRE(1935), ed; WHOLE TOWN'S TALKING, THE(1935), ed; CRAIG'S WIFE(1936), ed; KING STEPS OUT, THE(1936), ed; LADY OF SECRETS(1936), ed; LONE WOLF RETURNS, THE(1936), ed; DEVIL'S PLAYGROUND(1937), ed; LIFE BEGINS WITH LOVE(1937), ed; SPEED TO SPARE(1937), ed; CITY STREETS(1938), ed; I AM THE LAW(1938), ed; PENITENTIARY(1938), ed; SHE MARRIED AN ARTIST(1938), ed; THERE'S ALWAYS A WOMAN(1938), ed; THERE'S THAT WOMAN AGAIN(1938), ed; AMAZING MR. WILLIAMS(1939), ed; BLONDIE TAKES A VACATION(1939), ed; ONLY ANGELS HAVE WINGS(1939), ed; DOCTOR TAKES A WIFE(1940), ed; FIVE LITTLE PEPPERS AT HOME(1940), ed; GLAMOUR FOR SALE(1940), ed; HE STAYED FOR BREAKFAST(1940), ed; THIS THING CALLED

LOVE(1940), ed; BIG BOSS, THE(1941), ed; HERE COMES MR. JORDAN(1941), ed; LONE WOLF TAKES A CHANCE, THE(1941), ed; TWO IN A TAXI(1941), ed; YOU BELONG TO ME(1941), ed; BEDTIME STORY(1942), ed; MY SISTER EILEEN(1942), ed; THEY ALL KISSED THE BRIDE(1942), ed; TWO YANKS IN TRINIDAD(1942), ed; FIRST COMES COURAGE(1943), ed; ONE DANGEROUS NIGHT(1943), ed; COVER GIRL(1944), ed; SECRET COMMAND(1944), ed; FIGHTING GUARDSMAN, THE(1945), ed; HIT THE HAY(1945), ed; SHE WOULDN'T SAY YES(1945), ed; TONIGHT AND EVERY NIGHT(1945), ed; PERILOUS HOLIDAY(1946), ed; DOWN TO EARTH(1947), ed; DARK PAST, THE(1948), ed; GALLANT BLADE, THE(1948), ed; LADY FROM SHANGHAI, THE(1948), ed; LEATHER GLOVES(1948), ed; MARY LOU(1948), ed; AND BABY MAKES THREE(1949), ed; KNOCK ON ANY DOOR(1949), ed; TOKYO JOE(1949), ed; FLYING MISSILE(1950), ed; HARRIET CRAIG(1950), ed; IN A LONELY PLACE(1950), ed; TRAVELING SALESWOMAN(1950), ed; SIROCCO(1951), ed; AFFAIR IN TRINIDAD(1952), ed; FIRST TIME, THE(1952), ed; PAULA(1952), ed; MAN IN THE DARK(1953), ed; MISS SADIE THOMPSON(1953), ed; SALOME(1953), ed; JESSE JAMES VERSUS THE DALTONS(1954), ed; MIAMI STORY, THE(1954), ed; CHICAGO SYNDICATE(1955), ed; QUEEN BEE(1955), ed; THREE FOR THE SHOW(1955), ed; TIGHT SPOT(1955), ed; EDDY DUCHIN STORY, THE(1956), ed; JEANNE EAGELS(1957), ed; PAL JOEY(1957), ed; PEPE(1960), ed; WHO WAS THAT LADY?(1960), ed

Silents
NIGHT OF LOVE, THE(1927), ed; AWAKENING, THE(1928), ed; TWO LOVERS(1928), ed; QUEEN KELLY(1929), ed

W. E. Lawrence
Silents
HOME SWEET HOME(1914); INTOLERANCE(1916); OLD FOLKS AT HOME, THE(1916); NARROW PATH, THE(1918)

W.E. Lawrence
Silents
BATTLE OF THE SEXES, THE(1914)
Misc. Silents
JAPANESE NIGHTINGALE, A(1918)

Walter A. Lawrence
BECAUSE OF EVE(1948), w

Walter Lawrence
PAID TO DANCE(1937); SAPS AT SEA(1940); TRIAL OF MARY DUGAN, THE(1941); IT HAPPENS EVERY THURSDAY(1953)

Whitey Lawrence
WYOMING BANDIT, THE(1949), makeup

Wiliam A. Lawrence
Misc. Silents
CALEB PIPER'S GIRL(1919)

William E. Lawrence
SHE COULDN'T TAKE IT(1935)
Silents
FLIRTING WITH FATE(1916); FLYING TORPEDO, THE(1916); DUCKS AND DRAKES(1921); FRONT PAGE STORY, A(1922); LAW FORBIDS, THE(1924); RECKLESS AGE, THE(1924)
Misc. Silents
BEANS(1918); COMMON CLAY(1919); GIRL WOMAN, THE(1919); KISS, THE(1921); THEY LIKE 'EM ROUGH(1922); THRILL CHASER, THE(1923); WHISPERED NAME, THE(1924)

William Lawrence
HELL BOUND(1931); BEST OF ENEMIES(1933); RIDE 'EM COWBOY(1936); SILVER SPURS(1936); SUNSET OF POWER(1936); EMPTY SADDLES(1937); SUDDEN BILL DORN(1938); TONIGHT AND EVERY NIGHT(1945); DEAD RECKONING(1947); MAN, THE(1972)
Silents
GET YOUR MAN(1921); MORALS(1921); BLOOD AND SAND(1922); LOVE GAMBLER, THE(1922); MAN FOUR-SQUARE, A(1926)
Misc. Silents
BODY AND SOUL(1920); HARD BOILED(1926)

Wingold Lawrence
Silents
EUGENE ARAM(1914, Brit.); GIRL WHO TOOK THE WRONG TURNING, THE(1915, Brit.)
Misc. Silents
MYSTERIES OF LONDON, THE(1915, Brit.); TWO LANCASHIRE LASSES IN LONDON(1916, Brit.)

Zack Lawrence
ASSASSIN(1973, Brit.), m

Alma Lawrentz
MR. MAJESTYK(1974)

James H. Lawrie
PACIFIC DESTINY(1956, Brit.), p

James Lawrie
STRANGE AFFECTION(1959, Brit.), p

Charles Lawry
WANDA NEVADA(1979)

John Laws
NED KELLY(1970, Brit.); NICKEL QUEEN, THE(1971, Aus.)

Maury Laws
DAYDREAMER, THE(1966), m; MARCO(1973), m; BUSHIDO BLADE, THE(1982, Brit./U.S.), m

Sam Laws
COOL BREEZE(1972); HIT MAN(1972); SWEET JESUS, PREACHER MAN(1973); WALKING TALL(1973); DIRTY O'NEIL(1974); TRUCK TURNER(1974); DARKTOWN STRUTTERS(1975); WHITE LINE FEVER(1975, Can.); BINGO LONG TRAVELING ALL-STARS AND MOTOR KINGS, THE(1976); MR. BILLION(1977); FURY, THE(1978); WHITE DOG(1982); GET CRAZY(1983)

Er Lawshe
Silents
PATSY(1921), w

Alan Lawson
FORTUNATE FOOL, THE(1933, Brit.), ph

Anne Lawson
LAMP IN ASSASSIN MEWS, THE(1962, Brit.); DOUBLE, THE(1963, Brit)

Arthur Lawson
STAIRWAY TO HEAVEN(1946, Brit.), art d; RED SHOES, THE(1948, Brit.), art d; FIGHTING PIMPERNEL, THE(1950, Brit.), set d; TALES OF HOFFMANN, THE(1951, Brit.), prod d; STORY OF ROBIN HOOD, THE(1952, Brit.), art d; WILD HEART, THE(1952, Brit.), art d; FOLLY TO BE WISE(1953), prod d; TWICE UPON A TIME(1953, Brit.), prod d; HIGH TERRACE(1957, Brit.), art d; PURSUIT OF THE GRAF SPEE(1957, Brit.), prod d; SEA WIFE(1957, Brit.), art d; HARRY BLACK AND THE TIGER(1958, Brit.), art d; DAMN THE DEFIANT!(1962, Brit.), art d; VALIANT, THE(1962, Brit./Ital.), art d; BRAIN, THE(1965, Ger./Brit.), art d; LEATHER BOYS, THE(1965, Brit.), art d; DOUBLE MAN, THE(1967), art d; LOST CONTINENT, THE(1968, Brit.), art d; MIDAS RUN(1969), art d

Barbara Lawson
VISIT TO A SMALL PLANET(1960)

Bobby Lawson
DOWN THE WYOMING TRAIL(1939)

Brian Lawson
O LUCKY MAN!(1973, Brit.)

Carol Lawson
COFFY(1973); THIS IS A HIJACK(1973)

Charles Lawson
1984
FOUR DAYS IN JULY(1984)

Christine Lawson
SUMMER HOLIDAY(1963, Brit.); SHE(1965, Brit.), ch

Chuck Lawson
Misc. Talkies
SWEET GEORGIA(1972)

Daphne Lawson
OPTIMISTS, THE(1973, Brit.); UNDERCOVERS HERO(1975, Brit.)

Denis Lawson
PROVIDENCE(1977, Fr.); LOCAL HERO(1983, Brit.); RETURN OF THE JEDI(1983)

Dennis Lawson
STAR WARS(1977); EMPIRE STRIKES BACK, THE(1980)

Edward C. Lawson
1984
CHOOSE ME(1984)

Eleanor Lawson
PICK-UP(1933); MAN WITH TWO LIVES, THE(1942); TAKE CARE OF MY LITTLE GIRL(1951)
Silents
MERTON OF THE MOVIES(1924); IT(1927)
Misc. Silents
RENAISSANCE AT CHARLEROI, THE(1917)

Elsie Lawson
Silents
AMAZONS, THE(1917); DANCING MOTHERS(1926); SOCIAL CELEBRITY, A(1926)

Frank Lawson
EMPEROR'S CANDLESTICKS, THE(1937)

Gerald Lawson
WILD HEART, THE(1952, Brit.); HIGH TIDE AT NOON(1957, Brit.); MUMMY, THE(1959, Brit.); BECKET(1964, Brit.); GYPSY GIRL(1966, Brit.); GREAT CATHERINE(1968, Brit.); THAT RIVIERA TOUCH(1968, Brit.); VENGEANCE OF SHE, THE(1968, Brit.)

Gerald C. Lawson
NO WAY BACK(1949, Brit.); DUBLIN NIGHTMARE(1958, Brit.); DR. BLOOD'S COFFIN(1961)

Glyn Lawson
NOW BARABBAS WAS A ROBBER(1949, Brit.); GAY ADVENTURE, THE(1953, Brit.); SIMBA(1955, Brit.)

Henry Lawson
THREE IN ONE(1956, Aus.), w

Jay Lawson
THINGS ARE TOUGH ALL OVER(1982)

John H. Lawson
BLUSHING BRIDES(1930), w

John Howard Lawson
OUR BLUSHING BRIDES(1930), w; SEA BAT, THE(1930), w; SHIP FROM SHANGHAI, THE(1930), w; BACHELOR APARTMENT(1931), w; GOODBYE LOVE(1934), w; SUCCESS AT ANY PRICE(1934), w; TREASURE ISLAND(1934), w; PARTY WIRE(1935), w; ALGIERS(1938), w; BLOCKADE(1938), w; THEY SHALL HAVE MUSIC(1939), w; EARTHBOUND(1940), w; FOUR SONS(1940), w; ACTION IN THE NORTH ATLANTIC(1943), w; SAHARA(1943), w; COUNTER-ATTACK(1945), w; SMASH-UP, THE STORY OF A WOMAN(1947), w

John Lawson
Misc. Silents
KING OF CRIME, THE(1914, Brit.)

Jon Lawson
MODEL SHOP, THE(1969)

Kate Drain Lawson
CITY STREETS(1931); REMEMBER THE NIGHT(1940); WEST POINT WIDOW(1941); IT AIN'T HAY(1943); LOVES OF CARMEN, THE(1948); BRIDE OF VENGEANCE(1949); NEVADAN, THE(1950); ROCK ISLAND TRAIL(1950); GROOM WORE SPURS, THE(1951); JOURNEY INTO LIGHT(1951); FIRST TRAVELING SALESLADY, THE(1956)

Kate Lawson
LITTLE ORPHAN ANNIE(1932); GIRLS ON PROBATION(1938); TORCHY PLAYS WITH DYNAMITE(1939); GIRL FROM GOD'S COUNTRY(1940); LEOPARD MAN, THE(1943); PHANTOM OF THE OPERA(1943); RHYTHM OF THE ISLANDS(1943); WHITE SAVAGE(1943); SONG OF MY HEART(1947); EVERY GIRL SHOULD BE MARRIED(1948); JOAN OF ARC(1948); WHIPLASH(1948); THEY LIVE BY NIGHT(1949); FILE ON THELMA JORDAN, THE(1950); ON DANGEROUS GROUND(1951); STEEL FIST, THE(1952)

Larry Lawson
BEAU GESTE(1939); GREAT MAN'S LADY, THE(1942); MY FAVORITE SPY(1942); ROXIE HART(1942)

Leigh Lawson
BROTHER SUN, SISTER MOON(1973, Brit./Ital.); GHOST STORY(1974, Brit.); IT'S NOT THE SIZE THAT COUNTS(1979, Brit.); TESS(1980, Fr./Brit.)

1984
SWORD OF THE VALIANT(1984, Brit.)
Misc. Talkies
FIRE AND SWORD(1982, Brit.); BLACK CARRION(1984)

Len Lawson
CALIFORNIA SUITE(1978); IN GOD WE TRUST(1980); S.O.B.(1981); WAR-GAMES(1983)

Lillian Lawson
ONE WAY WAHINI(1965), makeup

Linda Lawson
THREAT, THE(1960); NIGHT TIDE(1963); APACHE RIFLES(1964); LET'S KILL UNCLE(1966); SOMETIMES A GREAT NOTION(1971)

Louise Lawson
PLAYGIRLS AND THE BELLBOY, THE(1962,Ger.)

Marie Lawson
HAPPIDROME(1943, Brit.)

Mary Lawson
COLONEL BLOOD(1934, Brit.); THINGS ARE LOOKING UP(1934, Brit.); YOUTH-FUL FOLLY(1934, Brit.); CAN YOU HEAR ME MOTHER?(1935, Brit.); FIRE HAS BEEN ARRANGED, A(1935, Brit.); RADIO PIRATES(1935, Brit.); SCROOGE(1935, Brit.); HOUSE BROKEN(1936, Brit.); TO CATCH A THIEF(1936, Brit.); TOILERS OF THE SEA(1936, Brit.); TROUBLE AHEAD(1936, Brit.); COTTON QUEEN(1937, Brit.); OH BOY!(1938, Brit.); CAPTAIN MOONLIGHT(1940, Brit.)

Mary Louise Lawson
ROSEMARY'S BABY(1968)

Nancy Lawson
Misc. Talkies
CONVENTION GIRLS(1978)

Peggy Lawson
BLAST OF SILENCE(1961), ed; YEAR OF THE HORSE, THE(1966), ed

Priscilla Lawson
GREAT IMPERSONATION, THE(1935); HIS NIGHT OUT(1935); DON'T GET PER-SONAL(1936); FLASH GORDON(1936); ROSE BOWL(1936); SUTTER'S GOLD(1936); DOUBLE WEDDING(1937); INTERNES CAN'T TAKE MONEY(1937); KING OF GAMBLERS(1937); LAST GANGSTER, THE(1937); ARSENE LUPIN RETURNS(1938); FIRST 100 YEARS, THE(1938); GIRL DOWNSTAIRS, THE(1938); GIRL OF THE GOLDEN WEST, THE(1938); HEROES OF THE HILLS(1938); TEST PILOT(1938); THREE COMRADES(1938); THREE LOVES HAS NANCY(1938); TOY WIFE, THE(1938); WOMEN, THE(1939)

Ralph Lawson
Silents
SNOB, THE(1924), ed

Reginald Lawson
Silents
FATE'S PLAYTHING(1920, Brit.), w

Richard Lawson
DIRTY HARRY(1971); SCREAM BLACULA SCREAM(1973); WILLIE DYNAMI-TE(1973); SUGAR HILL(1974); AUDREY ROSE(1977); MAIN EVENT, THE(1979); POLTERGEIST(1982)
1984
STREETS OF FIRE(1984)
Misc. Talkies
BLACK STREETFIGHTER(1976); BLACK FIST(1977)

Russell Lawson
BLOCKADE(1938), spec eff

Russell E. Lawson
DELUGE(1933), spec eff

Sarah Lawson
BROWNING VERSION, THE(1951, Brit.); NIGHT WON'T TALK, THE(1952, Brit.); BOTH SIDES OF THE LAW(1953, Brit.); THREE STEPS IN THE DARK(1953, Brit.); MEET MR. MALCOLM(1954, Brit.); YOU KNOW WHAT SAILORS ARE(1954, Brit.); IT'S NEVER TOO LATE(1958, Brit.); LINKS OF JUSTICE(1958); SOLITARY CHILD, THE(1958, Brit.); THREE CROOKED MEN(1958, Brit.); NAVY HEROES(1959, Brit.); NIGHT WITHOUT PITY(1961, Brit.); PUSSYCAT ALLEY(1965, Brit.); ON THE RUN(1967, Brit.); DEVIL'S BRIDE, THE(1968, Brit.); BATTLE OF BRITAIN, THE(1969, Brit.); ISLAND OF THE BURNING DAMNED(1971, Brit.); STUD, THE(1979, Brit.)

Capt. Ted W. Lawson
THIRTY SECONDS OVER TOKYO(1944), w

Thomas W. Lawson
Silents
FRIDAY THE 13TH(1916), w

Tony Lawson
STRAW DOGS(1971, Brit.), ed; BARRY LYNDON(1975, Brit.), ed; CROSS OF IRON(1977, Brit., Ger.), ed; DRAGONSLAYER(1981), ed; EUREKA(1983, Brit.), ed
1984
BOUNTY, THE(1984), ed

Vincent Lawson
TOO MANY MILLIONS(1934, Brit.); MONKEY'S PAW, THE(1948, Brit.); SUSPEND-ED ALIBI(1957, Brit.)

Wilfrid Lawson
EAST LYNNE ON THE WESTERN FRONT(1931, Brit.); STRIKE IT RICH(1933, Brit.); TURN OF THE TIDE(1935, Brit.); LADIES IN LOVE(1936); WHITE HUNTER(1936); MAN WHO MADE DIAMONDS, THE(1937, Brit.); BANK HOLIDAY(1938, Brit.); PYGMALION(1938, Brit.); YELLOW SANDS(1938, Brit.); ALLEGHENY UPRISING(1939); DEAD MAN'S SHOES(1939, Brit.); PHANTOM STRIKES, THE(1939, Brit.); STOLEN LIFE(1939, Brit.); LONG VOYAGE HOME, THE(1940); PASTOR HALL(1940, Brit.); DANNY BOY(1941, Brit.); FARMER'S WIFE, THE(1941, Brit.); GIRL IN DISTRESS(1941, Brit.); HARD STEEL(1941, Brit.); IT HAPPENED TO ONE MAN(1941, Brit.); TERROR, THE(1941, Brit.); GREAT MR. HANDEL, THE(1942, Brit.); TERROR HOUSE(1942, Brit.); TOWER OF TERROR, THE(1942, Brit.); THURSDAY'S CHILD(1943, Brit.); TURNERS OF PROSPECT ROAD, THE(1947, Brit.); MAN OF EVIL(1948, Brit.); MAKE ME AN OFFER(1954, Brit.); PRISONER, THE(1955, Brit.); NOW AND FOREVER(1956, Brit.); WAR AND PEACE(1956, Ital./U.S.); ALLIGATOR NAMED DAISY, AN(1957, Brit.); MIRACLE IN SOHO(1957, Brit.); HELL DRI-VERS(1958, Brit.); YOUR PAST IS SHOWING(1958, Brit.); EXPRESSO BONGO(1959, Brit.); ROOM AT THE TOP(1959, Brit.); TREAD SOFTLY STRANGER(1959, Brit.); NAKED EDGE, THE(1961); NOTHING BARRED(1961, Brit.); OVER THE ODDS(1961, Brit.); GO TO BLAZES(1962, Brit.); POSTMAN'S KNOCK(1962, Brit.); TOM JO-NES(1963, Brit.); WRONG BOX, THE(1966, Brit.); VIKING QUEEN, THE(1967, Brit.)

Alma Lawton
LADY POSSESSED(1952); MY COUSIN RACHEL(1952); MARY POPPINS(1964); MY FAIR LADY(1964)

Carol Lawton
TROJAN BROTHERS, THE(1946); WOMAN TO WOMAN(1946, Brit.); GREEN FIN-GERS(1947)

Charles Lawton
MIRACLES FOR SALE(1939), ph; NICK CARTER, MASTER DETECTIVE(1939), ph; WITHIN THE LAW(1939), ph; ANDY HARDY MEETS DEBUTANTE(1940), ph; CON-GO MAISIE(1940), ph; DULCY(1940), ph; FORTY LITTLE MOTHERS(1940), ph; GOLD RUSH MAISIE(1940), ph; HULLABALOO(1940), ph; SKY MURDER(1940), ph; BIG STORE, THE(1941), ph; FREE AND EASY(1941), ph; MAISIE WAS A LA-DY(1941), ph; RINGSIDE MAISIE(1941), ph; VANISHING VIRGINIAN, THE(1941), ph; AFFAIRS OF MARTHA, THE(1942), ph; EYES IN THE NIGHT(1942), ph; FIN-GERS AT THE WINDOW(1942), ph; JOE SMITH, AMERICAN(1942), ph; YANK AT ETON, A(1942), ph; YOUNG IDEAS(1943), ph; YOUNGEST PROFESSION, THE(1943), ph; ABROAD WITH TWO YANKS(1944), ph; SEE HERE, PRIVATE HAR-GROVE(1944), ph; BREWSTER'S MILLIONS(1945), ph; BLACK ARROW(1948), ph; GALLANT BLADE, THE(1948), ph; CARGO TO CAPETOWN(1950), ph; HER FIRST ROMANCE(1951), ph; FULL OF LIFE(1956), ph; COMANCHE STATION(1960), ph; ROME ADVENTURE(1962), ph; SPENCER'S MOUNTAIN(1963), ph; ENSIGN PUL-VER(1964), ph; RAGE TO LIVE, A(1965), ph

Charles Lawton, Jr.
MY DEAR MISS ALDRICH(1937), ph; CHASER, THE(1938), ph; LISTEN, DAR-LING(1938), ph; UP IN MABEL'S ROOM(1944), ph; 3 IS A FAMILY(1944), ph; GET-TING GERTIE'S GARTER(1945), ph; KISS AND TELL(1945), ph; ONE WAY TO LOVE(1946), ph; PERILOUS HOLIDAY(1946), ph; RETURN OF MONTE CRISTO, THE(1946), ph; THRILL OF BRAZIL, THE(1946), ph; MISS GRANT TAKES RICHMOND(1949), ph; MR. SOFT TOUCH(1949), ph; SHOCKPROOF(1949), ph; SLIGHTLY FRENCH(1949), ph; TOKYO JOE(1949), ph; WALKING HILLS, THE(1949), ph; FULLER BRUSH GIRL, THE(1950), ph; KILL THE UMPIRE(1950), ph; NEVADAN, THE(1950), ph; ROGUES OF SHERWOOD FOREST(1950), ph; STAGE TO TUCSON(1950), ph; MAN IN THE SADDLE(1951), ph; MASK OF THE AVEN-GER(1951), ph; SANTA FE(1951), ph; BOOTS MALONE(1952), ph; CAPTAIN PI-RATE(1952), ph; HANGMAN'S KNOT(1952), ph; HAPPY TIME, THE(1952), ph; LAST OF THE COMANCHES(1952), ph; PAULA(1952), ph; ALL ASHORE(1953), ph; CRUIS-IN' DOWN THE RIVER(1953), ph; FORT ALGIERS(1953), ph; LET'S DO IT AGAIN(1953), ph; MISS SADIE THOMPSON(1953), ph; DRIVE A CROOKED ROAD(1954), ph; THEY RODE WEST(1954), ph; THREE HOURS TO KILL(1954), ph; BRING YOUR SMILE ALONG(1955), ph; LONG GRAY LINE, THE(1955), ph; MY SISTER EILEEN(1955), ph ATI FULL OF LIFE (1956), ph; JUBAL(1956), ph; YOU CAN'T RUN AWAY FROM IT(1956), ph; OPERATION MAD BALL(1957), ph; TALL T, THE(1957), ph; 3:10 TO YUMA(1957), ph; GUNMAN'S WALK(1958), ph; LAST HUR-RAH, THE(1958), ph; GENE KRUPA STORY, THE(1959), ph; IT HAPPENED TO JANE(1959), ph; RIDE LONESOME(1959), ph; MAN ON A STRING(1960), ph; RAIS-IN IN THE SUN, A(1961), ph; TWO RODE TOGETHER(1961), ph; WACKIEST SHIP IN THE ARMY, THE(1961), ph; THIRTEEN WEST STREET(1962), ph; YOUNGB-LOOD HAWKE(1964), ph

David Lawton
KILL HER GENTLY(1958, Brit.); WOMAN EATER, THE(1959, Brit.)

Donald Lawton
GHOST CHASERS(1951); ROAD TO BALI(1952); TREASURE OF THE GOLDEN CONDOR(1953); KNOCK ON WOOD(1954); MAN WHO KNEW TOO MUCH, THE(1956); FUNNY FACE(1957)

Frank Lawton
YOUNG WOODLEY(1930, Brit.); PERFECT ALIBI, THE(1931, Brit.); SKIN GAME, THE(1931, Brit.); AFTER OFFICE HOURS(1932, Brit.); MICHAEL AND MARY(1932, Brit.); CAVALCADE(1933); CHARMING DECEIVER, THE(1933, Brit.); OUTSIDER, THE(1933, Brit.); FRIDAY THE 13TH(1934, Brit.); ONE MORE RIVER(1934); DAVID COPPERFIELD(1935); DEVIL DOLL, THE(1936); THE INVISIBLE RAY(1936); MILL ON THE FLOSS(1939, Brit.); SECRET FOUR, THE(1940, Brit.); 48 HOURS(1944, Brit.); WINSLOW BOY, THE(1950, Brit.); SHOOT FIRST(1953, Brit.); DOUBLE CROSS(1956, Brit.); RISING OF THE MOON, THE(1957, Ireland); NIGHT TO REMEMBER, A(1958, Brit.); GIDEON OF SCOTLAND YARD(1959, Brit.); QUEEN'S GUARDS, THE(1963, Brit.)

Harry Lawton
TELL THEM WILLIE BOY IS HERE(1969), d&w

Jack Lawton
Misc. Silents
DESERT HONEYMOON, A(1915); WESTERN GOVERNOR'S HUMANITY, A(1915)

Kenneth Lawton
GENTLEMAN FROM LOUISIANA(1936)

Leslie Lawton
RUN WITH THE WIND(1966, Brit.)

Mary Lawton
Silents
JOHN GLAYDE'S HONOR(1915)

Ralph Lawton
CHARIOTS OF FIRE(1981, Brit.)

Scott Lawton
NORMA RAE(1979)

Shaun Lawton
POSSESSION(1981, Fr./Ger.)

Shawn Lawton
1984
WOMAN IN FLAMES, A(1984, Ger.)

Tommy Lawton
GREAT GAME, THE(1953, Brit.)

Abe Lax
CATSKILL HONEYMOON(1950)

Frances Lax
ERRAND BOY, THE(1961); FAMILY JEWELS, THE(1965)

Frances Weintraub Lax
APARTMENT, THE(1960)

Francis Lax
VERY CURIOUS GIRL, A(1970, Fr.)

Leo Lax
AWFUL DR. ORLOFF, THE(1964, Span./Fr.), p
Robert Lax
SIREN OF ATLANTIS(1948), w
Pedro Laxaet
DARK RIVER(1956, Arg.)
Pedro Laxalt
DARK RIVER(1956, Arg.); SUMMERSKIN(1962, Arg.)
Andrey Laxinni
LA BALANCE(1983, Fr.)
Andre Lay
THEY CAME TO ROB LAS VEGAS(1969, Fr./Ital./Span./Ger.), w
Beirne Lay, Jr.
TWELVE O'CLOCK HIGH(1949), w; ABOVE AND BEYOND(1953), w; STRATEGIC AIR COMMAND(1955), w; TOWARD THE UNKNOWN(1956), w; GALLANT HOURS, THE(1960), w; YOUNG AND THE BRAVE, THE(1963), a, w
Lt. Beirne Lay, Jr.
I WANTED WINGS(1941), w
Eugene Lay
G.I. WAR BRIDES(1946); FAST ON THE DRAW(1950)
John Hunter Lay
SLIGHTLY HONORABLE(1940), w
Karen Lay
RETURN OF THE JEDI(1983)
Me Me Lay
Misc. Talkies
AU PAIR GIRLS(1973)
Ubaldo Lay
MONTE CASSINO(1948, Ital.); PIRATE AND THE SLAVE GIRL, THE(1961, Fr./Ital.); GUILT IS NOT MINE(1968, Ital.)
Mario Layco
YEAR OF LIVING DANGEROUSLY, THE(1982, Aus.)
Ada Laycock
Silents
DOWN TO THE SEA IN SHIPS(1923)
Pat Layde
NEVER PUT IT IN WRITING(1964); PADDY(1970, Irish); RYAN'S DAUGHTER(1970, Brit.)
Patrick Layde
HOME IS THE HERO(1959, Ireland)
Elmer Layden
SPIRIT OF NOTRE DAME, THE(1931)
Robert Layden
HOUSE OF DARK SHADOWS(1970), makeup
Claude Laydu
VOYAGE TO AMERICA(1952, Fr.); DIARY OF A COUNTRY PRIEST(1954, Fr.); ATTILA(1958, Ital.)
Dilys Laye
GAY LADY, THE(1949, Brit.); PAPER GALLOWS(1950, Brit.); DOCTOR AT LARGE(1957, Brit.); BLUE MURDER AT ST. TRINIAN'S(1958, Brit.); BRIDAL PATH, THE(1959, Brit.); IDOL ON PARADE(1959, Brit.); PLEASE TURN OVER(1960, Brit.); PETTICOAT PIRATES(1961, Brit.); UPSTAIRS AND DOWNSTAIRS(1961, Brit.); CARRY ON CRUISING(1962, Brit.); ON THE BEAT(1962, Brit.); CARRY ON SPYING(1964, Brit.); COUNTESS FROM HONG KONG, A(1967, Brit.); CARRY ON DOCTOR(1968, Brit.); CARRY ON CAMPING(1969, Brit.)
Evelyn Laye
ONE HEAVENLY NIGHT(1931); WALTZ TIME(1933, Brit.); EVENSONG(1934, Brit.); NIGHT IS YOUNG, THE(1935); PRINCESS CHARMING(1935, Brit.); I'LL TURN TO YOU(1946, Brit.); MAKE MINE A MILLION(1965, Brit.); THEATRE OF DEATH(1967, Brit.); SAY HELLO TO YESTERDAY(1971, Brit.); NEVER NEVER LAND(1982)
Misc. Silents
LUCK OF THE NAVY, THE(1927, Brit.)
Ruby Layfayette
Silents
KAISER, BEAST OF BERLIN, THE(1918)
Debora Layman
STUDENT BODY, THE(1976)
Fatty Layman
MEN OF AMERICA(1933)
Anne Layne
WINDSPLITTER, THE(1971)
Beverly Layne
HONEYMOON OF HORROR(1964)
Bill Layne
FEMALE JUNGLE, THE(1955); SLEEPING BEAUTY(1959), art d; ONE HUNDRED AND ONE DALMATIANS(1961), art d; SWORD IN THE STONE, THE(1963), art d; ARISTOCATS, THE(1970), anim
Bob Layne
$1,000 A TOUCHDOWN(1939)
G. Cornell Layne
ABBY(1974), w
Gordon C. Layne
ABBY(1974), p
Mary Layne
CACTUS IN THE SNOW(1972)
Michael Layne
NO MERCY MAN, THE(1975)
Rickie Layne
NORTH AVENUE IRREGULARS, THE(1979)
Shary Layne
LADIES MAN, THE(1961); RUNAWAY GIRL(1966)
Tracy Layne
TUMBLING TUMBLEWEEDS(1935); GUN SMOKE(1936); GUNS AND GUITARS(1936); LONELY TRAIL, THE(1936); SINGING COWBOY, THE(1936); WINDS OF THE WASTELAND(1936); GALLOPING DYNAMITE(1937); RIDERS OF THE WHISTLING SKULL(1937)
Donald Layne-Smith
DAVID COPPERFIELD(1970, Brit.)

Lissa Layng
WHOSE LIFE IS IT ANYWAY?(1981)
1984
NIGHT OF THE COMET(1984)
Tony Layng
IN A LONELY PLACE(1950); ONE TOO MANY(1950)
Joseph Layode
EAST OF SUDAN(1964, Brit.); GUNS AT BATASI(1964, Brit.)
Lorena Layson
GOLD DIGGERS OF 1933(1933); I LOVED A WOMAN(1933); 42ND STREET(1933); HERE COMES THE NAVY(1934); JIMMY THE GENT(1934); KANSAS CITY PRINCESS(1934); LOST LADY, A(1934); SIDE STREETS(1934)
Loretta Layson
LITTLE GIANT, THE(1933)
The Layson Brothers
CAROLINA BLUES(1944)
Dorothy Layton
PACK UP YOUR TROUBLES(1932); PICK-UP(1933)
Frank Layton
BIG SHAKEDOWN, THE(1934); VOICE IN THE NIGHT(1934); BAR 20 RIDES AGAIN(1936); TWO IN A CROWD(1936)
George Layton
HERE WE GO ROUND THE MULBERRY BUSH(1968, Brit.); MOSQUITO SQUADRON(1970, Brit.); STAND UP VIRGIN SOLDIERS(1977, Brit.)
Joe Layton
THOROUGHLY MODERN MILLIE(1967), ch
Ken Layton
MALIBU HIGH(1979)
Lord Layton
KING'S THIEF, THE(1955)
R. T. Layton
LONG VOYAGE HOME, THE(1940), spec eff
Scott Layton
Silents
KILTIES THREE(1918, Brit.)
Sheila Layton
HOW SWEET IT IS(1968)
Verne Layton
Misc. Silents
FINDERS KEEPERS(1921)
Vernon Layton
MC VICAR(1982, Brit.), ph
William Layton
MAN IN THE WILDERNESS(1971, U.S./Span.); TRAVELS WITH MY AUNT(1972, Brit.); OPEN SEASON(1974, U.S./Span.)
Frank Layva
WHERE DANGER LIVES(1950)
A. Lazaebnikoff
DESERTER(1934, USSR), w
Pedro Lazaga
GLADIATORS 7(1964, Span./Ital.), d
Stan Lazan
MIXED COMPANY(1974), ph
Ava Lazar
DEATH WISH II(1982); FAST TIMES AT RIDGEMONT HIGH(1982); NIGHT SHIFT(1982)
Lajos Lazar
BLUE IDOL, THE(1931, Hung.), d
Paul Lazar
STREAMERS(1983)
Veronica Lazar
LUNA(1979, Ital.); INFERNO(1980, Ital.); IDENTIFICATION OF A WOMAN(1983, Ital.)
Carol Lazare
ONE MAN(1979, Can.)
Carole Lazare
LIES MY FATHER TOLD ME(1975, Can.)
Corinne Lazare
1984
A NOS AMOURS(1984, Fr.), ed
Lazare and Castellanos
FOLLIES GIRL(1943)
Serge Lazareff
NED KELLY(1970, Brit.); THREE TO GO(1971, Aus.); SIDECAR RACERS(1975, Aus.); TRUE STORY OF ESKIMO NELL, THE(1975, Aus.); ELIZA FRASER(1976, Aus.)
Norma Lazareno
NIGHT OF THE BLOODY APES zero(1968, Mex.); VENGEANCE OF THE VAMPIRE WOMEN, THE(1969, Mex.); SURVIVE!(1977, Mex.)
Alexander Lazarev
CHEREZ TERNII K SVEZDAM(1981 USSR)
V. Lazarev
DAY THE WAR ENDED, THE(1961, USSR), lyrics; MARRIAGE OF BALZAMINOV, THE(1966, USSR)
R. Lazareva
Misc. Silents
IN THE KINGDOM OF OIL AND MILLIONS(1916, USSR)
Eusebio Lazaro
1984
DEMONS IN THE GARDEN(1984, Span.)
Nicolo Lazarri
MESSALINE(1952, Fr./Ital.), ed
Ashley Lazarus
FOREVER YOUNG, FOREVER FREE(1976, South Afr.), d, w; GOLDEN RENDEZVOUS(1977), d
Bill Lazarus
THIEVES(1977)
Erna Lazarus
ATLANTIC FLIGHT(1937), w; HE MARRIED HIS WIFE(1940), w; I'M NOBODY'S SWEETHEART NOW(1940), w; MARGIE(1940), w; BODY DISAPPEARS, THE(1941), w; CRACKED NUTS(1941), w; DOUBLE DATE(1941), w; MOONLIGHT IN HA-

WAII(1941), w; BLONDE FROM BROOKLYN(1945), w; DANCING IN MANHAT-
TAN(1945), w; GIRL OF THE LIMBERLOST, THE(1945), w; LET'S GO STEADY(1945),
w; JUNIOR PROM(1946), w; LITTLE MISS BIG(1946), w; SLIGHTLY SCANDAL-
OUS(1946), w; MICHAEL O'HALLORAN(1948), w; BLACK MIDNIGHT(1949), w;
MEET ME AFTER THE SHOW(1951), w; HOLLYWOOD OR BUST(1956), w

Frank Lazarus
SUPERMAN(1978)

Jeff Lazarus
GIVE ME A SAILOR(1938), p; RIDE A CROOKED MILE(1938), p; CAFE SOCIE-
TY(1939), p; HONEYMOON IN BALI(1939), p; LADY'S FROM KENTUCKY,
THE(1939), p; ST. LOUIS BLUES(1939), p

Jerry Lazarus
TREASURE OF THE FOUR CROWNS(1983, Span./U.S.), a, w
1984
BREAKIN' 2: ELECTRIC BOOGALOO(1984); OVER THE BROOKLYN BRID-
GE(1984)

Milton Lazarus
SUDDEN MONEY(1939), w; WHEN THE LIGHTS GO ON AGAIN(1944), w; FRESH
FROM PARIS(1955), w; PARIS FOLLIES OF 1956(1955), w; SONG OF NOR-
WAY(1970), w

Paul Lazarus III
FUTUREWORLD(1976), p

Paul N. Lazarus III
CAPRICORN ONE(1978), p; HANOVER STREET(1979, Brit.), p; BARBAROSA(1982),
p

Sidney Lazarus
BROTHERS(1930), w; DOUGH BOYS(1930), w
Silents
FLYING ROMEOS(1928), t; HEAD MAN, THE(1928), t; LADY BE GOOD(1928), t

Tom Lazarus
JUST YOU AND ME, KID(1979), w

William Lazarus
RUN ACROSS THE RIVER(1961)

Betty Lazebnik
1984
RENO AND THE DOC(1984, Can.), m

Perk Lazelle
SERENADE(1956)

Perk Lazello
MILDRED PIERCE(1945)

George Lazenby
ON HER MAJESTY'S SECRET SERVICE(1969, Brit.); UNIVERSAL SOLDIER(1971,
Brit.); MAN FROM HONG KONG(1975); KENTUCKY FRIED MOVIE, THE(1977);
SAINT JACK(1979)
Misc. Talkies
NEWMAN SHAME, THE(1977); FREEZE BOMB(1980)

David Lazer
GREAT MUPPET CAPER, THE(1981), p
1984
MUPPETS TAKE MANHATTAN, THE(1984), p

Joan Lazer
UNDERCOVER MAN, THE(1949)

Peter Lazer
NINE MILES TO NOON(1963); PINOCCHIO IN OUTER SPACE(1965, U.S./Bel.);
HOMBRE(1967)

William Lazerus
PETE KELLY'S BLUES(1955)

Vladislav Lazic
LOVE AFFAIR; OR THE CASE OF THE MISSING SWITCHBOARD OPERA-
TOR(1968, Yugo.), art d

Lee Lazich
HANGUP(1974), w

Gil Lazier
GAL YOUNG UN(1979)

Aladar Lazlo
BLOND CHEAT(1938), w

Alexander Lazlo
SONG OF INDIA(1949), m

Andrew Lazlo
TO FIND A MAN(1972), ph; THIEVES(1977), ph

Ernest Lazlo
MUTINY(1952), ph; SCARED STIFF(1953), ph; BIG MOUTH, THE(1967), ph

Jindrich Laznicka
SEVENTH CONTINENT, THE(1968, Czech./Yugo.)

Lilia Lazo
AFFAIR IN HAVANA(1957)

Ernest Lazslo
IMPACT(1949), ph; BABY, THE RAIN MUST FALL(1965), ph

Veronica Lazur
Misc. Talkies
SEVEN DOORS OF DEATH(1983)

Gabrielle Lazure
BEAUTIFUL PRISONER, THE(1983, Fr.)

Solomon Lazurin
DIARY OF A NAZI(1943, USSR), w

Paul N. Lazurus III
WESTWORLD(1973), p

Louis Lazzara
1984
NIGHT SHADOWS(1984), makeup

Gino Lazzari
PRIEST'S WIFE, THE(1971, Ital./Fr.)

Nicola Lazzari
ETERNAL MELODIES(1948, Ital.), ed

Nicolo Lazzari
MADAME BUTTERFLY(1955 Ital./Jap.), ed; CARTHAGE IN FLAMES(1961, Fr./
Ital.), ed; NEOPOLITAN CAROUSEL(1961, Ital.), ed; DAMON AND PYTHIAS(1962),
ed

Lorenza Lazzarini
Silents
THOU ART THE MAN(1920)
Misc. Silents
SINS OF ST. ANTHONY, THE(1920)

Tony Lazzarino
X-15(1961), p, w

Tony Lazzeri
Silents
SLIDE, KELLY, SLIDE(1927)

Joan Lazzerini
THIEF(1981)

Le Van Le
QUIET AMERICAN, THE(1958)

Dorothy Le Baire
HI, NELLIE!(1934)

Louis Le Barbenchon
NIGHTS OF SHAME(1961, Fr.), art d; VICE DOLLS(1961, Fr.), art d; WOMEN AND
WAR(1965, Fr.), art d; WITHOUT APPARENT MOTIVE(1972, Fr.), set d

Bert Le Baron
MRS. PARKINGTON(1944); MICHIGAN KID, THE(1947); CASBAH(1948); MADAME
BOVARY(1949); FRENCH LINE, THE(1954)

Boots Le Baron
ONE MILLION B.C.(1940); PAN-AMERICANA(1945)

Eddie Le Baron
LADY GAMBLES, THE(1949); MA AND PA KETTLE ON VACATION(1953); TO
CATCH A THIEF(1955); THIRD VOICE, THE(1960)

Patrick Le Barz
1984
LES COMPERES(1984, Fr.)

Arthur Le Bau
TRIAL OF JOAN OF ARC(1965, Fr.)

Henry Le Baubigny
PARIS AFTER DARK(1943)

Le Beal
DISCREET CHARM OF THE BOURGEOISIE, THE(1972, Fr.)

Robert Le Beal
DAY TO REMEMBER, A(1953, Brit.); SWORD AND THE ROSE, THE(1953); FO-
REIGN INTRIGUE(1956); PARIS DOES STRANGE THINGS(1957, Fr./Ital.); NIGHT
ENCOUNTER(1963, Fr./Ital.); TWO ARE GUILTY(1964, Fr.)

Bettine Le Beau
DEVIL'S DAFFODIL, THE(1961, Brit./Ger.); VILLAGE OF DAUGHTERS(1962, Brit.)

Betty Le Beau
TRUNK, THE(1961, Brit.)

Candy Le Beau
HOTEL PARADISO(1966, U.S./Brit.)

Gene le Bell
HAMMER(1972)
1984
MICKI AND MAUDE(1984)

Helene Le Berthon
MYSTIC CIRCLE MURDER(1939)

Lee le Blanc
NORTH BY NORTHWEST(1959), spec eff; ATLANTIS, THE LOST CON-
TINENT(1961), spec eff; SWEET BIRD OF YOUTH(1962), spec eff

Lionel Le Blanc
LOUISIANA STORY(1948)

Robert Le Blanc
1984
RIVER RAT, THE(1984)

Lee Le Blane
WRECK OF THE MARY DEAR, THE(1959), spec eff

Lisette Le Bon
TIGHT SKIRTS, LOOSE PLEASURES(1966, Fr.)

Reginald Le Borge
HOUSE OF THE BLACK DEATH(1965), d

Donna le Bourdais
BARNACLE BILL(1935, Brit.)

George Le Bow
GUNFIGHT, A(1971)

Gertrude Le Brandt
Silents
DOING THEIR BIT(1918); ROSE OF THE WORLD(1918)
Misc. Silents
YOUTH'S ENDEARING CHARM(1916); ANNIE-FOR-SPITE(1917); THROUGH THE
TOILS(1919)

Flora le Brenton
Misc. Silents
THROUGH FIRE AND WATER(1923, Brit.)

Auguste Le Breton
RIFIFI(1956, Fr.), w; RIFF RAFF GIRLS(1962, Fr./Ital.), w; RIFIFI IN TOKYO(1963,
Fr./Ital.), w; SICILIAN CLAN, THE(1970, Fr.), w

Flora Le Breton
CHARLEY'S AUNT(1930)
Silents
LA POUPEE(1920, Brit.); CRIMSON CIRCLE, THE(1922, Brit.); GLORIOUS ADVEN-
TURE, THE(1922, U.S./Brit.); ANOTHER SCANDAL(1924); LOVER'S ISLAND(1925)
Misc. Silents
GIPSY CAVALIER, A(1922, Brit.); SOUL'S AWAKENING, A(1922, Brit.); WHILE
LONDON SLEEPS(1922, Brit.); LITTLE MISS NOBODY(1923, Brit.); SWORDS AND
THE WOMAN(1923, Brit.); THOSE WHO JUDGE(1924); TONS OF MONEY(1924, Brit.);
ROLLING ROAD, THE(1927)

John le Breton
SISTER TO ASSIST'ER, A(1930, Brit.), w; SISTER TO ASSIST'ER, A(1938, Brit.), w;
SISTER TO ASSIST'ER, A(1948, Brit.), d&w
Silents
SISTER TO ASSIST 'ER, A(1922, Brit.), w; SISTER TO ASSIST 'ER, A(1927, Brit.), w

Kelly Le Brock
1984
 WOMAN IN RED, THE(1984)
Betty le Brocke
 HIS MAJESTY AND CO(1935, Brit.)
John Le Carre
 SPY WHO CAME IN FROM THE COLD, THE(1965, Brit.), w; DEADLY AFFAIR,
 THE(1967, Brit.), w; LOOKING GLASS WAR, THE(1970, Brit.), w
1984
 LITTLE DRUMMER GIRL, THE(1984), w
Emma Le Chanois
 PASSION FOR LIFE(1951, Fr.), ed; LOVE AND THE FRENCHWOMAN(1961, Fr.),
 ed; MONSIEUR(1964, Fr.), ed
Jean Paul Le Chanois
 TAXI(1953), w
Jean-Paul Le Chanois
 CARNIVAL OF SINNERS(1947, Fr.), w; PASSION FOR LIFE(1951, Fr.), d, w; CASE
 OF DR. LAURENT(1958, Fr.), d, w; LOVE AND THE FRENCHWOMAN(1961, Fr.), d,
 w; MONSIEUR(1964, Fr.), d
Charles Le Clainche
 MAN ESCAPED, A(1957, Fr.)
Blanche Le Clair
 LIGHTNIN'(1930)
Wayne Le Clos
 THREE TO GO(1971, Aus.), ed
Bernard Le Coq
 CESAR AND ROSALIE(1972, Fr.)
Le Corbusier
 LIFE BEGINS TOMORROW(1952, Fr.)
Catherine Le Couey
 WOMEN AND WAR(1965, Fr.)
Helen Le Counte
1984
 BIG MEAT EATER(1984, Can.)
Catherine Le Covey
 SEVENTH JUROR, THE(1964, Fr.)
Emile Le Croix
Silents
 MAN WORTH WHILE, THE(1921)
Sally le Cuyer
 STRANGE LOVERS(1963)
Gerard Le Du
1984
 TO CATCH A COP(1984, Fr.), ed
James le Fane
Misc. Silents
 PAIR OF SPECTACLES, A(1916, Brit.)
J. Sheridan Le Fanu
 VAMPIRE LOVERS, THE(1970, Brit.), w; TWINS OF EVIL(1971, Brit.), w
Joseph Sheridan Le Fanu
 VAMPYR(1932, Fr./Ger.), w
Sheridan Le Fanu
 INHERITANCE, THE(1951, Brit.), w
Robert Le Febre
 BALLERINA(1950, Fr.), ph
Robert Le Febvre
 LE MONDE TREMBLERA(1939, Fr.), ph; COLONEL CHABERT(1947, Fr.), ph;
 GAME OF LOVE, THE(1954, Fr.), ph; CASQUE D'OR(1956, Fr.), ph; GRAND MA-
 NEUVER, THE(1956, Fr.), ph; GATES OF PARIS(1958, Fr./Ital.), ph; NA-
 THALIE(1958, Fr.), ph; MICHAEL STROGOFF(1960, Fr./Ital./Yugo.), ph; NATHALIE,
 AGENT SECRET(1960, Fr.), ph; PLEASE, NOT NOW!(1963, Fr./Ital.), ph
Robert Le Fehvre
 ALI BABA(1954, Fr.), ph
Guy le Feuvre
 2,000 WOMEN(1944, Brit.); MAN OF EVIL(1948, Brit.); CHRISTOPHER COLUM-
 BUS(1949, Brit.)
Kit Le Fever
1984
 ULTIMATE SOLUTION OF GRACE QUIGLEY, THE(1984)
Michael Le Fevre
 UNDERCOVER AGENT(1935, Brit.), w
Pierre le Fevre
 HOUSE OF THE ARROW, THE(1953, Brit.)
Ralph Le Fevre
 LONE STAR RANGER, THE(1930)
Robert Le Fevre
 SEVEN DEADLY SINS, THE(1953, Fr./Ital.), ph
Marcel Le Floch
 DIARY OF A CHAMBERMAID(1964, Fr./Ital.)
Julius Le Flore
1984
 CITY HEAT(1984)
Renee Le Flore
1984
 LOVE STREAMS(1984)
Anne Le Fol
1984
 UNTIL SEPTEMBER(1984)
Robert Le Fort
 MOULIN ROUGE(1952); LE CIEL EST A VOUS(1957, Fr.)
Albert le Fre
 SHE KNEW WHAT SHE WANTED(1936, Brit.)
Eric Le Fre
 LETTING IN THE SUNSHINE(1933, Brit.)
Ian Le Frenais
 OTLEY(1969, Brit.), w
Gus Le Fuevre
 SO EVIL MY LOVE(1948, Brit.)

Eva Le Gallienne
 PRINCE OF PLAYERS(1955); DEVIL'S DISCIPLE, THE(1959)
Le Gallo
 AMOUR, AMOUR(1937, Fr.)
Kenneth Le Gallos
 JOY(1983, Fr./Can.)
Lance Le Gault
 SWINGER, THE(1966); YOUNG RUNAWAYS, THE(1968); SWEET CHARITY(1969);
 CATCH MY SOUL(1974); COMA(1978); FAST-WALKING(1982)
Sheila Le Gay
Misc. Silents
 CALL OF THE DESERT(1930)
Shelia Le Gay
Misc. Silents
 CANYON OF MISSING MEN, THE(1930)
Vou Le Giokaris
 ARNOLD(1973), cos
Jean-Louis Le Goff
 LOVE AT NIGHT(1961, Fr.); LES ABYSSES(1964, Fr.)
Sybil Le Goff
 WE'LL GROW THIN TOGETHER(1979, Fr.), p
Jeni le Gon
 DISHONOR BRIGHT(1936, Brit.); ALI BABA GOES TO TOWN(1937); SUN-
 DOWN(1941); ARABIAN NIGHTS(1942); TAKE MY LIFE(1942); HI-DE-HO(1947); I
 SHOT JESSE JAMES(1949)
Jennie Le Gon
 MY SON, THE HERO(1943)
Richard Le Grand
 GETTING GERTIE'S GARTER(1945)
George Le Guere
Silents
 ENVY(1917); WAY OF A WOMAN(1919); MISSING MILLIONS(1922)
Misc. Silents
 COMMUTORS, THE(1915); SEVENTH NOON, THE(1915); BLINDNESS OF LOVE,
 THE(1916); TURMOIL, THE(1916); UPSTART, THE(1916); PASSION(1917); SEVENTH
 SIN, THE(1917); WRATH(1917); BIRTH OF A RACE(1919); STRIFE(1919); BLIND
 LOVE, THE(1920); MAMA'S AFFAIR(1921)
George Le Guerre
 THREE-CORNERED MOON(1933)
Denis Le Guillou
 SOLO(1970, Fr.)
Victor Le Guillow
 THIEVES(1977)
Lois le Guriadec
 BREAK THE NEWS(1938, Brit.), w
Rene Le Henaff
 UNDER THE ROOFS OF PARIS(1930, Fr.), ed; A NOUS LA LIBERTE(1931, Fr.), ed;
 PORT OF SHADOWS(1938, Fr.), ed; DAYBREAK(1940, Fr.), ed; COLONEL CHAB-
 ERT(1947, Fr.), d; LAFAYETTE(1963, Fr.), ed; PLAYTIME(1963, Fr.), ed
John Le Mahin
 STAR IS BORN, A(1937), w
Charles Le Maire
 GEORGE WHITE'S 1935 SCANDALS(1935), cos; FOREVER AMBER(1947), cos;
 FAN, THE(1949), cos; HOUSE OF STRANGERS(1949), cos; WHIRLPOOL(1949), cos;
 MY BLUE HEAVEN(1950), cos; FIXED BAYONETS(1951), cos; YOU'RE IN THE
 NAVY NOW(1951), cos; DIPLOMATIC COURIER(1952), cos; WE'RE NOT MAR-
 RIED(1952), cos; PRINCE VALIANT(1954), cos; RIVER OF NO RETURN(1954), cos;
 WOMAN'S WORLD(1954), cos; LOVE IS A MANY-SPLENDORED THING(1955), cos;
 HILDA CRANE(1956), cos; TEENAGE REBEL(1956), cos; 23 PACES TO BAKER
 STREET(1956), cos; DESK SET(1957), cos; PEYTON PLACE(1957), cos; WOMAN OB-
 SESSED(1959), cos
George Le Maire
 TAXI 13(1928), w
William Le Maire
 ONLY THE BRAVE(1930); PENGUIN POOL MURDER, THE(1932); SILVER DOL-
 LAR(1932); CAPTURED(1933)
William Le Massena
 CAROUSEL(1956); WRONG MAN, THE(1956); WHERE'S POPPA?(1970)
Alan Le May
 ALONG CAME JONES(1945), w
Howard Le May
 TEENAGE MOTHER(1967)
Lester Le May
Misc. Silents
 UNDER THE TOP(1919)
Pierre Le May
Misc. Silents
 PLAYING WITH FIRE(1916)
John Le Mesurier
 COMING-OUT PARTY, A(; HELL, HEAVEN OR HOBOKEN(1958, Brit.); MATTER OF
 MURDER, A(1949, Brit.); DARK INTERVAL(1950, Brit.); BLIND MAN'S BLUFF(1952,
 Brit.); NEVER TAKE NO FOR AN ANSWER(1952, Brit./Ital.); OLD MOTHER
 RILEY(1952, Brit.); BLUE PARROT, THE(1953, Brit.); BLACK 13(1954, Brit.); DAN-
 GEROUS CARGO(1954, Brit.); STRANGER FROM VENUS, THE(1954, Brit.); POLICE
 DOG(1955, Brit.); TIME TO KILL, A(1955, Brit.); PRIVATE'S PROGRESS(1956, Brit.);
 BABY AND THE BATTLESHIP, THE(1957, Brit.); BROTHERS IN LAW(1957, Brit.);
 GOOD COMPANIONS, THE(1957, Brit.); HIGH FLIGHT(1957, Brit.); PURSUIT OF
 THE GRAF SPEE(1957, Brit.); ANOTHER TIME, ANOTHER PLACE(1958); BLIND
 SPOT(1958, Brit.); BLOOD OF THE VAMPIRE(1958, Brit.); DANGEROUS
 YOUTH(1958, Brit.); HAPPY IS THE BRIDE(1958, Brit.); LAW AND DISORDER(1958,
 Brit.); MAN WHO WOULDN'T TALK, THE(1958, Brit.); MAN WITH A GUN(1958,
 Brit.); MOONRAKER, THE(1958, Brit.); BEN HUR(1959); FOLLOW A STAR(1959,
 Brit.); GIDEON OF SCOTLAND YARD(1959, Brit.); HOUND OF THE BASKER-
 VILLES, THE(1959, Brit.); I'M ALL RIGHT, JACK(1959, Brit.); JACK THE RIP-
 PER(1959, Brit.); LADY IS A SQUARE, THE(1959, Brit.); SHAKE HANDS WITH THE
 DEVIL(1959, Ireland); TOO MANY CROOKS(1959, Brit.); WRECK OF THE MARY
 DEAR, THE(1959); BULLDOG BREED, THE(1960, Brit.); CAPTAIN'S TABLE,
 THE(1960, Brit.); DAY THEY ROBBED THE BANK OF ENGLAND, THE(1960, Brit.);
 DEAD LUCKY(1960, Brit.); DESERT MICE(1960, Brit.); DOCTOR IN LOVE(1960, Brit.);
 LET'S GET MARRIED(1960, Brit.); MAN IN A COCKED HAT(1960, Bri.); NEVER LET

GO(1960, Brit.); SCHOOL FOR SCOUNDRELS(1960, Brit.); CALL ME GENIUS(1961, Brit.); FIVE GOLDEN HOURS(1961, Brit.); INVASION QUARTET(1961, Brit.); NIGHT WE GOT THE BIRD, THE(1961, Brit.); PURE HELL OF ST. TRINIAN'S, THE(1961, Brit.); FLAT TWO(1962, Brit.); GO TO BLAZES(1962, Brit.); HAIR OF THE DOG(1962, Brit.); I LIKE MONEY(1962, Brit.); MAIN ATTRACTION, THE(1962, Brit.); MRS. GIBBONS' BOYS(1962, Brit.); ONLY TWO CAN PLAY(1962, Brit.); VILLAGE OF DAUGHTERS(1962, Brit.); WALTZ OF THE TOREADORS(1962, Brit.); WE JOINED THE NAVY(1962, Brit.); AGENT 8 3/4(1963, Brit.); IN THE COOL OF THE DAY(1963); MOUSE ON THE MOON, THE(1963, Brit.); MY SON, THE VAMPIRE(1963, Brit.); PUNCH AND JUDY MAN, THE(1963, Brit.); WRONG ARM OF THE LAW, THE(1963, Brit.); MOON-SPINNERS, THE(1964); NEVER PUT IT IN WRITING(1964); PINK PANTHER, THE(1964); WHY BOTHER TO KNOCK(1964, Brit.); CITY UNDER THE SEA(1965, Brit.); CUCKOO PATROL(1965, Brit.); EARLY BIRD, THE(1965, Brit.); JIG SAW(1965, Brit.); MASQUERADE(1965, Brit.); OPERATION SNAFU(1965, Brit.); THOSE MAGNIFICENT MEN IN THEIR FLYING MACHINES; OR HOW I FLEW FROM LONDON TO PARIS IN 25 HOURS AND 11 MINUTES(1965, Brit.); WHERE THE SPIES ARE(1965, Brit.); BANG, BANG, YOU'RE DEAD(1966); FINDERS KEEP-ERS(1966, Brit.); LIQUIDATOR, THE(1966, Brit.); SANDWICH MAN, THE(1966, Brit.); WRONG BOX, THE(1966, Brit.); EYE OF THE DEVIL(1967, Brit.); MISTER TEN PERCENT(1967, Brit.); 25TH HOUR, THE(1967, Fr./Ital./Yugo.); SALT & PEP-PER(1968, Brit.); ITALIAN JOB, THE(1969, Brit.); MIDAS RUN(1969); DOCTOR IN TROUBLE(1970, Brit.); MAGIC CHRISTIAN, THE(1970, Brit.); ON A CLEAR DAY YOU CAN SEE FOREVER(1970); DAD'S ARMY(1971, Brit.); CONFESSIONS OF A WIN-DOW CLEANER(1974, Brit.); ADVENTURES OF SHERLOCK HOLMES' SMARTER BROTHER, THE(1975, Brit.); BARRY MC KENZIE HOLDS HIS OWN(1975, Aus.); STAND UP VIRGIN SOLDIERS(1977, Brit.); WHO IS KILLING THE GREAT CHEFS OF EUROPE?(1978, US/Ger.); UNIDENTIFIED FLYING ODDBALL, THE(1979, Brit.); FIENDISH PLOT OF DR. FU MANCHU, THE(1980, Brit.); SHILLINGBURY BLOWERS, THE(1980, Brit.)
Misc. Talkies
ALF GARNETT SAGA, THE(1972)

Doug Le Mille
NEW YEAR'S EVIL(1980)

Raymond Le Moigne
DRAGON SKY(1964, Fr.), ph

Jean-Pierre Le Moine
WE'LL GROW THIN TOGETHER(1979, Fr.), p

Axeline Le Mon
LOVING COUPLES(1966, Swed.)

Henri Le Monnier
NO TIME FOR ECSTASY(1963, Fr.)

Michelle Le Mothe
CHILDREN, THE(1980)

Charles Le Moyne
Silents
HUMAN STUFF(1920); LAST STRAW, THE(1920); OVERLAND RED(1920); WAL-LOP, THE(1921); MAN TO MAN(1922); RIDERS OF THE PURPLE SAGE(1925); ROUGH SHOD(1925)
Misc. Silents
MR. LOGAN, USA(1918); HIS DIVORCED WIFE(1919); HEARTS UP!(1920); HEA-DIN' WEST(1922)

Charles J. Le Moyne
Silents
KICK BACK, THE(1922)

Rosetta Le Noire
1984
BROTHER FROM ANOTHER PLANET, THE(1984); MOSCOW ON THE HUD-SON(1984)

Pass Le Nori
HAPPY LAND(1943)

Don Le Page
MORE AMERICAN GRAFFITI(1979), makeup

Rick Le Parmentier
ROLLERBALL(1975)

Paul Le Paul
ETERNALLY YOURS(1939)

Marc Le Pelletier
ROOM UPSTAIRS, THE(1948, Fr.), p

Nicolette Le Pelley
STATUE, THE(1971, Brit.)

Pamela Le Pelley
STATUE, THE(1971, Brit.)

Paul Le Pere
IRON MAJOR, THE(1943)

Paul Le Person
MAN AND A WOMAN, A(1966, Fr.); LA VIE DE CHATEAU(1967, Fr.); THIEF OF PARIS, THE(1967, Fr./Ital.); VERY HAPPY ALEXANDER(1969, Fr.); TALL BLOND MAN WITH ONE BLACK SHOE, THE(1973, Fr.); HORSE OF PRIDE(1980, Fr.); SNOW(1983, Fr.)

Marcel Le Picard
SILENT ENEMY, THE(1930), ph; HOTEL VARIETY(1933), ph; LEGION OF MISS-ING MEN(1937), ph; OUTER GATE, THE(1937), ph; INTERNATIONAL CRIME(1938), ph; PRISON TRAIN(1938), ph; MAN FROM TEXAS, THE(1939), ph; MAD YOUTH(1940), ph; PALS OF THE SILVER SAGE(1940), ph; BORROWED HE-RO(1941), ph; BOWERY BLITZKRIEG(1941), ph; GENTLEMAN FROM DIXIE(1941), ph; INVISIBLE GHOST, THE(1941), ph; MURDER BY INVITATION(1941), ph; RIOT SQUAD(1941), ph; SPOOKS RUN WILD(1941), ph; ZIS BOOM BAH(1941), ph; COL-LEGE SWEETHEARTS(1942), ph; HILLBILLY BLITZKRIEG(1942), ph; NIGHT FOR CRIME, A(1942), ph; PANTHER'S CLAW, THE(1942), ph; PHANTOM KILLER(1942), ph; PRISON GIRL(1942), ph; SNUFFY SMITH, YARD BIRD(1942), ph; YANKS ARE COMING, THE(1942), ph; BEHIND PRISON WALLS(1943), ph; BLAZING GUNS(1943), ph; BOSS OF BIG TOWN(1943), ph; GIRL FROM MONTEREY, THE(1943), ph; LADY FROM CHUNGKING(1943), ph; LAW RIDES AGAIN, THE(1943), ph; MR. MUGGS STEPS OUT(1943), ph; OUTLAWS OF STAMPEDE PASS(1943), ph; SUBMARINE BASE(1943), ph; WILD HORSE STAMPEDE(1943), ph; BLOCK BUSTERS(1944), ph; FOLLOW THE LEADER(1944), ph; GHOST GUNS(1944), ph; MILLION DOLLAR KID(1944), ph; MINSTREL MAN(1944), ph; SHADOW OF SUSPICION(1944), ph; VOODOO MAN(1944), ph; GANGS OF THE WATER-FRONT(1945), ph; NAVAJO TRAIL, THE(1945), ph; NORTHWEST TRAIL(1945), ph; SONG OF OLD WYOMING(1945), ph; SPORTING CHANCE, A(1945), ph; WILD-

FIRE(1945), ph; DEATH VALLEY(1946), ph; FLIGHT TO NOWHERE(1946), ph; BOWERY BUCKAROOS(1947), ph; NEWS HOUNDS(1947), ph; SCARED TO DEATH(1947), ph; ANGELS ALLEY(1948), ph; JINX MONEY(1948), ph; SMUG-GLERS' COVE(1948), ph; TROUBLE MAKERS(1948), ph; ANGELS IN DIS-GUISE(1949), ph; ROARING WESTWARD(1949), ph; JOE PALOOKA IN THE SQUARED CIRCLE(1950), ph; LUCKY LOSERS(1950), ph; TRIPLE TROUBLE(1950), ph; BOWERY BATTALION(1951), ph; GHOST CHASERS(1951), ph; LET'S GO NA-VY(1951), ph; FEUDIN' FOOLS(1952), ph; HOLD THAT LINE(1952), ph
Silents
ONE LAW FOR BOTH(1917), ph; CONQUERED HEARTS(1918), ph; PERFECT LADY, A(1918), ph; ALMOST A HUSBAND(1919), ph; DAUGHTER OF MINE(1919), ph; JUBILO(1919), ph; DOUBLING FOR ROMEO(1921), ph; AMERICA(1924), ph

Vivian Le Picard
Misc. Silents
THOU SHALT NOT LOVE(1922)

Monique Le Poirier
PARIS BELONGS TO US(1962, Fr.)

Richard Le Pore
STORY ON PAGE ONE, THE(1959); IN HARM'S WAY(1965); SEVEN(1979)

Jean Le Poulain
DEADLY DECOYS, THE(1962, Fr.); BRAIN, THE(1969, Fr./US)

June le Pre
JOAN OF ARC(1948)

Carmen Le Roux
Silents
DON MIKE(1927)

Francois Le Roux
1984
BIZET'S CARMEN(1984, Fr./Ital.)

Madeline le Roux
Misc. Talkies
CRY UNCLE(1973)

Maurice Le Roux
VIEW FROM THE BRIDGE, A(1962, Fr./Ital.), m; NAKED AUTUMN(1963, Fr.), m

Gloria Le Roy
GANG THAT COULDN'T SHOOT STRAIGHT, THE(1971)

Jean Le Roy
TRIAL OF MADAM X, THE(1948, Brit.)

Mervyn Le Roy
HIGH PRESSURE(1932), d; HI, NELLIE!(1934), d
Silents
BROADWAY AFTER DARK(1924)

Rita Le Roy
LOVE TRAP, THE(1929); LEATHERNECKING(1930); FUGITIVE LADY(1934)

Michel Le Royer
LAFAYETTE(1963, Fr.); NUTTY, NAUGHTY CHATEAU(1964, Fr./Ital.)

Al Le Rue
ENCHANTED VALLEY, THE(1948)

Pierre Le Rumeur
HORSE OF PRIDE(1980, Fr.)

Bernadette Le Sache
HORSE OF PRIDE(1980, Fr.)

Claude Le Sache
1984
RAZOR'S EDGE, THE(1984); SUCCESS IS THE BEST REVENGE(1984, Brit.)

Bill Le Sage
TELL-TALE HEART, THE(1962, Brit.), m

Edward Le Saint
TALK OF HOLLYWOOD, THE(1929); FOR THE DEFENSE(1930); CITY STREETS(1931); DAWN TRAIL, THE(1931); LAST PARADE, THE(1931); MIRACLE WOMAN, THE(1931); DARING DANGER(1932); FIGHTING MARSHAL, THE(1932); LAST MAN(1932); VIRTUE(1932); HOLD THE PRESS(1933); MAN HUNT(1933); MEN ARE SUCH FOOLS(1933); NO MORE ORCHIDS(1933); WRECKER, THE(1933); CHAINED(1934); FUGITIVE LADY(1934); GAMBLING LADY(1934); GAY BRIDE, THE(1934); GEORGE WHITE'S SCANDALS(1934); GIRL IN DANGER(1934); GREEN EYES(1934); JEALOUSY(1934); LOST LADY, A(1934); OLD-FASHIONED WAY, THE(1934); ONCE TO EVERY WOMAN(1934); UPPER WORLD(1934); YOU'RE TELL-ING ME(1934); IN OLD KENTUCKY(1935); IN SPITE OF DANGER(1935); LIFE BEGINS AT 40(1935); PARTY WIRE(1935); PUBLIC OPINION(1935); RECK-LESS(1935); WOMAN IN RED, THE(1935); BULLDOG EDITION(1936); DANGEROUS INTRIGUE(1936); FURY(1936); LEGION OF TERROR(1936); MODERN TIMES(1936); MR. DEEDS GOES TO TOWN(1936); MYSTERIOUS AVENGER, THE(1936); PIGSKIN PARADE(1936); ROAD GANG(1936); WIFE VERSUS SECRETARY(1936); BREAK-FAST FOR TWO(1937); CODE OF THE RANGE(1937); COUNTERFEIT LADY(1937); GOLD RACKET, THE(1937); OH DOCTOR(1937); OLD WYOMING TRAIL, THE(1937); TOAST OF NEW YORK, THE(1937); LAW OF THE PLAINS(1938); ARIZONA LE-GION(1939); FIVE LITTLE PEPPERS AND HOW THEY GREW(1939); FRONTIER MARSHAL(1939); JESSE JAMES(1939); UNION PACIFIC(1939); FIVE LITTLE PEP-PERS AT HOME(1940)
Silents
SLEEPWALKER, THE(1922), d
Misc. Silents
MORE TO BE PITIED THAN SCORNED(1922), d; LOVE GAMBLE, THE(1925), d

Edward J. Le Saint
DESTRY RIDES AGAIN(1932); TOMORROW AT SEVEN(1933); LEMON DROP KID, THE(1934); LOST JUNGLE, THE(1934); GALLANT DEFENDER(1935); TOMORROW'S YOUTH(1935); WESTERNER, THE(1936); TRAPPED(1937); MY LUCKY STAR(1938); OUTLAWS OF THE PRAIRIE(1938); DISBARRED(1939); TELEVISION SPY(1939); THUNDERING WEST, THE(1939); STRANGER FROM TEXAS, THE(1940)
Misc. Talkies
TREASON(1933); RIDING WILD(1935)
Silents
NOBODY'S WIFE(1918), d; OATH-BOUND(1922), w; ONLY A SHOP GIRL(1922), d&w; INNOCENCE(1923), d; YESTERDAY'S WIFE(1923), d
Misc. Silents
SUPREME TEST, THE(1915), d; THREE GODFATHERS, THE(1916), d; VICTORIA CROSS, THE(1916), d; SQUAW MAN'S SON, THE(1917), d; STRANGE WOMAN, THE(1918), d; SPEED MANIAC, THE(1919), d; WILDERNESS TRAIL, THE(1919), d; TWO MOONS(1920); WHITE LIES(1920), d; MARRIAGE MARKET, THE(1923), d; DISCONTENTED HUSBANDS(1924), d; SPEED(1925), d; THREE KEYS(1925), d; UN-

WRITTEN LAW, THE(1925), d; BROODING EYES(1926), d; MILLIONAIRE POLICE-
MAN, THE(1926), d
Stella Le Saint
MAID OF SALEM(1937); JOAN OF ARC(1948)
Raymond Le Senechal
LA BONNE SOUPE(1964, Fr./Ital.), m; NUTTY, NAUGHTY CHATEAU(1964, Fr./
Ital.), m; FRIEND OF THE FAMILY(1965, Fr./Ital.), m
Hal Le Seuer
TOY WIFE, THE(1938); DANCING CO-ED(1939)
Joseph Le Shelle
CLAUDIA AND DAVID(1946), ph
Rene Le Somptier
Misc. Silents
LA SULTANE DE L'AMOUR(1919, Fr.), d; LA CROISADE(1920, Fr.), d; LA MONTEE
VERS L'ACROPOLE(1920, Fr.), d; LA PORTEUSE DE PAIN(1923, Fr.), d; LA FORET
QUI TUE(1924, Fr.), d; LES TERRES D'OR(1925, Fr.), d
Rene Le Stomptier
Misc. Silents
LA BETE TRAQUEE(1923, Fr.), d
Richard Le Strange
Misc. Silents
HIDDEN CODE, THE(1920), a, d
Pierre Le Stringuey
CLANDESTINE(1948, Fr.), w
Hal Le Sueur
SHADOW OF THE THIN MAN(1941); JEANNE EAGELS(1957)
Joan Le Sueur
MAYTIME(1937)
Lucille Le Sueur [Joan Crawford]
Silents
PRETTY LADIES(1925)
Robert Le Tet
CLINIC, THE(1983, Aus.), p; NEXT OF KIN(1983, Aus.), p
Margaret Le Van
MARRIED WOMAN, THE(1965, Fr.)
William Le Vanway
HIS GLORIOUS NIGHT(1929), ed; BISHOP MURDER CASE, THE(1930), ed;
DOUGH BOYS(1930), ed
Silents
BRIGHT LIGHTS(1925), ed; WANING SEX, THE(1926), ed; LITTLE JOURNEY,
A(1927), ed; TEA FOR THREE(1927), ed; DESERT RIDER, THE(1929), ed; MOR-
GAN'S LAST RAID(1929), ed; OVERLAND TELEGRAPH, THE(1929), ed; SIOUX
BLOOD(1929), ed
Lloyd Le Vasseur
ANATOMY OF A MURDER(1959)
Eddie Le Veque
WON TON TON, THE DOG WHO SAVED HOLLYWOOD(1976)
Le Vigan
DR. KNOCK(1936, Fr.)
Robert Le Vigan
GOLGOTHA(1937, Fr.); LOWER DEPTHS, THE(1937, Fr.); PORT OF SHA-
DOWS(1938, Fr.); ESCAPE FROM YESTERDAY(1939, Fr.); HEART OF A NATION,
THE(1943, Fr.)
Albert Shelby Le Vino
SHOPWORN ANGEL, THE(1928), w; CANARY MURDER CASE, THE(1929), w;
MAN FROM WYOMING, A(1930), w; WOMAN RACKET, THE(1930), w; RENE-
GADES OF THE WEST(1932), w; AFTER TONIGHT(1933), w; KEEP 'EM ROL-
LING(1934), w; HOLD'EM NAVY!(1937), w; TOMBSTONE, THE TOWN TOO TOUGH
TO DIE(1942), w; WESTBOUND(1959), w
Silents
ADOPTED SON, THE(1917), w; ALIAS MRS. JESSOP(1917), w; AMERICAN WID-
OW, AN(1917), w; ISLAND OF INTRIGUE, THE(1919), w; CAPPY RICKS(1921), w;
DON'T TELL EVERYTHING(1921), w; STRANGER THAN FICTION(1921), w; TEN
DOLLAR RAISE, THE(1921), w; MAKING A MAN(1922), w; MISSING MIL-
LIONS(1922), w; OVER THE BORDER(1922), w; WHILE SATAN SLEEPS(1922), w;
WORLD'S CHAMPION, THE(1922), w; MR. BILLINGS SPENDS HIS DIME(1923), w;
IN EVERY WOMAN'S LIFE(1924), w; CORPORAL KATE(1926), w; RUNAWAY,
THE(1926), w; NIGHT LIFE(1927), w; TRAGEDY OF YOUTH, THE(1928), w
Jean Le Vitte
DEVIL'S DAUGHTER(1949, Fr.), w
Jack Le White
FURTHER UP THE CREEK!(1958, Brit.)
1984
BLOODBATH AT THE HOUSE OF DEATH(1984, Brit.)
Catherine Le-Gouey
1984
ONE DEADLY SUMMER(1984, Fr.)
Olivia K. Le'Aauanae
SOUP FOR ONE(1982)
Ah Lea
BOOLOO(1938)
Andrea Lea
LAST DAYS OF DOLWYN, THE(1949, Brit.); HOUSE OF THE ARROW, THE(1953,
Brit.); LANDFALL(1953, Brit.)
Barbara Lea
CHIVATO(1961); REBELLION IN CUBA(1961)
Fanny Heaslip Lea
CHEATERS(1934), w
Fanny Measlip Lea
MAN-PROOF(1938), w
Jacque de Lane Lea
BLACK ICE, THE(1957, Brit.), p; IN THE WAKE OF A STRANGER(1960, Brit.), p
Jennie Lea
JEANNE EAGELS(1957)
Jennifer Lea
TALL STRANGER, THE(1957); HOSTAGE, THE(1966)
Jenny Lea
OKLAHOMAN, THE(1957)

Jim Lea
FLAME(1975, Brit.)
Jimmy Lea
FLAME(1975, Brit.), m
Mara Lea
ONE GIRL'S CONFESSION(1953)
Mari Lea
HIT AND RUN(1957)
Ron Lea
HAPPY BIRTHDAY TO ME(1981)
Sharan Lea
SOMETHING WICKED THIS WAY COMES(1983)
Terrea Lea
HIGH-POWERED RIFLE, THE(1960)
Timothy Lea
CONFESSIONS OF A WINDOW CLEANER(1974, Brit.), w; CONFESSIONS OF A
POP PERFORMER(1975, Brit.), w; CONFESSIONS FROM A HOLIDAY CAMP(1977,
Brit.), w
Tom Lea
BRAVE BULLS, THE(1951), w; WONDERFUL COUNTRY, THE(1959), a, w
William Lea, Jr.
MEN, THE(1950)
Leslie Gay Leace
MORE AMERICAN GRAFFITI(1979)
Al Leach
Silents
LOVE AUCTION, THE(1919), ph; WINNING STROKE, THE(1919), ph
Alan Leach
SO FINE(1981); TATTOO(1981)
1984
LONELY GUY, THE(1984)
Britt Leach
FUZZ(1972); INTERVAL(1973, Mex./U.S.); JACKSON COUNTY JAIL(1976); GOIN'
SOUTH(1978); HARDLY WORKING(1981)
1984
LAST STARFIGHTER, THE(1984); SILENT NIGHT, DEADLY NIGHT(1984)
Catherine Leach
NO HIGHWAY IN THE SKY(1951, Brit.)
Edith Leach
RIDERS OF THE BADLANDS(1941); KEEP YOUR POWDER DRY(1945)
George Leach
FFOLKES(1980, Brit.)
Harvey Leach
WHEN YOU'RE IN LOVE(1937)
Ken Leach
MY WAY(1974, South Africa)
Misc. Talkies
SUPER-JOCKS, THE(1980)
Paul Leach
DON'T LET THE ANGELS FALL(1969, Can.), ph
Richard Leach
CHILDREN GALORE(1954, Brit.)
Roger Murray Leach
1984
KILLING FIELDS, THE(1984, Brit.), art d
Rosemary Leach
FACE OF A STRANGER(1964, Brit.); THAT'LL BE THE DAY(1974, Brit.)
1984
PLAGUE DOGS, THE(1984, U.S./Brit.)
Susanne Leach
WUTHERING HEIGHTS(1939)
Wendy Leach
RAIDERS OF THE LOST ARK(1981); NEVER SAY NEVER AGAIN(1983)
Wilford Leach
WEDDING PARTY, THE(1969), p,d&w, ed; PIRATES OF PENZANCE, THE(1983),
d&w
Cloris Leachman
KISS ME DEADLY(1955); RACK, THE(1956); CHAPMAN REPORT, THE(1962);
BUTCH CASSIDY AND THE SUNDANCE KID(1969); LOVERS AND OTHER STRAN-
GERS(1970); PEOPLE NEXT DOOR, THE(1970); LAST PICTURE SHOW, THE(1971);
STEAGLE, THE(1971); CHARLEY AND THE ANGEL(1973); DILLINGER(1973); HAP-
PY MOTHER'S DAY... LOVE, GEORGE(1973); DAISY MILLER(1974); YOUNG FRAN-
KENSTEIN(1974); CRAZY MAMA(1975); HIGH ANXIETY(1977); MOUSE AND HIS
CHILD, THE(1977); MUPPET MOVIE, THE(1979); NORTH AVENUE IRREGULARS,
THE(1979); SCAVENGER HUNT(1979); FOOLIN' AROUND(1980); HERBIE GOES
BANANAS(1980); YESTERDAY(1980, Can.); HISTORY OF THE WORLD, PART
1(1981)
Misc. Talkies
THIS TIME FOREVER(1981)
Claudia Leacock
SKY PIRATE, THE(1970)
Philip Leacock
LIFE IN HER HANDS(1951, Brit.), d; BRAVE DON'T CRY, THE(1952, Brit.), d;
APPOINTMENT IN LONDON(1953, Brit.), d; LITTLE KIDNAPPERS, THE(1954,
Brit.), d; ESCAPADE(1955, Brit.), d; HIGH TIDE AT NOON(1957, Brit.), d; SPANISH
GARDENER, THE(1957, Span.), d; INNOCENT SINNERS(1958, Brit.), d; RABBIT
TRAP, THE(1959), d; TAKE A GIANT STEP(1959), d; HAND IN HAND(1960, Brit.), d;
LET NO MAN WRITE MY EPITAPH(1960), d; THIRTEEN WEST STREET(1962), d;
WAR LOVER, THE(1962, U.S./Brit.), d; REACH FOR GLORY(1963, Brit.), d; TAMA-
HINE(1964, Brit.), d; FIRECREEK(1968), p; ADAM'S WOMAN(1972, Austral.), d
Richard Leacock
LOUISIANA STORY(1948), ph; MAIDSTONE(1970), ph
William Leacock
I'M ALL RIGHT, JACK(1959, Brit.)
Bill Leadbitter
1984
LASSITER(1984)

Anton Leader
IT HAPPENS EVERY THURSDAY(1953), p
Anton M. Leader
GO, MAN, GO!(1954), p; CHILDREN OF THE DAMNED(1963, Brit.), d
Expedition Leader
STARK MAD(1929)
James Leader
Silents
BROKEN MELODY, THE(1929, Brit.), w
Tony Leader
COCKEYED COWBOYS OF CALICO COUNTY, THE(1970), d
Bonnie Leaders
BUFFALO BILL AND THE INDIANS, OR SITTING BULL'S HISTORY LESSON(1976)
Ernest Leadlay
CHEERS OF THE CROWD(1936), ed
Ernie Leadlay
DICK TRACY(1945), ed; FALCON IN SAN FRANCISCO, THE(1945), ed; CODE OF THE WEST(1947), ed
Ernie Leadley
MASTER RACE, THE(1944), ed
Allen Leaf
ACT ONE(1964)
Jack Leaf
GREY FOX, THE(1983, Can.)
Paul Leaf
HAIL(1973), p
Janet League
SPOOK WHO SAT BY THE DOOR, THE(1973)
Ruth League
DIVINE NYMPH, THE(1979, Ital.)
Lindy Leah
TERROR ON TOUR(1980)
Petra Leah
ROCKY HORROR PICTURE SHOW, THE(1975, Brit.)
Agnes Brand Leahy
ONLY THE BRAVE(1930), w; SOCIAL LION, THE(1930), w; SPOILERS, THE(1930), w; BELOVED BACHELOR, THE(1931), w; CAUGHT(1931), w; FIGHTING CARAVANS(1931), w; SIN SHIP(1931), w; EVENINGS FOR SALE(1932), w; FORGOTTEN COMMANDMENTS(1932), w; NIGHT OF JUNE 13(1932), w; NO ONE MAN(1932), w; SKY BRIDE(1932), w; HELL AND HIGH WATER(1933), w; PICK-UP(1933), w; LONE COWBOY(1934), w
Silents
RED HAIR(1928), w; STAIRS OF SAND(1929), w
Bernardette Leahy
MY HANDS ARE CLAY(1948, Irish)
Eugene Leahy
GENERAL JOHN REGAN(1933, Brit.); OVERNIGHT(1933, Brit.); CRIMSON CANDLE, THE(1934, Brit.); IRISH FOR LUCK(1936, Brit.); LOVE FROM A STRANGER(1937, Brit.); MEN OF IRELAND(1938, Ireland); HEART OF THE MATTER, THE(1954, Brit.); CURSE OF FRANKENSTEIN, THE(1957, Brit.)
Jeanette Leahy
LIVING VENUS(1961)
Joe Leahy
SANTA AND THE THREE BEARS(1970), md
Misc. Talkies
69 MINUTES(1977)
Margaret Leahy
CRY DR. CHICAGO(1971), p
Silents
THREE AGES, THE(1923)
Ronnie Leahy
ASCENDANCY(1983, Brit.), m
Frances Leak
SHE SHALL HAVE MURDER(1950, Brit.)
Jeniffer Leak
EYE OF THE CAT(1969)
Jennifer Leak
YOURS, MINE AND OURS(1968)
Barbara Leake
LOVES OF JOANNA GODDEN, THE(1947, Brit.); MY SISTER AND I(1948, Brit.); DON'T EVER LEAVE ME(1949, Brit.); KIND HEARTS AND CORONETS(1949, Brit.); SARABAND(1949, Brit.); HIS EXCELLENCY(1952, Brit.); YOU CAN'T ESCAPE(1955, Brit.); GENTLE TOUCH, THE(1956, Brit.); OUT OF THE CLOUDS(1957, Brit.); THREE SPARE WIVES(1962, Brit.); EYES OF ANNIE JONES, THE(1963, Brit.); STUDY IN TERROR, A(1966, Brit./Ger.); UNCLE, THE(1966, Brit.)
Cynthia Leake
GREAT MUPPET CAPER, THE(1981)
1984
BEAR, THE(1984)
Damien Leake
SERPICO(1973); APOCALYPSE NOW(1979)
1984
COTTON CLUB, THE(1984)
Grace S. Leake
BONDAGE(1933), w
Ian Leake
O LUCKY MAN!(1973, Brit.)
Jimmy Leake
FIVE LITTLE PEPPERS AND HOW THEY GREW(1939)
Joan Leake
ROOM AT THE TOP(1959, Brit.)
Phil Leakey
REVENGE OF FRANKENSTEIN, THE(1958, Brit.), makeup; IMMORAL CHARGE(1962, Brit.), makeup; ONLY TWO CAN PLAY(1962, Brit.), makeup; MYSTERY SUBMARINE(1963, Brit.), makeup; IPCRESS FILE, THE(1965, Brit.), makeup
Philip Leakey
X THE UNKNOWN(1957, Brit.), makeup; SPY WITH A COLD NOSE, THE(1966, Brit.), makeup; VIRGIN SOLDIERS, THE(1970, Brit.), makeup; THREE SISTERS(1974, Brit.), makeup

Manuel Leal
SANTO Y BLUE DEMON CONTRA LOS MONSTRUOS(1968, Mex.)
Nell Leaman
BEING THERE(1979)
David Lean
ESCAPE ME NEVER(1935, Brit.), ed; PYGMALION(1938, Brit.), ed; INVADERS, THE,(1941), ed; MAJOR BARBARA(1941, Brit.), ed; IN WHICH WE SERVE(1942, Brit.), d, ed; ONE OF OUR AIRCRAFT IS MISSING(1942, Brit.), ed; THIS HAPPY BREED(1944, Brit.), d, w; BLITHE SPIRIT(1945, Brit.), d, w; BRIEF ENCOUNTER(1945, Brit.), d, w; GREAT EXPECTATIONS(1946, Brit.), d, w; ONE WOMAN'S STORY(1949, Brit.), d, w; MADELEINE(1950, Brit.), d; OLIVER TWIST(1951, Brit.), d, w; BREAKING THE SOUND BARRIER(1952), p&d; HOBSON'S CHOICE(1954, Brit.), p&d, d; SUMMERTIME(1955), d, w; BRIDGE ON THE RIVER KWAI, THE(1957), d; LAWRENCE OF ARABIA(1962, Brit.), p, d; DOCTOR ZHIVAGO(1965), d; RYAN'S DAUGHTER(1970, Brit.), d
1984
PASSAGE TO INDIA, A(1984, Brit.), d&w, ed
Davis Lean
FRENCH WITHOUT TEARS(1939, Brit.), ed
Kathryn Lean
Misc. Silents
RULER OF THE ROAD(1918); GIRL OF THE SEA(1920)
Mike Leander
PRIVILEGE(1967, Brit.), m; TWO A PENNY(1968, Brit.), m; ADDING MACHINE, THE(1969), m
Zarah Leander
LA HABANERA(1937, Ger.); LIFE BEGINS ANEW(1938, Ger.)
Rino Leandri
WHITE SHEIK, THE(1956, Ital.)
Beto Leao
XICA(1982, Braz.)
Danuza Leao
EARTH ENTRANCED(1970, Braz.)
Jackie Leapman
LUST FOR A VAMPIRE(1971, Brit.)
Bill Lear
Misc. Talkies
MY NAME IS LEGEND(1975)
Evelyn Lear
BUFFALO BILL AND THE INDIANS, OR SITTING BULL'S HISTORY LESSON(1976)
Jerry Lear
TANK COMMANDOS(1959)
Norman Lear
SCARED STIFF(1953), w; COME BLOW YOUR HORN(1963), p, w; NEVER TOO LATE(1965), p; DIVORCE AMERICAN STYLE(1967), p, w; NIGHT THEY RAIDED MINSKY'S, THE(1968), p, W; COLD TURKEY(1971), p&d, w
Peter Lear
GOLDENGIRL(1979), w
W.P. Lear, Sr.
IN LIKE FLINT(1967)
Kelly Learman
HUNTER, THE(1980)
Richard Learman
DESPERATE WOMEN, THE(?)
Jimmy Learmouth
Misc. Silents
LADS OF THE VILLAGE, THE(1919, Brit.)
Bessie Learn
Misc. Silents
THROUGH TURBULENT WATERS(1915); GIRL OF THE GYPSY CAMP, THE(1925)
Michael Learned
TOUCHED BY LOVE(1980)
Michael Learner
BALTIMORE BULLET, THE(1980)
Brianne Leary
OFF THE WALL(1983)
Donna Leary
MA AND PA KETTLE(1949); MA AND PA KETTLE GO TO TOWN(1950); HAS ANYBODY SEEN MY GAL?(1952); MA AND PA KETTLE AT THE FAIR(1952); MA AND PA KETTLE ON VACATION(1953); MA AND PA KETTLE AT WAIKIKI(1955)
Eugene Leary
END OF THE ROAD, THE(1954, Brit.)
Helen Leary
MAKE WAY FOR TOMORROW(1937), w
Margaret Leary
BIRCH INTERVAL(1976)
Mildred Leary
Silents
WILD HONEY(1919)
Nolan Leary
MAKE WAY FOR TOMORROW(1937), w; AIR RAID WARDENS(1943); DAYS OF OLD CHEYENNE(1943); GHOST SHIP, THE(1943); CODE OF THE PRAIRIE(1944); EXPERIMENT PERILOUS(1944); MAN FROM FRISCO(1944); MRS. PARKINGTON(1944); MY BUDDY(1944); ONCE UPON A TIME(1944); OUTLAWS OF SANTA FE(1944); SHERIFF OF SUNDOWN(1944); TWO GIRLS AND A SAILOR(1944); GREAT JOHN L. THE(1945); LONE TEXAS RANGER(1945); SANTA FE SADDLEMATES(1945); STRANGLER OF THE SWAMP(1945); THIS LOVE OF OURS(1945); THOROUGHBREDS(1945); CROSS MY HEART(1946); DEVIL BAT'S DAUGHTER, THE(1946); GIRL ON THE SPOT(1946); HOODLUM SAINT, THE(1946); KILLERS, THE(1946); MURDER IN THE MUSIC HALL(1946); OUT CALIFORNIA WAY(1946); QUEEN OF BURLESQUE(1946); EGG AND I, THE(1947); LAST ROUND-UP, THE(1947); LOVE FROM A STRANGER(1947); SADDLE PALS(1947); SEA OF GRASS, THE(1947); EASTER PARADE(1948); HOLLOW TRIUMPH(1948); HOMECOMING(1948); I, JANE DOE(1948); ON AN ISLAND WITH YOU(1948); OUTLAW BRAND(1948); SECRET BEYOND THE DOOR, THE(1948); COME TO THE STABLE(1949); COWBOY AND THE INDIANS, THE(1949); FOLLOW ME QUIETLY(1949); RIDERS OF THE WHISTLING PINES(1949); ROARING WESTWARD(1949); TULSA(1949); WHITE HEAT(1949); FILE ON THELMA JORDAN, THE(1950); FURIES, THE(1950); SIDE STREET(1950); GENE AUTRY AND THE MOUNTIES(1951);

PRINCE WHO WAS A THIEF, THE(1951); CARBINE WILLIAMS(1952); CAR-
RIE(1952); HIGH NOON(1952); SCARLET ANGEL(1952); SNIPER, THE(1952); SCAN-
DAL AT SCOURIE(1953); THERE'S NO BUSINESS LIKE SHOW BUSINESS(1954);
TALL MAN RIDING(1955); MAN OF A THOUSAND FACES(1957); NO DOWN
PAYMENT(1957); PERSUADER, THE(1957); MONEY, WOMEN AND GUNS(1958); 10
NORTH FREDERICK(1958); POLLYANNA(1960); SWEET CHARITY(1969)
Misc. Talkies
BLAZING THE WESTERN TRAIL(1945); HEADING WEST(1946)
O'Mara Leary
DON'T GO IN THE HOUSE(1980)
Dr. Timothy Leary
CHEECH AND CHONG'S NICE DREAMS(1981)
Maria Lease
SCAVENGERS, THE(1969)
Misc. Talkies
SINTHIA THE DEVIL'S DOLL(1970)
Rex Lease
YOUNGER GENERATION(1929); BORROWED WIVES(1930); HOT CURVES(1930);
SUNNY SKIES(1930); TROOPERS THREE(1930); UTAH KID, THE(1930); WINGS OF
ADVENTURE(1930); CHINATOWN AFTER DARK(1931); IN OLD CHEYENNE(1931);
IS THERE JUSTICE?(1931); CANNONBALL EXPRESS(1932); LONE TRAIL,
THE(1932); MIDNIGHT MORALS(1932); MONSTER WALKS, THE(1932); INSIDE
INFORMATION(1934); COWBOY AND THE BANDIT, THE(1935); CYCLONE OF THE
SADDLE(1935); FIGHTING CABALLERO(1935); GHOST RIDER, THE(1935); PALS OF
THE RANGE(1935); ROUGH RIDING RANGER(1935); ACES AND EIGHTS(1936);
CAVALCADE OF THE WEST(1936); FAST BULLETS(1936); LIGHTNING BILL
CARSON(1936); MAN FROM GUN TOWN, THE(1936); ROARIN' GUNS(1936); RIDING
ON(1937); SILVER TRAIL, THE(1937); CODE OF THE RANGERS(1938); DESERT
PATROL(1938); FURY BELOW(1938); HEROES OF THE ALAMO(1938); LAND OF
FIGHTING MEN(1938); PROFESSOR BEWARE(1938); TEN LAPS TO GO(1938); IN
OLD MONTEREY(1939); SOUTH OF THE BORDER(1939); CHUMP AT OXFORD,
A(1940); GRAPES OF WRATH(1940); LONE STAR RAIDERS(1940); ONE MAN'S
LAW(1940); RANCHO GRANDE(1940); TRAIL BLAZERS, THE(1940); UNDER TEXAS
SKIES(1940); BILLY THE KID IN SANTA FE(1941); BILLY THE KID'S RANGE
WAR(1941); DEATH VALLEY OUTLAWS(1941); JESSE JAMES AT BAY(1941);
NEVADA CITY(1941); OUTLAWS OF THE CHEROKEE TRAIL(1941); OUTLAWS OF
THE RIO GRANDE(1941); PHANTOM COWBOY, THE(1941); RIDERS OF BLACK
MOUNTAIN(1941); SIERRA SUE(1941); TONTO BASIN OUTLAWS(1941); ARIZONA
TERRORS(1942); BOSS OF HANGTOWN MESA(1942); CYCLONE KID, THE(1942);
EAGLE SQUADRON(1942); HOME IN WYOMIN'(1942); IN OLD CALIFORNIA(1942);
LADY IN A JAM(1942); RAIDERS OF THE WEST(1942); SABOTEUR(1942); SHAD-
OWS ON THE SAGE(1942); SILVER BULLET, THE(1942); STARDUST ON THE
SAGE(1942); SUNSET SERENADE(1942); TOMORROW WE LIVE(1942); DEAD
MAN'S GULCH(1943); HAUNTED RANCH, THE(1943); HE'S MY GUY(1943); IDA-
HO(1943); KEEP 'EM SLUGGING(1943); SANTA FE SCOUTS(1943); SO'S YOUR
UNCLE(1943); TENTING TONIGHT ON THE OLD CAMP GROUND(1943);
CHEYENNE WILDCAT(1944); CODE OF THE PRAIRIE(1944); FIREBRANDS OF
ARIZONA(1944); MAN FROM FRISCO(1944); SHERIFF OF SUNDOWN(1944); YEL-
LOW ROSE OF TEXAS, THE(1944); CODE OF THE LAWLESS(1945); DAKOTA(1945);
FLAME OF THE BARBARY COAST(1945); FRONTIER GAL(1945); GREAT JOHN L.
THE(1945); LONE TEXAS RANGER(1945); NAUGHTY NINETIES, THE(1945); ON
STAGE EVERYBODY(1945); OREGON TRAIL(1945); ROUGH RIDERS OF
CHEYENNE(1945); SANTA FE SADDLEMATES(1945); CYCLOTRODE X(1946); DAYS
OF BUFFALO BILL(1946); HELLDORADO(1946); PLAINSMAN AND THE LA-
DY(1946); RUSTLER'S ROUNDUP(1946); SUN VALLEY CYCLONE(1946); TIME OF
THEIR LIVES, THE(1946); TWO YEARS BEFORE THE MAST(1946); WHITE TIE AND
TAILS(1946); BRUTE FORCE(1947); EASY COME, EASY GO(1947); PERILS OF
PAULINE, THE(1947); SLAVE GIRL(1947); WISTFUL WIDOW OF WAGON GAP,
THE(1947); WYOMING(1947); GALLANT LEGION, THE(1948); LETTER FROM AN
UNKNOWN WOMAN(1948); OUT OF THE STORM(1948); PLUNDERERS, THE(1948);
LADY GAMBLES, THE(1949); LAST BANDIT, THE(1949); MA AND PA KETT-
LE(1949); BELLS OF CORONADO(1950); CODE OF THE SILVER SAGE(1950); COP-
PER CANYON(1950); COVERED WAGON RAID(1950); CURTAIN CALL AT CACTUS
CREEK(1950); FRISCO TORNADO(1950); HILLS OF OKLAHOMA(1950); MA AND PA
KETTLE GO TO TOWN(1950); SINGING GUNS(1950); ABBOTT AND COSTELLO
MEET CAPTAIN KIDD(1952); LONE STAR(1952); LOST IN ALASKA(1952); MA AND
PA KETTLE AT THE FAIR(1952); MAN BEHIND THE GUN, THE(1952); MONTANA
BELLE(1952); WILD NORTH, THE(1952); ABBOTT AND COSTELLO GO TO
MARS(1953); RIDE, VAQUERO!(1953); PRODIGAL, THE(1955); RAWHIDE YEARS,
THE(1956)
Misc. Talkies
EVIL EYE OF KALINOR, THE(1934); RIDIN' ON(1936); SPRINGTIME IN TEX-
AS(1945)
Silents
EASY MONEY(1925); LAST EDITION, THE(1925); WOMAN WHO SINNED, A(1925);
LAST ALARM, THE(1926); CLANCY'S KOSHER WEDDING(1927); OUTLAW DOG,
THE(1927); LAW OF THE RANGE, THE(1928); MAKING THE VARSITY(1928); GIRLS
WHO DARE(1929)
Misc. Silents
RACE WILD(1926); SOMEBODY'S MOTHER(1926); TIMID TERROR, THE(1926);
CANCELLED DEBT, THE(1927); COLLEGE HERO, THE(1927); HEROES OF THE
NIGHT(1927); MOULDERS OF MEN(1927); NOT FOR PUBLICATION(1927); BROAD-
WAY DADDIES(1928); CANDY KID, THE(1928); LAST LAP(1928); PHANTOM OF
THE TURF(1928); QUEEN OF THE CHORUS(1928); RED RIDERS OF CANADA(1928);
RIDERS OF THE DARK(1928); SPEED CLASSIC, THE(1928); STOLEN LOVE(1928);
TWO SISTERS(1929); WHEN DREAMS COME TRUE(1929)
James Leasor
ONE THAT GOT AWAY, THE(1958, Brit.), w; WHERE THE SPIES ARE(1965,
Brit.), w; SEA WOLVES, THE(1981, Brit.), w
C. B. Leasure
Silents
COME ON OVER(1922)
Jean-Pierre Leaud
FOUR HUNDRED BLOWS, THE(1959); TESTAMENT OF ORPHEUS, THE(1962, Fr.);
LOVE AT TWENTY(1963, Fr./Ital./Jap./Pol./Ger.); MADE IN U.S.A.(1966, Fr.); MAS-
CULINE FEMININE(1966, Fr./Swed.); LA CHINOISE(1967, Fr.); LE GAI SA-
VOIR(1968, Fr.); OLDEST PROFESSION, THE(1968, Fr./Ital./Ger.); PIERROT LE
FOU(1968, Fr./Ital.); WEEKEND(1968, Fr./Ital.); STOLEN KISSES(1969, Fr.); BED
AND BOARD(1971, Fr.); TWO ENGLISH GIRLS(1972, Fr.); DAY FOR NIGHT(1973,
Fr.); MOTHER AND THE WHORE, THE(1973, Fr.); LOVE ON THE RUN(1980, Fr.)

Rosie Leavasa
PACIFIC DESTINY(1956, Brit.)
Philip Leaver
KATE PLUS TEN(1938, Brit.); LADY VANISHES, THE(1938, Brit.); SMILING
ALONG(1938, Brit.); TOO MANY HUSBANDS(1938, Brit.); INSPECTOR HORNLEIGH
ON HOLIDAY(1939, Brit.); THIS MAN IS NEWS(1939, Brit.); ALIBI, THE(1943, Brit.);
SILVER FLEET, THE(1945, Brit.); DR. MORELLE–THE CASE OF THE MISSING
HEIRESS(1949, Brit.); TALE OF FIVE WOMEN, A(1951, Brit.); TALES OF HOFF-
MANN, THE(1951, Brit.); MARTIN LUTHER(1953); SPACEWAYS(1953, Brit.); TALE
OF THREE WOMEN, A(1954, Brit.); GAMMA PEOPLE, THE(1956); KEY MAN,
THE(1957, Brit.); VIOLENT STRANGER(1957, Brit.); DUKE WORE JEANS, THE(1958,
Brit.); JACK THE RIPPER(1959, Brit.); MANIA(1961, Brit.); MY SON, THE VAM-
PIRE(1963, Brit.)
Robert Leaver
BECAUSE OF EVE(1948)
The Leaves
COOL ONES THE(1967)
Norman Leavett
IDEA GIRL(1946)
Billy Leavitt, Jr.
OPEN THE DOOR AND SEE ALL THE PEOPLE(1964)
Doug Leavitt
CAMPUS RYTHM(1943)
Douglas Leavitt
YOU WERE NEVER LOVELIER(1942); GOOD LUCK, MR. YATES(1943); IT'S A
GREAT LIFE(1943); LAW OF THE NORTHWEST(1943); MURDER IN TIMES
SQUARE(1943); POWER OF THE PRESS(1943); SHE HAS WHAT IT TAKES(1943);
TWO SENORITAS FROM CHICAGO(1943); REDHEAD FROM MANHATTAN(1954)
Frank "Man Mountain Dean" Leavitt
MIGHTY JOE YOUNG(1949)
Harry Leavitt
JANIE(1944)
Irving Leavitt
HALLIDAY BRAND, THE(1957), cos
Lane Leavitt
1984
ICE PIRATES, THE(1984)
Max Leavitt
PARADISE ALLEY(1978)
Melanie Leavitt
LINCOLN CONSPIRACY, THE(1977), makeup
Norm Leavitt
DAY OF THE LOCUST, THE(1975)
Norman Leavitt
HARVEY GIRLS, THE(1946); SPIDER WOMAN STRIKES BACK, THE(1946); TWO
SISTERS FROM BOSTON(1946); LUCK OF THE IRISH(1948); MUSIC MAN(1948);
THAT WONDERFUL URGE(1948); THREE MUSKETEERS, THE(1948); WALLS OF
JERICHO(1948); YELLOW SKY(1948); INSPECTOR GENERAL, THE(1949); RECK-
LESS MOMENTS, THE(1949); SLATTERY'S HURRICANE(1949); HARVEY(1950);
MULE TRAIN(1950); SIDE STREET(1950); COMIN' ROUND THE MOUNTAIN(1951);
ELOPEMENT(1951); LADY AND THE BANDIT, THE(1951); MR. BELVEDERE RINGS
THE BELL(1951); SHOW BOAT(1951); VENGEANCE VALLEY(1951); BUSHWHACK-
ERS, THE(1952); MUTINY(1952); O. HENRY'S FULL HOUSE(1952); STARS AND
STRIPES FOREVER(1952); COMBAT SQUAD(1953); HANNAH LEE(1953); MOON-
LIGHTER, THE(1953); OFF LIMITS(1953); RIDE, VAQUERO!(1953); LONG, LONG
TRAILER, THE(1954); INSIDE DETROIT(1955); BRASS LEGEND, THE(1956);
FRIENDLY PERSUASION(1956); STAGECOACH TO FURY(1956); WHEN GANG-
LAND STRIKES(1956); FURY AT SHOWDOWN(1957); GIRL IN BLACK STOCK-
INGS(1957); ROCKABILLY BABY(1957); SHOWDOWN AT BOOT HILL(1958);
TEENAGE MONSTER(1958); ROOKIE, THE(1959); YOUNG JESSE JAMES(1960);
JUMBO(1962); SAINTLY SINNERS(1962); SWINGIN' ALONG(1962); THREE
STOOGES IN ORBIT, THE(1962); SUMMER MAGIC(1963); PATSY, THE(1964); MC
HALE'S NAVY JOINS THE AIR FORCE(1965); MARRIAGE OF A YOUNG STOCKBR-
OKER, THE(1971)
Paul Leavitt
NAKED ALIBI(1954)
Sam Leavitt
THIEF, THE(1952), ph; CHINA VENTURE(1953), ph; MISSION OVER KO-
REA(1953), ph; CARMEN JONES(1954), ph; SOUTHWEST PASSAGE(1954), ph;
STAR IS BORN, A(1954), ph; ANNAPOLIS STORY, AN(1955), ph; COURT-MARTIAL
OF BILLY MITCHELL, THE(1955), ph; MAN WITH THE GOLDEN ARM, THE(1955),
ph; CRIME IN THE STREETS(1956), ph; HOT ROD GIRL(1956), ph; WILD PARTY,
THE(1956), ph; CARELESS YEARS, THE(1957), ph; EIGHTEEN AND ANXI-
OUS(1957), ph; HELL SHIP MUTINY(1957), ph; SIERRA STRANGER(1957), ph;
TIME LIMIT(1957), ph; DEFIANT ONES, THE(1958), ph; FEARMAKERS, THE(1958),
ph; SPANISH AFFAIR(1958, Span.), ph; ANATOMY OF A MURDER(1959), ph;
CRIMSON KIMONO, THE(1959), ph; FIVE GATES TO HELL(1959), ph; PORK CHOP
HILL(1959), ph; EXODUS(1960), ph; SEVEN THIEVES(1960), ph; RIGHT AP-
PROACH, THE(1961), ph; ADVISE AND CONSENT(1962), ph; DIAMOND
HEAD(1962), ph; JOHNNY COOL(1963), ph; SHOCK TREATMENT(1964), ph;
BRAINSTORM(1965), ph; DR. GOLDFOOT AND THE BIKINI MACHINE(1965), ph;
MAJOR DUNDEE(1965), ph; MY BLOOD RUNS COLD(1965), ph; TWO ON A GUIL-
LOTINE(1965), ph; AMERICAN DREAM, AN(1966), ph; I DEAL IN DANGER(1966),
ph; MURDERERS' ROW(1966), ph; GUESS WHO'S COMING TO DINNER(1967), ph;
WHERE ANGELS GO...TROUBLE FOLLOWS(1968), ph; WRECKING CREW,
THE(1968), ph; DESPERADOS, THE(1969), ph; GRASSHOPPER, THE(1970), ph;
STAR SPANGLED GIRL(1971), ph; MAN IN THE GLASS BOOTH, THE(1975), ph
Samuel Leavitt
BOLD AND THE BRAVE, THE(1956), ph; CAPE FEAR(1962), ph
Jack Leavy
KEEPER, THE(1976, Can.)
Leo Leavy
KEEPER, THE(1976, Can.)
Pam Leawood
SHOOT(1976, Can.)
John Lebar
ENCHANTED FOREST, THE(1945), w

Odette LeBarbenchon
MOUCHETTE(1970, Fr.), cos

Bert LeBaron
THEY WON'T BELIEVE ME(1947); STARDUST ON THE SAGE(1942); GIRL RUSH(1944); CARBINE WILLIAMS(1952); SCARAMOUCHE(1952); SCARLET ANGEL(1952); MISSISSIPPI GAMBLER, THE(1953)

Eddie LeBaron
LADY, LET'S DANCE(1944); DON'T TRUST YOUR HUSBAND(1948); SECOND CHANCE(1953); RACERS, THE(1955)

Lawrence LeBaron
SINGING BUCKAROO, THE(1937)

Pert LeBaron
DESIRE ME(1947)

William LeBaron
PERFECT CRIME, THE(1928), w; DELIGHTFUL HOGUE(1929), p; HALF-MARRIAGE(1929), p; JAZZ HEAVEN(1929), p; NIGHT PARADE(1929, Brit.), p; RIO RITA(1929), p; SIDE STREET(1929), p; STREET GIRL(1929), p; VERY IDEA, THE(1929), d, w; BEAU BANDIT(1930), p; CASE OF SERGEANT GRISCHA, THE(1930), p; DANGER LIGHTS(1930), p; DIXIANA(1930), p; FALL GUY, THE(1930), p; FRAMED(1930), p; INSIDE THE LINES(1930), p; LAWFUL LARCENY(1930), p; LOVIN' THE LADIES(1930), p, w; MIDNIGHT MYSTERY(1930), p; PAY OFF, THE(1930), p; SILVER HORDE, THE(1930), p; CIMARRON(1931), p; FRIENDS AND LOVERS(1931), p; KEPT HUSBANDS(1931), p; PEACH O' RENO(1931), p; TRANSGRESSION(1931), p; TRAVELING HUSBANDS(1931), p; WOMAN BETWEEN(1931), p; GIRL CRAZY(1932), p; LADIES OF THE JURY(1932), p; NIGHT AFTER NIGHT(1932), p; ROAR OF THE DRAGON(1932), p; I'M NO ANGEL(1933), p; SHE DONE HIM WRONG(1933), p; TERROR ABOARD(1933), p; TOO MUCH HARMONY(1933), p; BELLE OF THE NINETIES(1934), p; IT'S A GIFT(1934), p; LEMON DROP KID, THE(1934), p; YOU'RE TELLING ME(1934), p; ALL THE KING'S HORSES(1935), p; BABY FACE HARRINGTON(1935), w; CORONADO(1935), p; GOIN' TO TOWN(1935), p; HERE COMES COOKIE(1935), p; MAN ON THE FLYING TRAPEZE, THE(1935), p; RUMBA(1935), p; GENERAL DIED AT DAWN, THE(1936), p; GIVE US THIS NIGHT(1936), p; KLONDIKE ANNIE(1936), p; POPPY(1936), p; ROSE OF THE RANCHO(1936), p; TELEVISION SPY(1939), p; RHYTHM ON THE RIVER(1940), p; KISS THE BOYS GOODBYE(1941), p; LAS VEGAS NIGHTS(1941), p; WEEKEND IN HAVANA(1941), p; FOOTLIGHT SERENADE(1942), p; ICELAND(1942), p; ORCHESTRA WIVES(1942), p; SONG OF THE ISLANDS(1942), p; SPRINGTIME IN THE ROCKIES(1942), p; GANG'S ALL HERE, THE(1943), p; STORMY WEATHER(1943), p; WINTERTIME(1943), p; GREENWICH VILLAGE(1944), p; PIN UP GIRL(1944), p; SWEET AND LOWDOWN(1944), p; DON JUAN QUILLIGAN(1945), p; CARNEGIE HALL(1947), p
Silents
NOBODY'S MONEY(1923), w; ACE OF CADS, THE(1926), p; TIN GODS(1926), p; YOUNG WHIRLWIND(1928), p

Willian LeBaron
OLD-FASHIONED WAY, THE(1934), p

Philippe Lebas
COCKTAIL MOLOTOV(1980, Fr.)

Madeleine LeBeau
HOLD BACK THE DAWN(1941); CASABLANCA(1942); GENTLEMAN JIM(1942); PARIS AFTER DARK(1943); MUSIC FOR MILLIONS(1944); CAGE OF GOLD(1950, Brit.); CADET-ROUSSELLE(1954, Fr.); LA PARISIENNE(1958, Fr./Ital.); 8 ½(1963, Ital.); GUNMEN OF THE RIO GRANDE(1965, Fr./Ital./Span.)

Steve LeBeau
1984
NIGHT OF THE COMET(1984)

Ivan Lebedeff
STREET GIRL(1929); THEY HAD TO SEE PARIS(1929); VEILED WOMAN, THE(1929); CONSPIRACY(1930); CUCKOOS, THE(1930); MIDNIGHT MYSTERY(1930); BACHELOR APARTMENT(1931); GAY DIPLOMAT, THE(1931); LADY REFUSES, THE(1931); UNHOLY LOVE(1932); BOMBSHELL(1933); LAUGHING AT LIFE(1933); MADE ON BROADWAY(1933); SWEEPINGS(1933); KANSAS CITY PRINCESS(1934); MERRY FRINKS, THE(1934); MOULIN ROUGE(1934); CHINA SEAS(1935); GOIN' TO TOWN(1935); SHE COULDN'T TAKE IT(1935); STRANGE WIVES(1935); SWEEPSTAKE ANNIE(1935); GOLDEN ARROW, THE(1936); LOVE ON THE RUN(1936); PEPPER(1936); ANGEL(1937); ATLANTIC FLIGHT(1937); CONQUEST(1937); FAIR WARNING(1937); HISTORY IS MADE AT NIGHT(1937); MAMA STEPS OUT(1937); MAYTIME(1937); WISE GIRL(1937); STRAIGHT, PLACE AND SHOW(1938); HOTEL FOR WOMEN(1939); MYSTERY OF MR. WONG, THE(1939); TRAPPED IN THE SKY(1939); YOU CAN'T CHEAT AN HONEST MAN(1939); PUBLIC DEB NO. 1(1940); BLUE, WHITE, AND PERFECT(1941); SHANGHAI GESTURE, THE(1941); FOREIGN AGENT(1942); LURE OF THE ISLANDS(1942); MISSION TO MOSCOW(1943); ARE THESE OUR PARENTS?(1944); OH, WHAT A NIGHT(1944); RHAPSODY IN BLUE(1945); CALIFORNIA CONQUEST(1952); SNOWS OF KILIMANJARO, THE(1952); WAR OF THE WORLDS, THE(1953)
Misc. Talkies
WOMAN PURSUED(1931)
Silents
SORROWS OF SATAN(1926); ANGEL OF BROADWAY, THE(1927); LET 'ER GO GALLEGHER(1928); WALKING BACK(1928)
Misc. Silents
FORBIDDEN WOMAN, THE(1927); SIN TOWN(1929)

Olga Lebedeff
STALAG 17(1953)

A. Lebedev
SUN SHINES FOR ALL, THE(1961, USSR); FATHER OF A SOLDIER(1966, USSR); WAR AND PEACE(1968, USSR)

N. Lebedev
WAR AND PEACE(1968, USSR)

R. Lebedev
OVERCOAT, THE(1965, USSR)

V. Lebedev
OTHELLO(1960, U.S.S.R.); WHEN THE TREES WERE TALL(1965, USSR)

Vladik Lebedev
GORDEYEV FAMILY, THE(1961, U.S.S.R.)

Janine Lebedew
CLAY(1964 Aus.)

Ivan Lebedoff
PASSPORT TO ALCATRAZ(1940)

Vasyll Lebedyev-Kumach
SPRING(1948, USSR), m

Marie Lebee
ANNA(1981, Fr./Hung.)

Carole Lebel
TWO WEEKS IN SEPTEMBER(1967, Fr./Brit.)

Jean-Patrick Lebel
OLDEST PROFESSION, THE(1968, Fr./Ital./Ger.); TWO OR THREE THINGS I KNOW ABOUT HER(1970, Fr.)

David Gene Lebell
HEARTBEEPS(1981)

Gene LeBell
SPLIT, THE(1968); MELINDA(1972); SLAUGHTER'S BIG RIP-OFF(1973); WALKING TALL(1973); I WANNA HOLD YOUR HAND(1978); FOOLIN' AROUND(1980); GOING APE!(1981)
1984
CITY HEAT(1984)

Chris Lebenzon
WOLFEN(1981), ed
1984
BREED APART, A(1984), ed

Christopher Lebenzon
GOD TOLD ME TO(1976), ed; PRIVATE FILES OF J. EDGAR HOOVER, THE(1978), ed

Stanley Leber
DEADLY AFFAIR, THE(1967, Brit.)

Alfred Leberfeld
MIDDLE OF THE NIGHT(1959)

Joseph Leberman
ER LOVE A STRANGER(1958); PIE IN THE SKY(1964)

Patrick Leberre
1984
LE DERNIER COMBAT(1984, Fr.), set d

Maiwen Lebesco
1984
ONE DEADLY SUMMER(1984, Fr.)

Erin LeBessoniere
WIDOW IN SCARLET(1932)

Zalman Lebiush
HILL 24 DOESN'T ANSWER(1955, Israel)

Alice LeBlanc
CAT IN THE SACK, THE(1967, Can.); WOMEN AND BLOODY TERROR(1970)

Diane LeBlanc
THIRD WALKER, THE(1978, Can.)

Donal LeBlanc
PADDY(1970, Irish)

Georgette Leblanc
Misc. Silents
L'INHUMAINE(1923, Fr.)

Lee LeBlanc
CAT ON A HOT TIN ROOF(1958), spec eff; LAW AND JAKE WADE, THE(1958), spec eff; PARTY GIRL(1958), spec eff; GREEN MANSIONS(1959), spec eff; NEVER SO FEW(1959), spec eff; TARZAN, THE APE MAN(1959), spec eff; WORLD, THE FLESH, AND THE DEVIL, THE(1959), spec eff; CIMARRON(1960), spec eff; SUBTERRANEANS, THE(1960), spec eff; KING OF KINGS(1961), spec eff; FOUR HORSEMEN OF THE APOCALYPSE, THE(1962), spec eff; MUTINY ON THE BOUNTY(1962), spec eff

Libertad Leblanc
LOVE HUNGER(1965, Arg.); VIOLATED LOVE(1966, Arg.)

Maurice LeBlanc
ARSENE LUPIN(1932), w; ENTER ARSENE LUPIN(1944), w; ADVENTURES OF ARSENE LUPIN(1956, Fr./Ital.), w
Silents
ARSENE LUPIN(1916, Brit.), w; ARSENE LUPIN(1917), w

Raymon LeBlanc
GULLIVER'S TRAVELS(1977, Brit., Bel.), p

Rose LeBlanc
EASY RIDER(1969)

Lee LeBlank
HONEYMOON MACHINE, THE(1961), spec eff

Michel Leblond
RED(1970, Can.)

Lisette Lebon
VOYAGE TO AMERICA(1952, Fr.); NIGHTS OF SHAME(1961, Fr.); SUNDAYS AND CYBELE(1962, Fr.); FAREWELL, FRIEND(1968, Fr./Ital.)

Pierre Lebon
FRUSTRATIONS(1967, Fr./Ital.), ph

Yvette Lebon
ABUSED CONFIDENCE(1938, Fr. ABUS DE CONFIANCE); IT HAPPENED IN GIBRALTAR(1943, Fr.); NIGHT THEY KILLED RASPUTIN, THE(1962, Fr./Ital.); CLEOPATRA'S DAUGHTER(1963, Fr., Ital.); VISCOUNT, THE(1967, Fr./Span./Ital./Ger.)

Stanley Lebor
OH! WHAT A LOVELY WAR(1969, Brit.); HENNESSY(1975, Brit.); NOTHING BUT THE NIGHT(1975, Brit.); DEVIL WITHIN HER, THE(1976, Brit.); MEDUSA TOUCH, THE(1978, Brit.); FLASH GORDON(1980)

Reginald LeBorg
GREAT JASPER, THE(1933), d; ONE NIGHT OF LOVE(1934); MELODY LINGERS ON, THE(1935), ch; SWING IT SOLDIER(1941), ch; CALLING DR. DEATH(1943), d; SHE'S FOR ME(1943), d; DEAD MAN'S EYES(1944), d; DESTINY(1944), d; JUNGLE WOMAN(1944), d; MUMMY'S GHOST, THE(1944), d; SAN DIEGO, I LOVE YOU(1944), d; WEIRD WOMAN(1944), d; HONEYMOON AHEAD(1945), d; JOE PALOOKA, CHAMP(1946), d; LITTLE IODINE(1946), d; SUSIE STEPS OUT(1946), d, w; ADVENTURES OF DON COYOTE(1947), d; FALL GUY(1947), d; PHILO VANCE'S SECRET MISSION(1947), d; FIGHTING MAD(1948), d; JOE PALOOKA IN WINNER TAKE ALL(1948), d; PORT SAID(1948), d; TROUBLE MAKERS(1948), d; FIGHTING FOOLS(1949), d; HOLD THAT BABY!(1949), d; JOE PALOOKA IN THE COUNTERPUNCH(1949), d; JOE PALOOKA IN THE SQUARED CIRCLE(1950), d; WYOMING

MAIL(1950), d; YOUNG DANIEL BOONE(1950), d, w; G.I. JANE(1951); d; JOE PALOOKA IN TRIPLE CROSS(1951), d; MODELS, INC.(1952), d; BAD BLONDE(1953, Brit.), d; GREAT JESSE JAMES RAID, THE(1953), d; SINS OF JEZEBEL(1953), d; WHITE ORCHID, THE(1954), p&d, w; BLACK SLEEP, THE(1956), d; DALTON GIRLS, THE(1957), d; VOODOO ISLAND(1957), d; WAR DRUMS(1957), d; FLIGHT THAT DISAPPEARED, THE(1961), d; DEADLY DUO(1962), d; DIARY OF A MAD-MAN(1963), d; EYES OF ANNIE JONES, THE(1963, Brit.), d
Misc. Talkies
ADVENTURE IN MUSIC(1944), d; JOE PALOOKA IN THE KNOCKOUT(1947), d
Sha Lebosi
Misc. Silents
WHERE AMBITION LEADS(1919, Brit.)
Ray Leboursier
VISCOUNT, THE(1967, Fr./Span./Ital./Ger.), ed
Raymond Leboursier
LIGHT ACROSS THE STREET, THE(1957, Fr.), ed
Jean LeBouvier
ONE AND ONLY, THE(1978)
James A. Lebovitz
PERMANENT VACATION(1982), ph, ph
George LeBow
MOLLY AND LAWLESS JOHN(1972)
Hilary LeBow
CITY ON FIRE(1979 Can.)
Mary LeBow
LADIES MAN, THE(1961); ADVANCE TO THE REAR(1964)
Armand Lebowitz
INCIDENT, THE(1967), ed; Q(1982), ed
Armond Lebowitz
SATAN IN HIGH HEELS(1962), ed; LADYBUG, LADYBUG(1963), ed; MIDSUM-MER NIGHT'S DREAM, A(1966), ed
1984
PERFECT STRANGERS(1984), ed
Leo Lebowitz
HERCULES IN NEW YORK(1970), ph
Goyo Lebrero
BOY WHO STOLE A MILLION, THE(1960, Brit.)
Al LeBreton
DEATHTRAP(1982)
Jacques Lebreton
LOLA(1961, Fr./Ital.)
Larry LeBron
DR. BLACK AND MR. HYDE(1976), w
Daniele Lebrun
IT ONLY HAPPENS TO OTHERS(1971, Fr./Ital.)
Francoise Lebrun
MOTHER AND THE WHORE, THE(1973, Fr.)
Michel Lebrun
SHADOW OF EVIL(1967, Fr./Ital.), w
Mignon LeBrun
Misc. Silents
WANTED - A BROTHER(1918)
Madeline Lebueau
NAPOLEON(1955, Fr.)
Alan Lebuse
DIAMOND HEAD(1962); RIDE THE WILD SURF(1964)
Mark LeBuse
HAWAIIANS, THE(1970)
Alex Tang Lec
DEVIL WOMAN(1976, Phil.)
Yvon Lec
MURMUR OF THE HEART(1971, Fr./Ital./Ger.)
Gregory Lecakin
EDUCATION OF SONNY CARSON, THE(1974), cos
Arnault Lecarpentier
1984
LE BAL(1984, Fr./Ital./Algeria)
Andres LeCasa
REDS(1981)
Lou Leccese
LUGGAGE OF THE GODS(1983); WITHOUT A TRACE(1983)
1984
C.H.U.D.(1984)
Patricia Lecchi
SILVER BEARS(1978)
Francois Leccia
THIS SPECIAL FRIENDSHIP(1967, Fr.)
Yvon Lech
JUDGE AND THE ASSASSIN, THE(1979, Fr.)
Bee Lechat
YOUNG CYCLE GIRLS, THE(1979)
Bill Lechner
MISS GRANT TAKES RICHMOND(1949); TELL IT TO THE JUDGE(1949); CHICAGO CALLING(1951)
Billy Lechner
PENROD AND SAM(1937); PENROD AND HIS TWIN BROTHER(1938); FIVE LITTLE PEPPERS IN TROUBLE(1940); YOUNG AS YOU FEEL(1940); SPIRIT OF STANFORD, THE(1942); JUNIOR ARMY(1943); TWO GIRLS AND A SAILOR(1944); WING AND A PRAYER(1944); INCENDIARY BLONDE(1945); OVER 21(1945); O.S.S.(1946); SONS OF NEW MEXICO(1949); JACKPOT, THE(1950); TAKE CARE OF MY LITTLE GIRL(1951)
Dr. H. Lechner
SONG OF LIFE, THE(1931, Ger.), w
William Lechner
SUSAN AND GOD(1940); WE'VE NEVER BEEN LICKED(1943); LET'S GO NA-VY(1951); PHFFFT!(1954)
William G. Lechner
CHAIN GANG(1950)

Volker Lechtenbrink
BRIDGE, THE(1961, Ger.)
Raoul Lechuga
WHEN YOU'RE IN LOVE(1937); ONLY ANGELS HAVE WINGS(1939)
Derek Leckenby
HOLD ON(1966); MRS. BROWN, YOU'VE GOT A LOVELY DAUGHTER(1968, Brit.)
John Leckert
PLOT THICKENS, THE(1936), ed
Henry LeClair
NOBODY'S PERFEKT(1981)
Michael LeClair
BABY BLUE MARINE(1976)
Turk Leclair
FLOWER THIEF, THE(1962)
Georges Leclerc
PICNIC ON THE GRASS(1960, Fr.), ph; ELUSIVE CORPORAL, THE(1963, Fr.), ph; LE GAI SAVOIR(1968, Fr.), ph; RISE OF LOUIS XIV, THE(1970, Fr.), ph; LE PETIT THEATRE DE JEAN RENOIR(1974, Fr.), ph
Ginette Leclerc
BAKER'S WIFE, THE(1940, Fr.); LOUISE(1940, Fr.); TWO WOMEN(1940, Fr.); LE PLAISIR(1954, Fr.); LOVER'S NET(1957, Fr.); COUNTERFEITERS OF PARIS, THE(1962, Fr., Ital.); DOUBLE DECEPTION(1963, Fr.); POPSY POP(1971, Fr.); SPER-MULA(1976, Fr.)
Jean Leclerc
STRANGE SHADOWS IN AN EMPTY ROOM(1977, Can./Ital.)
John LeClerc
UNCANNY, THE(1977, Brit./Can.)
Martine Leclerc
THERESE AND ISABELLE(1968, U.S./Ger.)
Ruthene Leclerc
WALTZ TIME(1946, Brit.)
Ginette Leclere
RAVEN, THE(1948, Fr.)
Arthur Leclerq
ALF'S CARPET(1929, Brit.), w
Wayne LeClos
CARS THAT ATE PARIS, THE(1974, Aus.), ed
Charles Lecocq
DEVIL'S NIGHTMARE, THE(1971 Bel./Ital.), p, w
Maurice Lecoeur
1984
ERENDIRA(1984, Mex./Fr./Ger.), m
Serge Lecointe
PERFECTIONIST, THE(1952, Fr.); EARRINGS OF MADAME DE..., THE(1954, Fr.)
JoAnn LeCompte
PRIME TIME, THE(1960)
Yvon LeCompte
RABID(1976, Can.)
Claude Lecomte
ADORABLE LIAR(1962, Fr.), ph; BLONDE FROM PEKING, THE(1968, Fr.), ph; BYE BYE BARBARA(1969, Fr.), ph; FRENCH WAY, THE(1975, Fr.), ph; SUNDAY LOV-ERS(1980, Ital./Fr.), ph; BETTER LATE THAN NEVER(1983), ph
1984
JUST THE WAY YOU ARE(1984), ph
Germaine Lecomte
NAKED HEART, THE(1955, Brit.), cos
Jacqueline Lecomte
PLAYTIME(1973, Fr.)
Jean-Jacques Lecomte
TRAIN, THE(1965, Fr./Ital./U.S.); RISE OF LOUIS XIV, THE(1970, Fr.)
Lissette LeCorn
1984
SWING SHIFT(1984)
Jean-Jacques Lecot
TIME BOMB(1961, Fr./Ital.); PLEASURES AND VICES(1962, Fr.)
Helen LeCounte
1984
BIG MEAT EATER(1984, Can.), ch
Daniel Lecourtois
ADORABLE CREATURES(1956, Fr.); BEAR, THE(1963, Fr.); TRAIN, THE(1965, Fr./Ital./U.S.); JUST BEFORE NIGHTFALL(1975, Fr./Ital.); VERDICT(1975, Fr./Ital.)
Lisa LeCover
ZAPPED!(1982)
Lecuona
SONG OF MEXICO(1945), m
Ernesto Lecuona
CARNIVAL IN COSTA RICA(1947), m
Lecuona Cuban Boys
HEAT WAVE(1935, Brit.); CARNIVAL IN COSTA RICA(1947)
Ernest Lecuono
IT COMES UP LOVE(1943), m
Dina Ledani
1984
SAHARA(1984)
Bertha Ledbetter
THEY WON'T BELIEVE ME(1947)
Bud Ledbetter
Misc. Silents
PASSING OF THE OKLAHOMA OUTLAWS, THE(1915)
Gavino Ledda
PADRE PADRONE(1977, Ital.), d&w
Arthur D. Leddy
DALTONS RIDE AGAIN, THE(1945), set d
Rick Lede
MAN WHO WOULD NOT DIE, THE(1975)
Marie LeDeaux
SABOTEUR(1942)

Eugen Ledebur
WALK WITH LOVE AND DEATH, A(1969)
Frederick Ledebur
MR. BLANDINGS BUILDS HIS DREAM HOUSE(1948); BARABBAS(1962, Ital.)
Frederick Ledebur
ROYAL SCANDAL, A(1945); NOTORIOUS(1946); GREAT SINNER, THE(1949);
ALEXANDER THE GREAT(1956); MOBY DICK(1956, Brit.); MAN WHO TURNED TO
STONE, THE(1957); VOODOO ISLAND(1957); 27TH DAY, THE(1957); ENCHANTED
ISLAND(1958); ROOTS OF HEAVEN, THE(1958); JULIET OF THE SPIRITS(1965,
Fr./Ital./W.Ger.); BLUE MAX, THE(1966); OEDIPUS THE KING(1968, Brit.); CHRIST-
MAS TREE, THE(1969, Fr.); SLAUGHTERHOUSE-FIVE(1972); SORCERER(1977)
Mons. Ledebur
MOULIN ROUGE(1952)
Bruno Leder
VENUS IN FURS(1970, Ital./Brit./Ger.), w
Erwin Leder
DAS BOOT(1982)
Geraldine Leder
ROTTEN APPLE, THE(1963)
Herbert J. Leder
FIEND WITHOUT A FACE(1958), w; PRETTY BOY FLOYD(1960), d&w; NINE
MILES TO NOON(1963), p, d&w; FROZEN DEAD, THE(1967, Brit.), p,d&w; IT!(1967,
Brit.), p,d&w; CANDY MAN, THE(1969), p,d&w
Paul Leder
GRASS EATER, THE(1961), a, p; ROTTEN APPLE, THE(1963), a, w; FARMER'S
OTHER DAUGHTER, THE(1965), p; MARIGOLD MAN(1970), p, d; I DISMEMBER
MAMA(1974), d
Misc. Talkies
A(1976, U.S./Korea), d; I'M GOING TO BE FAMOUS(1981), d; MY FRIENDS NEED
KILLING(1984), d; VULTURES IN PARADISE(1984), d
Shelly Leder
NINE MILES TO NOON(1963)
Friedrich V. Lederbur
FREUD(1962)
Andrew J. Lederer
1984
THIS IS SPINAL TAP(1984)
Charles Lederer
FRONT PAGE, THE(1931), w; COCK OF THE AIR(1932), w; BABY FACE HARRING-
TON(1935), w; DOUBLE OR NOTHING(1937), w; MOUNTAIN MUSIC(1937), w;
BROADWAY SERENADE(1939), w; WITHIN THE LAW(1939), w; COMRADE
X(1940), w; HIS GIRL FRIDAY(1940), w; I LOVE YOU AGAIN(1940), w; LOVE
CRAZY(1941), w; FINGERS AT THE WINDOW(1942), d; SLIGHTLY DAN-
GEROUS(1943), w; YOUNGEST PROFESSION, THE(1943), w; HER HUSBAND'S
AFFAIRS(1947), w; KISS OF DEATH(1947), w; RIDE THE PINK HORSE(1947), w;
MACBETH(1948); I WAS A MALE WAR BRIDE(1949), w; OCEAN BREAKERS(1949,
Swed.), w; RED, HOT AND BLUE(1949), w; WABASH AVENUE(1950), w; ON THE
LOOSE(1951), d; THING, THE(1951), w; FEARLESS FAGAN(1952), w; MONKEY
BUSINESS(1952), w; GENTLEMEN PREFER BLONDES(1953), w; KISMET(1955), w;
GABY(1956), w; SPIRIT OF ST. LOUIS, THE(1957), w; TIP ON A DEAD JOCK-
EY(1957), w; FIEND WHO WALKED THE WEST, THE(1958), w; IT STARTED WITH
A KISS(1959), w; NEVER STEAL ANYTHING SMALL(1959), d, w; CAN-CAN(1960),
w; OCEAN'S ELEVEN(1960), w; FOLLOW THAT DREAM(1962), w; MUTINY ON THE
BOUNTY(1962), w; GLOBAL AFFAIR, A(1964), w
Emanuel Lederer
ARE YOU A MASON?(1934, Brit.), w
Forrest Lederer
LAS VEGAS STORY, THE(1952); OCEAN'S ELEVEN(1960)
Francis Lederer
MAN OF TWO WORLDS(1934); PURSUIT OF HAPPINESS, THE(1934); GAY DECEP-
TION, THE(1935); ROMANCE IN MANHATTAN(1935); MY AMERICAN WIFE(1936);
ONE RAINY AFTERNOON(1936); IT'S ALL YOURS(1937); LONE WOLF IN PARIS,
THE(1938); CONFESSIONS OF A NAZI SPY(1939); MIDNIGHT(1939); MAN I MAR-
RIED, THE(1940); PUDDIN' HEAD(1941); BRIDGE OF SAN LUIS REY, THE(1944);
VOICE IN THE WIND(1944); DIARY OF A CHAMBERMAID(1946); MADONNA'S
SECRET, THE(1946); MILLION DOLLAR WEEKEND(1948); CAPTAIN CAREY, U.S-
.A(1950); SURRENDER(1950); WOMAN OF DISTINCTION, A(1950); STOLEN IDENTI-
TY(1953); AMBASSADOR'S DAUGHTER, THE(1956); LISBON(1956);
MARACAIBO(1958); RETURN OF DRACULA, THE(1958); TERROR IS A MAN(1959,
U.S./Phil.)
Franz Lederer
Silents
PANDORA'S BOX(1929, Ger.)
George Lederer
Misc. Silents
RUNAWAY ROMANY(1917), d
George W. Lederer
Misc. Silents
FIGHT, THE(1915), d; DECOY, THE(1916), d
Gretchen Lederer
Silents
GREATER LAW, THE(1917); KENTUCKY CINDERELLA, A(1917); RESCUE,
THE(1917); KAISER, BEAST OF BERLIN, THE(1918); NEW LOVE FOR OLD(1918);
RED, RED HEART, THE(1918)
Misc. Silents
BUSINESS IS BUSINESS(1915); DR. NEIGHBOR(1916); GRASP OF GREED,
THE(1916); LITTLE EVE EDGARTON(1916); MORALS OF HILDA(1916); TWO
MEN OF SANDY BAR(1916); WAY OF THE WORLD, THE(1916); BONDAGE(1917);
LAIR OF THE WOLF, THE(1917); LITTLE ORPHAN, THE(1917); LITTLE PIRATE,
THE(1917); MY LITTLE BOY(1917); POLLY REDHEAD(1917); SILENT LADY,
THE(1917); SPOTTED LILY, THE(1917); RIDDLE GAWNE(1918); WIFE OR COUN-
TRY(1919)
Otto Lederer
JAZZ SINGER, THE(1927); FROM HEADQUARTERS(1929); ONE STOLEN
NIGHT(1929); SMILING IRISH EYES(1929); JAZZ BABIES(1932); SIGN OF THE
CROSS, THE(1932); FORGOTTEN(1933)
Silents
ALADDIN FROM BROADWAY(1917); BY RIGHT OF POSSESSION(1917); CAPTAIN
OF THE GRAY HORSE TROOP, THE(1917); BY THE WORLD FORGOT(1918);
MAKING THE GRADE(1921); STRUGGLE, THE(1921), d; HUNGRY HEARTS(1922);

POISON(1924); SWORD OF VALOR, THE(1924); BORROWED FINERY(1925); WIZ-
ARD OF OZ, THE(1925); KING OF KINGS, THE(1927); SAILOR IZZY MURPHY(1927);
CHICAGO(1928)
Misc. Silents
LAST MAN, THE(1916); FLAMING OMEN, THE(1917); MAGNIFICENT MEDDLER,
THE(1917); CAVANAUGH OF THE FOREST RANGERS(1918); CHANGING WOMAN,
THE(1918); WHEN MEN ARE TEMPTED(1918); WILD STRAIN, THE(1918); LITTLE
BOSS, THE(1919); OVER THE GARDEN WALL(1919); WITHOUT BENEFIT OF
CLERGY(1921); SOULS IN BONDAGE(1923); TURNED UP(1924)
Richard Lederer
EXORCIST II: THE HERETIC(1977), p; HOLLYWOOD KNIGHTS, THE(1980), p, w
W. J. Lederer
SKIPPER SURPRISED HIS WIFE, THE(1950), w
William J. Lederer
UGLY AMERICAN, THE(1963), w; MC HALE'S NAVY JOINS THE AIR FOR-
CE(1965), w
Franz Lederle
FOUNTAIN OF LOVE, THE(1968, Aust.), ph
Franz X. Lederle
DOCTOR OF ST. PAUL, THE(1969, Ger.), ph; PRIEST OF ST. PAULI, THE(1970,
Ger.), ph
Caz Lederman
WINTER OF OUR DREAMS(1982, Aus.)
1984
TAIL OF THE TIGER(1984, Aus.)
D. Lederman
DYBBUK THE(1938, Pol.)
D. Ross Lederman
MILLION DOLLAR COLLAR, THE(1929), d; BRANDED(1931), d; RANGE FEUD,
THE(1931), d; TEXAS RANGER, THE(1931), d; DARING DANGER(1932), d; END OF
THE TRAIL(1932), d; MC KENNA OF THE MOUNTED(1932), d; RIDIN' FOR JUS-
TICE(1932), d; RIDING TORNADO, THE(1932), d; TEXAS CYCLONE(1932), d; TWO-
FISTED LAW(1932), d; MARK IT PAID(1933), d; RUSTY RIDES ALONE(1933), d;
SOLDIERS OF THE STORM(1933), d; STATE TROOPER(1933), d; BEYOND THE
LAW(1934), d; CRIME OF HELEN STANLEY(1934), d; GIRL IN DANGER(1934), d;
HELL BENT FOR LOVE(1934), d; MAN'S GAME, A(1934), d; MURDER IN THE
CLOUDS(1934), d; CASE OF THE MISSING MAN, THE(1935), d; DINKY(1935), d;
RED HOT TIRES(1935), d; TOO TOUGH TO KILL(1935), d; ALIBI FOR MUR-
DER(1936), d; COME CLOSER, FOLKS(1936), d; FINAL HOUR, THE(1936), d; HELL-
SHIP MORGAN(1936), d; MOONLIGHT ON THE PRAIRIE(1936), d; PRIDE OF THE
MARINES(1936), d; COUNTERFEIT LADY(1937), d; DANGEROUS ADVENTURE,
A(1937), d; FRAME-UP THE(1937), d; GAME THAT KILLS, THE(1937), d; I PROMISE
TO PAY(1937), d; MOTOR MADNESS(1937), d; ADVENTURE IN SAHARA(1938), d;
JUVENILE COURT(1938), d; LITTLE ADVENTURESS, THE(1938), d; TARZAN'S
REVENGE(1938), d; NORTH OF SHANGHAI(1939), d; RACKETEERS OF THE
RANGE(1939), d; GLAMOUR FOR SALE(1940), d; MILITARY ACADEMY(1940), d;
THUNDERING FRONTIER(1940), d; ACROSS THE SIERRAS(1941), d; BODY DISAP-
PEARS, THE(1941), d; FATHER'S SON(1941), d; PASSAGE FROM HONG
KONG(1941), d; SHADOWS ON THE STAIRS(1941), d; STRANGE ALIBI(1941), d;
BULLET SCARS(1942), d; BUSSES ROAR(1942), d; ESCAPE FROM CRIME(1942), d;
GORILLA MAN(1942), d; I WAS FRAMED(1942), d; ADVENTURES IN IRAQ(1943),
d; FIND THE BLACKMAILER(1943), d; LAST RIDE, THE(1944), d; RACKET MAN,
THE(1944), d; BOSTON BLACKIE AND THE LAW(1946), d; DANGEROUS BUSI-
NESS(1946), d; NOTORIOUS LONE WOLF, THE(1946), d; OUT OF THE
DEPTHS(1946), d; PHANTOM THIEF, THE(1946), d; SING WHILE YOU DAN-
CE(1946), d; KEY WITNESS(1947), d; LONE WOLF IN MEXICO, THE(1947), d;
RETURN OF THE WHISTLER, THE(1948), d; MILITARY ACADEMY WITH THAT
TENTH AVENUE GANG(1950), d; TANKS ARE COMING, THE(1951), d
Misc. Talkies
SILENT MEN(1933), d; SPEED DEMON(1933), d; WHIRLWIND, THE(1933), d;
THREE OF A KIND(1944), d
Silents
SHADOWS OF THE NIGHT(1928), d&w
Misc. Silents
RACE FOR LIFE, A(1928), d; RINTY OF THE DESERT(1928), d
Ross Lederman
MAN HUNTER, THE(1930), d; FIGHTING MARSHAL, THE(1932), d; HIGH
SPEED(1932), d
Silents
DOG OF THE REGIMENT(1927), d
Lilla Ledersen
CHANGELING, THE(1980, Can.), ed
Enrique Ledesma
WARKILL(1968, U.S./Phil.), spec eff
Kuh Ledesma
YEAR OF LIVING DANGEROUSLY, THE(1982, Aus.)
Nena Ledesma
NO MAN IS AN ISLAND(1962)
Jonathan Ledford
AMAZING TRANSPARENT MAN, THE(1960); FREE, WHITE AND 21(1963); UN-
DER AGE(1964)
Bernard Ledger
PIRATE MOVIE, THE(1982, Aus.)
Jason Ledger
Misc. Talkies
BALLAD OF BILLIE BLUE(1972)
Lotte Ledi
HEIDI(1968, Aust.)
Stanislav Ledinak
PHANTOM OF SOHO, THE(1967, Ger.)
Stanislav Ledinek
THREE PENNY OPERA(1963, Fr./Ger.); MAD EXECUTIONERS, THE(1965, Ger.)
Lotte Ledl
TOMORROW IS MY TURN(1962, Fr./Ital./Ger.); YOUNG TORLESS(1968, Fr./Ger.)
Vadim Ledogorow
CHEREZ TERNII K SVEZDAM(1981 USSR)
Carmen Ledoux
WHEN YOU COMIN' BACK, RED RYDER?(1979)

Fernand Ledoux
LA BETE HUMAINE(1938, Fr.); IT HAPPENED AT THE INN(1945, Fr.); STORMY WATERS(1946, Fr.); BELLMAN, THE(1947, Fr.); DEVIL'S ENVOYS, THE(1947, Fr.); HER FIRST AFFAIR(1947, Fr.); VOLPONE(1947, Fr.); DEVIL'S DAUGHTER(1949, Fr.); MONSEIGNEUR(1950, Fr.); ACT OF LOVE(1953); DOCTORS, THE(1956, Fr.); CHRISTINE(1959, Fr.); BIG GAMBLE, THE(1961); CARTHAGE IN FLAMES(1961, Fr./Ital.); TRUTH, THE(1961, Fr./Ital.); FREUD(1962); I SPIT ON YOUR GRAVE(1962, Fr.); LONGEST DAY, THE(1962); TRIAL, THE(1963, Fr./Ital./Ger.); TWO ARE GUILTY(1964, Fr.); UP FROM THE BEACH(1965); DONKEY SKIN(1975, Fr.); ALICE, OR THE LAST ESCAPADE(1977, Fr.); LES MISERABLES(1982, Fr.)
Patrice Ledoux
1984
BIZET'S CARMEN(1984, Fr./Ital.), p
Germaine Ledoyen
APRES L'AMOUR(1948, Fr.); DEVIL IN THE FLESH, THE(1949, Fr.)
D.B. Ledrov
SHUTTERED ROOM, THE(1968, Brit.), w
Roger Ledru
HARVEST(1939, Fr.), ph
Willy Ledru
HARVEST(1939, Fr.), ph
Jean Ledrut
PORT OF DESIRE(1960, Fr.), m; TRIAL, THE(1963, Fr./Ital./Ger.), m, md; YOUNG REBEL, THE(1969, Fr./Ital./Span.), m
Kurt "Mello Cat" Ledterman
Misc. Talkies
SKATEBOARD MADNESS(1980)
Claudine LeDuc
SONG OF BERNADETTE, THE(1943)
Jean Leduc
GIRL ON A MOTORCYCLE, THE(1968, Fr./Brit.)
Michelle Leduc
QUEST FOR FIRE(1982, Fr./Can.)
Tito LeDuc
SON OF SAMSON(1962, Fr./Ital./Yugo.), ch
Violette Leduc
THERESE AND ISABELLE(1968, U.S./Ger.), w
Gennadiy Ledyakh
LITTLE HUMPBACKED HORSE, THE(1962, USSR)
Mme. Lee
SHE FREAK(1967)
Mrs. Lee
Silents
MIND OVER MOTOR(1923)
A'Lesha Lee
FEMALE BUNCH, THE(1969)
A'Leshia Lee
LOVE GOD?, THE(1969)
Ah Lee
DEVIL TIGER(1934)
Al Lee
I LIVE FOR LOVE(1935); STAGECOACH(1939)
Misc. Silents
MARRIAGES ARE MADE(1918)
Alan Lee
SISTER KENNY(1946); KING OF THE KHYBER RIFLES(1953); LONG, LONG TRAILER, THE(1954); REAR WINDOW(1954); ARTISTS AND MODELS(1955); SEA CHASE, THE(1955); HELL ON DEVIL'S ISLAND(1957); PETERSEN(1974, Aus.); EYES OF A STRANGER(1980)
Alan S. Lee
DESERT RAVEN, THE(1965), d, w
Albert Lee
Silents
NANCY FROM NOWHERE(1922)
Alberta Lee
Silents
BIRTH OF A NATION, THE(1915); LILY AND THE ROSE, THE(1915); INTOLERANCE(1916); MARTHA'S VINDICATION(1916); REGGIE MIXES IN(1916); ALIAS MARY BROWN(1918); REAL FOLKS(1918); LIVE WIRES(1921); NOT GUILTY(1921); WATCH YOUR STEP(1922); LOVE LETTER, THE(1923)
Misc. Silents
BRED IN THE BONE(1915); FALSE AMBITION(1918); ROAD TO DIVORCE, THE(1920); ROGUE AND RICHES(1920); MAGNIFICENT BRUTE, THE(1921); LITTLE MINISTER, THE(1922)
Alisa Lee
MAN WHO LOVED WOMEN, THE(1983)
Allan Lee
CRASHING BROADWAY(1933); MADEMOISELLE FIFI(1944); WEST OF THE PECOS(1945)
Alta Lee
Misc. Talkies
SWING, COWBOY, SWING(1944); TROUBLE AT MELODY MESA(1949)
Angela Lee
COUNTDOWN TO DANGER(1967, Brit.); UNCOMMON VALOR(1983)
Anita Lee
DEVIL AND DANIEL WEBSTER, THE(1941)
Ann Lee
CIMARRON(1931); DOCTOR TAKES A WIFE(1940); BOOTS MALONE(1952); TRIAL(1955)
Misc. Talkies
LARIATS AND SIXSHOOTERS(1931)
Anna Lee
EBB TIDE(1932, Brit.); SAY IT WITH MUSIC(1932, Brit.); CHELSEA LIFE(1933, Brit.); KING'S CUP, THE(1933, Brit.); MANNEQUIN(1933, Brit.); MAYFAIR GIRL(1933, Brit.); YES, MR. BROWN(1933, Brit.); CAMELS ARE COMING, THE(1934, Brit.); FACES(1934, Brit.); LUCKY LOSER(1934, Brit.); ROLLING IN MONEY(1934, Brit.); FIRST A GIRL(1935, Brit.); HEAT WAVE(1935, Brit.); MAN WHO LIVED AGAIN, THE(1936, Brit.); PASSING OF THE THIRD FLOOR BACK, THE(1936, Brit.); KING SOLOMON'S MINES(1937, Brit.); NON-STOP NEW YORK(1937, Brit.); YOU'RE IN THE ARMY NOW(1937, Brit.); RETURN TO YESTERDAY(1940, Brit.); SECRET

FOUR, THE(1940, Brit.); SEVEN SINNERS(1940); HOW GREEN WAS MY VALLEY(1941); MY LIFE WITH CAROLINE(1941); COMMANDOS STRIKE AT DAWN, THE(1942); FLYING TIGERS(1942); GHOST AND MRS. MUIR, THE(1942); FLESH AND FANTASY(1943); FOREVER AND A DAY(1943); HANGMEN ALSO DIE(1943); YOUNG MAN'S FANCY(1943, Brit.); SUMMER STORM(1944); BEDLAM(1946); G.I. WAR BRIDES(1946); HIGH CONQUEST(1947); BEST MAN WINS(1948); FORT APACHE(1948); PRISON WARDEN(1949); LAST HURRAH, THE(1958); CRIMSON KIMONO, THE(1959); GIDEON OF SCOTLAND YARD(1959, Brit.); HORSE SOLDIERS, THE(1959); THIS EARTH IS MINE(1959); BIG NIGHT, THE(1960); JET OVER THE ATLANTIC(1960); TWO RODE TOGETHER(1961); JACK THE GIANT KILLER(1962); MAN WHO SHOT LIBERTY VALANCE, THE(1962); WHATEVER HAPPENED TO BABY JANE?(1962); PRIZE, THE(1963); FOR THOSE WHO THINK YOUNG(1964); UNSINKABLE MOLLY BROWN, THE(1964); SOUND OF MUSIC, THE(1965); PICTURE MOMMY DEAD(1966); SEVEN WOMEN(1966); IN LIKE FLINT(1967); STAR!(1968)
Annabelle Lee
COMMON LAW WIFE(1963)
Silents
RIDIN' MAD(1924)
Misc. Silents
HEARTS OF THE WEST(1925)
Anne Lee
Silents
ALSTER CASE, THE(1915)
Arnold Lee
SINISTER MAN, THE(1965, Brit.)
Auriol Lee
ROYAL DIVORCE, A(1938, Brit.); SUSPICION(1941)
Baayork Lee
JESUS CHRIST, SUPERSTAR(1973)
Barbara Lee
BETRAYAL, THE(1948)
Misc. Silents
VARSITY(1930, Brit.)
Belinda Lee
BLACKOUT(1954, Brit.); FAMILY AFFAIR(1954, Brit.); MEET MR. CALLAGHAN(1954, Brit.); RUNAWAY BUS, THE(1954, Brit.); FOOTSTEPS IN THE FOG(1955, Brit.); MAN OF THE MOMENT(1955, Brit.); NO SMOKING(1955, Brit.); EYEWITNESS(1956, Brit.); GENTLE TOUCH, THE(1956, Brit.); WHO DONE IT?(1956, Brit.); MIRACLE IN SOHO(1957, Brit.); DANGEROUS EXILE(1958, Brit.); SECRET PLACE, THE(1958, Brit.); ELEPHANT GUN(1959, Brit.); GODDESS OF LOVE, THE(1960, Ital./Fr.); MARIE OF THE ISLES(1960, Fr.); NIGHTS OF LUCRETIA BORGIA, THE(1960, Ital.); BIG MONEY, THE(1962, Brit.); CONSTANTINE AND THE CROSS(1962, Ital.); STORY OF JOSEPH AND HIS BRETHREN THE(1962, Ital.); LOVE, THE ITALIAN WAY(1964, Ital.)
Benny Lee
KEEP IT CLEAN(1956, Brit.); MY WIFE'S FAMILY(1962, Brit.); NIGHT OF THE PROWLER(1962, Brit.); GIRL HUNTERS, THE(1963, Brit.); MAHLER(1974, Brit.)
Bernard Lee
DOUBLE EVENT, THE(1934, Brit.); RIVER HOUSE MYSTERY, THE(1935, Brit.); RHODES(1936, Brit.); BLACK TULIP, THE(1937, Brit.); FROZEN LIMITS, THE(1939, Brit.); LET GEORGE DO IT(1940, Brit.); MURDER IN THE NIGHT(1940, Brit.); SPARE A COPPER(1940, Brit.); ONCE A CROOK(1941, Brit.); TERROR, THE(1941, Brit.); THIS MAN IS MINE(1946 Brit.); COURTNEY AFFAIR, THE(1947, Brit.); ELIZABETH OF LADYMEAD(1949, Brit.); FALLEN IDOL, THE(1949, Brit.); BLUE LAMP, THE(1950, Brit.); CAGE OF GOLD(1950, Brit.); LAST HOLIDAY(1950, Brit.); THIRD MAN, THE(1950, Brit.); ADVENTURERS, THE(1951, Brit.); CALLING BULLDOG DRUMMOND(1951, Brit.); ODETTE(1951, Brit.); OPERATION DISASTER(1951, Brit.); GLORY AT SEA(1952, Brit.); ISLAND RESCUE(1952, Brit.); WHITE CORRIDORS(1952, Brit.); MR. DENNING DRIVES NORTH(1953, Brit.); SAILOR OF THE KING(1953, Brit.); YELLOW BALLOON, THE(1953, Brit.); CREST OF THE WAVE(1954, Brit.); DETECTIVE, THE(1954, Qit.); PURPLE PLAIN, THE(1954, Brit.); SHIP THAT DIED OF SHAME, THE(1956, Brit.); ACROSS THE BRIDGE(1957, Brit.); FIRE DOWN BELOW(1957, U.S./Brit.); HIGH FLIGHT(1957, Brit.); OUT OF THE CLOUDS(1957, Brit.); PURSUIT OF THE GRAF SPEE(1957, Brit.); SPANISH GARDENER, THE(1957, Span.); DUNKIRK(1958, Brit.); KEY, THE(1958, Brit.); BEYOND THIS PLACE(1959, Brit.); MAN UPSTAIRS, THE(1959, Brit.); NOWHERE TO GO(1959, Brit.); ANGRY SILENCE, THE(1960, Brit.); BREAKOUT(1960, Brit.); KIDNAPPED(1960); CLUE OF THE SILVER KEY, THE(1961, Brit.); SECRET PARTNER, THE(1961, Brit.); TROUBLE IN THE SKY(1961, Brit.); WHISTLE DOWN THE WIND(1961, Brit.); DR. NO(1962, Brit.); L-SHAPED ROOM, THE(1962, Brit.); FROM RUSSIA WITH LOVE(1963, Brit.); FURY AT SMUGGLERS BAY(1963, Brit.); GOLDFINGER(1964, Brit.); PLACE TO GO, A(1964, Brit.); RING OF SPIES(1964, Brit.); SATURDAY NIGHT OUT(1964, Brit.); WHO WAS MADDOX?(1964, Brit.); BRAIN, THE(1965, Ger./Brit.); DR. TERROR'S HOUSE OF HORRORS(1965, Brit.); SPY WHO CAME IN FROM THE COLD, THE(1965, Brit.); THUNDERBALL(1965, Brit.); TWO LEFT FEET(1965, Brit.); SHARE OUT, THE(1966, Brit.); OPERATION KID BROTHER(1967, Ital.); YOU ONLY LIVE TWICE(1967, Brit.); CLUE OF THE TWISTED CANDLE(1968, Brit.); CROSSPLOT(1969, Brit.); ON HER MAJESTY'S SECRET SERVICE(1969, Brit.); DIAMONDS ARE FOREVER(1971, Brit.); DULCIMA(1971, Brit.); LONG AGO, TOMORROW(1971, Brit.); LIVE AND LET DIE(1973, Brit.); FRANKENSTEIN AND THE MONSTER FROM HELL(1974, Brit.); MAN WITH THE GOLDEN GUN, THE(1974, Brit.); SPY WHO LOVED ME, THE(1977, Brit.); MOONRAKER(1979, Brit.); DANGEROUS DAVIES–THE LAST DETECTIVE(1981, Brit.)
Misc. Talkies
PARTNERS IN CRIME(1961, Brit.); MAN IN A LOOKING GLASS, A(1965, Brit.)
Bert Lee
THE BLACK HAND GANG(1930, Brit.), w; NO LADY(1931, Brit.), w; OUT OF THE BLUE(1931, Brit.), w; SPLINTERS IN THE NAVY(1931, Brit.), w; UP FOR THE CUP(1931, Brit.), w; JOSSER ON THE RIVER(1932, Brit.), w; LUCKY GIRL(1932, Brit.), w; MAYOR'S NEST, THE(1932, Brit.), d&w; IT'S A KING(1933, Brit.), w; THIS IS THE LIFE(1933, Brit.), w; TROUBLE(1933, Brit.), w; UP FOR THE DERBY(1933, Brit.), w; DOCTOR'S ORDERS(1934, Brit.), w; GIRLS PLEASE!(1934, Brit.), w; IT'S A COP(1934, Brit.), w; HOPE OF HIS SIDE(1935, Brit.), w; FAME(1936, Brit.), w; PLEASE TEACHER(1937, Brit.), w; SPLINTERS IN THE AIR(1937, Brit.), w; HOLD MY HAND(1938, Brit.), w; YES, MADAM?(1938, Brit.), w; SHE COULDN'T SAY NO(1939, Brit.), w; UP FOR THE CUP(1950, Brit.), w
Silents
WIZARD OF OZ, THE(1925), t

Betsy Lee
Misc. Silents
NIGHT BIRD, THE(1928)
Betty Lee
DARK HORSE, THE(1946)
Misc. Talkies
PECOS DANDY, THE(1934)
Misc. Silents
TRIUMPH OF VENUS, THE(1918)
Bill Lee
ONE HUNDRED AND ONE DALMATIANS(1961); YOUNG GIRLS OF ROCHEFORT, THE(1968, Fr.)
Billie Lee
FOLIES DERGERE(1935); RECKLESS(1935); SHE MARRIED HER BOSS(1935)
Billy Lee
WAGON WHEELS(1934); SILK HAT KID(1935); TWO FISTED(1935); AND SUDDEN DEATH(1936); ARIZONA MAHONEY(1936); BIG BROADCAST OF 1937, THE(1936); EASY TO TAKE(1936); ROSE BOWL(1936); SKY PARADE(1936); THREE CHEERS FOR LOVE(1936); TOO MANY PARENTS(1936); EXCLUSIVE(1937); MAKE A WISH(1937); THUNDER TRAIL(1937); WILD MONEY(1937); COCOANUT GROVE(1938); SAY IT IN FRENCH(1938); SONS OF THE LEGION(1938); AMBUSH(1939); BOY TROUBLE(1939); IN OLD MONTEREY(1939); JEEPERS CREEPERS(1939); LET US LIVE(1939); NIGHT WORK(1939); SUDDEN MONEY(1939); BISCUIT EATER, THE(1940); NOBODY'S CHILDREN(1940); PAROLE FIXER(1940); HOLD BACK THE DAWN(1941); NEVADA CITY(1941); REG'LAR FELLERS(1941); RELUCTANT DRAGON, THE(1941); MRS. WIGGS OF THE CABBAGE PATCH(1942); PRIDE OF THE ARMY(1942); ROAD TO HAPPINESS(1942); WAR DOGS(1942); EYES OF THE UNDERWORLD(1943); MACHINE GUN McCAIN(1970, Ital.); HOT LEAD AND COLD FEET(1978), spec eff
Billy Lee, Jr.
POWER DIVE(1941)
Bob Lee
PASSION HOLIDAY(1963); LET THE BALLOON GO(1977, Aus.)
Bobbie Lee
PAL JOEY(1957)
Brenda Lee
TWO LITTLE BEARS, THE(1961); SMOKEY AND THE BANDIT II(1980)
Brian Lee
MOUSE AND THE WOMAN, THE(1981, Brit.)
Bruce Lee
WRECKING CREW, THE(1968), tec adv; MARLOWE(1969), a, stunts; ENTER THE DRAGON(1973); FISTS OF FURY(1973, Chi.); RETURN OF THE DRAGON(1974, Chin.), a, d&w; CIRCLE OF IRON(1979, Brit.), w; GAME OF DEATH, THE(1979)
Misc. Silents
DRAGON DIES HARD, THE(1974)
Bruce A. Lee
BODY HEAT(1981)
Bryarly Lee
NAKED WITCH, THE(1964)
C.Y. Lee
FLOWER DRUM SONG(1961), w
Canada Lee
LIFEBOAT(1944); BODY AND SOUL(1947); LOST BOUNDARIES(1949); CRY, THE BELOVED COUNTRY(1952, Brit.)
Misc. Talkies
KEEP PUNCHING(1939)
Candace Lee
LOVE IS A MANY-SPLENDORED THING(1955); HUNTERS, THE(1958); SOUTH PACIFIC(1958)
Carey Lee
Misc. Silents
BONDMAN, THE(1916); REPUTATION(1917)
Miss Carey Lee
Silents
DARLING OF PARIS, THE(1917)
Carl Lee
AFRICA SCREAMS(1949), spec eff; HUMAN DESIRE(1954); CONNECTION, THE(1962); COOL WORLD, THE(1963); LANDLORD, THE(1970); WEREWOLVES ON WHEELS(1971); SUPERFLY(1972); GORDON'S WAR(1973); EXPOSED(1983)
Carol Ann Lee
CANDIDATE, THE(1964)
Mrs. Caroline Lee
Silents
ANNE OF GREEN GABLES(1919)
Carolyn Lee
HONEYMOON IN BALI(1939); BIRTH OF THE BLUES(1941); VIRGINIA(1941); MRS. WIGGS OF THE CABBAGE PATCH(1942)
Misc. Silents
LOTTERY MAN, THE(1916)
Catherine Lee
Misc. Silents
LAST OF THE MAFFIA, THE(1915)
Chai Lee
FOR YOUR EYES ONLY(1981); GREAT MUPPET CAPER, THE(1981)
Mrs. Chan Lee
KLONDIKE ANNIE(1936)
Charlene Lee
MICKEY ONE(1965)
Charles Lee
TENDER WARRIOR, THE(1971); TIME TO DIE, A(1983), p
Silents
SABLE LORCHA, THE(1915); OLD FOLKS AT HOME, THE(1916)
Misc. Silents
JIM BLUDSO(1917)
Charley Lee
DON'T BET ON LOVE(1933)
Chen Lee
TO KILL OR TO DIE(1973, Ital.)

Cherrylene Lee
STAGECOACH TO DANCER'S PARK(1962)
Cherylene Lee
FLOWER DRUM SONG(1961); DONOVAN'S REEF(1963)
China Lee
TROUBLEMAKER, THE(1964); DR. GOLDFOOT AND THE BIKINI MACHINE(1965); WHAT'S UP, TIGER LILY?(1966); GOOD TIMES(1967); MEDIUM COOL(1969)
Ching Wah Lee
DAUGHTER OF SHANGHAI(1937); THIRTY SECONDS OVER TOKYO(1944); FLOWER DRUM SONG(1961)
Chingwah Lee
GOOD EARTH, THE(1937); LITTLE MISTER JIM(1946)
Chingwha Lee
CHINA(1943)
Chistopher Lee
DR. TERROR'S HOUSE OF HORRORS(1965, Brit.)
Christopher Lee
CORRIDOR OF MIRRORS(1948, Brit.); HAMLET(1948, Brit.); ONE NIGHT WITH YOU(1948, Brit); SONG FOR TOMORROW, A(1948, Brit.); GAY LADY, THE(1949, Brit.); SARABAND(1949, Brit.); SCOTT OF THE ANTARCTIC(1949, Brit.); PRELUDE TO FAME(1950, Brit.); CAPTAIN HORATIO HORNBLOWER(1951, Brit.); THEY WERE NOT DIVIDED(1951, Brit.); CRIMSON PIRATE, THE(1952); MOULIN ROUGE(1952); PAUL TEMPLE RETURNS(1952, Brit.); VALLEY OF EAGLES(1952, Brit.); MR. POTTS GOES TO MOSCOW(1953, Brit.); DEATH OF MICHAEL TURBIN, THE(1954, Brit.); DESTINATION MILAN(1954, Brit.); COCKLESHELL HEROES, THE(1955); FINAL COLUMN, THE(1955, Brit.); INNOCENTS IN PARIS(1955, Brit.); STORM OVER THE NILE(1955, Brit.); THAT LADY(1955, Brit.); ALIAS JOHN PRESTON(1956); PORT AFRIQUE(1956, Brit.); BEYOND MOMBASA(1957); CURSE OF FRANKENSTEIN, THE(1957, Brit.); PURSUIT OF THE GRAF SPEE(1957, Brit.); SHE PLAYED WITH FIRE(1957, Brit.); ACCURSED, THE(1958, Brit.); BITTER VICTORY(1958, Fr.); HORROR OF DRACULA, THE(1958, Brit.); NIGHT AMBUSH(1958, Brit.); TALE OF TWO CITIES, A(1958, Brit.); TRUTH ABOUT WOMEN, THE(1958, Brit.); HOUND OF THE BASKERVILLES, THE(1959, Brit.); MAN WHO COULD CHEAT DEATH, THE(1959, Brit.); MUMMY, THE(1959, Brit.); HORROR HOTEL(1960, Brit.); MISSILE FROM HELL(1960, Brit.); DEVIL'S DAFFODIL, THE(1961, Brit./Ger.); HOUSE OF FRIGHT(1961); SCREAM OF FEAR(1961); TERROR OF THE TONGS, THE(1961, Brit.); TOO HOT TO HANDLE(1961, Brit.); CORRIDORS OF BLOOD(1962, Brit.); DEVIL'S AGENT, THE(1962, Brit.); HOT MONEY GIRL(1962, Brit./Ger.); LONGEST DAY, THE(1962); PIRATES OF BLOOD RIVER, THE(1962, Brit.); SHERLOCK HOLMES AND THE DEADLY NECKLACE(1962, Ger.); CASTLE OF THE LIVING DEAD(1964, Ital./Fr.); DEVIL-SHIP PIRATES, THE(1964, Brit.); GORGON, THE(1964, Brit.); HANDS OF ORLAC, THE(1964, Brit./Fr.); HERCULES IN THE HAUNTED WORLD(1964, Ital.); FACE OF FU MANCHU, THE(1965, Brit.); HORROR CASTLE(1965, Ital.); SHE(1965, Brit.); SKULL, THE(1965, Brit.); WHAT!(1965, Fr./Brit./Ital.); BRIDES OF FU MANCHU, THE(1966, Brit.); DRACULA-PRINCE OF DARKNESS(1966, Brit.); RASPUTIN-THE MAD MONK(1966, Brit.); BLOOD DEMON(1967, Ger.); FIVE GOLDEN DRAGONS(1967, Brit.); PSYCHO-CIRCUS(1967, Brit.); THEATRE OF DEATH(1967, Brit.); BLOOD OF FU MANCHU, THE(1968, Brit.); CASTLE OF FU MANCHU, THE(1968, Ger./Span./Ital./Brit.); DEVIL'S BRIDE, THE(1968, Brit.); DRACULA HAS RISEN FROM HIS GRAVE(1968, Brit.); EVE(1968, Brit./Span.); VENGEANCE OF FU MANCHU, THE(1968, Brit./Ger./Hong Kong/Ireland); OBLONG BOX, THE(1969, Brit.); CRIMSON CULT, THE(1970, Brit.); JULIUS CAESAR(1970, Brit.); MAGIC CHRISTIAN, THE(1970, Brit.); ONE MORE TIME(1970, Brit.); PRIVATE LIFE OF SHERLOCK HOLMES, THE(1970, Brit.); SCARS OF DRACULA, THE(1970, Brit.); SCREAM AND SCREAM AGAIN(1970, Brit.); TASTE THE BLOOD OF DRACULA(1970, Brit.); COUNT DRACULA(1971, Sp., Ital., Ger., Brit.); HANNIE CALDER(1971, Brit.); HOUSE THAT DRIPPED BLOOD, THE(1971, Brit.); I, MONSTER(1971, Brit.); ISLAND OF THE BURNING DAMNED(1971, Brit.); DRACULA A.D. 1972(1972, Brit.); HORROR EXPRESS(1972, Span./Brit.); CREEPING FLESH,THE(1973, Brit.); DEATHLINE(1973, Brit.); DARK PLACES(1974, Brit.); DIAGNOSIS: MURDER(1974, Brit.); MAN WITH THE GOLDEN GUN, THE(1974, Brit.); THREE MUSKETEERS, THE(1974, Panama); WICKER MAN, THE(1974, Brit.); FOUR MUSKETEERS, THE(1975); KILLER FORCE(1975, Switz./Ireland); NOTHING BUT THE NIGHT(1975, Brit.); DRACULA AND SON(1976, Fr.); KEEPER, THE(1976, Can.); TO THE DEVIL A DAUGHTER(1976, Brit./Ger.); AIRPORT '77(1977); END OF THE WORLD(1977); MEAT CLEAVER MASSACRE(1977); CARAVANS(1978, U.S./Iranian); COUNT DRACULA AND HIS VAMPIRE BRIDE(1978, Brit.); NIGHT OF THE ASKARI(1978, Ger./South African); RETURN FROM WITCH MOUNTAIN(1978); STARSHIP INVASIONS(1978, Can.); ARABIAN ADVENTURE(1979, Brit.); CIRCLE OF IRON(1979, Brit.); JAGUAR LIVES(1979); NUTCRACKER FANTASY(1979); PASSAGE, THE(1979); 1941(1979); BEAR ISLAND(1980, Brit.-Can.); SERIAL(1980); EYE FOR AN EYE, AN(1981); LAST UNICORN, THE(1982); SAFARI 3000(1982); HOUSE OF LONG SHADOWS, THE(1983, Brit.); RETURN OF CAPTAIN INVINCIBLE, THE(1983, Aus./U.S.); SALAMANDER, THE(1983, U.S./Ital./Brit.)
1984
ROSEBUD BEACH HOTEL(1984)
Misc. Talkies
TERROR IN THE CRYPT(1963, Span./Ital.); VENGEANCE OF VIRGO(1972); ALBINO(1980)
Cindy Lee
JET OVER THE ATLANTIC(1960)
Connie Lee
GALLOPING DYNAMITE(1937), m; ROUGH RIDIN' RHYTHM(1937), m; SWING IT, PROFESSOR(1937), w; THANKS FOR LISTENING(1937), md; WEST OF RAINBOW'S END(1938), m; MEXICALI ROSE(1939), w; MOUNTAIN RHYTHM(1939), w; CAROLINA MOON(1940), w; GHOST VALLEY RAIDERS(1940), w; RANCHO GRANDE(1940), w; RIDE, TENDERFOOT, RIDE(1940), w; ZIS BOOM BAH(1941), w; BLONDIE FOR VICTORY(1942), w; COLLEGE SWEETHEARTS(1942), w; DARING YOUNG MAN, THE(1942), w; FOOTLIGHT GLAMOUR(1943), w; IT'S A GREAT LIFE(1943), w; NINE GIRLS(1944), w; LEAVE IT TO BLONDIE(1945), w; BLONDIE'S LUCKY DAY(1946), w; LIFE WITH BLONDIE(1946), w; BLONDIE'S BIG MOMENT(1947), w; RETURN OF OCTOBER, THE(1948), w
Constance Lee
BLONDIE'S HOLIDAY(1947), w
Cora Lee
Misc. Silents
NURSE AND MARTYR(1915, Brit.)

Cosette Lee
CHANGE OF MIND(1969); FIRST TIME, THE(1969); MY SIDE OF THE MOUNTAIN(1969); DERANGED(1974, Can.)
Curry Lee
IMITATION OF LIFE(1934)
Cynthia Lee
1984
NEW YORK NIGHTS(1984)
Daisy Lee
GOLD IS WHERE YOU FIND IT(1938); LITTLE TOKYO, U.S.A.(1942); SECRET AGENT OF JAPAN(1942); BEHIND THE RISING SUN(1943)
Damien Lee
1984
RENO AND THE DOC(1984, Can.), a, w
Dan Lee
SWISS FAMILY ROBINSON(1960), spec eff
Dana Lee
FUTUREWORLD(1976)
Danny Lee
IT'S A MAD, MAD, MAD, MAD WORLD(1963), spec eff; MURDERERS' ROW(1966), spec eff; WHAT DID YOU DO IN THE WAR, DADDY?(1966), spec eff; BONNIE AND CLYDE(1967), spec eff; LOVE BUG, THE(1968), spec eff; SECRET OF SANTA VITTORIA, THE(1969), spec eff; PUSSYCAT, PUSSYCAT, I LOVE YOU(1970), spec eff; BEDKNOBS AND BROOMSTICKS(1971), spec eff; NOW YOU SEE HIM, NOW YOU DON'T(1972), spec eff; SNOWBALL EXPRESS(1972), spec eff; WORLD'S GREATEST ATHLETE, THE(1973), spec eff; HERBIE RIDES AGAIN(1974), spec eff; ISLAND AT THE TOP OF THE WORLD, THE(1974), spec eff; FREAKY FRIDAY(1976), spec eff; GUS(1976), spec eff; HERBIE GOES TO MONTE CARLO(1977), spec eff; PETE'S DRAGON(1977), spec eff; CAT FROM OUTER SPACE, THE(1978), spec eff; HOT LEAD AND COLD FEET(1978), spec eff; RETURN FROM WITCH MOUNTAIN(1978), spec eff; NORTH AVENUE IRREGULARS, THE(1979), spec eff; HERBIE GOES BANANAS(1980), spec eff; LAST FLIGHT OF NOAH'S ARK, THE(1980), spec eff; MIDNIGHT MADNESS(1980), spec eff
Dave Lee
RELUCTANT ASTRONAUT, THE(1967), spec eff; THINK DIRTY(1970, Brit.)
Davey Lee
FROZEN RIVER(1929); SAY IT WITH SONGS(1929); SKIN DEEP(1929); SONNY BOY(1929); SQUEALER, THE(1930)
David Lee
SINGING FOOL, THE(1928); KITCHEN, THE(1961, Brit.), m; VERY EDGE, THE(1963, Brit.), m; MASQUE OF THE RED DEATH, THE(1964, U.S./Brit.), m, md; WITH SIX YOU GET EGGROLL(1968), spec eff; EXIT THE DRAGON, ENTER THE TIGER(1977, Hong Kong)
1984
NIGHTSONGS(1984)
Deborah Lee
Misc. Talkies
FOLLOW ME(1969)
Dennis Lee
I'M DANCING AS FAST AS I CAN(1982)
DeWitt Lee
PURSUIT(1975), a, w
Diana K. Lee
YOUNG GIRLS OF ROCHEFORT, THE(1968, Fr.)
Dick Lee
Silents
SEVEN SISTERS, THE(1915); POLLY OF THE CIRCUS(1917); CARDIGAN(1922)
Dixie Lee
FOX MOVIETONE FOLLIES(1929); WHY LEAVE HOME?(1929); BIG PARTY, THE(1930); CHEER UP AND SMILE(1930); HAPPY DAYS(1930); HARMONY AT HOME(1930); LET'S GO PLACES(1930); NIGHT LIFE IN RENO(1931); NO LIMIT(1931); MANHATTAN LOVE SONG(1934); LOVE IN BLOOM(1935); REDHEADS ON PARADE(1935); ACE ELI AND RODGER OF THE SKIES(1973); LEGACY(1976)
Misc. Silents
DAD'S GIRL(1919); LAW OF NATURE, THE(1919); WHERE BONDS ARE LOOSED(1919); NOT FOR SALE(1924)
Don Lee
SMASH PALACE(1982, New Zealand)
Donald W. Lee
RULING VOICE, THE(1931), d; BOILING POINT, THE(1932), w; PARTNERS(1932), w; UNKNOWN VALLEY(1933), d&w
Silents
GENTLE JULIA(1923), w; LADIES TO BOARD(1924), w; OH, YOU TONY!(1924), w
Donivee Lee
STAR SPANGLED RHYTHM(1942); CRYSTAL BALL, THE(1943); GREAT MOMENT, THE(1944)
Donna Lee
BODY SNATCHER, THE(1945); SING YOUR WAY HOME(1945); STONE COLD DEAD(1980, Can.)
Doris Lee
MASTER OF BANKDAM, THE(1947, Brit.), cos
Silents
PLAYING THE GAME(1918)
Misc. Silents
HIS MOTHER'S BOY(1917); GREEN EYES(1918); HIRED MAN, THE(1918); LAW OF THE NORTH, THE(1918); HAY FOOT, STRAW FOOT(1919)
Doris Lee [Doris May]
Misc. Silents
GIRL DODGER, THE(1919)
Dorothy Lee
RIO RITA(1929); SYNCOPATION(1929); CUCKOOS, THE(1930); DIXIANA(1930); HALF SHOT AT SUNRISE(1930); HOOK, LINE AND SINKER(1930); CAUGHT PLASTERED(1931); CRACKED NUTS(1931); LAUGH AND GET RICH(1931); LOCAL BOY MAKES GOOD(1931); PEACH O' RENO(1931); TOO MANY COOKS(1931); GIRL CRAZY(1932); TAKE A CHANCE(1933); COCKEYED CAVALIERS(1934); HIPS, HIPS, HOORAY(1934); CURTAIN FALLS, THE(1935); OLD HOMESTEAD, THE(1935); RAINMAKERS, THE(1935); SCHOOL FOR GIRLS(1935); PENTHOUSE PARTY(1936); SILLY BILLIES(1936); S.O.S. TIDAL WAVE(1939); TWELVE CROWDED HOURS(1939); REPENT AT LEISURE(1941); ROAR OF THE PRESS(1941); TOO MANY BLONDES(1941)

Silents
HER ELEPHANT MAN(1920)
Misc. Silents
MAN FROM THE RIO GRANDE, THE(1926); PATHS OF FLAME(1926); SALT LAKE TRAIL(1926)
Dottie Lee
NEW ORLEANS AFTER DARK(1958)
Dudley Lee
GENERAL DIED AT DAWN, THE(1936)
Duke Lee
CONCENTRATIN' KID, THE(1930); HEADIN' FOR TROUBLE(1931); FIGHTING GENTLEMAN, THE(1932); SCARLET BRAND(1932); DEADWOOD PASS(1933); FLAMING GUNS(1933); FOURTH HORSEMAN, THE(1933); MAN OF THE FOREST(1933); JUDGE PRIEST(1934); DESERT GUNS(1936); PRISONER OF SHARK ISLAND, THE(1936); SWIFTY(1936); SANTA FE STAMPEDE(1938); STAGECOACH(1939); MY DARLING CLEMENTINE(1946)
Silents
OUTCASTS OF POKER FLAT, THE(1919); IF ONLY JIM(1921); JUST TONY(1922); WHITE OUTLAW, THE(1925); TONY RUNS WILD(1926); CIRCUS ACE, THE(1927); OUTLAWS OF RED RIVER(1927); CLEARING THE TRAIL(1928)
Misc. Silents
STRAIGHT SHOOTING(1917); CALL OF COURAGE, THE(1925); DON DARE DEVIL(1925)
Duke R. Lee
MARIE ANTOINETTE(1938); FEUD OF THE RANGE(1939)
Misc. Talkies
EVIL EYE OF KALINOR, THE(1934)
Silents
TRACKED TO EARTH(1922); RUSTLER'S RANCH(1926); TERROR OF BAR X, THE(1927)
Misc. Silents
HELL BENT(1918); ACE OF THE SADDLE(1919); JUST PALS(1920); FIGHTING FURY(1924); SKY HIGH CORRAL(1926); SON OF THE GOLDEN WEST(1928)
Earl Lee
FIVE(1951); ASSIGNMENT-PARIS(1952); STORY OF WILL ROGERS, THE(1952); TROPICAL HEAT WAVE(1952); GERALDINE(1953); SCANDAL AT SCOURIE(1953)
Ed Lee
SHE LEARNED ABOUT SAILORS(1934)
Eddie Lee
BORDERTOWN(1935); SUNSET RANGE(1935); WITHOUT REGRET(1935); COWBOY AND THE KID,THE(1936); WEST OF SHANGHAI(1937); MOONLIGHT IN HAWAII(1941); ACROSS THE PACIFIC(1942); PACIFIC RENDEZVOUS(1942); REUNION IN FRANCE(1942); HEADIN' FOR GOD'S COUNTRY(1943); JACK LONDON(1943); MAN FROM THUNDER RIVER, THE(1943); DESTINATION TOKYO(1944); PURPLE HEART, THE(1944); FRONTIER GAL(1945); SAIGON(1948); TO THE ENDS OF THE EARTH(1948); BELLS OF CORONADO(1950); MALAYA(1950); MISTER 880(1950); I WAS AN AMERICAN SPY(1951); MASK OF THE DRAGON(1951)
Eddie E. Lee
PEKING EXPRESS(1951)
Edgy Lee
LAST MARRIED COUPLE IN AMERICA, THE(1980); SWORD AND THE SORCERER, THE(1982)
Edna Lee
ALL THAT HEAVEN ALLOWS(1955), w; QUEEN BEE(1955), w
Elaine Lee
NO. 96(1974, Aus.)
Misc. Talkies
GONE TO GROUND(1976)
Elizabeth Lee
SOMETHING WEIRD(1967)
Eric Lee
GOING BERSERK(1983)
Misc. Talkies
WEAPONS OF DEATH(1982)
Esme Lee
SOLDIER, SAILOR(1944, Brit.)
Esther Lee
DRAGON'S GOLD(1954); D.C. CAB(1983)
Etta Lee
INTERNATIONAL HOUSE(1933); MYSTERIOUS MR. WONG(1935)
Silents
TALE OF TWO WORLDS, A(1921); THIEF OF BAGDAD, THE(1924); CAMILLE(1927); OUT WITH THE TIDE(1928)
Misc. Silents
UNTAMEABLE, THE(1923)
Eugene Lee
HAMMETT(1982), prod d; EASY MONEY(1983), prod d
Evan Lee
MEAT CLEAVER MASSACRE(1977), d
Misc. Talkies
REVENGE OF THE DEAD(1975), d
Florence Lee
Silents
ACROSS THE DEADLINE(1925); SPEED MAD(1925); CITY LIGHTS(1931)
Misc. Silents
DIVORCONS(1915); MARY OF THE MOVIES(1923); LUCK AND SAND(1925); MAN RUSTLIN'(1926); ILLUSION OF LOVE(1929)
Florence D. Lee
Silents
JACK O' CLUBS(1924)
Misc. Silents
TOP O' THE MORNING, THE(1922)
Frances Lee
CARNATION KID(1929); HER SPLENDID FOLLY(1933); PHANTOM THUNDERBOLT, THE(1933); FLIRTATION WALK(1934); THESE THIRTY YEARS(1934); TRAVELING SALESLADY, THE(1935)
Misc. Talkies
DIVORCE MADE EASY(1929)

Misc. Silents
GOOD AS GOLD(1927)
Franchesca Lee
CHILDREN OF THE DAMNED(1963, Brit.)
Frank Lee
Misc. Silents
CROWN JEWELS(1918); LOVE'S CONQUEST(1918)
Frankie Lee
Silents
QUICKSANDS(1918); MIRACLE MAN, THE(1919); JUDY OF ROGUES' HARBOUR(1920); MOON MADNESS(1920); NURSE MARJORIE(1920); OLD FASHIONED BOY, AN(1920); KILLER, THE(1921); POVERTY OF RICHES, THE(1921); SHAME(1921); SIN OF MARTHA QUEED, THE(1921); SWAMP, THE(1921); DESERTED AT THE ALTAR(1922); SCRAPPER, THE(1922); SHATTERED IDOLS(1922); THIRD ALARM, THE(1922); HERO, THE(1923)
Misc. Silents
BONDS OF LOVE(1919); CHILDREN OF DUST(1923); ROBIN HOOD, JR.(1923)
Master Frankie Lee
Silents
KAISER, BEAST OF BERLIN, THE(1918)
Franne Lee
BABY, IT'S YOU(1983), cos
Fred Lee
TOAST OF NEW YORK, THE(1937); CHRISTMAS STORY, A(1983)
Frederick Lee
SKINNER STEPS OUT(1929); PLAYBOY OF PARIS(1930); SPLENDOR(1935)
Misc. Silents
RAMBLIN' GALOOT, THE(1926); TWIN TRIGGERS(1926)
Galen Lee
1984
ROADHOUSE 66(1984), w
Garrett G. Lee
HARD PART BEGINS, THE(1973, Can.), p
Gavin Lee
FALL OF THE HOUSE OF USHER, THE(1952, Brit.)
Geoff Lee
1984
NIGHTSONGS(1984)
George A. Lee
GUNFIGHTERS OF CASA GRANDE(1965, U.S./Span.), ed
George Lee
SUBMARINE BASE(1943); FIRST YANK INTO TOKYO(1945); MISTER 880(1950); BIGAMIST,THE(1953); FORT TI(1953); LEFT HAND OF GOD, THE(1955); 10 RILLINGTON PLACE(1971, Brit.)
Mrs. George Griffin Lee
Silents
DOLLY'S VACATION(1918), w
George T. Lee
RAINBOW ISLAND(1944); UP IN ARMS(1944); NOB HILL(1945); PEKING EXPRESS(1951)
Georgia Lee
GOOD NEWS(1947); WIRETAPPERS(1956); PERSUADER, THE(1957); RESTLESS ONES, THE(1965); BIG BAD MAMA(1974)
Gerald Lee
GUERRILLA GIRL(1953); BLACK SHAMPOO(1976), m; SATAN'S CHEERLEADERS(1977), m; HI-RIDERS(1978), m; ANGELS BRIGADE(1980), m
Gertrude Lee
DAY OF THE ANIMALS(1977)
Gilbert Lee
HISTORY OF THE WORLD, PART 1(1981)
Gita Lee
SALAMANDER, THE(1983, U.S./Ital./Brit.)
Glenn Lee
NAKED ANGELS(1969)
Glita Lee
Silents
RIDERS OF VENGEANCE(1919)
Gloria Lee
Misc. Silents
PINTO KID, THE(1928)
Grace Lee
SILENCERS, THE(1966)
Gracia Lee
TWO-MINUTE WARNING(1976)
Gracie Lee
SCHIZOID(1980)
Guy Lee
GIDGET GOES HAWAIIAN(1961); GIRLS! GIRLS! GIRLS!(1962); ONE MORE TRAIN TO ROB(1971)
Gwen Lee
LADY OF CHANCE, A(1928); SHOW GIRL(1928); FAST COMPANY(1929); LUCKY BOY(1929); MAN AND THE MOMENT, THE(1929); UNTAMED(1929); CAUGHT SHORT(1930); CHASING RAINBOWS(1930); EXTRAVAGANCE(1930); FREE AND EASY(1930); LORD BYRON OF BROADWAY(1930); OUR BLUSHING BRIDES(1930); PAID(1930); INSPIRATION(1931); LAWLESS WOMAN, THE(1931); PAGAN LADY(1931); TRAVELING HUSBANDS(1931); WEST OF BROADWAY(1931); ALIAS MARY SMITH(1932); BROADWAY TO CHEYENNE(1932); INTRUDER, THE(1932); MIDNIGHT MORALS(1932); CORRUPTION(1933); CITY PARK(1934); ONE IN A MILLION(1935); DOUBLE WEDDING(1937); MANNEQUIN(1937); MY DEAR MISS ALDRICH(1937); MAN-PROOF(1938); PAROLED FROM THE BIG HOUSE(1938)
Misc. Talkies
EVIL EYE OF KALINOR, THE(1934)
Silents
HIS SECRETARY(1925); PRETTY LADIES(1925); ADAM AND EVIL(1927); AFTER MIDNIGHT(1927); TWELVE MILES OUT(1927); ACTRESS, THE(1928); LAUGH, CLOWN, LAUGH(1928); SHARP SHOOTERS(1928)
Misc. Silents
THERE YOU ARE!(1926); UPSTAGE(1926); HEAVEN ON EARTH(1927); HER WILD OAT(1927); ORCHIDS AND ERMINE(1927); BABY CYCLONE, THE(1928); DIAMOND HANDCUFFS(1928); THIEF IN THE DARK, A(1928)

Gypsy Rose Lee
LADY OF BURLESQUE(1943), w; STAGE DOOR CANTEEN(1943); BELLE OF THE YUKON(1944); BABES IN BAGDAD(1952); SCREAMING MIMI(1958); WIND ACROSS THE EVERGLADES(1958); GYPSY(1962), w; STRIPPER, THE(1963); TROUBLE WITH ANGELS, THE(1966)
Hanna Lee
Misc. Silents
SIDEWALKS OF NEW YORK(1923)
Hans William Lee
SEVEN WOMEN(1966); KILL A DRAGON(1967)
Harold Lee
DEADLY MANTIS, THE(1957)
Harper Lee
TO KILL A MOCKINGBIRD(1962), w
Harriet Lee
ZIEGFELD FOLLIES(1945)
Harry Lee
GENTLEMEN OF THE PRESS(1929); SUNNY SKIES(1930); ALL THAT HEAVEN ALLOWS(1955), w; TOO HOT TO HANDLE(1961, Brit.), w; PUZZLE OF A DOWNFALL CHILD(1970)
Silents
RAINBOW PRINCESS, THE(1916); ARMS AND THE GIRL(1917); MONSIEUR BEAUCAIRE(1924)
Misc. Silents
DESTINY'S TOY(1916); LITTLE LADY EILEEN(1916); LIQUID GOLD(1919)
Helen Lee
THREE WEIRD SISTERS, THE(1948, Brit.)
Irvin Lee
KEEPER OF THE FLAME(1942)
Irving Lee
HARRIGAN'S KID(1943)
Isobel Lee
Silents
OPEN COUNTRY(1922, Brit.)
J. C. Lee
COOL WORLD, THE(1963)
Jack Lee
BOMBAY CLIPPER(1942); APPOINTMENT IN BERLIN(1943); PASSPORT TO SUEZ(1943); GHOST THAT WALKS ALONE, THE(1944); ONCE UPON A TIME(1944); THEY WERE EXPENDABLE(1945); CRIME DOCTOR'S MAN HUNT(1946); SHADOWED(1946); VOICE OF THE TURTLE, THE(1947); SOUTHERN YANKEE, A(1948); COVER-UP(1949); LADY TAKES A SAILOR, THE(1949); WOMAN IN THE HALL, THE(1949, Brit.), d, w; BROKEN ARROW(1950); TWO FLAGS WEST(1950); HALLS OF MONTEZUMA(1951); MANIACS ON WHEELS(1951, Brit.), d, w; PEOPLE AGAINST O'HARA, THE(1951); WOODEN HORSE, THE(1951), d; GOLDEN MASK, THE(1954, Brit.), d; TURN THE KEY SOFTLY(1954, Brit.), d; ROBBERY UNDER ARMS(1958, Brit.), d; TOWN LIKE ALICE, A(1958, Brit.), d; CIRCLE OF DECEPTION(1961, Brit.), d; PURSUIT(1975), w
Jack G. Lee
WEB, THE(1947); RIVER LADY(1948); ROAD HOUSE(1948)
Jack H. Lee
IMPERFECT LADY, THE(1947)
Jack M. Lee
DESK SET(1957)
Jack S. Lee
BRUTE FORCE(1947)
James Lee
KENNEL MURDER CASE, THE(1933); CAREER(1959), w; ADVENTURES OF HUCKLEBERRY FINN, THE(1960), w; BANNING(1967), w; COUNTERPOINT(1967), w; CHANGE OF HABIT(1969), w; PURSUIT OF D.B. COOPER, THE(1981)
Jane Lee
KNOCK ON ANY DOOR(1949)
Silents
CLEMENCEAU CASE, THE(1915); SOUL OF BROADWAY, THE(1915); ROMEO AND JULIET(1916); AMERICAN BUDS(1918); DOING THEIR BIT(1918)
Misc. Silents
GALLEY SLAVE, THE(1915); DAUGHTER OF THE GODS, A(1916); LOVE AND HATE(1916); RAGGED PRINCESS, THE(1916); SMALL TOWN GIRL, A(1917); TROUBLEMAKERS(1917); TWO LITTLE IMPS(1917); SWAT THE SPY(1918); TELL IT TO THE MARINES(1918); WE SHOULD WORRY(1918); SMILES(1919)
Jennie Lee
THREE NUTS IN SEARCH OF A BOLT(1964)
Silents
BIRTH OF A NATION, THE(1915); INNOCENT MAGDALENE, AN(1916); INTOLERANCE(1916); LITTLE LIAR, THE(1916); CLEVER MRS. CARFAX, THE(1917); INNOCENT SINNER, THE(1917); NINA, THE FLOWER GIRL(1917); RIDERS OF VENGEANCE(1919); BIG PUNCH, THE(1921); NORTH OF HUDSON BAY(1923); HEARTS OF OAK(1924)
Misc. Silents
HER SHATTERED IDOL(1915); CHILD OF THE PARIS STREETS, A(1916); STAGE STRUCK(1917)
Jennifer Lee
ACT OF VENGEANCE(1974); SUNSHINE BOYS, THE(1975); WILD PARTY, THE(1975); DUCHESS AND THE DIRTWATER FOX, THE(1976); PRIVATE FILES OF J. EDGAR HOOVER, THE(1978)
Jennifer Ann Lee
CHU CHU AND THE PHILLY FLASH(1981)
Miss Jeri Lee
SWEET BEAT(1962, Brit.)
Joanna Lee
BRAIN EATERS, THE(1958); PLAN 9 FROM OUTER SPACE(1959)
1984
MAKING THE GRADE(1984)
Jocelyn Lee
BROADWAY BABIES(1929); LOVE TRAP, THE(1929); MARRIAGE PLAYGROUND, THE(1929); THREE LIVE GHOSTS(1929); TWIN BEDS(1929); YOUNG NOWHERES(1929); NO, NO NANETTE(1930); HER FIRST MATE(1933)
Silents
CAMPUS FLIRT, THE(1926); AFRAID TO LOVE(1927); BACKSTAGE(1927); MASKED ANGEL(1928)

Misc. Silents
LOVE THRILL, THE(1927); SAY IT WITH DIAMONDS(1927); DRY MARTINI(1928)
Joe E. Lee
WE'LL SMILE AGAIN(1942, Brit.)
John B. Lee
ANATOMY OF A PSYCHO(1961)
John Lee
BOTTOM OF THE BOTTLE, THE(1956); CAT GIRL(1957); MAILBAG ROBBERY(1957, Brit.); SPIRIT OF ST. LOUIS, THE(1957); SILENT ENEMY, THE(1959, Brit.); SECRET PARTNER, THE(1961, Brit.); SEVEN KEYS(1962, Brit.); DR. CRIPPEN(1963, Brit.); SPACEFLIGHT IC-1(1965, Brit.); KILL, THE(1968); CROSSPLOT(1969, Brit.); SAY HELLO TO YESTERDAY(1971, Brit.); BUGSY MALONE(1976, Brit.); FFOLKES(1980, Brit.)
Johnnie Lee
STORMY WEATHER(1943)
Johnny Lee
TALES OF MANHATTAN(1942); SONG OF THE SOUTH(1946); MY FORBIDDEN PAST(1951); NARROW MARGIN, THE(1952); FIRST TRAVELING SALESLADY, THE(1956); HOT SPELL(1958); NORTH TO ALASKA(1960); HINDENBURG, THE(1975); URBAN COWBOY(1980)
Misc. Talkies
COME ON, COWBOY!(1948); SHE'S TOO MEAN TO ME(1948)
Johnny Lee, Jr.
Misc. Talkies
BOARDING HOUSE BLUES(1948)
Johnny Scott Lee
MARRIAGE OF A YOUNG STOCKBROKER, THE(1971)
Jonathan Lee
HAIRY APE, THE(1944)
Jonna Lee
1984
LOVELINES(1984); SAM'S SON(1984)
Joseph Lee
GIRL ON THE RUN(1961), d
Joy Lee
SON OF SINBAD(1955); EMERGENCY HOSPITAL(1956)
Joyce Lee
NIGHT THEY ROBBED BIG BERTHA'S, THE zero(1975); GREAT WHITE, THE(1982, Ital.)
Judy Lee
STING OF DEATH(1966)
Misc. Talkies
BODYGUARD, THE(1976); QUEEN BOXER, THE(1973)
Juliet Lee
1984
MISSING IN ACTION(1984)
Kaaren Lee
RIGHT STUFF, THE(1983)
1984
ROADHOUSE 66(1984)
Kaiulani Lee
SEDUCTION OF JOE TYNAN, THE(1979); FAN, THE(1981); WORLD ACCORDING TO GARP, The(1982); CUJO(1983)
Karen Lee
POINT BLANK(1967); FUNNY GIRL(1968)
Karole Lee
JANIE(1944)
Karsen Lee
DEATH WISH II(1982)
Katherine Lee
Silents
NEPTUNE'S DAUGHTER(1914); SCALES OF JUSTICE, THE(1914); ROMEO AND JULIET(1916); AMERICAN BUDS(1918); DOING THEIR BIT(1918); SIDESHOW OF LIFE, THE(1924)
Misc. Silents
DAUGHTER OF THE GODS, A(1916); LOVE AND HATE(1916); TROUBLEMAKERS(1917); TWO LITTLE IMPS(1917); SWAT THE SPY(1918); TELL IT TO THE MARINES(1918); WE SHOULD WORRY(1918); SMILES(1919)
Kathy Lee
SILENT RAGE(1982)
Kay Lee
ONE FLEW OVER THE CUCKOO'S NEST(1975)
Keith Lee
WEEKEND OF SHADOWS(1978, Aus.)
Misc. Talkies
DEMOLITION(1977)
Ken Lee
SUDDEN IMPACT(1983)
Kendall Lee
SIN TAKES A HOLIDAY(1930); RAIN(1932); SECRETS OF THE FRENCH POLICE(1932); LADY IS WILLING, THE(1934, Brit.)
Kenneth Lee
JEREMIAH JOHNSON(1972), animal
Kim Lee
NO MAN'S LAND(1964)
Kwang Ho Lee
YONGKARI MONSTER FROM THE DEEP(1967 S.K.)
Lani Lee
PENNY SERENADE(1941)
Larry Lee
ANATOMY OF A PSYCHO(1961), w; GOSPEL ROAD, THE(1973)
Laura Lee
MAYBE IT'S LOVE(1930); TOP SPEED(1930); GOING WILD(1931); TIMBER FURY(1950); JESSE JAMES' WOMEN(1954)
Lavender Lee
MR. PERRIN AND MR. TRAILL(1948, Brit.)
Law Lee
Misc. Talkies
KUNG FU HALLOWEEN(1981)

Leon Lee
ARM OF THE LAW(1932), w; RECKONING, THE(1932), w
Silents
WIZARD OF OZ, THE(1925), w; IS YOUR DAUGHTER SAFE?(1927), d; LADIES AT EASE(1927), w
Leonard Lee
SINNER TAKE ALL(1936), w; BEG, BORROW OR STEAL(1937), w; ESPIONAGE(1937), w; STREET OF MISSING MEN(1939), w; ADVENTURE IN DIAMONDS(1940), w; CHOCOLATE SOLDIER, THE(1941), w; BOMBER'S MOON(1943), w; SO'S YOUR UNCLE(1943), w; PURSUIT TO ALGIERS(1945), w; THIS LOVE OF OURS(1945), w; DRESSED TO KILL(1946), w; TIME, THE PLACE AND THE GIRL, THE(1946), w; WHISPERING CITY(1947, Can.), w; SPY HUNT(1950), w; WYOMING MAIL(1950), w; FAT MAN, THE(1951), w; SMUGGLER'S ISLAND(1951), w; GLASS WEB, THE(1953), w; NEVER SAY GOODBYE(1956), w
Leslie Lee
1984
GO TELL IT ON THE MOUNTAIN(1984), w
Misc. Talkies
AXE(1977); LISA(1977)
Lester Lee
LOVE AT FIRST SIGHT(1930), w; SYMPHONY OF SIX MILLION(1932); MEN ARE SUCH FOOLS(1933); SYMPHONY OF LIVING(1935); ONE WAY TO LOVE(1946), w
Leyton Lee
EARL OF CHICAGO, THE(1940)
Lila Lee
ARGYLE CASE, THE(1929); DARK STREETS(1929); DRAG(1929); FLIGHT(1929); HONKY TONK(1929); LOVE, LIVE AND LAUGH(1929); QUEEN OF THE NIGHTCLUBS(1929); SACRED FLAME, THE(1929); DOUBLE CROSS ROADS(1930); MURDER WILL OUT(1930); SECOND WIFE(1930); THOSE WHO DANCE(1930); UNHOLY THREE, THE(1930); GORILLA, THE(1931); MISBEHAVING LADIES(1931); WOMAN HUNGRY(1931); FALSE FACES(1932); INTRUDER, THE(1932); NIGHT OF JUNE 13(1932); RADIO PATROL(1932); UNHOLY LOVE(1932); WAR CORRESPONDENT(1932); FACE IN THE SKY(1933); IRON MASTER, THE(1933); OFFICER 13(1933); I CAN'T ESCAPE(1934); IN LOVE WITH LIFE(1934); LONE COWBOY(1934); STAND UP AND CHEER(1934 80m FOX bw); WHIRLPOOL(1934); CHAMPAGNE FOR BREAKFAST(1935); PEOPLE'S ENEMY, THE(1935); EX-MRS. BRADFORD, THE(1936); COUNTRY GENTLEMEN(1937); NATION AFLAME(1937); TWO WISE MAIDS(1937); COTTONPICKIN' CHICKENPICKERS(1967)
Misc. Talkies
EXPOSURE(1932); MARRIAGE BARGAIN, THE(1935)
Silents
HAWTHORNE OF THE U.S.A.(1919); JANE GOES A' WOOING(1919); MALE AND FEMALE(1919); MIDSUMMER MADNESS(1920); SOUL OF YOUTH, THE(1920); AFTER THE SHOW(1921); CHARM SCHOOL, THE(1921); CRAZY TO MARRY(1921); EASY ROAD, THE(1921); GASOLINE GUS(1921); IF WOMEN ONLY KNEW(1921); BACK HOME AND BROKE(1922); BLOOD AND SAND(1922); DICTATOR, THE(1922); EBB TIDE(1922); ANOTHER MAN'S WIFE(1924); OLD HOME WEEK(1925); BROKEN HEARTS(1926); NEW KLONDIKE, THE(1926); ADORABLE CHEAT, THE(1928); JUST MARRIED(1928); LITTLE WILD GIRL, THE(1928); MAN IN HOBBLES, THE(1928)
Misc. Silents
CRUISE OF THE MAKE-BELIEVES, THE(1918); SUCH A LITTLE PIRATE(1918); DAUGHTER OF THE WOLF, A(1919); PUPPY LOVE(1919); ROSE OF THE RIVER(1919); RUSTLING A BRIDE(1919); SECRET GARDEN, THE(1919); HEART OF YOUTH, THE(1920); PRINCE CHAP, THE(1920); TERROR ISLAND(1920); DOLLAR-A-YEAR MAN, THE(1921); GHOST BREAKER, THE(1922); IS MATRIMONY A FAILURE?(1922); ONE GLORIOUS DAY(1922); RENT FREE(1922); HOMEWARD BOUND(1923); NE'ER-DO-WELL, THE(1923); WOMAN-PROOF(1923); LOVE'S WHIRLPOOL(1924); WANDERING HUSBANDS(1924); COMING THROUGH(1925); MIDNIGHT GIRL, THE(1925); MILLION DOLLAR MYSTERY(1927); ONE INCREASING PURPOSE(1927); BIT OF HEAVEN, A(1928); BLACK BUTTERFLIES(1928); BLACK PEARL, THE(1928); THUNDERGOD(1928); TOP SERGEANT MULLIGAN(1928); UNITED STATES SMITH(1928); YOU CAN'T BEAT THE LAW(1928)
Lillian Lee
Silents
NO MOTHER TO GUIDE HER(1923)
Lily Lee
FIGHT TO THE LAST(1938, Chi.)
Linda Lee
MOONSHINER'S WOMAN(1968); NIGHT IN HEAVEN, A(1983)
1984
FEAR CITY(1984)
Lisa Lee
HAPPIDROME(1943, Brit.); TROUBLE IN THE AIR(1948, Brit.); SCOTLAND YARD INSPECTOR(1952, Brit.); CIRCUMSTANIAL EVIDENCE(1954, Brit.); LADY GODIVA RIDES AGAIN(1955, Brit.); DANGEROUS EXILE(1958, Brit.); PURE HELL OF ST. TRINIAN'S, THE(1961, Brit.); GREAT ST. TRINIAN'S TRAIN ROBBERY, THE(1966, Brit.)
Lois Lee
Silents
PRISONER OF ZENDA, THE(1922)
Misc. Silents
LINCOLN HIGHWAYMAN, THE(1920)
London Lee
GAMBLER, THE(1974)
Lora Lee
THIS GUN FOR HIRE(1942)
Lou Anne Lee
JUKE BOX RACKET(1960)
Louise Lee
MILLION EYES OF SU-MURU, THE(1967, Brit.)
Silents
ON THE QUIET(1918)
Misc. Silents
DEVIL'S CONFESSION, THE(1921); WOMAN'S WOMAN, A(1922)
Luana Lee
THESE WILDER YEARS(1956); RAINTREE COUNTY(1957)
Mabel Lee
Misc. Talkies
SWANEE SHOWBOAT(1939); DREAMER, THE(1947)

Madeline Lee
PARADES(1972); SAVE THE TIGER(1973); ROSELAND(1977); LIANNA(1983)
Malachi Lee
Misc. Talkies
FORCE FOUR(1975)
Manfred Lee
ENEMY AGENTS MEET ELLERY QUEEN(1942), w
Manfred Bennington Lee
DESPERATE CHANCE FOR ELLERY QUEEN, A(1942), w
Manli Lee
MARINE BATTLEGROUND(1966, U.S/S.K.), d
Mannie Lee
1984
ALLEY CAT(1984), set d
Margaret Lee
FOLLOW THRU(1930); EVER SINCE EVE(1937), w; TWELVE-HANDED MEN OF MARS, THE(1964, Ital./Span.); CASANOVA '70(1965, Ital.); DOUBLE BED, THE(1965, Fr./Ital.); BANG, BANG, YOU'RE DEAD(1966); SECRET AGENT SUPER DRAGON(1966, Fr./Ital./Ger./Monaco); WEB OF VIOLENCE(1966, Ital./Span.); FIVE GOLDEN DRAGONS(1967, Brit.); KISS THE GIRLS AND MAKE THEM DIE(1967, U.S./Ital.); PSYCHO-CIRCUS(1967, Brit.); NO ROSES FOR OSS 117(1968, Fr.); VIOLENT FOUR, THE(1968, Ital.); GHOSTS, ITALIAN STYLE(1969, Ital./Fr.); LEATHER AND NYLON(1969, Fr./Ital.); SONS OF SATAN(1969, Ital./Fr./Ger.); DORIAN GRAY(1970, Ital./Brit./Ger./Liechtenstein); VENUS IN FURS(1970, Ital./Brit./Ger.); SLAUGHTER HOTEL(1971, Ital.)
Misc. Talkies
SAMSON AND THE SEA BEAST(1960); FURY ON THE BOSPHOROUS(1965, Brit.); ROGUE, THE(1976)
Margaret Jo Lee
CARNY(1980); LOVELESS, THE(1982)
Margo Lee
TIM(1981, Aus.); STARSTRUCK(1982, Aus.)
Margot Lee
INTO THE STRAIGHT(1950, Aus.)
Marie Lee
DYNAMITE JOHNSON(1978, Phil.)
Mark Lee
GALLIPOLI(1981, Aus.)
Marrie Lee
Misc. Talkies
PAY OR DIE(1982)
Mary Lee
NANCY DREW–REPORTER(1939); SOUTH OF THE BORDER(1939); BARNYARD FOLLIES(1940); CAROLINA MOON(1940); GAUCHO SERENADE(1940); MELODY AND MOONLIGHT(1940); MELODY RANCH(1940); RANCHO GRANDE(1940); RIDE, TENDERFOOT, RIDE(1940); SING, DANCE, PLENTY HOT(1940); ANGELS WITH BROKEN WINGS(1941); BACK IN THE SADDLE(1941); RIDIN' ON A RAINBOW(1941); SINGING HILL, THE(1941); NOBODY'S DARLING(1943); SHANTYTOWN(1943); COWBOY AND THE SENORITA(1944); SONG OF NEVADA(1944); THREE LITTLE SISTERS(1944)
Maurice Lee
HARD TO GET(1938), w
May Lee
LEFT HAND OF GOD, THE(1955); ROSE TATTOO, THE(1955)
Michael Lee
SKIN GAME, THE(1965, Brit.)
Michael D. Lee
KILL SQUAD(1982), p
Michael David Lee
FOUL PLAY(1978); DIE LAUGHING(1980)
Michele Lee
LOVE BUG, THE(1968); COMIC, THE(1969); HOW TO SUCCEED IN BUSINESS WITHOUT REALLY TRYING(1976); NUTCRACKER FANTASY(1979)
Mike Lee
JOHNNY GOT HIS GUN(1971)
Mildred Lee
Misc. Silents
GAME'S UP, THE(1919)
Milton Lee
BITTER TEA OF GENERAL YEN, THE(1933)
Moe Lee
Misc. Silents
GOOD-BAD WIFE, THE(1921)
Monroe Lee
INDIANAPOLIS SPEEDWAY(1939)
Monte Lee
RIGHT HAND OF THE DEVIL, THE(1963)
Nak Hoon Lee
INCHON(1981)
Nancy Lee
TEN SECONDS TO HELL(1959); FAME(1980)
Misc. Silents
FORTUNE HUNTER, THE(1920)
Noreen Lee
FIRST YANK INTO TOKYO(1945)
Norma Lee
WISE GIRLS(1930)
Misc. Silents
COUNTERFEIT LOVE(1923)
Norman Lee
DR. JOSSER KC(1931, Brit.), p,d&w; JOSSER IN THE ARMY(1932, Brit.), d; JOSSER JOINS THE NAVY(1932, Brit.), p&d; JOSSER ON THE RIVER(1932, Brit.), p&d; MONEY TALKS(1933, Brit.), d, w; POLITICAL PARTY, A(1933, Brit.), d; PRIDE OF THE FORCE, THE(1933, Brit.), p&d, w; DOCTOR'S ORDERS(1934, Brit.), d; OUTCAST, THE(1934, Brit.), d; SPRING IN THE AIR(1934, Brit.), d&w; REGAL CAVALCADE(1935, Brit.), d; DON'T RUSH ME(1936, Brit.), d; HAPPY DAYS ARE HERE AGAIN(1936, Brit.), d; NO ESCAPE(1936, Brit.), d; BULLDOG DRUMMOND AT BAY(1937, Brit.), d; FRENCH LEAVE(1937, Brit.), d; KNIGHTS FOR A DAY(1937, Brit.), d; SATURDAY NIGHT REVUE(1937, Brit.), d; ALMOST A HONEYMOON(1938, Brit.), d; KATHLEEN(1938, Ireland), d; SAVE A LITTLE SUNSHINE(1938, Brit.), d;

YES, MADAM?(1938, Brit.), d; NORTH SEA PATROL(1939, Brit.), d; WANTED BY SCOTLAND YARD(1939, Brit.), d; MEIN KAMPF–MY CRIMES(1940, Brit.), d; MURDER IN THE NIGHT(1940, Brit.), d; CHAMBER OF HORRORS(1941, Brit.), d, w; FARMER'S WIFE, THE(1941, Brit.), d, w; MY WIFE'S FAMILY(1941, Brit.), w; MYSTERY OF ROOM 13(1941, Brit.), d; SOUTH AMERICAN GEORGE(1941, Brit.), w; SPRING MEETING(1941, Brit.), w; HE SNOOPS TO CONQUER(1944, Brit.), w; I DIDN'T DO IT(1945, Brit.), w; THIS MAN IS MINE(1946 Brit.), w; IDOL OF PARIS(1948, Brit.), w; MONKEY'S PAW, THE(1948, Brit.), d, w; CASE OF CHARLES PEACE, THE(1949, Brit.), d, w; GIRL WHO COULDN'T QUITE, THE(1949, Brit.), d, w
Silents
PRIDE OF DONEGAL, THE(1929, Brit.), w
Misc. Silents
CITY OF SHADOWS(1929, Brit.), d; STREETS OF LONDON, THE(1929, Brit.), d
Owen Lee
ZORRO, THE GAY BLADE(1981)
Misc. Talkies
$20 A WEEK(1935)
P. C. Lee
MOUNTAIN ROAD, THE(1960)
Paige Lee
VOYAGE TO THE PLANET OF PREHISTORIC WOMEN(1966)
Palmer Lee
CIMARRON KID, THE(1951); BACK AT THE FRONT(1952); BATTLE AT APACHE PASS, THE(1952); FRANCIS GOES TO WEST POINT(1952); RAIDERS, THE(1952); RED BALL EXPRESS(1952); SALLY AND SAINT ANNE(1952); SON OF ALI BABA(1952); COLUMN SOUTH(1953); IT HAPPENS EVERY THURSDAY(1953); REDHEAD FROM WYOMING, THE(1953); VEILS OF BAGDAD, THE(1953)
Pami Lee
MOVE OVER, DARLING(1963)
Pat Lee
PORKY'S(1982)
1984
STARMAN(1984)
Patricia Lee
STAND UP AND CHEER(1934 80m FOX bw); MATTER OF WHO, A(1962, Brit.), w; COLOR ME BLOOD RED(1965)
Patti Lee
1984
SPLITZ(1984)
Patty Lee
STRAIT-JACKET(1964)
Peggy Lee
POWERS GIRL, THE(1942); MR. MUSIC(1950); JAZZ SINGER, THE(1953); LADY AND THE TRAMP(1955); PETE KELLY'S BLUES(1955)
Penelope Lee
TOMB OF LIGEIA, THE(1965, Brit.); SUPERMAN(1978)
1984
PLAGUE DOGS, THE(1984, U.S./Brit.)
Pinky Lee
LADY OF BURLESQUE(1943); BLONDE RANSOM(1945); EARL CARROLL'S VANITIES(1945); ONE EXCITING WEEK(1946); THAT'S MY GAL(1947); IN OLD AMARILLO(1951); SOUTH OF CALIENTE(1951); PALS OF THE GOLDEN WEST(1952)
Preston Lee
LADY FROM SHANGHAI, THE(1948)
Ralph Lee
JUMBO(1962); STRIPPER, THE(1963); SWEET RIDE, THE(1968)
Randee Lee
CYCLE SAVAGES(1969)
Raymond Lee
ROAD TO BALI(1952)
Silents
JACK AND THE BEANSTALK(1917); ALI BABA AND THE FORTY THIEVES(1918); KID, THE(1921); NO WOMAN KNOWS(1921); LONG LIVE THE KING(1923); PILGRIM, THE(1923); ABRAHAM LINCOLN(1924)
Richard Lee
HALF PAST MIDNIGHT(1948)
Misc. Silents
CYCLONE COWBOY, THE(1927)
Richardo Lee
JAGUAR(1980, Phil.), w
Robbie Lee
BIG BAD MAMA(1974); SWITCHBLADE SISTERS(1975)
Robert Lee
DESPERATE WOMEN, THE(?); SOMETHING TO SING ABOUT(1937), art d; DRAGON SEED(1944); WORLD OF SUZIE WONG, THE(1960); PASSPORT TO CHINA(1961, Brit.); SATAN NEVER SLEEPS(1962); SINISTER MAN, THE(1965, Brit.); DON'T RAISE THE BRIDGE, LOWER THE RIVER(1968, Brit.); CHAIRMAN, THE(1969); PROJECTIONIST, THE(1970); HIGH ROAD TO CHINA(1983)
1984
ALLEY CAT(1984), prod d
Robert E. Lee
AUNTIE MAME(1958), w; INHERIT THE WIND(1960), w; MAME(1974), w; FIRST MONDAY IN OCTOBER(1981), w; TRADING PLACES(1983)
Silents
ALIAS THE LONE WOLF(1927), art d; BY WHOSE HAND?(1927), art d; SALLY IN OUR ALLEY(1927), art d; STAGE KISSES(1927), art d; WARNING, THE(1927), art d; AFTER THE STORM(1928), art d; MATINEE IDOL, THE(1928), art d; SO THIS IS LOVE(1928), art d
Robert H. Lee
CAPTAIN KIDD(1945), w
Robert Lee [Robert Lee Johnson]
DUDE WRANGLER, THE(1930), w
Robert N. Lee
MIGHTY, THE(1929), w; LITTLE CAESAR(1931), w; 70,000 WITNESSES(1932), w; FROM HEADQUARTERS(1933), w; KENNEL MURDER CASE, THE(1933), w; MYSTERIOUS RIDER, THE(1933), w; DRAGON MURDER CASE, THE(1934), w; FOG OVER FRISCO(1934), w; WHILE THE PATIENT SLEPT(1935), w; ARMORED CAR(1937), w; DARK SANDS(1938, Brit.), w; TOWER OF LONDON(1939), w

Silents
SHIRLEY OF THE CIRCUS(1922), w; ALIAS THE NIGHT WIND(1923), w; ARIZONA EXPRESS, THE(1924), w; WESTERN LUCK(1924), w; OUTSIDER, THE(1926), w; ROUGH RIDERS, THE(1927), w; UNDERWORLD(1927), w; MIDNIGHT MADNESS(1928), w

Robert W. Lee
PEKING EXPRESS(1951); TARGET HONG KONG(1952)

Robin Lee
ICE-CAPADES REVUE(1942)

Rodney Lee, Jr.
THIEVES LIKE US(1974)

Rohama Lee
TONIGHT WE RAID CALAIS(1943), w

Roland Lee
Misc. Silents
TIME LOCKS AND DIAMONDS(1917)

Roland V. Lee
LADIES LOVE BRUTES(1930), d; RULING VOICE, THE(1931), d, d
Misc. Silents
WATER, WATER, EVERYWHERE(1920)

Ron Lee
TWILIGHT'S LAST GLEAMING(1977, U.S./Ger.)

Ronald Lee
RACKET, THE(1951); INN OF THE SIXTH HAPPINESS, THE(1958)

Rosalyn Lee
KISMET(1944); UP IN ARMS(1944)

Rosanna Lee
SON OF DRACULA(1974, Brit.)

Rose Lee
1984
NIGHTSONGS(1984)

Rosie Lee
DENTIST IN THE CHAIR(1960, Brit.)

Rowland Lee
Misc. Silents
MATERNAL SPARK, THE(1917); MOTHER INSTINCT, THE(1917); POLLY ANN(1917); STAINLESS BARRIER, THE(1917); THEY'RE OFF(1917); WILD WINSHIP'S WIDOW(1917); DANGEROUS DAYS(1920); HER HUSBAND'S FRIEND(1920); HIS OWN LAW(1920)

Rowland V. Lee
DANGEROUS WOMAN(1929), d; MYSTERIOUS DR. FU MANCHU, THE(1929), d; WOLF OF WALL STREET, THE(1929), d; DERELICT(1930), d; MAN FROM WYOMING, A(1930), d; RETURN OF DR. FU MANCHU, THE(1930), d; GUILTY GENERATION, THE(1931), d; SIGN OF FOUR, THE(1932, Brit.), p; OVERNIGHT(1933, Brit.), d; ZOO IN BUDAPEST(1933), d, w; COUNT OF MONTE CRISTO, THE(1934), d, w; GAMBLING(1934), d; I AM SUZANNE(1934), d, w; CARDINAL RICHELIEU(1935), d; THREE MUSKETEERS, THE(1935), d, w; ONE RAINY AFTERNOON(1936), d; LOVE FROM A STRANGER(1937, Brit.), d; TOAST OF NEW YORK, THE(1937), d; MOTHER CAREY'S CHICKENS(1938), d; SERVICE DE LUXE(1938), d; SON OF FRANKENSTEIN(1939), p&d; SUN NEVER SETS, THE(1939), p&d; TOWER OF LONDON(1939), p&d; SON OF MONTE CRISTO(1940), d; POWDER TOWN(1942), d; BRIDGE OF SAN LUIS REY, THE(1944), d; CAPTAIN KIDD(1945), d; BIG FISHERMAN, THE(1959), p, w
Silents
BLIND HEARTS(1921), d; SEA LION, THE(1921), d; DUST FLOWER, THE(1922), d; MIXED FACES(1922), d; SHIRLEY OF THE CIRCUS(1922), d; ALICE ADAMS(1923), d&w; GENTLE JULIA(1923), d; OUTSIDER, THE(1926), d; BARBED WIRE(1927), d, w; SECRET HOUR, THE(1928), d&w; THREE SINNERS(1928), d
Misc. Silents
THOUSAND TO ONE, A(1920), d; CUP OF LIFE, THE(1921), d; CUPID'S BRAND(1921), d; HIS BACK AGAINST THE WALL(1922), d; MEN OF ZANSIBAR, THE(1922), d; MONEY TO BURN(1922), d; SELF-MADE MAN, A(1922), d; DESIRE(1923), d; YOU CAN'T GET AWAY WITH IT(1923), d; IN LOVE WITH LOVE(1924), d; HAVOC(1925), d; MAN WITHOUT A COUNTRY, THE(1925), d; SILVER TREASURE, THE(1926), d; WHIRLPOOL OF YOUTH, THE(1927), d; DOOMSDAY(1928), d; FIRST KISS, THE(1928), d; LOVES OF AN ACTRESS(1928), d

Rudee Lee
IT HAPPENS EVERY THURSDAY(1953)

Rudy Lee
SKIPPER SURPRISED HIS WIFE, THE(1950); DARLING, HOW COULD YOU!(1951); MAN WITH A CLOAK, THE(1951); QUEEN FOR A DAY(1951); WHEN WORLDS COLLIDE(1951); MONKEY BUSINESS(1952); SKIRTS AHOY!(1952); SOMETHING TO LIVE FOR(1952); SON OF PALEFACE(1952); PRIVATE EYES(1953); SCANDAL AT SCOURIE(1953); SLIGHT CASE OF LARCENY, A(1953); SMALL TOWN GIRL(1953); STORY OF THREE LOVES, THE(1953); WAR OF THE WORLDS, THE(1953); BOWERY BOYS MEET THE MONSTERS, THE(1954); LAY THAT RIFLE DOWN(1955); THREE FOR THE SHOW(1955); GREAT AMERICAN PASTIME, THE(1956); STORM CENTER(1956)

Russell Lee
HOTEL FOR WOMEN(1939); ONCE A THIEF(1965)

Ruta Lee
TWINKLE IN GOD'S EYE, THE(1955); GABY(1956); FUNNY FACE(1957); WITNESS FOR THE PROSECUTION(1957); MARJORIE MORNINGSTAR(1958); OPERATION EICHMANN(1961); SERGEANTS 3(1962); GUN HAWK, THE(1963); HOOTENANNY HOOT(1963); BULLET FOR A BADMAN(1964); DOOMSDAY MACHINE(1967)

Ruth Lee
RICH ARE ALWAYS WITH US, THE(1932); MIDDLETON FAMILY AT THE N.Y. WORLD'S FAIR(1939); BEHIND THE EIGHT BALL(1942); GET HEP TO LOVE(1942); ADVENTURES OF A ROOKIE(1943); GOOD MORNING, JUDGE(1943); HERS TO HOLD(1943); MEXICAN SPITFIRE'S BLESSED EVENT(1943); MOONLIGHT IN VERMONT(1943); RHYTHM OF THE ISLANDS(1943); SHADOW OF A DOUBT(1943); SILVER SKATES(1943); GOIN' TO TOWN(1944); HI BEAUTIFUL(1944); SENSATIONS OF 1945(1944); TUCSON RAIDERS(1944); CORPUS CHRISTI BANDITS(1945); DALTONS RIDE AGAIN, THE(1945); DIVORCE(1945); G.I. HONEYMOON(1945); HERE COME THE CO-EDS(1945); I'LL TELL THE WORLD(1945); KEEP YOUR POWDER DRY(1945); MAMA LOVES PAPA(1945); MAN WHO WALKED ALONE, THE(1945); NAUGHTY NINETIES, THE(1945); ON STAGE EVERYBODY(1945); TOWN WENT WILD, THE(1945); WEEKEND AT THE WALDORF(1945); CUBAN PETE(1946); DARK HORSE, THE(1946); DING DONG WILLIAMS(1946); IDEA GIRL(1946); MAGNIFICENT DOLL(1946); MAGNIFICENT ROGUE, THE(1946); PARTNERS IN TIME(1946);

LARCENY(1948); COVER-UP(1949); HENRY, THE RAINMAKER(1949); IT HAPPENS EVERY SPRING(1949); LADY TAKES A SAILOR, THE(1949); WHIRLPOOL(1949); EYE WITNESS(1950, Brit.); AS YOU WERE(1951); INSURANCE INVESTIGATOR(1951); ON DANGEROUS GROUND(1951); PAYMENT ON DEMAND(1951); WHEN I GROW UP(1951); SKIRTS AHOY!(1952); CRIME WAVE(1954); LONG, LONG TRAILER, THE(1954); HELL'S OUTPOST(1955); HIGH SOCIETY(1956); THESE WILDER YEARS(1956); JET PILOT(1957); WILD IS THE WIND(1957); THREE ON A SPREE(1961, Brit.)

Sam Lee
NO LADY(1931, Brit.); MRS. WIGGS OF THE CABBAGE PATCH(1934); GRACIE ALLEN MURDER CASE(1939); JAMAICA INN(1939, Brit.); NEUTRAL PORT(1941, Brit.); MATTER OF MURDER, A(1949, Brit.), p; SKIPALONG ROSENBLOOM(1951)

Sammy Lee
CHILDREN OF PLEASURE(1930), ch; FREE AND EASY(1930), ch; LADY'S MORALS, A(1930), ch; LORD BYRON OF BROADWAY(1930), ch; LOVE IN THE ROUGH(1930), ch; MEN OF THE NORTH(1930), ch; THEY LEARNED ABOUT WOMEN(1930), ch; THOSE THREE FRENCH GIRLS(1930), ch; WOMAN RACKET, THE(1930), ch; ADORABLE(1933), ch; DANCING LADY(1933), ch; I LOVED YOU WEDNESDAY(1933), ch; IT'S GREAT TO BE ALIVE(1933), ch; LIFE IN THE RAW(1933), ch; MY LIPS BETRAY(1933), ch; I AM SUZANNE(1934), ch; STAND UP AND CHEER(1934 80m FOX bw), ch; TRANSATLANTIC MERRY-GO-ROUND(1934), ch; 365 NIGHTS IN HOLLYWOOD(1934), ch; HOORAY FOR LOVE(1935), ch; CAN THIS BE DIXIE?(1936), ch; KING OF BURLESQUE(1936), ch; STAR FOR A NIGHT(1936), ch; UNDER YOUR SPELL(1936), ch; LIFE OF THE PARTY, THE(1937), ch; NEW FACES OF 1937(1937), ch; HONOLULU(1939), ch; HOUSE ACROSS THE BAY, THE(1940), ch; WASHINGTON MELODRAMA(1941), ch; BORN TO SING(1942), ch; JACKASS MAIL(1942), ch; HIT THE ICE(1943), ch; MEET THE PEOPLE(1944), ch; TWO GIRLS AND A SAILOR(1944), ch; EARL CARROLL'S VANITIES(1945), ch; OUT OF THIS WORLD(1945), ch; ABILENE TOWN(1946), ch

Samuel Lee
LAST EXPRESS, THE(1938)

Sandra Lee
TWO GIRLS AND A SAILOR(1944); IT SHOULD HAPPEN TO YOU(1954); LA DOLCE VITA(1961, Ital./Fr.); PSYCHE 59(1964, Brit.)

Sanford Lee
STUDENT BODY, THE(1976)

Sarah Lee
ODD ANGRY SHOT, THE(1979, Aus.)

Scott Lee
KID FROM AMARILLO, THE(1951); WILD HORSE AMBUSH(1952); SEMINOLE(1953); DAWN AT SOCORRO(1954)

Senor Lee
SWING IT SOLDIER(1941); LITTLEST OUTLAW, THE(1955)

Shariaya Lee
MOONLIGHTING WIVES(1966)

Sharon Lee
SECRETS OF A MODEL(1940); ESCAPE TO BURMA(1955); CHICAGO CONFIDENTIAL(1957); REFORM SCHOOL GIRL(1957); PASSION HOLIDAY(1963); MOTOR PSYCHO(1965); HEART BEAT(1979)

Shaw and Lee
KING OF BURLESQUE(1936)

Sheldon Lee
MIGHTY GORGA, THE(1969); HELL'S BLOODY DEVILS(1970); PSYCHIC KILLER(1975); GETTING OVER(1981)

Soliga Lee
Silents
LOVES OF RICARDO, THE(1926)

Soonjai Lee
YONGKARI MONSTER FROM THE DEEP(1967 S.K.)

Stephen Lee
WARGAMES(1983)
1984
CRIMES OF PASSION(1984); PURPLE HEARTS(1984)

Stuart Lee
BORN AGAIN(1978)

Sung Lee
SAMURAI(1945)

Swim Lee
RETURN OF THE JEDI(1983)

Sylvan Lee
COCOANUTS, THE(1929)

Tammy Lee
WHAT'S THE MATTER WITH HELEN?(1971); UP THE SANDBOX(1972)

Tanya Lee
WHICH WAY IS UP?(1977)

Taras Lee
GLADIATORS, THE(1970, Swed.)

Teri Lee
QUEEN OF BLOOD(1966)

Terry Afton Lee
HARRY'S WAR(1981)

Thelma Lee
VOICES(1979); KING OF COMEDY, THE(1983)

Thomas Lee
GENERAL DIED AT DAWN, THE(1936)

Tim Lee
1984
HEART OF THE STAG(1984, New Zealand)

Timothy Lee
GOODBYE PORK PIE(1981, New Zealand); NATE AND HAYES(1983, U.S./New Zealand)

Tom Lee
MAROC 7(1967, Brit.)

Tommy H. Lee
EXPERIMENT IN TERROR(1962); LAST OF THE SECRET AGENTS?, THE(1966)

Tommy Lee
PACIFIC RENDEZVOUS(1942); REUNION IN FRANCE(1942); FIRST YANK INTO TOKYO(1945); HER HUSBAND'S AFFAIRS(1947); SAIGON(1948); MACAO(1952); SAND PEBBLES, THE(1966); ROOSTER COGBURN(1975)

Tony Lee
GOLDEN NEEDLES(1974)
Tracy Lee
SET, THE(1970, Aus.)
Vanessa Lee
SPLIT, THE(1968)
Venessa Lee
ADVENTURERS, THE(1970)
Vera Lee
HARVEY GIRLS, THE(1946); HOLIDAY RHYTHM(1950)
Vicki Lee
"X"–THE MAN WITH THE X-RAY EYES(1963)
Virginia Lee
PAROLE, INC.(1949); DAUGHTER OF ROSIE O'GRADY, THE(1950); D.O.A.(1950); ROYAL WEDDING(1951); ROBE, THE(1953); FLOWER DRUM SONG(1961); DIMENSION 5(1966)
Silents
LUCK AND PLUCK(1919); OH, JOHNNY(1919); IF WOMEN ONLY KNEW(1921); DESTINY'S ISLE(1922); ADORABLE CHEAT, THE(1928)
Misc. Silents
TERROR, THE(1917); BEYOND THE LAW(1918); SANDY BURKE OF THE U-BAR-U(1919); LOVE OR MONEY(1920); SERVANT QUESTION, THE(1920); WHITE MASKS, THE(1921); BEYOND THE RAINBOW(1922); ROAD TO ARCADY, THE(1922); IT HAPPENED OUT WEST(1923)
Virginia Ann Lee
HAWAIIANS, THE(1970); LOST HORIZON(1973)
Misc. Talkies
CHARLIE CHAN: HAPPINESS IS A WARM CLUE(1971)
Wah Lee
THIRTY SECONDS OVER TOKYO(1944)
Wang Lee
WELCOME DANGER(1929)
Waveney Lee
PASSIONATE SUMMER(1959, Brit.); TOUCH OF LARCENY, A(1960, Brit.); KONGA(1961, Brit.); FLOOD, THE(1963, Brit.)
Weaver Lee
SATAN NEVER SLEEPS(1962)
Wendy Lee
UNSUSPECTED, THE(1947); IT'S A GREAT FEELING(1949); LADY TAKES A SAILOR, THE(1949); I SHOT BILLY THE KID(1950)
Will Lee
BABES ON BROADWAY(1941); BALL OF FIRE(1941); MELODY LANE(1941); WHISTLING IN THE DARK(1941); ALMOST MARRIED(1942); SABOTEUR(1942); BRUTE FORCE(1947); CASBAH(1948); FORCE OF EVIL(1948); LETTER FROM AN UNKNOWN WOMAN(1948); SONG IS BORN, A(1948); LONE WOLF AND HIS LADY, THE(1949); THEY LIVE BY NIGHT(1949); SHAKEDOWN(1950); ST. BENNY THE DIP(1951); NARROW MARGIN, THE(1952); LITTLE FUGITIVE, THE(1953); HIT AND RUN(1982); DANIEL(1983)
Willard Lee
FLOWER DRUM SONG(1961); YOUNG AND THE BRAVE, THE(1963)
William A. Lee
EDGE OF THE CITY(1957)
William E. Lee
SWINGIN' SUMMER, A(1965), ed
Willie Lee
DREAM ON(1981), m
Winston Lee
CALIFORNIA SPLIT(1974)
Woody Lee
DRAGSTRIP GIRL(1957); NOTORIOUS CLEOPATRA, THE(1970); HOW COME NOBODY'S ON OUR SIDE?(1975)
Lee Allen and His Band
SWEET BEAT(1962, Brit.)
Richard Lee-Sung
APPLE DUMPLING GANG, THE(1975)
1984
SLAPSTICK OF ANOTHER KIND(1984)
J. Lee-Thompson
MIDDLE WATCH, THE(1939, Brit.), w; FOR THEM THAT TRESPASS(1949, Brit.), w; NO PLACE FOR JENNIFER(1950, Brit.), w; MURDER WITHOUT CRIME(1951, Brit.), d&w; GOOD COMPANIONS, THE(1957, Brit.), d; DESERT ATTACK(1958, Brit.), d
John Lee-Thompson
PRICE OF FOLLY, THE(1937, Brit.), w
Peter Lee-Thompson
NINTH CONFIGURATION, THE(1980), ed
1984
EVIL THAT MEN DO, THE(1984), ed
Pete Lee-Wilson
REMEMBRANCE(1982, Brit.)
1984
BOUNTY, THE(1984)
Vivienne Leebosh
TICKET TO HEAVEN(1981), p
Mary Pat Leece
NIGHTHAWKS(1978, Brit.), ed
George Leech
PORT AFRIQUE(1956, Brit.); COAST OF SKELETONS(1965, Brit.); MOZAMBIQUE(1966, Brit.); KISS THE GIRLS AND MAKE THEM DIE(1967, U.S./Ital.); ON HER MAJESTY'S SECRET SERVICE(1969, Brit.), stunts; PINK PANTHER STRIKES AGAIN, THE(1976, Brit.); WILD GEESE, THE(1978, Brit.)
Georgina Leech
NORAH O'NEALE(1934, Brit.)
Richard Leech
TEMPTRESS, THE(1949, Brit.); LEASE OF LIFE(1954, Brit.); PRISONER, THE(1955, Brit.); BATTLE HELL(1956, Brit.); GENTLE TOUCH, THE(1956, Brit.); GOOD COMPANIONS, THE(1957, Brit.); THIRD KEY, THE(1957, Brit.); TIME WITHOUT PITY(1957, Brit.); CURSE OF THE DEMON(1958); DANGEROUS YOUTH(1958, Brit.); DESERT ATTACK(1958, Brit.); DUBLIN NIGHTMARE(1958, Brit.); IT'S NEVER TOO LATE(1958, Brit.); LADY MISLAID, A(1958, Brit.); MOONRAKER, THE(1958, Brit.);

NIGHT TO REMEMBER, A(1958, Brit.); WIND CANNOT READ, THE(1958, Brit.); TUNES OF GLORY(1960, Brit.); TERROR OF THE TONGS, THE(1961, Brit.); I THANK A FOOL(1962, Brit.); WAR LOVER, THE(1962, U.S./Brit.); FLOOD, THE(1963, Brit.); WALK A TIGHTROPE(1964, U.S./Brit.); YOUNG AND WILLING(1964, Brit.); LIFE AT THE TOP(1965, Brit.); FIGHTING PRINCE OF DONEGAL, THE(1966, Brit.); RICOCHET(1966, Brit.); YOUNG WINSTON(1972, Brit.)
1984
CHAMPIONS(1984)
William K. Leech
GOING HOME(1971)
Alan Leeds
1984
PURPLE RAIN(1984)
Andrea Leeds
DANTE'S INFERNO(1935); COME AND GET IT(1936); MOON'S OUR HOME, THE(1936); IT COULD HAPPEN TO YOU(1937); STAGE DOOR(1937); GOLDWYN FOLLIES, THE(1938); LETTER OF INTRODUCTION(1938); YOUTH TAKES A FLING(1938); REAL GLORY, THE(1939); SWANEE RIVER(1939); THEY SHALL HAVE MUSIC(1939); EARTHBOUND(1940)
Charles Leeds
TWENTY QUESTIONS MURDER MYSTERY, THE(1950, Brit.), w; MASTER PLAN, THE(1955, Brit.), p; GUILTY?(1956, Brit.), p; SHADOW OF FEAR(1956, Brit.), p; MAN IN THE ROAD, THE(1957, Brit.), p; NO ROAD BACK(1957, Brit.), p, w; SURGEON'S KNIFE, THE(1957, Brit.), p; MENACE IN THE NIGHT(1958, Brit.), p; CROWNING TOUCH, THE(1959, Brit.), p; MURDER AT SITE THREE(1959, Brit.), p; LIES MY FATHER TOLD ME(1960, Brit.), p; FOLLOW THAT MAN(1961, Brit.), p; TICKET TO PARADISE(1961, Brit.), p; FREEDOM TO DIE(1962, Brit.), p; IN TROUBLE WITH EVE(1964, Brit.), prod d
David Leeds
Misc. Talkies
SHOOT THE SUN DOWN(1981), d
Dorothy Leeds
Silents
BURN 'EM UP BARNES(1921)
Elissa Leeds
EARTHBOUND(1981)
1984
WOMAN IN RED, THE(1984)
Herbert I. Leeds
ARIZONA WILDCAT(1938), d; FIVE OF A KIND(1938), d; ISLAND IN THE SKY(1938), d; KEEP SMILING(1938), d; LOVE ON A BUDGET(1938), d; CHARLIE CHAN IN THE CITY OF DARKNESS(1939), d; CHICKEN WAGON FAMILY(1939), d; CISCO KID AND THE LADY, THE(1939), d; MR. MOTO IN DANGER ISLAND(1939), d; RETURN OF THE CISCO KID(1939), d; YESTERDAY'S HEROES(1940), d; BLUE, WHITE, AND PERFECT(1941), d; RIDE ON VAQUERO(1941), d; ROMANCE OF THE RIO GRANDE(1941), d; JUST OFF BROADWAY(1942), d; MAN WHO WOULDN'T DIE, THE(1942), d; MANILA CALLING(1942), d; TIME TO KILL(1942), d; IT SHOULDN'T HAPPEN TO A DOG(1946), d; LET'S LIVE AGAIN(1948), d; BUNCO SQUAD(1950), d; FATHER'S WILD GAME(1950), d
Howard Leeds
SHERLOCK HOLMES(1932); VANESSA, HER LOVE STORY(1935)
Lila Leeds
SHOW-OFF, THE(1946); LADY IN THE LAKE(1947); MOONRISE(1948); WILD WEED(1949)
Misc. Talkies
SHE SHOULD HAVE SAID NO(1949)
Linda Leeds
YOU BETTER WATCH OUT(1980), ed
1984
CITY GIRL, THE(1984), ed
Marion Leeds
NAKED CITY, THE(1948); BUTTERFIELD 8(1960)
Max Leeds
IT'S IN THE BLOOD(1938, Brit.)
Maxine Leeds
SUDAN(1945)
Meredith Leeds
LIFE OF HER OWN, A(1950); BELLE OF NEW YORK, THE(1952)
Nancy Leeds
Misc. Silents
HUMAN TORNADO, THE(1925)
Peter Leeds
PUBLIC ENEMIES(1941); LADY BODYGUARD(1942); REUNION IN FRANCE(1942); TREAT EM' ROUGH(1942); LADY GAMBLES, THE(1949); MA AND PA KETTLE GO TO TOWN(1950); SADDLE TRAMP(1950); FROGMEN, THE(1951); KATIE DID IT(1951); MA AND PA KETTLE BACK ON THE FARM(1951); STALAG 17(1953); 99 RIVER STREET(1953); ATOMIC KID, THE(1954); LAST TIME I SAW PARIS, THE(1954); LONG, LONG TRAILER, THE(1954); BOBBY WARE IS MISSING(1955); I'LL CRY TOMORROW(1955); INTERRUPTED MELODY(1955); IT'S ALWAYS FAIR WEATHER(1955); LOVE ME OR LEAVE ME(1955); SIX BRIDGES TO CROSS(1955); TIGHT SPOT(1955); BEHIND THE HIGH WALL(1956); TEA AND SYMPATHY(1956); KISS THEM FOR ME(1957); GIRLS' TOWN(1959); ROOKIE, THE(1959); THIRTY FOOT BRIDE OF CANDY ROCK, THE(1959); FACTS OF LIFE, THE(1960); PLEASE DON'T EAT THE DAISIES(1960); SCARFACE MOB, THE(1962); WHEELER DEALERS, THE(1963); HARLOW(1965); OSCAR, THE(1966); EIGHT ON THE LAM(1967); WITH SIX YOU GET EGGROLL(1968)
Phil Leeds
ROSEMARY'S BABY(1968); DON'T DRINK THE WATER(1969); WON TON TON, THE DOG WHO SAVED HOLLYWOOD(1976); HISTORY OF THE WORLD, PART 1(1981)
Robert Leeds
KING OF THE GAMBLERS(1948), ed; FLAME OF YOUTH(1949), ed; ARMORED CAR ROBBERY(1950), w; LAST TIME I SAW ARCHIE, THE(1961), ed
Robert L. Leeds
DRAGNET(1954), ed
Robert M. Leeds
POWDER RIVER RUSTLERS(1949), ed; FRISCO TORNADO(1950), ed; MISSOURIANS, THE(1950), ed; PIONEER MARSHAL(1950), ed; RUSTLERS ON HORSEBACK(1950), ed; TARNISHED(1950), ed; UNMASKED(1950), ed; VIGILANTE HIDEOUT(1950), ed; MILLION DOLLAR PURSUIT(1951), ed; RODEO KING

AND THE SENORITA(1951), ed; SILVER CITY BONANZA(1951), ed; STORM-BOUND(1951, Ital.), ed; CAPTIVE OF BILLY THE KID(1952), ed; LEADVILLE GUNSLINGER(1952), ed; BREAKDOWN(1953), ed; PETE KELLY'S BLUES(1955), ed; D.I., THE(1957), ed; -30-(1959), ed

Robert W. Leeds
WELLS FARGO GUNMASTER(1951), ed

Thelma Leeds
FOLLOW THE FLEET(1936); NEW FACES OF 1937(1937); TOAST OF NEW YORK, THE(1937); MODERN ROMANCE(1981)

Glenn Leedy
SONG OF THE SOUTH(1946)

Dan Leegant
ESCAPE FROM ALCATRAZ(1979); PROMISE, THE(1979)
1984
SIGNAL 7(1984)

Daniel Leegant
TIME AFTER TIME(1979, Brit.)

Tiiu Leek
WHY ROCK THE BOAT?(1974, Can.); STARSHIP INVASIONS(1978, Can.)
1984
COVERGIRL(1984, Can.); MICKI AND MAUDE(1984)

Leelabhai
HEAT AND DUST(1983, Brit.)

Rene Leeland
WILD, FREE AND HUNGRY(1970)

Dicky Leeman
DATE WITH A DREAM, A(1948, Brit.), d, w

Garry Leeman
STRANGE AFFECTION(1959, Brit.)

Paulette Leeman
COUNTRY BOY(1966)

Peter Leeming
SLIPPER AND THE ROSE, THE(1976, Brit.)

Roger Leenhardt
LES DERNIERES VACANCES(1947, Fr.), d, w; MIDNIGHT MEETING(1962, Fr.), d, w; MARRIED WOMAN, THE(1965, Fr.); MAN WHO LOVED WOMEN, THE(1977, Fr.)

Grant Leenhouts
NO MORE WOMEN(1934), w

Evenda Leeper
PUFNSTUF(1970), puppeteer

Preben Leerdorff-Rye
1984
ELEMENT OF CRIME, THE(1984, Den.)

Carol Lees
MANNEQUIN(1933, Brit.); LAST WORD, THE(1979), m

Freddie Lees
HORROR HOUSE(1970, Brit.)

Ginger Lees
MONEY FOR SPEED(1933, Brit.); DAREDEVILS OF EARTH(1936, Brit.)

Hannah Lees
SHADOW ON THE WALL(1950), w

John Lees
GREAT GAME, THE(1930), w; FLASH GORDON(1980)

Michael Lees
WHISTLE DOWN THE WIND(1961, Brit.); SEANCE ON A WET AFTERNOON(1964 Brit.); KING RAT(1965); WRONG BOX, THE(1966, Brit.); WHISPERERS, THE(1967, Brit.); LONG AGO, TOMORROW(1971, Brit.); GIRO CITY(1982, Brit.)

Paul Lees
O.S.S.(1946); SUDDENLY IT'S SPRING(1947); BEYOND GLORY(1948); SEALED VERDICT(1948); CHICAGO DEADLINE(1949); HEIRESS, THE(1949); RED, HOT AND BLUE(1949); SORROWFUL JONES(1949); CAPTAIN CAREY, U.S.A(1950); COPPER CANYON(1950); GREAT MISSOURI RAID, THE(1950); MY FRIEND IRMA GOES WEST(1950); UNION STATION(1950); APPOINTMENT WITH DANGER(1951); HALLS OF MONTEZUMA(1951); PEOPLE WILL TALK(1951); WARPATH(1951)

Robert Lees
STREET OF MEMORIES(1940), w; BACHELOR DADDY(1941), w; BLACK CAT, THE(1941), w; HOLD THAT GHOST(1941), w; INVISIBLE WOMAN, THE(1941), w; JUKE BOX JENNY(1942), w; CRAZY HOUSE(1943), w; HIT THE ICE(1943), w; NO TIME FOR LOVE(1943), w; BUCK PRIVATES COME HOME(1947), w; WISTFUL WIDOW OF WAGON GAP, THE(1947), w; ABBOTT AND COSTELLO MEET FRANKENSTEIN(1948), w; HOLIDAY IN HAVANA(1949), w; ABBOTT AND COSTELLO MEET THE INVISIBLE MAN(1951), w; COMIN' ROUND THE MOUNTAIN(1951), w; JUMPING JACKS(1952), w

Tamara Lees
MARRY ME!(1949, Brit.); TAMING OF DOROTHY, THE(1950, Brit.); WHILE THE SUN SHINES(1950, Brit.); VERGINITA(1953, Ital.); FOUR WAYS OUT(1954, Ital.); QUEEN OF BABYLON, THE(1956, Ital.)

William Lees
Silents
SMASHING THROUGH(1928, Brit.), w

Antoinette Lees [Andrea Leeds]
SONG OF THE TRAIL(1936)

Elizabeth Leese
FORBIDDEN JOURNEY(1950, Can.)

Leeser
M(1933, Ger.)

Lois Leeson
MOLLY AND ME(1929), w; BRIGHT LIGHTS(1935), w
Silents
JOANNA(1925), w

Michael Leeson
SURVIVORS, THE(1983), w

Marjorie Leet
BIG TRAIL, THE(1930)

Tom Leetch
APPLE DUMPLING GANG RIDES AGAIN, THE(1979), p; NORTH AVENUE IRREGULARS, THE(1979), p; NIGHT CROSSING(1982), p

Carole Leete
MAN TO REMEMBER, A(1938)

Jack Leewood
HOLIDAY RHYTHM(1950), p; THUNDERING JETS(1958), p; ALLIGATOR PEOPLE, THE(1959), p; LITTLE SAVAGE, THE(1959), p; LONE TEXAN(1959), p; THIRTEEN FIGHTING MEN(1960), p; YOUNG JESSE JAMES(1960), p; 20,000 EYES(1961), p&d; SWINGIN' ALONG(1962), p; THUNDER ISLAND(1963), p&d

John Leezer
Silents
I'LL GET HIM YET(1919), ph; NUGGET NELL(1919), ph; JUST LIKE A WOMAN(1923), ph; OUT OF THE WEST(1926), ph; TOM AND HIS PALS(1926), ph

John W. Leezer
Silents
ACQUITTED(1916), ph; HELL-TO-PAY AUSTIN(1916), ph

Eleanor LeFaber
HOUSE OF USHER(1960)

Pierre Lefait
1984
L'ARGENT(1984, Fr./Switz.), art d, set d

Sheridan LeFanu
BLOOD AND ROSES(1961, Fr./Ital.), d&w

Andre Lefaur
ENTENTE CORDIALE(1939, Fr.); WITH A SMILE(1939, Fr.)

Charles Lefaux
CONQUEST OF THE AIR(1940)

Jean Lefaux
1984
THREE CROWNS OF THE SAILOR(1984, Fr.), p

Charles Lefeaux
LADY IN DANGER(1934, Brit.); BREAK THE NEWS(1938, Brit.); RETURN OF THE FROG, THE(1938, Brit.); SAVE A LITTLE SUNSHINE(1938, Brit.); YOU WILL REMEMBER(1941, Brit.)

Hans Lefebre
MARTIN LUTHER(1953)

Annie Lefebure
ARMY GAME, THE(1963, Fr.)

G. Lefebure
LA MARSEILLAISE(1938, Fr.)

Jean Lefebure
HIGHWAY PICKUP(1965, Fr./Ital.)

Jean Lefebvre
AND GOD CREATED WOMAN(1957, Fr.); BACK TO THE WALL(1959, Fr.); PORT OF DESIRE(1960, Fr.); GIGOT(1962); OF FLESH AND BLOOD(1964, Fr./Ital.); COUNTERFEIT CONSTABLE, THE(1966, Fr.); GENDARME OF ST. TROPEZ, THE(1966, Fr./Ital.); SLEEPING CAR MURDER THE(1966, Fr.); SUCKER, THE(1966, Fr./Ital.); MADMAN OF LAB 4, THE(1967, Fr.); BLUEBEARD(1972); TREASURE ISLAND(1972, Brit./Span./Fr./Ger.); MAGNIFICENT ONE, THE(1974, Fr./Ital.); SOME LIKE IT COOL(1979, Ger./Aust./Ital./Fr.)

Rene Lefebvre
MILLION, THE(1931, Fr.); LIGHT ACROSSS THE STREET, THE(1957, Fr.), w

Robert LeFebvre
LIFE AND LOVES OF BEETHOVEN, THE(1937, Fr.), ph; THREE HOURS(1944, Fr.), ph; FRIEND WILL COME TONIGHT, A(1948, Fr.), ph; ROYAL AFFAIR, A(1950), ph; EDWARD AND CAROLINE(1952, Fr.), ph; COME DANCE WITH ME(1960, Fr.), ph; LOVE AND THE FRENCHWOMAN(1961, Fr.), ph; DEADLY DECOYS, THE(1962, Fr.), ph; DOUBLE BED, THE(1965, Fr./Ital.), ph; FRIEND OF THE FAMILY(1965, Fr./Ital.), ph; HEAT OF MIDNIGHT(1966, Fr.), ph

Rolf Lefebvre
PAPER ORCHID(1949, Brit.); COUNT FIVE AND DIE(1958, Brit.); HAPPY IS THE BRIDE(1958, Brit.)

Yves Lefebvre
MARRIAGE CAME TUMBLING DOWN, THE(1968, Fr.); SECRET WORLD(1969, Fr.); MISTER FREEDOM(1970, Fr.); SICILIAN CLAN, THE(1970, Fr.)

Guy Lefeuve
BONNIE PRINCE CHARLIE(1948, Brit.)

Robert Lefevbre
DAUGHTERS OF DESTINY(1954, Fr./Ital.), ph; CANDIDE(1962, Fr.), ph

Rick LeFevour
ON THE RIGHT TRACK(1981)
1984
SIXTEEN CANDLES(1984)

LeFevre
KISS OF FIRE, THE(1940, Fr.), ph

Adam LeFevre
RETURN OF THE SECAUCUS SEVEN(1980)
1984
RECKLESS(1984)

Jim LeFevre
RIOT ON SUNSET STRIP(1967)

Louis Lefevre
L'ATALANTE(1947, Fr.)

Marjorie Lefevre, R.N.
NOT AS A STRANGER(1955), tech adv

Ned LeFevre
JOKER IS WILD, THE(1957)

Pierre Lefevre
MARTIN LUTHER(1953); FOREVER MY HEART(1954, Brit.)

Raymond Lefevre
GENDARME OF ST. TROPEZ, THE(1966, Fr./Ital.), m

Rene Lefevre
CRIME OF MONSIEUR LANGE, THE(1936, Fr.); THEY ARE NOT ANGELS(1948, Fr.); GORILLA GREETS YOU, THE(1958, Fr.); FINGERMAN, THE(1963, Fr.); DOULOS–THE FINGER MAN(1964, Fr./Ital.)

Abraham Leff
WHERE IS MY CHILD?(1937), p

Elva Leff
AUTHOR! AUTHOR!(1982)

Henry Leff
TAKE THE MONEY AND RUN(1969); STRAWBERRY STATEMENT, THE(1970); ONE IS A LONELY NUMBER(1972)
George Lefferts
MEAN DOG BLUES(1978), p
Jean Lefferty
Silents
MATINEE LADIES(1927); WHAT HAPPENED TO FATHER(1927)
Gary Leffew
J.W. COOP(1971)
Robert Leffingwell
GULLIVER'S TRAVELS(1939), anim d
Tom Leffingwell
STRANGE MR. GREGORY, THE(1945); HOODLUM SAINT, THE(1946); BUFFALO BILL RIDES AGAIN(1947); JOAN OF ARC(1948)
John Leffler
PAPERBACK HERO(1973, Can.)
Mark Leffler
FRATERNITY ROW(1977)
Camille Lefko
TEMPEST(1982)
Sonia Lefkova
DEVOTION(1946)
Nancy Lefkowith
HAIR(1979)
Ann Lefkowitz
LORDS OF FLATBUSH, THE(1974)
John Lefkowitz
HURRY UP OR I'LL BE 30(1973)
Luc Leflaquais
STRANGE SHADOWS IN AN EMPTY ROOM(1977, Can./Ital.), cos
Velma Lefler
Misc. Silents
HEART OF PAULA, THE(1916)
Joe LeFlore
1984
LOVE STREAMS(1984)
Julius Leflore
NIGHT SHIFT(1982)
Jonothan Leford
HIGH YELLOW(1965)
Nathalie LeForet
BLOOD AND ROSES(1961, Fr./Ital.)
Guy LeFranc
KNOCK(1955, Fr.), d, w; WOMAN OF SIN(1961, Fr.), d, w; ELUSIVE CORPORAL, THE(1963, Fr.), w
Jacques Lefrancois
ANOTHER MAN, ANOTHER CHANCE(1977 Fr/US), ph
Capt. W.S. LeFrancois
GUNG HO!(1943), w. Lucien Hubbard
Arthur Left
COLORADO(1940)
Abe Lefton
MELODY TRAIL(1935); OLD CORRAL, THE(1937)
Sue Lefton
TESS(1980, Fr./Brit.), ch
Alex Leftwich
JUAREZ(1939)
Alexander Leftwich
LIFE OF EMILE ZOLA, THE(1937); WAIKIKI WEDDING(1937); MIDNIGHT INTRUDER(1938); PRISON TRAIN(1938); RECKLESS LIVING(1938); ZAZA(1939); MELODY FOR THREE(1941); OUT OF THE FOG(1941); WOMAN'S FACE(1941)
Ed Leftwich
SQUAD CAR(1961), p&d
Ruby Leftwich
HUCKLEBERRY FINN(1974)
Alexander Leftwitch
DARK VICTORY(1939)
Lefty
LOOKING UP(1977)
Lefty Wild Eagle
1984
SACRED GROUND(1984)
Augusto Lega
UP THE MACGREGORS(1967, Ital./Span.), art d
Ernest Legal
INTERMEZZO(1937, Ger.)
Ernst Legal
LIFE BEGINS ANEW(1938, Ger.); DAY WILL COME, A(1960, Ger.)
Eva LeGallienne
RESURRECTION(1980)
Oliva Legare
LUCK OF GINGER COFFEY, THE(1964, U.S./Can.)
Ovila Legare
THIRTEENTH LETTER, THE(1951); I CONFESS(1953)
Ken Legarguant
SNOW(1983, Fr.), p
Romaine Legarguant
SNOW(1983, Fr.), p
Catherine Legault
1984
A NOS AMOURS(1984, Fr.), ed
Lance LeGault
ROUSTABOUT(1964); FRENCH QUARTER(1978); AMY(1981); STRIPES(1981)
Marc Legault
ONE MAN(1979, Can.)
Gilbert Legay
STUDENT PRINCE, THE(1954)

Sheila LeGay
CANYON OF MISSING MEN, THE(1930)
Johnny Legend
MY BREAKFAST WITH BLASSIE(1983), w,p&d, ed
Alain Legendre
MY UNCLE ANTOINE(1971, Can.)
Claude Leger
LUCKY STAR, THE(1980, Can.), p; ODYSSEY OF THE PACIFIC(1983, Can./Fr.), p
Fernand Leger
DREAMS THAT MONEY CAN BUY(1948), w
Guy Leger
MY NIGHT AT MAUD'S(1970, Fr.)
Jack Alain Leger
MY FIRST LOVE(1978, Fr.), w; MONSIGNOR(1982), w
Lucy Leger
OPEN ROAD, THE(1940, Fr.)
J. Gordon Legg
FANTASIA(1940), art d
Stuart Legg
Misc. Silents
VARSITY(1930, Brit.), d
Alison Leggart
THIS HAPPY BREED(1944, Brit.)
Alison Leggatt
NINE TILL SIX(1932, Brit.); BOY, A GIRL AND A BIKE, A(1949 Brit.); MARRY ME!(1949, Brit.); WATERLOO ROAD(1949, Brit.); MINIVER STORY, THE(1950, Brit./U.S.); ENCORE(1951, Brit.); PROMOTER, THE(1952, Brit.); NOOSE FOR A LADY(1953, Brit.); LIGHT TOUCH, THE(1955, Brit.); WOMAN POSSESSED, A(1958, Brit.); NEVER TAKE CANDY FROM A STRANGER(1961, Brit.); DAY OF THE TRIFFIDS, THE(1963); NOTHING BUT THE BEST(1964, Brit.); ONE WAY PENDULUM(1965, Brit.); FAR FROM THE MADDING CROWD(1967, Brit.); GOODBYE MR. CHIPS(1969, U.S./Brit.); HIRELING, THE(1973, Brit.); SEVEN-PER-CENT SOLUTION, THE(1977, Brit.)
Wg. Cdr. Claire Legge
BATTLE OF BRITAIN, THE(1969, Brit.), tech adv
David Legge
Misc. Talkies
SUNSHINE RUN(1979)
Janette Legge
HIDING PLACE, THE(1975)
Misc. Talkies
BEGGING THE RING(1979, Brit.)
Joan Legge
Silents
IF THOU WERT BLIND(1917, Brit.); ALL THE SAD WORLD NEEDS(1918, Brit.); ONCE UPON A TIME(1918, Brit.)
Misc. Silents
BLACKMAILERS, THE(1915, Brit.); WHEEL OF DEATH, THE(1916, Brit.); HAPPY WARRIOR, THE(1917, Brit.); SPLENDID COWARD, THE(1918, Brit.); TURF CONSPIRACY, A(1918, Brit.)
Arthur Legge-Willis
SECRETS OF CHINATOWN(1935)
Geoffrey Leggett
RAILWAY CHILDREN, THE(1971, Brit.), set d
Ronnie Leggett
CONRACK(1974)
Alfredo Legggi
HAWKS AND THE SPARROWS, THE(1967, Ital.)
Darling Legitimus
EGLANTINE(1972, Fr.)
1984
SUGAR CANE ALLEY(1984, Fr.)
Michael LeGlaire
IN THE HEAT OF THE NIGHT(1967)
Steve Legler
HOWLING, THE(1981), set d
Steven Legler
1984
CHOOSE ME(1984), prod d, art d; HOUSE WHERE DEATH LIVES, THE(1984), art d
Steven G. Legler
HELL NIGHT(1981), art d
Charles Legneur
THEY GOT ME COVERED(1943); WHERE THERE'S LIFE(1947)
Jani LeGon
BAHAMA PASSAGE(1941)
Jeni LeGon
HOORAY FOR LOVE(1935); FOOLS FOR SCANDAL(1938); I CAN'T GIVE YOU ANYTHING BUT LOVE, BABY(1940); I WALKED WITH A ZOMBIE(1943); EASTER PARADE(1948)
Misc. Talkies
DOUBLE DEAL(1939); WHILE THOUSANDS CHEER(1940)
Sarah Legor
NORSEMAN, THE(1978), ed
Claude LeGors
LA NUIT DE VARENNES(1983, Fr./Ital.)
Vladimir Legoshin
MILITARY SECRET(1945, USSR), d
E. Legouve
DEVIL MAY CARE(1929), w
Andre Legrand
SECRET DOCUMENT – VIENNA(1954, Fr.), w
Christiane Legrand
YOUNG GIRLS OF ROCHEFORT, THE(1968, Fr.)
Gaelle Legrand
COUSINS IN LOVE(1982)
H.A. Legrand
SYMPHONIE FANTASTIQUE(1947, Fr.), w

Lucienne Legrand
LITTLE ROMANCE, A(1979, U.S./Fr.)
Martha Legrand
GAMES MEN PLAY, THE(1968, Arg.)
Michel Legrand
CLEO FROM 5 TO 7(1961, Fr.), a, m, m; LOLA(1961, Fr./Ital.), m; WOMAN IS A WOMAN, A(1961, Fr./Ital.), m; COUNTERFEITERS OF PARIS, THE(1962, Fr., Ital.), m; EVA(1962, Fr./Ital.), m; SEVEN CAPITAL SINS(1962, Fr./Ital.), m; FRENCH GAME, THE(1963, Fr.), m; LOVE IS A BALL(1963), m; MY LIFE TO LIVE(1963, Fr.), m; BAY OF ANGELS(1964, Fr.), m; UMBRELLAS OF CHERBOURG, THE(1964, Fr./Ger.), m, md; BAND OF OUTSIDERS(1966, Fr.), m; PLASTIC DOME OF NORMA JEAN, THE(1966), m, md; RAVISHING IDIOT, A(1966, Ital./Fr.), m; LA VIE DE CHATEAU(1967, Fr.), m; TENDER SCOUNDREL(1967, Fr./Ital.), m; HOW TO SAVE A MARRIAGE–AND RUIN YOUR LIFE(1968), m; ICE STATION ZEBRA(1968), m, md; MATTER OF INNOCENCE, A(1968, Brit.), m; OLDEST PROFESSION, THE(1968, Fr./Ital./Ger.), m; SWEET NOVEMBER(1968), m; THOMAS CROWN AFFAIR, THE(1968), m; YOUNG GIRLS OF ROCHEFORT, THE(1968, Fr.), m; CASTLE KEEP(1969), m; HAPPY ENDING, THE(1969), m; PLAY DIRTY(1969, Brit.), m; LADY IN THE CAR WITH GLASSES AND A GUN, THE(1970, U.S./Fr.), m, md; PIECES OF DREAMS(1970), m; WUTHERING HEIGHTS(1970, Brit.), m; GO-BETWEEN, THE(1971, Brit.), m; LE MANS(1971), m; SUMMER OF '42(1971), m, md; TIME FOR LOVING, A(1971, Brit.), m; LADY SINGS THE BLUES(1972), m; ONE IS A LONELY NUMBER(1972), m, md; PORTNOY'S COMPLAINT(1972), m, md; BREEZY(1973), m; COPS AND ROBBERS(1973), m; DOLL'S HOUSE, A(1973, Brit.), m; FORTY CARATS(1973), m; IMPOSSIBLE OBJECT(1973, Fr.), m; NELSON AFFAIR, THE(1973, Brit.), m; OUTSIDE MAN, THE(1973, U.S./Fr.), m; OUR TIME(1974), m; THREE MUSKETEERS, THE(1974, Panama), m; DONKEY SKIN(1975, Fr.), m; FOUR MUSKETEERS, THE(1975, Fr.), m; SAVAGE, THE(1975, Fr.), m; SHEILA LEVINE IS DEAD AND LIVING IN NEW YORK(1975), m; GABLE AND LOMBARD(1976), m; ODE TO BILLY JOE(1976), m; GULLIVER'S TRAVELS(1977, Brit., Bel.), m;OTHER SIDE OF MIDNIGHT, THE(1977), m; LADY OSCAR(1979, Fr./Jap.), m; FALLING IN LOVE AGAIN(1980), m; HINOTORI(1980, Jap.), m; HUNTER, THE(1980), m; MOUNTAIN MEN, THE(1980), m; ATLANTIC CITY(1981, U.S./Can.), m; BEST FRIENDS(1982), m; BOLERO(1982, Fr.), m; GIFT, THE(1983, Fr./Ital.), m; NEVER SAY NEVER AGAIN(1983), m; YENTL(1983), m
1984
LOVE IN GERMANY, A(1984, Fr./Ger.), m; SECRET PLACES(1984, Brit.), m; SMURFS AND THE MAGIC FLUTE, THE(1984, Fr./Belg.), m
Raymond Legrand
MOST WANTED MAN, THE(1962, Fr./Ital.), m
Richard LeGrand
GILDERSLEEVE ON BROADWAY(1943); GILDERSLEEVE'S BAD DAY(1943); GILDERSLEEVE'S GHOST(1944)
Georges Legrande
RUY BLAS(1948, Fr.), p
Valerie Legrange
CAT AND MOUSE(1978, Fr.)
Jacques Legras
LA BELLE AMERICAINE(1961, Fr.); PEEK-A-BOO(1961, Fr.); LADY L(1965, Fr./Ital.); COUNTERFEIT CONSTABLE, THE(1966, Fr.); LADY IN THE CAR WITH GLASSES AND A GUN, THE(1970, U.S./Fr.)
Josephine LeGrice
Misc. Talkies
BLACK BIRD DESCENDING: TENSE ALIGNMENT(1977)
Malcolm LeGrice
Misc. Talkies
BLACK BIRD DESCENDING: TENSE ALIGNMENT(1977), d
R. Legris
UTOPIA(1952, Fr./Ital.)
Roger Legris
COURRIER SUD(1937, Fr.); PEPE LE MOKO(1937, Fr.); UN CARNET DE BAL(1938, Fr.); THREE HOURS(1944, Fr.); THANK HEAVEN FOR SMALL FAVORS(1965, Fr.)
Claude Legros
BLACK AND WHITE IN COLOR(1976, Fr.)
Guillaume LeGuellec
ENTRE NOUS(1983, Fr.)
George LeGuere
MEN WITHOUT WOMEN(1930)
Silents
ONE MILLION DOLLARS(1915)
Misc. Silents
BACHELOR'S ROMANCE, THE(1915); ONE MILLION DOLLARS(1915); SOUL OF A WOMAN, THE(1915)
Jonathan Lehan
HUMANOIDS FROM THE DEEP(1980)
Bertha Lehar
LOS PLATILLOS VOLADORES(1955, Mex.); LAST REBEL, THE(1961, Mex.)
Franz Lehar
ROGUE SONG, THE(1930), w; WHERE IS THIS LADY?(1932, Brit.), m; MERRY WIDOW, THE(1934), w, m; DREAMS COME TRUE(1936, Brit.), w, m; MERRY WIDOW, THE(1952), w, m
Silents
MERRY WIDOW, THE(1925), w
Zvi Lehat
JESUS CHRIST, SUPERSTAR(1973)
Alain LeHenry
COCKTAIL MOLOTOV(1980, Fr.), w
Gene Lehfeldt
MIDNIGHT MAN, THE(1974)
1984
KILLPOINT(1984), stunts
Al Lehman
WHY WOULD I LIE(1980), cos
Ari Lehman
FRIDAY THE 13TH(1980)
Augie Lehman
FALL GUY(1947), spec eff

Beatrix Lehman
RAT, THE(1938, Brit.)
Claude Lehman
DARK EYES(1938, Fr.)
Ernest Lehman
INSIDE STORY, THE(1948), w; EXECUTIVE SUITE(1954), w; SABRINA(1954), w; KING AND I, THE(1956), w; SOMEBODY UP THERE LIKES ME(1956), w; SWEET SMELL OF SUCCESS(1957), w; NORTH BY NORTHWEST(1959), w; FROM THE TERRACE(1960), w; WEST SIDE STORY(1961), w; PRIZE, THE(1963), w; SOUND OF MUSIC, THE(1965), w; WHO'S AFRAID OF VIRGINIA WOOLF?(1966), p, w; HELLO, DOLLY!(1969), p&w; PORTNOY'S COMPLAINT(1972), p, d&w; FAMILY PLOT(1976), w; BLACK SUNDAY(1977), w
Eunice Lehman
BIRCH INTERVAL(1976)
Gladys Lehman
BROADWAY HOOFER, THE(1929), w; CLEAR THE DECKS(1929), w; FALL OF EVE, THE(1929), w; HIS LUCKY DAY(1929), w; MEXICALI ROSE(1929), w; RED HOT SPEED ½(1929), w; CAT CREEPS, THE(1930), w; EMBARRASSING MOMENTS(1930), w; LADY SURRENDERS, A(1930), w; LITTLE ACCIDENT(1930), w; PERSONALITY(1930), w; MANY A SLIP(1931), w; SEED(1931), w; STRICTLY DISHONORABLE(1931), w; NICE WOMAN(1932), w; HOLD ME TIGHT(1933), w; THEY JUST HAD TO GET MARRIED(1933), w; WHITE WOMAN(1933), w; DEATH TAKES A HOLIDAY(1934), w; DOUBLE DOOR(1934), w; LITTLE MISS MARKER(1934), w; CAPTAIN JANUARY(1935), w; COUNTY CHAIRMAN, THE(1935), w; ENTER MADAME(1935), w; IN OLD KENTUCKY(1935), w; IT'S A SMALL WORLD(1935), w; MESSAGE TO GARCIA, A(1936), w; POOR LITTLE RICH GIRL(1936), w; REUNION(1936), w; MIDNIGHT MADONNA(1937), w; SLAVE SHIP(1937), w; LADY OBJECTS, THE(1938), w; SHE MARRIED AN ARTIST(1938), w; THERE'S ALWAYS A WOMAN(1938), w; THERE'S THAT WOMAN AGAIN(1938), w; BLONDIE BRINGS UP BABY(1939), w; GOOD GIRLS GO TO PARIS(1939), w; HIRED WIFE(1940), w; HER FIRST BEAU(1941), w; NICE GIRL?(1941), w; RIO RITA(1942), w; PRESENTING LILY MARS(1943), w; TWO GIRLS AND A SAILOR(1944), w; HER HIGHNESS AND THE BELLBOY(1945), w; THRILL OF A ROMANCE(1945), w; THIS TIME FOR KEEPS(1947), w; LUXURY LINER(1948), w; SORROWFUL JONES(1949), w; GOLDEN GIRL(1951), w
Silents
ICE FLOOD, THE(1926), w; OUT ALL NIGHT(1927), w; SHIELD OF HONOR, THE(1927), w
Lew Lehman
KING SOLOMON'S TREASURE(1978, Can.), m; PHOBIA(1980, Can.), w
Misc. Talkies
PIT, THE(1984), d
Lillian Lehman
SEVEN MINUTES, THE(1971)
Louis Lehman
Misc. Talkies
SOUTH OF HELL MOUNTAIN(1971), d
Maurice Lehman
PASTEUR(1936, Fr.), p
Milton Lehman
KILLER THAT STALKED NEW YORK, THE(1950), w
Paul Evan Lehman
IDAHO KID, THE(1937), w
Robin Lehman
TOMMY(1975, Brit.), ph
Ted Lehman
ONE DARK NIGHT(1983)
Trent Lehman
CHRISTINE JORGENSEN STORY, THE(1970)
Val Lehman
KITTY AND THE BAGMAN(1983, Aus.)
Veta Lehman
KNICKERBOCKER HOLIDAY(1944)
Beatrix Lehmann
PASSING OF THE THIRD FLOOR BACK, THE(1936, Brit.); STRANGERS ON A HONEYMOON(1937, Brit.); CANDLES AT NINE(1944, Brit.); KEY, THE(1958, Brit.); PSYCHE 59(1964, Brit.); OPERATION SNAFU(1965, Brit.); SPY WHO CAME IN FROM THE COLD, THE(1965, Brit.); FUNNY THING HAPPENED ON THE WAY TO THE FORUM, A(1966); STAIRCASE(1969 U.S./Brit./Fr.); WONDERWALL(1969, Brit.); CAT AND THE CANARY, THE(1979, Brit.)
Carla Lehmann
NORTH SEA PATROL(1939, Brit.); SO THIS IS LONDON(1940, Brit.); THREE COCKEYED SAILORS(1940, Brit.); BOMBSIGHT STOLEN(1941, Brit.); ONCE A CROOK(1941, Brit.); FLYING FORTRESS(1942, Brit.); TALK ABOUT JACQUELINE(1942, Brit.); CANDLELIGHT IN ALGERIA(1944, Brit.); SECRET MISSION(1944, Brit.); FAME IS THE SPUR(1947, Brit.); FACTS OF LOVE(1949, Brit.)
Claude Lehmann
FRIEND WILL COME TONIGHT, A(1948, Fr.)
Friedhelm Lehmann
JUST A GIGOLO(1979, Ger.); MALOU(1983)
Fritz Lehmann
LITTLE MELODY FROM VIENNA(1948, Aust.)
Helge Lehmann
RIVER CHANGES, THE(1956)
Joann Lehmann
NIGHT THEY RAIDED MINSKY'S, THE(1968)
Joanna Lehmann
SUNBURN(1979)
John Lehmann
FURY AT GUNSIGHT PASS(1956); PHANTOM STAGECOACH, THE(1957); MAGIC FOUNTAIN, THE(1961), w; MOUSE AND THE WOMAN, THE(1981, Brit.)
Lotte Lehmann
BIG CITY(1948)
Maurice Lehmann
BONNE CHANCE(1935, Fr.), p; COURIER OF LYONS(1938, Fr.), d; FRIC FRAC(1939, FR.), p
Olga Lehmann
ROBBERY UNDER ARMS(1958, Brit.), cos; VICTORS, THE(1963), cos; CAPTAIN NEMO AND THE UNDERWATER CITY(1969, Brit.), cos; KIDNAPPED(1971, Brit.), cos

Rosamond Lehmann
WEATHER IN THE STREETS, THE(1983, Brit.), w
Ted Lehmann
COTTONPICKIN' CHICKENPICKERS(1967); ROAD HUSTLERS, THE(1968); UNDER THE RAINBOW(1981)
Theodore F. Lehmann
ROUSTABOUT(1964)
Walter Lehmann
MERRY WIVES OF WINDSOR, THE(1952, Ger.), p
Louis Lehmans
ZERO IN THE UNIVERSE(1966)
Peter A. Lehmbrock
RESTLESS NIGHT, THE(1964, Ger.)
Erwin Lehn
HEAD, THE(1961, Ger.), md
Georg Lehn
MAN WHO WALKED THROUGH THE WALL, THE(1964, Ger.); CASTLE, THE(1969, Ger.); VERONIKA VOSS(1982, Ger.)
John Lehnberg
Misc. Silents
BIRD OF PREY, A(1916)
Fredric Lehne
FOXES(1980); ORDINARY PEOPLE(1980)
John Lehne
EFFECT OF GAMMA RAYS ON MAN-IN-THE-MOON MARIGOLDS, THE(1972); SERPICO(1973); WHO?(1975, Brit./Ger.); BOUND FOR GLORY(1976); FAMILY PLOT(1976); BROTHERS(1977); AMERICAN HOT WAX(1978); F.I.S.T.(1978); CARNY(1980); LADIES AND GENTLEMEN, THE FABULOUS STAINS(1982)
Helga Lehner
CITY OF FEAR(1965, Brit.); 24 HOURS TO KILL(1966, Brit.)
Helena Lehovcova
VOYAGE TO THE END OF THE UNIVERSE(1963, Czech.), ed
Andre Lehr
1984
SUGAR CANE ALLEY(1984, Fr.)
Anna Lehr
UNCONQUERED(1947)
Silents
RAMONA(1916); TARGET, THE(1916); MAN HATER, THE(1917); JUNGLE TRAIL, THE(1919); CHILD FOR SALE, A(1920); CHEATED HEARTS(1921); CRADLE, THE(1922); RUGGLES OF RED GAP(1923)
Misc. Silents
WHITE SCAR, THE(1915); BUGLE CALL, THE(1916); CIVILIZATION'S CHILD(1916); GRAFTERS(1917); LAUGHING BILL HYDE(1918); OTHER WOMAN, THE(1918); PARENTAGE(1918); FOR FREEDOM(1919); HOME WANTED(1919); THUNDERBOLTS OF FATE(1919); UPSIDE DOWN(1919); CHAINS OF EVIDENCE(1920); DARKEST HOUR, THE(1920); TRUTH ABOUT HUSBANDS, THE(1920); VALLEY OF DOUBT, THE(1920); VEILED MARRIAGE, THE(1920); MR. BARNES OF NEW YORK(1922); JESUS OF NAZARETH(1928)
Baby Ann Lehr [Ann Dvorak]
Silents
RAMONA(1916)
Lew Lehr
DEVIL TIGER(1934), w
Dennis Lehrer
GUNMAN HAS ESCAPED, A(1948, Brit.); SHOOT FIRST(1953, Brit.)
James Lehrer
VIVA MAX!(1969), w
Henry Lehrman
MOULIN ROUGE(1934), w; SHOW THEM NO MERCY(1935), w
Silents
REPORTED MISSING(1922), d, w; ON TIME(1924), d; FIGHTING EDGE(1926), d; HUSBANDS FOR RENT(1927), d; SAILOR IZZY MURPHY(1927), d; HOMESICK(1928), d; NEW YEAR'S EVE(1929), d
Misc. Silents
DOUBLE DEALING(1923), d; FIGHTING EDGE, THE(1926), d; CHICKEN A LA KING(1928), d; WHY SAILORS GO WRONG(1928), d
Melford Lehrman
DATE WITH DEATH, A(1959)
Matti Lehtela
MAKE LIKE A THIEF(1966, Fin.)
Emilio Lehurberg
LAZARILLO(1963, Span.), m
Chao Lei
MADAME WHITE SNAKE(1963, Hong Kong); MAGNIFICENT CONCUBINE, THE(1964, Hong Kong); EMPRESS WU(1965, Hong Kong); ENCHANTING SHADOW, THE(1965, Hong Kong)
Cheng Lei
TRIPLE IRONS(1973, Hong Kong); SACRED KNIVES OF VENGEANCE, THE(1974, Hong Kong)
Heng Ko Lei
GLADIATORS, THE(1970, Swed.)
Linda Lei
1984
CANNONBALL RUN II(1984)
Lydia Lei
INCHON(1981); HAMMETT(1982); VICE SQUAD(1982); DOCTOR DETROIT(1983)
Me Me Lei
1984
ELEMENT OF CRIME, THE(1984, Den.)
Pan Lei
LOVERS' ROCK(1966, Taiwan), d&w
Marshall Leib
HOMETOWN U.S.A.(1979), md
Vladimir Leib
RAMPAGE AT APACHE WELLS(1966, Ger./Yugo.)
Hans Leibelt
ROYAL WALTZ, THE(1936); MARRIAGE IN THE SHADOWS(1948, Ger.); SOMEWHERE IN BERLIN(1949, E. Ger.); GLASS OF WATER, A(1962, Cgr.); MAN WHO WALKED THROUGH THE WALL, THE(1964, Ger.)

Fritz Leiber
UNDER TWO FLAGS(1936); ANTHONY ADVERSE(1936); DOWN TO THE SEA(1936); HEARTS IN BONDAGE(1936); SINS OF MAN(1936); CHAMPAGNE WALTZ(1937); GREAT GARRICK, THE(1937); PRINCE AND THE PAUPER, THE(1937); FLIGHT INTO NOWHERE(1938); GATEWAY(1938); JURY'S SECRET, THE(1938); HUNCHBACK OF NOTRE DAME, THE(1939); NURSE EDITH CAVELL(1939); PACK UP YOUR TROUBLES(1939); THEY MADE HER A SPY(1939); ALL THIS AND HEAVEN TOO(1940); LADY WITH RED HAIR(1940); MORTAL STORM, THE(1940); SEA HAWK, THE(1940); WAY OF ALL FLESH, THE(1940); ALOMA OF THE SOUTH SEAS(1941); CROSSROADS(1942); DESERT SONG, THE(1943); FIRST COMES COURAGE(1943); PHANTOM OF THE OPERA(1943); SALUTE TO THE MARINES(1943); SONG OF BERNADETTE, THE(1943); COBRA WOMAN(1944); CRY OF THE WEREWOLF(1944); IMPOSTER, THE(1944); CISCO KID RETURNS, THE(1945); SCARLET STREET(1945); SPANISH MAIN, THE(1945); THIS LOVE OF OURS(1945); ANGEL ON MY SHOULDER(1946); HUMORESQUE(1946); SCANDAL IN PARIS, A(1946); STRANGE JOURNEY(1946); BELLS OF SAN ANGELO(1947); DANGEROUS VENTURE(1947); HIGH CONQUEST(1947); MONSIEUR VERDOUX(1947); WEB, THE(1947); ANOTHER PART OF THE FOREST(1948); TO THE ENDS OF THE EARTH(1948); BAGDAD(1949); BRIDE OF VENGEANCE(1949); SAMSON AND DELILAH(1949); SONG OF INDIA(1949); DEVIL'S DOORWAY(1950); EQUINOX(1970)
Silents
QUEEN OF SHEBA, THE(1921)
Misc. Silents
CLEOPATRA(1917); PRIMITIVE CALL, THE(1917); IF I WERE KING(1920); SONG OF THE SOUL, THE(1920)
Fritz Leiber, Jr.
CAMILLE(1937); GREAT GARRICK, THE(1937); WEIRD WOMAN(1944), w; BURN WITCH BURN(1962), w
Fritz Leiber, Sr.
TALE OF TWO CITIES, A(1935); STORY OF LOUIS PASTEUR, THE(1936)
Marianna Leibl
LA DOLCE VITA(1961, Ital./Fr.); STEPPE, THE(1963, Fr./Ital.); SENSO(1968, Ital.)
Marianne Leibl
WAR AND PEACE(1956, Ital./U.S.)
Avram Leibman
1984
LOVE STREAMS(1984)
Ron Leibman
WHERE'S POPPA?(1970); HOT ROCK, THE(1972); SLAUGHTERHOUSE-FIVE(1972); YOUR THREE MINUTES ARE UP(1973); SUPER COPS, THE(1974); WON TON TON, THE DOG WHO SAVED HOLLYWOOD(1976); NORMA RAE(1979); ZORRO, THE GAY BLADE(1981); ROMANTIC COMEDY(1983)
1984
PHAR LAP(1984, Aus.)
Meier Leibovitch
KID FOR TWO FARTHINGS, A(1956, Brit.)
Francis Leibowitz
UNSTRAP ME(1968)
Sol Leibowitz
UNHINGED(1982), prod d
Lela Leibrand
Silents
LITTLE PATRIOT, A(1917), w
Francois Legrand [Franz Antel]
SOME LIKE IT COOL(1979, Ger./Aust./Ital./Fr.), d
Ann Leicester
TOWERING INFERNO, THE(1974)
Ernest Leicester
Silents
IF(1916, Brit.)
Frederick Leicester
CRIMSON PIRATE, THE(1952)
Jack Leicester
DOUGHGIRLS, THE(1944), ph
James Leicester
CASABLANCA(1942), art d; EDGE OF DARKNESS(1943), set d; NORTHERN PURSUIT(1943), spec eff; ADVENTURES OF MARK TWAIN, THE(1944), ph; CONSPIRATORS, THE(1944), spec eff; MR. SKEFFINGTON(1944), p; APPOINTMENT IN HONDURAS(1953), ed; COUNT THE HOURS(1953), ed; SILVER LODE(1954), ed; ESCAPE TO BURMA(1955), ed; PEARL OF THE SOUTH PACIFIC(1955), ed; TENNESSEE'S PARTNER(1955), ed; SLIGHTLY SCARLET(1956), ed; RIVER'S EDGE, THE(1957), w, ed; ENCHANTED ISLAND(1958), ed; FROM THE EARTH TO THE MOON(1958), w, ed; JET OVER THE ATLANTIC(1960), ed; MOST DANGEROUS MAN ALIVE, THE(1961), w
Violet Leicester
Silents
ON THE BANKS OF ALLAN WATER(1916, Brit.)
William Leicester
STRANGE GAMBLE(1948); MYSTERY STREET(1950); SECRET OF CONVICT LAKE, THE(1951); YOU'RE IN THE NAVY NOW(1951); OPERATION SECRET(1952); FINGER MAN(1955); BEYOND A REASONABLE DOUBT(1956)
William P. Leicester
LAST MAN ON EARTH, THE(1964, U.S./Ital.), w
Harry Leichke
Misc. Silents
FORBIDDEN LOVE(1927, Brit.)
Larry Leichliter
BON VOYAGE, CHARLIE BROWN(AND DON'T COME BACK) (1980), anim; RACE FOR YOUR LIFE, CHARLIE BROWN(1977), anim
Mitchell Leichter
DESERT GUNS(1936), p
Barry Leichtling
CAPTAIN MILKSHAKE(1970), a, w
Jerry Leider
JAZZ SINGER, THE(1980), p; TRENCHCOAT(1983), p
Linda Leider
AROUSERS, THE(1973)

Harry Leidtke
Misc. Silents
SUMURUN(1921, Ger.)

Neil Leifer
YESTERDAY'S HERO(1979, Brit.), d

Don Leifert
FIEND(; NIGHTBEAST(1982)
1984
ALIEN FACTOR, THE(1984)
Misc. Talkies
ALIEN FACTOR, THE(1978); TERROR FROM THE UNKNOWN(1983)

Adele Leigh
DAVY(1958, Brit.)

Andrew Leigh
GREAT MR. HANDEL, THE(1942, Brit.); RUN FOR YOUR MONEY, A(1950, Brit.); PAUL TEMPLE'S TRIUMPH(1951, Brit.); PORTRAIT OF CLARE(1951, Brit.); DOUBLE CONFESSION(1953, Brit.); LANDFALL(1953, Brit.); FLAW, THE(1955, Brit.)

Anne Leigh
Misc. Silents
STING OF VICTORY, THE(1916)

Anthea Leigh
THEY WHO DARE(1954, Brit.)

Austin Leigh
Silents
ADVENTURES OF CAPTAIN KETTLE, THE(1922, Brit.), a, p; OLD BILL THROUGH THE AGES(1924, Brit.)
Misc. Silents
BEAU BROCADE(1916, Brit.)

Barbara Leigh
STUDENT NURSES, THE(1970); CHRISTIAN LICORICE STORE, THE(1971); PRETTY MAIDS ALL IN A ROW(1971); JUNIOR BONNER(1972); TERMINAL ISLAND(1973); BOSS NIGGER(1974); SEVEN(1979); MISTRESS OF THE APES(1981)

Benedicta Leigh
HANDS OF DESTINY(1954, Brit.)

Burt Leigh
BIRDS DO IT(1966)

Caroline Leigh
MAKE MINE MINK(1960, Brit.)

Charlotte Leigh
BROWN WALLET, THE(1936, Brit.); DISHONOR BRIGHT(1936, Brit.); SECOND BEST BED(1937, Brit.); YOU LIVE AND LEARN(1937, Brit.); THANK EVANS(1938, Brit.)

Constance Leigh
BLONDE BLACKMAILER(1955, Brit.)

Diana Leigh
1984
KILLPOINT(1984)

Dorna Leigh
Silents
HOLY ORDERS(1917, Brit.)

Eleanor Leigh
UNDERCOVER GIRL(1957, Brit.)

Frank Leigh
LOVE IN THE DESERT(1929); LOTUS LADY(1930); THIRTEENTH CHAIR, THE(1930); TEN NIGHTS IN A BARROOM(1931); WOMAN FROM MONTE CARLO, THE(1932); RESCUE SQUAD(1935); SPANISH CAPE MYSTERY(1935); LEGION OF MISSING MEN(1937); ARSENE LUPIN RETURNS(1938); BLACK SWAN, THE(1942); SONG OF BERNADETTE, THE(1943); RETURN OF THE APE MAN(1944); MINISTRY OF FEAR(1945); TONIGHT AND EVERY NIGHT(1945); GILDA(1946); UNDERCURRENT(1946)
Silents
LIFE'S WHIRLPOOL(1917); ALL OF A SUDDEN NORMA(1919); HELP WANTED–MALE(1920); NURSE MARJORIE(1920); BOB HAMPTON OF PLACER(1921); OUT OF THE SILENT NORTH(1922); ASHES OF VENGEANCE(1923); LONELY ROAD, THE(1923); NORTH OF HUDSON BAY(1923); ROSITA(1923); RECKLESS AGE, THE(1924); AS MAN DESIRES(1925); WINDING STAIR, THE(1925); ADORABLE DECEIVER, THE(1926); SOFT CUSHIONS(1927); SOMEWHERE IN SONORA(1927); NIGHT OF MYSTERY, A(1928)
Misc. Silents
HOMEBREAKER, THE(1919); LORD AND LADY ALGY(1919); REGULAR FELLOW, A(1919); ROSE OF THE WEST(1919); SNARES OF PARIS(1919); USURPER, THE(1919); MOTHER OF HIS CHILDREN, THE(1920); ONE HOUR BEFORE DAWN(1920); DOMESTIC RELATIONS(1922); TRUXTON KING(1923); FLAMES OF DESIRE(1924); HILL BILLY, THE(1924); HUTCH OF THE U.S.A.(1924); AMERICAN PLUCK(1925); FLAME OF THE ARGENTINE(1926); IMPOSTER, THE(1926); TIGRESS, THE(1927); BELOW THE DEADLINE(1929)

George Leigh
FATAL WITNESS, THE(1945); SALOME, WHERE SHE DANCED(1945); CHAMPAGNE FOR CAESAR(1950); NEVER A DULL MOMENT(1950); THREE CAME HOME(1950); DIAL M FOR MURDER(1954)

Gilbert Leigh
MAD DOG COLL(1961)

Grace Leigh
Silents
SEATS OF THE MIGHTY, THE(1914)

J.L.V. Leigh
Misc. Silents
QUICKSANDS OF LIFE(1915, Brit.), d; KEY OF THE WORLD, THE(1918, Brit.), d; FIRST MEN IN THE MOON, THE(1919, Brit.), d; PALLARD THE PUNTER(1919, Brit.), d

Jack Leigh
Silents
EUGENE ARAM(1914, Brit.)
Misc. Silents
WRECKER OF LIVES, THE(1914, Brit.); PALLARD THE PUNTER(1919, Brit.); TROUSERS(1920, Brit.)

Jacqueline Leigh
ROAD TO HONG KONG, THE(1962, U.S./Brit.)

James Leigh
MAKING IT(1971), w

Janet Leigh
IF WINTER COMES(1947); ROMANCE OF ROSY RIDGE, THE(1947); HILLS OF HOME(1948); ACT OF VIOLENCE(1949); DOCTOR AND THE GIRL, THE(1949); HOLIDAY AFFAIR(1949); LITTLE WOMEN(1949); RED DANUBE, THE(1949); THAT FORSYTE WOMAN(1949); ANGELS IN THE OUTFIELD(1951); IT'S A BIG COUNTRY(1951); STRICTLY DISHONORABLE(1951); TWO TICKETS TO BROADWAY(1951); FEARLESS FAGAN(1952); JUST THIS ONCE(1952); SCARAMOUCHE(1952); CONFIDENTIAL CONNIE(1953); HOUDINI(1953); NAKED SPUR, THE(1953); WALKING MY BABY BACK HOME(1953); BLACK SHIELD OF FALWORTH, THE(1954); LIVING IT UP(1954); PRINCE VALIANT(1954); ROGUE COP(1954); MY SISTER EILEEN(1955); PETE KELLY'S BLUES(1955); SAFARI(1956); JET PILOT(1957); PERFECT FURLOUGH, THE(1958); TOUCH OF EVIL(1958); VIKINGS, THE(1958); PEPE(1960); PSYCHO(1960); WHO WAS THAT LADY?(1960); MANCHURIAN CANDIDATE, THE(1962); BYE BYE BIRDIE(1963); WIVES AND LOVERS(1963); AMERICAN DREAM, AN(1966); HARPER(1966); KID RODELO(1966, U.S./Span.); SPY IN THE GREEN HAT, THE(1966); THREE ON A COUCH(1966); GRAND SLAM(1968, Ital., Span., Ger.); HELLO DOWN THERE(1969); NIGHT OF THE LEPUS(1972); ONE IS A LONELY NUMBER(1972); BOARDWALK(1979); FOG, THE(1980)

Jennifer Jason Leigh
EYES OF A STRANGER(1980); FAST TIMES AT RIDGEMONT HIGH(1982); WRONG IS RIGHT(1982); EASY MONEY(1983)
1984
GRANDVIEW, U.S.A.(1984)

Joy Leigh
SCROOGE(1970, Brit.)

Julian Leigh
CANTOR'S SON, THE(1937), titles; LOWER DEPTHS, THE(1937, Fr.), titles; ALEXANDER NEVSKY(1939), titles; TWO WOMEN(1940, Fr.), titles

Julien Leigh
OVERTURE TO GLORY(1940), titles

Laurie Leigh
DEAD MAN'S EVIDENCE(1962, Brit.); FREEDOM TO DIE(1962, Brit.); MARKED ONE, THE(1963, Brit.); PARANOIAC(1963, Brit.); DR. TERROR'S HOUSE OF HORRORS(1965, Brit.)

Leona Leigh
LOCKED DOOR, THE(1929)

Leslie Leigh
Silents
AMERICAN WAY, THE(1919)

Lisle Leigh
Silents
CAPRICE OF THE MOUNTAINS(1916)

Malcolm Leigh
GAMES THAT LOVERS PLAY(1971, Brit.), d&w
Misc. Talkies
LADY CHATTERLY VS. FANNY HILL(1980), d

Mike Leigh
BLEAK MOMENTS(1972, Brit.), d&w
1984
FOUR DAYS IN JULY(1984), d

Mitch Leigh
MAN OF LA MANCHA(1972), m; ONCE IN PARIS(1978), m

Nelson Leigh
FIRST COMES COURAGE(1943); LASSIE, COME HOME(1943); FOLLOW THE BOYS(1944); JAM SESSION(1944); LOUISIANA HAYRIDE(1944); MR. WINKLE GOES TO WAR(1944); TEXAS MASQUERADE(1944); U-BOAT PRISONER(1944); WHITE CLIFFS OF DOVER, THE(1944); CORNERED(1945); IDENTITY UNKNOWN(1945); IT'S A PLEASURE(1945); TONIGHT AND EVERY NIGHT(1945); BANDIT OF SHERWOOD FOREST, THE(1946); ANGELS ALLEY(1948); RACING LUCK(1948); BARBARY PIRATE(1949); JOLSON SINGS AGAIN(1949); LOST TRIBE, THE(1949); CAPTIVE GIRL(1950); ROGUES OF SHERWOOD FOREST(1950); HOME TOWN STORY(1951); HURRICANE ISLAND(1951); YUKON MANHUNT(1951); BUGLES IN THE AFTERNOON(1952); THIEF OF DAMASCUS(1952); JACK SLADE(1953); PRISONERS OF THE CASBAH(1953); SAVAGE MUTINY(1953); TEXAS BAD MAN(1953); VALLEY OF THE HEADHUNTERS(1953); JESSE JAMES VERSUS THE DALTONS(1954); OUTLAW'S DAUGHTER, THE(1954); SARACEN BLADE, THE(1954); CREATURE WITH THE ATOM BRAIN(1955); REBEL WITHOUT A CAUSE(1955); VIRGIN QUEEN, THE(1955); FIRST TEXAN, THE(1956); FRIENDLY PERSUASION(1956); HOLD BACK THE NIGHT(1956); TOWARD THE UNKNOWN(1956); WORLD WITHOUT END(1956); BOMBERS B-52(1957); GOD IS MY PARTNER(1957); GUNFIGHT AT THE O.K. CORRAL(1957); JET PILOT(1957); SPIRIT OF ST. LOUIS, THE(1957); IN LOVE AND WAR(1958); THESE THOUSAND HILLS(1959); DARK AT THE TOP OF THE STAIRS, THE(1960); GALLANT HOURS, THE(1960); MA BARKER'S KILLER BROOD(1960); LITTLE SHEPHERD OF KINGDOM COME(1961); LOVER COME BACK(1961); INCIDENT IN AN ALLEY(1962); GATHERING OF EAGLES, A(1963)
Misc. Talkies
MAGNIFICENT ADVENTURE, THE(1952)

Norman Leigh
BRINK'S JOB, THE(1978), ph; SCHIZOID(1980), ph; LOVE(1982, Can.), ph; DEADLY FORCE(1983), ph

Patric Dennis Leigh
NO PLACE TO LAND(1958); DOCTOR DEATH: SEEKER OF SOULS(1973)

Roland Leigh
KNICKERBOCKER HOLIDAY(1944), w; HEARTBEAT(1946), w; SIREN OF ATLANTIS(1948), w

Rowland Leigh
F.P. 1(1933, Brit.), m; CHARGE OF THE LIGHT BRIGADE, THE(1936), w; FIRST LADY(1937), w; SECRETS OF AN ACTRESS(1938), w; VIGIL IN THE NIGHT(1940), w; MASTER RACE, THE(1944), w; SUMMER STORM(1944), w; SONG FOR MISS JULIE, A(1945), w; HEAVEN ONLY KNOWS(1947), w; TARZAN AND THE HUNTRESS(1947), w

Suzanna Leigh
BOEING BOEING(1965); PARADISE, HAWAIIAN STYLE(1966); PLEASURE GIRLS, THE(1966, Brit.); DEADLIER THAN THE MALE(1967, Brit.); DEADLY BEES,THE(1967, Brit.); LOST CONTINENT, THE(1968, Brit.); SUBTERFUGE(1969, US/Brit.); LUST FOR A VAMPIRE(1971, Brit.); SON OF DRACULA(1974, Brit.)

Misc. Talkies
FIEND, THE(1971, Brit.); BEWARE MY BRETHREN(1972, Brit.)
Suzanne Leigh
BOMB IN THE HIGH STREET(1961, Brit.)
Vanessa Leigh
DUET FOR FOUR(1982, Aus.)
Vivian Leigh
THINGS ARE LOOKING UP(1934, Brit.)
Vivien Leigh
GENTLEMAN'S AGREEMENT(1935, Brit.); LOOK UP AND LAUGH(1935, Brit.); VILLAGE SQUIRE, THE(1935, Brit.); FIRE OVER ENGLAND(1937, Brit.); STORM IN A TEACUP(1937, Brit.); YANK AT OXFORD, A(1938); GONE WITH THE WIND(1939); SIDEWALKS OF LONDON(1940, Brit.); TWENTY-ONE DAYS TOGETHER(1940, Brit.); WATERLOO BRIDGE(1940); THAT HAMILTON WOMAN(1941); CAESAR AND CLEOPATRA(1946, Brit.); ANNA KARENINA(1948, Brit.); STREETCAR NAMED DESIRE, A(1951); ELEPHANT WALK(1954); DEEP BLUE SEA, THE(1955, Brit.); ROMAN SPRING OF MRS. STONE, THE(1961, U.S./Brit.); SHIP OF FOOLS(1965)
Wandisa Leigh
LIGHTNING BOLT(1967, Ital./Sp.)
Adele Leigh-Enderl
WAGNER(1983, Brit./Hung./Aust.)
Patrick Leigh-Fermor
ROOTS OF HEAVEN, THE(1958), w
Barbara Leigh-Hunt
MIDSUMMERS NIGHT'S DREAM, A(1961, Czech); FRENZY(1972, Brit.); HENRY VIII AND HIS SIX WIVES(1972, Brit.); NELSON AFFAIR, THE(1973, Brit.); OH, HEAVENLY DOG!(1980); WAGNER(1983, Brit./Hung./Aust.)
1984
PLAGUE DOGS, THE(1984, U.S./Brit.)
Ronald Leigh-Hunt
TREAD SOFTLY(1952, Brit.); FLANNELFOOT(1953, Brit.); WHITE FIRE(1953, Brit.); ZOO BABY(1957, Brit.); ACTION STATIONS(1959, Brit.); OSCAR WILDE(1960, Brit.); PRIVATE POOLEY(1962, Brit./E. Ger.); WE JOINED THE NAVY(1962, Brit.); SEVENTY DEADLY PILLS(1964, Brit.); THIRD SECRET, THE(1964, Brit.); KHARTOUM(1966, Brit.); LIQUIDATOR, THE(1966, Brit.); WHERE THE BULLETS FLY(1966, Brit.); LE MANS(1971); BAXTER(1973, Brit.); MOHAMMAD, MESSENGER OF GOD(1976, Lebanon/Brit.)
Judy Leigh-Johnson
1984
FINDERS KEEPERS(1984)
Kathryn Leigh-Scott
PROVIDENCE(1977, Fr.)
Warren D. Leight
MOTHER'S DAY(1980), w
Warren Leight
STUCK ON YOU(1983), w
1984
STUCK ON YOU(1984), w
Lolita Leighter
FOLLOW THE BOYS(1944)
Cynthia Leighton
STRANGERS WHEN WE MEET(1960)
Dan Leighton
Misc. Silents
PHANTOM'S SECRET, THE(1917)
Donrue Leighton
OH DOCTOR(1937)
Frank Leighton
HIDE-OUT(1934); OPERATOR 13(1934); SPLENDID FELLOWS(1934, Aus.); TWO MINUTES' SILENCE(1934, Brit.); THOROUGHBRED(1936, Aus.); LAST CHANCE, THE(1937, Brit.); TALL TIMBERS(1937, Aus.); I SEE ICE(1938); IT'S IN THE AIR(1940, Brit.)
Misc. Talkies
TIMBERLAND TERROR(1940, Aus.)
Isabel Leighton
FIGHT FOR YOUR LADY(1937), w
Jan Leighton
TRICK BABY(1973); ZAPPED!(1982)
Jim Leighton
PEGGY(1950); WILD BLUE YONDER, THE(1952)
Lee Leighton
STAR IN THE DUST(1956), w
Lillian Leighton
GRAND PARADE, THE(1930); LAST DANCE, THE(1930); SWEEPSTAKES(1931); SIGN OF THE CROSS, THE(1932); BITTER TEA OF GENERAL YEN, THE(1933); MAN FROM MONTEREY, THE(1933); SECRET SINNERS(1933); SPHINX, THE(1933); TWO FISTED(1935)
Silents
JOAN THE WOMAN(1916); PLOW GIRL, THE(1916); OLD WIVES FOR NEW(1918); LOUISIANA(1919); MALE AND FEMALE(1919); POOR RELATIONS(1919); JACK KNIFE MAN, THE(1920); MIDSUMMER MADNESS(1920); THOU ART THE MAN(1920); CRAZY TO MARRY(1921); PECK'S BAD BOY(1921); RED HOT ROMANCE(1922); SATURDAY NIGHT(1922); TILLIE(1922); CRINOLINE AND ROMANCE(1923); ETERNAL THREE, THE(1923); ONLY 38(1923); BEDROOM WINDOW, THE(1924); CODE OF THE SEA(1924); IN THE NAME OF LOVE(1925); TUMBLEWEEDS(1925); SANDY(1926); TORRENT, THE(1926); BY WHOSE HAND?(1927); CALIFORNIA(1927); FAIR CO-ED, THE(1927)
Misc. Silents
WITCHCRAFT(1916); BETTY TO THE RESCUE(1917); FRECKLES(1917); ALL OF A SUDDEN PEGGY(1920); CITY SPARROW, THE(1920); HOUSE OF TOYS, THE(1920); THIRTIETH PIECE OF SILVER, THE(1920); LOVE NEVER DIES(1921); UNDER THE LASH(1921); WASTED LIVES(1923); PARISIAN LOVE(1925); GOLDEN YUKON, THE(1927)
Lilliane Leighton
FIGHTING SHERIFF, THE(1931); SUBWAY EXPRESS(1931)
Lillianne Leighton
FEET FIRST(1930); MILLIONS IN THE AIR(1935); WHIPSAW(1936)

Louis D. Leighton
HERE IS MY HEART(1934), p
Silents
PENROD AND SAM(1923), w
Margaret Leighton
BONNIE PRINCE CHARLIE(1948, Brit.); UNDER CAPRICORN(1949); ASTONISHED HEART, THE(1950, Brit.); FIGHTING PIMPERNEL, THE(1950, Brit.); WINSLOW BOY, THE(1950); CALLING BULLDOG DRUMMOND(1951, Brit.); MURDER ON MONDAY(1953, Brit.); COURT MARTIAL(1954, Brit.); GOOD DIE YOUNG, THE(1954, Brit.); HOLLY AND THE IVY, THE(1954, Brit.); CONSTANT HUSBAND, THE(1955, Brit.); TECKMAN MYSTERY, THE(1955, Brit); NOVEL AFFAIR, A(1957, Brit.); SOUND AND THE FURY, THE(1959); WALTZ OF THE TOREADORS(1962, Brit.); BEST MAN, THE(1964); LOVED ONE, THE(1965); SEVEN WOMEN(1966); MADWOMAN OF CHAILLOT, THE(1969); GO-BETWEEN, THE(1971, Brit.); LADY CAROLINE LAMB(1972, Brit./Ital.); X Y & ZEE(1972, Brit.); NELSON AFFAIR, THE(1973, Brit.); GALILEO(1975, Brit.); GREAT EXPECTATIONS(1975, Brit.); DIRTY KNIGHT'S WORK(1976, Brit.)
Maxine Leighton
DON'T RAISE THE BRIDGE, LOWER THE RIVER(1968, Brit.), cos
Melinda Leighton
CODE OF THE OUTLAW(1942); COWBOY SERENADE(1942)
Michael Leighton
APPOINTMENT WITH CRIME(1945, Brit.), w; JOHNNY, YOU'RE WANTED(1956, Brit.), w
Michael W. Leighton
KILLER INSIDE ME, THE(1976), p
Miriam Leighton
KNIGHTS FOR A DAY(1937, Brit.)
Queenie Leighton
UNDER THE GREENWOOD TREE(1930, Brit.)
Robert Leighton
KILL AND KILL AGAIN(1981), ed; BLOOD TIDE(1982), ed; WAVELENGTH(1983), ed
1984
HOUSE WHERE DEATH LIVES, THE(1984), ed; THIS IS SPINAL TAP(1984), ed
Roberta Leighton
BARRACUDA(1978); STRIPES(1981)
1984
COVERGIRL(1984, Can.)
Sara Leighton
WOMAN EATER, THE(1959, Brit.)
Ted Leighton
HUNTER, THE(1980), w
Warner E. Leighton
GONE IN 60 SECONDS(1974), ed; JUNKMAN, THE(1982), ed
Warner Leighton
HEY THERE, IT'S YOGI BEAR(1964), ed; MAN CALLED FLINTSTONE, THE(1966), ed; SHINBONE ALLEY(1971), ed; C.H.O.M.P.S.(1979), ed
Will Leighton
SOPHIE'S PLACE(1970)
William R. Leighton
Silents
ABLEMINDED LADY, THE(1922), w
Winifred Leighton
Misc. Silents
SOCIAL PIRATE, THE(1919)
Leighton Noble and His Orchestra
IT AIN'T HAY(1943)
Leighton Noble Orchestra
CRAZY HOUSE(1943)
Chrisabel Leighton-Porter
ADVENTURES OF JANE, THE(1949, Brit.)
Leila
FROM RUSSIA WITH LOVE(1963, Brit.); KHARTOUM(1966, Brit.)
Dione Leilani
PAGAN LOVE SONG(1950)
Sandy Leim
MY BLOODY VALENTINE(1981, Can.)
Tom Leindecker
Misc. Talkies
CHEERING SECTION(1977)
Colin Leinster
OUTSIDER, THE(1980), d&w
Murray Leinster
MURDER WILL OUT(1930), w; TORCHY BLANE IN CHINATOWN(1938), w; NAVY VS. THE NIGHT MONSTERS, THE(1966), w; TERRORNAUTS, THE(1967, Brit.), w
Harald Leipnitz
ENDLESS NIGHT, THE(1963, Ger.); BRIDES OF FU MANCHU, THE(1966, Brit.); RAMPAGE AT APACHE WELLS(1966, Ger./Yugo.); THUNDER AT THE BORDER(1966, Ger./Yugo.); THAT WOMAN(1968, Ger./Ital./Fr.); LADY HAMILTON(1969, Ger./Ital./Fr.); 24-HOUR LOVER(1970, Ger.)
Harold Leipnitz
Misc. Talkies
RIVER OF EVIL(1964)
John Leipold
FIGHTING CARAVANS(1931), m; FAREWELL TO ARMS, A(1932), m; FOUR FRIGHTENED PEOPLE(1934), m; SOULS AT SEA(1937), m; STAGECOACH(1939), m; UNION PACIFIC(1939), m; OUTLAWS OF THE DESERT(1941), m; DARING YOUNG MAN, THE(1942), m; HEAT'S ON, THE(1943), m; MY KINGDOM FOR A COOK(1943), m; MASSACRE RIVER(1949), m
Justin Leir
1984
HEARTBREAKERS(1984)
John Leirier
IT FELL FROM THE SKY(1980)
Noelle Leiris
PARIS BELONGS TO US(1962, Fr.)

Leisen
TAKE A LETTER, DARLING(1942), cos; LADY IN THE DARK(1944), cos

Mitchell Leisen
SHOW FOLKS(1928), art d; GODLESS GIRL, THE(1929), art d; MADAME SA-TAN(1930), art d; SQUAW MAN, THE(1931), art d; CRADLE SONG(1933), d; DEATH TAKES A HOLIDAY(1934), d; MURDER AT THE VANITIES(1934), d; BEHOLD MY WIFE(1935), d; FOUR HOURS TO KILL(1935), d; HANDS ACROSS THE TA-BLE(1935), d; BIG BROADCAST OF 1937, THE(1936), d; THIRTEEN HOURS BY AIR(1936), d; BIG BROADCAST OF 1938, THE(1937), d; EASY LIVING(1937), d; SWING HIGH, SWING LOW(1937), d; ARTISTS AND MODELS ABROAD(1938), d; MIDNIGHT(1939), d; ARISE, MY LOVE(1940), d; REMEMBER THE NIGHT(1940), p&d; HOLD BACK THE DAWN(1941), a, d; I WANTED WINGS(1941), d; LADY IS WILLING, THE(1942), p&d; TAKE A LETTER, DARLING(1942), d; NO TIME FOR LOVE(1943), p, d; FRENCHMAN'S CREEK(1944), d; LADY IN THE DARK(1944), d; PRACTICALLY YOURS(1944), p&d; KITTY(1945), d; MASQUERADE IN MEX-ICO(1945), d; TO EACH HIS OWN(1946), d; DREAM GIRL(1947), d; GOLDEN EAR-RINGS(1947), d; SUDDENLY IT'S SPRING(1947), d; VARIETY GIRL(1947); MISS TATLOCK'S MILLIONS(1948); BRIDE OF VENGEANCE(1949), d; SONG OF SUR-RENDER(1949), d; CAPTAIN CAREY, U.S.A(1950), d; NO MAN OF HER OWN(1950), d; DARLING, HOW COULD YOU!(1951), d; MATING SEASON, THE(1951), d; YOUNG MAN WITH IDEAS(1952), d; TONIGHT WE SING(1953), d; BEDEVILLED(1955), d; GIRL MOST LIKELY, THE(1957), d
Silents
ROBIN HOOD(1922), cos; THIEF OF BAGDAD, THE(1924), cos; VOLGA BOATMAN, THE(1926), art d; ANGEL OF BROADWAY, THE(1927), art d; KING OF KINGS, THE(1927), art d; CHICAGO(1928), art d

John Leisenring
MONDO TRASHO(1970)

Mitchell R. Leiser
ROUND TRIP(1967), p

Frederick Leister
BRACELETS(1931, Brit.); DOWN RIVER(1931, Brit.); DREYFUS CASE, THE(1931, Brit.); WORLD, THE FLESH, AND THE DEVIL, THE(1932, Brit.); IRON DUKE, THE(1935, Brit.); DINNER AT THE RITZ(1937, Brit.); KING SOLOMON'S MINES(1937, Brit.); SHOW GOES ON, THE(1937, Brit.); YOU'RE IN THE ARMY NOW(1937, Brit.); SIXTY GLORIOUS YEARS(1938, Brit.); GOODBYE MR. CHIPS(1939, Brit.); FUGI-TIVE, THE(1940, Brit.); MOZART(1940, Brit.); OUTSIDER, THE(1940, Brit.); ATLAN-TIC FERRY(1941, Brit.); PRIME MINISTER, THE(1941, Brit.); NEXT OF KIN(1942, Brit.); WE'LL MEET AGAIN(1942, Brit.); YOUNG MR. PITT, THE(1942, Brit.); GENTLE SEX, THE(1943, Brit.); HUNDRED POUND WINDOW, THE(1943, Brit.); SHIPBUILD-ERS, THE(1943, Brit.); KISS THE BRIDE GOODBYE(1944, Brit.); RANDOLPH FAMI-LY, THE(1945, Brit.); SPELL OF AMY NUGENT, THE(1945, Brit.); YOU CAN'T DO WITHOUT LOVE(1946, Brit.); SO WELL REMEMBERED(1947, Brit.); CAPTIVE HEART, THE(1948, Brit.); ESCAPE(1948, Brit.); NIGHT BEAT(1948, Brit.); AGITATOR, THE(1949); ALL OVER THE TOWN(1949, Brit.); DEAR MR. PROHACK(1949, Brit.); FOR THEM THAT TRESPASS(1949, Brit.); FORBIDDEN(1949, Brit.); PAPER OR-CHID(1949, Brit.); QUARTET(1949, Brit.); MRS. FITZHERBERT(1950, Brit.); ROSSIT-ER CASE, THE(1950, Brit.); TWENTY QUESTIONS MURDER MYSTERY, THE(1950, Brit.); GREEN GROW THE RUSHES(1951, Brit.); LANDFALL(1953, Brit.); MR. POTTS GOES TO MOSCOW(1953, Brit.); CIRCUMSTANIAL EVIDENCE(1954, Brit.); END OF THE AFFAIR, THE(1955, Brit.); FOOTSTEPS IN THE FOG(1955, Brit.); SOULS IN CONFLICT(1955, Brit.); TIME OF HIS LIFE, THE(1955, Brit.); SHADOW OF FEAR(1956, Brit.); DANGEROUS EXILE(1958, Brit.); RX MURDER(1958, Brit.); LEFT, RIGHT AND CENTRE(1959); NAKED EDGE, THE(1961)

Norma Leistiko
LULU(1978)

Adeline Leitbach
NOTORIOUS BUT NICE(1934), w

Abbey Leitch
SWEET JESUS, PREACHER MAN(1973), w

Christopher Leitch
Misc. Talkies
HITTER, THE(1979), d

Sonya Leite
1984
SUPERGIRL(1984)

Eva Leiter
VIENNA WALTZES(1961, Aust.)

Richard Leiterman
MARRIED COUPLE, A(1969, Can.), ph; GOIN' DOWN THE ROAD(1970, Can.), ph; RIP-OFF(1971, Can.), ph; WEDDING IN WHITE(1972, Can.), ph; GET BACK(1973, Can.), ph; RECOMMENDATION FOR MERCY(1975, Can.), ph; FAR SHORE, THE(1976, Can.), ph; WILD HORSE HANK(1979, Can.), ph; WHO HAS SEEN THE WIND(1980, Can.), ph; SILENCE OF THE NORTH(1981, Can.), ph; TICKET TO HEAVEN(1981), ph; MOTHER LODE(1982), ph; UTILITIES(1983, Can.), ph

Audine Leith
ON THE BEACH(1959)

Virginia Leith
FEAR AND DESIRE(1953); BLACK WIDOW(1954); VIOLENT SATURDAY(1955); WHITE FEATHER(1955); KISS BEFORE DYING, A(1956); ON THE THRESHOLD OF SPACE(1956); TOWARD THE UNKNOWN(1956); BRAIN THAT WOULDN'T DIE, THE(1959); FIRST LOVE(1977)

Ronald Leith-Hunt
HOSTILE WITNESS(1968, Brit.)

Eberhard Leithoff
GOLD(1934, Ger.)

Jacques Leitienne
1984
CAGED WOMEN(1984, Ital./Fr.), p

Harry Leitke
Misc. Silents
BOHEMIAN DANCER(1929)

Amy Leitman
SMALL CIRCLE OF FRIENDS, A(1980)

Hermann Leitner
STORY OF VICKIE, THE(1958, Aust.), ed

Adeline Leitzbach
HOUSE OF SECRETS(1929), w

Silents
SUCCESS(1923), w; ONE SPLENDID HOUR(1929), w; PEACOCK FAN(1929), w

Adeline Leitzback
Silents
MANHATTAN KNIGHTS(1928), w

Zalman Leiviush
MY FATHER'S HOUSE(1947, Palestine)

Ewa Lejczak
CONSTANT FACTOR, THE(1980, Pol.)

Andree Lejon
Silents
IF I WERE QUEEN(1922)

Nico Lek
O. HENRY'S FULL HOUSE(1952)

Per LeKang
MY FATHER'S MISTRESS(1970, Swed.), cos

Jim Lekester
CATTLE QUEEN OF MONTANA(1954), ed

Dell Lekus
TERROR ON TOUR(1980), w

David Leland
HOUR BEFORE THE DAWN, THE(1944); NOTHING BUT TROUBLE(1944); JULIUS CAESAR(1970, Brit.); SCARS OF DRACULA, THE(1970, Brit.); UNDERGROUND(1970, Brit.); ONE BRIEF SUMMER(1971, Brit.); PIED PIPER, THE(1972, Brit.); TIME BANDITS(1981, Brit.); MISSIONARY, THE(1982)

Davil Leland
GAWAIN AND THE GREEN KNIGHT(1973, Brit.)

Fiona Leland
IT HAPPENED HERE(1966, Brit.)

Georgette Leland
Misc. Silents
IL TROVATORE(1914)

Harry Leland
CIRCLE CANYON(1934)

Jacques Leland
GIRL FROM LORRAINE, A(1982, Fr./Switz.)

Lea Leland
Silents
SHOULD A WOMAN DIVORCE?(1914)

Joanna Lelanow
CONTRACT, THE(1982, Pol.), art d

Indu Lele
HOUSEHOLDER, THE(1963, US/India)

Maurice Leloir
IRON MASK, THE(1929), prod d, cos

Natalie Lelong
PRIVATE LIFE OF DON JUAN, THE(1934, Brit.)

Christine Lelouch
CROOK, THE(1971, Fr.)

Claude Lelouch
MAN AND A WOMAN, A(1966, Fr.), p&d, w, ph, ed; LIVE FOR LIFE(1967, Fr./Ital.), d, w, ph, ed; TO BE A CROOK(1967, Fr.), p&d, w, ed; LES GAULOISES BLEUES(1969, Fr.), p; LIFE LOVE DEATH(1969, Fr./Ital.), d, w; LOVE IS A FUNNY THING(1970, Fr./Ital.), d&ph, w; CROOK, THE(1971, Fr.), d, w; IT ONLY HAPPENS TO OTHERS(1971, Fr./Ital.), p; AND NOW MY LOVE(1975, Fr.), d, w; ANOTHER MAN, ANOTHER CHANCE(1977 Fr./US), d&w; CAT AND MOUSE(1978, Fr.), p,d&w; BOLERO(1982, Fr.), p,d&w
1984
EDITH AND MARCEL(1984, Fr.), d, w

Colette Leloup
JE T'AIME, JE T'AIME(1972, Fr./Swed.), ed

Grace Lem
PACIFIC RENDEZVOUS(1942); PASSPORT TO SUEZ(1943); BLOOD ON THE SUN(1945); TOKYO ROSE(1945); LADY FROM SHANGHAI, THE(1948); SOUTH SEA WOMAN(1953)

Stanislas Lem
SOLARIS(1972, USSR), w

Stanislaw Lem
FIRST SPACESHIP ON VENUS(1960, Ger./Pol.), w; TEST OF PILOT PIRX, THE(1978, Pol./USSR), w

Walter Lem
GENERAL DIED AT DAWN, THE(1936)

Philippe Lemaaire
VICE AND VIRTUE(1965, Fr./Ital.)

Charles LeMaire
GEORGE WHITE'S SCANDALS(1934), cos; CAPTAIN FROM CASTILE(1947), cos; KISS OF DEATH(1947), cos; LUCK OF THE IRISH(1947), cos; PINKY(1949), cos; YOU'RE MY EVERYTHING(1949), cos; AMERICAN GUERRILLA IN THE PHILIP-PINES, AN(1950), cos; WHEN WILLIE COMES MARCHING HOME(1950), cos; WHERE THE SIDEWALK ENDS(1950), cos; HALLS OF MONTEZUMA(1951), cos; I CAN GET IT FOR YOU WHOLESALE(1951), cos; PEOPLE WILL TALK(1951), cos; DEADLINE–U.S.A.(1952), cos; MY PAL GUS(1952), cos; WAY OF A GAUCHO(1952), cos; WITH A SONG IN MY HEART(1952), cos; TREASURE OF THE GOLDEN CONDOR(1953), cos; VICKI(1953), cos; DEMETRIUS AND THE GLADIATORS(1954), cos; EGYPTIAN. THE(1954), cos; HELL AND HIGH WATER(1954), cos; SIEGE AT RED RIVER, THE(1954), cos; GIRL IN THE RED VELVET SWING, THE(1955), cos; HOUSE OF BAMBOO(1955), cos; SEVEN YEAR ITCH, THE(1955), cos; SOLDIER OF FORTUNE(1955), cos; D-DAY, THE SIXTH OF JUNE(1956), cos; GIRL CAN'T HELP IT, THE(1956), cos; MAN IN THE GREY FLANNEL SUIT, THE(1956), cos; BERNAR-DINE(1957), cos; FORTY GUNS(1957), cos; KISS THEM FOR ME(1957), cos; OH, MEN! OH, WOMEN!(1957), cos; TOP SECRET AFFAIR(1957), cos; WILL SUCCESS SPOIL ROCK HUNTER?(1957), cos; GIFT OF LOVE, THE(1958), cos; HUNTERS, THE(1958), cos; MARDI GRAS(1958), cos; RALLY 'ROUND THE FLAG, BOYS!(1958), cos; YOUNG LIONS, THE(1958), cos; 10 NORTH FREDERICK(1958), cos; COMPUL-SION(1959), cos; MAN WHO UNDERSTOOD WOMEN, THE(1959), cos; REMARKA-BLE MR. PENNYPACKER, THE(1959), cos; THUNDER IN THE SUN(1959), cos; WARLOCK(1959), cos; MARRIAGE-GO-ROUND, THE(1960), cos; WALK ON THE WILD SIDE(1962), cos

Gerard Lemaire
CATHERINE & CO.(1976, Fr.)
Martine Lemaire
DIARY OF A COUNTRY PRIEST(1954, Fr.)
Monique LeMaire
DOUBLE TROUBLE(1967)
Philippe Lemaire
NOUS IRONS A PARIS(1949, Fr.); MONTE CARLO BABY(1953, Fr.); SINGING TAXI DRIVER(1953, Ital.); STRANGE DECEPTION(1953, Ital.); FROU-FROU(1955, Fr.); NAKED HEART, THE(1955, Brit.); NIGHTS OF SHAME(1961, Fr.); VICE DOLLS(1961, Fr.); CARTOUCHE(1962, Fr./Ital.); GERMINAL(1963, Fr.); YOUR TURN, DARLING(1963, Fr.); SPIRITS OF THE DEAD(1969, Fr./Ital.); BLOOD ROSE, THE(1970, Fr.)
Rufus LeMaire
BROADWAY SCANDALS(1929), ch
William LeMaire
LIGHT OF WESTERN STARS, THE(1930); PAINTED DESERT, THE(1931); I AM A FUGITIVE FROM A CHAIN GANG(1932); 20,000 YEARS IN SING SING(1933); LONE COWBOY(1934)
Jean Lemaitre
LOVE IS A BALL(1963)
Isobel LeMall
THIRTEENTH GUEST, THE(1932)
Tania Lemani
HELL WITH HEROES, THE(1968); THAT TENDER TOUCH(1969)
Tanya Lemani
GLOBAL AFFAIR, A(1964); DEAD HEAT ON A MERRY-GO-ROUND(1966); LAST MOMENT, THE(1966); KING'S PIRATE(1967); BIG DADDY(1969)
Lucienne Lemarchand
CRIME AND PUNISHMENT(1935, Fr.)
Jacques Lemare
TEMPTATION(1962, Fr.), ph
Charles LeMarie
RAZOR'S EDGE, THE(1946), cos
Francis Lemarque
COUNTERFEITERS OF PARIS, THE(1962, Fr., Ital.), m; PLAYTIME(1973, Fr.), m
Oliver LeMat
1984
CAGED WOMEN(1984, Ital./Fr.), w
Paul LeMat
AMERICAN GRAFFITI(1973); ALOHA, BOBBY AND ROSE(1975); CITIZENS BAND(1977); MORE AMERICAN GRAFFITI(1979); MELVIN AND HOWARD(1980); DEATH VALLEY(1982); JIMMY THE KID(1982); STRANGE INVADERS(1983)
Misc. Talkies
ROCK 'N' RULE(1983)
Alan LeMay
NORTHWEST MOUNTED POLICE(1940), w; REAP THE WILD WIND(1942), w; ADVENTURES OF MARK TWAIN, THE(1944), w; STORY OF DR. WASSELL, THE(1944), w; SAN ANTONIO(1945), w; CHEYENNE(1947), w; GUNFIGHTERS, THE(1947), w; TAP ROOTS(1948), w; WALKING HILLS, THE(1949), w; HIGH LONESOME(1950), d&w; ROCKY MOUNTAIN(1950), w; SUNDOWNERS, THE(1950), p, w; QUEBEC(1951), p, w; BLACKBEARD THE PIRATE(1952), w; I DREAM OF JEANIE(1952), w; FLIGHT NURSE(1953), w; VANISHING AMERICAN, THE(1955), w; SEARCHERS, THE(1956), w; UNFORGIVEN, THE(1960), w
Pierre LeMay
Misc. Silents
REAPERS, THE(1916)
Stephan LeMay
HOME MOVIES(1979), w
Charles LeMayne
HELL FIRE AUSTIN(1932)
Harvey Lembeck
FINDERS KEEPERS(1951); FOURTEEN HOURS(1951); FROGMEN, THE(1951); YOU'RE IN THE NAVY NOW(1951); BACK AT THE FRONT(1952); JUST ACROSS THE STREET(1952); GIRLS IN THE NIGHT(1953); MISSION OVER KOREA(1953); STALAG 17(1953); COMMAND, THE(1954); BETWEEN HEAVEN AND HELL(1956); LAST TIME I SAW ARCHIE, THE(1961); SAIL A CROOKED SHIP(1961); VIEW FROM THE BRIDGE, A(1962, Fr./Ital.); BEACH PARTY(1963); LOVE WITH THE PROPER STRANGER(1963); BIKINI BEACH(1964); PAJAMA PARTY(1964); UNSINKABLE MOLLY BROWN, THE(1964); BEACH BLANKET BINGO(1965); DR. GOLDFOOT AND THE BIKINI MACHINE(1965); HOW TO STUFF A WILD BIKINI(1965); SERGEANT DEADHEAD(1965); FIREBALL 590(1966); GHOST IN THE INVISIBLE BIKINI(1966); SPIRIT IS WILLING, THE(1967); HELLO DOWN THERE(1969); THERE IS NO 13(1977); GONG SHOW MOVIE, THE(1980)
Michael Lembeck
BOYS IN COMPANY C, THE(1978, U.S./Hong Kong); IN-LAWS, THE(1979); GORP(1980); ON THE RIGHT TRACK(1981)
Grigori Lemberg
Misc. Silents
ABORTION(1924, USSR), d
Marc Lemberger
FLASHDANCE(1983)
Francine Lembi
CHU CHU AND THE PHILLY FLASH(1981); DREAM ON(1981)
1984
ADVENTURES OF BUCKAROO BANZAI: ACROSS THE 8TH DIMENSION, THE(1984)
Lilly Lembo
PHAROAH'S WOMAN, THE(1961, Ital.); DEATH SENTENCE(1967, Ital.)
Gary LeMel
MAIN EVENT, THE(1979), md
Roger Lemelin
ODYSSEY OF THE PACIFIC(1983, Can./Fr.), w
Roger LeMesurier
1984
SQUIZZY TAYLOR(1984, Aus.), p
David Lemieux
SPOOK WHO SAT BY THE DOOR, THE(1973)

Pierre Lemieux
GAS(1981, Can.)
Stanley Lemin
HAPPIEST DAYS OF YOUR LIFE(1950, Brit.); BRANDY FOR THE PARSON(1952, Brit.)
Odie Lemire
THIRTEENTH LETTER, THE(1951)
Klaus Lemke
48 HOURS TO ACAPULCO(1968, Ger.), d
Tutte Lemkow
LOST PEOPLE, THE(1950, Brit.); MOULIN ROUGE(1952); CAPTAIN'S PARADISE, THE(1953, Brit.), a, a, ch; I AM A CAMERA(1955, Brit.); IRON PETTICOAT, THE(1956, Brit.); FIRE DOWN BELOW(1957, U.S./Brit.), ch; HIGH FLIGHT(1957, Brit.), ch; BONJOUR TRISTESSE(1958), a, ch; BEN HUR(1959); TOO MANY CROOKS(1959, Brit.); BOY WHO STOLE A MILLION, THE(1960, Brit.); SIEGE OF SIDNEY STREET, THE(1960, Brit.); STRANGLERS OF BOMBAY, THE(1960, Brit.); TOMMY THE TOREADOR(1960, Brit.); GREEN HELMET, THE(1961, Brit.); GUNS OF NAVARONE, THE(1961); SECRET OF MONTE CRISTO, THE(1961, Brit.); WEEKEND WITH LULU, A(1961, Brit.); GUNS OF DARKNESS(1962, Brit.); CRACKSMAN, THE(1963, Brit.); HELLFIRE CLUB, THE(1963, Brit.); VICTORS, THE(1963); WRONG ARM OF THE LAW, THE(1963, Brit.); MOON-SPINNERS, THE(1964); MASQUERADE(1965, Brit.); SPYLARKS(1965, Brit.); WRONG BOX, THE(1966, Brit.); CASINO ROYALE(1967, Brit.), ch; FATHOM(1967); FEARLESS VAMPIRE KILLERS, OR PARDON ME BUT YOUR TEETH ARE IN MY NECK, THE(1967), ch; DUFFY(1968, Brit.); INSPECTOR CLOUSEAU(1968, Brit.); JUSTINE(1969); FIDDLER ON THE ROOF(1971); THEATRE OF BLOOD(1973, Brit.), a, ch; LOVE AND DEATH(1975); RAIDERS OF THE LOST ARK(1981); SPHINX(1981)
Fred Lemler
LUNCH WAGON(1981), ph
John Lemma
HORNET'S NEST(1970)
Willie Lemmey
BANG THE DRUM SLOWLY(1973)
Otto Lemming
WILD IS MY LOVE(1963), w
James Lemmo
ONE DOWN TWO TO GO(1982), ph; LAST FIGHT, THE(1983), ph; VIGILANTE(1983), ph
1984
FEAR CITY(1984), ph
Joan Lemmo
MARIGOLD MAN(1970); PARALLAX VIEW, THE(1974); SILENT SCREAM(1980)
1984
KARATE KID, THE(1984)
Chris Lemmon
HAPPY HOOKER GOES TO HOLLYWOOD, THE(1980); JUST BEFORE DAWN(1980)
Misc. Talkies
C.O.D.(1983)
Christopher Lemmon
1984
CANNONBALL RUN II(1984); SWING SHIFT(1984)
Jack Lemmon
YOU CAN'T RUN AWAY FROM IT(1956); TRIBUTE(1980, Can.); IT SHOULD HAPPEN TO YOU(1954); PHFFFT!(1954); MISTER ROBERTS(1955); MY SISTER EILEEN(1955); THREE FOR THE SHOW(1955); FIRE DOWN BELOW(1957, U.S./Brit.); OPERATION MAD BALL(1957); BELL, BOOK AND CANDLE(1958); COWBOY(1958); IT HAPPENED TO JANE(1959); SOME LIKE IT HOT(1959); APARTMENT, THE(1960); PEPE(1960); WACKIEST SHIP IN THE ARMY, THE(1961); DAYS OF WINE AND ROSES(1962); NOTORIOUS LANDLADY, THE(1962); STOWAWAY IN THE SKY(1962, Fr.); IRMA LA DOUCE(1963); UNDER THE YUM-YUM TREE(1963); GOOD NEIGHBOR SAM(1964); GREAT RACE, THE(1965); HOW TO MURDER YOUR WIFE(1965); FORTUNE COOKIE, THE(1966); LUV(1967); ODD COUPLE, THE(1968); APRIL FOOLS, THE(1969); OUT OF TOWNERS, THE(1970); KOTCH(1971), a, d; AVANTI!(1972); WAR BETWEEN MEN AND WOMEN, THE(1972); SAVE THE TIGER(1973); FRONT PAGE, THE(1974); ENTERTAINER, THE(1975); PRISONER OF SECOND AVENUE, THE(1975); ALEX AND THE GYPSY(1976); AIRPORT '77(1977); CHINA SYNDROME, THE(1979); TRIBUTE(1980, Can.); BUDDY BUDDY(1981); MISSING(1982)
1984
MASS APPEAL(1984)
John Uhler Lemmon II
NOTORIOUS LANDLADY, THE(1962)
C.B. Lemmond
MY DOG, BUDDY(1960)
Lilla Lemmond
MY DOG, BUDDY(1960)
Travis Lemmond
MY DOG, BUDDY(1960)
Michele Lemoigne
TESTAMENT OF ORPHEUS, THE(1962, Fr.)
Raymond Lemoigne
NO TIME FOR ECSTASY(1963, Fr.), ph; FANTOMAS STRIKES BACK(1965, Fr./Ital.), ph; SWEET SKIN(1965, Fr./Ital.), ph; MADMAN OF LAB 4, THE(1967, Fr.), ph; SHADOW OF EVIL(1967, Fr./Ital.), ph; TO COMMIT A MURDER(1970, Fr./Ital./Ger.), ph
Michael Lemoine
PLANETS AGAINST US, THE(1961, Ital./Fr.)
Michel Lemoine
FRUIT IS RIPE, THE(1961, Fr./Ital.); PRISONER OF THE IRON MASK(1962, Fr./Ital.); CONQUEST OF MYCENE(1965, Ital., Fr.); NIGHT OF LUST(1965, Fr.); ROAD TO FORT ALAMO, THE(1966, Fr./Ital.); WILD, WILD PLANET, THE(1967, Ital.)
Michele Lemoine
SIN ON THE BEACH(1964, Fr.)
Lisa Lemole
DRIVE-IN(1976)
Bob Lemon
KID FROM CLEVELAND, THE(1949); WINNING TEAM, THE(1952)

Brian B. Lemon
Silents
FLYING FIFTY-FIVE, THE(1924, Brit.)

C.O. Lemon
SANDERS OF THE RIVER(1935, Brit.), tech adv

Max Lemon
PICNIC AT HANGING ROCK(1975, Aus.), ed; F.J. HOLDEN, THE(1977, Aus.), ed; LAST WAVE, THE(1978, Aus.), ed; DAWN(1979, Aus.), ed; NEXT OF KIN(1983, Aus.), ed
1984
FOREVER YOUNG(1984, Brit.), ed

Meadowlark Lemon
FISH THAT SAVED PITTSBURGH, THE(1979); MODERN ROMANCE(1981)

Frenchie Lemond
DAYS OF HEAVEN(1978)

Meg Lemonnier
GREEN GLOVE, THE(1952); MAXIME(1962, Fr.)

Theopharis Lemonopoulos
DREAM OF KINGS, A(1969)

Charles Lemons
TOGETHER BROTHERS(1974)

John K. Lemons
ORGANIZATION, THE(1971), cos

Johenne Lemont
WILD WHEELS(1969)

John Lemont
GREEN BUDDHA, THE(1954, Brit.), d; WITNESS IN THE DARK(1959, Brit.), w; AND WOMEN SHALL WEEP(1960, Brit.), d, w; SHAKEDOWN, THE(1960, Brit.), d, w; FRIGHTENED CITY, THE(1961, Brit.), p, d, w; KONGA(1961, Brit.), d

Charles Lemontier
MR. ORCHID(1948, Fr.); ROOM UPSTAIRS, THE(1948, Fr.); RUY BLAS(1948, Fr.); UTOPIA(1952, Fr./Ital.); LOVE IN THE AFTERNOON(1957)

Jules Lemontier
Silents
HEARTS OF THE WORLD(1918)

Rusty Lemorande
YENTL(1983), p
1984
ELECTRIC DREAMS(1984), p, w

Vince Lemorocco
1984
MAKING THE GRADE(1984)

Carlos Lemos
HORROR OF THE ZOMBIES(1974, Span.)

Luis Lemos
1984
DEMONS IN THE GARDEN(1984, Span.)

Charles LeMoyne
DYNAMITE RANCH(1932); COWBOY AND THE KID,THE(1936); RIDE 'EM COWBOY(1936); DEVIL'S SADDLE LEGION(1937); EMPTY HOLSTERS(1937); EMPTY SADDLES(1937); LAW FOR TOMBSTONE(1937); LEFT-HANDED LAW(1937); OUTLAWS OF THE PRAIRIE(1938); SUDDEN BILL DORN(1938)
Silents
CRASHIN' THRU(1923)
Misc. Silents
LAD AND THE LION, THE(1917); TREAT 'EM ROUGH(1919)

James Lemp
MACHISMO–40 GRAVES FOR 40 GUNS(1970); VALDEZ IS COMING(1971)

Fay Lemport
Silents
DADDY LONG LEGS(1919); HUCKLEBERRY FINN(1920)

William Lemuels
HIS FAMILY TREE(1936); TOAST OF NEW YORK, THE(1937)

Conchita Lemus
APACHE ROSE(1947)

Koula Lemvessi
ASTERO(1960, Gr.)

Gunnar Lemvigh
WHILE THE ATTORNEY IS ASLEEP(1945, Den.); CHRISTINE KEELER AFFAIR, THE(1964, Brit.); CRAZY PARADISE(1965, Den.)

Paolo Lena
VOYAGE, THE(1974, Ital.)

Marcia Lenack
THREE RUSSIAN GIRLS(1943)

Peter Lenahan
EL CONDOR(1970)

Grace Lenard
GIRLS OF THE ROAD(1940); SECRETS OF A MODEL(1940); THEY KNEW WHAT THEY WANTED(1940); HONOLULU LU(1941); PARIS CALLING(1941); PLAYMATES(1941); BROADWAY(1942); MAN'S WORLD, A(1942); SILVER BULLET, THE(1942); STRICTLY IN THE GROOVE(1942); MAN FROM FRISCO(1944); ONCE UPON A TIME(1944); SUNDOWN VALLEY(1944); JOHNNY STOOL PIGEON(1949); I WAS A COMMUNIST FOR THE F.B.I.(1951); QUEEN FOR A DAY(1951); ABBOTT AND COSTELLO GO TO MARS(1953); FOXFIRE(1955)

Kay Lenard
CIMARRON KID, THE(1951), w; WINGS OF THE HAWK(1953), w; MA AND PA KETTLE AT HOME(1954), w; KETTLES IN THE OZARKS, THE(1956), w; NAVY WIFE(1956), w

L.G. Lenard
HOLLYWOOD ROUNDUP(1938), p

Mark Lenard
HANG'EM HIGH(1968); STAR TREK: THE MOTION PICTURE(1979)
1984
STAR TREK III: THE SEARCH FOR SPOCK(1984)

Melvyn Lenard
DESPERATE WOMEN, THE(?), m; RIDE THE HIGH IRON(1956), m; DAUGHTER OF DR. JEKYLL(1957), md

Ernest Lenart
INTERNATIONAL SQUADRON(1941)

Rena Lenart
DATE WITH JUDY, A(1948); SUMMER STOCK(1950)

Jean Lenauer
DANGER IS A WOMAN(1952, Fr.), titles; MY DINNER WITH ANDRE(1981)

Karen Lenay
ME AND THE COLONEL(1958)

Georges Lend
COUSIN, COUSINE(1976, Fr.), ph

Mary Lou Lender
COUNTY FAIR(1937); PROFESSOR BEWARE(1938)

Armand Lenders
Silents
AT THE VILLA ROSE(1920, Brit.)

William Lenders
Misc. Silents
BELONGING(1922, Brit.)

R. Lendruz
BAKER'S WIFE, THE(1940, Fr.), ph

Nancy Lenehan
SMOKEY AND THE BANDIT II(1980); JEKYLL AND HYDE...TOGETHER AGAIN(1982)

Mow Leng
1984
KILLING FIELDS, THE(1984, Brit.)

William C. Lengle
24 HOURS(1931), w

Suzanne Lenglen
THINGS ARE LOOKING UP(1934, Brit.)

Andre Lenglet
EXCUSE MY GLOVE(1936, Brit.)

Francesco Lengo
HEART AND SOUL(1950, Ital.)

Ivan Lengyel
CLOUDS OVER ISRAEL(1966, Israel), d

Melchior Lengyel
STRANGE CARGO(1929), w; CARAVAN(1934), w; CATHERINE THE GREAT(1934, Brit.), w; TEMPTATION(1935, Brit.), d&w; ANGEL(1937), w; NINOTCHKA(1939), w; TO BE OR NOT TO BE(1942), w; ROYAL SCANDAL, A(1945), w; SILK STOCKINGS(1957), w
Silents
TYPHOON, THE(1914), w

Melchoir Lengyel
DAYS OF GLORY(1944), w
Silents
FORBIDDEN PARADISE(1924), w

Billy Lenhardt
SPOTLIGHT SCANDALS(1943)

Bill Lenhart
UNDER-PUP, THE(1939)

Billy Lenhart
MELODY OF THE PLAINS(1937); IN THE NAVY(1941); MAN FROM MONTANA(1941); MELODY LANE(1941); NEVER GIVE A SUCKER AN EVEN BREAK(1941); CINDERELLA SWINGS IT(1942); ARMY WIVES(1944)

Buddy "Bull Fiddle Bill" Lenhart
TWO-GUN TROUBADOR(1939)

Paul Leni
LAST WARNING, THE(1929), d
Silents
CAT AND THE CANARY, THE(1927), d; MAN WHO LAUGHS, THE(1927), d
Misc. Silents
BACKSTAIRS(1921, Ger.), d; WAXWORKS(1924, Ger.), d; CHINESE PARROT, THE(1927), d

Christine Lenier
NUN, THE(1971, Fr.)

Deirdre Lenihan
GLASS HOUSES(1972)

Winifred Lenihan
WORKING GIRLS(1931), w

Winifrid Lenihan
JIGSAW(1949)

M. Lenin
Misc. Silents
FIGHT FOR THE 'ULTIMATUM' FACTORY(1923, USSR)

The Leningrad Philharmonic Orchestra
MORNING STAR(1962, USSR)

Boris Lenissevitch
UP TO HIS EARS(1966, Fr./Ital.)

Jean Lenivick
PALMY DAYS(1931)

E. Lenkers
FREUD(1962)

Philip Lenkowsky
JANE AUSTEN IN MANHATTAN(1980); ENDLESS LOVE(1981)
1984
AMADEUS(1984)

Patricia Lenn
TWO GIRLS AND A SAILOR(1944)

Arthur Lennard
Silents
FIRES OF INNOCENCE(1922, Brit.); LADY NOGGS-PEERESS(1929, Brit.)
Misc. Silents
SWEET AND TWENTY(1919, Brit.); LILAC SUNBONNET, THE(1922, Brit.)

Elizabeth Lennard
HELL ON EARTH(1934, Ger.)

Kay Lennard
RICOCHET ROMANCE(1954), w

Maria Lennard
PURE HELL OF ST. TRINIAN'S, THE(1961, Brit.); BILLIE(1965); MUNSTER, GO HOME(1966); KARATE KILLERS, THE(1967); TOP OF THE HEAP(1972)
Philip Lennard
UNHOLY FOUR, THE(1954, Brit.)
Phillip Lennard
SWORD AND THE ROSE, THE(1953)
Isobel Lennart
AFFAIRS OF MARTHA, THE(1942), w; STRANGER IN TOWN, A(1943), w; LOST ANGEL(1944), w; ANCHORS AWEIGH(1945), w; HOLIDAY IN MEXICO(1946), w; IT HAPPENED IN BROOKLYN(1947), w; KISSING BANDIT, THE(1948), w; EAST SIDE, WEST SIDE(1949), w; HOLIDAY AFFAIR(1949), w; LIFE OF HER OWN, A(1950), w; IT'S A BIG COUNTRY(1951), w; MY WIFE'S BEST FRIEND(1952), w; SKIRTS AHOY!(1952), w; GIRL NEXT DOOR, THE(1953), w; LATIN LOVERS(1953), w; LOVE ME OR LEAVE ME(1955), w; MEET ME IN LAS VEGAS(1956), w; THIS COULD BE THE NIGHT(1957), w; INN OF THE SIXTH HAPPINESS, THE(1958), w; MERRY ANDREW(1958), w; PLEASE DON'T EAT THE DAISIES(1960), w; SUNDOWNERS, THE(1960), w; PERIOD OF ADJUSTMENT(1962), w; TWO FOR THE SEESAW(1962), w; FITZWILLY(1967), w; FUNNY GIRL(1968), w
Rena Lennart
PRINCE OF FOXES(1949)
Julian Lenne
Silents
PENROD(1922)
Claudia Lennear
THUNDERBOLT AND LIGHTFOOT(1974)
Ann Lenner
GARRISON FOLLIES(1940, Brit.)
Shirley Lenner
THOSE KIDS FROM TOWN(1942, Brit.)
Roy Lennert
TRAUMA(1962)
Bill Lenney
UNHOLY FOUR, THE(1954, Brit.), ed
Ben Lennick
FLAMING FRONTIER(1958, Can.)
M. Lennick
LAST CHASE, THE(1981), spec eff
Michael Lennick
VIDEODROME(1983, Can.), spec eff
Angus Lennie
GREAT ESCAPE, THE(1963); V.I.P.s, THE(1963, Brit.); SQUADRON 633(1964, U.S./Brit.); 633 SQUADRON(1964); OH! WHAT A LOVELY WAR(1969, Brit.)
Bill Lennie
FUNNY MONEY(1983, Brit.), ed
Bert Lennon
Silents
FAMILY SKELETON, THE(1918), w
James F. Lennon
WORLD IN MY CORNER(1956)
James Lennon
IRON MAN, THE(1951); MOVIE MOVIE(1978)
Jim Lennon
ALIAS THE CHAMP(1949)
Jimmy Lennon
HAMMER(1972); TRAIN RIDE TO HOLLYWOOD(1975); MATILDA(1978); MAIN EVENT, THE(1979)
John Lennon
HARD DAY'S NIGHT, A(1964, Brit.), a, m; HELP!(1965, Brit.); HOW I WON THE WAR(1967, Brit.); OH! CALCUTTA!(1972), w
Joseph Lennon
HAIR(1979)
Percy Lennon
MILLION DOLLAR MERMAID(1952); SON OF THE RENEGADE(1953)
Terrence Lennon
BUGS BUNNY'S THIRD MOVIE–1001 RABBIT TALES(1982), anim
Terry Lennon
RACE FOR YOUR LIFE, CHARLIE BROWN(1977), anim
Thomas Lennon
GRAND JURY(1936), w; MURDER ON A BRIDLE PATH(1936), w; SECOND WIFE(1936), w; SILLY BILLIES(1936), w; SPECIAL INVESTIGATOR(1936), w; CRIMINAL LAWYER(1937), w; MAN WHO FOUND HIMSELF, THE(1937), w; RACING LADY(1937), w; CROWD ROARS, THE(1938), w; SPELLBINDER, THE(1939), w; WE GO FAST(1941), w; KNICKERBOCKER HOLIDAY(1944), w; KILLER McCOY(1947), w
Thomas Lloyd Lennon
MEN ARE SUCH FOOLS(1933), w
Toby Lennon
CONQUEROR WORM, THE(1968, Brit.); MUTATIONS, THE(1974, Brit.)
Tom Lennon
SECRETS OF A NURSE(1938), w
Tony Lennon
EMBEZZLER, THE(1954, Brit.)
Cosmo Gordon Lennox
Silents
MARRIAGE OF KITTY, THE(1915), w; PUPPET MAN, THE(1921, Brit.), w
Dora Lennox
Silents
BACHELORS' CLUB, THE(1921, Brit.)
Misc. Silents
CROXLEY MASTER, THE(1921, Brit.)
Doug Lennox
BREAKING POINT(1976); SIEGE(1983, Can.)
1984
POLICE ACADEMY(1984)
Misc. Talkies
KELLY(1981, Can.)

Gillian Lennox
OFFERING, THE(1966, Can.), w
Helen Lennox
KNACK ... AND HOW TO GET IT, THE(1965, Brit.)
John Lennox
NO HIGHWAY IN THE SKY(1951, Brit.)
Michael Lennox
WHISPERING CITY(1947, Can.), w
Mike Lennox
SMASHING TIME(1967 Brit.); BEST HOUSE IN LONDON, THE(1969, Brit.)
Pat Lennox
DANNY BOY(1941, Brit.)
Red Lennox
Silents
SPLITTING THE BREEZE(1927)
Vera Lennox
END OF THE ROAD, THE(1936, Brit.); QUEEN OF HEARTS(1936, Brit.); WHEN THE DEVIL WAS WELL(1937, Brit.); LASSIE FROM LANCASHIRE(1938, Brit.); IN THE WAKE OF A STRANGER(1960, Brit.)
Anthony Lenny
ALF 'N' FAMILY(1968, Brit.), ed
Bil Lenny
FURTHER UP THE CREEK!(1958, Brit.), ed
Bill Lenny
RACE FOR LIFE, A(1955, Brit.), ed; ABOMINABLE SNOWMAN OF THE HIMALAYAS, THE(1957, Brit.), ed; BREAK IN THE CIRCLE, THE(1957, Brit.), ed; CAMP ON BLOOD ISLAND, THE(1958, Brit.), ed; HORROR OF DRACULA, THE(1958, Brit.), ed; STEEL BAYONET, THE(1958, Brit.), ed; DENTIST IN THE CHAIR(1960, Brit.), ed; DAY THE EARTH CAUGHT FIRE, THE(1961, Brit.), ed; STOP ME BEFORE I KILL!(1961, Brit.), ed; LIFE IS A CIRCUS(1962, Brit.), ed; NEARLY A NASTY ACCIDENT(1962, Brit.), ed; RING-A-DING RHYTHM(1962, Brit.), ed; FRIENDS AND NEIGHBORS(1963, Brit.), ed; GET ON WITH IT(1963, Brit.), ed; MOUSE ON THE MOON, THE(1963, Brit.), ed; 80,000 SUSPECTS(1963, Brit.), ed; JIG SAW(1965, Brit.), ed; WHERE THE SPIES ARE(1965, Brit.), ed; BEAUTY JUNGLE, THE(1966, Brit.), ed; CASINO ROYALE(1967, Brit.), ed; DON'T RAISE THE BRIDGE, LOWER THE RIVER(1968, Brit.), ed; MACKENNA'S GOLD(1969), ed; CROMWELL(1970, Brit.), ed; PUPPET ON A CHAIN(1971, Brit.), ed; POPE JOAN(1972, Brit.), ed; CONFESSIONS OF A WINDOW CLEANER(1974, Brit.), ed; SHILLINGBURY BLOWERS, THE(1980, Brit.), ed; DANGEROUS DAVIES–THE LAST DETECTIVE(1981, Brit.), ed
Edith Lenny
BABES IN BAGDAD(1952), ed
Charles Leno
GREAT GAME, THE(1953, Brit.); PASSING STRANGER, THE(1954, Brit.); SOULS IN CONFLICT(1955, Brit.); DEVIL'S PASS, THE(1957, Brit.); WHITE TRAP, THE(1959, Brit.); TWO GENTLEMEN SHARING(1969, Brit.)
Jay Leno
AMERICAN HOT WAX(1978); SILVER BEARS(1978); AMERICATHON(1979)
Gabriel Lenoff
MISSION TO MOSCOW(1943); THIS LAND IS MINE(1943)
Jack Lenoir
LOVE AND DEATH(1975); ONCE IN PARIS(1978); DOGS OF WAR, THE(1980, Brit.); VICTORY(1981)
Misc. Talkies
BREAKFAST IN PARIS(1981)
Jean Lenoir
LILIOM(1935, Fr.), m; SECOND BUREAU(1936, Fr.), m; SACRIFICE OF HONOR(1938, Fr.), m; DEVIL IS AN EMPRESS, THE(1939, Fr.), m; DOUBLE CRIME IN THE MAGINOT LINE(1939, Fr.), m
Lee Lenoir
BLACK MAGIC(1949)
Leon Lenoir
BRAZIL(1944); CLOAK AND DAGGER(1946); CRIME DOCTOR'S MAN HUNT(1946); GILDA(1946); NIGHT AND DAY(1946); THRILL OF BRAZIL, THE(1946); CRIME DOCTOR'S GAMBLE(1947); ESCAPE ME NEVER(1947); IVY(1947); RIDE THE PINK HORSE(1947); SENATOR WAS INDISCREET, THE(1947); STALLION ROAD(1947); ARCH OF TRIUMPH(1948); TO THE ENDS OF THE EARTH(1948); MAN FROM CAIRO, THE(1953); STRANGER ON THE PROWL(1953, Ital.)
Lion Lenoir
CORPSE CAME C.O.D., THE(
Richelle LeNoir
GORDON'S WAR(1973)
Rudy Lenoir
DANIELLA BY NIGHT(1962, Fr/Ger.); VICE AND VIRTUE(1965, Fr./Ital.); FANTOMAS(1966, Fr./Ital.); DON'T LOOK NOW(1969, Brit./Fr.)
Rosetta Lenoire
ANNA LUCASTA(1958); SUNSHINE BOYS, THE(1975)
Janine Lenon
Misc. Talkies
AROUSED(1968)
Col. Lenone
Silents
JACK AND JILL(1917)
Lydia Lenosi
SUMMER LOVERS(1982)
Bernard Lenrow
HOUSE ON 92ND STREET, THE(1945)
Bernie Lenrow
VIOLATORS, THE(1957)
Terry Lens
RING OF BRIGHT WATER(1969, Brit.), prod d
Birger Lensander
SILENCE, THE(1964, Swed.); HERE'S YOUR LIFE(1968, Swed.)
Rula Lenska
ALFIE DARLING(1975, Brit.); CONFESSIONS OF A POP PERFORMER(1975, Brit.); UNDERCOVERS HERO(1975, Brit.); DEADLY FEMALES, THE(1976, Brit.)
A. Lenskaya
DAY THE EARTH FROZE, THE(1959, Fin./USSR)

O.G. Lenskaya
Misc. Silents
RIVALS(1933, USSR)
Leib Lensky
WHO SAYS I CAN'T RIDE A RAINBOW!(1971); RIVALS(1972); LOVE AND DEATH(1975); VERDICT, THE(1982); ECHOES(1983)
1984
OVER THE BROOKLYN BRIDGE(1984)
Lieb Lensky
BYE BYE BRAVERMAN(1968)
Judy Lenson
ROYAL WEDDING(1951)
Jill Lent
GIANT(1956)
Judy Lent
GIANT(1956)
Miklos Lente
U-TURN(1973, Can.), ph; INBREAKER, THE(1974, Can.), ph; IN PRAISE OF OLDER WOMEN(1978, Can.), ph; SUZANNE(1980, Can.), ph; AGENCY(1981, Can.), ph; HAPPY BIRTHDAY TO ME(1981), ph; JULIE DARLING(1982, Can./Ger.), ph; SCREWBALLS(1983), ph
1984
BEDROOM EYES(1984, Can.), ph
Bernard Lenteric
SPERMULA(1976, Fr.), p
Lara Lenti
HOUSE OF 1,000 DOLLS(1967, Ger./Span./Brit.)
Massimo Lentini
1990: THE BRONX WARRIORS(1983, Ital.), cos
1984
CONQUEST(1984, Ital./Span./Mex.), art d
Christian Lentretian
GREEN ROOM, THE(1979, Fr.); LOVE ON THE RUN(1980, Fr.)
Ya. Lents
UNCOMMON THIEF, AN(1967, USSR)
Irene Lentz
Silents
TAILOR MADE MAN, A(1922)
Adolfo Lenvell
PUT UP OR SHUT UP(1968, Arg.)
Lotte Lenya
THREEPENNY OPERA, THE(1931, Ger./U.S.); ROMAN SPRING OF MRS. STONE, THE(1961, U.S./Brit.); FROM RUSSIA WITH LOVE(1963, Brit.); APPOINTMENT, THE(1969); SEMI-TOUGH(1977)
A. Francis Lenz
Misc. Silents
BARKER, THE(1917)
Carolyn Lenz
WHITE RAT(1972)
Cliff Lenz
JOYRIDE(1977)
Kay Lenz
BREEZY(1973); WHITE LINE FEVER(1975, Can.); GREAT SCOUT AND CATHOUSE THURSDAY, THE(1976); MOVING VIOLATION(1976); MEAN DOG BLUES(1978); PASSAGE, THE(1979, Brit.); FAST-WALKING(1982)
Richard Lenz
SHOOTIST, THE(1976)
Rick Lenz
CACTUS FLOWER(1969); HOW DO I LOVE THEE?(1970); SCANDALOUS JOHN(1971); WHERE DOES IT HURT?(1972); LITTLE DRAGONS, THE(1980); MELVIN AND HOWARD(1980)
Rudolf Lenz
STORY OF VICKIE, THE(1958, Aust.); EFFI BRIEST(1974, Ger.); LILI MARLEEN(1981, Ger.)
Werner M. Lenz
RED-DRAGON(1967, Ital./Ger./US), ph, ed
Gerd Lenze
NOT RECONCILED, OR "ONLY VIOLENCE HELPS WHERE IT RULES"(1969, Ger.)
Don Lenzer
ROAD MOVIE(1974), ph
Bert Lenzi
Misc. Talkies
BRUTAL JUSTICE(1978), d
Bruno Lenzi
AMARCORD(1974, Ital.)
Giovanna Lenzi
CLIMAX, THE(1967, Fr., Ital.); GOD FORGIVES–I DON'T!(1969, Ital./Span.)
Laura Lenzi
BURNING YEARS, THE(1979, Ital.)
1984
BASILEUS QUARTET(1984, Ital.)
Umberto Lenzi
SAMSON AND THE SLAVE QUEEN(1963, Ital.), d, w; SANDOKAN THE GREAT(1964, Fr./Ital./Span.), d, w; TERROR OF THE BLACK MASK(1967, Fr./Ital.), d, w; ALMOST HUMAN(1974,Ital.), d; DEATH RACE(1978, Ital.), p; EYEBALL(1978, Ital.), d; FROM HELL TO VICTORY(1979, Fr./Ital./Span.), w; CITY OF THE WALKING DEAD(1983, Span./Ital.), d
Misc. Talkies
SPASMO(1976), d
Rosemary Lenzo
WINTER OF OUR DREAMS(1982, Aus.)
Connie Leo
BLONDIE'S BLESSED EVENT(1942), w
Eddie Leo
CALCUTTA(1947)
Franco Leo
JOHNNY HAMLET(1972, Ital.)

Frank Leo
INCIDENT IN AN ALLEY(1962); SHELL SHOCK(1964); ANGELS DIE HARD(1970)
Len Leo
Misc. Silents
LAW AND THE LADY, THE(1924)
Linda Leo
RESCUE SQUAD, THE(1963, Brit.)
Malcolm Leo
THIS IS ELVIS(1982), p,d&w
Maurice Leo
HOLLYWOOD HOTEL(1937), w; GOLD DIGGERS IN PARIS(1938), w; SWING YOUR LADY(1938), w; GOING PLACES(1939), w; FLIGHT ANGELS(1940), w; HIT PARADE OF 1941(1940), w; HELLO SUCKER(1941), w; THEY MEET AGAIN(1941), w; SO'S YOUR UNCLE(1943), w; HAT CHECK HONEY(1944), w; SWING IN THE SADDLE(1944), w
Robert Leo
YOUNG AND THE BRAVE, THE(1963), ed
Sandra Leo
LUNCH HOUR(1962, Brit.)
Leo Diamond and His Harmonaires
FOREVER YOURS(1945)
Leo Diamond and His Solitaires
SWEET ROSIE O'GRADY(1943)
Leo Diamond Quintet
HI' YA, SAILOR(1943); SWING OUT, SISTER(1945)
The Leo Lyons Orchestra
JAZZ BABIES(1932)
Leo Reisman Orchestra
STOLEN HEAVEN(1931), m
Jim Leom
DONKEY SKIN(1975, Fr.), art d
Alesia Leon
Misc. Silents
DEVIL'S PROFESSION, THE(1915, Brit.); CRIME AND THE PENALTY(1916, Brit.)
Anne Leon
APPOINTMENT IN LONDON(1953, Brit.); REACH FOR THE SKY(1957, Brit.); CARVE HER NAME WITH PRIDE(1958, Brit.); ROOM AT THE TOP(1959, Brit.); I LIKE MONEY(1962, Brit.)
Bob Leon
ROLLERBALL(1975)
Carlos Leon
LOS PLATILLOS VOLADORES(1955, Mex.), w
Charito Leon
SEPTEMBER STORM(1960)
Connie Leon
CLIVE OF INDIA(1935); GREAT GARRICK, THE(1937); HONEYMOON IN BALI(1939); LIGHT THAT FAILED, THE(1939); RAINS CAME, THE(1939); MY SON, MY SON!(1940); WESTERNER, THE(1940); SINGAPORE WOMAN(1941); WHERE DID YOU GET THAT GIRL?(1941); WOLF MAN, THE(1941); BOMBAY CLIPPER(1942); MRS. MINIVER(1942); TALES OF MANHATTAN(1942); THUNDER BIRDS(1942); BEHIND THE RISING SUN(1943); FOREVER AND A DAY(1943); SONG OF BERNADETTE, THE(1943); SWEET ROSIE O'GRADY(1943); AND NOW TOMORROW(1944); LODGER, THE(1944); MY BUDDY(1944); PEARL OF DEATH, THE(1944); HANGOVER SQUARE(1945); LOVE LETTERS(1945); MINISTRY OF FEAR(1945); ANNA AND THE KING OF SIAM(1946); LOCKET, THE(1946); THAT BRENNAN GIRL(1946); THREE STRANGERS(1946); MOSS ROSE(1947); SMASH-UP, THE STORY OF A WOMAN(1947); JULIA MISBEHAVES(1948)
Dorothy Leon
LOVE IN A TAXI(1980)
Eva Leon
HOUSE OF PSYCHOTIC WOMEN, THE zero(1973, Span.); I HATE MY BODY(1975, Span./Switz.)
Fernando Leon
UNSATISFIED, THE(1964, Span.)
Gary Leon
DANTE'S INFERNO(1935)
Jean Leon
TASTE FOR WOMEN, A(1966, Fr./Ital.), d, w
Jerry Leon
BOOK OF NUMBERS(1973); SEVEN UPS, THE(1973)
Joe Leon
IF EVER I SEE YOU AGAIN(1978)
1984
ALMOST YOU(1984)
Joseph Leon
SWEET SMELL OF SUCCESS(1957); ACT ONE(1964); PEOPLE NEXT DOOR, THE(1970); SHAFT(1971); HE KNOWS YOU'RE ALONE(1980); JUST TELL ME WHAT YOU WANT(1980); SOPHIE'S CHOICE(1982); DANIEL(1983)
1984
COLD FEET(1984)
Katherine Leon
Silents
LEECH, THE(1921)
Linda Leon
ROOM AT THE TOP(1959, Brit.)
Lita Leon
GUN RUNNERS, THE(1958)
Madeline Leon
KITCHEN, THE(1961, Brit.); TELL-TALE HEART, THE(1962, Brit.)
Michael Leon
HAWAIIANS, THE(1970); HERO AT LARGE(1980)
Nissim Leon
RABBI AND THE SHIKSE, THE(1976, Israel), ph
Peggie Leon
GAL WHO TOOK THE WEST, THE(1949)
Peggy Leon
MEN OF THE NIGHT(1934); OUR LEADING CITIZEN(1939); I TAKE THIS WOMAN(1940); GIRL CRAZY(1943); JEALOUSY(1945); SENORITA FROM THE WEST(1945); CUBAN PETE(1946); POSSESSED(1947); FATHER OF THE BRIDE(1950); WABASH AVENUE(1950); FRENCH LINE, THE(1954)

Romulo Leon
MIRAGE(1972, Peru)
Rubin Leon
STAKEOUT ON DOPE STREET(1958)
Valerie Leon
SMASHING TIME(1967 Brit.); CARRY ON AGAIN, DOCTOR(1969, Brit.); ITALIAN JOB, THE(1969, Brit.); CARRY ON UP THE JUNGLE(1970, Brit.); THIS, THAT AND THE OTHER(1970, Brit.); BLOOD FROM THE MUMMY'S TOMB(1972, Brit.); SPY WHO LOVED ME, THE(1977, Brit.); REVENGE OF THE PINK PANTHER(1978); NO SEX PLEASE—WE'RE BRITISH(1979, Brit.); NEVER SAY NEVER AGAIN(1983)
Valery Leon
SMASHING TIME(1967 Brit.)
Victor Leon
MERRY WIDOW, THE(1934), w; MERRY WIDOW, THE(1952), w
Virginia Leon
DESPERATE WOMEN, THE(?)
Leon Woizikowski Ballet
SHE SHALL HAVE MUSIC(1935, Brit.)
Ada Leonard
FORTY NAUGHTY GIRLS(1937); MEET THE MISSUS(1937); MUSIC FOR MADAME(1937); STAGE DOOR(1937); MY DREAM IS YOURS(1949)
Adeline Leonard
JENNIFER ON MY MIND(1971), prod d; SEVEN UPS, THE(1973)
Archie Leonard
MRS. MIKE(1949); SET-UP, THE(1949)
Arthur Leonard
POCOMANIA(1939), p&d; STRAIGHT TO HEAVEN(1939), d; BOY! WHAT A GIRL(1947), d; SEPIA CINDERELLA(1947), p, d
Audrey Leonard
LOVE, HONOR AND BEHAVE(1938)
Barbara Leonard
DRAKE CASE, THE(1929); MEN OF THE NORTH(1930); ONE ROMANTIC NIGHT(1930); SCOTLAND YARD(1930); SON OF THE GODS(1930); BEAUTY AND THE BOSS(1932); LOVE AFFAIR(1932); MAN FROM YESTERDAY, THE(1932); ONE HOUR WITH YOU(1932); SUCCESSFUL CALAMITY, A(1932); THE CRASH(1932); DESIRABLE(1934); MERRY WIDOW, THE(1934); FOLIES DERGERE(1935); SENORA CASADA NECEISITA MARIDO(1935); WHITE ANGEL, THE(1936); ESPIONAGE(1937); CHARLIE CHAN IN THE CITY OF DARKNESS(1939)
Misc. Silents
LADIES OF THE NIGHT CLUB(1928)
Bernard Leonard
COUNTRYMAN(1982, Jamaica), art d
Betty Leonard
HALF-BREED, THE(1952)
Bob Leonard
Silents
GOLD RUSH, THE(1925)
Bobby Leonard
BEHIND THE EIGHT BALL(1942)
Brian Leonard
TICKET TO HEAVEN(1981)
Charle Leonard
LUCKY JORDAN(1942), w
Christopher Leonard
FOURTEEN, THE(1973, Brit.)
Cyril Leonard
Misc. Silents
ONE WONDERFUL NIGHT(1914)
David Leonard
VICTIMS OF PERSECUTION(1933), a, w; DON RICARDO RETURNS(1946); RENDEZVOUS 24(1946); BELLS OF SAN FERNANDO(1947); DESIRE ME(1947); INTRIGUE(1947); PHILO VANCE'S SECRET MISSION(1947); SONG OF MY HEART(1947); UNSUSPECTED, THE(1947); SWORD OF THE AVENGER(1948); ADVENTURES OF DON JUAN(1949); BLONDE ICE(1949); DARING CABALLERO, THE(1949); BORDER TREASURE(1950); CAPTAIN CAREY, U.S.A(1950); PAYMENT ON DEMAND(1951); FIGHTER ATTACK(1953); FOREVER FEMALE(1953); ROBE, THE(1953); SALOME(1953); DESIREE(1954); PRODIGAL, THE(1955); TRIAL(1955); LUST FOR LIFE(1956); SOMEBODY UP THERE LIKES ME(1956); SAY ONE FOR ME(1959); OCEAN'S ELEVEN(1960)
Don Leonard
KIMBERLEY JIM(1965, South Africa); WILD SEASON(1968, South Africa); CREATURES THE WORLD FORGOT(1971, Brit.)
Douglas Leonard
1984
LIES(1984, Brit.)
Eddie Leonard
MELODY LANE(1929); IF I HAD MY WAY(1940)
Elmore Leonard
3:10 TO YUMA(1957), w; TALL T, THE(1957), w; BIG BOUNCE, THE(1969), w; MOONSHINE WAR, THE(1970), w; VALDEZ IS COMING(1971), w; JOE KIDD(1972), w; MR. MAJESTYK(1974), w
1984
AMBASSADOR, THE(1984), w
F. Leonard
PINOCCHIO IN OUTER SPACE(1965, U.S./Bel.), m
Francios Leonard
1984
SMURFS AND THE MAGIC FLUTE, THE(1984, Fr./Belg.), ph
Francois Leonard
LUCKY LUKE(1971, Fr./Bel.), ph
George Leonard
STREET WITH NO NAME, THE(1948)
Grace Leonard
NORTH STAR, THE(1943); COVER GIRL(1944); RED PLANET MARS(1952)
Gus Leonard
SMART MONEY(1931); MOVIE CRAZY(1932); BABES IN TOYLAND(1934); PAINTED VEIL, THE(1934); MILKY WAY, THE(1936); PETRIFIED FOREST, THE(1936); MAYTIME(1937)

Silents
SAILOR-MADE MAN, A(1921); TWO MINUTES TO GO(1921); GRANDMA'S BOY(1922); WATCH YOUR STEP(1922); SAFETY LAST(1923); SECOND HAND LOVE(1923); FRESHMAN, THE(1925); KID BROTHER, THE(1927); SPEEDY(1928)
Harry Leonard
STRANGE LOVE OF MARTHA IVERS, THE(1946)
Herbert Leonard
SWEET MUSIC(1935), ed; MURDER IN THE OLD RED BARN(1936, Brit.)
Herbert B. Leonard
PERILS OF PAULINE, THE(1967), p, d; POPI(1969), p; GOING HOME(1971), p&d
Howard Leonard
GOOSE AND THE GANDER, THE(1935), ed
Hugh Leonard
BROTH OF A BOY(1959, Brit.), w; GREAT CATHERINE(1968, Brit.), w; INTERLUDE(1968, Brit.), w; PERCY(1971, Brit.), w; OUR MISS FRED(1972, Brit.), w
Irene Leonard
Misc. Silents
GRAFTERS(1917)
Jack Leonard
STORMY(1935); HAUNTED HOUSE, THE(1940), w; GLAMOUR GIRL(1947); WHEN A GIRL'S BEAUTIFUL(1947); HIS KIND OF WOMAN(1951), w; MY MAN AND I(1952), w; NARROW MARGIN, THE(1952), w; CRY OF THE HUNTED(1953), w; MAN IN THE DARK(1953), w; HELL'S ISLAND(1955), w; MARAUDERS, THE(1955), w; GUN BATTLE AT MONTEREY(1957), w; DOULOS—THE FINGER MAN(1964, Fr./Ital.); GODSON, THE(1972, Ital./Fr.); TARGET: HARRY(1980)
Misc. Talkies
SWING THE WESTERN WAY(1947)
Jack E. Leonard
THREE SAILORS AND A GIRL(1953); DISORDERLY ORDERLY, THE(1964); FAT SPY(1966)
Jack R. Leonard
SECRET FURY, THE(1950), w
Jackie Leonard
JOURNEY BACK TO OZ(1974)
James Leonard
Silents
ALL ABOARD(1927)
Jamie Leonard
GIRO CITY(1982, Brit.), art d; REMEMBRANCE(1982, Brit.), art d; ASCENDANCY(1983, Brit.), art d
1984
LAUGHTER HOUSE(1984, Brit.), art d; LOOSE CONNECTIONS(1984, Brit.), art d
Joel Leonard
PSYCHIC KILLER(1975), art d
John R. Leonard, Sr.
NIGHTWING(1979)
Keith Leonard
CHARLEY-ONE-EYE(1973, Brit.), w
L.G. Leonard
HEADIN' EAST(1937), p; OVERLAND EXPRESS, THE(1938), p
Laurence Leonard
THEY'RE A WEIRD MOB(1966, Aus.), m, md
LaVerne Leonard
HAPPY DAYS(1930)
Leon Leonard
OMOO OMOO, THE SHARK GOD(1949), d, w
Lu Leonard
ANNIE(1982)
1984
BREAKIN' 2: ELECTRIC BOOGALOO(1984); MICKI AND MAUDE(1984); STARMAN(1984)
Marion Leonard
Misc. Silents
SIGHT UNSEEN, A(1914); VOW, THE(1915)
Mark Leonard
GREATEST STORY EVER TOLD, THE(1965)
Misc. Talkies
ATTACK AT NOON SUNDAY(1971); NOON SUNDAY(1971)
Mel Leonard
KATHY O'(1958); WILD AND THE INNOCENT, THE(1959)
Michael Leonard
BILLION DOLLAR HOBO, THE(1977), m; THEY WENT THAT-A-WAY AND THAT-A-WAY(1978), m
Murray Leonard
IN SOCIETY(1944); LOST IN A HAREM(1944); THOUSAND AND ONE NIGHTS, A(1945); NIGHT EDITOR(1946); QUEEN OF BURLESQUE(1946); WISTFUL WIDOW OF WAGON GAP, THE(1947); FIGHTING MAD(1948); NOOSE HANGS HIGH, THE(1948); WHITE HEAT(1949); YOUNG MAN WITH A HORN(1950); ABBOTT AND COSTELLO MEET THE KEYSTONE KOPS(1955); BRING YOUR SMILE ALONG(1955)
Pat Leonard
ADVENTURESS, THE(1946, Brit.)
Phillip Leonard
Misc. Talkies
DEADLINE(1984)
Queenie Leonard
ROMANCE IN RHYTHM(1934, Brit.); MILLIONS(1936, Brit.); SKYLARKS(1936, Brit.); BACKSTAGE(1937, Brit.); SHOW GOES ON, THE(1937, Brit.); KATE PLUS TEN(1938, Brit.); MOONLIGHT SONATA(1938, Brit.); CONFIRM OR DENY(1941); LADIES IN RETIREMENT(1941); EAGLE SQUADRON(1942); THIS ABOVE ALL(1942); FOREVER AND A DAY(1943); THUMBS UP(1943); LODGER, THE(1944); OUR HEARTS WERE YOUNG AND GAY(1944); UNINVITED, THE(1944); AND THEN THERE WERE NONE(1945); MOLLY AND ME(1945); MY NAME IS JULIA ROSS(1945); TONIGHT AND EVERY NIGHT(1945); CLUNY BROWN(1946); LOCKET, THE(1946); LIFE WITH FATHER(1947); LONE WOLF IN LONDON(1947); HOMECOMING(1948); MY OWN TRUE LOVE(1948); LIFE OF HER OWN, A(1950); ALICE IN WONDERLAND(1951); LORNA DOONE(1951); THUNDER ON THE HILL(1951); LES MISERABLES(1952); MILLION DOLLAR MERMAID(1952); NARROW MARGIN, THE(1952); THUNDER IN THE EAST(1953); KING'S THIEF, THE(1955); D-DAY, THE SIXTH OF JUNE(1956); 23 PACES TO BAKER STREET(1956); ONE HUNDRED AND

ONE DALMATIANS(1961); HATARI!(1962); NOTORIOUS LANDLADY, THE(1962); PRIZE, THE(1963); MY FAIR LADY(1964); WHAT A WAY TO GO(1964)

Robert Leonard
Silents
JUDGE NOT OR THE WOMAN OF MONA DIGGINGS(1915), d, w; SECRET LOVE(1916), d&w; TAILOR OF BOND STREET, THE(1916, Brit.); JUST DECEPTION, A(1917, Brit.)
Misc. Silents
HERITAGE(1915), a, d; SILENT COMMAND, THE(1915), a, d; CRIPPLED HAND, THE(1916), a, d; EAGLE'S WINGS, THE(1916), d; AT FIRST SIGHT(1917), d; MORMON MAID, A(1917), d; PRIMROSE RING, THE(1917), d; HER BODY IN BOND(1918), d; MODERN LOVE(1918), d

Robert E. Leonard
HEAVEN CAN WAIT(1978)

Robert Z. Leonard
LADY OF CHANCE, A(1928), d; MARIANNE(1929), d; DIVORCEE, THE(1930), p&d; IN GAY MADRID(1930), d; LET US BE GAY(1930), d; BACHELOR FATHER(1931), d; FIVE AND TEN(1931), d; IT'S A WISE CHILD(1931), d; SUSAN LENOX–HER FALL AND RISE(1931), d; LOVERS COURAGEOUS(1932), d; STRANGE INTERLUDE(1932), d; DANCING LADY(1933), d; PEG O' MY HEART(1933), d; OUTCAST LADY(1934), d; AFTER OFFICE HOURS(1935), d; ESCAPADE(1935), d; GREAT ZIEGFELD, THE(1936), d; PICCADILLY JIM(1936), d; FIREFLY, THE(1937), a, d; MAYTIME(1937), d; GIRL OF THE GOLDEN WEST, THE(1938), d; BROADWAY SERENADE(1939), p&d; NEW MOON(1940), p&d; PRIDE AND PREJUDICE(1940), d; THIRD FINGER, LEFT HAND(1940), d; WHEN LADIES MEET(1941), p, d; ZIEGFELD GIRL(1941), d; STAND BY FOR ACTION(1942), p, d; WE WERE DANCING(1942), p, d; MAN FROM DOWN UNDER, THE(1943), p, d; MARRIAGE IS A PRIVATE AFFAIR(1944), d; ABBOTT AND COSTELLO IN HOLLYWOOD(1945); WEEKEND AT THE WALDORF(1945), d; SECRET HEART, THE(1946), d; CYNTHIA(1947), d; B. F.'S DAUGHTER(1948), d; BRIBE, THE(1949), d; IN THE GOOD OLD SUMMERTIME(1949), d; DUCHESS OF IDAHO, THE(1950), d; GROUNDS FOR MARRIAGE(1950), d; NANCY GOES TO RIO(1950), d; TOO YOUNG TO KISS(1951), d; EVERYTHING I HAVE IS YOURS(1952), d; CLOWN, THE(1953), d; GREAT DIAMOND ROBBERY(1953), d; HER TWELVE MEN(1954), d; KING'S THIEF, THE(1955), d; KELLY AND ME(1957), d
Silents
LOVE GIRL, THE(1916), d&w; PLOW GIRL, THE(1916), d; ON RECORD(1917), d; BRIDE'S AWAKENING, THE(1918), d; WAY OF A WOMAN(1919), d; GILDED LILY, THE(1921), d; BROADWAY ROSE(1922), d; PEACOCK ALLEY(1922), d⊃ FRENCH DOLL, THE(1923), d; JAZZMANIA(1923), d; LOVE'S WILDERNESS(1924), d; MARRIED FLIRTS(1924); BRIGHT LIGHTS(1925), d; WANING SEX, THE(1926), d; ADAM AND EVIL(1927), d; LITTLE JOURNEY, A(1927), d; TEA FOR THREE(1927), d; BABY MINE(1928), d
Misc. Silents
LITTLE EVE EDGARTON(1916), d; PRINCESS VIRTUE(1917), d; DANGER, GO SLOW(1918), d; FACE VALUE(1918), d; BIG LITTLE PERSON, THE(1919), d; DELICIOUS LITTLE DEVIL, THE(1919), d; SCARLET SHADOW, THE(1919), d; WHAT AM I BID?(1919), d; APRIL FOLLY(1920), d; MIRACLE OF LOVE, THE(1920), d; RESTLESS SEX, THE(1920), d; HEEDLESS MOTHS(1921), d; FASCINATION(1922), d; FASHION ROW(1923), d; CIRCE THE ENCHANTRESS(1924), d; MADEMOISELLE MIDNIGHT(1924), d; CHEAPER TO MARRY(1925), d; TIME, THE COMEDIAN(1925), d; DANCE MADNESS(1926), d; MADEMOISELLE MODISTE(1926), d; DEMIBRIDE, THE(1927), d; CARDBOARD LOVER, THE(1928), d

Sarah Leonard
HOW TO BEAT THE HIGH COST OF LIVING(1980)

Sheldon Leonard
OUANGA(1936, Brit.); ANOTHER THIN MAN(1939); BUY ME THAT TOWN(1941); MARRIED BACHELOR(1941); PRIVATE NURSE(1941); RISE AND SHINE(1941); TALL, DARK AND HANDSOME(1941); WEEKEND IN HAVANA(1941); BORN TO SING(1942); LUCKY JORDAN(1942); PIERRE OF THE PLAINS(1942); STREET OF CHANCE(1942); TENNESSEE JOHNSON(1942); TORTILLA FLAT(1942); CITY WITHOUT MEN(1943); HARVEST MELODY(1943); HIT THE ICE(1943); PASSPORT TO SUEZ(1943); FALCON IN HOLLYWOOD, THE(1944); GAMBLER'S CHOICE(1944); KLONDIKE KATE(1944); TIMBER QUEEN(1944); TO HAVE AND HAVE NOT(1944); TROCADERO(1944); UNCERTAIN GLORY(1944); CAPTAIN KIDD(1945); CRIME, INC.(1945); FRONTIER GAL(1945); RADIO STARS ON PARADE(1945); RIVER GANG(1945); SHADOW OF TERROR(1945), w; WHY GIRLS LEAVE HOME(1945); ZOMBIES ON BROADWAY(1945); BOWERY BOMBSHELL(1946); DECOY(1946); GENTLEMAN MISBEHAVES, THE(1946); HER KIND OF MAN(1946); IT'S A WONDERFUL LIFE(1946); LAST CROOKED MILE, THE(1946); RAINBOW OVER TEXAS(1946); SOMEWHERE IN THE NIGHT(1946); GANGSTER, THE(1947); SINBAD THE SAILOR(1947); VIOLENCE(1947); ALIAS A GENTLEMAN(1948); FORCE OF EVIL(1948); IF YOU KNEW SUSIE(1948); JINX MONEY(1948); JOE PALOOKA IN WINNER TAKE ALL(1948); MADONNA OF THE DESERT(1948); OPEN SECRET(1948); DAUGHTER OF THE JUNGLE(1949); MY DREAM IS YOURS(1949); SHEP COMES HOME(1949); TAKE ONE FALSE STEP(1949); IROQUOIS TRAIL, THE(1950); ABBOTT AND COSTELLO MEET THE INVISIBLE MAN(1951); BEHAVE YOURSELF(1951); COME FILL THE CUP(1951); HERE COME THE NELSONS(1952); STOP, YOU'RE KILLING ME(1952); YOUNG MAN WITH IDEAS(1952); BREAKDOWN(1953); DIAMOND QUEEN(1953); MONEY FROM HOME(1953); GUYS AND DOLLS(1955); POCKETFUL OF MIRACLES(1961); BRINK'S JOB, THE(1978)

Terry Leonard
BARQUERO(1970); MAN CALLED HORSE, A(1970), a, stunts; SOMETIMES A GREAT NOTION(1971); LIFE AND TIMES OF JUDGE ROY BEAN, THE(1972); DILLINGER(1973); NIGHT MOVES(1975); RETURN TO MACON COUNTY(1975), stunts; 1941(1979), stunts; MOUNTAIN MEN, THE(1980); LEGEND OF THE LONE RANGER, THE(1981); RAIDERS OF THE LOST ARK(1981)
1984
ROMANCING THE STONE(1984), stunts; STARMAN(1984), stunts

Terry J. Leonard
USED CARS(1980), stunts

Vesta Leonard
Misc. Silents
SOME WAITER!(1916, Brit.)

William Leonard
LOVE CHILD(1982)

Leonard and Zolo
SEPIA CINDERELLA(1947)

Leonard Harper's Chorus
EXILE, THE(1931)

Leonard-Munson
WAY OUT WEST(1937), m

Antonio Leonardi
THIS WINE OF LOVE(1948, Ital.), w

Urylee Leonardos
NO SAD SONGS FOR ME(1950)

Ruggiero Leoncavallo
CLOWN MUST LAUGH, A(1936, Brit.), w; TAXI TO HEAVEN(1944, USSR), m; LAUGH PAGLIACCI(1948, Ital.), m

Guglielmo Leoncini
WHITE SHEIK, THE(1956, Ital.)

Jordan Leondopoulos
SAM'S SONG(1971), d; EXORCIST, THE(1973), ed

Alfred Leone
BARON BLOOD(1972, Ital.), p; HOUSE OF EXORCISM, THE(1976, Ital.), p, w

Danny Leone
HOUSE ON 92ND STREET, THE(1945)

Harry Leone
Silents
PRUNELLA(1918)

Henry Leone
Silents
SIN(1915); WOMAN AND WINE(1915); MY COUSIN(1918); SUCH A LITTLE QUEEN(1921)
Misc. Silents
MORTAL SIN, THE(1917); TO THE DEATH(1917); HER PRICE(1918); ORDEAL OF ROSETTA, THE(1918)

Ignazio Leone
LOVE AND LARCENY(1963, Fr./Ital.); MISSION BLOODY MARY(1967, Fr./Ital./Span.); DEATH RIDES A HORSE(1969, Ital.)

John Leone
GREAT SMOKEY ROADBLOCK, THE(1978), d&w; TOUGH ENOUGH(1983), w

Kathy Leone
HOUSE OF EXORCISM, THE(1976, Ital.)

Mr. Leone
Silents
ARSENE LUPIN(1917)

Roberti Sergio Leone
SIGN OF THE GLADIATOR(1959, Fr./Ger./Ital.), w

Sergio Leone
LAST DAYS OF POMPEII, THE(1960, Ital.), w; COLOSSUS OF RHODES, THE(1961, Ital., Fr., Span.), d, w; SODOM AND GOMORRAH(1962, U.S./Fr./Ital.), d; DUEL OF THE TITANS(1963, Ital.), w; FISTFUL OF DOLLARS, A(1964, Ital./Ger./Span.), d, w; FOR A FEW DOLLARS MORE(1967, Ital./Ger./Span.), d, w; GOOD, THE BAD, AND THE UGLY, THE(1967, Ital./Span.), d, w; SEVEN REVENGES, THE(1967, Ital.), w; ONCE UPON A TIME IN THE WEST(1969, U.S./Ital.), d, w; DUCK, YOU SUCKER!(1972, Ital.), d, w; MY NAME IS NOBODY(1974, Ital./Fr./Ger.), p
1984
ONCE UPON A TIME IN AMERICA(1984), a, d, w

Virgil C. Leone
FINE PAIR, A(1969, Ital.), w

Elisa Leonelli
LULU(1978)

Francesco Leonetti
GOSPEL ACCORDING TO ST. MATTHEW, THE(1966, Fr., Ital.); HAWKS AND THE SPARROWS, THE(1967, Ital.); CANNIBALS, THE(1970, Ital.)

Matthew F Leonetti
CHICKEN CHRONICLES, THE(1977), ph

Matthew F. Leonetti
MR. BILLION(1977), ph; BREAKING AWAY(1979), ph; RAISE THE TITANIC(1980, Brit.), ph; EYEWITNESS(1981), ph; POLTERGEIST(1982), ph
1984
BUDDY SYSTEM, THE(1984), ph; ICE PIRATES, THE(1984), ph; SONGWRITER(1984), ph

Matthew Leonetti
BAT PEOPLE, THE(1974), ph

Matthew R. Leonetti
FAST TIMES AT RIDGEMONT HIGH(1982), ph

Tommy Leonetti
HUMAN DUPLICATORS, THE(1965); SQUEEZE A FLOWER(1970, Aus.), m; MASSACRE AT CENTRAL HIGH(1976), m

Albert Leong
TWILIGHT ZONE–THE MOVIE(1983)
1984
PROTOCOL(1984)

Charles Leong
GENERAL DIED AT DAWN, THE(1936)

Harry Leong
GENERAL DIED AT DAWN, THE(1936)

James B. Leong
TANGLED DESTINIES(1932); SON OF KONG(1933); MANDALAY(1934); MYSTERIOUS MR. WONG(1935); WEST OF SHANGHAI(1937); INTERNATIONAL SETTLEMENT(1938); MR. MOTO TAKES A CHANCE(1938); THEY MET IN BOMBAY(1941); REMEMBER PEARL HARBOR(1942); HEADIN' FOR GOD'S COUNTRY(1943); DESTINATION TOKYO(1944); HER HUSBAND'S AFFAIRS(1947); PEKING EXPRESS(1951); MACAO(1952)
Silents
RANSOM(1928)
Misc. Silents
PURPLE DAWN(1923)

James Leong
WELCOME DANGER(1929); HATCHET MAN, THE(1932); HEART PUNCH(1932); SHANGHAI EXPRESS(1932); SHADOWS OF THE ORIENT(1937); THANK YOU, MR. MOTO(1937); ADVENTURES OF MARCO POLO, THE(1938); SOUTH OF PAGO PAGO(1940); ACROSS THE PACIFIC(1942); LADY FROM CHUNGKING(1943); KEYS OF THE KINGDOM, THE(1944); PURPLE HEART, THE(1944); FIRST YANK INTO TOKYO(1945); GREEN DOLPHIN STREET(1947); I WAS AN AMERICAN SPY(1951)

Jimmy Leong
SHANGHAI LADY(1929); LOTUS LADY(1930); TRICK FOR TRICK(1933)
Misc. Silents
SILK BOUQUET, THE(1926)
Shisuen Leong
REVENGE OF THE SHOGUN WOMEN(1982, Taiwan)
Terry Leong
PUZZLE OF A DOWNFALL CHILD(1970), cos
Marie Leonhard
Silents
PRIDE OF JENNICO, THE(1914)
Gustav Leonhardt
CHRONICLE OF ANNA MAGDALENA BACH(1968, Ital., Ger.)
Kathrien Leonhardt
CHRONICLE OF ANNA MAGDALENA BACH(1968, Ital., Ger.)
G. Leoni
RING AROUND THE CLOCK(1953, Ital.), w
Luigi Leoni
MANDRAGOLA(1966 Fr./Ital.); WITCHES, THE(1969, Fr./Ital.)
Roberto Leoni
MASTER TOUCH, THE(1974, Ital./Ger.), w; STREET PEOPLE(1976, U.S./Ital.), w
Leon Leonidof
WHEN YOU'RE IN LOVE(1937), ch
Leon Leonidoff
SUNNY(1941), ch
Leonidoff Ballet
TALK OF HOLLYWOOD, THE(1929)
G. Leonidov
CAPTAIN GRANT'S CHILDREN(1939, USSR), w
Leonid Leonidov
Misc. Silents
BREAD(1918, USSR); WINGS OF A SERF(1926, USSR), a, d; SEEDS OF FREE-DOM(1929, USSR)
Y. Leonidov
MAGIC VOYAGE OF SINBAD, THE(1962, USSR); HOUSE WITH AN ATTIC, THE(1964, USSR)
Yu. Leonidov
DUEL, THE(1964, USSR)
John Leoning
PIPE DREAMS(1976)
Nina Leonise
Misc. Silents
MAN WHO BOUGHT LONDON, THE(1916, Brit.)
Hedi Leonore
50,000 B.C.(BEFORE CLOTHING)* (1963)
N. Leonov
Misc. Silents
JEW AT WAR, A(1931, USSR)
Vladimir Leonov
DARK IS THE NIGHT(1946, USSR)
Ye. Leonov
SONG OVER MOSCOW(1964, USSR)
Yevgeny Leonov
AUTUMN MARATHON(1982, USSR)
K. Leonova
YOLANTA(1964, USSR)
Eugenie Leonovich
MEN IN HER LIFE, THE(1941)
Leontiev
Misc. Silents
BEAUTY AND THE BOLSHEVIK(1923, USSR)
Guido Leontini
VALACHI PAPERS, THE(1972, Ital./Fr.); CRAZY JOE(1974); THREE TOUGH GUYS(1974, U.S./Ital.)
Eugenie Leontovich
FOUR SONS(1940); ANYTHING CAN HAPPEN(1952); WORLD IN HIS ARMS, THE(1952); RAINS OF RANCHIPUR, THE(1955); HOMICIDAL(1961)
Maria Leontovitsch
DIVIDED HEART, THE(1955, Brit.)
Yura Leontyev
MOTHER AND DAUGHTER(1965, USSR)
Antonio Leonuiola
ATLAS AGAINST THE CYCLOPS(1963, Ital.), d
Antonio Leonviola
APPOINTMENT, THE(1969), w
Ethelreda Leopold
LOST LADY, A(1934); GREAT GUY(1936); SWEETHEARTS(1938); TRADE WINDS(1938); DANCING CO-ED(1939); YOU CAN'T CHEAT AN HONEST MAN(1939); ANGELS OVER BROADWAY(1940); HE STAYED FOR BREAKFAST(1940); MAD YOUTH(1940); BALL OF FIRE(1941); CITY, FOR CONQUEST(1941); MONSTER AND THE GIRL, THE(1941); VOODOO MAN(1944); GEORGE WHITE'S SCANDALS(1945); LITTLE GIANT(1946); LIKELY STORY, A(1947); MAD WEDNESDAY(1950)
Glenn Leopold
PROWLER, THE(1981), w
John Leopold
DISPUTED PASSAGE(1939), m; FLYING DEUCES, THE(1939), m; GERONI-MO(1939), m; SANTA FE MARSHAL(1940), m; SHOWDOWN, THE(1940), m; SE-CRETS OF THE WASTELANDS(1941), m; WIDE OPEN TOWN(1941), md; NINE GIRLS(1944), m
John M. Leopold
KNIGHTS OF THE RANGE(1940), m
Stratton Leopold
FARMER, THE(1977)
Tom Leopold
CHILD'S PLAY(1972); MR. MOM(1983)
Leopold Archduke of Austria
Silents
NIGHT LIFE(1927); FOUR SONS(1928)

Leopold Stokowski and his symphony orchestra
BIG BROADCAST OF 1937, THE(1936)
A. Leorov
Misc. Silents
WANDERING STARS(1927, USSR)
M. Leorov
Misc. Silents
LEAH'S SUFFERING(1917, USSR); WANDERING STARS(1927, USSR); SIMPLE TAILOR, THE(1934, USSR)
Philippe Leotard
TWO ENGLISH GIRLS(1972, Fr.); DAY OF THE JACKAL, THE(1973, Brit./Fr.); KAMOURASKA(1973, Can./Fr.); SUCH A GORGEOUS KID LIKE ME(1973, Fr.); FRENCH CONNECTION 11(1975); CAT AND MOUSE(1978, Fr.); PARADISE POUR TOUS(1982, Fr.); LA BALANCE(1983, Fr.)
1984
LA PETIT SIRENE(1984, Fr.)
Michel Leoup
GULLIVER'S TRAVELS(1977, Brit., Bel.), anim
Emelia Leovalli
ON AN ISLAND WITH YOU(1948)
J. Leoz
BABES IN BAGDAD(1952), m
Brent LePage
HALLOWEEN(1978)
Gaston Lepage
CORDELIA(1980, Fr., Can.)
Gerard Lepage
PARALLELS(1980, Can.)
Monique LePage
IN PRAISE OF OLDER WOMEN(1978, Can.)
Misc. Talkies
SEPARATION(1977, Brit.)
Rene Lepage
LOST COMMAND, THE(1966), adv
Katya Lepanova
IN THE NAME OF LIFE(1947, USSR)
Richard LeParmentier
STAR WARS(1977)
Ana Bertha Lepe
SANTO CONTRA EL CEREBRO DIABOLICO zero(1962, Mex.)
Ann Bertha Lepe
LA NAVE DE LOS MONSTRUOS(1959, Mex.)
Rosita Lepe
GUADALAJARA(1943, Mex.)
Bernd Lepel
CIRCLE OF DECEIT(1982, Fr./Ger.), set d
Kay Leperc
PILGRIMAGE(1972)
Paul Lepere
THEY KNEW WHAT THEY WANTED(1940); REPENT AT LEISURE(1941)
Ray LePere
TENDER MERCIES(1982)
Paul Leperson
PHANTOM OF LIBERTY, THE(1974, Fr.)
Marcel LePicard
DOWN THE WYOMING TRAIL(1939), ph; RIDERS OF THE FRONTIER(1939), ph; ROLL, WAGONS, ROLL(1939), ph; ROLLIN' WESTWARD(1939), ph; ARIZONA FRONTIER(1940), ph; COWBOY FROM SUNDOWN(1940), ph; GOLDEN TRAIL, THE(1940), ph; RAINBOW OVER THE RANGE(1940), ph; RHYTHM OF THE RIO GRANDE(1940), ph; WESTBOUND STAGE(1940), ph; DRIFTIN' KID, THE(1941), ph; PIONEERS, THE(1941), ph; RIDING THE CHEROKEE TRAIL(1941), ph; RIDING THE SUNSET TRAIL(1941), ph; ROLLIN' HOME TO TEXAS(1941), ph; SILVER STALLION(1941), ph; KING OF THE STALLIONS(1942), ph; MISS V FROM MOS-COW(1942), ph; ONE THRILLING NIGHT(1942), ph; WESTERN MAIL(1942), ph; MAN OF COURAGE(1943), ph; CRAZY KNIGHTS(1944), ph; LAW OF THE VAL-LEY(1944), ph; WESTWARD BOUND(1944), ph; WHAT A MAN!(1944), ph; LOST TRAIL, THE(1945), ph; CARAVAN TRAIL, THE(1946), ph; DRIFTIN' RIVER(1946), ph; HOME ON THE HANGE(1946), ph; ROMANCE OF THE WEST(1946), ph; SONG OF THE SIERRAS(1946), ph; RAINBOW OVER THE ROCKIES(1947), ph; SIX GUN SERENADE(1947), ph; INCIDENT(1948), ph; ALASKA PATROL(1949), ph; FORGOT-TEN WOMEN(1949), ph; MASTER MINDS(1949), ph; BLONDE DYNAMITE(1950), ph; BLUES BUSTERS(1950), ph; LOST VOLCANO, THE(1950), ph; CRAZY OVER HORSES(1951), ph; HERE COME THE MARINES(1952), ph; JET JOB(1952), ph
Eugene Lepicier
THERESE(1963, Fr.), p; MATA HARI(1965, Fr./Ital.), p; GODSON, THE(1972, Ital./Fr.), p
Benoit Lepine
WHY ROCK THE BOAT?(1974, Can.)
V. Lepke
CZAR WANTS TO SLEEP(1934, U.S., USSR)
Viktoria Lepko
LULLABY(1961, USSR)
Vladimar Lepko
SPRINGTIME ON THE VOLGA(1961, USSR)
Rene Leplat
HOUSE OF THE ARROW, THE(1953, Brit.); GOLDEN MASK, THE(1954, Brit.)
Marcel LePleard
ENCHANTED FOREST, THE(1945), ph
Robert Lepler
SIEGE OF SIDNEY STREET, THE(1960, Brit.); DEVIL'S AGENT, THE(1962, Brit.); MURDER IN EDEN(1962, Brit.)
Robin Lepler
OF HUMAN BONDAGE(1964, Brit.)
Harold Lepnvitz
CREATURE WITH THE BLUE HAND(1971, Ger.)
Enrique Leporace
TERRACE, THE(1964, Arg.)

Richard LePore
WHY MUST I DIE?(1960); GATHERING OF EAGLES, A(1963); QUICK, BEFORE IT
MELTS(1964); STACEY!(1973)
Hekki Leppanen
GORKY PARK(1983)
Raymond Leppard
LORD OF THE FLIES(1963, Brit.), m; ALFRED THE GREAT(1969, Brit.), m
Ivan Lepper
SCHLOCK(1973), spec eff
Robert Lepresle
WHO KILLED JOHN SAVAGE?(1937, Brit.), ph
Tina Lepri
GIDGET GOES TO ROME(1963)
Rene Leprince
Misc. Silents
LA VIE D'UNE REINE(1917, Fr.), d; LE NOEL D'UN VAGABOND(1918, Fr.), d; LE
CALVAIRE D'UNE REINE(1919, Fr.), d; LES LARMES DU PARDON(1919, Fr.), d;
FACE A L'OCEAN(1920, Fr.), d; FORCE DE LA VIE(1920, Fr.), d; LA LUTTE POUR LA
VIE(1920, Fr.), d; ETRE OU NE PAS ETRE(1922, Fr.), d; JEAN D'AGREVE(1922,
Fr.), d; LA FOLIE DU DOUTE(1923, Fr.), d; MON ONCLE BENJAMIN(1923, Fr.), d;
PAX DOMINE(1923, Fr.), d; UN BON PETIT DIABLE(1923, Fr.), d; VENT DE-
BOUT(1923, Fr.), d; LE JARDIN SUR L'ORONTE(1925, Fr.), d; PRINCESSE MA-
SHA(1927, Fr.), d; LA REVANCHE DU MAUDIT(1929, Fr.), d
Yves Leprince
TRIAL OF JOAN OF ARC(1965, Fr.)
Pierre Leproux
PICNIC ON THE GRASS(1960, Fr.); LA GUERRE EST FINIE(1967, Fr./Swed.)
Denise Lepvrier
LANDRU(1963, Fr./Ital)
Diana Lepvrier
LONG ABSENCE, THE(1962, Fr./Ital.); LANDRU(1963, Fr./Ital); TWO ARE GUILT-
Y(1964, Fr.)
Leray
BATTLE OF THE RAILS(1949, Fr.)
Georgia Lerch
WHOOPEE(1930)
Louis Lerch
CRIMSON CIRCLE, THE(1930, Brit.)
Misc. Silents
CARMEN(1928, Fr.)
Arnfried Lerche
WILLY(1963, U.S./Ger.)
Severine Lerczinska
LA MARSEILLAISE(1938, Fr.)
Severine Lerczynska
BOUDU SAVED FROM DROWNING(1967, Fr.)
Albert Lerda
CHARLES AND LUCIE(1982, Fr.)
Preben Lerdorff
DAY OF WRATH(1948, Den.)
Preben Lerdorff-Rye
ORDET(1957, Den.); STRANGER KNOCKS, A(1963, Den.)
Joe Lerer
EYE FOR AN EYE, AN(1981)
1984
BIRDY(1984); NO SMALL AFFAIR(1984)
Hans Henrik Lerfeldt
FANNY AND ALEXANDER(1983, Swed./Fr./Ger.)
James Leria
DELINQUENTS, THE(1957)
Irenee Leriche
THREE FACES OF SIN(1963, Fr./Ital.), p; SKY ABOVE HEAVEN(1964, Fr./Ital.), p
Roberto Lerici
VACATION, THE(1971, Ital.), w
Bob Lerick
SUCKER, THE(1966, Fr./Ital.)
April Lerman
ANNIE(1982)
Leo Lerman
TROUBLEMAKER, THE(1964)
Oscar S. Lerman
YESTERDAY'S HERO(1979, Brit.), p; WORLD IS FULL OF MARRIED MEN,
THE(1980, Brit.), p
Lerner
DRAGNET NIGHT(1931, Fr.); SUICIDE LEGION(1940, Brit.), m
Alan Jay Lerner
TRIBUTE(1980, Can.), m; AMERICAN IN PARIS, AN(1951), w; ROYAL WED-
DING(1951), w; BRIGADOON(1954), w; GIGI(1958), w; MY FAIR LADY(1964), w;
CAMELOT(1967), w; PAINT YOUR WAGON(1969), p, w; ON A CLEAR DAY YOU
CAN SEE FOREVER(1970), w; LITTLE PRINCE, THE(1974, Brit.), w
Carl Lerner
CRY MURDER(1936), ed; SO YOUNG, SO BAD(1950), ed; PATTERNS(1956), ed; 12
ANGRY MEN(1957), ed; GODDESS, THE(1958), ed; MIDDLE OF THE NIGHT(1959),
ed; FUGITIVE KIND, THE(1960), ed; SOMETHING WILD(1961), ed; NO EXIT(1962,
U.S./Arg.), ed; REQUIEM FOR A HEAVYWEIGHT(1962), ed; ALL THE WAY HO-
ME(1963), ed; GREENWICH VILLAGE STORY(1963), ed; BLACK LIKE ME(1964), d,
w; QUICK, LET'S GET MARRIED(1965), ed; MAN CALLED ADAM, A(1966), ed;
SWIMMER, THE(1968), ed; ANGEL LEVINE, THE(1970), ed; KLUTE(1971), ed
Dick Lerner
SKY COMMANDO(1953)
DiKi Lerner
LI'L ABNER(1959); IRMA LA DOUCE(1963); SWINGER, THE(1966); EASY COME,
EASY GO(1967); SWEET CHARITY(1969)
Fred Lerner
DIRTY HARRY(1971); SOMETIMES A GREAT NOTION(1971); LEGEND OF NIG-
GER CHARLEY, THE(1972); SOUL OF NIGGER CHARLEY, THE(1973); FOXY
BROWN(1974); HARD TIMES(1975)
1984
CITY HEAT(1984); GRANDVIEW, U.S.A.(1984); SPLASH(1984)

Fred M. Lerner
STERILE CUCKOO, THE(1969)
Gera Lerner
BLACK LIKE ME(1964), w
Geraldine Lerner
C-MAN(1949), ed; GUILTY BYSTANDER(1950), ed; MR. UNIVERSE(1951), ed
Irving Lerner
MAN CRAZY(1953), d; EDGE OF FURY(1958), d; MURDER BY CONTRACT(1958),
d; CITY OF FEAR(1959), d; STUDS LONIGAN(1960), d; CRY OF BATTLE(1963), d;
CUSTER OF THE WEST(1968, U.S., Span.), p; ROYAL HUNT OF THE SUN, THE(1969,
Brit.), d; EXECUTIVE ACTION(1973), ed; STEPPENWOLF(1974), ed; RIVER NIGER,
THE(1976), ed; NEW YORK, NEW YORK(1977), ed
Jacques Lerner
Silents
MONKEY TALKS, THE(1927)
Joseph Lerner
GUILTY BYSTANDER(1950), d; MR. UNIVERSE(1951), p&d
Ken Lerner
GRAND THEFT AUTO(1977); HOT TOMORROWS(1978)
1984
IRRECONCILABLE DIFFERENCES(1984)
Mary Lerner
Silents
BREAKING POINT, THE(1921), w
Michael Lerner
ALEX IN WONDERLAND(1970); CANDIDATE, THE(1972); BUSTING(1974); HANG-
UP(1974); NEWMAN'S LAW(1974); ST. IVES(1976); OTHER SIDE OF MIDNIGHT,
THE(1977); OUTLAW BLUES(1977); GOLDENGIRL(1979); BORDERLINE(1980);
COAST TO COAST(1980); POSTMAN ALWAYS RINGS TWICE, THE(1981); NATION-
AL LAMPOON'S CLASS REUNION(1982); STRANGE INVADERS(1983); THRE-
SHOLD(1983, Can.)
Murray Lerner
MARSHAL OF HELDORADO(1950), p; WEST OF THE BRAZOS(1950), p; G.I.
JANE(1951), p, w
Richard Lerner
REVENGE OF THE CHEERLEADERS(1976), p, d, w
1984
MASSIVE RETALIATION(1984), ph
Stephen Lerner
COWARDS(1970), m
Yafa Lerner
SCARECROW IN A GARDEN OF CUCUMBERS(1972)
Alexander Lernet-Holenia
STOLEN IDENTITY(1953), w
Rod LeRocque
PREVIEW MURDER MYSTERY(1936)
Jean-Paul Leroix
CADET-ROUSSELLE(1954, Fr.), w
M. Lerorov
Misc. Silents
BENNIE THE HOWL(1927, USSR)
Alain Leroux
SHADES OF SILK(1979, Can.), m
Bobby Leroux
NIGHT THE LIGHTS WENT OUT IN GEORGIA, THE(1981)
Gaston Leroux
PHANTOM OF THE OPERA, THE(1929), w; PHANTOM OF PARIS, THE(1931), w;
COMPLIMENTS OF MR. FLOW(1941, Fr.), w; PHANTOM OF THE OPERA(1943), w;
PHANTOM OF THE OPERA, THE(1962, Brit.), w
Silents
PHANTOM OF THE OPERA, THE(1925), w
Jean-Pierre Leroux
JUDGE AND THE ASSASSIN, THE(1979, Fr.)
Maurice LeRoux
BITTER VICTORY(1958, Fr.), m; LE PETIT SOLDAT(1965, Fr.), m; KAMOURAS-
KA(1973, Can./Fr.), m
Tiphaine Leroux
ATTENTION, THE KIDS ARE WATCHING(1978, Fr.)
Yvon Leroux
ONE MAN(1979, Can.)
Allan Leroy
REASON TO LIVE, A REASON TO DIE, A(1974, Ital./Fr./Ger./Span.)
Baby LeRoy
ALICE IN WONDERLAND(1933); BEDTIME STORY, A(1933); TORCH SIN-
GER(1933); IT'S A GIFT(1934); LEMON DROP KID, THE(1934); MISS FANE'S BABY
IS STOLEN(1934); OLD-FASHIONED WAY, THE(1934); IT'S A GREAT LIFE(1936)
Dickie Leroy
JOE PALOOKA IN TRIPLE CROSS(1951); MASK OF THE AVENGER(1951)
Eddie Leroy
VICIOUS CIRCLE, THE(1948); HAPPY YEARS, THE(1950); LOOKING FOR DAN-
GER(1957); SPOOK CHASERS(1957); UP IN SMOKE(1957); IN THE MONEY(1958)
Elsa Leroy
MASCULINE FEMININE(1966, Fr./Swed.)
Florence LeRoy
BED AND BREAKFAST(1936, Brit.)
Gloria LeRoy
NIGHT THEY RAIDED MINSKY'S, THE(1968); COLD TURKEY(1971); DAY OF THE
LOCUST, THE(1975); TENDER FLESH(1976); BLOODBROTHERS(1978); HONKY
TONK FREEWAY(1981); PENNIES FROM HEAVEN(1981)
Hal LeRoy
HAROLD TEEN(1934); WONDER BAR(1934); START CHEERING(1938); TOO MANY
GIRLS(1940)
Irving Leroy
CHICK(1936, Brit.), w; GYPSY MELODY(1936, Brit.), w
Jacques Leroy
GODSON, THE(1972, Ital./Fr.)
Kenneth LeRoy
BACK DOOR TO HEAVEN(1939); PAJAMA GAME, THE(1957)

Mervyn LeRoy
WITHOUT RESERVATIONS(1946), a, d; BROADWAY BABIES(1929), d; HOT STUFF(1929), d; LITTLE JOHNNY JONES(1930), d; NUMBERED MEN(1930), d; PLAYING AROUND(1930), d; SHOW GIRL IN HOLLYWOOD(1930), d; TOP SPEED(1930), d; BROADMINDED(1931), d; FIVE STAR FINAL(1931), d; GENTLEMAN'S FATE(1931), d; LITTLE CAESAR(1931), d; LOCAL BOY MAKES GOOD(1931), d; TONIGHT OR NEVER(1931), d; TOO YOUNG TO MARRY(1931), d; BIG CITY BLUES(1932), p; HEART OF NEW YORK(1932), d; I AM A FUGITIVE FROM A CHAIN GANG(1932), d; THREE ON A MATCH(1932), d; TWO SECONDS(1932), d; ELMER THE GREAT(1933), d; GOLD DIGGERS OF 1933(1933), d; HARD TO HANDLE(1933), d; TUGBOAT ANNIE(1933), d; HAPPINESS AHEAD(1934), d; HEAT LIGHTNING(1934), d; I FOUND STELLA PARISH(1935), d; OIL FOR THE LAMPS OF CHINA(1935), d; PAGE MISS GLORY(1935), d; SWEET ADELINE(1935), d; ANTHONY ADVERSE(1936), d; THREE MEN ON A HORSE(1936), d; GREAT GARRICK, THE(1937), p; KING AND THE CHORUS GIRL, THE(1937), p&d; MR. DODD TAKES THE AIR(1937), p; THEY WON'T FORGET(1937), p&d; DRAMATIC SCHOOL(1938), p; FOOLS FOR SCANDAL(1938), p&d; AT THE CIRCUS(1939), p; STAND UP AND FIGHT(1939), p; WIZARD OF OZ, THE(1939), p; ESCAPE(1940), p&d; WATERLOO BRIDGE(1940), d; BLOSSOMS IN THE DUST(1941), d; UNHOLY PARTNERS(1941), d; JOHNNY EAGER(1942), d; RANDOM HARVEST(1942), d; MADAME CURIE(1943), d; THIRTY SECONDS OVER TOKYO(1944), d; DESIRE ME(1947), d; HOMECOMING(1948), d; ANY NUMBER CAN PLAY(1949), d; EAST SIDE, WEST SIDE(1949), d; LITTLE WOMEN(1949), p&d; LOVELY TO LOOK AT(1952), d; MILLION DOLLAR MERMAID(1952), d; LATIN LOVERS(1953), d; ROSE MARIE(1954), p&d; MISTER ROBERTS(1955), d; STRANGE LADY IN TOWN(1955), p&d; BAD SEED, THE(1956), p&d; TOWARD THE UNKNOWN(1956), p&d; HOME BEFORE DARK(1958), p&d; NO TIME FOR SERGEANTS(1958), p&d; FBI STORY, THE(1959), p&d; WAKE ME WHEN IT'S OVER(1960), p&d; DEVIL AT FOUR O'CLOCK, THE(1961), d; MAJORITY OF ONE, A(1961), p&d; GYPSY(1962), p&d; MARY, MARY(1963), p&d; MOMENT TO MOMENT(1966), p&d
Misc. Talkies
BROKEN DISHES(1930), d
Silents
ELLA CINDERS(1926), w; IRENE(1926), w; FLYING ROMEOS(1928), d; HAROLD TEEN(1928), d; OH, KAY(1928), d; NAUGHTY BABY(1929), d
Misc. Silents
NO PLACE TO GO(1927), d

Pauline Leroy
1984
HERE COMES SANTA CLAUS(1984), ed

Philippe Leroy
FRUIT IS RIPE, THE(1961, Fr./Ital.); ALONE AGAINST ROME(1963, Ital.); 55 DAYS AT PEKING(1963); CASTLE OF THE LIVING DEAD(1964, Ital./Fr.); NAKED HOURS, THE(1964, Ital.); NIGHT WATCH, THE(1964, Fr./Ital.); LOVE IN 4 DIMENSIONS(1965 Fr./Ital.); MARRIED WOMAN, THE(1965, Fr.); WHITE VOICES(1965, Fr./Ital.); LOVE AND MARRIAGE(1966, Ital.); MANDRAGOLA(1966 Fr./Ital.); MAIDEN FOR A PRINCE, A(1967, Fr./Ital.); BUONA SERA, MRS. CAMPBELL(1968, Ital.); WILD EYE, THE(1968, Ital.); SEVEN GOLDEN MEN(1969, Fr./Ital./Span.); NIGHT PORTER, THE(1974, Ital./U.S.); COVERT ACTION(1980, Ital.)
1984
BEYOND GOOD AND EVIL(1984, Ital./Fr./Ger.)

Rita LeRoy
DYNAMITE(1930); HOLLYWOOD SPEAKS(1932); YOU'RE MY EVERYTHING(1949)
Misc. Talkies
WOMAN PURSUED(1931)

Serge Leroy
ATTENTION, THE KIDS ARE WATCHING(1978, Fr.), d, w

Zoaunne LeRoy
THE RUNNER STUMBLES(1979)

Leroy & Skillet
PETEY WHEATSTRAW(1978)

Michel LeRoyer
PLAYMATES(1969, Fr./Ital.)

The Leroys
SEASIDE SWINGERS(1965, Brit.)

Paul K. Lerpae
HERE COME THE WAVES(1944), spec eff; LADY IN THE DARK(1944), spec eff; MURDER, HE SAYS(1945), spec eff; BLUE SKIES(1946), spec eff; DARK MIRROR, THE(1946), spec eff; ROAD TO RIO(1947), spec eff; UNCONQUERED(1947), spec eff; SAMSON AND DELILAH(1949), spec eff; GREATEST SHOW ON EARTH, THE(1952), spec eff; SON OF PALEFACE(1952), spec eff; SCARED STIFF(1953), spec eff; WAR OF THE WORLDS, THE(1953), spec eff; ELEPHANT WALK(1954), spec eff; CONQUEST OF SPACE(1955), spec eff; COME BLOW YOUR HORN(1963), spec eff; DONOVAN'S REEF(1963), spec eff; FUN IN ACAPULCO(1963), spec eff; HUD(1963), spec eff; NUTTY PROFESSOR, THE(1963), spec eff; PAPA'S DELICATE CONDITION(1963), spec eff; WHO'S MINDING THE STORE?(1963), spec eff; CARPETBAGGERS, THE(1964), spec eff; DISORDERLY ORDERLY, THE(1964), spec eff; LADY IN A CAGE(1964), spec eff; LAW OF THE LAWLESS(1964), spec eff; PARIS WHEN IT SIZZLES(1964), spec eff; ROUSTABOUT(1964), spec eff; WHERE LOVE HAS GONE(1964), spec eff; FAMILY JEWELS, THE(1965), spec eff; RED LINE 7000(1965), spec eff; SYLVIA(1965), spec eff; LAST OF THE SECRET AGENTS?, THE(1966), spec eff; NEVADA SMITH(1966), spec eff; OSCAR, THE(1966), spec eff; SWINGER, THE(1966), spec eff; THIS PROPERTY IS CONDEMNED(1966), spec eff; EASY COME, EASY GO(1967), spec eff; EL DORADO(1967), spec eff; FORT UTAH(1967), spec eff; GUNN(1967), spec eff; HOSTILE GUNS(1967), spec eff; SPIRIT IS WILLING, THE(1967), spec eff; WATERHOLE NO. 3(1967), spec eff; ODD COUPLE, THE(1968), spec eff; PROJECT X(1968), spec eff; WILL PENNY(1968), spec eff

Rocco Lerro
1990: THE BRONX WARRIORS(1983, Ital.)

I. Lersky
Misc. Silents
CONGESTION(1918, USSR)

Richard Lert
SERENADE(1956)

Joseph Lertora
Silents
ROMANCE OF THE AIR, A(1919)

Pierre Lerumeur
BEAU PERE(1981, Fr.)

Les Brown and His Band of Renown
NUTTY PROFESSOR, THE(1963)

Les Brown and His Orchestra
SEVEN DAYS LEAVE(1942)

Les Compagnons de la Chanson
SCHOOL FOR BRIDES(1952, Brit.)

Les Flambeaux Steele Band
TWO GENTLEMEN SHARING(1969, Brit.)

Les Hite and the Cotton Club Orchestra
Misc. Talkies
BARGAIN WITH BULLETS(1937)

Les Petits Chanteurs De L'Abbaye
LAST METRO, THE(1981, Fr.)

Michele Hamel Les Productiones de l'Ordinaire
1984
DREAM ONE(1984, Brit./Fr.), cos

Roland Lesaffre
CASQUE D'OR(1956, Fr.); ADULTERESS, THE(1959, Fr.); CHEATERS, THE(1961, Fr.); NO TIME FOR ECSTASY(1963, Fr.); LIARS, THE(1964, Fr.); EROTIQUE(1969, Fr.); PLAYMATES(1969, Fr./Ital.)

Edward LeSaign
I AM A FUGITIVE FROM A CHAIN GANG(1932)

Ed LeSaint
RANGE FEUD, THE(1931); HELL BENT FOR LOVE(1934); CASE AGAINST MRS. AMES, THE(1936); TRAIL OF THE LONESOME PINE, THE(1936)

Edward J. LeSaint
CAUGHT(1931); ONE-MAN LAW(1932); TEXAS BAD MAN(1932); THRILL HUNTER, THE(1933); TORCH SINGER(1933); LAST TRAIL, THE(1934); THIS SIDE OF HEAVEN(1934); FIGHTING SHADOWS(1935); ON PROBATION(1935); THUNDER MOUNTAIN(1935); OREGON TRAIL, THE(1936); SHADOW, THE(1937); TWO GUN LAW(1937); COLLEGE SWING(1938); I AM THE LAW(1938); TEXANS, THE(1938); WEST OF CHEYENNE(1938); WEST OF SANTA FE(1938); MAN FROM SUNDOWN, THE(1939); RIO GRANDE(1939); MAN FROM TUMBLEWEEDS, THE(1940); RETURN OF WILD BILL, THE(1940); TEXAS STAGECOACH(1940)
Silents
EACH TO HIS KIND(1917), d; FLAMES OF THE FLESH(1920), d; GIRL OF MY HEART(1920), d&w; TEMPTATION(1923), d&w
Misc. Silents
CIRCULAR STAIRCASE, THE(1915), d; LONG CHANCE, THE(1915), d; HONORABLE FRIEND, THE(1916), d; SOUL OF KURA SAN(1916), d; FIGHTING MAD(1917), d; GOLDEN FETTER, THE(1917), d; HEIR OF THE AGES, THE(1917), d; LONESOME CHAP, THE(1917), d; BIRD OF PREY, THE(1918), d; CUPID'S ROUND-UP(1918), d; DEVIL'S WHEEL, THE(1918), d; HER ONE MISTAKE(1918), d; KULTUR(1918), d; PAINTED LIPS(1918), d; SCARLET ROAD, THE(1918), d; WOLF AND HIS MATE, THE(1918), d; CALL OF THE SOUL, THE(1919), d; FEUD, THE(1919), d; FIGHTING FOR GOLD(1919), d; HELL ROARIN' REFORM(1919), d; SNEAK, THE(1919), d; MERELY MARY ANN(1920), d; MOTHER OF HIS CHILDREN, THE(1920), d; ROSE OF NOME(1920), d; SISTER TO SALOME, A(1920), d

Edward LeSaint
SHADOW OF THE LAW(1930); CENTRAL PARK(1932); DEADLINE, THE(1932); NIGHT OF JUNE 13(1932); THIRTEEN WOMEN(1932); BIG SHAKEDOWN, THE(1934); FRONTIER MARSHAL(1934); SHE LEARNED ABOUT SAILORS(1934); STUDENT TOUR(1934); FRISCO KID(1935); JUSTICE OF THE RANGE(1935); RUGGLES OF RED GAP(1935); SCHOOL FOR GIRLS(1935); SONS OF STEEL(1935); BUNKER BEAN(1936); END OF THE TRAIL(1936); WITNESS CHAIR, THE(1936); DAY AT THE RACES, A(1937); MARRIED BEFORE BREAKFAST(1937); PAID TO DANCE(1937); SHE'S DANGEROUS(1937); CALL OF THE ROCKIES(1938); CATTLE RAIDERS(1938); COLORADO TRAIL(1938); JUVENILE COURT(1938); SQUADRON OF HONOR(1938); SPOILERS OF THE RANGE(1939); BULLETS FOR RUSTLERS(1940); RANGERS OF FORTUNE(1940)
Misc. Talkies
DRAGNET, THE(1936)

Stella LeSaint
YOU CAN'T TAKE IT WITH YOU(1938); UNDERCOVER MAN, THE(1949)

Stella LeSant
WIFE TAKES A FLYER, THE(1942)

Luisa Leschin
TRUE CONFESSIONS(1981)
1984
SAVAGE STREETS(1984)

Jean Lescot
LES GAULOISES BLEUES(1969, Fr.); CONFESSION, THE(1970, Fr.)

Jack Lescoulie
OKLAHOMA RENEGADES(1940); EMERGENCY LANDING(1941); GIRL, A GUY AND A GOB, A(1941); SLEEPING CITY, THE(1950)

Rudolpho Lesey
MACUMBA LOVE(1960), ph

Dmitri Leshchenko
Misc. Silents
CONGESTION(1918, USSR)

E. D. Leshin
MURDER, HE SAYS(1945), p

E.D. Leshin
AND THE ANGELS SING(1944), p; RAINBOW ISLAND(1944), p; SALTY O'ROURKE(1945), p

Harry Leshner
SONG AND THE SILENCE, THE(1969)

Zbigniew Lesien
TEST OF PILOT PIRX, THE(1978, Pol./USSR)

Witold Lesiewicz
PASSENGER, THE(1970, Pol.), ed

Stan Lesk
THRESHOLD(1983, Can.)

Kaarina Leskinen
  MAKE LIKE A THIEF(1966, Fin.)
Joe Lesko
  MURDER IN MISSISSIPPI(1965), m
Nikolai Leskov
  KATERINA IZMAILOVA(1969, USSR), w
Vladimir Leskovar
  ISADORA(1968, Brit.)
Carol Lesley
  GAY LADY, THE(1949, Brit.)
Carole Lesley
  SILVER DARLINGS, THE(1947, Brit.); WOMEN IN A DRESSING GOWN(1957, Brit.); DANGEROUS YOUTH(1958, Brit.); DOCTOR IN LOVE(1960, Brit.); THREE ON A SPREE(1961, Brit.); WHAT A WHOPPER(1961, Brit.); POT CARRIERS, THE(1962, Brit.); OPERATION BULLSHINE(1963, Brit.); NO TREE IN THE STREET(1964, Brit.)
Dawn Lesley
  MELODY IN THE DARK(1948, Brit.)
Elgin Lesley
Silents
  NAVIGATOR, THE(1924), ph
Frank Lesley
  SPOOK WHO SAT BY THE DOOR, THE(1973)
Janine Lesley
  MISSIONARY, THE(1982)
Lorna Lesley
  JUST OUT OF REACH(1979, Aus.); CHAIN REACTION(1980, Aus.)
Misc. Talkies
  LITTLE FELLER, THE(1979)
Rosamund Lesley
  NIGHT TRAIN FOR INVERNESS(1960, Brit.)
Rosemund Lesley
  BULLDOG BREED, THE(1960, Brit.)
Sylvia Lesley
  WOMEN WHO PLAY(1932, Brit.)
Leslie
  L-SHAPED ROOM, THE(1962, Brit.)
Aleen Leslie
  DOCTOR TAKES A WIFE(1940), w; AFFECTIONATELY YOURS(1941), w; STORK PAYS OFF, THE(1941), w; HENRY ALDRICH GETS GLAMOUR(1942), w; IT COMES UP LOVE(1943), w; HENRY ALDRICH PLAYS CUPID(1944), w; HENRY ALDRICH'S LITTLE SECRET(1944), w; ROSIE THE RIVETER(1944), w; DATE WITH JUDY, A(1948), w; FATHER WAS A FULLBACK(1949), w; FATHER IS A BACHELOR(1950), w
Avril Leslie
  REVENGE OF FRANKENSTEIN, THE(1958, Brit.); 6.5 SPECIAL(1958, Brit.)
Bernard Leslie
  SEDUCERS, THE(1962), ed
Bethel Leslie
  RABBIT TRAP, THE(1959); CAPTAIN NEWMAN, M.D.(1963); RAGE TO LIVE, A(1965); MOLLY MAGUIRES, THE(1970); OLD BOYFRIENDS(1979)
Bob Leslie
  DIRTYMOUTH(1970); FIRE SALE(1977)
Colin Leslie
  GHOST GOES WEST, THE(1936)
D. S. Leslie
  MARINES COME THROUGH, THE(1943), w
David Stuart Leslie
  TWO LEFT FEET(1965, Brit.), w; TWO GENTLEMEN SHARING(1969, Brit.), w
Desmond Leslie
  STRANGER AT MY DOOR(1950, Brit.), d, w; STRANGER FROM VENUS, THE(1954, Brit.), w
Don Leslie
  PRINCE OF THE CITY(1981)
Dudley Leslie
  LIVING DANGEROUSLY(1936, Brit.), w; SENSATION(1936, Brit.), w; STAR FELL FROM HEAVEN, A(1936, Brit.), w; GLAMOROUS NIGHT(1937, Brit.), w; RIVER OF UNREST(1937, Brit.), w; TENTH MAN, THE(1937, Brit.), w; BLACK LIME-LIGHT(1938, Brit.), w; HOUSEMASTER(1938, Brit.), w; JANE STEPS OUT(1938, Brit.), w; MARIGOLD(1938, Brit.), w; OH BOY!(1938, Brit.), w; BLACK EYES(1939, Brit.), w; DANGEROUS CARGO(1939, Brit.), w; OUTSIDER, THE(1940, Brit.), w; THREE SILENT MEN(1940, Brit.), w; FALSE RAPTURE(1941), w; FRIGHTENED BRIDE, THE(1952, Brit.), w; PORTRAIT OF A SINNER(1961, Brit.), w
Eddie Leslie
  MEET MR. LUCIFER(1953, Brit.); LADY GODIVA RIDES AGAIN(1955, Brit.); TROUBLE IN STORE(1955, Brit.); JUST MY LUCK(1957, Brit.); UP IN THE WORLD(1957, Brit.); SQUARE PEG, THE(1958, Brit.), a, w; FOLLOW A STAR(1959, Brit.); ECHO OF BARBARA(1961, Brit.); ON THE BEAT(1962, Brit.), w; FAST LADY, THE(1963, Brit.); EARLY BIRD, THE(1965, Brit.); PRESS FOR TIME(1966, Brit.), w; STITCH IN TIME, A(1967, Brit.), w
Edith Leslie
  GREEN DOLPHIN STREET(1947); JIGGS AND MAGGIE IN SOCIETY(1948); LULLABY OF BROADWAY, THE(1951); PRIVATE EYES(1953); SHE COULDN'T SAY NO(1954)
Edward Leslie
  TRIAL OF MADAM X, THE(1948, Brit.); PANDORA AND THE FLYING DUTCHMAN(1951, Brit.); MY DEATH IS A MOCKERY(1952, Brit.); SAADIA(1953); DEVIL'S JEST, THE(1954, Brit.)
Elgin Leslie
Silents
  ALIAS MARY BROWN(1918), ph
Elinor Leslie
  CLEAR THE DECKS(1929)
Silents
  DREAM MELODY, THE(1929)
Erika Leslie
  FLASHDANCE(1983)
Ethel Leslie
  BILL'S LEGACY(1931, Brit.)

Fred Leslie
  DEPUTY DRUMMER, THE(1935, Brit.); TRUST THE NAVY(1935, Brit.); HOT NEWS(1936, Brit.)
Gene Leslie
  MR. BLANDINGS BUILDS HIS DREAM HOUSE(1948); EASY LIVING(1949)
George Leslie
Silents
  GOLD RUSH, THE(1925)
Geraldine Leslie
Silents
  GOLD RUSH, THE(1925); REDHEADS PREFERRED(1926)
Gladys Leslie
Silents
  RANSON'S FOLLY(1915); FORTUNE'S CHILD(1919); MISS DULCIE FROM DIXIE(1919); CHILD FOR SALE, A(1920); JIM THE PENMAN(1921); STRAIGHT IS THE WAY(1921); SISTERS(1922); TIMOTHY'S QUEST(1922); DARLING OF THE RICH, THE(1923); HALDANE OF THE SECRET SERVICE(1923); ENEMIES OF YOUTH(1925)
Misc. Silents
  BETRAYED!(1916); AMATEUR ORPHAN, AN(1917); HER BELOVED ENEMY(1917); IT HAPPENED TO ADELE(1917); VICAR OF WAKEFIELD, THE(1917); BELOVED IMPOSTER, THE(1918); HIS OWN PEOPLE(1918); LITTLE MISS NO-ACCOUNT(1918); LITTLE RUNAWAY, THE(1918); MATING, THE(1918); NYMPH OF THE FOOTHILLS, A(1918); SOAP GIRL, THE(1918); WILD PRIMROSE(1918); WOOING OF PRINCESS PAT, THE(1918); GIRL WOMAN, THE(1919); GOLDEN SHOWER, THE(1919); GRAY TOWERS MYSTERY, THE(1919); STITCH IN TIME, A(1919); TOO MANY CROOKS(1919); MIDNIGHT BRIDE, THE(1920); GOD'S COUNTRY AND THE LAW(1921); SNITCHING HOUR, THE(1922); BROADWAY BROKE(1923); MAN AND WIFE(1923); PEARL OF LOVE, THE(1925)
Gloria Leslie
  TIME TRAVELERS, THE(1964)
Helen Leslie
Misc. Silents
  IF MY COUNTRY SHOULD CALL(1916)
Herbert Leslie
  THISTLEDOWN(1938, Brit.)
Hubert Leslie
  EASY MONEY(1934, Brit.); PRISONER OF CORBAL(1939, Brit.); NIGHT BOAT TO DUBLIN(1946, Brit.)
J. Hubert Leslie
  OTHER PEOPLE'S SINS(1931, Brit.); LOVE ON THE SPOT(1932, Brit.); DOSS HOUSE(1933, Brit.); WHEN LONDON SLEEPS(1934, Brit.); IMMORTAL GENTLEMAN(1935, Brit.); HEARTS OF HUMANITY(1936, Brit.); OLD MOTHER RILEY(1937, Brit.); DRAGON OF PENDRAGON CASTLE, THE(1950, Brit.)
Jack Leslie
  GREAT POWER, THE(1929); RANDOLPH FAMILY, THE(1945, Brit.)
Jean Leslie
Misc. Silents
  PAYING THE PRICE(1924)
Jimmie Leslie
  HERE'S GEORGE(1932, Brit.)
Joan Leslie
  SERGEANT YORK(; MEN WITH WINGS(1938); LOVE AFFAIR(1939); NANCY DREW-REPORTER(1939); STAR DUST(1940); SUSAN AND GOD(1940); YOUNG AS YOU FEEL(1940); GREAT MR. NOBODY, THE(1941); HIGH SIERRA(1941); THIEVES FALL OUT(1941); WAGONS ROLL AT NIGHT, THE(1941); HARD WAY, THE(1942); MALE ANIMAL, THE(1942); YANKEE DOODLE DANDY(1942); SKY'S THE LIMIT, THE(1943); THANK YOUR LUCKY STARS(1943); THIS IS THE ARMY(1943); HOLLYWOOD CANTEEN(1944); RHAPSODY IN BLUE(1945); TOO YOUNG TO KNOW(1945); WHERE DO WE GO FROM HERE?(1945); CINDERELLA JONES(1946); JANIE GETS MARRIED(1946); REPEAT PERFORMANCE(1947); NORTHWEST STAMPEDE(1948); BORN TO BE BAD(1950); SKIPPER SURPRISED HIS WIFE, THE(1950); MAN IN THE SADDLE(1951); HELLGATE(1952); TOUGHEST MAN IN ARIZONA(1952); FLIGHT NURSE(1953); WOMAN THEY ALMOST LYNCHED, THE(1953); JUBILEE TRAIL(1954); HELL'S OUTPOST(1955); REVOLT OF MAMIE STOVER, THE(1956)
John Leslie
  SAFARI 3000(1982)
Misc. Talkies
  DRACULA SUCKS(1979)
Silents
  WINNING STROKE, THE(1919)
June Leslie
  WAR IS A RACKET(1934)
Karen Leslie
  TOMCAT, THE(1968, Brit.); DEATH PLAY(1976)
Katherine Leslie
  MY LIFE WITH CAROLINE(1941)
Kay Leslie
  BUCK PRIVATES(1941); INVISIBLE WOMAN, THE(1941); TEXAS MARSHAL, THE(1941); WHERE DID YOU GET THAT GIRL?(1941)
Kevin Leslie
  TIM(1981, Aus.)
Misc. Talkies
  LOVELETTERS FROM TERALBA ROAD(1977)
Kim Leslie
1984
  UNFAITHFULLY YOURS(1984)
Laurie Leslie
Silents
  PREHISTORIC MAN, THE(1924, Brit.)
Lawrence Leslie
  GENTLEMEN OF THE PRESS(1929); WHY BRING THAT UP?(1929)
Lila Leslie
Silents
  JOHNNY-ON-THE-SPOT(1919); KEEPING UP WITH LIZZIE(1921); FRONT PAGE STORY, A(1922); GAY AND DEVILISH(1922); HUNTRESS, THE(1923); WHAT WIVES WANT(1923); LAST EDITION, THE(1925); FOREVER AFTER(1926); SKINNER'S DRESS SUIT(1926)

Misc. Silents
GRAY HORROR, THE(1915); LOVE OF WOMEN, THE(1915); RATED AT $10.000.000(1915); VOICES FROM THE PAST(1915); WARNING, THE(1915); SILENT WOMAN, THE(1918); LITTLE BROTHER OF THE RICH, A(1919); BEST OF LUCK, THE(1920); BLUE STREAK MCCOY(1920); LOVE'S HARVEST(1920); MOLLY AND I(1920); WOULD YOU FORGIVE?(1920); GUILTY CONSCIENCE, A(1921); ANY NIGHT(1922); HOTTENTOT, THE(1922)

Lindop Leslie
FRIGHTENED BRIDE, THE(1952, Brit.), w

Lisa Leslie
PIPE DREAMS(1976)

Lorna Leslie
NEWSFRONT(1979, Aus.)

Marguerite Leslie
Silents
QUESTION, THE(1916)
Misc. Silents
JIM, THE PENMAN(1915)

Maude Leslie
KING'S VACATION, THE(1933); CAPTAIN BLOOD(1935)

Maxine Leslie
OVERLAND MAIL(1939); RIDERS OF THE FRONTIER(1939); EAST SIDE KIDS(1940); HOUSE ACROSS THE BAY, THE(1940); LAUGHING AT DANGER(1940); ON THE SPOT(1940); CAUGHT IN THE ACT(1941); LONE RIDER AMBUSHED, THE(1941); ROAR OF THE PRESS(1941); I MARRIED AN ANGEL(1942); PARDON MY STRIPES(1942); SHERIFF OF SAGE VALLEY(1942); SHE'S IN THE ARMY(1942); MY SON, THE HERO(1943)
Misc. Talkies
FUGITIVE OF THE PLAINS(1943)

Minna Leslie
Silents
DON QUIXOTE(1923, Brit.); REST CURE, THE(1923, Brit.); NOT FOR SALE(1924, Brit.)
Misc. Silents
PEACEMAKER, THE(1922, Brit.)

Nan Leslie
GEORGE WHITE'S SCANDALS(1945); I'LL REMEMBER APRIL(1945); UNDER WESTERN SKIES(1945); FALCON'S ALIBI, THE(1946); FROM THIS DAY FORWARD(1946); SISTER KENNY(1946); SUNSET PASS(1946); DEVIL THUMBS A RIDE, THE(1947); UNDER THE TONTO RIM(1947); WILD HORSE MESA(1947); WOMAN ON THE BEACH, THE(1947); ARIZONA RANGER, THE(1948); GUNS OF HATE(1948); INDIAN AGENT(1948); WESTERN HERITAGE(1948); RIM OF THE CANYON(1949); PIONEER MARSHAL(1950); TRAIN TO TOMBSTONE(1950); IRON MOUNTAIN TRAIL(1953); PROBLEM GIRLS(1953); MIRACLE OF THE HILLS, THE(1959); CROWDED SKY, THE(1960); BAMBOO SAUCER, THE(1968)

Noel Leslie
SEARCH FOR BRIDEY MURPHY, THE(1956)

Patricia Leslie
MISSING NOTE, THE(1961, Brit.)

Ralph Leslie
VAGABOND QUEEN, THE(1931, Brit.)

Robert Leslie
Misc. Talkies
WHISKEY MOUNTAIN(1977); SUNSHINE RUN(1979)

Robert Franklin Leslie
BEARS AND I, THE(1974), w

Rolf Leslie
LAST POST, THE(1929, Brit.)
Silents
EAST LYNNE(1913, Brit.); JO THE CROSSING SWEEPER(1918, Brit.); ON LEAVE(1918, Brit.); ROYAL OAK, THE(1923, Brit.); NELL GWYNNE(1926, Brit.); MUMSIE(1927, Brit.)
Misc. Silents
FAITH OF A CHILD, THE(1915, Brit.)

Sylvia Leslie
SWEET DEVIL(1937, Brit.)

Valerie Leslie
KEY, THE(1958, Brit.), cos

Vilma Ann Leslie
SEA WIFE(1957, Brit.); TOO MANY CROOKS(1959, Brit.); TOP FLOOR GIRL(1959, Brit.); PROFESSIONALS, THE(1960, Brit.); SONS AND LOVERS(1960, Brit.)

William Leslie
FOREVER FEMALE(1953); JOHNNY DARK(1954); MAGNIFICENT OBSESSION(1954); TAZA, SON OF COCHISE(1954); BRING YOUR SMILE ALONG(1955); LONG GRAY LINE, THE(1955); QUEEN BEE(1955); BATTLE STATIONS(1956); SEVENTH CAVALRY(1956); WHITE SQUAW, THE(1956); HELLCATS OF THE NAVY(1957); NIGHT THE WORLD EXPLODED, THE(1957); OPERATION MAD BALL(1957); SHADOW ON THE WINDOW, THE(1957); ANDY HARDY COMES HOME(1958); BUCHANAN RIDES ALONE(1958); COWBOY(1958); LAST HURRAH, THE(1958); LINEUP, THE(1958); RETURN TO WARBOW(1958); HORSE SOLDIERS, THE(1959); UP PERISCOPE(1959); COUCH, THE(1962); MUTINY IN OUTER SPACE(1965)
Misc. Talkies
SCORCHING FURY(1952)

The Leslie Horton Dancers
RHYTHM OF THE ISLANDS(1943)

The Leslie Roberts Television Girls
FORCES' SWEETHEART(1953, Brit.)

Karen Leslie-Lyttle
TOY, THE(1982)

Kenneth Leslie-Smith
SINGING COP, THE(1938, Brit.), w

Mark Lesly
WANDERERS, THE(1979)

Gus Lesnevich
REQUIEM FOR A HEAVYWEIGHT(1962)

Emilia Lesniak
1984
FEAR CITY(1984)

Lesnie
1984
FANTASY MAN(1984, Aus.), ph

Pierre Lesou
FINGERMAN, THE(1963, Fr.), d&w; DOULOS–THE FINGER MAN(1964, Fr./Ital.), d&w

Mrs. Lesovosky
MARK OF THE VAMPIRE(1935)

Arthur Lessac
1984
MICKI AND MAUDE(1984)

Roland Lessaffre
TO CATCH A THIEF(1955)

Sherrie Lessard
PARTNERS(1982)

Anton Lesser
MISSIONARY, THE(1982)

Arthur Lesser
LA BELLE AMERICAINE(1961, Fr.), p

Bob Lesser
DAVID HOLZMAN'S DIARY(1968); HOT TIMES(1974)

Bobby Lesser
YOU BETTER WATCH OUT(1980)

Budd Lesser
BANDIT QUEEN(1950), w Victor West

Julian Lesser
MICHAEL O'HALLORAN(1948), p; MASSACRE RIVER(1949), p; DEATH OF AN ANGEL(1952, Brit.), p; WHISPERING SMITH VERSUS SCOTLAND YARD(1952, Brit.), p; SAINT'S GIRL FRIDAY, THE(1954, Brit.), p

Len Lesser
SHACK OUT ON 101(1955); CRIME AND PUNISHMENT, U.S.A.(1959); SOME CAME RUNNING(1959); PLEASE DON'T EAT THE DAISIES(1960); HOW TO STUFF A WILD BIKINI(1965); MC HALE'S NAVY JOINS THE AIR FORCE(1965); FIREBALL 590(1966); KELLY'S HEROES(1970, U.S./Yugo.); BLOOD AND LACE(1971); DIRTY LITTLE BILLY(1972); PAPILLON(1973); SLITHER(1973); RUBY(1977); SUPER VAN(1977); HOUSE CALLS(1978); MAIN EVENT, THE(1979); DEATH HUNT(1981); TAKE THIS JOB AND SHOVE IT(1981)
1984
DUBEAT-E-O(1984)
Misc. Talkies
JOY RIDE TO NOWHERE(1978); BABY DOLLS(1982)

Michele Lesser
CONCORDE, THE–AIRPORT '79(

Robert Lesser
GOODBYE GIRL, THE(1977)
1984
2010(1984)

Sol Lesser
EYES OF THE WORLD, THE(1930), p; LONE RIDER, THE(1930), p; MEN WITHOUT LAW(1930), p; AVENGER, THE(1931), p; DESERT VENGEANCE(1931), p; FIGHTING SHERIFF, THE(1931), p; TEXAS RANGER, THE(1931), p; JAWS OF JUSTICE(1933), p; ROBBERS' ROOST(1933), p; TARZAN THE FEARLESS(1933), p; DUDE RANGER, THE(1934), p; FEROCIOUS PAL(1934), p; FRONTIER MARSHAL(1934), p; PECK'S BAD BOY(1934), p; COWBOY MILLIONAIRE(1935), p; HARD ROCK HARRIGAN(1935), p; THUNDER MOUNTAIN(1935), p; WHEN A MAN'S A MAN(1935), p; WHISPERING SMITH SPEAKS(1935), p; BORDER PATROLMAN, THE(1936), p; DAN MATTHEWS(1936), p; KING OF THE ROYAL MOUNTED(1936), p; LET'S SING AGAIN(1936), p; MINE WITH THE IRON DOOR, THE(1936), p; O'MALLEY OF THE MOUNTED(1936), p; RAINBOW ON THE RIVER(1936), p; WILD BRIAN KENT(1936), p; CALIFORNIAN, THE(1937), p; IT HAPPENED OUT WEST(1937), p; MAKE A WISH(1937), p; SECRET VALLEY(1937), p; WESTERN GOLD(1937), p; BREAKING THE ICE(1938), p; HAWAII CALLS(1938), p; HAWAIIAN BUCKAROO(1938), p; PANAMINT'S BAD MAN(1938), p; PECK'S BAD BOY WITH THE CIRCUS(1938), p; RAWHIDE(1938), p; ROLL ALONG, COWBOY(1938), p; TARZAN'S REVENGE(1938), p; EVERYTHING'S ON ICE(1939), p; FISHERMAN'S WHARF(1939), p; WAY DOWN SOUTH(1939), p; OUR TOWN(1940), p; TUTTLES OF TAHITI(1942), p; STAGE DOOR CANTEEN(1943), p; TARZAN TRIUMPHS(1943), p; TARZAN'S DESERT MYSTERY(1943), p; 3 IS A FAMILY(1944), p; TARZAN AND THE AMAZONS(1945), p; TARZAN AND THE LEOPARD WOMAN(1946), p; RED HOUSE, THE(1947), p; TARZAN AND THE HUNTRESS(1947), p; TARZAN AND THE MERMAIDS(1948), p; TARZAN'S MAGIC FOUNTAIN(1949), p; TARZAN AND THE SLAVE GIRL(1950), p; TARZAN'S PERIL(1951), p; TARZAN'S SAVAGE FURY(1952), p; TARZAN AND THE SHE-DEVIL(1953), p; TARZAN'S HIDDEN JUNGLE(1955), p; TARZAN'S FIGHT FOR LIFE(1958), p
Silents
MY BOY(1922), p; DADDY(1923), p; DRUG TRAFFIC, THE(1923), p; HELEN'S BABIES(1924), p

Ted Lesser
SOULS AT SEA(1937), w; COLLEGE SWING(1938), w

George Lessey
ANDY HARDY MEETS DEBUTANTE(1940); BOOM TOWN(1940); DR. KILDARE'S STRANGE CASE(1940); EDISON, THE MAN(1940); GALLANT SONS(1940); GO WEST(1940); GOLDEN FLEECING, THE(1940); HULLABALOO(1940); SKY MURDER(1940); SPORTING BLOOD(1940); STRIKE UP THE BAND(1940); BIG BOSS, THE(1941); BLONDE INSPIRATION(1941); BLOSSOMS IN THE DUST(1941); MEN OF BOYS TOWN(1941); MOON OVER MIAMI(1941); SWEETHEART OF THE CAMPUS(1941); WE GO FAST(1941); YOU BELONG TO ME(1941); GAY SISTERS, THE(1942); GIRL TROUBLE(1942); NOW, VOYAGER(1942); PRIDE OF THE YANKEES, THE(1942); ROXIE HART(1942); DIXIE DUGAN(1943); LAUGH YOUR BLUES AWAY(1943); MISSION TO MOSCOW(1943); OLD ACQUAINTANCE(1943); PISTOL PACKIN' MAMA(1943); SOMEONE TO REMEMBER(1943); ADVENTURES OF MARK TWAIN, THE(1944); BUFFALO BILL(1944); CHARLIE CHAN IN THE SECRET SERVICE(1944); COVER GIRL(1944); NONE SHALL ESCAPE(1944); ROGER TOUHY, GANGSTER!(1944); EADIE WAS A LADY(1945)
Silents
RAINBOW(1921); SCHOOL DAYS(1921); SILENT COMMAND, THE(1923); IT IS THE LAW(1924)
Misc. Silents
TWILIGHT(1919); DIVORCE OF CONVENIENCE, A(1921); IS LIFE WORTH LIVING?(1921); WHITE THUNDER(1925)

George Lessey, Sr.
RINGS ON HER FINGERS(1942)
George A. Lessey
Silents
SUBURBAN, THE(1915), d
Misc. Silents
PURPLE LADY, THE(1916), d; HARVEST MOON, THE(1920)
Arnold Lessing
BEACH GIRLS AND THE MONSTER, THE(1965); GIRLS ON THE BEACH(1965)
Bruno Lessing
Silents
SCARLET ROAD, THE(1916), d
Doris Lessing
MEMOIRS OF A SURVIVOR(1981, Brit.), w; GRASS IS SINGING, THE(1982, Brit./Swed.), d&w
1984
KILLING HEAT(1984), d&w Michael Raeburn
Florence Lessing
JUST FOR YOU(1952)
Gotthold Ephraim Lessing
HELDINNEN(1962, Ger.), w
Lilly Lessing
SAVAGES(1972)
Marian Lessing
MISSION TO MOSCOW(1943)
Marion Lessing
SEAS BENEATH, THE(1931); WOMEN OF ALL NATIONS(1931); DOWN-STAIRS(1932); RED-HAIRED ALIBI, THE(1932); DOCTOR MONICA(1934); ONE NIGHT OF LOVE(1934); MILDRED PIERCE(1945)
Mona Lessing
Misc. Talkies
FIGHTING LADY(1935)
Norman Lessing
ARTISTS AND MODELS(1955), w; JOY IN THE MORNING(1965), w
Elgin Lessley
Silents
ATOM, THE(1918), ph; OUR HOSPITALITY(1923), ph; THREE AGES, THE(1923), ph; SHERLOCK, JR.(1924), ph; GO WEST(1925), ph; SEVEN CHANCES(1925), ph; STRONG MAN, THE(1926), ph; TRAMP, TRAMP, TRAMP(1926), ph; LONG PANTS(1927), ph; THREE'S A CROWD(1927), ph; CAMERAMAN, THE(1928), ph; CHASER, THE(1928), ph
Colin Lesslie
ALL AT SEA(1935, Brit.); THAT'S MY UNCLE(1935, Brit.); TAMING OF DOROTHY, THE(1950, Brit.), p; NO RESTING PLACE(1952, Brit.), p, w; HORSE'S MOUTH, THE(1953, Brit.), p; FIRE OVER AFRICA(1954, Brit.), p; CHARLEY MOON(1956, Brit.), p; BREAKOUT(1960, Brit.), p; TUNES OF GLORY(1960, Brit.), p
Michael Lesson
JEKYLL AND HYDE...TOGETHER AGAIN(1982), w
Adam Lessuck
LAW AND DISORDER(1974)
Ben Lessy
WOMAN OF THE YEAR(1942); THOUSANDS CHEER(1943); YOUTH ON PARADE(1943); MUSIC FOR MILLIONS(1944); HER HIGHNESS AND THE BELL-BOY(1945); DARK DELUSION(1947); PIRATE, THE(1948); JACKIE ROBINSON STORY, THE(1950); PURPLE HEART DIARY(1951); JUST FOR YOU(1952); GYPSY(1962); IT'S A MAD, MAD, MAD, MAD WORLD(1963); I'D RATHER BE RICH(1964); PAJAMA PARTY(1964); THAT DARN CAT(1965); THAT FUNNY FEELING(1965); LAST OF THE SECRET AGENTS?, THE(1966); FASTEST GUITAR ALIVE, THE(1967); LOVE MACHINE, THE,(1971); BUDDY BUDDY(1981)
George Lessy
SWEET AND LOWDOWN(1944)
Andrea Virginia Lester
PAINTED HILLS, THE(1951)
Bill Lester
FEDERAL MAN(1950); GIRL FROM SAN LORENZO, THE(1950); I WAS A COMMUNIST FOR THE F.B.I.(1951)
Billy Lester
Silents
BACK TRAIL, THE(1924)
Bruce Lester
BOY MEETS GIRL(1938); IF I WERE KING(1938); WITNESS VANISHES, THE(1939); BRITISH INTELLIGENCE(1940); INVISIBLE MAN RETURNS, THE(1940); LETTER, THE(1940); MY SON, MY SON!(1940); PRIDE AND PREJUDICE(1940); MAN HUNT(1941); SHADOWS ON THE STAIRS(1941); SHINING VICTORY(1941); SINGAPORE WOMAN(1941); YANK IN THE R.A.F., A(1941); DESPERATE JOURNEY(1942); EAGLE SQUADRON(1942); ABOVE SUSPICION(1943); FLESH AND FANTASY(1943); MYSTERIOUS DOCTOR, THE(1943); CLOAK AND DAGGER(1946); STRANGE JOURNEY(1946); GOLDEN EARRINGS(1947); FOOL AND THE PRINCESS, THE(1948, Brit.); I WALK ALONE(1948); LORNA DOONE(1951); SECRETS OF MONTE CARLO(1951); SON OF DR. JEKYLL, THE(1951); TALES OF ROBIN HOOD(1951); PATHFINDER, THE(1952); ROGUE'S MARCH(1952); CHARADE(1953); ROYAL AFRICAN RIFLES, THE(1953); KING RICHARD AND THE CRUSADERS(1954); SOMETHING OF VALUE(1957)
Buddy Lester
GENE KRUPA STORY, THE(1959); OCEAN'S ELEVEN(1960); LADIES MAN, THE(1961); SERGEANTS 3(1962); NUTTY PROFESSOR, THE(1963); PATSY, THE(1964); THREE ON A COUCH(1966); BIG MOUTH, THE(1967); PARTY, THE(1968); HARDLY WORKING(1981); SMORGASBORD(1983)
Carole Lester [Lesley]
LUCKY MASCOT, THE(1951, Brit.)
Charles Lester
SO PROUDLY WE HAIL(1943)
Dan Lester
GREEN BUDDHA, THE(1954, Brit.)
David Lester
WIND AND THE LION, THE(1975)
Donna Jean Lester
UNTAMED(1940)

Eleese Lester
1984
CLOAK AND DAGGER(1984)
Elliot Lester
SOUTH SEA ROSE(1929), w; CITY GIRL(1930), w; TWO SECONDS(1932), w
Elliott Lester
HARMONY AT HOME(1930), w; MEDICINE MAN, THE(1930), w; ROUGH ROMANCE(1930), w
Ernest Lester
GUILT(1930, Brit.); WRITTEN LAW, THE(1931, Brit.); WONDERFUL STORY, THE(1932, Brit.)
Ferrell Lester
TEXAN MEETS CALAMITY JANE, THE(1950)
Frank Lester
ROCKY HORROR PICTURE SHOW, THE(1975, Brit.)
Henry Lester
STUDY IN TERROR, A(1966, Brit./Ger.), p; ADVENTURES OF GERARD, THE(1970, Brit.), p, w
Howard Lester
NAKED ANGELS(1969)
Jack Lester
LOVE ON SKIS(1933, Brit.); NON-STOP NEW YORK(1937, Brit.); MAN WITH 100 FACES, THE(1938, Brit.); ROSE OF TRALEE(1938, Ireland); NO ORCHIDS FOR MISS BLANDISH(1948, Brit.); PORT OF ESCAPE(1955, Brit.); ACROSS THE BRIDGE(1957, Brit.); FLOODS OF FEAR(1958, Brit.); SHERIFF OF FRACTURED JAW, THE(1958, Brit.); TWO LITTLE BEARS, THE(1961); DEADWOOD'76(1965); RAT FINK(1965); ROAD HUSTLERS, THE(1968); INCREDIBLE TWO-HEADED TRANSPLANT, THE(1971)
Misc. Talkies
JENNIE, WIFE/CHILD(1968)
Jan Lester
HEART OF THE RIO GRANDE(1942)
Jean Lester
ROAD TO FORTUNE, THE(1930, Brit.); PUBLIC LIFE OF HENRY THE NINTH, THE(1934, Brit.)
Jeff Lester
1984
LITTLE DRUMMER GIRL, THE(1984)
Jerry Lester
ARIZONA TO BROADWAY(1933); SLEEPYTIME GAL(1942); ROOKIE, THE(1959); SMOKEY AND THE BANDIT II(1980); HARDLY WORKING(1981)
Jim Lester
MAD DOG COLL(1961)
Judy Lester
DESIREE(1954)
Kate Lester
Silents
KISS, THE(1916); SOCIAL SECRETARY, THE(1916); ADVENTURES OF CAROL, THE(1917); DIVORCE GAME, THE(1917); TODAY(1917); DOING THEIR BIT(1918); STOP THIEF(1920); BEAUTIFUL LIAR, THE(1921); MADE IN HEAVEN(1921); ONE WEEK OF LOVE(1922); TAILOR MADE MAN, A(1922); GIMMIE(1923); HUNCHBACK OF NOTRE DAME, THE(1923); RENDEZVOUS, THE(1923); GOLDFISH, THE(1924); MEDDLER, THE(1925); RAFFLES, THE AMATEUR CRACKSMAN(1925)
Misc. Silents
REWARD OF PATIENCE, THE(1916); GOD'S MAN(1917); GOOD FOR NOTHING, THE(1917); HEART OF A GIRL(1918); HIS ROYAL HIGHNESS(1918); UNBELIEVER, THE(1918); WAY OUT, THE(1918); MAN AND HIS MONEY, A(1919); STRONGER VOW, THE(1919); SIMPLE SOULS(1920); DON'T NEGLECT YOUR WIFE(1921); FOURTEENTH LOVER, THE(1922); GLORIOUS FOOL, THE(1922); REMEMBRANCE(1922); CAN A WOMAN LOVE TWICE?(1923); LOVE TRAP, THE(1923); MARRIAGE MARKET, THE(1923); BEAUTIFUL SINNER, THE(1924); LEAVE IT TO GERRY(1924); WIFE OF THE CENTAUR(1924); PRICE OF PLEASURE, THE(1925)
Kathy Lester
PHANTASM(1979)
Ken Lester
FRAMED(1975)
Ketty Lester
JUST FOR FUN(1963, Brit.); UPTIGHT(1968); BLACULA(1972); UPTOWN SATURDAY NIGHT(1974)
Kevin Lester
1984
NATURAL, THE(1984)
Larry D. Lester
TAMMY AND THE MILLIONAIRE(1967), ed
Leonie Lester
Silents
MAN AND MAID(1925)
Loren Lester
ROCK 'N' ROLL HIGH SCHOOL(1979); SWAP MEET(1979)
Louise Lester
STRAIGHT FROM THE HEART(1935)
Silents
RECKONING DAY, THE(1918); OUTCASTS OF POKER FLAT, THE(1919)
Misc. Silents
APRIL(1916); DESERT HAWK, THE(1924); GALLOPING ON(1925)
Margie Lester
Misc. Talkies
HOW TO MAKE A DOLL(1967)
Mark Lester
SHADOWS(1931, Brit.); THINGS ARE LOOKING UP(1934, Brit.); CAR OF DREAMS(1935, Brit.); CASE OF GABRIEL PERRY, THE(1935, Brit.); DOMMED CARGO(1936, Brit.); LAMBETH WALK, THE(1940, Brit.); MAD MEN OF EUROPE(1940, Brit.); ASKING FOR TROUBLE(1942, Brit.); SPACEFLIGHT IC-1(1965, Brit.); FAHRENHEIT 451(1966, Brit.); OUR MOTHER'S HOUSE(1967, Brit.); OLIVER!(1968, Brit.); RUN WILD, RUN FREE(1969, Brit.); SUDDEN TERROR(1970, Brit.); BLACK BEAUTY(1971, Brit./Ger./Span.); MELODY(1971, Brit.); NIGHT HAIR CHILD(1971, Brit.); WHO SLEW AUNTIE ROO?(1971, U.S./Brit.); SCALAWAG(1973, Yugo.); REDNECK(1975, Ital./Span.); CROSSED SWORDS(1978); CLASS OF 1984(1982, Can.), d, w

Misc. Talkies
LOVE UNDER THE ELMS(1973)
Mark L. Lester
STEEL ARENA(1973), p, d&w; TRUCK STOP WOMEN(1974), p&d, w; BOBBIE JO AND THE OUTLAW(1976), p&d; STUNTS(1977), d; ROLLER BOOGIE(1979), d
1984
FIRESTARTER(1984), d
Marvin Lester
SCUM OF THE EARTH(1963), ph
Neil Lester
GHOST GOES WEST, THE(1936)
Ray Lester
MACHISMO–40 GRAVES FOR 40 GUNS(1970)
Richard Lester
RING-A-DING RHYTHM(1962, Brit. 73m Amicus/COL bw (G.B: IT'S TRAD, DAD!), p&d; MOUSE ON THE MOON, THE(1963, Brit.), d; HARD DAY'S NIGHT, A(1964, Brit.), d; HELP!(1965, Brit.), d; KNACK ... AND HOW TO GET IT, THE(1965, Brit.), d; FUNNY THING HAPPENED ON THE WAY TO THE FORUM, A(1966), d; HOW I WON THE WAR(1967, Brit.), p&d; PETULIA(1968, U.S./Brit.), d; BED SITTING ROOM, THE(1969, Brit.), p&d;JUGGERNAUT(1974, Brit.), d; THREE MUSKETEERS, THE(1974, Panama), d; FOUR MUSKETEERS, THE(1975), d; ROYAL FLASH(1975, Brit.), d; RITZ, THE(1976), d; ROBIN AND MARIAN(1976, Brit.), d; BUTCH AND SUNDANCE: THE EARLY DAYS(1979), d; CUBA(1979), d; SUPERMAN II(1980), d; SUPERMAN III(1983), d
1984
FINDERS KEEPERS(1984), d
Roy Lester
RINGSIDE MAISIE(1941)
Seelag Lester
WINNING TEAM, THE(1952), w
Seeleg Lester
CHECKERED COAT, THE(1948), w; IRON SHERIFF, THE(1957), w; CHANGE OF MIND(1969), p, w
Seeler Lester
SERGEANT RYKER(1968), w
Seelig Lester
REINCARNATE, THE(1971, Can.), p, w
Stephen Lester
CORPSE GRINDERS, THE(1972)
Susan Lester
TREE GROWS IN BROOKLYN, A(1945)
Tom Lester
BENJI(1974)
Vicki Lester
MAD MISS MANTON, THE(1938); MAID'S NIGHT OUT(1938); PATIENT IN ROOM 18, THE(1938); SKY GIANT(1938); THIS MARRIAGE BUSINESS(1938); GREAT PLANE ROBBERY, THE(1940); TALL, DARK AND HANDSOME(1941); TOM, DICK AND HARRY(1941); YOU'RE OUT OF LUCK(1941); I LIVE ON DANGER(1942); LONE RIDER AND THE BANDIT, THE(1942); MIRACLE KID(1942); SLEEPYTIME GAL(1942); YOU'RE TELLING ME(1942)
Vonne Lester
KID FROM BOOKLYN, THE(1946); SUNSET PASS(1946); SINBAD THE SAILOR(1947); GIRL FROM JONES BEACH, THE(1949); DESERT HAWK, THE(1950); SON OF SINBAD(1955); THERE'S ALWAYS TOMORROW(1956)
William Lester
BAD BOY(1949); SKY LINER(1949); TWILIGHT IN THE SIERRAS(1950); SINGIN' IN THE RAIN(1952); ABOVE AND BEYOND(1953)
Silents
MARSHAL OF MONEYMINT, THE(1922); GENTLE JULIA(1923); BARRIERS OF THE LAW(1925), w; FIGHTING BOOB, THE(1926), w; AIR PATROL, THE(1928), w; ARIZONA CYCLONE(1928), w; SLIM FINGERS(1929), w
Misc. Silents
DOUBLE O, THE(1921); BARB WIRE(1922); FORBIDDEN TRAIL, THE(1923); WOLVES OF THE BORDER(1923)
Lester Cole and the Debutantes
SOUTH OF DIXIE(1944)
The Lester Horton Dancers
CALYPSO JOE(1957)
Adolph Lestina
Silents
GIRL WHO STAYED AT HOME, THE(1919)
Adolphe Lestina
Silents
FRUITS OF DESIRE, THE(1916); GREATEST THING IN LIFE, THE(1918); HEARTS OF THE WORLD(1918); HUN WITHIN, THE(1918); GIRL WHO STAYED AT HOME, THE(1919); ROMANCE OF HAPPY VALLEY, A(1919); SCARLET DAYS(1919); IDOL DANCER, THE(1920); LOVE FLOWER, THE(1920); ORPHANS OF THE STORM(1922)
Misc. Silents
MARY ELLEN COMES TO TOWN(1920)
Humphrey Lestocq
STOP PRESS GIRL(1949, Brit.); FAKE'S PROGRESS(1950, Brit.); COME BACK PETER(1952, Brit.); ONCE A SINNER(1952, Brit.); SCHOOL FOR BRIDES(1952, Brit.); GOOD BEGINNING, THE(1953, Brit.); MEET MR. LUCIFER(1953, Brit.); FUSS OVER FEATHERS(1954, Brit.); SON OF ROBIN HOOD(1959, Brit.); NOT A HOPE IN HELL(1960, Brit.); BOMB IN THE HIGH STREET(1961, Brit.); COURT MARTIAL OF MAJOR KELLER, THE(1961, Brit.); LONG SHADOW, THE(1961, Brit.); PIT OF DARKNESS(1961, Brit.); THIRD ALIBI, THE(1961, Brit.); TWO WIVES AT ONE WEDDING(1961, Brit.); UNSTOPPABLE MAN, THE(1961, Brit.); DESIGN FOR LOVING(1962, Brit.); GOLDEN RABBIT, THE(1962, Brit.); WALTZ OF THE TOREADORS(1962, Brit.); LIFE IN DANGER(1964, Brit.)
Leon Lestocq-Prayne
HALF A SIXPENCE(1967, Brit.)
David Lestrange
Silents
WHEN BOYS LEAVE HOME(1928, Brit.), w
Pierre Lestringuez
MONSEIGNEUR(1950, Fr.), p,d&w

Sauncey LeSuer
SHE DANCES ALONE(1981, Aust./U.S.)
Hal LeSueur
MUTINY ON THE BOUNTY(1935)
Daniel Lesur
NIGHTS OF SHAME(1961, Fr.), m
J. Leszczynski
BORDER STREET(1950, Pol.)
Witold Leszczynski
MAN WHO THOUGHT LIFE, THE(1969, Den.), ph
Henry LeTang
1984
COTTON CLUB, THE(1984), ch
David Letch
NATE AND HAYES(1983, U.S./New Zealand)
Eileen Letchworth
LAST SUMMER(1969)
Jacques Letellier
DIE GANS VON SEDAN(1962, Fr./Ger.), ph
Catherine Leterrier
PROVIDENCE(1977, Fr.), cos; FRENCH POSTCARDS(1979), cos
1984
LIFE IS A BED OF ROSES(1984, Fr.), cos
Francois Leterrier
MAN ESCAPED, A(1957, Fr.); NAKED AUTUMN(1963, Fr.), d, w; GOODBYE EMMANUELLE(1980, Fr.), d, w
Ronald Letham
HANOVER STREET(1979, Brit.)
Hugh Lethbridge
WISHBONE, THE(1933, Brit.)
Lori Lethin
1984
PREY, THE(1984)
Misc. Talkies
BLOODY BIRTHDAY(1980)
Sam Lethrone
AND NOW MY LOVE(1975, Fr.)
Alik Letichevsky
RAINBOW, THE(1944, USSR)
Jodi Letizia
ROCKY(1976)
Dennis Letkeman
1984
ICEMAN(1984)
Ken Letner
GOING BERSERK(1983)
Phil Leto
JUST TELL ME WHAT YOU WANT(1980)
Henri Letondal
MAGNIFICENT DOLL(1946); RAZOR'S EDGE, THE(1946); CRIME DOCTOR'S GAMBLE(1947); FOXES OF HARROW, THE(1947); APARTMENT FOR PEGGY(1948); BIG CLOCK, THE(1948); COME TO THE STABLE(1949); MADAME BOVARY(1949); MOTHER IS A FRESHMAN(1949); PLEASE BELIEVE ME(1950); ACROSS THE WIDE MISSOURI(1951); KIND LADY(1951); ON THE RIVERA(1951); ROYAL WEDDING(1951); TEN TALL MEN(1951); BIG SKY, THE(1952); MONKEY BUSINESS(1952); WHAT PRICE GLORY?(1952); WILD NORTH, THE(1952); DANGEROUS WHEN WET(1953); DESERT LEGION(1953); GENTLEMEN PREFER BLONDES(1953); LITTLE BOY LOST(1953); SOUTH SEA WOMAN(1953); DEEP IN MY HEART(1954); GAMBLER FROM NATCHEZ, THE(1954); BULLET FOR JOEY, A(1955)
Louise Letourneau
END, THE(1978)
Pierre Letourneau
LOVE IN A FOUR LETTER WORLD(1970, Can.)
Nathalie Letrosne
1984
A NOS AMOURS(1984, Fr.), ed
Zh. Letskiy
DON QUIXOTE(1961, USSR)
Dan Lett
1984
MRS. SOFFEL(1984)
Kathy Lette
PUBERTY BLUES(1983, Aus.), w
Catherine Letterier
L'ETOILE DU NORD(1983, Fr.), cos
Amy Letterman
YOU LIGHT UP MY LIFE(1977)
Barry Lettes
SCOTT OF THE ANTARCTIC(1949, Brit.)
Anthony Lettier
DARK INTRUDER(1965); WILD SEED(1965)
Louis Lettiere
BUCKSKIN LADY, THE(1957)
Al Lettieri
TOWN CALLED HELL, A(1971, Span./Brit.); VILLAIN(1971, Brit.), w; GETAWAY, THE(1972); GODFATHER, THE(1972); PULP(1972, Brit.); DEADLY TRACKERS(1973); DON IS DEAD, THE(1973); MC Q(1974); MR. MAJESTYK(1974)
Alfredo Lettieri
BOBO, THE(1967, Brit.); NIGHT OF THE FOLLOWING DAY, THE(1969, Brit.)
Louis Lettieri
CYCLONE FURY(1951); ENFORCER, THE(1951); HOLLYWOOD STORY(1951); STRANGERS ON A TRAIN(1951); MONKEY BUSINESS(1952); STOP, YOU'RE KILLING ME(1952); FIGHTER ATTACK(1953); DESPERATE HOURS, THE(1955)
Louis Michael Lettieri
THREE RING CIRCUS(1954)
Tony Lettieri
KING OF THE MOUNTAIN(1981)

Rudolf Lettinger
Silents
CABINET OF DR. CALIGARI, THE(1921, Ger.)
Barry Letts
FRIEDA(1947, Brit.); SAN DEMETRIO, LONDON(1947, Brit.); CRUEL SEA, THE(1953)
Dom Letts
KING OF COMEDY, THE(1983)
Pauline Letts
PINK STRING AND SEALING WAX(1950, Brit.); GIRL ON APPROVAL(1962, Brit.); EYE OF THE DEVIL(1967, Brit.); GAWAIN AND THE GREEN KNIGHT(1973, Brit.)
Fred Letuli
MISS SADIE THOMPSON(1953); SALOME(1953)
Freddie Letuli
ONE WAY STREET(1950)
Uluao Letuli
ON AN ISLAND WITH YOU(1948); MALAYA(1950)
Freddie Letull
HOLIDAY RHYTHM(1950)
George Letz [George Montgomery]
SINGING VAGABOND, THE(1935); SPRINGTIME IN THE ROCKIES(1937); GOLD MINE IN THE SKY(1938); FRONTIER PONY EXPRESS(1939); ROUGH RIDERS' ROUNDUP(1939); HI-YO SILVER(1940)
Mike Letz
EL DORADO(1967)
Misc. Talkies
UTAH KID, THE(1944)
Raoul Letzer
5 SINNERS(1961, Ger.)
Clair Leucart
POLTERGEIST(1982)
Clair E. Leucart
1984
FOOTLOOSE(1984)
Chow Fook Leung
EXIT THE DRAGON, ENTER THE TIGER(1977, Hong Kong), m
Man Chi Leung
SECRET, THE(1979, Hong Kong)
Tony Leung
FORCED VENGEANCE(1982), set d
Heidi Leupolt
FAUST(1963, Ger.)
Gino Leurini
HEART AND SOUL(1950, Ital.); QUEEN OF SHEBA(1953, Ital.); ANITA GARIBAL-DI(1954, Ital.)
Borys Leurn
THE DIRTY GAME(1966, Fr./Ital./Ger.), ed
Jean-Pierre Leursse
STORY OF ADELE H., THE(1975, Fr.)
Leurville
GERVAISE(1956, Fr.)
Jack Leustig
BREATHLESS(1983)
E.B. Leuthege
DIPLOMATIC LOVER, THE(1934, Brit.), w
Eric Leutzinger
BIBLE...IN THE BEGINNING, THE(1966)
Ina Leuvennink
SPOTS ON MY LEOPARD, THE(1974, S. Africa), m
Inno Leuvennink
SPOTS ON MY LEOPARD, THE(1974, S. Africa), m
Ruth Leuwerik
TRAPP FAMILY, THE(1961, Ger.); DISORDER AND EARLY TORMENT(1977, Ger.)
Benjamin Lev
SERAFINO(1970, Fr./Ital.); FAMILY, THE(1974, Fr./Ital.)
Donald Lev
PUTNEY SWOPE(1969)
Martin Lev
BUGSY MALONE(1976, Brit.)
Carlo Leva
ONCE UPON A TIME IN THE WEST(1969, U.S./Ital.), set d; SPIRITS OF THE DEAD(1969, Fr./Ital.), art d, cos; CAT O'NINE TAILS(1971, Ital./Ger./Fr.), art d
Juan Levaggi
LOVE HUNGER(1965, Arg.), ph
Kate Levan
TREASURE OF THE FOUR CROWNS(1983, Span./U.S.)
Michael Levanios, Jr.
UNCLE SCAM(1981), p&d, w, ed
Michael Levanios III
UNCLE SCAM(1981), m
Daniel Levans
GOODBYE GIRL, THE(1977); TURNING POINT, THE(1977)
Hus Levant
DARK CRYSTAL, THE(1982, Brit.)
Mark Levant
TRAIL TO VENGEANCE(1945), md; WOMAN IN GREEN, THE(1945), md; GUN TOWN(1946), md; TERROR BY NIGHT(1946), md
Oscar Levant
DANCE OF LIFE, THE(1929); JAZZ HEAVEN(1929), m; LEATHERNECKING(1930), m; ORIENT EXPRESS(1934), w; BLACK SHEEP(1935), m; NOTHING SACRED(1937), m; RHYTHM ON THE RIVER(1940); KISS THE BOYS GOODBYE(1941); RHAPSODY IN BLUE(1945); HUMORESQUE(1946); ROMANCE ON THE HIGH SEAS(1948); YOU WERE MEANT FOR ME(1948); BARKLEYS OF BROADWAY, THE(1949); AMERICAN IN PARIS, AN(1951); I DON'T CARE GIRL, THE(1952); O. HENRY'S FULL HOUSE(1952); BAND WAGON, THE(1953); COBWEB, THE(1955)
Rene LeVant
SAVAGE HARVEST(1981)

William LeVanway
WONDER OF WOMEN(1929), ed; FREE AND EASY(1930), ed; GOOD NEWS(1930), ed; WAR NURSE(1930), ed; PARLOR, BEDROOM AND BATH(1931), ed; POSSESSED(1931), ed; REDUCING(1931), ed; SHIPMATES(1931), ed; THIS MODERN AGE(1931), ed; EMMA(1932), ed; PROSPERITY(1932), ed; SPEAK EASILY(1932), ed; BAND PLAYS ON, THE(1934), ed; LAZY RIVER(1934), ed; OUTCAST LADY(1934), ed; CHINA SEAS(1935), ed; NIGHT AT THE OPERA, A(1935), ed
Anne Levaslot
TWO ENGLISH GIRLS(1972, Fr.)
Andre Levasseur
FLEA IN HER EAR, A(1968, Fr.), cos
Palmyre Levasseur
FRENCH CANCAN(1956, Fr.); PARIS DOES STRANGE THINGS(1957, Fr./Ital.)
Sylvester Levay
1984
BODY ROCK(1984), m; WHERE THE BOYS ARE '84(1984), m
Volodia Levcenko
WATERLOO(1970, Ital./USSR)
Levchenko
Silents
BATTLESHIP POTEMKIN, THE(1925, USSR)
V. Levchenko
WAR AND PEACE(1968, USSR)
Yu. Levchenko
FORTY-NINE DAYS(1964, USSR)
M. C. Levee
Silents
IN EVERY WOMAN'S LIFE(1924), p
Michael Levee
BLACK BIRD, THE(1975), p; SLOW DANCING IN THE BIG CITY(1978), p
Claude Leveilles
TROUBLE-FETE(1964, Can.), m
Maurice Level
ROADHOUSE MURDER, THE(1932), w
Calvin Levels
RAGTIME(1981)
Bert Leven
HOUSE BY THE RIVER(1950), art d
Boris Leven
ALEXANDER'S RAGTIME BAND(1938), art d; DOWN ON THE FARM(1938), art d; ROAD DEMON(1938), art d; FLYING DEUCES, THE(1939), art d; SHANGHAI GESTURE, THE(1941), art d; GIRL TROUBLE(1942), art d; LIFE BEGINS AT 8:30(1942), art d; TALES OF MANHATTAN(1942), art d; HELLO, FRISCO, HELLO(1943), art d; DOLL FACE(1945), art d; HOME SWEET HOMICIDE(1946), art d; SHOCK(1946), art d; I WONDER WHO'S KISSING HER NOW(1947), art d; SHOCKING MISS PILGRIM, THE(1947), art d; MR. PEABODY AND THE MERMAID(1948), art d; CRISS CROSS(1949), art d; LOVABLE CHEAT, THE(1949), art d; SEARCH FOR DANGER(1949), art d; DESTINATION MURDER(1950), art d; EXPERIMENT ALCATRAZ(1950), art d; MILLIONAIRE FOR CHRISTY, A(1951), art d; PROWLER, THE(1951), art d; SECOND WOMAN, THE(1951), prod d; TWO DOLLAR BETTOR(1951), art d; SUDDEN FEAR(1952), art d; DONOVAN'S BRAIN(1953), art d; FORT ALGIERS(1953), art d; INVADERS FROM MARS(1953), art d; LONG WAIT, THE(1954), art d; SILVER CHALICE, THE(1954), art d; GIANT(1956), prod d; THUNDER IN THE SUN(1959), art d; SEPTEMBER STORM(1960), art d; WEST SIDE STORY(1961), prod d; TWO FOR THE SEESAW(1962), prod d; STRAIT-JACKET(1964), prod d; SOUND OF MUSIC, THE(1965), prod d; SAND PEBBLES, THE(1966), prod d; STAR!(1968), prod d; DREAM OF KINGS, A(1969), prod d, art d; ANDROMEDA STRAIN, THE(1971), prod d; HAPPY BIRTHDAY, WANDA JUNE(1971), prod d; NEW CENTURIONS, THE(1972), prod d; JONATHAN LIVINGSTON SEAGULL(1973), prod d; SHANKS(1974), prod d; MANDINGO(1975), prod d; NEW YORK, NEW YORK(1977), prod d; KING OF COMEDY, THE(1983), prod d
1984
FLETCH(1984), prod d
Edward Leven
CRY MURDER(1936), p; PROJECT X(1949), p
Edward J. Leven
SECOND FACE, THE(1950), p
Mel Leven
MOUSE AND HIS CHILD, THE(1977)
Richard Leven
MALTA STORY(1954, Brit.)
Sid Leven
CALIFORNIA DREAMING(1979), ed
John Levene
DARK PLACES(1974, Brit.); PERMISSION TO KILL(1975, U.S./Aust.)
Philip Levene
DEADLY STRANGERS(1974, Brit.), w; DIAGNOSIS: MURDER(1974, Brit.), w
Sam Levene
YELLOW JACK(1938); AFTER THE THIN MAN(1936); THREE MEN ON A HORSE(1936); MAD MISS MANTON, THE(1938); SHOPWORN ANGEL(1938); GOLDEN BOY(1939); MARRIED BACHELOR(1941); SHADOW OF THE THIN MAN(1941); BIG STREET, THE(1942); DESTINATION UNKNOWN(1942); GRAND CENTRAL MURDER(1942); SING YOUR WORRIES AWAY(1942); SUNDAY PUNCH(1942); ACTION IN THE NORTH ATLANTIC(1943); GUNG HO!(1943); I DOOD IT(1943); WHISTLING IN BROOKLYN(1943); PURPLE HEART, THE(1944); BOOMERANG(1947); BRUTE FORCE(1947); CROSSFIRE(1947); KILLER McCOY(1947); LIKELY STORY, A(1947); BABE RUTH STORY, THE(1948); LEATHER GLOVES(1948); DIAL 1119(1950); GUILTY BYSTANDER(1950); THREE SAILORS AND A GIRL(1953); OPPOSITE SEX, THE(1956); DESIGNING WOMAN(1957); SLAUGHTER ON TENTH AVENUE(1957); SWEET SMELL OF SUCCESS(1957); KATHY O'(1958); ACT ONE(1964); DREAM OF KINGS, A(1969); SUCH GOOD FRIENDS(1971); MONEY, THE(1975); GOD TOLD ME TO(1976); ...AND JUSTICE FOR ALL(1979); LAST EMBRACE(1979)
Terry Levene
WOMEN IN CELL BLOCK 7(1977, Ital./U.S.), p; FIST OF FEAR, TOUCH OF DEATH(1980), p
Knowlton Levenick
TEST PILOT(1938)

Lew Levenson
24 HOURS(1931), w; EAST OF FIFTH AVE.(1933), w

S. B. Levenson
IT HAPPENED IN PARIS(1953, Fr.), w

Fannie Levenstein
Misc. Talkies
JEWISH KING LEAR(1935)

Alain Levent
OBJECTIVE 500 MILLION(1966, Fr.), ph; SIX IN PARIS(1968, Fr.), ph; LES
GAULOISES BLEUES(1969, Fr.), ph; SABRA(1970, Fr./Ital./Israel), ph; NUN,
THE(1971, Fr.), ph; DRACULA AND SON(1976, Fr.), ph; QUESTION, THE(1977,
Fr.), ph

Pierre Levent
UN CARNET DE BAL(1938, Fr.), ph; SUITOR, THE(1963, Fr.), ph

V. Levental
FAREWELL, DOVES(1962, USSR), art d

Harold Leventhal
BOUND FOR GLORY(1976), p

Thomas Leventhal
GOSPEL ROAD, THE(1973)

Annabel Leventon
THINK DIRTY(1970, Brit.); COME BACK PETER(1971, Brit.)
1984
REAL LIFE(1984, Brit.)

William Levenway
FELLER NEEDS A FRIEND(1932), ed

Claude Leveque
ZITA(1968, Fr.)

Lady Arthur Lever
BROWN SUGAR(1931, Brit.), w

Connie Lever
Silents
JO THE CROSSING SWEEPER(1918, Brit.)

Philip Lever
JOHN WESLEY(1954, Brit.)

Reg Lever
SCROOGE(1970, Brit.); LOLA(1971, Brit./Ital.)

Carey Leverett
WHAT DID YOU DO IN THE WAR, DADDY?(1966), ch

Carole Leverett
HI, MOM!(1970)

Carey Leverette
FROM HERE TO ETERNITY(1953)

Harry Leverette
TAKE MY LIFE(1942)

Frank Levering
PARASITE(1982), w

Jack Levering
Misc. Silents
VERY IDEA, THE(1920)

James Levering
Silents
IDOL OF THE STAGE, THE(1916); KIDNAPPED(1917)
Misc. Silents
DEAD ALIVE, THE(1916); FEATHERTOP(1916); MY OWN UNITED STATES(1918)

Joseph Levering
DEFENDERS OF THE LAW(1931), d; SEA DEVILS(1931), d; SPORTING CHAN-
CE(1931); CHEATING BLONDES(1933), d; LAW OF THE RANGER(1937), w; RANG-
ERS STEP IN, THE(1937), w; RECKLESS RANGER(1937), w; IN EARLY
ARIZONA(1938), d; PHANTOM GOLD(1938), d; PIONEER TRAIL(1938), d; ROLLING
CARAVANS(1938), d; STAGECOACH DAYS(1938), d; FRONTIERS OF '49(1939), d;
LAW COMES TO TEXAS, THE(1939), d; LONE STAR PIONEERS(1939), d; RIDERS
OF THE FRONTIER(1939), w
Silents
FINGER PRINTS(1923), d; TIE THAT BINDS, THE(1923), d
Misc. Silents
FIGHT FOR MILLIONS, THE(1913); TEMPTATIONS OF SATAN, THE(1914); LIT-
TLE MISS FORTUNE(1917), d; LITTLE SAMARITAN, THE(1917), d; ROAD BE-
TWEEN, THE(1917), d; VICTIM, THE(1917), d; TRANSGRESSOR, THE(1918), d; HIS
TEMPORARY WIFE(1920), d; HUSBANDS AND WIVES(1920), d; LURING SHAD-
OWS(1920), d; DETERMINATION(1922), d; FLESH AND SPIRIT(1922), d; LILLIES
OF THE STREETS(1925), d; UNRESTRAINED YOUTH(1925), d

Shelby Leverington
HOT TOMORROWS(1978); LONG RIDERS, THE(1980); WORLDS APART(1980, U.S.,
Israel); S.O.B.(1981); LOVE LETTERS(1983)
1984
CLOAK AND DAGGER(1984)

Loretta Leversee
PLAYGROUND, THE(1965); UP THE DOWN STAIRCASE(1967)

Glenis Leverstam
SKIN DEEP(1978, New Zealand)

Ted Leversuch
TANGIER ASSIGNMENT(1954, Brit.), d&w; ADULTEROUS AFFAIR(1966), d&w

Dominique Levert
WILD CHILD, THE(1970, Fr.)

Jacques Levert [Jacques Mortier]
TONI(1968, Fr.), w

Rene Levert
WILD CHILD, THE(1970, Fr.)

Suzanne Levesi
LADY GODIVA RIDES AGAIN(1955, Brit.)

Benoit Levesque
QUEST FOR FIRE(1982, Fr./Can.)

Marcel Levesque
CRIME OF MONSIEUR LANGE, THE(1936, Fr.); LUMIERE D'ETE(1943, Fr.)
Misc. Silents
LA SULTANE DE L'AMOUR(1919, Fr.)

Mariette Levesque
TANYA'S ISLAND(1981, Can.)

Michael Levesque
INCREDIBLE MELTING MAN, THE(1978), art d; FOXES(1980), art d

Michel Levesque
WEREWOLVES ON WHEELS(1971), d, w; SWEET SUGAR(1972), d; CANNON-
BALL(1976, U.S./Hong Kong), art d

Susanne Levesey
RICE GIRL(1963, Fr./Ital.)

Bill Levey
1984
NIGHT PATROL(1984), w

Charles Levey
KITTY(1929, Brit.); WINDJAMMER, THE(1931, Brit.)
Silents
SHADOW OF EGYPT, THE(1924, Brit.)

Ethel Levey
HIGH STAKES(1931)

Gerry Levey
OPERATION CONSPIRACY(1957, Brit.)

Jules Levey
BOYS FROM SYRACUSE(1940), p; TIGHT SHOES(1941), p; BUTCH MINDS THE
BABY(1942), p; HAIRY APE, THE(1944), p; NEW ORLEANS(1947), p

William A. Levey
HAPPY HOOKER GOES TO WASHINGTON, THE(1977), p&d; SLUMBER PARTY
'57(1977), p, d, w; SKATETOWN, U.S.A.(1979), p, d, w

Alan J. Levi
Misc. Talkies
BLOOD SONG(1982), d

Ben Levi
INCIDENT, THE(1967)

Carlo Levi
EBOLI(1980, Ital.), w

Eitan Levi
1984
DRIFTING(1984, Israel), art d

Juda Levi
FAITHFUL CITY(1952, Israel)

M. Levi
OUTCRY(1949, Ital.)

Paolo Levi
RED LIPS(1964, Fr./Ital.), w; OPERATION KID BROTHER(1967, Ital.), w

Robert Levi
HOME FREE ALL(1983), ph
1984
HOME FREE ALL(1984), ph

Shaika Levi
SALLAH(1965, Israel); CLOUDS OVER ISRAEL(1966, Israel)

Yona Levi
IMPOSSIBLE ON SATURDAY(1966, Fr./Israel)

Klara Leviczki
FORBIDDEN RELATIONS(1983, Hung.)

Philip Levien
DIFFERENT STORY, A(1978)
1984
BEVERLY HILLS COP(1984)

Sonya Levien
BEHIND THAT CURTAIN(1929), w; FROZEN JUSTICE(1929), w; LUCKY
STAR(1929), w; SOUTH SEA ROSE(1929), w; THEY HAD TO SEE PARIS(1929), w;
YOUNGER GENERATION(1929), w; LIGHTNIN'(1930), w; LILIOM(1930), w; SO
THIS IS LONDON(1930), w; SONG O' MY HEART(1930), w; BRAT, THE(1931), w;
DADDY LONG LEGS(1931), w; DELICIOUS(1931), w; SURRENDER(1931), w; AFT-
ER TOMORROW(1932), w; REBECCA OF SUNNYBROOK FARM(1932), w; SHE
WANTED A MILLIONAIRE(1932), w; TESS OF THE STORM COUNTRY(1932), w;
BERKELEY SQUARE(1933), w; MR. SKITCH(1933), w; STATE FAIR(1933), w; WAR-
RIOR'S HUSBAND, THE(1933), w; AS HUSBANDS GO(1934), w; CHANGE OF
HEART(1934), w; WHITE PARADE, THE(1934), w; HERE'S TO ROMANCE(1935), w;
COUNTRY DOCTOR, THE(1936), w; NAVY WIFE(1936), w; REUNION(1936), w;
COWBOY AND THE LADY, THE(1938), w; FOUR MEN AND A PRAYER(1938), w; IN
OLD CHICAGO(1938), w; KIDNAPPED(1938), w; DRUMS ALONG THE MO-
HAWK(1939), w; HUNCHBACK OF NOTRE DAME, THE(1939), w; ZIEGFELD
GIRL(1941), w; RHAPSODY IN BLUE(1945), w; STATE FAIR(1945), w; VALLEY OF
DECISION, THE(1945), w; GREEN YEARS, THE(1946), w; THREE DARING DAUGH-
TERS(1948), w; GREAT CARUSO, THE(1951), w; MERRY WIDOW, THE(1952), w;
STUDENT PRINCE, THE(1954), w; HIT THE DECK(1955), w; INTERRUPTED MELO-
DY(1955), w; OKLAHOMA(1955), w; BHOWANI JUNCTION(1956), w; JEANNE EA-
GELS(1957), w; PEPE(1960), w; STATE FAIR(1962), w
Silents
EXCITERS, THE(1923), w; TOP OF NEW YORK, THE(1925), w; PRINCESS FROM
HOBOKEN, THE(1927), w; POWER OF THE PRESS, THE(1928), w

Milcho Leviev
DETOUR, THE(1968, Bulgarian), m

Josef Levigard
Silents
GRIT WINS(1929), d; SLIM FINGERS(1929), d
Misc. Silents
BORN TO THE SADDLE(1929), d; SMILING TERROR, THE(1929), d

Emile Levigne
TARAS BULBA(1962), makeup

Marina Levikova
LIQUID SKY(1982), prod d, cos

Albert Levin
BORN TO SPEED(1947), m

Alvin Levin
GAS HOUSE KIDS GO WEST(1947), m; IT'S A JOKE, SON!(1947), m; KILLER AT
LARGE(1947), m; RAILROADED(1947), m; TOO MANY WINNERS(1947), m

Ben Levin
1984
DRIFTING(1984, Israel)

Bernard Levin
NOTHING BUT THE BEST(1964, Brit.)
Boris Levin
JUST AROUND THE CORNER(1938), art d; SECOND CHORUS(1940), art d; SENATOR WAS INDISCREET, THE(1947), art d; WOMAN ON THE RUN(1950), art d; ROSE OF CIMARRON(1952), art d; STAR, THE(1953), art d; MY GUN IS QUICK(1957), art d; MATILDA(1978), prod d
Charles Levin
ANNIE HALL(1977); BETWEEN THE LINES(1977); MANHATTAN(1979); SEDUCTION OF JOE TYNAN, THE(1979); HONEYSUCKLE ROSE(1980); DEAL OF THE CENTURY(1983)
1984
THIS IS SPINAL TAP(1984)
Edwina Levin
Silents
HELP WANTED–MALE!(1920), w; REPUTATION(1921), w
Erma E. Levin
PROJECTIONIST, THE(1970), m
Erma Levin
MIGHTY JUNGLE, THE(1965, U.S./Mex.), ed
Ethel Levin
LOVE AND MARRIAGE(1966, Ital.)
Henry Levin
CORPSE CAME C.O.D., THE(, d; GENGHIS KHAN(U.S./Brit./Ger./Yugo), d; CRY OF THE WEREWOLF(1944, d; DANCING IN MANHATTAN(1945), d; FIGHTING GUARDSMAN, THE(1945), d; I LOVE A MYSTERY(1945), d; SERGEANT MIKE(1945), d; BANDIT OF SHERWOOD FOREST, THE(1946), d; DEVIL'S MASK, THE(1946), d; NIGHT EDITOR(1946), d; RETURN OF MONTE CRISTO, THE(1946), d; UNKNOWN, THE(1946), d; GUILT OF JANET AMES, THE(1947), d; GALLANT BLADE, THE(1948), d; MAN FROM COLORADO, THE(1948), d; MATING OF MILLIE, THE(1948), d; AND BABY MAKES THREE(1949), d; JOLSON SINGS AGAIN(1949), d; MR. SOFT TOUCH(1949), d; CONVICTED(1950), d; FLYING MISSILE(1950), d; PETTY GIRL, THE(1950), d; FAMILY SECRET, THE(1951), d; TWO OF A KIND(1951), d; BELLES ON THEIR TOES(1952), d; FARMER TAKES A WIFE, THE(1953), d; MR. SCOUTMASTER(1953), d; PRESIDENT'S LADY, THE(1953), d; GAMBLER FROM NATCHEZ, THE(1954), d; THREE YOUNG TEXANS(1954), d; WARRIORS, THE(1955), d; APRIL LOVE(1957), d; BERNARDINE(1957), d; LET'S BE HAPPY(1957, Brit.), d; LONELY MAN, THE(1957), d; NICE LITTLE BANK THAT SHOULD BE ROBBED, A(1958), d; HOLIDAY FOR LOVERS(1959), d; JOURNEY TO THE CENTER OF THE EARTH(1959), d; REMARKABLE MR. PENNYPACKER, THE(1959), d; WHERE THE BOYS ARE(1960), d; WONDERS OF ALADDIN, THE(1961, Fr./Ital.), d; IF A MAN ANSWERS(1962), d; WONDERFUL WORLD OF THE BROTHERS ERIMM, THE(1962), d; COME FLY WITH ME(1963), d; HONEYMOON HOTEL(1964), d; MURDERERS' ROW(1966), d; AMBUSHERS, THE(1967), d; KISS THE GIRLS AND MAKE THEM DIE(1967, U.S./Ital.), d; DESPERADOS, THE(1969), d; THAT MAN BOLT(1973), d; RUN FOR THE ROSES(1978), d
Misc. Talkies
JAMAICAN GOLD(1971), d; THOROUGHBREDS, THE(1977), d
Ira Levin
KISS BEFORE DYING, A(1956), w; NO TIME FOR SERGEANTS(1958), w; CRITIC'S CHOICE(1963), w; ROSEMARY'S BABY(1968), d&w; STEPFORD WIVES, THE(1975), w; BOYS FROM BRAZIL, THE(1978), w
Iran Levin
DEATHTRAP(1982), w
Irving H. Levin
HELL TO ETERNITY(1960), p
Jack Levin
ENGLAND MADE ME(1973, Brit.), p
John Levin
DRACULA'S DOG(1978); ENEMY OF THE PEOPLE, AN(1978)
Lear Levin
TERMS OF ENDEARMENT(1983)
Lesley Levin
1984
HOLLYWOOD HOT TUBS(1984), cos
Margaret Levin
QUEEN CHRISTINA(1933), w
Meyer Levin
MY FATHER'S HOUSE(1947, Palestine), p, w; COMPULSION(1959), w
Miguel Levin
BULLET FOR PRETTY BOY, A(1970), ed
Nat Levin
HIT PARADE, THE(1937), p
Richard Levin
HALLS OF ANGER(1970)
Robert Levin
UNDER FIRE(1957); JOY RIDE(1958); LAST HURRAH, THE(1958)
Sam Levin
WINK OF AN EYE(1958)
Sid Levin
SOUNDER(1972), ed; MEAN STREETS(1973), ed; SOUNDER, PART 2(1976), ed
Sidney Levin
MARYJANE(1968), ed; MINI-SKIRT MOB, THE(1968), ed; NASHVILLE(1975), ed; FRONT, THE(1976), ed; CASEY'S SHADOW(1978), ed; CHEAP DETECTIVE, THE(1978), ed; GREAT BRAIN, THE(1978), ed; NORMA RAE(1979), ed; HERO AT LARGE(1980), ed; WHOLLY MOSES(1980), ed; BACK ROADS(1981), ed; I OUGHT TO BE IN PICTURES(1982), ed; CROSS CREEK(1983), ed
1984
RIVER, THE(1984), ed
Tony Levin
ONE-TRICK PONY(1980)
Alan Levine
IN THE HEAT OF THE NIGHT(1967), cos; THOMAS CROWN AFFAIR, THE(1968), cos; REIVERS, THE(1969), cos
Amy Levine
NIGHT IN HEAVEN, A(1983)
Anna Levine
TWO SISTERS(1938); HEAVEN'S GATE(1980)

1984
POPE OF GREENWICH VILLAGE, THE(1984)
Ben Levine
1984
LITTLE DRUMMER GIRL, THE(1984)
Bob Levine
FAST BREAK(1979); LOVING COUPLES(1980); TOOTSIE(1982)
Borys Levine
MATA HARI'S DAUGHTER(1954, Fr./Ital), ed
Bruce Levine
CRUISING(1980)
Charles Levine
LUPE(1967)
Darryl Levine
HOLLYWOOD KNIGHTS, THE(1980), cos
1984
SLAPSTICK OF ANOTHER KIND(1984), cos
Floyd Levine
DEATH WISH(1974); DOG DAY AFTERNOON(1975); BLOODBROTHERS(1978); BORDER, THE(1982); NIGHT SHIFT(1982)
Hank Levine
YOUNG SWINGERS, THE(1963), m; RAIDERS FROM BENEATH THE SEA(1964), m
Harvey Levine
M(1970); MURPH THE SURF(1974); SKATEBOARD(1978)
Issac Don Levine
REDS(1981)
James Levine
LA TRAVIATA(1982), md
Jeffrey Levine
1984
NIGHTMARE ON ELM STREET, A(1984)
Joe Levine
NOTHING BUT THE BEST(1964, Brit.)
Joel Levine
1984
NIGHT OF THE COMET(1984)
John Levine
UP YOUR TEDDY BEAR(1970), ed
Joseph E. Levine
FABULOUS WORLD OF JULES VERNE, THE(1961, Czech.), p; WONDERS OF ALADDIN, THE(1961, Fr./Ital.), p; SEVEN CAPITAL SINS(1962, Fr./Ital.), p; CONTEMPT(1963, Fr./Ital.), p; CARPETBAGGERS, THE(1964), p; WHERE LOVE HAS GONE(1964), p; HARLOW(1965), p; BRIDGE TOO FAR, A(1977, Brit.), p; MAGIC(1978), p; TATTOO(1981), p
Jules Levine
STEPCHILD(1947), w
Louise Levine
DAVID HOLZMAN'S DIARY(1968)
Lucy Levine
Misc. Talkies
HIS WIFE'S LOVER(1931)
Michael Levine
RENALDO AND CLARA(1978), ph
Michel Levine
DARK EYES(1938, Fr.), m; COMPLIMENTS OF MR. FLOW(1941, Fr.), md; DEAD RUN(1961, Fr./Ital./Ger.), w; NO ROSES FOR OSS 117(1968, Fr.), w; EROTIQUE(1969, Fr.), w
Mike Levine
DAVID HOLZMAN'S DIARY(1968); DON'T ANSWER THE PHONE(1980)
Nat Levine
CRIMSON ROMANCE(1934), p; LOST JUNGLE, THE(1934), p; BEHIND GREEN LIGHTS(1935), p; HARMONY LANE(1935), p; IN OLD SANTA FE(1935), p; LADIES CRAVE EXCITEMENT(1935), p; MARINES ARE COMING, THE(1935), p; MELODY TRAIL(1935), p; ONE FRIGHTENED NIGHT(1935), p; SAGEBRUSH TROUBADOR(1935), p; TUMBLING TUMBLEWEEDS(1935), p; WATERFRONT LADY(1935), p; $1,000 A MINUTE(1935), p; BOLD CABALLERO(1936), p; BULLDOG EDITION(1936), p; COMIN' ROUND THE MOUNTAIN(1936), p; DOUGHNUTS AND SOCIETY(1936), p; DOWN TO THE SEA(1936), p; FOLLOW YOUR HEART(1936), p; GENTLEMAN FROM LOUISIANA(1936), p; GIRL FROM MANDALAY(1936), p; GUNS AND GUITARS(1936), p; HARVESTER, THE(1936), p; HEARTS IN BONDAGE(1936), p; HITCH HIKE LADY(1936), p; HOUSE OF A THOUSAND CANDLES, THE(1936), p; LONELY TRAIL, THE(1936), p; NAVY BORN(1936), p; PRESIDENT'S MYSTERY, THE(1936), p; RIDE, RANGER, RIDE(1936), p; SINGING COWBOY, THE(1936), p; SITTING ON THE MOON(1936), p; THREE MESQUITEERS, THE(1936), p; TICKET TO PARADISE(1936), p; WINDS OF THE WASTELAND(1936), p; BEWARE OF LADIES(1937), p; BIG SHOW, THE(1937), p; CIRCUS GIRL(1937), p; COUNTRY GENTLEMEN(1937), p; GHOST TOWN GOLD(1937), p; HAPPY-GO-LUCKY(1937), p; HIT THE SADDLE(1937), p; JOIN THE MARINES(1937), p; LARCENY ON THE AIR(1937), p; MANDARIN MYSTERY, THE(1937), p; OH, SUSANNA(1937), p; PARADISE EXPRESS(1937), p; RIDERS OF THE WHISTLING SKULL(1937), p; ROARIN' LEAD(1937), p; ROUNDUP TIME IN TEXAS(1937), p; TWO WISE MAIDS(1937), p; FOUR GIRLS IN WHITE(1939), p
Philip Levine
FIRECHASERS, THE(1970, Brit.), w
Richard Levine
BRIDGE TOO FAR, A(1977, Brit.), p
Richard P. Levine
MAGIC(1978), p; TATTOO(1981), p
Robert Levine
UP THE DOWN STAIRCASE(1967); HOT ROCK, THE(1972)
Ron Levine
NESTING, THE(1981); ONLY WHEN I LAUGH(1981)
Rose Levine
LONE COWBOY(1934)
Sam Levine
KILLERS, THE(1946); FAREWELL TO ARMS, A(1957)

Saul Levine
GREEN FIELDS(1937)
Sheldon Levine
AUDREY ROSE(1977), cos
Sidney H. Levine
WOMAN INSIDE, THE(1981), p
Susan Levine
PARDON MY SARONG(1942); PRIVATE BUCKAROO(1942); WHAT'S COO-KIN'?(1942); SOMEONE TO REMEMBER(1943)
Terry Levine
DR. BUTCHER, M.D.(1982, Ital.), p
Jack Levine [Jack Jevne]
GHOST RIDER, THE(1935), d
Carl Leviness
LIVE, LOVE AND LEARN(1937); SLEEPYTIME GAL(1942); FEAR(1946); HER HUSBAND'S AFFAIRS(1947); IT HAPPENED ON 5TH AVENUE(1947); ON AN ISLAND WITH YOU(1948)
Carl M. Leviness
DONOVAN'S REEF(1963)
John Levingston
KING RAT(1965)
Kermit Levinsky
TAKE THE MONEY AND RUN(1969), md
Arthur Levinson
FACE BEHIND THE MASK, THE(1941), w
Barry Levinson
FIRST LOVE(1970, Ger./Switz.), p; INTERNECINE PROJECT, THE(1974, Brit.), p, w; WHO?(1975, Brit./Ger.), p; SILENT MOVIE(1976), a, w; HIGH ANXIETY(1977), a, w; ...AND JUSTICE FOR ALL(1979), w; INSIDE MOVES(1980), w; HISTORY OF THE WORLD, PART 1(1981); BEST FRIENDS(1982), w; DINER(1982), d&w
1984
NATURAL, THE(1984), d; UNFAITHFULLY YOURS(1984), w
Bill Levinson
FINNEY(1969)
Charles Levinson
ADVICE TO THE LOVELORN(1933); EASY TO TAKE(1936)
Danny Levinson
1984
TEACHERS(1984)
Fred Levinson
HAIL(1973), d
Gary Levinson
SHOCK WAVES(1977)
Janice Levinson
HOW TO STUFF A WILD BIKINI(1965)
Leonard L. Levinson
LOOK WHO'S LAUGHING(1941), w
Leslie Levinson
KING OF COMEDY, THE(1983)
Lew Levinson
MYSTERIOUS MR. WONG(1935), w
Mark Levinson
1984
ROADHOUSE 66(1984), p
Richard Levinson
ROLLERCOASTER(1977), w
Richard A. Levinson
HINDENBURG, THE(1975), w
Selwyn Levinson
ROAD TO THE BIG HOUSE(1947), p
Harry Levinthal
Misc. Talkies
CLOSE SHAVE(1981)
Marc Levinthal
VALLEY GIRL(1983), m
1984
CITY GIRL, THE(1984), m
Carl Levinus
TWIN BEDS(1929)
Mika Levio
TELEFON(1977)
Charles Levison "Lane"
TWO FOR TONIGHT(1935)
Carroll Levis
DISCOVERIES(1939, Brit.), a, w; LUCKY MASCOT, THE(1951, Brit.); DEPRAVED, THE(1957, Brit.)
Cyril Levis
DISCOVERIES(1939, Brit.)
Dora Levis
LOVE'S OLD SWEET SONG(1933, Brit.); SISTER TO ASSIST'ER, A(1938, Brit.); THREE WEIRD SISTERS, THE(1948, Brit.)
James Levis
SOUTH OF SUEZ(1940)
Charles Levison
LOVE AT FIRST SIGHT(1930), w; GRAND SLAM(1933); MY WOMAN(1933); I'LL FIX IT(1934)
Ken Levison
IN SEARCH OF GREGORY(1970, Brit./Ital.), w; MADHOUSE(1974, Brit.), w
Nat Levison
INN OF THE DAMNED(1974, Aus.)
Gladys Levitan
REUBEN, REUBEN(1983)
Amy Levitar
ANNIE HALL(1977)
Willard Levitas
LOVELY WAY TO DIE, A(1968), art d
Joe Levitch
BELLBOY, THE(1960)

Robert Levithan
HAIR(1979)
V. Levitin
SON OF MONGOLIA(1936, USSR), ph
Yuri Levitin
AND QUIET FLOWS THE DON(1960 USSR), m
Yuriy Levitin
SOUND OF LIFE, THE(1962, USSR), m
Abe Levitow
1001 ARABIAN NIGHTS(1959), anim d; GAY PURR-EE(1962), d; MR. MAGOO'S HOLIDAY FESTIVAL(1970), d; PHANTOM TOLLBOOTH, THE(1970), p, d
Al Levitsky
MARTIN(1979); NIGHTHAWKS(1981)
Alfred Lewis Levitt
BOY WITH THE GREEN HAIR, THE(1949), w; MRS. MIKE(1949), w; SHAKE-DOWN(1950), w; DREAM WIFE(1953), w
Amy Levitt
WHO IS HARRY KELLERMAN AND WHY IS HE SAYING THOSE TERRIBLE THINGS ABOUT ME?(1971); DOG DAY AFTERNOON(1975); AMERICAN POP(1981)
David Levitt
RECKLESS MOMENTS, THE(1949)
Dee Dee Levitt
FANTASM(1976, Aus.)
Ed Levitt
BOY NAMED CHARLIE BROWN, A(1969), anim
Edward Levitt
GAY PURR-EE(1962), prod d
Gene Levitt
FOREIGN INTRIGUE(1956), w; BEYOND MOMBASA(1957), w; NIGHT RUNNER, THE(1957), w; UNDERWATER WARRIOR(1958), w; DARING GAME(1968), p
Harriet Levitt
IN COLD BLOOD(1967)
Helen Levitt
SAVAGE EYE, THE(1960), ph; AFFAIR OF THE SKIN, AN(1964), p
John Levitt
JOHNNY ON THE RUN(1953, Brit.)
Karen Levitt
TIME WALKER(1982), w
Lou Levitt
APPRENTICESHIP OF DUDDY KRAVITZ, THE(1974, Can.)
Neil Levitt
THREE RING CIRCUS(1954)
Paul Levitt
WHEN I GROW UP(1951); HELL'S HORIZON(1955); ONE DESIRE(1955); TOUGH-EST MAN ALIVE(1955); HOUSTON STORY, THE(1956); THREE VIOLENT PEO-PLE(1956); MY MAN GODFREY(1957); CAPE FEAR(1962)
Robert R. Levitt
NEW YORK, NEW YORK(1977), set d
Robin Levitt
TAKE A HARD RIDE(1975, U.S./Ital.)
Ruby Levitt
MR. PEABODY AND THE MERMAID(1948), set d; TAKE ONE FALSE STEP(1949), set d; PILLOW TALK(1959), set d; FORTY POUNDS OF TROUBLE(1962), set d; FOR LOVE OR MONEY(1963), set d; WILD AND WONDERFUL(1964), set d; SOUND OF MUSIC, THE(1965), set d; COLOSSUS: THE FORBIN PROJECT(1969), set d; TELL THEM WILLIE BOY IS HERE(1969), set d; ANDROMEDA STRAIN, THE(1971), set d; HAPPY BIRTHDAY, WANDA JUNE(1971), set d; OTHER, THE(1972), set d; FREE-BIE AND THE BEAN(1974), set d; ONCE IS NOT ENOUGH(1975), set d; HARRY AND WALTER GO TO NEW YORK(1976), set d; STAR IS BORN, A(1976), set d; LOOKING FOR MR. GOODBAR(1977), set d; ONE AND ONLY, THE(1978), set d; JAZZ SINGER, THE(1980), set d
Ruby R. Levitt
SMASH-UP, THE STORY OF A WOMAN(1947), set d; KISS THE BLOOD OFF MY HANDS(1948), set d; LETTER FROM AN UNKNOWN WOMAN(1948), set d; TAP ROOTS(1948), set d; YOU GOTTA STAY HAPPY(1948), set d; ABANDONED(1949), set d; ONCE MORE, MY DARLING(1949), set d; WOMAN IN HIDING(1949), set d; PEGGY(1950), set d; SHAKEDOWN(1950), set d; WEEKEND WITH FATHER(1951), set d; MEET ME AT THE FAIR(1952), set d; NO ROOM FOR THE GROOM(1952), set d; UNTAMED FRONTIER(1952), set d; MAGNIFICENT OBSESSION(1954), set d; INCREDIBLE SHRINKING MAN, THE(1957), set d; THIS EARTH IS MINE(1959), set d; LET'S DO IT AGAIN(1975), set d
Saul Levitt
COVENANT WITH DEATH, A(1966), w; TRIAL OF THE CATONSVILLE NINE, THE(1972), w
Stan Levitt
CARNIVAL OF SOULS(1962); IN COLD BLOOD(1967)
Steve Levitt
THOSE LIPS, THOSE EYES(1980); PRIVATE SCHOOL(1983)
Jean Levitte
MY WIFE'S HUSBAND(1965, Fr./Ital.), w; VICE AND VIRTUE(1965, Fr./Ital.)
Zalman Leviush
SIMCHON FAMILY, THE(1969, Israel)
Uta Levka
DEFECTOR, THE(1966, Ger./Fr.); CARMEN, BABY(1967, Yugo./Ger.); OPERATION ST. PETER'S(1968, Ital.); DE SADE(1969); OBLONG BOX, THE(1969, Brit.); SCREAM AND SCREAM AGAIN(1970, Brit.)
Sonia Levkova
IN OUR TIME(1944)
G. Levkoyev
Misc. Silents
FROM SPARKS–FLAMES(1924, USSR)
Marjorie Levoe
HAPPY DAYS(1930)
M. Levor
EAST OF KILIMANJARO(1962, Brit./Ital.), w
Albert E. Levoy
JIM HANVEY, DETECTIVE(1937), p; LADY BEHAVE(1937), p; PORTIA ON TRIAL(1937), p; GHOST COMES HOME, THE(1940), p; SPORTING BLOOD(1940), p

Alan Levson
SECOND WIND(1976, Can.)
Allan Levson
MEATBALLS(1979, Can.)
Vida Levstik
WARRIORS FIVE(1962)
Albert M. Levy
FOLIES DERGERE(1935), cos
Alfred Levy
DILLINGER IS DEAD(1969, Ital.), p
Allan Levy
HOW WILLINGLY YOU SING(1975, Aus.)
Anne Levy
ENTRE NOUS(1983, Fr.)
Art Levy
MADE FOR EACH OTHER(1971)
Arthur Levy
ROUSTABOUT(1964)
Asher Levy
FLYING MATCHMAKER, THE(1970, Israel)
Barbara Levy
MADE FOR EACH OTHER(1971)
Benn Levy
TEMPORARY WIDOW, THE(1930, Ger./Brit.), w; DEVIL AND THE DEEP(1932), w;
EVERGREEN(1934, Brit.), m; DICTATOR, THE(1935, Brit./Ger.), w; UNFINISHED
SYMPHONY, THE(1953, Aust./Brit.), w
Benn W. Levy
WATERLOO BRIDGE(1931), w; BLACKMAIL(1929, Brit.), w; INFORMER,
THE(1929, Brit.), w; KITTY(1929, Brit.), w; GAY DIPLOMAT, THE(1931), w; TRANS-
GRESSION(1931), w; LORD CAMBER'S LADIES(1932, Brit.), d, w; OLD DARK
HOUSE, THE(1932), w; TOPAZE(1933), w; EVERGREEN(1934, Brit.), w; MELODY IN
SPRING(1934), w; SPRINGTIME FOR HENRY(1934), w
Bert Levy
CENTRAL PARK(1932), ed; TWO AGAINST THE WORLD(1932), ed; I LOVED A
WOMAN(1933), ed; LIFE OF JIMMY DOLAN, THE(1933), ed; NARROW CORNER,
THE(1933), ed; GENTLEMEN ARE BORN(1934), ed; MADAME DU BARRY(1934), ed
Bob Levy
Misc. Talkies
IF YOU DON'T STOP IT, YOU'LL GO BLIND(1977), d
Charles Christian Levy, Sr.
CARNY(1980)
Dafna Levy
HANNAH K.(1983, Fr.)
David S. Levy
BANK ALARM(1937), w; GOLD RACKET, THE(1937), w
Delphine Levy
FIRST TIME, THE(1978, Fr.)
Don Levy
PIRATES OF BLOOD RIVER, THE(1962, Brit.); HEROSTRATUS(1968, Brit.), p,
d&w; PAT GARRETT AND BILLY THE KID(1973)
Donald J. Levy
Misc. Talkies
BELT AND SUSPENDERS MAN, THE(1970), d
Edward Levy
BEAST WITHIN, THE(1982), w
Eugene Levy
CANNIBAL GIRLS(1973); RUNNING(1979, Can.); NOTHING PERSONAL(1980,
Can.); HEAVY METAL(1981, Can.); GOING BERSERK(1983); NATIONAL LAM-
POON'S VACATION(1983)
1984
SPLASH(1984)
Gary Levy
LUNCH WAGON(1981)
Gene Levy
HYSTERICAL(1983), p
Georges Levy
ROAD TO SHAME, THE(1962, Fr.), art d; MISTRESS FOR THE SUMMER, A(1964,
Fr./Ital.), art d; TWO OF US, THE(1968, Fr.), art d
Gerry Levy
FLAW, THE(1955, Brit.); WHERE HAS POOR MICKEY GONE?(1964, Brit.), p&d;
BODY STEALERS, THE(1969), d
Misc. Talkies
OUT OF THIN AIR(1969), d
Hal Levy
FIRST TRAVELING SALESLADY, THE(1956), m
Harold Levy
ROYAL BOX, THE(1930), m
Herbert Levy
WEEK-END MARRIAGE(1932), ed; DARK HAZARD(1934), ed; SIDE
STREETS(1934), ed; DIMPLES(1936), ed; HALF ANGEL(1936), ed; MESSAGE TO
GARCIA, A(1936), ed
I. Robert Levy
Misc. Talkies
CAN I DO IT 'TIL I NEED GLASSES?(1977), d
J. Levy
TRAITORS, THE(1963, Brit.), w
Jacques Levy
OH! CALCUTTA!(1972), w
Jeremy Levy
RICH KIDS(1979)
Jerome Levy
THREE IN ONE(1956, Aus.)
Jerry Levy
MURDER REPORTED(1958, Brit.), ed
Joan Levy
Misc. Talkies
DAWN OF THE MUMMY(1981)

Joel Levy, Jr.
ARMY WIVES(1944), w
Jules Levy
HELLZAPOPPIN'(1941), p; ABILENE TOWN(1946), p; WITHOUT WARNING(1952),
p; VAMPIRE, THE(1957), p; GLORY GUYS, THE(1965), p; CLAMBAKE(1967), p;
SCALPHUNTERS, THE(1968), p; SAM WHISKEY(1969), p; MC KENZIE BREAK,
THE(1970), p; UNDERGROUND(1970, Brit.), p; HONKERS, THE(1972), p; WHITE
LIGHTNING(1973), p; MC Q(1974), p; BRANNIGAN(1975, Brit.), p; GATOR(1976), p
Jules V. Levy
VICE SQUAD(1953), p; DOWN THREE DARK STREETS(1954), p; MONSTER THAT
CHALLENGED THE WORLD, THE(1957), p; FLAME BARRIER, THE(1958), p; RE-
TURN OF DRACULA, THE(1958), p; SAFARI 3000(1982), p, w
Julien Levy
DREAMS THAT MONEY CAN BUY(1948)
Katharine Levy
LORDS OF DISCIPLINE, THE(1983)
Katherine Levy
WATCHER IN THE WOODS, THE(1980, Brit.)
Lois Levy
REMARKABLE MR. KIPPS(1942, Brit.), md
Louis Levy
LOVE IN MOROCCO(1933, Fr.), md; WALTZ TIME(1933, Brit.), w; CHU CHIN
CHOW(1934, Brit.), md; LITTLE FRIEND(1934, Brit.), md; WOMAN IN COMMAND,
THE(1934 Brit.), md; FIRST A GIRL(1935, Brit.), md; MAN WHO KNEW TOO MUCH,
THE(1935, Brit.), md; MY SONG FOR YOU(1935, Brit.), md; PHANTOM LIGHT,
THE(1935, Brit.), md; PRINCESS CHARMING(1935, Brit.), md; 39 STEPS, THE(1935,
Brit.), m; DOMMED CARGO(1936, Brit.), md; MISTER HOBO(1936, Brit.), md; PASS-
ING OF THE THIRD FLOOR BACK, THE(1936, Brit.), m; SECRET AGENT, THE(1936,
Brit.), m; WHERE THERE'S A WILL(1936, Brit), md; DOCTOR SYN(1937, Brit.), md;
HEAD OVER HEELS IN LOVE(1937, Brit.), md; SABOTAGE(1937, Brit.), m; WIND-
BAG THE SAILOR(1937, Brit.), md; ALF'S BUTTON AFLOAT(1938, Brit.), md; CITA-
DEL, THE(1938), m; CONVICT 99(1938, Brit.), md; LADY VANISHES, THE(1938,
Brit.), m; MAN WITH 100 FACES, THE(1938, Brit.), md; TO THE VICTOR(1938,
Brit.), md; YOUNG AND INNOCENT(1938, Brit.), m; GOODBYE MR. CHIPS(1939,
Brit.), md; MAD MEN OF EUROPE(1940, Brit.), md; NIGHT TRAIN(1940, Brit.), m;
SHIPYARD SALLY(1940, Brit.), md; SPARE A COPPER(1940, Brit.), m; GIRL IN THE
NEWS, THE(1941, Brit.), m; MAIL TRAIN(1941, Brit.), m; YOUNG MR. PITT,
THE(1942, Brit.), md; MAN IN GREY, THE(1943, Brit.), md; WE DIVE AT
DAWN(1943, Brit.), md; UNCENSORED(1944, Brit.), md; I'LL BE YOUR SWEET-
HEART(1945, Brit.), p; MADONNA OF THE SEVEN MOONS(1945, Brit.), m; PLACE
OF ONE'S OWN, A(1945, Brit.), md; RANDOLPH FAMILY, THE(1945, Brit.), md;
THEY WERE SISTERS(1945, Brit.), m; CARAVAN(1946, Brit.), md; WICKED LADY,
THE(1946, Brit.), m; HOLIDAY CAMP(1947, Brit.), md; LADY SURRENDERS, A(1947,
Brit.), md; ROOT OF ALL EVIL, THE(1947, Brit.), md; JASSY(1948, Brit.), md; MAN
OF EVIL(1948, Brit.), md; QUEEN OF SPADES(1948, Brit.), md; HASTY HEART,
THE(1949), md; UNDER CAPRICORN(1949, Brit.), md; WATERLOO ROAD(1949, Brit.),
md; LAST HOLIDAY(1950, Brit.), md; NO PLACE FOR JENNIFER(1950, Brit.), md;
STAGE FRIGHT(1950, Brit.), md; HAPPY GO LOVELY(1951, Brit.), md; MURDER
WITHOUT CRIME(1951, Brit.), md; PORTRAIT OF CLARE(1951, Brit.), md; WHE-
RE'S CHARLEY?(1952, Brit.), md; SO LITTLE TIME(1953, Brit.), m; YOUNG WIVES'
TALE(1954, Brit.), md; DAM BUSTERS, THE(1955, Brit.), m; WARRIORS, THE(1955),
md; IT'S GREAT TO BE YOUNG(1956, Brit.), md; MOBY DICK(1956, Brit.), md;
1984(1956, Brit.), md; LET'S BE HAPPY(1957, Brit.), md; TARZAN AND THE LOST
SAFARI(1957, Brit.), md; WOMEN IN A DRESSING GOWN(1957, Brit.), m; MARK OF
THE HAWK, THE(1958), md
Marcy Levy
SGT. PEPPER'S LONELY HEARTS CLUB BAND(1978)
Marga Rubia Levy
Misc. Silents
DAUGHTER OF ENGLAND, A(1915, Brit.)
Mark C. Levy
YOUR THREE MINUTES ARE UP(1973), p
Meir Levy
EVERY BASTARD A KING(1968, Israel)
Melvin Levy
ROBIN HOOD OF EL DORADO(1936), w; HIDEAWAY(1937), w; FIRST COMES
COURAGE(1943), w; HITLER'S MADMAN(1943), w; SHE'S A SOLDIER TOO(1944),
w; SUNDAY DINNER FOR A SOLDIER(1944), w; BANDIT OF SHERWOOD FOREST,
THE(1946), w; RENEGADES(1946), w; CALAMITY JANE AND SAM BASS(1949), w;
GREAT SIOUX UPRISING, THE(1953), w; CRY BABY KILLER, THE(1958), w;
PIRATES OF TORTUGA(1961), w; WHO FEARS THE DEVIL(1972), w
Morris Levy
Silents
INTOLERANCE(1916)
Newman A. Levy
JURY'S SECRET, THE(1938), w
Ori Levy
EVERY BASTARD A KING(1968, Israel); BEFORE WINTER COMES(1969, Brit.);
CHAIRMAN, THE(1969); MOON ZERO TWO(1970, Brit.); JERUSALEM FILE,
THE(1972, U.S./Israel); ROSEBUD(1975); SELL OUT, THE(1976); OPERATION THUN-
DERBOLT(1978, ISRAEL)
1984
AMBASSADOR, THE(1984); LITTLE DRUMMER GIRL, THE(1984)
P.H. Levy
WRECKER, THE(1933)
Parke Levy
GEORGE WHITE'S SCANDALS(1945), w; HAVING WONDERFUL CRIME(1945), w;
EARL CARROLL SKETCHBOOK(1946), w; HIT PARADE OF 1947(1947), w; MY
FRIEND IRMA(1949), w; MY FRIEND IRMA GOES WEST(1950), w
Paul Levy [Paolo Levi]
UP THE MACGREGORS(1967, Ital./Span.), w
Ralph Levy
BEDTIME STORY(1964), d; DO NOT DISTURB(1965), d
Raoul J. Levy
AND GOD CREATED WOMAN(1957, Fr.), p, w; NIGHT HEAVEN FELL, THE(1958,
Fr.), p; LOVE IS MY PROFESSION(1959, Fr.), p; BABETTE GOES TO WAR(1960,
Fr.), p, w; TRUTH, THE(1961, Fr./Ital.), p; MODERATO CANTABILE(1964, Fr./Ital.),
p; HAIL MAFIA(1965, Fr./Ital.), p&d, w; DEFECTOR, THE(1966, Ger./Fr.), p&d, w;
MARCO THE MAGNIFICENT(1966, Ital./Fr./Yugo./Egypt/Afghanistan), p, w; TWO
OR THREE THINGS I KNOW ABOUT HER(1970, Fr.), a, p

Robert L. Levy
SMOKEY AND THE BANDIT(1977), w; SMOKEY AND THE BANDIT II(1980), w; SMOKEY AND THE BANDIT–PART 3(1983), w

Simon Levy
ROAD TO HONG KONG, THE(1962, U.S./Brit.)

Stephanie Ann Levy
WITHOUT A TRACE(1983)

Stephen Levy
THIN RED LINE, THE(1964); SILENT PARTNER, THE(1979, Can.)

Stuart Levy
CARRY ON SERGEANT(1959, Brit.), p

Stuart Levy [Peter Rogers]
DUKE WORE JEANS, THE(1958, Brit.), p

Wayne Levy
TRUE STORY OF ESKIMO NELL, THE(1975, Aus.)

Weaver Levy
FIRST YANK INTO TOKYO(1945); NIGHT HAS A THOUSAND EYES(1948); MALAYA(1950); CHINA CORSAIR(1951); I WAS AN AMERICAN SPY(1951); PEKING EXPRESS(1951); JAPANESE WAR BRIDE(1952); MACAO(1952); TARGET HONG KONG(1952); FORBIDDEN(1953); FROM HERE TO ETERNITY(1953); PRISONER OF WAR(1954); BAMBOO PRISON, THE(1955); LOVE IS A MANY-SPLENDORED THING(1955); KING AND I, THE(1956); CHINA GATE(1957); 27TH DAY, THE(1957); JET ATTACK(1958); FLOWER DRUM SONG(1961); YOUNG AND THE BRAVE, THE(1963); WRECKING CREW, THE(1968); GIRL WHO KNEW TOO MUCH, THE(1969); M(1970); SHARKY'S MACHINE(1982)

William A. Levy
BLACKENSTEIN(1973), d

Yaacov Levy
EVERY BASTARD A KING(1968, Israel)

Pierre Levy-Corti
MY WIFE'S HUSBAND(1965, Fr./Ital.), w; IMPOSSIBLE ON SATURDAY(1966, Fr./Israel), w; VERY HAPPY ALEXANDER(1969, Fr.), w

Frank Levya
GUNGA DIN(1939)

I. Levyanu
SANDU FOLLOWS THE SUN(1965, USSR)

James Lew
GOING BERSERK(1983)
1984
KILLPOINT(1984)

Joycelyne Lew
BIG BRAWL, THE(1980)

Shirley Lew
BEHIND THE RISING SUN(1943); FLIGHT FOR FREEDOM(1943); WEEKEND AT THE WALDORF(1945); CALCUTTA(1947); KEY TO THE CITY(1950)

Warren Lew
BLUE HAWAII(1961), ed

Lew Diamond and His Harmonaires
WEEKEND PASS(1944)

Lew Preston and His Ranch Hands
PRAIRIE STRANGER(1941)

Lew Stone and His Band
KING'S CUP, THE(1933, Brit.); INTIMATE RELATIONS(1937, Brit.); STREET SINGER, THE(1937, Brit.)

Lew Stone and the Monseigneur Orchestra
IT'S A KING(1933, Brit.)

Eric Lewald
Misc. Talkies
INCOMING FRESHMEN(1979), d

Margaret LeWars
DR. NO(1962, Brit.)

Bunny Lewbel
I'LL SEE YOU IN MY DREAMS(1951); ROAD TO BALI(1952)

Fewlass Lewellyn
Silents
FLAG LIEUTENANT, THE(1926, Brit.)

H.K. Lewenhak
WINGS OF MYSTERY(1963, Brit.), w

Count Lewenhaupt
Misc. Silents
BLACK BUTTERFLY, THE(1916)

Oscar Lewenstein
GIRL WITH GREEN EYES(1964, Brit.), p; KNACK ... AND HOW TO GET IT, THE(1965, Brit.), p; MADEMOISELLE(1966, Fr./Brit.), p; SAILOR FROM GIBRALTAR, THE(1967, Brit.), p

Bettyna Lewertoff
BENJAMIN(1973, Ger.), ed

Jose Lewgoy
ROSE FOR EVERYONE, A(1967, Ital.); EARTH ENTRANCED(1970, Braz.); FITZCARRALDO(1982)
1984
BLAME IT ON RIO(1984)

Albert Lewin
GUARDSMAN, THE(1931), p; CHINA SEAS(1935), p; GOOD EARTH, THE(1937), p; TRUE CONFESSION(1937), p; SPAWN OF THE NORTH(1938), p; SO ENDS OUR NIGHT(1941), p; MOON AND SIXPENCE, THE(1942), d, w; PICTURE OF DORIAN GRAY, THE(1945), d, w; PRIVATE AFFAIRS OF BEL AMI, THE(1947), d&w; ALICE IN WONDERLAND(1951, Fr.), w; PANDORA AND THE FLYING DUTCHMAN(1951, Brit.), p, d&w; DOWN AMONG THE SHELTERING PALMS(1953), w; SAADIA(1953), p&d, w; LIVING IDOL, THE(1957), p, d&w
Silents
LITTLE JOURNEY, A(1927), w; QUALITY STREET(1927), w

Albert E. Lewin
CALL ME MISTER(1951), w; BOY, DID I GET A WRONG NUMBER!(1966), w; EIGHT ON THE LAM(1967), w; WICKED DREAMS OF PAULA SCHULTZ, THE(1968), w; I WILL ...I WILL ...FOR NOW(1976), w

Ben Lewin
Misc. Silents
FOR YOU MY BOY(1923)

Bill Lewin
THREE DARING DAUGHTERS(1948); PAT AND MIKE(1952); SINGIN' IN THE RAIN(1952)

Borys Lewin
RED AND THE BLACK, THE(1954, Fr./Ital.), ed; FRENCH CANCAN(1956, Fr.), ed; HAPPY ROAD, THE(1957), ed; PARIS DOES STRANGE THINGS(1957, Fr./Ital.), ed; BIG CHIEF, THE(1960, Fr.), ed; FROM A ROMAN BALCONY(1961, Fr./Ital.), ed; LOVE AND THE FRENCHWOMAN(1961, Fr.), ed; TOMORROW IS MY TURN(1962, Fr./Ital./Ger.), ed; THREE FABLES OF LOVE(1963, Fr./Ital./Span.), ed

Ch. Lewin
YIDDLE WITH HIS FIDDLE(1937, Pol.)

Irwin Lewin
PSYCHOTRONIC MAN, THE(1980)

J.D. Lewin
SONG OF THE FORGE(1937, Brit.), w

Max Lewin
GAMES(1967)

Michel Lewin
ZITA(1968, Fr.), ed; WISE GUYS(1969, Fr./Ital.), ed; SOME LIKE IT COOL(1979, Ger./Aust./Ital./Fr.), ed; JOY(1983, Fr./Can.), ed

Robert Lewin
BOLD AND THE BRAVE, THE(1956), w; THIRD OF A MAN(1962), p, d&w

William Lewin
COURAGE OF LASSIE(1946); NEPTUNE'S DAUGHTER(1949)

Bob Lewine
PUNISHMENT PARK(1971)

Ken Lewington
RISE AND RISE OF MICHAEL RIMMER, THE(1970, Brit.), cos

Lothar Lewinsohn
GORBALS STORY, THE(1950, Brit.)

Joel Lewinson
YOU HAVE TO RUN FAST(1961)

Al Lewis
ZIEGFELD FOLLIES(1945), w; MA AND PA KETTLE(1949), w; OUR MISS BROOKS(1956), d, w; PRETTY BOY FLOYD(1960); WORLD OF HENRY ORIENT, THE(1964); MUNSTER, GO HOME(1966); THEY SHOOT HORSES, DON'T THEY?(1969); BOATNIKS, THE(1970); THEY MIGHT BE GIANTS(1971); USED CARS(1980)

Alan Lewis
JAMAICA INN(1939, Brit.); CAESAR AND CLEOPATRA(1946, Brit.)

Albert Lewis
NO MAN OF HER OWN(1933), p; TORCH SINGER(1933), p; COME ON, MARINES(1934), p; SHOOT THE WORKS(1934), p; COLLEGE SCANDAL(1935), p; GILDED LILY, THE(1935), p; MEN WITHOUT NAMES(1935), p; ONE HOUR LATE(1935), p; STOLEN HARMONY(1935), p; FLORIDA SPECIAL(1936), p; MY AMERICAN WIFE(1936), p; SON COMES HOME, A(1936), p; TILL WE MEET AGAIN(1936), p; FIGHT FOR YOUR LADY(1937), p; MEET THE MISSUS(1937), p; THERE GOES THE GROOM(1937), p; WOMAN I LOVE, THE(1937), p; SHE'S GOT EVERYTHING(1938), p; SHOW-OFF, THE(1946), p; MERTON OF THE MOVIES(1947), p; GOLDEN GIRL(1951), w
Silents
ROYAL FAMILY, A(1915); ACTRESS, THE(1928), w

Alfred Lewis
Silents
SHATTERED REPUTATIONS(1923)

Alfred Henry Lewis
LIGHT FINGERS(1929), w

Allan Lewis
SIERRA BARON(1958)

Althea Lewis
JETLAG(1981, U.S./Span.)

Alun Lewis
GIRO CITY(1982, Brit.); EXPERIENCE PREFERRED... BUT NOT ESSENTIAL(1983, Brit.)

Andy Lewis
UNDERGROUND(1970, Brit.), w

Ann Lewis
IN THE FRENCH STYLE(1963, U.S./Fr.); PARIS IN THE MONTH OF AUGUST(1968, Fr.)

Anthony Lewis
THREE BRAVE MEN(1957), w

Art Lewis
PICKUP(1951); STRIP, THE(1951); DECKS RAN RED, THE(1958); THREAT, THE(1960); WHAT DID YOU DO IN THE WAR, DADDY?(1966)

Arthur Lewis
OH, YOU BEAUTIFUL DOLL(1949), w; GOLDEN GIRL(1951), w; CONQUEST OF COCHISE(1953), w; JOKER IS WILD, THE(1957); LOOT(1971, Brit.), p; BAXTER(1973, Brit.), p; KILLER ELITE, THE(1975), p; BRASS TARGET(1978), p
Silents
AMERICAN WIDOW, AN(1917)

Arthur H. Lewis
MOLLY MAGUIRES, THE(1970), w

Artie Lewis
WHICH WAY TO THE FRONT?(1970); STAR SPANGLED GIRL(1971); HOT STUFF(1979)

B. A. Lewis
Silents
HOODLUM THE(1919)

B. M. Lewis
STRAUSS' GREAT WALTZ(1934, Brit.)

Ben Lewis
PAGAN, THE(1929), ed; MAN IN POSSESSION, THE(1931), ed; NEVER THE TWAIN SHALL MEET(1931), ed; TRADER HORN(1931), ed; MASK OF FU MANCHU, THE(1932), ed; NIGHT COURT(1932), ed; TARZAN, THE APE MAN(1932), ed; WASHINGTON MASQUERADE(1932), ed; BROADWAY TO HOLLYWOOD(1933), ed; DINNER AT EIGHT(1933), ed; FAST WORKERS(1933), ed; STRANGER'S RETURN(1933), ed; WHISTLING IN THE DARK(1933), ed; HAVE A HEART(1934), ed; MANHATTAN MELODRAMA(1934), ed; WICKED WOMAN, A(1934), ed; YOU CAN'T BUY EVERYTHING(1934), ed; MARK OF THE VAMPIRE(1935), ed; SOCIETY DOCTOR(1935), ed; WOMAN WANTED(1935), ed; GARDEN MURDER CASE,

THE(1936), ed; MOONLIGHT MURDER(1936), ed; BAD GUY(1937), ed; LAST GANG-
STER, THE(1937), ed; PERSONAL PROPERTY(1937), ed; THEY GAVE HIM A
GUN(1937), ed; UNDER COVER OF NIGHT(1937), ed; WESTLAND CASE, THE(1937);
YOU'RE A SWEETHEART(1937); ARSENE LUPIN RETURNS(1938), ed; HOLD THAT
KISS(1938), ed; JUDGE HARDY'S CHILDREN(1938), ed; LOVE FINDS ANDY
HARDY(1938), ed; OUT WEST WITH THE HARDYS(1938), ed; VACATION FROM
LOVE(1938), ed; ANDY HARDY GETS SPRING FEVER(1939), ed; BURN 'EM UP
O'CONNER(1939), ed; FORGOTTEN WOMAN, THE(1939); HARDYS RIDE HIGH,
THE(1939), ed; HERO FOR A DAY(1939); HOUSE OF FEAR, THE(1939); JUDGE
HARDY AND SON(1939), ed; FORTY LITTLE MOTHERS(1940), ed; GALLANT
SONS(1940), ed; GIVE US WINGS(1940); STRIKE UP THE BAND(1940), ed; BUGLE
SOUNDS, THE(1941), ed; DOWN IN SAN DIEGO(1941), ed; LOVE CRAZY(1941), ed;
MARRIED BACHELOR(1941), ed; FOR ME AND MY GAL(1942), ed; PACIFIC
RENDEZVOUS(1942), ed; RIO RITA(1942), ed; LASSIE, COME HOME(1943), ed;
WHISTLING IN BROOKLYN(1943), ed; KISMET(1944), ed; ABBOTT AND COSTEL-
LO IN HOLLYWOOD(1945), ed; SON OF LASSIE(1945), ed; BAD BASCOMB(1946),
ed; COCKEYED MIRACLE, THE(1946), ed; MIGHTY MCGURK, THE(1946), ed; UN-
DERCOVER MAISIE(1947), ed; ALIAS A GENTLEMAN(1948), ed; SOUTHERN YAN-
KEE, A(1948), ed; STRATTON STORY, THE(1949), ed; AMBUSH(1950), ed;
MALAYA(1950), ed; THREE LITTLE WORDS(1950), ed; IT'S A BIG COUNTRY(1951),
ed; RED BADGE OF COURAGE, THE(1951), ed; SHADOW IN THE SKY(1951), ed;
UNKNOWN MAN, THE(1951), ed; DEVIL MAKES THREE, THE(1952), ed; BIG
LEAGUER(1953), ed; GIRL WHO HAD EVERYTHING, THE(1953), ed; SLIGHT CASE
OF LARCENY, A(1953), ed; TENNESSEE CHAMP(1954), ed; MANY RIVERS TO
CROSS(1955), ed; SCARLET COAT, THE(1955), ed; LAST HUNT, THE(1956), ed;
THESE WILDER YEARS(1956), ed; HOT SUMMER NIGHT(1957), ed; TIP ON A
DEAD JOCKEY(1957), ed; VINTAGE, THE(1957), ed; HANDLE WITH CARE(1958),
ed; HIGH SCHOOL CONFIDENTIAL(1958), ed; BEAT GENERATION, THE(1959), ed;
BIG OPERATOR, THE(1959), ed; NIGHT OF THE QUARTER MOON(1959), ed;
SUBTERRANEANS, THE(1960), ed; ATLANTIS, THE LOST CONTINENT(1961), ed;
HONEYMOON MACHINE, THE(1961), ed; FOUR HORSEMEN OF THE APOCA-
LYPSE, THE(1962), ed; DRUMS OF AFRICA(1963), ed; GET YOURSELF A COLLEGE
GIRL(1964), ed; KISSIN' COUSINS(1964), ed; YOUR CHEATIN' HEART(1964), ed;
HARUM SCARUM(1965), ed; WHEN THE BOYS MEET THE GIRLS(1965), ed; HOLD
ON(1966), ed; FASTEST GUITAR ALIVE, THE(1967), ed; HOT RODS TO HELL(1967),
ed; LOVE-INS, THE(1967), ed; RIOT ON SUNSET STRIP(1967), ed; FOR SINGLES
ONLY(1968), ed; TIME TO SING, A(1968), ed; YOUNG RUNAWAYS, THE(1968), ed
Silents
FLAMES OF CHANCE, THE(1918); MR. WU(1927), ed; QUALITY STREET(1927), ed;
ACROSS THE SINGAPORE(1928), ed; HONEYMOON(1929), ed; KISS, THE(1929), ed;
SINGLE MAN, A(1929), ed; THUNDER(1929), ed
Misc. Silents
SISTER OF SIX, A(1916)
Bernard Lewis
UNDERCOVER GIRL(1957, Brit.), w
Bernie Kaai Lewis
CAT MURKIL AND THE SILKS(1976), m
Bernie Lewis
GIRL IN A MILLION, A(1946, Brit.), ph; DIAMOND CITY(1949, Brit.), ph
Blayney Lewis
ESCAPE IN THE DESERT(1945); TENDER YEARS, THE(1947); JOHNNY BELIN-
DA(1948)
Bobo Lewis
INTERNS, THE(1962); HOOTENANNY HOOT(1963); IT'S A MAD, MAD, MAD, MAD
WORLD(1963); KISS ME, STUPID(1964); WAY...WAY OUT(1966); WHICH WAY TO
THE FRONT?(1970); WILD PARTY, THE(1975); CAN'T STOP THE MUSIC(1980);
ARTHUR(1981); NESTING, THE(1981)
Bruce Lewis
80,000 SUSPECTS(1963, Brit.)
Bud Lewis
CHICAGO CONFIDENTIAL(1957)
Buddy Lewis
TARAWA BEACHHEAD(1958); ROUSTABOUT(1964); HARLOW(1965); SWEET
CHARITY(1969); 2000 YEARS LATER(1969); WOMEN AND BLOODY TERROR(1970);
LAST OF THE RED HOT LOVERS(1972)
C. James Lewis
1984
CANNONBALL RUN II(1984)
Carlo Lewis
MEN, THE(1950)
Carol Jean Lewis
GIRLS ON THE BEACH(1965); FORTY DEUCE(1982)
1984
MIXED BLOOD(1984)
Carroll Lewis
LAW OF THE PAMPAS(1939), ed; HIDDEN GOLD(1940), ed; KNIGHTS OF THE
RANGE(1940), ed; SHOWDOWN, THE(1940), ed; THREE MEN FROM TEXAS(1940),
ed; BORDER VIGILANTES(1941), ed; DOOMED CARAVAN(1941), ed; IN OLD
COLORADO(1941), ed; OUTLAWS OF THE DESERT(1941), ed; ROUNDUP,
THE(1941), ed; WIDE OPEN TOWN(1941), ed; AMERICAN EMPIRE(1942), ed;
TOMBSTONE, THE TOWN TOO TOUGH TO DIE(1942), ed; BAR 20(1943), ed; KAN-
SAN, THE(1943), ed; LEATHER BURNERS, THE(1943), ed; WOMAN OF THE TOWN,
THE(1943), ed; FORTY THIEVES(1944), ed; BORDER BANDITS(1946), ed; DRIFT-
ING ALONG(1946), ed
Catherine Lewis
DOUBLE TROUBLE(1941); MODEL WIFE(1941); KID GLOVE KILLER(1942);
SLIGHTLY DANGEROUS(1943)
Cathy Lewis
STORY OF MOLLY X, THE(1949); PARTY CRASHERS, THE(1958); DEVIL AT FOUR
O'CLOCK, THE(1961)
Cecil Lewis
CARMEN(1931, Brit.), d&w; ARMS AND THE MAN(1932, Brit.), d&w; INDISCRE-
TIONS OF EVE(1932, Brit.), p,d&w; LEAVE IT TO ME(1933, Brit.), w; CAFE MAS-
COT(1936, Brit.), w; PYGMALION(1938, Brit.), w
Charles Lewis
BOOK OF NUMBERS(1973)
Constance Lewis
LAST DAYS OF DOLWYN, THE(1949, Brit.); MR. H. C. ANDERSEN(1950, Brit.)

Cpl. Harry Lewis
WINGED VICTORY(1944)
Cullin Lewis
DESERT TRAIL(1935), d
Curigwen Lewis
JOHN WESLEY(1954, Brit.)
Cyril Lewis
Misc. Talkies
BROKEN STRINGS(1940)
D. David Lewis
FAN, THE(1981)
D.B. Wyndham Lewis
CARDINAL, THE(1936, Brit.), w; BOMBS OVER LONDON(1937, Brit.), w
Daniel Day Lewis
GANDHI(1982)
Danny Lewis
SHORT CUT TO HELL(1957); ROCK-A-BYE BABY(1958)
Dave Lewis
SECOND FIDDLE TO A STEEL GUITAR(1965); MORE(1969, Luxembourg), p;
KLUTE(1971), w
David Lewis
FLYING DEVILS(1933), p; SON OF THE BORDER(1933), p; TWO ALONE(1934), p;
MEN ARE SUCH FOOLS(1938), p; SECRETS OF AN ACTRESS(1938), p; SISTERS,
THE(1938), p; DARK VICTORY(1939), p; EACH DAWN I DIE(1939), p; ALL THIS
AND HEAVEN TOO(1940), p; IN THIS OUR LIFE(1942), p; 'TILL WE MEET
AGAIN(1944), p; IT'S A PLEASURE(1945), p; TOMORROW IS FOREVER(1946), p;
OTHER LOVE, THE(1947), p; ARCH OF TRIUMPH(1948), p; END OF THE AFFAIR,
THE(1955, Brit.), p; SCARLET HOUR, THE(1956); THAT CERTAIN FEELING(1956);
RAINTREE COUNTY(1957), p; SEVENTH SIN, THE(1957), p; APARTMENT,
THE(1960); ABSENT-MINDED PROFESSOR, THE(1961); KID GALAHAD(1962); SPI-
RAL ROAD, THE(1962); HONEYMOON HOTEL(1964); JOHN GOLDFARB, PLEASE
COME HOME(1964); GENERATION(1969)
Silents
SINNER'S PARADE(1928), w
David P Lewis
CITY ON FIRE(1979 Can.), w
Davis Lewis
GIRL NAMED TAMIRO, A(1962)
Derrick Lewis
LIVING BETWEEN TWO WORLDS(1963)
Diana Lewis
IT'S A GIFT(1934); ENTER MADAME(1935); ONE HOUR LATE(1935); HE
COULDN'T SAY NO(1938); FIRST OFFENDERS(1939); ANDY HARDY MEETS
DEBUTANTE(1940); BITTER SWEET(1940); FORTY LITTLE MOTHERS(1940); GO
WEST(1940); PEOPLE VS. DR. KILDARE, THE(1941); JOHNNY EAGER(1942); SEV-
EN SWEETHEARTS(1942); SOMEWHERE I'LL FIND YOU(1942); WHISTLING IN
DIXIE(1942); CRY HAVOC(1943); ROCKY(1976)
Misc. Talkies
GIRLS OF 42ND STREET(1974)
Diane Lewis
BODY HEAT(1981)
Don Lewis
THEY WERE EXPENDABLE(1945)
1984
BREAKIN' 2: ELECTRIC BOOGALOO(1984)
Donald S. Lewis
HIGH BARBAREE(1947)
Dorothy Lewis
ICE-CAPADES(1941)
Duncan Lewis
LOVE IN WAITING(1948, Brit.); STRONGROOM(1962, Brit.); V.I.P.s, THE(1963,
Brit.); ACT OF MURDER(1965, Brit.); PANIC(1966, Brit.)
Ed Lewis
IT'S A DEAL(1930); PRESIDENT VANISHES, THE(1934); PRIVATE BEN-
JAMIN(1980)
Ed "Strangler" Lewis
THAT NAZTY NUISANCE(1943); BODYHOLD(1950)
Eddie Lewis
JOHNNY ANGEL(1945); MR. SYCAMORE(1975)
Edgar Lewis
UNMASKED(1929), d; LADIES IN LOVE(1930), d; LOVE AT FIRST SIGHT(1930), d;
HUMAN TARGETS(1932); MADAME RACKETEER(1932); TEXAS GUN FIGHT-
ER(1932)
Misc. Talkies
UNMASKED(1929), d
Silents
CAPTAIN SWIFT(1914), d; PLUNDERER, THE(1915), d; THIEF, THE(1915), d&w;
LIGHT AT DUSK, THE(1916), d; BAR SINISTER, THE(1917), d; ONE GLORIOUS
SCRAP(1927), d; ARIZONA CYCLONE(1928), d; GUN RUNNER, THE(1928), d;
STORMY WATERS(1928), d
Misc. Silents
NORTHERN LIGHTS(1914), d; SAMSON(1915), d; BONDMAN, THE(1916), d;
FLAMES OF JOHANNIS, THE(1916), d; GREAT DIVIDE, THE(1916), d; SOULS IN
BONDAGE(1916), d; THOSE WHO TOIL(1916), d; SIGN INVISIBLE, THE(1918), d;
CALIBRE 38(1919), d; LOVE AND THE LAW(1919), d; BEGGAR IN PURPLE, A(1920),
d; LAHOMA(1920), d; OTHER MEN'S SHOES(1920), d; SHERRY(1920), d; SAGE
HEN, THE(1921), d; STRENGTH OF THE PINES(1922), d; YOU ARE GUILTY(1923),
d; RIGHT OF THE STRONGEST, THE(1924), d; RED LOVE(1925), d; ONE GLORIOUS
SCRAP(1927), d; FEARLESS RIDER, THE(1928), d; LIFE'S CROSSROADS(1928), d;
MADE-TO-ORDER HERO, A(1928), d; PUT 'EM UP(1928), d; UNMASKED(1929), d
Edgar P. Lewis
Misc. Silents
WIVES OF MEN(1918)
Edward Lewis
LOVABLE CHEAT, THE(1949), p, w; CARELESS YEARS, THE(1957), p, w; SPAR-
TACUS(1960), p; LAST SUNSET, THE(1961), p; LONELY ARE THE BRAVE(1962), p;
LIST OF ADRIAN MESSENGER, THE(1963), p; SEVEN DAYS IN MAY(1964), p;
GRAND PRIX(1966), p; SECONDS(1966), p; FIXER, THE(1968), p; EXTRAORDI-
NARY SEAMAN, THE(1969), p; HORSEMEN, THE(1971), p; EXECUTIVE AC-
TION(1973), p; BROTHERS(1977), p, w; MISSING(1982), p

1984
CRACKERS(1984), p; RIVER, THE(1984), p
Edwin Lewis
WHAT EVERY WOMAN WANTS(1954, Brit.), w
Elliott Lewis
STORY OF MOLLY X, THE(1949); MA AND PA KETTLE GO TO TOWN(1950); SATURDAY'S HERO(1951)
Eric Lewis
Misc. Silents
BROWN SUGAR(1922, Brit.)
Ernest Lewis
LOYAL HEART(1946, Brit.), w
Esme Lewis
FATHER O'FLYNN(1938, Irish); HOME SWEET HOME(1945, Brit.); THINGS HAPPEN AT NIGHT(1948, Brit.)
Ethelreda Lewis
TRADER HORN(1931), w; TRADER HORN(1973), w
Eugene Lewis
Silents
CLEAN UP, THE(1923), w
Eugene B. Lewis
Silents
RIDERS OF VENGEANCE(1919), w; DR. JIM(1921), w; LITTLE CLOWN, THE(1921), w
Eva Lewis
RIDING SHOTGUN(1954)
Silents
HUNCHBACK OF NOTRE DAME, THE(1923)
Fiona Lewis
FEARLESS VAMPIRE KILLERS, OR PARDON ME BUT YOUR TEETH ARE IN MY NECK, THE(1967); JOANNA(1968, Brit.); OTLEY(1969, Brit.); WHERE'S JACK?(1969, Brit.); VILLAIN(1971, Brit.); DOCTOR PHIBES RISES AGAIN(1972, Brit.); BLUE BLOOD(1973, Brit.); LISZTOMANIA(1975, Brit.); DRUM(1976); STUNTS(1977); TINTORERA...BLOODY WATERS(1977, Brit./Mex.); FURY, THE(1978); WANDA NEVADA(1979); DEAD KIDS(1981 Aus./New Zealand); STRANGE INVADERS(1983)
Forrest Lewis
I'LL TELL THE WORLD(1945); WEEKEND WITH FATHER(1951); HAS ANYBODY SEEN MY GAL?(1952); IT GROWS ON TREES(1952); LAWLESS BREED, THE(1952); CLOWN, THE(1953); ESCAPE FROM FORT BRAVO(1953); FRANCIS COVERS THE BIG TOWN(1953); GUN FURY(1953); STAND AT APACHE RIVER, THE(1953); TAKE ME TO TOWN(1953); APACHE AMBUSH(1955); SPOILERS, THE(1955); MAN IN THE SHADOW(1957); THING THAT COULDN'T DIE, THE(1958); MONSTER OF PIEDRAS BLANCAS, THE(1959); SHAGGY DOG, THE(1959); ABSENT-MINDED PROFESSOR, THE(1961); POSSE FROM HELL(1961); SON OF FLUBBER(1963); TAMMY AND THE DOCTOR(1963); MAN'S FAVORITE SPORT[?](1964); RED LINE 7000(1965); OUT OF SIGHT(1966); RIOT ON SUNSET STRIP(1967); SKIN GAME(1971); TODD KILLINGS, THE(1971)
Fran Lewis
MORE(1969, Luxembourg), art d
Franklin Lewis
MISTER ANTONIO(1929); KID FROM CLEVELAND, THE(1949)
Fred Lewis
HOUR OF GLORY(1949, Brit.); MY BLUE HEAVEN(1950)
Silents
ONCE ABOARD THE LUGGER(1920, Brit.); GAME OF LIFE, THE(1922, Brit.)
Misc. Silents
ENEMY TO THE KING, AN(1916)
Fredeick Lewis
Misc. Silents
MORAL SINNER, THE(1924)
Frederic Lewis
STORM IN A TEACUP(1937, Brit.), m; JAMAICA INN(1939, Brit.), md; TWICE UPON A TIME(1953, Brit.), md; FIEND WITHOUT A FACE(1958), md; NIGHT AMBUSH(1958, Brit.), md
Frederick Lewis
PURSUIT OF THE GRAF SPEE(1957, Brit.), md; HAUNTED STRANGLER, THE(1958, Brit.), md; CORRIDORS OF BLOOD(1962, Brit.), md
Misc. Silents
LILY OF POVERTY FLAT, THE(1915)
Furry Lewis
W. W. AND THE DIXIE DANCEKINGS(1975); THIS IS ELVIS(1982)
Gabe Lewis
SIGN OF AQUARIUS(1970)
Garrett Lewis
STAR!(1968); GOOD GUYS AND THE BAD GUYS, THE(1969); FUNNY LADY(1975); OH, HEAVENLY DOG!(1980), prod d
1984
AGAINST ALL ODDS(1984), set d
Gary Lewis
ROCK-A-BYE BABY(1958); IT'S ONLY MONEY(1962); NUTTY PROFESSOR, THE(1963)
Gene Lewis
HONEYMOON LANE(1931); SHE-WOLF, THE(1931), w; OUT ALL NIGHT(1933); COUNTESS OF MONTE CRISTO, THE(1934), w; COBRA WOMAN(1944), w; GYPSY WILDCAT(1944), w; BLONDE RANSOM(1945), w; SONG OF THE SARONG(1945), p, w; TRAIL STREET(1947), w; ALBUQUERQUE(1948), w; LONELY HEARTS BANDITS(1950), w; WOMAN FROM HEADQUARTERS(1950), w; FLAMING FEATHER(1951)
Geoffrey Lewis
BAD COMPANY(1972); CULPEPPER CATTLE COMPANY, THE(1972); WELCOME HOME, SOLDIER BOYS(1972); DILLINGER(1973); HIGH PLAINS DRIFTER(1973); MACON COUNTY LINE(1974); MY NAME IS NOBODY(1974, Ital./Fr./Ger.); THUNDERBOLT AND LIGHTFOOT(1974); GREAT WALDO PEPPER(1975); LUCKY LADY(1975); SMILE(1975); WIND AND THE LION, THE(1975); RETURN OF A MAN CALLED HORSE, THE(1976); EVERY WHICH WAY BUT LOOSE(1978); TILT(1979); ANY WHICH WAY YOU CAN(1980); BRONCO BILLY(1980); HEAVEN'S GATE(1980); HUMAN EXPERIMENTS(1980); TOM HORN(1980); I, THE JURY(1982); 10 TO MIDNIGHT(1983)

1984
NIGHT OF THE COMET(1984)
Misc. Talkies
SHOOT THE SUN DOWN(1981)
George Lewis
COLLEGE LOVE(1929); GIVE AND TARE(1929); TONIGHT AT TWELVE(1929); HEART PUNCH(1932); PARISIAN ROMANCE, A(1932); HER RESALE VALUE(1933); LAZY RIVER(1934); MERRY WIDOW, THE(1934); TWO HEADS ON A PILLOW(1934); HEADLINE WOMAN, THE(1935); RED MORNING(1935); STORM OVER THE ANDES(1935); UNDER THE PAMPAS MOON(1935); CAPTAIN CALAMITY(1936); BACK DOOR TO HEAVEN(1939); MEN AGAINST THE SKY(1940); OUTSIDE THE 3-MILE LIMIT(1940); NO HANDS ON THE CLOCK(1941); OUTLAWS OF THE DESERT(1941); THEY MET IN ARGENTINA(1941); FALCON'S BROTHER, THE(1942); OUTLAWS OF PINE RIDGE(1942); PHANTOM KILLER(1942); SIN TOWN(1942); YANK IN LIBYA, A(1942); BLACK HILLS EXPRESS(1943); FLESH AND FANTASY(1943); CHARLIE CHAN IN THE SECRET SERVICE(1944); FALCON IN MEXICO, THE(1944); OH, WHAT A NIGHT(1944); SHADOW OF SUSPICION(1944); LADY ON A TRAIN(1945); SONG OF MEXICO(1945); MISSING LADY, THE(1946); WISTFUL WIDOW OF WAGON GAP, THE(1947); LULU BELLE(1948); TAP ROOTS(1948); CRASHING THRU(1949); DALTON GANG, THE(1949); CAPTAIN CAREY, U.S.A(1950); COLORADO RANGER(1950); CRISIS(1950); CROOKED RIVER(1950); FAST ON THE DRAW(1950); MARSHAL OF HELDORADO(1950); ONE WAY STREET(1950); WEST OF THE BRAZOS(1950); KID FROM AMARILLO, THE(1951); SADDLE LEGION(1951); BAD AND THE BEAUTIFUL, THE(1952); HOLD THAT LINE(1952); IRON MISTRESS(1952); PRISONER OF ZENDA, THE(1952); RAIDERS, THE(1952); BANDITS OF CORSICA, THE(1953); COW COUNTRY(1953); BORDER RIVER(1954); DRUM BEAT(1954); SASKATCHEWAN(1954); PRODIGAL, THE(1955); DAVY CROCKETT AND THE RIVER PIRATES(1956); COMANCHEROS, THE(1961); HAPPY BIRTHDAY, DAVY(1970), art d
Misc. Talkies
BLOCKED TRAIL, THE(1943); BORDER CITY RUSTLERS(1953)
Silents
OLD SOAK, THE(1926); HONEYMOON FLATS(1928); JAZZ MAD(1928); 13 WASHINGTON SQUARE(1928)
Misc. Silents
HIS PEOPLE(1925); DEVIL'S ISLAND(1926); FOURFLUSHER, THE(1928); WE AMERICANS(1928)
George B. Lewis
HUMANOID, THE(1979, Ital.), d
George "Beetlepuss" Lewis
WHEN MY BABY SMILES AT ME(1948)
George J. Lewis
SOUTH OF THE RIO GRANDE(1932); RIDE, RANGER, RIDE(1936); BEWARE SPOOKS(1939); MIDDLETON FAMILY AT THE N.Y. WORLD'S FAIR(1939); DEATH VALLEY OUTLAWS(1941); KANSAS CYCLONE(1941); RIDERS OF THE BADLANDS(1941); LARAMIE TRAIL, THE(1944); TEXAS KID, THE(1944); SOUTH OF THE RIO GRANDE(1945); BEAUTY AND THE BANDIT(1946); GILDA(1946); PASSKEY TO DANGER(1946); RAINBOW OVER TEXAS(1946); TARZAN AND THE LEOPARD WOMAN(1946); THRILL OF BRAZIL, THE(1946); UNDER NEVADA SKIES(1946); BLACKMAIL(1947); PIRATES OF MONTEREY(1947); SLAVE GIRL(1947); TWILIGHT ON THE RIO GRANDE(1947); CASBAH(1948); DOCKS OF NEW ORLEANS(1948); FEATHERED SERPENT, THE(1948); OKLAHOMA BLUES(1948); ONE TOUCH OF VENUS(1948); RENEGADES OF SONORA(1948); SILVER TRAILS(1948); BIG SOMBRERO, THE(1949); LOST TRIBE, THE(1949); HOSTILE COUNTRY(1950); KING OF THE BULLWHIP(1950); SHORT GRASS(1950); ABBOTT AND COSTELLO MEET THE INVISIBLE MAN(1951); AL JENNINGS OF OKLAHOMA(1951); APPOINTMENT WITH DANGER(1951); BANDITS OF EL DORADO(1951); VIVA ZAPATA!(1952); WAGON TEAM(1952); DESERT LEGION(1953); DEVIL'S CANYON(1953); SHANE(1953); THUNDER IN THE EAST(1953); VEILS OF BAGDAD, THE(1953); CRY IN THE NIGHT, A(1956); HELL ON FRISCO BAY(1956); SANTIAGO(1956); WAGON WHEELS WESTWARD(1956); BIG LAND, THE(1957); JEANNE EAGELS(1957); TALL STRANGER, THE(1957); GHOST OF ZORRO(1959); SIGN OF ZORRO, THE(1960); INDIAN PAINT(1965)
Misc. Talkies
PECOS DANDY, THE(1934); SHERIFF OF MEDICINE BOW, THE(1948)
George Wells Lewis
MAN BEAST(1956)
Gilbert Lewis
PURSUIT OF HAPPINESS, THE(1971); WHO KILLED MARY WHAT'SER NAME?(1971); ACROSS 110TH STREET(1972); HOT ROCK, THE(1972); TOGETHER FOR DAYS(1972); GORDON'S WAR(1973); FORT APACHE, THE BRONX(1981); TOUCHED(1983)
Gillian Lewis
RING OF SPIES(1964, Brit.); FAHRENHEIT 451(1966, Brit.); SPY WITH A COLD NOSE, THE(1966, Brit.)
Glenn Charles Lewis
SWARM, THE(1978)
Greg Lewis
1984
ANGEL(1984)
Grover Lewis
LAST PICTURE SHOW, THE(1971); CANDIDATE, THE(1972)
Gwen Lewis
FAMILY AFFAIR(1954, Brit.); LYONS IN PARIS, THE(1955, Brit.); OVER THE ODDS(1961, Brit.); EYES OF A STRANGER(1980)
Harold Lewis
EIGHT GIRLS IN A BOAT(1934), m; SENSATION HUNTERS(1934), m
Harrison Lewis
PROUD ONES, THE(1956); CRIMSON KIMONO, THE(1959); FACE OF A FUGITIVE(1959); CASE OF PATTY SMITH, THE(1962)
Harry Lewis
DIVE BOMBER(1941); INTERNATIONAL SQUADRON(1941); YOU'RE IN THE ARMY NOW(1941); ALWAYS IN MY HEART(1942); BUSSES ROAR(1942); DESPERATE JOURNEY(1942); SECRET ENEMIES(1942); THEY DIED WITH THEIR BOOTS ON(1942); LAST RIDE, THE(1944); HER KIND OF MAN(1946); UNSUSPECTED, THE(1947); INCIDENT(1948), p, w; KEY LARGO(1948); WHIPLASH(1948); WINTER MEETING(1948); GUN CRAZY(1949); JOE PALOOKA IN THE COUNTERPUNCH(1949); BLONDE DYNAMITE(1950); FAT MAN, THE(1951); RUN FOR THE HILLS(1953); ACCUSED OF MURDER(1956); MAN IS ARMED, THE(1956); PENDULUM(1969)

Harvey Lewis
ALMOST SUMMER(1978); TILT(1979); HOW TO BEAT THE HIGH COST OF LIVING(1980); RAISE THE TITANIC(1980, Brit.)

Hedgemon Lewis
TOP OF THE HEAP(1972); NICKELODEON(1976)

Helen Lewis
THUNDERBOLT(1929), ed; WIVES BEWARE(1933, Brit.), ed; TALK OF THE DEVIL(1937, Brit.), ed; LADY SINGS THE BLUES(1972)
Silents
DRAGNET, THE(1928), ed

Helen Prothero Lewis
Silents
AS GOD MADE HER(1920, Brit.), w

Henry Lewis
BOMBA ON PANTHER ISLAND(1949)

Herbert Clyde Lewis
ESCAPE TO PARADISE(1939), w; FISHERMAN'S WHARF(1939), w; DON JUAN QUILLIGAN(1945), w; LADY LUCK(1946), w; IT HAPPENED ON 5TH AVENUE(1947), w; FREE FOR ALL(1949), w; ONE LAST FLING(1949), w

Herschell Gordon Lewis
LIVING VENUS(1961), p&d; BLOOD FEAST(1963), p, d, ph&m, spec eff; MOONSHINE MOUNTAIN(1964), p&d; TWO THOUSAND MANIACS!(1964), d&w, ph, m; COLOR ME BLOOD RED(1965), d,w&ph; GIRL, THE BODY, AND THE PILL, THE(1967), p&d; SOMETHING WEIRD(1967), d, ph; TASTE OF BLOOD, A(1967), p&d; GRUESOME TWOSOME(1968), p&d; JUST FOR THE HELL OF IT(1968), p&d; SHE-DEVILS ON WHEELS(1968), p&d; WIZARD OF GORE, THE(1970), p&d; THIS STUFF'LL KILL YA!(1971), p,d&w; YEAR OF THE YAHOO(1971), p&d
Misc. Talkies
ADVENTURES OF LUCKY PIERRE, THE(1961), d; JIMMY, THE BOY WONDER(1966), d; BLAST-OFF GIRLS(1967), d; HOW TO MAKE A DOLL(1967), d; JUST FOR THE HELL OF IT(1968), d

Hilda Lewis
CRASH OF SILENCE(1952, Brit.), w

Howard L. Lewis
MOUSE AND THE WOMAN, THE(1981, Brit.)

Hugh X. Lewis
FORTY ACRE FEUD(1965); GOLD GUITAR, THE(1966); COTTONPICKIN' CHICKENPICKERS(1967)

Ida Lewis
SINNERS IN THE SUN(1932)
Silents
INSIDE THE LINES(1918); MORE TROUBLE(1918); PARIS GREEN(1920); SWEET ADELINE(1926)
Misc. Silents
PAINTED LIE, THE(1917); WHITHER THOU GOEST(1917); BELLS, THE(1918); DANGEROUS WATERS(1919)

Ira Lewis
SOFT SKIN ON BLACK SILK(1964, Fr./Span.); WHAT'S SO BAD ABOUT FEELING GOOD?(1968); ROLLOVER(1981)

Jack Lewis
LAUGH YOUR BLUES AWAY(1943); KING OF THE BULLWHIP(1950), w; OUTLAW GOLD(1950), w; WHISTLING HILLS(1951), w; MANFISH(1956); NAKED GUN, THE(1956), w; AMAZING TRANSPARENT MAN, THE(1960), w; SECRET FILE: HOLLYWOOD(1962), w; YANK IN VIET-NAM, A(1964), w; WHAT'S UP, TIGER LILY?(1966), m; COME SPY WITH ME(1967)

Jacqueline A. Lewis
SECOND THOUGHTS(1983)

Jacqueline Lewis
CARRY ON TEACHER(1962, Brit.)
Misc. Talkies
GOD'S STEPCHILDREN(1937)

James Lewis
JAZZ BABIES(1932), md; SHARKY'S MACHINE(1982)

James E. Lewis
EVERYTHING IN LIFE(1936, Brit.), w

James H. Lewis
Misc. Silents
FORBIDDEN FRUIT(1916)

James P. Lewis
RECOMMENDATION FOR MERCY(1975, Can.), p

Jarma Lewis
WAC FROM WALLA WALLA, THE(1952); MAGNETIC MONSTER, THE(1953); FRENCH LINE, THE(1954); PRINCE VALIANT(1954); RIVER OF NO RETURN(1954); SEVEN BRIDES FOR SEVEN BROTHERS(1954); WOMAN'S WORLD(1954); BAR SINISTER, THE(1955); COBWEB, THE(1955); MARAUDERS, THE(1955); PRODIGAL, THE(1955); TENDER TRAP, THE(1955); RAINTREE COUNTY(1957)

Jay Gardner Lewis
MAN'S AFFAIR, A(1949, Brit.), p&d, w

Jay Lewis
OPERATION DISASTER(1951, Brit.), p; FRONT PAGE STORY(1954, Brit.), p, w; BABY AND THE BATTLESHIP, THE(1957, Brit.), p, d, w; INVASION QUARTET(1961, Brit.), d; LIVE NOW–PAY LATER(1962, Brit.), d

Jean Ann Lewis
JOURNEY TO FREEDOM(1957); STORM RIDER, THE(1957); BRIDE AND THE BEAST, THE(1958)

Jean Lewis
BRIDE WORE RED, THE(1937); AFFAIR IN TRINIDAD(1952), cos; FEMALE JUNGLE, THE(1955); GARMENT JUNGLE, THE(1957)

Jeffrys Lewis
Silents
PEACOCK ALLEY(1922)

Jerry Lee Lewis
JAMBOREE(1957); HIGH SCHOOL CONFIDENTIAL(1958); AMERICAN HOT WAX(1978); MIDDLE AGE CRAZY(1980, Can.), w

Jerry Lewis
MY FRIEND IRMA(1949); AT WAR WITH THE ARMY(1950); MILKMAN, THE(1950); MY FRIEND IRMA GOES WEST(1950); SAILOR BEWARE(1951); THAT'S MY BOY(1951); JUMPING JACKS(1952); ROAD TO BALI(1952); STOOGE, THE(1952); CADDY, THE(1953); MONEY FROM HOME(1953); SCARED STIFF(1953); LIVING IT UP(1954); THREE RING CIRCUS(1954); ARTISTS AND MODELS(1955); YOU'RE NEVER TOO YOUNG(1955); HOLLYWOOD OR BUST(1956); DELICATE DELINQUENT, THE(1957), a, p; SAD SACK, THE(1957); GEISHA BOY, THE(1958), a, p; ROCK-A-BYE BABY(1958), a, p; DON'T GIVE UP THE SHIP(1959); BELLBOY, THE(1960), a, p,d&w; CINDERFELLA(1960), a, p; VISIT TO A SMALL PLANET(1960); ERRAND BOY, THE(1961), a, d, w; LADIES MAN, THE(1961), a, p&d, w; IT'S ONLY MONEY(1962); IT'S A MAD, MAD, MAD, MAD WORLD(1963); NUTTY PROFESSOR, THE(1963), a, p, d, w; WHO'S MINDING THE STORE?(1963); DISORDERLY ORDERLY, THE(1964), a, p; PATSY, THE(1964), a, d, w; BOEING BOEING(1965); FAMILY JEWELS, THE(1965), a, p&d, w; THREE ON A COUCH(1966), a, p&d; WAY...WAY OUT(1966); BIG MOUTH, THE(1967), a, p&d, w; DON'T RAISE THE BRIDGE, LOWER THE RIVER(1968, Brit.); HOOK, LINE AND SINKER(1969), a, p; ONE MORE TIME(1970, Brit.), d; WHICH WAY TO THE FRONT?(1970), a, p&d; HARDLY WORKING(1981), a, d, w; KING OF COMEDY, THE(1983); SMORGASBORD(1983), a, d, w
1984
PAR OU T'ES RENTRE? ON T'A PAS VUE SORTIR(1984, Fr./Tunisia); SLAPSTICK OF ANOTHER KIND(1984); TO CATCH A COP(1984, Fr.)

Jerry Lewis, Jr.
PARDNERS(1956)

Jessie Lewis
Silents
CUB, THE(1915); FAMILY CUPBOARD, THE(1915); BALLET GIRL, THE(1916); BROKEN CHAINS(1916)
Misc. Silents
BUTTERFLY, THE(1915)

Jim Lewis
NEON PALACE, THE(1970, Can.), ph, ed; CANNONBALL RUN, THE(1981); MAN WHO LOVED WOMEN, THE(1983); STROKER ACE(1983)
1984
CITY HEAT(1984)

Jimmy Lewis
SOLOMON KING(1974), m

Joe Lewis
PRIVATE NUMBER(1936); BOYS OF THE CITY(1940), d; JAGUAR LIVES(1979), a, ch; FORCE: FIVE(1981)
Misc. Talkies
DEATH ON CREDIT(1976)

Joe E. Lewis
HOLY TERROR, THE(1937); PRIVATE BUCKAROO(1942); LADY IN CEMENT(1968)

John Lewis
DEVIL'S HARBOR(1954, Brit.); HAPPINESS OF THREE WOMEN, THE(1954, Brit.); ODDS AGAINST TOMORROW(1959), m; NO BLADE OF GRASS(1970, Brit.)

John E. Lewis
LIVE WIRE, THE(1937, Brit.), w

John Martin Lewis
ROBBERY WITH VIOLENCE(1958, Brit.)

Joseph Lewis
HARMONY LANE(1935), ed; HEADLINE WOMAN, THE(1935), ed; LADIES CRAVE EXCITEMENT(1935), ed; STREAMLINE EXPRESS(1935), ed; CRIMINALS WITHIN(1941), d; DESPERATE SEARCH(1952), d; BIG COMBO, THE(1955), d

Joseph H. Lewis
ONE FRIGHTENED NIGHT(1935), ed; DEVIL ON HORSEBACK, THE(1936), ed; KING OF THE PECOS(1936), ed; LAUGHING IRISH EYES(1936), ed; COURAGE OF THE WEST(1937), d; SINGING OUTLAW(1937), d; BORDER WOLVES(1938), d; LAST STAND, THE(1938), d; SPY RING, THE(1938), d; BLAZING SIX SHOOTERS(1940), d; BOYS OF THE CITY(1940), d; MAN FROM TUMBLEWEEDS, THE(1940), d; RETURN OF WILD BILL, THE(1940), d; TEXAS STAGECOACH(1940), d; THAT GANG OF MINE(1940), d; TWO-FISTED RANGERS(1940), d; ARIZONA CYCLONE(1941), d; INVISIBLE GHOST, THE(1941), d; PRIDE OF THE BOWERY(1941), d; BOMBS OVER BURMA(1942), d, w; BOSS OF HANGTOWN MESA(1942), d; MAD DOCTOR OF MARKET STREET, THE(1942), d; SECRETS OF A CO-ED(1942), d; SILVER BULLET, THE(1942), d; MINSTREL MAN(1944), d; FALCON IN SAN FRANCISCO, THE(1945), d; MY NAME IS JULIA ROSS(1945), d; JOLSON STORY, THE(1946), ch; SO DARK THE NIGHT(1946), d; SWORDSMAN, THE(1947), d; RETURN OF OCTOBER, THE(1948), d; GUN CRAZY(1949), d; UNDERCOVER MAN, THE(1949), d; LADY WITHOUT PASSPORT, A(1950), d; CRY OF THE HUNTED(1953), d; LAWLESS STREET, A(1955), d; SEVENTH CAVALRY(1956), d; HALLIDAY BRAND, THE(1957), d; TERROR IN A TEXAS TOWN(1958), d

Joshua Hill Lewis
BAD COMPANY(1972); TOM SAWYER(1973)

Joy Lewis
Misc. Silents
SON OF A GUN, THE(1919)

Judy Lewis
OPERATION BIKINI(1963); THUNDER IN DIXIE(1965)
Misc. Talkies
SOUTHERN DOUBLE CROSS(1973)

Julia Lewis
1984
SUPERGIRL(1984)

Karl Lewis
ONE PLUS ONE(1969, Brit.)

Katherine Lewis
Silents
KENNEDY SQUARE(1916); TWIN BEDS(1920); WHEN THE DEVIL DRIVES(1922); RECOMPENSE(1925); NUT-CRACKER, THE(1926); YOUR WIFE AND MINE(1927)
Misc. Silents
INDISCRETION(1917); SOUL MASTER, THE(1917); EVERYTHING BUT THE TRUTH(1920); UNFORTUNATE SEX, THE(1920)

Kathleen Hope Lewis
EASY LIVING(1937)

Kay Lewis
FACE AT THE WINDOW, THE(1939, Brit.); THREE SILENT MEN(1940, Brit.); FRONT LINE KIDS(1942, Brit.); DEMOBBED(1944, Brit.); LADY SINGS THE BLUES(1972)

Kim Lewis
1984
SQUIZZY TAYLOR(1984, Aus.)

Kitty Lewis
Misc. Talkies
MISS LESLIE'S DOLLS(1972)
Lalage Lewis
ESTHER WATERS(1948, Brit.); MAN ON THE RUN(1949, Brit.)
Larry Lewis
1984
LOUISIANE(1984, Fr./Can.)
Laurie Lewis
ON THE RUN(1983, Aus.), m
Leo Lewis
TIME AFTER TIME(1979, Brit.)
Linda Lewis
IT FELL FROM THE SKY(1980)
Livingston Lewis
MEDIUM COOL(1969)
Lloyd Lewis
Silents
JUST FOR TONIGHT(1918), ph
Lolita Lewis
CLARENCE AND ANGEL(1981)
Lonney Lewis
ALL WOMAN(1967)
Louise Lewis
BLOOD OF DRACULA(1957); I WAS A TEENAGE WEREWOLF(1957); VAMPIRE, THE(1957)
Mabel Terry Lewis
JAMAICA INN(1939, Brit.); ADVENTURES OF TARTU(1943, Brit.)
Mae Evlyn Lewis
Misc. Silents
GREATEST SIN, THE(1922)
Maizie Lewis
TROUBLE IN TEXAS(1937), cos
Maj. Henry B. Lewis
Silents
CLASSMATES(1924)
Marcia Lewis
1984
ICE PIRATES, THE(1984)
Mark Lewis
1984
SECRET PLACES(1984, Brit.)
Martin J. Lewis
GOLEM, THE(1937, Czech./Fr.), ed
Martin Lewis
LATIN LOVE(1930, Brit.); STRONGER SEX, THE(1931, Brit.); DANGEROUS GROUND(1934, Brit.); RIVERSIDE MURDER, THE(1935, Brit.); SHADOW OF MIKE EMERALD, THE(1935, Brit.); HEIRLOOM MYSTERY, THE(1936, Brit.); CURTAIN RISES, THE(1939, Fr.), titles
Martin M. Lewis
Misc. Talkies
NAUGHTY GIRLS ON THE LOOSE(1976), d
Mary Margaret Lewis
FOXES(1980)
Maude Lewis
Misc. Silents
SLAVE OF VANITY, A(1920)
Max Lewis
HARRY'S WAR(1981)
Maxine Lewis
RAINBOW OVER BROADWAY(1933); SHE COULDN'T TAKE IT(1935); GAMBLER'S CHOICE(1944)
Meade Lux Lewis
NEW ORLEANS(1947)
Mel Lewis
KINGS GO FORTH(1958)
Mettlepuss Lewis
HALF PAST MIDNIGHT(1948)
Michael Lewis
RECOMMENDATION FOR MERCY(1975, Can.)
Michael J. Lewis
MADWOMAN OF CHAILLOT, THE(1969), m; JULIUS CAESAR(1970, Brit.), m; MAN WHO HAUNTED HIMSELF, THE(1970, Brit.), m, md; UNMAN, WITTERING AND ZIGO(1971, Brit.), m; RUNNING SCARED(1972, Brit.), m; BAXTER(1973, Brit.), m; THEATRE OF BLOOD(1973, Brit.), m; 11 HARROWHOUSE(1974, Brit.), m; RUSSIAN ROULETTE(1975), m; 92 IN THE SHADE(1975, U.S./Brit.), m, md; MEDUSA TOUCH, THE(1978, Brit.), m; STICK UP, THE(1978, Brit.), m; LEGACY, THE(1979, Brit.), m; PASSAGE, THE(1979, Brit.), m; FFOLKES(1980, Brit.), m; SPHINX(1981), m; UNSEEN, THE(1981), m; HOUND OF THE BASKERVILLES, THE(1983, Brit.), m
1984
BAD MANNERS(1984), m; NAKED FACE, THE(1984), m
Mildred Lewis
BROTHERS(1977), p, w; MISSING(1982), p
Milo Lewis
EGGHEAD'S ROBOT(1970, Brit.), d; TROUBLESOME DOUBLE, THE(1971, Brit.), d
Mitchell Lewis
TENDERLOIN(1928); BLACK WATCH, THE(1929); BRIDGE OF SAN LUIS REY, THE(1929); LEATHERNECK, THE(1929); MADAME X(1929); ONE STOLEN NIGHT(1929); BAD ONE, THE(1930); BEAU BANDIT(1930); CUCKOOS, THE(1930); GIRL OF THE PORT(1930); MAMMY(1930); SEE AMERICA THIRST(1930); NEVER THE TWAIN SHALL MEET(1931); SON OF INDIA(1931); SQUAW MAN, THE(1931); KONGO(1932); MC KENNA OF THE MOUNTED(1932); NEW MORALS FOR OLD(1932); WORLD AND THE FLESH, THE(1932); ANN VICKERS(1933); SECRET OF MADAME BLANCHE, THE(1933); COUNT OF MONTE CRISTO, THE(1934); FARMER TAKES A WIFE, THE(1935); RED MORNING(1935); TALE OF TWO CITIES, A(1935); BOHEMIAN GIRL, THE(1936); DANCING PIRATE(1936); MUMMY'S BOYS(1936); SUTTER'S GOLD(1936); DOUBLE WEDDING(1937); EMPEROR'S CANDLESTICKS, THE(1937); ESPIONAGE(1937); WAIKIKI WEDDING(1937); ARSENE LUPIN RETURNS(1938); MYSTERIOUS MR. MOTO(1938); RICH MAN, POOR GIRL(1938); THREE COMRADES(1938); BAD LITTLE ANGEL(1939); BLACKMAIL(1939); HENRY

GOES ARIZONA(1939); IDIOT'S DELIGHT(1939); LET FREEDOM RING(1939); WIZARD OF OZ, THE(1939); GO WEST(1940); STRANGE CARGO(1940); BILLY THE KID(1941); I'LL WAIT FOR YOU(1941); MEET JOHN DOE(1941); CAIRO(1942); I MARRIED AN ANGEL(1942); RIO RITA(1942); DU BARRY WAS A LADY(1943); KISMET(1944); THIN MAN GOES HOME, THE(1944); BLUE SIERRA(1946); COURAGE OF LASSIE(1946); HARVEY GIRLS, THE(1946); DESIRE ME(1947); IT HAPPENED IN BROOKLYN(1947); JULIA MISBEHAVES(1948); KISSING BANDIT, THE(1948); STRATTON STORY, THE(1949); TAKE ME OUT TO THE BALL GAME(1949); MAN WITH A CLOAK, THE(1951); MR. IMPERIUM(1951); SCARAMOUCHE(1952); ALL THE BROTHERS WERE VALIANT(1953); KISS ME KATE(1953); LILI(1953); SUN SHINES BRIGHT, THE(1953); TORCH SONG(1953); TRIAL(1955)
Silents
BAR SINISTER, THE(1917); KING SPRUCE(1920); ON THE HIGH SEAS(1922); SALOME(1922); SIREN CALL, THE(1922); GOLD MADNESS(1923); MIRACLE MAKERS, THE(1923); RUPERT OF HENTZAU(1923); BEN-HUR(1925); CRIMSON RUNNER, THE(1925); MISS NOBODY(1926); OLD IRONSIDES(1926); TELL IT TO THE MARINES(1926); WILD OATS LANE(1926); BEAU SABREUR(1928); OUT WITH THE TIDE(1928); WAY OF THE STRONG, THE(1928); LINDA(1929)
Misc. Silents
FLOWER OF NO MAN'S LAND, THE(1916); NINE-TENTHS OF THE LAW(1918); SIGN INVISIBLE, THE(1918); CALIBRE 38(1919); CHILDREN OF BANISHMENT(1919); CODE OF THE YUKON(1919); FAITH OF THE STRONG(1919); FOOL'S GOLD(1919); JACQUES OF THE SILVER NORTH(1919); LAST OF HIS PEOPLE, THE(1919); LIFE'S GREATEST PROBLEM(1919); BURNING DAYLIGHT(1920); MUTINY OF THE ELSINORE, THE(1920); AT THE END OF THE WORLD(1921); WOMAN CONQUERS, THE(1922); HER ACCIDENTAL HUSBAND(1923); LITTLE GIRL NEXT DOOR, THE(1923); HALF-A-DOLLAR BILL(1924); MYSTIC, THE(1925); TRACKED IN THE SNOW COUNTRY(1925); TYPHOON LOVE(1926); BACK TO GOD'S COUNTRY(1927); HARD BOILED HAGGERTY(1927); HAWK'S NEST, THE(1928); SPEED CLASSIC, THE(1928)
Monica Lewis
CONCORDE, THE–AIRPORT '79(; EXCUSE MY DUST(1951); INSIDE STRAIGHT(1951); STRIP, THE(1951); EVERYTHING I HAVE IS YOURS(1952); AFFAIR WITH A STRANGER(1953); D.I., THE(1957); CHARLEY VARRICK(1973); EARTHQUAKE(1974); AIRPORT '77(1977); ROLLERCOASTER(1977); NUNZIO(1978); BOXOFFICE(1982); STING II, THE(1983)
Morton Lewis
SUBURBAN WIVES(1973, Brit.), p; GIRL FROM STARSHIP VENUS, THE(1975, Brit.), p
Morton M. Lewis
WALLET, THE(1952, Brit.), p&d
Nancy Lewis
INTENT TO KILL(1958, Brit.); LOVE AND KISSES(1965)
Netta Lewis
DREAMS COME TRUE(1936, Brit.)
Nicholas Lewis
HOMEBODIES(1974)
Misc. Talkies
DISCO 9000(1977)
Oscar Lewis
CHILDREN OF SANCHEZ, THE(1978, U. S./Mex.), w
Pamela Lewis
SO FINE(1981)
Patricia Lewis
EXPRESSO BONGO(1959, Brit.)
Patricia Finn Lewis
JOURNEY THROUGH ROSEBUD(1972), ed
Paul Lewis
GLASS CAGE, THE(1964), p; LAST MOVIE, THE(1971), p; WEREWOLVES ON WHEELS(1971), p; THIS IS A HIJACK(1973), p; VAN, THE(1977), p
Pauline Lewis
Silents
DAWN(1917, Brit.), w
Peter Lewis
MELODY(1971, Brit.)
Misc. Silents
SHATTERED IDYLL, A(1916, Brit.)
Ralph Lewis
GIRL IN THE GLASS CAGE, THE(1929); ABRAHAM LINCOLN(1930); BAD ONE, THE(1930); FOURTH ALARM, THE(1930); SOMEWHERE IN SONORA(1933); SUCKER MONEY(1933); BADGE OF HONOR(1934); FIGHTING HERO(1934); MYSTERY LINER(1934); READY FOR LOVE(1934); DR. SOCRATES(1935); SUNSET RANGE(1935); SAN FRANCISCO(1936); SWIFTY(1936); MAID OF SALEM(1937); MAKE WAY FOR TOMORROW(1937); MUSIC FOR MADAME(1937); SINGING OUTLAW(1937); ARMY WIVES(1944); MARKED TRAILS(1944); SHADOW OF SUSPICION(1944); CHINA'S LITTLE DEVILS(1945); DILLINGER(1945); G.I. HONEYMOON(1945); JADE MASK, THE(1945); DANNY BOY(1946); FLYING SERPENT, THE(1946)
Misc. Talkies
TRIGGER LAW(1944); UTAH KID, THE(1944)
Silents
AVENGING CONSCIENCE, THE(1914); ESCAPE, THE(1914); FLOOR ABOVE, THE(1914); GANGSTERS OF NEW YORK, THE(1914); GREAT LEAP, THE(1914); HOME SWEET HOME(1914); BIRTH OF A NATION, THE(1915); JORDAN IS A HARD ROAD(1915); FLYING TORPEDO, THE(1916); GRETCHEN, THE GREENHORN(1916); HELL-TO-PAY AUSTIN(1916); INTOLERANCE(1916); MARTHA'S VINDICATION(1916); JACK AND THE BEANSTALK(1917); TALE OF TWO CITIES, A(1917); HOODLUM THE(1919); WHEN THE CLOUDS ROLL BY(1920); CONQUERING POWER, THE(1921); OUTSIDE THE LAW(1921); PRISONERS OF LOVE(1921); PRIVATE SCANDAL, A(1921); SALVAGE(1921); ENVIRONMENT(1922); THIRD ALARM, THE(1922); FOG, THE(1923); MAILMAN, THE(1923); DANTE'S INFERNO(1924); EAST OF BROADWAY(1924); IN EVERY WOMAN'S LIFE(1924); LAST EDITION, THE(1925); ONE OF THE BRAVEST(1925); OVERLAND LIMITED, THE(1925); LADY FROM HELL, THE(1926); SILENT POWER, THE(1926); HELD BY THE LAW(1927); SHIELD OF HONOR, THE(1927); SUNSET DERBY, THE(1927)
Misc. Silents
WOLF-MAN, THE(1915); CHILDREN PAY, THE(1916); GOING STRAIGHT(1916); LET KATHY DO IT(1916); SISTER OF SIX, A(1916); HER TEMPTATION(1917); SILENT LIE, THE(1917); THIS IS THE LIFE(1917); CHEATING THE PUBLIC(1918);

Ralph S. Lewis
FIRES OF YOUTH(1918); KID IS CLEVER, THE(1918); REVENGE(1918); DUB, THE(1919); "813"(1920); COMMON SENSE(1920); WHAT WOMEN LOVE(1920); MAN-WOMAN-MARRIAGE(1921); SOWING THE WIND(1921); BROAD DAYLIGHT(1922); FIVE DOLLAR BABY, THE(1922); IN THE NAME OF THE LAW(1922); BLOW YOUR OWN HORN(1923); TEA-WITH A KICK(1923); VENGEANCE OF THE DEEP(1923); WESTBOUND LIMITED, THE(1923); MAN WHO CAME BACK, THE(1924); UN-TAMED YOUTH(1924); MILLION DOLLAR HANDICAP, THE(1925); BIGGER THAN BARNUM'S(1926); BLOCK SIGNAL, THE(1926); FALSE ALARM, THE(1926); SHAD-OW OF THE LAW, THE(1926); CASEY JONES(1927); CROOKS CAN'T WIN(1928); OUTCAST SOULS(1928)

Ralph S. Lewis
FIGHTING MAD(1948), w

Ray Lewis
GIRLS IN THE STREET(1937, Brit.), w; GIRL IN THE STREET(1938, Brit.), w

Reg Lewis
DON'T MAKE WAVES(1967)

Rhoda Lewis
UNDER MILK WOOD(1973, Brit.)

Richard Lewis
LOVELY WAY TO DIE, A(1968), p; SIDELONG GLANCES OF A PIGEON KICKER, THE(1970), p
Misc. Silents
YANKEE SPEED(1924)

Richard Warren Lewis
SEVEN MINUTES, THE(1971), w

Rivers Lewis
SIX GUN SERENADE(1947); SONG OF THE WASTELAND(1947)

Robert Lewis
BOMBER'S MOON(1943); PARIS AFTER DARK(1943); TONIGHT WE RAID CALAIS(1943); DRAGON SEED(1944); HIDDEN EYE, THE(1945); SON OF LAS-SIE(1945); MONSIEUR VERDOUX(1947); LOST VOLCANO, THE(1950)

Robert E. Lewis
PUBLIC AFFAIR, A(1962), p

Robert Lewis
ZIEGRELD FOLLIES(1945), d, w; ANYTHING GOES(1956), d

SHE-DEVILS ON WHEELS(1968), m

Robert Q. Lewis
AFFAIR TO REMEMBER, AN(1957); GOOD NEIGHBOR SAM(1964); SKI PAR-TY(1965); RIDE BEYOND VENGEANCE(1966); EVERYTHING YOU ALWAYS WANTED TO KNOW ABOUT SEX, BUT WE'RE AFRAID TO ASK(1972); HOW TO SUCCEED IN BUSINESS WITHOUT REALLY TRYING(1976)

Roger Lewis
PAWNBROKER, THE(1965), p; SWIMMER, THE(1968), p; SHAFT'S BIG SCO-RE(1972), p; SHAFT IN AFRICA(1973), p; NIGHT GAMES(1980), p

Ronald Lewis
PRISONER, THE(1955, Brit.); SQUARE RING, THE(1955, Brit.); STORM OVER THE NILE(1955, Brit.); THE BEACHCOMBER(1955, Brit.); HELEN OF TROY(1956, Ital); HELL IN KOREA(1956, Brit.); PANIC IN THE PARLOUR(1957, Brit.); BACHELOR OF HEARTS(1958, Brit.); ROBBERY UNDER ARMS(1958, Brit.); SECRET PLACE, THE(1958, Brit.); WIND CANNOT READ, THE(1958, Brit.); CONSPIRACY OF HEARTS(1960, Brit.); MR. SARDONICUS(1961); SCREAM OF FEAR(1961, Brit.); STOP ME BEFORE I KILL!(1961, Brit.); BILLY BUDD(1962); TWICE AROUND THE DAFFODILS(1962, Brit.); SIEGE OF THE SAXONS(1963, Brit.); NURSE ON WHEELS(1964, Brit.); BRIGAND OF KANDAHAR, THE(1965, Brit.); JIG SAW(1965, Brit.); WHICH WAY TO THE FRONT?(1970); FRIENDS(1971, Brit.); PAUL AND MICHELLE(1974, Fr./Brit.)

Russell Lewis
BECKY SHARP(1935), ch; DANCING PIRATE(1936), ch; LOOKING GLASS WAR, THE(1970, Brit.); SUNDAY BLOODY SUNDAY(1971, Brit.); IT'S A 2"6" ABOVE THE GROUND WORLD(1972, Brit.); YOUNG WINSTON(1972, Brit.); TALES THAT WIT-NESS MADNESS(1973, Brit.); VOICES(1973, Brit.)

Ruth Lewis
LADY TAKES A SAILOR, THE(1949); WHERE DANGER LIVES(1950)

Sagan Lewis
LITTLE SEX, A(1982)

Sam Lewis
STUDENT TOUR(1934)
Silents
SQUIBS WINS THE CALCUTTA SWEEP(1922, Brit.)

Sandy Lewis
CARMEN JONES(1954)

Sharon Lewis
LETTER OF INTRODUCTION(1938); SWEETHEARTS(1938); SOCIETY LA-WYER(1939); IF YOU COULD SEE WHAT I HEAR(1982)

Sheldon Lewis
RIVER WOMAN, THE(1928); SEVEN FOOTPRINTS TO SATAN(1929); FIREBRAND JORDAN(1930); MONSTER WALKS, THE(1932); TEX TAKES A HOLIDAY(1932); TOMBSTONE CANYON(1932); GUN JUSTICE(1934); CATTLE THIEF, THE(1936)
Misc. Talkies
RIDERS OF RIO(1931)
Silents
CHARITY?(1916); KING'S GAME, THE(1916); PURSUING VENGEANCE, THE(1916); IMPOSSIBLE CATHERINE(1919); ORPHANS OF THE STORM(1922); JACQUELINE, OR BLAZING BARRIERS(1923); ENEMY SEX, THE(1924); IN FAST COMPANY(1924); BASHFUL BUCCANEER(1925); NEW LIVES FOR OLD(1925); BRIDE OF THE STORM(1926); DON JUAN(1926); GILDED HIGHWAY, THE(1926); DRIVEN FROM HOME(1927); HAZARDOUS VALLEY(1927); LADYBIRD, THE(1927); LITTLE WILD GIRL, THE(1928); SKY RIDER, THE(1928)
Misc. Silents
AFFAIR OF THREE NATIONS, AN(1915); HOUSE OF FEAR, THE(1915); WARFARE OF THE FLESH, THE(1917); BISHOP'S EMERALDS, THE(1919); SILENT BARRIER, THE(1920); WHEN THE DESERT CALLS(1922); DARLING OF NEW YORK, THE(1923); LITTLE RED SCHOOLHOUSE, THE(1923); DANGEROUS FLIRT, THE(1924); HONOR AMONG MEN(1924); DEFEND YOURSELF(1925); KIT CARSON OVER THE GREAT DIVIDE(1925); LURE OF THE TRACK(1925); MYSTERIOUS STRANGER, THE(1925); SUPER SPEED(1925); BEYOND THE TRAIL(1926); BUF-FALO BILL ON THE U.P. TRAIL(1926); DESPERATE MOMENT, A(1926); MORAN OF THE MOUNTED(1926); SELF STARTER, THE(1926); SKY PIRATE, THE(1926); TWO-GUN MAN, THE(1926); BURNING GOLD(1927); CRUISE OF THE HELLION,

THE(1927); OVERLAND STAGE, THE(1927); SEVEN FOOTPRINTS TO SATAN(1929); DANGER MAN, THE(1930)

Sherry Lewis
KLONDIKE FEVER(1980)

Sinclair Lewis
ARROWSMITH(1931), w; NEWLY RICH(1931), w; ANN VICKERS(1933), w; BAB-BITT(1934), w; DODSWORTH(1936), w; I MARRIED A DOCTOR(1936), w; UN-TAMED(1940), w; THIS IS THE LIFE(1944), w; CASS TIMBERLANE(1947), w; FUN AND FANCY FREE(1947), w; ELMER GANTRY(1960), d&w
Silents
BABBITT(1924), w

Stephen Lewis
PRIZE OF ARMS, A(1962, Brit.); SPARROWS CAN'T SING(1963, Brit.), a, w; STAIR-CASE(1969 U.S./Brit./Fr.); ON THE BUSES(1972, Brit.); LAST REMAKE OF BEAU GESTE, THE(1977)

Stephen L. Lewis
DREAMS OF GLASS(1969), ed

Steven Lewis
NEGATIVES(1968, Brit.)

Strangler Lewis
PRIZEFIGHTER AND THE LADY, THE(1933)

Suzanne Lewis
CRATER LAKE MONSTER, THE(1977)

Sybil Lewis
AM I GUILTY?(1940); REVENGE OF THE ZOMBIES(1943); BOY! WHAT A GIRL(1947); MIRACLE IN HARLEM(1948)

Sybyl Lewis
GOING MY WAY(1944)

Sylvia Lewis
LAS VEGAS STORY, THE(1952); DRUMS OF TAHITI(1954); CHA-CHA-CHA BOOM(1956); HOT BLOOD(1956), ch; LIEUTENANT WORE SKIRTS, THE(1956); JET PILOT(1957); SPRING REUNION(1957), ch; LADIES MAN, THE(1961); HOOK, LINE AND SINKER(1969)

Ted Lewis
IS EVERYBODY HAPPY?(1929); HERE COMES THE BAND(1935); MANHATTAN MERRY-GO-ROUND(1937); HOLD THAT GHOST(1941); IS EVERYBODY HAP-PY?(1943)

Ted Lewis
GET CARTER(1971, Brit.), w; HIT MAN(1972), d&w

Terina Lewis
UNION CITY(1980)

Terry Lewis
PILGRIM, FAREWELL(1980), ed

Texas Jim Lewis
PARDON MY GUN(1942)

Therese Lewis
WHAT A WOMAN!(1943), w

Tim Lewis
JOE(1970); PRAISE MARX AND PASS THE AMMUNITION(1970, Brit.), ed; LONE-LY HEARTS(1983, Aus.), ed
1984
MAN OF FLOWERS(1984, Aus.), ed

Tom Lewis
CAUSE FOR ALARM(1951), p, w

Tom Lewis
CAUSE FOR ALARM(1951), p, w
Silents
ENCHANTMENT(1921); ADAM AND EVA(1923); CALLAHANS AND THE MUR-PHYS, THE(1927); STEAMBOAT BILL, JR.(1928)
Misc. Silents
GO-GETTER, THE(1923); GREAT WHITE WAY, THE(1924)

Tommy Lewis
TERESA(1951)

Tommy Lewis
CHANT OF JIMMIE BLACKSMITH, THE(1980, Aus.); WE OF THE NEVER NE-VER(1983, Aus.)

Tony Lewis
GET OUTTA TOWN(1960)

V. C. Lewis
WAKAMBA!(1955), ed

Vance Lewis
Misc. Talkies
SILENT STRANGER, THE(1975), d

Vance Lewis [Luigi Vanzi]
SHOOT FIRST, LAUGH LAST(1967, Ital./Ger./U.S.), d; STRANGER IN TOWN, A(1968, U.S./Ital.), d; STRANGER RETURNS, THE(1968, U.S./Ital./Ger./Span.), d

Vera Lewis
HOME TOWNERS, THE(1928); IRON MASK, THE(1929); WIDE OPEN(1930); COM-MAND PERFORMANCE(1931); NIGHT NURSE(1931); KING KONG(1933); MAN ON THE FLYING TRAPEZE, THE(1935); PADDY O'DAY(1935); WAY DOWN EAST(1935); DANCING PIRATE(1936); DON'T GET PERSONAL(1936); MAID OF SALEM(1937); NOTHING SACRED(1937); AMAZING DR. CLITTERHOUSE, THE(1938); ANGELS WITH DIRTY FACES(1938); BOY MEETS GIRL(1938); COMET OVER BROAD-WAY(1938); FOUR DAUGHTERS(1938); HARD TO GET(1938); IN OLD CHICA-GO(1938); NANCY DREW-DETECTIVE(1938); SISTERS, THE(1938); DODGE CITY(1939); EACH DAWN I DIE(1939); ESPIONAGE AGENT(1939); FOUR WI-VES(1939); HELL'S KITCHEN(1939); KING OF THE UNDERWORLD(1939); MR. SMITH GOES TO WASHINGTON(1939); NANCY DREW AND THE HIDDEN STAIR-CASE(1939); NAUGHTY BUT NICE(1939); ON TRIAL(1939); PRIVATE DETEC-TIVE(1939); RETURN OF DR. X, THE(1939); ROARING TWENTIES, THE(1939); SWEEPSTAKES WINNER(1939); TORCHY PLAYS WITH DYNAMITE(1939); WOM-EN IN THE WIND(1939); ADVENTURE IN DIAMONDS(1940); COURAGEOUS DR. CHRISTIAN, THE(1940); FATHER IS A PRINCE(1940); GRANNY GET YOUR GUN(1940); MAN WHO TALKED TOO MUCH, THE(1940); NIGHT AT EARL CAR-ROLL'S, A(1940); THEY DRIVE BY NIGHT(1940); WOMEN IN WAR(1940); BODY DISAPPEARS, THE(1941); FOUR MOTHERS(1941); HERE COMES HAP-PINESS(1941); KNOCKOUT(1941); MANPOWER(1941); MODEL WIFE(1941); NINE LIVES ARE NOT ENOUGH(1941); ONE FOOT IN HEAVEN(1941); REMEMBER THE DAY(1941); SHE COULDN'T SAY NO(1941); THREE GIRLS ABOUT TOWN(1941); BUSSES ROAR(1942); GAY SISTERS, THE(1942); LADY GANGSTER(1942); LARCE-

NY, INC.(1942); MAN WHO CAME TO DINNER, THE(1942); MOONTIDE(1942); THEY DIED WITH THEIR BOOTS ON(1942); EDGE OF DARKNESS(1943); PRINCESS O'ROURKE(1943); SOMEONE TO REMEMBER(1943); MR. SKEFFINGTON(1944); HOLLYWOOD AND VINE(1945); CAT CREEPS, THE(1946); KILLERS, THE(1946); SPOOK BUSTERS(1946); IT HAD TO BE YOU(1947); IT'S A JOKE, SON!(1947); STALLION ROAD(1947)
Misc. Talkies
NEVER TOO LATE(1935)
Silents
CAPRICES OF KITTY, THE(1915); MADCAP BETTY(1915); INTOLERANCE(1916); JACK AND THE BEANSTALK(1917); AS THE SUN WENT DOWN(1919); NURSE MARJORIE(1920); NANCY FROM NOWHERE(1922); LONG LIVE THE KING(1923); BROADWAY AFTER DARK(1924); IN EVERY WOMAN'S LIFE(1924); EVE'S SECRET(1925); STELLA DALLAS(1925); ELLA CINDERS(1926); GILDED BUTTERFLY, THE(1926); TAKE IT FROM ME(1926); THUMBS DOWN(1927); WHAT HAPPENED TO FATHER(1927); RAMONA(1928)
Misc. Silents
BIT OF JADE, A(1918); YVONNE FROM PARIS(1919); POOR SIMP, THE(1920); SHE COULDN'T HELP IT(1921); GLORIOUS FOOL, THE(1922); HOW TO EDUCATE A WIFE(1924); ENTICEMENT(1925); KING OF THE PACK(1926); SATAN AND THE WOMAN(1928)

Victor Lewis
TAKE IT BIG(1944), ed; SKIPALONG ROSENBLOOM(1951), ed

W. Michael Lewis
NEW YEAR'S EVIL(1980), m; SHOGUN ASSASSIN(1980, Jap.), m; ENTER THE NINJA(1982), m; BALLAD OF GREGORIO CORTEZ, THE(1983), m; REVENGE OF THE NINJA(1983), m

W. P. Lewis
Silents
OUT OF A CLEAR SKY(1918)

Walter Lewis
Silents
ETERNAL SAPHO, THE(1916); STEADFAST HEART, THE(1923); DOWN UPON THE SUWANNEE RIVER(1925)
Misc. Silents
WHITE MOLL, THE(1920); LONESOME CORNERS(1922)

Walter P. Lewis
ARIZONA KID, THE(1930)
Silents
AVENGING TRAIL, THE(1918); TOL'ABLE DAVID(1921)

Walter Pratt Lewis
Silents
JOAN OF THE WOODS(1918)

Webster Lewis
HEARSE, THE(1980), m; BODY AND SOUL(1981), m; MY TUTOR(1983), m
1984
GO TELL IT ON THE MOUNTAIN(1984), m

Willard Lewis
Silents
BIG GAME(1921)

William W. Lewis
1984
BRADY'S ESCAPE(1984, U.S./Hung.), w

Lewis &Vaughn
1984
PURPLE RAIN(1984), cos

Lewis and Clarke Expedition
FOR SINGLES ONLY(1968)

Lewis Lymon Teenchords
JAMBOREE(1957)

Denis Lewiston
CRIME AND PASSION(1976, U.S., Ger.), ph; SWALLOWS AND AMAZONS(1977, Brit.), ph; SIGN OF FOUR, THE(1983, Brit.), ph

Dennis Lewiston
SQUEEZE, THE(1977, Brit.), ph; NIGHT GAMES(1980), ph

Peter Lewiston
ROCK AROUND THE WORLD(1957, Brit.); WOMAN EATER, THE(1959, Brit.)

Bella Lewitsky
PREHISTORIC WOMEN(1950), ch

Bella Lewitzky
WHITE SAVAGE(1943)

Daniel Lewk
CHINA SYNDROME, THE(1979)

Patrick Lewsley
1984
COMFORT AND JOY(1984, Brit.)

Rick Lewson
1984
RENO AND THE DOC(1984, Can.)

Bill Lewthaite
SUBTERFUGE(1969, US/Brit.), ed

Bill Lewthwaite
LADY WITH A LAMP, THE(1951, Brit.), ed; MAN IN THE DINGHY, THE(1951, Brit.), ed; FOUR AGAINST FATE(1952, Brit.), ed; TRENT'S LAST CASE(1953, Brit.), ed; FRONT PAGE STORY(1954, Brit.), ed; 1984(1956, Brit.), ed; TARZAN AND THE LOST SAFARI(1957, Brit.), ed; YOUR PAST IS SHOWING(1958, Brit.), ed; FIVE GOLDEN HOURS(1961, Brit.), ed; ON THE BEAT(1962, Brit.), ed; MYSTERY SUBMARINE(1963, Brit.), ed; PANIC(1966, Brit.), ed; HALF A SIXPENCE(1967, Brit.), ed; CAPTAIN NEMO AND THE UNDERWATER CITY(1969, Brit.), ed; DULCIMA(1971, Brit.), ed

Mill Lewthwaite
TOO MANY CROOKS(1959, Brit.), ed

W. J. Lewthwaite
MELBA(1953, Brit.), ed

W. Lewthwaite
ODETTE(1951, Brit.), ed

William Lewthwaite
PRIZE OF GOLD, A(1955), ed

Charles Lewton
THIS TIME FOR KEEPS(1942), ph

Val Lewton
TALE OF TWO CITIES, A(1935), staging; CAT PEOPLE(1942), p; GHOST SHIP, THE(1943), p; I WALKED WITH A ZOMBIE(1943), p; LEOPARD MAN, THE(1943), p; SEVENTH VICTIM, THE(1943), p; CURSE OF THE CAT PEOPLE, THE(1944), p; MADEMOISELLE FIFI(1944), p; YOUTH RUNS WILD(1944), p; BODY SNATCHER, THE(1945), p; ISLE OF THE DEAD(1945), p, w; BEDLAM(1946), p; MY OWN TRUE LOVE(1948), p; PLEASE BELIEVE ME(1950), p; APACHE DRUMS(1951), p

Boris Lewyn
EARRINGS OF MADAME DE..., THE(1954, Fr.), ed

Jake Lexa
FUZZ(1972)

Pedro Lexalt
TERRACE, THE(1964, Arg.)

Edward Lexy
SECOND BEST BED(1937, Brit.); DRUMS(1938, Brit.); KATE PLUS TEN(1938, Brit.); MANY TANKS MR. ATKINS(1938, Brit.); NIGHT JOURNEY(1938, Brit.); SOUTH RIDING(1938, Brit.); ANYTHING TO DECLARE?(1939, Brit.); MRS. PYM OF SCOTLAND YARD(1939, Brit.); THIS MAN IN PARIS(1939, Brit.); THIS MAN IS NEWS(1939, Brit.); TOO DANGEROUS TO LIVE(1939, Brit.); CONVOY(1940); LAUGH IT OFF(1940, Brit.); OUTSIDER, THE(1940, Brit.); SIDEWALKS OF LONDON(1940, Brit.); SPARE A COPPER(1940, Brit.); SPIDER, THE(1940, Brit.); TORSO MURDER MYSTERY, THE(1940, Brit.); LARCENY STREET(1941, Brit.); PROUD VALLEY, THE(1941, Brit.); TERROR, THE(1941, Brit.); UNDER SECRET ORDERS(1943, Brit.); GIRL IN A MILLION, A(1946, Brit.); SCHOOL FOR SECRETS(1946, Brit.); CAPTAIN BOYCOTT(1947, Brit.); GHOSTS OF BERKELEY SQUARE(1947, Brit.); WHILE I LIVE(1947, Brit.); BLANCHE FURY(1948, Brit.); BONNIE PRINCE CHARLIE(1948, Brit.); MARK OF CAIN, THE(1948, Brit.); CHILDREN OF CHANCE(1949, Brit.); FOR THEM THAT TRESPASS(1949, Brit.); IT'S NOT CRICKET(1949, Brit.); TEMPTATION HARBOR(1949, Brit.); GOOD TIME GIRL(1950, Brit.); TWENTY QUESTIONS MURDER MYSTERY, THE(1950, Brit.); WINSLOW BOY, THE(1950); LADY WITH A LAMP, THE(1951, Brit.); NIGHT WAS OUR FRIEND(1951, Brit.); SMART ALEC(1951, Brit.); CLOUDBURST(1952, Brit.); MISS ROBIN HOOD(1952, Brit.); MR. LORD SAYS NO(1952, Brit.); YOU'RE ONLY YOUNG TWICE(1952, Brit.); GAY ADVENTURE, THE(1953, Brit.); GOLDEN LINK, THE(1954, Brit.); CAPTAIN LIGHTFOOT(1955); WHERE THERE'S A WILL(1955, Brit.); RISING OF THE MOON, THE(1957, Ireland); MAN WHO WOULDN'T TALK, THE(1958, Brit.); ORDERS ARE ORDERS(1959, Brit.)

Fritz Ley
TREMENDOUSLY RICH MAN, A(1932, Ger.)

Grita Ley
Misc. Silents
BERLIN AFTER DARK(1929, Ger.)

John Ley
MAD MAX(1979, Aus.); BMX BANDITS(1983); ESCAPE 2000(1983, Aus.)

Jonathan Ley
NO TIME FOR TEARS(1957, Brit.)

Margot Ley
CAPTAIN NEMO AND THE UNDERWATER CITY(1969, Brit.)

Tabu Ley
1984
WHITE ELEPHANT(1984, Brit.), m

Willy Ley
CONQUEST OF SPACE(1955), w

J. Ley-On
FLAME OF LOVE, THE(1930, Brit.)

Claire Leyba
ANNA LUCASTA(1958)

Tommy Leyba
TIMERIDER(1983)

Laura Leycester
Silents
MOTHERHOOD(1915, Brit.)

Jay Leyda
MISSION TO MOSCOW(1943), tech adv

Leo Leyden
MASK, THE(1961, Can.); LUCK OF GINGER COFFEY, THE(1964, U.S./Can.); 1776(1972); QUIET DAY IN BELFAST, A(1974, Can.)

William Leyden
PATSY, THE(1964)

Martin Leyder
ON HER MAJESTY'S SECRET SERVICE(1969, Brit.)

Noel Leyland
FIRST MRS. FRASER, THE(1932, Brit.)

Pierre Leymarie
PICKPOCKET(1963, Fr.)

Monique Leyrac
ACT OF THE HEART(1970, Can.)

Willy Leyrer
GIRL AND THE LEGEND, THE(1966, Ger.)

Paul Leyssac
PARIS CALLING(1941)

Johan Leysen
GIRL WITH THE RED HAIR, THE(1983, Neth.)

Helen Leyser
LONE WOLF RETURNS, THE(1936)

Emrys Leyshon
LAST DAYS OF DOLWYN, THE(1949, Brit.); MEN ARE CHILDREN TWICE(1953, Brit.); DELAYED ACTION(1954, Brit.); UNSTOPPABLE MAN, THE(1961, Brit.); NEARLY A NASTY ACCIDENT(1962, Brit.)

Emyra Leyshon
HAPPINESS OF THREE WOMEN, THE(1954, Brit.)

Paul Leyssac
VICTORIA THE GREAT(1937, Brit.); HEAD OVER HEELS IN LOVE(1937, Brit.); ARISE, MY LOVE(1940); TWO-FACED WOMAN(1941)

Josef Leytes
VALLEY OF MYSTERY(1967), d; COUNTERFEIT KILLER, THE(1968), d

Joseph Leytes
FAITHFUL CITY(1952, Israel), p,d&w; PASSION(1954), w

Drue Leyton
CHANGE OF HEART(1934); CHARLIE CHAN IN LONDON(1934); CHARLIE CHAN'S COURAGE(1934); ALIBI FOR MURDER(1936); BLACKMAILER(1936); CHARLIE CHAN AT THE CIRCUS(1936); SMALL TOWN GIRL(1936); MURDER IN THE NIGHT(1940, Brit.)

George Leyton
Misc. Silents
BOYS OF THE OLD BRIGADE, THE(1916, Brit.); IT'S NEVER TOO LATE TO MEND(1917, Brit.); MAN WHO MADE GOOD, THE(1917, Brit.); LAND OF MY FATHERS(1921, Brit.)

John Leyton
RING-A-DING RHYTHM(1962, Brit. 73m Amicus/COL bw (G.B: IT'S TRAD, DAD!); GREAT ESCAPE, THE(1963); GUNS AT BATASI(1964, Brit.); SEASIDE SWINGERS(1965, Brit.); VON RYAN'S EXPRESS(1965); IDOL, THE(1966, Brit.); KRAKATOA, EAST OF JAVA(1969); SCHIZO(1977, Brit.); DANGEROUS DAVIES–THE LAST DETECTIVE(1981, Brit.)

Laurence Leyton
Silents
PATRICIA BRENT, SPINSTER(1919, Brit.)

Saul N. Leyton
WEEKEND OF FEAR(1966), ph

Frank Leyuda
WHERE DANGER LIVES(1950)

Chiek Leyva
Silents
JOYOUS TROUBLEMAKERS, THE(1920)

Frank Leyva
LAST TRAIN FROM MADRID, THE(1937); WHEN YOU'RE IN LOVE(1937); MASQUERADE IN MEXICO(1945); GILDA(1946); TYCOON(1947); FEATHERED SERPENT, THE(1948); TALL MEN, THE(1955); MARACAIBO(1958); EL DORADO(1967)

Laura Leyva
ZOOT SUIT(1981)

Roberto Leyva
NIGHT OF THE IGUANA, THE(1964)

Sara Lezana
GRINGO(1963, Span./Ital.); MURIETA(1965, Span.)

Cecile Lezard
AVENGERS, THE(1950); NATIVE SON(1951, U.S., Arg.)

Zurab Lezhava
LAST HILL, THE(1945, USSR)

E. Lezhdey
ITALIANO BRAVA GENTE(1965, Ital./USSR)

Mme. Lherbay
END OF A DAY, THE(1939, Fr.)

Thierry Lhermitte
MEN PREFER FAT GIRLS(1981, Fr.)
1984
MY BEST FRIEND'S GIRL(1984, Fr.); MY NEW PARTNER(1984, Fr.); UNTIL SEPTEMBER(1984)

Anita Lhoest
CAPTIVE GIRL(1950)

Pierre Lhomme
LA VIE DE CHATEAU(1967, Fr.), ph; LAST MAN, THE(1968, Fr.), ph; L'ARMEE DES OMBRES(1969, Fr./Ital.), ph; MISTER FREEDOM(1970, Fr.), ph; SOMEONE BEHIND THE DOOR(1971, Fr./Brit.), ph; FOUR NIGHTS OF A DREAMER(1972, Fr.), ph; SAVAGE, THE(1975, Fr.), ph; QUARTET(1981, Brit./Fr.), ph

Jean Lhote
COUNTERFEIT CONSTABLE, THE(1966, Fr.), w

Alicia Li
CONFESSIONS OF AN OPIUM EATER(1962); STAGECOACH TO DANCER'S PARK(1962); OPERATION BIKINI(1963)

Bruce Li
POWERFORCE(1983)
Misc. Talkies
RETURN OF THE TIGER(1979)

Change Li
Misc. Talkies
RETURN OF THE TIGER(1979)

Chu'eng Li
RETURN OF THE DRAGON(1974, Chin.)

Kao Li
MERMAID, THE(1966, Hong Kong), d

Lily Li
CALL HIM MR. SHATTER(1976, Hong Kong)

Pat Li
MISTER BUDDWING(1966); DREAMS OF GLASS(1969)

Jose Li-Ho
ROBOT VS. THE AZTEC MUMMY, THE(1965, Mex.), ed

Li Li-hua
MAGNIFICENT CONCUBINE, THE(1964, Hong Kong); EMPRESS WU(1965, Hong Kong); GRAND SUBSTITUTION, THE(1965, Hong Kong); VERMILION DOOR(1969, Hong Kong)

Lia
1984
SUPERGIRL(1984)

Ron Liace
Misc. Talkies
BLAST-OFF GIRLS(1967)

Thierry Liagre
1984
UNTIL SEPTEMBER(1984)

Peter Liakakis
HANGAR 18(1980)

Jewell Lian
SUICIDE BATTALION(1958)

Chow Foo Liang
BRUCE LEE–TRUE STORY(1976, Chi.), m

Theo Lianos
FORTY THOUSAND HORSEMEN(1941, Aus.)

Peter Liapis
1984
SWORDKILL(1984)

Peter Paul Liapis
STARHOPS(1978)

Demetrios Liappas
POSTMAN ALWAYS RINGS TWICE, THE(1981)

Elie Liardet
PRIVATE BENJAMIN(1980)

Sven Libaek
SET, THE(1970, Aus.), m; NICKEL QUEEN, THE(1971, Aus.), m

Dorothy Libaire
CONFESSIONS OF A CO-ED(1931); MADAME BUTTERFLY(1932); MAN WHO PLAYED GOD, THE(1932); BONDAGE(1933); JENNIE GERHARDT(1933); ZOO IN BUDAPEST(1933); AFFAIRS OF A GENTLEMAN(1934); BABY, TAKE A BOW(1934); PICTURE BRIDES(1934); BABY FACE HARRINGTON(1935); HOOSIER SCHOOLMASTER(1935); MURDER ON A HONEYMOON(1935); PERFECT CLUE, THE(1935)

Jiri Libal
FIREMAN'S BALL, THE(1968, Czech.)

Renato Libassi
CRAZY DESIRE(1964, Ital.), p; FASCIST, THE(1965, Ital.), p; HOURS OF LOVE, THE(1965, Ital.), p

Salvo Libassi
MY WIFE'S ENEMY(1967, Ital.)

Harvey Libbert
JOURNEY'S END(1930), art d

Hervey Libbert
LUCKY BOY(1929), art d; PEACOCK ALLEY(1930), art d
Silents
BACHELOR'S PARADISE(1928), art d; GRAIN OF DUST, THE(1928), art d; LINGERIE(1928), art d; MAN IN HOBBLES, THE(1928), art d; SCARLET DOVE, THE(1928), art d; STORMY WATERS(1928), art d; TOILERS, THE(1928), art d

J. Libbey
Silents
GREED(1925)

Robert Libbott
GROOM WORE SPURS, THE(1951), w; CAPTAIN PIRATE(1952), w

Brian Libby
SILENT RAGE(1982)
1984
DREAMSCAPE(1984)

Diane Libby
HOUSE IS NOT A HOME, A(1964)

Dianne Libby
ROUSTABOUT(1964)

Fred Libby
MY DARLING CLEMENTINE(1946); CAPTAIN FROM CASTILE(1947); THREE GODFATHERS, THE(1948); EVERYBODY DOES IT(1949); SHE WORE A YELLOW RIBBON(1949); WAKE OF THE RED WITCH(1949); CARIBOO TRAIL, THE(1950); DESERT HAWK, THE(1950); FATHER'S WILD GAME(1950); WAGONMASTER(1950); CALL ME MISTER(1951); WHAT PRICE GLORY?(1952); SERGEANT RUTLEDGE(1960)

Freddy Libby
BELLE STARR'S DAUGHTER(1947)

Linda Libera
WE SHALL RETURN(1963)

Liberace
SOUTH SEA SINNER(1950); SINCERELY YOURS(1955); LOVED ONE, THE(1965); WHEN THE BOYS MEET THE GIRLS(1965)

Margarita Liberaki
PHAEDRA(1962, U.S./Gr./Fr.), w

Alberto Liberati
SON OF THE RED CORSAIR(1963, Ital.), w; KNIVES OF THE AVENGER(1967, Ital.), w; DESERTER AND THE NOMADS, THE(1969, Czech./Ital.), w

Mario Liberati
AMARCORD(1974, Ital.)

Pietro Liberati
WOMAN ON FIRE, A(1970, Ital.), art d

Ugo Liberatore
PHAROAH'S WOMAN, THE(1961, Ital.), w; AVENGER, THE(1962, Fr./Ital.), w; NIGHT THEY KILLED RASPUTIN, THE(1962, Fr./Ital.), w; TROJAN HORSE, THE(1962, Fr./Ital.), w; 300 SPARTANS, THE(1962), w; ARTURO'S ISLAND(1963, Ital.), w; MILL OF THE STONE WOMEN(1963, Fr./Ital.), w; EMPTY CANVAS, THE(1964, Fr./Ital.), w; IDOL, THE(1966, Brit.), w; TRAMPLERS, THE(1966, Ital.), w; HELLBENDERS, THE(1967, U.S./Ital./Span.), w; JOURNEY BENEATH THE DESERT(1967, Fr./Ital.), w; MAIDEN FOR A PRINCE, A(1967, Fr./Ital.), w; CHASTITY BELT, THE(1968, Ital.), w; MINUTE TO PRAY, A SECOND TO DIE, A(1968, Ital.), w; WITCH, THE(1969, Ital.), w; NO WAY OUT(1975, Ital./Fr.), w
Misc. Talkies
MAY MORNING(1970), d

Leon Liberman
WIND AND THE LION, THE(1975); CONFESSIONS OF AMANS, THE(1977)

Wili Liberman
SHAPE OF THINGS TO COME, THE(1979, Can.)

Anne Libert
VICE AND VIRTUE(1965, Fr./Ital.)

Beatrice Libert
MOONRAKER(1979, Brit.)

Jacob Libert
Misc. Silents
SLAUGHTER, THE(1913, USSR); STRANGER, THE(1913, USSR)

Richard Libertini
NIGHT THEY RAIDED MINSKY'S, THE(1968); DON'T DRINK THE WATER(1969); CATCH-22(1970); OUT OF TOWNERS, THE(1970); LADY LIBERTY(1972, Ital./Fr.); FIRE SALE(1977); DAYS OF HEAVEN(1978); IN-LAWS, THE(1979); POPEYE(1980); BEST FRIENDS(1982); SHARKY'S MACHINE(1982); SOUP FOR ONE(1982); DEAL OF

THE CENTURY(1983); GOING BERSERK(1983)
1984
ALL OF ME(1984); FLETCH(1984); UNFAITHFULLY YOURS(1984)
Ray Liberto
HONEYSUCKLE ROSE(1980)
Richard Liberty
THE CRAZIES(1973); FINAL COUNTDOWN, THE(1980); LOVE CHILD(1982); PORKY'S II: THE NEXT DAY(1983)
Liberty Horses
GREATEST SHOW ON EARTH, THE(1952)
Robert Yale Libett
ALL-AMERICAN, THE(1953), w
L. Libgold
DYBBUK THE(1938, Pol.)
Armando Libianchi
WHITE SHEIK, THE(1956, Ital.)
Jan Libicek
90 DEGREES IN THE SHADE(1966, Czech./Brit.); NIGHTS OF PRAGUE, THE(1968, Czech.); SIGN OF THE VIRGIN(1969, Czech.); END OF A PRIEST(1970, Czech.)
Jan Libieck
SIR, YOU ARE A WIDOWER(1971, Czech.)
Z. Libin
Silents
BROKEN HEARTS(1926), w
Marek M. Libkov
THE CATMAN OF PARIS(1946), p
M. Libman
DYBBUK THE(1938, Pol.)
Syd Libman
LUCKY STAR, THE(1980, Can.)
Alain Libolt
L'ARMEE DES OMBRES(1969, Fr./Ital.); WANDERER, THE(1969, Fr.)
Dana Libonati
1984
AMERICAN TABOO(1984), m
Jan Libora
CAPRICIOUS SUMMER(1968, Czech.), p
Robert Libott
STRANGE MRS. CRANE, THE(1948), w; AIR HOSTESS(1949), w; BARBARY PIRATE(1949), w; CHINATOWN AT MIDNIGHT(1949), w; FLAME OF YOUTH(1949), w; LAW OF THE BARBARY COAST(1949), w; FORTUNES OF CAPTAIN BLOOD(1950), w; STAGE TO TUCSON(1950), w; STATE PENITENTIARY(1950), w; TYRANT OF THE SEA(1950), w; LADY AND THE BANDIT, THE(1951), w
Robert Yale Libott
LAST TRAIN FROM BOMBAY(1952), w
Herwig Libowitsky
PRISONER OF ZENDA, THE(1979), art d
Dennis Libscomb
PENITENTIARY II(1982)
Glaus Libucaberger
BLUE LIGHT, THE(1932, Ger.), ph
Lawrence Licaizi
Silents
BOY OF MINE(1923)
Carlo Licari
FAREWELL TO ARMS, A(1957)
Rodolfo Licari
BLACK VEIL FOR LISA, A(1969 Ital./Ger.)
Giuseppe Licastro
INVESTIGATION OF A CITIZEN ABOVE SUSPICION(1970, Ital.)
Marty Licata
1984
ONCE UPON A TIME IN AMERICA(1984)
Vincenzo Licata
SEDUCED AND ABANDONED(1964, Fr./Ital.)
Irving L. Lichenstein
EQUINOX(1970)
Rosa Lichenstein
M(1933, Ger.)
David Lichine
HEAT'S ON, THE(1943), ch; NORTH STAR, THE(1943), ch; SOMETHING TO SHOUT ABOUT(1943), ch; SONG OF RUSSIA(1943), ch; SENSATIONS OF 1945(1944), a, ch; MAKE MINE MUSIC(1946); UNFINISHED DANCE,THE(1947), ch; TONIGHT WE SING(1953), ch
A.E. Licho
1914(1932, Ger.); TESTAMENT OF DR. MABUSE, THE(1943, Ger.)
Adolf Edgar Licho
Misc. Silents
DEVIL'S PAWN, THE(1922, Ger.)
Eddie Licho
ONCE UPON A HONEYMOON(1942)
Edgar Licho
MAN HUNT(1941); REUNION IN FRANCE(1942); TO BE OR NOT TO BE(1942); MISSION TO MOSCOW(1943); DAYS OF GLORY(1944); MASK OF DIMITRIOS, THE(1944)
Lichorshin
ROMEO AND JULIET(1955, USSR), ed
E.A. Lichs
DAUGHTER OF EVIL(1930, Ger.)
Jeremy Licht
NEXT ONE, THE(1982, U.S./Gr.); TWILIGHT ZONE–THE MOVIE(1983)
Louis Lichtenfield
SPIRIT OF ST. LOUIS, THE(1957), spec eff; NO TIME FOR SERGEANTS(1958), spec eff
Fritz Lichtenhahn
SISTERS, OR THE BALANCE OF HAPPINESS(1982, Ger.)
1984
GERMANY PALE MOTHER(1984, Ger.)

Mitchell Lichtenstein
LORDS OF DISCIPLINE, THE(1983); STREAMERS(1983)
1984
CRACKERS(1984)
Rose Lichtenstein
Silents
KRIEMHILD'S REVENGE(1924, Ger.); METROPOLIS(1927, Ger.)
Baron James Lichter
ACCORDING TO MRS. HOYLE(1951)
Baron Lichter
FURIES, THE(1950)
Zeev Lichter
EVERY BASTARD A KING(1968, Israel), set d
Marvin Lichterman
JOHN AND MARY(1969); FRIENDS OF EDDIE COYLE, THE(1973); FRONT, THE(1976); IF EVER I SEE YOU AGAIN(1978); STARTING OVER(1979)
Renee Lichtig
PICNIC ON THE GRASS(1960, Fr.), ed; KING OF KINGS(1961), ed; ELUSIVE CORPORAL, THE(1963, Fr.), ed; IN THE FRENCH STYLE(1963, U.S./Fr.), ed; DAY THE HOTLINE GOT HOT, THE(1968, Fr./Span.), ed; KAMOURASKA(1973, Can./Fr.), ed
Reny Lichtig
EXTERMINATORS, THE(1965 Fr.), ed
Scott Lichtig
LIFEGUARD(1976)
Al Lichtman
YOUNG LIONS, THE(1958), p
Paul Lichtman
YOUR THREE MINUTES ARE UP(1973)
Robert Lickens
NO HIGHWAY IN THE SKY(1951, Brit.)
Martin Lickert
TWO HUNDRED MOTELS(1971, Brit.)
Jose Licneraki
MARGIN, THE,(1969, Braz.)
Margo Lico
ALIBI, THE(1939, Fr.)
Gabriella Licudi
FALL OF THE ROMAN EMPIRE, THE(1964); UNEARTHLY STRANGER, THE(1964, Brit.); YOU MUST BE JOKING!(1965, Brit.); LIQUIDATOR, THE(1966, Brit.); CASINO ROYALE(1967, Brit.); JOKERS, THE(1967, Brit.); LAST SAFARI, THE(1967, Brit.); HEROSTRATUS(1968, Brit.); UNDERCOVERS HERO(1975, Brit.)
Choko Lida
DRUNKEN ANGEL(1948, Jap.); HONOLULU-TOKYO-HONG KONG(1963, Hong Kong/Jap.)
Anna Lidakova
DESERTER AND THE NOMADS, THE(1969, Czech./Ital.), cos
Eric Lidberg
HELLCATS, THE(1968); FIVE THE HARD WAY(1969)
Don Liddel
PRELUDE TO FAME(1950, Brit.)
Alvar Liddell
WE'LL MEET AGAIN(1942, Brit.); SCHOOL FOR SECRETS(1946, Brit.); YANK IN LONDON, A(1946, Brit.); IT HAPPENED HERE(1966, Brit.)
Jane Liddell
ROGUE RIVER(1951); SMALL TOWN GIRL(1953); WESTWARD HO THE WAGONS!(1956)
Laura Liddell
SHAKESPEARE WALLAH(1966, India)
Francesca Liddi
SENSUALITA(1954, Ital.)
Gary Liddiard
WAY WE WERE, THE(1973), makeup; MORE DEAD THAN ALIVE(1968), makeup; SUPPOSE THEY GAVE A WAR AND NOBODY CAME?(1970), makeup; JEREMIAH JOHNSON(1972), makeup; LADY ICE(1973), makeup; GREAT WALDO PEPPER, THE(1975), makeup
Gary D. Liddiard
WAR BETWEEN MEN AND WOMEN, THE(1972), makeup
1984
MICKI AND MAUDE(1984), makeup
Keith Liddiard
MC KENZIE BREAK, THE(1970), set d
Gail Liddle
TROUBLE WITH ANGELS, THE(1966); WILD RIDERS(1971)
Ralph Liddle
SPIRIT OF THE WIND(1979), d, w
Bill Liddy
1984
VIGIL(1984, New Zealand)
James Liddy
LAST OF THE LONE WOLF(1930)
Alvar Lidell
THEY MET IN THE DARK(1945, Brit.); COUNTERFEIT PLAN, THE(1957, Brit.)
Katarina Lidfeldt
STATUE, THE(1971, Brit.)
Gary Lidiard
CANDIDATE, THE(1972), makeup
Bruce Lidington
1984
SWORD OF THE VALIANT(1984, Brit.)
Pini Lido
EVIL EYE(1964 Ital.)
Jon Lidolt
CRIMES OF THE FUTURE(1969, Can.)
Ferdinando Lidonni
MADAME BUTTERFLY(1955 Ital./Jap.)
Anna Marie Lie
OPERATION LOVEBIRDS(1968, Den.)

Henry Lie
MURDER IN THE MUSIC HALL(1946)

Harry Lieb
SKINNER STEPS OUT(1929), ed; DAMES AHOY(1930), ed; LITTLE AC-CIDENT(1930), ed; HOMICIDE SQUAD(1931), ed

Harry W. Lieb
MANY A SLIP(1931), ed; RECKLESS LIVING(1931), ed; AIR MAIL(1932), ed

Henry Lieb
RADIO PATROL(1932), ed

Herman Lieb
Misc. Silents
DAYBREAK(1918)

Morris Lieb
TWO GALS AND A GUY(1951)

Robert Lieb
SOMEBODY UP THERE LIKES ME(1956); PORTRAIT IN BLACK(1960); BRASS BOTTLE, THE(1964); READY FOR THE PEOPLE(1964); CLAMBAKE(1967); ANGEL IN MY POCKET(1969); LOVE GOD?, THE(1969)

Robert P. Lieb
UNDERWORLD U.S.A.(1961); FORTUNE COOKIE, THE(1966); HOW TO FRAME A FIGG(1971)

Tom Lieb
TOUCHDOWN!(1931)

W. Harry Lieb
SEE AMERICA THIRST(1930), ed

Warren Lieb
TWIST ALL NIGHT(1961), ph

Hapsburg Liebe
Silents
DOWN UPON THE SUWANNEE RIVER(1925), w

Wolfgang Liebeneiner
ONE APRIL 2000(1952, Aust.), d; APRIL 1, 2000(1953, Aust.), d; DANCING HEART, THE(1959, Ger.), d&w; TRAPP FAMILY, THE(1961, Ger.), d

Jorg von Liebenfels
JAIL BAIT(1977, Ger.)

Fritz Lieber
YOUTH RUNS WILD(1944); ADVENTURES OF CASANOVA(1948); INNER SANC-TUM(1948)

Joel Lieber
MOVE(1970), w

Marvin Lieber
HUNGRY WIVES(1973)

Mimi Lieber
NIGHT SHIFT(1982)

Paul Lieber
GURU, THE MAD MONK(1971); LOOKING UP(1977)

Art Lieberman
Misc. Talkies
UP YOUR ALLEY(1975), d; MELON AFFAIR, THE(1979), d

Bradley Lieberman
HOMETOWN U.S.A.(1979); PANDEMONIUM(1982)

Frank Lieberman
MOUSE ON THE MOON, THE(1963, Brit.); DUTCHMAN(1966, Brit.); BATTLE BENEATH THE EARTH(1968, Brit.)

Jeff Lieberman
BLADE(1973), w; SQUIRM(1976), d&w; BLUE SUNSHINE(1978), d&w; JUST BEFORE DAWN(1980), d

Leo Lieberman
YANK IN KOREA, A(1951), w; BONZO GOES TO COLLEGE(1952), w; CARNIVAL ROCK(1957), w

Lou Lieberman
SORORITY GIRL(1957), w

Manny Lieberman
HERE COME THE TIGERS(1978)

Rick Lieberman
SO FINE(1981); SOUP FOR ONE(1982)

Robert Lieberman
TABLE FOR FIVE(1983), d

Rolf Liebermann
DER FREISCHUTZ(1970, Ger.), p; FIDELIO(1970, Ger.), p; MARRIAGE OF FIGARO, THE(1970, Ger.), p

Goddard Lieberson
THREE FOR BEDROOM C(1952), d&w

Sandy Lieberson
LAST DAYS OF MAN ON EARTH, THE(1975, Brit.), p; JABBERWOCKY(1977, Brit.), p; LONG SHOT(1981, Brit.)

Sanford Lieberson
PIED PIPER, THE(1972, Brit.), p; STARDUST(1974, Brit.), p; THAT'LL BE THE DAY(1974, Brit.), p

Bertrand Liebert
1984
FIRST NAME: CARMEN(1984, Fr.)

Billy Liebert
HANG YOUR HAT ON THE WIND(1969), m

Else Liebesburg
LIFE AND LOVES OF MOZART, THE(1959, Ger.)

B. Liebgold
YIDDLE WITH HIS FIDDLE(1937, Pol.)

L. Liebgold
YIDDLE WITH HIS FIDDLE(1937, Pol.)

Leon Liebgold
TEVYA(1939)
Misc. Talkies
KOL NIDRE(1939)

Franziska Liebing
UNWILLING AGENT(1968, Ger.); WILLY WONKA AND THE CHOCOLATE FACTO-RY(1971)

Theodore A. Liebler, Jr.
Silents
SUCCESS(1923), w

A.J. Liebling
RING AROUND THE CLOCK(1953, Ital.), titles

Joe Liebman
I COULD NEVER HAVE SEX WITH ANY MAN WHO HAS SO LITTLE REGARD FOR MY HUSBAND(1973), m

Joseph Liebman
FORCE OF IMPULSE(1961), m; LIGHT FANTASTIC(1964), m

Max Liebman
ZIEGFELD FOLLIES(1945), w

Robert Liebman
HEART SONG(1933, Brit.), w; CARAVAN(1934), w; LILIOM(1935, Fr.), w

Ron Liebman
UP THE ACADEMY(1980)
1984
DOOR TO DOOR(1984); RHINESTONE(1984)

Norm Liebmann
DISORDERLY ORDERLY, THE(1964), w

Robert Liebmann
BLUE ANGEL, THE(1930, Ger.), w; LOVE WALTZ, THE(1930, Ger.), w; IMMORTAL VAGABOND(1931, Ger.), w; CONGRESS DANCES(1932, Ger.), w; TEMPEST(1932, Ger.), w; EARLY TO BED(1933, Brit./Ger.), w; EMPRESS AND I, THE(1933, Ger.), w; BLUE ANGEL, THE(1959), w

Wieland Liebske
END OF THE GAME(1976, Ger./Ital.)

James Liecester
ENCHANTED ISLAND(1958), w

Hans Liechti
DEATH OF MARIO RICCI, THE(1983, Ital.), ph

Uldis Liedldidzh
CHEREZ TERNII K SVEZDAM(1981 USSR)

Jose Liedra
POLITICAL ASYLUM(1975, Mex./Guatemalan)

Harry Liedtke
Silents
PASSION(1920, Ger.); ONE ARABIAN NIGHT(1921, Ger.)
Misc. Silents
OYSTER PRINCESS, THE(1919, Ger.); GYPSY BLOOD(1921, Ger.); VENDETTA(1921, Ger.); DEVIL'S PAWN, THE(1922, Ger.); WIFE OF THE PHARAOH, THE(1922, Ger.); LITTLE NAPOLEON, THE(1923, Ger.); MADAME WANTS NO CHILDREN(1927, Ger.)

Henry Liedtke
Misc. Silents
LAST PAYMENT(1921, Ger.)

Hillary Lief
HUMAN FACTOR, THE(1975)

J.O. Lief
TWO FOR TONIGHT(1935), w

Max Lief
UNEXPECTED FATHER(1932), w; CONVENTION GIRL(1935), w; TWO FOR TO-NIGHT(1935), w; SLEEPYTIME GAL(1942), w

Henry Lieferant
DOCTORS' WIVES(1931), w

Sylva Lieferant
DOCTORS' WIVES(1931), w

Karl Lieffen
BEGGAR STUDENT, THE(1958, Ger.); ONE, TWO, THREE(1961); HAMLET(1962, Ger.); MAN WHO WALKED THROUGH THE WALL, THE(1964, Ger.); PHONY AMERICAN, THE(1964, Ger.); DEFECTOR, THE(1966, Ger./Fr.); JACK OF DIA-MONDS(1967, U.S./Ger.)

Don Liegerman
WATER RUSTLERS(1939), p

Lo Lieh
FIVE FINGERS OF DEATH(1973, Hong Kong)

Didi Liekov
JESUS CHRIST, SUPERSTAR(1973)

Cecile Lieman
NESTING, THE(1981)

Frode Lien
DOLL'S HOUSE, A(1973, Brit.)

Mai Thi Lien
DON'T CRY, IT'S ONLY THUNDER(1982)

Robert Liensol
SNOW(1983, Fr.)

Fritz Liepe
1984
NIGHTSONGS(1984), ed

Karl Liepinsc
WATERLOO(1970, Ital./USSR)

Karel Lier
MURDER CZECH STYLE(1968, Czech.), art d

Wolfried Lier
GREAT BRITISH TRAIN ROBBERY, THE(1967, Ger.); SOMETHING FOR EVERY-ONE(1970)

Hal Lierley
CHICAGO DEADLINE(1949), makeup; RETURN OF THE FLY(1959), makeup; TWO LITTLE BEARS, THE(1961), makeup; PICTURE MOMMY DEAD(1966), makeup; WICKED DREAMS OF PAULA SCHULTZ, THE(1968), makeup

Hal Lierly
HEIRESS, THE(1949), makeup

Harold Lierly
SAMSON AND DELILAH(1949), makeup

Ernest Liesenhoff
PIPPI IN THE SOUTH SEAS(1974, Swed./Ger.), p

Ernst Liesenhoff
JIMMY ORPHEUS(1966, Ger.), p

Geoffrey Liesik
  NIGHT CROSSING(1982)
Michael Liesik
  NIGHT CROSSING(1982)
Trude Lieske
  RENDEZ-VOUS(1932, Ger.)
Wera Liessem
  TESTAMENT OF DR. MABUSE, THE(1943, Ger.)
Virginia Lieth
  HERE COME THE GIRLS(1953)
Brian Lietz
  GAL YOUNG UN(1979)
Mario Lieu
  SKATETOWN, U.S.A.(1979)
Albert Lieven
  VICTORIA THE GREAT(1937, Brit.); SPY FOR A DAY(1939, Brit.); CONVOY(1940); FOR FREEDOM(1940, Brit.); LET GEORGE DO IT(1940, Brit.); NIGHT TRAIN(1940, Brit.); GIRL IN DISTRESS(1941, Brit.); NEUTRAL PORT(1941, Brit.); BIG BLOCKADE, THE(1942, Brit.); YOUNG MR. PITT, THE(1942, Brit.); YELLOW CANARY, THE(1944, Brit.); COLONEL BLIMP(1945, Brit.); BEWARE OF PITY(1946, Brit.); SEVENTH VEIL, THE(1946, Brit.); FRIEDA(1947, Brit.); HER MAN GILBEY(1949, Brit.); SLEEPING CAR TO TRIESTE(1949, Brit.); DARK LIGHT, THE(1951, Brit.); HOTEL SAHARA(1951, Brit.); DESPERATE MOMENT(1953, Brit.); LOSER TAKES ALL(1956, Brit.); DEVIL'S GENERAL, THE(1957, Ger.); HOUSE OF INTRIGUE, THE(1959, Ital.); SUBWAY IN THE SKY(1959, Brit.); CONSPIRACY OF HEARTS(1960, Brit.); FOXHOLE IN CAIRO(1960, Brit.); THREE MOVES TO FREEDOM(1960, Ger.); BRAINWASHED(1961, Ger.); DEVIL'S DAFFODIL, THE(1961, Brit./Ger.); GUNS OF NAVARONE, THE(1961); DEATH TRAP(1962, Brit.); MYSTERY SUBMARINE(1963, Brit.); SANDERS(1963, Brit.); VICTORS, THE(1963); CITY OF FEAR(1965, Brit.); TRAITOR'S GATE(1966, Brit./Ger.); RIDE THE HIGH WIND(1967, South Africa)
Domenic Lieven
  TOWN LIKE ALICE, A(1958, Brit.)
Tatiana Lieven
  YELLOW CANARY, THE(1944, Brit.)
Fred Liewehr
  STORY OF VICKIE, THE(1958, Aust.); EMBEZZLED HEAVEN(1959,Ger.)
Eva Liewellyn
Silents
  PRIDE OF THE NORTH, THE(1920, Brit.)
Boris Lifanov
Misc. Silents
  KATORGA(1928, USSR)
Jose Ruis Lifante
  DON'T OPEN THE WINDOW(1974, Ital.)
Serge Lifar
  LIVING CORPSE, THE(1940, Fr.), ch; CRIME DOES NOT PAY(1962, Fr.); TESTAMENT OF ORPHEUS, THE(1962, Fr.)

Joel Lifschultz
  SWEET ECSTASY(1962, Fr.), p
Joel Lifschutz
  EROTIQUE(1969, Fr.), p; PLAYMATES(1969, Fr./Ital.), p
Amnon Lifshitz
  FAITHFUL CITY(1952, Israel)
Bob Lifton
  IF EVER I SEE YOU AGAIN(1978)
Robert K. Lifton
  EDDIE AND THE CRUISERS(1983), p
Gyorgi Ligeti
1984
  2010(1984), m
Gyorgy Ligeti
  SHINING, THE(1980), m
Juliska Ligeti
  SUN SHINES, THE(1939, Hung.)
Grover Liggen
  ST. LOUIS KID, THE(1934)
Amelia Liggett
  SARATOGA TRUNK(1945)
Louis Liggett
  STREET ANGEL(1928)
Tommy G. Liggins
1984
  SOLDIER'S STORY, A(1984)
Grover Liggon
  MILLION DOLLAR COLLAR, THE(1929); FATHER'S SON(1931); TIME OUT FOR ROMANCE(1937)
Blanche Light
Silents
  PENROD(1922)
James Light
  NAGANA(1933), w
Joe Light
  CHASTITY(1969)
Letty Light
  WHERE THERE'S LIFE(1947)
Pamela Light
  UNTIL THEY SAIL(1957); IN THE MONEY(1958); MIDNIGHT LACE(1960); ON THE DOUBLE(1961)
Robert Light
  GENTLEMEN ARE BORN(1934); MURDER IN THE CLOUDS(1934); CEILNG ZERO(1935); MARY JANE'S PA(1935); RECKLESS(1935); SHIPMATES FOREVER(1935); WOMEN MUST DRESS(1935); DOUGHNUTS AND SOCIETY(1936); MY MAN GODFREY(1936)
Light Crust Doughboys Band
  OH, SUSANNA(1937)

Fletcher Lightfoot
  GLIMPSE OF PARADISE, A(1934, Brit.); MADNESS OF THE HEART(1949, Brit.); LONG DARK HALL, THE(1951, Brit.); PENNY PRINCESS(1953, Brit.)
Gordon Lightfoot
  HARRY TRACY-DESPERADO(1982, Can.)
Leonard C. Lightfoot
  TENTACLES(1977, Ital.)
Leonard Lightfoot
  CUTTER AND BONE(1981)
Linda Lightfoot
  TONIGHT FOR SURE(1962)
William Lightfoot
  TOMBOY AND THE CHAMP(1961), p, w
Stephen Lighthill
  OVER-UNDER, SIDEWAYS-DOWN(1977), ph
Lighting
Misc. Silents
  ONE SHOT RANGER(1925)
Frances Lightner
Silents
  PUPPETS(1926), w
Fred Lightner
  BABE RUTH STORY, THE(1948)
Richard Lightner
  SPRINGFIELD RIFLE(1952)
Winnie Lightner
  GOLD DIGGERS OF BROADWAY(1929); HOLD EVERYTHING(1930); LIFE OF THE PARTY, THE(1930); SHE COULDN'T SAY NO(1930); GOLD DUST GERTIE(1931); MANHATTAN PARADE(1931); SIDE SHOW(1931); SIT TIGHT(1931); PLAY GIRL(1932); DANCING LADY(1933); SHE HAD TO SAY YES(1933); I'LL FIX IT(1934)
Lightning
  DOG OF FLANDERS, A(1935); WHITE FANG(1936)
Silents
  LURE OF THE WILD, THE(1925)
Lightning the Dog
  TWO IN REVOLT(1936); RENFREW OF THE ROYAL MOUNTED(1937)
Lightning the Horse
Misc. Talkies
  MAN'S BEST FRIEND(1935)
Duryea Lighton
Silents
  APRIL SHOWERS(1923), w
Louis Lighton
  ALL OF ME(1934), p
Louis B. Lighton
Silents
  EAST SIDE–WEST SIDE(1923), w
Louis D. Lighton
  SHOPWORN ANGEL, THE(1928), p; DANGEROUS WOMAN(1929), p; VIRGINIAN, THE(1929), p; SEVEN DAYS LEAVE(1930), p; TOM SAWYER(1930), p; SKIPPY(1931), p; IF I HAD A MILLION(1932), p; ALICE IN WONDERLAND(1933), p; ONE SUNDAY AFTERNOON(1933), p; ELMER AND ELSIE(1934), p; NOW AND FOREVER(1934), p; YOU BELONG TO ME(1934), p; ANNAPOLIS FAREWELL(1935), p; LIVES OF A BENGAL LANCER(1935), p; PETER IBBETSON(1935), p; COLLEGIATE(1936), p; TROUBLE FOR TWO(1936), p; CAPTAINS COURAGEOUS(1937), p; MAN-PROOF(1938), p; TEST PILOT(1938), p; LUCKY NIGHT(1939), p; BELL FOR ADANO, A(1945), p; TREE GROWS IN BROOKLYN, A(1945), p; ANNA AND THE KING OF SIAM(1946), p; HOME SWEET HOMICIDE(1946), p; DOWN TO THE SEA IN SHIPS(1949), p; BLACK ROSE, THE(1950), p; NO HIGHWAY IN THE SKY(1951, Brit.), p
Silents
  BOY OF MINE(1923), w, t; DON'T MARRY FOR MONEY(1923), w; VIRGINIAN, THE(1923), w; HELEN'S BABIES(1924), w; K-THE UNKNOWN(1924), w; LULLABY, THE(1924), w; HIS SECRETARY(1925), w; LITTLE ANNIE ROONEY(1925), w; RANGER OF THE BIG PINES(1925), w; CAT'S PAJAMAS, THE(1926), w; CHILDREN OF DIVORCE(1927), w; IT(1927), w; TWO FLAMING YOUTHS(1927), sup; WINGS(1927), w
Louis Duryea Lighton
Silents
  PAID BACK(1922), w; BLIND GODDESS, THE(1926), w; RAINMAKER, THE(1926), w
Leonard Lightstone
  IDOL, THE(1966, Brit.), p; SPY WITH A COLD NOSE, THE(1966, Brit.), p
Marilyn Lightstone
  LIES MY FATHER TOLD ME(1975, Can.); IN PRAISE OF OLDER WOMEN(1978, Can.); HEAVY METAL(1981, Can.); SPASMS(1983, Can.)
1984
  SURROGATE, THE(1984, Can.)
Peter Lightstone
  TOYS ARE NOT FOR CHILDREN(1972)
Jack Lightsy
  48 HOURS(1982)
Hamid Lighvani
  CARAVANS(1978, U.S./Iranian)
Guy Ligier
  GRAND PRIX(1966)
Laurence Ligneres
  SUITOR, THE(1963, Fr.); MY WIFE'S HUSBAND(1965, Fr./Ital.); FRENCH POSTCARDS(1979)
G. G. Ligon
Silents
  TILLIE'S PUNCTURED ROMANCE(1914)
Tom Ligon
  NOTHING BUT A MAN(1964); PAINT YOUR WAGON(1969); JUMP(1971); BANG THE DRUM SLOWLY(1973); LAST AMERICAN HERO, THE(1973); JOYRIDE(1977); YOUNG DOCTORS IN LOVE(1982)
Al Ligouri
Silents
  EMBARRASSMENT OF RICHES, THE(1918), ph; ROMANCE OF THE AIR, A(1919), ph; STRAIGHT IS THE WAY(1921), ph; WOMAN GOD CHANGED, THE(1921), ph;

TIMOTHY'S QUEST(1922), ph

Mitsos Liguisos
NEVER ON SUNDAY(1960, Gr.)

Alfonso Liguori
SHE-DEVIL ISLAND(1936, Mex.), w
Silents
INNOCENT LIE, THE(1916), ph

Emilie Lihou
FIVE DAYS ONE SUMMER(1982)

Lucita Lijertwood
LEO THE LAST(1970, Brit.); PRESSURE(1976, Brit.); SQUEEZE, THE(1977, Brit.)

Robert Likala
NAKED WITCH, THE(1964)

Ralph Like
FIRST AID(1931), p

Ralph M. Like
ANYBODY'S BLONDE(1931), p; CHINATOWN AFTER DARK(1931), p; SOUL OF THE SLUMS(1931), p; DOCKS OF SAN FRANCISCO(1932), p; DRAGNET PATROL(1932), p; GORILLA SHIP, THE(1932), p; NIGHT BEAT(1932), p; SIN'S PAYDAY(1932), p; TANGLED DESTINIES(1932), p; WIDOW IN SCARLET(1932), p

Don Likes
Silents
WOODEN SHOES(1917)

V.A. Likhachov
WATERLOO(1970, Ital./USSR), spec eff

Vladimir Likhachyov
WAR AND PEACE(1968, USSR)

Tatyana Likhachyova
DESTINY OF A MAN(1961, USSR), ed; WAR AND PEACE(1968, USSR), ed

N. Likhobabina
MEET ME IN MOSCOW(1966, USSR)

John Likoxitch
SHIRLEY THOMPSON VERSUS THE ALIENS(1968, Aus.)

Princess Lilamani
ROMAN HOLIDAY(1953)

Suzanne Lilar
BENVENUTA(1983, Fr.), w

Prinya Lilason
1 2 3 MONSTER EXPRESS(1977, Thai.), d

James Lilburn
QUIET MAN, THE(1952); WHAT PRICE GLORY?(1952); DESERT RATS, THE(1953); SAN ANTONE(1953); TITANIC(1953); FIRE OVER AFRICA(1954, Brit.); JUBILEE TRAIL(1954); AT GUNPOINT(1955); FORT YUMA(1955); HELL'S OUTPOST(1955); SEA CHASE, THE(1955); BATTLE STATIONS(1956); MOHAWK(1956)

Jim Lilburn
SUDDENLY(1954)

Ford Lile
HARD RIDE, THE(1971)

John Lilern
BIG TOWN(1932)

James Liles
LAST CHASE, THE(1981), spec eff

Myrna Liles
DEVIL SHIP(1947)

Randy Liles
SHADOWS(1960), set d

Ronald Liles
GAOLBREAK(1962, Brit.), p; SHADOW OF FEAR(1963, Brit.), w; SICILIANS, THE(1964, Brit.), p, w; BLOOD BEAST FROM OUTER SPACE(1965, Brit.), p; ISLAND OF THE BURNING DAMNED(1971, Brit.), w

Ronald C. Liles
DANGER BY MY SIDE(1962, Brit.), w

Lloyd Lilford
GOLD(1974, Brit.)

Lili
1984
SCARRED(1984)

Mona Lilian
SLEEPING CAR TO TRIESTE(1949, Brit.); TRACK THE MAN DOWN(1956, Brit.); LIST OF ADRIAN MESSENGER, THE(1963)

Lili Liliana
DYBBUK THE(1938, Pol.)
Misc. Talkies
KOL NIDRE(1939)

Kurt Lilien
CASE VAN GELDERN(1932, Ger.); JOHNNY STEALS EUROPE(1932, Ger.)

Nat Lilienstein
NAKED HEARTS(1970, Fr.)

David Lilienthal
NORMAN LOVES ROSE(1982, Aus.)

Peter Lilienthal
AMERICAN FRIEND, THE(1977, Ger.); DAVID(1979, Ger.), d, w; DEAR MR. WONDERFUL(1983, Ger.), d

E. Lilina
ON HIS OWN(1939, USSR)

Eve Lilith
STACY'S KNIGHTS(1983)

Liliveva
Misc. Silents
ABORTION(1924, USSR)

Staffan Liljander
EMIGRANTS, THE(1972, Swed.)

Synnove Liljeback
DEAR JOHN(1966, Swed.)

Marie Liljedahl
DORIAN GRAY(1970, Ital./Brit./Ger./Liechtenstein)

Denis Lill
EAGLE HAS LANDED, THE(1976, Brit.)

Lill-Acke
WALPURGIS NIGHT(1941, Swed.)

Lillane & Mario
EARL CARROLL'S VANITIES(1945)

Tom Lillard
Misc. Talkies
BRIG, THE(1965)

Clint Lilley
USED CARS(1980)

Edward Lilley
HONEYMOON LODGE(1943), d; LARCENY WITH MUSIC(1943), d; MOONLIGHT IN VERMONT(1943), d; NEVER A DULL MOMENT(1943), d; SING A JINGLE(1943), p&d; YOU'RE A LUCKY FELLOW, MR. SMITH(1943), p; BABES ON SWING STREET(1944), d; MY GAL LOVES MUSIC(1944), p&d; HER LUCKY NIGHT(1945), d; SWING OUT, SISTER(1945), d

Edward C. Lilley
SWEET SURRENDER(1935), w; HI, GOOD-LOOKIN'(1944), d

Edward Clark Lilley
LADIES' DAY(1943), w

Jack Lilley
METEOR(1979)

Joe Lilley
GIRLS! GIRLS! GIRLS!(1962), m

Joseph Lilley
LI'L ABNER(1959), md; BLUE HAWAII(1961), m

Joseph J. Lilley
FOREST RANGERS, THE(1942), m; VARIETY GIRL(1947), md; ISN'T IT ROMANTIC?(1948), md; GREAT LOVER, THE(1949), m&md; RED, HOT AND BLUE(1949), md; MR. MUSIC(1950), m; HERE COMES THE GROOM(1951), md; MATING SEASON, THE(1951), m; SAILOR BEWARE(1951), md; ROAD TO BALI(1952), md; STOOGE, THE(1952), md; CADDY, THE(1953), md; SCARED STIFF(1953), md; RED GARTERS(1954), md; WHITE CHRISTMAS(1954), md; SEVEN LITTLE FOYS, THE(1955), md; THAT CERTAIN FEELING(1956), m, md; BEAU JAMES(1957), m; ALIAS JESSE JAMES(1959), md; G.I. BLUES(1960), md; FUN IN ACAPULCO(1963), m; PAPA'S DELICATE CONDITION(1963), m, md; WHO'S MINDING THE STORE?(1963), m; DISORDERLY ORDERLY, THE(1964), m; PARADISE, HAWAIIAN STYLE(1966), m; EASY COME, EASY GO(1967), m; HOW TO COMMIT MARRIAGE(1969), m, md, md

Joseph L. Lilley
CROSS MY HEART(1946), md; PARIS HOLIDAY(1958), m, md; ROUSTABOUT(1964), m

Katie Lilley
CHANT OF JIMMIE BLACKSMITH, THE(1980, Aus.)

Merv Lilley
LAST WAVE, THE(1978, Aus.)

Peter Lilley
MAN WITH THE MAGNETIC EYES, THE(1945, Brit.); CAESAR AND CLEOPATRA(1946, Brit.)

Rose Lilley
JOURNEY AMONG WOMEN(1977, Aus.)

Rosie Lilley
CHANT OF JIMMIE BLACKSMITH, THE(1980, Aus.)

Val Lilley
1984
SCRUBBERS(1984, Brit.)

Harry Lillford
Silents
$5,000,000 COUNTERFEITING PLOT, THE(1914)

Lillian
LIFE BEGINS AT 40(1935), cos; MAEVA(1961)

Anna Lillian
WHERE IS MY CHILD?(1937)

DeWitt Lillibridge
Silents
OUT OF THE DRIFTS(1916)

W. Lillibridge
Silents
WHERE THE TRAIL DIVIDES(1914), w

Beatrice Lillie
THOROUGHLY MODERN MILLIE(1967); ARE YOU THERE?(1930); DR. RHYTHM(1938); ON APPROVAL(1944, Brit.); AROUND THE WORLD IN 80 DAYS(1956)
Silents
EXIT SMILING(1926)

George Lillie
PAPER MOON(1973)

Torsten Lilliecrona
LESSON IN LOVE, A(1960, Swed.)

Jane Lillig
1984
LIES(1984, Brit.)

Ursula Lillig
GIRL FROM HONG KONG(1966, Ger.); IN A YEAR OF THIRTEEN MOONS(1980, Ger.)

Jo Ann Lilliquist
SPOILERS OF THE FOREST(1957)

James Lillis
SIN OF MONA KENT, THE(1961), ph

Lisa Lillot
MOONLIGHTING WIVES(1966)

Lilly
INCREDIBLY STRANGE CREATURES WHO STOPPED LIVING AND BECAME CRAZY MIXED-UP ZOMBIES, THE(1965), makeup

Andra Lilly
THOMASINE AND BUSHROD(1974), cos

Edward Lilly
ALLERGIC TO LOVE(1943), d

Paul Lilly
KISS OF DEATH(1947)
Susan Lilly
GETTING EVEN(1981), cos
Peter Lily
HOLIDAYS WITH PAY(1948, Brit.)
Lilyan and Malo
KING OF HEARTS(1936, Brit.)
Leonard Lilyholm
ICE CASTLES(1978)
Jang Lim
SISTERS, THE(1938)
Jing Lim
ONCE UPON A TIME(1944)
Judy Lim
SAINT JACK(1979)
Jung Lim
PEKING EXPRESS(1951)
Kwam Hi Lim
SEVEN(1979)
Kwan Hi Lim
UNCOMMON VALOR(1983)
Mabel Lim
HUNTERS, THE(1958)
Nona Jane Lim
Misc. Talkies
I REMEMBER LOVE(1981)
Pik-Sen Lim
GLADIATORS, THE(1970, Swed.)
Swee Lim
DARK CRYSTAL, THE(1982, Brit.)
Altair Lima
XICA(1982, Braz.)
Ana Lucia Lima
1984
BLAME IT ON RIO(1984)
Brian Lima
TWO PEOPLE(1973)
1984
FIRSTBORN(1984)
Carlo Lima
MYTH, THE(1965, Ital.)
Danny Lima
1984
POLICE ACADEMY(1984)
Elyane Lima
DEVOTION(1946)
Jim Adhi Lima
1984
PERILS OF GWENDOLINE, THE(1984, Fr.)
Jose Maria Lima
BYE-BYE BRASIL(1980, Braz.)
Walter Lima, Jr.
BRASIL ANNO 2,000(1968, Braz.), p,d&w
Jim Adhi Limas
DIVA(1982, Fr.)
Limau the Tiger
JUNGLE PRINCESS, THE(1936)
Bobby Limb
SUNSTRUCK(1973, Aus.)
Harold Lime
DEATHMASTER, THE(1972), ed
Yvonne Lime
RAINMAKER, THE(1956); I WAS A TEENAGE WEREWOLF(1957); LOVING
YOU(1957); UNTAMED YOUTH(1957); DRAGSTRIP RIOT(1958); HIGH SCHOOL
HELLCATS(1958); SPEED CRAZY(1959)
Annalena Limentani
PAISAN(1948, Ital.), w
Angel Arturo Limon
TOM THUMB(1967, Mex.)
W.P. Limpscomb
TILLY OF BLOOMSBURY(1931, Brit.), w
Beru-Bera Lin
GODZILLA VERSUS THE COSMIC MONSTER(1974, Jap.)
F. Kenneth Lin
WAR OF THE WIZARDS(1983, Taiwan), w
Louise Lin
INN OF THE SIXTH HAPPINESS, THE(1958)
Nandrea Lin
1984
ALPHABET CITY(1984)
Tung Lin
FIVE FINGERS OF DEATH(1973, Hong Kong)
Yao Lin-shum
1984
AH YING(1984, Hong Kong)
Kay Linaker
EASY MONEY(1936); GIRL FROM MANDALAY(1936); MURDER OF DR. HARRI-
GAN, THE(1936); ROAD GANG(1936); BLACK ACES(1937); CHARLIE CHAN AT
MONTE CARLO(1937); CRACK-UP, THE(1937); OUTER GATE, THE(1937); LAST
WARNING, THE(1938); PERSONAL SECRETARY(1938); TRADE WINDS(1938);
CHARLIE CHAN IN RENO(1939); DRUMS ALONG THE MOHAWK(1939); GIRL
FROM RIO, THE(1939); HEAVEN WITH A BARBED WIRE FENCE(1939); HOTEL
FOR WOMEN(1939); I AM A CRIMINAL(1939); MAN ABOUT TOWN(1939); YOUNG
MR. LINCOLN(1939); BUCK BENNY RIDES AGAIN(1940); CHARLIE CHAN'S MUR-
DER CRUISE(1940); FREE, BLONDE AND 21(1940); GREEN HELL(1940); HIDDEN
ENEMY(1940); KITTY FOYLE(1940); MYSTERY SEA RAIDER(1940); BLOOD AND
SAND(1941); CHARLIE CHAN IN RIO(1941); INVISIBLE WOMAN, THE(1941);
PRIVATE NURSE(1941); REMEMBER THE DAY(1941); THEY DARE NOT LO-
VE(1941); CINDERELLA SWINGS IT(1942); CLOSE CALL FOR ELLERY QUEEN,

A(1942); MEN OF TEXAS(1942); NIGHT BEFORE THE DIVORCE, THE(1942); PRIDE
OF THE ARMY(1942); WAR DOGS(1942); HAPPY GO LUCKY(1943); LET'S FACE
IT(1943); MORE THE MERRIER, THE(1943); TWO WEEKS TO LIVE(1943); WINTER-
TIME(1943); HERE COME THE WAVES(1944); LADY IN THE DARK(1944); LAU-
RA(1944); MEN ON HER MIND(1944)
Misc. Talkies
BEHIND PRISON BARS(1937)
Ninette Linar
THEY WERE TEN(1961, Israel)
Antonio Navarro Linares
SWORD OF EL CID, THE(1965, Span./Ital.), w
Nancy Linari
UNCOMMON VALOR(1983)
John Lince
Silents
DEVIL DODGER, THE(1917); BY PROXY(1918); I LOVE YOU(1918); STOP
THIEF(1920); GUILE OF WOMEN(1921); HUNTRESS, THE(1923)
Misc. Silents
REGENERATES, THE(1917); ALL AROUND FRYING PAN(1925)
Tom Lincir
MY SISTER EILEEN(1942); THEY ALL KISSED THE BRIDE(1942)
A. Lincoln
Misc. Silents
MASTER PASSION, THE(1917)
Abbey Lincoln
GIRL CAN'T HELP IT, THE(1956); NOTHING BUT A MAN(1964); FOR LOVE OF
IVY(1968)
Alpheus Lincoln
Misc. Silents
DETERMINATION(1922)
Caryl Lincoln
LAND OF MISSING MEN, THE(1930); AT THE RIDGE(1931); CYCLONE KID(1931);
MAN FROM NEW MEXICO, THE(1932); OKAY AMERICA(1932); THRILL OF
YOUTH(1932); WAR OF THE RANGE(1933); KID MILLIONS(1934); MERRY WIDOW,
THE(1934); GOLDEN EARRINGS(1947); JACKPOT, THE(1950); MOTHER DIDN'T
TELL ME(1950); LOVE NEST(1951)
Misc. Talkies
QUICK TRIGGER LEE(1931); TANGLED FORTUNES(1932); MAN OF ACTION(1933)
Silents
GIRL IN EVERY PORT, A(1928)
Misc. Silents
WOLF FANGS(1927); HELLO CHEYENE(1928); TRACKED(1928); WILD WEST
ROMANCE(1928)
Charles Lincoln
KNIGHT IN LONDON, A(1930, Brit./Ger.), w; MURDER TOMORROW(1938, Brit.);
TREACHERY ON THE HIGH SEAS(1939, Brit.), w
Misc. Silents
STREETS OF LONDON, THE(1929, Brit.)
E.K. [Elmo] Lincoln
Silents
WOMAN GOD CHANGED, THE(1921); LIGHT IN THE DARK, THE(1922)
Misc. Silents
LITTLEST REBEL, THE(1914); ALMIGHTY DOLLAR, THE(1916); WORLD
AGAINST HIM, THE(1916); FOR THE FREEDOM OF THE WORLD(1917); BELOVED
TRAITOR, THE(1918); LAFAYETTE, WE COME!(1918); DESERT GOLD(1919); PAINT-
ED WORLD, THE(1919); SHADOWS OF THE PAST(1919); UNKNOWN LOVE,
THE(1919); VIRTUOUS MEN(1919); INNER VOICE, THE(1920); DEVOTION(1921);
MAN OF COURAGE(1922); WOMEN MEN MARRY(1922); LITTLE RED SCHOOL-
HOUSE, THE(1923); WOMAN IN CHAINS, THE(1923); RIGHT OF THE STRONGEST,
THE(1924); MY NEIGHBOR'S WIFE(1925)
Elmo Lincoln
COLORADO SUNSET(1939); REAL GLORY, THE(1939); TIMBER STAMPEDE(1939);
UNION PACIFIC(1939); WYOMING OUTLAW(1939); STAGE TO CHINO(1940); TAR-
ZAN'S NEW YORK ADVENTURE(1942); STORY OF DR. WASSELL, THE(1944);
WHEN THE LIGHTS GO ON AGAIN(1944); MAN WHO WALKED ALONE, THE(1945);
DOUBLE LIFE, A(1947); TAP ROOTS(1948)
Silents
BIRTH OF A NATION, THE(1915); INTOLERANCE(1916); GREATEST THING IN
LIFE, THE(1918); KAISER, BEAST OF BERLIN, THE(1918); ROMANCE OF TARZAN,
THE(1918); TARZAN OF THE APES(1918); RENDEZVOUS, THE(1923); RUPERT OF
HENTZAU(1923)
Misc. Silents
MIGHT AND THE MAN(1917); UNDER CRIMSON SKIES(1920); WHOM SHALL I
MARRY(1926)
Fred Lincoln
LAST HOUSE ON THE LEFT(1972); HERE COME THE TIGERS(1978)
George Lincoln
SUNDOWN(1941)
Henry Lincoln
CRIMSON CULT, THE(1970, Brit.), w; SHADOWMAN(1974, Fr./Ital.)
Joseph Lincoln
GARBAGE MAN, THE(1963)
Joseph Crosby Lincoln
Silents
PARTNERS OF THE TIDE(1921), w; NO TRESPASSING(1922), w; RUGGED WA-
TER(1925), w
Marianne Lincoln
DEMOBBED(1944, Brit.); HONEYMOON HOTEL(1946, Brit.)
Mary Lincoln
Misc. Silents
LITTLE WOMEN(1917, Brit.)
Pamela Lincoln
TINGLER, THE(1959); ANATOMY OF A PSYCHO(1961); TOOTSIE(1982)
Richard Lincoln
HERE COME THE TIGERS(1978)
Rosa Lee Lincoln
Silents
ABSENT(1928)

Rosalie Lincoln
TELL NO TALES(1939)
Steve Lincoln
Misc. Talkies
FOX AFFAIR, THE(1978)
Tony Lincoln
1984
GRANDVIEW, U.S.A.(1984); TEACHERS(1984)
Victoria Lincoln
PRIMROSE PATH(1940), w
Warren Lincoln
1984
POWER, THE(1984)
Jack Lincy
DARK MANHATTAN(1937)
Art Lind
FAT MAN, THE(1951)
Birger Lind
VENOM(1968, Den.), ed
Bob Lind
WORLD IS JUST A 'B' MOVIE, THE(1971), m
Brit Lind
PLAY MISTY FOR ME(1971)
Charles Lind
ADAM HAD FOUR SONS(1941); ADVENTURE IN WASHINGTON(1941); SCATTER-GOOD RIDES HIGH(1942); JUNIOR ARMY(1943); FIGHTER SQUADRON(1948); PERFECT STRANGERS(1950); ON THE THRESHOLD OF SPACE(1956)
Chickie Lind
SERGEANT WAS A LADY, THE(1961)
Christian Lind
SHOW BOAT(1951)
Dagny Lind
BREAD OF LOVE, THE(1954, Swed.)
Della Lind
SWISS MISS(1938)
Gillian Lind
CONDEMNED TO DEATH(1932, Brit.); DICK TURPIN(1933, Brit.); MAN OUTSIDE, THE(1933, Brit.); OPEN ALL NIGHT(1934, Brit.); DEATH CROONS THE BLUES(1937, Brit.); HORSE'S MOUTH, THE(1953, Brit.); AUNT CLARA(1954, Brit.); HEART OF THE MATTER, THE(1954, Brit.); DON'T TALK TO STRANGE MEN(1962, Brit.); FEAR IN THE NIGHT(1972, Brit.); AND NOW THE SCREAMING STARTS(1973, Brit.)
Gitta Lind
SCHLAGER-PARADE(1953)
Graham Lind
STONE(1974, Aus.), ph; REMOVALISTS, THE(1975, Aus.), ph
Harts Lind
MARIE ANTOINETTE(1938)
Herta Lind
LOVE IS LIKE THAT(1933); HIDE-OUT(1934); MAYTIME(1937)
Jane Lind
WOLFEN(1981)
Jean Lind
SINBAD THE SAILOR(1947)
John Lind
WILD DUCK, THE(1983, Aus.), w
Karen Lind
WEEKEND AT THE WALDORF(1945); HARD ROAD, THE(1970); GLASS HOUSES(1972)
Lard Lind
BRINK OF LIFE(1960, Swed.)
Lars Lind
SEVENTH SEAL, THE(1958, Swed.); SWEDISH WEDDING NIGHT(1965, Swed.); OBSESSION(1968, Swed.)
M. Lind
Misc. Silents
JOCKEY OF DEATH, THE(1916, Ital.), d
Moira Lind
RIGHT AGE TO MARRY, THE(1935, Brit.)
Myrtle Lind
Silents
NANCY COMES HOME(1918)
Randi Lind
ADVENTURERS, THE(1970)
Steffany Lind
DR. FRANKENSTEIN ON CAMPUS(1970, Can.)
Viola Lind
Silents
IN FOLLY'S TRAIL(1920)
Linda
LOVE MATES(1967, Swed.), cos; FLASH GORDON(1980)
Anita Linda
JAGUAR(1980, Phil.)
Boguslaw Linda
MAN OF IRON(1981, Pol.); DANTON(1983)
Hala Linda
LEGION OF MISSING MEN(1937)
Tove Lindan
CIRCLE OF DEATH(1935)
Rolf Lindau
ESPIONAGE AGENT(1939); DESPERATE JOURNEY(1942); SECRET ENE-MIES(1942); EDGE OF DARKNESS(1943); FIRST COMES COURAGE(1943); MISSION TO MOSCOW(1943)
Rudolph Lindau
YANKS AHOY(1943); TAMPICO(1944)
Jack Lindauer
ONE FROM THE HEART(1982)
Margaret Linday
BROADWAY MUSKETEERS(1938)

Augusta Lindberg
Misc. Silents
CHARLES XII, PARTS 1 & 2(1927, Swed.)
Christina Lindberg
THEY CALL HER ONE EYE(1974, Swed.)
Don Lindberg
HEARTS OF HUMANITY(1932), ed
Donna Lindberg
MARS NEEDS WOMEN(1966)
Erick Lindberg
Misc. Talkies
MARK OF THE GUN(1969)
Goran Lindberg
HERE'S YOUR LIFE(1968, Swed.)
Helge Lindberg
SWEDENHIELMS(1935, Swed.), m
Lasse Lindberg
GORKY PARK(1983)
Lennart Lindberg
BREAD OF LOVE, THE(1954, Swed.); MATTER OF MORALS, A(1961, U.S./Swed.)
Monica Lindberg
SHAME(1968, Swed.)
Per Lindberg
NIGHT IN JUNE, A(1940, Swed.), d
Stig Lindberg
SHAME(1968, Swed.); GLADIATORS, THE(1970, Swed.), spec eff
Sven Lindberg
DREAMS(1960, Swed.); NIGHT IS MY FUTURE(1962, Swed.); LOVE MATES(1967, Swed.), p; FACE TO FACE(1976, Swed.)
Charles A. Lindbergh
SPIRIT OF ST. LOUIS, THE(1957), w
Jon Lindbergh
UNDERWATER WARRIOR(1958)
Arne Lindblad
LESSON IN LOVE, A(1960, Swed.); LOVING COUPLES(1966, Swed.)
Miss E.O. Lindblom
Misc. Silents
BLACK HEART, THE(1915)
Gunnel Lindblom
SEVENTH SEAL, THE(1958, Swed.); WILD STRAWBERRIES(1959, Swed.); VIRGIN SPRING, THE(1960, Swed.); WINTER LIGHT, THE(1963, Swed.); SILENCE, THE(1964, Swed.); RAPTURE(1965); LOVING COUPLES(1966, Swed.); HUNGER(1968, Den./Norway/Swed.); WOMAN OF DARKNESS(1968, Swed.); GIRLS, THE(1972, Swed.); SCENES FROM A MARRIAGE(1974, Swed.)
Misc. Talkies
BROTHER CARL(1972)
M. Lindblom
ESCAPED FROM DARTMOOR(1930, Brit.), ph
Margareta Lindblom
"RENT-A-GIRL"(1965)
Vera Lindby
OCEAN BREAKERS(1949, Swed.)
Laurie Linde
ALIMONY(1949)
Liv Lindeland
DIRTY O'NEIL(1974)
Jack Lindell
KING OF THE SIERRAS(1938)
Rod Lindeman
ORGY OF THE DEAD(1965)
The Lindeman Sisters
TRIPLE JUSTICE(1940)
Eric Lindemann
RAW FORCE(1982), ed
Mitch Lindemann
WAY WEST, THE(1967), w
Anne Linden
GHASTLY ONES, THE(1968); VIXENS, THE(1969)
Barbara Linden
KING, MURRAY(1969)
Bert Linden
BOB'S YOUR UNCLE(1941, Brit.)
Brayden Linden
BUNNY O'HARE(1971)
Brooke Linden
MAN CALLED FLINTSTONE, THE(1966), spec eff
Carol Linden
Misc. Talkies
CONVENTION GIRLS(1978)
Debbie Linden
1984
BLOODBATH AT THE HOUSE OF DEATH(1984, Brit.)
Delia Linden
OH! WHAT A LOVELY WAR(1969, Brit.)
Doris Linden
HILLBILLY BLITZKRIEG(1942); SNUFFY SMITH, YARD BIRD(1942); LADIES COURAGEOUS(1944)
Ed Linden
WEST OF PINTO BASIN(1940), ph
Eddie Linden
SON OF KONG(1933), ph; CRUSADE AGAINST RACKETS(1937), ph; CALIFORNIA FRONTIER(1938), ph; LAW OF THE TEXAN(1938), ph; PAROLED FROM THE BIG HOUSE(1938), ph; STRANGER FROM ARIZONA, THE(1938), ph; WOLVES OF THE SEA(1938), ph; SKY BANDITS, THE(1940), ph; HARD GUY(1941), ph; DAWN EX-PRESS, THE(1942), ph; LAST OF THE DESPERADOES(1956), ph
Silents
LAZY LIGHTNING(1926), ph; RUSTLER'S RANCH(1926), ph; ACTION CRAVER, THE(1927), ph; ONE GLORIOUS SCRAP(1927), ph; RANGE RIDERS, THE(1927), ph; WESTERN COURAGE(1927), ph; ARIZONA CYCLONE(1928), ph

Eddie Linden, Jr.
LAST DAYS OF POMPEII, THE(1935), ph
Edward Linden
WITHOUT HONORS(1932), ph; KING KONG(1933), ph; CRASHING THRU(1939), ph; ISLE OF DESTINY(1940), ph; RANGE BUSTERS, THE(1940), ph; TRAILING DOUBLE TROUBLE(1940), ph; CITY OF MISSING GIRLS(1941), ph; SWAMP WOMAN(1941), ph; YANK IN LIBYA, A(1942), ph; ADVENTURES OF MARK TWAIN, THE(1944), ph
Edwin Linden
WEREWOLF, THE(1956), ph
Silents
MASK, THE(1921), ph; WESTERN ROVER, THE(1927), ph
Einar Linden
Silents
ETERNAL SAPHO, THE(1916); ROMEO AND JULIET(1916)
Misc. Silents
CARMEN(1915); IRON WOMAN, THE(1916); HEDDA GABLER(1917)
Eric Linden
ARE THESE OUR CHILDREN?(1931); AFRAID TO TALK(1932); AGE OF CONSENT(1932); BIG CITY BLUES(1932); CROWD ROARS, THE(1932); LIFE BEGINS(1932); ROADHOUSE MURDER, THE(1932); YOUNG BRIDE(1932); FLYING DEVILS(1933); NO OTHER WOMAN(1933); PAST OF MARY HOLMES, THE(1933); SILVER CORD(1933); SWEEPINGS(1933); I GIVE MY LOVE(1934); AH, WILDERNESS!(1935); BORN TO GAMBLE(1935); LADIES CRAVE EXCITEMENT(1935); LET 'EM HAVE IT(1935); CAREER WOMAN(1936); IN HIS STEPS(1936); OLD HUTCH(1936); ROBIN HOOD OF EL DORADO(1936); VOICE OF BUGLE ANN(1936); FAMILY AFFAIR, A(1937); GIRL LOVES BOY(1937); GOOD OLD SOAR, THE(1937); HERE'S FLASH CASEY(1937); SWEETHEART OF THE NAVY(1937); MIDNIGHT INTRUDER(1938); ROMANCE OF THE LIMBERLOST(1938); EVERYTHING'S ON ICE(1939); GONE WITH THE WIND(1939); CRIMINALS WITHIN(1941)
Hal Linden
WHEN YOU COMIN' BACK, RED RYDER?(1979)
Jemmie Linden
WOMEN IN LOVE(1969, Brit.)
Jennie Linden
NIGHTMARE(1963, Brit.); DR. WHO AND THE DALEKS(1965, Brit.); SEVERED HEAD, A(1971, Brit.); HEDDA(1975, Brit.); OLD DRACULA(1975, Brit.)
Jo Linden
ENTERTAINER, THE(1960, Brit.)
Joyce Linden
WALTZ TIME(1946, Brit.); DARK ROAD, THE(1948, Brit.); MAN'S AFFAIR, A(1949, Brit.); DICK BARTON AT BAY(1950, Brit.)
Judith Linden
HER FIRST ROMANCE(1940); LONG VOYAGE HOME, THE(1940); KING OF DODGE CITY(1941); SING FOR YOUR SUPPER(1941); LADY IS WILLING, THE(1942)
Liane Linden
ARSENAL STADIUM MYSTERY, THE(1939, Brit.)
Lionel Linden
MONSIEUR BEAUCAIRE(1946), ph; O.S.S.(1946), ph; ISN'T IT ROMANTIC?(1948), ph; DRUMS IN THE DEEP SOUTH(1951), ph; CARIBBEAN(1952), ph; SCARLET HOUR, THE(1956), ph; YOUNG SAVAGES, THE(1961), ph; GENERATION(1969), ph
Margaret Linden
UNDER CAPRICORN(1949), w
Silents
NEW YORK IDEA, THE(1920)
Misc. Silents
WANTED - A HUSBAND(1919); HIS HOUSE IN ORDER(1920)
Marguerite Linden
Silents
WOMAN'S PLACE(1921)
Marta Linden
RANDOM HARVEST(1942); STAND BY FOR ACTION(1942); YANK AT ETON, A(1942); SWING SHIFT MAISIE(1943); THOUSANDS CHEER(1943); THREE HEARTS FOR JULIA(1943); YOUNGEST PROFESSION, THE(1943); ANDY HARDY'S BLONDE TROUBLE(1944); MAISIE GOES TO RENO(1944); SEE HERE, PRIVATE HARGROVE(1944); KEEP YOUR POWDER DRY(1945)
Nat S. Linden
YELLOWNECK(1955), w
Olga Linden
ASSIGNMENT K(1968, Brit.)
Rita Linden
STEPPING TOES(1938, Brit.)
Robert Linden
SUBWAY EXPRESS(1931); WHEN YOU'RE IN LOVE(1937)
Stella Linden
TWO A PENNY(1968, Brit.), w
Sue Linden
SWEET CHARITY(1969)
Virginia Linden
SECOND CHANCE(1953); DANGEROUS MISSION(1954)
Walter Linden
OPERATION EICHMANN(1961); VON RYAN'S EXPRESS(1965)
Warris Linden
Silents
MAN'S SHADOW, A(1920, Brit.)
Elaine Lindenbaum
ONE WAY TICKET TO HELL(1955)
Alfred Linder
HOUSE ON 92ND STREET, THE(1945); 13 RUE MADELEINE(1946); BRASHER DOUBLOON, THE(1947); CANON CITY(1948); I WAS A MALE WAR BRIDE(1949); GUILTY OF TREASON(1950); DIPLOMATIC COURIER(1952); LES MISERABLES(1952); TIGHT SPOT(1955); GIRL IN THE KREMLIN, THE(1957); INVISIBLE BOY, THE(1957); TROOPER HOOK(1957)
Allan Linder
DOLLAR(1938, Swed.)
Cec Linder
SUBWAY IN THE SKY(1959, Brit.); CRACK IN THE MIRROR(1960); S.O.S. PACIFIC(1960, Brit.); TOO YOUNG TO LOVE(1960, Brit.); JET STORM(1961, Brit.); LOLITA(1962); GOLDFINGER(1964, Brit.); VERDICT, THE(1964, Brit.); HIRED KILLER, THE(1967, Fr./Ital.); EXPLOSION(1969, Can.); INNOCENT BYSTANDERS(1973, Brit.);

TOUCH OF CLASS, A(1973, Brit.); WHY ROCK THE BOAT?(1974, Can.); SUNDAY IN THE COUNTRY(1975, Can.); CLOWN MURDERS, THE(1976, Can.); SECOND WIND(1976, Can.); AGE OF INNOCENCE(1977, Can.); TOMORROW NEVER COMES(1978, Brit./Can.); CITY ON FIRE(1979 Can.); SOMETHING'S ROTTEN(1979, Can.); ATLANTIC CITY(1981, U.S./Can.); DEADLY EYES(1982)
Cecil Linder
FLAMING FRONTIER(1958, Can.); LOST AND FOUND(1979)
Cecil [Cec] Linder
VIRUS(1980, Jap.)
Christa Linder
FOUNTAIN OF LOVE, THE(1968, Aust.); DAY OF ANGER(1970, Ital./Ger.); INCREDIBLE INVASION, THE(1971, Mex./U.S.); NIGHT OF A THOUSAND CATS(1974, Mex.)
Crista Linder
TALL WOMEN, THE(1967, Aust./Ital./Span.)
Jenny Linder
MA AND PA KETTLE AT THE FAIR(1952); MA AND PA KETTLE ON VACATION(1953); MA AND PA KETTLE AT WAIKIKI(1955)
Leslie Linder
GREAT MANHUNT, THE(1951, Brit.); GREEN BUDDHA, THE(1954, Brit.); PRIZE OF GOLD, A(1955); WARRIORS, THE(1955); STAR OF INDIA(1956, Brit.); MEN OF SHERWOOD FOREST(1957, Brit.); MOONRAKER, THE(1958, Brit.); SEPARATION(1968, Brit.); SEE NO EVIL(1971, Brit.), p; 10 RILLINGTON PLACE(1971, Brit.), p
Mark Linder
SQUEALER, THE(1930), w
Max Linder
Misc. Silents
LE PETIT CAFE(1919, Fr.); BE MY WIFE(1921), d; SEVEN YEARS BAD LUCK(1921), a, d; THREE MUST-GET-THERES, THE(1922), a, d; LE ROI DE CIRQUE(1925, Fr.)
Slawomir Linder
SARAGOSSA MANUSCRIPT, THE(1972, Pol.)
Stewart Linder
BLUE(1968), ed
Stu Linder
FORTUNE, THE(1975), ed; FIRST FAMILY(1980), ed; MY BODYGUARD(1980), ed; DINER(1982), ed; SIX WEEKS(1982), ed
1984
NATURAL, THE(1984), ed
Jan Lindestrom
RAVEN'S END(1970, Swed.), ph
Olaf Lindfors
OPERATION LOVEBIRDS(1968, Den.)
Viveca Lindfors
WAY WE WERE, THE(1973); APPASSIONATA(1946, Swed.); TO THE VICTOR(1948); ADVENTURES OF DON JUAN(1949); NIGHT UNTO NIGHT(1949); BACKFIRE(1950); DARK CITY(1950); FLYING MISSILE(1950); GYPSY FURY(1950, Fr.); NO SAD SONGS FOR ME(1950); THIS SIDE OF THE LAW(1950); FOUR IN A JEEP(1951, Switz.); JOURNEY INTO LIGHT(1951); NO TIME FOR FLOWERS(1952); RAIDERS, THE(1952); MOONFLEET(1955); RUN FOR COVER(1955); HALLIDAY BRAND, THE(1957); I ACCUSE(1958, Brit.); TEMPEST(1958, Ital./Yugo./Fr.); STORY OF RUTH, THE(1960); WEDDINGS AND BABIES(1960); KING OF KINGS(1961); NO EXIT(1962, U.S./Arg.); AFFAIR OF THE SKIN, AN(1964); BRAINSTORM(1965); SYLVIA(1965); THESE ARE THE DAMNED(1965, Brit.); PUZZLE OF A DOWNFALL CHILD(1970); CAULDRON OF BLOOD(1971, Span.); WELCOME TO L.A.(1976); GIRLFRIENDS(1978); WEDDING, A(1978); NATURAL ENEMIES(1979); VOICES(1979); HAND, THE(1981); CREEPSHOW(1982)
1984
SILENT MADNESS(1984)
Misc. Talkies
COMING APART(1969); NIGHTKILLERS(1983)
Aron Lindgren
Misc. Silents
INGEBORG HOLM(1913, Swed.)
Astrid Lindgren
PIPPI IN THE SOUTH SEAS(1974, Swed./Ger.), w
Goran Lindgren
DEAR JOHN(1966, Swed.), p; LOVING COUPLES(1966, Swed.), p; HUGS AND KISSES(1968, Swed.), p; LE VIOL(1968, Fr./Swed.), p; PEOPLE MEET AND SWEET MUSIC FILLS THE HEART(1969, Den./Swed.), p; GLADIATORS, THE(1970, Swed.), p; GIRLS, THE(1972, Swed.), p
Hans Lindgren
JOHANSSON GETS SCOLDED(1945, Swed.); CHILDREN, THE(1949, Swed.)
Lars Magnus Lindgren
DEAR JOHN(1966, Swed.), d, w
Lars-Magnus Lindgren
LOVE MATES(1967, Swed.), d&w
Orley Lindgren
HITLER'S CHILDREN(1942); GREAT LOVER, THE(1949); SADDLE TRAMP(1950); UNDER MY SKIN(1950); YOUNG MAN WITH A HORN(1950); LORNA DOONE(1951); JAPANESE WAR BRIDE(1952); RED PLANET MARS(1952); WILD STALLION(1952); MR. SCOUTMASTER(1953); SAVAGE, THE(1953)
Misc. Talkies
BEHIND SOUTHERN LINES(1952)
Peter Lindgren
NEW LAND, THE(1973, Swed.)
Sten Lindgren
OCEAN BREAKERS(1949, Swed.); VALLEY OF EAGLES(1952, Brit.)
Andy Lindhoff
PRIME TIME, THE(1960)
Eileen Lindhoff
PRIME TIME, THE(1960)
Eric Lindholm
Misc. Silents
GIVE US THIS DAY(1913, Swed.); INGEBORG HOLM(1913, Swed.)
Kristen Lindholm
TWINS OF EVIL(1971, Brit.)
Manne Lindholm
SEVENTH SEAL, THE(1958, Swed.), cos

Marita Lindholm
POSSESSION OF JOEL DELANEY, THE(1972)

Jilian Lindig
EYES OF A STRANGER(1980)

Edward Lindin
TODAY I HANG(1942), ph

Hugo Lindinger
MIRACLE OF THE WHITE STALLIONS(1963)

Birgit Lindkvist
DEVIL'S WANTON, THE(1962, Swed.)

Audra Lindley
WHEN YOU COMIN' BACK, RED RYDER?(1979); DANGEROUSLY THEY LIVE(1942); MALE ANIMAL, THE(1942); TAKING OFF(1971); HEARTBREAK KID, THE(1972); BEST FRIENDS(1982); CANNERY ROW(1982)

Bert Lindley
POCATELLO KID(1932); ARE WE CIVILIZED?(1934); MISSISSIPPI(1935); ROSE MARIE(1936)
Silents
ALIAS THE NIGHT WIND(1923)
Misc. Silents
BRINGIN' HOME THE BACON(1924); $50,000 Reward(1924)

Daryle Ann Lindley
1984
FEAR CITY(1984)

David Lindley
1984
PARIS, TEXAS(1984, Ger./Fr.), m

Gisele Lindley
S.O.B.(1981)

John Lindley
1984
GOODBYE PEOPLE, THE(1984), ph

Ken Lindley
TOMORROW(1972)

Mona Lindley
TANGLED DESTINIES(1932)

Monaei Lindley
Misc. Talkies
HER SECRET(1933)

Virginia Lindley
DRAGONWYCH(1946)

Ake Lindman
PRELUDE TO ECSTASY(1963, Fin.); MAKE LIKE A THIEF(1966, Fin.); MOONWOLF(1966, Fin./Ger.); TELEFON(1977); REDS(1981)

Wilma Lindmar
Misc. Talkies
RAMON(1972)

Robert Lindner
BETWEEN TIME AND ETERNITY(1960, Ger.); PRESSURE POINT(1962), w

Dr. Robert M. Lindner
REBEL WITHOUT A CAUSE(1955), w

Oskar Lindner
CANARIS(1955, Ger.)

Delroy Lindo
MORE AMERICAN GRAFFITI(1979)

L. Lindo
ROCKERS(1980)

Olga Lindo
SHADOW BETWEEN, THE(1932, Brit.); CASE OF GABRIEL PERRY, THE(1935, Brit.); DARK WORLD(1935, Brit.); REGAL CAVALCADE(1935, Brit.); LAST JOURNEY, THE(1936, Brit.); NORTH SEA PATROL(1939, Brit.); LOST ON THE WESTERN FRONT(1940, Brit.); RETURN TO YESTERDAY(1940, Brit.); STARS LOOK DOWN, THE(1940, Brit.); ALIBI, THE(1943, Brit.); WHEN WE ARE MARRIED(1943, Brit.); GIVE ME THE STARS(1944, Brit.); TIME FLIES(1944, Brit.); NOTORIOUS GENTLEMAN(1945, Brit.); ADVENTURESS, THE(1946, Brit.); BEDELIA(1946, Brit.); NIGHT BOAT TO DUBLIN(1946, Brit.); THINGS HAPPEN AT NIGHT(1948, Brit.); HIDDEN ROOM, THE(1949, Brit.); TWENTY QUESTIONS MURDER MYSTERY, THE(1950, Brit.); TRAIN OF EVENTS(1952, Brit.); INSPECTOR CALLS, AN(1954, Brit.); BLONDE SINNER(1956, Brit.); EXTRA DAY, THE(1956, Brit.); RAISING A RIOT(1957, Brit.); WOMEN IN A DRESSING GOWN(1957, Brit.); SAPPHIRE(1959, Brit.); OUT OF THE FOG(1962, Brit.); DR. CRIPPEN(1963, Brit.); MAKE MINE A MILLION(1965, Brit.)

Jennie Lindon
VALENTINO(1977, Brit.)

Lionel Lindon
LET'S FACE IT(1943), ph; GOING MY WAY(1944), ph; DUFFY'S TAVERN(1945), ph; MASQUERADE IN MEXICO(1945), ph; MEDAL FOR BENNY, A(1945), ph; ROAD TO UTOPIA(1945), ph; BLUE DAHLIA, THE(1946), ph; MY FAVORITE BRUNETTE(1947), ph; TROUBLE WITH WOMEN, THE(1947), ph; VARIETY GIRL(1947), ph; WELCOME STRANGER(1947), ph; SAINTED SISTERS, THE(1948), ph; TAP ROOTS(1948), ph; ALIAS NICK BEAL(1949), ph; TOP O' THE MORNING(1949), ph; WITHOUT HONOR(1949), ph; DESTINATION MOON(1950), ph; GREAT RUPERT, THE(1950), ph; PREHISTORIC WOMEN(1950), ph; QUICKSAND(1950), ph; SUN SETS AT DAWN, THE(1950), ph; HONG KONG(1951), ph; ONLY THE VALIANT(1951), ph; RHUBARB(1951), ph; SUBMARINE COMMAND(1951), ph; BLAZING FOREST, THE(1952), ph; JAPANESE WAR BRIDE(1952), ph; TURNING POINT, THE(1952), ph; HERE COME THE GIRLS(1953), ph; JAMAICA RUN(1953), ph; SANGAREE(1953), ph; STARS ARE SINGING, THE(1953), ph; THOSE REDHEADS FROM SEATTLE(1953), ph; TROPIC ZONE(1953), ph; VANQUISHED, THE(1953), ph; CASANOVA'S BIG NIGHT(1954), ph; JIVARO(1954), ph; SECRET OF THE INCAS(1954), ph; CONQUEST OF SPACE(1955), ph; HELL'S ISLAND(1955), ph; LUCY GALLANT(1955), ph; MAN ALONE, A(1955), ph; AROUND THE WORLD IN 80 DAYS(1956), ph; BLACK SCORPION, THE(1957), ph; LONELY MAN, THE(1957), ph; I WANT TO LIVE!(1958), ph; ALIAS JESSE JAMES(1959), ph; ALL FALL DOWN(1962), ph; MANCHURIAN CANDIDATE, THE(1962), ph; TOO LATE BLUES(1962), ph; MC HALE'S NAVY JOINS THE AIR FORCE(1965), ph; BOY, DID I GET A WRONG NUMBER!(1966), ph; DEAD HEAT ON A MERRY-GO-ROUND(1966), ph; GRAND PRIX(1966), ph; TROUBLE WITH ANGELS, THE(1966), ph; THREE GUNS FOR TEXAS(1968), ph; EXTRAORDINARY SEAMAN, THE(1969), ph; PENDULUM(1969), ph

Audrey Erskine Lindop
BLANCHE FURY(1948, Brit.), w; SINGER NOT THE SONG, THE(1961, Brit.), w; I THANK A FOOL(1962, Brit.), w; I START COUNTING(1970, Brit.), w

Zofia Lindorf
KANAL(1961, Pol.)

Lone Lindorff
Z.P.G.(1972)
1984
ZAPPA(1984, Den.)

Leon Lindos
TWO FOR DANGER(1940, Brit.)

Jack Lindquist
MAJOR AND THE MINOR, THE(1942); JOAN OF ARC(1948)

Ake Lindqvist
KONGI'S HARVEST(1971, U.S./Nigeria), ph

Frej Lindqvist
SEA GULL, THE(1968); SHAME(1968, Swed.)

Gunnar Lindqvist
DUET FOR CANNIBALS(1969, Swed.)

Jan-Erik Lindqvist
TO LOVE(1964, Swed.); LOVING COUPLES(1966, Swed.); HERE'S YOUR LIFE(1968, Swed.)

Helen Lindroth
Silents
FROM THE MANGER TO THE CROSS(1913); AUDREY(1916); INNOCENT LIE, THE(1916); SPIDER, THE(1916); KILDARE OF STORM(1918); FIGHTER, THE(1921); RIGHT WAY, THE(1921); WAY OF A MAID, THE(1921); JAVA HEAD(1923)
Misc. Silents
LURING LIGHTS(1915); DAUGHTER OF MACGREGOR, A(1916); LITTLE MISS NOBODY(1917); HOUSE OF GOLD, THE(1918); WOMAN AND WIFE(1918); SHADOWS OF SUSPICION(1919); POOR, DEAR MARGARET KIRBY(1921)

Louise Lindroth
Silents
FLAPPER, THE(1920)

Horace Lindrum
COUNTERFEIT PLAN, THE(1957, Brit.)

Carol Lindsay
SHE-GODS OF SHARK REEF(1958)

Clare Lindsay
LAUGHING LADY, THE(1950, Brit.)

Delia Lindsay
SCARS OF DRACULA, THE(1970, Brit.)

Earl Lindsay
SWEETIE(1929), ch; GOLDEN CALF, THE(1930), ch; HAPPY DAYS(1930), ch

Enid Lindsay
TICKET OF LEAVE(1936, Brit.)

Eric Lindsay
WOMAN TO WOMAN(1946, Brit.)

Col. Fred Lindsay
Silents
ROUGH RIDERS, THE(1927)

Gary Lindsay
PRINCESS AND THE MAGIC FROG, THE(1965), ed

George Lindsay
ARISTOCATS, THE(1970); ROBIN HOOD(1973); TAKE THIS JOB AND SHOVE IT(1981)

Grant Lindsay
SQUATTER'S DAUGHTER(1933, Aus.)

Helen Lindsay
DUBLIN NIGHTMARE(1958, Brit.); DARLING(1965, Brit.); PARTNER, THE(1966, Brit.); ONE BRIEF SUMMER(1971, Brit.)
1984
SECRETS(1984, Brit.)

Howard Lindsay
SHE'S MY WEAKNESS(1930), w; LOVE, HONOR, AND OH BABY!(1933), w; SHE LOVES ME NOT(1934), w; YOUR UNCLE DUDLEY(1935), w; ANYTHING GOES(1936), w; SWING TIME(1936), w; BIG BROADCAST OF 1938, THE(1937), w; ARTISTS AND MODELS ABROAD(1938), w; SLIGHT CASE OF MURDER, A(1938), w; TRUE TO THE ARMY(1942), w; LIFE WITH FATHER(1947), w; STATE OF THE UNION(1948), w; HASTY HEART, THE(1949), p; STOP, YOU'RE KILLING ME(1952), w; REMAINS TO BE SEEN(1953), w; WOMAN'S WORLD(1954), w; HOW TO BE VERY, VERY, POPULAR(1955), w; ANYTHING GOES(1956), w; TALL STORY(1960), w; SOUND OF MUSIC, THE(1965), w

James Lindsay
Silents
ALONE IN LONDON(1915, Brit.); GIRL WHO LOVES A SOLDIER, THE(1916, Brit.); ALL THE WORLD'S A STAGE(1917, Brit.); ADMIRABLE CRICHTON, THE(1918, Brit.); MISSING THE TIDE(1918, Brit.); SNARE, THE(1918, Brit.); DOUBLE LIFE OF MR. ALFRED BURTON, THE(1919, Brit.); EDGE O'BEYOND(1919, Brit.); MRS. THOMPSON(1919, Brit.); AUNT RACHEL(1920, Brit.); ALL SORTS AND CONDITIONS OF MEN(1921, Brit.); BACHELORS' CLUB, THE(1921, Brit.); GAME OF LIFE, THE(1922, Brit.); FORBIDDEN CARGOES(1925, Brit.); RAT, THE(1925, Brit.); ONE OF THE BEST(1927, Brit.)
Misc. Silents
THROUGH THE VALLEY OF SHADOWS(1914, Brit.); DUNGEON OF DEATH, THE(1915, Brit.); PORT OF MISSING WOMEN, THE(1915, Brit.); DR. WAKE'S PATIENT(1916, Brit.); HER GREATEST PERFORMANCE(1916, Brit.); LYONS MAIL, THE(1916, Brit.); GAMBLE FOR LOVE, A(1917, Brit.); FORTUNE AT STAKE, A(1918, Brit.); TINKER, TAILOR, SOLDIER, SAILOR(1918, Brit.); CITY OF BEAUTIFUL NONSENSE, THE(1919); DAMAGED GOODS(1919, Brit.); DISAPPEARANCE OF THE JUDGE, THE(1919, Brit.); LIFE OF A LONDON ACTRESS, THE(1919, Brit.); THUNDERCLOUD, THE(1919, Brit.); GRIP OF IRON, THE(1920, Brit.); HONEYPOT, THE(1920, Brit.); NANCE(1920, Brit.); FOR HER FATHER'S SAKE(1921, Brit.); LOVE MAGGY(1921, Brit.); AFTERGLOW(1923, Brit.); M'LORD OF THE WHITE ROAD(1923, Brit.); ROGUES OF THE TURF(1923, Brit.); TEMPTATION OF CARLTON EARLYE, THE(1923, Brit.); WHAT PRICE LOVING CUP?(1923, Brit.); COST OF BEAUTY, THE(1924, Brit.)

Joan Lindsay
PICNIC AT HANGING ROCK(1975, Aus.), w
Joanne Lindsay
TELL ME LIES(1968, Brit.)
John V. Lindsay
ROSEBUD(1975)
Kirsty Lindsay
1984
SHEENA(1984)
Lara Lindsay
SWEET RIDE, THE(1968); THE BOSTON STRANGLER, THE(1968); LOGAN'S RUN(1976)
Les Lindsay
Misc. Talkies
MAN FROM ARIZONA, THE(1932)
Lex Lindsay
SOB SISTER(1931)
Lois Lindsay
GOLD DIGGERS OF 1937(1936)
Louis Lindsay
MACBETH(1948), ed
Magaret Lindsay
CLOSE CALL FOR ELLERY QUEEN, A(1942)
Margaret Lindsay
ALL-AMERICAN, THE(1932); OKAY AMERICA(1932); ONCE IN A LIFETIME(1932); BABY FACE(1933); CAPTURED(1933); CAVALCADE(1933); CHRISTOPHER STRONG(1933); FOURTH HORSEMAN, THE(1933); FROM HEADQUARTERS(1933); HOUSE ON 56TH STREET, THE(1933); LADY KILLER(1933); PADDY, THE NEXT BEST THING(1933); PRIVATE DETECTIVE 62(1933); VOLTAIRE(1933); WEST OF SINGAPORE(1933); WORLD CHANGES, THE(1933); DRAGON MURDER CASE, THE(1934); FOG OVER FRISCO(1934); GENTLEMEN ARE BORN(1934); MERRY WIVES OF RENO, THE(1934); BORDERTOWN(1935); CASE OF THE CURIOUS BRIDE, THE(1935); DEVIL DOGS OF THE AIR(1935); FLORENTINE DAGGER, THE(1935); FRISCO KID(1935); G-MEN(1935); PERSONAL MAID'S SECRET(1935); DANGEROUS(1936); ISLE OF FURY(1936); LADY CONSENTS, THE(1936); LAW IN HER HANDS, THE(1936); PUBLIC ENEMY'S WIFE(1936); SINNER TAKE ALL(1936); BACK IN CIRCULATION(1937); GREEN LIGHT(1937); SLIM(1937); SONG OF THE CITY(1937); GARDEN OF THE MOON(1938); GOLD IS WHERE YOU FIND IT(1938); JEZEBEL(1938); THERE'S THAT WOMAN AGAIN(1938); WHEN WERE YOU BORN?(1938); HELL'S KITCHEN(1939); ON TRIAL(1939); UNDER-PUP, THE(1939); 20,000 MEN A YEAR(1939); BRITISH INTELLIGENCE(1940); DOUBLE ALIBI(1940); ELLERY QUEEN. MASTER DETECTIVE(1940); HONEYMOON DEFERRED(1940); HOUSE OF THE SEVEN GABLES, THE(1940); MEET THE WILDCAT(1940); ELLERY QUEEN AND THE MURDER RING(1941); ELLERY QUEEN AND THE PERFECT CRIME(1941); ELLERY QUEEN'S PENTHOUSE MYSTERY(1941); THERE'S MAGIC IN MUSIC(1941); DESPERATE CHANCE FOR ELLERY QUEEN, A(1942); ENEMY AGENTS MEET ELLERY QUEEN(1942); SPOILERS, THE(1942); TRAGEDY AT MIDNIGHT, A(1942); CRIME DOCTOR(1943); NO PLACE FOR A LADY(1943); ALASKA(1944); ADVENTURES OF RUSTY(1945); SCARLET STREET(1945); CLUB HAVANA(1946); HER SISTER'S SECRET(1946); CASS TIMBERLANE(1947); LOUISIANA(1947); SEVEN KEYS TO BALDPATE(1947); VIGILANTES RETURN, THE(1947); B. F.'S DAUGHTER(1948); BOTTOM OF THE BOTTLE, THE(1956); EMERGENCY HOSPITAL(1956); RESTLESS YEARS, THE(1958); JET OVER THE ATLANTIC(1960); PLEASE DON'T EAT THE DAISIES(1960); TAMMY AND THE DOCTOR(1963)
Misc. Talkies
LET'S HAVE FUN(1943)
Mark Lindsay
SGT. PEPPER'S LONELY HEARTS CLUB BAND(1978); SHOGUN ASSASSIN(1980, Jap.), m
Mary Lindsay
NEW YORK, NEW YORK(1977)
Minnie Lindsay
1984
CHOOSE ME(1984)
Norman Lindsay
ADVENTURES OF SADIE, THE(1955, Brit.), w; AGE OF CONSENT(1969, Austral.), w
Peter Lindsay
DEVIL ON HORSEBACK(1954, Brit.)
Philip Lindsay
UNDER THE RED ROBE(1937, Brit.), w; SONG OF FREEDOM(1938, Brit.), w
Phillip Lindsay
ONLY WHEN I LAUGH(1981)
Powell Lindsay
Misc. Talkies
THAT MAN OF MINE(1947); SOULS OF SIN(1949), d
Richard Lindsay
Silents
NEW CLOWN, THE(1916, Brit.); PLEYDELL MYSTERY, THE(1916, Brit.)
Robert Lindsay
THAT'LL BE THE DAY(1974, Brit.); MANIAC(1980), ph
Robin Lindsay
WIRE SERVICE(1942), set d
Vera Lindsay
SPELL OF AMY NUGENT, THE(1945, Brit.)
Walter Lindsay
FOR VALOR(1937, Brit.)
Lindsay Kemp and Troupe
JUBILEE(1978, Brit.)
Michael Lindsay-Hogg
NASTY HABITS(1976, Brit.), d
Lillian Lindsco
MISSISSIPPI RHYTHM(1949)
Stuart Lindsdell
BONNIE PRINCE CHARLIE(1948, Brit.)
R. Stuart Lindsell
BROKEN JOURNEY(1948, Brit.); CHRISTOPHER COLUMBUS(1949, Brit.); MAN ON THE RUN(1949, Brit.); MY BROTHER JONATHAN(1949, Brit.); HIGH TREASON(1951, Brit.); ONCE A SINNER(1952, Brit.); WEST OF ZANZIBAR(1954, Brit.)

Stuart Lindsell
YOUNG MR. PITT, THE(1942, Brit.); MAN IN GREY, THE(1943, Brit.); UNCENSORED(1944, Brit.); MAN FROM MOROCCO, THE(1946, Brit.); NIGHT BOAT TO DUBLIN(1946, Brit.); ESCAPE(1948, Brit.); HATTER'S CASTLE(1948, Brit.); MAN OF EVIL(1948, Brit.); GIRL WHO COULDN'T QUITE, THE(1949, Brit.); PASSPORT TO PIMLICO(1949, Brit.); LILLI MARLENE(1951, Brit.); MANIACS ON WHEELS(1951, Brit.); FOREVER MY HEART(1954, Brit.); PROFILE(1954, Brit.)
Judge Ben Lindsey
Silents
SOUL OF YOUTH, THE(1920)
Judge Ben B. Lindsey
ONE MILE FROM HEAVEN(1937), w
Mrs. Ben Lindsey
Silents
SOUL OF YOUTH, THE(1920)
Dr. Charles Frederick Lindsley
KEEPER OF THE FLAME(1942)
Dan Lindsey
SILKWOOD(1983)
Enid Lindsey
BELLES OF ST. CLEMENTS, THE(1936, Brit.); PRISON WITHOUT BARS(1939, Brit.); MAN WHO KNEW TOO MUCH, THE(1956); LIFE IN EMERGENCY WARD 10(1959, Brit.)
Francis Lindsey
SAVAGE(1962)
Gene Lindsey
SANTA CLAUS CONQUERS THE MARTIANS zero(1964); COTTON COMES TO HARLEM(1970); ALL THE PRESIDENT'S MEN(1976)
George Lindsey
SNOWBALL EXPRESS(1972); CHARLEY AND THE ANGEL(1973); RESCUERS, THE(1977)
1984
CANNONBALL RUN II(1984)
George T. Lindsey
DEVONSVILLE TERROR, THE(1983), w
Howard Lindsey
CALL ME MADAM(1953), w
Jack Lindsey
LIVE NOW–PAY LATER(1962, Brit.), w
John Lindsey
WHERE THE RED FERN GROWS(1974)
Larry Lindsey
NEW YEAR'S EVIL(1980); ROADIE(1980)
Lois Lindsey
FEATHER IN HER HAT, A(1935); SHE COULDN'T TAKE IT(1935); LONE WOLF RETURNS, THE(1936)
Marilyn Lindsey
WOMAN THEY ALMOST LYNCHED, THE(1953)
Minnie E. Lindsey
VAN NUYS BLVD.(1979)
Minnie Lindsey
1984
CITY HEAT(1984); IRRECONCILABLE DIFFERENCES(1984)
Mort Lindsey
FORTY POUNDS OF TROUBLE(1962), m; SEDUCERS, THE(1962), m; I COULD GO ON SINGING(1963), m, md; STOLEN HOURS(1963), m; BEST MAN, THE(1964), m; REAL LIFE(1979), a, m
Nina Lindsey
Silents
MASQUERADERS, THE(1915)
Peter Lindsey
PRIVATE LIFE OF HENRY VIII, THE(1933), tech adv
Frederick Lindsley
ESPIONAGE AGENT(1939)
Vincent Lindsley
1984
REVENGE OF THE NERDS(1984)
Pierre Lindstedt
ADALEN 31(1969, Swed.); EMIGRANTS, THE(1972, Swed.); NEW LAND, THE(1973, Swed.)
Fred Lindstrand
MEN OF AMERICA(1933)
Ake Lindstrom
TOUCH, THE(1971, U.S./Swed.); GIRLS, THE(1972, Swed.)
Bengt Lindstrom
NO TIME TO KILL(1963, Brit./Swed./Ger.), ph
Bibi Lindstrom
NAKED NIGHT, THE(1956, Swed.), art d; BRINK OF LIFE(1960, Swed.), set d; MATTER OF MORALS, A(1961, U.S./Swed.), set d; TWO LIVING, ONE DEAD(1964, Brit./Swed.), art d; PERSONA(1967, Swed.), prod d, art d
Jorgen Lindstrom
SILENCE, THE(1964, Swed.); NIGHT GAMES(1966, Swed.); PERSONA(1967, Swed.)
Lief Lindstrom
CASE OF PATTY SMITH, THE(1962)
Pia Lindstrom
MARRIAGE–ITALIAN STYLE(1964, Fr./Ital.); QUEENS, THE(1968, Ital./Fr.)
Richard Lindstrom
DOLLAR(1938, Swed.)
Rune Lindstrom
RAILROAD WORKERS(1948, Swed.), w; AFFAIRS OF A MODEL(1952, Swed.), w; NIGHT GAMES(1966, Swed.); SHAME(1968, Swed.); WOMAN OF DARKNESS(1968, Swed.)
Karl Lindt
THIS ISLAND EARTH(1955); FIVE STEPS TO DANGER(1957)
Karl Ludwig Lindt
DANGEROUS CROSSING(1953); TIME TO LOVE AND A TIME TO DIE, A(1958); ONE, TWO, THREE(1961); DEEP END(1970 Ger./U.S.)

Leopold Lindtberg
LAST CHANCE, THE(1945, Switz.), d; FOUR DAYS LEAVE(1950, Switz.), d, w; FOUR IN A JEEP(1951, Switz.), d; VILLAGE, THE(1953, Brit./Switz.), d, w

Eli Lindtner
SONG OF NORWAY(1970)

David Lindup
GAMES THAT LOVERS PLAY(1971, Brit.), m; SPIRAL STAIRCASE, THE(1975, Brit.), m; CALL HIM MR. SHATTER(1976, Hong Kong), m; RISING DAMP(1980, Brit.), m

The Lindy Hoppers
Misc. Talkies
SWANEE SHOWBOAT(1939)

Bruce Line
NEWLY RICH(1931); GREAT JASPER, THE(1933); NO GREATER GLORY(1934)

Helga Line
KILL OR BE KILLED(1950); NIGHTMARE CASTLE(1966, Ital.); SECRET SEVEN, THE(1966, Ital./Span.); MISSION BLOODY MARY(1967, Fr./Ital./Span.); WEEKEND, ITALIAN STYLE(1967, Fr./Ital./Span.); ONE STEP TO HELL(1969, U.S./Ital./Span.); OPEN SEASON(1974, U.S./Span.); SANTO CONTRA EL DOCTOR MUERTE(1974, Span./Mex.); SAGA OF DRACULA, THE(1975, Span.)

John Line
YOUNG, WILLING AND EAGER(1962, Brit.)
1984
ANOTHER COUNTRY(1984, Brit.)

Mary Jane Line
Misc. Talkies
HIDEOUT IN THE SUN(1960)

Pipe Line
SEARCHERS, THE(1956)

Lloyd Linean
STEEL(1980), set d

Richard Lineback
JONI(1980); HARD COUNTRY(1981)

James Lineberger
TAPS(1981), w

Hardee Lineham
DEAD ZONE, THE(1983)

Barry Linehan
DEATH TRAP(1962, Brit.); RIVALS, THE(1963, Brit.); DEVIL-SHIP PIRATES, THE(1964, Brit.); WITCHCRAFT(1964, Brit.); SUBURBAN WIVES(1973, Brit.); DARK PLACES(1974, Brit.)

Rosaleen Linehan
ULYSSES(1967, U.S./Brit.)

Jeannie Linero
GODFATHER, THE(1972); HEAVEN CAN WAIT(1978)
Misc. Talkies
FLUSH(1981, Brit.)

Barry Lines
FIDDLER ON THE ROOF(1971)

Chris Lines
GOODBYE PORK PIE(1981, New Zealand)

David Lines
MR. PERRIN AND MR. TRAILL(1948, Brit.); TROUBLE IN THE AIR(1948, Brit.); FOOLS RUSH IN(1949, Brit.); GAY LADY, THE(1949, Brit.); IT ALWAYS RAINS ON SUNDAY(1949, Brit.); SCOTT OF THE ANTARCTIC(1949, Brit.)

Graham Lines
ULYSSES(1967, U.S./Brit.); SUBTERFUGE(1969, US/Brit.)

Stephen J. Lineweaver
1984
ALPHABET CITY(1984), art d, spec eff; BROTHER FROM ANOTHER PLANET, THE(1984), art d

Dee Linford
MAN WITHOUT A STAR(1955), w; MAN CALLED GANNON, A(1969), w

Denis Linford
ROOM AT THE TOP(1959, Brit.)

Ling
MEN OF AMERICA(1933)

Bo Ling
CALLING PHILO VANCE(1940)
Silents
RED WINE(1928)

Chen Man Ling
LET'S GO, YOUNG GUY!(1967, Jap.)

Eugene Ling
WITHIN THESE WALLS(1945), w; IT SHOULDN'T HAPPEN TO A DOG(1946), w; SHOCK(1946), w; ASSIGNED TO DANGER(1948), p, w; BEHIND LOCKED DOORS(1948), p, w; LOST BOUNDARIES(1949), w; PORT OF NEW YORK(1949), w; BETWEEN MIDNIGHT AND DAWN(1950), w; LOAN SHARK(1952), w; SCANDAL SHEET(1952), w; MAN FROM CAIRO, THE(1953), w; MISSION OVER KOREA(1953), w; HAND OF DEATH(1962), p, w

F. Ling
FIGHT TO THE LAST(1938, Chi.)

Fiesta Mei Ling
REVENGE OF THE PINK PANTHER(1978)

Frank Ling
GREEN FOR DANGER(1946, Brit.); DULCIMER STREET(1948, Brit.); MADNESS OF THE HEART(1949, Brit.)

James B. Ling
TARZAN, THE APE MAN(1981), ed

Ka Ling
Misc. Talkies
KUNG FU HALLOWEEN(1981)

Lai Ling
TASTE THE BLOOD OF DRACULA(1970, Brit.)

Mai Ling
CHAIRMAN, THE(1969)

Mei Ling
ROAD TO HONG KONG, THE(1962, U.S./Brit.)

Nien Son Ling
Misc. Silents
SURVIVAL(1930, Ger.)

Richie Ling
Silents
SENTIMENTAL LADY, THE(1915); IMPOSTER, THE(1918)
Misc. Silents
WOMAN NEXT DOOR, THE(1915)

Soong Ling
55 DAYS AT PEKING(1963)

Suzanne Ling
KISS OF THE TARANTULA(1975)

Thomas G. Lingham
Silents
JUDITH OF THE CUMBERLANDS(1916); HUNTED MEN(1930); OKLAHOMA SHERIFF, THE(1930)
Misc. Silents
MEDICINE BEND(1916); MY LADY FRIENDS(1921); LIGHTING RIDER, THE(1924); HEARTLESS HUSBANDS(1925); SET-UP, THE(1926); COWBOY AND THE OUTLAW, THE(1929)

Tiko Ling
OPERATION BOTTLENECK(1961)

Wen Ling
LOVERS' ROCK(1966, Taiwan)

Wesley Ling
STALAG 17(1953)

Yai Tsui Ling
METEOR(1979)

Shangkuan Ling-feng
DRAGON INN(1968, Chi.)

Edward Lingard
Silents
ALONE IN LONDON(1915, Brit.)
Misc. Silents
DEAD HEART, THE(1914, Brit.); THROUGH THE VALLEY OF SHADOWS(1914, Brit.); LOST AND WON(1915, Brit.)

Theo Lingen
DOLLY GETS AHEAD(1931, Ger.); M(1933, Ger.); TESTAMENT OF DR. MABUSE, THE(1943, Ger.); HELP I'M INVISIBLE(1952, Ger.); HEIDI(1954, Switz.); HEIDI AND PETER(1955, Switz.); DIE GANS VON SEDAN(1962, Fr/Ger.); TONIO KROGER(1968, Fr./Ger.)

Thomas Lingham
Silents
ACROSS THE DEADLINE(1925); INVADERS, THE(1929)
Misc. Silents
PITFALL, THE(1915); DIAMOND RUNNERS, THE(1916); DARING DEEDS(1927)

Tom Lingham
STAR PACKER, THE(1934)
Silents
WESTERN LUCK(1924); RIDERS OF MYSTERY(1925); BANDIT'S SON, THE(1927); SPLITTING THE BREEZE(1927); BANTAM COWBOY, THE(1928); DESERT PIRATE, THE(1928); FANGS OF THE WILD(1928); INTO THE NIGHT(1928); MAN IN THE ROUGH(1928); ORPHAN OF THE SAGE(1928); RAWHIDE KID, THE(1928); YOUNG WHIRLWIND(1928); AMAZING VAGABOND(1929); FRECKLED RASCAL, THE(1929); PALS OF THE PRAIRIE(1929)
Misc. Silents
FIRE EATER, THE(1921); CROW'S NEST, THE(1922); SON OF THE GOLDEN WEST(1928); TRAIL OF COURAGE, THE(1928); TWO SISTERS(1929)

Wendy Lingham
PRIVATE LIFE OF SHERLOCK HOLMES, THE(1970, Brit.); DEMONSTRATOR(1971, Aus.)

Emil A. Linghelm
PIMPERNEL SVENSSON(1953, Swed.), d

Thomas Lingston
CONVICTED(1950)

Linh-Nam
SHANGHAI DRAMA, THE(1945, Fr.)

Rosaleen Linhan
PORTRAIT OF THE ARTIST AS A YOUNG MAN, A(1979, Ireland)

Buzzy Linhart
DEALING: OR THE BERKELEY-TO-BOSTON FORTY-BRICK LOST-BAG BLUES(1971); GROOVE TUBE, THE(1974); MODERN PROBLEMS(1981)

Jan Linhart
LUDWIG(1973, Ital./Ger./Fr.)

George Linjeris
COWARDS(1970)

Andre Link
YESTERDAY(1980, Can.), p; HAPPY BIRTHDAY TO ME(1981), p; MY BLOODY VALENTINE(1981, Can.), p; SPACEHUNTER: ADVENTURES IN THE FORBIDDEN ZONE(1983), p

John Link
CARNIVAL BOAT(1932), ed; BORN TO THE WEST(1937), ed; FORLORN RIVER(1937), ed; THUNDER TRAIL(1937), ed; GERONIMO(1939), ed; FOR WHOM THE BELL TOLLS(1943), ed; BOWERY CHAMPS(1944), ed; CHARLIE CHAN IN BLACK MAGIC(1944), ed; I'M FROM ARKANSAS(1944), ed; IDENTITY UNKNOWN(1945), ed; JEALOUSY(1945), ed; WOMAN WHO CAME BACK(1945), ed; BORDERLINE(1980), ed
Misc. Talkies
CALL OF THE FOREST(1949), d

John F. Link
KNICKERBOCKER HOLIDAY(1944), ed; GREAT FLAMARION, THE(1945), ed; GLASS ALIBI, THE(1946), ed; STRANGE IMPERSONATION(1946), ed; PRETENDER, THE(1947), ed; YANKEE FAKIR(1947), ed; DEVIL'S CARGO, THE(1948), d; VICIOUS CIRCLE, THE(1948), ed; GOLD FEVER(1952), ed; STORM RIDER, THE(1957), ed; ESCAPE FROM RED ROCK(1958), ed; SPACE MASTER X-7(1958), ed; SERGEANT WAS A LADY, THE(1961), ed; SHAME OF THE SABINE WOMEN, THE(1962, Mex.), ed; DESERT RAVEN, THE(1965), ed

John F. Link II
KING OF MARVIN GARDENS, THE(1972), ed; CHOSEN SURVIVORS(1974 U.S.-Mex.), ed; STAY HUNGRY(1976), ed; CITIZENS BAND(1977), ed
Johnny Link
ARE THESE OUR PARENTS?(1944), ed; QUEEN OF THE AMAZONS(1947), ed
Peter Link [Riggs O'Hara]
SIDELONG GLANCES OF A PIGEON KICKER, THE(1970)
William Link
HINDENBURG, THE(1975), w; ROLLERCOASTER(1977), w
Vladimir Linka
TRANSPORT FROM PARADISE(1967, Czech.)
Paul Linke
BABY MAKER, THE(1970); BIG BAD MAMA(1974); GRAND THEFT AUTO(1977); MOTEL HELL(1980); HEART LIKE A WHEEL(1983)
Oscar Linkenhelt
Misc. Silents
BUCKSHOT JOHN(1915)
Eduard Linkers
THEY WERE SO YOUNG(1955); FAREWELL TO ARMS, A(1957); QUESTION 7(1961, U.S./Ger.); MATTER OF WHO, A(1962, Brit.); JACK OF DIAMONDS(1967, U.S./Ger.); DEEP END(1970 Ger./U.S.); STEPPENWOLF(1974)
Edward Linkers
KRAKATIT(1948, Czech.); SALZBURG CONNECTION, THE(1972)
William Linkie
MY FAIR LADY(1964)
Eric Linklater
POET'S PUB(1949, Brit.), w; PRIVATE ANGELO(1949, Brit.), w; MAN BETWEEN, THE(1953, Brit.), w; SCOTCH ON THE ROCKS(1954, Brit.), w
Art Linkletter
PEOPLE ARE FUNNY(1945); CHAMPAGNE FOR CAESAR(1950); SNOW QUEEN, THE(1959, USSR)
Ludwig Linkmann
CITY OF TORMENT(1950, Ger.); GLASS TOWER, THE(1959, Ger.)
Dan Linkmeyer
SEED OF INNOCENCE(1980), art d
Eva Linkova
MISTRESS FOR THE SUMMER, A(1964, Fr./Ital.)
Paul Linkson
GALLIPOLI(1981, Aus.)
Betty Linley
HEIRESS, THE(1949)
Bambi Linn
OKLAHOMA(1955)
Frank Linn
SHERIFF OF REDWOOD VALLEY(1946)
James Linn
ALIAS BILLY THE KID(1946); TANGIER(1946); ONCE MORE, MY DARLING(1949)
Jim Linn
POCKET MONEY(1972), cos; CLOSE ENCOUNTERS OF THE THIRD KIND(1977), cos
Margaret Linn
KLUTE(1971)
Ralph Linn
GOVERNMENT GIRL(1943); MY BUDDY(1944); RAINBOW ISLAND(1944); WILSON(1944); CAPTAIN TUGBOAT ANNIE(1945); THERE GOES KELLY(1945)
Ray Linn, Jr.
SHE'S WORKING HER WAY THROUGH COLLEGE(1952)
Roberta Linn
GET YOURSELF A COLLEGE GIRL(1964)
Mark Linn-Baker
END OF AUGUST, THE(1982); MY FAVORITE YEAR(1982)
Joe Linnane
FIVE ANGLES ON MURDER(1950, Brit.); PENNY POINTS TO PARADISE(1951, Brit.); SECRET PEOPLE(1952, Brit.); SOMETHING MONEY CAN'T BUY(1952, Brit.); STRANGER IN BETWEEN, THE(1952, Brit.); YOU CAN'T BEAT THE IRISH(1952, Brit.); NOOSE FOR A LADY(1953, Brit.); ANGEL WHO PAWNED HER HARP, THE(1956, Brit.)
Isabelle Linnartz
1984
LOVE ON THE GROUND(1984,Fr.)
Bertil Linne
HERE'S YOUR LIFE(1968, Swed.)
Gees Linnebank
SPETTERS(1983, Holland)
Bob Linnell
CHRISTINA(1974, Can.), prod d
Susanna Linnman
VICTOR FRANKENSTEIN(1975, Swed./Ireland), ed
Edilson Lino
PIXOTE(1981, Braz.)
Hector Valentin Lino, Jr.
HI, MOM!(1970)
Patricia Linova
BLESS 'EM ALL(1949, Brit.)
Ivan Linow
RIVER, THE(1928); COCK-EYED WORLD, THE(1929); IN OLD ARIZONA(1929); SPEAKEASY(1929); JUST IMAGINE(1930); MADONNA OF THE STREETS(1930); NUMBERED MEN(1930); SHIP FROM SHANGHAI, THE(1930); SILVER HORDE, THE(1930); SONG OF THE FLAME(1930); TEMPLE TOWER(1930); UNHOLY THREE, THE(1930); GOLDIE(1931 58m FOX bw); MIRACLE WOMAN, THE(1931); TIP-OFF, THE(1931); IT'S TOUGH TO BE FAMOUS(1932); JEWEL ROBBERY(1932); RACKETY RAX(1932); SCARLET DAWN(1932); SPORT PARADE, THE(1932); TILLIE AND GUS(1933); KID MILLIONS(1934); MERRY FRINKS, THE(1934); WHARF ANGEL(1934)
Silents
CAPPY RICKS(1921); ENEMIES OF WOMEN, THE(1923); LOVER'S ISLAND(1925); FAR CALL, THE(1929)
Misc. Silents
THREE MILES OUT(1924); WAGES OF VIRTUE(1924); PLASTERED IN PARIS(1928); RED DANCE, THE(1928)

Rudy Linschoten
MASK, THE(1961, Can.)
Lester Linsk
COVER ME BABE(1970), p; GAMES, THE(1970), p
Art Linson
RAFFERTY AND THE GOLD DUST TWINS(1975), p; CARWASH(1976), p; AMERICAN HOT WAX(1978), p; MELVIN AND HOWARD(1980), p; WHERE THE BUFFALO ROAM(1980), p&d; FAST TIMES AT RIDGEMONT HIGH(1982), p
1984
WILD LIFE, THE(1984), p, d
Harry Linson
Misc. Silents
TRUTH ABOUT HELEN, THE(1915)
John Linson
CARWASH(1976)
1984
WILD LIFE, THE(1984)
Axel Linstadt
KINGS OF THE ROAD(1976, Ger.), m
Alec Linstead
RICHARD'S THINGS(1981, Brit.)
Hilary Linstead
HEATWAVE(1983, Aus.), p
Soren Linsted
VICTORY(1981)
Helen Linstrom
SNIPER, THE(1952)
Illona Linthwaite
1984
LITTLE DRUMMER GIRL, THE(1984)
Betty Hyatt Linton
I EAT YOUR SKIN(1971)
Cora Linton
Misc. Silents
RING OF THE BORGIAS, THE(1915)
Donald Linton
AROUND THE WORLD UNDER THE SEA(1966)
Harry B. Linton
MY WIFE'S FAMILY(1932, Brit.), w
Jean-Peter Linton
SOMETHING'S ROTTEN(1979, Can.)
John Linton
Misc. Talkies
KNOCKING AT HEAVEN'S DOOR(1980), d
John Peter Linton
HEAD ON(1981, Can.)
Jon Linton
PUFNSTUF(1970); 10(1979)
Sydney Linton
INTRUDER, THE(1955, Brit.)
Ken Lintott
KING LEAR(1971, Brit./Den.), makeup
Albert Linville
DAMN YANKEES(1958)
Joan Linville
GODDESS, THE(1958)
Joanne Linville
SCORPIO(1973); GABLE AND LOMBARD(1976); STAR IS BORN, A(1976); SEDUCTION, THE(1982)
Larry Linville
Misc. Talkies
STEPMOTHER, THE(1973)
Lawrence Linville
KOTCH(1971)
Conrad Linz
RASPUTIN(1932, Ger.), w
Lewis Linzee
TOUCH OF DEATH(1962, Brit.), p
Gustl Linzer
WHERE IS THIS LADY?(1932, Brit.)
Fernand Lion [Fernando Di Leo]
UP THE MACGREGORS(1967, Ital./Span.), w; SEVEN GUNS FOR THE MACGREGORS(1968, Ital./Span.), w
Leon M. Lion
BOAT FROM SHANGHAI(1931, Brit.); MANY WATERS(1931, Brit.), w; CHINESE PUZZLE, THE(1932, Brit.), a, w; NUMBER SEVENTEEN(1932, Brit.); LADY IN DANGER(1934, Brit.); ROMANCE AND RICHES(1937, Brit.); MAN WITH 100 FACES, THE(1938, Brit.); STRANGE BOARDERS(1938, Brit.)
Silents
HARD TIMES(1915, Brit.); HANGING JUDGE, THE(1918, Brit.), w; AS HE WAS BORN(1919, Brit.), w
Misc. Silents
GRIP(1915, Brit.); WOMAN WHO WAS NOTHING, THE(1917, Brit.); CHINESE PUZZLE, THE(1919, Brit.)
Margo Lion
THREEPENNY OPERA, THE(1931, Ger./U.S.); TRUNKS OF MR. O.F., THE(1932, Ger.); FROM TOP TO BOTTOM(1933, Fr.); ESCAPE FROM YESTERDAY(1939, Fr.); LOLA(1961, Fr./Ital.); JULIE THE REDHEAD(1963, Fr.); MADMAN OF LAB 4, THE(1967, Fr.)
Mickey Lion [Mario Bava]
HOUSE OF EXORCISM, THE(1976, Ital.), d
Roger Lion
Misc. Silents
CHANSON FILMEES(1918, Fr.), d; LA FLAMME CACHE(1918, Fr.), d; L'ETERNEL FEMININE(1921, Fr.), d; LA SIRENE DE PIERRE(1922, Fr.), d; LES YEUX D L'AIME(1922, Fr.), d; FIDELITE(1924, Fr.), d; J'AI TUE(1924, Fr.), d; LA FONTAINE DES AMOURS(1924, Fr.), d; LA CLE DE VOUTE(1925, Fr.), d; FIANCAILLES(1926, Fr.), d; LA NUIT EST A NOUS(1927, Fr.), d; LES CHASSEUR DE CHEZ MAXIM'S(1927, Fr.), d; LE VENENOSA(1928, Fr.), d

Lionel
JONAH–WHO WILL BE 25 IN THE YEAR 2000(1976, Switz.)
Alain Lionel
PROSTITUTION(1965, Fr.)
C.J. Lionel
Misc. Silents
LAND OF LONG SHADOWS(1917)
Guy Lionel
GUNMEN OF THE RIO GRANDE(1965, Fr./Ital./Span.), w
Lionel Blair and His Dancers
PLAY IT COOL(1963, Brit.)
Lionel Hampton and his Band
MISTER ROCK AND ROLL(1957)
Alberto Lionello
LOVE IN 4 DIMENSIONS(1965 Fr./Ital.); BIRDS, THE BEES AND THE ITALIANS, THE(1967); TILL MARRIAGE DO US PART(1979, Ital.)
Gabriel Lionoff
SUMMER STORM(1944)
Louis Lions
PANIQUE(1947, Fr.)
Anne-Severine Liotard
1984
FULL MOON IN PARIS(1984, Fr.)
Therese Liotard
ONE SINGS, THE OTHER DOESN'T(1977, Fr.); DEATHWATCH(1980, Fr./Ger.)
Ray Liotta
LONELY LADY, THE(1983)
Anna Liotti
MORE THAN A MIRACLE(1967, Ital./Fr.); STORY OF A WOMAN(1970, U.S./Ital.)
Tony Lip
1984
POPE OF GREENWICH VILLAGE, THE(1984)
K. Lipanov
HOUSE ON THE FRONT LINE, THE(1963, USSR)
G. Lipari
MAN COULD GET KILLED, A(1966)
Victor Lipari
Z.P.G.(1972)
The Lipham Four
SONG OF THE OPEN ROAD(1944)
Dieter Liphardt
KENNER(1969), ph
Arnold Lipin
EVEL KNIEVEL(1971), cos
Arnold M. Lipin
THEY ONLY KILL THEIR MASTERS(1972), cos
Arny Lipin
KING KONG(1976), cos
Marta Lipinska
SALTO(1966, Pol.)
Eugene Lipinski
HANOVER STREET(1979, Brit.); YANKS(1979); SUPERMAN II(1980); OUTLAND(1981); SHOCK TREATMENT(1981); FIREFOX(1982); MOONLIGHTING(1982, Brit.); SOPHIE'S CHOICE(1982)
Stanley Lipinski
TANGIER ASSIGNMENT(1954, Brit.), ph; ADULTEROUS AFFAIR(1966), ph; OFFERING, THE(1966, Can.), ph
Clara Lipman
SINS OF THE CHILDREN(1930), w
David Lipman
EXTERMINATOR, THE(1980); SOLDIER, THE(1982)
Jerzy Lipman
EIGHTH DAY OF THE WEEK, THE(1959, Pol./Ger.), ph; KANAL(1961, Pol.), ph; KNIFE IN THE WATER(1963, Pol.), ph; LOVE AT TWENTY(1963, Fr./Ital./Jap./Pol./Ger.), ph; LOTNA(1966, Pol.), ph; BEAUTIFUL SWINDLERS, THE(1967, Fr./Ital./Jap./Neth.), ph; DEAD PIGEON ON BEETHOVEN STREET(1972, Ger.), ph; MARTYR, THE(1976, Ger./Israel), ph
Maureen Lipman
UP THE JUNCTION(1968, Brit.); GUMSHOE(1972, Brit.); SCHOOL FOR UNCLAIMED GIRLS(1973, Brit.); WILDCATS OF ST. TRINIAN'S, THE(1980, Brit.); DANGEROUS DAVIES–THE LAST DETECTIVE(1981, Brit.); EDUCATING RITA(1983)
Nicola Lipman
MADELEINE IS(1971, Can.)
William K. Lipman
GOOD DAME(1934), w
William R. Lipman
DOUBLE CROSS ROADS(1930), w; BROADWAY BAD(1933), w; LITTLE MISS MARKER(1934), w; MILLION DOLLAR RANSOM(1934), w; YOURS FOR THE ASKING(1936), w; LOVE IS NEWS(1937), w; ON SUCH A NIGHT(1937), w; DANGEROUS TO KNOW(1938), w; HUNTED MEN(1938), w; LOVE IS A HEADACHE(1938), w; ISLAND OF LOST MEN(1939), w; PERSONS IN HIDING(1939), w; TELEVISION SPY(1939), w; UNDERCOVER DOCTOR(1939), w; GALLANT SONS(1940), w; PAROLE FIXER(1940), w; PHANTOM RAIDERS(1940), w; QUEEN OF THE MOB(1940), w; SKY MURDER(1940), w; TEXAS RANGERS RIDE AGAIN(1940), w; WOMEN WITHOUT NAMES(1940), w; TARZAN'S NEW YORK ADVENTURE(1942), w; SWEET ROSIE O'GRADY(1943), w; BARBARY COAST GENT(1944), w; RATIONING(1944), w; BAD BASCOMB(1946), w; MIGHTY MCGURK, THE(1946), w; ALIAS A GENTLEMAN(1948), w; THAT WONDERFUL URGE(1948), w; SORROWFUL JONES(1949), w
Amanda Hope Lipnick
NUNZIO(1978)
Anina Lipoldva
FIREMAN'S BALL, THE(1968, Czech.)
Nahum Lipovsky
Misc. Silents
STRANGER, THE(1913, USSR), d

Arnold Lipp
SAVAGE BRIGADE(1948, Fr.), w
Dave Lipp
PATSY, THE(1964); BIG MOUTH, THE(1967)
Wilma Lipp
CARDINAL, THE(1963)
Jeffrey Lippa
AMERICAN POP(1981)
Charles Lippcott
BABY MAKER, THE(1970)
Dr. Edouard Lippe
NAUGHTY MARIETTA(1935)
Jonathan Lippe
ACT ONE(1964); HANG'EM HIGH(1968); ICE STATION ZEBRA(1968); ONE IS A LONELY NUMBER(1972)
Steve Lippe
1984
BIRDY(1984)
Albert Lippert
FINAL CHORD, THE(1936, Ger.)
Egon Lippert
DECISION BEFORE DAWN(1951)
Gerhart Lippert
TOWN WITHOUT PITY(1961, Ger./Switz./U.S.)
Robert Lippert
WITCHCRAFT(1964, Brit.), p; CURSE OF THE FLY(1965, Brit.), p
Robert L. Lippert
LAST OF THE WILD HORSES(1948), p, d; EARTH DIES SCREAMING, THE(1964, Brit.), p; LAST MAN ON EARTH, THE(1964, U.S./Ital.), p; NIGHT TRAIN TO PARIS(1964, Brit.), p; RETURN OF MR. MOTO, THE(1965, Brit.), p; SPACEFLIGHT IC-1(1965, Brit.), p; MURDER GAME, THE(1966, Brit.), p
Robert L. Lippert, Jr.
GREAT JASPER, THE(1933), p; GREAT JESSE JAMES RAID, THE(1953), p; TALL TEXAN, THE(1953), p; BIG CHASE, THE(1954), p; BLACK PIRATES, THE(1954, Mex.), p; FANGS OF THE WILD(1954), p; MASSACRE(1956), p
Alena Lippertova
END OF AUGUST AT THE HOTEL OZONE, THE(1967, Czech.)
Jack Lippiatt
MAN-TRAP(1961), ed
Renee Lippin
PORTNOY'S COMPLAINT(1972); UP THE SANDBOX(1972); LITTLE SEX, A(1982)
Norman Lippincott
MURDER AT GLEN ATHOL(1936), w
Irmgard Lippman
PINOCCHIO(1969, E. Ger.), makeup
Irving Lippman
DOMINO KID(1957), ph; HELLCATS OF THE NAVY(1957), ph; 20 MILLION MILES TO EARTH(1957), ph; APACHE TERRITORY(1958), ph; GUNMEN FROM LAREDO(1959), ph; SAFE AT HOME(1962), ph; THREE STOOGES GO AROUND THE WORLD IN A DAZE, THE(1963), ph; GREAT SIOUX MASSACRE, THE(1965), ph; OUTLAWS IS COMING, THE(1965), ph; TARZAN AND THE VALLEY OF GOLD(1966 U.S./Switz.), ph; TARZAN AND THE GREAT RIVER(1967, U.S./Switz.), ph; ANGEL UNCHAINED(1970), ph; LONERS, THE(1972), ph
Paul E. Lippman
PLAY MISTY FOR ME(1971)
Julie M. Lippmann
Silents
HOODLUM THE(1919), w
Mirko Lippo
GREH(1962, Ger./Yugo.), art d
Nancy Lippold
1984
SUPERGIRL(1984)
Cathy Lipps
ONE FOOT IN HEAVEN(1941)
Herbert Lippschitz
SHOT AT DAWN, A(1934, Ger.), art d
George Lipschulta
HAT CHECK GIRL(1932), md
George Lipschultz
DISORDERLY CONDUCT(1932), md; SHE WANTED A MILLIONAIRE(1932), md; SOCIETY GIRL(1932), md; YOUNG AMERICA(1932), md
Irving Lipschultz
DOUBLE WEDDING(1937)
Dennis Lipscomb
UNION CITY(1980); LOVE CHILD(1982); WARGAMES(1983)
1984
EYES OF FIRE(1984); SOLDIER'S STORY, A(1984)
Gwen Lipscomb
WITCHMAKER, THE(1969)
W.P. Lipscomb
UNDER TWO FLAGS(1936), w; SPLINTERS(1929, Brit.), w; GREAT GAME, THE(1930), w; ON APPROVAL(1930, Brit.), w; ONE EMBARRASSING NIGHT(1931, Brit.), w; CHANCE OF A NIGHT-TIME, THE(1931, Brit), w; FRENCH LEAVE(1931, Brit.), w; MISCHIEF(1931, Brit.), w; PLUNDER(1931, Brit.), w; SPECKLED BAND, THE(1931, Brit.), w; NIGHT LIKE THIS, A(1932, Brit.), w; SIGN OF FOUR, THE(1932, Brit.), w; GOOD COMPANIONS(1933, Brit.), w; MAN FROM TORONTO, THE(1933, Brit.), w; NIGHT AND DAY(1933, Brit.), w; THERE GOES THE BRIDE(1933, Brit.), w; CAMELS ARE COMING, THE(1934, Brit.), w; CHANNEL CROSSING(1933, Brit.), w; COLONEL BLOOD(1934, Brit.), d&w; I WAS A SPY(1934, Brit.), w; KING OF PARIS, THE(1934, Brit.), w; LOYALTIES(1934, Brit.), w; WOMAN IN COMMAND, THE(1934 Brit.), w; CARDINAL RICHELIEU(1935), w; CLIVE OF INDIA(1935), w; LES MISERABLES(1935), w; ME AND MARLBOROUGH(1935, Brit.), w; TALE OF TWO CITIES, A(1935), w; GARDEN OF ALLAH, THE(1936), w; MESSAGE TO GARCIA, A(1936), w; TROUBLED WATERS(1936, Brit.), w; PYGMALION(1938, Brit.), w; SUN NEVER SETS, THE(1939), w; MOON OVER BURMA(1940), w; MIDNIGHT ANGEL(1941), w; PACIFIC BLACKOUT(1942), w; FOREVER AND A DAY(1943), w; BEWARE OF PITY(1946, Brit.), w; MARK OF CAIN, THE(1948, Brit.), w; BITTER SPRINGS(1950, Aus.), w; HIS EXCELLENCY(1952, Brit.), w; IVORY HUNTER(1952, Brit.), w; MAKE ME AN OFFER(1954, Brit.), p, w; DUNKIRK(1958, Brit.), w; ROBBERY UNDER

ARMS(1958, Brit.), w; TOWN LIKE ALICE, A(1958, Brit.), w
Alan Lipscott
 SNOW QUEEN, THE(1959, USSR), w
George Lipshultz
 PAINTED WOMAN(1932), md
Harold B. Lipsitz
 LAST OF THE DUANES(1930), p
Silents
 SILVER VALLEY(1927), w
Morris Lipsius
 FINGER MAN(1955), w
Scott Lipsker
1984
 JOY OF SEX(1984), m
Eleazar Lipsky
 KISS OF DEATH(1947), w; PEOPLE AGAINST O'HARA, THE(1951), w; FIEND WHO WALKED THE WEST, THE(1958), w; READY FOR THE PEOPLE(1964), w
L. Lipsky
 I KILLED EINSTEIN, GENTLEMEN(1970, Czech.)
Lubomir Lipsky
 MAN FROM THE FIRST CENTURY, THE(1961, Czech.)
Oldrich Lipsky
 MAN FROM THE FIRST CENTURY, THE(1961, Czech.), d&w; LEMONADE JOE(1966, Czech.), d; HAPPY END(1968, Czech.), d, w; I KILLED EINSTEIN, GENTLEMEN(1970, Czech.), d, w; ADELE HASN'T HAD HER SUPPER YET(1978, Czech.), d
Arthur Lipson
 STRUGGLE, THE(1931)
Burke Lipson
 WIRE SERVICE(1942), makeup
Cecelia Lipson
 MIDNIGHT COWBOY(1969)
Doreen Lipson
 STARSHIP INVASIONS(1978, Can.)
Jack Lipson
 SKINNER STEPS OUT(1929); MANHATTAN MELODRAMA(1934); NIGHT AT THE OPERA, A(1935); ONE MAN JUSTICE(1937); CHOCOLATE SOLDIER, THE(1941); THREE DARING DAUGHTERS(1948)
Jack "Tiny" Lipson
 NEVER GIVE A SUCKER AN EVEN BREAK(1941); I MARRIED AN ANGEL(1942); KISMET(1944)
John Lipson
 FLASH GORDON(1936)
Larry Lipson
 IT'S A DEAL(1930), ed
Mark Lipson
1984
 ALMOST YOU(1984), p
Paul Lipson
 PRETTY BOY FLOYD(1960)
Tiny Lipson
 SUSPENSE(1946)
Aaron Lipstadt
 ANDROID(1982), d; SLUMBER PARTY MASSACRE, THE(1982), a, d
Harold Lipstein
 AMBUSH(1950), ph; SKIPPER SURPRISED HIS WIFE, THE(1950), ph; BANNERLINE(1951), ph; NO QUESTIONS ASKED(1951), ph; PAINTED HILLS, THE(1951), ph; FEARLESS FAGAN(1952), ph; CONFIDENTIAL CONNIE(1953), ph; FAST COMPANY(1953), ph; ADVENTURES OF HAJJI BABA(1954), ph; DRUMS ACROSS THE RIVER(1954), ph; GYPSY COLT(1954), ph; THREE YOUNG TEXANS(1954), ph; CHIEF CRAZY HORSE(1955), ph; MAN CALLED PETER, THE(1955), ph; PRIVATE WAR OF MAJOR BENSON, THE(1955), ph; WICHITA(1955), ph; FOREVER DARLING(1956), ph; PILLARS OF THE SKY(1956), ph; WALK THE PROUD LAND(1956), ph; GREAT MAN, THE(1957), ph; PAL JOEY(1957), ph; RIVER'S EDGE, THE(1957), ph; SPRING REUNION(1957), ph; DAMN YANKEES(1958), ph; RIDE A CROOKED TRAIL(1958), ph; NEVER STEAL ANYTHING SMALL(1959), ph; NO NAME ON THE BULLET(1959), ph; WILD AND THE INNOCENT, THE(1959), ph; HELLER IN PINK TIGHTS(1960), ph; CHAPMAN REPORT, THE(1962), ph; HELL IS FOR HEROES(1962), ph; PALM SPRINGS WEEKEND(1963), ph; RAMPAGE(1963), ph; HONEYMOON HOTEL(1964), ph; NONE BUT THE BRAVE(1965, U.S./Jap.), ph; ANY WEDNESDAY(1966), ph; LET'S KILL UNCLE(1966), ph; NIGHT OF THE GRIZZLY, THE(1966), ph; ASSIGNMENT TO KILL(1968), ph
Harry Lipstein
 CRY OF THE HUNTED(1953), ph
Robert Lipsyte
 THAT'S THE WAY OF THE WORLD(1975), w
1984
 ACT, THE(1984), w
Miles Liptak
 TO ALL A GOODNIGHT(1980), makeup
Albert Lipton
Misc. Talkies
 MIRELE EFROS(1939); KISS HER GOODBYE(1959), d
Celia Lipton
 CALLING PAUL TEMPLE(1948, Brit.); THIS WAS A WOMAN(1949, Brit.); FRIGHTENED BRIDE, THE(1952, Brit.)
Gene Lipton
Misc. Talkies
 BRIG, THE(1965)
Laurence Lipton
 ALIMONY(1949), w
Lawrence Lipton
 THE HYPNOTIC EYE(1960)
Lew Lipton
 MAN FROM WYOMING, A(1930), w; SUICIDE FLEET(1931), w; SWEEPSTAKES(1931), w; MUMMY'S BOYS(1936), w; BROADWAY SERENADE(1939), w
Silents
 BRIGHT LIGHTS(1925), w; IN OLD KENTUCKY(1927), w; BABY MINE(1928), w; CAMERAMAN, THE(1928), w; HONEYMOON(1929), w; SPITE MARRIAGE(1929), w

Lou Lipton
 HOLD'EM JAIL(1932), w; IT'S IN THE AIR(1935), w
Louis R. Lipton
 HERITAGE OF THE DESERT(1939), md
Lynn Lipton
 MONITORS, THE(1969); RICHARD(1972)
Lynne Lipton
 I COULD NEVER HAVE SEX WITH ANY MAN WHO HAS SO LITTLE REGARD FOR MY HUSBAND(1973)
Michael Lipton
 MAN CALLED ADAM, A(1966); HERCULES IN NEW YORK(1970); NETWORK(1976); WINDOWS(1980)
Rex Lipton
 GIGANTIS(1959, Jap./U.S.), m; THUNDER IN CAROLINA(1960), ed; FLIGHT OF THE LOST BALLOON(1961), ed; GUN HAWK, THE(1963), ed; TERRIFIED!(1963), ed
Richard Lipton
 FEMALE RESPONSE, THE(1972), a, p
Robert Lipton
 BLUE(1968); BULLITT(1968); MARYJANE(1968); TELL THEM WILLIE BOY IS HERE(1969); GOD'S GUN(1977)
Sandy Lipton
 T.R. BASKIN(1971); SEEMS LIKE OLD TIMES(1980)
1984
 BREAKIN' 2: ELECTRIC BOOGALOO(1984); NIGHTMARE ON ELM STREET, A(1984)
Jiri Lir
 LEMONADE JOE(1966, Czech.)
Constanza Lira
 MALOU(1983)
Georges Liron
 MARRIED WOMAN, THE(1965, Fr.); HOA-BINH(1971, Fr.), ph
Anna Lisa
 BEASTS OF BERLIN(1939); HOLD THAT WOMAN(1940)
Mona Lisa
 SUCKER MONEY(1933)
Silents
 SILVER CAR, THE(1921); NOTORIETY(1922)
Misc. Silents
 TOO WISE WIVES(1921); WHAT'S WORTH WHILE?(1921); DIVORCE COUPONS(1922)
Ronald Lisa
 MEN OF THE FIGHTING LADY(1954)
Edward Lisak
 SCOTT OF THE ANTARCTIC(1949, Brit.)
Lisat
 DREAM OF BUTTERFLY, THE(1941, Ital.), m
Steven Lisberger
 TRON(1982), d&w
Natalia Lisenko
Misc. Silents
 PUBLIC PROSECUTOR(1917, USSR); SATAN TRIUMPHANT(1917, USSR); FATHER SERGIUS(1918, USSR)
Stefan Lisewski
 FLOWERS FOR THE MAN IN THE MOON(1975, Ger.)
Tania Lish
 TERROR IN THE JUNGLE(1968)
Harold Lishman
 SONG OF THE ISLANDS(1942); WAKE OF THE RED WITCH(1949)
Gaetano Lisi
 SUMMER WISHES, WINTER DREAMS(1973)
Joe Lisi
1984
 HOME FREE ALL(1984)
Virna Lisi
 LOST SOULS(1961, Ital.); EVA(1962, Fr./Ital.); DUEL OF THE TITANS(1963, Ital.); DON'T TEMPT THE DEVIL(1964, Fr./Ital.); BAMBOLE!(1965, Ital.); CASANOVA '70(1965, Ital.); DOLL THAT TOOK THE TOWN, THE(1965, Ital.); HOW TO MURDER YOUR WIFE(1965); ASSAULT ON A QUEEN(1966); NOT WITH MY WIFE, YOU DON'T!(1966); BIRDS, THE BEES AND THE ITALIANS, THE(1967); GIRL AND THE GENERAL, THE(1967, Fr./Ital.); MADE IN ITALY(1967, Fr./Ital.); MAIDEN FOR A PRINCE, A(1967, Fr./Ital.); 25TH HOUR, THE(1967, Fr./Ital./Yugo.); ANYONE CAN PLAY(1968, Ital.); KISS THE OTHER SHEIK(1968, Fr./Ital.); ARABELLA(1969, U.S./Ital.); BETTER A WIDOW(1969, Ital.); CHRISTMAS TREE, THE(1969, Fr.); GIRL WHO COULDN'T SAY NO, THE(1969, Ital.); IF IT'S TUESDAY, THIS MUST BE BELGIUM(1969); SECRET OF SANTA VITTORIA, THE(1969); TIME OF THE WOLVES(1970, Fr.); STATUE, THE(1971, Brit.); BLUEBEARD(1972); SERPENT, THE(1973, Fr./Ital./Ger.); ERNESTO(1979, Ital.); HEIST, THE(1979, Ital.)
1984
 BEYOND GOOD AND EVIL(1984, Ital./Fr./Ger.)
Salvatore Lisitano
 DAISY MILLER(1974)
Pavel Lisitsian
 YOLANTA(1964, USSR)
Stephen Liska
1984
 STAR TREK III: THE SEARCH FOR SPOCK(1984)
Zdenek Liska
 BARON MUNCHAUSEN(1962, Czech.), m; DEVIL'S TRAP, THE(1964, Czech.), m; SHOP ON MAIN STREET, THE(1966, Czech.), m; MARKETA LAZAROVA(1968, Czech.), m; MURDER CZECH STYLE(1968, Czech.), m; ADRIFT(1971, Czech.), m; DIVINE EMMA, THE(1983, Czech,), m
Holly Lisker
 JAWS 3-D(1983)
Betsy Ann Lisle
Silents
 WAY OF ALL FLESH, THE(1927)
David Lisle
Silents
 IMPOSSIBLE MRS. BELLEW, THE(1922), w

Edward Lisle
SOMEWHERE IN FRANCE(1943, Brit.)
Josephine Lisle
GIRLS AT SEA(1958, Brit.)
Lucille Lisle
EXPERT'S OPINION(1935, Brit.); MIDNIGHT AT THE WAX MUSEUM(1936, Brit.); TWICE BRANDED(1936, Brit.); MINSTREL BOY, THE(1937, Brit.); SPECIAL EDITION(1938, Brit.)
Dennis R. Lisonbee
Misc. Talkies
TWO CATCH TWO(1979), d
JoAnn Lisosky
STACY'S KNIGHTS(1983)
Benjamin Liss
NO PLACE TO GO(1939), ed; CALLING PHILO VANCE(1940), ed
Bennett Liss
ZAPPED!(1982)
Henry Liss
FABULOUS WORLD OF JULES VERNE, THE(1961, Czech.), anim
Ted Liss
MAHOGANY(1975); SOMEWHERE IN TIME(1980)
Zvi Liss
DREAM NO MORE(1950, Palestine)
Leon Lissek
PERSECUTION AND ASSASSINATION OF JEAN-PAUL MARAT AS PERFORMED BY THE INMATES OF THE ASYLUM OF CHARENTON UNDER THE DIRECTION OF THE MARQUIS DE SADE, THE(1967, Brit.); TELL ME LIES(1968, Brit.); WHERE'S JACK?(1969, Brit.); UNDERGROUND(1970, Brit.); HORSEMEN, THE(1971); LAST VALLEY, THE(1971, Brit.); NICHOLAS AND ALEXANDRA(1971, Brit.); COUNTESS DRACULA(1972, Brit.); TALES THAT WITNESS MADNESS(1973, Brit.); BLOCK-HOUSE, THE(1974, Brit.); ELIZA FRASER(1976, Aus.); SWEENEY 2(1978, Brit.); TIME BANDITS(1981, Brit.)
Natalie Lissenko
Misc. Silents
QUEEN'S SECRET, THE(1919, USSR); LE BRASIER ARDENT(1923, Fr.); LES OMBRES QUI PASSANT(1924, Fr.); L'AFFICHE(1925, Fr.); EN RADE(1927, Fr.)
Lissette
WINTER KILLS(1979)
Elvy Lissiak
FROM A ROMAN BALCONY(1961, Fr./Ital.); SHIP OF CONDEMNED WOMEN, THE(1963, ITAL.); RED LIPS(1964, Fr./Ital.); GUILT IS NOT MINE(1968, Ital.)
Dan List
CHAFED ELBOWS(1967); PUT UP OR SHUT UP(1968, Arg.), spec eff; PUTNEY SWOPE(1969), spec eff
Danny List
VOYAGE TO THE END OF THE UNIVERSE(1963, Czech.), m
Eugene List
BACHELOR'S DAUGHTERS, THE(1946)
Liesbeth List
MYSTERIES(1979, Neth.)
Bruce Lister
BADGER'S GREEN(1934, Brit.); DEATH AT A BROADCAST(1934, Brit.); THIRD CLUE, THE(1934, Brit.); TO BE A LADY(1934, Brit.); OLD FAITHFUL(1935, Brit.); OLD ROSES(1935, Brit.); CRIME OVER LONDON(1936, Brit.); HAIL AND FARE-WELL(1936, Brit.); HEAD OFFICE(1936, Brit.); HEIRLOOM MYSTERY, THE(1936, Brit.); STAR FELL FROM HEAVEN, A(1936, Brit.); CHANGE FOR A SOVE-REIGN(1937, Brit.); MAYFAIR MELODY(1937, Brit.); RIVER OF UNREST(1937, Brit.); TENTH MAN, THE(1937, Brit.); WINDMILL, THE(1937, Brit.); QUIET PLEASE(1938, Brit.); THISTLEDOWN(1938, Brit.); HOME FROM HOME(1939, Brit.); BUT NOT IN VAIN(1948, Brit.); CELIA(1949, Brit.)
Clem Lister
MARCH HARE, THE(1956, Brit.)
Eva Lister
DEMON BARBER OF FLEET STREET, THE(1939, Brit.)
Eve Lister
GIRL IN THE CROWD, THE(1934, Brit.); GLIMPSE OF PARADISE, A(1934, Brit.); BIRDS OF A FEATHER(1935, Brit.); CITY OF BEAUTIFUL NONSENSE, THE(1935, Brit.); COCK O' THE NORTH(1935, Brit.); NO LIMIT(1935, Brit.); MEN OF YESTER-DAY(1936, Brit.); SUNSHINE AHEAD(1936, Brit.)
Francis Lister
ATLANTIC(1929 Brit.); MYSTERY AT THE VILLA ROSE(1930, Brit.); BROWN SUGAR(1931, Brit.); UNEASY VIRTUE(1931, Brit.); COUNSEL'S OPINION(1933, Brit.); HAWLEY'S OF HIGH STREET(1933, Brit.); NIGHT AND DAY(1933, Brit.); UP TO THE NECK(1933, Brit.); CARDINAL RICHELIEU(1935); CLIVE OF INDIA(1935); MUTINY ON THE BOUNTY(1935); LIVING DANGEROUSLY(1936, Brit.); SENSATION(1936, Brit.); RETURN OF THE SCARLET PIMPERNEL(1938, Brit.); MURDER IN THE NIGHT(1940, Brit.); HUNDRED POUND WINDOW, THE(1943, Brit.); HENRY V(1946, Brit.); WICKED LADY, THE(1946, Brit.); CHRISTOPHER COLUMBUS(1949, Brit.); HOME TO DANGER(1951, Brit.)
Silents
OLD WIVES' TALE, THE(1921, Brit.); UNWANTED, THE(1924, Brit.)
Misc. Silents
BRANDED(1920, Brit.); FORTUNE OF CHRISTINA MCNAB, THE(1921, Brit.); BODEN'S BOY(1923, Brit.); SHOULD A DOCTOR TELL?(1923, Brit.); CHAPPY - THAT'S ALL(1924, Brit.)
Gabrial Lister
FRANCHETTE; LES INTRIGUES(1969), ph
Irene Lister
TECKMAN MYSTERY, THE(1955, Brit)
Jean Lister
QUEEN OF HEARTS(1936, Brit.)
Margot Lister
MADE IN HEAVEN(1952, Brit.); ISN'T LIFE WONDERFUL!(1953, Brit.); PRINCE AND THE SHOWGIRL, THE(1957, Brit.); TEARS FOR SIMON(1957, Brit.); THREE MEN IN A BOAT(1958, Brit.)
Moira Lister
SHIPBUILDERS, THE(1943, Brit.); MY AIN FOLK(1944, Brit.); DON CHICAGO(1945, Brit.); WANTED FOR MURDER(1946, Brit.); LADY SURRENDERS, A(1947, Brit.); ANOTHER SHORE(1948, Brit.); SO EVIL MY LOVE(1948, Brit.); UNEASY TERMS(1948, Brit.); AGITATOR, THE(1949, Brit.); MRS. FITZHERBERT(1950, Brit.); RUN

FOR YOUR MONEY, A(1950, Brit.); FILES FROM SCOTLAND YARD(1951, Brit.); MANIACS ON WHEELS(1951, Brit.); POOL OF LONDON(1951, Brit.); SOMETHING MONEY CAN'T BUY(1952, Brit.); WHITE CORRIDORS(1952, Brit.); CRUEL SEA, THE(1953); LIMPING MAN, THE(1953, Brit.); DEEP BLUE SEA, THE(1955, Brit.); TROUBLE IN STORE(1955, Brit.); WICKED WIFE(1955, Brit.); ABANDON SHIP(1957, Brit.); JOHN AND JULIE(1957, Brit.); JOEY BOY(1965, Brit.); YELLOW ROLLS-ROYCE, THE(1965, Brit.); COP-OUT(1967, Brit.); DOUBLE MAN, THE(1967); NOT NOW DARLING(1975, Brit.)
Renny Lister
CURSE OF THE WEREWOLF, THE(1961); TOUCH OF THE OTHER, A(1970, Brit.)
Rupert Lister
SPLINTERS IN THE NAVY(1931, Brit.)
Ryan Listman
EVENTS(1970)
Ian Liston
EMPIRE STRIKES BACK, THE(1980)
Frank Liston [Franco Lauteri]
JOHNNY YUMA(1967, Ital.)
Melba Liston
SMILE ORANGE(1976, Jamaican), m
Millie Liston
Silents
NEPTUNE'S DAUGHTER(1914)
Sonny Liston
HARLOW(1965); HEAD(1968); MOONFIRE(1970)
Giorgio Listuzzi
WHITE NIGHTS(1961, Ital./Fr.)
Mary Liswood
PANIC IN THE STREETS(1950)
A. Lisyanskaya
TWELFTH NIGHT(1956, USSR)
Anna Lisyanskaya
RAINBOW, THE(1944, USSR); DAYS AND NIGHTS(1946, USSR); PORTRAIT OF LENIN(1967, Pol./USSR)
Rudy Liszcak.
SMALL CIRCLE OF FRIENDS, A(1980), spec eff
Rudi Liszczak
DOGS OF WAR, THE(1980, Brit.), spec eff
Franz Liszt
SONG OF LOVE(1947), m; RHAPSODY(1954), m; INTERLUDE(1957), m; ONCE MORE, WITH FEELING(1960), m; SONG WITHOUT END(1960), m; LISZTOMANIA(1975, Brit.), m
Margie Liszt
TWO WEEKS IN ANOTHER TOWN(1962); BLONDIE'S LUCKY DAY(1946); AS YOU WERE(1951); CALLAWAY WENT THATAWAY(1951); WE'RE NOT MARRIED(1952); DREAM WIFE(1953)
Marjorie Liszt
SIDE STREET(1950); VALLEY OF FIRE(1951); DEEP IN MY HEART(1954)
R. Liszt
WILD WOMEN OF WONGO, THE(1959), makeup
Rudolph Liszt
PROJECT X(1949), makeup; WILD HARVEST(1962), makeup; PASSION HOLI-DAY(1963), makeup
John Litel
WAYWARD(1932); ALCATRAZ ISLAND(1937); BACK IN CIRCULATION(1937); BLACK LEGION, THE(1937); FUGITIVE IN THE SKY(1937); LIFE OF EMILE ZOLA, THE(1937); MARKED WOMAN(1937); MIDNIGHT COURT(1937); MISSING WIT-NESSES(1937); SLIM(1937); AMAZING DR. CLITTERHOUSE, THE(1938); BROAD-WAY MUSKETEERS(1938); COMET OVER BROADWAY(1938); GOLD IS WHERE YOU FIND IT(1938); JEZEBEL(1938); LITTLE MISS THOROUGHBRED(1938); LOVE, HONOR AND BEHAVE(1938); MY BILL(1938); NANCY DREW-DETECTIVE(1938); OVER THE WALL(1938); SLIGHT CASE OF MURDER, A(1938); VALLEY OF THE GIANTS(1938); DEAD END KIDS ON DRESS PARADE(1939); DODGE CITY(1939); DUST BE MY DESTINY(1939); NANCY DREW-REPORTER(1939); NANCY DREW AND THE HIDDEN STAIRCASE(1939); NANCY DREW, TROUBLE SHOOTER(1939); ON TRIAL(1939); ONE HOUR TO LIVE(1939); RETURN OF DR. X, THE(1939); SECRET SERVICE OF THE AIR(1939); WINGS OF THE NAVY(1939); YOU CAN'T GET AWAY WITH MURDER(1939); ANGEL FROM TEXAS, AN(1940); CASTLE ON THE HUDSON(1940); CHILD IS BORN, A(1940); FATHER IS A PRINCE(1940); FIGHTING 69TH, THE(1940); FLIGHT ANGELS(1940); GAMBLING ON THE HIGH SEAS(1940); IT ALL CAME TRUE(1940); KNUTE ROCKNE-ALL AMERICAN(1940); LADY WITH RED HAIR(1940); MAN WHO TALKED TOO MUCH, THE(1940); MEN WITHOUT SOULS(1940); MONEY AND THE WOMAN(1940); MURDER IN THE AIR(1940); SANTA FE TRAIL(1940); THEY DRIVE BY NIGHT(1940); VIRGINIA CITY(1940); BIG BOSS, THE(1941); FATHER'S SON(1941); GREAT MR. NOBODY, THE(1941); HENRY ALDRICH FOR PRESIDENT(1941); SEALED LIPS(1941); THIEVES FALL OUT(1941); TRIAL OF MARY DUGAN, THE(1941); DESPERATE CHANCE FOR ELLERY QUEEN, A(1942); HENRY ALDRICH, EDITOR(1942); HENRY ALDRICH GETS GLAMOUR(1942); HENRY AND DIZZY(1942); INVISIBLE AGENT(1942); KID GLOVE KILLER(1942); MADAME SPY(1942); MEN OF TEX-AS(1942); MISSISSIPPI GAMBLER(1942); MYSTERY OF MARIE ROGET, THE(1942); THEY DIED WITH THEIR BOOTS ON(1942); BOSS OF BIG TOWN(1943); CRIME DOCTOR(1943); HENRY ALDRICH HAUNTS A HOUSE(1943); HENRY ALDRICH SWINGS IT(1943); MURDER IN TIMES SQUARE(1943); SO PROUDLY WE HAIL(1943); SUBMARINE BASE(1943); WHERE ARE YOUR CHILDREN?(1943); FACES IN THE FOG(1944); HENRY ALDRICH, BOY SCOUT(1944); HENRY AL-DRICH PLAYS CUPID(1944); HENRY ALDRICH'S LITTLE SECRET(1944); LAKE PLACID SERENADE(1944); MURDER IN THE BLUE ROOM(1944); MY BUDDY(1944); BREWSTER'S MILLIONS(1945); CRIME DOCTOR'S WARNING(1945); CRIMSON CANARY(1945); DALTONS RIDE AGAIN, THE(1945); ENCHANTED FOREST, THE(1945); NORTHWEST TRAIL(1945); SALOME, WHERE SHE DANCED(1945); SAN ANTONIO(1945); MADONNA'S SECRET, THE(1946); NIGHT IN PARADISE, A(1946); SHE WROTE THE BOOK(1946); SISTER KENNY(1946); SMOOTH AS SILK(1946); SWELL GUY(1946); BEGINNING OR THE END, THE(1947); CASS TIMBER-LANE(1947); CHRISTMAS EVE(1947); EASY COME, EASY GO(1947); GUILTY, THE(1947); HEAVEN ONLY KNOWS(1947); LIGHTHOUSE(1947); I, JANE DOE(1948); MY DOG RUSTY(1948); PITFALL(1948); RUSTY LEADS THE WAY(1948); SMART WOMAN(1948); TRIPLE THREAT(1948); VALIANT HOMBRE(1948); GAL WHO TOOK THE WEST, THE(1949); MARY RYAN, DETECTIVE(1949); OUTPOST IN MOROCCO(1949); RUSTY SAVES A LIFE(1949); RUSTY'S BIRTHDAY(1949); SHAM-

ROCK HILL(1949); WOMAN IN HIDING(1949); FULLER BRUSH GIRL, THE(1950); KISS TOMORROW GOODBYE(1950); SUNDOWNERS, THE(1950); CUBAN FIRE-BALL(1951); FLIGHT TO MARS(1951); GROOM WORE SPURS, THE(1951); LITTLE EGYPT(1951); TAKE CARE OF MY LITTLE GIRL(1951); TEXAS RANGERS, THE(1951); TWO DOLLAR BETTOR(1951); JET JOB(1952); MONTANA BELLE(1952); SCARAMOUCHE(1952); JACK SLADE(1953); SITTING BULL(1954); KENTUCKIAN, THE(1955); TEXAS LADY(1955); COMANCHE(1956); WILD DAKOTAS, THE(1956); DECISION AT SUNDOWN(1957); HIRED GUN, THE(1957); RUNAWAY DAUGH-TERS(1957); HOUSEBOAT(1958); LOVER COME BACK(1961); POCKETFUL OF MIRACLES(1961); VOYAGE TO THE BOTTOM OF THE SEA(1961); GUN HAWK, THE(1963); SONS OF KATIE ELDER, THE(1965); NEVADA SMITH(1966)

Misc. Talkies
RETURN OF RUSTY, THE(1946)

Carlo Liten
Misc. Silents
STRONGEST, THE(1920)

Stanislav Litera
LEMONADE JOE(1966, Czech.)

Marek Litewka
CONSTANT FACTOR, THE(1980, Pol.); CAMERA BUFF(1983, Pol.)

John Lithgow
DEALING: OR THE BERKELEY-TO-BOSTON FORTY-BRICK LOST-BAG BLUES(1971); OBSESSION(1976); BIG FIX, THE(1978); ALL THAT JAZZ(1979); RICH KIDS(1979); BLOW OUT(1981); I'M DANCING AS FAST AS I CAN(1982); WORLD ACCORDING TO GARP, The(1982); TERMS OF ENDEARMENT(1983)
1984
ADVENTURES OF BUCKAROO BANZAI: ACROSS THE 8TH DIMENSION, THE(1984); FOOTLOOSE(1984); 2010(1984)

Lorraine Lithgow
MY WAY(1974, South Africa)

Tom Lithgow
WHITE HUNTRESS(1957, Brit.)

Ben Lithman
UNDERDOG, THE(1943), w

Massimo Liti
1984
ONCE UPON A TIME IN AMERICA(1984)

Marti Litis
HOW SWEET IT IS(1968)

Boris Litkin
Misc. Silents
CHILDREN OF THE NEW DAY(1930, USSR)

Phil Lito
WINTER KILLS(1979)

Angela Litolff
FIND THE LADY(1936, Brit.)

Oliver Litondo
1984
SHEENA(1984)

Benjamin Litrenta
JOAN OF ARC(1948)

Richard Litt
ZELIG(1983)

Joseph Littau
MOLLY AND ME(1929), md
Silents
TOILERS, THE(1928), md

William Littauer
KING OF COMEDY, THE(1983)

Guy Littaye
LA FEMME INFIDELE(1969, Fr./Ital.), art d; LES GAULOISES BLEUES(1969, Fr.), art d; THIS MAN MUST DIE(1970, Fr./Ital.), art d; DOCTEUR POPAUL(1972, Fr.), art d; TEN DAYS' WONDER(1972, Fr.), art d; JUST BEFORE NIGHTFALL(1975, Fr./Ital.), art d

Phillip Littell
FIREFOX(1982)

Robert Littell
AMATEUR, THE(1982), w

Giampiero Littera
VIOLENT SUMMER(1961, Fr./Ital.); EIGHTEEN IN THE SUN(1964, Ital.)

Herman Littin
ALSINO AND THE CONDOR(1983, Nicaragua), p

M. Littin
ALSINO AND THE CONDOR(1983, Nicaragua), w

Miguel Littin
ALSINO AND THE CONDOR(1983, Nicaragua), d

Ann Little
Silents
NAN OF MUSIC MOUNTAIN(1917); ALIAS MIKE MORAN(1919); ROARING ROAD, THE(1919); EXCUSE MY DUST(1920); CHAIN LIGHTNING(1922)
Misc. Silents
BELIEVE ME, XANTIPPE(1918); FIREFLY OF FRANCE, THE(1918); HOUSE OF SILENCE, THE(1918); LESS THAN KIN(1918); MAN FROM FUNERAL RANGE, THE(1918); RIMROCK JONES(1918); SOURCE, THE(1918); SQUAW MAN, THE(1918); WORLD FOR SALE, THE(1918); SOMETHING TO DO(1919); SQUARE DEAL SAND-ERSON(1919); TOLD IN THE HILLS(1919); CRADLE OF COURAGE, THE(1920); HAIR TRIGGER CASEY(1922); GREATEST MENACE, THE(1923)

Anna Little
Silents
BATTLE OF GETTYSBURG(1914); DAMON AND PYTHIAS(1914); OPENED SHUT-TERS, THE(1914); IMMEDIATE LEE(1916)
Misc. Silents
CALLED BACK(1914); LAND O' LIZARDS(1916); SILENT MASTER, THE(1917); UNDER HANDICAP(1917)

Arthur Little, Jr.
IROQUOIS TRAIL, THE(1950); HARD, FAST, AND BEAUTIFUL(1951)

Carol Little
Misc. Talkies
HIDEOUT IN THE SUN(1960)

Caryl Little
HALF A SIXPENCE(1967, Brit.); BOY FRIEND, THE(1971, Brit.); LUST FOR A VAMPIRE(1971, Brit.)

Charles Little
THEY'RE A WEIRD MOB(1966, Aus.)

Cleavon Little
WHAT'S SO BAD ABOUT FEELING GOOD?(1968); JOHN AND MARY(1969); COTTON COMES TO HARLEM(1970); VANISHING POINT(1971); BLAZING SAD-DLES(1974); GREASED LIGHTNING(1977); FM(1978); SCAVENGER HUNT(1979); HIGH RISK(1981); DOUBLE EXPOSURE(1982); JIMMY THE KID(1982); SALA-MANDER, THE(1983, U.S./Ital./Brit.)
1984
SURF II(1984); TOY SOLDIERS(1984)
Misc. Talkies
TOY SOLDIERS(1983)

David Little
KING OF THE GYPSIES(1978)

Don Little
WAR AND PEACE(1956, Ital./U.S.)

Ed Little
VILLAIN, THE(1979)

Eddie Little
APACHE WARRIOR(1957); REVOLT AT FORT LARAMIE(1957); TOMAHAWK TRAIL(1957); GUN FEVER(1958); MISSOURI TRAVELER, THE(1958); RIDE A CROOKED TRAIL(1958)

Edwetta Little
SAMMY STOPS THE WORLD zero(1978)

George Little
NIGHT TRAIN TO PARIS(1964, Brit.); FIDDLER ON THE ROOF(1971)

George Simpson Little
LONG JOHN SILVER(1954, Aus.)

Gordon Little
TWO HEARTS IN HARMONY(1935, Brit.); SHIPMATES O' MINE(1936, Brit.); ON VELVET(1938, Brit.)

Herbert Little, Jr.
TROOPER HOOK(1957), w

Jack Little
FULLER BRUSH GIRL, THE(1950)

James Little
HOUSE OF STRANGERS(1949); SLEEPING CITY, THE(1950); TAXI(1953)

Jimmy Little
HEY, ROOKIE(1944); EADIE WAS A LADY(1945); TALK ABOUT A LADY(1946)

Jonathon Little
DRYLANDERS(1963, Can.)

Little Jack Little
NASTY RABBIT, THE(1964); DEADWOOD'76(1965)

Lyle Little
THUNDERHEAD-SON OF FLICKA(1945), art d

Mark Little
STARSTRUCK(1982, Aus.); CLINIC, THE(1983, Aus.)

Michael Little
MISTER 880(1950)

Michele Little
OUT OF THE BLUE(1982)

Mickey Little
PURSUED(1947); DARING CABALLERO, THE(1949); GUN CRAZY(1949); CALLA-WAY WENT THATAWAY(1951); DARLING, HOW COULD YOU!(1951); IT'S A BIG COUNTRY(1951); GLORY ALLEY(1952); MONKEY BUSINESS(1952); CLOWN, THE(1953); MR. SCOUTMASTER(1953); TAKE ME TO TOWN(1953); PRIVATE WAR OF MAJOR BENSON, THE(1955)

Rich Little
PHYNX, THE(1970); LUCKY LUKE(1971, Fr./Bel.); DIRTY TRICKS(1981, Can.)

Stan Little
OFF THE DOLE(1935, Brit.); HOME SWEET HOME(1945, Brit.); GLASS TOMB, THE(1955, Brit.)

Thomas Little
KING KONG(1933), set d; MONKEY'S PAW, THE(1933), set d; SON OF KONG(1933), set d; WORLD MOVES ON, THE(1934), set d; TOP HAT(1935), set d; BANJO ON MY KNEE(1936), set d; DIMPLES(1936), set d; GIRLS' DORMITORY(1936), set d; KING OF BURLESQUE(1936), set d; LADIES IN LOVE(1936), set d; LLOYDS OF LON-DON(1936), set d; MESSAGE TO GARCIA, A(1936), set d; PRISONER OF SHARK ISLAND, THE(1936), set d; ROAD TO GLORY, THE(1936), set d; SING, BABY, SING(1936), set d; STOWAWAY(1936), set d; ALI BABA GOES TO TOWN(1937), set d; CAFE METROPOLE(1937), set d; LOVE AND HISSES(1937), art d; LOVE IS NEWS(1937), set d; ON THE AVENUE(1937), set d; SECOND HONEYMOON(1937), set d; THIN ICE(1937), set d; THIS IS MY AFFAIR(1937), set d; WAKE UP AND LIVE(1937), set d; WEE WILLIE WINKIE(1937), set d; YOU CAN'T HAVE EVERY-THING(1937), set d; ALEXANDER'S RAGTIME BAND(1938), set d; ALWAYS GOOD-BYE(1938), set d; BARONESS AND THE BUTLER, THE(1938), set d; FOUR MEN AND A PRAYER(1938), set d; IN OLD CHICAGO(1938), set d; JOSETTE(1938), set d; REBECCA OF SUNNYBROOK FARM(1938), set d; SALLY, IRENE AND MARY(1938), set d; SUBMARINE PATROL(1938), set d; SUEZ(1938), set d; BARRICADE(1939), set d; DAY-TIME WIFE(1939), set d; DRUMS ALONG THE MOHAWK(1939), set d; FRONTIER MARSHAL(1939), set d; HOLLYWOOD CAVALCADE(1939), set d; RAINS CAME, THE(1939), set d; ROSE OF WASHINGTON SQUARE(1939), set d; SECOND FIDDLE(1939), set d; STANLEY AND LIVINGSTONE(1939), set d; TAIL SPIN(1939), set d; WIFE, HUSBAND AND FRIEND(1939), set d; YOUNG MR. LINCOLN(1939), set d; BRIGHAM YOUNG-FRONTIERSMAN(1940), set d; GRAPES OF WRATH(1940), set d; I WAS AN ADVENTURESS(1940), set d; JOHNNY APOLLO(1940), set d; LILLIAN RUSSELL(1940), set d; LITTLE OLD NEW YORK(1940), set d; MARK OF ZORRO, THE(1940), set d; RETURN OF FRANK JAMES, THE(1940), set d; TIN PAN ALLEY(1940), set d; BLOOD AND SAND(1941), set d; CHARLEY'S AUNT(1941), set d; GREAT AMERICAN BROADCAST, THE(1941), set d; GREAT GUNS(1941), set d; HOW GREEN WAS MY VALLEY(1941), set d; MAN HUNT(1941), set d; SWAMP WATER(1941), art d; THAT NIGHT IN RIO(1941), set d; TOBACCO ROAD(1941), set d; WEEKEND IN HAVANA(1941), set d; WESTERN UNION(1941), set d; YANK IN THE R.A.F., A(1941), set d; A-HAUNTING WE WILL GO(1942), set d; BLACK SWAN, THE(1942), set d; GHOST AND MRS. MUIR, THE(1942), set d; I WAKE UP SCREAM-ING(1942), set d; LIFE BEGINS AT 8:30(1942), set d; MOONTIDE(1942), set d; MY GAL SAL(1942), set d; PIED PIPER, THE(1942), set d; RINGS ON HER FIN-

GERS(1942), set d; ROXIE HART(1942), set d; SON OF FURY(1942), set d; TALES OF MANHATTAN(1942), set d; THIS ABOVE ALL(1942), set d; CRASH DIVE(1943), set d; GANG'S ALL HERE, THE(1943), set d; HEAVEN CAN WAIT(1943), art d; HELLO, FRISCO, HELLO(1943), set d; HOLY MATRIMONY(1943), set d; JITTERBUGS(1943), set d; MARGIN FOR ERROR(1943), set d; MOON IS DOWN, THE(1943), set d; OX-BOW INCIDENT, THE(1943), set d; SONG OF BERNADETTE, THE(1943), set d; SWEET ROSIE O'GRADY(1943), set d; THEY CAME TO BLOW UP AMERICA(1943), set d; WINTERTIME(1943), set d; BIG NOISE, THE(1944), set d; FOUR JILLS IN A JEEP(1944), set d; IN THE MEANTIME, DARLING(1944), set d; JANE EYRE(1944), set d; KEYS OF THE KINGDOM, THE(1944), set d; LAURA(1944), prod d, set d; LODGER, THE(1944), set d; PURPLE HEART, THE(1944), set d; ROGER TOUHY, GANGSTER!(1944), set d; TAMPICO(1944), set d; WILSON(1944), set d; COLONEL EFFINGHAM'S RAID(1945), set d; DOLL FACE(1945), set d; DON JUAN QUILLIGAN(1945), set d; FALLEN ANGEL(1945), set d; HOUSE ON 92ND STREET, THE(1945), set d; NOB HILL(1945), set d; ROYAL SCANDAL, A(1945), set d; STATE FAIR(1945), set d; TREE GROWS IN BROOKLYN, A(1945), set d; WHERE DO WE GO FROM HERE?(1945), set d; WITHIN THESE WALLS(1945), set d; ANNA AND THE KING OF SIAM(1946), set d; CENTENNIAL SUMMER(1946), set d; CLUNY BROWN(1946), set d; DARK CORNER, THE(1946), set d; DO YOU LOVE ME?(1946), set d; LEAVE HER TO HEAVEN(1946), set d; MY DARLING CLEMENTINE(1946), set d; RAZOR'S EDGE, THE(1946), set d; SENTIMENTAL JOURNEY(1946), set d; SHOCK(1946), set d; SMOKY(1946), set d; SOMEWHERE IN THE NIGHT(1946), set d; STRANGE TRIANGLE(1946), set d; 13 RUE MADELEINE(1946), set d; BRASHER DOUBLOON, THE(1947), set d; CAPTAIN FROM CASTILE(1947), set d; DAISY KENYON(1947), set d; FOREVER AMBER(1947), set d; FOXES OF HARROW, THE(1947), set d; HOMESTRETCH, THE(1947), set d; KISS OF DEATH(1947), set d; MIRACLE ON 34TH STREET, THE(1947), set d; MOTHER WORE TIGHTS(1947), set d; NIGHTMARE ALLEY(1947), set d; APARTMENT FOR PEGGY(1948), set d; CALL NORTHSIDE 777(1948), set d; CRY OF THE CITY(1948), set d; FURY AT FURNACE CREEK(1948), set d; IRON CURTAIN, THE(1948), set d; LETTER TO THREE WIVES, A(1948), set d; LUCK OF THE IRISH(1948), set d; ROAD HOUSE(1948), set d; SITTING PRETTY(1948), set d; SNAKE PIT, THE(1948), set d; STREET WITH NO NAME, THE(1948), set d; THAT LADY IN ERMINE(1948), set d; THAT WONDERFUL URGE(1948), set d; UNFAITHFULLY YOURS(1948), set d; WALLS OF JERICHO(1948), set d; YELLOW SKY(1948), set d; DANCING IN THE DARK(1949), set d; FAN, THE(1949), set d; FATHER WAS A FULLBACK(1949), set d; HOUSE OF STRANGERS(1949), set d; I WAS A MALE WAR BRIDE(1949), set d; IT HAPPENS EVERY SPRING(1949), set d; MOTHER IS A FRESHMAN(1949), set d; PINKY(1949), set d; PRINCE OF FOXES(1949), set d; SAND(1949), set d; THIEVES' HIGHWAY(1949), set d; WHIRLPOOL(1949), set d; YOU'RE MY EVERYTHING(1949), set d; AMERICAN GUERRILLA IN THE PHILIPPINES, AN(1950), set d; PANIC IN THE STREETS(1950), set d; THREE CAME HOME(1950), set d; UNDER MY SKIN(1950), set d; WHEN WILLIE COMES MARCHING HOME(1950), set d; WHERE THE SIDEWALK ENDS(1950), set d; DAVID AND BATHSHEBA(1951), set d; DESERT FOX, THE(1951), set d; FIXED BAYONETS(1951), set d; HOUSE ON TELEGRAPH HILL(1951), set d; I CAN GET IT FOR YOU WHOLESALE(1951), set d; I'D CLIMB THE HIGHEST MOUNTAIN(1951), set d; PEOPLE WILL TALK(1951), set d; RAWHIDE(1951), set d; THIRTEENTH LETTER, THE(1951), set d; YOU'RE IN THE NAVY NOW(1951), set d; DEADLINE—U.S.A.(1952), set d; DIPLOMATIC COURIER(1952), set d; DON'T BOTHER TO KNOCK(1952), set d; DREAMBOAT(1952), set d; LES MISERABLES(1952), set d; LURE OF THE WILDERNESS(1952), set d; MONKEY BUSINESS(1952), set d; MY PAL GUS(1952), set d; MY WIFE'S BEST FRIEND(1952), set d; NIGHT WITHOUT SLEEP(1952), set d; O. HENRY'S FULL HOUSE(1952), set d; PHONE CALL FROM A STRANGER(1952), set d; PONY SOLDIER(1952), set d; RED SKIES OF MONTANA(1952), set d; SOMETHING FOR THE BIRDS(1952), set d; STARS AND STRIPES FOREVER(1952), set d; WAY OF A GAUCHO(1952), set d; WE'RE NOT MARRIED(1952), set d; WHAT PRICE GLORY?(1952), set d; WITH A SONG IN MY HEART(1952), set d

Thomas K. Little
LITTLEST REBEL, THE(1935), set d; ROBERTA(1935), set d

Vera Little
YOUNG LORD, THE(1970, Ger.)

The Little Angels
INCHON(1981)

George Little Buffalo
LAST CHALLENGE, THE(1967)

Little Elsa
LIVING FREE(1972, Brit.)

Little Fred's Football Dogs
AROUND THE WORLD(1943)

Little Rex
Silents
FATHER O'FLYNN(1919, Brit.)

Little Sam
SPECIAL DELIVERY(1955, Ger.)

Beau Little Sky
JOURNEY THROUGH ROSEBUD(1972)

Dawn Little Sky
CIMARRON(1960); TEN WHO DARED(1960); APPLE DUMPLING GANG, THE(1975)

Eddie Little Sky
CIMARRON(1960); HELL BENT FOR LEATHER(1960); HELLER IN PINK TIGHTS(1960); SEVEN FACES OF DR. LAO(1964); PROFESSIONALS, THE(1966); LAST CHALLENGE, THE(1967); VALLEY OF MYSTERY(1967); WAY WEST, THE(1967); PAINT YOUR WAGON(1969); SOLDIER BLUE(1970), tech adv; JOURNEY THROUGH ROSEBUD(1972); BREAKHEART PASS(1976); CAR, THE(1977)

Edward Little Sky
MAN CALLED HORSE, A(1970)

Robert Little Star
LITTLE BIG MAN(1970)

The Little Vagabonds
TUXEDO JUNCTION(1941)

Lennie Little-White
CHILDREN OF BABYLON(1980, Jamaica), p,d&w, ed

Bianca Littlebaum
1984
SPLITZ(1984), w

Larry Littlebird
MAN WHO LOVED CAT DANCING, THE(1973)

John Littlechild
RUNNING BRAVE(1983, Can.)

Anabel Littledale
ASSAULT(1971, Brit.)

Richard Littledale
SLEEPING CAR(1933, Brit.); GIRL IN THE CROWD, THE(1934, Brit.); LUCKY JADE(1937, Brit.); GABLES MYSTERY, THE(1938, Brit.); MISS PILGRIM'S PROGRESS(1950, Brit.); RUN FOR YOUR MONEY, A(1950, Brit.); LONG DARK HALL, THE(1951, Brit.)

Sacheen Littlefeather
TRIAL OF BILLY JACK, THE(1974); WINTERHAWK(1976)
Misc. Talkies
JOHNNY FIRECLOUD(1975); SHOOT THE SUN DOWN(1981)

Bob Littlefield
PHANTOM EXPRESS, THE(1932)

Jack Littlefield
IT CAME FROM BENEATH THE SEA(1955); BLACKJACK KETCHUM, DESPERADO(1956); GANG WAR(1958)

Jack V. Littlefield
HOUSTON STORY, THE(1956)

L. D. Littlefield
Silents
EVERYMAN'S PRICE(1921), ph; MAN FROM BEYOND, THE(1922), ph

Lucien Littlefield
MOTHER KNOWS BEST(1928); CLEAR THE DECKS(1929); DARK STREETS(1929); DRAG(1929); GIRL IN THE GLASS CAGE, THE(1929); MAKING THE GRADE(1929); SATURDAY'S CHILDREN(1929); THIS IS HEAVEN(1929); CLANCY IN WALL STREET(1930); GREAT DIVIDE, THE(1930); HIGH SOCIETY BLUES(1930); NO, NO NANETTE(1930); SEVEN KEYS TO BALDPATE(1930); SHE'S MY WEAKNESS(1930); TOM SAWYER(1930); IT PAYS TO ADVERTISE(1931); MISBEHAVING LADIES(1931); REDUCING(1931); SCANDAL SHEET(1931); YOUNG AS YOU FEEL(1931); BROKEN LULLABY(1932); DEVIL AND THE DEEP(1932); DOWNSTAIRS(1932); EVENINGS FOR SALE(1932); HIGH PRESSURE(1932); IF I HAD A MILLION(1932); JAZZ BABIES(1932); MISS PINKERTON(1932); PRIDE OF THE LEGION, THE(1932); RASPUTIN AND THE EMPRESS(1932); SHOPWORN(1932); SPEED MADNESS(1932); STRANGERS IN LOVE(1932); STRANGERS OF THE EVENING(1932); THAT'S MY BOY(1932); ALICE IN WONDERLAND(1933); BIG BRAIN, THE(1933); BIG PAYOFF, THE(1933); BITTER TEA OF GENERAL YEN, THE(1933); CHANCE AT HEAVEN(1933); EAST OF FIFTH AVE.(1933); PROFESSIONAL SWEETHEART(1933); RAINBOW OVER BROADWAY(1933); SAILOR'S LUCK(1933); SKYWAY(1933); SONS OF THE DESERT(1933); SWEEPINGS(1933); KISS AND MAKE UP(1934); LOVE TIME(1934); MANDALAY(1934); MARRYING WIDOWS(1934); STAND UP AND CHEER(1934 80m FOX bw); THIRTY-DAY PRINCESS(1934); WHEN STRANGERS MEET(1934); CAPPY RICKS RETURNS(1935); GRIDIRON FLASH(1935); I DREAM TOO MUCH(1935); MAGNIFICENT OBSESSION(1935); MAN ON THE FLYING TRAPEZE, THE(1935); MURDER MAN(1935); ONE FRIGHTENED NIGHT(1935); RETURN OF PETER GRIMM, THE(1935); RUGGLES OF RED GAP(1935); SWEEPSTAKE ANNIE(1935); EARLY TO BED(1936), a, w; LET'S SING AGAIN(1936); MOON'S OUR HOME, THE(1936); ROSE MARIE(1936); BORN TO THE WEST(1937); BULLDOG DRUMMOND'S REVENGE(1937); HIGH, WIDE AND HANDSOME(1937); HOTEL HAYWIRE(1937); PARTNERS IN CRIME(1937); SOULS AT SEA(1937); WELLS FARGO(1937); WILD MONEY(1937); GLADIATOR, THE(1938); HOLLYWOOD STADIUM MYSTERY(1938); I AM THE LAW(1938); NIGHT HAWK, THE(1938); RECKLESS LIVING(1938); SCANDAL STREET(1938); WIDE OPEN FACES(1938); JEEPERS CREEPERS(1939); MYSTERY PLANE(1939); PIRATES OF THE SKIES(1939); SABOTAGE(1939); UNMARRIED(1939); WHAT A LIFE(1939); LI'L ABNER(1940); MONEY TO BURN(1940); THOSE WERE THE DAYS(1940); WESTERNER, THE(1940); GREAT AMERICAN BROADCAST, THE(1941); HENRY ALDRICH FOR PRESIDENT(1941); LIFE WITH HENRY(1941); LITTLE FOXES, THE(1941); MAN AT LARGE(1941); MR. AND MRS. NORTH(1941); MURDER AMONG FRIENDS(1941); BELLS OF CAPISTRANO(1942); CASTLE IN THE DESERT(1942); GREAT MAN'S LADY, THE(1942); HENRY ALDRICH GETS GLAMOUR(1942); HILLBILLY BLITZKRIEG(1942); LARCENY, INC.(1942); WHISTLING IN DIXIE(1942); HENRY ALDRICH HAUNTS A HOUSE(1943); JOHNNY COME LATELY(1943); CASANOVA IN BURLESQUE(1944); COWBOY AND THE SENORITA(1944); GOODNIGHT SWEETHEART(1944); LADY, LET'S DANCE(1944); LIGHTS OF OLD SANTA FE(1944); ONE BODY TOO MANY(1944); CARIBBEAN MYSTERY, THE(1945); SCARED STIFF(1945); IN OLD SACRAMENTO(1946); LOVE LAUGHS AT ANDY HARDY(1946); RENDEZVOUS WITH ANNIE(1946); THAT BRENNAN GIRL(1946); DOWN TO EARTH(1947); HOLLOW TRIUMPH(1948); JINX MONEY(1948); LET'S LIVE A LITTLE(1948); LIGHTNIN' IN THE FOREST(1948); SUSANNA PASS(1949); AT SWORD'S POINT(1951); ROAR OF THE CROWD(1953); CASANOVA'S BIG NIGHT(1954); SUDDEN DANGER(1955); WINK OF AN EYE(1958)
Misc. Talkies
SWEET GENEVIEVE(1947)
Silents
MARRIAGE OF KITTY, THE(1915); TEMPTATION(1915); WARRENS OF VIRGINIA, THE(1915); WILD GOOSE CHASE, THE(1915); JOAN THE WOMAN(1916); ON RECORD(1917); EYES OF THE HEART(1920); JACK STRAW(1920); ROUND UP, THE(1920); AFFAIRS OF ANATOL(1921); CRAZY TO MARRY(1921); LITTLE CLOWN, THE(1921); SHEIK, THE(1921); TOO MUCH SPEED(1921); ACROSS THE CONTINENT(1922); OUR LEADING CITIZEN(1922); SIREN CALL, THE(1922); TILLIE(1922); TO HAVE AND TO HOLD(1922); FRENCH DOLL, THE(1923); MR. BILLINGS SPENDS HIS DIME(1923); RENDEZVOUS, THE(1923); THREE WISE FOOLS(1923); TIGER'S CLAW, THE(1923); BABBITT(1924); NEVER SAY DIE(1924); GOLD AND THE GIRL(1925); RAINBOW TRAIL, THE(1925); SOUL MATES(1925); TUMBLEWEEDS(1925); WOMAN WHO SINNED, A(1925); TAKE IT FROM ME(1926); TONY RUNS WILD(1926); TORRENT, THE(1926); TWINKLETOES(1926); CAT AND THE CANARY, THE(1927); CHEATING CHEATERS(1927); MY BEST GIRL(1927); TAXI! TAXI!(1927); TEXAS STEER, A(1927); DO YOUR DUTY(1928); HAROLD TEEN(1928); HEAD MAN, THE(1928); MAN IN HOBBLES, THE(1928)
Misc. Silents
GUTTER MAGDALENE, THE(1916); WILD GOOSE CHASE(1919); HER FIRST ELOPEMENT(1920); HER HUSBAND'S TRADEMARK(1922); GOLD HEELS(1924); CHARLEY'S AUNT(1925); SMALL BACHELOR, THE(1927); HEART TO HEART(1928); CLEAR THE DECKS(1929)

Ralph Littlefield
APE MAN, THE(1943); VOODOO MAN(1944); ALONG CAME JONES(1945); SCARLET STREET(1945); THIS LOVE OF OURS(1945); SEA OF GRASS, THE(1947); STALLION ROAD(1947); SECRET BEYOND THE DOOR, THE(1948); WALLS OF JERICHO(1948); SMOKY MOUNTAIN MELODY(1949)

Robert Littlefield
INFERNAL MACHINE(1933); WITCHING HOUR, THE(1934); MAN ON THE FLYING TRAPEZE, THE(1935); ONE HOUR LATE(1935)
Silents
SHATTERED IDOLS(1922)

Scott Littlefield
SPY TRAIN(1943), w

Bill Littlejohn
BON VOYAGE, CHARLIE BROWN(AND DON'T COME BACK)*** (1980), anim; BOY NAMED CHARLIE BROWN, A(1969), anim; PHANTOM TOLLBOOTH, THE(1970), anim; RACE FOR YOUR LIFE, CHARLIE BROWN(1977), anim

Garry LittleJohn
SPEEDWAY(1968)

Gary Littlejohn
HELL'S ANGELS ON WHEELS(1967); SAVAGE SEVEN, THE(1968); CYCLE SAVAGES(1969); ANGELS DIE HARD(1970); ANGELS HARD AS THEY COME(1971); C. C. AND COMPANY(1971); BURY ME AN ANGEL(1972); LIMIT, THE(1972); BADLANDS(1974); RENEGADE GIRLS(1974)

Mimi Littlejohn
WINNING(1969)

William Littlejohn
OF STARS AND MEN(1961), anim d

Stuart Littlemore
MONEY MOVERS(1978, Aus.)

Craig Littler
MORE DEAD THAN ALIVE(1968); MODEL SHOP, THE(1969); BARQUERO(1970); SUPERBEAST(1972); SHEILA LEVINE IS DEAD AND LIVING IN NEW YORK(1975)

Susan Littler
LOVERS, THE(1972, Brit.); ROUGH CUT(1980, Brit.)

Tiny Littler
SHAMUS(1959, Brit.)

Dawn Littlesky
BILLY TWO HATS(1973, Brit.)

Eddie Littlesky
SERGEANTS 3(1962)

Bill Littleton
I WALK THE LINE(1970); DEADHEAD MILES(1982)

Carol Littleton
LEGACY(1976), ed; MAFU CAGE, THE(1978), ed; FRENCH POSTCARDS(1979), ed; ROADIE(1980), ed; BODY HEAT(1981), ed; E.T. THE EXTRA-TERRESTRIAL(1982), ed; BIG CHILL, THE(1983), ed
1984
PLACES IN THE HEART(1984), ed

Scott Littleton
FOURTH ALARM, THE(1930), w; WORLDLY GOODS(1930), w; SEA DEVILS(1931), w; TORCHY PLAYS WITH DYNAMITE(1939), w; LURE OF THE ISLANDS(1942), w; NIGHT EDITOR(1946), w; STEEL CAGE, THE(1954), w

Twyla Littleton
DEATH WISH II(1982)

Frank Littlewood
TERROR SHIP(1954, Brit.)

Harry Littlewood
FINAL CONFLICT, THE(1981)

Jaon Littlewood
SPARROWS CAN'T SING(1963, Brit.), w

Joan Littlewood
SPARROWS CAN'T SING(1963, Brit.), d; OH! WHAT A LOVELY WAR(1969, Brit.), w

Ray Littlewood
SMASH PALACE(1982, New Zealand)

Tom Littlewood
ROCK AROUND THE WORLD(1957, Brit.)

Brett Littman
WORLD ACCORDING TO GARP, The(1982)

Gordon Littman
RED SHOES, THE(1948, Brit.); MADNESS OF THE HEART(1949, Brit.)

Julian Littman
Misc. Talkies
BLACK CARRION(1984)

Lynne Littman
TESTAMENT(1983), p, d

Dr. Laszlo Littmann
CONFIDENCE(1980, Hung.)

George Litto
OBSESSION(1976), p; OVER THE EDGE(1979), p; DRESSED TO KILL(1980), p; BLOW OUT(1981), p

Maria Litto
Misc. Talkies
APE CREATURE(1968, Ger.)

Morgia Litton
Misc. Silents
IL TROVATORE(1914)

Anatol Litvak
DOLLY GETS AHEAD(1931, Ger.), d

Anatole Litvak
BE MINE TONIGHT(1933, Brit.), d; SLEEPING CAR(1933, Brit.), d; MAYERLING(1937, Fr.), d; TOVARICH(1937), d; WOMAN I LOVE, THE(1937), d; AMAZING DR. CLITTERHOUSE, THE(1938), p, d; SISTERS, THE(1938), d; CONFESSIONS OF A NAZI SPY(1939), d; ROARING TWENTIES, THE(1939), d; ALL THIS AND HEAVEN TOO(1940), d; CASTLE ON THE HUDSON(1940), d; BLUES IN THE NIGHT(1941), d; CITY, FOR CONQUEST(1941), p&d; OUT OF THE FOG(1941), d; THIS ABOVE ALL(1942), d; LONG NIGHT, THE(1947), p, d; MEET ME AT DAWN(1947, Brit.), w; SNAKE PIT, THE(1948), p, d; SORRY, WRONG NUMBER(1948), p, d; DECISION BEFORE DAWN(1951), p, d; ACT OF LOVE(1953), p&d; DEEP BLUE SEA, THE(1955, Brit.), p, d; ANASTASIA(1956), d; JOURNEY, THE(1959, U.S./Aust.), p&d; GOODBYE AGAIN(1961), p&d; FIVE MILES TO MIDNIGHT(1963, U.S./Fr./Ital.), p&d; 10:30

P.M. SUMMER(1966, U.S./Span.), p; NIGHT OF THE GENERALS, THE(1967, Brit./Fr.), d; LADY IN THE CAR WITH GLASSES AND A GUN, THE(1970, U.S./Fr.), p, d; ONE DOWN TWO TO GO(1982)

Berta Litvina
DREAMER, THE(1970, Israel)

T. Litvinenko
KIEV COMEDY, A(1963, USSR)

Taisa Litvinenko
SKY CALLS, THE(1959, USSR)

Si Litvinoff
WALKABOUT(1971, Aus./U.S.), p

N. Litvinov
CITY OF YOUTH(1938, USSR)

Sidney Z. Litwack
HEAD(1968), art d

Syd Litwack
GOLDENGIRL(1979), art d

Sydney Litwack
WHITE LINE FEVER(1975, Can.), art d

Sydney Z. Litwack
LOVED ONE, THE(1965), art d; MAD ROOM, THE(1969), art d; GETTING STRAIGHT(1970), art d; WATERMELON MAN(1970), art d; WHOSE LIFE IS IT ANYWAY?(1981), art d
1984
PLACES IN THE HEART(1984), art d

Krzystof Litwin
WALKOVER(1969, Pol.)

Krzysztof Litwin
SARAGOSSA MANUSCRIPT, THE(1972, Pol.)

Berta Litwina
LONG IS THE ROAD(1948, Ger.)

Felix Litzendorf
HOUSE OF LIFE(1953, Ger.), w

Anne Liu
DEEP THRUST-THE HAND OF DEATH(1973, Hong Kong)

Benjamin Liu
LIQUID SKY(1982)

Dan Liu
BIG JIM McLAIN(1952)

Frank Michael Liu
FORCED VENGEANCE(1982)

Irene Liu
LOVE IS A MANY-SPLENDORED THING(1955)

Kalen Liu
WELCOME TO HARD TIMES(1967); MATTER OF INNOCENCE, A(1968, Brit.)

Lotus Liu
I FOUND STELLA PARISH(1935); OIL FOR THE LAMPS OF CHINA(1935); ADVENTURES OF MARCO POLO, THE(1938); TRADE WINDS(1938)

Maurice Liu
DAUGHTER OF SHANGHAI(1937); WAIKIKI WEDDING(1937)

Mia Liu
STRANDED(1935)

Paul Liu
SOUTH SEA WOMAN(1953)

Terry Liu
INFRA-MAN(1975, Hong Kong)

Tony Liu
FISTS OF FURY(1973, Chi.)

P. Liubeshkin
LAD FROM OUR TOWN(1941, USSR)

Yuri Liubimoff
DAYS AND NIGHTS(1946, USSR)

V. Liubimov
TRAIN GOES EAST, THE(1949, USSR)

Liutz-Morat
Misc. Silents
PETIT ANGE(1920, Fr.), d

Giuseppe Liuzzi
DIARY OF A SCHIZOPHRENIC GIRL(1970, Ital.)

Paul Livadery
STUDENT TEACHERS, THE(1973)

Boris Livanov
DESERTER(1934, USSR); ENEMIES OF PROGRESS(1934, USSR); BALTIC DEPUTY(1937, USSR); MEN OF THE SEA(1938, USSR); SOUND OF LIFE, THE(1962, USSR)
Silents
TEN DAYS THAT SHOOK THE WORLD(1927, USSR)
Misc. Silents
FATHER FROST(1924, USSR)

Vasili Livanov
WATERLOO(1970, Ital./USSR)

Vasiliy Livanov
LETTER THAT WAS NEVER SENT, THE(1962, USSR); RESURRECTION(1963, USSR)

Vasily Livanov
SOUND OF LIFE, THE(1962, USSR)

Bill Lively
DEATH RIDES THE RANGE(1940), w; PHANTOM RANCHER(1940), w

Bob Lively
ENLIGHTEN THY DAUGHTER(1934), w; INSIDE INFORMATION(1934), w

Brenda Lively
ON THE RIGHT TRACK(1981)

Gene Lively
SUGARLAND EXPRESS, THE(1974)

Jason Lively
BRAINSTORM(1983)

Robert Lively
GIRL SAID NO, THE(1937), w; RHYTHM RACKETEER(1937, Brit.), w; DANGER ON THE AIR(1938), w; PERSONAL SECRETARY(1938), w; GREAT VICTOR HERBERT, THE(1939), w; EAST SIDE KIDS(1940), w; ISLE OF DESTINY(1940), w; THERE'S MAGIC IN MUSIC(1941), w

William Lively
FIGHTING DEPUTY, THE(1937), w; UNASHAMED(1938), w; FEDERAL MAN-HUNT(1939), w; FIGHTING RENEGADE(1939), w; BOYS OF THE CITY(1940), w; FRONTIER CRUSADER(1940), w; MERCY PLANE(1940), w; SAGEBRUSH FAMILY TRAILS WEST, THE(1940), w; THAT GANG OF MINE(1940), w; BILLY THE KID'S RANGE WAR(1941), w; LONE RIDER CROSSES THE RIO, THE(1941), w; PRIDE OF THE BOWERY(1941), w; TEXAS MARSHAL, THE(1941), w; TEXAS MAN HUNT(1942), w; ARIZONA TRAIL(1943), w; WAGON TRACKS WEST(1943), w; MAR-SHAL OF GUNSMOKE(1944), w; OLD TEXAS TRAIL, THE(1944), w; DAYS OF BUFFALO BILL(1946), w; GUN TOWN(1946), w; GUNMAN'S CODE(1946), w; RANGE RENEGADES(1948), w; TORNADO RANGE(1948), w; DAUGHTER OF THE JUNGLE(1949), w; ARIZONA MANHUNT(1951), w; DAKOTA KID, THE(1951), w; HOT LEAD(1951), w; COLORADO SUNDOWN(1952), w; GOLD RAIDERS, THE(1952), w; TRAIL GUIDE(1952), w; WILD HORSE AMBUSH(1952), w; IRON MOUNTAIN TRAIL(1953), w; PHANTOM OF THE JUNGLE(1955), w; TARZAN'S HIDDEN JUN-GLE(1955), w; GHOST OF ZORRO(1959), w

Gene Livermore
MOONSHINE COUNTY EXPRESS(1977)

Paul Livermore
AT WAR WITH THE ARMY(1950); TRIPOLI(1950); CONFIDENCE GIRL(1952); HOODLUM EMPIRE(1952); WILD BLUE YONDER, THE(1952); WOMAN THEY ALMOST LYNCHED, THE(1953)

Richard Livernoin
DON'T GAMBLE WITH LOVE(1936)

Barrie Livesey
COMMISSIONAIRE(1933, Brit.); HIS GRACE GIVES NOTICE(1933, Brit.); BLUE SQUADRON, THE(1934, Brit.); BREAKERS AHEAD(1935, Brit.); THEY WERE SIS-TERS(1945, Brit.)

Barry Livesey
PARIS PLANE(1933, Brit.); SOMETHING ALWAYS HAPPENS(1934, Brit.); VARIE-TY(1935, Brit.); MR. COHEN TAKES A WALK(1936, Brit.); REMBRANDT(1936, Brit.)
Silents
OLD CURIOSITY SHOP, THE(1921, Brit.)

Cassie Livesey
VARIETY(1935, Brit.)

Dave Livesey
YELLOW SUBMARINE(1958, Brit.), animation

Jack Livesey
COUNTY FAIR(1933, Brit.); VARIETY(1935, Brit.); WANDERING JEW, THE(1935, Brit.); HOWARD CASE, THE(1936, Brit.); PASSING OF THE THIRD FLOOR BACK, THE(1936, Brit.); REMBRANDT(1936, Brit.); BEHIND YOUR BACK(1937, Brit.); FIRST NIGHT(1937, Brit.); IT'S NEVER TOO LATE TO MEND(1937, Brit.); BEDTIME STORY(1938, Brit.); MURDER TOMORROW(1938, Brit.); OLD BONES OF THE RIVER(1938, Brit.); PENNY PARADISE(1938, Brit.); WORLD OWES ME A LIVING, THE(1944, Brit.); AFFAIRS OF A ROGUE, THE(1949, Brit.); MYSTERY AT THE BURLESQUE(1950, Brit.); PAUL TEMPLE'S TRIUMPH(1951, Brit.); MIDNIGHT LACE(1960); NOTORIOUS LANDLADY, THE(1962); THAT TOUCH OF MINK(1962)
Misc. Silents
DIVINE GIFT, THE(1918, Brit.)

Roger Livesey
EAST LYNNE ON THE WESTERN FRONT(1931, Brit.); CUCKOO IN THE NEST, THE(1933, Brit.); BLIND JUSTICE(1934, Brit.); LORNA DOONE(1935, Brit.); PRICE OF WISDOM, THE(1935, Brit.); REMBRANDT(1936, Brit.); DRUMS(1938, Brit.); SMILING ALONG(1938, Brit.); REBEL SON, THE ½(1939, Brit.); SPIES OF THE AIR(1940, Brit.); GIRL IN THE NEWS, THE(1941, Brit.); COLONEL BLIMP(1945, Brit.); STAIRWAY TO HEAVEN(1946, Brit.); I KNOW WHERE I'M GOING(1947, Brit.); VICE VERSA(1948, Brit.); IF THIS BE SIN(1950, Brit.); GREEN GROW THE RUSHES(1951, Brit.); MEN OF THE SEA(1951, Brit.); MASTER OF BALLANTRAE, THE(1953, U.S./Brit.); FINGER OF GUILT(1956, Brit.); ENTERTAINER, THE(1960, Brit.); IT HAPPENED IN BROAD DAYLIGHT(1960, Ger./Switz.); LEAGUE OF GENTLEMEN, THE(1961, Brit.); NO, MY DARLING DAUGHTER(1964, Brit.); OF HUMAN BONDAGE(1964, Brit.); AMOROUS ADVENTURES OF MOLL FLANDERS, THE(1965); OEDIPUS THE KING(1968, Brit.); HAMLET(1969, Brit.)

Sam Livesey
ONE FAMILY(1930, Brit.); RAISE THE ROOF(1930); YOUNG WOODLEY(1930, Brit.); DREYFUS CASE, THE(1931, Brit.); GIRL IN THE NIGHT, THE(1931, Brit.); JEAL-OUSY(1931, Brit.); MANY WATERS(1931, Brit.); UP FOR THE CUP(1931, Brit.); WICKHAM MYSTERY, THE(1931, Brit.); FLAG LIEUTENANT, THE(1932, Brit.); HOUND OF THE BASKERVILLES(1932, Brit.); INSULT(1932, Brit.); WONDERFUL STORY, THE(1932, Brit.); COMMISSIONAIRE(1933, Brit.); MAN WHO WON, THE(1933, Brit.); PRIVATE LIFE OF HENRY VIII, THE(1933); GREAT DEFENDER, THE(1934, Brit.); POWER(1934, Brit.); TANGLED EVIDENCE(1934, Brit.); DRAKE THE PIRATE(1935, Brit.); HOPE OF HIS SIDE(1935, Brit.); REGAL CAVAL-CADE(1935, Brit.); TURN OF THE TIDE(1935, Brit.); VARIETY(1935, Brit.); CALLING THE TUNE(1936, Brit.); MEN OF YESTERDAY(1936, Brit.); REMBRANDT(1936, Brit.); SHADOW, THE(1936, Brit.); DARK JOURNEY(1937, Brit.); WINGS OF THE MORN-ING(1937, Brit.); MILL ON THE FLOSS(1939, Brit.)
Silents
ONE SUMMER'S DAY(1917, Brit.); ALL THE WINNERS(1920, Brit.); ZERO(1928, Brit.)
Misc. Silents
MIDNIGHT GAMBOLS(1919, Brit.); SINS OF YOUTH, THE(1919, Brit.); BLACK SPIDER, THE(1920, Brit.); BURNT IN(1920, Brit.); MARRIAGE LINES, THE(1921, Brit.); FOOLISH MONTE CARLO(1922); MAISIE'S MARRIAGE(1923, Brit.); WAIT AND SEE(1928, Brit.); YOUNG WOODLEY(1929, Brit.)

Jean-Louis Livi
CHLOE IN THE AFTERNOON(1972, Fr.)

Ilia Livikou
ANTIGONE(1962 Gr.)

Members of the Living Theater
WHEEL OF ASHES(1970, Fr.)

Henry Livings
WORK IS A FOUR LETTER WORD(1968, Brit.), w

Jock Livingstom
ZERO IN THE UNIVERSE(1966), p

Barry Livingston
ERRAND BOY, THE(1961); MY SIX LOVES(1963); LOVE AND KISSES(1965); SIDEWINDER ONE(1977)

Bob Livingston
CIRCUS GIRL(1937); RANGE DEFENDERS(1937); RIDERS OF THE WHISTLING SKULL(1937); CALL THE MESQUITEERS(1938); KING OF THE NEWSBOYS(1938); OUTLAWS OF SONORA(1938); PURPLE VIGILANTES, THE(1938); RIDERS OF THE BLACK HILLS(1938); WILD HORSE RODEO(1938); OVERLAND STAGE-COACH(1942); WILD HORSE RUSTLERS(1943); WOLVES OF THE RANGE(1943); BENEATH WESTERN SKIES(1944); DEATH RIDES THE PLAINS(1944); LAW OF THE SADDLE(1944); RAIDERS OF RED GAP(1944); ONCE UPON A HORSE(1958)
Misc. Talkies
ARSON RACKET SQUAD(1938)

Ed Livingston
COUNTRY BOY(1966); THAT TENNESSEE BEAT(1966); TRACK OF THUN-DER(1967)

H.A. Livingston
Silents
TRUTH WAGON, THE(1914)
Misc. Silents
JACK CHANTY(1915)

Harold Livingston
STREET IS MY BEAT, THE(1966), w; HELL WITH HEROES, THE(1968), w; STAR TREK: THE MOTION PICTURE(1979), w

Ivy Livingston
Silents
JOSSELYN'S WIFE(1926)

Jack Livingston
Silents
ASHES OF HOPE(1917); DARK ROAD, THE(1917); WOODEN SHOES(1917); JUDGE HER NOT(1921); SAPHEAD, THE(1921); MAN'S LAW AND GOD'S(1922)
Misc. Silents
AMERICAN BEAUTY, THE(1916); HEART OF PAULA, THE(1916); SON OF ERIN, A(1916); BECAUSE OF THE WOMAN(1917); EYES OF THE WORLD, THE(1917); FLYING COLORS(1917); IN SLUMBERLAND(1917); TEN OF DIAMONDS(1917); HARD ROCK BREED, THE(1918); HIS ENEMY THE LAW(1918); INNOCENT'S PROGRESS(1918); PRICE OF APPLAUSE, THE(1918); WHO IS TO BLAME?(1918); COWARDICE COURT(1919); GOLDEN TRAIL, THE(1920); TOKIO SIREN, A(1920); WOLVES OF THE RANGE(1921); CRASHING COURAGE(1923); FRAME UP, THE(1923); POWER DIVINE, THE(1923); RANGE PATROL, THE(1923); SCARS OF HATE(1923); VOW OF VENGEANCE, THE(1923); BEATEN(1924); WHAT THREE MEN WANTED(1924)

Jay Livingston
SUNSET BOULEVARD(1950); LEMON DROP KID, THE(1951), m

Jock Livingston
ZERO IN THE UNIVERSE(1966), a, w; STAR!(1968)

Mae Livingston
WITHOUT RESERVATIONS(1946), w

Margaret Livingston
ACQUITTED(1929); BELLAMY TRIAL, THE(1929); CHARLATAN, THE(1929); INNO-CENTS OF PARIS(1929); LAST WARNING, THE(1929); MORGAN'S MARAU-DERS(1929); OFFICE SCANDAL, THE(1929); TONIGHT AT TWELVE(1929); BIG MONEY(1930); FOR THE LOVE O'LIL(1930); MURDER ON THE ROOF(1930); SEVEN KEYS TO BALDPATE(1930); WHAT A WIDOW(1930); BROADMINDED(1931); GOD'S GIFT TO WOMEN(1931); KIKI(1931); LADY REFUSES, THE(1931); SMART MO-NEY(1931); SOCIAL REGISTER(1934)
Silents
ALL WRONG(1919); HAIRPINS(1920); LYING LIPS(1921); DIVORCE(1923); AFTER MARRIAGE(1925); WAGES FOR WIVES(1925); WOMANPOWER(1926); YANKEE SENOR, THE(1926); AMERICAN BEAUTY(1927); MARRIED ALIVE(1927); SLAVES OF BEAUTY(1927); SUNRISE-A SONG OF TWO HUMANS(1927); APACHE, THE(1928); SCARLET DOVE, THE(1928); WAY OF THE STRONG, THE(1928)
Misc. Silents
BUSHER, THE(1919); BRUTE MASTER, THE(1920); HAUNTING SHADOWS(1920); COLORADO PLUCK(1921); EDEN AND RETURN(1921); HOME STRETCH, THE(1921); CHORUS LADY, THE(1924); HER MARRIAGE VOW(1924); WANDERING HUSBANDS(1924); GREATER THAN A CROWN(1925); UP THE LADDER(1925); WHEEL, THE(1925); WHEN THE DOOR OPENED(1925); BREED OF THE SEA(1926); HELL'S 400(1926); TRIP TO CHINATOWN, A(1926); LIGHTING(1927); STREETS OF SHANGHAI(1927); HIS PRIVATE LIFE(1928); SAY IT WITH SABLES(1928); THROUGH THE BREAKERS(1928); WOMAN'S WAY, A(1928)

Mildred Livingston
WORDS AND MUSIC(1929)

Patricia Livingston
GUNS OF FORT PETTICOAT, THE(1957)

Pickles Livingston
THINGS TO COME(1936, Brit.)

Princess Livingston
ROPE OF FLESH(1965); PUFNSTUF(1970)

Ramon Livingston
SPOOK WHO SAT BY THE DOOR, THE(1973)

Ray Livingston
SHADOW OF TERROR(1945), ed; BLUE BLOOD(1951), ed

Robert Livingston
DANCE, FOOLS, DANCE(1931); BAND PLAYS ON, THE(1934); DEATH OF THE DIAMOND(1934); MUTINY ON THE BOUNTY(1935); WEST POINT OF THE AIR(1935); ABSOLUTE QUIET(1936); BOLD CABALLERO(1936); SMALL TOWN GIRL(1936); SPEED(1936); SUZY(1936); THREE GODFATHERS(1936); THREE MES-QUITEERS, THE(1936); COME ON, COWBOYS(1937); GHOST TOWN GOLD(1937); GUNSMOKE RANCH(1937); HEART OF THE ROCKIES(1937); HIT THE SAD-DLE(1937); LARCENY ON THE AIR(1937); ROARIN' LEAD(1937); ARSON GANG BUSTERS(1938); HEROES OF THE HILLS(1938); LADIES IN DISTRESS(1938); NIGHT HAWK, THE(1938); COWBOYS FROM TEXAS(1939); FEDERAL MAN-HUNT(1939); KANSAS TERRORS, THE(1939); ORPHANS OF THE STREET(1939); COVERED WAGON DAYS(1940); HEROES OF THE SADDLE(1940); LONE STAR RAIDERS(1940); OKLAHOMA RENEGADES(1940); PIONEERS OF THE WEST(1940); ROCKY MOUNTAIN RANGERS(1940); TRAIL BLAZERS, THE(1940); UNDER TEXAS SKIES(1940); GANGS OF SONORA(1941); PALS OF THE PECOS(1941); PRAIRIE PIONEERS(1941); SADDLEMATES(1941); PISTOL PACKIN' MAMA(1943); BIG BONANZA, THE(1944); BRAZIL(1944); GOODNIGHT SWEETHEART(1944); LAKE PLACID SERENADE(1944); LARAMIE TRAIL, THE(1944); PRIDE OF THE PLAINS(1944); STORM OVER LISBON(1944); BELLS OF ROSARITA(1945); CHEAT-ERS, THE(1945); DAKOTA(1945); DON'T FENCE ME IN(1945); STEPPIN' IN SOCIE-

TY(1945); TELL IT TO A STAR(1945); UNDERCOVER WOMAN, THE(1946); VALLEY OF THE ZOMBIES(1946); DAREDEVILS OF THE CLOUDS(1948); FEATHERED SERPENT, THE(1948); GRAND CANYON TRAIL(1948); MYSTERIOUS DESPERADO, THE(1949); RIDERS IN THE SKY(1949); LAW OF THE BADLANDS(1950); MULE TRAIN(1950); SADDLE LEGION(1951); NIGHT STAGE TO GALVESTON(1952); SOMETHING FOR THE BIRDS(1952); WINNING OF THE WEST(1953)

Roy Livingston
DANGEROUS HOLIDAY(1937), ed; NAVY BLUES(1937), ed; CRIME, INC.(1945), ed; ENCHANTED FOREST, THE(1945), ed; AMBUSH TRAIL(1946), ed; MASK OF DIIJON, THE(1946), ed; NAVAJO KID, THE(1946), ed; SECRETS OF A SORORITY GIRL(1946), ed; SIX GUN MAN(1946), ed; THUNDER TOWN(1946), ed; BLACK GOLD(1947), ed; ARTHUR TAKES OVER(1948), ed; FIGHTING MAD(1948), ed; I WOULDN'T BE IN YOUR SHOES(1948), ed; KING OF THE BANDITS(1948), ed; BOMBA THE JUNGLE BOY(1949), ed; FORGOTTEN WOMEN(1949), ed; SKY DRAG-ON(1949), ed; TROUBLE PREFERRED(1949), ed; BLUE GRASS OF KENTUCK-Y(1950), ed; BOMBA AND THE HIDDEN CITY(1950), ed; HOT ROD(1950), ed; HOUSE ON HAUNTED HILL(1958), ed; SIGN OF ZORRO, THE(1960), ed; OPERA-TION EICHMANN(1961), ed; BRUSHFIRE(1962), ed; CONFESSIONS OF AN OPIUM EATER(1962), ed; BILLY THE KID VS. DRACULA(1966), ed; JESSE JAMES MEETS FRANKENSTEIN'S DAUGHTER(1966), ed; HILLBILLYS IN A HAUNTED HOUSE(1967), ed

Roy V. Livingston
JIGGS AND MAGGIE OUT WEST(1950), ed; ACCORDING TO MRS. HOYLE(1951), ed; NO ESCAPE(1953), ed; HELL TO ETERNITY(1960), ed

Sandy Livingston
CERTAIN SMILE, A(1958); MARJORIE MORNINGSTAR(1958)

Shelby Livingston
TWO THOUSAND MANIACS!(1964)

Stanley Livingston
BONNIE PARKER STORY, THE(1958); RALLY 'ROUND THE FLAG, BOYS!(1958); PLEASE DON'T EAT THE DAISIES(1960); X-15(1961); PRIVATE PARTS(1972)
Misc. Talkies
SMOKEY AND THE HOTWIRE GANG(1980)

Tyrone Livingston
SPOOK WHO SAT BY THE DOOR, THE(1973)

Bob Livingstone
Misc. Talkies
BLAZING STEWARDESSES(1975)

Douglas Livingstone
KIND OF LOVING, A(1962, Brit.); PASSWORD IS COURAGE, THE(1962, Brit.)

Jack Livingstone
Misc. Silents
STAINLESS BARRIER, THE(1917)

Leonard Livingstone
Misc. Silents
PITFALLS OF PASSION(1927), d

Mary Livingstone
THIS WAY PLEASE(1937)

Jack Livington
Misc. Silents
DESERT MAN, THE(1917)

Bert Livitt
BEAST WITHIN, THE(1982), ed

Sam Livneh
1984
BREAKIN' 2: ELECTRIC BOOGALOO(1984)

Samuel Livneh
DR. HECKYL AND MR. HYPE(1980)

Tere Livrano
GODFATHER, THE(1972); GODFATHER, THE, PART II(1974)

Titus Livus
Silents
CABIRIA(1914, Ital.), w

Vincente Liwanag
NO MAN IS AN ISLAND(1962)

Germaine Lix
DAYBREAK(1940, Fr.)

Luda Lizengevich
TARAS FAMILY, THE(1946, USSR)

Kari Lizer
SMOKEY BITES THE DUST(1981); PRIVATE SCHOOL(1983)

Laura Lizer
SMOKEY AND THE BANDIT(1977)

Vera Liznerova
90 DEGREES IN THE SHADE(1966, Czech./Brit.), art d

Carlo Lizzani
GERMANY, YEAR ZERO(1949, Ger.), w; OUTCRY(1949, Ital.), a, w; BITTER RI-CE(1950, Ital.), w; HUNCHBACK OF ROME, THE(1963, Ital.), d, w; VERONA TRIAL, THE(1963, Ital.), d; DUEL OF CHAMPIONS(1964 Ital./Span.), w; THE DIRTY GA-ME(1966, Fr./Ital./Ger.), d; WAKE UP AND DIE(1967, Fr./Ital.), p, d, w; VIOLENT FOUR, THE(1968, Ital.), a, d, w; CRAZY JOE(1974), d; LAST DAYS OF MUS-SOLINI(1974, Ital.), d, w

Nicolo Lizzari
MICHAEL STROGOFF(1960, Fr./Ital./Yugo.), ed

Martin Ljund
PIPPI IN THE SOUTH SEAS(1974, Swed./Ger.)

Martin Ljung
Misc. Talkies
GROOVE ROOM, THE(1974, Brit.)

Oscar Ljung
MAGICIAN, THE(1959, Swed.); VIRGIN SPRING, THE(1960, Swed.); NEW LAND, THE(1973, Swed.)

Leonor Llausas
CRIMINAL LIFE OF ARCHIBALDO DE LA CRUZ, THE(1962, Mex.); UNDER FIRE(1983)

Alastair Llewellyn
FFOLKES(1980, Brit.)

Desmond Llewellyn
THEY WERE NOT DIVIDED(1951, Brit.); MEN ARE CHILDREN TWICE(1953, Brit.); FURTHER UP THE CREEK!(1958, Brit.); SILENT PLAYGROUND, THE(1964, Brit.); MAN WITH THE GOLDEN GUN, THE(1974, Brit.)

Doris Llewellyn
BITTER TEA OF GENERAL YEN, THE(1933); MENACE(1934)

Dryhurst Llewellyn
SILK NOOSE, THE(1950, Brit.), w

Eva Llewellyn
DANCE PRETTY LADY(1932, Brit.)
Silents
ROB ROY(1922, Brit.)

Eve Llewellyn
GLIMPSE OF PARADISE, A(1934, Brit.); KISS THE BRIDE GOODBYE(1944, Brit.)

Fewlass Llewellyn
OFFICER'S MESS, THE(1931, Brit.); ASK BECCLES(1933, Brit.); OUTSIDER, THE(1933, Brit.); SEEING IS BELIEVING(1934, Brit.); STRIKE!(1934, Brit.); LAZY-BONES(1935, Brit.); PHANTOM LIGHT, THE(1935, Brit.); STORMY WEATHER(1935, Brit.); ALL IN(1936, Brit.); EVERYTHING OKAY(1936, Brit.); BRIEF ECSTASY(1937, Brit.); IT'S A GRAND OLD WORLD(1937, Brit.); SECOND BUREAU(1937, Brit.); WHERE THERE'S A WILL(1937, Brit.); MAN WITH 100 FACES, THE(1938, Brit.); SPECIAL EDITION(1938, Brit.); SPOT OF BOTHER, A(1938, Brit.); TWO OF US, THE(1938, Brit.); STOLEN LIFE(1939, Brit.); OUTSIDER, THE(1940, Brit.)
Silents
FURTHER ADVENTURES OF THE FLAG LIEUTENANT(1927, Brit.); AFTER-WARDS(1928, Brit.); VIRGINIA'S HUSBAND(1928, Brit.)

Josephine Llewellyn
CURSE OF THE WEREWOLF, THE(1961)

Len Llewellyn
PORT OF ESCAPE(1955, Brit.)

Leonard Llewellyn
CAESAR AND CLEOPATRA(1946, Brit.)

Richard Llewellyn
CATCH AS CATCH CAN(1937, Brit.), w; INSPECTOR HORNLEIGH(1939$c Brit.), w; HOW GREEN WAS MY VALLEY(1941), w; POISON PEN(1941, Brit.), w; NONE BUT THE LONELY HEART(1944), w; SILK NOOSE, THE(1950, Brit.), w; TALE OF FIVE WOMEN, A(1951, Brit.), w; QUIET MAN, THE(1952), w; GET OUTTA TOWN(1960), ed

Sylvia Llewellyn
IMPROPER CHANNELS(1981, Can.)

Tracy Llewellyn
OCTOPUSSY(1983, Brit.)

Tony Llewellyn-Jones
ILLUMINATIONS(1976, Aus.); INSIDE LOOKING OUT(1977, Aus.); LONELY HEARTS(1983, Aus.)
1984
MAN OF FLOWERS(1984, Aus.)

John Llewellyn-Rhys
WORLD OWES ME A LIVING, THE(1944, Brit.), w

Daniel Llewelyn
1984
GREMLINS(1984)

Desmond Llewelyn
SWORD OF SHERWOOD FOREST(1961, Brit.); PIRATES OF BLOOD RIVER, THE(1962, Brit.); FROM RUSSIA WITH LOVE(1963, Brit.); GOLDFINGER(1964, Brit.); THUNDERBALL(1965, Brit.); YOU ONLY LIVE TWICE(1967, Brit.); CHITTY CHITTY BANG BANG(1968, Brit.); ON HER MAJESTY'S SECRET SERVICE(1969, Brit.); DIAMONDS ARE FOREVER(1971, Brit.); SPY WHO LOVED ME, THE(1977, Brit.); MOONRAKER(1979, Brit.); FOR YOUR EYES ONLY(1981); OCTOPUSSY(1983, Brit.)

Doug Llewelyn
SMALL CIRCLE OF FRIENDS, A(1980)

Sylvia Llewelyn
STONE COLD DEAD(1980, Can.)

Sylvia Llore
GIDGET GOES TO ROME(1963)

Tony Llorens
WEDDING, A(1978)

Angel Llorente
TO BEGIN AGAIN(1982, Span.), w

Juanita Llosa
DAUGHTER OF THE SUN GOD(1962)

Enrique Llouet
TEN LITTLE INDIANS(1975, Ital./Fr./Span./Ger.), w

Enrique Llovet
YOUNG REBEL, THE(1969, Fr./Ital./Span.), w

Al Lloyd
ANGELS WITH DIRTY FACES(1938); CODE OF THE SECRET SERVICE(1939); EACH DAWN I DIE(1939); ESPIONAGE AGENT(1939); THEY MADE ME A CRIMI-NAL(1939); TUGBOAT ANNIE SAILS AGAIN(1940); MEET JOHN DOE(1941); SHE COULDN'T SAY NO(1941); MALE ANIMAL, THE(1942); SOLDIER, SAILOR(1944, Brit.), w

Albert Lloyd
CONFESSION(1937); SECRET SERVICE OF THE AIR(1939); SWAPPERS, THE(1970, Brit.), ph

Alice Lloyd
REGAL CAVALCADE(1935, Brit.)

Alma Lloyd
JIMMY AND SALLY(1933); BIG NOISE, THE(1936); BRIDES ARE LIKE THAT(1936); BULLETS OR BALLOTS(1936); COLLEEN(1936); FRESHMAN LO-VE(1936); GOLDEN ARROW, THE(1936); I MARRIED A DOCTOR(1936); SNOWED UNDER(1936); SONG OF THE SADDLE(1936); WHITE ANGEL, THE(1936); IF I WERE KING(1938)

Andrea Lloyd
UP POMPEII(1971, Brit.)

Anthony Lloyd
OPERATION EICHMANN(1961), makeup

Art Lloyd
PACK UP YOUR TROUBLES(1932), ph; DEVIL'S BROTHER, THE(1933), ph; BABES IN TOYLAND(1934), ph; BONNIE SCOTLAND(1935), ph; BOHEMIAN GIRL, THE(1936), ph; KELLY THE SECOND(1936), ph; GENERAL SPANKY(1937), ph; PICK A STAR(1937), ph; WAY OUT WEST(1937), ph; BLOCKHEADS(1938), ph;

SWISS MISS(1938), ph; FLYING DEUCES, THE(1939), ph; CHUMP AT OXFORD, A(1940), ph; SAPS AT SEA(1940), ph

Betty Lloyd
WILD HORSE ROUND-UP(1937)

Beverly Lloyd
SILENT PARTNER(1944); SING, NEIGHBOR, SING(1944); EARL CARROLL'S VANITIES(1945)

Bill Lloyd
WILD GUITAR(1962); DESERT RAVEN, THE(1965)

Bob Lloyd
OLD MOTHER RILEY OVERSEAS(1943, Brit.)

Brian Lloyd
OLIVER!(1968, Brit.)

Charles Lloyd
OPERATOR 13(1934); ALMOST SUMMER(1978), m

Chris Lloyd
BUTCH AND SUNDANCE: THE EARLY DAYS(1979)

Christine Lloyd
GOODBYE PORK PIE(1981, New Zealand)

Christopher Lloyd
ONE FLEW OVER THE CUCKOO'S NEST(1975); GOIN' SOUTH(1978); LADY IN RED, THE(1979); ONION FIELD, THE(1979); PILGRIM, FAREWELL(1980); SCHIZOID(1980); LEGEND OF THE LONE RANGER, THE(1981); POSTMAN ALWAYS RINGS TWICE, THE(1981); MR. MOM(1983); TO BE OR NOT TO BE(1983)
1984
ADVENTURES OF BUCKAROO BANZAI: ACROSS THE 8TH DIMENSION, THE(1984); JOY OF SEX(1984); STAR TREK III: THE SEARCH FOR SPOCK(1984)

Cosmo Lloyd
WILD REBELS, THE(1967)

Dan Lloyd
YANKS AHOY(1943)

Danny Lloyd
SHINING, THE(1980)

David Lloyd
JIM, THE WORLD'S GREATEST(1976)

Dian Lloyd
SIN YOU SINNERS(1963)

Dora Lloyd
SCREAM OF FEAR(1961, Brit.), cos

Doris Lloyd
WATERLOO BRIDGE(1931); CARELESS AGE(1929); DISRAELI(1929); DRAKE CASE, THE(1929); CHARLEY'S AUNT(1930); OLD ENGLISH(1930); RENO(1930); SARAH AND SON(1930); WAY FOR A SAILOR(1930); BACHELOR FATHER(1931); BOUGHT(1931); DEVOTION(1931); ONCE A LADY(1931); TRANSGRESSION(1931); BACK STREET(1932); TARZAN, THE APE MAN(1932); LOOKING FORWARD(1933); OLIVER TWIST(1933); PEG O' MY HEART(1933); ROBBERS' ROOST(1933); SECRETS(1933); STUDY IN SCARLET, A(1933); VOLTAIRE(1933); BRITISH AGENT(1934); GLAMOUR(1934); KISS AND MAKE UP(1934); LONG LOST FATHER(1934); MADAME DU BARRY(1934); SHE WAS A LADY(1934); SISTERS UNDER THE SKIN(1934); BECKY SHARP(1935); CHASING YESTERDAY(1935); CLIVE OF INDIA(1935); DANGEROUS CORNER(1935); FEATHER IN HER HAT, A(1935); KIND LADY(1935); MAN WHO RECLAIMED HIS HEAD, THE(1935); MOTIVE FOR REVENGE(1935); MUTINY ON THE BOUNTY(1935); ONE EXCITING ADVENTURE(1935); PERFECT GENTLEMAN, THE(1935); PETER IBBETSON(1935); SHOT IN THE DARK, A(1935); STRAIGHT FROM THE HEART(1935); STRANGE WIVES(1935); TWO FOR TONIGHT(1935); WOMAN IN RED, THE(1935); BRILLIANT MARRIAGE(1936); DON'T GET PERSONAL(1936); FOLLOW THE FLEET(1936); MARY OF SCOTLAND(1936); PLOUGH AND THE STARS, THE(1936); TOO MANY PARENTS(1936); ALCATRAZ ISLAND(1937); BULLDOG DRUMMOND ESCAPES(1937); TOVARICH(1937); BLACK DOLL, THE(1938); LETTER OF INTRODUCTION(1938); PORT OF SEVEN SEAS(1938); BARRICADE(1939); FIRST LOVE(1939); I'M FROM MISSOURI(1939); MURDER IS NEWS(1939); OLD MAID, THE(1939); PRIVATE LIVES OF ELIZABETH AND ESSEX, THE(1939); THEY MADE ME A CRIMINAL(1939); UNDER-PUP, THE(1939); WE ARE NOT ALONE(1939); GREAT PLANE ROBBERY, THE(1940); LADY WITH RED HAIR(1940); LETTER, THE(1940); 'TIL WE MEET AGAIN(1940); VIGIL IN THE NIGHT(1940); DR. JEKYLL AND MR. HYDE(1941); GREAT LIE, THE(1941); INTERNATIONAL SQUADRON(1941); KEEP 'EM FLYING(1941); LIFE WITH HENRY(1941); SCOTLAND YARD(1941); SHINING VICTORY(1941); WOLF MAN, THE(1941); GHOST OF FRANKENSTEIN, THE(1942); JOURNEY FOR MARGARET(1942); NIGHT MONSTER(1942); THIS ABOVE ALL(1942); CONSTANT NYMPH, THE(1943); FLESH AND FANTASY(1943); FOREVER AND A DAY(1943); FRANKENSTEIN MEETS THE WOLF MAN(1943); MISSION TO MOSCOW(1943); NO PLACE FOR A LADY(1943); TWO TICKETS TO LONDON(1943); WHAT A WOMAN!(1943); CONSPIRATORS, THE(1944); FOLLOW THE BOYS(1944); INVISIBLE MAN'S REVENGE(1944); LODGER, THE(1944); PHANTOM LADY(1944); WHITE CLIFFS OF DOVER, THE(1944); HOUSE OF FEAR, THE(1945); KITTY(1945); MOLLY AND ME(1945); MY NAME IS JULIA ROSS(1945); SCOTLAND YARD INVESTIGATOR(1945, Brit.); DEVOTION(1946); G.I. WAR BRIDES(1946); HOLIDAY IN MEXICO(1946); OF HUMAN BONDAGE(1946); SISTER KENNY(1946); TARZAN AND THE LEOPARD WOMAN(1946); THREE STRANGERS(1946); TO EACH HIS OWN(1946); ESCAPE ME NEVER(1947); IMPERFECT LADY, THE(1947); SECRET LIFE OF WALTER MITTY, THE(1947); SIGN OF THE RAM, THE(1948); RED DANUBE, THE(1949); TYRANT OF THE SEA(1950); ALICE IN WONDERLAND(1951); KIND LADY(1951); SON OF DR. JEKYLL, THE(1951); PRISONER OF ZENDA, THE(1952); YOUNG BESS(1953); INTERRUPTED MELODY(1955); MAN CALLED PETER, THE(1955); SWAN, THE(1956); JEANNE EAGELS(1957); MIDNIGHT LACE(1960; Brit./U.S.); TIME MACHINE, THE(1960; Brit./U.S.); NOTORIOUS LANDLADY, THE(1962); MARY POPPINS(1964); SOUND OF MUSIC, THE(1965); ROSIE!(1967)
Silents
BLACK BIRD, THE(1926); EXIT SMILING(1926); AUCTIONEER, THE(1927); BRONCHO TWISTER(1927); IS ZAT SO?(1927); TRAIL OF '98, THE(1929)
Misc. Silents
SHADOW BETWEEN, THE(1920, Brit.); MIDNIGHT KISS, THE(1926); LONESOME LADIES(1927)

Dorothy Lloyd
GARRISON FOLLIES(1940, Brit.); LOOK WHO'S LAUGHING(1941); SUSPICION(1941); TOM, DICK AND HARRY(1941)

E. Lloyd
DARK INTERVAL(1950, Brit.), ph

E. James Lloyd
BORN LOSERS(1967), w

Edward Lloyd
GIRL IN THE PICTURE, THE(1956, Brit.), p; INN FOR TROUBLE(1960, Brit.), p

Eileen Lloyd
GAME OF CHANCE, A(1932, Brit.)

Ethel Lloyd
Silents
FLORIDA ENCHANTMENT, A(1914); LITTLE MISS BROWN(1915); RANSOM, THE(1916)

Euan Lloyd
POPPY IS ALSO A FLOWER, THE(1966), p; SHALAKO(1968, Brit.), p; CATLOW(1971, Span.), p; MAN CALLED NOON, THE(1973, Brit.), p; PAPER TIGER(1975, Brit.), p; WILD GEESE, THE(1978, Brit.), p; SEA WOLVES, THE(1981, Brit.), p; FINAL OPTION, THE(1983, Brit.), p

Evie Lloyd
CONSTANT HUSBAND, THE(1955, Brit.)

Frank Lloyd
UNDER TWO FLAGS(1936), d; DARK STREETS(1929), d; DRAG(1929), d; WEARY RIVER(1929), d; YOUNG NOWHERES(1929), d; LASH, THE(1930), d; SON OF THE GODS(1930), d; WAY OF ALL MEN, THE(1930), d; AGE FOR LOVE, THE(1931), d, w; EAST LYNNE(1931), d; RIGHT OF WAY, THE(1931), d; PASSPORT TO HELL(1932), d; BERKELEY SQUARE(1933), d; CAVALCADE(1933), d; HOOPLA(1933), d; SERVANTS' ENTRANCE(1934), d; MUTINY ON THE BOUNTY(1935), d; BIG NOISE, THE(1936), d; MAID OF SALEM(1937), p&d; WELLS FARGO(1937), p&d; IF I WERE KING(1938), p&d; RULERS OF THE SEA(1939), p&d; HOWARDS OF VIRGINIA, THE(1940), p&d; LADY FROM CHEYENNE(1941), p&d; THIS WOMAN IS MINE(1941), p&d; INVISIBLE AGENT(1942), p; SABOTEUR(1942), p; SPOILERS, THE(1942), p; FOREVER AND A DAY(1943), p&d; BLOOD ON THE SUN(1945), d; SHANGHAI STORY, THE(1954), d; LAST COMMAND, THE(1955), p&d; CADDIE(1976, Aus.)
Misc. Talkies
DIVINE LADY, THE(1929), d
Silents
DAMON AND PYTHIAS(1914); OPENED SHUTTERS, THE(1914); CODE OF MARCIA GRAY(1916), d, w; TONGUES OF MEN, THE(1916), d; AMERICAN METHODS(1917), d, w; TALE OF TWO CITIES, A(1917), d&w; KINGDOM OF LOVE, THE(1918), d&w; LES MISERABLES(1918), d&w; INVISIBLE POWER, THE(1921), p&d; TALE OF TWO WORLDS, A(1921), d; VOICE IN THE DARK(1921), d; OLIVER TWIST(1922), d, w; ASHES OF VENGEANCE(1923), d, w; SPLENDID ROAD, THE(1925), d; CHILDREN OF DIVORCE(1927), d; ADORATION(1928), d
Misc. Silents
SPY, THE(1914), d; CALL OF THE CUMBERLANDS, THE(1915), d; GENTLEMAN FROM INDIANA, A(1915), d; JANE(1915), d; REFORM CANDIDATE, THE(1915), d; DAVID GARRICK(1916), d; INTERNATIONAL MARRIAGE, AN(1916), d; INTRIGUE(1916), d; MADAME LA PRESIDENTE(1916), d; MAKING OF MADDALENA, THE(1916), d; SINS OF HER PARENT(1916), d; STRONGER LOVE, THE(1916), a, d; PRICE OF SILENCE, THE(1917), d; WHEN A MAN SEES RED(1917), d; BLINDNESS OF DIVORCE, THE(1918), d; HEART OF A LION, THE(1918), d; RAINBOW TRAIL, THE(1918), d; RIDERS OF THE PURPLE SAGE(1918), d; TRUE BLUE(1918), d; FOR FREEDOM(1919), d; MAN HUNTER, THE(1919), d; PITFALLS OF A BIG CITY(1919), d; WORLD AND ITS WOMAN, THE(1919), d; GREAT LOVER, THE(1920), d; LOVES OF LETTY, THE(1920), d; MADAME X(1920), d; SILVER HORDE, THE(1920), d; WOMAN IN ROOM 13, THE(1920), d; GRIM COMEDIAN, THE(1921), d; MAN FROM LOST RIVER, THE(1921), d; ROADS OF DESTINY(1921), d; ETERNAL FLAME, THE(1922), d; SIN FLOOD, THE(1922), d; VOICE FROM THE MINARET, THE(1923), d; WITHIN THE LAW(1923), d; BLACK OXEN(1924), d; SILENT WATCHER, THE(1924), d; HER HUSBAND'S SECRET(1925), d; WINDS OF CHANCE(1925), d; EAGLE OF THE SEA, THE(1926), d; WISE GUY, THE(1926), d

Fred Lloyd
MAN FROM CHICAGO, THE(1931, Brit.)

Frederick Lloyd
TEMPORARY WIDOW, THE(1930, Ger./Brit.); "W" PLAN, THE(1931, Brit.); BATTLE OF GALLIPOLI(1931, Brit.); BEGGAR STUDENT, THE(1931,Brit.); GENTLEMAN OF PARIS, A(1931); GREAT GAY ROAD, THE(1931, Brit.); PERFECT LADY, THE(1931, Brit.); ARMS AND THE MAN(1932, Brit.); HOUND OF THE BASKERVILLES(1932, Brit.); CRIME AT BLOSSOMS, THE(1933, Brit.); MIXED DOUBLES(1933, Brit.); SLEEPLESS NIGHTS(1933, Brit.); UP FOR THE DERBY(1933, Brit.); SONG YOU GAVE ME, THE(1934, Brit.); LIEUTENANT DARING, RN(1935, Brit.); RADIO PIRATES(1935, Brit.); REGAL CAVALCADE(1935, Brit.); EVERYTHING IS THUNDER(1936, Brit.); APRIL BLOSSOMS(1937, Brit.); I MARRIED A SPY(1938); WEDDINGS ARE WONDERFUL(1938, Brit.); TWENTY-ONE DAYS TOGETHER(1940, Brit.); UNDER SECRET ORDERS(1943, Brit.); OLIVER TWIST(1951, Brit.)

Gabrielle Lloyd
GREAT TRAIN ROBBERY, THE(1979, Brit.)

Gaylord Lloyd
Silents
WHY WORRY(1923)

George Lloyd
SILENCE OF DEAN MAITLAND, THE(1934, Aus.); FRECKLES(1935); GRANDAD RUDD(1935, Aus.); MEN WITHOUT NAMES(1935); MISSISSIPPI(1935); ONE HOUR LATE(1935); SHE COULDN'T TAKE IT(1935); SHE GETS HER MAN(1935); BIG NOISE, THE(1936); BULLDOG EDITION(1936); BULLETS OR BALLOTS(1936); RETURN OF JIMMY VALENTINE, THE(1936); ROAD GANG(1936); CASE OF THE STUTTERING BISHOP, THE(1937); GIRLS CAN PLAY(1937); IDOL OF THE CROWDS(1937); LAST TRAIN FROM MADRID, THE(1937); PAID TO DANCE(1937); SAN QUENTIN(1937); SLIM(1937); SMART BLONDE(1937); THANKS FOR LISTENING(1937); THEY WON'T FORGET(1937); MR. WONG, DETECTIVE(1938); PRISON TRAIN(1938); SLIGHT CASE OF MURDER, A(1938); SMASHING THE RACKETS(1938); BEHIND PRISON GATES(1939); FIVE LITTLE PEPPERS AND HOW THEY GREW(1939); GOLDEN BOY(1939); GOOD GIRLS GO TO PARIS(1939); HOMICIDE BUREAU(1939); OKLAHOMA KID, THE(1939); SWEEPSTAKES WINNER(1939); TORCHY PLAYS WITH DYNAMITE(1939); WATERFRONT(1939); CAPTAIN CAUTION(1940); DEVIL'S ISLAND(1940); FLORIAN(1940); FUGITIVE FROM JUSTICE, A(1940); GAUCHO SERENADE(1940); I LOVE YOU AGAIN(1940); INVISIBLE MAN RETURNS, THE(1940); LEATHER-PUSHERS, THE(1940); NEW MOON(1940); RETURN OF WILD BILL, THE(1940); THEY DRIVE BY NIGHT(1940); CITY, FOR CONQUEST(1941); FATHER'S SON(1941); GIRL, A GUY AND A GOB,

A(1941); HIGH SIERRA(1941); IN OLD CHEYENNE(1941); OBLIGING YOUNG LADY(1941); SHADOW OF THE THIN MAN(1941); WILDCAT OF TUCSON(1941); ZIEGFELD GIRL(1941); IN OLD CALIFORNIA(1942); MISS ANNIE ROONEY(1942); MOKEY(1942); RINGS ON HER FINGERS(1942); ROAD TO MOROCCO(1942); VALLEY OF THE SUN(1942); DANCING MASTERS, THE(1943); FALLEN SPARROW, THE(1943); HELLO, FRISCO, HELLO(1943); LARCENY WITH MUSIC(1943); OX-BOW INCIDENT, THE(1943); SHE HAS WHAT IT TAKES(1943); DESTINATION TOKYO(1944); MAN FROM FRISCO(1944); MISSING JUROR, THE(1944); MY BUDDY(1944); SAN DIEGO, I LOVE YOU(1944); SINCE YOU WENT AWAY(1944); WHEN STRANGERS MARRY(1944); WHISTLER, THE(1944); BOSTON BLACKIE BOOKED ON SUSPICION(1945); FOG ISLAND(1945); FRISCO SAL(1945); GREAT JOHN L. THE(1945); I ACCUSE MY PARENTS(1945); LADY ON A TRAIN(1945); NOB HILL(1945); OUR VINES HAVE TENDER GRAPES(1945); PATRICK THE GREAT(1945); PENTHOUSE RHYTHM(1945); SCARLET STREET(1945); SHE GETS HER MAN(1945); UNDER WESTERN SKIES(1945); WHITE PONGO(1945); HOME IN OKLAHOMA(1946); YOUNG WIDOW(1946); EGG AND I, THE(1947); IT HAPPENED ON 5TH AVENUE(1947); JOHNNY O'CLOCK(1947); MY FAVORITE BRUNETTE(1947); NIGHTMARE ALLEY(1947); ROAD TO RIO(1947); SECRET LIFE OF WALTER MITTY, THE(1947); SINBAD THE SAILOR(1947); SINGAPORE(1947); VIGILANTES OF BOOMTOWN(1947); WHERE THERE'S LIFE(1947); DENVER KID, THE(1948); FRENCH LEAVE(1948); ON OUR MERRY WAY(1948); RED RIVER(1948); BLONDIE'S BIG DEAL(1949); BOSTON BLACKIE'S CHINESE VENTURE(1949); LARAMIE(1949); FULLER BRUSH GIRL, THE(1950); MAN IN THE SADDLE(1951); I'LL CRY TOMORROW(1955)
Misc. Talkies
LET GEORGE DO IT(1938, Aus.)

George H. Lloyd
UNDER CALIFORNIA STARS(1948); BANDIT KING OF TEXAS(1949); DEATH VALLEY GUNFIGHTER(1949); FRONTIER INVESTIGATOR(1949); ARIZONA COWBOY, THE(1950); BODYHOLD(1950); IRON MOUNTAIN TRAIL(1953)

George W. Lloyd
OUTCASTS OF THE TRAIL(1949)

Gerrit Lloyd
LADY OF THE PAVEMENTS(1929), w
Silents
BATTLE OF THE SEXES, THE(1928), w, t

Gerrit J. Lloyd
SECRET SERVICE(1931), w

Gladys Lloyd
FIVE STAR FINAL(1931); SMART MONEY(1931); HATCHET MAN, THE(1932); TWO SECONDS(1932)

Gloria Lloyd
TEMPTATION(1946)

Grace Lloyd
Misc. Silents
UNDER THE WESTERN SKIES(1921)

Gwyneth Lloyd
FALLING FOR YOU(1933, Brit.); ARE YOU A MASON?(1934, Brit.)

Gwynneth Lloyd
WILD BOY(1934, Brit.); ADMIRALS ALL(1935, Brit.)

Harold Lloyd
WELCOME DANGER(1929), a, p; FEET FIRST(1930); MOVIE CRAZY(1932), a, p; CAT'S PAW, THE(1934), a, p; MILKY WAY, THE(1936); PROFESSOR BEWARE(1938), a, p; GIRL, A GUY AND A GOB, A(1941), p; MY FAVORITE SPY(1942), p; MAD WEDNESDAY(1950)
Silents
SAMSON(1914); SAILOR-MADE MAN, A(1921); DOCTOR JACK(1922); GRANDMA'S BOY(1922), a, w; SAFETY LAST(1923); WHY WORRY(1923); GIRL SHY(1924); HOT WATER(1924); FRESHMAN, THE(1925); FOR HEAVEN'S SAKE(1926); KID BROTHER, THE(1927); SPEEDY(1928)

Harold Lloyd
PROFESSIONALS, THE(1966), makeup

Harold Lloyd, Jr.
OUR VERY OWN(1950); YANK IN ERMINE, A(1955, Brit.); FRANKENSTEIN'S DAUGHTER(1958); GIRLS' TOWN(1959); PLATINUM HIGH SCHOOL(1960); SEX KITTENS GO TO COLLEGE(1960); MARRIED TOO YOUNG(1962); MUTINY IN OUTER SPACE(1965)
Misc. Talkies
FLAMING URGE, THE(1953)

Harry Lloyd
Silents
JUDITH OF THE CUMBERLANDS(1916)

Hugh Lloyd
RING-A-DING RHYTHM(1962, Brit.); JUST FOR FUN(1963, Brit.); MAID FOR MURDER(1963, Brit.); MOUSE ON THE MOON, THE(1963, Brit.); PUNCH AND JUDY MAN, THE(1963, Brit.); FATHER CAME TOO(1964, Brit.); RUNAWAY RAILWAY(1965, Brit.); VENOM(1982, Brit.)

Hugh Russell Lloyd
UNFORGIVEN, THE(1960), ed

J. Lloyd
DANTE'S INFERNO(1935)

James Lloyd
LOVE-INS, THE(1967); WRECKING CREW, THE(1968)

Jeremy Lloyd
SCHOOL FOR SCOUNDRELS(1960, Brit.); MAN IN THE MOON(1961, Brit.); WHAT A WHOPPER(1961, Brit.), w; OPERATION SNATCH(1962, Brit.); TWO AND TWO MAKE SIX(1962, Brit.); WE JOINED THE NAVY(1962, Brit.); JUST FOR FUN(1963, Brit.); SANDERS(1963, Brit.); HELP!(1965, Brit.); THOSE MAGNIFICENT MEN IN THEIR FLYING MACHINES; OR HOW I FLEW FROM LONDON TO PARIS IN 25 HOURS AND 11 MINUTES(1965, Brit.); THREE HATS FOR LISA(1965, Brit.); LIQUIDATOR, THE(1966, Brit.); WRONG BOX, THE(1966, Brit.); CARNABY, M.D.(1967, Brit.); LONG DUEL, THE(1967, Brit.); SMASHING TIME(1967 Brit.); SALT & PEPPER(1968, Brit.); ASSASSINATION BUREAU, THE(1969, Brit.); GOODBYE MR. CHIPS(1969, U.S./Brit.); MAGIC CHRISTIAN, THE(1970, Brit.); GAMES THAT LOVERS PLAY(1971, Brit.); MURDER ON THE ORIENT EXPRESS(1974, Brit.); OLD DRACULA(1975, Brit.), w; BAWDY ADVENTURES OF TOM JONES, THE(1976, Brit.), a, w

Jimmy Lloyd
SHE'S A SWEETHEART(1944); TOGETHER AGAIN(1944); LET'S GO STEADY(1945); SNAFU(1945); STORY OF G.I. JOE, THE(1945); TEN CENTS A DANCE(1945); BANDIT OF SHERWOOD FOREST, THE(1946); GALLANT JOURNEY(1946); GENTLEMAN MISBEHAVES, THE(1946); IT'S GREAT TO BE YOUNG(1946); JOLSON STORY, THE(1946); NIGHT EDITOR(1946); CIGARETTE GIRL(1947); GLAMOUR GIRL(1947); KEY WITNESS(1947); TWO BLONDES AND A REDHEAD(1947); FULLER BRUSH MAN(1948); MANHATTAN ANGEL(1948); MY DOG RUSTY(1948); WALK A CROOKED MILE(1948); MARY RYAN, DETECTIVE(1949); MISS GRANT TAKES RICHMOND(1949); RIDERS OF THE WHISTLING PINES(1949); SHOCKPROOF(1949); SLIGHTLY FRENCH(1949); BEAUTY ON PARADE(1950); BLONDIE'S HERO(1950); COUNTERSPY MEETS SCOTLAND YARD(1950); DAVID HARDING, COUNTERSPY(1950); WHEN YOU'RE SMILING(1950); GASOLINE ALLEY(1951); G.I. JANE(1951); JOE PALOOKA IN TRIPLE CROSS(1951); BATTLE OF ROGUE RIVER(1954); 6.5 SPECIAL(1958, Brit.)

John Lloyd
LAST JOURNEY, THE(1936, Brit.); STOLEN LIFE(1939, Brit.)

John Lloyd
MUNSTER, GO HOME(1966), art d; HOW TO FRAME A FIGG(1971), art d; AT LONG LAST LOVE(1975), art d; DAY OF THE LOCUST, THE(1975), art d; SWASHBUCKLER(1976), prod d; PLAYERS(1979); RAGGEDY MAN(1981), art d

John J. Lloyd
HELL WITH HEROES, THE(1968), art d; SERGEANT RYKER(1968), art d; COLOSSUS: THE FORBIN PROJECT(1969), art d; WINNING(1969), art d; MAC ARTHUR(1977), prod d; NATIONAL LAMPOON'S ANIMAL HOUSE(1978), art d; PRISONER OF ZENDA, THE(1979), prod d; THING, THE(1982), prod d; D.C. CAB(1983), prod d, set d
1984
CRACKERS(1984), prod d; RIVER RAT, THE(1984), prod d

John Robert Lloyd
NIGHT THEY RAIDED MINSKY'S, THE(1968), art d; SWEET NOVEMBER(1968), art d; JOHN AND MARY(1969), prod d; MIDNIGHT COWBOY(1969), prod d; BOYS IN THE BAND, THE(1970), prod d; OWL AND THE PUSSYCAT, THE(1970), prod d; THEY MIGHT BE GIANTS(1971), prod d; HOT ROCK, THE(1972), prod d; THIEVES(1977), prod d

Josie Lloyd
STUDS LONIGAN(1960)

Julie Lloyd
1984
OH GOD! YOU DEVIL(1984)

Kari Lloyd
1984
JUNGLE WARRIORS(1984, U.S./Ger./Mex.)

Kathleen Lloyd
MISSOURI BREAKS, THE(1976); CAR, THE(1977); IT LIVES AGAIN(1978); SKATEBOARD(1978); TAKE DOWN(1979)

Keith Lloyd
WOMAN TO WOMAN(1946, Brit.)

Kevin Lloyd
DIRTY KNIGHT'S WORK(1976, Brit.); BRITTANIA HOSPITAL(1982, Brit.)
1984
DON'T OPEN TILL CHRISTMAS(1984, Brit.)

Kit Lloyd
FOLLOW ME, BOYS!(1966)

Lala Lloyd
DULCIMER STREET(1948, Brit.)
1984
SECRET PLACES(1984, Brit.)

Lola Lloyd
ADDING MACHINE, THE(1969)

Lonnie Lloyd
WHY WOULD I LIE(1980)

M. J. Lloyd
JAWS 3-D(1983)

Margaret Lloyd
WHEN I GROW UP(1951); LOVE IS BETTER THAN EVER(1952)

Margo Lloyd
ADVENTURES OF BARRY McKENZIE(1972, Austral.)

Marie Lloyd, Jr.
VARIETY JUBILEE(1945, Brit.)

Michael Lloyd
POM POM GIRLS, THE(1976), m; VAN, THE(1977), md; NORTH AVENUE IRREGULARS, THE(1979); BEACH GIRLS(1982), m; TOUGH ENOUGH(1983), m
1984
LOVELINES(1984), a, p, w; SAVAGE STREETS(1984), m

Norman Lloyd
SABOTEUR(1942); LETTER FOR EVIE, A(1945); SOUTHERNER, THE(1945); SPELLBOUND(1945); UNSEEN, THE(1945); WALK IN THE SUN, A(1945); WITHIN THESE WALLS(1945); GREEN YEARS, THE(1946); YOUNG WIDOW(1946); NO MINOR VICES(1948); BLACK BOOK, THE(1949); CALAMITY JANE AND SAM BASS(1949); SCENE OF THE CRIME(1949); BUCCANEER'S GIRL(1950); FLAME AND THE ARROW, THE(1950); HE RAN ALL THE WAY(1951); LIGHT TOUCH, THE(1951); M(1951); LIMELIGHT(1952); FLAME OF STAMBOUL(1957); AUDREY ROSE(1977); FM(1978); JAWS OF SATAN(1980); NUDE BOMB, THE(1980)

Peggy Lloyd
COVER GIRL(1944)

Richard Lloyd
HERCULES, SAMSON & ULYSSES(1964, Ital.)

Robert Lloyd
SHE COULDN'T SAY NO(1930), w; PERSECUTION AND ASSASSINATION OF JEAN-PAUL MARAT AS PERFORMED BY THE INMATES OF THE ASYLUM OF CHARENTON UNDER THE DIRECTION OF THE MARQUIS DE SADE, THE(1967, Brit.); COMMITTEE, THE(1968, Brit.); TELL ME LIES(1968, Brit.); KING LEAR(1971, Brit./Den.); PARSIFAL(1983, Fr.)

Robin Lloyd
TROUBLE IN THE GLEN(1954, Brit.); ISADORA(1968, Brit.)

Rollo Lloyd
OKAY AMERICA(1932); PRESTIGE(1932), a, w; CARNIVAL LADY(1933); DESTINATION UNKNOWN(1933); OUT ALL NIGHT(1933); SITTING PRETTY(1933); STRICTLY PERSONAL(1933); TODAY WE LIVE(1933); FLAMING GOLD(1934);

MADAME SPY(1934); PARTY'S OVER, THE(1934); PRIVATE SCANDAL(1934); BARBARY COAST(1935); GILDED LILY, THE(1935); HIS NIGHT OUT(1935); LIVES OF A BENGAL LANCER(1935); MAD LOVE(1935); MAGNIFICENT OBSESSION(1935); MAN WHO RECLAIMED HIS HEAD, THE(1935); MURDER ON A HONEYMOON(1935); MYSTERY MAN, THE(1935), w; STRAIGHT FROM THE HEART(1935); ANTHONY ADVERSE(1936); COME AND GET IT(1936); DESIRE(1936); DEVIL DOLL, THE(1936); EX-MRS. BRADFORD, THE(1936); FOUR DAYS WONDER(1936); HELLSHIP MORGAN(1936); I CONQUER THE SEA(1936), w; LOVE LETTERS OF A STAR(1936); MAN I MARRY, THE(1936); PROFESSIONAL SOLDIER(1936); REVOLT OF THE ZOMBIES(1936), w; STRAIGHT FROM THE SHOULDER(1936); WHITE LEGION, THE(1936); YELLOWSTONE(1936); ARMORED CAR(1937); EMPEROR'S CANDLESTICKS, THE(1937); GIRL LOVES BOY(1937); LAST TRAIN FROM MADRID, THE(1937); LIVE, LOVE AND LEARN(1937); SEVENTH HEAVEN(1937); SOULS AT SEA(1937); WESTLAND CASE, THE(1937); WOMEN MEN MARRY, THE(1937); ARSENE LUPIN RETURNS(1938); GOODBYE BROADWAY(1938); LADY IN THE MORGUE(1938); NIGHT SPOT(1938); SPAWN OF THE NORTH(1938); MAN FROM HEADQUARTERS(1942), w

Rosalind Lloyd
WILD GEESE, THE(1978, Brit.); HORROR PLANET(1982, Brit.); FINAL OPTION, THE(1983, Brit.)

Russell Lloyd
MURDER ON DIAMOND ROW(1937, Brit.), ed; MAN ABOUT THE HOUSE, A(1947, Brit.), ed; ANNA KARENINA(1948, Brit.), ed; LUCKY NICK CAIN(1951), ed; ISLAND OF DESIRE(1952, Brit.), ed; DECAMERON NIGHTS(1953, Brit.), ed; SEA SHALL NOT HAVE THEM, THE(1955, Brit.), ed; MOBY DICK(1956, Brit.), ed; STAR OF INDIA(1956, Brit.), ed; HEAVEN KNOWS, MR. ALLISON(1957), ed; COUNT FIVE AND DIE(1958, Brit.), ed; NAKED EARTH, THE(1958, Brit.), ed; ROOTS OF HEAVEN, THE(1958), ed; WHIRLPOOL(1959, Brit.), ed; LION, THE(1962, Brit.), ed; BITTER HARVEST(1963, Brit.), ed; OF HUMAN BONDAGE(1964, Brit.), ed; RETURN FROM THE ASHES(1965, U.S./Brit.), ed; AFTER THE FOX(1966, U.S./Brit./Ital.), ed; WILD AFFAIR, THE(1966, Brit.), ed; 90 DEGREES IN THE SHADE(1966, Czech./Brit.), ed; REFLECTIONS IN A GOLDEN EYE(1967), ed; SINFUL DAVEY(1969, Brit.), ed; WALK WITH LOVE AND DEATH, A(1969), ed; KREMLIN LETTER, THE(1970), ed; LAST RUN, THE(1971), ed; LOVE AND PAIN AND THE WHOLE DAMN THING(1973), ed; MACKINTOSH MAN, THE(1973, Brit.), ed; IN CELEBRATION(1975, Brit.), ed; MAN WHO WOULD BE KING, THE(1975, Brit.), ed; FIENDISH PLOT OF DR. FU MANCHU, THE(1980), ed; LADY VANISHES, THE(1980, Brit.), ed
1984
WHERE IS PARSIFAL?(1984, Brit.), ed

Sherman Lloyd
NEIGHBORS(1981)

Sherman G. Lloyd
W. W. AND THE DIXIE DANCEKINGS(1975)

Shirley Lloyd
CHINA CLIPPER(1936); COLLEEN(1936); GOLD DIGGERS OF 1937(1936); GOLDEN ARROW, THE(1936); POLO JOE(1936); SNOWED UNDER(1936); GOD'S COUNTRY AND THE WOMAN(1937); GREEN LIGHT(1937)

Stanley Lloyd
MC VICAR(1982, Brit.)
1984
FOREVER YOUNG(1984, Brit.)

Sue Lloyd
HYSTERIA(1965, Brit.); IPCRESS FILE, THE(1965, Brit.); ATTACK ON THE IRON COAST(1968, U.S./Brit.); CORRUPTION(1968, Brit.); WHERE'S JACK?(1969, Brit.); SQUEEZE A FLOWER(1970, Aus.); PERCY(1971, Brit.); INNOCENT BYSTANDERS(1973, Brit.); STONE(1974, Aus.); SPANISH FLY(1975, Brit.); REVENGE OF THE PINK PANTHER(1978); STUD, THE(1979, Brit.); ROUGH CUT(1980, Brit.)
Misc. Talkies
MAN IN A LOOKING GLASS, A(1965, Brit.); DOUBLE TAKE(1972, Brit.); GO FOR A TAKE(1972, Brit.); BITCH, THE(1979)

Susan Lloyd
NED KELLY(1970, Brit.)

Suzanne Lloyd
PEPE(1960); SEVEN WAYS FROM SUNDOWN(1960); WHO WAS MADDOX?(1964, Brit.); RETURN OF MR. MOTO, THE(1965, Brit.); CHAMPAGNE MURDERS, THE(1968, Fr.); THAT RIVIERA TOUCH(1968, Brit.)

Ted Lloyd
CHELSEA STORY(1951, Brit.), ph; BLIND MAN'S BLUFF(1952, Brit.), ph; HOT ICE(1952, Brit.), ph; NO HAUNT FOR A GENTLEMAN(1952, Brit.), ph; ALF'S BABY(1953, Brit.), ph; LIFE IN EMERGENCY WARD 10(1959, Brit.), p; WEEKEND WITH LULU, A(1961, Brit.), p, w; TRAITOR'S GATE(1966, Brit./Ger.), p

Tom Lloyd
RUSTLERS(1949)

Trevor Lloyd
WILD GEESE, THE(1978, Brit.)

Viola Lloyd
SAVAGES FROM HELL(1968)

Vivianne Lloyd
MAN IN THE VAULT(1956)

Warren Lloyd
NAVAL ACADEMY(1941)

William Lloyd
Silents
COUNTY CHAIRMAN, THE(1914); LITTLE PAL(1915); PRETTY SISTER OF JOSE(1915)
Misc. Silents
$5,000 REWARD(1918)

Beti Lloyd-Jones
MIKADO, THE(1967, Brit.)

Charles Lloyd-Pack
CURSE OF THE DEMON(1958); BOBBIKINS(1959, Brit.); MAN WHO COULD CHEAT DEATH, THE(1959, Brit.); DAY THEY ROBBED THE BANK OF ENGLAND, THE(1960, Brit.); MY SON, THE VAMPIRE(1963, Brit.); FRANKENSTEIN AND THE MONSTER FROM HELL(1974, Brit.); MIRROR CRACK'D, THE(1980, Brit.)

Roger Lloyd-Pack
HAMLET(1969, Brit.)

Joseph Luis Lluch
TREASURE OF MAKUBA, THE(1967, U.S./Span.)

Lita Lluch-Piero
THAT OBSCURE OBJECT OF DESIRE(1977, Fr./Span.)

Kenneth Lo
GLADIATORS, THE(1970, Swed.)

Y Sa Lo
MOTHER KUSTERS GOES TO HEAVEN(1976, Ger.); DESPAIR(1978, Ger.); LOLA(1982, Ger.); QUERELLE(1983, Ger./Fr.)

Francesco Lo Briglio
MAFIOSO(1962, Ital.)

Francesco Lo Como
MORE THAN A MIRACLE(1967, Ital./Fr.)

Julius Lo Iacono
CHILD'S PLAY(1972)

Severio Lo Medico
PURPLE GANG, THE(1960)

Joe Lo Presti
WHAT DID YOU DO IN THE WAR, DADDY?(1966)

Ed Lo Russo
BULLET FOR PRETTY BOY, A(1970)

Larry Lo Verde
KISS THEM FOR ME(1957)

Ken Loach
FAMILY LIFE(1971, Brit.), d

Kenneth Loach
POOR COW(1968, Brit.), d, w; KES(1970, Brit.), d, w; BLACK JACK(1979, Brit.), d, w; GAMEKEEPER, THE(1980, Brit.), d, w; LOOKS AND SMILES(1982, Brit.), d

Meat Loaf
AMERICATHON(1979)

Demetris Loakimides
DAY THE FISH CAME OUT, THE(1967. Brit./Gr.)

H. H. Van Loan
Silents
BRING HIM IN(1921), w

Theano Ioannidou
ELECTRA(1962, Gr.)

John Ioannou
GREEK TYCOON, THE(1978)

Karl Lob
APRIL 1, 2000(1953, Aust.), ph; THOUSAND EYES OF DR. MABUSE, THE(1960, Fr./Ital./Ger.), ph; RETURN OF DR. MABUSE, THE(1961, Ger./Fr./Ital.), ph; AMONG VULTURES(1964, Ger./Ital./Fr./Yugo.), ph; THUNDER AT THE BORDER(1966, Ger./Yugo.), ph

Marvin Lobach
OLD-FASHIONED WAY, THE(1934)

Marvin Loback
IT HAPPENED ONE NIGHT(1934)

P. Lobanov
OVERCOAT, THE(1965, USSR)

Ebar Lobato
SCREAM OF THE BUTTERFLY(1965), d

Nelida Lobato
SCREAM OF THE BUTTERFLY(1965)

Georgette Lobbe
LOVERS, THE(1959, Fr.)

Madame Lobegue
SCREAM OF FEAR(1961, Brit.)

Bruni Lobel
BIG LIFT, THE(1950); ALMOST ANGELS(1962); CITY OF SECRETS(1963, Ger.)

Elektrah Lobel
TWO VOICES(1966)

Malvine Lobel
Misc. Silents
UNWELCOME WIFE, THE(1915)

Marc Lobell
ORIENT EXPRESS(1934)

Michael Lobell
DREAMER(1979), p; WINDOWS(1980), p

Mike Lobell
SO FINE(1981), p

David Lober
HAPPY GO LOVELY(1951, Brit.)

Joy Lober
ADIOS AMIGO(1975)

Tony LoBianco
HONEYMOON KILLERS, THE(1969); FRENCH CONNECTION, THE(1971); SEVEN UPS, THE(1973); GOD TOLD ME TO(1976); MEAN FRANK AND CRAZY TONY(1976, Ital.); BLOODBROTHERS(1978); SEPARATE WAYS(1981)
1984
CITY HEAT(1984)

Lotte Lobinger
M(1933, Ger.)

Bela Loblov
REUNION IN VIENNA(1933)

Bella Loblov
MERRY WIDOW, THE(1934)

Mira Lobo
KILL OR BE KILLED(1950)

Rene Lobo
1984
QUESTION OF SILENCE(1984, Neth.)

Lobo the Dog
GUARD THAT GIRL(1935)

Lobo the Marvel Dog
THUNDERBOLT(1936)

T. Lobova
GENERAL SUVOROV(1941, USSR), ph; ADMIRAL NAKHIMOV(1948, USSR), ph; DRAGONFLY, THE(1955 USSR), ph

Ann-Christin Lobraten
TOUCH, THE(1971, U.S./Swed.)
Jane Lobre
GENTLE CREATURE, A(1971, Fr.); SMALL CHANGE(1976, Fr.); GREEN ROOM, THE(1979, Fr.)
Jeanne Lobre
TWO ENGLISH GIRLS(1972, Fr.)
Vitya Lobzov
SUN SHINES FOR ALL, THE(1961, USSR)
Hoang Vinh Loc
YANK IN VIET-NAM, A(1964)
Locafilms
ZAZIE(1961, Fr.), spec eff
Locarno
KID FOR TWO FARTHINGS, A(1956, Brit.)
Joseph Locastro
QUICK AND THE DEAD, THE(1963)
Carol Locatell
PATERNITY(1981); BEST FRIENDS(1982); SHARKY'S MACHINE(1982)
Al Locatelli
MC CABE AND MRS. MILLER(1971), art d
Albert Locatelli
TONIGHT FOR SURE(1962), set d; DEMENTIA 13(1963), art d; YOUNG RACERS, THE(1963), art d; QUEEN OF BLOOD(1966), art d
Alfredo Locatelli
UNDER THE SUN OF ROME(1949, Ital.)
Laura Locatelli
TREE OF WOODEN CLOGS, THE(1979, Ital.)
Capt. E. Erskine Loch
MAN HUNTERS OF THE CARIBBEAN(1938)
Laurence Lochard
GETTING OVER(1981), art d
David Lochary
MONDO TRASHO(1970); FEMALE TROUBLE(1975)
Lochavoff
Silents
NAPOLEON(1927, Fr.), art d
Marcel Loche
BEAR, THE(1963, Fr.)
Charles Locher [Jon Hall]
WINDS OF THE WASTELAND(1936)
Felix Locher
HELL SHIP MUTINY(1957); CURSE OF THE FACELESS MAN(1958); DESERT HELL(1958); FRANKENSTEIN'S DAUGHTER(1958); THUNDER IN THE SUN(1959); WALK TALL(1960); FIREBRAND, THE(1962); CALIFORNIA(1963)
Anita Lochner
DEEP END(1970 Ger./U.S.)
Richard S. Lochte
ESCAPE TO ATHENA(1979, Brit.), w
Nicholas Locise
SCROOGE(1970, Brit.)
Carsta Lock
FOUR COMPANIONS, THE(1938, Ger.); FILM WITHOUT A NAME(1950, Ger.)
E. A. Lock
Silents
MASTER CRACKSMAN, THE(1914)
Gary Lock
SAILOR WHO FELL FROM GRACE WITH THE SEA, THE(1976, Brit.)
Gerry Lock
COMPULSION(1959)
Ong Ah Lock
MATTER OF INNOCENCE, A(1968, Brit.)
Peter Lock
OLIVER!(1968, Brit.); SCROOGE(1970, Brit.)
Stuart Lock
SCRAMBLE(1970, Brit.)
Lenny Lockabaugh
DRIVE, HE SAID(1971)
Arnold Locke
SQUADRON 633(1964, U.S./Brit.); 633 SQUADRON(1964); OLIVER!(1968, Brit.); VAMPIRE CIRCUS(1972, Brit.)
Ashley T. Locke
Silents
ALIMONY(1924), w; GAMBLING WIVES(1924), w
Charles O. Locke
FROM HELL TO TEXAS(1958), w
Daisy Locke
YOU'VE GOT TO WALK IT LIKE YOU TALK IT OR YOU'LL LOSE THAT BEAT(1971)
Doreen Locke
STOCK CAR(1955, Brit.)
Edward Locke
CLIMAX, THE(1930), w; CLIMAX, THE(1944), w
Harry Locke
PICCADILLY INCIDENT(1948, Brit.); PASSPORT TO PIMLICO(1949, Brit.); PRIVATE ANGELO(1949, Brit.); NO ROOM AT THE INN(1950, Brit.); TREASURE ISLAND(1950, Brit.); FATHER'S DOING FINE(1952, Brit.); JUDGMENT DEFERRED(1952, Brit.); TREAD SOFTLY(1952, Brit.); TERROR ON A TRAIN(1953); ANGELS ONE FIVE(1954, Brit.); DEVIL ON HORSEBACK(1954, Brit.); DOCTOR IN THE HOUSE(1954, Brit.); PARATROOPER(1954, Brit.); NAKED HEART, THE(1955, Brit.); TECKMAN MYSTERY, THE(1955, Brit); YANK IN ERMINE, A(1955, Brit.); BLONDE SINNER(1956, Brit.); BABY AND THE BATTLESHIP, THE(1957, Brit.); DOCTOR AT LARGE(1957, Brit.); REACH FOR THE SKY(1957, Brit.); SILKEN AFFAIR, THE(1957, Brit.); THIRD KEY, THE(1957, Brit.); TOWN ON TRIAL(1957, Brit.); WOMEN IN A DRESSING GOWN(1957, Brit.); ALL AT SEA(1958, Brit.); CARRY ON NURSE(1959, Brit.); I'M ALL RIGHT, JACK(1959, Brit.); NOWHERE TO GO(1959, Brit.); CAPTAIN'S TABLE, THE(1960, Brit.); LIGHT UP THE SKY(1960, Brit.); MAN IN A COCKED HAT(1960, Bri.); MAN IN THE BACK SEAT, THE(1961, Brit.); KILL OR CURE(1962, Brit.); L-SHAPED ROOM, THE(1962, Brit.); TWO AND TWO MAKE SIX(1962, Brit.); HEAVENS ABOVE!(1963, Brit.); MAID FOR MURDER(1963, Brit.); SMALL WORLD

OF SAMMY LEE, THE(1963, Brit.); DEVIL-SHIP PIRATES, THE(1964, Brit.); GO KART GO(1964, Brit.); IN THE DOGHOUSE(1964, Brit.); YOUNG AND WILLING(1964, Brit.); AMOROUS MR. PRAWN, THE(1965, Brit.); EARLY BIRD, THE(1965, Brit.); OPERATION SNAFU(1965, Brit.); FAMILY WAY, THE(1966, Brit.); HALF A SIXPENCE(1967, Brit.); NEVER BACK LOSERS(1967, Brit.); SKY BIKE, THE(1967, Brit.); CLUE OF THE TWISTED CANDLE(1968, Brit.); CARRY ON AGAIN, DOCTOR(1969, Brit.); OH! WHAT A LOVELY WAR(1969, Brit.); ON THE RUN(1969, Brit.); SUBTERFUGE(1969, US/Brit.); TALES FROM THE CRYPT(1972, Brit.)
Silents
WHILE NEW YORK SLEEPS(1920)
Joe Locke
SCARLET COAT, THE(1955); LIEUTENANT WORE SKIRTS, THE(1956); MAGNIFICENT ROUGHNECKS(1956); ON THE THRESHOLD OF SPACE(1956); CINDERELLA LIBERTY(1973)
Jon Locke
WESTWARD HO THE WAGONS!(1956); UNDER FIRE(1957); FIVE GUNS TO TOMBSTONE(1961); GUN FIGHT(1961)
Josef Locke
HOLIDAYS WITH PAY(1948, Brit.); SOMEWHERE IN POLITICS(1949, Brit.); WHAT A CARRY ON!(1949, Brit.)
Katherine Locke
STRAIGHT FROM THE SHOULDER(1936); SEVENTH CROSS, THE(1944); WILSON(1944); SNAKE PIT, THE(1948); SOUND OF FURY, THE(1950); PEOPLE WILL TALK(1951); FLESH AND FURY(1952); CERTAIN SMILE, A(1958)
Martin Locke
SECRETS OF SEX(1970, Brit.), w
Michael Locke
RAW WEEKEND(1964), w
Peter Locke
YOU'VE GOT TO WALK IT LIKE YOU TALK IT OR YOU'LL LOSE THAT BEAT(1971), a, p,d&w, ed; HILLS HAVE EYES, THE(1978), p
Misc. Talkies
KITTY CAN'T HELP IT(1975), d; CARHOPS(1980), d
Philip Locke
GIRL ON THE BOAT, THE(1962, Brit.); FACE OF A STRANGER(1964, Brit.); FATHER CAME TOO(1964, Brit.); THUNDERBALL(1965, Brit.); INCIDENT AT MIDNIGHT(1966, Brit.); ON THE RUN(1967, Brit.); HITLER: THE LAST TEN DAYS(1973, Brit./Ital.); ESCAPE TO ATHENA(1979, Ital./Fr.); AND THE SHIP SAILS ON(1983, Ital./Fr.); ASCENDANCY(1983, Brit.)
1984
PLAGUE DOGS, THE(1984, U.S./Brit.)
Poodie Locke
1984
SONGWRITER(1984)
Ralph J. Locke
Misc. Silents
PUTTING ONE OVER(1919)
Randy Locke
HONEYSUCKLE ROSE(1980)
Raymond Friday Locke
ROPE OF FLESH(1965), w
Richard Locke
Misc. Talkies
TAKE ONE(1977)
Ruth Locke
YOU'VE GOT TO WALK IT LIKE YOU TALK IT OR YOU'LL LOSE THAT BEAT(1971)
Shamus Locke
HUNGRY HILL(1947, Brit.); TURNERS OF PROSPECT ROAD, THE(1947, Brit.); YOU CAN'T FOOL AN IRISHMAN(1950, Ireland); IT'S ALIVE(1974)
Sharyl Locke
FATHER GOOSE(1964); ONE MAN'S WAY(1964); I SAW WHAT YOU DID(1965)
Sondra Locke
HEART IS A LONELY HUNTER, THE(1968); COVER ME BABE(1970); WILLARD(1971); REFLECTION OF FEAR, A(1973); SECOND COMING OF SUZANNE, THE(1974); OUTLAW JOSEY WALES, THE(1976); DEATH GAME(1977); GAUNTLET, THE(1977); EVERY WHICH WAY BUT LOOSE(1978); WISHBONE CUTTER(1978); ANY WHICH WAY YOU CAN(1980); BRONCO BILLY(1980); SUDDEN IMPACT(1983)
Tammy Locke
ONCE A THIEF(1965)
Terrence Locke
GOODBYE, NORMA JEAN(1976); WHICH WAY IS UP?(1977)
William J. Locke
STRANGERS IN LOVE(1932), w; BELOVED VAGABOND, THE(1936, Brit.), w; MORALS OF MARCUS, THE(1936, Brit.), w
Silents
SIMON THE JESTER(1915), w; STELLA MARIS(1918), w; MORALS(1921), w
William Locke
Silents
WHILE NEW YORK SLEEPS(1920)
William John Locke
Silents
SIDESHOW OF LIFE, THE(1924), w; COMING OF AMOS, THE(1925), w; STELLA MARIS(1925), w
Gerlinde Locker
$100 A NIGHT(1968, Ger.)
Judith Suzanne Locker
NAKED CITY, THE(1948)
Kenneth Locker
PLEASANTVILLE(1976), d&w
Maud Locker
BIRDS OF A FEATHER(1935, Brit.)
Beth Lockerbie
INCREDIBLE JOURNEY, THE(1963)
John Lockert
NITWITS, THE(1935), ed; MUMMY'S BOYS(1936), ed; SILLY BILLIES(1936), ed; FORTY NAUGHTY GIRLS(1937), ed; HIGH FLYERS(1937), ed; ON AGAIN–OFF AGAIN(1937), ed; GUNGA DIN(1939), ed; GREAT GILDERSLEEVE, THE(1942), ed; PIRATES OF THE PRAIRIE(1942), ed; RAIDERS OF THE RANGE(1942), ed; AVENGING RIDER, THE(1943), ed; GHOST SHIP, THE(1943), ed; SAGEBRUSH LAW(1943),

ed; SEVENTH VICTIM, THE(1943), ed; YOUTH RUNS WILD(1944), ed

Ray Lockert
TARZAN'S DESERT MYSTERY(1943), ed; MESA OF LOST WOMEN, THE(1956), ed

Kim Lockett
PROSTITUTE(1980, Brit.)

Anne Lockhart
JORY(1972); JOYRIDE(1977); YOUNG WARRIORS(1983)
1984
HAMBONE AND HILLIE(1984); OASIS, THE(1984)

Araby Lockhart
1984
POLICE ACADEMY(1984)

Calvin Lockhart
DANDY IN ASPIC, A(1968, Brit.); DARK OF THE SUN(1968, Brit.); HIGH COMMISSIONER, THE(1968, U.S./Brit.); JOANNA(1968, Brit.); ONLY WHEN I LARF(1968, Brit.); SALT & PEPPER(1968, Brit.); COTTON COMES TO HARLEM(1970); HALLS OF ANGER(1970); LEO THE LAST(1970, Brit.); MELINDA(1972); BEAST MUST DIE, THE(1974, Brit.); HONEYBABY, HONEYBABY(1974); UPTOWN SATURDAY NIGHT(1974); LET'S DO IT AGAIN(1975); BALTIMORE BULLET, THE(1980)

Caroline Lockhart
DUDE WRANGLER, THE(1930), w

Gene Lockhart
BY YOUR LEAVE(1935); CAPTAIN HURRICANE(1935); CRIME AND PUNISHMENT(1935); I'VE BEEN AROUND(1935); STAR OF MIDNIGHT(1935); STORM OVER THE ANDES(1935); THUNDER IN THE NIGHT(1935); BRIDES ARE LIKE THAT(1936); CAREER WOMAN(1936); COME CLOSER, FOLKS(1936); DEVIL IS A SISSY, THE(1936); EARTHWORM TRACTORS(1936); FIRST BABY(1936); GARDEN MURDER CASE, THE(1936); GORGEOUS HUSSY, THE(1936); TIMES SQUARE PLAYBOY(1936); WEDDING PRESENT(1936); MAKE WAY FOR TOMORROW(1937); MAMA STEPS OUT(1937); MIND YOUR OWN BUSINESS(1937); SHEIK STEPS OUT, THE(1937); SOMETHING TO SING ABOUT(1937); TOO MANY WIVES(1937); ALGIERS(1938); BLONDIE(1938); CHRISTMAS CAROL, A(1938); LISTEN, DARLING(1938); MEET THE GIRLS(1938); MEN ARE SUCH FOOLS(1938); OF HUMAN HEARTS(1938); PENROD'S DOUBLE TROUBLE(1938); SINNERS IN PARADISE(1938); SWEETHEARTS(1938); BLACKMAIL(1939); BRIDAL SUITE(1939); GERONIMO(1939); HOTEL IMPERIAL(1939); I'M FROM MISSOURI(1939); OUR LEADING CITIZEN(1939); STORY OF ALEXANDER GRAHAM BELL, THE(1939); TELL NO TALES(1939); ABE LINCOLN IN ILLINOIS(1940); DISPATCH FROM REUTERS, A(1940); DR. KILDARE GOES HOME(1940); EDISON, THE MAN(1940); HIS GIRL FRIDAY(1940); SOUTH OF PAGO PAGO(1940); WE WHO ARE YOUNG(1940); BILLY THE KID(1941); DEVIL AND DANIEL WEBSTER, THE(1941); INTERNATIONAL LADY(1941); KEEPING COMPANY(1941); MEET JOHN DOE(1941); ONE FOOT IN HEAVEN(1941); SEA WOLF, THE(1941); STEEL AGAINST THE SKY(1941); GAY SISTERS, THE(1942); JUKE GIRL(1942); THEY DIED WITH THEIR BOOTS ON(1942); YOU CAN'T ESCAPE FOREVER(1942); DESERT SONG, THE(1943); FIND THE BLACKMAILER(1943); FOREVER AND A DAY(1943); HANGMEN ALSO DIE(1943); MISSION TO MOSCOW(1943); NORTHERN PURSUIT(1943); ACTION IN ARABIA(1944); GOING MY WAY(1944); MAN FROM FRISCO(1944); HOUSE ON 92ND STREET, THE(1945); THAT'S THE SPIRIT(1945); LEAVE HER TO HEAVEN(1946); MEET ME ON BROADWAY(1946); SCANDAL IN PARIS, A(1946); STRANGE WOMAN, THE(1946); CYNTHIA(1947); FOXES OF HARROW, THE(1947); HER HUSBAND'S AFFAIRS(1947); HONEYMOON(1947); MIRACLE ON 34TH STREET, THE(1947); SHOCKING MISS PILGRIM, THE(1947); APARTMENT FOR PEGGY(1948); I, JANE DOE(1948); INSIDE STORY, THE(1948); JOAN OF ARC(1948); THAT WONDERFUL URGE(1948); DOWN TO THE SEA IN SHIPS(1949); INSPECTOR GENERAL, THE(1949); MADAME BOVARY(1949); RED LIGHT(1949); BIG HANGOVER, THE(1950); RIDING HIGH(1950); I'D CLIMB THE HIGHEST MOUNTAIN(1951); LADY FROM TEXAS, THE(1951); RHUBARB(1951); ANDROCLES AND THE LION(1952); APACHE WAR SMOKE(1952); BONZO GOES TO COLLEGE(1952); FACE TO FACE(1952); GIRL IN EVERY PORT, A(1952); HOODLUM EMPIRE(1952); SEEDS OF DESTRUCTION(1952); CONFIDENTIAL CONNIE(1953); DOWN AMONG THE SHELTERING PALMS(1953); FRANCIS COVERS THE BIG TOWN(1953); LADY WANTS MINK, THE(1953); WORLD FOR RANSOM(1954); VANISHING AMERICAN, THE(1955); CAROUSEL(1956); MAN IN THE GREY FLANNEL SUIT, THE(1956); JEANNE EAGELS(1957)
Misc. Talkies
STORM OVER THE ANDES(1935)

Harry Lockhart
ONE THAT GOT AWAY, THE(1958, Brit.); ONCE MORE, WITH FEELING(1960); TAMAHINE(1964, Brit.)

John Lockhart
HAPPY DAYS(1930)

June Lockhart
ALL THIS AND HEAVEN TOO(1940); ADAM HAD FOUR SONS(1941); SERGEANT YORK(1941); MISS ANNIE ROONEY(1942); FOREVER AND A DAY(1943); MEET ME IN ST. LOUIS(1944); WHITE CLIFFS OF DOVER, THE(1944); KEEP YOUR POWDER DRY(1945); SON OF LASSIE(1945); EASY TO WED(1946); SHE-WOLF OF LONDON(1946); YEARLING, THE(1946); BURY ME DEAD(1947); IT'S A JOKE, SON!(1947); T-MEN(1947); TIME LIMIT(1957); LASSIE'S GREAT ADVENTURE(1963); BUTTERFLY(1982); STRANGE INVADERS(1983)
Misc. Talkies
JUST TELL ME YOU LOVE ME(1979)

Kathleen Lockhart
BRIDES ARE LIKE THAT(1936); CAREER WOMAN(1936); DEVIL IS A SISSY, THE(1936); MISTER CINDERELLA(1936); TIMES SQUARE PLAYBOY(1936); SOMETHING TO SING ABOUT(1937); BLONDIE(1938); CHRISTMAS CAROL, A(1938); GIVE ME A SAILOR(1938); MEN ARE SUCH FOOLS(1938); PENROD'S DOUBLE TROUBLE(1938); SWEETHEARTS(1938); MAN OF CONQUEST(1939); OUR LEADING CITIZEN(1939); OUTSIDE THESE WALLS(1939); WHAT A LIFE(1939); LOVE CRAZY(1941); ARE HUSBANDS NECESSARY?(1942); GOOD FELLOWS, THE(1943); MISSION TO MOSCOW(1943); LOST ANGEL(1944); ROUGHLY SPEAKING(1945); TWO YEARS BEFORE THE MAST(1946); GENTLEMAN'S AGREEMENT(1947); LADY IN THE LAKE(1947); MOTHER WORE TIGHTS(1947); I'D CLIMB THE HIGHEST MOUNTAIN(1951); PLYMOUTH ADVENTURE(1952); GLENN MILLER STORY, THE(1953); WALKING MY BABY BACK HOME(1953); PURPLE GANG, THE(1960)

Laura Lockhart
Misc. Silents
TWIN TRIGGERS(1926)

Marshall Lockhart
ROAD HUSTLERS, THE(1968)

R.H. Bruce Lockhart
BRITISH AGENT(1934), w

Ray Lockhart
SEA SPOILERS, THE(1936), ed

Danny Lockin
GYPSY(1962); HELLO, DOLLY!(1969)

Heather Locklear
1984
FIRESTARTER(1984)

Ormer L. Locklear
Misc. Silents
GREAT AIR ROBBERY, THE(1920)

Ormer Locklear
Misc. Silents
SKYWAYMAN, THE(1920)

Sydney Locklynne
Silents
OLD CURIOSITY SHOP, THE(1913, Brit.)

Richard Lockmiller
JACKSON COUNTY JAIL(1976); RATTLERS(1976); OUTLAW BLUES(1977)

J.P. Lockney
WHEN YOU'RE IN LOVE(1937)
Silents
EYE OF THE NIGHT, THE(1916); JIM GRIMSBY'S BOY(1916); CRAB, THE(1917); JUST TONY(1922); MAKING A MAN(1922); SEEING'S BELIEVING(1922); WHILE SATAN SLEEPS(1922); PRISONER, THE(1923); SKY RIDER, THE(1928); SMOKE BELLEW(1929)
Misc. Silents
IN SLUMBERLAND(1917); SILENT MAN, THE(1917); FLARE-UP SAL(1918); GUILTY MAN, THE(1918); BROADWAY COWBOY, THE(1920); HIS NIBS(1921); KISS, THE(1921); WESTERN SPEED(1922); DANGER AHEAD(1923); DOUBLE ACTION DANIELS(1925); DEUCE HIGH(1926); DOUBLE DARING(1926); GALLOPING THUNDER(1927); SODA WATER COWBOY(1927); FLYING BUCKAROO, THE(1928)

John Lockney
Misc. Silents
POLLY ANN(1917)

John P. Lockney
Silents
TAR HEEL WARRIOR, THE(1917); YELLOW STAIN, THE(1922); SWEET ADELINE(1926)
Misc. Silents
DESERT WOOING, A(1918); FUSS AND FEATHERS(1918); STRING BEANS(1918); EGG CRATE WALLOP, THE(1919); PARTNERS THREE(1919); SHERIFF'S SON, THE(1919); HICKVILLE TO BROADWAY(1921)

L.P. Lockney
Silents
PARTNERS OF THE TIDE(1921); RUGGED WATER(1925)

Dee Lockood
Misc. Talkies
AFFAIRS OF ROBIN HOOD, THE(1981)

Ray Lockrem
SNOW WHITE AND THE SEVEN DWARFS(1937), anim

Frances Lockridge
MR. AND MRS. NORTH(1941), w

Richard Lockridge
MR. AND MRS. NORTH(1941), w

Ross Lockridge, Jr.
RAINTREE COUNTY(1957), w

Joan Lockton
Misc. Silents
DISAPPEARANCE OF THE JUDGE, THE(1919, Brit.); MISS CHARITY(1921, Brit.); PORT OF LOST SOULS(1924, Brit.); SINS YE DO, THE(1924, Brit.); CONFESSIONS(1925, Brit.); KING'S HIGHWAY, THE(1927, Brit.); WOMAN REDEEMED, A(1927, Brit.)

JoAnn Locktov
STACY'S KNIGHTS(1983), p

Alex Lockwood
SABOTEUR(1942)

Alexander Lockwood
ANGELS WITH DIRTY FACES(1938); MURDER IN THE AIR(1940); DIVE BOMBER(1941); FLIGHT FROM DESTINY(1941); JUST OFF BROADWAY(1942); MADAME SPY(1942); JIGSAW(1949); WRONG MAN, THE(1956); HELL CANYON OUTLAWS(1957); INVISIBLE BOY, THE(1957); STORY OF MANKIND, THE(1957); TARNISHED ANGELS, THE(1957); TATTERED DRESS, THE(1957); MONSTER ON THE CAMPUS(1958); EDGE OF ETERNITY(1959); NORTH BY NORTHWEST(1959); THIS EARTH IS MINE(1959); WALK ON THE WILD SIDE(1962); BEAUTY AND THE BEAST(1963); MONKEY'S UNCLE, THE(1965); FAMILY PLOT(1976); MAKING LOVE(1982); ROMANTIC COMEDY(1983)

Alyn Lockwood
BLONDIE KNOWS BEST(1946); BLONDIE'S ANNIVERSARY(1947); BLONDIE'S BIG MOMENT(1947); BLONDIE'S HOLIDAY(1947); BLONDIE'S REWARD(1948); BLONDIE'S SECRET(1948); BLONDIE HITS THE JACKPOT(1949); BLONDIE'S BIG DEAL(1949); BEWARE OF BLONDIE(1950); BLONDIE'S HERO(1950); BORDER RANGERS(1950); BADMAN'S GOLD(1951), a, w; CATTLE QUEEN(1951); JEANNE EAGELS(1957)

Charles A. Lockwood
HELLCATS OF THE NAVY(1957), w

Dee Lockwood
PRECIOUS JEWELS(1969)

Douglas Lockwood
HALF PINT, THE(1960)

Gary Lockwood
CALL ME GENIUS(1961, Brit.); SPLENDOR IN THE GRASS(1961); WILD IN THE COUNTRY(1961); MAGIC SWORD, THE(1962); IT HAPPENED AT THE WORLD'S FAIR(1963); KITTEN WITH A WHIP(1964); FIRECREEK(1968); 2001: A SPACE ODYSSEY(1968, U.S./Brit.); MODEL SHOP, THE(1969); THEY CAME TO ROB LAS VEGAS(1969, Fr./Ital./Span./Ger.); R.P.M.(1970); STAND UP AND BE COUNTED(1972); PROJECT: KILL(1976)

Misc. Talkies
MANHUNT IN SPACE(1954); BAD GEORGIA ROAD(1977)

Harold Lockwood
NO ROOM FOR THE GROOM(1952)
Silents
CONSPIRACY, THE(1914); COUNTY CHAIRMAN, THE(1914); HEARTS ADRIFT(1914); SCALES OF JUSTICE, THE(1914); SUCH A LITTLE QUEEN(1914); TESS OF THE STORM COUNTRY(1914); ARE YOU A MASON?(1915); DAVID HARUM(1915); BIG TREMAINE(1916); HAUNTED PAJAMAS(1917); PARADISE GARDEN(1917); AVENGING TRAIL, THE(1918)
Misc. Silents
CRUCIBLE, THE(1914); MAN FROM MEXICO, THE(1914); UNWELCOME MRS. HATCH, THE(1914); WILDFLOWER(1914); BUZZARD'S SHADOW, THE(1915); END OF THE ROAD, THE(1915); JIM, THE PENMAN(1915); LOVE ROUTE, THE(1915); LURE OF THE MASK, THE(1915); SECRETARY OF FRIVOLOUS AFFAIRS, THE(1915); COME-BACK, THE(1916); LIFE'S BLIND ALLEY(1916); MASKED RIDER, THE(1916); MISTER 44(1916); OTHER SIDE OF THE DOOR, THE(1916); PIDGIN ISLAND(1916); RIVER OF ROMANCE, THE(1916); HIDDEN CHILDREN, THE(1917); HIDDEN SPRING, THE(1917); PROMISE, THE(1917); SQUARE DECEIVER, THE(1917); UNDER HANDICAP(1917); BROADWAY BILL(1918); LANDLOPER, THE(1918); LEND ME YOUR NAME(1918); PALS FIRST(1918); GREAT ROMANCE, THE(1919); MAN OF HONOR, A(1919); SHADOWS OF SUSPICION(1919)

J. R. Lockwood
WARE CASE, THE(1939, Brit.)
Silents
SMALL TOWN IDOL, A(1921), ph

J.H. Lockwood
FATAL HOUR, THE(1937, Brit.)

Jale Lockwood
FEMALE BUNCH, THE(1969), w

Johnny Lockwood
NO. 96(1974, Aus.); NORMAN LOVES ROSE(1982, Aus.)

Julia Lockwood
FLYING EYE, THE(1955, Brit.); SOLITARY CHILD, THE(1958, Brit.); TEENAGE BAD GIRL(1959, Brit.); PLEASE TURN OVER(1960, Brit.); BEWARE OF CHILDREN(1961, Brit.)

King Lockwood
MAN IN THE GREY FLANNEL SUIT, THE(1956); TATTERED DRESS, THE(1957); DONOVAN'S REEF(1963)

Lyn Lockwood
IT'S NOT CRICKET(1949, Brit.), w

Margaret Lockwood
CASE OF GABRIEL PERRY, THE(1935, Brit.); HONOURS EASY(1935, Brit.); LORNA DOONE(1935, Brit.); MAN OF THE MOMENT(1935, Brit.); SOME DAY(1935, Brit.); AMATEUR GENTLEMAN(1936, Brit.); BELOVED VAGABOND, THE(1936, Brit.); IRISH FOR LUCK(1936, Brit.); JURY'S EVIDENCE(1936, Brit.); DOCTOR SYN(1937, Brit.); MELODY AND ROMANCE(1937, Brit.); STREET SINGER, THE(1937, Brit.); WHO'S YOUR LADY FRIEND?(1937, Brit.); BANK HOLIDAY(1938, Brit.); LADY VANISHES, THE(1938, Brit.); TO THE VICTOR(1938, Brit.); RULERS OF THE SEA(1939); SUSANNAH OF THE MOUNTIES(1939); NIGHT TRAIN(1940, Brit.); STARS LOOK DOWN, THE(1940, Brit.); GIRL IN THE NEWS, THE(1941, Brit.); GIRL MUST LIVE, A(1941, Brit.); QUIET WEDDING(1941, Brit.); ALIBI, THE(1943, Brit.); MAN IN GREY, THE(1943, Brit.); GIVE US THE MOON(1944, Brit.); I'LL BE YOUR SWEETHEART(1945, Brit.); PLACE OF ONE'S OWN, A(1945, Brit.); RANDOLPH FAMILY, THE(1945, Brit.); BEDELIA(1946, Brit.); WICKED LADY, THE(1946, Brit.); BAD SISTER(1947, Brit.); HUNGRY HILL(1947, Brit.); LADY SURRENDERS, A(1947, Brit.); JASSY(1948, Brit.); LOOK BEFORE YOU LOVE(1948, Brit.); CARDBOARD CAVALIER, THE(1949, Brit.); MADNESS OF THE HEART(1949, Brit.); HIGHLY DANGEROUS(1950, Brit.); MEN OF THE SEA(1951, Brit.); TRENT'S LAST CASE(1953, Brit.); LAUGHING ANNE(1954, Brit./U.S.); TROUBLE IN THE GLEN(1954, Brit.); CAST A DARK SHADOW(1958, Brit.); SLIPPER AND THE ROSE, THE(1976, Brit.)

Paul Lockwood
FINDERS KEEPERS, LOVERS WEEPERS(1968)

Preston Lockwood
JULIUS CAESAR(1970, Brit.); LADY CAROLINE LAMB(1972, Brit./Ital.); BLACK WINDMILL, THE(1974, Brit.); TERRORISTS, THE(1975, Brit.); ABSOLUTION(1981, Brit.); TIME BANDITS(1981, Brit.)
1984
ELECTRIC DREAMS(1984); SCANDALOUS(1984)

Renaud Lockwood
HOWARD CASE, THE(1936, Brit.)

Rick Lockwood
NIGHT MOVES(1975)

Roy Lockwood
PEARLS BRING TEARS(1937, Brit.), w; YOU'RE THE DOCTOR(1938, Brit.), d; MUTINY OF THE ELSINORE, THE(1939, Brit.), d; JAMBOREE(1957), d

Toots Lockwood
BAD SISTER(1947, Brit.)

Victoria Lockwood
SILENCERS, THE(1966)

William H. Lockwood
WEEKEND OF FEAR(1966), m

Tom Lockyear
TEENAGERS FROM OUTER SPACE(1959)

Malcolm Lockyer
STRICTLY CONFIDENTIAL(1959, Brit.), m; SWEET BEAT(1962, Brit.), md; BE MY GUEST(1965, Brit.), m; DR. WHO AND THE DALEKS(1965, Brit.), m, md; LITTLE ONES, THE(1965, Brit.), md; TEN LITTLE INDIANS(1965, Brit.), m, md; PLEASURE GIRLS, THE(1966, Brit.), m, md; DEADLIER THAN THE MALE(1967, Brit.), m; FIVE GOLDEN DRAGONS(1967, Brit.), m; ISLAND OF TERROR(1967, Brit.), m, md; EVE(1968, Brit./Span.), m; VENGEANCE OF FU MANCHU, THE(1968, Brit./Ger./Hong Kong/Ireland), m&md; ISLAND OF THE BURNING DAMNED(1971, Brit.), m, md

C. D. Locock
DANCE OF DEATH, THE(1971, Brit.), w

H. Lisle Locoque
Misc. Silents
SHE(1916, Brit.), d

Matthew J. Locricchio
ESCAPE FROM ALCATRAZ(1979)

Loris Loddi
CLEOPATRA(1963); HERCULES, SAMSON & ULYSSES(1964, Ital.); HILLS RUN RED, THE(1967, Ital.); ADVENTURERS, THE(1970)

Adolph Lodel
DECISION BEFORE DAWN(1951)

Barbara Loden
WILD RIVER(1960); SPLENDOR IN THE GRASS(1961); WANDA(1971), a, d&w
Misc. Talkies
FADE-IN(1968)

Edith Loder
PANIC IN THE CITY(1968)

John Loder
BLACK WATERS(1929); DOCTOR'S SECRET(1929); RACKETEER, THE(1929); RICH PEOPLE(1929); UNHOLY NIGHT, THE(1929); HER PRIVATE AFFAIR(1930); LILIES OF THE FIELD(1930); MAN HUNTER, THE(1930); ONE NIGHT AT SUSIE'S(1930); SECOND FLOOR MYSTERY, THE(1930); SWEETHEARTS AND WIVES(1930); SEAS BENEATH, THE(1931); MONEY MEANS NOTHING(1932, Brit.); WEDDING REHEARSAL(1932, Brit.); MONEY FOR SPEED(1933, Brit.); PARIS PLANE(1933, Brit.); PRIVATE LIFE OF HENRY VIII, THE(1933); BATTLE, THE(1934, Fr.); LOVE, LIFE AND LAUGHTER(1934, Brit.); MY SONG GOES ROUND THE WORLD(1934, Brit.); ROLLING IN MONEY(1934, Brit.); SING AS WE GO(1934, Brit.); WARN LONDON!(1934, Brit.); YOU MADE ME LOVE YOU(1934, Brit.); IT HAPPENED IN PARIS(1935, Brit.); JAVA HEAD(1935, Brit.); LORNA DOONE(1935, Brit.); SILENT PASSENGER, THE(1935, Brit.); 18 MINUTES(1935, Brit.); DAREDEVILS OF EARTH(1936, Brit.); GUILTY MELODY(1936, Brit.); MAN WHO LIVED AGAIN, THE(1936, Brit.); QUEEN OF HEARTS(1936, Brit.); DOCTOR SYN(1937, Brit.); KING SOLOMON'S MINES(1937, Brit.); NON-STOP NEW YORK(1937, Brit.); RIVER OF UNREST(1937, Brit.); SABOTAGE(1937, Brit.); TO THE VICTOR(1938, Brit.); CONTINENTAL EXPRESS(1939, Brit.); MURDER WILL OUT(1939, Brit.); ADVENTURE IN DIAMONDS(1940); DIAMOND FRONTIER(1940); MOZART(1940, Brit.); TIN PAN ALLEY(1940); CONFIRM OR DENY(1941); HOW GREEN WAS MY VALLEY(1941); ONE NIGHT IN LISBON(1941); SCOTLAND YARD(1941); EAGLE SQUADRON(1942); GENTLEMAN JIM(1942); GORILLA MAN(1942); MAXWELL ARCHER, DETECTIVE(1942, Brit.); NOW, VOYAGER(1942); ADVENTURES IN IRAQ(1943); MURDER ON THE WATERFRONT(1943); MYSTERIOUS DOCTOR, THE(1943); OLD ACQUAINTANCE(1943); UNDER SECRET ORDERS(1943, Brit.); ABROAD WITH TWO YANKS(1944); HAIRY APE, THE(1944); PASSAGE TO MARSEILLE(1944); BRIGHTON STRANGLER, THE(1945); FIGHTING GUARDSMAN, THE(1945); GAME OF DEATH, A(1945); JEALOUSY(1945); WOMAN WHO CAME BACK(1945); ONE MORE TOMORROW(1946); WIFE OF MONTE CRISTO, THE(1946); DISHONORED LADY(1947); SMALL HOTEL(1957, Brit.); STORY OF ESTHER COSTELLO, THE(1957, Brit.); WOMAN AND THE HUNTER, THE(1957); SECRET MAN, THE(1958, Brit.); GIDEON OF SCOTLAND YARD(1959, Brit.); FIRECHASERS, THE(1970, Brit.)
Silents
SUNSET PASS(1929)
Misc. Silents
FIRST BORN, THE(1928, Brit.); SUNSET PASS(1929)

Kathryn Loder
NIGHT OF THE WITCHES(1970); BIG DOLL HOUSE, THE(1971); FOXY DROWN(1974)

Lotti Loder
OH! SAILOR, BEHAVE!(1930); MEN OF THE SKY(1931); SIT TIGHT(1931); SOLDIER'S PLAYTHING, A(1931)

Peggi Loder
ONE PLUS ONE(1961, Can.); WILLIE MCBEAN AND HIS MAGIC MACHINE(1965, U.S./Jap.); MY SIDE OF THE MOUNTAIN(1969)

Sydney Loder
MASSACRE HILL(1949, Brit.)

Andrew Lodge
LAST ESCAPE, THE(1970, Brit.); BEAST MUST DIE, THE(1974, Brit.); CONDUCT UNBECOMING(1975, Brit.); LAND THAT TIME FORGOT, THE(1975, Brit.); REVENGE OF THE PINK PANTHER(1978); PRIEST OF LOVE(1981, Brit.)

Bernard Lodge
ALIEN(1979), spec eff

Bill Lodge
SAFECRACKER, THE(1958, Brit.), makeup; SWISS FAMILY ROBINSON(1960), makeup; SPARROWS CAN'T SING(1963, Brit.), makeup; HORROR OF IT ALL, THE(1964, Brit.), makeup; HIGH WIND IN JAMAICA, A(1965), makeup; MAROC 7(1967, Brit.), makeup; OUR MOTHER'S HOUSE(1967, Brit.), makeup; GREAT CATHERINE(1968, Brit.), makeup; LION IN WINTER, THE(1968, Brit.), makeup; WUTHERING HEIGHTS(1970, Brit.), makeup; MAN FRIDAY(1975, Brit.), makeup

David Lodge
HELL, HEAVEN OR HOBOKEN(1958, Brit.); YESTERDAY'S ENEMY(1959, Brit.); COCKLESHELL HEROES, THE(1955); FINGER OF GUILT(1956, Brit.); PRIVATE'S PROGRESS(1956, Brit.); COUNTERFEIT PLAN, THE(1957, Brit.); STRANGER'S MEETING(1957, Brit.); DANGEROUS YOUTH(1958, Brit.); DESERT ATTACK(1958, Brit.); FURTHER UP THE CREEK!(1958, Brit.); GIRLS AT SEA(1958, Brit.); I ONLY ASKED!(1958, Brit.); SAFECRACKER, THE(1958, Brit.); TANK FORCE(1958, Brit.); UP THE CREEK(1958, Brit.); YOUR PAST IS SHOWING(1958, Brit.); BOBBIKINS(1959, Brit.); IDOL ON PARADE(1959, Brit.); I'M ALL RIGHT, JACK(1959, Brit.); LIFE IN EMERGENCY WARD 10(1959, Brit.); SILENT ENEMY, THE(1959, Brit.); UGLY DUCKLING, THE(1959, Brit.); BULLDOG BREED, THE(1960, Brit.); JAZZ BOAT(1960, Brit.); NEVER LET GO(1960, Brit.); CARRY ON REGARDLESS(1961, Brit.); LEAGUE OF GENTLEMEN, THE(1961, Brit.); TWO-WAY STRETCH(1961, Brit.); WATCH YOUR STERN(1961, Brit.); GO TO BLAZES(1962, Brit.); KILL OR CURE(1962, Brit.); MRS. GIBBONS' BOYS(1962, Brit.); NIGHT CREATURES(1962, Brit.); ON THE BEAT(1962, Brit.); PIRATES OF BLOOD RIVER, THE(1962, Brit.); ROOMMATES(1962, Brit.); TIME TO REMEMBER(1962, Brit.); TRIAL AND ERROR(1962, Brit.); HELLFIRE CLUB, THE(1963, Brit.); GUNS AT BATASI(1964, Brit.); LONG SHIPS, THE(1964, Brit./Yugo.); NO, MY DARLING DAUGHTER(1964, Brit.); SATURDAY NIGHT OUT(1964, Brit.); SHOT IN THE DARK, A(1964); AMOROUS ADVENTURES OF MOLL FLANDERS, THE(1965); HAVING A WILD WEEKEND(1965, Brit.); SAN FERRY ANN(1965, Brit.); SPYLARKS(1965, Brit.); TWO LEFT FEET(1965, Brit.); ALPHABET MURDERS, THE(1966); PRESS FOR TIME(1966, Brit.); SKY BIKE, THE(1967, Brit.); SMASHING TIME(1967 Brit.); CORRUPTION(1968, Brit.); FIXER, THE(1968); HEADLINE HUNTERS(1968, Brit.); OH! WHAT A LOVELY WAR(1969, Brit.); WHAT'S GOOD FOR THE GOOSE(1969, Brit.); HOFFMAN(1970, Brit.); INCENSE FOR THE DAMNED(1970, Brit.); MAGIC CHRISTIAN, THE(1970, Brit.); SCRAMBLE(1970, Brit.); SCREAM AND

SCREAM AGAIN(1970, Brit.); SOPHIE'S PLACE(1970); SUDDEN TERROR(1970, Brit.); RAILWAY CHILDREN, THE(1971, Brit.); AMAZING MR. BLUNDEN, THE(1973, Brit.); CHARLEY-ONE-EYE(1973, Brit.); SCHOOL FOR UNCLAIMED GIRLS(1973, Brit.); RETURN OF THE PINK PANTHER, THE(1975, Brit.); CARRY ON ENGLAND(1976, Brit.)
1984
BLOODBATH AT THE HOUSE OF DEATH(1984, Brit.); SAHARA(1984)
Misc. Talkies
RAISING THE ROOF(1971, Brit.)
David S. Lodge
CUP FEVER(1965, Brit.)
Edward Lodge
SCHOOL FOR SECRETS(1946, Brit.)
Jean Lodge
DICK BARTON STRIKES BACK(1949, Brit.); DR. MORELLE–THE CASE OF THE MISSING HEIRESS(1949, Brit.); HIGH JINKS IN SOCIETY(1949, Brit.); BRANDY FOR THE PARSON(1952, Brit.); DEATH OF AN ANGEL(1952, Brit.); WHITE CORRIDORS(1952, Brit.); GLAD TIDINGS(1953, Brit.); BLACK KNIGHT, THE(1954); FINAL APPOINTMENT(1954, Brit.); JOHNNY ON THE SPOT(1954, Brit.); TERROR SHIP(1954, Brit.); EYES OF ANNIE JONES, THE(1963, Brit.); HELLFIRE CLUB, THE(1963, Brit.); MASQUE OF THE RED DEATH, THE(1964, U.S./Brit.); CURSE OF THE VOODOO(1965, Brit.); INVASION(1965, Brit.)
Misc. Talkies
ACCUSED, THE(1953)
Jimmy Lodge
LONG DUEL, THE(1967, Brit.); WHEN DINOSAURS RULED THE EARTH(1971, Brit.)
Joan Lodge
ACCIDENTAL DEATH(1963, Brit.)
John Lodge
MURDERS IN THE ZOO(1933); UNDER THE TONTO RIM(1933); WOMAN ACCUSED(1933); MENACE(1934); SCARLET EMPRESS, THE(1934); KOENIGSMARK(1935, Fr.); LITTLE COLONEL, THE(1935); SENSATION(1936, Brit.); BULLDOG DRUMMOND AT BAY(1937, Brit.); RIVER OF UNREST(1937, Brit.); TENTH MAN, THE(1937, Brit.); BANK HOLIDAY(1938, Brit.); LIGHTNING CONDUCTOR(1938, Brit.); JUST LIKE A WOMAN(1939, Brit.); ONE NIGHT IN PARIS(1940, Brit.); PIRATES OF THE SEVEN SEAS(1941, Brit.)
John Lodge
OUT OF SIGHT(1966); IN LIKE FLINT(1967); JUDY'S LITTLE NO-NO(1969); WITCHMAKER, THE(1969)
John Davis Lodge
LITTLE WOMEN(1933)
Reg Lodge
YELLOW SUBMARINE(1958, Brit.), animation
Ruth Lodge
MY BROTHER JONATHAN(1949, Brit.); NO PLACE FOR JENNIFER(1950, Brit.); HOUSE OF THE ARROW, THE(1953, Brit.)
Stephen Lodge
HONKERS, THE(1972), w
Terence Lodge
AMOROUS ADVENTURES OF MOLL FLANDERS, THE(1965)
William Lodge
TANK FORCE(1958, Brit.), makeup; MAN IN THE WILDERNESS(1971, U.S./Span.), makeup
Elvira Lodi
LITTLE RED RIDING HOOD AND HER FRIENDS(1964, Mex.)
Fronco Lodi
LUXURY GIRLS(1953, Ital.)
Rodolfo Lodi
WILD, WILD PLANET, THE(1967, Ital.); SABATA(1969, Ital.); WATERLOO(1970, Ital./USSR); ASH WEDNESDAY(1973); DAISY MILLER(1974); LUNA(1979, Ital.)
Theodore Lodi
GENERAL CRACK(1929); THEY HAD TO SEE PARIS(1929); AMBASSADOR BILL(1931); ONCE A SINNER(1931); DOWN TO EARTH(1932); STAMBOUL QUEST(1934); MAN WHO BROKE THE BANK AT MONTE CARLO, THE(1935)
Maurizio Lodi-Fe
MAN WHO CAME FOR COFFEE, THE(1970, Ital.), p; CONFORMIST, THE(1971, Ital., Fr.), p; BREAD AND CHOCOLATE(1978, Ital.), p
Luigi Filippo Lodoli
1984
RUSH(1984, Ital.)
M.C.S. Lodolo
QUEENS, THE(1968, Ital./Fr.), anim
Hugo Lodrini
PURPLE TAXI, THE(1977, Fr./Ital./Ireland), p
Sabine Lods
MADWOMAN OF CHAILLOT, THE(1969)
Joe LoDuca
EVIL DEAD, THE(1983), m
Peter Lodwick
MIKADO, THE(1967, Brit.)
A. Lodzinski
PORTRAIT OF LENIN(1967, Pol./USSR)
Judy Loe
MONTY PYTHON'S THE MEANING OF LIFE(1983, Brit.)
Art Loeb
SANTA FE(1951)
Arthur Loeb
CHELSEA GIRLS, THE(1967)
Caroline Loeb
QUARTET(1981, Brit./Fr.)
Harold Loeb
SOLDIER BLUE(1970), p
Jerome Loeb
FIRST TIME, THE(1978, Fr.)
Karl Loeb
DARK EYES OF LONDON(1961, Ger.), ph; FRONTIER HELLCAT(1966, Fr./Ital./Ger./Yugo.), ph; FLAMING FRONTIER(1968, Ger./Yugo.), ph

Lee Loeb
CASE OF THE MISSING MAN, THE(1935), w; BLACKMAILER(1936), w; COME CLOSER, FOLKS(1936), w; DON'T GAMBLE WITH LOVE(1936), w; TRAPPED BY TELEVISION(1936), w; TROUBLE AHEAD(1936, Brit.), w; COUNSEL FOR CRIME(1937), w; DEVIL IS DRIVING, THE(1937), w; IT CAN'T LAST FOREVER(1937), w; SHALL WE DANCE(1937), w; MAIN EVENT, THE(1938), w; SWING THAT CHEER(1938), w; THREE LOVES HAS NANCY(1938), w; FORGED PASSPORT(1939), w; HAWAIIAN NIGHTS(1939), w; LAUGH IT OFF(1939), w; MELODY FOR THREE(1941), w; PERFECT SNOB, THE(1941), w; REMEDY FOR RICHES(1941), w; GENTLEMAN AT HEART, A(1942), w; IT HAPPENED IN FLATBUSH(1942), w; DIXIE DUGAN(1943), w; NATIONAL BARN DANCE(1944), w; LOVE, HONOR AND GOODBYE(1945), w; AFFAIRS OF GERALDINE(1946), w; CALENDAR GIRL(1947), w; SEVEN KEYS TO BALDPATE(1947), w; UNDERTOW(1949), w; SUNNY SIDE OF THE STREET(1951), w; ABBOTT AND COSTELLO MEET DR. JEKYLL AND MR. HYDE(1954), w; FIREMAN SAVE MY CHILD(1954), w; ABBOTT AND COSTELLO MEET THE MUMMY(1955), w; MOBS INC(1956), w
Philip Loeb
ROOM SERVICE(1938); GOLDBERGS, THE(1950)
Phillip Loeb
DOUBLE LIFE, A(1947)
Bruni Loebel
SPECIAL DELIVERY(1955, Ger.)
Marc Loebell
GREAT COMMANDMENT, THE(1941)
A. V. Loeben
FREUD(1962)
Carsta Loeck
ETERNAL LOVE(1960, Ger.)
George Loeffler
Silents
CARDIGAN(1922)
John Loeffler
1984
SAM'S SON(1984), ed
Louis Loeffler
IN OLD ARIZONA(1929), ed; THRU DIFFERENT EYES(1929), ed; LIGHTNIN'(1930), ed; ONE MAD KISS(1930), ed; AMATEUR DADDY(1932), ed; ARIZONA TO BROADWAY(1933), ed; YOUR UNCLE DUDLEY(1935), ed; CAN THIS BE DIXIE?(1936), ed; CAREER WOMAN(1936), ed; EDUCATING FATHER(1936), ed; HERE COMES TROUBLE(1936), ed; HIGH TENSION(1936), ed; HUMAN CARGO(1936), ed; THIRTY SIX HOURS TO KILL(1936), ed; FAIR WARNING(1937), ed; LANCER SPY(1937), ed; LIFE BEGINS IN COLLEGE(1937), ed; SHE HAD TO EAT(1937), ed; FOUR MEN AND A PRAYER(1938), ed; HAPPY LANDING(1938), ed; HOLD THAT CO-ED(1938), ed; I'LL GIVE A MILLION(1938), ed; HERE I AM A STRANGER(1939), ed; HOTEL FOR WOMEN(1939), ed; LITTLE PRINCESS, THE(1939), ed; ROSE OF WASHINGTON SQUARE(1939), ed; SWANEE RIVER(1939), ed; EARTHBOUND(1940), ed; GIRL FROM AVENUE A(1940), ed; GIRL IN 313(1940), ed; MURDER OVER NEW YORK(1940), ed; DANCE HALL(1941), ed; MARRY THE BOSS' DAUGHTER(1941), ed; RIDE, KELLY, RIDE(1941), ed; RIDE ON VAQUERO(1941), ed; JUST OFF BROADWAY(1942), ed; QUIET PLEASE, MURDER(1942), ed; RIGHT TO THE HEART(1942), ed; THRU DIFFERENT EYES(1942), ed; WHO IS HOPE SCHUYLER?(1942), ed; YOUNG AMERICA(1942), ed; HE HIRED THE BOSS(1943), ed; MARGIN FOR ERROR(1943), ed; MOON IS DOWN, THE(1943), ed; WINTERTIME(1943), ed; IN THE MEANTIME, DARLING(1944), ed; LAURA(1944), ed; SULLIVANS, THE(1944), ed; HOME SWEET HOMICIDE(1946), ed; DAISY KENYON(1947), ed; FOREVER AMBER(1947), ed; I WONDER WHO'S KISSING HER NOW(1947), ed; IRON CURTAIN, THE(1948), ed; THAT WONDERFUL URGE(1948), ed; DANCING IN THE DARK(1949), ed; FAN, THE(1949), ed; OH, YOU BEAUTIFUL DOLL(1949), ed; TWO FLAGS WEST(1950), ed; WHERE THE SIDEWALK ENDS(1950), ed; CALL ME MISTER(1951), ed; GOLDEN GIRL(1951), ed; THIRTEENTH LETTER, THE(1951), ed; I DON'T CARE GIRL, THE(1952), ed; MY COUSIN RACHEL(1952), ed; RETURN OF THE TEXAN(1952), ed; WE'RE NOT MARRIED(1952), ed; DOWN AMONG THE SHELTERING PALMS(1953), ed; FARMER TAKES A WIFE, THE(1953), ed; HOW TO MARRY A MILLIONAIRE(1953), ed; TITANIC(1953), ed; RIVER OF NO RETURN(1954), ed; WOMAN'S WORLD(1954), ed; HOW TO BE VERY, VERY, POPULAR(1955), ed; TALL MEN, THE(1955), ed; VIOLENT SATURDAY(1955), ed; BIGGER THAN LIFE(1956), ed; KING AND FOUR QUEENS, THE(1956), ed; REVOLT OF MAMIE STOVER, THE(1956), ed; NO DOWN PAYMENT(1957), ed; WAYWARD BUS, THE(1957), ed; HOUND-DOG MAN(1959), ed; ANGEL WORE RED, THE(1960), ed; COMANCHEROS, THE(1961), ed; FRANCIS OF ASSISI(1961), ed; ADVISE AND CONSENT(1962), ed; PLEASURE SEEKERS, THE(1964), ed; HURRY SUNDOWN(1967), ed
Louis R. Loeffler
PILGRIMAGE(1933), ed; WHIRLPOOL(1949), ed; MOON IS BLUE, THE(1953), ed; CARMEN JONES(1954), ed; MAN WITH THE GOLDEN ARM, THE(1955), ed; CERTAIN SMILE, A(1958), ed; LONG, HOT SUMMER, THE(1958), ed; RALLY 'ROUND THE FLAG, BOYS!(1958), ed; ANATOMY OF A MURDER(1959), ed; EXODUS(1960), ed; CARDINAL, THE(1963), ed; SHOCK TREATMENT(1964), ed
Clive Loehnis
ROYAL EAGLE(1936, Brit.), p
Dolly Loehr [Diana Lynn]
THEY SHALL HAVE MUSIC(1939); THERE'S MAGIC IN MUSIC(1941)
Hans Loehr
EMIL AND THE DETECTIVE(1931, Ger.)
Georg Loekkeberg
WHALERS, THE(1942, Swed.)
Art Loel
MISTER ROBERTS(1955), art d; GREEN-EYED BLONDE, THE(1957), art d; SPIRIT OF ST. LOUIS, THE(1957), art d; STORY OF MANKIND, THE(1957), art d; UNTAMED YOUTH(1957), art d; LEFT-HANDED GUN, THE(1958), art d; OLD MAN AND THE SEA, THE(1958), art d; TWO ON A GUILLOTINE(1965), art d; CHAMBER OF HORRORS(1966), art d; FIRST TO FIGHT(1967), art d; ONCE YOU KISS A STRANGER(1969), art d; FLAP(1970), prod d
Arthur Loel
OMEGA MAN, THE(1971), art d
J. Arthur Loel
MORE DEAD THAN ALIVE(1968), art d

Mark Loerering
STRANGLEHOLD(1962, Brit.)
Billy Loes
ROOGIE'S BUMP(1954)
Hanna Loeser
DON JUAN(1956, Aust.)
Frank Loesser
FIGHT FOR YOUR LADY(1937), m; ST. LOUIS BLUES(1939), m; ZAZA(1939), m; JOHNNY APOLLO(1940), m; QUARTERBACK, THE(1940), m; FOREST RANGERS, THE(1942), m; PRIORITIES ON PARADE(1942), w; RED, HOT AND BLUE(1949); HANS CHRISTIAN ANDERSEN(1952), m; WHERE'S CHARLEY?(1952, Brit.), w
Arthur Loew, Jr.
LIFE OF HER OWN, A(1950); SUMMER STOCK(1950); TO PLEASE A LADY(1950); ARENA(1953), w; PENELOPE(1966), p
Arthur M. Loew
TERESA(1951), p
Arthur M. Loew, Jr.
AFFAIRS OF DOBIE GILLIS, THE(1953), p; ARENA(1953), p; MARAUDERS, THE(1955), p; RACK, THE(1956), p
David L. Loew
FIT FOR A KING(1937), p; RIDING ON AIR(1937), p; FLIRTING WITH FATE(1938), p; GLADIATOR, THE(1938), p; SO ENDS OUR NIGHT(1941), p; MOON AND SIXPENCE, THE(1942), p; SOUTHERNER, THE(1945), p; NIGHT IN CASABLANCA, A(1946), p; PRIVATE AFFAIRS OF BEL AMI, THE(1947), p
Edward T. Loew, Jr.
Silents
PRISONER, THE(1923), w; SOCIAL HIGHWAYMAN, THE(1926), w
David Loew
WIDE OPEN FACES(1938), p
Evan Loew
SO BIG(1953)
Jean Loew
Silents
JOURNEY'S END(1918)
Jim Loew
DELIRIUM(1979), w
Marcus Loew
Silents
SAPHEAD, THE(1921), p
Paola Loew
GREAT WALTZ, THE(1972)
Sherman Loew
ROAD AGENT(1941), w
Frederick Loewe
BRIGADOON(1954), w; GIGI(1958), m; MY FAIR LADY(1964), w, m; CAMELOT(1967), w, m; PAINT YOUR WAGON(1969), w, m; LITTLE PRINCE, THE(1974, Brit.), m
Dr. Fritz Loewe
S.O.S. ICEBERG(1933), tech adv
Rose Loewenger
STUDY IN SCARLET, A(1933), ed; TOMORROW AT SEVEN(1933), ed
Carolyn Loewenstein
PRIVATE FILES OF J. EDGAR HOOVER, THE(1978), set d
Dan Loewenthal
BIG SCORE, THE(1983), ed
1984
HARD CHOICES(1984), ed
Daniel Loewenthal
ONE DOWN TWO TO GO(1982), ed; HOME FREE ALL(1983), ed; LAST FIGHT, THE(1983), ed
1984
FRIDAY THE 13TH-THE FINAL CHAPTER(1984), ed; HOME FREE ALL(1984), ed; MISSING IN ACTION(1984), ed
Rose Loewinger
SALVATION NELL(1931), ed; FALSE FACES(1932), ed; LAST MILE, THE(1932), ed; THOSE WE LOVE(1932), ed; UPTOWN NEW YORK(1932), ed; WHISTLIN' DAN(1932), ed; BIG BRAIN, THE(1933), ed; DEATH KISS, THE(1933), ed; DELUGE(1933), ed; RACETRACK(1933), ed
Klaus Loewitsch
BREAKTHROUGH(1978, Ger.)
Raymond Lofaro
STUNTS(1977), p, w
Jeanette Loff
RACKETEER, THE(1929); SOPHOMORE, THE(1929); BOUDOIR DIPLOMAT(1930); PARTY GIRL(1930); FIGHTING THRU(1931); HIDE-OUT(1934); MILLION DOLLAR BABY(1935)
Misc. Talkies
ST. LOUIS WOMAN(1935)
Silents
ANNAPOLIS(1928); HOLD 'EM YALE!(1928); MAN-MADE WOMEN(1928)
Misc. Silents
BLACK ACE, THE(1928); LOVE OVER NIGHT(1928)
Carlo Loffredo
LOVE AND MARRIAGE(1966, Ital.)
Juli Loffredo
GREEN FIRE(1955)
George Lofgren
MIGHTY JOE YOUNG(1949), spec eff
Marianne Lofgren
ON THE SUNNYSIDE(1936, Swed.); NIGHT IN JUNE, A(1940, Swed.); ONLY ONE NIGHT(1942, Swed.); AFFAIRS OF A MODEL(1952, Swed.); TIME OF DESIRE, THE(1957, Swed.); DEVIL'S WANTON, THE(1962, Swed.)
Nils Lofgren
SGT. PEPPER'S LONELY HEARTS CLUB BAND(1978)
Gianni Lofredo
ASSASSINATION OF TROTSKY, THE(1972 Fr./Ital.)
Arthur Loft
UNCLE HARRY(1945); STAND UP AND CHEER(1934 80m FOX bw); DANGER AHEAD(1935); KID COURAGEOUS(1935); ON PROBATION(1935); WESTERN JUSTICE(1935); WHAT PRICE CRIME?(1935); BARS OF HATE(1936); KING OF THE ROYAL MOUNTED(1936); LEGION OF TERROR(1936); LONE WOLF RETURNS, THE(1936); M'LISS(1936); NIGHT WAITRESS(1936); PAROLE(1936); POSTAL INSPECTOR(1936); PRISONER OF SHARK ISLAND, THE(1936); ROGUES' TAVERN, THE(1936); WHIPSAW(1936); WINTERSET(1936); WITHOUT ORDERS(1936); ALL-AMERICAN SWEETHEART(1937); GAME THAT KILLS, THE(1937); IT HAPPENED IN HOLLYWOOD(1937); MOTOR MADNESS(1937); PAID TO DANCE(1937); PARADISE EXPRESS(1937); PUBLIC COWBOY NO. 1(1937); SHADOW, THE(1937); SILENT BARRIERS(1937, Brit.); WOMAN IN DISTRESS(1937); CITY STREETS(1938); DOWN IN ARKANSAW(1938); EXTORTION(1938); GANG BULLETS(1938); HIGHWAY PATROL(1938); I AM THE LAW(1938); LADY OBJECTS, THE(1938); MAIN EVENT, THE(1938); NO TIME TO MARRY(1938); RAWHIDE(1938); RHYTHM OF THE SADDLE(1938); SQUADRON OF HONOR(1938); START CHEERING(1938); THERE'S ALWAYS A WOMAN(1938); WHO KILLED GAIL PRESTON?(1938); WOMEN IN PRISON(1938); DAYS OF JESSE JAMES(1939); EVERYBODY'S BABY(1939); HELL'S KITCHEN(1939); ICE FOLLIES OF 1939(1939); LET US LIVE(1939); PRIDE OF THE BLUEGRASS(1939); RISKY BUSINESS(1939); ROARING TWENTIES, THE(1939); SMUGGLED CARGO(1939); SOUTHWARD HO!(1939); WOMAN IS THE JUDGE, A(1939); CAFE HOSTESS(1940); CARSON CITY KID(1940); CROOKED ROAD, THE(1940); GLAMOUR FOR SALE(1940); RIDERS OF PASCO BASIN(1940); TEXAS TERRORS(1940); YOU'RE NOT SO TOUGH(1940); BACK IN THE SADDLE(1941); BLUE, WHITE, AND PERFECT(1941); CAUGHT IN THE DRAFT(1941); DOWN MEXICO WAY(1941); HOLD BACK THE DAWN(1941); LIFE BEGINS FOR ANDY HARDY(1941); NORTH FROM LONE STAR(1941); STORK PAYS OFF, THE(1941); THREE GIRLS ABOUT TOWN(1941); WE GO FAST(1941); YOU BELONG TO ME(1941); BROADWAY(1942); DR. BROADWAY(1942); FLY BY NIGHT(1942); FOREST RANGERS, THE(1942); GIRL TROUBLE(1942); GLASS KEY, THE(1942); HENRY ALDRICH GETS GLAMOUR(1942); LADY HAS PLANS, THE(1942); LUCKY JORDAN(1942); MAGNIFICENT DOPE, THE(1942); MAN IN THE TRUNK, THE(1942); MEET THE STEWARTS(1942); NIGHT IN NEW ORLEANS, A(1942); PRIORITIES ON PARADE(1942); SECRET AGENT OF JAPAN(1942); SOUTH OF SANTA FE(1942); SPIRIT OF STANFORD, THE(1942); STAR SPANGLED RHYTHM(1942); STREET OF CHANCE(1942); TAKE A LETTER, DARLING(1942); THEY DIED WITH THEIR BOOTS ON(1942); TRUE TO THE ARMY(1942); DR. GILLESPIE'S CRIMINAL CASE(1943); FLESH AND FANTASY(1943); FOOTLIGHT GLAMOUR(1943); FRONTIER BADMEN(1943); GILDERSLEEVE'S BAD DAY(1943); HANGMEN ALSO DIE(1943); HAPPY GO LUCKY(1943); IN OLD OKLAHOMA(1943); JACK LONDON(1943); LET'S FACE IT(1943); MEANEST MAN IN THE WORLD, THE(1943); MISSION TO MOSCOW(1943); MY FRIEND FLICKA(1943); NO TIME FOR LOVE(1943); OUTLAW, THE(1943); SCREAM IN THE DARK, A(1943); SILVER SPURS(1943); WINTERTIME(1943); AND THE ANGELS SING(1944); CHARLIE CHAN IN THE SECRET SERVICE(1944); HENRY ALDRICH PLAYS CUPID(1944); HITLER GANG, THE(1944); LEAVE IT TO THE IRISH(1944); LIGHTS OF OLD SANTA FE(1944); LOUISIANA HAYRIDE(1944); MY BUDDY(1944); PRACTICALLY YOURS(1944); ROSIE THE RIVETER(1944); STANDING ROOM ONLY(1944); WILSON(1944); ALONG CAME JONES(1945); ARSON SQUAD(1945); BLONDE FROM BROOKLYN(1945); BLOOD ON THE SUN(1945); HONEYMOON AHEAD(1945); INCENDIARY BLONDE(1945); IT'S A PLEASURE(1945); MAN FROM OKLAHOMA, THE(1945); MEN IN HER DIARY(1945); NAUGHTY NINETIES, THE(1945); NOB HILL(1945); ON STAGE EVERYBODY(1945); ROAD TO UTOPIA(1945); SCARLET STREET(1945); SHANGHAI COBRA, THE(1945); SHE GETS HER MAN(1945); WOMAN IN THE WINDOW, THE(1945); BLONDIE KNOWS BEST(1946); BLUE DAHLIA, THE(1946); CAT CREEPS, THE(1946); CROSS MY HEART(1946); JOLSON STORY, THE(1946); LITTLE MISS BIG(1946); ONE EXCITING WEEK(1946); OUR HEARTS WERE GROWING UP(1946); SEARCHING WIND, THE(1946); SHERIFF OF REDWOOD VALLEY(1946); TO EACH HIS OWN(1946); TRAFFIC IN CRIME(1946); TWO YEARS BEFORE THE MAST(1946); CIGARETTE GIRL(1947); WHIRLWIND RAIDERS(1948); REDHEAD FROM MANHATTAN(1954)
Misc. Talkies
LONE STAR MOONLIGHT(1946)
Christopher Lofthouse
NO BLADE OF GRASS(1970, Brit.)
Carey Loftin
LOST IN A HAREM(1944); TRAIL TO VENGEANCE(1945); TROUBLE MAKERS(1948); MILKMAN, THE(1950); JALOPY(1953); STEEL JUNGLE, THE(1956); RISE AND FALL OF LEGS DIAMOND, THE(1960); SPARTACUS(1960); THUNDER IN CAROLINA(1960); HATARI!(1962), stunts; IT'S A MAD, MAD, MAD, MAD WORLD(1963), stunts; DR. GOLDFOOT AND THE BIKINI MACHINE(1965); PATTON(1970); GETAWAY, THE(1972), stunts; HOT ROCK, THE(1972), stunts; WALKING TALL(1973), a, stunts; FRAMED(1975), stunts; NIGHT MOVES(1975); WALKING TALL, PART II(1975, Can.), stunt; WHITE LINE FEVER(1975, Can.), stunt; SPECIAL DELIVERY(1976), stunts; HERBIE GOES TO MONTE CARLO(1977); OUTLAW BLUES(1977), stunts; PROMISE, THE(1979)
1984
AGAINST ALL ODDS(1984); CITY HEAT(1984); HIGHPOINT(1984, Can.), stunts
Cary Loftin
SIX BRIDGES TO CROSS(1955); VANISHING POINT(1971), stunts; SUGARLAND EXPRESS, THE(1974), stunts
Dixie Loftin
KEY, THE(1934)
Harry Loftin
JOHNNY ROCCO(1958)
Jay Loftin
PICKUP ON SOUTH STREET(1953)
Harry Lofting
Silents
KENT, THE FIGHTING MAN(1916, Brit.); TATTERLY(1919, Brit.)
Misc. Silents
ON THE STEPS OF THE ALTAR(1916, Brit.)
Hugh Lofting
DOCTOR DOLITTLE(1967), d
Morgan Lofting
JOYSTICKS(1983)
William Loftos
MAVERICK QUEEN, THE(1956)
Norah Lofts
JASSY(1948, Brit.), w; SEVEN WOMEN(1966), w
B.T. Loftus
STONE OF SILVER CREEK(1935), ed

Bernard Loftus
IVORY-HANDLED GUN(1935), ed; OUTLAWED GUNS(1935), ed; THROWBACK, THE(1935), ed; SUNSET OF POWER(1936), ed; BLACK ACES(1937), ed; SANDFLOW(1937), ed; CIPHER BUREAU(1938), ed; SHADOWS OVER SHANGHAI(1938), ed; LONG SHOT, THE(1939), ed; PANAMA PATROL(1939), ed; COVERED WAGON DAYS(1940), ed

Bryan Loftus
2001: A SPACE ODYSSEY(1968, U.S./Brit.), spec eff

Cecilia Loftus
DOCTORS' WIVES(1931); EAST LYNNE(1931); YOUNG SINNERS(1931); ONCE IN A BLUE MOON(1936); DEAD END KIDS ON DRESS PARADE(1939); OLD MAID, THE(1939); IT'S A DATE(1940); LUCKY PARTNERS(1940); BLACK CAT, THE(1941)
Silents
PRIDE OF JENNICO, THE(1914)
Misc. Silents
LADY OF QUALITY, A(1913); DIANA OF DOBSON'S(1917, Brit.)

Laura Loftus
ONE DOWN TWO TO GO(1982)

Chris Lofven
20TH CENTURY OZ(1977, Aus.), p, d&w

H. G. Logalton
Silents
SPIDER WEBS(1927), w

Anna Logan
Silents
GOVERNOR'S BOSS, THE(1915)

Andrew Logan
Misc. Talkies
ALTERNATIVE MISS WORLD, THE(1980)

Annabelle Logan
PRESENTING LILY MARS(1943)

Anne Logan
CHAMP, THE(1979)

Barbara Logan
TWO DOLLAR BETTOR(1951); TWO TICKETS TO BROADWAY(1951); TELL ME THAT YOU LOVE ME, JUNIE MOON(1970)

Bill Logan
JOHNNY IN THE CLOUDS(1945, Brit.)

Brad Logan
MADAME X(1966)

Bruce Logan
2001: A SPACE ODYSSEY(1968, U.S./Brit.), spec eff; HOWZER(1973), ph; THIS IS A HIJACK(1973), ph; BIG BAD MAMA(1974), ph; CRAZY MAMA(1975), ph; IDAHO TRANSFER(1975), ph; CAT MURKIL AND THE SILKS(1976), ph; JACKSON COUNTY JAIL(1976), ph; I NEVER PROMISED YOU A ROSE GARDEN(1977), ph; STUNTS(1977), ph; DRACULA'S DOG(1978), ph; AIRPLANE!(1980), spec eff; INCREDIBLE SHRINKING WOMAN, THE(1981), ph, spec eff; TRON(1982), ph

Christopher Logan
DEATH WISH(1974)

Danny Logan
DATE BAIT(1960)

Ella Logan
FLYING HOSTESS(1936); TOP OF THE TOWN(1937); WOMAN CHASES MAN(1937); 52ND STREET(1937); GOLDWYN FOLLIES, THE(1938)

Frank Logan
AROUND THE WORLD UNDER THE SEA(1966); GENTLE GIANT(1967); HELLO DOWN THERE(1969); HOW DO I LOVE THEE?(1970); LIMBO(1972)

Gary Logan
HUMAN FACTOR, THE(1979, Brit.), m

Gwendolen Logan
MAN FROM BLANKLEY'S, THE(1930); ONCE A LADY(1931); ANGEL(1937); NORTHWEST PASSAGE(1940); JANE EYRE(1944)
Silents
EAST IS EAST(1916, Brit.), w

Gwendolin Logan
ALEXANDER HAMILTON(1931)

Gwendolyn Logan
UNDER TWO FLAGS(1936); DISRAELI(1929); CHRISTOPHER STRONG(1933); WE LIVE AGAIN(1934); SYLVIA SCARLETT(1936); FOREIGN CORRESPONDENT(1940); RINGS ON HER FINGERS(1942); IMPERFECT LADY, THE(1947)

Helen Logan
CHARLIE CHAN IN EGYPT(1935), w; HAPPINESS C.O.D.(1935), w; LADIES LOVE DANGER(1935), w; LADY IN SCARLET, THE(1935), w; BACK TO NATURE(1936), w; CHARLIE CHAN AT THE CIRCUS(1936), w; CHARLIE CHAN AT THE RACE TRACK(1936), w; CHARLIE CHAN'S SECRET(1936), w; HERE COMES TROUBLE(1936), w; HITCH HIKE TO HEAVEN(1936), w; BIG BUSINESS(1937), w; BIG TOWN GIRL(1937), w; BORN RECKLESS(1937), w; CHARLIE CHAN AT MONTE CARLO(1937), w; CHARLIE CHAN AT THE OLYMPICS(1937), w; CHARLIE CHAN ON BROADWAY(1937), w; LAUGHING AT TROUBLE(1937), w; OFF TO THE RACES(1937), w; DOWN ON THE FARM(1938), w; LOVE ON A BUDGET(1938), w; RASCALS(1938), w; ROAD DEMON(1938), w; SHARPSHOOTERS(1938), w; SPEED TO BURN(1938), w; TRIP TO PARIS, A(1938), w; CHARLIE CHAN IN THE CITY OF DARKNESS(1939), w; CHASING DANGER(1939), w; ESCAPE, THE(1939), w; PARDON OUR NERVE(1939), w; SUSANNAH OF THE MOUNTIES(1939), w; TOO BUSY TO WORK(1939), w; HIGH SCHOOL(1940), w; LUCKY CISCO KID(1940), w; MAN WHO WOULDN'T TALK, THE(1940), w; STAR DUST(1940), w; TIN PAN ALLEY(1940), w; GREAT AMERICAN BROADCAST, THE(1941), w; SUN VALLEY SERENADE(1941), w; FOOTLIGHT SERENADE(1942), w; ICELAND(1942), w; SONG OF THE ISLANDS(1942), w; HELLO, FRISCO, HELLO(1943), w; FOUR JILLS IN A JEEP(1944), w; PIN UP GIRL(1944), w; SOMETHING FOR THE BOYS(1944), w; DO YOU LOVE ME?(1946), w; IF I'M LUCKY(1946), w; THREE LITTLE GIRLS IN BLUE(1946), w; I'LL GET BY(1950), w

Horace Logan
CARNIVAL ROCK(1957)

Jacqueline Logan
RIVER WOMAN, THE(1928); BACHELOR GIRL, THE(1929); GENERAL CRACK(1929); STARK MAD(1929); MIDDLE WATCH, THE(1930, Brit.); SYMPHONY IN TWO FLATS(1930, Brit.); SHADOWS(1931, Brit.)
Silents
MOLLY O'(1921); PERFECT CRIME, A(1921); WHITE AND UNMARRIED(1921); BLIND BARGAIN, A(1922); BURNING SANDS(1922); EBB TIDE(1922); GAY AND DEVILISH(1922); TAILOR MADE MAN, A(1922); JAVA HEAD(1923); MR. BILLINGS SPENDS HIS DIME(1923); SALOMY JANE(1923); SIXTY CENTS AN HOUR(1923); CODE OF THE SEA(1924); FLAMING BARRIERS(1924); HOUSE OF YOUTH, THE(1924); MANHATTAN(1924); WAGES FOR WIVES(1925); OUTSIDER, THE(1926); TONY RUNS WILD(1926); KING OF KINGS, THE(1927); ONE HOUR OF LOVE(1927); LEOPARD LADY, THE(1928); MIDNIGHT MADNESS(1928); NOTHING TO WEAR(1928); STOCKS AND BLONDES(1928)
Misc. Silents
SAVED BY RADIO(1922); LIGHT THAT FAILED, THE(1923); DAWN OF A TOMORROW, THE(1924); DYNAMITE SMITH(1924); IF MARRIAGE FAILS(1925); MAN MUST LIVE, THE(1925); PEACOCK FEATHERS(1925); PLAYING WITH SOULS(1925); SKY RAIDER, THE(1925); THANK YOU(1925); WHEN THE DOOR OPENED(1925); FOOTLOOSE WIDOWS(1926); OUT OF THE STORM(1926); WHITE MICE(1926); BLOOD SHIP, THE(1927); FOR LADIES ONLY(1927); WISE WIFE, THE(1927); BROADWAY DADDIES(1928); CHARGE OF THE GAUCHOS, THE(1928); COP, THE(1928); LOOK OUT GIRL, THE(1928); POWER(1928); SHIPS OF THE NIGHT(1928); FAKER, THE(1929); RIVER WOMAN(1929)

James Logan
NOTORIOUS(1946); BLONDE SAVAGE(1947); EXILE, THE(1947); JOAN OF ARC(1948); JULIA MISBEHAVES(1948); KISS THE BLOOD OFF MY HANDS(1948); MR. PEABODY AND THE MERMAID(1948); NOOSE HANGS HIGH, THE(1948); SOUTHERN YANKEE, A(1948); ROGUES OF SHERWOOD FOREST(1950); THREE CAME HOME(1950); LORNA DOONE(1951); MAN WITH A CLOAK, THE(1951); SON OF DR. JEKYLL, THE(1951); PLYMOUTH ADVENTURE(1952); LOOSE IN LONDON(1953); ROSE MARIE(1954); KING'S THIEF, THE(1955); MOLE PEOPLE, THE(1956); ABDUCTORS, THE(1957); DINOSAURUS(1960); NOTORIOUS LANDLADY, THE(1962); MARY POPPINS(1964)

James E. Logan
FLASHING GUNS(1947)

Janice Logan
UNDERCOVER DOCTOR(1939); WHAT A LIFE(1939); DR. CYCLOPS(1940); OPENED BY MISTAKE(1940)

Jesse Logan
LOOKER(1981)

Jim Logan
REBEL ROUSERS(1970)

Jimmy Logan
FULLER BRUSH MAN(1948); FLOODTIDE(1949, Brit.); WILD AFFAIR, THE(1966, Brit.)

John Logan
MAN BEHIND THE GUN, THE(1952); OPERATION SECRET(1952); TALL MAN RIDING(1955); MORITURI(1965); BOY WHO CRIED WEREWOLF, THE(1973)

Joshua Logan
I MET MY LOVE AGAIN(1938), d; HIGHER AND HIGHER(1943), w; MAIN STREET TO BROADWAY(1953); MISTER ROBERTS(1955), w; PICNIC(1955), d; BUS STOP(1956), d; SAYONARA(1957), d; SOUTH PACIFIC(1958), d, w; TALL STORY(1960), p&d; FANNY(1961), p&d, w; ENSIGN PULVER(1964), p&d, w; CAMELOT(1967), d; PAINT YOUR WAGON(1969), d

Laurie V. Logan
ABSENCE OF MALICE(1981)

Lillian Logan
Silents
HOUSE OF TEMPERLEY, THE(1913, Brit.)

M. Logan
SOME LIKE IT HOT(1959), w

Marc Logan
BIG PUNCH, THE(1948)

Mark Logan
GRIM REAPER, THE(1981, Ital.)

Michael Logan
DICTATOR, THE(1935, Brit./Ger.), w; MARK OF CAIN, THE(1948, Brit.); QUESTION OF ADULTERY, A(1959, Brit.); SNAKE WOMAN, THE(1961, Brit.); THIS SPORTING LIFE(1963, Brit.); APPLE, THE(1980 U.S./Ger.)

Minnie C. Logan
NEW KIND OF LOVE, A(1963)

Pete Logan
HANG YOUR HAT ON THE WIND(1969)

Peter Logan
Misc. Talkies
ALTERNATIVE MISS WORLD, THE(1980)

Phoebe Logan
FIGHTING DEPUTY, THE(1937)

Phyllis Logan
ANOTHER TIME, ANOTHER PLACE(1983, Brit.)
1984
ANOTHER TIME, ANOTHER PLACE(1984, Brit.); EVERY PICTURE TELLS A STORY(1984, Brit.); 1984(1984, Brit.)

Richard Logan
HUMAN FACTOR, THE(1979, Brit.), m
Misc. Talkies
ALTERNATIVE MISS WORLD, THE(1980)

Robert Logan
CLAUDELLE INGLISH(1961); BEACH BALL(1965); BRIDGE AT REMAGEN, THE(1969); ACROSS THE GREAT DIVIDE(1976); FURTHER ADVENTURES OF THE WILDERNESS FAMILY-PART TWO(1978); SEA GYPSIES, THE(1978); MOUNTAIN FAMILY ROBINSON(1979); NIGHT IN HEAVEN, A(1983)
Misc. Talkies
KELLY(1981, Can.)

Robert F. Logan
ADVENTURES OF THE WILDERNESS FAMILY, THE(1975)

Ruby Logan
ONE DARK NIGHT(1939)

Samantha Logan
1984
COVERGIRL(1984, Can.)

Sidney Logan
Misc. Talkies
GANGSTER'S DEN(1945)
Stanley Logan
CONFESSION(1937), w; FIRST LADY(1937), d; LOVE, HONOR AND BEHAVE(1938), d; WOMEN ARE LIKE THAT(1938), d; WE ARE NOT ALONE(1939); ARISE, MY LOVE(1940); ESCAPE TO GLORY(1940); MY SON, MY SON!(1940); SOUTH OF SUEZ(1940); WOMEN IN WAR(1940); SINGAPORE WOMAN(1941); COUNTER-ESPIONAGE(1942); FALCON'S BROTHER, THE(1942), d; NIGHTMARE(1942); HIGHER AND HIGHER(1943); TWO TICKETS TO LONDON(1943); SHERLOCK HOLMES AND THE SPIDER WOMAN(1944); WILSON(1944); HOME SWEET HOMICIDE(1946); THREE STRANGERS(1946); CHALLENGE, THE(1948); SWORD IN THE DESERT(1949); THAT FORSYTE WOMAN(1949); DOUBLE CROSSBONES(1950); YOUNG DANIEL BOONE(1950); LAW AND THE LADY, THE(1951); PRIDE OF MARYLAND(1951); FIVE FINGERS(1952); PRISONER OF ZENDA, THE(1952); WITH A SONG IN MY HEART(1952)
Silents
AS HE WAS BORN(1919, Brit.)
Misc. Silents
WHAT WOULD A GENTLEMAN DO?(1918, Brit.)
Susan Logan
MEAL, THE(1975)
Sydney Logan
UNDERCURRENT(1946)
Thomas Logan
MASSACRE AT CENTRAL HIGH(1976)
Tom Logan
WHERE ANGELS GO...TROUBLE FOLLOWS(1968)
Vincent Logan
SUMMER HOLIDAY(1963, Brit.)
Virginia Logan
CARNY(1980)
Yvonne Logan
Misc. Silents
CLOUDED NAME, A(1923)
Logan Costume
KINFOLK(1970), cos
Rota Logapoulou
ELECTRA(1962, Gr.)
Bengt Logardt
LAUGHING IN THE SUNSHINE(1953, Brit./Swed.); NIGHT IS MY FUTURE(1962, Swed.)
Raymond Logeart
VICE DOLLS(1961, Fr.), p
Simone Logeart
NIGHTS OF SHAME(1961, Fr.)
John Loggia
VORTEX(1982), set d
Robert Loggia
SOMEBODY UP THERE LIKES ME(1956); GARMENT JUNGLE, THE(1957); COP HATER(1958); LOST MISSILE, THE(1958, U.S./Can.); CATTLE KING(1963); GREATEST STORY EVER TOLD, THE(1965); CHE!(1969); FIRST LOVE(1977); THREE SISTERS, THE(1977); REVENGE OF THE PINK PANTHER(1978); SPEEDTRAP(1978); NINTH CONFIGURATION, THE(1980); S.O.B.(1981); OFFICER AND A GENTLEMAN, AN(1982); TRAIL OF THE PINK PANTHER, THE(1982); CURSE OF THE PINK PANTHER(1983); PSYCHO II(1983); SCARFACE(1983)
Art Loggins
KISS ME DEADLY(1955)
Seymour Logie
YOUNG AND THE GUILTY, THE(1958, Brit.), ed; WOMAN EATER, THE(1959, Brit.), ed
Ye Loginov
FORTY-NINE DAYS(1964, USSR)
N. Loginova
WHEN THE TREES WERE TALL(1965, USSR), ed
T. Loginova
GARNET BRACELET, THE(1966, USSR); TSAR'S BRIDE, THE(1966, USSR)
Dimitri Logothetis
NEW YORK, NEW YORK(1977)
Charles Logue
DRAKE CASE, THE(1929), w; WHISPERING WINDS(1929), w; DECEIVER, THE(1931), w; HOMICIDE SQUAD(1931), w; FAST COMPANIONS(1932), w; MENACE, THE(1932), w; EMBARRASSING MOMENTS(1934), w; WAGON WHEELS(1934), w; HOME ON THE RANGE(1935), w; HOOSIER SCHOOLMASTER(1935), w; MAKE A MILLION(1935), w; SING SING NIGHTS(1935), w; RENFREW OF THE ROYAL MOUNTED(1937), w; CRIME TAKES A HOLIDAY(1938), w; MARINES ARE HERE, THE(1938), w; ON THE GREAT WHITE TRAIL(1938), w
Silents
LONELY ROAD, THE(1923), w; ARIZONA SWEEPSTAKES(1926), w; LOVE TOY, THE(1926), w; MICHIGAN KID, THE(1928), w
Misc. Silents
MAN AND WOMAN(1921), d
Charles A. Logue
SHAKEDOWN, THE(1929), w; STORM, THE(1930), w; TICKET TO CRIME(1934), w; CONFLICT(1937), w; WILDCATTER, THE(1937), w
Silents
OUTWITTED(1917), w; JUST FOR TONIGHT(1918), w; MY FOUR YEARS IN GERMANY(1918), w; AMAZING LOVERS(1921), w; WHAT WOMEN WILL DO(1921), w; GAY AND DEVILISH(1922), w; WOMAN WHO FOOLED HERSELF, THE(1922), d, w; BELOW THE LINE(1925), w; MAN ON THE BOX, THE(1925), w; HIS JAZZ BRIDE(1926), w; CHEATING CHEATERS(1927), w; HELD BY THE LAW(1927), w; HEART OF A FOLLIES GIRL, THE(1928), w
Misc. Silents
MAN AND WOMAN(1920), d; TENTS OF ALLAH, THE(1923), d
Christopher Logue
SAVAGE MESSIAH(1972, Brit.), w; MOONLIGHTING(1982, Brit.)
Elizabeth Logue
NEW FACES(1954); NUDE ODYSSEY(1962, Fr./Ital.); HAWAII(1966)

John Logue
SPIRIT OF THE WIND(1979), w, ph
M. Logvinov
PEACE TO HIM WHO ENTERS(1963, USSR)
Gerald Loham
JOHN WESLEY(1954, Brit.)
Gerard Lohan
LAUGHING ANNE(1954, Brit./U.S.); DECISION AGAINST TIME(1957, Brit.); ZOO BABY(1957, Brit.)
Lohde
M(1933, Ger.)
Sigurd Lohde
NEUTRAL PORT(1941, Brit.); QUESTION 7(1961, U.S./Ger.); FROZEN ALIVE(1966, Brit./Ger.)
A.J. Lohman
PAT GARRETT AND BILLY THE KID(1973), spec eff
Angie Lohman
ESCAPE FROM EAST BERLIN(1962), spec eff
Augie Lohman
HARD BOILED MAHONEY(1947), spec eff; LOST CONTINENT(1951), spec eff; JUNGLE GENTS(1954), spec eff; SPOOK CHASERS(1957), spec eff; HORSE SOLDIERS, THE(1959), spec eff; LONGEST DAY, THE(1962), spec eff; CAPTAIN SINDBAD(1963), spec eff; DOCTOR FAUSTUS(1967, Brit.), spec eff; KISS THE GIRLS AND MAKE THEM DIE(1967, U.S./Ital.), spec eff; REFLECTIONS IN A GOLDEN EYE(1967), spec eff; TAMING OF THE SHREW, THE(1967, U.S./Ital.), spec eff; CANDY(1968, Ital./Fr.), spec eff; KREMLIN LETTER, THE(1970), spec eff; BREAKOUT(1975), spec eff; THREE DAYS OF THE CONDOR(1975), spec eff; FROM NOON TO THREE(1976), spec eff; MURDER BY DEATH(1976), spec eff; SHOOTIST, THE(1976), spec eff; ELECTRIC HORSEMAN, THE(1979), spec eff
August Lohman
MAJOR DUNDEE(1965), spec eff; DESERTER, THE(1971 Ital./Yugo.), spec eff
Gladys Lohman
BACK STREET(1932), w
Glase Lohman
PRINCE OF PIRATES(1953); PURPLE MASK, THE(1955)
Gus Lohman
MOBY DICK(1956, Brit.), spec eff
Carolyn Lohmann
CALIFORNIA SPLIT(1974)
Dietrich Lohmann
AMERICAN SOLDIER, THE(1970 Ger.), ph; EFFI BRIEST(1974, Ger.), ph; JAIL BAIT(1977, Ger.), ph; WHY DOES HERR R. RUN AMOK?(1977, Ger.), ph; GERMANY IN AUTUMN(1978, Ger.), ph; OUR HITLER, A FILM FROM GERMANY(1980, Ger.), ph
Paul Lohmann
COFFY(1973), ph; CALIFORNIA SPLIT(1974), ph; NASHVILLE(1975), ph; BUFFALO BILL AND THE INDIANS, OR SITTING BULL'S HISTORY LESSON(1976), ph; SILENT MOVIE(1976), ph; HIGH ANXIETY(1977), ph; WHITE BUFFALO, THE(1977), ph; ENEMY OF THE PEOPLE, AN(1978), ph; METEOR(1979), ph; NORTH DALLAS FORTY(1979), ph; TIME AFTER TIME(1979, Brit.), ph; HIDE IN PLAIN SIGHT(1980), ph; CHARLIE CHAN AND THE CURSE OF THE DRAGON QUEEN(1981), ph; LOOKER(1981), ph; MOMMIE DEAREST(1981), ph; ENDANGERED SPECIES(1982), ph
1984
KIDCO(1984), ph
Fritz Lohner
STUDENT'S ROMANCE, THE(1936, Brit.), w
Helmut Lohner
MRS. WARREN'S PROFESSION(1960, Ger.); KING IN SHADOW(1961, Ger.); SPESSART INN, THE(1961, Ger.); HANNIBAL BROOKS(1969, Brit.)
Helmuth Lohner
HOUSE OF THE THREE GIRLS, THE(1961, Aust.)
Fritz Lohner-Beda
BALL AT SAVOY(1936, Brit.), w
Vaclav Lohnisky
SWEET LIGHT IN A DARK ROOM(1966, Czech.); TRANSPORT FROM PARADISE(1967, Czech.); ADELE HASN'T HAD HER SUPPER YET(1978, Czech.); DIVINE EMMA, THE(1983, Czech,)
Yurij Lohovy
TULIPS(1981, Can), ed
Marie Lohr
ARENT WE ALL?(1932, Brit.); LADY IN DANGER(1934, Brit.); ROAD HOUSE(1934, Brit.); COCK O' THE NORTH(1935, Brit.); FIGHTING STOCK(1935, Brit.); FOREIGN AFFAIRES(1935, Brit.); MY HEART IS CALLING(1935, Brit.); OH DADDY!(1935, Brit.); REGAL CAVALCADE(1935, Brit.); DREAMS COME TRUE(1936, Brit.); IT'S YOU I WANT(1936, Brit.); REASONABLE DOUBT(1936, Brit.); PYGMALION(1938, Brit.); SOUTH RIDING(1938, Brit.); GENTLEMAN'S GENTLEMAN, A(1939, Brit.); GEORGE AND MARGARET(1940, Brit.); MOZART(1940, Brit.); MAJOR BARBARA(1941, Brit.); KISS THE BRIDE GOODBYE(1944, Brit.); TWILIGHT HOUR(1944, Brit.); 48 HOURS(1944, Brit.); NOTORIOUS GENTLEMAN(1945, Brit.); GHOSTS OF BERKELEY SQUARE(1947, Brit.); MAGIC BOW, THE(1947, Brit.); ANNA KARENINA(1948, Brit.); COUNTER BLAST(1948, Brit.); DEVIL'S PLOT, THE(1948, Brit.); SILENT DUST(1949, Brit.); WINSLOW BOY, THE(1950); LITTLE BIG SHOT(1952, Brit.); ALWAYS A BRIDE(1954, Brit.); ESCAPADE(1955, Brit.); ABANDON SHIP(1957, Brit.); OUT OF THE CLOUDS(1957, Brit.); SMALL HOTEL(1957, Brit.); TOWN LIKE ALICE, A(1958, Brit.); MAN IN A COCKED HAT(1960, Bri.); GREAT CATHERINE(1968, Brit.)
Misc. Silents
VICTORY AND PEACE(1918, Brit.)
Kahren Lohren
GREAT MUPPET CAPER, THE(1981)
Barbara Lohrman
FRENCH LINE, THE(1954); SON OF SINBAD(1955)
Luisa Loiano
MAMMA ROMA(1962, Ital.)
Eduard Loibner
FOUR IN A JEEP(1951, Switz.); MAN WHO WALKED THROUGH THE WALL, THE(1964, Ger.)

Florence Loinod
GAME FOR SIX LOVERS, A(1962, Fr.); IMMORAL MOMENT, THE(1967, Fr.)
Jocelyne Loiseau
SUNDAYS AND CYBELE(1962, Fr.)
Olivier Loiseau
1984
LE BAL(1984, Fr./Ital./Algeria)
Julien Loisel
THIEF OF PARIS, THE(1967, Fr./Ital.)
Jacques Loiseleux
LOULOU(1980, Fr.), ph
1984
A NOS AMOURS(1984, Fr.), ph
Helene Loiselle
MY UNCLE ANTOINE(1971, Can.); ORDERS, THE(1977, Can.)
Mayo Loizeau
BAND OF ANGELS(1957)
Kathy Lojac
TIMES SQUARE(1980)
Catherine Lojacono
PUTNEY SWOPE(1969)
Adele Angela Lojodice
CASANOVA(1976, Ital.)
Christine Lok
MILLION EYES OF SU-MURU, THE(1967, Brit.)
Chang Lok-yee
1984
AH YING(1984, Hong Kong), ph
Ben Lokey
1984
BREAKIN'(1984)
Hicks Lokey
FANTASIA(1940), anim; DUMBO(1941), anim; MAN CALLED FLINTSTONE, THE(1966), anim
Georg Lokkeberg
AUTUMN SONATA(1978, Swed.)
Pal Lokkeberg
PASSIONATE DEMONS, THE(1962, Norway), w
Vibeke Lokkeberg
1984
KAMILLA(1984, Norway), a, d, w
Aleksandr Lokshin
HUNTING IN SIBERIA(1962, USSR), m
Aleksey Loktev
FAREWELL, DOVES(1962, USSR); MEET ME IN MOSCOW(1966, USSR)
Lola
PLAINSMAN AND THE LADY(1946)
Lyda Lola
Silents
HAS THE WORLD GONE MAD!(1923)
Lola and Luis
Silents
ARCADIANS, THE(1927, Brit.)
Myrtle Elizabeth Lolatte
LOOKIN' TO GET OUT(1982)
Alberto C. Lolli
MONTE CASSINO(1948, Ital.)
Alberto Carlo Lolli
WAR AND PEACE(1956, Ital./U.S.)
Alberto Lolli
WHEN IN ROME(1952)
Carlo Lolli
LEOPARD, THE(1963, Ital.)
Franco Lolli
LUCKY TO BE A WOMAN(1955, Ital.), art d; HOUSE OF INTRIGUE, THE(1959, Ital.), art d; CONSTANTINE AND THE CROSS(1962, Ital.), art d; HERCULES AND THE CAPTIVE WOMEN(1963, Fr./Ital.), art d; FRIENDS FOR LIFE(1964, Ital.), art d; HERCULES IN THE HAUNTED WORLD(1964, Ital.), art d; MISSION BLOODY MARY(1967, Fr./Ital./Span.), art d
Giovanni Lolli
RED DESERT(1965, Fr./Ital.)
George Lollier
ACE OF ACES(1933); HOLD'EM NAVY!(1937); PAID TO DANCE(1937); I LOVE YOU AGAIN(1940); THREE MEN FROM TEXAS(1940); TWO GIRLS ON BROADWAY(1940); I WANTED WINGS(1941); LOVE CRAZY(1941); TWO-FACED WOMAN(1941); PACIFIC RENDEZVOUS(1942); THREE HEARTS FOR JULIA(1943)
Gianna Lollini
LA TRAVIATA(1968, Ital.)
Gina Lollobrigida
CHILDREN OF CHANCE(1950, Ital.); TALE OF FIVE WOMEN, A(1951, Brit.); FANFAN THE TULIP(1952, Fr.); LES BELLES-DE-NUIT(1952, Fr.); WHITE LINE, THE(1952, Ital.); BEAT THE DEVIL(1953); BREAD, LOVE AND DREAMS(1953, Ital.); TIMES GONE BY(1953, Ital.); CROSSED SWORDS(1954); FLESH AND THE WOMAN(1954, Fr./Ital.); FOUR WAYS OUT(1954, Ital.); FRISKY(1955, Ital.); TRAPEZE(1956); WOMAN OF ROME(1956, Ital.); HUNCHBACK OF NOTRE DAME, THE(1957, Fr.); ANNA OF BROOKLYN(1958, Ital.); NEVER SO FEW(1959); FAST AND SEXY(1960, Fr./Ital.); UNFAITHFULS, THE(1960, Ital.); WHERE THE HOT WIND BLOWS(1960, Fr., Ital.); COME SEPTEMBER(1961); GO NAKED IN THE WORLD(1961); IMPERIAL VENUS(1963, Ital./Fr.); WOMAN OF STRAW(1964, Brit.); BAMBOLE!(1965, Ital.); STRANGE BEDFELLOWS(1965); HOTEL PARADISO(1966, U.S./Brit.); BUONA SERA, MRS. CAMPBELL(1968, Ital.); PRIVATE NAVY OF SGT. O'FARRELL, THE(1968); PLUCKED(1969, Fr./Ital.); YOUNG REBEL, THE(1969, Fr./Ital./Span.); THAT SPLENDID NOVEMBER(1971, Ital./Fr.); BAD MAN'S RIVER(1972, Span.); KING, QUEEN, KNAVE(1972, Ger./U.S.)
Guido Lollobrigida
OPERATION KID BROTHER(1967, Ital.); ROME WANTS ANOTHER CAESAR(1974, Ital.)

Herbert Lom
MEIN KAMPF–MY CRIMES(1940, Brit.); YOUNG MR. PITT, THE(1942, Brit.); DARK TOWER, THE(1943, Brit.); SECRET MISSION(1944, Brit.); APPOINTMENT WITH CRIME(1945, Brit.); HOTEL RESERVE(1946, Brit.); NIGHT BOAT TO DUBLIN(1946, Brit.); SEVENTH VEIL, THE(1946, Brit.); DUAL ALIBI(1947, Brit.); GIRL IN THE PAINTING, THE(1948, Brit.); SNOWBOUND(1949, Brit.); BLACK ROSE, THE(1950); CAGE OF GOLD(1950, Brit.); GOLDEN SALAMANDER(1950, Brit.); GOOD TIME GIRL(1950, Brit.); NIGHT AND THE CITY(1950, Brit.); GREAT MANHUNT, THE(1951, Brit.); HELL IS SOLD OUT(1951, Brit.); LUCKY MASCOT, THE(1951, Brit.); SCHOOL FOR BRIDES(1952, Brit.); WHISPERING SMITH VERSUS SCOTLAND YARD(1952, Brit.); MR. DENNING DRIVES NORTH(1953, Brit.); PROJECT M7(1953, Brit.); RINGER, THE(1953, Brit.); SHOOT FIRST(1953, Brit.); BEAUTIFUL STRANGER(1954, Brit.); LOVE LOTTERY, THE(1954, Brit.); LADYKILLERS, THE(1954, Brit.); STAR OF INDIA(1956, Brit.); WAR AND PEACE(1956, Ital./U.S.); ACTION OF THE TIGER(1957); FIRE DOWN BELOW(1957, U.S./Brit.); CHASE A CROOKED SHADOW(1958, Brit.); HELL DRIVERS(1958, Brit.); I ACCUSE(1958, Brit.); INTENT TO KILL(1958, Brit.); ROOTS OF HEAVEN, THE(1958); BIG FISHERMAN, THE(1959); ROOM 43(1959, Brit.); THIRD MAN ON THE MOUNTAIN(1959); FLAME OVER INDIA(1960, Brit.); I AIM AT THE STARS(1960); SPARTACUS(1960); EL CID(1961, U.S./Ital.); FRIGHTENED CITY, THE(1961, Brit.); MYSTERIOUS ISLAND(1961, U.S./Brit.); I LIKE MONEY(1962, Brit.); PHANTOM OF THE OPERA, THE(1962, Brit.); TIARA TAHITI(1962, Brit.); NO TREE IN THE STREET(1964, Brit.); SHOT IN THE DARK, A(1964); RETURN FROM THE ASHES(1965, U.S./Brit.); TREASURE OF SILVER LAKE(1965, Fr./Ger./Yugo.); BANG, BANG, YOU'RE DEAD(1966); GAMBIT(1966); KARATE KILLERS, THE(1967); ASSIGNMENT TO KILL(1968); EVE(1968, Brit./Span.); VILLA RIDES(1968); JOURNEY TO THE FAR SIDE OF THE SUN(1969, Brit.); UNCLE TOM'S CABIN(1969, Fr./Ital./Ger./Yugo.); DORIAN GRAY(1970, Ital./Brit./Ger./Liechtenstein); MARK OF THE DEVIL(1970, Ger./Brit.); COUNT DRACULA(1971, Sp., Ital., Ger., Brit.); MURDERS IN THE RUE MORGUE(1971); ASYLUM(1972, Brit.); AND NOW THE SCREAMING STARTS(1973, Brit.); DARK PLACES(1974, Brit.); RETURN OF THE PINK PANTHER, THE(1975, Brit.); TEN LITTLE INDIANS(1975, Ital./Fr./Span./Ger.); PINK PANTHER STRIKES AGAIN, THE(1976, Brit.); CHARLESTON(1978, Ital.); REVENGE OF THE PINK PANTHER(1978); HOPSCOTCH(1980); LADY VANISHES, THE(1980, Brit.); MAN WITH BOGART'S FACE, THE(1980); TRAIL OF THE PINK PANTHER, THE(1982); CURSE OF THE PINK PANTHER(1983); DEAD ZONE, THE(1983)
1984
MEMED MY HAWK(1984, Brit.)
Misc. Talkies
99 WOMEN(1969, Brit./Span./Ger./Ital.)
Herbert Lom, Jr.
PARIS EXPRESS, THE(1953, Brit.)
Grace Loman
CHICAGO CALLING(1951)
Jack Loman
STORY OF SEABISCUIT, THE(1949)
Paul Loman
HELL'S ANGELS '69(1969), ph
Bonnie Lomann
CATALINA CAPER, THE(1967)
Brenda Lomas
JEANNE EAGELS(1957)
Herbert Lomas
HOBSON'S CHOICE(1931, Brit.); MANY WATERS(1931, Brit.); FRAIL WOMEN(1932, Brit.); MISSING REMBRANDT, THE(1932, Brit.); SIGN OF FOUR, THE(1932, Brit.); WHEN LONDON SLEEPS(1932, Brit.); DAUGHTERS OF TODAY(1933, Brit.); MAN FROM TORONTO, THE(1933, Brit.); BLACK MASK(1935, Brit.); FIGHTING STOCK(1935, Brit.); JAVA HEAD(1935, Brit.); LORNA DOONE(1935, Brit.); PHANTOM LIGHT, THE(1935, Brit.); FAME(1936, Brit.); GHOST GOES WEST, THE(1936); REMBRANDT(1936, Brit.); FIRE OVER ENGLAND(1937, Brit.); KNIGHT WITHOUT ARMOR(1937, Brit.); SOUTH RIDING(1938, Brit.); ASK A POLICEMAN(1939, Brit.); INQUEST(1939, Brit.); JAMAICA INN(1939, Brit.); LION HAS WINGS, THE(1940, Brit.); OVER THE MOON(1940, Brit.); COURAGEOUS MR. PENN, THE(1941, Brit.); GHOST TRAIN, THE(1941, Brit.); SOUTH AMERICAN GEORGE(1941, Brit.); WELCOME, MR. WASHINGTON(1944, Brit.); THEY MET IN THE DARK(1945, Brit.); I KNOW WHERE I'M GOING(1947, Brit.); MASTER OF BANKDAM(1947, Brit.); BONNIE PRINCE CHARLIE(1948, Brit.); SMUGGLERS, THE(1948, Brit.); OUTSIDER, THE(1949, Brit.); MAGIC BOX, THE(1952, Brit.); PROJECT M7(1953, Brit.)
Jack Lomas
DESPERATE JOURNEY(1942); DAUGHTER OF ROSIE O'GRADY, THE(1950); OPERATION SECRET(1952); APRIL IN PARIS(1953); GLASS WEB, THE(1953); SEVEN ANGRY MEN(1955); REPRISAL(1956); THAT CERTAIN FEELING(1956); THERE'S ALWAYS TOMORROW(1956); NIGHT RUNNER, THE(1957); SHADOW ON THE WINDOW, THE(1957); CATTLE EMPIRE(1958); TOO MUCH, TOO SOON(1958); LAST TRAIN FROM GUN HILL(1959)
Jack M. Lomas
COPPER SKY(1957)
James Lomas
RANDOLPH FAMILY, THE(1945, Brit.); LOVE IN WAITING(1948, Brit.); GALLOPING MAJOR, THE(1951, Brit.); KID FOR TWO FARTHINGS, A(1956, Brit.); THUNDER OVER TANGIER(1957, Brit.)
Pauline Lomas
ENTITY, THE(1982); TESTAMENT(1983)
Raoul Lomas
STACY'S KNIGHTS(1983), ph; YOUNG GIANTS(1983), ph
1984
CHILDREN OF THE CORN(1984), ph
Hosei Lomatsu
KURAGEJIMA–LEGENDS FROM A SOUTHERN ISLAND(1970, Jap.)
Bliss Lomax
SECRETS OF THE WASTELANDS(1941), w; LEATHER BURNERS, THE(1943), w
Felix Lomax
HENTAI(1966, Jap.), p
Harry Lomax
OTHELLO(1965, Brit.); THREE SISTERS(1974, Brit.)
Jackie Lomax
SGT. PEPPER'S LONELY HEARTS CLUB BAND(1978)

Joseph Warren Lomax, U.S.N.
YOU'RE IN THE NAVY NOW(1951), tech adv
Louis Lomax
WILD IN THE STREETS(1968)
Rosemary Lomax
WEAKER SEX, THE(1949, Brit.)
Michael Lomazow
PSYCHO II(1983)
Cyrena Lomba
HAIR(1979)
Carole Lombard
SHOW FOLKS(1928); BIG NEWS(1929); HIGH VOLTAGE(1929); RACKETEER, THE(1929); ARIZONA KID, THE(1930); FAST AND LOOSE(1930); SAFETY IN NUMBERS(1930); I TAKE THIS WOMAN(1931); IT PAYS TO ADVERTISE(1931); LADIES' MAN(1931); MAN OF THE WORLD(1931); UP POPS THE DEVIL(1931); NO ONE MAN(1932); SINNERS IN THE SUN(1932); VIRTUE(1932); BRIEF MOMENT(1933); EAGLE AND THE HAWK, THE(1933); FROM HELL TO HEAVEN(1933); NO MAN OF HER OWN(1933); NO MORE ORCHIDS(1933); SUPERNATURAL(1933); WHITE WOMAN(1933); BOLERO(1934); GAY BRIDE, THE(1934); LADY BY CHOICE(1934); NOW AND FOREVER(1934); TWENTIETH CENTURY(1934); WE'RE NOT DRESSING(1934); HANDS ACROSS THE TABLE(1935); RUMBA(1935); LOVE BEFORE BREAKFAST(1936); MY MAN GODFREY(1936); PRINCESS COMES ACROSS, THE(1936); NOTHING SACRED(1937); SWING HIGH, SWING LOW(1937); TRUE CONFESSION(1937); FOOLS FOR SCANDAL(1938); IN NAME ONLY(1939); MADE FOR EACH OTHER(1939); THEY KNEW WHAT THEY WANTED(1940); VIGIL IN THE NIGHT(1940); MR. AND MRS. SMITH(1941); TO BE OR NOT TO BE(1942)
Silents
NED MCCOBB'S DAUGHTER(1929)
Misc. Silents
HEARTS AND SPURS(1925); MARRIAGE IN TRANSIT(1925)
Claus Benton Lombard
DEVIL MAKES THREE, THE(1952)
Linda Lombard
MOONRISE(1948)
Michael Lombard
WHO?(1975, Brit./Ger.); NETWORK(1976); FATSO(1980); SO FINE(1981)
1984
GARBO TALKS(1984)
Peter Lombard
TEMPEST(1982)
Pushface Lombard
LOVE BEFORE BREAKFAST(1936)
Robert Lombard
LE PLAISIR(1954, Fr.); HUNCHBACK OF NOTRE DAME, THE(1957, Fr.); SPUTNIK(1960, Fr.); ROAD TO SHAME, THE(1962, Fr.); HEAT OF MIDNIGHT(1966, Fr.); EROTIQUE(1969, Fr.); HIT(1973)
Ron Lombard
CHINA SYNDROME, THE(1979); FOXES(1980)
Tony Lombard
LILITH(1964)
Yvonne Lombard
LESSON IN LOVE, A(1960, Swed.); SWEDISH WEDDING NIGHT(1965, Swed.)
Juan Lombardero
WIDOWS' NEST(1977, U.S./Span.)
Angel Lombardi
TEXICAN, THE(1966, U.S./Span.)
Carlo Lombardi
BALL AT THE CASTLE(1939, Ital.); HUNS, THE(1962, Fr./Ital.), p
Dillo Lombardi
Misc. Silents
LOST IN THE DARK(1914, Ital.); TERESA RAQUIN(1915, Ital.)
Ettore Lombardi
SOUND OF TRUMPETS, THE(1963, Ital.), art d; FIANCES, THE(1964, Ital.), art d
Frank Lombardi
VOICES(1979)
G. Lombardi
VOICE IN YOUR HEART, A(1952, Ital.), ph
Joe Lombardi
WAR PARTY(1965), spec eff; GODFATHER, THE(1972), spec eff; HICKEY AND BOGGS(1972), spec eff; RAGE(1972), spec eff; ELECTRA GLIDE IN BLUE(1973), spec eff; HIT(1973), spec eff; GODFATHER, THE, PART II(1974), spec eff; THREE THE HARD WAY(1974), spec eff; SEVEN(1979), spec eff; SMALL CIRCLE OF FRIENDS, A(1980), spec eff; ENTITY, THE(1982), spec eff
Leigh Lombardi
1984
WILD LIFE, THE(1984)
Paul Lombardi
RAGE(1972), spec eff
Rodolfo Lombardi
WHITE DEVIL, THE(1948, Ital.), ph; RETURN OF THE BLACK EAGLE(1949, Ital.), ph; VOICE IN YOUR HEART, A(1952, Ital.), w; MIGHTY CRUSADERS, THE(1961, Ital.), ph
Steve Lombardi
DOGS OF WAR, THE(1980, Brit.), spec eff
Vince Lombardi
ANGELS WITH DIRTY FACES(1938)
Vince Lombardi
PAPER LION(1968)
Elizabeth Lombardo
LAST RITES(1980), ed
Francis Lombardo
CONVOY(1978), art d
Francisco Lombardo
SPY IN THE GREEN HAT, THE(1966), set d; SILENT RUNNING(1972), set d
Frank Lombardo
PURPLE GANG, THE(1960), set d; CRAZY WORLD OF JULIUS VROODER, THE(1974), set d; RIVER NIGER, THE(1976), set d
1984
REVENGE OF THE NERDS(1984), set d

Goffredo Lombardo
NAKED MAJA, THE(1959, Ital./U.S.), p; ANGEL WORE RED, THE(1960), p; SODOM AND GOMORRAH(1962, U.S./Fr./Ital.), p; FAMILY DIARY(1963 Ital.), p; FOUR DAYS OF NAPLES, THE(1963, US/Ital.), p; LEOPARD, THE(1963, Ital.), p; FIANCES, THE(1964, Ital.), p; GOLDEN ARROW, THE(1964, Ital.), p; TIKO AND THE SHARK(1966, U.S./Ital./Fr.), p
Guy Lombardo
MANY HAPPY RETURNS(1934); PHYNX, THE(1970)
James Lombardo
VICIOUS YEARS, THE(1950)
Lance Lombardo
1984
REVENGE OF THE NERDS(1984)
Leon Lombardo
BLUE DAHLIA, THE(1946)
Lou Lombardo
UP IN SMOKE(1978), p, ed; BALLAD OF CABLE HOGUE, THE(1970), ed; LONG GOODBYE, THE(1973), ed; THIEVES LIKE US(1974), ed; BLACK BIRD, THE(1975), p, ed; RUSSIAN ROULETTE(1975), d; LATE SHOW, THE(1977), ed
Louis Lombardo
NAME OF THE GAME IS KILL, THE(1968), ed; WILD BUNCH, THE(1969), ed; BREWSTER McCLOUD(1970), ed; MC CABE AND MRS. MILLER(1971), ed; ACE ELI AND RODGER OF THE SKIES(1973), ed; CALIFORNIA SPLIT(1974), ed
Miroslawa Lombardo
SARAGOSSA MANUSCRIPT, THE(1972, Pol.)
Sal Lombardo
TWO TICKETS TO PARIS(1962)
Tony Lombardo
WEDDING, A(1978), ed; PERFECT COUPLE, A(1979), ed; POPEYE(1980), ed
1984
BLAME IT ON THE NIGHT(1984), ed
Lombos
WAJAN(1938, South Bali)
Sam Lomburg
WELCOME TO THE CLUB(1971), p
Saverio Lomedico
SEPTEMBER AFFAIR(1950); PATCH OF BLUE, A(1965)
Luis Lomeli
EXTERMINATING ANGEL, THE(1967, Mex.)
Celine Lomez
FAR SHORE, THE(1976, Can.); PLAGUE(1978, Can.); SILENT PARTNER, THE(1979, Can.)
Misc. Talkies
M3: THE GEMINI STRAIN(1980)
Dan Lomino
CLOSE ENCOUNTERS OF THE THIRD KIND(1977), art d; FAST TIMES AT RIDGEMONT HIGH(1982), art d
Daniel Lomino
CHU CHU AND THE PHILLY FLASH(1981), art d
1984
STARMAN(1984), prod d
Sol Lomita
ZELIG(1983)
John Lomma
BADLANDS OF MONTANA(1957); SABU AND THE MAGIC RING(1957); HARD RIDE, THE(1971)
Chris Lomme
GIRL WITH THE RED HAIR, THE(1983, Neth.)
Ulli Lommel
FANNY HILL: MEMOIRS OF A WOMAN OF PLEASURE zero(1965); AMERICAN SOLDIER, THE(1970 Ger.); EFFI BRIEST(1974, Ger.); CHINESE ROULETTE(1977, Ger.); COCAINE COWBOYS(1979), d, w; BOOGEY MAN, THE(1980), p,d&w; BOOGEYMAN II(1983), a, p, d; BRAINWAVES(1983), p&d, w; DEVONSVILLE TERROR, THE(1983), p&d, w, ph; TASTE OF SIN, A(1983), a, p&d, w, ph
Merry Lommis
LITTLE SEX, A(1982)
Jacek Lomnicki
MAN OF MARBLE(1979, Pol.)
Tadeusz Lomnicki
EIGHTH DAY OF THE WEEK, THE(1959, Pol./Ger.); BARRIER(1966, Pol.); EROICA(1966, Pol.); MAN OF MARBLE(1979, Pol.); CONTRACT, THE(1982, Pol.)
Chief Lomoiro
VISIT TO A CHIEF'S SON(1974)
Britt Lomond
TONKA(1958); SIGN OF ZORRO, THE(1960)
Ada Lonati
BED AND BOARD(1971, Fr.)
Peggy Lonaty
MURDER AT 45 R.P.M.(1965, Fr.)
France Lonbard
DANIELLA BY NIGHT(1962, Fr/Ger.)
Beba Loncar
NINTH CIRCLE, THE(1961, Yugo.); LONG SHIPS, THE(1964, Brit./Yugo.); CASANOVA '70(1965, Ital.); BOY CRIED MURDER, THE(1966, Ger./Brit./Yugo.); SUCKER, THE(1966, Fr./Ital.); BIRDS, THE BEES AND THE ITALIANS, THE(1967); LISTEN, LET'S MAKE LOVE(1969, Fr./Ital.); SOME GIRLS DO(1969, Brit.); PUSSYCAT, PUSSYCAT, I LOVE YOU(1970); SUNDAY LOVERS(1980, Ital./Fr.)
Misc. Talkies
FULLER REPORT, THE(1966)
Janet Loncar
Misc. Talkies
THREE WAY LOVE(1977)
Linda Loncar
GENGHIS KHAN(U.S./Brit./Ger./Yugo)
Richard Loncraine
SUNDAY BLOODY SUNDAY(1971, Brit.); FLAME(1975, Brit.), d; HAUNTING OF JULIA, THE(1981, Brit./Can.), d; BRIMSTONE AND TREACLE(1982, Brit.), d; MISSIONARY, THE(1982), d

London
MY DOG, BUDDY(1960)
London the Dog
LITTLEST HOBO, THE(1958)
Andrew London
PSYCHO II(1983), ed
1984
CLOAK AND DAGGER(1984), ed
Arthur London
CONFESSION, THE(1970, Fr.), w
Babe London
JACKASS MAIL(1942); THIS TIME FOR KEEPS(1942); CRYSTAL BALL, THE(1943); HERE COME THE WAVES(1944); ROAD TO RIO(1947); HAZARD(1948); HOLLOW TRIUMPH(1948); JOAN OF ARC(1948); PALEFACE, THE(1948); SEX KITTENS GO TO COLLEGE(1960)
Silents
IS THAT NICE?(1926); AIN'T LOVE FUNNY?(1927); ALL ABOARD(1927); FORTUNE HUNTER, THE(1927); PRINCESS FROM HOBOKEN, THE(1927); TILLIE'S PUNCTURED ROMANCE(1928)
Barbara London
PAD, THE(AND HOW TO USE IT)* (1966, Brit.); MOVING FINGER, THE(1963); PSYCH-OUT(1968); CHASTITY(1969) CALIFORNIA SPLIT(1974)
Barbara M. London
1984
WILD LIFE, THE(1984)
Charmian London
JACK LONDON(1943), w
Chet London
GROUP, THE(1966)
Damian London
GUIDE FOR THE MARRIED MAN, A(1967); STAR!(1968); I LOVE MY WIFE(1970)
Dirk London
LONELY MAN, THE(1957); AMBUSH AT CIMARRON PASS(1958); PURPLE GANG, THE(1960)
Franco London
GAMBLER, THE(1958, Fr.), p
Francois London
KAMOURASKA(1973, Can./Fr.), ed
Francoise London
PICNIC ON THE GRASS(1960, Fr.), ed
Frank London
QUICK, BEFORE IT MELTS(1964); MORITURI(1965)
George London
MAYTIME(1937)
Jack London
SEA WOLF, THE(1930), w; CALL OF THE WILD(1935), w; WHITE FANG(1936), w; CONFLICT(1937), w; OLD BONES OF THE RIVER(1938, Brit.); MUTINY OF THE ELSINORE, THE(1939, Brit.), w; ROMANCE OF THE REDWOODS(1939), w; TORTURE SHIP(1939), w; WOLF CALL(1939), w; QUEEN OF THE YUKON(1940), w; SEA WOLF, THE(1941), w; SIGN OF THE WOLF(1941), w; ADVENTURES OF MARTIN EDEN, THE(1942), w; NORTH TO THE KLONDIKE(1942), w; ALASKA(1944), w; FIGHTER, THE(1952), w; WOLF LARSEN(1958), w; ASSASSINATION BUREAU, THE(1969, Brit.), w; PUNISHMENT PARK(1971); CALL OF THE WILD(1972, Ger./Span./Ital./Fr.), w
Silents
SEA-WOLF, THE(1913), w; JOHN BARLEYCORN(1914), w; ODYSSEY OF THE NORTH, AN(1914), w; IT'S NO LAUGHING MATTER(1915), w; SON OF THE WOLF, THE(1922), w; ABYSMAL BRUTE, THE(1923), w; CALL OF THE WILD, THE(1923), w; ADVENTURE(1925), w; STORMY WATERS(1928), w; SMOKE BELLEW(1929), w
James London
JESSE AND LESTER, TWO BROTHERS IN A PLACE CALLED TRINITY(1972, Ital.), d
Misc. Talkies
TRINITY(1975), d
Jean London
SINGLE ROOM FURNISHED(1968); DIRTY DINGUS MAGEE(1970)
Jean "Babe" London
DANCING IN THE DARK(1949); MOTHER DIDN'T TELL ME(1950)
Jim London
Misc. Silents
COWBOY MUSKETEER, THE(1925)
John London
NEW YEAR'S EVIL(1980)
Julie London
NABONGA(1944); ON STAGE EVERYBODY(1945); NIGHT IN PARADISE, A(1946); RED HOUSE, THE(1947); TAP ROOTS(1948); TASK FORCE(1949); RETURN OF THE FRONTIERSMAN(1950); FAT MAN, THE(1951); FIGHTING CHANCE, THE(1955); CRIME AGAINST JOE(1956); GIRL CAN'T HELP IT, THE(1956); DRANGO(1957); GREAT MAN, THE(1957); MAN OF THE WEST(1958); SADDLE THE WIND(1958); VOICE IN THE MIRROR(1958); NIGHT OF THE QUARTER MOON(1959); QUESTION OF ADULTERY, A(1959, Brit.); WONDERFUL COUNTRY, THE(1959); THIRD VOICE, THE(1960); GEORGE RAFT STORY, THE(1961); HELICOPTER SPIES, THE(1968)
Kitty London
PRINCESS OF THE NILE(1954)
Laurene London
AIRPLANE II: THE SEQUEL(1982)
Len London
1984
CAREFUL, HE MIGHT HEAR YOU(1984, Aus.)
Lisa London
H.O.T.S.(1979); SUDDEN IMPACT(1983)
Lise London
CONFESSION, THE(1970, Fr.), w
Louis London
WOMANHOOD(1934, Brit.), p
Lynette London
SONG OF THE TRAIL(1936)

Maggie London
HIDE AND SEEK(1964, Brit.); MAROC 7(1967, Brit.)
Marc London
DON'T MAKE WAVES(1967)
Mark London
PRIVILEGE(1967, Brit.); FIRST LOVE(1970, Ger./Switz.), m
1984
BLOODBATH AT THE HOUSE OF DEATH(1984, Brit.), m
Melody London
1984
STRANGER THAN PARADISE(1984, U.S./Ger.), ed
Pauline London
TELL NO TALES(1939), w
Roy London
HARDCORE(1979)
Samuel London
STRIP, THE(1951)
Sarah London
PARTY PARTY(1983, Brit.); RUNNERS(1983, Brit.)
Steve London
ZERO HOUR!(1957); I MARRIED A MONSTER FROM OUTER SPACE(1958)
Susan London
Misc. Talkies
CHORUS CALL(1979)
Tom London
BORROWED WIVES(1930); FIREBRAND JORDAN(1930); STORM, THE(1930); THIRD ALARM, THE(1930); TROOPERS THREE(1930); WOMAN RACKET, THE(1930); AIR POLICE(1931); PLATINUM BLONDE(1931); RANGE LAW(1931); SECRET SIX, THE(1931); TWO GUN MAN, THE(1931); UNDER TEXAS SKIES(1931); WESTWARD BOUND(1931); BEYOND THE ROCKIES(1932); BOILING POINT, THE(1932); GOLD(1932); HIDDEN VALLEY(1932); HONOR OF THE MOUNTED(1932); HUMAN TARGETS(1932); NIGHT RIDER, THE(1932); THIRTEENTH GUEST, THE(1932); TRAILING THE KILLER(1932); TRIAL OF VIVIENNE WARE, THE(1932); WITHOUT HONORS(1932); FUGITIVE, THE(1933); I'M NO ANGEL(1933); IRON MASTER, THE(1933); ONE YEAR LATER(1933); OUTLAW JUSTICE(1933); SUNSET PASS(1933); CAT'S PAW, THE(1934); FEROCIOUS PAL(1934); FIGHTING HERO(1934); HOLLYWOOD PARTY(1934); JEALOUSY(1934); MEN OF THE NIGHT(1934); BARBARY COAST(1935); GALLANT DEFENDER(1935); GOIN' TO TOWN(1935); HONG KONG NIGHTS(1935); JUSTICE OF THE RANGE(1935); LAST OF THE CLINTONS, THE(1935); LAW BEYOND THE RANGE(1935); RED SALUTE(1935); SAGEBRUSH TROUBADOR(1935); TIMBER TERRORS(1935); TUMBLING TUMBLEWEEDS(1935); WHOLE TOWN'S TALKING, THE(1935); BORDER PATROLMAN, THE(1936); GUN PLAY(1936); GUNS AND GUITARS(1936); HEROES OF THE RANGE(1936); LAWLESS NINETIES, THE(1936); O'MALLEY OF THE MOUNTED(1936); PRESCOTT KID, THE(1936); RAMONA(1936); TOLL OF THE DESERT(1936); ANGEL'S HOLIDAY(1937); BAR Z BAD MEN(1937); LAW OF THE RANGER(1937); OLD WYOMING TRAIL, THE(1937); RECKLESS RANGER(1937); RIO GRANDE RANGER(1937); ROARING TIMBER(1937); SILVER TRAIL, THE(1937); SPRINGTIME IN THE ROCKIES(1937); THIS IS MY AFFAIR(1937); WESTERN GOLD(1937); IN EARLY ARIZONA(1938); JUVENILE COURT(1938); OUTLAWS OF SONORA(1938); PAINTED TRAIL, THE(1938); PHANTOM RANGER(1938); PIONEER TRAIL(1938); PRAIRIE MOON(1938); RENEGADE RANGER(1938); RHYTHM OF THE SADDLE(1938); RIDERS OF THE BLACK HILLS(1938); SANTA FE STAMPEDE(1938); SIX SHOOTIN' SHERIFF(1938); SKULL AND CROWN(1938); SUNSET TRAIL(1938); FLAMING LEAD(1939); JESSE JAMES(1939); LET US LIVE(1939); LURE OF THE WASTELAND(1939); MADE FOR EACH OTHER(1939); MAN FROM TEXAS, THE(1939); MEXICALI ROSE(1939); MOUNTAIN RHYTHM(1939); NIGHT RIDERS, THE(1939); NORTH OF THE YUKON(1939); ROLL, WAGONS, ROLL(1939); ROLLIN' WESTWARD(1939); SONG OF THE BUCKAROO(1939); SOUTHWARD HO!(1939); TIMBER STAMPEDE(1939); DARK COMMAND, THE(1940); FIVE LITTLE PEPPERS AT HOME(1940); GAUCHO SERENADE(1940); GHOST VALLEY RAIDERS(1940); HI-YO SILVER(1940); KID FROM SANTA FE, THE(1940); LILLIAN RUSSELL(1940); LONE STAR RAIDERS(1940); MELODY RANCH(1940); NORTHWEST PASSAGE(1940); PHANTOM RANCHER(1940); RIDERS FROM NOWHERE(1940); SHOOTING HIGH(1940); STAGE TO CHINO(1940); TRAILING DOUBLE TROUBLE(1940); WESTBOUND STAGE(1940); WHEN THE DALTONS RODE(1940); ACROSS THE SIERRAS(1941); DUDE COWBOY(1941); DYNAMITE CANYON(1941); FUGITIVE VALLEY(1941); LAND OF THE OPEN RANGE(1941); LAST OF THE DUANES(1941); LONE WOLF TAKES A CHANCE, THE(1941); PALS OF THE PECOS(1941); RIDIN' ON A RAINBOW(1941); RIDING THE SUNSET TRAIL(1941); ROBBERS OF THE RANGE(1941); ROMANCE OF THE RIO GRANDE(1941); SAN FRANCISCO DOCKS(1941); SON OF DAVY CROCKETT, THE(1941); STICK TO YOUR GUNS(1941); TWILIGHT ON THE TRAIL(1941); UNDERGROUND RUSTLERS(1941); WANDERERS OF THE WEST(1941); WILD GEESE CALLING(1941); ARIZONA TERRORS(1942); BANDIT RANGER(1942); COWBOY SERENADE(1942); DOWN TEXAS WAY(1942); GHOST TOWN LAW(1942); LONE STAR RANGER(1942); RIDERS OF THE WEST(1942); SHADOWS ON THE SAGE(1942); SONS OF THE PIONEERS(1942); STARDUST ON THE SAGE(1942); VALLEY OF THE SUN(1942); WEST OF TOMBSTONE(1942); BAD MEN OF THUNDER GAP(1943); CANYON CITY(1943); CARSON CITY CYCLONE(1943); FALSE COLORS(1943); FIGHTING FRONTIER(1943); HAIL TO THE RANGERS(1943); IDAHO(1943); IN OLD OKLAHOMA(1943); MAN FROM THE RIO GRANDE, THE(1943); OVERLAND MAIL ROBBERY(1943); OX-BOW INCIDENT, THE(1943); RED RIVER ROBIN HOOD(1943); SANTA FE SCOUTS(1943); SILVER SPURS(1943); SONG OF TEXAS(1943); STRANGER FROM PECOS, THE(1943); TENTING TONIGHT ON THE OLD CAMP GROUND(1943); WAGON TRACKS WEST(1943); WEST OF TEXAS(1943); WILD HORSE STAMPEDE(1943); WOMAN OF THE TOWN, THE(1943); BENEATH WESTERN SKIES(1944); CHEYENNE WILDCAT(1944); CODE OF THE PRAIRIE(1944); FACES IN THE FOG(1944); FIREBRANDS OF ARIZONA(1944); HIDDEN VALLEY OUTLAWS(1944); LADY AND THE MONSTER, THE(1944); MAN FROM FRISCO(1944); MARSHAL OF RENO(1944); MOJAVE FIREBRAND(1944); SAN ANTONIO KID, THE(1944); SHERIFF OF SUNDOWN(1944); SILVER CITY KID(1944); STAGECOACH TO MONTEREY(1944); THREE LITTLE SISTERS(1944); TUCSON RAIDERS(1944); VIGILANTES OF DODGE CITY(1944); YELLOW ROSE OF TEXAS, THE(1944); BEHIND CITY LIGHTS(1945); CHEROKEE FLASH, THE(1945); COLORADO PIONEERS(1945); CORPUS CHRISTI BANDITS(1945); DON'T FENCE ME IN(1945); EARL CARROLL'S VANITIES(1945); GREAT STAGECOACH ROBBERY(1945); GRISSLY'S MILLIONS(1945); MARSHAL OF LAREDO(1945); OREGON TRAIL(1945); PHANTOM OF THE PLAINS(1945); ROUGH RIDERS OF CHEYENNE(1945); SHERIFF OF CIMARRON(1945); SUNSET IN EL DORADO(1945);

THOROUGHBREDS(1945); THREE'S A CROWD(1945); TOPEKA TERROR, THE(1945); TRAIL OF KIT CARSON(1945); ALIAS BILLY THE KID(1946); CONQUEST OF CHEYENNE(1946); CRIME OF THE CENTURY(1946); DAYS OF BUFFALO BILL(1946); INVISIBLE INFORMER(1946); MAN FROM RAINBOW VALLEY, THE(1946); MURDER IN THE MUSIC HALL(1946); OUT CALIFORNIA WAY(1946); PASSKEY TO DANGER(1946); RED RIVER RENEGADES(1946); RIO GRANDE RAIDERS(1946); ROLL ON TEXAS MOON(1946); SANTA FE UPRISING(1946); SHERIFF OF REDWOOD VALLEY(1946); STAGECOACH TO DENVER(1946); SUN VALLEY CYCLONE(1946); UNDERCOVER WOMAN, THE(1946); DICK TRACY'S DILEMMA(1947); HOMESTEADERS OF PARADISE VALLEY(1947); LAST FRONTIER UPRISING(1947); MARSHAL OF CRIPPLE CREEK, THE(1947); RUSTLERS OF DEVIL'S CANYON(1947); SADDLE PALS(1947); TWILIGHT ON THE RIO GRANDE(1947); UNDER COLORADO SKIES(1947); WILD FRONTIER, THE(1947); WYOMING(1947); MARK OF THE LASH(1948); MARSHAL OF AMARILLO(1948); BRAND OF FEAR(1949); FAR FRONTIER, THE(1949); FRONTIER INVESTIGATOR(1949); RED DESERT(1949); RIDERS IN THE SKY(1949); SAN ANTONE AMBUSH(1949); SAND(1949); SOUTH OF RIO(1949); BLAZING SUN, THE(1950); OLD FRONTIER, THE(1950); HILLS OF UTAH(1951); ROUGH RIDERS OF DURANGO(1951); SECRET OF CONVICT LAKE, THE(1951); APACHE COUNTRY(1952); BLUE CANADIAN ROCKIES(1952); HIGH NOON(1952); OLD WEST, THE(1952); TRAIL GUIDE(1952); MARSHAL'S DAUGHTER, THE(1953); PACK TRAIN(1953); TARANTULA(1955); TRIBUTE TO A BADMAN(1956); WAGON WHEELS WESTWARD(1956); STORM RIDER, THE(1957); TALL STRANGER, THE(1957); GOOD DAY FOR A HANGING(1958); LONE TEXAN(1959); UNDERWORLD U.S.A.(1961)
Misc. Talkies
LIGHTNIN' SMITH RETURNS(1931); TRAILS OF THE GOLDEN WEST(1931); CACTUS KID, THE(1934); OUTLAWS' HIGHWAY(1934); COURAGE OF THE NORTH(1935); RIO RATTLER(1935)
Silents
LOSER'S END, THE(1924); GREY DEVIL, THE(1926); WEST OF THE RAINBOW'S END(1926); KING OF KINGS, THE(1927); APACHE RAIDER, THE(1928); HARVEST OF HATE(1929)
Misc. Silents
DEMON RIDER, THE(1925); THREE IN EXILE(1925); CHASING TROUBLE(1926); CODE OF THE NORTHWEST(1926); DANGEROUS TRAFFIC(1926); BOSS OF RUSTLER'S ROOST, THE(1928); BRONC STOMPER, THE(1928); PRICE OF FEAR, THE(1928); PUT 'EM UP(1928); YELLOW CONTRABAND(1928); BORDER WILDCAT, THE(1929)

Tony London
CLASS OF MISS MAC MICHAEL, THE(1978, Brit./U.S.); THAT SUMMER(1979, Brit.); ELEPHANT MAN, THE(1980, Brit.)
1984
SECRET PLACES(1984, Brit.)
Vicki London
VILLAGE OF THE GIANTS(1965)
Walter London
NIGHT CARGO(1936), ph
The London Babes
OFF THE DOLE(1935, Brit.)
London Brass Band
PLAY UP THE BAND(1935, Brit.)
London Festival Ballet
NEVER LET ME GO(1953, U.S./Brit.)
London Fog
IDOLMAKER, THE(1980)
The London Lovelies
MELODY IN THE DARK(1948, Brit.)
London Symphony Orchestra
I'LL WALK BESIDE YOU(1943, Brit.); FOR YOU ALONE(1945, Brit.); I'LL TURN TO YOU(1946, Brit.)
W.J. Londregan
RAMPARTS WE WATCH, THE(1940)
John Lone
KING KONG(1976)
1984
ICEMAN(1984)
Philip Lonegran
Silents
PENALTY, THE(1920), w
Ed Lonehill
LAST HUNT, THE(1956)
Arthur Lonergan
BLACK BEAUTY(1946), art d; INTRIGUE(1947), art d; SONG OF MY HEART(1947), art d; TENDER YEARS, THE(1947), art d; MAN-EATER OF KUMAON(1948), art d; PITFALL(1948), art d; MRS. MIKE(1949), art d; OUTPOST IN MOROCCO(1949), art d; LIFE OF HER OWN, A(1950), art d; MAGNIFICENT YANKEE, THE(1950), art d; CAUSE FOR ALARM(1951), art d; IT'S A BIG COUNTRY(1951), art d; MAN WITH A CLOAK, THE(1951), art d; RICH, YOUNG AND PRETTY(1951), art d; SELLOUT, THE(1951), art d; HOLIDAY FOR SINNERS(1952), ait d; YOUNG MAN WITH IDEAS(1952), art d; ACTRESS, THE(1953), art d; RIDE, VAQUERO!(1953), art d; IT'S ALWAYS FAIR WEATHER(1955), art d; TENDER TRAP, THE(1955), art d; FORBIDDEN PLANET(1956), art d; GUN BROTHERS(1956), art d; RANSOM(1956), art d; SEARCH FOR BRIDEY MURPHY, THE(1956), art d; ERRAND BOY, THE(1961), art d; ON THE DOUBLE(1961), art d; MY GEISHA(1962), art d; WHO'S GOT THE ACTION?(1962), art d; NEW KIND OF LOVE, A(1963), art d; PAPA'S DELICATE CONDITION(1963), art d; WHO'S BEEN SLEEPING IN MY BED?(1963), art d; FOR THOSE WHO THINK YOUNG(1964), art d; ROBINSON CRUSOE ON MARS(1964), art d; BILLIE(1965), art d; RED LINE 7000(1965), art d; TICKLE ME(1965), art d; YOUNG FURY(1965), art d; OSCAR, THE(1966), art d; HOW SWEET IT IS(1968), art d; YOURS, MINE AND OURS(1968), art d; CHE!(1969), art d; M(1970), art d; PLAZA SUITE(1971), art d; TODD KILLINGS, THE(1971), art d
Lenore Lonergan
TOM, DICK AND HARRY(1941); LADY SAYS NO, THE(1951); WESTWARD THE WOMEN(1951); WHISTLE AT EATON FALLS(1951)
Lester Lonergan
SEVEN FACES(1929); BOOMERANG(1947)
Lloyd Lonergan
Silents
NET, THE(1916), w; TRAFFIC COP, THE(1916), w; MODERN MONTE CRISTO, A(1917), w; NEGLECTED WIVES(1920), w

Philip Lonergan
MAN FROM GALVESTON, THE(1964), w
Silents
KING LEAR(1916), w; STEADFAST HEART, THE(1923), w; ON THE STROKE OF THREE(1924), w; PRIVATE IZZY MURPHY(1926), w
Col. Tim Lonergan
FLIRTATION WALK(1934)
Grigore ‡onescu
FANTASTIC COMEDY, A(1975, Rum.), ph
Ralph Lonewolf
GOOD MORNING, JUDGE(1943)
R. Loney
POCKET MONEY(1972)
Alan Long
Misc. Talkies
PICK-UP(1975)
Alexi Long
NED KELLY(1970, Brit.)
Amelia Reynolds Long
FIEND WITHOUT A FACE(1958), w
Ann Long
NEST OF THE CUCKOO BIRDS, THE(1965)
Audrey Long
ADVENTURES OF GALLANT BESS(1948); EAGLE SQUADRON(1942); GREAT IMPERSONATION, THE(1942); MALE ANIMAL, THE(1942); PARDON MY SARONG(1942); YANKEE DOODLE DANDY(1942); NIGHT OF ADVENTURE, A(1944); TALL IN THE SADDLE(1944); GAME OF DEATH, A(1945); PAN-AMERICANA(1945); WANDERER OF THE WASTELAND(1945); PERILOUS HOLIDAY(1946); BORN TO KILL(1947); DESPERATE(1947); SONG OF MY HEART(1947); HOMICIDE FOR THREE(1948); MIRACULOUS JOURNEY(1948); PERILOUS WATERS(1948); STAGE STRUCK(1948); ALIAS THE CHAMP(1949); DUKE OF CHICAGO(1949); POST OFFICE INVESTIGATOR(1949); RED DANUBE, THE(1949); DAVID HARDING, COUNTERSPY(1950); PETTY GIRL, THE(1950); TRIAL WITHOUT JURY(1950); BLUE BLOOD(1951); CAVALRY SCOUT(1951); INDIAN UPRISING(1951); INSURANCE INVESTIGATOR(1951); SUNNY SIDE OF THE STREET(1951)
Misc. Talkies
IN SELF DEFENSE(1947)
Avon Long
ZIEGFELD FOLLIES(1945); CENTENNIAL SUMMER(1946); ROMANCE ON THE HIGH SEAS(1948); FINIAN'S RAINBOW(1968); STING, THE(1973); HARRY AND TONTO(1974); BYE BYE MONKEY(1978, Ital/Fr.); TRADING PLACES(1983)
Barbara Long
GEORGE(1973, U.S./Switz.), art d
Beverly Long
REBEL WITHOUT A CAUSE(1955); GREEN-EYED BLONDE, THE(1957); AS YOUNG AS WE ARE(1958)
Bobby Long
IT HAPPENED IN BROOKLYN(1947)
Chris Long
SO LONG, BLUE BOY(1973), w
Constance Ullman Long
EDGE, THE(1968)
David Long
SO LONG, BLUE BOY(1973), w
Dick Long
DARK MIRROR, THE(1946); HE LAUGHED LAST(1956)
Doris Long
LURE, THE(1933, Brit.)
Dwight Long
TANGA-TIKA(1953), p, d, ph
Ed Long
WILD ROVERS(1971)
Edmund Long
ROWDYMAN, THE(1973, Can.), ph
Elisabeth Long
STORY WITHOUT WORDS(1981, Ital.)
Elizabeth Long
ONE PLUS ONE(1969, Brit.)
Francesca Long
WHEN TOMORROW DIES(1966, Can.)
Frederick Long
Silents
LOST PATROL, THE(1929, Brit.)
Gerald Long
IN THE COUNTRY(1967); EDGE, THE(1968)
Hal Long
BLOOD MONEY(1933), w; FOLIES DERGERE(1935), w; WHITE FANG(1936), w; BAD GUY(1937), w; NANCY STEELE IS MISSING(1937), w; STANLEY AND LIVINGSTONE(1939), w; JOHNNY APOLLO(1940), w; VIVA CISCO KID(1940), w; ROBIN HOOD OF THE PECOS(1941), w; THAT NIGHT IN RIO(1941), w; KING OF THE COWBOYS(1943), w; FABULOUS TEXAN, THE(1947), w
Harry Long
DEATH IS A NUMBER(1951, Brit.), ph
Helen Long
Misc. Silents
HEART'S REVENGE, A(1918)
Hilary Long
FAKE'S PROGRESS(1950, Brit.), p, w
Horace Long
NIGHT SHIFT(1982)
Misc. Talkies
JOE'S BED-STUY BARBERSHOP: WE CUT HEADS(1983)
Jack Long
MAN FROM NEW MEXICO, THE(1932); MASON OF THE MOUNTED(1932); SCARLET BRAND(1932); POLICE CAR 17(1933); SPEED WINGS(1934); JUVENILE COURT(1938); LAW OF THE PLAINS(1938)
Misc. Talkies
WHIRLWIND RIDER, THE(1935)

Jerry Long
WILD, WILD WINTER(1966), m; CATALINA CAPER, THE(1967), m

Jimmie Long
SON OF DR. JEKYLL, THE(1951)

Jimmy Long
LAS VEGAS STORY, THE(1952)

Jo Long
RAVAGER, THE(1970)

Joan Long
CADDIE(1976, Aus.), w; PICTURE SHOW MAN, THE(1980, Aus.), p, w; PUBERTY BLUES(1983, Aus.), p

Jodi Long
ROLLOVER(1981)
1984
SPLASH(1984)

John Luther Long
MADAME BUTTERFLY(1932), w
Silents
MADAME BUTTERFLY(1915), w

Johnny Long
HIT THE ICE(1943); MAD DOCTOR OF BLOOD ISLAND, THE(1969, Phil./U.S.); BEAST OF BLOOD(1970, U.S./Phil.); TWILIGHT PEOPLE(1972, Phil.)

Julius Long
JUDGE, THE(1949), w

Keny Long
KING KONG(1976); HERO AIN'T NOTHIN' BUT A SANDWICH, A(1977); DOCTOR DETROIT(1983)

L. Long
FASHIONS IN LOVE(1929), w

Lily Long
OLD CURIOSITY SHOP, THE(1935, Brit.)

Lionel Long
AMOROUS ADVENTURES OF MOLL FLANDERS, THE(1965); INN OF THE DAMNED(1974, Aus.)

Lotus Long
MYSTERIOUS MR. WONG(1935); SING SING NIGHTS(1935); LAST OF THE PAGANS(1936); SEA SPOILERS, THE(1936); CHINA PASSAGE(1937); THINK FAST, MR. MOTO(1937); MR. WONG IN CHINATOWN(1939); MYSTERY OF MR. WONG, THE(1939); PHANTOM OF CHINATOWN(1940); FOR BEAUTY'S SAKE(1941); TOKYO ROSE(1945); ROSE OF THE YUKON(1949); TAHITIAN, THE(1956), p, w
Silents
PEACOCK FAN(1929)

Louis Long
Silents
WHAT A NIGHT!(1928), w

Louise Long
GREENE MURDER CASE, THE(1929), w; WOMAN TRAP(1929), w; VIRTUOUS SIN, THE(1930), w; ZOO IN BUDAPEST(1933), w; THIS LOVE OF OURS(1945)
Silents
CAMPUS FLIRT, THE(1926), w; ROUGH HOUSE ROSIE(1927), w; LOVE AND LEARN(1928), w

Marcia Long
ROSE BOWL STORY, THE(1952)

Mark Long
1984
KILLING FIELDS, THE(1984, Brit.)

Mary Long
CLASS OF '44(1973); STONE COLD DEAD(1980, Can.)

Matthew Long
ZEPPELIN(1971, Brit.); MEDUSA TOUCH, THE(1978, Brit.); YESTERDAY'S HE-RO(1979, Brit.); GIRO CITY(1982, Brit.)

Michael Long
DEMONSTRATOR(1971, Aus.); CHAIN REACTION(1980, Aus.)
1984
CAREFUL, HE MIGHT HEAR YOU(1984, Aus.); SQUIZZY TAYLOR(1984, Aus.)

Nate Long
WHITE LINE FEVER(1975, Can.), stunt; SCORCHY(1976)

Nguyen Long
1984
LE CRABE TAMBOUR(1984, Fr.), ed

Nicholas Long
Silents
ADVENTURES OF CAROL, THE(1917)

Nick Long
Silents
SHORE LEAVE(1925)

Nick Long, Jr.
BROADWAY MELODY OF 1936(1935); KING OF BURLESQUE(1936)

Norman Long
NEW HOTEL, THE(1932, Brit.); REGAL CAVALCADE(1935, Brit.)

Pierre Long
LE PETIT THEATRE DE JEAN RENOIR(1974, Fr.), p

Reginald Long
DEPUTY DRUMMER, THE(1935, Brit.), a, w; TRUST THE NAVY(1935, Brit.), a, w; WHO'S YOUR FATHER?(1935, Brit.), w; AVENGING HAND, THE(1936, Brit.), a, w; BALL AT SAVOY(1936, Brit.), w; HOT NEWS(1936, Brit.), a, w; VARIETY PARA-DE(1936, Brit.), p; MAKE-UP(1937, Brit.), w; SECOND BUREAU(1937, Brit.), w; WIFE OF GENERAL LING, THE(1938, Brit.), w; ALL AT SEA(1939, Brit.), w; FACE BEHIND THE SCAR(1940, Brit.), w; SPIDER, THE(1940, Brit.), w; LOOK BEFORE YOU LOVE(1948, Brit.), w; AFFAIRS OF A ROGUE, THE(1949, Brit.), w; TO HAVE AND TO HOLD(1951, Brit.), w; DEATH OF AN ANGEL(1952, Brit.), w; LIMPING MAN, THE(1953, Brit.), w

Richard Long
STRANGER THE(1946); TOMORROW IS FOREVER(1946); EGG AND I, THE(1947); TAP ROOTS(1948); CRISS CROSS(1949); LIFE OF RILEY, THE(1949); MA AND PA KETTLE(1949); KANSAS RAIDERS(1950); MA AND PA KETTLE GO TO TOWN(1950); AIR CADET(1951); MA AND PA KETTLE BACK ON THE FARM(1951); BACK AT THE FRONT(1952); ALL-AMERICAN, THE(1953); ALL I DESIRE(1953); PLAYGIRL(1954); SASKATCHEWAN(1954); CULT OF THE COBRA(1955); FURY AT GUNSIGHT PASS(1956); HOUSE ON HAUNTED HILL(1958); TOKYO AFTER DARK(1959); FOL-

LOW THE BOYS(1963); MAKE LIKE A THIEF(1966, Fin.), a, d

Robert Long
LIFE IN HER HANDS(1951, Brit.); STREET BANDITS(1951); CAPTAIN KIDD AND THE SLAVE GIRL(1954); RETURN TO TREASURE ISLAND(1954)

Ronald Long
TWO LOVES(1961); NOTORIOUS LANDLADY, THE(1962); MAN FROM THE DIN-ERS' CLUB, THE(1963); ASSAULT ON A QUEEN(1966)

Sally Long
COCK O' THE WALK(1930)
Silents
HIS DARKER SELF(1924); KID SISTER, THE(1927)
Misc. Silents
BORDER WHIRLWIND, THE(1926); FIGHTING BUCKAROO, THE(1926); GOING THE LIMIT(1926); THRILL SEEKERS, THE(1927); WHEN DANGER CALLS(1927)

Sarah Long
VILLAGE OF THE DAMNED(1960, Brit.); HENRY VIII AND HIS SIX WIVES(1972, Brit.)

Shelley Long
SMALL CIRCLE OF FRIENDS, A(1980); NIGHT SHIFT(1982); LOSIN' IT(1983)
1984
IRRECONCILABLE DIFFERENCES(1984)

Shelly Long
CAVEMAN(1981)

Stanley Long
SECRETS OF A WINDMILL GIRL(1966, Brit.), p; SORCERERS, THE(1967, Brit.), ph; I AM A GROUPIE(1970, Brit.), p, ph; SWAPPERS, THE(1970, Brit.), p, w; THIS, THAT AND THE OTHER(1970, Brit.), p, ph

Stanley A. Long
SKIN GAME, THE(1965, Brit.), p, ph; TOMCAT, THE(1968, Brit.), ph

Sumner A. Long
GOING STEADY(1958), w

Sumner Arthur Long
LASSIE'S GREAT ADVENTURE(1963), w; NEVER TOO LATE(1965), w

Thelma Long
KISS THE BOYS GOODBYE(1941)

Tim Long
Misc. Talkies
DARK DREAMS(1971)

Trisha Long
1984
JOHNNY DANGEROUSLY(1984)

W. H. Long
Silents
HOME SWEET HOME(1914)

Walter Long
GANG WAR(1928); BLACK WATCH, THE(1929); BEAU BANDIT(1930); CONSPIRA-CY(1930); MOBY DICK(1930); MALTESE FALCON, THE(1931); OTHER MEN'S WOM-EN(1931); PARDON US(1931); SEA DEVILS(1931); SOUL OF THE SLUMS(1931); CORNERED(1932); DRAGNET PATROL(1932); ESCAPADE(1932); I AM A FUGITIVE FROM A CHAIN GANG(1932); SILVER DOLLAR(1932); EASY MILLIONS(1933); WOMEN WON'T TELL(1933); LAZY RIVER(1934); OPERATOR 13(1934); SIX OF A KIND(1934); THIN MAN, THE(1934); FRISCO KID(1935); LIGHTNING STRIKES TWICE(1935); NAUGHTY MARIETTA(1935); WHOLE TOWN'S TALKING, THE(1935); BOLD CABALLERO(1936); DRIFT FENCE(1936); WEDDING PRESENT(1936); GLO-RY TRAIL, THE(1937); NORTH OF THE RIO GRANDE(1937); PICK A STAR(1937); BAR 20 JUSTICE(1938); MAN'S COUNTRY(1938); PAINTED TRAIL, THE(1938); SIX SHOOTIN' SHERIFF(1938); FIGHTING MAD(1939); FLAMING LEAD(1939); UNION PACIFIC(1939); WILD HORSE CANYON(1939); HIDDEN GOLD(1940); WHEN THE DALTONS RODE(1940); CITY OF MISSING GIRLS(1941); SILVER STALLION(1941); WABASH AVENUE(1950)
Misc. Talkies
DARK ENDEAVOUR(1933)
Silents
TRAFFIC IN SOULS(1913); BIRTH OF A NATION, THE(1915); JORDAN IS A HARD ROAD(1915); MARTYRS OF THE ALAMO, THE(1915); DAPHNE AND THE PIRA-TE(1916); INTOLERANCE(1916); JOAN THE WOMAN(1916); ROMANCE OF THE REDWOODS, A(1917); ADVENTURE IN HEARTS, AN(1919); SCARLET DAYS(1919); EXCUSE MY DUST(1920); SHEIK, THE(1921); WHITE AND UNMARRIED(1921); ACROSS THE CONTINENT(1922); BEAUTIFUL AND DAMNED, THE(1922); BLOOD AND SAND(1922); DICTATOR, THE(1922); KICK IN(1922); MORAN OF THE LADY LETTY(1922); SHADOWS(1922); SOUTH OF SUVA(1922); TO HAVE AND TO HOLD(1922); CALL OF THE WILD, THE(1923); HUNTRESS, THE(1923); ISLE OF LOST SHIPS, THE(1923); LITTLE CHURCH AROUND THE CORNER(1923); MY AMERICAN WIFE(1923); SHOCK, THE(1923); RAFFLES, THE AMATEUR CRACKS-MAN(1925); RECKLESS SEX, THE(1925); RED DICE(1926); JEWELS OF DESI-RE(1927); JIM THE CONQUEROR(1927); WHITE PANTS WILLIE(1927); YANKEE CLIPPER, THE(1927)
Misc. Silents
LET KATHY DO IT(1916); SOLD FOR MARRIAGE(1916); YEARS OF THE LOCUST, THE(1916); WINNING OF SALLY TEMPLE, THE(1917); FIGHTING SHEPHERDESS, THE(1920); HELD IN TRUST(1920); FIRE CAT, THE(1921); GIANT OF HIS RACE, A(1921); BROKEN WING, THE(1923); SHOT IN THE NIGHT, A(1923); DARING LOVE(1924); WHITE MAN(1924); YANKEE MADNESS(1924); EVE'S LEAVES(1926); WEST OF BROADWAY(1926); BACK TO GOD'S COUNTRY(1927); THUNDER-GOD(1928); BLACK CARGOES OF THE SOUTH SEAS(1929)

Walter R. Long
BROADWAY RHYTHM(1944)

Will Long
ODE TO BILLY JOE(1976)

William Long, Jr.
CANDIDATE, THE(1964)

The Long & The Short
GONKS GO BEAT(1965, Brit.)

Long Beach Boys' Choir
SAN FRANCISCO(1936)

Remy Longa
HOW TO STEAL A MILLION(1966); THERESE AND ISABELLE(1968, U.S./Ger.)

Rachel Longacker
OH, GOD!(1977)
Frank Longacre
Misc. Silents
HEARTS OF MEN(1915); WARNING, THE(1915)
Renee Longarini
LA DOLCE VITA(1961, Ital./Fr.); CLIMAX, THE(1967, Fr., Ital.)
Frederick Longbridge
Silents
ONLY WAY, THE(1926, Brit.), w
Richard Longcraine
FULL CIRCLE(1977, Brit./Can.), d
John Longden
ATLANTIC(1929 Brit.); BLACKMAIL(1929, Brit.); LAST POST, THE(1929, Brit.); CHILDREN OF CHANCE(1930, Brit.); FLAME OF LOVE, THE(1930, Brit.); JUNO AND THE PAYCOCK(1930, Brit.); TWO WORLD(1930, Brit.); SKIN GAME, THE(1931, Brit.); WICKHAM MYSTERY, THE(1931, Brit.); BORN LUCKY(1932, Brit.); LUCKY SWEEP, A(1932, Brit.); MURDER ON THE SECOND FLOOR(1932, Brit.); RINGER, THE(1932, Brit.); SILENCE OF DEAN MAITLAND, THE(1934, Aus.); THOROUGHBRED(1936, Aus.); FRENCH LEAVE(1937, Brit.); IT ISN'T DONE(1937, Aus.); JENIFER HALE(1937, Brit.); LITTLE MISS SOMEBODY(1937, Brit.); BAD BOY(1938, Brit.); YOUNG AND INNOCENT(1938, Brit.); CLOUDS OVER EUROPE(1939, Brit.); GOODBYE MR. CHIPS(1939, Brit.); JAMAICA INN(1939, Brit.); PHANTOM STRIKES, THE(1939, Brit.); LION HAS WINGS, THE(1940, Brit.); COMMON TOUCH, THE(1941, Brit.); OLD MOTHER RILEY'S CIRCUS(1941, Brit.); ROSE OF TRALEE(1942, Brit.); TOWER OF TERROR, THE(1942, Brit.); UNPUBLISHED STORY(1942, Brit.); YELLOW CANARY, THE(1944, Brit.); SILVER FLEET, THE(1945, Brit.); GHOSTS OF BERKELEY SQUARE(1947, Brit.); ANNA KARENINA(1948, Brit.); BONNIE PRINCE CHARLIE(1948, Brit.); LAST LOAD, THE(1948, Brit.); FIGHTING PIMPERNEL, THE(1950, Brit.); LADY CRAVED EXCITEMENT, THE(1950, Brit.); BLACK WIDOW(1951, Brit.); DARK LIGHT, THE(1951, Brit.); POOL OF LONDON(1951, Brit.); WALLET, THE(1952, Brit.); DANGEROUS CARGO(1954, Brit.); MEET MR. CALLAGHAN(1954, Brit.); COUNT OF TWELVE(1955, Brit.); FINAL COLUMN, THE(1955, Brit.); ALIAS JOHN PRESTON(1956, Brit.); SHIP THAT DIED OF SHAME, THE(1956, Brit.); ENEMY FROM SPACE(1957, Brit.); THREE SUNDAYS TO LIVE(1957, Brit.); HONOURABLE MURDER, AN(1959, Brit.); SO EVIL SO YOUNG(1961, Brit.); SWORD OF LANCELOT(1963, Brit.); FROZEN ALIVE(1966, Brit./Ger.)
Silents
ARCADIANS, THE(1927, Brit.); PALAIS DE DANSE(1928, Brit.), a, w
Misc. Silents
HOUSE OF MARNEY(1926, Brit.); YOU KNOW WHAT SAILORS ARE(1928, Brit.); FLYING SQUAD, THE(1929)
Johnny Longden
WINNER'S CIRCLE, THE(1948)
Robert Longden
STICK UP, THE(1978, Brit.); AGATHA(1979, Brit.)
1984
GIVE MY REGARDS TO BROAD STREET(1984, Brit.)
Terence Longden
ISLAND RESCUE(1952, Brit.); MAN WHO NEVER WAS, THE(1956, Brit.); BEN HUR(1959)
John Longdon
TRAPPED BY THE TERROR(1949, Brit.); MAGIC BOX, THE(1952, Brit.); WOMAN'S TEMPTATION, A(1959, Brit.)
Robert Longdon
CONFESSIONS OF A WINDOW CLEANER(1974, Brit.)
Terence Longdon
NEVER LOOK BACK(1952, Brit.); WOMAN FOR JOE, THE(1955, Brit.); HELEN OF TROY(1956, Ital); JUMPING FOR JOY(1956, Brit.); SIMON AND LAURA(1956, Brit.); DOCTOR AT LARGE(1957, Brit.); DANGEROUS EXILE(1958, Brit.); CARRY ON NURSE(1959, Brit.); CARRY ON SERGEANT(1959, Brit.); SILENT ENEMY, THE(1959, Brit.); CARRY ON CONSTABLE(1960, Brit.); CARRY ON REGARDLESS(1961, Brit.); WHAT A WHOPPER(1961, Brit.); MURDER ON THE CAMPUS(1963, Brit.); ESCAPE BY NIGHT(1965, Brit.); OPERATION SNAFU(1965, Brit.); RETURN OF MR. MOTO, THE(1965, Brit.); SEA WOLVES, THE(1981, Brit.)
Terrence Longdon
ANOTHER TIME, ANOTHER PLACE(1958)
Franco Longelia
ALONE IN THE STREETS(1956, Ital.), m
Malvina Longellow
Misc. Silents
STRONG MAN'S WEAKNESS, A(1917, Brit.)
Bert Longenecker
CRIME PATROL, THE(1936), ph; BOOTHILL BRIGADE(1937), ph; DESERT PHANTOM(1937), ph; DOOMED AT SUNDOWN(1937), ph; GAMBLING TERROR, THE(1937), ph; GOD'S COUNTRY AND THE MAN(1937), ph; GUN LORDS OF STIRRUP BASIN(1937), ph; GUN RANGER, THE(1937), ph; GUNS IN THE DARK(1937), ph; LAWMAN IS BORN, A(1937), ph; LIGHTNIN' CRANDALL(1937), ph; RECKLESS RANGER(1937), ph; RED ROPE, THE(1937), ph; RIDERS OF THE DAWN(1937), ph; STARS OVER ARIZONA(1937), ph; TRAIL OF VENGEANCE(1937), ph; TRUSTED OUTLAW, THE(1937), ph; DANGER VALLEY(1938), ph; GUN PACKER(1938), ph; MAN'S COUNTRY(1938), ph; MEXICALI KID, THE(1938), ph; PAINTED TRAIL, THE(1938), ph; ROMANCE OF THE ROCKIES(1938), ph; ACROSS THE PLAINS(1939), ph; DRIFTING WESTWARD(1939), ph; OKLAHOMA TERROR(1939), ph; SUNDOWN ON THE PRAIRIE(1939), ph; SCREAM IN THE NIGHT(1943), ph
Silents
AIR HAWK, THE(1924), ph; DYNAMITE DAN(1924), ph; IN HIGH GEAR(1924), ph; RIDERS OF MYSTERY(1925), ph
Robert Longer
DEATM GOES TO SCHOOL(1953, Brit.)
Claudine Longet
MC HALE'S NAVY(1964); PARTY, THE(1968)
Emma Longfellow
PINK FLOYD–THE WALL(1982, Brit.)
Henry Longfellow
Silents
WOMAN'S SECRET, A(1924, Brit.), w

Henry Wadsworth Longfellow
EVANGELINE(1929), w; HIAWATHA(1952), w
Silents
COURTSHIP OF MILES STANDISH, THE(1923), w; EVANGELINE(1929), w&t
Malvina Longfellow
Silents
HOLY ORDERS(1917, Brit.); ADAM BEDE(1918, Brit.); NELSON(1918, Brit.); MARY LATIMER, NUN(1920, Brit.); INDIAN LOVE LYRICS, THE(1923, Brit.)
Misc. Silents
FOR ALL ETERNITY(1917, Brit.); BETTA THE GYPSY(1918, Brit.); THELMA(1918, Brit.); ROMANCE OF LADY HAMILTON, THE(1919, Brit.); GAMBLE IN LIVES, A(1920, Brit.); GRIP OF IRON, THE(1920, Brit.); STORY OF THE ROSARY, THE(1920, Brit.); UNMARRIED(1920, Brit.); MOTH AND RUST(1921, Brit.); NIGHT HAWK, THE(1921, Brit.); WANDERING JEW, THE(1923, Brit.); CELESTIAL CITY, THE(1929, Brit.)
Michael Longfield
TAPS(1981)
Charlie Longfoot
RIO LOBO(1970)
Raymond Longford
Misc. Silents
BLUE MOUNTAIN MYSTERY, THE(1922), d
The Longhairs
RIOT ON SUNSET STRIP(1967)
Roberta Longhi
SQUARE ROOT OF ZERO, THE(1964)
Donald Longhurst
THX 1138(1971), cos
Graham Longhurst
PINK FLOYD–THE WALL(1982, Brit.), spec eff
H. B. Longhurst
CROOKED LADY, THE(1932, Brit.)
Henry Longhurst
LET ME EXPLAIN, DEAR(1932); LETTING IN THE SUNSHINE(1933, Brit.); MY LUCKY STAR(1933, Brit.); DANGEROUS GROUND(1934, Brit.); WHEN LONDON SLEEPS(1934, Brit.); ALIAS BULLDOG DRUMMOND(1935, Brit.); MR. WHAT'S-HIS-NAME(1935, Brit.); MURDER AT MONTE CARLO(1935, Brit.); HOT NEWS(1936, Brit.); UNDER PROOF(1936, Brit.); FOR VALOR(1937, Brit.); OLD MOTHER RILEY MP(1939, Brit.); LONG DARK HALL, THE(1951, Brit.); HIS EXCELLENCY(1952, Brit.); CAPTAIN'S PARADISE, THE(1953, Brit.); TIME GENTLEMEN PLEASE!(1953, Brit.); DIPLOMATIC PASSPORT(1954, Brit.); MAD ABOUT MEN(1954, Brit.); PARATROOPER(1954, Brit.); LADY GODIVA RIDES AGAIN(1955, Brit.); LIGHT TOUCH, THE(1955, Brit.); KEEP IT CLEAN(1956, Brit.); PRIVATE'S PROGRESS(1956, Brit.); BROTHERS IN LAW(1957, Brit.); LUCKY JIM(1957, Brit.); GIDEON OF SCOTLAND YARD(1959, Brit.); FRENCH MISTRESS(1960, Brit.); HEAVENS ABOVE!(1963, Brit.); MURDER AHOY(1964, Brit.); PSYCHO-CIRCUS(1967, Brit.)
Henry B. Longhurst
THIS ACTING BUSINESS(1933, Brit.); VANDERGILT DIAMOND MYSTERY, THE(1936); MAN WITH 100 FACES, THE(1938, Brit.); SAILOR'S DON'T CARE(1940, Brit.); OLD MOTHER RILEY'S GHOSTS(1941, Brit.); VACATION FROM MARRIAGE(1945, Brit.)
Jeremy Longhurst
LUCKY JIM(1957, Brit.); CRAWLING EYE, THE(1958, Brit.); STEEL BAYONET, THE(1958, Brit.); GORGON, THE(1964, Brit.); SPACEFLIGHT IC-1(1965, Brit.)
Sue Longhurst
LUST FOR A VAMPIRE(1971, Brit.); CONFESSIONS OF A WINDOW CLEANER(1974, Brit.)
Misc. Talkies
GROOVE ROOM, THE(1974, Brit.); NAUGHTY WIVES(1974); KEEP IT UP, JACK!(1975)
Zoran Longinovic
FRAULEIN DOKTOR(1969, Ital./Yugo.)
Sally Longley
MURDERS IN THE RUE MORGUE(1971)
Yves Longlois
JACQUES BREL IS ALIVE AND WELL AND LIVING IN PARIS(1975), ed
Alix Longman
GETTING OF WISDOM, THE(1977, Aus.)
E. G. Longman
Silents
ALL FOR A GIRL(1915)
Adele Longmire
BULLET SCARS(1942); PEOPLE WILL TALK(1951); TURNING POINT, THE(1952); BATTLE CIRCUS(1953)
Roy Longmire
FOUR FOR THE MORGUE(1962)
Susan Longmire
RUNNING(1979, Can.), art d; SILENCE OF THE NORTH(1981, Can.), art d; TICKET TO HEAVEN(1981), prod d; FUNERAL HOME(1982, Can.), prod d
Bert Longnecker
BETWEEN MEN(1935), ph; FIRETRAP, THE(1935), ph; LAST OF THE WARRENS, THE(1936), ph; SUNDOWN SAUNDERS(1937), ph; WHERE TRAILS DIVIDE(1937), ph; WANTED BY THE POLICE(1938), ph; OVERLAND MAIL(1939), ph; TRIGGER SMITH(1939), ph; WILD HORSE CANYON(1939), ph
Barbara J. Longo
LIFE AND TIMES OF JUDGE ROY BEAN, THE(1972)
Germano Longo
NIGHTS OF LUCRETIA BORGIA, THE(1960, Ital.); GUNS OF THE BLACK WITCH(1961, Fr./Ital.); PIRATE OF THE BLACK HAWK, THE(1961, Fr./Ital.); ATLAS AGAINST THE CYCLOPS(1963, Ital.); DUEL OF THE TITANS(1963, Ital.); REVENGE OF THE GLADIATORS(1965, Ital.); SEVEN SLAVES AGAINST THE WORLD(1965, Ital.); GIRL WHO COULDN'T SAY NO, THE(1969, Ital.); SUNFLOWER(1970, Fr./Ital.)
Gisella Longo
MATCHLESS(1967, Ital.), set d; FIST IN HIS POCKET(1968, Ital.), art d
Malisa Longo
THREE STOOGES VS. THE WONDER WOMEN(1975, Ital./Chi.)
Marisa Longo
YOUNG, THE EVIL AND THE SAVAGE, THE(1968, Ital.)

Christopher Loomis
NESTING, THE(1981); SO FINE(1981); TWO OF A KIND(1983)
Deborah Loomis
HERCULES IN NEW YORK(1970); FOREPLAY(1975)
Dr. Frederic M. Loomis
PAID IN FULL(1950), w
John Loomis
JACK AND THE BEANSTALK(1970)
Judith Loomis
LORD LOVE A DUCK(1966)
Margaret Loomis
Silents
ALWAYS AUDACIOUS(1920); KISS IN TIME, A(1921); STRANGER'S BAN-
QUET(1922); LAW OF THE LAWLESS, THE(1923); MONEY! MONEY! MONEY!(1923)
Misc. Silents
SHE LEFT WITHOUT HER TRUNKS(1916); BOTTLE IMP, THE(1917); CALL OF
THE EAST, THE(1917); HASHIMURA TOGO(1917); HIDDEN PEARLS(1918); SINS OF
ST. ANTHONY, THE(1920); THREE GOLD COINS(1920); WHAT HAPPENED TO
JONES(1920); WHEN A MAN LOVES(1920); BELL BOY 13(1923)
Nancy Loomis
ASSAULT ON PRECINCT 13(1976); HALLOWEEN(1978); FOG, THE(1980); HAL-
LOWEEN 11(1981)
Rod Loomis
BEASTMASTER, THE(1982)
1984
BODY DOUBLE(1984)
Sally Loomis
YOU'RE IN THE ARMY NOW(1941); DARK HORSE, THE(1946)
Stephen Loomis
FOG, THE(1980), cos; ESCAPE FROM NEW YORK(1981), cos
Terry Loomis
SPRING AFFAIR(1960)
Virginia Loomis
Silents
RENO(1923); BABBITT(1924)
Keith Loone
KING OF THE CORAL SEA(1956, Aus.), ph
Jere Looney
Silents
KILDARE OF STORM(1918), w
Peter Looney
OLIVER'S STORY(1978)
Jame Loonfboeurrow
TRUE CONFESSION(1937)
Staci Loop
ICE CASTLES(1978)
Friedl Loor
ETERNAL WALTZ, THE(1959, Ger.)
Anita Loos
FALL OF EVE, THE(1929), w; EX-BAD BOY(1931), w; STRUGGLE, THE(1931), w;
BLONDIE OF THE FOLLIES(1932), w; RED HEADED WOMAN(1932), w; BARBARI-
AN, THE(1933), w; HOLD YOUR MAN(1933), w; MIDNIGHT MARY(1933), w; GIRL
FROM MISSOURI, THE(1934), w; SOCIAL REGISTER(1934), w; BIOGRAPHY OF A
BACHELOR GIRL(1935), w; RIFF-RAFF(1936), w; SAN FRANCISCO(1936), w;
MAMA STEPS OUT(1937), w; SARATOGA(1937), w; WOMEN, THE(1939), w;
STRANGE CARGO(1940), w; SUSAN AND GOD(1940), w; BLOSSOMS IN THE
DUST(1941), w; THEY MET IN BOMBAY(1941), w; WHEN LADIES MEET(1941), w;
I MARRIED AN ANGEL(1942), w; PIRATE, THE(1948), w; GENTLEMEN PREFER
BLONDES(1953), w; GENTLEMEN MARRY BRUNETTES(1955), w
Silents
GANGSTERS OF NEW YORK, THE(1914), w; AMERICAN ARISTOCRACY(1916),
w; LITTLE LIAR, THE(1916), w; MATRIMANIAC, THE(1916), w; SOCIAL SECRE-
TARY, THE(1916), w; AMERICANO, THE(1917), w; DOWN TO EARTH(1917), w; IN
AGAIN-OUT AGAIN(1917), w; REACHING FOR THE MOON(1917), w; WILD AND
WOOLLY(1917), w; GETTING MARY MARRIED(1919), w; GOOD-BYE, BILL(1919),
w; ISLE OF CONQUEST(1919), w; BRANDED WOMAN, THE(1920), w; IN SEARCH
OF A SINNER(1920), w; WOMAN'S PLACE(1921), w; RED HOT ROMANCE(1922), w;
DULCY(1923), w; LEARNING TO LOVE(1925), w; STRANDED(1927), w; GENTLE-
MEN PREFER BLONDES(1928), w, t
Anne Loos
HITLER'S CHILDREN(1942); TWO SENORITAS FROM CHICAGO(1943); EVER
SINCE VENUS(1944); JAM SESSION(1944); MR. WINKLE GOES TO WAR(1944);
ONCE UPON A TIME(1944); ONE MYSTERIOUS NIGHT(1944); TOGETHER
AGAIN(1944); LEAVE IT TO BLONDIE(1945); OVER 21(1945); PILLOW TO
POST(1945); WOMAN IN THE WINDOW, THE(1945); TOMORROW IS FORE-
VER(1946); HANNAH LEE(1953); PUSHOVER(1954); NEVER SAY GOODBYE(1956);
SOLID GOLD CADILLAC, THE(1956); MUSIC MAN, THE(1962)
Mary Anita Loos
STUDENT TOUR(1934); ROSE MARIE(1936)
Mary Loos
RENDEZVOUS WITH ANNIE(1946), w; CALENDAR GIRL(1947), w; DRIFT-
WOOD(1947), w; HIT PARADE OF 1947(1947), w; DUDE GOES WEST, THE(1948), w;
INSIDE STORY, THE(1948), w; FATHER WAS A FULLBACK(1949), w; MOTHER IS
A FRESHMAN(1949), w; MR. BELVEDERE GOES TO COLLEGE(1949), w; I'LL GET
BY(1950), w, art d; TICKET TO TOMAHAWK(1950), w; WHEN WILLIE COMES
MARCHING HOME(1950), w; LET'S DO IT AGAIN(1953), w; FRENCH LINE,
THE(1954), w; WOMAN'S WORLD(1954), w; GENTLEMEN MARRY BRUNET-
TES(1955), w; OVER-EXPOSED(1956), w
Peter Loos
5 SINNERS(1961, Ger.), w; TURKISH CUCUMBER, THE(1963, Ger.), w
Theodor Loos
GREAT YEARNING, THE(1930, Ger.); ARIANE(1931, Ger.); EIGHT GIRLS IN A
BOAT(1932, Ger.); RASPUTIN(1932, Ger.); 1914(1932, Ger.); M(1933, Ger.); SHOT AT
DAWN, A(1934, Ger.); GIRL FROM THE MARSH CROFT(1935, Ger.); FINAL
CHORD, THE(1936, Ger.); TESTAMENT OF DR. MABUSE, THE(1943, Ger.)
Silents
KRIEMHILD'S REVENGE(1924, Ger.); SIEGFRIED(1924, Ger.); METROPOLIS(1927,
Ger.)

Bill Loose
SWEET SUZY(1973), m
William Loose
SHOOT OUT AT BIG SAG(1962), m; MAN IN THE WATER, THE(1963), m; DEVIL'S
BEDROOM, THE(1964), m; LOVE AND KISSES(1965), m; NAVAJO RUN(1966), m;
TARZAN AND THE GREAT RIVER(1967, U.S./Switz.), m, md; TARZAN AND THE
JUNGLE BOY(1968, US/Switz.), m, md; JONIKO AND THE KUSH TA KA(1969), m;
TRADER HORNEE(1970), md; BIG BIRD CAGE, THE(1972), m; LEGEND OF COU-
GAR CANYON(1974), m; WRESTLER, THE(1974), m
1984
MYSTERY MANSION(1984), m
Jinx Lootens
1984
RAZORBACK(1984, Aus.)
Rosanna Lopapero
MAFIA(1969, Fr./Ital.)
Valya Lopatina
Misc. Silents
EXTRAORDINARY ADVENTURES OF MR. WEST IN THE LAND OF THE BOL-
SHEVIKS(1924, USSR)
Ludmila Lopato
INNOCENTS IN PARIS(1955, Brit.)
Anna Lopatowska
CONDUCTOR, THE(1981, Pol.)
Don Loper
THOUSANDS CHEER(1943); BELLE OF THE YUKON(1944), ch; FOUR JILLS IN A
JEEP(1944), ch; LADY IN THE DARK(1944), a, ch; TWO GIRLS AND A SAI-
LOR(1944), ch; IT'S A PLEASURE(1945), a, ch; ZIEGFELD FOLLIES(1945), w; SO-
FIA(1948), cos; RANCHO NOTORIOUS(1952), cos; MOON IS BLUE, THE(1953), cos;
BIG COMBO, THE(1955), cos; FRESH FROM PARIS(1955), cos; NOT AS A STRAN-
GER(1955), cos; SPRING REUNION(1957), cos; LOOKING FOR LOVE(1964), cos
Robert Loper
JOYRIDE(1977)
Miguel Loperana
OLIVER'S STORY(1978)
I.E. Lopert
GOLGOTHA(1937, Fr.), w
I.K. Lopert
NO GREATER LOVE(1944, USSR), w
Ilya Lopert
SUMMERTIME(1955), p
Tanya Lopert
SOMETHING WILD(1961); MY SON, THE HERO(1963, Ital./Fr.); LADY L(1965,
Fr./Ital.); MALE HUNT(1965, Fr./Ital.); WHAT'S NEW, PUSSYCAT?(1965, U.S./Fr.);
SLEEPING CAR MURDER THE(1966, Fr.); YOUNG WORLD, A(1966, Fr./Ital.);
NAVAJO JOE(1967, Ital./Span.); DEVIL BY THE TAIL, THE(1969, Fr./Ital.); FELLINI
SATYRICON(1969, Fr./Ital.); LES GAULOISES BLEUES(1969, Fr.); LISTEN, LET'S
MAKE LOVE(1969, Fr./Ital.); PROVIDENCE(1977, Fr.); ONCE IN PARIS(1978); TALES
OF ORDINARY MADNESS(1983, Ital.)
1984
EDITH AND MARCEL(1984, Fr.)
Adolfo Lopez
1984
ALLEY CAT(1984)
Al Lopez
1984
LOVE STREAMS(1984)
Alberto Lopez
SANTO EN EL MUSEO DE CERA(1963, Mex.), p
Alejandro Lopez
SCALPHUNTERS, THE(1968)
Alvaro Lopez
1984
FEAR CITY(1984)
Anita Lopez
Misc. Silents
DEAD LINE, THE(1920)
Antonio Lopez
VOYAGE OF SILENCE(1968, Fr.)
Atilio Lopez
1984
MIDSUMMER NIGHT'S DREAM, A(1984, Brit./Span.)
Augustina Lopez
WOLF SONG(1929)
Carlos Lopez
RANCHO GRANDE(1938, Mex.)
Carmen Lopez
GREAT FLAMARION, THE(1945); PAN-AMERICANA(1945); RIFFRAFF(1947)
Caroline Lopez
MEXICAN HAYRIDE(1948)
Cecilia Lopez
WALLS OF HELL, THE(1964, U.S./Phil.)
Chel Lopez
SOFIA(1948); MY BROTHER, THE OUTLAW(1951); ADVENTURES OF ROBINSON
CRUSOE, THE(1954); EXTERMINATING ANGEL, THE(1967, Mex.)
Danny Lopez
TROUBLE MAN(1972)
Eddie "El Animal" Lopez
CHAMP, THE(1979); MAIN EVENT, THE(1979); ROCKY II(1979)
Elsa Lopez
Silents
SECRETS OF PARIS, THE(1922), art d; MODERN MARRIAGE(1923), art d
Estrellita Lopez
ONLY ONCE IN A LIFETIME(1979)
Evita Lopez
PAN-AMERICANA(1945)
Famille Lopez
1984
CHEECH AND CHONG'S THE CORSICAN BROTHERS(1984)

Fernando Lopez
DEFIANCE(1980)
Gerry Lopez
CONAN THE BARBARIAN(1982)
Inez Lopez
VIRGINIA JUDGE, THE(1935), w
Irene Olga Lopez
MAX DUGAN RETURNS(1983)
1984
FLETCH(1984)
J. Victor Lopez
10(1979); MEGAFORCE(1982); DEADLY FORCE(1983)
Joaquin Lopez
1984
YELLOW HAIR AND THE FORTRESS OF GOLD(1984)
Joe Lopez
NORSEMAN, THE(1978)
John Lopez
PROFESSIONALS, THE(1966)
John S. Lopez
Silents
OUT OF THE PAST(1927), w
Misc. Silents
SINS OF THE CHILDREN(1918), d; DEVIL'S CONFESSION, THE(1921), d; WHY NOT MARRY?(1922), d
Jose Lopez
STRANGE LADY IN TOWN(1955); VILLA!(1958); MAIDEN, THE(1961, Fr.)
Jose Antonio Lopez
MERCENARY, THE(1970, Ital./Span.)
Julio Lopez
CREATURE FROM THE BLACK LAGOON(1954)
Lorenzo Lopez
TWO SMART PEOPLE(1946)
Luis Lopez
WIDOWS' NEST(1977, U.S./Span.), cos
Manny Lopez
CHA-CHA-CHA BOOM(1956)
Manuel Lopez
TORRID ZONE(1940); ADVENTURES IN IRAQ(1943); FOR WHOM THE BELL TOLLS(1943); SCREAM IN THE NIGHT(1943); JUBILEE TRAIL(1954); HELL'S ISLAND(1955); MARACAIBO(1958); LA NAVE DE LOS MONSTRUOS(1959, Mex.); DEADLY DUO(1962)
Manuel Villegas Lopez
DESERT WARRIOR(1961 Ital./Span.), w
Marga Lopez
NAZARIN(1968, Mex.)
Mary Lopez
Silents
PAINTED PONIES(1927)
Paul Lopez
RIDERS OF THE ROCKIES(1937); TROPIC HOLIDAY(1938); ARIZONA(1940)
Pedro Lopez
DRUMS O' VOODOO(1934)
Pepe Lopez
BRAVE BULLS, THE(1951)
Perry Lopez
DRUM BEAT(1954); JUBILEE TRAIL(1954); BATTLE FLAME(1955); I DIED A THOUSAND TIMES(1955); LONE RANGER, THE(1955); MC CONNELL STORY, THE(1955); MISTER ROBERTS(1955); HELL ON FRISCO BAY(1956); STEEL JUNGLE, THE(1956); YOUNG GUNS, THE(1956); OMAR KHAYYAM(1957); DEEP SIX, THE(1958); VIOLENT ROAD(1958); CRY TOUGH(1959); FLAMING STAR(1960); MANTRAP(1961); TARAS BULBA(1962); MC LINTOCK!(1963); RARE BREED, THE(1966); BANDOLERO!(1968); DARING GAME(1968); SOL MADRID(1968); CHE!(1969); KELLY'S HEROES(1970, U.S./Yugo.); LADY ICE(1973); CHINATOWN(1974)
Primo Lopez
OUT OF THE PAST(1947)
Priscilla Lopez
CHEAPER TO KEEP HER(1980)
Rafael Lopez
DIME WITH A HALO(1963); REWARD, THE(1965); TRACKDOWN(1976)
Rafael E. Lopez
WALK PROUD(1979)
Raphael Lopez
YOUNG SAVAGES, THE(1961)
Raymond Lopez
GIRL FROM HAVANA, THE(1929)
Rico Lopez
GUNS FOR SAN SEBASTIAN(1968, U.S./Fr./Mex./Ital.)
Ronnie A. Lopez
1984
KILLPOINT(1984)
Rose Marie Lopez
HOMESTRETCH, THE(1947); RIDE THE PINK HORSE(1947); MEXICAN HAYRIDE(1948)
Rosemary Lopez
WITHOUT RESERVATIONS(1946)
Sal Lopez
ZOOT SUIT(1981)
Santiago Lopez
1984
BIZET'S CARMEN(1984, Fr./Ital.)
Severo Lopez
CARNIVAL IN COSTA RICA(1947)
Soledad Lopez
HATCHET FOR A HONEYMOON(1969, Span./Ital.), ed
Sylvia Lopez
HERCULES UNCHAINED(1960, Ital./Fr.); HEROD THE GREAT(1960, Ital.); SON OF THE RED CORSAIR(1963, Ital.); MORALIST, THE(1964, Ital.)

Trini Lopez
MARRIAGE ON THE ROCKS(1965); POPPY IS ALSO A FLOWER, THE(1966); DIRTY DOZEN, THE(1967, Brit.); PHYNX, THE(1970)
Sergio Lopez-Cal
FAN, THE(1981)
Humberto Lopez-Pineda
RETURN OF A MAN CALLED HORSE, THE(1976)
Jorge Lopez-Portillo
FIVE BOLD WOMEN(1960), d
Dorian Lopinto
HE KNOWS YOU'RE ALONE(1980)
Lydia Lopokova
DARK RED ROSES(1930, Brit.)
Phil LoPresti
1984
PREPPIES(1984)
Bill Lopresto
WALK PROUD(1979)
P. Lopukhin
Misc. Silents
CHRISTMAS EVE(1913, USSR); VOLGA AND SIBERIA(1914, USSR); NATASHA ROSTOVA(1915, USSR)
Santo Loquasto
SAMMY STOPS THE WORLD zero(1978), set d, cos; SIMON(1980), cos; STARDUST MEMORIES(1980), prod d; FAN, THE(1981), prod d; SO FINE(1981), prod d; MIDSUMMER NIGHT'S SEX COMEDY, A(1982), cos; ZELIG(1983), cos
1984
FALLING IN LOVE(1984), prod d
Franco Loquenzi
HERCULES, SAMSON & ULYSSES(1964, Ital.), set d
Denise Lor
DIARY OF A BACHELOR(1964)
Joan Lora
LURE OF THE SWAMP(1957)
Corine Lorain
NIGHTHAWKS(1981)
Amy Loraine
Silents
DOORSTEPS(1916, Brit.)
Emily Loraine
Silents
CAPTAIN SWIFT(1914)
Louise Loraine
Silents
BABY MINE(1928)
Mr. Loraine
Silents
JUST JIM(1915)
Nita Loraine
CRIMSON CULT, THE(1970, Brit.)
Oscar Loraine
STRICTLY IN THE GROOVE(1942); THIS LAND IS MINE(1943); RHAPSODY IN BLUE(1945)
Philip Loraine
EYE OF THE DEVIL(1967, Brit.), w
Robert Loraine
OUTCAST LADY(1934); FATHER BROWN, DETECTIVE(1935)
Misc. Silents
BENTLEY'S CONSCIENCE(1922, Brit.); S.O.S.(1928, Brit.)
Violet Loraine
BRITANNIA OF BILLINGSGATE(1933, Brit.); ROAD HOUSE(1934, Brit.)
Auric Lorand
THE BEACHCOMBER(1955, Brit.); PORT AFRIQUE(1956, Brit.)
M.E. Lorange
PROMISES IN THE DARK(1979)
Gail Lorber
HOT TIMES(1974)
Steve Lorber
RAINBOW OVER THE RANGE(1940)
Alberto Lorca
NAKED MAJA, THE(1959, Ital./U.S.), ch
Federico Garcia Lorca
BLOOD WEDDING(1981, Sp.), w
Nana Lorca
PROUD AND THE DAMNED, THE(1972)
Luciano Lorcas
CONFESSIONS OF A POLICE CAPTAIN(1971, Ital.)
Theodore Lorch
SHOW BOAT(1929); RUNAWAY BRIDE(1930); WHOOPEE(1930); HONOR OF THE MOUNTED(1932); TENDERFOOT, THE(1932); TEXAS BAD MAN(1932); FUGITIVE, THE(1933); GALLANT FOOL, THE(1933); JEALOUSY(1934); KID MILLIONS(1934); WE LIVE AGAIN(1934); ANNIE OAKLEY(1935); HIS FIGHTING BLOOD(1935); HOLD'EM YALE(1935); MYSTERIOUS MR. WONG(1935); RECKLESS(1935); RUSTLER'S PARADISE(1935); FLASH GORDON(1936); ROMANCE RIDES THE RANGE(1936); SHOW BOAT(1936); WILDCAT TROOPER(1936); ACES WILD(1937); CHEYENNE RIDES AGAIN(1937); LOST RANCH(1937); ORPHAN OF THE PECOS(1938); PROFESSOR BEWARE(1938); REBELLION(1938); RED RIVER RANGE(1938); STAGECOACH(1939); LADY IN QUESTION, THE(1940)
Misc. Talkies
EVIL EYE OF KALINOR, THE(1934); GUNFIRE(1935); TONTO KID, THE(1935)
Silents
LAST OF THE MOHICANS, THE(1920); GASOLINE GUS(1921); WESTBOUND(1924); MAN ON THE BOX, THE(1925); ACROSS THE PACIFIC(1926); BETTER 'OLE, THE(1926); GINSBERG THE GREAT(1927); KING OF KINGS, THE(1927); SAILOR IZZY MURPHY(1927); ROYAL RIDER, THE(1929); WILD BLOOD(1929)
Misc. Silents
ONCE IN A LIFETIME(1925); BLACK JACK(1927); CANYON OF ADVENTURE, THE(1928)

E.P. Lorchagima-Alexandrovskaya
Misc. Silents
CHILDREN OF THE NEW DAY(1930, USSR)
Albert Lord
FRANCES(1982)
Anthony Lord
YOU SAID A MOUTHFUL(1932)
Arline Lord
ROMANCE OF SEVILLE, A(1929, Brit.), w
Barbara Lord
BLOODY BROOD, THE(1959, Can.)
Basil Lord
MISS PILGRIM'S PROGRESS(1950, Brit.); NIGHT WE GOT THE BIRD, THE(1961, Brit.); TERROR FROM UNDER THE HOUSE(1971, Brit.)
Beatrice Lord
GUNS(1980, Fr.)
Bill Lord
1984
LISTEN TO THE CITY(1984, Can.)
Billy Lord
PENROD AND SAM(1931); TOGETHER AGAIN(1944); MY FOOLISH HEART(1949)
Byron Lord
IN THE YEAR 2889(1966); MARS NEEDS WOMEN(1966)
Carleen Lord
SONG FOR TOMORROW, A(1948, Brit.)
Chad Stuart Lord
JUNGLE BOOK, THE(1967)
David Lord
JOHNNY TROUBLE(1957), w
Del Lord
BARNUM WAS RIGHT(1929), d; TRAPPED BY TELEVISION(1936), d; WHAT PRICE VENGEANCE?(1937), d; KANSAS CITY KITTY(1944), d; SHE'S A SWEETHEART(1944), d; BLONDE FROM BROOKLYN(1945), d; HIT THE HAY(1945), d; I LOVE A BANDLEADER(1945), d; LET'S GO STEADY(1945), d; ROUGH, TOUGH AND READY(1945), d; IN FAST COMPANY(1946), d; IT'S GREAT TO BE YOUNG(1946), d; SINGIN' IN THE CORN(1946), d
Misc. Silents
LOST AT THE FRONT(1927), d; TOPSY AND EVA(1927), d
Derek Lord
BLACK WINDMILL, THE(1974, Brit.); CONFESSIONS OF A WINDOW CLEANER(1974, Brit.)
Doug Lord
TOUGH ENOUGH(1983)
Fred Lord
MR. WINKLE GOES TO WAR(1944)
Gayle Lord
COLT COMRADES(1943)
Grace Lord
Silents
SOULS AFLAME(1928)
Misc. Silents
FAGASA(1928)
Jack Lord
CRY MURDER(1936); PROJECT X(1949); COURT-MARTIAL OF BILLY MITCHELL, THE(1955); VAGABOND KING, THE(1956); TIP ON A DEAD JOCKEY(1957); GOD'S LITTLE ACRE(1958); MAN OF THE WEST(1958); TRUE STORY OF LYNN STUART, THE(1958); HANGMAN, THE(1959); WALK LIKE A DRAGON(1960); DR. NO(1962, Brit.); RIDE TO HANGMAN'S TREE, THE(1967); COUNTERFEIT KILLER, THE(1968); NAME OF THE GAME IS KILL, THE(1968)
Jean Claude Lord
VISITING HOURS(1982, Can.), d, ed
Jean-Claude Lord
TROUBLE-FETE(1964, Can.), p, w
1984
COVERGIRL(1984, Can.), d
Jeff Lord
PUTNEY SWOPE(1969)
Jon Lord
LAST REBEL, THE(1971), m
Justine Lord
LIVE NOW–PAY LATER(1962, Brit.); WAR LOVER, THE(1962, U.S./Brit.); MANIAC(1963, Brit.); RING OF SPIES(1964, Brit.); TAMAHINE(1964, Brit.); ACT OF MURDER(1965, Brit.); INCIDENT AT MIDNIGHT(1966, Brit.); CARNABY, M.D.(1967, Brit.); DEADLIER THAN THE MALE(1967, Brit.); MISTER TEN PERCENT(1967, Brit.); NIGHT AFTER NIGHT AFTER NIGHT(1970, Brit.)
Leon Lord
LONELY TRAIL, THE(1936)
Louis Lord
HEAVEN IS ROUND THE CORNER(1944, Brit.); IF THIS BE SIN(1950, Brit.)
Louise Lord
WELCOME, MR. WASHINGTON(1944, Brit.); HER MAN GILBEY(1949, Brit.)
Marion Lord
BROADWAY(1929); ONE HEAVENLY NIGHT(1931); GIRL FROM MISSOURI, THE(1934); STRAIGHT FROM THE HEART(1935)
Marjorie Lord
BORDER CAFE(1937); FORTY NAUGHTY GIRLS(1937); HIDEAWAY(1937); HIGH FLYERS(1937); ON AGAIN–OFF AGAIN(1937); MIDDLETON FAMILY AT THE N.Y. WORLD'S FAIR(1939); ABOUT FACE(1942); ESCAPE FROM HONG KONG(1942); MOONLIGHT IN HAVANA(1942); TIMBER(1942); FLESH AND FANTASY(1943); HI, BUDDY(1943); JOHNNY COME LATELY(1943); SHANTYTOWN(1943); SHERLOCK HOLMES IN WASHINGTON(1943); NEW ORLEANS(1947); ARGYLE SECRETS, THE(1948); STRANGE MRS. CRANE, THE(1948); AIR HOSTESS(1949); MASKED RAIDERS(1949); CHAIN GANG(1950); LOST VOLCANO, THE(1950); RIDING HIGH(1950); STOP THAT CAB(1951); BLADES OF THE MUSKETEERS(1953); DOWN LAREDO WAY(1953); MEXICAN MANHUNT(1953); REBEL CITY(1953); PORT OF HELL(1955); THUNDER OVER SANGOLAND(1955); BOY, DID I GET A WRONG NUMBER!(1966)

Martin Lord
JANIE(1944)
Mary Lord
VALLEY OF DECISION, THE(1945); HOODLUM SAINT, THE(1946)
Mildred Lord
BIG BLUFF, THE(1955), w
Mindret Lord
GLASS ALIBI, THE(1946), w; STRANGE IMPERSONATION(1946), w; YANKEE FAKIR(1947), w; SAINTED SISTERS, THE(1948), w; ALIAS NICK BEAL(1949), w; VIRGIN QUEEN, THE(1955), w
Nora Lord
KING, MURRAY(1969)
Olga Lord
PEPE LE MOKO(1937, Fr.)
Pauline Lord
MRS. WIGGS OF THE CABBAGE PATCH(1934); FEATHER IN HER HAT, A(1935)
Peter Lord
CAESAR AND CLEOPATRA(1946, Brit.); NEXT OF KIN(1983, Aus.)
Philip Lord
CALL NORTHSIDE 777(1948)
Phillips H. Lord
WAY BACK HOME(1932); MR. DISTRICT ATTORNEY(1941), w; MR. DISTRICT ATTORNEY(1946), w; DAVID HARDING, COUNTERSPY(1950), w; GANG BUSTERS(1955), w
Misc. Talkies
OBEAH(1935)
Mrs. Phillips Lord
WAY BACK HOME(1932)
Pierre Lord
ROYAL AFFAIRS IN VERSAILLES(1957, Fr.)
Rene Lord
MY UNCLE(1958, Fr.)
Robert Lord
LION AND THE MOUSE, THE(1928), w; MY MAN(1928), w; ON TRIAL(1928), w; WOMEN THEY TALK ABOUT(1928), w; AVIATOR, THE(1929), w; GOLD DIGGERS OF BROADWAY(1929), w; HARDBOILED ROSE(1929), w; KID GLOVES(1929), w; MILLION DOLLAR COLLAR, THE(1929), w; NO DEFENSE(1929), w; ON WITH THE SHOW(1929), w; SAP, THE(1929), w; SO LONG LETTY(1929), w; SONNY BOY(1929), w; TIME, THE PLACE AND THE GIRL, THE(1929), w; HOLD EVERYTHING(1930), w; BIG BUSINESS GIRL(1931), w; FINGER POINTS, THE(1931), w; FIVE STAR FINAL(1931), w; HER MAJESTY LOVE(1931), w; LITTLE CAESAR(1931), w; LOCAL BOY MAKES GOOD(1931), p, w; MANHATTAN PARADE(1931), w; RECKLESS HOUR, THE(1931), w; RULING VOICE, THE(1931), d; CONQUERORS, THE(1932), w; FIREMAN, SAVE MY CHILD(1932), w; IT'S TOUGH TO BE FAMOUS(1932), w; MAN WANTED(1932), w; ONE WAY PASSAGE(1932), w; PURCHASE PRICE, THE(1932), w; SO BIG(1932), w; WINNER TAKE ALL(1932), w; YOU SAID A MOUTHFUL(1932), w; COLLEGE COACH(1933), p; CONVENTION CITY(1933), w; FRISCO JENNY(1933), w; GOLD DIGGERS OF 1933(1933), p; HARD TO HANDLE(1933), w; HAVANA WIDOWS(1933), p; HEROES FOR SALE(1933), w; LITTLE GIANT, THE(1933), w; MARY STEVENS, M.D.(1933), w; MIND READER, THE(1933), w; WORLD CHANGES, THE(1933), p; 20,000 YEARS IN SING SING(1933), p; w; DAMES(1934), w; FLIRTATION WALK(1934), p; FOG OVER FRISCO(1934), p; HE WAS HER MAN(1934), w; HOUSEWIFE(1934), w; JIMMY THE GENT(1934), p; MAN WITH TWO FACES, THE(1934), p; MERRY WIVES OF RENO, THE(1934), p, w; UPPER WORLD(1934), p; VERY HONORABLE GUY, A(1934), p; WONDER BAR(1934), b; BLACK FURY(1935), p; BORDERTOWN(1935), p, w; DR. SOCRATES(1935), p, w; GOLD DIGGERS OF 1935(1935), w; OIL FOR THE LAMPS OF CHINA(1935), p; PAGE MISS GLORY(1935), w; COLLEEN(1936), w; SINGING KID, THE(1936), p, w; STAGE STRUCK(1936), p, w; BLACK LEGION, THE(1937), p, w; THAT CERTAIN WOMAN(1937), p; TOVARICH(1937), p; AMAZING DR. CLITTERHOUSE, THE(1938), p; BROTHER RAT(1938), p; DAWN PATROL, THE(1938), p; WOMEN ARE LIKE THAT(1938), p; CONFESSIONS OF A NAZI SPY(1939), p; DODGE CITY(1939), p; ON YOUR TOES(1939), p; BROTHER RAT AND A BABY(1940), p; LETTER, THE(1940), p; 'TIL WE MEET AGAIN(1940), w; FOOTSTEPS IN THE DARK(1941), p; SHINING VICTORY(1941), p; WINGS FOR THE EAGLE(1942), p; HIGH WALL, THE(1947), p; AND BABY MAKES THREE(1949), p; KNOCK ON ANY DOOR(1949), p; TOKYO JOE(1949), p; IN A LONELY PLACE(1950), p; FAMILY SECRET, THE(1951), p; SIROCCO(1951), p; PICTURES(1982, New Zealand), w
Silents
LUCKY HORSESHOE, THE(1925), w; JOHNSTOWN FLOOD, THE(1926), w; TONY RUNS WILD(1926), w; IF I WERE SINGLE(1927), w; SWELL-HEAD, THE(1927), w; MATINEE IDOL, THE(1928), w; POWDER MY BACK(1928), w
Rosemary Lord
DEADLY AFFAIR, THE(1967, Brit.); DR. JEKYLL AND SISTER HYDE(1971, Brit.)
Ruth Lord
Silents
NOOSE, THE(1928)
Stephen Lord
TARZAN AND THE JUNGLE BOY(1968, US/Switz.), w; BEYOND AND BACK(1978), w; FALL OF THE HOUSE OF USHER, THE(1980), w
Steve Lord
NEW ORLEANS AFTER DARK(1958)
Walter Lord
NIGHT TO REMEMBER, A(1958, Brit.), w
Lord Flea and his Calypsonians
CALYPSO JOE(1957)
Athena Lorde
FIRECREEK(1968); ANGEL IN MY POCKET(1969); HOW TO FRAME A FIGG(1971); FUZZ(1972); MECHANIC, THE(1972); DOCTOR DEATH: SEEKER OF SOULS(1973)
Colden Lore
Silents
ALL SORTS AND CONDITIONS OF MEN(1921, Brit.), w
Tony Lorea
FIVE THE HARD WAY(1969); BAD CHARLESTON CHARLIE(1973); WONDER WOMEN(1973, Phil.)
Misc. Talkies
SUPERCOCK(1975); SMOKEY AND THE HOTWIRE GANG(1980)

Al Loring
Silents
SHACKLES OF GOLD(1922)
Alfred Loring
Misc. Silents
STRUGGLE, THE(1916)
Ann Loring
ABSOLUTE QUIET(1936); ROBIN HOOD OF EL DORADO(1936)
Cleo Loring
Silents
KINKAID, GAMBLER(1916)
David Loring
READY FOR LOVE(1934)
Eugene Loring
NATIONAL VELVET(1944); YOLANDA AND THE THIEF(1945), ch; ZIEGFELD FOLLIES(1945), a, w; THRILL OF BRAZIL, THE(1946), ch; FIESTA(1947), ch; MEXICAN HAYRIDE(1948), ch; TOAST OF NEW ORLEANS, THE(1950), ch; MARK OF THE RENEGADE(1951), ch; GOLDEN BLADE, THE(1953), ch; TORCH SONG(1953); VEILS OF BAGDAD, THE(1953), ch; 5,000 FINGERS OF DR. T. THE(1953), ch; DEEP IN MY HEART(1954), ch; MEET ME IN LAS VEGAS(1956), ch; FUNNY FACE(1957), ch; SILK STOCKINGS(1957), ch; PEPE(1960), ch
Frantisek Loring
DO YOU KEEP A LION AT HOME?(1966, Czech.); TRANSPORT FROM PARADISE(1967, Czech.)
Hope Loring
INTERFERENCE(1928), w; PARIS(1929), w; THIS IS HEAVEN(1929), w; FATHER'S SON(1931), w
Silents
CABARET GIRL, THE(1919), w; BEAUTIFUL GAMBLER, THE(1921), w; PAID BACK(1922), w; SHADOWS(1922), w; THORNS AND ORANGE BLOSSOMS(1922), w; APRIL SHOWERS(1923), w; BOY OF MINE(1923), w; DON'T MARRY FOR MONEY(1923), w; EAST SIDE–WEST SIDE(1923), w; MONEY! MONEY! MONEY!(1923), w; PENROD AND SAM(1923), w; VIRGINIAN, THE(1923), w; HELEN'S BABIES(1924), w; K–THE UNKNOWN(1924), w; LULLABY, THE(1924), w; HIS SECRETARY(1925), w; LITTLE ANNIE ROONEY(1925), w; RANGER OF THE BIG PINES(1925), w; BLIND GODDESS, THE(1926), w; CAT'S PAJAMAS, THE(1926), w; RAINMAKER, THE(1926), w; CHILDREN OF DIVORCE(1927), w; IT(1927), w; MY BEST GIRL(1927), w; WE'RE ALL GAMBLERS(1927), w; WINGS(1927), w; WOMAN ON TRIAL, THE(1927), w; FOUR FEATHERS(1929), w
Jane Loring
SATURDAY NIGHT KID, THE(1929), ed; ANYBODY'S WOMAN(1930), ed; LIGHT OF WESTERN STARS, THE(1930), ed; POINTED HEELS(1930), ed; GANG BUSTER, THE(1931), ed; HER BODYGUARD(1933), ed; WHITE WOMAN(1933), w; GOOD DAME(1934), ed; ALICE ADAMS(1935), ed; MARY OF SCOTLAND(1936), ed; SYLVIA SCARLETT(1936), ed
Silents
AVALANCHE(1928), ed; SUNSET PASS(1929), ed
Joan Loring
LOST MOMENT, THE(1947)
John Loring
GORGO(1961, Brit.), w
John R. Loring
KENNER(1969), w
June Loring
THIRTY-DAY PRINCESS(1934), ed
Ken Loring
WARKILL(1968, U.S./Phil.)
Lotte Loring
Misc. Silents
HER GREATEST BLUFF(1927, Ger.)
Luke J. Loring
Silents
FORGIVEN, OR THE JACK O'DIAMONDS(1914)
Lynn Loring
SPLENDOR IN THE GRASS(1961); PRESSURE POINT(1962); JOURNEY TO THE FAR SIDE OF THE SUN(1969, Brit.); MR. MOM(1983), p
Marjorie Loring
KNOWING MEN(1930, Brit.); NOT SO QUIET ON THE WESTERN FRONT(1930, Brit.); PRICE OF THINGS, THE(1930, Brit.)
Michael Loring
FLYING HOSTESS(1936); POSTAL INSPECTOR(1936); YELLOWSTONE(1936); BREEZING HOME(1937); WINGS OVER HONOLULU(1937)
Mike Loring
GROUND ZERO(1973)
Nancy Loring
SABOTEUR(1942)
Pauline Loring
WARNING TO WANTONS, A(1949, Brit.); I'VE GOTTA HORSE(1965, Brit.)
Phyllis Loring
MIDDLE WATCH, THE(1930, Brit.); MY FRIEND THE KING(1931, Brit.)
Ray Loring
RUBY(1971), w, m
Richard Loring
OH! WHAT A LOVELY WAR(1969, Brit.); MY WAY(1974, South Africa); KILLER FORCE(1975, Switz./Ireland)
Misc. Talkies
SUPER-JOCKS, THE(1980)
Teala Loring
BLUEBEARD(1944); DELINQUENT DAUGHTERS(1944); ALLOTMENT WIVES, INC.(1945); BLACK MARKET BABIES(1946); BOWERY BOMBSHELL(1946); DARK ALIBI(1946); GAS HOUSE KIDS(1946); PARTNERS IN TIME(1946); WIFE WANTED(1946); FALL GUY(1947); HARD BOILED MAHONEY(1947); ARIZONA COWBOY, THE(1950)
Misc. Talkies
RIDING THE CALIFORNIA TRAIL(1947)
Thomas Z. Loring
THRU DIFFERENT EYES(1942), d; WHO IS HOPE SCHUYLER?(1942), d; HE HIRED THE BOSS(1943), d

Loriot
MY UNCLE(1958, Fr.)
Noelle Loriot
NO TIME FOR BREAKFAST(1978, Fr.), w
Diana Loris
SUPERARGO(1968, Ital./Span.)
Fabien Loris
CRIME OF MONSIEUR LANGE, THE(1936, Fr.); CHILDREN OF PARADISE(1945, Fr.)
Janine Loris
CRIME OF MONSIEUR LANGE, THE(1936, Fr.)
Joyce Lorme
HAPPY DAYS(1930)
Jon Lormer
GIRLS ON THE LOOSE(1958); MATCHMAKER, THE(1958); RALLY 'ROUND THE FLAG, BOYS!(1958); ONE MAN'S WAY(1964); ZEBRA IN THE KITCHEN(1965); DIMENSION 5(1966); FINE MADNESS, A(1966); IF HE HOLLERS, LET HIM GO(1968); LEARNING TREE, THE(1969); GETTING STRAIGHT(1970); DOCTORS' WIVES(1971); ROOSTER COGBURN(1975); BOOGENS, THE(1982)
Constance Lorne
ONE WILD OAT(1951, Brit.); CURTAIN UP(1952, Brit.); SEVERED HEAD, A(1971, Brit.)
Marion Lorne
STRANGERS ON A TRAIN(1951); GIRL RUSH, THE(1955); GRADUATE, THE(1967)
Jon Lorner
CREEPSHOW(1982)
Hedda Lornie
1984
FOURTH MAN, THE(1984, Neth.)
George Loros
GANG THAT COULDN'T SHOOT STRAIGHT, THE(1971); W.C. FIELDS AND ME(1976); ON THE NICKEL(1980)
Peter Lorr
TORN CURTAIN(1966)
Francoise Lorrain
HOA-BINH(1971, Fr.), w
Amy Lorraine
Silents
ALONE IN LONDON(1915, Brit.); GREAT ADVENTURE, THE(1915, Brit.); MY OLD DUTCH(1915, Brit.); AYLWIN(1920, Brit.)
Betty Lorraine
BEDTIME STORY, A(1933); SOULS AT SEA(1937)
Silents
RED WINE(1928)
Emily Lorraine
Misc. Silents
PAY DAY(1918); GAY OLD DOG, THE(1919)
Guido Lorraine
ONE WOMAN'S STORY(1949, Brit.); ENCORE(1951, Brit.); GREAT MANHUNT, THE(1951, Brit.); HOTEL SAHARA(1951, Brit.); MR. POTTS GOES TO MOSCOW(1953, Brit.); SAILOR OF THE KING(1953, Brit.); VILLAGE, THE(1953, Brit./Switz.); DETECTIVE, THE(1954, Qit.); PARATROOPER(1954, Brit.); GENTLEMEN MARRY BRUNETTES(1955); THEY CAN'T HANG ME(1955, Brit.); ABOVE US THE WAVES(1956, Brit.); LOSER TAKES ALL(1956, Brit.); PORT AFRIQUE(1956, Brit.); BREAK IN THE CIRCLE, THE(1957, Brit.); CITY AFTER MIDNIGHT(1957, Brit.); GREAT VAN ROBBERY, THE(1963, Brit.)
Harriet Lorraine
BITTER TEA OF GENERAL YEN, THE(1933)
Harry Lorraine
Silents
IF THOU WERT BLIND(1917, Brit.); KISMET(1920); LAST OF THE MOHICANS, THE(1920); HUNCH, THE(1921); LAVENDER BATH LADY, THE(1922); LITTLE EVA ASCENDS(1922); SLAVE OF DESIRE(1923)
Misc. Silents
STOLEN HEIRLOOMS, THE(1915, Brit.); WIRELESS(1915, Brit.), a, d; BIG MONEY(1918, Brit.), d; FURTHER EXPLOITS OF SEXTON BLAKE, THE - MYSTERY OF THE S.S. OLYMPIC, THE(1919, Brit.), d; LADS OF THE VILLAGE, THE(1919, Brit.), d; WOMAN AND OFFICER 26, THE(1920, Brit.), a, d; DON'T WRITE LETTERS(1922); UNTO EACH OTHER(1929, Brit.)
Jean Lorraine
WILD PARTY, THE(1929); WORDS AND MUSIC(1929); GREAT DIVIDE, THE(1930); MILDRED PIERCE(1945)
Keith Lorraine
FALL OF THE HOUSE OF USHER, THE(1952, Brit.)
Leota Lorraine
RUGGLES OF RED GAP(1935); YOUNGEST PROFESSION, THE(1943); THEY WERE EXPENDABLE(1945); NIGHT AND DAY(1946); NOTORIOUS(1946); SEA OF GRASS, THE(1947); SHAKEDOWN(1950); IMITATION OF LIFE(1959)
Silents
KAISER'S SHADOW, THE(1918); PLAYING THE GAME(1918); PEST, THE(1919); HER FIVE-FOOT HIGHNESS(1920)
Misc. Silents
MARTINACHE MARRIAGE, THE(1917); DAUGHTER OF THE WEST, A(1918); DESERT LAW(1918); HER AMERICAN HUSBAND(1918); LUCK IN PAWN(1919); TURNING POINT, THE(1920); BOWERY BISHOP, THE(1924); WOMAN I LOVE, THE(1929)
Lillian Lorraine
Silents
SHOULD A WIFE FORGIVE?(1915)
Louise Lorraine
MOUNTED STRANGER, THE(1930); NEAR THE RAINBOW'S END(1930)
Misc. Talkies
BEYOND THE LAW(1930)
Silents
ALTAR STAIRS, THE(1922); BORROWED FINERY(1925); WILD GIRL, THE(1925); BLUE STREAK, THE(1926); EXIT SMILING(1926); SHADOWS OF THE NIGHT(1928)
Misc. Silents
FIRE EATER, THE(1921); UP IN THE AIR ABOUT MARY(1922); GENTLEMAN FROM AMERICA, THE(1923); MCGUIRE OF THE MOUNTED(1923); PALS(1925); THREE IN EXILE(1925); VERDICT, THE(1925); SILENT GUARDIAN, THE(1926);

STOLEN RANCH, THE(1926); HARD FISTS(1927); LEGIONNAIRES IN PARIS(1927); ROOKIES(1927); CHINATOWN CHARLIE(1928); CIRCUS ROOKIES(1928); WRIGHT IDEA, THE(1928)

Marie Lorraine
TWO MINUTES' SILENCE(1934, Brit.)

Nita Lorraine
VIKING QUEEN, THE(1967, Brit.); ALL NEAT IN BLACK STOCKINGS(1969, Brit.)

Ola Lorraine
HIGHER AND HIGHER(1943); WOMAN'S VENGEANCE, A(1947); KISS THE BLOOD OFF MY HANDS(1948); MR. PEABODY AND THE MERMAID(1948); MISS GRANT TAKES RICHMOND(1949); SON OF DR. JEKYLL, THE(1951); MY COUSIN RACHEL(1952)

Oscar Lorraine
ONCE UPON A HONEYMOON(1942); TO HAVE AND HAVE NOT(1944); GILDA(1946)

Philip Lorraine
BREAK IN THE CIRCLE, THE(1957, Brit.), w

Robert Lorraine
PERFECT ALIBI, THE(1931, Brit.); LIMEHOUSE BLUES(1934); MARIE GALANTE(1934); MILDRED PIERCE(1945)

Robert L. Lorraine
CASBAH(1948)

Robert Locke Lorraine
THREE RING CIRCUS(1954)

Tui Lorraine
THIN MAN, THE(1934)

Lorraine and Rognan
FLEET'S IN, THE(1942)

Betty Lorraise
PALMY DAYS(1931)

Ruth Lorran
PAN-AMERICANA(1945)

Vyvyan Lorrayne
1984
TOP SECRET!(1984)

Lolita Lorre
1984
SCREAM FOR HELP(1984)

Peter Lorre
BOMBARDMENT OF MONTE CARLO, THE(1931, Ger.); JAZZBAND FIVE, THE(1932, Ger.); TRUNKS OF MR. O.F., THE(1932, Ger.); WHITE DEMON, THE(1932, Ger.); F.P. 1 DOESN'T ANSWER(1933, Ger.); FROM TOP TO BOTTOM(1933, Fr.); INVISIBLE OPPONENT(1933, Ger.); M(1933, Ger.); WHAT WOMEN DREAM(1933, Ger.); SHOT AT DAWN, A(1934, Ger.); CRIME AND PUNISHMENT(1935); MAD LOVE(1935); MAN WHO KNEW TOO MUCH, THE(1935, Brit.); SECRET AGENT, THE(1936, Brit.); CRACK-UP, THE(1937); LANCER SPY(1937); NANCY STEELE IS MISSING(1937); THANK YOU, MR. MOTO(1937); THINK FAST, MR. MOTO(1937); I'LL GIVE A MILLION(1938); MR. MOTO TAKES A CHANCE(1938); MR. MOTO TAKES A VACATION(1938); MR. MOTO'S GAMBLE(1938); MYSTERIOUS MR. MOTO(1938); MR. MOTO IN DANGER ISLAND(1939); MR. MOTO'S LAST WARNING(1939); I WAS AN ADVENTURESS(1940); ISLAND OF DOOMED MEN(1940); STRANGE CARGO(1940); STRANGER ON THE THIRD FLOOR(1940); YOU'LL FIND OUT(1940); FACE BEHIND THE MASK, THE(1941); MALTESE FALCON, THE(1941); MR. DISTRICT ATTORNEY(1941); THEY MET IN BOMBAY(1941); ALL THROUGH THE NIGHT(1942); BOOGIE MAN WILL GET YOU, THE(1942); CASABLANCA(1942); IN THIS OUR LIFE(1942); INVISIBLE AGENT(1942); BACKGROUND TO DANGER(1943); CONSTANT NYMPH, THE(1943); CROSS OF LORRAINE, THE(1943); ARSENIC AND OLD LACE(1944); CONSPIRATORS, THE(1944); HOLLYWOOD CANTEEN(1944); MASK OF DIMITRIOS, THE(1944); PASSAGE TO MARSEILLE(1944); CONFIDENTIAL AGENT(1945); HOTEL BERLIN(1945); BEAST WITH FIVE FINGERS, THE(1946); BLACK ANGEL(1946); CHASE, THE(1946); THREE STRANGERS(1946); VERDICT, THE(1946); MY FAVORITE BRUNETTE(1947); CASBAH(1948); ROPE OF SAND(1949); QUICKSAND(1950); LOST ONE, THE(1951, Ger.), a, d, w; BEAT THE DEVIL(1953); DOUBLE CONFESSION(1953, Brit.); 20,000 LEAGUES UNDER THE SEA(1954); AROUND THE WORLD IN 80 DAYS(1956); CONGO CROSSING(1956); MEET ME IN LAS VEGAS(1956); BUSTER KEATON STORY, THE(1957); HELL SHIP MUTINY(1957); SAD SACK, THE(1957); SILK STOCKINGS(1957); STORY OF MANKIND, THE(1957); BIG CIRCUS, THE(1959); SCENT OF MYSTERY(1960); VOYAGE TO THE BOTTOM OF THE SEA(1961); FIVE WEEKS IN A BALLOON(1962); TALES OF TERROR(1962); RAVEN, THE(1963); COMEDY OF TERRORS, THE(1964); MUSCLE BEACH PARTY(1964); PATSY, THE(1964)

Peter Lorre, Jr.
FRASIER, THE SENSUOUS LION(1973)

Vivi Lorre
1984
MEATBALLS PART II(1984)

John Lorrell
PROJECT M7(1953, Brit.)

Jose Maria E. Lorrieta
WITCH WITHOUT A BROOM, A(1967, U.S./Span.), w

Elsa Lorrimer
Silents
JUNGLE CHILD, THE(1916)

Enid Lorrimer
COUNT OF TWELVE(1955, Brit.)

Louise Lorrimer
GLASS MENAGERIE, THE(1950)

Shirley Lorrimer
YOU KNOW WHAT SAILORS ARE(1954, Brit.)

Joan Lorring
BRIDGE OF SAN LUIS REY, THE(1944); CORN IS GREEN, THE(1945); THREE STRANGERS(1946); VERDICT, THE(1946); GANGSTER, THE(1947); OTHER LOVE, THE(1947); GOOD SAM(1948); BIG NIGHT, THE(1951); STRANGER ON THE PROWL(1953, Ital.); MIDNIGHT MAN, THE(1974)

Lotte Lorring
Misc. Silents
DANGERS OF THE ENGAGEMENT PERIOD(1929, Ger.)

Marianna Lors
JOY(1983, Fr./Can.)

Rene Lorsay
Misc. Silents
RAMUNTCHO(1919, Fr.)

Alexandra Lorska
1984
AMERICAN DREAMER(1984)

Richard Lortz
VOICES(1973, Brit.), w

Eddie LoRusso
SLAUGHTER(1972); SLAUGHTER'S BIG RIP-OFF(1973); HOW COME NOBODY'S ON OUR SIDE?(1975)

Jacques Lory
MERRY WIDOW, THE(1934); ROAD TO GLORY, THE(1936); CAFE METROPOLE(1937); FIREFLY, THE(1937); I MET HIM IN PARIS(1937); KING AND THE CHORUS GIRL, THE(1937); MAYTIME(1937); FOOLS FOR SCANDAL(1938); MARIE ANTOINETTE(1938); SUEZ(1938); FIGHTING 69TH, THE(1940); LEOPARD MAN, THE(1943); PARIS AFTER DARK(1943); FALCON IN HOLLYWOOD, THE(1944); CORNERED(1945)

Jeanne Lory
BIZARRE BIZARRE(1939, Fr.)

Robin Lory
GIDGET GOES HAWAIIAN(1961)

Denise Lorys
Silents
LIFE(1928, Brit.)
Misc. Silents
LA MORT DU SOLEIL(1922, Fr.); PEAU DE PECHE(1929, Fr.)

Diana Lorys
AWFUL DR. ORLOFF, THE(1964, Span./Fr.); BACKFIRE(1965, Fr.); GUNFIGHTERS OF CASA GRANDE(1965, U.S./Span.); MURIETA(1965, Span.); TEXICAN, THE(1966, U.S./Span.); DEVIL'S MAN, THE(1967, Ital.); LIGHTNING BOLT(1967, Ital./Sp.); VILLA RIDES(1968); BAD MAN'S RIVER(1972, Span.); MALENKA, THE VAMPIRE(1972, Span./Ital.); HOUSE OF PSYCHOTIC WOMEN, THE zero(1973, Span.); CHINO(1976, Ital., Span., Fr.)

Los Angeles Ballet
MAN WHO LOVED WOMEN, THE(1983)

The Los Angeles Dodgers
GEISHA BOY, THE(1958)

The Los Angeles Rams
EASY LIVING(1949); CRAZYLEGS, ALL AMERICAN(1953)

Los Angeles Troop No. 107
MIND YOUR OWN BUSINESS(1937)

Losada
VALDEZ IS COMING(1971)

Candida Losada
HOUSE THAT SCREAMED, THE(1970, Span.); TRISTANA(1970, Span./Ital./Fr.)

Rolf Losansky
FLOWERS FOR THE MAN IN THE MOON(1975, Ger.), d, w

Donald Losby
RAINTREE COUNTY(1957); MATING GAME, THE(1959); REMARKABLE MR. PENNYPACKER, THE(1959); TOWER OF LONDON(1962); CRITIC'S CHOICE(1963); YOUR CHEATIN' HEART(1964); HOW SWEET IT IS(1968)

Vincent Loscalzo
SQUARE ROOT OF ZERO, THE(1964), cos, makeup; DEAR, DEAD DELILAH(1972), makeup

Tilly Losch
GARDEN OF ALLAH, THE(1936); GOOD EARTH, THE(1937); DUEL IN THE SUN(1946), a, ch; SONG OF SCHEHERAZADE(1947), ch

Frank Losee
Silents
ETERNAL CITY, THE(1915); MASQUERADERS, THE(1915); ASHES OF EMBERS(1916); SPIDER, THE(1916); BAB'S BURGLAR(1917); BAB'S DIARY(1917); GREAT EXPECTATIONS(1917); ON THE QUIET(1918); RIDDLE: WOMAN, THE(1920); SUCH A LITTLE QUEEN(1921); MISSING MILLIONS(1922); ORPHANS OF THE STORM(1922); SEVENTH DAY, THE(1922); AS A MAN LIVES(1923)
Misc. Silents
HELENE OF THE NORTH(1915); DIPLOMACY(1916); EVIL THEREOF, THE(1916); HULDA FROM HOLLAND(1916); LESS THAN THE DUST(1916); MISS GEORGE WASHINGTON(1916); MOMENT BEFORE, THE(1916); OLD HOMESTEAD, THE(1916); UNDER COVER(1916); DUMMY, THE(1917); SAPHO(1917); VALENTINE GIRL, THE(1917); IN PURSUIT OF POLLY(1918); LA TOSCA(1918); MADAME JEALOUSY(1918); MRS. DANE'S DEFENSE(1918); REASON WHY, THE(1918); SONG OF SONGS, THE(1918); UNCLE TOM'S CABIN(1918); HIS PARISIAN WIFE(1919); MARIE, LTD.(1919); PAID IN FULL(1919); FEAR MARKET, THE(1920); HALF AN HOUR(1920); LADY ROSE'S DAUGHTER(1920); RIGHT TO LOVE, THE(1920); DANGEROUS TOYS(1921); FALSE FRONTS(1922); MAN SHE BROUGHT BACK, THE(1922); MAN WANTED(1922)

Frank Losee, Jr.
FOUR HOURS TO KILL(1935); ONE HOUR LATE(1935); MURDER WITH PICTURES(1936); HIDEAWAY GIRL(1937)

Harry Losee
SHALL WE DANCE(1937), ch; THIN ICE(1937), ch; YOU CAN'T HAVE EVERYTHING(1937), ch; HAPPY LANDING(1938), ch; SECOND FIDDLE(1939), ch; HIT THE ICE(1943), ch

Richard Losee
CANNONBALL RUN, THE(1981)

Mara Loseff
SKY'S THE LIMIT, THE(1937, Brit.)

Anna Losen
SONG FROM MY HEART, THE(1970, Jap.)

Garvik Losey
AGATHA(1979, Brit.), p

Gavric Losey
LITTLE MALCOLM(1974, Brit.), p

Gavrik Losey
FLAME(1975, Brit.), p; BABYLON(1980, Brit.), p

Joseph Losey
BOY WITH THE GREEN HAIR, THE(1949), d; LAWLESS, THE(1950), d; BIG NIGHT, THE(1951), d, w; M(1951), d; PROWLER, THE(1951), d; TIME WITHOUT PITY(1957, Brit.), d; GYPSY AND THE GENTLEMAN, THE(1958, Brit.), d; CHANCE MEETING(1960, Brit.), d; CONCRETE JUNGLE, THE(1962, Brit.), d; EVA(1962, Fr./Ital.), a, d; KING AND COUNTRY(1964, Brit.), d; SERVANT, THE(1964, Brit.), p, d; THESE ARE THE DAMNED(1965, Brit.), d; MODESTY BLAISE(1966, Brit.), d; ACCIDENT(1967, Brit.), p, d; BOOM!(1968), d; SECRET CEREMONY(1968, Brit.), d; FIGURES IN A LANDSCAPE(1970, Brit.), d; GO-BETWEEN, THE(1971, Brit.), d; ASSASSINATION OF TROTSKY, THE(1972 Fr./Ital.), d; DOLL'S HOUSE, A(1973, Brit.), p&d; GALILEO(1975, Brit.), d, w; ROMANTIC ENGLISHWOMAN, THE(1975, Brit./Fr.), d; MR. KLEIN(1976, Fr.), d; DON GIOVANNI(1979, Fr./Ital./Ger.), d, w; TROUT, THE(1982, Fr.), d, w

Patricia Losey
DON GIOVANNI(1979, Fr./Ital./Ger.), w

Mario Losi
KILLING KIND, THE(1973), ph

Guido Iosia
DRAMA OF THE RICH(1975, Ital./Fr.), art d

Lina Lossen
LIFE BEGINS ANEW(1938, Ger.)

Katia Losser
FICKLE FINGER OF FATE, THE(1967, Span./U.S.)

Larry Lossing
YELLOWNECK(1955), art d

Ed Lossman
SHOOT OUT AT BIG SAG(1962), cos

The Lost Wandering Band
CAN SHE BAKE A CHERRY PIE?(1983)

Sally Loswijk
1984
QUESTION OF SILENCE(1984, Neth.)

Ila Loth
FATHER(1967, Hung.)

Pauline Loth
MR. BUG GOES TO TOWN(1941)

Stanislaw Loth
GUESTS ARE COMING(1965, Pol.), ph

Ernst Lothar
LITTLE FRIEND(1934, Brit.), w; CLAIRVOYANT, THE(1935, Brit.), w; ACT OF MURDER, AN(1948), w

Hanns Lothar
ONE, TWO, THREE(1961); GIRL FROM HONG KONG(1966, Ger.); UNWILLING AGENT(1968, Ger.)

John Lothar
MAXWELL ARCHER, DETECTIVE(1942, Brit.)

Mark Lothar
MARTIN LUTHER(1953), m; AFFAIRS OF DR. HOLL(1954, Ger.), m; FAUST(1963, Ger.), m; DEVIL IN SILK(1968, Ger.), m

Rudolph Lothar
BOUDOIR DIPLOMAT(1930), w; FOLIES DERGERE(1935), w; FACE BEHIND THE SCAR(1940, Brit.), w; THAT NIGHT IN RIO(1941), w; ON THE RIVERA(1951), w

Stanley Lothbury
BELLS GO DOWN, THE(1943, Brit.)

Ralph Lother
CITY OF TORMENT(1950, Ger.)

Elisa Loti
VILLA!(1958); CODE OF SILENCE(1960); CLAUDINE(1974)

Gianni Loti
GIANT OF MARATHON, THE(1960, Ital.); NIGHTS OF LUCRETIA BORGIA, THE(1960, Ital.)

Ernest Lotinga
DR. JOSSER KC(1931, Brit.), p,d&w; LOVE UP THE POLE(1936, Brit.), w

Ernie Lotinga
DR. JOSSER KC(1931, Brit.); P.C. JOSSER(1931, Brit.), a, w; JOSSER IN THE ARMY(1932, Brit.); JOSSER JOINS THE NAVY(1932, Brit.); JOSSER ON THE RIVER(1932, Brit.); JOSSER ON THE FARM(1934, Brit.); SMITH'S WIVES(1935, Brit.); LOVE UP THE POLE(1936, Brit.)

R.W. Lotinga
UNHOLY QUEST, THE(1934, Brit.), d

Dennis Lotis
EXTRA DAY, THE(1956, Brit.); IT'S A WONDERFUL WORLD(1956, Brit.); INBE-TWEEN AGE, THE(1958, Brit.); HORROR HOTEL(1960, Brit.); SWORD OF SHER-WOOD FOREST(1961, Brit.); WHAT EVERY WOMAN WANTS(1962, Brit.); MAID FOR MURDER(1963, Brit.); MAKE MINE A MILLION(1965, Brit.)

Leo Lotito
GETTING STRAIGHT(1970), makeup; STAND UP AND BE COUNTED(1972), make-up; OH, GOD!(1977), makeup

Barbara Lott
THREE SILENT MEN(1940, Brit.); PARTY'S OVER, THE(1966, Brit.); UNMAN, WITTERING AND ZIGO(1971, Brit.)

Dale Lott
ZAPPED!(1982)

Jack Lott
Misc. Silents
MOUNTAIN MADNESS(1920)

Lawrence Lott
1984
PHILADELPHIA EXPERIMENT, THE(1984)

Milton Lott
LAST HUNT, THE(1956), w

Perrie Lott
HAMMER(1972)

Robert Lott
Misc. Talkies
CHAIN GANG WOMEN(1972)

Tina Lottanzi
LOYALTY OF LOVE(1937, Ital.)

Angelo Lotti
RED SHEIK, THE(1963, Ital.), ph; SANDOKAN THE GREAT(1964, Fr./Ital./Span.), ph; BLACK VEIL FOR LISA, A(1969 Ital./Ger.), ph; VENUS IN FURS(1970, Ital./Brit./Ger.), ph

Franco Lotti
CENTO ANNI D'AMORE(1954, Ital.), art d & set d

Mariella Lotti
PIRATES OF CAPRI, THE(1949); HIS LAST TWELVE HOURS(1953, Ital.)

Maso Lotti
HIS LAST TWELVE HOURS(1953, Ital.)

Barclay Lottimer
TOUCHED(1983), p

Eb Lottimer
1984
BREAKIN'(1984)

Evan Lottman
MAN FROM O.R.G.Y., THE(1970), ed; PUZZLE OF A DOWNFALL CHILD(1970), ed; PANIC IN NEEDLE PARK(1971), ed; EFFECT OF GAMMA RAYS ON MAN-IN-THE-MOON MARIGOLDS, THE(1972), ed; EXORCIST, THE(1973), ed; SCARE-CROW(1973), ed; DANDY, THE ALL AMERICAN GIRL(1976), a, ed; ON THE YARD(1978), ed; PILOT, THE(1979), ed; SEDUCTION OF JOE TYNAN, THE(1979), ed; HONEYSUCKLE ROSE(1980), ed; ROLLOVER(1981), ed; SOPHIE'S CHOICE(1982), ed
1984
MUPPETS TAKE MANHATTAN, THE(1984), ed

Claire Lotto
Misc. Silents
MASTER OF BEASTS, THE(1922)

Family Lotus
CATCH MY SOUL(1974)

Patty Lotz
1984
BODY DOUBLE(1984)

Louisiana Lou
WALL STREET COWBOY(1939)

Marie Lou
J'ACCUSE(1939, Fr.)

Louanne
OH GOD! BOOK II(1980)

Patrick Loubert
125 ROOMS OF COMFORT(1974, Can.), d, w

Jean Loubignac
BARBER OF SEVILLE(1949, Fr.), d; PEEK-A-BOO(1961, Fr.), d

Dabket Loubna
MADAME ROSA(1977, Fr.), m

Ralph Loubser
KIMBERLEY JIM(1965, South Africa)

Sophie Loucachevski
PASSION(1983, Fr./Switz.)

Lance Loud
SUBWAY RIDERS(1981)

Sherman Loud
ZELIG(1983)

Colin Loudan
MALTA STORY(1954, Brit.)

Jay Louden
YOUNG GIANTS(1983)

Robert Louden
Misc. Talkies
BURNOUT(1979)

Thomas Louden
HONEYMOON IN BALI(1939); OUR LEADING CITIZEN(1939); SAFARI(1940); VIRGINIA(1941); MRS. MINIVER(1942); PIED PIPER, THE(1942); THIS ABOVE ALL(1942); HOLY MATRIMONY(1943); HOUR BEFORE THE DAWN, THE(1944); JANE EYRE(1944); TWO GIRLS AND A SAILOR(1944); CORN IS GREEN, THE(1945); DANGEROUS PARTNERS(1945); MINISTRY OF FEAR(1945); DARK CORNER, THE(1946); STRANGE LOVE OF MARTHA IVERS, THE(1946); TILL THE CLOUDS ROLL BY(1946); TOMORROW IS FOREVER(1946); WHEN A GIRL'S BEAUTI-FUL(1947)

Thomas Louden
Silents
WORLD'S CHAMPION, THE(1922), w

Romaine Loudermilk
RAINBOW OVER THE RANGE(1940)

Sherman Loudermilk
MOVING VIOLATION(1976), art d; ONE ON ONE(1977), art d

Loudiche
THINGS OF LIFE, THE(1970, Fr./Ital./Switz.)

Carolyn Loudon
FRIDAY THE 13TH PART II(1981)

Dorothy Loudon
1984
GARBO TALKS(1984)

Norman Loudon
REUNION(1932, Brit.), p; EYES OF FATE(1933, Brit.), p; GOLDEN CAGE, THE(1933, Brit.), p; COLONEL BLOOD(1934, Brit.), p; DESIGNING WOMEN(1934, Brit.), p; DIPLOMATIC LOVER, THE(1934, Brit.), p; LEST WE FORGET(1934, Brit.), p; WHEN LONDON SLEEPS(1934, Brit.), p; YOUTHFUL FOLLY(1934, Brit.), p; RADIO PI-RATES(1935, Brit.), p; ROLLING HOME(1935, Brit.), p

Tom Loudon
COVERED WAGON DAYS(1940)

Joan Lougee
STARFIGHTERS, THE(1964)

Carmel Lougene
HARRY AND WALTER GO TO NEW YORK(1976)

James Lough
BABY BLUE MARINE(1976)

David Loughery
1984
DREAMSCAPE(1984), w
Jackie Loughery
ABBOTT AND COSTELLO GO TO MARS(1953); MISSISSIPPI GAMBLER, THE(1953); TAKE ME TO TOWN(1953); VEILS OF BAGDAD, THE(1953); ESCAPE TO BURMA(1955); NAKED STREET, THE(1955); PARDNERS(1956); D.I., THE(1957); EIGHTEEN AND ANXIOUS(1957); HOT ANGEL, THE(1958)
Jacqueline Loughery
PUBLIC AFFAIR, A(1962)
Lori Loughlin
AMITYVILLE 3-D(1983)
Paul Loughlin
ONE MAN(1979, Can.)
Donald Loughman
HAPPY DEATHDAY(1969, Brit.), p
Lee Loughnane
ELECTRA GLIDE IN BLUE(1973)
John Loughney
BEYOND THE TIME BARRIER(1960)
Tom Loughney
STATE FAIR(1962)
Bebe Louie
LT. ROBIN CRUSOE, U.S.N.(1966); HELLFIGHTERS(1968); I SAILED TO TAHITI WITH AN ALL GIRL CREW(1969); JESUS TRIP, THE(1971)
Bill Louie
Misc. Talkies
BODYGUARD, THE(1976)
Billie Louie
MISSION TO MOSCOW(1943); WEEKEND AT THE WALDORF(1945)
Billy Louie
LADY FROM SHANGHAI, THE(1948); SAIGON(1948)
Ducky Louie
BACK TO BATAAN(1945); CHINA SKY(1945); CHINA'S LITTLE DEVILS(1945); BLACK GOLD(1947); SMUGGLER'S ISLAND(1951)
Eugene Louie
KEYS OF THE KINGDOM, THE(1944)
John Louie
OH GOD! BOOK II(1980)
1984
GREMLINS(1984)
Ronald Louie
INTRIGUE(1947)
Sweet Louie
Misc. Talkies
BLACK CONNECTION, THE(1974)
Viola Louie
GODLESS GIRL, THE(1929)
Silents
KING OF KINGS, THE(1927)
William Louie
INTRIGUE(1947)
Louie and the Rockets
UNHOLY ROLLERS(1972)
Louiguy
ANATOMY OF A MARRIAGE(MY DAYS WITH JEAN-MARC AND MY NIGHTS WITH FRANCOISE)**1/2 (1964 Fr.), m; FROU-FROU(1955, Fr.), m; MIRROR HAS TWO FACES, THE(1959, Fr.), m; FIRST TASTE OF LOVE(1962, Fr.), m; RIFF RAFF GIRLS(1962, Fr./Ital.), m; TOMORROW IS MY TURN(1962, Fr./Ital./Ger.), m; PARIS OOH-LA-LA!(1963, U.S./Fr.), m; SIN ON THE BEACH(1964, Fr.), m; TWO ARE GUILTY(1964, Fr.), m; HEAT OF MIDNIGHT(1966, Fr.), m; VERDICT(1975, Fr./Ital.), m
Alika Louis
CRIME AGAINST JOE(1956)
Alyce Louis
HARPOON(1948); FORBIDDEN JUNGLE(1950)
Bill Louis
FIST OF FEAR, TOUCH OF DEATH(1980)
Francois Louis
NOT RECONCILED, OR "ONLY VIOLENCE HELPS WHERE IT RULES"(1969, Ger.), md
Grace Louis
LOVE AT FIRST SIGHT(1977, Can.)
Greg Louis
MICKEY ONE(1965)
Hermina Louis
Silents
END OF THE TRAIL, THE(1916)
J. Louis
LA MARSEILLAISE(1938, Fr.), ph
Jean Louis
YOU CAN'T RUN AWAY FROM IT(1956), cos; 3:10 TO YUMA(1957), cos; THOROUGHLY MODERN MILLIE(1967), cos; STRANGE AFFAIR(1944), cos; TOGETHER AGAIN(1944), cos; KISS AND TELL(1945), cos; OVER 21(1945), cos; THOUSAND AND ONE NIGHTS, A(1945), cos; TONIGHT AND EVERY NIGHT(1945), cos; GILDA(1946), cos; JOLSON STORY, THE(1946), cos; MR. DISTRICT ATTORNEY(1946), cos; ONE WAY TO LOVE(1946), cos; THRILL OF BRAZIL, THE(1946), cos; TOMORROW IS FOREVER(1946), cos; DEAD RECKONING(1947), cos; DOWN TO EARTH(1947), cos; FRAMED(1947), cos; IT HAD TO BE YOU(1947), cos; JOHNNY O'CLOCK(1947), cos; SWORDSMAN, THE(1947), cos; DARK PAST, THE(1948), cos; LADY FROM SHANGHAI, THE(1948), cos; LOVES OF CARMEN, THE(1948), cos; LUXURY LINER(1948), cos; MAN FROM COLORADO, THE(1948), cos; MATING OF MILLIE, THE(1948), cos; RETURN OF OCTOBER, THE(1948), cos; YOU GOTTA STAY HAPPY(1948), cos; JOHNNY ALLEGRO(1949), cos; JOLSON SINGS AGAIN(1949), cos; KNOCK ON ANY DOOR(1949), cos; LUST FOR GOLD(1949), cos; MISS GRANT TAKES RICHMOND(1949), cos; MR. SOFT TOUCH(1949), cos; SHOCKPROOF(1949), cos; SLIGHTLY FRENCH(1949), cos; TELL IT TO THE JUDGE(1949), cos; TOKYO JOE(1949), cos; UNDERCOVER MAN, THE(1949), cos; WALKING HILLS, THE(1949), cos; WE WERE STRANGERS(1949), cos; IN A LONELY PLACE(1950), cos; TRAVELING SALESWOMAN(1950), cos; WOMAN OF DISTINCTION, A(1950), cos; BORN

YESTERDAY(1951), cos; MASK OF THE AVENGER(1951), cos; SATURDAY'S HERO(1951), cos; MARRYING KIND, THE(1952), cos; PAULA(1952), cos; SCANDAL SHEET(1952), cos; BIG HEAT, THE(1953), cos; FROM HERE TO ETERNITY(1953), cos; LET'S DO IT AGAIN(1953), cos; MISS SADIE THOMPSON(1953), cos; SALOME(1953), cos; SERPENT OF THE NILE(1953), cos; IT SHOULD HAPPEN TO YOU(1954), cos; PHFFFT!(1954), cos; PUSHOVER(1954), cos; STAR IS BORN, A(1954), cos; FIVE AGAINST THE HOUSE(1955), cos; PICNIC(1955), cos; QUEEN BEE(1955), cos; THREE FOR THE SHOW(1955), cos; TIGHT SPOT(1955), cos; VIOLENT MEN, THE(1955), cos; EDDY DUCHIN STORY, THE(1956), cos; JUBAL(1956), cos; NIGHTFALL(1956), cos; OVER-EXPOSED(1956), cos; SOLID GOLD CADILLAC, THE(1956), cos; BROTHERS RICO, THE(1957), cos; GARMENT JUNGLE, THE(1957), cos; JEANNE EAGELS(1957), cos; MONTE CARLO STORY, THE(1957, Ital.), cos; PAL JOEY(1957), cos; STORY OF ESTHER COSTELLO, THE(1957, Brit.), cos; IMITATION OF LIFE(1959), cos; LAST ANGRY MAN, THE(1959), cos; MIDDLE OF THE NIGHT(1959), cos; PILLOW TALK(1959), cos; SUDDENLY, LAST SUMMER(1959, Brit.), cos; THEY CAME TO CORDURA(1959), cos; SONG WITHOUT END(1960), cos; STRANGERS WHEN WE MEET(1960), cos; WHO WAS THAT LADY?(1960), cos; BACK STREET(1961), cos; IF A MAN ANSWERS(1962), cos; FOR LOVE OR MONEY(1963), cos; THRILL OF IT ALL, THE(1963), cos; SEND ME NO FLOWERS(1964), cos; BUS RILEY'S BACK IN TOWN(1965), cos; MIRAGE(1965), cos; SHIP OF FOOLS(1965), cos; STRANGE BEDFELLOWS(1965), cos; GAMBIT(1966), cos; MADAME X(1966), cos; GUESS WHO'S COMING TO DINNER(1967), cos; HELL WITH HEROES, THE(1968), cos; P.J.(1968), cos; TREASURE OF SAN GENNARO(1968, Fr./Ital./Ger.); HOUSE OF CARDS(1969); WATERLOO(1970, Ital./USSR); TRINITY IS STILL MY NAME(1971, Ital.); FORTY CARATS(1973), cos; LOST HORIZON(1973), cos
Misc. Talkies
RAMON(1972)
Joe Louis
SPIRIT OF YOUTH(1937); THIS IS THE ARMY(1943); JOE PALOOKA, CHAMP(1946); SQUARE JUNGLE, THE(1955); PHYNX, THE(1970)
Misc. Talkies
FIGHT NEVER ENDS, THE(1947)
Lee Louis
Q(1982)
Mrs. Willard Louis
THEY SHALL HAVE MUSIC(1939)
Pierre Louis
THEY ARE NOT ANGELS(1948, Fr.); DANGER IS A WOMAN(1952, Fr.); MARTIAN IN PARIS, A(1961, Fr.)
Pira Louis
GHOST DIVER(1957)
Sam T. Louis
THIEF(1981)
St. Louis
YOU'VE GOT TO WALK IT LIKE YOU TALK IT OR YOU'LL LOSE THAT BEAT(1971)
Willard Louis
Silents
END OF THE TRAIL, THE(1916); FIRES OF CONSCIENCE(1916); AMERICAN METHODS(1917); TALE OF TWO CITIES, A(1917); JUBILO(1919); DOLLARS AND SENSE(1920); ONLY A SHOP GIRL(1922); ROBIN HOOD(1922); DADDY(1923); FRENCH DOLL, THE(1923); BABBITT(1924); BEAU BRUMMEL(1924); BROADWAY AFTER DARK(1924); EVE'S LOVER(1925); HIS SECRETARY(1925); KISS ME AGAIN(1925); DON JUAN(1926); LOVE TOY, THE(1926)
Misc. Silents
BATTLE OF HEARTS(1916); ISLAND OF DESIRE, THE(1917); ONE TOUCH OF SIN(1917); BIRD OF PREY, THE(1918); FOR LIBERTY(1918); HER ONE MISTAKE(1918); KULTUR(1918); WHAT AM I BID?(1919); GREAT ACCIDENT, THE(1920); LOVES OF LETTY, THE(1920); SLAVE OF VANITY, A(1920); MOONLIGHT AND HONEYSUCKLE(1921); MCGUIRE OF THE MOUNTED(1923); AGE OF INNOCENCE, THE(1924); HER MARRIAGE VOW(1924); LOVER OF CAMILLE, THE(1924); PAL O'MINE(1924); BROADWAY BUTTERFLY, A(1925); HOGAN'S ALLEY(1925); LIMITED MAIL, THE(1925); LOVE HOUR, THE(1925); MAN WITHOUT A CONSCIENCE, THE(1925); THREE WEEKS IN PARIS(1925); HONEYMOON EXPRESS, THE(1926); MADEMOISELLE MODISTE(1926); PASSIONATE QUEST, THE(1926)
Mrs. Louis
Misc. Silents
AFTER HIS OWN HEART(1919)
Louis Armstrong and Band
STRIP, THE(1951)
Louis Armstrong and His All Stars
NEW ORLEANS(1947)
Louis Armstrong and His Jazz Band
EX-FLAME(1931)
Louis Armstrong and His Orchestra
ATLANTIC CITY(1944)
Louis Armstrong and Orchestra
ARTISTS AND MODELS(1937); SONG IS BORN, A(1948)
Louis Armstrong Band
PENNIES FROM HEAVEN(1936)
Louis Armstrong Orchestra
JAM SESSION(1944); PILLOW TO POST(1945)
Louis Jordan and His Orchestra
FOLLOW THE BOYS(1944)
Louis Jordan and the Tympany Five
MEET MISS BOBBY SOCKS(1944)
Misc. Talkies
REET, PETITE AND GONE(1947)
Louis Prima & Co
RAFFERTY AND THE GOLD DUST TWINS(1975)
Louis Prima and His Band
MANHATTAN MERRY-GO-ROUND(1937)
Louis Prima with His Band
START CHEERING(1938)
Louis-MichelCarpentier
1984
SMURFS AND THE MAGIC FLUTE, THE(1984, Fr./Belg.), anim

Madame Louise
STORY OF ADELE H., THE(1975, Fr.)

Anita Louise
MARRIAGE PLAYGROUND, THE(1929); SQUARE SHOULDERS(1929); FLORODO-
RA GIRL, THE(1930); JUST LIKE HEAVEN(1930); THIRD ALARM, THE(1930); WHAT
A MAN(1930); EVERYTHING'S ROSIE(1931); GREAT, MEADOW, THE(1931); HEAV-
EN ON EARTH(1931); MILLIE(1931); WOMAN BETWEEN(1931); PHANTOM OF
CRESTWOOD, THE(1932); OUR BETTERS(1933); CROSS STREETS(1934); FIREBIRD,
THE(1934); I GIVE MY LOVE(1934); JUDGE PRIEST(1934); MADAME DU BAR-
RY(1934); MOST PRECIOUS THING IN LIFE(1934); BACHELOR OF ARTS(1935);
HERE'S TO ROMANCE(1935); MIDSUMMER'S NIGHT'S DREAM, A(1935); PERSON-
AL MAID'S SECRET(1935); ANTHONY ADVERSE(1936); BRIDES ARE LIKE
THAT(1936); STORY OF LOUIS PASTEUR, THE(1936); CALL IT A DAY(1937); FIRST
LADY(1937); GO-GETTER, THE(1937); GREEN LIGHT(1937); THAT CERTAIN WOM-
AN(1937); TOVARICH(1937); MARIE ANTOINETTE(1938); MY BILL(1938); SISTERS,
THE(1938); GOING PLACES(1939); GORILLA, THE(1939); HERO FOR A DAY(1939);
LITTLE PRINCESS, THE(1939); MAIN STREET LAWYER(1939); RENO(1939); THESE
GLAMOUR GIRLS(1939); GLAMOUR FOR SALE(1940); VILLAIN STILL PURSUED
HER, THE(1940); WAGONS WESTWARD(1940); HARMON OF MICHIGAN(1941);
PHANTOM SUBMARINE, THE(1941); TWO IN A TAXI(1941); DANGEROUS
BLONDES(1943); CASANOVA BROWN(1944); NINE GIRLS(1944); FIGHTING
GUARDSMAN, THE(1945); LOVE LETTERS(1945); BANDIT OF SHERWOOD FOR-
EST, THE(1946); DEVIL'S MASK, THE(1946); PERSONALITY KID(1946); SHAD-
OWED(1946); BLONDIE'S BIG MOMENT(1947)
Misc. Talkies
BULLDOG DRUMMOND AT BAY(1947)

Helen Louise
WORDS AND MUSIC(1929)

Helli Louise
CONFESSIONS OF A POP PERFORMER(1975, Brit.)

Jenna Louise
CURTAINS(1983, Can.)

Little Mary Louise
Misc. Silents
BIRDS' CHRISTMAS CAROL, THE(1917)

Marie Louise
ARENA, THE(1973)

Tina Louise
GOD'S LITTLE ACRE(1958); DAY OF THE OUTLAW(1959); HANGMAN, THE(1959);
TRAP, THE(1959); ARMORED COMMAND(1961); WARRIOR EMPRESS, THE(1961,
Ital./Fr.); SIEGE OF SYRACUSE(1962, Fr./Ital.); FOR THOSE WHO THINK
YOUNG(1964); WRECKING CREW, THE(1968); GOOD GUYS AND THE BAD GUYS,
THE(1969); HAPPY ENDING, THE(1969); HOW TO COMMIT MARRIAGE(1969);
STEPFORD WIVES, THE(1975); MEAN DOG BLUES(1978)
1984
DOG DAY(1984, Fr.)
Misc. Talkies
EVILS OF THE NIGHT(1983)

Louise Massey's Westerners
WHERE THE BUFFALO ROAM(1938)

Louise Selkirk's Ladies Orchestra
PLAY UP THE BAND(1935, Brit.)

Nicholas Loukes
DOCTOR FAUSTUS(1967, Brit.); UNDERCOVERS HERO(1975, Brit.)

I. Loukovsky
ADMIRAL NAKHIMOV(1948, USSR), w

Michel Loulergue
1984
SUGAR CANE ALLEY(1984, Fr.), p

Loumel Morgan Trio
MELODY PARADE(1943)

Helen Lounck
NOTHING BUT A MAN(1964)

The Lounge Lizards
UNDERGROUND U.S.A.(1980), m

John Lounsberry
PINOCCHIO(1940), anim; SONG OF THE SOUTH(1946), anim; SO DEAR TO MY
HEART(1949), anim; ALICE IN WONDERLAND(1951), anim d; ARISTOCATS,
THE(1970), anim d; ROBIN HOOD(1973), anim d

John Lounsbery
FANTASIA(1940), anim; DUMBO(1941), anim d; THREE CABALLEROS, THE(1944),
anim; MAKE MINE MUSIC(1946), anim; FUN AND FANCY FREE(1947), anim d;
PETER PAN(1953), anim; LADY AND THE TRAMP(1955), anim d; ONE HUNDRED
AND ONE DALMATIANS(1961), anim; SWORD IN THE STONE, THE(1963), anim;
MARY POPPINS(1964), anim; JUNGLE BOOK, THE(1967), anim d; RESCUERS,
THE(1977), d

Jim Lounsbury
TWIST ALL NIGHT(1961)

Christine Hopf de Loup
MARRIAGE OF MARIA BRAUN, THE(1979, Ger.)

Daniel Louradour
WANDERER, THE(1969, Fr.), art d

Athena Lourde
SKIN GAME(1971)

Oswaldo Loureiro
ROSE FOR EVERYONE, A(1967, Ital.)

David Lourie
PALM BEACH(1979, Aus.)

Eugene Lourie
UNCLE HARRY(1945), art d; LA BETE HUMAINE(1938, Fr.), set d; RULES OF THE
GAME, THE(1939, Fr.), set d; SAHARA(1943), art d; THIS LAND IS MINE(1943), prod
d; THREE RUSSIAN GIRLS(1943), art d; IMPOSTER, THE(1944), art d; IN SOCIE-
TY(1944), art d; SOUTHERNER, THE(1945), set d; DIARY OF A CHAMBER-
MAID(1946), prod d & art d; LONG NIGHT, THE(1947), prod d; WOMAN'S
VENGEANCE, A(1947), art d; ADVENTURES OF CAPTAIN FABIAN(1951), set d;
BEAST FROM 20,000 FATHOMS, THE(1953), d; DIAMOND QUEEN, THE(1953), prod
d; SO THIS IS PARIS(1954), art d; COLOSSUS OF NEW YORK, THE(1958), d;
REVOLT IN THE BIG HOUSE(1958), w; BEHEMOTH, THE SEA MONSTER(1959,
Brit.), d, w; GORGO(1961, Brit.), d; CONFESSIONS OF AN OPIUM EATER(1962), art
d; SHOCK CORRIDOR(1963), art d; FLIGHT FROM ASHIYA(1964, U.S./Jap.), prod d;

NAKED KISS, THE(1964), art d; STRANGLER, THE(1964), art d; CRACK IN THE
WORLD(1965), art d; CUSTER OF THE WEST(1968, U.S., Span.), art d; KRAKATOA,
EAST OF JAVA(1969), prod d; ROYAL HUNT OF THE SUN, THE(1969, Brit.), art d;
WHAT'S THE MATTER WITH HELEN?(1971), prod d; ENEMY OF THE PEOPLE,
AN(1978), prod d; BREATHLESS(1983)
Silents
NAPOLEON(1927, Fr.), art d

John Lourie
ISLAND OF DESIRE(1952, Brit.)

Michele Lourie
DEADLY TRAP, THE(1972, Fr./Ital.)

Norman Lourie
DREAM NO MORE(1950, Palestine), p

Eric Louro
ROOM AT THE TOP(1959, Brit.)

Jacques Loussier
LIFE UPSIDE DOWN(1965, Fr.), m; DARK OF THE SUN(1968, Brit.), m; KILLING
GAME, THE(1968, Fr.), m; YOU ONLY LIVE ONCE(1969, Fr.), m; SNOW JOB(1972),
m

Genevieve Louveau
BIQUEFARRE(1983, Fr.), ed

Louvigny
SYMPHONIE PASTORALE(1948, Fr.)

Charlie Louvin
GOLD GUITAR, THE(1966)

Paul Louyet
TRANS-EUROP-EXPRESS(1968, Fr.)

Pierre Louys
DEVIL IS A WOMAN, THE(1935), w; FEMALE, THE(1960, Fr.), w; THAT OBSCURE
OBJECT OF DESIRE(1977, Fr./Span.), w

Oswaldo Louzada
VIOLENT AND THE DAMNED, THE(1962, Braz.); TRAIN ROBBERY CONFIDEN-
TIAL(1965, Braz.)

Jose Louzeiro
PIXOTE(1981, Braz.), w

Geoffrey Lovat
CONSTANT HUSBAND, THE(1955, Brit.)

Beto Lovato
1984
BREAKIN' 2: ELECTRIC BOOGALOO(1984)

Grant Lovatt
HE WHO RIDES A TIGER(1966, Brit.)

Jack Lovatt
Misc. Silents
CRIME AND THE PENALTY(1916, Brit.)

Alan Love
THAT SINKING FEELING(1979, Brit.); APPLE, THE(1980 U.S./Ger.); GREGORY'S
GIRL(1982, Brit.)
Misc. Talkies
BLACK CARRION(1984)

Bessie Love
BROADWAY MELODY, THE(1929); GIRL IN THE SHOW, THE(1929); IDLE RICH,
THE(1929); CHASING RAINBOWS(1930); CONSPIRACY(1930); GOOD NEWS(1930);
SEE AMERICA THIRST(1930); THEY LEARNED ABOUT WOMEN(1930); MORALS
FOR WOMEN(1931); LIVE AGAIN(1936, Brit.); ATLANTIC FERRY(1941, Brit.); JOUR-
NEY TOGETHER(1946, Brit.); MAGIC BOX, THE(1952, Brit.); BAREFOOT CONTESSA,
THE(1954); WEAK AND THE WICKED, THE(1954, Brit.); LIGHT TOUCH, THE(1955,
Brit.); STORY OF ESTHER COSTELLO, THE(1957, Brit.); NOWHERE TO GO(1959,
Brit.); NEXT TO NO TIME(1960, Brit.); TOO YOUNG TO LOVE(1960, Brit.); LOSS OF
INNOCENCE(1961, Brit.); ROMAN SPRING OF MRS. STONE, THE(1961, U.S./Brit.);
PROMISE HER ANYTHING(1966, Brit.); WILD AFFAIR, THE(1966, Brit.); BATTLE
BENEATH THE EARTH(1968, Brit.); ISADORA(1968, Brit.); ON HER MAJESTY'S
SECRET SERVICE(1969, Brit.); CATLOW(1971, Span.); SUNDAY BLOODY SUN-
DAY(1971, Brit.); RITZ, THE(1976); GULLIVER'S TRAVELS(1977, Brit., Bel.); VAM-
PYRES, DAUGHTERS OF DRACULA(1977, Brit.); LADY CHATTERLEY'S
LOVER(1981, Fr./Brit.); RAGTIME(1981); REDS(1981); HUNGER, THE(1983)
Silents
BIRTH OF A NATION, THE(1915); ACQUITTED(1916); ARYAN, THE(1916); FLYING
TORPEDO, THE(1916); GOOD BAD MAN, THE(1916); HELL-TO-PAY AUSTIN(1916);
INTOLERANCE(1916); REGGIE MIXES IN(1916); NINA, THE FLOWER GIRL(1917);
GREAT ADVENTURE, THE(1918); CAROLYN OF THE CORNERS(1919); SEA LION,
THE(1921); SWAMP, THE(1921); BULLDOG COURAGE(1922); DESERTED AT THE
ALTAR(1922); NIGHT LIFE IN HOLLYWOOD(1922); ETERNAL THREE, THE(1923);
GENTLE JULIA(1923); SLAVE OF DESIRE(1923); SOULS FOR SALE(1923); ST.
ELMO(1923); TORMENT(1924); LOST WORLD, THE(1925); NEW BROOMS(1925);
DRESS PARADE(1927); RUBBER TIRES(1927); MATINEE IDOL, THE(1928); SALLY
OF THE SCANDALS(1928)
Misc. Silents
SISTER OF SIX, A(1916); STRANDED(1916); CHEERFUL GIVERS(1917); DAUGH-
TER OF THE POOR, A(1917); HEIRESS AT "COFFEE DAN'S", THE(1917); POLLY
ANN(1917); SAWDUST RING, THE(1917); WEE LADY BETTY(1917); DAWN OF
UNDERSTANDING, THE(1918); HOW COULD YOU, CAROLINE?(1918); LITTLE
SISTER OF EVERYBODY, A(1918); CUPID FORECLOSES(1919); FIGHTING COL-
LEEN, A(1919); LITTLE BOSS, THE(1919); OVER THE GARDEN WALL(1919);
WISHING RING MAN, THE(1919); YANKEE PRINCESS, A(1919); BONNIE
MAY(1920); MIDLANDERS, THE(1920); PEGEEN(1920); PENNY OF TOP HILL
TRAIL(1921); FORGET-ME-NOT(1922); GHOST PATROL, THE(1923); HUMAN
WRECKAGE(1923); THREE WHO PAID(1923); DYNAMITE SMITH(1924); SILENT
WATCHER, THE(1924); SUNDOWN(1924); THOSE WHO DANCE(1924); TONGUES
OF FLAME(1924); WOMAN ON THE JURY, THE(1924); KING ON MAIN STREET,
THE(1925); SON OF HIS FATHER, A(1925); SOUL-FIRE(1925); GOING CROO-
KED(1926); LOVEY MARY(1926); SONG AND DANCE MAN(1926); YOUNG
APRIL(1926); HARP IN HOCK, A(1927); ANYBODY HERE SEEN KELLY?(1928)

Bill Love
THX 1138(1971)

Bloodstone "Charles" Love
TRAIN RIDE TO HOLLYWOOD(1975)

Bobby Love
NOTORIOUS CLEOPATRA, THE(1970)
Bruce Love
NIGHT TRAIN TO MUNDO FINE(1966)
Buddy Love
STEEL ARENA(1973)
Burt Love
NIGHT OF BLOODY HORROR zero(1969)
David Love
TEENAGERS FROM OUTER SPACE(1959)
Dickie Love
TOP MAN(1943); THIS LOVE OF OURS(1945)
Dorothea Love
Silents
"THAT ROYLE GIRL"(1925)
Dorothy Love
RENEGADE GIRLS(1974); INCREDIBLE MELTING MAN, THE(1978)
Edmund Love
Misc. Silents
MY LADY'S LATCHKEY(1921)
Edmund G. Love
DESTINATION GOBI(1953), w
Edward Love
FANTASIA(1940), anim
Geoff Love
DREAM MAKER, THE(1963, Brit.); FOLLOW THE BOYS(1963), md
Ian Love
SECRET INVASION, THE(1964), set d
June Love
Misc. Talkies
COURAGE OF THE NORTH(1935)
Karyn Love
STONE(1974, Aus.)
Kenneth Love
DON'T RUSH ME(1936, Brit.)
Lenita Love
DEVIL ON WHEELS, THE(1947)
Liz Love
MY BODY HUNGERS(1967)
Lucinda Love
UNSTRAP ME(1968)
Lucretia Love
ARENA, THE(1973); BATTLE OF THE AMAZONS(1973, Ital./Span.); TORMENTED, THE(1978, Ital.); DR. HECKYL AND MR. HYPE(1980)
Mable Love
Misc. Silents
IN ANOTHER GIRL'S SHOES(1917, Brit.)
Marilyn Love
BANK MESSENGER MYSTERY, THE(1936, Brit.)
Mary Love
GREED OF WILLIAM HART, THE(1948, Brit.); PRODUCERS, THE(1967)
Michael Love
GIRLS ON THE BEACH(1965)
Montagu Love
HAUNTED HOUSE, THE(1928); WIND, THE(1928); BULLDOG DRUMMOND(1929); CHARMING SINNERS(1929); HER PRIVATE LIFE(1929); LAST WARNING, THE(1929); MIDSTREAM(1929); MOST IMMORAL LADY, A(1929); MYSTERIOUS ISLAND(1929); BACK PAY(1930); CAT CREEPS, THE(1930); DOUBLE CROSS ROADS(1930); INSIDE THE LINES(1930); KISMET(1930); LOVE COMES ALONG(1930); NOTORIOUS AFFAIR, A(1930); OUTWARD BOUND(1930); RENO(1930); ALEXANDER HAMILTON(1931); LION AND THE LAMB(1931); LOVE BOUND(1932); MIDNIGHT LADY(1932); OUT OF SINGAPORE(1932); RIDING TORNADO, THE(1932); SILVER LINING(1932); STOWAWAY(1932); VANITY FAIR(1932); HIS DOUBLE LIFE(1933); LIMEHOUSE BLUES(1934); MENACE(1934); MYSTIC HOUR, THE(1934); CLIVE OF INDIA(1935); CRUSADES, THE(1935); MAN WHO BROKE THE BANK AT MONTE CARLO, THE(1935); CHAMPAGNE CHARLIE(1936); COUNTRY DOCTOR, THE(1936); HI GAUCHO!(1936); LLOYDS OF LONDON(1936); ONE IN A MILLION(1936); REUNION(1936); SING, BABY, SING(1936); SUTTER'S GOLD(1936); WHITE ANGEL, THE(1936); ADVENTURE'S END(1937); DAMSEL IN DISTRESS, A(1937); LIFE OF EMILE ZOLA, THE(1937); LONDON BY NIGHT(1937); PARNELL(1937); PRINCE AND THE PAUPER, THE(1937); PRISONER OF ZENDA, THE(1937); TOVARICH(1937); ADVENTURES OF ROBIN HOOD, THE(1938); BUCCANEER, THE(1938); IF I WERE KING(1938); KIDNAPPED(1938); PROFESSOR BEWARE(1938); GUNGA DIN(1939); JUAREZ(1939); MAN IN THE IRON MASK, THE(1939); RULERS OF THE SEA(1939); WE ARE NOT ALONE(1939); ALL THIS AND HEAVEN TOO(1940); DISPATCH FROM REUTERS, A(1940); DR. EHRLICH'S MAGIC BULLET(1940); HUDSON'S BAY(1940); LONE WOLF STRIKES, THE(1940); MARK OF ZORRO, THE(1940); NORTHWEST MOUNTED POLICE(1940); NORTHWEST PASSAGE(1940); PRIVATE AFFAIRS(1940); SEA HAWK, THE(1940); SON OF MONTE CRISTO(1940); DEVIL AND MISS JONES, THE(1941); LADY FOR A NIGHT(1941); SHINING VICTORY(1941); REMARKABLE ANDREW, THE(1942); SHERLOCK HOLMES AND THE VOICE OF TERROR(1942); TENNESSEE JOHNSON(1942); CONSTANT NYMPH, THE(1943); FOREVER AND A DAY(1943); HOLY MATRIMONY(1943); WINGS OVER THE PACIFIC(1943); DEVOTION(1946)
Misc. Talkies
VOICE WITHIN, THE(1929); FIGHTING DEVIL DOGS(1938); MURDER ON THE HIGH SEAS(1938)
Silents
ROYAL FAMILY, A(1915); FRIDAY THE 13TH(1916); GILDED CAGE, THE(1916); HIDDEN SCAR, THE(1916); MEN SHE MARRIED, THE(1916); AWAKENING, THE(1917); DANCER'S PERIL, THE(1917); CABARET, THE(1918); RIDDLE: WOMAN, THE(1920); LOVE'S REDEMPTION(1921); SHAMS OF SOCIETY(1921); SECRETS OF PARIS, THE(1922); DARLING OF THE RICH, THE(1923); ROULETTE(1924); SINNERS IN HEAVEN(1924); ANCIENT HIGHWAY(1925); DESERT'S PRICE, THE(1926); DON JUAN(1926); HANDS UP(1926); SILENT LOVER, THE(1926); SOCIAL HIGHWAYMAN, THE(1926); SON OF THE SHEIK(1926); JESSE JAMES(1927); KING OF KINGS, THE(1927); NIGHT OF LOVE, THE(1927); ONE HOUR OF LOVE(1927); TENDER HOUR, THE(1927); NOOSE, THE(1928); SILKS AND SADDLES(1929)

Misc. Silents
SUICIDE CLUB, THE(1914, Brit.); ANTIQUE DEALER, THE(1915); GREATER WILL, THE(1915); BOUGHT AND PAID FOR(1916); CHALLENGE, THE(1916); DEVIL'S TOY, THE(1916); WOMAN'S WAY, A(1916); BRAND OF SATAN, THE(1917); DORMANT POWER, THE(1917); FORGET-ME-NOTS(1917); GUARDIAN, THE(1917); RASPUTIN, THE BLACK MONK(1917); YANKEE PLUCK(1917); BROKEN TIES(1918); CROSS BEARER, THE(1918); STOLEN ORDERS(1918); TO HIM THAT HATH(1918); VENGEANCE(1918); BROADWAY SAINT, A(1919); HAND INVISIBLE, THE(1919); QUICKENING FLAME, THE(1919); ROUGHNECK, THE(1919); STEEL KING, THE(1919); THREE GREEN EYES(1919); THROUGH THE TOILS(1919); MAN'S PLAYTHING(1920); PLACE OF THE HONEYMOONS, THE(1920); WORLD AND HIS WIFE, THE(1920); WRONG WOMAN, THE(1920); CASE OF BECKY, THE(1921); FOREVER(1921); WHAT'S WRONG WITH THE WOMEN?(1922); LEOPARDESS, THE(1923); LOVE OF WOMEN(1924); RESTLESS WIVES(1924); WEEK END HUSBANDS(1924); BROODING EYES(1926); OUT OF THE STORM(1926); GOOD TIME CHARLEY(1927); HAUNTED SHIP, THE(1927); ROSE OF THE GOLDEN WEST(1927); DEVIL'S SKIPPER, THE(1928); HAWK'S NEST, THE(1928)
Nicholas Love
BOOGEYMAN II(1983); BRAINWAVES(1983); TASTE OF SIN, A(1983)
Misc. Talkies
KILLING TOUCH, THE(1983)
Patti Love
BUTLEY(1974, Brit.); THAT'LL BE THE DAY(1974, Brit.); TERROR(1979, Brit.); LONG GOOD FRIDAY, THE(1982, Brit.)
Phyllis Love
FRIENDLY PERSUASION(1956); YOUNG DOCTORS, THE(1961)
Richard Love
SING A JINGLE(1943)
1984
ADERYN PAPUR(1984, Brit.)
Robert Love
I COVER CHINATOWN(1938)
Sandi Love
1984
MEATBALLS PART II(1984), cos
Sherman Love
OLD CORRAL, THE(1937), w
Suki Love
HAIR(1979)
Susanna Love
COCAINE COWBOYS(1979)
Suzanna Love
BOOGEY MAN, THE(1980); BOOGEYMAN II(1983); BRAINWAVES(1983), a, w; DEVONSVILLE TERROR, THE(1983), a, w; TASTE OF SIN, A(1983)
Tony Love
SANTA AND THE THREE BEARS(1970), anim
Ula Love
SPRINGTIME IN THE ROCKIES(1937); YOUTH ON PAROLE(1937)
Wayne Love
BOOGEYMAN II(1983), m
Yolanda Love
Misc. Talkies
BLACK LOLITA(1975)
H.P. Lovecraft
HAUNTED PALACE, THE(1963), w; DIE, MONSTER, DIE(1965, Brit.), w; SHUTTERED ROOM, THE(1968, Brit.), w; DUNWICH HORROR, THE(1970), w
Denise Loveday
1984
BODY DOUBLE(1984)
Arthur Lovegrove
YESTERDAY'S ENEMY(1959, Brit.); MEET SIMON CHERRY(1949, Brit.); SILK NOOSE, THE(1950, Brit.); GALLOPING MAJOR, THE(1951, Brit.); MURDER AT 3 A.M.(1953, Brit.); STEEL KEY, THE(1953, Brit.); WHITE FIRE(1953, Brit.); DEVIL ON HORSEBACK(1954, Brit.); RUNAWAY BUS, THE(1954, Brit.); PASSAGE HOME(1955, Brit.); SECRET OF THE FOREST, THE(1955, Brit.); THEY CAN'T HANG ME(1955, Brit.); KID FOR TWO FARTHINGS, A(1956, Brit.); SAFARI(1956); WAY OUT, THE(1956, Brit.); BREAK IN THE CIRCLE, THE(1957, Brit.); CARRY ON ADMIRAL(1957, Brit.); TEARS FOR SIMON(1957, Brit.); WEAPON, THE(1957, Brit.); STEEL BAYONET, THE(1958, Brit.); NAKED FURY(1959, Brit.); WRONG NUMBER(1959, Brit.); NEXT TO NO TIME(1960, Brit.); SHAKEDOWN, THE(1960, Brit.); HOUSE OF FRIGHT(1961); WE JOINED THE NAVY(1962, Brit.); CROOKS ANONYMOUS(1963, Brit.); MARKED ONE, THE(1963, Brit.); PLEASURE LOVERS, THE(1964, Brit.); ESCAPE BY NIGHT(1965, Brit.); SMASHING TIME(1967 Brit.); INSPECTOR CLOUSEAU(1968, Brit.); RISE AND RISE OF MICHAEL RIMMER, THE(1970, Brit.); EYE OF THE NEEDLE(1981); MEMOIRS OF A SURVIVOR(1981, Brit.)
Vincent Lovegrove
MONKEY GRIP(1983, Aus.)
Alec Lovejoy
Misc. Talkies
BRAND OF CAIN, THE(1935); SWING(1938); BIRTHRIGHT(1939); MOON OVER HARLEM(1939); MURDER ON LENOX AVENUE(1941); SUNDAY SINNERS(1941)
Alice Lovejoy
Misc. Talkies
GOD'S STEPCHILDREN(1937)
Arthur Lovejoy
NIGHT WORK(1930); LETTER FROM AN UNKNOWN WOMAN(1948); FULL OF LIFE(1956); 27TH DAY, THE(1957); MATCHMAKER, THE(1958)
Frank Lovejoy
BLACK BART(1948); HOME OF THE BRAVE(1949); BREAKTHROUGH(1950); IN A LONELY PLACE(1950); SOUND OF FURY, THE(1950); SOUTH SEA SINNER(1950); THREE SECRETS(1950); FORCE OF ARMS(1951); GOODBYE, MY FANCY(1951); I WAS A COMMUNIST FOR THE F.B.I.(1951); I'LL SEE YOU IN MY DREAMS(1951); STARLIFT(1951); WINNING TEAM, THE(1952); CHARGE AT FEATHER RIVER, THE(1953); HITCH-HIKER, THE(1953); HOUSE OF WAX(1953); SHE'S BACK ON BROADWAY(1953); SYSTEM, THE(1953); BEACHHEAD(1954); MEN OF THE FIGHTING LADY(1954); AMERICANO, THE(1955); CROOKED WEB, THE(1955); FINGER MAN(1955); MAD AT THE WORLD(1955); SHACK OUT ON 101(1955); STRATEGIC AIR COMMAND(1955); TOP OF THE WORLD(1955); JULIE(1956); THREE BRAVE MEN(1957); COLE YOUNGER, GUNFIGHTER(1958)

Harry Lovejoy
NO RETURN ADDRESS(1961); FARMER'S OTHER DAUGHTER, THE(1965); BLACK KLANSMAN, THE(1966); GIRL IN GOLD BOOTS(1968); CORPSE GRINDERS, THE(1972)

Ray Lovejoy
2001: A SPACE ODYSSEY(1968, U.S./Brit.), ed; DAY IN THE DEATH OF JOE EGG, A(1972, Brit.), ed; RULING CLASS, THE(1972, Brit.), ed; FEAR IS THE KEY(1973), ed; LITTLE MALCOLM(1974, Brit.), ed; SHINING, THE(1980), ed; DRESSER, THE(1983), ed; KRULL(1983), ed
1984
SHEENA(1984), ed

Stephen Lovejoy
1984
SONGWRITER(1984), ed

Jenny Lovelace
NIGHT INVADER, THE(1943, Brit)

Linda Lovelace
Misc. Talkies
LINDA LOVELACE FOR PRESIDENT(1975)

Richard Lovelace [Julio Buchs]
SUPERARGO(1968, Ital./Span.), w

David Loveless
END OF AUGUST, THE(1982), cos

Nita Loveless
MARRIED TOO YOUNG(1962)

Jim Lovelett
PHANTOM OF THE PARADISE(1974); SOMEBODY KILLED HER HUSBAND(1978); DEATH VENGEANCE(1982); LITTLE SEX, A(1982)

Angela Lovell
HAND OF NIGHT, THE(1968, Brit.)

Dudley Lovell
WHEN THE BOUGH BREAKS(1947, Brit.), ph; BLIND GODDESS, THE(1948, Brit.), ph; DON'T EVER LEAVE ME(1949, Brit.), ph; GOLDEN SALAMANDER(1950, Brit.), ph; MY SON, THE VAMPIRE(1963, Brit.), ph

Dyson Lovell
PANIC(1966, Brit.); ROMEO AND JULIET(1968, Brit./Ital.); CHAMP, THE(1979), p; ENDLESS LOVE(1981), p

Capt. James Lovell
MAN WHO FELL TO EARTH, THE(1976, Brit.)

Jenny Lovell
PICNIC AT HANGING ROCK(1975, Aus.); GALLIPOLI(1981, Aus.)

John Lovell
LIAR'S DICE(1980)

Judy Lovell
YEAR OF LIVING DANGEROUSLY, THE(1982, Aus.), makeup

Margot Lovell
DON'T SAY DIE(1950, Brit.), p

Mike Lovell
2001: A SPACE ODYSSEY(1968, U.S./Brit.)

Nigel Lovell
MASSACRE HILL(1949, Brit.); WHEREVER SHE GOES(1953, Aus.); NED KELLY(1970, Brit.); LET THE BALLOON GO(1977, Aus.)

Pat Lovell
BREAK OF DAY(1977, Aus.), p; SUMMERFIELD(1977, Aus.), p

Patricia Lovell
GALLIPOLI(1981, Aus.), p; MONKEY GRIP(1983, Aus.), p

Pedro Lovell
ROCKY(1976)

Raymond Lovell
THIRD CLUE, THE(1934, Brit.); WARN LONDON!(1934, Brit.); CASE OF GABRIEL PERRY, THE(1935, Brit.); CRIME UNLIMITED(1935, Brit.); SEXTON BLAKE AND THE MADEMOISELLE(1935, Brit.); SOME DAY(1935, Brit.); FAIR EXCHANGE(1936, Brit.); GAOL BREAK(1936, Brit.); GYPSY MELODY(1936, Brit.); KING OF THE DAMNED(1936, Brit.); NOT SO DUSTY(1936, Brit.); TROUBLED WATERS(1936, Brit.); BEHIND YOUR BACK(1937, Brit.); BOMBS OVER LONDON(1937, Brit.); I MARRIED A SPY(1938); MURDER TOMORROW(1938, Brit.); BLACKOUT(1940, Brit.); COMMON TOUCH, THE(1941, Brit.); HE FOUND A STAR(1941, Brit.); INVADERS, THE,(1941); GOOSE STEPS OUT, THE(1942, Brit.); YOUNG MR. PITT, THE(1942, Brit.); ALIBI, THE(1943, Brit.); MAN IN GREY, THE(1943, Brit.); UNDER SECRET ORDERS(1943, Brit.); WARN THAT MAN(1943, Brit.); CANDLELIGHT IN ALGERIA(1944, Brit.); UNCENSORED(1944, Brit.); APPOINTMENT WITH CRIME(1945, Brit.); WAY AHEAD, THE(1945, Brit.); CAESAR AND CLEOPATRA(1946, Brit.); HOTEL RESERVE(1946, Brit.); NIGHT BOAT TO DUBLIN(1946, Brit.); END OF THE RIVER, THE(1947, Brit.); BLIND GODDESS, THE(1948, Brit.); BUT NOT IN VAIN(1948, Brit.); CALENDAR, THE(1948, Brit.); EASY MONEY(1948, Brit.); SO EVIL MY LOVE(1948, Brit.); THREE WEIRD SISTERS, THE(1948, Brit.); BAD LORD BYRON, THE(1949, Brit.); FOOLS RUSH IN(1949, Brit.); MADNESS OF THE HEART(1949, Brit.); MY BROTHER'S KEEPER(1949, Brit.); ONCE UPON A DREAM(1949, Brit.); QUARTET(1949, Brit.); MUDLARK, THE(1950, Brit.); NAUGHTY ARLETTE(1951, Brit.); PICKWICK PAPERS, THE(1952, Brit.); STEEL KEY, THE(1953, Brit.); TIME GENTLEMEN PLEASE!(1953, Brit.); WHO KILLED VAN LOON?(1984, Brit.)

Roderick Lovell
SO EVIL MY LOVE(1948, Brit.); HOUR OF GLORY(1949, Brit.); UNDER CAPRICORN(1949); IVANHOE(1952, Brit.); MY SON, THE VAMPIRE(1963, Brit.)

Rosemary Lovell
YOU LIGHT UP MY LIFE(1977)

Simone Lovell
HARASSED HERO, THE(1954, Brit.); MEET MR. MALCOLM(1954, Brit.)

Maurice Lovelle
Silents
ANNE OF GREEN GABLES(1919)

Ray Lovelock
DON'T OPEN THE WINDOW(1974, Ital.); FROM HELL TO VICTORY(1979, Fr./Ital./Span.)
Misc. Talkies
AUTOPSY(1980, Ital.)

Raymond Lovelock
DJANGO KILL(1967, Ital./Span.); VIOLENT FOUR, THE(1968, Ital.); FIDDLER ON THE ROOF(1971); ALMOST HUMAN(1974,Ital.); CASSANDRA CROSSING, THE(1977)

Misc. Talkies
OASIS OF FEAR(1973); ONE RUSSIAN SUMMER(1973)

Louise Lovely
Silents
GILDED SPIDER, THE(1916); MEASURE OF A MAN, THE(1916); GIRL WHO WOULDN'T QUIT, THE(1918); NOBODY'S WIFE(1918); JOHNNY-ON-THE-SPOT(1919); JOYOUS TROUBLEMAKERS, THE(1920); POVERTY OF RICHES, THE(1921); SHATTERED IDOLS(1922)
Misc. Silents
BETTINA LOVED A SOLDIER(1916); BOBBIE OF THE BALLET(1916); GRASP OF GREED, THE(1916); GRIP OF JEALOUSY, THE(1916); SOCIAL BUCCANEER, THE(1916); TANGLED HEARTS(1916); FIELD OF HONOR, THE(1917); GIFT GIRL, THE(1917); REED CASE, THE(1917); SIRENS OF THE SEA(1917); PAINTED LIPS(1918); RICH MAN'S DAUGHTER, A(1918); WOLF AND HIS MATE, THE(1918); LAST OF THE DUANES, THE(1919); LIFE'S A FUNNY PROPOSITION(1919); LONE STAR RANGER, THE(1919); MAN HUNTER, THE(1919); USURPER, THE(1919); WINGS OF THE MORNING, THE(1919); WOLVES OF THE NIGHT(1919); LITTLE GREY MOUSE, THE(1920); ORPHAN, THE(1920); SKYWAYMAN, THE(1920); THIRD WOMAN, THE(1920); TWINS OF SUFFERING CREEK(1920); LIFE'S GREATEST QUESTION(1921); PARTNERS OF FATE(1921); WHILE THE DEVIL LAUGHS(1921)

Charles Loventhal
HOME MOVIES(1979), w

Charlie Loventhal
FIRST TIME, THE(1983), d, w

Evelyn Lovequist
TWO TICKETS TO BROADWAY(1951); LAS VEGAS STORY, THE(1952); SON OF SINBAD(1955)

Anthony Lover
MY BODY HUNGERS(1967), ph; DISTANCE(1975), d, ph&ed

Brian Lover
1984
REVENGE OF THE NERDS(1984)

Samuel Lover
Silents
HANDY ANDY(1921, Brit.), w

Frank Loverde
LAST OF THE RED HOT LOVERS(1972)

Frank Loverede
EVEL KNIEVEL(1971)

Marguerite Loveridge
Silents
WITHOUT HOPE(1914)

Otho Lovering
WILD PARTY, THE(1929), ed; MIGHTY, THE(1929), ed; WHEEL OF LIFE, THE(1929), ed; MANSLAUGHTER(1930), ed; SOCIAL LION, THE(1930), ed; STREET OF CHANCE(1930), ed; VIRTUOUS SIN, THE(1930), ed; CONQUERING HORDE, THE(1931), ed; DEVIL AND THE DEEP(1932), ed; FAREWELL TO ARMS, A(1932), ed; BEDTIME STORY, A(1933), ed; I'M NO ANGEL(1933), ed; ALL OF ME(1934), ed; WE LIVE AGAIN(1934), ed; YOU'RE TELLING ME(1934), ed; ACCENT ON YOUTH(1935), ed; GILDED LILY, THE(1935), ed; SHANGHAI(1935), ed; STOLEN HARMONY(1935), ed; WANDERER OF THE WASTELAND(1935), d; BORDER FLIGHT(1936), d; DRIFT FENCE(1936), d; SKY PARADE(1936), d; VALIANT IS THE WORD FOR CARRIE(1936), ed; I MET HIM IN PARIS(1937), ed; STAND-IN(1937), ed; VOGUES OF 1938(1937), ed; 52ND STREET(1937), ed; ALGIERS(1938), ed; I MET MY LOVE AGAIN(1938), ed; TRADE WINDS(1938), ed; FOREIGN CORRESPONDENT(1940), ed; SLIGHTLY HONORABLE(1940), ed; LADY IN A JAM(1942), w; DILLINGER(1945), ed; PARDON MY PAST(1945), ed; STORY OF G.I. JOE, THE(1945), ed; ABILENE TOWN(1946), ed; SUSPENSE(1946), ed; JOE PALOOKA IN WINNER TAKE ALL(1948), ed; SHANGHAI CHEST, THE(1948), ed; SMUGGLERS' COVE(1948), ed; BOMBA THE JUNGLE BOY(1949), ed; FORGOTTEN WOMEN(1949), ed; BLUE GRASS OF KENTUCKY(1950), ed; HUMPHREY TAKES A CHANCE(1950), ed; JOE PALOOKA MEETS HUMPHREY(1950), ed; LUCKY LOSERS(1950), ed; SHORT GRASS(1950), ed; DISC JOCKEY(1951), ed; LION HUNTERS, THE(1951), ed; NAVY BOUND(1951), ed; JACK AND THE BEANSTALK(1952), ed; MAN WHO SHOT LIBERTY VALANCE, THE(1962), ed; MODERN MARRIAGE, A(1962), ed; DONOVAN'S REEF(1963), ed; MC LINTOCK!(1963), ed; CHEYENNE AUTUMN(1964), ed; LAW OF THE LAWLESS(1964), ed; SHENANDOAH(1965), ed; LAST OF THE SECRET AGENTS?, THE(1966), ed; RIDE BEYOND VENGEANCE(1966), ed; WAY WEST, THE(1967), ed; GREEN BERETS, THE(1968), ed; GOOD GUYS AND THE BAD GUYS, THE(1969), ed; YOUNG BILLY YOUNG(1969), ed
Silents
EASY COME, EASY GO(1928), ed; SPORTING GOODS(1928), ed; TAKE ME HOME(1928), ed; WARMING UP(1928), ed

Otho S. Lovering
SEVEN WOMEN(1966), ed; BALLAD OF JOSIE(1968), ed

Lis Lovert
WOODEN HORSE, THE(1951)

Henry Lovet
THOSE DIRTY DOGS(1974, U.S./Ital./Span.), w

Robert Q. Lovet
COTTON COMES TO HARLEM(1970), ed

Alden Lovett
Misc. Silents
TRAFFIC(1915, Brit.)

Bill Lovett
SONG OF OLD WYOMING(1945)

Dorothy Lovett
MEET DR. CHRISTIAN(1939); STORY OF VERNON AND IRENE CASTLE, THE(1939); THAT'S RIGHT–YOU'RE WRONG(1939); COURAGEOUS DR. CHRISTIAN, THE(1940); DR. CHRISTIAN MEETS THE WOMEN(1940); LOOK WHO'S LAUGHING(1941); LUCKY DEVILS(1941); REMEDY FOR RICHES(1941); THEY MEET AGAIN(1941); CALL OUT THE MARINES(1942); POWDER TOWN(1942); SING YOUR WORRIES AWAY(1942); MANTRAP, THE(1943); WHY MUST I DIE?(1960)

Frank Lovett
Silents
ONLY A MILL GIRL(1919, Brit.)

Helen Lovett
STREET SCENE(1931)

Joseph Lovett
CAPTAIN HURRICANE(1935), w
Josephine Lovett
OUR MODERN MAIDENS(1929), w; WHAT A WIDOW(1930), w; CORSAIR(1931), w; ROAD TO RENO(1931), w; MADAME BUTTERFLY(1932), w; THUNDER BE-LOW(1932), w; TOMORROW AND TOMORROW(1932), w; JENNIE GER-HARDT(1933), w; TWO ALONE(1934), w
Silents
AWAY GOES PRUDENCE(1920), w; RENDEZVOUS, THE(1923), w; CLASS-MATES(1924), w; ENCHANTED COTTAGE, THE(1924), w; SHORE LEAVE(1925), w; ANNIE LAURIE(1927), w; OUR DANCING DAUGHTERS(1928), w; OUR MODERN MAIDENS(1929), w; SINGLE STANDARD, THE(1929), w
Misc. Silents
NINETY AND NINE, THE(1916)
Marjorie Lovett
TOOTSIE(1982)
Monica Lovett
CHILDRENS GAMES(1969)
Patricia Lovett
HALF A SIXPENCE(1967, Brit.)
Peter Lovett
SUMMER CAMP(1979)
Robert Lovett
NEXT MAN, THE(1976), ed
Robert Q. Lovett
TAKING OF PELHAM ONE, TWO, THREE, THE(1974), ed; PSYCHOMANIA(1964), ed; DESPERATE CHARACTERS(1971), ed; ONCE IN PARIS(1978), ed; HAM-METT(1982), ed; GOLDEN SEAL, THE(1983), ed
1984
COTTON CLUB, THE(1984), ed
Regine Lovi
NUDE IN HIS POCKET(1962, Fr.)
Pearl Lovici
Silents
LITTLE COMRADE(1919)
Rodney Lovick
GREAT MUPPET CAPER, THE(1981)
The Lovin' Spoonful
WHAT'S UP, TIGER LILY?(1966), a, m
Lisa Loving
1984
ALPHABET CITY(1984)
The Loving Spoonful
ONE-TRICK PONY(1980)
B. Lovitt
NEW YORK, NEW YORK(1977), ed; HARRY'S WAR(1981), ed
Bert Lovitt
FORCE OF ONE, A(1979), ed
Celia Lovsky
MAN WHO KNEW TOO MUCH, THE(1935, Brit.); FOXES OF HARROW, THE(1947); LETTER FROM AN UNKNOWN WOMAN(1948); SEALED VERDICT(1948); SNAKE PIT, THE(1948); CHICAGO DEADLINE(1949); FLAMING FURY(1949); CAPTAIN CAREY, U.S.A(1950); KILLER THAT STALKED NEW YORK, THE(1950); NIGHT INTO MORNING(1951); PEOPLE AGAINST O'HARA, THE(1951); SCARF, THE(1951); BECAUSE YOU'RE MINE(1952); LAST TIME I SAW PARIS, THE(1954); RHAP-SODY(1954); THREE COINS IN THE FOUNTAIN(1954); DUEL ON THE MISSISSIP-PI(1955); FOXFIRE(1955); NEW YORK CONFIDENTIAL(1955); TEXAS LADY(1955); DEATH OF A SCOUNDREL(1956); OPPOSITE SEX, THE(1956); RUMBLE ON THE DOCKS(1956); WHILE THE CITY SLEEPS(1956); GARMENT JUNGLE, THE(1957); MAN OF A THOUSAND FACES(1957); TROOPER HOOK(1957); CRASH LAND-ING(1958); ME AND THE COLONEL(1958); TWILIGHT FOR THE GODS(1958); GENE KRUPA STORY, THE(1959); I, MOBSTER(1959); HITLER(1962); GREATEST STORY EVER TOLD, THE(1965); HARLOW(1965); 36 HOURS(1965); ST. VALENTINE'S DAY MASSACRE, THE(1967); POWER, THE(1968); SOYLENT GREEN(1973)
Peter Lovstrom
MONTY PYTHON'S THE MEANING OF LIFE(1983, Brit.); PARTY PARTY(1983, Brit.)
Alex Lovy
MAN CALLED FLINTSTONE, THE(1966), w
Andrew Low
ANASTASIA(1956), set d; LOLITA(1962), set d; WAR LOVER, THE(1962, U.S./Brit.), set d; STORK TALK(1964, Brit.), set d; DEADLY BEES,THE(1967, Brit.), set d; TERRORNAUTS, THE(1967, Brit.), set d; CONQUEROR WORM, THE(1968, Brit.), set d; SALT & PEPPER(1968, Brit.), set d; TORTURE GARDEN(1968, Brit.), set d; MIND OF MR. SOAMES, THE(1970, Brit.), set d
Belinda Low
BUTLEY(1974, Brit.)
Ben Low
13 RUE MADELEINE(1946); ONE MAN(1979, Can.), m
Bruce Low
FOX AND HIS FRIENDS(1976, Ger.); MARRIAGE OF MARIA BRAUN, THE(1979, Ger.)
Carl Low
WILD IS MY LOVE(1963)
Chuck L. Low
KING OF COMEDY, THE(1983)
Frances Low
1984
LOOSE CONNECTIONS(1984, Brit.)
Graeme Low
Silents
PRIDE OF DONEGAL, THE(1929, Brit.)
Jack Low
DON'T BET ON BLONDES(1935); MODERN TIMES(1936); SLAVE SHIP(1937); DARK COMMAND, THE(1940); OUTLAWS OF THE PANHANDLE(1941); MAN FROM FRISCO(1944); CARRIE(1952); SALOME(1953); PROUD ONES, THE(1956)
Lorna Low
ROBERTA(1935)

Martin L. Low
HOT ROD HULLABALOO(1966), p
Sally Low
SPY WITH A COLD NOSE, THE(1966, Brit.)
Stephen Low
1984
SPLITZ(1984), p
Warren Low
ISLE OF FURY(1936), ed; WHITE ANGEL, THE(1936), ed; GREAT GARRICK, THE(1937), ed; GREAT O'MALLEY, THE(1937), ed; KID COMES BACK, THE(1937), ed; MARRY THE GIRL(1937), ed; AMAZING DR. CLITTERHOUSE, THE(1938), ed; JEZEBEL(1938), ed; SISTERS, THE(1938), ed; DUST BE MY DESTINY(1939), ed; JUAREZ(1939), ed; WE ARE NOT ALONE(1939), ed; ALL THIS AND HEAVEN TOO(1940), ed; DISPATCH FROM REUTERS, A(1940), ed; DR. EHRLICH'S MAGIC BULLET(1940), ed; ONE FOOT IN HEAVEN(1941), ed; OUT OF THE FOG(1941), ed; SHINING VICTORY(1941), ed; GAY SISTERS, THE(1942), ed; JUKE GIRL(1942), ed; NOW, VOYAGER(1942), ed; PRINCESS O'ROURKE(1943), ed; SEARCHING WIND, THE(1946), ed; DESERT FURY(1947), ed; JOHNNY O'CLOCK(1947), ed; SORRY, WRONG NUMBER(1948), ed; ACCUSED, THE(1949), ed; ROPE OF SAND(1949), ed; DARK CITY(1950), ed; FILE ON THELMA JORDAN, THE(1950), ed; MY FRIEND IRMA GOES WEST(1950), ed; PAID IN FULL(1950), ed; SEPTEMBER AFFAIR(1950), ed; PEKING EXPRESS(1951), ed; RED MOUNTAIN(1951), ed; SAILOR BEWA-RE(1951), ed; THAT'S MY BOY(1951), ed; COME BACK LITTLE SHEBA(1952), ed; STOOGE, THE(1952), ed; CADDY, THE(1953), ed; MONEY FROM HOME(1953), ed; SCARED STIFF(1953), ed; ABOUT MRS. LESLIE(1954), ed; THREE RING CIR-CUS(1954), ed; ARTISTS AND MODELS(1955), ed; ROSE TATTOO, THE(1955), ed; BAD SEED, THE(1956), ed; RAINMAKER, THE(1956), ed; GUNFIGHT AT THE O.K. CORRAL(1957), ed; WILD IS THE WIND(1957), ed; HOT SPELL(1958), ed; KING CREOLE(1958), ed; CAREER(1959), ed; DON'T GIVE UP THE SHIP(1959), ed; LAST TRAIN FROM GUN HILL(1959), ed; G.I. BLUES(1960), ed; VISIT TO A SMALL PLANET(1960), ed; SUMMER AND SMOKE(1961), ed; GIRL NAMED TAMIRO, A(1962), ed; WIVES AND LOVERS(1963), ed; ROUSTABOUT(1964), ed; BOEING BOEING(1965), ed; SONS OF KATIE ELDER, THE(1965), ed; PARADISE, HAWAII-AN STYLE(1966), ed; OH DAD, POOR DAD, MAMA'S HUNG YOU IN THE CLOSET AND I'M FEELIN' SO SAD(1967), ed; WATERHOLE NO. 3(1967), ed; FIVE CARD STUD(1968), ed; WILL PENNY(1968), ed; KRAKATOA, EAST OF JAVA(1969), ed; TRUE GRIT(1969), ed; NORWOOD(1970), ed; WILLARD(1971), ed
John Lowall
Misc. Silents
CAPTAIN COWBOY(1929)
Morton Lowater
DAWN PATROL, THE(1938)
John Lowdell
TWO HUNDRED MOTELS(1971, Brit.)
Alice Lowe
Silents
SHOULD A WIFE WORK?(1922)
Arthur Lowe
DULCIMER STREET(1948, Brit.); FLOODTIDE(1949, Brit.); KIND HEARTS AND CORONETS(1949, Brit.); POET'S PUB(1949, Brit.); STOP PRESS GIRL(1949, Brit.); SPIDER AND THE FLY, THE(1952, Brit.); FINAL APPOINTMENT(1954, Brit.); WINDFALL(1955 Brit.); WOMAN FOR JOE, THE(1955, Brit.); WHO DONE IT?(1956, Brit.); GREEN MAN, THE(1957, Brit.); HIGH TERRACE(1957, Brit.); STRANGER IN TOWN(1957, Brit.); TWO GROOMS FOR A BRIDE(1957, Brit.); STORMY CROSSING(1958, Brit.); BOY AND THE BRIDGE, THE(1959, Brit.); FOLLOW THAT HORSE!(1960, Brit.); THIS SPORTING LIFE(1963, Brit.); YOU MUST BE JOKING!(1965, Brit.); IF ...(1968, Brit.); BED SITTING ROOM, THE(1969, Brit.); RISE AND RISE OF MICHAEL RIMMER, THE(1970, Brit.); SOME WILL, SOME WON'T(1970, Brit.); SPRING AND PORT WINE(1970, Brit.); DAD'S ARMY(1971, Brit.); FRAGMENT OF FEAR(1971, Brit.); RULING CLASS, THE(1972, Brit.); ADOLF HITLER—MY PART IN HIS DOWN-FALL(1973, Brit.); O LUCKY MAN!(1973, Brit.); THEATRE OF BLOOD(1973, Brit.); BAWDY ADVENTURES OF TOM JONES, THE(1976, Brit.); NO SEX PLEASE–WE'RE BRITISH(1979, Brit.); LADY VANISHES, THE(1980, Brit.); SWEET WILLIAM(1980, Brit.); WAGNER(1983, Brit./Hung./Aust.)
Arthur Lowe, Jr.
MYSTERY STREET(1950); NEW MEXICO(1951)
Barbara Lowe
LILITH(1964)
Barry Lowe
YESTERDAY'S ENEMY(1959, Brit.); THEY CAN'T HANG ME(1955, Brit.); HELL IN KOREA(1956, Brit.); STOWAWAY GIRL(1957, Brit.); STEEL BAYONET, THE(1958, Brit.); UP THE CREEK(1958, Brit.); EXPRESSO BONGO(1959, Brit.); CASH ON DEMAND(1962, Brit.); SANDS OF THE KALAHARI(1965, Brit.); TORTURE GAR-DEN(1968, Brit.); START THE REVOLUTION WITHOUT ME(1970); HANDS OF THE RIPPER(1971, Brit.)
Bill Lowe
DATE WITH A DREAM, A(1948, Brit.); MELODY CLUB(1949, Brit.); RECOIL(1953); WHITE FIRE(1953, Brit.)
Claudia Lowe
1984
DREAMSCAPE(1984)
David Lowe
MARINE BATTLEGROUND(1966, U.S/S.K.)
Debbie Lowe
Misc. Talkies
CHEERLEADERS, THE(1973)
Dennis Lowe
REVENGE OF THE PINK PANTHER(1978), spec eff
Donna Lowe
SAMMY STOPS THE WORLD zero(1978)
E. T. Lowe
ESCAPADE(1932), w
E. T. Lowe, Jr.
LITTLE WILDCAT, THE(1928), w; STATE STREET SADIE(1928), w
Silents
SCRAPPER, THE(1922), w
Edmund Lowe
COCK-EYED WORLD, THE(1929); IN OLD ARIZONA(1929); MAKING THE GRA-DE(1929); PAINTED ANGEL, THE(1929); THIS THING CALLED LOVE(1929); THRU DIFFERENT EYES(1929); BAD ONE, THE(1930); BORN RECKLESS(1930); GOOD

INTENTIONS(1930); HAPPY DAYS(1930); PART TIME WIFE(1930); SCOTLAND YARD(1930); CISCO KID(1931); DON'T BET ON WOMEN(1931); MEN ON CALL(1931); SPIDER, THE(1931); TRANSATLANTIC(1931); WOMEN OF ALL NATIONS(1931); ATTORNEY FOR THE DEFENSE(1932); CHANDU THE MAGICIAN(1932); DEVIL IS DRIVING, THE(1932); GUILTY AS HELL(1932); MISLEADING LADY, THE(1932); DINNER AT EIGHT(1933); HER BODYGUARD(1933); HOT PEPPER(1933); I LOVE THAT MAN(1933); BOMBAY MAIL(1934); GIFT OF GAB(1934); LET'S FALL IN LOVE(1934); NO MORE WOMEN(1934); BEST MAN WINS, THE(1935); BLACK SHEEP(1935); GRAND EXIT(1935); GREAT HOTEL MURDER(1935); GREAT IMPERSONATION, THE(1935); KING SOLOMON OF BROADWAY(1935); MR. DYNAMITE(1935); THUNDER IN THE NIGHT(1935); UNDER PRESSURE(1935); DOMMED CARGO(1936, Brit.); GARDEN MURDER CASE, THE(1936); GIRL ON THE FRONT PAGE, THE(1936); MAD HOLIDAY(1936); ESPIONAGE(1937); MURDER ON DIAMOND ROW(1937, Brit.); UNDER COVER OF NIGHT(1937); EVERY DAY'S A HOLIDAY(1938); SECRETS OF A NURSE(1938); NEWSBOY'S HOME(1939); OUR NEIGHBORS–THE CARTERS(1939); WITNESS VANISHES, THE(1939); CROOKED ROAD, THE(1940); HONEYMOON DEFERRED(1940); I LOVE YOU AGAIN(1940); MEN AGAINST THE SKY(1940); WOLF OF NEW YORK(1940); DOUBLE DATE(1941); FLYING CADETS(1941); CALL OUT THE MARINES(1942); KLONDIKE FURY(1942); DANGEROUS BLONDES(1943); MURDER IN TIMES SQUARE(1943); GIRL IN THE CASE(1944); OH, WHAT A NIGHT(1944); DILLINGER(1945); ENCHANTED FOREST, THE(1945); STRANGE MR. GREGORY, THE(1945); GOOD SAM(1948); INTRUDER IN THE DUST(1949); AROUND THE WORLD IN 80 DAYS(1956); WINGS OF EAGLES, THE(1957); LAST HURRAH, THE(1958); PLUNDERERS OF PAINTED FLATS(1959); HELLER IN PINK TIGHTS(1960)

Silents
SPREADING DAWN, THE(1917); MADONNAS AND MEN(1920); WOMAN'S BUSINESS, A(1920); PEACOCK ALLEY(1922); SILENT COMMAND, THE(1923); WHITE FLOWER, THE(1923); NELLIE, THE BEAUTIFUL CLOAK MODEL(1924); CHAMPION OF LOST CAUSES(1925); EAST OF SUEZ(1925); KISS BARRIER, THE(1925); PORTS OF CALL(1925); SOUL MATES(1925); WINDING STAIR, THE(1925); SIBERIA(1926); WHAT PRICE GLORY(1926); IS ZAT SO?(1927); OUTCAST(1928)

Misc. Silents
VIVE LA FRANCE(1918); SOMEONE IN THE HOUSE(1920); WOMAN GIVES, THE(1920); DEVIL, THE(1921); LIVING LIES(1922); IN THE PALACE OF THE KING(1923); WIFE IN NAME ONLY(1923); BARBARA FRIETCHIE(1924); BRASS BOWL, THE(1924); HONOR AMONG MEN(1924); EAST LYNNE(1925); FOOL, THE(1925); GREATER THAN A CROWN(1925); MARRIAGE IN TRANSIT(1925); BLACK PARADISE(1926); PALACE OF PLEASURE, THE(1926); ONE INCREASING PURPOSE(1927); PUBLICITY MADNESS(1927); WIZARD, THE(1927); DRESSED TO KILL(1928); HAPPINESS AHEAD(1928)

Edward T. Lowe
ALIAS MARY SMITH(1932), w; CRUSADER, THE(1932), w; DISCARDED LOVERS(1932), w; FORBIDDEN COMPANY(1932), w; HEARTS OF HUMANITY(1932), w; MIDNIGHT LADY(1932), w; PROBATION(1932), w; RED-HAIRED ALIBI, THE(1932), w; SHOP ANGEL(1932), w; TANGLED DESTINIES(1932), w; THRILL OF YOUTH(1932), w; UNWRITTEN LAW, THE(1932), w; PENAL CODE, THE(1933), w; SING SINNER, SING(1933), w; VAMPIRE BAT, THE(1933), w; WORLD GONE MAD, THE(1933), w; CURTAIN AT EIGHT(1934), w; CHARLIE CHAN IN EGYPT(1935), p; CHARLIE CHAN IN PARIS(1935), w; CHARLIE CHAN IN SHANGHAI(1935), w; LADIES LOVE DANGER(1935), p; YOUR UNCLE DUDLEY(1935), p; CHAMPAGNE CHARLIE(1936), p; CHARLIE CHAN AT THE RACE TRACK(1936), w; EDUCATING FATHER(1936), w; NAVY WIFE(1936), w; BULLDOG DRUMMOND COMES BACK(1937), w; BULLDOG DRUMMOND ESCAPES(1937), w; BULLDOG DRUMMOND'S REVENGE(1937), w; WILD MONEY(1937), w; TIP-OFF GIRLS(1938), p; TOUCHDOWN, ARMY(1938), p; ALL WOMEN HAVE SECRETS(1939), p; BULLDOG DRUMMOND'S SECRET POLICE(1939), p; PERSONS IN HIDING(1939), p; TELEVISION SPY(1939), p; UNDERCOVER DOCTOR(1939), p; TEXAS RANGERS RIDE AGAIN(1940), p; PUBLIC ENEMIES(1941), w; SCATTERGOOD BAINES(1941), w; GIRL FROM ALASKA(1942), w; MAN'S WORLD, A(1942), w; SHERLOCK HOLMES AND THE SECRET WEAPON(1942), w; MINESWEEPER(1943), w; TARZAN'S DESERT MYSTERY(1943), w; HOUSE OF FRANKENSTEIN(1944), w; TIMBER QUEEN(1944); HOUSE OF DRACULA(1945), w; ROUGH, TOUGH AND READY(1945), w; PIRATES OF MONTEREY(1947), w

Silents
SLIM PRINCESS, THE(1915), w

Edward T. Lowe, Jr.
LONESOME(1928), w; TENDERLOIN(1928), w; BROADWAY(1929), w; MISSISSIPPI GAMBLER(1929), w; ONE STOLEN NIGHT(1929), w; STOLEN KISSES(1929), w; NIGHT RIDE(1930), w; UNDERTOW(1930), w; THREE ON A HONEYMOON(1934), w

Silents
BIG GAME(1921), w; RIDIN' WILD(1922), w; HUNCHBACK OF NOTRE DAME, THE(1923), w; WHAT WIVES WANT(1923), w; ROSE OF PARIS, THE(1924), w; COMPROMISE(1925), w; FIGHTING EDGE(1926), w; SAILOR IZZY MURPHY(1927), w; TILLIE THE TOILER(1927), w

Ellen E. Lowe
KING OF BURLESQUE(1936); RANCHO GRANDE(1940)

Ellen Lowe
CHRISTOPHER BEAN(1933); DANCING PIRATE(1936); SMALL TOWN GIRL(1936); BELOVED BRAT(1938); WAGON TRAIN(1940); SADDLEMATES(1941); TOM, DICK AND HARRY(1941); YOU BELONG TO ME(1941); HI DIDDLE DIDDLE(1943); SLEEPY LAGOON(1943); GOODNIGHT SWEETHEART(1944); PORT OF 40 THIEVES, THE(1944); ROSIE THE RIVETER(1944); NIGHT AND DAY(1946); OPEN SECRET(1948); SITTING PRETTY(1948); SNAKE PIT, THE(1948); BLACK BOOK, THE(1949); SIDE STREET(1950)

Misc. Talkies
BORDERTOWN TRAIL(1944)

Enid Lowe
LOOT(1971, Brit.)

Ephraim Lowe
INTRUDER IN THE DUST(1949)

Ernie Lowe
BILLY IN THE LOWLANDS(1979)

Evan Lowe
RIDING SHOTGUN(1954)

Frances Lowe
MUSIC MACHINE, THE(1979, Brit.)

Grant Lowe
RABID(1976, Can.)

Harry Lowe, Jr.
SEQUOIA(1934)

Harvey Lowe
MC CABE AND MRS. MILLER(1971)

Heather Lowe
BATTLE FOR THE PLANET OF THE APES(1973); SPIRAL STAIRCASE, THE(1975, Brit.)

Irma Lowe
SHANGHAI LADY(1929)

Jack Lowe
ONLY ANGELS HAVE WINGS(1939); HE STAYED FOR BREAKFAST(1940); MAN FROM TUMBLEWEEDS, THE(1940); TALK OF THE TOWN(1942)

James Lowe
Misc. Silents
UNCLE TOM'S CABIN(1927)

K. Elmo Lowe
THESE THIRTY YEARS(1934); KID FROM CLEVELAND, THE(1949); TRIAL WITHOUT JURY(1950); WOMAN FROM HEADQUARTERS(1950)

Kevin Lowe
MOTHER'S DAY(1980)

Len Lowe
DATE WITH A DREAM, A(1948, Brit.); MELODY CLUB(1949, Brit.); COUNTESS FROM HONG KONG, A(1967, Brit.); CARRY ON LOVING(1970, Brit.)

Leslie Lowe
1984
SCREAM FOR HELP(1984)

Lorna Lowe
DANTE'S INFERNO(1935); RECKLESS(1935)

Mundell Lowe
SATAN IN HIGH HEELS(1962), m, md; TIME FOR KILLING, A(1967), m, md; BILLY JACK(1971), m; EVERYTHING YOU ALWAYS WANTED TO KNOW ABOUT SEX, BUT WE'RE AFRAID TO ASK(1972), m; SIDEWINDER ONE(1977), m, md

Olga Lowe
GREAT MANHUNT, THE(1951, Brit.); HOTEL SAHARA(1951, Brit.); SO LITTLE TIME(1953, Brit.); OH ROSALINDA(1956, Brit.); NIJINSKY(1980, Brit.)
1984
RIDDLE OF THE SANDS, THE(1984, Brit.)

Pearl Lowe
Silents
OLIVER TWIST, JR.(1921)

Penny Lowe
UP POMPEII(1971, Brit.), cos

Rob Lowe
CLASS(1983); OUTSIDERS, THE(1983)
1984
HOTEL NEW HAMPSHIRE, THE(1984); OXFORD BLUES(1984)

Roger Lowe
MEGAFORCE(1982)

Sherman L. Lowe
ON PROBATION(1935), w; NIGHT CARGO(1936), w; HIGH HAT(1937), w; LEGION OF MISSING MEN(1937), w; TOUGH TO HANDLE(1937), w; WITH LOVE AND KISSES(1937), w; I DEMAND PAYMENT(1938), w; MYSTERY HOUSE(1938), w; INVISIBLE INFORMER(1946), w; MAGNIFICENT ROGUE, THE(1946), w; THE CAT-MAN OF PARIS(1946), w; UNDERCOVER WOMAN, THE(1946), w; VALLEY OF THE ZOMBIES(1946), w; ALIMONY(1949), w; PAROLE, INC.(1949), w; WHITE GODDESS(1953), w; PHANTOM OF THE JUNGLE(1955), w; THUNDER OVER SANGOLAND(1955), w

Sherman Lowe
DAMES AHOY(1930), w; THEY NEVER COME BACK(1932), w; DIAMOND TRAIL(1933), w; CRIMSON ROMANCE(1934), w; LOST JUNGLE, THE(1934), w; MELODY TRAIL(1935), w; TRAPPED BY TELEVISION(1936), w; ARIZONA DAYS(1937), w; GALLOPING DYNAMITE(1937), w; HEADLINE CRASHER(1937), w; SING WHILE YOU'RE ABLE(1937), w; DAREDEVIL DRIVERS(1938), w; CRASHING THRU(1939), w; EVERYTHING'S ON ICE(1939), w; AM I GUILTY?(1940), w; LAW AND ORDER(1940), w; PONY POST(1940), w; RAGTIME COWBOY JOE(1940), w; SECRETS OF A MODEL(1940), w; WEST OF CARSON CITY(1940), w; ARIZONA CYCLONE(1941), w; BURY ME NOT ON THE LONE PRAIRIE(1941), w; MASKED RIDER, THE(1941), w; KING OF THE STALLIONS(1942), w; LITTLE JOE, THE WRANGLER(1942), w; MISS V FROM MOSCOW(1942), w; NIGHT FOR CRIME, A(1942), w; YANK IN LIBYA, A(1942), w; YANKS ARE COMING, THE(1942), w; SWEETHEARTS OF THE U.S.A.(1944), w; DESERT HORSEMAN(1946), w; GUNMAN'S CODE(1946), w; RUSTLER'S ROUNDUP(1946), w; KANGAROO KID, THE(1950, Aus./U.S.), w

Skip Lowe
BLACK SHAMPOO(1976)

Stanja Lowe
1984
SILENT MADNESS(1984)

Susan Lowe
FEMALE TROUBLE(1975); POLYESTER(1981)

Tom Rov Lowe
POCO...LITTLE DOG LOST(1977)

Trina Lowe
THEY WERE EXPENDABLE(1945)

Walter Lowe
SPOOK WHO SAT BY THE DOOR, THE(1973)

Warren Lowe
LIFE OF EMILE ZOLA, THE(1937), ed

William Lowe
SLAUGHTER IN SAN FRANCISCO(1981), d&w

Lowe the Dog
WONDER BOY(1951, Brit./Aust.)

Rose Loweinger
HOTEL CONTINENTAL(1932), ed

Art Lowel
NUMBER ONE(1969), art d

William Paul Lowery
WINGS OF EAGLES, THE(1957)
Curt Lowgren
NAKED NIGHT, THE(1956, Swed.)
Mark Lowhead
SATIN MUSHROOM, THE(1969)
Jack Lowin
RETURN OF THE JEDI(1983), ph
Robert Lowing
Silents
RAMSHACKLE HOUSE(1924)
Paul Lowinger
Misc. Talkies
NAUGHTY NYMPHS(1974)
Arthur Lowis
EARTH DIES SCREAMING, THE(1964, Brit.), ph
Klaus Lowitsch
ODESSA FILE, THE(1974, Brit./Ger.); ROSEBUD(1975); CROSS OF IRON(1977, Brit., Ger.); JAIL BAIT(1977, Ger.); DESPAIR(1978, Ger.); MARRIAGE OF MARIA BRAUN, THE(1979, Ger.); DESIRE, THE INTERIOR LIFE(1980, Ital./Ger.); FIREFOX(1982); NIGHT CROSSING(1982)
Jackie Lowitt
GOODBYE PORK PIE(1981, New Zealand)
Siegfried Lowitz
SINS OF ROSE BERND, THE(1959, Ger.); CONFESS DR. CORDA(1960, Ger.); IT HAPPENED IN BROAD DAYLIGHT(1960, Ger./Switz.); KING IN SHADOW(1961, Ger.); BRAIN, THE(1965, Ger./Brit.); INVISIBLE DR. MABUSE, THE(1965, Ger.); GIRL AND THE LEGEND, THE(1966, Ger.); GREAT BRITISH TRAIN ROBBERY, THE(1967, Ger.)
Brian Lown
SPARE THE ROD(1961, Brit.)
Marie Belloc Lowndes
LETTY LYNTON(1932), w; LODGER, THE(1944), w; IVY(1947), w; MAN IN THE ATTIC(1953), w
Victor Lowndes
FLEDGLINGS(1965, Brit)
Peter Lownds
KRAMER VS. KRAMER(1979)
Richard Lownes
THISTLEDOWN(1938, Brit.)
Victor Lownes
AND NOW FOR SOMETHING COMPLETELY DIFFERENT(1972, Brit.), p
Raymond Lowney
Silents
AWFUL TRUTH, THE(1925)
Dan Lownsberry
PROWLER, THE(1981)
Peanuts Lowrey
WINNING TEAM, THE(1952)
Eugene Lowrie
HOUSE OF FEAR, THE(1945), art d
Ted Lowrie
INCIDENT, THE(1967)
A. Hunt Lowry
HUMANOIDS FROM THE DEEP(1980), p
Bob Lowry
COW COUNTRY(1953)
Brick Lowry
GETAWAY, THE(1972)
Chuck Lowry
LUXURY LINER(1948)
Dick Lowry
SMOKEY AND THE BANDIT–PART 3(1983), a, d
Ed Lowry
HOUSE OF MYSTERY(1934)
Emily Lowry
AS THE EARTH TURNS(1934)
Emma Lowry
Silents
CONQUERED HEARTS(1918)
Misc. Silents
BLUEBIRD, THE(1918)
George Lowry
THAT CHAMPIONSHIP SEASON(1982)
Helen Lowry
YANK IN LONDON, A(1946, Brit.)
Hunt Lowry
GET CRAZY(1983), p
1984
TOP SECRET!(1984), p
Ira M. Lowry
Silents
OH, JOHNNY(1919), d
Misc. Silents
FOR THE FREEDOM OF THE WORLD(1917), d; FOR THE FREEDOM OF THE EAST(1918), d; HIGH POCKETS(1919), d; ROAD CALLED STRAIGHT, THE(1919), d; SANDY BURKE OF THE U-BAR-U(1919), d; SPEEDY MEADE(1919), d
Ira W. Lowry
Misc. Silents
MISFIT EARL, A(1919), d
Jane Lowry
ALICE, SWEET ALICE(1978)
Joe Lowry
MAGIC(1978); CHINA SYNDROME, THE(1979); FINAL COUNTDOWN, THE(1980)
Judith Lowry
MIRACLE OF MORGAN'S CREEK, THE(1944); 13 RUE MADELEINE(1946); MIRACLE WORKER, THE(1962); LADYBUG, LADYBUG(1963); TROUBLE WITH ANGELS, THE(1966); VALLEY OF THE DOLLS(1967); NIGHT THEY RAIDED MINSKY'S, THE(1968); POPI(1969); HUSBANDS(1970); ANDERSON TAPES, THE(1971); COLD TURKEY(1971); EFFECT OF GAMMA RAYS ON MAN-IN-THE-MOON MARIGOLDS,

THE(1972); SUPERDAD(1974)
L. Lowry
Silents
HEARTS OF THE WORLD(1918)
Lisa Lowry
MRS. O'MALLEY AND MR. MALONE(1950)
Ludwig Lowry
NEXT TIME WE LOVE(1936)
Silents
MAN FROM HEADQUARTERS(1928)
Lynn Lowry
BATTLE OF LOVE'S RETURN, THE(1971); I DRINK YOUR BLOOD(1971); THE CRAZIES(1973); FIGHTING MAD(1976); THEY CAME FROM WITHIN(1976, Can.); CAT PEOPLE(1982)
Misc. Talkies
SCORE(1973)
Malcolm Lowry
1984
UNDER THE VOLCANO(1984), w
Marcella Lowry
ARTHUR(1981)
Mark Lowry
BLOOD BATH(1966), m
Morton Lowry
HOUND OF THE BASKERVILLES, THE(1939); TARZAN FINDS A SON!(1939); WINTER CARNIVAL(1939); HUDSON'S BAY(1940); CHARLEY'S AUNT(1941); HOW GREEN WAS MY VALLEY(1941); YANK IN THE R.A.F., A(1941); CAPTAINS OF THE CLOUDS(1942); COUNTER-ESPIONAGE(1942); LOVES OF EDGAR ALLAN POE, THE(1942); PIED PIPER, THE(1942); THIS ABOVE ALL(1942); IMMORTAL SERGEANT, THE(1943); NO TIME FOR LOVE(1943); HOUR BEFORE THE DAWN, THE(1944); MAN IN HALF-MOON STREET, THE(1944); NONE BUT THE LONELY HEART(1944); STORY OF DR. WASSELL, THE(1944); PICTURE OF DORIAN GRAY, THE(1945); PURSUIT TO ALGIERS(1945); VERDICT, THE(1946); CALCUTTA(1947); TOO HOT TO HANDLE(1961, Brit.)
Murray Lowry
SHADOW OF THE HAWK(1976, Can.)
Peter Lowry
GIVE ME THE STARS(1944, Brit.)
Robert Lowry
HOMESTEADERS, THE(1953); THAT KIND OF WOMAN(1959), w
Roger Lowry
NEGATIVES(1968, Brit.), w
Tony Lowry
MAGIC NIGHT(1932, Brit.), m; NOT WANTED ON VOYAGE(1957, Brit.), m; UP THE CREEK(1958, Brit.), m
Viola Lowry
COLLEEN(1936); GOLDEN ARROW, THE(1936)
Lowry and Richardson
MY AIN FOLK(1944, Brit.)
Janice Lowthian
DICK BARTON–SPECIAL AGENT(1948, Brit.)
Louis Lowy
SEARCHING WIND, THE(1946)
Louis Ludwig Lowy
STORM OVER LISBON(1944)
Otto Lowy
CHRISTINA(1974, Can.)
Robert E. Lowy
FADE TO BLACK(1980), set d
Robert Lowy
1984
SURF II(1984), set d
D.A. Loxley
BAD BASCOMB(1946), w
James Loxley
THRESHOLD(1983, Can.)
Violet Loxley
FIND THE LADY(1936, Brit.); MUSIC MAKER, THE(1936, Brit.)
Barbara Loy
WAR ITALIAN STYLE(1967, Ital.)
Loo Loy
GENERAL DIED AT DAWN, THE(1936); IT HAD TO HAPPEN(1936)
Mino Loy
SECRET AGENT FIREBALL(1965, Fr./Ital.), p; 10,000 DOLLARS BLOOD MONEY(1966, Ital.), p; SWEET BODY OF DEBORAH, THE(1969, Ital./Fr.), p; WOLF LARSEN(1978, Ital.), p
Myrna Loy
JAZZ SINGER, THE(1927); MIDNIGHT TAXI, THE(1928); NOAH'S ARK(1928); STATE STREET SADIE(1928); BLACK WATCH, THE(1929); DESERT SONG, THE(1929); EVIDENCE(1929); FANCY BAGGAGE(1929); HARDBOILED ROSE(1929); SQUALL, THE(1929); BRIDE OF THE REGIMENT(1930); CAMEO KIRBY(1930); COCK O' THE WALK(1930); DEVIL TO PAY, THE(1930); GREAT DIVIDE, THE(1930); ISLE OF ESCAPE(1930); JAZZ CINDERELLA(1930); LAST OF THE DUANES(1930); RENEGADES(1930); ROGUE OF THE RIO GRANDE(1930); TRUTH ABOUT YOUTH, THE(1930); UNDER A TEXAS MOON(1930); ARROWSMITH(1931); BODY AND SOUL(1931); CONNECTICUT YANKEE, A(1931); CONSOLATION MARRIAGE(1931); HUSH MONEY(1931); NAUGHTY FLIRT, THE(1931); REBOUND(1931); SKYLINE(1931); TRANSATLANTIC(1931); ANIMAL KINGDOM, THE(1932); EMMA(1932); LOVE ME TONIGHT(1932); MASK OF FU MANCHU(1932); NEW MORALS FOR OLD(1932); THIRTEEN WOMEN(1932); VANITY FAIR(1932); WET PARADE, THE(1932); WOMAN IN ROOM 13, THE(1932); BARBARIAN, THE(1933); NIGHT FLIGHT(1933); PENTHOUSE(1933); PRIZEFIGHTER AND THE LADY, THE(1933); SCARLET RIVER(1933); TOPAZE(1933); WHEN LADIES MEET(1933); BROADWAY BILL(1934); EVELYN PRENTICE(1934); MANHATTAN MELODRAMA(1934); MEN IN WHITE(1934); STAMBOUL QUEST(1934); THIN MAN, THE(1934); WINGS IN THE DARK(1935); AFTER THE THIN MAN(1936); GREAT ZIEGFELD, THE(1936); LIBELED LADY(1936); PETTICOAT FEVER(1936); TO MARY-WITH LOVE(1936); WHIPSAW(1936); WIFE VERSUS SECRETARY(1936); DOUBLE WEDDING(1937); PARNELL(1937); MAN-PROOF(1938); TEST PILOT(1938); TOO HOT TO HANDLE(1938); ANOTHER THIN MAN(1939); LUCKY NIGHT(1939); RAINS CAME,

THE(1939); I LOVE YOU AGAIN(1940); THIRD FINGER, LEFT HAND(1940); LOVE CRAZY(1941); SHADOW OF THE THIN MAN(1941); THIN MAN GOES HOME, THE(1944); BEST YEARS OF OUR LIVES, THE(1946); SO GOES MY LOVE(1946); BACHELOR AND THE BOBBY-SOXER, THE(1947); SENATOR WAS INDISCREET, THE(1947); SONG OF THE THIN MAN(1947); MR. BLANDINGS BUILDS HIS DREAM HOUSE(1948); RED PONY, THE(1949); IF THIS BE SIN(1950, Brit.); BELLES ON THEIR TOES(1952); AMBASSADOR'S DAUGHTER, THE(1956); LONELY-HEARTS(1958); FROM THE TERRACE(1960); MIDNIGHT LACE(1960); AIRPORT 1975(1974); END, THE(1978); JUST TELL ME WHAT YOU WANT(1980)

Silents

ACROSS THE PACIFIC(1926); CAVEMAN, THE(1926); DON JUAN(1926); EXQUISITE SINNER, THE(1926); GILDED HIGHWAY, THE(1926); SO THIS IS PARIS(1926); GIRL FROM CHICAGO, THE(1927); HAM AND EGGS AT THE FRONT(1927); IF I WERE SINGLE(1927); SAILOR'S SWEETHEART, A(1927); CRIMSON CITY, THE(1928)

Misc. Silents

WHY GIRLS GO BACK HOME(1926); BITTER APPLES(1927); FINGER PRINTS(1927); SIMPLE SIS(1927); BEWARE OF MARRIED MEN(1928); PAY AS YOU ENTER(1928); TURN BACK THE HOURS(1928)

Nanni Loy
FIASCO IN MILAN(1963, Fr./Ital.), d, w; FOUR DAYS OF NAPLES, THE(1963, US/Ital.), d, w; HEAD OF THE FAMILY(1967, Ital./Fr.), d, w; MADE IN ITALY(1967, Fr./Ital.), d, w; GOODNIGHT, LADIES AND GENTLEMEN(1977, Ital.), d&w; CAFE EXPRESS(1980, Ital.), d, w

Misc. Talkies

OPERATION SNAFU(1970, Ital./Yugo.), d

Sonny Loy
Silents
MR. WU(1927)

Carlow Loya
PONY SOLDIER(1952)

Javier Loya
QUEEN'S SWORDSMEN, THE(1963, Mex.); EXTERMINATING ANGEL, THE(1967, Mex.); CURSE OF THE DOLL PEOPLE, THE(1968, Mex.)

Alison Loyd "Thelma Todd"
CORSAIR(1931)

Beverly Loyd
TIGER WOMAN, THE(1945); UTAH(1945); HERE COMES TROUBLE(1948); JOAN OF ARC(1948)

Jeremy Loyd
COMING-OUT PARTY, A(

Lala Loyd
FIEND WITHOUT A FACE(1958)

Russell Loyd
SCHOOL FOR SECRETS(1946, Brit.), ed

George Loyer
Silents
HEARTS OF THE WORLD(1918)

Raymond Loyer
TIME BOMB(1961, Fr./Ital.); CRIME DOES NOT PAY(1962, Fr.)

Jeff Loynes
YELLOW SUBMARINE(1958, Brit.), animation

Roberto Loyola
SONNY AND JED(1974, Ital.), p

Mieczyslaw Loza
LOTNA(1966, Pol.)

Ray Loza
PROPER TIME, THE(1959)

Lozach
BATTLE OF THE RAILS(1949, Fr.)

Irma Lozano
GIGANTES PLANETARIOS(1965, Mex.)

Margareta Lozano
THAT SPLENDID NOVEMBER(1971, Ital./Fr.)

Margarita Lozano
VIRIDIANA(1962, Mex./Span.); LAZARILLO(1963, Span.); FISTFUL OF DOLLARS, A(1964, Ital./Ger./Span.); DIARY OF A SCHIZOPHRENIC GIRL(1970, Ital.); LADY OF MONZA, THE(1970, Ital.); NIGHT OF THE SHOOTING STARS, THE(1982, Ital.)

Margherita Lozano
VACATION, THE(1971, Ital.)

Mario Lozano
SAVAGE PAMPAS(1967, Span./Arg.)

Salvador Lozano
AZTEC MUMMY, THE(1957, Mex.)

Curtis Lozer
HELL SQUAD(1958)

Zorica Lozic
TWO OF US, THE(1968, Fr.); MAN WITH CONNECTIONS, THE(1970, Fr.); FIRST TIME, THE(1978, Fr.)

John Lozier
LIKE A CROW ON A JUNE BUG(1972)

Edmondo Lozzi
GOLIATH AGAINST THE GIANTS(1963, Ital./Span.), ed; SABATA(1969, Ital.), ed

Lisa Lu
MOUNTAIN ROAD, THE(1960); RIDER ON A DEAD HORSE(1962); WOMAN HUNT(1962); TERROR IN THE WAX MUSEUM(1973); DEMON SEED(1977); SAINT JACK(1979); DON'T CRY, IT'S ONLY THUNDER(1982); HAMMETT(1982)

Ho Lu-ying
ENCHANTING SHADOW, THE(1965, Hong Kong), ph

Adriano Lualdi
MONTE CASSINO(1948, Ital.), m

Antonella Lualdi
HIS LAST TWELVE HOURS(1953, Ital.); RED AND THE BLACK, THE(1954, Fr./Ital.); YOUNG HUSBANDS(1958, Ital./Fr.); WEB OF PASSION(1961, Fr.); END OF DESIRE(1962 Fr./Ital.); I SPIT ON YOUR GRAVE(1962, Fr.); LA NOTTE BRAVA(1962, Fr./Ital.); MY SON, THE HERO(1963, Ital./Fr.); RUN WITH THE DEVIL(1963, Fr./Ital.); DISORDER(1964, Fr./Ital.); LET'S TALK ABOUT WOMEN(1964, Fr./Ital.); MONGOLS, THE(1966, Fr./Ital.); SEA PIRATE, THE(1967, Fr./Span./Ital.); HOW TO SEDUCE A PLAYBOY(1968, Aust./Fr./Ital.)

Antonella Lualdl
ADORABLE CREATURES(1956, Fr.)

Luukia Luana
ROAD TO BALI(1952)

Luao
SANDERS OF THE RIVER(1935, Brit.)

Hank Luba
GOING HOME(1971)

Milton Luban
GRAND CANYON(1949), w; TOUGH ASSIGNMENT(1949), w

Edward Lubaszenko
CONTRACT, THE(1982, Pol.)

Henry H. Lube
DALTON THAT GOT AWAY(1960), p

Jack Lubell
STUDENT TOUR(1934); SWISS MISS(1938); HOUSE ACROSS THE BAY, THE(1940)

Paula Lubelska
MOTHERS OF TODAY(1939); TEVYA(1939); ELI ELI(1940)

Bernard Luber
LOAN SHARK(1952), p; I'LL GET YOU(1953, Brit.), p; MAN FROM CAIRO, THE(1953), p; QUEEN OF SHEBA(1953, Ital.), w; SWORD OF LANCELOT(1963, Brit.), p

Madeline Lubetty
Silents
CARDIGAN(1922)

Ivan Lubeznov
SIX P.M.(1946, USSR)

Claude Lubicki
FIRST TIME, THE(1978, Fr.)

Christina Lubicz
SECOND FIDDLE(1957, Brit.); TIME WITHOUT PITY(1957, Brit.); NIGHT TO REMEMBER, A(1958, Brit.); CHANCE MEETING(1960, Brit.)

Karolina Lubienska
Misc. Silents
10 CONDEMNED(1932, Pol.)

A. Ronald Lubin
CONVICTS FOUR(1962), p; OUTRAGE, THE(1964), p; GUNFIGHT, A(1971), p

Arthur Lubin
TIMES SQUARE(1929); SUCCESSFUL FAILURE, A(1934), d; FRISCO WATERFRONT(1935), d; GREAT GOD GOLD(1935), d; TWO SINNERS(1935), d; HONEYMOON LIMITED(1936), d; HOUSE OF A THOUSAND CANDLES, THE(1936), d; YELLOWSTONE(1936), d; ADVENTURE'S END(1937), d; CALIFORNIA STRAIGHT AHEAD(1937), d; I COVER THE WAR(1937), d; IDOL OF THE CROWDS(1937), d; MYSTERIOUS CROSSING(1937), d; BELOVED BRAT(1938), d; MIDNIGHT INTRUDER(1938), d; PRISON BREAK(1938), d; SECRETS OF A NURSE(1938), d; BIG GUY, THE(1939), d; BIG TOWN CZAR(1939), d; CALL A MESSENGER(1939), d; MICKEY, THE KID(1939), d; RISKY BUSINESS(1939), d; BLACK FRIDAY(1940), d; GANGS OF CHICAGO(1940), d; I'M NOBODY'S SWEETHEART NOW(1940), d; MEET THE WILDCAT(1940), d; WHO KILLED AUNT MAGGIE?(1940), d; BUCK PRIVATES(1941), d; HOLD THAT GHOST(1941), d; IN THE NAVY(1941), d; KEEP 'EM FLYING(1941), d; SAN FRANCISCO DOCKS(1941), d; WHERE DID YOU GET THAT GIRL?(1941), d; EAGLE SQUADRON(1942), d; RIDE 'EM COWBOY(1942), d; PHANTOM OF THE OPERA(1943), d; WHITE SAVAGE(1943), d; ALI BABA AND THE FORTY THIEVES(1944), d; DELIGHTFULLY DANGEROUS(1945), d; NIGHT IN PARADISE, A(1946), d; SPIDER WOMAN STRIKES BACK, THE(1946), d; NEW ORLEANS(1947), d; FRANCIS(1949), d; IMPACT(1949), d; FRANCIS GOES TO THE RACES(1951), d; QUEEN FOR A DAY(1951), d; RHUBARB(1951), d; FRANCIS GOES TO WEST POINT(1952), d; IT GROWS ON TREES(1952), d; FRANCIS COVERS THE BIG TOWN(1953), d; SOUTH SEA WOMAN(1953), d; FRANCIS JOINS THE WACS(1954), d; FOOTSTEPS IN THE FOG(1955, Brit.), d; FRANCIS IN THE NAVY(1955), d; LADY GODIVA(1955), d; FIRST TRAVELING SALESLADY, THE(1956), p, d; STAR OF INDIA(1956, Brit.), d; THIEF OF BAGHDAD, THE(1961, Ital./Fr.), d; INCREDIBLE MR. LIMPET, THE(1964), d; SWORD OF ALI BABA, THE(1965), d; HOLD ON(1966), d; RAIN FOR A DUSTY SUMMER(1971, U.S./Span.), d

Silents
AFRAID TO LOVE(1927); EYES OF THE UNDERWORLD(1929)

Misc. Silents
BUSHRANGER, THE(1928)

Harry Lubin
MR. RECKLESS(1948), m; WATERFRONT AT MIDNIGHT(1948), m

Lon Lubin
WHEN STRANGERS MARRY(1944)

Lou Lubin
SHADOW OF THE THIN MAN(1941); A-HAUNTING WE WILL GO(1942); HARD WAY, THE(1942); JOHNNY EAGER(1942); SABOTEUR(1942); FIND THE BLACKMAILER(1943); HI'YA, CHUM(1943); LADY OF BURLESQUE(1943); SEVENTH VICTIM, THE(1943); THEY GOT ME COVERED(1943); HI BEAUTIFUL(1944); DILLINGER(1945); SCARLET STREET(1945); CROSS MY HEART(1946); NIGHT EDITOR(1946); EASY COME, EASY GO(1947); FALL GUY(1947); RIFFRAFF(1947); JOE PALOOKA IN THE BIG FIGHT(1949); CRY DANGER(1951); PEOPLE AGAINST O'HARA, THE(1951); JUST ACROSS THE STREET(1952); MODELS, INC.(1952); PAT AND MIKE(1952); TROPICAL HEAT WAVE(1952); CLOWN, THE(1953); MONEY FROM HOME(1953); PRIVATE EYES(1953)

Ronald Lubin
LIBERATION OF L.B. JONES, THE(1970), p

Shellen Lubin
TAKING OFF(1971)

Tibi Lubin
Misc. Silents
PRINCE AND THE PAUPER, THE(1929, Aust./Czech.)

Ernest Lubitsch
Misc. Silents
DECEPTION(1921, Ger.), d; THREE WOMEN(1924), d

Ernst Lubitsch
THAT UNCERTAIN FEELING(1941), p&d; PATRIOT, THE(1928), d, ed; LOVE PARADE, THE(1929), p&d; MONTE CARLO(1930), d; SMILING LIEUTENANT, THE(1931), p&d, w; BROKEN LULLABY(1932); IF I HAD A MILLION(1932), d, w; ONE HOUR WITH YOU(1932), p, d; TROUBLE IN PARADISE(1932), p&d; DESIGN FOR LIVING(1933), p&d; MERRY WIDOW, THE(1934), d; DESIRE(1936), p; ANGEL(1937), p&d; BLUEBEARD'S EIGHTH WIFE(1938), p&d; NINOTCHKA(1939),

p&d; SHOP AROUND THE CORNER, THE(1940), p&d; TO BE OR NOT TO BE(1942), p&d, w; HEAVEN CAN WAIT(1943), p&d; ROYAL SCANDAL, A(1945), p; CLUNY BROWN(1946), p&d; THAT LADY IN ERMINE(1948), p, d; TO BE OR NOT TO BE(1983), w

Silents

PASSION(1920, Ger.), d; ONE ARABIAN NIGHT(1921, Ger.), a, d, w; ROSITA(1923), d; FORBIDDEN PARADISE(1924), d; MARRIAGE CIRCLE, THE(1924), d; KISS ME AGAIN(1925), d; LADY WINDERMERE'S FAN(1925), d; SO THIS IS PARIS(1926), d; ETERNAL LOVE(1929), d

Misc. Silents

OYSTER PRINCESS, THE(1919, Ger.), d; GYPSY BLOOD(1921, Ger.), d; SUMU-RUN(1921, Ger.), a, d; VENDETTA(1921, Ger.), d; WIFE OF THE PHARAOH, THE(1922, Ger.), d; STUDENT PRINCE IN OLD HEIDELBERG, THE(1927), d

N. Lubko
THREE SISTERS, THE(1969, USSR)

Vera Lubov
MOTHERS OF TODAY(1939)

Sid Lubow
FIVE(1951), ph

Dave Lubritsky
Misc. Talkies
JEWISH MELODY, THE(1940)

Jean-Claude Lubtchansky
LORD OF THE FLIES(1963, Brit.), ed

Nicole Lubtchansky
IT ONLY HAPPENS TO OTHERS(1971, Fr./Ital.), ed; NATHALIE GRANGER(1972, Fr.), ed; CELINE AND JULIE GO BOATING(1974, Fr.), ed
1984
LOVE ON THE GROUND(1984,Fr.), ed

William Lubtchansky
EVERY MAN FOR HIMSELF(1980, Fr.), ph; WOMAN NEXT DOOR, THE(1981, Fr.), ph; SNOW(1983, Fr.), ph
1984
LOVE ON THE GROUND(1984,Fr.), ph

Willy Lubtchansky
IT ONLY HAPPENS TO OTHERS(1971, Fr./Ital.), ph

Ray Luby
BAD BOY(1939), ed

Roy Luby
POCATELLO KID(1932), ed; HER SPLENDID FOLLY(1933), ed; MAN FROM HELL, THE(1934), ed; RIDER OF THE LAW, THE(1935), ed; TOUGH TO HANDLE(1937), d; DELINQUENT PARENTS(1938), ed; SLANDER HOUSE(1938), ed; CRASHING THRU(1939), ed; FIGHTING MAD(1939), ed; TRIGGER PALS(1939), ed; MR. WALKIE TALKIE(1952), ed

S. Roy Luby
GOLD(1932), ed; OUT OF SINGAPORE(1932), ed; PHANTOM EXPRESS, THE(1932), ed; SHOTGUN PASS(1932), ed; SUNSET TRAIL(1932), ed; SUCKER MONEY(1933), ed; FRONTIER DAYS(1934), ed; MOTH, THE(1934), ed; MURDER IN THE MUSEUM(1934), ed; ROAD TO RUIN(1934), ed; TEXAS TORNADO(1934), ed; ARIZONA BADMAN(1935), d; COURAGEOUS AVENGER, THE(1935), ed; KID COURAGEOUS(1935), ed; SMOKEY SMITH(1935), ed; WHAT PRICE CRIME?(1935), ed; CROOKED TRAIL, THE(1936), d; LAST OF THE WARRENS, THE(1936), ed; BORDER PHANTOM(1937), d; DESERT PHANTOM(1937), d; GAMBLING TERROR, THE(1937), ed; GUN LORDS OF STIRRUP BASIN(1937), ed; GUNS IN THE DARK(1937), ed; LAWLESS LAND(1937), ed; LIGHTNIN' CRANDALL(1937), ed; RED ROPE, THE(1937), d; RIDIN' THE LONE TRAIL(1937), ed; ROGUE OF THE RANGE(1937), d; SUNDOWN SAUNDERS(1937), ed; TRAIL OF VENGEANCE(1937), ed; TRUSTED OUTLAW, THE(1937), ed; COLORADO KID(1938), ed; THUNDER IN THE DESERT(1938), ed; RANGE BUSTERS, THE(1940), d; TRAILING DOUBLE TROUBLE(1940), d; WEST OF PINTO BASIN(1940), d; FUGITIVE VALLEY(1941), d; KID'S LAST RIDE, THE(1941), d; SADDLE MOUNTAIN ROUNDUP(1941), d; TONTO BASIN OUTLAWS(1941), d; TRAIL OF THE SILVER SPURS(1941), d; TUMBLEDOWN RANCH IN ARIZONA(1941), d; UNDERGROUND RUSTLERS(1941), d; WRANGLER'S ROOST(1941), d; ARIZONA STAGECOACH(1942), d; PRIDE OF THE ARMY(1942), d; ROCK RIVER RENEGADES(1942), d; THUNDER RIVER FEUD(1942), d; WAR DOGS(1942), d; BLACK MARKET RUSTLERS(1943), d; COWBOY COMMANDOS(1943), d; LAND OF HUNTED MEN(1943), d; PARTNERS IN TIME(1946), ed

Misc. Talkies
LIGHTNING TRIGGERS(1935), d; OUTLAW RULE(1935), d; RANGE WARFARE(1935), d; BOOT HILL BANDITS(1942), d; TEXAS TROUBLE SHOOTERS(1942), d

Jean Bernard Luc
APRES L'AMOUR(1948, Fr.), w; MONSIEUR VINCENT(1949, Fr.), w

Jean-Bernard Luc
LAFAYETTE(1963, Fr.), w

Dia Luca
DON JUAN(1956, Aust.), ch

Gio Vagni Luca
CONFORMIST, THE(1971, Ital., Fr)

Loes Luca
GIRL WITH THE RED HAIR, THE(1983, Neth.)

Maria Eugenia Luca
VAMPIRES, THE(1969, Mex.), makeup

Denise Lucadamo
1984
MUPPETS TAKE MANHATTAN, THE(1984)

Arthur Lucan
OLD MOTHER RILEY(1937, Brit.); KATHLEEN(1938, Ireland); OLD MOTHER RILEY IN PARIS(1938, Brit.); OLD MOTHER RILEY JOINS UP(1939, Brit.); OLD MOTHER RILEY MP(1939, Brit.); OLD MOTHER RILEY IN BUSINESS(1940, Brit.); OLD MOTHER RILEY IN SOCIETY(1940, Brit.); OLD MOTHER RILEY'S CIRCUS(1941, Brit.), a, w; OLD MOTHER RILEY'S GHOSTS(1941, Brit.), a, w; OLD MOTHER RILEY, DETECTIVE(1943, Brit.), a, w; OLD MOTHER RILEY OVERSEAS(1943, Brit.), a, w; OLD MOTHER RILEY AT HOME(1945, Brit.); OLD MOTHER RILEY, HEADMISTRESS(1950, Brit.); OLD MOTHER RILEY'S JUNGLE TREASURE(1951, Brit.); OLD MOTHER RILEY(1952, Brit.); MY SON, THE VAMPIRE(1963, Brit.)

Alberto Lucantoni
BIBLE...IN THE BEGINNING, THE(1966)

Marco Lucantoni
ASSASSINATION OF TROTSKY, THE(1972 Fr./Ital.)

Bert Lucarelli
VERY NATURAL THING, A(1974), m

Gianni Hecht Lucari
WARRIOR EMPRESS, THE(1961, Ital./Fr.), p; RUN WITH THE DEVIL(1963, Fr./Ital.), p; BAMBOLE!(1965, Ital.), p; HIGH INFIDELITY(1965, Fr./Ital.), p; MADE IN ITALY(1967, Fr./Ital.), p; ANYONE CAN PLAY(1968, Ital.), p; GIRL WITH A PISTOL, THE(1968, Ital.), p; QUEENS, THE(1968, Ital./Fr.), p; GARDEN OF THE FINZI-CONTINIS, THE(1976, Ital./Ger.), p; INHERITANCE, THE(1978, Ital.), p

Lucas
PICNIC ON THE GRASS(1960, Fr.)

Alex Lucas
HAMMERSMITH IS OUT(1972), p

Andres Lucas
I WAS AN AMERICAN SPY(1951)

Arthur Lucas
NO HIGHWAY IN THE SKY(1951, Brit.)

Cary Lucas
MACABRE(1958), w

Cleo Lucas
MERRILY WE GO TO HELL(1932), w

Cornel Lucas
QUEEN'S GUARDS, THE(1963, Brit.)

Curt Lucas
SHOT AT DAWN, A(1934, Ger.)

Dick Lucas
ONE HUNDRED AND ONE DALMATIANS(1961), anim; SWORD IN THE STONE, THE(1963), anim; ARISTOCATS, THE(1970), anim

Dick Lucas
MICKEY ONE(1965), anim.

F.R. Lucas
Misc. Silents
WOODPIGEON PATROL, THE(1930, Brit.), d

Frank J. Lucas
SIMON(1980)

George Lucas
THX 1138(1971), d, w, ed; AMERICAN GRAFFITI(1973), d, w; STAR WARS(1977), d&w; MORE AMERICAN GRAFFITI(1979), w; EMPIRE STRIKES BACK, THE(1980), w; RAIDERS OF THE LOST ARK(1981), w; RETURN OF THE JEDI(1983), p, w
1984
INDIANA JONES AND THE TEMPLE OF DOOM(1984), w
Misc. Silents
DECEIT(1923)

Glenn Lucas
WYOMING(1940)

Henry Lucas [Kanner]
1984
KINGS AND DESPERATE MEN(1984, Brit.), ph, ed

Isabelle Lucas
OUTLAND(1981)

Isobel Lucas
LOLITA(1962)

J. Frank Lucas
CURSE OF THE LIVING CORPSE, THE(1964); LAW AND DISORDER(1974); LITTLE SEX, A(1982)

Jack Lucas
BOY WHO CRIED WEREWOLF, THE(1973)

James Lucas
YOU CAN'T CHEAT AN HONEST MAN(1939); JOURNEY TO THE BEGINNING OF TIME(1966, Czech)

Jerry Lucas
FUNNY FACE(1957)

Jim Lucas
SABOTEUR(1942); STRICTLY IN THE GROOVE(1942)

Jimmie Lucas
ADVENTURE'S END(1937); PRESCRIPTION FOR ROMANCE(1937); MIDNIGHT INTRUDER(1938); HELL'S KITCHEN(1939); ONE HOUR TO LIVE(1939); DANGER ON WHEELS(1940); I TAKE THIS WOMAN(1940); STRIKE UP THE BAND(1940); SAN FRANCISCO DOCKS(1941); MYSTERY OF MARIE ROGET, THE(1942)

Jimmy Lucas
GIRL WITH IDEAS, A(1937); SUDAN(1945); GIRL ON THE SPOT(1946)

John Lucas
ANGEL(1982, Irish), art d; LIGHT YEARS AWAY(1982, Fr./Switz.), art d
1984
ANNE DEVLIN(1984, Ireland), prod d

John Meredyth Lucas
DARK CITY(1950), w; PEKING EXPRESS(1951), w; RED MOUNTAIN(1951), w; CAPTAIN PIRATE(1952), w; TUMBLEWEED(1953), w; SCARLET HOUR, THE(1956), w; SIGN OF ZORRO, THE(1960), w; MY BLOOD RUNS COLD(1965), w

Jonathan Lucas
TROUBLE WITH GIRLS(AND HOW TO GET INTO IT), THE*1/2 (1969), ch; TWO LITTLE BEARS, THE(1961), ch; MARRIAGE ON THE ROCKS(1965), ch

Jonathon Lucas
HAPPY GO LOVELY(1951, Brit.)

Karen Lucas
Misc. Talkies
ZOO ROBBERY(1973, Brit.)

Kirke Lucas
Silents
SMILES ARE TRUMPS(1922)

L. Lucas
TEACHER AND THE MIRACLE, THE(1961, Ital./Span.), w

Lauren Lucas
FIRST NUDIE MUSICAL, THE(1976)

Leighton Lucas
NOW BARABBAS WAS A ROBBER(1949, Brit.), m; STAGE FRIGHT(1950, Brit.), m; PORTRAIT OF CLARE(1951, Brit.), m; YOU CAN'T BEAT THE IRISH(1952, Brit.), m; DAM BUSTERS, THE(1955, Brit.), m; DESERT ATTACK(1958, Brit.), m; SON OF ROBIN HOOD(1959, Brit.), m; I LIKE MONEY(1962, Brit.), md; IMMORAL CHARGE(1962, Brit.), m

Lisa Lucas
TURNING POINT, THE(1977); UNMARRIED WOMAN, AN(1978)
1984
HADLEY'S REBELLION(1984)

Luke Lucas
Silents
MADNESS OF YOUTH(1923)

Marcia Lucas
AMERICAN GRAFFITI(1973), ed; ALICE DOESN'T LIVE HERE ANYMORE(1975), ed; TAXI DRIVER(1976), ed; NEW YORK, NEW YORK(1977), ed; STAR WARS(1977), ed; RETURN OF THE JEDI(1983), ed

Michel Lucas
GATES OF PARIS(1958, Fr./Ital.)

Monique Lucas
DARK OF THE SUN(1968, Brit.)

Nick Lucas
GOLD DIGGERS OF BROADWAY(1929); THIS IS THE LIFE(1935); DISC JOCKEY(1951)

Paul Lucas
SING SINNER, SING(1933)

Ralph Lucas
CHILD, THE(1977), w; PLANET OF DINOSAURS(1978), w

Rodney Lucas [Radovan Lukavsky]
VOYAGE TO THE END OF THE UNIVERSE(1963, Czech.)

Roger Lucas
MOSES AND AARON(1975, Ger./Fr./Ital.)

Sam Lucas
Silents
UNCLE TOM'S CABIN(1914)

Scott Lucas
MOTHER'S DAY(1980)

Sissy Lucas
COAL MINER'S DAUGHTER(1980)

Tom Lucas
TREASURE ISLAND(1950, Brit.); OUTLAW BLUES(1977), makeup

Victor Lucas
UNDER CAPRICORN(1949); BLUE PARROT, THE(1953, Brit.)

Victoria Lucas
1984
SPLASH(1984)

Virginia Lucas
RAINBOW ISLAND(1944)

Wilfred Lucas
ARIZONA KID, THE(1930); COCK O' THE WALK(1930); HELLO SISTER(1930); JUST IMAGINE(1930); MADAME SATAN(1930); THOSE WHO DANCE(1930); CONVICTED(1931); CRACKED NUTS(1931); DISHONORED(1931); PARDON US(1931); YOUNG DONOVAN'S KID(1931); CROSS-EXAMINATION(1932); DEVIL AND THE DEEP(1932); INTRUDER, THE(1932); MIDNIGHT PATROL(1932); SIGN OF THE CROSS, THE(1932); TENDERFOOT, THE(1932); UNWRITTEN LAW, THE(1932); YOU SAID A MOUTHFUL(1932); BREED OF THE BORDER(1933); DAY OF RECKONING(1933); DEVIL'S BROTHER, THE(1933); I COVER THE WATERFRONT(1933); LAWYER MAN(1933); LUCKY LARRIGAN(1933); MARY STEVENS, M.D.(1933); MAYOR OF HELL, THE(1933); PHANTOM THUNDERBOLT, THE(1933); RACETRACK(1933); SPHINX, THE(1933); STRANGE PEOPLE(1933); CLEOPATRA(1934); HOUSE OF ROTHSCHILD, THE(1934); MOTH, THE(1934); NOTORIOUS BUT NICE(1934); ONE NIGHT OF LOVE(1934); OPERATOR 13(1934); ST. LOUIS KID, THE(1934); UPPER WORLD(1934); FRISCO KID(1935); NAUGHTY MARIETTA(1935); SECRET BRIDE, THE(1935); SHOW THEM NO MERCY(1935); STORMY(1935); STRANDED(1935); CHARGE OF THE LIGHT BRIGADE, THE(1936); HUMAN CARGO(1936); MARY OF SCOTLAND(1936); MODERN TIMES(1936); PRISONER OF SHARK ISLAND, THE(1936); STORY OF LOUIS PASTEUR, THE(1936); BLAZING SIXES(1937); CALIFORNIA MAIL, THE(1937); CRIME AFLOAT(1937); CRIMINAL LAWYER(1937); EMPTY HOLSTERS(1937); LAND BEYOND THE LAW(1937); MILE A MINUTE LOVE(1937); PERFECT SPECIMEN, THE(1937); PRAIRIE THUNDER(1937); SHE LOVED A FIREMAN(1937); ACCIDENTS WILL HAPPEN(1938); ANGELS WITH DIRTY FACES(1938); BARONESS AND THE BUTLER, THE(1938); GOLD IS WHERE YOU FIND IT(1938); SERGEANT MURPHY(1938); DODGE CITY(1939); EACH DAWN I DIE(1939); MARSHAL OF MESA CITY, THE(1939); RACKETEERS OF THE RANGE(1939); RAFFLES(1939); WOMEN IN THE WIND(1939); BROTHER ORCHID(1940); CHUMP AT OXFORD, A(1940); FIGHTING 69TH, THE(1940); LEGION OF THE LAWLESS(1940); RAGTIME COWBOY JOE(1940); SANTA FE TRAIL(1940); THEY DRIVE BY NIGHT(1940); TRIPLE JUSTICE(1940); VIRGINIA CITY(1940); WATERLOO BRIDGE(1940); WOMEN WITHOUT NAMES(1940); SEA WOLF, THE(1941); IT'S A GREAT FEELING(1949)
Misc. Talkies
SISTER TO JUDAS(1933)
Silents
LILY AND THE ROSE, THE(1915); ACQUITTED(1916); HELL-TO-PAY AUSTIN(1916); RED, RED HEART, THE(1918), d; ROMANCE OF TARZAN, THE(1918), d; BEAUTIFUL LIAR, THE(1921); BREAKING POINT, THE(1921); FIGHTING BREED, THE(1921), a, d&w; ACROSS THE DEAD-LINE(1922); KENTUCKY DERBY, THE(1922); PAID BACK(1922); GIRL OF THE GOLDEN WEST, THE(1923); INNOCENCE(1923); JAZZMANIA(1923); LIGHTNING ROMANCE(1924); NORTH OF NEVADA(1924); ON PROBATION(1924); RACING FOR LIFE(1924), w; EASY MONEY(1925); RIDERS OF THE PURPLE SAGE(1925); WAS IT BIGAMY?(1925); NEST, THE(1927)
Misc. Silents
SOULS TRIUMPHANT(1915); SPANISH JADE, THE(1915), d; MACBETH(1916); MICROSCOPE MYSTERY, THE(1916); RUMMY, THE(1916); WILD GIRL OF THE SIERRAS, A(1916); WOOD NYMPH, THE(1916); CO-RESPONDENT, THE(1917); FOOD GAMBLERS(1917); HANDS UP!(1917); JIM BLUDSO(1917), a, d; JUDGEMENT HOUSE, THE(1917); LOVE SUBLIME, A(1917), a, d; MORGAN'S RAIDERS(1918), d; RETURN OF MARY, THE(1918), d; TESTING OF MILDRED VANE, THE(1918), d; GIRL FROM NOWHERE, THE(1919), a, d; WHAT EVERY WOMAN WANTS(1919);

WOMAN OF PLEASURE, A(1919); HUSHED HOUR, THE(1920); BETTER MAN, THE(1921), a, d; SHADOW OF LIGHTING RIDGE, THE(1921), a, d; THROUGH THE BACK DOOR(1921); BARNSTORMER, THE(1922); BARRIERS OF FOLLY(1922); GREATEST MENACE, THE(1923); FATAL MISTAKE, THE(1924); FIGHTING SAP, THE(1924); MASK OF LOPEZ, THE(1924); PASSION'S PATHWAY(1924); VALLEY OF HATE, THE(1924); BAD LANDS, THE(1925); CYCLONE CAVALIER(1925); HOW BAXTER BUTTED IN(1925); SNOB BUSTER, THE(1925); YOUTH'S GAMBLE(1925); HER SACRIFICE(1926), d; BURNT FINGERS(1927)

Wilfrid Lucas
DEVIL DOLL, THE(1936)

William Lucas
POSTMARK FOR DANGER(1956, Brit.); HIGH FLIGHT(1957, Brit.); TEARS FOR SIMON(1957, Brit.); UP IN THE WORLD(1957, Brit.); X THE UNKNOWN(1957, Brit.); CRACK IN THE MIRROR(1960); PROFESSIONALS, THE(1960, Brit.); SONS AND LOVERS(1960, Brit.); DEVIL'S DAFFODIL, THE(1961, Brit./Ger.); SHADOW OF THE CAT, THE(1961, Brit.); BREAK, THE(1962, Brit.); PAYROLL(1962, Brit.); TOUCH OF DEATH(1962, Brit.); BITTER HARVEST(1963, Brit.); CALCULATED RISK(1963, Brit.); MARKED ONE, THE(1963, Brit.); VERY EDGE, THE(1963, Brit.); DATELINE DIAMONDS(1966, Brit.); SKY BIKE, THE(1967, Brit.); SCRAMBLE(1970, Brit.); ISLAND OF THE BURNING DAMNED(1971, Brit.); MAN AT THE TOP(1973, Brit.); OPERATION DAYBREAK(1976, U.S./Brit./Czech.); BEYOND THE FOG(1981, Brit.)
1984
PLAGUE DOGS, THE(1984, U.S./Brit.)

Tony Lucatorto
JIM, THE WORLD'S GREATEST(1976)

Nick Lucats
SPIRIT OF STANFORD, THE(1942), w

Vincent Lucchesi
FRANCES(1982)

Deborah Lucchessi
BODY HEAT(1981)

Virginia Lucchetti
Misc. Silents
SHEPHERD KING, THE(1923)

Maurizio Lucci
DAISY MILLER(1974)

Mike Lucci
PAPER LION(1968)

Anna Maria Lucciani
LAW IS THE LAW, THE(1959, Fr.)

Micheline Luccioni
GERVAISE(1956, Fr.); MAXIME(1962, Fr.); EGLANTINE(1972, Fr.)

Aime Luce
ONE WAY WAHINI(1965); KING'S PIRATE(1967)

Angela Luce
HUNCHBACK OF ROME, THE(1963, Ital.); SHOOT LOUD, LOUDER... I DON'T UNDERSTAND(1966, Ital.); STRANGER, THE(1967, Algeria/Fr./Ital.); 'TIS A PITY SHE'S A WHORE(1973, Ital.); MALICIOUS(1974, Ital.)

Claire Luce
UP THE RIVER(1930); LAZYBONES(1935, Brit.); VINTAGE WINE(1935, Brit.); LET'S MAKE A NIGHT OF IT(1937, Brit.); OVER SHE GOES(1937, Brit.); UNDER SECRET ORDERS(1943, Brit.)

Clare Boothe Luce
COME TO THE STABLE(1949), w

Deborah Luce
MOTHER'S DAY(1980)

George Luce
Misc. Talkies
DANNY(1979)

Polly Luce
MAID HAPPY(1933, Brit.)

Ralph Luce
WILD WHEELS(1969), w, ed

Richard Luce
UP GOES MAISIE(1946), art d

Julio Lucena
EAGLE'S WING(1979, Brit.)

Ernesto Lucente
CUCKOO CLOCK, THE(1938, Ital.), ed

Ignazio Luceri
REBEL GLADIATORS, THE(1963, Ital.), p

Carl Lucerne
OPERATION EICHMANN(1961)

Armando Lucero
ONCE BEFORE I DIE(1967, U.S./Phil.); LOSERS, THE(1970)

Enrique Lucero
SIERRA BARON(1958); VILLA!(1958); MACARIO(1961, Mex.); LOVE HAS MANY FACES(1965); MAJOR DUNDEE(1965); TARZAN AND THE VALLEY OF GOLD(1966 U.S./Switz.); GUNS FOR SAN SEBASTIAN(1968, U.S./Fr./Mex./Ital.); CURSE OF THE CRYING WOMAN, THE(1969, Mex.); SHARK(1970, U.S./Mex.); TWO MULES FOR SISTER SARA(1970); SOMETHING BIG(1971); BUCK AND THE PREACHER(1972); WRATH OF GOD, THE(1972); LONG GOODBYE, THE(1973); MARY, MARY, BLOODY MARY(1975, U.S./Mex.); RETURN OF A MAN CALLED HORSE, THE(1976); EAGLE'S WING(1979, Brit.); UNDER FIRE(1983)
1984
EVIL THAT MEN DO, THE(1984)

Gilbert Lucero
WINTERHAWK(1976)

Oscar Lucero
WAY OF A GAUCHO(1952)

E.C. Lucey
RAMPARTS WE WATCH, THE(1940)

Bob Luchaire
DANIELLA BY NIGHT(1962, Fr/Ger.), set d; SWEET ECSTASY(1962, Fr.), art d

Corinne Luchaire
AFFAIR LAFONT, THE(1939, Fr.); CONFLICT(1939, Fr.); PRISON WITHOUT BARS(1939, Brit.); THREE HOURS(1944, Fr.)

Robert Luchaire
MAN AND A WOMAN, A(1966, Fr.), art d; EXPOSED(1983), art d
Milton Luchan
PIE IN THE SKY(1964)
Ceriano Luchetti
FITZCARRALDO(1982)
Fabrice Luchini
CLAIRE'S KNEE(1971, Fr.); VIOLETTE(1978, Fr.); AVIATOR'S WIFE, THE(1981, Fr.)
1984
FULL MOON IN PARIS(1984, Fr.)
Katya Luchko
TWELFTH NIGHT(1956, USSR)
Klara Luchko
HOUSE ON THE FRONT LINE, THE(1963, USSR)
Tami Luchow
BUSTIN' LOOSE(1981)
Darlene Lucht
HAUNTED PALACE, THE(1963); MUSCLE BEACH PARTY(1964); PATSY, THE(1964)
Chip Lucia
HOSPITAL MASSACRE(1982); MAKING LOVE(1982)
1984
HOSPITAL MASSACRE(1984)
S.A. Luciani
DEFEAT OF HANNIBAL, THE(1937, Ital.), w
Felipe Luciano
BADGE 373(1973)
Fulvio Luciano
DR. GOLDFOOT AND THE GIRL BOMBS(1966, Ital.), p; PRIMITIVE LOVE(1966, Ital.), p
Michael Luciano
GANG WAR(1940), ed; STOP THAT CAB(1951), ed; WORLD FOR RANSOM(1954), ed; BIG KNIFE, THE(1955), ed; KISS ME DEADLY(1955), ed; ATTACK!(1956), ed; AUTUMN LEAVES(1956), ed; RIDE BACK, THE(1957), ed; BLOOD ARROW(1958), ed; WONDERFUL COUNTRY, THE(1959), ed; ATLAS(1960), ed; WHATEVER HAPPENED TO BABY JANE?(1962), ed; BLACK ZOO(1963), ed; FOUR FOR TEXAS(1963), ed; HUSH... HUSH, SWEET CHARLOTTE(1964), ed; FLIGHT OF THE PHOENIX, THE(1965), ed; DIRTY DOZEN, THE(1967, Brit.), ed; LEGEND OF LYLAH CLARE, THE(1968), ed; TOO LATE THE HERO(1970), ed; GRISSOM GANG, THE(1971), ed; ULZANA'S RAID(1972), ed; EMPEROR OF THE NORTH POLE(1973), ed; LONGEST YARD, THE(1974), ed; HUSTLE(1975), ed; BOBBIE JO AND THE OUTLAW(1976), ed; SCORCHY(1976), ed; EMPIRE OF THE ANTS(1977), ed; TWILIGHT'S LAST GLEAMING(1977, U.S./Ger.), ed; HARDLY WORKING(1981), ed; STRIPES(1981), ed
Elvira Lucianti
MADAME SATAN(1930)
Robert Lucid
MAIDSTONE(1970)
Mario Lucidi
LET'S TALK ABOUT WOMEN(1964, Fr./Ital.); STRANGER IN TOWN, A(1968, U.S./Ital.), ed
Maurice Lucidi
STREET PEOPLE(1976, U.S./Ital.), d, w
Maurizio Lucidi
GOLIATH AND THE DRAGON(1961, Ital./Fr.), ed; MORGAN THE PIRATE(1961, Fr./Ital.), ed; TARTARS, THE(1962, Ital./Yugo.), ed; EASY LIFE, THE(1963, Ital.), ed; HERCULES AND THE CAPTIVE WOMEN(1963, Fr./Ital.), ed; CHRISMAS THAT ALMOST WASN'T. THE(1966, Ital.), ed; MY NAME IS PECOS(1966, Ital.), d&w; TRAMPLERS, THE(1966, Ital.), ed; OPIATE '67(1967, Fr./Ital.), ed; PUSSYCAT, PUSSYCAT, I LOVE YOU(1970), ed; BIG AND THE BAD, THE(1971, Ital./Fr./Span.), d; STATELINE MOTEL(1976, Ital.), d
Renzo Lucidi
THIEF OF VENICE, THE(1952), ed; OTHELLO(1955, U.S./Fr./Ital.), ed; ROMANOFF AND JULIET(1961), ed; JESSICA(1962, U.S./Ital./Fr.), ed; MR. ARKADIN(1962, Brit./Fr./Span.), ed; MY SON, THE HERO(1963, Ital./Fr.), ed; DUEL OF CHAMPIONS(1964 Ital./Span.), ed; EMPTY CANVAS, THE(1964, Fr./Ital.), ed; STRANGER RETURNS, THE(1968, U.S./Ital./Ger./Span.), ed; MADRON(1970, U.S./Israel), ed; MAN CALLED SLEDGE, A(1971, Ital.), ed; STREET PEOPLE(1976, U.S./Ital.), ed
Marcel Lucien
LOVE IN MOROCCO(1933, Fr.), ph; SECOND BUREAU(1936, Fr.), ph; STORY OF A CHEAT, THE(1938, Fr.), ph; FIRE IN THE STRAW(1943), ph
Lucienne and Ashour
OKAY FOR SOUND(1937, Brit.); AROUND THE WORLD(1943)
Alvin Lucier
CRY DR. CHICAGO(1971)
Luciano Lucignani
LOVE PROBLEMS(1970, Ital.), w
Lucilla
END OF DESIRE(1962 Fr./Ital.), cos
Lucille
TELL ME IN THE SUNLIGHT(1967); LIQUID SKY(1982)
Lucille Walker and the Texas Rangers
LAW OF THE RANGE(1941)
Mario Lucinni
ROMAN HOLIDAY(1953)
Jose Lucio
Silents
LIFE(1928, Brit.)
Jose Lucioni
CATHERINE & CO.(1976, Fr.)
Fulvio Lucisano
HEAVEN ON EARTH(1960, Ital./U.S.), p; WARRIORS FIVE(1962), p; PLANET OF THE VAMPIRES(1965, U.S./Ital./Span.), p; SPY IN YOUR EYE(1966, Ital.), p; WAR ITALIAN STYLE(1967, Ital.), p; COBRA, THE(1968), p; GLASS SPHINX, THE(1968, Egypt/Ital./Span.), p; DOWN THE ANCIENT STAIRCASE(1975, Ital.), p
Lucita
SEA CHASE, THE(1955); MIRACLE IN THE RAIN(1956); UNTAMED YOUTH(1957); SPEED CRAZY(1959)

Olive Lucius
SILK NOOSE, THE(1950, Brit.)
Courtney Luck
MILLIONS LIKE US(1943, Brit.)
George Luck
CAESAR AND CLEOPATRA(1946, Brit.)
Harry Luck
THOMASINE AND BUSHROD(1974)
James Luck
CAUGHT IN THE NET(1960, Brit.); ROCKETS IN THE DUNES(1960, Brit.); REACH FOR GLORY(1963, Brit.)
Lucky Luck
DEVIL AT FOUR O'CLOCK, THE(1961); KONA COAST(1968)
Max Lucke
GOIN' TO TOWN(1935); DAY AT THE RACES, A(1937); ESPIONAGE(1937); HITLER'S CHILDREN(1942)
Rosemarie Lucke
TONIO KROGER(1968, Fr./Ger.)
Edith Luckett
Misc. Silents
COMING POWER, THE(1914)
Willene Luckett
I'LL BE YOURS(1947)
Euna Luckey
Silents
STEELHEART(1921)
Max Luckey
FOUR JACKS AND A JILL(1941)
Susan Luckey
CAROUSEL(1956); MUSIC MAN, THE(1962)
Suzanne Luckey
DEEP IN MY HEART(1954); TEENAGE REBEL(1956)
W.L. Luckey
EAT MY DUST!(1976); HOLLYWOOD BOULEVARD(1976)
William Luckey
CRAZY MAMA(1975); MOONSHINE COUNTY EXPRESS(1977)
Cyril Luckham
MURDER IN REVERSE(1946, Brit.); STRANGER FROM VENUS, THE(1954, Brit.); HOSTAGE, THE(1956, Brit.); BIRTHDAY PRESENT, THE(1957, Brit.); HOW TO MURDER A RICH UNCLE(1957, Brit.); OUT OF THE CLOUDS(1957, Brit.); INVASION QUARTET(1961, Brit.); PUMPKIN EATER, THE(1964, Brit.); SOME PEOPLE(1964, Brit.); ALPHABET MURDERS, THE(1966); MAN FOR ALL SEASONS, A(1966, Brit.); NAKED RUNNER, THE(1967, Brit.); ANNE OF THE THOUSAND DAYS(1969, Brit.); HAPPY DEATHDAY(1969, Brit.); ONE MORE TIME(1970, Brit.); CRY OF THE PENGUINS(1972, Brit.); PROVIDENCE(1977, Fr.)
Laurence Luckinbill
BOYS IN THE BAND, THE(1970); SUCH GOOD FRIENDS(1971); CORKY(1972); MONEY, THE(1975); PROMISE, THE(1979)
1984
NOT FOR PUBLICATION(1984)
Bill Lucking
DOC SAVAGE... THE MAN OF BRONZE(1975); BIRCH INTERVAL(1976); RETURN OF A MAN CALLED HORSE, THE(1976); 10(1979); COAST TO COAST(1980); MOUNTAIN MEN, THE(1980); STRIPES(1981)
William Lucking
HELL'S BELLES(1969); HAROLD AND MAUDE(1971); TODD KILLINGS, THE(1971); WILD ROVERS(1971); MAGNIFICENT SEVEN RIDE, THE(1972); OKLAHOMA CRUDE(1973)
Sid Luckman
TRIPLE THREAT(1948)
Bill Luckwell
MISS TULIP STAYS THE NIGHT(1955, Brit.), p, w; SEE HOW THEY RUN(1955, Brit.), p; NOT SO DUSTY(1956, Brit.), p; BOOBY TRAP(1957, Brit.), p, w; CROOKED SKY, THE(1957, Brit.), p; UNDERCOVER GIRL(1957, Brit.), w; NOBODY IN TOYLAND(1958, Brit.), w; STRANGE CASE OF DR. MANNING, THE(1958, Brit.), p, w; HIDDEN HOMICIDE(1959, Brit.), w; HAND, THE(1960, Brit.), p; ENTER INSPECTOR DUVAL(1961, Brit.), p; QUESTION OF SUSPENSE, A(1961, Brit.), p; AMBUSH IN LEOPARD STREET(1962, Brit.), p; BREATH OF LIFE(1962, Brit.), p; GUY CALLED CAESAR, A(1962, Brit.), p; MURDER IN EDEN(1962, Brit.), p; RUNAWAY, THE(1964, Brit.), p
Kay Luckwell
FIGHTING WILDCATS, THE(1957, Brit.), p; UNDERCOVER GIRL(1957, Brit.), p; NOBODY IN TOYLAND(1958, Brit.), p
Michael Luckwell
NOBODY IN TOYLAND(1958, Brit.), w
Lucky the Chimp
TARZAN'S HIDDEN JUNGLE(1955)
Fred Lucky
RESCUERS, THE(1977), w
The Lucky Seven Choir
FRESHMAN YEAR(1938)
Bruce L. Lucoff
NEW YORK, NEW YORK(1977)
H. Lisle Lucoque
Silents
DAWN(1917, Brit.), d; TATTERLY(1919, Brit.), d
Misc. Silents
CASTLES IN SPAIN(1920, Brit.), d; LORNA DOONE(1920, Brit.), d; WHERE THE RAINBOW ENDS(1921, Brit.), d
Nellie E. Lucoque
Silents
TATTERLY(1919, Brit.), w
Arnold Lucy
GHOST TALKS, THE(1929); MASQUERADE(1929); ALL QUIET ON THE WESTERN FRONT(1930); MANSLAUGHTER(1930); PRINCESS AND THE PLUMBER, THE(1930); SCOTLAND YARD(1930); MERELY MARY ANN(1931); UNFAITHFUL(1931); YOUNG SINNERS(1931); ALIAS THE DOCTOR(1932); DR. JEKYLL AND MR. HYDE(1932); GUILTY AS HELL(1932); LADY WITH A PAST(1932); SHERLOCK HOLMES(1932); LOYALTIES(1934, Brit.); LUCK OF A SAILOR, THE(1934, Brit.); ROLLING IN MONEY(1934, Brit.); WANDERING JEW, THE(1935, Brit.); MORALS OF

MARCUS, THE(1936, Brit.); MEMBER OF THE JURY(1937, Brit.); MEN OF THE SEA(1951, Brit.)
Silents
IN AGAIN-OUT AGAIN(1917); COST, THE(1920); IN SEARCH OF A SINNER(1920); SCHOOL DAYS(1921); MODERN MARRIAGE(1923)
Misc. Silents
LOVE EXPERT, THE(1920)
Queenie Lucy
ON VELVET(1938, Brit.)
Gianni Luda
WAR AND PEACE(1956, Ital./U.S.)
Werner Jorg Luddecke
JOURNEY TO THE LOST CITY(1960, Ger./Fr./Ital.), w
Allen Ludden
FUTUREWORLD(1976)
Barbara Luddy
HEADIN' NORTH(1930); LADY AND THE TRAMP(1955); SLEEPING BEAUTY(1959); ONE HUNDRED AND ONE DALMATIANS(1961); TERRIFIED!(1963)
Silents
ROSE OF THE WORLD(1925)
Misc. Silents
SEE YOU LATER(1928)
Edward Luddy
GIRL FROM WOOLWORTH'S, THE(1929), w; COHENS AND KELLYS IN AFRICA, THE(1930), w; VIRTUOUS HUSBAND(1931), w
Silents
IRRESISTIBLE LOVER, THE(1927), w
Edward I. Luddy
SEE AMERICA THIRST(1930), w; SO IT'S SUNDAY(1932), d; STEADY COMPANY(1932), w
Silents
JAKE THE PLUMBER(1927), d, w
Misc. Silents
MAN WHO WAITED, THE(1922), d
Christian Lude
PRIZE, THE(1952, Fr.); LETTERS FROM MY WINDMILL(1955, Fr.); TRUTH, THE(1961, Fr./Ital.); DOULOS–THE FINGER MAN(1964, Fr./Ital.); MALE COMPANION(1965, Fr./Ital.); THIEF OF PARIS, THE(1967, Fr./Ital.)
Jack Luden
WILD PARTY, THE(1929); SINS OF THE FATHERS(1928); DANGEROUS CURVES(1929); INNOCENTS OF PARIS(1929); STUDIO MURDER MYSTERY, THE(1929); WHY BRING THAT UP?(1929); WOLF OF WALL STREET, THE(1929); YOUNG EAGLES(1930); KING OF THE ROYAL MOUNTED(1936); TOAST OF NEW YORK, THE(1937); PHANTOM GOLD(1938); PIONEER TRAIL(1938); STAGECOACH DAYS(1938); SUSANNAH OF THE MOUNTIES(1939); FLIGHT COMMAND(1940); FLORIAN(1940); NORTHWEST MOUNTED POLICE(1940); CAUGHT IN THE DRAFT(1941); I WANTED WINGS(1941); WEST POINT WIDOW(1941); GLASS KEY, THE(1942); I MARRIED A WITCH(1942); MY FAVORITE BLONDE(1942); REAP THE WILD WIND(1942); GUADALCANAL DIARY(1943); SO PROUDLY WE HAIL(1943); LADY IN THE DARK(1944); SEE HERE, PRIVATE HARGROVE(1944); STORY OF DR. WASSELL, THE(1944); DANGEROUS PARTNERS(1945); INCENDIARY BLONDE(1945); ROUGH RIDERS OF CHEYENNE(1945); THEY WERE EXPENDABLE(1945); WEEKEND AT THE WALDORF(1945)
Silents
IT'S THE OLD ARMY GAME(1926); AFLAME IN THE SKY(1927); SHOOTIN' IRONS(1927); TWO FLAMING YOUTHS(1927); PARTNERS IN CRIME(1928)
Misc. Silents
FASCINATING YOUTH(1926); JADE CUP, THE(1926); LAST OUTLAW, THE(1927); TELL IT TO SWEENEY(1927); UNEASY PAYMENTS(1927); FOOLS FOR LUCK(1928)
John Luden
ROLLING CARAVANS(1938)
Hans Ludermilk
WORLD IS JUST A 'B' MOVIE, THE(1971)
Gunther Luders
GIRL AND THE LEGEND, THE(1966, Ger.); TONIO KROGER(1968, Fr./Ger.)
Gustav Luders
Silents
PRINCE OF PILSEN, THE(1926), w
Edwin E. Ludig
MIDDLETON FAMILY AT THE N.Y. WORLD'S FAIR(1939), md
Charles Ludlam
LUPE(1967); IMPOSTORS(1979)
Helen Ludlam
SIDELONG GLANCES OF A PIGEON KICKER, THE(1970); SUMMER WISHES, WINTER DREAMS(1973); ANNIE HALL(1977)
Jenny Ludlam
WINTER OF OUR DREAMS(1982, Aus.)
Glen Ludlow
LOVE IN A FOUR LETTER WORLD(1970, Can.), ed
Glenn Ludlow
TAKE HER BY SURPRISE(1967, Can.), ed
Patrick Ludlow
BACHELOR'S BABY(1932, Brit.); BLUE DANUBE(1932, Brit.); HIS LORDSHIP(1932, Brit.); LOVE ON THE SPOT(1932, Brit.); WATCH BEVERLY(1932, Brit.); CHELSEA LIFE(1933, Brit.); EVERGREEN(1934, Brit.); FACES(1934, Brit.), w; DOMMED CARGO(1936, Brit.); JURY'S EVIDENCE(1936, Brit.); KING OF HEARTS(1936, Brit.); THEY DIDN'T KNOW(1936, Brit.); GANGWAY(1937, Brit.); OLD MOTHER RILEY(1937, Brit.); ROSE OF TRALEE(1938, Ireland); GOODBYE MR. CHIPS(1939, Brit.); OLD MOTHER RILEY MP(1939, Brit.); WE'LL SMILE AGAIN(1942, Brit.); MODESTY BLAISE(1966, Brit.)
Misc. Silents
NAUGHTY HUSBANDS(1930, Brit.)
Susan Ludlow
JOYRIDE(1977)
1984
PRODIGAL, THE(1984)
Helen Ludlum
MIRACLE WORKER, THE(1962)

Robert Ludlum
OSTERMAN WEEKEND, THE(1983), w
Cesare Vico Ludovici
MERCHANT OF SLAVES(1949, Ital.), w
Vicky Ludovisi
FIASCO IN MILAN(1963, Fr./Ital.)
Archie Ludski
CARRY ON CABBIE(1963, Brit.), ed; CARRY ON JACK(1963, Brit.), ed; SWINGIN' MAIDEN, THE(1963, Brit.), ed; CARRY ON CLEO(1964, Brit.), ed; CARRY ON SPYING(1964, Brit.), ed; NURSE ON WHEELS(1964, Brit.), ed; DECLINE AND FALL... OF A BIRD WATCHER(1969, Brit.), ed; LAND RAIDERS(1969), ed
Karen Ludwi
YOU'VE GOT TO WALK IT LIKE YOU TALK IT OR YOU'LL LOSE THAT BEAT(1971)
Rex Ludwick
HONEYSUCKLE ROSE(1980)
1984
BLAME IT ON THE NIGHT(1984)
Adam Ludwig
SCANNERS(1981, Can.)
Alan Ludwig
TUMBLING TUMBLEWEEDS(1935), w
Alice Ludwig
MARRIAGE IN THE SHADOWS(1948, Ger.), ed; TOXI(1952, Ger.), ed
Arthur Ludwig
Silents
OLD IRONSIDES(1926)
Charles Ludwig
O'SHAUGHNESSY'S BOY(1935)
Chris Ludwig
BLACK OAK CONSPIRACY(1977), ph
David Ludwig
GREAT MUPPET CAPER, THE(1981)
Edward Ludwig
STEADY COMPANY(1932), d; THEY JUST HAD TO GET MARRIED(1933), d; FRIENDS OF MR. SWEENEY(1934), d; LET'S BE RITZY(1934), d; AGE OF INDISCRETION(1935), d; MAN WHO RECLAIMED HIS HEAD, THE(1935), d; OLD MAN RHYTHM(1935), d; THREE KIDS AND A QUEEN(1935), d; ADVENTURE IN MANHATTAN(1936), d; FATAL LADY(1936), d; HER HUSBAND LIES(1937), d; LAST GANGSTER, THE(1937), d; THAT CERTAIN AGE(1938), d; COAST GUARD(1939), d; SWISS FAMILY ROBINSON(1940), d; MAN WHO LOST HIMSELF, THE(1941), d; BORN TO SING(1942), d; THEY CAME TO BLOW UP AMERICA(1943), d; FIGHTING SEABEES, THE(1944), d; 3 IS A FAMILY(1944), d; FABULOUS TEXAN, THE(1947), d; BIG WHEEL, THE(1949), d; WAKE OF THE RED WITCH(1949), d; SMUGGLER'S ISLAND(1951), d; BIG JIM McLAIN(1952), d; BLAZING FOREST, THE(1952), d; CARIBBEAN(1952), d, w; SANGAREE(1953), d; VANQUISHED, THE(1953), d; JIVARO(1954), d; FLAME OF THE ISLANDS(1955), p&d; BLACK SCORPION, THE(1957), d; GUN HAWK, THE(1963), d
Misc. Talkies
WOMAN'S MAN, A(1934), d
Emil Ludwig
HITLER'S MADMAN(1943), w
Fred Ludwig
NAKED AMONG THE WOLVES(1967, Ger.)
Hermann Ludwig
FREDDY UNTER FREMDEN STERNEN(1962, Ger.), ed
Jerry Ludwig
THREE THE HARD WAY(1974), w; TAKE A HARD RIDE(1975, U.S./Ital.), w
Julian Ludwig
GOG(1954)
Karen Ludwig
MANHATTAN(1979); DEAR MR. WONDERFUL(1983, Ger.)
Kurt Ludwig
SEVEN DARING GIRLS(1962, Ger.)
Leopold Ludwig
DER FREISCHUTZ(1970, Ger.), md
Marlene Ludwig
RESTLESS ONES, THE(1965)
Otto Ludwig
LOVE DOCTOR, THE(1929), ed; SHOOTING STRAIGHT(1930), ed; SILVER HORDE, THE(1930), ed; DRUMS OF JEOPARDY(1931), ed; SIGN OF FOUR, THE(1932, Brit.), ed; EVENSONG(1934, Brit.), ed; MAN WHO RECLAIMED HIS HEAD, THE(1935), d; POWER(1934, Brit.), ed; ALIAS BULLDOG DRUMMOND(1935, Brit.), ed; BORN FOR GLORY(1935, Brit.), ed; KING OF THE DAMNED(1936, Brit.), ed; HAWAIIAN NIGHTS(1939), ed; YOU CAN'T CHEAT AN HONEST MAN(1939), ed; BEYOND TOMORROW(1940), ed; DREAMING OUT LOUD(1940), ed; FRAMED(1940), ed; DOUBLE DATE(1941), ed; FLYING CADETS(1941), ed; HORROR ISLAND(1941), ed; MELODY LANE(1941), ed; TIGHT SHOES(1941), ed; BOMBAY CLIPPER(1942), ed; FRISCO LILL(1942), ed; SABOTEUR(1942), ed; SHERLOCK HOLMES AND THE SECRET WEAPON(1942), ed; TIMBER(1942), ed; CHEYENNE ROUNDUP(1943), ed; SHERLOCK HOLMES IN WASHINGTON(1943), ed; CUBAN PETE(1946), ed; IDEA GIRL(1946), ed; INSIDE JOB(1946), ed; I'LL BE YOURS(1947), ed; SOMETHING IN THE WIND(1947), ed; ONE TOUCH OF VENUS(1948), ed; RIVER LADY(1948), ed; UP IN CENTRAL PARK(1948), ed; ARCTIC MANHUNT(1949), ed; RED CANYON(1949), ed; SWORD IN THE DESERT(1949), ed; BUCCANEER'S GIRL(1950), ed; DESERT HAWK, THE(1950), ed; I WAS A SHOPLIFTER(1950), ed; WOMAN ON THE RUN(1950), ed; GROOM WORE SPURS, THE(1951), ed; ACTORS AND SIN(1952), ed; RANCHO NOTORIOUS(1952), ed; SAN FRANCISCO STORY, THE(1952), ed; STEEL TRAP, THE(1952), ed; MOON IS BLUE, THE(1953), ed; STAR, THE(1953), ed; BULLET IS WAITING, A(1954), ed; THIS IS MY LOVE(1954), ed; FIRST TRAVELING SALESLADY, THE(1956), ed; HOT BLOOD(1956), ed; STORM FEAR(1956), ed; PUBLIC PIGEON NO. 1(1957), ed; I MARRIED A WOMAN(1958), ed; ESCORT WEST(1959), ed; TAMMY, TELL ME TRUE(1961), ed; JOHNNY COOL(1963), ed
Pamela Ludwig
OVER THE EDGE(1979); SPLIT IMAGE(1982); TEX(1982)
Phyllis Ludwig
IT HAPPENED IN NEW YORK(1935)

Richard Ludwig
FINAL CHORD, THE(1936, Ger.)
Rolf Ludwig
TINDER BOX, THE(1968, E. Ger.)
Salem Ludwig
ER LOVE A STRANGER(1958); AMERICA, AMERICA(1963); I LOVE YOU, ALICE B. TOKLAS!(1968); WHAT'S SO BAD ABOUT FEELING GOOD?(1968); NEXT MAN, THE(1976); THREE SISTERS, THE(1977); ENDLESS LOVE(1981)
Ursula Ludwig
NIGHT CROSSING(1982)
1984
GERMANY PALE MOTHER(1984, Ger.), p
William Ludwig
LOVE FINDS ANDY HARDY(1938), w; OUT WEST WITH THE HARDYS(1938), w; BLACKMAIL(1939), w; HARDYS RIDE HIGH, THE(1939), w; STRONGER THAN DESIRE(1939), w; LOVE CRAZY(1941), w; JOURNEY FOR MARGARET(1942), w; AMERICAN ROMANCE, AN(1944), w; ANDY HARDY'S BLONDE TROUBLE(1944), w; BOYS' RANCH(1946), w; LOVE LAUGHS AT ANDY HARDY(1946), w; HILLS OF HOME(1948), w; JULIA MISBEHAVES(1948), w; CHALLENGE TO LASSIE(1949), w; SUN COMES UP, THE(1949), w; SHADOW ON THE WALL(1950), w; GREAT CARUSO, THE(1951), w; IT'S A BIG COUNTRY(1951), w; MERRY WIDOW, THE(1952), w; ATHENA(1954), w; STUDENT PRINCE, THE(1954), w; HIT THE DECK(1955), w; INTERRUPTED MELODY(1955), w; OKLAHOMA(1955), w; GUN GLORY(1957), w; TEN THOUSAND BEDROOMS(1957), w; BACK STREET(1961), w
Alice Ludwig-Rasch
WORLD IN MY POCKET, THE(1962, Fr./Ital./Ger.), ed
Peter Luechinger
BLACK SPIDER, THE(1983, Swit.)
Werne Joerg Luedecke
MORITURI(1965), w
Guenther Lueders
ETERNAL LOVE(1960, Ger.)
Gunther Lueders
SPESSART INN, THE(1961, Ger.)
Toni Luedi
GERMANY IN AUTUMN(1978, Ger.), set d
Cindy Luedke
AVALANCHE(1978)
Kurt Luedtke
ABSENCE OF MALICE(1981), w
David Luell
PERFECT COUPLE, A(1979)
Walo Lueoend
BLACK SPIDER, THE(1983, Swit.)
Christina Luescher
NEVER CRY WOLF(1983), w
Felix Luetzkendorf
THEY WERE SO YOUNG(1955), w
Laurette Luez
UNFAITHFULLY YOURS(1948); D.O.A.(1950); KILLER SHARK(1950); KIM(1950); PREHISTORIC WOMEN(1950); AFRICAN TREASURE(1952); PARIS MODEL(1953); SIREN OF BAGDAD(1953); JUNGLE GENTS(1954); FLOWER DRUM SONG(1961)
June Lufboro
Silents
YOUR WIFE AND MINE(1927)
Beverly Luff
ROARIN' LEAD(1937)
Jeff Luff
SATURN 3(1980), spec eff
W. Luff
BRIDE OF THE LAKE(1934, Brit.), ph
William Luff
CONDEMNED TO DEATH(1932, Brit.), ph; ANNIE, LEAVE THE ROOM(1935, Brit.), ph; COCK O' THE NORTH(1935, Brit.), ph; DEPARTMENT STORE(1935, Brit.), ph; INSIDE THE ROOM(1935, Brit.), ph; PRIVATE SECRETARY, THE(1935, Brit.), ph; SCROOGE(1935, Brit.), ph; SHE SHALL HAVE MUSIC(1935, Brit.), ph; TRIUMPH OF SHERLOCK HOLMES, THE(1935, Brit.), ph; ELIZA COMES TO STAY(1936, Brit.), ph; HEAD OFFICE(1936, Brit.), ph; LAST JOURNEY, THE(1936, Brit.), ph; MURDER ON THE SET(1936, Brit.), ph; BEAUTY AND THE BARGE(1937, Brit.), ph; JUGGERNAUT(1937, Brit.), ph; VICAR OF BRAY, THE(1937, Brit.), ph; WHO KILLED FEN MARKHAM?(1937, Brit.), ph; LOST ON THE WESTERN FRONT(1940, Brit.), ph; MURDER AT THE BASKERVILLES(1941, Brit.), ph
Silents
GLORIOUS ADVENTURE, THE(1922, U.S./Brit.)
Sam Lufkin
PART TIME WIFE(1930); PARDON US(1931); SONS OF THE DESERT(1933); SIX OF A KIND(1934); MAN ON THE FLYING TRAPEZE, THE(1935); MYSTERY MAN, THE(1935); SHE GETS HER MAN(1935); OUR RELATIONS(1936); PICK A STAR(1937); WAY OUT WEST(1937); SWISS MISS(1938); FLYING DEUCES, THE(1939); SAPS AT SEA(1940); MIRACLE KID(1942); CRACK-UP(1946); LADY LUCK(1946); LIKELY STORY, A(1947); TRAIL STREET(1947); TYCOON(1947); LAW OF THE BADLANDS(1950)
Silents
WHY WORRY(1923); FIGHTING BOOB, THE(1926); SPEEDY(1928)
Herbert G. Luft
HONG KONG AFFAIR(1958), w
Lorna Luft
GREASE 2(1982)
1984
WHERE THE BOYS ARE '84(1984)
Sid Luft
FRENCH LEAVE(1948), p
Sidney Luft
KILROY WAS HERE(1947), p; STAR IS BORN, A(1954), p
Uriel Luft
NIKKI, WILD DOG OF THE NORTH(1961, U.S./Can.)
Francoise Lugagne
LANDRU(1963, Fr./Ital); DIARY OF A CHAMBERMAID(1964, Fr./Ital.)

Alfred Lugg
Silents
QUEEN OF MY HEART(1917, Brit.)
Eric Lugg
Silents
FALSE EVIDENCE(1922, Brit.)
William Lugg
Silents
AVE MARIA(1918, Brit.); OLD CURIOSITY SHOP, THE(1921, Brit.)
Misc. Silents
DADDY(1917, Brit.); DOWN UNDER DONOVAN(1922, Brit.)
Bob Lugo
CASBAH(1948); DREAM WIFE(1953)
Robert Lugo
MEXICAN HAYRIDE(1948); CRISIS(1950)
Bela Lugosi
PRISONERS(1929); OH, FOR A MAN!(1930); RENEGADES(1930); SUCH MEN ARE DANGEROUS(1930); THIRTEENTH CHAIR, THE(1930); VIENNESE NIGHTS(1930); WILD COMPANY(1930); BLACK CAMEL, THE(1931); BROADMINDED(1931); DRACULA(1931); FIFTY MILLION FRENCHMEN(1931); WOMEN OF ALL NATIONS(1931); CHANDU THE MAGICIAN(1932); MURDERS IN THE RUE MORGUE(1932); WHITE ZOMBIE(1932); DEATH KISS, THE(1933); DEVIL'S IN LOVE, THE(1933); INTERNATIONAL HOUSE(1933); ISLAND OF LOST SOULS(1933); NIGHT OF TERROR(1933); BLACK CAT, THE(1934); GIFT OF GAB(1934); BEST MAN WINS, THE(1935); MARK OF THE VAMPIRE(1935); MURDER BY TELEVISION(1935); MYSTERIOUS MR. WONG(1935); RAVEN, THE(1935); POSTAL INSPECTOR(1936); THE INVISIBLE RAY(1936); PHANTOM SHIP(1937, Brit.); GORILLA, THE(1939); NINOTCHKA(1939); SON OF FRANKENSTEIN(1939); BLACK FRIDAY(1940); HUMAN MONSTER, THE(1940, Brit.); SAINT'S DOUBLE TROUBLE, THE(1940); YOU'LL FIND OUT(1940); BLACK CAT, THE(1941); DEVIL BAT, THE(1941); INVISIBLE GHOST, THE(1941); SPOOKS RUN WILD(1941); WOLF MAN, THE(1941); BLACK DRAGONS(1942); BOWERY AT MIDNIGHT(1942); CORPSE VANISHES, THE(1942); GHOST OF FRANKENSTEIN, THE(1942); NIGHT MONSTER(1942); APE MAN, THE(1943); FRANKENSTEIN MEETS THE WOLF MAN(1943); GHOSTS ON THE LOOSE(1943); ONE BODY TOO MANY(1944); RETURN OF THE APE MAN(1944); RETURN OF THE VAMPIRE, THE(1944); VOODOO MAN(1944); BODY SNATCHER, THE(1945); ZOMBIES ON BROADWAY(1945); GENIUS AT WORK(1946); SCARED TO DEATH(1947); ABBOTT AND COSTELLO MEET FRANKENSTEIN(1948); BELA LUGOSI MEETS A BROOKLYN GORILLA(1952); GLEN OR GLENDA(1953); BRIDE OF THE MONSTER(1955); BLACK SLEEP, THE(1956); PLAN 9 FROM OUTER SPACE(1959); MY SON, THE VAMPIRE(1963, Brit.)
Misc. Talkies
CHANDU ON THE MAGIC ISLAND(1934); S.O.S. COAST GUARD(1937)
Silents
SILENT COMMAND, THE(1923); REJECTED WOMAN, THE(1924)
Misc. Silents
HEAD OF JANUS, THE(1920, Ger.)
James Lugton
BMX BANDITS(1983)
Andre Luguet
MAD GENIUS, THE(1931); AMERICAN LOVE(1932, Fr.); JEWEL ROBBERY(1932); LOVE IS A RACKET(1932); MAN WHO PLAYED GOD, THE(1932); MADAME DU BARRY(1954 Fr./Ital.); FRENCH, THEY ARE A FUNNY RACE, THE(1956, Fr.); LA PARISIENNE(1958, Fr./Ital.); ROOTS OF HEAVEN, THE(1958); PARIS BLUES(1961); LOVE IS A BALL(1963); MALE COMPANION(1965, Fr./Ital.); RAVISHING IDIOT, A(1966, Ital./Fr.); LA PRISONNIERE(1969, Fr./Ital.)
Rosine Luguet
HER FIRST AFFAIR(1947, Fr.); SYMPHONIE PASTORALE(1948, Fr.); PEEK-A-BOO(1961, Fr.); MADEMOISELLE(1966, Fr./Brit.)
Hermanos Lugunas
PRIEST OF LOVE(1981, Brit.)
Peter Luhr
DECISION BEFORE DAWN(1951); UNWILLING AGENT(1968, Ger.); OUR HITLER, A FILM FROM GERMANY(1980, Ger.); VERONIKA VOSS(1982, Ger.)
Baz Luhrmann
WINTER OF OUR DREAMS(1982, Aus.)
Bill Luhrs
SO FINE(1981)
1984
SLAYGROUND(1984, Brit.)
Wolfgang Luhrse
THAT WOMAN(1968, Ger.), ph
Lotus Lui
GOOD EARTH, THE(1937)
Maurice Lui
WEST OF SHANGHAI(1937)
Roland Lui
GOOD EARTH, THE(1937)
Wonci Lui
KISMET(1955)
Earl Luick
ON TRIAL(1928), cos; OLD ENGLISH(1930), cos; OUTWARD BOUND(1930), cos; ILLICIT(1931), cos; LAST FLIGHT, THE(1931), cos; LITTLE CAESAR(1931), cos; NIGHT NURSE(1931), cos; OTHER MEN'S WOMEN(1931), cos; PUBLIC ENEMY, THE(1931), cos; SAFE IN HELL(1931), cos; MOUTHPIECE, THE(1932), cos; PASSPORT TO HELL(1932), cos; TOO BUSY TO WORK(1932), cos; WEEK-ENDS ONLY(1932), cos; WILD GIRL(1932), cos; EVER IN MY HEART(1933), cos; PILGRIMAGE(1933), cos; WORLD CHANGES, THE(1933), cos; BLACK SWAN, THE(1942), cos; CRASH DIVE(1943), cos; OX-BOW INCIDENT, THE(1943), cos
Luigi
THINGS OF LIFE, THE(1970, Fr./Ital./Switz.)
Hans Luigi
INDECENT(1962, Ger.), set d
Mario Luillard
FRENCH CANCAN(1956, Fr.)
Jacqueline Luis
EL TOPO(1971, Mex.)

"Hank" Luisetti
CAMPUS CONFESSIONS(1938)
James Luisi
TIGER MAKES OUT, THE(1967); BEN(1972); TAKE, THE(1974); STUNTS(1977); MOMENT BY MOMENT(1978); NORMA RAE(1979); FADE TO BLACK(1980); STAR 80(1983)
Misc. Talkies
SPORTS KILLER, THE(1976); KILLER'S DELIGHT(1978)
Jean Luisi
LONG ABSENCE, THE(1962, Fr./Ital.)
Luitz-Morat
Misc. Silents
LES CINQ GENTLEMEN MAUDITS(1919, Fr.), d; MONSIEUR LEBUREAU(1920, Fr.), d; LA TERRE DU DIABLE(1921, Fr.), d; AU SEUIL DU HAREM(1922, Fr.), d; LE SANG D'ALLAH(1922, Fr.), d; PETIT ANGE ET SON PANTIN(1923, Fr.), d; LA CITE FOUDROYEE(1924, Fr.), d; LA COURSE AU FLAMBEAU(1925, Fr.), d; LE JUIF ERRANT(1926, Fr.), d; LA RONDE INFERNALE(1927, Fr.), d; LA VIERGE FOLLE(1929, Fr.), d
Loretta Luiz
STORY OF DR. WASSELL, THE(1944)
Luthero Luiz
1984
GABRIELA(1984, Braz.)
Armando Lujan
LITTLE RED RIDING HOOD AND HER FRIENDS(1964, Mex.)
Kath Ann Lujan
DEAD END(1937)
Geta Luka
KAZABLAN(1974, Israel)
Jetta Luka
FLYING MATCHMAKER, THE(1970, Israel)
M. Lukach
THERE WAS AN OLD COUPLE(1967, USSR)
Sandor Lukacs
MEPHISTO(1981, Ger.)
Jaromir Lukas
SHOP ON MAIN STREET, THE(1966, Czech.), p
Josef Lukas
JOURNEY TO THE BEGINNING OF TIME(1966, Czech)
Karel Lukas
MATTER OF DAYS, A(1969, Fr./Czech.), set d
Karl Lukas
LONG, LONG TRAILER, THE(1954); UNDER FIRE(1957); ONIONHEAD(1958); TRUE STORY OF LYNN STUART, THE(1958); TALL STORY(1960); THERE WAS A CROOKED MAN(1970); TORA! TORA! TORA!(1970, U.S./Jap.); WATERMELON MAN(1970); EMPEROR OF THE NORTH POLE(1973); OKLAHOMA CRUDE(1973); 99 AND 44/100% DEAD(1974); HUSTLE(1975); LAS VEGAS LADY(1976); SHAGGY D.A., THE(1976); TWO-MINUTE WARNING(1976)
Paul Lukas
MANHATTAN COCKTAIL(1928); SHOPWORN ANGEL, THE(1928); HALF WAY TO HEAVEN(1929); ILLUSION(1929); WOLF OF WALL STREET, THE(1929); ANYBODY'S WOMAN(1930); BEHIND THE MAKEUP(1930); BENSON MURDER CASE, THE(1930); DEVIL'S HOLIDAY, THE(1930); GRUMPY(1930); SLIGHTLY SCARLET(1930); YOUNG EAGLES(1930); BELOVED BACHELOR, THE(1931); CITY STREETS(1931); RIGHT TO LOVE, THE(1931); STRICTLY DISHONORABLE(1931); UNFAITHFUL(1931); VICE SQUAD, THE(1931); WOMEN LOVE ONCE(1931); WORKING GIRLS(1931); DOWNSTAIRS(1932); NO ONE MAN(1932); PASSPORT TO HELL(1932); ROCKABYE(1932); THUNDER BELOW(1932); TOMORROW AND TOMORROW(1932); CAPTURED(1933); GRAND SLAM(1933); KISS BEFORE THE MIRROR, THE(1933); LITTLE WOMEN(1933); SECRET OF THE BLUE ROOM(1933); AFFAIRS OF A GENTLEMAN(1934); BY CANDLELIGHT(1934); COUNTESS OF MONTE CRISTO, THE(1934); FOUNTAIN, THE(1934); GIFT OF GAB(1934); GLAMOUR(1934); I GIVE MY LOVE(1934); AGE OF INDISCRETION(1935); CASINO MURDER CASE, THE(1935); FATHER BROWN, DETECTIVE(1935); I FOUND STELLA PARISH(1935); THREE MUSKETEERS, THE(1935); DODSWORTH(1936); LADIES IN LOVE(1936); BRIEF ECSTASY(1937, Brit.); DINNER AT THE RITZ(1937, Brit.); ESPIONAGE(1937); DANGEROUS SECRETS(1938, Brit.); LADY VANISHES, THE(1938, Brit.); CAPTAIN FURY(1939); CONFESSIONS OF A NAZI SPY(1939); MUTINY OF THE ELSINORE, THE(1939, Brit.); CHINESE DEN, THE(1940, Brit.); GHOST BREAKERS, THE(1940); STRANGE CARGO(1940); MONSTER AND THE GIRL, THE(1941); THEY DARE NOT LOVE(1941); LADY IN DISTRESS(1942, Brit.); HOSTAGES(1943); WATCH ON THE RHINE(1943); ADDRESS UNKNOWN(1944); EXPERIMENT PERILOUS(1944); UNCERTAIN GLORY(1944); DEADLINE AT DAWN(1946); TEMPTATION(1946); WHISPERING CITY(1947, Can.); BERLIN EXPRESS(1948); KIM(1950); 20,000 LEAGUES UNDER THE SEA(1954); ROOTS OF HEAVEN, THE(1958); SCENT OF MYSTERY(1960); TENDER IS THE NIGHT(1961); FOUR HORSEMEN OF THE APOCALYPSE, THE(1962); FUN IN ACAPULCO(1963); 55 DAYS AT PEKING(1963); LORD JIM(1965, Brit.); SOL MADRID(1968)
Silents
HOT NEWS(1928); NIGHT WATCH, THE(1928); THREE SINNERS(1928); TWO LOVERS(1928)
Misc. Silents
SAMSON AND DELILAH(1922, Aust.); MANHATTAN COCKTAIL(1928); WOMAN FROM MOSCOW, THE(1928)
Peter Lukas
STUD, THE(1979, Brit.)
Wilfred Lukas
SILVER DOLLAR(1932)
Misc. Silents
HER EXCELLENCY, THE GOVERNOR(1917)
Rudolf Lukasek
DIAMONDS OF THE NIGHT(1968, Czech.)
T. Lukashevich
BRIDE WITH A DOWRY(1954, USSR), d
Tatyana Lukashevitch
SOUND OF LIFE, THE(1962, USSR), d
G. Lukashov
MOTHER AND DAUGHTER(1965, USSR), spec eff

Dorys Lukather
PHANTOM FROM 10,000 LEAGUES, THE(1956), w
Marie Curie Lukather
1984
ROSEBUD BEACH HOTEL(1984)
Paul Lukather
DRANGO(1957); JOHNNY TROUBLE(1957); DINOSAURUS(1960); HANDS OF A STRANGER(1962); FATE IS THE HUNTER(1964); I'D RATHER BE RICH(1964); ALVAREZ KELLY(1966); WAY WEST, THE(1967); HOT LEAD AND COLD FEET(1978)
1984
FRIDAY THE 13TH-THE FINAL CHAPTER(1984)
Nick Lukats
COLLEGE HOLIDAY(1936); MURDER WITH PICTURES(1936); ROSE BOWL(1936); STRIKE ME PINK(1936); VALIANT IS THE WORD FOR CARRIE(1936); BORN TO THE WEST(1937); CHAMPAGNE WALTZ(1937); EASY LIVING(1937); HOTEL HAYWIRE(1937); INTERNES CAN'T TAKE MONEY(1937); KING OF GAMBLERS(1937); MAKE WAY FOR TOMORROW(1937); MURDER GOES TO COLLEGE(1937); SOPHIE LANG GOES WEST(1937); SWING HIGH, SWING LOW(1937); WAIKIKI WEDDING(1937); WILD MONEY(1937); DUKE OF WEST POINT, THE(1938); EXTORTION(1938); I AM THE LAW(1938); REBELLIOUS DAUGHTERS(1938); START CHEERING(1938); KNUTE ROCKNE-ALL AMERICAN(1940), a, tech adv
Radovan Lukavsky
MAN FROM THE FIRST CENTURY, THE(1961, Czech.)
Benny Luke
LA CAGE AUX FOLLES(1979, Fr./Ital.); LA CAGE AUX FOLLES II(1981, Ital./Fr.)
Cressida Luke
OEDIPUS THE KING(1968, Brit.)
Eddie Luke
FIRST YANK INTO TOKYO(1945); KING AND I, THE(1956)
Edwin Luke
JADE MASK, THE(1945)
Jorge Luke
REVENGERS, THE(1972, U.S./Mex.); ULZANA'S RAID(1972); RETURN OF A MAN CALLED HORSE, THE(1976); FOXTROT(1977, Mex./Swiss); EAGLE'S WING(1979, Brit.); SUNBURN(1979)
1984
EVIL THAT MEN DO, THE(1984)
Keye Luke
PAINTED VEIL, THE(1934); CASINO MURDER CASE, THE(1935); CHARLIE CHAN IN PARIS(1935); CHARLIE CHAN IN SHANGHAI(1935); MAD LOVE(1935); OIL FOR THE LAMPS OF CHINA(1935); SHANGHAI(1935); CHARLIE CHAN AT THE CIRCUS(1936); CHARLIE CHAN AT THE OPERA(1936); CHARLIE CHAN AT THE RACE TRACK(1936); KING OF BURLESQUE(1936); CHARLIE CHAN AT MONTE CARLO(1937); CHARLIE CHAN AT THE OLYMPICS(1937); CHARLIE CHAN ON BROADWAY(1937); GOOD EARTH, THE(1937); INTERNATIONAL SETTLEMENT(1938); MR. MOTO'S GAMBLE(1938); BARRICADE(1939); DISPUTED PASSAGE(1939); NORTH OF SHANGHAI(1939); NO, NO NANETTE(1940); PHANTOM OF CHINATOWN(1940); SUED FOR LIBEL(1940); BOWERY BLITZKRIEG(1941); BURMA CONVOY(1941); GANG'S ALL HERE(1941); LET'S GO COLLEGIATE(1941); MR. AND MRS. NORTH(1941); NO HANDS ON THE CLOCK(1941); THEY MET IN BOMBAY(1941); ACROSS THE PACIFIC(1942); DESTINATION UNKNOWN(1942); DR. GILLESPIE'S NEW ASSISTANT(1942); FALCON'S BROTHER, THE(1942); INVISIBLE AGENT(1942); JOURNEY FOR MARGARET(1942); MEXICAN SPITFIRE'S ELEPHANT(1942); NORTH TO THE KLONDIKE(1942); SOMEWHERE I'LL FIND YOU(1942); SPY SHIP(1942); TRAGEDY AT MIDNIGHT, A(1942); YANK ON THE BURMA ROAD, A(1942); DR. GILLESPIE'S CRIMINAL CASE(1943); SALUTE TO THE MARINES(1943); ANDY HARDY'S BLONDE TROUBLE(1944); BETWEEN TWO WOMEN(1944); THREE MEN IN WHITE(1944); FIRST YANK INTO TOKYO(1945); TOKYO ROSE(1945); HOW DO YOU DO?(1946); DARK DELUSION(1947); FEATHERED SERPENT, THE(1948); SLEEP, MY LOVE(1948); WATERFRONT AT MIDNIGHT(1948); SKY DRAGON(1949); YOUNG MAN WITH A HORN(1950); FAIR WIND TO JAVA(1953); SOUTH SEA WOMAN(1953); HELL'S HALF ACRE(1954); WORLD FOR RANSOM(1954); BAMBOO PRISON, THE(1955); LOVE IS A MANY-SPLENDORED THING(1955); BATTLE HELL(1956, Brit.); NOBODY'S PERFECT(1968); PROJECT X(1968); CHAIRMAN, THE(1969); HAWAIIANS, THE(1970); WON TON TON, THE DOG WHO SAVED HOLLYWOOD(1976); AMSTERDAM KILL, THE(1978, Hong Kong); JUST YOU AND ME, KID(1979)
1984
GREMLINS(1984)
Lucas C. Luke
Silents
WHITE YOUTH(1920)
Michael Luke
PUSSYCAT ALLEY(1965, Brit.), p; OEDIPUS THE KING(1968, Brit.), p, w
Norman Luke
Misc. Silents
BOOTS AND SADDLES(1916)
Oenone Luke
OEDIPUS THE KING(1968, Brit.)
Patricia Luke
DOMINO PRINCIPLE, THE(1977)
Sherrill Luke
SOUTH OF DIXIE(1944)
George E. Lukens, Jr.
SOURDOUGH(1977), p
Victor Lukens
BLACK LIKE ME(1964), ph
Mark Luker
LOVES OF JOANNA GODDEN, THE(1947, Brit.), cos
Oldrich Lukes
FIRST SPACESHIP ON VENUS(1960, Ger./Pol.); LEMONADE JOE(1966, Czech.)
Jirina Lukesova
CLOSELY WATCHED TRAINS(1967, Czech.), ed; DEATH OF TARZAN, THE(1968, Czech.), ed; INTIMATE LIGHTING(1969, Czech.), ed; MOST BEAUTIFUL AGE, THE(1970, Czech.), ed
Sergei Lukianov
MILITARY SECRET(1945, USSR)

Vladimir Lukin
DEFENSE OF VOLOTCHAYEVSK, THE(1938, USSR)
Yuriy Lukin
DESTINY OF A MAN(1961, USSR), w
Annabel Lukins
JUST TELL ME WHAT YOU WANT(1980)
A. Lukovsky
Misc. Silents
LEAH'S SUFFERING(1917, USSR)
Peter Lukoye
BORN FREE(1966); LIVING FREE(1972, Brit.)
Wolfgang Lukschy
AFFAIRS OF JULIE, THE(1958, Ger.); ETERNAL LOVE(1960, Ger.); DARK EYES OF LONDON(1961, Ger.); GIRL OF THE MOORS, THE(1961, Ger.); LONGEST DAY, THE(1962); ROMMEL'S TREASURE(1962, Ital.); SHERLOCK HOLMES AND THE DEADLY NECKLACE(1962, Ger.); FISTFUL OF DOLLARS, A(1964, Ital./Ger./Span.); FROZEN ALIVE(1966, Brit./Ger.); PLACE CALLED GLORY, A(1966, Span./Ger.); THE DIRTY GAME(1966, Fr./Ital./Ger.); 24 HOURS TO KILL(1966, Brit.); FLAMING FRONTIER(1968, Ger./Yugo.); INSIDE OUT(1975, Brit.)
S. Lukyanov
TWELFTH NIGHT(1956, USSR); ITALIANO BRAVA GENTE(1965, Ital./USSR)
Sergey Lukyanov
GORDEYEV FAMILY, THE(1961, U.S.S.R.)
Folco Lulli
BANDIT, THE(1949, Ital.); WITHOUT PITY(1949, Ital.); TIMES GONE BY(1953, Ital.); GREAT HOPE, THE(1954, Ital.); COUNT OF MONTE-CRISTO(1955, Fr., Ital.); WAGES OF FEAR, THE(1955, Fr./Ital.); HOUSE OF INTRIGUE, THE(1959, Ital.); SIGN OF THE GLADIATOR(1959, Fr./Ger./Ital.); ALWAYS VICTORIOUS(1960, Ital.); ESTHER AND THE KING(1960, U.S./Ital.); MARIE OF THE ISLES(1960, Fr.); UNDER TEN FLAGS(1960, U.S./Ital.); GREAT WAR, THE(1961, Fr., Ital.); NEOPOLITAN CAROUSEL(1961, Ital.); DULCINEA(1962, Span.); HUNS, THE(1962, Fr./Ital.); TARTARS, THE(1962, Ital./Yugo.); WARRIORS FIVE(1962); ERIK THE CONQUEROR(1963, Fr./Ital.); LAFAYETTE(1963, Fr.); RICE GIRL(1963, Fr./Ital.); ORGANIZER, THE(1964, Fr./Ital./Yugo.); VARIETY LIGHTS(1965, Ital.); MARCO THE MAGNIFICENT(1966, Ital./Fr./Yugo./Egypt/Afghanistan); ALL THE OTHER GIRLS DO!(1967, Ital.); LIGHTNING BOLT(1967, Ital./Sp.)
Piero Lulli
ANNA(1951, Ital.); ULYSSES(1955, Ital.); ALWAYS VICTORIOUS(1960, Ital.); HUNS, THE(1962, Fr./Ital.); LAST OF THE VIKINGS, THE(1962, Fr./Ital.); DUEL OF THE TITANS(1963, Ital.); GLADIATOR OF ROME(1963, Ital.); HERO OF BABYLON(1963, Ital.); GOLIATH AND THE SINS OF BABYLON(1964, Ital.); HERCULES VS THE GIANT WARRIORS(1965 Fr./Ital.); KILL BABY KILL(1966, Ital.); SECRET SEVEN, THE(1966, Ital./Span.); DJANGO KILL(1967, Ital./Span.); NO ROSES FOR OSS 117(1968, Fr.); BOLDEST JOB IN THE WEST, THE(1971, Ital.); DIRTY OUTLAWS, THE(1971, Ital.); MY NAME IS NOBODY(1974, Ital./Fr./Ger.)
Jean-Baptiste Lully
WOULD-BE GENTLEMAN, THE(1960, Fr.), m; PICKPOCKET(1963, Fr.), m
Lulu [Marie Lawrie]
TO SIR, WITH LOVE(1967, Brit.)
Lulu & The Lovers
GONKS GO BEAT(1965, Brit.)
Lulu and Tonio
TRAPEZE(1956)
Lulubelle and Scotty
SHINE ON, HARVEST MOON(1938); VILLAGE BARN DANCE(1940); HI, NEIGHBOR(1942); SWING YOUR PARTNER(1943); NATIONAL BARN DANCE(1944); SING, NEIGHBOR, SING(1944)
Alvin Lum
YEAR OF THE HORSE, THE(1966)
Gladys Lum
Misc. Talkies
ABAR–THE FIRST BLACK SUPERMAN(1977)
Harry Lum
LIQUID SKY(1982)
Franca Lumachi
MASOCH(1980, Ital.)
Bob Luman
CARNIVAL ROCK(1957)
Raoul Lumas
PROWLER, THE(1981), ph
Carl Lumbly
CAVEMAN(1981)
1984
ADVENTURES OF BUCKAROO BANZAI: ACROSS THE 8TH DIMENSION, THE(1984)
Carl Lumby
ESCAPE FROM ALCATRAZ(1979)
Baruch Lumet
ONE THIRD OF A NATION(1939); KILLER SHREWS, THE(1959); INTERNS, THE(1962); PAWNBROKER, THE(1965); GROUP, THE(1966); EVERYTHING YOU ALWAYS WANTED TO KNOW ABOUT SEX, BUT WE'RE AFRAID TO ASK(1972); WILD PARTY, THE(1975)
Jenny Lumet
DEATHTRAP(1982)
Sidney Lumet
WIZ, THE(1978), d; ONE THIRD OF A NATION(1939); 12 ANGRY MEN(1957), d; STAGE STRUCK(1958), d; THAT KIND OF WOMAN(1959), d; FUGITIVE KIND, THE(1960), d; LONG DAY'S JOURNEY INTO NIGHT(1962), d; VIEW FROM THE BRIDGE, A(1962, Fr./Ital.), d; FAIL SAFE(1964), d; HILL, THE(1965, Brit.), d; PAWNBROKER, THE(1965), d; GROUP, THE(1966), d; DEADLY AFFAIR, THE(1967, Brit.), p&d; BYE BYE BRAVERMAN(1968), p&d; SEA GULL, THE(1968), p&d; APPOINTMENT, THE(1969), d; ANDERSON TAPES, THE(1971), d; CHILD'S PLAY(1972), d; OFFENSE, THE(1973, Brit.), d; SERPICO(1973), d; LOVIN' MOLLY(1974), d; MURDER ON THE ORIENT EXPRESS(1974, Brit.), d; DOG DAY AFTERNOON(1975), d; NETWORK(1976), d; "EQUUS"(1977), d; JUST TELL ME WHAT YOU WANT(1980), p, d; PRINCE OF THE CITY(1981), d; DEATHTRAP(1982), d; VERDICT, THE(1982), d; DANIEL(1983), d
1984
GARBO TALKS(1984), d

Sal Lumetta
1984
SPLATTER UNIVERSITY(1984)
Arthur Lumley
Silents
NOTORIOUS MRS. CARRICK, THE(1924, Brit.)
Joanna Lumley
ON HER MAJESTY'S SECRET SERVICE(1969, Brit.); GAMES THAT LOVERS PLAY(1971, Brit.); DON'T JUST LIE THERE, SAY SOMETHING!(1973, Brit.); COUNT DRACULA AND HIS VAMPIRE BRIDE(1978, Brit.); TRAIL OF THE PINK PANTHER, THE(1982); CURSE OF THE PINK PANTHER(1983); WEATHER IN THE STREETS, THE(1983, Brit.)
Misc. Talkies
BREAKING OF BUMBO(1972, Brit.)
Joanne Lumley
DEVIL'S WIDOW, THE(1972, Brit.)
Misc. Talkies
LADY CHATTERLY VS. FANNY HILL(1980)
Ralph Lumley
IN THE SOUP(1936, Brit.), w
Dayton Lummis
LES MISERABLES(1952); ALL I DESIRE(1953); CHINA VENTURE(1953); GLENN MILLER STORY, THE(1953); GOLDEN BLADE, THE(1953); HOW TO MARRY A MILLIONAIRE(1953); JULIUS CAESAR(1953); MAN IN THE DARK(1953); MISSISSIPPI GAMBLER, THE(1953); PORT SINISTER(1953); PRESIDENT'S LADY, THE(1953); TANGIER INCIDENT(1953); DEMETRIUS AND THE GLADIATORS(1954); DRAGON'S GOLD(1954); LOOPHOLE(1954); RETURN TO TREASURE ISLAND(1954); YELLOW MOUNTAIN, THE(1954); COURT-MARTIAL OF BILLY MITCHELL, THE(1955); HIGH SOCIETY(1955); PRINCE OF PLAYERS(1955); PRODIGAL, THE(1955); SPOILERS, THE(1955); SUDDEN DANGER(1955); VIEW FROM POMPEY'S HEAD, THE(1955); DAY OF FURY, A(1956); FIRST TEXAN, THE(1956); OVER-EXPOSED(1956); SHOWDOWN AT ABILENE(1956); WRONG MAN, THE(1956); MONKEY ON MY BACK(1957); MUSIC BOX KID, THE(1960); SPARTACUS(1960); FLIGHT THAT DISAPPEARED, THE(1961); DEADLY DUO(1962); JACK THE GIANT KILLER(1962); BEAUTY AND THE BEAST(1963); MOONFIRE(1970)
John Lummis
FLASH GORDON(1980)
John Lummiss
RETURN OF THE JEDI(1983)
Roger Lumont
TRAIN, THE(1965, Fr./Ital./U.S.); IS PARIS BURNING?(1966, U.S./Fr.); MAYERLING(1968, Brit./Fr.); LADY IN THE CAR WITH GLASSES AND A GUN, THE(1970, U.S./Fr.); ALFIE DARLING(1975, Brit.); LOVE AND DEATH(1975)
Lumpy the Camel
SLAVE GIRL(1947)
Geoffrey Lumsden
STORY OF ROBIN HOOD, THE(1952, Brit.); DATELINE DIAMONDS(1966, Brit.); DANDY IN ASPIC, A(1968, Brit.); HOSTILE WITNESS(1968, Brit.); SALT & PEPPER(1968, Brit.)
Norman Lumsden
RUNNERS(1983, Brit.)
Sue Lumsden
SILENT PARTNER, THE(1979, Can.)
Luna
SKIDOO(1968)
Barbara Luna
TANK BATTALION(1958); CRY TOUGH(1959); DEVIL AT FOUR O'CLOCK, THE(1961); FIVE WEEKS IN A BALLOON(1962); DIME WITH A HALO(1963); MAIL ORDER BRIDE(1964); SHIP OF FOOLS(1965); SYNANON(1965); FIRECREEK(1968); CHE!(1969); GATLING GUN, THE(1972); CONCRETE JUNGLE, THE(1982)
Misc. Talkies
CAMPER JOHN(1973); WOMAN IN THE RAIN(1976)
Charito Luna
STEEL CLAW, THE(1961)
Donyale Luna
FELLINI SATYRICON(1969, Fr./Ital.)
Manuel Luna
CARMEN(1949, Span.); MAD QUEEN, THE(1950, Span.)
Margarita Luna
MY BROTHER, THE OUTLAW(1951)
Margarito Luna
TREASURE OF THE SIERRA MADRE, THE(1948); TORCH, THE(1950); LITTLEST OUTLAW, THE(1955); BANDIDO(1956); BEAST OF HOLLOW MOUNTAIN, THE(1956); RUN FOR THE SUN(1956); VAMPIRE, THE(1968, Mex.); TWO MULES FOR SISTER SARA(1970)
Mike Luna
WONDERFUL COUNTRY, THE(1959)
Ricardo Luna
HAND IN THE TRAP, THE(1963, Arg./Span.), w; TERRACE, THE(1964, Arg.), art d
The Luna Boys
SIDEWALKS OF LONDON(1940, Brit.)
Charles Lunard
ZIEGFELD FOLLIES(1945); SWEET CHARITY(1969)
Lydia Lunch
OFFENDERS, THE(1980), a, m; VORTEX(1982), a, m
Alan Lund
MEET THE NAVY(1946, Brit.)
Anna Lena Lund
PRIZE, THE(1963)
Annalena Lund
MR. SARDONICUS(1961); FREE, WHITE AND 21(1963)
Art Lund
MOLLY MAGUIRES, THE(1970); HEAD ON(1971); BLACK CAESAR(1973); LAST AMERICAN HERO, THE(1973); BUCKTOWN(1975); BABY BLUE MARINE(1976)
Misc. Talkies
BOOTS TURNER(1973)
Deanna Lund
DR. GOLDFOOT AND THE BIKINI MACHINE(1965); ONCE UPON A COFFEE HOUSE(1965); DIMENSION 5(1966); JOHNNY TIGER(1966); OUT OF SIGHT(1966); RUN FOR YOUR WIFE(1966, Fr./Ital.); STING OF DEATH(1966); TONY ROME(1967);

PANIC IN THE CITY(1968); HARDLY WORKING(1981)

Eddie Lund
TAHITIAN, THE(1956), m

Gail Lund
LOVING YOU(1957)

Gary Lund
SHINBONE ALLEY(1971), prod d

Jana Lund
DON'T KNOCK THE ROCK(1956); LOVING YOU(1957); FRANKENSTEIN 1970(1958); HIGH SCHOOL HELLCATS(1958); HOT CAR GIRL(1958); MARRIED TOO YOUNG(1962)

John Lund
TO EACH HIS OWN(1946); PERILS OF PAULINE, THE(1947); VARIETY GIRL(1947); FOREIGN AFFAIR, A(1948); MISS TATLOCK'S MILLIONS(1948); NIGHT HAS A THOUSAND EYES(1948); BRIDE OF VENGEANCE(1949); MY FRIEND IRMA(1949); DUCHESS OF IDAHO, THE(1950); MY FRIEND IRMA GOES WEST(1950); NO MAN OF HER OWN(1950); DARLING, HOW COULD YOU!(1951); MATING SEASON, THE(1951); BATTLE AT APACHE PASS, THE(1952); BRONCO BUSTER(1952); JUST ACROSS THE STREET(1952); STEEL TOWN(1952); LATIN LOVERS(1953); WOMAN THEY ALMOST LYNCHED, THE(1953); CHIEF CRAZY HORSE(1955); FIVE GUNS WEST(1955); WHITE FEATHER(1955); BATTLE STATIONS(1956); DAKOTA INCIDENT(1956); HIGH SOCIETY(1956); AFFAIR IN RENO(1957); WACKIEST SHIP IN THE ARMY, THE(1961); IF A MAN ANSWERS(1962)

Larry Lund
IRON MAJOR, THE(1943)

Lucille Lund
HORSEPLAY(1933); SATURDAY'S MILLIONS(1933); BLACK CAT, THE(1934); KISS AND MAKE UP(1934); YOUNG AND BEAUTIFUL(1934); FOLIES DERGERE(1935); DON'T GET PERSONAL(1936); PRISON SHADOWS(1936); PUT ON THE SPOT(1936); RIO GRANDE ROMANCE(1936); TIMBER WAR(1936); CRIMINALS OF THE AIR(1937); FIGHT TO THE FINISH, A(1937); GIRLS CAN PLAY(1937); WHAT PRICE VENGEANCE?(1937); THERE'S THAT WOMAN AGAIN(1938)
Misc. Talkies
FIGHTING THROUGH(1934); RANGE WARFARE(1935)

Margareta Lund
PRIZE, THE(1963)

Marie Lund
MADEMOISELLE FIFI(1944)

Martin Lund
DOUBLES(1978), m

O.A.C. Lund
Silents
DOLLAR MARK, THE(1914), d, w; WHEN BROADWAY WAS A TRAIL(1914), d&w; PEG OF THE PIRATES(1918), d&w
Misc. Silents
MARKED WOMAN, THE(1914), d; M'LISS(1915), a, d; AUTUMN(1916), d; DORIAN'S DIVORCE(1916), d; PRICE OF MALICE, THE(1916), d; HER NEW YORK(1917), d; MOTHER LOVE AND THE LAW(1917); PAINTED MADONNA, THE(1917), d; DEBT OF HONOR, THE(1918), d; HEART'S REVENGE, A(1918), d; TOGETHER(1918), d; NATURE GIRL, THE(1919), d

Oscar Lund
Misc. Silents
LOVE'S OLD SWEET SONG(1923), d; FOR WOMAN'S FAVOR(1924), d

Oscar A. C. Lund
Silents
JUST JIM(1915), d&w; TRAIL OF THE SHADOW, THE(1917), w

Otto Lund
JOURNEY TO THE SEVENTH PLANET(1962, U.S./Swed.), art d; REPTILICUS(1962, U.S./Den.), set d; ERIC SOYA'S "17"(1967, Den.), art d

P. Lund
PRIME CUT(1972)

Richard Lund
NIGHT IN JUNE, A(1940, Swed.)
Misc. Silents
LOVE AND JOURNALISM(1916, Swed.); SIR ARNE'S TREASURE(1920, Swed.)

Rickard Lund
WALPURGIS NIGHT(1941, Swed.)

Tina Lund
SUMMER RUN(1974)
Misc. Talkies
SUMMER RUN(1974)

Wilhelm Lund
HUNGER(1968, Den./Norway/Swed.)

Wulff Lund
WILD STRAWBERRIES(1959, Swed.)

Dan Lundberg
PARTY CRASHERS, THE(1958), w; RAW WIND IN EDEN(1958), w

Lasse Lundberg
ELVIS! ELVIS!(1977, Swed.), ed

Raymond Lundberg
SHAME(1968, Swed.)

Ann Lundeen
MARRIAGE IS A PRIVATE AFFAIR(1944)

Florence Lundeen
MEET THE PEOPLE(1944); UP IN ARMS(1944)

Kenneth Lundeen
TENTACLES(1977, Ital.)

Peggy Lundeen
Silents
EMBARRASSMENT OF RICHES, THE(1918)

Erik Lundegard
JOHANSSON GETS SCOLDED(1945, Swed.), w

Kert Lundell
THEY ALL LAUGHED(1981), art d

Niles Lundell
Misc. Silents
KARIN, INGMAR'S DAUGHTER(1920, Swed.)

Jack Lunden
Misc. Silents
UNDER THE TONTO RIM(1928)

Gerda Lundeqvist
Misc. Silents
SAGA OF GOSTA BERLING, THE(1924, Fr.)

Lyn Lundgren
STRAIT-JACKET(1964)
Misc. Talkies
PLEASE DON'T EAT MY MOTHER(1972)

P.A. Lundgren
SMILES OF A SUMMER NIGHT(1957, Swed.), art d; SEVENTH SEAL, THE(1958, Swed.), set d; MAGICIAN, THE(1959, Swed.), art d; DEVIL'S EYE, THE(1960, Swed.), art d; LESSON IN LOVE, A(1960, Swed.), set d; VIRGIN SPRING, THE(1960, Swed.), art d; DEVIL'S WANTON, THE(1962, Swed.), art d; NIGHT IS MY FUTURE(1962, Swed.), art d; THROUGH A GLASS DARKLY(1962, Swed.), art d; JUST ONCE MORE(1963, Swed.), set d; WINTER LIGHT, THE(1963, Swed.), set d; SILENCE, THE(1964, Swed.), art d; SWEDISH MISTRESS, THE(1964, Swed.), set d; HAGBARD AND SIGNE(1968, Den./Iceland/Swed.), art d; SHAME(1968, Swed.), art d; PEOPLE MEET AND SWEET MUSIC FILLS THE HEART(1969, Den./Swed.), art d; NIGHT VISITOR, THE(1970, Swed./U.S.), prod d; PASSION OF ANNA, THE(1970, Swed.), prod d; TOUCH, THE(1971, U.S./Swed.), prod d; EMIGRANTS, THE(1972, Swed.), art d; NEW LAND, THE(1973, Swed.), art d

Siv Lundgren
SCENES FROM A MARRIAGE(1974, Swed.), ed; FACE TO FACE(1976, Swed.), ed

Borje Lundh
DEVIL'S EYE, THE(1960, Swed.); WINTER LIGHT, THE(1963, Swed.), makeup; SILENCE, THE(1964, Swed.), makeup; PERSONA(1967, Swed.), makeup; SHAME(1968, Swed.); TOUCH, THE(1971, U.S./Swed.), makeup

Lisa Lundholm
SMILES OF A SUMMER NIGHT(1957, Swed.)

Monika Lundi
24-HOUR LOVER(1970, Ger.)

Ted Lundigan
THEY WERE EXPENDABLE(1945); WHAT NEXT, CORPORAL HARGROVE?(1945)

William Lundigan
ARMORED CAR(1937); GIRL WITH IDEAS, A(1937); LADY FIGHTS BACK(1937); PRESCRIPTION FOR ROMANCE(1937); THAT'S MY STORY(1937); WESTBOUND LIMITED(1937); BLACK DOLL, THE(1938); DANGER ON THE AIR(1938); FRESHMAN YEAR(1938); MISSING GUEST, THE(1938); RECKLESS LIVING(1938); STATE POLICE(1938); WIVES UNDER SUSPICION(1938); DODGE CITY(1939); FORGOTTEN WOMAN, THE(1939); LEGION OF LOST FLYERS(1939); OLD MAID, THE(1939); THEY ASKED FOR IT(1939); THREE SMART GIRLS GROW UP(1939); EAST OF THE RIVER(1940); FIGHTING 69TH, THE(1940); MAN WHO TALKED TOO MUCH, THE(1940); SANTA FE TRAIL(1940); SEA HAWK, THE(1940); THREE CHEERS FOR THE IRISH(1940); BUGLE SOUNDS, THE(1941); CASE OF THE BLACK PARROT, THE(1941); GREAT MR. NOBODY, THE(1941); HIGHWAY WEST(1941); INTERNATIONAL SQUADRON(1941); SAILORS ON LEAVE(1941); SHOT IN THE DARK, THE(1941); ANDY HARDY'S DOUBLE LIFE(1942); APACHE TRAIL(1942); COURTSHIP OF ANDY HARDY, THE(1942); NORTHWEST RANGERS(1942); SUNDAY PUNCH(1942); DR. GILLESPIE'S CRIMINAL CASE(1943); HEADIN' FOR GOD'S COUNTRY(1943); SALUTE TO THE MARINES(1943); DISHONORED LADY(1947); FABULOUS DORSEYS, THE(1947); INSIDE STORY, THE(1948); MYSTERY IN MEXICO(1948); FOLLOW ME QUIETLY(1949); PINKY(1949); STATE DEPARTMENT-FILE 649(1949); I'LL GET BY(1950); MOTHER DIDN'T TELL ME(1950); ELOPEMENT(1951); HOUSE ON TELEGRAPH HILL(1951); I'D CLIMB THE HIGHEST MOUNTAIN(1951); LOVE NEST(1951); DOWN AMONG THE SHELTERING PALMS(1953); INFERNO(1953); SERPENT OF THE NILE(1953); RIDERS TO THE STARS(1954); TERROR SHIP(1954, Brit.); WHITE ORCHID, THE(1954); UNDERWATER CITY, THE(1962); WAY WEST, THE(1967); WHERE ANGELS GO...TROUBLE FOLLOWS(1968)

Goran Lundin
EMIGRANTS, THE(1972, Swed.)

Richard Lundin
HAWMPS!(1976)

Vic Lundin
MA BARKER'S KILLER BROOD(1960); TWO FOR THE SEESAW(1962); ISLAND OF LOVE(1963); PROMISES, PROMISES(1963); ROBINSON CRUSOE ON MARS(1964); BEAU GESTE(1966)

Walter Lundin
WELCOME DANGER(1929), ph; FEET FIRST(1930), ph; MOVIE CRAZY(1932), ph; CAT'S PAW, THE(1934), ph; BONNIE SCOTLAND(1935), ph; GENERAL SPANKY(1937), ph; WAY OUT WEST(1937), ph; AIR RAID WARDENS(1943), ph; HARRIGAN'S KID(1943), ph
Silents
SAILOR-MADE MAN, A(1921), ph; DOCTOR JACK(1922), ph; GRANDMA'S BOY(1922), ph; SAFETY LAST(1923), ph; WHY WORRY(1923), ph; GIRL SHY(1924), ph; HOT WATER(1924), ph; FRESHMAN, THE(1925), ph; KID BROTHER, THE(1927), ph; SPEEDY(1928), ph

Bill Lundmark
MAN CRAZY(1953); PEYTON PLACE(1957)

William Lundmark
FROM HERE TO ETERNITY(1953)

Arthur Lundquist
TIME OF DESIRE, THE(1957, Swed.), d&w

Goran Lundquist
WILD STRAWBERRIES(1959, Swed.)

Torbjorn Lundquist
MATTER OF MORALS, A(1961, U.S./Swed.), md; JUST ONCE MORE(1963, Swed.), m; LOVE MATES(1967, Swed.), m

Ralph Lundsten
ELVIS! ELVIS!(1977, Swed.), m

Rune Lundstrom
MY FATHER'S MISTRESS(1970, Swed.)

Dick Lundy
SNOW WHITE AND THE SEVEN DWARFS(1937), anim

Ken Lundy
PUBLIC ENEMIES(1941); MAJOR AND THE MINOR, THE(1942); SIOUX CITY SUE(1946)

Kenneth Lundy
TUXEDO JUNCTION(1941); WHERE DID YOU GET THAT GIRL?(1941); MAYOR OF 44TH STREET, THE(1942); TROUBLE MAKERS(1948)

Richard Lundy
MAN CALLED FLINTSTONE, THE(1966), anim

Rocky Lundy
STORM RIDER, THE(1957)

Wayne Lundy
WILD GYPSIES(1969)

William Lundy
TEXAS CARNIVAL(1951)

Margarite Lune
WAR WAGON, THE(1967)

Ted Lune
LADY IS A SQUARE, THE(1959, Brit.); BERSERK(1967)

Gene Luneska
Silents
SENATOR, THE(1915)

Charles Lung
DESTINATION UNKNOWN(1942); BEHIND THE RISING SUN(1943); FALLEN SPARROW, THE(1943); FLIGHT FOR FREEDOM(1943); GHOST SHIP, THE(1943); LEOPARD MAN, THE(1943); DRAGON SEED(1944); SECRETS OF MONTE CARLO(1951); JIVARO(1954); MA AND PA KETTLE AT WAIKIKI(1955)

Charlie Lung
HONOLULU LU(1941); HEADIN' FOR GOD'S COUNTRY(1943); JACK LONDON(1943); SIREN OF BAGDAD(1953); THUNDER IN THE EAST(1953); BOWERY TO BAGDAD(1955)

Chiang Lung
DEADLY CHINA DOLL(1973, Hong Kong), ed

Clarence Lung
DRAGON SEED(1944); KEYS OF THE KINGDOM, THE(1944); PURPLE HEART, THE(1944); FIRST YANK INTO TOKYO(1945); SONG OF THE SARONG(1945); PRISONER OF WAR(1954); WORLD FOR RANSOM(1954); RAWHIDE YEARS, THE(1956); EXPERIMENT IN TERROR(1962)

Clarence E. Lung
OPERATION PETTICOAT(1959)

Jimmy Lung
SALOME, WHERE SHE DANCED(1945)

K. Lung
MURDER IN REVERSE(1946, Brit.)

Ti Lung
TRIPLE IRONS(1973, Hong Kong); CALL HIM MR. SHATTER(1976, Hong Kong)

Romilly Lunge
PERFECT FLAW, THE(1934, Brit.); ROAD HOUSE(1934, Brit.); KOENIGSMARK(1935, Fr.); WHILE PARENTS SLEEP(1935, Brit.); ANNIE LAURIE(1936, Brit.); FOR VALOR(1937, Brit.); MAN OF AFFAIRS(1937, Brit.); TWO WHO DARED(1937, Brit.); ROYAL DIVORCE, A(1938, Brit.); MYSTERIOUS MR. REEDER, THE(1940, Brit.); SIDEWALKS OF LONDON(1940, Brit.); TORSO MURDER MYSTERY, THE(1940, Brit.); CHAMBER OF HORRORS(1941, Brit.)

Cherie Lunghi
EXCALIBUR(1981); PRAYING MANTIS(1982, Brit.); SIGN OF FOUR, THE(1983, Brit.)

Ludovico Lunghi
CALL OF THE BLOOD(1948, Brit.), m

Elsa Lunghini
INQUISITOR, THE(1982, Fr.)

Isabelle Lunghini
LOLA(1961, Fr./Ital.); DE L'AMOUR(1968, Fr./Ital.)

S. Lungin
WELCOME KOSTYA!(1965, USSR), w

Olga Lunick
GOLDEN BLADE, THE(1953); SON OF SINBAD(1955), ch

Stanley Lunin
HEART OF THE MATTER, THE(1954, Brit.)

Kitty Lunn
EYES OF A STRANGER(1980)

Nina Lunn
SENATOR WAS INDISCREET, THE(1947); UP IN CENTRAL PARK(1948)

Brendon Lunney
KILLING OF ANGEL STREET, THE(1983, Aus.)

David Lunney
HOW TO BEAT THE HIGH COST OF LIVING(1980)

Beverly Lunsford
THAT NIGHT(1957); INTRUDER, THE(1962); CRAWLING HAND, THE(1963)
Misc. Talkies
JENNIE, WIFE/CHILD(1968)

Larry Lunsford
1984
KILLPOINT(1984)

Alfred Lunt
GUARDSMAN, THE(1931); STAGE DOOR CANTEEN(1943)
Silents
RAGGED EDGE, THE(1923); SECOND YOUTH(1924); SALLY OF THE SAWDUST(1925)
Misc. Silents
BACKBONE(1923); LOVERS IN QUARANTINE(1925)

Francis Lunt
WAY WE LIVE, THE(1946, Brit.)

Edouard Luntz
NAKED HEARTS(1970, Fr.), d&w

Walo Luond
INVISIBLE DR. MABUSE, THE(1965, Ger.)

Ham Chao Luong
GAME IS OVER, THE(1967, Fr.)

Nam Luong
YANK IN VIET-NAM, A(1964)

Luong-Ham-Chau
SAMSON AND THE SEVEN MIRACLES OF THE WORLD(1963, Fr./Ital.)

Gene Luotto
GUNMEN OF THE RIO GRANDE(1965, Fr./Ital./Span.), w

Y. Lupandin
NIGHT BEFORE CHRISTMAS, A(1963, USSR), spec eff

Mario Lupi
BEBO'S GIRL(1964, Ital.)

Renato Lupi
QUIET PLACE IN THE COUNTRY, A(1970, Ital./Fr.)

Roldano Lupi
WHITE DEVIL, THE(1948, Ital.); DEVOTION(1953, Ital.); DUEL WITHOUT HONOR(1953, Ital.); TIMES GONE BY(1953, Ital.); CROSSED SWORDS(1954); QUEEN OF BABYLON, THE(1956, Ital.); BUFFALO BILL, HERO OF THE FAR WEST(1962, Ital.); GIANT OF METROPOLIS, THE(1963, Ital.); MONGOLS, THE(1966, Fr./Ital.); SEVEN REVENGES, THE(1967, Ital.)

Lupe Lupien
LADY LUCK(1936)

Lauri Lupina-Lane
KING IN NEW YORK, A(1957, Brit.)

Andrew Lupino
WHILE THE CITY SLEEPS(1956)

Antoinette Lupino
HIS BROTHER'S KEEPER(1939, Brit.)

Barry Lupino
NEVER TROUBLE TROUBLE(1931, Brit.); MASTER AND MAN(1934, Brit.); BED AND BREAKFAST(1936, Brit.); SKY'S THE LIMIT, THE(1937, Brit.); GARRISON FOLLIES(1940, Brit.); I'LL BE YOUR SWEETHEART(1945, Brit.); WHAT DO WE DO NOW?(1945, Brit.)

Constance Lupino
WOMAN REBELS, A(1936)

Dicky Lupino
JUST WILLIAM(1939, Brit.)

Henry Richard Lupino
STRATEGIC AIR COMMAND(1955)

Ida Lupino
HER FIRST AFFAIRE(1932, Brit.); GHOST CAMERA, THE(1933, Brit.); HIGH FINANCE(1933, Brit.); I LIVED WITH YOU(1933, Brit.); MONEY FOR SPEED(1933, Brit.); PRINCE OF ARCADIA(1933, Brit.); COME ON, MARINES(1934); READY FOR LOVE(1934); SEARCH FOR BEAUTY(1934); PARIS IN SPRING(1935); PETER IBBETSON(1935); SMART GIRL(1935); ANYTHING GOES(1936); DAREDEVILS OF EARTH(1936, Brit.); GAY DESPERADO, THE(1936); ONE RAINY AFTERNOON(1936); YOURS FOR THE ASKING(1936); ARTISTS AND MODELS(1937); FIGHT FOR YOUR LADY(1937); LET'S GET MARRIED(1937); SEA DEVILS(1937); ADVENTURES OF SHERLOCK HOLMES, THE(1939); LADY AND THE MOB, THE(1939); LIGHT THAT FAILED, THE(1939); LONE WOLF SPY HUNT, THE(1939); THEY DRIVE BY NIGHT(1940); HIGH SIERRA(1941); LADIES IN RETIREMENT(1941); OUT OF THE FOG(1941); SEA WOLF, THE(1941); HARD WAY, THE(1942); LIFE BEGINS AT 8:30(1942); MOONTIDE(1942); FOREVER AND A DAY(1943); THANK YOUR LUCKY STARS(1943); HOLLYWOOD CANTEEN(1944); IN OUR TIME(1944); PILLOW TO POST(1945); DEVOTION(1946); MAN I LOVE, THE(1946); DEEP VALLEY(1947); ESCAPE ME NEVER(1947); ROAD HOUSE(1948); LUST FOR GOLD(1949); NOT WANTED(1949), p, w; WOMAN IN HIDING(1949); NEVER FEAR(1950), p&d, w; OUTRAGE(1950), d, w; HARD, FAST, AND BEAUTIFUL(1951), d; ON DANGEROUS GROUND(1951); BEWARE, MY LOVELY(1952); BIGAMIST,THE(1953), a, d; HITCHHIKER, THE(1953), d, w; JENNIFER(1953); PRIVATE HELL 36(1954), a, w; BIG KNIFE, THE(1955); WOMEN'S PRISON(1955); STRANGE INTRUDER(1956); WHILE THE CITY SLEEPS(1956); TROUBLE WITH ANGELS(1966), d; BACKTRACK(1969); JUNIOR BONNER(1972); DEVIL'S RAIN, THE(1975, U.S./Mex.); FOOD OF THE GODS, THE(1976); MY BOYS ARE GOOD BOYS(1978); DEADHEAD MILES(1982)

Richard Lupino
THAT FORSYTE WOMAN(1949); KIM(1950); RHAPSODY(1954); MARAUDERS, THE(1955); NEVER SO FEW(1959); MIDNIGHT LACE(1960); FATHER GOOSE(1964)

Rita Lupino
MASQUERADE IN MEXICO(1945); DEVOTION(1946); NOT WANTED(1949); RED, HOT AND BLUE(1949); NEVER FEAR(1950); OUTRAGE(1950); WILD SCENE, THE(1970)

Stanley Lupino
LOVE LIES(1931, Brit.), a, p, w; LOVE RACE, THE(1931, Brit.), a, p, w; FACING THE MUSIC(1933, Brit.), a, w; KING OF THE RITZ(1933, Brit.); SLEEPLESS NIGHTS(1933, Brit.), a, w; HAPPY(1934, Brit.), a, w; YOU MADE ME LOVE YOU(1934, Brit.), a, w; HONEYMOON FOR THREE(1935, Brit.), a, p, w; CHEER UP!(1936, Brit.), a, p, w; SPORTING LOVE(1936, Brit.), a, w; OVER SHE GOES(1937, Brit.), a, w; HOLD MY HAND(1938, Brit.), a, w; LUCKY TO ME(1939, Brit.), a, w

Toni Lupino
SOMEWHERE IN CAMP(1942, Brit.); SOMEWHERE ON LEAVE(1942, Brit.)

Wallace Lupino
CHILDREN OF CHANCE(1930, Brit.); YELLOW MASK, THE(1930, Brit.); LOVE LIES(1931, Brit.); LOVE RACE, THE(1931, Brit.); NEVER TROUBLE TROUBLE(1931, Brit.); NO LADY(1931, Brit.); JOSSER ON THE RIVER(1932, Brit.); MAID OF THE MOUNTAINS, THE(1932, Brit.); OLD SPANISH CUSTOMERS(1932, Brit.); WHY SAPS LEAVE HOME(1932, Brit.); MELODY MAKER, THE(1933, Brit.); MASTER AND MAN(1934, Brit.), a, w; DEPUTY DRUMMER, THE(1935, Brit.); TRUST THE NAVY(1935, Brit.); HOT NEWS(1936, Brit.); LOVE UP THE POLE(1936, Brit.); SHIPMATES O' MINE(1936, Brit.); STUDENT'S ROMANCE, THE(1936, Brit.); MAN WHO COULD WORK MIRACLES, THE(1937, Brit.); LAMBETH WALK, THE(1940, Brit.); TWENTY-ONE DAYS TOGETHER(1940, Brit.); WATERLOO ROAD(1949, Brit.)

Ed Lupinski
LINCOLN CONSPIRACY, THE(1977); HOT STUFF(1979)

Alberto Lupo
GIANT OF MARATHON, THE(1960, Ital.); HEROD THE GREAT(1960, Ital.); ATOM AGE VAMPIRE(1961, Ital.); MINOTAUR, THE(1961, Ital.); SWORDSMAN OF SIENA, THE(1962, Fr./Ital.); BACCHANTES, THE(1963, Fr./Ital.); TORPEDO BAY(1964, Ital./Fr.); AGONY AND THE ECSTASY, THE(1965)

Carlo Lupo
Misc. Talkies
LAST FEELINGS(1981)

Chuck Lupo
ABSENCE OF MALICE(1981)

Frank Lupo
CONQUEST OF THE EARTH(1980), p
George Lupo
QUADROON(1972)
Michele Lupo
GOLIATH AND THE SINS OF BABYLON(1964, Ital.), d; ARIZONA COLT(1965, It./Fr./Span.), d; REVENGE OF THE GLADIATORS(1965, Ital.), d; SEVEN SLAVES AGAINST THE WORLD(1965, Ital.), d, w; WEEKEND MURDERS, THE(1972, Ital.), d; MASTER TOUCH, THE(1974, Ital./Ger.), d, w; MEAN FRANK AND CRAZY TONY(1976, Ital.), d
Misc. Talkies
SEVEN TIMES SEVEN(1973, Ital.), d
Patti LuPone
KING OF THE GYPSIES(1978); 1941(1979); DEATH VENGEANCE(1982)
Robert LuPone
JESUS CHRIST, SUPERSTAR(1973)
Rupert Lupone
SONG OF NORWAY(1970)
Sandro Luporini
LOVE NOW...PAY LATER(1966, Ital.)
Marcel Lupovici
CRIME OF MONSIEUR LANGE, THE(1936, Fr.); RIFIFI(1956, Fr.)
John Lupton
SHADOW IN THE SKY(1951); ROGUE'S MARCH(1952); ALL THE BROTHERS WERE VALIANT(1953); BAND WAGON, THE(1953); DRAGONFLY SQUADRON(1953); ESCAPE FROM FORT BRAVO(1953); JULIUS CAESAR(1953); SCANDAL AT SCOURIE(1953); STORY OF THREE LOVES, THE(1953); PRISONER OF WAR(1954); BATTLE FLAME(1955); DIANE(1955); GLORY(1955); MAN WITH THE GUN(1955); GREAT LOCOMOTIVE CHASE, THE(1956); DRANGO(1957); TAMING SUTTON'S GAL(1957); GUN FEVER(1958); BLOOD AND STEEL(1959); MAN IN THE NET, THE(1959); REBEL SET, THE(1959); THREE CAME TO KILL(1960); CLOWN AND THE KID, THE(1961); DEVIL'S BEDROOM, THE(1964); GREATEST STORY EVER TOLD, THE(1965); JESSE JAMES MEETS FRANKENSTEIN'S DAUGHTER(1966); COOL BREEZE(1972); NAPOLEON AND SAMANTHA(1972); PRIVATE PARTS(1972); WORLD'S GREATEST ATHLETE, THE(1973)
Peter Lupus
Misc. Talkies
MODERN DAY HOUDINI(1983)
Peter Lupus, Jr.
MUSCLE BEACH PARTY(1964)
Ignacia Farias Luque
THIRTEEN FRIGHTENED GIRLS(1963)
Jesus Luque
ALEXANDER THE GREAT(1956)
Sammy Luquis
1984
DELIVERY BOYS(1984)
Tony Luraschi
OUTSIDER, THE(1980), d&w
Doris Luray
GRUMPY(1930)
Walter Lure
OFFENDERS, THE(1980)
Peter Luria
JESUS CHRIST, SUPERSTAR(1973)
Tom Lurich
FLYING DOCTOR, THE(1936, Aus.); SEASON OF PASSION(1961, Aus./Brit.)
Allan Lurie
PLUNDERERS OF PAINTED FLATS(1959); THEN THERE WERE THREE(1961), w
Evan Lurie
OFFENDERS, THE(1980)
John Lurie
OFFENDERS, THE(1980), a, m; UNDERGROUND U.S.A.(1980); SUBWAY RIDERS(1981); PERMANENT VACATION(1982), a, m
1984
PARIS, TEXAS(1984, Ger./Fr.); STRANGER THAN PARADISE(1984, U.S./Ger.), a, m; VARIETY(1984), m
Larry Lurin
BLACK CAESAR(1973), art d; HELL UP IN HARLEM(1973), prod d
Werner Luring
WAR AND PEACE(1983, Ger.), ph
Don Lurio
BOBO, THE(1967, Brit.); CANDY(1968, Ital./Fr.), ch
Lurville
OPEN ROAD, THE(1940, Fr.); RUY BLAS(1948, Fr.)
Bob Lusby
SKYDIVERS, THE(1963), ed
Lucia Lusca
WINGS OVER HONOLULU(1937)
Volodya Luschik
ADVENTURE IN ODESSA(1954, USSR)
Doel Luscombe
DATELINE DIAMONDS(1966, Brit.); REMEMBRANCE(1982, Brit.)
1984
ORDEAL BY INNOCENCE(1984, Brit.)
George Luscombe
PASSING STRANGER, THE(1954, Brit.)
Tito Lusiardo
TANGO BAR(1935)
Andro Lusicic
SEVENTH CONTINENT, THE(1968, Czech./Yugo.), w
Dane Lusier
MAGNIFICENT ROGUE, THE(1946), w
Don Lusk
FANTASIA(1940), anim, anim; PINOCCHIO(1940), anim; SONG OF THE SOUTH(1946), anim; MELODY TIME(1948), animators; SO DEAR TO MY HEART(1949), anim; CINDERELLA(1950), anim; ALICE IN WONDERLAND(1951), anim; PETER PAN(1953), anim; LADY AND THE TRAMP(1955), anim; SLEEPING BEAUTY(1959), anim; ONE HUNDRED AND ONE DALMATIANS(1961), anim; GAY PURR-EE(1962), anim; HEY THERE, IT'S YOGI BEAR(1964), anim; MAN CALLED

FLINTSTONE, THE(1966), anim; RACE FOR YOUR LIFE, CHARLIE BROWN(1977), anim
Freeman Lusk
MAGNIFICENT YANKEE, THE(1950); DAY THE EARTH STOOD STILL, THE(1951); DESERT FOX, THE(1951); HALF ANGEL(1951); LITTLE EGYPT(1951); WHEN WORLDS COLLIDE(1951); PHONE CALL FROM A STRANGER(1952); PRIDE OF ST. LOUIS, THE(1952); WILD BLUE YONDER, THE(1952); CADDY, THE(1953); FROM HERE TO ETERNITY(1953); WAR OF THE WORLDS, THE(1953); GIRL RUSH, THE(1955); TO THE SHORES OF HELL(1966)
Skip Lusk
TOOLBOX MURDERS, THE(1978), ed; REUBEN, REUBEN(1983), ed
Hamilton Luske
SNOW WHITE AND THE SEVEN DWARFS(1937), anim; FANTASIA(1940), d; PINOCCHIO(1940), d; RELUCTANT DRAGON, THE(1941), cartoon d; MAKE MINE MUSIC(1946), d; FUN AND FANCY FREE(1947), d; MELODY TIME(1948), d; SO DEAR TO MY HEART(1949), anim d; CINDERELLA(1950), d; ALICE IN WONDERLAND(1951), d; PETER PAN(1953), d; LADY AND THE TRAMP(1955), d
Hamilton S. Luske
ONE HUNDRED AND ONE DALMATIANS(1961), d; MARY POPPINS(1964), anim d
Jimmy Luske
RELUCTANT DRAGON, THE(1941)
Tommy Luske
PETER PAN(1953)
Capt. L. Lussier
APPRENTICESHIP OF DUDDY KRAVITZ, THE(1974, Can.)
Dane Lussier
LADIES' DAY(1943), w; MEXICAN SPITFIRE'S BLESSED EVENT(1943), w; MYSTERY BROADCAST(1943), w; FALCON OUT WEST, THE(1944), w; LADY AND THE MONSTER, THE(1944), w; PORT OF 40 THIEVES, THE(1944), w; STORM OVER LISBON(1944), w; SPORTING CHANCE, A(1945), w; THREE'S A CROWD(1945), w; DICK TRACY VS. CUEBALL(1946), w; FALCON'S ALIBI, THE(1946), w; SMOOTH AS SILK(1946), w; PILGRIM LADY, THE(1947), w; FAMILY HONEYMOON(1948), w; MY DREAM IS YOURS(1949), w; LET'S DANCE(1950), w; FIRST TIME, THE(1952), w; IT HAPPENS EVERY THURSDAY(1953), w; LADY WANTS MINK, THE(1953), w
Doris Lussier
BIG RED(1962)
John Paul Lussier
1984
BAD MANNERS(1984)
Robert Lussier
SILENT MOVIE(1976); FUN WITH DICK AND JANE(1977); MR. MOM(1983)
Carmen Luster
LOVE NOW...PAY LATER(1966, Ital.)
Mary Luster
TOY WIFE, THE(1938)
Robert Luster
COOL HAND LUKE(1967); WILL PENNY(1968); CHARRO(1969)
Edgar Lustgarten
LONG DARK HALL, THE(1951, Brit.), w; MAD LITTLE ISLAND(1958, Brit.); MAN WHO WOULDN'T TALK, THE(1958, Brit.), w; GAME FOR THREE LOSERS(1965, Brit.), w
Steve Lustgarten
1984
AMERICAN TABOO(1984), p, d, w, ph, ed
Arnost Lustig
TRANSPORT FROM PARADISE(1967, Czech.), w; DIAMONDS OF THE NIGHT(1968, Czech.), w
Branko Lustig
KAYA, I'LL KILL YOU(1969, Yugo./Fr.), p
Florence Lustig
PROJECT X(1949), cos; DR. COPPELIUS(1968, U.S./Span.), prod d
H.G. Lustig
DICTATOR, THE(1935, Brit./Ger.), w; HEART OF PARIS(1939, Fr.), w; LADY IN QUESTION, THE(1940), w
Jan Lustig
REUNION IN FRANCE(1942), w; WHITE CLIFFS OF DOVER, THE(1944), w; HOMECOMING(1948), w; THAT FORSYTE WOMAN(1949), w; KNIGHTS OF THE ROUND TABLE(1953), w; STORY OF THREE LOVES, THE(1953), w; TORCH SONG(1953), w; YOUNG BESS(1953), w; MOONFLEET(1955), w; TOWN WITHOUT PITY(1961, Ger./Switz./U.S.), w; SITUATION HOPELESS–BUT NOT SERIOUS(1965), w
Jean Lustig
DANCING ON A DIME(1940), w
Konrad Lustig
SNOW WHITE(1965, Ger.), w; SNOW WHITE AND ROSE RED(1966, Ger.), w
William Lustig
MANIAC(1980), p, d; VIGILANTE(1983), p, d
Marlena Lustik
SCREAM BLOODY MURDER(1972)
Lou Lusty
AFFAIRS OF ANNABEL(1938), p; ANNABEL TAKES A TOUR(1938), p; FUGITIVES FOR A NIGHT(1938), p; WILDCAT BUS(1940), w
Lutchiline
ROMEO AND JULIET(1955, USSR)
Don K. Lutenbacher
PRETTY BABY(1978)
Don Lutenbacher
1984
TIGHTROPE(1984)
Ingrid Luterkort
CHILDREN, THE(1949, Swed.)
Robert Luthardt
SIX BLACK HORSES(1962), art d; KISS ME, STUPID(1964), art d; CHASE, THE(1966), art d; FORTUNE COOKIE, THE(1966), art d; FUNNY GIRL(1968), art d; APRIL FOOLS, THE(1969), art d; CARNAL KNOWLEDGE(1971), art d; HEARTS OF THE WEST(1975), art d; LIPSTICK(1976), prod d; FIRST LOVE(1977), prod d; 9/30/55(1977), art d; CHEAP DETECTIVE, THE(1978), prod d

Luther
COUP DE GRACE(1978, Ger./Fr.), ph
Ann Luther
EASY TO LOVE(1953)
Misc. Silents
SOUL AND BODY(1921); WOMAN WHO BELIEVED, THE(1922); GOVERNOR'S LADY, THE(1923); TRUTH ABOUT WIVES, THE(1923); FATAL PLUNGE, THE(1924)
Anna Luther
CASANOVA BROWN(1944)
Silents
JUNGLE TRAIL, THE(1919)
Misc. Silents
BEAST, THE(1916); ISLAND OF DESIRE, THE(1917); MELTING MILLIONS(1917); HER MOMENT(1918)
Anne Luther
Silents
NEGLECTED WIVES(1920)
Misc. Silents
MORAL SUICIDE(1918)
Barbara Luther
TICKLISH AFFAIR, A(1963), w
David Luther
PARSIFAL(1983, Fr.)
Frank Luther
HIGH HAT(1937), a, m
Igor Luther
MAN WHO LIES, THE(1970, Czech./Fr.), ph; SLAVERS(1977, Ger.), ph; TIN DRUM, THE(1979, Ger./Fr./Yugo./Pol.), ph; CIRCLE OF DECEIT(1982, Fr./Ger.), ph; DANTON(1983), ph; PARSIFAL(1983, Fr.), ph; WAR AND PEACE(1983, Ger.), ph
1984
LOVE IN GERMANY, A(1984, Fr./Ger.), ph
Ingeborg Luther
DECISION BEFORE DAWN(1951)
John Luther
STORMY(1935)
Lester Luther
MASQUERADE IN MEXICO(1945); ADAM'S RIB(1949); RED MENACE, THE(1949)
Michael Luther
MALIBU BEACH(1978)
Phillip Luther
INSIDE AMY(1975)
Subhash Luthra
PRIVATE ENTERPRISE, A(1975, Brit.)
Bernard Lutic
AVIATOR'S WIFE, THE(1981, Fr.), ph; MEN PREFER FAT GIRLS(1981, Fr.), ph; LE BEAU MARIAGE(1982, Fr.), ph; ENTRE NOUS(1983, Fr.), ph
1984
HEAT OF DESIRE(1984, Fr.), ph
Gustaw Lutkiewicz
EVE WANTS TO SLEEP(1961, Pol.); PORTRAIT OF LENIN(1967, Pol./USSR)
Guy Lutman
FIDDLER ON THE ROOF(1971)
Lew Luton
MOON ZERO TWO(1970, Brit.); CRY OF THE PENGUINS(1972, Brit.)
Luton Girls Choir
OLD MOTHER RILEY, HEADMISTRESS(1950, Brit.)
Mara Lutra
FANTASM(1976, Aus.)
Helen Lutrell
Misc. Silents
GRETNA GREEN(1915); WHEN WE WERE TWENTY-ONE(1915)
V. Lutsekovich
WAR AND PEACE(1968, USSR)
Tina Luttanzi
BURIED ALIVE(1951, Ital.)
Lelio Luttazzi
IT HAPPENED IN ROME(1959, Ital.), m; L'AVVENTURA(1960, Ital.); TRAPPED IN TANGIERS(1960, Ital./Span.), m; PASSIONATE THIEF, THE(1963, Ital.), m; VISIT, THE(1964, Ger./Fr./Ital./U.S.); WEEKEND, ITALIAN STYLE(1967, Fr./Ital./Span.), a, m; KISS THE OTHER SHEIK(1968, Fr./Ital.); SNOW JOB(1972)
Geraldine Lutten
NO GREATER LOVE(1944, USSR), ed
Max Luttenberg
ELEPHANT STAMPEDE(1951), spec eff; RAYMIE(1960), spec eff
Alfred Lutter
ALICE DOESN'T LIVE HERE ANYMORE(1975); BAD NEWS BEARS IN BREAKING TRAINING, THE(1977)
Alfred Lutter III
LOVE AND DEATH(1975)
Alfred W. Lutter
BAD NEWS BEARS, THE(1976)
Ellen Lutter
FRIDAY THE 13TH PART II(1981), cos
Charles Luttrell
RED RUNS THE RIVER(1963)
Martha Luttrell
MAN CALLED DAGGER, A(1967)
Phillip Luttrell
RED RUNS THE RIVER(1963)
Robert Luttrell
CITY NEWS(1983), spec eff
Al Luttringer
SONG TO REMEMBER, A(1945)
Edward N. Luttwak
POWER PLAY(1978, Brit./Can.), d&w
Paul Luty
WATER BABIES, THE(1979, Brit.); DRESSER, THE(1983)

Elisabeth Lutyens
NEVER TAKE CANDY FROM A STRANGER(1961, Brit.), m; PARANOIAC(1963, Brit.), m; EARTH DIES SCREAMING, THE(1964, Brit.), m; WHY BOTHER TO KNOCK(1964, Brit.), m; DR. TERROR'S HOUSE OF HORRORS(1965, Brit.), m; SKULL, THE(1965, Brit.), m; SPACEFLIGHT IC-1(1965, Brit.), m; PSYCHOPATH, THE(1966, Brit.), m; MALPAS MYSTERY, THE(1967, Brit.), m; TERRORNAUTS, THE(1967, Brit.), m
Gillian Lutyens
COMPANIONS IN CRIME(1954, Brit.); VALUE FOR MONEY(1957, Brit.)
Catherine Lutz
LOLA(1961, Fr./Ital.); SHOOT THE PIANO PLAYER(1962, Fr.); STOLEN KISSES(1969, Fr.)
Dan Lutz
ONE FROM THE HEART(1982)
Ingrid Lutz
MOONWOLF(1966, Fin./Ger.)
Pieter Lutz
LIFT, THE(1983, Neth.)
Regine Lutz
LOST HONOR OF KATHARINA BLUM, THE(1975, Ger.)
Thuy An Luu
DIVA(1982, Fr.)
Luukiuluana
MA AND PA KETTLE AT WAIKIKI(1955)
Martin Luvat
JENNY(1969), w
Lillian Lux
FLYING MATCHMAKER, THE(1970, Israel)
Bert Luxford
TWINS OF EVIL(1971, Brit.), spec eff; TWO HUNDRED MOTELS(1971, Brit.), spec eff; DEVIL WITHIN HER, THE(1976, Brit.), spec eff
Les Luxford
20TH CENTURY OZ(1977, Aus.), ed
Mark Luxford
Misc. Talkies
FRIEND OR FOE(1982, Brit.)
Nola Luxford
SUCCESSFUL CALAMITY, A(1932); IRON MASTER, THE(1933); RIP TIDE(1934); KIND LADY(1935); SYLVIA SCARLETT(1936)
Silents
MAD MARRIAGE, THE(1921); KING OF THE HERD(1927)
Misc. Silents
FLYING DUTCHMAN, THE(1923); ROUGED LIPS(1923); BORDER JUSTICE(1925); PRINCE OF PEP, THE(1925); THAT DEVIL QUEMADO(1925); LADIES BEWARE(1927); MEDDLIN' STRANGER, THE(1927)
Dora Luz
THREE CABALLEROS, THE(1944)
Ernst Luz
Silents
LOVE(1927), m
Franc Luz
VOICES(1979)
Alberto Luza
YOUR UNCLE DUDLEY(1935), cos
Larisa Luzhina
HOUSE ON THE FRONT LINE, THE(1963, USSR); SANDU FOLLOWS THE SUN(1965, USSR)
Maria Pia Luzi
LA NOTTE(1961, Fr./Ital.); PLANETS AGAINST US, THE(1961, Ital./Fr.); WHITE SLAVE SHIP(1962, Fr./Ital.); STOP TRAIN 349(1964, Fr./Ital./Ger.)
Avi Luzia
WORLDS APART(1980, U.S., Israel)
Alejandro Perez Luzin
IN GAY MADRID(1930), w
Sara Luzita
WHY BOTHER TO KNOCK(1964, Brit.)
Sari Luzita
MOULIN ROUGE(1952)
Beth Luzuka
UP THE SANDBOX(1972)
Guido Luzzato
CARTHAGE IN FLAMES(1961, Fr./Ital.), p
Enrico Luzzi
YOR, THE HUNTER FROM THE FUTURE(1983, Ital.), cos
Ludmilla Lvova
YOUNG, THE EVIL AND THE SAVAGE, THE(1968, Ital.)
Archibald Lyall
WAR AND PEACE(1956, Ital./U.S.)
Archie Lyall
JOHN PAUL JONES(1959)
Edna Lyall
SHE MARRIED HER BOSS(1935)
Gavin Lyall
MOON ZERO TWO(1970, Brit.), w
C. B. Lyars
SOLOMON KING(1974)
Alyosha Lyarsky
CHILDHOOD OF MAXIM GORKY(1938, Russ.)
Eustace Lyatt
GUS(1976), spec eff
B. Lyaush
RESURRECTION(1963, USSR)
Joan Lybrook
EVERY GIRL SHOULD BE MARRIED(1948)
George W. Lycan
RED SUN(1972, Fr./Ital./Span.)
Georges Lycan
GOLD FOR THE CAESARS(1964); GIRL CAN'T STOP, THE(1966, Fr./Gr.); TRAMPLERS, THE(1966, Ital.); SELLERS OF GIRLS(1967, Fr.); TRIPLE CROSS(1967, Fr./Brit.); DESTRUCTORS, THE(1974, Brit.)

1984
PERILS OF GWENDOLINE, THE(1984, Fr.)
Eustace Lycett
DARBY O'GILL AND THE LITTLE PEOPLE(1959), spec eff; ABSENT-MINDED PROFESSOR, THE(1961), spec eff; MOON PILOT(1962), spec eff; SAVAGE SAM(1963), spec eff; SON OF FLUBBER(1963), spec eff; MARY POPPINS(1964), spec eff; THOSE CALLOWAYS(1964), spec eff; MONKEY'S UNCLE, THE(1965), spec eff; THAT DARN CAT(1965), spec eff; FOLLOW ME, BOYS!(1966), spec eff; LT. ROBIN CRUSOE, U.S.N.(1966), spec eff; UGLY DACHSHUND, THE(1966), spec eff; GNOME-MOBILE, THE(1967), spec eff; HAPPIEST MILLIONAIRE, THE(1967), spec eff; BLACKBEARD'S GHOST(1968), spec eff; LOVE BUG, THE(1968), spec eff; NEVER A DULL MOMENT(1968), spec eff; RASCAL(1969), spec eff; BEDKNOBS AND BROOMSTICKS(1971), spec eff; $1,000,000 DUCK(1971), spec eff; NOW YOU SEE HIM, NOW YOU DON'T(1972), spec eff; SNOWBALL EXPRESS(1972), spec eff; WORLD'S GREATEST ATHLETE, THE(1973), spec eff; HERBIE RIDES AGAIN(1974), spec eff; FREAKY FRIDAY(1976), spec eff; HERBIE GOES TO MONTE CARLO(1977), spec eff; PETE'S DRAGON(1977), spec eff; CAT FROM OUTER SPACE, THE(1978), spec eff; HOT LEAD AND COLD FEET(1978), spec eff; RETURN FROM WITCH MOUNTAIN(1978), spec eff; NORTH AVENUE IRREGULARS, THE(1979), spec eff; LAST FLIGHT OF NOAH'S ARK, THE(1980), spec eff
Benita Lydal
HIGH TERRACE(1957, Brit.)
Howard Lydecker
ONE FRIGHTENED NIGHT(1935), spec eff; HOUSE OF A THOUSAND CANDLES, THE(1936), spec eff; MAN OF CONQUEST(1939), spec eff; WOMEN IN WAR(1940), spec eff; FLYING TIGERS(1942), spec eff; REMEMBER PEARL HARBOR(1942), spec eff; CHATTERBOX(1943), spec eff; FIGHTING SEABEES, THE(1944), d; LAKE PLACID SERENADE(1944), spec eff; DAKOTA(1945), spec eff; FLAME OF THE BARBARY COAST(1945), spec eff; GIRLS OF THE BIG HOUSE(1945), spec eff; GRISSLY'S MILLIONS(1945), spec eff; MAN FROM OKLAHOMA, THE(1945), spec eff; MEXICANA(1945), spec eff; ROAD TO ALCATRAZ(1945), spec eff; SCOTLAND YARD INVESTIGATOR(1945, Brit.), spec eff; TELL IT TO A STAR(1945), spec eff; TIGER WOMAN, THE(1945), spec eff; TRAIL OF KIT CARSON(1945), spec eff; EARL CARROLL SKETCHBOOK(1946), spec eff; GAY BLADES(1946), spec eff; HELLDORADO(1946), spec eff; HOME ON THE HANGE(1946), spec eff; I'VE ALWAYS LOVED YOU(1946), spec eff; LAST CROOKED MILE, THE(1946), ph; MADONNA'S SECRET, THE(1946), spec eff; MAGNIFICENT ROGUE, THE(1946), spec eff; MURDER IN THE MUSIC HALL(1946), spec eff; MY PAL TRIGGER(1946), spec eff; NIGHT TRAIN TO MEMPHIS(1946), spec eff; ONE EXCITING WEEK(1946), spec eff; PASSKEY TO DANGER(1946), spec eff; PLAINSMAN AND THE LADY(1946), spec eff; RENDEZVOUS WITH ANNIE(1946), spec eff; RIO GRANDE RAIDERS(1946), spec eff; SANTA FE UPRISING(1946), spec eff; SIOUX CITY SUE(1946), spec eff; THAT BRENNAN GIRL(1946), spec eff; UNDERCOVER WOMAN, THE(1946), spec eff; VALLEY OF THE ZOMBIES(1946), spec eff; DRIFTWOOD(1947), spec eff; HOMESTEADERS OF PARADISE VALLEY(1947), spec eff; NORTHWEST OUTPOST(1947), spec eff; ON THE OLD SPANISH TRAIL(1947), spec eff; OREGON TRAIL SCOUTS(1947), spec eff; OTHER LOVE, THE(1947), spec eff; SPOILERS OF THE NORTH(1947), spec eff; THAT'S MY MAN(1947), spec eff; UNDER COLORADO SKIES(1947), spec eff; WEB OF DANGER, THE(1947), spec eff; WYOMING(1947), spec eff; ANGEL ON THE AMAZON(1948), spec eff; LIGHTNIN' IN THE FOREST(1948), spec eff; MACBETH(1948), spec eff; MOONRISE(1948), spec eff; NIGHT TIME IN NEVADA(1948), spec eff; OKLAHOMA BADLANDS(1948), spec eff; OLD LOS ANGELES(1948), spec eff; OUT OF THE STORM(1948), spec eff; SONS OF ADVENTURE(1948), spec eff; TIMBER TRAIL, THE(1948), spec eff; UNDER CALIFORNIA STARS(1948), spec eff; FIGHTING KENTUCKIAN, THE(1949), spec eff; RED MENACE, THE(1949), spec eff; RED PONY, THE(1949), spec eff; SAN ANTONE AMBUSH(1949), spec eff; SHERIFF OF WICHITA(1949), spec eff; SOUTH OF RIO(1949), spec eff; STREETS OF SAN FRANCISCO(1949), spec eff; TOO LATE FOR TEARS(1949), spec eff; WAKE OF THE RED WITCH(1949), spec eff; HOUSE BY THE RIVER(1950), spec eff; RIO GRANDE(1950), spec eff; SUNSET IN THE WEST(1950), spec eff; SURRENDER(1950), spec eff; TRAIL OF ROBIN HOOD(1950), spec eff; HONEYCHILE(1951), spec eff; SPOILERS OF THE PLAINS(1951), spec eff; MONTANA BELLE(1952), spec eff; OKLAHOMA ANNIE(1952), spec eff; WAC FROM WALLA WALLA, THE(1952), spec eff; WILD BLUE YONDER, THE(1952), spec eff; CITY THAT NEVER SLEEPS(1953), spec eff; FAIR WIND TO JAVA(1953), spec eff; INVADERS FROM MARS(1953), spec eff; SEA OF LOST SHIPS(1953), spec eff; JOHNNY GUITAR(1954), spec eff; UNTAMED HEIRESS(1954), spec eff; CAROLINA CANNONBALL(1955), spec eff; LAY THAT RIFLE DOWN(1955), spec eff; MAVERICK QUEEN, THE(1956), spec eff; SATAN'S SATELLITES(1958), spec eff; GHOST OF ZORRO(1959), spec eff; SINK THE BISMARCK!(1960, Brit.), spec eff; DAMN THE DEFIANT!(1962, Brit.), spec eff; UNDERWATER CITY, THE(1962), spec eff; FLIGHT OF THE PHOENIX, THE(1965), sp eff; WAY...WAY OUT(1966), spec eff; DOCTOR DOLITTLE(1967), spec eff
Howard Lydecker, Jr.
IN OLD OKLAHOMA(1943), spec eff
Theodore Lydecker
FIGHTING SEABEES, THE(1944), spec eff; LADY AND THE MONSTER, THE(1944), spec eff; LAKE PLACID SERENADE(1944), spec eff; STORM OVER LISBON(1944), spec eff; DAKOTA(1945), spec eff; FLAME OF THE BARBARY COAST(1945), spec eff; GIRLS OF THE BIG HOUSE(1945), spec eff; GRISSLY'S MILLIONS(1945), spec eff; MAN FROM OKLAHOMA, THE(1945), spec eff; MEXICANA(1945), spec eff; ROAD TO ALCATRAZ(1945), spec eff; SCOTLAND YARD INVESTIGATOR(1945, Brit.), spec eff; TIGER WOMAN, THE(1945), spec eff; TRAIL OF KIT CARSON(1945), spec eff; EARL CARROLL SKETCHBOOK(1946), spec eff; GAY BLADES(1946), spec eff; HELLDORADO(1946), spec eff; HOME ON THE HANGE(1946), spec eff; IN OLD SACRAMENTO(1946), spec eff; I'VE ALWAYS LOVED YOU(1946), spec eff; LAST CROOKED MILE, THE(1946), ph; MADONNA'S SECRET, THE(1946), spec eff; MAGNIFICENT ROGUE, THE(1946), spec eff; MURDER IN THE MUSIC HALL(1946), spec eff; MY PAL TRIGGER(1946), spec eff; NIGHT TRAIN TO MEMPHIS(1946), spec eff; ONE EXCITING WEEK(1946), spec eff; PASSKEY TO DANGER(1946), spec eff; PLAINSMAN AND THE LADY(1946), spec eff; RENDEZVOUS WITH ANNIE(1946), spec eff; RIO GRANDE RAIDERS(1946), spec eff; SANTA FE UPRISING(1946), spec eff; SIOUX CITY SUE(1946), spec eff; THAT BRENNAN GIRL(1946), spec eff; UNDERCOVER WOMAN, THE(1946), spec eff; VALLEY OF THE ZOMBIES(1946), spec eff; DRIFTWOOD(1947), spec eff; HOMESTEADERS OF PARADISE VALLEY(1947), spec eff; NORTHWEST OUTPOST(1947), spec eff; ON THE OLD SPANISH TRAIL(1947), spec eff; OREGON TRAIL SCOUTS(1947), spec eff; OTHER LOVE, THE(1947), spec eff; SPOILERS OF THE NORTH(1947), spec eff; THAT'S MY MAN(1947), spec eff; UNDER COLORADO SKIES(1947), spec eff; WEB OF DANGER, THE(1947), spec eff; WYOMING(1947), spec eff; ANGEL ON THE AMAZON(1948), spec eff; LIGHTNIN' IN THE FOREST(1948), spec eff; MACBETH(1948), spec eff; MOONRISE(1948), spec eff; NIGHT TIME IN NEVADA(1948), spec eff; OKLAHOMA BADLANDS(1948), spec eff; OLD LOS ANGELES(1948), spec eff; OUT OF THE STORM(1948), spec eff; SONS OF ADVENTURE(1948), spec eff; TIMBER TRAIL, THE(1948), spec eff; UNDER CALIFORNIA STARS(1948), spec eff; FIGHTING KENTUCKIAN, THE(1949), spec eff; RED MENACE, THE(1949), spec eff; RED PONY, THE(1949), spec eff; SAN ANTONE AMBUSH(1949), spec eff; SHERIFF OF WICHITA(1949), spec eff; SOUTH OF RIO(1949), spec eff; STREETS OF SAN FRANCISCO(1949), spec eff; TOO LATE FOR TEARS(1949), spec eff; WAKE OF THE RED WITCH(1949), spec eff; HOUSE BY THE RIVER(1950), spec eff; RIO GRANDE(1950), spec eff; SUNSET IN THE WEST(1950), spec eff; SURRENDER(1950), spec eff; TRAIL OF ROBIN HOOD(1950), spec eff; HONEYCHILE(1951), spec eff; SPOILERS OF THE PLAINS(1951), spec eff; MONTANA BELLE(1952), spec eff; OKLAHOMA ANNIE(1952), spec eff; WAC FROM WALLA WALLA, THE(1952), spec eff; WILD BLUE YONDER, THE(1952), spec eff; CITY THAT NEVER SLEEPS(1953), spec eff; FAIR WIND TO JAVA(1953), spec eff; SEA OF LOST SHIPS(1953), spec eff; JOHNNY GUITAR(1954), spec eff; UNTAMED HEIRESS(1954), spec eff; CAROLINA CANNONBALL(1955), spec eff; LAY THAT RIFLE DOWN(1955), spec eff; MAVERICK QUEEN, THE(1956), spec eff; SATAN'S SATELLITES(1958), spec eff; GHOST OF ZORRO(1959), spec eff
Al Lydell
WAY DOWN EAST(1935); EAGLE'S BROOD, THE(1936); ANGEL'S HOLIDAY(1937)
Benita Lydell
IT'S IN THE BAG(1943, Brit.); LOVE IN PAWN(1953, Brit.)
Marlene Lyden
MIRACLE ON 34TH STREET, THE(1947); CARBINE WILLIAMS(1952); SNIPER, THE(1952)
Pierce Lyden
KING OF DODGE CITY(1941); BABY FACE MORGAN(1942); ONE THRILLING NIGHT(1942); THEY RAID BY NIGHT(1942); UNDERCOVER MAN(1942); BLACK HILLS EXPRESS(1943); CANYON CITY(1943); CHATTERBOX(1943); DEAD MAN'S GULCH(1943); DEATH VALLEY MANHUNT(1943); FALSE COLORS(1943); FUGITIVE FROM SONORA(1943); GOOD MORNING, JUDGE(1943); RIDERS OF THE DEADLINE(1943); CALIFORNIA JOE(1944); FIREBRANDS OF ARIZONA(1944); LUMBERJACK(1944); MYSTERY MAN(1944); OUTLAWS OF SANTA FE(1944); SAN FERNANDO VALLEY(1944); TEXAS MASQUERADE(1944); BAD MEN OF THE BORDER(1945); CHEROKEE FLASH, THE(1945); CODE OF THE LAWLESS(1945); TRAIL TO VENGEANCE(1945); ALIAS BILLY THE KID(1946); GENTLEMAN FROM TEXAS(1946); RAINBOW OVER TEXAS(1946); ROLL ON TEXAS MOON(1946); WILD BEAUTY(1946); ADVENTURES OF DON COYOTE(1947); FABULOUS TEXAN, THE(1947); RAIDERS OF THE SOUTH(1947); RUSTLERS OF DEVIL'S CANYON(1947); SIX GUN SERENADE(1947); SONG OF THE WASTELAND(1947); BACK TRAIL(1948); COUNTESS OF MONTE CRISTO, THE(1948); CROSSED TRAILS(1948); DEAD MAN'S GOLD(1948); RANGERS RIDE, THE(1948); SILVER TRAILS(1948); SIX-GUN LAW(1948); BIG SOMBRERO, THE(1949); GAL WHO TOOK THE WEST, THE(1949); ILLEGAL ENTRY(1949); SHADOWS OF THE WEST(1949); SONS OF NEW MEXICO(1949); COVERED WAGON RAID(1950); MARK OF THE GORILLA(1950); PYGMY ISLAND(1950); TWILIGHT IN THE SIERRAS(1950); FURY OF THE CONGO(1951); NEVADA BADMEN(1951); STAGE TO BLUE RIVER(1951); TEXAS LAWMEN(1951); WHISTLING HILLS(1951); CANYON AMBUSH(1952); KANSAS TERRITORY(1952); MONTANA BELLE(1952); TEXAS CITY(1952); WACO(1952); WAGON TEAM(1952); FIRST TRAVELING SALESLADY, THE(1956); FRONTIER GAMBLER(1956); PHANTOM FROM 10,000 LEAGUES, THE(1956); CALYPSO HEAT WAVE(1957); WOMEN OF PITCAIRN ISLAND, THE(1957); WILD WESTERNERS, THE(1962)
Robert Lyden
HOLIDAY AFFAIR(1949); I'LL SEE YOU IN MY DREAMS(1951); WRITTEN ON THE WIND(1956); MAN OF A THOUSAND FACES(1957)
Martin Lyder
ROCK YOU SINNERS(1957, Brit.); DEVIL'S DAFFODIL, THE(1961, Brit./Ger.)
Sylvia Lydi
GREAT BRITISH TRAIN ROBBERY, THE(1967, Ger.)
Bob Lydiard
PAPER CHASE, THE(1973)
Eithne Lydon
MURDER IN EDEN(1962, Brit.); PLAYBOY OF THE WESTERN WORLD, THE(1963, Ireland)
James Lydon
TIME OF YOUR LIFE, THE(1948); MIDDLETON FAMILY AT THE N.Y. WORLD'S FAIR(1939); HENRY ALDRICH FOR PRESIDENT(1941); STRANGE ILLUSION(1945); TOWN WENT WILD, THE(1945); AFFAIRS OF GERALDINE(1946); CYNTHIA(1947); JOAN OF ARC(1948); OUT OF THE STORM(1948); BAD BOY(1949); DESTINATION BIG HOUSE(1950); HOT ROD(1950); MAGNIFICENT YANKEE, THE(1950); TARNISHED(1950); WHEN WILLIE COMES MARCHING HOME(1950); OH! SUSANNA(1951); ISLAND IN THE SKY(1953); BATTLE STATIONS(1956); CHAIN OF EVIDENCE(1957); I PASSED FOR WHITE(1960); THE HYPNOTIC EYE(1960); LAST TIME I SAW ARCHIE, THE(1961); DEATH OF A GUNFIGHTER(1969); SCANDALOUS JOHN(1971); VIGILANTE FORCE(1976)
Misc. Talkies
BEYOND THE MOON(1964)
James J. Lydon
DESPERADO, THE(1954)
Jimmy Lydon
BACK DOOR TO HEAVEN(1939); TWO THOROUGHBREDS(1939); BOWERY BOY(1940); LITTLE MEN(1940); TOM BROWN'S SCHOOL DAYS(1940); NAVAL ACADEMY(1941); HENRY ALDRICH, EDITOR(1942); HENRY ALDRICH GETS GLAMOUR(1942); HENRY AND DIZZY(1942); MAD MARTINDALES, THE(1942); STAR SPANGLED RHYTHM(1942); AERIAL GUNNER(1943); HENRY ALDRICH HAUNTS A HOUSE(1943); HENRY ALDRICH SWINGS IT(1943); HENRY ALDRICH, BOY SCOUT(1944); HENRY ALDRICH PLAYS CUPID(1944); HENRY ALDRICH'S LITTLE SECRET(1944); MY BEST GAL(1944); WHEN THE LIGHTS GO ON AGAIN(1944); TWICE BLESSED(1945); LIFE WITH FATHER(1947); OLD-FASHIONED GIRL, AN(1948); MISS MINK OF 1949(1949); TUCSON(1949); SEPTEMBER AFFAIR(1950); CORKY OF GASOLINE ALLEY(1951); GASOLINE ALLEY(1951)
Misc. Talkies
CADETS ON PARADE(1942); SWEET GENEVIEVE(1947)
John Lydon
1984
CORRUPT(1984, Ital.)

Misc. Talkies
COP KILLERS(1984)
Richard Lydon
COLORADO PIONEERS(1945)
Reg Lye
SHIRALEE, THE(1957, Brit.); SMILEY(1957, Brit.); SMILEY GETS A GUN(1959, Brit.); WRONG ARM OF THE LAW, THE(1963, Brit.); AMOROUS MR. PRAWN, THE(1965, Brit.); KING RAT(1965); WRONG BOX, THE(1966, Brit.); FATHOM(1967); CHALLENGE FOR ROBIN HOOD, A(1968, Brit.); DANGER ROUTE(1968, Brit.); LOST CONTINENT, THE(1968, Brit.); GAMES, THE(1970); 10 RILLINGTON PLACE(1971, Brit.); SUNDAY TOO FAR AWAY(1975, Aus.); UNIDENTIFIED FLYING ODDBALL, THE(1979, Brit.); KILLING OF ANGEL STREET, THE(1983, Aus.)
Reginald Lye
KING OF THE CORAL SEA(1956, Aus.); WALK INTO HELL(1957, Aus.)
Willie Lye
MOUSE AND HIS CHILD, THE(1977), anim
Viola Lyel
LORD RICHARD IN THE PANTRY(1930, Brit.); HOBSON'S CHOICE(1931, Brit.); AFTER OFFICE HOURS(1932, Brit.); LET ME EXPLAIN, DEAR(1932); MARRY ME(1932, Brit.); MAROONED(1933, Brit.); POLITICAL PARTY, A(1933, Brit.); CHANNEL CROSSING(1934, Brit.); OVER THE GARDEN WALL(1934, Brit.); PASSING SHADOWS(1934, Brit.); NIGHT MAIL(1935, Brit.); FARMER'S WIFE, THE(1941, Brit.); QUIET WEDDING(1941, Brit.); WANTED FOR MURDER(1946, Brit.); PATIENT VANISHES, THE(1947, Brit.); MR. PERRIN AND MR. TRAILL(1948, Brit.); IT'S NOT CRICKET(1949, Brit.); NO PLACE FOR JENNIFER(1950, Brit.); ISN'T LIFE WONDERFUL!(1953, Brit.); BLACK 13(1954, Brit.); FABIAN OF THE YARD(1954, Brit.); SEE HOW THEY RUN(1955, Brit.); LITTLE HUT, THE(1957); SUSPENDED ALIBI(1957, Brit.)
David Lyell
CONQUEROR WORM, THE(1968, Brit.)
Richard Lyford
ISLAND OF ALLAH(1956), p&d
Danos Lygizos
GREEK TYCOON, THE(1978)
1984
BLIND DATE(1984)
Mitsos Lygizos
ISLAND OF LOVE(1963)
Lisa Lyke
TWO-MINUTE WARNING(1976)
Karen Lykkehus
LURE OF THE JUNGLE, THE(1970, Den.)
Alexander Lykourezos
DAY THE FISH CAME OUT, THE(1967. Brit./Gr.)
Frances Lyland
IN OLD SACRAMENTO(1946), w
Barbara Ellen Lyle
FRATERNITY ROW(1977)
Barbara Lyle
SEED OF INNOCENCE(1980)
Bessie Lyle
ILLUSION(1929); BLONDE VENUS(1932); LITTLEST REBEL, THE(1935)
Clinton Lyle
PAINTED FACES(1929); MURDER IN THE MUSEUM(1934); SPLENDOR(1935)
Dylan Lyle
1984
TAIL OF THE TIGER(1984, Aus.)
Edith Lyle
Silents
ENCHANTMENT(1921); SCARLET LILY, THE(1923)
Misc. Silents
GIRL WITH THE GREEN EYES, THE(1916)
Eugene P. Lyle, Jr.
Silents
AMERICANO, THE(1917), w; MODERN MUSKETEER, A(1917), w
Gerald Lyle
NOT SO QUIET ON THE WESTERN FRONT(1930, Brit.)
Lyston Lyle
Silents
PLACE IN THE SUN, A(1916, Brit.); GAY LORD QUEX, THE(1917, Brit.)
Misc. Silents
VAGABOND'S REVENGE, A(1915, Brit.)
Capt. R. C. Lyle
WINGS OF THE MORNING(1937, Brit.)
Suzanne Lyle
TOO MANY HUSBANDS(1938, Brit.)
Warren E. Lyle
Misc. Silents
FOLLY OF REVENGE, THE(1916)
A.C. Lyles
SHORT CUT TO HELL(1957), p; RAYMIE(1960), p; YOUNG AND THE BRAVE, THE(1963), p; LAW OF THE LAWLESS(1964), p; STAGE TO THUNDER ROCK(1964), p; BLACK SPURS(1965), p; TOWN TAMER(1965), p, w; YOUNG FURY(1965), p, w; APACHE UPRISING(1966), p; JOHNNY RENO(1966), p, w; WACO(1966), p; FORT UTAH(1967), p; HOSTILE GUNS(1967), p; RED TOMAHAWK(1967), p; ARIZONA BUSHWHACKERS(1968), p; BUCKSKIN(1968), p; NIGHT OF THE LEPUS(1972), p
Chuck Lyles
SWEET JESUS, PREACHER MAN(1973)
1984
ANGEL(1984)
Jerry Lyles
CARNY(1980)
Tracee Lyles
LADY SINGS THE BLUES(1972); NEW CENTURIONS, THE(1972)
Gerard Lyley
LOOSE ENDS(1930, Brit.); WHY SAILORS LEAVE HOME(1930, Brit.); UNEASY VIRTUE(1931, Brit.); WOMEN WHO PLAY(1932, Brit.)

Abe Lyman
SWEET SURRENDER(1935); JUNIOR PROM(1946), md; SARGE GOES TO COLLEGE(1947); SINGING GUNS(1950), p
Brandy Lyman
Misc. Talkies
SCREAM IN THE STREETS, A(1972)
Dana Lyman
1984
BREAKIN'(1984), cos; NIGHTMARE ON ELM STREET, A(1984), cos
Dorothy Lyman
300 YEAR WEEKEND(1971); NIGHT OF THE JUGGLER(1980)
Frank Lyman, Jr.
TRAIL OF TERROR(1935)
Joni Lyman
WINTER A GO-GO(1965)
Lila Lyman
RAMPARTS WE WATCH, THE(1940)
Margaret Lyman
NOTHING SACRED(1937); THIN ICE(1937)
Mary-Fran Lyman
REUBEN, REUBEN(1983)
John Lymington
ISLAND OF THE BURNING DAMNED(1971, Brit.), w
F. Lymons
Silents
HARD TIMES(1915, Brit.)
David Lyn
1984
YR ALCOHOLIG LION(1984, Brit.)
Dawin Lyn
DEVIL TIMES FIVE(1974)
Dawn Lyn
I LOVE MY WIFE(1970); SHOOT OUT(1971); WALKING TALL(1973); WALKING TALL, PART II(1975); FINAL CHAPTER–WALKING TALL zero(1977)
Jacquie Lyn
PACK UP YOUR TROUBLES(1932); PROSPERITY(1932)
Rhonda Lyn
THIS IS ELVIS(1982)
Sandy Lyn
VIOLENT WOMEN(1960)
Ursula Lyn
FREUD(1962)
Margaret Lynar
LIVE, LOVE AND LEARN(1937)
Jeffrey Lynas
LIES MY FATHER TOLD ME(1975, Can.); BREAKING POINT(1976)
Sid Lynas
STRANGE BREW(1983)
Alfred Lynch
LOOK BACK IN ANGER(1959); PASSWORD IS COURAGE, THE(1962, Brit.); TWO AND TWO MAKE SIX(1962, Brit.); WEST 11(1963, Brit.); 55 DAYS AT PEKING(1963); HILL, THE(1965, Brit.); OPERATION SNAFU(1965, Brit.); TAMING OF THE SHREW, THE(1967, U.S./Ital.); SEA GULL, THE(1968); BLOCKHOUSE, THE(1974, Brit.); LOOPHOLE(1981, Brit.)
Beatrice Lynch
I'M DANCING AS FAST AS I CAN(1982)
Becky Jo Lynch
1984
RIVER, THE(1984)
Billy Lynch
EDDIE MACON'S RUN(1983)
Brid Lynch
PROFESSOR TIM(1957, Ireland); POACHER'S DAUGHTER, THE(1960, Brit.)
Catherine Lynch
PIRATE MOVIE, THE(1982, Aus.)
David Lynch
ERASERHEAD(1978), p,d&w, ed, art d; ELEPHANT MAN, THE(1980, Brit.), d, w
1984
DUNE(1984), d, w
Debbie Lynch
FUGITIVE KIND, THE(1960)
Don Lynch
PRAIRIE, THE(1948)
Doris Lynch
STEEL(1980), cos
Ed Lynch
WATCHED(1974), ph
Edward Lynch
PLAYBOY OF PARIS(1930); SCAREHEADS(1931)
Edwin Lynch
BRIGHT LIGHTS(1931)
Hal Lynch
STAGECOACH(1966); ROSIE!(1967); WAY WEST, THE(1967); WILD ROVERS(1971)
Heidi Lynch
WARRIORS, THE(1979)
Helen Lynch
IN OLD ARIZONA(1929); SPEAKEASY(1929); EMERGENCY CALL(1933); WOMEN WITHOUT NAMES(1940)
Silents
WHAT'S A WIFE WORTH?(1921); DANGEROUS AGE, THE(1922); ETERNAL THREE, THE(1923); AMERICAN MANNERS(1924); IN HIGH GEAR(1924); OH, DOCTOR(1924); ON PROBATION(1924); AFTER MARRIAGE(1925); SMILIN' AT TROUBLE(1925); ARIZONA SWEEPSTAKES(1926); TOM AND HIS PALS(1926); AVENGING FANGS(1927); CHEATERS(1927); HUSBANDS FOR RENT(1927); LITTLE BIG HORN(1927); UNDERWORLD(1927); LADIES OF THE MOB(1928); LOVE AND LEARN(1928)
Misc. Silents
HOUSE THAT JAZZ BUILT, THE(1921); MY LADY FRIENDS(1921); GLASS HOUSES(1922); OTHER SIDE, THE(1922); CAUSE FOR DIVORCE(1923); BUSTIN' THRU(1925); THREE WEEKS IN PARIS(1925); GENERAL CUSTER AT LITTLE BIG

HORN(1926); SPEEDING THROUGH(1926); STOLEN LOVE(1928); THUNDER-GOD(1928)

Helene Lynch
WHY BRING THAT UP?(1929); ELMER AND ELSIE(1934)

Jimmy Lynch
HUMAN TORNADO, THE(1976); PETEY WHEATSTRAW(1978)

Joe Lynch
TOUGH KID(1939); NIGHT FIGHTERS, THE(1960); SIEGE OF SIDNEY STREET, THE(1960, Brit.); LIST OF ADRIAN MESSENGER, THE(1963); RUNNING MAN, THE(1963, Brit.); GIRL WITH GREEN EYES(1964, Brit.); JOHNNY NOBODY(1965, Brit.); YOUNG CASSIDY(1965, U.S./Brit.); ULYSSES(1967, U.S./Brit.); LOOT(1971, Brit.)
Misc. Talkies
SAINT AND THE BRAVE GOOSE, THE(1981, Brit.)

John Lynch
CUBAN LOVE SONG,THE(1931), w
1984
CAL(1984, Ireland)
Silents
BRIDE OF HATE, THE(1917), w; DARK ROAD, THE(1917), w; LAST OF THE INGRAHAMS, THE(1917), w; QUICKSANDS(1918), w; EXTRAVAGANCE(1919), w; DARLING MINE(1920), w; EVERYBODY'S SWEETHEART(1920), w; AFTER MID-NIGHT(1921), w; PRIDE OF PALOMAR, THE(1922), w; VALLEY OF SILENT MEN, THE(1922), w; ENEMIES OF WOMEN, THE(1923), w; KENTUCKY DAYS(1923), w; LAWFUL LARCENY(1923), w; REJECTED WOMAN, THE(1924), w; SECOND YOUTH(1924), w; GRAND DUCHESS AND THE WAITER, THE(1926), w

Joy Lynch
OUTSIDER, THE(1980)

Kate Lynch
MEATBALLS(1979, Can.); SUMMER'S CHILDREN(1979, Can.); NOTHING PERSON-AL(1980, Can.); IMPROPER CHANNELS(1981, Can.); SOUP FOR ONE(1982); CUR-TAINS(1983, Can.)

Kathy Lynch
TOUGH ENOUGH(1983)

Ken Lynch
WHEN WILLIE COMES MARCHING HOME(1950); BONNIE PARKER STORY, THE(1958); I MARRIED A MONSTER FROM OUTER SPACE(1958); MAN OR GUN(1958); RUN SILENT, RUN DEEP(1958); UNWED MOTHER(1958); VOICE IN THE MIRROR(1958); YOUNG AND WILD(1958); ANATOMY OF A MURDER(1959); LEGEND OF TOM DOOLEY, THE(1959); NORTH BY NORTHWEST(1959); PARA-TROOP COMMAND(1959); PORK CHOP HILL(1959); DARK AT THE TOP OF THE STAIRS, THE(1960); SEVEN WAYS FROM SUNDOWN(1960); HONEYMOON MA-CHINE, THE(1961); PORTRAIT OF A MOBSTER(1961); DAYS OF WINE AND ROSES(1962); WALK ON THE WILD SIDE(1962); APACHE RIFLES(1964); DEAD RINGER(1964); DEAR HEART(1964); FBI CODE 98(1964); MISTER BUDDWING(1966); HOTEL(1967); NEVER A DULL MOMENT(1968); P.J.(1968); BAD CHARLESTON CHARLIE(1973); WILLIE DYNAMITE(1973); W(1974)

Kenneth Lynch
Misc. Talkies
MY PLEASURE IS MY BUSINESS(1974, Can.)

Kenny Lynch
JUST FOR FUN(1963, Brit.); DR. TERROR'S HOUSE OF HORRORS(1965, Brit.); PLANK, THE(1967, Brit.); CARRY ON LOVING(1970, Brit.)

Maria Lynch
SUDDEN IMPACT(1983)

Mark Lynch
TOM SAWYER(1973)

Owen Lynch
Misc. Silents
PAYING THE PRICE(1924)

Paul Lynch
HARD PART BEGINS, THE(1973, Can.), d; BLOOD AND GUTS(1978, Can.), d; PROM NIGHT(1980), d; HUMONGOUS(1982, Can.), d; CROSS COUNTRY(1983, Can.), d

Raymond Lynch
1984
NIGHT OF THE COMET(1984)

Richard Lynch
SCARECROW(1973); SEVEN UPS, THE(1973); OPEN SEASON(1974, U.S./Span.); HAPPY HOOKER, THE(1975); GOD TOLD ME TO(1976); PREMONITION, THE(1976); STUNTS(1977); DEATHSPORT(1978); DELTA FOX(1979); FORMULA, THE(1980); NINTH CONFIGURATION, THE(1980); STEEL(1980); SWORD AND THE SORCERER, THE(1982)
1984
SAVAGE DAWN(1984)

Roland Lynch
COWBOY FROM SUNDOWN(1940), w; GOLDEN TRAIL, THE(1940), w; RAINBOW OVER THE RANGE(1940), w

Sean Lynch
SLASHER, THE(1953, Brit./U.S.); LAUGHING ANNE(1954, Brit./U.S.); VIOLENT PLAY-GROUND(1958, Brit.); INNOCENT MEETING(1959, Brit.); KITCHEN, THE(1961, Brit.); TRAITORS, THE(1963, Brit.); BRIGAND OF KANDAHAR, THE(1965, Brit.); JOEY BOY(1965, Brit.); KALEIDOSCOPE(1966, Brit.); PANIC(1966, Brit.); SALT & PEP-PER(1968, Brit.); ONE PLUS ONE(1969, Brit.); WONDERWALL(1969, Brit.); AT THE EARTH'S CORE(1976, Brit.)

Sharon Lynch
DON'T GO IN THE HOUSE(1980), cos

Sheila Lynch
MARINES COME THROUGH, THE(1943); QUICK AND THE DEAD, THE(1963), w

Skipp Lynch
SURVIVORS, THE(1983)

Susan Lynch
NORTHERN LIGHTS(1978)

T.B. Lynch
LEAP OF FAITH(1931, Brit.), ph

Theodora Lynch
LOST WEEKEND, THE(1945); SONG OF SCHEHERAZADE(1947); FORGOTTEN WOMEN(1949)

Tracey Lynch
ACCEPTABLE LEVELS(1983, Brit.)

W. L. Lynch
Silents
PEACEFUL PETERS(1922)

Walter Lynch
Silents
KID, THE(1921); SCARS OF JEALOUSY(1923)
Misc. Silents
BORDER RAIDERS, THE(1921)

Warren Lynch
IRON MASK, THE(1929), ph; MURDER IN THE CLOUDS(1934), ph; SIX-DAY BIKE RIDER(1934), ph; RED HOT TIRES(1935), ph; WIDOW FROM MONTE CARLO, THE(1936), ph; DANCE, CHARLIE, DANCE(1937), ph; FLY-AWAY BABY(1937), ph; MIDNIGHT COURT(1937), ph; OVER THE GOAL(1937), ph; PRAIRIE THUN-DER(1937), ph; SMART BLONDE(1937), ph; THAT MAN'S HERE AGAIN(1937), ph; BLONDES AT WORK(1938), ph; TORCHY BLANE IN CHINATOWN(1938), ph; TORCHY GETS HER MAN(1938), ph; TORCHY RUNS FOR MAYOR(1939), ph; BACKGROUND TO DANGER(1943), spec eff; VERY THOUGHT OF YOU, THE(1944), spec eff; PILLOW TO POST(1945), spec eff; TANKS ARE COMING, THE(1951), ph

Warren E. Lynch
BULLETS OR BALLOTS(1936), spec eff; PETRIFIED FOREST, THE(1936), spec eff

William Lynch
JANIE(1944), spec eff

Samantha Lynche
HURRY UP OR I'LL BE 30(1973)

Eva Lynd
THE HYPNOTIC EYE(1960)

Eve Lynd
MOUNTAINS O'MOURNE(1938, Brit.); TORSO MURDER MYSTERY, THE(1940, Brit.)

Helen Lynd
MELODY IN SPRING(1934); SWEET SURRENDER(1935); HATS OFF(1937); THE-RE'S THAT WOMAN AGAIN(1938); CAFE SOCIETY(1939); FLIGHT AT MID-NIGHT(1939); KID FROM TEXAS, THE(1939); LONE WOLF SPY HUNT, THE(1939); OF MICE AND MEN(1939); WHEN TOMORROW COMES(1939); KITTY FOYLE(1940); LUCKY PARTNERS(1940); MURDER IN THE AIR(1940); ROAD TO SIN-GAPORE(1940); HERE COMES HAPPINESS(1941); STRAWBERRY BLONDE, THE(1941); UNFINISHED BUSINESS(1941); GREAT MAN'S LADY, THE(1942); MOONLIGHT IN HAVANA(1942); YOU'RE TELLING ME(1942); SO PROUDLY WE HAIL(1943)

Herta Lynd
YOU AND ME(1938)

Michael Lynd
OLD MOTHER RILEY, DETECTIVE(1943, Brit.)

Moira Lynd
PERFECT LADY, THE(1931, Brit.); ILLEGAL(1932, Brit.); VERDICT OF THE SEA(1932, Brit.); GOING STRAIGHT(1933, Brit.); SWINGING THE LEAD(1934, Brit.); VANITY(1935); VILLAGE SQUIRE, THE(1935, Brit.); ALL THAT GLITTERS(1936, Brit.); FULL SPEED AHEAD(1936, Brit.); LUCK OF THE TURF(1936, Brit.); NOTHING LIKE PUBLICITY(1936, Brit.); PRISONER OF CORBAL(1939, Brit.); SPIDER, THE(1940, Brit.)

Patty Lou Lynd
TEN NIGHTS IN A BARROOM(1931)

Janice Lynde
BEYOND EVIL(1980)

Paul Lynde
NEW FACES(1954), a, w; BYE BYE BIRDIE(1963); SON OF FLUBBER(1963); UN-DER THE YUM-YUM TREE(1963); FOR THOSE WHO THINK YOUNG(1964); SEND ME NO FLOWERS(1964); BEACH BLANKET BINGO(1965); GLASS BOTTOM BOAT, THE(1966); HOW SWEET IT IS(1968); CHARLOTTE'S WEB(1973); JOURNEY BACK TO OZ(1974); HUGO THE HIPPO(1976, Hung./U.S.); RABBIT TEST(1978); VILLAIN, THE(1979)

Alice Lyndon
BULLETS OR BALLOTS(1936); MOUNTAIN JUSTICE(1937)

Barre Lyndon
AMAZING DR. CLITTERHOUSE, THE(1938), w; THEY CAME BY NIGHT(1940, Brit.), w; SUNDOWN(1941), w; LODGER, THE(1944), w; MAN IN HALF-MOON STREET, THE(1944), w; HANGOVER SQUARE(1945), w; HOUSE ON 92ND STREET, THE(1945), w; NIGHT HAS A THOUSAND EYES(1948), w; TO PLEASE A LA-DY(1950), w; MAN IN THE ATTIC(1953), w; WAR OF THE WORLDS, THE(1953), w; SIGN OF THE PAGAN(1954), w; CONQUEST OF SPACE(1955), w; OMAR KHAYYAM(1957), w; MAN WHO COULD CHEAT DEATH, THE(1959, Brit.), w; LITTLE SHEPHERD OF KINGDOM COME(1961), w; DARK INTRUDER(1965), w

Michael Lyndon
1984
SUCCESS IS THE BEST REVENGE(1984, Brit.), a, w

Victor Lyndon
JOHNNY ON THE RUN(1953, Brit.), p; STOCK CAR(1955, Brit.), w; IT'S A GREAT DAY(1956, Brit.), p; SPARE THE ROD(1961, Brit.), p; DEVIL'S AGENT, THE(1962, Brit.), p; STATION SIX-SAHARA(1964, Brit./Ger.), p; OPTIMISTS, THE(1973, Brit.), p

Tommy Lyndon-Hayes
UGLY DUCKLING, THE(1959, Brit.), p

Tom Lyndon-Haynes
SCRAMBLE(1970, Brit.), p

Ernest Lynds
TRIUMPH OF SHERLOCK HOLMES, THE(1935, Brit.)

Thor Lyndthal
TIME IN THE SUN, A(1970, Swed.)

Adrian Lyne
FOXES(1980), d; FLASHDANCE(1983), d

Robert Lynen
POIL DE CAROTTE(1932, Fr.); THEY WERE FIVE(1938, Fr.); UN CARNET DE BAL(1938, Fr.); MAN OF THE HOUR, THE(1940, Fr.); HATRED(1941, Fr.)

Jim Lyness
KING OF COMEDY, THE(1983)

Carol Lynley
LIGHT IN THE FOREST, THE(1958); BLUE DENIM(1959); HOLIDAY FOR LO-VERS(1959); HOUND-DOG MAN(1959); LAST SUNSET, THE(1961); RETURN TO PEYTON PLACE(1961); CARDINAL, THE(1963); STRIPPER, THE(1963); UNDER THE

YUM-YUM TREE(1963); PLEASURE SEEKERS, THE(1964); SHOCK TREATMENT(1964); BUNNY LAKE IS MISSING(1965); HARLOW(1965); DANGER ROUTE(1968, Brit.); HELICOPTER SPIES, THE(1968); SHUTTERED ROOM, THE(1968, Brit.); MALTESE BIPPY, THE(1969); ONCE YOU KISS A STRANGER(1969); NORWOOD(1970); BEWARE! THE BLOB(1972); POSEIDON ADVENTURE, THE(1972); FOUR DEUCES, THE(1976); CAT AND THE CANARY, THE(1979, Brit.); SHAPE OF THINGS TO COME, THE(1979, Can.); VIGILANTE(1983)
Misc. Talkies
COTTER(1972); BAD GEORGIA ROAD(1977); WASHINGTON AFFAIR, THE(1978)

Darlyn Ann Lynley
BOOTLEGGERS(1974)

Ann Lynn
JOHNNY, YOU'RE WANTED(1956, Brit.); MOMENT OF INDISCRETION(1958, Brit.); NAKED FURY(1959, Brit.); PICCADILLY THIRD STOP(1960, Brit.); FLAME IN THE STREETS(1961, Brit.); STRIP TEASE MURDER(1961, Brit.); WIND OF CHANGE, THE(1961, Brit.); DAMN THE DEFIANT!(1962, Brit.); STRONGROOM(1962, Brit.); DOCTOR IN DISTRESS(1963, Brit.); PLEASURE LOVERS, THE(1964, Brit.); SHOT IN THE DARK, A(1964); BLACK TORMENT, THE(1965, Brit.); FOUR IN THE MORNING(1965, Brit.); GIRL GETTERS, THE(1966, Brit.); PARTY'S OVER, THE(1966, Brit.); UNCLE, THE(1966, Brit.); I'LL NEVER FORGET WHAT'S 'IS NAME(1967, Brit.); SEPARATION(1968, Brit.); BABY LOVE(1969, Brit.); OTHER SIDE OF THE UNDERNEATH, THE(1972, Brit.); HITLER: THE LAST TEN DAYS(1973, Brit./Ital.)

April Lynn
SINISTER URGE, THE(1961)
Misc. Talkies
BODY IS A SHELL, THE(1957)

Barbara Lynn
THAT NIGHT IN RIO(1941); TALES OF MANHATTAN(1942); FALCON AND THE CO-EDS, THE(1943); HIGH EXPLOSIVE(1943); GODZILLA VERSUS THE COSMIC MONSTER(1974, Jap.)

Basil Lynn
BRITISH AGENT(1934); FOR VALOR(1937, Brit.)

Betty Lynn
APARTMENT FOR PEGGY(1948); JUNE BRIDE(1948); FATHER WAS A FULLBACK(1949); MOTHER IS A FRESHMAN(1949); CHEAPER BY THE DOZEN(1950); PAYMENT ON DEMAND(1951); TAKE CARE OF MY LITTLE GIRL(1951); BEHIND THE HIGH WALL(1956); MEET ME IN LAS VEGAS(1956); GUN FOR A COWARD(1957); LOUISIANA HUSSY(1960)

Betty Ann Lynn
SITTING PRETTY(1948)

Bill Lynn
1984
HIGHPOINT(1984, Can.); POLICE ACADEMY(1984)

Billy Lynn
OUTCASTS OF POKER FLAT, THE(1952); TWONKY, THE(1953)

Carey Lynn
HOW SWEET IT IS(1968)

Carole Lynn
GHOST TRAIN, THE(1941, Brit.)

Cathy Lynn
TOYS ARE NOT FOR CHILDREN(1972), m

Christy Lynn
RAYMIE(1960)

Cynthia Lynn
BEDTIME STORY(1964)

Dani Lynn
CASE OF PATTY SMITH, THE(1962); IF A MAN ANSWERS(1962); BLACK ZOO(1963); THEY SAVED HITLER'S BRAIN(1964)

Denise Lynn
INCREDIBLY STRANGE CREATURES WHO STOPPED LIVING AND BECAME CRAZY MIXED-UP ZOMBIES, THE(1965); JUD(1971)

Diana Lynn
HENRY ALDRICH GETS GLAMOUR(1942); MAJOR AND THE MINOR, THE(1942); AND THE ANGELS SING(1944); HENRY ALDRICH PLAYS CUPID(1944); MIRACLE OF MORGAN'S CREEK, THE(1944); OUR HEARTS WERE YOUNG AND GAY(1944); DUFFY'S TAVERN(1945); OUT OF THIS WORLD(1945); BRIDE WORE BOOTS, THE(1946); OUR HEARTS WERE GROWING UP(1946); EASY COME, EASY GO(1947); VARIETY GIRL(1947); EVERY GIRL SHOULD BE MARRIED(1948); RUTHLESS(1948); TEXAS, BROOKLYN AND HEAVEN(1948); MY FRIEND IRMA(1949); MY FRIEND IRMA GOES WEST(1950); PAID IN FULL(1950); PEGGY(1950); ROGUES OF SHERWOOD FOREST(1950); BEDTIME FOR BONZO(1951); PEOPLE AGAINST O'HARA, THE(1951); MEET ME AT THE FAIR(1952); PLUNDER OF THE SUN(1953); TRACK OF THE CAT(1954); ANNAPOLIS STORY, AN(1955); KENTUCKIAN, THE(1955); YOU'RE NEVER TOO YOUNG(1955); COMPANY OF KILLERS(1970)

Don Lynn
LADY OF BURLESQUE(1943)

Donna Lynn
1984
HOLLYWOOD HIGH PART II(1984)

Doris Lynn
THAT TOUCH OF MINK(1962)

Eddie Lynn
REFORM SCHOOL(1939); TAKE MY LIFE(1942)

Edward Lynn
THRILL OF BRAZIL, THE(1946)

Eleanor Lynn
AS HUSBANDS GO(1934); FIRST 100 YEARS, THE(1938); FUGITIVES FOR A NIGHT(1938); SHOPWORN ANGEL(1938); YOU'RE ONLY YOUNG ONCE(1938)

Emmett Lynn
GRANDPA GOES TO TOWN(1940); SCATTERBRAIN(1940); WAGON TRAIN(1940); ALONG THE RIO GRANDE(1941); FARGO KID, THE(1941); ROAD AGENT(1941); ROBBERS OF THE RANGE(1941); CITY OF SILENT MEN(1942); FRISCO LILL(1942); IN OLD CALIFORNIA(1942); JOAN OF OZARK(1942); OUTLAWS OF PINE RIDGE(1942); QUEEN OF BROADWAY(1942); STAGECOACH EXPRESS(1942); SUNDOWN KID, THE(1942); TOMORROW WE LIVE(1942); WESTWARD HO(1942); YOU'RE TELLING ME(1942); CARSON CITY CYCLONE(1943); DAYS OF OLD CHEYENNE(1943); DEAD MAN'S GULCH(1943); GIRLS IN CHAINS(1943); HANGMEN ALSO DIE(1943); LAW RIDES AGAIN, THE(1943); RETURN OF THE RANGERS, THE(1943); BLUEBEARD(1944); COWBOY CANTEEN(1944); FRONTIER OUTLAWS(1944); GOODNIGHT SWEETHEART(1944); JOHNNY DOESN'T LIVE HERE ANY MORE(1944); LARAMIE TRAIL, THE(1944); NEVADA(1944); OUTLAWS OF SANTA FE(1944); SWING HOSTESS(1944); WHEN THE LIGHTS GO ON AGAIN(1944); CISCO KID RETURNS, THE(1945); HOLLYWOOD AND VINE(1945); SHADOW OF TERROR(1945); SHADOWS OF DEATH(1945); SONG OF OLD WYOMING(1945); TOWN WENT WILD, THE(1945); CARAVAN TRAIL, THE(1946); CONQUEST OF CHEYENNE(1946); LANDRUSH(1946); MAN FROM RAINBOW VALLEY, THE(1946); ROMANCE OF THE WEST(1946); SANTA FE UPRISING(1946); STAGECOACH TO DENVER(1946); CODE OF THE WEST(1947); NIGHTMARE ALLEY(1947); OREGON TRAIL SCOUTS(1947); RUSTLERS OF DEVIL'S CANYON(1947); WISTFUL WIDOW OF WAGON GAP, THE(1947); GRAND CANYON TRAIL(1948); RELENTLESS(1948); WEST OF SONORA(1948); WESTERN HERITAGE(1948); LAST BANDIT, THE(1949); RIDE, RYDER, RIDE!(1949); ROLL, THUNDER, ROLL!(1949); COWBOY AND THE PRIZEFIGHTER(1950); FIGHTING REDHEAD, THE(1950); TRAVELING SALESWOMAN(1950); BADMAN'S GOLD(1951); BEST OF THE BADMEN(1951); CALLAWAY WENT THATAWAY(1951); JOURNEY INTO LIGHT(1951); MILLIONAIRE FOR CHRISTY, A(1951); RED BADGE OF COURAGE, THE(1951); SCARF, THE(1951); TEXAS CARNIVAL(1951); APACHE WAR SMOKE(1952); DESERT PURSUIT(1952); LONE STAR(1952); LUSTY MEN, THE(1952); MONKEY BUSINESS(1952); OKLAHOMA ANNIE(1952); SKIRTS AHOY!(1952); SKY FULL OF MOON(1952); HOMESTEADERS, THE(1953); NORTHERN PATROL(1953); PICKUP ON SOUTH STREET(1953); ROBE, THE(1953); BAIT(1954); JUBILEE TRAIL(1954); LIVING IT UP(1954); RING OF FEAR(1954); MAN CALLED PETER, THE(1955); TEN COMMANDMENTS, THE(1956); WAGON WHEELS WESTWARD(1956)
Misc. Talkies
BOTH BARRELS BLAZING(1945); GANGSTER'S DEN(1945)

Emmy Lynn
Misc. Silents
MATER DOLOROSA(1917, Fr.); LA DIXIEME SYMPHONIE(1918, Fr.); LA FAUTE D'ODETTE MARECHAL(1920, Fr.); VISAGES VIOLES...AMES CLOSES(1921, Fr.); LA VIERGE FOLLE(1929, Fr.)

Evanna Lynn
WILD SCENE, THE(1970)

Florence Lynn
PORTRAIT OF A WOMAN(1946, Fr.)

Frank Lynn
1984
DELIVERY BOYS(1984)

George Lynn
SINNER TAKE ALL(1936); CHARLIE CHAN AT MONTE CARLO(1937); DUKE COMES BACK, THE(1937); INTERNES CAN'T TAKE MONEY(1937); CITY GIRL(1938); A-HAUNTING WE WILL GO(1942); GRAND CENTRAL MURDER(1942); TO BE OR NOT TO BE(1942); CRIME DOCTOR'S STRANGEST CASE(1943); NORTH STAR, THE(1943); NORTHERN PURSUIT(1943); THEY CAME TO BLOW UP AMERICA(1943); TONIGHT WE RAID CALAIS(1943); HOUSE OF FRANKENSTEIN(1944); TWO-MAN SUBMARINE(1944); SHADY LADY(1945); SHE GETS HER MAN(1945); GIRL ON THE SPOT(1946); NOTORIOUS(1946); UNDER NEVADA SKIES(1946); KILLER AT LARGE(1947); SUDDENLY IT'S SPRING(1947); BEST MAN WINS(1948); HOMICIDE FOR THREE(1948); NAKED CITY, THE(1948); CRISS CROSS(1949); TAKE ONE FALSE STEP(1949); SIDE STREET(1950); DAY THE EARTH STOOD STILL, THE(1951); MY FAVORITE SPY(1951); SHOW BOAT(1951); BUSHWHACKERS, THE(1952); MAGNIFICENT OBSESSION(1954); BOSS, THE(1956); DEADLY MANTIS, THE(1957); HALLIDAY BRAND, THE(1957); MAN WHO TURNED TO STONE, THE(1957); GIRL IN THE WOODS(1958); I WAS A TEENAGE FRANKENSTEIN(1958)

George M. Lynn
UNION STATION(1950); ATOMIC CITY, THE(1952); SOMETHING TO LIVE FOR(1952); WEREWOLF, THE(1956)

Gillian Lynn
HALF A SIXPENCE(1967, Brit.), ch

Grace Lynn
Misc. Talkies
ALL MEN ARE APES(1965)

Henry Lynn
MOTHERS OF TODAY(1939), d
Misc. Talkies
JEWISH FATHER(1934), d; SONG OF SONGS(1935), d; POWER OF LIFE, THE(1938), d; PEOPLE THAT SHALL NOT DIE, A(1939), d

Hilary Lynn
HOLLYWOOD CAVALCADE(1939), w; GREAT PROFILE, THE(1940), w; WHERE ARE YOUR CHILDREN?(1943), w; ARE THESE OUR PARENTS?(1944), w

Jack Lynn
NEVER TAKE CANDY FROM A STRANGER(1961, Brit.); CONQUEROR WORM, THE(1968, Brit.); YENTL(1983)

James Lynn
CHEROKEE FLASH, THE(1945)

Jane Lynn
NIGHTFALL(1956)

Janet Lynn
COOL IT, CAROL!(1970, Brit.); ASSAULT(1971, Brit.)
Misc. Talkies
DIRTIEST GIRL I EVER MET, THE(1973)

Jeffrey Lynn
COWBOY FROM BROOKLYN(1938); FOUR DAUGHTERS(1938); WHEN WERE YOU BORN?(1938); DAUGHTERS COURAGEOUS(1939); ESPIONAGE AGENT(1939); FOUR WIVES(1939); ROARING TWENTIES, THE(1939); YES, MY DARLING DAUGHTER(1939); ALL THIS AND HEAVEN TOO(1940); CHILD IS BORN, A(1940); FIGHTING 69TH, THE(1940); IT ALL CAME TRUE(1940); MONEY AND THE WOMAN(1940); MY LOVE CAME BACK(1940); BODY DISAPPEARS, THE(1941); FLIGHT FROM DESTINY(1941); FOUR MOTHERS(1941); LAW OF THE TROPICS(1941); MILLION DOLLAR BABY(1941); UNDERGROUND(1941); BLACK BART(1948); FOR THE LOVE OF MARY(1948); LETTER TO THREE WIVES, A(1948); WHIPLASH(1948); CAPTAIN CHINA(1949); STRANGE BARGAIN(1949); HOME TOWN STORY(1951); UP FRONT(1951); LOST LAGOON(1958), a, w; BUTTERFIELD 8(1960); TONY ROME(1967)
Misc. Talkies
THAT I MAY SEE(1953)

Jennie Lynn
SNOW QUEEN, THE(1959, USSR)

Jenny Lynn
TICKET OF LEAVE MAN, THE(1937, Brit.); GREED OF WILLIAM HART, THE(1948, Brit.)
Jimmy Lynn
IN SEARCH OF GREGORY(1970, Brit./Ital.)
Jody Lynn
MOONLIGHTING WIVES(1966)
Joe Lynn
WIZ, THE(1978)
1984
COTTON CLUB, THE(1984); MOSCOW ON THE HUDSON(1984)
Jonathan Lynn
PRUDENCE AND THE PILL(1968, Brit.); INTERNECINE PROJECT, THE(1974, Brit.), w
Judy Lynn
FIVE LITTLE PEPPERS IN TROUBLE(1940); TOP BANANA(1954)
Kane Lynn
TERROR IS A MAN(1959, U.S./Phil.), p
Kane W. Lynn
RAVAGERS, THE(1965, U.S./Phil.), p; BRAIN OF BLOOD(1971, Phil.), w
Kary Lynn
Misc. Talkies
SWEET COUNTRY ROAD(1981)
Kathy Lynn
WITCHMAKER, THE(1969)
Kerry Lynn
MY BOYS ARE GOOD BOYS(1978)
Lee Lynn
LIFE OF HER OWN, A(1950)
Leni Lynn
BABES IN ARMS(1939); HULLABALOO(1940); I LOVE YOU AGAIN(1940); ANGELS WITH BROKEN WINGS(1941); GIVE ME THE STARS(1944, Brit.); HEAVEN IS ROUND THE CORNER(1944, Brit.); SHOWTIME(1948, Brit.); SPRINGTIME(1948, Brit.)
Loretta Lynn
FORTY ACRE FEUD(1965); NASHVILLE REBEL(1966); COAL MINER'S DAUGHTER(1980), w
Mara Lynn
PREHISTORIC WOMEN(1950); G.I. JANE(1951); LEAVE IT TO THE MARINES(1951); SKY HIGH(1952); TOP BANANA(1954); LAST TRAIN FROM GUN HILL(1959); LET'S MAKE LOVE(1960); QUICK, LET'S GET MARRIED(1965); WILD 90(1968); MAIDSTONE(1970)
Misc. Talkies
RETURN OF GILBERT AND SULLIVAN(1952)
Mari Lynn
SERGEANT WAS A LADY, THE(1961); EXPERIMENT IN TERROR(1962); INTERNS, THE(1962); SON OF FLUBBER(1963)
Marianne Lynn
PARIS PLAYBOYS(1954)
Mary Lynn
BEYOND THE LAW(1968)
Mauri Lynn
BIG NIGHT, THE(1951); NIGHT WITHOUT SLEEP(1952); CARMEN JONES(1954)
May Lynn
Misc. Silents
COAL KING, THE(1915, Brit.); DEVIL'S PROFESSION, THE(1915, Brit.)
Nancy Lynn
KID FROM SPAIN, THE(1932)
Natalie Lynn
THIS MAN IS MINE(1946 Brit.); INTENT TO KILL(1958, Brit.)
Misc. Talkies
FOR MEMBERS ONLY(1960)
Neva Lynn
PALMY DAYS(1931)
Nikki Lynn
Misc. Talkies
TEENAGE HITCHHIKERS(1975)
Nina Lynn
Silents
GIRL WHO TOOK THE WRONG TURNING, THE(1915, Brit.); SHOPSOILED GIRL, THE(1915, Brit.); QUEEN OF THE WICKED(1916, Brit.)
Misc. Silents
BEGGAR GIRL'S WEDDING, THE(1915, Brit.)
Pat Lynn
PAL JOEY(1957); INCREDIBLY STRANGE CREATURES WHO STOPPED LIVING AND BECAME CRAZY MIXED-UP ZOMBIES, THE(1965)
Patricia Lynn
NARCOTICS STORY, THE(1958)
Peggy Lynn
OUTLAWS OF THE CHEROKEE TRAIL(1941); THEY GOT ME COVERED(1943)
Silents
NOTORIOUS MRS. CARRICK, THE(1924, Brit.)
Peter George Lynn
MR. WONG IN CHINATOWN(1939); MYSTERY PLANE(1939); SOCIETY SMUGGLERS(1939); WOLF CALL(1939); DRUMS OF THE DESERT(1940); NORTHWEST PASSAGE(1940); SADDLEMATES(1941); SUDAN(1945); TANGIER(1946)
Peter Lynn
CIPHER BUREAU(1938); TIME OUT FOR MURDER(1938); BURIED ALIVE(1939); LET US LIVE(1939); NEWSBOY'S HOME(1939); QUICK MILLIONS(1939); GREAT DICTATOR, THE(1940); KIT CARSON(1940); LONE WOLF STRIKES, THE(1940); SAINT IN PALM SPRINGS, THE(1941); BOMBAY CLIPPER(1942)
Ralph Lynn
ONE EMBARRASSING NIGHT(1930, Brit.); CHANCE OF A NIGHT-TIME, THE(1931, Brit), a, d; MISCHIEF(1931, Brit.); PLUNDER(1931, Brit.); TONS OF MONEY(1931, Brit.), a, w; NIGHT LIKE THIS, A(1932, Brit.); THARK(1932, Brit.); CUCKOO IN THE NEST, THE(1933, Brit.); JUST MY LUCK(1933, Brit.); SUMMER LIGHTNING(1933, Brit.); TURKEY TIME(1933, Brit.); UP TO THE NECK(1933, Brit.); CUP OF KINDNESS, A(1934, Brit.); DIRTY WORK(1934, Brit.); FIGHTING STOCK(1935, Brit.); FOREIGN AFFAIRES(1935, Brit.); STORMY WEATHER(1935, Brit.); ALL IN(1936, Brit.); IN THE SOUP(1936, Brit.); POT LUCK(1936, Brit.); FOR

VALOR(1937, Brit.); THEY DRIVE BY NIGHT(1940); WOMEN IN BONDAGE(1943); PRACTICALLY YOURS(1944)
Randee Lynn
SATAN'S SADISTS(1969)
Richard Lynn
Misc. Talkies
SUPERBUG, THE WILD ONE(1977)
Misc. Silents
HER GREAT HOUR(1916)
Rita Lynn
MR. HEX(1946); CODE OF THE WEST(1947); EAST SIDE, WEST SIDE(1949); JOE DAKOTA(1957); WAYWARD GIRL, THE(1957); CAST A LONG SHADOW(1959); MADIGAN(1968)
Robert Lynn
MIRACLE ON 34TH STREET, THE(1947); BAREFOOT MAILMAN, THE(1951); TEXAS LADY(1955); SHOOT-OUT AT MEDICINE BEND(1957); RETURN OF DRACULA, THE(1958); INFORMATION RECEIVED(1962, Brit.), d; INVITATION TO MURDER(1962, Brit.), d; POSTMAN'S KNOCK(1962, Brit.), d; TWO LETTER ALIBI(1962), d; BLAZE OF GLORY(1963, Brit.), d; DR. CRIPPEN(1963, Brit.), d; TAKE ME OVER(1963, Brit.), d; CODE 7, VICTIM 5(1964, Brit.), d; CHANGE PARTNERS(1965, Brit.), d; COAST OF SKELETONS(1965, Brit.), d; MOZAMBIQUE(1966, Brit.), d; EVE(1968, Brit./Span.), d; SANDY THE SEAL(1969, Brit.), d; RAILWAY CHILDREN, THE(1971, Brit.), p
Misc. Talkies
KILLER'S CARNIVAL(1965), d
Robert Lynn, Sr.
GOOD MORNING, MISS DOVE(1955)
Ron Lynn
PICTURES(1982, New Zealand)
Ross Lynn
UNASHAMED(1938)
Sandra Lynn
MOVIE STAR, AMERICAN STYLE, OR, LSD I HATE YOU!(1966); ON HER BED OF ROSES(1966)
Sharon Lynn
FOX MOVIETONE FOLLIES(1929); GIVE AND TARE(1929); SPEAKEASY(1929); SUNNY SIDE UP(1929); CRAZY THAT WAY(1930); HAPPY DAYS(1930); LET'S GO PLACES(1930); LIGHTNIN'(1930); MAN TROUBLE(1930); UP THE RIVER(1930); WILD COMPANY(1930); MEN ON CALL(1931); TOO MANY COOKS(1931); BIG BROADCAST, THE(1932); DISCARDED LOVERS(1932); SO IT'S SUNDAY(1932); BIG EXECUTIVE(1933)
Silents
AFLAME IN THE SKY(1927); CLANCY'S KOSHER WEDDING(1927); COWARD, THE(1927); JAKE THE PLUMBER(1927); NONE BUT THE BRAVE(1928); RED WINE(1928)
Misc. Silents
CHEROKEE KID, THE(1927); TOM'S GANG(1927); SON OF THE GOLDEN WEST(1928); ONE WOMAN IDEA, THE(1929)
Sherry Lynn
SHEPHERD OF THE HILLS, THE(1964); I WANNA HOLD YOUR HAND(1978)
Stella Lynn
LEFT HAND OF GOD, THE(1955); LOVE IS A MANY-SPLENDORED THING(1955); JET ATTACK(1958)
Sydney Lynn
ATLANTIC(1929 Brit.); PLUNDER(1931, Brit.)
Ted Lynn
DEATHMASTER, THE(1972)
Tracy Lynn
DEVIL'S SLEEP, THE(1951)
Vera Lynn
WE'LL MEET AGAIN(1942, Brit.); RHYTHM SERENADE(1943, Brit.); YOU CAN'T DO WITHOUT LOVE(1946, Brit.)
Vicky Lynn
JUMP(1971)
Victoria Lynn
TWO TICKETS TO BROADWAY(1951)
William Lynn
HARVEY(1950); KATIE DID IT(1951); MR. BELVEDERE RINGS THE BELL(1951)
Winifred Lynn
FLORIAN(1940)
Lynn Proctor Trio
MIRACLE IN HARLEM(1948)
Lynn Royce and Vanya
SEVEN DAYS LEAVE(1942)
Rick Lynn-Thomas
WINTER KILLS(1979)
Andrea Lynne
Silents
ALIEN, THE(1915)
Betty Lynne
GIRL IN THE CROWD, THE(1934, Brit.); FRENCH LEAVE(1937, Brit.); IT'S NOT CRICKET(1937, Brit.); PATRICIA GETS HER MAN(1937, Brit.); SATURDAY NIGHT REVUE(1937, Brit.); TAKE IT FROM ME(1937, Brit.); GLAMOUR GIRL(1938, Brit.); MR. SATAN(1938, Brit.); VIPER, THE(1938, Brit.); DEAD MEN ARE DANGEROUS(1939, Brit.); WANTED BY SCOTLAND YARD(1939, Brit.); THAT'S THE TICKET(1940, Brit.); GIRL IN THE PAINTING, THE(1948, Brit.); BAD LORD BYRON, THE(1949, Brit.); ONCE UPON A DREAM(1949, Brit.)
Carol Lynne
ASKING FOR TROUBLE(1942, Brit.)
Donna Lynne
PRIVATE LIVES OF ADAM AND EVE, THE(1961)
Elisabeth Lynne
GIRO CITY(1982, Brit.)
Ethel Lynne
Silents
AMAZING WIFE, THE(1919)
Misc. Silents
BIGGEST SHOW ON EARTH, THE(1918)

Eve Lynne
FLAME OF THE BARBARY COAST(1945)
Gillian Lynne
MASTER OF BALLANTRAE, THE(1953, U.S./Brit.); LAST MAN TO HANG, THE(1956, Brit.); MAKE MINE A MILLION(1965, Brit.); SEASIDE SWINGERS(1965, Brit.), ch; SWINGER'S PARADISE(1965, Brit.), ch; THREE HATS FOR LISA(1965, Brit.), ch; TWO HUNDRED MOTELS(1971, Brit.), ch; MAN OF LA MANCHA(1972), ch; MR. QUILP(1975, Brit.), ch; YENTL(1983), ch
Jerrie Lynne
YANKEE DOODLE DANDY(1942)
Juli Lynne
NIGHT IN PARADISE, A(1946)
Randee Lynne
GAY DECEIVERS, THE(1969)
Sharon Lynne
ENTER MADAME(1935); GO INTO YOUR DANCE(1935); WAY OUT WEST(1937); THISTLEDOWN(1938, Brit.); REG'LAR FELLERS(1941); WEST POINT WIDOW(1941)
Doug Lynner
1984
KILLERS, THE(1984), m
Francis D. Lynon
GREAT PROFILE, THE(1940), ed
Eve Lyntett
HAIL AND FAREWELL(1936, Brit.)
Chris Lynton
Silents
KISS FOR SUSIE, A(1917)
Christian Lynton
Silents
PUPPET CROWN, THE(1915)
Maggie Lynton
WHEN DINOSAURS RULED THE EARTH(1971, Brit.)
Mayme Lynton
Silents
SEVEN SISTERS, THE(1915)
Mayne Lynton
IN THE WAKE OF THE BOUNTY(1933, Aus.); MAN WHO KNEW TOO MUCH, THE(1956)
Ardda Lynwood
WHO KILLED "DOC" ROBBIN?(1948)
Burt Lynwood
FIRETRAP, THE(1935), d; MOTIVE FOR REVENGE(1935), d; SHADOWS OF THE ORIENT(1937), d
Burt P. Lynwood
RECKLESS ROADS(1935), d
Agnes Lyon
DIFFERENT STORY, A(1978), cos; MANITOU, THE(1978), cos
Alice Lyon
HORROR OF PARTY BEACH, THE(1964)
Barbara Lyon
FAMILY AFFAIR(1954, Brit.); LYONS IN PARIS, THE(1955, Brit.)
Ben Lyon
FLYING MARINE, THE(1929); ALIAS FRENCH GERTIE(1930); HELL'S AN-GELS(1930); LUMMOX(1930); WHAT MEN WANT(1930); ALOHA(1931); BOUGHT(1931); COMPROMISED(1931); HER MAJESTY LOVE(1931); HOT HEI-RESS(1931); INDISCREET(1931); MISBEHAVING LADIES(1931); MY PAST(1931); NIGHT NURSE(1931); SOLDIER'S PLAYTHING, A(1931); WEST OF THE ROCK-IES(1931); BY WHOSE HAND?(1932); CROOKED CIRCLE(1932); HAT CHECK GIRL(1932); LADY WITH A PAST(1932); WEEK-ENDS ONLY(1932); GIRL MIS-SING(1933); I COVER THE WATERFRONT(1933); I SPY(1933, Brit.); CRIMSON ROMANCE(1934); WOMEN IN HIS LIFE, THE(1934); FRISCO WATERFRONT(1935); LIGHTNING STRIKES TWICE(1935); TOGETHER WE LIVE(1935); DANCING FEET(1936); DOWN TO THE SEA(1936); NAVY WIFE(1936); HE LOVED AN AC-TRESS(1938, Brit.); CONFIDENTIAL LADY(1939, Brit.); TREACHERY ON THE HIGH SEAS(1939, Brit.); WHO IS GUILTY?(1940, Brit.); HI, GANG!(1941, Brit.), a, w; THIS WAS PARIS(1942, Brit.); DARK TOWER, THE(1943, Brit.); FAMILY AFFAIR(1954, Brit.); LYONS IN PARIS, THE(1955, Brit.)
Misc. Talkies
CALL OF THE ROCKIES(1931); BIG TIMER(1932); BEAUTY'S DAUGHTER(1935)
Silents
OPEN YOUR EYES(1919); HEART OF MARYLAND, THE(1921); PAINTED PEO-PLE(1924); SO BIG(1924); NECESSARY EVIL, THE(1925); NEW COMMANDMENT, THE(1925); PACE THAT THRILLS, THE(1925); BLUEBEARD'S SEVEN WIVES(1926); RECKLESS LADY, THE(1926); TENDER HOUR, THE(1927); AIR LEGION, THE(1929)
Misc. Silents
TRANSGRESSOR, THE(1918); LILY OF THE DUST(1924); WAGES OF VIR-TUE(1924); WHITE MOTH, THE(1924); ONE WAY STREET(1925); WINDS OF CHANCE(1925); GREAT DECEPTION, THE(1926); PRINCE OF TEMPTERS, THE(1926); SAVAGE, THE(1926); DANCE MAGIC(1927); FOR THE LOVE OF MI-KE(1927); HIGH HAT(1927); PERFECT SAP, THE(1927); QUITTER, THE(1929); CALL OF THE ROCKIES(1931)
Betty Lyon
INTERVAL(1973, Mex./U.S.)
Chester Lyon
BOMBSHELL(1933), ph
Cliff Lyon
DONOVAN'S REEF(1963)
Dana Lyon
HOUSE ON TELEGRAPH HILL(1951), w; MACABRE(1958), w
David Lyon
1984
PLOUGHMAN'S LUNCH, THE(1984, Brit.)
Earle Lyon
FLYING SAUCER, THE(1950); SILENT RAIDERS(1954), a, p; LONESOME TRAIL, THE(1955), a, p; SILVER STAR, THE(1955), a, p; STAGECOACH TO FURY(1956), p, w; TWO-GUN LADY(1956); QUIET GUN, THE(1957), p; RAWHIDE TRAIL, THE(1958), p; REBEL SET, THE(1959), p; CYBORG 2087(1966), p; DESTINATION INNER SPACE(1966), p; DIMENSION 5(1966), p; CASTLE OF EVIL(1967), p; DESTRUC-TORS, THE(1968), p; MONEY JUNGLE, THE(1968), p; PANIC IN THE CITY(1968), p; GIRL WHO KNEW TOO MUCH, THE(1969), p

1984
INVISIBLE STRANGLER(1984), p, w
Francis Lyon
HYPNOTIZED(1933), ed; I STAND CONDEMNED(1936, Brit.), ed; REM-BRANDT(1936, Brit.), ed; THINGS TO COME(1936, Brit.), ed; DAKOTA LIL(1950), ed
Francis D. Lyon
INTERMEZZO: A LOVE STORY(1939), ed; FOUR SONS(1940), ed; I WAS AN ADVENTURESS(1940), ed; ADAM HAD FOUR SONS(1941), ed; MEN IN HER LIFE, THE(1941), ed; RUTHLESS(1948), ed; BASKETBALL FIX(1951), ed; BRIDE OF THE GORILLA(1951), ed; FIRST LEGION, THE(1951), ed; HE RAN ALL THE WAY(1951), ed; SWORD OF MONTE CRISTO, THE(1951), ed; BUSHWHACKERS, THE(1952), ed; RED PLANET MARS(1952), ed; CRAZYLEGS, ALL AMERICAN(1953), d; DIAMOND QUEEN, THE(1953), ed; BOB MATHIAS STORY, THE(1954), d; CULT OF THE COBRA(1955), d; GREAT LOCOMOTIVE CHASE, THE(1956), d; BAILOUT AT 43,000(1957), d; GUNSIGHT RIDGE(1957), d; OKLAHOMAN, THE(1957), d; ES-CORT WEST(1959), d; TOMBOY AND THE CHAMP(1961), d; YOUNG AND THE BRAVE, THE(1963), d; DESTINATION INNER SPACE(1966), d; CASTLE OF EVIL(1967), d; DESTRUCTORS, THE(1968), d; MONEY JUNGLE, THE(1968), d; GIRL WHO KNEW TOO MUCH, THE(1969), d; TIGER BY THE TAIL(1970), p
Frank Lyon
BIG POND, THE(1930); PARIS AFTER DARK(1943)
Frank A. Lyon
Silents
JUST A SONG AT TWILIGHT(1922)
Misc. Silents
MAGIC SKIN, THE(1915)
Joel Lyon
DEATH FROM A DISTANCE(1936)
Lisa Lyon
1984
THREE CROWNS OF THE SAILOR(1984, Fr.)
Nelson Lyon
Misc. Talkies
TELEPHONE BOOK, THE(1971), d
Priscilla Lyon
DRAEGERMAN COURAGE(1937); BELOVED BRAT(1938); LADY IN THE DARK(1944); STRANGE HOLIDAY(1945)
Rachel Lyon
TELL ME A RIDDLE(1980), p
Richard Lyon
SECRET COMMAND(1944); UNSEEN, THE(1945); ANNA AND THE KING OF SIAM(1946); GREEN YEARS, THE(1947); TENDER YEARS, THE(1947); SMART WOMAN(1948); BOY WITH THE GREEN HAIR, THE(1949); GREAT LOVER, THE(1949); FAMILY AFFAIR(1954, Brit.); LYONS IN PARIS, THE(1955, Brit.); HEADLESS GHOST, THE(1959, Brit.)
Sue Lyon
LOLITA(1962); NIGHT OF THE IGUANA, THE(1964); SEVEN WOMEN(1966); FLIM-FLAM MAN, THE(1967); TONY ROME(1967); FOUR RODE OUT(1969, US/Span.); EVEL KNIEVEL(1971); CRASH(1977); END OF THE WORLD(1977); TO-WING(1978); ALLIGATOR(1980)
1984
INVISIBLE STRANGLER(1984)
Misc. Talkies
TO LOVE, PERHAPS TO DIE(1975)
Theresa Lyon
STRANGLER OF THE SWAMP(1945); LATE GEORGE APLEY, THE(1947); APART-MENT FOR PEGGY(1948); SNAKE PIT, THE(1948)
Therese Lyon
LETTER FOR EVIE, A(1945); LOVE, HONOR AND GOODBYE(1945); KILLERS, THE(1946); ALL MY SONS(1948); HALF ANGEL(1951); MUSIC MAN, THE(1962)
Virginia Lyon
SPY WITH A COLD NOSE, THE(1966, Brit.)
Wanda Lyon
Misc. Silents
GREATEST LOVE OF ALL, THE(1925)
William Lyon
COWBOY STAR, THE(1936), ed; CODE OF THE RANGE(1937), ed; FIND THE WITNESS(1937), ed; I'LL TAKE ROMANCE(1937), ed; OLD WYOMING TRAIL, THE(1937), ed; TRAPPED(1937), ed; TWO-FISTED SHERIFF(1937), ed; TWO GUN LAW(1937), ed; CALL OF THE ROCKIES(1938), ed; OUTLAWS OF THE PRAI-RIE(1938), ed; SOUTH OF ARIZONA(1938), ed; WEST OF CHEYENNE(1938), ed; MAN FROM SUNDOWN, THE(1939), ed; MAN THEY COULD NOT HANG, THE(1939), ed; NORTH OF THE YUKON(1939), ed; RIDERS OF BLACK RI-VER(1939), ed; RIO GRANDE(1939), ed; SPOILERS OF THE RANGE(1939), ed; THUNDERING WEST, THE(1939), ed; WESTERN CARAVANS(1939), ed; ARIZO-NA(1940), ed; MY SON IS GUILTY(1940), ed; SCANDAL SHEET(1940), ed; TOO MANY HUSBANDS(1940), ed; NAVAL ACADEMY(1941), ed; PHANTOM SUBMA-RINE, THE(1941), ed; SWEETHEART OF THE CAMPUS(1941), ed; TEXAS(1941), ed; HARVARD, HERE I COME(1942), ed; LAWLESS PLAINSMEN(1942), ed; SABOTAGE SQUAD(1942), ed; SUBMARINE RAIDER(1942), ed; TRAMP, TRAMP, TRAMP(1942), ed; YOU WERE NEVER LOVELIER(1942), ed; JOLSON STORY, THE(1946), ed; MR. DISTRICT ATTORNEY(1946), ed; LONE WOLF IN MEXICO, THE(1947), ed; TO THE ENDS OF THE EARTH(1948), ed; JOLSON SINGS AGAIN(1949), ed; WALKING HILLS, THE(1949), ed; CARGO TO CAPETOWN(1950), ed; FULLER BRUSH GIRL, THE(1950), ed; NO SAD SONGS FOR ME(1950), ed; SATURDAY'S HERO(1951), ed; TEN TALL MEN(1951), ed; DEATH OF A SALESMAN(1951), ed; MEMBER OF THE WEDDING, THE(1952), ed; THIEF OF DAMASCUS(1952), ed; FROM HERE TO ETERNITY(1953), ed; CAINE MUTINY, THE(1954), ed; LONG GRAY LINE, THE(1955), ed; MAN FROM LARAMIE, THE(1955), ed; GARMENT JUNGLE, THE(1957), ed; HARD MAN, THE(1957), ed; DEAD HEAT ON A MERRY-GO-ROUND(1966), ed; SECRET OF SANTA VITTORIA, THE(1969), ed
William A. Lyon
HAPPY TIME, THE(1952), ed; FORT TI(1953), ed; FORTY-NINTH MAN, THE(1953), ed; SLAVES OF BABYLON(1953), ed; HUMAN DESIRE(1954), ed; PICNIC(1955), ed; NIGHTFALL(1956), ed; STORM CENTER(1956), ed; SHADOW ON THE WINDOW, THE(1957), ed; COWBOY(1958), ed; ME AND THE COLONEL(1958), ed; GID-GET(1959), ed; THEY CAME TO CORDURA(1959), ed; SONG WITHOUT END(1960), ed; GIDGET GOES HAWAIIAN(1961), ed; RAISIN IN THE SUN, A(1961), ed; SAIL A CROOKED SHIP(1961), ed; DIAMOND HEAD(1962), ed; FIVE FINGER EXER-CISE(1962), ed; GIDGET GOES TO ROME(1963), ed; MAN FROM THE DINERS'

CLUB, THE(1963), ed; YOUNG LOVERS, THE(1964), ed; MAJOR DUNDEE(1965), ed; LORD LOVE A DUCK(1966), ed; R.P.M.(1970), ed

William H. Lyon
BAREFOOT IN THE PARK(1967), ed

William Lyon-Brown
DAVID COPPERFIELD(1970, Brit.)

Brand Lyonell
MISSION BLOODY MARY(1967, Fr./Ital./Span.)

Emma Lyonnel
LADIES OF THE PARK(1964, Fr.)

Louis Lyonnet
LIVE FOR LIFE(1967, Fr./Ital.)

A. Neil Lyons
RETURN OF THE RAT, THE(1929, Brit.), w

Arthur Lyons
Silents
LONDON PRIDE(1920, Brit.), w

Arthur S. Lyons
RUTHLESS(1948), p

Chester A. Lyons
SEQUOIA(1934), ph
Silents
PRIDE OF PALOMAR, THE(1922), ph; BACHELOR'S PARADISE(1928), ph

Chester Lyons
LUCKY STAR(1929), ph; THEY HAD TO SEE PARIS(1929), ph; LIGHTNIN'(1930), ph; LILIOM(1930), ph; SONG O' MY HEART(1930), ph; YOUNG AS YOU FEEL(1931), ph; MAD LOVE(1935), ph; THREE LIVE GHOSTS(1935), ph; UNDER THE PAMPAS MOON(1935), ph; RAMONA(1936), ph; ROBIN HOOD OF EL DORADO(1936), ph; WHITE HUNTER(1936), ph
Silents
FAMILY SKELETON, THE(1918), ph; ALARM CLOCK ANDY(1920), ph; NINE-TEEN AND PHYLLIS(1920), ph; OLD FASHIONED BOY, AN(1920), ph; PARIS GREEN(1920), ph; RED HOT DOLLARS(1920), ph; SISTERS(1922), ph; VALLEY OF SILENT MEN, THE(1922), ph; JUST LIKE A WOMAN(1923), ph; NTH COMMAND-MENT, THE(1923), ph; FIRST YEAR, THE(1926), ph; LOVE MAKES 'EM WILD(1927), ph; NIGHT LIFE(1927), ph; GATEWAY OF THE MOON, THE(1928), ph; NAMELESS MEN(1928), ph; FUGITIVES(1929), ph

Chester L. Lyons
Silents
PLAYING THE GAME(1918), ph

Chet Lyons
NOT DAMAGED(1930), ph; DECEPTION(1933), ph
Silents
MAN AND MAID(1925), ph; POWER OF THE PRESS, THE(1928), ph

Christian Lyons
WEDDING NIGHT(1970, Ireland)

Cliff Lyons
WEST OF THE ROCKIES(1929); CANYON HAWKS(1930); CANYON OF MISSING MEN, THE(1930); FIREBRAND JORDAN(1930); OKLAHOMA CYCLONE(1930); RED FORK RANGE(1931); DYNAMITE RANCH(1932); NIGHT RIDER, THE(1932); GUN JUSTICE(1934); DANTE'S INFERNO(1935); OUTLAWED GUNS(1935); TUMBLING TUMBLEWEEDS(1935); LAWLESS NINETIES, THE(1936); DESPERATE TRAILS(1939); DARK COMMAND, THE(1940); WAGON TRACKS WEST(1943); DAKOTA(1945); FRONTIER GAL(1945); SAN ANTONIO(1945); THREE GODFA-THERS, THE(1948); FIGHTING KENTUCKIAN, THE(1949); SHE WORE A YELLOW RIBBON(1949); MILKMAN, THE(1950); RIO GRANDE(1950); WAGONMASTER(1950); BEND OF THE RIVER(1952); SEARCHERS, THE(1956); WINGS OF EAGLES, THE(1957); BEN HUR(1959); HORSE SOLDIERS, THE(1959); YOUNG LAND, THE(1959); SERGEANT RUTLEDGE(1960); SPARTACUS(1960); TWO RODE TOGETHER(1961); MARCO THE MAGNIFICENT(1966, Ital./Fr./Yugo./Egypt/Afghanistan), d; TRAIN ROBBERS, THE(1973), stunts
Silents
WEST OF THE LAW(1926); LAW OF THE MOUNTED(1928); MANHATTAN COW-BOY(1928); OLD CODE, THE(1928); ARIZONA KID, THE(1929); FIGHTING TERROR, THE(1929); HEADIN' WESTWARD(1929); LAST ROUNDUP, THE(1929); OKLAHOMA SHERIFF, THE(1930)
Misc. Silents
FLASHING HOOFS(1928); MASTER OF THE RANGE(1928); RIDDLE TRAIL, THE(1928); GALLOPING LOVER, THE(1929); SADDLE KING, THE(1929); SHERIFF'S LASH, THE(1929), d; CALL OF THE DESERT(1930); RED GOLD(1930)

Colette Lyons
WABASH AVENUE(1950); REBEL SET, THE(1959)

Collette Lyons
DANCE, CHARLIE, DANCE(1937); HOTEL HAYWIRE(1937); 52ND STREET(1937); WOMAN AGAINST THE WORLD(1938); THREE TEXAS STEERS(1939); BLONDE RANSOM(1945); DOLLY SISTERS, THE(1945); FRISCO SAL(1945); BLONDIE'S BIG DEAL(1949); LONE WOLF AND HIS LADY, THE(1949); WHEN YOU'RE SMI-LING(1950); RETURN TO PEYTON PLACE(1961)

Donald Lyons
CHELSEA GIRLS, THE(1967)

Donna Lyons
SATAN'S MISTRESS(1982), makeup

Eddie Lyons
Silents
ONCE A PLUMBER(1920), a, d; SHOCKING NIGHT, A(1921), a, d; LODGE IN THE WILDERNESS, THE(1926)
Misc. Silents
MRS. PLUM'S PUDDING(1915); EVERYTHING BUT THE TRUTH(1920), a, d; FIXED BY GEORGE(1920), a, d; LA LA LUCILLE(1920), a, d

Edgar Lyons
FIGHTING TROOPER, THE(1935), ph; NORTHERN FRONTIER(1935), ph; RACING LUCK(1935), ph; SINGING COWBOY, THE(1936), ph; BIG SHOW, THE(1937), ph; OLD CORRAL, THE(1937), ph; DEATH VALLEY OUTLAWS(1941), ph; SHADOWS ON THE SAGE(1942), ph; EL PASO KID, THE(1946), ph; STAGECOACH TO DEN-VER(1946), ph
Silents
WESTERN DEMON, A(1922), ph; RECKLESS SEX, THE(1925), ph

Frances Lyons
COLLEGE COQUETTE, THE(1929)

Francis Lyons
DAY-TIME WIFE(1939), ed; TWIN BEDS(1942), ed

Gene Lyons
YOUNG DON'T CRY, THE(1957); SYLVIA(1965); DADDY'S GONE A-HUN-TING(1969)

Genevieve Lyons
STORK TALK(1964, Brit.)

Glen Lyons
Silents
IS MONEY EVERYTHING?(1923), d&w
Misc. Silents
FIRST WOMAN, THE(1922), d

Graham Lyons
STOP THE WORLD–I WANT TO GET OFF(1966, Brit.)

H. Agar Lyons
DR. SIN FANG(1937, Brit.); CHINATOWN NIGHTS(1938, Brit.)
Silents
LITTLE LORD FAUNTLEROY(1914, Brit.); MAN THE ARMY MADE, A(1917, Brit.); KNAVE OF HEARTS, THE(1919, Brit.); MARY LATIMER, NUN(1920, Brit.); FRAIL-TY(1921, Brit.); PREHISTORIC MAN, THE(1924, Brit.); SLAVES OF DESTINY(1924, Brit.)
Misc. Silents
GRIP OF IRON, THE(1913, Brit.); CHANCE OF A LIFETIME, THE(1916, Brit.); WARRIOR STRAIN, THE(1919, Brit.); BRANDED SOUL, THE(1920, Brit.); SEN YAN'S DEVOTION(1924, Brit.); THOROUGHBRED, THE(1928, Brit.)

Heather Lyons
ROCKETS IN THE DUNES(1960, Brit.)

Ivan Lyons
WHO IS KILLING THE GREAT CHEFS OF EUROPE?(1978, US/Ger.), w

Pvt. James Lyons, USAR
TOKYO FILE 212(1951)

Jarold Clifford Lyons
STORY OF ALEXANDER GRAHAM BELL, THE(1939)

Jeffrey Lyons
DEATHTRAP(1982)

John Lyons
DR. JEKYLL AND SISTER HYDE(1971, Brit.); SWEENEY 2(1978, Brit.)

Katherine Lyons
1984
NO SMALL AFFAIR(1984)

Leonard Lyons
DAISY KENYON(1947); JIGSAW(1949)

Linda Lee Lyons
ANOTHER MAN, ANOTHER CHANCE(1977 Fr/US); NORTH AVENUE IRREGU-LARS, THE(1979)

Lori Lyons
PHANTOM PLANET, THE(1961)

Lurline Lyons
Silents
RAMONA(1916)

Lynn Lyons
CLOAK AND DAGGER(1946)

Lynne Lyons
MONSIEUR BEAUCAIRE(1946)

Margaret Lyons
ROMEO AND JULIET(1966, Brit.)

Martin Lyons
WEDDING NIGHT(1970, Ireland)

Nan Lyons
WHO IS KILLING THE GREAT CHEFS OF EUROPE?(1978, US/Ger.), w

Paul Lyons
TAPS(1981)

Reginald Lyons
Silents
BLACK BEAUTY(1921), ph; SO THIS IS ARIZONA(1922), ph; JUST LIKE A WOM-AN(1923), ph; DESERT'S PRICE, THE(1926), ph; MAN FOUR-SQUARE, A(1926), ph; WAR HORSE, THE(1927), ph

Richard E. Lyons
FRONTIER GUN(1958), p; MIRACLE OF THE HILLS, THE(1959), p; SAD HORSE, THE(1959), p; RIDE THE HIGH COUNTRY(1962), p; MAIL ORDER BRIDE(1964), p; ROUNDERS, THE(1965), p; PLAINSMAN, THE(1966), p; DEATH OF A GUNFIGHT-ER(1969), p

Robert Lyons
BLACK OAK CONSPIRACY(1977); 10 TO MIDNIGHT(1983)

Robert F. Lyons
PENDULUM(1969); GETTING STRAIGHT(1970); DEALING: OR THE BERKELEY-TO-BOSTON FORTY-BRICK LOST-BAG BLUES(1971); SHOOT OUT(1971); TODD KILLINGS, THE(1971); DEATH WISH II(1982)

Ruth Lyons
NIGHT WORK(1930); LADIES OF THE BIG HOUSE(1932); OKAY AMERICA(1932)

Spencer Lyons
TELL THEM WILLIE BOY IS HERE(1969)

Steve Lyons
TOWN THAT DREADED SUNDOWN, THE(1977)

Stuart Lyons
SLIPPER AND THE ROSE, THE(1976, Brit.), p; MEETINGS WITH REMARKABLE MEN(1979, Brit.), p

Therese Lyons
MILKMAN, THE(1950)

Toby Lyons
1984
WHERE THE BOYS ARE '84(1984)

Tom Lyons
BURN(1970)

Tony Lyons
Misc. Talkies
SUPERSONIC SAUCER(1956, Brit.)

Virginia Lyons
Misc. Silents
MODERN DAUGHTERS(1927)
Warren Lyons
SOMETHING WILD(1961)
Alexander Lyovshin
Silents
BATTLESHIP POTEMKIN, THE(1925, USSR)
Carlos Lyra
PRETTY BUT WICKED(1965, Braz.), m
Dan Lyra
TORTURE DUNGEON(1970)
Agata Lys
1984
HOLY INNOCENTS, THE(1984, Span.)
Lya Lys
CLEAR ALL WIRES(1933); JIMMY AND SALLY(1933); LIVES OF A BENGAL
LANCER(1935); GREAT GAMBINI, THE(1937); MY DEAR MISS ALDRICH(1937);
YOUNG IN HEART, THE(1938); CONFESSIONS OF A NAZI SPY(1939); RETURN OF
DR. X, THE(1939); MURDER IN THE AIR(1940); L'AGE D'OR(1979, Fr.)
Anastasia Lysak
SIX P.M.(1946, USSR)
Piotr Lysak
1984
LOVE IN GERMANY, A(1984, Fr./Ger.)
Andreas Lysandrou
KITCHEN, THE(1961, Brit.)
Olga Lysenko
DIMKA(1964, USSR)
L. Lysenkova
MEET ME IN MOSCOW(1966, USSR), ed
Anna Lyslanskaya
LUCKY BRIDE, THE(1948, USSR)
Fotheringham Lysons
Silents
ELUSIVE PIMPERNEL, THE(1919, Brit.)
Sam Lysons
MADNESS OF THE HEART(1949, Brit.)
Mrs. Hudson Lyston
Silents
TRAFFIC IN SOULS(1913)
Tom Lytel
YEAR OF THE YAHOO(1971)
Andrew Lytele
NAME FOR EVIL, A(1970), w
Bert Lytell
ON TRIAL(1928); LONE WOLF'S DAUGHTER, THE(1929); BROTHERS(1930); LAST
OF THE LONE WOLF(1930); SINGLE SIN(1931); ALONG CAME LOVE(1937), d;
STAGE DOOR CANTEEN(1943)
Silents
EASY TO MAKE MONEY(1919); ALIAS JIMMY VALENTINE(1920); IDLE RICH,
THE(1921); MAN WHO, THE(1921); SHERLOCK BROWN(1922); KICK IN(1922);
RIGHT THAT FAILED, THE(1922); TO HAVE AND TO HOLD(1922); RUPERT OF
HENTZAU(1923); EVE'S LOVER(1925); LADY WINDERMERE'S FAN(1925); NEVER
THE TWAIN SHALL MEET(1925); GILDED BUTTERFLY, THE(1926); ALIAS THE
LONE WOLF(1927)
Misc. Silents
LONE WOLF, THE(1917); BOSTON BLACKIE'S LITTLE PAL(1918); EMPTY POCK-
ETS(1918); HITTING THE HIGH SPOTS(1918); NO MAN'S LAND(1918); TRAIL TO
YESTERDAY, THE(1918); UNEXPECTED PLACES(1918); BLACKIE'S REDEMP-
TION(1919); BLIND MAN'S EYES(1919); FAITH(1919); IT'S EASY TO MAKE MO-
NEY(1919); LION'S DEN, THE(1919); LOMBARDI, LTD.(1919);
ONE-THING-AT-A-TIME O'DAY(1919); SPENDER, THE(1919); MISLEADING LADY,
THE(1920); PRICE OF REDEMPTION, THE(1920); RIGHT OF WAY, THE(1920);
LADYFINGERS(1921); MESSAGE FROM MARS, A(1921); TRIP TO PARADISE,
A(1921); FACE BETWEEN, THE(1922); ETERNAL CITY, THE(1923); BORN
RICH(1924); SON OF THE SAHARA, A(1924); SANDRA(1924); BOOMERANG,
THE(1925); SHIP OF SOULS(1925); SPORTING LIFE(1925); STELLE OF THE ROYAL
MOUNTED(1925); LONE WOLF RETURNS, THE(1926); OBEY THE LAW(1926); THAT
MODEL FROM PARIS(1926); FIRST NIGHT, THE(1927); WOMEN'S WARES(1927)
Berty Lytell
Misc. Silents
MEANEST MAN IN THE WORLD, THE(1923)
Ed Lytell
Misc. Silents
SELL 'EM COWBOY(1924)
Marjorie Lytell
FINISHING SCHOOL(1934); JOURNAL OF A CRIME(1934); PARTY'S OVER,
THE(1934)
Pat Lytell
PUFNSTUF(1970)
Wilfred Lytell
Silents
OUR MRS. McCHESNEY(1918); KENTUCKIANS, THE(1921); KNOW YOUR
MEN(1921); WARRENS OF VIRGINIA, THE(1924); BLUEBEARD'S SEVEN WI-
VES(1926)
Misc. Silents
THUNDERBOLTS OF FATE(1919); FATAL HOUR, THE(1920); HARVEST MOON,
THE(1920); HELIOTROPE(1920); MAN WHO PAID, THE(1922); WOLF'S FANGS,
THE(1922); FAIR CHEAT, THE(1923); LEAVENWORTH CASE, THE(1923); TRAIL OF
THE LAW(1924)
William Lytell, Jr.
Misc. Silents
CONFLICT, THE(1916)
Natash Lytess
ONCE UPON A HONEYMOON(1942)
Natasha Lytess
COMRADE X(1940); HOUSE ON TELEGRAPH HILL(1951); ANYTHING CAN
HAPPEN(1952)

Nigel Lythgoe
APPLE, THE(1980 U.S./Ger.), ch
Ole Lytken
OPERATION CAMEL(1961, Den.), ph; ERIC SOYA'S "17"(1967, Den.), ph
Alev Lytle
TELL ME A RIDDLE(1980), w
Bill Lytle
UNDER THE RAINBOW(1981)
Katherine Lytle
LIKELY STORY, A(1947)
Steve Lytle
PACK, THE(1977)
T.E. Lytle
NO MAN'S LAND(1964), tech adv
Tom Lytle
NO MAN'S LAND(1964)
Humphrey Lyttelton
IT'S GREAT TO BE YOUNG(1956, Brit.)
Yngve Lyttkens
WOMAN OF DARKNESS(1968, Swed.), w
The Lyttle Sisters
ABBOTT AND COSTELLO IN HOLLYWOOD(1945)
Bart Lytton
TOMORROW WE LIVE(1942), w; HITLER'S MADMAN(1943), w; SPY TRAIN(1943),
w; BOWERY TO BROADWAY(1944), w; SING YOUR WAY HOME(1945), w
Debbie Lytton
VIGILANTE FORCE(1976); HOT LEAD AND COLD FEET(1978)
Doris Lytton
Silents
SINGLE MAN, THE(1919, Brit.); MUTINY(1925, Brit.)
Misc. Silents
BRASS BOTTLE, THE(1914, Brit.)
Edward Bulwer Lytton
Silents
EUGENE ARAM(1914, Brit.), w; EUGENE ARAM(1915), w
Herb Lytton
NAVY BOUND(1951); SPIRIT OF ST. LOUIS, THE(1957)
Herbert Lytton
CHAMPAGNE FOR CAESAR(1950); WHERE THE SIDEWALK ENDS(1950); GREAT-
EST SHOW ON EARTH, THE(1952); SOMETHING FOR THE BIRDS(1952); STEEL
TOWN(1952); BIG HEAT, THE(1953); MARSHAL OF CEDAR ROCK(1953); WAR OF
THE WORLDS, THE(1953); CITY STORY(1954); IT SHOULD HAPPEN TO YOU(1954);
JET PILOT(1957); PARTY GIRL(1958); GALLANT HOURS, THE(1960)
Herbert C. Lytton
GLASS WEB, THE(1953); I'LL CRY TOMORROW(1955); BEHIND THE HIGH
WALL(1956)
J. Courtland Lytton
LAST DAYS OF BOOT HILL(1947)
J.C. Lytton
OKLAHOMA BLUES(1948); PARTNERS OF THE SUNSET(1948)
L. Roger Lytton
Misc. Silents
PANTHEA(1917)
L. Rogers Lytton
Silents
BATTLE CRY OF PEACE, THE(1915)
Misc. Silents
WIN(K)SOME WIDOW, THE (1914); HEARTS AND THE HIGHWAY(1915); MAKING
OVER OF GEOFFREY MANNING, THE(1915); PRICE OF FAME, THE(1916); TARAN-
TULA, THE(1916); MESSAGE OF THE MOUSE, THE(1917); ON-THE-SQUARE GIRL,
THE(1917); FORBIDDEN CITY, THE(1918); LEST WE FORGET(1918); BELLE OF
NEW YORK, THE(1919); REGULAR GIRL, A(1919); THIN ICE(1919)
Lord Lytton
NIGHT COMES TOO SOON(1948, Brit.), w
Silents
ERNEST MALTRAVERS(1920, Brit.), w
Mrs. Henry Lytton
Silents
GAME OF LIFE, THE(1922, Brit.)
Phyllip Lytton
FLYING DOCTOR, THE(1936, Aus.)
Phyllis Lytton
Silents
NOT FOR SALE(1924, Brit.)
Robert Lytton
COSMIC MAN, THE(1959)
Roger Lytton
Silents
SILVER WINGS(1922)
Misc. Silents
HIGH SPEED(1920); LOVE OR MONEY(1920); ROAD TO ARCADY, THE(1922); WHO
ARE MY PARENTS?(1922)
Rogers Lytton
Silents
SAINTED DEVIL, A(1924)
Misc. Silents
HIS BROTHER'S KEEPER(1921)
L. Lyubashevsky
NEW HORIZONS(1939, USSR)
P. Lyubeshkin
MUMU(1961, USSR); HUNTING IN SIBERIA(1962, USSR); SHE-WOLF, THE(1963,
USSR); FATHER OF A SOLDIER(1966, USSR)
I. Lyubeznov
IDIOT, THE(1960, USSR)
V. Lyubimova
KATERINA IZMAILOVA(1969, USSR)
Ye. Lyutsau
WAR AND PEACE(1968, USSR)

Al Lyx
PRISONER OF THE VOLGA(1960, Fr./Ital.), w

M

Luisa Sanchez M
UNDER FIRE(1983)
Vincent M
VIGILANTE TERROR(1953), p
Walter M
RALLY 'ROUND THE FLAG, BOYS!(1958), set d; VON RYAN'S EXPRESS(1965), set d
M'Beti Tribe of French Equatorial Africa
MOGAMBO(1953)
Ambroise M'Bia
MYSTERIOUS ISLAND OF CAPTAIN NEMO, THE(1973, Fr./Ital./ Span./Cameroon)
Christophe M'Doulabia [Christophe Colomb]
MANDABI(1970, Fr./Senegal)
M'Viguier
Silents
NAPOLEON(1927, Fr.)
Dan Ma
CHRISTMAS STORY, A(1983)
James Ma
CALL HIM MR. SHATTER(1976, Hong Kong)
Tzi Ma
THEY ALL LAUGHED(1981)
Jose Ma Aguinaco
MERCENARY, THE(1970, Ital./Span.)
Jose MaAlarcon
ANTONY AND CLEOPATRA(1973, Brit.), art d
Peter Maalberg
CASE OF THE 44'S, THE(1964 Brit./Den.)
Sybille Maar
24-HOUR LOVER(1970, Ger.)
Audrey Maas
ALICE DOESN'T LIVE HERE ANYMORE(1975), p
Dick Maas
LIFT, THE(1983, Neth.), d&w
Ernest Maas
SHOCKING MISS PILGRIM, THE(1947), w
Frederica Maas
SHOCKING MISS PILGRIM, THE(1947), w
Gary Maas
PORKY'S(1982)
Peter Maas
VALACHI PAPERS, THE(1972, Ital./Fr.), w; SERPICO(1973), w; KING OF THE GYPSIES(1978), w
Sybil Maas
COUSIN, COUSINE(1976, Fr.)
Reinet Maasdorf
AFTER YOU, COMRADE(1967, S. Afr.)
Ise Maassen
NOT RECONCILED, OR "ONLY VIOLENCE HELPS WHERE IT RULES"(1969, Ger.)
Lincoln Maazel
MARTIN(1979)
Lorin Maazel
1984
BIZET'S CARMEN(1984, Fr./Ital.), md
Carlos Mabarek
TIME AND THE TOUCH, THE(1962), m
Byron Mabe
1,000 SHAPES OF A FEMALE(1963); SMELL OF HONEY, A SWALLOW OF BRINE! A(1966), ed; SHE FREAK(1967), d, ed; DOBERMAN GANG, THE(1972); I HATE MY BODY(1975, Span./Switz.)
Alvis Maben
BLACKOUT(1954, Brit.)
Alvys Maben
UNHOLY FOUR, THE(1954, Brit.)
Mary Mabery
Silents
CAPTAIN CARELESS(1928); DOG LAW(1928)
Misc. Silents
LIGHTING SPEED(1928)
Judith Mabey
PARALLELS(1980, Can.)
Mabille
KAMIKAZE '89(1983, Ger.), set d
Jackie "Moms" Mabley
Misc. Talkies
BIG TIMERS(1947); BOARDING HOUSE BLUES(1948)
Moms Mabley
AMAZING GRACE(1974)
Misc. Talkies
KILLER DILLER(1948)
Ernst Maboe
ONE APRIL 2000(1952, Aust.), w
Greg Mabrey
ROOMMATES, THE(1973); OTHER SIDE OF THE MOUNTAIN, THE(1975)
Anna Mabry
VIEW FROM POMPEY'S HEAD, THE(1955)
Moss Mabry
WAY WE WERE, THE(1973), cos; SOUTH SEA WOMAN(1953), cos; THUNDER OVER THE PLAINS(1953), cos; DIAL M FOR MURDER(1954), cos; I DIED A THOUSAND TIMES(1955), cos; ILLEGAL(1955), cos; MISTER ROBERTS(1955), cos; REBEL WITHOUT A CAUSE(1955), cos; SEA CHASE, THE(1955), cos; TALL MAN RIDING(1955), cos; TARGET ZERO(1955), cos; BAD SEED, THE(1956), cos; CRY IN THE NIGHT, A(1956), cos; GIANT(1956), cos; GIRL HE LEFT BEHIND, THE(1956), cos; HELL ON FRISCO BAY(1956), cos; SANTIAGO(1956), cos; TOWARD THE UN-

KNOWN(1956), cos; STAGE STRUCK(1958), cos; SUBTERRANEANS, THE(1960), cos; MANCHURIAN CANDIDATE, THE(1962), cos; MUTINY ON THE BOUNTY(1962), cos; CEREMONY, THE(1963, U.S./Span.), cos; MOVE OVER, DARLING(1963), cos; FATE IS THE HUNTER(1964), cos; SHOCK TREATMENT(1964), cos; WHAT A WAY TO GO(1964), cos; DEAR BRIGETTE(1965), cos; HOW TO MURDER YOUR WIFE(1965), cos; MORITURI(1965), cos; REWARD, THE(1965), cos; MURDERERS' ROW(1966), cos; SILENCERS, THE(1966), cos; THREE ON A COUCH(1966), cos; WAY...WAY OUT(1966), cos; GUIDE FOR THE MARRIED MAN, A(1967), cos; TONY ROME(1967), cos; DETECTIVE, THE(1968), cos; HOW TO SAVE A MARRIAGE–AND RUIN YOUR LIFE(1968), cos; LADY IN CEMENT(1968), cos; SOL MADRID(1968), cos; WHERE ANGELS GO...TROUBLE FOLLOWS(1968), cos; WRECKING CREW, THE(1968), cos; BOB AND CAROL AND TED AND ALICE(1969), cos; GREAT BANK ROBBERY, THE(1969), cos; MAD ROOM, THE(1969), cos; MALTESE BIPPY, THE(1969), cos; ALEX IN WONDERLAND(1970); CHRISTINE JORGENSEN STORY, THE(1970), cos; HOW DO I LOVE THEE?(1970), cos; R.P.M.(1970), cos; DOCTORS' WIVES(1971), cos; LOVE MACHINE, THE,(1971), cos; MEPHISTO WALTZ, THE(1971), cos; BUTTERFLIES ARE FREE(1972), cos; PORTNOY'S COMPLAINT(1972), cos; STAND UP AND BE COUNTED(1972), cos; TRIAL OF BILLY JACK, THE(1974), cos; ONCE IS NOT ENOUGH(1975), cos; FROM NOON TO THREE(1976), cos; KING KONG(1976), cos; SHOOTIST, THE(1976), cos; CASEY'S SHADOW(1978), cos; SUNBURN(1979), cos; TOUCHED BY LOVE(1980), cos; CONTINENTAL DIVIDE(1981), cos; TOY, THE(1982), cos
Kaoru Mabuchi
FRANKENSTEIN CONQUERS THE WORLD(1964, Jap./US), w; KING KONG ESCAPES(1968, Jap.), w; DESTROY ALL MONSTERS(1969, Jap.), w; WAR OF THE GARGANTUAS, THE(1970, Jap.), w; GODZILLA VERSUS THE SMOG MONSTER(1972, Jap.), w
Romeo Mabutol
TWILIGHT PEOPLE(1972, Phil.)
Jenny Mac
WHISTLING IN THE DARK(1941); TISH(1942)
Jimmy Mac
1984
FOREVER YOUNG(1984, Brit.)
Johnny Mac
1984
COMFORT AND JOY(1984, Brit.)
Riley Mac
COOL WORLD, THE(1963)
John Mac Burnie
BELLS OF CORONADO(1950), ph
Mac Niles and the Calypsonians
CALYPSO HEAT WAVE(1957)
Pierre Mac Orlan [Pierre Dumarchais]
PORT OF SHADOWS(1938, Fr.), w
George Mac Quarrie
DESIRE(1936)
Earl Mac Rauch
1984
ADVENTURES OF BUCKAROO BANZAI: ACROSS THE 8TH DIMENSION, THE(1984), w
E. M. Mac-Manigal
COURAGEOUS AVENGER, THE(1935), ph
Jack Macadam
1984
LOUISIANE(1984, Fr./Can.), prod d
Annabelle Macadams
IT'S ALIVE(1968)
Anne MacAdams
COMMON LAW WIFE(1963); UNDER AGE(1964); HIGH YELLOW(1965); STREET IS MY BEAT, THE(1966); BULLET FOR PRETTY BOY, A(1970)
Jack MacAdams
ECHOES OF A SUMMER(1976), art d
Rhea MacAdams
DON'T LOOK IN THE BASEMENT(1973)
Amos Macadi
PILLAR OF FIRE, THE(1963, Israel)
Florence MacAfee
MAN CALLED PETER, THE(1955); JEANNE EAGELS(1957)
Paddy Macafee
1984
RENO AND THE DOC(1984, Can.)
Dorothy Macaill
Misc. Silents
WHIP, THE(1928)
Jiri Macak
END OF AUGUST AT THE HOTEL OZONE, THE(1967, Czech.), ph; VISITORS FROM THE GALAXY(1981, Yugo.), ph
David Macalister
COUNTDOWN TO DANGER(1967, Brit.)
Patrick MacAllister
IT'S ALIVE(1974)
Phillip MacAllister
GREATEST, THE(1977, U.S./Brit.)
A.V. Macaluso
GREAT DAWN, THE(1947, Ital.), titles
Armando Macaluso
TO LIVE IN PEACE(1947, Ital.), titles; LADY IS FICKLE, THE(1948, Ital.), titles
Armando V. Macaluso
KING'S JESTER, THE(1947, Ital.), titles
Ray MacAnally
PROFESSOR TIM(1957, Ireland); OUTSIDER, THE(1980)
John MacAndrews
Silents
FAR FROM THE MADDING CROWD(1915, Brit.); MOLLY BAWN(1916, Brit.); PLACE IN THE SUN, A(1916, Brit.); ONCE ABOARD THE LUGGER(1920, Brit.)
Misc. Silents
WHITE HOPE, THE(1915, Brit.)

Jac MacAnelly
1984
REPO MAN(1984)
Thomas MacAnna
ULYSSES(1967, U.S./Brit.)
George Burr MacAnnan
SUPERNATURAL(1933); WE LIVE AGAIN(1934); SHERLOCK HOLMES AND THE SECRET WEAPON(1942)
Donald Macardle
CARNIVAL(1931, Brit.), w; KING'S CUP, THE(1933, Brit.), d; THURSDAY'S CHILD(1943, Brit.), w
Misc. Silents
WEE MACGREGOR'S SWEETHEART, THE(1922, Brit.)
Dorothy Macardle
UNINVITED, THE(1944), w
Macari and His Dutch Accordion Serenaders
MUSIC HALL PARADE(1939, Brit.)
Macari and His Dutch Serenaders
PENNY POOL, THE(1937, Brit.)
Macari's Dutch Serenaders
MUSIC HALL(1934, Brit.)
Nina Macarova
REDS(1981)
Alex MacArthur
THEY ALL LAUGHED(1981)
Charles MacArthur
GIRL SAID NO, THE(1930), w; PAID(1930), w; WAY FOR A SAILOR(1930), w; FRONT PAGE, THE(1931), w; NEW ADVENTURES OF GET-RICH-QUICK WALLINGFORD, THE(1931), w; SIN OF MADELON CLAUDET, THE(1931), w; UNHOLY GARDEN, THE(1931), w; RASPUTIN AND THE EMPRESS(1932), w; CRIME WITHOUT PASSION(1934), a, p,d&w; TWENTIETH CENTURY(1934), w; BARBARY COAST(1935), w; SCOUNDREL, THE(1935), p,d&w; ONCE IN A BLUE MOON(1936), p,d&w; SOAK THE RICH(1936), p,d&w; GONE WITH THE WIND(1939), w; GUNGA DIN(1939), w; WUTHERING HEIGHTS(1939), w; HIS GIRL FRIDAY(1940), w; I TAKE THIS WOMAN(1940), w; SENATOR WAS INDISCREET, THE(1947), w; LULU BELLE(1948), w; PERFECT STRANGERS(1950), w; JUMBO(1962), w; FRONT PAGE, THE(1974), w
Courtney MacArthur
WEDDING, A(1978)
Cynthia Macarthur
NEW YEAR'S EVIL(1980)
Douglas MacArthur
EXTRAORDINARY SEAMAN, THE(1969)
Harold H. MacArthur
PICTURE BRIDES(1934), art d; MURDER IN THE BLUE ROOM(1944), art d; OLD TEXAS TRAIL, THE(1944), art d; RECKLESS AGE(1944), art d; SOUTH OF DIXIE(1944), art d; DALTONS RIDE AGAIN, THE(1945), art d; NAUGHTY NINETIES, THE(1945), art d; PENTHOUSE RHYTHM(1945), art d; SLIGHTLY SCANDALOUS(1946), art d
Harold MacArthur
HI, BUDDY(1943), art d; MR. BIG(1943), art d; SHERLOCK HOLMES FACES DEATH(1943), art d; DANGER WOMAN(1946), art d; DARK HORSE, THE(1946), art d; HER ADVENTUROUS NIGHT(1946), art d; KEEPER OF THE BEES(1947), art d; KEY WITNESS(1947), art d; LAST ROUND-UP, THE(1947), art d; MILLERSON CASE, THE(1947), art d; LOADED PISTOLS(1948), art d; STRAWBERRY ROAN, THE(1948), art d; CRIME DOCTOR'S DIARY, THE(1949), art d; DEVIL'S HENCHMEN, THE(1949), art d; LAW OF THE BARBARY COAST(1949), art d; RIDERS IN THE SKY(1949), art d; RIDERS OF THE WHISTLING PINES(1949), art d; RIM OF THE CANYON(1949), art d; RUSTY'S BIRTHDAY(1949), art d; SONS OF NEW MEXICO(1949), art d; DAVID HARDING, COUNTERSPY(1950), art d; ROGUES OF SHERWOOD FOREST(1950), art d; WHEN YOU'RE SMILING(1950), art d; LORNA DOONE(1951), art d; MASK OF THE AVENGER(1951), art d; TEXAS RANGERS, THE(1951), art d
James MacArthur
SPOILERS, THE(1955), w; YOUNG STRANGER, THE(1957); LIGHT IN THE FOREST, THE(1958); THIRD MAN ON THE MOUNTAIN(1959); KIDNAPPED(1960); SWISS FAMILY ROBINSON(1960); INTERNS, THE(1962); CRY OF BATTLE(1963); SPENCER'S MOUNTAIN(1963); BATTLE OF THE BULGE(1965); BEDFORD INCIDENT, THE(1965, Brit.); TRUTH ABOUT SPRING, THE(1965, Brit.); RIDE BEYOND VENGEANCE(1966); LOVE-INS, THE(1967); HANG'EM HIGH(1968); ANGRY BREED, THE(1969)
Silents
SPOILERS, THE(1914), w
Jane MacArthur
SOMETHING WILD(1961)
Roy MacArthur
LIQUID SKY(1982)
Thalia C. MacArthur
1984
UNFAITHFULLY YOURS(1984), cos
Carol Macartney
GREGORY'S GIRL(1982, Brit.)
Sydney Macartney
PARTY PARTY(1983, Brit.), ph
Xavier Saint Macary
HERBIE GOES TO MONTE CARLO(1977)
Antonio Macasoli
TEACHER AND THE MIRACLE, THE(1961, Ital./Span.), ph; FINGER ON THE TRIGGER(1965, US/Span.), ph; FICKLE FINGER OF FATE, THE(1967, Span./U.S.), ph; BANG BANG KID, THE(1968 U.S./Span./Ital.), ph; GRAND SLAM(1968, Ital., Span., Ger.), ph; GUNS OF THE MAGNIFICENT SEVEN(1969), ph; CANNON FOR CORDOBA(1970), ph
Alan Macateer
JIGSAW(1949)
Armando V. Macatuso
BEFORE HIM ALL ROME TREMBLED(1947, Ital.), titles
Charles Macaulay
HEAD(1968); DIRT GANG, THE(1972); TWILIGHT PEOPLE(1972, Phil.); HINDENBURG, THE(1975); BIG RED ONE, THE(1980); RAISE THE TITANIC(1980, Brit.)

1984
SPLASH(1984)
Charles Macauley
Misc. Talkies
BLOODLESS VAMPIRE, THE(1965)
Jack Macaulay
Misc. Silents
VALLEY OF FEAR, THE(1916, Brit.)
Joseph Macaulay
LOTTERY BRIDE, THE(1930)
Richard Macaulay
EARTHWORM TRACTORS(1936), w; MELODY FOR TWO(1937), w; READY, WILLING AND ABLE(1937), w; RIDING ON AIR(1937), w; VARSITY SHOW(1937), w; BROTHER RAT(1938), w; GARDEN OF THE MOON(1938), w; GOLD DIGGERS IN PARIS(1938), w; NAUGHTY BUT NICE(1939), w; ON YOUR TOES(1939), w; ROARING TWENTIES, THE(1939), w; BROTHER RAT AND A BABY(1940), w; THEY DRIVE BY NIGHT(1940), w; TORRID ZONE(1940), w; MANPOWER(1941), w; MILLION DOLLAR BABY(1941), w; NAVY BLUES(1941), w; OUT OF THE FOG(1941), w; ACROSS THE PACIFIC(1942), w; CAPTAINS OF THE CLOUDS(1942), w; WINGS FOR THE EAGLE(1942), w; TAMPICO(1944), w; YOUNG WIDOW(1946), w; BORN TO KILL(1947), w
Tom Macaulay
AMAZING MR. BEECHAM, THE(1949, Brit.)
Tony Macaulay
IT'S NOT THE SIZE THAT COUNTS(1979, Brit.), m
Carl Macauley
MAN FROM GALVESTON, THE(1964), art d
Ed MacAuley
KID FROM CLEVELAND, THE(1949)
Richard Macauley
FRONT PAGE WOMAN(1935), w; HOLLYWOOD HOTEL(1937), w; HARD TO GET(1938), w; KID FROM KOKOMO, THE(1939), w; FLIGHT ANGELS(1940), w; THREE CHEERS FOR THE IRISH(1940), w; HELLO, FRISCO, HELLO(1943), w; BUCK PRIVATES COME HOME(1947), w; GOOD DIE YOUNG, THE(1954, Brit.), w
Ted Macauley
THIN RED LINE, THE(1964)
Tom Macauley
ADVENTURESS, THE(1946, Brit.); FIVE ANGLES ON MURDER(1950, Brit.); LONG DARK HALL, THE(1951, Brit.); OUTPOST IN MALAYA(1952, Brit.); SKID KIDS(1953, Brit.)
Misc. Talkies
MURDER AT SCOTLAND YARD(1952)
Tony Macauley
BEAST IN THE CELLAR, THE(1971, Brit.), m
Jose MacAvin
SEVENTH DAWN, THE(1964), set d
Josie Macavin
SHAKE HANDS WITH THE DEVIL(1959, Ireland), set d; CARRY ON REGARDLESS(1961, Brit.), set d; MARK, THE(1961, Brit.), set d; LONELINESS OF THE LONG DISTANCE RUNNER, THE(1962, Brit.), set d; TOM JONES(1963, Brit.), set d; PSYCHE 59(1964, Brit.), set d; SPY WHO CAME IN FROM THE COLD, THE(1965, Brit.), set d; MAN FOR ALL SEASONS, A(1966, Brit.), set d; HANNIBAL BROOKS(1969, Brit.), set d; SINFUL DAVEY(1969, Brit.), set d; WALK WITH LOVE AND DEATH, A(1969), set d; RYAN'S DAUGHTER(1970, Brit.), set d; WUTHERING HEIGHTS(1970, Brit.), set d
1984
CAL(1984, Ireland), art d
Gene MacAvoy
RECORD CITY(1978), art d
Cmdr. Merle MacBain,
MISTER ROBERTS(1955), tech adv
L.C. MacBean
Misc. Silents
ANSWER THE CALL(1915, Brit.), d; INFELICE(1915, Brit.), d; WAYS OF THE WORLD, THE(1915, Brit.), d; LOVE TRAIL, THE(1916, Brit.), d; BLADYS OF THE STEWPONY(1919, Brit.), d; DAWN OF THE TRUTH, THE(1920, Brit.), d
Robert Macbeth
1984
MOSCOW ON THE HUDSON(1984)
MacBeth's Calypso Band
Misc. Talkies
HOUSE RENT PARTY(1946)
Bonnie MacBird
TRON(1982), d&w
Donald MacBride
MISLEADING LADY, THE(1932); ROOM SERVICE(1938); AMAZING MR. WILLIAMS(1939); BLONDIE TAKES A VACATION(1939); CHARLIE CHAN AT TREASURE ISLAND(1939); GIRL AND THE GAMBLER, THE(1939); GIRL FROM MEXICO, THE(1939); GRACIE ALLEN MURDER CASE(1939); GREAT MAN VOTES, THE(1939); STORY OF VERNON AND IRENE CASTLE, THE(1939); TWELVE CROWDED HOURS(1939); CURTAIN CALL(1940); HIT PARADE OF 1941(1940); MICHAEL SHAYNE, PRIVATE DETECTIVE(1940); MURDER OVER NEW YORK(1940); MY FAVORITE WIFE(1940); NORTHWEST PASSAGE(1940); SAINT'S DOUBLE TROUBLE, THE(1940); WYOMING(1940); HERE COMES MR. JORDAN(1941); HIGH SIERRA(1941); INVISIBLE WOMAN, THE(1941); LOUISIANA PURCHASE(1941); LOVE CRAZY(1941); RISE AND SHINE(1941); TOPPER RETURNS(1941); YOU'LL NEVER GET RICH(1941); YOU'RE IN THE ARMY NOW(1941); GLASS KEY, THE(1942); JUKE GIRL(1942); LADY BODYGUARD(1942); MEXICAN SPITFIRE SEES A GHOST(1942); MY SISTER EILEEN(1942); NIGHT TO REMEMBER, A(1942); TWO YANKS IN TRINIDAD(1942); BEST FOOT FORWARD(1943); STRANGER IN TOWN, A(1943); THEY GOT ME COVERED(1943); DOUGHGIRLS, THE(1944); PRACTICALLY YOURS(1944); THIN MAN GOES HOME, THE(1944); ABBOTT AND COSTELLO IN HOLLYWOOD(1945); HOLD THAT BLONDE(1945); OUT OF THIS WORLD(1945); SHE GETS HER MAN(1945); BLONDE ALIBI(1946); BRUTE MAN, THE(1946); DARK CORNER, THE(1946); DARK HORSE, THE(1946); GIRL ON THE SPOT(1946); KILLERS, THE(1946); LITTLE GIANT(1946); TIME OF THEIR LIVES, THE(1946); BEAT THE BAND(1947); BUCK PRIVATES COME HOME(1947); EGG AND I, THE(1947); GOOD NEWS(1947); CAMPUS SLEUTH(1948); JINX MONEY(1948); SMART POLITICS(1948); STORY OF SEABISCUIT, THE(1949); JOE PALOOKA MEETS HUMPHREY(1950); BOWERY BATTALION(1951); CUBAN FIREBALL(1951);

RHUBARB(1951); SAILOR BEWARE(1951); TEXAS CARNIVAL(1951); TWO TICKETS TO BROADWAY(1951); GOBS AND GALS(1952); MEET DANNY WILSON(1952); SEVEN YEAR ITCH, THE(1955)
Misc. Silents
    HESPER OF THE MOUNTAINS(1916)
John MacBride
    HALLOWEEN III: SEASON OF THE WITCH(1982)
Lilyan MacBride
    SUPERCHICK(1973); MITCHELL(1975)
Phyllis MacBride
    FEMALE RESPONSE, THE(1972)
Jack MacBurnie
    NIGHT RIDERS OF MONTANA(1951), ph
John MacBurnie
    TEXAS TERRORS(1940), ph; TULSA KID, THE(1940), ph; JESSE JAMES, JR.(1942), ph; STAGECOACH EXPRESS(1942), ph; CANYON CITY(1943), ph; MAN FROM THE RIO GRANDE, THE(1943), ph; OVERLAND MAIL ROBBERY(1943), ph; RAIDERS OF SUNSET PASS(1943), ph; PRIDE OF THE PLAINS(1944), ph; BANDITS OF DARK CANYON(1947), ph; MAIN STREET KID, THE(1947), ph; CAMPUS HONEY-MOON(1948), ph; DAREDEVILS OF THE CLOUDS(1948), ph; DENVER KID, THE(1948), ph; DESPERADOES OF DODGE CITY(1948), ph; HEART OF VIR-GINIA(1948), ph; HOMICIDE FOR THREE(1948), ph; KING OF THE GAM-BLERS(1948), ph; LIGHTNIN' IN THE FOREST(1948), ph; MADONNA OF THE DESERT(1948), ph; MARSHAL OF AMARILLO(1948), ph; OKLAHOMA BAD-LANDS(1948), ph; RENEGADES OF SONORA(1948), ph; SECRET SERVICE INVES-TIGATOR(1948), ph; SLIPPY MCGEE(1948), ph; SON OF GOD'S COUNTRY(1948), ph; SONS OF ADVENTURE(1948), ph; SUNDOWN IN SANTA FE(1948), ph; ALIAS THE CHAMP(1949), ph; BANDIT KING OF TEXAS(1949), ph; DAUGHTER OF THE JUNGLE(1949), ph; DUKE OF CHICAGO(1949), ph; FLAME OF YOUTH(1949), ph; FLAMING FURY(1949), ph; HIDEOUT(1949), ph; NAVAJO TRAIL RAIDERS(1949), ph; POST OFFICE INVESTIGATOR(1949), ph; POWDER RIVER RUSTLERS(1949), ph; RED MENACE, THE(1949), ph; ROSE OF THE YUKON(1949), ph; SAN ANTONE AMBUSH(1949), ph; SHERIFF OF WICHITA(1949), ph; SOUTH OF RIO(1949), ph; STREETS OF SAN FRANCISCO(1949), ph; WYOMING BANDIT, THE(1949), ph; CALIFORNIA PASSAGE(1950), ph; CODE OF THE SILVER SAGE(1950), ph; COV-ERED WAGON RAID(1950), ph; DESTINATION BIG HOUSE(1950), ph; FEDERAL AGENT AT LARGE(1950), ph; FRISCO TORNADO(1950), ph; HARBOR OF MISSING MEN(1950), ph; MISSOURIANS, THE(1950), ph; PIONEER MARSHAL(1950), ph; REDWOOD FOREST TRAIL(1950), ph; RUSTLERS ON HORSEBACK(1950), ph; SALT LAKE RAIDERS(1950), ph; TARNISHED(1950), ph; TRAIL OF ROBIN HOOD(1950), ph; TRIAL WITHOUT JURY(1950), ph; UNDER MEXICALI STARS(1950), ph; VIGILANTE HIDEOUT(1950), ph; WOMAN FROM HEADQUARTERS(1950), ph; ARIZONA MANHUNT(1951), ph; BUCKAROO SHERIFF OF TEXAS(1951), ph; DAKOTA KID, THE(1951), ph; DESERT OF LOST MEN(1951), ph; FORT DODGE STAMPEDE(1951), ph; INSURANCE INVES-TIGATOR(1951), ph; MISSING WOMEN(1951), ph; PRIDE OF MARYLAND(1951), ph; ROUGH RIDERS OF DURANGO(1951), ph; SILVER CITY BONANZA(1951), ph; STREET BANDITS(1951), ph; THUNDER IN GOD'S COUNTRY(1951), ph; UTAH WAGON TRAIN(1951), ph; WELLS FARGO GUNMASTER(1951), ph; BORDER SAD-DLEMATES(1952), ph; CAPTIVE OF BILLY THE KID(1952), ph; COLORADO SUN-DOWN(1952), ph; DESPERADOES OUTPOST(1952), ph; GOBS AND GALS(1952), ph; LAST MUSKETEER, THE(1952), ph; OLD OKLAHOMA PLAINS(1952), ph; SOUTH PACIFIC TRAIL(1952), ph; THUNDERING CARAVANS(1952), ph; TROPICAL HEAT WAVE(1952), ph; WILD HORSE AMBUSH(1952), ph; WOMAN IN THE DARK(1952), ph; DOWN LAREDO WAY(1953), ph; EL PASO STAMPEDE(1953), ph; MARSHAL OF CEDAR ROCK(1953), ph; OLD OVERLAND TRAIL(1953), ph; SATAN'S SATEL-LITES(1958), ph; GHOST OF ZORRO(1959), ph
Jerzy Macc
    NEW LIFE STYLE, THE(1970, Ger.), d, w
Crawford MacCallum
    TRACK OF THE MOONBEAST(1976)
R. H. MacCandless
    LUCK OF THE IRISH, THE(1937, Ireland)
Roberto Maccanti
    1900(1976, Ital.)
Maccari
    DONATELLA(1956, Ital.), w; HERCULES' PILLS(1960, Ital.), w
Ruggero Maccari
    EASY LIFE, THE(1963, Ital.), w; LET'S TALK ABOUT WOMEN(1964, Fr./Ital.), w; HIGH INFIDELITY(1965, Fr./Ital.), w; LOVE A LA CARTE(1965, Ital.), w; MAGNIFI-CENT CUCKOLD, THE(1965, Fr./Ital.), w; ONE MILLION DOLLARS(1965, Ital.), w; LA VISITA(1966, Ital./Fr.), w; HEAD OF THE FAMILY(1967, Ital./Fr.), w; MADE IN ITALY(1967, Fr./Ital.), w; OPIATE '67(1967, Fr./Ital.), w; ANYONE CAN PLAY(1968, Ital.), w; DEVIL IN LOVE, THE(1968, Ital.), w; QUEENS, THE(1968, Ital./Fr.), w; PRIEST'S WIFE, THE(1971, Ital./Fr.), w; WHITE SISTER(1973, Ital./Span./Fr.), w; ROCCO PAPALEO(1974, Ital.), w; SCENT OF A WOMAN(1976, Ital.), w; GOOD-NIGHT, LADIES AND GENTLEMEN(1977, Ital.), d&w; SPECIAL DAY, A(1977, Ital./Can.), w; VIVA ITALIA(1978, Ital.), w; PASSION OF LOVE(1982, Ital./Fr.), w
1984
    LE BAL(1984, Fr./Ital./Algeria), w
Nino Maccari [Ruggero Maccari]
    TWO NIGHTS WITH CLEOPATRA(1953, Ital.), w
Barbara Lee Maccarone
1984
    ICE PIRATES, THE(1984), cos
Frank MacCarroll
    LAWLESS CODE(1949)
Anne MacCauley
    HIGH ANXIETY(1977), set d
Alice MacChesney
Silents
    TRAIL OF THE SHADOW, THE(1917)
Egisto Macchi
    ASSASSINATION OF TROTSKY, THE(1972 Fr./Ital.), m; MR. KLEIN(1976, Fr.), m; PADRE PADRONE(1977, Ital.), m
Giulio Macchi
    GOLDEN COACH, THE(1953, Fr./Ital.), w; DEFEND MY LOVE(1956, Ital.), d

Valentino Macchi
    ARIZONA COLT(1965, It./Fr./Span.); SUPERARGO VERSUS DIABOLICUS(1966, Ital./Span.); WEB OF VIOLENCE(1966, Ital./Span.); BULLET FOR THE GENERAL, A(1967, Ital.); GIRL AND THE GENERAL, THE(1967, Fr./Ital.); MORE THAN A MIRACLE(1967, Ital./Fr.); STRANGER, THE(1967, Algeria/Fr./Ital.); TALL WOMEN, THE(1967, Aust./Ital./Span.); GRAND SLAM(1968, Ital., Span., Ger.); YOUNG, THE EVIL AND THE SAVAGE, THE(1968, Ital.); GHOSTS, ITALIAN STYLE(1969, Ital./Fr.); ONE STEP TO HELL(1969, U.S./Ital./Span.); SWEET BODY OF DEBORAH, THE(1969, Ital./Fr.); WITCHES, THE(1969, Fr./Ital.); DIRTY HEROES(1971, Ital./Fr./Ger.)
Gianni Macchia
    WOMAN ON FIRE, A(1970, Ital.); ITALIAN CONNECTION, THE(1973, U.S./Ital./Ger.)
John Macchia
    DISORDERLY ORDERLY, THE(1964); PATSY, THE(1964); FAMILY JEWELS, THE(1965); HOW TO STUFF A WILD BIKINI(1965); SERGEANT DEADHEAD(1965); GHOST IN THE INVISIBLE BIKINI(1966); PINK MOTEL(1983)
Nicolette Macchiavelli
1984
    BEYOND GOOD AND EVIL(1984, Ital./Fr./Ger.)
Ralph Macchio
    UP THE ACADEMY(1980); OUTSIDERS, THE(1983)
1984
    KARATE KID, THE(1984); TEACHERS(1984)
Aldo Maccione
    LOVES AND TIMES OF SCARAMOUCHE, THE(1976, Ital.); FRANKENSTEIN-ITALIAN STYLE(1977, Ital.)
Misc. Talkies
    INSTANT COFFEE(1974)
Fred MacClean
    MY MAN AND I(1952), set d
Donald MacClennan
Misc. Silents
    AWAKENING OF RUTH, THE(1917)
June MacCloy
    BIG GAMBLE, THE(1931); JUNE MOON(1931); REACHING FOR THE MOON(1931); GLAMOUR FOR SALE(1940); GO WEST(1940); UNHOLY PARTNERS(1941)
Gladys MacClure
Silents
    LOVE AUCTION, THE(1919)
Victor MacClure
    GREAT, MEADOW, THE(1931), w; MURDER ON THE SET(1936, Brit.), w; GREAT MR. HANDEL, THE(1942, Brit.), a, w; THEY KNEW MR. KNIGHT(1945, Brit.), w
Catriona Maccoll
    LADY OSCAR(1979, Fr./Jap.); HAWK THE SLAYER(1980, Brit.)
1984
    HOUSE BY THE CEMETERY, THE(1984, Ital.)
James MacColl
    THIS IS THE ARMY(1943); EXECUTIVE ACTION(1973)
Katherine MacColl
Misc. Talkies
    SEVEN DOORS OF DEATH(1983)
Kendall MacComak
    DADDY LONG LEGS(1931)
Ron Maccone
    PRINCE OF THE CITY(1981); LITTLE SEX, A(1982)
Ronald Maccone
    SHADOWS(1960)
1984
    BROADWAY DANNY ROSE(1984); POPE OF GREENWICH VILLAGE, THE(1984)
Ronnie Maccone
    GLORIA(1980)
Keith MacConnell
    WRONG IS RIGHT(1982)
Simon MacCorkindale
    DEATH ON THE NILE(1978, Brit.); QUATERMASS CONCLUSION(1980, Brit.); CABOBLANCO(1981); SWORD AND THE SORCERER, THE(1982); JAWS 3-D(1983)
1984
    RIDDLE OF THE SANDS, THE(1984, Brit.)
Misc. Talkies
    FALCON'S GOLD(1982)
Joanne MacCormack
    DIARY OF A BACHELOR(1964)
Merrill MacCormack
    MAN'S LAND, A(1932)
William M. MacCormack
    CRISIS(1950)
Don MacCracken
    DECOY(1946); KISS THE BLOOD OFF MY HANDS(1948); RIVER LADY(1948)
Frank MacCready
    RETURN OF SOPHIE LANG, THE(1936)
George MacCready
    WILSON(1944)
William MacCrow
    UNMAN, WITTERING AND ZIGO(1971, Brit.), art d
Verna MacCurran
    SIX BRIDGES TO CROSS(1955), ed
Etta MacDaniel
    KING KONG(1933)
Galt MacDermot
    COTTON COMES TO HARLEM(1970), m; FORTUNE AND MEN'S EYES(1971, U.S./Can.), m; GOLDEN APPLES OF THE SUN(1971, Can.), m; RHINOCEROS(1974), m; HAIR(1979), w, m; MOON OVER THE ALLEY(1980, Brit.), m
Rory MacDermot
    ROOT OF ALL EVIL, THE(1947, Brit.); AGAINST THE WIND(1948, Brit.); WATCH YOUR STERN(1961, Brit.)
John MacDermott
Silents
    DINTY(1920), d

Marc MacDermott
Silents
EUGENE ARAM(1915); RANSON'S FOLLY(1915); NEW MOON, THE(1919); WHILE NEW YORK SLEEPS(1920); HE WHO GETS SLAPPED(1924); IN EVERY WOMAN'S LIFE(1924); GOOSE WOMAN, THE(1925); FLESH AND THE DEVIL(1926); KIKI(1926); TEMPTRESS, THE(1926); TAXI DANCER, THE(1927)
Misc. Silents
NECKLACE OF RAMESES, THE(1914); DESTROYING ANGEL, THE(1915); MYSTERY OF ROOM 13, THE(1915); SALLY CASTLETON, SOUTHERNER(1915); SHADOWS FROM THE PAST(1915); CATSPAW, THE(1916); FOOTLIGHTS OF FATE, THE(1916); PRICE OF FAME, THE(1916); WHOM THE GODS DESTROY(1916); BABETTE(1917); BUILDERS OF CASTLES(1917); INTRIGUE(1917); LAST SENTENCE, THE(1917); MARY JANE'S PA(1917); SIXTEENTH WIFE, THE(1917); WOMAN BETWEEN FRIENDS, THE(1918); BLIND WIVES(1920); FOOTLIGHTS(1921); LIGHTS OF NEW YORK, THE(1922); LUCRETIA LOMBARD(1923); SATIN GIRL, THE(1923); DOROTHY VERNON OF HADDON HALL(1924); THREE MILES OUT(1924); GRAUSTARK(1925); SIEGE(1925); LOVE THIEF, THE(1926); LUCKY LADY, THE(1926); MAN, WOMAN AND SIN(1927); RESURRECTION(1927); ROAD TO ROMANCE, THE(1927); YELLOW LILY, THE(1928)

Charles Macdona
Silents
ONCE UPON A TIME(1918, Brit.)

Mrs. Charles Macdona
Silents
LABOUR LEADER, THE(1917, Brit.)

John MacDonagh
Misc. Silents
CASEY'S MILLIONS(1922, Brit.), d; CRUISKEEN LAWN(1922, Brit.), d

Paulette MacDonagh
TWO MINUTES' SILENCE(1934, Brit.), p&d

A.C. MacDonald
THE CRAZIES(1973)

Aimi MacDonald
TAKE A GIRL LIKE YOU(1970, Brit,); OLD DRACULA(1975, Brit.)

Aleida MacDonald
QUIET DAY IN BELFAST, A(1974, Can.), cos

Alexander MacDonald
MR. PATMAN(1980, Can.), p
Misc. Silents
KINGDOM OF TWILIGHT, THE(1929, Brit.), d

Archer MacDonald
GEISHA GIRL(1952); KID MONK BARONI(1952); SOMETHING FOR THE BIRDS(1952); GLORY BRIGADE, THE(1953); LATIN LOVERS(1953); POWDER RIVER(1953); THREE SAILORS AND A GIRL(1953); STUDENT PRINCE, THE(1954); ANYTHING GOES(1956)

Audrey MacDonald
NAKED MAJA, THE(1959, Ital./U.S.)

Ballard MacDonald
DEEP IN MY HEART(1954), lyrics

Betty MacDonald
EGG AND I, THE(1947), d
1984
BAY BOY(1984, Can.)

Bruce MacDonald
WHEN WILLIE COMES MARCHING HOME(1950), set d; O. HENRY'S FULL HOUSE(1952), set d; PHONE CALL FROM A STRANGER(1952), set d; SOMETHING FOR THE BIRDS(1952), set d; WAY OF A GAUCHO(1952), set d; DIME WITH A HALO(1963), set d; RETURN OF THE SECAUCUS SEVEN(1980)

Catherine MacDonald
Silents
HEADIN' SOUTH(1918)

Cheryl MacDonald
FORT COURAGEOUS(1965)

Dan MacDonald
CHANGE OF MIND(1969); NEPTUNE FACTOR, THE(1973, Can.)

David H. MacDonald
1984
JOY OF SEX(1984)

David MacDonald
DEATH CROONS THE BLUES(1937, Brit.), d; IT'S NEVER TOO LATE TO MEND(1937, Brit.), d; LAST CURTAIN, THE(1937, Brit.), d; RIDING HIGH(1937, Brit.), d; SPECIAL AGENT K-7(1937); MAKE IT THREE(1938, Brit.), d; MEET MR. PENNY(1938, Brit.), d; SPOT OF BOTHER, A(1938, Brit.), d; DEAD MEN TELL NO TALES(1939, Brit.), d; THIS MAN IN PARIS(1939, Brit.), d; THIS MAN IS NEWS(1939, Brit.), d; LAW AND DISORDER(1940, Brit.), d; MIDAS TOUCH, THE(1940, Brit.), d; SPIES OF THE AIR(1940, Brit.), d; THIS ENGLAND(1941, Brit.), d; BROTHERS, THE(1948, Brit.), d, w; BAD LORD BYRON, THE(1949, Brit.), d; CHRISTOPHER COLUMBUS(1949, Brit.), d; DIAMOND CITY(1949, Brit.), d; SNOWBOUND(1949, Brit.), d; CAIRO ROAD(1950, Brit.), d; GOOD TIME GIRL(1950, Brit.), d; ADVENTURERS, THE(1951, Brit.), d; TREAD SOFTLY(1952, Brit.), d; BIG FRAME, THE(1953, Brit.), d; DEVIL GIRL FROM MARS(1954, Brit.), d; THREE CORNERED FATE(1954, Brit.), d; YELLOW ROBE, THE(1954, Brit.), d; FINAL COLUMN, THE(1955, Brit.), d; ONE JUST MAN(1955, Brit.), d; ALIAS JOHN PRESTON(1956), d; SMALL HOTEL(1957, Brit.), d; LADY MISLAID, A(1958, Brit.), d; MOONRAKER, THE(1958, Brit.), d; PETTICOAT PIRATES(1961, Brit.), d; GOLDEN RABBIT, THE(1962, Brit.), d

Don MacDonald
HAIL, HERO!(1969), cos

Donald MacDonald
THESE THIRTY YEARS(1934); MA AND PA KETTLE AT HOME(1954); KENTUCKIAN, THE(1955); LAY THAT RIFLE DOWN(1955)
Misc. Talkies
DEMOLITION(1977)
Silents
EXTRAVAGANCE(1919); PARIS GREEN(1920); SKY PILOT, THE(1921); ONE CLEAR CALL(1922); ALIAS THE NIGHT WIND(1923); STEPPING FAST(1923); LORNA DOONE(1927)
Misc. Silents
ABANDONMENT, THE(1916), d; APRIL(1916), d; TRUE NOBILITY(1916), d; WHITE ROSETTE, THE(1916), d; DESERT WOOING, A(1918); MARKET OF SOULS, THE(1919); SILVER GIRL, THE(1919); GREATER THAN LOVE(1920); VILLAGE

SLEUTH, A(1920); YELLOW TAIFUN, THE(1920); MIDNIGHT BELL, A(1921); WOMAN HE MARRIED, THE(1922)

Edmund MacDonald
ENLIGHTEN THY DAUGHTER(1934); PRISON BREAK(1938); COAST GUARD(1939); DESTRY RIDES AGAIN(1939); I STOLE A MILLION(1939); BLACK FRIDAY(1940); BRIDE WORE CRUTCHES, THE(1940); GAY CABALLERO, THE(1940); INVISIBLE MAN RETURNS, THE(1940); MANHATTAN HEARTBEAT(1940); SAILOR'S LADY(1940); YESTERDAY'S HEROES(1940); GREAT GUNS(1941); TEXAS(1941); CALL OF THE CANYON(1942); CASTLE IN THE DESERT(1942); FLYING TIGERS(1942); HEART OF THE GOLDEN WEST(1942); MADAME SPY(1942); STRANGE CASE OF DR. RX, THE(1942); TIMBER(1942); TO THE SHORES OF TRIPOLI(1942); WHISPERING GHOSTS(1942); WHO DONE IT?(1942); CORVETTE K-225(1943); HANGMEN ALSO DIE(1943); HI'YA, CHUM(1943); MANTRAP, THE(1943); SHERLOCK HOLMES IN WASHINGTON(1943); ROGER TOUHY, GANGSTER!(1944); SAILOR'S HOLIDAY(1944); STORY OF DR. WASSELL, THE(1944); TIMBER QUEEN(1944); DETOUR(1945); HOLD THAT BLONDE(1945); INCENDIARY BLONDE(1945); LADY CONFESSES, THE(1945); BLONDIE'S ANNIVERSARY(1947); SHOOT TO KILL(1947); BLACK EAGLE(1948); THAT LADY IN ERMINE(1948); RED CANYON(1949)

Farrell MacDonald
FOUR DEVILS(1929)

Flora MacDonald
Misc. Silents
FALL OF A NATION, THE(1916)

Francis J. MacDonald
Misc. Silents
IN THE WEB OF THE GRAFTERS(1916)

Francis MacDonald
BROTHERS(1930); IN THE LINE OF DUTY(1931); SADIE MCKEE(1934); EVERY DAY'S A HOLIDAY(1938); GUN LAW(1938); TEXANS, THE(1938); CARSON CITY KID(1940); BLOOD AND SAND(1941); WILD BILL HICKOK RIDES(1942); RAIDERS, THE(1952); SAGA OF HEMP BROWN, THE(1958)
Silents
DIVORCE TRAP, THE(1919)

Frank MacDonald
BARNYARD FOLLIES(1940), d; OLD HOMESTEAD, THE(1942), d; TWO SENORITAS FROM CHICAGO(1943), p; APACHE CHIEF(1949), d

Fred MacDonald
ON OUR SELECTION(1930, Aus.)

George MacDonald
PRIDE OF THE YANKEES, THE(1942); DANCING IN THE DARK(1949); PRIDE OF ST. LOUIS, THE(1952)

Grant MacDonald
CONVICTED(1938); WOMAN AGAINST THE WORLD(1938); SPECIAL INSPECTOR(1939)

Gregory MacDonald
RUNNING SCARED(1972, Brit.), w

Greta MacDonald
Misc. Silents
MATT(1918, Brit.)

Harry MacDonald
HELLO SISTER(1930)

Helen MacDonald
Misc. Silents
YOUNG AMERICA(1918)

Ian MacDonald
MADAME GUILLOTINE(1931, Brit.); ADVENTURES OF MARTIN EDEN, THE(1942); THEY DIED WITH THEIR BOOTS ON(1942); DARK PASSAGE(1947); DEEP VALLEY(1947); PURSUED(1947); MAN FROM COLORADO, THE(1948); MR. RECKLESS(1948); ROAD HOUSE(1948); SIXTEEN FATHOMS DEEP(1948); SOUTHERN YANKEE, A(1948); WOMAN FROM TANGIER, THE(1948); BATTLEGROUND(1949); COME TO THE STABLE(1949); JOE PALOOKA IN THE BIG FIGHT(1949); STREETS OF SAN FRANCISCO(1949); WHIRLPOOL(1949); WHITE HEAT(1949); COLT .45(1950); COMMANCHE TERRITORY(1950); DESERT HAWK, THE(1950); LAWLESS, THE(1950); MALAYA(1950); MONTANA(1950); WHERE THE SIDEWALK ENDS(1950); FLAMING FEATHER(1951); NEW MEXICO(1951); SHOW BOAT(1951); TEN TALL MEN(1951); TEXAS RANGERS, THE(1951); THUNDER IN GOD'S COUNTRY(1951); BRIGAND, THE(1952); HIAWATHA(1952); HIGH NOON(1952); THIS WOMAN IS DANGEROUS(1952); TOUGHEST MAN IN ARIZONA(1952); BLOWING WILD(1953); PERILOUS JOURNEY, A(1953); SAVAGE, THE(1953); SILVER WHIP, THE(1953); APACHE(1954); EGYPTIAN, THE(1954); JOHNNY GUITAR(1954); TAZA, SON OF COCHISE(1954); LONESOME TRAIL, THE(1955), a, w; SILVER STAR, THE(1955), w; SON OF SINBAD(1955); TIMBERJACK(1955); STAGECOACH TO FURY(1956); TWO-GUN LADY(1956); DUEL AT APACHE WELLS(1957); MONEY, WOMEN AND GUNS(1958); WARLOCK(1959)

Inez MacDonald
Misc. Silents
MAN WHO WAITED, THE(1922)

J. Farrell MacDonald
TRUE TO LIFE(1943); ABIE'S IRISH ROSE(1928); IN OLD ARIZONA(1929); MASQUERADE(1929); PAINTED ANGEL, THE(1929); SOUTH SEA ROSE(1929); GIRL OF THE GOLDEN WEST(1930); HAPPY DAYS(1930); MEN WITHOUT WOMEN(1930); SONG O' MY HEART(1930); TRUTH ABOUT YOUTH, THE(1930); BRAT, THE(1931); EASIEST WAY, THE(1931); MALTESE FALCON, THE(1931); MILLIONAIRE, THE(1931); OTHER MEN'S WOMEN(1931); PAINTED DESERT, THE(1931); SPORTING BLOOD(1931); SQUAW MAN, THE(1931); TOO YOUNG TO MARRY(1931); TOUCHDOWN!(1931); WOMAN HUNGRY(1931); DISCARDED LOVERS(1932); HEARTS OF HUMANITY(1932); HOTEL CONTINENTAL(1932); MADAME RACKETEER(1932); ME AND MY GAL(1932); PRIDE OF THE LEGION, THE(1932); PROBATION(1932); SCANDAL FOR SALE(1932); SO IT'S SUNDAY(1932); STEADY COMPANY(1932); THIRTEENTH GUEST, THE(1932); THIS SPORTING AGE(1932); UNDER EIGHTEEN(1932); VANISHING FRONTIER, THE(1932); WEEK-END MARRIAGE(1932); 70,000 WITNESSES(1932); BIG PAYOFF, THE(1933); HERITAGE OF THE DESERT(1933); I LOVED A WOMAN(1933); IRON MASTER, THE(1933); LAUGHING AT LIFE(1933); MEN ARE SUCH FOOLS(1933); NO MAN OF HER OWN(1933); PEG O' MY HEART(1933); POWER AND THE GLORY, THE(1933); RACING STRAIN, THE(1933); UNDER SECRET ORDERS(1933); WORKING MAN, THE(1933); CAT'S PAW, THE(1934); CRIME DOCTOR, THE(1934); CROSBY CASE, THE(1934); MAN OF TWO WORLDS(1934); MURDER ON THE CAMPUS(1934); MYRT AND MARGE(1934); ONCE TO EVERY WOMAN(1934); CAPTAIN HURRICANE(1935); DANGER

AHEAD(1935); FARMER TAKES A WIFE, THE(1935); FIGHTING YOUTH(1935); FRONT PAGE WOMAN(1935); HEALER, THE(1935); IRISH IN US, THE(1935); LET 'EM HAVE IT(1935); MAYBE IT'S LOVE(1935); NORTHERN FRONTIER(1935); OUR LITTLE GIRL(1935); ROMANCE IN MANHATTAN(1935); STAR OF MID-NIGHT(1935); STORMY(1935); SWELL-HEAD(1935); WATERFRONT LADY(1935); WHOLE TOWN'S TALKING, THE(1935); EXCLUSIVE STORY(1936); FLORIDA SPE-CIAL(1936); HITCH HIKE LADY(1936); RIFF-RAFF(1936); SHOW BOAT(1936); COUN-TY FAIR(1937); COURAGE OF THE WEST(1937); GAME THAT KILLS, THE(1937); HIT PARADE, THE(1937); MAID OF SALEM(1937); MY DEAR MISS ALDRICH(1937); MYSTERIOUS CROSSING(1937); PARNELL(1937); ROARING TIMBER(1937); SHAD-OWS OF THE ORIENT(1937); SILENT BARRIERS(1937, Brit.); SLAVE SHIP(1937); SLIM(1937); TOPPER(1937); CROWD ROARS, THE(1938); EXTORTION(1938); FLY-ING FISTS, THE(1938); GANG BULLETS(1938); LITTLE ORPHAN ANNIE(1938); MY OLD KENTUCKY HOME(1938); STATE POLICE(1938); THERE GOES MY HEART(1938); WHITE BANNERS(1938); COME ON RANGERS(1939); CON-SPIRACY(1939); EAST SIDE OF HEAVEN(1939); HOUSEKEEPER'S DAUGHT-ER(1939); MICKEY, THE KID(1939); SUSANNAH OF THE MOUNTIES(1939); THEY SHALL HAVE MUSIC(1939); ZENOBIA(1939); DARK COMMAND, THE(1940); FRIENDLY NEIGHBORS(1940); GENTLEMAN FROM ARIZONA, THE(1940); I TAKE THIS OATH(1940); KNIGHTS OF THE RANGE(1940); LIGHT OF WESTERN STARS, THE(1940); PRAIRIE LAW(1940); STAGECOACH WAR(1940); UNTAMED(1940); GREAT LIE, THE(1941); IN OLD CHEYENNE(1941); LAW OF THE TIMBER(1941); MEET JOHN DOE(1941); SULLIVAN'S TRAVELS(1941); BOWERY AT MID-NIGHT(1942); CAPTAINS OF THE CLOUDS(1942); LITTLE TOKYO, U.S.A.(1942); LIVING GHOST, THE(1942); ONE THRILLING NIGHT(1942); PALM BEACH STORY, THE(1942); PHANTOM KILLER(1942); REAP THE WILD WIND(1942); SNUFFY SMITH, YARD BIRD(1942); WILD BILL HICKOK RIDES(1942); APE MAN, THE(1943); CLANCY STREET BOYS(1943); TIGER FANGS(1943); FOLLOW THE LEADER(1944); GREAT MOMENT, THE(1944); IRISH EYES ARE SMILING(1944); LADIES OF WASHINGTON(1944); MIRACLE OF MORGAN'S CREEK, THE(1944); PIN UP GIRL(1944); SHADOW OF SUSPICION(1944); TEXAS MASQUERADE(1944); DOLLY SISTERS, THE(1945); HANGOVER SQUARE(1945); JOHNNY ANGEL(1945); NOB HILL(1945); PILLOW OF DEATH(1945); TREE GROWS IN BROOKLYN, A(1945); WOMAN WHO CAME BACK(1945); IT'S A WONDERFUL LIFE(1946); MY DARLING CLEMENTINE(1946); SMOKY(1946); KEEPER OF THE BEES(1947); WEB OF DAN-GER, THE(1947); FURY AT FURNACE CREEK(1948); IF YOU KNEW SUSIE(1948); LUCK OF THE IRISH(1948); PANHANDLE(1948); SITTING PRETTY(1948); UN-FAITHFULLY YOURS(1948); WALLS OF JERICHO(1948); WHEN MY BABY SMILES AT ME(1948); WHISPERING SMITH(1948); DALTON GANG, THE(1949); FIGHTING MAN OF THE PLAINS(1949); LAW OF THE BARBARY COAST(1949); SHEP COMES HOME(1949); STREETS OF SAN FRANCISCO(1949); TOUGH ASSIGNMENT(1949); YOU'RE MY EVERYTHING(1949); DAKOTA LIL(1950); DALTON'S WOMEN, THE(1950); HOSTILE COUNTRY(1950); MAD WEDNESDAY(1950); WHEN WILLIE COMES MARCHING HOME(1950); WOMAN ON THE RUN(1950); ELOPE-MENT(1951); HERE COMES THE GROOM(1951); MR. BELVEDERE RINGS THE BELL(1951); SUPERMAN AND THE MOLE MEN(1951)
Misc. Talkies
BROKEN DISHES(1930); BEGGAR'S HOLIDAY(1934); NUMBERED WOMAN(1938); LAST ALARM, THE(1940)
Silents
LAST EGYPTIAN, THE(1914); PATCHWORK GIRL OF OZ, THE(1914), d; RAGS(1915); MOLLY OF THE FOLLIES(1919); OUTCASTS OF POKER FLAT, THE(1919); RIDERS OF VENGEANCE(1919); THIS HERO STUFF(1919); RIDING WITH DEATH(1921); WALLOP, THE(1921); COME ON OVER(1922); OVER THE BORDER(1922); SKY HIGH(1922); RACING HEARTS(1923); IRON HORSE, THE(1924); SIGNAL TOWER, THE(1924); STORM DAUGHTER, THE(1924); WESTERN LUCK(1924); LUCKY HORSESHOE, THE(1925); FIRST YEAR, THE(1926); ANKLES PREFERRED(1927); BERTHA, THE SEWING MACHINE GIRL(1927); LOVE MAKES 'EM WILD(1927); SUNRISE—A SONG OF TWO HUMANS(1927); COHENS AND THE KELLYS IN PARIS(1928); NONE BUT THE BRAVE(1928); RILEY THE COP(1928); MASKED EMOTIONS(1929); STRONG BOY(1929)
Misc. Silents
HIS MAJESTY, THE SCARECROW OF OZ(1914), d; HEART OF MARYLAND, THE(1915); PRICE OF POWER, THE(1916); $5,000 REWARD(1918); SPORTING CHANCE, A(1919); HITCHIN' POSTS(1920); MARKED MEN(1920); PATH SHE CHOSE, THE(1920); ACTION(1921); DESPERATE YOUTH(1921); BONDED WOMAN, THE(1922); DRIFTING(1923); FASHIONABLE FAKERS(1923); BRASS BOWL, THE(1924); FAIR WEEK(1924); FIGHTING HEART, THE(1925); KENTUCKY PRI-DE(1925); LIGHTNIN'(1925); SCARLET HONEYMOON, THE(1925); THANK YOU(1925); COUNTRY BEYOND, THE(1926); DIXIE MERCHANT, THE(1926); FAMI-LY UPSTAIRS, THE(1926); SHAMROCK HANDICAP, THE(1926); THREE BAD MEN(1926); TRIP TO CHINATOWN, A(1926); COLLEEN(1927); CRADLE SNATCH-ERS, THE(1927); EAST SIDE, WEST SIDE(1927); BRINGING UP FATHER(1928)

Mrs. J. Farrell MacDonald
Silents
JAZZMANIA(1923)
Jack MacDonald
Silents
NE'ER-DO-WELL, THE(1916); REBECCA OF SUNNYBROOK FARM(1917); KAISER, BEAST OF BERLIN, THE(1918)
Misc. Silents
BETTER TIMES(1919); DO THE DEAD TALK?(1920), d
James MacDonald
CINDERELLA(1950); ALICE IN WONDERLAND(1951); RESCUERS, THE(1977)
Jay MacDonald
WOLF DOG(1958, Can.)
Jeanette MacDonald
LOVE PARADE, THE(1929); LET'S GO NATIVE(1930); LOTTERY BRIDE, THE(1930); MONTE CARLO(1930); OH, FOR A MAN!(1930); VAGABOND KING, THE(1930); ANNABELLE'S AFFAIRS(1931); DON'T BET ON WOMEN(1931); LOVE ME TONIGHT(1932); ONE HOUR WITH YOU(1932); CAT AND THE FIDDLE(1934); MERRY WIDOW, THE(1934); NAUGHTY MARIETTA(1935); ROSE MARIE(1936); SAN FRANCISCO(1936); FIREFLY, THE(1937); MAYTIME(1937); GIRL OF THE GOLDEN WEST, THE(1938); SWEETHEARTS(1938); BROADWAY SERENADE(1939); BITTER SWEET(1940); NEW MOON(1940); SMILIN' THROUGH(1941); CAIRO(1942); I MARRIED AN ANGEL(1942); FOLLOW THE BOYS(1944); THREE DARING DAUGHTERS(1948); SUN COMES UP, THE(1949)

Jessica MacDonald
RETURN OF THE SECAUCUS SEVEN(1980)
Jessica Wight MacDonald
LIANNA(1983)
Jim Macdonald
SNOW WHITE AND THE SEVEN DWARFS(1937)
Joe MacDonald
WINTERTIME(1943), ph; BIG NOISE, THE(1944), ph; IN THE MEANTIME, DAR-LING(1944), ph; SUNDAY DINNER FOR A SOLDIER(1944), ph; CAPTAIN ED-DIE(1945), ph; BEHIND GREEN LIGHTS(1946), ph; DARK CORNER, THE(1946), ph; SHOCK(1946), ph; MOSS ROSE(1947), ph; CALL NORTHSIDE 777(1948), ph; STREET WITH NO NAME, THE(1948), ph; YELLOW SKY(1948), ph; IT HAPPENS EVERY SPRING(1949), ph; PINKY(1949), ph; PANIC IN THE STREETS(1950), ph; STEL-LA(1950), ph; AS YOUNG AS YOU FEEL(1951), ph; FOURTEEN HOURS(1951), ph; YOU'RE IN THE NAVY NOW(1951), ph; O. HENRY'S FULL HOUSE(1952), ph; VIVA ZAPATA!(1952), ph; HOW TO MARRY A MILLIONAIRE(1953), ph; NIAGARA(1953), ph; PICKUP ON SOUTH STREET(1953), ph; TITANIC(1953), ph; BROKEN LAN-CE(1954), ph; HELL AND HIGH WATER(1954), ph; WOMAN'S WORLD(1954), ph; HOUSE OF BAMBOO(1955), ph; RACERS, THE(1955), ph; VIEW FROM POMPEY'S HEAD, THE(1955), ph; BIGGER THAN LIFE(1956), ph; HILDA CRANE(1956), ph; ON THE THRESHOLD OF SPACE(1956), ph; TEENAGE REBEL(1956), ph; HATFUL OF RAIN, A(1957), ph; TRUE STORY OF JESSE JAMES, THE(1957), ph; WILL SUCCESS SPOIL ROCK HUNTER?(1957), ph; FIEND WHO WALKED THE WEST, THE(1958), ph; YOUNG LIONS, THE(1958), ph; 10 NORTH FREDERICK(1958), ph; WAR-LOCK(1959), ph; GALLANT HOURS, THE(1960), ph; PEPE(1960), ph; WALK ON THE WILD SIDE(1962), ph; LIST OF ADRIAN MESSENGER, THE(1963), ph; RIO CON-CHOS(1964), ph
John D. MacDonald
MAN-TRAP(1961), w; CAPE FEAR(1962), w; KONA COAST(1968), w; DARKER THAN AMBER(1970), w
1984
FLASH OF GREEN, A(1984), d&w
John MacDonald
SUMMER HOLIDAY(1963, Brit.); HALF A SIXPENCE(1967, Brit.); YOUNG GIRLS OF ROCHEFORT, THE(1968, Fr.); MY BLOODY VALENTINE(1981, Can.)
1984
CITY GIRL, THE(1984), w
Misc. Silents
MASKED RIDER, THE(1916)
Joseph MacDonald
LITTLE TOKYO, U.S.A.(1942), ph; POSTMAN DIDN'T RING, THE(1942), ph; QUIET PLEASE, MURDER(1942), ph; THAT OTHER WOMAN(1942), ph; DOWN TO THE SEA IN SHIPS(1949), ph; WHAT PRICE GLORY?(1952), ph; LAST TIME I SAW ARCHIE, THE(1961), ph; FORTY POUNDS OF TROUBLE(1962), ph; TARAS BUL-BA(1962), ph; KINGS OF THE SUN(1963), ph; CARPETBAGGERS, THE(1964), ph; FLIGHT FROM ASHIYA(1964, U.S./Jap.), ph; WHERE LOVE HAS GONE(1964), ph; MIRAGE(1965), ph; REWARD, THE(1965), ph; ALVAREZ KELLY(1966), ph; BLIND-FOLD(1966), ph; SAND PEBBLES, THE(1966), ph; GUIDE FOR THE MARRIED MAN, A(1967), ph; MACKENNA'S GOLD(1969), ph
Joseph P. MacDonald
CHARLIE CHAN IN RIO(1941), ph; MAN WHO WOULDN'T DIE, THE(1942), ph; MY DARLING CLEMENTINE(1946), ph
Karen MacDonald
TERROR EYES(1981)
Karl MacDonald
GIRL IN BLACK STOCKINGS(1957); RIDE A VIOLENT MILE(1957); CONVICT STAGE(1965)
Katharine MacDonald
Misc. Silents
INFIDEL, THE(1922)
Katherine MacDonald
Silents
MR. FIX-IT(1918); NOTORIOUS MISS LISLE, THE(1920); BEAUTIFUL LIAR, THE(1921); STRANGER THAN FICTION(1921); LONELY ROAD, THE(1923); MONEY! MONEY! MONEY!(1923); SCARLET LILY, THE(1923); OLD LOVES AND NEW(1926)
Misc. Silents
BATTLING JANE(1918); HIS OWN HOME TOWN(1918); RIDDLE GAWNE(1918); SHARK MONROE(1918); SPIRIT OF '17, THE(1918); SQUAW MAN, THE(1918); HIGH POCKETS(1919); SPEEDY MEADE(1919); THUNDERBOLT, THE(1919); WOMAN THOU GAVEST ME, THE(1919); BEAUTY MARKET, THE(1920); CURTAIN(1920); PASSION'S PLAYGROUND(1920); TURNING POINT, THE(1920); HER SOCIAL VAL-UE(1921); MY LADY'S LATCHKEY(1921); TRUST YOUR WIFE(1921); DOMESTIC RELATIONS(1922); HEROES AND HUSBANDS(1922); WHITE SHOULDERS(1922); WOMAN CONQUERS(1922); WOMAN'S SIDE, THE(1922); CHASTITY(1923); REFUGE(1923); UNNAMED WOMAN, THE(1925)
Ken MacDonald
JOHNNY O'CLOCK(1947); HELLFIRE(1949); BORDER TREASURE(1950); MY FORBIDDEN PAST(1951); LAW AND ORDER(1953)
Kenneth MacDonald
LAST MILE, THE(1932); FRONTIER VENGEANCE(1939); OUTPOST OF THE MOUNTIES(1939); SPOILERS OF THE RANGE(1939); TAMING OF THE WEST, THE(1939); BULLETS FOR RUSTLERS(1940); DURANGO KID, THE(1940); TEXAS STAGECOACH(1940); TWO-FISTED RANGERS(1940); DEVIL COMMANDS, THE(1941); MYSTERY SHIP(1941); SON OF DAVY CROCKETT, THE(1941); WILD-CAT OF TUCSON(1941); MAN WHO RETURNED TO LIFE, THE(1942); RIDERS OF THE NORTHLAND(1942); SABOTAGE SQUAD(1942); TRAMP, TRAMP, TRAMP(1942); UNDERGROUND AGENT(1942); ROBIN HOOD OF THE RAN-GE(1943); SIX GUN GOSPEL(1943); WE'VE NEVER BEEN LICKED(1943); COWBOY FROM LONESOME RIVER(1944); PRIDE OF THE PLAINS(1944); U-BOAT PRISON-ER(1944); LOST TRAIL, THE(1945); SHADOW OF TERROR(1945); BELLE STARR'S DAUGHTER(1947); CHEYENNE(1947); FABULOUS TEXAN, THE(1947); FRA-MED(1947); FALSE PARADISE(1948); FEUDIN', FUSSIN' AND A-FIGHTIN'(1948); FRONTIER AGENT(1948); TRAIN TO ALCATRAZ(1948); GAY AMIGO, THE(1949); MYSTERIOUS DESPERADO, THE(1949); STAGECOACH KID(1949); DAKOTA LIL(1950); EXPERIMENT ALCATRAZ(1950); FEDERAL AGENT AT LARGE(1950); LAW OF THE BADLANDS(1950); SALT LAKE RAIDERS(1950); STORM OVER WYOMING(1950); DESERT OF LOST MEN(1951); HOT LEAD(1951); SUGAR-FOOT(1951); LEADVILLE GUNSLINGER(1952); MONTANA BELLE(1952); TRAIL GUIDE(1952); MARSHAL OF CEDAR ROCK(1953); SAVAGE FRONTIER(1953); SOUTHWEST PASSAGE(1954); CAPTAIN LIGHTFOOT(1955); GUN THAT WON THE

WEST, THE(1955); SEMINOLE UPRISING(1955); SHE-CREATURE, THE(1956); THREE VIOLENT PEOPLE(1956); GUNFIGHTERS OF ABILENE(1960); ERRAND BOY, THE(1961); RETURN TO PEYTON PLACE(1961); 40 GUNS TO APACHE PASS(1967)
1984
LAUGHTER HOUSE(1984, Brit.)
Misc. Talkies
BORDER VENGEANCE(1935); HANDS ACROSS THE ROCKIES(1941)
Silents
AFTER A MILLION(1924)
Kenneth R. MacDonald
BRUTE FORCE(1947); SOMEBODY LOVES ME(1952)
M. MacDonald
WHAT'S NEW, PUSSYCAT?(1965, U.S./Fr.), spec eff
Mac MacDonald
1984
TOP SECRET!(1984)
Marcia MacDonald
SLAVERS(1977, Ger.), w
Marie MacDonald
YOU'RE TELLING ME(1942)
Mary MacDonald
Misc. Silents
FLASH OF FATE, THE(1918)
Mary MacDonald [MacLaren]
Misc. Silents
SHOES(1916)
May MacDonald
MARK OF CAIN, THE(1948, Brit.); MR. PERRIN AND MR. TRAILL(1948, Brit.)
Michael MacDonald
BEST MAN, THE(1964)
Mike MacDonald
FUNNY FARM, THE(1982, Can.)
Moira MacDonald
RETURN TO PARADISE(1953); PACIFIC DESTINY(1956, Brit.)
Neil MacDonald
1984
BIG MEAT EATER(1984, Can.)
Nesta MacDonald
JOHNNY THE GIANT KILLER(1953, Fr.), w
Norman MacDonald
SQUAD CAR(1961)
Misc. Silents
CHRISTIE JOHNSTONE(1921, Brit.), d; LOUDWATER MYSTERY, THE(1921, Brit.), d
Peter Macdonald
1984
SECRET PLACES(1984, Brit.), ph
Philip MacDonald
C.O.D.(1932, Brit.), w; HOTEL SPLENDIDE(1932, Brit.), w; CHARLIE CHAN IN LONDON(1934), w; LOST PATROL, THE,(1934), w; MENACE(1934), w; MYSTERY OF MR. X, THE(1934), w; CHARLIE CHAN IN PARIS(1935), w; LAST OUTPOST, THE(1935), w; YOURS FOR THE ASKING(1936), w; RIVER OF UNREST(1937, Brit.), w; WHO KILLED JOHN SAVAGE?(1937, Brit.), w; MR. MOTO TAKES A VACATION(1938), w; MYSTERIOUS MR. MOTO(1938), w; GENTLEMAN'S GENTLE-MAN, A(1939, Brit.), w; MR. MOTO'S LAST WARNING(1939), w; NURSEMAID WHO DISAPPEARED, THE(1939, Brit.), w; REBECCA(1940), w; NIGHTMARE(1942), w; SAHARA(1943), w; ACTION IN ARABIA(1944), w; BODY SNATCHER, THE(1945), w; DANGEROUS INTRUDER(1945), w; LOVE FROM A STRANGER(1947), w; DARK PAST, THE(1948), w; CIRCLE OF DANGER(1951, Brit.), w; MAN WHO CHEATED HIMSELF, THE(1951), w; MASK OF THE AVENGER(1951), w; HOUR OF THIR-TEEN, THE(1952), w; RING OF FEAR(1954), w; 23 PACES TO BAKER STREET(1956), w; LIST OF ADRIAN MESSENGER, THE(1963), w
Phillip MacDonald
MYSTERY WOMAN(1935), w; PRINCESS COMES ACROSS, THE(1936), w; BLIND ALLEY(1939), w; STRANGERS IN THE NIGHT(1944), w; TOBOR THE GREAT(1954), w
Silents
LOST PATROL, THE(1929, Brit.), w
Philo MacDonald
Silents
EXTRAVAGANCE(1919)
Pirie MacDonald
NETWORK(1976)
Richard MacDonald
GYPSY AND THE GENTLEMAN, THE(1958, Brit.), prod d; CHANCE MEE-TING(1960, Brit.), prod d; CONCRETE JUNGLE, THE(1962, Brit.), prod d; EVA(1962, Fr./Ital.), art d; KING AND COUNTRY(1964, Brit.), prod d; SERVANT, THE(1964, Brit.), prod d; MODESTY BLAISE(1966, Brit.), prod d; BOOM!(1968), prod d; SECRET CEREMONY(1968, Brit.), prod d; SEVERED HEAD, A(1971, Brit.), prod d; JESUS CHRIST, SUPERSTAR(1973), prod d; DAY OF THE LOCUST, THE(1975), prod d; ROMANTIC ENGLISHWOMAN, THE(1975, Brit./Fr.), art d; MARATHON MAN(1976), prod d; EXORCIST II: THE HERETIC(1977), prod d; F.I.S.T.(1978), prod d; ...AND JUSTICE FOR ALL(1979), set d; ROSE, THE(1979), prod d; SOMETHING WICKED THIS WAY COMES(1983), prod d
1984
CRIMES OF PASSION(1984), prod d; ELECTRIC DREAMS(1984), prod d; SUPER-GIRL(1984), prod d; TEACHERS(1984), prod d
Robert MacDonald
BEN HUR(1959), spec eff; IS PARIS BURNING?(1966, U.S./Fr.), spec eff; CHARGE OF THE LIGHT BRIGADE, THE(1968, Brit.), spec eff; FLEA IN HER EAR, A(1968, Fr.), spec eff; RYAN'S DAUGHTER(1970, Brit.), spec eff; WHAT'S UP, DOC?(1972), spec eff; MARCH OR DIE(1977, Brit.), spec eff; HEAVEN CAN WAIT(1978), spec eff
Robert MacDonald, Jr.
MAGIC(1978), spec eff
Robert A. MacDonald
ALFRED THE GREAT(1969, Brit.), spec eff

Roger MacDonald
LAW AND DISORDER(1940, Brit.), w
Ronald MacDonald
HER TWELVE MEN(1954)
Ross MacDonald
HARPER(1966), w; DROWNING POOL, THE(1975), w; DOUBLE NEGATIVE(1980, Can.), w
Sherwood MacDonald
Misc. Silents
BAB THE FIXER(1917), d; BETTY BE GOOD(1917), d; BIT OF KINDLING, A(1917), d; CHECKMATE, THE(1917), d; SUNNY JANE(1917), d; WILDCAT, THE(1917), d
Susan MacDonald
MIDNIGHT MAN, THE(1974)
1984
BLAME IT ON THE NIGHT(1984)
Thomas H. MacDonald
Silents
IN THE HANDS OF THE LONDON CROOKS(1913, Brit.); ROAD TO RUIN, THE(1913, Brit.); JACK TAR(1915, Brit.); HARD WAY, THE(1916, Brit.); TAILOR OF BOND STREET, THE(1916, Brit.); ODDS AGAINST HER, THE(1919, Brit.)
Thos H. MacDonald
Misc. Silents
FIVE NIGHTS(1915, Brit.); STRIFE ETERNAL, THE(1915, Brit.)
Thos. H. MacDonald
Misc. Silents
WOMAN WHO DID, THE(1915, Brit.)
Tom H. MacDonald
Misc. Silents
LIGHTS O' LONDON, THE(1914, Brit.); DO UNTO OTHERS(1915, Brit.); BURNT WINGS(1916, Brit.)
Wallace MacDonald
BLOCKADE(1929); DARKENED ROOMS(1929); FANCY BAGGAGE(1929); SWEE-TIE(1929); DARKENED SKIES(1930); HIT THE DECK(1930); BRANDED(1931); DRUMS OF JEOPARDY(1931); FIFTY FATHOMS DEEP(1931); FIGHTING THRU(1931); PAGAN LADY(1931); RANGE FEUD, THE(1931); SMART MONEY(1931); BETWEEN FIGHTING MEN(1932); CORNERED(1932), w; HELLO TROUBLE(1932); HIGH SPEED(1932); RIDING TORNADO, THE(1932); TEX TAKES A HOLIDAY(1932); TEXAS CYCLONE(1932); TWO-FISTED LAW(1932); VANISHING FRONTIER, THE(1932); FLYING DOWN TO RIO(1933); GOLD DIGGERS OF 1933(1933); MARY STEVENS, M.D.(1933); MAYOR OF HELL, THE(1933); KING OF THE WILD HORSES, THE(1934); IN OLD SANTA FE(1935), w; DOUGHNUTS AND SOCIETY(1936), w; HITCH HIKE LADY(1936), w; SHADOW, THE(1937), p; WHEN G-MEN STEP IN(1938), p; KONGA, THE WILD STALLION(1939), p; MAN THEY COULD NOT HANG, THE(1939), p; BEFORE I HANG(1940), p; ISLAND OF DOOMED MEN(1940), p; MAN WITH NINE LIVES, THE(1940), p; BIG BOSS, THE(1941), p; DEVIL COM-MANDS, THE(1941), p; HARMON OF MICHIGAN(1941), p; HONOLULU LU(1941), p; I WAS A PRISONER ON DEVIL'S ISLAND(1941), p; NAVAL ACADEMY(1941), p; TWO LATINS FROM MANHATTAN(1941), p; BOSTON BLACKIE GOES HOLLY-WOOD(1942), p; COUNTER-ESPIONAGE(1942), p; HARVARD, HERE I COME(1942), p; HELLO ANNAPOLIS(1942), p; MAN WHO RETURNED TO LIFE, THE(1942), p; MAN'S WORLD, A(1942), p; PARACHUTE NURSE(1942), p; SUBMARINE RAI-DER(1942), p; TRAMP, TRAMP, TRAMP(1942), p; CHANCE OF A LIFETIME, THE(1943), p; PASSPORT TO SUEZ(1943), p; CRY OF THE WEREWOLF(1944), p; MISSING JUROR, THE(1944), p; RACKET MAN, THE(1944), p; SAILOR'S HOLI-DAY(1944), p; STARS ON PARADE(1944), p; U-BOAT PRISONER(1944), p; DANCING IN MANHATTAN(1945), p; ESCAPE IN THE FOG(1945), p; GUY, A GAL AND A PAL, A(1945), p; I LOVE A MYSTERY(1945), p; MY NAME IS JULIA ROSS(1945), p; DEVIL'S MASK, THE(1946), p; OUT OF THE DEPTHS(1946), p; PERSONALITY KID(1946), p; UNKNOWN, THE(1946), p; WHEN A GIRL'S BEAUTIFUL(1947), p; MY DOG RUSTY(1948), p; PORT SAID(1948), p; AIR HOSTESS(1949), p; LAW OF THE BARBARY COAST(1949), p; RUSTY SAVES A LIFE(1949), p; RUSTY'S BIRT-HDAY(1949), p; BEAUTY ON PARADE(1950), p; COUNTERSPY MEETS SCOTLAND YARD(1950), p; GIRLS' SCHOOL(1950), p; MILITARY ACADEMY WITH THAT TENTH AVENUE GANG(1950), p; ON THE ISLE OF SAMOA(1950), p; TOUGHER THEY COME, THE(1950), p; BIG GUSHER, THE(1951), p; CHAIN OF CIRCUM-STANCE(1951), p; CORKY OF GASOLINE ALLEY(1951), p; HAREM GIRL(1952), p; OKINAWA(1952), p; TARGET HONG KONG(1952), p; MAN IN THE DARK(1953), p; NEBRASKAN, THE(1953), p; BLACK DAKOTAS, THE(1954), p; EL ALAMEIN(1954), p; MASSACRE CANYON(1954), p; OUTLAW STALLION, THE(1954), p; REDHEAD FROM MANHATTAN(1954), p; APACHE AMBUSH(1955), p; CELL 2455, DEATH ROW(1955), p; WYOMING RENEGADES(1955), p; FURY AT GUNSIGHT PASS(1956), p; SECRET OF TREASURE MOUNTAIN(1956), p; WHITE SQUAW, THE(1956), p; FLAME OF STAMBOUL(1957), p; NO TIME TO BE YOUNG(1957), p; PHANTOM STAGECOACH, THE(1957), p; RETURN TO WARBOW(1958), p; GUNMEN FROM LAREDO(1959), p&d
Silents
TILLIE'S PUNCTURED ROMANCE(1914); NANETTE OF THE WILDS(1916); FOL-LIES GIRL, THE(1919); ARE ALL MEN ALIKE?(1920); MOON MADNESS(1920); GIRL FROM THE WEST(1923), d; ROARING RAILS(1924); CHARMER, THE(1925); LEARN-ING TO LOVE(1925); NEW LIVES FOR OLD(1925); TUMBLING RIVER(1927); YOUR WIFE AND MINE(1927); FREE LIPS(1928), d
Misc. Silents
YOUTH'S ENDEARING CHARM(1916); MARRIAGE SPECULATION, THE(1917); PRINCESS OF PARK ROW, THE(1917); MADAME SPHINX(1918); MARKED CARDS(1918); MLLE PAULETTE(1918); SHOES THAT DANCED, THE(1918); BROTH-ERS DIVIDED(1919); LEAVE IT TO SUSAN(1919); LITTLE BOSS, THE(1919); SPOT-LIGHT SADIE(1919); FIGHTING SHEPHERDESS, THE(1920); SILK HOSIERY(1920); TRUMPET ISLAND(1920); POOR RELATION, A(1921); SAGE HEN, THE(1921); CAUGHT BLUFFING(1922); UNDERSTUDY, THE(1922); YOUTH MUST HAVE LOVE(1922); DAY OF FAITH, THE(1923); CURLYTOP(1924); HEART BANDIT, THE(1924); LOVE AND GLORY(1924); SEA HAWK, THE(1924); THY NAME IS WOMAN(1924); LIGHTNIN'(1925); PRIMROSE PATH, THE(1925); WANDERING FIRES(1925); BAR-C MYSTERY, THE(1926); CHECKERED FLAG, THE(1926); FAITH-FUL WIVES(1926); TWO CAN PLAY(1926); DRUMS OF THE DESERT(1927); HIS FOREIGN WIFE(1927)
Wilfred MacDonald
Silents
CONNECTICUT YANKEE AT KING ARTHUR'S COURT, A(1921)

William MacDonald
MOVIE CRAZY(1932), art d
William C. MacDonald
ALONG THE NAVAJO TRAIL(1945), w
William Colt MacDonald
RIDING TORNADO, THE(1932), w; TEXAS CYCLONE(1932), w; TWO-FISTED LAW(1932), w; POWDERSMOKE RANGE(1935), w; THREE MESQUITEERS, THE(1936), w; TOO MUCH BEEF(1936), w; GHOST TOWN GOLD(1937), w; HIT THE SADDLE(1937), w; ONE MAN JUSTICE(1937), w; RIDERS OF THE WHISTLING SKULL(1937), w; TWO-FISTED SHERIFF(1937), w; OUTLAWS OF SONORA(1938), w; PALS OF THE SADDLE(1938), w; PURPLE VIGILANTES, THE(1938), w; RED RIVER RANGE(1938), w; SANTA FE STAMPEDE(1938), w; COWBOYS FROM TEXAS(1939), w; THREE TEXAS STEERS(1939), w; WYOMING OUTLAW(1939), w; COVERED WAGON DAYS(1940), w; OKLAHOMA RENEGADES(1940), w; TRAIL BLAZERS, THE(1940), w; UNDER TEXAS SKIES(1940), w; GANGS OF SONORA(1941), w; GAUCHOS OF EL DORADO(1941), w; OUTLAWS OF THE CHEROKEE TRAIL(1941), w; PALS OF THE PECOS(1941), w; SADDLEMATES(1941), w; RAIDERS OF THE RANGE(1942), w; SHADOWS ON THE SAGE(1942), w; VALLEY OF HUNTED MEN(1942), w; SANTA FE SCOUTS(1943), w; THUNDERING TRAILS(1943), w
Peter Macdonell
KID FROM CANADA, THE(1957, Brit.)
Frankie MacDonncha
POITIN(1979, Irish), art d
A.G. MacDonnell
PIMPERNEL SMITH(1942, Brit.), w
Claude MacDonnell
CITY OF PLAY(1929, Brit.), ph; HIGH SEAS(1929, Brit.), ph; CROOKED BILLET, THE(1930, Brit.), ph
Fergus Macdonnell
I MET A MURDERER(1939, Brit.), ed
Gordon MacDonnell
LUCKY DAYS(1935, Brit.), w; TO CATCH A THIEF(1936, Brit.), w
Kyle MacDonnell
THAT HAGEN GIRL(1947); TAXI(1953)
Margaret MacDonnell
LUCKY DAYS(1935, Brit.), w; TO CATCH A THIEF(1936, Brit.), w
Norman MacDonnell
BALLAD OF JOSIE(1968), p
Peter MacDonnell
FLESH AND BLOOD(1951, Brit.)
Ron MacDonnell
TARZAN THE MAGNIFICENT(1960, Brit.)
Glen MacDonough
BABES IN TOYLAND(1961), w
Roger MacDougal
LET'S BE FAMOUS(1939, Brit.), w; THIS MAN IS NEWS(1939, Brit.), w
Allan Ross MacDougall
SOAK THE RICH(1936)
Joanne MacDougall
LEARNING TREE, THE(1969), set d
Kenneth MacDougall
Misc. Silents
BULLDOGS OF THE TRAIL, THE(1915), a, d
Ranald MacDougall
MILDRED PIERCE(1945), w; OBJECTIVE, BURMA!(1945), w; POSSESSED(1947), w; UNSUSPECTED, THE(1947), w; DECISION OF CHRISTOPHER BLAKE, THE(1948), p, w; JUNE BRIDE(1948), w; HASTY HEART, THE(1949), w; BREAKING POINT, THE(1950), w; BRIGHT LEAF(1950), w; STAGE FRIGHT(1950, Brit.), w; I'LL NEVER FORGET YOU(1951), w; NAKED JUNGLE, THE(1953), w; SECRET OF THE INCAS(1954), w; QUEEN BEE(1955), d, w; WE'RE NO ANGELS(1955), w; MOUNTAIN, THE(1956), w; MAN ON FIRE(1957), d&w; WORLD, THE FLESH, AND THE DEVIL, THE(1959), d, w; GO NAKED IN THE WORLD(1961), w; CLEOPATRA(1963), w; JIGSAW(1968), p; COCKEYED COWBOYS OF CALICO COUNTY, THE(1970), p, w
Robin Macdougall
Misc. Silents
BLUEBIRD, THE(1918)
Roger Macdougall
MIDNIGHT AT THE WAX MUSEUM(1936, Brit.), w; BOMBS OVER LONDON(1937, Brit.), w; CHEER BOYS CHEER(1939, Brit.), w; THIS MAN IN PARIS(1939, Brit.), w; SPARE A COPPER(1940, Brit.), w; BELLS GO DOWN, THE(1943, Brit.), w; GENTLE GUNMAN, THE(1952, Brit.), w; MAN IN THE WHITE SUIT, THE(1952), w; ESCAPADE(1955, Brit.), w; CASH ON DELIVERY(1956, Brit.), w; MOUSE THAT ROARED, THE(1959, Brit.), w; TOUCH OF LARCENY, A(1960, Brit.), w
Ronald MacDougall
MR. BELVEDERE RINGS THE BELL(1951), w; GO NAKED IN THE WORLD(1961), d
John MacDouglas
SULEIMAN THE CONQUEROR(1963, Ital.)
Andie MacDowell
1984
GREYSTOKE: THE LEGEND OF TARZAN, LORD OF THE APES(1984)
Bill MacDowell
ROAD HUSTLERS, THE(1968)
Claire MacDowell
IT'S TOUGH TO BE FAMOUS(1932)
Fred MacDowell
RING OF FEAR(1954), ed; TRACK OF THE CAT(1954), ed; GOODBYE, MY LADY(1956), ed; I'VE LIVED BEFORE(1956), ed; JOE DAKOTA(1957), ed; LAND UNKNOWN, THE(1957), ed; QUANTEZ(1957), ed
J. B. MacDowell
Silents
LIEUTENANT DARING RN AND THE WATER RATS(1924, Brit.), p
John MacDowell
YOUNG MAN OF MANHATTAN(1930)
Melbourne MacDowell
Silents
PLAYING THE GAME(1918); ALL OF A SUDDEN NORMA(1919); GO WEST, YOUNG MAN(1919); DIAMONDS ADRIFT(1921); OUTSIDE THE LAW(1921); GEARED TO GO(1924); SPEED MAD(1925); BEHIND THE FRONT(1926); RAINMAK-

ER, THE(1926); WHAT HAPPENED TO JONES(1926); DRIVEN FROM HOME(1927); OLD CODE, THE(1928)
Misc. Silents
GOLDEN SNARE, THE(1921); BOOTLEGGER'S DAUGHTER, THE(1922); FLAMING HOUR, THE(1922); LOVE PIRATE, THE(1923); BANDITS OF THE AIR(1925); FIGHTING COURAGE(1925); SAVAGES OF THE SEA(1925); SKY'S THE LIMIT(1925); OUTLAW EXPRESS, THE(1926); STICK TO YOUR STORY(1926); CODE OF THE COW COUNTRY(1927); FEEL MY PULSE(1928)
Nelson MacDowell
Silents
LOST WORLD, THE(1925)
Ewan MacDuff
FOUR DESPERATE MEN(1960, Brit.)
Sean MacDuff
TOO LATE THE HERO(1970)
Tyler MacDuff
BOUNTY HUNTER, THE(1954); BOY FROM OKLAHOMA, THE(1954); CELL 2455, DEATH ROW(1955); BURNING HILLS, THE(1956); CYBORG 2087(1966)
Alain Mace
DANTON(1983)
Borden Mace
ANIMAL FARM(1955, Brit.), w
Fred Mace
Silents
WITHOUT HOPE(1914), d
Misc. Silents
WHAT HAPPENED TO JONES(1915)
Patricia Mace
POWERS GIRL, THE(1942); RIDING HIGH(1943)
Patsy Mace
DISPUTED PASSAGE(1939); OUR NEIGHBORS–THE CARTERS(1939); $1,000 A TOUCHDOWN(1939); ALOMA OF THE SOUTH SEAS(1941); ARABIAN NIGHTS(1942); ROAD TO MOROCCO(1942)
Paul Mace
HOSPITAL, THE(1971); PANIC IN NEEDLE PARK(1971); LORDS OF FLATBUSH, THE(1974); PARADISE ALLEY(1978)
Terry Mace
BURY ME AN ANGEL(1972)
Victor Mace
Misc. Talkies
FIGHTING PILOT, THE(1935)
Warren Mace
EMERGENCY WEDDING(1950); DREAMBOAT(1952); THEM!(1954)
William Mace
GIRL IN THE RED VELVET SWING, THE(1955), ed; D-DAY, THE SIXTH OF JUNE(1956), ed; TEENAGE REBEL(1956), ed; BOY ON A DOLPHIN(1957), ed; SUN ALSO RISES, THE(1957), ed; SING, BOY, SING(1958), ed; DIARY OF ANNE FRANK, THE(1959), ed; REMARKABLE MR. PENNYPACKER, THE(1959), ed
Wynn Mace
Silents
CHASING THE MOON(1922); SKY HIGH(1922); ROMANCE LAND(1923)
Rita Macedo
CRIMINAL LIFE OF ARCHIBALDO DE LA CRUZ, THE(1962, Mex.); EMPTY STAR, THE(1962, Mex.); SPIRITISM(1965, Mex.); NAZARIN(1968, Mex.); CURSE OF THE CRYING WOMAN, THE(1969, Mex.); CASTLE OF PURITY(1974, Mex.)
Romollo Macellini
TALE OF FIVE WOMEN, A(1951, Brit.), d
Carla Macelloni
FAST AND SEXY(1960, Fr./Ital.)
Sandy Macera
WOMEN AND BLOODY TERROR(1970)
Ted Macero
FRIDAY THE 13TH... THE ORPHAN(1979), m
Teo Macero
VIRUS(1980, Jap.), m
Frank Macetta
ANDERSON TAPES, THE(1971)
Walter MacEwan
MAN IN HALF-MOON STREET, THE(1944), p
Linda MacEwen
THEY ALL LAUGHED(1981)
1984
FOOTLOOSE(1984)
Walter MacEwen
ALWAYS IN MY HEART(1942), p; BIG SHOT, THE(1942), p; HENRY ALDRICH GETS GLAMOUR(1942), p; NIGHT PLANE FROM CHUNGKING(1942), p; GOOD FELLOWS, THE(1943), p; HENRY ALDRICH SWINGS IT(1943), p; SALUTE FOR THREE(1943), p; HENRY ALDRICH'S LITTLE SECRET(1944), p; NATIONAL BARN DANCE(1944), p; MIRACLE OF THE BELLS, THE(1948), p
Betty Macey
LOCAL HERO(1983, Brit.)
Carleton Macey
Silents
DESTRUCTION(1915)
Misc. Silents
CITY OF ILLUSION, THE(1916); SCARLET OATH, THE(1916)
Cora Macey
Silents
IRENE(1926)
Elizabeth Macey
BOUND FOR GLORY(1976)
Michael Macey
GREAT SINNER, THE(1949)
Hamilton MacFadden
CRAZY THAT WAY(1930), d&w; HARMONY AT HOME(1930), d; CHARLIE CHAN CARRIES ON(1931), d; RIDERS OF THE PURPLE SAGE(1931), d; CHEATERS AT PLAY(1932), d; CHARLIE CHAN'S GREATEST CASE(1933), d; FOURTH HORSEMAN, THE(1933), d; SECOND HAND WIFE(1933), d&w; TRICK FOR TRICK(1933), d; HOLD THAT GIRL(1934), d; SHE WAS A LADY(1934), d; STAND UP AND CHEER(1934 80m FOX bw), d; ELINOR NORTON(1935), d; FIGHTING YOUTH(1935),

d, w; IT CAN'T LAST FOREVER(1937), d; LEGION OF MISSING MEN(1937), d; THREE LEGIONNAIRES, THE(1937), d; FIVE OF A KIND(1938); SHARP-SHOOTERS(1938); TARNISHED ANGEL(1938); CHARLIE CHAN IN RENO(1939); HONEYMOON'S OVER, THE(1939), w; JONES FAMILY IN HOLLYWOOD, THE(1939); LADY IN QUESTION, THE(1940); SHOOTING HIGH(1940); CHARLIE CHAN IN RIO(1941); DRESSED TO KILL(1941); RIDE, KELLY, RIDE(1941); SLEEP-ERS WEST(1941); INSIDE THE LAW(1942), d

Misc. Talkies
THEIR MAD MOMENT(1931), d

Ivor MacFadden
Silents
MEASURE OF A MAN, THE(1916)

Dorothea MacFarland
NIGHT THEY RAIDED MINSKY'S, THE(1968)

Frank MacFarland
WINNING TEAM, THE(1952)

George MacFarland
VARSITY SHOW(1937)

Mike MacFarland
GOODBYE FRANKLIN HIGH(1978), p&d; HI-RIDERS(1978), p

Spanky MacFarland
PECK'S BAD BOY WITH THE CIRCUS(1938); I ESCAPED FROM THE GES-TAPO(1943)

Bruce MacFarlane
COME ON, LEATHERNECKS(1938); COME ON RANGERS(1939); FORGED PASS-PORT(1939); TORCHY PLAYS WITH DYNAMITE(1939)

Cassie MacFarlane
BURNING AN ILLUSION(1982, Brit.)

Debra MacFarlane
HANGAR 18(1980)

Frank MacFarlane
PARDON MY GUN(1930)

George MacFarlane
NIX ON DAMES(1929); PAINTED ANGEL, THE(1929); SOUTH SEA ROSE(1929); WALL STREET(1929); DOUBLE CROSS ROADS(1930); HALF SHOT AT SUN-RISE(1930); HAPPY DAYS(1930); UP THE RIVER(1930); HEART OF NEW YORK(1932); TAXI!(1932)

Janet Macfarlane
MAN WHO KNEW TOO MUCH, THE(1956)

Jim Macfarlane
SKIN DEEP(1978, New Zealand)

John MacFarlane
Silents
PATSY(1921)

Louella MacFarlane
GUILT OF JANET AMES, THE(1947), w; MATING OF MILLIE, THE(1948), w

Pascoe MacFarlane
BROTHERS AND SISTERS(1980, Brit.), ph

Peter Clark MacFarlane
Silents
MOLLY OF THE FOLLIES(1919), w; GUILE OF WOMEN(1921), w; HELD TO ANSWER(1923), w

Peter MacFarlane
BLACK ROSES(1936, Ger.), w

Tom MacFarlane
PARDON MY GUN(1930)

Wendy Macfarlane
SKIN DEEP(1978, New Zealand)

Rory Macfarquhar
1984
DARK ENEMY(1984, Brit.)

Gavin MacFayden
THIEF(1981)

Jim MacGeorge
WORLD OF HANS CHRISTIAN ANDERSEN, THE(1971, Jap.)

Harriet E. MacGibbon
CRY FOR HAPPY(1961)

Harriet MacGibbon
MAJORITY OF ONE, A(1961); FOUR HORSEMEN OF THE APOCALYPSE, THE(1962); SON OF FLUBBER(1963); FLUFFY(1965)

Bernard MacGill
BREWSTER'S MILLIONS(1935, Brit.), ph

Gay MacGill
SILENCERS, THE(1966)

Moyna MacGill
UNCLE HARRY(1945); FOREVER AND A DAY(1943); FRENCHMAN'S CREEK(1944); JANE EYRE(1944); NATIONAL VELVET(1944); UNINVITED, THE(1944); WINGED VICTORY(1944); PICTURE OF DORIAN GRAY, THE(1945); BLACK BEAUTY(1946); GREEN DOLPHIN STREET(1947); THREE DARING DAUGHTERS(1948); BRIDE OF THE GORILLA(1951); KIND LADY(1951); MY FAIR LADY(1964); UNSINKABLE MOLLY BROWN, THE(1964)

Patrick MacGill
SUSPENSE(1930, Brit.), w

Sheila MacGill
CAVALCADE(1933)

Niall Macginnis
TURN OF THE TIDE(1935, Brit.); EDGE OF THE WORLD, THE(1937, Brit.); LUCK OF THE IRISH, THE(1937, Ireland); RIVER OF UNREST(1937, Brit.); MOUNTAINS O'MOURNE(1938, Brit.); INVADERS, THE(1941); HUNDRED POUND WINDOW, THE(1943, Brit.); WE DIVE AT DAWN(1943, Brit.); UNDERGROUND GUERRIL-LAS(1944, Brit.); HENRY V(1946, Brit.); TAWNY PIPIT(1947, Brit.); ANNA KARENI-NA(1948, Brit.); CHRISTOPHER COLUMBUS(1949, Brit.); DIAMOND CITY(1949, Brit.); CHANCE OF A LIFETIME(1950, Brit.); NO ROOM AT THE INN(1950, Brit.); NO HIGHWAY IN THE SKY(1951, Brit.); MURDER IN THE CATHEDRAL(1952, Brit.); KNIGHTS OF THE ROUND TABLE(1953); MARTIN LUTHER(1953); BE-TRAYED(1954, Brit.); FUSS OVER FEATHERS(1954, Brit.); HELL BELOW ZERO(1954, Brit.); SPECIAL DELIVERY(1955, Ger.); ALEXANDER THE GREAT(1956); HELEN OF TROY(1956, Ital); LUST FOR LIFE(1956); SHIRALEE, THE(1957, Brit.); BEHIND THE MASK(1958, Brit.); CURSE OF THE DEMON(1958); SHAKE HANDS WITH THE DEVIL(1959, Ireland); TARZAN'S GREATEST ADVENTURE(1959, Brit.); THIS OTH-

ER EDEN(1959, Brit.); FOXHOLE IN CAIRO(1960, Brit.); IN THE NICK(1960, Brit.); KIDNAPPED(1960); NIGHT FIGHTERS, THE(1960); NEVER TAKE CANDY FROM A STRANGER(1961, Brit.); SWORD OF SHERWOOD FOREST(1961, Brit.); BILLY BUDD(1962); SHE DIDN'T SAY NO!(1962, Brit.); WEBSTER BOY, THE(1962, Brit.); JASON AND THE ARGONAUTS(1963, Brit.); BECKET(1964, Brit.); JOHNNY NO-BODY(1965, Brit.); SPY WHO CAME IN FROM THE COLD, THE(1965, Brit.); TRUTH ABOUT SPRING, THE(1965, Brit.); WAR LORD, THE(1965); MAN COULD GET KILLED, A(1966); ISLAND OF TERROR(1967, Brit.); VIKING QUEEN, THE(1967, Brit.); SHOES OF THE FISHERMAN, THE(1968); TORTURE GARDEN(1968, Brit.); KRAKATOA, EAST OF JAVA(1969); SINFUL DAVEY(1969, Brit.); DARLING LILI(1970); KREMLIN LETTER, THE(1970); MACKINTOSH MAN, THE(1973, Brit.)

Misc. Talkies
PLAY IT COOLER(1961)

John MacGloan
STEEL CLAW, THE(1961)

J.P. MacGowan
FIGHTING HERO(1934)

Kenneth Macgowan
IF I WERE FREE(1933), p; LITTLE WOMEN(1933), p; MURDER ON THE BLACK-BOARD(1934), p; WEDNESDAY'S CHILD(1934), p; BECKY SHARP(1935), p; EN-CHANTED APRIL(1935), p; JALNA(1935), p; MURDER ON A HONEYMOON(1935), p; RETURN OF PETER GRIMM, THE(1935), p; LLOYDS OF LONDON(1936), p; SINS OF MAN(1936), p; RETURN OF THE CISCO KID(1939), p; STORY OF ALEXANDER GRAHAM BELL, THE(1939), p; SUSANNAH OF THE MOUNTIES(1939), p; YOUNG MR. LINCOLN(1939), p; HUDSON'S BAY(1940), p; STAR DUST(1940), p; TIN PAN ALLEY(1940), p; BELLE STARR(1941), p; HAPPY LAND(1943), p; LIFEBOAT(1944), p; EASY COME, EASY GO(1947), p

Norman MacGowan
LUST FOR LIFE(1956)

Jack MacGowran
PANIC IN THE PARLOUR(1957, Brit.); RISING OF THE MOON, THE(1957, Ireland); ROONEY(1958, Brit.); BOY AND THE BRIDGE, THE(1959, Brit.); DARBY O'GILL AND THE LITTLE PEOPLE(1959); CHANCE MEETING(1960, Brit.); MIX ME A PER-SON(1962, Brit.); NIGHT CREATURES(1962, Brit.); SHE DIDN'T SAY NO!(1962, Brit.); TWO AND TWO MAKE SIX(1962, Brit.); TOM JONES(1963, Brit.); BRAIN, THE(1965, Ger./Brit.); DOCTOR ZHIVAGO(1965); LORD JIM(1965, Brit.); YOUNG CAS-SIDY(1965, U.S./Brit.); CUL-DE-SAC(1966, Brit.); FEARLESS VAMPIRE KILLERS, OR PARDON ME BUT YOUR TEETH ARE IN MY NECK, THE(1967); HOW I WON THE WAR(1967, Brit.); AGE OF CONSENT(1969, Austral.); WONDERWALL(1969, Brit.); START THE REVOLUTION WITHOUT ME(1970); KING LEAR(1971, Brit./Den.); EXORCIST, THE(1973)

Tara MacGowran
MEMOIRS OF A SURVIVOR(1981, Brit.)
1984
SECRET PLACES(1984, Brit.)

Harold MacGrath
DRUMS OF JEOPARDY(1931), w
Silents
NOT GUILTY(1921), w; RAGGED EDGE, THE(1923), w; MAN ON THE BOX, THE(1925), w; WOMANPOWER(1926), w

Leueen MacGrath
PYGMALION(1938, Brit.); SAINT'S VACATION, THE(1941, Brit.); MAXWELL ARCHER, DETECTIVE(1942, Brit.); EDWARD, MY SON(1949, U.S./Brit.); THREE CASES OF MURDER(1955, Brit.)

Margaret MacGrath
CIRCUS WORLD(1964)

Ali MacGraw
LOVELY WAY TO DIE, A(1968); GOODBYE COLUMBUS(1969); LOVE STORY(1970); CONVOY(1978)

Oliver MacGreevey
LEATHER BOYS, THE(1965, Brit.); FLASH GORDON(1980)

Oliver MacGreevy
GIRL WITH GREEN EYES(1964, Brit.); IPCRESS FILE, THE(1965, Brit.); SECOND BEST SECRET AGENT IN THE WHOLE WIDE WORLD, THE(1965, Brit.); INCIDENT AT MIDNIGHT(1966, Brit.); MODESTY BLAISE(1966, Brit.); FROZEN DEAD, THE(1967, Brit.); KISS THE GIRLS AND MAKE THEM DIE(1967, U.S./Ital.); GREAT CATHERINE(1968, Brit.); SALT & PEPPER(1968, Brit.); WHEN EIGHT BELLS TOLL(1971, Brit.); RULING CLASS, THE(1972, Brit.); TALES FROM THE CRYPT(1972, Brit.)

Barry MacGregor
NIGHT TO REMEMBER, A(1958, Brit.)

Casey MacGregor
LADY IN A JAM(1942); KNICKERBOCKER HOLIDAY(1944); SEVEN DOORS TO DEATH(1944); BORDER FEUD(1947); WEST TO GLORY(1947); BUCKAROO FROM POWDER RIVER(1948); MOONRISE(1948); MAN WITHOUT A STAR(1955); FIRST TRAVELING SALESLADY, THE(1956); STUDS LONIGAN(1960)

Charles MacGregor
THAT'S THE WAY OF THE WORLD(1975)

Chummy MacGregor
SUN VALLEY SERENADE(1941); GLENN MILLER STORY, THE(1953), tech adv

Doreen MacGregor
CONVICTED(1938)

Edgar J. MacGregor
GOOD NEWS(1930), d

Frank MacGregor
FAMILY HONEYMOON(1948)

Harmon MacGregor
Silents
SLAVE OF DESIRE(1923)
Misc. Silents
VENGEANCE OF THE DEEP(1923)

Hector MacGregor
STAGE FRIGHT(1950, Brit.); FLESH AND BLOOD(1951, Brit.); NO HIGHWAY IN THE SKY(1951, Brit.); RELUCTANT WIDOW, THE(1951, Brit.); 13 EAST STREET(1952, Brit.)

Ian MacGregor
JE T'AIME, JE T'AIME(1972, Fr./Swed.); WORLD ACCORDING TO GARP, The(1982)

Isabelle Macgregor
Misc. Silents
HEART OF NEW YORK, THE(1916)
Jack MacGregor
AMBUSH IN LEOPARD STREET(1962, Brit.), p
James MacGregor
Silents
BREWSTER'S MILLIONS(1914)
Jock MacGregor
ENTER INSPECTOR DUVAL(1961, Brit.), p; QUESTION OF SUSPENSE, A(1961, Brit.), p; MURDER IN EDEN(1962, Brit.), p; MAN WHO COULDN'T WALK, THE(1964, Brit.), p
John MacGregor
WICKER MAN, THE(1974, Brit.)
K.C. MacGregor
DALTON GIRLS, THE(1957)
Kenneth MacGregor
1984
MUPPETS TAKE MANHATTAN, THE(1984)
Lee MacGregor
MOTHER WORE TIGHTS(1947); ROAD HOUSE(1948); SCUDDA-HOO! SCUDDA-HAY!(1948); WHEN MY BABY SMILES AT ME(1948); YOU WERE MEANT FOR ME(1948); FATHER WAS A FULLBACK(1949); MOTHER IS A FRESHMAN(1949); MR. BELVEDERE GOES TO COLLEGE(1949); SLATTERY'S HURRICANE(1949); TWELVE O'CLOCK HIGH(1949); THREE CAME HOME(1950); TICKET TO TOMAHAWK(1950); TWO FLAGS WEST(1950); WHERE THE SIDEWALK ENDS(1950); BEST OF THE BADMEN(1951); HOT LEAD(1951); SEALED CARGO(1951); HALF-BREED, THE(1952); TOUGHEST MAN IN ARIZONA(1952); ABOVE AND BEYOND(1953)
Malcolm MacGregor
HAPPINESS C.O.D.(1935); SPECIAL AGENT K-7(1937)
Mary MacGregor
WIFE VERSUS SECRETARY(1936)
Norval MacGregor
Silents
TARGET, THE(1916), d; CHAIN LIGHTNING(1922); IMPULSE(1922), d; COURTSHIP OF MILES STANDISH, THE(1923); LOVER'S LANE(1924)
Misc. Silents
COLORADO(1915), d; CHILDREN OF BANISHMENT(1919), d; JACQUES OF THE SILVER NORTH(1919), d; STEPPING LIVELY(1924)
Park MacGregor
YUKON VENGEANCE(1954)
Parke MacGregor
MILKMAN, THE(1950)
Sandra MacGregor
GREAT MACARTHY, THE(1975, Aus.)
Scott MacGregor
MASTER PLAN, THE(1955, Brit.), art d; FIRE MAIDENS FROM OUTER SPACE(1956, Brit.), art d; DR. BLOOD'S COFFIN(1961), art d; JET STORM(1961, Brit.), art d; CONCRETE JUNGLE, THE(1962, Brit.), art d; HEIGHTS OF DANGER(1962, Brit.), set d; DREAM MAKER, THE(1963), art d; PARTNER, THE(1966, Brit.), art d; 24 HOURS TO KILL(1966, Brit.), art d; FROZEN DEAD, THE(1967, Brit.), art d; IT!(1967, Brit.), art d; MAN WHO FINALLY DIED, THE(1967, Brit.), art d; MILLION EYES OF SU-MURU, THE(1967, Brit.), art d; VENGEANCE OF FU MANCHU, THE(1968, Brit./Ger./Hong Kong/Ireland), art d; LIMBO LINE, THE(1969, Brit.), art d; MOON ZERO TWO(1970, Brit.), art d; SCARS OF DRACULA, THE(1970, Brit.), art d; TASTE THE BLOOD OF DRACULA(1970, Brit.), art d; VAMPIRE LOVERS, THE(1970, Brit.), art d; CRESCENDO(1972, Brit.), art d; VAMPIRE CIRCUS(1972, Brit.), art d; FRANKENSTEIN AND THE MONSTER FROM HELL(1974, Brit.), art d; STRAIGHT ON TILL MORNING(1974, Brit.), art d
Scottie MacGregor
STUDENT NURSES, THE(1970); TRAVELING EXECUTIONER, THE(1970)
Scotty MacGregor
Silents
TIPPED OFF(1923)
Sean MacGregor
FOR LOVE OR MONEY(1963); CRY BLOOD, APACHE(1970), w
Stuart MacGregor
1984
CLOAK AND DAGGER(1984)
Warren MacGregor
DISTANT DRUMS(1951); LONE STAR(1952); IT CAME FROM OUTER SPACE(1953)
Peter MacGregor-Scott
STILL SMOKIN'(1983), p
1984
CHEECH AND CHONG'S THE CORSICAN BROTHERS(1984), p
N. MacGregory
Silents
SPOILERS, THE(1914)
George MacGrill
I WAS A COMMUNIST FOR THE F.B.I.(1951)
Erie MacGruder
SINGLE ROOM FURNISHED(1968)
Jack MacGuire
HIGH AND DRY(1954, Brit.)
Marlena MacGuire
FIVE EASY PIECES(1970)
Michael MacGuire
DOG AND THE DIAMONDS, THE(1962, Brit.); STOLEN AIRLINER, THE(1962, Brit.)
Robert MacGunigle
WHISTLING IN THE DARK(1941), w
Milan Mach
FIFTH HORSEMAN IS FEAR, THE(1968, Czech.); MATTER OF DAYS, A(1969, Fr./Czech.)
Miroslav Machacek
DEVIL'S TRAP, THE(1964, Czech.); FIFTH HORSEMAN IS FEAR, THE(1968, Czech.)
Jose Machado
GOODBYE GIRL, THE(1977); SO FINE(1981)

Maria Machado
IS PARIS BURNING?(1966, U.S./Fr.); PROMISE AT DAWN(1970, U.S./Fr.); ROSE-BUD(1975)
1984
ONE DEADLY SUMMER(1984, Fr.)
Mario Machado
CONCORDE, THE–AIRPORT '79(; ROCKY III(1982); BLUE THUNDER(1983); SCARFACE(1983)
Roberto Machado
ROSE FOR EVERYONE, A(1967, Ital.), prod d
Oleg Machajlov
WATERLOO(1970, Ital./USSR)
Christian Machalet
FREDDY UNTER FREMDEN STERNEN(1962, Ger.)
Jiri Machane
NINTH HEART, THE(1980, Czech.), ph
Alfred Machard
TRAPEZE(1932, Ger.), w
Melinda Machard
GUN RUNNER(1969)
A. Macharet
CONCENTRATION CAMP(1939, USSR), d, w
William Briggs MacHarg
Silents
PRICE OF A PARTY, THE(1924), w; ROULETTE(1924), w
Gustav Machaty
WITHIN THE LAW(1939), d; ECSTASY(1940, Czech.), p, w; JEALOUSY(1945), p&d, w
Misc. Silents
EROTIKON(1929, Czech.), d
J. Macher
KID MILLIONS(1934)
Jim Macher
NOTORIOUS CLEOPATRA, THE(1970), w
A. Macheret
DAY THE EARTH FROZE, THE(1959, Fin./USSR)
Paul Machette
Silents
JUDGE NOT OR THE WOMAN OF MONA DIGGINGS(1915)
Niccolo Machiavelli
MANDRAGOLA(1966 Fr./Ital.), w
Nicholetta Machiavelli
NO ROOM TO DIE(1969, Ital.)
Nicoletta Machiavelli
HILLS RUN RED, THE(1967, Ital.); KISS THE GIRLS AND MAKE THEM DIE(1967, U.S./Ital.); MATCHLESS(1967, Ital.); NAVAJO JOE(1967, Ital./Span.); CANDY(1968, Ital./Fr.); MINUTE TO PRAY, A SECOND TO DIE, A(1968, Ital.); THOSE DARING YOUNG MEN IN THEIR JAUNTY JALOPIES(1969, Fr./Brit./ Ital.); MAN WITH THE TRANSPLANTED BRAIN, THE(1972, Fr./Ital./Ger.); NO WAY OUT(1975, Ital./Fr.)
Kyosuke Machida
GANGSTER VIP, THE(1968, Jap.)
Machiguengas
FITZCARRALDO(1982)
Alfred Machin
Misc. Silents
MOI AUSSI, J'ACCUSE(1920, Fr.), d; UNE NUIT AGITEE(1920, Fr.), d; BETES..-.COMES LES HOMMES(1923, Fr.), d; LE CABINET DE L'HOMME NOIR(1924, Fr.), d; L'ENIGME DU MONT AGEL(1924, Fr.), d; LES HERITIERS DE L'ONCLE JAMES(1924, Fr.), d; LE COUR DES GUEUX(1925, Fr.); LE MANOIR DE LA PEUR(1927, Fr.), d
Beryl Machin
SILVER CHALICE, THE(1954)
Peter Machin
BRITTANIA HOSPITAL(1982, Brit.)
Will Machin
Silents
NE'ER-DO-WELL, THE(1916)
Misc. Silents
COUNTRY THAT GOD FORGOT, THE(1916); LAD AND THE LION, THE(1917); CORSICAN BROTHERS, THE(1920)
William Machin
Misc. Silents
WEB OF CHANCE, THE(1919); FORGET-ME-NOT(1922)
Tonia Machinga
MADIGAN(1968)
Arthur Machley
Silents
HURRICANE KID, THE(1925)
Milt Machlin
WILD 90(1968)
Karen Machon
MOLLY MAGUIRES, THE(1970); BLADE(1973)
Olga Machoninova
DO YOU KEEP A LION AT HOME?(1966, Czech.)
Robert Machover
IN THE COUNTRY(1967), ph, ed; EDGE, THE(1968), p, ph&ed; ICE(1970), ph
Ignacy Machowski
FIRST SPACESHIP ON VENUS(1960, Ger./Pol.); ASHES AND DIAMONDS(1961, Pol.); YELLOW SLIPPERS, THE(1965, Pol.); EROICA(1966, Pol.); CONTRACT, THE(1982, Pol.)
Stephen Macht
CHOIRBOYS, THE(1977); NIGHTWING(1979); GALAXINA(1980); MOUNTAIN MEN, THE(1980)
Misc. Talkies
LAST WINTER, THE(1983)
Mimi Machu
HELL'S ANGELS ON WHEELS(1967)

Emmanuel Machuel
SECOND WIND, A(1978, Fr.), ph
1984
L'ARGENT(1984, Fr./Switz.), ph
Augustin MacHugh
MEANEST MAN IN THE WORLD, THE(1943), w
Jan Machulski
SARAGOSSA MANUSCRIPT, THE(1972, Pol.)
Juliusz Machulski
CONSTANT FACTOR, THE(1980, Pol.)
Karl Machus
Silents
PASSION(1920, Ger.), set d
Ernest Macias
WALK THE ANGRY BEACH(1961)
Norma Jean Macias
COME FILL THE CUP(1951)
Phil J. Macias
HOLLYWOOD HIGH(1977)
Bill MacIlwraith
BIG DAY, THE(1960, Brit.), w; LINDA(1960, Brit.), w; THIS IS MY STREET(1964, Brit.), w; ANNIVERSARY, THE(1968, Brit.), w
Frances MacInerney
WATERLOO BRIDGE(1940)
Angus MacInnes
ROLLERBALL(1975); FORCE 10 FROM NAVARONE(1978, Brit.); ATLANTIC CITY(1981, U.S./Can.); OUTLAND(1981); SENDER, THE(1982, Brit.); SPASMS(1983, Can.); STRANGE BREW(1983)
Helen MacInnes
ABOVE SUSPICION(1943), w; ASSIGNMENT IN BRITTANY(1943), w; VENETIAN AFFAIR, THE(1967), w; SALZBURG CONNECTION, THE(1972), w
Alex MacIntosh
THERE'S ALWAYS A THURSDAY(1957, Brit.); HELP!(1965, Brit.); BOY CRIED MURDER, THE(1966, Ger./Brit./Yugo.)
Frank MacIntosh
TORTURE ME KISS ME(1970)
Fraser MacIntosh
BOY CRIED MURDER, THE(1966, Ger./Brit./Yugo.)
Jane MacIntosh
TOMCAT, THE(1968, Brit.)
Jay MacIntosh
J.W. COOP(1971)
Jay W. MacIntosh
SGT. PEPPER'S LONELY HEARTS CLUB BAND(1978); JONI(1980)
Joan MacIntosh
1984
FLASH OF GREEN, A(1984)
Louise MacIntosh
UP THE RIVER(1930); DOCTORS' WIVES(1931); LAUGH AND GET RICH(1931); AIR MAIL(1932)
Woods MacIntosh
ONE-TRICK PONY(1980), art d
Carl MacIntre
WORLD IS JUST A 'B' MOVIE, THE(1971)
Alastair Macintyre
WHO GOES NEXT?(1938, Brit.)
Alistair MacIntyre
CUL-DE-SAC(1966, Brit.), ed
Christine Macintyre
DAWN ON THE GREAT DIVIDE(1942); RIDERS OF THE WEST(1942); BORDER BUCKAROOS(1943); CRIMSON CANARY(1945)
Don MacIntyre
WHY ROCK THE BOAT?(1974, Can.)
Duncan MacIntyre
HIGH AND DRY(1954, Brit.)
George MacIntyre
Silents
SONG OF THE WAGE SLAVE, THE(1915)
Wayne MacIntyre
TOP BANANA(1954)
Macio
WILD PACK, THE(1972)
Fred MacIsaacs
MYSTERIOUS CROSSING(1937), w
M. Alvarez Maciste
GAY DESPERADO, THE(1936)
Manuel Alvarez Maciste
FIREFLY, THE(1937)
Manuel Maciste
ONLY ANGELS HAVE WINGS(1939), a, m
Derek MacIver
ATLANTIC FERRY(1941, Brit.), w
Wynne MacIver
ATLANTIC FERRY(1941, Brit.), w
Al Mack
CLARENCE, THE CROSS-EYED LION(1965), m
Alan Mack
HOODLUM PRIEST, THE(1961)
Alfred Mack
Silents
IRON MAN, THE(1925)
Andrew Mack
Silents
BLUEBEARD'S SEVEN WIVES(1926)
Misc. Silents
RAGGED EARL, THE(1914)
Arthur Mack
RETURN OF SHERLOCK HOLMES(1936); HANGMAN WAITS, THE(1947, Brit.)

Baby Mack
CLOSE HARMONY(1929); GHOST TALKS, THE(1929); CRAZY THAT WAY(1930)
Betty Mack
GOD'S COUNTRY AND THE MAN(1931); HEADIN' FOR TROUBLE(1931); LAW OF THE RIO GRANDE(1931); MAN FROM DEATH VALLEY, THE(1931); PARTNERS OF THE TRAIL(1931); BEAUTY PARLOR(1932); FORTY-NINERS, THE(1932); GALLOPING THRU(1932); SCARLET BRAND(1932); FIGHTING TEXANS(1933); LOVE IS LIKE THAT(1933); WOMEN WON'T TELL(1933); LIFE OF VERGIE WINTERS, THE(1934); LAST OF THE CLINTONS, THE(1935); PUBLIC OPINION(1935); EASY MONEY(1936); TOLL OF THE DESERT(1936); LOVE IN A BUNGALOW(1937); ROUGH RIDIN' RHYTHM(1937); ACCIDENTS WILL HAPPEN(1938); MR. BOGGS STEPS OUT(1938); PRISON FARM(1938); LITTLE ACCIDENT(1939); OFF THE RECORD(1939); PAL FROM TEXAS, THE(1939); CONFESSIONS OF BOSTON BLACKIE(1941)
Misc. Talkies
OUTLAW RULE(1935); RECKLESS BUCKAROO, THE(1935); HAIR-TRIGGER CASEY(1936); SENOR JIM(1936)
Billy Mack
Silents
BLACK BIRD, THE(1926)
Bobby Mack
EVANGELINE(1929)
Silents
HUMAN STUFF(1920); BLACK BEAUTY(1921); MAN'S LAW AND GOD'S(1922); WHILE SATAN SLEEPS(1922); PORTS OF CALL(1925); WOMAN WHO SINNED, A(1925); BANDIT'S SON, THE(1927); EVANGELINE(1929)
Brice Mack
FUN AND FANCY FREE(1947), art d; LADY AND THE TRAMP(1955), art d; MARA OF THE WILDERNESS(1966), p; JENNIFER(1978), d; SWAP MEET(1979), d
Misc. Talkies
HALF A HOUSE(1979), d
Buck Mack
ONE HOUR LATE(1935); PLOUGH AND THE STARS, THE(1936); ROSE BOWL(1936); SOMETHING TO SING ABOUT(1937); BRINGING UP BABY(1938); MAD MISS MANTON, THE(1938); GREAT MAN'S LADY, THE(1942)
Cactus Mack
MOONLIGHT ON THE PRAIRIE(1936); MAN FROM MUSIC MOUNTAIN(1938); ROLLING CARAVANS(1938); FIGHTING GRINGO, THE(1939); IN OLD MONTANA(1939); KNIGHT OF THE PLAINS(1939); MARSHAL OF MESA CITY, THE(1939); NEW FRONTIER(1939); NIGHT RIDERS, THE(1939); RACKETEERS OF THE RANGE(1939); SAGA OF DEATH VALLEY(1939); ONE MAN'S LAW(1940); TULSA KID, THE(1940); IN OLD CHEYENNE(1941); KANSAS CYCLONE(1941); OUTLAWS OF THE CHEROKEE TRAIL(1941); SINGING HILL, THE(1941); WEST OF CIMARRON(1941); WYOMING WILDCAT(1941); CODE OF THE OUTLAW(1942); HEART OF THE GOLDEN WEST(1942); OUTLAWS OF PINE RIDGE(1942); RAIDERS OF THE RANGE(1942); OUTLAWS OF STAMPEDE PASS(1943); OVERLAND MAIL ROBBERY(1943); SAGEBRUSH LAW(1943); THUNDERING TRAILS(1943); HIDDEN VALLEY OUTLAWS(1944); SHERIFF OF SUNDOWN(1944); OREGON TRAIL(1945); ROUGH RIDERS OF CHEYENNE(1945); LAND OF THE LAWLESS(1947); RAIDERS OF THE SOUTH(1947); SIX GUN SERENADE(1947); GALLANT LEGION, THE(1948); GUN TALK(1948); RANGE RENEGADES(1948); RANGERS RIDE, THE(1948); DALTON GANG, THE(1949); FIRST TRAVELING SALESLADY, THE(1956)
Charles Mack
WHY BRING THAT UP?(1929); ANYBODY'S WAR(1930)
Charles E. Mack
Silents
ONE EXCITING NIGHT(1922)
Charles Emmett Mack
Silents
DREAM STREET(1921); WHITE ROSE, THE(1923); AMERICA(1924); YOUTH FOR SALE(1924); DOWN UPON THE SUWANNEE RIVER(1925); OLD SAN FRANCISCO(1927); ROUGH RIDERS, THE(1927)
Misc. Silents
DARING YEARS, THE(1923); DRIVEN(1923); WOMAN OF THE WORLD, A(1925); DEVIL'S CIRCUS, THE(1926); UNKNOWN SOLDIER, THE(1926); FIRST AUTO, THE(1927)
Charles W. Mack
Silents
MASKED AVENGER, THE(1922), sup; NIGHT SHIP, THE(1925); NIGHT WATCH, THE(1926)
Misc. Silents
BLUE BLAZES(1922), d
Charlie Mack
HYPNOTIZED(1933)
Donald Mack
Misc. Silents
IN THE WATER(1923)
Earle Mack
SHE DANCES ALONE(1981, Aust./U.S.), p
Eric Mack
WINDOW, THE(1949); STORM BOY(1976, Aus.)
Erick Mack
Silents
COLLEGE(1927)
Frances Mack
SET-UP, THE(1949)
Frederick A. Mack
STRONGHOLD(1952, Mex.)
Gene Mack
1984
POLICE ACADEMY(1984); RENO AND THE DOC(1984, Can.)
George E. Mack
Silents
RED WIDOW, THE(1916)
Georgie Mack
Misc. Silents
WILDFIRE(1915)

Gertrude Mack
YOU'RE TELLING ME(1942)
Harry Mack
Silents
MILLION DOLLAR ROBBERY, THE(1914)
Hayward Mack
Silents
CINDERELLA(1915); FOUR FEATHERS(1915); MISTRESS NELL(1915); GILDED SPIDER, THE(1916); SPINDLE OF LIFE, THE(1917); ALL THE WORLD TO NOTHING(1919); LIVE WIRES(1921); OLIVER TWIST, JR.(1921)
Misc. Silents
FATHER AND THE BOYS(1915); ISLE OF LIFE, THE(1916); DOUBLE-ROOM MYSTERY, THE(1917); FLAME OF YOUTH, THE(1917); HIGH SIGN, THE(1917); PHANTOM'S SECRET, THE(1917); STORMY KNIGHT, A(1917); GODDESS OF LOST LAKE, THE(1918); IMPOSSIBLE SUSAN(1918); WINDING TRAIL, THE(1918); IT HAPPENED IN PARIS(1919); PUT UP YOUR HANDS!(1919); SPEED MANIAC, THE(1919); THIEVES(1919); GAMESTERS, THE(1920); PAYMENT GUARANTEED(1921); PLAY SQUARE(1921); PLAYING WITH FIRE(1921)
Haywood Mack
Misc. Silents
SOME LIAR(1919)
Helen Mack
STRUGGLE, THE(1931); SILENT WITNESS, THE(1932); WHILE PARIS SLEEPS(1932); BLIND ADVENTURE(1933); CALIFORNIA TRAIL, THE(1933); CHRISTOPHER BEAN(1933); FARGO EXPRESS(1933); MELODY CRUISE(1933); SON OF KONG(1933); SWEEPINGS(1933); ALL OF ME(1934); COLLEGE RHYTHM(1934); KISS AND MAKE UP(1934); LEMON DROP KID, THE(1934); YOU BELONG TO ME(1934); CAPTAIN HURRICANE(1935); FOUR HOURS TO KILL(1935); RETURN OF PETER GRIMM, THE(1935); SHE(1935); MILKY WAY, THE(1936); FIT FOR A KING(1937); I PROMISE TO PAY(1937); LAST TRAIN FROM MADRID, THE(1937); WRONG ROAD, THE(1937); YOU CAN'T BUY LUCK(1937); I STAND ACCUSED(1938); KING OF THE NEWSBOYS(1938); SECRETS OF A NURSE(1938); CALLING ALL MARINES(1939); GAMBLING SHIP(1939); MYSTERY OF THE WHITE ROOM(1939); GIRLS OF THE ROAD(1940); HIS GIRL FRIDAY(1940); POWER DIVE(1941); AND NOW TOMORROW(1944); DIVORCE(1945); STRANGE HOLIDAY(1945)
Howard Mack
Misc. Silents
LOVE IS LOVE(1919)
Hughie Mack
Silents
NIGHT OUT, A(1916); RENO(1923); GREED(1925); MERRY WIDOW, THE(1925); MARE NOSTRUM(1926); WEDDING MARCH, THE(1927); FOUR SONS(1928)
Misc. Silents
WIN(K)SOME WIDOW, THE (1914); C.O.D.(1915); DUST OF EGYPT, THE(1915); ARIZONA WHIRLWIND, THE(1927); WHERE TRAILS BEGIN(1927)
Irene Mack
ROBIN OF TEXAS(1947)
Jack Mack
NIGHT WORK(1930); LOVER COME BACK(1931); EVELYN PRENTICE(1934); JEALOUSY(1934); MEN OF THE NIGHT(1934); RED HEAD(1934); LOST IN THE STRATOSPHERE(1935); RETURN OF JIMMY VALENTINE, THE(1936); I COVER THE WAR(1937); TEST PILOT(1938)
James Mack
ARSENE LUPIN(1932); ONE YEAR LATER(1933); BONNIE SCOTLAND(1935); MARY BURNS, FUGITIVE(1935); STOLEN HARMONY(1935)
Silents
FRUITS OF DESIRE, THE(1916); HUSBAND HUNTERS(1927)
James T Mack
CHARLIE CHAN'S SECRET(1936)
James T. Mack
HOME TOWNERS, THE(1928); QUEEN OF THE NIGHTCLUBS(1929); ANNA CHRISTIE(1930); HELLO SISTER(1930); IN LOVE WITH LIFE(1934); G-MEN(1935); LIBELED LADY(1936); THEODORA GOES WILD(1936); ADVENTURE'S END(1937); LOVE IN A BUNGALOW(1937); TEXANS, THE(1938)
Jimmy Mack
BLACK KLANSMAN, THE(1966)
Joe Mack
FOLIES DERGERE(1935); LOVE ON THE RUN(1936); WOMAN REBELS, A(1936)
Joseph Mack
ONE NIGHT OF LOVE(1934)
Silents
NEVER SAY QUIT(1919); CROSS BREED(1927); MAN FROM HEADQUARTERS(1928)
Joseph P Mack
CANYON PASSAGE(1946)
Joseph W. Mack
Silents
WILD HONEY(1919)
Kerry Mack
1984
FANTASY MAN(1984, Aus.)
L.E. Mack
TERROR(1979, Brit.)
Leonard Mack
MY BODYGUARD(1980)
Lester Mack
ROCK, ROCK, ROCK!(1956)
Lonnie Mack
COME BACK BABY(1968), m
Marion Mack
Silents
ONE OF THE BRAVEST(1925); CARNIVAL GIRL, THE(1926); GENERAL, THE(1927)
Misc. Silents
MARY OF THE MOVIES(1923)
Max Mack
YOU BELONG TO ME(1934); SINGING THROUGH(1935, Brit.), p&d
Misc. Talkies
BE CAREFUL, MR. SMITH(1935), d

Misc. Silents
OTHER, THE(1912, Ger.), d
Molly Mack
BASHFUL ELEPHANT, THE(1962, Aust.)
Odell Mack
Misc. Talkies
ABAR–THE FIRST BLACK SUPERMAN(1977)
Richard Mack
SAVAGE GOLD(1933), w; CHARLIE MC CARTHY, DETECTIVE(1939), w; YOU CAN'T CHEAT AN HONEST MAN(1939), w
Roy Mack
LILIES OF THE FIELD(1930), ch; LOOSE ANKLES(1930), ch; HILLBILLY BLITZKRIEG(1942), d
Russell Mack
RIO RITA(1929), w; BIG MONEY(1930), d, w; NIGHT WORK(1930), d; SECOND WIFE(1930), d; HEAVEN ON EARTH(1931), d; LONELY WIVES(1931), d; SPIRIT OF NOTRE DAME, THE(1931), d; ALL-AMERICAN, THE(1932), d; ONCE IN A LIFETIME(1932), d; SCANDAL FOR SALE(1932), d; PRIVATE JONES(1933), d; BAND PLAYS ON, THE(1934), d; MEANEST GAL IN TOWN, THE(1934), d, w
Sally Mack
LOVE KISS, THE(1930)
Stanley Mack
GUN SMOKE(1931); GAMBLING LADY(1934); JEALOUSY(1934); JIMMY THE GENT(1934); ST. LOUIS KID, THE(1934); SHE COULDN'T TAKE IT(1935); PAID TO DANCE(1937); WOMEN OF GLAMOUR(1937); JUVENILE COURT(1938); THOSE WERE THE DAYS(1940); TAKE A LETTER, DARLING(1942)
Stephen Mack
ANGELO MY LOVE(1983), ed
Tom Mack
EVERYTHING YOU ALWAYS WANTED TO KNOW ABOUT SEX, BUT WE'RE AFRAID TO ASK(1972)
Tommy Mack
NEW FACES OF 1937(1937); LAW OF THE TEXAN(1938); LADY AND THE MOB, THE(1939); ZENOBIA(1939); SHADOW OF THE THIN MAN(1941); COWBOY IN MANHATTAN(1943); JUNIOR MISS(1945); SMART POLITICS(1948); SUNSTRUCK(1973, Aus.)
Wanda Mack
COTTONPICKIN' CHICKENPICKERS(1967), cos
Wayne Mack
WACKY WORLD OF DR. MORGUS, THE(1962); OUTLAWS IS COMING, THE(1965); MARDI GRAS MASSACRE(1978)
Silents
NO MAN'S WOMAN(1921), d
Misc. Silents
BUBBLES(1920), d; NINE POINTS OF THE LAW(1922), d
Wilbur Mack
ARGYLE CASE, THE(1929); HONKY TONK(1929); CZAR OF BRODWAY, THE(1930); REMOTE CONTROL(1930); SCARLET PAGES(1930); SPRING IS HERE(1930); SWEETHEARTS ON PARADE(1930); ANNABELLE'S AFFAIRS(1931); LAWYER'S SECRET, THE(1931); STRANGERS MAY KISS(1931); STREET OF WOMEN(1932); GOLD DIGGERS OF 1933(1933); EVELYN PRENTICE(1934); GAY BRIDE, THE(1934); LOUDSPEAKER, THE(1934); READY FOR LOVE(1934); STAND UP AND CHEER(1934 80m FOX bw); MILLION DOLLAR BABY(1935); NIGHT AT THE OPERA, A(1935); REDHEADS ON PARADE(1935); CRIME PATROL, THE(1936); HITCH HIKE LADY(1936); OLD HUTCH(1936); SAN FRANCISCO(1936); DAY AT THE RACES, A(1937); LARCENY ON THE AIR(1937); LIVE, LOVE AND LEARN(1937); PICK A STAR(1937); PLAINSMAN, THE(1937); ANGELS WITH DIRTY FACES(1938); MR. WONG, DETECTIVE(1938); NEW FRONTIER(1939); TOUGH KID(1939); UNION PACIFIC(1939); DOOMED TO DIE(1940); HALF A SINNER(1940); THAT GANG OF MINE(1940); FOOTLIGHT SERENADE(1942); LADY BODYGUARD(1942); NAZI AGENT(1942); RINGS ON HER FINGERS(1942); YOU'RE TELLING ME(1942); DIXIE(1943); SHE HAS WHAT IT TAKES(1943); SOMEONE TO REMEMBER(1943); TWO SENORITAS FROM CHICAGO(1943); HEAVENLY DAYS(1944); SHADOW OF SUSPICION(1944); DICK TRACY(1945); CROSS MY HEART(1946); SHE WROTE THE BOOK(1946); WIFE WANTED(1946); DOWN TO EARTH(1947); SECRET LIFE OF WALTER MITTY, THE(1947); STAGE STRUCK(1948); TRAIL OF THE YUKON(1949); MAD WEDNESDAY(1950); ACCORDING TO MRS. HOYLE(1951); CRAZY OVER HORSES(1951); RHUBARB(1951); LOOSE IN LONDON(1953); UP IN SMOKE(1957); IN THE MONEY(1958); WHO'S GOT THE ACTION?(1962)
Silents
AVENGING SHADOW, THE(1928); BEAUTY AND BULLETS(1928); SLIM FINGERS(1929)
Misc. Silents
LOVE OF PAQUITA, THE(1927); SHOOTING STRAIGHT(1927); CRIMSON CANYON, THE(1928); QUICK TRIGGERS(1928); BODY PUNCH, THE(1929)
Willard Mack
HIS GLORIOUS NIGHT(1929), w; MADAME X(1929), w; UNTAMED(1929), w; VOICE OF THE CITY(1929), a, d&w; CAUGHT SHORT(1930), w; IT'S A GREAT LIFE(1930), w; LORD BYRON OF BROADWAY(1930), w; MEN OF THE NORTH(1930), w; TIGER ROSE(1930), w; FREE SOUL, A(1931), w; HIGH STAKES(1931), w; KICK IN(1931), w; REDUCING(1931), w; SPORTING BLOOD(1931), w; BILLION DOLLAR SCANDAL(1932), w; GIRL OF THE RIO(1932), w; BROADWAY TO HOLLYWOOD(1933), d, w; NIGHT OF TERROR(1933), w; SONG OF THE EAGLE(1933), w; STRICTLY PERSONAL(1933), w; WHAT PRICE INNOCENCE?(1933), a, d&w; NANA(1934), w; TOGETHER WE LIVE(1935), a, d&w; I'D GIVE MY LIFE(1936), w; GIRL AND THE GAMBLER, THE(1939), w
Silents
BATTLE OF GETTYSBURG(1914); EDGE OF THE ABYSS, THE(1915); ALL MAN(1916), w; LOST BRIDEGROOM, THE(1916), w; NANETTE OF THE WILDS(1916), a, w; ALADDIN'S OTHER LAMP(1917), w; KICK IN(1917), w; GO WEST, YOUNG MAN(1919), w; KICK IN(1922), w; WELCOME STRANGER(1924), w; MONSTER, THE(1925), w; OLD CLOTHES(1925), w; RAG MAN, THE(1925), w; NOOSE, THE(1928), w
Misc. Silents
ALOHA OE(1915); CONQUEROR, THE(1916); CORNER, THE(1916); WOMAN ON THE INDEX, THE(1919); YOUR FRIEND AND MINE(1923)
William B. Mack
Silents
MISSING MILLIONS(1922); STEADFAST HEART, THE(1923); AMERICAN VENUS, THE(1926)

Misc. Silents
BACKBONE(1923)
Dorothy Mackaill
BARKER, THE(1928); HARD TO GET(1929); HIS CAPTIVE WOMAN(1929); LOVE RACKET, THE(1929); TWO WEEKS OFF(1929); FLIRTING WIDOW, THE(1930); GREAT DIVIDE, THE(1930); MAN TROUBLE(1930); OFFICE WIFE, THE(1930); STRICTLY MODERN(1930); BRIGHT LIGHTS(1931); KEPT HUSBANDS(1931); ONCE A SINNER(1931); PARTY HUSBAND(1931); RECKLESS HOUR, THE(1931); SAFE IN HELL(1931); LOVE AFFAIR(1932); CHIEF, THE(1933); NEIGHBORS' WIVES(1933); NO MAN OF HER OWN(1933); CHEATERS(1934); CURTAIN AT EIGHT(1934); PICTURE BRIDES(1934); BULLDOG DRUMMOND AT BAY(1937, Brit.)
Misc. Talkies
THEIR MAD MOMENT(1931)
Silents
INNER MAN, THE(1922); STREETS OF NEW YORK, THE(1922); JOANNA(1925); ONE YEAR TO LIVE(1925); SHORE LEAVE(1925); RANSON'S FOLLY(1926); CONVOY(1927); CRYSTAL CUP, THE(1927); MAN CRAZY(1927); SMILE, BROTHER, SMILE(1927); LADY BE GOOD(1928)
Misc. Silents
ISLE OF DOUBT(1922); FAIR CHEAT, THE(1923); HIS CHILDREN'S CHILDREN(1923); TWENTY-ONE(1923); MAN WHO CAME BACK, THE(1924); MINE WITH THE IRON DOOR, THE(1924); NEXT CORNER, THE(1924); PAINTED LADY, THE(1924); WHAT SHALL I DO?(1924); BRIDGE OF SIGHS, THE(1925); CHICKIE(1925); MAKING OF O'MALLEY, THE(1925); DANCER OF PARIS, THE(1926); SUBWAY SADIE(1926); LUNATIC AT LARGE, THE(1927); LADIES' NIGHT IN A TURKISH BATH(1928); WATERFRONT(1928); CHILDREN OF THE RITZ(1929)
Lawton Mackall
IF I HAD A MILLION(1932), w
Barton MacKane
STORM, THE(1938)
David MacKane
SWINGING THE LEAD(1934, Brit.), d; GORBALS STORY, THE(1950, Brit.), d, w
Mike MacKane
X-15(1961)
Shayla MacKarvich
1984
SPLASH(1984)
Fulton Mackaw
MYSTERY SUBMARINE(1963, Brit.)
Alan Mackay
MYSTERY ON BIRD ISLAND(1954, Brit.)
Angus MacKay
NOTHING BUT THE BEST(1964, Brit.); DARLING(1965, Brit.); MORGAN!(1966, Brit.); PERCY(1971, Brit.); TERROR FROM UNDER THE HOUSE(1971, Brit.)
Barry Mackay
EVERGREEN(1934, Brit.); PASSING SHADOWS(1934, Brit.); PRIVATE LIFE OF DON JUAN, THE(1934, Brit.); ME AND MARLBOROUGH(1935, Brit.); OH DADDY!(1935, Brit.); PRIVATE SECRETARY, THE(1935, Brit.); GANGWAY(1937, Brit.); GLAMOROUS NIGHT(1937, Brit.); SILENT BARRIERS(1937, Brit.); WHO KILLED JOHN SAVAGE?(1937, Brit.); CHRISTMAS CAROL, A(1938); FORBIDDEN TERRITORY(1938, Brit.); SAILING ALONG(1938, Brit.); SMUGGLED CARGO(1939); PICKWICK PAPERS, THE(1952, Brit.); KNIGHTS OF THE ROUND TABLE(1953); ATOMIC MAN, THE(1955, Brit.); WICKED WIFE(1955, Brit.); ORDERS ARE ORDERS(1959, Brit.)
Bob Mackay
Misc. Talkies
SUPERBUG, THE WILD ONE(1977)
Brigid Mackay
PROSTITUTE(1980, Brit.)
Bruce Mackay
PROLOGUE(1970, Can.)
Charles Mackay
Silents
OAKDALE AFFAIR, THE(1919); DIANE OF STAR HOLLOW(1921); INNER MAN, THE(1922), w; WITHOUT FEAR(1922)
Misc. Silents
STEEL KING, THE(1919); WOMAN OF LIES(1919); PEGGY PUTS IT OVER(1921); TEN NIGHTS IN A BAR ROOM(1921); MAN SHE BROUGHT BACK, THE(1922)
Dana MacKay
THIS IS ELVIS(1982)
David Mackay
1984
NUMBER ONE(1984, Brit.), m
Don Mackay
FIRST BLOOD(1982); GREY FOX, THE(1983, Can.)
Edward Mackay
Misc. Silents
MAN AND HIS ANGEL(1916)
Elsie Mackay
SYLVIA SCARLETT(1936)
Fred MacKay
LAST PERFORMANCE, THE(1929)
Fulton Mackay
BRAVE DON'T CRY, THE(1952, Brit.); I'M A STRANGER(1952, Brit.); LAST MOMENT, THE(1954, Brit.); SCOTCH ON THE ROCKS(1954, Brit.); PRIZE OF ARMS, A(1962, Brit.); GUMSHOE(1972, Brit.); NOTHING BUT THE NIGHT(1975, Brit.); DOING TIME(1979, Brit.); BRITTANIA HOSPITAL(1982, Brit.); LOCAL HERO(1983, Brit.)
Hamish MacKay
TELL ME IN THE SUNLIGHT(1967)
Harper MacKay
GUESS WHAT WE LEARNED IN SCHOOL TODAY?(1970), m
Jeff MacKay
1984
SONGWRITER(1984)
John MacKay
CUBAN REBEL GIRLS(1960); LINCOLN CONSPIRACY, THE(1977)
Misc. Silents
WEAKER VESSEL, THE(1919)

John Victor Mackay
ESCAPE BY NIGHT(1937), art d; HIT THE SADDLE(1937), art d; LADY BEHAVE(1937), art d; GANGS OF NEW YORK(1938), art d; I STAND ACCUSED(1938), art d; MAMA RUNS WILD(1938), art d; NIGHT HAWK, THE(1938), art d; FORGED PASSPORT(1939), art d; MAN OF CONQUEST(1939), art d; MICKEY, THE KID(1939), art d; PRIDE OF THE NAVY(1939), art d; SHE MARRIED A COP(1939), art d; S.O.S. TIDAL WAVE(1939), art d; WOMAN DOCTOR(1939), art d; ZERO HOUR, THE(1939), art d; DARK COMMAND, THE(1940), art d; FORGOTTEN GIRLS(1940), art d; GANGS OF CHICAGO(1940), art d; GIRL FROM GOD'S COUNTRY(1940), art d; GRANDPA GOES TO TOWN(1940), art d; HIT PARADE OF 1941(1940), art d; SCATTERBRAIN(1940), art d; SING, DANCE, PLENTY HOT(1940), art d; THREE FACES WEST(1940), art d; VILLAGE BARN DANCE(1940), art d; WHO KILLED AUNT MAGGIE?(1940), art d; WOMEN IN WAR(1940), art d; DEVIL PAYS OFF, THE(1941), art d; GAY VAGABOND, THE(1941), art d; ICE-CAPADES(1941), art d; LADY FROM LOUISIANA(1941), art d; MAN BETRAYED, A(1941), art d; MR. DISTRICT ATTORNEY(1941), art d; PETTICOAT POLITICS(1941), art d; PITTSBURGH KID, THE(1941), art d; PUDDIN' HEAD(1941), art d; RAGS TO RICHES(1941), art d; SIS HOPKINS(1941), art d; PARDON MY STRIPES(1942), art d
Joseph Victor Mackay
MELODY RANCH(1940), art d
Ken MacKay
THIRD SECRET, THE(1964, Brit.), makeup; PLEASURE GIRLS, THE(1966, Brit.), makeup
Lynne MacKay
HAPPY BIRTHDAY, GEMINI(1980), cos
Mary MacKay
CADDIE(1976, Aus.)
Nancy MacKay
PANIC IN NEEDLE PARK(1971)
Norman MacKay
UNTAMED FURY(1947)
Phoebe Mackay
BURGLAR, THE(1956); SPLENDOR IN THE GRASS(1961)
Ruth Mackay
Silents
EAST IS EAST(1916, Brit.); INNOCENT(1921, Brit.); PLACE OF HONOUR, THE(1921, Brit.)
Tanya Mackay
PROLOGUE(1970, Can.)
Yvonne Mackay
1984
SILENT ONE, THE(1984, New Zealand), d
The Mackay Twins
JIMMY BOY(1935, Brit.)
Bronwyn Mackay-Payne
DAWN(1979, Aus.)
Dorothy Mackaye
LADIES THEY TALK ABOUT(1933), w; LADY GANGSTER(1942), w
Silents
JACK AND THE BEANSTALK(1917)
Edward Mackaye
Silents
SECRET ORCHARD(1915)
Misc. Silents
CLUE, THE(1915)
Elsie Mackaye
Silents
NOTHING BUT THE TRUTH(1920)
Fred MacKaye
BROADWAY HOOFER, THE(1929); CHARLATAN, THE(1929); GIRL OVERBOARD(1929); KING OF THE ARENA(1933); BLACK ACES(1937)
Frederic MacKaye
FIREFLY, THE(1937)
Marshall Mackaye
Silents
KILMENY(1915)
Norman MacKaye
SPELL OF THE HYPNOTIST(1956); HOODLUM PRIEST, THE(1961)
Theo Mackeben
JAZZBAND FIVE, THE(1932, Ger,), m; TREMENDOUSLY RICH MAN, A(1932, Ger.), m; INTERMEZZO(1937, Ger.), m; BIMBO THE GREAT(1961, Ger.), m
Cromwell MacKechnie
PERSONALITY KID(1946), w
James MacKechnie
2,000 WOMEN(1944, Brit.)
Scott MacKee
2001: A SPACE ODYSSEY(1968, U.S./Brit.)
Helen MacKellar
PAST OF MARY HOLMES, THE(1933); HIGH SCHOOL GIRL(1935); TWO AGAINST THE WORLD(1936); CASE OF THE STUTTERING BISHOP, THE(1937); DRAEGERMAN COURAGE(1937); FEDERAL BULLETS(1937); CRIME SCHOOL(1938); LITTLE TOUGH GUY(1938); VALLEY OF THE GIANTS(1938); BAD BOY(1939); DISBARRED(1939); WHEN TOMORROW COMES(1939); DARK COMMAND, THE(1940); NORTHWEST PASSAGE(1940); THREE FACES WEST(1940); WOMEN WITHOUT NAMES(1940); DOWN MEXICO WAY(1941); GANGS OF SONORA(1941); GREAT MR. NOBODY, THE(1941); GREAT TRAIN ROBBERY, THE(1941); MAN WHO RETURNED TO LIFE, THE(1942); POWERS GIRL, THE(1942); STREET OF CHANCE(1942); SUNDOWN KID, THE(1942)
Helen MacKeller
BAREFOOT BOY(1938); DELINQUENT PARENTS(1938); CHEERS FOR MISS BISHOP(1941)
Jock MacKelvie
PENDULUM(1969)
Walter Macken
HOME IS THE HERO(1959, Ireland), a, w; QUARE FELLOW, THE(1962, Brit.); FLIGHT OF THE DOVES(1971), w
Ray Mackender
LITTLE OF WHAT YOU FANCY, A(1968, Brit.), w

Alexander Mackendrick
BOMBS OVER LONDON(1937, Brit.), w; SARABAND(1949, Brit.), w; TIGHT LITTLE ISLAND(1949, Brit.), d; DANCE HALL(1950, Brit.), w; CRASH OF SILENCE(1952, Brit.), d; MAN IN THE WHITE SUIT, THE(1952), d, w; HIGH AND DRY(1954, Brit.), d, w; LADYKILLERS, THE(1956, Brit.), d; SWEET SMELL OF SUCCESS(1957), d; BOY TEN FEET TALL, A(1965, Brit.), d; HIGH WIND IN JAMAICA, A(1965), d; DON'T MAKE WAVES(1967), d; OH DAD, POOR DAD, MAMA'S HUNG YOU IN THE CLOSET AND I'M FEELIN' SO SAD(1967), d

Kate MacKenna
SO ENDS OUR NIGHT(1941); WIFE TAKES A FLYER, THE(1942); SUMMER STORM(1944); GANG BUSTERS(1955)

Kenneth MacKenna
LOVE, LIVE AND LAUGH(1929); PLEASURE CRAZED(1929); SOUTH SEA ROSE(1929); CRAZY THAT WAY(1930); MAN TROUBLE(1930); MEN WITHOUT WOMEN(1930); SIN TAKES A HOLIDAY(1930); TEMPLE TOWER(1930); THREE SISTERS, THE(1930); VIRTUOUS SIN, THE(1930); ALWAYS GOODBYE(1931), d; GOOD SPORT(1931), d; MAN WHO CAME BACK, THE(1931); SPIDER, THE(1931), d; CARELESS LADY(1932), d; THOSE WE LOVE(1932); WALLS OF GOLD(1933), d; SENSATION HUNTERS(1934); SLEEPERS EAST(1934), d; HIGH TIME(1960); JUDGMENT AT NUREMBERG(1961); THIRTEEN WEST STREET(1962)
Silents
KISS IN THE DARK, A(1925); MISS BLUEBEARD(1925); AMERICAN VENUS, THE(1926)

Stephen MacKenna
EYE OF THE NEEDLE(1981)

Mackenzie
LOVES OF THREE QUEENS, THE(1954, Ital./Fr.), w

Aeneas Mackenzie
JUAREZ(1939), w; PRIVATE LIVES OF ELIZABETH AND ESSEX, THE(1939), w; NAVY COMES THROUGH, THE(1942), w; THEY DIED WITH THEIR BOOTS ON(1942), w; WOMAN OF THE TOWN, THE(1943), w; BUFFALO BILL(1944), w; FIGHTING SEABEES, THE(1944), w; BACK TO BATAAN(1945), w; SPANISH MAIN, THE(1945), w; BLACK BOOK, THE(1949), w; AVENGERS, THE(1950), w; CAPTAIN HORATIO HORNBLOWER(1951, Brit.), w; PRINCE WHO WAS A THIEF, THE(1951), w; AGAINST ALL FLAGS(1952), w; FACE TO FACE(1952), w; TEN COMMANDMENTS, THE(1956), w; KING'S PIRATE(1967), w

Alastair Mackenzie
DAVID COPPERFIELD(1970, Brit.); MAN WHO HAUNTED HIMSELF, THE(1970, Brit.)

Alex Mackenzie
HIGH AND DRY(1954, Brit.); WEE GEORDIE(1956, Brit.); KID FROM CANADA, THE(1957, Brit.); MAD LITTLE ISLAND(1958, Brit.); BRIDAL PATH, THE(1959, Brit.); BATTLE OF THE SEXES, THE(1960, Brit.); KIDNAPPED(1960); THREE LIVES OF THOMASINA, THE(1963, U.S./Brit.); THAT SINKING FEELING(1979, Brit.)

Alexander Mackenzie
GREYFRIARS BOBBY(1961, Brit.)

Alice MacKenzie
SUMMER HOLIDAY(1948)

Boyd MacKenzie
TOO HOT TO HANDLE(1961, Brit.)

Colin MacKenzie
WORLD IS JUST A 'B' MOVIE, THE(1971)

Compton Mackenzie
DANCE PRETTY LADY(1932, Brit.), d&w; SYLVIA SCARLETT(1936), w; CARNIVAL(1946, Brit.), w; TIGHT LITTLE ISLAND(1949, Brit.), a, w; CHANCE OF A LIFETIME(1950, Brit.); MAD LITTLE ISLAND(1958, Brit.), w
Silents
BALLET GIRL, THE(1916), w

Diana MacKenzie
MAIDSTONE(1970)

Donald MacKenzie
MYSTERIOUS DR. FU MANCHU, THE(1929); STUDIO MURDER MYSTERY, THE(1929); CONSPIRACY(1930); GIRL OF THE PORT(1930); SCARLET PAGES(1930); FIGHTING CARAVANS(1931); KICK IN(1931); UNFAITHFUL(1931); NOWHERE TO GO(1959, Brit.), d
Misc. Silents
DETECTIVE CRAIG'S COUP(1914), d; HAND OF DESTINY, THE(1914), d; LEAVES OF MEMORY(1914), d; GALLOPER, THE(1915), d; MARY'S LAMB(1915), d; SPENDER OR THE FORTUNES OF PETER, THE(1915), d; CHALLENGE, THE(1916), d; PRECIOUS PACKET, THE(1916), d

Gordon Mackenzie
MIKADO, THE(1967, Brit.)

Hugh MacKenzie
NO ESCAPE(1953), p; MAN WHO HAUNTED HIMSELF, THE(1970, Brit.)

Jack Mackenzie
DANCE HALL(1929), ph; JAZZ HEAVEN(1929), ph; RAINBOW MAN(1929), ph; WHISPERING WINDS(1929), ph; BEAU BANDIT(1930), ph; ESCAPE(1930, Brit.), ph; CAUGHT PLASTERED(1931), ph; KEPT HUSBANDS(1931), ph; LAUGH AND GET RICH(1931), ph; PEACH O' RENO(1931), ph; SHOULD A DOCTOR TELL?(1931, Brit.), ph; WHITE SHOULDERS(1931), ph; LADIES OF THE JURY(1932), ph; ONE MAN'S JOURNEY(1933), ph; GAMBLING(1934), ph; ANOTHER FACE(1935), ph; HOT TIP(1935), ph; TOMORROW'S YOUTH(1935), ph; VAGABOND LADY(1935), ph; DON'T TURN'EM LOOSE(1936), ph; HI GAUCHO!(1936), ph; LAST OUTLAW, THE(1936), ph; MUMMY'S BOYS(1936), ph; TWO IN REVOLT(1936), ph; FIGHT FOR YOUR LADY(1937), ph; MEET THE MISSUS(1937), ph; ON AGAIN–OFF AGAIN(1937), ph; 23 ½ HOURS LEAVE(1937), ph; BREAKING THE ICE(1938), ph; CRIME RING(1938), ph; GO CHASE YOURSELF(1938), ph; PECK'S BAD BOY WITH THE CIRCUS(1938), ph; RADIO CITY REVELS(1938), ph; DAY THE BOOKIES WEPT, THE(1939), ph; GIRL FROM MEXICO, THE(1939), ph; MEXICAN SPITFIRE(1939), ph; LET'S MAKE MUSIC(1940), ph; MEXICAN SPITFIRE OUT WEST(1940), ph; MILLIONAIRE PLAYBOY(1940), ph; POP ALWAYS PAYS(1940), ph; SUED FOR LIBEL(1940), ph; WILDCAT BUS(1940), ph; MEXICAN SPITFIRE'S BABY(1941), ph; SCATTERGOOD BAINES(1941), ph; SCATTERGOOD MEETS BROADWAY(1941), ph; SCATTERGOOD PULLS THE STRINGS(1941), ph; MEXICAN SPITFIRE AT SEA(1942), ph; MEXICAN SPITFIRE'S ELEPHANT(1942), ph; SCATTERGOOD RIDES HIGH(1942), ph; SCATTERGOOD SURVIVES A MURDER(1942), ph; FALCON STRIKES BACK, THE(1943), ph; GILDERSLEEVE ON BROADWAY(1943), ph; GILDERSLEEVE'S BAD DAY(1943), ph; HI' YA, SAILOR(1943), ph; LADIES' DAY(1943), ph; MEXICAN SPITFIRE'S BLESSED EVENT(1943), ph; TWO WEEKS TO LIVE(1943), ph; GILDERSLEEVE'S

GHOST(1944), ph; JUNGLE WOMAN(1944), ph; MY PAL, WOLF(1944), ph; PASSPORT TO DESTINY(1944), ph; DIXIE JAMBOREE(1945), ph; ISLE OF THE DEAD(1945), ph; MAMA LOVES PAPA(1945), ph; TWO O'CLOCK COURAGE(1945), ph; CHILD OF DIVORCE(1946), ph; PARTNERS IN TIME(1946), ph; CODE OF THE WEST(1947), ph; SEVEN KEYS TO BALDPATE(1947), ph; THUNDER MOUNTAIN(1947), ph; MASSACRE RIVER(1949), ph; BOY FROM INDIANA(1950), ph; MARSHAL'S DAUGHTER, THE(1953), ph; RETURN OF DRACULA, THE(1958), ph
Silents
ETERNAL LOVE(1917), ph; PURPLE CIPHER, THE(1920), ph; BRING HIM IN(1921), ph; DIAMONDS ADRIFT(1921), ph; IT CAN BE DONE(1921), ph; JOLT, THE(1921), ph; SECRET OF THE HILLS, THE(1921), ph; SILVER CAR, THE(1921), ph; THELMA(1922), ph; DIVORCE(1923), ph; LULLABY, THE(1924), ph; NEVER SAY DIE(1924), ph; HIS MASTER'S VOICE(1925), ph; INTRODUCE ME(1925), ph; OVERLAND LIMITED, THE(1925), ph; LODGE IN THE WILDERNESS, THE(1926), ph; NUT-CRACKER, THE(1926), ph; THAT'S MY BABY(1926), ph; LET IT RAIN(1927), ph; SOFT CUSHIONS(1927), ph; TEXAS STEER, A(1927), ph

Jacqueline Mackenzie
YOU'RE ONLY YOUNG TWICE(1952, Brit.); TERROR STREET(1953); WEDDING OF LILLI MARLENE, THE(1953, Brit.); YOU CAN'T ESCAPE(1955, Brit.)

Jimmie MacKenzie
WICKER MAN, THE(1974, Brit.)

John E.A. Mackenzie
SEPARATE PEACE, A(1972)

John MacKenzie
HIGH FLYERS(1937), ph; TUNES OF GLORY(1960, Brit.); ONE BRIEF SUMMER(1971, Brit.), d; UNMAN, WITTERING AND ZIGO(1971, Brit.), d; MADE(1972, Brit.), d; LONG GOOD FRIDAY, THE(1982, Brit.), d; BEYOND THE LIMIT(1983), d

Joyce MacKenzie
KID FROM BOOKLYN, THE(1946); TOMORROW IS FOREVER(1946); BROKEN ARROW(1950); DESTINATION MURDER(1950); STELLA(1950); TICKET TO TOMAHAWK(1950); MODEL AND THE MARRIAGE BROKER, THE(1951); ON THE RIVERA(1951); PEOPLE WILL TALK(1951); RACKET, THE(1951); DEADLINE–U.S.A.(1952); NIGHT WITHOUT SLEEP(1952); O. HENRY'S FULL HOUSE(1952); WAIT 'TIL THE SUN SHINES, NELLIE(1952); TARZAN AND THE SHE-DEVIL(1953); FRENCH LINE, THE(1954); RAILS INTO LARAMIE(1954)

Julio Mackenzie
XICA(1982, Braz.)

Keith MacKenzie
SONS OF THE LEGION(1938)

Kenneth Rose MacKenzie
RIDE THE PINK HORSE(1947)

Kent MacKenzie
EXILES, THE(1966), p,d&w, ed

Lewis MacKenzie
NATIVE SON(1951, U.S., Arg.)

Mary Mackenzie
WANTED FOR MURDER(1946, Brit.); LADY WITH A LAMP, THE(1951, Brit.); SCOTLAND YARD INSPECTOR(1952, Brit.); STOLEN FACE(1952, Brit.); LONG MEMORY, THE(1953, Brit.); PARIS EXPRESS, THE(1953, Brit.); DUEL IN THE JUNGLE(1954, Brit.); HARASSED HERO, THE(1954, Brit.); TROUBLE IN THE GLEN(1954, Brit.); MASTER PLAN, THE(1955, Brit.); BLONDE SINNER(1956, Brit.); TRACK THE MAN DOWN(1956, Brit.); DECISION AGAINST TIME(1957, Brit.); OPERATION CONSPIRACY(1957, Brit.); MAN WHO LIKED FUNERALS, THE(1959, Brit.); QUESTION OF ADULTERY, A(1959, Brit.)

N'Was Mackenzie
MISSING WITNESSES(1937), cos

Patch Mackenzie
GOODBYE, NORMA JEAN(1976); HOUSE CALLS(1978); SERIAL(1980); GRADUATION DAY(1981)

Phil MacKenzie
DOUBLE LIFE, A(1947)

Philip Charles Mackenzie
DOG DAY AFTERNOON(1975)

Robert Mackenzie
HAPPINESS C.O.D.(1935); BLIND SPOT(1958, Brit.); FIEND WITHOUT A FACE(1958); FLOODS OF FEAR(1958, Brit.); SECRET MAN, THE(1958, Brit.); WOMAN EATER, THE(1959, Brit.)

Sidney Ann MacKenzie
FRIDAY THE 13TH... THE ORPHAN(1979), art d

Tandy MacKenzie
SAN FRANCISCO(1936); THERE'S MAGIC IN MUSIC(1941)

Will MacKenzie
HARVEY MIDDLEMAN, FIREMAN(1965)

Anna Mackeown
1984
SCRUBBERS(1984, Brit.)

Bonnie Macker
ONE FROM THE HEART(1982)

Vivian Mackerall
GHOST STORY(1974, Brit.)

Evelyn Mackert
FUGITIVE LADY(1934)

Beatrix Mackey
RAILWAY CHILDREN, THE(1971, Brit.)

Bruce Mackey
THX 1138(1971); STEEL ARENA(1973)

Charles D. Mackey
Misc. Silents
WEAKNESS OF MAN, THE(1916)

Clarke Mackey
ONLY THING YOU KNOW, THE(1971, Can.), p,d&w

Edward Mackey
Misc. Silents
COMING POWER, THE(1914), d; SPAN OF LIFE, THE(1914), d

Elizabeth Mackey
Silents
FAMILY SECRET, THE(1924)

Fletcher Mackey
1984
 LAST NIGHT AT THE ALAMO(1984), art d
Gloria Mackey
 YOUNGEST PROFESSION, THE(1943)
James Mackey
 NOBODY'S CHILDREN(1940)
John Mackey
 MACKENNA'S GOLD(1969), spec eff; GREAT MCGONAGALL, THE(1975, Brit.), ph
John Victor Mackey
 MELODY AND MOONLIGHT(1940), art d; LADY FOR A NIGHT(1941), art d
Kathleen Mackey
 EGG AND I, THE(1947)
Mary Mackey
 SILENCE(1974), w
Percival Mackey
 RESERVED FOR LADIES(1932, Brit.), m; ACCUSED(1936, Brit.), md; WHEN THIEF MEETS THIEF(1937, Brit.), m; THIS MAN IS NEWS(1939, Brit.), md; HONEYMOON HOTEL(1946, Brit.); HILLS OF DONEGAL, THE(1947, Brit.), md; WHEN YOU COME HOME(1947, Brit.), m
Bob Mackichan
 ENTERTAINER, THE(1975), art d
Robert C. MacKichan
 DID YOU HEAR THE ONE ABOUT THE TRAVELING SALESLADY?(1968), art d
Bob Mackie
 DIVORCE AMERICAN STYLE(1967), cos; LADY SINGS THE BLUES(1972), cos; FUNNY LADY(1975), cos; ...ALL THE MARBLES(1981), cos; PENNIES FROM HEAVEN(1981), cos; STAYING ALIVE(1983), cos
Leslie Mackie
 WICKER MAN, THE(1974, Brit.)
Philip Mackie
 WHOLE TRUTH, THE(1958, Brit.), w; CLUE OF THE SILVER KEY, THE(1961, Brit.), w; MAN AT THE CARLTON TOWER(1961, Brit.), w; NUMBER SIX(1962, Brit.), w; 20,000 POUNDS KISS, THE(1964, Brit.), w; SHARE OUT, THE(1966, Brit.), w; CLUE OF THE TWISTED CANDLE(1968, Brit.), w; ALL THE WAY UP(1970, Brit.), p, w; PRAYING MANTIS(1982, Brit.), w
Philo Mackie
 CLUE OF THE NEW PIN, THE(1961, Brit.), w
Richard Mackie
 GHOST GOES WEST, THE(1936)
Sharon Mackie
 SCATTERGOOD MEETS BROADWAY(1941)
Robert MacKiehan
 COOGAN'S BLUFF(1968), art d
Harry Mackin
 COWBOY AND THE INDIANS, THE(1949); SONS OF NEW MEXICO(1949); TEXANS NEVER CRY(1951); LAST OF THE PONY RIDERS(1953)
John Mackin
 FAR COUNTRY, THE(1955); GREAT VAN ROBBERY, THE(1963, Brit.)
Silents
 IDOL OF THE STAGE, THE(1916); NEW YORK PEACOCK, THE(1917)
John E. Mackin
Misc. Silents
 COMMON SENSE BRACKETT(1916); LOTUS WOMAN, THE(1916)
Ray Mackin
 SMASHING TIME(1967 Brit.)
Allan Mackinnon
 CHEER BOYS CHEER(1939, Brit.), w; LET'S BE FAMOUS(1939, Brit.), w; THIS MAN IN PARIS(1939, Brit.), w; THIS MAN IS NEWS(1939, Brit.), w; UNPUBLISHED STORY(1942, Brit.), w; VOTE FOR HUGGETT(1948, Brit.), w; SLEEPING CAR TO TRIESTE(1949, Brit.), w; SHE SHALL HAVE MURDER(1950, Brit.), w; BLACK WIDOW(1951, Brit.), w; TRAVELLER'S JOY(1951, Brit.), w; BACHELOR IN PARIS(1953, Brit.), w; BLUE PARROT, THE(1953, Brit.), w; HOUSE OF BLACKMAIL(1953, Brit.), w; CIRCUMSTANIAL EVIDENCE(1954, Brit.), w; GOLDEN LINK, THE(1954, Brit.), w; SAINT'S GIRL FRIDAY, THE(1954, Brit.), w; HORNET'S NEST, THE(1955, Brit.), w; BEHIND THE HEADLINES(1956, Brit.), w; MARCH HARE, THE(1956, Brit.), w; MEN OF SHERWOOD FOREST(1957, Brit.), w; SECOND FIDDLE(1957, Brit.), w; TIME IS MY ENEMY(1957, Brit.), w
Armand MacKinnon
Misc. Talkies
 PINOCCHIO'S STORYBOOK ADVENTURES(1979)
Derek MacKinnon
 TERROR TRAIN(1980, Can.)
Errol MacKinnon
 HIGH TIDE AT NOON(1957, Brit.)
Georgina Mackinnon
 HI, GANG!(1941, Brit.)
John MacKinnon
Silents
 FORBIDDEN WOMAN, THE(1920); KISSES(1922); WOMAN WHO WALKED ALONE, THE(1922)
Mary MacKinnon
1984
 BAY BOY(1984, Can.)
Alex Mackintosh
 DEAD MAN'S EVIDENCE(1962, Brit.)
Angus Duncan Mackintosh
 HOW TO SEDUCE A WOMAN(1974)
Estella Mackintosh
Misc. Silents
 SYRIAN IMMIGRANT, THE(1921)
Kenneth Mackintosh
 PRIZE OF ARMS, A(1962, Brit.); OTHELLO(1965, Brit.); THREE SISTERS(1974, Brit.)
Louise Mackintosh
 BLACK CAMEL, THE(1931); BRAT, THE(1931); DOWN TO EARTH(1932); PHANTOM PRESIDENT, THE(1932); HARD TO HANDLE(1933); LITTLE GIANT, THE(1933); SAILOR BE GOOD(1933); THEY JUST HAD TO GET MARRIED(1933)
Misc. Silents
 FEAR-BOUND(1925)

Woods Mackintosh
 WORLD ACCORDING TO GARP, The(1982), art d; JAWS 3-D(1983), prod d
1984
 NOTHING LASTS FOREVER(1984), art d
Woody Mackintosh
 FIRST DEADLY SIN, THE(1980), art d
Laura Macklan
Misc. Silents
 HEART OF NEW YORK, THE(1916)
Arthur Mackley
Silents
 HONOR SYSTEM, THE(1917); SHOOTIN' FOR LOVE(1923)
J. Arthur Mackley
Misc. Silents
 FEUD, THE(1919)
Mrs. Arthur Mackley
Silents
 INTOLERANCE(1916)
Albert Macklin
 STREAMERS(1983)
Silents
 ACCORDING TO LAW(1916); DRIFTER, THE(1916)
Clifton Macklin
 MARK OF THE HAWK, THE(1958)
David Macklin
 GUNPOINT(1966); TAMMY AND THE MILLIONAIRE(1967); BORN WILD(1968); MIDWAY(1976); TENDER FLESH(1976)
Hughes Macklin
 BRIDE OF THE LAKE(1934, Brit.); MELODY OF MY HEART(1936, Brit.)
James Macklin
 SAN FRANCISCO(1936); VOICE OF BUGLE ANN(1936); MOVIE STUNTMEN(1953); NO PLACE TO LAND(1958)
Misc. Talkies
 HOLLYWOOD THRILL-MAKERS(1954)
Mary Macklin
 CAESAR AND CLEOPATRA(1946, Brit.)
Harrison Macklyn
 CARELESS AGE(1929), w
Denny Macko
 DRIVER, THE(1978)
Peter MacKriel
1984
 SWORD OF THE VALIANT(1984, Brit.)
Helen Macks
Silents
 SUCCESS(1923)
Moe Macky
 PRECIOUS JEWELS(1969), ed
Andrew MacLachlan
 MONTY PYTHON'S LIFE OF BRIAN(1979, Brit.); TIME BANDITS(1981, Brit.); MONTY PYTHON'S THE MEANING OF LIFE(1983, Brit.)
Janet MacLachlan
 UPTIGHT(1968); CHANGE OF MIND(1969); DARKER THAN AMBER(1970); HALLS OF ANGER(1970); MAN, THE(1972); SOUNDER(1972); MAURIE(1973)
1984
 TIGHTROPE(1984)
Misc. Talkies
 MAURIE(1973)
Kyle MacLachlan
1984
 DUNE(1984)
Robert MacLachlan
 DOSS HOUSE(1933, Brit.); JOY RIDE(1935, Brit.)
Angus MacLahlan
 REUBEN, REUBEN(1983)
Ian Maclaine
 BOY AND THE BRIDGE, THE(1959, Brit.)
Shirley MacLaine
 ARTISTS AND MODELS(1955); TROUBLE WITH HARRY, THE(1955); AROUND THE WORLD IN 80 DAYS(1956); HOT SPELL(1958); MATCHMAKER, THE(1958); SHEEPMAN, THE(1958); ASK ANY GIRL(1959); CAREER(1959); SOME CAME RUNNING(1959); APARTMENT, THE(1960); CAN-CAN(1960); OCEAN'S ELEVEN(1960); ALL IN A NIGHT'S WORK(1961); CHILDREN'S HOUR, THE(1961); TWO LOVES(1961); MY GEISHA(1962); TWO FOR THE SEESAW(1962); IRMA LA DOUCE(1963); JOHN GOLDFARB, PLEASE COME HOME(1964); WHAT A WAY TO GO(1964); YELLOW ROLLS-ROYCE, THE(1965, Brit.); GAMBIT(1966); WOMAN TIMES SEVEN(1967, U.S./Fr./Ital.); BLISS OF MRS. BLOSSOM, THE(1968, Brit.); SWEET CHARITY(1969); TWO MULES FOR SISTER SARA(1970); DESPERATE CHARACTERS(1971); POSSESSION OF JOEL DELANEY, THE(1972); TURNING POINT, THE(1977); BEING THERE(1979); CHANGE OF SEASONS, A(1980); LOVING COUPLES(1980); TERMS OF ENDEARMENT(1983)
1984
 CANNONBALL RUN II(1984)
Barton MacLane
 COCOANUTS, THE(1929); HIS WOMAN(1931); BIG EXECUTIVE(1933); HELL AND HIGH WATER(1933); MAN OF THE FOREST(1933); TILLIE AND GUS(1933); TO THE LAST MAN(1933); LAST ROUND-UP, THE(1934); LONE COWBOY(1934); THUNDERING HERD, THE(1934); BLACK FURY(1935); CASE OF THE CURIOUS BRIDE, THE(1935); CASE OF THE LUCKY LEGS, THE(1935); CEILNG ZERO(1935); DR. SOCRATES(1935); FRISCO KID(1935); G-MEN(1935); GO INTO YOUR DANCE(1935); I FOUND STELLA PARISH(1935); MAN OF IRON(1935); PAGE MISS GLORY(1935); STRANDED(1935); BENGAL TIGER(1936); BULLETS OR BALLOTS(1936); JAILBREAK(1936); TIMES SQUARE PLAYBOY(1936); WALKING DEAD, THE(1936); ADVENTUROUS BLONDE(1937); BORN RECKLESS(1937); EVER SINCE EVE(1937); FLY-AWAY BABY(1937); GOD'S COUNTRY AND THE WOMAN(1937); KID COMES BACK, THE(1937); PRINCE AND THE PAUPER, THE(1937); SAN QUENTIN(1937); SMART BLONDE(1937); WINE, WOMEN AND HORSES(1937); YOU ONLY LIVE ONCE(1937); BLONDES AT WORK(1938); GOLD IS WHERE YOU FIND IT(1938); PRISON BREAK(1938); TORCHY BLANE IN CHINATOWN(1938); TORCHY GETS HER MAN(1938); YOU AND ME(1938); BIG TOWN CZAR(1939); I WAS A CON-

VICT(1939); MUTINY IN THE BIG HOUSE(1939); STAND UP AND FIGHT(1939); TORCHY RUNS FOR MAYOR(1939); GANGS OF CHICAGO(1940); MELODY RANCH(1940); MEN WITHOUT SOULS(1940); SECRET SEVEN, THE(1940); BARNACLE BILL(1941); COME LIVE WITH ME(1941); DR. JEKYLL AND MR. HYDE(1941); HIGH SIERRA(1941); HIT THE ROAD(1941); MALTESE FALCON, THE(1941); MANPOWER(1941); WESTERN UNION(1941); WILD GEESE CALLING(1941); ALL THROUGH THE NIGHT(1942); BIG STREET, THE(1942); HIGHWAYS BY NIGHT(1942); IN THIS OUR LIFE(1942); BOMBARDIER(1943); CRIME DOCTOR'S STRANGEST CASE(1943); GENTLE GANGSTER, A(1943); MAN OF COURAGE(1943), a, w; SONG OF TEXAS(1943); UNDERDOG, THE(1943); CRY OF THE WEREWOLF(1944); GENTLE ANNIE(1944); MARINE RAIDERS(1944); MUMMY'S GHOST, THE(1944); NABONGA(1944); SECRET COMMAND(1944); SCARED STIFF(1945); SPANISH MAIN, THE(1945); TARZAN AND THE AMAZONS(1945); MYSTERIOUS INTRUDER(1946); SAN QUENTIN(1946); SANTA FE UPRISING(1946); CHEYENNE(1947); JUNGLE FLIGHT(1947); TARZAN AND THE HUNTRESS(1947); ANGEL IN EXILE(1948); DUDE GOES WEST, THE(1948); RELENTLESS(1948); SILVER RIVER(1948); TREASURE OF THE SIERRA MADRE, THE(1948); UNKNOWN ISLAND(1948); WALLS OF JERICHO(1948); RED LIGHT(1949); BANDIT QUEEN(1950); KISS TOMORROW GOODBYE(1950); LET'S DANCE(1950); ROOKIE FIREMAN(1950); BEST OF THE BADMEN(1951); DRUMS IN THE DEEP SOUTH(1951); BUGLES IN THE AFTERNOON(1952); HALF-BREED, THE(1952); THUNDERBIRDS(1952); COW COUNTRY(1953); GLENN MILLER STORY, THE(1953); JACK SLADE(1953); KANSAS PACIFIC(1953); SEA OF LOST SHIPS(1953); JUBILEE TRAIL(1954); RAILS INTO LARAMIE(1954); FOXFIRE(1955); HELL'S OUTPOST(1955); JAIL BUSTERS(1955); SILVER STAR, THE(1955); TREASURE OF RUBY HILLS(1955); BACKLASH(1956); JAGUAR(1956); LAST OF THE DESPERADOES(1956); MAN IS ARMED, THE(1956); NAKED GUN, THE(1956); THREE VIOLENT PEOPLE(1956); HELL'S CROSSROADS(1957); NAKED IN THE SUN(1957); SIERRA STRANGER(1957); FRONTIER GUN(1958); GEISHA BOY, THE(1958); GIRL IN THE WOODS(1958); GUNFIGHTERS OF ABILENE(1960); NOOSE FOR A GUNMAN(1960); POCKETFUL OF MIRACLES(1961); LAW OF THE LAWLESS(1964); ROUNDERS, THE(1965); TOWN TAMER(1965); ARIZONA BUSHWHACKERS(1968); BUCKSKIN(1968)

Kerry MacLane
JOHNNY GOT HIS GUN(1971)

Mary MacLane
Misc. Silents
MEN WHO HAVE MADE LOVE TO ME(1918)

Ian Maclaren
JOURNEY'S END(1930); BODY AND SOUL(1931); CONQUERING HORDE, THE(1931); AFRAID TO TALK(1932); PRESTIGE(1932); CLEOPATRA(1934); LET 'EM HAVE IT(1935); HOUSE OF SECRETS, THE(1937); LANCER SPY(1937); PORTIA ON TRIAL(1937); PRINCE AND THE PAUPER, THE(1937); PRISONER OF ZENDA, THE(1937); INVISIBLE ENEMY(1938); LITTLE ORPHAN ANNIE(1938); HOUND OF THE BASKERVILLES, THE(1939); LET US LIVE(1939); MAN IN THE IRON MASK, THE(1939); DOCTOR TAKES A WIFE(1940); HILLS OF HOME(1948), w
Silents
UNDER THE RED ROBE(1923); MONSIEUR BEAUCAIRE(1924)

Ivor MacLaren
EVERGREEN(1934, Brit.)

John MacLaren
WELCOME, MR. WASHINGTON(1944, Brit.); DIPLOMATIC PASSPORT(1954, Brit.); YANK IN ERMINE, A(1955, Brit.)

Katherine MacLaren
Misc. Silents
TEARS AND SMILES(1917)

Mary MacLaren
HEADLINE SHOOTER(1933); PHANTOM BROADCAST, THE(1933); ESCAPADE(1935); HANDS ACROSS THE TABLE(1935); NEW FRONTIER, THE(1935); THEODORA GOES WILD(1936); DAY AT THE RACES, A(1937); LAWMAN IS BORN, A(1937); RECKLESS RANGER(1937); DUKE OF WEST POINT, THE(1938); I STOLE A MILLION(1939); IN NAME ONLY(1939); UNION PACIFIC(1939); 'TIL WE MEET AGAIN(1940); SAINT IN PALM SPRINGS, THE(1941); LEOPARD MAN, THE(1943); SIX GUN GOSPEL(1943); LADY IN THE DARK(1944); FRONTIER FEUD(1945); KITTY(1945); NAVAJO TRAIL, THE(1945); CROSSED TRAILS(1948); MY OWN TRUE LOVE(1948)
Silents
SAVING THE FAMILY NAME(1916); BREAD(1918); AMAZING WIFE, THE(1919); PETAL ON THE CURRENT, THE(1919); THREE MUSKETEERS, THE(1921); WILD GOOSE, THE(1921); ACROSS THE CONTINENT(1922); ON THE BANKS OF THE WABASH(1923); UNDER THE RED ROBE(1923)
Misc. Silents
IDLE WIVES(1916); WANTED - A HOME(1916); MONEY MADNESS(1917); MYSTERIOUS MRS. M, THE(1917); PLOW WOMAN, THE(1917); MODEL'S CONFESSION, THE(1918); VANITY POOL, THE(1918); BONNIE, BONNIE LASSIE(1919); CREAKING STAIRS(1919); POINTING FINGER, THE(1919); SECRET MARRIAGE(1919); UNPAINTED WOMAN, THE(1919); WEAKER VESSEL, THE(1919); FORGED BRIDE, THE(1920); ROAD TO DIVORCE, THE(1920); ROGUE AND RICHES(1920); COURAGEOUS COWARD, THE(1924); UNINVITED GUEST, THE(1924)

Jerry MacLauchlin
VOICES(1979)

Janet MacLaughlin
...TICK...TICK...TICK...(1970)

Michael MacLaverty
TANYA'S ISLAND(1981, Can.), ed; CURTAINS(1983, Can.), ed

Otis Maclay
SQUARE ROOT OF ZERO, THE(1964), ed, spec eff

Alistair MacLean
GUNS OF NAVARONE, THE(1961), w; SECRET WAYS, THE(1961), w; WHERE EAGLES DARE(1968, Brit.), w; PUPPET ON A CHAIN(1971), w; WHEN EIGHT BELLS TOLL(1971, Brit.), w; FEAR IS THE KEY(1973), w; CARAVAN TO VACCARES(1974, Brit./Fr), w; BREAKHEART PASS(1976), w; GOLDEN RENDEZVOUS(1977), w; FORCE 10 FROM NAVARONE(1978, Brit.), w; BEAR ISLAND(1980, Brit.-Can.), w

Ann MacLean
YOUNGEST PROFESSION, THE(1943)

Barbara MacLean
BARONESS AND THE BUTLER, THE(1938), ed; LITTLE OLD NEW YORK(1940), ed

Douglas MacLean
CARNATION KID(1929); CAUGHT PLASTERED(1931), p, w; CRACKED NUTS(1931), p, w; LAUGH AND GET RICH(1931), p, w; TOO MANY COOKS(1931), p; MAMA LOVES PAPA(1933), w; TILLIE AND GUS(1933), p; LADIES SHOULD LISTEN(1934), p; MELODY IN SPRING(1934), p; MRS. WIGGS OF THE CABBAGE PATCH(1934), p; SIX OF A KIND(1934), w; ACCENT ON YOUTH(1935), p; PEOPLE WILL TALK(1935), p; TWO FOR TONIGHT(1935), p; GREAT GUY(1936), p; 23 ½ HOURS LEAVE(1937), p
Misc. Talkies
DIVORCE MADE EASY(1929)
Silents
AS YE SOW(1914); HUN WITHIN, THE(1918); JAILBIRD, THE(1920); CHICKENS(1921); ONE A MINUTE(1921); ROOKIE'S RETURN, THE(1921); SUNSHINE TRAIL, THE(1923); NEVER SAY DIE(1924); INTRODUCE ME(1925); THAT'S MY BABY(1926); LET IT RAIN(1927); SOFT CUSHIONS(1927)
Misc. Silents
LOVE'S CRUCIBLE(1916); WOMAN'S POWER, A(1916); FAIR BARBARIAN, THE(1917); SOULS IN PAWN(1917); UPPER CRUST, THE(1917); FUSS AND FEATHERS(1918); MIRANDY SMILES(1918); VAMP, THE(1918); CAPTAIN KIDD, JR.(1919); HAPPY THOUGH MARRIED(1919); HOMEBREAKER, THE(1919); WHAT'S YOUR HUSBAND DOING?(1919); 23 ½ HOURS ON LEAVE(1919); LET'S BE FASHIONABLE(1920); MARY'S ANKLE(1920); HOME STRETCH, THE(1921); PASSING THRU(1921); HOTTENTOT, THE(1922); BELL BOY 13(1923); GOING UP(1923); MAN OF ACTION, THE(1923); YANKEE CONSUL, THE(1924); SEVEN KEYS TO BALDPATE(1925); HOLD THAT LION(1926)

Duncan Maclean
JOYRIDE(1977)

Fred MacLean
OLD ACQUAINTANCE(1943), set d; MR. SKEFFINGTON(1944), set d; SARATOGA TRUNK(1945), set d; BIG SLEEP, THE(1946), set d; WINTER MEETING(1948), set d; MOONLIGHTER, THE(1953), set d; SOMBRERO(1953), set d; BAD DAY AT BLACK ROCK(1955), set d; TRIAL(1955), set d; RACK, THE(1956), set d; TRIBUTE TO A BADMAN(1956), set d; JOHNNY TREMAIN(1957), set d; OLD YELLER(1957), set d; LIGHT IN THE FOREST, THE(1958), set d; DARBY O'GILL AND THE LITTLE PEOPLE(1959), set d; SHAGGY DOG, THE(1959), set d; POLLYANNA(1960), set d; TOBY TYLER(1960), set d; RETURN TO PEYTON PLACE(1961), set d; RIGHT APPROACH, THE(1961), set d; SANCTUARY(1961), set d

Fred M. MacLean
CORN IS GREEN, THE(1945), set d; STOLEN LIFE, A(1946), set d; ESCAPE ME NEVER(1947), set d; POSSESSED(1947), set d; THAT WAY WITH WOMEN(1947), set d; KEY LARGO(1948), set d; TREASURE OF THE SIERRA MADRE, THE(1948), set d; WHITE HEAT(1949), set d; LION IS IN THE STREETS, A(1953), set d

Grace MacLean
Misc. Silents
HERO OF THE HOUR, THE(1917); TERROR, THE(1917)

Hugh Maclean
Silents
OWD BOB(1924, Brit.), w

Ian MacLean
STREET SINGER, THE(1937, Brit.); MARIGOLD(1938, Brit.); RETURN OF CAROL DEANE, THE(1938, Brit.); SINGING COP, THE(1938, Brit.); THANK EVANS(1938, Brit.); THISTLEDOWN(1938, Brit.); ARSENAL STADIUM MYSTERY, THE(1939, Brit.); GENTLEMAN'S GENTLEMAN, A(1939, Brit.); MURDER WILL OUT(1939, Brit.); NURSEMAID WHO DISAPPEARED, THE(1939, Brit.); TOO DANGEROUS TO LIVE(1939, Brit.); SAILOR'S DON'T CARE(1940, Brit.); THAT'S THE TICKET(1940, Brit.); TWO FOR DANGER(1940, Brit.); YOUNG MR. PITT, THE(1942, Brit.); HEADLINE(1943, Brit.); SHIPBUILDERS, THE(1943, Brit.); DREAMING(1944, Brit.); TWILIGHT HOUR(1944, Brit.); WORLD OWES ME A LIVING, THE(1944, Brit.); HERE COMES THE SUN(1945, Brit.); STORY OF SHIRLEY YORKE, THE(1948, Brit.); FLOODTIDE(1949, Brit.); VALDEZ IS COMING(1971)

Lorraine Eddy MacLean
FOOLS FOR SCANDAL(1938)

Lorraine MacLean
IF I WERE FREE(1933); SUNBONNET SUE(1945), cos; VIOLENCE(1947), Cos

Monica MacLean
DEMON SEED(1977)

Nancy MacLean
RETURN OF THE JEDI(1983)

Peter MacLean
CARDINAL, THE(1963); PLAYGROUND, THE(1965); FRIENDS OF EDDIE COYLE, THE(1973); SQUIRM(1976); FORCE: FIVE(1981)
1984
BREAKIN' 2: ELECTRIC BOOGALOO(1984)

Richard MacLean
DEATH RACE 2000(1975), spec eff

Rob MacLean
HOUNDS... OF NOTRE DAME, THE(1980, Can.)

Stephen Maclean
STARSTRUCK(1982, Aus.), w

Scott MacLellan
LITTLE DARLINGS(1980); NIGHT THE LIGHTS WENT OUT IN GEORGIA, THE(1981)

Susan MacLenachan
HERO(1982, Brit.), cos

Andy MacLennan
Silents
BLACK BIRD, THE(1926)

Donald MacLennan
FIDDLER ON THE ROOF(1971)

Elizabeth MacLennan
JOANNA(1968, Brit.); HANDS OF THE RIPPER(1971, Brit.)

Jack Maclennan
HONEYMOON IN BALI(1939)

Susan MacLennan
GUEST AT STEENKAMPSKRAAL, THE(1977, South Africa)
1984
GUEST, THE(1984, Brit.)

Gavin Macleod
I WANT TO LIVE!(1958); COMPULSION(1959); OPERATION PETTICOAT(1959); HIGH TIME(1960); WAR HUNT(1962); MC HALE'S NAVY(1964); MC HALE'S NAVY JOINS THE AIR FORCE(1965); SWORD OF ALI BABA, THE(1965); SAND PEBBLES, THE(1966); PARTY, THE(1968); COMIC, THE(1969); MAN CALLED GANNON, A(1969); 1,000 PLANE RAID, THE(1969)

Gordon MacLeod
SPITFIRE(1943, Brit.)

Ian MacLeod
DINGAKA(1965, South Africa), art d; KIMBERLEY JIM(1965, South Africa), art d

Jane MacLeod
GUESS WHAT WE LEARNED IN SCHOOL TODAY?(1970)

Janet MacLeod
Silents
TAKE ME HOME(1928); VAMPING VENUS(1928)

Kelty Macleod
BRAVE DON'T CRY, THE(1952, Brit.)

Mary MacLeod
IF ...(1968, Brit.); O LUCKY MAN!(1973, Brit.); BRITTANIA HOSPITAL(1982, Brit.)

Murray MacLeod
STRAWBERRY STATEMENT, THE(1970); CAHILL, UNITED STATES MAR-SHAL(1973); BIG FIX, THE(1978)

Robert MacLeod
APPALOOSA, THE(1966), w; 100 RIFLES(1969), w; OMEN, THE(1976); TWILIGHT'S LAST GLEAMING(1977, U.S./Ger.); SUPERMAN(1978)

Roland MacLeod
LAST REMAKE OF BEAU GESTE, THE(1977)

Virginia MacLeod
ONE PLUS ONE(1961, Can.)

Harold MacLernon
WHITE ZOMBIE(1932), ed

Michael MacLiammoir
OTHELLO(1955, U.S./Fr./Ital.); TOM JONES(1963, Brit.); 30 IS A DANGEROUS AGE, CYNTHIA(1968, Brit.); KREMLIN LETTER, THE(1970)

Micheal MacLiammoir
WHAT'S THE MATTER WITH HELEN?(1971)

Frances MacInerney
GIRL CRAZY(1943)

Elli Maclure
ALVIN PURPLE(1974, Aus.); TRUE STORY OF ESKIMO NELL, THE(1975, Aus.)

Lionel MacLyn
CRY MURDER(1936)

Aline MacMahon
FIVE STAR FINAL(1931); HEART OF NEW YORK(1932); LIFE BEGINS(1932); ONCE IN A LIFETIME(1932); ONE WAY PASSAGE(1932); SILVER DOLLAR(1932); WEEK-END MARRIAGE(1932); GOLD DIGGERS OF 1933(1933); HEROES FOR SALE(1933); LIFE OF JIMMY DOLAN, THE(1933); WORLD CHANGES, THE(1933); BABBITT(1934); HEAT LIGHTNING(1934); MERRY FRINKS, THE(1934); SIDE STREETS(1934); AH, WILDERNESS!(1935); I LIVE MY LIFE(1935); KIND LA-DY(1935); MARY JANE'S PA(1935); WHILE THE PATIENT SLEPT(1935); WHEN YOU'RE IN LOVE(1937); OUT OF THE FOG(1941); LADY IS WILLING, THE(1942); TISH(1942); SEEDS OF FREEDOM(1943, USSR); STAGE DOOR CANTEEN(1943); DRAGON SEED(1944); GUEST IN THE HOUSE(1944); MIGHTY MCGURK, THE(1946); SEARCH, THE(1948); ROSEANNA McCOY(1949); FLAME AND THE ARROW, THE(1950); EDDIE CANTOR STORY, THE(1953); MAN FROM LARAMIE, THE(1955); CIMARRON(1960); YOUNG DOCTORS, THE(1961); DIAMOND HEAD(1962); ALL THE WAY HOME(1963); I COULD GO ON SINGING(1963)

Clair MacMahon
YOICKS!(1932, Brit.), cos

David MacMahon
PEGGY(1950); I WAS A COMMUNIST FOR THE F.B.I.(1951)

Horace MacMahon
EXCLUSIVE(1937); GIRL WITH IDEAS, A(1937); KID GALAHAD(1937); NAVY BLUES(1937); PUBLIC WEDDING(1937); WRONG ROAD, THE(1937); BROADWAY MUSKETEERS(1938); KING OF THE NEWSBOYS(1938); LADIES IN DIS-TRESS(1938); MARIE ANTOINETTE(1938); SECRETS OF A NURSE(1938); TENTH AVENUE KID(1938); WHEN G-MEN STEP IN(1938); ANOTHER THIN MAN(1939); BACHELOR MOTHER(1939); BIG TOWN CZAR(1939); FEDERAL MAN-HUNT(1939); FOR LOVE OR MONEY(1939); GRACIE ALLEN MURDER CASE(1939); I WAS A CONVICT(1939); NEWSBOY'S HOME(1939); PIRATES OF THE SKIES(1939); PRIDE OF THE NAVY(1939); QUICK MILLIONS(1939); ROSE OF WASHINGTON SQUA-RE(1939); SABOTAGE(1939); SERGEANT MADDEN(1939); SHE MARRIED A COP(1939); 6000 ENEMIES(1939); BRIDE WORE CRUTCHES, THE(1940); DR. KIL-DARE'S CRISIS(1940); DR. KILDARE'S STRANGE CASE(1940); GANGS OF CHICA-GO(1940); I CAN'T GIVE YOU ANYTHING BUT LOVE, BABY(1940); LEATHER-PUSHERS, THE(1940); MARGIE(1940); MARINES FLY HIGH, THE(1940); MELODY RANCH(1940); MILLIONAIRES IN PRISON(1940); MY FAVORITE WI-FE(1940); OH JOHNNY, HOW YOU CAN LOVE!(1940); BUY ME THAT TOWN(1941); LADY SCARFACE(1941); ROOKIES ON PARADE(1941); STORK PAYS OFF, THE(1941); JAIL HOUSE BLUES(1942); ROGER TOUHY, GANGSTER!(1944); RE-TURN OF OCTOBER, THE(1948); FAST COMPANY(1953); TEXAS LADY(1955); NEVER STEAL ANYTHING SMALL(1959)

J.G. MacMahon
I AM THE LAW(1938)

Leo MacMahon
HILLS OF OLD WYOMING(1937); TEXAS TRAIL(1937); HEART OF ARIZONA(1938)

Thomas MacMahon
ROAD DEMON(1938)

Dan MacManus
ALICE IN WONDERLAND(1951), anim; PETER PAN(1953), anim; ARISTOCATS, THE(1970), anim

Daniel MacManus
FANTASIA(1940), anim, spec eff

Florence MacMichael
YOUNG AND WILLING(1943); WOMAN OBSESSED(1959); CHILDREN'S HOUR, THE(1961); HORSE IN THE GRAY FLANNEL SUIT, THE(1968); WELCOME HOME, SOLDIER BOYS(1972)

Allan MacMillan
SILENCE OF THE NORTH(1981, Can.), m

Gloria MacMillan
OUR MISS BROOKS(1956)

Joseph MacMillan
FOREVER FEMALE(1953), art d

Kenneth MacMillan
EXPRESSO BONGO(1959, Brit.), ch; ROMEO AND JULIET(1966, Brit.), w, ch; TURNING POINT, THE(1977), ch; HIDE IN PLAIN SIGHT(1980)

M. MacMillan
Silents
ONLY SON, THE(1914)

Norma MacMillan
Misc. Talkies
ALICE OF WONDERLAND IN PARIS(1966)

Roddy MacMillan
YOU'RE ONLY YOUNG TWICE(1952, Brit.)

Ronnie MacMillan
1941(1979)

Susannah MacMillan
CONFESSIONS OF AMANS, THE(1977)

Tonie MacMillan
CURE FOR LOVE, THE(1950, Brit.); WHAT THE BUTLER SAW(1950, Brit.); GIRDLE OF GOLD(1952, Brit.); CHALK GARDEN, THE(1964, Brit.)

Violet MacMillan
Silents
PATCHWORK GIRL OF OZ, THE(1914)
Misc. Silents
MAGIC CLOAK OF OZ, THE(1914); SAVED FROM THE HAREM(1915); GIRL WHO WON OUT, THE(1917)

Alain MacMoy
JE T'AIME, JE T'AIME(1972, Fr./Swed.)

Hugh MacMullan
YANKEE DOODLE DANDY(1942), d

Hugh MacMullen
FOOTSTEPS IN THE DARK(1941), d

Charles MacMurphy
YOU CAN'T TAKE IT WITH YOU(1938)

Fred MacMurray
TIGER ROSE(1930); ALICE ADAMS(1935); CAR 99(1935); GILDED LILY, THE(1935); GRAND OLD GIRL(1935); HANDS ACROSS THE TABLE(1935); MEN WITHOUT NAMES(1935); BRIDE COMES HOME(1936); PRINCESS COMES ACROSS, THE(1936); TEXAS RANGERS, THE(1936); THIRTEEN HOURS BY AIR(1936); TRAIL OF THE LONESOME PINE, THE(1936); CHAMPAGNE WALTZ(1937); EXCLUSIVE(1937); MAID OF SALEM(1937); SWING HIGH, SWING LOW(1937); TRUE CONFES-SION(1937); COCOANUT GROVE(1938); MEN WITH WINGS(1938); SING YOU SIN-NERS(1938); CAFE SOCIETY(1939); HONEYMOON IN BALI(1939); INVITATION TO HAPPINESS(1939); LITTLE OLD NEW YORK(1940); RANGERS OF FORTUNE(1940); REMEMBER THE NIGHT(1940); TOO MANY HUSBANDS(1940); DIVE BOM-BER(1941); NEW YORK TOWN(1941); ONE NIGHT IN LISBON(1941); VIR-GINIA(1941); FOREST RANGERS, THE(1942); LADY IS WILLING, THE(1942); STAR SPANGLED RHYTHM(1942); TAKE A LETTER, DARLING(1942); ABOVE SUSPI-CION(1943); FLIGHT FOR FREEDOM(1943); NO TIME FOR LOVE(1943); AND THE ANGELS SING(1944); DOUBLE INDEMNITY(1944); PRACTICALLY YOURS(1944); STANDING ROOM ONLY(1944); CAPTAIN EDDIE(1945); MURDER, HE SAYS(1945); PARDON MY PAST(1945); WHERE DO WE GO FROM HERE?(1945); SMOKY(1946); EGG AND I, THE(1947); SINGAPORE(1947); SUDDENLY IT'S SPRING(1947); DON'T TRUST YOUR HUSBAND(1948); FAMILY HONEYMOON(1948); MIRACLE OF THE BELLS, THE(1948); ON OUR MERRY WAY(1948); FATHER WAS A FULLBACK(1949); BORDERLINE(1950); NEVER A DULL MOMENT(1950); CALLAWAY WENT THATA-WAY(1951); MILLIONAIRE FOR CHRISTY, A(1951); FAIR WIND TO JAVA(1953); MOONLIGHTER, THE(1953); CAINE MUTINY, THE(1954); PUSHOVER(1954); WOM-AN'S WORLD(1954); AT GUNPOINT(1955); FAR HORIZONS, THE(1955); RAINS OF RANCHIPUR, THE(1955); THERE'S ALWAYS TOMORROW(1956); GUN FOR A COWARD(1957); QUANTEZ(1957); DAY OF THE BAD MAN(1958); GOOD DAY FOR A HANGING(1958); FACE OF A FUGITIVE(1959); OREGON TRAIL, THE(1959); SHAGGY DOG, THE(1959); APARTMENT, THE(1960); ABSENT-MINDED PROFES-SOR, THE(1961); BON VOYAGE(1962); SON OF FLUBBER(1963); KISSES FOR MY PRESIDENT(1964); FOLLOW ME, BOYS!(1966); CHARLEY AND THE ANGEL(1973); SWARM, THE(1978)

Katherine MacMurray
S.O.B.(1981)

Myrna MacMurray
EL DORADO(1967)

Maeve MacMurrough
THUNDER IN THE EAST(1953)

Arch Macnair
CAUGHT IN THE DRAFT(1941)

Diana Macnamara
DON'T LOSE YOUR HEAD(1967, Brit.)

Ed MacNamara
SHOOT(1976, Can.)

Major James H. MacNamara
LADY FROM LOUISIANA(1941)

P. Macnamara
BIRDS OF A FEATHER(1931, Brit.), p

W. P. MacNamara
Silents
SUPREME TEST, THE(1923), d&w

Walter MacNamara
Misc. Silents
HEART OF NEW YORK, THE(1916), d

Alan MacNaughton
VICTIM(1961, Brit.); DOUBLE, THE(1963, Brit); FRANKENSTEIN CREATED WOM-AN(1965, Brit.); PATTON(1970)

Ian MacNaughtan
IDOL ON PARADE(1959, Brit.)

Alan MacNaughton
FAMILY LIFE(1971, Brit.)
Dorothea MacNaughton
I AM THE CHEESE(1983)
Grace MacNaughton
WHERE DANGER LIVES(1950)
Gus MacNaughton
GIRL IN DISTRESS(1941, Brit.)
Ian MacNaughton
SCOTCH ON THE ROCKS(1954, Brit.); X THE UNKNOWN(1957, Brit.); SAFE-CRACKER, THE(1958, Brit.); AND NOW FOR SOMETHING COMPLETELY DIFFERENT(1972, Brit.), d
Jack MacNaughton
NO HAUNT FOR A GENTLEMAN(1952, Brit.); PICKWICK PAPERS, THE(1952, Brit.); WAY OUT, THE(1956, Brit.)
Robert MacNaughton
E.T. THE EXTRA-TERRESTRIAL(1982); I AM THE CHEESE(1983)
Wendell MacNeal
RACHEL, RACHEL(1968)
Patrick MacNee
UNTIL THEY SAIL(1957); FATAL NIGHT, THE(1948, Brit.); DICK BARTON AT BAY(1950, Brit.); FIGHTING PIMPERNEL, THE(1950, Brit.); GIRL IS MINE, THE(1950, Brit.); FLESH AND BLOOD(1951, Brit.); LES GIRLS(1957); PURSUIT OF THE GRAF SPEE(1957, Brit.); INCENSE FOR THE DAMNED(1970, Brit.); KING SOLOMON'S TREASURE(1978, Can.); CREATURE WASN'T NICE,THE(1981); HOWLING, THE(1981); SEA WOLVES, THE(1981, Brit.); YOUNG DOCTORS IN LOVE(1982); SWEET SIXTEEN(1983)
1984
THIS IS SPINAL TAP(1984)
Misc. Talkies
BILLION DOLLAR THREAT, THE(1979, Brit.)
Howard Louis MacNeely
JACKIE ROBINSON STORY, THE(1950)
Louis MacNeice
GIRL ON THE CANAL, THE(1947, Brit.), w
Cornell MacNeil
LA TRAVIATA(1982)
Francis MacNeil
1984
BAY BOY(1984, Can.)
Jennie MacNeil
FIST IN HIS POCKET(1968, Ital.)
John MacNeil
SHAGGY(1948), set d
Peter MacNeil
STRANGE SHADOWS IN AN EMPTY ROOM(1977, Can./Ital.); ONE MAN(1979, Can.)
Peter MacNeill
WHY ROCK THE BOAT?(1974, Can.)
Peter MacNicol
DRAGONSLAYER(1981); SOPHIE'S CHOICE(1982)
King Charles MacNiles
P.J.(1968)
Joan Fay Macoboy
THRILL OF A ROMANCE(1945)
Barry Macollum
HOLE IN THE WALL(1929); INTERNES CAN'T TAKE MONEY(1937); MURDER IN GREENWICH VILLAGE(1937); IF I WERE KING(1938); BEAU GESTE(1939); RULERS OF THE SEA(1939); ARKANSAS JUDGE(1941); REMEDY FOR RICHES(1941); IT AIN'T HAY(1943); REVENGE OF THE ZOMBIES(1943); JANE EYRE(1944); KISMET(1944); MARINE RAIDERS(1944); NATIONAL VELVET(1944); TWO YEARS BEFORE THE MAST(1946); DOUBLE LIFE, A(1947); ON THE WATERFRONT(1954); TROUBLE WITH HARRY, THE(1955); TEN COMMANDMENTS, THE(1956); 36 HOURS(1965)
Misc. Silents
FURY(1922)
Milos Macourek
HAPPY END(1968, Czech.), w; VISITORS FROM THE GALAXY(1981, Yugo.), w
Norman MacOwan
TIGHT LITTLE ISLAND(1949, Brit.); DARK LIGHT, THE(1951, Brit.); CASTLE IN THE AIR(1952, Brit.); SCOTCH ON THE ROCKS(1954, Brit.); FOOTSTEPS IN THE FOG(1955, Brit.); WHERE THERE'S A WILL(1955, Brit.); ACTION OF THE TIGER(1957); X THE UNKNOWN(1957, Brit.); HEART OF A CHILD(1958, Brit.); BOY AND THE BRIDGE, THE(1959, Brit.); HORROR HOTEL(1960, Brit.); KIDNAPPED(1960)
Norman MacOwen
TREAD SOFTLY STRANGER(1959, Brit.)
Taylor MacPeters [Cactus Mack]
RANGER'S ROUNDUP, THE(1938)
Angus Macphail
CITY OF PLAY(1929, Brit.), w; TAXI FOR TWO(1929, Brit.), w; CROOKED BILLET, THE(1930, Brit.), w; SYMPHONY IN TWO FLATS(1930, Brit.), w; WARM CORNER, A(1930, Brit.), w; HINDLE WAKES(1931, Brit.), w; NIGHT IN MONTMARTE, A(1931, Brit.), w; SPORT OF KINGS, THE(1931, Brit.), w; THIRD TIME LUCKY(1931, Brit.), w; CRIMINAL AT LARGE(1932, Brit.), w; LORD BABS(1932, Brit.), w; LOVE ON WHEELS(1932, Brit.), w; MARRY ME(1932, Brit.), w; MICHAEL AND MARY(1932, Brit.), w; RINGER, THE(1932, Brit.), w; CUCKOO IN THE NEST, THE(1933, Brit.), p; FAITHFUL HEART(1933, Brit.), w; GHOST TRAIN, THE(1933, Brit.), w; GOOD COMPANIONS(1933, Brit.), w; MAN THEY COULDN'T ARREST, THE(1933, Brit.), w; WHITE FACE(1933, Brit.), w; CHANNEL CROSSING(1934, Brit.), p, w; YANK AT OXFORD, A(1938), w; BUSMAN'S HONEYMOON(1940, Brit.), w; LET GEORGE DO IT(1940, Brit.), w; RETURN TO YESTERDAY(1940, Brit.), w; SALOON BAR(1940, Brit.), w; SECRET FOUR, THE(1940, Brit.), w; THREE COCKEYED SAILORS(1940, Brit.), w; BLACK SHEEP OF WHITEHALL, THE(1941 Brit.), w; GHOST OF ST. MICHAEL'S. THE(1941, Brit.), w; BIG BLOCKADE, THE(1942, Brit.), w; GOOSE STEPS OUT, THE(1942, Brit.), w; PLAYBOY, THE(1942, Brit.), w; CHAMPAGNE CHARLIE(1944, Brit.), w; FIDDLERS THREE(1944, Brit.), w; HALF-WAY HOUSE, THE(1945, Brit.), w; SPELLBOUND(1945), w; DEAD OF NIGHT(1946, Brit.), w; FRIEDA(1947, Brit.), w; LOVES OF JOANNA GODDEN, THE(1947, Brit.), w; CAPTIVE HEART, THE(1948, Brit.), w; TIGHT LITTLE ISLAND(1949, Brit.), w; TRAIN OF EVENTS(1952, Brit.), w; WRONG MAN, THE(1956), w

Silents
LADY OF THE LAKE, THE(1928, Brit.), w
Angus Macphaill
OFFICE GIRL, THE(1932, Brit.), w
J. L. DuRocher Macphearson
Silents
EVIDENCE(1915), w
Duncan MacPhee
HELL BOATS(1970, Brit.), cos
Denyse MacPherson
ORDERS TO KILL(1958, Brit.)
Don MacPherson
BAWDY ADVENTURES OF TOM JONES, THE(1976, Brit.), w
Donald MacPherson
Silents
DARK MIRROR, THE(1920)
Douglas MacPherson
Silents
JIM THE PENMAN(1921); LET'S GET MARRIED(1926)
Gordon MacPherson
ELEPHANT GUN(1959, Brit.)
Harry MacPherson
STARLIGHT OVER TEXAS(1938), w
J. Du Rocher MacPherson
EVIDENCE(1929), w
Jack MacPherson
HAUNTING OF M, THE(1979)
Jeanie MacPherson
GODLESS GIRL, THE(1929), w; DYNAMITE(1930), w; MADAME SATAN(1930), w; DEVIL'S BROTHER, THE(1933), w; PLAINSMAN, THE(1937), w; BUCCANEER, THE(1938), w; REAP THE WILD WIND(1942), w; BUCCANEER, THE(1958), w
Silents
OUTLAW REFORMS, THE(1914); ROSE OF THE RANCHO(1914); CAPTIVE, THE(1915), a, w; CARMEN(1915); CHIMMIE FADDEN OUT WEST(1915), w; GIRL OF THE GOLDEN WEST, THE(1915); GOLDEN CHANCE, THE(1915), w; JOAN THE WOMAN(1916), w; ROMANCE OF THE REDWOODS, A(1917), w; OLD WIVES FOR NEW(1918), w; MALE AND FEMALE(1919), w; SOMETHING TO THINK ABOUT(1920), w; AFFAIRS OF ANATOL, THE(1921), w; SATURDAY NIGHT(1922), w; ADAM'S RIB(1923), w; TEN COMMANDMENTS, THE(1923), w; RED DICE(1926), w, ed; KING OF KINGS, THE(1927), w
Joe MacPherson
1984
BAY BOY(1984, Can.)
L. du Rocher Macpherson
WASHINGTON MELODRAMA(1941), w
Lottie MacPherson
Silents
KING, QUEEN, JOKER(1921)
Patricia MacPherson
BAWDY ADVENTURES OF TOM JONES, THE(1976, Brit.)
Peter MacPherson
1984
JOY OF SEX(1984)
Quinton MacPherson
ROMANCE AND RICHES(1937, Brit.); TALK OF THE DEVIL(1937, Brit.)
Sandy Macpherson
COMMON TOUCH, THE(1941, Brit.); I'LL TURN TO YOU(1946, Brit.)
Stewart MacPherson
TWENTY QUESTIONS MURDER MYSTERY, THE(1950, Brit.)
Al MacQuarrie
Silents
CHEATED HEARTS(1921); LAVENDER BATH LADY, THE(1922); SCRAPPER, THE(1922)
Albert MacQuarrie
Silents
MANHATTAN MADNESS(1916); TARGET, THE(1916); HIGH SPEED(1917); HIS MAJESTY THE AMERICAN(1919); KNICKERBOCKER BUCKAROO, THE(1919); MARK OF ZORRO(1920); MOLLYCODDLE, THE(1920); WHEN THE CLOUDS ROLL BY(1920); BULLDOG COURAGE(1922); ONE CLEAR CALL(1922); SUPER-SEX, THE(1922); DON Q, SON OF ZORRO(1925); GAUCHO, THE(1928)
Misc. Silents
(; FRAME-UP, THE(1915)
Clarice Manning MacQuarrie
Silents
NANCY'S BIRTHRIGHT(1916), w
Frank MacQuarrie
Misc. Silents
TWO MEN OF SANDY BAR(1916); MAN TRAP, THE(1917); MADAME SPHINX(1918)
George MacQuarrie
BEDTIME STORY, A(1933); KING KONG(1933); MIGHTY BARNUM, THE(1934); YOU'RE TELLING ME(1934); CRUSADES, THE(1935); WINGS IN THE DARK(1935); BORDER PATROLMAN, THE(1936); PLAINSMAN, THE(1937); HOTEL IMPERIAL(1939); THIS LAND IS MINE(1943); FOURTEEN HOURS(1951)
Silents
ETERNAL SAPHO, THE(1916); ADVENTURES OF CAROL, THE(1917); IRON RING, THE(1917); APPEARANCE OF EVIL(1918); CABARET, THE(1918); JOAN OF THE WOODS(1918); LOVE IN A HURRY(1919); IDOL DANCER, THE(1920); LOVE FLOWER, THE(1920); CITY OF SILENT MEN(1921); HUNCHBACK OF NOTRE DAME, THE(1923); RAGGED EDGE, THE(1923); REJECTED WOMAN, THE(1924)
Misc. Silents
FORGET-ME-NOTS(1917); HER HOUR(1917); HUNGRY HEART, A(1917); MAID OF BELGIUM, THE(1917); SOCIAL LEPER, THE(1917); STOLEN PARADISE, THE(1917); TENTH CASE, THE(1917); DIAMONDS AND PEARLS(1918); GATES OF GLADNESS(1918); MERELY PLAYERS(1918); WANTED - A MOTHER(1918); BLUFFER, THE(1919); LITTLE INTRUDER, THE(1919); MANDARIN'S GOLD(1919); UNVEILING HAND, THE(1919); WHISPER MARKET, THE(1920); FORBIDDEN LOVE(1921); FIND THE WOMAN(1922)

Melanie Morse MacQuarrie
PROM NIGHT(1980)
Mudock MacQuarrie
Misc. Silents
FORBIDDEN ROOM, THE(1914)
Murdock MacQuarrie
COMMAND PERFORMANCE(1931); DRUMS OF JEOPARDY(1931); DEVIL PAYS, THE(1932); DR. JEKYLL AND MR. HYDE(1932); WILD GIRL(1932); MAN FROM HELL, THE(1934); DARK ANGEL, THE(1935); STONE OF SILVER CREEK(1935); FURY(1936); GREAT GUY(1936); NEVADA(1936); PRISONER OF SHARK ISLAND, THE(1936); PICK A STAR(1937); PHANTOM STAGE, THE(1939); SMOKY TRAILS(1939); CAPTAIN IS A LADY, THE(1940); HOUSE OF THE SEVEN GABLES, THE(1940); MAN FROM MONTANA(1941); RETURN OF DANIEL BOONE, THE(1941); RICHEST MAN IN TOWN(1941); WILDCAT OF TUCSON(1941); ARABIAN NIGHTS(1942); JACKASS MAIL(1942)
Silents
NANCY'S BIRTHRIGHT(1916), a, d; KINGDOM OF LOVE, THE(1918); GAMBLING IN SOULS(1919); CHEATED HEARTS(1921); IF I WERE QUEEN(1922); ASHES OF VENGEANCE(1923); ONLY WOMAN, THE(1924); HAIR TRIGGER BAXTER(1926); JAZZ GIRL, THE(1926); MAN FROM HARDPAN, THE(1927); APACHE RAIDER, THE(1928)
Misc. Silents
RICHELIEU(1914); IN THE WEB OF THE GRAFTERS(1916), d; SIGN OF THE SPADE, THE(1916), d; STAIN IN THE BLOOD, THE(1916), a, d; FEAR NOT(1917); LOYALTY(1918); JACQUES OF THE SILVER NORTH(1919); WHEN A WOMAN STRIKES(1919); HIDDEN WOMAN, THE(1922); HIGH HAND, THE(1926)
William MacQuitty
BLUE SCAR(1949, Brit.), p; MR. LORD SAYS NO(1952, Brit.), p; BOTH SIDES OF THE LAW(1953, Brit.), p; THE BEACHCOMBER(1955, Brit.), p; ABOVE US THE WAVES(1956, Brit.), p; BLACK TENT, THE(1956, Brit.), p; UNDERWORLD INFORMERS(1965, Brit.), p
Alison Macrae
1984
GREYSTOKE: THE LEGEND OF TARZAN, LORD OF THE APES(1984)
Arthur Macrae
HOUSE OPPOSITE, THE(1931, Brit.); PRIVATE SECRETARY, THE(1935, Brit.), w; SHE SHALL HAVE MUSIC(1935, Brit.), w; GAIETY GIRLS, THE(1938, Brit.), w; HIDEOUT IN THE ALPS(1938, Brit.); GEORGE AND MARGARET(1940, Brit.); UNDER YOUR HAT(1940, Brit.), w; MURDER AT THE BASKERVILLES(1941, Brit.); SAINT'S VACATION, THE(1941, Brit.); ENCORE(1951, Brit.), w; HAPPY GO LOVELY(1951, Brit.), w; TRAVELLER'S JOY(1951, Brit.); HORSE'S MOUTH, THE(1953, Brit.); HORSE'S MOUTH, THE(1958, Brit.)
Charles MacRae
CRY, THE BELOVED COUNTRY(1952, Brit.)
Duncan Macrae
BROTHERS, THE(1948, Brit.); TIGHT LITTLE ISLAND(1949, Brit.); FIVE ANGLES ON MURDER(1950, Brit.); YOU'RE ONLY YOUNG TWICE(1952, Brit.); LITTLE KIDNAPPERS, THE(1954, Brit.); WEE GEORDIE(1956, Brit.); MAD LITTLE ISLAND(1958, Brit.); BRIDAL PATH, THE(1959, Brit.); KIDNAPPED(1960); OUR MAN IN HAVANA(1960, Brit.); TUNES OF GLORY(1960, Brit.); GREYFRIARS BOBBY(1961, Brit.); BEST OF ENEMIES, THE(1962); JOLLY BAD FELLOW, A(1964, Brit.); MODEL MURDER CASE, THE(1964, Brit.); 30 IS A DANGEROUS AGE, CYNTHIA(1968, Brit.)
Silents
AUCTION MART, THE(1920, Brit.), d
Misc. Silents
USURPER, THE(1919, Brit.), d; BURNT IN(1920, Brit.), d; MONEY(1921), d
Elizabeth MacRae
LOVE IN A GOLDFISH BOWL(1961); WILD WESTERNERS, THE(1962); FOR LOVE OR MONEY(1963); WILD IS MY LOVE(1963); INCREDIBLE MR. LIMPET, THE(1964); CONVERSATION, THE(1974)
Gordon MacRae
BIG PUNCH, THE(1948); LOOK FOR THE SILVER LINING(1949); BACKFIRE(1950); DAUGHTER OF ROSIE O'GRADY, THE(1950); RETURN OF THE FRONTIERSMAN(1950); TEA FOR TWO(1950); WEST POINT STORY, THE(1950); ON MOONLIGHT BAY(1951); STARLIFT(1951); ABOUT FACE(1952); BY THE LIGHT OF THE SILVERY MOON(1953); DESERT SONG, THE(1953); THREE SAILORS AND A GIRL(1953); OKLAHOMA(1955); BEST THINGS IN LIFE ARE FREE, THE(1956); CAROUSEL(1956); PILOT, THE(1979)
Heather MacRae
RECESS(1967); WHO SAYS I CAN'T RIDE A RAINBOW!(1971); EVERYTHING YOU ALWAYS WANTED TO KNOW ABOUT SEX, BUT WE'RE AFRAID TO ASK(1972); BANG THE DRUM SLOWLY(1973); PERFECT COUPLE, A(1979)
Henry MacRae
STORMY(1935), p; FLASH GORDON(1936), p; WESTBOUND LIMITED(1937), p
Silents
RACING FOR LIFE(1924), d; FEARLESS LOVER, THE(1925), d; HARVEST OF HATE, THE(1929), d; HOOFBEATS OF VENGEANCE(1929), d; KING OF THE RODEO(1929), d; PLUNGING HOOFS(1929), d; WILD BLOOD(1929), d
Misc. Silents
GOD'S CRUCIBLE(1921), d; MAN FROM GLENGARRY, THE(1923), d; FIGHT FOR HONOR, A(1924), d; PRICE SHE PAID, THE(1924), d; TAINTED MONEY(1924), d; WILD BEAUTY(1927), d; DANGER RIDER, THE(1928), d; GUARDIANS OF THE WILD(1928), d; TWO OUTLAWS, THE(1928), d; BURNING THE WIND(1929), d; SMILIN' GUNS(1929), d
Jean MacRae
BILLIE(1965)
Lesley MacRae
FEMALE BUNCH, THE(1969)
Meredith MacRae
BIKINI BEACH(1964); NORWOOD(1970); EARTHBOUND(1981)
1984
CENSUS TAKER, THE(1984)
Misc. Talkies
SKETCHES OF A STRANGLER(?); GRAND JURY(1977); I'M GOING TO BE FAMOUS(1981); MY FRIENDS NEED KILLING(1984); VULTURES IN PARADISE(1984)
Michael MacRae
COMA(1978)

Misc. Talkies
GREAT RIDE, THE(1978); MADHOUSE(1982)
Earl MacRauch
NEW YORK, NEW YORK(1977), w; STRANGER IS WATCHING, A(1982), w
John Victor Macray
TRAGEDY AT MIDNIGHT, A(1942), art d
Arthur Macrea
HIDEOUT IN THE ALPS(1938, Brit.), w
James Macreading
ABDUCTION(1975), ed
Carol Macready
PIRATES OF PENZANCE, THE(1983)
1984
FOREVER YOUNG(1984, Brit.)
Erica Macready
COUNT YORGA, VAMPIRE(1970)
George Macready
TWO WEEKS IN ANOTHER TOWN(1962); COMMANDOS STRIKE AT DAWN, THE(1942); CONSPIRATORS, THE(1944); FOLLOW THE BOYS(1944); MISSING JUROR, THE(1944); SEVENTH CROSS, THE(1944); SOUL OF A MONSTER, THE(1944); STORY OF DR. WASSELL, THE(1944); COUNTER-ATTACK(1945); DON JUAN QUILLIGAN(1945); FIGHTING GUARDSMAN, THE(1945); I LOVE A MYSTERY(1945); MY NAME IS JULIA ROSS(1945); SONG TO REMEMBER, A(1945); BANDIT OF SHERWOOD FOREST, THE(1946); GILDA(1946); MAN WHO DARED, THE(1946); RETURN OF MONTE CRISTO, THE(1946); WALLS CAME TUMBLING DOWN, THE(1946); DOWN TO EARTH(1947); SWORDSMAN, THE(1947); BEYOND GLORY(1948); BIG CLOCK, THE(1948); BLACK ARROW(1948); CORONER CREEK(1948); GALLANT BLADE, THE(1948); ALIAS NICK BEAL(1949); DOOLINS OF OKLAHOMA, THE(1949); JOHNNY ALLEGRO(1949); KNOCK ON ANY DOOR(1949); DESERT HAWK, THE(1950); FORTUNES OF CAPTAIN BLOOD(1950); LADY WITHOUT PASSPORT, A(1950); NEVADAN, THE(1950); ROGUES OF SHERWOOD FOREST(1950); DESERT FOX, THE(1951); DETECTIVE STORY(1951); GOLDEN HORDE, THE(1951); TARZAN'S PERIL(1951); GREEN GLOVE, THE(1952); GOLDEN BLADE, THE(1953); JULIUS CAESAR(1953); STRANGER WORE A GUN, THE(1953); TREASURE OF THE GOLDEN CONDOR(1953); DUFFY OF SAN QUENTIN(1954); VERA CRUZ(1954); KISS BEFORE DYING, A(1956); THUNDER OVER ARIZONA(1956); ABDUCTORS, THE(1957); GUNFIRE AT INDIAN GAP(1957); PATHS OF GLORY(1957); ALLIGATOR PEOPLE, THE(1959); PLUNDERERS OF PAINTED FLATS(1959); JET OVER THE ATLANTIC(1960); TARAS BULBA(1962); DEAD RINGER(1964); SEVEN DAYS IN MAY(1964); WHERE LOVE HAS GONE(1964); GREAT RACE, THE(1965); HUMAN DUPLICATORS, THE(1965); COUNT YORGA, VAMPIRE(1970); TORA! TORA! TORA!(1970, U.S./Jap.); RETURN OF COUNT YORGA, THE(1971)
Misc. Talkies
ASYLUM FOR A SPY(1967)
Michael Macready
COUNT YORGA, VAMPIRE(1970), a, p; RETURN OF COUNT YORGA, THE(1971), p; TERROR HOUSE(1972), a, p
Rene Macready
HOUSE OPPOSITE, THE(1931, Brit.)
Renee Macready
GIRL OF THE PORT(1930); LOVIN' THE LADIES(1930); MANY WATERS(1931, Brit.); SALLY IN OUR ALLEY(1931, Brit.); FOR THE LOVE OF MIKE(1933, Brit.); MY OLD DUCHESS(1933, Brit.); WISHBONE, THE(1933, Brit.); BORROWED CLOTHES(1934, Brit.); REGAL CAVALCADE(1935, Brit.)
Silents
PEEP BEHIND THE SCENES, A(1929, Brit.)
Susan Macready
PROMISE, THE(1969, Brit.); DARWIN ADVENTURE, THE(1972, Brit.); POPE JOAN(1972, Brit.)
Renee Macredy
SCARLET PIMPERNEL, THE(1935, Brit.)
Antonio Macri
THREE BROTHERS(1982, Ital.), p; IDENTIFICATION OF A WOMAN(1983, Ital.), p
Alma Macrorie
SING YOU SINNERS(1938), ed; THANKS FOR THE MEMORY(1938), ed; BOY TROUBLE(1939), ed; INVITATION TO HAPPINESS(1939), ed; STAR MAKER, THE(1939), ed; NIGHT AT EARL CARROLL'S, A(1940), ed; QUARTERBACK, THE(1940), ed; TYPHOON(1940), ed; NOTHING BUT THE TRUTH(1941), ed; ROAD TO ZANZIBAR(1941), ed; MY HEART BELONGS TO DADDY(1942), ed; SWEATER GIRL(1942), ed; TRUE TO THE ARMY(1942), ed; NO TIME FOR LOVE(1943), ed; FRENCHMAN'S CREEK(1944), ed; LADY IN THE DARK(1944), ed; KITTY(1945), ed; MASQUERADE IN MEXICO(1945), ed; TO EACH HIS OWN(1946), a, ed; DREAM GIRL(1947), ed; GOLDEN EARRINGS(1947), ed; SUDDENLY IT'S SPRING(1947), ed; VARIETY GIRL(1947), ed; EMPEROR WALTZ, THE(1948), ed; SEALED VERDICT(1948), ed; BRIDE OF VENGEANCE(1949), ed; SONG OF SURRENDER(1949), ed; CAPTAIN CAREY, U.S.A(1950), ed; NO MAN OF HER OWN(1950), ed; BRANDED(1951), ed; DARLING, HOW COULD YOU!(1951), ed; DEAR BRAT(1951), ed; RHUBARB(1951), ed; ANYTHING CAN HAPPEN(1952), ed; BOTANY BAY(1953), ed; LITTLE BOY LOST(1953), ed; BRIDGES AT TOKO-RI, THE(1954), ed; KNOCK ON WOOD(1954), ed; TROUBLE WITH HARRY, THE(1955), ed; ANYTHING GOES(1956); PROUD AND THE PROFANE, THE(1956), ed; THREE VIOLENT PEOPLE(1956), ed; TIN STAR, THE(1957), ed; GEISHA BOY, THE(1958), ed; ROCK-A-BYE BABY(1958), ed; TEACHER'S PET(1958), ed; BUT NOT FOR ME(1959), ed; RAT RACE, THE(1960), ed; PLEASURE OF HIS COMPANY, THE(1961), ed; COUNTERFEIT TRAITOR, THE(1962), ed; CAPTAIN NEWMAN, M.D.(1963), ed; FOR LOVE OR MONEY(1963), ed; LOVE HAS MANY FACES(1965), ed; GAMBIT(1966), ed; MAN COULD GET KILLED, A(1966), ed; WHAT'S SO BAD ABOUT FEELING GOOD?(1968), ed
Lon MacSunday
SMILING LIEUTENANT, THE(1931)
Wally MacSween
INBREAKER, THE(1974, Can.)
John MacSweeney
Silents
WILD OATS LANE(1926)
James MacTaggart
ALL THE WAY UP(1970, Brit.), d

Ruth MacTammany
Misc. Silents
  ALMA, WHERE DO YOU LIVE?(1917)
Ruth MacTammay
Misc. Silents
  GIRL FROM RECTOR'S, THE(1917)
Mactavish
  ECHOES OF SILENCE(1966)
Angeles Macua
  SON OF CAPTAIN BLOOD, THE(1964, U.S./Ital./Span.)
Giovanna Maculani
  DAMON AND PYTHIAS(1962)
Giulio Maculani
  WAR OF THE ZOMBIES, THE(1965 Ital.)
Guilio Maculani
  PAYMENT IN BLOOD(1968, Ital.)
John Macurdy
  DON GIOVANNI(1979, Fr./Ital./Ger.)
Sue MacVeigh
  GRAND CENTRAL MURDER(1942), w
Archie N. MacVicar
  TOMAHAWK(1951)
Martha MacVicar
  CAPTIVE WILD WOMAN(1943)
Martha MacVicar [Vickers]
  FALCON IN MEXICO, THE(1944); MARINE RAIDERS(1944)
Bill MacWilliams "Williams"
  MURDER IN THE BLUE ROOM(1944)
Bruce MacVittie
1984
  COTTON CLUB, THE(1984)
Glen MacWilliams
  HEARTS IN DIXIE(1929), ph; PLEASURE CRAZED(1929), ph; VALIANT, THE(1929), ph; ARIZONA KID, THE(1930), ph; COMMON CLAY(1930), ph; SEA WOLF, THE(1930), ph; BODY AND SOUL(1931), ph; HAT CHECK GIRL(1932), ph; REBECCA OF SUNNYBROOK FARM(1932), ph; WHILE PARIS SLEEPS(1932), ph; CUCKOO IN THE NEST, THE(1933, Brit.), ph; EVERGREEN(1934, Brit.), ph; ORDERS IS ORDERS(1934, Brit.), ph; STRAUSS' GREAT WALTZ(1934, Brit.), ph; THINGS ARE LOOKING UP(1934, Brit.), ph; FIRST A GIRL(1935, Brit.), ph; HEAT WAVE(1935, Brit.), ph; MY HEART IS CALLING(1935, Brit.), ph; IT'S LOVE AGAIN(1936, Brit.), ph; GANGWAY(1937, Brit.), ph; HEAD OVER HEELS IN LOVE(1937, Brit.), ph; SILENT BARRIERS(1937, Brit.), ph; SAILING ALONG(1938, Brit.), ph; BLUE, WHITE, AND PERFECT(1941), ph; DRESSED TO KILL(1941), ph; GREAT GUNS(1941), ph; PROUD VALLEY, THE(1941, Brit.), ph; A-HAUNTING WE WILL GO(1942), ph; MAN IN THE TRUNK, THE(1942), ph; SUNDOWN JIM(1942), ph; YOUNG AMERICA(1942), ph; CHETNIKS(1943), ph; HE HIRED THE BOSS(1943), ph; WINTERTIME(1943), ph; LIFEBOAT(1944), ph; ROGER TOUHY, GANGSTER!(1944), ph; WING AND A PRAYER(1944), ph; WINGED VICTORY(1944), ph; SPIDER, THE(1945), ph; WITHIN THESE WALLS(1945), ph; IF I'M LUCKY(1946), ph; IT SHOULDN'T HAPPEN TO A DOG(1946), ph; SHOCK(1946), ph
Silents
  ARIZONA(1918), ph; SAY! YOUNG FELLOW(1918), ph; HIS MAJESTY THE AMERICAN(1919), ph; KNICKERBOCKER BUCKAROO, THE(1919), ph; LAMPLIGHTER, THE(1921), ph; WING TOY(1921), ph; DESERTED AT THE ALTAR(1922), ph; MY BOY(1922), ph; OLIVER TWIST(1922), ph; TROUBLE(1922), ph; RUPERT OF HENTZAU(1923), ph; SPIDER AND THE ROSE, THE(1923), ph; CAPTAIN JANUARY(1924), ph; HELEN'S BABIES(1924), ph; LAZYBONES(1925), ph; RETURN OF PETER GRIMM, THE(1926), ph; SIBERIA(1926), ph; ANKLES PREFERRED(1927), ph; LADIES MUST DRESS(1927), ph; PAJAMAS(1927), ph; STAGE MADNESS(1927), ph
Paul MacWilliams
  KING OF THE UNDERWORLD(1939); HELL ON DEVIL'S ISLAND(1957); UNEARTHLY, THE(1957)
Paul M. MacWilliams
  DISPUTED PASSAGE(1939)
Ian MacWolfe
  SON OF MONTE CRISTO(1940)
Bill Macy
  OH! CALCUTTA!(1972); LATE SHOW, THE(1977); JERK, THE(1979); SERIAL(1980); MY FAVORITE YEAR(1982)
Carleton Macy
  SEVEN KEYS TO BALDPATE(1930)
Silents
  PEG OF THE PIRATES(1918)
Misc. Silents
  FIREBRAND, THE(1918); HER MAN(1918)
Dora Macy
  MY PAST(1931), w
Dora Macy [Grace Perkins Oursler]
  NIGHT NURSE(1931), w
H. R. Macy
Silents
  TESS OF THE STORM COUNTRY(1914)
Jack Macy
  OTHER WOMAN, THE(1954); UNTAMED(1955)
Maud Hall Macy
Misc. Silents
  MOTHER'S HEART, A(1914)
Mike Macy
  LAKE PLACID SERENADE(1944); WHERE THERE'S LIFE(1947)
W. H. Macy
  FOOLIN' AROUND(1980); SOMEWHERE IN TIME(1980); WITHOUT A TRACE(1983)
Debbie Madalina
1984
  NIGHT PATROL(1984), set d
Celeste Madamba
  I WAS AN AMERICAN SPY(1951)

Madame Sul-te-Wan
  LADIES THEY TALK ABOUT(1933)
John Madara
  HEY, GOOD LOOKIN'(1982), m
Jozsef Madaras
  FATHER(1967, Hung.); RED AND THE WHITE, THE(1969, Hung./USSR); ROUND UP, THE(1969, Hung.); WINTER WIND(1970, Fr./Hung.); FORTRESS, THE(1979, Hung.)
Enrique Madariaga
  PASSION IN THE SUN(1964), w
Robert Madaris
  MAKO: THE JAWS OF DEATH(1976), w
Pierrette Madd
Misc. Silents
  MILADY(1923, Fr.)
Giorgio Mecchia Maddalena
  THANK YOU, AUNT(1969, Ital.), art d
Julie Maddalena
1984
  CHILDREN OF THE CORN(1984)
Betty Pecha Madden
  BEASTMASTER, THE(1982), cos
Ciaran Madden
  GAWAIN AND THE GREEN KNIGHT(1973, Brit.); BEAST MUST DIE, THE(1974, Brit.)
Dave Madden
  CHARLOTTE'S WEB(1973); EAT MY DUST!(1976)
Dennis Madden
  HOT TOMORROWS(1978)
1984
  BEVERLY HILLS COP(1984)
Donald Madden
  1776(1972)
Doreen Madden
  RISING OF THE MOON, THE(1957, Ireland); GIDEON OF SCOTLAND YARD(1959, Brit.)
George Madden
Silents
  LURE OF THE YUKON(1924), ph; JUSTICE OF THE FAR NORTH(1925), ph
Golda Madden
Misc. Silents
  FLYING COLORS(1917); JILTED JANET(1918)
Goldie Madden
Silents
  IMPULSE(1922); MARSHAL OF MONEYMINT, THE(1922)
Harry Madden
  GOODBYE CHARLIE(1964)
Henry Madden
  SMALL HOURS, THE(1962)
Jarry Madden
  PENROD AND HIS TWIN BROTHER(1938)
Jean Madden
  STAGE STRUCK(1936)
Jeanne Madden
  SEA RACKETEERS(1937); TALENT SCOUT(1937)
Jerry Madden
  DR. SOCRATES(1935); BULLETS OR BALLOTS(1936); PENROD AND SAM(1937)
Joe Madden
  LANDLORD, THE(1970); OWL AND THE PUSSYCAT, THE(1970); GREASER'S PALACE(1972); NEXT STOP, GREENWICH VILLAGE(1976)
Lee Madden
  HELL'S ANGELS '69(1969), d; ANGEL UNCHAINED(1970), p, d, w; NIGHT GOD SCREAMED, THE(1975), d; NIGHT CREATURE(1979), d, w
Misc. Talkies
  MANHANDLERS, THE(1975), d
M. Stuart Madden
  SWEET JESUS, PREACHER MAN(1973), w
Michael Madden
  MARY HAD A LITTLE(1961, Brit.)
Peter Madden
  RHYTHM SERENADE(1943, Brit.); DEVIL'S PLOT, THE(1948, Brit.); MATTER OF MURDER, A(1949, Brit.); TOM BROWN'S SCHOOLDAYS(1951, Brit.); FIEND WITHOUT A FACE(1958); FLOODS OF FEAR(1958, Brit.); EXODUS(1960); HELL IS A CITY(1960, Brit.); MISSILE FROM HELL(1960, Brit.); SATURDAY NIGHT AND SUNDAY MORNING(1961, Brit.); KIND OF LOVING, A(1962, Brit.); LONELINESS OF THE LONG DISTANCE RUNNER, THE(1962, Brit.); ROAD TO HONG KONG, THE(1962, U.S./Brit.); FROM RUSSIA WITH LOVE(1963, Brit.); KISS OF EVIL(1963, Brit.); STOLEN HOURS(1963); NOTHING BUT THE BEST(1964, Brit.); WOMAN OF STRAW(1964, Brit.); DOCTOR ZHIVAGO(1965); DR. TERROR'S HOUSE OF HORRORS(1965, Brit.); FRANKENSTEIN CREATED WOMAN(1965, Brit.); HE WHO RIDES A TIGER(1966, Brit.); PRIVATE LIFE OF SHERLOCK HOLMES, THE(1970, Brit.); HENRY VIII AND HIS SIX WIVES(1972, Brit.); MOHAMMAD, MESSENGER OF GOD(1976, Lebanon/Brit.); ONE MAN(1979, Can.), w
Tommy Madden
  SWAMP THING(1982)
Tony Madden
  SMALL HOURS, THE(1962)
Victor Madden
  EXODUS(1960)
Sara Maddern
  MELODY(1971, Brit.)
Sarah Maddern
  SECOND BEST SECRET AGENT IN THE WHOLE WIDE WORLD, THE(1965, Brit.)
Victor Maddern
  HELL, HEAVEN OR HOBOKEN(1958, Brit.); SEVEN DAYS TO NOON(1950, Brit.); I'LL NEVER FORGET YOU(1951, Brit.); OPERATION DISASTER(1951, Brit.); POOL OF LONDON(1951, Brit.); FRANCHISE AFFAIR, THE(1952, Brit.); HIS EXCELLENCY(1952, Brit.); OUTPOST IN MALAYA(1952, Brit.); GOOD BEGINNING, THE(1953, Brit.); MR. POTTS GOES TO MOSCOW(1953, Brit.); SAILOR OF THE KING(1953, Brit.); SHADOW MAN(1953, Brit.); TERROR ON A TRAIN(1953); COURT MARTIAL(1954,

Brit.); FABIAN OF THE YARD(1954, Brit.); PARATROOPER(1954, Brit.); COCKLE-SHELL HEROES, THE(1955); FOOTSTEPS IN THE FOG(1955, Brit.); JOSEPHINE AND MEN(1955, Brit.); NIGHT MY NUMBER CAME UP, THE(1955, Brit.); SEA SHALL NOT HAVE THEM, THE(1955, Brit.); CHILD IN THE HOUSE(1956, Brit.); HELL IN KOREA(1956, Brit.); IT'S A GREAT DAY(1956, Brit.); LAST MAN TO HANG, THE(1956, Brit.); PRIVATE'S PROGRESS(1956, Brit.); ROTTEN TO THE CORE(1956, Brit.); ABANDON SHIP(1957, Brit.); DECISION AGAINST TIME(1957, Brit.); RAISING A RIOT(1957, Brit.); SAINT JOAN(1957); SON OF A STRANGER(1957, Brit.); STRANGER'S MEETING(1957, Brit.); ALL AT SEA(1958, Brit.); BLOOD OF THE VAMPIRE(1958, Brit.); CAT AND MOUSE(1958, Brit); DUNKIRK(1958, Brit.); HAPPY IS THE BRIDE(1958, Brit.); MENACE IN THE NIGHT(1958, Brit.); SAFECRACKER, THE(1958, Brit.); I'M ALL RIGHT, JACK(1959, Brit.); CARRY ON CONSTABLE(1960, Brit.); CROSSROADS TO CRIME(1960, Brit.); FOUR DESPERATE MEN(1960, Brit.); LET'S GET MARRIED(1960, Brit.); LIGHT UP THE SKY(1960, Brit.); PLEASE TURN OVER(1960, Brit.); PETTICOAT PIRATES(1961, Brit.); WATCH YOUR STERN(1961, Brit.); DAMN THE DEFIANT!(1962, Brit.); ROOMMATES(1962, Brit.); CARRY ON CLEO(1964, Brit.); BUNNY LAKE IS MISSING(1965); CUCKOO PATROL(1965, Brit.); OPERATION SNAFU(1965, Brit.); MAGNIFICENT TWO, THE(1967, Brit.); PSYCHO-CIRCUS(1967, Brit.); CHITTY CHITTY BANG BANG(1968, Brit.); LOST CONTINENT, THE(1968, Brit.); RUN LIKE A THIEF(1968, Span.); DECLINE AND FALL... OF A BIRD WATCHER(1969, Brit.); BUSHBABY, THE(1970); MAGIC CHRISTIAN, THE(1970, Brit.); STEPTOE AND SON(1972, Brit.); DIGBY, THE BIGGEST DOG IN THE WORLD(1974, Brit.)

Marilyn Madderom
STAR 80(1983)

Ginette Maddie
Misc. Silents
L'INONDATION(1924, Fr.)

Burt Maddock
Silents
MASKED AVENGER, THE(1922)

Ben Maddow
FRAMED(1947), w; KISS THE BLOOD OFF MY HANDS(1948), w; MAN FROM COLORADO, THE(1948), w; INTRUDER IN THE DUST(1949), w; ASPHALT JUNGLE, THE(1950), w; SHADOW IN THE SKY(1951), w; SAVAGE EYE(1960), p,d&w; UNFORGIVEN, THE(1960), w; TWO LOVES(1961), w; BALCONY, THE(1963), p, w; AFFAIR OF THE SKIN, AN(1964), p, d&w; WAY WEST, THE(1967), w; CHAIRMAN, THE(1969), w; SECRET OF SANTA VITTORIA, THE(1969), w; MEPHISTO WALTZ, THE(1971), w

Daphne Maddox
MURDER AT 3 A.M.(1953, Brit.)

Dean Maddox, Jr.
IT CAME FROM BENEATH THE SEA(1955)

Diana Maddox
PEACE KILLERS, THE(1971), w; CHANGELING, THE(1980, Can.), w; AMATEUR, THE(1982), w

Gloria Maddox
Misc. Talkies
DANNY(1979)

Jean Maddox
HOLLYWOOD HOTEL(1937); SHE COULDN'T SAY NO(1941)

Layne Maddox
PATSY, THE(1964)

Mary Maddox
WATERSHIP DOWN(1978, Brit.); LONG SHOT(1981, Brit.)

Muriel Maddox
EMERGENCY WEDDING(1950); RED SNOW(1952)

William Maddox
DOCTORS' WIVES(1931)

Jim Maddux
DAVY CROCKETT, KING OF THE WILD FRONTIER(1955)

Rachel Maddux
WALK IN THE SPRING RAIN, A(1970), w

Mady Made
CURTAIN RISES, THE(1939, Fr.)

Humberto Madeira
LISBON(1956)

Paul Madeira
BACHELOR PARTY, THE(1957), m

Eva Madelung
WHY DOES HERR R. RUN AMOK?(1977, Ger.)

Bruno Maderna
PLUCKED(1969, Fr./Ital.), m

Marquita Madero
TWO LATINS FROM MANHATTAN(1941)

Robert Madero
MAUSOLEUM(1983), p, w

G. D. Madgulkar
TWO EYES, TWELVE HANDS(1958, India), w

The Madhyma Lanka Mandala Dancers
ELEPHANT WALK(1954)

Stefano Madia
ERNESTO(1979, Ital.)

Amy Madigan
LOVE CHILD(1982); LOVE LETTERS(1983)
1984
PLACES IN THE HEART(1984); STREETS OF FIRE(1984)

M. Sharon Madigan
I, THE JURY(1982)

Sharon Madigan
TRUCK TURNER(1974)

Susan Madigan
HAROLD AND MAUDE(1971); STUDENT TEACHERS, THE(1973)

Thomas F. Madigan
Z.P.G.(1972), p

Virginia Madigan
Silents
BABY MINE(1917)

Linda Madikisa
PENNYWHISTLE BLUES, THE(1952, South Africa)

Shannon Madill
1984
SIXTEEN CANDLES(1984)

Arne Madin
TOMORROW IS MY TURN(1962, Fr./Ital./Ger.)

C. Madison
FURY OF HERCULES, THE(1961, Ital.), w; SAMSON(1961, Ital.), w

Chad Madison
WHEN WORLDS COLLIDE(1951)

Cleo Madison
Silents
DAMON AND PYTHIAS(1914); ROMANCE OF TARZAN, THE(1918); LURE OF YOUTH(1921); DANGEROUS AGE, THE(1922); GOLD MADNESS(1923); LULLA-BY, THE(1924); ROUGHNECK, THE(1924)
Misc. Silents
CHALICE OF SORROW, THE(1916); HEART'S CRUCIBLE, A(1916); HER BITTER CUP(1916), a, d; SOUL ENSLAVED, A(1916), a, d; BLACK ORCHIDS(1917); GIRL FROM NOWHERE, THE(1919); PRICE OF REDEMPTION, THE(1920); SOULS IN BONDAGE(1923); DISCONTENTED HUSBANDS(1924); TRUE AS STEEL(1924)

Dana Madison
WORLD'S GREATEST SINNER, THE(1962)

Daniel Madison
VALLEY OF THE REDWOODS(1960), w

Elaine Madison
Silents
DOUBLE LIFE OF MR. ALFRED BURTON, THE(1919, Brit.); FANCY DRESS(1919, Brit.)

Ellen Madison
GOLDSTEIN(1964)

Fred Madison
GAY PURR-EE(1962), anim

Gloria Madison
NATIVE SON(1951, U.S., Arg.)

Guy Madison
SINCE YOU WENT AWAY(1944); TILL THE END OF TIME(1946); HONEYMOON(1947); TEXAS, BROOKLYN AND HEAVEN(1948); MASSACRE RIVER(1949); DRUMS IN THE DEEP SOUTH(1951); RED SNOW(1952); CHARGE AT FEATHER RIVER, THE(1953); COMMAND, THE(1954); FIVE AGAINST THE HOUSE(1955); LAST FRONTIER, THE(1955); BEAST OF HOLLOW MOUNTAIN, THE(1956); HILDA CRANE(1956); ON THE THRESHOLD OF SPACE(1956); REPRISAL(1956); HARD MAN, THE(1957); BULLWHIP(1958); JET OVER THE ATLANTIC(1960); SWORD OF THE CONQUEROR(1962, Ital.); GUNMEN OF THE RIO GRANDE(1965, Fr./Ital./Span.); FIVE GIANTS FROM TEXAS(1966, Ital./Span.); MYSTERY OF THUG ISLAND, THE(1966, Ital./Ger.); DEVIL'S MAN, THE(1967, Ital.); BANG BANG KID, THE(1968 U.S./Span./Ital.); OLD SHATTERHAND(1968, Ger./Yugo./Fr./Ital.); PAYMENT IN BLOOD(1968, Ital.); SUPERARGO(1968, Ital./Span.); THIS MAN CAN'T DIE(1970, Ital.); WON TON TON, THE DOG WHO SAVED HOLLYWOOD(1976)
Misc. Talkies
BEHIND SOUTHERN LINES(1952); GHOST OF CROSSBONES CANYON, THE(1952); TRAIL OF THE ARROW(1952); YELLOW HAIRED KID, THE(1952); BORDER CITY RUSTLERS(1953); SECRET OF OUTLAW FLATS(1953); SIX-GUN DECISION(1953); MARSHALS IN DISGUISE(1954); OUTLAW'S SON(1954); TROUBLE ON THE TRAIL(1954); HELL IN NORMANDY(1968, Brit.); WHERE'S WILLIE?(1978)

Helene Madison
WARRIOR'S HUSBAND, THE(1933)

James Madison
Silents
APRIL FOOL(1926), t

Jerry Madison
1984
SUBURBIA(1984)

John Madison
YOUNG FRANKENSTEIN(1974)

Julian Madison
COLLEGE RHYTHM(1934); COME ON, MARINES(1934); IT'S A GIFT(1934); WAGON WHEELS(1934); PRIVATE WORLDS(1935); SHOT IN THE DARK, A(1935); WINGS IN THE DARK(1935); GUNS IN THE DARK(1937); DESERT PATROL(1938); DURANGO VALLEY RAIDERS(1938); TORTURE SHIP(1939); DEATH RIDES THE RANGE(1940); MY SON IS GUILTY(1940)

Julien Madison
SECRETS OF A MODEL(1940)

Laura Madison
HARD COUNTRY(1981)

Leigh Madison
6.5 SPECIAL(1958, Brit.); BEHEMOTH, THE SEA MONSTER(1959, Brit.); CARRY ON NURSE(1959, Brit.); HIGH JUMP(1959, Brit.); NAKED FURY(1959, Brit.); PLEASE TURN OVER(1960, Brit.); IMMORAL CHARGE(1962, Brit.); PLEASURE LOVERS, THE(1964, Brit.)

Mae Madison
WORDS AND MUSIC(1929); BOUGHT(1931); EXPENSIVE WOMEN(1931); HER MAJESTY LOVE(1931); MAD GENIUS, THE(1931); RECKLESS HOUR, THE(1931); SMART MONEY(1931); BIG STAMPEDE, THE(1932); MISS PINKERTON(1932); MOUTHPIECE, THE(1932); PLAY GIRL(1932); RICH ARE ALWAYS WITH US, THE(1932); SO BIG(1932); TENDERFOOT, THE(1932); UNION DEPOT(1932); NOW I'LL TELL(1934); FOLIES DERGERE(1935); RECKLESS(1935)

Marilyn Madison
CURFEW BREAKERS(1957)

Martha Madison
SUBWAY EXPRESS(1931), w
Silents
MISS BLUEBEARD(1925); NECESSARY EVIL, THE(1925)

Martha Madison [Martha O'Dwyer]
RECKLESS LIVING(1931), w

Miles Madison
YOICKS!(1932, Brit.)

Noel Madison
DOORWAY TO HELL(1930); SINNER'S HOLIDAY(1930); FINGER POINTS, THE(1931); LITTLE CAESAR(1931); STAR WITNESS(1931); HAT CHECK GIRL(1932); LAST MILE, THE(1932); MAN ABOUT TOWN(1932); ME AND MY GAL(1932); PLAY GIRL(1932); SYMPHONY OF SIX MILLION(1932); TRIAL OF VIVIENNE WARE, THE(1932); DESTINATION UNKNOWN(1933); HUMANITY(1933); IMPORTANT WITNESS, THE(1933); LAUGHTER IN HELL(1933); WEST OF SINGAPORE(1933); CAT'S PAW, THE(1934); HOUSE OF ROTHSCHILD, THE(1934); I LIKE IT THAT WAY(1934); JOURNAL OF A CRIME(1934); MANHATTAN MELODRAMA(1934); FOUR HOURS TO KILL(1935); G-MEN(1935); GIRL WHO CAME BACK, THE(1935); THREE KIDS AND A QUEEN(1935); WHAT PRICE CRIME?(1935); WOMAN WANTED(1935); CHAMPAGNE CHARLIE(1936); EASY MONEY(1936); MISSING GIRLS(1936); MORALS OF MARCUS, THE(1936, Brit.); MURDER AT GLEN ATHOL(1936); MUSS 'EM UP(1936); MY MARRIAGE(1936); OUR RELATIONS(1936); STRAIGHT FROM THE SHOULDER(1936); GANGWAY(1937, Brit.); HOUSE OF SECRETS, THE(1937); MAN OF THE PEOPLE(1937); MAN WHO MADE DIAMONDS, THE(1937, Brit.); NATION AFLAME(1937); CLIMBING HIGH(1938, Brit.); KATE PLUS TEN(1938, Brit.); MAN WITH 100 FACES, THE(1938, Brit.); SAILING ALONG(1938, Brit.); CHARLIE CHAN IN THE CITY OF DARKNESS(1939); MISSING EVIDENCE(1939); GREAT PLANE ROBBERY, THE(1940); ELLERY QUEEN'S PENTHOUSE MYSTERY(1941); FOOTSTEPS IN THE DARK(1941); HIGHWAY WEST(1941); SHOT IN THE DARK, THE(1941); BOMBS OVER BURMA(1942); DESPERATE CHANCE FOR ELLERY QUEEN, A(1942); JOE SMITH, AMERICAN(1942); MISS V FROM MOSCOW(1942); SECRET AGENT OF JAPAN(1942); BLACK RAVEN, THE(1943); FOREVER AND A DAY(1943); JITTERBUGS(1943); SHANTYTOWN(1943); GENTLEMAN FROM NOWHERE, THE(1948)
Misc. Talkies
COCAINE FIENDS(1937)
Noel N. Madison
HATCHET MAN, THE(1932)
Rock Madison
MAN BEAST(1956); CREATURE OF THE WALKING DEAD(1960, Mex.)
V. Madison
Silents
KID, THE(1921)
Virginia Madison
Silents
BLIND BARGAIN, A(1922); FIRST YEAR, THE(1926)
Jim Madland
J.W. COOP(1971)
Philip Madoc
HIGH WIND IN JAMAICA, A(1965); QUILLER MEMORANDUM, THE(1966, Brit.); BERSERK(1967); DEADFALL(1968, Brit.); JOURNEY TO THE FAR SIDE OF THE SUN(1969, Brit.); HELL BOATS(1970, Brit.); DR. JEKYLL AND SISTER HYDE(1971, Brit.); OPERATION DAYBREAK(1976, U.S./Brit./Czech.)
Ruth Madoc
FIDDLER ON THE ROOF(1971); UNDER MILK WOOD(1973, Brit.)
Barbara Madock
MR. H. C. ANDERSEN(1950, Brit.)
Steve Madoff
DEVIL'S EXPRESS(1975), p
Hiram Mino Madonia
RED DESERT(1965, Fr./Ital.)
Douglas Madore
ADVENTURES OF RUSTY(1945); DANGEROUS PARTNERS(1945); PAN-AMERICANA(1945)
Bert Madrid
HOW COME NOBODY'S ON OUR SIDE?(1975)
Cornejo Madrid
CHIMES AT MIDNIGHT(1967, Span.,Switz.), cos
Francesco Madrid
DOLORES(1949, Span.), w
Joe Madrid
UNHOLY ROLLERS(1972)
Mark Madrid
PORKY'S II: THE NEXT DAY(1983)
Miguel Madrid
GRAVEYARD OF HORROR(1971, Span.), d&w
Mitzou of Madrid
PYRO(1964, U.S./Span.), cos
Felix Bussio Madrigal
1984
ERENDIRA(1984, Mex./Fr./Ger.)
Charles Madrin
WEEKEND AT THE WALDORF(1945); TILL THE CLOUDS ROLL BY(1946)
Teresa Madruga
IN THE WHITE CITY(1983, Switz./Portugal)
Bill Madsen
OUR RELATIONS(1936)
Chris Madsen
Misc. Silents
PASSING OF THE OKLAHOMA OUTLAWS, THE(1915)
Ed Madsen
LAW AND DISORDER(1974); WINTER KILLS(1979)
Gerda Madsen
Misc. Talkies
SINFUL DWARF, THE(1973)
Harry Madsen
WIZ, THE(1978); CLAUDINE(1974); GOD TOLD ME TO(1976); WARRIORS, THE(1979); PRINCE OF THE CITY(1981)
1984
ALMOST YOU(1984); ALPHABET CITY(1984), a, stunts; FLAMINGO KID, THE(1984), stunts; GARBO TALKS(1984)
Holger Madsen
Silents
JUDGE NOT(1920, Brit.), w
Michael Madsen
WARGAMES(1983)

1984
NATURAL, THE(1984); RACING WITH THE MOON(1984)
Peter Madsen
MARYJANE(1968)
Tex Madsen
MIGHTY BARNUM, THE(1934)
Virginia Madsen
CLASS(1983)
1984
DUNE(1984); ELECTRIC DREAMS(1984)
Prince Madupe
SOUTH OF SUEZ(1940)
Madura
ELECTRA GLIDE IN BLUE(1973)
Gonzalo Madurga
SHAFT(1971)
Brenda Maduzia
STUDENT BODIES(1981)
Hans Maebus
FIVE GRAVES TO CAIRO(1943)
Maechivinko
EAST SIDE SADIE(1929)
Beverly Maeda
SON OF GODZILLA(1967, Jap.)
Bibari Maeda
LET'S GO, YOUNG GUY!(1967, Jap.)
Gin Maeda
NO GREATER LOVE THAN THIS(1969, Jap.); TORA-SAN PART 2(1970, Jap.)
Masahiro Maeda
1984
WARRIORS OF THE WIND(1984, Jap.), anim
Yoneo Maeda
1984
FAMILY GAME, THE(1984, Jap.), ph
Jay Maeder
SHOCK WAVES(1977)
Norman Maen
YOUNG GIRLS OF ROCHEFORT, THE(1968, Fr.), ch
Jacqueline Maeppiel
LAST ADVENTURE, THE(1968, Fr./Ital.), ed
W. Maertens
TOXI(1952, Ger.)
Ursula Maes
MAN ON A TIGHTROPE(1953), cos
Mae Maeshire
HUNTERS, THE(1958)
Jack Maeshiro
HOUSE OF BAMBOO(1955)
J. Maesso
CON MEN, THE(1973, Ital.,Span.), w
Joe Maesso
CAULDRON OF DEATH, THE(1979, Ital.), w
Jose G. Maesso
SCHEHERAZADE(1965, Fr./Ital./Span.), w; DJANGO(1966 Ital./Span.), w; SIX DAYS A WEEK(1966, Fr./Ital./Span.), w; HELLBENDERS, THE(1967, U.S./Ital./Span.), w; UGLY ONES, THE(1968, Ital./Span.), w
Jose Maesso
SAVAGE GUNS, THE(1962, U.S./Span.), p
Misc. Talkies
ORDER TO KILL(1974), d
Walter Maestosi
SECRET SEVEN, THE(1966, Ital./Span.)
Ann Maestri
BITTER RICE(1950, Ital.)
Anna Maestri
COME SEPTEMBER(1961)
Antonio Maestri
CONFORMIST, THE(1971, Ital., Fr)
Ubaldo Maestri
GOLD OF NAPLES(1957, Ital.)
John Maestro
HAIR(1979)
Maurice Maeterlinck
BLUE BIRD, THE(1940), w; BLUE BIRD, THE(1976), w
Kurt Maetzig
MARRIAGE IN THE SHADOWS(1948, Ger.), d&w; FIRST SPACESHIP ON VENUS(1960, Ger./Pol.), d, w
Hannalore Maeusel
GENGHIS KHAN(U.S./Brit./Ger./Yugo)
Giulia Mafai
PIRATE OF THE BLACK HAWK, THE(1961, Fr./Ital.), cos
Guiulia Mafai
LOVE, THE ITALIAN WAY(1964, Ital.), cos
Paul Mafela
GOLD(1974, Brit.)
Tony Maffatone
NIGHTHAWKS(1981)
Buck Maffei
ATLANTIS, THE LOST CONTINENT(1961)
Gianpaolo Maffei
ROMANOFF AND JULIET(1961)
Mildred Maffei
FEELIN' GOOD(1966), w
Robert Maffei
MAGIC CHRISTMAS TREE(1964)
Robert "Big Buck" Maffei
CHEECH AND CHONG'S NICE DREAMS(1981)

Gianni Maffeo
LA BOHEME(1965, Ital.)
Roma Maffia
SMITHEREENS(1982)
Giuseppe Maffioli
PIZZA TRIANGLE, THE(1970, Ital./Span.); PRIEST'S WIFE, THE(1971, Ital./Fr.); MOST WONDERFUL EVENING OF MY LIFE, THE(1972, Ital./Fr.); WHITE SISTER(1973, Ital./Span./Fr.)
Julia Maffre
NIGHTS OF SHAME(1961, Fr.)
Jacques Mafioly
ROYAL AFFAIRS IN VERSAILLES(1957, Fr.)
Sousso Abdel Mafiz
CIRCLE OF DECEIT(1982, Fr./Ger.)
Mag-Avril
MY BABY IS BLACK!(1965, Fr.); MY WIFE'S HUSBAND(1965, Fr./Ital.)
Conrad Maga
BACK DOOR TO HELL(1964)
Mickey Maga
DIANE(1955); EDDY DUCHIN STORY, THE(1956); LUST FOR LIFE(1956); MAN IN THE GREY FLANNEL SUIT, THE(1956); RAINTREE COUNTY(1957)
Micky Maga
ONE HUNDRED AND ONE DALMATIANS(1961)
Robert Magahay
HARLOW(1965), cos; CAPER OF THE GOLDEN BULLS, THE(1967), cos; SLAVES(1969), cos
O. Magakyan
FATHER OF A SOLDIER(1966, USSR), spec eff
Lourdes Magalhaes
FITZCARRALDO(1982)
Ramiro Magalhaes
VIOLENT AND THE DAMNED, THE(1962, Braz.)
Nicholas Magallanes
MIDSUMMER NIGHT'S DREAM, A(1966)
Enrique Magalona
HOOK, THE(1962); YANK IN VIET-NAM, A(1964)
Pancho Magalona
CRY FREEDOM(1961, Phil.); CAVALRY COMMAND(1963, U.S./Phil.); MORO WITCH DOCTOR(1964, U.S./Phil.)
Paolo Magalotti
HILLS RUN RED, THE(1967, Ital.); MINUTE TO PRAY, A SECOND TO DIE, A(1968, Ital.)
Angel Magana
GAMES MEN PLAY, THE(1968, Arg.)
Sergio Magana
PUSS 'N' BOOTS(1964, Mex.), w; LITTLE RED RIDING HOOD AND THE MONSTERS(1965, Mex.), w
William MaGann
CASE OF THE BLACK CAT, THE(1936), d
Aiko Magara
TRADE WINDS(1938)
Sophie Magaril
DIARY OF A REVOLUTIONIST(1932, USSR)
S. Magarill
CZAR WANTS TO SLEEP(1934, U.S., USSR)
Sophie Magarill
Misc. Silents
NEW BABYLON, THE(1929, USSR); CITIES AND YEARS(1931, USSR)
Polli Magaro
PARADISE ALLEY(1978)
Polly Magaro
EASY MONEY(1983)
Magda
PALACE OF NUDES(1961, Fr./Ital.); FLASH GORDON(1980)
Mauricio Magdaleno
PORTRAIT OF MARIA(1946, Mex.), w
Zale Magder
SHOOT(1976, Can.), ph; PHOBIA(1980, Can.), p
David Mage
GINA(1961, Fr./Mex.), p; DEATH IN THE GARDEN(1977, Fr./Mex.), p
Jacques Mage
HEAD, THE(1961, Ger.), w; RIFF RAFF GIRLS(1962, Fr./Ital.), p, w
Anita Magee
BACK DOOR TO HEAVEN(1939)
Frank Magee
CASE OF THE BLACK CAT, THE(1936), ed; TWO AGAINST THE WORLD(1936), ed; ADVENTUROUS BLONDE(1937), ed; DANCE, CHARLIE, DANCE(1937), ed; MIDNIGHT COURT(1937), ed; SMART BLONDE(1937), ed; MY BILL(1938), ed; MYSTERY HOUSE(1938), ed; NANCY DREW-DETECTIVE(1938), ed; OVER THE WALL(1938), ed; EVERYBODY'S HOBBY(1939), ed; SMASHING THE MONEY RING(1939), ed; SWEEPSTAKES WINNER(1939), ed; ALWAYS A BRIDE(1940), ed; CALLING ALL HUSBANDS(1940), ed; DEVIL'S ISLAND(1940), ed; FATHER IS A PRINCE(1940), ed; MONEY AND THE WOMAN(1940), ed; MURDER IN THE AIR(1940), ed; FATHER'S SON(1941), ed; STRANGE ALIBI(1941), ed; YOU'RE IN THE ARMY NOW(1941), ed; ACROSS THE PACIFIC(1942), ed; I WAS FRAMED(1942), ed; YOU CAN'T ESCAPE FOREVER(1942), ed; DESERT SONG, THE(1943), ed; CHRISTMAS IN CONNECTICUT(1945), ed; DANGER SIGNAL(1945), ed; BEAST WITH FIVE FINGERS, THE(1946), ed; BIG PUNCH, THE(1948), ed; WHIPLASH(1948), ed; FLAXY MARTIN(1949), ed; HOUSE ACROSS THE STREET, THE(1949), ed; COLT .45(1950), ed; GREAT JEWEL ROBBER, THE(1950), ed; RETURN OF THE FRONTIERSMAN(1950), ed; THIS SIDE OF THE LAW(1950), ed
Gordon Magee
LOVE IN THE DESERT(1929); TIGER ROSE(1930)
Honor Magee
FLAME IN THE HEATHER(1935, Brit.)
Ken Magee
PATERNITY(1981); POSTMAN ALWAYS RINGS TWICE, THE(1981); BEST LITTLE WHOREHOUSE IN TEXAS, THE(1982)

1984
STONE BOY, THE(1984)
Kenneth Magee
1984
ADVENTURES OF BUCKAROO BANZAI: ACROSS THE 8TH DIMENSION, THE(1984)
Michael Magee
MERRY WIVES OF TOBIAS ROUKE, THE(1972, Can.); CLOWN MURDERS, THE(1976, Can.)
Noel Magee
POACHER'S DAUGHTER, THE(1960, Brit.)
Pati Magee
VIOLENT WOMEN(1960)
Patricia Magee
Silents
CHARM SCHOOL, THE(1921)
Patrick Magee
BOYS, THE(1962, Brit.); CONCRETE JUNGLE, THE(1962, Brit.); PRIZE OF ARMS, A(1962, Brit.); YOUNG, WILLING AND EAGER(1962, Brit.); DEMENTIA 13(1963); VERY EDGE, THE(1963, Brit.); YOUNG RACERS, THE(1963); MASQUE OF THE RED DEATH, THE(1964, U.S./Brit.); SEANCE ON A WET AFTERNOON(1964 Brit.); SERVANT, THE(1964, Brit.); ZULU(1964, Brit.); PORTRAIT IN TERROR(1965); SKULL, THE(1965, Brit.); RICOCHET(1966, Brit.); NEVER BACK LOSERS(1967, Brit.); PERSECUTION AND ASSASSINATION OF JEAN-PAUL MARAT AS PERFORMED BY THE INMATES OF THE ASYLUM OF CHARENTON UNDER THE DIRECTION OF THE MARQUIS DE SADE, THE(1967, Brit.); ANZIO(1968, Ital.); DECLINE AND FALL... OF A BIRD WATCHER(1969, Brit.); HARD CONTRACT(1969); CROMWELL(1970, Brit.); YOU CAN'T WIN 'EM ALL(1970, Brit.); CLOCKWORK ORANGE, A(1971, Brit.); KING LEAR(1971, Brit./Den.); TROJAN WOMEN, THE(1971); ASYLUM(1972, Brit.); DEMONS OF THE MIND(1972, Brit.); POPE JOAN(1972, Brit.); TALES FROM THE CRYPT(1972, Brit.); YOUNG WINSTON(1972, Brit.); AND NOW THE SCREAMING STARTS(1973, Brit.); LADY ICE(1973, Brit.); LUTHER(1974); BARRY LYNDON(1975, Brit.); GALILEO(1975, Brit.); LAST DAYS OF MAN ON EARTH, THE(1975, Brit.); TELEFON(1977); BRONTE SISTERS, THE(1979, Fr.); HAWK THE SLAYER(1980, Brit.); ROUGH CUT(1980, Brit.); SIR HENRY AT RAWLINSON END(1980, Brit.); CHARIOTS OF FIRE(1981, Brit.); MONSTER CLUB, THE(1981, Brit.)
1984
BLACK CAT, THE(1984, Ital./Brit.)
Misc. Talkies
FIEND, THE(1971, Brit.); BEWARE MY BRETHREN(1972, Brit.)
Virginia Magee
Silents
SONNY(1922)
J. R. Mageean
LUCK OF THE IRISH, THE(1937, Ireland)
James Mageean
TONIGHT'S THE NIGHT(1954, Brit.)
Jimmy Mageean
EARLY BIRD, THE(1936, Brit.); AGAINST THE TIDE(1937, Brit.); BEHIND YOUR BACK(1937, Brit.); CATCH AS CATCH CAN(1937, Brit.); LANDSLIDE(1937, Brit.); MACUSHLA(1937, Brit.); MY WIFE'S FAMILY(1962, Brit.)
Jimmy Mageen
IRISH AND PROUD OF IT(1938, Ireland)
Anne Magel
DON'T TRUST YOUR HUSBAND(1948)
Giovanni Magello
HELL RAIDERS OF THE DEEP(1954, Ital.)
Ralph Magelssen
THIS IS THE ARMY(1943)
Maggie Magennis
GALLANT HOURS, THE(1960)
Guy Magenta
DEVIL AND THE TEN COMMANDMENTS, THE(1962, Fr.), m; SELLERS OF GIRLS(1967, Fr.), m
Kitty Mager
BEAT GENERATION, THE(1959), cos; KEY WITNESS(1960), cos; WHERE THE BOYS ARE(1960), cos; THUNDER OF DRUMS, A(1961), cos
Alan P. Magerman
STREET IS MY BEAT, THE(1966), p
William Magerman
STIGMA(1972); TRADING PLACES(1983)
Duffy Caesar Magesis
STUCK ON YOU(1983), w
1984
STUCK ON YOU(1984), w
Adriano Magestretti
SOMEONE BEHIND THE DOOR(1971, Fr./Brit.)
Brandon Maggart
MAGIC GARDEN OF STANLEY SWEETHART, THE(1970); DRESSED TO KILL(1980); YOU BETTER WATCH OUT(1980); WORLD ACCORDING TO GARP, THE(1982)
Larry Maggart
1984
STRANGERS KISS(1984)
Brandon Maggert
HAIL(1973)
Del Maggert
RACKETEERS OF THE RANGE(1939)
Amina Pirani Maggi
WHEN IN ROME(1952); NAKED MAJA, THE(1959, Ital./U.S.)
Mike Maggi
SUBJECT WAS ROSES, THE(1968), makeup; POPI(1969), makeup; LANDLORD, THE(1970), makeup; UNMARRIED WOMAN, AN(1978), makeup
Stefano Maggi
VERY HANDY MAN, A(1966, Fr./Ital.)
Dante Maggie
MELODY OF LOVE(1954, Ital.)

Kathleen Magginetti
GUNFIRE(1950)
William Magginetti
THEY WON'T BELIEVE ME(1947), set d; SHAGGY(1948), set d; MERRILL'S MA-RAUDERS(1962), art d
Angelo Maggio
ANGELO IN THE CROWD(1952, Ital.)
Beniamino Maggio
MELODY OF LOVE(1954, Ital.)
Dante Maggio
ANGELO IN THE CROWD(1952, Ital.); DAVID AND GOLIATH(1961, Ital.); BOC-CACCIO '70(1962/Ital./Fr.); RIFIFI IN TOKYO(1963, Fr./Ital.); VISIT, THE(1964, Ger./Fr./Ital./U.S.); VARIETY LIGHTS(1965, Ital.); OPERATION ST. PETER'S(1968, Ital.); SAUL AND DAVID(1968, Ital./Span.); TREASURE OF SAN GENNARO(1968, Fr./Ital./Ger.)
Enzio Maggio
FOUR WAYS OUT(1954, Ital.)
Enzo Maggio
WHITE SHEIK, THE(1956, Ital.); PIRATE AND THE SLAVE GIRL, THE(1961, Fr./Ital.)
Mimmo Maggio
FALL OF ROME, THE(1963, Ital.)
Pupella Maggio
TWO WOMEN(1961, Ital./Fr.); FOUR DAYS OF NAPLES, THE(1963, US/Ital.); BIBLE...IN THE BEGINNING, THE(1966); VALACHI PAPERS, THE(1972, Ital./Fr.); AMARCORD(1974, Ital.)
Lamberto Maggiorani
BICYCLE THIEF, THE(1949, Ital.)
Charles Maggiore
GREEK TYCOON, THE(1978)
Magic Lantern
ST. HELENS(1981), spec eff
Magic Tramp Midnight Opera Company
INJUN FENDER(1973), m
Allan Magicovsky
MAN, A WOMAN, AND A BANK, A(1979, Can.)
1984
KILLERS, THE(1984)
Aaron Magidow
SECONDS(1966)
Herb Magidson
GLAMOUR FOR SALE(1940), m/l Oakland
M. Magidson
LOSS OF FEELING(1935, USSR), ph
Dan Magiera
1984
WOMAN IN RED, THE(1984)
Eddie Magill
HURRICANE SMITH(1952)
James Magill
IRON MAJOR, THE(1943); CANON CITY(1948); TRAIL OF ROBIN HOOD(1950); HE RAN ALL THE WAY(1951); LET'S MAKE IT LEGAL(1951); VALLEY OF FIRE(1951)
Jim Magill
SILVER CANYON(1951)
1984
SCANDALOUS(1984)
Jimmie Magill
TWO SMART PEOPLE(1946)
Jimmy Magill
CRIMSON KEY, THE(1947)
Mark Magill
1984
FAR FROM POLAND(1984), p&d
Michael Magill
ONE FROM THE HEART(1982)
Moyna Magill
TEXAS, BROOKLYN AND HEAVEN(1948)
Margherita Magilone
DOCTOR BEWARE(1951, Ital.), w
Maria D. Magisano
1984
TEACHERS(1984)
Franco Magli
UNA SIGNORA DELL'OVEST(1942, Ital), p; LITTLE MARTYR, THE(1947, Ital.), p
Marguerite Maglione
LITTLE MARTYR, THE(1947, Ital.), w
Licia Magna
LOLLIPOP(1966, Braz.)
Janine Magnan
TO BE A CROOK(1967, Fr.); LIFE LOVE DEATH(1969, Fr./Ital.)
Anna Magnani
OPEN CITY(1946, Ital.); BEFORE HIM ALL ROME TREMBLED(1947, Ital.); AN-GELINA(1948, Ital.), a, w; BANDIT, THE(1949, Ital.); PEDDLIN' IN SOCIETY(1949, Ital.); DOCTOR BEWARE(1951, Ital.); BELLISSIMA(1952, Ital.); GOLDEN COACH, THE(1953, Fr./Ital.); VOLCANO(1953, Ital.); ANITA GARIBALDI(1954, Ital.); ROSE TATTOO, THE(1955); WILD IS THE WIND(1957); AWAKENING, THE(1958, Ital.); FUGITIVE KIND, THE(1960); AND THE WILD, WILD WOMEN(1961, Ital.); MAMMA ROMA(1962, Ital.); PASSIONATE THIEF, THE(1963, Ital.); MADE IN ITALY(1967, Fr./Ital.); SECRET OF SANTA VITTORIA, THE(1969); ROMA(1972, Ital./Fr.)
Silvana Magnano
1984
DUNE(1984)
Mariana Magnasco
EXPOSED(1983)
Ann Magnasen
VORTEX(1982)
Hildy Magnasun
PIRANHA II: THE SPAWNING(1981, Neth.)

Michael Magne
TWO WEEKS IN SEPTEMBER(1967, Fr./Brit.), m; COLD SWEAT(1974, Ital., Fr.), m
Michel Magne
FRUIT IS RIPE, THE(1961, Fr./Ital.), m; DEADLY DECOYS, THE(1962, Fr.), m; DEVIL AND THE TEN COMMANDMENTS, THE(1962, Fr.), m; GIGOT(1962), md; MONKEY IN WINTER, A(1962, Fr.), m; PRICE OF FLESH, THE(1962, Fr.), m; ANY NUMBER CAN WIN(1963 Fr.), m; LOVE ON A PILLOW(1963, Fr./Ital.), m; OF FLESH AND BLOOD(1964, Fr./Ital.), m; CIRCLE OF LOVE(1965, Fr.), m; EXTERMINATORS, THE(1965 Fr.), m; MALE HUNT(1965, Fr./Ital.), m; MY BABY IS BLACK!(1965, Fr.), m; SYMPHONY FOR A MASSACRE(1965, Fr./Ital.), m; VICE AND VIR-TUE(1965, Fr./Ital.), m; FANTOMAS(1966, Fr./Ital.), m; GALIA(1966, Fr./Ital.), m; GREAT SPY CHASE, THE(1966, Fr.), m; MAN FROM COCODY(1966, Fr/Ital.), m; OSS 117–MISSION FOR A KILLER(1966, Fr./Ital.), m; SLEEPING CAR MURDER THE(1966, Fr.), m; SHADOW OF EVIL(1967, Fr./Ital.), m; SERGEANT, THE(1968), m; SHOCK TROOPS(1968, Ital./Fr.), m; JOHNNY BANCO(1969, Fr./Ital./Ger.), m; SONS OF SATAN(1969, Ital./Fr./Ger.), md
Don Magner
SAILOR FROM GIBRALTAR, THE(1967, Brit.), w
Jack Magner
AMITYVILLE II: THE POSSESSION(1982)
1984
FIRESTARTER(1984)
Kerry Magness
NIGHT OF THE COBRA WOMAN(1974, U.S./Phil.), p, w
Tommy Magness
SMOKY MOUNTAIN MELODY(1949)
Cecile Magnet
GIFT, THE(1983, Fr./Ital.)
Gianni Magni
TAMING OF THE SHREW, THE(1967, U.S./Ital.); WHITE SISTER(1973, Ital./Span./Fr.)
Luigi Magni
WHITE VOICES(1965, Fr./Ital.), w; EL GRECO(1966, Ital., Fr.), w; MAN-DRAGOLA(1966 Fr./Ital.), w; CHASTITY BELT, THE(1968, Ital.), w; DROP DEAD, MY LOVE(1968, Italy), w; GIRL WITH A PISTOL, THE(1968, Ital.), w; GOODNIGHT, LADIES AND GENTLEMEN(1977, Ital.), d&w
Claude Magnier
WHERE WERE YOU WHEN THE LIGHTS WENT OUT?(1968), w
P. Magnier
RUY BLAS(1948, Fr.)
Pierre Magnier
SECOND BUREAU(1936, Fr.); DOUBLE CRIME IN THE MAGINOT LINE(1939, Fr.); END OF A DAY, THE(1939, Fr.); RULES OF THE GAME, THE(1939, Fr.); NAKED WOMAN, THE(1950, Fr.)
Misc. Silents
LA ROUE(1923, Fr.)
The Magnificent Force
1984
BEAT STREET(1984)
Claire Magnin
1984
CHEECH AND CHONG'S THE CORSICAN BROTHERS(1984)
Cyril Magnin
FOUL PLAY(1978)
I. Magnin
$1,000 A MINUTE(1935), cos
Franco Magno
AMARCORD(1974, Ital.)
Carlotta Magnoff
Z.P.G.(1972)
Barbara Magnolfi
SUSPIRIA(1977, Ital.)
Albert Magnoli
1984
PURPLE RAIN(1984), d, w, ed; RECKLESS(1984), ed
Lou Magnolia
MADISON SQUARE GARDEN(1932)
Vic Magnotta
WHO'S THAT KNOCKING AT MY DOOR?(1968), a, art d; TAXI DRIVER(1976)
1984
BEAT STREET(1984)
Victor Magnotta
WORLD ACCORDING TO GARP, The(1982)
Alexis Magnotti
I SPIT ON YOUR GRAVE(1983)
Annabelle Magnus
Silents
ORPHAN OF THE SAGE(1928)
Misc. Silents
HIS DOG(1927)
Harry Magnus
WILD GEESE, THE(1978, Brit.)
Ann Magnuson
HUNGER, THE(1983)
1984
PERFECT STRANGERS(1984)
Ann-Christine Magnussen
VIBRATION(1969, Swed.)
Barbara Magnusson
SCALPS(1983)
Leif Magnusson
1984
ELEMENT OF CRIME, THE(1984, Den.)
Sven Magnusson
RAILROAD WORKERS(1948, Swed.)
Michele Magny
DON'T LET THE ANGELS FALL(1969, Can.)

Michelle Magny
DISAPPEARANCE, THE(1981, Brit./Can.)
Nicole Magny
SPECIAL DAY, A(1977, Ital./Can.)
Mago
SMILES OF A SUMMER NIGHT(1957, Swed.), cos; THROUGH A GLASS DARK-
LY(1962, Swed.), cos; WINTER LIGHT, THE(1963, Swed.), cos; ALL THESE WO-
MEN(1964, Swed.), cos; SWEDISH MISTRESS, THE(1964, Swed.), cos; TO LOVE(1964,
Swed.), cos; PERSONA(1967, Swed.), cos; HOUR OF THE WOLF, THE(1968, Swed.),
cos; SHAME(1968, Swed.), cos; PASSION OF ANNA, THE(1970, Swed.), cos; RITUAL,
THE(1970, Swed.), cos; TOUCH, THE(1971, U.S./Swed.), cos
Susan Magolier
INTERNECINE PROJECT, THE(1974, Brit.)
Pancho Magolona
MERRILL'S MARAUDERS(1962)
Brian Magowan
Silents
KNOCKNAGOW(1918, Ireland); IRISH DESTINY(1925, Brit.)
Misc. Silents
WHEN LOVE CAME TO GAVIN BURKE(1918); WILLY REILLY AND HIS COL-
LEEN BAWN(1918, Brit.)
Tom Magrane
Misc. Silents
MUTE APPEAL, A(1917)
Paul Magranville
LITTLE BOY LOST(1953)
Eileen Magrath
Silents
SHOEBLACK OF PICCADILLY, THE(1920, Brit.)
Misc. Silents
BY BERWIN BANKS(1920, Brit.); CHILDREN OF GIBEON, THE(1920, Brit.); HIS
OTHER WIFE(1921, Brit.)
James Magrath
FIGHTING PLAYBOY(1937)
Judith Magre
LOVERS, THE(1959, Fr.); MODIGLIANI OF MONTPARNASSE(1961, Fr./Ital.);
SECRET WORLD(1969, Fr.); CROOK, THE(1971, Fr.); AND NOW MY LOVE(1975, Fr.);
ASSOCIATE, THE(1982 Fr./Ger.)
George Magrill
YELLOW JACK(1938); DEVIL AND THE DEEP(1932); LAST MAN(1932); TEXAS
BAD MAN(1932); CAT'S PAW, THE(1934); MERRY WIDOW, THE(1934); DANTE'S
INFERNO(1935); WEDDING NIGHT, THE(1935); FOLLOW THE FLEET(1936); SAN
FRANCISCO(1936); UNDER YOUR SPELL(1936); LAST GANGSTER, THE(1937);
MAID OF SALEM(1937); MIDNIGHT MADONNA(1937); OUTCAST(1937); ROSA-
LIE(1937); SHALL WE DANCE(1937); BORN TO BE WILD(1938); CITY GIRL(1938);
MAD MISS MANTON, THE(1938); MR. MOTO'S GAMBLE(1938); SAY IT IN
FRENCH(1938); WHO KILLED GAIL PRESTON?(1938); HOTEL IMPERIAL(1939);
KING OF CHINATOWN(1939); OKLAHOMA FRONTIER(1939); OUR LEADING
CITIZEN(1939); TELL NO TALES(1939); WINTER CARNIVAL(1939); 6000 ENE-
MIES(1939); NEW MOON(1940); SLIGHTLY HONORABLE(1940); DESIGN FOR
SCANDAL(1941); LOVE CRAZY(1941); MEET BOSTON BLACKIE(1941); SEA WOLF,
THE(1941); SOUTH OF TAHITI(1941); NAZI AGENT(1942); SABOTAGE SQUAD(1942);
TORTILLA FLAT(1942); UNDERGROUND AGENT(1942); COBRA WOMAN(1944);
DOUBLE INDEMNITY(1944); LOUISIANA HAYRIDE(1944); UP IN ARMS(1944);
DICK TRACY(1945); JOHNNY ANGEL(1945); SANTA FE SADDLEMATES(1945);
SUDAN(1945); THEY WERE EXPENDABLE(1945); FROM THIS DAY FOR-
WARD(1946); JOLSON STORY, THE(1946); PHANTOM THIEF, THE(1946); TWO
SMART PEOPLE(1946); HIGH BARBAREE(1947); LADY IN THE LAKE(1947); LIKE-
LY STORY, A(1947); PIRATES OF MONTEREY(1947); SEA OF GRASS, THE(1947);
SECRET LIFE OF WALTER MITTY, THE(1947); TWILIGHT ON THE RIO GRAN-
DE(1947); WHERE THERE'S LIFE(1947); FORCE OF EVIL(1948); JOAN OF
ARC(1948); RIVER LADY(1948); ADAM'S RIB(1949); CHICAGO DEADLINE(1949);
FLAXY MARTIN(1949); SCENE OF THE CRIME(1949); WHEN WILLIE COMES
MARCHING HOME(1950); WOMAN ON PIER 13, THE(1950); PEOPLE AGAINST
O'HARA, THE(1951); PRINCE WHO WAS A THIEF, THE(1951); OPERATION SE-
CRET(1952)
Silents
NORTH OF NEVADA(1924); FIGHTING SMILE, THE(1925); LORD JIM(1925);
ENCHANTED HILL, THE(1926)
Misc. Silents
FAST AND FEARLESS(1924)
Jimmy Magrill
THEY WERE EXPENDABLE(1945)
Ramona Magrill
FRENCH LINE, THE(1954)
Gitt Magrini
LA NOTTE(1961, Fr./Ital.); RED DESERT(1965, Fr./Ital.), cos; WILD CHILD,
THE(1970, Fr.), a, cos; CONFORMIST, THE(1971, Ital., Fr) cos; IT ONLY HAPPENS
TO OTHERS(1971, Fr./Ital.), art d&cos; NUN, THE(1971, Fr.), cos; PULP(1972, Brit.),
cos; TWO ENGLISH GIRLS(1972, Fr.), cos; 1900(1976, Ital.), cos; MARCH OR DIE(1977,
Brit.), cos
Rosa Chira Magrini
IT ONLY HAPPENS TO OTHERS(1971, Fr./Ital.)
Anthony Magro
FIGHTING MAD(1976), ed
Rene Magron
RIVER CHANGES, THE(1956)
Ann Magruder
SIDE SHOW(1931)
Anna Magruder
ILLUSION(1929)
Silents
TWO FLAMING YOUTHS(1927)
Melonie Magruder
SEMI-TOUGH(1977)
Robert Magruder
FIVE DAYS FROM HOME(1978)

Pierre Maguelon
MILKY WAY, THE(1969, Fr./Ital.); VERY HAPPY ALEXANDER(1969, Fr.); BED
AND BOARD(1971, Fr.); DISCREET CHARM OF THE BOURGEOISIE, THE(1972, Fr.);
PHANTOM OF LIBERTY, THE(1974, Fr.); INQUISITOR, THE(1982, Fr.)
Al Maguire
TERROR HOUSE(1972), ed
Andrew Maguire
IRISHMAN, THE(1978, Aus.)
Barry Maguire
PORK CHOP HILL(1959); PRESIDENT'S ANALYST, THE(1967)
Billy Maguire
PRINCE AND THE PAUPER, THE(1937)
Brian Maguire
1984
STRANGERS KISS(1984)
Charles Maguire
I LOVE YOU, ALICE B. TOKLAS!(1968), p
Fred Maguire
GENTLEMAN FROM TEXAS(1946), ed; LIVE WIRES(1946), ed; UNDER ARIZONA
SKIES(1946), ed; FLASHING GUNS(1947), ed; PRAIRIE EXPRESS(1947), ed; RAID-
ERS OF THE SOUTH(1947), ed; SONG OF THE WASTELAND(1947), ed; CROSSED
TRAILS(1948), ed; FRONTIER AGENT(1948), ed; GUN TALK(1948), ed; OKLAHOMA
BLUES(1948), ed; SONG OF THE DRIFTER(1948), ed; JOE PALOOKA IN THE BIG
FIGHT(1949), ed; JUDGE, THE(1949), ed; OUTLAW GOLD(1950), ed; COLORADO
AMBUSH(1951), ed; MONTANA DESPERADO(1951), ed
Gerard Maguire
DEMONSTRATOR(1971, Aus.)
Misc. Talkies
COUNTRY TOWN(1971)
Hal Maguire
LEGEND OF LYLAH CLARE, THE(1968); ULZANA'S RAID(1972)
Hugh Maguire
GOING MY WAY(1944); THIS LOVE OF OURS(1945); LEAVE HER TO HEA-
VEN(1946)
Jack Maguire
THEATRE OF BLOOD(1973, Brit.)
Jeff Maguire
VICTORY(1981), w
Joan Maguire
MC CABE AND MRS. MILLER(1971)
John Maguire
HIGHWAYS BY NIGHT(1942); MAGNIFICENT AMBERSONS, THE(1942); MEXI-
CAN SPITFIRE AT SEA(1942); NAVY COMES THROUGH, THE(1942); POWDER
TOWN(1942)
1984
MUPPETS TAKE MANHATTAN, THE(1984)
Johnny Maguire
DEAD OF NIGHT(1946, Brit.)
Kathleen Maguire
CONCORDE, THE–AIRPORT '79(; EDGE OF THE CITY(1957); FLIPPER(1963);
WILLIE AND PHIL(1980)
Leo Maguire
FLYING SORCERER, THE(1974, Brit.), w; KADOYNG(1974, Brit.), a, w
Leonard Maguire
AWAKENING, THE(1980)
Les Maguire
FERRY ACROSS THE MERSEY(1964, Brit.)
Lupe Maguire
MAN IN GREY, THE(1943, Brit.)
Mady Maguire
KINFOLK(1970)
Misc. Talkies
JEKYLL AND HYDE PORTFOLIO, THE(1972)
Mary Maguire
FLYING DOCTOR, THE(1936, Aus.); ALCATRAZ ISLAND(1937); CONFES-
SION(1937); THAT MAN'S HERE AGAIN(1937); MYSTERIOUS MR. MOTO(1938);
SERGEANT MURPHY(1938); SMILING ALONG(1938, Brit.); BLACK EYES(1939,
Brit.); MAD MEN OF EUROPE(1940, Brit.); OUTSIDER, THE(1940, Brit.); FALSE
RAPTURE(1941); THIS WAS PARIS(1942, Brit.)
Neil Maguire
SULTAN'S DAUGHTER, THE(1943), art d
Nina Maguire
SINGING PRINCESS, THE(1967, Ital.), w
Oliver Maguire
BUTLEY(1974, Brit.); HENNESSY(1975, Brit.); NASTY HABITS(1976, Brit.); EMPIRE
STRIKES BACK, THE(1980); EDUCATING RITA(1983)
Peggy Maguire
HERITAGE(1935, Aus.)
Sinead MaGuire
1984
MUPPETS TAKE MANHATTAN, THE(1984)
Thomas Maguire
Silents
STARDUST(1921)
Tom Maguire
CITY GIRL(1930)
Misc. Silents
SAVAGE, THE(1926); COLLEEN(1927); SAWDUST PARADISE, THE(1928)
Tony Maguire
SINGING PRINCESS, THE(1967, Ital.), w
Tucker Maguire
TWO GROOMS FOR A BRIDE(1957); GET CHARLIE TULLY(1976, Brit.)
Paul Magwood
CHANDLER(1971), d, w
Laurence Mah
CLINIC, THE(1983, Aus.)
Capt. Hamish Mahaddie
BATTLE OF BRITAIN, THE(1969, Brit.), tech adv

Anita Mahadervan
NUTCRACKER(1982, Brit.)
Antranig Mahakian
LAST MOVIE, THE(1971), ed; HEX(1973), ed; INNERVIEW, THE(1974); SUMMER RUN(1974), ed
Carl Mahakian
HALF PINT, THE(1960), ed; NUN AND THE SERGEANT, THE(1962), ed; WORLD'S GREATEST SINNER, THE(1962), ed
Billy Mahan
BACK TO NATURE(1936); BIG BUSINESS(1937); BORROWING TROUBLE(1937); HOT WATER(1937); OFF TO THE RACES(1937); DOWN ON THE FARM(1938); LOVE ON A BUDGET(1938); SAFETY IN NUMBERS(1938); TRIP TO PARIS, A(1938); EVERYBODY'S BABY(1939); JONES FAMILY IN HOLLYWOOD, THE(1939); QUICK MILLIONS(1939); TOO BUSY TO WORK(1939); ON THEIR OWN(1940)
Larry Mahan
J.W. COOP(1971); HONKERS, THE(1972); MACKINTOSH & T.J.(1975); SIX PACK ANNIE(1975)
Wayne Mahan
FAT CITY(1972)
William Mahan
EDUCATING FATHER(1936); EVERY SATURDAY NIGHT(1936); YOUNG AS YOU FEEL(1940); STRANGE LOVERS(1963), p, w
William A. Mahan
TAKE CARE OF MY LITTLE GIRL(1951)
Floyd Mahaney
LAST PICTURE SHOW, THE(1971); PAPER MOON(1973)
Christopher Mahar
1984
BEST DEFENSE(1984)
Dan Mahar
DIFFERENT STORY, A(1978)
Ralph Maharaj
Misc. Talkies
BIM(1976)
Maharajah of Hakwar
SONG OF INDIA(1949)
George Maharis
EXODUS(1960); QUICK, BEFORE IT MELTS(1964); SATAN BUG, THE(1965); SYLVIA(1965); COVENANT WITH DEATH, A(1966); HAPPENING, THE(1967); DESPERADOS, THE(1969); LAND RAIDERS(1969); LAST DAY OF THE WAR, THE(1969, U.S./Ital./Span.); SWORD AND THE SORCERER, THE(1982)
Michele Mahaut
FIRE WITHIN, THE(1964, Fr./Ital.)
Timothy Mahen
THOROUGHBREDS(1945)
Bill Maher
D.C. CAB(1983)
Bob Maher
WHISTLE AT EATON FALLS(1951)
Claude Maher
TI-CUL TOUGAS(1977, Can.)
Dan Maher
Silents
JACQUELINE, OR BLAZING BARRIERS(1923), ph
Frank Maher
INNOCENT BYSTANDERS(1973, Brit.), a, stunts
James Maher
1984
NINJA III–THE DOMINATION(1984)
Joe Maher
FINNEGANS WAKE(1965); FOR PETE'S SAKE(1977); I'M DANCING AS FAST AS I CAN(1982)
John C. Maher
DEVIL GIRL FROM MARS(1954, Brit.), w
Joseph Maher
IT AIN'T EASY(1972); HEAVEN CAN WAIT(1978); TIME AFTER TIME(1979, Brit.); JUST TELL ME WHAT YOU WANT(1980); THOSE LIPS, THOSE EYES(1980); GOING APE!(1981); UNDER THE RAINBOW(1981)
1984
EVIL THAT MEN DO, THE(1984)
Kerry Lee Maher
1984
PHILADELPHIA EXPERIMENT, THE(1984)
Marty Maher
LONG GRAY LINE, THE(1955), w
Mohammad Ali Maher
MOHAMMAD, MESSENGER OF GOD(1976, Lebanon/Brit.), w
Patrick Maher
1984
THIS IS SPINAL TAP(1984)
Terry Maher
SECOND BEST SECRET AGENT IN THE WHOLE WIDE WORLD, THE(1965, Brit.), ph; NAKED WORLD OF HARRISON MARKS, THE(1967, Brit.), w; DAD'S ARMY(1971, Brit.), ph; ADOLF HITLER–MY PART IN HIS DOWNFALL(1973, Brit.), ph
Wally Maher
RENDEZVOUS(1935); FURY(1936); LIBELED LADY(1936); RIFF-RAFF(1936); HOLLYWOOD HOTEL(1937); HOTEL HAYWIRE(1937); MOUNTAIN MUSIC(1937); SUBMARINE D-1(1937); 23½ HOURS LEAVE(1937); FIRST 100 YEARS, THE(1938); TEST PILOT(1938); HONEYMOON IN BALI(1939); NICK CARTER, MASTER DETECTIVE(1939); OUR LEADING CITIZEN(1939); STAR MAKER, THE(1939); STRANGE HOLIDAY(1945); JOHNNY STOOL PIGEON(1949); STORY OF MOLLY X, THE(1949); MYSTERY STREET(1950); REFORMER AND THE REDHEAD, THE(1950); RIGHT CROSS(1950)
Pierre Maheu
CAT IN THE SACK, THE(1967, Can.)
Mark Mahez
BATTLE OF BRITAIN, THE(1969, Brit.)

Slim Mahfoudh
L'ETOILE DU NORD(1983, Fr.)
Ted Mahgean
SHADOW, THE(1937)
Kimo Mahi
TWILIGHT FOR THE GODS(1958)
Don Mahin
MARRYING KIND, THE(1952)
Graham Lee Mahin
MOVIE STAR, AMERICAN STYLE, OR, LSD I HATE YOU!(1966), w; BLACK GIRL(1972), ed
John Mahin
RED DUST(1932), w
John Lee Mahin
BEAST OF THE CITY, THE(1932), w; SCARFACE(1932), w; WET PARADE, THE(1932), w; BOMBSHELL(1933), w; HELL BELOW(1933), a, w; CHAINED(1934), w; LAUGHING BOY(1934), w; TREASURE ISLAND(1934), w; NAUGHTY MARIETTA(1935), w; DEVIL IS A SISSY, THE(1936), w; LOVE ON THE RUN(1936), w; SMALL TOWN GIRL(1936), w; WIFE VERSUS SECRETARY(1936), w; CAPTAINS COURAGEOUS(1937), w; LAST GANGSTER, THE(1937), w; TOO HOT TO HANDLE(1938), w; GONE WITH THE WIND(1939), w; BOOM TOWN(1940), w; DR. JEKYLL AND MR. HYDE(1941), w; JOHNNY EAGER(1942), w; TORTILLA FLAT(1942), w; ADVENTURES OF TARTU(1943, Brit.), w; DOWN TO THE SEA IN SHIPS(1949), w; LOVE THAT BRUTE(1950), w; SHOW BOAT(1951), w; MY SON, JOHN(1952), w; MOGAMBO(1953), w; ELEPHANT WALK(1954), w; LUCY GALLANT(1955), w; BAD SEED, THE(1956), w; HEAVEN KNOWS, MR. ALLISON(1957), w; NO TIME FOR SERGEANTS(1958), w; HORSE SOLDIERS, THE(1959), p, w; NORTH TO ALASKA(1960), w; SPIRAL ROAD, THE(1962), w; MOMENT TO MOMENT(1966), w
John Lee Mahin, Jr.
PRIZEFIGHTER AND THE LADY, THE(1933), w
Hildur Mahl
HILDUR AND THE MAGICIAN(1969)
William Mahlen
LAW OF THE TONG(1931)
Bruce Mahler
1984
FRIDAY THE 13TH–THE FINAL CHAPTER(1984); POLICE ACADEMY(1984)
Gustav Mahler
DUET FOR CANNIBALS(1969, Swed.), m; HONEYMOON KILLERS, THE(1969), m; GLADIATORS, THE(1970, Swed.), m; DEATH IN VENICE(1971, Ital./Fr.), m; GAMBLER, THE(1974), m; HAUNTING OF M, THE(1979), m
1984
EL NORTE(1984), m
Horst Mahler
GERMANY IN AUTUMN(1978, Ger.)
Michael Mahler
CITIZENS BAND(1977)
Miriam Mahler
ODESSA FILE, THE(1974, Brit./Ger.)
Ruth Mahler
KING LEAR(1971, Brit./Den.), makeup
Zdenek Mahler
DIVINE EMMA, THE(1983, Czech,), w
Hans Mahlich
NAKED AMONG THE WOLVES(1967, Ger.), p
Knut Mahlke
TRAPP FAMILY, THE(1961, Ger.)
David Mahlowe
KIND OF LOVING, A(1962, Brit.)
Barry Mahn
Misc. Talkies
BEAST THAT KILLED WOMEN(1965), d
Gustav Mahnke
MOSCOW SHANGHAI(1936, Ger.)
Hans Mahnke
DAY WILL COME, A(1960, Ger.)
Paul Maho
CHARRIOTS OF FIRE(1981, Brit.)
Ahmed Ben Mahomed
ANOTHER SKY(1960 Brit.)
Sheik Mahomet
Silents
WHITE SISTER, THE(1923)
Anthony Mahon
PREMONITION, THE(1976), w
Barry Mahon
CUBAN REBEL GIRLS(1960), p&d; JUKE BOX RACKET(1960), d; VIOLENT WOMEN(1960), p&d; DEAD ONE, THE(1961), p,d&w; PAGAN ISLAND(1961), p&d; ROCKET ATTACK, U.S.A.(1961), p&d; 1,000 SHAPES OF A FEMALE(1963), p&d; GIRL SMUGGLERS(1967), p; PROWL GIRLS(1968), p; WONDERFUL LAND OF OZ, THE(1969), p,d&w; JACK AND THE BEANSTALK(1970), p,d&w; MUSICAL MUTINY(1970), p; THUMBELINA(1970), p&d
Carl Mahon
EXILE, THE(1931)
Cassandra Mahon
PEOPLE MEET AND SWEET MUSIC FILLS THE HEART(1969, Den./Swed.)
Channy Mahon
WONDERFUL LAND OF OZ, THE(1969)
Clelle Mahon
CUBAN REBEL GIRLS(1960); PAGAN ISLAND(1961), w
Isabelle Mahon
SPLENDID FELLOWS(1934, Aus.)
J. Barrett Mahon
CROSSED SWORDS(1954), p
John Mahon
Misc. Silents
LURE OF HEART'S DESIRE, THE(1916)

Kevin Mahon
RAGING BULL(1980)
Michael Mahon
1984
FLAMINGO KID, THE(1984)
Peggy Mahon
FUNERAL HOME(1982, Can.)
Sharon Mahon
Misc. Talkies
DEVIL RIDER(1971)
Thomas Lee Mahon
1984
BLAME IT ON RIO(1984)
William Mahon
FATHER OF THE BRIDE(1950)
Juanita Mahone
LOVE CHILD(1982)
1984
MOSCOW ON THE HUDSON(1984)
Billie Mahoney
NIGHT THEY RAIDED MINSKY'S, THE(1968); BELOW THE BELT(1980)
Elizabeth Mahoney
Silents
EYES OF JULIA DEEP, THE(1918), w; FAIR ENOUGH(1918), w
Ernestine Mahoney
WHOOPEE(1930)
Francis X. Mahoney
SHOW BOAT(1936)
Jack Mahoney
LOVE BUG, THE(1968)
Jack [Jock] Mahoney
PECOS RIVER(1951); HAWK OF WILD RIVER, THE(1952); JUNCTION CITY(1952); KID FROM BROKEN GUN, THE(1952); LARAMIE MOUNTAINS(1952); ROUGH, TOUGH WEST, THE(1952); SMOKY CANYON(1952); OVERLAND PACIFIC(1954)
Janet Mahoney
CARRY ON LOVING(1970, Brit.); DOCTOR IN TROUBLE(1970, Brit.)
Jean Mahoney
G.I. JANE(1951)
Jock Mahoney
JOLSON SINGS AGAIN(1949); SMOKY MOUNTAIN MELODY(1949); AWAY ALL BOATS(1956); DAY OF FURY, A(1956); I'VE LIVED BEFORE(1956); SHOWDOWN AT ABILENE(1956); BATTLE HYMN(1957); JOE DAKOTA(1957); LAND UNKNOWN, THE(1957); SLIM CARTER(1957); LAST OF THE FAST GUNS, THE(1958); MONEY, WOMEN AND GUNS(1958); TIME TO LOVE AND A TIME TO DIE, A(1958); TARZAN THE MAGNIFICENT(1960, Brit.); THREE BLONDES IN HIS LIFE(1961); TARZAN GOES TO INDIA(1962, U.S./Brit./Switz.); CALIFORNIA(1963); TARZAN'S THREE CHALLENGES(1963); MORO WITCH DOCTOR(1964, U.S./Phil.); WALLS OF HELL, THE(1964, U.S./Phil.); MARINE BATTLEGROUND(1966, U.S/S.K.); RUNAWAY GIRL(1966); GLORY STOMPERS, THE(1967); BANDOLERO!(1968); TARZAN'S DEADLY SILENCE(1970); TOM(1973); END, THE(1978)
Misc. Talkies
BAD BUNCH, THE(1976); THEIR ONLY CHANCE(1978)
John Mahoney
MORE DEADLY THAN THE MALE(1961, Brit.)
Kathy Mahoney
ALL-AMERICAN BOY, THE(1973)
Louis Mahoney
PLAGUE OF THE ZOMBIES, THE(1966, Brit.); PREHISTORIC WOMEN(1967, Brit.); FINAL CONFLICT, THE(1981); AMIN-THE RISE AND FALL(1982, Kenya)
1984
SHEENA(1984)
Luis Mahoney
PRAISE MARX AND PASS THE AMMUNITION(1970, Brit.)
Maggie Mahoney
OUR HEARTS WERE GROWING UP(1946); BLACKJACK KETCHUM, DESPERADO(1956); SLIM CARTER(1957); DESIRE IN THE DUST(1960)
Michael Mahoney
COURT JESTER, THE(1956); PATSY, THE(1964)
Mike Mahoney
FATHER WAS A FULLBACK(1949); I WAS A MALE WAR BRIDE(1949); RECKLESS MOMENTS, THE(1949); DARK CITY(1950); MY FRIEND IRMA GOES WEST(1950); UNION STATION(1950); BORN YESTERDAY(1951); DETECTIVE STORY(1951); MY FAVORITE SPY(1951); PLACE IN THE SUN, A(1951); SAILOR BEWARE(1951); CARRIE(1952); RED SKIES OF MONTANA(1952); SCANDAL SHEET(1952); BIG HEAT, THE(1953); OFF LIMITS(1953); WAR OF THE WORLDS, THE(1953); DRIVE A CROOKED ROAD(1954); REAR WINDOW(1954); GIRL RUSH, THE(1955); DEVIL'S HAIRPIN, THE(1957); KISS THEM FOR ME(1957); LAST TRAIN FROM GUN HILL(1959); ROUSTABOUT(1964)
Richard Mahoney
HOUSE OF THE BLACK DEATH(1965), w
Slim Mahoney
Silents
IS YOUR DAUGHTER SAFE?(1927)
Tom Mahoney
LOVE RACKET, THE(1929); LOVE TRADER(1930); TREASURE ISLAND(1934); FURY(1936); LIBELED LADY(1936); SWORN ENEMY(1936); WIFE VERSUS SECRETARY(1936); GREAT HOSPITAL MYSTERY, THE(1937); GIRL OF THE GOLDEN WEST, THE(1938); EDISON, THE MAN(1940); SISTER-IN-LAW, THE(1975); COACH(1978); MALIBU BEACH(1978); AIRPLANE!(1980), ch; ON THE NICKEL(1980); CANNERY ROW(1982); ESCAPE ARTIST, THE(1982); NIGHT SHIFT(1982)
Tommy Mahoney
BABES IN TOYLAND(1961), ch
Trish Mahoney
SWEET CHARITY(1969); EVEL KNIEVEL(1971)
Wilkie Mahoney
SOME LIKE IT HOT(1939), w; PANAMA HATTIE(1942), w; WHISTLING IN DIXIE(1942), w; DU BARRY WAS A LADY(1943), w; WHISTLING IN BROOKLYN(1943), w; ABROAD WITH TWO YANKS(1944), w; BREWSTER'S MILLIONS(1945), w; ZIEGFELD FOLLIES(1945), w; PIRATE, THE(1948), w; THREE ON A SPREE(1961, Brit.), w

Will Mahoney
SEZ O'REILLY TO MACNAB(1938, Brit.); ANTS IN HIS PANTS(1940, Aus.)
Frank Mahony
FOR LOVE OR MONEY(1963)
Maria Mahor
LEGIONS OF THE NILE(1960, Ital.); TALL WOMEN, THE(1967, Aust./Ital./Span.)
Diane Mahree
MANOS, THE HANDS OF FATE(1966)
Preben Mahrt
HIDDEN FEAR(1957)
Misc. Talkies
CYNTHIA'S SISTER(1975)
Carola Mai
WAR AND PEACE(1983, Ger.), ed
Jin Jin Mai
OPERATION BOTTLENECK(1961)
Irenio Maia
1984
MEMOIRS OF PRISON(1984, Braz.), art d
Leonor Maia
KILL OR BE KILLED(1950)
Marise Maia
Silents
ITALIAN STRAW HAT, AN(1927, Fr.)
Nuno Leal Maia
1984
GABRIELA(1984, Braz.)
A. G. Maiano
MELODY OF LOVE(1954, Ital.), w
Charles Maibaum
GHOST COMES HOME, THE(1940), w
Richard Maibaum
GOLD DIGGERS OF 1937(1936), w; WE WENT TO COLLEGE(1936), w; LIVE, LOVE AND LEARN(1937), w; THEY GAVE HIM A GUN(1937), w; STABLEMATES(1938), w; LADY AND THE MOB, THE(1939), w; I WANTED WINGS(1941), w; TEN GENTLEMEN FROM WEST POINT(1942), w; SEE MY LAWYER(1945), w; O.S.S.(1946), p, w; BIG CLOCK, THE(1948), p; SAINTED SISTERS, THE(1948), p; BRIDE OF VENGEANCE(1949), p; DEAR WIFE(1949), p; GREAT GATSBY, THE(1949), p, w; SONG OF SURRENDER(1949), p, w; NO MAN OF HER OWN(1950), p; HELL BELOW ZERO(1954, Brit.), w; COCKLESHELL HEROES, THE(1955), w; BIGGER THAN LIFE(1956), w; RANSOM(1956), w; ZARAK(1956, Brit.), w; MAN INSIDE, THE(1958, Brit.), w; TANK FORCE(1958, Brit.), w; BANDIT OF ZHOBE, THE(1959); DAY THEY ROBBED THE BANK OF ENGLAND, THE(1960, Brit.), w; KILLERS OF KILIMANJARO(1960, Brit.), w; BATTLE AT BLOODY BEACH(1961), p, w; DR. NO(1962, Brit.), w; FROM RUSSIA WITH LOVE(1963, Brit.), w; GOLDFINGER(1964, Brit.), w; THUNDERBALL(1965, Brit.), w; CHITTY CHITTY BANG BANG(1968, Brit.), w; ON HER MAJESTY'S SECRET SERVICE(1969, Brit.), w; DIAMONDS ARE FOREVER(1971, Brit.), w; GREAT GATSBY, THE(1974), p, w; MAN WITH THE GOLDEN GUN, THE(1974, Brit.), w; SPY WHO LOVED ME, THE(1977, Brit.), w; FOR YOUR EYES ONLY(1981), w; OCTOPUSSY(1983, Brit.), w
Grant Maiben
WALK IN THE SUN, A(1945)
Richard Maibum
TWENTY MULE TEAM(1940), w
Michael Maichle
1984
CHINESE BOXES(1984, Ger./Brit.)
Elda Maida
GODFATHER, THE, PART II(1974)
Cecil Maiden
BLIND MAN'S BLUFF(1936, Brit.), w; SHOW FLAT(1936, Brit.), w; FORBIDDEN JOURNEY(1950, Can.), p,d&w; CULT OF THE COBRA(1955), w
Rita Maiden
MARRIED WOMAN, THE(1965, Fr.); MADE IN U.S.A.(1966, Fr.); LIFE LOVE DEATH(1969, Fr./Ital.); MILKY WAY, THE(1969, Fr./Ital.); MISTER FREEDOM(1970, Fr.); RISE OF LOUIS XIV, THE(1970, Fr.); WE ARE ALL NAKED(1970, Can./Fr.); PLAYTIME(1973, Fr.)
Sharon Maiden
PARTY PARTY(1983, Brit.)
Tony Maiden
SPACED OUT(1981, Brit.)
Kenneth L. Maidment
VILLAGE, THE(1953, Brit./Switz.), p
Terence Maidment
MURDER CAN BE DEADLY(1963, Brit.); ONE MILLION YEARS B.C.(1967, Brit./U.S.); O LUCKY MAN!(1973, Brit.); PASSAGE, THE(1979, Brit.)
Tailor Maids
SO'S YOUR UNCLE(1943)
Michael Maien
MARK OF THE DEVIL(1970, Ger./Brit.)
Barbara Maier
Silents
SPEED GIRL, THE(1921)
F.X. Maier
SWITCHBLADE SISTERS(1975), w
Pat Maier
YOU'RE TELLING ME(1942)
Patricia Maier
ANGELS OVER BROADWAY(1940); KITTY FOYLE(1940)
Sigrid Maier
G.I. BLUES(1960)
Tim Maier
PSYCHO II(1983)
1984
RAW COURAGE(1984)
William Maier
GIRLS OF PLEASURE ISLAND, THE(1953), w

Joe Maierhouser
INCREDIBLE PETRIFIED WORLD, THE(1959); OPERATION DAMES(1959)
Achille Maieroni
LOYALTY OF LOVE(1937, Ital.); CONJUGAL BED, THE(1963, Ital.)
Annie Maiers
MAGIC FACE, THE(1951, Aust.)
Charles Maigne
Silents
BRAND OF COWARDICE, THE(1916), w; RISE OF JENNIE CUSHING, THE(1917), w; DOLL'S HOUSE, A(1918), w; HER GREAT CHANCE(1918), d&w; KNIFE, THE(1918), w; OUT OF A CLEAR SKY(1918), w; PRUNELLA(1918), w; ROSE OF THE WORLD(1918), w; CUMBERLAND ROMANCE, A(1920), d&w; HUSH MONEY(1921), d&w; KENTUCKIANS, THE(1921), d; ISLE OF LOST SHIPS, THE(1923), w; SILENT PARTNER, THE(1923), d; WAR PAINT(1926), w; CLEARING THE TRAIL(1928), w
Misc. Silents
IN THE HOLLOW OF HER HAND(1918), d; FIRING LINE, THE(1919), d; INDE-STRUCTIBLE WIFE, THE(1919), d; REDHEAD(1919), d; WORLD TO LIVE IN, THE(1919), d; COPPERHEAD, THE(1920), d; FIGHTING CHANCE, THE(1920), d; INVISIBLE BOND, THE(1920), d; FRONTIER OF THE STARS, THE(1921), d; COW-BOY AND THE LADY, THE(1922), d; RECEIVED PAYMENT(1922), d; DRUMS OF FATE(1923), d; TRAIL OF THE LONESOME, THE(1923), d
Liliane Maigne
RAVEN, THE(1948, Fr.)
Robert Maigne
Silents
DANGER MARK, THE(1918), w
Henri Maik
TIME BOMB(1961, Fr./Ital.)
Sam Maikai
PAGAN LOVE SONG(1950)
Gilda Maiken
YOUNG GIRLS OF ROCHEFORT, THE(1968, Fr.)
Leone Mail
WOULD-BE GENTLEMAN, THE(1960, Fr.), ch
Richard Mailbaum
BAD MAN OF BRIMSTONE(1938), w
Lev Mailer
FIREFOX(1982)
Norman Mailer
NAKED AND THE DEAD, THE(1958), w; AMERICAN DREAM, AN(1966), w; BEYOND THE LAW(1968), a, p, d, w, ed; WILD 90(1968), a, p&d, ed; MAID-STONE(1970), a, p, d&w, ed; RAGTIME(1981)
Charles Mailes
LILIES OF THE FIELD(1930)
Silents
RED HOT DOLLARS(1920); CHICKENS(1921); LYING TRUTH, THE(1922); HELD TO ANSWER(1923); HEARTS AND FISTS(1926); PLAY SAFE(1927)
Misc. Silents
SEEKERS, THE(1916); FIND YOUR MAN(1924); THUNDERING HOOFS(1924); MIDNIGHT FLYER, THE(1925); MAN IN THE SADDLE, THE(1926); PHANTOM CITY, THE(1928)
Charles H. Mailes
Silents
GIRL WHO WOULDN'T QUIT, THE(1918)
Misc. Silents
FIGHTING GRIN, THE(1918); MAGIC EYE, THE(1918)
Charles Hill Mailes
BELLAMY TRIAL, THE(1929); CARNATION KID(1929); ONE STOLEN NIGHT(1929); MOTHERS CRY(1930); UNHOLY GARDEN, THE(1931); SO IT'S SUN-DAY(1932); NO MORE ORCHIDS(1933); WOMEN WON'T TELL(1933); MURDER BY TELEVISION(1935)
Misc. Talkies
BROKEN HEARTS(1933)
Silents
JUDITH OF BETHULIA(1914); OUTCASTS OF POKER FLAT, THE(1919); MARK OF ZORRO(1920); TREASURE ISLAND(1920); COURAGE(1921); TEN DOLLAR RAISE, THE(1921); CRASHIN' THRU(1923); EAST SIDE-WEST SIDE(1923); TOWN SCAN-DAL, THE(1923); LIGHTHOUSE BY THE SEA, THE(1924); CRIMSON RUNNER, THE(1925); OVERLAND LIMITED, THE(1925); BLUE STREAK, THE(1926); OLD IRONSIDES(1926); SOCIAL HIGHWAYMAN, THE(1926); AIN'T LOVE FUN-NY?(1927); CITY GONE WILD, THE(1927); GREAT MAIL ROBBERY, THE(1927); SOMEWHERE IN SONORA(1927); WHAT A NIGHT!(1928)
Misc. Silents
WOMAN IN BLACK, THE(1914); BRONZE BRIDE, THE(1917); GIRL WHO WON OUT, THE(1917); LASH OF POWER, THE(1917); SPOTTED LILY, THE(1917); WINGED MYSTERY, THE(1917); OUR BETTER SELVES(1919); HAUNTING SHAD-OWS(1920); BOND BOY, THE(1922); MAN FROM DOWNING STREET, THE(1922); BITTER APPLES(1927); MAN POWER(1927)
Maxence Mailfort
DISCREET CHARM OF THE BOURGEOISIE, THE(1972, Fr.); DRIVER'S SEAT, THE(1975, Ital.)
Jacqueline Maillan
GRAND MANEUVER, THE(1956, Fr.); PEEK-A-BOO(1961, Fr.); CANDIDE(1962, Fr.); MAGNIFICENT TRAMP, THE(1962, Fr./Ital.)
Anne-Sophie Maille
1984
A NOS AMOURS(1984, Fr.)
Maite Maille
1984
A NOS AMOURS(1984, Fr.)
Marie-Paul Mailleux
SYMPTOMS(1976, Brit.)
Jean-Marie Maillols
LA MARSEILLAISE(1938, Fr.), ph
Maurice Maillot
TESTAMENT OF DR. MABUSE, THE(1943, Ger.)
Michael Maillot
QUINTET(1979)

Michel Maillot
ONE MAN(1979, Can.)
Fernand Mailly
Silents
MARE NOSTRUM(1926)
Alex Maimon
TWO KOUNEY LEMELS(1966, Israel), w; FLYING MATCHMAKER, THE(1970, Israel), w
David Main
IT SEEMED LIKE A GOOD IDEA AT THE TIME(1975, Can.), w; SUNDAY IN THE COUNTRY(1975, Can.), w; IMPROPER CHANNELS(1981, Can.); TICKET TO HEAV-EN(1981)
Ian Main
SUBWAY IN THE SKY(1959, Brit.), w
Laurie Main
YELLOW BALLOON, THE(1953, Brit.); DELAVINE AFFAIR, THE(1954, Brit.); MASTER PLAN, THE(1955, Brit.); WHOLE TRUTH, THE(1958, Brit.); MY WIFE'S FAMILY(1962, Brit.); PUNCH AND JUDY MAN, THE(1963, Brit.); I'D RATHER BE RICH(1964); MY FAIR LADY(1964); DARLING LILI(1970); ON A CLEAR DAY YOU CAN SEE FOREVER(1970); PRIVATE PARTS(1972); FREAKY FRIDAY(1976); HER-BIE GOES TO MONTE CARLO(1977); TIME AFTER TIME(1979, Brit.)
Marjorie Main
HOT SATURDAY(1932); HOUSE DIVIDED, A(1932); TAKE A CHANCE(1933); CRIME WITHOUT PASSION(1934); MUSIC IN THE AIR(1934); NAUGHTY MARIET-TA(1935); BOY OF THE STREETS(1937); DEAD END(1937); LOVE IN A BUN-GALOW(1937); MAN WHO CRIED WOLF, THE(1937); SHADOW, THE(1937); STELLA DALLAS(1937); WRONG ROAD, THE(1937); CITY GIRL(1938); GIRLS' SCHOOL(1938); KING OF THE NEWSBOYS(1938); LITTLE TOUGH GUY(1938); PENITEN-TIARY(1938); PRISON FARM(1938); ROMANCE OF THE LIMBERLOST(1938); TEST PILOT(1938); THERE GOES MY HEART(1938); THREE COMRADES(1938); TOO HOT TO HANDLE(1938); UNDER THE BIG TOP(1938); ANGELS WASH THEIR FA-CES(1939); ANOTHER THIN MAN(1939); LUCKY NIGHT(1939); THEY SHALL HAVE MUSIC(1939); TWO THOROUGHBREDS(1939); WOMEN, THE(1939); CAPTAIN IS A LADY, THE(1940); DARK COMMAND, THE(1940); I TAKE THIS WOMAN(1940); SUSAN AND GOD(1940); TURNABOUT(1940); WOMEN WITHOUT NAMES(1940); WYOMING(1940); BARNACLE BILL(1941); BUGLE SOUNDS, THE(1941); HONKY TONK(1941); SHEPHERD OF THE HILLS, THE(1941); TRIAL OF MARY DUGAN, THE(1941); WILD MAN OF BORNEO, THE(1941); WOMAN'S FACE(1941); AFFAIRS OF MARTHA, THE(1942); JACKASS MAIL(1942); TENNESSEE JOHNSON(1942); TISH(1942); WE WERE DANCING(1942); HEAVEN CAN WAIT(1943); JOHNNY COME LATELY(1943); GENTLE ANNIE(1944); MEET ME IN ST. LOUIS(1944); RATIONING(1944); MURDER, HE SAYS(1945); BAD BASCOMB(1946); HARVEY GIRLS, THE(1946); SHOW-OFF, THE(1946); UNDERCURRENT(1946); EGG AND I, THE(1947); WISTFUL WIDOW OF WAGON GAP, THE(1947); FEUDIN', FUSSIN' AND A-FIGHTIN'(1948); BIG JACK(1949); MA AND PA KETTLE(1949); MA AND PA KETTLE GO TO TOWN(1950); MRS. O'MALLEY AND MR. MALONE(1950); SUMMER STOCK(1950); IT'S A BIG COUNTRY(1951); LAW AND THE LADY, THE(1951); MA AND PA KETTLE BACK ON THE FARM(1951); MR. IMPERIUM(1951); BELLE OF NEW YORK, THE(1952); MA AND PA KETTLE AT THE FAIR(1952); FAST COMPA-NY(1953); MA AND PA KETTLE ON VACATION(1953); LONG, LONG TRAILER, THE(1954); MA AND PA KETTLE AT HOME(1954); RICOCHET ROMANCE(1954); ROSE MARIE(1954); MA AND PA KETTLE AT WAIKIKI(1955); FRIENDLY PERSUA-SION(1956); KETTLES IN THE OZARKS, THE(1956); KETTLES ON OLD MAC-DONALD'S FARM, THE(1957)
Elisa Mainardi
FELLINI SATYRICON(1969, Fr./Ital.); ROMA(1972, Ital./Fr.)
Renato Mainardi
OF WAYWARD LOVE(1964, Ital./Ger.), w
Charles Eric Maine
SPACEWAYS(1953, Brit.), w; ATOMIC MAN, THE(1955, Brit.), w; ELECTRONIC MONSTER. THE(1960, Brit.), w; MIND OF MR. SOAMES, THE(1970, Brit.), w
Al Maini
IMPROPER CHANNELS(1981, Can.)
Maxi Mainka
SIGNS OF LIFE(1981, Ger.), ed
Maximiliane Mainka
GERMANY IN AUTUMN(1978, Ger.), d
Beate Mainka-Jellinghaus
EVERY MAN FOR HIMSELF AND GOD AGAINST ALL(1975, Ger.), ed; AGUIRRE, THE WRATH OF GOD(1977, W. Ger.), ed; GERMANY IN AUTUMN(1978, Ger.), d; NOSFERATU, THE VAMPIRE(1979, Fr./Ger.), ed; SIGNS OF LIFE(1981, Ger.), ed; FITZCARRALDO(1982), ed; WAR AND PEACE(1983, Ger.), ed
Maria Paola Maino
LUNA(1979, Ital.), art d
Laurie Mains
TARZAN, THE APE MAN(1981)
Marlene Mains
HEAVEN CAN WAIT(1943); WOMAN OF THE TOWN, THE(1943)
Cash Maintenant
SUNSET COVE(1978), w
Pierre Maintigneux
LEONOR(1977, Fr./Span./Ital.), w
Bernard Mainwaring
NEW HOTEL, THE(1932, Brit.), p&d; CRIMSON CANDLE, THE(1934, Brit.), p,d&w; PUBLIC LIFE OF HENRY THE NINTH, THE(1934, Brit.), d&w; WHISPERING TONGUES(1934, Brit.), w; LINE ENGAGED(1935, Brit.), d; OLD ROSES(1935, Brit.), p&d; SHOW FLAT(1936, Brit.), d; CROSS MY HEART(1937, Brit.), d; JENIFER HALE(1937, Brit.), d, w; MEMBER OF THE JURY(1937, Brit.), d; VILLIERS DIA-MOND, THE(1938, Brit.), d; WOMEN AREN'T ANGELS(1942, Brit.), w
Cecil Mainwaring
FIRE OVER ENGLAND(1937, Brit.)
Daniel Mainwaring
HITCH-HIKER, THE(1953), w; PHENIX CITY STORY, THE(1955), w; INVASION OF THE BODY SNATCHERS(1956), w; THUNDERSTORM(1956), w; BABY FACE NEL-SON(1957), w; COLE YOUNGER, GUNFIGHTER(1958), w; GUN RUNNERS, THE(1958), w; SPACE MASTER X-7(1958), w; WALK LIKE A DRAGON(1960), w; ATLANTIS, THE LOST CONTINENT(1961), w; MINOTAUR, THE(1961, Ital.), w; EAST OF KILIMANJARO(1962, Brit./Ital.), w; CONVICT STAGE(1965), w; WOMAN WHO WOULDN'T DIE, THE(1965, Brit.), w

1984
AGAINST ALL ODDS(1984), w
Ernest Mainwaring
UMBRELLA, THE(1933, Brit.); FIRST NIGHT(1937, Brit.)
Pat Mainwaring
SWISS HONEYMOON(1947, Brit.)
Friedrich A. Mainz
AFFAIRS OF DR. HOLL(1954, Ger.), d
Arthur Mainzer
JAZZBAND FIVE, THE(1932, Ger.); TRUNKS OF MR. O.F., THE(1932, Ger.)
John Maio
1984
LAST STARFIGHTER, THE(1984)
Maria Gabriella Maione
DISCREET CHARM OF THE BOURGEOISIE, THE(1972, Fr.)
John Mair
CROSS-UP(1958), w
Martha Mair
BLUE LIGHT, THE(1932, Ger.)
Pegeen Mair
GENERAL JOHN REGAN(1933, Brit.); NORAH O'NEALE(1934, Brit.)
Marise Maire
NAKED HEARTS(1970, Fr.)
Sophie Maire
PASSION(1983, Fr./Switz.)
Guy Mairesse
TAMANGO(1959, Fr.); RED CLOAK, THE(1961, Ital./Fr.); DIABOLICAL DR. Z, THE(1966 Span./Fr.); Z(1969, Fr./Algeria); CONFESSION, THE(1970, Fr.); MARCH OR DIE(1977, Brit.)
Valerie Mairesse
ONE SINGS, THE OTHER DOESN'T(1977, Fr.); BANZAI(1983, Fr.)
Max Mairich
UNWILLING AGENT(1968, Ger.)
Michele Mais
TRADING PLACES(1983)
Suzet Mais
ANGEL AND SINNER(1947, Fr.); UTOPIA(1952, Fr./Ital.)
Suzette Mais
AMERICAN LOVE(1932, Fr.)
Herbert Maisch
BOCCACCIO(1936, Ger.), d; ROYAL WALTZ, THE(1936), d
Sam Maisel
Z.P.G.(1972)
Susan Maisey
MIKADO, THE(1967, Brit.)
Maisie
MELODY AND ROMANCE(1937, Brit.)
Alice Maison
Silents
LAWFUL LARCENY(1923)
Edna Maison
Misc. Silents
SPY, THE(1914); UNDINE(1916); RICH MAN'S DAUGHTER, A(1918)
Miss Edna Maison
Silents
DUMB GIRL OF PORTICI(1916)
Luis A. Maisonet
HEROINA(1965), ph
Francois Maisongrosse
TRAFFIC(1972, Fr.)
Francois Maistre
JOKER, THE(1961, Fr.); PARIS BELONGS TO US(1962, Fr.); OSS 117-MISSION FOR A KILLER(1966, Fr./Ital.); SHAMELESS OLD LADY, THE(1966, Fr.); IMMORAL MOMENT, THE(1967, Fr.); BELLE DE JOUR(1968, Fr.); MILKY WAY, THE(1969, Fr./Ital.); DISCREET CHARM OF THE BOURGEOISIE, THE(1972, Fr.); SERPENT, THE(1973, Fr./Ital./Ger.); PHANTOM OF LIBERTY, THE(1974, Fr.); DIRTY HANDS(1976, Fr/Ital./Ger.); VIOLETTE(1978, Fr.)
O. Maisurian
Misc. Silents
NAMUS(1926, USSR)
Christine Maitland
Silents
NOBODY'S CHILD(1919, Brit.)
Misc. Silents
TEMPTRESS, THE(1920, Brit.)
Colin Maitland
DURING ONE NIGHT(1962, Brit.); LOLITA(1962); VICTORS, THE(1963); BEDFORD INCIDENT, THE(1965, Brit.); DIRTY DOZEN, THE(1967, Brit.)
Dexter Maitland
NIGHT THEY RAIDED MINSKY'S, THE(1968)
Gertrude Maitland
Silents
ON RECORD(1917)
Ian Maitland
NOCTURNA(1979), ed
Lauderdale Maitland
Silents
REBECCA THE JEWESS(1913, Brit.); QUEEN'S EVIDENCE(1919, Brit.)
Misc. Silents
BEGGAR GIRL'S WEDDING, THE(1915, Brit.); WHAT'S BRED...COMES OUT IN THE FLESH(1916, Brit.); RIGHT TO STRIKE, THE(1923, Brit.); WOMAN IN PAWN, A(1927, Brit.)
Lena Maitland
MONEY TALKS(1933, Brit.)
Lorna Maitland
ROPE OF FLESH(1965)
Marine Maitland
STATUE, THE(1971, Brit.)

Marne Maitland
HELL, HEAVEN OR HOBOKEN(1958, Brit.); CAIRO ROAD(1950, Brit.); OUTCAST OF THE ISLANDS(1952, Brit.); SAADIA(1953); DETECTIVE, THE(1954, Brit.); DIPLOMATIC PASSPORT(1954, Brit.); FLAME AND THE FLESH(1954); GOLDEN MASK, THE(1954, Brit.); SVENGALI(1955, Brit.); BHOWANI JUNCTION(1956); RAMSBOTTOM RIDES AGAIN(1956, Brit.); BREAK IN THE CIRCLE, THE(1957, Brit.); HOUR OF DECISION(1957, Brit.); PICKUP ALLEY(1957, Brit.); I ONLY ASKED!(1958, Brit.); MARK OF THE HAWK, THE(1958); WIND CANNOT READ, THE(1958, Brit.); WINDOM'S WAY(1958, Brit.); I'M ALL RIGHT, JACK(1959, Brit.); TIGER BAY(1959, Brit.); MAN IN A COCKED HAT(1960, Bri.); SANDS OF THE DESERT(1960, Brit.); STRANGLERS OF BOMBAY, THE(1960, Brit.); MIDDLE COURSE, THE(1961, Brit.); PASSPORT TO CHINA(1961, Brit.); TERROR OF THE TONGS, THE(1961, Brit.); THREE ON A SPREE(1961, Brit.); TROUBLE IN THE SKY(1961, Brit.); PHANTOM OF THE OPERA, THE(1962, Brit.); CLEOPATRA(1963); NINE HOURS TO RAMA(1963, U.S./Brit.); FIRST MEN IN THE MOON(1964, Brit.); MASTER SPY(1964, Brit.); BOY TEN FEET TALL, A(1965, Brit.); LORD JIM(1965, Brit.); RETURN OF MR. MOTO, THE(1965, Brit.); KHARTOUM(1966, Brit.); PANIC(1966, Brit.); REPTILE, THE(1966, Brit.); BOBO, THE(1967, Brit.); DUFFY(1968, Brit.); SHOES OF THE FISHERMAN, THE(1968); ANNE OF THE THOUSAND DAYS(1969, Brit.); DECLINE AND FALL... OF A BIRD WATCHER(1969, Brit.); BUSHBABY, THE(1970); MAN OF LA MANCHA(1972); ROMA(1972, Ital./Fr.); SHAFT IN AFRICA(1973); MAN WITH THE GOLDEN GUN, THE(1974, Brit.); MARCH OR DIE(1977, Brit.); TRAIL OF THE PINK PANTHER, THE(1982)
1984
MEMED MY HAWK(1984, Brit.)
Norman Maitland
BONNIE PRINCE CHARLIE(1948, Brit.)
Richard Maitland
Silents
IS ZAT SO?(1927)
Ruth Maitland
BED AND BREAKFAST(1930, Brit.); TIN GODS(1932, Brit.); HEART SONG(1933, Brit.); KISS ME GOODBYE(1935, Brit.); ROLLING HOME(1935, Brit.); AREN'T MEN BEASTS?(1937, Brit.); SPOT OF BOTHER, A(1938, Brit.); OLD MOTHER RILEY IN BUSINESS(1940, Brit.); OLD MOTHER RILEY IN SOCIETY(1940, Brit.); SECOND MR. BUSH, THE(1940, Brit.); HOUSE OF MYSTERY(1941, Brit.); IT HAPPENED TO ONE MAN(1941, Brit.); WE'LL SMILE AGAIN(1942, Brit.)
Scott Maitland
CHRISTINA(1974, Can.)
Bernard Maitre
DANTON(1983)
Albert Maitz
SEEDS OF FREEDOM(1943, USSR), w
Andrino Maiuri
DOCTOR CRIMEN(1953, Mex.), w
Arduino Maiuri
BLOOD IN THE STREETS(1975, Ital./Fr.), w
Dino Maiuri
KISS THE GIRLS AND MAKE THEM DIE(1967, U.S./Ital.), d, w; DANGER: DIABOLIK(1968, Ital./Fr.), w; VIOLENT FOUR, THE(1968, Ital.), w; COMPANEROS(1970 Ital./Span./Ger.), w; DON'T TURN THE OTHER CHEEK(1974, Ital./Ger./Span.), w; FAMILY, THE(1974, Fr./Ital.), w; CHINO(1976, Ital., Span., Fr.), w
Toshiro Maiyuzumi
DAPHNE, THE(1967), m
Lillian Taft Maize
Silents
HANDSOME BRUTE, THE(1925), w
Leonard Maizola
HIT(1973), set d
Zelma Maja
Silents
AFFAIRS OF ANATOL, THE(1921); LITTLE CLOWN, THE(1921)
Ana Maria Majalca
GIANT(1956); BON VOYAGE(1962)
Juan Majan
LEGIONS OF THE NILE(1960, Ital.); GUNMEN OF THE RIO GRANDE(1965, Fr./Ital./Span.); OPEN SEASON(1974, U.S./Span.), stunts; MARCH OR DIE(1977, Brit.), Stunts
A.G. Majano
CITY OF PAIN(1951, Ital.), w
Anton Giulio Majano
WANDERING JEW, THE(1948, Ital.), w
Anton Guilio Majano
ATOM AGE VAMPIRE(1961, Ital.), d, w
Krzysztof Majchrzak
GOLEM(1980, Pol.)
Maria Majczen
DIALOGUE(1967, Hung.)
Wojciech Majda
MAN OF MARBLE(1979, Pol.), prod d
Katja Majer
EVENT, AN(1970, Yugo.), ed
Renata Majer
WAITRESS(1982)
Tom Majer
POSTMAN ALWAYS RINGS TWICE, THE(1981)
Achille Majerone
VITELLONI(1956, Ital./Fr.)
Achille Majeroni
APE WOMAN, THE(1964, Ital.)
George Majeroni
Silents
ETERNAL CITY, THE(1915); MY LADY INCOG(1916); ALL MAN(1918); KING OF DIAMONDS, THE(1918); DIANE OF STAR HOLLOW(1921); WHAT WOMEN WILL DO(1921)
Misc. Silents
FEUD GIRL, THE(1916); STRANDED IN ARCADY(1917); CAILLAUX CASE, THE(1918); GREEN GOD, THE(1918); HOARDED ASSETS(1918); BEATING THE ODDS(1919); BEAUTY PROOF(1919); FIGHTING DESTINY(1919); MARRIAGE FOR CONVENIENCE(1919)

Georgio Majeroni
Misc. Silents
BELGIAN, THE(1917)
Mario Majeroni
Silents
NIGHTINGALE, THE(1914); PARTNERS OF THE NIGHT(1920); VALLEY OF SILENT MEN, THE(1922); ENEMIES OF WOMEN, THE(1923); STEADFAST HEART, THE(1923); ARGENTINE LOVE(1924)
Misc. Silents
HEART'S DESIRE(1917); SLEEPING MEMORY, A(1917); FROM NOW ON(1920); LOVE WITHOUT QUESTION(1920); SNOW BRIDE, THE(1923)
Majesta
MY THIRD WIFE GEORGE(1968)
Hans Martin Majewski
BRIDGE, THE(1961, Ger.), m
Hans-Martin Majewski
CONFESSIONS OF FELIX KRULL, THE(1957, Ger.), m; THREE MOVES TO FREEDOM(1960, Ger.), m; BRAINWASHED(1961, Ger.), m; QUESTION 7(1961, U.S./Ger.), m; ESCAPE FROM EAST BERLIN(1962), m; END OF MRS. CHENEY(1963, Ger.), m; RESTLESS NIGHT, THE(1964, Ger.), m; VISIT, THE(1964, Ger./Fr./Ital./U.S.), m, md; UNWILLING AGENT(1968, Ger.), m
Milorad Majic
STEPPE, THE(1963, Fr./Ital.)
Mitsura Majima
NIGHT OF THE SEAGULL, THE(1970, Jap.), w
Joseph Majinsky
FOREIGN INTRIGUE(1956), makeup
Juan Majon
TAKE A HARD RIDE(1975, U.S./Ital.), stunts
Louis Majoney
CURSE OF THE VOODOO(1965, Brit.)
Anthony Major
SUPER SPOOK(1975), d, w
Charles Major
SWORD AND THE ROSE, THE(1953), w
Silents
WHEN KNIGHTHOOD WAS IN FLOWER(1922), w
Doug Major
BANG THE DRUM SLOWLY(1973)
Robert Major
PRIME TIME, THE(1960)
Ross Major
DAWN(1979, Aus.), art d; HOODWINK(1981, Aus.), prod d; BMX BANDITS(1983), prod d; HEATWAVE(1983, Aus.), prod d
Tamas Major
MEPHISTO(1981, Ger.)
Tony Major
FOR LOVE OF IVY(1968); NO WAY TO TREAT A LADY(1968); LANDLORD, THE(1970); KLUTE(1971); BANG THE DRUM SLOWLY(1973)
William Major
STILL OF THE NIGHT(1982)
Major, the Lion
NAPOLEON AND SAMANTHA(1972)
Stefano Majore
ROMA(1972, Ital./Fr.)
George Majorim
Silents
AS IN A LOOKING GLASS(1916)

Eddie Majors
WEST OF THE ALAMO(1946); OUTLAW BRAND(1948); GUN LAW JUSTICE(1949); GUN RUNNER(1949); TRAIL'S END(1949)
Lee Majors
WILL PENNY(1968); LIBERATION OF L.B. JONES, THE(1970); NORSEMAN, THE(1978); KILLER FISH(1979, Ital./Braz.); STEEL(1980); AGENCY(1981, Can.); LAST CHASE, THE(1981)
Steve Majstorovic
HEAVEN'S GATE(1980)
Robin Majumder
MUSIC ROOM, THE(1963, India), m
Suzanne Majure
THIEVES LIKE US(1974)
Mirjana Majurec
RAT SAVIOUR, THE(1977, Yugo.)
Majuto
MAN'S HOPE(1947, Span.)
Marii Mak
1984
DREAMSCAPE(1984)
Marri Mak
SEDUCTION, THE(1982)
Nani Maka
PAGAN ISLAND(1961)
Dorothy Makaill
Misc. Silents
WOMAN'S WOMAN, A(1922)
Moti Makan
VENOM(1982, Brit.)
1984
PASSAGE TO INDIA, A(1984, Brit.)
Halcyon Makapagal
Misc. Talkies
BELT AND SUSPENDERS MAN, THE(1970)
David Makarenke
TEVYA(1939)
Dan Makarenko
Misc. Silents
FLAME OF THE ARGENTINE(1926)

Daniel Makarenko
Silents
ADORABLE DECEIVER, THE(1926); SIBERIA(1926)
A. Makarov
DAY THE EARTH FROZE, THE(1959, Fin./USSR), set d
V. Makarov
IMMORTAL GARRISON, THE(1957, USSR); PEACE TO HIM WHO ENTERS(1963, USSR)
Inna Makarova
MARRIAGE OF BALZAMINOV, THE(1966, USSR)
T. Makarova
SEVEN BRAVE MEN(1936, USSR)
Tamara Makarova
DESERTER(1934, USSR); CITY OF YOUTH(1938, USSR); THEY WANTED PEACE(1940, USSR); NEW TEACHER, THE(1941, USSR)
A. Makasheva
VIOLIN AND ROLLER(1962, USSR), makeup
Natalia Makasova
SLEEPING BEAUTY, THE(1966, USSR)
Marge Makau
DON'T WORRY, WE'LL THINK OF A TITLE(1966), cos
Dusan Makavejev
LOVE AFFAIR; OR THE CASE OF THE MISSING SWITCHBOARD OPERATOR(1968, Yugo.), d&w; INNOCENCE UNPROTECTED(1971, Yugo.), d&w; MONTENEGRO(1981, Brit./Swed.), d, w
Arpad Makay
LOOKING UP(1977), ph
Butros Makdissy
LIAR'S DICE(1980), p
Issam B. Makdissy
LIAR'S DICE(1980), a, d, ed
Blaidsell Makee
Misc. Talkies
MANSON MASSACRE, THE(1976)
Eliot Makeham
HOME, SWEET HOME(1933, Brit.); I LIVED WITH YOU(1933, Brit.); I'M AN EXPLOSIVE(1933, Brit.); ROME EXPRESS(1933, Brit.); ROOF, THE(1933, Brit.); BYPASS TO HAPPINESS(1934, Brit.); CRIMSON CANDLE, THE(1934, Brit.); FRIDAY THE 13TH(1934, Brit.); ORDERS IS ORDERS(1934, Brit.); HER LAST AFFAIRE(1935, Brit.); LORNA DOONE(1935, Brit.); ONCE IN A NEW MOON(1935, Brit.); TWO HEARTS IN HARMONY(1935, Brit.); BROWN WALLET, THE(1936, Brit.); CALLING THE TUNE(1936, Brit.); EAST MEETS WEST(1936, Brit.); LAST JOURNEY, THE(1936, Brit.); PEG OF OLD DRURY(1936, Brit.); SOMEONE AT THE DOOR(1936, Brit.); STAR FELL FROM HEAVEN, A(1936, Brit.); TO CATCH A THIEF(1936, Brit.); TOMORROW WE LIVE(1936, Brit.); BORN THAT WAY(1937, Brit.); DARK JOURNEY(1937, Brit.); HEAD OVER HEELS IN LOVE(1937, Brit.); LOST CHORD, THE(1937, Brit.); RACING ROMANCE(1937, Brit.); STORM IN A TEACUP(1937, Brit.); TAKE MY TIP(1937, Brit.); BEDTIME STORY(1938, Brit.); CITADEL, THE(1938); COMING OF AGE(1938, Brit.); DARTS ARE TRUMPS(1938, Brit.); EVERYTHING HAPPENS TO ME(1938, Brit.); MERELY MR. HAWKINS(1938, Brit.); TROOPSHIP(1938, Brit.); YOU'RE THE DOCTOR(1938, Brit.); INSPECTOR HORNLEIGH(1939, Brit.); ME AND MY PAL(1939, Brit.); MILL ON THE FLOSS(1939, Brit.); NURSEMAID WHO DISAPPEARED, THE(1939, Brit.); SPY FOR A DAY(1939, Brit.); NIGHT TRAIN(1940, Brit.); PASTOR HALL(1940, Brit.); SALOON BAR(1940, Brit.); SECRET FOUR, THE(1940, Brit.); SPARE A COPPER(1940, Brit.); COMMON TOUCH, THE(1941, Brit.); FACING THE MUSIC(1941, Brit.); LET THE PEOPLE SING(1942, Brit.); WINGS AND THE WOMAN(1942, Brit.); BELL-BOTTOM GEORGE(1943, Brit.); SUSPECTED PERSON(1943, Brit.); CANDLES AT NINE(1944, Brit.); CANTERBURY TALE, A(1944, Brit.); GIVE US THE MOON(1944, Brit.); UNCENSORED(1944, Brit.); YELLOW CANARY, THE(1944, Brit.); HALF-WAY HOUSE, THE(1945, Brit.); I'LL BE YOUR SWEETHEART(1945, Brit.); MADONNA OF THE SEVEN MOONS(1945, Brit.); VACATION FROM MARRIAGE(1945, Brit.); MAGIC BOW, THE(1947, Brit.); NICHOLAS NICKLEBY(1947, Brit.); DAYDREAM(1948, Brit.); LOVE IN WAITING(1948, Brit.); VOTE FOR HUGGETT(1948, Brit.); CHILDREN OF CHANCE(1949, Brit.); FORBIDDEN(1949, Brit.); MINIVER STORY, THE(1950, Brit./U.S.); NO ROOM AT THE INN(1950, Brit.); TRIO(1950, Brit.); CHRISTMAS CAROL, A(1951, Brit.); GREEN GROW THE RUSHES(1951, Brit.); LITTLE BALLERINA, THE(1951, Brit.); SCARLET THREAD(1951, Brit.); CRIMSON PIRATE, THE(1952); DECAMERON NIGHTS(1953, Brit.); FAKE, THE(1953, Brit.); MEET MR. LUCIFER(1953, Brit.); UNFINISHED SYMPHONY, THE(1953, Aust./Brit.); COMPANIONS IN CRIME(1954, Brit.); DOCTOR IN THE HOUSE(1954, Brit.); FAST AND LOOSE(1954, Brit.); MAN WITH A MILLION(1954, Brit.); RAINBOW JACKET, THE(1954, Brit.); WEAK AND THE WICKED, THE(1954, Brit.); PANIC IN THE PARLOUR(1957, Brit.)
Elliot Makeham
THE BEACHCOMBER(1938, Brit.); IT'S IN THE AIR(1940, Brit.); MYSTERY AT THE BURLESQUE(1950, Brit.); NIGHT AND THE CITY(1950, Brit.); YELLOW BALLOON, THE(1953, Brit.)
Joseph F. Makel
HEAVEN CAN WAIT(1978)
Helena Makela
TENTACLES(1977, Ital.); HYSTERICAL(1983)
Toivo Makela
PRELUDE TO ECSTASY(1963, Fin.)
Hal R. Makelim
MAN OF CONFLICT(1953), p&d; PEACEMAKER, THE(1956), p; VALERIE(1957), p
Chris Makepeace
MEATBALLS(1979, Can.); MY BODYGUARD(1980); LAST CHASE, THE(1981)
1984
OASIS, THE(1984)
Christopher Makepeace
Misc. Talkies
MYSTERIOUS STRANGER(1982)
Paul Makgoba
DINGAKA(1965, South Africa)
Ye. Makhankova
DON QUIXOTE(1961, USSR), ed; HAMLET(1966, USSR), ed
T. Makharova
VOW, THE(1947, USSR.)

V. Makhov
RESURRECTION(1963, USSR)
T. Makhova
WAR AND PEACE(1968, USSR)
Fusako Maki
PERFORMERS, THE(1970, Jap.)
Kim Maki
JUNGLE PRINCESS, THE(1936)
Taugendo Maki
MY GEISHA(1962)
Tsjundo Maki
COMPLIMENTS OF MR. FLOW(1941, Fr.)
Tsugundo Maki
MY GEISHA(1962)
Harry Makin
CROWD INSIDE, THE(1971, Can.), ph; FAN'S NOTES, A(1972, Can.), ph; NEPTUNE FACTOR, THE(1973, Can.), ph; QUIET DAY IN BELFAST, A(1974, Can.), ph; IT SEEMED LIKE A GOOD IDEA AT THE TIME(1975, Can.), ph; IF YOU COULD SEE WHAT I HEAR(1982), ph
W. J. Makin
MURDER AT COVENT GARDEN(1932, Brit.), w
William J. Makin
RETURN OF DR. X, THE(1939), w
Marie Makine
MAIL TRAIN(1941, Brit.)
Yutaka Makino
TEMPTRESS AND THE MONK, THE(1963, Jap.), m
Chishi Makiura
SHOWDOWN FOR ZATOICHI(1968, Jap.), ph; HIKEN YABURI(1969, Jap.), ph; SECRETS OF A WOMAN'S TEMPLE(1969, Jap.), ph; ZATOICHI CHALLENGED(1970, Jap.), ph
Chriski Makiura
SHOGUN ASSASSIN(1980, Jap.), ph
Karoly Makk
LOVE(1972, Hung.), d
Zdzislaw Maklakiewicz
SALTO(1966, Pol.); SARAGOSSA MANUSCRIPT, THE(1972, Pol.)
Maklary
BLUE IDOL, THE(1931, Hung.)
Zoltan Maklary
DIALOGUE(1967, Hung.)
David M. Makler
FORBIDDEN ZONE(1980), art d
M. Maklyarsky
SECRET MISSION(1949, USSR), w
Mako
SAND PEBBLES, THE(1966); UGLY DACHSHUND, THE(1966); PRIVATE NAVY OF SGT. O'FARRELL, THE(1968); GREAT BANK ROBBERY, THE(1969); FOOLS(1970); HAWAIIANS, THE(1970); ISLAND AT THE TOP OF THE WORLD, THE(1974); KILLER ELITE, THE(1975); BIG BRAWL, THE(1980); EYE FOR AN EYE, AN(1981); UNDER THE RAINBOW(1981); BUSHIDO BLADE, THE(1982 Brit./U.S.); CONAN THE BARBARIAN(1982); TESTAMENT(1983)
1984
CONAN THE DESTROYER(1984)
Rhoda Makoff
E.T. THE EXTRA-TERRESTRIAL(1982)
Rudy Makoul
TEENAGE THUNDER(1957), w; GEISHA BOY, THE(1958), w
Milos Makourek
WHO KILLED JESSIE?(1965, Czech.), w; I KILLED EINSTEIN, GENTLEMEN(1970, Czech.), w; SIR, YOU ARE A WIDOWER(1971, Czech.), w; WHAT WOULD YOU SAY TO SOME SPINACH(1976, Czech.), d&w
Milos Makovec
EMPEROR AND THE NIGHTINGALE, THE(1949, Czech.), d
Milos Makovek
NIGHTS OF PRAGUE, THE(1968, Czech.), d
S. Makovskaya
WAR AND PEACE(1968, USSR)
Claude Makovski
BAND OF OUTSIDERS(1966, Fr.); VERY CURIOUS GIRL, A(1970, Fr.), a, p, w; CHARLES AND LUCIE(1982, Fr.), p
Orestis Makris
AUNT FROM CHICAGO(1960, Gr.); GROUCH, THE(1961, Gr.); MIDWIFE, THE(1961, Greece)
Lyudmila Maksamova
THERE WAS AN OLD COUPLE(1967, USSR)
V. Maksimenko
SONG OF THE FOREST(1963, USSR)
V. Maksimov
DON QUIXOTE(1961, USSR); OVERCOAT, THE(1965, USSR)
A. Maksimova
FAREWELL, DOVES(1962, USSR); VIOLIN AND ROLLER(1962, USSR); GIRL AND THE BUGLER, THE(1967, USSR); UNCOMMON THIEF, AN(1967, USSR)
Ekaterina Maksimova
LA TRAVIATA(1982)
Yelena Maksimova
HOME FOR TANYA, A(1961, USSR); SUN SHINES FOR ALL, THE(1961, USSR); FATHER OF A SOLDIER(1966, USSR)
Dragan Maksimovic
MEETINGS WITH REMARKABLE MEN(1979, Brit.); TWILIGHT TIME(1983, U.S./Yugo.)
Dzemal Maksut
1984
MEMED MY HAWK(1984, Brit.)
Jimmy Makulis
$100 A NIGHT(1968, Ger.)
Eseka Makumbi
KISENGA, MAN OF AFRICA(1952, Brit.)

Thony Maky [Adriano Mikahtoni]
TOMB OF TORTURE(1966, Ital.)
Isabelle Mal
PATRICK THE GREAT(1945)
Rose Mal
HELL ON EARTH(1934, Ger.)
Mala
LAST OF THE PAGANS(1936); CALL OF THE YUKON(1938); MUTINY ON THE BLACKHAWK(1939); DEVIL'S PIPELINE, THE(1940); GIRL FROM GOD'S COUNTRY(1940); TUTTLES OF TAHITI(1942)
Mala [Ray Mala]
UNION PACIFIC(1939)
Ray Mala
JUNGLE PRINCESS, THE(1936); GREEN HELL(1940); NORTHWEST MOUNTED POLICE(1940); ZANZIBAR(1940); HOLD BACK THE DAWN(1941); HONOLULU LU(1941); GIRL FROM ALASKA(1942); MAD DOCTOR OF MARKET STREET, THE(1942); SON OF FURY(1942); RED SNOW(1952)
Malabar
LAST GUNFIGHTER, THE(1961, Can.), cos
George Malaby
SPY WHO LOVED ME, THE(1977, Brit.)
Marisa Malachini
RUN FOR YOUR WIFE(1966, Fr./Ital.)
Dino Malacrida
MORGAN THE PIRATE(1961, Fr./Ital.)
Andreas Maladrinos
OBLONG BOX, THE(1969, Brit.)
Milo Malagoli
MINOTAUR, THE(1961, Ital.)
Stefania Malagu
BARBER OF SEVILLE, THE(1973, Ger./Fr.)
Bruna Malaguti
LOVE AND MARRIAGE(1966, Ital.), ed
Patrick Malahide
1984
COMFORT AND JOY(1984, Brit.); KILLING FIELDS, THE(1984, Brit.)
Malalene
FISTS OF FURY(1973, Chi.)
Sara Malament
FAME(1980)
Bernard Malamud
FIXER, THE(1968), w; ANGEL LEVINE, THE(1970), w
1984
NATURAL, THE(1984), w
Wendy Malan
FOREVER YOUNG, FOREVER FREE(1976, South Afr.), art d
William Malan
Silents
ONE PUNCH O'DAY(1926)
Misc. Silents
RED HOT LEATHER(1926); THREE MILES UP(1927); BORDER WILDCAT, THE(1929)
Andrea Malandrinos
RAISE THE ROOF(1930); GOLDEN CAGE, THE(1933, Brit.); MEDICINE MAN, THE(1933, Brit.); ADMIRAL'S SECRET, THE(1934, Brit.); BROKEN MELODY, THE(1934, Brit.); DIPLOMATIC LOVER, THE(1934, Brit.); VIRGINIA'S HUSBAND(1934, Brit.); LATE EXTRA(1935, Brit.); PHANTOM FIEND, THE(1935, Brit.); PLAY UP THE BAND(1935, Brit.); VINTAGE WINE(1935, Brit.); GAY ADVENTURE, THE(1936, Brit.); OLD SPANISH CUSTOM, AN(1936, Brit.); PRISON BREAKER(1936, Brit.); SECRET AGENT, THE(1936, Brit.); SECRET OF STAMBOUL, THE(1936, Brit.); TROPICAL TROUBLE(1936, Brit.); UNDER PROOF(1936, Brit.); GYPSY(1937, Brit.); NON-STOP NEW YORK(1937, Brit.); PRICE OF FOLLY, THE(1937, Brit.); ROMANCE AND RICHES(1937, Brit.); SHOW GOES ON, THE(1937, Brit.); SKY'S THE LIMIT, THE(1937, Brit.); HE LOVED AN ACTRESS(1938, Brit.); LAST BARRICADE, THE(1938, Brit.); MAN WITH 100 FACES, THE(1938, Brit.); WHAT WOULD YOU DO, CHUMS?(1939, Brit.); CROOKS TOUR(1940, Brit.); LOST ON THE WESTERN FRONT(1940, Brit.); ROOM FOR TWO(1940, Brit.); FLYING FORTRESS(1942, Brit.); WE'LL SMILE AGAIN(1942, Brit.); CHAMPAGNE CHARLIE(1944, Brit.); THUNDER ROCK(1944, Brit.); END OF THE RIVER, THE(1947, Brit.); MAN ABOUT THE HOUSE, A(1947, Brit.); HER MAN GILBEY(1949, Brit.); MY BROTHER JONATHAN(1949, Brit.); SLEEPING CAR TO TRIESTE(1949, Brit.); WHILE THE SUN SHINES(1950, Brit.); CHELSEA STORY(1951, Brit.); LAVENDER HILL MOB, THE(1951, Brit.); MEN OF THE SEA(1951, Brit.); HAMMER THE TOFF(1952, Brit.); PAUL TEMPLE RETURNS(1952, Brit.); SALUTE THE TOFF(1952, Brit.); SPIDER AND THE FLY, THE(1952, Brit.); CAPTAIN'S PARADISE, THE(1953, Brit.); LOVE LOTTERY, THE(1954, Brit.); BLONDE BLACKMAILER(1955, Brit.); INNOCENTS IN PARIS(1955, Brit.); TECKMAN MYSTERY, THE(1955, Brit.); PORT AFRIQUE(1956, Brit.); CHECKPOINT(1957, Brit.); PRINCE AND THE SHOWGIRL, THE(1957, Brit.); THERE'S ALWAYS A THURSDAY(1957, Brit.); LINKS OF JUSTICE(1958); ORDERS TO KILL(1958, Brit.); BOY WHO STOLE A MILLION, THE(1960, Brit.); TOMMY THE TOREADOR(1960, Brit.)
Andreas Malandrinos
IMPROPER DUCHESS, THE(1936, Brit.); I SEE ICE(1938); TANK FORCE(1958, Brit.); BOY AND THE BRIDGE, THE(1959, Brit.); WEEKEND WITH LULU, A(1961, Brit.); IN SEARCH OF THE CASTAWAYS(1962, Brit.); HELP!(1965, Brit.); YELLOW ROLLS-ROYCE, THE(1965, Brit.); FEARLESS VAMPIRE KILLERS, OR PARDON ME BUT YOUR TEETH ARE IN MY NECK, THE(1967, Brit.); MAGNIFICENT TWO, THE(1967, Brit.); MUMMY'S SHROUD, THE(1967, Brit.); MAGUS, THE(1968, Brit.); HELL BOATS(1970, Brit.); MAN OF VIOLENCE(1970, Brit.); UNDERGROUND(1970, Brit.)
Gerard Malanga
CHELSEA GIRLS, THE(1967); ILLIAC PASSION, THE(1968)
Joe Malanga
SCARECROW IN A GARDEN OF CUCUMBERS(1972)
P. Malaniksev
SILVER DUST(1953, USSR), spec eff
Vera Malanovskaya
Misc. Silents
MARRIAGE OF THE BEAR, THE(1928, USSR)

Zygmunt Malanowicz
KNIFE IN THE WATER(1963, Pol.); NAKED AMONG THE WOLVES(1967, Ger.)
Curzio Malaparte
STRANGE DECEPTION(1953, Ital.), d&w, m
Louisette Malapert
DIVA(1982, Fr.)
Jose Malar
MAGIC VOYAGE OF SINBAD, THE(1962, USSR), makeup
Tay Malarkey
CLOSE HARMONY(1929), ed; NO LIMIT(1931), ed
Silents
HOT NEWS(1928), ed
Ilario Malaschini
UNDER THE SUN OF ROME(1949, Ital.)
Nunsio Malasomma
WHITE DEVIL, THE(1948, Ital.), d, w
Michele Malaspina
PIRATE AND THE SLAVE GIRL, THE(1961, Fr./Ital.); NIGHT THEY KILLED RASPUTIN, THE(1962, Fr./Ital.)
Daniele Malat
CHLOE IN THE AFTERNOON(1972, Fr.)
Jan Malat
STOLEN DIRIGIBLE, THE(1966, Czech.)
Fred Malatesa
CAUGHT CHEATING(1931)
Fered Malatesta
ESPIONAGE(1937)
Fred Malatesta
UNDER TWO FLAGS(1936); WINGS OF ADVENTURE(1930); FAREWELL TO ARMS, A(1932); GET THAT GIRL(1932); GAY BRIDE, THE(1934); PICTURE BRIDES(1934); STUDENT TOUR(1934); THIN MAN, THE(1934); WHAT'S YOUR RACKET?(1934); CRUSADES, THE(1935); ENTER MADAME(1935); UNDER THE PAMPAS MOON(1935); DODSWORTH(1936); LONE WOLF RETURNS, THE(1936); GOLD RACKET, THE(1937); ARTISTS AND MODELS ABROAD(1938); PORT OF SEVEN SEAS(1938); SUEZ(1938); JUAREZ(1939); ARISE, MY LOVE(1940); MARK OF ZORRO, THE(1940); RANGERS OF FORTUNE(1940); ROAD TO SINGAPORE(1940); BLOOD AND SAND(1941); THAT NIGHT IN RIO(1941)
Misc. Talkies
SENOR JIM(1936)
Silents
GREATEST THING IN LIFE, THE(1918); SINS OF ROZANNE(1920); ALL DOLLED UP(1921); LITTLE LORD FAUNTLEROY(1921); MASK, THE(1921); FORBIDDEN PARADISE(1924); LULLABY, THE(1924); RECKLESS AGE, THE(1924); GATE CRASHER, THE(1928); PEACOCK FAN(1929)
Misc. Silents
LEGION OF DEATH, THE(1918); FULL OF PEP(1919); BEST OF LUCK, THE(1920); BIG HAPPINESS(1920); VALLEY OF TOMORROW, THE(1920); GIRL WHO CAME BACK, THE(1923); MAN BETWEEN, THE(1923); NIGHT HAWK, THE(1924); WAGON SHOW, THE(1928)
Fred M. Malatesta
Silents
DEVIL'S TRAIL, THE(1919)
Fred W. Malatesta
RIP TIDE(1934); LOVE ON THE RUN(1936)
Guido Malatesta
FURY OF THE PAGANS(1963, Ital.), d; GOLIATH AGAINST THE GIANTS(1963, Ital./Span.), d; SAMSON AND THE SLAVE QUEEN(1963, Ital.), w; TERROR OF THE BLACK MASK(1967, Fr./Ital.), w
Lafayette Malatsun
CHAFED ELBOWS(1967)
Renato Malavasi
VARIETY LIGHTS(1965, Ital.)
Chu Chu Malave
DOG DAY AFTERNOON(1975); FORCE OF ONE, A(1979); MAIN EVENT, THE(1979)
Kelvin Malave
JOE HILL(1971, Swed./U.S.)
Groupe Malavoi
1984
SUGAR CANE ALLEY(1984, Fr.), m
Christophe Malavoy
LA BALANCE(1983, Fr.)
Zygmunt Malawski
JOAN OF THE ANGELS(1962, Pol.); YELLOW SLIPPERS, THE(1965, Pol.)
Richard Malbaum
COAST GUARD(1939), w
Anna Malberg
GERTRUD(1966, Den.)
Henrik Malberg
ORDET(1957, Den.)
Isabelle Malbrun
PARSIFAL(1983, Fr.)
Tatyana Malchenko
THREE SISTERS, THE(1969, USSR)
Edelweiss Malchin
MAN ON A TIGHTROPE(1953); PRIZE OF GOLD, A(1955)
Georges Malchior
Misc. Silents
L'ATLANTIDE(1921, Fr.)
Paolo Malco
MASOCH(1980, Ital.)
1984
HOUSE BY THE CEMETERY, THE(1984, Ital.)
Bill Malcolm
LAST WAVE, THE(1978, Aus.), set d
Chris Malcolm
ADVENTURES OF BARRY McKENZIE(1972, Austral.); SHOCK TREATMENT(1981); SUPERMAN III(1983)

Christopher Malcolm
DESPERADOS, THE(1969); FIGURES IN A LANDSCAPE(1970, Brit.); WELCOME TO THE CLUB(1971); SPIRAL STAIRCASE, THE(1975, Brit.); FORCE 10 FROM NAVARONE(1978, Brit.); DOGS OF WAR, THE(1980, Brit.); EMPIRE STRIKES BACK, THE(1980); RAGTIME(1981); REDS(1981)
1984
LASSITER(1984)
David Malcolm
BEACH BALL(1965), w; GIRLS ON THE BEACH(1965), w; WILD, WILD WINTER(1966), w
Doris Malcolm
OH, HEAVENLY DOG!(1980)
George Malcolm
SPLENDID FELLOWS(1934, Aus.), ph; TYPHOON TREASURE(1939, Brit.), ph; ALWAYS ANOTHER DAWN(1948, Aus.), ph
George D. Malcolm
LITTLE AUSTRALIANS(1940, Aus.), ph
Gina Malcolm
MISCHIEF(1969, Brit.)
Harry Malcolm
TYPHOON TREASURE(1939, Brit.), ph; GLENROWAN AFFAIR, THE(1951, Aus.), ph
James Malcolm
MERRY CHRISTMAS MR. LAWRENCE(1983, Jap./Brit.)
Joe Malcolm
1984
UTU(1984, New Zealand)
John Malcolm
WHERE HAS POOR MICKEY GONE?(1964, Brit.); RECKONING, THE(1971, Brit.)
Mary Malcolm
DESIGN FOR LOVING(1962, Brit.)
Maude Malcolm
Silents
SCARAB RING, THE(1921)
Misc. Silents
CALL OF THE HILLS, THE(1923)
Otis Malcolm
TIME OF YOUR LIFE, THE(1948), makeup; MACOMBER AFFAIR, THE(1947), makeup; DAMNED DON'T CRY, THE(1950), makeup; KISS TOMORROW GOODBYE(1950), makup; WEST POINT STORY, THE(1950), makeup; LION IS IN THE STREETS, A(1953), makeup; HORSE IN THE GRAY FLANNEL SUIT, THE(1968), makeup; LOVE BUG, THE(1968), makeup; RASCAL(1969), makeup; SMITH(1969), makeup; GUNFIGHT, A(1971), makeup
Paul Malcolm
HELL'S BELLES(1969), makeup
Robert Malcolm
UNCLE HARRY(1945); CAPTAIN EDDIE(1945); DANGEROUS PARTNERS(1945); SCARLET STREET(1945); TREE GROWS IN BROOKLYN, A(1945); CARAVAN TRAIL, THE(1946); CENTENNIAL SUMMER(1946); DRAGONWYCH(1946); MASK OF DIJON, THE(1946); NOCTURNE(1946); STRANGE TRIANGLE(1946); DEVIL THUMBS A RIDE, THE(1947); SEA OF GRASS, THE(1947); FOREIGN AFFAIR, A(1948); RETURN OF OCTOBER, THE(1948); TO THE ENDS OF THE EARTH(1948); BLAZING TRAIL, THE(1949); LADY TAKES A SAILOR, THE(1949); UNDERCOVER MAN, THE(1949); WE WERE STRANGERS(1949); WOMAN'S SECRET, A(1949); CONVICTED(1950); MAGNIFICENT YANKEE, THE(1950); ONE TOO MANY(1950); SIDE STREET(1950); WOMAN OF DISTINCTION, A(1950); MR. BELVEDERE RINGS THE BELL(1951); PLACE IN THE SUN, A(1951); STRIP, THE(1951); HANS CHRISTIAN ANDERSEN(1952); SNIPER, THE(1952); LOVE ME OR LEAVE ME(1955); WRITTEN ON THE WIND(1956); TATTERED DRESS, THE(1957)
Roy Malcolm
GREAT DAY(1945, Brit.)
Malcolm Mitchell Trio
STAR OF MY NIGHT(1954, Brit.)
Clinton Malcome
SPOOK WHO SAT BY THE DOOR, THE(1973)
Ronald Malcomson
IRELAND'S BORDER LINE(1939, Ireland)
Malda and Ray
YOU'RE A SWEETHEART(1937)
Francesco Maldacea
FAREWELL TO LOVE(1931, Brit.)
Franz Maldacea
BLUE LIGHT, THE(1932, Ger.)
Bertha Maldanado
TUNDRA(1936)
Otto Malde
SPARTACUS(1960)
Karl Malden
THEY KNEW WHAT THEY WANTED(1940); 13 RUE MADELEINE(1946); BOOMERANG(1947); KISS OF DEATH(1947); GUNFIGHTER, THE(1950); WHERE THE SIDEWALK ENDS(1950); HALLS OF MONTEZUMA(1951); SELLOUT, THE(1951); STREETCAR NAMED DESIRE, A(1951); DIPLOMATIC COURIER(1952); OPERATION SECRET(1952); RUBY GENTRY(1952); I CONFESS(1953); TAKE THE HIGH GROUND(1953); ON THE WATERFRONT(1954); PHANTOM OF THE RUE MORGUE(1954); BABY DOLL(1956); BOMBERS B-52(1957); FEAR STRIKES OUT(1957); TIME LIMIT(1957), d; HANGING TREE, THE(1959); GREAT IMPOSTOR, THE(1960); POLLYANNA(1960); ONE-EYED JACKS(1961); PARRISH(1961); ALL FALL DOWN(1962); BIRDMAN OF ALCATRAZ(1962); GYPSY(1962); HOW THE WEST WAS WON(1962); COME FLY WITH ME(1963); CHEYENNE AUTUMN(1964); DEAD RINGER(1964); CINCINNATI KID, THE(1965); MURDERERS' ROW(1966); NEVADA SMITH(1966); ADVENTURES OF BULLWHIP GRIFFIN, THE(1967); BILLION DOLLAR BRAIN(1967, Brit.); HOTEL(1967); BLUE(1968); HOT MILLIONS(1968, Brit.); PATTON(1970); CAT O'NINE TAILS(1971, Ital./Ger./Fr.); WILD ROVERS(1971); SUMMERTIME KILLER(1973); BEYOND THE POSEIDON ADVENTURE(1979); METEOR(1979); STING II, THE(1983); TWILIGHT TIME(1983, U.S./Yugo.)
Cpl. Karl Malden
WINGED VICTORY(1944)

Maria Malden-Madsen
PLAYGIRLS AND THE BELLBOY, THE(1962,Ger.)
Roberto Maldera
NIGHT EVELYN CAME OUT OF THE GRAVE, THE(1973, Ital.)
Sheldon Maldoff
MARCO POLO JUNIOR(1973, Aus.), w, m/1
Angel Maldonado
MASSACRE(1956)
Joseph Maldonado
1984
DELIVERY BOYS(1984)
Ruben Maldonado
HAWAII CALLS(1938)
Ruth Maleczech
1984
FAR FROM POLAND(1984)
Irina Maleeva
UNION CITY(1980)
Lena Malena
HELL'S ANGELS(1930); WAY FOR A SAILOR(1930)
Silents
TEMPEST(1928)
Misc. Silents
DIAMOND HANDCUFFS(1928); TROPIC MADNESS(1928)
Andrea Malendrinas
COCKLESHELL HEROES, THE(1955)
Maleno Malenotti
LOVE SPECIALIST, THE(1959, Ital.), p; SAVAGE INNOCENTS, THE(1960, Brit.), p; MADAME(1963, Fr./Ital./Span.), p; ARABELLA(1969, U.S./Ital.), p
Patrick Maleon
GREEN ROOM, THE(1979, Fr.)
Luigi Malerba
GIRL AND THE GENERAL, THE(1967, Fr./Ital.), w; MATCHLESS(1967, Ital.), w; CATCH AS CATCH CAN(1968, Ital.), w
Art Malesci
1984
WHERE THE BOYS ARE '84(1984)
Arti Malesci
SPRING BREAK(1983), stunts
Telo Malese
1984
SILENT ONE, THE(1984, New Zealand)
Arthur Malet
CONVICTS FOUR(1962); MAN FROM GALVESTON, THE(1964); MARY POP-PINS(1964); KING RAT(1965); LT. ROBIN CRUSOE, U.S.N.(1966); MUNSTER, GO HOME(1966); PENELOPE(1966); IN THE HEAT OF THE NIGHT(1967); VANISHING POINT(1971); CULPEPPER CATTLE COMPANY, THE(1972); ACE ELI AND RODGER OF THE SKIES(1973); YOUNG FRANKENSTEIN(1974); HALLOWEEN(1978); HEAV-EN CAN WAIT(1978); SAVAGE HARVEST(1981); SECRET OF NIMH, THE(1982)
1984
CITY HEAT(1984); OH GOD! YOU DEVIL(1984)
Frank Malet
DESERT HAWK, THE(1950); MILKMAN, THE(1950)
Laurent Malet
BLOOD RELATIVES(1978, Fr./Can.); ANGRY MAN, THE(1979 Fr./Can.); QUE-RELLE(1983, Ger./Fr.)
Pierre Malet
LA NUIT DE VARENNES(1983, Fr./Ital.)
1984
BASILEUS QUARTET(1984, Ital.)
Roget Malet
BIQUEFARRE(1983, Fr.)
Irinia Maleva
WEB OF THE SPIDER(1972, Ital./Fr./Ger.)
Alan Maley
COMING-OUT PARTY, A(, set d; LOVE BUG, THE(1968), spec eff; BEDKNOBS AND BROOMSTICKS(1971), spec eff; HERBIE RIDES AGAIN(1974), spec eff
D. Maley
Misc. Silents
LURE OF THE WEST(1925); CYCLONE BOB(1926)
Denman Maley
Misc. Silents
OLD HOMESTEAD, THE(1916); ROLLING STONES(1916)
Gloria Maley
HORROR PLANET(1982, Brit.), w
Laila Maley
LITTLEST OUTLAW, THE(1955)
Len Maley
GIVE A DOG A BONE(1967, Brit.)
Nick Maley
SUPERMAN(1978), makeup; HORROR PLANET(1982, Brit.), w, makeup; KRULL(1983), makeup
Peggy June Maley
MIDNIGHT STORY, THE(1957)
Peggy Maley
MEET THE PEOPLE(1944); SINCE YOU WENT AWAY(1944); THIRTY SECONDS OVER TOKYO(1944); TWO GIRLS AND A SAILOR(1944); ANCHORS AWEIGH(1945); HARVEY GIRLS, THE(1946); THRILL OF BRAZIL, THE(1946); DOWN TO EARTH(1947); I WANT YOU(1951); LADY SAYS NO, THE(1951); BIGA-MIST,THE(1953); WILD ONE, THE(1953); DRIVE A CROOKED ROAD(1954); GYPSY COLT(1954); HUMAN DESIRE(1954); I DIED A THOUSAND TIMES(1955); MOON-FLEET(1955); BROTHERS RICO, THE(1957); GUNS OF FORT PETTICOAT, THE(1957); MAN ON THE PROWL(1957); GUN RUNNERS, THE(1958); LIVE FAST, DIE YOUNG(1958); OKEFENOKEE(1960)
Sean Maley
DIRTY HARRY(1971)
Marina Malfatti
MISTRESS FOR THE SUMMER, A(1964, Fr./Ital.); MORE THAN A MIRACLE(1967, Ital./Fr.); NIGHT EVELYN CAME OUT OF THE GRAVE, THE(1973, Ital.)

Malia
RETURN TO PARADISE(1953)
Vasiliki Maliaros
EXORCIST, THE(1973)
John Jack Malick
2001: A SPACE ODYSSEY(1968, U.S./Brit.), spec eff
Terence Malick
DEADHEAD MILES(1982), w
Terrance Malick
DAYS OF HEAVEN(1978), d&w
Terrence Malick
BADLANDS(1974), p,d&w
Terry Malick
POCKET MONEY(1972), a, w
Wendie Malick
LITTLE SEX, A(1982)
Mark Malicz
DESPERATE ONES, THE(1968 U.S./Span.); BEFORE WINTER COMES(1969, Brit.); BROTHERLY LOVE(1970, Brit.); FIDDLER ON THE ROOF(1971); PUPPET ON A CHAIN(1971, Brit.)
Lisette Malidor
TROUT, THE(1982, Fr.)
Jean-Louis Maligne
SLOGAN(1970, Fr.), ph
Art Malik
1984
PASSAGE TO INDIA, A(1984, Brit.)
Athar Malik
ARABIAN ADVENTURE(1979, Brit.); RICHARD'S THINGS(1981, Brit.)
Kunlan Malik
NINE HOURS TO RAMA(1963, U.S./Brit.)
Myra Malik
WALK WITH LOVE AND DEATH, A(1969)
Serge Malik
INQUISITOR, THE(1982, Fr.)
H. Malikoff
Misc. Silents
SPY OF MME. POMPADOUR(1929, Ger.)
Nicholas Malikoff
Misc. Silents
APACHES OF PARIS(1928, Fr.), d
Nikolai Malikoff
Misc. Silents
RASPUTIN(1930)
Kevork Malikyan
MAN WHO HAUNTED HIMSELF, THE(1970, Brit.); MIDNIGHT EXPRESS(1978, Brit.); TRENCHCOAT(1983)
Eddie Malin
KID FOR TWO FARTHINGS, A(1956, Brit.); NIGHT TO REMEMBER, A(1958, Brit.); OPERATION CUPID(1960, Brit.); HARD DAY'S NIGHT, A(1964, Brit.); HOW TO STEAL A MILLION(1966)
Edward Malin
GREED OF WILLIAM HART, THE(1948, Brit.); END OF THE ROAD, THE(1954, Brit.); TWO-HEADED SPY, THE(1959, Brit.); INN FOR TROUBLE(1960, Brit.); PER-CY(1971, Brit.)
Harold Malin
HARASSED HERO, THE(1954, Brit.)
Howard Malin
JUBILEE(1978, Brit.), p
Kym Malin
JOYSTICKS(1983)
1984
MIKE'S MURDER(1984)
Judith Malina
DOG DAY AFTERNOON(1975)
Luba Malina
MEXICAN HAYRIDE(1948)
Margh Malina
PLAYGIRLS AND THE BELLBOY, THE(1962,Ger.), w
Thomas Malinari
LOVES OF CARMEN, THE(1948)
Charles Malinda
AFRICA–TEXAS STYLE!(1967 U.S./Brit.)
Jim Malinda
ONCE(1974)
Alain Maline
1984
LA PETIT SIRENE(1984, Fr.), m
Ardeta Malino
Silents
STEELHEART(1921)
Vera Malinovskava
Misc. Silents
BEAR'S WEDDING, THE(1926, USSR)
L. Malinovskaya
KATERINA IZMAILOVA(1969, USSR)
Vera Malinovskaya
Misc. Silents
STATION MASTER, THE(1928, USSR)
Geoffrey H. Malins
LONDON MELODY(1930, Brit.), p,d&w
Silents
GIRL FROM DOWNING STREET, THE(1918, Brit.), d&w; PEEP BEHIND THE SCENES, A(1918, Brit.), d; PATRICIA BRENT, SPINSTER(1919 Brit.), d; ALL THE WINNERS(1920, Brit.), d; SAFETY FIRST(1926, Brit.), w
Misc. Silents
GREATER LOVE, THE(1919, Brit.), d; GOLDEN WEB, THE(1920, Brit.), d; BLUFF(1921, Brit.), d; WATCHING EYES(1921, Brit.), a, d; FORTUNE'S FOOL(1922, Brit.), d; RECOIL, THE(1922, Brit.), d; WAY OF A WOMAN, THE(1925, Brit.), d

Mark Malinsuskee
DRIVE, HE SAID(1971)

Adele Malis
KINGDOM OF THE SPIDERS(1977)

Claire Malis
HUSBANDS(1970)
1984
HEARTBREAKERS(1984)

Cy Malis
LADIES' DAY(1943); DESTINATION TOKYO(1944); NIGHT EDITOR(1946); FRAMED(1947); JOHNNY O'CLOCK(1947); LIKELY STORY, A(1947); WHIPLASH(1948); UNDERCOVER MAN, THE(1949); FULLER BRUSH GIRL, THE(1950); COURT-MARTIAL OF BILLY MITCHELL, THE(1955)

Ivan Malishevsky
MILITARY SECRET(1945, USSR)

N. Malishyovskiy
MAGIC VOYAGE OF SINBAD, THE(1962, USSR)

Martin Malivoire
HUMONGOUS(1982, Can.), spec eff; INCUBUS, THE(1982, Can.), spec eff; QUEST FOR FIRE(1982, Fr./Can.), spec eff; STRANGE INVADERS(1983), spec eff
1984
BAY BOY(1984, Can.), spec eff

Don Malkames
VICTIMS OF PERSECUTION(1933), ph; CRY MURDER(1936), ph; BEWARE(1946), ph; HI-DE-HO(1947), ph; MIRACLE IN HARLEM(1948), ph; JIGSAW(1949), ph; PROJECT X(1949), ph; SARUMBA(1950), ph; SO YOUNG, SO BAD(1950), ph; ST. BENNY THE DIP(1951), ph; THAT MAN FROM TANGIER(1953), ph; BURGLAR, THE(1956), ph

Donald Malkames
PIE IN THE SKY(1964), ph

Karl Malkames
HARVEY MIDDLEMAN, FIREMAN(1965), ph

Don Malkaunes
CITIZEN SAINT(1947), ph

Jack Malken
NESTING, THE(1981), m

Malkevich-Khodakovskaya
Misc. Silents
BEILIS CASE, THE(1917, USSR)

Irena Malkiewicz
LOTNA(1966, Pol.); PASSENGER, THE(1970, Pol.)

Barry Malkin
FAT SPY(1966), ed; WHO IS HARRY KELLERMAN AND WHY IS HE SAYING THOSE TERRIBLE THINGS ABOUT ME?(1971), ed; COPS AND ROBBERS(1973), ed; GODFATHER, THE, PART II(1974), ed; ONE SUMMER LOVE(1976), ed; SOMEBODY KILLED HER HUSBAND(1978), ed; LAST EMBRACE(1979), ed; ONE-TRICK PONY(1980), ed; WINDOWS(1980), ed; FOUR FRIENDS(1981), ed, ed; HAMMETT(1982), ed; RUMBLE FISH(1983), ed
1984
COTTON CLUB, THE(1984), ed

Blackie Malkin
RAIN PEOPLE, THE(1969), ed

Sam Malkin
VIDEODROME(1983, Can.)

Vicki Malkin
HARUM SCARUM(1965)

George Malkine
FIRST OFFENCE(1936, Brit.)

George Malko
ALIEN THUNDER(1975, US/Can.), w; LUNA(1979, Ital.), w; DOGS OF WAR, THE(1980, Brit.), w

John Malkovich
1984
KILLING FIELDS, THE(1984, Brit.); PLACES IN THE HEART(1984)

David Mall
SPRING FEVER(1983, Can.)

A. Malla
TEXICAN, THE(1966, U.S./Span.)

Cedric Mallabey
MAN IN GREY, THE(1943, Brit.), m; MAN OF EVIL(1948, Brit.), m

George Mallaby
PETERSEN(1974, Aus.); END PLAY(1975, Aus.); ELIZA FRASER(1976, Aus.)
Misc. Talkies
OUTBREAK OF HOSTILITIES(1979)

Vivian Mallah
YOUNG MAN WITH A HORN(1950)

Aubrey Mallalieu
WHAT HAPPENED TO HARKNESS(1934, Brit.); CROSS CURRENTS(1935, Brit.); MUSIC HATH CHARMS(1935, Brit.); RIVERSIDE MURDER, THE(1935, Brit.); ALL THAT GLITTERS(1936, Brit.); LOVE AT SEA(1936, Brit.); NOT SO DUSTY(1936, Brit.); NOTHING LIKE PUBLICITY(1936, Brit.); PRISON BREAKER(1936, Brit.); STAR FELL FROM HEAVEN, A(1936, Brit.); SUCH IS LIFE(1936, Brit.); TOUCH OF THE MOON, A(1936, Brit.); BLACK TULIP, THE(1937, Brit.); CHANGE FOR A SOVEREIGN(1937, Brit.); FIFTY-SHILLING BOXER(1937, Brit.); HOLIDAY'S END(1937, Brit.); KEEP FIT(1937, Brit.); LAST CHANCE, THE(1937, Brit.); MAYFAIR MELODY(1937, Brit.); PATRICIA GETS HER MAN(1937, Brit.); PEARLS BRING TEARS(1937, Brit.); STRANGE ADVENTURES OF MR. SMITH, THE(1937, Brit.); TALK OF THE DEVIL(1937, Brit.); TENTH MAN, THE(1937, Brit.); WEEKEND MILLIONAIRE(1937, Brit.); WHEN THE DEVIL WAS WELL(1937, Brit.); ALMOST A HONEYMOON(1938, Brit.); CLAYDON TREASURE MYSTERY, THE(1938, Brit.); COMING OF AGE(1938, Brit.); DANGEROUS MEDICINE(1938, Brit.); GABLES MYSTERY, THE(1938, Brit.); HIS LORDSHIP REGRETS(1938, Brit.); MIRACLES DO HAPPEN(1938, Brit.); PAID IN ERROR(1938, Brit.); RAT, THE(1938, Brit.); RETURN OF CAROL DEANE, THE(1938, Brit.); RETURN OF THE FROG, THE(1938, Brit.); REVERSE BE MY LOT, THE(1938, Brit.); SAVE A LITTLE SUNSHINE(1938, Brit.); SIMPLY TERRIFIC(1938, Brit.); THANK EVANS(1938, Brit.); YOU'RE THE DOCTOR(1938, Brit.); ALL AT SEA(1939, Brit.); DEAD MEN ARE DANGEROUS(1939, Brit.); FACE AT THE WINDOW, THE(1939, Brit.); HIS LORDSHIP GOES TO PRESS(1939, Brit.); ME AND MY PAL(1939, Brit.); MURDER WILL OUT(1939, Brit.); BRIGGS FAMILY, THE(1940, Brit.); BULLDOG SEES IT THROUGH(1940, Brit.); SO

THIS IS LONDON(1940, Brit.); TWENTY-ONE DAYS TOGETHER(1940, Brit.); WHO IS GUILTY?(1940, Brit.); CHAMBER OF HORRORS(1941, Brit.); COURAGEOUS MR. PENN, THE(1941, Brit.); FACING THE MUSIC(1941, Brit.); GERT AND DAISY'S WEEKEND(1941, Brit.); ASKING FOR TROUBLE(1942, Brit.); GOOSE STEPS OUT, THE(1942, Brit.); LET THE PEOPLE SING(1942, Brit.); PIMPERNEL SMITH(1942, Brit.); UNPUBLISHED STORY(1942, Brit.); WE'LL MEET AGAIN(1942, Brit.); WINGS AND THE WOMAN(1942, Brit.); YOUNG MR. PITT, THE(1942, Brit.); ADVENTURE IN BLACKMAIL(1943, Brit.); LAMP STILL BURNS, THE(1943, Brit.); MY LEARNED FRIEND(1943, Brit.); RHYTHM SERENADE(1943, Brit.); SQUADRON LEADER X(1943, Brit.); CHAMPAGNE CHARLIE(1944, Brit.); HE SNOOPS TO CONQUER(1944, Brit.); KISS THE BRIDE GOODBYE(1944, Brit.); UNCENSORED(1944, Brit.); YELLOW CANARY, THE(1944, Brit.); ADVENTURE FOR TWO(1945, Brit.); FOR YOU ALONE(1945, Brit.); GIRL IN A MILLION, A(1946, Brit.); HONEYMOON HOTEL(1946, Brit.); I'LL TURN TO YOU(1946, Brit.); MURDER IN REVERSE(1946, Brit.); SCHOOL FOR SECRETS(1946, Brit.); YANK IN LONDON, A(1946, Brit.); FRIEDA(1947, Brit.); GHOSTS OF BERKELEY SQUARE(1947, Brit.); MASTER OF BANKDAM, THE(1947, Brit.); MEET ME AT DAWN(1947, Brit.); COUNTER BLAST(1948, Brit.); DEVIL'S PLOT, THE(1948, Brit.); FATAL NIGHT, THE(1948, Brit.); HATTER'S CASTLE(1948, Brit.); QUEEN OF SPADES(1948, Brit.); FACTS OF LOVE(1949, Brit.); SARABAND(1949, Brit.); WHILE THE SUN SHINES(1950, Brit.); WINSLOW BOY, THE(1950)

Alf Malland
ONE DAY IN THE LIFE OF IVAN DENISOVICH(1971, U.S./Brit./Norway); TERRORISTS, THE(1975, Brit.)

Grahame Mallard
LAND THAT TIME FORGOT, THE(1975, Brit.)

Mario Mallarno
LA DOLCE VITA(1961, Ital./Fr.)

Stephen Mallatratt
CHARRIOTS OF FIRE(1981, Brit.)

Louis Malle
LOVERS, THE(1959, Fr.), d, w; FRANTIC(1961, Fr.), d, w; ZAZIE(1961, Fr.), p&d, w; VERY PRIVATE AFFAIR, A(1962, Fr./Ital.), a, d, w; FIRE WITHIN, THE(1964, Fr./Ital.), d&w; VIVA MARIA(1965, Fr./Ital.), p, d, w; THIEF OF PARIS, THE(1967, Fr./Ital.), p&d, w; SPIRITS OF THE DEAD(1969, Fr./Ital.), d, w; VERY CURIOUS GIRL, A(1970, Fr.); MURMUR OF THE HEART(1971, Fr./Ital./Ger.), d&w; LACOMBE, LUCIEN(1974), p&d, w; BLACK MOON(1975, Fr.), p&d, w; PRETTY BABY(1978), p&d, w; ATLANTIC CITY(1981, U.S./Can.), d; MY DINNER WITH ANDRE(1981), d
1984
CRACKERS(1984), d

Martine Malle
LISTEN, LET'S MAKE LOVE(1969, Fr./Ital.)
1984
ALPHABET CITY(1984)

Vincent Malle
MURMUR OF THE HEART(1971, Fr./Ital./Ger.), p

Werner Malle
IT HAPPENED HERE(1966, Brit.)

Meetook Mallee
WHITE DAWN, THE(1974)

Bruce Mallen
HIGH COUNTRY, THE(1981, Can.), p

Clarke Mallery
1001 ARABIAN NIGHTS(1959), anim

Miles Malleso
WOMAN DECIDES, THE(1932, Brit.), w

Miles Malleson
VICTORIA THE GREAT(1937, Brit.), a, w; CHILDREN OF CHANCE(1930, Brit.), w; TWO WORLD(1930, Brit.), w; YELLOW MASK, THE(1930, Brit.), w; "W" PLAN, THE(1931, Brit.), w; FAREWELL TO LOVE(1931, Brit.), a, w; NIGHT BIRDS(1931, Brit.), w; NIGHT IN MONTMARTE, A(1931, Brit.), w; SALLY IN OUR ALLEY(1931, Brit.), w; BLUE DANUBE(1932, Brit.), w; LOVE CONTRACT, THE(1932, Brit.); LOVE ON WHEELS(1932, Brit.); MAYOR'S NEST, THE(1932, Brit.); MONEY MEANS NOTHING(1932, Brit.), a, w; SIGN OF FOUR, THE(1932, Brit.); WATER GYPSIES, THE(1932, Brit.), w; PERFECT UNDERSTANDING(1933, Brit.), w; STRANGE EVIDENCE(1933, Brit.), a, w; SUMMER LIGHTNING(1933, Brit.), a, w; LAZYBONES(1935, Brit.); LORNA DOONE(1935, Brit.), w; NELL GWYN(1935, Brit.), a, w; RUNAWAY QUEEN, THE(1935, Brit.), a, w; VINTAGE WINE(1935, Brit.); 39 STEPS, THE(1935, Brit.); LADY JANE GREY(1936, Brit.), a, w; PEG OF OLD DRURY(1936, Brit.), w; RHODES(1936, Brit.), w; TROUBLE AHEAD(1936, Brit.), w; ACTION FOR SLANDER(1937, Brit.), w; KNIGHT WITHOUT ARMOR(1937, Brit.), w; RAT, THE(1938, Brit.), w; ROYAL DIVORCE, A(1938, Brit.), w; SIXTY GLORIOUS YEARS(1938, Brit.), w; FOR FREEDOM(1940, Brit.), w; LION HAS WINGS, THE(1940, Brit.); THIEF OF BAGHDAD, THE(1940, Brit.), a, w; MAJOR BARBARA(1941, Brit.); THIS WAS PARIS(1942, Brit.); UNPUBLISHED STORY(1942, Brit.); WINGS AND THE WOMAN(1942, Brit.), a, w; ADVENTURES OF TARTU(1943, Brit.), w; GENTLE SEX, THE(1943, Brit.); SPITFIRE(1943, Brit.), a, w; SQUADRON LEADER X(1943, Brit.), w; THUNDER ROCK(1944, Brit.); YELLOW CANARY, THE(1944, Brit.), w; ADVENTURE FOR TWO(1945, Brit.); SPELL OF AMY NUGENT(1945, Brit.), w; THEY MET IN THE DARK(1945, Brit.), w; DEAD OF NIGHT(1946, Brit.); JOURNEY TOGETHER(1946, Brit.); IDOL OF PARIS(1948, Brit.); MARK OF CAIN, THE(1948, Brit.); ONE NIGHT WITH YOU(1948, Brit); QUEEN OF SPADES(1948, Brit.); CARDBOARD CAVALIER, THE(1949, Brit.); HISTORY OF MR. POLLY, THE(1949, Brit.); KIND HEARTS AND CORONETS(1949, Brit.); SARABAND(1949, Brit.); WOMAN HATER(1949, Brit.); GOLDEN SALAMANDER(1950, Brit.); PERFECT WOMAN, THE(1950, Brit.); STAGE FRIGHT(1950, Brit.); WHILE THE SUN SHINES(1950, Brit.); CHRISTMAS CAROL, A(1951, Brit.); IMPORTANCE OF BEING EARNEST, THE(1952, Brit.); MAGIC BOX, THE(1952, Brit.); MAN IN THE WHITE SUIT, THE(1952); MR. LORD SAYS NO(1952, Brit.); TRAIN OF EVENTS(1952, Brit.); TREASURE HUNT(1952, Brit.); ASSASSIN, THE(1953, Brit.); CAPTAIN'S PARADISE, THE(1953, Brit.); FOLLY TO BE WISE(1953); TRENT'S LAST CASE(1953, Brit.); WOMAN'S ANGLE, THE(1954, Brit.); KING'S RHAPSODY(1955, Brit.); DRY ROT(1956, Brit.); MAN WHO NEVER WAS, THE(1956, Brit.); PRIVATE'S PROGRESS(1956, Brit.); WEE GEORDIE(1956, Brit.); ADMIRABLE CRICHTON, THE(1957, Brit.); BROTHERS IN LAW(1957, Brit.); SILKEN AFFAIR, THE(1957, Brit.); ALL AT SEA(1958, Brit.); BACHELOR OF HEARTS(1958, Brit.); BEHIND THE MASK(1958, Brit.); HAPPY IS THE BRIDE(1958, Brit.); HORROR OF DRACULA, THE(1958, Brit.); THREE MEN IN A BOAT(1958, Brit.); YOUR PAST IS SHOWING(1958, Brit.); GIDEON OF SCOTLAND YARD(1959, Brit.); HOUND OF THE BASKERVILLES, THE(1959, Brit.); I'M ALL RIGHT, JACK(1959, Brit.); AND THE SAME TO YOU(1960, Brit.); BRIDES OF

DRACULA, THE(1960, Brit.); CAPTAIN'S TABLE, THE(1960, Brit.); DAY THEY ROBBED THE BANK OF ENGLAND, THE(1960, Brit.); KIDNAPPED(1960); MAN IN A COCKED HAT(1960, Bri.); PEEPING TOM(1960, Brit.); DOUBLE BUNK(1961, Brit.); GO TO BLAZES(1962, Brit.); PHANTOM OF THE OPERA, THE(1962, Brit.); POSTMAN'S KNOCK(1962, Brit.); FURY AT SMUGGLERS BAY(1963, Brit.); HEAVENS ABOVE!(1963, Brit.); HELLFIRE CLUB, THE(1963, Brit.); CIRCUS WORLD(1964); FIRST MEN IN THE MOON(1964, Brit.); JOLLY BAD FELLOW, A(1964, Brit.); MURDER AHOY(1964, Brit.); BRAIN, THE(1965, Ger./Brit.); YOU MUST BE JOKING!(1965, Brit.)
Misc. Silents
HEADMASTER, THE(1921, Brit.)

Harold Mallet
HOT ANGEL, THE(1958)

Jane Mallet
UTILITIES(1983, Can.)

Robert Mallet
VALIANT, THE(1962, Brit./Ital.), w

Sophie Mallet
INNOCENTS IN PARIS(1955, Brit.); PEEK-A-BOO(1961, Fr.)

Bob Mallett
BOYS IN COMPANY C, THE(1978, U.S./Hong Kong); NIGHT GAMES(1980)

George Mallett
Silents
SINGLE MAN, THE(1919, Brit.)

Jack Arundel Mallett
IVORY HUNTER(1952, Brit.)

Jane Mallett
LOVE AT FIRST SIGHT(1977, Can.); IMPROPER CHANNELS(1981, Can.)

Stephen Mallett
SCRAMBLE(1970, Brit.); MELODY(1971, Brit.)

Steven Mallett
ALL AT SEA(1970, Brit.)

Tania Mallett
GOLDFINGER(1964, Brit.)

Gaston Malletti
MINIVER STORY, THE(1950, Brit./U.S.), cos

Bill Malley
LATE LIZ, THE(1971), art d; STEAGLE, THE(1971), art d; PRIME CUT(1972), art d; EXORCIST, THE(1973), prod d; ALEX AND THE GYPSY(1976), prod d; CITIZENS BAND(1977), art d; DEFIANCE(1980), prod d; NINTH CONFIGURATION, THE(1980), prod d; MOMMIE DEAREST(1981), prod d; DEAL OF THE CENTURY(1983), prod d; STAR CHAMBER, THE(1983), prod d
1984
HOUSE OF GOD, THE(1984), prod d; PROTOCOL(1984), prod d

Billy Malley
FURY, THE(1978), prod d

Doris Malley
CORREGIDOR(1943), w

Pat O. Malley
THRU DIFFERENT EYES(1942)

William Malley
GET TO KNOW YOUR RABBIT(1972), art d

Giuseppe Mallia
PULP(1972, Brit.)

Aris Malliagross
LOVE CYCLES(1969, Gr.)

Umesh Mallick
GUY CALLED CAESAR, A(1962, Brit.), w; MAN WHO COULDN'T WALK, THE(1964, Brit.), p, w

Umesh Mallik
GUY CALLED CAESAR, A(1962, Brit.), p

Dan Mallinger
HUNGRY WIVES(1973)

Geoffrey H. Mallins
Silents
WATCHING EYES(1921)

Matthew Mallinson
FIST OF FEAR, TOUCH OF DEATH(1980), d, w, ed

Rory Mallinson
PRIDE OF THE MARINES(1945); CLOAK AND DAGGER(1946); CRY WOLF(1947); DARK PASSAGE(1947); DEEP VALLEY(1947); FOR YOU I DIE(1947); NORA PRENTISS(1947); POSSESSED(1947); ROAD TO THE BIG HOUSE(1947); CHECKERED COAT, THE(1948); DOCKS OF NEW ORLEANS(1948); HE WALKED BY NIGHT(1948); I WOULDN'T BE IN YOUR SHOES(1948); KING OF THE BANDITS(1948); LAST OF THE WILD HORSES(1948); OPEN SECRET(1948); PANHANDLE(1948); BLONDE ICE(1949); EL DORADO PASS(1949); PRINCE OF THE PLAINS(1949); ROSEANNA McCOY(1949); SOUTH OF RIO(1949); TASK FORCE(1949); TRAPPED(1949); WAKE OF THE RED WITCH(1949); WOMAN'S SECRET, A(1949); COUNTY FAIR(1950); DAMNED DON'T CRY, THE(1950); SALT LAKE RAIDERS(1950); SHORT GRASS(1950); CAVALRY SCOUT(1951); FINGERPRINTS DON'T LIE(1951); FORT DODGE STAMPEDE(1951); PURPLE HEART DIARY(1951); RODEO KING AND THE SENORITA(1951); THREE DESPERATE MEN(1951); YOU'RE IN THE NAVY NOW(1951); BRAVE WARRIOR(1952); HELLGATE(1952); LARAMIE MOUNTAINS(1952); MAN BEHIND THE GUN, THE(1952); MONTANA BELLE(1952); SNIPER, THE(1952); SPRINGFIELD RIFLE(1952); WACO(1952); YANK IN INDO-CHINA, A(1952); COW COUNTRY(1953); GREAT JESSE JAMES RAID, THE(1953); KILLER APE(1953); SAFARI DRUMS(1953); JESSE JAMES VERSUS THE DALTONS(1954); KILLER LEOPARD(1954); SEMINOLE UPRISING(1955); SHOTGUN(1955); KENTUCKY RIFLE(1956); SHOOT-OUT AT MEDICINE BEND(1957); SPOILERS OF THE FOREST(1957); KING OF THE WILD STALLIONS(1959); WESTBOUND(1959)

Roy Mallinson
COUNTY FAIR(1950)

Rory Mallison
UNSUSPECTED, THE(1947); DENVER KID, THE(1948); RIM OF THE CANYON(1949); ACCORDING TO MRS. HOYLE(1951)

G.R. Malloch
DEVIL'S MAZE, THE(1929, Brit.), w

Yannick Malloire
INNOCENTS IN PARIS(1955, Brit.)

John Mallon
WHERE THERE'S LIFE(1947); SORROWFUL JONES(1949)

Wil Mallone
DEATHLINE(1973, Brit.), m

Jose Mallorqui
FEW BULLETS MORE, A(1968, Ital./Span.), w

Barbara Mallory
IS THIS TRIP REALLY NECESSARY?(1970); TODD KILLINGS, THE(1971); JONI(1980)
Misc. Talkies
BLOOD OF THE IRON MAIDEN(1969)

Bolton Mallory
YOU SAID A MOUTHFUL(1932), w

Boots Mallory
HANDLE WITH CARE(1932); CARNIVAL LADY(1933); HELLO SISTER!(1933); HUMANITY(1933); BIG RACE, THE(1934); POWDERSMOKE RANGE(1935); SING SING NIGHTS(1935); HERE'S FLASH CASEY(1937)

Carole Mallory
STEPFORD WIVES, THE(1975); TAKE THIS JOB AND SHOVE IT(1981)

Chad Mallory
KID MONK BARONI(1952); SEA TIGER(1952); THEM!(1954)

Dolores Mallory
LYDIA BAILEY(1952)

Doris C. Mallory
Misc. Silents
CLOTHES(1924)

Drue Mallory
PLEASE BELIEVE ME(1950); THREE CAME HOME(1950)

Edward Mallory
DIAMOND HEAD(1962); EXPERIMENT IN TERROR(1962); UNDERWATER CITY, THE(1962); WALK ON THE WILD SIDE(1962)

Jay Mallory [Joyce Carey]
GIVE ME YOUR HEART(1936), w

Joan Mallory
LAS VEGAS STORY, THE(1952)

John Mallory
FLYING LEATHERNECKS(1951); ONE MINUTE TO ZERO(1952); PACE THAT THRILLS, THE(1952)

Kay Mallory
BLONDIE KNOWS BEST(1946)

Monica Mallory
LATE AT NIGHT(1946, Brit.)

Shawn Mallory
SPRING AFFAIR(1960)

Wayne Mallory
REPRISAL(1956); STORM RIDER, THE(1957); BULLWHIP(1958)

Yolande Mallott
DEVIL BAT, THE(1941)

Ace Malloy
LAWLESS COWBOYS(1952)

Doris Malloy
MAD PARADE, THE(1931), w; AMATEUR DADDY(1932), w; BONDAGE(1933), w; GAMBLING LADY(1934), w; DIAMOND JIM(1935), w; HIS NIGHT OUT(1935), w; I AM A THIEF(1935), w; KING SOLOMON OF BROADWAY(1935), w; MR. DYNAMITE(1935), w; PRINCESS O'HARA(1935), w; REMEMBER LAST NIGHT(1935), w; HUMAN CARGO(1936), w; TOO MANY PARENTS(1936), w; TWO IN A CROWD(1936), w; LOVE ON TOAST(1937), w; MIDNIGHT MADONNA(1937), w; ON SUCH A NIGHT(1937), w; OUTCAST(1937), w; MICKEY, THE KID(1939), w; NOBODY'S CHILDREN(1940), w; RIDIN' ON A RAINBOW(1941), w; HITLER'S MADMAN(1943), w; MY SON, THE HERO(1943), w; SWING OUT THE BLUES(1943), w

Francetta Malloy
LAS VEGAS NIGHTS(1941)

J.L. Malloy
IT COMES UP LOVE(1943), m

James Malloy
LONG NIGHT, THE(1976), ph

John Malloy
STORK TALK(1964, Brit.); FINAL CHAPTER–WALKING TALL zero(1977); I WANNA HOLD YOUR HAND(1978); CANNERY ROW(1982)

Les Malloy
DISC JOCKEY(1951)

Marilyn Malloy
FEAR STRIKES OUT(1957)

Mickey Malloy
TILL THE CLOUDS ROLL BY(1946)

Mike Malloy
1984
REFLECTIONS(1984, Brit.), ph

Peggy Malloy
WORDS AND MUSIC(1929)

Thomas Malloy
UNMASKED(1929), ph
Silents
CLIMBERS, THE(1919), ph; NO MOTHER TO GUIDE HER(1923), ph; AVENGING SHADOW, THE(1928), ed; HARVEST OF HATE, THE(1929), ed; HOOFBEATS OF VENGEANCE(1929), ed; PLUNGING HOOFS(1929), ed; WILD BLOOD(1929), ed

Tom Malloy
Silents
ADVENTURE SHOP, THE(1918), ph; HEART OF MARYLAND, THE(1921), ph; ANY WIFE(1922), ph; MOONSHINE VALLEY(1922), ph; SHACKLES OF GOLD(1922), ph; WITHOUT FEAR(1922), ph

Olga Mallsnerd
1984
2010(1984)

Dimo Mally
DIVA(1982, Fr.)

Leo Mally
CASTLE, THE(1969, Ger.)
Veneta Mally
DIVA(1982, Fr.)
Gunnar Malm
DRIVE, HE SAID(1971)
Mona Malm
SMILES OF A SUMMER NIGHT(1957, Swed.); ALL THESE WOMEN(1964, Swed.); FANNY AND ALEXANDER(1983, Swed./Fr./Ger.)
Bertil Malmberg
CRIME AND PUNISHMENT(1948, Swed.), w
Mark Malmborg
PRETTY MAIDS ALL IN A ROW(1971)
Lennart Malmer
ELVIRA MADIGAN(1967, Swed.)
Sixten Malmerfelt
Misc. Silents
SAGA OF GOSTA BERLING, THE(1924, Fr.)
Jan Malmsjo
LOVING COUPLES(1966, Swed.); SCENES FROM A MARRIAGE(1974, Swed.)
Jan Malmsjoe
FANNY AND ALEXANDER(1983, Swed./Fr./Ger.)
Vertil Malmstedt
Misc. Silents
KARIN, INGMAR'S DAUGHTER(1920, Swed.)
Berger Malmsten
TIME OF DESIRE, THE(1957, Swed.)
Birger Malmsten
48 HOURS TO LIVE(1960, Brit./Swed.); SECRETS OF WOMEN(1961, Swed.); DEVIL'S WANTON, THE(1962, Swed.); MAKE WAY FOR LILA(1962, Swed./Ger.); NIGHT IS MY FUTURE(1962, Swed.); SILENCE, THE(1964, Swed.); MASCULINE FEMININE(1966, Fr./Swed.)
Bruce Malmuth
FOREPLAY(1975), d; NIGHTHAWKS(1981), d; MAN WHO WASN'T THERE, THE(1983), a, d
1984
KARATE KID, THE(1984)
Rava Malmuth
RED, WHITE AND BLACK, THE(1970)
Matt Malneck
TO BEAT THE BAND(1935), m
Matty Malneck
QUARTERBACK, THE(1940), m
Matty Malnick
WITNESS FOR THE PROSECUTION(1957), m
Michael Malnick
DARWIN ADVENTURE, THE(1972, Brit.)
Susan Malnick
LENNY(1974)
Susie Malnik
FUNHOUSE, THE(1981)
Tony Malnowski
1984
ALIEN FACTOR, THE(1984)
Frank Malo
BOY SLAVES(1938)
Gina Malo
MAGIC NIGHT(1932, Brit.); KING OF THE RITZ(1933, Brit.); STRIKE IT RICH(1933, Brit.); WALTZ TIME(1933, Brit.); BRIDE OF THE LAKE(1934, Brit.); PRIVATE LIFE OF DON JUAN, THE(1934, Brit.); IN A MONASTERY GARDEN(1935); MY SONG FOR YOU(1935, Brit.); ALL IN(1936, Brit.); SOUTHERN ROSES(1936, Brit.); WHERE THERE'S A WILL(1936, Brit); IT'S A GRAND OLD WORLD(1937, Brit.); OVER SHE GOES(1937, Brit.); GANG, THE(1938, Brit.); HIS LORDSHIP REGRETS(1938, Brit.); TWO OF US, THE(1938, Brit.); CHAMBER OF HORRORS(1941, Brit.)
Jesse Malo
STAR DUST(1940), w
Pierre Malodon
Misc. Silents
SALAMMBO(1925, Fr.), d; LES DIEUX ONT SOIF(1926, Fr.), d
Peter Malof
1984
INITIATION, THE(1984)
Angus Malone
1984
RAZORBACK(1984, Aus.)
Cavan Malone
WHEN THE BOUGH BREAKS(1947, Brit.); MR. PERRIN AND MR. TRAILL(1948, Brit.); FURTHER UP THE CREEK!(1958, Brit.); LINDA(1960, Brit.); SQUADRON 633(1964, U.S./Brit.); 633 SQUADRON(1964)
Cindy Malone
WILD ON THE BEACH(1965)
Clancy Malone
JAIL BAIT(1954)
Dale Malone
HONEYMOON HOTEL(1964); QUICK, BEFORE IT MELTS(1964); WHERE WERE YOU WHEN THE LIGHTS WENT OUT?(1968)
Dan Malone
BOOTS OF DESTINY(1937), ed
Danny Malone
ROSE OF TRALEE(1938, Ireland)
Dorothy Malone
HIGHER AND HIGHER(1943); HOLLYWOOD CANTEEN(1944); SEVEN DAYS ASHORE(1944); SHOW BUSINESS(1944); STEP LIVELY(1944); TOO YOUNG TO KNOW(1945); BIG SLEEP, THE(1946); JANIE GETS MARRIED(1946); NIGHT AND DAY(1946); ONE SUNDAY AFTERNOON(1948); TO THE VICTOR(1948); TWO GUYS FROM TEXAS(1948); COLORADO TERRITORY(1949); FLAXY MARTIN(1949); SOUTH OF ST. LOUIS(1949); CONVICTED(1950); KILLER THAT STALKED NEW YORK, THE(1950); MRS. O'MALLEY AND MR. MALONE(1950); NEVADAN, THE(1950); SADDLE LEGION(1951); BUSHWHACKERS, THE(1952); JACK SLADE(1953); LAW AND ORDER(1953); SCARED STIFF(1953); TORPEDO ALLEY(1953);

FAST AND THE FURIOUS, THE(1954); LONE GUN, THE(1954); LOOPHOLE(1954); PRIVATE HELL 36(1954); PUSHOVER(1954); SECURITY RISK(1954); ARTISTS AND MODELS(1955); AT GUNPOINT(1955); BATTLE FLAME(1955); FIVE GUNS WEST(1955); SINCERELY YOURS(1955); TALL MAN RIDING(1955); YOUNG AT HEART(1955); PILLARS OF THE SKY(1956); TENSION AT TABLE ROCK(1956); WRITTEN ON THE WIND(1956); MAN OF A THOUSAND FACES(1957); QUANTEZ(1957); TARNISHED ANGELS, THE(1957); TIP ON A DEAD JOCKEY(1957); TOO MUCH, TOO SOON(1958); WARLOCK(1959); LAST VOYAGE, THE(1960); LAST SUNSET, THE(1961); BEACH PARTY(1963); FATE IS THE HUNTER(1964); ABDUCTION(1975); MAN WHO WOULD NOT DIE, THE(1975); GOLDEN RENDEZVOUS(1977); GOOD LUCK, MISS WYCKOFF(1979); WINTER KILLS(1979); DAY TIME ENDED, THE(1980, Span.); BEING, THE(1983)
Misc. Talkies
OFF YOUR ROCKER(1980)
Dudley Field Malone
MISSION TO MOSCOW(1943)
Florence Malone
Misc. Silents
STRONGEST, THE(1920)
Hal Malone
THIS LAND IS MINE(1943); BRUTE FORCE(1947)
Helen Malone
Silents
SUBURBAN, THE(1915)
Jessica Malone
UNCIVILISED(1937, Aus.)
Joe Malone
BIG FIX, THE(1947), w
Joel Malone
CRIME BY NIGHT(1944), w; SLIGHTLY SCANDALOUS(1946), w; APPOINTMENT WITH MURDER(1948), w; ARCTIC MANHUNT(1949), w; ILLEGAL ENTRY(1949), w; SOUTH SEA SINNER(1950), w; JUST ACROSS THE STREET(1952), w
John Malone
1984
DREAMSCAPE(1984)
Leigh Malone
GREAT MUPPET CAPER, THE(1981), art d
Micki Malone
WEEKEND OF FEAR(1966)
Mike Malone
PROFESSOR TIM(1957, Ireland)
Molly Malone
Silents
RESCUE, THE(1917); STOP THIEF(1920); JUST OUT OF COLLEGE(1921); MADE IN HEAVEN(1921); NOT GUILTY(1921); ACROSS THE DEAD-LINE(1922); FRESHIE, THE(1922); WESTBOUND(1924); KNOCKOUT KID, THE(1925)
Misc. Silents
CAR OF CHANCE, THE(1917); MARKED MAN, A(1917); PULSE OF LIFE, THE(1917); STRAIGHT SHOOTING(1917); BUCKING BROADWAY(1918); PHANTOM RIDERS, THE(1918); SCARLET DROP, THE(1918); THIEVES' GOLD(1918); WILD WOMEN(1918); WOMAN'S FOOL, A(1918); IT'S A GREAT LIFE(1920); BUCKING THE LINE(1921); RED COURAGE(1921); SURE FIRE(1921); UNWILLING HERO, AN(1921); BLAZE AWAY(1922); TRAIL OF HATE(1922); BATTLING BUNYON(1925); BAD MAN'S BLUFF(1926); BANDIT BUSTER, THE(1926); RAWHIDE(1926); DARING DEEDS(1927)
Nancy Malone
SPELL OF THE HYPNOTIST(1956); VIOLATORS, THE(1957); AFFAIR OF THE SKIN, AN(1964); INTIMACY(1966); TRIAL OF THE CATONSVILLE NINE, THE(1972); MAN WHO LOVED CAT DANCING, THE(1973)
Pat Malone
GASLIGHT(1944); LOCKET, THE(1946); KISS OF DEATH(1947)
Ralph Malone
LOVE BEFORE BREAKFAST(1936); THEODORA GOES WILD(1936); WOMAN TRAP(1936); PICK A STAR(1937); SWEETHEARTS(1938)
Ray Malone
MOONLIGHT IN VERMONT(1943); SLIGHTLY TERRIFIC(1944)
Richard Malone
OTHER SIDE OF THE MOUNTAIN, THE(1975)
Tom Malone
GRAND PARADE, THE(1930); BLUES BROTHERS, THE(1980)
Violet Malone
Silents
LITTLE ANGEL OF CANYON CREEK, THE(1914); ALIEN SOULS(1916)
Misc. Silents
DESERT HONEYMOON, A(1915)
William Malone
SCARED TO DEATH(1981), d&w, spec eff
Coleen Maloney
YOUNG DOCTORS IN LOVE(1982)
Dorothy Maloney [Malone]
FALCON AND THE CO-EDS, THE(1943)
Dorothy [Malone] Maloney
ONE MYSTERIOUS NIGHT(1944)
James Maloney
DETECTIVE STORY(1951); HELL CANYON OUTLAWS(1957); LURE OF THE SWAMP(1957); TWO LITTLE BEARS, THE(1961); THIRD OF A MAN(1962)
Jim Maloney
WAIT 'TIL THE SUN SHINES, NELLIE(1952)
Joe Maloney
OVERLAND BOUND(1929)
Leo Maloney
OVERLAND BOUND(1929), a, p&d
Silents
ARIZONA CATCLAW, THE(1919); SPITFIRE OF SEVILLE, THE(1919); NO MAN'S WOMAN(1921), a, d; WOLVERINE, THE(1921); WESTERN MUSKETEER, THE(1922); KING'S CREEK LAW(1923), a, d; LOSER'S END, THE(1924); ACROSS THE DEADLINE(1925), a, d; MAN FROM HARDPAN, THE(1927); APACHE RAIDER, THE(1928)

Misc. Silents
GHOST CITY(1921); NINE POINTS OF THE LAW(1922); RUM RUNNERS, THE(1923); BUILT FOR RUNNING(1924); NOT BUILT FOR RUNNIN'(1924), a, d; PAYABLE ON DEMAND(1924), a, d; PERFECT ALIBI, THE(1924); RIDING DOUBLE(1924), a, d; BLOOD BOND, THE(1925); FLASH O'LIGHTING(1925), a, d; LUCK AND SAND(1925), a, d; RANCHERS AND RASCALS(1925); SHIELD OF SILENCE, THE(1925), a, d; TROUBLE BUSTER, THE(1925), a, d; WIN, LOSE OR DRAW(1925), a, d; BLIND TRAIL(1926), a, d; HIGH HAND, THE(1926), a, d; OUTLAW EXPRESS, THE(1926); WITHOUT ORDERS(1926), a, d; BORDER BLACKBIRDS(1927), a, d; DEVIL'S TWIN, THE(1927), a, d; DON DESPERADO(1927), a, d; LONG LOOP ON THE PECOS, THE(1927), a, d; TWO-GUN OF THE TUMBLEWEED(1927), a, d; BOSS OF RUSTLER'S ROOST, THE(1928), d; YELLOW CONTRABAND(1928), a, d; .45 CALIBRE WAR(1929), d

Leo D. Maloney
Silents
JUDITH OF THE CUMBERLANDS(1916); MAN FROM HARDPAN, THE(1927), d; APACHE RAIDER, THE(1928), d
Misc. Silents
DIAMOND RUNNERS, THE(1916); MANAGER OF THE B&A, THE(1916); HEADIN' THROUGH(1924), a, d; HUNTIN' TROUBLE(1924), a, d; OUTLAW EXPRESS, THE(1926), d; BLACK ACE, THE(1928), d; BRONC STOMPER, THE(1928), d

Michael Maloney
RICHARD'S THINGS(1981, Brit.)
1984
ORDEAL BY INNOCENCE(1984, Brit.)

Pam Maloney
HAREM BUNCH; OR WAR AND PIECE, THE(1969)

Patty Maloney
UNDER THE RAINBOW(1981)
1984
ICE PIRATES, THE(1984); SWING SHIFT(1984)

Paul Maloney
ON THE BEACH(1959)

Peter Maloney
PUTNEY SWOPE(1969); HI, MOM!(1970); CAPONE(1975); BREAKING AWAY(1979); LITTLE ROMANCE, A(1979, U.S./Fr.); HIDE IN PLAIN SIGHT(1980); THING, THE(1982)

Sally Maloney
END OF AUGUST, THE(1982)

Tom Maloney
OFFICER O'BRIEN(1930)

Harry Malonie
Silents
HUNTINGTOWER(1927, Brit.)

Zygmunt Malonowicz
BARRIER(1966, Pol.)

John Maloon
BEYOND THE LAW(1968); MAIDSTONE(1970)

Thomas Malory
SWORD OF LANCELOT(1963, Brit.), w; EXCALIBUR(1981), w

Sir Thomas Malory
KNIGHTS OF THE ROUND TABLE(1953), w

Chris Malott
FIRST NUDIE MUSICAL, THE(1976)

Albert Hay Malotte
GIRL FROM CALGARY(1932), m; DR. CYCLOPS(1940), m; ENCHANTED FOREST, THE(1945), m; BIG FISHERMAN, THE(1959), m

Stan Malotte
MR. SCOUTMASTER(1953); IT SHOULD HAPPEN TO YOU(1954); BULLET FOR JOEY, A(1955)

Malou
DOLL, THE(1964, Swed.)

Jacqueline Malouf
DONOVAN'S REEF(1963)

Joseph Malouf
LOVES OF CARMEN, THE(1948)

Karen Malouf
ANGRY BREED, THE(1969)

La Rue Malouf
SON OF SINBAD(1955)

LaRue Malouf
WALK THE DARK STREET(1956)

I. Malov
CHILDHOOD OF MAXIM GORKY(1938, Russ.), ph

Anna Malova
NINTH HEART, THE(1980, Czech.)

Z. Malowski
GREAT BIG WORLD AND LITTLE CHILDREN, THE(1962, Pol.)

Doris Maloy
SHADOWS OF SING SING(1934), w

Mickey Maloy
UP IN ARMS(1944); WONDER MAN(1945)

George Malpas
1984
LASSITER(1984)

Andre Malraux
MAN'S HOPE(1947, Span.), p,d&w

Linda Malson
GREEN SLIME, THE(1969)

Berger Malsten
ILLICIT INTERLUDE(1954, Swed.)

Eva Maltagliati
CATCH-22(1970)

Evi Maltagliati
ULYSSES(1955, Ital.); SULEIMAN THE CONQUEROR(1963, Ital.); HEAD OF THE FAMILY(1967, Ital./Fr.)

Evi Maltaglisti
BURIED ALIVE(1951, Ital.)

H. F. Maltby
FOR THE LOVE OF MIKE(1933, Brit.), w; I SPY(1933, Brit.); JUST MY LUCK(1933, Brit.), w; LOVE NEST, THE(1933, Brit.), w; POLITICAL PARTY, A(1933, Brit.); FREEDOM OF THE SEAS(1934, Brit.); GIRLS WILL BE BOYS(1934, Brit.); JOSSER ON THE FARM(1934, Brit.); LOST IN THE LEGION(1934, Brit.); LUCK OF A SAILOR, THE(1934, Brit.); OVER THE GARDEN WALL(1934, Brit.), w; THOSE WERE THE DAYS(1934, Brit.); DEPARTMENT STORE(1935, Brit.), w; IT HAPPENED IN PARIS(1935, Brit.), w; LITTLE BIT OF BLUFF, A(1935, Brit.), a, w; OLD FAITHFUL(1935, Brit.), w; RIGHT AGE TO MARRY, THE(1935, Brit.), a, w; VANITY(1935); BUSMAN'S HOLIDAY(1936, Brit.), a, w; CALLING THE TUNE(1936, Brit.); CRIMES OF STEPHEN HAWKE, THE(1936, Brit.), w; EVERYTHING IN LIFE(1936, Brit.); EVERYTHING IS THUNDER(1936, Brit.); FAME(1936, Brit.); HEAD OFFICE(1936, Brit.); HEIRLOOM MYSTERY, THE(1936, Brit.); HOWARD CASE, THE(1936, Brit.), w; KING OF THE CASTLE(1936, Brit.); MORALS OF MARCUS, THE(1936, Brit.); NOT SO DUSTY(1936, Brit.), a, w; NOTHING LIKE PUBLICITY(1936, Brit.); QUEEN OF HEARTS(1936, Brit.), a, w; REASONABLE DOUBT(1936, Brit.); TO CATCH A THIEF(1936, Brit.), a, w; TOUCH OF THE MOON, A(1936, Brit.), w; TROUBLE AHEAD(1936, Brit.); WHERE THERE'S A WILL(1936, Brit.); BOYS WILL BE GIRLS(1937, Brit.), w; CAPTAIN'S ORDERS(1937, Brit.); FAREWELL TO CINDERELLA(1937, Brit.), w; IT'S NEVER TOO LATE TO MEND(1937, Brit.), w; LIVE WIRE, THE(1937, Brit.); MR. SMITH CARRIES ON(1937, Brit.); OKAY FOR SOUND(1937, Brit.); PEARLS BRING TEARS(1937, Brit.); SING AS YOU SWING(1937, Brit.); SKY'S THE LIMIT, THE(1937, Brit.); SONG OF THE ROAD(1937, Brit.); STRANGE ADVENTURES OF MR. SMITH, THE(1937, Brit.), w; TAKE MY TIP(1937, Brit.); TICKET OF LEAVE MAN, THE(1937, Brit.); WAKE UP FAMOUS(1937, Brit.); WANTED(1937, Brit.), w; WHAT A MAN!(1937, Brit.); WHY PICK ON ME?(1937, Brit.), w; DARTS ARE TRUMPS(1938, Brit.), a, w; EVERYTHING HAPPENS TO ME(1938, Brit.); GAIETY GIRLS, THE(1938, Brit.); HIS LORDSHIP REGRETS(1938, Brit.), w; PAID IN ERROR(1938, Brit.), w; PYGMALION(1938, Brit.); TO THE VICTOR(1938, Brit.); TWO OF US, THE(1938, Brit.); WEDDINGS ARE WONDERFUL(1938, Brit.), w; YOUNG AND INNOCENT(1938, Brit.); YOU'RE THE DOCTOR(1938, Brit.), w; BLIND FOLLY(1939, Brit.), w; DEMON BARBER OF FLEET STREET, THE(1939, Brit.), w; GOOD OLD DAYS, THE(1939, Brit.); HIS LORDSHIP GOES TO PRESS(1939, Brit.), a, w; OLD MOTHER RILEY JOINS UP(1939, Brit.); TWO'S COMPANY(1939, Brit.); CRIMES AT THE DARK HOUSE(1940, Brit.), a, w; GARRISON FOLLIES(1940, Brit.), a, w; RETURN TO YESTERDAY(1940, Brit.); UNDER YOUR HAT(1940, Brit.); BOB'S YOUR UNCLE(1941, Brit.); FACING THE MUSIC(1941, Brit.); GERT AND DAISY'S WEEKEND(1941, Brit.), w; FRONT LINE KIDS(1942, Brit.), w; GERT AND DAISY CLEAN UP(1942, Brit.), w; GREAT MR. HANDEL, THE(1942, Brit.), w; ROSE OF TRALEE(1942, Brit.), w; OLD MOTHER RILEY, DETECTIVE(1943, Brit.); SOMEWHERE IN CIVVIES(1943, Brit.); HOME SWEET HOME(1945, Brit.); CAESAR AND CLEOPATRA(1946, Brit.); GAY INTRUDERS, THE(1946, Brit.); TROJAN BROTHERS, THE(1946); SOMETHING IN THE CITY(1950, Brit.), w; IT'S A GRAND LIFE(1953, Brit.), w; NOT SO DUSTY(1956, Brit.), w
Silents
PROFIT AND THE LOSS(1917, Brit.), w

Wendy Maltby
JESUS CHRIST, SUPERSTAR(1973)

Felicitas Malten
Misc. Silents
MYSTIC MIRROR, THE(1928, Ger.)

William Malten
T-MEN(1947)

Daniel Maltese
HISTORY OF THE WORLD, PART 1(1981), set d

Mike Maltese
GREAT AMERICAN BUGS BUNNY-ROAD RUNNER CHASE(1979), w

Fred Maltesta
MODERN TIMES(1936)

Leslie Malton
POSSESSION(1981, Fr./Ger.)

M. Maltseva
TSAR'S BRIDE, THE(1966, USSR)

Albert Maltz
AFRAID TO TALK(1932), w; THIS GUN FOR HIRE(1942), w; DESTINATION TOKYO(1944), w; PRIDE OF THE MARINES(1945), w; CLOAK AND DAGGER(1946), w; NAKED CITY, THE(1948), w; TWO MULES FOR SISTER SARA(1970), w; SCALAWAG(1973, Yugo.), w

Della Maltzahn
GIRL IN THE KREMLIN, THE(1957)

Sofie Maltzeff
LES GAULOISES BLEUES(1969, Fr.)

Clardy Malugen
ABSENCE OF MALICE(1981)

L. Malughin
TRAIN GOES EAST, THE(1949, USSR), w

Elaine Malus
PROLOGUE(1970, Can.)

Corinne Malvern
Misc. Silents
LURING LIGHTS(1915)

Dan Malvern
GALLOPING MAJOR, THE(1951, Brit.)

Gerald Malvern
Silents
FACE AT THE WINDOW, THE(1920, Brit.), p

Henry Malvern
Misc. Silents
VARMINT, THE(1917)

Paul Malvern
BREED OF THE BORDER(1933), p; CRASHING BROADWAY(1933), p; FUGITIVE, THE(1933), p; RIDERS OF DESTINY(1933), p; BLUE STEEL(1934), p; HOUSE OF MYSTERY(1934), p; LUCKY TEXAN, THE(1934), p; MAN FROM UTAH, THE(1934), p; MONTE CARLO NIGHTS(1934), p; MOONSTONE, THE(1934), p; MYSTERY LINER(1934), p; 'NEATH THE ARIZONA SKIES(1934), p; RANDY RIDES ALONE(1934), p; SAGEBRUSH TRAIL(1934), p; SIXTEEN FATHOMS DEEP(1934), p; STAR PACKER, THE(1934), p; TRAIL BEYOND, THE(1934), p; WEST OF THE DIVIDE(1934), p; DAWN RIDER(1935), p; DESERT TRAIL(1935), p; LAWLESS FRONTIER, THE(1935), p; LAWLESS RANGE(1935), p; NEW FRONTIER, THE(1935), p; PARADISE CANYON(1935), p; RAINBOW VALLEY(1935), p; TEXAS TERROR(1935), p; KING OF

THE PECOS(1936), p; LAWLESS NINETIES, THE(1936), p; OREGON TRAIL, THE(1936), p; WESTWARD HO(1936), p; COURAGE OF THE WEST(1937), p; IDOL OF THE CROWDS(1937), p; SINGING OUTLAW(1937), p; BORDER WOLVES(1938), p; PRAIRIE JUSTICE(1938), p; WESTERN TRAILS(1938), p; DANGER FLIGHT(1939), p; MYSTERY PLANE(1939), p; PHANTOM STAGE, THE(1939), p; SKY PATROL(1939), p; STUNT PILOT(1939), p; DOOMED TO DIE(1940), p; DRUMS OF THE DESERT(1940), p; PHANTOM OF CHINATOWN(1940), p; QUEEN OF THE YUKON(1940), p; FLYING CADETS(1941), p; SIGN OF THE WOLF(1941), p; FRISCO LILL(1942), p; GREAT IMPERSONATION, THE(1942), p; HALF WAY TO SHANGHAI(1942), p; MAD DOCTOR OF MARKET STREET, THE(1942), p; MISSISSIPPI GAMBLER(1942), p; MYSTERY OF MARIE ROGET, THE(1942), p; NORTH TO THE KLONDIKE(1942), p; COWBOY IN MANHATTAN(1942), p; FOLLOW THE BAND(1943), p; GOOD MORNING, JUDGE(1943), p; HI, BUDDY(1943), p; ALI BABA AND THE FORTY THIEVES(1944), p; HOUSE OF FRANKENSTEIN(1944), p; HOUSE OF DRACULA(1945), p; SUDAN(1945), p; TANGIER(1946), p; PIRATES OF MONTEREY(1947), p; ROCK ISLAND TRAIL(1950), p

Paul R. Malvern
WOLF CALL(1939), p

Marcello Malvestiti
LET'S TALK ABOUT WOMEN(1964, Fr./Ital.), ed; ONE MILLION DOLLARS(1965, Ital.), m; TIGER AND THE PUSSYCAT, THE(1967, U.S., Ital.), ed; CATCH AS CATCH CAN(1968, Ital.), ed; KISS THE OTHER SHEIK(1968, Fr./Ital.), ed; DETECTIVE BELLI(1970, Ital.), ed

Marcello Malvestitit
ACE HIGH(1969, Ital.), ed

Patricia Malvoisin
L'ETOILE DU NORD(1983, Fr.)

Gero Maly
SUN SHINES, THE(1939, Hung.)

Ludvik Maly
LEMONADE JOE(1966, Czech.), spec eff

Walter Maly
Silents
PROWLERS OF THE NIGHT(1926); BULLDOG PLUCK(1927); GALLOPING GOBS, THE(1927); TERROR OF BAR X, THE(1927); DOG LAW(1928)
Misc. Silents
RIDIN' WILD(1925); WHITE PEBBLES(1927); SILENT SENTINEL(1929); WHITE OUTLAW, THE(1929)

Pavel Grigoryevich Malyarevskiy
LITTLE HUMPBACKED HORSE, THE(1962, USSR), w

N. Malyavina
GARNET BRACELET, THE(1966, USSR)

V. Malyavina
MY NAME IS IVAN(1963, USSR)

Hans-Gunther Malyjurek
HEIDI(1968, Aust.), art d

Ray Malyneaux
CISCO PIKE(1971), set d

Eily Malyon
GREAT EXPECTATIONS(1934); HIS GREATEST GAMBLE(1934); LIMEHOUSE BLUES(1934); LITTLE MINISTER, THE(1934); NANA(1934); CLIVE OF INDIA(1935); FLAME WITHIN, THE(1935); FLORENTINE DAGGER, THE(1935); KIND LADY(1935); LES MISERABLES(1935); MARK OF THE VAMPIRE(1935); MELODY LINGERS ON, THE(1935); ROMANCE IN MANHATTAN(1935); STRANDED(1935); TALE OF TWO CITIES, A(1935); ANTHONY ADVERSE(1936); CAIN AND MABEL(1936); CAREER WOMAN(1936); DEVIL DOLL, THE(1936); DRACULA'S DAUGHTER(1936); LITTLE LORD FAUNTLEROY(1936); ONE RAINY AFTERNOON(1936); THREE MEN ON A HORSE(1936); WHITE ANGEL, THE(1936); WIDOW FROM MONTE CARLO, THE(1936); WOMAN REBELS, A(1936); ANOTHER DAWN(1937); GOD'S COUNTRY AND THE WOMAN(1937); NIGHT MUST FALL(1937); KIDNAPPED(1938); REBECCA OF SUNNYBROOK FARM(1938); YOUNG IN HEART, THE(1938); BARRICADE(1939); CONFESSIONS OF A NAZI SPY(1939); HOUND OF THE BASKERVILLES, THE(1939); LITTLE PRINCESS, THE(1939); ON BORROWED TIME(1939); WE ARE NOT ALONE(1939); FOREIGN CORRESPONDENT(1940); UNTAMED(1940); YOUNG TOM EDISON(1940); ARKANSAS JUDGE(1941); HIT THE ROAD(1941); MAN HUNT(1941); REACHING FOR THE SUN(1941); I MARRIED A WITCH(1942); MAN IN THE TRUNK, THE(1942); SCATTERGOOD SURVIVES A MURDER(1942); UNDYING MONSTER, THE(1942); YOU'RE TELLING ME(1942); ABOVE SUSPICION(1943); SHADOW OF A DOUBT(1943); GOING MY WAY(1944); JANE EYRE(1944); SEVENTH CROSS, THE(1944); GRISSLY'S MILLIONS(1945); PARIS UNDERGROUND(1945); ROUGHLY SPEAKING(1945); SCARED STIFF(1945); SHE WOULDN'T SAY YES(1945); SON OF LASSIE(1945); SECRET HEART, THE(1946); SHE-WOLF OF LONDON(1946); CHALLENGE, THE(1948)

G. Malyshev
DON QUIXOTE(1961, USSR)

Y. Malyutin
SECRET BRIGADE, THE(1951 USSR)

Gunther Malzacher
SERPENT'S EGG, THE(1977, Ger./U.S.)

Della Malzahn
HIGH SCHOOL CONFIDENTIAL(1958)

Della Malzarn
FLOOD TIDE(1958)

N. Mamaeva
THEY CALL ME ROBERT(1967, USSR)

Pete Mamakos
BLADES OF THE MUSKETEERS(1953)

Peter Mamakos
TRAIL OF THE YUKON(1949); TUNA CLIPPER(1949); BETWEEN MIDNIGHT AND DAWN(1950); CARGO TO CAPETOWN(1950); KIM(1950); MALAYA(1950); CHINA CORSAIR(1951); COMIN' ROUND THE MOUNTAIN(1951); LET'S GO NAVY(1951); PEOPLE AGAINST O'HARA, THE(1951); PIER 23(1951); SILVER CANYON(1951); HORIZONS WEST(1952); PRISONER OF ZENDA, THE(1952); VIVA ZAPATA!(1952); BANDITS OF CORSICA, THE(1953); CITY BENEATH THE SEA(1953); GLORY BRIGADE, THE(1953); PRIVATE EYES(1953); ADVENTURES OF HAJJI BABA(1954); DEMETRIUS AND THE GLADIATORS(1954); EL ALAMEIN(1954); GAMBLER FROM NATCHEZ, THE(1954); AIN'T MISBEHAVIN'(1955); DESERT SANDS(1955); I COVER THE UNDERWORLD(1955); MARAUDERS, THE(1955); PIRATES OF TRIPOLI(1955); CONQUEROR, THE(1956); QUINCANNON, FRONTIER SCOUT(1956); SEARCHERS, THE(1956); WHEN GANGLAND STRIKES(1956); FLAME OF STAMBOUL(1957);

LOOKING FOR DANGER(1957); MY GUN IS QUICK(1957); SABU AND THE MAGIC RING(1957); SPOOK CHASERS(1957); CROOKED CIRCLE, THE(1958); FORT BOWIE(1958); MERRY ANDREW(1958); SCARFACE MOB, THE(1962); TERROR AT BLACK FALLS(1962); DRUMS OF AFRICA(1963); ISLAND OF LOVE(1963); SHIP OF FOOLS(1965); CATALINA CAPER, THE(1967); HEART IS A LONELY HUNTER, THE(1968); DREAM OF KINGS, A(1969); JUSTINE(1969); RESURRECTION OF ZACHARY WHEELER, THE(1971); FOR PETE'S SAKE(1977); OTHER SIDE OF MIDNIGHT, THE(1977); MAN WITH BOGART'S FACE, THE(1980)

Peter J. Mamakos
FORBIDDEN(1953)

N. Mamangakis
CANNON AND THE NIGHTINGALE, THE(1969, Gr.), m

Renato Mambor
CLEOPATRA'S DAUGHTER(1963, Fr., Ital.); LIPSTICK(1965, Fr./Ital.); STRANGER RETURNS, THE(1968, U.S./Ital./Ger./Span.)

Valerie Mamches
CHILDREN SHOULDN'T PLAY WITH DEAD THINGS(1972)

Gladys Mamer
Silents
EVERY MOTHER'S SON(1926, Brit.)

Pauline Mameson
ESTHER WATERS(1948, Brit.)

David Mamet
POSTMAN ALWAYS RINGS TWICE, THE(1981), w

Henry Mamet
PANIC IN THE STREETS(1950)

Yoshio Mamiya
WEIRD LOVE MAKERS, THE(1963, Jap.), ph

Fulvia Mammi
QUEEN OF SHEBA(1953, Ital.)

Maurizio Mammi
1984
CAGED WOMEN(1984, Ital./Fr.), art d

John Mamo
CONFESSIONS OF AN OPIUM EATER(1962); GIRL NAMED TAMIRO, A(1962); MC HALE'S NAVY(1964); M(1970)

Peter Mamoks
HAREM GIRL(1952)

A. Mamontove
MOTHER AND DAUGHTER(1965, USSR), art d

Rouben Mamoulian
APPLAUSE(1929), d; CITY STREETS(1931), d; DR. JEKYLL AND MR. HYDE(1932), p&d; LOVE ME TONIGHT(1932), p&d; QUEEN CHRISTINA(1933), d; SONG OF SONGS(1933), p&d; WE LIVE AGAIN(1934), d; BECKY SHARP(1935), d; GAY DESPERADO, THE(1936), d; HIGH, WIDE AND HANDSOME(1937), d; GOLDEN BOY(1939), d; MARK OF ZORRO, THE(1940), d; BLOOD AND SAND(1941), d; RINGS ON HER FINGERS(1942), d; SUMMER HOLIDAY(1948), d; SILK STOCKINGS(1957), d

Mamounah
SHARK WOMAN, THE(1941)

Manolo Mampaso
DOC(1971), set d

Manuel Mampaso
LIGHT AT THE EDGE OF THE WORLD, THE(1971, U.S./Span./Lichtenstein), cos

I. Mamporiya
Misc. Silents
ELISO(1928, USSR)

Chariot Man
SINS OF JEZEBEL(1953)

Christopher Man
CHILD'S PLAY(1972)

David Man
WESTWORLD(1973)

Edward J. Man
CARRIE(1952)

Frankie Man
LENNY(1974); ALL THAT JAZZ(1979)

Hank Man
MEET JOHN DOE(1941)

Iris Man
KISS OF DEATH(1947)

Tso Yee Man
GOLDEN GATE GIRL(1941)

Man O'War
WINNER'S CIRCLE, THE(1948)

Yuan Man-Tzu
INFRA-MAN(1975, Hong Kong)

Riichiro Manabe
NAKED YOUTH(1961, Jap.), m; NO GREATER LOVE THAN THIS(1969, Jap.), m; SUN ABOVE, DEATH BELOW(1969, Jap.), m; GODZILLA VERSUS THE SMOG MONSTER(1972, Jap.), m

Yoshihiko Manabe
GAMERA VERSUS ZIGRA(1971, Jap.), p

Albert Manachi
CHARLES AND LUCIE(1982, Fr.)

Harvey Manager
BRIDGE OF SAN LUIS REY, THE(1944), ed

Anna Manahan
SHE DIDN'T SAY NO!(1962, Brit.); OF HUMAN BONDAGE(1964, Brit.); ULYSSES(1967, U.S./Brit.); VIKING QUEEN, THE(1967, Brit.); CLASH OF THE TITANS(1981)

Bob Manahan
YOU LIGHT UP MY LIFE(1977)

Sheila Manahan
ANOTHER SHORE(1948, Brit.); SAINTS AND SINNERS(1949, Brit.); SEVEN DAYS TO NOON(1950, Brit.); FOOTSTEPS IN THE FOG(1955, Brit.); LAST MAN TO HANG, THE(1956, Brit.); STORY OF ESTHER COSTELLO, THE(1957, Brit.); ONLY TWO CAN PLAY(1962, Brit.)

Manalpuy
BUSH CHRISTMAS(1983, Aus.)
Alan Manaon
BANG THE DRUM SLOWLY(1973)
Cuciano Manara
LITTLE WORLD OF DON CAMILLO, THE(1953, Fr./Ital.)
Biff Manard
SHANKS(1974); LUNCH WAGON(1981); OFF THE WALL(1983)
Bill Manard
BUDDY BUDDY(1981)
Gabe Manarino
1984
GOODBYE PEOPLE, THE(1984)
Jean Manaroux
PARIS PICK-UP(1963, Fr./Ital.), art d
Alfredo Manas
BLOOD WEDDING(1981, Sp.), w
Steve Manasian
PIECES(1983, Span./Puerto Rico), p
George Manasse
WHO KILLED MARY WHAT'SER NAME?(1971), p; BLADE(1973), p; SQUIRM(1976), p; BLUE SUNSHINE(1978), p; HE KNOWS YOU'RE ALONE(1980), p
Benjamin Manaster
GOLDSTEIN(1964), d&w
Janine Manatis
I, MAUREEN(1978, Can.), d&w
1984
HOTEL NEW HAMPSHIRE, THE(1984)
John Manazanet
MAIDSTONE(1970)
Donna Manbeck
1984
COUNTRY(1984)
Edwin Manbeck
1984
COUNTRY(1984)
David Manber
HAIL, HERO!(1969), w
Maurice Manbson
WRONG MAN, THE(1956)
Lidia Mancani
SERAFINO(1970, Fr./Ital.)
Ann Manceer
OF HUMAN BONDAGE(1964, Brit.)
Valerie Manches
WANDA(1971)
Percy Manchester
DANNY BOY(1941, Brit.)
Manchester Tribe of the Poma Nation
ISLAND OF THE BLUE DOLPHINS(1964)
Manchester United Football Team
CUP FEVER(1965, Brit.)
Jean-Patrick Manchette
NADA GANG, THE(1974, Fr./Ital.), w; THREE MEN TO DESTROY(1980, Fr.), w; LES MAITRES DU TEMPS(1982, Fr./Switz./Ger.), w
Carlo Manchini
WALKABOUT(1971, Aus./U.S.)
Shirleena Manchur
SOMETHING BIG(1971)
Jorge Mancilla
MISSING(1982)
Mario Mancilla
TREASURE OF THE SIERRA MADRE, THE(1948)
Franco Mancinelli
FAREWELL TO ARMS, A(1957)
Mancini
MY UNCLE(1958, Fr.)
Al Mancini
DIRTY DOZEN, THE(1967, Brit.); DON'T RAISE THE BRIDGE, LOWER THE RIVER(1968, Brit.); WELCOME TO THE CLUB(1971)
Belarmino Mancini
MARGIN, THE,(1969, Braz.), ph
Carla Mancini
BLACK BELLY OF THE TARANTULA, THE(1972, Ital.); LUDWIG(1973, Ital./Ger./Fr.); DON'T TURN THE OTHER CHEEK(1974, Ital./Ger./Span.)
Claudio Mancini
MY NAME IS NOBODY(1974, Ital./Fr./Ger.), p; GENIUS, THE(1976, Ital./Fr./Ger.), p; ALIEN CONTAMINATION(1982, Ital.), p
Dennis Mancini
FORCE: FIVE(1981)
Don Francesco Mancini
CARDINAL, THE(1963)
Elsa Mancini
TWO WOMEN(1961, Ital./Fr.)
Henry Mancini
GLENN MILLER STORY, THE(1953), m; TARANTULA(1955), m; BENNY GOODMAN STORY, THE(1956), m; ROCK, PRETTY BABY(1956), m; MAN AFRAID(1957), m; DAMN CITIZEN(1958), m; FLOOD TIDE(1958), m; SUMMER LOVE(1958), m; TOUCH OF EVIL(1958), m; VOICE IN THE MIRROR(1958), m; GREAT IMPOSTOR, THE(1960), m; HIGH TIME(1960), m; BACHELOR IN PARADISE(1961), m; BREAKFAST AT TIFFANY'S(1961), m; SECOND TIME AROUND, THE(1961), m/l; DAYS OF WINE AND ROSES(1962), m; EXPERIMENT IN TERROR(1962), m; HATARI!(1962), m; MR. HOBBS TAKES A VACATION(1962), m; CHARADE(1963), m; SOLDIER IN THE RAIN(1963), m, md; DEAR HEART(1964), m; MAN'S FAVORITE SPORT [?](1964), m; PINK PANTHER, THE(1964), m; SHOT IN THE DARK, A(1964), m; GREAT RACE, THE(1965), m; ARABESQUE(1966), m; MOMENT TO MOMENT(1966), m; WHAT DID YOU DO IN THE WAR, DADDY?(1966), m; GUNN(1967), m; TWO FOR THE ROAD(1967, Brit.), m; WAIT UNTIL DARK(1967), m; PARTY, THE(1968), m; GAILY, GAILY(1969), m; ME, NATALIE(1969), m; DARLING LILI(1970), m; HAWAIIANS, THE(1970), m; MOLLY MAGUIRES, THE(1970), m; NIGHT VISITOR,

THE(1970, Swed./U.S.), m; SUNFLOWER(1970, Fr./Ital.), m; SOMETIMES A GREAT NOTION(1971), m, md; OKLAHOMA CRUDE(1973), m; THIEF WHO CAME TO DINNER, THE(1973), m; GIRL FROM PETROVKA, THE(1974), m; WHITE DAWN, THE(1974), m; 99 AND 44/100% DEAD(1974), m; GREAT WALDO PEPPER, THE(1975), m; ONCE IS NOT ENOUGH(1975), m; RETURN OF THE PINK PANTHER, THE(1975, Brit.), m; ALEX AND THE GYPSY(1976), m; PINK PANTHER STRIKES AGAIN, THE(1976, Brit.), m; SILVER STREAK(1976), m; W.C. FIELDS AND ME(1976), m; ANGELA(1977, Can.), m; HOUSE CALLS(1978), m; REVENGE OF THE PINK PANTHER(1978), m; WHO IS KILLING THE GREAT CHEFS OF EUROPE?(1978, US/Ger.), m; NIGHTWING(1979), m; PRISONER OF ZENDA, THE(1979), m; 10(1979), m; CHANGE OF SEASONS, A(1980), m; LITTLE MISS MARKER(1980), m; BACK ROADS(1981), m; CONDORMAN(1981), m; MOMMIE DEAREST(1981), m; S.O.B.(1981), m; TRAIL OF THE PINK PANTHER, THE(1982), m; VICTOR/VICTORIA(1982), m; BETTER LATE THAN NEVER(1983), m; CURSE OF THE PINK PANTHER(1983), m; MAN WHO LOVED WOMEN, THE(1983), m; SECOND THOUGHTS(1983), m
1984
HARRY AND SON(1984), m
Hugh Mancini
WAY OF A GAUCHO(1952)
Liliana Mancini
UNDER THE SUN OF ROME(1949, Ital.)
Lucien Mancini
LA CHIENNE(1975, Fr.)
Misc. Silents
MARQUITTA(1927, Fr.)
Mauro Mancini
FALL OF ROME, THE(1963, Ital.), w
Michael Mancini
JONI(1980); WOMAN INSIDE, THE(1981)
Ric Mancini
BADGE 373(1973); SHAMUS(1973); GAMBLER, THE(1974); NICKELODEON(1976); BELOW THE BELT(1980)
1984
BREAKIN'(1984); GHOSTBUSTERS(1984)
Misc. Talkies
TEENAGE HITCHHIKERS(1975)
Tony Mancini
HIDE IN PLAIN SIGHT(1980)
Harry Mancke
SEALED CARGO(1951)
Ermanno Manco
ITALIANO BRAVA GENTE(1965, Ital./USSR), set d
Alvaro Mancori
LADY DOCTOR, THE(1963, Fr./Ital./Span.), ph; SECRET MARK OF D'ARTAGNAN, THE(1963, Fr./Ital.), ph; GOLIATH AND THE VAMPIRES(1964, Ital.), ph; MORALIST, THE(1964, Ital.), ph; TIGER OF THE SEVEN SEAS(1964, Fr./Ital.), ph; CHRISMAS THAT ALMOST WASN'T. THE(1966, Ital.), ph; TRAMPLERS, THE(1966, Ital.), p, ph; LION OF ST. MARK(1967, Ital.), ph
Guglielmo Mancori
GUNMEN OF THE RIO GRANDE(1965, Fr./Ital./Span.), ph; REVENGE OF THE GLADIATORS(1965, Ital.), ph; SEVEN SLAVES AGAINST THE WORLD(1965, Ital.), ph; MYSTERY OF THUG ISLAND, THE(1966, Ital./Ger.), ph; WEEKEND MURDERS, THE(1972, Ital.), ph; TO KILL OR TO DIE(1973, Ital.), ph
Sandro Mancori
SABATA(1969, Ital.), ph; ADIOS SABATA(1971, Ital./Span.), ph; RETURN OF SABATA(1972, Ital./Fr./Ger.), ph; WEB OF THE SPIDER(1972, Ital./Fr./Ger.), ph; YETI(1977, Ital.), ph
1984
HUNTERS OF THE GOLDEN COBRA, THE(1984, Ital.), ph
Frank Mancuso
OFF THE WALL(1983), p
Frank Mancuso, Jr.
FRIDAY THE 13TH PART III(1982), p; MAN WHO WASN'T THERE, THE(1983), p
1984
FRIDAY THE 13TH–THE FINAL CHAPTER(1984), p
M. Mancuso
STRANGER'S GUNDOWN, THE(1974, Ital.), m
Nick Mancuso
NIGHTWING(1979); DEATH SHIP(1980, Can.); TICKET TO HEAVEN(1981); MOTHER LODE(1982)
1984
BLAME IT ON THE NIGHT(1984); HEARTBREAKERS(1984)
Misc. Talkies
TELL ME THAT YOU LOVE ME(1983)
Mons. Mandaille
Misc. Silents
JADE CASKET, THE(1929, Fr.)
Robert Mandan
LIGHT FANTASTIC(1964); CAREY TREATMENT, THE(1972); HICKEY AND BOGGS(1972); MAC ARTHUR(1977); BEST LITTLE WHOREHOUSE IN TEXAS, THE(1982); ZAPPED!(1982)
Ashok Mandanna
1984
PASSAGE TO INDIA, A(1984, Brit.)
Players of the Mandarin Theatre of San Francisco
LADY FROM SHANGHAI, THE(1948)
Jean Mandaroux
LOVE IN A HOT CLIMATE(1958, Fr./Span.), set d; FRANTIC(1961, Fr.), art d; TRIAL, THE(1963, Fr./Ital./Ger.), art d; DON'T TEMPT THE DEVIL(1964, Fr./Ital.), art d; MURDER AT 45 R.P.M.(1965, Fr.), art d; COUNTERFEIT CONSTABLE, THE(1966, Fr.), art d; WILD CHILD, THE(1970, Fr.), a, art d; BED AND BOARD(1971, Fr.), art d
Mandel
NO, NO NANETTE(1930), ed
Alan Mandel
SMOKEY AND THE BANDIT(1977), w; GOIN' SOUTH(1978), w; HOUSE CALLS(1978), w

Babaloo Mandel
NIGHT SHIFT(1982), w
1984
SPLASH(1984), a, w
Daniel Mandel
UNDERTOW(1930), ed
Frank Mandel
DESERT SONG, THE(1929), w; FOLLOW THRU(1930), p; GOOD NEWS(1930), w; NEW MOON(1930), w; NO, NO NANETTE(1930), w; QUEEN HIGH(1930), p, w; NEW MOON(1940), w; NO, NO NANETTE(1940), w; DESERT SONG, THE(1943), w; GOOD NEWS(1947), w; TEA FOR TWO(1950), w; DESERT SONG, THE(1953), w
Harold Mandel
TATTOO(1981)
Howie Mandel
GAS(1981, Can.); FUNNY FARM, THE(1982, Can.)
John Mandel
I WANT TO LIVE!(1958), m&md; SAILOR WHO FELL FROM GRACE WITH THE SEA, THE(1976, Brit.), m; BEING THERE(1979), m
Johnny Mandel
THIRD VOICE, THE(1960), m; DRUMS OF AFRICA(1963), m; AMERICANIZATION OF EMILY, THE(1964), m; SANDPIPER, THE(1965), m; AMERICAN DREAM, AN(1966), m; HARPER(1966), m; RUSSIANS ARE COMING, THE RUSSIANS ARE COMING, THE(1966), m; POINT BLANK(1967), m; PRETTY POISON(1968), m; HEAVEN WITH A GUN(1969), m; SOME KIND OF A NUT(1969), m; THAT COLD DAY IN THE PARK(1969, U.S./Can.), m; M(1970), m; JOURNEY THROUGH ROSEBUD(1972), m; MOLLY AND LAWLESS JOHN(1972), m; LAST DETAIL, THE(1973), m; SUMMER WISHES, WINTER DREAMS(1973), m; W(1974), m; FREAKY FRIDAY(1976), m; AGATHA(1979, Brit.), m; BALTIMORE BULLET, THE(1980), m; CADDY SHACK(1980), m; DEATHTRAP(1982), m; LOOKIN' TO GET OUT(1982), m; SOUP FOR ONE(1982), m; VERDICT, THE(1982), m; STAYING ALIVE(1983), m
Joseph C. Mandel
TELL THEM WILLIE BOY IS HERE(1969)
Joy Mandel
T.R. BASKIN(1971)
Linda Mandel
PUNISHMENT PARK(1971)
Loring Mandel
COUNTDOWN(1968), w; PROMISES IN THE DARK(1979), w
1984
LITTLE DRUMMER GIRL, THE(1984), w
Rena Mandel
VAMPYR(1932, Fr./Ger.)
Robert Mandel
INDEPENDENCE DAY(1983), d
Steve Mandel
DELIVERANCE(1972), song
Suzy Mandel
PRIVATE EYES, THE(1980)
Tommy Mandel
DEADLY HERO(1976), m
Issac Mandelbaum
DREAMER, THE(1970, Israel)
Arthur Mandelberg
GOD TOLD ME TO(1976), ed
Dan Mandell
DEVOTION(1931), ed; REBOUND(1931), ed; WOMAN COMMANDS, A(1932), ed
Daniel Mandell
MELODY LANE(1929), ed; SHOW BOAT(1929), ed; HOLIDAY(1930), ed; SIN TAKES A HOLIDAY(1930), ed; SWING HIGH(1930), ed; BEYOND VICTORY(1931), ed; ANIMAL KINGDOM, THE(1932), ed; COUNSELLOR-AT-LAW(1933), ed; I'LL TELL THE WORLD(1934), ed; WAKE UP AND DREAM(1934), ed; GOOD FAIRY, THE(1935), ed; HIS NIGHT OUT(1935), ed; KING SOLOMON OF BROADWAY(1935), ed; DODSWORTH(1936), ed; THESE THREE(1936), ed; DEAD END(1937), ed; WOMAN CHASES MAN(1937), ed; YOU ONLY LIVE ONCE(1937), ed; REAL GLORY, THE(1939), ed; WUTHERING HEIGHTS(1939), ed; WESTERNER, THE(1940), ed; LITTLE FOXES, THE(1941), ed; MEET JOHN DOE(1941), ed; PRIDE OF THE YANKEES, THE(1942), ed; NORTH STAR, THE(1943), ed; THEY GOT ME COVERED(1943), ed; ARSENIC AND OLD LACE(1944), ed; PRINCESS AND THE PIRATE, THE(1944), ed; UP IN ARMS(1944), ed; WONDER MAN(1945), ed; BEST YEARS OF OUR LIVES, THE(1946), ed; KID FROM BOOKLYN, THE(1946), ed; ENCHANTMENT(1948), ed; SONG IS BORN, A(1948), ed; MY FOOLISH HEART(1949), ed; ROSEANNA McCOY(1949), ed; EDGE OF DOOM(1950), ed; I WANT YOU(1951), ed; MILLIONAIRE FOR CHRISTY, A(1951), ed; VALENTINO(1951), ed; HANS CHRISTIAN ANDERSEN(1952), ed; RETURN TO PARADISE(1953), ed; GUYS AND DOLLS(1955), ed; SHARKFIGHTERS, THE(1956), ed; WITNESS FOR THE PROSECUTION(1957), ed; PORGY AND BESS(1959), ed; APARTMENT, THE(1960), ed; ONE, TWO, THREE(1961), ed; IRMA LA DOUCE(1963), ed; KISS ME, STUPID(1964), ed; FORTUNE COOKIE, THE(1966), ed; ONE-TRICK PONY(1980), ed
Silents
LOVE ME AND THE WORLD IS MINE(1928), ed; SILKS AND SADDLES(1929), ed
Ethel Mandell
LOVE BIRDS(1934)
Harry L. Mandell
GIRL IN THE WOODS(1958), p
Johnny Mandell
ESCAPE TO WITCH MOUNTAIN(1975), m
Lori Mandell
MY BODYGUARD(1980)
Pamela Mandell
SUPERMAN II(1980); SUPERMAN III(1983)
Peter Mandell
RETURN OF THE JEDI(1983); XTRO(1983, Brit.)
Robyn Mandell
MOONLIGHTING(1982, Brit.); LONELY LADY, THE(1983)
1984
SCREAM FOR HELP(1984); SUPERGIRL(1984)
Sol Mandelsohn
WINTER KEPT US WARM(1968, Can.)

Charles Mander
ROOM TO LET(1949, Brit.)
Jerry Mander
CRAZY QUILT, THE(1966); FUNNYMAN(1967)
Kay Mander
KID FROM CANADA, THE(1957, Brit.), d
Melanie Mander
MURDER A LA MOD(1968)
Miles Mander
CROOKED BILLET, THE(1930, Brit.); LOOSE ENDS(1930, Brit.); MURDER(1930, Brit.); FASCINATION(1931, Brit.), d; FRAIL WOMEN(1932, Brit.); LILY CHRISTINE(1932, Brit.); MISSING REMBRANDT, THE(1932, Brit.); BITTER SWEET(1933, Brit.); MATINEE IDOL(1933, Brit.); OVERNIGHT(1933, Brit.); PRIVATE LIFE OF HENRY VIII, THE(1933); BATTLE, THE(1934, Fr.); CASE FOR THE CROWN, THE(1934, Brit.); FOUR MASKED MEN(1934, Brit.); LOYALTIES(1934, Brit.); YOUTHFUL FOLLY(1934, Brit.), d; DEATH DRIVES THROUGH(1935, Brit.); DON QUIXOTE(1935, Fr.); PHANTOM FIEND, THE(1935, Brit.), w; THREE MUSKETEERS, THE(1935); FLYING DOCTOR, THE(1936, Aus.), p&d; LLOYDS OF LONDON(1936); MORALS OF MARCUS, THE(1936, Brit.), d, w; SLAVE SHIP(1937); WAKE UP AND LIVE(1937); YOUTH ON PAROLE(1937); KIDNAPPED(1938); MAD MISS MANTON, THE(1938); SUEZ(1938); LITTLE PRINCESS, THE(1939); MAN IN THE IRON MASK, THE(1939); STANLEY AND LIVINGSTONE(1939); THREE MUSKETEERS, THE(1939); TOWER OF LONDON(1939); WUTHERING HEIGHTS(1939); BABIES FOR SALE(1940); CAPTAIN CAUTION(1940); EARL OF CHICAGO, THE(1940); HOUSE OF THE SEVEN GABLES, THE(1940); LADDIE(1940); PRIMROSE PATH(1940); ROAD TO SINGAPORE(1940); SOUTH OF SUEZ(1940); DR. KILDARE'S WEDDING DAY(1941); SHADOWS ON THE STAIRS(1941); THAT HAMILTON WOMAN(1941); APACHE TRAIL(1942); CAPTAINS OF THE CLOUDS(1942); FINGERS AT THE WINDOW(1942); FLY BY NIGHT(1942); LUCKY JORDAN(1942); MRS. MINIVER(1942); SOMEWHERE I'LL FIND YOU(1942); TARZAN'S NEW YORK ADVENTURE(1942); THIS ABOVE ALL(1942); TO BE OR NOT TO BE(1942); TRAGEDY AT MIDNIGHT, A(1942); WAR AGAINST MRS. HADLEY, THE(1942); ASSIGNMENT IN BRITTANY(1943); FALLEN SPARROW, THE(1943); FIRST COMES COURAGE(1943); FIVE GRAVES TO CAIRO(1943); GUADALCANAL DIARY(1943); MADAME CURIE(1943); PHANTOM OF THE OPERA(1943); SECRETS OF THE UNDERGROUND(1943); ENTER ARSENE LUPIN(1944); FOUR JILLS IN A JEEP(1944); PEARL OF DEATH, THE(1944); RETURN OF THE VAMPIRE, THE(1944); SCARLET CLAW, THE(1944); STORY OF DR. WASSELL, THE(1944); WHITE CLIFFS OF DOVER, THE(1944); BRIGHTON STRANGLER, THE(1945); CAPTAIN KIDD(1945); CONFIDENTIAL AGENT(1945); CRIME DOCTOR'S WARNING(1945); MURDER, MY SWEET(1945); PICTURE OF DORIAN GRAY, THE(1945); WEEKEND AT THE WALDORF(1945); WALLS CAME TUMBLING DOWN, THE(1946); IMPERFECT LADY, THE(1947)
Silents
HALF A TRUTH(1922, Brit.); OPEN COUNTRY(1922, Brit.); PRUDES FALL, THE(1924, Brit.); PLEASURE GARDEN, THE(1925, Brit./Ger.); FAKE, THE(1927, Brit.); PHYSICIAN, THE(1928, Brit.)
Misc. Silents
LOVERS IN ARABY(1924, Brit.); FIRST BORN, THE(1928, Brit.), a, d; JAWS OF HELL(1928, Brit.)
Tommie Manderson
1984
KILLING FIELDS, THE(1984, Brit.), makeup
Tommy Manderson
HUSBANDS(1970), makeup
William Manderville
Misc. Silents
WHAT HAPPENED TO JONES(1915)
J. P. Mandes
THIS IS THE ARMY(1943)
Miles Mandet
WOMAN DECIDES, THE(1932, Brit.), d&w
Leopoldo Mandeville
PUTNEY SWOPE(1969); EMMA MAE(1976)
Michael Mandeville
HUMAN FACTOR, THE(1975)
William Mandeville
Silents
WITHOUT HOPE(1914)
Misc. Silents
CALL OF HER PEOPLE, THE(1917)
Geraldo A. Mandia
WAY TO THE GOLD, THE(1957)
Ricardo Mandia
ON THE AVENUE(1937); SWING HIGH, SWING LOW(1937)
Veljko Mandic
HOROSCOPE(1950, Yugo.)
Frantizek Mandik
PASSION(1983, Fr./Switz.)
Fred Mandl
SEVEN MINUTES, THE(1971), ph
Percy G. Mandley
EIGHT BELLS(1935), w
Adina Mandlova
MERRY WIVES, THE(1940, Czech.); FOOL AND THE PRINCESS, THE(1948, Brit.)
Luciano Mandolfo
MAIDEN FOR A PRINCE, A(1967, Fr./Ital.)
Joyce Mandre
CRY OF THE BANSHEE(1970, Brit.)
Harry Mandredini
KIRLIAN WITNESS, THE(1978), m
Barbara Mandrell
Misc. Talkies
COUNTRY MUSIC(1972)
Charles Mandru
Misc. Silents
LA BOURASQUE(1920, Fr.), d
Pierre Mandru
FRUSTRATIONS(1967, Fr./Ital.), w

Cornelia Mandry
PASSION(1983, Fr./Switz.)

Joe Manduke
ALICE'S RESTAURANT(1969), p; JUMP(1971), d; NEW LEAF, A(1971), p; CORN-
BREAD, EARL AND ME(1975), p&d; KID VENGEANCE(1977), d

Mandy
GENTLE TOUCH, THE(1956, Brit.)

Jerry Mandy
LOVE, LIVE AND LAUGH(1929); SAP, THE(1929); DOORWAY TO HELL(1930);
GIRLS DEMAND EXCITEMENT(1931); PARDON US(1931); SAILOR'S LUCK(1933);
STRANGE PEOPLE(1933); IT'S A GIFT(1934); FRONT PAGE WOMAN(1935); HANDS
ACROSS THE TABLE(1935); MC FADDEN'S FLATS(1935); TWO FOR TO-
NIGHT(1935); UNKNOWN WOMAN(1935); BRIDE COMES HOME(1936); KING OF
BURLESQUE(1936); POSTAL INSPECTOR(1936); SPENDTHRIFT(1936); TWO IN A
CROWD(1936); BEHIND THE MIKE(1937); EVER SINCE EVE(1937); THAT'S MY
STORY(1937); HAWAII CALLS(1938); KID NIGHTINGALE(1939); NAUGHTY BUT
NICE(1939); ONE NIGHT IN THE TROPICS(1940); ONE NIGHT IN LISBON(1941);
SHADOW OF THE THIN MAN(1941); SKY'S THE LIMIT, THE(1943); THANK YOUR
LUCKY STARS(1943)
Silents
BEHIND THE FRONT(1926); UNDERWORLD(1927); HOLD 'EM YALE!(1928); LOVE
AND LEARN(1928)
Misc. Silents
GAY DEFENDER, THE(1927)

Samba Mane
COUP DE TORCHON(1981, Fr.)

Maneaters
JUBILEE(1978, Brit.), m

Barbara Maneff
WILD SCENE, THE(1970)

Sabine Manela
LIZZIE(1957), cos; FLIGHT THAT DISAPPEARED, THE(1961), cos; GUN
FIGHT(1961), cos; LAST TIME I SAW ARCHIE, THE(1961), cos; SECRET OF DEEP
HARBOR(1961), cos; DEADLY DUO(1962), cos; GUN STREET(1962), cos

Daniel Manell
BALL OF FIRE(1941), ed

Louis Manella
MY WIFE'S HUSBAND(1965, Fr./Ital.), p; CHECKERBOARD(1969, Fr.), prod d

Bianca Manenti
LUXURY GIRLS(1953, Ital.)

Wally Maner
TRUE CONFESSION(1937)

Luisa Maneri
LA CAGE AUX FOLLES(1979, Fr./Ital.)

Sal Maneri
NUNZIO(1978)

Jose Manero
DOWN MEXICO WAY(1941)

Douglas Manes
1984
LIES(1984, Brit.)

Fritz Manes
ESCAPE FROM ALCATRAZ(1979); ANY WHICH WAY YOU CAN(1980), p; FIRE-
FOX(1982)
1984
CITY HEAT(1984), a, p; TIGHTROPE(1984), a, p

Gina Manes
MAYERLING(1937, Fr.); NIGHTS OF SHAME(1961, Fr.); PALACE OF NUDES(1961,
Fr./Ital.)
Silents
NAPOLEON(1927, Fr.)
Misc. Silents
COEUR FIDELE(1923, Fr.); L'AUBERGE ROUGE(1923, Fr.); SABLES(1928, Fr.);
THERESE RAQUIN(1928, Fr./Ger.)

Griffith Manes
AVENGERS, THE(1942, Brit.)

Stephen Manes
MOTHER, JUGS & SPEED(1976), w

Violet Manes
1984
THEY'RE PLAYING WITH FIRE(1984)

Sherman Maness
RABID(1976, Can.)

Helene Manesse
RISE OF LOUIS XIV, THE(1970, Fr.)

Elisabeth Manet
MIRROR HAS TWO FACES, THE(1959, Fr.)

Jeanne Manet
SLIGHTLY FRENCH(1949); OPERATION MAD BALL(1957); PEPE(1960)

Juliette Manet
BATTLEAXE, THE(1962, Brit.)

G.D. Manetta
BLAME THE WOMAN(1932, Brit.)

Larry Manetti
TWO-MINUTE WARNING(1976)

Lido Manetti
Silents
EVENING CLOTHES(1927)

B. Manevich
LADY WITH THE DOG, THE(1962, USSR), art d; OVERCOAT, THE(1965, USSR), art
d

Iosif Manevich
SOUND OF LIFE, THE(1962, USSR), w

Joseph Manevich
HYPERBOLOID OF ENGINEER GARIN, THE(1965, USSR), w

Virginia P. Maney
NIGHTWING(1979)

Lowell Manfall
ON THE YARD(1978)

Carole Manferdini
NEXT STOP, GREENWICH VILLAGE(1976)

Guy Manford
FLESH MERCHANT, THE(1956)

Fran Manfred
ROCK, ROCK, ROCK!(1956)

Harry Manfredi
SPRING BREAK(1983), m

Nino Manfredi
HERCULES' PILLS(1960, Ital.); FIASCO IN MILAN(1963, Fr./Ital.); AND SUDDEN-
LY IT'S MURDER!(1964, Ital.); OF WAYWARD LOVE(1964, Ital./Ger.), d; BAM-
BOLE!(1965, Ital.); HIGH INFIDELITY(1965, Fr./Ital.); NOT ON YOUR LIFE(1965,
Ital./Span.); HEAD OF THE FAMILY(1967, Ital./Fr.); MADE IN ITALY(1967, Fr./Ital.);
ROSE FOR EVERYONE, A(1967, Ital.), a, w; ITALIAN SECRET SERVICE(1968, Ital.);
TREASURE OF SAN GENNARO(1968, Fr./Ital./Ger.), a, w; GOODNIGHT, LADIES
AND GENTLEMEN(1977, Ital.); BREAD AND CHOCOLATE(1978, Ital.), a, w; CAFE
EXPRESS(1980, Ital.), a, w
Misc. Talkies
OPERATION SNAFU(1970, Ital./Yugo.)

Harry Manfredini
HERE COME THE TIGERS(1978), m; NIGHT FLOWERS(1979), m; FRIDAY THE
13TH(1980), m; FRIDAY THE 13TH PART II(1981), m; FRIDAY THE 13TH PART
III(1982), m; SWAMP THING(1982), m; RETURNING, THE(1983), m

Henry Manfredini
CHILDREN, THE(1980), m
1984
FRIDAY THE 13TH–THE FINAL CHAPTER(1984), m

Guido Manfrino
SWORD OF THE CONQUEROR(1962, Ital.)

Vittorio Manfrino
SANDRA(1966, Ital.)

Jone Mang
STRANGER IN TOWN, A(1968, U.S./Ital.), w; STRANGER RETURNS, THE(1968,
U.S./Ital./Ger./Span.), w

Anna Manga
TWO OR THREE THINGS I KNOW ABOUT HER(1970, Fr.)

Elaine Mangan
MANGANINNIE(1982, Aus.)

Richard Mangan
PROSTITUTE(1980, Brit.)

The Mangan Tillerettes
LOVE CONTRACT, THE(1932, Brit.)

Richard Mangana
VOYAGE, THE(1974, Ital.)

Aldo Manganaro
SHARE OUT, THE(1966, Brit.), makeup; WHERE THE BULLETS FLY(1966, Brit.),
makeup

Gino Manganello
ORGANIZER, THE(1964, Fr./Ital./Yugo.)

Natascia Mangano
ANNA(1951, Ital.)

Patrizia Mangano
ANNA(1951, Ital.); RING AROUND THE CLOCK(1953, Ital.)

Roy Mangano
BARABBAS(1962, Ital.)

Silvana Mangano
BITTER RICE(1950, Ital.); ANNA(1951, Ital.); MAMBO(1955, Ital.); ULYSSES(1955,
Ital.); GOLD OF NAPLES(1957, Ital.); TEMPEST(1958, Ital./Yugo./Fr.); THIS ANGRY
AGE(1958, Ital./Fr.); FIVE BRANDED WOMEN(1960); BARABBAS(1962, Ital.); VERO-
NA TRIAL, THE(1963, Ital.); TEOREMA(1969, Ital.); WITCHES, THE(1969, Fr./Ital.);
DEATH IN VENICE(1971, Ital./Fr.); SCIENTIFIC CARDPLAYER, THE(1972, Ital.);
LUDWIG(1973, Ital./Ger./Fr.); CONVERSATION PIECE(1976, Ital., Fr.)

Silvano Mangano
FLYING SAUCER, THE(1964, Ital.)

Sylvana Mangano
AND SUDDENLY IT'S MURDER!(1964, Ital.)

Silvana Mangaro
GREAT WAR, THE(1961, Fr., Ital.)

Ted Mangean
MEXICAN SPITFIRE OUT WEST(1940)

Teddy Mangean
THIRTEEN WOMEN(1932); HILLBILLY BLITZKRIEG(1942); LADIES' DAY(1943);
LOUISIANA HAYRIDE(1944); BLUEPRINT FOR MURDER, A(1953); JALOPY(1953);
LOOSE IN LONDON(1953); SHE COULDN'T SAY NO(1954)

Elaine Mangel
MADE FOR EACH OTHER(1971), cos

Harvey Manger
HI DIDDLE DIDDLE(1943), ed; AND THEN THERE WERE NONE(1945), ed; DE-
LIGHTFULLY DANGEROUS(1945), ed; GUNFIGHTERS, THE(1947), ed; SPIRIT OF
WEST POINT, THE(1947), ed; BIG CAT, THE(1949), ed; NEVER FEAR(1950), ed;
OUTRAGE(1950), ed

Frank Mangiapane
Misc. Talkies
ADVERSARY, THE(1970)

Aurelio Mangiarotti
FIST IN HIS POCKET(1968, Ital.), ed

Noel Mangin
MARRIAGE OF FIGARO, THE(1970, Ger.)

Joe Mangine
PLEASURE PLANTATION(1970), ph; BLACK PANTHER, THE(1977, Brit.), ph;
MOTHER'S DAY(1980), ph

Joseph Mangine
LORDS OF FLATBUSH, THE(1974), ph; SQUIRM(1976), ph; VAN NUYS
BLVD.(1979), ph; ALLIGATOR(1980), ph; LOVE IN A TAXI(1980), ph; ALONE IN
THE DARK(1982), ph; SWORD AND THE SORCERER, THE(1982), ph
1984
EXTERMINATOR 2(1984), ph

Gino Mangini
GOLIATH AND THE BARBARIANS(1960, Ital.), w; DAVID AND GOLIATH(1961, Ital.), w; ATLAS AGAINST THE CYCLOPS(1963, Ital.), w; FURY OF THE PAGANS(1963, Ital.), w; THIS MAN CAN'T DIE(1970, Ital.), w

Palma Mangini
8 ½(1963, Ital.)

Chuck Mangione
CHILDREN OF SANCHEZ, THE(1978, U. S./Mex.), m

Giuseppe Mangione
ANGELS OF DARKNESS(1956, Ital.), w; QUEEN OF BABYLON, THE(1956, Ital.), w; SIGN OF THE GLADIATOR(1959, Fr./Ger./Ital.), w; COMMANDO(1962, Ital., Span., Bel., Ger.), w; MIGHTY URSUS(1962, Ital./Span.), w; EYE OF THE NEEDLE, THE(1965, Ital./Fr.), w; HYPNOSIS(1966, Ger./Sp./Ital.), w
1984
MISUNDERSTOOD(1984), m

Raniero Mangione
GRAN VARIETA(1955, Ital.), ed

Tony Mangis
CITY NEWS(1983)

Giorgio Manglamele
CLAY(1964 Aus.), p,d,w,ph,ed

Mary Jane Mangler
MURDERERS' ROW(1966); SILENCERS, THE(1966); FUNNY GIRL(1968)

Alec Mango
FIDDLERS THREE(1944, Brit.); CAPTAIN HORATIO HORNBLOWER(1951, Brit.); HIS EXCELLENCY(1952, Brit.); GOLDEN MASK, THE(1954, Brit.); THEY WHO DARE(1954, Brit.); UP TO HIS NECK(1954, Brit.); LUST FOR LIFE(1956); ZARAK(1956, Brit.); PICKUP ALLEY(1957, Brit.); SHIRALEE, THE(1957, Brit.); COSMIC MONSTERS(1958, Brit.); MAN INSIDE, THE(1958, Brit.); SEVENTH VOYAGE OF SINBAD, THE(1958); ANGRY HILLS, THE(1959, Brit.); THREE WORLDS OF GULLIVER, THE(1960, Brit.); WE SHALL SEE(1964, Brit.); FRANKENSTEIN CREATED WOMAN(1965, Brit.); KHARTOUM(1966, Brit.); SOME MAY LIVE(1967, Brit.); LION OF THE DESERT(1981, Libya/Brit.)
Misc. Talkies
CRAWLING TERROR, THE(1958, Brit.)

Alex Mango
RACE FOR LIFE, A(1955, Brit.)

Alexander Mango
FREUD(1962)

Ernie Mangold
MRS. WARREN'S PROFESSION(1960, Ger.)

Lisi Mangold
SERPENT'S EGG, THE(1977, Ger./U.S.); GERMANY IN AUTUMN(1978, Ger.)

Armando Mangolini
STRANGER RETURNS, THE(1968, U.S./Ital./Ger./Span.)

Babette Mangolte
Misc. Talkies
WHAT MAISIE KNEW(1976), d

Alf Mangon
DRAGONSLAYER(1981)

Sune Mangs
MY FATHER'S MISTRESS(1970, Swed.); FANNY AND ALEXANDER(1983, Swed./Fr./Ger.)

Alf Mangun
WRONG BOX, THE(1966, Brit.)

Peter Manhardt
RIO 70(1970, U.S./Ger./Span.), art d

The Manhattan Twisters
TWIST ALL NIGHT(1961)

Emanuel Manheim
GAMBLING SHIP(1939), w

Kate Manheim
KING OF THE GYPSIES(1978)
Misc. Talkies
WHAT MAISIE KNEW(1976); STRONG MEDICINE(1981)

Mannie Manheim
DOUBLE DYNAMITE(1951), Harry Crane

Albert Manheimer
DANCING CO-ED(1939), w

Bill Manhoff
OWL AND THE PUSSYCAT, THE(1970), w

Eltore Mani
LA GRANDE BOURGEOISE(1977, Ital.)

Karin Mani
1984
ALLEY CAT(1984)

Gentle Maniacs
SWING IT, PROFESSOR(1937)

Alexandros Maniatakis
OEDIPUS THE KING(1968, Brit.)

Belle K. Maniates
Silents
AMARILLY OF CLOTHESLINE ALLEY(1918), w

John Manier
AMBUSH AT CIMARRON PASS(1958)

Antonio Manifredi
UNDER THE PAMPAS MOON(1935)

Phillip Manikum
CORRUPTION(1968, Brit.)

Barry Manilow
TRIBUTE(1980, Can.), m

Bianco Manini
BULLET FOR THE GENERAL, A(1967, Ital.), p; PRICE OF POWER, THE(1969, Ital./Span.), p

Cindy Manion
1984
PREPPIES(1984)

Gloria Manion
I LOVE MY WIFE(1970)

Guglielmo Maniori
ARIZONA COLT(1965, It./Fr./Span.), ph

Sandro Maniori
BOUNTY HUNTERS, THE(1970, Ital.), ph

Stelios Manios
Misc. Talkies
RIP OFF(1977)

James Manis
LOVING(1970); GOING IN STYLE(1979); FAME(1980)

Tony Maniscalco
SIX PACK(1982)

Girolamo Manisco
HELL RAIDERS OF THE DEEP(1954, Ital.)

Joe Maniscola
IT HAPPENED IN CANADA(1962, Can.)

Indira Manjrekar
SURVIVORS, THE(1983)

Chaw Mank
VALENTINO(1977, Brit.), w

Joseph L. Mankiewcz
MILLION DOLLAR LEGS(1932), w

Tom Mankiewcz
DIAMONDS ARE FOREVER(1971, Brit.), w

Don M. Mankiewicz
TRIAL(1955), w; CHAPMAN REPORT, THE(1962), w

Don Mankiewicz
FAST COMPANY(1953), w; HOUSE OF NUMBERS(1957), w; I WANT TO LIVE!(1958), w; BLACK BIRD, THE(1975), w

Francis Mankiewicz
FOND MEMORIES(1982, Can.), d

Herman Mankiewicz
ABIE'S IRISH ROSE(1928), w; BARKER, THE(1928), w; MIGHTY, THE(1929), w; ROYAL FAMILY OF BROADWAY, THE(1930), w; VAGABOND KING, THE(1930), w; DUDE RANCH(1931), w; DUCK SOUP(1933), p; STAMBOUL QUEST(1934), w; LOVE IN EXILE(1936, Brit.), w; SHOW GOES ON, THE(1938, Brit.), w; GOOD FELLOWS, THE(1943), w
Silents
ROAD TO MANDALAY, THE(1926), w; CITY GONE WILD, THE(1927), t; AVALANCHE(1928), w, t; GENTLEMEN PREFER BLONDES(1928), t; TAKE ME HOME(1928), t

Herman J. Mankiewicz
CANARY MURDER CASE, THE(1929), w; DUMMY, THE(1929), w; LOVE DOCTOR, THE(1929), w; MAN I LOVE, THE(1929), w; THUNDERBOLT(1929), w; HONEY(1930), w; LADIES LOVE BRUTES(1930), w; LOVE AMONG THE MILLIONAIRES(1930), w; MEN ARE LIKE THAT(1930), w; TRUE TO THE NAVY(1930), w; LADIES' MAN(1931), w; MAN OF THE WORLD(1931), w; DANCERS IN THE DARK(1932), w; GIRL CRAZY(1932), w; LOST SQUADRON, THE(1932), w; MILLION DOLLAR LEGS(1932), p; ANOTHER LANGUAGE(1933), w; DINNER AT EIGHT(1933), w; MEET THE BARON(1933), w; SHOW-OFF, THE(1934), w; AFTER OFFICE HOURS(1935), w; ESCAPADE(1935), w; JOHN MEADE'S WOMAN(1937), w; MY DEAR MISS ALDRICH(1937), p, w; IT'S A WONDERFUL WORLD(1939), w; CITIZEN KANE(1941), w; KEEPING COMPANY(1941), w; RISE AND SHINE(1941), w; WILD MAN OF BORNEO, THE(1941), w; PRIDE OF THE YANKEES, THE(1942), w; STAND BY FOR ACTION(1942), w; THIS TIME FOR KEEPS(1942), w; CHRISTMAS HOLIDAY(1944), w; ENCHANTED COTTAGE, THE(1945), w; SPANISH MAIN, THE(1945), w; WOMAN'S SECRET, A(1949), p, w; PRIDE OF ST. LOUIS, THE(1952), w
Silents
TWO FLAMING YOUTHS(1927), t; DRAGNET, THE(1928), t; LAST COMMAND, THE(1928), t; LOVE AND LEARN(1928), t; MAGNIFICENT FLIRT, THE(1928), t; NIGHT OF MYSTERY, A(1928), t; WHAT A NIGHT!(1928), t

Joseph Mankiewicz
FORSAKING ALL OTHERS(1935), w; I LIVE MY LIFE(1935), w; GORGEOUS HUSSY, THE(1936), p

Joseph L. Mankiewicz
DUMMY, THE(1929), w; FAST COMPANY(1929), w; VIRGINIAN, THE(1929), titles; WOMAN TRAP(1929), w; ONLY SAPS WORK(1930), w; SOCIAL LION, THE(1930), w; FINN AND HATTIE(1931), w; GANG BUSTER, THE(1931), w; JUNE MOON(1931), w; NEWLY RICH(1931), w; SKIPPY(1931), w; SOOKY(1931), w; IF I HAD A MILLION(1932), w; SKY BRIDE(1932), w; THIS RECKLESS AGE(1932), w; ALICE IN WONDERLAND(1933), w; DIPLOMANIACS(1933), w; EMERGENCY CALL(1933), w; TOO MUCH HARMONY(1933), w; MANHATTAN MELODRAMA(1934), w; OUR DAILY BREAD(1934), w; FURY(1936), p; LOVE ON THE RUN(1936), p; THREE GODFATHERS(1936), p; BRIDE WORE RED, THE(1937), p; DOUBLE WEDDING(1937), p; MANNEQUIN(1937), p; CHRISTMAS CAROL, A(1938), p; SHINING HOUR, THE(1938), p; SHOPWORN ANGEL(1938), p; THREE COMRADES(1938), p; HUCKLEBERRY FINN(1939), p; PHILADELPHIA STORY, THE(1940), p; STRANGE CARGO(1940), p; FEMININE TOUCH, THE(1941), p; WILD MAN OF BORNEO, THE(1941), p; GHOST AND MRS. MUIR, THE(1942), p; REUNION IN FRANCE(1942), p; WOMAN OF THE YEAR(1942), p; KEYS OF THE KINGDOM, THE(1944), p, w; DRAGONWYCH(1946), d, w; SOMEWHERE IN THE NIGHT(1946), d, w; LATE GEORGE APLEY, THE(1947), d; ESCAPE(1948, Brit.), d; LETTER TO THREE WIVES, A(1948), d, w; PIRATE, THE(1948), w; HOUSE OF STRANGERS(1949), d; ALL ABOUT EVE(1950), d, w; NO WAY OUT(1950), d, w; PEOPLE WILL TALK(1951), d&w; FIVE FINGERS(1952), d; JULIUS CAESAR(1953), d&w; BAREFOOT CONTESSA, THE(1954), p,d&w; GUYS AND DOLLS(1955), d&w; QUIET AMERICAN, THE(1958), p,d&w; SUDDENLY, LAST SUMMER(1959, Brit.), d; CLEOPATRA(1963), d, w; HONEY POT, THE(1967, Brit.), p, d&w; THERE WAS A CROOKED MAN(1970), p&d; SLEUTH(1972, Brit.), d

Tom Mankiewicz
SWEET RIDE, THE(1968), w; LIVE AND LET DIE(1973, Brit.), w; MAN WITH THE GOLDEN GUN, THE(1974, Brit.), w; EAGLE HAS LANDED, THE(1976, Brit.), w; MOTHER, JUGS & SPEED(1976), p, w; CASSANDRA CROSSING, THE(1977), w

Reg Mankin
TILLY OF BLOOMSBURY(1940, Brit.)

Roxie Mankins
Misc. Silents
FLAMES OF WRATH(1923)
Isidore Mankofsky
JUD(1971), ph; WEREWOLVES ON WHEELS(1971), ph; SCREAM BLACULA SCREAM(1973), ph; TRICK BABY(1973), ph; HOMEBODIES(1974), ph; SECOND COMING OF SUZANNE, THE(1974), ph; ULTIMATE THRILL, THE(1974), ph; MUPPET MOVIE, THE(1979), ph; JAZZ SINGER, THE(1980), ph; SOMEWHERE IN TIME(1980), ph
Wolf Mankowitz
MAKE ME AN OFFER(1954, Brit.), w; KID FOR TWO FARTHINGS, A(1956, Brit.), w; EXPRESSO BONGO(1959, Brit.), a, w; MILLIONAIRESS, THE(1960, Brit.), w; DAY THE EARTH CAUGHT FIRE, THE(1961, Brit.), w; HOUSE OF FRIGHT(1961), w; LONG AND THE SHORT AND THE TALL, THE(1961, Brit.), w; WALTZ OF THE TOREADORS(1962, Brit.), w; WHERE THE SPIES ARE(1965, Brit.), w; CASINO ROYALE(1967, Brit.), w; 25TH HOUR, THE(1967, Fr./Ital./Yugo.), w; BLACK BEAUTY(1971, Brit./Ger./Span.), w; BLOOMFIELD(1971, Brit./Israel), p, w; TREASURE ISLAND(1972, Brit./Span./Fr./Ger.), w; HIRELING, THE(1973, Brit.), w
Philip Mankowski
1984
NATURAL, THE(1984)
Vivianne Manku
CONFESSIONS OF AN OPIUM EATER(1962)
Blu Mankuma
1984
FINDERS KEEPERS(1984)
Dave Manley
STRUGGLE, THE(1931)
David Manley
PRIDE OF THE YANKEES, THE(1942); MORITURI(1965)
Doug Manley
SPRING FEVER(1983, Can.)
Jerry Manley
YOUNG GIRLS OF ROCHEFORT, THE(1968, Fr.); PIRATES OF PENZANCE, THE(1983)
Lou Manley
KNICKERBOCKER HOLIDAY(1944); WOMAN OBSESSED(1959)
Louis Manley
KISMET(1944); TILL THE CLOUDS ROLL BY(1946); MILLION DOLLAR MERMAID(1952)
Stephen Manley
KANSAS CITY BOMBER(1972); HINDENBURG, THE(1975)
1984
STAR TREK III: THE SEARCH FOR SPOCK(1984)
Walter H. Manley
GREEN SLIME, THE(1969), p
Walter Manley
EMBALMER, THE(1966, Ital.), p; WAR BETWEEN THE PLANETS(1971, Ital.), p, d
William Ford Manley
BIG BROADCAST, THE(1932), w
Manley and Austin
DUMMY TALKS, THE(1943, Brit.)
Dudley Manlove
10 NORTH FREDERICK(1958); PLAN 9 FROM OUTER SPACE(1959); CREATION OF THE HUMANOIDS(1962)
Fred Manly
Silents
ABRAHAM LINCOLN(1924)
J.Burnell Manly
Misc. Silents
THROUGH THE WRONG DOOR(1919)
Abby Mann
PORT OF ESCAPE(1955, Brit.), w; JUDGMENT AT NUREMBERG(1961), w; CHILD IS WAITING, A(1963), w; CONDEMNED OF ALTONA, THE(1963), w; SHIP OF FOOLS(1965), w; DETECTIVE, THE(1968), w; REPORT TO THE COMMISSIONER(1975), w
Adolph Mann
WITHOUT A HOME(1939, Pol.), p
Alan Mann
Misc. Talkies
HILARY'S BLUES(1983)
Alex Mann
I DRINK YOUR BLOOD(1971)
Misc. Talkies
GREAT SKYCOPTER RESCUE, THE(1982)
Alice Mann
Silents
PAIR OF SIXES, A(1918)
Misc. Silents
FRUITS OF PASSION(1919); WATER LILY, THE(1919); FAMILY CLOSET, THE(1921); PERJURY(1921)
Angela Mann
MONTY PYTHON'S THE MEANING OF LIFE(1983, Brit.)
Anita Mann
LOVE AND KISSES(1965); GREAT MUPPET CAPER, THE(1981), ch
Anthony Mann
DR. BROADWAY(1942), d; MOONLIGHT IN HAVANA(1942), d; NOBODY'S DARLING(1943), d; MY BEST GAL(1944), d; STRANGERS IN THE NIGHT(1944), d; GREAT FLAMARION, THE(1945), d; SING YOUR WAY HOME(1945), d; TWO O'CLOCK COURAGE(1945), d; BAMBOO BLONDE, THE(1946), d; STRANGE IMPERSONATION(1946), d; DESPERATE(1947), d, w; RAILROADED(1947), d; T-MEN(1948), d; HE WALKED BY NIGHT(1948), d; RAW DEAL(1948), d; BLACK BOOK, THE(1949), d; BORDER INCIDENT(1949), d; FOLLOW ME QUIETLY(1949), w; DEVIL'S DOORWAY(1950), d; FURIES, THE(1950), d; SIDE STREET(1950), d; WINCHESTER '73(1950), d; TALL TARGET, THE(1951), d; BEND OF THE RIVER(1952), d; GLENN MILLER STORY, THE(1953), d; NAKED SPUR, THE(1953), d; THUNDER BAY(1953), d; FAR COUNTRY, THE(1955), d; LAST FRONTIER, THE(1955), d; MAN FROM LARAMIE, THE(1955), d; STRATEGIC AIR COMMAND(1955), d; SERENADE(1956), d; MEN IN WAR(1957), d; TIN STAR, THE(1957), d; GOD'S LITTLE ACRE(1958), d; MAN OF THE WEST(1958), d; CIMARRON(1960),

d; SPARTACUS(1960), d; EL CID(1961, U.S./Ital.), p, d; FALL OF THE ROMAN EMPIRE, THE(1964), d; HEROES OF TELEMARK, THE(1965, Brit.), d; DANDY IN ASPIC, A(1968, Brit.), p&d
Arthur Mann
JACKIE ROBINSON STORY, THE(1950), w
Barry Mann
I NEVER SANG FOR MY FATHER(1970), m
Bernadene Mann
SIDEWINDER ONE(1977), cos
Bertha Mann
ALL QUIET ON THE WESTERN FRONT(1930); FREE LOVE(1930); LITTLE ACCIDENT(1930); CAUGHT CHEATING(1931); FATHER'S SON(1931); WOMAN OF EXPERIENCE, A(1931); BEHIND THE MASK(1932); FINAL EDITION(1932)
Misc. Silents
BLINDNESS OF DIVORCE, THE(1918)
Billy Mann
LADY BY CHOICE(1934); SHE SHALL HAVE MUSIC(1935, Brit.); THANKS A MILLION(1935); UNHOLY PARTNERS(1941)
Brian Mann
1984
SAVAGE STREETS(1984)
Burch Mann
TREASURE OF MATECUMBE(1976), ch
Cathleen Mann
SHOW GOES ON, THE(1938, Brit.), cos
Cherina Mann
STRAW DOGS(1971, Brit.)
Cindy Mann
SWEET BEAT(1962, Brit.)
Claude Mann
BAY OF ANGELS(1964, Fr.); SLEEPING CAR MURDER THE(1966, Fr.); L'ARMEE DES OMBRES(1969, Fr./Ital.); SACCO AND VANZETTI(1971, Ital./Fr.); INNOCENT, THE(1979, Ital.)
Colin Mann
HAPPY ROAD, THE(1957); GOODBYE AGAIN(1961); ADVENTURES OF SCARAMOUCHE, THE(1964, Fr.), w
Collette Mann
KITTY AND THE BAGMAN(1983, Aus.)
Daniel Mann
COME BACK LITTLE SHEBA(1952), d; ABOUT MRS. LESLIE(1954), d; I'LL CRY TOMORROW(1955), d; ROSE TATTOO, THE(1955), d; TEAHOUSE OF THE AUGUST MOON, THE(1956), d; HOT SPELL(1958), d; LAST ANGRY MAN, THE(1959), d; BUTTERFIELD 8(1960), d; MOUNTAIN ROAD, THE(1960), d; ADA(1961), d; FIVE FINGER EXERCISE(1962), d; WHO'S BEEN SLEEPING IN MY BED?(1963), d; JUDITH(1965), d; OUR MAN FLINT(1966), d; FOR LOVE OF IVY(1968), d; DREAM OF KINGS, A(1969), d; WILLARD(1971), d; REVENGERS, THE(1972, U.S./Mex.), d; INTERVAL(1973, Mex./U.S.), d; MAURIE(1973), d; LOST IN THE STARS(1974), d; JOURNEY INTO FEAR(1976, Can), d; MATILDA(1978), d
Misc. Talkies
MAURIE(1973), d
Dara Mann
WHO SAYS I CAN'T RIDE A RAINBOW!(1971)
Dave Mann
NEPTUNE FACTOR, THE(1973, Can.)
David Mann
WHO SAYS I CAN'T RIDE A RAINBOW!(1971); BREAKING POINT(1976)
Delbert Mann
MARTY(1955), d; BACHELOR PARTY, THE(1957), d; DESIRE UNDER THE ELMS(1958), d; SEPARATE TABLES(1958), d; MIDDLE OF THE NIGHT(1959), d; DARK AT THE TOP OF THE STAIRS, THE(1960), d; LOVER COME BACK(1961), d; OUTSIDER, THE(1962), d; THAT TOUCH OF MINK(1962), d; GATHERING OF EAGLES, A(1963), d; DEAR HEART(1964), d; QUICK, BEFORE IT MELTS(1964), p, d; MISTER BUDDWING(1966), p, d; FITZWILLY(1967), d; PINK JUNGLE, THE(1968), d; DAVID COPPERFIELD(1970, Brit.), d; JANE EYRE(1971, Brit.), d; KIDNAPPED(1971, Brit.), d; BIRCH INTERVAL(1976), d; NIGHT CROSSING(1982), d
Silents
IRON HORSE, THE(1924)
Dina Mann
PETERSEN(1974, Aus.)
Dolores Mann
WHEN WORLDS COLLIDE(1951); NO ROOM FOR THE GROOM(1952)
Dorothy Mann
SINCE YOU WENT AWAY(1944)
E. B. Mann
BOSS RIDER OF GUN CREEK(1936), w; STORMY TRAILS(1936), w; DESERT PHANTOM(1937), w; GUNS IN THE DARK(1937), w; LIGHTNIN' CRANDALL(1937), w; RIDIN' THE LONE TRAIL(1937), w; TRAIL OF VENGEANCE(1937), w
Ed Mann
CHASE, THE(1946), ed
Misc. Talkies
HOOCH(1977), d
Eddie Mann
RETURN OF RIN TIN TIN, THE(1947), ed; RIOT IN JUVENILE PRISON(1959), ed
Edward Mann
BILL CRACKS DOWN(1937), ed; LARCENY ON THE AIR(1937), ed; MICHAEL O'HALLORAN(1937), ed; RHYTHM IN THE CLOUDS(1937), ed; ARSON GANG BUSTERS(1938), ed; COME ON, LEATHERNECKS(1938), ed; HOLLYWOOD STADIUM MYSTERY(1938), ed; I MET MY LOVE AGAIN(1938), ed; MAMA RUNS WILD(1938), ed; COME ON RANGERS(1939), ed; FORGED PASSPORT(1939), ed; FRONTIER VENGEANCE(1939), ed; IN OLD CALIENTE(1939), ed; IN OLD MONTEREY(1939), ed; MAN OF CONQUEST(1939), ed; MEET DR. CHRISTIAN(1939), ed; PRIDE OF THE NAVY(1939), ed; BORDER LEGION, THE(1940), ed; BOWERY BOY(1940), ed; COLORADO(1940), ed; COURAGEOUS DR. CHRISTIAN, THE(1940), ed; DR. CHRISTIAN MEETS THE WOMEN(1940), ed; SING, DANCE, PLENTY HOT(1940), ed; WHO KILLED AUNT MAGGIE?(1940), ed; WOMEN IN WAR(1940), ed; DOCTORS DON'T TELL(1941), ed; LADY FROM LOUISIANA(1941), ed; MELODY FOR THREE(1941), ed; MR. DISTRICT ATTORNEY(1941), ed; PETTICOAT POLITICS(1941), ed; PUBLIC ENEMIES(1941), ed; SAILORS ON LEAVE(1941), ed; BELLS OF CAPISTRANO(1942), ed; CALL OF THE CANYON(1942), ed; HOME IN WYO-

MIN'(1942), ed; HURRICANE SMITH(1942), ed; MOONLIGHT MASQUERADE(1942), ed; RIDIN' DOWN THE CANYON(1942), ed; STARDUST ON THE SAGE(1942), ed; TRAGEDY AT MIDNIGHT, A(1942), ed; YOKEL BOY(1942), ed; DILLINGER(1945), ed; MAN FROM RAINBOW VALLEY, THE(1946), ed; UNDER NEVADA SKIES(1946), ed; CARTER CASE, THE(1947), ed; HEAVEN ONLY KNOWS(1947), ed; FOUR FACES WEST(1948), ed; HIGHWAY 13(1948), ed; ARSON, INC.(1949), ed; DEPUTY MARSHAL(1949), ed; SKY LINER(1949), ed; EVERYBODY'S DANCIN'(1950), ed; HI-JACKED(1950), ed; ONE TOO MANY(1950), ed; BIG NIGHT, THE(1951), ed; M(1951), ed; WHEN I GROW UP(1951), ed; ABBOTT AND COSTELLO MEET CAPTAIN KIDD(1952), ed; FIGHTER, THE(1952), ed; BLUE GARDENIA, THE(1953), ed; MARRY ME AGAIN(1953), ed; SCANDAL INCORPORATED(1956), d, ed; ATTACK OF THE 50 FOOT WOMAN(1958), ed; HONG KONG CONFIDENTIAL(1958), ed; WILD HERITAGE(1958), ed; FOUR SKULLS OF JONATHAN DRAKE, THE(1959), ed; GUNFIGHTERS OF ABILENE(1960), ed; TWELVE TO THE MOON(1960), ed; LAST SUNSET, THE(1961), ed; BIRDMAN OF ALCATRAZ(1962), ed; LONELY ARE THE BRAVE(1962), ed; HOTHEAD(1963), d; SCUM OF THE EARTH(1963); TARZAN AND THE GREAT RIVER(1967, U.S./Switz.), ed; LOST MAN, THE(1969), ed; WHO SAYS I CAN'T RIDE A RAINBOW!(1971), d, w; GATLING GUN, THE(1972), ed; MUTATIONS, THE(1974, Brit.), w; SEIZURE(1974), w; KILLER INSIDE ME, THE(1976), w

Edward A. Mann
HALLUCINATION GENERATION(1966), d&w, spec eff
Edward Andrew Mann
ISLAND OF TERROR(1967, Brit.), w
Edward Beverly Mann
STAMPEDE(1949), w
Elizabeth Mann
AVENGERS, THE(1942, Brit.)
Ellen Mann
INADMISSIBLE EVIDENCE(1968, Brit.)
Ellika Mann
SHAME(1968, Swed.)
Erika Mann
CONFESSIONS OF FELIX KRULL, THE(1957, Ger.), w; TONIO KROGER(1968, Fr./Ger.), w
Frances Mann
Silents
FORTUNE'S CHILD(1919)
Misc. Silents
FRUITS OF PASSION(1919); ROOT OF EVIL, THE(1919)
Frances R. Mann
WHO GOES NEXT?(1938, Brit.)
Frank Mann
DIAMONDS ARE FOREVER(1971, Brit.)
Frankie Mann
DIRTYMOUTH(1970)
Silents
CLIMBERS, THE(1915); JOHN SMITH(1922); SHADOWS OF THE SEA(1922); ON TIME(1924)
Misc. Silents
SEX LURE, THE(1916); PLACE OF THE HONEYMOONS, THE(1920); UNCONQUERED WOMAN(1922)
George Mann
YEARLING, THE(1946); NEPTUNE'S DAUGHTER(1949); COLD TURKEY(1971)
George K. Mann
SENATOR WAS INDISCREET, THE(1947); TOO LATE FOR TEARS(1949)
Grace Mann
SPECTER OF THE ROSE(1946)
Greta Mann
CAUGHT SHORT(1930)
Gus Mann
SHARKY'S MACHINE(1982)
Hank Mann
DONOVAN AFFAIR, THE(1929); FALL OF EVE, THE(1929); ARIZONA KID, THE(1930); SINNER'S HOLIDAY(1930); ANNABELLE'S AFFAIRS(1931); DAWN TRAIL, THE(1931); MILLION DOLLAR LEGS(1932); RIDIN' FOR JUSTICE(1932); SCARFACE(1932); STRANGE LOVE OF MOLLY LOUVAIN, THE(1932); BIG CHANCE, THE(1933); FOURTH HORSEMAN, THE(1933); SMOKY(1933); FUGITIVE ROAD(1934); BARBARY COAST(1935); DEVIL IS A WOMAN, THE(1935); CALL OF THE PRAIRIE(1936); MODERN TIMES(1936); ON THE AVENUE(1937); SARATOGA(1937); YOU CAN'T HAVE EVERYTHING(1937); STRANGER FROM ARIZONA, THE(1938); FRONTIER MARSHAL(1939); HOLLYWOOD CAVALCADE(1939); GREAT DICTATOR, THE(1940); BULLETS FOR O'HARA(1941); HONOLULU LU(1941); MALTESE FALCON, THE(1941); NINE LIVES ARE NOT ENOUGH(1941); BULLET SCARS(1942); GAY SISTERS, THE(1942); GEORGE WASHINGTON SLEPT HERE(1942); KING'S ROW(1942); LARCENY, INC.(1942); MALE ANIMAL, THE(1942); MAN WHO CAME TO DINNER, THE(1942); DANCING MASTERS, THE(1943); MYSTERIOUS DOCTOR, THE(1943); PHANTOM OF THE OPERA(1943); THANK YOUR LUCKY STARS(1943); ARSENIC AND OLD LACE(1944); CRIME BY NIGHT(1944); PERILS OF PAULINE, THE(1947); WHEN MY BABY SMILES AT ME(1948); ROSEANNA McCOY(1949); HUMPHREY TAKES A CHANCE(1950); MY FAVORITE SPY(1951); ON MOONLIGHT BAY(1951); SON OF PALEFACE(1952); THREE HOURS TO KILL(1954); ABBOTT AND COSTELLO MEET THE KEYSTONE KOPS(1955); ABBOTT AND COSTELLO MEET THE MUMMY(1955); HOW TO BE VERY, VERY, POPULAR(1955); PARDNERS(1956); MAN OF A THOUSAND FACES(1957); ROCK-A-BYE BABY(1958); DADDY-O(1959); LAST TRAIN FROM GUN HILL(1959)
Silents
TILLIE'S PUNCTURED ROMANCE(1914); DON'T MARRY FOR MONEY(1923); NEAR LADY, THE(1923); NOISE IN NEWBORO, A(1923); WANTERS, THE(1923); EMPTY HANDS(1924); ARIZONA ROMEO, THE(1925); WOMAN WHO SINNED, A(1925); SKYROCKET, THE(1926); WINGS OF THE STORM(1926); LADYBIRD, THE(1927); SMILE, BROTHER, SMILE(1927); MORGAN'S LAST RAID(1929); SPITE MARRIAGE(1929); CITY LIGHTS(1931)
Misc. Silents
MODERN ENOCH ARDEN, A(1916); MAN WHO PLAYED SQUARE, THE(1924); SCORCHER, THE(1927)

Harry Mann
Silents
KINKAID, GAMBLER(1916); AFRAID TO FIGHT(1922); ABYSMAL BRUTE, THE(1923); STORM DAUGHTER, THE(1924)
Misc. Silents
BATTLING BUNYON(1925)
Heinrich Mann
BLUE ANGEL, THE(1930, Ger.), w; BLUE ANGEL, THE(1959), w
Helen Mann
HAPPY DAYS(1930); JUST IMAGINE(1930); EMPLOYEE'S ENTRANCE(1933); LADIES THEY TALK ABOUT(1933); LITTLE GIANT, THE(1933); FOLIES DERGERE(1935)
Howard Mann
WHOLLY MOSES(1980); GOING APE!(1981); HISTORY OF THE WORLD, PART 1(1981)
Iris Mann
ROOM FOR ONE MORE(1952)
Jack Mann
FLIGHT THAT DISAPPEARED, THE(1961); POLICE DOG STORY, THE(1961); YOU HAVE TO RUN FAST(1961)
Jane Mann
UNEARTHLY, THE(1957), w; ANATOMY OF A PSYCHO(1961), w
Jay Mann
NIGHT THEY ROBBED BIG BERTHA'S, THE(1975)
Jerry Mann
UNDERWORLD U.S.A.(1961); MALTESE BIPPY, THE(1969); SWEET CHARITY(1969); HOW TO SEDUCE A WOMAN(1974)
Jodie Mann
NEW YEAR'S EVIL(1980)
John Mann
SUCH IS LIFE(1936, Brit.); IT'S NOT CRICKET(1949, Brit.)
Klaus Mann
PAISAN(1948, Ital.), w; MEPHISTO(1981, Ger.), w
Kurt Mann
CHECKMATE(1973)
Misc. Talkies
DYNAMITE(1972)
Larry Mann
FLAMING FRONTIER(1958, Can.); SPENCER'S MOUNTAIN(1963); ROBIN AND THE SEVEN HOODS(1964); BLACK EYE(1974)
Larry D. Mann
QUICK AND THE DEAD, THE(1963); WILLIE MCBEAN AND HIS MAGIC MACHINE(1965, U.S./Jap.); APPALOOSA, THE(1966); COVENANT WITH DEATH, A(1966); SINGING NUN, THE(1966); SWINGER, THE(1966); CAPRICE(1967); IN THE HEAT OF THE NIGHT(1967); WICKED DREAMS OF PAULA SCHULTZ, THE(1968); ANGEL IN MY POCKET(1969); LIBERATION OF L.B. JONES, THE(1970); THERE WAS A CROOKED MAN(1970); SCANDALOUS JOHN(1971); GET TO KNOW YOUR RABBIT(1972); CHARLEY AND THE ANGEL(1973); OKLAHOMA CRUDE(1973); STING, THE(1973); PONY EXPRESS RIDER(1976); OCTAGON, THE(1980)
Laura Mann
PHANTASM(1979)
Lawrence Mann
WILD COUNTRY, THE(1971)
Lawrence D. Mann
DEAD HEAT ON A MERRY-GO-ROUND(1966)
Leonard Mann
UNHOLY FOUR, THE(1969, Ital.); HUMANOID, THE(1979, Ital.); WIFEMISTRESS(1979, Ital.); NIGHT SCHOOL(1981); TERROR EYES(1981)
1984
CORRUPT(1984, Ital.); UNFAITHFULLY YOURS(1984)
Lisa Mann
LILIES OF THE FIELD(1963)
Lothar Mann
ORDERED TO LOVE(1963, Ger.); STOP TRAIN 349(1964, Fr./Ital./Ger.)
Lou Mann
1984
MEATBALLS PART II(1984), set d
Louis Mann
SINS OF THE CHILDREN(1930)
Louis Mann [Luigi Carpentieri]
HORRIBLE DR. HICHCOCK, THE(1964, Ital.), p; GHOST, THE(1965, Ital.), p
Luigi Mann
WITCHES, THE(1969, Fr./Ital.), w
Manfred Mann
UP THE JUNCTION(1968, Brit.), m; VENUS IN FURS(1970, Ital./Brit./Ger.), m
Marcia Mann
TOP BANANA(1954)
Margaret Mann
RIVER, THE(1928); DISRAELI(1929); BRAT, THE(1931); SECRET MENACE(1931); IF I HAD A MILLION(1932); BACHELOR MOTHER(1933); CHARLIE CHAN IN LONDON(1934); JUDGE PRIEST(1934); PAINTED VEIL, THE(1934); KENTUCKY BLUE STREAK(1935); LITTLE MEN(1935); MAN WHO RECLAIMED HIS HEAD, THE(1935); LAW RIDES, THE(1936); UNDERCOVER MAN(1936); CONFLICT(1937); YOU CAN'T TAKE IT WITH YOU(1938); FEDERAL MAN-HUNT(1939); MR. SMITH GOES TO WASHINGTON(1939)
Silents
RED LANE, THE(1920); BLACK BEAUTY(1921); DESERT BLOSSOMS(1921); MILLIONAIRE, THE(1921); NEW DISCIPLE, THE(1921); FOUR SONS(1928)
Misc. Silents
ONCE TO EVERY WOMAN(1920); MAN–WOMAN–MARRIAGE(1921); CALL OF HOME, THE(1922); HER SISTER FROM PARIS(1925)
Michael Mann
ROOGIE'S BUMP(1954); NOW THAT APRIL'S HERE(1958, Can.); SMOKEY AND THE BANDIT(1977); HOUSE CALLS(1978); CHINA SYNDROME, THE(1979); THIEF(1981), d&w; KEEP, THE(1983), d&w
Milton Mann
SCANDAL INCORPORATED(1956), p, w; HOTHEAD(1963), p, w; MARINE BATTLEGROUND(1966, U.S/S.K.), d, w, ed; TARZAN AND THE JUNGLE BOY(1968, US/Switz.), ed

Ned Mann
LADY OF THE PAVEMENTS(1929), spec. eff; DELUGE(1933), spec eff; SCARLET PIMPERNEL, THE(1935, Brit.), spec eff; GHOST GOES WEST, THE(1936), spec eff; REMBRANDT(1936, Brit.), spec eff; THINGS TO COME(1936, Brit.), spec eff; DARK JOURNEY(1937, Brit.), spec eff; FIRE OVER ENGLAND(1937, Brit.), spec eff; KNIGHT WITHOUT ARMOR(1937, Brit.), spec eff; MAN WHO COULD WORK MIRACLES, THE(1937, Brit.), spec eff; MEN ARE NOT GODS(1937, Brit.), spec eff; STORM IN A TEACUP(1937, Brit.), spec eff; DIVORCE OF LADY X. THE(1938, Brit.), spec eff; BEYOND TOMORROW(1940), spec eff; MIRACLE IN MILAN(1951, Ital.), spec eff
Silents
DON Q, SON OF ZORRO(1925), spec eff
Norman Mann
PLAGUE OF THE ZOMBIES, THE(1966, Brit.); VENOM(1982, Brit.)
P.J. Mann
LITTLE SEX, A(1982)
Pat Mann
MOONRUNNERS(1975), art d; LOVE CHILD(1982)
Patrick Mann
1984
NEW YORK NIGHTS(1984), art d
Paul Mann
QUARTERBACK, THE(1940), m; AMERICA, AMERICA(1963); FIDDLER ON THE ROOF(1971)
Peter Mann
POCKETFUL OF MIRACLES(1961); LIVELY SET, THE(1964); GREATEST STORY EVER TOLD, THE(1965); SWORD OF ALI BABA, THE(1965); HEAD ON(1981, Can.), m
R. Mann
LAST STOP, THE(1949, Pol.), set d
Ray Mann
Misc. Talkies
KING FRAT(1979)
Roman Mann
ASHES AND DIAMONDS(1961, Pol.), art d; EVE WANTS TO SLEEP(1961, Pol.), art d; KANAL(1961, Pol.), art d; JOAN OF THE ANGELS(1962, Pol.), art d; KNIGHTS OF THE TEUTONIC ORDER, THE(1962, Pol.), art d
Ron Mann
1984
LISTEN TO THE CITY(1984, Can.), p&d, w
Sheri Mann
MAUSOLEUM(1983)
Stanely Mann
METEOR(1979), w
Stanley Mann
RIP TIDE(1934); GILDED LILY, THE(1935); MRS. MINIVER(1942); ANNA AND THE KING OF SIAM(1946); CRIMSON KEY, THE(1947); IMPERFECT LADY, THE(1947); MOSS ROSE(1947); THIRTEENTH LETTER, THE(1951); ANOTHER TIME, ANOTHER PLACE(1958), w; MOUSE THAT ROARED, THE(1959, Brit.), w; HIS AND HERS(1961, Brit.), w; MARK, THE(1961, Brit.), w; WOMAN OF STRAW(1964, Brit.), w; COLLECTOR, THE(1965), w; HIGH WIND IN JAMAICA, A(1965), w; RAPTURE(1965), w; UP FROM THE BEACH(1965), w; NAKED RUNNER, THE(1967, Brit.), w; STRANGE AFFAIR, THE(1968, Brit.), p, w; FRAULEIN DOKTOR(1969, Ital./Yugo.), w; DEVIL'S WIDOW, THE(1972, Brit.), p; THEATRE OF BLOOD(1973, Brit.), p; RUSSIAN ROULETTE(1975), w; BREAKING POINT(1976), w; SKY RIDERS(1976, U.S./Gr.), w; DAMIEN–OMEN II(1978), w; CIRCLE OF IRON(1979, Brit.), w; EYE OF THE NEEDLE(1981), w
1984
CONAN THE DESTROYER(1984), w; FIRESTARTER(1984), a, w
Stately Mann
METEOR(1979)
Sugar Ray Mann
ABSENCE OF MALICE(1981)
Suzy Mann
FEMALE RESPONSE, THE(1972)
Ted Mann
ILLUSTRATED MAN, THE(1969), p
Thomas Mann
CONFESSIONS OF FELIX KRULL, THE(1957, Ger.), w; TONIO KROGER(1968, Fr./Ger.), w; DEATH IN VENICE(1971, Ital./Fr.), w; DISORDER AND EARLY TORMENT(1977, Ger.), w
Tracey Mann
HARD KNOCKS(1980, Aus.)
Tracy Mann
SCARECROW, THE(1982, New Zealand)
Vincent Mann
STRANGE SHADOWS IN AN EMPTY ROOM(1977, Can./Ital.), w
Werner Mann
MOSES AND AARON(1975, Ger./Fr./Ital.)
Winifred Mann
TELL ME A RIDDLE(1980)
Yanka Mann
ETERNAL SUMMER(1961); PASSION HOLIDAY(1963); HONEYMOON OF HORROR(1964); FLESH FEAST(1970)
Henry Manna
CHAMPAGNE WALTZ(1937)
Beppe Mannaiuolo
BEAUTIFUL SWINDLERS, THE(1967, Fr./Ital./Jap./Neth.)
Russ Mannarelli
RED, WHITE AND BLACK, THE(1970), ed
Guido Mannari
SHE AND HE(1969, Ital.); DRIVER'S SEAT, THE(1975, Ital.)
Mauro Mannatrizio
HILLS RUN RED, THE(1967, Ital.)
Manne
YOUNG BILLY YOUNG(1969), m/l
Daniel Manne
WHO'S GOT THE ACTION?(1962), d

M.C. Manne
SUMMER'S CHILDREN(1979, Can.), ed
Max Manne
FOLLOW THE LEADER(1930), m
Michael Manne
ROWDYMAN, THE(1973, Can.), ed
Shelley Manne
FIVE PENNIES, THE(1959); GENE KRUPA STORY, THE(1959); T-BIRD GANG(1959), m
Shelly Manne
MAN WITH THE GOLDEN ARM, THE(1955); I WANT TO LIVE!(1958); PROPER TIME, THE(1959), m; SUBTERRANEANS, THE(1960); LIKE FATHER LIKE SON(1961), m; WILD AND WONDERFUL(1964); YOUNG SINNER, THE(1965), m; YOUNG BILLY YOUNG(1969), m; TRIAL OF THE CATONSVILLE NINE, THE(1972), m; TRADER HORN(1973), m; MAN WHO LOVED WOMEN, THE(1983)
Mannejuolo
AUGUSTINE OF HIPPO(1973, Ital.)
Maria Mannelli
OPIATE '67(1967, Fr./Ital.)
Cecil Mannering
MERRY COMES TO STAY(1937, Brit.); STORM IN A TEACUP(1937, Brit.)
Silents
GRIT OF A JEW, THE(1917, Brit.); SINGLE MAN, THE(1919, Brit.); TATTERLY(1919, Brit.); OLD ARM CHAIR, THE(1920, Brit.)
Misc. Silents
KISSING CUP(1913, Brit.); BEAU BROCADE(1916, Brit.); MILL-OWNER'S DAUGHTER, THE(1916, Brit.); DUCHESS OF SEVEN DIALS, THE(1920, Brit.); IN FULL CRY(1921, Brit.)
Lewin Mannering
CARMEN(1931, Brit.)
Silents
LAND OF HOPE AND GLORY(1927, Brit.)
Moya Mannering
Misc. Silents
LES CLOCHES DE CORNEVILLE(1917, Brit.)
Peter Mannering
TIME LOCK(1959, Brit.)
Audrey Manners
GUNGA DIN(1939); MY SON, MY SON!(1940); ONE MILLION B.C.(1940); MARINE RAIDERS(1944); PEARL OF DEATH, THE(1944); PICTURE OF DORIAN GRAY, THE(1945)
David Manners
HE KNEW WOMEN(1930); JOURNEY'S END(1930); KISMET(1930); MOTHERS CRY(1930); SWEET MAMA(1930); TRUTH ABOUT YOUTH, THE(1930); DRACULA(1931); LAST FLIGHT, THE(1931); MILLIONAIRE, THE(1931); MIRACLE WOMAN, THE(1931); RIGHT TO LOVE, THE(1931); RULING VOICE, THE(1931); BILL OF DIVORCEMENT, A(1932); CROONER(1932); GREEKS HAD A WORD FOR THEM(1932); LADY WITH A PAST(1932); MAN WANTED(1932); MUMMY, THE(1932); STRANGER IN TOWN(1932); THEY CALL IT SIN(1932); DEATH KISS, THE(1933); DEVIL'S IN LOVE, THE(1933); FROM HELL TO HEAVEN(1933); GIRL IN 419(1933); ROMAN SCANDALS(1933); TORCH SINGER(1933); WARRIOR'S HUSBAND, THE(1933); BLACK CAT, THE(1934); GREAT FLIRTATION, THE(1934); LUCK OF A SAILOR, THE(1934, Brit.); MOONSTONE, THE(1934); JALNA(1935); MYSTERY OF EDWIN DROOD, THE(1935); PERFECT CLUE, THE(1935); HEARTS IN BONDAGE(1936); WOMAN REBELS, A(1936)
Diana Manners
IT COULDN'T HAVE HAPPENED–BUT IT DID(1936)
Silents
GLORIOUS ADVENTURE, THE(1922, U.S./Brit.)
Dorothy Manners
Silents
PAWN TICKET 210(1922); GARRISON'S FINISH(1923)
Misc. Silents
VICTOR, THE(1923)
J. Hartley Manners
PEG O' MY HEART(1933), w
Silents
HOUSE NEXT DOOR, THE(1914), w
Jane Manners
1984
BOSTONIANS, THE(1984)
Jayne Manners
CEILNG ZERO(1935)
John Manners
Silents
LONDON(1926, Brit.); GHOST TRAIN, THE(1927, Brit.); HUNTINGTOWER(1927, Brit.)
Misc. Silents
TIPTOES(1927, Brit.)
Kim Manners
HALLS OF ANGER(1970)
Lady Diana Manners
Silents
GREAT LOVE, THE(1918)
Misc. Silents
VIRGIN QUEEN, THE(1923, Brit.)
Marcia Manners
CAUGHT(1931); IT PAYS TO ADVERTISE(1931)
Margery Manners
MRS. BROWN, YOU'VE GOT A LOVELY DAUGHTER(1968, Brit.)
Marian Manners
LET'S MAKE LOVE(1960)
Marjorie Manners
NIGHT FOR CRIME, A(1942); RUBBER RACKETEERS(1942); TEXAS TO BATAAN(1942); HARVEST MELODY(1943); WESTERN CYCLONE(1943); BLAZING FRONTIER(1944); THAT'S MY BABY(1944); TROCADERO(1944); BIG SHOW-OFF, THE(1945); IDENTITY UNKNOWN(1945); ACCOMPLICE(1946); FRENCH KEY, THE(1946)

Misc. Talkies
OUTLAWS OF BOULDER PASS(1942); TUMBLEWEED TRAIL(1942); FRONTIER FIGHTERS(1947)

Marlene Manners
SHOCK CORRIDOR(1963)

Mary Manners
Silents
EUGENE ARAM(1914, Brit.)

Mickey Manners
ERRAND BOY, THE(1961); WHICH WAY TO THE FRONT?(1970)

Rose Manners
Misc. Silents
BIG MONEY(1918, Brit.); DECEPTION(1918, Brit.)

Scott Manners
SGT. PEPPER'S LONELY HEARTS CLUB BAND(1978)

Sheila Manners
TEN NIGHTS IN A BARROOM(1931); LAND OF WANTED MEN(1932)
Misc. Talkies
PLAYTHINGS OF HOLLYWOOD(1931)

Yvonne Manners
UP THE JUNCTION(1968, Brit.); LEOPARD IN THE SNOW(1979, Brit./Can.)

Zeke Manners
REAL LIFE(1979)

Gerard Manneveau
STATE OF SIEGE(1973, Fr./U.S./Ital./Ger.)

Dorothy Manney
SAFETY IN NUMBERS(1938), w

Renate Mannhardt
LOST ONE, THE(1951, Ger.); RIVER CHANGES, THE(1956); DAY WILL COME, A(1960, Ger.); BIG SHOW, THE(1961)

Lucie Mannheim
DANTON(1931, Ger.); 39 STEPS, THE(1935, Brit.); EAST MEETS WEST(1936, Brit.); YELLOW CANARY, THE(1944, Brit.); HOTEL RESERVE(1946, Brit.); TAWNY PIPIT(1947, Brit.); PARIS EXPRESS, THE(1953, Brit.); SO LITTLE TIME(1953, Brit.); BEYOND THE CURTAIN(1960, Brit.); CONFESS DR. CORDA(1960, Ger.); CITY OF SECRETS(1963, Ger.); BUNNY LAKE IS MISSING(1965)
Misc. Silents
STONE RIDER, THE(1923, Ger.)

Lucy Mannheim
HIGH COMMAND(1938, Brit.)

Albert Mannheimer
KID FROM TEXAS, THE(1939), w; DULCY(1940), w; SPORTING BLOOD(1940), w; WHISTLING IN THE DARK(1941), w; DU BARRY WAS A LADY(1943), w; SONG OF THE OPEN ROAD(1944), w; THREE DARING DAUGHTERS(1948), w; BORN YESTERDAY(1950), w; HER FIRST ROMANCE(1951), w

Ettore Manni
FATAL DESIRE(1953); TWO NIGHTS WITH CLEOPATRA(1953, Ital.); ATTILA(1958, Ital.); WARRIOR AND THE SLAVE GIRL, THE(1959, Ital.); AUSTERLITZ(1960, Fr./Ital./Yugo.); LEGIONS OF THE NILE(1960, Ital.); PIRATE OF THE BLACK HAWK, THE(1961, Fr./Ital.); REVOLT OF THE SLAVES, THE(1961, Ital./Span./Ger.); LE AMICHE(1962, Ital.); VALIANT, THE(1962, Brit./Ital.); CLEOPATRA'S DAUGHTER(1963, Fr., Ital.); HERCULES AND THE CAPTIVE WOMEN(1963, Fr./Ital.); RED SHEIK, THE(1963, Ital.); SHIP OF CONDEMNED WOMEN, THE(1963, ITAL.); GOLD FOR THE CAESARS(1964); BATTLE OF THE VILLA FIORITA, THE(1965, Brit.); WAR OF THE ZOMBIES, THE(1965 Ital.); MADEMOISELLE(1966, Fr./Brit.); RINGO AND HIS GOLDEN PISTOL(1966, Ital.); DEVIL IN LOVE, THE(1968, Ital.); STRANGER RETURNS, THE(1968, U.S./Ital./Span.); DRAMA OF THE RICH(1975, Ital./Fr.); CHINO(1976, Ital., Span., Fr.); STREET PEOPLE(1976, U.S./Ital.); DIVINE NYMPH, THE(1979, Ital.); CITY OF WOMEN(1980, Ital./Fr.)

Jack Mannick
CALL NORTHSIDE 777(1948)

Ethel Mannin
BELOVED IMPOSTER(1936, Brit.), w

Hamilton Mannin
Silents
ADVENTUROUS SEX, THE(1925), w

Aileen Manning
SWEETIE(1929); THIRD ALARM, THE(1930); WEDDING RINGS(1930); HUCKLEBERRY FINN(1931); RANGE LAW(1931); UP FOR MURDER(1931)
Silents
EVERYBODY'S SWEETHEART(1920); HOME STUFF(1921); MIXED FACES(1922); RAGS TO RICHES(1922); TAILOR MADE MAN, A(1922); NOBODY'S MONEY(1923); HOUSE OF YOUTH, THE(1924); LOVER'S LANE(1924); SNOB, THE(1924); STELLA MARIS(1925); OLYMPIC HERO, THE(1928); SINGLE MAN, A(1929)
Misc. Silents
POWER OF LOVE, THE(1922); HOME JAMES(1928)

Albert Manning
THREE DARING DAUGHTERS(1948), w

Ambrose Manning
SONG OF FREEDOM(1938, Brit.)
Silents
SQUIBS(1921, Brit.)

Amy Manning
Silents
RAINBOW PRINCESS, THE(1916)

Art Manning
Misc. Silents
SPEED DEMON, THE(1925)

Audrey Manning
JUST WILLIAM'S LUCK(1948, Brit.)

Barry Manning
DOWN OUR ALLEY(1939, Brit.)

Bruce Manning
NINTH GUEST, THE(1934), w; PRIVATE SCANDAL(1934), w; AFTER THE DANCE(1935), w; EIGHT BELLS(1935), w; GRAND EXIT(1935), w; PARTY WIRE(1935), w; COUNTERFEIT(1936), w; DEVIL'S SQUADRON(1936), w; LONE WOLF RETURNS, THE(1936), w; MEET NERO WOLFE(1936), w; ROAMING LADY(1936), w; GIRL WITH IDEAS, A(1937), w; LET THEM LIVE(1937), w; WE HAVE OUR MOMENTS(1937), w; 100 MEN AND A GIRL(1937), w; MAD ABOUT MUSIC(1938), w; RAGE OF PARIS, THE(1938), w; SERVICE DE LUXE(1938), w; THAT CERTAIN AGE(1938), w; FIRST LOVE(1939), w; THREE SMART GIRLS GROW UP(1939), w; SPRING PARADE(1940), w; APPOINTMENT FOR LOVE(1941), p, w; BACK STREET(1941), w; BROADWAY(1942), w; AMAZING MRS. HOLLIDAY(1943), p&d; GUEST WIFE(1945), w; THIS LOVE OF OURS(1945), w; MAGNIFICENT DOLL(1946), p; SO GOES MY LOVE(1946), p, w; BRIDE FOR SALE(1949), w; THAT MIDNIGHT KISS(1949), w; SECRET FURY, THE(1950), p; PAYMENT ON DEMAND(1951), p, w; HOODLUM EMPIRE(1952), w; JUBILEE TRAIL(1954), w; FLAME OF THE ISLANDS(1955), w; NEVER SAY GOODBYE(1956), w; SPOILERS OF THE FOREST(1957), w

Bruce Manning [Frank Shaw]
BROADWAY(1942), p

Buck Manning
Misc. Silents
WINDING TRAIL, THE(1921)

Edward Manning
1984
DREAMSCAPE(1984), anim

George Manning
DOUBLE LIFE, A(1947)

George M. Manning
T-MEN(1947)

Guy Manning
DRESSER, THE(1983)

Hallie Manning
Silents
NEW KLONDIKE, THE(1926)

Hobart Manning
HOMECOMING(1948)

Hope Manning
ANY MAN'S WIFE(1936); MICHAEL O'HALLORAN(1937); OLD CORRAL, THE(1937); TWO WISE MAIDS(1937)

Hugh Manning
SECRET PLACE, THE(1958, Brit.); OUR MAN IN HAVANA(1960, Brit.); MIDSUMMERS NIGHT'S DREAM, A(1961, Czech.); FIVE MILLION YEARS TO EARTH(1968, Brit.); MACKINTOSH MAN, THE(1973, Brit.); ELEPHANT MAN, THE(1980, Brit.)

Irene Manning
BIG SHOT, THE(1942); SPY SHIP(1942); YANKEE DOODLE DANDY(1942); DESERT SONG, THE(1943); DOUGHGIRLS, THE(1944); HOLLYWOOD CANTEEN(1944); MAKE YOUR OWN BED(1944); SHINE ON, HARVEST MOON(1944); ESCAPE IN THE DESERT(1945); YANK IN LONDON, A(1946, Brit.)

Jack Manning
WALK EAST ON BEACON(1952); OWL AND THE PUSSYCAT, THE(1970); WHERE'S POPPA?(1970); GREAT NORTHFIELD, MINNESOTA RAID, THE(1972); MELINDA(1972); THIEF WHO CAME TO DINNER, THE(1973); SUPERDAD(1974); GREAT WALDO PEPPER, THE(1975); FRANCES(1982)
Silents
LOVE FLOWER, THE(1920)

Jean Manning
DON'T GO IN THE HOUSE(1980)

Joseph Manning
Silents
LITTLE PAL(1915); RAGS(1915); KINGDOM OF LOVE, THE(1918)

Judy Manning
OUTSIDER, THE(1949, Brit.)

Katy Manning
1984
MELVIN, SON OF ALVIN(1984, Aus.)

Knox Manning
FLYING IRISHMAN, THE(1939); CHEERS FOR MISS BISHOP(1941); MEET JOHN DOE(1941); TANKS A MILLION(1941); TOM, DICK AND HARRY(1941); SPIRIT OF STANFORD, THE(1942); TO THE SHORES OF TRIPOLI(1942); YANK ON THE BURMA ROAD, A(1942); UP IN ARMS(1944); KID FROM BOOKLYN, THE(1946); HIT PARADE OF 1947(1947); BABE RUTH STORY, THE(1948); LAWTON STORY, THE(1949); WILD WEED(1949); JOE PALOOKA MEETS HUMPHREY(1950)

Lainie Manning
GOING BERSERK(1983); TO BE OR NOT TO BE(1983)

Lucky Manning
SONG OF THE LOON(1970)

Marcia Manning
HOUSE OF SECRETS(1929)

Marilyn Manning
EEGAH!(1962); SADIST, THE(1963); WHAT'S UP FRONT(1964)

Marjorie Manning
WATERLOO BRIDGE(1940)
Silents
COST, THE(1920)

Mary Manning
FINNEGANS WAKE(1965), w

Max Manning
ROUSTABOUT(1964); YOUNG GRADUATES, THE(1971)
Misc. Talkies
CINDY AND DONNA(1971)

Mildred Manning
Misc. Silents
MARRIAGE SPECULATION, THE(1917); MARY JANE'S PA(1917); PRINCESS OF PARK ROW, THE(1917); WESTERNERS, THE(1919); FOOLISH MATRONS, THE(1921); WHILE PARIS SLEEPS(1923)

Monroe Manning
LASSIE'S GREAT ADVENTURE(1963), w; FACE OF TERROR(1964, Span.), w; THEY RAN FOR THEIR LIVES(1968), w

Nona Manning
RUMBLE FISH(1983)

Patricia Manning
HIDEOUS SUN DEMON, THE(1959); GRASS EATER, THE(1961); REBEL ANGEL(1962); HOUSE IS NOT A HOME, A(1964)

Philip Manning
F.P. 1 DOESN'T ANSWER(1933, Ger.)

Dr. Philip Manning
F.P. 1(1933, Brit.)
Philipp Manning
WORLD WITHOUT A MASK, THE(1934, Ger.)
Dr. Philipp Manning
INHERITANCE IN PRETORIA(1936, Ger.)
R. Manning
POCKET MONEY(1972)
Robert Manning
SIGN OF THE CROSS, THE(1932); SINGLE-HANDED SANDERS(1932); EAGLE AND THE HAWK, THE(1933); CLEOPATRA(1934); FEROCIOUS PAL(1934); WOMAN ON THE BEACH, THE(1947); FIGHTER SQUADRON(1948)
Roger Manning
Misc. Talkies
DAY IT CAME TO EARTH, THE(1979)
Roger James Manning
Misc. Silents
BRAWN OF THE NORTH(1922)
Ruth Manning
CAT MURKIL AND THE SILKS(1976); AUDREY ROSE(1977); YOU LIGHT UP MY LIFE(1977); LAST FLIGHT OF NOAH'S ARK, THE(1980); WHOLLY MOSES(1980); DEVIL AND MAX DEVLIN, THE(1981); LOOKIN' TO GET OUT(1982)
Stacy Manning
APPLE DUMPLING GANG, THE(1975)
T H. Manning
COUNSELLOR-AT-LAW(1933)
Terry Manning
VERY NATURAL THING, A(1974), ed
Thelma Manning
IN OLD CHICAGO(1938)
Thomas Manning
1984
WHERE THE BOYS ARE '84(1984)
Tom Manning
MISS PACIFIC FLEET(1935); NEXT TIME WE LOVE(1936); ROAD GANG(1936); SINGING KID, THE(1936)
Tom H. Manning
STREET SCENE(1931)
Tony Manning
YOUNG GIRLS OF ROCHEFORT, THE(1968, Fr.)
William Manning
GUY NAMED JOE, A(1943); WING AND A PRAYER(1944)
Nancy Manningham
OMEN, THE(1976)
1984
SECRETS(1984, Brit.)
Elena Mannini
DEEP RED(1976, Ital.), cos
Al Mannino
MALIBU HIGH(1979)
Anthony Mannino
YOUNG GRADUATES, THE(1971); ALL THE PRESIDENT'S MEN(1976); LOOKING UP(1977); STARHOPS(1978); THOSE LIPS, THOSE EYES(1980); TATTOO(1981)
Franco Mannino
BELLISSIMA(1952, Ital.), m; BEAT THE DEVIL(1953), m; SEVEN SEAS TO CALAIS(1963, Ital.), m, md; GOLD FOR THE CAESARS(1964), m; LOVE IN 4 DIMENSIONS(1965 Fr./Ital.), m; LUDWIG(1973, Ital./Ger./Fr.), md; DRIVER'S SEAT, THE(1975, Ital.), m; INNOCENT, THE(1979, Ital.), m
Vincenzo Mannino
OPERATION KID BROTHER(1967, Ital.), w; TEMPTER, THE(1978, Ital.), w
Anne Mannion
DRESSER, THE(1983)
Suzanne Mannion
Misc. Talkies
BELOW THE HILL(1974)
Tom Mannion
THAT SINKING FEELING(1979, Brit.); RETURN OF THE JEDI(1983)
France Mannireo
MORGAN THE PIRATE(1961, Fr./Ital.), md
Franco Mannireo
MORGAN THE PIRATE(1961, Fr./Ital.), m
Kevin Mannis
STUDENT BODIES(1981)
Sammy Mannis
NIGHT OF EVIL(1962)
Bobbie Mannix
AT LONG LAST LOVE(1975), cos; UNCLE JOE SHANNON(1978), cos; WARRIORS, THE(1979), cos; LONG RIDERS, THE(1980), cos; XANADU(1980), cos
Dan P. Mannix
KILLERS OF KILIMANJARO(1960, Brit.), w
Daniel P. Mannix
FOX AND THE HOUND, THE(1981), w
E. J. Mannix
IT'S IN THE AIR(1935), p; MARK OF THE VAMPIRE(1935), p
Edward J. Mannix
DEVIL DOLL, THE(1936), p
Julie Mannix
TUNNELVISION(1976)
Peggy Mannix
LUNCH WAGON(1981)
Sgt. Roy Mannix
FORTY THOUSAND HORSEMEN(1941, Aus.)
Dana Manno
LEADBELLY(1976)
Franco Manno
CONVERSATION PIECE(1976, Ital., Fr.), m
P. L. Mannock
Silents
DEAD CERTAINTY, A(1920, Brit.), w

Patrick L. Mannock
AULD LANG SYNE(1929, Brit.), w
Silents
RANK OUTSIDER(1920, Brit.), w; CRIMSON CIRCLE, THE(1922, Brit.), w; FLAG LIEUTENANT, THE(1926, Brit.), w; ONE OF THE BEST(1927, Brit.), w; HIS HOUSE IN ORDER(1928, Brit.), w
Terrance Winston Mannock
GOSPEL ROAD, THE(1973)
Pirkko Mannola
MAKE LIKE A THIEF(1966, Fin.)
Al Mannon
FIGHTING PIONEERS(1935), p
Alfred T. Mannon
SEA GHOST, THE(1931), p
Jan Eisner Mannon
PIRANHA II: THE SPAWNING(1981, Neth.)
Wingy Mannone
TROCADERO(1944)
Sheila Mannors
DADDY LONG LEGS(1931); SCARLET WEEKEND, A(1932); TEXAS GUN FIGHTER(1932); TEXAS PIONEERS(1932); COWBOY COUNSELOR(1933); MERRY WIDOW, THE(1934); THAT'S GRATITUDE(1934); BEHIND THE EVIDENCE(1935); DANGER AHEAD(1935); LAWLESS RANGE(1935); TOGETHER WE LIVE(1935); KELLY OF THE SECRET SERVICE(1936); MOONLIGHT ON THE PRAIRIE(1936); PRESCOTT KID, THE(1936); WESTWARD HO(1936); DESERT PHANTOM(1937)
Misc. Talkies
COCAINE FIENDS(1937)
Alessandra Mannoukine
JULIET OF THE SPIRITS(1965, Fr./Ital./W.Ger.)
Eigrid Mannson
DAY THE EARTH FROZE, THE(1959, Fin./USSR), cos
Otto Mannstaedt
Misc. Silents
PEST IN FLORENZ(1919, Ger.)
Laura Mannucchi
NIGHT OF THE SHOOTING STARS, THE(1982, Ital.)
Armando Mannuzzi
LA CAGE AUX FOLLES(1979, Fr./Ital.), ph
Liz Manny
PRIVATE PARTS(1972), cos
Manny Klein and His Trumpet
FROM HERE TO ETERNITY(1953)
Shigeo Mano
WAY OUT, WAY IN(1970, Jap.), art d
Bahram Manocheri
1984
NUMBER ONE(1984, Brit.), ph
Yoichi Manoda
SPACE AMOEBA, THE(1970, Jap.), spec eff; YOG-MONSTER FROM SPACE(1970, Jap.), ph; GODZILLA VERSUS THE SMOG MONSTER(1972, Jap.), ph
Arnold Manoff
MAN FROM FRISCO(1944), w; MY BUDDY(1944), w; CASBAH(1948), w; NO MINOR VICES(1948), w
Dinah Manoff
GREASE(1978); ORDINARY PEOPLE(1980); I OUGHT TO BE IN PICTURES(1982)
Tom Manoff
PRISM(1971), m
Yvonne Manoff
HIT PARADE, THE(1937)
Bobby Manogoff
ALIAS THE CHAMP(1949)
Manohargin
NINE HOURS TO RAMA(1963, U.S./Brit.)
Gloria Manon
MAD ROOM, THE(1969); WOMAN INSIDE, THE(1981)
Marcia Manon
LOVE, LIVE AND LAUGH(1929); THEY HAD TO SEE PARIS(1929)
Silents
OLD WIVES FOR NEW(1918); ONE MORE AMERICAN(1918); IN OLD KENTUCKY(1920); ALL'S FAIR IN LOVE(1921); JUSTICE OF THE FAR NORTH(1925)
Misc. Silents
CLAW, THE(1918); SAVAGE WOMAN, THE(1918); TEST OF HONOR, THE(1919); WOMAN MICHAEL MARRIED, THE(1919); FORBIDDEN THING, THE(1920); SKIN DEEP(1922); WOMAN HE LOVED, THE(1922)
Wingy Manone
RHYTHM ON THE RIVER(1940); SARGE GOES TO COLLEGE(1947)
Bahram Manoochehri
BLEAK MOMENTS(1972, Brit.), ph
Betzi Manoogian
WHO'S THAT KNOCKING AT MY DOOR?(1968), p, w
Haig Manoogian
WHO'S THAT KNOCKING AT MY DOOR?(1968), p
Michael Manoogian
NEIGHBORS(1981)
Chris Manor
KING OF THE GYPSIES(1978); WOLFEN(1981)
Doyle Manor
HE WALKED BY NIGHT(1948)
Stella Manors
BORN TO FIGHT(1938)
George J. Manos
HEAVEN CAN WAIT(1978); RAGTIME(1981)
George Manos
HAIR(1979)
Gloria Manos
LOOKIN' TO GET OUT(1982)
Joseph Manoth
CELESTE(1982, Ger.)

Edward Manouk
TO CATCH A THIEF(1955); MAN WHO KNEW TOO MUCH, THE(1956)
Kostas Manoussakis
FEAR, THE(1967, Gr.), d&w
Jean Manoussi
PURPLE MASK, THE(1955), w
Manolo Manpaso
CHATO'S LAND(1972), art d
Arturo Manrique
BANDIDO(1956)
Lorenzo Mans
DAVID HOLZMAN'S DIARY(1968); SKY PIRATE, THE(1970); PROWLER, THE(1981), prod d
Roy Mansano
1984
BREAKIN' 2: ELECTRIC BOOGALOO(1984)
Sam Mansaray
BEAST MUST DIE, THE(1974, Brit.)
Claude Mansard
BREATHLESS(1959, Fr.); FOUR HUNDRED BLOWS, THE(1959); LOVERS, THE(1959, Fr.); SHOOT THE PIANO PLAYER(1962, Fr.); LANDRU(1963, Fr./Ital)
Marie Mansart
ROYAL AFFAIRS IN VERSAILLES(1957, Fr.); TWO ENGLISH GIRLS(1972, Fr.)
John B. Mansbridge
TENSION AT TABLE ROCK(1956), art d; PUBLIC PIGEON NO. 1(1957), art d; YOUNG STRANGER, THE(1957), art d; YOUNG JESSE JAMES(1960), art d; IN-CREDIBLE JOURNEY, THE(1963), art d; THOSE CALLOWAYS(1964), art d; HAPPI-EST MILLIONAIRE, THE(1967), art d; MONKEYS, GO HOME!(1967), art d; HORSE IN THE GRAY FLANNEL SUIT, THE(1968), art d; LOVE BUG, THE(1968), art d; NEVER A DULL MOMENT(1968), art d; RASCAL(1969), art d; SMITH(1969), art d; BAREFOOT EXECUTIVE, THE(1971), art d; SCANDALOUS JOHN(1971), art d; WILD COUNTRY, THE(1971), art d; $1,000,000 DUCK(1971), art d; BISCUIT EATER, THE(1972), art d; NAPOLEON AND SAMANTHA(1972), art d; NOW YOU SEE HIM, NOW YOU DON'T(1972), art d; SNOWBALL EXPRESS(1972), art d; CHARLEY AND THE ANGEL(1973), art d; ONE LITTLE INDIAN(1973), art d; WORLD'S GREATEST ATHLETE, THE(1973), art d; BEARS AND I, THE(1974), art d; CASTAWAY COW-BOY, THE(1974), art d; HERBIE RIDES AGAIN(1974), art d; ISLAND AT THE TOP OF THE WORLD, THE(1974), art d; SUPERDAD(1974), art d; APPLE DUMPLING GANG, THE(1975), art d; STRONGEST MAN IN THE WORLD, THE(1975), art d; FREAKY FRIDAY(1976), art d; GUS(1976), art d; NO DEPOSIT, NO RETURN(1976), art d; SHAGGY D.A., THE(1976), art d; TREASURE OF MATECUMBE(1976), art d; HERBIE GOES TO MONTE CARLO(1977), art d; PETE'S DRAGON(1977), art d; CAT FROM OUTER SPACE, THE(1978), art d; RETURN FROM WITCH MOUNTAIN(1978), art d; APPLE DUMPLING GANG RIDES AGAIN, THE(1979), art d; BLACK HOLE, THE(1979), art d; NORTH AVENUE IRREGULARS, THE(1979), art d; HERBIE GOES BANANAS(1980), art d; LAST FLIGHT OF NOAH'S ARK, THE(1980), art d; MID-NIGHT MADNESS(1980), art d; AMY(1981), art d; DEVIL AND MAX DEVLIN, THE(1981), art d; TEX(1982), art d; SOMETHING WICKED THIS WAY COMES(1983), art d; TRENCHCOAT(1983), art d
1984
COUNTRY(1984), art d; SPLASH(1984), art d
John Mansbridge
FORTY GUNS(1957), art d; GANG WAR(1958), art d; SHOWDOWN AT BOOT HILL(1958), art d; SIERRA BARON(1958), art d; THUNDERING JETS(1958), art d; VILLA!(1958), art d; ALLIGATOR PEOPLE, THE(1959), art d; FIVE GATES TO HELL(1959), art d; HERE COME THE JETS(1959), art d; LITTLE SAVAGE, THE(1959), art d; MIRACLE OF THE HILLS, THE(1959), art d; RETURN OF THE FLY(1959), art d; ROOKIE, THE(1959), art d; VERBOTEN!(1959), art d; DESIRE IN THE DUST(1960), art d; JET OVER THE ATLANTIC(1960), art d; TWELVE HOURS TO KILL(1960), art d; LITTLE SHEPHERD OF KINGDOM COME(1961), art d; LONG ROPE, THE(1961), art d; PURPLE HILLS, THE(1961), art d; SILENT CALL, THE(1961), art d; SNIPER'S RIDGE(1961), art d; TESS OF THE STORM COUN-TRY(1961), art d; TWO LITTLE BEARS(1961), art d; 20,000 EYES(1961), art d; BEDKNOBS AND BROOMSTICKS(1971), art d; ESCAPE TO WITCH MOUN-TAIN(1975), art d; HOT LEAD AND COLD FEET(1978), art d; TRON(1982), art d
John R. Mansbridge
COMPUTER WORE TENNIS SHOES, THE(1970), art d
Mark Mansbridge
SMOKEY AND THE BANDIT(1977), art d; MAN WITH TWO BRAINS, THE(1983), art d
Mark W. Mansbridge
AMY(1981), art d
Jean Manse
FERNANDEL THE DRESSMAKER(1957, Fr.), w; FORBIDDEN FRUIT(1959, Fr.), w; BIG CHIEF, THE(1960, Fr.), w; COW AND I, THE(1961, Fr., Ital., Ger.), w; DYNAMITE JACK(1961, Fr.), w; MOST WANTED MAN, THE(1962, Fr./Ital.), w
Jean Manse,Scarpelli
LAW IS THE LAW, THE(1959, Fr.), w
Barbara Mansell
TWELVE HOURS TO KILL(1960); WALKING TARGET, THE(1960); BLUEPRINT FOR ROBBERY(1961); FRONTIER UPRISING(1961); FIREBRAND, THE(1962); MR. HOBBS TAKES A VACATION(1962); POLICE NURSE(1963); YOUNG GUNS OF TEXAS(1963)
C. Hargreave Mansell
Misc. Silents
HER CROSS(1919, Brit.)
Charles Mansell
STRANGER AT MY DOOR(1950, Brit.)
Colstan Mansell
Silents
GENERAL POST(1920, Brit.)
Doris Mansell
Silents
APACHE, THE(1925, Brit.)
Hargrave Mansell
Silents
AUTUMN OF PRIDE, THE(1921, Brit.)
Misc. Silents
DICK'S FAIRY(1921, Brit.); LITTLE MEG'S CHILDREN(1921, Brit.)

Hargreave Mansell
Silents
ENCHANTMENT(1920, Brit.); GAMBLE WITH HEARTS, A(1923, Brit.)
Janet Mansell
HAUNTING, THE(1963)
Juliet Mansell
TOMORROW WE LIVE(1936, Brit.)
William Mansell
EXCLUSIVE(1937)
Mansell & Ling
RIDING HIGH(1937, Brit.)
James T. Mansen
FOOLS(1970), set d
Valda Mansen
CAIN'S WAY(1969)
Alan Manser
RAGING BULL(1980), art d
Kevin Manser
COUNTESS FROM HONG KONG, A(1967, Brit.)
Michael Mansfeld
BRIDGE, THE(1961, Ger.), w
Alma Mansfield
I WAS A COMMUNIST FOR THE F.B.I.(1951)
David Mansfield
HEAVEN'S GATE(1980), m
Silents
LAST CHANCE, THE(1921)
Ducan Mansfield
Silents
WHITE SISTER, THE(1923)
Duncan Mansfield
EMBARRASSING MOMENTS(1930), ed; I'D GIVE MY LIFE(1936), ed; IN HIS STEPS(1936), ed; WHITE LEGION, THE(1936), ed; GIRL LOVES BOY(1937), d, w; SWEETHEART OF THE NAVY(1937), d; PROFESSOR BEWARE(1938), ed; ONE THIRD OF A NATION(1939), ed; BASHFUL BACHELOR, THE(1942), ed; SO THIS IS WASHINGTON(1943), ed; TWO WEEKS TO LIVE(1943), ed; WHERE ARE YOUR CHILDREN?(1943), ed; AND NOW TOMORROW(1944), ed; GIRL RUSH(1944), ed; BETRAYAL FROM THE EAST(1945), ed; WALK IN THE SUN, A(1945), ed; BACHE-LOR'S DAUGHTERS, THE(1946), ed; IMPERFECT LADY, THE(1947), ed; PROFES-SIONALS, THE(1966), ed
Silents
TOL'ABLE DAVID(1921), ed; SEVENTH DAY, THE(1922), ed; SONNY(1922), ed; WHITE SISTER, THE(1923), ed; KIT CARSON(1928), ed; PIONEER SCOUT, THE(1928), ed; SUNSET LEGION(1928), ed
Elizabeth Mansfield
SLIPPER AND THE ROSE, THE(1976, Brit.)
George Mansfield
FOOLS RUSH IN(1949, Brit.)
Jayne Mansfield
FEMALE JUNGLE, THE(1955); ILLEGAL(1955); PETE KELLY'S BLUES(1955); BURGLAR, THE(1956); GIRL CAN'T HELP IT, THE(1956); HELL ON FRISCO BAY(1956); KISS THEM FOR ME(1957); WAYWARD BUS, THE(1957); WILL SUC-CESS SPOIL ROCK HUNTER?(1957); SHERIFF OF FRACTURED JAW, THE(1958, Brit.); IT TAKES A THIEF(1960, Brit.); LOVES OF HERCULES, THE(1960); GEORGE RAFT STORY, THE(1961); TOO HOT TO HANDLE(1961, Brit.); IT HAPPENED IN ATHENS(1962); DOG EAT DOG(1963, U.S./Ger./Ital.); PROMISES, PROMISES(1963); PANIC BUTTON(1964); FAT SPY(1966); LAS VEGAS HILLBILLYS(1966); PRIMITIVE LOVE(1966, Ital.); GUIDE FOR THE MARRIED MAN, A(1967); SINGLE ROOM FURNISHED(1968)
John Mansfield
MAN-EATER OF KUMAON(1948); TOO LATE FOR TEARS(1949); SAVAGE DRUMS(1951); SILVER CITY(1951); WARPATH(1951); NAKED JUNGLE, THE(1953); PONY EXPRESS(1953); PRISONERS OF THE CASBAH(1953); WAR OF THE WORLDS, THE(1953); DUEL ON THE MISSISSIPPI(1955); ESCAPE TO BURMA(1955); TENNESSEE'S PARTNER(1955); BOSS, THE(1956)
Kay Mansfield
HOMECOMING(1948); GIRL FROM JONES BEACH, THE(1949); NEPTUNE'S DAUGHTER(1949)
Keith Mansfield
FIST OF FEAR, TOUCH OF DEATH(1980), m
Ken Mansfield
VAN NUYS BLVD.(1979), m
Marian Mansfield
HERE IS MY HEART(1934); LOVE IN BLOOM(1935)
Martha Mansfield
Silents
PERFECT LOVER, THE(1919); DR. JEKYLL AND MR. HYDE(1920); IS MONEY EVERYTHING?(1923); SILENT COMMAND, THE(1923); WARRENS OF VIRGINIA, THE(1924)
Misc. Silents
BROADWAY BILL(1918); CIVILIAN CLOTHES(1920); MOTHERS OF MEN(1920); WONDERFUL CHANCE, THE(1920); GILDED LIES(1921); HIS BROTHER'S KEEP-ER(1921); MAN OF STONE, THE(1921); WOMEN MEN LOVE(1921); QUEEN OF THE MOULIN ROUGE(1922); FOG BOUND(1923); LEAVENWORTH CASE, THE(1923); LITTLE RED SCHOOLHOUSE, THE(1923); POTASH AND PERLMUTTER(1923); WOMAN IN CHAINS, THE(1923); YOUTHFUL CHEATERS(1923)
Mercia Mansfield
GREAT ARMORED CAR SWINDLE, THE(1964); THAT LUCKY TOUCH(1975, Brit.)
Michael Mansfield
WITNESS OUT OF HELL(1967, Ger./Yugo.), w
Monte Mansfield
NAKED KISS, THE(1964)
Rankin Mansfield
HOW TO MARRY A MILLIONAIRE(1953); HUMAN JUNGLE, THE(1954); DIAL RED O(1955); TO HELL AND BACK(1955); WORLD WITHOUT END(1956); BAD-LANDS OF MONTANA(1957); OKLAHOMAN, THE(1957); FACE OF A FUGITI-VE(1959)

Ray Mansfield
EXECUTIVE SUITE(1954)
Richard Mansfield
OUT OF THE DEPTHS(1946), set d; INTERNS, THE(1962), set d; THREE STOOGES IN ORBIT, THE(1962), set d; NEW INTERNS, THE(1964), set d; IN HARM'S WAY(1965), set d; ROOMMATES, THE(1973)
1984
MISSION, THE(1984)
Sally Mansfield
FOREVER FEMALE(1953); PHFFFFT!(1954); ERRAND BOY, THE(1961)
Misc. Talkies
BEYOND THE MOON(1964)
Scott Mansfield
Misc. Talkies
DEADLY GAMES(1980), d
Victor Mansfield
HERE COMES THE BAND(1935), w
W. Duncan Mansfield
FRONT PAGE, THE(1931), ed; COCK OF THE AIR(1932), ed; RAIN(1932), ed
Wilda Mansfield
OUR BLUSHING BRIDES(1930)
George Manship
GOOD COMPANIONS(1933, Brit.); MAROONED(1933, Brit.)
John Mansi
HAMMER THE TOFF(1952, Brit.); SECRET PEOPLE(1952, Brit.)
Louis Mansi
HELP!(1965, Brit.); ITALIAN JOB, THE(1969, Brit.); TALES FROM THE CRYPT(1972, Brit.); GET CHARLIE TULLY(1976, Brit.)
Annie Mansicalco
1984
EYES OF FIRE(1984), makeup
Eric Mansker
PROPHECY(1979); NINE TO FIVE(1980); THING, THE(1982)
Susan Manskey
PRETTY BABY(1978)
Roberta Manski
RAMPARTS WE WATCH, THE(1940)
Juanita Manso
MANOLETE(1950, Span.)
Leonor Manso
Misc. Talkies
HOUSE OF SHADOWS(1977, Arg.)
Alan Manson
THIS IS THE ARMY(1943); COP HATER(1958); RAIN PEOPLE, THE(1969); LET'S SCARE JESSICA TO DEATH(1971); WHIFFS(1975); LEADBELLY(1976)
Eddy Lawrence Manson
WOMAN INSIDE, THE(1981), ph
Eddy Manson
LITTLE FUGITIVE, THE(1953), m; LOVERS AND LOLLIPOPS(1956), md; WEDDINGS AND BABIES(1960), m; THREE BITES OF THE APPLE(1967), m
Elena Manson
STRANGER ON THE PROWL(1953, Ital.)
Lt. Emmet L. Manson, USN
BACK TO BATAAN(1945)
Helena Manson
ETERNAL HUSBAND, THE(1946, Fr.); RAVEN, THE(1948, Fr.); STRANGERS IN THE HOUSE(1949, Fr.); MANON(1950, Fr.); ADVENTURES OF CAPTAIN FABIAN(1951); LE PLAISIR(1954, Fr.); LOLA MONTES(1955, Fr./Ger.); NUDE IN A WHITE CAR(1960, Fr.); TWO ARE GUILTY(1964, Fr.); PARIS IN THE MONTH OF AUGUST(1968, Fr.); TENANT, THE(1976, Fr.); MON ONCLE D'AMERIQUE(1980, Fr.)
Janet Manson
DOUBLE LIFE, A(1947)
Jean Manson
YOUNG NURSES, THE(1973); DIRTY O'NEIL(1974)
Jeane Manson
10 TO MIDNIGHT(1983)
Mary Manson
LIFE IN DANGER(1964, Brit.); CURSE OF THE FLY(1965, Brit.)
Maurice Manson
CLOSE-UP(1948); AUTUMN LEAVES(1956); CREATURE WALKS AMONG US, THE(1956); NAVY WIFE(1956); SOLID GOLD CADILLAC, THE(1956); GIRL IN THE KREMLIN, THE(1957); HELLCATS OF THE NAVY(1957); KELLY AND ME(1957); SPIRIT OF ST. LOUIS, THE(1957); HELL'S FIVE HOURS(1958); LIFE BEGINS AT 17(1958); PORGY AND BESS(1959); THREE STOOGES IN ORBIT, THE(1962); ROBIN AND THE SEVEN HOODS(1964); CHASE, THE(1966); NICKELODEON(1976)
Pamela Manson
ROOM AT THE TOP(1959, Brit.); CLASS OF MISS MAC MICHAEL, THE(1978, Brit./U.S.)
Malek Abdul Mansour
FISH THAT SAVED PITTSBURGH, THE(1979)
Philip Mansour
STAKEOUT ON DOPE STREET(1958)
Phillip A. Mansour
YOUNG CAPTIVES, THE(1959)
Salah Mansour
CAIRO(1963)
Mathe Mansoura
WHERE THE TRUTH LIES(1962, Fr.)
Margit Manstead
Silents
ALLEY CAT, THE(1929, Brit.)
A. Mansvetov
VOW, THE(1947, USSR.)
Pamela Mant
RUNNING MAN, THE(1963, Brit.); STORK TALK(1964, Brit.); ULYSSES(1967, U.S./Brit.)
Ann Mantee
MANITOU, THE(1978)

Paul Mantee
BLOOD ON THE ARROW(1964); ROBINSON CRUSOE ON MARS(1964); AMERICAN DREAM, AN(1966); MAN CALLED DAGGER, A(1967); THEY SHOOT HORSES, DON'T THEY?(1969); BREAKOUT(1975); FRAMED(1975); W.C. FIELDS AND ME(1976); DAY OF THE ANIMALS(1977); GREATEST, THE(1977, U.S./Brit.); MANITOU, THE(1978); GREAT SANTINI, THE(1979)
Joe Mantegna
TOWING(1978); SECOND THOUGHTS(1983)
Bronwen Mantel
IN PRAISE OF OLDER WOMEN(1978, Can.); CITY ON FIRE(1979 Can.); ONE MAN(1979, Can.); OF UNKNOWN ORIGIN(1983, Can.)
1984
COVERGIRL(1984, Can.)
Michael Albert Mantel
1984
BROTHER FROM ANOTHER PLANET, THE(1984)
Arthur Mantell
THIS IS HEAVEN(1929), w
Ethel Mantell
Misc. Silents
ROMEO AND JULIET(1916)
James Mantell
CLONUS HORROR, THE(1979)
Joe Mantell
BARBARY PIRATE(1949); UNDERCOVER MAN, THE(1949); MARTY(1955); STORM CENTER(1956); BEAU JAMES(1957); SAD SACK, THE(1957); ONIONHEAD(1958); CROWDED SKY, THE(1960); SCARFACE MOB, THE(1962); BIRDS, THE(1963); MISTER BUDDWING(1966); CHINATOWN(1974)
1984
BLAME IT ON THE NIGHT(1984)
Mary Mantell
Misc. Silents
MY PARTNER(1916)
Richard Mantell
SCHOOL FOR SECRETS(1946, Brit.)
Robert Mantell
CAT ATE THE PARAKEET, THE(1972)
Misc. Talkies
POT! PARENTS! POLICE!(1975)
Misc. Silents
BLINDNESS OF DEVOTION(1915); SPIDER AND THE FLY, THE(1916)
Robert Mantell, Jr.
Misc. Silents
WHEN YOU AND I WERE YOUNG(1918)
Robert B. Mantell
Silents
UNDER THE RED ROBE(1923)
Misc. Silents
UNFAITHFUL WIFE, THE(1915); GREEN-EYED MONSTER, THE(1916); WIFE'S SACRIFICE, A(1916); TANGLED LIVES(1917)
Robert B. Mantell, Jr.
Silents
SINS OF SOCIETY(1915)
Maria Mantella
SPRING AND PORT WINE(1970, Brit.)
Alexis Mantheakis
DAY THE FISH CAME OUT, THE(1967. Brit./Gr.); OEDIPUS THE KING(1968, Brit.)
Raymond Manthorpe
ALIVE AND KICKING(1962, Brit.); SHE DIDN'T SAY NO!(1962, Brit.)
Margit Mantical
MY TRUE STORY(1951), w
Christian Mantilla
FITZCARRALDO(1982)
Burns Mantle
Silents
HOW MOLLY MADE GOOD(1915), w
Clive Mantle
PARTY PARTY(1983, Brit.)
Doreen Mantle
PRIVILEGE(1967, Brit.); FRENCH LIEUTENANT'S WOMAN, THE(1981); YENTL(1983)
Mickey Mantle
SAFE AT HOME(1962); THAT TOUCH OF MINK(1962)
John Mantley
SECRET FURY, THE(1950); THREE CAME HOME(1950); PARSON AND THE OUTLAW, THE(1957), w; 27TH DAY, THE(1957), w; WOMAN OBSESSED(1959), w; MY BLOOD RUNS COLD(1965), w; FIRECREEK(1968), p
Lillian Manton
COMPULSORY HUSBAND, THE(1930, Brit.)
Marcus Manton
FUNNY FARM, THE(1982, Can.), ed
1984
EXTERMINATOR 2(1984), ed
Percy Manton
Silents
MOLLY BAWN(1916, Brit.)
Don Mantooth
UNCOMMON VALOR(1983)
Donald Mantooth
EARTHQUAKE(1974)
Lilly Mantovani
WARRIOR EMPRESS, THE(1961, Ital./Fr.)
Stella Mantovani
VINTAGE WINE(1935, Brit.)
Mantovani and His Tipicas
SING AS YOU SWING(1937, Brit.)
Patrick Mantoya
LEGEND OF THE LONE RANGER, THE(1981)

Christina Mantt
SUEZ(1938)
Mario Mantuori
UNHOLY FOUR, THE(1969, Ital.), ph
Mike Manty
Misc. Talkies
BLOOD DEBTS(1983)
A. F. Mantz
Silents
HOME STUFF(1921), art d; OFF-SHORE PIRATE, THE(1921), art d; SHERLOCK BROWN(1921), art d; SEEING'S BELIEVING(1922), art d
Paul Mantz
AIR MAIL(1932), stunts; CEILNG ZERO(1935), a, tech adv; MEN WITH WINGS(1938); TEST PILOT(1938), ph; ONLY ANGELS HAVE WINGS(1939), stunts&tech adv; DIVE BOMBER(1941), chief pilot; THUNDER BIRDS(1942), stunts; BLAZE OF NOON(1947), spec eff; WINGS OF EAGLES, THE(1957), stunts
Anna Mantzourani
LAND OF THE MINOTAUR(1976, Gr.)
Max Manudian
Misc. Silents
VENUS(1929, Fr.)
Manuel
TEARS OF HAPPINESS(1974)
Delia Manuel
VIOLATED LOVE(1966, Arg.), ed
Denis Manuel
MILKY WAY, THE(1969, Fr./Ital.)
Jacques Manuel
JUST A BIG, SIMPLE GIRL(1949, Fr.), d
Luis Manuel
ZOOT SUIT(1981); MAYA(1982)
Richard Manuel
ELIZA'S HOROSCOPE(1975, Can.)
Robert Manuel
RIFIFI(1956, Fr.); DEADLIER THAN THE MALE(1957, Fr.); GORILLA GREETS YOU, THE(1958, Fr.); WOULD-BE GENTLEMAN, THE(1960, Fr.); NIGHT AFFAIR(1961, Fr.); THREE PENNY OPERA(1963, Fr./Ger.); EXTERMINATORS, THE(1965 Fr.); HOW NOT TO ROB A DEPARTMENT STORE(1965, Fr./Ital.)
1984
LIFE IS A BED OF ROSES(1984, Fr.); RAZOR'S EDGE, THE(1984)
Roland Manuel
ESCAPE FROM YESTERDAY(1939, Fr.), m; LUMIERE D'ETE(1943, Fr.), m
Tony Manufo
COCAINE COWBOYS(1979)
Guido Manuli
ALLEGRO NON TROPPO(1977, Ital.), w, anim
Martin Manulis
DAYS OF WINE AND ROSES(1962), p; DEAR HEART(1964), p; LUV(1967), p; DUFFY(1968, Brit.), p
Vittorio Manunta
NEVER TAKE NO FOR AN ANSWER(1952, Brit./Ital.); STRANGER ON THE PROWL(1953, Ital.)
George Manupelli
CRY DR. CHICAGO(1971), d&w&ph
Manushka
WOMAN TO WOMAN(1946, Brit.)
Manver
POR MIS PISTOLAS(1969, Mex.)
Anita Manville
MARIZINIA(1962, U.S./Braz.), w
Kate Manx
PRIVATE PROPERTY(1960); HERO'S ISLAND(1962)
Jose Many [Giuseppe Mangione]
SHOOT FIRST, LAUGH LAST(1967, Ital./Ger./U.S.), w
Bob Many Mules
SEARCHERS, THE(1956)
Many Mules Son
SEARCHERS, THE(1956)
Many Treaties
BUFFALO BILL RIDES AGAIN(1947); SEA OF GRASS, THE(1947)
Alexandra Manys
GERMANY, YEAR ZERO(1949, Ger.)
Joe Manz
ICE FOLLIES OF 1939(1939)
Linda Manz
DAYS OF HEAVEN(1978); KING OF THE GYPSIES(1978); WANDERERS, THE(1979); OUT OF THE BLUE(1982)
Misc. Talkies
LONGSHOT(1982)
Michael Manza
FRANKENSTEIN'S BLOODY TERROR(1968, Span.)
Ralph Manza
ENEMY BELOW, THE(1957); GANG WAR(1958); HUNTERS, THE(1958); TOO SOON TO LOVE(1960); SECRET OF DEEP HARBOR(1961); THAT TOUCH OF MINK(1962); WHAT DID YOU DO IN THE WAR, DADDY?(1966); THREE GUNS FOR TEXAS(1968); WILD PARTY, THE(1975); CAT FROM OUTER SPACE, THE(1978); ONE AND ONLY, THE(1978); APPLE DUMPLING GANG RIDES AGAIN, THE(1979); LITTLE MISS MARKER(1980)
1984
PHILADELPHIA EXPERIMENT, THE(1984)
Armando Manzanero
INTERVAL(1973, Mex./U.S.), m
1984
ON THE LINE(1984, Span.), m
Manzanita
1984
SKYLINE(1984, Spain), m

Llovety Manzano
MANOLETE(1950, Span.), w
Miguel Manzano
LA CUCARACHA(1961, Mex.); LITTLE ANGEL(1961, Mex.); QUEEN'S SWORDSMEN, THE(1963, Mex.); SPIRITISM(1965, Mex.); ILLUSION TRAVELS BY STREETCAR, THE(1977, Mex.)
Nicola Manzari
MERCHANT OF SLAVES(1949, Ital.), w
Marvine Manzel
DELICIOUS(1931)
Homero Manzi
SAVAGE PAMPAS(1967, Span./Arg.), w
Jim Manzie
F.J. HOLDEN, THE(1977, Aus.), m
Italia Almirante Manzini
Silents
CABIRIA(1914, Ital.)
Diane Manzo
DEATH WISH II(1982)
Gilbert Manzon
TWO FOR THE ROAD(1967, Brit.), spec eff
Alessandro Manzoni
SPIRIT AND THE FLESH, THE(1948, Ital.), w
Achille Manzotti
GIRL FROM TRIESTE, THE(1983, Ital.), p
Natalia Manzuelas
MANHUNT IN THE JUNGLE(1958)
Zecharia Manzur
EVERY BASTARD A KING(1968, Israel)
David Manzy
BABY, THE(1973); WORLD'S GREATEST ATHLETE, THE(1973)
Angela Mao
DEADLY CHINA DOLL(1973, Hong Kong); DEEP THRUST-THE HAND OF DEATH(1973, Hong Kong)
Misc. Talkies
RETURN OF THE TIGER(1979)
Agnes Mapes
Misc. Silents
IL TROVATORE(1914)
Jacque Mapes
PAROLE, INC.(1949), set d; DESTINATION MURDER(1950), set d; PEOPLE AGAINST O'HARA, THE(1951), set d
Jacques Mapes
WOMAN WHO CAME BACK(1945), set d; CHAMPAGNE FOR CAESAR(1950), set d; WOMAN ON THE RUN(1950), set d; PROWLER, THE(1951), set d; SECOND WOMAN, THE(1951), set d; UNKNOWN MAN, THE(1951), set d; EVERYTHING I HAVE IS YOURS(1952), set d; SINGIN' IN THE RAIN(1952), set d; LATIN LOVERS(1953), set d; ROSIE!(1967), p
Ted Mapes
LAW RIDES, THE(1936); SECRET PATROL(1936); STAMPEDE(1936); ONE MAN JUSTICE(1937); RIO GRANDE(1939); THREE TEXAS STEERS(1939); WALL STREET COWBOY(1939); CARSON CITY KID(1940); RANGER AND THE LADY, THE(1940); UNDER TEXAS SKIES(1940); IN OLD CHEYENNE(1941); RIDERS OF THE BADLANDS(1941); ROYAL MOUNTED PATROL, THE(1941); TONTO BASIN OUTLAWS(1941); BELOW THE BORDER(1942); HOME IN WYOMIN'(1942); PARDON MY GUN(1942); THUNDER RIVER FEUD(1942); CALLING WILD BILL ELLIOTT(1943); LAND OF HUNTED MEN(1943); OUTLAW, THE(1943); CYCLONE PRAIRIE RANGERS(1944); DEAD OR ALIVE(1944); DEATH RIDES THE PLAINS(1944); FUZZY SETTLES DOWN(1944); JAM SESSION(1944); LAST HORSEMAN, THE(1944); LAW MEN(1944); PARTNERS OF THE TRAIL(1944); INCENDIARY BLONDE(1945); CONQUEST OF CHEYENNE(1946); DRIFTING ALONG(1946); MY PAL TRIGGER(1946); UNDER ARIZONA SKIES(1946); FABULOUS TEXAN, THE(1947); WILD FRONTIER, THE(1947); BLACK EAGLE(1948); DESPERADOES OF DODGE CITY(1948); FURY AT FURNACE CREEK(1948); PALEFACE, THE(1948); STRAWBERRY ROAN, THE(1948); SUNDOWN RIDERS(1948); DESERT VIGILANTE(1949); EL DORADO PASS(1949); LOOK FOR THE SILVER LINING(1949); OUTCASTS OF THE TRAIL(1949); SAMSON AND DELILAH(1949); BLONDIE'S HERO(1950); COW TOWN(1950); RAIDERS OF TOMAHAWK CREEK(1950); WINCHESTER '73(1950); THUNDER BAY(1953); TOPEKA(1953); FAR COUNTRY, THE(1955); NIGHT PASSAGE(1957); MAN WHO SHOT LIBERTY VALANCE, THE(1962); NEW KIND OF LOVE, A(1963); CHEYENNE AUTUMN(1964); DEAR BRIGETTE(1965); RARE BREED, THE(1966)
Victor Mapes
HOTTENTOT, THE(1929), w; LOVE DOCTOR, THE(1929), w; HIGH FLYERS(1937), w; GOING PLACES(1939), w
Silents
SAPHEAD, THE(1921), w
Audrey Maple
ENLIGHTEN THY DAUGHTER(1934)
Christine Maple
WHOOPEE(1930); BIG SHOW, THE(1937); MAN BETRAYED, A(1937); ROARIN' LEAD(1937)
Chrystine Maple
GOOD SPORT(1931)
John E. Maple
Misc. Silents
BEFORE THE WHITE MAN CAME(1920), d
Terence Maple
STORY OF DAVID, A(1960, Brit.), w
Maple City Four
GIT ALONG, LITTLE DOGIES(1937); OLD BARN DANCE, THE(1938); UNDER WESTERN STARS(1938)
Virginia Maples
WILDFIRE(1945); BLACK WIDOW(1954)
Jim Mapp
TRICK BABY(1973)
Lucille Mapp
NO TIME FOR TEARS(1957, Brit.)

Neville Mapp
DEMOBBED(1944, Brit.); SOLDIER, SAILOR(1944, Brit.); COLONEL BLIMP(1945, Brit.); SILVER FLEET, THE(1945, Brit.); YANK IN LONDON, A(1946, Brit.); SAN DEMETRIO, LONDON(1947, Brit.); PICCADILLY INCIDENT(1948, Brit.)
Jefferson Mappan
STONE COLD DEAD(1980, Can.)
Jacqueline Mappiel
HO(1968, Fr.), ed
Jeff Mappin
CITY ON FIRE(1979 Can.)
Jefferson Mappin
HEARTACHES(1981, Can.)
1984
JUST THE WAY YOU ARE(1984)
Tasneem Maqsood
STORIES FROM A FLYING TRUNK(1979, Brit.)
George Maquire
SECOND THOUGHTS(1983)
Oliver Maquire
THIRTY NINE STEPS, THE(1978, Brit.)
Ben Mar, Jr.
SONG OF MEXICO(1945); RANCHO DELUXE(1975)
Helen Mar
RUNAWAY QUEEN, THE(1935, Brit.)
Lo Mar
BRUCE LEE AND I(1976, Chi.), d
Adele Mara
ALIAS BOSTON BLACKIE(1942); BLONDIE GOES TO COLLEGE(1942); LUCKY LEGS(1942); SHUT MY BIG MOUTH(1942); YOU WERE NEVER LOVELIER(1942); REVEILLE WITH BEVERLY(1943); RIDERS OF THE NORTHWEST MOUNTED(1943); ATLANTIC CITY(1944); CALL OF THE SOUTH SEAS(1944); FACES IN THE FOG(1944); BELLS OF ROSARITA(1945); FLAME OF THE BARBARY COAST(1945); GIRLS OF THE BIG HOUSE(1945); GRISSLY'S MILLIONS(1945); THOROUGHBREDS(1945); TIGER WOMAN, THE(1945); VAMPIRE'S GHOST, THE(1945); GUY COULD CHANGE, A(1946); INNER CIRCLE, THE(1946); INVISIBLE INFORMER(1946); I'VE ALWAYS LOVED YOU(1946); LAST CROOKED MILE, THE(1946); MAGNIFICENT ROGUE, THE(1946); NIGHT TRAIN TO MEMPHIS(1946); PASSKEY TO DANGER(1946); THE CATMAN OF PARIS(1946); TRAFFIC IN CRIME(1946); BLACKMAIL(1947); EXPOSED(1947); MAIN STREET KID, THE(1947); ROBIN OF TEXAS(1947); TRESPASSER, THE(1947); TWILIGHT ON THE RIO GRANDE(1947); WEB OF DANGER, THE(1947); ANGEL IN EXILE(1948); CAMPUS HONEYMOON(1948); GALLANT LEGION, THE(1948); I, JANE DOE(1948); NIGHT TIME IN NEVADA(1948); SANDS OF IWO JIMA(1949); WAKE OF THE RED WITCH(1949); AVENGERS, THE(1950); CALIFORNIA PASSAGE(1950); ROCK ISLAND TRAIL(1950); SEA HORNET, THE(1951); COUNT THE HOURS(1953); REDHEAD FROM MANHATTAN(1954); BACK FROM ETERNITY(1956); BLACK WHIP, THE(1956); CURSE OF THE FACELESS MAN(1958); BIG CIRCUS, THE(1959)
Misc. Talkies
VENGEANCE OF THE WEST(1942)
Lya Mara
CRIMSON CIRCLE, THE(1930, Brit.)
Misc. Silents
BOHEMIAN DANCER(1929)
Maurice Maraac
LAFAYETTE ESCADRILLE(1958)
Carmelita Maracci
THREE CABALLEROS, THE(1944), ch
Vincent Maracecchi
KELLY'S HEROES(1970, U.S./Yugo.)
Heinz Maracek
LITTLE NIGHT MUSIC, A(1977, Aust./U.S./Ger.)
Steve Marachuk
EYES OF LAURA MARS(1978); PIRANHA II: THE SPAWNING(1981, Neth.)
Lucille Maracini
PRODIGAL, THE(1955)
Ettore M. Maragadonna
MORALIST, THE(1964, Ital.), w
Dacia Maraini
CERTAIN, VERY CERTAIN, AS A MATTER OF FACT... PROBABLE(1970, Ital.), w; LOVE PROBLEMS(1970, Ital.), w
Fosco Maraini
VIOLATED PARADISE(1963, Ital./Jap.), w, ph
Jean Marais
ETERNAL RETURN, THE(1943, Fr.); CARMEN(1946, Ital.); BEAUTY AND THE BEAST(1947, Fr.); EAGLE WITH TWO HEADS(1948, Fr.); RUY BLAS(1948, Fr.); LES PARENTS TERRIBLES(1950, Fr.); ORPHEUS(1950, Fr.); COUNT OF MONTE-CRISTO(1955, Fr., Ital.); NAPOLEON(1955, Fr.); IF PARIS WERE TOLD TO US(1956, Fr.); JULIETTA(1957, Fr.); PARIS DOES STRANGE THINGS(1957, Fr./Ital.); ROYAL AFFAIRS IN VERSAILLES(1957, Fr.); AUSTERLITZ(1960, Fr./Ital./Yugo.); WHITE NIGHTS(1961, Ital./Fr.); NUDE IN HIS POCKET(1962, Fr.); TESTAMENT OF ORPHEUS, THE(1962, Fr.); FANTOMAS STRIKES BACK(1965, Fr./Ital.); FRIEND OF THE FAMILY(1965, Fr./Ital.); FANTOMAS(1966, Fr./Ital.); MAN FROM COCODY(1966, Fr/Ital.); PONTIUS PILATE(1967, Fr./Ital.); DONKEY SKIN(1975, Fr.)
Josef Marais
ROPE OF SAND(1949)
Marc Marais
HOUSE OF THE LIVING DEAD(1973, S. Afr.), w; CRASH(1977), w
Georges Marakoff
TWO WORLD(1930, Brit.)
Y. Maralon
FREUD(1962)
Evaristo Maran
WITCH'S CURSE, THE(1963, Ital.)
Francesco Maran
MELODY LINGERS ON, THE(1935); UNDER THE PAMPAS MOON(1935); ESPIONAGE(1937); I MET HIM IN PARIS(1937); SHOPWORN ANGEL(1938)
Francisco Maran
YELLOW JACK(1938); LAST WARNING, THE(1929); UNDER A TEXAS MOON(1930); FLYING DOWN TO RIO(1933); RIP TIDE(1934); MAN WHO BROKE THE BANK AT MONTE CARLO, THE(1935); MAYTIME(1937); WE'RE IN THE LEGION NOW(1937); ARTISTS AND MODELS ABROAD(1938); RICH MAN, POOR GIRL(1938); MUTINY ON THE BLACKHAWK(1939); ONLY ANGELS HAVE WINGS(1939); GHOST BREAKERS, THE(1940); HOLD BACK THE DAWN(1941); ONE NIGHT IN LISBON(1941); SIX LESSONS FROM MADAME LA ZONGA(1941); SKYLARK(1941); THEY MET IN ARGENTINA(1941); LADY HAS PLANS, THE(1942)
Jaroslav Maran
LEMONADE JOE(1966, Czech.)
G. Maranadzhyan
OVERCOAT, THE(1965, USSR), ph
Eva Marandi
GIDGET GOES TO ROME(1963)
Evi Marandi
FRANCIS OF ASSISI(1961); PARIS WHEN IT SIZZLES(1964); PLANET OF THE VAMPIRES(1965, U.S./Ital./Span.)
Misc. Talkies
OUR MEN IN BAGHDAD(1967, Ital.)
Marandy
COMIN' ROUND THE MOUNTAIN(1940)
Luiza Maranhao
TRAIN ROBBERY CONFIDENTIAL(1965, Braz.)
Erminia Marani
1984
NOSTALGHIA(1984, USSR/Ital.), ed
Imelde Marani
VALACHI PAPERS, THE(1972, Ital./Fr.)
Jose Maranio
MC MASTERS, THE(1970)
Andre Maranne
LOSER TAKES ALL(1956, Brit.); PORT AFRIQUE(1956, Brit.); HARRY BLACK AND THE TIGER(1958, Brit.); SQUARE PEG, THE(1958, Brit.); LOSS OF INNOCENCE(1961, Brit.); MIDDLE COURSE, THE(1961, Brit.); TWO WIVES AT ONE WEDDING(1961, Brit.); DAMN THE DEFIANT!(1962, Brit.); SILENT INVASION, THE(1962, Brit.); NIGHT TRAIN TO PARIS(1964, Brit.); SHOT IN THE DARK, A(1964); RETURN FROM THE ASHES(1965, U.S./Brit.); TERRORNAUTS, THE(1967, Brit.); DUFFY(1968, Brit.); GIRL ON A MOTORCYCLE, THE(1968, Fr./Brit.); BATTLE OF BRITAIN, THE(1969, Brit.); DARLING LILI(1970); NELSON AFFAIR, THE(1973, Brit.); GOLD(1974, Brit.); PAUL AND MICHELLE(1974, Fr./Brit.); RETURN OF THE PINK PANTHER, THE(1975, Brit.); PINK PANTHER STRIKES AGAIN, THE(1976, Brit.); REVENGE OF THE PINK PANTHER(1978); AMIN–THE RISE AND FALL(1982, Kenya); TRAIL OF THE PINK PANTHER, THE(1982); CURSE OF THE PINK PANTHER(1983)
1984
RAZOR'S EDGE, THE(1984)
Ezio Marano
THEY CALL ME TRINITY(1971, Ital.); BLACK BELLY OF THE TARANTULA, THE(1972, Ital.)
Mario Marano
Silents
OUT OF THE PAST(1927)
Coco Marantha
YEAR OF LIVING DANGEROUSLY, THE(1982, Aus.)
Mario Maranzana
GOODBYE MR. CHIPS(1969, U.S./Brit.); LONG RIDE FROM HELL, A(1970, Ital.); DEAD ARE ALIVE, THE(1972, Yugo./Ger./Ital.); LADY CAROLINE LAMB(1972, Brit./Ital.)
Lew Marao
KID FOR TWO FARTHINGS, A(1956, Brit.)
V. Mararov
FORTY-NINE DAYS(1964, USSR)
Bob Maras
RUMBLE FISH(1983)
Dimitri Maras
SERENITY(1962)
Pietro Marascalchi
BEST OF ENEMIES, THE(1962)
Lance Maraschal
DETECTIVE, THE(1954, Qit.); VIOLENT STRANGER(1957, Brit.)
Launce Maraschal
GREEN SCARF, THE(1954, Brit.); ATOMIC MAN, THE(1955, Brit.); JOE MACBETH(1955); MURDER ON APPROVAL(1956, Brit.); SECOND FIDDLE(1957, Brit.); FIEND WITHOUT A FACE(1958); ORDERS TO KILL(1958, Brit.); TEENAGE BAD GIRL(1959, Brit.)
Frank Marasco
PAN-AMERICANA(1945)
Robert Marasco
CHILD'S PLAY(1972), w; BURNT OFFERINGS(1976), w
Horace Marassi
1984
DEATHSTALKER, THE(1984)
Alan Maraton
UNTAMED(1955)
Franco Maratta
I HATE BLONDES(1981, Ital.), w
"Pistol" Pete Maravich
Misc. Talkies
SCORING(1980)
Mirella Maravidi
THREE BITES OF THE APPLE(1967)
Elke Maravilha
XICA(1982, Braz.)
Charles Marawood
IRISHMAN, THE(1978, Aus.), m; WEEKEND OF SHADOWS(1978, Aus.), m
J. S. Marba
UNDER TEXAS SKIES(1931)
Joe Marba
CARNIVAL BOAT(1932); SHOTGUN PASS(1932)
Joe Smith Marba
STAND UP AND CHEER(1934 80m FOX bw); FRISCO KID(1935); LOVE IS NEWS(1937)

Bertram Marbaugh
Silents
WHISPERS(1920)
Jacqueline Marbaux
MAGNIFICENT SINNER(1963, Fr.)
Fay Marbe
TALK OF HOLLYWOOD, THE(1929)
Gilbert Marbe
TALK OF HOLLYWOOD, THE(1929)
Ginette Marbeauf
GENERALS WITHOUT BUTTONS(1938, Fr.)
Alice Marble
PAT AND MIKE(1952)
Scott Marble
Silents
TENNESSEE'S PARDNER(1916), w
Ernst Marboe
APRIL 1, 2000(1953, Aust.), w
Bertram Marburgh
FOR THE DEFENSE(1930); MELODY MAN(1930); THEY JUST HAD TO GET
MARRIED(1933); LADY EVE, THE(1941); THERE'S MAGIC IN MUSIC(1941); CROSS-
ROADS(1942); TOO MANY WOMEN(1942); HEAVENLY BODY, THE(1943)
Silents
TIMOTHY'S QUEST(1922); OUTSIDER, THE(1926); AFFAIR OF THE FOLLIES,
AN(1927); KING OF KINGS, THE(1927); WOMAN ON TRIAL, THE(1927)
Misc. Silents
RAIL RIDER, THE(1916); YOU NEVER KNOW YOUR LUCK(1919); STREAK OF
LUCK, A(1925); SILKEN SHACKLES(1926); UNKNOWN TREASURES(1926)
Jane Marbury
MR. BELVEDERE RINGS THE BELL(1951)
Agnes Marc
Silents
PERFECT LADY, A(1918)
Alice Marc
Silents
JUNGLE, THE(1914); NAN OF MUSIC MOUNTAIN(1917)
Joseph Marc [Jose Marco]
SECRET SEVEN, THE(1966, Ital./Span.)
Marie Marc
LA VIE DE CHATEAU(1967, Fr.); VERY HAPPY ALEXANDER(1969, Fr.); ME(1970,
Fr.)
Peter Marc
LUNCH WAGON(1981)
Sebastien Marc
SMALL CHANGE(1976, Fr.)
Ted Marc
GOOD MORNING, MISS DOVE(1955); STORM CENTER(1956)
Theodore Marc
LADY IN THE DARK(1944)
Xavier Marc
TIME AND THE TOUCH, THE(1962); TWO MULES FOR SISTER SARA(1970)
Ellen Marca
SATURDAY NIGHT FEVER(1977)
Augusto Marcacci
FEDORA(1946, Ital.); MERCHANT OF SLAVES(1949, Ital.)
Pierre Marcade
NIGHT OF THE FOLLOWING DAY, THE(1969, Brit.), cos
Marthe Marcadier
OBSESSION(1954, Fr./Ital.)
Joss Marcano
1984
DELIVERY BOYS(1984)
Dominique Marcas
1984
PERILS OF GWENDOLINE, THE(1984, Fr.)
Marceau
LA BETE HUMAINE(1938, Fr.)
Bill Marceau
RECKLESS LIVING(1938)
Emily Marceau
Silents
OPEN YOUR EYES(1919)
Felicien Marceau
LOVE AND THE FRENCHWOMAN(1961, Fr.), w; SEVEN CAPITAL SINS(1962,
Fr./Ital.), w; DISORDER(1964, Fr./Ital.), d; LA BONNE SOUPE(1964, Fr./Ital.), w
Marcel Marceau
BARBARELLA(1968, Fr./Ital.); SHANKS(1974), a, ch; SILENT MOVIE(1976)
Michele Marceau
GREAT SPY CHASE, THE(1966, Fr.)
Sophie Marceau
LA BOUM(1983, Fr.)
Violette Marceau
POPPY IS ALSO A FLOWER, THE(1966); THE DIRTY GAME(1966, Fr./Ital./Ger.);
RISE OF LOUIS XIV, THE(1970, Fr.)
Marcel
CARNIVAL OF SINNERS(1947, Fr.)
Alain Marcel
DIVA(1982, Fr.)
Inez Marcel
Silents
MISCHIEF MAKER, THE(1916); APPEARANCE OF EVIL(1918)
Misc. Silents
VICTIM, THE(1917); TRANSGRESSOR, THE(1918); BURNING QUESTION,
THE(1919); GAY OLD DOG, THE(1919)
Isadore Marcel
Silents
JANICE MEREDITH(1924)

Len Marcel
HIRED HAND, THE(1971)
Nino Marcel
HINDU, THE(1953, Brit.)
Sonia Marcel
Silents
ELUSIVE ISABEL(1916)
Terence Marcel
THERE GOES THE BRIDE(1980, Brit.), d, w
Terry Marcel
HAWK THE SLAYER(1980, Brit.), d, w
James Marcelino
48 HOURS(1982)
Mario Marcelino
LOSIN' IT(1983)
1984
STAR TREK III: THE SEARCH FOR SPOCK(1984)
Micki Marcelino
WHIPLASH(1948), makeup
Muzzy Marcelino
SWEETHEART OF SIGMA CHI(1933)
Shari Marcell
GOING HOME(1971)
Lou Marcelle
CASABLANCA(1942); BACKGROUND TO DANGER(1943); THANK YOUR LUCKY
STARS(1943); DESTINATION TOKYO(1944); DOUGHGIRLS, THE(1944); I
WOULDN'T BE IN YOUR SHOES(1948); PERFECT STRANGERS(1950)
Sonia Marcelle
Silents
BABY MINE(1917); DIANE OF STAR HOLLOW(1921)
Filippo Pompa Marcelli
APE WOMAN, THE(1964, Ital.)
Marta Marcelli
LOVE ON THE RIVIERA(1964, Fr./Ital.)
Sioux Marcelli
DOCTOR DETROIT(1983); GOING BERSERK(1983)
Romolo Marcellini
ROMMEL'S TREASURE(1962, Ital.), d, w
Siro Marcellini
HERO OF BABYLON(1963, Ital.), d; SECRET MARK OF D'ARTAGNAN, THE(1963,
Fr./Ital.), d, w
Muzzy Marcellino
TWENTY MILLION SWEETHEARTS(1934); ROBERTA(1935)
Nick Marcellino
SSSSSSSS(1973), makeup
Vince Marcellino
Misc. Talkies
MORALS SQUAD(1960)
The Marcels
TWIST AROUND THE CLOCK(1961)
Alex March
PAPER LION(1968), d; BIG BOUNCE, THE(1969), d; MASTERMIND(1977), d
Allen March
PIRATES OF TRIPOLI(1955), w
Anthony March
ROMEO AND JULIET(1936); ONCE BEFORE I DIE(1967, U.S./Phil.), w
Barbara March
DESERTERS(1983, Can.)
Catherine March
1984
CAGED FURY(1984, Phil.)
Charles March
BIG PUNCH, THE(1948)
Craig March
SECRET INVASION, THE(1964)
David March
JAPANESE WAR BRIDE(1952); CRY BABY KILLER, THE(1958), p
Dennis March
PSYCHO FROM TEXAS(1982), makeup
Doria March
ROAD TO FORTUNE, THE(1930, Brit.); ETERNAL FEMININE, THE(1931, Brit.)
Ellen March
SOMETHING SHORT OF PARADISE(1979); URBAN COWBOY(1980); SOUP FOR
ONE(1982)
Elspeth March
MR. EMMANUEL(1945, Brit.); QUO VADIS(1951); HIS EXCELLENCY(1952, Brit.);
MIRACLE, THE(1959); MIDNIGHT LACE(1960); FOLLOW THAT MAN(1961, Brit.);
ROMAN SPRING OF MRS. STONE, THE(1961, U.S./Brit.); DR. CRIPPEN(1963, Brit.);
PLAYBOY OF THE WESTERN WORLD, THE(1963, Ireland); THREE LIVES OF
THOMASINA, THE(1963, U.S./Brit.); PSYCHE 59(1964, Brit.); WOMAN TIMES SEV-
EN(1967, U.S./Fr./Ital.); GOODBYE MR. CHIPS(1969, U.S./Br.); TWO GENTLEMEN
SHARING(1969, Brit.); PROMISE AT DAWN(1970, U.S./Fr.); RISE AND RISE OF
MICHAEL RIMMER, THE(1970, Brit.); LOLA(1971, Brit./Ital.)
Eve March
HOW GREEN WAS MY VALLEY(1941); BROADWAY(1942); CALLING WILD BILL
ELLIOTT(1943); SEVENTH VICTIM, THE(1943); SONG OF TEXAS(1943); CURSE OF
THE CAT PEOPLE, THE(1944); THEY WERE EXPENDABLE(1945); DANNY
BOY(1946); GUILT OF JANET AMES, THE(1947); KILLER McCOY(1947); CANON
CITY(1948); JOAN OF ARC(1948); ADAM'S RIB(1949); STREETS OF SAN FRANCIS-
CO(1949); MODEL AND THE MARRIAGE BROKER, THE(1951); SUN SHINES
BRIGHT, THE(1953); WILD ONE, THE(1953); LAST HURRAH, THE(1958)
Frances March
MERRY WIDOW, THE(1934), ed
Frederic March
SIGN OF THE CROSS, THE(1932); SMILIN' THROUGH(1932); NOTHING SAC-
RED(1937); TRADE WINDS(1938)
Fredric March
WILD PARTY, THE(1929); DUMMY, THE(1929); FOOTLIGHTS AND FOOLS(1929);
JEALOUSY(1929); MARRIAGE PLAYGROUND, THE(1929); PARIS BOUND(1929);
STUDIO MURDER MYSTERY, THE(1929); LADIES LOVE BRUTES(1930); LAUGH-

Hal March-
TER(1930); MANSLAUGHTER(1930); ROYAL FAMILY OF BROADWAY, THE(1930); SARAH AND SON(1930); TRUE TO THE NAVY(1930); HONOR AMONG LOVERS(1931); MY SIN(1931); NIGHT ANGEL, THE(1931); DR. JEKYLL AND MR. HYDE(1932); MAKE ME A STAR(1932); MERRILY WE GO TO HELL(1932); STRANGERS IN LOVE(1932); DESIGN FOR LIVING(1933); EAGLE AND THE HAWK, THE(1933); TONIGHT IS OURS(1933); AFFAIRS OF CELLINI, THE(1934); ALL OF ME(1934); BARRETTS OF WIMPOLE STREET, THE(1934); DEATH TAKES A HOLIDAY(1934); GOOD DAME(1934); WE LIVE AGAIN(1934); ANNA KARENINA(1935); DARK ANGEL, THE(1935); LES MISERABLES(1935); ANTHONY ADVERSE(1936); MARY OF SCOTLAND(1936); ROAD TO GLORY, THE(1936); STAR IS BORN, A(1937); THERE GOES MY HEART(1938); SUSAN AND GOD(1940); VICTORY(1940); ONE FOOT IN HEAVEN(1941); SO ENDS OUR NIGHT(1941); BEDTIME STORY(1942); I MARRIED A WITCH(1942); ADVENTURES OF MARK TWAIN, THE(1944); TOMORROW THE WORLD(1944); BEST YEARS OF OUR LIVES, THE(1946); ACT OF MURDER, AN(1948); ANOTHER PART OF THE FOREST(1948); CHRISTOPHER COLUMBUS(1949, Brit.); IT'S A BIG COUNTRY(1951); DEATH OF A SALESMAN(1952); MAN ON A TIGHTROPE(1953); BRIDGES AT TOKO-RI, THE(1954); EXECUTIVE SUITE(1954); DESPERATE HOURS, THE(1955); ALEXANDER THE GREAT(1956); ISLAND OF ALLAH(1956); MAN IN THE GREY FLANNEL SUIT, THE(1956); MIDDLE OF THE NIGHT(1959); INHERIT THE WIND(1960); YOUNG DOCTORS, THE(1961); CONDEMNED OF ALTONA, THE(1963); SEVEN DAYS IN MAY(1964); HOMBRE(1967); ...TICK...TICK...TICK...(1970); ICEMAN COMETH, THE(1973)

Hal March
MA AND PA KETTLE GO TO TOWN(1950); OUTRAGE(1950); COMBAT SQUAD(1953); EDDIE CANTOR STORY, THE(1953); ATOMIC KID, THE(1954); YANKEE PASHA(1954); IT'S ALWAYS FAIR WEATHER(1955); MY SISTER EILEEN(1955); HEAR ME GOOD(1957); SEND ME NO FLOWERS(1964); GUIDE FOR THE MARRIED MAN, A(1967)

Iris March
MAROONED(1933, Brit.); THREE MEN IN A BOAT(1933, Brit.); COLLEEN(1936); SNOWED UNDER(1936); WELL DONE, HENRY(1936, Brit.); LEAVE IT TO ME(1937, Brit.)

J.M. March
HOOPLA(1933), w

Joseph M. March
HER JUNGLE LOVE(1938), w; WAGONS WESTWARD(1940), w

Joseph Moncure March
HELL'S ANGELS(1930), w; JOURNEY'S END(1930), w; MAN FROM WYOMING, A(1930), w; MADAME BUTTERFLY(1932), w; SKY DEVILS(1932), w; JENNIE GERHARDT(1933), w; TRANSATLANTIC MERRY-GO-ROUND(1934), w; TWO ALONE(1934), w; LET 'EM HAVE IT(1935), w; AND SUDDEN DEATH(1936), w; HIDEAWAY GIRL(1937), w; FLIRTING WITH FATE(1938), w; WOMAN DOCTOR(1939), w; FORGOTTEN GIRLS(1940), w; LONE STAR RAIDERS(1940), w; THREE FACES WEST(1940), w; SET-UP, THE(1949), w; WILD PARTY, THE(1975), w

Karin March
MOONSHINE MOUNTAIN(1964)

Lee March
IN THE MEANTIME, DARLING(1944)

Linda March
LIKE FATHER LIKE SON(1961); YOUNG SINNER, THE(1965)

Liska March
TRUNKS OF MR. O.F., THE(1932, Ger.); JOE HILL(1971, Swed./U.S.)

Lori March
LOVERS AND LOLLIPOPS(1956); RANSOM(1956)

Marvin March
YOU'RE A BIG BOY NOW(1966), set d; ILLUSTRATED MAN, THE(1969), set d; LOVE GOD?, THE(1969), set d; TAKE THE MONEY AND RUN(1969), set d; RABBIT, RUN(1970), set d; DOCTORS' WIVES(1971), set d; FOOLS' PARADE(1971), set d; ORGANIZATION, THE(1971), set d; SUMMER OF '42(1971), set d; EVERYTHING YOU ALWAYS WANTED TO KNOW ABOUT SEX, BUT WE'RE AFRAID TO ASK(1972), set d; TERMINAL MAN, THE(1974), set d; DOC SAVAGE... THE MAN OF BRONZE(1975), set d; PEEPER(1975), set d; PRISONER OF SECOND AVENUE, THE(1975), set d; SUNSHINE BOYS, THE(1975), set d; BIRCH INTERVAL(1976), set d; FUTUREWORLD(1976), set d; MISSOURI BREAKS, THE(1976), set d; MURDER BY DEATH(1976), set d; SILVER STREAK(1976), set d; TURNING POINT, THE(1977), set d; SGT. PEPPER'S LONELY HEARTS CLUB BAND(1978), set d; STRAIGHT TIME(1978), set d; FRISCO KID, THE(1979), set d; TRUE CONFESSIONS(1981), set d; FLASHDANCE(1983), set d
1984
FLETCH(1984), set d; GHOSTBUSTERS(1984), set d

Myron March [Miroslav Machacek]
VOYAGE TO THE END OF THE UNIVERSE(1963, Czech.)

Nadine March
AFTER OFFICE HOURS(1932, Brit.); IT'S A BET(1935, Brit.); GIVE HER A RING(1936, Brit.); WEEKEND MILLIONAIRE(1937, Brit.); RAT, THE(1938, Brit.); WANTED BY SCOTLAND YARD(1939, Brit.); BULLDOG SEES IT THROUGH(1940, Brit.); PRIME MINISTER, THE(1941, Brit.)

Oliver T. March
FLORODORA GIRL, THE(1930), ph

Peter March
SCHOOL FOR SECRETS(1946, Brit.)

Philippe March
WINTER WIND(1970, Fr./Hung.); TWO PEOPLE(1973)

Phillippe March
ONCE IN PARIS(1978)

Ruth March
SUNRISE AT CAMPOBELLO(1960)

Sally March
ARIZONA KID, THE(1939)

Taylor March
STRANGE FETISHES, THE(1967)

Thomas March
WAR AND PEACE(1983, Ger.), ph

Timothy March
LET'S DO IT AGAIN(1975), w; PIECE OF THE ACTION, A(1977), w

Tony March
PARTNERS(1982); WRONG IS RIGHT(1982)

William March
BAD SEED, THE(1956), w

John Marchak
RED, HOT AND BLUE(1949)

Arlette Marchal
ENTENTE CORDIALE(1939, Fr.); FIGHTING PIMPERNEL, THE(1950, Brit.)
Silents
CAT'S PAJAMAS, THE(1926); WINGS(1927)
Misc. Silents
BORN TO THE WEST(1926); DIPLOMACY(1926); FORLORN RIVER(1926); LA CHATELAINE DU LIBAN(1926, Fr.); BLONDE OR BRUNETTE(1927); GENTLEMAN OF PARIS, A(1927); HULA(1927); MOON OF ISRAEL(1927, Aust.); SPOTLIGHT, THE(1927)

Franck Marchal
NATHALIE, AGENT SECRET(1960, Fr.), w

Frank Marchal
NATHALIE(1958, Fr.), w

Georges Marchal
LUMIERE D'ETE(1943, Fr.); HER FIRST AFFAIR(1947, Fr.); FRENCH WAY, THE(1952, Fr.); JUPITER(1952, Fr.); AFFAIRS OF MESSALINA, THE(1954, Ital.); ROYAL AFFAIRS IN VERSAILLES(1957, Fr.); WARRIOR AND THE SLAVE GIRL, THE(1959, Ital.); AUSTERLITZ(1960, Fr./Ital./Yugo.); LEGIONS OF THE NILE(1960, Ital.); COLOSSUS OF RHODES, THE(1961, Ital., Fr., Span.); GINA(1961, Fr./Mex.); SECRET MARK OF D'ARTAGNAN, THE(1963, Fr./Ital.); SEVEN DWARFS TO THE RESCUE, THE(1965, Ital.); THE DIRTY GAME(1966, Fr./Ital./Ger.); SELLERS OF GIRLS(1967, Fr.); BELLE DE JOUR(1968, Fr.); MILKY WAY, THE(1969, Fr./Ital.); DEATH IN THE GARDEN(1977, Fr./Mex.)

Isabelle Marchal
VALACHI PAPERS, THE(1972, Ital./Fr.)

Lynda Marchal
DRAUGHTSMAN'S CONTRACT, THE(1983, Brit.); HIGH ROAD TO CHINA(1983)

Georges Marchalk
SIN ON THE BEACH(1964, Fr.), ed

Anne-Marie Marchand
FANNY(1961), cos; RETURN OF MARTIN GUERRE, THE(1983, Fr.), cos

Cathy Marchand
PASSION(1983, Fr./Switz.)

Claude Marchand
RABID(1976, Can.), art d; CITY ON FIRE(1979 Can.), art d

Colette Marchand
MOULIN ROUGE(1952)

Corinne Marchand
CLEO FROM 5 TO 7(1961, Fr.); LOLA(1961, Fr./Ital.); SEVEN CAPITAL SINS(1962, Fr./Ital.); ARIZONA COLT(1965, It./Fr./Span.); BORSALINO(1970, Fr.); RIDER ON THE RAIN(1970, Fr./Ital.); TRAVELS WITH MY AUNT(1972, Brit.); LIZA(1976, Fr./Ital.)

Ernest Marchand
FABULOUS WORLD OF JULES VERNE, THE(1961, Czech.), anim

Eve Marchand
GLORY BOY(1971)

Guy Marchand
SUCH A GORGEOUS KID LIKE ME(1973, Fr.); COUSIN, COUSINE(1976, Fr.); DEAR DETECTIVE(1978, Fr.); LOULOU(1980, Fr.); COUP DE TORCHON(1981, Fr.); INQUISITOR, THE(1982, Fr.); ENTRE NOUS(1983, Fr.)
1984
HEAT OF DESIRE(1984, Fr.)

Henri Marchand
A NOUS LA LIBERTE(1931, Fr.); AMOUR, AMOUR(1937, Fr.)

J. Marchand
PORTRAIT OF LENIN(1967, Pol./USSR)

Jean Marchand
STRANGE SHADOWS IN AN EMPTY ROOM(1977, Can./Ital.)

Jean-Pierre Marchand
FIRE IN THE FLESH(1964, Fr.), w

Leopold Marchand
LOVE ME TONIGHT(1932), w; TOPAZE(1935, Fr.), w; LUCREZIA BORGIA(1937, Fr.), w

Lucienne Marchand
CLEO FROM 5 TO 7(1961, Fr.)

Michelle Marchand
SEIZURE(1974), set d

Nancy Marchand
BACHELOR PARTY, THE(1957); LADYBUG, LADYBUG(1963); ME, NATALIE(1969); TELL ME THAT YOU LOVE ME, JUNIE MOON(1970); HOSPITAL, THE(1971)
1984
BOSTONIANS, THE(1984)

Claude Marchant
SIGN OF THE GLADIATOR(1959, Fr./Ger./Ital.), ch

Jay Marchant
Silents
FIGHTING SMILE, THE(1925), d; SPEED MAD(1925), d
Misc. Silents
GREAT SENSATION, THE(1925), d

Laurence Marchant
2001: A SPACE ODYSSEY(1968, U.S./Brit.)

Shirley Marchant
TIME AFTER TIME(1979, Brit.)

William Marchant
DESK SET(1957), w; TRIPLE CROSS(1967, Fr./Brit.), w; MY LOVER, MY SON(1970, Brit.), w

Jean Marchat
CROISIERES SIDERALES(1941, Fr.); STORMY WATERS(1946, Fr.); MOST WANTED MAN, THE(1962, Fr./Ital.); TOMORROW IS MY TURN(1962, Fr./Ital./Ger.); LADIES OF THE PARK(1964, Fr.); TWO ARE GUILTY(1964, Fr.)

Gazelle Marche
Silents
ARGYLE CASE, THE(1917)

Arlette Marchel
Misc. Silents
L'IMAGE(1926, Fr.)
Suzanne Marchellier
THERESE AND ISABELLE(1968, U.S./Ger.)
Lyudmila Marchenko
HOME FOR TANYA, A(1961, USSR); SONG OF THE FOREST(1963, USSR)
Carlos Romero Marchent
SANTO CONTRA EL DOCTOR MUERTE(1974, Span./Mex.)
Rafael Romero Marchent
SANTO CONTRA EL DOCTOR MUERTE(1974, Span./Mex.), d, w
Joseph Marchese
WHY RUSSIANS ARE REVOLTING(1970)
Marcello Marchesi
LADY DOCTOR, THE(1963, Fr./Ital./Span.), w
Pia Marchesi
IL GRIDO(1962, U.S./Ital.), cos
Emilio Marchesini
CAT O'NINE TAILS(1971, Ital./Ger./Fr.)
Alfredo Marchetti
SWORD OF THE CONQUEROR(1962, Ital.)
Gianni Marchetti
WILD EYE, THE(1968, Ital.), m; ONE STEP TO HELL(1969, U.S./Ital./Span.), m
Giulio Marchetti
STRANGER ON THE PROWL(1953, Ital.); SWORDSMAN OF SIENA, THE(1962, Fr./Ital.); SECRET MARK OF D'ARTAGNAN, THE(1963, Fr./Ital.); QUEEN OF THE NILE(1964, Ital.); SECRET INVASION, THE(1964); LION OF ST. MARK(1967, Ital.)
Giuseppe Marchetti
ORGANIZER, THE(1964, Fr./Ital./Yugo.)
Goanni Marchetti
ONE STEP TO HELL(1969, U.S./Ital./Span.), md
Guilio Marchetti
FUGITIVE LADY(1951)
Milo Marchetti, Jr.
FISHERMAN'S WHARF(1939)
Nino Marchetti
CARTOUCHE(1957, Ital./US); DESERT DESPERADOES(1959); PRISONER OF THE VOLGA(1960, Fr./Ital.); PHAROAH'S WOMAN, THE(1961, Ital.); LIPSTICK(1965, Fr./Ital.); QUEENS, THE(1968, Ital./Fr.)
Alex Marchevsky
MAN OUTSIDE, THE(1968, Brit.)
Eve Marchew
Silents
GREAT GAME, THE(1918, Brit.); PRIDE OF THE NORTH, THE(1920, Brit.)
Misc. Silents
I HEAR YOU CALLING ME(1919, Brit.)
Maria Marchi
EL GRECO(1966, Ital., Fr.); WHITE SISTER(1973, Ital./Span./Fr.)
Pier Vittorio Marchi
TROJAN HORSE, THE(1962, Fr./Ital.), art d; FURY OF THE PAGANS(1963, Ital.), art d; GOLIATH AND THE SINS OF BABYLON(1964, Ital.), art d; REVENGE OF THE GLADIATORS(1965, Ital.), art d; SEVEN SLAVES AGAINST THE WORLD(1965, Ital.), art d
Virgilio Marchi
INDISCRETION OF AN AMERICAN WIFE(1954, U.S./Ital.), art d; LOVES OF THREE QUEENS, THE(1954, Ital./Fr.), art d; MATA HARI'S DAUGHTER(1954, Fr./Ital), art d; UMBERTO D(1955, Ital.), prod d; ANGELS OF DARKNESS(1956, Ital.), art d
Virgillio Marchi
GREATEST LOVE, THE(1954, Ital.), set d
Maria Marchiali
Silents
NERO(1922, U.S./Ital.)
David Marchick
MIDNIGHT(1983)
Carlo Marchini
OUTBACK(1971, Aus.)
Dorothy Marchini
GIVE HER THE MOON(1970, Fr./Ital.)
Ron Marchini
DEATH MACHINES(1976)
Fanny Marchio
WHITE SHEIK, THE(1956, Ital.); VARIETY LIGHTS(1965, Ital.)
Gilda Marchio
SPIRIT AND THE FLESH, THE(1948, Ital.)
Marchioness of Queensbury
THINGS TO COME(1936, Brit.), cos
Mignon Marchland
MELODY OF MY HEART(1936, Brit.)
George Marci
TOP BANANA(1954)
Georges Marci
WILD EYE, THE(1968, Ital.), p
Danilo Marciani
MINNESOTA CLAY(1966, Ital./Fr./Span.), p
Consolato Marciano
TENTACLES(1977, Ital.)
Francesca Marciano
SEVEN BEAUTIES(1976, Ital.)
Rocky Marciano
DELICATE DELINQUENT, THE(1957); COLLEGE CONFIDENTIAL(1960)
Shoshi Marciano
1984
LITTLE DRUMMER GIRL, THE(1984)
Andreja Marcic
GENGHIS KHAN(U.S./Brit./Ger./Yugo)
Isidor Marcil
Misc. Silents
PLAYING DEAD(1915)

Max Marcin
GHOST TALKS, THE(1929), w; THREE LIVE GHOSTS(1929), p, w; BE YOURSELF(1930), w; DERELICT(1930), w; SHADOW OF THE LAW(1930), d, w; CITY STREETS(1931), w; LAWYER'S SECRET, THE(1931), d, w; SCANDAL SHEET(1931), w; SILENCE(1931), d, w; CASE OF CLARA DEANE, THE(1932), d, w; STRANGE CASE OF CLARA DEANE, THE(1932), d, w; WOMAN IN ROOM 13, THE(1932), w; GAMBLING SHIP(1933), d, w; KING OF THE JUNGLE(1933), d, w; CHEATING CHEATERS(1934), w; LOVE CAPTIVE, THE(1934), d, w; THREE LIVE GHOSTS(1935), w; JUNGLE PRINCESS, THE(1936), w; SLIGHTLY TEMPTED(1940), w
Silents
TOWER OF LIES, THE(1925), w; CHEATING CHEATERS(1927), w; ROUGH HOUSE ROSIE(1927), w
Natalie Marcin
ANCHORS AWEIGH(1945), w
O. Marcin
MOST BEAUTIFUL AGE, THE(1970, Czech.)
Angelo Marcini
FRANCHETTE; LES INTRIGUES(1969)
Judy Marcione
GET TO KNOW YOUR RABBIT(1972)
Grazia Marciso
TIME OF YOUR LIFE, THE(1948)
Anton Marco
ZELIG(1983)
Armand Marco
TOUT VA BIEN(1973, Fr.), ph
Henry Marco
I SHOT BILLY THE KID(1950); ON THE ISLE OF SAMOA(1950); MARA MARU(1952)
Jose Marco
ALEXANDER THE GREAT(1956); ROMEO AND JULIET(1968, Ital./Span.)
Joseph Marco
GLADIATORS 7(1964, Span./Ital.)
Luis Marco
GOLIATH AGAINST THE GIANTS(1963, Ital./Span.)
Marya Marco
CLAY PIGEON, THE(1949); CUSTOMS AGENT(1950); CHINA CORSAIR(1951); I WAS AN AMERICAN SPY(1951); NEVER WAVE AT A WAC(1952); CITY BENEATH THE SEA(1953); TOP OF THE WORLD(1955)
Paul Marco
BRIDE OF THE MONSTER(1955); PLAN 9 FROM OUTER SPACE(1959)
Raoul Marco
MAN STOLEN(1934, Fr.); LILIOM(1935, Fr.); LE CIEL EST A VOUS(1957, Fr.); UP FROM THE BEACH(1965)
Sally Marco
IN CALIENTE(1935)
Senor Marco
1984
BLOOD SIMPLE(1984)
Silvia Marco
MAN WHO WAGGED HIS TAIL, THE(1961, Ital./Span.)
Tony Marco
IN CALIENTE(1935)
Marconi
TIGER AND THE FLAME, THE(1955, India)
Chris Marconi
BLOOD MANIA(1971), p; POINT OF TERROR(1971), p, w
Lana Marconi
NAPOLEON(1955, Fr.); IF PARIS WERE TOLD TO US(1956, Fr.); ROYAL AFFAIRS IN VERSAILLES(1957, Fr.)
Nadia Marconi
HATE FOR HATE(1967, Ital.)
Saverio Marconi
PADRE PADRONE(1977, Ital.)
Yannis Marcopoulos
APOLLO GOES ON HOLIDAY(1968, Ger./Swed.), m
Jose Luis Hernandez Marcos
NUN AT THE CROSSROADS, A(1970, Ital./Span.), w
William Marcos
PENITENTE MURDER CASE, THE(1936); DEVIL'S SISTERS, THE(1966); DEATH CURSE OF TARTU(1967)
Benoit Marcoux
MY UNCLE ANTOINE(1971, Can.)
Robin Marcoux
MY UNCLE ANTOINE(1971, Can.)
Vanni Marcoux
Silents
SCANDAL, THE(1923, Brit.)
Misc. Silents
DON JUAN ET FAUST(1923, Fr.); MIRACLE OF WOLVES, THE(1925, Fr.)
Andrea Marcovicci
CONCORDE, THE–AIRPORT '79(; FRONT, THE(1976); HAND, THE(1981); SPACE-HUNTER: ADVENTURES IN THE FORBIDDEN ZONE(1983)
1984
KINGS AND DESPERATE MEN(1984, Brit.)
Ron Marcroft
CUTTER AND BONE(1981)
Bob Marcucci
IDOLMAKER, THE(1980), tech adv
Robert P. Marcucci
1984
RAZOR'S EDGE, THE(1984), p
Al Marcus
RING-A-DING RHYTHM(1962, Brit. 73m Amicus/COL bw (G.B: IT'S TRAD, DAD!), prod d
Alan Marcus
MARAUDERS, THE(1955), w; KILL SQUAD(1982)

Alex Marcus
GENTLE CREATURE, A(1971, Fr.), makeup

Alexandre Marcus
TIME BOMB(1961, Fr./Ital.), makeup; LAST YEAR AT MARIENBAD(1962, Fr./Ital.), makeup; NUDE IN HIS POCKET(1962, Fr.), makeup; LA GUERRE EST FINIE(1967, Fr./Swed.), makeup

Bernie Marcus
OUTRAGE(1950)

David Marcus
SPEED LOVERS(1968)

Deborah Marcus
YOUNG CYCLE GIRLS, THE(1979)

DeVera Marcus
HARPER VALLEY, P.T.A.(1978); I'M DANCING AS FAST AS I CAN(1982)
1984
JOY OF SEX(1984)

Ed Marcus
DESTRUCTORS, THE(1974, Brit.); LOVE AND DEATH(1975); HERBIE GOES TO MONTE CARLO(1977)

Eliane Marcus
LA GUERRE EST FINIE(1967, Fr./Swed.), makeup

Elisabeth Marcus
ELUSIVE CORPORAL, THE(1963, Fr.)

Ellen Marcus
ECHOES OF SILENCE(1966)

Ellis Marcus
RIDE CLEAR OF DIABLO(1954), w

Frank Marcus
PRIEST OF LOVE(1981, Brit.)

Jacques Marcus
1984
DESIREE(1984, Neth.), ed

James Marcus
EVANGELINE(1929); IN OLD ARIZONA(1929); WHISPERING WINDS(1929); BACK PAY(1930); BILLY THE KID(1930); LILIOM(1930); TEXAN, THE(1930); ARROWS-MITH(1931); FIGHTING CARAVANS(1931); HELL'S HOUSE(1932); LAND OF WANT-ED MEN(1932); MASON OF THE MOUNTED(1932); ME AND MY GAL(1932); KING OF THE ARENA(1933); LONE AVENGER, THE(1933); SONG OF SONGS(1933); STRAWBERRY ROAN(1933); HONOR OF THE RANGE(1934); OPERATOR 13(1934); SCARLET EMPRESS, THE(1934); TRAIL BEYOND, THE(1934); WAGON WHEELS(1934); WE LIVE AGAIN(1934); LIFE BEGINS AT 40(1935); RED MOR-NING(1935); STEAMBOAT ROUND THE BEND(1935); LONELY TRAIL, THE(1936); PRISONER OF SHARK ISLAND, THE(1936); MAID OF SALEM(1937); WRONG ROAD, THE(1937); CLOCKWORK ORANGE, A(1971, Brit.); LITTLEST HORSE THIEVES, THE(1977); MC VICAR(1982, Brit.)
1984
NUMBER ONE(1984, Brit.)
Silents
MEDIATOR, THE(1916); SERPENT, THE(1916); LITTLE LORD FAUNT-LEROY(1921); COME ON OVER(1922); OLIVER TWIST(1922); STRANGER'S BAN-QUET(1922); SCARAMOUCHE(1923); IRON HORSE, THE(1924); DICK TURPIN(1925); EAGLE, THE(1925); ISLE OF HOPE, THE(1925); SIBERIA(1926); BACHELOR'S BABY, THE(1927); CAPTAIN SALVATION(1927); KING OF KINGS, THE(1927); ISLE OF LOST MEN(1928); EVANGELINE(1929)
Misc. Silents
BETRAYED(1917); ON THE JUMP(1918); PRUSSIAN CUR, THE(1918); EVANGE-LINE(1919); ALL AROUND FRYING PAN(1925); TEXAS STREAK, THE(1926); TRAF-FIC COP, THE(1926); BUCK PRIVATES(1928); REVENGE(1928)

James A. Marcus
Silents
HONOR SYSTEM, THE(1917); BEAU BRUMMEL(1924); SCARLET LETTER, THE(1926); SADIE THOMPSON(1928)
Misc. Silents
CARMEN(1915); BLUE BLOOD AND RED(1916); CONQUEROR, THE(1917); PRIDE OF NEW YORK, THE(1917); THIS IS THE LIFE(1917); HEADIN' HOME(1920); SERENADE(1921)

Jeff Marcus
ENDLESS LOVE(1981)

Jim Marcus
WESTERN FRONTIER(1935); ON SUCH A NIGHT(1937)

John Marcus
NAKED PREY, THE(1966, U.S./South Africa)

Julie Marcus
WESTWORLD(1973)

Larry Marcus
BACKFIRE(1950), w; DARK CITY(1950), w; CAUSE FOR ALARM(1951), w; PAU-LA(1952), w; BIGAMIST,THE(1953), w; THREE'S COMPANY(1953, Brit.), w; DEATH OF MICHAEL TURBIN, THE(1954, Brit.), w; FOREVER MY HEART(1954, Brit.), w; RED DRESS, THE(1954, Brit.), w; UNGUARDED MOMENT, THE(1956), w; WITNESS FOR THE PROSECUTION(1957), w; DIAMOND SAFARI(1958), w; VOICE IN THE MIRROR(1958), w; BRAINSTORM(1965), w

Larry B. Marcus
COVENANT WITH DEATH, A(1966), w

Lawrence B. Marcus
VALLEY OF MYSTERY(1967), w; PETULIA(1968, U.S./Brit.), w; JUSTINE(1969), w; GOING HOME(1971), w; ALEX AND THE GYPSY(1976), w; STUNT MAN, THE(1980), w

Lee Marcus
LIGHTNING STRIKES TWICE(1935), p; NITWITS, THE(1935), p; RAINMAKERS, THE(1935), p; GRAND JURY(1936), p; LOVE ON A BET(1936), p; MUMMY'S BOYS(1936), p; SECOND WIFE(1936), p; SILLY BILLIES(1936), p; ON AGAIN–OFF AGAIN(1937), p; WE'RE ON THE JURY(1937), p; BILL OF DIVORCEMENT(1940), p; MEXICAN SPITFIRE OUT WEST(1940), p; POP ALWAYS PAYS(1940), p; STRAN-GER ON THE THIRD FLOOR(1940), p; FATHER TAKES A WIFE(1941), p; DANCING MASTERS, THE(1943), p; THEY CAME TO BLOW UP AMERICA(1943), p; ROGER TOUHY, GANGSTER!(1944), p; LOST HONEYMOON(1947), p

Les Marcus
HIGH FLYERS(1937), p

Marlene Marcus
1984
SCREAM FOR HELP(1984)

Perle Marcus
TEVYA(1939)

Peter Marcus
WHERE HAS POOR MICKEY GONE?(1964, Brit.), w; BODY STEALERS, THE(1969), w; HORROR HOUSE(1970, Brit.), w

Rachel Marcus
OPERATION THUNDERBOLT(1978, ISRAEL)

Raymond Marcus
HELLCATS OF THE NAVY(1957), w

Raymond T. Marcus
EARTH VS. THE FLYING SAUCERS(1956), w; CHICAGO CONFIDENTIAL(1957), w; ESCAPE FROM SAN QUENTIN(1957), w; ZOMBIES OF MORA TAU(1957), w; CASE AGAINST BROOKLYN, THE(1958), w

Reg Marcus
GLIMPSE OF PARADISE, A(1934, Brit.); SOMETHING ALWAYS HAPPENS(1934, Brit.); MR. WHAT'S-HIS-NAME(1935, Brit.)

Ruth Marcus
WILD GYPSIES(1969)

Sparky Marcus
FREAKY FRIDAY(1976); MAN WITH TWO BRAINS, THE(1983)

Susan Marcus
CLASS OF '44(1973)

T. Marcus
SUMMERSPELL(1983), m

Vicki Marcus
TEVYA(1939)

Vicky Marcus
CANTOR'S SON, THE(1937)

Vitina Marcus
LOST WORLD, THE(1960); TARAS BULBA(1962)

Wade Marcus
FINAL COMEDOWN, THE(1972), m

Ted Marcuse
JEANNE EAGELS(1957)

Theo Marcuse
TWO LITTLE BEARS, THE(1961); CINCINNATI KID, THE(1965); HARUM SCA-RUM(1965); LAST OF THE SECRET AGENTS?, THE(1966); MARA OF THE WILDER-NESS(1966); WICKED DREAMS OF PAULA SCHULTZ, THE(1968)

Theodore Marcuse
DESPERATE WOMEN, THE(?); 27TH DAY, THE(1957); OPERATION EICH-MANN(1961); HITLER(1962); FOR LOVE OR MONEY(1963); REBELS AGAINST THE LIGHT(1964); TIGER WALKS, A(1964); SANDS OF BEERSHEBA(1966, U.S./Israel)

Elia Marcuzzo
OSSESSIONE(1959, Ital.)

Lucio Marcuzzo
SPY IN YOUR EYE(1966, Ital.), p, w

Claude Marcy
SYLVIA AND THE PHANTOM(1950, Fr.)

Eve Marcy
42ND STREET(1933)

George Marcy
LAST MILE, THE(1959)

Teresa Marczewska
1984
SHIVERS(1984, Pol.)

Wojciech Marczewski
1984
SHIVERS(1984, Pol.), d&w

Christl Mardayn
STORY OF VICKIE, THE(1958, Aust.)

Christiane Mardayne
SHANGHAI DRAMA, THE(1945, Fr.)

Diana V. Marde
Misc. Silents
LA VIRGEN DE LA CARIDAD(1930, Cuba)

Regina Mardeck
AMERICAN SUCCESS COMPANY, THE(1980)

Adrienne Marden
MILLIONS IN THE AIR(1935); F MAN(1936); STAR FOR A NIGHT(1936); THIRTEEN HOURS BY AIR(1936); FOR THE LOVE OF MARY(1948); SUPERMAN AND THE MOLE MEN(1951); SNIPER, THE(1952); DANGEROUS CROSSING(1953); INFER-NO(1953); COUNT THREE AND PRAY(1955); ONE DESIRE(1955); SHRIKE, THE(1955); MAN FROM DEL RIO(1956); WALK ON THE WILD SIDE(1962); KISSES FOR MY PRESIDENT(1964)

Benes Marden
IS THIS TRIP REALLY NECESSARY?(1970)

Mabel Marden
MADAME SPY(1934)

Nona Marden
Misc. Silents
SILAS MARNER(1922)

Richard Marden
FRIENDS AND NEIGHBORS(1963, Brit.), set d; SOLDIER'S TALE, THE(1964, Brit.), ed; OTHELLO(1965, Brit.), ed; BEDAZZLED(1967, Brit.), ed; TWO FOR THE ROAD(1967, Brit.), ed; HOT MILLIONS(1968, Brit.), ed; ANNE OF THE THOUSAND DAYS(1969, Brit.), ed; STAIRCASE(1969 U.S./Brit./Fr.), ed; MARY, QUEEN OF SCOTS(1971, Brit.), ed; SUNDAY BLOODY SUNDAY(1971, Brit.), ed; MALPERTI-US(1972, Bel./Fr.), ed; SLEUTH(1972, Brit.), ed; RUSSIAN ROULETTE(1975), ed; CARRY ON ENGLAND(1976, Brit.), ed; LITTLEST HORSE THIEVES, THE(1977), ed; HOUND OF THE BASKERVILLES, THE(1980, Brit.), ed; MIRROR CRACK'D, THE(1980, Brit.), ed; SATURN 3(1980), ed; EVIL UNDER THE SUN(1982, Brit.), ed
1984
BLAME IT ON RIO(1984), ed; SWORD OF THE VALIANT(1984, Brit.), ed

Barry Marder
1984
WHERE THE BOYS ARE '84(1984)

Bruce Marder
1984
  MIKE'S MURDER(1984)
Linda Marder
  REAL LIFE(1979), art d
Rebecca Marder
1984
  MIKE'S MURDER(1984)
Nick Mardi
1984
  HOTEL NEW HAMPSHIRE, THE(1984)
Aurora Mardiganian
Misc. Silents
  AUCTION OF SOULS(1922)
Tom Mardirosian
  TOOTSIE(1982); TRADING PLACES(1983)
1984
  ALPHABET CITY(1984)
Al Mardo
  THAT'S MY BABY(1944)
Estelle Mardo
Silents
  FAMILY CUPBOARD, THE(1915)
Jimmell Mardorne
1984
  PURPLE RAIN(1984), cos
Heinz Marecek
  GIRL FROM PETROVKA, THE(1974)
Arlette Marechal
Misc. Silents
  VENETIAN LOVERS(1925, Brit.)
Georges Marechal
  MESSALINE(1952, Fr./Ital.)
Joseph Marechal
  STRANGER, THE(1967, Algeria/Fr./Ital.)
Lynne Maree
  HOUSE OF THE LIVING DEAD(1973, S. Afr.)
Tanya Maree
  PSYCHO A GO-GO!(1965)
Matiu Mareikura
  PICTURES(1982, New Zealand)
1984
  WILD HORSES(1984, New Zealand)
Andrezj Marek
Misc. Silents
  HARSH FATHER, THE(1911, USSR), d
Andrzej Marek
Misc. Silents
  MIRELE EFROS(1912, USSR), d
Liane Marelli
  IT TAKES A THIEF(1960, Brit.)
Otello Marelli
  ANNA(1951, Ital.), ph; BOCCACCIO '70(1962/Ital./Fr.), ph
Grete Maren
  STORM IN A WATER GLASS(1931, Aust.)
Jerry Maren
  FLESH AND FANTASY(1943); JOHNNY DOESN'T LIVE HERE ANY MORE(1944);
  SHOW BUSINESS(1944); DUFFY'S TAVERN(1945); WHEN MY BABY SMILES AT
  ME(1948); DIRTY HARRY(1971); LITTLE CIGARS(1973); WHERE THE BUFFALO
  ROAM(1980)
Sylvia Marenco
  SINISTER URGE, THE(1961)
Jerry Marenghi
  AT THE CIRCUS(1939)
V. Marenkov
  MY NAME IS IVAN(1963, USSR); PEACE TO HIM WHO ENTERS(1963, USSR);
  RESURRECTION(1963, USSR)
Jaroslav Mares
  LEMONADE JOE(1966, Czech.)
John Mares [Jaroslav Mares]
  VOYAGE TO THE END OF THE UNIVERSE(1963, Czech.)
Karel Mares
  FIREMAN'S BALL, THE(1968, Czech.), m; MARTYRS OF LOVE(1968, Czech.), m;
  REPORT ON THE PARTY AND THE GUESTS, A(1968, Czech.), a, m; MOST BEAUTI-
  FUL AGE, THE(1970, Czech.), m
Maria Grazia Marescalchi
  SACCO AND VANZETTI(1971, Ital./Fr.); ASH WEDNESDAY(1973)
Simone Marescat
  TRUTH, THE(1961, Fr./Ital.), w
Harald Maresch
  RIVER CHANGES, THE(1956); THREE MOVES TO FREEDOM(1960, Ger.); BRAIN-
  WASHED(1961, Ger.); IT'S HOT IN PARADISE(1962, Ger./Yugo.)
Harold D. Maresch
  STALAG 17(1953)
Alberto Mareschalchi
  INVASION 1700(1965, Fr./Ital./Yugo.)
Marie Maresova
  SWEET LIGHT IN A DARK ROOM(1966, Czech.)
Harry Maret
  CRY OF THE CITY(1948), makeup; SEPARATE TABLES(1958), makeup; TWENTY
  PLUS TWO(1961), makeup; SHOCK TREATMENT(1964), makeup; GLASS BOTTOM
  BOAT, THE(1966), makeup; GRADUATE, THE(1967), makeup; WHERE WERE YOU
  WHEN THE LIGHTS WENT OUT?(1968), makeup; WITH SIX YOU GET EG-
  GROLL(1968), makeup
Jacques Maret
  STORY OF THREE LOVES, THE(1953), w; STATION SIX-SAHARA(1964, Brit./Ger.),
  w

Paul Maret
  AMOUR, AMOUR(1937, Fr.), w
Glenville Mareth
  SANTA CLAUS CONQUERS THE MARTIANS(1964), w
Vera Maretskaya
  MOTHER AND DAUGHTER(1965, USSR)
Misc. Silents
  HOUSE ON TRUBNAYA SQUARE(1928, USSR)
Sandro Maretti
  GOLIATH AND THE DRAGON(1961, Ital./Fr.)
Colette Mareuil
  PLEASURES AND VICES(1962, Fr.)
Philippe Mareuil
  JUDEX(1966, Fr./Ital.); CHANEL SOLITAIRE(1981)
Simone Mareuil
Misc. Silents
  LA GALERIE DES MONSTRES(1924, Fr.); PEAU DE PECHE(1929, Fr.)
Janie Mareze
  LA CHIENNE(1975, Fr.)
Dwight Marfield
  TROUBLE WITH HARRY, THE(1955); SKI BUM, THE(1971); ONE FLEW OVER THE
  CUCKOO'S NEST(1975)
Irena Marga
Misc. Silents
  ASIAN SUN, THE(1921, Ger.)
Marga And Deighton
  SEVEN THIEVES(1960)
E.M. Margadonna
  BANDIT, THE(1949, Ital.), w; FRISKY(1955, Ital.), w; FAST AND SEXY(1960, Fr./
  Ital.), w
Ettore M. Margadonna
  WITHOUT PITY(1949, Ital.), w; WHITE SHEIK, THE(1956, Ital.)
Ettore Margadonna
  UNDER THE SUN OF ROME(1949, Ital.), w; BREAD, LOVE AND DREAMS(1953,
  Ital.), w; SCANDAL IN SORRENTO(1957, Ital./Fr.), w; ANNA OF BROOKLYN(1958,
  Ital.), w
Meir Margalit
  SIMCHON FAMILY, THE(1969, Israel)
Juan Margallo
  SPIRIT OF THE BEEHIVE, THE(1976, Span.)
Lillian Margarejo
  LOSERS, THE(1970)
Gilles Margaritis
  L'ATALANTE(1947, Fr.)
Marge
  ESCAPE TO BURMA(1955)
Charles Margelis
Silents
  MERRY WIDOW, THE(1925)
James Margellos
  PAPERBACK HERO(1973, Can.), p; INBREAKER, THE(1974, Can.), p; SLIP-
  STREAM(1974, Can.), p; SECOND WIND(1976, Can.), p; SEARCH AND DE-
  STROY(1981), p
Gilbert Margerie
  LION IN WINTER, THE(1968, Brit.), art d; SINGAPORE, SINGAPORE(1969, Fr./
  Ital.), art d; LE PETIT THEATRE DE JEAN RENOIR(1974, Fr.), prod d
Arthur Margetson
  WOLVES(1930, Brit.); MANY WATERS(1931, Brit.); OTHER PEOPLE'S SINS(1931,
  Brit.); HIS GRACE GIVES NOTICE(1933, Brit.); GREAT DEFENDER, THE(1934, Brit.);
  LITTLE FRIEND(1934, Brit.); DIVINE SPARK, THE(1935, Brit./Ital.); MUSIC HATH
  CHARMS(1935, Brit.); REGAL CAVALCADE(1935, Brit.); BROKEN BLOSSOMS(1936,
  Brit.); CLOWN MUST LAUGH, A(1936, Brit.); HEAD OFFICE(1936, Brit.); ACTION
  FOR SLANDER(1937, Brit.); JUGGERNAUT(1937, Brit.); PHANTOM SHIP(1937, Brit.);
  LOVES OF MADAME DUBARRY, THE(1938, Brit.); RETURN OF CAROL DEANE,
  THE(1938, Brit.); ME AND MY PAL(1939, Brit.); NURSEMAID WHO DISAPPEARED,
  THE(1939, Brit.); RETURN TO YESTERDAY(1940, Brit.); LARCENY STREET(1941,
  Brit.); COMMANDOS STRIKE AT DAWN, THE(1942); RANDOM HARVEST(1942);
  SHERLOCK HOLMES FACES DEATH(1943); THUMBS UP(1943)
Monty Margetts
  ANY WEDNESDAY(1966); ANGEL IN MY POCKET(1969); SUPPOSE THEY GAVE
  A WAR AND NOBODY CAME?(1970); NAPOLEON AND SAMANTHA(1972)
Antonella Margheriti
  YOR, THE HUNTER FROM THE FUTURE(1983, Ital.), spec eff
Antonio Margheriti
  ASSIGNMENT OUTER SPACE(1960, Ital.), d; GOLDEN ARROW, THE(1964, Ital.), d;
  HORROR CASTLE(1965, Ital.), w; SNOW DEVILS, THE(1965, Ital.), p, d; WILD, WILD
  PLANET, THE(1967, Ital.), p; WAR BETWEEN THE PLANETS(1971, Ital.), p; WEB OF
  THE SPIDER(1972, Ital./Fr./Ger.), w; BLOOD MONEY(1974, U.S./Hong Kong/Ital./
  Span.), d; YOR, THE HUNTER FROM THE FUTURE(1983, Ital.), spec eff
Antonio Margheriti [Anthony Dawson]
  CASTLE OF BLOOD(1964, Fr./Ital.), d; CANNIBALS IN THE STREETS(1982, Ital./
  Span.), d, w
Eduardo Margheriti
  YOR, THE HUNTER FROM THE FUTURE(1983, Ital.), spec eff
Lee Margill
  FOR LOVE AND MONEY(1967)
Marco Margine
  SEED OF MAN, THE(1970, Ital.)
Margo
  CRIME WITHOUT PASSION(1934); RUMBA(1935); ROBIN HOOD OF EL DORA-
  DO(1936); WINTERSET(1936); LOST HORIZON(1937); MIRACLE ON MAIN STREET,
  A(1940); BEHIND THE RISING SUN(1943); GANGWAY FOR TOMORROW(1943);
  LEOPARD MAN, THE(1943); VIVA ZAPATA!(1952); I'LL CRY TOMORROW(1955);
  FROM HELL TO TEXAS(1958); WHO'S GOT THE ACTION?(1962); TAFFY AND THE
  JUNGLE HUNTER(1965)
George Margo
  HELL IS SOLD OUT(1951, Brit.); PARATROOPER(1954, Brit.); JOE MACBETH(1955);
  LET'S MAKE UP(1955, Brit.); TOUCH OF THE SUN, A(1956, Brit.); WHO DONE
  IT?(1956, Brit.); ZARAK(1956, Brit.); AFTER THE BALL(1957, Brit.); KEY MAN,
  THE(1957, Brit.); MARK OF THE PHOENIX(1958, Brit.); WINDOM'S WAY(1958, Brit.);

MOUSE THAT ROARED, THE(1959, Brit.); MAKE MINE A MILLION(1965, Brit.); ADDING MACHINE, THE(1969); CAPTAIN APACHE(1971, Brit.)

Larry Margo
1984
IRRECONCILABLE DIFFERENCES(1984)

Peter Margo
BALTIMORE BULLET, THE(1980)

Bill Margold
FANTASM(1976, Aus.)

E.M. Margolese
PAWNBROKER, THE(1965)

Debra Margolies
DOZENS, THE(1981)

Herbert Margolies
FOR MEN ONLY(1952), w

Alan Margolin
BLOODSUCKING FREAKS(1982), p

Arnold Margolin
STAR SPANGLED GIRL(1971), w; SNOWBALL EXPRESS(1972), w; RUSSIAN ROULETTE(1975), w

James Margolin
WARRIORS, THE(1979); STAR CHAMBER, THE(1983)

Janet Margolin
DAVID AND LISA(1962); BUS RILEY'S BACK IN TOWN(1965); GREATEST STORY EVER TOLD, THE(1965); MORITURI(1965); NEVADA SMITH(1966); THE EAVESDROPPER(1966, U.S./Arg.); ENTER LAUGHING(1967); BUONA SERA, MRS. CAMPBELL(1968, Ital.); TAKE THE MONEY AND RUN(1969); YOUR THREE MINUTES ARE UP(1973); ANNIE HALL(1977); LAST EMBRACE(1979)

Stuart Margolin
WOMEN OF THE PREHISTORIC PLANET(1966); DON'T JUST STAND THERE(1968); GAMBLERS, THE(1969); KELLY'S HEROES(1970, U.S./Yugo.); LIMBO(1972); STONE KILLER, THE(1973); DEATH WISH(1974); GAMBLER, THE(1974); BIG BUS, THE(1976); FUTUREWORLD(1976); DAYS OF HEAVEN(1978); MAN, A WOMAN, AND A BANK, A(1979, Can.), w; S.O.B.(1981); CLASS(1983)
1984
HIGHWAY TO HELL(1984); RUNNING HOT(1984)

Margolion
NO TIME FOR BREAKFAST(1978, Fr.)

Edward Margolis
JOHNNY O'CLOCK(1947)

Herbert F. Margolis
LARCENY(1948), w

Herbert Margolis
SMART WOMAN(1948), w; MA AND PA KETTLE(1949), w; DANGER ZONE(1951), w; PIER 23(1951), w; ROARING CITY(1951), w; SMUGGLER'S ISLAND(1951), w; FRANCIS IN THE HAUNTED HOUSE(1956), w; ROCK, PRETTY BABY(1956), w; KETTLES ON OLD MACDONALD'S FARM, THE(1957), w; ROCK BABY, ROCK IT(1957), w; SUMMER LOVE(1958), w; WACKIEST SHIP IN THE ARMY, THE(1961), w

Jack Margolis
I LOVE YOU, ALICE B. TOKLAS!(1968)

Mark Margolis
SHORT EYES(1977); DINER(1982); EDDIE MACON'S RUN(1983); SCARFACE(1983)
1984
FAR FROM POLAND(1984)

Zora Margolis
CALIFORNIA SUITE(1978); HUNTER, THE(1980)

Sylvianne Margolle
MONKEY IN WINTER, A(1962, Fr.)

Mariam Margolyes
1984
ELECTRIC DREAMS(1984)

Miriam Margolyes
APPLE, THE(1980 U.S./Ger.); AWAKENING, THE(1980); YENTL(1983)

Mikki Margorian
MC VICAR(1982, Brit.)

Creta Margos
STRANGERS IN THE CITY(1962)

Herta Margot
MEXICAN SPITFIRE OUT WEST(1940)

Lena Margot
ROAD TO HONG KONG, THE(1962, U.S./Brit.)

Rosa Margot
MISSION TO MOSCOW(1943)

Michael Margotta
MARYJANE(1968); WILD IN THE STREETS(1968); COVER ME BABE(1970); STRAWBERRY STATEMENT, THE(1970); DRIVE, HE SAID(1971); PARTNERS(1976, Can.); TIMES SQUARE(1980); CAN SHE BAKE A CHERRY PIE?(1983)

Jean Margouleff
CIAO MANHATTAN(1973)

Robert Margouleff
CIAO MANHATTAN(1973), p

Richard Margowitz
OPERATION DAMES(1959), m

Miriam Margoyles
STAND UP VIRGIN SOLDIERS(1977, Brit.)
1984
SCRUBBERS(1984, Brit.)

Tom Margraviti
ACROSS THE RIVER(1965), ph

Marguerite
COW AND I, THE(1961, Fr., Ital., Ger.)

Marguertie
Misc. Silents
DESERT DRIVEN(1923)

Desmond Marguette
MEN AGAINST THE SKY(1940), ed

Michael Marguiles
RIVER NIGER, THE(1976), ph

William Marguiles
HOT CARS(1956), ph

David Margulies
TIMES SQUARE(1980)

Lynne Margulies
MY BREAKFAST WITH BLASSIE(1983), ed

William Margulies
TOKYO AFTER DARK(1959), ph; GUNPOINT(1966), ph

Martin Margules
CAT ATE THE PARAKEET, THE(1972)
Misc. Talkies
POT! PARENTS! POLICE!(1975)

David Margulies
SCARECROW IN A GARDEN OF CUCUMBERS(1972); FRONT, THE(1976); ALL THAT JAZZ(1979); LAST EMBRACE(1979); DRESSED TO KILL(1980); HIDE IN PLAIN SIGHT(1980); DANIEL(1983)
1984
GHOSTBUSTERS(1984)

Lynne Margulies
Misc. Talkies
AFTERMATH, THE(1980)

Mark Margulies
DIRTY MARY, CRAZY LARRY(1974), ph

Michael D. Margulies
MY BODYGUARD(1980), ph; SIX WEEKS(1982), ph
1984
POLICE ACADEMY(1984), ph

Michael Margulies
MINNIE AND MOSKOWITZ(1971), ph

Stan Margulies
FORTY POUNDS OF TROUBLE(1962), p; THOSE MAGNIFICENT MEN IN THEIR FLYING MACHINES; OR HOW I FLEWFROM LONDON TO PARIS IN 25 HOURS AND 11 MINUTES(1965, Brit.), p; DON'T JUST STAND THERE(1968), p; PINK JUNGLE, THE(1968), p; IF IT'S TUESDAY, THIS MUST BE BELGIUM(1969), p; I LOVE MY WIFE(1970), p; WILLY WONKA AND THE CHOCOLATE FACTORY(1971), p; ONE IS A LONELY NUMBER(1972), p

Thomas Margulies
GENGHIS KHAN(U.S./Brit./Ger./Yugo)

William Margulies
BROKEN STAR, THE(1956), ph; CRIME AGAINST JOE(1956), ph; EMERGENCY HOSPITAL(1956), ph; GIRL IN BLACK STOCKINGS(1957), ph; JUNGLE HEAT(1957), ph; OUTLAW'S SON(1957), ph; PHARAOH'S CURSE(1957), ph; REVOLT AT FORT LARAMIE(1957), ph; TOMAHAWK TRAIL(1957), ph; VOODOO ISLAND(1957), ph; WAR DRUMS(1957), ph; JOHNNY ROCCO(1958), ph; REVOLT IN THE BIG HOUSE(1958), ph; ARSON FOR HIRE(1959), ph; MC HALE'S NAVY(1964), ph; TAGGART(1964), ph; SWORD OF ALI BABA, THE(1965), ph; GHOST AND MR. CHICKEN, THE(1966), ph; INCIDENT AT PHANTOM HILL(1966), ph; EASY COME, EASY GO(1967), ph; ANGEL IN MY POCKET(1969), ph; LOVE GOD?, THE(1969), ph; MAN CALLED GANNON, A(1969), ph; HOW TO FRAME A FIGG(1971), ph

William Margulis
CLAMBAKE(1967), ph

Margutti
ONE WISH TOO MANY(1956, Brit.), spec eff

Regina Marheineke
DER FREISCHUTZ(1970, Ger.)

Angelita Mari
THANK YOUR LUCKY STARS(1943)

Fiorella Mari
DAY THE SKY EXPLODED, THE(1958, Fr./Ital.)

George Mari
EAGLE'S BROOD, THE(1936)

Gina Mari
SLUMBER PARTY MASSACRE, THE(1982)

Isa Mari
AND THE WILD, WILD WOMEN(1961, Ital.), w

John Mari
TORRID ZONE(1940), tech adv

Keiko Mari
GODZILLA VERSUS THE SMOG MONSTER(1972, Jap.)

Paul Mari
NUTCRACKER(1982, Brit.); BLOODY KIDS(1983, Brit.); PARTY PARTY(1983, Brit.)

Pedro Mari
SECRET SEVEN, THE(1966, Ital./Span.)

Sergio Mari
Silents
MAN WITHOUT DESIRE, THE(1923, Brit.)

Ditte Maria
Z.P.G.(1972)

Elsa Maria
VAMPIRES, THE(1969, Mex.)

Inga Maria
Misc. Talkies
BLUE MONEY(1975)

Maria-Pia
Misc. Talkies
DOUBLE INITIATION(1970)

G. Mariamov
OTHELLO(1960, U.S.S.R.), ed

Ferdinand Marian
LA HABANERA(1937, Ger.)

Mark Marian [Marco Mariani]
TOMB OF TORTURE(1966, Ital.)

Howard Marian-Crawford
CHARGE OF THE LIGHT BRIGADE, THE(1968, Brit.)

Andy Mariani
FORCE OF ARMS(1951)

Fiorella Mariani
SONG OF NORWAY(1970), cos
Giuseppe Mariani
GLADIATOR OF ROME(1963, Ital.), w; TAMING OF THE SHREW, THE(1967, U.S./Ital.), art d
Jacopo Mariani
SUSPIRIA(1977, Ital.)
Marcella Mariani
SENSO(1968, Ital.); AUGUSTINE OF HIPPO(1973, Ital.), w; AGE OF THE MEDICI, THE(1979, Ital.), w
Marcello Mariani
YEAR ONE(1974, Ital.), w
Marco Mariani
REBEL GLADIATORS, THE(1963, Ital.); HERCULES, SAMSON & ULYSSES(1964, Ital.); GIRL AND THE GENERAL, THE(1967, Fr./Ital.); PAYMENT IN BLOOD(1968, Ital.)
Mario Mariani
LA FUGA(1966, Ital.), p
Marianna
GUERRILLA GIRL(1953)
Luis Mariano
NAPOLEON(1955, Fr.); CANDIDE(1962, Fr.)
Nick Mariano
FIGHT FOR YOUR LIFE(1977)
Maurice Mariaud
Misc. Silents
LA MARCHE TRIOMPHALE(1916, Fr.), d; LARMES DE CROCODILE(1916, Fr.), d; LE CREPUSCULE DE COEUR(1916, Fr.), d; LA CALOMNIE(1917, Fr.), d; LA DAN-SEUSE VOILEE(1917, Fr.), d; LE NOCTURNE(1917, Fr.), d; L'EPAVE(1917, Fr.), d; LES DAMES DE CROIX-MORT(1917, Fr.), d; LES MOUTTES(1919, Fr.), d; L'ETAU(1920, Fr.), d; L'IDOLE BRISEE(1920, Fr.), d; L'HOMME ET LA POU-PEE(1921, Fr.), d; LA GOUTTE DE SANG(1924, Fr.), d; L'AVENTURIER(1924, Fr.), d; MON ONCLE(1925, Fr.), d; LE SECRET DE CARGO(1929, Fr.), d
Ethel Marical
MADE FOR EACH OTHER(1939)
Leona Marical
COMET OVER BROADWAY(1938)
Jean-Pierre Marichal
MATTER OF DAYS, A(1969, Fr./Czech.)
Veljko Maricic
DESPERADO TRAIL, THE(1965, Ger./Yugo.); RAMPAGE AT APACHE WELLS(1966, Ger./Yugo.)
Leona Maricle
WITHOUT RESERVATIONS(1946); O'SHAUGHNESSY'S BOY(1935); THEODORA GOES WILD(1936); LIFE BEGINS WITH LOVE(1937); PAROLE RACKET(1937); WOMAN CHASES MAN(1937); WOMEN OF GLAMOUR(1937); LONE WOLF IN PARIS, THE(1938); MAD MISS MANTON, THE(1938); BEAUTY FOR THE AS-KING(1939); JUDGE HARDY AND SON(1939); CURTAIN CALL(1940); DR. KILDARE GOES HOME(1940); THIS THING CALLED LOVE(1940); UNDER AGE(1941); HARD WAY, THE(1942); JOHNNY EAGER(1942); OLD ACQUAINTANCE(1943); SOMEONE TO REMEMBER(1943); MY PAL, WOLF(1944); MY REPUTATION(1946); SCANDAL IN PARIS, A(1946)
Marijane Maricle
OUR TIME(1974)
Michali Maridalis
MANOLIS(1962, Brit.)
Alice Marie
KAREN, THE LOVEMAKER(1970)
Ann Marie
CHROME AND HOT LEATHER(1971)
Anna Marie
JUST WILLIAM'S LUCK(1948, Brit.)
Anne Marie
STOOLIE, THE(1972)
Arnold Marie
ABOMINABLE SNOWMAN OF THE HIMALAYAS, THE(1957, Brit.)
Benaud Marie
BERNADETTE OF LOURDES(1962, Fr.)
Connie Lisa Marie
VAN, THE(1977)
Deena Marie
1984
SWING SHIFT(1984)
Dominique Marie
MY UNCLE(1958, Fr.)
Else Marie
OPERATION LOVEBIRDS(1968, Den.)
Francois Marie
VERY PRIVATE AFFAIR, A(1962, Fr./Ital.)
Jean Marie
ANGEL UNCHAINED(1970)
Jo Marie
HOUSE ON SKULL MOUNTAIN, THE(1974)
Lisa Marie
DEAD AND BURIED(1981)
Louisa Marie
1984
SPLASH(1984)
Norma Marie
Silents
DON MIKE(1927)
Rose Marie
TOP BANANA(1954); BIG BEAT, THE(1958); DON'T WORRY, WE'LL THINK OF A TITLE(1966); MEMORY OF US(1974); CHEAPER TO KEEP HER(1980); LUNCH WAGON(1981)
Tina Marie
MOONLIGHTING WIVES(1966)

The Marie Louise Sisters
PENNY POOL, THE(1937, Brit.)
Marie Rambert's Corps de Ballet
DANCE PRETTY LADY(1932, Brit.)
Marie-Antoinette
LILITH(1964)
Marie-France
1984
PURPLE RAIN(1984), cos
Jeanne Marie-Laurent
CALL, THE(1938, Fr.)
Marie-Lise
HELP!(1965, Brit.)
Marie-Therese
LOVE IS A BALL(1963), cos
Marieka
WHO'S THAT KNOCKING AT MY DOOR?(1968)
Jean Pierre Marielle
FOUR FLIES ON GREY VELVET(1972, Ital.)
Jean-Pierre Marielle
SWEET AND SOUR(1964, Fr./Ital.); BACKFIRE(1965, Fr.); BANANA PEEL(1965, Fr.); HOW NOT TO ROB A DEPARTMENT STORE(1965, Fr./Ital.); MALE COMPAN-ION(1965, Fr./Ital.); WEEKEND AT DUNKIRK(1966, Fr./Ital.); TENDER SCOUN-DREL(1967, Fr./Ital.); DEVIL BY THE TAIL, THE(1969, Fr./Ital.); GIVE HER THE MOON(1970, Fr./Ital.); MAN WITH CONNECTIONS, THE(1970, Fr.); WITHOUT APPARENT MOTIVE(1972, Fr.); LET JOY REIGN SUPREME(1977, Fr.); COUP DE TORCHON(1981, Fr.)
Mike Marienthal
GUY WHO CAME BACK, THE(1951)
Capt. Victor Marier [D.W. Griffith]
Silents
GREAT LOVE, THE(1918), w; GREATEST THING IN LIFE, THE(1918), w; HEARTS OF THE WORLD(1918), w; ROMANCE OF HAPPY VALLEY, A(1919), w
Marietta
NAUGHTY MARIETTA(1935)
Mariettino
VERY HANDY MAN, A(1966, Fr./Ital.)
Marietto
IT STARTED IN NAPLES(1960); PIGEON THAT TOOK ROME, THE(1962); STORY OF JOSEPH AND HIS BRETHREN THE(1962, Ital.); GIANT OF METROPOLIS, THE(1963, Ital.)
Joseph Marievsky
MAN WHO BROKE THE BANK AT MONTE CARLO, THE(1935); THREE GODFA-THERS(1936); HOTEL IMPERIAL(1939); SECOND CHORUS(1940)
Maria Marigliano
LA DOLCE VITA(1961, Ital./Fr.)
Martine Marignac
1984
LOVE ON THE GROUND(1984,Fr.), p
Renzo Marignano
GIRL WITH A PISTOL, THE(1968, Ital.), art d
Tod Hunter Marigold
Silents
CYCLONE, THE(1920), w
Tammy Marihugh
SNOW QUEEN, THE(1959, USSR); LAST VOYAGE, THE(1960); BACK STREET(1961); THUNDER OF DRUMS, A(1961); WONDERFUL WORLD OF THE BROTHERS ERIMM, THE(1962)
Marin Marija
STORY OF JOSEPH AND HIS BRETHREN THE(1962, Ital.)
Bojana Marijan
MONTENEGRO(1981, Brit./Swed.), w
Lucette Marimar
YOU PAY YOUR MONEY(1957, Brit.); GUTTER GIRLS(1964, Brit.)
The Marimba Merry Makers
SAILOR BEWARE(1951)
Marimba Merrymakers
SKIRTS AHOY!(1952)
Andrew Peter Marin
HOG WILD(1980, Can.), w
Antoine Marin
LOVERS OF TERUEL, THE(1962, Fr.); MADEMOISELLE(1966, Fr./Brit.)
Arturo Marin
MAD QUEEN, THE(1950, Span.)
Carlos Marin
MAN AND THE BEAST, THE(1951, Arg.), w
Chinita Marin
PAN-AMERICANA(1945)
Christian Marin
LA BELLE AMERICAINE(1961, Fr.); GENDARME OF ST. TROPEZ, THE(1966, Fr./Ital.); SLEEPING CAR MURDER THE(1966, Fr.); STORY OF A THREE DAY PASS, THE(1968, Fr.)
Edward L. Marin
SWEETHEART OF SIGMA CHI(1933), d; AFFAIRS OF A GENTLEMAN(1934), d
Edwin L. Marin
AVENGER, THE(1933), d; DEATH KISS, THE(1933), d; STUDY IN SCARLET, A(1933), d; BOMBAY MAIL(1934), d; CROSBY CASE, THE(1934), d; PARIS INTER-LUDE(1934), d; CASINO MURDER CASE, THE(1935), d; PURSUIT(1935), d; ALL-AMERICAN CHUMP(1936), d; GARDEN MURDER CASE, THE(1936), d; I'D GIVE MY LIFE(1936), d; MOONLIGHT MURDER(1936), d; SPEED(1936), d; SWORN ENE-MY(1936), d; MAN OF THE PEOPLE(1937), d; MARRIED BEFORE BREAK-FAST(1937), d; CHASER, THE(1938), d; CHRISTMAS CAROL, A(1938), d; EVERYBODY SING(1938), d; HOLD THAT KISS(1938), d; LISTEN, DARLING(1938), d; FAST AND LOOSE(1939), d; HENRY GOES ARIZONA(1939), d; MAISIE(1939), d; SOCIETY LAWYER(1939), d; FLORIAN(1940), d; GOLD RUSH MAISIE(1940), d; HULLABALOO(1940), d; MAISIE WAS A LADY(1941), d; PARIS CALLING(1941), d; RINGSIDE MAISIE(1941), d; INVISIBLE AGENT(1942), d; MISS ANNIE ROO-NEY(1942), d; TWO TICKETS TO LONDON(1943), p&d; SHOW BUSINESS(1944), d; TALL IN THE SADDLE(1944), d; JOHNNY ANGEL(1945), d; ABILENE TOWN(1946), d; LADY LUCK(1946), d; MR. ACE(1946), d; NOCTURNE(1946), d; YOUNG WI-

Francis Marin- (cont.)
DOW(1946), d; CHRISTMAS EVE(1947), d; INTRIGUE(1947), d; RACE STREET(1948), d; CANADIAN PACIFIC(1949), d; FIGHTING MAN OF THE PLAINS(1949), d; YOUNGER BROTHERS, THE(1949), d; CARIBOO TRAIL, THE(1950), d; COLT .45(1950), d; FORT WORTH(1951), d; RATON PASS(1951), d; SUGARFOOT(1951), d

Francis Marin
TEXICAN, THE(1966, U.S./Span.), ph

Francisco Marin
LAST TOMAHAWK, THE(1965, Ger./Ital./Span.), ph; SWORD OF EL CID, THE(1965, Span./Ital.), ph; PISTOL FOR RINGO, A(1966, Ital./Span.), ph; RETURN OF RINGO, THE(1966, Ital./Span.), ph; SUNSCORCHED(1966, Span./Ger.), ph; SUPERARGO VERSUS DIABOLICUS(1966, Ital./Span.), ph

George Marin
Misc. Talkies
REVOLT IN CANADA(1964)

Guglielmo Marin
LAST DAYS OF POMPEII, THE(1960, Ital.)

Ivan Marin
THERE WAS AN OLD COUPLE(1967, USSR)

Jacques Marin
FORBIDDEN GAMES(1953, Fr.); FRENCH CANCAN(1956, Fr.); GATES OF PARIS(1958, Fr./Ital.); ROOTS OF HEAVEN, THE(1958); CRACK IN THE MIRROR(1960); ENEMY GENERAL, THE(1960); BIG GAMBLE, THE(1961); COUNTERFEITERS OF PARIS, THE(1962, Fr., Ital.); GIGOT(1962); TIARA TAHITI(1962, Brit.); CHARADE(1963); FIVE MILES TO MIDNIGHT(1963, U.S./Fr./Ital.); TRAIN, THE(1965, Fr./Ital./U.S.); WOMEN AND WAR(1965, Fr.); HOW TO STEAL A MILLION(1966); LOST COMMAND, THE(1966); 25TH HOUR, THE(1967, Fr./Ital./Yugo.); GIRL ON A MOTORCYCLE, THE(1968, Fr./Brit.); PARIS IN THE MONTH OF AUGUST(1968, Fr.); MADWOMAN OF CHAILLOT, THE(1969); NIGHT OF THE FOLLOWING DAY, THE(1969, Brit.); DARLING LILI(1970, Fr.); VERY CURIOUS GIRL, A(1970, Fr.); SHAFT IN AFRICA(1973); ISLAND AT THE TOP OF THE WORLD, THE(1974); S(1974); CATHERINE & CO.(1976, Fr.); MARATHON MAN(1976); HERBIE GOES TO MONTE CARLO(1977); WHO IS KILLING THE GREAT CHEFS OF EUROPE?(1978, US/Ger.)

Jesus Marin
YANCO(1964, Mex.), w

Jose Marin
UNDER FIRE(1983)

Lina Marin
MAN CALLED HORSE, A(1970)

Luciano Marin
LAW IS THE LAW, THE(1959, Fr.); GOLIATH AND THE BARBARIANS(1960, Ital.); SIEGE OF SYRACUSE(1962, Fr./Ital.); TARTARS, THE(1962, Ital./Yugo.); FURY OF THE PAGANS(1963, Ital.); HERCULES AND THE CAPTIVE WOMEN(1963, Fr./Ital.); SON OF THE RED CORSAIR(1963, Ital.); SULEIMAN THE CONQUEROR(1963, Ital.); DUEL OF CHAMPIONS(1964 Ital./Span.)

Luis Marin
WHITE SISTER(1973, Ital./Span./Fr.)
Misc. Talkies
REVOLT IN CANADA(1964)

Ned Marin
DARK STREETS(1929), p; GIRL IN THE GLASS CAGE, THE(1929), p; GOLDEN CALF, THE(1930), p; WOMEN EVERYWHERE(1930), p; PURSUIT(1935), p; GARDEN MURDER CASE, THE(1936), p; MOONLIGHT MURDER(1936), p; UNDER COVER OF NIGHT(1937), p
Silents
ISLE OF LOST SHIPS, THE(1923), p; NIGHT WATCH, THE(1928), sup

Paul Marin
ONE MAN'S WAY(1964); DOCTORS' WIVES(1971); HARDCORE(1979)

Richard "Cheech" Marin
UP IN SMOKE(1978), w; THINGS ARE TOUGH ALL OVER(1982), w; CHEECH AND CHONG'S NEXT MOVIE(1980), w; CHEECH AND CHONG'S NICE DREAMS(1981), w; STILL SMOKIN'(1983), a, w; YELLOWBEARD(1983)
1984
CHEECH AND CHONG'S THE CORSICAN BROTHERS(1984), a, w

Rikki Marin
THINGS ARE TOUGH ALL OVER(1982); CHEECH AND CHONG'S NEXT MOVIE(1980); CHEECH AND CHONG'S NICE DREAMS(1981)
1984
CHEECH AND CHONG'S THE CORSICAN BROTHERS(1984)

Russ Marin
KANSAS CITY BOMBER(1972); SLAUGHTER'S BIG RIP-OFF(1973); CAPONE(1975); DARK, THE(1979); SEED OF INNOCENCE(1980); MOMMIE DEAREST(1981); SWORD AND THE SORCERER, THE(1982)
1984
BODY DOUBLE(1984)

Marina
PARDON MY FRENCH(1951, U.S./Fr.)

Terence Marinan
FAN, THE(1981)

Giancarlo Marinangeli
NEST OF VIPERS(1979, Ital.)

Elisa Marinardi
AND THE SHIP SAILS ON(1983, Ital./Fr.)

Ed Marinaro
FINGERS(1978); GONG SHOW MOVIE, THE(1980)

Ivan Marincek
NINTH CIRCLE, THE(1961, Yugo.), ph

John [Juan] Marine
SUPERSONIC MAN(1979, Span.), ph

Bill Marinella
1984
TEACHERS(1984)

Iole Marinelli
ARRIVEDERCI, BABY!(1966, Brit.); WHERE'S JACK?(1969, Brit.)

Larry Marinelli
MINX, THE(1969), ed

Lawrence Marinelli
HAPPY HOOKER GOES TO WASHINGTON, THE(1977), ed

Lorenzo Marinelli
MANIAC(1980), ed; VIGILANTE(1983), ed

Rudolph Marinelli
WAR OF THE WIZARDS(1983, Taiwan), w

Carmen Marineo
GIRL IN ROOM 13(1961, U.S./Braz.)

Rudolph Mariner
Silents
WHAT FOOLS MEN ARE(1922), ph

Misty Maring
HELLCATS, THE(1968), cos

Jose Marinho
EARTH ENTRANCED(1970, Braz.)

Giovanna Marini
CAFE EXPRESS(1980, Ital.), m

Leandro Marini
FACTS OF MURDER, THE(1965, Ital.)

Lou Marini
BLUES BROTHERS, THE(1980)

Pir Marini
SHADOWS(1960)

Tullio Marini
WILD EYE, THE(1968, Ital.)

Peter Marinker
FEAR IS THE KEY(1973)

Art Marino
FIRST NUDIE MUSICAL, THE(1976)

Ben Marino
UP IN SMOKE(1978); FRENCH CONNECTION, THE(1971)

Benedetto Marino
SEVEN UPS, THE(1973)

Benny Marino
KILLING OF A CHINESE BOOKIE, THE(1976)

Don Marino
THEY ALL LAUGHED(1981)

Joan Jose Marino
FOOL KILLER, THE(1965), ed

Juan Jose Marino
TWO MULES FOR SISTER SARA(1970), ed; REVENGERS, THE(1972, U.S./Mex.), ed
1984
JUNGLE WARRIORS(1984, U.S./Ger./Mex.), ed

Juan Marino
PIECES(1983, Span./Puerto Rico), ph

Kenny Marino
PRINCE OF THE CITY(1981)
1984
ALPHABET CITY(1984)

Luis Marino
ROMAN HOLIDAY(1953)

Ralph Marino
FUNHOUSE, THE(1981)

Silvia Marino
SHIP OF FOOLS(1965)

Vincent Marino
FIRST TIME, THE(1969); GAS(1981, Can.)

Brenda Marinoff
HILLS HAVE EYES, THE(1978)

Fania Marinoff
Silents
ONE OF OUR GIRLS(1914); LIFE'S WHIRLPOOL(1916); NEW YORK(1916); RISE OF JENNIE CUSHING, THE(1917)
Misc. Silents
GALLOPER, THE(1915); NEDRA(1915)

Eleni Marinou
ELECTRA(1962, Gr.)

Luciana Marinucci
CONJUGAL BED, THE(1963, Ital.), cos; LOVE AND MARRIAGE(1966, Ital.), cos; WE STILL KILL THE OLD WAY(1967, Ital.), cos; DANGER: DIABOLIK(1968, Ital./Fr.), cos

Vinicio Marinucci
GRAN VARIETA(1955, Ital.), w

Gino Marinuzzi
RED CLOAK, THE(1961, Ital./Fr.), m; HERCULES AND THE CAPTIVE WOMEN(1963, Fr./Ital.), m

Gino Marinuzzi, Jr.
APPOINTMENT FOR MURDER(1954, Ital.), m; PLANET OF THE VAMPIRES(1965, U.S./Ital./Span.), m; WHITE VOICES(1965, Fr./Ital.), m; MANDRAGOLA(1966 Fr./Ital.), m; MATCHLESS(1967, Ital.), m

Talleri Mario
SONNY AND JED(1974, Ital.)

Wolfranco Coccia Mario
YETI(1977, Ital.), p

Albert Marion
Misc. Silents
FEAST OF LIFE, THE(1916), d

Baby Marion
Misc. Silents
TOLL OF THE SEA, THE(1922)

Beth Marion
BETWEEN MEN(1935); TRAIL OF TERROR(1935); AVENGING WATERS(1936); EVERYMAN'S LAW(1936); FOR THE SERVICE(1936); FUGITIVE SHERIFF, THE(1936); RIP ROARIN' BUCKAROO(1936); SILVER SPURS(1936); PHANTOM GOLD(1938); PHANTOM OF THE RANGE, THE(1938); FRONTIER SCOUT(1939)

Betty Marion
HANDS ACROSS THE BORDER(1943); WONDER MAN(1945)

Charles B. Marion
ANGELS IN DISGUISE(1949), w; HOLD THAT BABY!(1949), w

Charles H. Marion
GOIN' TO TOWN(1944), w

Charles Marion
SPOOKS RUN WILD(1941), w; GALS, INCORPORATED(1943), w; MELODY PARADE(1943), w; MYSTERY OF THE 13TH GUEST, THE(1943), w; RHYTHM PARADE(1943), w; HOT RHYTHM(1944), w; TRAPPED BY BOSTON BLACKIE(1948), w; BLONDE DYNAMITE(1950), w; HOLD THAT LINE(1952), w

Charles R. Marion
CAMPUS RYTHM(1943), w; SARONG GIRL(1943), w; SMART GUY(1943), w; HIT THE HAY(1945), w; DARK HORSE, THE(1946), w; IDEA GIRL(1946), w; MASTER MINDS(1949), w; BLUES BUSTERS(1950), w; LUCKY LOSERS(1950), w; TRIPLE TROUBLE(1950), w; BOWERY BATTALION(1951), w; GHOST CHASERS(1951), w; FABULOUS SENORITA, THE(1952), w; HERE COME THE MARINES(1952), w; JET JOB(1952), w; RODEO(1952), w; ROSE BOWL STORY, THE(1952), w; CLIPPED WINGS(1953), w; HOT NEWS(1953), w; ROAR OF THE CROWD(1953), w; WHITE LIGHTNING(1953), w; APACHE TERRITORY(1958), w

Don Marion
GODLESS GIRL, THE(1929); COURAGE(1930); SECOND HONEYMOON(1937); COW-BOY FROM BROOKLYN(1938); FRONTIER TOWN(1938)
Silents
JEALOUS HUSBANDS(1923); CHILDREN OF DIVORCE(1927)
Misc. Silents
TRAFFIC IN HEARTS(1924)

Edna Marion
SKINNER STEPS OUT(1929); TODAY(1930)
Silents
DESERT'S PRICE, THE(1926); SINNER'S PARADE(1928)
Misc. Silents
CALL OF THE WILDERNESS, THE(1926); READIN''RITIN''RITHMETIC(1926); STILL ALARM, THE(1926); FOR LADIES ONLY(1927)

Ellen Marion
LOVE IS A CAROUSEL(1970)

Frances Marion
WIND, THE(1928), w; ANNA CHRISTIE(1930), w; BIG HOUSE, THE(1930), w; GOOD NEWS(1930), w; LET US BE GAY(1930), w; MIN AND BILL(1930), w; ROGUE SONG, THE(1930), w; CHAMP, THE(1931), w; SECRET SIX, THE(1931), w; BLONDIE OF THE FOLLIES(1932), w; EMMA(1932), w; DINNER AT EIGHT(1933), w; GOING HOLLYWOOD(1933), w; PRIZEFIGHTER AND THE LADY, THE(1933), w; SE-CRETS(1933), w; RIFF-RAFF(1936), w; CAMILLE(1937), w; KNIGHT WITHOUT AR-MOR(1937, Brit.), w; LOVE FROM A STRANGER(1937, Brit.), w; GREEN HELL(1940), w; MOLLY AND ME(1945), w; CLOWN, THE(1953), w; CHAMP, THE(1979), w
Silents
DAUGHTER OF THE SEA, A(1915), w; DAWN OF A TOMORROW, THE(1915), w; ESMERALDA(1915), w; FANCHON THE CRICKET(1915), w; LITTLE PAL(1915), w; MISTRESS NELL(1915), w; RAGS(1915), w; ALL MAN(1916), w; FRIDAY THE 13TH(1916), w; HIDDEN SCAR, THE(1916), w; TANGLED FATES(1916), w; AMA-ZONS, THE(1917), w; CRIMSON DOVE, THE(1917), w; GIRL'S FOLLY, A(1917), w; POOR LITTLE RICH GIRL, A(1917), w; REBECCA OF SUNNYBROOK FARM(1917), w; TILLIE WAKES UP(1917), w; AMARILLY OF CLOTHESLINE ALLEY(1918), w; M'LISS(1918), w; STELLA MARIS(1918), w; ANNE OF GREEN GABLES(1919), w; FLAPPER, THE(1920), w; POLLYANNA(1920), w; JUST AROUND THE COR-NER(1921), d&w; LITTLE LORD FAUNTLEROY(1921); LOVE LIGHT, THE(1921), d&w; STRAIGHT IS THE WAY(1921), w; EAST IS WEST(1922), w; SONNY(1922), w; FRENCH DOLL, THE(1923), w; NTH COMMANDMENT, THE(1923), w; SONG OF LOVE, THE(1923), d, w; ABRAHAM LINCOLN(1924), w; CYTHEREA(1924), w; IN HOLLYWOOD WITH POTASH AND PERLMUTTER(1924), w; DARK ANGEL, THE(1925), w; LAZYBONES(1925), w; STELLA DALLAS(1925), w; ZANDER THE GREAT(1925), w; FIRST YEAR, THE(1926), w; PARTNERS AGAIN(1926), w; SCAR-LET LETTER, THE(1926), w, t; SON OF THE SHEIK(1926), w; WINNING OF BAR-BARA WORTH, THE(1926), w; CALLAHANS AND THE MURPHYS, THE(1927), w; LOVE(1927), w; MADAME POMPADOUR(1927, Brit.), w; RED MILL, THE(1927), w; AWAKENING, THE(1928), w; EXCESS BAGGAGE(1928), w

Francis Marion
CYNARA(1932), w; PEG O' MY HEART(1933), w
Silents
GILDED CAGE, THE(1916), w; DIVORCE GAME, THE(1917), w; HEARTS OF THE WORLD(1918)
Misc. Silents
WORLD AND ITS WOMAN, THE(1919)

Frank Marion
Misc. Silents
WRECK OF THE HESPERUS, THE(1927)

George Marion
SHOW GIRL(1928), w; BISHOP MURDER CASE, THE(1930); SEA LEGS(1930), w; SIX HOURS TO LIVE(1932); HER FIRST MATE(1933); PORT OF LOST DREAMS(1935)
Silents
JUST MARRIED(1928), t; LADIES OF THE MOB(1928), t; SPORTING GOODS(1928), t; WARMING UP(1928), t
Misc. Silents
ROBINSON CRUSOE(1916), d

George Marion, Jr.
WILD PARTY, THE(1929), w; DANGEROUS CURVES(1929), w; SWEETIE(1929), w; THIS IS HEAVEN(1929), w; LET'S GO NATIVE(1930), w; SAFETY IN NUM-BERS(1930), w; ALONG CAME YOUTH(1931), w; NO LIMIT(1931), w; BIG BROAD-CAST, THE(1932), w; LOVE ME TONIGHT(1932), w; THIS IS THE NIGHT(1932), w; ADORABLE(1933), w; COLLEGE RHYTHM(1934), w; GAY DIVORCEE, THE(1934), w; KISS AND MAKE UP(1934), w; WE'RE NOT DRESSING(1934), w; METROPOLI-TAN(1935), w; TO BEAT THE BAND(1935), w; TWO FOR TONIGHT(1935), w; THREE CHEERS FOR LOVE(1936), w; FIFTY ROADS TO TOWN(1937), w; GLADIATOR, THE(1938), w; YOU CAN'T CHEAT AN HONEST MAN(1939), w; TOO MANY GIRLS(1940), w
Silents
BEAUTIFUL LIAR, THE(1921), w; EAGLE, THE(1925), t; WEDDING SONG, THE(1925), t; BAT, THE(1926), t; ELLA CINDERS(1926), t; IRENE(1926), t; KID BOOTS(1926), t; LADIES AT PLAY(1926), t; MISS NOBODY(1926), t; SON OF THE SHEIK(1926), t; SPARROWS(1926), t; CAMILLE(1927), t; EVENING CLOTHES(1927), t; IT(1927), t; LITTLE JOURNEY, A(1927), t; NOW WE'RE IN THE AIR(1927), t; ONE WOMAN TO ANOTHER(1927), t; ROUGH HOUSE ROSIE(1927), t; ROUGH RIDERS, THE(1927), t; SHE'S A SHEIK(1927), t; SPECIAL DELIVERY(1927), t; UNDER-

WORLD(1927), t; WEDDING BILL$(1927), t; EASY COME, EASY GO(1928), t; PART-NERS IN CRIME(1928), t; RED HAIR(1928), t; WIFE SAVERS(1928), t

George Marion, Sr.
EVANGELINE(1929); MAN TO MAN(1931); SAFE IN HELL(1931); METROPOLI-TAN(1935); ROCKY MOUNTAIN MYSTERY(1935); DEATH FROM A DISTAN-CE(1936)
Silents
TEXAS STEER, A(1927); EVANGELINE(1929)

George F. Marion
ANNA CHRISTIE(1930); BIG HOUSE, THE(1930); LADY'S MORALS, A(1930); PAY OFF, THE(1930); SEA BAT, THE(1930); LAUGHING SINNERS(1931)
Silents
ANNA CHRISTIE(1923); CLOTHES MAKE THE PIRATE(1925); ON THE GO(1925); TUMBLEWEEDS(1925); ROLLING HOME(1926); KING OF KINGS, THE(1927)
Misc. Silents
EXCUSE ME(1916); MADAME X(1916), d; WHITE MONKEY, THE(1925); WISE GUY, THE(1926); SKEDADDLE GOLD(1927)

George F. Marion, Sr.
HOOK, LINE AND SINKER(1930)

Jean Marion
ROYAL AFFAIR, A(1950), m; SIMPLE CASE OF MONEY, A(1952, Fr.), m; CADET-ROUSSELLE(1954, Fr.), m; LOVE AT NIGHT(1961, Fr.), m; MY WIFE'S HUS-BAND(1965, Fr./Ital.), m

Joan Marion
HER NIGHT OUT(1932, Brit.); RIVER HOUSE GHOST, THE(1932, Brit.); GOING STRAIGHT(1933, Brit.); LORD OF THE MANOR(1933, Brit.); MELODY MAKER, THE(1933, Brit.); OUT OF THE PAST(1933, Brit.); TANGLED EVIDENCE(1934, Brit.); SENSATION(1936, Brit.); FOR VALOR(1937, Brit.); BLACK LIMELIGHT(1938, Brit.); DEAD MAN'S SHOES(1939, Brit.); ONE NIGHT IN PARIS(1940, Brit.); SPIES OF THE AIR(1940, Brit.); MISSING TEN DAYS(1941, Brit.); TONS OF TROUBLE(1956, Brit.)

Manuel Marion
COUNT DRACULA(1971, Sp., Ital., Ger., Brit.), ph

Paul Marion
IN OLD CALIENTE(1939); COVERED WAGON DAYS(1940); GHOST SHIP, THE(1943); PHANTOM OF THE OPERA(1943); MADEMOISELLE FIFI(1944); TO HAVE AND HAVE NOT(1944); GALLANT JOURNEY(1946); SO DARK THE NIGHT(1946); THE CATMAN OF PARIS(1946); DEVIL'S CARGO, THE(1948); LOVES OF CARMEN, THE(1948); DEVIL'S HENCHMEN, THE(1949); FLAMING FURY(1949); LOST TRIBE, THE(1949); SECRET OF ST. IVES, THE(1949); SWORD IN THE DESERT(1949); UNDERCOVER MAN, THE(1949); WE WERE STRANGERS(1949); BANDIT QUEEN(1950); HARBOR OF MISSING MEN(1950); LAST OF THE BUCCA-NEERS(1950); RAIDERS OF TOMAHAWK CREEK(1950); SIDE STREET(1950); FURY OF THE CONGO(1951); HOT LEAD(1951); SAVAGE DRUMS(1951); TEN TALL MEN(1951); FIGHTER, THE(1952); HAREM GIRL(1952); PRISONER OF ZENDA, THE(1952); SNIPER, THE(1952); FORT VENGEANCE(1953); HINDU, THE(1953, Brit.); KILLER APE(1953); SAFARI DRUMS(1953); SAVAGE MUTINY(1953); SCARED STIFF(1953); KING RICHARD AND THE CRUSADERS(1954); BOWERY TO BAG-DAD(1955); GREEN FIRE(1955); HELL'S ISLAND(1955); SHOTGUN(1955); FLAME OF STAMBOUL(1957)

Richard Marion
ROADIE(1980)
1984
CHOOSE ME(1984)

Ruth Marion
OLD-FASHIONED WAY, THE(1934); SERVANTS' ENTRANCE(1934)

Sid Marion
MAGNIFICENT OBSESSION(1935); LADY OF BURLESQUE(1943); EVERYBODY DOES IT(1949); LOVE THAT BRUTE(1950); PEGGY(1950); TRIAL WITHOUT JU-RY(1950); WOMAN FROM HEADQUARTERS(1950); MY FAIR LADY(1964)

Sidney Marion
HOW DO YOU DO?(1946); CALL ME MADAM(1953); OUTLAWS IS COMING, THE(1965)
Silents
WINNING STROKE, THE(1919)

William Marion
Silents
DEVIL TO PAY, THE(1920); ACROSS THE DEAD-LINE(1922); ONE CLEAR CALL(1922); HUNTRESS, THE(1923)
Misc. Silents
BOSS, THE(1915); WANTED AT HEADQUARTERS(1920)

Marion Morgan Dancers
Silents
NIGHT OF LOVE, THE(1927)

Howard Marion-Crawford
13 MEN AND A GUN(1938, Brit.); VOICE IN THE NIGHT, A(1941, Brit.); MR. DRAKE'S DUCK(1951, Brit.); TOP OF THE FORM(1953, Brit.); DECISION AGAINST TIME(1957, Brit.); SILKEN AFFAIR, THE(1957, Brit.); GIDEON OF SCOTLAND YARD(1959, Brit.); MODEL FOR MURDER(1960, Brit.); NEXT TO NO TIME(1960, Brit.); FACE OF FU MANCHU, THE(1965, Brit.); SINGING PRINCESS, THE(1967, Ital.); SMASHING TIME(1967 Brit.)

Ray Marioni
FILE OF THE GOLDEN GOOSE, THE(1969, Brit.)

Moore Mariott
DAREDEVILS OF EARTH(1936, Brit.)

Frederick Mariotti
Silents
MARE NOSTRUM(1926)

Aurora Maris
BOBBY DEERFIELD(1977)

Giannis Maris
LISA, TOSCA OF ATHENS(1961, Gr.), w; YOU CAME TOO LATE(1962, Gr.), w

Mona Maris
ROMANCE OF THE RIO GRANDE(1929); ARIZONA KID, THE(1930); DEVIL WITH WOMEN, A(1930); ONE MAD KISS(1930); UNDER A TEXAS MOON(1930); SEAS BENEATH, THE(1931); MAN CALLED BACK(1932); ONCE IN A LIFETI-ME(1932); PASSIONATE PLUMBER(1932); SOUTH OF THE RIO GRANDE(1932); DEATH KISS, THE(1933); IO ... TU ... Y ... ELLA(1933); QUANDO EL AMOR RIE(1933); SECRETS(1933); KISS AND MAKE UP(1934); WHITE HEAT(1934); LOVE ON THE RUN(1936); DATE WITH THE FALCON, A(1941); FLIGHT FROM DESTINY(1941); LAW OF THE TROPICS(1941); UNDERGROUND(1941); BERLIN CORRESPON-

DENT(1942); I MARRIED AN ANGEL(1942); MY GAL SAL(1942); PACIFIC RENDEZ-VOUS(1942); FALCON IN MEXICO, THE(1944); TAMPICO(1944); HEARTBEAT(1946); MONSIEUR BEAUCAIRE(1946); AVENGERS, THE(1950)

Silents
APACHE, THE(1925, Brit.)
Misc. Silents
LITTLE PEOPLE, THE(1926, Brit.); SPY OF MME. POMPADOUR(1929, Ger.)

Peter Maris
DELIRIUM(1979), p, d

Roger Maris
SAFE AT HOME(1962); THAT TOUCH OF MINK(1962)

Stella Maris
NELLY'S VERSION(1983, Brit.)
1984
ELECTRIC DREAMS(1984); SUCCESS IS THE BEST REVENGE(1984, Brit.)

Alberto Mariscal
DOCTOR CRIMEN(1953, Mex.); SIERRA BARON(1958); RETURN OF A MAN CALLED HORSE, THE(1976)

Ana Mariscal
LADY DOCTOR, THE(1963, Fr./Ital./Span.), d

Ernst Marischa
RUNAWAY QUEEN, THE(1935, Brit.), w

Ernest Marischka
ETERNAL MELODIES(1948, Ital.), w; FOREVER MY LOVE(1962), p,d&w

Ernst Marischka
STRAUSS' GREAT WALTZ(1934, Brit.), w; MY HEART IS CALLING(1935, Brit.), w; MY SONG FOR YOU(1935, Brit.), w; KING STEPS OUT, THE(1936), w; SPRING PARADE(1940), w; SONG TO REMEMBER, A(1945), w; STORY OF VICKIE, THE(1958, Aust.), p,d&w; EMBEZZLED HEAVEN(1959,Ger.), d&w; HOUSE OF THE THREE GIRLS, THE(1961, Aust.), d&w; YOU ARE THE WORLD FOR ME(1964, Aust.), d&w

Franz Marischka
SMALL TOWN STORY(1953, Brit.), w

Georg Marischka
ODESSA FILE, THE(1974, Brit./Ger.)

Hubert Marischka
KING STEPS OUT, THE(1936), w

Marisenka
PYRO(1964, U.S./Span.)

Marishka
GAY DECEIVERS, THE(1969)

Georg Marishka
BOYS FROM BRAZIL, THE(1978)

Maresco Marisini
Misc. Silents
MY LORD CONCEIT(1921, Brit.)

Marisol
EVERY DAY IS A HOLIDAY(1966, Span.); CORRUPTION OF CHRIS MILLER, THE(1979, Span.)
Misc. Talkies
BEHIND THE SHUTTERS(1976, Span.)

Anne Marisse
HAUNTS(1977), w; BEYOND EVIL(1980); GRADUATION DAY(1981), w

Mike Marita
GIRL MISSING(1933)

Mike Marito
THEY CALL IT SIN(1932)

Rita Maritt
SKY'S THE LIMIT, THE(1943)

Maritza
Misc. Talkies
MORALS SQUAD(1960)

Sari Maritza
BED AND BREAKFAST(1930, Brit.); LATIN LOVE(1930, Brit.); NO LADY(1931, Brit.); EVENINGS FOR SALE(1932); FORGOTTEN COMMANDMENTS(1932); WATER GYPSIES, THE(1932, Brit.); INTERNATIONAL HOUSE(1933); LADY'S PROFESSION, A(1933); RIGHT TO ROMANCE(1933); CRIMSON ROMANCE(1934)
Misc. Talkies
HER SECRET(1933)

Maritza Dancers
SLIGHTLY TERRIFIC(1944)

Marius B. Winter and His Orchestra
INDISCRETIONS OF EVE(1932, Brit.)

Giorgio Mariuzzo
1984
HOUSE BY THE CEMETERY, THE(1984, Ital.), w

Leo Marjane
PARIS DOES STRANGE THINGS(1957, Fr./Ital.)

Don Marjarian
SINCE YOU WENT AWAY(1944)

Mario Marjeroni
Silents
DESTINY'S ISLE(1922)

"Marjorie"
PROPERTY(1979)

Bob Mark
NORTHWEST OUTPOST(1947), makeup; I, JANE DOE(1948), makeup; MAC-BETH(1948), makeup; MOONRISE(1948), makeup; OKLAHOMA BADLANDS(1948), makeup; OLD LOS ANGELES(1948), makeup; SUNDOWN IN SANTA FE(1948), makeup; UNDER CALIFORNIA STARS(1948), makeup; FIGHTING KENTUCKIAN, THE(1949), makeup; KID FROM CLEVELAND, THE(1949), makeup; TOO LATE FOR TEARS(1949), makeup; CITY THAT NEVER SLEEPS(1953), makeup; JUBILEE TRAIL(1954), ch; CROOKED CIRCLE, THE(1958), makeup; MAN WHO DIED TWICE, THE(1958), makeup; NOTORIOUS MR. MONKS, THE(1958), makeup; GHOST OF ZORRO(1959), makeup; PAY OR DIE(1960), spec eff; PURPLE HILLS, THE(1961), makeup; HAND OF DEATH(1962), makeup; THUNDER ISLAND(1963), makeup; YELLOW CANARY, THE(1963), makeup; YOUNG GUNS OF TEXAS(1963), makeup; HUMAN DUPLICATORS, THE(1965), makeup; MARYJANE(1968), makeup

Brown Mark
1984
PURPLE RAIN(1984)

David Mark
Misc. Talkies
SUPERBUG, THE WILD ONE(1977), d

Flip Mark
JOURNEY, THE(1959, U.S./Aust.); PLEASE DON'T EAT THE DAISIES(1960); SAFE AT HOME(1962); MARRIAGE ON THE ROCKS(1965)

Gene Mark
OFFERING, THE(1966, Can.)

John Mark
HURRY SUNDOWN(1967)

Mae Mark
MONKEY'S PAW, THE(1933), makeup

Mary Mark
VOYAGE TO THE PLANET OF PREHISTORIC WOMEN(1966)

Michael Mark
FRANKENSTEIN(1931); RESURRECTION(1931); WORLD AND THE FLESH, THE(1932); ROMAN SCANDALS(1933); SHE DONE HIM WRONG(1933); ONE NIGHT OF LOVE(1934); CRIME AND PUNISHMENT(1935); GLASS KEY, THE(1935); PARIS IN SPRING(1935); GARDEN OF ALLAH, THE(1936); SONS O' GUNS(1936); CONFESSION(1937); MISSING WITNESSES(1937); PRESCRIPTION FOR ROMANCE(1937); THAT GIRL FROM PARIS(1937); SWISS MISS(1938); SOCIETY SMUGGLERS(1939); SON OF FRANKENSTEIN(1939); TOWER OF LONDON(1939); ARISE, MY LO-VE(1940); MA, HE'S MAKING EYES AT ME(1940); MUMMY'S HAND, THE(1940); CASABLANCA(1942); GHOST OF FRANKENSTEIN, THE(1942); MEN OF SAN QUENTIN(1942); ROAD TO MOROCCO(1942); BACKGROUND TO DANGER(1943); MISSION TO MOSCOW(1943); HOUSE OF FRANKENSTEIN(1944); UNCERTAIN GLORY(1944); CORNERED(1945); GREAT FLAMARION, THE(1945); JEALOU-SY(1945); JOE PALOOKA, CHAMP(1946); EXILE, THE(1947); NORTHWEST OUT-POST(1947); PRETENDER, THE(1947); APPOINTMENT WITH MURDER(1948); FIGHTING MAD(1948); LETTER FROM AN UNKNOWN WOMAN(1948); VICIOUS CIRCLE, THE(1948); SEARCH FOR DANGER(1949); ONCE A THIEF(1950); PEOPLE AGAINST O'HARA, THE(1951); DESERT PASSAGE(1952); PHANTOM FROM SPA-CE(1953); SALOME(1953); BIG COMBO, THE(1955); SON OF SINBAD(1955); EDGE OF HELL(1956); JET PILOT(1957); LIZZIE(1957); ATTACK OF THE PUPPET PEO-PLE(1958); TOO MUCH, TOO SOON(1958); BIG FISHERMAN, THE(1959); RETURN OF THE FLY(1959)
Silents
FOUR SONS(1928)

Robert Mark
KILL OR BE KILLED(1967, Ital.); SUPERBUG, SUPER AGENT(1976, Ger.)
Misc. Talkies
SUPER BUG(1975)

Robert Mark [Rudolf Zehetgruber]
MADDEST CAR IN THE WORLD, THE(1974, Ger.)

Ted Mark
MAN FROM O.R.G.Y., THE(1970), w

Valerie Mark
JACKPOT, THE(1950)

Zane Mark
1984
COTTON CLUB, THE(1984)

Ann Markall
PARACHUTE NURSE(1942)

Raymond Markam
BAD CHARLESTON CHARLIE(1973), art d

Annie Markart
WORLD WITHOUT A MASK, THE(1934, Ger.)

George Markas
SHOOT(1976, Can.)

Maritta Marke
NIGHT IN JUNE, A(1940, Swed.)

Dave Markee
O LUCKY MAN!(1973, Brit.)

Markee the Horse
Silents
HOOFBEATS OF VENGEANCE(1929)

Louis Markein
LARCENY(1948), w

Jean Markell
SKATEBOARD(1978)

Robert Markell
12 ANGRY MEN(1957), art d

Jane Markem
THREEPENNY OPERA, THE(1931, Ger./U.S.)

Jane Marken
LIFE AND LOVES OF BEETHOVEN, THE(1937, Fr.); LUMIERE D'ETE(1943, Fr.); ETERNAL HUSBAND, THE(1946, Fr.); CONFESSIONS OF A ROGUE(1948, Fr.); DEDEE(1949, Fr.); CHEAT, THE(1950, Fr.); JUST ME(1950, Fr.); KNOCK(1955, Fr.); MIRROR HAS TWO FACES, THE(1959, Fr.); CRAZY FOR LOVE(1960, Fr.); MAX-IME(1962, Fr.); ROAD TO SHAME, THE(1962, Fr.); LA BONNE SOUPE(1964, Fr./Ital.); FRIEND OF THE FAMILY(1965, Fr./Ital.)

Jeanne Marken
OPEN ROAD, THE(1940, Fr.); CHILDREN OF PARADISE(1945, Fr.); WAYS OF LOVE(1950, Ital./Fr.); LA MARIE DU PORT(1951, Fr.); AND GOD CREATED WO-MAN(1957, Fr.)

Harry Marker
EAST IS WEST(1930), ed; HELL'S HEROES(1930), ed; HIDE-OUT, THE(1930), ed; SECRET OF THE CHATEAU(1935), ed; BEHIND THE HEADLINES(1937), ed; CRASHING HOLLYWOOD(1937), ed; FLIGHT FROM GLORY(1937), ed; LIVING ON LOVE(1937), ed; ANNABEL TAKES A TOUR(1938), ed; NIGHT SPOT(1938), ed; SAINT IN NEW YORK, THE(1938), ed; SKY GIANT(1938), ed; SMASHING THE RACKETS(1938), ed; THIS MARRIAGE BUSINESS(1938), ed; FIVE CAME BACK(1939), ed; FULL CONFESSION(1939), ed; LIFE RETURNS(1939), ed; PACIFIC LINER(1939), ed; RENO(1939), ed; SORORITY HOUSE(1939), ed; THEY MADE HER A SPY(1939), ed; TWELVE CROWDED HOURS(1939), ed; BILL OF DIVOR-CEMENT(1940), ed; CROSS COUNTRY ROMANCE(1940), ed; CURTAIN CALL(1940), ed; MARRIED AND IN LOVE(1940), ed; PLAY GIRL(1940), ed; STRANGER ON THE

THIRD FLOOR(1940), ed; WAGON TRAIN(1940), ed; DATE WITH THE FALCON, A(1941), ed; LADY SCARFACE(1941), ed; MEXICAN SPITFIRE'S BABY(1941), ed; REPENT AT LEISURE(1941), ed; FALCON TAKES OVER, THE(1942), ed; HIGHWAYS BY NIGHT(1942), ed; MEXICAN SPITFIRE'S ELEPHANT(1942), ed; ADVENTURES OF A ROOKIE(1943), ed; LADIES' DAY(1943), ed; MEXICAN SPITFIRE'S BLESSED EVENT(1943), ed; ROOKIES IN BURMA(1943), ed; MUSIC IN MANHATTAN(1944), ed; MY PAL, WOLF(1944), ed; SEVEN DAYS ASHORE(1944), ed; BELLS OF ST. MARY'S, THE(1945), ed; PAN-AMERICANA(1945), ed; SING YOUR WAY HOME(1945), ed; SPIRAL STAIRCASE, THE(1946), ed; FARMER'S DAUGHTER, THE(1947), ed; LIKELY STORY, A(1947), ed; NIGHT SONG(1947), ed; EVERY GIRL SHOULD BE MARRIED(1948), ed; MR. BLANDINGS BUILDS HIS DREAM HOUSE(1948), ed; HOLIDAY AFFAIR(1949), ed; SECRET FURY, THE(1950), ed; DOUBLE DYNAMITE(1951), ed; PAYMENT ON DEMAND(1951), ed; TWO TICKETS TO BROADWAY(1951), ed; PLUNDER OF THE SUN(1953), ed; SUSAN SLEPT HERE(1954), ed; AMERICANO, THE(1955), ed; RAGE AT DAWN(1955), ed; TREASURE OF PANCHO VILLA, THE(1955), ed; BUNDLE OF JOY(1956), ed; GREAT DAY IN THE MORNING(1956), ed; TENSION AT TABLE ROCK(1956), ed; GIRL MOST LIKELY, THE(1957), ed; JET PILOT(1957), ed; THUNDER ROAD(1958), ed; VOICE OF THE HURRICANE(1964), ed
Silents
MICHIGAN KID, THE(1928), ed; SKY SKIDDER, THE(1929), ed; SLIM FINGERS(1929), ed

Martha Marker
WEREWOLF IN A GIRL'S DORMITORY(1961, Ital./Aust.)

Russ Marker
DEMON FROM DEVIL'S LAKE, THE(1964), p,d&w

Russell Marker
BEYOND THE TIME BARRIER(1960)

Russell Markert
MOULIN ROUGE(1934), ch

George Markes
RICH ARE ALWAYS WITH US, THE(1932), ed

Larry Markes
FOR LOVE OR MONEY(1963), w; WILD AND WONDERFUL(1964), w

Tony Markes
VALLEY GIRL(1983)

Jeanne Market
ETERNAL RETURN, THE(1943, Fr.)

I. Markevich
FAREWELL, DOVES(1962, USSR)

Enid Markey
SNAFU(1945); NAKED CITY, THE(1948); TAKE ONE FALSE STEP(1949)
Silents
BATTLE OF GETTYSBURG(1914); DESPOILER, THE(1915); CAPTIVE GOD, THE(1916); CIVILIZATION(1916); JIM GRIMSBY'S BOY(1916); LIEUT. DANNY, U.S.A.(1916); FEMALE OF THE SPECIES(1917); ROMANCE OF TARZAN, THE(1918); TARZAN OF THE APES(1918)
Misc. Silents
ALOHA OE(1915); DARKENING TRAIL, THE(1915); IRON STRAIN, THE(1915); BETWEEN MEN(1916); CONQUEROR, THE(1916); DEVIL'S DOUBLE, THE(1916); NO-GOOD GUY, THE(1916); PHANTOM, THE(1916); SHELL FORTY-THREE(1916); WAR'S WOMEN(1916); BLOOD WILL TELL(1917); YANKEE WAY, THE(1917); CHEATING THE PUBLIC(1918); MOTHER, I NEED YOU(1918); SIX-SHOOTER ANDY(1918); FOOLISH MOTHERS(1923)

Gene Markey
BATTLE OF PARIS, THE(1929), w; CLOSE HARMONY(1929), w; LUCKY IN LOVE(1929), w; MOTHER'S BOY(1929), w; SYNCOPATION(1929), w; FLORODORA GIRL, THE(1930), w; PRINCE OF DIAMONDS(1930), w; GREAT LOVER, THE(1931), w; INSPIRATION(1931), w; WEST OF BROADWAY(1931), w; AS YOU DESIRE ME(1932), w; BABY FACE(1933), w; FEMALE(1933), w; LILLY TURNER(1933), w; LUXURY LINER(1933), w; MIDNIGHT MARY(1933), w; FASHIONS OF 1934(1934), w; LOST LADY, A(1934), w; MERRY FRINKS, THE(1934), w; MODERN HERO, A(1934), w; LET'S LIVE TONIGHT(1935), w; BIG NOISE, THE(1936, Brit.), w; GIRLS' DORMITORY(1936), w; KING OF BURLESQUE(1936), w; LOVE IN EXILE(1936, Brit.), w; PRIVATE NUMBER(1936), w; WHITE HUNTER(1936), w; ON THE AVENUE(1937), w; WEE WILLIE WINKIE(1937), p; JOSETTE(1938), p; KENTUCKY(1938), p; SUEZ(1938), p; ADVENTURES OF SHERLOCK HOLMES, THE(1939), p; HOUND OF THE BASKERVILLES, THE(1939), p; SECOND FIDDLE(1939), p; MARYLAND(1940), p; PUBLIC DEB NO. 1(1940), p; YOU'RE THE ONE(1941), p, w; MOSS ROSE(1947), p; IF THIS BE SIN(1950, Brit.), w; WONDER BOY(1951, Brit./Aust.), w; MEET ME AT THE FAIR(1952), w; GLORY(1955), w

Harry Markey
RENDEZVOUS AT MIDNIGHT(1935), ed

Melinda Markey
TITANIC(1953); ADVENTURES OF HAJJI BABA(1954); OTHER WOMAN, THE(1954); WOMAN'S WORLD(1954); CRASHOUT(1955); PRINCE OF PLAYERS(1955)

Zoli Markey
DEMON, THE(1981, S. Africa)

Wallace Markfield
BYE BYE BRAVERMAN(1968), w

Alice Markham
SHOW BOAT(1951)

Barbara Markham
AIRBORNE(1962); HOUSE OF WHIPCORD(1974, Brit.); LADY VANISHES, THE(1980, Brit.)

Brian Markham
PIRATES OF PENZANCE, THE(1983)

Daisy Markham
Silents
SHIPS THAT PASS IN THE NIGHT(1921, Brit.)

David Markham
MURDER IN THE FAMILY(1938, Brit.); STARS LOOK DOWN, THE(1940, Brit.); TWO GENTLEMEN SHARING(1969, Brit.); BLOOD FROM THE MUMMY'S TOMB(1972, Brit.); TALES FROM THE CRYPT(1972, Brit.); TWO ENGLISH GIRLS(1972, Fr.); Z.P.G.(1972); DAY FOR NIGHT(1973, Fr.); MEETINGS WITH REMARKABLE MEN(1979, Brit.); TESS(1980, Fr./Brit.); RICHARD'S THINGS(1981, Brit.)

Dewey "Pigmeat" Markham
Misc. Talkies
SWANEE SHOWBOAT(1939); WRONG MR. RIGHT, THE(1939); MR. SMITH GOES GHOST(1940); HOUSE RENT PARTY(1946); SHUT MY BIG MOUTH(1946)

Edwin Markham
Misc. Silents
LOVE'S REDEMPTION(1921)

Harry Markham
THIS SPORTING LIFE(1963, Brit.); MR. QUILP(1975, Brit.)

Henry Markham
KIND OF LOVING, A(1962, Brit.)

Joe Markham
Misc. Talkies
FIRST TIME ROUND(1972)

Kika Markham
BUNNY LAKE IS MISSING(1965); TWO ENGLISH GIRLS(1972, Fr.); OUTLAND(1981)

Mansfield Markham
MADAME GUILLOTINE(1931, Brit.), p; WRITTEN LAW, THE(1931, Brit.), p; RETURN OF RAFFLES, THE(1932, Brit.), p&d; LOVE IN MOROCCO(1933, Fr.), p; MAID HAPPY(1933, Brit.), p&d

Marcella Markham
ROMANTIC ENGLISHWOMAN, THE(1975, Brit./Fr.); VALENTINO(1977, Brit.)

Monte Markham
HOUR OF THE GUN(1967); PROJECT X(1968); GUNS OF THE MAGNIFICENT SEVEN(1969); ONE IS A LONELY NUMBER(1972); GINGER IN THE MORNING(1973); MIDWAY(1976); AIRPORT '77(1977); SEPARATE WAYS(1981); OFF THE WALL(1983)

Petra Markham
DEADLY AFFAIR, THE(1967, Brit.); FRAGMENT OF FEAR(1971, Brit.); GET CARTER(1971, Brit.); LONG AGO, TOMORROW(1971, Brit.); HIRELING, THE(1973, Brit.)

"Pigmeat" Markham
AM I GUILTY?(1940); THAT'S MY BABY(1944)

Ray Markham
NAME OF THE GAME IS KILL, THE(1968), art d; IS THIS TRIP REALLY NECESSARY?(1970), art d; INCREDIBLE TWO-HEADED TRANSPLANT, THE(1971), art d; SEVEN ALONE(1975), prod d; CHICKEN CHRONICLES, THE(1977), art d

Ronald Markham
1984
RIDDLE OF THE SANDS, THE(1984, Brit.)

Janis Markhouse
FINNEGANS WAKE(1965)

Eleni Marki
ELECTRA(1962, Gr.)

Anton Markic
MOONWOLF(1966, Fin./Ger.), ph

V. Markin
DESTINY OF A MAN(1961, USSR); LULLABY(1961, USSR); HOUSE ON THE FRONT LINE, THE(1963, USSR); SHE-WOLF(1963, USSR); SANDU FOLLOWS THE SUN(1965, USSR); THERE WAS AN OLD COUPLE(1967, USSR)

Ted Markland
HALLELUJAH TRAIL, THE(1965); WATERHOLE NO. 3(1967); ANGELS FROM HELL(1968); HIRED HAND, THE(1971); LAST MOVIE, THE(1971); JORY(1972); PLAY IT AGAIN, SAM(1972); ULZANA'S RAID(1972); WELCOME HOME, SOLDIER BOYS(1972); ONE FLEW OVER THE CUCKOO'S NEST(1975); FIGHTING MAD(1976); WHICH WAY IS UP?(1977); WANDA NEVADA(1979); KING OF THE MOUNTAIN(1981)

Fletcher Markle
JOURNEY TOGETHER(1946, Brit.); JIGSAW(1949), a, d, w; MAN WITH A CLOAK, THE(1951), d; NIGHT INTO MORNING(1951), d; INCREDIBLE JOURNEY, THE(1963), d

Lois Markle
SPORTING CLUB, THE(1971)
Misc. Talkies
COMING APART(1969)

Peter Markle
PERSONALS, THE(1982), d&w, ph
1984
HOT DOG...THE MOVIE(1984), d

Stephen Markle
TICKET TO HEAVEN(1981)
Misc. Talkies
TOMORROW MAN, THE(1979)

Peter Marklin
SUMMER WISHES, WINTER DREAMS(1973)

Lew Markman
DATE WITH DEATH, A(1959)

Larry Marko
BODY HEAT(1981)

Nicole Marko
LIFE UPSIDE DOWN(1965, Fr.), ed; KILLING GAME, THE(1968, Fr.), ed

Zekial Marko
ONCE A THIEF(1965), a, w

Diane Markoff
DEATH WISH II(1982)

Gregory J. Markopolous
TWICE A MAN(1964), p,d, ed

Iannis Markopolous
DREAM OF PASSION, A(1978, Gr.), m

Gregory J. Markopoulos
SERENITY(1962), p,d&w; ILLIAC PASSION, THE(1968), a, p,d,w&ph, ed

Yannis Markopoulos
YOUNG APHRODITES(1966, Gr.), m; FEAR, THE(1967, Gr.), m; LOVE CYCLES(1969, Gr.), m; SISTERS, THE(1969, Gr.), m

Andreas Markos
KITCHEN, THE(1961, Brit.); IN THE COOL OF THE DAY(1963)

Sandra Markota
SOPHIE'S CHOICE(1982)

Margaret Markov
RUN, ANGEL, RUN(1969); STERILE CUCKOO, THE(1969); PRETTY MAIDS ALL IN A ROW(1971); HOT BOX, THE(1972, U.S./Phil.); ARENA, THE(1973); THERE IS NO 13(1977)

Alicia Markova
SONG FOR MISS JULIE, A(1945)

Sonia Markova
Silents
LES MISERABLES(1918)
Misc. Silents
PAINTED MADONNA, THE(1917); HEART'S REVENGE, A(1918)

V. Markova
LAST GAME, THE(1964, USSR)

Milorad Markovic
BOY CRIED MURDER, THE(1966, Ger./Brit./Yugo.), ph

Milored Markovic
WITNESS OUT OF HELL(1967, Ger./Yugo.), ph

Rade Markovic
PEACH THIEF, THE(1969, Bulgaria); ADRIFT(1971, Czech.)
1984
SECRET DIARY OF SIGMUND FREUD, THE(1984)

Slobodanka Markovic
TWILIGHT TIME(1983, U.S./Yugo.)

Joseph Markovitch
POWER(1934, Brit.)

Larry Markow
SECRET OF THE PURPLE REEF, THE(1960)

Margaret Markow
BLACK MAMA, WHITE MAMA(1973)

Mark S. Markowicz
STRIPES(1981)

Abraham Markowitz
DREAMER, THE(1970, Israel)

Charles Markowitz
I MISS YOU, HUGS AND KISSES(1978, Can.), p

Cheryl Markowitz
PRETTY BABY(1978)

Dick Markowitz
BLACK VEIL FOR LISA, A(1969 Ital./Ger.), m

H. Benny Markowitz
FUZZ(1972)

Mike Markowitz
1984
FLAMINGO KID, THE(1984)

Murray Markowitz
RECOMMENDATION FOR MERCY(1975, Can.), p, d, w; I MISS YOU, HUGS AND KISSES(1978, Can.), p, d&w

Richard Markowitz
HOT ANGEL, THE(1958), m; STAKEOUT ON DOPE STREET(1958), m, md; ROADRACERS, THE(1959), m; YOUNG CAPTIVES, THE(1959), m; HOODLUM PRIEST, THE(1961), m; MAGIC SWORD, THE(1962), m; CRY OF BATTLE(1963), m; FACE IN THE RAIN, A(1963), m; ONE MAN'S WAY(1964), m; BUS RILEY'S BACK IN TOWN(1965), m; WILD SEED(1965), m; RIDE BEYOND VENGEANCE(1966), m; SHOOTING, THE(1971), m; BOSS'S SON, THE(1978), m

Robert Markowitz
VOICES(1979), d

Alfred Marks
PENNY POINTS TO PARADISE(1951, Brit.); JOHNNY, YOU'RE WANTED(1956, Brit.); DESERT MICE(1960, Brit.); FRIGHTENED CITY, THE(1961, Brit.); WEEKEND WITH LULU, A(1961, Brit.); THERE WAS A CROOKED MAN(1962, Brit.); MAID FOR MURDER(1963, Brit.); SCRAMBLE(1970, Brit.); SCREAM AND SCREAM AGAIN(1970, Brit.); OUR MISS FRED(1972, Brit.); VALENTINO(1977, Brit.)
Misc. Talkies
MISSION: MONTE CARLO(1981, Brit.)

Arthur Marks
DETROIT 9000(1973), p&d, w; ROOMMATES, THE(1973), d, w; BUCKTOWN(1975), d; FRIDAY FOSTER(1975), p&d, w; J.D.'S REVENGE(1976), p&d; MONKEY HUSTLE, THE(1976), p&d
Misc. Talkies
TOGETHERNESS(1970), d; CLASS OF '74(1972), d; BONNIE'S KIDS(1973), d; WOMAN FOR ALL MEN, A(1975), d

Arthur D. Marks
FEMALE RESPONSE, THE(1972), ph, ed

Aviva Marks
SINAI COMMANDOS: THE STORY OF THE SIX DAY WAR(1968, Israel/Ger.); PARADISE(1982)

Barbara Marks
ONE WAY TICKET TO HELL(1955)

C.J. Marks
FAST COMPANIONS(1932), w

Chris Marks
DREAM OF KINGS, A(1969); SEVEN MINUTES, THE(1971)

Clarence Marks
SHAKEDOWN, THE(1929), w; TOM BROWN OF CULVER(1932), w; HER FIRST MATE(1933), w; HORSEPLAY(1933), w; HALF A SINNER(1934), w; LOVE BIRDS(1934), w; AFFAIR OF SUSAN(1935), w; DON'T GET PERSONAL(1936), w; RAINBOW ON THE RIVER(1936), w; SWING IT SAILOR(1937), w; TERROR OF TINY TOWN, THE(1938), w; WIDE OPEN FACES(1938), w; SPIRIT OF CULVER, THE(1939), w; BROOKLYN ORCHID(1942), d; THAT NAZTY NUISANCE(1943), w

Clarence E. Marks
FIGHTING THOROUGHBREDS(1939), w

Clarence J. Marks
LOVE TRAP, THE(1929), w

Eddie Marks
TOP OF THE HEAP(1972), cos; COMA(1978), cos; WHERE THE BUFFALO ROAM(1980), cos

Eduard Marks
FAUST(1963, Ger.)

Edward Marks
MAN CALLED HORSE, A(1970), cos; ZIGZAG(1970), cos

Franklyn Marks
LIGHT IN THE FOREST, THE(1958), md; CHARLIE, THE LONESOME COUGAR(1967), m

Gareth Marks
SCRAMBLE(1970, Brit.)

Garnet Marks
G.I. JANE(1951); TAKE CARE OF MY LITTLE GIRL(1951)

Garnett Marks
MAGNIFICENT DOLL(1946); PHILO VANCE'S GAMBLE(1947); GUY WHO CAME BACK, THE(1951); PAINTING THE CLOUDS WITH SUNSHINE(1951)

George Marks
LITTLE WILDCAT, THE(1928), ed; STATE STREET SADIE(1928), ed; KID GLOVES(1929), ed; SKIN DEEP(1929), ed; STOLEN KISSES(1929), ed; SONG OF THE WEST(1930), ed; BOUGHT(1931), ed; MALTESE FALCON, THE(1931), ed; MAN TO MAN(1931), ed; DARK HORSE, THE(1932), ed; FIREMAN, SAVE MY CHILD(1932), ed; LIFE BEGINS(1932), ed; SILVER DOLLAR(1932), ed; UNDER EIGHTEEN(1932), ed; LITTLE GIANT, THE(1933), ed

George Harrison Marks
NAKED WORLD OF HARRISON MARKS, THE(1967, Brit.), p&d, w

Guy Marks
PEEPER(1975); TRAIN RIDE TO HOLLYWOOD(1975)

Harrison Marks
NAKED WORLD OF HARRISON MARKS, THE(1967, Brit.)

Harvey Marks
MARCH OF THE SPRING HARE(1969); ROOMMATES(1971); NIGHT OF THE COBRA WOMAN(1974, U.S./Phil.), p

Herman Marks
MEN OF THE NIGHT(1934); BULLETS OR BALLOTS(1936); MARKED WOMAN(1937); TALK OF THE TOWN(1942); GILDA(1946); NIGHT EDITOR(1946)

I. Marks
WHEN THE TREES WERE TALL(1965, USSR)

Jack Marks
SPLINTERS IN THE NAVY(1931, Brit.), w; MAYOR'S NEST, THE(1932, Brit.), d&w; IT'S A KING(1933, Brit.), w; THIS WEEK OF GRACE(1933, Brit.), w; TROUBLE(1933, Brit.), w; UP FOR THE DERBY(1933, Brit.), w; GIRLS PLEASE!(1934, Brit.), w; IT'S A COP(1934, Brit.), w; HOPE OF HIS SIDE(1935, Brit.), w; KISS ME GOODBYE(1935, Brit.), w; SAY IT WITH DIAMONDS(1935, Brit.), w; WHILE PARENTS SLEEP(1935, Brit.), w; FAME(1936, Brit.), w; SPLINTERS IN THE AIR(1937, Brit.), w; WHAT A MAN!(1937, Brit.), w; WHY PICK ON ME?(1937, Brit.), w; MIRACLES DO HAPPEN(1938, Brit.), w; OLD MOTHER RILEY JOINS UP(1939, Brit.), w; TILLY OF BLOOMSBURY(1940, Brit.), w; OLD MOTHER RILEY, HEADMISTRESS(1950, Brit.), w; UP FOR THE CUP(1950, Brit.), w; WORM'S EYE VIEW(1951, Brit.), w; OLD MOTHER RILEY(1952, Brit.), w; NOT WANTED ON VOYAGE(1957, Brit.), p, w; FRIDAY THE 13TH PART II(1981)
1984
FRIDAY THE 13TH–THE FINAL CHAPTER(1984)

Jack R. Marks
FAN, THE(1981)

Jennifer Marks
MIKADO, THE(1967, Brit.)

Joe Marks
SO ENDS OUR NIGHT(1941)

Joe E. Marks
OUTSIDE OF PARADISE(1938); LI'L ABNER(1959); NIGHT THEY RAIDED MINSKY'S, THE(1968)

John Marks
PRUDENCE AND THE PILL(1968, Brit.), cos

Kurt Marks
SIGNALS-AN ADVENTURE IN SPACE(1970, E. Ger./Pol.), spec eff

Lambert Marks
LOOKING FOR LOVE(1964), cos; GIRL HAPPY(1965), cos; SUPPORT YOUR LOCAL GUNFIGHTER(1971), cos; MECHANIC, THE(1972), cos; THUMB TRIPPING(1972), cos; WAR BETWEEN MEN AND WOMEN, THE(1972), cos; SLITHER(1973), cos; PARADISE ALLEY(1978), cos

Lambert E. Marks
FUN WITH DICK AND JANE(1977), cos

Larry Marks
ONE WAY TO LOVE(1946), w

Lee Marks
PUNISHMENT PARK(1971)

Leo Marks
GIRL WHO COULDN'T QUITE, THE(1949, Brit.), w; CLOUDBURST(1952, Brit.), w; PEEPING TOM(1960, Brit.), w; WEBSTER BOY, THE(1962, Brit.), w; GUNS AT BATASI(1964, Brit.), w; SEBASTIAN(1968, Brit.), w; TWISTED NERVE(1969, Brit.), w; UNDERCOVERS HERO(1975, Brit.), w

Libby Marks
FOLIES DERGERE(1935)

Lou Marks
MISTER ROCK AND ROLL(1957); COUNTRY MUSIC HOLIDAY(1958)

Louis Marks
MAN WHO FINALLY DIED, THE(1967, Brit.), w

Marianne Marks
WRONG IS RIGHT(1982)

Marie Marks
TOAST OF NEW YORK, THE(1937)

Maurice Marks
WHAT NEXT, CORPORAL HARGROVE?(1945); HOT CARS(1956); TATTERED DRESS, THE(1957); BAD NEWS BEARS, THE(1976); CHEAP DETECTIVE, THE(1978); HOUSE CALLS(1978); LITTLE MISS MARKER(1980)

Michael Marks
WASP WOMAN, THE(1959)
1984
MY KIND OF TOWN(1984, Can.)

Mrs. Marks
FREUD(1962)
Myron Marks
CRISIS(1950); MY FAVORITE SPY(1951)
Owen Marks
LAND OF THE SILVER FOX(1928), ed; MIDNIGHT TAXI, THE(1928), ed; MY MAN(1928), ed; DISRAELI(1929), ed; FANCY BAGGAGE(1929), ed; SAY IT WITH SONGS(1929), ed; SONNY BOY(1929), ed; OLD ENGLISH(1930), ed; DIVORCE AMONG FRIENDS(1931), ed; MILLIONAIRE, THE(1931), ed; HATCHET MAN, THE(1932), ed; PLAY GIRL(1932), ed; TENDERFOOT, THE(1932), ed; YOU SAID A MOUTHFUL(1932), ed; CONVENTION CITY(1933), ed; EVER IN MY HEART(1933), ed; KING'S VACATION, THE(1933), ed; VOLTAIRE(1933), ed; WORKING MAN, THE(1933), ed; LOST LADY, A(1934), ed; RETURN OF THE TERROR(1934), ed; UPPER WORLD(1934), ed; FRISCO KID(1935), ed; GIRL FROM TENTH AVENUE, THE(1935), ed; SECRET BRIDE, THE(1935), ed; TRAVELING SALESLADY, THE(1935), ed; WE'RE IN THE MONEY(1935), ed; WHILE THE PATIENT SLEPT(1935), ed; CHINA CLIPPER(1936), ed; I MARRIED A DOCTOR(1936), ed; PETRIFIED FOREST, THE(1936), ed; BLACK LEGION, THE(1937), ed; IT'S LOVE I'M AFTER(1937), ed; SLIM(1937), ed; ANGELS WITH DIRTY FACES(1938), ed; LOVE, HONOR AND BEHAVE(1938), ed; SECRETS OF AN ACTRESS(1938), ed; CONFESSIONS OF A NAZI SPY(1939), ed; OKLAHOMA KID, THE(1939), ed; PRIVATE LIVES OF ELIZABETH AND ESSEX, THE(1939), ed; FIGHTING 69TH, THE(1940), ed; NO TIME FOR COMEDY(1940), ed; SATURDAY'S CHILDREN(1940), ed; AFFECTIONATELY YOURS(1941), ed; BLUES IN THE NIGHT(1941), ed; FOOTSTEPS IN THE DARK(1941), ed; CASABLANCA(1942), ed; WINGS FOR THE EAGLE(1942), ed; MISSION TO MOSCOW(1943), ed; JANIE(1944), ed; PASSAGE TO MARSEILLE(1944), ed; ESCAPE IN THE DESERT(1945), ed; PRIDE OF THE MARINES(1945), ed; MAN I LOVE, THE(1946), ed; DEEP VALLEY(1947), ed; NORA PRENTISS(1947), ed; JUNE BRIDE(1948), ed; TREASURE OF THE SIERRA MADRE, THE(1948), ed; WINTER MEETING(1948), ed; COLORADO TERRITORY(1949), ed; WHITE HEAT(1949), ed; BRIGHT LEAF(1950), ed; CAGED(1950), ed; HIGHWAY 301(1950), ed; WEST POINT STORY, THE(1950), ed; FORCE OF ARMS(1951), ed; I'LL SEE YOU IN MY DREAMS(1951), ed; INSIDE THE WALLS OF FOLSOM PRISON(1951), ed; MAN BEHIND THE GUN, THE(1952), ed; STOP, YOU'RE KILLING ME(1952), ed; THREE SAILORS AND A GIRL(1953), ed; TROUBLE ALONG THE WAY(1953), ed; LUCKY ME(1954), ed; EAST OF EDEN(1955), ed; MC CONNELL STORY, THE(1955), ed; SINCERELY YOURS(1955), ed; SANTIAGO(1956), ed; DARBY'S RANGERS(1958), ed; LAFAYETTE ESCADRILLE(1958), ed; TOO MUCH, TOO SOON(1958), ed; HANGING TREE, THE(1959), ed; SUMMER PLACE, A(1959), ed; SINS OF RACHEL CADE, THE(1960), ed; PARRISH(1961), ed
Silents
HELEN'S BABIES(1924), ed; POWDER MY BACK(1928), ed
Owens Marks
SAFE IN HELL(1931), ed
Patricia Marks
NEVER TAKE CANDY FROM A STRANGER(1961, Brit.)
Patsy Marks
Silents
MY BOY(1922)
Percy Marks
Silents
PLASTIC AGE, THE(1925), w; RED LIPS(1928), w
Richard Marks
PARADES(1972), ed; BANG THE DRUM SLOWLY(1973), ed; SERPICO(1973), ed; GODFATHER, THE, PART II(1974), ed; THREE TOUGH GUYS(1974, U.S./Ital.), ed; LIES MY FATHER TOLD ME(1975, Can.), ed; LAST TYCOON, THE(1976), ed; APOCALYPSE NOW(1979), w; HAND, THE(1981), ed; PENNIES FROM HEAVEN(1981), ed; MAX DUGAN RETURNS(1983), ed; TERMS OF ENDEARMENT(1983), ed
1984
ADVENTURES OF BUCKAROO BANZAI: ACROSS THE 8TH DIMENSION, THE(1984), ed
Robert Marks
VILLAGE OF THE DAMNED(1960, Brit.)
Robin Marks
LOVE MERCHANT, THE(1966)
Sherry Marks
SATAN'S CHEERLEADERS(1977); HOMETOWN U.S.A.(1979)
Sherry Lee Marks
MALIBU BEACH(1978)
Shirley Marks
STORMY(1935)
Slash Marks
NIGHT OF THE COBRA WOMAN(1974, U.S./Phil.)
Walter Marks
WILD PARTY, THE(1975), w
Wes Marks
SAVAGE WILD, THE(1970), ph
William Marks
SHAKEDOWN(1950); LITTLEST HOBO, THE(1958); WAR PARTY(1965), w; DON'T WORRY, WE'LL THINK OF A TITLE(1966), w; KILL A DRAGON(1967), w; BARQUERO(1970), w
Willis Marks
REBECCA OF SUNNYBROOK FARM(1932)
Silents
SECRET LOVE(1916); JACK KNIFE MAN, THE(1920); BEAUTIFUL GAMBLER, THE(1921); CHICKENS(1921); TRAVELIN' ON(1922); NIGHT SHIP, THE(1925)
Misc. Silents
PEOPLE VS. JOHN DOE, THE(1916); MYSTERIOUS MRS. M, THE(1917); MAN FROM FUNERAL RANGE, THE(1918); GREASED LIGHTING(1919); TREMBLING HOUR, THE(1919); VIRTUOUS THIEF, THE(1919); YOU NEVER SAID SUCH A GIRL(1919); DANCIN' FOOL, THE(1920); GREATER PROFIT, THE(1921); WHICH SHALL IT BE?(1924); ON THE THRESHOLD(1925); SILENT PAL(1925)
Ben Markson
HALF-NAKED TRUTH, THE(1932), w; IS MY FACE RED?(1932), w; RACKETY RAX(1932), w; WHAT PRICE HOLLYWOOD?(1932), w; GIRL MISSING(1933), w; GOLD DIGGERS OF 1933(1933), w; GOODBYE AGAIN(1933), w; LADY KILLER(1933), w; LUCKY DEVILS(1933), w; PICTURE SNATCHER(1933), w; SILK EXPRESS(1933), w; BIG HEARTED HERBERT(1934), w; CASE OF THE HOWLING DOG, THE(1934), w; HERE COMES THE NAVY(1934), w; UPPER WORLD(1934), w; BRIGHT LIGHTS(1935), w; CASE OF THE LUCKY LEGS, THE(1935), w; WHITE COCKATOO(1935), w; BRIDES ARE LIKE THAT(1936), w; NOBODY'S FOOL(1936), w; DANGER–LOVE AT WORK(1937), w; SING AND BE HAPPY(1937), w; THAT I MAY LIVE(1937), w; WOMAN-WISE(1937), w; I WAS A CONVICT(1939), w; PRIDE OF THE NAVY(1939), w; GREAT MR. NOBODY, THE(1941), w; THIEVES FALL OUT(1941), w; HE HIRED THE BOSS(1943), w; FALCON IN SAN FRANCISCO, THE(1945), w; PRISON SHIP(1945), w; BEAUTIFUL CHEAT, THE(1946), w; CLOSE CALL FOR BOSTON BLACKIE, A(1946), w; EDGE OF ETERNITY(1959), w
Benjamin Markson
Silents
MASKED EMOTIONS(1929), w
David Markson
DIRTY DINGUS MAGEE(1970), w; COUNT YOUR BULLETS(1972), w
Morley Markson
Misc. Talkies
OFF YOUR ROCKER(1980), d
George Markstein
ROBBERY(1967, Brit.), w; ODESSA FILE, THE(1974, Brit./Ger.), w; FINAL OPTION, THE(1983, Brit.), w
Rachel Markus
FAITHFUL CITY(1952, Israel)
Sahbra Markus
DAYS OF HEAVEN(1978)
Tarja Markus
TIME OF ROSES(1970, Fin.)
Tibor Markus
ILLUMINATIONS(1976, Aus.), a, p
Winnie Markus
MOZART STORY, THE(1948, Aust.); DEVIL IN SILK(1968, Ger.)
Keld Markuslund
CRAZY PARADISE(1965, Den.)
Milton Markwell
Silents
HIGH HEELS(1921)
Paul Markwitz
DEVIL MAKES THREE, THE(1952), art d; MARTIN LUTHER(1953), art d; ORDERED TO LOVE(1963, Ger.), art d; TERROR OF DR. MABUSE, THE(1965, Ger.), art d
Richard Markwitz
COUNT YOUR BULLETS(1972), m
Bob Markworth
KARATE, THE HAND OF DEATH(1961)
Norma Marla
UGLY DUCKLING, THE(1959, Brit.); HOUSE OF FRIGHT(1961)
Philippe Marlaud
AVIATOR'S WIFE, THE(1981, Fr.)
Helen Marlborough
Silents
WILD GOOSE CHASE, THE(1915)
Miss Marlborough
Silents
TONGUES OF MEN, THE(1916)
Anni Marle
SLEEPING BEAUTY(1965, Ger.)
Arnold Marle
ONE OF OUR AIRCRAFT IS MISSING(1942, Brit.); MR. EMMANUEL(1945, Brit.); HIGH FURY(1947, Brit.); GIRL IN THE PAINTING, THE(1948, Brit.); GLASS MOUNTAIN, THE(1950, Brit.); KISENGA, MAN OF AFRICA(1952, Brit.); FLOATING DUTCHMAN, THE(1953, Brit.); GREEN BUDDHA, THE(1954, Brit.); CASE OF THE RED MONKEY(1955, Brit.); CROSS CHANNEL(1955, Brit.); GLASS TOMB, THE(1955, Brit.); THEY CAN'T HANG ME(1955, Brit.); ZARAK(1956, Brit.); BREAK IN THE CIRCLE, THE(1957, Brit.); MAN WHO COULD CHEAT DEATH, THE(1959, Brit.); SNAKE WOMAN, THE(1961, Brit.)
Louise Marleau
ADOLESCENTS, THE(1967, Can.); IN PRAISE OF OLDER WOMEN(1978, Can.); ALIEN CONTAMINATION(1982, Ital.)
Lucien Marleau
TROUBLE-FETE(1964, Can.), ed
Gloria Marlen
BORDER FEUD(1947)
Misc. Talkies
SWEET GENEVIEVE(1947)
Marlene
JUDY'S LITTLE NO-NO(1969)
Christine Marler
TRUMAN CAPOTE'S TRILOGY(1969)
Helen Marler
NEW KIND OF LOVE, A(1963)
Franco Marletta
SABATA(1969, Ital.); INVESTIGATION OF A CITIZEN ABOVE SUSPICION(1970, Ital.)
Ben Marley
JAWS II(1978); STEEL(1980)
Eve Marley
LOVE IN THE AFTERNOON(1957)
J. Peverell Marley
SHOW FOLKS(1928), ph; DYNAMITE(1930), ph; IT'S A GREAT LIFE(1930), ph; THIS DAY AND AGE(1933), ph; COUNT OF MONTE CRISTO, THE(1934), ph; LET 'EM HAVE IT(1935), ph; IT HAD TO HAPPEN(1936), ph; SUEZ(1938), ph; JOHN LOVES MARY(1949), ph; GREATEST SHOW ON EARTH, THE(1952), ph; OFF LIMITS(1953), ph; DRUM BEAT(1954), ph; KING RICHARD AND THE CRUSADERS(1954), ph; PHANTOM OF THE RUE MORGUE(1954), ph; ILLEGAL(1955), ph; JUMP INTO HELL(1955), ph; SERENADE(1956), ph; STEEL JUNGLE, THE(1956), ph; JOHNNY TROUBLE(1957), ph; SPIRIT OF ST. LOUIS, THE(1957), ph; LEFT-HANDED GUN, THE(1958), ph; WESTBOUND(1959), ph; SINS OF RACHEL CADE, THE(1960), ph; FEVER IN THE BLOOD, A(1961), ph
Silents
TEN COMMANDMENTS, THE(1923), ph

Jean Marley
WONDER MAN(1945)

John Marley
TRIBUTE(1980, Can.); KISS OF DEATH(1947); NAKED CITY, THE(1948); MOB, THE(1951); MY SIX CONVICTS(1952); JOE LOUIS STORY, THE(1953); SQUARE JUNGLE, THE(1955); TIMETABLE(1956); I WANT TO LIVE!(1958); PAY OR DIE(1960); AMERICA, AMERICA(1963); WHEELER DEALERS, THE(1963); NIGHTMARE IN THE SUN(1964); CAT BALLOU(1965); LOLLIPOP COVER, THE(1965); FACES(1968); IN ENEMY COUNTRY(1968); LOVE STORY(1970); CLAY PIGEON(1971); MAN CALLED SLEDGE, A(1971, Ital.); DEAD ARE ALIVE, THE(1972, Yugo./Ger./Ital.); DEATHDREAM(1972, Can.); GODFATHER, THE(1972); JORY(1972); BLADE(1973); FRAMED(1975); W.C. FIELDS AND ME(1976); CAR, THE(1977); GREATEST, THE(1977, U.S./Brit.); KID VENGEANCE(1977); HOOPER(1978); IT LIVES AGAIN(1978); PRIVATE FILES OF J. EDGAR HOOVER, THE(1978); AMATEUR, THE(1982); MOTHER LODE(1982); THRESHOLD(1983, Can.); UTILITIES(1983, Can.)
Misc. Talkies
FALCON'S GOLD(1982)

Peverell Marley
LADY OF CHANCE, A(1928), ph; GODLESS GIRL, THE(1929), ph; THIS MAD WORLD(1930), ph; WOMAN RACKET, THE(1930), ph; WICKED(1931), ph; SPRING SHOWER(1932, Hung.), ph; FAST WORKERS(1933), ph; BULLDOG DRUMMOND STRIKES BACK(1934), ph; GALLANT LADY(1934), ph; HOUSE OF ROTHSCHILD, THE(1934), ph; MIGHTY BARNUM, THE(1934), ph; CARDINAL RICHELIEU(1935), ph; CLIVE OF INDIA(1935), ph; FOLIES DERGERE(1935), ph; THANKS A MILLION(1935), ph; THREE MUSKETEERS, THE(1935), ph; KING OF BURLESQUE(1936), ph; ONE RAINY AFTERNOON(1936), ph; PRIVATE NUMBER(1936), ph; SING, BABY, SING(1936), ph; WINTERSET(1936), ph; TOAST OF NEW YORK, THE(1937), ph; WISE GIRL(1937), ph; WOMEN OF GLAMOUR(1937), ph; ALEXANDER'S RAGTIME BAND(1938), ph; IN OLD CHICAGO(1938), ph; SALLY, IRENE AND MARY(1938), ph; UP THE RIVER(1938), ph; DAY-TIME WIFE(1939), ph; HOTEL FOR WOMEN(1939), ph; HOUND OF THE BASKERVILLES, THE(1939), ph; THREE MUSKETEERS, THE(1939), ph; HUDSON'S BAY(1940), ph; MAN I MARRIED, THE(1940), ph; STAR DUST(1940), ph; ADAM HAD FOUR SONS(1941), ph; CHARLEY'S AUNT(1941), ph; GREAT AMERICAN BROADCAST, THE(1941), ph; MOON OVER MIAMI(1941), ph; SLEEPERS WEST(1941), ph; SWAMP WATER(1941), ph; MAGNIFICENT DOPE, THE(1942), ph; NIGHT BEFORE THE DIVORCE, THE(1942), ph; DIXIE DUGAN(1943), ph; MEANEST MAN IN THE WORLD, THE(1943), ph; FOUR JILLS IN A JEEP(1944), ph; SENSATIONS OF 1945(1944), ph; PRIDE OF THE MARINES(1945), ph; NIGHT AND DAY(1946), ph; OF HUMAN BONDAGE(1946), ph; LIFE WITH FATHER(1947), ph; TWO MRS. CARROLLS, THE(1947), ph; WHIPLASH(1948), ph; HOMICIDE(1949), ph; LOOK FOR THE SILVER LINING(1949), ph; NIGHT UNTO NIGHT(1949), ph; KISS TOMORROW GOODBYE(1950), ph; PERFECT STRANGERS(1950), ph; PRETTY BABY(1950), ph; RETURN OF THE FRONTIERSMAN(1950), ph; GROOM WORE SPURS, THE(1951), ph; CHARGE AT FEATHER RIVER, THE(1953), ph; HOUSE OF WAX(1953), ph; TEN COMMANDMENTS, THE(1956), ph
Silents
FORTY WINKS(1925), ph; NIGHT CLUB, THE(1925), ph; VOLGA BOATMAN, THE(1926), ph; DRESS PARADE(1927), ph; KING OF KINGS, THE(1927), ph; CHICAGO(1928), ph

Warren Marley
SIDELONG GLANCES OF A PIGEON KICKER, THE(1970), m

Rene Marlic
CARTOUCHE(1962, Fr./Ital.)

John Marlieb
NATIVE LAND(1942)

Carla Marlier
ZAZIE(1961, Fr.); AVENGER, THE(1962, Fr./Ital.); GIRL WITH THE GOLDEN EYES, THE(1962, Fr.); ANY NUMBER CAN WIN(1963 Fr.); MATA HARI(1965, Fr./Ital.); SPIRITS OF THE DEAD(1969, Fr./Ital.); JE T'AIME, JE T'AIME(1972, Fr./Swed.)

Billie Joe Marlin
SECOND-HAND HEARTS(1981)

Gloria Marlin
LAURA(1944)

Mary Marlind
THREE KIDS AND A QUEEN(1935), w; LITTLE MISS BIG(1946), w

Rand Marlis
SCARED TO DEATH(1981), p

Frank Marlo
RUSTLER'S ROUNDUP(1946); KNOCK ON ANY DOOR(1949)

George Marlo
Misc. Silents
FUGITIVE, THE(1916); PILLORY, THE(1916); WOMAN IN POLITICS, THE(1916); POTS AND PANS PEGGIE(1917)

Helga Marlo
FOUNTAIN OF LOVE, THE(1968, Aust.)

Mary Marlo
SECOND GREATEST SEX, THE(1955)

Steve Marlo
W.I.A.(WOUNDED IN ACTION)*1/2 (1966); SLENDER THREAD, THE(1965); SWARM, THE(1978)

Steven Marlo
BUCCANEER, THE(1958); YOUNG CAPTIVES, THE(1959); ARNOLD(1973); TERROR IN THE WAX MUSEUM(1973); WHEN TIME RAN OUT(1980)

Tony Marlo
MR. IMPERIUM(1951)
Silents
RACKET, THE(1928)

Vic Marlo
SPEED CRAZY(1959)

Charles R. Marlon
HERE COMES KELLY(1943), w

Mary Marlon [Maria Luisa Merlo]
MIGHTY URSUS(1962, Ital./Span.)

Allen Marlow
LADY IN QUESTION, THE(1940)

Anthony Marlow
PHANTOM OF THE OPERA(1943)

Armor Marlow
PHILO VANCE RETURNS(1947), set d; CANON CITY(1948), set d

Brian Marlow
COCK O' THE WALK(1930), w; HELLO SISTER(1930), w; GIRLS ABOUT TOWN(1931), w; ROAD TO RENO(1931), w; DANCERS IN THE DARK(1932), w, w; NIGHT OF JUNE 13(1932), w; BRIEF MOMENT(1933), w; CRIME OF THE CENTURY, THE(1933), w; SUPERNATURAL(1933), w; HAPPINESS AHEAD(1934), w; ACCUSING FINGER, THE(1936), w; FORGOTTEN FACES(1936), w; PREVIEW MURDER MYSTERY(1936), w; RETURN OF SOPHIE LANG, THE(1936), w; TILL WE MEET AGAIN(1936), w; MURDER GOES TO COLLEGE(1937), w; BEWARE SPOOKS(1939), w; UNMARRIED(1939), w; MANHATTAN HEARTBEAT(1940), w; JUMPING JACKS(1952), w

Derek Marlow
DISAPPEARANCE, THE(1981, Brit./Can.), w

Don Marlow
SQUAD CAR(1961)

Dwan Marlow
HONEYMOON OF TERROR(1961)

Estelle Marlow
PRIVATE BENJAMIN(1980)

Frank Marlow
ANYTHING FOR A THRILL(1937); WISTFUL WIDOW OF WAGON GAP, THE(1947); JOHNNY GUITAR(1954)

Fred Marlow
KISS IN THE DARK, A(1949); PARRISH(1961)

Hans Marlow
CRIMSON CIRCLE, THE(1930, Brit.)

Helen Marlow
Silents
ALBANY NIGHT BOAT, THE(1928)

Jean Marlow
UNSTOPPABLE MAN, THE(1961, Brit.); LITTLE ONES, THE(1965, Brit.); TAKE A GIRL LIKE YOU(1970, Brit,); LOOT(1971, Brit.)

Jo Ann Marlow
YANKEE DOODLE DANDY(1942)

John Marlow
WONDER BAR(1934)

Joyce Marlow
FACES IN THE DARK(1960, Brit.)

Judy Marlow
Misc. Talkies
SWINGING COEDS, THE(1976)

June Marlow
Silents
ALIAS THE DEACON(1928); FREE LIPS(1928)
Misc. Silents
MAN WITHOUT A CONSCIENCE, THE(1925)

Linda Marlow
AMERICANIZATION OF EMILY, THE(1964)
Misc. Talkies
BIG ZAPPER(1974)

Lucy Marlow
LUCKY ME(1954); STAR IS BORN, A(1954); BRING YOUR SMILE ALONG(1955); MY SISTER EILEEN(1955); QUEEN BEE(1955); TIGHT SPOT(1955); HE LAUGHED LAST(1956)

Mariann Marlow
LIQUID SKY(1982)

Nancy Marlow
HAVING WONDERFUL CRIME(1945); SING YOUR WAY HOME(1945); TWO O'CLOCK COURAGE(1945)

Ray Marlow
COUNTESS FROM HONG KONG, A(1967, Brit.)

Rex Marlow
DEADWOOD'76(1965)

Ric Marlow
YOU HAVE TO RUN FAST(1961); ON HER BED OF ROSES(1966)

T. Tom Marlow
MIDNIGHT COWBOY(1969)

Tony Marlow
MUMMY, THE(1932); BLACK CAT, THE(1934)

William Marlow
ZEPPELIN(1971, Brit.)

Zada Marlow
Misc. Silents
GIRL WHO DOESN'T KNOW, THE(1917)

Alona Marlowe
ARGYLE CASE, THE(1929); WAY OF ALL MEN, THE(1930)

Amor Marlowe
HOLLOW TRIUMPH(1948), set d

Anna Marlowe
MICROWAVE MASSACRE(1983)

Anthony Marlowe
FLAME OF NEW ORLEANS, THE(1941); GREAT COMMANDMENT, THE(1941); IS EVERYBODY HAPPY?(1943); GHOSTS OF BERKELEY SQUARE(1947, Brit.); GHOST SHIP(1953, Brit.); SAADIA(1953); DOCTOR IN THE HOUSE(1954, Brit.); ROOM IN THE HOUSE(1955, Brit.)

Armor Marlowe
NIGHT AND DAY(1946), set d; BIG FIX, THE(1947), set d; OUT OF THE BLUE(1947), set d; PHILO VANCE'S GAMBLE(1947), set d; PHILO VANCE'S SECRET MISSION(1947), set d; RAILROADED(1947), set d; REPEAT PERFORMANCE(1947), set d; STEPCHILD(1947), set d; T-MEN(1947), set d; BEHIND LOCKED DOORS(1948), set d; HE WALKED BY NIGHT(1948), set d; LET'S LIVE A LITTLE(1948), set d; NOOSE HANGS HIGH, THE(1948), set d; NORTHWEST STAMPEDE(1948), set d; RAW DEAL(1948), set d; SPIRITUALIST, THE(1948), set d; BLACK BOOK, THE(1949), set d; PORT OF NEW YORK(1949), set d; RED STALLION IN THE ROCKIES(1949), set d; TRAPPED(1949), set d; TULSA(1949), set d

Armor E. Marlowe
WEST POINT STORY, THE(1950), set d; ONLY THE VALIANT(1951), set d

Brian Marlowe
MY WOMAN(1933), w; SKY PARADE(1936), w; WOMAN TRAP(1936), w; SOPHIE LANG GOES WEST(1937), w; ROAD TO RENO, THE(1938), w; AMONG THE LIVING(1941), w

Charles Marlowe
WHEN KNIGHTS WERE BOLD(1942, Brit.), w

Christopher Marlowe
DOCTOR FAUSTUS(1967, Brit.), w
Silents
FAUST(1926, Ger.), w

David Marlowe
RISING OF THE MOON, THE(1957, Ireland)

Derek Marlowe
DANDY IN ASPIC, A(1968, Brit.), w

Diana Pat Marlowe
NAKED CITY, THE(1948)

Don Marlowe
CRASHING LAS VEGAS(1956); JOURNEY TO FREEDOM(1957); OKLAHOMAN, THE(1957)

Faye Marlowe
HANGOVER SQUARE(1945); JUNIOR MISS(1945); SPIDER, THE(1945); JOHNNY COMES FLYING HOME(1946); RENDEZVOUS WITH ANNIE(1946); THIEF OF VENICE, THE(1952)

Frank Marlowe
HIDE-OUT(1934); MEN OF THE NIGHT(1934); NOW I'LL TELL(1934); G-MEN(1935); GLASS KEY, THE(1935); SHE COULDN'T TAKE IT(1935); SHIPMATES FOREVER(1935); STRANDED(1935); WE'RE IN THE MONEY(1935); MURDER WITH PICTURES(1936); LIVE, LOVE AND LEARN(1937); WINGS OVER HONOLULU(1937); BRINGING UP BABY(1938); LITTLE ACCIDENT(1939); ONE HOUR TO LIVE(1939); MY FAVORITE WIFE(1940); CAUGHT IN THE DRAFT(1941); SERGEANT YORK(1941); MADAME SPY(1942); MY FAVORITE BLONDE(1942); NAZI AGENT(1942); SABOTEUR(1942); THEY ALL KISSED THE BRIDE(1942); IRISH EYES ARE SMILING(1944); MAN FROM FRISCO(1944); MURDER IN THE BLUE ROOM(1944); MY BUDDY(1944); RAINBOW ISLAND(1944); WING AND A PRAYER(1944); IDENTITY UNKNOWN(1945); IN FAST COMPANY(1946); LIVE WIRES(1946); MIGHTY MCGURK, THE(1946); NIGHT AND DAY(1946); NOTORIOUS(1946); SIOUX CITY SUE(1946); SMOOTH AS SILK(1946); BRUTE FORCE(1947); HIGH WALL, THE(1947); POSSESSED(1947); JOAN OF ARC(1948); THEY LIVE BY NIGHT(1949); WITHOUT HONOR(1949); BARRICADE(1950); IN A LONELY PLACE(1950); KISS TOMORROW GOODBYE(1950); NO MAN OF HER OWN(1950); PERFECT STRANGERS(1950); STORM WARNING(1950); TRIPLE TROUBLE(1950); CATTLE QUEEN(1951); I WAS A COMMUNIST FOR THE F.B.I.(1951); IRON MAN, THE(1951); ROADBLOCK(1951); BUSHWHACKERS, THE(1952); MY PAL GUS(1952); STEEL TOWN(1952); WINNING TEAM, THE(1952); ABBOTT AND COSTELLO GO TO MARS(1953); FRENCH LINE, THE(1954); LONG WAIT, THE(1954); AMERICANO, THE(1955); LUCY GALLANT(1955); MAN WITH THE GOLDEN ARM, THE(1955); SQUARE JUNGLE, THE(1955); HOT SHOTS(1956); CHICAGO CONFIDENTIAL(1957); GARMENT JUNGLE, THE(1957); ROCKABILLY BABY(1957); ESCAPE FROM RED ROCK(1958); LONE TEXAN(1959); NORTH BY NORTHWEST(1959)

Gene Marlowe
APACHE WOMAN(1955)

Geoff Marlowe
CHAMP, THE(1979)

Gloria Marlowe
ANYTHING CAN HAPPEN(1952)

Hugh Marlowe
BETWEEN TWO WOMEN(1937); MARRIED BEFORE BREAKFAST(1937); MARRIAGE IS A PRIVATE AFFAIR(1944); MEET ME IN ST. LOUIS(1944); MRS. PARKINGTON(1944); COME TO THE STABLE(1949); TWELVE O'CLOCK HIGH(1949); ALL ABOUT EVE(1950); NIGHT AND THE CITY(1950, Brit.); DAY THE EARTH STOOD STILL, THE(1951); MR. BELVEDERE RINGS THE BELL(1951); RAWHIDE(1951); BUGLES IN THE AFTERNOON(1952); DIPLOMATIC COURIER(1952); MONKEY BUSINESS(1952); WAIT 'TIL THE SUN SHINES, NELLIE(1952); WAY OF A GAUCHO(1952); STAND AT APACHE RIVER, THE(1953); CASANOVA'S BIG NIGHT(1954); GARDEN OF EVIL(1954); ILLEGAL(1955); BLACK WHIP, THE(1956); EARTH VS. THE FLYING SAUCERS(1956); WORLD WITHOUT END(1956); ELMER GANTRY(1960); LONG ROPE, THE(1961); BIRDMAN OF ALCATRAZ(1962); THIRTEEN FRIGHTENED GIRLS(1963); SEVEN DAYS IN MAY(1964); CASTLE OF EVIL(1967); LAST SHOT YOU HEAR, THE(1969, Brit.); VIOLENT ENEMY, THE(1969, Brit.), w

Jackie Marlowe
HEART IS A LONELY HUNTER, THE(1968)

James Marlowe
Silents
BACK HOME AND BROKE(1922)

Jerry Marlowe
FOR LOVE OR MONEY(1939); HERO FOR A DAY(1939); I STOLE A MILLION(1939); LEGION OF LOST FLYERS(1939); WHEN TOMORROW COMES(1939); HONEYMOON DEFERRED(1940); MAN FROM MONTREAL, THE(1940); BORROWED HERO(1941); OUT OF THE BLUE(1947); HOLLOW TRIUMPH(1948); NOOSE HANGS HIGH, THE(1948); ONE TOUCH OF VENUS(1948)

Jo Ann Marlowe
MILDRED PIERCE(1945); ROUGHLY SPEAKING(1945); LITTLE IODINE(1946); MAN FROM RAINBOW VALLEY, THE(1946); SCANDAL IN PARIS, A(1946); KEEPER OF THE BEES(1947); NEVER A DULL MOMENT(1950)

JoAnn Marlowe
DANGEROUS INTRUDER(1945); NIGHT AND DAY(1946)

John Marlowe
BRILLIANT MARRIAGE(1936); IT COULDN'T HAVE HAPPENED–BUT IT DID(1936); TELL NO TALES(1939); WHEN LADIES MEET(1941); I MARRIED AN ANGEL(1942); MASQUERADE IN MEXICO(1945); SILVER CHALICE, THE(1954); PATSY, THE(1964)

Jonas Marlowe
1984
CHILDREN OF THE CORN(1984)

Joyce Marlowe
INNOCENTS IN PARIS(1955, Brit.)

June Marlowe
PARDON US(1931); SLAVE GIRL(1947)
Misc. Talkies
DEVIL ON DECK(1932); RIDDLE RANCH(1936)
Silents
LOST LADY, A(1924); BELOW THE LINE(1925); DON JUAN(1926); FANGS OF JUSTICE(1926); NIGHT CRY, THE(1926); OLD SOAK, THE(1926)
Misc. Silents
FIND YOUR MAN(1924); TENTH WOMAN, THE(1924); WHEN A MAN'S A MAN(1924); CLASH OF THE WOLVES(1925); PLEASURE BUYERS, THE(1925); TRACKED IN THE SNOW COUNTRY(1925); FOURTH COMMANDMENT, THE(1927); LIFE OF RILEY, THE(1927); ON THE STROKE OF TWELVE(1927); WILD BEAUTY(1927); BRANDED MAN(1928); CODE OF THE AIR(1928); GRIP OF THE YUKON, THE(1928); THEIR HOUR(1928)

Katharine Marlowe
DOUBLE LIFE, A(1947)

Katherine Marlowe
FALL GUY(1947); ROCKETSHIP X-M(1950); PHENIX CITY STORY, THE(1955)

Kathryn Marlowe
DODSWORTH(1936)

Kathy Marlowe
ILLEGAL(1955); FIRST TRAVELING SALESLADY, THE(1956); LIEUTENANT WORE SKIRTS, THE(1956); REVOLT OF MAMIE STOVER, THE(1956); GARMENT JUNGLE, THE(1957); PAJAMA GAME, THE(1957); QUEEN OF OUTER SPACE(1958); FIVE BOLD WOMEN(1960)

Kay Marlowe
YOU CAN'T CHEAT AN HONEST MAN(1939); MY FOOLISH HEART(1949)

Linda Marlowe
IMPACT(1963, Brit.); THAT KIND OF GIRL(1963, Brit.); BECKET(1964, Brit.); PUSSYCAT ALLEY(1965, Brit.); SPACEFLIGHT IC-1(1965, Brit.); ROBBERY(1967, Brit.); MAN OUTSIDE, THE(1968, Brit.); NIGHT AFTER NIGHT AFTER NIGHT(1970, Brit.)

Maxine Marlowe
PHFFFT!(1954)

Mercedes Marlowe
MAN IN THE WATER, THE(1963)

Mia Marlowe
Misc. Talkies
ALL MEN ARE APES(1965)

Mr. Marlowe
STARS OVER BROADWAY(1935)

Nancy Marlowe
FALCON IN HOLLYWOOD, THE(1944); PAN-AMERICANA(1945); CHICAGO CONFIDENTIAL(1957)

Nora Marlowe
I'LL CRY TOMORROW(1955); AFFAIR TO REMEMBER, AN(1957); NORTH BY NORTHWEST(1959); BRASS BOTTLE, THE(1964); KITTEN WITH A WHIP(1964); THAT FUNNY FEELING(1965); HOSTAGE, THE(1966); TEXAS ACROSS THE RIVER(1966); THOMAS CROWN AFFAIR, THE(1968); GAILY, GAILY(1969); WESTWORLD(1973)

Norma Jane Marlowe
NAKED CITY, THE(1948)

Patricia Marlowe
FM(1978)

Patricial Marlowe
JOAN OF ARC(1948)

Robert Marlowe
ON THE LOOSE(1951)

S. Victoria Marlowe
NIGHT THE LIGHTS WENT OUT IN GEORGIA, THE(1981)

Sally Marlowe
TRAPEZE(1956)

Sally-Ann Marlowe
Misc. Talkies
BLINKER'S SPY-SPOTTER(1971)

Scott Marlowe
GABY(1956); SCARLET HOUR, THE(1956); YOUNG GUNS, THE(1956); MEN IN WAR(1957); RESTLESS BREED, THE(1957); COOL AND THE CRAZY, THE(1958); YOUNG AND WILD(1958); RIOT IN JUVENILE PRISON(1959); SUBTERRANEANS, THE(1960); COLD WIND IN AUGUST(1961); LONNIE(1963); JOURNEY INTO FEAR(1976, Can)

William Marlowe
TUNES OF GLORY(1960, Brit.); PLACE TO GO, A(1964, Brit.); HEROES OF TELEMARK, THE(1965, Brit.); UNCLE, THE(1966, Brit.); ROBBERY(1967, Brit.); AMSTERDAM AFFAIR, THE(1968 Brit.); ROYAL HUNT OF THE SUN, THE(1969, Brit.); WHERE'S JACK?(1969, Brit.)

Florence Marly
CAFE DE PARIS(1938, Fr.); ALIBI, THE(1939, Fr.); DAMNED, THE(1948, Fr.); KRAKATIT(1948, Czech.); SEALED VERDICT(1948); TOKYO JOE(1949); TOKYO FILE 212(1951); GOBS AND GALS(1952); UNDERSEA GIRL(1957); QUEEN OF BLOOD(1966); GAMES(1967); DOCTOR DEATH: SEEKER OF SOULS(1973)

Guy Marly
LA FEMME INFIDELE(1969, Fr./Ital.); THIS MAN MUST DIE(1970, Fr./Ital.); MARCH OR DIE(1977, Brit.)

Marmalade
LIFE AND TIMES OF JUDGE ROY BEAN, THE(1972), m/1

Heinrich Marmann
SISTERS, OR THE BALANCE OF HAPPINESS(1982, Ger.)

Roy Marmara
PULP(1972, Brit.)

Lea Marmer
WALK THE ANGRY BEACH(1961); WHAT AM I BID?(1967); EASY RIDER(1969); WAR BETWEEN MEN AND WOMEN, THE(1972)

Steve Marmer
ON THE RIGHT TRACK(1981)

Joe Marmo
SCARFACE(1983)

Edward Marmolejo
ARABIAN NIGHTS(1942)
Patricia Marmont
LOYAL HEART(1946, Brit.); CROWDED DAY, THE(1954, Brit.); FRONT PAGE
STORY(1954, Brit.); NO TIME FOR TEARS(1957, Brit.); SHE PLAYED WITH FI-
RE(1957, Brit.); SUDDENLY, LAST SUMMER(1959, Brit.); MARY HAD A LITT-
LE(1961, Brit.)
Percy Marmont
CROSS ROADS(1930, Brit.); SQUEAKER, THE(1930, Brit.); YELLOW STOCK-
INGS(1930, Brit.); WRITTEN LAW, THE(1931, Brit.); BLIND SPOT(1932, Brit.); RICH
AND STRANGE(1932, Brit.); SAY IT WITH MUSIC(1932, Brit.); HER IMAGINARY
LOVER(1933, Brit.); VANITY(1935); WHITE LILAC(1935, Brit.); CAPTAIN'S TABLE,
THE(1936, Brit.), a, d; DAVID LIVINGSTONE(1936, Brit.); SECRET AGENT,
THE(1936, Brit.); ACTION FOR SLANDER(1937, Brit.); PEARLS OF THE
CROWN(1938, Fr.); YOUNG AND INNOCENT(1938, Brit.); CONQUEST OF THE
AIR(1940); COURAGEOUS MR. PENN, THE(1941, Brit.); THOSE KIDS FROM
TOWN(1942, Brit.); I'LL WALK BESIDE YOU(1943, Brit.); LOYAL HEART(1946, Brit.);
SWISS HONEYMOON(1947, Brit.); NO ORCHIDS FOR MISS BLANDISH(1948, Brit.);
DARK SECRET(1949, Brit.); GAMBLER AND THE LADY, THE(1952, Brit.); FOUR
SIDED TRIANGLE(1953, Brit.); FOOTSTEPS IN THE FOG(1955, Brit.); LOVERS,
HAPPY LOVERS!(1955, Brit.); LISBON(1956); HOSTILE WITNESS(1968, Brit.)
Silents
ROSE OF THE WORLD(1918); CLIMBERS, THE(1919); AWAY GOES PRUDEN-
CE(1920); BRANDED WOMAN, THE(1920); LOVE'S PENALTY(1921); WIFE AGAINST
WIFE(1921); ENEMY SEX, THE(1924); K-THE UNKNOWN(1924); LEGEND OF
HOLLYWOOD, THE(1924); JUST A WOMAN(1925); LORD JIM(1925); ALOMA OF
THE SOUTH SEAS(1926); LADY OF THE LAKE, THE(1928, Brit.)
Misc. Silents
IN THE HOLLOW OF HER HAND(1918); TURN OF THE WHEEL, THE(1918);
THREE MEN AND A GIRL(1919); VENGEANCE OF DURAND, THE(1919); WIN-
CHESTER WOMAN, THE(1919); DEAD MEN TELL NO TALES(1920); SLAVES OF
PRIDE(1920); SPORTING DUCHESS, THE(1920); WHAT'S YOUR REPUTATION
WORTH?(1921); FIRST WOMAN, THE(1922); MARRIED PEOPLE(1922); BROADWAY
BROKE(1923); IF WINTER COMES(1923); LIGHT THAT FAILED, THE(1923); MAN
LIFE PASSED BY, THE(1923); MIDNIGHT ALARM, THE(1923); YOU CAN'T GET
AWAY WITH IT(1923); BROKEN LAWS(1924); CLEAN HEART, THE(1924); IDLE
TONGUES(1924); MARRIAGE CHEAT, THE(1924); SHOOTING OF DAN MCGREW,
THE(1924); WHEN A GIRL LOVES(1924); WINNING A CONTINENT(1924); DADDY'S
GONE A-HUNTING(1925); FINE CLOTHES(1925); INFATUATION(1925); SHINING
ADVENTURE, THE(1925); STREET OF FORGOTTEN MEN, THE(1925); WOMAN'S
FAITH, A(1925); MANTRAP(1926); MIRACLE OF LIFE, THE(1926); SAN FRANCISCO
NIGHTS(1928); SIR OR MADAM(1928, Brit.); STRONGER WILL, THE(1928); WARN-
ING, THE(1928, Brit.); YELLOW STOCKINGS(1928, Brit.); SILVER KING, THE(1929,
Brit.)
Larry Marmorstein
PRETTY MAIDS ALL IN A ROW(1971)
Mal Marmorstein
S(1974), w
Malcolm Marmorstein
MARY, MARY, BLOODY MARY(1975, U.S./Mex.), w; WHIFFS(1975), w; PETE'S
DRAGON(1977), w; RETURN FROM WITCH MOUNTAIN(1978), w
Patricia Marmount
HELEN OF TROY(1956, Ital)
Lorens Marmstedt
GYPSY FURY(1950, Fr.), p; DEVIL'S WANTON, THE(1962, Swed.), p; NIGHT IS MY
FUTURE(1962, Swed.), p; DOLL, THE(1964, Swed.), p; GORILLA(1964, Swed.), p;
SWEDISH WEDDING NIGHT(1965, Swed.), p; WOMAN OF DARKNESS(1968, Swed.),
p
Jacland Marmur
RETURN FROM THE SEA(1954), w
E. Marn
GUNMEN OF THE RIO GRANDE(1965, Fr./Ital./Span.)
Marcelle Marnay
UNCIVILISED(1937, Aus.)
Richard Marner
AFRICAN QUEEN, THE(1951, U.S./Brit.); ISLAND RESCUE(1952, Brit.); MR. POTTS
GOES TO MOSCOW(1953, Brit.); NORMAN CONQUEST(1953, Brit.); MASTER PLAN,
THE(1955, Brit.); RACE FOR LIFE, A(1955, Brit.); OH ROSALINDA(1956, Brit.);
MIRACLE IN SOHO(1957, Brit.); DESERT ATTACK(1958, Brit.); ONE THAT GOT
AWAY, THE(1958, Brit.); SAFECRACKER, THE(1958, Brit.); CIRCLE OF DECEP-
TON(1961, Brit.); PASSWORD IS COURAGE, THE(1962, Brit.); MOUSE ON THE
MOON, THE(1963, Brit.); RING OF SPIES(1964, Brit.); SPY WHO CAME IN FROM THE
COLD, THE(1965, Brit.); WHERE THE SPIES ARE(1965, Brit.); ISADORA(1968, Brit.);
GIRL FROM PETROVKA, THE(1974); INTERNECINE PROJECT, THE(1974, Brit.);
BOYS FROM BRAZIL, THE(1978); NUTCRACKER(1982, Brit.)
Elizabeth Marner-Brooks
I DRINK YOUR BLOOD(1971)
Richard Marnery
LILLI MARLENE(1951, Brit.)
Marcelle Marney
LOVERS AND LUGGERS(1938, Aus.); VENGEANCE OF THE DEEP(1940, Aus.)
Erwin Marno
INDECENT(1962, Ger.), p, w
Marc Marno
MAJORITY OF ONE, A(1961); DIAMOND HEAD(1962)
Pierre Marodon
Misc. Silents
LE DIAMANT VERT(1917, Fr.), d; QUI A TUE(1919, Fr.), d; LA FEE DES NEI-
GES(1920, Fr.), d; LA FEMME AUX DEUX VISAGES(1920, Fr.), d; LE TOCSIN(1920,
Fr.), d; LES FEMMES DES AUTRES(1920, Fr.), d; LES MORTS QUI PARLENT(1920,
Fr.), d; LES TROIS GANTS DE LA DAMES EN NOIR(1920, Fr.), d; BURIDAN, LE
HEROS DE LA TOUR DE NESLE(1924, Fr.), d; LES VOLEURS DE GLOIRE(1926,
Fr.), d
Bob Maroff
ANNIE HALL(1977); SHORT EYES(1977); I WANNA HOLD YOUR HAND(1978);
GOING IN STYLE(1979); STARDUST MEMORIES(1980); PATERNITY(1981)
1984
RACING WITH THE MOON(1984)

Mike Maroff
CATTLE ANNIE AND LITTLE BRITCHES(1981)
Robert Maroff
TAXI DRIVER(1976)
John Marolakos
TEMPEST(1982)
Daniel Marolen
DINGAKA(1965, South Africa)
Annie Marolt
TEMPTATION(1962, Fr.), cos
Alfred Maron
HELL, HEAVEN OR HOBOKEN(1958, Brit.); HARASSED HERO, THE(1954, Brit.);
MAN IN THE ROAD, THE(1957, Brit.); CLUE OF THE TWISTED CANDLE(1968, Brit.);
FIDDLER ON THE ROOF(1971)
Francisco Maron
DOWN TO THE SEA(1936)
Franz Maron
WHY DOES HERR R. RUN AMOK?(1977, Ger.)
Kelli Maroney
FAST TIMES AT RIDGEMONT HIGH(1982)
1984
NIGHT OF THE COMET(1984); SLAYGROUND(1984, Brit.)
Madeleine Maroou
MEDIUM COOL(1969)
Basil Maros
ATLAS(1960), ph
Mircea Marosin
HAMLET(1976, Brit.), cos
Joe Maross
RUN SILENT, RUN DEEP(1958); ELMER GANTRY(1960); ZIGZAG(1970); SOME-
TIMES A GREAT NOTION(1971); SALZBURG CONNECTION, THE(1972); SIXTH
AND MAIN(1977); RICH AND FAMOUS(1981)
Irene Marot
1984
LITTLE DRUMMER GIRL, THE(1984)
Kathy Marothy
FIVE DAYS ONE SUMMER(1982)
Franco Marotta
BINGO BONGO(1983, Ital.), w
Giuseppe Marotta
GOLD OF NAPLES(1957, Ital.), w; NEOPOLITAN CAROUSEL(1961, Ital.), w
Carl Marotte
GAS(1981, Can.); MY BLOODY VALENTINE(1981, Can.); PICK-UP SUMMER(1981)
Misc. Talkies
HARD FEELINGS(1981)
Leonida Maroulis
STRANGE DECEPTION(1953, Ital.), art d
Barney Marovitz
WHO SAYS I CAN'T RIDE A RAINBOW!(1971)
Lucian Maroweck
NEW MEXICO(1951), m
Fred Marpeaux
PLEASURES AND VICES(1962, Fr.), art d
Jim Marples
MILKY WAY, THE(1936)
Michele Marquais
RISE OF LOUIS XIV, THE(1970, Fr.)
Carol Marquand
IT ONLY HAPPENS TO OTHERS(1971, Fr./Ital.), ed
Christian Marquand
LUCRECE BORGIA(1953, Ital./Fr.); AND GOD CREATED WOMAN(1957, Fr.);
ATTILA(1958, Ital.); LOVE AT NIGHT(1961, Fr.); CRIME DOES NOT PAY(1962, Fr.);
END OF DESIRE(1962 Fr./Ital.); I SPIT ON YOUR GRAVE(1962, Fr.); LONGEST DAY,
THE(1962); TALES OF PARIS(1962, Fr./Ital.); TEMPTATION(1962, Fr.); PLAYTI-
ME(1963, Fr.); BEHOLD A PALE HORSE(1964); LA BONNE SOUPE(1964, Fr./Ital.); OF
FLESH AND BLOOD(1964, Fr./Ital.), d, w; FLIGHT OF THE PHOENIX, THE(1965);
LORD JIM(1965, Brit.); CORRUPT ONES, THE(1967, Ger.); CANDY(1968, Ital./Fr.), d;
SENSO(1968, Ital.); WHO'S GOT THE BLACK BOX?(1970, Fr./Gr./Ital.); OTHER SIDE
OF MIDNIGHT, THE(1977)
J. P. Marquand
MR. MOTO TAKES A CHANCE(1938), w; MR. MOTO TAKES A VACATION(1938),
w; MR. MOTO IN DANGER ISLAND(1939), w
John Marquand
ROCKY HORROR PICTURE SHOW, THE(1975, Brit.)
John P. Marquand
THANK YOU, MR. MOTO(1937), w; THINK FAST, MR. MOTO(1937), w; MR.
MOTO'S GAMBLE(1938), w; H.M. PULHAM, ESQ.(1941), w; LATE GEORGE APLEY,
THE(1947), w; B. F.'S DAUGHTER(1948), w; STOPOVER TOKYO(1957), w; TOP
SECRET AFFAIR(1957), w; RETURN OF MR. MOTO, THE(1965, Brit.), w
John Phillips Marquand
Silents
RIGHT THAT FAILED, THE(1922), w
Nadine Marquand
GAME FOR SIX LOVERS, A(1962, Fr.), ed; FRENCH GAME, THE(1963, Fr.), ed; LE
PETIT SOLDAT(1965, Fr.), ed
Richard Marquand
LEGACY, THE(1979, Brit.), d; EYE OF THE NEEDLE(1981), d; RETURN OF THE
JEDI(1983), d
1984
UNTIL SEPTEMBER(1984), d
Serge Marquand
BLOOD AND ROSES(1961, Fr./Ital.); TALES OF PARIS(1962, Fr./Ital.); PLEASE,
NOT NOW!(1963, Fr./Ital.); OF FLESH AND BLOOD(1964, Fr./Ital.); VICE AND
VIRTUE(1965, Fr./Ital.); DROP THEM OR I'LL SHOOT(1969, Fr./Ger./Span.); SONS
OF SATAN(1969, Ital./Fr./Ger.); SPIRITS OF THE DEAD(1969, Fr./Ital.); SOPHIE'S
WAYS(1970, Fr.); IT ONLY HAPPENS TO OTHERS(1971, Fr./Ital.); CARAVAN TO
VACCARES(1974, Brit./Fr); BIG RED ONE, THE(1980); QUARTET(1981, Brit./Fr.)

Tina Marquand
MODESTY BLAISE(1966, Brit.); TEXAS ACROSS THE RIVER(1966); GAME IS OVER, THE(1967, Fr.)
Christian Marquant
DOCTORS, THE(1956, Fr.)
Brick Marquard
THIS IS NOT A TEST(1962), ph; DESTINATION INNER SPACE(1966), ph; DON'T WORRY, WE'LL THINK OF A TITLE(1966), ph; CASTLE OF EVIL(1967), ph; DAYTON'S DEVILS(1968), ph; WHERE DOES IT HURT?(1972), ph; ACT OF VENGEANCE(1974), ph; FOXY DROWN(1974), ph
Carl F. Marquard
PICKUP ON 101(1972), ph
Kurt Marquardt
DECISION BEFORE DAWN(1951)
Paul Marquardt
FAREWELL TO ARMS, A(1932), m; SWEETHEARTS(1938)
Sigrid Marquardt
HIPPODROME(1961, Aust./Ger.)
Tim Marquart
NIGHTHAWKS(1981)
Gilbert Marques
SALOME(1953)
Gilberto Marques
GIVEN WORD, THE(1964, Braz.)
Maria Elena Marques
PEARL, THE(1948, U.S./Mex.); ACROSS THE WIDE MISSOURI(1951); TOM THUMB(1967, Mex.)
Marie Elena Marques
AMBUSH AT TOMAHAWK GAP(1953)
Henri Marquet
JOUR DE FETE(1952, Fr.), w; MR. HULOT'S HOLIDAY(1954, Fr.), w
Maite Marquet
1984
SUGAR CANE ALLEY(1984, Fr.)
Marie Marquet
ROYAL AFFAIRS IN VERSAILLES(1957, Fr.)
Mary Marquet
DOCTORS, THE(1956, Fr.); LANDRU(1963, Fr./Ital); LA VIE DE CHATEAU(1967, Fr.); MARRIAGE CAME TUMBLING DOWN, THE(1968, Fr.); DON'T LOOK NOW(1969, Brit./Fr.)
Desmond Marquette
FRECKLES(1935), ed; SEVEN KEYS TO BALDPATE(1935), ed; LOVE ON A BET(1936), ed; NIGHT WAITRESS(1936), ed; WITHOUT ORDERS(1936), ed; CHINA PASSAGE(1937), ed; HITTING A NEW HIGH(1937), ed; MUSIC FOR MADAME(1937), ed; THERE GOES MY GIRL(1937), ed; THEY WANTED TO MARRY(1937), ed; TOO MANY WIVES(1937), ed; BOY SLAVES(1938), ed; DOUBLE DANGER(1938), ed; FUGITIVES FOR A NIGHT(1938), ed; GO CHASE YOURSELF(1938), ed; TARNISHED ANGEL(1938), ed; ALMOST A GENTLEMAN(1939), ed; DAY THE BOOKIES WEPT, THE(1939), ed; GIRL AND THE GAMBLER, THE(1939), ed; GIRL FROM MEXICO, THE(1939), ed; MEXICAN SPITFIRE(1939), ed; LET'S MAKE MUSIC(1940), ed; MEXICAN SPITFIRE OUT WEST(1940), ed; MILLIONAIRE PLAYBOY(1940), ed; POP ALWAYS PAYS(1940), ed; SAINT TAKES OVER, THE(1940), ed; SUED FOR LIBEL(1940), ed; SCATTERGOOD PULLS THE STRINGS(1941), ed; THEY MET IN ARGENTINA(1941), ed; WEEKEND FOR THREE(1941), ed; HERE WE GO AGAIN(1942), ed; MY FAVORITE SPY(1942), ed; VALLEY OF THE SUN(1942), ed; WILD HORSE MESA(1947), ed; ARIZONA RANGER, THE(1948), ed; GUNS OF HATE(1948), ed; WESTERN HERITAGE(1948), ed; ARMORED CAR ROBBERY(1950), ed; BORDER TREASURE(1950), ed; BUNCO SQUAD(1950), ed; LAW OF THE BADLANDS(1950), ed; RIO GRANDE PATROL(1950), ed; BEST OF THE BADMEN(1951), ed; ON THE LOOSE(1951), ed; SADDLE LEGION(1951), ed
Jack Marquette
BUCKET OF BLOOD, A(1959), ph; LAST WOMAN ON EARTH, THE(1960), ph; VARAN THE UNBELIEVABLE(1962, U.S./Jap.), ph; YOUNG SWINGERS, THE(1963), ph; WILD ON THE BEACH(1965), ph; MORE DEAD THAN ALIVE(1968), ph
Jacques Marquette
TROUBLE WITH GIRLS(AND HOW TO GET INTO IT), THE*1/2 (1969), ph; TEENAGE THUNDER(1957), p, ph; BRAIN FROM THE PLANET AROUS, THE(1958), p, ph; TEENAGE MONSTER(1958), p&d; BATTLE OF BLOOD ISLAND(1960), ph; CREATURE FROM THE HAUNTED SEA(1961), ph; FLIGHT OF THE LOST BALLOON(1961), ph; TRAUMA(1962), ph; STRANGLER, THE(1964), ph; WAR IS HELL(1964), ph; ARIZONA RAIDERS(1965), ph; WINTER A GO-GO(1965), ph; FRANKIE AND JOHNNY(1966), ph; 40 GUNS TO APACHE PASS(1967), ph; WICKED DREAMS OF PAULA SCHULTZ, THE(1968), ph; ONCE YOU KISS A STRANGER(1969), ph; CHRISTINE JORGENSEN STORY, THE(1970), ph; FUZZ(1972), ph; GATLING GUN, THE(1972), ph; RETURN TO MACON COUNTY(1975), ph; BURNT OFFERINGS(1976), ph
Jacques R. Marquette
ATTACK OF THE 50 FOOT WOMAN(1958), ph
Susy Marquette
PURPLE GANG, THE(1960)
Bill Marquez
STANLEY(1973)
Evaristo Marquez
BURN(1970)
Gabriel Garcia Marquez
1984
ERENDIRA(1984, Mex./Fr./Ger.), w
Gilberto Marquez
WILD PACK, THE(1972), makeup
Luz Marquez
TEXICAN, THE(1966, U.S./Span.); SAUL AND DAVID(1968, Ital./Span.)
Ricardo Marquez
ABSENCE OF MALICE(1981)
Ruth Marquez
COOL AND THE CRAZY, THE(1958)
William Marquez
DEAL OF THE CENTURY(1983)

1984
BEST DEFENSE(1984); CLOAK AND DAGGER(1984)
Luis Marquina
GIRL FROM VALLADOLIO(1958, Span.), w
Andre Marquis
PROUD AND THE DAMNED, THE(1972)
Misc. Talkies
PACO(1976)
Arnold Marquis
KAMIKAZE '89(1983, Ger.)
Dixie Marquis
DETECTIVE, THE(1968)
Don Marquis
SKIPPY(1931), w; GOOD OLD SOAR, THE(1937), w; SHINBONE ALLEY(1971), w
Silents
OLD SOAK, THE(1926), w
Misc. Silents
BLOOD TEST(1923), d
Eric Marquis
SHAMUS(1959, Brit.), d&w
Joseph Marquis
Silents
RIGHT WAY, THE(1921); ARE CHILDREN TO BLAME?(1922)
Kathy Marquis
FLASH GORDON(1980)
Margareet Marquis
STRIKE UP THE BAND(1940)
Margaret Marquis
PENROD AND SAM(1931); EIGHT GIRLS IN A BOAT(1934); LAST OF THE WARRENS, THE(1936); LOVE ON THE RUN(1936); FAMILY AFFAIR, A(1937); CASSIDY OF BAR 20(1938); MY OLD KENTUCKY HOME(1938); GOOD MORNING, JUDGE(1943)
Misc. Talkies
BRAND OF THE OUTLAWS(1936)
Max Marquis
STRONGROOM(1962, Brit.), w
Robert Marquis
CRAZY QUILT, THE(1966)
Rosalind Marquis
BULLETS OR BALLOTS(1936); GOLD DIGGERS OF 1937(1936); STAGE STRUCK(1936); MARKED WOMAN(1937); TALENT SCOUT(1937); THAT CERTAIN WOMAN(1937)
Suzy Marquis
HEAVEN IS ROUND THE CORNER(1944, Brit.)
The Marquis Family
TOBY TYLER(1960)
Marquis of Ely
EVERYTHING IN LIFE(1936, Brit.), p
Marquis the Chimpanzee
WILLIAM COMES TO TOWN(1948, Brit.)
Marquis Trio
COME DANCE WITH ME(1950, Brit.)
"Marquis"
KING OF THE WILD HORSES, THE(1934)
Alice Marr
ST. LOUIS KID, THE(1934)
Bill Marr
NEXT OF KIN(1983, Aus.)
Dick Marr
JULIA(1977)
Eddie Marr
DANGEROUS TO KNOW(1938); SPAWN OF THE NORTH(1938); MR. MOTO IN DANGER ISLAND(1939); SUDDEN MONEY(1939); TORCHY PLAYS WITH DYNAMITE(1939); EARL OF CHICAGO, THE(1940); HOUSE ACROSS THE BAY, THE(1940); JOHNNY APOLLO(1940); PAROLE FIXER(1940); YOUTH WILL BE SERVED(1940); GLASS KEY, THE(1942); HI DIDDLE DIDDLE(1943); ONE DANGEROUS NIGHT(1943); HOLLYWOOD CANTEEN(1944); CIRCUMSTANTIAL EVIDENCE(1945); RHAPSODY IN BLUE(1945); TELL IT TO A STAR(1945); I LOVE TROUBLE(1947); IT HAPPENED ON 5TH AVENUE(1947); DAMNED DON'T CRY, THE(1950); CLOSE TO MY HEART(1951); ON MOONLIGHT BAY(1951); CONFIDENCE GIRL(1952); STEEL TRAP, THE(1952); DANCE WITH ME, HENRY(1956); I WAS A TEENAGE WEREWOLF(1957); HOW TO MAKE A MONSTER(1958); ROUSTABOUT(1964)
Edward Marr
FORTY NAUGHTY GIRLS(1937); LAST GANGSTER, THE(1937); CITY GIRL(1938); MR. MOTO'S GAMBLE(1938); ROAD DEMON(1938); SKY GIANT(1938); TIME OUT FOR MURDER(1938); DISBARRED(1939); GRAND JURY SECRETS(1939); OUR NEIGHBORS-THE CARTERS(1939); CHARLIE CHAN AT THE WAX MUSEUM(1940); CITY OF CHANCE(1940); SCANDAL SHEET(1940); LUCKY LEGS(1942); DEADLINE FOR MURDER(1946); CLOWN, THE(1953); 20,000 LEAGUES UNDER THE SEA(1954); NIGHT HOLDS TERROR, THE(1955)
Edward [Eddie] Marr
KING OF ALCATRAZ(1938); KING OF CHINATOWN(1939)
Edward M. Marr
STAR SPANGLED RHYTHM(1942)
Gordon Marr
Silents
ISLAND OF INTRIGUE, THE(1919)
Hans Marr
Misc. Silents
MOVING IMAGE, THE(1920, Ger.)
Joe Marr
PORTLAND EXPOSE(1957); RISE AND FALL OF LEGS DIAMOND, THE(1960)
Joseph Marr
MY OWN TRUE LOVE(1948); ENSIGN PULVER(1964)
Oceana Marr
MAN WITH TWO BRAINS, THE(1983)
1984
SWING SHIFT(1984)

Sadja Marr
DRIFTER, THE(1966)
Sally Marr
EVERY LITTLE CROOK AND NANNY(1972)
Sally K. Marr
FIRE SALE(1977); HOUSE CALLS(1978); CHEECH AND CHONG'S NICE DREAMS(1981); DEVIL AND MAX DEVLIN, THE(1981)
Irene Marra
BOTTOMS UP(1934), ed
Luciano Della Marra
AIDA(1954, Ital.)
Luigi Marra
BEN HUR(1959)
Rosana Marra
DESIRE, THE INTERIOR LIFE(1980, Ital./Ger.)
Sheila Marra
TAPS(1981)
Mike Marracino
THERE'S ALWAYS VANILLA(1972), a, m
Beatrice Marraden
Silents
SHIPS THAT PASS IN THE NIGHT(1921, Brit.), w
Alberto Marrama
FIST IN HIS POCKET(1968, Ital.), ph
Franco Marras
PLUCKED(1969, Fr./Ital.), p
Fred Marratto
NARCOTICS STORY, THE(1958)
Suzanne Marre
TOUCH OF HER FLESH, THE(1967)
Dave Marrell
Misc. Silents
TRACY THE OUTLAW(1928)
Marta Marrero
1984
BREAKIN' 2: ELECTRIC BOOGALOO(1984)
Sonia Marrero
CHIVATO(1961); REBELLION IN CUBA(1961)
Stephanie Marrian
HISTORY OF THE WORLD, PART 1(1981)
J.J. Marric [John Creasey]
GIDEON OF SCOTLAND YARD(1959, Brit.), w
George Moor Marriett
ACCUSED(1936, Brit.)
Tony Marrill
MY FAVORITE SPY(1942)
Kim Marrimer
1984
IRRECONCILABLE DIFFERENCES(1984)
Gene Marrin
TEENAGE GANG DEBS(1966)
John Marriner
JAVA HEAD(1935, Brit.)
Kim Marriner
1984
IRRECONCILABLE DIFFERENCES(1984); MISSING IN ACTION(1984)
Neville Marriner
1984
AMADEUS(1984), md
Sadie Marriner
1984
VIGIL(1984, New Zealand)
Gitt Marrini
TWO OR THREE THINGS I KNOW ABOUT HER(1970, Fr.), cos
Charles Marriot
Silents
IT'S NO LAUGHING MATTER(1915); TONGUES OF MEN, THE(1916)
John Marriot
DEAR, DEAD DELILAH(1972)
Moore Marriot
Silents
AFRAID OF LOVE(1925, Brit.)
Robert Marriot
ROOGIE'S BUMP(1954)
Sandee Marriot
HILDA CRANE(1956)
Stephen Marriot
BE MY GUEST(1965, Brit.)
Misc. Talkies
NIGHT CARGOES(1963)
Violet Marriot
Silents
ASTHORE(1917, Brit.)
Elsie Marriot-Watson
Silents
PREHISTORIC MAN, THE(1924, Brit.)
Anne-Marie Marriott
MISSIONARY, THE(1982)
Anthony Marriott
SEASIDE SWINGERS(1965, Brit.), w; DEADLY BEES,THE(1967, Brit.), w; NO SEX PLEASE-WE'RE BRITISH(1979, Brit.), w
Brett Marriott
Misc. Talkies
SINS OF RACHEL, THE(1975)
Charles Marriott
Silents
FALSE COLORS(1914)
Misc. Silents
BETTY AND THE BUCCANEERS(1917)

Craig Marriott
GOODBYE MR. CHIPS(1969, U.S./Brit.); MELODY(1971, Brit.)
Crittenden Marriott
ISLE OF LOST SHIPS(1929), w
Silents
ISLE OF LOST SHIPS, THE(1923), w
George Moore Marriott
IT HAPPENED ONE SUNDAY(1944, Brit.)
Jack Marriott
GAME OF CHANCE, A(1932, Brit.); THOROUGHBRED(1932, Brit.)
John Marriott
LITTLE FOXES, THE(1941); JOE LOUIS STORY, THE(1953); COOL WORLD, THE(1963); BLACK LIKE ME(1964); BADGE 373(1973); DOG DAY AFTERNOON(1975)
Moore Marriott
VICTORIA THE GREAT(1937, Brit.); CHARLEY'S(BIG-HEARTED) AUNT*1/2(1940); FLYING SCOTSMAN, THE(1929, Brit.); KITTY(1929, Brit.); LADY FROM THE SEA, THE(1929, Brit.); KISSING CUP'S RACE(1930, Brit.); LYONS MAIL, THE(1931, Brit.); UP FOR THE CUP(1931, Brit.); CROOKED LADY, THE(1932, Brit.); DANCE PRETTY LADY(1932, Brit.); NINE TILL SIX(1932, Brit.); WATER GYPSIES, THE(1932, Brit.); WONDERFUL STORY, THE(1932, Brit.); CRIME AT BLOSSOMS, THE(1933, Brit.); HAWLEY'S OF HIGH STREET(1933, Brit.); HOUSE OF TRENT, THE(1933, Brit.); LOVE'S OLD SWEET SONG(1933, Brit.); MAN WHO WON, THE(1933, Brit.); MONEY FOR SPEED(1933, Brit.); POLITICAL PARTY, A(1933, Brit.); FACES(1934, Brit.); FEATHERED SERPENT, THE(1934, Brit.); GIRLS PLEASE!(1934, Brit.); SCOOP, THE(1934, Brit.); DANDY DICK(1935, Brit.); DRAKE THE PIRATE(1935, Brit.); MAN WITHOUT A FACE, THE(1935, Brit.); NELL GWYN(1935, Brit.); TURN OF THE TIDE(1935, Brit.); GAY OLD DOG(1936, Brit.); LUCK OF THE TURF(1936, Brit.); STRANGE CARGO(1936, Brit.); WEDNESDAY'S LUCK(1936, Brit.); FATAL HOUR, THE(1937, Brit.); FEATHER YOUR NEST(1937, Brit.); FIFTY-SHILLING BOXER(1937, Brit.); INTIMATE RELATIONS(1937, Brit.); NIGHT RIDE(1937, Brit.); OH, MR. PORTER!(1937, Brit.); ROMANCE AND RICHES(1937, Brit.); TALK OF THE DEVIL(1937, Brit.); WINDBAG THE SAILOR(1937, Brit.); OLD BONES OF THE RIVER(1938, Brit.); TO THE VICTOR(1938, Brit.); ASK A POLICEMAN(1939, Brit.); CHEER BOYS CHEER(1939, Brit.); FROZEN LIMITS, THE(1939, Brit.); WHERE'S THAT FIRE?(1939, Brit.); BAND WAGGON(1940, Brit.); GASBAGS(1940, Brit.); GIRL MUST LIVE, A(1941, Brit.); HI, GANG!(1941, Brit.); I THANK YOU(1941, Brit.); BACK ROOM BOY(1942, Brit.); WHEN KNIGHTS WERE BOLD(1942, Brit.); MILLIONS LIKE US(1943, Brit.); DON'T TAKE IT TO HEART(1944, Brit.); TIME FLIES(1944, Brit.); I'LL BE YOUR SWEETHEART(1945, Brit.); PLACE OF ONE'S OWN, A(1945, Brit.); GREEN FOR DANGER(1946, Brit.); GREEN FINGERS(1947); HILLS OF DONEGAL, THE(1947, Brit.); ROOT OF ALL EVIL, THE(1947, Brit.); AGITATOR, THE(1949); HIGH JINKS IN SOCIETY(1949, Brit.); HISTORY OF MR. POLLY, THE(1949, Brit.)
Silents
MARY LATIMER, NUN(1920, Brit.); FOUR MEN IN A VAN(1921, Brit.); HEAD OF THE FAMILY, THE(1922, Brit.); MONKEY'S PAW, THE(1923, Brit.); NOT FOR SALE(1924, Brit.); KING OF THE CASTLE(1925, Brit.); QUALIFIED ADVENTURER, THE(1925, Brit.); EVERY MOTHER'S SON(1926, Brit.); HUNTINGTOWER(1927, Brit.); PASSION ISLAND(1927, Brit.); BARNES MURDER CASE, THE(1930, Brit.)
Misc. Silents
BY THE SHORTEST OF HEADS(1915, Brit.); SECOND TO NONE(1926, Brit.); CARRY ON!(1927, Brit.); SWEENEY TODD(1928, Brit.); TONI(1928, Brit.); VICTORY(1928, Brit.)
Ronald Marriott
TEXAN MEETS CALAMITY JANE, THE(1950)
Steven Marriott
SING AND SWING(1964, Brit.)
Sylvia Marriott
IT'S NOT CRICKET(1937, Brit.); CRIMES AT THE DARK HOUSE(1940, Brit.); FACE BEHIND THE SCAR(1940, Brit.); I'LL WALK BESIDE YOU(1943, Brit.); ONE HUNDRED AND ONE DALMATIANS(1961); HAND OF NIGHT, THE(1968, Brit.); TWO ENGLISH GIRLS(1972, Fr.); STORY OF ADELE H., THE(1975, Fr.); CLASS OF MISS MAC MICHAEL, THE(1978, Brit./U.S.); NEVER SAY NEVER AGAIN(1983)
Thomas Marriott
Silents
SKIPPER'S WOOING, THE(1922, Brit.)
Will Marriott
FINAL RECKONING, THE(1932, Brit.)
Jane Marrison
Misc. Talkies
TWO WORLDS OF ANGELITA, THE(1982), d
Rene Marrison
RICH AND STRANGE(1932, Brit.), ed
Gino Marrocco
1984
POLICE ACADEMY(1984)
Paulette Marron
PUTNEY SWOPE(1969)
Mark Marrone
1984
MUPPETS TAKE MANHATTAN, THE(1984)
Franco Marrottax
NIGHT CHILD(1975, Brit./Ital.), w
Hyla Marrow
MANIAC(1980); SO FINE(1981)
Marlene Marrow
MY FAIR LADY(1964)
Stella Marrs
WHERE'S POPPA?(1970)
Michelle Marrus
1984
SIGNAL 7(1984)
Captain Marryat
MEN OF THE SEA(1951, Brit.), w
Frederick Marryat
LITTLE SAVAGE, THE(1959), w
Betty Mars
PIAF–THE EARLY YEARS(1982, U.S./Fr.)

Bruce Mars
STAGECOACH(1966); MARYJANE(1968)
Douglas Mars
Misc. Silents
WHEN LONDON SLEEPS(1914, Brit.)
Janice Mars
FUGITIVE KIND, THE(1960); UP THE DOWN STAIRCASE(1967)
Kenneth Mars
PRODUCERS, THE(1967); APRIL FOOLS, THE(1969); BUTCH CASSIDY AND THE SUNDANCE KID(1969); VIVA MAX!(1969); DESPERATE CHARACTERS(1971); WHAT'S UP, DOC?(1972); PARALLAX VIEW, THE(1974); YOUNG FRANKENSTEIN(1974); NIGHT MOVES(1975); GOIN' COCONUTS(1978); APPLE DUMPLING GANG RIDES AGAIN, THE(1979); FULL MOON HIGH(1982); YELLOWBEARD(1983)
1984
FLETCH(1984); PROTOCOL(1984)
Marjorie Mars
YELLOW STOCKINGS(1930, Brit.); SHADOW OF MIKE EMERALD, THE(1935, Brit.); CROUCHING BEAST, THE(1936, U. S./Brit.); SPY OF NAPOLEON(1939, Brit.); BRIEF ENCOUNTER(1945, Brit.); TAKE MY LIFE(1948, Brit.)
Misc. Silents
YELLOW STOCKINGS(1928, Brit.)
Marjory Mars
MAID HAPPY(1933, Brit.)
Monica Mars
DEVIL BAT'S DAUGHTER, THE(1946)
Severin Mars
Misc. Silents
J'ACCUSE(1919, Fr.)
Jean Marsac
EDWARD AND CAROLINE(1952, Fr.)
Maurice Marsac
PARIS AFTER DARK(1943); OUR HEARTS WERE YOUNG AND GAY(1944); THIS IS THE LIFE(1944); TO HAVE AND HAVE NOT(1944); SEARCHING WIND, THE(1946); ROGUES' REGIMENT(1948); WOMAN FROM TANGIER, THE(1948); ONCE MORE, MY DARLING(1949); SECRET OF ST. IVES, THE(1949); TAKE ONE FALSE STEP(1949); THREE HUSBANDS(1950); TYRANT OF THE SEA(1950); AGAINST ALL FLAGS(1952); CAPTAIN PIRATE(1952); HAPPY TIME, THE(1952); ONE MINUTE TO ZERO(1952); CADDY, THE(1953); HOW TO MARRY A MILLIONAIRE(1953); JUMP INTO HELL(1955); FOUR GIRLS IN TOWN(1956); RIDE THE HIGH IRON(1956); CHINA GATE(1957); LES GIRLS(1957); ME AND THE COLONEL(1958); TWILIGHT FOR THE GODS(1958); SCENT OF MYSTERY(1960); ARMORED COMMAND(1961); KING OF KINGS(1961); WEREWOLF IN A GIRL'S DORMITORY(1961, Ital./Aust.); CAPTAIN SINDBAD(1963); COME FLY WITH ME(1963); TAKE HER, SHE'S MINE(1963); PLEASURE SEEKERS, THE(1964); WHAT A WAY TO GO(1964); WILD AND WONDERFUL(1964); ART OF LOVE, THE(1965); CLARENCE, THE CROSS-EYED LION(1965); GAMBIT(1966); CAPRICE(1967); DOUBLE TROUBLE(1967); MONKEYS, GO HOME!(1967); HOW DO I LOVE THEE?(1970); BIG RED ONE, THE(1980); DEAL OF THE CENTURY(1983)
Roberto Marsach
PIE IN THE SKY(1964)
Michele Marsala
YOR, THE HUNTER FROM THE FUTURE(1983, Ital.), p
Charles . Marsan
Misc. Silents
PRES DE CRIME(1921, Fr.), d
Guido A. Marsan
LA NOTTE(1961, Fr./Ital.)
Jean Marsan
GRAND MANEUVER, THE(1956, Fr.), w; TONIGHT THE SKIRTS FLY(1956, Fr.), w
Claudia Marsani
CONVERSATION PIECE(1976, Ital., Fr.)
Andre Marsauden
THIS LOVE OF OURS(1945); ARCH OF TRIUMPH(1948)
Andre Marsaudo
ARTISTS AND MODELS ABROAD(1938)
Andre Marsaudon
FOOLS FOR SCANDAL(1938); HOTEL IMPERIAL(1939); SO DARK THE NIGHT(1946)
Andre P. Marsaudon
DAUGHTER OF SHANGHAI(1937)
George Marschalk
NIGHT OF LUST(1965, Fr.), ed
Inge Marschall
DUCK RINGS AT HALF PAST SEVEN, THE(1969, Ger./Ital.)
Archie Marschek
LAST DAYS OF POMPEII, THE(1935), ed
Kurt Marschner
FIDELIO(1970, Ger.); MARRIAGE OF FIGARO, THE(1970, Ger.)
Finanziaria S. Marsco
ACE HIGH(1969, Ital.), p
Aileen Pitt Marsden
WATCH BEVERLY(1932, Brit.)
Beatrice Marsden
SKY RAIDERS, THE(1938, Brit.); MILL ON THE FLOSS(1939, Brit.); KISS THE BRIDE GOODBYE(1944, Brit.); NIGHT COMES TOO SOON(1948, Brit.); MY BROTHER JONATHAN(1949, Brit.); WINSLOW BOY, THE(1950)
Beatrice "Betty" Marsden
RAT, THE(1938, Brit.)
Betty Marsden
SHIPS WITH WINGS(1942, Brit.); CHANCE MEETING(1954, Brit.); RAMSBOTTOM RIDES AGAIN(1956, Brit.); BIG DAY, THE(1960, Brit.); LET'S GET MARRIED(1960, Brit.); CARRY ON REGARDLESS(1961, Brit.); BOYS, THE(1962, Brit.); LEATHER BOYS, THE(1965, Brit.); WILD AFFAIR, THE(1966, Brit.); BEST HOUSE IN LONDON, THE(1969, Brit.); CARRY ON CAMPING(1969, Brit.); SUDDEN TERROR(1970, Brit.); DRESSER, THE(1983)
Frances Marsden
NO ORCHIDS FOR MISS BLANDISH(1948, Brit.); MISS PILGRIM'S PROGRESS(1950, Brit.)

Fred Marsden
FERRY ACROSS THE MERSEY(1964, Brit.)
Gerry Marsden
FERRY ACROSS THE MERSEY(1964, Brit.)
Philip Marsden
DULCIMA(1971, Brit.)
Robert Marsden
SECOND BEST SECRET AGENT IN THE WHOLE WIDE WORLD, THE(1965, Brit.)
Roy Marsden
TOOMORROW(1970, Brit.); SQUEEZE, THE(1977, Brit.)
Simeta Marsden
SAILING ALONG(1938, Brit.)
Vicki Marsden
LOVE ISLAND(1952)
Trudi Marsdon
DANCE HALL(1941)
Fred Marsell
DELTA FACTOR, THE(1970)
Tita Marsell
DIMENSION 5(1966)
Adolfo Marsellach
MUSHROOM EATER, THE(1976, Mex.)
Anthony Marsh
SOCIETY FEVER(1935); PORTIA ON TRIAL(1937); DAWN PATROL, THE(1938); OVERLAND STAGE RAIDERS(1938); MILLION DOLLAR LEGS(1939); TEN GENTLEMEN FROM WEST POINT(1942); WE WERE DANCING(1942); IMMORTAL SERGEANT, THE(1943); PRACTICALLY YOURS(1944); LOVE LETTERS(1945); O.S.S.(1946); TILL THE END OF TIME(1946); GREATEST SHOW ON EARTH, THE(1952); SCARAMOUCHE(1952); YOUNG RACERS, THE(1963); GRAND PRIX(1966)
Betty Marsh
Silents
HOME SWEET HOME(1914)
Bill Marsh
LINEUP, THE(1958)
Bryan Marsh
EAGLE ROCK(1964, Brit.)
Caren Marsh
NAVAJO KID, THE(1946); SECRETS OF A SORORITY GIRL(1946); WILD HARVEST(1947)
Carol Marsh
BRIGHTON ROCK(1947, Brit.); HELTER SKELTER(1949, Brit.); MARRY ME!(1949, Brit.); ALICE IN WONDERLAND(1951, Fr.); CHRISTMAS CAROL, A(1951, Brit.); NAUGHTY ARLETTE(1951, Brit.); PRIVATE INFORMATION(1952, Brit.); SALUTE THE TOFF(1952, Brit.); HORROR OF DRACULA, THE(1958, Brit.); MAN ACCUSED(1959)
Misc. Talkies
BRIGHTHAVEN EXPRESS(1950)
Charles Marsh
JEALOUSY(1934); NAVY BORN(1936); ANGELS WITH DIRTY FACES(1938); CHILD IS BORN, A(1940); AFFECTIONATELY YOURS(1941); MILLION DOLLAR BABY(1941); SIN TOWN(1942); NORTHERN PURSUIT(1943); ATLANTIC CITY(1944); LOUISIANA HAYRIDE(1944); SHINE ON, HARVEST MOON(1944); TOGETHER AGAIN(1944); DON JUAN QUILLIGAN(1945); HIT THE HAY(1945); I'LL TELL THE WORLD(1945); OVER 21(1945); CLOAK AND DAGGER(1946); NIGHT EDITOR(1946); SOMEWHERE IN THE NIGHT(1946); WIFE WANTED(1946); JOHNNY O'CLOCK(1947); MY WILD IRISH ROSE(1947); NORA PRENTISS(1947); UNFAITHFUL, THE(1947); WALLS OF JERICHO(1948); WHIPLASH(1948); RECKLESS MOMENTS, THE(1949); SHOCKPROOF(1949); STORM WARNING(1950); I WANT YOU(1951); MOB, THE(1951); SHE'S WORKING HER WAY THROUGH COLLEGE(1952); SNIPER, THE(1952)
Charles L. Marsh
MISS GRANT TAKES RICHMOND(1949)
D'Arcy Marsh
BILLY IN THE LOWLANDS(1979), ph, ed; DARK END OF THE STREET, THE(1981), ph
David Marsh
JOURNEY INTO LIGHT(1951)
Dennis Marsh
HAREM BUNCH; OR WAR AND PIECE, THE(1969), makeup; SCAVENGERS, THE(1969), makeup, makeup; MACHISMO–40 GRAVES FOR 40 GUNS(1970), makeup
Edward Marsh
JULIE(1956)
Eve Marsh
CANON CITY(1948)
Frances Marsh
SINS OF THE FATHERS(1928), ed; DARKENED ROOMS(1929), ed
Silents
MAGNIFICENT FLIRT, THE(1928), ed; NIGHT OF MYSTERY, A(1928), ed; STAIRS OF SAND(1929), ed
Francis Marsh
DESIGN FOR LIVING(1933), ed
Garry Marsh
DREYFUS CASE, THE(1931, Brit.); ETERNAL FEMININE, THE(1931, Brit.); KEEPERS OF YOUTH(1931, Brit.); NIGHT BIRDS(1931, Brit.); P.C. JOSSER(1931, Brit.); STAMBOUL(1931, Brit.); STRANGLEHOLD(1931, Brit.); THIRD TIME LUCKY(1931, Brit.); UNEASY VIRTUE(1931, Brit.); AFTER OFFICE HOURS(1932, Brit.); C.O.D.(1932, Brit.); DON'T BE A DUMMY(1932, Brit.); FIRES OF FATE(1932, Brit.); MAID OF THE MOUNTAINS, THE(1932, Brit.); NUMBER SEVENTEEN(1932, Brit.); ASK BECCLES(1933, Brit.); FALLING FOR YOU(1933, Brit.); LOVE NEST, THE(1933, Brit.); MAN THEY COULDN'T ARREST, THE(1933, Brit.); THAT'S A GOOD GIRL(1933, Brit.); GREEN PACK, THE(1934, Brit.); IT'S A COP(1934, Brit.); JOSSER ON THE FARM(1934, Brit.); MONEY MAD(1934, Brit.); ROLLING IN MONEY(1934, Brit.); SILVER SPOON, THE(1934, Brit.); WARN LONDON!(1934, Brit.); WIDOW'S MIGHT(1934, Brit.); CHARING CROSS ROAD(1935, Brit.); DEPARTMENT STORE(1935, Brit.); FULL CIRCLE(1935, Brit.); INSIDE THE ROOM(1935, Brit.); MR. WHAT'S-HIS-NAME(1935, Brit.); NIGHT MAIL(1935, Brit.); SCROOGE(1935, Brit.); THREE WITNESSES(1935, Brit.); WIFE OR TWO, A(1935, Brit.); ALL IN(1936, Brit.); DEBT OF HONOR(1936, Brit.); GAY LOVE(1936, Brit.); MAN IN THE MIRROR,

THE(1936, Brit.); MURDER ON THE SET(1936, Brit.); INTIMATE RELATIONS(1937, Brit.); IT'S A GRAND OLD WORLD(1937, Brit.); LEAVE IT TO ME(1937, Brit.); LOST CHORD, THE(1937, Brit.); MELODY AND ROMANCE(1937, Brit.); VICAR OF BRAY, THE(1937, Brit.); WHO KILLED FEN MARKHAM?(1937, Brit.); BANK HOLIDAY(1938, Brit.); BREAK THE NEWS(1938, Brit.); CLAYDON TREASURE MYSTERY, THE(1938, Brit.); CONVICT 99(1938, Brit.); DARK STAIRWAY, THE(1938, Brit.); I SEE ICE(1938); HOOTS MON!(1939, Brit.); LET'S BE FAMOUS(1939, Brit.); OLD MOTHER RILEY JOINS UP(1939, Brit.); THIS MAN IN PARIS(1939, Brit.); THIS MAN IS NEWS(1939, Brit.); TROUBLE BREWING(1939, Brit.); IT'S IN THE AIR(1940, Brit.); LET GEORGE DO IT(1940, Brit.); LOST ON THE WESTERN FRONT(1940, Brit.); RETURN TO YESTERDAY(1940, Brit.); SECRET FOUR, THE(1940, Brit.); WHEN KNIGHTS WERE BOLD(1942, Brit.); I'LL BE YOUR SWEETHEART(1945, Brit.); NOTORIOUS GENTLEMAN(1945, Brit.); ADVENTURESS, THE(1946, Brit.); DEAD OF NIGHT(1946, Brit.); GIRL IN A MILLION, A(1946, Brit.); DANCING WITH CRIME(1947, Brit.); FRIEDA(1947, Brit.); CODE OF SCOTLAND YARD(1948); JUST WILLIAM'S LUCK(1948, Brit.); THINGS HAPPEN AT NIGHT(1948, Brit.); WILLIAM COMES TO TOWN(1948, Brit.); BADGER'S GREEN(1949, Brit.); FORBIDDEN(1949, Brit.); MY BROTHER'S KEEPER(1949, Brit.); PAPER ORCHID(1949, Brit.); GOOD TIME GIRL(1950, Brit.); MISS PILGRIM'S PROGRESS(1950, Brit.); MYSTERY AT THE BURLESQUE(1950, Brit.); PINK STRING AND SEALING WAX(1950, Brit.); SOMEONE AT THE DOOR(1950, Brit.); SOMETHING IN THE CITY(1950, Brit.); WHILE THE SUN SHINES(1950, Brit.); MADAME LOUISE(1951, Brit.); OLD MOTHER RILEY'S JUNGLE TREASURE(1951, Brit.); WORM'S EYE VIEW(1951, Brit.); MAGIC BOX, THE(1952, Brit.); THOSE PEOPLE NEXT DOOR(1952, Brit.); BIG FRAME, THE(1953, Brit.); MURDER WILL OUT(1953, Brit.); AUNT CLARA(1954, Brit.); DOUBLE EXPOSURE(1954, Brit.); MAN OF THE MOMENT(1955, Brit.); JOHNNY, YOU'RE WANTED(1956, Brit.); WHO DONE IT?(1956, Brit.); IN TROUBLE WITH EVE(1964, Brit.); RING OF SPIES(1964, Brit.); WHERE THE BULLETS FLY(1966, Brit.); CAMELOT(1967)

Gary Alan Marsh
THX 1138(1971)

George Marsh
JAZZ HEAVEN(1929), ed; VERY IDEA, THE(1929), ed; HE KNEW WOMEN(1930), ed; OFFICE WIFE, THE(1930), ed; RUNAROUND, THE(1931), ed; GIRL ON THE RUN(1961)
Silents
YOUNG WHIRLWIND(1928), ed; FRECKLED RASCAL, THE(1929), ed; LITTLE SAVAGE, THE(1929), ed; PALS OF THE PRAIRIE(1929), ed

H.R. Marsh
SWING YOUR LADY(1938), w

Hal Marsh
PASSION HOLIDAY(1963), p

Harry Marsh
Silents
LONG ODDS(1922, Brit.)

Jack Marsh
Misc. Silents
LAW'S LASH, THE(1928)

James Marsh
STIR(1980, Aus.)

Jamie Marsh
MONTENEGRO(1981, Brit./Swed.)

Jean Marsh
CLEOPATRA(1963); FACE OF A STRANGER(1964, Brit.); UNEARTHLY STRANGER, THE(1964, Brit.); LIMBO LINE, THE(1969, Brit.); JANE EYRE(1971, Brit.); FRENZY(1972, Brit.); DARK PLACES(1974, Brit.); EAGLE HAS LANDED, THE(1976, Brit.); CHANGELING, THE(1980, Can.)

Jesse Marsh
MAKE MINE MUSIC(1946), w; MELODY TIME(1948), w

Joan Marsh
ALL QUIET ON THE WESTERN FRONT(1930); LITTLE ACCIDENT(1930); DANCE, FOOLS, DANCE(1931); GOD IS MY WITNESS(1931); INSPIRATION(1931); MAKER OF MEN(1931); MEET THE WIFE(1931); POLITICS(1931); SHIPMATES(1931); TAILOR MADE MAN, A(1931); THREE GIRLS LOST(1931); ARE YOU LISTENING?(1932); BACHELOR'S AFFAIRS(1932); WET PARADE, THE(1932); DARING DAUGHTERS(1933); HIGH GEAR(1933); IT'S GREAT TO BE ALIVE(1933); MAN WHO DARED, THE(1933); MARK IT PAID(1933); RAINBOW OVER BROADWAY(1933); THREE-CORNERED MOON(1933); MANY HAPPY RETURNS(1934); WE'RE RICH AGAIN(1934); YOU'RE TELLING ME(1934); ANNA KARENINA(1935); CHAMPAGNE FOR BREAKFAST(1935); BRILLIANT MARRIAGE(1936); DANCING FEET(1936); CHARLIE CHAN ON BROADWAY(1937); HOT WATER(1937); LIFE BEGINS IN COLLEGE(1937); LADY OBJECTS, THE(1938); FAST AND LOOSE(1939); IDIOT'S DELIGHT(1939); ROAD TO ZANZIBAR(1941); MAN IN THE TRUNK, THE(1942); POLICE BULLETS(1942); KEEP 'EM SLUGGING(1943); MR. MUGGS STEPS OUT(1943); FOLLOW THE LEADER(1944)
Misc. Talkies
SPEED DEMON(1933)

Joe [Tiger] Marsh
REBEL SET, THE(1959)

John P. Marsh
TASTE OF SIN, A(1983), w

Judy Marsh
WONDERFUL COUNTRY, THE(1959)

Julian Marsh
SATAN'S BED(1965), ph; TOUCH OF HER FLESH, THE(1967), p, d, ed

Keith Marsh
OTHELLO(1965, Brit.); DALEKS–INVASION EARTH 2155 A.D.(1966, Brit.); FIVE MILLION YEARS TO EARTH(1968, Brit.); SCROOGE(1970, Brit.); TASTE THE BLOOD OF DRACULA(1970, Brit.); HUMAN FACTOR, THE(1979, Brit.)

Linda Marsh
AMERICA, AMERICA(1963); CHE!(1969); FREEBIE AND THE BEAN(1974); HOMEBODIES(1974)

Lois Marsh
MAN WITH TWO HEADS, THE(1972), makeup; RATS ARE COMING! THE WEREWOLVES ARE HERE!, THE(1972), makeup

Lou Marsh
HARDLY WORKING(1981)

Mae Marsh
OVER THE HILL(1931); REBECCA OF SUNNYBROOK FARM(1932); THAT'S MY BOY(1932); ALICE IN WONDERLAND(1933); LITTLE MAN, WHAT NOW?(1934); BACHELOR OF ARTS(1935); BLACK FURY(1935); HOLLYWOOD BOULEVARD(1936); DRUMS ALONG THE MOHAWK(1939); GRAPES OF WRATH(1940); MAN WHO WOULDN'T TALK, THE(1940); YOUNG PEOPLE(1940); BLUE, WHITE, AND PERFECT(1941); GREAT GUNS(1941); REMEMBER THE DAY(1941); SWAMP WATER(1941); LOVES OF EDGAR ALLAN POE, THE(1942); QUIET PLEASE, MURDER(1942); SON OF FURY(1942); TALES OF MANHATTAN(1942); DIXIE DUGAN(1943); SONG OF BERNADETTE, THE(1943); IN THE MEANTIME, DARLING(1944); JANE EYRE(1944); SULLIVANS, THE(1944); DOLLY SISTERS, THE(1945); TREE GROWS IN BROOKLYN, A(1945); LEAVE HER TO HEAVEN(1945); MY DARLING CLEMENTINE(1946); LATE GEORGE APLEY, THE(1947); APARTMENT FOR PEGGY(1948); DEEP WATERS(1948); FORT APACHE(1948); SNAKE PIT, THE(1948); THREE GODFATHERS(1948); EVERYBODY DOES IT(1949); FIGHTING KENTUCKIAN, THE(1949); IMPACT(1949); IT HAPPENS EVERY SPRING(1949); GUNFIGHTER, THE(1950); MY BLUE HEAVEN(1950); WHEN WILLIE COMES MARCHING HOME(1950); MODEL AND THE MARRIAGE BROKER, THE(1951); NIGHT WITHOUT SLEEP(1952); QUIET MAN, THE(1952); BLUEPRINT FOR MURDER, A(1953); ROBE, THE(1953); SUN SHINES BRIGHT, THE(1953); TITANIC(1953); STAR IS BORN, A(1954); GOOD MORNING, MISS DOVE(1955); PRINCE OF PLAYERS(1955); GIRLS IN PRISON(1956); HELL ON FRISCO BAY(1956); JULIE(1956); SEARCHERS, THE(1956); WHILE THE CITY SLEEPS(1956); WINGS OF EAGLES, THE(1957); CRY TERROR(1958); FROM THE TERRACE(1960); SERGEANT RUTLEDGE(1960); TWO RODE TOGETHER(1961); DONOVAN'S REEF(1963)
Silents
AVENGING CONSCIENCE, THE(1914); ESCAPE, THE(1914); GREAT LEAP, THE(1914); HOME SWEET HOME(1914); JUDITH OF BETHULIA(1914); BIRTH OF A NATION, THE(1915); LITTLE LIAR, THE(1916); POLLY OF THE CIRCUS(1917); ALL WOMAN(1918); LITTLE 'FRAID LADY, THE(1920); NOBODY'S KID(1921); FLAMES OF PASSION(1922, Brit.); PADDY, THE NEXT BEST THING(1923, Brit.); WHITE ROSE, THE(1923); RAT, THE(1925, Brit.)
Misc. Silents
VICTIM, THE(1914); HER SHATTERED IDOL(1915); OUTCAST, THE(1915); CHILD OF THE PARIS STREETS, A(1916); HOODOO ANN(1916); MARRIAGE OF MOLLY-O, THE(1916); WHARF RAT, THE(1916); WILD GIRL OF THE SIERRAS, A(1916); SUNSHINE ALLEY(1917); BELOVED TRAITOR, THE(1918); CINDERELLA MAN, THE(1918); FACE IN THE DARK, THE(1918); FIELDS OF HONOR(1918); GLORIOUS ADVENTURE, THE(1918); HIDDEN FIRES(1918); MONEY MAD(1918); BONDAGE OF BARBARA, THE(1919); RACING STRAIN(1919); SPOTLIGHT SADIE(1919); TILL WE MEET AGAIN(1922); DADDIES(1924); TIDES OF PASSION(1925)

Margaret Marsh
Silents
ETERNAL MAGDALENE, THE(1919)

Marguerite Marsh
Silents
INTOLERANCE(1916); CONQUERED HEARTS(1918); OUR LITTLE WIFE(1918); IDOL OF THE NORTH, THE(1921); LION'S MOUSE, THE(1922, Brit.)
Misc. Silents
DEVIL'S NEEDLE, THE(1916); PRICE OF POWER, THE(1916); FIELDS OF HONOR(1918); PHANTOM HONEYMOON, THE(1919); ROYAL DEMOCRAT, A(1919); FACE TO FACE(1920); WITS VS. WITS(1920); WOMEN MEN LOVE(1921); BOOMERANG BILL(1922); IRON TO GOLD(1922)

Marian Marsh
FIVE STAR FINAL(1931); MAD GENIUS, THE(1931); ROAD TO SINGAPORE(1931); SVENGALI(1931); ALIAS THE DOCTOR(1932); BEAUTY AND THE BOSS(1932); SPORT PARADE, THE(1932); STRANGE JUSTICE(1932); UNDER EIGHTEEN(1932); DARING DAUGHTERS(1933); ELEVENTH COMMANDMENT(1933); MAN OF SENTIMENT, A(1933); GIRL OF THE LIMBERLOST(1934); I LIKE IT THAT WAY(1934); NOTORIOUS BUT NICE(1934); OVER THE GARDEN WALL(1934, Brit.); BLACK ROOM, THE(1935); CRIME AND PUNISHMENT(1935); IN SPITE OF DANGER(1935); UNKNOWN WOMAN(1935); COME CLOSER, FOLKS(1936); COUNTERFEIT(1936); LADY OF SECRETS(1936); MAN WHO LIVED TWICE(1936); GREAT GAMBINI, THE(1937); SATURDAY'S HEROES(1937); WHEN'S YOUR BIRTHDAY?(1937); YOUTH ON PAROLE(1937); DESPERATE ADVENTURE, A(1938); GIRL THIEF, THE(1938); PRISON NURSE(1938); MISSING DAUGHTERS(1939); FUGITIVE FROM A PRISON CAMP(1940); GENTLEMAN FROM DIXIE(1941); MURDER BY INVITATION(1941); HOUSE OF ERRORS(1942)

Marion Marsh
PRODIGAL SON, THE(1935)

Marvin Marsh
BUTTERFLIES ARE FREE(1972), set d

Mary Marsh
I LIVE FOR LOVE(1935)

Maude Marsh
MONEY TALKS(1933, Brit.), cos

Michele Marsh
FIDDLER ON THE ROOF(1971)

Mildred Marsh
Misc. Silents
COUNTRY FLAPPER, THE(1922)

Myra Marsh
PADDY O'DAY(1935); GENTLE JULIA(1936); LIBELED LADY(1936); MORE THAN A SECRETARY(1936); NAVY BORN(1936); WIFE VERSUS SECRETARY(1936); CAPTAINS COURAGEOUS(1937); NIGHT OF MYSTERY(1937); RASCALS(1938); BOY FRIEND(1939); INVITATION TO HAPPINESS(1939); KANSAS TERRORS(1939); DOCTOR TAKES A WIFE(1940); GLAMOUR FOR SALE(1940); FATHER'S SON(1941); PRIVATE NURSE(1941); HITLER–DEAD OR ALIVE(1942); YOUNG AMERICA(1942); ROSEANNA McCOY(1949); THEY LIVE BY NIGHT(1949); RUBY GENTRY(1952); MAN FROM THE ALAMO, THE(1953); MOONLIGHTER, THE(1953); DOWN THREE DARK STREETS(1954); COBWEB, THE(1955)

Oliver Marsh
MARIANNE(1929), ph; OUR MODERN MAIDENS(1929), ph; UNTAMED(1929), ph; DU BARRY, WOMAN OF PASSION(1930), ph; IN GAY MADRID(1930), ph; NOT SO DUMB(1930), ph; STRICTLY UNCONVENTIONAL(1930), ph; SWEETHEARTS(1938), ph; IT'S A WONDERFUL WORLD(1939), ph; RAGE IN HEAVEN(1941), ph
Silents
IN SEARCH OF A SINNER(1920), ph; WOMAN'S PLACE(1921), ph; BROADWAY ROSE(1922), ph; PEACOCK ALLEY(1922), ph; LOVE'S WILDERNESS(1924), ph; MARRIED FLIRTS(1924), ph; MERRY WIDOW, THE(1925), ph; SOUL MATES(1925),

ph; KIKI(1926), ph; LOVE'S BLINDNESS(1926), ph; ANNIE LAURIE(1927), ph; ENE-MY, THE(1927), ph; DIVINE WOMAN, THE(1928), ph; SADIE THOMPSON(1928), ph; SMART SET, THE(1928), ph; ETERNAL LOVE(1929), ph; OUR MODERN MAI-DENS(1929), ph; SINGLE STANDARD, THE(1929), ph

Oliver T. Marsh
LADY OF SCANDAL, THE(1930), ph; NEW MOON(1930), ph; BACHELOR FA-THER(1931), ph; IT'S A WISE CHILD(1931), ph; JUST A GIGOLO(1931), ph; MAN IN POSSESSION, THE(1931), ph; NEW ADVENTURES OF GET-RICH-QUICK WAL-LINGFORD, THE(1931), ph; PHANTOM OF PARIS, THE(1931), ph; POSSES-SED(1931), ph; SIN OF MADELON CLAUDET, THE(1931), ph; ARSENE LUPIN(1932), ph; BUT THE FLESH IS WEAK(1932), ph; DIVORCE IN THE FAMI-LY(1932), ph; EMMA(1932), ph; FAITHLESS(1932), ph; LETTY LYNTON(1932), ph; RAIN(1932), ph; SON-DAUGHTER, THE(1932), ph; DANCING LADY(1933), ph; LOOKING FORWARD(1933), ph; NIGHT FLIGHT(1933), ph; TODAY WE LIVE(1933), ph; MERRY WIDOW, THE(1934), ph; MYSTERY OF MR. X, THE(1934), ph; SADIE MCKEE(1934), ph; BABY FACE HARRINGTON(1935), ph; DAVID COPPER-FIELD(1935), ph; NO MORE LADIES(1935), ph; ONE NEW YORK NIGHT(1935), ph; TALE OF TWO CITIES, A(1935), ph; AFTER THE THIN MAN(1936), ph; GREAT ZIEGFELD, THE(1936), ph; HIS BROTHER'S WIFE(1936), ph; LOVE ON THE RUN(1936), ph; SAN FRANCISCO(1936), ph; WOMEN ARE TROUBLE(1936), ph; FIREFLY, THE(1937), ph; MAYTIME(1937), ph; ROSALIE(1937), ph; GIRL OF THE GOLDEN WEST, THE(1938), ph; TOY WIFE, THE(1938), ph; ANOTHER THIN MAN(1939), ph; BROADWAY SERENADE(1939), ph; ICE FOLLIES OF 1939(1939), ph; WOMEN, THE(1939), ph; BITTER SWEET(1940), ph; BROADWAY MELODY OF 1940(1940), ph; I LOVE YOU AGAIN(1940), ph; BLONDE INSPIRATION(1941), ph; LADY BE GOOD(1941), ph; WILD MAN OF BORNEO, THE(1941), ph
Silents
ALL WOMAN(1918), ph; JOAN OF PLATTSBURG(1918), ph; LESSONS IN LO-VE(1921), ph; RED HOT ROMANCE(1922), ph; FRENCH DOLL, THE(1923), ph; JAZZ-MANIA(1923), ph; CAMILLE(1927), ph

Ray Marsh
NO DRUMS, NO BUGLES(1971); LAST PORNO FLICK, THE(1974), d

Raymond Marsh
LORD SHANGO(1975), d

Reginald Marsh
UGLY DUCKLING, THE(1959, Brit.); SHADOW OF FEAR(1963, Brit.); SICILIANS, THE(1964, Brit.); JIG SAW(1965, Brit.); IT HAPPENED HERE(1966, Brit.); BER-SERK(1967); HEADLINE HUNTERS(1968, Brit.); YOUNG WINSTON(1972, Brit.); NO LONGER ALONE(1978)

Ronald Marsh
ONCE A SINNER(1952, Brit.), w

Sam Marsh
Silents
LONG ODDS(1922, Brit.)

Sandra Marsh
1984
FINDERS KEEPERS(1984), p

Stephen Marsh
1984
ANGEL(1984), art d; CRIMES OF PASSION(1984), art d

Tani Marsh
MAD DOCTOR OF MARKET STREET, THE(1942); FROM HELL IT CAME(1957)

Terence Marsh
DOCTOR ZHIVAGO(1965), art d; MAN FOR ALL SEASONS, A(1966, Brit.), art d; WILD AFFAIR, THE(1966, Brit.), art d; OLIVER!(1968, Brit.), art d; LOOKING GLASS WAR, THE(1970, Brit.), art d; PERFECT FRIDAY(1970, Brit.), prod d; SCROOGE(1970, Brit.), prod d; MARY, QUEEN OF SCOTS(1971, Brit.), prod d; PUBLIC EYE, THE(1972, Brit.), prod d; JUGGERNAUT(1974, Brit.), prod d; ROYAL FLASH(1975, Brit.), prod d; WORLD'S GREATEST LOVER, THE(1977), prod d; MAGIC(1978), prod d; FRISCO KID, THE(1979), prod d; ABSENCE OF MALICE(1981), prod d; SPHINX(1981), prod d; TO BE OR NOT TO BE(1983), a, prod d
1984
FINDERS KEEPERS(1984), p, w, prod d

Terry Marsh
MACKINTOSH MAN, THE(1973, Brit.), prod d; TOUCH OF CLASS, A(1973, Brit.), prod d

Tiger Marsh
HERE COME THE JETS(1959)

Tiger Joe Marsh
PANIC IN THE STREETS(1950); EGYPTIAN. THE(1954); VENGEANCE(1964); C'MON, LET'S LIVE A LITTLE(1967); CACTUS IN THE SNOW(1972); TOP OF THE HEAP(1972); ESCAPE TO WITCH MOUNTAIN(1975); CAT FROM OUTER SPACE, THE(1978)

Tony Marsh
FOLLOW THE BOYS(1944); TONIGHT AND EVERY NIGHT(1945)

Vera Marsh
GOOD NEWS(1930); MADAME SATAN(1930); WAY OUT WEST(1930); BEDSIDE MANNER(1945); MISS MINK OF 1949(1949)

Vernon Marsh
1,000 SHAPES OF A FEMALE(1963)

Wally Marsh
RUSSIAN ROULETTE(1975)

Walter Marsh
TRAP, THE(1967, Can./Brit.); MAN, A WOMAN, AND A BANK, A(1979, Can.)

Yvonne Marsh
COME DANCE WITH ME(1950, Brit.); LITTLE BALLERINA, THE(1951, Brit.); BOTH SIDES OF THE LAW(1953, Brit.); GREAT GILBERT AND SULLIVAN, THE(1953, Brit.)

Archie Marshak
BLACK SPURS(1965), ed

Philip Marshak
Misc. Talkies
DRACULA SUCKS(1979), d; CATACLYSM(1980), d

Adam Marshal
TRUE STORY OF JESSE JAMES, THE(1957)

Alan Marshal
PARNELL(1937); DRAMATIC SCHOOL(1938); I MET MY LOVE AGAIN(1938); INVISIBLE ENEMY(1938); ADVENTURES OF SHERLOCK HOLMES, THE(1939); EXILE EXPRESS(1939); FOUR GIRLS IN WHITE(1939); HUNCHBACK OF NOTRE DAME, THE(1939); HE STAYED FOR BREAKFAST(1940); HOWARDS OF VIRGINIA, THE(1940); IRENE(1940); MARRIED AND IN LOVE(1940); TOM, DICK AND HAR-RY(1941); BRIDE BY MISTAKE(1944); OPPOSITE SEX, THE(1956); HOUSE ON HAUNTED HILL(1958); DAY OF THE OUTLAW(1959)

Scott Marshal
RAIDERS OF THE LOST ARK(1981), anim

Tully Marshal
Silents
ANYTHING ONCE(1925)

Vivian Marshal
OPPOSITE SEX, THE(1956)

William C. Marshal
Silents
AMAZONS, THE(1917), ph

Marshall
Misc. Talkies
CYCLES SOUTH(1971), d

A. David Marshall
FIRE AND ICE(1983), ed

Al Marshall
ROBBER SYMPHONY, THE(1937, Brit.)

Alan Marshall
AFTER THE THIN MAN(1936); GARDEN OF ALLAH, THE(1936); CONQUEST(1937); NIGHT MUST FALL(1937); ROAD TO RENO, THE(1938); LYDIA(1941); WHITE CLIFFS OF DOVER, THE(1944); BUGSY MALONE(1976, Brit.), p; MIDNIGHT EX-PRESS(1978, Brit.), p; FAME(1980), p; PINK FLOYD–THE WALL(1982, Brit.), p; SHOOT THE MOON(1982), p; 10 TO MIDNIGHT(1983), makeup
1984
ANOTHER COUNTRY(1984, Brit.), p; BIRDY(1984), p

Alfonso Marshall
PARRISH(1961)

Andrea Marshall
PUTNEY SWOPE(1969)

Ann Marshall
SUPERDAD(1974)

Anne T. Marshall
GOIN' SOUTH(1978)

Annette Marshall
PUTNEY SWOPE(1969)

Anthony Marshall
SWORDSMAN OF SIENA, THE(1962, Fr./Ital.), w
Misc. Talkies
BULLETS AND SADDLES(1943), d

Armina Marshall
PURSUIT OF HAPPINESS, THE(1934), w

Art Marshall
OTHER WOMAN, THE(1954)

Arthur Marshall
FOR MEN ONLY(1952); HIGH SCHOOL HELLCATS(1958); ONE MAN'S WAY(1964)

Belinda Marshall
THREE WEIRD SISTERS, THE(1948, Brit.)

Betty Marshall
Misc. Silents
MAN WHO BEAT DAN DOLAN, THE(1915)

Bill Marshall
FIRE IN THE FLESH(1964, Fr.); DR. FRANKENSTEIN ON CAMPUS(1970, Can.), p, w; WILD HORSE HANK(1979, Can.), p; MR. PATMAN(1980, Can.), p

Billy Marshall
I ESCAPED FROM THE GESTAPO(1943)

Boyd Marshall
Silents
KING LEAR(1916); MODERN MONTE CRISTO, A(1917)
Misc. Silents
HIDDEN VALLEY, THE(1916); WORLD AND THE WOMAN, THE(1916); VICAR OF WAKEFIELD, THE(1917); WHEN LOVE WAS BLIND(1917)

Brenda Marshall
ESPIONAGE AGENT(1939); EAST OF THE RIVER(1940); MAN WHO TALKED TOO MUCH, THE(1940); MONEY AND THE WOMAN(1940); SEA HAWK, THE(1940); SOUTH OF SUEZ(1940); FOOTSTEPS IN THE DARK(1941); HIGHWAY WEST(1941); SINGAPORE WOMAN(1941); SMILING GHOST, THE(1941); CAPTAINS OF THE CLOUDS(1942); YOU CAN'T ESCAPE FOREVER(1942); BACKGROUND TO DAN-GER(1943); CONSTANT NYMPH, THE(1943); PARIS AFTER DARK(1943); STRANGE IMPERSONATION(1946); WHISPERING SMITH(1948); IROQUOIS TRAIL(1950)

Brian Marshall
BMX BANDITS(1983)

Bruce Marshall
RED DANUBE, THE(1949), w

Bryan Marshall
DEVIL'S OWN, THE(1967, Brit.); VIKING QUEEN, THE(1967, Brit.); FIVE MILLION YEARS TO EARTH(1968, Brit.); I START COUNTING(1970, Brit.); MOSQUITO SQUADRON(1970, Brit.); MAN IN THE WILDERNESS(1971, U.S./Span.); TAMARIND SEED, THE(1974, Brit.); SPY WHO LOVED ME, THE(1977, Brit.); LONG GOOD FRIDAY, THE(1982, Brit.)
Misc. Talkies
BECAUSE OF THE CATS(1974)

Bud Marshall
NO DEFENSE(1929)

Burt Marshall
BUCK ROGERS IN THE 25TH CENTURY(1979)

Catherine Marshall
MAN CALLED PETER, THE(1955), w

Charles Marshall
AIR EAGLES(1932), ph; GOLD(1932), ph; SKY BRIDE(1932), ph; NIGHT FLIGHT(1933), ph; WEST POINT OF THE AIR(1935), ph; MEN WITH WINGS(1938), ph; 20,000 MEN A YEAR(1939), ph; DIVE BOMBER(1941), aerial ph; TOWN LIKE ALICE, A(1958, Brit.)

Charles A. Marshall
Silents
FLYING FEET, THE(1929), air ph

Charles "Red" Marshall
WAVE, A WAC AND A MARINE, A(1944); SPECTER OF THE ROSE(1946)
Chester Marshall
RAINBOW 'ROUND MY SHOULDER(1952)
Chet Marshall
DANGEROUS MISSION(1954); D-DAY, THE SIXTH OF JUNE(1956)
Claire Marshall
SPARE THE ROD(1961, Brit.); SAVAGE MESSIAH(1972, Brit.)
Clark Marshall
VOICE OF THE CITY(1929); CRIMINAL CODE(1931); SIDEWALKS OF NEW YORK(1931); POLLY OF THE CIRCUS(1932)
Misc. Silents
WORLD AFLAME, THE(1919)
Connie Marshall
SUNDAY DINNER FOR A SOLDIER(1944); DRAGONWYCH(1946); HOME SWEET HOMICIDE(1946); SENTIMENTAL JOURNEY(1946); WAKE UP AND DREAM(1946); DAISY KENYON(1947); MOTHER WORE TIGHTS(1947); MR. BLANDINGS BUILDS HIS DREAM HOUSE(1948); GREEN PROMISE, THE(1949); KILL THE UMPIRE(1950); SAGINAW TRAIL(1953); ROGUE COP(1954)
Conrad Marshall
PURSUIT OF D.B. COOPER, THE(1981)
Darrah Marshall
TEENAGE CAVEMAN(1958)
David R. Marshall
OFFICER AND A GENTLEMAN, AN(1982)
Desmond Marshall
BEHIND YOUR BACK(1937, Brit.)
Diana Marshall
COLONEL BLIMP(1945, Brit.)
Dodie Marshall
SPINOUT(1966); EASY COME, EASY GO(1967)
Don Marshall
SERGEANT RYKER(1968); THING WITH TWO HEADS, THE(1972); TERMINAL ISLAND(1973); UPTOWN SATURDAY NIGHT(1974)
Misc. Talkies
CYCLES SOUTH(1971)
E. G. Marshall
UNTAMED FURY(1947); CALL NORTHSIDE 777(1948); DIPLOMATIC COURIER(1952); BROKEN LANCE(1954); CAINE MUTINY, THE(1954); PUSHOVER(1954); SILVER CHALICE, THE(1954); BAMBOO PRISON, THE(1955); LEFT HAND OF GOD, THE(1955); MOUNTAIN, THE(1956); SCARLET HOUR, THE(1956); BACHELOR PARTY, THE(1957); MAN ON FIRE(1957); 12 ANGRY MEN(1957); BUCCANEER, THE(1958); COMPULSION(1959); JOURNEY, THE(1959, U.S./Aust.); CASH McCALL(1960); TOWN WITHOUT PITY(1961, Ger./Switz./U.S.); CHASE, THE(1966); IS PARIS BURNING?(1966, U.S./Fr.); POPPY IS ALSO A FLOWER, THE(1966); BRIDGE AT REMAGEN, THE(1969); TORA! TORA! TORA!(1970, U.S./Jap.); PURSUIT OF HAPPINESS, THE(1971); BILLY JACK GOES TO WASHINGTON(1977); INTERIORS(1978); SUPERMAN II(1980); CREEPSHOW(1982)
Earl Marshall
NOTORIOUS CLEOPATRA, THE(1970), art d; GRAVE OF THE VAMPIRE(1972), art d
Ed Marshall
HAND, THE(1981)
Edison Marshall
SON OF FURY(1942), w; TREASURE OF THE GOLDEN CONDOR(1953), d&w; YANKEE PASHA(1954), w; VIKINGS, THE(1958), w
Silents
ISLE OF RETRIBUTION, THE(1926), w; FAR CALL, THE(1929), w
Edward Marshall
HOUSE ON 92ND STREET, THE(1945); PUMPKIN EATER, THE(1964, Brit.), art d; LIFE AT THE TOP(1965, Brit.), art d; SPY WHO CAME IN FROM THE COLD, THE(1965, Brit.), art d; UNCLE, THE(1966, Brit.), art d; BIRTHDAY PARTY, THE(1968, Brit.), art d; CHARGE OF THE LIGHT BRIGADE, THE(1968, Brit.), art d; CHARLIE BUBBLES(1968, Brit.), art d; SOME GIRLS DO(1968, Brit.), art d; EXECUTIONER, THE(1970, Brit.), art d; DARKTOWN STRUTTERS(1975); DIRTY KNIGHT'S WORK(1976, Brit.), prod d; JACKSON COUNTY JAIL(1976); NICKELODEON(1976); FUN WITH DICK AND JANE(1977); SILVER BEARS(1978), art d; NINE TO FIVE(1980); CARBON COPY(1981)
1984
ULTIMATE SOLUTION OF GRACE QUIGLEY, THE(1984)
Silents
GAY RETREAT, THE(1927), w
Edwin Marshall
BRIGHAM YOUNG–FRONTIERSMAN(1940)
Elizabeth Marshall
HELLFIRE(1949); GREATEST, THE(1977, U.S./Brit.)
Ellye Marshall
CHAMPAGNE FOR CAESAR(1950); ROGUE RIVER(1951); CAT WOMEN OF THE MOON(1953); FRENCH LINE, THE(1954)
Misc. Talkies
SECOND CHANCE(1950)
Eric Marshall
GLAMOUR(1931, Brit.)
Everett G. Marshall
13 RUE MADELEINE(1946)
Everett Marshall
DIXIANA(1930); I LIVE FOR LOVE(1935)
Frank Marshall
FEET OF CLAY(1960, Brit.), d; IDENTITY UNKNOWN(1960, Brit.), d; GANG WAR(1962, Brit.), d; GENTLE TERROR, THE(1962, Brit.), d; GUY CALLED CAESAR, A(1962, Brit.), d; TARGETS(1968); LAST PICTURE SHOW, THE(1971); NICKELODEON(1976); RAIDERS OF THE LOST ARK(1981), a, p; POLTERGEIST(1982), p
Fred Marshall
HAPPIEST DAYS OF YOUR LIFE(1950, Brit.); POPDOWN(1968, Brit.), a, p,d&w
G. K. Marshall
ESCAPE ARTIST, THE(1982)
Garry Marshall
HOW SWEET IT IS(1968), p, w; MARYJANE(1968); PSYCH-OUT(1968); GRASSHOPPER, THE(1970), p, w; YOUNG DOCTORS IN LOVE(1982), d

1984
FLAMINGO KID, THE(1984), d, w
Gary K. Marshall
GRAND THEFT AUTO(1977)
Gary Marshall
PHONY AMERICAN, THE(1964, Ger.); CAMELOT(1967); 1,000 PLANE RAID, THE(1969)
Gene Marshall
TWO TICKETS TO BROADWAY(1951)
Misc. Talkies
TWO CATCH TWO(1979), d
George Marshall
TRUE TO LIFE(1943), d; PACK UP YOUR TROUBLES(1932), a, d; CALL IT LUCK(1934), w; EVER SINCE EVE(1934), d; SHE LEARNED ABOUT SAILORS(1934), d; WILD GOLD(1934), d; 365 NIGHTS IN HOLLYWOOD(1934), d; IN OLD KENTUCKY(1935), d; LIFE BEGINS AT 40(1935), d; MUSIC IS MAGIC(1935), d; SHOW THEM NO MERCY(1935), d; $10 RAISE(1935), d; CAN THIS BE DIXIE?(1936), d, w; CRIME OF DR. FORBES(1936), d; MESSAGE TO GARCIA, A(1936), d; LOVE UNDER FIRE(1937), d; NANCY STEELE IS MISSING(1937), d; BATTLE OF BROADWAY(1938), d; GOLDWYN FOLLIES, THE(1938), d; HOLD THAT CO-ED(1938), d; DESTRY RIDES AGAIN(1939), d; YOU CAN'T CHEAT AN HONEST MAN(1939), d; GHOST BREAKERS, THE(1940), d; WHEN THE DALTONS RODE(1940), d; POT O' GOLD(1941), d; TEXAS(1941), d; FOREST RANGERS, THE(1942), d; STAR SPANGLED RHYTHM(1942), d; VALLEY OF THE SUN(1942), d; RIDING HIGH(1943), d; HOLD THAT BLONDE(1945), d; INCENDIARY BLONDE(1945), d; MURDER, HE SAYS(1945), d; BLUE DAHLIA, THE(1946), d; MONSIEUR BEAUCAIRE(1946), d; PERILS OF PAULINE, THE(1947), d; VARIETY GIRL(1947), a, d; HAZARD(1948), d; TAP ROOTS(1948), d; MY FRIEND IRMA(1949), d; FANCY PANTS(1950), d; NEVER A DULL MOMENT(1950), d; MILLIONAIRE FOR CHRISTY, A(1951), d; HOUDINI(1953), d; MONEY FROM HOME(1953), d; OFF LIMITS(1953), d; SAVAGE, THE(1953), d; SCARED STIFF(1953), d; DESTRY(1954), d; DUEL IN THE JUNGLE(1954, Brit.), d; RED GARTERS(1954), d; SECOND GREATEST SEX, THE(1955), d; TIMBERJACK(1955); PILLARS OF THE SKY(1956), d; BEYOND MOMBASA(1957), d; GUNS OF FORT PETTICOAT, THE(1957), d; SAD SACK, THE(1957), d; IMITATION GENERAL(1958), d; SHEEPMAN, THE(1958), d; GAZEBO, THE(1959), d; IT STARTED WITH A KISS(1959), d; MATING GAME, THE(1959), d; CRY FOR HAPPY(1961), d; HAPPY THIEVES, THE(1962), d; HOW THE WEST WAS WON(1962), d; PAPA'S DELICATE CONDITION(1963), d; ADVANCE TO THE REAR(1964), d; DARK PURPOSE(1964), d; BOY, DID I GET A WRONG NUMBER!(1966), d; EIGHT ON THE LAM(1967), d; WICKED DREAMS OF PAULA SCHULTZ, THE(1968), d; HOOK, LINE AND SINKER(1969), d; PUTNEY SWOPE(1969); CRAZY WORLD OF JULIUS VROODER, THE(1974)
Silents
MAN FROM MONTANA, THE(1917), d, w
Misc. Silents
PRAIRIE TRAILS(1920), d
George Marshall [Georges Marshell]
SIGN OF THE GLADIATOR(1959, Fr./Ger./Ital.)
George E. Marshall
Silents
JOLT, THE(1921), d; SMILES ARE TRUMPS(1922), d; GAY RETREAT, THE(1927), sup
Misc. Silents
LOVE'S LARIAT(1916), d; AFTER YOUR OWN HEART(1921), d; HANDS OFF(1921), d; LADY FROM LONGACRE, THE(1921), d; RIDIN' ROMEO, A(1921), d; WHY TRUST YOUR HUSBAND?(1921), d; DON QUICKSHOT OF THE RIO GRANDE(1923), d; MEN IN THE RAW(1923), d; WHERE IS THIS WEST?(1923), d
George F. Marshall
Silents
JOLT, THE(1921), w
Geroge Marshall
OLSEN'S BIG MOMENT(1934), w
Glen Leigh Marshall
STRIPES(1981)
Glen Marshall
LITTLE SHEPHERD OF KINGDOM COME(1961); AIR PATROL(1962); POLICE NURSE(1963)
Gloria Marshall
ESCAPE TO BURMA(1955); ROADRACERS, THE(1959)
Gregory Marshall
BANDITS OF DARK CANYON(1947); STEPCHILD(1947); THAT'S MY MAN(1947); JOAN OF ARC(1948); ADVENTURE IN BALTIMORE(1949); FULLER BRUSH GIRL, THE(1950); BLUE VEIL, THE(1951); WASHINGTON STORY(1952); TANGANYIKA(1954); TEENAGE THUNDER(1957)
Hal Marshall
ANGELS HARD AS THEY COME(1971); RENEGADE GIRLS(1974); CRAZY MAMA(1975); MELVIN AND HOWARD(1980)
Helene Marshall
LIEUTENANT WORE SKIRTS, THE(1956); INCREDIBLE SHRINKING MAN, THE(1957); TATTERED DRESS, THE(1957)
Herbert Marshall
LETTER, THE(1929); MURDER(1930, Brit.); CALENDAR, THE(1931, Brit.); SECRETS OF A SECRETARY(1931); BLONDE VENUS(1932); EVENINGS FOR SALE(1932); MICHAEL AND MARY(1932, Brit.); TROUBLE IN PARADISE(1932); FAITHFUL HEART(1933, Brit.); SOLITAIRE MAN, THE(1933); FOUR FRIGHTENED PEOPLE(1934); I WAS A SPY(1934, Brit.); OUTCAST LADY(1934); PAINTED VEIL, THE(1934); RIP TIDE(1934); ACCENT ON YOUTH(1935); DARK ANGEL, THE(1935); FLAME WITHIN, THE(1935); GOOD FAIRY, THE(1935); FORGOTTEN FACES(1936); GIRLS' DORMITORY(1936); IF YOU COULD ONLY COOK(1936); LADY CONSENTS, THE(1936); MAKE WAY FOR A LADY(1936); TILL WE MEET AGAIN(1936); WOMAN REBELS, A(1936); ANGEL(1937); BREAKFAST FOR TWO(1937); ALWAYS GOODBYE(1938); MAD ABOUT MUSIC(1938); WOMAN AGAINST WOMAN(1938); ZAZA(1939); BILL OF DIVORCEMENT(1940); FOREIGN CORRESPONDENT(1940); LETTER, THE(1940); ADVENTURE IN WASHINGTON(1941); KATHLEEN(1941); LITTLE FOXES, THE(1941); PROUD VALLEY, THE(1941, Brit.), w; WHEN LADIES MEET(1941); MOON AND SIXPENCE(1942); FLIGHT FOR FREEDOM(1943); FOREVER AND A DAY(1943); YOUNG IDEAS(1943); ANDY HARDY'S BLONDE TROUBLE(1944); ENCHANTED COTTAGE, THE(1945); UNSEEN, THE(1945); CRACK-UP(1946); DUEL IN THE SUN(1946); RAZOR'S EDGE, THE(1946); HIGH WALL, THE(1947); IVY(1947); SECRET GARDEN, THE(1949); WHIPPED, THE(1950);

ANNE OF THE INDIES(1951); CAPTAIN BLACK JACK(1952, U.S./Fr.); ANGEL FACE(1953); BLACK SHIELD OF FALWORTH, THE(1954); GOG(1954); RIDERS TO THE STARS(1954); VIRGIN QUEEN, THE(1955); PORTRAIT IN SMOKE(1957, Brit.); WEAPON, THE(1957, Brit.); FLY, THE(1958); STAGE STRUCK(1958); COLLEGE CONFIDENTIAL(1960); MIDNIGHT LACE(1960); FEVER IN THE BLOOD, A(1961); FIVE WEEKS IN A BALLOON(1962); CARETAKERS, THE(1963); LIST OF ADRIAN MESSENGER, THE(1963); THIRD DAY, THE(1965)

Misc. Talkies
TINKER(1950, Brit.)
Silents
MUMSIE(1927, Brit.)
Herbert P.J. Marshall
TINKER(1949, Brit.), p&w, d
Iris Marshall
COLOR ME BLOOD RED(1965)
J. D. Marshall
COTTONPICKIN' CHICKENPICKERS(1967)
Jack Marshall
SLIGHTLY SCANDALOUS(1946); MISSOURI TRAVELER, THE(1958), m; THUNDER ROAD(1958), m; GIANT GILA MONSTER, THE(1959), m; RABBIT TRAP, THE(1959), m; TAKE A GIANT STEP(1959), m; MY DOG, BUDDY(1960), m; MUNSTER, GO HOME(1966), m; TAMMY AND THE MILLIONAIRE(1967), m; KONA COAST(1968), m; STAY AWAY, JOE(1968), m; BACKTRACK(1969), m
James Marshall
SANTA FE(1951), w
James Vance Marshall
WALKABOUT(1971, Aus./U.S.), w; GOLDEN SEAL, THE(1983), w
Jane Marshall
GOLD DIGGERS OF 1937(1936)
Jerry Marshall
ROAR(1981)
Jo Ann Marshall
1984
PREPPIES(1984)
Jo-Ann Marshall
1984
DELIVERY BOYS(1984)
Joan Marshall
LIVE FAST, DIE YOUNG(1958); TAMMY AND THE DOCTOR(1963); LOOKING FOR LOVE(1964); HAPPIEST MILLIONAIRE, THE(1967); HORSE IN THE GRAY FLANNEL SUIT, THE(1968)
Joel Marshall
ROAR(1981), prod d
John Marshall
EASY LIVING(1937); HIGH, WIDE AND HANDSOME(1937); TOAST OF NEW YORK, THE(1937); WHERE THE SIDEWALK ENDS(1950); OPERATION SECRET(1952); PRISONERS OF THE CASBAH(1953); SECRET OF THE INCAS(1954); TIGHT SPOT(1955); MAN WHO KNEW TOO MUCH, THE(1956); FRONTIER UPRISING(1961); GREATEST, THE(1977, U.S./Brit.), p; ROAR(1981)
Julian Marshall
1984
OLD ENOUGH(1984), m
Juliette Marshall
XANADU(1980); KING OF THE MOUNTAIN(1981)
Karen Marshall
MICROWAVE MASSACRE(1983)
Kathi Marshall
1984
FLAMINGO KID, THE(1984)
Ken Marshall
TILT(1979); KRULL(1983)
Kristina Marshall
NEXT OF KIN(1983, Aus.)
Larry Marshall
PANIC IN NEEDLE PARK(1971); ROADIE(1980)
1984
COTTON CLUB, THE(1984)
Larry T. Marshall
JESUS CHRIST, SUPERSTAR(1973)
Linda Marshall
GIRLS ON THE BEACH(1965); TAMMY AND THE MILLIONAIRE(1967)
Lois Marshall
Misc. Talkies
CAMERONS, THE(1974)
Lorraine Marshall
I'VE GOT YOUR NUMBER(1934)
Lyn Marshall
SUBTERFUGE(1969, US/Brit.)
M.T. Marshall
GUNN(1967)
Madeline Marshall
Misc. Silents
LOADED DICE(1918)
Marion Marshall
DAISY KENYON(1947); APARTMENT FOR PEGGY(1948); LUCK OF THE IRISH(1948); ROAD HOUSE(1948); SITTING PRETTY(1948); STREET WITH NO NAME, THE(1948); UNFAITHFULLY YOURS(1948); WHEN MY BABY SMILES AT ME(1948); YOU WERE MEANT FOR ME(1948); DANCING IN THE DARK(1949); I WAS A MALE WAR BRIDE(1949); LOVE THAT BRUTE(1950); MY BLUE HEAVEN(1950); STELLA(1950); TICKET TO TOMAHAWK(1950); WABASH AVENUE(1950); HALLS OF MONTEZUMA(1951); I CAN GET IT FOR YOU WHOLESALE(1951); SAILOR BEWARE(1951); THAT'S MY BOY(1951); STOOGE, THE(1952); I WANT TO LIVE!(1958); RUN WITH THE DEVIL(1963, Fr./Ital.)
Mary Marshall
PREJUDICE(1949); NED KELLY(1970, Brit.)
Maurice Marshall
COOLEY HIGH(1975); MARIE-ANN(1978, Can.), m; HOUNDS... OF NOTRE DAME, THE(1980, Can.), m

Misc. Silents
WIFE'S RELATIONS, THE(1928), d
Melvia Marshall
PUTNEY SWOPE(1969)
Michael Marshall
PHANTOM PLANET, THE(1961); MOONRAKER(1979, Brit.)
Mike Marshall
FRIEND OF THE FAMILY(1965, Fr./Ital.); DON'T LOOK NOW(1969, Brit./Fr.); HELLO–GOODBYE(1970); LITTLE ROMANCE, A(1979, U.S./Fr.)
1984
UNTIL SEPTEMBER(1984)
Monica Marshall
TOO HOT TO HANDLE(1961, Brit.)
Mort Marshall
GO, MAN, GO!(1954); SILVER CHALICE, THE(1954); TARGET EARTH(1954); KISS ME DEADLY(1955); PETE KELLY'S BLUES(1955); GAMERA THE INVINCIBLE(1966, Jap.); LOVERS AND OTHER STRANGERS(1970); SKULLDUGGERY(1970); GRISSOM GANG, THE(1971); LONGEST YARD, THE(1974); W. W. AND THE DIXIE DANCEKINGS(1975); STARTING OVER(1979)
Muriel Marshall
LOVE IS A CAROUSEL(1970)
Nancy Marshall
TO KILL A MOCKINGBIRD(1962); FRANKENSTEIN MEETS THE SPACE MONSTER(1965)
Neal Marshall
1984
FLAMINGO KID, THE(1984), w
Noel Marshall
ROAR(1981), a, p,d&w
Norman Marshall
SHAMUS(1973); FOR PETE'S SAKE(1977)
Norman Thomas Marshall
REVENGE OF THE CHEERLEADERS(1976)
Pat Marshall
LIEUTENANT WORE SKIRTS, THE(1956)
Patricia Marshall
GOOD NEWS(1947)
Paul Marshall
JACQUES BREL IS ALIVE AND WELL AND LIVING IN PARIS(1975), p
Peggy Marshall
TIM DRISCOLL'S DONKEY(1955, Brit.); WOMAN OF STRAW(1964, Brit.); FIGHTING PRINCE OF DONEGAL, THE(1966, Brit.)
1984
JIGSAW MAN, THE(1984, Brit.)
Penny Marshall
HOW SWEET IT IS(1968); SAVAGE SEVEN, THE(1968); HOW COME NOBODY'S ON OUR SIDE?(1975); 1941(1979)
Pete Marshall
FBI GIRL(1951); ROOKIE, THE(1959); SWINGIN' ALONG(1962)
Peter L. Marshall
ENSIGN PULVER(1964); CAVERN, THE(1965, Ital./Ger.)
Peter Marshall
HOLIDAY RHYTHM(1950); FORTY-NINTH MAN, THE(1953); MARYJANE(1968), a, w; LONG AGO, TOMORROW(1971, Brit.), w; BLACK JACK(1973), w; AMERICATHON(1979); ANNIE(1982)
Ray Marshall
CADDIE(1976, Aus.); MONEY MOVERS(1978, Aus.); STIR(1980, Aus.)
Red Marshall
QUEEN OF BURLESQUE(1946)
Robert Marshall
DEAD MAN'S EVIDENCE(1962, Brit.)
Roger Marshall
TWO LETTER ALIBI(1962), w; FIVE TO ONE(1963, Brit.), w; SET-UP, THE(1963, Brit.), w; WHO WAS MADDOX?(1964, Brit.), w; GAME FOR THREE LOSERS(1965, Brit.), w; INVASION(1965, Brit.), w; RICOCHET(1966, Brit.), w; SOLO FOR SPARROW(1966, Brit.), w; THEATRE OF DEATH(1967, Brit.), w; MAN OUTSIDE, THE(1968, Brit.), w; TWISTED NERVE(1969, Brit.), w; HELLO–GOODBYE(1970), w; WHAT BECAME OF JACK AND JILL?(1972, Brit.), w; AND NOW THE SCREAMING STARTS(1973, Brit.), w
Rosalyn Marshall
ST. IVES(1976)
Rosamond Marshall
ALL THE FINE YOUNG CANNIBALS(1960), w
Rosamund Marshall
KITTY(1945), w
Rose Marshall
HOT TOMORROWS(1978)
Ruby Marshall
Silents
FIGHTING FOR LOVE(1917)
S.L.A. Marshall
PORK CHOP HILL(1959), w
Sarah Marshall
LONG, HOT SUMMER, THE(1958); WILD AND WONDERFUL(1964); RAGE TO LIVE, A(1965); LORD LOVE A DUCK(1966); EMBASSY(1972, Brit.)
Scott Marshall
1984
FLAMINGO KID, THE(1984)
Sean Marshall
DEADLY TRACKERS(1973); PETE'S DRAGON(1977)
Sharon Marshall
ADAM AT 6 A.M.(1970)
Shary Marshall
PANIC IN YEAR ZERO!(1962); YOUR CHEATIN' HEART(1964); TAFFY AND THE JUNGLE HUNTER(1965); STREET IS MY BEAT, THE(1966); TELL ME IN THE SUNLIGHT(1967)
Sidney Marshall
MR. DISTRICT ATTORNEY(1946), w

Stacey Marshall
GANG WAR(1958); SHOWDOWN AT BOOT HILL(1958)
Stephen Marshall
CAT PEOPLE(1982)
Ted Marshall
STEEL BAYONET, THE(1958, Brit.), art d; ENTERTAINER, THE(1960, Brit.), art d; TOUCH OF FLESH, THE(1960); SATURDAY NIGHT AND SUNDAY MORNING(1961, Brit.), art d; LONELINESS OF THE LONG DISTANCE RUNNER, THE(1962, Brit.), art d; QUARE FELLOW, THE(1962, Brit.), art d; TWO AND TWO MAKE SIX(1962, Brit.), art d; TOM JONES(1963, Brit.), art d; GIRL WITH GREEN EYES(1964, Brit.), art d; PERSECUTION AND ASSASSINATION OF JEAN-PAUL MARAT AS PERFORMED BY THE INMATES OF THE ASYLUM OF CHARENTON UNDER THE DIRECTION OF THE MARQUIS DE SADE, THE(1967, Brit.), art d; MACHO CALLAHAN(1970), prod d
Tina Marshall
STAND UP AND CHEER(1934 80m FOX bw); ONE MORE SPRING(1935); JUVENILE COURT(1938); YOU CAN'T TAKE IT WITH YOU(1938)
Silents
CHARM SCHOOL, THE(1921)
Misc. Silents
HONOR OF MARY BLAKE, THE(1916); MAN INSIDE, THE(1916)
Tom Marshall
TERROR FROM UNDER THE HOUSE(1971, Brit.)
Misc. Talkies
KILLER'S MOON(1978)
Tony Marshall
I WAS A TEENAGE WEREWOLF(1957); ROCKABILLY BABY(1957)
Trudi Marshall
ONCE IS NOT ENOUGH(1975)
Trudy Marshall
FOOTLIGHT SERENADE(1942); GIRL TROUBLE(1942); SPRINGTIME IN THE ROCKIES(1942); CRASH DIVE(1943); DANCING MASTERS, THE(1943); HEAVEN CAN WAIT(1943); LADIES OF WASHINGTON(1944); PURPLE HEART, THE(1944); ROGER TOUHY, GANGSTER!(1944); SULLIVANS, THE(1944); CIRCUMSTANTIAL EVIDENCE(1945); DOLLY SISTERS, THE(1945); BOSTON BLACKIE AND THE LAW(1946); DRAGONWYCH(1946); SENTIMENTAL JOURNEY(1946); TALK ABOUT A LADY(1946); KEY WITNESS(1947); TOO MANY WINNERS(1947); DISASTER(1948); FULLER BRUSH MAN(1948); BARBARY PIRATE(1949); SHAMROCK HILL(1949); MARK OF THE GORILLA(1950); PRESIDENT'S LADY, THE(1953); FULL OF LIFE(1956); MARRIED TOO YOUNG(1962)
Misc. Talkies
JOE PALOOKA IN THE KNOCKOUT(1947)
Tully Marshall
ALIAS JIMMY VALENTINE(1928); PERFECT CRIME, THE(1928); BRIDGE OF SAN LUIS REY, THE(1929); CONQUEST(1929); MYSTERIOUS DR. FU MANCHU, THE(1929); SKIN DEEP(1929); THUNDERBOLT(1929); BIG TRAIL, THE(1930); BURNING UP(1930); COMMON CLAY(1930); DANCING SWEETIES(1930); MAMMY(1930); MURDER WILL OUT(1930); NUMBERED MEN(1930); ONE NIGHT AT SUSIE'S(1930); REDEMPTION(1930); SHE COULDN'T SAY NO(1930); TIGER ROSE(1930); TOM SAWYER(1930); UNDER A TEXAS MOON(1930); FIGHTING CARAVANS(1931); MILLIONAIRE, THE(1931); UNHOLY GARDEN, THE(1931); VIRTUOUS HUSBAND(1931); AFRAID TO TALK(1932); ARSENE LUPIN(1932); BEAST OF THE CITY, THE(1932); BROKEN LULLABY(1932); CABIN IN THE COTTON(1932); GRAND HOTEL(1932); HATCHET MAN, THE(1932); KLONDIKE(1932); NIGHT COURT(1932); RED DUST(1932); SCANDAL FOR SALE(1932); SCARFACE(1932); STRANGERS OF THE EVENING(1932); TWO-FISTED LAW(1932); CORRUPTION(1933); LAUGHING AT LIFE(1933); NIGHT OF TERROR(1933); MASSACRE(1934); MURDER ON THE BLACKBOARD(1934); BLACK FURY(1935); DIAMOND JIM(1935); TALE OF TWO CITIES, A(1935); CALIFORNIA STRAIGHT AHEAD(1937); HOLD'EM NAVY!(1937); SHE ASKED FOR IT(1937); SOULS AT SEA(1937); STAND-IN(1937); ARSENE LUPIN RETURNS(1938); COLLEGE SWING(1938); MAKING THE HEADLINES(1938); MR. BOGGS STEPS OUT(1938); YANK AT OXFORD, A(1938); BLUE MONTANA SKIES(1939); KID FROM TEXAS, THE(1939); BRIGHAM YOUNG--FRONTIERSMAN(1940); CHAD HANNA(1940); GO WEST(1940); INVISIBLE STRIPES(1940); YOUTH WILL BE SERVED(1940); FOR BEAUTY'S SAKE(1941); SERGEANT YORK(1941); MOONTIDE(1942); TEN GENTLEMEN FROM WEST POINT(1942); THIS GUN FOR HIRE(1942); BEHIND PRISON WALLS(1943); HITLER'S MADMAN(1943)
Misc. Talkies
EXPOSURE(1932)
Silents
PAINTED SOUL, THE(1915); SABLE LORCHA, THE(1915); INTOLERANCE(1916); JOAN THE WOMAN(1916); MARTHA'S VINDICATION(1916); OLIVER TWIST(1916); MODERN MUSKETEER, A(1917); ROMANCE OF THE REDWOODS, A(1917); ARIZONA(1918); M'LISS(1918); OLD WIVES FOR NEW(1918); DAUGHTER OF MINE(1919); GIRL WHO STAYED AT HOME, THE(1919); GRIM GAME, THE(1919); HAWTHORNE OF THE U.S.A.(1919); EXCUSE MY DUST(1920); LITTLE 'FRAID LADY, THE(1920); WHAT HAPPENED TO ROSA?(1921); BEAUTIFUL AND DAMNED, THE(1922); DESERTED AT THE ALTAR(1922); FOOLS OF FORTUNE(1922); LYING TRUTH, THE(1922); ONLY A SHOP GIRL(1922); PENROD(1922); SUPER-SEX, THE(1922); TOO MUCH BUSINESS(1922); COVERED WAGON, THE(1923); HUNCHBACK OF NOTRE DAME, THE(1923); LAW OF THE LAWLESS, THE(1923); TEMPORARY MARRIAGE(1923); ALONG CAME RUTH(1924); HE WHO GETS SLAPPED(1924); RECKLESS ROMANCE(1924); STRANGER, THE(1924); CLOTHES MAKE THE PIRATE(1925); MERRY WIDOW, THE(1925); PACE THAT THRILLS, THE(1925); OLD LOVES AND NEW(1926); TORRENT, THE(1926); TWINKLETOES(1926); CAT AND THE CANARY, THE(1927); JIM THE CONQUEROR(1927); QUEEN KELLY(1929); TRAIL OF '98, THE(1929)
Misc. Silents
PAID IN FULL(1914); CHILD OF THE PARIS STREETS, A(1916); DEVIL'S NEEDLE, THE(1916); LET KATHY DO IT(1916); DEVIL STONE, THE(1917); GOLDEN FETTER, THE(1917); UNCONQUERED(1917); BOUND IN MOROCCO(1918); THINGS WE LOVE, THE(1918); TOO MANY MILLIONS(1918); CRIMSON GARDENIA, THE(1919); LADY OF RED BUTTE, THE(1919); MAGGIE PEPPER(1919); DOUBLE SPEED(1920); HONEST HUTCH(1920); SLIM PRINCESS, THE(1920); CUP OF LIFE, THE(1921); LOTUS BLOSSOM(1921); SILENT YEARS(1921); ANY NIGHT(1922); LADDER JINX, THE(1922); MARRIAGE CHANCE, THE(1922); WITHOUT COMPROMISE(1922); BRASS BOTTLE, THE(1923); BROKEN HEARTS OF BROADWAY, THE(1923); DANGEROUS TRAILS(1923); DEFYING DESTINY(1923); FOOLS AND RICHES(1923); HER TEMPORARY HUSBAND(1923); LET'S GO(1923); PONJOLA(1923); HOLD YOUR BREATH(1924); PASSION'S PATHWAY(1924); RIDIN' KID FROM POWDER RIVER,

THE(1924); HALF-WAY GIRL, THE(1925); SMOULDERING FIRES(1925); HER BIG NIGHT(1926); GORILLA, THE(1927); DRUMS OF LOVE(1928)
Vicky Marshall
UGLY DUCKLING, THE(1959, Brit.)
Virginia Marshall
Silents
LAZYBONES(1925); OUTLAWS OF RED RIVER(1927)
Misc. Silents
DADDY'S GONE A-HUNTING(1925); MY OWN PAL(1926)
Vivian Marshall
THREE YOUNG TEXANS(1954); GOOD MORNING, MISS DOVE(1955); WOMEN'S PRISON(1955); GIDGET GOES HAWAIIAN(1961)
Wendy Marshall
ONE BRIEF SUMMER(1971, Brit.), w
William C. Marshall
Silents
ARMS AND THE GIRL(1917), ph; GREAT EXPECTATIONS(1917), ph
William Marshall
NIGHT PARADE(1929, Brit.), ph; SIDE STREET(1929), ph; AMOS 'N' ANDY(1930), ph; SECOND WIFE(1930), ph; FLOWING GOLD(1940); KNUTE ROCKNE--ALL AMERICAN(1940); MONEY AND THE WOMAN(1940); SANTA FE TRAIL(1940); FLYING WITH MUSIC(1942); TOMORROW WE LIVE(1942); BELLE OF THE YUKON(1944); STATE FAIR(1945); EARL CARROLL SKETCHBOOK(1946); MURDER IN THE MUSIC HALL(1946); THAT BRENNAN GIRL(1946); BLACKMAIL(1947); CALENDAR GIRL(1947); ADVENTURES OF CAPTAIN FABIAN(1951), p&d; HELLO GOD(1951, U.S./Ital.), a, p,d&w; LYDIA BAILEY(1952); DEMETRIUS AND THE GLADIATORS(1954); SABU AND THE MAGIC RING(1957); SOMETHING OF VALUE(1957); PHANTOM PLANET, THE(1961), d; QUICK, LET'S GET MARRIED(1965), p; TO TRAP A SPY(1966); HELL WITH HEROES, THE(1968); THE BOSTON STRANGLER, THE(1968); SKULLDUGGERY(1970); TARZAN'S JUNGLE REBELLION(1970); ZIGZAG(1970); HONKY(1971); BLACULA(1972); SCREAM BLACULA SCREAM(1973); ABBY(1974); OUTRAGEOUS!(1977, Can.), p; TWILIGHT'S LAST GLEAMING(1977, U.S./Ger.); HANK WILLIAMS: THE SHOW HE NEVER GAVE(1982, Can.), p; CURTAINS(1983, Can.)
Misc. Talkies
GREAT SKYCOPTER RESCUE, THE(1982)
Silents
LITTLE MISS HOOVER(1918), ph; CROOKED STREETS(1920), ph; EYES OF THE HEART(1920), ph; LADY IN LOVE, A(1920), ph; SHEIK, THE(1921), ph; WISE FOOL, A(1921), ph; JILT, THE(1922), ph; MORAN OF THE LADY LETTY(1922), ph; OUR LEADING CITIZEN(1922), ph; AMERICAN MANNERS(1924), ph; IN FAST COMPANY(1924), ph; LAUGHING AT DANGER(1924), ph; ON TIME(1924), ph; FLAMING WATERS(1925), ph; ISLE OF HOPE, THE(1925), ph; JIMMIE'S MILLIONS(1925), ph; WET PAINT(1926), ph; TIME TO LOVE(1927), ph; WEDDING BILL$(1927), ph; HOT NEWS(1928), ph; PARTNERS IN CRIME(1928), ph
Misc. Silents
DUST(1916)
Zena Marshall
CAESAR AND CLEOPATRA(1946, Brit.); END OF THE RIVER, THE(1947, Brit.); SO EVIL MY LOVE(1948, Brit.); BAD LORD BYRON, THE(1949, Brit.); HELTER SKELTER(1949, Brit.); MARRY ME!(1949, Brit.); MEET SIMON CHERRY(1949, Brit.); MIRANDA(1949, Brit.); SLEEPING CAR TO TRIESTE(1949, Brit.); SNOWBOUND(1949, Brit.); DARK INTERVAL(1950, Brit.); GOOD TIME GIRL(1950, Brit.); LOST PEOPLE, THE(1950, Brit.); HELL IS SOLD OUT(1951, Brit.); OPERATION DISASTER(1951, Brit.); SO LONG AT THE FAIR(1951, Brit.); SOHO CONSPIRACY(1951, Brit.); BLIND MAN'S BLUFF(1952, Brit.); CARETAKERS DAUGHTER, THE(1952, Brit.); DEADLY NIGHTSHADE(1953, Brit.); MEN AGAINST THE SUN(1953, Brit.); EMBEZZLER, THE(1954, Brit.); SCARLET WEB, THE(1954, Brit.); THREE CASES OF MURDER(1955, Brit.); BERMUDA AFFAIR(1956, Brit.); FOOTSTEPS IN THE NIGHT(1957); LET'S BE HAPPY(1957, Brit.); STORY OF DAVID, A(1960, Brit.); BACKFIRE!(1961, Brit.); CROSSTRAP(1962, Brit.); DR. NO(1962, Brit.); MY WIFE'S FAMILY(1962, Brit.); SWITCH, THE(1963, Brit.); VERDICT, THE(1964, Brit.); THOSE MAGNIFICENT MEN IN THEIR FLYING MACHINES; OR HOW I FLEWFROM LONDON TO PARIS IN 25 HOURS AND 11 MINUTES(1965, Brit.); TERRORNAUTS, THE(1967, Brit.)
Boris Marshalov
PIE IN THE SKY(1964)
Julia S. Marshbanks
INTRUDER IN THE DUST(1949)
Sheena Marshe
OVER THE ODDS(1961, Brit.); GET ON WITH IT(1963, Brit.); ACT OF MURDER(1965, Brit.)
Tony Marshe
ABBOTT AND COSTELLO MEET DR. JEKYLL AND MR. HYDE(1954)
Vera Marshe
OBLIGING YOUNG LADY(1941); AFFAIRS OF SUSAN(1945); GETTING GERTIE'S GARTER(1945); PHANTOM OF 42ND STREET, THE(1945); THOSE ENDEARING YOUNG CHARMS(1945); BLUE DAHLIA, THE(1946); CRIMSON KEY, THE(1947); HUCKSTERS, THE(1947); MONSIEUR VERDOUX(1947); WHERE THERE'S LIFE(1947); HOLLOW TRIUMPH(1948); YOU GOTTA STAY HAPPY(1948); BIG SOMBRERO, THE(1949); POST OFFICE INVESTIGATOR(1949); DAVY CROCKETT, INDIAN SCOUT(1950); WESTERN PACIFIC AGENT(1950); SCARLET ANGEL(1952); MC CONNELL STORY, THE(1955); TORMENTED(1960)
Archie Marshek
GANG WAR(1928), ed; BLOCKADE(1929), ed; HALF-MARRIAGE(1929), ed; TANNED LEGS(1929), ed; DANGER LIGHTS(1930), ed; FALL GUY, THE(1930), ed; HOOK, LINE AND SINKER(1930), ed; LOVE COMES ALONG(1930), ed; RUNAWAY BRIDE(1930), ed; PUBLIC DEFENDER, THE(1931), ed; MEN OF CHANCE(1932), ed; MOST DANGEROUS GAME, THE(1932), ed; SYMPHONY OF SIX MILLION(1932), ed; MURDER ON THE BLACKBOARD(1934), ed; BECKY SHARP(1935), ed; DANGEROUS CORNER(1935), ed; WEST OF THE PECOS(1935), ed; DANCING PIRATE(1936), ed; HIGH, WIDE AND HANDSOME(1937), ed; NIGHT CLUB SCANDAL(1937), ed; TROPIC HOLIDAY(1938), ed; CAT AND THE CANARY, THE(1939), ed; DEATH OF A CHAMPION(1939), ed; I'M FROM MISSOURI(1939), ed; PARIS HONEYMOON(1939), ed; FARMER'S DAUGHTER, THE(1940), ed; MYSTERY SEA RAIDER(1940), ed; MAD DOCTOR, THE(1941), ed; WEST POINT WIDOW(1941), ed; WORLD PREMIERE(1941), ed; YOU'RE THE ONE(1941), ed; GLASS KEY, THE(1942), ed; LUCKY JORDAN(1942), ed; REMARKABLE ANDREW, THE(1942), ed; THIS GUN FOR HIRE(1942), ed; HENRY ALDRICH SWINGS IT(1943), ed; HOSTAGES(1943), ed; INCENDIARY BLONDE(1945), ed; MINISTRY OF

FEAR(1945), ed; MISS SUSIE SLAGLE'S(1945), ed; STRANGE LOVE OF MARTHA IVERS, THE(1946), ed; CALCUTTA(1947), ed; DEAR RUTH(1947), ed; WHERE THERE'S LIFE(1947), ed; WHISPERING SMITH(1948), ed; CONNECTICUT YANKEE IN KING ARTHUR'S COURT, A(1949), ed; DEAR WIFE(1949), ed; STREETS OF LAREDO(1949), ed; FANCY PANTS(1950), ed; FURIES, THE(1950), ed; LEMON DROP KID, THE(1951), ed; AARON SLICK FROM PUNKIN CRICK(1952), ed; ATOMIC CITY, THE(1952), ed; ROAD TO BALI(1952), ed; FOREVER FEMALE(1953), ed; THOSE REDHEADS FROM SEATTLE(1953), ed; ALASKA SEAS(1954), ed; LIVING IT UP(1954), ed; HELL'S ISLAND(1955), ed; YOU'RE NEVER TOO YOUNG(1955), ed; PARDNERS(1956), ed; BUSTER KEATON STORY, THE(1957), ed; FUZZY PINK NIGHTGOWN, THE(1957), ed; SAD SACK, THE(1957), ed; BUCCANEER, THE(1958), ed; ONE-EYED JACKS(1961), ed; CABINET OF CALIGARI, THE(1962), ed; MY GEISHA(1962), ed; ADVANCE TO THE REAR(1964), ed; LIVELY SET, THE(1964), ed; PARIS WHEN IT SIZZLES(1964), ed; BIRDS AND THE BEES, THE(1965), ed; BOEING BOEING(1965), ed; HARLOW(1965), ed; TICKLE ME(1965), ed; ASSAULT ON A QUEEN(1966), ed; EASY COME, EASY GO(1967), ed; WARNING SHOT(1967), ed; NO WAY TO TREAT A LADY(1968), ed; ILLUSTRATED MAN, THE(1969), ed; RABBIT, RUN(1970), ed; SHOOT OUT(1971), ed
Silents
SALLY OF THE SCANDALS(1928), ed; SINNERS IN LOVE(1928), ed; SKINNER'S BIG IDEA(1928), ed; AIR LEGION, THE(1929), ed

Archie F. Marshek
PERFECT CRIME, THE(1928), ed; BEAU BANDIT(1930), ed; WE'RE ONLY HUMAN(1936), ed; PERFECT COUPLE, A(1979), ed

Archie S. Marshek
SON OF KONG(1933), p

D. M. Marshman, Jr.
SUNSET BOULEVARD(1950), w; SECOND CHANCE(1953), w; TAXI(1953), w

Joanne Marsic
PORKY'S(1982)

Vittorio Marsiglia
CAFE EXPRESS(1980, Ital.)

Antonio Marsina
STRANGER IN TOWN, A(1968, U.S./Ital.)

Joel Marsion
FEARMAKERS, THE(1958)

James Marsland
MIKADO, THE(1967, Brit.)

Francisco Marso
ERNESTO(1979, Ital.)

Aileen Marson
GREEN PACK, THE(1934, Brit.); LUCKY LOSER(1934, Brit.); PASSING SHADOWS(1934, Brit.); ROAD HOUSE(1934, Brit.); WAY OF YOUTH, THE(1934, Brit.); BLACK MASK(1935, Brit.); HONEYMOON FOR THREE(1935, Brit.); MY SONG FOR YOU(1935, Brit.); REGAL CAVALCADE(1935, Brit.); TEN MINUTE ALIBI(1935, Brit.); LIVING DANGEROUSLY(1936, Brit.); SOMEONE AT THE DOOR(1936, Brit.); SPRING HANDICAP(1937, Brit.); TENTH MAN, THE(1937, Brit.)

Ania Marson
NICHOLAS AND ALEXANDRA(1971, Brit.); PUPPET ON A CHAIN(1971, Brit.); ABDICATION, THE(1974, Brit.)

Joel Marson
THERE'S A GIRL IN MY HEART(1949)

Lionel Marson
HORSE'S MOUTH, THE(1953, Brit.)

Trudy Marson
SINGING MARINE, THE(1937)

Joel Marstan
STAR TREK II: THE WRATH OF KHAN(1982)

Kenneth Marstella
CONQUEROR, THE(1956), ed; I MARRIED A WOMAN(1958), ed

Lawrence Marsten
Silents
IRON MAN, THE(1925), w

Ann Marsters
EXCLUSIVE(1937); THIRD FINGER, LEFT HAND(1940)

Rosita Marstina
I COVER THE WATERFRONT(1933)

Marie Marstini
Silents
BLOOD AND SAND(1922)

Rosia Marstini
HOLIDAY IN MEXICO(1946)

Rosita Marstini
HOT FOR PARIS(1930); FOURTH HORSEMAN, THE(1933); IN LOVE WITH LIFE(1934); THIS LOVE OF OURS(1945); CASBAH(1948)
Silents
CLEVER MRS. CARFAX, THE(1917); INNOCENT SINNER, THE(1917); TALE OF TWO CITIES, A(1917); GOOD NIGHT, PAUL(1918); FLAMES OF THE FLESH(1920); OUTSIDE WOMAN, THE(1921); ENTER MADAME(1922); BIG PARADE, THE(1925); PROUD FLESH(1925); REDEEMING SIN, THE(1925); NO OTHER WOMAN(1928)
Misc. Silents
HIGH FINANCE(1917); MORAL LAW, THE(1918); SERENADE(1921)

Alan Marston
TITANIC(1953)

Allen Marston
NIGHT AND DAY(1946)

Christine Marston
DIZZY DAMES(1936)

Joel Marston
FORGOTTEN WOMEN(1949); MISSISSIPPI RHYTHM(1949); WEST POINT STORY, THE(1950); FBI GIRL(1951); PURPLE HEART DIARY(1951); RED BADGE OF COURAGE, THE(1951); OLD OKLAHOMA PLAINS(1952); TURNING POINT, THE(1952); CRAZYLEGS, ALL AMERICAN(1953); FIGHTER ATTACK(1953); FOREVER FEMALE(1953); WAR OF THE WORLDS, THE(1953); WHITE LIGHTNING(1953); BATTLE TAXI(1955); NIGHT HOLDS TERROR, THE(1955); DISEMBODIED, THE(1957); DECKS RAN RED, THE(1958); LAST VOYAGE, THE(1960); RING OF FIRE(1961); HARLOW(1965); POINT OF TERROR(1971); HEAVEN CAN WAIT(1978)

John Marston
LOVE IS A RACKET(1932); SCARLET DAWN(1932); SILVER DOLLAR(1932); SKYSCRAPER SOULS(1932); THREE ON A MATCH(1932); HELL AND HIGH WATER(1933); HEROES FOR SALE(1933); LADY KILLER(1933); LITTLE GIANT, THE(1933); MARY STEVENS, M.D.(1933); MAYOR OF HELL, THE(1933); SON OF A SAILOR(1933); SON OF KONG(1933); ALL OF ME(1934); BORN TO BE BAD(1934); GOOD DAME(1934); LOVE PAST THIRTY(1934); MANHATTAN MELODRAMA(1934); PURSUIT OF HAPPINESS, THE(1934); SERVANTS' ENTRANCE(1934); WAGON WHEELS(1934); CHINA CLIPPER(1936); WHIPSAW(1936); ANGELS WITH DIRTY FACES(1938); UNION PACIFIC(1939); EMERGENCY SQUAD(1940); NOBODY'S CHILDREN(1940); THOSE WERE THE DAYS(1940); TWO-FACED WOMAN(1941); BROKEN ARROW(1950)

Lawrence Marston
Misc. Silents
WOMAN IN BLACK, THE(1914), d; DORA THORNE(1915), d; MILLIONAIRE BABY, THE(1915), d; PRIMROSE PATH, THE(1915), d; LOVE'S PILGRIMAGE TO AMERICA(1916), d; MARRIAGE BOND, THE(1916), d; WALL STREET TRAGEDY, A(1916), d

Theodore Marston
Silents
WHEELS OF JUSTICE(1915), d
Misc. Silents
ROBIN HOOD(1913), d; CAVEMAN, THE(1915), d; MORTMAIN(1915), d; PAWNS OF MARS(1915), d; DAWN OF FREEDOM, THE(1916), d; SUPRISES OF AN EMPTY HOTEL, THE(1916), d; GREED(1917), d; RAGGEDY QUEEN, THE(1917), d; SEVENTH SIN, THE(1917), d; SLOTH(1917), d; WRATH(1917), d; BEYOND THE LAW(1918), d; GIRL BY THE ROADSIDE, THE(1918), d; BLACK GATE, THE(1919), d

Michael Marszalek
INVISIBLE MAN, THE(1963, Ger.), ph

Gunter Marszinkowsky
NAKED AMONG THE WOLVES(1967, Ger.), ph

Gin Mart
CLEOPATRA(1963); EMBALMER, THE(1966, Ital.)

Paul Mart
MARINE BATTLEGROUND(1966, U.S/S.K.), p; WILD GYPSIES(1969), p
Misc. Talkies
BEAUTY AND THE BODY(1963), d

Marta
NIGHT OF THE WITCHES(1970)

Jack A. Marta
PERILS OF PAULINE, THE(1967), ph; YOU'LL LIKE MY MOTHER(1972), ph; WALKING TALL(1973), ph; TRIAL OF BILLY JACK, THE(1974), ph; FRAMED(1975), ph; MASTER GUNFIGHTER, THE(1975), ph

Jack Marta
BEHIND GREEN LIGHTS(1935), ph; HARMONY LANE(1935), ph; SAGEBRUSH TROUBADOR(1935), ph; WATERFRONT LADY(1935), ph; $1,000 A MINUTE(1935), ph; ANY MAN'S WIFE(1936), ph; BOLD CABALLERO(1936), ph; BULLDOG EDITION(1936), ph; DANCING FEET(1936), ph; GENTLEMAN FROM LOUISIANA(1936), ph; GIRL FROM MANDALAY(1936), ph; HEARTS IN BONDAGE(1936), ph; HITCH HIKE LADY(1936), ph; HOUSE OF A THOUSAND CANDLES, THE(1936), ph; KING OF THE PECOS(1936), ph; LEATHERNECKS HAVE LANDED, THE(1936), ph; LEAVENWORTH CASE, THE(1936), ph; NAVY BORN(1936), ph; CIRCUS GIRL(1937), ph; GHOST TOWN GOLD(1937), ph; HEART OF THE ROCKIES(1937), ph; HIT THE SADDLE(1937), ph; IT COULD HAPPEN TO YOU(1937), ph; JIM HANVEY, DETECTIVE(1937), ph; LARCENY ON THE AIR(1937), ph; MANDARIN MYSTERY, THE(1937), ph; MANHATTAN MERRY-GO-ROUND(1937), ph; MICHAEL O'HALLORAN(1937), ph; NAVY BLUES(1937), ph; PARADISE EXPRESS(1937), ph; PUBLIC COWBOY NO. 1(1937), ph; RANGE DEFENDERS(1937), ph; RIDERS OF THE WHISTLING SKULL(1937), ph; SHEIK STEPS OUT, THE(1937), ph; BORN TO BE WILD(1938), ph; DESPERATE ADVENTURE, A(1938), ph; HE LOVED AN ACTRESS(1938, Brit.), ph; HIGGINS FAMILY, THE(1938), ph; I STAND ACCUSED(1938), ph; INVISIBLE ENEMY(1938), ph; KING OF THE NEWSBOYS(1938), ph; LADIES IN DISTRESS(1938), ph; MAN FROM MUSIC MOUNTAIN(1938), ph; NIGHT HAWK, THE(1938), ph; OUTSIDE OF PARADISE(1938), ph; RED RIVER RANGE(1938), ph; RHYTHM OF THE SADDLE(1938), ph; UNDER WESTERN STARS(1938), ph; BLUE MONTANA SKIES(1939), ph; FIGHTING THOROUGHBREDS(1939), ph; FORGED PASSPORT(1939), ph; MAIN STREET LAWYER(1939), ph; MICKEY, THE KID(1939), ph; MY WIFE'S RELATIVES(1939), ph; NIGHT RIDERS, THE(1939), ph; PRIDE OF THE NAVY(1939), ph; ROUGH RIDERS' ROUNDUP(1939), ph; SAGA OF DEATH VALLEY(1939), ph; SHOULD HUSBANDS WORK?(1939), ph; SMUGGLED CARGO(1939), ph; S.O.S. TIDAL WAVE(1939), ph; SOUTHWARD HO!(1939), ph; THOU SHALT NOT KILL(1939), ph; WALL STREET COWBOY(1939), ph; BORDER LEGION, THE(1940), ph; COLORADO(1940), ph; DARK COMMAND, THE(1940), ph; EARL OF PUDDLESTONE(1940), ph; GIRL FROM GOD'S COUNTRY(1940), ph; GRAND OLE OPRY(1940), ph; HIT PARADE OF 1941(1940), ph; PIONEERS OF THE WEST(1940), ph; RIDE, TENDERFOOT, RIDE(1940), ph; ROCKY MOUNTAIN RANGERS(1940), ph; WOMEN IN WAR(1940), ph; BEHIND THE NEWS(1941), ph; DOWN MEXICO WAY(1941), ph; ICE-CAPADES(1941), ph; LADY FROM LOUISIANA(1941), ph; MAN BETRAYED, A(1941), ph; PETTICOAT POLITICS(1941), ph; PUDDIN' HEAD(1941), ph; RED RIVER VALLEY(1941), ph; ROBIN HOOD OF THE PECOS(1941), ph; SIERRA SUE(1941), ph; SIS HOPKINS(1941), ph; COWBOY SERENADE(1942), ph; FLYING TIGERS(1942), ph; GIRL FROM ALASKA(1942), ph; HEART OF THE GOLDEN WEST(1942), ph; IN OLD CALIFORNIA(1942), ph; LONDON BLACKOUT MURDERS(1942), ph; MISSOURI OUTLAW, A(1942), ph; RIDIN' DOWN THE CANYON(1942), ph; SLEEPYTIME GAL(1942), ph; X MARKS THE SPOT(1942), ph; BORDERTOWN GUNFIGHTERS(1943), ph; HIT PARADE OF 1943(1943), ph; IN OLD OKLAHOMA(1943), ph; NOBODY'S DARLING(1943), ph; SOMEONE TO REMEMBER(1943), ph; TAHITI HONEY(1943), ph; WEST SIDE KID(1943), ph; WHISPERING FOOTSTEPS(1943), ph; BRAZIL(1944), ph; MAN FROM FRISCO(1944), ph; MY BEST GAL(1944), ph; PORT OF 40 THIEVES, THE(1944), ph; SONG OF NEVADA(1944), ph; YELLOW ROSE OF TEXAS, THE(1944), ph; ANGEL COMES TO BROOKLYN, AN(1945), ph; DAKOTA(1945), ph; EARL CARROLL'S VANITIES(1945), ph; HITCH-HIKE TO HAPPINESS(1945), ph; MEXICANA(1945), ph; EARL CARROLL SKETCHBOOK(1946), ph; IN OLD SACRAMENTO(1946), ph; MURDER IN THE MUSIC HALL(1946), ph; THAT BRENNAN GIRL(1946), ph; APACHE ROSE(1947), ph; BELLS OF SAN ANGELO(1947), ph; BILL AND COO(1947), ph; ON THE OLD SPANISH TRAIL(1947), ph; SPRINGTIME IN THE SIERRAS(1947), ph; EYES OF TEXAS(1948), ph; GALLANT LEGION, THE(1948), ph; GAY RANCHERO, THE(1948), ph; NIGHT TIME IN NEVADA(1948), ph; PLUNDERERS, THE(1948), ph; UNDER

CALIFORNIA STARS(1948), ph; BRIMSTONE(1949), ph; FAR FRONTIER, THE(1949), ph; GOLDEN STALLION, THE(1949), ph; HELLFIRE(1949), ph; KID FROM CLEVELAND, THE(1949), ph; BELLE OF OLD MEXICO(1950), ph; ROCK ISLAND TRAIL(1950), ph; SUNSET IN THE WEST(1950), ph; TRIGGER, JR.(1950), ph; HONEYCHILE(1951), ph; IN OLD AMARILLO(1951), ph; OH! SUSANNA(1951), ph; SOUTH OF CALIENTE(1951), ph; SPOILERS OF THE PLAINS(1951), ph; FABULOUS SENORITA, THE(1952), ph; MONTANA BELLE(1952), ph; OKLAHOMA ANNIE(1952), ph; PALS OF THE GOLDEN WEST(1952), ph; RIDE THE MAN DOWN(1952), ph; WAC FROM WALLA WALLA, THE(1952), ph; WOMAN OF THE NORTH COUNTRY(1952), ph; FAIR WIND TO JAVA(1953), ph; PERILOUS JOURNEY, A(1953), ph; JUBILEE TRAIL(1954), ph; SHANGHAI STORY, THE(1954), ph; HELL'S OUTPOST(1955), ph; LAST COMMAND, THE(1955), ph; TIMBERJACK(1955), ph; COME NEXT SPRING(1956), ph; LISBON(1956), ph; MAVERICK QUEEN, THE(1956), ph; AFFAIR IN RENO(1957), ph; DUEL AT APACHE WELLS(1957), ph; GUNFIRE AT INDIAN GAP(1957), ph; LAST STAGECOACH WEST, THE(1957), ph; LAWLESS EIGHTIES, THE(1957), ph; PANAMA SAL(1957), ph; SPOILERS OF THE FOREST(1957), ph; TAMING SUTTON'S GAL(1957), ph; BONNIE PARKER STORY, THE(1958), ph; CROOKED CIRCLE, THE(1958), ph; EARTH VS. THE SPIDER(1958), ph; GIRL IN THE WOODS(1958), ph; MAN OR GUN(1958), ph; MAN WHO DIED TWICE, THE(1958), ph; NOTORIOUS MR. MONKS, THE(1958), ph; SPIDER, THE(1958), ph; WAR OF THE COLOSSAL BEAST(1958), ph; YOUNG AND WILD(1958), ph; ANGEL BABY(1961), ph; CAT BALLOU(1965), ph; COMPANY OF KILLERS(1970), ph; PLAZA SUITE(1971), ph

John Marta
Silents
WHAT PRICE GLORY(1926), ph
Lynn Marta
Misc. Talkies
PETTY STORY, THE(1974)
Lynne Marta
RED SKY AT MORNING(1971); JOE KIDD(1972); BLOOD BEACH(1981)
1984
FOOTLOOSE(1984)
Nita Martan
TWIN BEDS(1929); BORDER ROMANCE(1930); BORROWED WIVES(1930); CHASING RAINBOWS(1930); THIRD ALARM, THE(1930); UNDER MONTANA SKIES(1930); WOMAN RACKET, THE(1930); CAUGHT CHEATING(1931)
Misc. Silents
ROYAL AMERICAN, THE(1927); DOG JUSTICE(1928)
Manilla Martans
Misc. Silents
WOLF'S FANGS, THE(1922)
Henri Marteau
LA FEMME INFIDELE(1969, Fr./Ital.); CONFESSION, THE(1970, Fr.)
Alphonse Martel
GIGOLETTES OF PARIS(1933), d&w; COWBOY AND THE BANDIT, THE(1935); MAN WHO BROKE THE BANK AT MONTE CARLO, THE(1935); COLLEEN(1936); GIVE ME YOUR HEART(1936); LIBELED LADY(1936); LOVE ON THE RUN(1936); GIRL FROM SCOTLAND YARD, THE(1937); KING AND THE CHORUS GIRL, THE(1937); MARKED WOMAN(1937); SOMETHING TO SING ABOUT(1937); WHEN YOU'RE IN LOVE(1937); ARTISTS AND MODELS ABROAD(1938); COLLEGE SWING(1938); KING OF THE NEWSBOYS(1938); SUEZ(1938); ANOTHER THIN MAN(1939); I'M NOBODY'S SWEETHEART NOW(1940); MEET JOHN DOE(1941); PARIS CALLING(1941); GIVE OUT, SISTERS(1942); GIRL CRAZY(1943); FALCON'S ALIBI, THE(1946); SO DARK THE NIGHT(1946); HOMECOMING(1948); STRATTON STORY, THE(1949); WOMAN'S SECRET, A(1949); ZAMBA(1949); DREAMBOAT(1952); DREAM WIFE(1953)
Silents
NAUGHTY NANETTE(1927)
Alphouse Martel
WONDER BAR(1934)
Arlene Martel
ANGELS FROM HELL(1968)
Christiane Martel
SO THIS IS PARIS(1954); ADAM AND EVE(1958, Mex.); LITTLE SAVAGE, THE(1959)
Christiane Martel "Miss Universe"
YANKEE PASHA(1954)
Donna Martel
LAST OF THE DESPERADOES(1956)
Gene Martel
DIPLOMATIC PASSPORT(1954, Brit.), p, d; STRANGER FROM VENUS, THE(1954, Brit.), p
Misc. Talkies
BLACK FOREST, THE(1954), d
Jeanne Martel
LOST RANCH(1937); SANTA FE BOUND(1937); TWO MINUTES TO PLAY(1937); BRINGING UP BABY(1938); FLYING FISTS, THE(1938); ORPHAN OF THE PECOS(1938)
John Martel
JUST WILLIAM'S LUCK(1948, Brit.)
June Martel
DR. SOCRATES(1935); FIGHTING YOUTH(1935); FRONT PAGE WOMAN(1935); GOING HIGHBROW(1935); ARIZONA MAHONEY(1936); SITTING ON THE MOON(1936); FORLORN RIVER(1937); HER HUSBAND LIES(1937); NIGHT OF MYSTERY(1937); SANTA FE STAMPEDE(1938); WILD HORSE RODEO(1938)
K.C. Martel
E.T. THE EXTRA-TERRESTRIAL(1982)
Max Martel
MY UNCLE(1958, Fr.)
Michaelina Martel
STILETTO(1969)
Michele Martel
CHARLES, DEAD OR ALIVE(1972, Switz.)
Philip Martel
MYSTERY AT THE BURLESQUE(1950, Brit.), m
Ray Martel
SCARFACE(1983)

Saul Z. Martel
GILDA(1946)
William Martel
RED MENACE, THE(1949); VIOLATED(1953); SIMON, KING OF THE WITCHES(1971); FUZZ(1972); SKYJACKED(1972); BABY BLUE MARINE(1976); MARATHON MAN(1976)
Alphonse Martell
SWEETHEARTS AND WIVES(1930); BLACK CAT, THE(1934); GAY DIVORCEE, THE(1934); KANSAS CITY PRINCESS(1934); NOTORIOUS SOPHIE LANG, THE(1934); CAPTAIN BLOOD(1935); WEDDING NIGHT, THE(1935); LOVE BEFORE BREAKFAST(1936); SATAN MET A LADY(1936); WIDOW FROM MONTE CARLO, THE(1936); KING OF GAMBLERS(1937); LOVE UNDER FIRE(1937); SEVENTH HEAVEN(1937); SHALL WE DANCE(1937); THIN ICE(1937); TOVARICH(1937); WE HAVE OUR MOMENTS(1937); LETTER OF INTRODUCTION(1938); CHARLIE CHAN IN THE CITY OF DARKNESS(1939); FOR LOVE OR MONEY(1939); MIRACLES FOR SALE(1939); TOPPER TAKES A TRIP(1939); ARISE, MY LOVE(1940); BRIDE CAME C.O.D., THE(1941); GREAT LIE, THE(1941); YANK IN THE R.A.F., A(1941); CROSSROADS(1942); I MARRIED AN ANGEL(1942); MOONLIGHT IN HAVANA(1942); PACIFIC RENDEZVOUS(1942); PITTSBURGH(1942); HONEYMOON LODGE(1943); PHANTOM OF THE OPERA(1943); SONG OF BERNADETTE, THE(1943); ENTER ARSENE LUPIN(1944); MASK OF DIMITRIOS, THE(1944); OUR HEARTS WERE YOUNG AND GAY(1944); PARDON MY RHYTHM(1944); STORM OVER LISBON(1944); SWINGTIME JOHNNY(1944); DICK TRACY(1945); NOB HILL(1945); GILDA(1946); THE CATMAN OF PARIS(1946); FRENCH LEAVE(1948); JULIA MISBEHAVES(1948); FAN, THE(1949); CONVICTED(1950); UNDER MY SKIN(1950); MY FAVORITE SPY(1951); SHOW BOAT(1951); PRISONER OF ZENDA, THE(1952); FORBIDDEN(1953); GENTLEMEN PREFER BLONDES(1953); TREASURE OF THE GOLDEN CONDOR(1953); PARIS PLAYBOYS(1954); PHFFFT!(1954); SEVEN THIEVES(1960); WHO'S GOT THE ACTION?(1962); NEW KIND OF LOVE, A(1963)
Silents
AFTER A MILLION(1924)
Misc. Silents
SCARLET YOUTH(1928); UNGUARDED GIRLS(1929)
Anita Martell
NEVER WAVE AT A WAC(1952)
Arleen Martell
DRACULA'S DOG(1978)
Chris Martell
WILD REBELS, THE(1967); GRUESOME TWOSOME(1968); MY THIRD WIFE GEORGE(1968); HOOKED GENERATION, THE(1969), m; SCREAM, BABY, SCREAM(1969); FLESH FEAST(1970)
David Martell
IT HAPPENED ON 5TH AVENUE(1947)
Donna Martell
TWILIGHT ON THE RIO GRANDE(1947); SAXON CHARM, THE(1948); ABBOTT AND COSTELLO MEET THE KILLER, BORIS KARLOFF(1949); ILLEGAL ENTRY(1949); KIM(1950); PEGGY(1950); ELEPHANT STAMPEDE(1951); HILLS OF UTAH(1951); GOLDEN HAWK, THE(1952); LAST TRAIN FROM BOMBAY(1952); GIVE A GIRL A BREAK(1953); PROJECT MOONBASE(1953); EGYPTIAN, THE(1954); LOVE IS A MANY-SPLENDORED THING(1955); TEN WANTED MEN(1955); HELL ON DEVIL'S ISLAND(1957)
Donne Martell
SECRET BEYOND THE DOOR, THE(1948)
Eve Martell
CLOWN, THE(1953)
Greg Martell
KISS OF DEATH(1947); ALASKA PASSAGE(1959)
Gregg Martell
RED MENACE, THE(1949); UNDERTOW(1949); DOUBLE CROSSBONES(1950); I WAS A SHOPLIFTER(1950); MA AND PA KETTLE GO TO TOWN(1950); SIERRA(1950); WINCHESTER '73(1950); LEAVE IT TO THE MARINES(1951); UNDER THE GUN(1951); AFFAIR IN TRINIDAD(1952); WORLD IN HIS ARMS, THE(1952); DEVIL'S CANYON(1953); GLORY BRIGADE, THE(1953); MASTERSON OF KANSAS(1954); BETWEEN HEAVEN AND HELL(1956); GUNFIGHT AT THE O.K. CORRAL(1957); THIS COULD BE THE NIGHT(1957); SPACE MASTER X-7(1958); TONKA(1958); CAGE OF EVIL(1960); DINOSAURUS!(1960); SERGEANT WAS A LADY, THE(1961); VALLEY OF THE DRAGONS(1961); SWINGIN' ALONG(1962); THREE STOOGES MEET HERCULES, THE(1962); CINCINNATI KID, THE(1965)
Jack Martell
GALLANT HOURS, THE(1960), cos; PROFESSIONALS, THE(1966), cos; IN COLD BLOOD(1967), cos; MAN CALLED HORSE, A(1970), cos; BAD NEWS BEARS IN BREAKING TRAINING, THE(1977), cos; MATILDA(1978), cos
John Martell
WILLIAM COMES TO TOWN(1948, Brit.); SILK NOOSE, THE(1950, Brit.)
K.C. Martell
AMITYVILLE HORROR, THE(1979)
Karl Martell
LA HABANERA(1937, Ger.)
Kurt Martell
STEEL TRAP, THE(1952); ONE WAY TICKET TO HELL(1955)
Lou Martell
SHAMUS(1973)
Neva Martell
CLOWN, THE(1953)
Peter Martell
MYTH, THE(1965, Ital.); SNOW DEVILS, THE(1965, Ital.); COBRA, THE(1968); VIOLENT FOUR, THE(1968, Ital.); THIS MAN CAN'T DIE(1970, Ital.)
Philip Martell
MISS PILGRIM'S PROGRESS(1950, Brit.), m; PENNY PRINCESS(1953, Brit.), m; TROUBLE IN STORE(1955, Brit.), md; POSTMARK FOR DANGER(1956, Brit.), md; MAN IN THE ROAD, THE(1957, Brit.), md; MENACE IN THE NIGHT(1958, Brit.), md; HOME IS THE HERO(1959, Ireland), md; MARY HAD A LITTLE(1961, Brit.), md; SNAKE WOMAN, THE(1961, Brit.), md; THREE ON A SPREE(1961, Brit.), md; HOT MONEY GIRL(1962, Brit./Ger.), m; NIGHT CREATURES(1962, Brit.), md; SMALL WORLD OF SAMMY LEE, THE(1963, Brit.), md; HORROR OF IT ALL, THE(1964, Brit.), md; MASTER SPY(1964, Brit.), md; CURSE OF THE MUMMY'S TOMB, THE(1965, Brit.), md; DIE, MONSTER, DIE(1965, Brit.), md; DR. TERROR'S HOUSE OF HORRORS(1965, Brit.), md; ESCAPE BY NIGHT(1965, Brit.), md; FRANKENSTEIN CREATED WOMAN(1965, Brit.), md; NANNY, THE(1965, Brit.), md; SKULL, THE(1965, Brit.), md; SPACEFLIGHT IC-1(1965, Brit.), md; PSYCHOPATH, THE(1966,

Brit.), m, md; REPTILE, THE(1966, Brit.), md; WHERE THE BULLETS FLY(1966, Brit.), md; DEVIL'S OWN, THE(1967, Brit.), md; FROZEN DEAD, THE(1967, Brit.), md; IT!(1967, Brit.), md; TO SIR, WITH LOVE(1967, Brit.), md; ANNIVERSARY, THE(1968, Brit.), m; DANGER ROUTE(1968, Brit.), md; FILE OF THE GOLDEN GOOSE, THE(1969, Brit.), md; FRANKENSTEIN MUST BE DESTROYED!(1969, Brit.), md; SCARS OF DRACULA, THE(1970, Brit.), md; TASTE THE BLOOD OF DRACULA(1970, Brit.), md; DR. JEKYLL AND SISTER HYDE(1971, Brit.), md; LUST FOR A VAMPIRE(1971, Brit.), md; VAMPIRE CIRCUS(1972, Brit.), md; GHOUL, THE(1975, Brit.), md; NOTHING BUT THE NIGHT(1975, Brit.), md

Phillip Martell
HELLO LONDON(1958, Brit.), md; NIGHT TRAIN TO PARIS(1964, Brit.), md

Ray Martell
CHE!(1969); TIGER BY THE TAIL(1970)

Saul Martell
HIGH BARBAREE(1947); THIEVES' HIGHWAY(1949); MISSISSIPPI GAMBLER, THE(1953); SALOME(1953); EMERGENCY HOSPITAL(1956)

Vern Martell
SNIPER, THE(1952)

William Martell
SLEEPING CITY, THE(1950)

Attilio Martella
SEDUCED AND ABANDONED(1964, Fr./Ital.); FACTS OF MURDER, THE(1965, Ital.)

Pietro Martellanz
STREET PEOPLE(1976, U.S./Ital.)

Anna Martelli
Misc. Silents
TOILER, THE(1932, Ital.)

Carlo Martelli
WITCHCRAFT(1964, Brit.), m; CURSE OF THE MUMMY'S TOMB, THE(1965, Brit.), m; WOMAN WHO WOULDN'T DIE, THE(1965, Brit.), m; MURDER GAME, THE(1966, Brit.), m; IT!(1967, Brit.), m; PREHISTORIC WOMEN(1967, Brit.), m

Marissa Martelli
MODESTY BLAISE(1966, Brit.), cos, makeup

Norma Martelli
NIGHT OF THE SHOOTING STARS, THE(1982, Ital.)

Otella Martelli
NIGHTS OF CABIRIA(1957, Ital.), ph

Otello Martelli
PAISAN(1948, Ital.), ph; GOLDEN MADONNA, THE(1949, Brit.), ph; BITTER RICE(1950, Ital.), ph; STROMBOLI(1950, Ital.), ph; WOMAN OF THE RIVER(1954, Fr./Ital.), ph; LUCKY TO BE A WOMAN(1955, Ital.), ph; LA STRADA(1956, Ital.), ph; VITELLONI(1956, Ital./Fr.), ph; GOLD OF NAPLES(1957, Ital.), ph; THIS ANGRY AGE(1958, Ital./Fr.), ph; WHERE THE HOT WIND BLOWS(1960, Fr., Ital.), ph; LA DOLCE VITA(1961, Ital./Fr.), ph; SWINDLE, THE(1962, Fr./Ital.), ph; THREE FACES OF A WOMAN(1965, Ital.), ph; VARIETY LIGHTS(1965, Ital.), ph

Phillip Martelli
MR. DRAKE'S DUCK(1951, Brit.), md

Tony Martelli
DANCE, GIRL, DANCE(1940)

Alexander Marten
WITHOUT A HOME(1939, Pol.), a, d

Collette Marten
CLEAR THE DECKS(1929)

Felix Marten
NATHALIE, AGENT SECRET(1960, Fr.); FRANTIC(1961, Fr.); MAXIME(1962, Fr.); LA BONNE SOUPE(1964, Fr./Ital.); IS PARIS BURNING?(1966, U.S./Fr.)
Misc. Talkies
ATOMIC AGENT(1959, Fr.)

Florence Marten
Misc. Silents
MISS GEORGE WASHINGTON(1916)

Helen Marten
Silents
ACCORDING TO LAW(1916); IDOL OF THE STAGE, THE(1916)
Misc. Silents
I ACCUSE(1916); MAN FROM NOWHERE, THE(1916)

Jurgen Marten
PINOCCHIO(1969, E. Ger.)

Richard Marten
CARAVANS(1978, U.S./Iranian), ed

Sarah Marten
1984
STREETS OF FIRE(1984)

Rodger Martencen
LIQUID SKY(1982)

Edward Martendel
LOVER COME BACK(1946)

Ondes Martenot
END OF THE WORLD, THE(1930, Fr.), m

Layton Martens
1984
TIGHTROPE(1984)

Lily Martens
80 STEPS TO JONAH(1969)

Mary Martens
1984
ALIEN FACTOR, THE(1984)

Mona Martenson
Misc. Silents
CHARLES XII, PARTS 1 & 2(1927, Swed.); LEGEND OF GOSTA BERLING(1928, Swed.)

Ian Marter
DOCTOR FAUSTUS(1967, Brit.); MEDUSA TOUCH, THE(1978, Brit.)

Frank Marth
SPELL OF THE HYPNOTIST(1956); LOVE WITH THE PROPER STRANGER(1963); MADAME X(1966); MADIGAN(1968); LOST MAN, THE(1969); MAROONED(1969); PENDULUM(1969); TELEFON(1977)

Peter Marthesheimer
DESPAIR(1978, Ger.), p; MARRIAGE OF MARIA BRAUN, THE(1979, Ger.), w; LOLA(1982, Ger.), w; VERONIKA VOSS(1982, Ger.), w

Francois Marthouret
CONFESSION, THE(1970, Fr.)

Michel Marti
MAN WHO LOVED WOMEN, THE(1977, Fr.)

Syra Marti
EDGE OF HELL(1956)

Martial
LAST OF SHEILA, THE(1973)

J. F. Martial
PANIQUE(1947, Fr.); MY UNCLE(1958, Fr.)

Jacques Martial
BROKEN ENGLISH(1981)

Elva Martien
TIMBUKTU(1959), cos; GIRL HAPPY(1965), cos

Norman Martien
20,000 LEAGUES UNDER THE SEA(1954), cos; NEW YORK CONFIDENTIAL(1955), cos; LIZZIE(1957), cos

Robert Martien
BLOOD ON THE SUN(1945), cos

Gerd Martienzen
DAY WILL COME, A(1960, Ger.)

Walter Martigli
ATOM AGE VAMPIRE(1961, Ital.), art d

A. E. Martin
GLASS TOMB, THE(1955, Brit.), w

A. Z. Martin
MAD ROOM, THE(1969), w

Al Martin
RIDER OF DEATH VALLEY(1932), w; CRIMSON ROMANCE(1934), w; LOST JUNGLE, THE(1934), w; YOUNG AND BEAUTIFUL(1934), w; DANGER AHEAD(1935), w; WHAT PRICE CRIME?(1935), w; BARS OF HATE(1936), w; FACE IN THE FOG, A(1936), w; KELLY OF THE SECRET SERVICE(1936), w; LAW RIDES, THE(1936), w; PRISON SHADOWS(1936), w; PUT ON THE SPOT(1936), w; RIO GRANDE ROMANCE(1936), w; ROGUES' TAVERN, THE(1936), w; TRAIL DUST(1936), w; TRAPPED BY TELEVISION(1936), w; ISLAND CAPTIVES(1937), w; SHADOW STRIKES, THE(1937), w; TAMING THE WILD(1937), w; WITH LOVE AND KISSES(1937), w; PECK'S BAD BOY WITH THE CIRCUS(1938), w; CAUGHT IN THE ACT(1941), w; FLYING WILD(1941), w; INVISIBLE GHOST, THE(1941), w; DEVIL WITH HITLER, THE(1942), w; MAD DOCTOR OF MARKET STREET, THE(1942), w; MISSISSIPPI GAMBLER(1942), w; STAGECOACH BUCKAROO(1942), w; GENTLE GANGSTER, A(1943), w; CAROLINA BLUES(1944), w; HAT CHECK HONEY(1944), w; RECKLESS AGE(1944), w; STANDING ROOM ONLY(1944), w; ADVENTURES OF RUSTY(1945), w; BLONDIE KNOWS BEST(1946), w; GUY COULD CHANGE, A(1946), w; MONEY MADNESS(1948), w; RACING LUCK(1948), w; RUSTY LEADS THE WAY(1948), w; STRANGE MRS. CRANE, THE(1948), w; AMAZON QUEST(1949), w; RUSTY SAVES A LIFE(1949), w; RUSTY'S BIRTHDAY(1949), w; SMUGGLER'S GOLD(1951), w; ARMY BOUND(1952), w; INVASION OF THE SAUCER MEN(1957), w; IN THE MONEY(1958), w
Silents
ALBANY NIGHT BOAT, THE(1928), t; DEVIL DOGS(1928), t; HEROIC LOVER, THE(1929), t

Alberto Martin
GREATEST, THE(1977, U.S./Brit.)

Allen Martin, Jr.
JOHNNY HOLIDAY(1949); HER FIRST ROMANCE(1951)

Alice Manougian Martin
LOVE STORY(1970), cos

Alma Martin
Misc. Silents
SPENDER OR THE FORTUNES OF PETER, THE(1915)

Ana Martin
BLUE DEMON VERSUS THE INFERNAL BRAINS(1967, Mex.)

Andra Martin
BIG BEAT, THE(1958); LADY TAKES A FLYER, THE(1958); THING THAT COULDN'T DIE, THE(1958); UP PERISCOPE(1959); YELLOWSTONE KELLY(1959); FEVER IN THE BLOOD, A(1961)

Andrea Martin
CANNIBAL GIRLS(1973); BLACK CHRISTMAS(1974, Can.); WHOLLY MOSES(1980); SOUP FOR ONE(1982)

Andrew Martin
PUBERTY BLUES(1983, Aus.)

Andy Martin
JAMBOREE(1957); OCEAN'S ELEVEN(1960)

Angela Martin
ANNIE(1982)

Ann Martin
ODE TO BILLY JOE(1976); SHADES OF SILK(1979, Can.), w

Anne Martin
SKIN GAME, THE(1965, Brit.)

Anne-Marie Martin
SAVAGE HARVEST(1981); BOOGENS, THE(1982)
1984
RUNAWAY(1984)

Annette Martin
10(1979)

Anthony Martin
BANJO ON MY KNEE(1936); HOLY TERROR, THE(1937)

Anthony [Tony] Martin
PIGSKIN PARADE(1936); SING AND BE HAPPY(1937)

Antonio Martin
PANDORA AND THE FLYING DUTCHMAN(1951, Brit.)

Ashlyn Martin
BLOOD FEAST(1963)

Aubrey Martin
THIS IS NOT A TEST(1962)

Barney Martin
LOVE WITH THE PROPER STRANGER(1963); PRODUCERS, THE(1967); CHAR-LY(1968); MOVIE MOVIE(1978); HOT STUFF(1979); ARTHUR(1981)
Barry Martin
HOUSE OF WHIPCORD(1974, Brit.)
Bern Martin
MAN IN THE WATER, THE(1963)
Beverley Martin
BURNING AN ILLUSION(1982, Brit.)
Bill Martin
ONCE UPON A HONEYMOON(1942); JOE PALOOKA IN WINNER TAKE ALL(1948); SATURDAY'S HERO(1951); THREE NUTS IN SEARCH OF A BOLT(1964), ed
Bob Martin
SHOULD A DOCTOR TELL?(1931, Brit.), ph; NINE TILL SIX(1932, Brit.), ph; SING AS WE GO(1934, Brit.), ph; LORNA DOONE(1935, Brit.), ph
Bonni Martin
FIGHT FOR YOUR LIFE(1977)
Breck Martin
JET OVER THE ATLANTIC(1960)
Brian Martin
1984
SILENT MADNESS(1984), art d
Buddy Martin
FATHER WAS A FULLBACK(1949)
Burt Martin
HAPPY AS THE GRASS WAS GREEN(1973), p; HAZEL'S PEOPLE(1978), p
Buzz Martin
FBI STORY, THE(1959); PORK CHOP HILL(1959); CIMARRON(1960); PT 109(1963)
Carla Martin
WESTERN PACIFIC AGENT(1950); MASK OF THE DRAGON(1951); STOP THAT CAB(1951)
Carlos Martin
FURY(1936)
Carmen Martin
REVOLT OF THE SLAVES, THE(1961, Ital./Span./Ger.), makeup; PYRO(1964, U.S./Span.), makeup; SON OF A GUNFIGHTER(1966, U.S./Span.), makeup; TAKE A HARD RIDE(1975, U.S./Ital.), makeup
Carol Martin
HERO AT LARGE(1980)
Carolyn Martin
END, THE(1978)
Cass Martin
TOWN CALLED HELL, A(1971, Span./Brit.); TRAVELS WITH MY AUNT(1972, Brit.)
Charles Martin
RICH AND STRANGE(1932, Brit.), ph; PARIS IN SPRING(1935); BIG BROWN EYES(1936); HOUSE OF A THOUSAND CANDLES, THE(1936); HEART OF THE WEST(1937); MISSING GUEST, THE(1938), w; I'LL BE SEEING YOU(1944), w; NO LEAVE, NO LOVE(1946), d, w; MY DEAR SECRETARY(1948), d&w; ON AN ISLAND WITH YOU(1948), w; PROJECT X(1949); DEATH OF A SCOUNDREL(1956), p,d&w; TOUCH OF FLESH, THE(1960); SECRET DOOR, THE(1964), w; GENTLE GIANT(1967); IF HE HOLLERS, LET HIM GO(1968), p,d&w; HELLO DOWN THE-RE(1969); LIMBO(1972); HOW TO SEDUCE A WOMAN(1974), p,d&w; ONE MAN JURY(1978), d&w
Misc. Talkies
FIGHTING BLACK KINGS(1977)
Misc. Silents
MORE TRUTH THAN POETRY(1917); WHO LOVED HIM BEST?(1918)
Charles G. Martin
CLOWN AND THE KID, THE(1961); INCIDENT IN AN ALLEY(1962); SAFE AT HOME(1962); CHECKERED FLAG, THE(1963); RACING FEVER(1964)
Charles H. Martin
Misc. Silents
WOMAN OF REDEMPTION, A(1918)
Charles M. Martin
LAW FOR TOMBSTONE(1937), w; LEFT-HANDED LAW(1937), w
Charles W. Martin
Misc. Silents
UNDYING FLAME, THE(1917)
Chris Martin
CISCO KID(1931); STOKER, THE(1932); FLIRTING WITH FATE(1938); ESPIONAGE AGENT(1939)
Silents
GOLD RUSH, THE(1925)
Chris Pin Martin
FOUR FRIGHTENED PEOPLE(1934); IN CALIENTE(1935); TROPIC HOLI-DAY(1938); STAGECOACH(1939); SECRET LIFE OF WALTER MITTY, THE(1947); MEXICAN HAYRIDE(1948)
Chris-Pin Martin
SQUAW MAN, THE(1931); BROKEN WING, THE(1932); GIRL CRAZY(1932); PAINT-ED WOMAN(1932); SOUTH OF SANTA FE(1932); WINNER TAKE ALL(1932); CALI-FORNIA TRAIL, THE(1933); OUTLAW JUSTICE(1933); CHAINED(1934); HEAT LIGHTNING(1934); VIVA VILLA!(1934); BORDERTOWN(1935); CAPTAIN BLOOD(1935); RED SALUTE(1935); UNDER THE PAMPAS MOON(1935); GAY DE-SPERADO, THE(1936); STAR IS BORN, A(1937); SWING HIGH, SWING LOW(1937); TENDERFOOT GOES WEST, A(1937); WHEN YOU'RE IN LOVE(1937); FOUR MEN AND A PRAYER(1938); RENEGADE RANGER(1938); TEXANS, THE(1938); CISCO KID AND THE LADY, THE(1939); CODE OF THE SECRET SERVICE(1939); FIGHT-ING GRINGO, THE(1939); FRONTIER MARSHAL(1939); GIRL AND THE GAMBLER, THE(1939); RETURN OF THE CISCO KID(1939); CHARLIE CHAN IN PANAMA(1940); DOWN ARGENTINE WAY(1940); GAY CABALLERO, THE(1940); LLANO KID, THE(1940); LUCKY CISCO KID(1940); MARK OF ZORRO, THE(1940); VIVA CISCO KID(1940); BAD MAN, THE(1941); RIDE ON VAQUERO(1941); ROMANCE OF THE RIO GRANDE(1941); WEEKEND IN HAVANA(1941); AMERICAN EMPIRE(1942); TOMBSTONE, THE TOWN TOO TOUGH TO DIE(1942); UNDERCOVER MAN(1942); OX-BOW INCIDENT, THE(1943); SULTAN'S DAUGHTER, THE(1943); ALI BABA AND THE FORTY THIEVES(1944); TAMPICO(1944); ALONG CAME JONES(1945); SAN ANTONIO(1945); GALLANT JOURNEY(1946); PERILOUS HOLIDAY(1946); SUSPENSE(1946); FUGITIVE, THE(1947); PIRATES OF MONTEREY(1947); KING OF THE BANDITS(1948); RETURN OF WILDFIRE, THE(1948); BEAUTIFUL BLONDE

FROM BASHFUL BEND, THE(1949); RIMFIRE(1949); ARIZONA COWBOY, THE(1950); LADY FROM TEXAS, THE(1951); MILLIONAIRE FOR CHRISTY, A(1951); MESA OF LOST WOMEN, THE(1956)
Misc. Talkies
ROBIN HOOD OF MONTEREY(1947)
Christiane Martin
FOUR DAYS LEAVE(1950, Switz.)
Christopher Martin
DARWIN ADVENTURE, THE(1972, Brit.)
Silents
RESCUE, THE(1929)
Claude Martin
BLOOD AND ROSES(1961, Fr./Ital.), d&w
Claudia Martin
FOR THOSE WHO THINK YOUNG(1964); GHOST IN THE INVISIBLE BIKI-NI(1966); SKI FEVER(1969, U.S./Aust./Czech.)
Clay Martin
NORTHERN PURSUIT(1943); JANIE(1944)
Clyde Martin
ONLY WAY HOME, THE(1972)
Colette Martin
SERVANT, THE(1964, Brit.)
Conrado S. Martin
MAD QUEEN, THE(1950, Span.)
D'Urville Martin
GUESS WHO'S COMING TO DINNER(1967); ROSEMARY'S BABY(1968); TIME TO SING, A(1968); WATERMELON MAN(1970); FINAL COMEDOWN, THE(1972); HAM-MER(1972); LEGEND OF NIGGER CHARLEY, THE(1972); BLACK CAESAR(1973); BOOK OF NUMBERS(1973); FIVE ON THE BLACK HAND SIDE(1973); HELL UP IN HARLEM(1973); SOUL OF NIGGER CHARLEY, THE(1973); BOSS NIGGER(1974); DOLEMITE(1975), a, d; SHEBA BABY(1975); BIG SCORE, THE(1983)
1984
BEAR, THE(1984)
Misc. Talkies
DEATH JOURNEY(1976); DISCO 9000(1977), d; BLIND RAGE(1978)
Dale Martin
SPACEHUNTER: ADVENTURES IN THE FORBIDDEN ZONE(1983), spec eff
Dan Martin
DEADLIEST SIN, THE(1956, Brit.), w; LAST TOMAHAWK, THE(1965, Ger./Ital./Span.)
Daniel Martin
GRINGO(1963, Span./Ital.); FISTFUL OF DOLLARS, A(1964, Ital./Ger./Span.); MI-NUTE TO PRAY, A SECOND TO DIE, A(1968, Ital.); MISSION STARDUST(1968, Ital./Span./Ger.); THEY CAME TO ROB LAS VEGAS(1969, Fr./Ital./Span./Ger.); BAD MAN'S RIVER(1972, Span.)
1984
YELLOW HAIR AND THE FORTRESS OF GOLD(1984)
Danny Martin
Misc. Talkies
JOEY(1977)
David Martin
STRONGER THAN THE SUN(1980, Brit.), ed
1984
LAUGHTER HOUSE(1984, Brit.), ed; PLOUGHMAN'S LUNCH, THE(1984, Brit.), ed
Dean Martin, Jr.
PARDNERS(1956)
Dean Martin, Jr. [Dean Paul Martin]
ROUGH NIGHT IN JERICHO(1967)
Dean Martin
TOYS IN THE ATTIC(1963); MY FRIEND IRMA(1949); AT WAR WITH THE ARMY(1950); MY FRIEND IRMA GOES WEST(1950); SAILOR BEWARE(1951); THAT'S MY BOY(1951); JUMPING JACKS(1952); ROAD TO BALI(1952); STOOGE, THE(1952); CADDY, THE(1953); MONEY FROM HOME(1953); SCARED STIFF(1953); LIVING IT UP(1954); THREE RING CIRCUS(1954); ARTISTS AND MODELS(1955); YOU'RE NEVER TOO YOUNG(1955); HOLLYWOOD OR BUST(1955); TEN THOU-SAND BEDROOMS(1957); YOUNG LIONS, THE(1958); CAREER(1959); RIO BRA-VO(1959); SOME CAME RUNNING(1959); BELLS ARE RINGING(1960); OCEAN'S ELEVEN(1960); PEPE(1960); WHO WAS THAT LADY?(1960); ADA(1961); ALL IN A NIGHT'S WORK(1961); ROAD TO HONG KONG, THE(1962, U.S./Brit.); SERGEANTS 3(1962); WHO'S GOT THE ACTION?(1962); COME BLOW YOUR HORN(1963); FOUR FOR TEXAS(1963); WHO'S BEEN SLEEPING IN MY BED?(1963); KISS ME, STU-PID(1964); ROBIN AND THE SEVEN HOODS(1964); WHAT A WAY TO GO(1964); MARRIAGE ON THE ROCKS(1965); SONS OF KATIE ELDER, THE(1965); MURDER-ERS' ROW(1966); SILENCERS, THE(1966); TEXAS ACROSS THE RIVER(1966); AMBUSHERS, THE(1967); ROUGH NIGHT IN JERICHO(1967); BANDOLERO!(1968); FIVE CARD STUD(1968); HOW TO SAVE A MARRIAGE–AND RUIN YOUR LI-FE(1968); WRECKING CREW, THE(1968); AIRPORT(1970); SOMETHING BIG(1971); SHOWDOWN(1973); MR. RICCO(1975); CANNONBALL RUN, THE(1981)
1984
CANNONBALL RUN II(1984)
Dean Paul Martin
HEART LIKE A WHEEL(1983)
Dean-Paul Martin
PLAYERS(1979)
Deana Martin
YOUNG BILLY YOUNG(1969)
Misc. Talkies
STRANGERS AT SUNRISE(1969)
Denine Martin
MALE SERVICE(1966)
Denis Martin
TONIGHT'S THE NIGHT(1954, Brit.); BAMBOO PRISON, THE(1955)
Denny Martin
HOT SPUR(1968), m
Derek Martin
EVIL OF FRANKENSTEIN, THE(1964, Brit.); BIG SWITCH, THE(1970, Brit.); PRIEST OF LOVE(1981, Brit.)

Dewey Martin

KNOCK ON ANY DOOR(1949); GOLDEN GLOVES STORY, THE(1950); KANSAS RAIDERS(1950); FLAME OF ARABY(1951); THING, THE(1951); BIG SKY, THE(1952); MEN OF THE FIGHTING LADY(1954); PRISONER OF WAR(1954); TENNESSEE CHAMP(1954); DESPERATE HOURS, THE(1955); LAND OF THE PHARAOHS(1955); PROUD AND THE PROFANE, THE(1956); TEN THOUSAND BEDROOMS(1957); LONGEST DAY, THE(1962); SAVAGE SAM(1963); FLIGHT TO FURY(1966, U.S./Phil.); SEVEN ALONE(1975)

Diana Martin

TILL WE MEET AGAIN(1944); MINNESOTA CLAY(1966, Ital./Fr./Span.)

Misc. Talkies

SIGMA III(1966)

Dick Martin

ONCE UPON A HORSE(1958); GLASS BOTTOM BOAT, THE(1966); MALTESE BIPPY, THE(1969); ZERO TO SIXTY(1978); CARBON COPY(1981)

Dino Martin, Jr.

BOY...A GIRL, A(1969)

Don Martin

LIGHTHOUSE(1947), w; PRETENDER, THE(1947), w; APPOINTMENT WITH MURDER(1948), w; CREEPER, THE(1948), w; DEVIL'S CARGO, THE(1948), w; SHED NO TEARS(1948), w; TRIPLE THREAT(1948), w; LOST TRIBE, THE(1949), w; SEARCH FOR DANGER(1949), w; DESTINATION MURDER(1950), w; SHAKEDOWN(1950), w; ARROW IN THE DUST(1954), w; LONE GUN, THE(1954), w; DOUBLE JEOPARDY(1955), w; NO MAN'S WOMAN(1955), w; STRANGER ON HORSEBACK(1955), w; BRASS LEGEND, THE(1956), w; EMERGENCY HOSPITAL(1956), w; HOT CARS(1956), w; MAN IS ARMED, THE(1956), w; QUINCANNON, FRONTIER SCOUT(1956), w; STORM RIDER, THE(1957), w; VIOLENT ROAD(1958), w; FOUR DEUCES, THE(1976), w

Dorothea Knox Martin

HOLLYWOOD BARN DANCE(1947), w

Douglas Brian Martin

FAST TIMES AT RIDGEMONT HIGH(1982)

Duke Martin

MARRIAGE BY CONTRACT(1928); IN OLD ARIZONA(1929); LOST ZEPPELIN(1930)

Silents

CITY GONE WILD, THE(1927); FORTUNE HUNTER, THE(1927); NOW WE'RE IN THE AIR(1927); ONE CHANCE IN A MILLION(1927); ACROSS THE SINGAPORE(1928); ALBANY NIGHT BOAT, THE(1928); FLYING ROMEOS(1928)

Misc. Silents

DANGER STREET(1928); LOST ZEPPELIN, THE(1929)

Dwight Martin

SET-UP, THE(1949)

E. A. Martin

Silents

FALSE FATHERS(1929)

Misc. Silents

HEART OF TEXAS RYAN, THE(1917), d

Ed Martin

YOUNG SINNER, THE(1965), ph

Eddie Martin

M'BLIMEY(1931, Brit.)

Edgar Martin

HI-DE-HO(1947)

Edie Martin

UNDER THE RED ROBE(1937, Brit.); BAD BOY(1938, Brit.); SPOT OF BOTHER, A(1938, Brit.); TROOPSHIP(1938, Brit.); OLD MOTHER RILEY IN BUSINESS(1940, Brit.); UNPUBLISHED STORY(1942, Brit.); IT'S IN THE BAG(1943, Brit.); DON'T TAKE IT TO HEART(1944, Brit.); ADVENTURE FOR TWO(1945, Brit.); HERE COMES THE SUN(1945, Brit.); PLACE OF ONE'S OWN, A(1945, Brit.); THEY WERE SISTERS(1945, Brit.); GREAT EXPECTATIONS(1946, Brit.); WHEN THE BOUGH BREAKS(1947, Brit.); ELIZABETH OF LADYMEAD(1949, Brit.); HISTORY OF MR. POLLY, THE(1949, Brit.); IT ALWAYS RAINS ON SUNDAY(1949, Brit.); MY BROTHER'S KEEPER(1949, Brit.); LADY WITH A LAMP, THE(1951, Brit.); LAVENDER HILL MOB, THE(1951, Brit.); NIGHT WAS OUR FRIEND(1951, Brit.); OLIVER TWIST(1951, Brit.); MAN IN THE WHITE SUIT, THE(1952, Brit.); GENEVIEVE(1953, Brit.); MEET MR. LUCIFER(1953, Brit.); TIME GENTLEMEN PLEASE!(1953, Brit.); TITFIELD THUNDERBOLT, THE(1953, Brit.); END OF THE ROAD, THE(1954, Brit.); LEASE OF LIFE(1954, Brit.); ROOM IN THE HOUSE(1955, Brit.); LADYKILLERS, THE(1956, Brit.); RAMSBOTTOM RIDES AGAIN(1956, Brit.); AS LONG AS THEY'RE HAPPY(1957, Brit.); PANIC IN THE PARLOUR(1957, Brit.); I'M ALL RIGHT, JACK(1959, Brit.); TEENAGE BAD GIRL(1959, Brit.); TOO MANY CROOKS(1959, Brit.); KIDNAPPED(1960); WEEKEND WITH LULU, A(1961, Brit.)

Edward Martin

Silents

JULES OF THE STRONG HEART(1918); GRIM GAME, THE(1919)

Edward R. Martin

OPERATION DAMES(1959), ph

Edwin L. Martin

GENTLEMAN AFTER DARK, A(1942), d

Eleanor Martin

GREAT POWER, THE(1929)

Ellen Martin

OPEN THE DOOR AND SEE ALL THE PEOPLE(1964)

Emile Martin

MOUCHETTE(1970, Fr.), md

Eric Martin

Misc. Talkies

FIRST TIME ROUND(1972)

Ernest Martin

WHERE'S CHARLEY?(1952, Brit.), p; CATAMOUNT KILLING, THE(1975, Ger.)

Ernie Martin

PIAF–THE EARLY YEARS(1982, U.S./Fr.), p

Ethel Martin

ON THE RIVERA(1951); FUNNY THING HAPPENED ON THE WAY TO THE FORUM, A(1966), ch

Silents

ROSE OF THE WORLD(1918)

Eugene Martin

TERROR IN A TEXAS TOWN(1958); THIS REBEL BREED(1960); TOWER OF LONDON(1962); PANCHO VILLA(1975, Span.), d

Eugenio Martin

HYPNOSIS(1966, Ger./Sp./Ital.), d, w; UGLY ONES, THE(1968, Ital./Span.), d, w; HORROR EXPRESS(1972, Span./Brit.), d; THAT HOUSE IN THE OUTSKIRTS(1980, Span.), d, w

Euline Martin

TENDER COMRADE(1943)

Eva Martin

ANNA(1981, Fr./Hung.), art d

1984

DIARY FOR MY CHILDREN(1984, Hung.), prod d

Fay Martin

WHITE LIGHTNING(1973)

Florence Evelyn Martin

Misc. Silents

UNDERCURRENT, THE(1919)

Florence Martin

Silents

TIGER WOMAN, THE(1917); SILENT COMMAND, THE(1923)

Misc. Silents

WHEN MEN DESIRE(1919); MILLIONAIRE FOR A DAY, A(1921); SCRAMBLED WIVES(1921)

Frances Martin

COLLEGE RHYTHM(1934), w; WAIKIKI WEDDING(1937), w

Francis Martin

DISGRACED(1933), w; INTERNATIONAL HOUSE(1933), w; TILLIE AND GUS(1933), d, w; WE'RE NOT DRESSING(1934), w; BIG BROADCAST OF 1936, THE(1935), w; MISSISSIPPI(1935), w; TWO FISTED(1935), w; BIG BROADCAST OF 1937, THE(1936), w; COLLEGIATE(1936), w; PRINCESS COMES ACROSS, THE(1936), w; RHYTHM ON THE RANGE(1936), w; STRIKE ME PINK(1936), w; ARTISTS AND MODELS(1937), w; BIG BROADCAST OF 1938, THE(1937), w; COLLEGE SWING(1938), w; ONE NIGHT IN THE TROPICS(1940), w; TILLIE THE TOILER(1941), w; SHUT MY BIG MOUTH(1942), w

Frank Martin [Franco Martinelli]

DR. BUTCHER, M.D.(1982, Ital.), d

Fred S. Martin

RIDERS OF THE WHISTLING PINES(1949); WAGON TEAM(1952); ON TOP OF OLD SMOKY(1953)

Freddy Martin

MAYOR OF 44TH STREET, THE(1942); WHAT'S BUZZIN COUSIN?(1943)

Frederick Martin

2001: A SPACE ODYSSEY(1968, U.S./Brit.), spec eff

Gary Martin

SHOCK TREATMENT(1981)

Gene Martin

BAD MAN'S RIVER(1972, Span.), d, w

George A. Martin

1984

SONGWRITER(1984), ed

George Martin

PALS OF THE SILVER SAGE(1940), w; ON THE RIVERA(1951); YELLOW SUBMARINE(1958, Brit.), md; V.D.(1961); FERRY ACROSS THE MERSEY(1964, Brit.), md; HARD DAY'S NIGHT, A(1964, Brit.), md; FUNNY THING HAPPENED ON THE WAY TO THE FORUM, A(1966), ch; ISLAND OF THE DOOMED(1968, Span./Ger.); PULP(1972, Brit.), m, md; LIVE AND LET DIE(1973, Brit.), m; OPTIMISTS, THE(1973, Brit.), md; SGT. PEPPER'S LONELY HEARTS CLUB BAND(1978), md; DARK END OF THE STREET, THE(1981); HONKY TONK FREEWAY(1981), m

1984

C.H.U.D.(1984); FALLING IN LOVE(1984); GIVE MY REGARDS TO BROAD STREET(1984, Brit.), a, md

Misc. Talkies

TWO VIOLENT MEN(1964)

Misc. Silents

UNDER THE WESTERN SKIES(1921), d; WINDING TRAIL, THE(1921), d

George Victor Martin

OUR VINES HAVE TENDER GRAPES(1945), w

George Martin [Jorge Martin]

PISTOL FOR RINGO, A(1966, Ital./Span.)

Georges Andre Martin

ROBBER SYMPHONY, THE(1937, Brit.)

Grady Martin

HONEYSUCKLE ROSE(1980)

1984

SONGWRITER(1984)

Greg Martin

GREAT WALDO PEPPER, THE(1975)

Gregg Martin

ONCE BEFORE I DIE(1967, U.S./Phil.)

Grek Martin

LOS AUTOMATAS DE LA MUERTE(1960, Mex.)

Guy Martin

GIRL WITH THE GOLDEN EYES, THE(1962, Fr.)

Gwen Martin

OUR HEARTS WERE GROWING UP(1946)

H. Kinley Martin

Silents

FOOD FOR SCANDAL(1920), ph; OH, LADY, LADY(1920), ph; AMATEUR DEVIL, AN(1921), ph; DUCKS AND DRAKES(1921), ph; ONE WILD WEEK(1921), ph; SPEED GIRL, THE(1921), ph; SLEEPWALKER, THE(1922), ph; EVE'S SECRET(1925), ph; PATHS TO PARADISE(1925), ph; CAMPUS FLIRT, THE(1926), ph; HANDS UP(1926), ph; MISS BREWSTER'S MILLIONS(1926), ph; RAINMAKER, THE(1926), ph; FIREMAN, SAVE MY CHILD(1927), ph; TWO FLAMING YOUTHS(1927), ph; WIFE SAVERS(1928), ph

Hal Martin

Silents

SQUIBS WINS THE CALCUTTA SWEEP(1922, Brit.); WOMAN'S SECRET, A(1924, Brit.)

Misc. Silents
PREY OF THE DRAGON, THE(1921, Brit.); BELLS OF ST. MARY'S, THE(1928, Brit.)
Harry Martin
FANCY PANTS(1950); THREE CAME HOME(1950); UNDER MY SKIN(1950); SOL-DIERS THREE(1951); SON OF DR. JEKYLL, THE(1951)
Helen Martin
INVISIBLE GHOST, THE(1941), w; LADY CONFESSES, THE(1945), w; PHENIX CITY STORY, THE(1955); COTTON COMES TO HARLEM(1970); WHERE'S POP-PA?(1970); DEATH WISH(1974); HERO AIN'T NOTHIN' BUT A SANDWICH, A(1977)
1984
REPO MAN(1984)
Silents
SONG OF THE WAGE SLAVE, THE(1915)
Helen R. Martin
Silents
ERSTWHILE SUSAN(1919), w
Helen Reimensyder Martin
Silents
SNOB, THE(1924), w
Henry Martin
STAGE STRUCK(1936); CROOKS ANONYMOUS(1963, Brit.), ed
Herbert Martin
DAWN OVER IRELAND(1938, Irish)
Hiram Martin
KING OF THE CASTLE(1936, Brit.)
Hugh Martin
ABBOTT AND COSTELLO IN HOLLYWOOD(1945), m/l Ralph Blane; ZIEGFELD FOLLIES(1945), w
I.C. Martin
PERFECT ALIBI, THE(1931, Brit.), ph
Ian Martin
THIEVES(1977); STARTING OVER(1979)
Ian Kennedy Martin
MITCHELL(1975), w; SWEENEY(1977, Brit.), w
Ida Martin
1984
BLAME IT ON THE NIGHT(1984)
Irene Martin
UNDERCOVER MAN, THE(1949); SAILOR BEWARE(1951); SUPERMAN AND THE MOLE MEN(1951); TAKE CARE OF MY LITTLE GIRL(1951); ACTORS AND SIN(1952); JUST FOR YOU(1952); VERY SPECIAL FAVOR, A(1965); HELLCATS, THE(1968)
Irvin J. Martin
Silents
ROBIN HOOD(1922), art d
J. Lockard Martin
LOST IN A HAREM(1944)
J.D. Martin
TOY, THE(1982)
Jack Martin
REGAL CAVALCADE(1935, Brit.), p; ONCE UPON A HONEYMOON(1942); THIS LAND IS MINE(1943); LIFE WITH FATHER(1947); LAST BANDIT, THE(1949), ph
Jacky Martin
INDEPENDENCE DAY(1983)
Jacqueline Martin
1984
KIDCO(1984), set d
James Martin
VIVA VILLA!(1934); GUY NAMED JOE, A(1943); PINTO BANDIT, THE(1944); RENEGADE GIRL(1946); HARPOON(1948); BABES IN TOYLAND(1961)
Jane Martin
EXPERIENCE PREFERRED... BUT NOT ESSENTIAL(1983, Brit.), art d
Janet Martin
HANDS ACROSS THE BORDER(1943); CALL OF THE SOUTH SEAS(1944); LADY AND THE MONSTER, THE(1944); LAKE PLACID SERENADE(1944); YELLOW ROSE OF TEXAS, THE(1944); BELLS OF ROSARITA(1945); SPORTING CHANCE, A(1945); CALENDAR GIRL(1947); MAIN STREET KID, THE(1947); TRESPASSER, THE(1947); HEART OF VIRGINIA(1948); KING OF THE GAMBLERS(1948); TRAIN TO ALCA-TRAZ(1948)
Jared Martin
MURDER A LA MOD(1968); WEDDING PARTY, THE(1969); MISSISSIPPI SUM-MER(1971); WESTWORLD(1973); SECOND COMING OF SUZANNE, THE(1974); LONELY LADY, THE(1983)
Jaye Martin
SOMETHING TO SHOUT ABOUT(1943)
Jean Martin
LAST CHANCE, THE(1945, Switz.); JAMBOREE(1957); PARIS BELONGS TO US(1962, Fr.); ADIOS GRINGO(1967, Ital./Fr./Span.); BATTLE OF ALGIERS, THE(1967, Ital./Alger.); MANON 70(1968, Fr.); PROMISE AT DAWN(1970, U.S./Fr.); JE T'AIME, JE T'AIME(1972, Fr./Swed.); DAY OF THE JACKAL, THE(1973, Brit./Fr.); MY NAME IS NOBODY(1974, Ital./Fr./Ger.)
Jean-Claude Martin
1984
LES COMPERES(1984, Fr.)
Jennifer Martin
WICKER MAN, THE(1974, Brit.)
Jerry Martin
LAST HUNT, THE(1956); SEX AND THE SINGLE GIRL(1964); WHAT DID YOU DO IN THE WAR, DADDY?(1966); PARTY, THE(1968); MAN WHO LOVED WOMEN, THE(1983)
1984
MICKI AND MAUDE(1984)
Jill Martin
TRIGGER FINGERS ½(1939); SCANDAL AT SCOURIE(1953)
Jim Martin
THUNDERING TRAIL, THE(1951); BLACK EYE(1974), w
Jimmie Martin
SIX GUN MAN(1946); SIX GUN SERENADE(1947); FRONTIER REVENGE(1948); RINGSIDE(1949); DALTON'S WOMEN, THE(1950); KING OF THE BULLWHIP(1950)

Jimmy Martin
FOUR JILLS IN A JEEP(1944); WEST TO GLORY(1947); MARK OF THE LASH(1948); COLORADO RANGER(1950); CROOKED RIVER(1950); HOSTILE COUNTRY(1950); MARSHAL OF HELDORADO(1950); WEST OF THE BRAZOS(1950); BLACK LASH, THE(1952); FROM THE TERRACE(1960)
Joe Martin
SCOBIE MALONE(1975, Aus.)
John Martin
BLACK DIAMONDS(1932, Brit.); SAVAGE GOLD(1933); WOMAN TRAP(1936); GEORGE WASHINGTON CARVER(1940); FIVE ANGLES ON MURDER(1950, Brit.); OUTPOST IN MALAYA(1952, Brit.); SEA TIGER(1952), ph; STORY OF ROBIN HOOD, THE(1952, Brit.); YUKON GOLD(1952), ph; LAUGHING IN THE SUNSHINE(1953, Brit./Swed.), p; PROJECT M7(1953, Brit.); HIGHWAY DRAGNET(1954), ph; RACING BLOOD(1954), ph; SECURITY RISK(1954), ph; BETRAYED WOMEN(1955), ph; BIG TIP OFF, THE(1955), ph; LAS VEGAS SHAKEDOWN(1955), ph; PORT OF HELL(1955), ph; TOUGHEST MAN ALIVE(1955), ph; TREASURE OF RUBY HILLS(1955), ph; MESA OF LOST WOMEN, THE(1956); YAQUI DRUMS(1956), ph; WEB OF SUSPICION(1959, Brit.); TELL-TALE HEART, THE(1962, Brit.); JUST FOR FUN(1963, Brit.); DR. TERROR'S HOUSE OF HORRORS(1965, Brit.); WINDSPLITTER, THE(1971); SILKWOOD(1983)
1984
EL NORTE(1984)
Misc. Talkies
DISCIPLES OF DEATH(1975); ENTER THE DEVIL(1975)
John Bartlow Martin
SCENE OF THE CRIME(1949), w
John J. Martin
BULLWHIP(1958), ph; LEGION OF THE DOOMED(1958), ph; SEVEN GUNS TO MESA(1958), ph
John L. Martin
EDDIE MACON'S RUN(1983)
Jose Manuel Martin
SPANISH AFFAIR(1958, Span.); SAVAGE GUNS, THE(1962, U.S./Span.); VIRIDIA-NA(1962, Mex./Span.); CEREMONY, THE(1963, U.S./Span.); GUNFIGHTERS OF CASA GRANDE(1965, U.S./Span.); SCHEHERAZADE(1965, Fr./Ital./Span.); MIN-NESOTA CLAY(1966, Ital./Fr./Span.); OPERATION DELILAH(1966, U.S./Span.); PIS-TOL FOR RINGO, A(1966, Ital./Span.); BULLET FOR THE GENERAL, A(1967, Ital.); VISCOUNT, THE(1967, Fr./Span./Ital./Ger.); CASTLE OF FU MANCHU, THE(1968, Ger./Span./Ital./Brit.); MINUTE TO PRAY, A SECOND TO DIE, A(1968, Ital.); GOD FORGIVES-I DON'T(1969, Ital./Span.); 100 RIFLES(1969); BULLET FOR SANDO-VAL, A(1970, Ital./Span.); ANTONY AND CLEOPATRA(1973, Brit.)
Joseph Martin
DADDY-O(1959); INVASION OF THE STAR CREATURES(1962)
Judy Martin
SCARECROW IN A GARDEN OF CUCUMBERS(1972)
Jules Martin
HAWAIIANS, THE(1970)
Julie Martin
GUTTER GIRLS(1964, Brit.); WHERE THE BULLETS FLY(1966, Brit.); OCTOPUS-SY(1983, Brit.)
June Martin
LOVE MATCH, THE(1955, Brit.); STUCK ON YOU(1983)
1984
STUCK ON YOU(1984)
Jurgen Martin
CELESTE(1982, Ger.), ph
Justin Martin
CURIOUS DR. HUMPP(1967, Arg.)
Karen Martin
RECOMMENDATION FOR MERCY(1975, Can.)
Kathy Martin
CLEOPATRA(1963); LAST OF THE SECRET AGENTS?, THE(1966)
Katy Martin
THOMASINE AND BUSHROD(1974)
Keith Martin
PETER RABBIT AND TALES OF BEATRIX POTTER(1971, Brit.)
Kent Martin
BLACK GIRL(1972)
Kiel Martin
UNDEFEATED, THE(1969); PANIC IN NEEDLE PARK(1971); LOLLY-MADONNA XXX(1973); TRICK BABY(1973); MOONRUNNERS(1975)
Kinley Martin
Silents
IT(1927), ph
Kirk Martin
DAYLIGHT ROBBERY(1964, Brit.)
Kreg Martin
CONVICTS FOUR(1962)
L. Martin
TWELVE-HANDED MEN OF MARS, THE(1964, Ital./Span.), d&w
Larry Martin
GREAT ST. TRINIAN'S TRAIN ROBBERY, THE(1966, Brit.)
Lawrence Martin
SCREAMERS(1978, Ital.), p; GREAT ALLIGATOR(1980, Ital.), p
Leila Martin
SANTA CLAUS CONQUERS THE MARTIANS(1964); GOD TOLD ME TO(1976)
Lenee Martin
STARS AND STRIPES FOREVER(1952)
Leo Martin
TNT JACKSON(1975)
Leon Martin
JOKER IS WILD, THE(1957)
Leonardo Martin
CALABUCH(1956, Span./Ital.), w; MISSION BLOODY MARY(1967, Fr./Ital./Span.), w
Lewis Martin
COUNTERSPY MEETS SCOTLAND YARD(1950); EXPERIMENT ALCATRAZ(1950); BIG CARNIVAL, THE(1951); CRIMINAL LAWYER(1951); DRUMS IN THE DEEP SOUTH(1951); OPERATION PACIFIC(1951); THREE GUYS NAMED MIKE(1951); WHIP HAND, THE(1951); RED PLANET MARS(1952); WILD NORTH, THE(1952);

ARROWHEAD(1953); CADDY, THE(1953); HOUDINI(1953); NO ESCAPE(1953); PONY EXPRESS(1953); WAR OF THE WORLDS, THE(1953); CRY VENGEANCE(1954); KNOCK ON WOOD(1954); MEN OF THE FIGHTING LADY(1954); PRISONER OF WAR(1954); WITNESS TO MURDER(1954); LAS VEGAS SHAKEDOWN(1955); NIGHT FREIGHT(1955); SEVEN LITTLE FOYS, THE(1955); COURT JESTER, THE(1956); MAN WHO KNEW TOO MUCH, THE(1956); MAN OF THE FIGHTING LADY(1954) DUST(1956); THESE WILDER YEARS(1956); LAST STAGECOACH WEST, THE(1957); QUIET GUN, THE(1957); ROCKABILLY BABY(1957); CRASH LANDING(1958); SUMMER PLACE, A(1959); DIARY OF A MADMAN(1963)

Liam Martin
RACE FOR YOUR LIFE, CHARLIE BROWN(1977)

Lily Martin
1984
BLAME IT ON THE NIGHT(1984)·

Lock Martin
DAY THE EARTH STOOD STILL, THE(1951); INVADERS FROM MARS(1953)

Lori Martin
CAPE FEAR(1962); CHASE, THE(1966); ANGRY BREED, THE(1969)

Lorna Martin
MY AIN FOLK(1944, Brit.)

Lorraine Martin
UNDER FIRE(1957)

Louis Martin
GAME OF TRUTH, THE(1961, Fr.), w; MAIDEN, THE(1961, Fr.), w; NIGHT ENCOUNTER(1963, Fr./Ital.), w; FIRE IN THE FLESH(1964, Fr.), w

Lucy Martin
COPS AND ROBBERS(1973)

Lydia Martin
SATAN'S BED(1965)

Madeleine Martin
ZIEGFELD GIRL(1941)

Malaika Martin
TASTE THE BLOOD OF DRACULA(1970, Brit.)

Manuel Martin
NUN AT THE CROSSROADS, A(1970, Ital./Span.), makeup

Marcella Martin
GONE WITH THE WIND(1939); WEST OF TOMBSTONE(1942)

Marcela Martin [Marcela Martinkova]
VOYAGE TO THE END OF THE UNIVERSE(1963, Czech.)

Marcelle Martin
MAN WHO RETURNED TO LIFE, THE(1942)

Mardik Martin
MEAN STREETS(1973), w,Martin Scorsese; NEW YORK, NEW YORK(1977), a, w; VALENTINO(1977, Brit.), w; RAGING BULL(1980), w; KING OF COMEDY, THE(1983)

Margaret Martin
ROAD TO SINGAPORE(1931); TAMPICO(1944); MY DARLING CLEMENTINE(1946); SIREN OF ATLANTIS(1948); CRISIS(1950); EAGLE AND THE HAWK, THE(1950)
1984
FINDERS KEEPERS(1984)
Silents
GOLD RUSH, THE(1925)

Margarita Martin
STREETS OF LAREDO(1949); JEOPARDY(1953); FAR HORIZONS, THE(1955); ONE-EYED JACKS(1961)

Marguerita Martin
HELL'S ISLAND(1955)

Marguerite Martin
MEN, THE(1950); ONE WAY STREET(1950)

Maria Martin
DOCTOR ZHIVAGO(1965); BANDIDOS(1967, Ital.); FLAME OVER VIETNAM(1967, Span./Ger.); HELLBENDERS, THE(1967, U.S./Ital./Span.); FOUR RODE OUT(1969, US/Span.); MURDERS IN THE RUE MORGUE(1971)

Marian Martin
HIS EXCITING NIGHT(1938); MAN IN THE IRON MASK, THE(1939); ELLERY QUEEN. MASTER DETECTIVE(1940); HIS GIRL FRIDAY(1940); GREAT MIKE, THE(1944); IRISH EYES ARE SMILING(1944); GANGS OF THE WATERFRONT(1945); GIRLS OF THE BIG HOUSE(1945); PHANTOM SPEAKS, THE(1945); CINDERELLA JONES(1946); DEADLINE FOR MURDER(1946); QUEEN OF BURLESQUE(1946); SUSPENSE(1946); THAT BRENNAN GIRL(1946); LIGHTHOUSE(1947); THAT'S MY GAL(1947); THUNDER IN THE PINES(1949); JOURNEY INTO LIGHT(1951); MIKADO, THE(1967, Brit.)

Maribel Martin
HOUSE THAT SCREAMED, THE(1970, Span.); BLOOD SPATTERED BRIDE, THE(1974, Span.)
1984
HOLY INNOCENTS, THE(1984, Span.)

Marion Martin
SINNERS IN PARADISE(1938); STORM, THE(1938); YOUTH TAKES A FLING(1938); INVITATION TO HAPPINESS(1939); PIRATES OF THE SKIES(1939); SERGEANT MADDEN(1939); BOOM TOWN(1940); UNTAMED(1940); WOMEN IN WAR(1940); BIG STORE, THE(1941); BLONDE INSPIRATION(1941); CRACKED NUTS(1941); LADY FROM CHEYENNE(1941); LADY SCARFACE(1941); MEXICAN SPITFIRE'S BABY(1941); NEW WINE(1941); TALL, DARK AND HANDSOME(1941); WEEKEND FOR THREE(1941); BIG STREET, THE(1942); MEXICAN SPITFIRE AT SEA(1942); MEXICAN SPITFIRE'S ELEPHANT(1942); POWDER TOWN(1942); STAR SPANGLED RHYTHM(1942); TALES OF MANHATTAN(1942); LADY OF BURLESQUE(1943); THEY GOT ME COVERED(1943); WOMAN OF THE TOWN, THE(1943); GILDERSLEEVE'S GHOST(1944); IT HAPPENED TOMORROW(1944); MERRY MONAHANS, THE(1944); SWEETHEARTS OF THE U.S.A.(1944); SWINGTIME JOHNNY(1944); ABBOTT AND COSTELLO IN HOLLYWOOD(1945); EADIE WAS A LADY(1945); ON STAGE EVERYBODY(1945); PENTHOUSE RHYTHM(1945); ANGEL ON MY SHOULDER(1946); NOBODY LIVES FOREVER(1946); STATE OF THE UNION(1948); COME TO THE STABLE(1949); MY DREAM IS YOURS(1949); OH, YOU BEAUTIFUL DOLL(1949); DAKOTA LIL(1950); KEY TO THE CITY(1950); OKLAHOMA ANNIE(1952)

Marty Martin
MILKY WAY, THE(1936)

Mary Martin
TRUE TO LIFE(1943); RAGE OF PARIS, THE(1938); GREAT VICTOR HERBERT, THE(1939); LOVE THY NEIGHBOR(1940); RHYTHM ON THE RIVER(1940); BIRTH OF THE BLUES(1941); KISS THE BOYS GOODBYE(1941); NEW YORK TOWN(1941); STAR SPANGLED RHYTHM(1942); HAPPY GO LUCKY(1943); NIGHT AND DAY(1946); MAIN STREET TO BROADWAY(1953); ACTION STATIONS(1959, Brit.)
Silents
ETERNAL SAPHO, THE(1916); TIGER WOMAN, THE(1917)
Misc. Silents
GREATER LOVE HATH NO MAN(1915); DAREDEVIL KATE(1916); VIXEN, THE(1916); DERELICT, THE(1917); SCARLET LETTER, THE(1917); HEART OF A LION, THE(1918)

Mary G. Martin
Misc. Silents
WONDERFUL ADVENTURE, THE(1915)

Maryse Martin
NOUS IRONS A PARIS(1949, Fr.); HAPPY ROAD, THE(1957)

Melvyn Martin
LES ENFANTS TERRIBLES(1952, Fr.)

Mia Martin
SUBURBAN WIVES(1973, Brit.)

Michael Martin
UP THE JUNCTION(1968, Brit.); ALAMBRISTA!(1977), m

Michelle Martin
1984
TOP SECRET!(1984)

Mickey Martin
THROWBACK, THE(1935); STRIKE UP THE BAND(1940); KEEPER OF THE FLAME(1942); FOREVER AND A DAY(1943); HARRIGAN'S KID(1943); SEA OF GRASS, THE(1947); B. F.'S DAUGHTER(1948); RACE STREET(1948); IT'S A BIG COUNTRY(1951); GNOME-MOBILE, THE(1967); BEST FRIENDS(1982)

Micky Martin
DEAD END(1937)

Midge Martin
TOO MANY GIRLS(1940)

Mike Martin
TRAITORS, THE(1963, Brit.)

Millicent Martin
LIBEL(1959, Brit.); INVASION QUARTET(1961, Brit.); GIRL ON THE BOAT, THE(1962, Brit.); NOTHING BUT THE BEST(1964, Brit.); THOSE MAGNIFICENT MEN IN THEIR FLYING MACHINES; OR HOW I FLEWFROM LONDON TO PARIS IN 25 HOURS AND 11 MINUTES(1965, Brit.); ALFIE(1966, Brit.); STOP THE WORLD–I WANT TO GET OFF(1966, Brit.)

Mimi Martin
MONEY MOVERS(1978, Aus.)

Mitch Martin
HOG WILD(1980, Can.)

Nan Martin
TOYS IN THE ATTIC(1963); MAN IN THE GREY FLANNEL SUIT, THE(1956); BUSTER KEATON STORY, THE(1957); MUGGER, THE(1958); BUS RILEY'S BACK IN TOWN(1965); FOR LOVE OF IVY(1968); THREE IN THE ATTIC(1968); GOODBYE COLUMBUS(1969); YOUNG NURSES, THE(1973); OTHER SIDE OF THE MOUNTAIN, THE(1975); JACKSON COUNTY JAIL(1976); OTHER SIDE OF THE MOUNTAIN–PART 2, THE(1978); LOVING COUPLES(1980); SMALL CIRCLE OF FRIENDS, A(1980); SOME KIND OF HERO(1982); DOCTOR DETROIT(1983)
1984
ALL OF ME(1984)

Nancy Martin
ART OF LOVE, THE(1965)

Ned Martin
HER PRIVATE LIFE(1929), p

Nell Martin
LORD BYRON OF BROADWAY(1930), w

Neville Martin
ONE BRIEF SUMMER(1971, Brit.)

Nita Martin
ANYBODY'S BLONDE(1931); TWO GUN MAN, THE(1931)
Silents
LADY BE GOOD(1928)

Nora Martin
HOLLYWOOD CANTEEN(1944)

Nora Lou Martin
BOSS OF HANGTOWN MESA(1942); SILVER BULLET, THE(1942)

Orlando Martin
AMERICAN GUERRILLA IN THE PHILIPPINES, AN(1950)

Owen Martin
PAJAMA GAME, THE(1957)

P.J. Martin
ZAPPED!(1982)

Pamela Sue Martin
POSEIDON ADVENTURE, THE(1972); TO FIND A MAN(1972); OUR TIME(1974); LADY IN RED, THE(1979)
1984
TORCHLIGHT(1984), a, w
Misc. Talkies
BUSTER AND BILLIE(1974)

Paul Martin
HAPPY EVER AFTER(1932, Ger./Brit.), d; ORIENT EXPRESS(1934), d, w; BLACK ROSES(1936, Ger.), d, w; FACING THE MUSIC(1941, Brit.); COUNTDOWN TO DANGER(1967, Brit.); ESCAPE FROM THE SEA(1968, Brit.); SMUGGLERS, THE(1969, Fr.)

Paul A. Martin
LIFE AT THE TOP(1965, Brit.)

Paula Martin
GYPSY(1962); DIRTY HARRY(1971)
Misc. Talkies
NAUGHTY GIRLS ON THE LOOSE(1976)

Penelope Martin
MUSIC MAN, THE(1962)

Pepper Martin
ANGELS FROM HELL(1968); IF HE HOLLERS, LET HIM GO(1968); WRECKING CREW, THE(1968); ANIMALS, THE(1971); CAHILL, UNITED STATES MARSHAL(1973); WALKING TALL(1973); LONGEST YARD, THE(1974); MURPH THE SURF(1974); SUPERMAN II(1980)

Perry Martin
HAWMPS!(1976)

Peter J. Martin
DEATHCHEATERS(1976, Aus.), m

Peter Martin
MATTER OF INNOCENCE, A(1968, Brit.)

Philip Martin
RIFFRAFF(1947), ed; THUNDER MOUNTAIN(1947), ed; IF YOU KNEW SUSIE(1948), ed; CANADIAN PACIFIC(1949), ed; FIGHTING MAN OF THE PLAINS(1949), ed; GREAT MISSOURI RAID, THE(1950), ed; WARPATH(1951), ed; LONELINESS OF THE LONG DISTANCE RUNNER, THE(1962, Brit.)

Philip Martin, Jr.
IRON MAJOR, THE(1943), ed; MARINE RAIDERS(1944), ed; TALL IN THE SADDLE(1944), ed; FIRST YANK INTO TOKYO(1945), ed; ZOMBIES ON BROADWAY(1945), ed; BADMAN'S TERRITORY(1946), ed; DICK TRACY VS. CUEBALL(1946), ed; FALCON'S ALIBI, THE(1946), ed

Phillip Martin
CARIBOO TRAIL, THE(1950), ed

Phillip Martin, Jr.
FALCON OUT WEST, THE(1944), ed; TWO O'CLOCK COURAGE(1945), ed

Pierre Martin
ARABESQUE(1966), w

Quinn Martin
BLONDIE GOES LATIN(1941), w; SCARFACE MOB, THE(1962), p; MEPHISTO WALTZ, THE(1971), p

Ray Martin
GREEN PASTURES(1936); HEADLINE CRASHER(1937); DUKE IS THE TOPS, THE(1938); BLONDE SINNER(1956, Brit.), m; IT'S GREAT TO BE YOUNG(1956, Brit.), m; YOUNG GRADUATES, THE(1971), m; HOAX, THE(1972), m; BALTIMORE BULLET, THE(1980)

Reni Martin
NIGHTMARE IN WAX(1969)

Reuben Martin
GREAT CATHERINE(1968, Brit.); CARRY ON UP THE JUNGLE(1970, Brit.)

Rhea Martin
Misc. Silents
COQUETTE, THE(1915)

Ricci Martin
Misc. Talkies
JUST TELL ME YOU LOVE ME(1979)

Richard Martin
ARMY SURGEON(1942); FALCON'S BROTHER, THE(1942); HITLER'S CHILDREN(1942); MAYOR OF 44TH STREET, THE(1942); MEXICAN SPITFIRE AT SEA(1942); MEXICAN SPITFIRE SEES A GHOST(1942); SEVEN DAYS LEAVE(1942); ADVENTURES OF A ROOKIE(1943); BOMBARDIER(1943); FALCON IN DANGER, THE(1943); GANGWAY FOR TOMORROW(1943); IRON MAJOR, THE(1943); LADIES' DAY(1943); LEOPARD MAN, THE(1943); TENDER COMRADE(1943); MARINE RAIDERS(1944); NEVADA(1944); HAVING WONDERFUL CRIME(1945); WANDERER OF THE WASTELAND(1945); WEST OF THE PECOS(1945); BAMBOO BLONDE, THE(1946); ADVENTURES OF DON COYOTE(1947); THUNDER MOUNTAIN(1947); UNDER THE TONTO RIM(1947); WILD HORSE MESA(1947); ARIZONA RANGER, THE(1948); GUN SMUGGLERS(1948); GUNS OF HATE(1948); INDIAN AGENT(1948); WESTERN HERITAGE(1948); BROTHERS IN THE SADDLE(1949); MASKED RAIDERS(1949); MYSTERIOUS DESPERADO, THE(1949); RIDERS OF THE RANGE(1949); RUSTLERS(1949); STAGECOACH KID(1949); BORDER TREASURE(1950); DYNAMITE PASS(1950); LAW OF THE BADLANDS(1950); RIDER FROM TUCSON(1950); RIO GRANDE PATROL(1950); STORM OVER WYOMING(1950); GUNPLAY(1951); HOT LEAD(1951); OVERLAND TELEGRAPH(1951); PISTOL HARVEST(1951); SADDLE LEGION(1951); DESERT PASSAGE(1952); RAIDERS, THE(1952); ROAD AGENT(1952); TARGET(1952); TRAIL GUIDE(1952); HELL BOUND(1957); FOUR FAST GUNS(1959)
Misc. Talkies
KING MONSTER(1977), d

Robert Martin
BLOCKADE(1929), ph; LOOKING ON THE BRIGHT SIDE(1932, Brit.), ph; WATER GYPSIES, THE(1932, Brit.), ph; WOMAN IN CHAINS(1932, Brit.), ph; HOUSE OF TRENT, THE(1933, Brit.), ph; OVERNIGHT(1933, Brit.), ph; STRANGE EVIDENCE(1933, Brit.), ph; THREE MEN IN A BOAT(1933, Brit.), ph; TIGER BAY(1933, Brit.), ph; AUTUMN CROCUS(1934, Brit.), ph; FOR LOVE OR MONEY(1934, Brit.), ph; LOYALTIES(1934, Brit.), ph; SHIPMATES O' MINE(1936, Brit.), ph; SILENT BARRIERS(1937, Brit.), ph; SOAPBOX DERBY(1958, Brit.), w; LAST VOYAGE, THE(1960); GEEK MAGGOT BINGO(1983)
Silents
GIRLS DON'T GAMBLE(1921), ph; MAKING THE GRADE(1921), ph; MY BOY(1922), ph; OLIVER TWIST(1922), ph; TROUBLE(1922), ph; CIRCUS DAYS(1923), ph; DADDY(1923), ph; RAG MAN, THE(1925), ph; SIBERIA(1926), ph; PRINCESS FROM HOBOKEN, THE(1927), ph; HEY RUBE!(1928), ph; HARDBOILED(1929), ph

Robert G. Martin
ESCAPE(1930, Brit.), ph; SALLY IN OUR ALLEY(1931, Brit.), ph; SIGN OF FOUR, THE(1932, Brit.), ph; JAVA HEAD(1935, Brit.), ph; LOOK UP AND LAUGH(1935, Brit.), ph; NO LIMIT(1935, Brit.), ph

Roberto Martin
PLACE CALLED GLORY, A(1966, Span./Ger.)

Roger Martin
STORY OF ADELE H., THE(1975, Fr.)

Roland Martin
LE PETIT THEATRE DE JEAN RENOIR(1974, Fr.)

Ron Martin
GOIN' DOWN THE ROAD(1970, Can.)

Rosemary Martin
MORE THAN A MIRACLE(1967, Ital./Fr.); WILD, WILD PLANET, THE(1967, Ital.); ALL THINGS BRIGHT AND BEAUTIFUL(1979, Brit.); TESS(1980, Fr./Brit.)
1984
LAUGHTER HOUSE(1984, Brit.); SECRET PLACES(1984, Brit.); SLAYGROUND(1984, Brit.)

Ross Martin
CONQUEST OF SPACE(1955); COLOSSUS OF NEW YORK, THE(1958); UNDERWATER WARRIOR(1958); EXPERIMENT IN TERROR(1962); GERONIMO(1962); CEREMONY, THE(1963, U.S./Span.); GREAT RACE, THE(1965); MAN FROM BUTTON WILLOW, THE(1965)
Misc. Talkies
CHARLIE CHAN: HAPPINESS IS A WARM CLUE(1971)

Roy Martin
WILD SEASON(1968, South Africa), m

Ruth Martin
VOGUES OF 1938(1937)

Sally Martin
JUNGLE PRINCESS, THE(1936); TIMOTHY'S QUEST(1936); BARRIER, THE(1937); NOBODY'S CHILDREN(1940)

Sam Martin
BEYOND THE REEF(1981), ph

Sandra Martin
1984
SUPERGIRL(1984)

Sandy Martin
SCALPEL(1976); 48 HOURS(1982)

Sarah Martin
Misc. Talkies
VOICE OVER(1983)

Scoop Martin
STABLEMATES(1938); TEXANS, THE(1938); LAW AND ORDER(1940); RAIDERS OF SAN JOAQUIN(1943); CROOKED RIVER(1950)

Sheila Martin
SLEEPING CAR TO TRIESTE(1949, Brit.); YOU CAN'T FOOL AN IRISHMAN(1950, Ireland)

Shelley Martin
Misc. Talkies
FOR MEMBERS ONLY(1960)

Shirley Martin
CANON CITY(1948)

Shirley Vance Martin
Silents
MY BOY(1922), t

Simon Michael Martin
HEARTACHES(1981, Can.), m

Skip Martin
I LOVE MELVIN(1953), m; OPPOSITE SEX, THE(1956), md; HELLFIRE CLUB, THE(1963, Brit.); MASQUE OF THE RED DEATH, THE(1964, U.S./Brit.); GUESS WHO'S COMING TO DINNER(1967); PSYCHO-CIRCUS(1967, Brit.); WHERE'S JACK?(1969, Brit.); VAMPIRE CIRCUS(1972, Brit.); HORROR HOSPITAL(1973, Brit.)

Slim Martin
JOSETTE(1938)

Speer Martin
CRASHING LAS VEGAS(1956); CASE OF PATTY SMITH, THE(1962)

Stan Martin
HAPPY AS THE GRASS WAS GREEN(1973), ph; HAZEL'S PEOPLE(1978), ph

Stanley Martin
YOUNG DON'T CRY, THE(1957)

Stephen Martin
INADMISSIBLE EVIDENCE(1968, Brit.); SECRETS(1971); SHADES OF SILK(1979, Can.), ed

Steve Martin
IRON MAN, THE(1951); SGT. PEPPER'S LONELY HEARTS CLUB BAND(1978); JERK, THE(1979), a, w; MUPPET MOVIE, THE(1979); PENNIES FROM HEAVEN(1981); DEAD MEN DON'T WEAR PLAID(1982), a, w; MAN WITH TWO BRAINS, THE(1983), a, w
1984
ALL OF ME(1984); LONELY GUY, THE(1984)

Steven M. Martin
FAST TIMES AT RIDGEMONT HIGH(1982)

Strother Martin
UP IN SMOKE(1978); RHUBARB(1951); STORM OVER TIBET(1952); MAGNETIC MONSTER, THE(1953); SOUTH SEA WOMAN(1953); DRUM BEAT(1954); BIG KNIFE, THE(1955); KISS ME DEADLY(1955); STRATEGIC AIR COMMAND(1955); TARGET ZERO(1955); ATTACK!(1956); BLACK WHIP, THE(1956); BLACK PATCH(1957); COPPER SKY(1957); HORSE SOLDIERS, THE(1959); SHAGGY DOG, THE(1959); WILD AND THE INNOCENT, THE(1959); DEADLY COMPANIONS, THE(1961); SANCTUARY(1961); MAN WHO SHOT LIBERTY VALANCE, THE(1962); MC LINTOCK!(1963); SHOWDOWN(1963); INVITATION TO A GUNFIGHTER(1964); BRAINSTORM(1965); SHENANDOAH(1965); SONS OF KATIE ELDER, THE(1965); EYE FOR AN EYE, AN(1966); HARPER(1966); COOL HAND LUKE(1967); FLIM-FLAM MAN, THE(1967); BUTCH CASSIDY AND THE SUNDANCE KID(1969); TRUE GRIT(1969); WILD BUNCH, THE(1969); BALLAD OF CABLE HOGUE, THE(1970); BROTHERHOOD OF SATAN, THE(1971); FOOLS' PARADE(1971); HANNIE CALDER(1971, Brit.); RED SKY AT MORNING(1971); POCKET MONEY(1972); SSSSSSSS(1973); HARD TIMES(1975); ROOSTER COGBURN(1975); GREAT SCOUT AND CATHOUSE THURSDAY, THE(1976); SLAP SHOT(1977); END, THE(1978); CHAMP, THE(1979); LOVE AND BULLETS(1979, Brit.); NIGHTWING(1979); VILLAIN, THE(1979)
Misc. Talkies
HOTWIRE(1980)

Susan Martin
PUNISHMENT PARK(1971), p; THRESHOLD(1983, Can.), ed

Sylvia Martin
PROM NIGHT(1980)

Tantoo Martin
MARIE-ANN(1978, Can.); DEATH HUNT(1981); RUNNING BRAVE(1983, Can.)

Ted Martin
PUNISHMENT PARK(1971)

Teddy Martin
SLEUTH(1972, Brit.)

Terry Martin
CRY OF THE BANSHEE(1970, Brit.); SHAPE OF THINGS TO COME, THE(1979, Can.); PHOBIA(1980, Can.)

Thomas Martin
DARK CORNER, THE(1946)
Thomas F. Martin
EMERGENCY WEDDING(1950)
Todd Martin
CRACK IN THE WORLD(1965); FINGER ON THE TRIGGER(1965, US/Span.); TREASURE OF MAKUBA, THE(1967, U.S./Span.); IF HE HOLLERS, LET HIM GO(1968); THOMAS CROWN AFFAIR, THE(1968); BAD COMPANY(1972); JORY(1972); HIT(1973); ALEX AND THE GYPSY(1976)
Tom Martin
DRAGONWYCH(1946); IMPACT(1949); HOW TO MARRY A MILLIONAIRE(1953)
Misc. Talkies
PSI FACTOR(1980, Brit.)
Tommy Martin
WUTHERING HEIGHTS(1939)
Tony Martin
BACK TO NATURE(1936); FARMER IN THE DELL, THE(1936); FOLLOW THE FLEET(1936); SING, BABY, SING(1936); ALI BABA GOES TO TOWN(1937); LIFE BEGINS IN COLLEGE(1937); YOU CAN'T HAVE EVERYTHING(1937); KENTUCKY MOONSHINE(1938); SALLY, IRENE AND MARY(1938); UP THE RIVER(1938); WINNER TAKE ALL(1939); MUSIC IN MY HEART(1940); BIG STORE, THE(1941); ZIEGFELD GIRL(1941); TILL THE CLOUDS ROLL BY(1946); CASBAH(1948); TWO TICKETS TO BROADWAY(1951); EASY TO LOVE(1953); HERE COME THE GIRLS(1953); DEEP IN MY HEART(1954); HIT THE DECK(1955); MEET ME IN LAS VEGAS(1956); QUINCANNON, FRONTIER SCOUT(1956); LET'S BE HAPPY(1957, Brit.); DEAR MR. WONDERFUL(1983, Ger.); WICKED LADY, THE(1983, Brit.)
Townsend Martin
MOST IMMORAL LADY, A(1929), w
Silents
CRADLE BUSTER, THE(1922); SECOND FIDDLE(1923); GRIT(1924); KISS IN THE DARK, A(1925), w; AMERICAN VENUS, THE(1926), w; KISS FOR CINDERELLA, A(1926), w
Trade Martin
MADE FOR EACH OTHER(1971), m; HAIL(1973), m
Trevor Martin
OTHELLO(1965, Brit.); ABSOLUTION(1981, Brit.)
Troy Kennedy Martin
ITALIAN JOB, THE(1969, Brit.), w; KELLY'S HEROES(1970, U.S./Yugo.), w; JERUSALEM FILE, THE(1972, U.S./Israel), w; SWEENEY 2(1978, Brit.), w
Vance Martin
LULU(1978), art d
Vera Martin
NOOSE HANGS HIGH, THE(1948)
Vince Martin
TOUCH AND GO(1955); ONCE UPON A COFFEE HOUSE(1965)
Misc. Talkies
MAMA'S GONE A-HUNTING(1976)
Vincent Martin
ISLAND WOMEN(1958)
1984
SWANN IN LOVE(1984, Fr.Ger.)
Vivian Martin
FOLIES DERGERE(1935)
Silents
WISHING RING, THE(1914); ARRIVAL OF PERPETUA, THE(1915); LITTLE MADEMOISELLE, THE(1915); LITTLE MISS BROWN(1915); KISS FOR SUSIE, A(1917); MOLLY ENTANGLED(1917); JANE GOES A' WOOING(1919); LITTLE COMRADE(1919); LOUISIANA(1919)
Misc. Silents
OVER NIGHT(1915); HER FATHER'S SON(1916); MERELY MARY ANN(1916); MODERN THELMA, A(1916); RIGHT DIRECTION, THE(1916); STRONGER LOVE, THE(1916); FAIR BARBARIAN, THE(1917); FORBIDDEN PATHS(1917); GIRL AT HOME, THE(1917); GIVING BECKY A CHANCE(1917); LITTLE MISS OPTIMIST(1917); SPIRIT OF ROMANCE, THE(1917); SUNSET TRAIL(1917); TROUBLE BUSTER, THE(1917); WAX MODEL, THE(1917); HER COUNTRY FIRST(1918); MIRANDY SMILES(1918); PETTICOAT PILOT, A(1918); UNCLAIMED GOODS(1918); VIVIETTE(1918); HIS OFFICIAL FIANCEE(1919); HOME TOWN GIRL, THE(1919); INNOCENT ADVENTURESS, AN(1919); THIRD KISS, THE(1919); YOU NEVER SAID SUCH A GIRL(1919); HUSBANDS AND WIVES(1920); SONG OF THE SOUL, THE(1920); MOTHER ETERNAL(1921); PARDON MY FRENCH(1921); SOILED(1924)
Vivienne Martin
BELLES OF ST. TRINIAN'S, THE(1954, Brit.); COURT MARTIAL(1954, Brit.); SECRET VENTURE(1955, Brit.)
W. Thorton Martin
BAND PLAYS ON, THE(1934), w
Wally Martin
IN PRAISE OF OLDER WOMEN(1978, Can.)
Wally Martin [Marshall Smith]
SATAN'S BED(1965)
Wendy Martin
MAN IN THE DARK(1963, Brit.)
William Martin
FIRST COMES COURAGE(1943); JACKTOWN(1962), p,d&w; CANDIDATE, THE(1964), ed; HELL'S ANGELS ON WHEELS(1967), ed; ANGELS FROM HELL(1968), ed; CHOIRBOYS, THE(1977), ed
Misc. Silents
YELLOWBACK, THE(1929)
Willis Martin
CAIN'S WAY(1969); WILD WHEELS(1969)
Wyndham Martin
Silents
SILVER CAR, THE(1921), w
Yves Martin
1984
L'ARGENT(1984, Fr./Switz.)
Yvonne Martin
PERSONAL COLUMN(1939, Fr.), ed; ANGELS OF THE STREETS(1950, Fr.), ed; MONSEIGNEUR(1950, Fr.), ed; AUSTERLITZ(1960, Fr./Ital./Yugo.), ed; TRIAL, THE(1963, Fr./Ital./Ger.), ed

Michael Martin-Harvey
DRUMS(1938, Brit.); MUTINY OF THE ELSINORE, THE(1939, Brit.); LET THE PEOPLE SING(1942, Brit.); SILVER DARLINGS, THE(1947, Brit.); PAPER GALLOWS(1950, Brit.); THIRD VISITOR, THE(1951, Brit.); JUDGMENT DEFERRED(1952, Brit.); LONG MEMORY, THE(1953, Brit.); TONIGHT'S THE NIGHT(1954, Brit.)
Muriel Martin-Harvey
Silents
ANSWER, THE(1916, Brit.)
Hans Martin-Majewski
BOOMERANG(1960, Ger.), m
Denis Martin-Sisteron
POURQUOI PAS!(1979, Fr.), art d
Edward Martindale
RAIN OR SHINE(1930)
Silents
COMPROMISE(1925)
Larry Martindale
HARD TIMES(1975); ST. IVES(1976); WHITE BUFFALO, THE(1977)
Wink Martindale
LET'S ROCK(1958)
Edward Martindel
ON TRIAL(1928); SINGING FOOL, THE(1928); AVIATOR, THE(1929); DESERT SONG, THE(1929); HARDBOILED ROSE(1929); MODERN LOVE(1929); PHANTOM OF THE OPERA, THE(1929); AMOS 'N' ANDY(1930); GOLDEN DAWN(1930); MAMBA(1930); SECOND CHOICE(1930); SONG O' MY HEART(1930); SONG OF THE WEST(1930); DIVORCE AMONG FRIENDS(1931); GAY DIPLOMAT, THE(1931); HIGH STAKES(1931); AFRAID TO TALK(1932); AMERICAN MADNESS(1932); FALSE FACES(1932); BY APPOINTMENT ONLY(1933); TWO HEADS ON A PILLOW(1934); CHAMPAGNE FOR BREAKFAST(1935); GIRL WHO CAME BACK, THE(1935); MAN WHO RECLAIMED HIS HEAD, THE(1935)
Silents
DUCKS AND DRAKES(1921); LITTLE EVA ASCENDS(1922); NICE PEOPLE(1922); ORDEAL, THE(1922); WHITE FLOWER, THE(1923); LADY WINDERMERE'S FAN(1925); TONY RUNS WILD(1926); CHILDREN OF DIVORCE(1927); IN OLD KENTUCKY(1927); TAXI! TAXI!(1927); WOMAN WHO DID NOT CARE, THE(1927); DEVIL'S APPLE TREE(1929); WHY BE GOOD?(1929)
Misc. Silents
FOUNDLING, THE(1916); SCARLET WOMAN, THE(1916); RICH MAN'S PLAYTHING, A(1917); VANITY(1917); YOU NEVER CAN TELL(1920); GLORY OF CLEMENTINA, THE(1922); DUCHESS OF BUFFALO, THE(1926); YOU'D BE SURPRISED(1926); FASHIONS FOR WOMEN(1927); LOVERS?(1927); VENUS OF VENICE(1927); COMPANIONATE MARRIAGE, THE(1928); DESERT BRIDE, THE(1928)
Edward Martindell
FOOTLIGHTS AND FOOLS(1929)
Gayna Martine
1984
LASSITER(1984)
Gigi Martine
PLAYGIRLS AND THE BELLBOY, THE(1962,Ger.)
Marie Martine
LA GUERRE EST FINIE(1967, Fr./Swed.), cos
Mortimer Martine
Misc. Silents
OLIVER TWIST(1912)
H.O. Martinek
Misc. Silents
FALSE WIRELESS, THE(1914, Brit.), a, d; IN THE GRIP OF SPIES(1914, Brit.), a, d; MYSTERY OF THE OLD MILL, THE(1914, Brit.), a, d; STOLEN MASTERPIECE, THE(1914, Brit.), a, d; AT THE TORRENT'S MERCY(1915, Brit.), d; CLUE OF THE CIGAR BAND, THE(1915, Brit.), a, d
Ivy Martinek
Misc. Silents
WHEN PARIS SLEEPS(1917, Brit.)
Coco Martinel
HEAT(1970, Arg.)
Arthur Martineli
BECAUSE OF EVE(1948), ph
Alfredo Martinelli
MATCHLESS(1967, Ital.)
Silents
WHITE SISTER, THE(1923); ROMOLA(1925)
Arthur Martinelli
WHITE ZOMBIE(1932), ph; SUPERNATURAL(1933), ph; I CONQUER THE SEA(1936), ph; REVOLT OF THE ZOMBIES(1936), ph; COUNTY FAIR(1937), ph; CRIME AFLOAT(1937), ph; DRUMS OF DESTINY(1937), ph; GLORY TRAIL, THE(1937), ph; MILE A MINUTE LOVE(1937), ph; NATION AFLAME(1937), ph; RAW TIMBER(1937), ph; UNDER STRANGE FLAGS(1937), ph; CIPHER BUREAU(1938), ph; FEMALE FUGITIVE(1938), ph; GANG BULLETS(1938), ph; LAW COMMANDS, THE(1938), ph; MY OLD KENTUCKY HOME(1938), ph; OLD LOUISIANA(1938), ph; REBELLION(1938), ph; SHADOWS OVER SHANGHAI(1938), ph; TEN LAPS TO GO(1938), ph; CONVICT'S CODE(1939), ph; COVERED TRAILER, THE(1939), ph; INSIDE INFORMATION(1939), ph; LONG SHOT, THE(1939), ph; PANAMA PATROL(1939), ph; STAR REPORTER(1939), ph; UNDERCOVER AGENT(1939), ph; WITNESS VANISHES, THE(1939), ph; MAD EMPRESS, THE(1940), ph; CRIMINALS WITHIN(1941), ph; DEADLY GAME, THE(1941), ph; DEVIL BAT, THE(1941), ph; DOUBLE CROSS(1941), ph; DOUBLE TROUBLE(1941), ph; FEDERAL FUGITIVES(1941), ph; PAPER BULLETS(1941), ph; SECRET EVIDENCE(1941), ph; CINDERELLA SWINGS IT(1942), ph; INSIDE THE LAW(1942), ph; MIRACLE KID(1942), ph; MR. CELEBRITY(1942), ph; DEERSLAYER(1943), ph; HERE COMES KELLY(1943), ph; SWING OUT THE BLUES(1943), ph; CALL OF THE JUNGLE(1944), ph; CHARLIE CHAN IN BLACK MAGIC(1944), ph; IN OLD NEW MEXICO(1945), ph
Silents
HER FIGHTING CHANCE(1917), ph; TRAIL OF THE SHADOW, THE(1917), ph; KILDARE OF STORM(1918), ph; AMATEUR ADVENTURESS, THE(1919), ph; LOVE, HONOR AND OBEY(1920), ph; IDLE RICH, THE(1921), ph; MAN WHO, THE(1921), ph; SHERLOCK BROWN(1921), ph; RIGHT THAT FAILED, THE(1922), ph; YOUTH TO YOUTH(1922), ph; EAST SIDE–WEST SIDE(1923), ph; ELLA CINDERS(1926), ph

Billy Martinelli
J.W. COOP(1971)
Brad Martinelli
DATE BAIT(1960)
Elsa Martinelli
INDIAN FIGHTER, THE(1955); DONATELLA(1956, Ital.); FOUR GIRLS IN TOWN(1956); STOWAWAY GIRL(1957, Brit.); PRISONER OF THE VOLGA(1960, Fr./Ital.); BLOOD AND ROSES(1961, Fr./Ital.); HATARI!(1962); LA NOTTE BRAVA(1962, Fr./Ital.); PIGEON THAT TOOK ROME, THE(1962); RAMPAGE(1963); RICE GIRL(1963, Fr./Ital.); TRIAL, THE(1963, Fr./Ital./Ger.); V.I.P.s, THE(1963, Brit.); HAIL MAFIA(1965, Fr./Ital.); TENTH VICTIM, THE(1965, Fr./Ital.); MARCO THE MAGNIFICENT(1966, Ital./Fr./Yugo./Egypt/Afghanistan); MAROC 7(1967, Brit.); WOMAN TIMES SEVEN(1967, U.S./Fr./Ital.); CANDY(1968, Ital./Fr.); DE L'AMOUR(1968, Fr./Ital.); MANON 70(1968, Fr.); OLDEST PROFESSION, THE(1968, Fr./Ital./Ger.); IF IT'S TUESDAY, THIS MUST BE BELGIUM(1969); MADIGAN'S MILLIONS(1970, Span./Ital)
Enzo A. Martinelli
TAMMY AND THE MILLIONAIRE(1967), ph; JOURNEY TO SHILOH(1968), ph
Franco Martinelli
DR. BUTCHER, M.D.(1982, Ital.), w
Frank Martinelli
DATE WITH THE FALCON, A(1941); FOUR JACKS AND A JILL(1941); SEVEN DAYS LEAVE(1942)
Jean Martinelli
RED AND THE BLACK, THE(1954, Fr./Ital.); TO CATCH A THIEF(1955); STORY OF THE COUNT OF MONTE CRISTO, THE(1962, Fr./Ital.)
John A. Martinelli
MAN AND BOY(1972), ed; HARD COUNTRY(1981), ed
John Martinelli
EMBRYO(1976), ed
Natalie Martinelli
GOODBYE CHARLIE(1964)
Tony Martinelli
YELLOW CARGO(1936), ed; GIT ALONG, LITTLE DOGIES(1937), ed; IT'S LOVE I'M AFTER(1937), ed; LOVE TAKES FLIGHT(1937), ed; NAVY SPY(1937), ed; RIDERS OF THE WHISTLING SKULL(1937), ed; ROOTIN' TOOTIN' RHYTHM(1937), ed; TRIGGER TRIO, THE(1937), ed; HEROES OF THE HILLS(1938), ed; OUTLAWS OF SONORA(1938), ed; OVERLAND STAGE RAIDERS(1938), ed; PALS OF THE SADDLE(1938), ed; RED RIVER RANGE(1938), ed; SANTA FE STAMPEDE(1938), ed; COWBOYS FROM TEXAS(1939), ed; DAYS OF JESSE JAMES(1939), ed; KANSAS TERRORS, THE(1939), ed; MEXICALI ROSE(1939), ed; NEW FRONTIER(1939), ed; ROVIN' TUMBLEWEEDS(1939), ed; THREE TEXAS STEERS(1939), ed; WYOMING OUTLAW(1939), ed; CAROLINA MOON(1940), ed; GAUCHO SERENADE(1940), ed; LONE STAR RAIDERS(1940), ed; OKLAHOMA RENEGADES(1940), ed; PIONEERS OF THE WEST(1940), ed; RANCHO GRANDE(1940), ed; TEXAS TERRORS(1940), ed; TRAIL BLAZERS, THE(1940), ed; UNDER TEXAS SKIES(1940), ed; YOUNG BUFFALO BILL(1940), ed; BACK IN THE SADDLE(1941), ed; DEATH VALLEY OUTLAWS(1941), ed; JESSE JAMES AT BAY(1941), ed; PHANTOM COWBOY, THE(1941), ed; RIDIN' ON A RAINBOW(1941), ed; SADDLEMATES(1941), ed; SHERIFF OF TOMBSTONE(1941), ed; SUNSET IN WYOMING(1941), ed; TWO GUN SHERIFF(1941), ed; UNDER FIESTA STARS(1941), ed; HANDS ACROSS THE BORDER(1943), ed; MAN FROM MUSIC MOUNTAIN(1943), ed; PISTOL PACKIN' MAMA(1943), ed; SILVER SPURS(1943), ed; SONG OF TEXAS(1943), ed; BIG BONANZA, THE(1944), ed; COWBOY AND THE SENORITA(1944), ed; FACES IN THE FOG(1944), ed; HIDDEN VALLEY OUTLAWS(1944), ed; MY BUDDY(1944), ed; SAN ANTONIO KID, THE(1944), ed; SONG OF NEVADA(1944), ed; YELLOW ROSE OF TEXAS, THE(1944), ed; ALONG THE NAVAJO TRAIL(1945), ed; ANGEL COMES TO BROOKLYN, AN(1945), ed; MAN FROM OKLAHOMA, THE(1945), ed; SHERIFF OF CIMARRON(1945), ed; SUNSET IN EL DORADO(1945), ed; THREE'S A CROWD(1945), ed; VAMPIRE'S GHOST, THE(1945), ed; AFFAIRS OF GERALDINE(1946), ed; GAY BLADES(1946), ed; G.I. WAR BRIDES(1946), ed; INNER CIRCLE, THE(1946), ed; NIGHT TRAIN TO MEMPHIS(1946), ed; BLACKMAIL(1947), ed; HIT PARADE OF 1947(1947), ed; MAIN STREET KID, THE(1947), ed; ON THE OLD SPANISH TRAIL(1947), ed; SPRINGTIME IN THE SIERRAS(1947), ed; CALIFORNIA FIREBRAND(1948), ed; CARSON CITY RAIDERS(1948), ed; EYES OF TEXAS(1948), ed; GAY RANCHERO, THE(1948), ed; GRAND CANYON TRAIL(1948), ed; NIGHT TIME IN NEVADA(1948), ed; RENEGADES OF SONORA(1948), ed; TIMBER TRAIL, THE(1948), ed; UNDER CALIFORNIA STARS(1948), ed; DOWN DAKOTA WAY(1949), ed; FAR FRONTIER, THE(1949), ed; FLAMING FURY(1949), ed; GOLDEN STALLION, THE(1949), ed; HELLFIRE(1949), ed; OUTCASTS OF THE TRAIL(1949), ed; SAN ANTONE AMBUSH(1949), ed; SHERIFF OF WICHITA(1949), ed; SUSANNA PASS(1949), ed; BELLS OF CORONADO(1950), ed; DESTINATION BIG HOUSE(1950), ed; SUNSET IN THE WEST(1950), ed; TRAIL OF ROBIN HOOD(1950), ed; TRIGGER, JR.(1950), ed; TWILIGHT IN THE SIERRAS(1950), ed; CUBAN FIREBALL(1951), ed; HAVANA ROSE(1951), ed; HEART OF THE ROCKIES(1951), ed; IN OLD AMARILLO(1951), ed; SEA HORNET, THE(1951), ed; SPOILERS OF THE PLAINS(1951), ed; BAL TABARIN(1952), ed; BLACK HILLS AMBUSH(1952), ed; COLORADO SUNDOWN(1952), ed; DESPERADOES OUTPOST(1952), ed; FABULOUS SENORITA, THE(1952), ed; OLD OKLAHOMA PLAINS(1952), ed; WAC FROM WALLA WALLA, THE(1952), ed; BANDITS OF THE WEST(1953), ed; EL PASO STAMPEDE(1953), ed; GERALDINE(1953), ed; IRON MOUNTAIN TRAIL(1953), ed; MARSHAL OF CEDAR ROCK(1953), ed; SAN ANTONE(1953), ed; OUTCAST, THE(1954), ed; SHANGHAI STORY, THE(1954), ed; CAROLINA CANNONBALL(1955), ed; CITY OF SHADOWS(1955), ed; I COVER THE UNDERWORLD(1955), ed; LAST COMMAND, THE(1955), ed; SANTA FE PASSAGE(1955), ed; TWINKLE IN GOD'S EYE, THE(1955), ed; COME NEXT SPRING(1956), ed; MAN IS ARMED, THE(1956), ed; TERROR AT MIDNIGHT(1956), ed; THUNDER OVER ARIZONA(1956), ed; WHEN GANGLAND STRIKES(1956), ed; AFFAIR IN RENO(1957), ed; HELL'S CROSSROADS(1957), ed; JOHNNY TROUBLE(1957), ed; TAMING SUTTON'S GAL(1957), ed; SAGA OF HEMP BROWN, THE(1958), ed; SUMMER LOVE(1958), ed; TWILIGHT FOR THE GODS(1958), ed; SEVEN WAYS FROM SUNDOWN(1960), ed; THIS REBEL BREED(1960), ed; TAGGART(1964), ed; COUNTERFEIT KILLER, THE(1968), ed; SHAKIEST GUN IN THE WEST, THE(1968), ed
Italo Martinenghi
FANTASTIC THREE, THE(1967, Ital./Ger./Fr./Yugo.), p
A. Martinez
COWBOYS, THE(1972); ONCE UPON A SCOUNDREL(1973); TAKE, THE(1974); JOE PANTHER(1976); BEYOND THE LIMIT(1983)

Misc. Talkies
STARBIRD AND SWEET WILLIAM(1975); ADVENTURES OF STAR BIRD(1978)
Adalberto Martinez
SANTO Y BLUE DEMON CONTRA LOS MONSTRUOS(1968, Mex.)
Agapito Martinez
PARTNERS OF THE SUNSET(1948); RANGE RENEGADES(1948)
Albert Martinez
SUDDEN IMPACT(1983)
Alejandro Martinez
CAPTAIN'S PARADISE, THE(1953, Brit.)
Alma Martinez
BARBAROSA(1982); UNDER FIRE(1983)
Alma Rose Martinez
ZOOT SUIT(1981)
Andrew Martinez
FIREBALL JUNGLE(1968)
Arturo Martinez
AZTEC MUMMY, THE(1957, Mex.); BLACK SCORPION, THE(1957); CURSE OF THE AZTEC MUMMY, THE(1965, Mex.); ROBOT VS. THE AZTEC MUMMY, THE(1965, Mex.)
Carmen Martinez
HEARTBREAKER(1983)
Chico Martinez
VISITORS, THE(1972); BADGE 373(1973); SORCERER(1977); UNMARRIED WOMAN, AN(1978)
Claudio Martinez
DARING DOBERMANS, THE(1973); WALK PROUD(1979); GUNS(1980, Fr.), ed
1984
THREE CROWNS OF THE SAILOR(1984, Fr.)
Conception Martinez
SANTO EN EL MUSEO DE CERA(1963, Mex.)
Cuca Martinez
T-MEN(1947)
Elena Martinez
TEXAS RANGERS, THE(1936); LONG VOYAGE HOME, THE(1940)
Elisa Martinez
SECOND-HAND HEARTS(1981)
Enrique Martinez
TURNING POINT, THE(1977)
Feiga Martinez
FAN, THE(1981)
Felix Miron Martinez
GLASS SPHINX, THE(1968, Egypt/Ital./Span.), ph
Fernando Martinez
DANIEL BOONE, TRAIL BLAZER(1957), ed; LA CUCARACHA(1961, Mex.), ed; LITTLE ANGEL(1961, Mex.), ed; KID RODELO(1966, U.S./Span.), makeup
Flavio Martinez III
NIGHTWING(1979)
Gisela Martinez
VILLA!(1958)
Hector Martinez
EL TOPO(1971, Mex.); SOME OF MY BEST FRIENDS ARE...(1971)
J. Martinez
POCKET MONEY(1972)
Jimmy Martinez
TUNNELVISION(1976); FUN WITH DICK AND JANE(1977); BLUE COLLAR(1978)
Joaquin Martinez
STALKING MOON, THE(1969); MOONFIRE(1970); JEREMIAH JOHNSON(1972); JOE KIDD(1972); ULZANA'S RAID(1972); EXECUTIVE ACTION(1973)
Misc. Talkies
HE IS MY BROTHER(1976)
Jorge Martinez
1984
REPO MAN(1984)
Jose Martinez
SCALPHUNTERS, THE(1968)
1984
LONELY GUY, THE(1984)
Jose Santiago Martinez
SHIP OF FOOLS(1965)
Leo Martinez
SECRET OF THE SACRED FOREST, THE(1970); ENTER THE NINJA(1982)
Louise Martinez
LIANNA(1983), cos
Luciana Martinez
Misc. Talkies
ALTERNATIVE MISS WORLD, THE(1980)
Luis Antonio Martinez
HARBOR LIGHTS(1963); STILETTO(1969)
Mark Martinez
PENNIES FROM HEAVEN(1981)
Mary Martinez
VOODOO HEARTBEAT(1972)
Melecio Martinez
1984
EL NORTE(1984), m
Mina Martinez
MADIGAN(1968); DIRTY DINGUS MAGEE(1970)
Miriam Martinez
PIECES OF DREAMS(1970)
Nina Martinez
ONE-EYED JACKS(1961)
Pablo Martinez
ALSINO AND THE CONDOR(1983, Nicaragua), ph
Praxedes Martinez
THAT MAN IN ISTANBUL(1966, Fr./Ital./Span.), makeup
Ramon Martinez
PAL JOEY(1957)

Raul Martinez
RAGE(1966, U.S./Mex.); SCALPHUNTERS, THE(1968); GREEN ICE(1981, Brit.)
Rene Martinez
Misc. Talkies
ROAD OF DEATH(1977), d
Rene Martinez, Jr.
Misc. Talkies
GUY FROM HARLEM, THE(1977), d
Richard Martinez
MC MASTERS, THE(1970)
Rita Martinez
BLONDE PICKUP(1955)
Robert Martinez
RAINBOW ISLAND(1944)
Roman Martinez
FORTY POUNDS OF TROUBLE(1962)
Salvador Martinez
ALAMBRISTA!(1977)
Santiago Martinez
WE WERE STRANGERS(1949)
Slavio Martinez
RUNNING WILD(1973)
Tony Martinez
ANGEL ON THE AMAZON(1948); BARRICADE(1950); RING, THE(1952); SECOND CHANCE(1953)
Tony R. Martinez
1984
ALLEY CAT(1984)
Val Martinez
NO MAN'S LAND(1964)
Velia Martinez
BIG BOODLE, THE(1957); DEVIL'S SISTERS, THE(1966)
Vic Martinez
1984
MEATBALLS PART II(1984)
Vicente Martinez
TRISTANA(1970, Span./Ital./Fr.), makeup
Antonio Martini
SEVEN SEAS TO CALAIS(1963, Ital.), set d
Bobby Martini
1984
RHINESTONE(1984)
David Martini
WARM IN THE BUD(1970)
Depy Martini
PHAEDRA(1962, U.S./Gr./Fr.)
Elena Martini
LOVE IN 4 DIMENSIONS(1965 Fr./Ital.)
Ferdinand Martini
Silents
PLEASURE GARDEN, THE(1925, Brit./Ger.)
Grazia Martini
SIX DAYS A WEEK(1966, Fr./Ital./Span.)
Lou Martini
ODDS AGAINST TOMORROW(1959); HOODLUM PRIEST, THE(1961)
Louise Martini
ENDLESS NIGHT, THE(1963, Ger.); DEEP END(1970 Ger./U.S.)
Luciano Martini
WARRIOR EMPRESS, THE(1961, Ital./Fr.), w
Mauro Martini
FIST IN HIS POCKET(1968, Ital.)
Mortimer Martini
Silents
PORT OF MISSING MEN(1914)
Misc. Silents
OTHER GIRL, THE(1916)
Nino Martini
HERE'S TO ROMANCE(1935); GAY DESPERADO, THE(1936); MUSIC FOR MADAME(1937); ONE NIGHT WITH YOU(1948, Brit)
Otto Martini
HIDEOUT IN THE ALPS(1938, Brit.), ph
Richard Martini
PERSONAL BEST(1982)
Robert Martini
STAYING ALIVE(1983)
Rossana Martini
SEVEN DWARFS TO THE RESCUE, THE(1965, Ital.); EL GRECO(1966, Ital., Fr.)
Wolfgang Martini
DEVIL IN SILK(1968, Ger.)
Claudio Martiniz
CHINATOWN(1974)
Susanna Martinkova
DETECTIVE BELLI(1970, Ital.)
Martino
YOUNG HUSBANDS(1958, Ital./Fr.), w
Adriana Martino
LA BOHEME(1965, Ital.)
Al Martino
GODFATHER, THE(1972)
Alberto Martino
SECRET SEVEN, THE(1966, Ital./Span.), d, w
Antonietta Martino
IT HAPPENED IN CANADA(1962, Can.)
Antonio Torres Martino
HARBOR LIGHTS(1963); THUNDER ISLAND(1963)
Chris Martino
PSYCHO A GO-GO!(1965), w

Giovanni Martino
LADY'S MORALS, A(1930)
John Martino
GODFATHER, THE(1972); DILLINGER(1973); TRUCK STOP WOMEN(1974)
Kenny Martino
1984
EXTERMINATOR 2(1984)
Luciano Martino
COLOSSUS OF RHODES, THE(1961, Ital., Fr., Span.), w; GUNS OF THE BLACK WITCH(1961, Fr./Ital.), w; PIRATE AND THE SLAVE GIRL, THE(1961, Fr./Ital.), w; BUFFALO BILL, HERO OF THE FAR WEST(1962, Ital.), w; DUEL OF THE TITANS(1963, Ital.), w; SECRET AGENT FIREBALL(1965, Fr./Ital.), p; MONGOLS, THE(1966, Fr./Ital.), w; 10,000 DOLLARS BLOOD MONEY(1966, Ital.), p, w; SWEET BODY OF DEBORAH, THE(1969, Ital./Fr.), p, w; NEXT!(1971, Ital./Span.), p; ALMOST HUMAN(1974,Ital.), p; NO WAY OUT(1975, Ital./Fr.), p
1984
AFTER THE FALL OF NEW YORK(1984, Ital./Fr.), p
Marie Martino
LADY CHASER(1946)
Paul Martino
SHORT EYES(1977), cos
Ray Martino
GOLIATH AGAINST THE GIANTS(1963, Ital./Span.); SON OF CAPTAIN BLOOD, THE(1964, U.S./Ital./Span.)
Sergio Martino
NEXT!(1971, Ital./Span.), d; TORSO(1974, Ital.), d, w; SCREAMERS(1978, Ital.), d, w; SLAVE OF THE CANNIBAL GOD(1979, Ital.), d; GREAT ALLIGATOR(1980, Ital.), d&w
1984
AFTER THE FALL OF NEW YORK(1984, Ital./Fr.), d
Misc. Talkies
THEY'RE COMING TO GET YOU(1976), d
V. Martino
BURIED ALIVE(1951, Ital.), w
Vittorio Martino
DEAD WOMAN'S KISS, A(1951, Ital.), w; PSYCOSISSIMO(1962, Ital.), p
Petar Martinovitch
BACKFIRE(1965, Fr.)
Danny Martins
HOSTAGE, THE(1966)
Orlando Martins
SANDERS OF THE RIVER(1935, Brit.); MAN FROM MOROCCO, THE(1946, Brit.); END OF THE RIVER, THE(1947, Brit.); HASTY HEART, THE(1949); GOOD TIME GIRL(1950, Brit.); IVORY HUNTER(1952, Brit.); KISENGA, MAN OF AFRICA(1952, Brit.); HEART OF THE MATTER, THE(1954, Brit.); WEST OF ZANZIBAR(1954, Brit.); SIMBA(1955, Brit.); SAFARI(1956); ABANDON SHIP(1957, Brit.); TARZAN AND THE LOST SAFARI(1957, Brit.); NAKED EARTH, THE(1958, Brit.); NUN'S STORY, THE(1959); SAPPHIRE(1959, Brit.); KILLERS OF KILIMANJARO(1960, Brit.); CALL ME BWANA(1963, Brit.); BOY TEN FEET TALL, A(1965, Brit.); MISTER MOSES(1965); KONGI'S HARVEST(1971, U.S./Nigeria)
Peter Martins
TURNING POINT, THE(1977)
Richard Martinsen
BRANDED A COWARD(1935), w
A. Martinson
VIOLIN AND ROLLER(1962, USSR), cos; FORTY-NINE DAYS(1964, USSR), cos
David Martinson
SISTER KENNY(1946)
Henry Martinson
NORTHERN LIGHTS(1978)
Leslie Martinson
HOT ROD RUMBLE(1957), d; BLACK GOLD(1963), d; MRS. POLLIFAX-SPY(1971), d; AND MILLIONS WILL DIE(1973), d
Misc. Talkies
CHARLIE CHAN: HAPPINESS IS A WARM CLUE(1971), d; ESCAPE FROM ANGOLA(1976), d
Leslie H. Martinson
ATOMIC KID, THE(1954), d; HOT ROD GIRL(1956), d; LAD: A DOG(1962), d; PT 109(1963), d; FBI CODE 98(1964), d; FOR THOSE WHO THINK YOUNG(1964), d; BATMAN(1966), d; FATHOM(1967), d
Misc. Talkies
CHALLENGERS, THE(1968), d
S. Martinson
SECRET MISSION(1949, USSR); IDIOT, THE(1960, USSR); MAGIC VOYAGE OF SINBAD, THE(1962, USSR); NIGHT BEFORE CHRISTMAS, A(1963, USSR)
S.A. Martinson
DIARY OF A REVOLUTIONIST(1932, USSR)
Sergei Martinson
ARMED AND DANGEROUS(1977, USSR)
Misc. Silents
ADVENTURES OF AN OCTOBERITE, THE(1924, USSR)
Ditte Martinsson
EMIGRANTS, THE(1972, Swed.)
Lasse Martinsson
EMIGRANTS, THE(1972, Swed.)
Pelle Martinsson
EMIGRANTS, THE(1972, Swed.)
Mary Martlew
GHOSTS OF BERKELEY SQUARE(1947, Brit.); ANNA KARENINA(1948, Brit.); AFFAIRS OF ADELAIDE(1949, U. S./Brit); LAUGHING LADY, THE(1950, Brit.)
Nino Martoglio
Misc. Silents
LOST IN THE DARK(1914, Ital.), d; TERESA RAQUIN(1915, Ital.), d
Ana Marton
FOREIGNER, THE(1978)
Andre Marton
MISS PRESIDENT(1935, Hung.), d

Andrew Marton
REBEL, THE(1933, Ger.), ed; S.O.S. ICEBERG(1933), ed; SECRET OF STAMBOUL, THE(1936, Brit.), d; WOLF'S CLOTHING(1936, Brit.), d; SCHOOL FOR HUSBANDS(1939, Brit.), d; LITTLE BIT OF HEAVEN, A(1940, U.S.); TWO-FACED WOMAN(1941), d; GENTLE ANNIE(1944), d; GALLANT BESS(1946), d; KING SOLOMON'S MINES(1950), d; DEVIL MAKES THREE, THE(1952), d; STORM OVER TIBET(1952), d; WILD NORTH, THE(1952), d; GYPSY COLT(1954), d; MEN OF THE FIGHTING LADY(1954), d; PRISONER OF WAR(1954), d; GREEN FIRE(1955), d; UNDERWATER WARRIOR(1958), d; IT HAPPENED IN ATHENS(1962), d; LONGEST DAY, THE(1962), d; 55 DAYS AT PEKING(1963), d; THIN RED LINE, THE(1964), d; CLARENCE, THE CROSS-EYED LION(1965), d; CRACK IN THE WORLD(1965), d; AROUND THE WORLD UNDER THE SEA(1966), p&d; BIRDS DO IT(1966), d; AFRICA-TEXAS STYLE!(1967 U.S./Brit.), p, d
Silents
ETERNAL LOVE(1929), ed
George Marton
WHISPERING CITY(1947, Can.), p; PLAY DIRTY(1969, Brit.), w; CATCH ME A SPY(1971, Brit./Fr.), w
Jarmila Marton
STORM OVER TIBET(1952)
John Marton
GOLD RAIDERS, THE(1952)
Paul Marton
COUNTERSPY MEETS SCOTLAND YARD(1950)
Pierre Marton [Peter Stone]
SKIN GAME(1971), w
Elaine Martone
HANDS OF A STRANGER(1962); WALK ON THE WILD SIDE(1962); ZOTZ!(1962); HALLELUJAH TRAIL, THE(1965)
Vincent Martorano
CORNBREAD, EARL AND ME(1975)
Misc. Talkies
CANDY SNATCHERS, THE(1974)
Andres Martorell
NEW LOVE(1968, Chile), ph
F. Martos
PRINCESS CHARMING(1935, Brit.), w
Joseph Martov
THREE TALES OF CHEKHOV(1961, USSR), ph
M. Martov
Misc. Silents
SLAVE OF PASSION, SLAVE OF VICE(1914, USSR), d
Jack Marts
CONFIDENTIAL(1935), ph
Robert Martsch
SNOW WHITE AND THE SEVEN DWARFS(1937), anim; PINOCCHIO(1940), anim
Eduard Martsevich
FATHERS AND SONS(1960, USSR); WAR AND PEACE(1968, USSR)
Y. Martsinchik
BALLAD OF COSSACK GLOOTA(1938, USSR)
Ray Martucci
BIG FIX, THE(1978)
Amerigo Martufi
HEART AND SOUL(1950, Ital.)
Guido Martufi
WESTWARD THE WOMEN(1951); WHEN IN ROME(1952); FAREWELL TO ARMS, A(1957); MONTE CARLO STORY, THE(1957, Ital.)
Gino Marturano
LA DOLCE VITA(1961, Ital./Fr.); RAGE OF THE BUCCANEERS(1963, Ital.); SANDOKAN THE GREAT(1964, Fr./Ital./Span.); SABATA(1969, Ital.)
Luigi Marturano
QUEEN OF THE PIRATES(1961, Ital./Ger.); GOLIATH AGAINST THE GIANTS(1963, Ital./Span.); QUEEN OF THE NILE(1964, Ital.)
Guido Marturi
VITELLONI(1956, Ital./Fr.)
Amalia Marty
1984
DEATHSTALKER, THE(1984)
Ellen Marty
SPRING AFFAIR(1960)
Jack Marty
DRIVE-IN(1976), set d; OUTLAW BLUES(1977), art d; DEADLY BLESSING(1981), art d; SILENT RAGE(1982), art d; SPLIT IMAGE(1982), art d
Marthe Marty
POIL DE CAROTTE(1932, Fr.); LA MARSEILLAISE(1938, Fr.)
Syra Marty
FINGERPRINTS DON'T LIE(1951); FANNY HILL: MEMOIRS OF A WOMAN OF PLEASURE zero(1965)
Dickie Martyn
MACBETH(1971, Brit.)
Hilary Martyn
FAMILY LIFE(1971, Brit.)
John Martyn
WHILE I LIVE(1947, Brit.)
Joyce Martyn
NO ROOM AT THE INN(1950, Brit.)
Kathleen Martyn
Silents
BLUEBEARD'S SEVEN WIVES(1926)
Misc. Silents
SIXTH COMMANDMENT, THE(1924)
Larry Martyn
TOO YOUNG TO LOVE(1960, Brit.); BREATH OF LIFE(1962, Brit.); THESE ARE THE DAMNED(1965, Brit.); NEVER BACK LOSERS(1967, Brit.); UP THE JUNCTION(1968, Brit.); TROUBLESOME DOUBLE, THE(1971, Brit.); FINAL CONFLICT, THE(1981)
Marty Martyn
NIGHT AFTER NIGHT(1932)

Peter Martyn
ISLAND RESCUE(1952, Brit.); MR. LORD SAYS NO(1952, Brit.); FOLLY TO BE WISE(1953); CHILD'S PLAY(1954, Brit.); MAD ABOUT MEN(1954, Brit.); YOU KNOW WHAT SAILORS ARE(1954, Brit.); INTRUDER, THE(1955, Brit.); LADY GODIVA RIDES AGAIN(1955, Brit.); NO SMOKING(1955, Brit.); ORDERS ARE ORDERS(1959, Brit.)
Vera Martyn
FIND THE LADY(1936, Brit.)
Wyndham Martyn
Silents
ALL THE WORLD TO NOTHING(1919), w
Ken Martyne
TOO HOT TO HANDLE(1961, Brit.)
Gene Martynec
RIP-OFF(1971, Can.), m
Kurt Martynow
LITTLE NIGHT MUSIC, A(1977, Aust./U.S./Ger.)
Grigoriy Martynyuk
THERE WAS AN OLD COUPLE(1967, USSR)
Taro Marui
GAMERA VERSUS GAOS(1967, Jap.)
Eugene Marum
ONCE UPON A HONEYMOON(1942)
Takashi Marumo
KUROENKO(1968, Jap.), art d
Marusov
Silents
BATTLESHIP POTEMKIN, THE(1925, USSR)
Horace Marussi
DEATHSTALKER(1983, Arg./U.S.)
V. Maruta
UNIVERSITY OF LIFE(1941, USSR)
Keiji Maruyama
PERFORMERS, THE(1970, Jap.), ph
Merv Maruyama
1984
FLETCH(1984)
Michiro Maruyama
ANATAHAN(1953, Jap.), d&ph
Toshiya Maruyama
HOUSE WHERE EVIL DWELLS, THE(1982)
Tom Maruzzi
MAN BEAST(1956); SILENT CALL, THE(1961), w; SNIPER'S RIDGE(1961), w
Joe Maruzzo
KING OF THE GYPSIES(1978)
Eleanor Marvak
JOLSON SINGS AGAIN(1949)
J. Marvan
INSPECTOR GENERAL, THE(1937, Czech.)
Jaroslav Marvan
ADRIFT(1971, Czech.)
Christian Marvel
EMBALMER, THE(1966, Ital.), p
Holt Marvel
MAGIC NIGHT(1932, Brit.), w
Paul Marvel
PSYCHOTRONIC MAN, THE(1980)
Holt Marvell
DEATH AT A BROADCAST(1934, Brit.), w; INVITATION TO THE WALTZ(1935, Brit.), w; REGAL CAVALCADE(1935, Brit.), w
The Marvelous Sylvesters
Silents
FINAL CURTAIN, THE(1916)
Jean Marvey
THREE MESQUITEERS, THE(1936)
Alice Marvin
Silents
HUCK AND TOM(1918)
Misc. Silents
TOM SAWYER(1917)
Allan Marvin
SNIPER'S RIDGE(1961)
Chris Marvin
BOOTS AND SADDLES(1937)
Frank Marvin
RED RIVER VALLEY(1936); SONS OF NEW MEXICO(1949); OLD WEST, THE(1952)
Frankie Marvin
SAGEBRUSH TROUBADOR(1935); TUMBLING TUMBLEWEEDS(1935); GUNS AND GUITARS(1936); HEARTS IN BONDAGE(1936); RIDE, RANGER, RIDE(1936); SINGING COWBOY, THE(1936); BOOTS AND SADDLES(1937); GIT ALONG, LITTLE DOGIES(1937); OH, SUSANNA(1937); OLD CORRAL, THE(1937); PUBLIC COWBOY NO. 1(1937); ROOTIN' TOOTIN' RHYTHM(1937); ROUNDUP TIME IN TEXAS(1937); SPRINGTIME IN THE ROCKIES(1937); YODELIN' KID FROM PINE RIDGE(1937); GOLD MINE IN THE SKY(1938); MAN FROM MUSIC MOUNTAIN(1938); OLD BARN DANCE, THE(1938); UNDER WESTERN STARS(1938); COLORADO SUNSET(1939); MOUNTAIN RHYTHM(1939); RACKETEERS OF THE RANGE(1939); SAGA OF DEATH VALLEY(1939); GAUCHO SERENADE(1940); MELODY RANCH(1940); SIERRA SUE(1941); UNDER FIESTA STARS(1941); COWBOY SERENADE(1942); HEART OF THE RIO GRANDE(1942); STARDUST ON THE SAGE(1942); SIOUX CITY SUE(1946); LAST ROUND-UP, THE(1947); ROBIN OF TEXAS(1947); TWILIGHT ON THE RIO GRANDE(1947); RIM OF THE CANYON(1949); BLAZING SUN, THE(1950); COW TOWN(1950); INDIAN TERRITORY(1950); SILVER CANYON(1951); VALLEY OF FIRE(1951); WHIRLWIND(1951); PACK TRAIN(1953)
Grace Marvin
PHANTOM OF THE OPERA, THE(1929)
Silents
LOVE GIRL, THE(1916); NO WOMAN KNOWS(1921); LONG CHANCE, THE(1922); PHANTOM OF THE OPERA, THE(1925)

Misc. Silents
  MASK, THE(1918)
Hank B. Marvin
  FINDERS KEEPERS(1966, Brit.)
Jack Marvin
  MUG TOWN(1943)
Jerry Marvin
  SUPERMAN AND THE MOLE MEN(1951)
Lee Marvin
  YOU'RE IN THE NAVY NOW(1951); DIPLOMATIC COURIER(1952); DUEL AT
  SILVER CREEK, THE(1952); EIGHT IRON MEN(1952); HANGMAN'S KNOT(1952);
  WE'RE NOT MARRIED(1952); BIG HEAT, THE(1953); DOWN AMONG THE SHEL-
  TERING PALMS(1953); GLORY BRIGADE, THE(1953); GUN FURY(1953); SEMI-
  NOLE(1953); STRANGER WORE A GUN, THE(1953); WILD ONE, THE(1953); CAINE
  MUTINY, THE(1954); GORILLA AT LARGE(1954); RAID, THE(1954); BAD DAY AT
  BLACK ROCK(1955); I DIED A THOUSAND TIMES(1955); LIFE IN THE BALANCE,
  A(1955); NOT AS A STRANGER(1955); PETE KELLY'S BLUES(1955); SHACK OUT ON
  101(1955); VIOLENT SATURDAY(1955); ATTACK!(1956); PILLARS OF THE
  SKY(1956); RACK, THE(1956); SEVEN MEN FROM NOW(1956); RAINTREE COUN-
  TY(1957); MISSOURI TRAVELER, THE(1958); RIDE LONESOME(1959); COMAN-
  CHEROS, THE(1961); MAN WHO SHOT LIBERTY VALANCE, THE(1962);
  DONOVAN'S REEF(1963); KILLERS, THE(1964); CAT BALLOU(1965); SHIP OF
  FOOLS(1965); PROFESSIONALS, THE(1966); DIRTY DOZEN, THE(1967, Brit.); POINT
  BLANK(1967); HELL IN THE PACIFIC(1968); SERGEANT RYKER(1968); PAINT
  YOUR WAGON(1969); MONTE WALSH(1970); POCKET MONEY(1972); PRIME
  CUT(1972); EMPEROR OF THE NORTH POLE(1973); ICEMAN COMETH, THE(1973);
  KLANSMAN, THE(1974); SPIKES GANG, THE(1974); GREAT SCOUT AND CAT-
  HOUSE THURSDAY, THE(1976); SHOUT AT THE DEVIL(1976, Brit.); AVALANCHE
  EXPRESS(1979); BIG RED ONE, THE(1980); DEATH HUNT(1981); GORKY
  PARK(1983)
1984
  DOG DAY(1984, Fr.)
Marion Marvin
Misc. Silents
  CACTUS CRANDALL(1918)
Marji Marvin
  GOING APE!(1981)
Mia Marvin
  PUBLIC ENEMY, THE(1931); YOU SAID A MOUTHFUL(1932)
Michelle Marvin
  REFLECTION OF FEAR, A(1973)
Mike Marvin
  SIX PACK(1982), w
1984
  HOT DOG...THE MOVIE(1984), a, p, w
Miss Marvin
Silents
  ETERNAL LOVE(1917)
Nicolette Marvin
  VALENTINO(1977, Brit.)
Ronn Marvin
  GAS HOUSE KIDS GO WEST(1947)
Kay Marvis
  BLOCK BUSTERS(1944)
Stuart Marwick
  GOIN' DOWN THE ROAD(1970, Can.)
Arthur Marx
  BLONDIE IN THE DOUGH(1947), w; WINTER WONDERLAND(1947), w; GLOBAL
  AFFAIR, A(1964), w; I'LL TAKE SWEDEN(1965), w; EIGHT ON THE LAM(1967), w;
  IMPOSSIBLE YEARS, THE(1968), w; CANCEL MY RESERVATION(1972), w
Bill Marx
  WALK THE ANGRY BEACH(1961), m; RETURN OF COUNT YORGA, THE(1971),
  m; DEATHMASTER, THE(1972), m; TERROR HOUSE(1972), m; JOHNNY VIK(1973),
  m; SCREAM BLACULA SCREAM(1973), m; ACT OF VENGEANCE(1974), m
Brett Marx
  BAD NEWS BEARS, THE(1976); BAD NEWS BEARS IN BREAKING TRAINING,
  THE(1977); BAD NEWS BEARS GO TO JAPAN, THE(1978); LUCKY STAR, THE(1980,
  Can.)
Chico Marx
  COCOANUTS, THE(1929); ANIMAL CRACKERS(1930); MONKEY BUSINESS(1931);
  HORSE FEATHERS(1932); DUCK SOUP(1933); NIGHT AT THE OPERA, A(1935); DAY
  AT THE RACES, A(1937); ROOM SERVICE(1938); AT THE CIRCUS(1939); GO
  WEST(1940); BIG STORE, THE(1941); NIGHT IN CASABLANCA, A(1946); LOVE
  HAPPY(1949); STORY OF MANKIND, THE(1957)
Chris Marx
  DARK ODYSSEY(1961)
David Marx
  PAPER LION(1968), ph
Debra Marx
  SUMMER CAMP(1979)
Gilda Marx
  MAIN EVENT, THE(1979)
Groucho Marx
  COCOANUTS, THE(1929); ANIMAL CRACKERS(1930); MONKEY BUSINESS(1931);
  HORSE FEATHERS(1932); DUCK SOUP(1933); NIGHT AT THE OPERA, A(1935);
  YOURS FOR THE ASKING(1936); DAY AT THE RACES, A(1937); KING AND THE
  CHORUS GIRL, THE(1937), w; ROOM SERVICE(1938); AT THE CIRCUS(1939); GO
  WEST(1940); BIG STORE, THE(1941); NIGHT IN CASABLANCA(1946);
  COPACABANA(1947); LOVE HAPPY(1949); MR. MUSIC(1950); DOUBLE DYNAMI-
  TE(1951); GIRL IN EVERY PORT, A(1952); STORY OF MANKIND, THE(1957); WILL
  SUCCESS SPOIL ROCK HUNTER?(1957); SKIDOO(1968)
Harpo Marx
  COCOANUTS, THE(1929); ANIMAL CRACKERS(1930); MONKEY BUSINESS(1931);
  HORSE FEATHERS(1932); DUCK SOUP(1933); NIGHT AT THE OPERA, A(1935); DAY
  AT THE RACES, A(1937); ROOM SERVICE(1938); AT THE CIRCUS(1939); GO
  WEST(1940); BIG STORE, THE(1941); STAGE DOOR CANTEEN(1943); NIGHT IN
  CASABLANCA, A(1946); LOVE HAPPY(1949), a, w; STORY OF MANKIND,
  THE(1957)

Herman Marx
  RIFF-RAFF(1936)
Jack Marx
  BLONDIE IN THE DOUGH(1947), w
Jozsef Marx
  FORBIDDEN RELATIONS(1983, Hung.), p
Judith Marx
1984
  BLAME IT ON THE NIGHT(1984)
L. Michelle Marx
  WILD HARVEST(1962)
Mary Marx
  MAN FROM O.R.G.Y., THE(1970)
Max Marx
  TOUGH KID(1939); NEW MOON(1940); HOLD THAT BABY!(1949)
Maxine Marx
  DRAMATIC SCHOOL(1938); DANCING CO-ED(1939)
Melinda Marx
  STORY OF MANKIND, THE(1957); VIOLENT ONES, THE(1967)
Misc. Talkies
  HILARY'S BLUES(1983)
Neyle Marx
  DRUMS OF THE DESERT(1940); THREE MEN FROM TEXAS(1940); PHANTOM
  COWBOY, THE(1941); RAIDERS OF THE DESERT(1941); DANGER IN THE PACI-
  FIC(1942); WHERE ARE YOUR CHILDREN?(1943); SINCE YOU WENT AWAY(1944)
Rick Marx
1984
  PREPPIES(1984), w
Sam Marx
  NIGHT MAYOR, THE(1932), w; NIGHT AT THE OPERA, A(1935); DUEL IN THE
  JUNGLE(1954, Brit.), w; DAMON AND PYTHIAS(1962), w
Samuel Marx
  STUDENT TOUR(1934), w; SOCIETY DOCTOR(1935), w; LONGEST NIGHT,
  THE(1936), p; SINNER TAKE ALL(1936), p; FAMILY AFFAIR, A(1937), p; GIRLS'
  SCHOOL(1938), p; KEEPING COMPANY(1941), p; UNHOLY PARTNERS(1941), p;
  APACHE TRAIL(1942), p; NORTHWEST RANGERS(1942), p; THIS TIME FOR
  KEEPS(1942), p; YANK ON THE BURMA ROAD, A(1942), p; LASSIE, COME HO-
  ME(1943), p; SON OF LASSIE(1945), p; THIS MAN'S NAVY(1945), p; MY BROTHER
  TALKS TO HORSES(1946), p; BEGINNING OR THE END, THE(1947), p; GROUNDS
  FOR MARRIAGE(1950), p, w; LADY WITHOUT PASSPORT, A(1950), p; ASSIGN-
  MENT-PARIS(1952), p; AIN'T MISBEHAVIN'(1955), p; KISS OF FIRE(1955), p
Solly Marx
1984
  SILENT MADNESS(1984)
William Marx
  COUNT YORGA, VAMPIRE(1970), m
Zeppo Marx
  COCOANUTS, THE(1929); ANIMAL CRACKERS(1930); MONKEY BUSINESS(1931);
  HORSE FEATHERS(1932); DUCK SOUP(1933)
Mary
  ESCAPE TO BURMA(1955); CLARENCE, THE CROSS-EYED LION(1965)
Miz Mary
  PRETTY BABY(1978)
Renaud Mary
  PARIS DOES STRANGE THINGS(1957, Fr./Ital.); CRIME DOES NOT PAY(1962, Fr.);
  MADAME(1963, Fr./Ital./Span.); MATHIAS SANDORF(1963, Fr.)
Antonina Shuranova Princess Marya
  WAR AND PEACE(1968, USSR)
Donald Marye
  ALICE'S RESTAURANT(1969); WHO KILLED MARY WHAT'SER NAME?(1971)
V. Maryev
  SECRET BRIGADE, THE(1951 USSR)
Michael Maryk
  SPASMS(1983, Can.), w
Martha Maryman
  BIG CARNIVAL, THE(1951)
Susan Maryott
  SOLO FOR SPARROW(1966, Brit.)
Osamu Maryuama
  BUDDHA(1965, Jap.)
Carolyn Marz
  DRILLER KILLER(1979)
Josef Marz
  MAGIC FOUNTAIN, THE(1961)
Mario Marzac
  NIGHT OF A THOUSAND CATS(1974, Mex.), w
Girolamo Marzano
  THREE BROTHERS(1982, Ital.)
Joseph Marzano
Misc. Talkies
  MAN OUTSIDE(1965), a, d
Joey Marzella
1984
  ONCE UPON A TIME IN AMERICA(1984)
Vincent Marzello
  SPY WHO LOVED ME, THE(1977, Brit.); SUPERMAN(1978); NEVER SAY NEVER
  AGAIN(1983)
Harold J. Marzerati
  SLANDER(1956), ph
Edward Marzevic
  RED TENT, THE(1971, Ital./USSR)
Franca Marzi
  PIRATES OF CAPRI, THE(1949); ISLAND OF PROCIDA, THE(1952, Ital.); DEVO-
  TION(1953, Ital.); VERGINITA(1953, Ital.); NIGHTS OF CABIRIA(1957, Ital.); PSYCO-
  SISSIMO(1962, Ital.); LOVE ON THE RIVIERA(1964, Fr./Ital.)
Franco Marzi
  MONSTER OF THE ISLAND(1953, Ital.)

Serge Marzolff
PASSION(1983, Fr./Switz.), art d
Harold J. Marzorati
GUN GLORY(1957), ph; HIRED GUN, THE(1957), ph; HOT SUMMER NIGHT(1957), ph; HANDLE WITH CARE(1958), ph; HIGH SCHOOL CONFIDENTIAL(1958), ph; WORLD, THE FLESH, AND THE DEVIL, THE(1959), ph
Harold Marzorati
MARAUDERS, THE(1955), ph
Vera Marzot
MARRIAGE–ITALIAN STYLE(1964, Fr./Ital.), cos; MY NAME IS NOBODY(1974, Ital./Fr./Ger.), cos
Claudio Marzulli
REBEL GLADIATORS, THE(1963, Ital.)
Antonia Mas
HATCHET FOR A HONEYMOON(1969, Span./Ital.)
Carlos Mas
BIG BOODLE, THE(1957)
Guy Mas
NEXT OF KIN(1942, Brit.)
Jean Mas
MATTER OF TIME, A(1976, Ital./U.S.)
Jean-Pierre Mas
POURQUOI PAS!(1979, Fr.), m
Uno Masaaki
MEET ME IN MOSCOW(1966, USSR)
People of Masai Tribe in Kenya, East Africa
VISIT TO A CHIEF'S SON(1974)
Masai Tribe Wakamba Tribal Dancers
LAST SAFARI, THE(1967, Brit.)
Ron Masak
ICE STATION ZEBRA(1968); DADDY'S GONE A-HUNTING(1969); TORA! TORA! TORA!(1970, U.S./Jap.); EVEL KNIEVEL(1971); MARRIAGE OF A YOUNG STOCKBROKER, THE(1971); HARPER VALLEY, P.T.A.(1978); LASERBLAST(1978)
Misc. Talkies
WOMAN IN THE RAIN(1976)
Goro Masaki
ALMOST TRANSPARENT BLUE(1980, Jap.)
Annalisa Masalli-Rocca
BOBBY DEERFIELD(1977), cos
Jan Masaryk
SCHWEIK'S NEW ADVENTURES(1943, Brit.)
Masashige
WHIRLPOOL OF WOMAN(1966, Jap.), w
Peter Masbacher
CANARIS(1955, Ger.)
Heidy Masbury
CAFE SOCIETY(1939)
Pietro Mascagni
FATAL DESIRE(1953), w
Bob Mascagno
IMMORTAL SERGEANT, THE(1943); MUSIC IN MANHATTAN(1944); WONDER MAN(1945)
Mil Mascaras
VAMPIRES, THE(1969, Mex.)
Tana Mascarelli
RAT(1960, Yugo.)
Rose Mascari
BLADE RUNNER(1982)
Pierrino Mascarino
IT AIN'T EASY(1972); BANG THE DRUM SLOWLY(1973); TRUE CONFESSIONS(1981)
1984
MISSING IN ACTION(1984)
Gary Mascaro
ROOMMATES, THE(1973)
M.F. Mascaro
HU-MAN(1975, Fr.), p
Marie-Francois Mascaro
BIQUEFARRE(1983, Fr.), p
Joseph V. Mascelli
WILD GUITAR(1962), ph; INCREDIBLY STRANGE CREATURES WHO STOPPED LIVING AND BECAME CRAZY MIXED-UP ZOMBIES, THE(1965), ph; THRILL KILLERS, THE(1965), ph; STREET IS MY BEAT, THE(1966), ph
Philip Mascellino
SILVER BEARS(1978)
Frank Mascetta
ACROSS 110TH STREET(1972); SEVEN UPS, THE(1973)
Gina Mascetti
WHITE SHEIK, THE(1956, Ital.); THIEF OF BAGHDAD, THE(1961, Ital./Fr.); WITCH'S CURSE, THE(1963, Ital.); VARIETY LIGHTS(1965, Ital.)
Rina Mascetti
PIRATE AND THE SLAVE GIRL, THE(1961, Fr./Ital.); HERCULES, SAMSON & ULYSSES(1964, Ital.); FACTS OF MURDER, THE(1965, Ital.)
Mascheck
M(1933, Ger.)
Dude Maschemeyer
DARK PASSAGE(1947)
Gabriele Mascher
QUESTION 7(1961, U.S./Ger.)
John Maschino
SPRING FEVER(1983, Can.)
Paul F. Maschke
Silents
NEW COMMANDMENT, THE(1925), ed; RECKLESS LADY, THE(1926), ed; WILDERNESS WOMAN, THE(1926), ed
Alice Maschler
FRENCH LIEUTENANT'S WOMAN, THE(1981)

Eric Maschwitz
INVITATION TO THE WALTZ(1935, Brit.), w; REGAL CAVALCADE(1935, Brit.), w; CAFE COLETTE(1937, Brit.), w; BALALAIKA(1939), w; GOODBYE MR. CHIPS(1939, Brit.), w; CARNIVAL(1946, Brit.), w; CASE OF THE RED MONKEY(1955, Brit.), w
Tony Mascia
MAN WHO FELL TO EARTH, THE(1976, Brit.); SILVER BEARS(1978)
Peer Mascini
LIFT, THE(1983, Neth.)
Marcel Masciocchi
ALL THE WAY, BOYS(1973, Ital.), ph
Marcello Masciocchi
ASSIGNMENT OUTER SPACE(1960, Ital.), ph; SHOOT FIRST, LAUGH LAST(1967, Ital./Ger./U.S.), ph; REVENGE AT EL PASO(1968, Ital./Span.), ph; STRANGER IN TOWN, A(1968, U.S./Ital.), ph; STRANGER RETURNS, THE(1968, U.S./Ital./Ger./Span.), ph; WILD EYE, THE(1968, Ital.), ph; ACE HIGH(1969, Ital.), ph; SWEET BODY OF DEBORAH, THE(1969, Ital./Fr.), ph; TREASURE OF THE FOUR CROWNS(1983, Span./U.S.), ph; YOR, THE HUNTER FROM THE FUTURE(1983, Ital.), ph
R. Masciocchi
HANNIBAL(1960, Ital.), ph
Raffaele Masciocchi
QUEEN OF THE PIRATES(1961, Ital./Ger.), ph; PRISONER OF THE IRON MASK(1962, Fr./Ital.), ph; SWORD OF THE CONQUEROR(1962, Ital.), ph; GOLD FOR THE CAESARS(1964), ph; WILD EYE, THE(1968, Ital.), ph
Raffaello Masciocchi
BATTLE OF THE WORLDS(1961, Ital.), ph
Dionys Mascolo
NATHALIE GRANGER(1972, Fr.)
Joe Mascolo
HAPPY MOTHER'S DAY... LOVE, GEORGE(1973)
Joseph Mascolo
HOT SPUR(1968); SHAFT'S BIG SCORE(1972); SPOOK WHO SAT BY THE DOOR, THE(1973); JAWS II(1978); SHARKY'S MACHINE(1982); YES, GIORGIO(1982)
Valerie Mascolo
NATHALIE GRANGER(1972, Fr.)
Jeddu Mascorieto
HEROINA(1965)
Laurence Mascott
TEN DAYS TO TULARA(1958), w
Laurence E. Mascott
LOOK IN ANY WINDOW(1961), p, w
Mascotte
PENNY POOL, THE(1937, Brit.)
Marino Mase
LEOPARD, THE(1963, Ital.); LOVE AND MARRIAGE(1966, Ital.); OPIATE '67(1967, Fr./Ital.); FIST IN HIS POCKET(1968, Ital.); LES CARABINIERS(1968, Fr./Ital.); CANNIBALS, THE(1970, Ital.); FIVE MAN ARMY, THE(1970); PUSSYCAT, PUSSYCAT, I LOVE YOU(1970); NIGHT PORTER, THE(1974, Ital./U.S.); ALIEN CONTAMINATION(1982, Ital.); SALAMANDER, THE(1983, U.S./Ital./Brit.)
Martin Mase
Misc. Talkies
ALIEN CONTAMINATION(1981)
Joseph Masefield
DON'T GO IN THE HOUSE(1980), w
Fulvio Masella
MY NAME IS NOBODY(1974, Ital./Fr./Ger.), w
Francesco Maselli
DOLL THAT TOOK THE TOWN, THE(1965, Ital.), d, w; TIME OF INDIFFERENCE(1965, Fr./Ital.), d, w; FINE PAIR, A(1969, Ital.), d, w; LADY WITHOUT CAMELLIAS, THE(1981, Ital.), w
Terry Masengale
HAPPY LAND(1943)
Gerhard Maser
SHE MAN, THE(1967), ph; ROAD HUSTLERS, THE(1968), ph
Enso Masetti
FABIOLA(1951, Ital.), m
Enzio Masetti
SENSUALITA(1954, Ital.), m
Enzo Masetti
BULLET FOR STEFANO(1950, Ital.), m; VOLCANO(1953, Ital.), m; ATTILA(1958, Ital.), m; HERCULES(1959, Ital.), m; HERCULES UNCHAINED(1960, Ital./Fr.), m
V. Masevich
SOUND OF LIFE, THE(1962, USSR), ph
Tom Mashall
OH! WHAT A LOVELY WAR(1969, Brit.)
Tully Mashall
Misc. Silents
HER BELOVED VILLIAN(1920)
V. Mashchenko
WAR AND PEACE(1968, USSR)
Kyosuke Mashida
YAKUZA, THE(1975, U.S./Jap.)
Yoichi Mashio
WE WILL REMEMBER(1966, Jap.)
Richard Mashiya
NAKED PREY, THE(1966, U.S./South Africa)
Ye. Mashkara
TRAIN GOES TO KIEV, THE(1961, USSR)
A. Mashkov
SUBWAY RIDERS(1981)
Mac Mashourian
EASY RIDER(1969)
Bill Masi
JUST TELL ME WHAT YOU WANT(1980)
Chic Masi
36 HOURS(1965)
Victor Masi
STRANGLER, THE(1964)

Joe Masiell
JACQUES BREL IS ALIVE AND WELL AND LIVING IN PARIS(1975)
Giuletta Masina
CENTO ANNI D'AMORE(1954, Ital.)
Giulietta Masina
BEHIND CLOSED SHUTTERS(1952, Ital.); GREATEST LOVE, THE(1954, Ital.); ANGELS OF DARKNESS(1956, Ital.); LA STRADA(1956, Ital.); WHITE SHEIK, THE(1956, Ital.); AND THE WILD, WILD WOMEN(1961, Ital.); SWINDLE, THE(1962, Fr./Ital.); JULIET OF THE SPIRITS(1965, Fr./Ital./W.Ger.); VARIETY LIGHTS(1965, Ital.); MADWOMAN OF CHAILLOT, THE(1969)
Guilietta Masina
WITHOUT PITY(1949, Ital.)
Masine and Nikitina
BLUE DANUBE(1932, Brit.)
Esther Masing
YOUNG, THE EVIL AND THE SAVAGE, THE(1968, Ital.)
Ben Masinga
SAFARI 3000(1982)
Giuseppe Masini
JOURNEY BENEATH THE DESERT(1967, Fr./Ital.), d; GUILT IS NOT MINE(1968, Ital.), d, w
Mario Masini
PADRE PADRONE(1977, Ital.), ph
Tito Masini
8 ½(1963, Ital.)
Stephen Masino
GANG WAR(1958)
Steve Masino
MASTER OF THE WORLD(1961)
Paulino Masip
MADCAP OF THE HOUSE(1950, Mex.), w
Lauretta Masiro
GRAN VARIETA(1955, Ital.)
Johnny Mask
TOMORROW(1972)
Glenn Maska
1984
WHERE THE BOYS ARE '84(1984)
K. Maskalenko
SPACE SHIP, THE(1935, USSR)
Jasper Maskeleyne
TERROR ON TIPTOE(1936, Brit.)
Misc. Silents
DIZZY LIMIT, THE(1930, Brit.)
Dan Maskell
PLAYERS(1979)
Trevor Maskell
WHITE TRAP, THE(1959, Brit.); SING AND SWING(1964, Brit.); MARRIAGE OF CONVENIENCE(1970, Brit.)
Virginia Maskell
HAPPY IS THE BRIDE(1958, Brit.); MAN UPSTAIRS, THE(1959, Brit.); DOCTOR IN LOVE(1960, Brit.); VIRGIN ISLAND(1960, Brit.); JET STORM(1961, Brit.); RISK, THE(1961, Brit.); ONLY TWO CAN PLAY(1962, Brit.); YOUNG AND WILLING(1964, Brit.); INTERLUDE(1968, Brit.)
Paul Maslansky
CASTLE OF THE LIVING DEAD(1964, Ital./Fr.), p; SHE BEAST, THE(1966, Brit./Ital./Yugo.), p; SUDDEN TERROR(1970, Brit.), p; DEATHLINE(1973, Brit.), p; SUGAR HILL(1974), d; BLUE BIRD, THE(1976), p; DAMNATION ALLEY(1977), p; CIRCLE OF IRON(1979, Brit.), p; SCAVENGER HUNT(1979), p; RUCKUS(1981), p; LOVE CHILD(1982), p; SALAMANDER, THE(1983, U.S./Ital./Brit.), p
1984
POLICE ACADEMY(1984), p
V. Maslatsov
WAR AND PEACE(1968, USSR)
A. Maslennikov
SHE-WOLF, THE(1963, USSR), ph
L. Maslov
QUEEN OF SPADES(1961, USSR)
Natalie Maslovova
END OF AUGUST AT THE HOTEL OZONE, THE(1967, Czech.)
W. Maslow
HERE COME THE JETS(1959)
Walter Maslow
UNDER FIRE(1957); SUICIDE BATTALION(1958); COSMIC MAN, THE(1959); ATLAS(1960); PURPLE GANG, THE(1960); FRANCIS OF ASSISI(1961); RAIDERS FROM BENEATH THE SEA(1964); WINTER A GO-GO(1965); VAN, THE(1977); MALIBU BEACH(1978)
Karl Maslowski
MYSTERY LAKE(1953), ph
L. Masokha
ITALIANO BRAVA GENTE(1965, Ital./USSR)
Pyotr Masokha
THIRTEEN, THE(1937, USSR)
Silents
ARSENAL(1929, USSR); EARTH(1930, USSR)
Cathy Masom
ONE FROM THE HEART(1982)
A. E. W. Mason
HOUSE OF THE ARROW, THE(1930, Brit.), w; MYSTERY AT THE VILLA ROSE(1930, Brit.), w; MYSTERY OF THE PINK VILLA, THE(1930, Fr.), w; HER IMAGINARY LOVER(1933, Brit.), w; WIDOW FROM MONTE CARLO, THE(1936), w; FIRE OVER ENGLAND(1937, Brit.), w; DRUMS(1938, Brit.), w; FOUR FEATHERS, THE(1939, Brit.), w; CASTLE OF CRIMES(1940, Brit.), w; HOUSE OF MYSTERY(1941, Brit.), w; HOUSE OF THE ARROW, THE(1953, Brit.), w; STORM OVER THE NILE(1955, Brit.), w
Silents
FOUR FEATHERS(1915), w; AT THE VILLA ROSE(1920, Brit.), w; RUNNING WATER(1922, Brit.), w; SLAVES OF DESTINY(1924, Brit.), w; FOUR FEATHERS(1929), w

Alfred Edward Woodley Mason
FLIRTING WIDOW, THE(1930), w
Silents
WINDING STAIR, THE(1925), w
Ann Mason
TOP OF THE HEAP(1972)
B. J. Mason
WUSA(1970)
Basil Mason
ARENT WE ALL?(1932, Brit.), w; EBB TIDE(1932, Brit.), w; INSULT(1932, Brit.), w; WOMEN WHO PLAY(1932, Brit.), w; JEWEL, THE(1933, Brit.), w; BRIDES TO BE(1934, Brit.), w; DEATH AT A BROADCAST(1934, Brit.), w; EASY MONEY(1934, Brit.), w; GIRLS PLEASE!(1934, Brit.), w; LUCKY LOSER(1934, Brit.), w; PRIMROSE PATH, THE(1934, Brit.), w; SCOOP(1934, Brit.), w; CHECKMATE(1935, Brit.), w; GENTLEMAN'S AGREEMENT(1935, Brit.), w; KEY TO HARMONY(1935, Brit.), w; ONCE A THIEF(1935, Brit.), w; PRICE OF WISDOM, THE(1935, Brit.), w; SILENT PASSENGER, THE(1935, Brit.), w; CALLING THE TUNE(1936, Brit.), w; HOUSE OF THE SPANIARD, THE(1936, Brit.), w; BRIEF ECSTASY(1937, Brit.), w; WAKE UP FAMOUS(1937, Brit.), w; WHAT A MAN!(1937, Brit.), w; DANGEROUS SECRETS(1938, Brit.), w; I MARRIED A SPY(1938), w; IF I WERE BOSS(1938, Brit.), w; MAN WITH 100 FACES, THE(1938, Brit.), w; PAID IN ERROR(1938, Brit.), w; LILAC DOMINO, THE(1940, Brit.), w; CANDLES AT NINE(1944, Brit.), w; CALL OF THE BLOOD(1948, Brit.), w
Bernice Mason
UNDER YOUR SPELL(1936), w
Bert Mason
RHYTHM SERENADE(1943, Brit.), ph; GIRL IN A MILLION, A(1946, Brit.), ph; YEARS BETWEEN, THE(1947, Brit.), ph; WILLIAM COMES TO TOWN(1948, Brit.), ph; BODY SAID NO!, THE(1950, Brit.), ph; MISS PILGRIM'S PROGRESS(1950, Brit.), ph; MYSTERY AT THE BURLESQUE(1950, Brit.), ph; LUCKY MASCOT, THE(1951, Brit.), ph; ACCURSED, THE(1958, Brit.), ph; MURDER AT SITE THREE(1959, Brit.), ph; ELECTRONIC MONSTER. THE(1960, Brit.), ph; ATTEMPT TO KILL(1961, Brit.), ph; DEATH TRAP(1962, Brit.), ph; SINISTER MAN, THE(1965, Brit.), ph; CANDIDATE FOR MURDER(1966, Brit.), ph; INCIDENT AT MIDNIGHT(1966, Brit.), ph; SHARE OUT, THE(1966, Brit.), ph; SOLO FOR SPARROW(1966, Brit.), ph; NEVER BACK LOSERS(1967, Brit.), ph
Bill Mason
YELLOWNECK(1955)
Billy Mason
Silents
PRINCE OF INDIA, A(1914)
Misc. Silents
TASTE OF LIFE, A(1919); IT MIGHT HAPPEN TO YOU(1920)
Bob Mason
OFFENDERS, THE(1980), m; TRAP DOOR, THE(1980), m; MOUSE AND THE WOMAN, THE(1981, Brit.)
Brewster Mason
MACBETH(1963); PRIVATE POTTER(1963, Brit.); QUATERMASS CONCLUSION(1980, Brit.)
Buddy Mason
INVASION OF THE SAUCER MEN(1957); YOUNG AND DANGEROUS(1957); COMEDY OF TERRORS, THE(1964)
Silents
COLLEGE(1927)
C. E. Mason
Silents
COME ON OVER(1922)
Misc. Silents
BOYS WILL BE BOYS(1921)
C.W. Mason
Misc. Silents
HARD BOILED(1919)
Cain Mason
REVOLT AT FORT LARAMIE(1957)
Caldwell Mason
WARNING TO WANTONS, A(1949, Brit.)
Carolyn Mason
TOP OF THE TOWN(1937)
Charles Mason
Silents
CLARION, THE(1916); LOVE AUCTION, THE(1919)
Misc. Silents
HIS LAST HAUL(1928)
Chris Mason
FOLLOW ME, BOYS!(1966)
Chuck Mason
WARRIORS, THE(1979)
Cilla Mason
LOOKS AND SMILES(1982, Brit.)
Connie Mason
BLOOD FEAST(1963); TWO THOUSAND MANIACS!(1964)
Dan Mason
MARCH OF THE SPRING HARE(1969); ROOMMATES(1971)
1984
LAST STARFIGHTER, THE(1984)
Silents
BRAVE AND BOLD(1918); JACK SPURLOCK, PRODIGAL(1918); ON THE QUIET(1918); SALLY(1925); WAGES FOR WIVES(1925); HEARTS AND FISTS(1926); STEPPING ALONG(1926); OUT ALL NIGHT(1927)
Misc. Silents
BROADWAY SPORT, THE(1917); SCARLET LETTER, THE(1917); SLAVE, THE(1917); LURE OF AMBITION(1919); CONDUCTOR 1492(1924); DARWIN WAS RIGHT(1924); FORBIDDEN WATERS(1926); RAINBOW RILEY(1926)
Dave Mason
SKATETOWN, U.S.A.(1979), a, m
David Mason
MANSTER, THE(1962, Jap.), ph

Dick Mason
HE WALKED BY NIGHT(1948)

Don Mason
MORE DEADLY THAN THE MALE(1961, Brit.)

Dorothy Mason
Misc. Silents
BOYS OF THE OTTER PATROL(1918, Brit.)

Durey Mason
Misc. Talkies
BLACK HOOKER(1974)

Edward Mason
DOZENS, THE(1981); VERDICT, THE(1982)

Edward J. Mason
DICK BARTON–SPECIAL AGENT(1948, Brit.), w; CELIA(1949, Brit.), w; DICK BARTON STRIKES BACK(1949, Brit.), w; DICK BARTON AT BAY(1950, Brit.), w; LADY CRAVED EXCITEMENT, THE(1950, Brit.), w; WHAT THE BUTLER SAW(1950, Brit.), w

Eliot Mason
TO THE VICTOR(1938, Brit.)

Elliot Mason
GAOL BREAK(1936, Brit.); GHOST GOES WEST, THE(1936); BLACK LIMELIGHT(1938, Brit.); BREAK THE NEWS(1938, Brit.); MARIGOLD(1938, Brit.); WARE CASE, THE(1939, Brit.); RETURN TO YESTERDAY(1940, Brit.); TWENTY-ONE DAYS TOGETHER(1940, Brit.); TURNED OUT NICE AGAIN(1941, Brit.); ON APPROVAL(1944, Brit.); VACATION FROM MARRIAGE(1945, Brit.); CAPTIVE HEART, THE(1948, Brit.)

Elliott Mason
BORN THAT WAY(1937, Brit.); BLIND FOLLY(1939, Brit.); GHOST OF ST. MICHAEL'S. THE(1941, Brit.); GENTLE SEX, THE(1943, Brit.); AGITATOR, THE(1949)

Elsie Mason
Misc. Silents
MUTE APPEAL, A(1917)

Eric Mason
THEY MET IN THE DARK(1945, Brit.); CANDIDATE, THE(1964); FAHRENHEIT 451(1966, Brit.); MAN FOR ALL SEASONS, A(1966, Brit.); LIMBO LINE, THE(1969, Brit.); MACKINTOSH MAN, THE(1973, Brit.); SCREAM BLACULA SCREAM(1973); KISS OF THE TARANTULA(1975); FFOLKES(1980, Brit.)
Misc. Talkies
BLACK STARLET(1974)

Ethelmae Mason
ENDLESS LOVE(1981)

Felicity Mason
GIRL WHO COULDN'T SAY NO, THE(1969, Ital.); SHE AND HE(1969, Ital.); SACCO AND VANZETTI(1971, Ital./Fr.)

Flora Mason
Silents
EARL OF PAWTUCKET, THE(1915)

Frank Mason
Silents
APARTMENT 29(1917)

Frank Mason [Franco DeMasi]
MURDER CLINIC, THE(1967, Ital./Fr.), m

Frank Van Wyck Mason
SPY RING, THE(1938), w

Fred Mason
SINISTER URGE, THE(1961)

Gabriel Mason
YEAR OF THE HORSE, THE(1966)

George Mason
WINNING(1969); POWERFORCE(1983), p

George O'Mara Mason
YOUNG WARRIORS(1983)

Gladys Mason
HOWARD CASE, THE(1936, Brit.)
Silents
QUEEN MOTHER, THE(1916, Brit.); VEILED WOMAN, THE(1917, Brit.); MAN'S SHADOW, A(1920, Brit.); AMAZING PARTNERSHIP, THE(1921, Brit.); DAUGHTER OF LOVE, A(1925, Brit.)
Misc. Silents
ROSE IN THE DUST(1921, Brit.); SHADOW OF EVIL(1921, Brit.)

Glen Mason
MAN WITH A GUN(1958, Brit.); SPY WITH A COLD NOSE, THE(1966, Brit.)

Glenn Mason
COOL MIKADO, THE(1963, Brit.)

Grace Sartwell Mason
HONEYMOON IN BALI(1939), w
Silents
MAN CRAZY(1927), w

Guthrie Mason
BRAVE DON'T CRY, THE(1952, Brit.)

Haddon Mason
LONDON MELODY(1930, Brit.); YELLOW MASK, THE(1930, Brit.); BIRDS OF A FEATHER(1931, Brit.); CONTRABAND LOVE(1931, Brit.); FRENCH LEAVE(1931, Brit.); INQUEST(1931, Brit.); TO OBLIGE A LADY(1931, Brit.); CASTLE SINISTER(1932, Brit.); SHADOW BETWEEN, THE(1932, Brit.); VILLAGE SQUIRE, THE(1935, Brit.); UNDER THE RED ROBE(1937, Brit.)
Silents
EVERY MOTHER'S SON(1926, Brit.); DAWN(1928, Brit.); LADY OF THE LAKE, THE(1928, Brit.); PEEP BEHIND THE SCENES, A(1929, Brit.); PAINTED PICTURES(1930, Brit.)
Misc. Silents
PALAVER(1926, Brit.); GOD'S CLAY(1928, Brit.); WOMAN IN WHITE, THE(1929, Brit.)

Hal Mason
BOY TEN FEET TALL, A(1965, Brit.), p

Harry Mason
Silents
LOOKING FOR TROUBLE(1926), ph

Helen Mason
NUTCRACKER(1982, Brit.)
1984
DARK ENEMY(1984, Brit.)

Herbert Mason
EAST MEETS WEST(1936, Brit.), d; FIRST OFFENCE(1936, Brit.), d; MAN OF AFFAIRS(1937, Brit.), d; TAKE MY TIP(1937, Brit.), d; STRANGE BOARDERS(1938, Brit.), d; CONTINENTAL EXPRESS(1939, Brit.), d; BRIGGS FAMILY, THE(1940, Brit.), d; DR. O'DOWD(1940, Brit.), d; FINGERS(1940, Brit.), d; ONCE A CROOK(1941, Brit.), d; BACK ROOM BOY(1942, Brit.), d; LADY IN DISTRESS(1942, Brit.), d; IT'S IN THE BAG(1943, Brit.), d; NIGHT INVADER, THE(1943, Brit), d; FLIGHT FROM FOLLY(1945, Brit.), p&d; BACKGROUND(1953, Brit.), p; TIME GENTLEMEN PLEASE!(1953, Brit.), p; FUSS OVER FEATHERS(1954, Brit.), p; JOHN AND JULIE(1957, Brit.), p; NAVY HEROES(1959, Brit.), p

Hilary Mason
ROCKETS IN THE DUNES(1960, Brit.); GUTTER GIRLS(1964, Brit.); DON'T LOOK NOW(1973, Brit./Ital.); DEVIL WITHIN HER, THE(1976, Brit.); RETURN OF THE SOLDIER, THE(1983, Brit.)

Howard Mason
FOLLOW THAT HORSE!(1960, Brit.), w

Ingrid Mason
PICNIC AT HANGING ROCK(1975, Aus.); ELIZA FRASER(1976, Aus.); BREAK OF DAY(1977, Aus.)

Isobel Mason
1984
DARK ENEMY(1984, Brit.)

J. M. Mason
Silents
LITTLE MISS HOOVER(1918)

Jackie Mason
OPERATION DELILAH(1966, U.S./Span.); STOOLIE, THE(1972); JERK, THE(1979); HISTORY OF THE WORLD, PART 1(1981)

James Mason
GENGHIS KHAN(U.S./Brit./Ger./Yugo); LONG, LONG TRAIL, THE(1929); VIRGINIAN, THE(1929); WELCOME DANGER(1929); CONCENTRATIN' KID, THE(1930); LAST OF THE DUANES(1930); BORDER LAW(1931); CAUGHT(1931); PAINTED DESERT, THE(1931); CARNIVAL BOAT(1932); PACK UP YOUR TROUBLES(1932); RENEGADES OF THE WEST(1932); TEXAS GUN FIGHTER(1932); SCARLET RIVER(1933); STORY OF TEMPLE DRAKE, THE(1933); SUNSET PASS(1933); CAT'S PAW, THE(1934); DUDE RANGER, THE(1934); LAST ROUND-UP, THE(1934); TREASURE ISLAND(1934); HOPALONG CASSIDY(1935); LATE EXTRA(1935, Brit.); POWDERSMOKE RANGE(1935); BLIND MAN'S BLUFF(1936, Brit.); PRISON BREAKER(1936, Brit.); ROSE MARIE(1936); SECRET OF STAMBOUL, THE(1936, Brit.); TROUBLED WATERS(1936, Brit.); TWICE BRANDED(1936, Brit.); CATCH AS CATCH CAN(1937, Brit.); FIRE OVER ENGLAND(1937, Brit.); HEADIN' FOR THE RIO GRANDE(1937); HILLS OF OLD WYOMING(1937); PLAINSMAN, THE(1937); PUBLIC COWBOY NO. 1(1937); WAY OUT WEST(1937); WHERE TRAILS DIVIDE(1937); GUN LAW(1938); HIGH COMMAND(1938, Brit.); PAINTED DESERT, THE(1938); RENEGADE RANGER(1938); RETURN OF THE SCARLET PIMPERNEL(1938, Brit.); RHYTHM OF THE SADDLE(1938); YOUNG DR. KILDARE(1938); I MET A MURDERER(1939, Brit.), a, p, w; IN OLD MONTEREY(1939); LET FREEDOM RING(1939); MILL ON THE FLOSS(1939, Brit.); BILLY THE KID TRAPPED(1942); TERROR HOUSE(1942, Brit.); ALIBI, THE(1943, Brit.); BELLS GO DOWN, THE(1943, Brit.); MAN IN GREY, THE(1943, Brit.); CANDLELIGHT IN ALGERIA(1944, Brit.); SECRET MISSION(1944, Brit.); THUNDER ROCK(1944, Brit.); PLACE OF ONE'S OWN, A(1945, Brit.); THEY MET IN THE DARK(1945, Brit.); THEY WERE SISTERS(1945, Brit.); HOTEL RESERVE(1946, Brit.); SEVENTH VEIL, THE(1946, Brit.); WICKED LADY, THE(1946, Brit.); ODD MAN OUT(1947, Brit.); PATIENT VANISHES, THE(1947, Brit.); UPTURNED GLASS, THE(1947, Brit.), a, p; HATTER'S CASTLE(1948, Brit.); MAN OF EVIL(1948, Brit.); CAUGHT(1949); EAST SIDE, WEST SIDE(1949); MADAME BOVARY(1949); RECKLESS MOMENTS, THE(1949); ONE WAY STREET(1950); DESERT FOX, THE(1951); PANDORA AND THE FLYING DUTCHMAN(1951, Brit.); SANTA FE(1951); FACE TO FACE(1952); FIVE FINGERS(1952); LADY POSSESSED(1952), a, p, w; PRISONER OF ZENDA, THE(1952); BOTANY BAY(1953); CHARADE(1953), a, p, w; DESERT RATS, THE(1953); JULIUS CAESAR(1953); MAN BETWEEN, THE(1953, Brit.); STORY OF THREE LOVES, THE(1953); PRINCE VALIANT(1954); STAR IS BORN, A(1954); 20,000 LEAGUES UNDER THE SEA(1954); BIGGER THAN LIFE(1956), a, p; FOREVER DARLING(1956); ISLAND IN THE SUN(1957); CRY TERROR(1958); DECKS RAN RED, THE(1958); JOURNEY TO THE CENTER OF THE EARTH(1959); NORTH BY NORTHWEST(1959); MAN WITH THE GREEN CARNATION, THE(1960, Brit.); MARRIAGE-GO-ROUND(1960); TOUCH OF LARCENY, A(1960, Brit.); ESCAPE FROM ZAHRAIN(1962); HERO'S ISLAND(1962), a, p; LOLITA(1962); TIARA TAHITI(1962, Brit.); FALL OF THE ROMAN EMPIRE, THE(1964); PUMPKIN EATER, THE(1964, Brit.); TORPEDO BAY(1964, Ital./Fr.); LORD JIM(1965, Brit.); BLUE MAX, THE(1966); GEORGY GIRL(1966, Brit.); COP-OUT(1967, Brit.); DEADLY AFFAIR, THE(1967, Brit.); DUFFY(1968, Brit.); MAYERLING(1968, Brit./Fr.); SEA GULL, THE(1968); UNINHIBITED, THE(1968, Fr./Ital./Span.); AGE OF CONSENT(1969, Austral.), a, p; SPRING AND PORT WINE(1970, Brit.); BAD MAN'S RIVER(1972, Span.); CHILD'S PLAY(1972); KILL! KILL! KILL!(1972, Fr./Ger./Ital./Span.); LAST OF SHEILA, THE(1973); MACKINTOSH MAN, THE(1973, Brit.); COLD SWEAT(1974, Ital., Fr.); DESTRUCTORS, THE(1974, Brit.); 11 HARROWHOUSE(1974, Brit.); GREAT EXPECTATIONS(1975, Brit.); INSIDE OUT(1975, Brit.); MANDINGO(1975); VOYAGE OF THE DAMNED(1976, Brit.); CROSS OF IRON(1977, Brit., Ger.); BOYS FROM BRAZIL, THE(1978); HEAVEN CAN WAIT(1978); BLOODLINE(1979); MURDER BY DECREE(1979, Brit.); PASSAGE, THE(1979, Brit.); WATER BABIES, THE(1979, Brit.); FFOLKES(1980, Brit.); EVIL UNDER THE SUN(1982, Brit.); VERDICT, THE(1982); YELLOWBEARD(1983)
Misc. Talkies
YIN AND YANG OF DR. GO, THE(1972)
Silents
HEADIN' SOUTH(1918); JUBILO(1919); KNICKERBOCKER BUCKAROO, THE(1919); PENALTY, THE(1920); RED LANE, THE(1920); SOMETHING TO THINK ABOUT(1920); SILENT CALL, THE(1921); LIGHTS OF THE DESERT(1922); SCARS OF JEALOUSY(1923); WHY WORRY(1923); BEGGAR ON HORSEBACK(1925); OLD CLOTHES(1925); RUGGED WATER(1925); FOR HEAVEN'S SAKE(1926); NIGHT OWL, THE(1926); UNKNOWN CAVALIER, THE(1926); WHISPERING SMITH(1926); ALIAS THE LONE WOLF(1927); KING OF KINGS, THE(1927); LET IT RAIN(1927); ACROSS THE SINGAPORE(1928); CHICAGO AFTER MIDNIGHT(1928); DEAD MAN'S CURVE(1928); SUNSET PASS(1929)

Misc. Silents
BORDER WIRELESS, THE(1918); PETTIGREW'S GIRL(1919); STRANGE BORDER, THE(1920); GODLESS MEN(1921); MYSTERIOUS RIDER(1921); TWO WEEKS WITH PAY(1921); FAST MAIL, THE(1922); FOOTLIGHT RANGER, THE(1923); MILE-A-MINUTE ROMEO(1923); FLAMING FORTIES, THE(1924); PLUNDERER, THE(1924); DASHING THRU(1925); UNDER THE ROUGE(1925); BRED IN OLD KENTUCKY(1926); PHANTOM OF THE FOREST, THE(1926); PHANTOM CITY, THE(1928); SINGAPORE MUTINY, THE(1928); SPEED CLASSIC, THE(1928)

James P. Mason
Silents
NAN OF MUSIC MOUNTAIN(1917)

Jana Mason
WOMEN'S PRISON(1955); WILD PARTY, THE(1956)

Jean Mason
SHIPS OF HATE(1931)

Jeanette Mason
WOMEN OF DESIRE(1968)

Jeff Mason
1984
MISSING IN ACTION(1984)

Jim Mason
DRUM TAPS(1933); CALL OF THE PRAIRIE(1936); STAGECOACH(1939)

Jimmy Mason
Misc. Silents
OLD FOOL, THE(1923)

John Mason
HARLEM IS HEAVEN(1932)
Misc. Silents
JIM, THE PENMAN(1915); LIBERTINE, THE(1916); REAPERS, THE(1916); MORAL SUICIDE(1918)

Julianne Mason
1984
MAJDHAR(1984, Brit.)

Kathleen Mason
MY COUSIN RACHEL(1952)

Kaye Mason
DR. SIN FANG(1937, Brit.), w

Kenneth Mason
ROMEO AND JULIET(1966, Brit.)

Larry Mason
Misc. Talkies
ADVENTURES OF THE MASKED PHANTOM, THE(1939)

Laura Mason
BOWERY BOYS MEET THE MONSTERS, THE(1954); KHYBER PATROL(1954); SERENADE(1956); QUEEN OF OUTER SPACE(1958)

Le Roy Mason
GOLD MINE IN THE SKY(1938); FIGHTING GRINGO, THE(1939)

LeRoy Mason
BRIDE OF THE DESERT(1929); CLIMAX, THE(1930); SEE AMERICA THIRST(1930); MASON OF THE MOUNTED(1932); MERRILY WE GO TO HELL(1932); TEXAS PIONEERS(1932); KING KONG(1933); MONKEY'S PAW, THE(1933); SMOKY(1933); ARE WE CIVILIZED?(1934); DUDE RANGER, THE(1934); RED HEAD(1934); WHEN A MAN SEES RED(1934); FIGHTING TROOPER, THE(1935); MYSTERY MAN, THE(1935); NORTHERN FRONTIER(1935); RAINBOW VALLEY(1935); TEXAS TERROR(1935); CALIFORNIA STRAIGHT AHEAD(1937); GHOST TOWN GOLD(1937); IT HAPPENED OUT WEST(1937); ROUNDUP TIME IN TEXAS(1937); SINGING OUTLAW(1937); WESTERN GOLD(1937); YODELIN' KID FROM PINE RIDGE(1937); AIR DEVILS(1938); FURY BELOW(1938); HEROES OF THE HILLS(1938); OUTLAW EXPRESS(1938); PAINTED TRAIL, THE(1938); RHYTHM OF THE SADDLE(1938); SANTA FE STAMPEDE(1938); SPY RING, THE(1938); WEST OF SANTA FE(1938); LURE OF THE WASTELAND(1939); MEXICALI ROSE(1939); NEW FRONTIER(1939); SKY PATROL(1939); WYOMING OUTLAW(1939); GHOST VALLEY RAIDERS(1940); KILLERS OF THE WILD(1940); NEW MOON(1940); ON THE SPOT(1940); RANGE BUSTERS, THE(1940); ROCKY MOUNTAIN RANGERS(1940); TRIPLE JUSTICE(1940); ACROSS THE SIERRAS(1941); APACHE KID, THE(1941); LAST OF THE DUANES(1941); PERFECT SNOB, THE(1941); RIDERS OF THE PURPLE SAGE(1941); ROBBERS OF THE RANGE(1941); SILVER STALLION(1941); SIX GUN GOLD(1941); BANDIT RANGER(1942); IT HAPPENED IN FLATBUSH(1942); JACKASS MAIL(1942); MAN WHO WOULDN'T DIE, THE(1942); SILVER BULLET(1942); SUNDOWN JIM(1942); TIME TO KILL(1942); WESTERN MAIL(1942); BLAZING GUNS(1943); CANYON CITY(1943); CHETNIKS(1943); HANDS ACROSS THE BORDER(1943); IN OLD OKLAHOMA(1943); MAN FROM THE RIO GRANDE, THE(1943); OVERLAND MAIL ROBBERY(1943); RAIDERS OF SUNSET PASS(1943); BENEATH WESTERN SKIES(1944); CALIFORNIA JOE(1944); FIREBRANDS OF ARIZONA(1944); HIDDEN VALLEY OUTLAWS(1944); MARSHAL OF RENO(1944); MOJAVE FIREBRAND(1944); OUTLAWS OF SANTA FE(1944); SAN ANTONIO KID, THE(1944); SAN FERNANDO VALLEY(1944); SONG OF NEVADA(1944); STAGECOACH TO MONTEREY(1944); TUCSON RAIDERS(1944); VIGILANTES OF DODGE CITY(1944); LONE TEXAS RANGER(1945); HELLDORADO(1946); HOME ON THE RANGE(1946); MURDER IN THE MUSIC HALL(1946); MY PAL TRIGGER(1946); NIGHT TRAIN TO MEMPHIS(1946); RED RIVER RENEGADES(1946); SIOUX CITY SUE(1946); UNDER NEVADA SKIES(1946); VALLEY OF THE ZOMBIES(1946); ALONG THE OREGON TRAIL(1947); APACHE ROSE(1947); BANDITS OF DARK CANYON(1947); SADDLE PALS(1947); UNDER COLORADO SKIES(1947); CALIFORNIA FIREBRAND(1948); GAY RANCHERO, THE(1948)
Misc. Talkies
VALLEY OF WANTED MEN(1935); GO-GET-'EM HAINES(1936); TOPA TOPA(1938)
Silents
TOM AND HIS PALS(1926); AVENGING SHADOW, THE(1928)
Misc. Silents
FLYING HIGH(1926); GOLDEN SHACKLES(1928); REVENGE(1928); VIKING, THE(1929); WOMAN WHO WAS FORGOTTEN, THE(1930)

Lesley Mason
SENOR AMERICANO(1929), w; WAGON MASTER, THE(1929), w; MOUNTAIN JUSTICE(1930), w; PARADE OF THE WEST(1930), w; SONG OF THE CABELLERO, w; SONS OF THE SADDLE(1930), w; MAN FROM MONTEREY, THE(1933), w
Silents
RUSH HOUR, THE(1927), t; LAWLESS LEGION, THE(1929), t; ROYAL RIDER, THE(1929), t

Leslie Mason
SENOR AMERICANO(1929), titles; CLIMAX, THE(1930), w; FIGHTING LEGION, THE(1930), w; ALOHA(1931), w
Silents
STORMY WATERS(1928), t

Lew Mason
DESIRE ME(1947)

Lewis Mason
Silents
CUB REPORTER, THE(1922)

Lola Mason
BRAIN THAT WOULDN'T DIE, THE(1959); FAREWELL, MY LOVELY(1975)

Lou Mason
EGG AND I, THE(1947); WALLS OF JERICHO(1948)

Louis Mason
JUDGE PRIEST(1934); SPITFIRE(1934); THIS MAN IS MINE(1934); FARMER TAKES A WIFE, THE(1935); IN PERSON(1935); KENTUCKY KERNELS(1935); MARY JANE'S PA(1935); STEAMBOAT ROUND THE BEND(1935); BANJO ON MY KNEE(1936); GIRL OF THE OZARKS(1936); M'LISS(1936); ROSE BOWL(1936); MARRY THE GIRL(1937); TROUBLE AT MIDNIGHT(1937); STAGECOACH(1939); THEY SHALL HAVE MUSIC(1939); YOUNG MR. LINCOLN(1939); CHAD HANNA(1940); GOLD RUSH MAISIE(1940); GRAPES OF WRATH(1940); RETURN OF FRANK JAMES, THE(1940); SEA WOLF, THE(1941); JACKASS MAIL(1942); KEEPER OF THE FLAME(1942); WHISTLING IN DIXIE(1942); WHAT'S BUZZIN COUSIN?(1943); BROADWAY RHYTHM(1944); LOUISIANA HAYRIDE(1944); SEE HERE, PRIVATE HARGROVE(1944); GRISSLY'S MILLIONS(1945); HIT THE HAY(1945); DECOY(1946); SOMEWHERE IN THE NIGHT(1946); SPORT OF KINGS(1947); GOOD SAM(1948); VELVET TOUCH, THE(1948); ADAM'S RIB(1949); I CHEATED THE LAW(1949); RECKLESS MOMENTS, THE(1949); NEVADAN, THE(1950); TRAVELING SALESWOMAN(1950); SANTA FE(1951); PAT AND MIKE(1952); FRANCIS COVERS THE BIG TOWN(1953)

Madison Mason
1984
DREAMSCAPE(1984); FEAR CITY(1984)

Marcia Mason
BEYOND THE LAW(1968)

Margery Mason
CHARLIE BUBBLES(1968, Brit.); WALK A CROOKED PATH(1969, Brit.); LONG AGO, TOMORROW(1971, Brit.); MADE(1972, Brit.); HENNESSY(1975, Brit.)

Marian Mason
GUIDE FOR THE MARRIED MAN, A(1967)

Marie Mason
LOOKS AND SMILES(1982, Brit.)

Marilyn Mason
TROUBLE WITH GIRLS(AND HOW TO GET INTO IT), THE*1/2 (1969)

Marjorie Mason
PINK FLOYD–THE WALL(1982, Brit.)

Marlyn Mason
MAKING IT(1971); CHRISTINA(1974, Can.)

Marsha Mason
HOT ROD HULLABALOO(1966); BLUME IN LOVE(1973); CINDERELLA LIBERTY(1973); AUDREY ROSE(1977); GOODBYE GIRL, THE(1977); CHEAP DETECTIVE, THE(1978); CHAPTER TWO(1979); PROMISES IN THE DARK(1979); ONLY WHEN I LAUGH(1981); MAX DUGAN RETURNS(1983)

Martin Mason
PLACE IN THE SUN, A(1951); SHANE(1953)

Marty Mason
FIGHTING FOOLS(1949)

Mary Mason
PENGUIN POOL MURDER, THE(1932); CHEYENNE KID, THE(1933); MAD GAME, THE(1933); WALLS OF GOLD(1933)
Silents
EXTRA GIRL, THE(1923)

Melissa Mason
RADIO CITY REVELS(1938)

Michael Mason
SHOWDOWN AT BOOT HILL(1958)

Mike Mason
UNDERSEA GIRL(1957); LET'S MAKE LOVE(1960)

Monica Mason
ROMEO AND JULIET(1966, Brit.); NIJINSKY(1980, Brit.)

Morgan Mason
HERO'S ISLAND(1962); SANDPIPER, THE(1965)

Muriel Mason
COLD RIVER(1982)

Myra Mason
HAPPY DAYS(1930)

Nan Mason
TOWING(1978)

Nellie Mason
Silents
THREE MUSKETEERS, THE(1921), ed

Noel Mason
DANCING DYNAMITE(1931), d; SCAREHEADS(1931), d; YANKEE DON(1931), d
Misc. Talkies
FIGHTING PILOT, THE(1935), d
Silents
BLUE STREAK, THE(1926), d; HEROIC LOVER, THE(1929), d
Misc. Silents
BROADWAY GALLANT, THE(1926), d; FLYING MAIL, THE(1926), d; MERRY CAVALIER, THE(1926), d; SNARL OF HATE, THE(1927), d; DANGER TRAIL(1928), d; MARLIE THE KILLER(1928), d; BACHELOR'S CLUB, THE(1929), d; BACK FROM SHANGHAI(1929), d

Pamela Mason
CHARADE(1953), a, w; COLLEGE CONFIDENTIAL(1960); SEX KITTENS GO TO COLLEGE(1960); FIVE MINUTES TO LIVE(1961); NAVY VS. THE NIGHT MONSTERS, THE(1966); WILD IN THE STREETS(1968); EVERYTHING YOU ALWAYS WANTED TO KNOW ABOUT SEX, BUT WE'RE AFRAID TO ASK(1972)

Patricia Mason
MACBETH(1971, Brit.)
Paul Mason
ANGEL BABY(1961), w; KING KONG VERSUS GODZILLA(1963, Jap.), w
Peter Mason
SIEGE OF THE SAXONS(1963, Brit.)
Phil Mason
LOVE MERCHANT, THE(1966)
Portland Mason
BIGGER THAN LIFE(1956); MAN IN THE GREY FLANNEL SUIT, THE(1956); CRY TERROR(1958); GREAT ST. TRINIAN'S TRAIN ROBBERY, THE(1966, Brit.); SEBASTIAN(1968, Brit.)
Ralph Mason
MIKADO, THE(1967, Brit.)
Ray Mason
SWIMMER, THE(1968)
Raymond Mason
BARTLEBY(1970, Brit.); YOUNG WINSTON(1972, Brit.)
Reginald Mason
LIFE BEGINS(1932); BEDTIME STORY, A(1933); BIG BRAIN, THE(1933); BRIEF MOMENT(1933); EMERGENCY CALL(1933); KISS BEFORE THE MIRROR, THE(1933); MARY STEVENS, M.D.(1933); SHANGHAI MADNESS(1933); TOPAZE(1933); CALL IT LUCK(1934); CHARLIE CHAN'S COURAGE(1934); WHOM THE GODS DESTROY(1934); YOU CAN'T BUY EVERYTHING(1934); MY MAN GODFREY(1936); SUZY(1936); 13 RUE MADELEINE(1946)
Misc. Silents
TWO WEEKS(1920)
Renee Mason
TRAUMA(1962)
Richard Mason
PACIFIC DESTINY(1956, Brit.), w; TOWN LIKE ALICE, A(1958, Brit.), w; WIND CANNOT READ, THE(1958, Brit.), w; PASSIONATE SUMMER(1959, Brit.), w; WORLD OF SUZIE WONG, THE(1960), w; TORTURE DUNGEON(1970); LET THE BALLOON GO(1977, Aus.), p, w; WINTER OF OUR DREAMS(1982, Aus.), p
1984
BIRDY(1984)
Rick Mason
HISTORY OF THE WORLD, PART 1(1981)
Roy Mason
BORDER PATROLMAN, THE(1936); COMIN' ROUND THE MOUNTAIN(1936); MAN ON A SWING(1974)
Misc. Talkies
MEN OF ACTION(1935)
Sara Y. Mason
GOLDEN BOY(1939), w
Sarah Y. Mason
ALIAS JIMMY VALENTINE(1928), w; GIRL SAID NO, THE(1930), w; LOVE IN THE ROUGH(1930), w; THEY LEARNED ABOUT WOMEN(1930), w; MAN IN POSSESSION, THE(1931), w; AGE OF CONSENT(1932), w; SHOPWORN(1932), w; CHANCE AT HEAVEN(1933), w; LITTLE WOMEN(1933), w; AGE OF INNOCENCE(1934), w; LITTLE MINISTER, THE(1934), w; BREAK OF HEARTS(1935), w; MAGNIFICENT OBSESSION(1935), w; STELLA DALLAS(1937), w; LITTLE WOMEN(1949), w; MAGNIFICENT OBSESSION(1954), w
Silents
BACKSTAGE(1927), w; ONE HOUR OF LOVE(1927), w
Scott Mason
RIDE HIM, COWBOY(1932), w
Sheila Mason
AIRPORT '77(1977), cos
Shirely Mason
Silents
RUNAWAY GIRLS(1928)
Shirley Mason
FLYING MARINE, THE(1929)
Silents
ENVY(1917); GOOD-BYE, BILL(1919); PUTTING IT OVER(1919); GIRL OF MY HEART(1920); HER ELEPHANT MAN(1920); TREASURE ISLAND(1920); LAMPLIGHTER, THE(1921); QUEENIE(1921); WING TOY(1921); LIGHTS OF THE DESERT(1922); LITTLE MISS SMILES(1922); NEW TEACHER, THE(1922); PAWN TICKET 210(1922); RAGGED HEIRESS, THE(1922); SHIRLEY OF THE CIRCUS(1922); ELEVENTH HOUR, THE(1923); SOUTH SEA LOVE(1923); MY HUSBAND'S WIVES(1924); LORD JIM(1925); WHAT FOOLS MEN(1925); LET IT RAIN(1925); SALLY IN OUR ALLEY(1927); STRANDED(1927); SO THIS IS LOVE(1928); ANNE AGAINST THE WORLD(1929)
Misc. Silents
APPLE-TREE GIRL, THE(1917); AWAKENING OF RUTH, THE(1917); CY WHITTAKER'S WARD(1917); GREED(1917); LADY OF THE PHOTOGRAPH, THE(1917); LAW OF THE NORTH, THE(1917); LIGHT IN DARKNESS(1917); LITTLE CHEVALIER, THE(1917); PASSION(1917); PRIDE(1917); SEVENTH SIN, THE(1917); TELL-TALE STEP, THE(1917); WHERE LOVE IS(1917); WRATH(1917); COME ON IN(1918); FINAL CLOSEUP, THE(1919); RESCUING ANGEL, THE(1919); UNWRITTEN CODE, THE(1919); WINNING GIRL, THE(1919); FLAME OF YOUTH(1920); LITTLE WANDERER, THE(1920); LOVE'S HARVEST(1920); MERELY MARY ANN(1920); MOLLY AND I(1920); EVER SINCE EVE(1921); JACKIE(1921); LOVETIME(1921); MOTHER HEART, THE(1921); VERY TRULY YOURS(1922); YOUTH MUST HAVE LOVE(1922); LOVEBOUND(1923); CURLYTOP(1924); GREAT DIAMOND MYSTERY, THE(1924); LOVE LETTERS(1924); STAR DUST TRAIL, THE(1924); THAT FRENCH LADY(1924); SCANDAL PROOF(1925); SCARLET HONEYMOON, THE(1925); TALKER, THE(1925); DESERT GOLD(1926); DON JUAN'S THREE NIGHTS(1926); ROSE OF THE TENEMENTS(1926); SIN CARGO(1926); SWEET ROSIE O'GRADY(1926); RICH MEN'S SONS(1927); WRECK, THE(1927); WIFE'S RELATIONS, THE(1928)
Sidney L. Mason
Silents
MODERN SALOME, A(1920)
Sidney Mason
MOB, THE(1951); PAULA(1952)
Silents
JOHN GLAYDE'S HONOR(1915); PEG OF THE PIRATES(1918)

Misc. Silents
DAUGHTER OF MACGREGOR, A(1916); DEAD ALIVE, THE(1916); HONOR OF MARY BLAKE, THE(1916); LITTLE MISS NOBODY(1917); LITTLE TERROR, THE(1917); PAINTED MADONNA, THE(1917); PEDDLER, THE(1917); BONNIE ANNIE LAURIE(1918); FORBIDDEN PATH, THE(1918); FALLEN IDOL, A(1919); TRAP, THE(1919); GOOD-BAD WIFE, THE(1921); ORPHAN SALLY(1922)
Stan Mason
VOODOO HEARTBEAT(1972)
Steve Mason
KID NIGHTINGALE(1939)
Sully Mason
THAT'S RIGHT-YOU'RE WRONG(1939); YOU'LL FIND OUT(1940); PLAYMATES(1941); MY FAVORITE SPY(1942); AROUND THE WORLD(1943); SWING FEVER(1943); CAROLINA BLUES(1944)
Syd Mason
SECRET FILE: HOLLYWOOD(1962)
Sydney Mason
EMERGENCY WEDDING(1950); BRIGHT VICTORY(1951); THREE GUYS NAMED MIKE(1951); APACHE COUNTRY(1952); HOODLUM EMPIRE(1952); SOMEBODY LOVES ME(1952); LADY WANTS MINK, THE(1953); WAR OF THE WORLDS, THE(1953); CREATURE FROM THE BLACK LAGOON(1954); TEEN-AGE CRIME WAVE(1955); BLACKJACK KETCHUM, DESPERADO(1956); DAY OF FURY, A(1956); FRONTIER GUN(1958)
Silents
SEVEN SISTERS, THE(1915)
Misc. Silents
UNBROKEN PROMISE, THE(1919)
Todd Mason
THOROUGHLY MODERN MILLIE(1967)
Tom Mason
KING OF THE GYPSIES(1978)
Vivian Mason
THAT NIGHT IN RIO(1941); KANSAS CITY KITTY(1944); GEORGE WHITE'S SCANDALS(1945); SUDAN(1945); THOUSAND AND ONE NIGHTS, A(1945); FRENCH LEAVE(1948); SAXON CHARM, THE(1948); EMERGENCY WEDDING(1950); HAREM GIRL(1952); CHARGE AT FEATHER RIVER, THE(1953); HERE COME THE GIRLS(1953); SIREN OF BAGDAD(1953); PHFFFT!(1954)
Vivien Mason
ZIEGFELD GIRL(1941)
Walter Mason
BLACK LIKE ME(1964)
William Mason
BETTY CO-ED(1946)
Michael Masone
1984
DELIVERY BOYS(1984)
Masoni
PASSPORT TO PIMLICO(1949, Brit.)
Curt Masreliez
DEVIL'S WANTON, THE(1962, Swed.)
Steve Mass
UNDERGROUND U.S.A.(1980)
Vadim Mass
YOLANTA(1964, USSR), ph
Vladimir Zakharovich Mass
SONG OVER MOSCOW(1964, USSR), w
Bennie Massa
HEY, GOOD LOOKIN'(1982)
Bernie Massa
HEAVEN CAN WAIT(1978)
Roberto Massa
CONDEMNED OF ALTONA, THE(1963)
Aristide Massaccesi
TEMPTER, THE(1978, Ital.), ph; GRIM REAPER, THE(1981, Ital.), w
1984
BURIED ALIVE(1984, Ital.), ph
Misc. Talkies
DEATH SMILES ON A MURDER(1974), d; ABSURD-ANTROPOPHAGOUS 2(1982), d
Aristide Massacessi
ARENA, THE(1973), ph
Louis Massad
QUICK AND THE DEAD, THE(1963)
Nabil Massad
1984
MISUNDERSTOOD(1984)
Oswaldo Massaini
GIVEN WORD, THE(1964, Braz.), p
N. Massalitinov
Misc. Silents
YEKATERINA IVANOVNA(1915, USSR)
V.O. Massalitinova
CHILDHOOD OF MAXIM GORKY(1938, Russ.); ALEXANDER NEVSKY(1939); ON HIS OWN(1939, USSR)
Varvara Massalitinova
THUNDERSTORM(1934, USSR)
Misc. Silents
FATHER FROST(1924, USSR)
Pavel Massalskiy
RESURRECTION(1963, USSR); GARNET BRACELET, THE(1966, USSR)
Pavel Massalsky
IVAN THE TERRIBLE(Part I, 1947, USSR)
Natal Massara
TREASURE ISLAND(1972, Brit./Span./Fr./Ger.), m
Natale Massara
TEX(1982), md
Natalie Massara
DRESSED TO KILL(1980), md

Yves Massard
 MAIN STREET(1956, Span.); ONCE IN PARIS(1978)
Aristide Massari
 SEVEN TASKS OF ALI BABA, THE(1963, Ital.)
Lea Massari
 DREAMS IN A DRAWER(1957, Fr./Ital.); L'AVVENTURA(1960, Ital.); COLOSSUS OF RHODES, THE(1961, Ital., Fr., Span.); FROM A ROMAN BALCONY(1961, Fr./Ital.); CAPTIVE CITY, THE(1963, Ital.); FOUR DAYS OF NAPLES, THE(1963, US/Ital.); PARIS PICK-UP(1963, Fr./Ital.); CONQUERED CITY(1966, Ital.); MADE IN ITALY(1967, Fr./Ital.); THINGS OF LIFE, THE(1970, Fr./Ital./Switz.); MURMUR OF THE HEART(1971, Fr./Ital./Ger.); AND HOPE TO DIE(1972 Fr/US); IMPOSSIBLE OBJECT(1973, Fr.); EBOLI(1980, Ital.)
Mounir Massari
 EMBASSY(1972, Brit.)
Mary Massart
 Misc. Silents
 BROKEN ROAD, THE(1921, Brit.); FOUR FEATHERS, THE(1921, Brit.); KNAVE OF DIAMONDS, THE(1921, Brit.); WOMAN WITH THE FAN, THE(1921, Brit.)
Javier Masse
 EXTERMINATING ANGEL, THE(1967, Mex.); TWO MULES FOR SISTER SARA(1970)
Osa Massen
 HONEYMOON IN BALI(1939); ACCENT ON LOVE(1941); HONEYMOON FOR THREE(1941); WOMAN'S FACE(1941); YOU'LL NEVER GET RICH(1941); ICELAND(1942); BACKGROUND TO DANGER(1943); JACK LONDON(1943); BLACK PARACHUTE, THE(1944); CRY OF THE WEREWOLF(1944); MASTER RACE, THE(1944); TOKYO ROSE(1945); DEADLINE AT DAWN(1946); GENTLEMAN MISBEHAVES, THE(1946); STRANGE JOURNEY(1946); NIGHT UNTO NIGHT(1949); ROCKETSHIP X-M(1950); OUTCASTS OF THE CITY(1958)
Oso Massen
 DEVIL PAYS OFF, THE(1941)
Carol Massenberg
 FAME(1980)
Joseph Massengale
 STIR CRAZY(1980)
Pierino Massenzi
 LOVE SLAVES OF THE AMAZONS(1957, art d; GIRL IN ROOM 13(1961, U.S./Braz.), art d; TRAIN ROBBERY CONFIDENTIAL(1965, Braz.), art d
Michael Masser
 MAHOGANY(1975), m; GREATEST, THE(1977, U.S./Brit.), m
 1984
 CHOOSE ME(1984), m/l "Choose Me," Luther Vandross
Andrew Masset
 HERO AT LARGE(1980)
Jean Masset
 CAFE METROPOLE(1937)
Gene Massett
 SEVENTH HEAVEN(1937)
Enzo Massetti
 WANDERING JEW, THE(1948, Ital.), m
Anna Massey
 GIDEON OF SCOTLAND YARD(1959, Brit.); PEEPING TOM(1960, Brit.); BUNNY LAKE IS MISSING(1965); DE SADE(1969); DAVID COPPERFIELD(1970, Brit.); LOOKING GLASS WAR, THE(1970, Brit.); FRENZY(1972, Brit.); DOLL'S HOUSE, A(1973); VAULT OF HORROR, THE(1973, Brit.); LITTLE ROMANCE, A(1979, U.S./Fr.); SWEET WILLIAM(1980, Brit.); FIVE DAYS ONE SUMMER(1982)
 1984
 ANOTHER COUNTRY(1984, Brit.); LITTLE DRUMMER GIRL, THE(1984); SACRED HEARTS(1984, Brit.)
Arthur Massey
 HIGH TIDE AT NOON(1957, Brit.)
Bebe Drake Massey
 OH GOD! BOOK II(1980)
Curt Massey
 WHERE THE BUFFALO ROAM(1938)
Daniel Massey
 IN WHICH WE SERVE(1942, Brit.); GIRLS AT SEA(1958, Brit.); ENTERTAINER, THE(1960, Brit.); UPSTAIRS AND DOWNSTAIRS(1961, Brit.); GO TO BLAZES(1962, Brit.); OPERATION BULLSHINE(1963, Brit.); QUEEN'S GUARDS, THE(1963, Brit.); AMOROUS ADVENTURES OF MOLL FLANDERS, THE(1965); JOKERS, THE(1967, Brit.); STAR!(1968); FRAGMENT OF FEAR(1971, Brit.); MARY, QUEEN OF SCOTS(1971, Brit.); VAULT OF HORROR, THE(1973, Brit.); INCREDIBLE SARAH, THE(1976, Brit.); WARLORDS OF ATLANTIS(1978, Brit.); CAT AND THE CANARY, THE(1979, Brit.); VICTORY(1981)
Daria Massey
 CARRIE(1952); IRON MISTRESS, THE(1952); SABU AND THE MAGIC RING(1957); MIRACLE, THE(1959); HIGH SCHOOL CAESAR(1960); LADIES MAN, THE(1961)
Edith Massey
 FEMALE TROUBLE(1975); POLYESTER(1981)
Emily Massey
 WHITE CLIFFS OF DOVER, THE(1944); PICTURE OF DORIAN GRAY, THE(1945); WITHOUT LOVE(1945)
Gene Massey
 GOLDEN BOX, THE(1970)
Ilona Massey
 ROSALIE(1937); BALALAIKA(1939); INTERNATIONAL LADY(1941); NEW WINE(1941); INVISIBLE AGENT(1942); FRANKENSTEIN MEETS THE WOLF MAN(1943); HOLIDAY IN MEXICO(1946); NORTHWEST OUTPOST(1947); PLUNDERERS, THE(1948); LOVE HAPPY(1949); JET OVER THE ATLANTIC(1960)
Jamila Massey
 LONG DUEL, THE(1967, Brit.); THAT LUCKY TOUCH(1975, Brit.)
Jayne Massey
 DESTRUCTORS, THE(1968)
Michael Massey
 NIGHT THE LIGHTS WENT OUT IN GEORGIA, THE(1981)
Raymond Massey
 SPECKLED BAND, THE(1931, Brit.); FACE AT THE WINDOW, THE(1932, Brit.); OLD DARK HOUSE, THE(1932); SCARLET PIMPERNEL, THE(1935, Brit.); THINGS TO COME(1936, Brit.); DREAMING LIPS(1937, Brit.); FIRE OVER ENGLAND(1937, Brit.); HURRICANE, THE(1937); PRISONER OF ZENDA, THE(1937); UNDER THE RED ROBE(1937, Brit.); BLACK LIMELIGHT(1938, Brit.); DRUMS(1938, Brit.); ABE LINCOLN IN ILLINOIS(1940); SANTA FE TRAIL(1940); INVADERS, THE,(1941); DANGEROUSLY THEY LIVE(1942); DESPERATE JOURNEY(1942); REAP THE WILD WIND(1942); ACTION IN THE NORTH ATLANTIC(1943); ARSENIC AND OLD LACE(1944); GOD IS MY CO-PILOT(1945); HOTEL BERLIN(1945); WOMAN IN THE WINDOW, THE(1945); STAIRWAY TO HEAVEN(1946, Brit.); MOURNING BECOMES ELECTRA(1947); POSSESSED(1947); FOUNTAINHEAD, THE(1949); ROSEANNA McCOY(1949); BARRICADE(1950); CHAIN LIGHTNING(1950); DALLAS(1950); COME FILL THE CUP(1951); DAVID AND BATHSHEBA(1951); SUGARFOOT(1951); CARSON CITY(1952); DESERT SONG, THE(1953); BATTLE FLAME(1955); EAST OF EDEN(1955); PRINCE OF PLAYERS(1955); SEVEN ANGRY MEN(1955); OMAR KHAYYAM(1957); NAKED AND THE DEAD, THE(1958); GREAT IMPOSTOR, THE(1960); FIERCEST HEART, THE(1961); HOW THE WEST WAS WON(1962); QUEEN'S GUARDS, THE(1963, Brit.); MACKENNA'S GOLD(1969)
Richard Massey
 Misc. Talkies
 ANDREA(1979)
Tom Massey
 MAKE MINE MUSIC(1946), anim; SONG OF THE SOUTH(1946), anim
Vic Massey
 G.I. JANE(1951)
Walter Massey
 NOW THAT APRIL'S HERE(1958, Can.); TOMORROW NEVER COMES(1978, Brit./Can.); GAS(1981, Can.); HAPPY BIRTHDAY TO ME(1981)
 1984
 HOTEL NEW HAMPSHIRE, THE(1984); MRS. SOFFEL(1984)
P. Massi
 Silents
 AS IN A LOOKING GLASS(1916)
Stelvio Massi
 PRICE OF POWER, THE(1969, Ital./Span.), ph
Stevio Massi
 BLOOD, SWEAT AND FEAR(1975, Ital.), d
Phyliss Massicot
 LOUISIANA TERRITORY(1953)
Steve Massicotte
 HAIR(1979)
Chris Massie
 LOVE LETTERS(1945), w; CORRIDOR OF MIRRORS(1948, Brit.), w
Julie Massie
 CURTAINS(1983, Can.)
Paul Massie
 HIGH TIDE AT NOON(1957, Brit.); ORDERS TO KILL(1958, Brit.); LIBEL(1959, Brit.); SAPPHIRE(1959, Brit.); CALL ME GENIUS(1961, Brit.); HOUSE OF FRIGHT(1961); POT CARRIERS, THE(1962, Brit.); ROOMMATES(1962, Brit.)
Robert K. Massie
 NICHOLAS AND ALEXANDRA(1971, Brit.), w
Gerald Massie-Collier
 MAN UPSTAIRS, THE(1959, Brit.), ph
Giulio Massimi
 FURY OF THE PAGANS(1963, Ital.)
Pierre Massimi
 SELLERS OF GIRLS(1967, Fr.); VISCOUNT, THE(1967, Fr./Span./Ital./Ger.); FEMMINA(1968 Fr./Ital./Ger.)
Vittorio Massimo
 ROMMEL'S TREASURE(1962, Ital.)
Massimo Vitalo
 PHAROAH'S WOMAN, THE(1961, Ital.), w
Janine Massina
 HEAT OF THE SUMMER(1961, Fr.)
Noelle Massina
 CARNY(1980)
Leonide Massine
 CARNIVAL IN COSTA RICA(1947), ch; RED SHOES, THE(1948, Brit.); TALES OF HOFFMANN, THE(1951, Brit.); HUNCHBACK OF NOTRE DAME, THE(1957, Fr.), ch; NEOPOLITAN CAROUSEL(1961, Ital.), a, ch
Richard Massingham
 TURN THE KEY SOFTLY(1954, Brit.); WILL ANY GENTLEMAN?(1955, Brit.)
Mia Massini
 SECRET INVASION, THE(1964)
M. Masso
 NO WAY OUT(1975, Ital./Fr.), ed
Lionello Massobrio
 CONJUGAL BED, THE(1963, Ital.), ed
Askell Masson
 OUTLAW: THE SAGE OF GISLI(1982, Iceland), m
Beatrice Masson
 1984
 JUST THE WAY YOU ARE(1984)
Diego Masson
 SPIRITS OF THE DEAD(1969, Fr./Ital.), m
Jacques Masson
 YOUNG WORLD, A(1966, Fr./Ital.); THIS MAN MUST DIE(1970, Fr./Ital.); VERY CURIOUS GIRL, A(1970, Fr.)
Jean-Pierre Masson
 WHY ROCK THE BOAT?(1974, Can.)
Louis Masson
 LIFE AND LOVES OF BEETHOVEN, THE(1937, Fr.), m, md
Luis Masson
 WALK WITH LOVE AND DEATH, A(1969)
Marjorie Masson
 IN THE MEANTIME, DARLING(1944)
Rene Masson
 LIGHT ACROSSS THE STREET, THE(1957, Fr.), w
Rudy Masson
 RAINBOW ISLAND(1944)
Tom Masson
 HANGMAN'S WHARF(1950, Brit.)

Yvette Masson
HEAD OF A TYRANT(1960, Fr./Ital.)
James Massong
SEVENTH DAWN, THE(1964)
Claude Massot
SUITOR, THE(1963, Fr.)
Joe Massot
WONDERWALL(1969, Brit.), d; ZACHARIAH(1971), w
Misc. Talkies
SPACE RIDERS(1984), d
Jean-Claude Massoulier
SEVEN CAPITAL SINS(1962, Fr./Ital.)
Marjorie Massow
TAKE IT OR LEAVE IT(1944)
Gerry Massy-Collier
STOLEN PLANS, THE(1962, Brit.), ph
Howard Master
BILLY THE KID'S RANGE WAR(1941)
David Masterman
GREEK TYCOON, THE(1978)
Joe Masteroff
CABARET(1972), w
Anthony Masters
CORRIDORS OF BLOOD(1962, Brit.), art d; PAPILLON(1973), prod d
1984
DUNE(1984), prod d
Ben Masters
MANDINGO(1975)
Daryl Masters
FLAMING FRONTIER(1958, Can.); WOLF DOG(1958, Can.); ONE PLUS ONE(1961, Can.)
E. Lanning Masters
Silents
VALLEY OF BRAVERY, THE(1926), w
George Masters
TRAIN ROBBERS, THE(1973), makeup; TOOTSIE(1982), makeup
Howard Masters
BILLY THE KID WANTED(1941); LONE RIDER CROSSES THE RIO, THE(1941); SECRET EVIDENCE(1941); GHOST TOWN LAW(1942)
Ian Masters
OSTERMAN WEEKEND, THE(1983), w
J. T. Masters
MIDNIGHT COWBOY(1969)
Jack Masters
SUDDENLY(1954), cos; WITNESS TO MURDER(1954), cos; HONG KONG CONFIDENTIAL(1958), cos; BEYOND THE TIME BARRIER(1960), cos
James Masters
Misc. Talkies
RIP OFF(1977)
John Masters
BHOWANI JUNCTION(1956), w
Judy Masters
DEVIL'S BEDROOM, THE(1964), set d
Marie Masters
1984
SCREAM FOR HELP(1984); SLAYGROUND(1984, Brit.)
Mary Masters
Silents
DEAD CERTAINTY, A(1920, Brit.)
Michael Masters
SSSSSSSS(1973); CHEECH AND CHONG'S NICE DREAMS(1981)
Mike Masters
SERGEANT WAS A LADY, THE(1961); MANCHURIAN CANDIDATE, THE(1962); YOUNG DILLINGER(1965); MACHO CALLAHAN(1970); APPLE DUMPLING GANG RIDES AGAIN, THE(1979); MAN WITH BOGART'S FACE, THE(1980)
Miss Masters
WALK ON THE WILD SIDE(1962)
Monte Masters
DRAGNET(1954)
Natalie Masters
BIGGER THAN LIFE(1956); SANTIAGO(1956); NIGHT RUNNER, THE(1957); VAMPIRE, THE(1957); MUSIC MAN, THE(1962); BEST MAN, THE(1964)
Natalie Park Masters
ROSEMARY'S BABY(1968)
Quentin Masters
THUMB TRIPPING(1972), d; STUD, THE(1979, Brit.), d
Misc. Talkies
PSI FACTOR(1980, Brit.), d
Richard Masters
STARFIGHTERS, THE(1964)
Ruth Masters
BRIDGE TO THE SUN(1961)
Sharon Masters
FIRST TIME, THE(1969); LAST TYCOON, THE(1976)
Misc. Talkies
YOUNG AND WILD(1975); DEADLINE(1984)
Silvia Masters
SORCERESS(1983)
Steve Masters
MOTOR PSYCHO(1965)
Tammy Masters
FM(1978)
Tony Masters
STORY OF ESTHER COSTELLO, THE(1957, Brit.), art d; SPANIARD'S CURSE, THE(1958, Brit.), art d; WHOLE TRUTH, THE(1958, Brit.), art d; EXPRESSO BONGO(1959, Brit.), art d; FACES IN THE DARK(1960, Brit.), art d; DAY THE EARTH CAUGHT FIRE, THE(1961, Brit.), art d; STOP ME BEFORE I KILL!(1961, Brit.), art d; UNSTOPPABLE MAN, THE(1961, Brit.), art d; LIFE IS A CIRCUS(1962, Brit.), art d; GET ON WITH IT(1963, Brit.), art d; MOON-SPINNERS, THE(1964), art d; TAMAHINE(1964, Brit.), art d; WHY BOTHER TO KNOCK(1964, Brit.), art d; HEROES OF

TELEMARK, THE(1965, Brit.), art d; 2001: A SPACE ODYSSEY(1968, U.S./Brit.), prod d; ADVENTURERS, THE(1970), prod d; CRY OF THE PENGUINS(1972, Brit.), art d; Z.P.G.(1972), prod d; THAT LUCKY TOUCH(1975, Brit.), prod d; DEEP, THE(1977), prod d
Debora Masterson
SAMMY STOPS THE WORLD zero(1978)
Graham Masterson
MANITOU, THE(1978), w
Natalie Masterson
MAN IN THE NET, THE(1959)
Paul Masterson
DISC JOCKEY(1951)
Pete Masterson
AMBUSH BAY(1966); COUNTERPOINT(1967)
Peter Masterson
IN THE HEAT OF THE NIGHT(1967); VON RICHTHOFEN AND BROWN(1970); TOMORROW(1972); MAN ON A SWING(1974); STEPFORD WIVES, THE(1975); BEST LITTLE WHOREHOUSE IN TEXAS, THE(1982), w
Rod Masterson
WALK PROUD(1979)
1984
TIGHTROPE(1984)
Sean Masterson
Misc. Talkies
FATAL GAMES(1983); KILLING TOUCH, THE(1983)
Valerie Masterson
MIKADO, THE(1967, Brit.)
Whit Masterson
CRY IN THE NIGHT, A(1956), w; TOUCH OF EVIL(1958), w; YELLOW CANARY, THE(1963), w; WARNING SHOT(1967), w
Willy Masterson
KENNY AND CO.(1976)
Kim Masterton
THAT SINKING FEELING(1979, Brit.)
Luigi Mastoianni
TURN ON TO LOVE(1969)
Nico Mastorakis
GREEK TYCOON, THE(1978), w; BLOOD TIDE(1982), p, w; NEXT ONE, THE(1982, U.S./Gr.), d&w
1984
BLIND DATE(1984), p&d, w
Leo Mastovoy
ONE GIRL'S CONFESSION(1953)
Augusto Mastrantoni
HEART AND SOUL(1950, Ital.); PRIEST'S WIFE, THE(1971, Ital./Fr.)
Mario Mastrantonio
SEVEN DWARFS TO THE RESCUE, THE(1965, Ital.)
Mary Elizabeth Mastrantonio
SCARFACE(1983)
Francesco Mastriani
BURIED ALIVE(1951, Ital.), w; DEAD WOMAN'S KISS, A(1951, Ital.), w
Ruggero Mastroianni
QUIET PLACE IN THE COUNTRY, A(1970, Ital./Fr.), ed
Dick Mastro
GOLDEN GLOVES STORY, THE(1950)
Ruggero Mastroainni
WE STILL KILL THE OLD WAY(1967, Ital.), ed
Camilio Mastrocinque
DUEL WITHOUT HONOR(1953, Ital.), d, w; LADY DOCTOR, THE(1963, Fr./Ital./Span.), d
Camille Mastrocinque
FEDORA(1946, Ital.), d
Camillio Mastrocinque
CUCKOO CLOCK, THE(1938, Ital.), d
Camillo Mastrocinque
EIGHTEEN IN THE SUN(1964, Ital.), d
Misc. Talkies
TERROR IN THE CRYPT(1963, Span./Ital.), d; ANGEL FOR SATAN, AN(1966, Ital.), d
Armand Mastroianni
HE KNOWS YOU'RE ALONE(1980), d; KILLING HOUR, THE(1982), d
Joe Mastroianni
1984
CITY GIRL, THE(1984)
Marcello Mastroianni
SENSUALITA(1954, Ital.); TOO BAD SHE'S BAD(1954, Ital.); LUCKY TO BE A WOMAN(1955, Ital.); MILLER'S WIFE, THE(1957, Ital.); ANATOMY OF LOVE(1959, Ital.); BIG DEAL ON MADONNA STREET, THE(1960); WHERE THE HOT WIND BLOWS(1960, Fr., Ital.); ASSASSIN, THE(1961, Ital./Fr.); LA DOLCE VITA(1961, Ital./Fr.); LA NOTTE(1961, Fr./Ital.); WHITE NIGHTS(1961, Ital.); BELL' ANTONIO(1962, Ital.); DIVORCE, ITALIAN STYLE(1962, Ital.); VERY PRIVATE AFFAIR, A(1962, Fr./Ital.); FAMILY DIARY(1963 Ital.); 8 ½(1963, Ital.); LOVE ON THE RIVIERA(1964, Fr./Ital.); MARRIAGE–ITALIAN STYLE(1964, Fr./Ital.); ORGANIZER, THE(1964, Fr./Ital./Yugo.); YESTERDAY, TODAY, AND TOMORROW(1964, Ital./Fr.); CASANOVA '70(1965, Ital.); LOVE A LA CARTE(1965, Ital.); TENTH VICTIM, THE(1965, Fr./Ital.); POPPY IS ALSO A FLOWER, THE(1966); SHOOT LOUD, LOUDER... I DON'T UNDERSTAND(1966, Ital.); MY WIFE'S ENEMY(1967, Ital.); STRANGER, THE(1967, Algeria/Fr./Ital.); DIAMONDS FOR BREAKFAST(1968, Brit.); KISS THE OTHER SHEIK(1968, Fr./Ital.); MAN WITH THE BALLOONS, THE(1968, Ital./Fr.); GHOSTS, ITALIAN STYLE(1969, Ital./Fr.); PLACE FOR LOVERS, A(1969, Ital./Fr.); LEO THE LAST(1970, Brit.); MOTIVE WAS JEALOUSY, THE(1970 Ital./Span.); PIZZA TRIANGLE, THE(1970, Ital./Span.); SUNFLOWER(1970, Fr./Ital.); IT ONLY HAPPENS TO OTHERS(1971, Fr./Ital.); PRIEST'S WIFE, THE(1971, Ital./Fr.); ROMA(1972, Ital./Fr.); CHE?(1973, Ital./Fr./Ger.); LA GRANDE BOUFFE(1973, Fr.); MASSACRE IN ROME(1973, Ital.); DON'T TOUCH WHITE WOMEN!(1974, Fr.); ROCCO PAPALEO(1974, Ital./Fr.); DOWN THE ANCIENT STAIRCASE(1975, Ital.); LIZA(1976, Fr./Ital.); GOODNIGHT, LADIES AND GENTLEMEN(1977, Ital.); SPECIAL DAY, A(1977, Ital./Can.); BLOOD FEUD(1979, Ital.); DIVINE NYMPH, THE(1979, Ital.); WIFEMISTRESS(1979, Ital.); CITY OF WOMEN(1980, Ital./Fr.); LA NUIT DE VARENNES(1983, Fr./Ital.)

1984
GABRIELA(1984, Braz.)
Ruggero Mastroianni
ASSASSIN, THE(1961, Ital./Fr.), ed; FOUR DAYS OF NAPLES, THE(1963, US/Ital.), ed; SLAVE, THE(1963, Ital.), ed; DISORDER(1964, Fr./Ital.), ed; ORGANIZER, THE(1964, Fr./Ital./Yugo.), ed; JULIET OF THE SPIRITS(1965, Fr./Ital./W.Ger.), ed; TENTH VICTIM, THE(1965, Fr./Ital.), ed; TIME OF INDIFFERENCE(1965, Fr./Ital.), ed; WHITE VOICES(1965, Fr./Ital.), ed; SHOOT LOUD, LOUDER... I DON'T UNDERSTAND(1966, Ital.), ed; MADE IN ITALY(1967, Fr./Ital.), ed; MAIDEN FOR A PRINCE, A(1967, Fr./Ital.), ed; STRANGER, THE(1967, Algeria/Fr./Ital.), ed; GIRL WITH A PISTOL, THE(1968, Ital.), ed; QUEENS, THE(1968, Ital./Fr.), ed; FELLINI SATYRICON(1969, Fr./Ital.), ed; LISTEN, LET'S MAKE LOVE(1969, Fr./Ital.), ed; SPIRITS OF THE DEAD(1969, Fr./Ital.), ed; INVESTIGATION OF A CITIZEN ABOVE SUSPICION(1970, Ital.), ed; DEATH IN VENICE(1971, Ital./Fr.), ed; LADY LIBERTY(1972, Ital./Fr.), ed; ROMA(1972, Ital./Fr.), ed; LUDWIG(1973, Ital./Ger./Fr.), ed; DON'T TOUCH WHITE WOMEN!(1974, Fr.), ed; RE: LUCKY LUCIANO(1974, Fr./Ital.), ed; ROCCO PAPALEO(1974, Ital./Fr.), ed; CONVERSATION PIECE(1976, Ital., Fr.), ed; INNOCENT, THE(1979, Ital.), ed; CITY OF WOMEN(1980, Ital./Fr.), ed; EBOLI(1980, Ital.), ed; LOVERS AND LIARS(1981, Ital.), ed; THREE BROTHERS(1982, Ital.), ed; AND THE SHIP SAILS ON(1983, Ital./Fr.), ed; TALES OF ORDINARY MADNESS(1983, Ital.), ed
1984
BIZET'S CARMEN(1984, Fr./Ital.), ed
Ruggiero Mastroianni
CASANOVA '70(1965, Ital.), ed; AMARCORD(1974, Ital.), ed; CASANOVA(1976, Ital.), ed; BYE BYE MONKEY(1978, Ital/Fr.), ed
Frank R. Mastroly
GREAT JOHN L. THE(1945), p
Jerry Masucci
LAST FIGHT, THE(1983), p, w
Aiko Masuda
LAKE, THE(1970, Jap.)
Hiroko Masuda
LAKE, THE(1970, Jap.)
Toshio Masuda
GANGSTER VIP, THE(1968, Jap.), d; TORA! TORA! TORA!(1970, U.S./Jap.), d; PROPHECIES OF NOSTRADAMUS(1974, Jap.), d
Alberto Masulli
SAVAGE PAMPAS(1967, Span./Arg.), ch
Yasuzo Masumura
PASSION(1968, Jap.), d; THOUSAND CRANES(1969, Jap.), d; PLAY IT COOL(1970, Jap.), d&w; VIXEN(1970, Jap.), d, w
Richard Masur
WHIFFS(1975); BITTERSWEET LOVE(1976); SEMI-TOUGH(1977); WHO'LL STOP THE RAIN?(1978); HANOVER STREET(1979, Brit.); SCAVENGER HUNT(1979); HEAVEN'S GATE(1980); I'M DANCING AS FAST AS I CAN(1982); THING, THE(1982); RISKY BUSINESS(1983); TIMERIDER(1983); UNDER FIRE(1983)
Zenzo Masuyama
DIFFERENT SONS(1962, Jap.), w; DAPHNE, THE(1967), w
Antonio Mata, Jr.
UNDER FIRE(1983)
Cosmo Mata
1984
REPO MAN(1984)
Mata & Hari
MEET THE PEOPLE(1944)
The Matadors
VENOM(1968, Den.), m
The Matadors Band
SATIN MUSHROOM, THE(1969)
Matahi
Silents
TABU(1931)
Virginia Mataix
1984
ESCAPE FROM SEGOVIA(1984, Span.)
Michael Mataka
DUEL IN THE JUNGLE(1954, Brit.)
Eddy Matalon
CATHY'S CURSE(1977, Can.), p, d, w; BLACKOUT(1978, Fr./Can.), p, d
Vivan Matalon
WEAPON, THE(1957, Brit.)
Vivian Matalon
FIRE DOWN BELOW(1957, U.S./Brit.); FLOODS OF FEAR(1958, Brit.); SUBWAY IN THE SKY(1959, Brit.); CRACK IN THE MIRROR(1960); TOO YOUNG TO LOVE(1960, Brit.); KING AND COUNTRY(1964, Brit.)
Richard Matamoros
SHORT EYES(1977)
Clelia Matania
MELODY OF MY HEART(1936, Brit.); NIGHT RIDE(1937, Brit.); CHILDREN OF CHANCE(1950, Ital.); NEVER TAKE NO FOR AN ANSWER(1952, Brit./Ital.); INDISCRETION OF AN AMERICAN WIFE(1954, U.S./Ital.); WAR AND PEACE(1956, Ital./U.S.); FAREWELL TO ARMS, A(1957); MONTE CARLO STORY, THE(1957, Ital.); SEVEN HILLS OF ROME, THE(1958); FAST AND SEXY(1960, Fr./Ital.); FIVE GOLDEN HOURS(1961, Brit.); NEOPOLITAN CAROUSEL(1961, Ital.); CAPTIVE CITY, THE(1963, Ital.); WASTREL, THE(1963, Ital.); QUEEN OF THE NILE(1964, Ital.); BATTLE OF THE VILLA FIORITA, THE(1965, Brit.); CONQUERED CITY(1966, Ital.); SECRET OF SANTA VITTORIA, THE(1969); DON'T LOOK NOW(1973, Brit./Ital.); NELSON AFFAIR, THE(1973, Brit.); JUST BEFORE NIGHTFALL(1975, Fr./Ital.)
Larry Matanski
WINGS OF CHANCE(1961, Can.), p; NAKED FLAME, THE(1970, Can.), p&d
Raffaello Matarazzo
RICE GIRL(1963, Fr./Ital.), d; SHIP OF CONDEMNED WOMEN, THE(1963, ITAL.), d, w
Lawrence Matarese
LOVELESS, THE(1982)
Matasburo
BUDDHA(1965, Jap.)

Barbara Matatian
Misc. Silents
POWER OF EVIL(1929, USSR/Armenian)
Mamea Mataumua
RETURN TO PARADISE(1953)
John Matautani
NAVY WIFE(1956)
Jim Mataya
BALTIMORE BULLET, THE(1980)
Earl Matcalfe
Misc. Silents
DARKNESS BEFORE DAWN, THE(1915)
Matchbox
DIMBOOLA(1979, Aus.)
Christie Matchett
ILLUSTRATED MAN, THE(1969)
Cryn Matchinga
UP THE SANDBOX(1972)
Guy Matchoro
1984
LES COMPERES(1984, Fr.)
Jeno Mate
DIME WITH A HALO(1963); LILITH(1964)
Rudloph Mate
IT HAD TO BE YOU(1947), ph
Rudolf Mate
SAHARA(1943), ph
Rudolph Mate
ARENT WE ALL?(1932, Brit.), ph; VAMPYR(1932, Fr./Ger.), ph; LE DENIER MILLIARDAIRE(1934, Fr.), ph; DANTE'S INFERNO(1935), ph; DRESSED TO THRILL(1935), ph; LILIOM(1935, Fr.), ph; METROPOLITAN(1935), ph; CHARLIE CHAN'S SECRET(1936), ph; COME AND GET IT(1936), ph; DODSWORTH(1936), ph; MESSAGE TO GARCIA, A(1936), ph; NAVY WIFE(1936), ph; OUR RELATIONS(1936), ph; PROFESSIONAL SOLDIER(1936), ph; OUTCAST(1937), ph; STELLA DALLAS(1937), ph; ADVENTURES OF MARCO POLO, THE(1938), ph; TRADE WINDS(1938), ph; YOUTH TAKES A FLING(1938), ph; LOVE AFFAIR(1939), ph; REAL GLORY, THE(1939), ph; FOREIGN CORRESPONDENT(1940), ph; MY FAVORITE WIFE(1940), ph; SEVEN SINNERS(1940), ph; FLAME OF NEW ORLEANS, THE(1941), ph; IT STARTED WITH EVE(1941), ph; THAT HAMILTON WOMAN(1941), ph; PRIDE OF THE YANKEES, THE(1942), ph; TO BE OR NOT TO BE(1942), ph; THEY GOT ME COVERED(1943), ph; ADDRESS UNKNOWN(1944), ph; COVER GIRL(1944), ph; OVER 21(1945), ph; DOWN TO EARTH(1947), ph; IT HAD TO BE YOU(1947), d; DARK PAST, THE(1948), d; RETURN OF OCTOBER, THE(1948), p; D.O.A.(1950), d; NO SAD SONGS FOR ME(1950), d; UNION STATION(1950), d; BRANDED(1951), d; PRINCE WHO WAS A THIEF, THE(1951), d; WHEN WORLDS COLLIDE(1951), d; GREEN GLOVE, THE(1952), d; PAULA(1952), d; SALLY AND SAINT ANNE(1952), d; FORBIDDEN(1953), d; MISSISSIPPI GAMBLER, THE(1953), d; SECOND CHANCE(1953), d; BLACK SHIELD OF FALWORTH, THE(1954), d; SIEGE AT RED RIVER, THE(1954), d; FAR HORIZONS, THE(1955), d; VIOLENT MEN, THE(1955), d; MIRACLE IN THE RAIN(1956), d; PORT AFRIQUE(1956, Brit.), d; RAWHIDE YEARS, THE(1956), d; THREE VIOLENT PEOPLE(1956), d; DEEP SIX, THE(1958), d; FOR THE FIRST TIME(1959, U.S./Ger./Ital.), d; 300 SPARTANS, THE(1962), p, d; SEVEN SEAS TO CALAIS(1963, Ital.), d
Misc. Talkies
ALIKI-MY LOVE(1963, U.S./Gr.), d
Silents
PASSION OF JOAN OF ARC, THE(1928, Fr.), ph
Rudy Mate
BLOCKADE(1938), ph; TONIGHT AND EVERY NIGHT(1945), ph; GILDA(1946), ph
Michael Matee
SHOCK WAVES(1977), set d
Adam Matejka
SHOP ON MAIN STREET, THE(1966, Czech.)
Pavla Matejovska
OPERATION DAYBREAK(1976, U.S./Brit./Czech.)
Robert Matek
ENSIGN PULVER(1964)
Matthew C. Matenazo
WORLD ACCORDING TO GARP, The(1982)
Miguel "Miguelin" Mateo
MOMENT OF TRUTH, THE(1965, Ital./Span.)
Antonio Mateos
RETURN OF THE SEVEN(1966, Span.), set d; KRAKATOA, EAST OF JAVA(1969), set d; PATTON(1970), set d
Antonios Mateos
SPIKES GANG, THE(1974), set d
Julian Mateos
UNSATISFIED, THE(1964, Span.); RETURN OF THE SEVEN(1966, Span.); 10:30 P.M. SUMMER(1966, U.S./Span.); HELLBENDERS, THE(1967, U.S./Ital./Span.); SHALAKO(1968, Brit.); FOUR RODE OUT(1969, US/Span.); CATLOW(1971, Span.); DEMON WITCH CHILD(1974, Span.); GOLDEN VOYAGE OF SINBAD, THE(1974, Brit.), set d; MARCH OR DIE(1977, Brit.), set d
1984
HOLY INNOCENTS, THE(1984, Span.), p
Sara Mateos
SLAUGHTER(1972), makeup
Giovanni Materassi
PRISONER OF THE IRON MASK(1962, Fr./Ital.); LEOPARD, THE(1963, Ital.)
Jose Luis Matesanz
NEST, THE(1982, Span.), ed
1984
IT'S NEVER TOO LATE(1984, Span.), ed
Alberto Mateu
DANCERS IN THE DARK(1932)
Maureen Math
BURY ME AN ANGEL(1972)
Edouard Mathe
Misc. Silents
VENDEMIAIRE(1919, Fr.)

Rose Mathe
MONEY ON THE STREET(1930, Aust.)
Jack Matheis
Misc. Silents
HEART SPECIALIST, THE(1922)
Rene Mathelin
ADIEU PHILLIPINE(1962, Fr./Ital.), ph; DON'T PLAY WITH MARTIANS(1967, Fr.), ph; VERY HAPPY ALEXANDER(1969, Fr.), ph; TALL BLOND MAN WITH ONE BLACK SHOE, THE(1973, Fr.), ph; MAGNIFICENT ONE, THE(1974, Fr./Ital.), ph
Mahdu Mathen
CHILDREN OF THE DAMNED(1963, Brit.)
Jerry Matheny
TENDER MERCIES(1982)
Nicos Matheos
ANNA OF RHODES(1950, Gr.)
Anna Mather
Misc. Silents
CHARLATAN, THE(1916, Brit.)
Anne Mather
LEOPARD IN THE SNOW(1979, Brit./Can.), w
Aubrey Mather
YOUNG WOODLEY(1930, Brit.); ARENT WE ALL?(1932, Brit.); LOVE ON THE SPOT(1932, Brit.); WOMAN IN CHAINS(1932, Brit.); BE MINE TONIGHT(1933, Brit.); ADMIRAL'S SECRET, THE(1934, Brit.); LASH, THE(1934, Brit.); MAN WHO CHANGED HIS NAME, THE(1934, Brit.); ANYTHING MIGHT HAPPEN(1935, Brit.); SILENT PASSENGER, THE(1935, Brit.); AS YOU LIKE IT(1936, Brit.); BALL AT SAVOY(1936, Brit.); CHICK(1936, Brit.); MAN IN THE MIRROR, THE(1936, Brit.); RED WAGON(1936); LIFE BEGINS WITH LOVE(1937); SABOTAGE(1937, Brit.); UNDERNEATH THE ARCHES(1937, Brit.); JAMAICA INN(1939, Brit.); JUST WILLIAM(1939, Brit.); ARISE, MY LOVE(1940); CAPTAIN CAUTION(1940); EARL OF PUDDLESTONE(1940); NO, NO NANETTE(1940); BALL OF FIRE(1941); DR. JEKYLL AND MR. HYDE(1941); RAGE IN HEAVEN(1941); SUSPICION(1941); AFFAIRS OF MARTHA, THE(1942); CAREFUL, SOFT SHOULDERS(1942); GREAT IMPERSONATION, THE(1942); MRS. MINIVER(1942); RANDOM HARVEST(1942); THIS ABOVE ALL(1942); UNDYING MONSTER, THE(1942); WHEN KNIGHTS WERE BOLD(1942, Brit.); WIFE TAKES A FLYER, THE(1942); YANK AT ETON, A(1942); FOREVER AND A DAY(1943); HEAVEN CAN WAIT(1943); HELLO, FRISCO, HELLO(1943); SONG OF BERNADETTE, THE(1943); JANE EYRE(1944); LODGER, THE(1944); NATIONAL VELVET(1944); WILSON(1944); HOUSE OF FEAR, THE(1945); MIGHTY MCGURK, THE(1946); TEMPTATION(1946); FOR THE LOVE OF RUSTY(1947); HUCKSTERS, THE(1947); IT HAPPENED IN BROOKLYN(1947); JOAN OF ARC(1948); JULIA MISBEHAVES(1948); ADVENTURES OF DON JUAN(1949); EVERYBODY DOES IT(1949); SECRET GARDEN, THE(1949); SECRET OF ST. IVES, THE(1949); THAT FORSYTE WOMAN(1949); IMPORTANCE OF BEING EARNEST, THE(1952, Brit.); FAST AND LOOSE(1954, Brit.); GOLDEN MASK, THE(1954, Brit.); CASH ON DELIVERY(1956, Brit.)
Berkely Mather
GENGHIS KHAN(U.S./Brit./Ger./Yugo), w; INFORMATION RECEIVED(1962, Brit.), w; LONG SHIPS, THE(1964, Brit./Yugo.), w
Berkley Mather
DR. NO(1962, Brit.), w
Charles Mather
Misc. Silents
RIGHT OFF THE BAT(1915)
George Mather
OUTSIDE THE LAW(1956); HELL BOUND(1957); RING OF TERROR(1962)
George E. Mather
GALAXINA(1980)
George Edward Mather
BLACKJACK KETCHUM, DESPERADO(1956)
Jack Mather
JACKPOT, THE(1950); LET'S MAKE IT LEGAL(1951); DREAMBOAT(1952); VICKI(1953); BROKEN LANCE(1954); DESIREE(1954); RIVER OF NO RETURN(1954); HOW TO BE VERY, VERY, POPULAR(1955); TALL MEN, THE(1955); VIEW FROM POMPEY'S HEAD, THE(1955); FOUR GIRLS IN TOWN(1956); MAN IN THE GREY FLANNEL SUIT, THE(1956); REVOLT OF MAMIE STOVER, THE(1956); DEADLY MANTIS, THE(1957); KISS THEM FOR ME(1957); MY MAN GODFREY(1957); BRAVADOS, THE(1958); THIS EARTH IS MINE(1959); SQUARES(1972); DERANGED(1974, Can.); SILVER STREAK(1976); MIDDLE AGE CRAZY(1980, Can.)
1984
MRS. SOFFEL(1984)
Jerry Mather
MEN OF THE FIGHTING LADY(1954); BIGGER THAN LIFE(1956)
John Mather
CONFESSION(1937); JUNGLE BOOK(1942); THEY GOT ME COVERED(1943)
John C. Mather
SATELLITE IN THE SKY(1956), w
Marian Mather
BEWARE OF CHILDREN(1961, Brit.)
Graham Matherick
ELIZA FRASER(1976, Aus.), a, spec eff
Don Mathers
TOUGHEST MAN ALIVE(1955)
James Mathers
DR. JEKYLL'S DUNGEON OF DEATH(1982), a, w
Jerry Mathers
THIS IS MY LOVE(1954); SEVEN LITTLE FOYS, THE(1955); TROUBLE WITH HARRY, THE(1955); THAT CERTAIN FEELING(1956); SHADOW ON THE WINDOW, THE(1957); DEEP SIX, THE(1958)
Jimmy Mathers
SUMMER MAGIC(1963); MAIL ORDER BRIDE(1964); NEW INTERNS, THE(1964)
Susie Mathers
THIS IS MY LOVE(1954)
Arno Mathes
MARRIAGE OF MARIA BRAUN, THE(1979, Ger.), set d
Marissa Mathes
PHANTOM PLANET, THE(1961); BLOOD BATH(1966); RIDE BEYOND VENGEANCE(1966)

Peter Mathes
BEFORE WINTER COMES(1969, Brit.)
Prof. Mathesius
INSPECTOR GENERAL, THE(1937, Czech.), w
Ali Matheson
SOMEWHERE IN TIME(1980)
Bryan Matheson
MEMOIRS OF A SURVIVOR(1981, Brit.)
C.M. Matheson
FEATHER, THE(1929, Brit.), w
Don Matheson
MURPH THE SURF(1974)
Doug Matheson
HARD RIDE, THE(1971)
Joan Matheson
CLEANING UP(1933, Brit.); WHEN LONDON SLEEPS(1934, Brit.)
Judy Matheson
LUST FOR A VAMPIRE(1971, Brit.); TWINS OF EVIL(1971, Brit.); CONFESSIONS OF A WINDOW CLEANER(1974, Brit.); HOUSE THAT VANISHED, THE(1974, Brit.)
Margaret Matheson
ALL THINGS BRIGHT AND BEAUTIFUL(1979, Brit.), p; STRONGER THAN THE SUN(1980, Brit.), p
Muir Matheson
KNIGHT WITHOUT ARMOR(1937, Brit.), md; ON APPROVAL(1944, Brit.), md; BEDEVILLED(1955), md; AFTER THE BALL(1957, Brit.), m; NIGHT TO REMEMBER, A(1958, Brit.), md; HIDE AND SEEK(1964, Brit.), m; LORD JIM(1965, Brit.), md; MC GUIRE, GO HOME!(1966, Brit.), md; YOU CAN'T WIN 'EM ALL(1970, Brit.), md
Murray Matheson
JOHNNY IN THE CLOUDS(1945, Brit.); JOURNEY TOGETHER(1946, Brit.); SCHOOL FOR SECRETS(1946, Brit.); FOOL AND THE PRINCESS, THE(1948, Brit.); HURRICANE SMITH(1952); PLYMOUTH ADVENTURE(1952); BOTANY BAY(1953); FLIGHT TO TANGIER(1953); JAMAICA RUN(1953); KING OF THE KHYBER RIFLES(1953); BAMBOO PRISON, THE(1955); LOVE IS A MANY-SPLENDORED THING(1955); WALL OF NOISE(1963); SIGNPOST TO MURDER(1964); ASSAULT ON A QUEEN(1966); IN ENEMY COUNTRY(1968); STAR!(1968); EXPLOSION(1969, Can.); HOW TO SUCCEED IN BUSINESS WITHOUT REALLY TRYING(1976); RABBIT TEST(1978); TWILIGHT ZONE–THE MOVIE(1983)
Richard Matheson
INCREDIBLE SHRINKING MAN, THE(1957), w; BEAT GENERATION, THE(1959), w; HOUSE OF USHER(1960), w; MASTER OF THE WORLD(1961), w; PIT AND THE PENDULUM, THE(1961), w; BURN WITCH BURN(1962), w; RAVEN, THE(1963), w; COMEDY OF TERRORS, THE(1964), p, w; LAST MAN ON EARTH, THE(1964, U.S./Ital.), w; DIE, DIE, MY DARLING(1965, Brit.), w; YOUNG WARRIORS, THE(1967), w; DEVIL'S BRIDE, THE(1968, Brit.), w; IT'S ALIVE(1968), w; DE SADE(1969), w; OMEGA MAN, THE(1971), w; LEGEND OF HELL HOUSE, THE(1973, Brit.), w; COLD SWEAT(1974, Ital., Fr.), w; SOMEWHERE IN TIME(1980), a, w; INCREDIBLE SHRINKING WOMAN, THE(1981), w; JAWS 3-D(1983), w; TWILIGHT ZONE–THE MOVIE(1983), w
Tim Matheson
MAGNUM FORCE(1973); ALMOST SUMMER(1978); NATIONAL LAMPOON'S ANIMAL HOUSE(1978); APPLE DUMPLING GANG RIDES AGAIN, THE(1979); DREAMER(1979); 1941(1979); LITTLE SEX, A(1982); TO BE OR NOT TO BE(1983)
1984
FLETCH(1984); HOUSE OF GOD, THE(1984); IMPULSE(1984); UP THE CREEK(1984)
Misc. Talkies
HOUSE OF GOD, THE(1979)
Ray Mathew
SAY HELLO TO YESTERDAY(1971, Brit.), w
A. E. Mathews
GREAT MR. HANDEL, THE(1942, Brit.); AROUND THE WORLD IN 80 DAYS(1956)
Al Mathews
HIGH CONQUEST(1947)
Allen Mathews
LAST GANGSTER, THE(1937); SHE LOVED A FIREMAN(1937); JOHNNY O'CLOCK(1947); KILROY WAS HERE(1947); BLONDIE'S SECRET(1948); FORCE OF EVIL(1948); SIXTEEN FATHOMS DEEP(1948); SOUTHERN YANKEE, A(1948); HOLIDAY AFFAIR(1949); MUTINEERS, THE(1949); SCENE OF THE CRIME(1949); UNDERCOVER MAN, THE(1949); DAVID HARDING, COUNTERSPY(1950); WELL, THE(1951); MY SIX CONVICTS(1952); LAS VEGAS SHAKEDOWN(1955)
Arthur Mathews
Misc. Silents
COURAGE AND THE MAN(1915)
Arthur W. Mathews
Misc. Silents
IGNORANCE(1916)
Bobby Mathews
SHE FREAK(1967)
Brendan Mathews
OF HUMAN BONDAGE(1964, Brit.); VIKING QUEEN, THE(1967, Brit.); MC KENZIE BREAK, THE(1970); QUACKSER FORTUNE HAS A COUSIN IN THE BRONX(1970); UNDERGROUND(1970, Brit.)
Carl Mathews
FIGHTING CABALLERO(1935); RED BLOOD OF COURAGE(1935); ROUGH RIDING RANGER(1935); MOONLIGHT ON THE RANGE(1937); SINGING BUCKAROO, THE(1937); ON THE GREAT WHITE TRAIL(1938); RANGER'S ROUNDUP, THE(1938); SIX SHOOTIN' SHERIFF(1938); SONGS AND BULLETS(1938); CODE OF THE CACTUS(1939); CODE OF THE FEARLESS(1939); FEUD OF THE RANGE(1939); FLAMING LEAD(1939); IN OLD MONTANA(1939); KNIGHT OF THE PLAINS(1939); OUTLAW'S PARADISE(1939); SIX-GUN RHYTHM(1939); TEXAS WILDCATS(1939); TRIGGER FINGERS ½(1939); TWO-GUN TROUBADOR(1939); ARIZONA GANGBUSTERS(1940); KID FROM SANTA FE, THE(1940); LAND OF THE SIX GUNS(1940); LIGHTNING STRIKES WEST(1940); RIDERS FROM NOWHERE(1940); SAGEBRUSH FAMILY TRAILS WEST, THE(1940); STRAIGHT SHOOTER(1940); TRAILING DOUBLE TROUBLE(1940); WEST OF PINTO BASIN(1940); KID'S LAST RIDE, THE(1941); LONE RIDER AMBUSHED, THE(1941); RIDERS OF BLACK MOUNTAIN(1941); SADDLE MOUNTAIN ROUNDUP(1941); TONTO BASIN OUTLAWS(1941); TRAIL OF THE SILVER SPURS(1941); TUMBLEDOWN RANCH IN ARIZONA(1941); UNDERGROUND RUSTLERS(1941); WRANGLER'S ROOST(1941); ARIZONA STAGECOACH(1942); BILLY THE KID TRAPPED(1942); HEART OF THE GOLDEN WEST(1942); LAWLESS PLAINSMEN(1942); PRAIRIE PALS(1942); RANGERS TAKE

OVER, THE(1942); ROCK RIVER RENEGADES(1942); TEXAS TO BATAAN(1942); THUNDER RIVER FEUD(1942); BLACK MARKET RUSTLERS(1943); FIGHTING VALLEY(1943); HAUNTED RANCH, THE(1943); LONE STAR TRAIL, THE(1943); TWO FISTED JUSTICE(1943); LOST TRAIL, THE(1945); STARS OVER TEXAS(1946); TUMBLEWEED TRAIL(1946); BUFFALO BILL RIDES AGAIN(1947); FIGHTING VIGILANTES, THE(1947); LAW OF THE LASH(1947); PRAIRIE EXPRESS(1947); RETURN OF THE LASH(1947); SHADOW VALLEY(1947); STAGE TO MESA CITY(1947); WEST TO GLORY(1947); GUN TALK(1948); HAWK OF POWDER RIVER, THE(1948); RANGE RENEGADES(1948); SONG OF THE DRIFTER(1948); WESTWARD TRAIL, THE(1948); RANGE LAND(1949); ARIZONA TERRITORY(1950); FENCE RIDERS(1950); GUNSLINGERS(1950); MARSHAL OF HELDORADO(1950); OUTLAW GOLD(1950); WEST OF WYOMING(1950); MONTANA DESPERADO(1951); NEVADA BADMEN(1951); OKLAHOMA JUSTICE(1951); SKIPALONG ROSEN-BLOOM(1951); ESCAPE TO BURMA(1955)
Misc. Talkies
SIX GUN MESA(1950)

Carmen Mathews
RAGE TO LIVE, A(1965); RABBIT, RUN(1970); SOUNDER(1972)

Carole Mathews
CRY MURDER(1936); GIRL IN THE CASE(1944); MISSING JUROR, THE(1944); SHE'S A SWEETHEART(1944); STRANGE AFFAIR(1944); SWING IN THE SADDLE(1944); TOGETHER AGAIN(1944); I LOVE A MYSTERY(1945); OUTLAWS OF THE ROCKIES(1945); OVER 21(1945); TAHITI NIGHTS(1945); TEN CENTS A DANCE(1945); THOUSAND AND ONE NIGHTS, A(1945); SEALED VERDICT(1948); ACCUSED, THE(1949); CHICAGO DEADLINE(1949); GREAT GATSBY, THE(1949); MASSACRE RIVER(1949); SPECIAL AGENT(1949); NO MAN OF HER OWN(1950); PAID IN FULL(1950); MAN WITH MY FACE, THE(1951); MEET ME AT THE FAIR(1952); RED SNOW(1952); CITY OF BAD MEN(1953); SHARK RIVER(1953); BETRAYED WOMEN(1955); PORT OF HELL(1955); TREASURE OF RUBY HILLS(1955); SWAMP WOMEN(1956); FEMALE FIENDS(1958, Brit.); SHOWDOWN AT BOOT HILL(1958); THIRTEEN FIGHTING MEN(1960); LOOK IN ANY WINDOW(1961); TENDER IS THE NIGHT(1961); MILLION DOLLAR MANHUNT(1962, Brit.)
Misc. Talkies
BLAZING THE WESTERN TRAIL(1945)

David Mathews
SLIGHTLY SCANDALOUS(1946), w; HURRICANE ISLAND(1951), w

Dorcas Mathews
Silents
CAPTIVE GOD, THE(1916)

Dorothy Mathews
DOORWAY TO HELL(1930); SON OF THE GODS(1930); TRUTH ABOUT YOUTH, THE(1930); WAY OF ALL MEN, THE(1930); WIDOW FROM CHICAGO, THE(1930)
Silents
GIRL IN EVERY PORT, A(1928)

Duke [Carl] Mathews
RANGE BUSTERS, THE(1940)

Forrest Mathews
WILD COUNTRY(1947)

Geoffrey Mathews
1984
PLAGUE DOGS, THE(1984, U.S./Brit.)

George Mathews
UP IN ARMS(1944); WILSON(1944); WING AND A PRAYER(1944); CORN IS GREEN, THE(1945); GREAT JOHN L. THE(1945); MOTHER IS A FRESHMAN(1949); LAST OF THE COMANCHES(1952); PAT AND MIKE(1952); SALLY AND SAINT ANNE(1952); YANKEE BUCCANEER(1952); ACT OF LOVE(1953); CITY BENEATH THE SEA(1953); GREAT DIAMOND ROBBERY(1953); MAN WITH THE GOLDEN ARM, THE(1955); LAST WAGON, THE(1956); PROUD ONES, THE(1956); GUNFIGHT AT THE O.K. CORRAL(1957); HELLER IN PINK TIGHTS(1960); GOING HOME(1971)

Gisella Mathews
GOLDEN COACH, THE(1953, Fr./Ital.); FAREWELL TO ARMS, A(1957)

Harriet Mathews
IN NAME ONLY(1939)

Harry C. Mathews
Silents
WELCOME CHILDREN(1921), d

Horace Mathews
SONG OF THE SIERRAS(1946)

James V. Mathews
1984
HOTEL NEW HAMPSHIRE, THE(1984)

Jessie Mathews
FOREVER AND A DAY(1943)

John Mathews
SHOCK CORRIDOR(1963)

Joseph Mathews [Pino Mattei]
SABATA(1969, Ital.)

Joyce Mathews
ARTISTS AND MODELS ABROAD(1938); COCOANUT GROVE(1938); TIP-OFF GIRLS(1938); YOU AND ME(1938); CAFE SOCIETY(1939); MIDNIGHT(1939); MILLION DOLLAR LEGS(1939); NIGHT WORK(1939); SUDDEN MONEY(1939); $1,000 A TOUCHDOWN(1939); THOSE WERE THE DAYS(1940)

June Mathews
CIRCLE CANYON(1934)

Junius Mathews
LINEUP, THE(1958)
Misc. Silents
SILENT WITNESS, THE(1917)

Kerwin Mathews
FIVE AGAINST THE HOUSE(1955); GARMENT JUNGLE, THE(1957); LAST BLITZKRIEG, THE(1958); SEVENTH VOYAGE OF SINBAD, THE(1958); TARAWA BEACHHEAD(1958); MAN ON A STRING(1960); THREE WORLDS OF GULLIVER, THE(1960, Brit.); WARRIOR EMPRESS, THE(1961, Ital./Fr.); JACK THE GIANT KILLER(1962); PIRATES OF BLOOD RIVER, THE(1962, Brit.); MANIAC(1963, Brit.); SHADOW OF EVIL(1967, Fr./Ital.); VISCOUNT, THE(1967, Fr./Span./Ital./Ger.); BOY...A GIRL, A(1969); BARQUERO(1970)

Laura J. Mathews
DEVIL'S PARTNER, THE(1958), w

Lester Mathews
RAVEN, THE(1935); LANCER SPY(1937); EVERYTHING HAPPENS AT NIGHT(1939); NORTHWEST PASSAGE(1940); MAN HUNT(1941); SON OF FURY(1942); STORY OF DR. WASSELL, THE(1944); I LOVE A MYSTERY(1945); MALAYA(1950); WOMAN ON PIER 13, THE(1950); FIVE FINGERS(1952); SANGAREE(1953); DESIREE(1954); PRIZE, THE(1963); GLOBAL AFFAIR, A(1964)
Misc. Talkies
TUGBOAT PRINCESS(1936)

Martin Mathews
LEATHER BOYS, THE(1965, Brit.)

Mary Jo Mathews
TWENTIETH CENTURY(1934)

Nita Mathews
THRILL OF BRAZIL, THE(1946); MISS GRANT TAKES RICHMOND(1949)

Richard Mathews
NELSON AFFAIR, THE(1973, Brit.); COUNT DRACULA AND HIS VAMPIRE BRIDE(1978, Brit.)

Sheila Mathews
STATE FAIR(1962); POSEIDON ADVENTURE, THE(1972); TOWERING INFERNO, THE(1974)

Susan Mathews
80 STEPS TO JONAH(1969)

Tony Mathews
DOGS OF WAR, THE(1980, Brit.); REMEMBRANCE(1982, Brit.)

Walter Mathews
NAKED KISS, THE(1964); LAWYER, THE(1969); NIGHTHAWKS(1981); CANNERY ROW(1982)

Anna Mathias
EATING RAOUL(1982)
1984
NIGHT OF THE COMET(1984)

Bob Mathias
BOB MATHIAS STORY, THE(1954); CHINA DOLL(1958); MINOTAUR, THE(1961, Ital.); IT HAPPENED IN ATHENS(1962)

Frank Mathias
FOR MEN ONLY(1952)

Melba Mathias
BOB MATHIAS STORY, THE(1954)

Reginald Mathias
1984
YR ALCOHOLIG LION(1984, Brit.)

Sean Mathias
PRIEST OF LOVE(1981, Brit.)

Marion Mathie
HONOURABLE MURDER, AN(1959, Brit.); LOLITA(1962); DRACULA HAS RISEN FROM HIS GRAVE(1968, Brit.)

Jack Mathies
Silents
IT CAN BE DONE(1921)

Mattis Mathiesen
SUICIDE MISSION(1956, Brit.), ph

Dock Mathieson
DIVIDED HEART, THE(1955, Brit.), md; SQUARE RING, THE(1955, Brit.), m, md; GENTLE TOUCH, THE(1956, Brit.), md; SHIP THAT DIED OF SHAME, THE(1956, Brit.), md; DECISION AGAINST TIME(1957, Brit.), md; OUT OF THE CLOUDS(1957, Brit.), md; DUNKIRK(1958, Brit.), md; NIGHT FIGHTERS, THE(1960), md; LIGHT IN THE PIAZZA(1962), md

Johanna Mathieson
BROADWAY(1929), cos; MELODY LANE(1929), cos

Muir Mathieson
CATHERINE THE GREAT(1934, Brit.), md; PRIVATE LIFE OF DON JUAN, THE(1934, Brit.), md; SANDERS OF THE RIVER(1935, Brit.), md; SCARLET PIMPERNEL, THE(1935, Brit.), md; GHOST GOES WEST, THE(1936), md; I STAND CONDEMNED(1936, Brit.), md; REMBRANDT(1936, Brit.), md; THINGS TO COME(1936, Brit.), md; ACTION FOR SLANDER(1937, Brit.), m; DARK JOURNEY(1937, Brit.), md; ELEPHANT BOY(1937, Brit.), md; FIRE OVER ENGLAND(1937, Brit.), md; FOREVER YOURS(1937, Brit.), md; MAN WHO COULD WORK MIRACLES, THE(1937, Brit.), md; MEN ARE NOT GODS(1937, Brit.), md; MURDER ON DIAMOND ROW(1937, Brit.), md; STORM IN A TEACUP(1937, Brit.), md; UNDER THE RED ROBE(1937, Brit.), md; DIVORCE OF LADY X. THE(1938, Brit.), md; DRUMS(1938, Brit.), md; GAIETY GIRLS, THE(1938, Brit.), md; RETURN OF THE SCARLET PIMPERNEL(1938, Brit.), md; SOUTH RIDING(1938, Brit.), md; TROOP-SHIP(1938, Brit.), md; CLOUDS OVER EUROPE(1939, Brit.), md; FOUR FEATHERS, THE(1939, Brit.), md; PRISON WITHOUT BARS(1939, Brit.), md; U-BOAT 29(1939, Brit.), md; CONQUEST OF THE AIR(1940), m; LION HAS WINGS, THE(1940), md; OLD BILL AND SON(1940, Brit.), md; OVER THE MOON(1940, Brit.), md; SIDEWALKS OF LONDON(1940, Brit.), md; THIEF OF BAGHDAD, THE(1940, Brit.), md; TWENTY-ONE DAYS TOGETHER(1940, Brit.), md; INVADERS, THE,(1941, Brit.), md; PIMPERNEL SMITH(1942, Brit.), md; SUICIDE SQUADRON(1942, Brit.), md; SPITFIRE(1943, Brit.), md; THIS HAPPY BREED(1944, Brit.), m, md; BLITHE SPIRIT(1945, Brit.), md; VACATION FROM MARRIAGE(1945, Brit.), md; WAY AHEAD, THE(1945, Brit.), md; GREEN FOR DANGER(1946, Brit.), md; HENRY V(1946, Brit.), md; SEVENTH VEIL, THE(1946, Brit.), a, md; CAPTAIN BOYCOTT(1947, Brit.), md; DEAR MURDERER(1947, Brit.), md; END OF THE RIVER, THE(1947, Brit.), md; HUNGRY HILL(1947, Brit.), md; MASTER OF BANKDAM, THE(1947, Brit.), md; ODD MAN OUT(1947, Brit.), md; SCHOOL FOR DANGER(1947, Brit.), md; SILVER DARLINGS, THE(1947, Brit.), md; TAWNY PIPIT(1947, Brit.), md; UPTURNED GLASS, THE(1947, Brit.), md; DULCIMER STREET(1948, Brit.), md; ESCAPE(1948, Brit.), md; GIRL IN THE PAINTING, THE(1948, Brit.), md; HAMLET(1948, Brit.), md; MARK OF CAIN, THE(1948, Brit.), md; MR. PERRIN AND MR. TRAILL(1948, Brit.), md; OCTOBER MAN, THE(1948, Brit.), md; ONE NIGHT WITH YOU(1948, Brit.), md; SMUGGLERS, THE(1948, Brit.), md; SO EVIL MY LOVE(1948, Brit.), md; TAKE MY LIFE(1948, Brit.), md; TROUBLE IN THE AIR(1948, Brit.), md; VICE VERSA(1948, Brit.), md; FACTS OF LOVE(1949, Brit.), md; GAY LADY, THE(1949, Brit.), md; MADNESS OF THE HEART(1949, Brit.), md; ONE WOMAN'S STORY(1949, Brit.), md; QUARTET(1949, Brit.), md; SLEEPING CAR TO TRIESTE(1949, Brit.), md; WEAKER SEX, THE(1949, Brit.), md; WOMAN HATER(1949, Brit.), md; WOMAN IN THE HALL, THE(1949, Brit.), md; BLACK ROSE, THE(1950), md; CURE FOR LOVE,

THE(1950, Brit.), md; GOLDEN SALAMANDER(1950, Brit.), md; MADELEINE(1950, Brit.), md; MINIVER STORY, THE(1950, Brit./U.S.), md; MUDLARK, THE(1950, Brit.), md; PRELUDE TO FAME(1950, Brit.), m; ROCKING HORSE WINNER, THE(1950, Brit.), md; TREASURE ISLAND(1950, Brit.), md; GREAT MANHUNT, THE(1951, Brit.), md; I'LL NEVER FORGET YOU(1951), md; OLIVER TWIST(1951, Brit.), md; THEY WERE NOT DIVIDED(1951, Brit.), md; TOM BROWN'S SCHOOLDAYS(1951, Brit.), md; WOODEN HORSE, THE(1951), md; FAITHFUL CITY(1952, Israel), md; KISENGA, MAN OF AFRICA(1952, Brit.), m; MAGIC BOX, THE(1952, Brit.); PASSIONATE SENTRY, THE(1952, Brit.), m, md; PROMOTER, THE(1952, Brit.), md; STORY OF ROBIN HOOD, THE(1952, Brit.), md; VALLEY OF EAGLES(1952, Brit.), md; WATERFRONT WOMEN(1952, Brit.), md; CAPTAIN'S PARADISE, THE(1953, Brit.), md; MAN BETWEEN, THE(1953, Brit.), md; MASTER OF BALLANTRAE, THE(1953, U.S./Brit.), md; MELBA(1953, Brit.), md; MURDER ON MONDAY(1953, Brit.), md; RINGER, THE(1953, Brit.), md; SAILOR OF THE KING(1953, Brit.), md; VILLAGE, THE(1953, Brit./Switz.), md; DANCE LITTLE LADY(1954, Brit.), md; DOCTOR IN THE HOUSE(1954, Brit.), md; HOBSON'S CHOICE(1954, Brit.), md; HOLLY AND THE IVY, THE(1954, Brit.), md; MALTA STORY(1954, Brit.), md; PURPLE PLAIN, THE(1954, Brit.), md; ROB ROY, THE HIGHLAND ROGUE(1954, Brit.), md; SLEEPING TIGER, THE(1954, Brit.), md; ADVENTURES OF SADIE, THE(1955, Brit.), md; CONSTANT HUSBAND, THE(1955, Brit.), md; DEEP BLUE SEA, THE(1955, Brit.), md; DOCTOR AT SEA(1955, Brit.), md; I AM A CAMERA(1955, Brit.), md; LADY GODIVA RIDES AGAIN(1955, Brit.), md; LAND OF FURY(1955 Brit.), md; PRIZE OF GOLD, A(1955), md; SEA SHALL NOT HAVE THEM, THE(1955, Brit.), md; TECKMAN MYSTERY, THE(1955, Brit.), md; THREE CASES OF MURDER(1955, Brit.), md; WICKED WIFE(1955, Brit.), md; JACQUELINE(1956, Brit.), md; MAN WHO NEVER WAS, THE(1956, Brit.), m; PORT AFRIQUE(1956, Brit.), md; RICHARD III(1956, Brit.), md; SAFARI(1956), md; STAR OF INDIA(1956, Brit.), md; WEE GEORDIE(1956, Brit.), md; ZARAK(1956, Brit.), md; FIRE DOWN BELOW(1957, U.S./Brit.), md; HIGH FLIGHT(1957, Brit.), md; PICKUP ALLEY(1957, Brit.), md; PORTRAIT IN SMOKE(1957, Brit.), md; PRINCE AND THE SHOWGIRL, THE(1957, Brit.), md; REACH FOR THE SKY(1957, Brit.), md; SHE PLAYED WITH FIRE(1957, Brit.), md; SMALLEST SHOW ON EARTH, THE(1957, Brit.), md; SMILEY(1957, Brit.), ed&md; STOWAWAY GIRL(1957, Brit.), md; VALUE FOR MONEY(1957, Brit.), md; ANOTHER TIME, ANOTHER PLACE(1958), md; DANGEROUS EXILE(1958, Brit.), md; HARRY BLACK AND THE TIGER(1958, Brit.), md; HORSE'S MOUTH, THE(1958, Brit.), md; I ACCUSE(1958, Brit.), md; INDISCREET(1958), md; INTENT TO KILL(1958, Brit.), md; LAW AND DISORDER(1958, Brit.), md; MAD LITTLE ISLAND(1958, Brit.), md; MAN INSIDE, THE(1958, Brit.), md; ROONEY(1958, Brit.), md; SAFECRACKER, THE(1958, Brit.), md; SECRET PLACE, THE(1958, Brit.), md; SHERIFF OF FRACTURED JAW, THE(1958, Brit.), md; TALE OF TWO CITIES, A(1958, Brit.), md; TANK FORCE(1958, Brit.), md; TOM THUMB(1958, Brit./U.S.), md; TRUTH ABOUT WOMEN, THE(1958, Brit.), md; WINDOM'S WAY(1958, Brit.), md; BANDIT OF ZHOBE, THE(1959), md; GIDEON OF SCOTLAND YARD(1959, Brit.), md; HORRORS OF THE BLACK MUSEUM(1959, U.S./Brit.), md; SHAKE HANDS WITH THE DEVIL(1959, Ireland), md; SILENT ENEMY, THE(1959, Brit.), md; TWO-HEADED SPY(1959, Brit.), md; CIRCUS OF HORRORS(1960, Brit.), m; GRASS IS GREENER, THE(1960), md; KIDNAPPED(1960), md; KILLERS OF KILIMANJARO(1960, Brit.), md; ONCE MORE, WITH FEELING(1960), md; SINK THE BISMARCK!(1960, Brit.), md; SWISS FAMILY ROBINSON(1960), md; CANADIANS, THE(1961, Brit.), m; KONGA(1961, Brit.), md; LOSS OF INNOCENCE(1961, Brit.), md; NAKED EDGE, THE(1961), md; PORTRAIT OF A SINNER(1961, Brit.), md; SECRET OF MONTE CRISTO, THE(1961, Brit.), md; DESERT PATROL(1962, Brit.), md; HELLIONS, THE(1962, Brit.), md; IN SEARCH OF THE CASTAWAYS(1962, Brit.), md; MAIN ATTRACTION, THE(1962, Brit.), md; ONLY TWO CAN PLAY(1962, Brit.), md; SATAN NEVER SLEEPS(1962), md; WALTZ OF THE TOREADORS(1962, Brit.), md; WAR LOVER, THE(1962, U.S./Brit.), md; WHAT A CARVE UP!(1962, Brit.), m; CALL ME BWANA(1963, Brit.), m; CROOKS ANONYMOUS(1963, Brit.), m, md; HELLFIRE CLUB, THE(1963, Brit.), md; MACBETH(1963), md; MIND BENDERS, THE(1963, Brit.), md; RUNNING MAN, THE(1963, Brit.), md; WOMAN OF STRAW(1964, Brit.), md; UNDERWORLD INFORMERS(1965, Brit.), md; WALK IN THE SHADOW(1966, Brit.), md; MALPAS MYSTERY, THE(1967, Brit.), md; SHALAKO(1968, Brit.), md; MY SIDE OF THE MOUNTAIN(1969), md

William Mathieson
YOU CAN'T HAVE EVERYTHING(1937)

Ginette Mathieu
BLUE COUNTRY, THE(1977, Fr.)

N. Mathieu
CATHY'S CURSE(1977, Can.), p

M. Mathillon
Silents
NAPOLEON(1927, Fr.)

Alfunso Mathis
CHEATERS, THE(1961, Fr.)

Alphonse Mathis
HOUSE OF INTRIGUE, THE(1959, Ital.)

Chris Mathis
Misc. Talkies
WEEKEND LOVER(1969)

Edith Mathis
DER FREISCHUTZ(1970, Ger.); MARRIAGE OF FIGARO, THE(1970, Ger.); YOUNG LORD, THE(1970, Ger.)

Emile Mathis
LES ENFANTS TERRIBLES(1952, Fr.)

Jack Mathis
Silents
BLIND HUSBANDS(1919); DEVIL'S PASSKEY, THE(1920); POISON(1924)

Johnny Mathis
LIZZIE(1957)

June Mathis
Silents
GOD'S HALF ACRE(1916), w; ALADDIN'S OTHER LAMP(1917), w; HIS FATHER'S SON(1917), w; POWER OF DECISION, THE(1917), w; TRAIL OF THE SHADOW, THE(1917), w; EYE FOR EYE(1918), w; KILDARE OF STORM(1918), w; ALMOST MARRIED(1919), w; AMATEUR ADVENTURESS, THE(1919), w; BRAT, THE(1919), w; ISLAND OF INTRIGUE, THE(1919), w; JOHNNY-ON-THE-SPOT(1919), w; CONQUERING POWER, THE(1921), w; FOUR HORSEMEN OF THE APOCALYPSE, THE(1921), w; IDLE RICH, THE(1921), w; MAN WHO, THE(1921), w; SAPHEAD, THE(1921), w; GOLDEN GIFT, THE(1922), w; KISSES(1922), w; SOULS FOR SALE(1923); THREE WISE FOOLS(1923), w; BEN-HUR(1925), w; DESERT FLOWER,

THE(1925), w; GREED(1925), w, t; SALLY(1925), w; FAR CRY, THE(1926), w; IRENE(1926), w; AFFAIR OF THE FOLLIES, AN(1927), w
Misc. Silents
HER SECOND CHANCE(1926), d

Milly Mathis
FROM TOP TO BOTTOM(1933, Fr.); MARIUS(1933, Fr.); CESAR(1936, Fr.); WITH A SMILE(1939, Fr.); WELL-DIGGER'S DAUGHTER, THE(1946, Fr.); FANNY(1948, Fr.)

Sherry Mathis
W. W. AND THE DIXIE DANCEKINGS(1975)

Steve Mathis
WITHOUT WARNING(1980), w

Helen Mathison
HOTEL PARADISO(1966, U.S./Brit.)

Melissa Mathison
BLACK STALLION, THE(1979), w; E.T. THE EXTRA-TERRESTRIAL(1982), w

Mellissa Mathison
ESCAPE ARTIST, THE(1982), w

Paul Mathison
THIRD OF A MAN(1962), art d; NIGHT TIDE(1963), prod d

Vivian Mathison
KID FROM SPAIN, THE(1932)

Jenny Mathot
OLD MOTHER RILEY, HEADMISTRESS(1950, Brit.); PAUL TEMPLE'S TRIUMPH(1951, Brit.)

Leon Mathot
MYSTERY OF THE PINK VILLA, THE(1930, Fr.)
Misc. Silents
LE DROIT A LA VIE(1917, Fr.); EMPIRE OF DIAMONDS, THE(1920); L'AMI FRITZ(1920, Fr.); TRAVAIL(1920, Fr.); BLANCHETTE(1921, Fr.); COEUR FIDELE(1923, Fr.); L'AUBERGE ROUGE(1923, Fr.); YASMINA(1926, Fr.); APPASSIONATA(1929, Fr.), a, d

Oliver Mathot
LAS RATAS NO DUERMEN DE NOCHE(1974, Span./Fr.)

Olivier Mathot
ROYAL AFFAIRS IN VERSAILLES(1957, Fr.); ROAD TO SHAME, THE(1962, Fr.)

Graham Mathrick
PETERSEN(1974, Aus.)

Otto Matiesen
PRISONERS(1929); STRANGE CARGO(1929); CONSPIRACY(1930)
Silents
SCARAMOUCHE(1923); REVELATION(1924); SALVATION HUNTERS, THE(1925); BRIDE OF THE STORM(1926); BELOVED ROGUE, THE(1927); SCARLET LADY, THE(1928)
Misc. Silents
SACKCLOTH AND SCARLET(1925); CHRISTINE OF THE BIG TOPS(1926); DESERT BRIDE, THE(1928); LAST MOMENT, THE(1928); WOMAN FROM MOSCOW, THE(1928); BEHIND CLOSED DOORS(1929)

Otto Matieson
GENERAL CRACK(1929); GOLDEN DAWN(1930); LAST OF THE LONE WOLF(1930); BEAU IDEAL(1931); MALTESE FALCON, THE(1931); MEN OF THE SKY(1931); SOLDIER'S PLAYTHING, A(1931)
Silents
ALIAS THE NIGHT WIND(1923); YELLOW FINGERS(1926)
Misc. Silents
BOSTON BLACKIE(1923); MORALS FOR MEN(1925); WHISPERING WIRES(1926); SURRENDER(1927)

Giovanna Matili
GOLIATH AND THE BARBARIANS(1960, Ital.), cos

Steven Matilla
1984
LAST NIGHT AT THE ALAMO(1984)

Samuel Matiovsky
BIRDS DO IT(1966), m

Bernard Matis
JOHNNY RENO(1966), ed; WACO(1966), ed

Anna Matisse
LOVE IS A SPLENDID ILLUSION(1970, Brit.); PRIVATE LIFE OF SHERLOCK HOLMES, THE(1970, Brit.)

V. Matissen
WAR AND PEACE(1968, USSR)

Arne Matisson
RAILROAD WORKERS(1948, Swed.), d

Kyalo Mativo
ROAR(1981)

Manuel Matji
THAT HOUSE IN THE OUTSKIRTS(1980, Span.), w
1984
HOLY INNOCENTS, THE(1984, Span.), w

George Matkovich
LOVE IS BETTER THAN EVER(1952)

Matty Matlock
PETE KELLY'S BLUES(1955)

Norman Matlock
DANDY, THE ALL AMERICAN GIRL(1976); TAXI DRIVER(1976); THIEVES(1977); FORT APACHE, THE BRONX(1981)
1984
GHOSTBUSTERS(1984)

Spider Matlock
CROWD ROARS, THE(1932)

Samuel Matlofsky
FISH HAWK(1981, Can.), m

Samuel Matlovsky
THIRD OF A MAN(1962), m; NAMU, THE KILLER WHALE(1966), m; GAMES(1967), m; GENTLE GIANT(1967), m, md

Harvey Matofsky
ZANDY'S BRIDE(1974), p

Jeri Matos
SEASIDE SWINGERS(1965, Brit.), w

Michael Matou
1984
MIDSUMMER NIGHT'S DREAM, A(1984, Brit./Span.)
Lida Matouskova
FIFTH HORSEMAN IS FEAR, THE(1968, Czech.)
V. Matov
THEY WANTED PEACE(1940, USSR); WAR AND PEACE(1968, USSR)
Leo V. Matranga
HELLER IN PINK TIGHTS(1960)
Christian Matras
CAFE DE PARIS(1938, Fr.), ph; GRAND ILLUSION(1938, Fr.), ph; END OF A DAY, THE(1939, Fr.), ph; ANGEL AND SINNER(1947, Fr.), ph; LES JEUX SONT FAITS(1947, Fr.), ph; IDIOT, THE(1948, Fr.), ph; GYPSY FURY(1950, Fr.), ph; FAN-FAN THE TULIP(1952, Fr.), ph; LUCRECE BORGIA(1953, Ital./Fr.), ph; DAUGH-TERS OF DESTINY(1954, Fr./Ital.), ph; EARRINGS OF MADAME DE..., THE(1954, Fr.), ph; LA RONDE(1954, Fr.), ph; LE PLAISIR(1954, Fr.), ph; MADAME DU BAR-RY(1954 Fr./Ital.), ph; SECRETS D'ALCOVE(1954, Fr./Ital.), ph; LOLA MON-TES(1955, Fr./Ger.), ph; ADORABLE CREATURES(1956, Fr.), ph; FRENCH, THEY ARE A FUNNY RACE, THE(1956, Fr.), ph; NANA(1957, Fr./Ital.), ph; CHRIS-TINE(1959, Fr.), ph; MIRROR HAS TWO FACES, THE(1959, Fr.), ph; GAME OF TRUTH, THE(1961, Fr.), ph; MODIGLIANI OF MONTPARNASSE(1961, Fr./Ital.), ph; PARIS BLUES(1961), ph; CARTOUCHE(1962, Fr./Ital.), ph; CRIME DOES NOT PAY(1962, Fr.), ph; MAXIME(1962, Fr.), ph; DOUBLE DECEPTION(1963, Fr.), ph; FRENCH GAME, THE(1963, Fr.), ph; THERESE(1963, Fr.), ph; SCHEHERAZA-DE(1965, Fr./Ital./Span.), ph; THIS SPECIAL FRIENDSHIP(1967, Fr.), ph; WOMAN TIMES SEVEN(1967, U.S./Fr./Ital.), ph; BIRDS COME TO DIE IN PERU(1968, Fr.), ph; DESPERATE ONES, THE(1968 U.S./Span.), ph; MILKY WAY, THE(1969, Fr./Ital.), ph
Ernest Matray
WHITE CARGO(1942), ch; STEP LIVELY(1944), ch; GEORGE WHITE'S SCAN-DALS(1945), ch
Misc. Talkies
ADVENTURE IN MUSIC(1944), d
Ernst Matray
BITTER SWEET(1940), ch; DANCE, GIRL, DANCE(1940), ch; FLORIAN(1940), ch; PRIDE AND PREJUDICE(1940), ch; WATERLOO BRIDGE(1940), ch; CHOCOLATE SOLDIER, THE(1941), ch; DR. JEKYLL AND MR. HYDE(1941), ch; I MARRIED AN ANGEL(1942), ch; SEVEN SWEETHEARTS(1942), ch; HIGHER AND HIGHER(1943), ch; HUMAN COMEDY, THE(1943), ch; PRESENTING LILY MARS(1943), ch; SWING FEVER(1943), ch
Maria Matray
SWING FEVER(1943), ch; MURDER IN THE MUSIC HALL(1946), w
Christian Matraz
EAGLE WITH TWO HEADS(1948, Fr.), ph
Leonore Matre
Silents
ON THE STROKE OF THREE(1924)
Matthew Matron
Silents
LADYBIRD, THE(1927)
the Matron
NO TIME FOR TEARS(1957, Brit.)
K. Matrossov
MEN OF THE SEA(1938, USSR)
Patricia Matsdorff
ABSENCE OF MALICE(1981)
Curt Matson
CORPSE GRINDERS, THE(1972)
Harry Matson
THEY ALL LAUGHED(1981)
Norman Matson
HE COULDN'T SAY NO(1938), w; I MARRIED A WITCH(1942), w
Robert Matson
LIFE AND TIMES OF CHESTER-ANGUS RAMSGOOD, THE(1971, Can.)
Chieko Matsubara
GANGSTER VIP, THE(1968, Jap.)
Shue Matsubayashi
I BOMBED PEARL HARBOR(1961, Jap.), d; LAST WAR, THE(1962, Jap.), d
Hiroo Matsuda
MESSAGE FROM SPACE(1978, Jap.), w
Sadatsugu Matsuda
TRAITORS(1957, Jap.), d
Tommy Matsuda
WAR HUNT(1962)
Yusaku Matsuda
1984
FAMILY GAME, THE(1984, Jap.)
Yoichi Matsue
WIND CANNOT READ, THE(1958, Brit.)
George Matsui
HELL TO ETERNITY(1960); WALK, DON'T RUN(1966)
Hachiro Matsui
NIGHT IN HONG KONG, A(1961, Jap.), m; STAR OF HONG KONG(1962, Jap.), m; HONOLULU-TOKYO-HONG KONG(1963, Hong Kong/Jap.), m; SIEGE OF FORT BISMARK(1968, Jap.), m
Kenzo Matsui
SANJURO(1962, Jap.)
S. Matsui
HELL AND HIGH WATER(1933)
Suisei Matsui
TOKYO FILE 212(1951)
Yasuko Matsui
KURAGEJIMA-LEGENDS FROM A SOUTHERN ISLAND(1970, Jap.)
Hiroki Matsukata
HIKEN YABURI(1969, Jap.)
Yasuo Matsukawa
SILENCE HAS NO WINGS(1971, Jap.), p, w

Jack Matsumoto
DIAMOND HEAD(1962)
Kaoru Matsumoto
RICKSHAW MAN, THE(1960, Jap.)
Koshiro Matsumoto
CHUSHINGURA(1963, Jap.); SAMURAI ASSASSIN(1965, Jap.); EMPEROR AND A GENERAL, THE(1968, Jap.)
Leiji Matsumoto
GALAXY EXPRESS(1982, Jap.), w
Megumi Matsumoto
NIGHT OF THE SEAGULL, THE(1970, Jap.)
Noriko Matsumoto
WEIRD LOVE MAKERS, THE(1963, Jap.)
Seicho Matsumoto
DEATH ON THE MOUNTAIN(1961, Jap.), w
Susie Matsumoto
JAPANESE WAR BRIDE(1952)
Narahiro Matsumura
JUDO SHOWDOWN(1966, Jap.), w
Tatsuo Matsumura
KING KONG VERSUS GODZILLA(1963, Jap.); REBELLION(1967, Jap.); HIKEN YABURI(1969, Jap.)
Teizo Matsumura
SILENCE HAS NO WINGS(1971, Jap.), m
Yasuyo Matsumura
SECRETS OF A WOMAN'S TEMPLE(1969, Jap.)
Craig Matsunaga
WALK, DON'T RUN(1966)
Kayo Matsuo
GATE OF FLESH(1964, Jap.); GANGSTER VIP, THE(1968, Jap.); SHOGUN ASSAS-SIN(1980, Jap.)
Toshi Matsuo
EYES OF LAURA MARS(1978)
Eisaku Matsura
ISLAND, THE(1962, Jap.), p
Tsukie Matsura
LIFE OF OHARU(1964, Jap.)
David Matsushama
THREE CAME HOME(1950)
Harris Matsushige
HOUSE OF BAMBOO(1955)
Kenro Matsuura
KOJIRO(1967, Jap.), w; BAND OF ASSASSINS(1971, Jap.), w
Takero Matsuura
MAN IN THE STORM, THE(1969, Jap.), w
Shoji Matsuyama
LIVE YOUR OWN WAY(1970, Jap.)
So Matsuyama
RASHOMON(1951, Jap.), art d; SEVEN SAMURAI, THE(1956, Jap.), art d; IKI-RU(1960, Jap.), art d; IDIOT, THE(1963, Jap.), art d; STRAY DOG(1963, Jap.), art d
Takashi Matsuyama
TEMPTRESS AND THE MONK, THE(1963, Jap.), art d; SCARLET CAMELLIA, THE(1965, Jap.), art d
Yoko Matsuyama
JUDO SHOWDOWN(1966, Jap.)
Zenzo Matsuyama
HUMAN CONDITION, THE(1959, Jap.), w; ETERNITY OF LOVE(1961, Jap.), w; HAPPINESS OF US ALONE(1962, Jap.), d&w; ROAD TO ETERNITY(1962, Jap.), w; WISER AGE(1962, Jap.), w; HONOLULU-TOKYO-HONG KONG(1963, Hong Kong/Jap.), w; MY HOBO(1963, Jap.), d&w; YOUTH AND HIS AMULET, THE(1963, Jap.), w; YEARNING(1964, Jap.), w; WE WILL REMEMBER(1966, Jap.), d, w; RIVER OF FOREVER(1967, Jap.), w; MOMENT OF TERROR(1969, Jap.), w; OUR SILENT LOVE(1969, Jap.), d&w; SOLDIER'S PRAYER, A(1970, Jap.), w
Shinjiro Matsuzaki
NAKED YOUTH(1961, Jap.)
Sharon Matt
Misc. Talkies
HANG-UP, THE(1969)
Matt Davidson and Adele
STRANGE CARGO(1936, Brit.)
Paloma Matta
IS PARIS BURNING?(1966, U.S./Fr.)
Arne Mattaon
BREAD OF LOVE, THE(1954, Swed.), d
Ghassan Mattar
CIRCLE OF DECEIT(1982, Fr./Ger.)
Dietrich Mattausch
1984
LOVE IN GERMANY, A(1984, Fr./Ger.)
Mattei
GREAT WHITE, THE(1982, Ital.), ph
Bruno Mattei
1984
CAGED WOMEN(1984, Ital./Fr.), ed
Bruno Mattei [Vincent Dawn or Darum]
NIGHT OF THE ZOMBIES(1983, Span./Ital.), d
Claire Mattei
ANTOINE ET ANTOINETTE(1947 Fr.)
Raifaele Mattela
ACE HIGH(1969, Ital.), w
Anthony Matteo
1984
DELIVERY BOYS(1984); PREPPIES(1984)
Dom Matteo
1984
BROADWAY DANNY ROSE(1984)
Alex Matter
DRIFTER, THE(1966), d&w; SCRATCH HARRY(1969), d, w&ph; SIX PACK(1982), w

Fred Matter
BITTER VICTORY(1958, Fr.)

Lino Mattera
YESTERDAY, TODAY, AND TOMORROW(1964, Ital./Fr.); AFTER THE FOX(1966, U.S./Brit./Ital.)

Kitti Mattern
OLD SHATTERHAND(1968, Ger./Yugo./Fr./Ital.)

Dollie Ledgerwood Matters
Misc. Silents
MOTHER LOVE AND THE LAW(1917)

Graham Matters
20TH CENTURY OZ(1977, Aus.)

Doris Mattes
FEAR EATS THE SOUL(1974, Ger.); WHY DOES HERR R. RUN AMOK?(1977, Ger.)

Eva Mattes
BITTER TEARS OF PETRA VON KANT, THE(1972, Ger.); EFFI BRIEST(1974, Ger.); JAIL BAIT(1977, Ger.); DAVID(1979, Ger.); IN A YEAR OF THIRTEEN MOONS(1980, Ger.); CELESTE(1982, Ger.)
1984
GERMANY PALE MOTHER(1984, Ger.)

Willy Mattes
HEAD, THE(1961, Ger.), m; IT'S HOT IN PARADISE(1962, Ger./Yugo.), m

Ruth Matteson
BIRTH OF A BABY(1938)

Gaetano Matteucci
IL GRIDO(1962, U.S./Ital.)

Robert A. Mattey
ABSENT-MINDED PROFESSOR, THE(1961), spec eff; SON OF FLUBBER(1963), spec eff; MARY POPPINS(1964), spec eff; MONKEY'S UNCLE, THE(1965), spec eff; LT. ROBIN CRUSOE, U.S.N.(1966), spec eff; GNOME-MOBILE, THE(1967), spec eff; LOST CONTINENT, THE(1968, Brit.), spec eff; NEVER A DULL MOMENT(1968), spec eff; SCANDALOUS JOHN(1971), spec eff; WILD COUNTRY, THE(1971), spec eff; JAWS(1975), spec eff; JAWS II(1978), spec eff

Robert Mattey
BLACKBEARD'S GHOST(1968), spec eff

RobertA. Mattey
LOVE BUG, THE(1968), spec eff

Charles Matthau
CHARLEY VARRICK(1973)

Charlie Matthau
HOUSE CALLS(1978)

David Matthau
CONCORDE, THE–AIRPORT '79(; GOODBYE GIRL, THE(1977); CALIFORNIA SUITE(1978); CHEAP DETECTIVE, THE(1978); FM(1978); BATTLESTAR GALACTICA(1979); HOPSCOTCH(1980)

Walter Matthau
TAKING OF PELHAM ONE, TWO, THREE, THE(1974); INDIAN FIGHTER, THE(1955); KENTUCKIAN, THE(1955); BIGGER THAN LIFE(1956); FACE IN THE CROWD, A(1957); SLAUGHTER ON TENTH AVENUE(1957); KING CREOLE(1958); ONIONHEAD(1958); RIDE A CROOKED TRAIL(1958); VOICE IN THE MIRROR(1958); GANGSTER STORY(1959), a, d; STRANGERS WHEN WE MEET(1960); LONELY ARE THE BRAVE(1962); WHO'S GOT THE ACTION?(1962); CHARADE(1963); ISLAND OF LOVE(1963); ENSIGN PULVER(1964); FAIL SAFE(1964); GOODBYE CHARLIE(1964); MIRAGE(1965); FORTUNE COOKIE, THE(1966); GUIDE FOR THE MARRIED MAN, A(1967); CANDY(1968, Ital./Fr.); ODD COUPLE, THE(1968); SECRET LIFE OF AN AMERICAN WIFE, THE(1968); CACTUS FLOWER(1969); HELLO, DOLLY!(1969); NEW LEAF, A(1971); PLAZA SUITE(1971); PETE 'N' TILLIE(1972); CHARLEY VARRICK(1973); LAUGHING POLICEMAN, THE(1973); FRONT PAGE, THE(1974); SUNSHINE BOYS, THE(1975); BAD NEWS BEARS, THE(1976); CALIFORNIA SUITE(1978); CASEY'S SHADOW(1978); HOUSE CALLS(1978); HOPSCOTCH(1980); LITTLE MISS MARKER(1980); BUDDY BUDDY(1981); FIRST MONDAY IN OCTOBER(1981); I OUGHT TO BE IN PICTURES(1982); SURVIVORS, THE(1983)

Walther Matthau
KOTCH(1971)

Mark Matthew
ONE PLUS ONE(1969, Brit.)

Mary Matthew
QUIET WEEKEND(1948, Brit.)

A.E. Matthews
IRON DUKE, THE(1935, Brit.); MEN ARE NOT GODS(1937, Brit.); QUIET WEDDING(1941, Brit.); THIS ENGLAND(1941, Brit.); PIMPERNEL SMITH(1942, Brit.); ESCAPE TO DANGER(1943, Brit.); MAN IN GREY, THE(1943, Brit.); THEY CAME TO A CITY(1944, Brit.); THUNDER ROCK(1944, Brit.); TWILIGHT HOUR(1944, Brit.); COLONEL BLIMP(1945, Brit.); FLIGHT FROM FOLLY(1945, Brit.); WAY AHEAD, THE(1945, Brit.); GHOSTS OF BERKELEY SQUARE(1947, Brit.); LADY SURRENDERS, A(1947, Brit.); JUST WILLIAM'S LUCK(1948, Brit.); PICCADILLY INCIDENT(1948, Brit.); WILLIAM COMES TO TOWN(1948, Brit.); AFFAIRS OF ADELAIDE(1949, U. S./Brit); AMAZING MR. BEECHAM, THE(1949, Brit.); TIGHT LITTLE ISLAND(1949, Brit.); GALLOPING MAJOR, THE(1951, Brit.); LAUGHTER IN PARADISE(1951, Brit.); MR. DRAKE'S DUCK(1951, Brit.); CASTLE IN THE AIR(1952, Brit.); MADE IN HEAVEN(1952, Brit.); MAGIC BOX, THE(1952, Brit.); PASSIONATE SENTRY, THE(1952, Brit.); SOMETHING MONEY CAN'T BUY(1952, Brit.); LANDFALL(1953, Brit.); PENNY PRINCESS(1953, Brit.); SKID KIDS(1953, Brit.); AUNT CLARA(1954, Brit.); MAN WITH A MILLION(1954, Brit.); TONIGHT'S THE NIGHT(1954, Brit.); WEAK AND THE WICKED, THE(1954, Brit.); MISS TULIP STAYS THE NIGHT(1955, Brit.); JUMPING FOR JOY(1956, Brit.); LOSER TAKES ALL(1956, Brit.); CARRY ON ADMIRAL(1957, Brit.); DOCTOR AT LARGE(1957, Brit.); THREE MEN IN A BOAT(1958, Brit.); INN FOR TROUBLE(1960, Brit.)
Silents
ONCE UPON A TIME(1918, Brit.)
Misc. Silents
WANTED - A WIDOW(1916, Brit.); CASTLE OF DREAMS(1919, Brit.)

Adelaide Matthews
Silents
JUST MARRIED(1928), w

Al Matthews
MEET NERO WOLFE(1936); YANKS(1979); ROUGH CUT(1980, Brit.); FINAL CONFLICT, THE(1981); SENDER, THE(1982, Brit.); FUNNY MONEY(1983, Brit.); SUPERMAN III(1983)

Alan Matthews
TWO IN A CROWD(1936)

Allen Matthews
SONS O' GUNS(1936); MARKED WOMAN(1937); DR. RHYTHM(1938); WHERE DANGER LIVES(1950); NEW MEXICO(1951); RACKET, THE(1951); JET PILOT(1957)

Arthur Matthews
Silents
NATION'S PERIL, THE(1915)
Misc. Silents
PATH TO THE RAINBOW, THE(1915)

Bill Matthews
NEW ORLEANS AFTER DARK(1958)

Billy Matthews
WALTZ TIME(1946, Brit.)

Bob Matthews
ROUSTABOUT(1964)

Brian Matthews
BURNING, THE(1981)

Burt Matthews
LOVE AT FIRST SIGHT(1930)

Carl Matthews
MELODY OF THE PLAINS(1937); FIGHTING RENEGADE(1939); FRONTIER SCOUT(1939); PHANTOM RANCHER(1940); PINTO CANYON(1940); FUGITIVE VALLEY(1941); CHEYENNE TAKES OVER(1947); PARTNERS OF THE SUNSET(1948); CROOKED RIVER(1950); LONGHORN, THE(1951)

Carmen Matthews
BUTTERFIELD 8(1960); DANIEL(1983)

Carole Matthews
AMAZON QUEST(1949)

Chip Matthews
DEMENTED(1980)

Chrisopher Matthews
SEE NO EVIL(1971, Brit.)

Christopher Matthews
SCARS OF DRACULA, THE(1970, Brit.); SCREAM AND SCREAM AGAIN(1970, Brit.); COME BACK PETER(1971, Brit.)

"Coots" Matthews
HELLFIGHTERS(1968), tech adv

David Matthews
MAGIC CARPET, THE(1951), w; STONY ISLAND(1978), m

Dorcas Matthews
Silents
JUNGLE CHILD, THE(1916); LITTLE BROTHER, THE(1917); PRICE MARK, THE(1917); TAR HEEL WARRIOR, THE(1917); NINE O'CLOCK TOWN, A(1918); OUT OF THE DUST(1920); BLOOD AND SAND(1922)
Misc. Silents
IDOLATORS(1917); LOVE LETTERS(1917); MADCAP MADGE(1917); MILLIONAIRE VAGRANT, THE(1917); STRANGE TRANSGRESSOR, A(1917); THOSE WHO PAY(1918); HAUNTED BEDROOM, THE(1919); LAW OF MEN, THE(1919); LUCK OF GERALDINE LAIRD, THE(1920); WOMAN IN THE SUITCASE, THE(1920)

Doreas Matthews
Misc. Silents
BORROWED PLUMAGE(1917)

E. C. Matthews
Silents
AYLWIN(1920, Brit.); KING OF THE CASTLE(1925, Brit.)

Eddie Matthews
FLAMINGO AFFAIR, THE(1948, Brit.)

Eleanor Matthews
THIEVES LIKE US(1974)

Eric Matthews
Misc. Talkies
END OF AUGUST(1974)

Forrest Matthews
DEADLINE(1948); DOCKS OF NEW ORLEANS(1948); JOE PALOOKA IN WINNER TAKE ALL(1948); BATTLING MARSHAL(1950); RED ROCK OUTLAW(1950)
Misc. Talkies
FIGHTING MUSTANG(1948)

Francis Matthews
BHOWANI JUNCTION(1956); SMALL HOTEL(1957, Brit.); I ONLY ASKED!(1958, Brit.); MARK OF THE HAWK, THE(1958); REVENGE OF FRANKENSTEIN, THE(1958, Brit.); WOMAN POSSESSED, A(1958, Brit.); SENTENCED FOR LIFE(1960, Brit.); PURSUERS, THE(1961, Brit.); SECRET OF MONTE CRISTO, THE(1961, Brit.); BATTLEAXE, THE(1962, Brit.); CORRIDORS OF BLOOD(1962, Brit.); LAMP IN ASSASSIN MEWS, THE(1962, Brit.); HELLFIRE CLUB, THE(1963, Brit.); NINE HOURS TO RAMA(1963, U.S./Brit.); MURDER AHOY(1964, Brit.); SPYLARKS(1965, Brit.); BEAUTY JUNGLE, THE(1966, Brit.); DRACULA–PRINCE OF DARKNESS(1966, Brit.); RASPUTIN–THE MAD MONK(1966, Brit.); JUST LIKE A WOMAN(1967, Brit.); STITCH IN TIME, A(1967, Brit.); CROSSPLOT(1969, Brit.); TASTE OF EXCITEMENT(1969, Brit.)

Frederick Matthews
BOYS IN COMPANY C, THE(1978, U.S./Hong Kong)

Geoffrey Matthews
DAY OF THE TRIFFIDS, THE(1963)

George Matthews
EVE OF ST. MARK, THE(1944); NIGHTMARE ALLEY(1947); UNFAITHFULLY YOURS(1948); BUCCANEER, THE(1958)

Glenn H. Matthews
EDDIE MACON'S RUN(1983)

Grace Matthews
FROM HELL IT CAME(1957); FLAME BARRIER, THE(1958)

Harriet Matthews
UNSUSPECTED, THE(1947); RACKET, THE(1951)

Hope Matthews
MARK OF CAIN, THE(1948, Brit.)

James Matthews
TECKMAN MYSTERY, THE(1955, Brit), w; RAISING A RIOT(1957, Brit.), w

Jessie Matthews
OUT OF THE BLUE(1931, Brit.); MIDSHIPMAID GOB(1932, Brit.); GOOD COMPAN-IONS(1933, Brit.); MAN FROM TORONTO, THE(1933, Brit.); THERE GOES THE BRIDE(1933, Brit.); EVERGREEN(1934, Brit.); FRIDAY THE 13TH(1934, Brit.); STRAUSS' GREAT WALTZ(1934, Brit.); FIRST A GIRL(1935, Brit.); IT'S LOVE AGAIN(1936, Brit.); GANGWAY(1937, Brit.); HEAD OVER HEELS IN LOVE(1937, Brit.); CLIMBING HIGH(1938, Brit.); SAILING ALONG(1938, Brit.); CANDLES AT NINE(1944, Brit.); TOM THUMB(1958, Brit./U.S.)

Jo Scott Matthews
HAUNTING OF M, THE(1979)

Joan Matthews
THANK YOUR LUCKY STARS(1943)

John Matthews
BLOOD ON THE ARROW(1964); CANDIDATE, THE(1964); GREAT SIOUX MAS-SACRE, THE(1965); SLEUTH(1972, Brit.)

Jon Matthews
WHERE THE BUFFALO ROAM(1980)

Jorge Matthews
SELLERS OF GIRLS(1967, Fr.)

Joyce Matthews
SITTING PRETTY(1933); THRILL OF A LIFETIME(1937); SAY IT IN FRENCH(1938); BOY TROUBLE(1939); DOUBLE LIFE, A(1947); MR. UNIVERSE(1951)

Jude Matthews
STONE(1974, Aus.)

Julius Matthews
SEEDS OF FREEDOM(1943, USSR)

Junius Matthews
WITHOUT RESERVATIONS(1946); SHOCKING MISS PILGRIM, THE(1947); CHICK-EN EVERY SUNDAY(1948); HALF ANGEL(1951); MY WIFE'S BEST FRIEND(1952); GOOD MORNING, MISS DOVE(1955); JEANNE EAGELS(1957); SUMMER PLACE, A(1959); SWORD IN THE STONE, THE(1963)

Kerwin Matthews
DEVIL AT FOUR O'CLOCK, THE(1961); BATTLE BENEATH THE EARTH(1968, Brit.); OCTAMAN(1971); BOY WHO CRIED WEREWOLF, THE(1973); NIGHTMARE IN BLOOD(1978)

Kevin Matthews
WILD PARTY, THE(1975)

LaMonica Matthews
TOY, THE(1982)

Lester Matthews
CARMEN(1931, Brit.); GABLES MYSTERY, THE(1931, Brit.); LIMPING MAN, THE(1931, Brit.); WICKHAM MYSTERY, THE(1931, Brit.); FIRES OF FATE(1932, Brit.); HER NIGHT OUT(1932, Brit.); INDISCRETIONS OF EVE(1932, Brit.); OLD MAN, THE(1932, Brit.); CALLED BACK(1933, Brit.); FACING THE MUSIC(1933, Brit.); MELODY MAKER, THE(1933, Brit.); OUT OF THE PAST(1933, Brit.); SECRET AGENT(1933, Brit.); SHE WAS ONLY A VILLAGE MAIDEN(1933, Brit.); BOOME-RANG(1934, Brit.); BORROWED CLOTHES(1934, Brit.); NORAH O'NEALE(1934, Brit.); POISONED DIAMOND, THE(1934, Brit.); SONG AT EVENTIDE(1934, Brit.); SONG YOU GAVE ME, THE(1934, Brit.); WEREWOLF OF LONDON, THE(1935); FIFTEEN MAIDEN LANE(1936); LLOYDS OF LONDON(1936); PROFESSIONAL SOL-DIER(1936); SONG AND DANCE MAN, THE(1936); THANK YOU, JEEVES(1936); TOO MANY PARENTS(1936); APRIL BLOSSOMS(1937, Brit.); CRACK-UP, THE(1937); PRINCE AND THE PAUPER, THE(1937); ADVENTURES OF ROBIN HOOD, THE(1938); IF I WERE KING(1938); MYSTERIOUS MR. MOTO(1938); THERE'S ALWAYS A WOMAN(1938); THREE LOVES HAS NANCY(1938); TIME OUT FOR MURDER(1938); CONSPIRACY(1939); I AM A CRIMINAL(1939); RULERS OF THE SEA(1939); SHOULD A GIRL MARRY?(1939); SUSANNAH OF THE MOUN-TIES(1939); THREE MUSKETEERS, THE(1939); BISCUIT EATER, THE(1940); BRIT-ISH INTELLIGENCE(1940); GAUCHO SERENADE(1940); LONE WOLF KEEPS A DATE, THE(1940); SEA HAWK, THE(1940); SING, DANCE, PLENTY HOT(1940); WOMEN IN WAR(1940); LIFE BEGINS FOR ANDY HARDY(1941); SCOTLAND YARD(1941); YANK IN THE R.A.F., A(1941); ACROSS THE PACIFIC(1942); DESPER-ATE JOURNEY(1942); LONDON BLACKOUT MURDERS(1942); MANILA CAL-LING(1942); NOW, VOYAGER(1942); PIED PIPER, THE(1942); SUNDAY PUNCH(1942); CORVETTE K-225(1943); MYSTERIOUS DOCTOR, THE(1943); NORTH-ERN PURSUIT(1943); TONIGHT WE RAID CALAIS(1943); TWO TICKETS TO LON-DON(1943); BETWEEN TWO WORLDS(1944); FOUR JILLS IN A JEEP(1944); INVISIBLE MAN'S REVENGE(1944); NINE GIRLS(1944); SHADOWS IN THE NIGHT(1944); MINISTRY OF FEAR(1945); OBJECTIVE, BURMA!(1945); SALTY O'ROURKE(1945); SON OF LASSIE(1945); TWO O'CLOCK COURAGE(1945); BEAUTI-FUL CHEAT, THE(1946); DARK DELUSION(1947); EXILE, THE(1947); FIGHTING FATHER DUNNE(1948); FREE FOR ALL(1949); MONTANA(1950); ROGUES OF SHERWOOD FOREST(1950); TYRANT OF THE SEA(1950); ANNE OF THE IN-DIES(1951); CORKY OF GASOLINE ALLEY(1951); DESERT FOX, THE(1951); LORNA DOONE(1951); SON OF DR. JEKYLL, THE(1951); TALES OF ROBIN HOOD(1951); AGAINST ALL FLAGS(1952); BRIGAND, THE(1952); CAPTAIN PIRATE(1952); JUN-GLE JIM IN THE FORBIDDEN LAND(1952); LADY IN THE IRON MASK(1952); LES MISERABLES(1952); OPERATION SECRET(1952); ROGUE'S MARCH(1952); STARS AND STRIPES FOREVER(1952); CHARGE OF THE LANCERS(1953); FORT TI(1953); JAMAICA RUN(1953); MAN IN THE ATTIC(1953); NIAGARA(1953); SAVAGE MUTI-NY(1953); TROUBLE ALONG THE WAY(1953); YOUNG BESS(1953); BAD FOR EACH OTHER(1954); JUNGLE MAN-EATERS(1954); KING RICHARD AND THE CRUSAD-ERS(1954); FAR HORIZONS, THE(1955); FLAME OF THE ISLANDS(1955); MOON-FLEET(1955); SEVEN LITTLE FOYS, THE(1955); TEN WANTED MEN(1955); SOMETHING OF VALUE(1957); MIRACLE, THE(1959); MARY POPPINS(1964); AS-SAULT ON A QUEEN(1966); STAR!(1968)
Misc. Talkies
HOUSE OF DREAMS(1933)

Lewter Matthews
PARADINE CASE, THE(1947)

Linda Matthews
WARGAMES(1983), cos
1984
GREMLINS(1984), cos

M. J. Matthews
NO BLADE OF GRASS(1970, Brit.)

Marie Matthews
MR. MAGOO'S HOLIDAY FESTIVAL(1970)

Martin Matthews
CURSE OF THE WEREWOLF, THE(1961); FFOLKES(1980, Brit.)

Mary Jo Matthews
SOCIETY DOCTOR(1935)

Mary Matthews
GALLOPING MAJOR, THE(1951, Brit.)

Nancy Matthews
NEVER SAY GOODBYE(1956); SUMMER PLACE, A(1959)

Pamela Matthews
SCHOOL FOR SECRETS(1946, Brit.)

Patrick Matthews
OPERATION DIAMOND(1948, Brit.), p

Paul Matthews
LITTLE MEN(1940); TOM BROWN'S SCHOOL DAYS(1940); HENRY ALDRICH FOR PRESIDENT(1941)
Misc. Talkies
GIRLS OF 42ND STREET(1974)

Peter Matthews
HIGH(1968, Can.)

Randy Matthews
1984
FIRST TURN-ON!, THE(1984)

Robert Matthews
JIGSAW(1949), ed; FRATERNITY ROW(1977)

Ross Matthews
JUST OUT OF REACH(1979, Aus.), p

Russel Matthews
1984
FIRST TURN-ON!, THE(1984)

Ruth Matthews
NIGHT AND DAY(1946)

Seymour Matthews
HANOVER STREET(1979, Brit.)

Stephanie Matthews
SKY RIDERS(1976, U.S./Gr.)

Tony Matthews
CUBA(1979)

Walter Matthews
1984
RACING WITH THE MOON(1984)

William Matthews
FOR LOVE OF IVY(1968)
Silents
SQUIBS(1921, Brit.); TIPPED OFF(1923), p

Ernest Matthewson
Silents
IN THE DAYS OF SAINT PATRICK(1920, Brit.)

Peter Matthey
1984
NEW YORK NIGHTS(1984)

Mathias Matthies
YOUNG GO WILD, THE(1962, Ger.), art d; WILLY(1963, U.S./Ger.), art d; GREAT BRITISH TRAIN ROBBERY, THE(1967, Ger.), art d

Thomas Matthiesen
IDAHO TRANSFER(1975), w

Tim Matthieson
DIVORCE AMERICAN STYLE(1967); YOURS, MINE AND OURS(1968); HOW TO COMMIT MARRIAGE(1969)

Luke Matthiessen
WILD PARTY, THE(1975)

Peter Matthiessen
YOUNG ONE, THE(1961, Mex.), w

Martial Matthieu
THIRD LOVER, THE(1963, Fr./Ital.), w; OPHELIA(1964, Fr.), w

Matthis
M(1933, Ger.)

June Matthis
Silents
BLOOD AND SAND(1922), w

Chela Matthison
BATTLE BENEATH THE EARTH(1968, Brit.)

Ettore Mattia
MAGNIFICENT CUCKOLD, THE(1965, Fr./Ital.); MONSIGNOR(1982)

Pattie Mattick
BEGUILED, THE(1971)

Billie Matticks
NIGHT OF THE IGUANA, THE(1964)

Van Mattimore
Misc. Silents
VENGEANCE OF THE DEEP(1923)

Darlene Mattingly
Misc. Talkies
FIVE ANGRY WOMEN(1975)

David Mattingly
WATCHER IN THE WOODS, THE(1980, Brit.), spec eff

Hedley Mattingly
THRILL OF IT ALL, THE(1963); SIGNPOST TO MURDER(1964); KING RAT(1965); MARRIAGE ON THE ROCKS(1965); STRANGE BEDFELLOWS(1965); TORN CUR-TAIN(1966); CLEOPATRA JONES(1973); LOST HORIZON(1973)
1984
ALL OF ME(1984)

Phil Mattingly
IN HARM'S WAY(1965); STROKER ACE(1983)

Burny Mattinson
ROBIN HOOD(1973), anim; RESCUERS, THE(1977), w; FOX AND THE HOUND, THE(1981), w

Guilano Mattioli
ROME WANTS ANOTHER CAESAR(1974, Ital.), ed

Luisa Mattioli
EIGHTEEN IN THE SUN(1964, Ital.)
Raf Mattioli
YOUNG HUSBANDS(1958, Ital./Fr.); WHERE THE HOT WIND BLOWS(1960, Fr., Ital.); VIOLENT SUMMER(1961, Fr./Ital.)
Dee Jay Mattis
PATSY, THE(1964); FRANKIE AND JOHNNY(1966)
Jack Mattis
THREE COINS IN THE FOUNTAIN(1954); GLASS HOUSES(1972)
Frank Mattison
Silents
OLD AGE HANDICAP(1928), d
Frank S. Mattison
Misc. Talkies
BROKEN HEARTED(1929), d; BYE-BYE BUDDY(1929), d
Silents
LONE WAGON, THE(1924), d&w; KING OF THE HERD(1927), d; LITTLE WILD GIRL, THE(1928), d; GIRLS WHO DARE(1929), d, w
Misc. Silents
BETTER MAN WINS, THE(1922), d; SHELL SHOCKED SAMMY(1923), d; CIRCUS LURE(1924), d; LAST WHITE MAN, THE(1924), d; MILE A MINUTE MORGAN(1924), d; NORTH OF ALASKA(1924), d; RAGGED ROBIN(1924), d; FLYING FOOL(1925), d; KIT CARSON OVER THE GREAT DIVIDE(1925), d; SLOW DYNAMITE(1925), d; BUFFALO BILL ON THE U.P. TRAIL(1926), d; CODE OF THE NORTHWEST(1926), d; DANIEL BOONE THRU THE WILDERNESS(1926), d; BETTER DAYS(1927), d; MUST WE MARRY?(1928), d; CHINA SLAVER(1929), d
Frank Mattison, Jr.
Silents
OLD AGE HANDICAP(1928)
John Mattison
BROADWAY(1942), ch; GIVE OUT, SISTERS(1942), ch; PRIVATE BUCKAROO(1942), ch
Johnny Mattison
WHAT'S COOKIN'?(1942), ch
Matty Mattison
Silents
LONE WAGON, THE(1924)
Misc. Silents
SHELL SHOCKED SAMMY(1923); CIRCUS LURE(1924); LAST WHITE MAN, THE(1924); MILE A MINUTE MORGAN(1924); NORTH OF ALASKA(1924); RAGGED ROBIN(1924); SLOW DYNAMITE(1925)
Jenine Matto
DEATM GOES TO SCHOOL(1953, Brit.)
Lou Matto
WEDDING OF LILLI MARLENE, THE(1953, Brit.)
Most Mattoe
Silents
PRIDE OF PALOMAR, THE(1922)
Mario Mattoli
DESTINY(1938), d; ANYTHING FOR A SONG(1947, Ital.), w; SCHOOLGIRL DIARY(1947, Ital.), p,d&w; LADY IS FICKLE, THE(1948, Ital.), d; TWO NIGHTS WITH CLEOPATRA(1953, Ital.), d
Charles Matton
SPERMULA(1976, Fr.), d&w, art d
Sarah Matton
SPERMULA(1976, Fr.), ed
Angelo Mattos
1984
BLAME IT ON RIO(1984)
Laure Mattos
1984
C.H.U.D.(1984)
Michael Mattos
CONNECTION, THE(1962)
Bruce Mattox
1984
MIKE'S MURDER(1984), spec eff
Martha Mattox
LOVE RACKET, THE(1929); EXTRAVAGANCE(1930); NIGHT WORK(1930); BORN TO LOVE(1931); MISBEHAVING LADIES(1931); MURDER BY THE CLOCK(1931); CARELESS LADY(1932); DYNAMITE RANCH(1932); HAUNTED GOLD(1932); MONSTER WALKS, THE(1932); MURDER AT DAWN(1932); NO GREATER LOVE(1932); SHOPWORN(1932); SILVER LINING(1932); SO BIG(1932); BITTER TEA OF GENERAL YEN, THE(1933); FOURTH HORSEMAN, THE(1933)
Silents
CAPRICES OF KITTY, THE(1915); ROUGH LOVER, THE(1918); CUMBERLAND ROMANCE, A(1920); EVERYBODY'S SWEETHEART(1920); GIRL OF MY HEART(1920); HUCKLEBERRY FINN(1920); CONFLICT, THE(1921); ANGEL OF CROOKED STREET, THE(1922); RICH MEN'S WIVES(1922); HERO, THE(1923); PENROD AND SAM(1923); THREE WISE FOOLS(1923); FAMILY SECRET, THE(1924); OH, DOCTOR(1924); NUT-CRACKER, THE(1926); RAINMAKER, THE(1926); TORRENT, THE(1926); WANING SEX, THE(1926); YANKEE SENOR, THE(1926); CAT AND THE CANARY, THE(1927); HEAD MAN, THE(1928); LOVE ME AND THE WORLD IS MINE(1928)
Misc. Silents
CHARMER, THE(1917); CLEAN-UP, THE(1917); POLLY PUT THE KETTLE ON(1917); SCARLET SHADOW, THE(1919); FIREBRAND TREVISON(1920); GAME CHICKEN, THE(1922); RESTLESS SOULS(1922); TIMES HAVE CHANGED(1923); KEEPER OF THE BEES, THE(1925); FOREST HAVOC(1926); SHAMEFUL BEHAVIOR?(1926); THIRTEENTH JUROR, THE(1927); BIT OF HEAVEN, A(1928); LITTLE SHEPHERD OF KINGDOM COME, THE(1928); BIG DIAMOND ROBBERY, THE(1929)
Matt Mattox
DREAMBOAT(1952); GLORY BRIGADE, THE(1953), ch; SEVEN BRIDES FOR SEVEN BROTHERS(1954); GIRL RUSH, THE(1955); HOT BLOOD(1956), ch; PEPE(1960)
Walt Mattox
WHITE STALLION(1947), p; DEADLINE(1948), p; BATTLING MARSHAL(1950), p

Scott Mattraw
ESCAPADE(1935); UNDER YOUR SPELL(1936)
Scotty Mattraw
SNOW WHITE AND THE SEVEN DWARFS(1937); WEE WILLIE WINKIE(1937); IN OLD CHICAGO(1938)
Silents
THIEF OF BAGDAD, THE(1924); ONE GLORIOUS SCRAP(1927); ARIZONA CYCLONE(1928); TWO LOVERS(1928)
Frank Matts
CAPTURE, THE(1950); SILVER CANYON(1951); APACHE COUNTRY(1952); MONTANA TERRITORY(1952); ESCAPE FROM FORT BRAVO(1953); THUNDER OVER THE PLAINS(1953)
Bart Mattson
STORY OF MANKIND, THE(1957)
Denver Mattson
DOMINO PRINCIPLE, THE(1977); HOUSE BY THE LAKE, THE(1977, Can.), a, stunts; MR. BILLION(1977); MAIN EVENT, THE(1979), a, stunts; THING, THE(1982)
Denver R. Mattson
MOVIE MOVIE(1978)
Per Mattson
FANNY AND ALEXANDER(1983, Swed./Fr./Ger.)
Robin Mattson
NAMU, THE KILLER WHALE(1966); RETURN TO MACON COUNTY(1975)
Misc. Talkies
BONNIE'S KIDS(1973); CANDY STRIPE NURSES(1974)
Steve Mattson
1984
REPO MAN(1984)
Arne Mattsson
DOLL, THE(1964, Swed.), d; WOMAN OF DARKNESS(1968, Swed.), d; MY FATHER'S MISTRESS(1970, Swed.), d, w
Gunnar Mattsson
TIME IN THE SUN, A(1970, Swed.), w
Sten Mattsson
SWEDISH WEDDING NIGHT(1965, Swed.)
Matty Malneck and his Orchestra
ST. LOUIS BLUES(1939); YOU'RE IN THE ARMY NOW(1941); SHANTYTOWN(1943)
Matty Malneck and Orchestra
SCATTERBRAIN(1940)
Matty Malneck Orchestra
MAN ABOUT TOWN(1939)
The Matty Malneck Orchestra
TROCADERO(1944)
I. Mattyasovsky
Misc. Silents
PAUL STREET BOYS(1929)
Niko Matul
TWILIGHT TIME(1983, U.S./Yugo.), art d
Hans Matula
SOME LIKE IT COOL(1979, Ger./Aust./Ital./Fr.), ph
Peter Matulavich
Misc. Talkies
JUPITER MENACE, THE(1982), d
Gino Maturano
JESSE AND LESTER, TWO BROTHERS IN A PLACE CALLED TRINITY(1972, Ital.)
Victor Mature
HOUSEKEEPER'S DAUGHTER(1939); CAPTAIN CAUTION(1940); NO, NO NANETTE(1940); SHANGHAI GESTURE, THE(1941); FOOTLIGHT SERENADE(1942); I WAKE UP SCREAMING(1942); MY GAL SAL(1942); SEVEN DAYS LEAVE(1942); SONG OF THE ISLANDS(1942); MY DARLING CLEMENTINE(1946); KISS OF DEATH(1947); MOSS ROSE(1947); CRY OF THE CITY(1948); FURY AT FURNACE CREEK(1948); EASY LIVING(1949); RED, HOT AND BLUE(1949); SAMSON AND DELILAH(1949); GAMBLING HOUSE(1950); I'LL GET BY(1950); STELLA(1950); WABASH AVENUE(1950); ANDROCLES AND THE LION(1952); LAS VEGAS STORY, THE(1952); MILLION DOLLAR MERMAID(1952); SOMETHING FOR THE BIRDS(1952); AFFAIR WITH A STRANGER(1953); GLORY BRIGADE, THE(1953); ROBE, THE(1953); VEILS OF BAGDAD, THE(1953); BETRAYED(1954); DANGEROUS MISSION(1954); DEMETRIUS AND THE GLADIATORS(1954); EGYPTIAN. THE(1954); CHIEF CRAZY HORSE(1955); LAST FRONTIER, THE(1955); VIOLENT SATURDAY(1955); SAFARI(1956); SHARKFIGHTERS, THE(1956); ZARAK(1956, Brit.); LONG HAUL, THE(1957, Brit.); PICKUP ALLEY(1957, Brit.); CHINA DOLL(1958); TANK FORCE(1958, Brit.); BANDIT OF ZHOBE, THE(1959); BIG CIRCUS, THE(1959); ESCORT WEST(1959); TIMBUKTU(1959); HANNIBAL(1960, Ital.); TARTARS, THE(1962, Ital./Yugo.); AFTER THE FOX(1966, U.S./Ital./Ital.); HEAD(1968); EVERY LITTLE CROOK AND NANNY(1972); WON TON TON, THE DOG WHO SAVED HOLLYWOOD(1976); FIREPOWER(1979, Brit.)
Victure Mature
ONE MILLION B.C.(1940)
Eric Maturin
BEYOND THE CITIES(1930, Brit.); SQUEAKER, THE(1930, Brit.); GIRL IN THE NIGHT, THE(1931, Brit.); FACE AT THE WINDOW, THE(1932, Brit.); FLAW, THE(1933, Brit.); LOVE, LIFE AND LAUGHTER(1934, Brit.); YOUTHFUL FOLLY(1934, Brit.); CITY OF BEAUTIFUL NONSENSE, THE(1935, Brit.); PRICE OF A SONG, THE(1935, Brit.); SANDERS OF THE RIVER(1935, Brit.); SOMEWHERE IN FRANCE(1943, Brit.); COLONEL BLIMP(1945, Brit.); LAST HOLIDAY(1950, Brit.)
Silents
HIS HOUSE IN ORDER(1928, Brit.)
Misc. Silents
WISP O' THE WOODS(1919, Brit.)
Charlene Matus
NIGHT OF THE ZOMBIES(1981)
Walter Matuschanskayasky [Matthau]
EARTHQUAKE(1974)
Tamara Matusian
URBAN COWBOY(1980)
Waldemar Matuska
LEMONADE JOE(1966, Czech.)

M. Matusova
SONG OVER MOSCOW(1964, USSR), makeup
John Matuszak
NORTH DALLAS FORTY(1979); CAVEMAN(1981)
1984
ICE PIRATES, THE(1984)
Marinka Matuszewski
MOTHER AND THE WHORE, THE(1973, Fr.)
Jerzy Matuszkiewicz
LOVE AT TWENTY(1963, Fr./Ital./Jap./Pol./Ger.), m
Alvaro Matute
REBELLION OF THE HANGED, THE(1954, Mex.)
Ivan Matveyev
COUNTRY BRIDE(1938, USSR)
Yevgeniy Matveyev
RESURRECTION(1963, USSR)
A. Matveyeva
CITY OF YOUTH(1938, USSR)
Stefan Matyjaszkiewicz
EVE WANTS TO SLEEP(1961, Pol.), ph
Bob Matz
BOY NAMED CHARLIE BROWN, A(1969), anim; RACE FOR YOUR LIFE, CHARLIE BROWN(1977), anim; BUGS BUNNY'S THIRD MOVIE–1001 RABBIT TALES(1982), anim
James Matz
Misc. Talkies
EVIDENCE OF POWER(1979)
Johanna Matz
MOON IS BLUE, THE(1953); THEY WERE SO YOUNG(1955); CONGRESS DANCES(1957, Ger.); LIFE AND LOVES OF MOZART, THE(1959, Ger.); WHITE HORSE INN, THE(1959, Ger.); MRS. WARREN'S PROFESSION(1960, Ger.); HOUSE OF THE THREE GIRLS, THE(1961, Aust.)
Peter Matz
BYE BYE BRAVERMAN(1968), m; MARLOWE(1969), m, md; RIVALS(1972), m, md; FUNNY LADY(1975), md; PRIZE FIGHTER, THE(1979), m; PRIVATE EYES, THE(1980), m
Madeline Matzen
Silents
BULLDOG PLUCK(1927), w
Margaret Matzenauer
MR. DEEDS GOES TO TOWN(1936)
Charles Mau
NUDE ODYSSEY(1962, Fr./Ital.)
Doan Chau Mau
YANK IN VIET-NAM, A(1964)
Maria Mauban
CAGE OF GOLD(1950, Brit.); CAIRO ROAD(1950, Brit.); DANGER IS A WOMAN(1952, Fr.); STRANGERS, THE(1955, Ital.); VICE DOLLS(1961, Fr.); LE GENDARME ET LES EXTRATERRESTRES(1978, Fr.)
Maria Mauben
MIDNIGHT FOLLY(1962, Fr.)
Pat Mauceri
NATURAL ENEMIES(1979)
Bill Mauch
HE WALKED BY NIGHT(1948); STREET WITH NO NAME, THE(1948); ACCUSED, THE(1949); BEDTIME FOR BONZO(1951)
Billy Mauch
ANTHONY ADVERSE(1936); WHITE ANGEL, THE(1936); PENROD AND SAM(1937); PRINCE AND THE PAUPER, THE(1937); PENROD AND HIS TWIN BROTHER(1938); PENROD'S DOUBLE TROUBLE(1938)
Bobby Mauch
PRINCE AND THE PAUPER, THE(1937); PENROD AND HIS TWIN BROTHER(1938); PENROD'S DOUBLE TROUBLE(1938)
Gene Mauch
WINNING TEAM, THE(1952)
Thomas Mauch
AGUIRRE, THE WRATH OF GOD(1977, W. Ger.), ph; SIGNS OF LIFE(1981, Ger.), ph; FITZCARRALDO(1982), ph
William Mauch
ROSEANNA McCOY(1949); PEOPLE WILL TALK(1951)
Jacques Mauclair
FEMALE, THE(1960, Fr.); DON'T TEMPT THE DEVIL(1964, Fr./Ital.); SHADOW OF EVIL(1967, Fr./Ital.)
Monique Mauclair
QUARTET(1981, Brit./Fr.)
Jean Maucorps
THAT SPLENDID NOVEMBER(1971, Ital./Fr.)
Jean-Pierre Maud
ZIG-ZAG(1975, Fr/Ital.)
Arthur Maude
CLUE OF THE NEW PIN, THE(1929, Brit.), d; LYONS MAIL, THE(1931, Brit.), d; WATCH BEVERLY(1932, Brit.), d; CALL ME MAME(1933, Brit.); HEAD OF THE FAMILY(1933, Brit.); LURE, THE(1933, Brit.), p&d; SHE WAS ONLY A VILLAGE MAIDEN(1933, Brit.), d; THIRTEENTH CANDLE, THE(1933, Brit.); WISHBONE, THE(1933, Brit.), d; BOOMERANG(1934, Brit.), d; BORROWED CLOTHES(1934, Brit.), d; LIVE AGAIN(1936, Brit.), d; CONTINENTAL EXPRESS(1939, Brit.); COMMON TOUCH, THE(1941, Brit.); SABOTAGE AT SEA(1942, Brit.)
Silents
THAIS(1914), a, d, w; MAN FROM BEYOND, THE(1922); POPPIES OF FLANDERS(1927, Brit.), d; RINGER, THE(1928, Brit.), d
Misc. Silents
BRINK, THE(1915); FATAL NIGHT, THE(1915); COURTESAN, THE(1916), d; EMBERS(1916), a, d; LORD LOVELAND DISCOVERS AMERICA(1916), a, d; POWDER(1916), a, d; REVELATIONS(1916), a, d; BORROWED PLUMAGE(1917); BLINDING TRAIL, THE(1919); MICROBE, THE(1919); TONI(1928, Brit.), d; CLUE OF THE NEW PIN, THE(1929, Brit.), d; FLYING SQUAD, THE(1929), d
Authur Maude
Silents
REWARD, THE(1915)

Beatrice Maude
DODSWORTH(1936); ARKANSAS JUDGE(1941); MR. AND MRS. SMITH(1941); ICE-CAPADES REVUE(1942); LAWLESS CODE(1949); SLAVES OF BABYLON(1953); LUCY GALLANT(1955); INVASION OF THE BODY SNATCHERS(1956)
Misc. Silents
FINAL JUDGEMENT, THE(1915)
Charles Maude
Silents
HOUSE OF TEMPERLEY, THE(1913, Brit.)
Cyril Maude
GRUMPY(1930); THESE CHARMING PEOPLE(1931, Brit.); COUNSEL'S OPINION(1933, Brit.); GIRLS WILL BE BOYS(1934, Brit.); ORDERS IS ORDERS(1934, Brit.); HEAT WAVE(1935, Brit.); WHILE THE SUN SHINES(1950, Brit.)
Misc. Silents
ANTIQUE DEALER, THE(1915); GREATER WILL, THE(1915); PEER GYNT(1915); HEADMASTER, THE(1921, Brit.)
Edna Maude
Silents
JOHN HALIFAX, GENTLEMAN(1915, Brit.); PRINCESS OF HAPPY CHANCE, THE(1916, Brit.)
Elizabeth Maude
THREE WEIRD SISTERS, THE(1948, Brit.); MY BROTHER JONATHAN(1949, Brit.)
Gillian Maude
TANGLED EVIDENCE(1934, Brit.); LEND ME YOUR WIFE(1935, Brit.); SEXTON BLAKE AND THE BEARDED DOCTOR(1935, Brit.); DICK BARTON–SPECIAL AGENT(1948, Brit.); MADNESS OF THE HEART(1949, Brit.); PICCADILLY THIRD STOP(1960, Brit.)
Jacqueline Maude
GALLOPING MAJOR, THE(1951, Brit.)
Joan Maude
ONE FAMILY(1930, Brit.); HOBSON'S CHOICE(1931, Brit.); IT'S A KING(1933, Brit.); KING OF PARIS, THE(1934, Brit.); LASH, THE(1934, Brit.); POWER(1934, Brit.); WHEN LONDON SLEEPS(1934, Brit.); IN A MONASTERY GARDEN(1935); TURN OF THE TIDE(1935, Brit.); WANDERING JEW, THE(1935, Brit.); LAMP STILL BURNS, THE(1943, Brit.); GREAT DAY(1945, Brit.); NOTORIOUS GENTLEMAN(1945, Brit.); STRAWBERRY ROAN(1945, Brit.); THEY KNEW MR. KNIGHT(1945, Brit.); NIGHT BOAT TO DUBLIN(1946, Brit.); STAIRWAY TO HEAVEN(1946, Brit.); CORRIDOR OF MIRRORS(1948, Brit.); TEMPTRESS, THE(1949, Brit.); LIFE IN HER HANDS(1951, Brit.)
Misc. Silents
CHAMBER OF HORRORS(1929, Brit.)
Margery Maude
YOU'RE NEVER TOO YOUNG(1955); BIRDS AND THE BEES, THE(1965)
Mary Maude
HOUSE THAT SCREAMED, THE(1970, Span.); CRUCIBLE OF TERROR(1971, Brit.); MAN AT THE TOP(1973, Brit.); SCORPIO(1973); TERROR(1979, Brit.)
Roddy Maude-Roxby
PARTY'S OVER, THE(1966, Brit.); CARNABY, M.D.(1967, Brit.); ARISTOCATS, THE(1970)
1984
GREYSTOKE: THE LEGEND OF TARZAN, LORD OF THE APES(1984)
Caroline Maudling
IT'S ALL OVER TOWN(1963, Brit.)
Charles Maudru
Misc. Silents
RENONCEMENT(1917, Fr.), d; LA MASCOTTE DES POILUS(1918, Fr.), d; LE DROIT DE TUER(1920, Fr.), d; LE LYS ROUGE(1920, Fr.), d; LA FIANCEE DU DISPARU(1921, Fr.), d; L'ASSOMOIR(1921, Fr.), d; LE MERCHANT HOMME(1921, Fr.), d; LE TALISON(1921, Fr.), d; L'INCONNU(1921, Fr.), d; PRES DE CRIME(1921, Fr.), d; UN AVENTUERIER(1921, Fr.), d; SERGE PANIN(1922, Fr.), d; L'HOMME DU TRAIN 117(1923, Fr.), d; ROCAMBOLE(1923, Fr.), d; LES AMOURS DE ROCAMBOLE(1924, Fr.), d; LES PREMIERES ARMES DE ROCAMBOLE(1924, Fr.), d
Pierre Maudru
MARIE OF THE ISLES(1960, Fr.), w
Craig Maudsley, Jr.
BLOOD FEAST(1963); SCUM OF THE EARTH(1963)
Cheri Maugans
FRIDAY THE 13TH PART III(1982)
Roger Mauge
BEAR, THE(1963, Fr.), w
Gaston Mauger
ACCUSED–STAND UP(1930, Fr.)
Andrea Maugeri
GODFATHER, THE, PART II(1974)
Claudine Maugey
DEVIL AND THE TEN COMMANDMENTS, THE(1962, Fr.); TWO ARE GUILTY(1964, Fr.)
Robin Maugham
INTRUDER, THE(1955, Brit.), w; BLACK TENT, THE(1956, Brit.), w; PORTRAIT OF A SINNER(1961, Brit.), w; SERVANT, THE(1964, Brit.), w
Robina Maugham
Silents
PRIDE OF DONEGAL, THE(1929, Brit.)
Somerset Maugham
CHARMING SINNERS(1929), w; LETTER, THE(1929), w; STRICTLY UNCONVENTIONAL(1930), w; ADORABLE JULIA(1964, Fr./Aust.), w
W. Somerset Maugham
SACRED FLAME, THE(1929), w; RAIN(1932), w; NARROW CORNER, THE(1933), w; OUR BETTERS(1933), w; OF HUMAN BONDAGE(1934), w; PAINTED VEIL, THE(1934), w; RIGHT TO LIVE, THE(1935), w; ISLE OF FURY(1936), w; SECRET AGENT, THE(1936, Brit.), w; TENTH MAN, THE(1937, Brit.), w; THE BEACHCOMBER(1938, Brit.), w; LETTER, THE(1940), w; TOO MANY HUSBANDS(1940), w; MOON AND SIXPENCE, THE(1942), w; CHRISTMAS HOLIDAY(1944), w; HOUR BEFORE THE DAWN(1944), w; OF HUMAN BONDAGE(1946), w; RAZOR'S EDGE, THE(1946), w; UNFAITHFUL(1947), w; QUARTET(1949, Brit.), w; TRIO(1950, Brit.), w; ENCORE(1951, Brit.), w; MISS SADIE THOMPSON(1953), w; THE BEACHCOMBER(1955, Brit.), w; THREE CASES OF MURDER(1955, Brit.), w; THREE FOR THE SHOW(1955), w; SEVENTH SIN, THE(1957), w; OF HUMAN BONDAGE(1964, Brit.), w

1984
RAZOR'S EDGE, THE(1984), w
Silents
JACK STRAW(1920), w; ORDEAL, THE(1922), w
William Somerset Maugham
Silents
EAST OF SUEZ(1925), w; SADIE THOMPSON(1928), w
Monica Maughan
WINTER'S TALE, THE(1968, Brit.); GETTING OF WISDOM, THE(1977, Aus.)
Myrtle Maughan
Silents
AT THE STAGE DOOR(1921)
Susan Maughan
WHAT A CRAZY WORLD(1963, Brit.)
Guy Maugin
TEN DAYS' WONDER(1972, Fr.), set d
Betty Mauk
GOLD DIGGERS OF 1937(1936); UNHOLY ROLLERS(1972)
Katharine Mauk
ROMAN SCANDALS(1933)
William Mauk
UNHOLY ROLLERS(1972)
Bill Mauldin
RED BADGE OF COURAGE, THE(1951); TERESA(1951); UP FRONT(1951), w
John Mauldin
MAGIC SWORD, THE(1962)
Annabel Maule
SAVE A LITTLE SUNSHINE(1938, Brit.); DANGER TOMORROW(1960, Brit.); MODEL FOR MURDER(1960, Brit.)
Brad Maule
LAST MARRIED COUPLE IN AMERICA, THE(1980)
Esson Maule
FLAME IN THE HEATHER(1935, Brit.), w
Hamilton Maule
BANNING(1967), w
Vee Maule
HAPPY DAYS(1930)
Georges Mauloy
HER FIRST AFFAIR(1947, Fr.)
Jean Maumy
EXTERMINATORS, THE(1965 Fr.), p; INVASION 1700(1965, Fr./Ital./Yugo.), prod d; SELLERS OF GIRLS(1967, Fr.), p; MANDABI(1970, Fr./Senegal), p
Wayne Maunder
SEVEN MINUTES, THE(1971); PORKY'S(1982)
Charles Maunsell
GIDEON OF SCOTLAND YARD(1959, Brit.); SENTENCED FOR LIFE(1960, Brit.); NEVER TAKE CANDY FROM A STRANGER(1961, Brit.)
David Maunsell
FRANCIS OF ASSISI(1961); QUIET PLACE IN THE COUNTRY, A(1970, Ital./Fr.)
Jacques Mauny
CHARLES AND LUCIE(1982, Fr.)
Ernest Maupain
Silents
BREAKER, THE(1916); EFFICIENCY EDGAR'S COURTSHIP(1917)
Misc. Silents
MAN TRAIL, THE(1915); RAVEN, THE(1915); DISCARD, THE(1916); PRINCE OF GRAUSTARK, THE(1916); SHERLOCK HOLMES(1916); THAT SORT(1916); VULTURES OF SOCIETY(1916); TRUFFLERS, THE(1917); MOTHER'S SIN, A(1918); TRAIL TO YESTERDAY, THE(1918)
Maupi
MARIUS(1933, Fr.); CESAR(1936, Fr.); FIRST OFFENCE(1936, Brit.); CROISIERES SIDERALES(1941, Fr.); FANNY(1948, Fr.)
Ernest Maupian
Misc. Silents
MAN WHO WAS AFRAID, THE(1917)
Andre Mauprey
THREEPENNY OPERA, THE(1931, Ger./U.S.), w
Meinhardt Maur
TRUNKS OF MR. O.F., THE(1932, Ger.)
Misc. Silents
HARAKIRI(1919, Ger.)
Meinhart Maur
REMBRANDT(1936, Brit.); DOCTOR SYN(1937, Brit.); OKAY FOR SOUND(1937, Brit.); SECOND BUREAU(1937, Brit.); LAST BARRICADE, THE(1938, Brit.); RETURN OF THE FROG, THE(1938, Brit.); WHO GOES NEXT?(1938, Brit.); MAD MEN OF EUROPE(1940, Brit.); PACK UP YOUR TROUBLES(1940, Brit.); THREE SILENT MEN(1940, Brit.); TWENTY-ONE DAYS TOGETHER(1940, Brit.); GIRL IN DISTRESS(1941, Brit.); WE'LL SMILE AGAIN(1942, Brit.); CANDLELIGHT IN ALGERIA(1944, Brit.); HUGGETTS ABROAD, THE(1949, Brit.); IT'S NOT CRICKET(1949, Brit.); DICK BARTON AT BAY(1950, Brit.); TALES OF HOFFMANN, THE(1951, Brit.); WOODEN HORSE, THE(1951); DECAMERON NIGHTS(1953, Brit.); NEVER LET ME GO(1953, U.S./Brit.); FIRE OVER AFRICA(1954, Brit.)
Carmen Maura
THAT HOUSE IN THE OUTSKIRTS(1980, Span.)
Silvio Maurano
DEFEAT OF HANNIBAL, THE(1937, Ital.), w
Mike Maurantonio
GROUND ZERO(1973)
David Maure
SURVIVAL(1976)
Michael Mauree
SECRET LIFE OF WALTER MITTY, THE(1947)
Maureen
ASTOUNDING SHE-MONSTER, THE(1958), cos
Mollie Maureen
PRIVATE LIFE OF SHERLOCK HOLMES, THE(1970, Brit.); CURSE OF THE PINK PANTHER(1983); WICKED LADY, THE(1983, Brit.)

Raymond Maurel
DIXIANA(1930)
Friedrich Maurer
JUDGE AND THE SINNER, THE(1964, Ger.); CASTLE, THE(1969, Ger.)
Geoffrey A. Maurer
THREE STOOGES GO AROUND THE WORLD IN A DAZE, THE(1963)
Georges Maurer
GREEN GLOVE, THE(1952), p
Ken Maurer
1984
ICE PIRATES, THE(1984)
Lisa Maurer
WARRIORS, THE(1979); JAWS 3-D(1983)
Michael Maurer
SUDDEN IMPACT(1983)
1984
CITY HEAT(1984)
Norman Maurer
ANGRY RED PLANET, THE(1959), p; THREE STOOGES IN ORBIT, THE(1962), p, w; THREE STOOGES MEET HERCULES, THE(1962), p; THREE STOOGES GO AROUND THE WORLD IN A DAZE, THE(1963), p&d, w; OUTLAWS IS COMING, THE(1965), p&d; WHO'S MINDING THE MINT?(1967), p; MAD ROOM, THE(1969), p
Peggy Maurer
I BURY THE LIVING(1958)
Ralph Maurer
JIGSAW(1968)
Viktor Maurer
DEATH OF TARZAN, THE(1968, Czech)
Ellet Mauret
NO LOVE FOR JUDY(1955, Brit.)
Marc Maurette
ALI BABA(1954, Fr.), w
Marcelle Maurette
ANASTASIA(1956), w
Yolande Maurette
IMMORTAL STORY, THE(1969, Fr.), ed; GODSON, THE(1972, Ital./Fr.), ed
Nicole Maurey
LITTLE BOY LOST(1953); DIARY OF A COUNTRY PRIEST(1954, Fr.); SECRET OF THE INCAS(1954); CONSTANT HUSBAND, THE(1955, Brit.); BOLD AND THE BRAVE, THE(1956); ROGUE'S YARN(1956, Brit.); ROYAL AFFAIRS IN VERSAILLES(1957, Fr.); WEAPON, THE(1957, Brit.); ME AND THE COLONEL(1958); HOUSE OF THE SEVEN HAWKS, THE(1959); JAYHAWKERS, THE(1959); SCAPEGOAT, THE(1959, Brit.); HIGH TIME(1960); HIS AND HERS(1961, Brit.); MOST WANTED MAN, THE(1962, Fr./Ital.); DAY OF THE TRIFFIDS, THE(1963); VERY EDGE, THE(1963, Brit.); WHY BOTHER TO KNOCK(1964, Brit.); CHANEL SOLITAIRE(1981)
Francisco Mauri
ZORRO, THE GAY BLADE(1981)
1984
ERENDIRA(1984, Mex./Fr./Ger.)
Glauco Mauri
CHINA IS NEAR(1968, Ital.); DEEP RED(1976, Ital.)
Paco Mauri
PRIEST OF LOVE(1981, Brit.)
Roberto Mauri
LOST SOULS(1961, Ital.), a, d&w; CURSE OF THE BLOOD GHOULS(1969, Ital.), d&w
Claude Mauriac
SEVEN CAPITAL SINS(1962, Fr./Ital.), w; THERESE(1963, Fr.), w
Francois Mauriac
THERESE(1963, Fr.), w
Maurice
GANGSTER, THE(1947), p
Andre Maurice
TRIAL OF JOAN OF ARC(1965, Fr.)
Celia Maurice
SMITHEREENS(1982)
Frank Maurice
PEPE LE MOKO(1937, Fr.); BAD MEN OF TOMBSTONE(1949), p
John Maurice
WARRIORS, THE(1979)
Marjorie Maurice
Misc. Silents
DEUCE OF SPADES, THE(1922)
Mary Maurice
Silents
BATTLE CRY OF PEACE, THE(1915); SINS OF THE MOTHERS(1915)
Misc. Silents
RETURN OF MAURICE DONNELLY, THE(1915); ROSE OF THE SOUTH(1916); SUPREME TEMPTATION, THE(1916); FOR FRANCE(1917); HER SECRET(1917); I WILL REPAY(1917); TRANSGRESSION(1917); WHO GOES THERE?(1917); LITTLE RUNAWAY, THE(1918)
Maurice Maurice
ARISE, MY LOVE(1940)
Paula Maurice
BRAIN THAT WOULDN'T DIE, THE(1959)
Peggy Maurice
Silents
MARCH HARE, THE(1919, Brit.)
Rex Maurice
KITTY(1929, Brit.); LATIN LOVE(1930, Brit.); SUCH IS THE LAW(1930, Brit.)
Misc. Silents
CHICK(1928, Brit.); PRICE OF DIVORCE, THE(1928, Brit.)
Rita Maurice
Silents
DARLING OF THE RICH, THE(1923)
Maurice Winnick and His Band
PICCADILLY NIGHTS(1930, Brit.); AROUND THE TOWN(1938, Brit.)

Maurice Winnick's Ciro's Club Band
GIVE HER A RING(1936, Brit.)
Mauricet
FROM TOP TO BOTTOM(1933, Fr.)
Giovanni Mauriello
ANOTHER TIME, ANOTHER PLACE(1983, Brit.)
1984
ANOTHER TIME, ANOTHER PLACE(1984, Brit.)
Tami Mauriello
ON THE WATERFRONT(1954)
Claire Maurier
LA PARISIENNE(1958, Fr./Ital.); BACK TO THE WALL(1959, Fr.); FOUR HUN-
DRED BLOWS, THE(1959); DANIELLA BY NIGHT(1962, Fr/Ger.); SWEET EC-
STASY(1962, Fr.); MISTRESS FOR THE SUMMER, A(1964, Fr./Ital.); MY WIFE'S
HUSBAND(1965, Fr./Ital.); VERY CURIOUS GIRL, A(1970, Fr.); LA CAGE AUX
FOLLES(1979, Fr./Ital.)
Serge Mauriet
ICE PALACE(1960)
Delphi Maurin
MURDER CLINIC, THE(1967, Ital./Fr.)
Dominique Maurin
RIFIFI(1956, Fr.); SUNDAYS AND CYBELE(1962, Fr.)
J.P. Maurin
AMAZING MONSIEUR FABRE, THE(1952, Fr.)
Jean-Francois Maurin
SECRET WORLD(1969, Fr.)
Marie Veronique Maurin
PEPPERMINT SODA(1979, Fr.)
Fritz Maurischat
COURT CONCERT, THE(1936, Ger.), set d; LIFE BEGINS ANEW(1938, Ger.), set d;
DEVIL MAKES THREE, THE(1952), art d; MARTIN LUTHER(1953), art d; FOR THE
FIRST TIME(1959, U.S./Ger./Ital.), art d
Maurishka
STAY AWAY, JOE(1968); RED, WHITE AND BLACK, THE(1970)
Albert M. Mauro
NATIONAL LAMPOON'S ANIMAL HOUSE(1978)
David Mauro
BEAU GESTE(1966); AMBUSHERS, THE(1967); DON'T JUST STAND THERE(1968);
MACK, THE(1973); HINDENBURG, THE(1975)
Donatella Mauro
LET'S TALK ABOUT WOMEN(1964, Fr./Ital.)
Humberto Mauro
Misc. Silents
BRASA DORMIDA(1928, Braz.), d
Jole Mauro
FRANCIS OF ASSISI(1961); EVERYBODY GO HOME!(1962, Fr./Ital.); INVINCIBLE
GLADIATOR, THE(1963, c.u. Ital./Span.); DISORDER(1964, Fr./Ital.); EMPTY CAN-
VAS, THE(1964, Fr./Ital.); HERCULES, SAMSON & ULYSSES(1964, Ital.)
Ralph Mauro
IT'S MY TURN(1980); THEY CALL ME BRUCE(1982)
Renata Mauro
NAKED MAJA, THE(1959, Ital./U.S.)
Andre Maurois
ENTENTE CORDIALE(1939, Fr.), w
Alfred Maurstad
VALLEY OF EAGLES(1952, Brit.); MAKE WAY FOR LILA(1962, Swed./Ger.)
Toralv Maurstad
PASSIONATE DEMONS, THE(1962, Norway); SONG OF NORWAY(1970)
Tordis Maurstad
SONG OF NORWAY(1970)
Gerda Maurus
WHITE DEMON, THE(1932, Ger.); INVISIBLE OPPONENT(1933, Ger.)
Silents
SPIES(1929, Ger.); WOMAN ON THE MOON, THE(1929, Ger.)
Alfred Maury
'TILL WE MEET AGAIN(1944), w
Charlotte Maury
1984
LES COMPERES(1984, Fr.)
Darrel Maury
LOOKER(1981)
Derrel Maury
CAT MURKIL AND THE SILKS(1976); MASSACRE AT CENTRAL HIGH(1976)
Jacques Maury
GENERALS WITHOUT BUTTONS(1938, Fr.), w; START THE REVOLUTION WITH-
OUT ME(1970); LOVE AND DEATH(1975); OTHER SIDE OF MIDNIGHT, THE(1977);
LITTLE ROMANCE, A(1979, U.S./Fr.)
1984
AMERICAN DREAMER(1984); LES COMPERES(1984, Fr.)
Jean-Louis Maury
LANDRU(1963, Fr./Ital); OPHELIA(1964, Fr.); BEAUTIFUL SWINDLERS,
THE(1967, Fr./Ital./Jap./Neth.); THIS MAN MUST DIE(1970, Fr./Ital.)
Gordon Maus
WILD PARTY, THE(1975)
Rodger Maus
SEVEN MINUTES, THE(1971), art d; UP THE SANDBOX(1972), set d; 10(1979), prod
d; HERBIE GOES BANANAS(1980), art d; VICTOR/VICTORIA(1982), prod d;
TRENCHCOAT(1983), prod d
1984
BUDDY SYSTEM, THE(1984), prod d; MICKI AND MAUDE(1984), prod d
Roger Maus
S.O.B.(1981), prod d; MAN WHO LOVED WOMEN, THE(1983), prod d
Roger E. Maus
MECHANIC, THE(1972), art d
Charles Mauu
PAGAN LOVE SONG(1950); ROAD TO BALI(1952); HELL SHIP MUTINY(1957)
Tetoa Mauu
TAHITIAN, THE(1956)

Jacques Mavae
LOVE AT NIGHT(1961, Fr.), ed
Jacques Mavel
PEEK-A-BOO(1961, Fr.), ed; PLEASURES AND VICES(1962, Fr.), ed
Daniel Maves
HOW TO BEAT THE HIGH COST OF LIVING(1980)
Milivoje Pepovic Mavid
TEMPEST(1958, Ital./Yugo./Fr.)
Adela Mavis
THIRD CLUE, THE(1934, Brit.)
Perry Mavrelis
RACING FEVER(1964)
Toni Maw
CIRCLE OF DECEIT(1982, Fr./Ger.)
Jacques Mawart
EXTERMINATORS, THE(1965 Fr.), art d
Angella Mawby
MAN FROM BLANKLEY'S, THE(1930)
Robert Mawdesley
LOYALTIES(1934, Brit.)
Marilyn Mawn
CAPTIVATION(1931, Brit)
J. P. Mawra
MURDER IN MISSISSIPPI(1965), d, ed
Misc. Talkies
ALL MEN ARE APES(1965), d
Joseph P. Mawra
OLGA'S GIRLS(1964), d
Edward Mawson
Misc. Silents
RETURN OF EVE, THE(1916)
Ed Max
STRANGE HOLIDAY(1945); EVERYBODY DOES IT(1949); HARVEY(1950); MISTER
880(1950); SIDE STREET(1950); FAT MAN, THE(1951); FRANCIS GOES TO THE
RACES(1951); I CAN GET IT FOR YOU WHOLESALE(1951); JIM THORPE–ALL
AMERICAN(1951); WELL, THE(1951); HERE COME THE NELSONS(1952); MODELS,
INC.(1952); WE'RE NOT MARRIED(1952); TWONKY, THE(1953)
Edwin Max
STAIRWAY TO HEAVEN(1946, Brit.); COME TO THE STABLE(1949); FOLLOW ME
QUIETLY(1949); JOHNNY STOOL PIGEON(1949); LAW OF THE BARBARY
COAST(1949); RED LIGHT(1949); RIDE, RYDER, RIDE!(1949); SET-UP, THE(1949);
THIEVES' HIGHWAY(1949); UNDERCOVER MAN, THE(1949); LOVE THAT BRU-
TE(1950); HALF ANGEL(1951); MEET ME AFTER THE SHOW(1951); RHU-
BARB(1951); BLOODHOUNDS OF BROADWAY(1952); JUMPING JACKS(1952);
TROPICAL HEAT WAVE(1952); INCREDIBLE MELTING MAN, THE(1978)
Harry Max
MODIGLIANI OF MONTPARNASSE(1961, Fr./Ital.)
Jason Max
SIMON, KING OF THE WITCHES(1971)
Jean Max
DARK EYES(1938, Fr.); J'ACCUSE(1939, Fr.)
Jerome Max
TENTACLES(1977, Ital.), w
Marilyn Max
SPRING BREAK(1983)
Maurice Max
WHEN THE GIRLS TAKE OVER(1962), ed
Ron Max
FORCED ENTRY(1975); BIG BRAWL, THE(1980); REACHING OUT(1983)
Max Rivers Girls
CLEANING UP(1933, Brit.)
The Max Rivers Girls
OVERNIGHT(1933, Brit.)
Max Rivers' Trocadero Girls
LATIN LOVE(1930, Brit.)
Bill Maxam
BUNNY LAKE IS MISSING(1965)
Louella Maxam
Misc. Silents
BECAUSE OF THE WOMAN(1917); DEUCE DUNCAN(1918)
The Maxellos
INCENDIARY BLONDE(1945); GREATEST SHOW ON EARTH, THE(1952)
Paul Maxey
THEY WON'T BELIEVE ME(1947); I'LL SELL MY LIFE(1941); LET'S GO COLLEGI-
ATE(1941); SWEET ROSIE O'GRADY(1943); BELOW THE DEADLINE(1946); PER-
SONALITY KID(1946); TILL THE CLOUDS ROLL BY(1946); BRASHER DOUBLOON,
THE(1947); MAGIC TOWN(1947); MILLIE'S DAUGHTER(1947); PHILO VANCE'S
SECRET MISSION(1947); RIDE THE PINK HORSE(1947); LET'S LIVE A LITT-
LE(1948); NOOSE HANGS HIGH, THE(1948); RIVER LADY(1948); SMART WO-
MAN(1948); THREE MUSKETEERS, THE(1948); BRIDE FOR SALE(1949);
DANGEROUS PROFESSION, A(1949); FIGHTING FOOLS(1949); MISSISSIPPI
RHYTHM(1949); MY DREAM IS YOURS(1949); SKY DRAGON(1949); REFORMER
AND THE REDHEAD, THE(1950); RETURN OF JESSE JAMES, THE(1950); ABBOTT
AND COSTELLO MEET THE INVISIBLE MAN(1951); AMERICAN IN PARIS,
AN(1951); BRIDE OF THE GORILLA(1951); CASA MANANA(1951); DREAM-
BOAT(1952); HERE COME THE MARINES(1952); KID MONK BARONI(1952); MON-
KEY BUSINESS(1952); NARROW MARGIN, THE(1952); SHE'S WORKING HER WAY
THROUGH COLLEGE(1952); SOMETHING TO LIVE FOR(1952); STARS AND
STRIPES FOREVER(1952); BIG HEAT, THE(1953); LATIN LOVERS(1953); RUN FOR
THE HILLS(1953); STORY OF THREE LOVES, THE(1953); STRANGER WORE A
GUN, THE(1953); BLACK TUESDAY(1955); CITY OF SHADOWS(1955); IT'S ALWAYS
FAIR WEATHER(1955); JUPITER'S DARLING(1955); TEN WANTED MEN(1955);
SHOWDOWN AT BOOT HILL(1958); NORTH TO ALASKA(1960); 20,000 EYES(1961);
WALK ON THE WILD SIDE(1962)
Paul Regan Maxey
MR. DODD TAKES THE AIR(1937)
Virginia Maxey
Misc. Talkies
TRAIL TO LAREDO(1948)

Harold Maxfield
CHANGE OF MIND(1969), art d
Harry Maxfield
REINCARNATE, THE(1971, Can.), art d
Henry S. Maxfield
DOUBLE MAN, THE(1967), w
Hiram Percy Maxim
SO GOES MY LOVE(1946), w
Hudson Maxim
Silents
BATTLE CRY OF PEACE, THE(1915), w
John Maxim
MARY HAD A LITTLE(1961, Brit.); FRANKENSTEIN CREATED WOMAN(1965, Brit.); SHE(1965, Brit.); DRACULA–PRINCE OF DARKNESS(1966, Brit.)
Max Maximilian
Silents
WOMAN ON THE MOON, THE(1929, Ger.)
Maximiliene
BAKER'S WIFE, THE(1940, Fr.)
Maximilienne
LILIOM(1935, Fr.); RECORD 413(1936, Fr.); PARDON MY FRENCH(1951, U.S./Fr.)
Maximillienne
MURDERER LIVES AT NUMBER 21, THE(1947, Fr.)
E. Maximov
BOUNTIFUL SUMMER(1951, USSR)
V. Maximov
Misc. Silents
THIEF(1916, USSR); LIVING CORPSE, A(1918, USSR); WOMAN WHO INVENTED LOVE, THE(1918, USSR); INFINITE SORROW(1922, USSR); LOCKSMITH AND CHANCELLOR(1923, USSR); DECEMBRISTS(1927, USSR)
A. Maximova
OTHELLO(1960, U.S.S.R.)
A.M. Maximova
HEROES OF THE SEA(1941)
Antonina Maximova
BALLAD OF A SOLDIER(1960, USSR)
E. Maximova
Silents
EARTH(1930, USSR)
Raia Maximova
IDIOT, THE(1960, USSR)
Yelena Maximova
Misc. Silents
WOMEN OF RYAZAN(1927, USSR)
Ita Maximovna
FIDELIO(1970, Ger.), set d; MARRIAGE OF FIGARO, THE(1970, Ger.), art d
Franz Maxman
ELEPHANT WALK(1954), m
Eric Maxon
Misc. Silents
AFTER DARK(1915)
Len Maxsell
WHAT'S UP, TIGER LILY?(1966), w
Jack Maxsted
MAN WITH A MILLION(1954, Brit.), art d; PURPLE PLAIN, THE(1954, Brit.), art d; DANGEROUS EXILE(1958, Brit.), art d; MAD LITTLE ISLAND(1958, Brit.), art d; ROONEY(1958, Brit.), art d; MAN IN THE MOON(1961, Brit.), art d; IMPERSONATOR, THE(1962, Brit.), art d; JASON AND THE ARGONAUTS(1963, Brit.), art d; SWORD OF LANCELOT(1963, Brit.), art d; BATTLE OF BRITAIN, THE(1969, Brit.), art d; DIAMONDS ARE FOREVER(1971, Brit.), art d; NICHOLAS AND ALEXANDRA(1971, Brit.), art d; PAPILLON(1973), art d; THAT LUCKY TOUCH(1975, Brit.), art d; DEEP, THE(1977), art d; WARLORDS OF ATLANTIS(1978, Brit.), art d; ARABIAN ADVENTURE(1979, Brit.), art d
David Maxt
SUPERMAN(1978)
Claude Maxted
OTHER PEOPLE'S SINS(1931, Brit.)
Jack Maxted
JACQUELINE(1956, Brit.), art d; ADVENTURERS, THE(1970), art d; WHEN EIGHT BELLS TOLL(1971, Brit.), art d
Stanley Maxted
FINAL TEST, THE(1953, Brit.); LAUGHING IN THE SUNSHINE(1953, Brit./Swed.); NEVER LET ME GO(1953, U.S./Brit.); PROJECT M7(1953, Brit.); LOVE LOTTERY, THE(1954, Brit.); I AM A CAMERA(1955, Brit.); ACROSS THE BRIDGE(1957, Brit.); CAMPBELL'S KINGDOM(1957, Brit.); WEAPON, THE(1957, Brit.); FEMALE FIENDS(1958, Brit.); FIEND WITHOUT A FACE(1958); IT'S NEVER TOO LATE(1958, Brit.)
Claude Maxten
TAXI FOR TWO(1929, Brit.)
Maxudian
Silents
ARAB, THE(1924)
Misc. Silents
LA TERRE PROMISE(1925, Fr.)
Max Maxudian
Silents
NAPOLEON(1927, Fr.)
Misc. Silents
POSSESSION(1922, Brit.)
Maxudian and Paulais
DARK EYES(1938, Fr.)
Aymer Maxwell
ANOTHER SKY(1960 Brit.), p
Barbara Maxwell
CLOWN AND THE KID, THE(1961), cos; YOU HAVE TO RUN FAST(1961), cos; INCIDENT IN AN ALLEY(1962), cos
Bill Maxwell
CONQUEROR WORM, THE(1968, Brit.)

Bob Maxwell
RAMRODDER, THE(1969), ph; SCAVENGERS, THE(1969), ph; WILD RIDERS(1971), ph
1984
CITY HEAT(1984)
Silents
OLYMPIC HERO, THE(1928)
Carolyn Maxwell
GAS(1981, Can.)
Charles Maxwell
CALM YOURSELF(1935), m; WEST POINT OF THE AIR(1935), m; GIRLS' DORMITORY(1936), m; SAN QUENTIN(1937), m; WINGS AND THE WOMAN(1942, Brit.); ALONG CAME JONES(1945), m; SCOTLAND YARD INVESTIGATOR(1945, Brit.), m; GROOM WORE SPURS, THE(1951), m; FINGER MAN(1955); SEARCH FOR BRIDEY MURPHY, THE(1956)
Dan Maxwell
MRS. MINIVER(1942)
Daphne Maxwell
1984
PROTOCOL(1984)
Don Maxwell
HUMANOIDS FROM THE DEEP(1980)
Dusty Maxwell
1984
BOSTONIANS, THE(1984)
E. C. Maxwell
Silents
OLD CODE, THE(1928), w
Ed Maxwell
GIRL FROM CALGARY(1932)
Edwin Maxwell
TAMING OF THE SHREW, THE(1929); ALL QUIET ON THE WESTERN FRONT(1930); DU BARRY, WOMAN OF PASSION(1930); TOP SPEED(1930); AMBASSADOR BILL(1931); DADDY LONG LEGS(1931); DAYBREAK(1931); GORILLA, THE(1931); INSPIRATION(1931); KIKI(1931); MEN OF THE SKY(1931); YELLOW TICKET, THE(1931); AMERICAN MADNESS(1932); COHENS, AND KELLYS IN HOLLYWOOD, THE(1932); GRAND HOTEL(1932); MERRILY WE GO TO HELL(1932); SCARFACE(1932); SHOPWORN(1932); SIX HOURS TO LIVE(1932); THOSE WE LOVE(1932); TIGER SHARK(1932); TRIAL OF VIVIENNE WARE, THE(1932); TWO KINDS OF WOMEN(1932); YOU SAID A MOUTHFUL(1932); ANN VICKERS(1933); DINNER AT EIGHT(1933); DUCK SOUP(1933); EMERGENCY CALL(1933); GAMBLING SHIP(1933); HEROES FOR SALE(1933); LADY KILLER(1933); MAYOR OF HELL, THE(1933); MYSTERY OF THE WAX MUSEUM, THE(1933); NIGHT OF TERROR(1933); POLICE CAR 17(1933); STATE TROOPER(1933); TONIGHT IS OURS(1933); WOMAN I STOLE, THE(1933); BIG TIME OR BUST(1934); CAT'S PAW, THE(1934); CLEOPATRA(1934); DANCING MAN(1934); FOG(1934); GIFT OF GAB(1934); HOLLYWOOD PARTY(1934); MISS FANE'S BABY IS STOLEN(1934); MYSTERY LINER(1934); NINTH GUEST, THE(1934); THIS SIDE OF HEAVEN(1934); CRUSADES, THE(1935); DEVIL IS A WOMAN, THE(1935); GREAT GOD GOLD(1935); HAPPINESS C.O.D.(1935); LAST DAYS OF POMPEII, THE(1935); MOTIVE FOR REVENGE(1935); THANKS A MILLION(1935); BIG BROWN EYES(1936); COME AND GET IT(1936); DANGEROUS WATERS(1936); FURY(1936); GREAT ZIEGFELD, THE(1936); MR. DEEDS GOES TO TOWN(1936); LOVE IS NEWS(1937); LOVE TAKES FLIGHT(1937); MAN BETRAYED, A(1937); NIGHT KEY(1937); PLAINSMAN, THE(1937); ROAD BACK,THE(1937); SLAVE SHIP(1937); SLIM(1937); STAR IS BORN, A(1937); 100 MEN AND A GIRL(1937); PARADISE FOR THREE(1938); RICH MAN, POOR GIRL(1938); ROMANCE ON THE RUN(1938); YOU CAN'T TAKE IT WITH YOU(1938); DRUMS ALONG THE MOHAWK(1939); MADE FOR EACH OTHER(1939); NINOTCHKA(1939); WAY DOWN SOUTH(1939); YOUNG MR. LINCOLN(1939); BLUE BIRD, THE(1940); HIS GIRL FRIDAY(1940); KIT CARSON(1940); NEW MOON(1940); PAROLE FIXER(1940); SHOP AROUND THE CORNER, THE(1940); BLOSSOMS IN THE DUST(1941); DEVIL AND MISS JONES, THE(1941); MIDNIGHT ANGEL(1941); RIDE ON VAQUERO(1941); I LIVE ON DANGER(1942); STREET OF CHANCE(1942); TEN GENTLEMEN FROM WEST POINT(1942); BEHIND PRISON WALLS(1943); HEAVEN CAN WAIT(1943); HOLY MATRIMONY(1943); GREAT MOMENT, THE(1944); PRACTICALLY YOURS(1944); SINCE YOU WENT AWAY(1944); WATERFRONT(1944); WILSON(1944); GREAT JOHN L. THE(1945); MAMA LOVES PAPA(1945); JOLSON STORY, THE(1946); SWAMP FIRE(1946); GANGSTER, THE(1947); SECOND CHANCE(1947); CAMPUS HONEYMOON(1948); VICIOUS CIRCLE, THE(1948)
Misc. Talkies
BACK PAGE(1934); MEN OF ACTION(1935)
Eileen Maxwell
WOMAN'S WORLD(1954); SON OF SINBAD(1955)
Elsa Maxwell
HOTEL FOR WOMEN(1939), a, w; PUBLIC DEB NO. 1(1940); STAGE DOOR CANTEEN(1943)
Everett C. Maxwell
Silents
NORTHERN CODE(1925), w
Frank Maxwell
VIOLATORS, THE(1957); LONELYHEARTS(1958); MOUNTAIN ROAD, THE(1960); ADA(1961); BY LOVE POSSESSED(1961); INTRUDER, THE(1962); HAUNTED PALACE, THE(1963); RAGE TO LIVE, A(1965); MADAME X(1966); WILD ANGELS, THE(1966); MR. MAJESTYK(1974)
Gavin Maxwell
RING OF BRIGHT WATER(1969, Brit.), w
Geraldine Maxwell
Misc. Silents
PEARLS OF DEATH(1914, Brit.); STOLEN HONOURS(1914, Brit.)
Ivor Maxwell
LOVE'S OLD SWEET SONG(1933, Brit.)
James Maxwell
SUBWAY IN THE SKY(1959, Brit.); DESIGN FOR LOVING(1962, Brit.); GIRL ON APPROVAL(1962, Brit.); PRIVATE POTTER(1963, Brit.); TRAITORS, THE(1963, Brit.); EVIL OF FRANKENSTEIN, THE(1964, Brit.); THIRD SECRET, THE(1964, Brit.); THESE ARE THE DAMNED(1965, Brit.); OTLEY(1969, Brit.); CONNECTING ROOMS(1971, Brit.); ONE DAY IN THE LIFE OF IVAN DENISOVICH(1971, U.S./Brit./Norway); TERRORISTS, THE(1975, Brit.)

Jane Maxwell
MYSTERY OF THE BLACK JUNGLE(1955)
Jennie Maxwell
BLUE DENIM(1959)
Jenny Maxwell
BLUE HAWAII(1961); SHOTGUN WEDDING, THE(1963); TAKE HER, SHE'S MINE(1963)
John Maxwell
BLACKMAIL(1929, Brit.), p; COMPULSORY HUSBAND, THE(1930, Brit.), p; JUNO AND THE PAYCOCK(1930, Brit.), p; KISS ME, SERGEANT(1930, Brit.), p; MIDDLE WATCH, THE(1930, Brit.), p; MURDER(1930, Brit.), p; SONG OF SOHO(1930, Brit.), p; WHY SAILORS LEAVE HOME(1930, Brit.), p; YELLOW MASK, THE(1930, Brit.), p; COMPROMISED!(1931, Brit.), p; HER STRANGE DESIRE(1931, Brit.), p; HOBSON'S CHOICE(1931, Brit.), p; KEEPERS OF YOUTH(1931, Brit.), p; LOVE HABIT, THE(1931, Brit.), p; MAN FROM CHICAGO, THE(1931, Brit.), p; OUT OF THE BLUE(1931, Brit.), p; SKIN GAME, THE(1931, Brit.), p; JOSSER IN THE ARMY(1932, Brit.), p; LAST COUPON, THE(1932, Brit.), p; LET ME EXPLAIN, DEAR(1932, Brit.), p; LUCKY GIRL(1932, Brit.), p; MAID OF THE MOUNTAINS, THE(1932, Brit.), p; MY WIFE'S FAMILY(1932, Brit.), p; NUMBER SEVENTEEN(1932, Brit.), p; OLD SPANISH CUSTOMERS(1932, Brit.), p; RICH AND STRANGE(1932, Brit.), p; SHADOW BETWEEN, THE(1932, Brit.), p; WOMAN DECIDES, THE(1932, Brit.), p; FACING THE MUSIC(1933, Brit.), p; LEAVE IT TO ME(1933, Brit.), p; LETTING IN THE SUNSHINE(1933, Brit.), p; SECRET AGENT(1933, Brit.), p; SONG YOU GAVE ME, THE(1934, Brit.), p; YOU MADE ME LOVE YOU(1934, Brit.), p; BORROWED HERO(1941); FLYING CADETS(1941); HONKY TONK(1941); NINE LIVES ARE NOT ENOUGH(1941); ARIZONA TERRORS(1942); BROADWAY(1942); LONE PRAIRIE, THE(1942); MAN FROM HEADQUARTERS(1942); MURDER IN THE BIG HOUSE(1942); MYSTERY OF MARIE ROGET, THE(1942); SPY SHIP(1942); BOSS OF BIG TOWN(1943); FALSE FACES(1943); MISSION TO MOSCOW(1943); MURDER ON THE WATERFRONT(1943); PAYOFF, THE(1943); RHYTHM OF THE ISLANDS(1943); SILVER SKATES(1943); TRUCK BUSTERS(1943); ALASKA(1944); KISMET(1944); LADY IN THE DEATH HOUSE(1944); LAST HORSEMAN, THE(1944); MAN I LOVE, THE(1946), d; MONSIEUR BEAUCAIRE(1946); O.S.S.(1946); PALEFACE, THE(1948); MASTERSON OF KANSAS(1954); THEM!(1954); COURT-MARTIAL OF BILLY MITCHELL, THE(1955); ETERNAL SEA, THE(1955); THEY CAN'T HANG ME(1955, Brit.); TRIAL(1955); YOUNG AT HEART(1955); FRANCIS IN THE HAUNTED HOUSE(1956); SHOWDOWN AT ABILENE(1956); STRANGE ADVENTURE, A(1956); TERROR AT MIDNIGHT(1956); THESE WILDER YEARS(1956); GUNFIGHT AT THE O.K. CORRAL(1957); WAYWARD GIRL, THE(1957); FLOOD TIDE(1958); LINEUP, THE(1958); MAN WHO DIED TWICE, THE(1958); CAGE OF EVIL(1960)
Silents
RING, THE(1927, Brit.), p; CHAMPAGNE(1928, Brit.), p; FARMER'S WIFE, THE(1928, Brit.), p; WOMAN TEMPTED, THE(1928, Brit.), p; MANXMAN, THE(1929, Brit.), p
Joseph Maxwell
Misc. Silents
FRIVOLOUS WIVES(1920), d
Len Maxwell
WHAT'S UP, TIGER LILY?(1966); HUGO THE HIPPO(1976, Hung./U.S.)
Lisa Maxwell
DARK CRYSTAL, THE(1982, Brit.); REMEMBRANCE(1982, Brit.)
Lois Maxwell
THAT HAGEN GIRL(1947); BIG PUNCH, THE(1948); CORRIDOR OF MIRRORS(1948, Brit.); DARK PAST, THE(1948); DECISION OF CHRISTOPHER BLAKE, THE(1948); CRIME DOCTOR'S DIARY, THE(1949); KAZAN(1949); BRIEF RAPTURE(1952, Ital.); SCOTLAND YARD INSPECTOR(1952, Brit.); TWILIGHT WOMEN(1953, Brit.); WOMAN IN HIDING(1953, Brit.); AIDA(1954, Ital.); GREAT HOPE, THE(1954, Ital.); WOMAN'S ANGLE, THE(1954, Brit.); PASSPORT TO TREASON(1956, Brit.); SATELLITE IN THE SKY(1956); HIGH TERRACE(1957, Brit.); TIME WITHOUT PITY(1957, Brit.); KILL ME TOMORROW(1958, Brit.); FACE OF FIRE(1959, U.S./Brit.); UNSTOPPABLE MAN, THE(1961, Brit.); DR. NO(1962, Brit.); LOLITA(1962); COME FLY WITH ME(1963); FROM RUSSIA WITH LOVE(1963, Brit.); HAUNTING, THE(1963); GOLDFINGER(1964, Brit.); THUNDERBALL(1965, Brit.); OPERATION KID BROTHER(1967, Ital.); YOU ONLY LIVE TWICE(1967, Brit.); ON HER MAJESTY'S SECRET SERVICE(1969, Brit.); ADVENTURERS, THE(1970); DIAMONDS ARE FOREVER(1971, Brit.); ENDLESS NIGHT(1971, Brit.); LIVE AND LET DIE(1973, Brit.); MAN WITH THE GOLDEN GUN, THE(1974, Brit.); AGE OF INNOCENCE(1977, Can.); SPY WHO LOVED ME, THE(1977, Brit.); LOST AND FOUND(1979); MOONRAKER(1979, Brit.); MR. PATMAN(1980, Can.); FOR YOUR EYES ONLY(1981); OCTOPUSSY(1983, Brit.)
Lucien Maxwell
PRAIRIE SCHOONERS(1940)
M. Maxwell
Misc. Silents
REGENERATION(1923)
Maggie Maxwell
MUSIC LOVERS, THE(1971, Brit.); GOODBYE PORK PIE(1981, New Zealand)
Maggy Maxwell
SAVAGE MESSIAH(1972, Brit.); SITTING TARGET(1972, Brit.)
Margaret Maxwell
MOULIN ROUGE(1952)
Marilyn Maxwell
STAND BY FOR ACTION(1942); DR. GILLESPIE'S CRIMINAL CASE(1943); DU BARRY WAS A LADY(1943); PILOT NO. 5(1943); PRESENTING LILY MARS(1943); SALUTE TO THE MARINES(1943); SWING FEVER(1943); THOUSANDS CHEER(1943); BETWEEN TWO WOMEN(1944); LOST IN A HAREM(1944); THREE MEN IN WHITE(1944); SHOW-OFF, THE(1946); HIGH BARBAREE(1947); RACE STREET(1948); SUMMER HOLIDAY(1948); CHAMPION(1949); KEY TO THE CITY(1950); OUTSIDE THE WALL(1950); LEMON DROP KID, THE(1951); NEW MEXICO(1951); EAST OF SUMATRA(1953); OFF LIMITS(1953); PARIS MODEL(1953); NEW YORK CONFIDENTIAL(1955); ROCK-A-BYE BABY(1958); CRITIC'S CHOICE(1963);

LIVELY SET, THE(1964); STAGE TO THUNDER ROCK(1964); ARIZONA BUSHWHACKERS(1968); FROM NASHVILLE WITH MUSIC(1969); PHYNX, THE(1970)
Morton Maxwell, M.D.
NOT AS A STRANGER(1955), tech adv
Nora Maxwell
GIRL IN GOLD BOOTS(1968), cos; POINT OF TERROR(1971), makeup
Norman Maxwell
PORT OF LOST DREAMS(1935), w; FORTY THOUSAND HORSEMEN(1941, Aus.)
Paisley Maxwell
FLAMING FRONTIER(1958, Can.); NOW THAT APRIL'S HERE(1958, Can.)
Patricia Maxwell
LINE, THE(1982), w
Paul Maxwell
TOUCH AND GO(1955), ed; BLOOD OF DRACULA(1957); HOW TO MAKE A MONSTER(1958); SUBMARINE SEAHAWK(1959); FREEDOM TO DIE(1962, Brit.); WE JOINED THE NAVY(1962, Brit.); FOLLOW THE BOYS(1963); HAUNTING, THE(1963); SHADOW OF FEAR(1963, Brit.); MAN IN THE MIDDLE(1964, U.S./Brit.); CITY OF FEAR(1965, Brit.); UP FROM THE BEACH(1965); DEVIL'S MAN, THE(1967, Ital.), d; IT!(1967, Brit.); 25TH HOUR, THE(1967, Fr./Ital./Yugo.); MAN OUTSIDE, THE(1968, Brit.); THUNDERBIRDS ARE GO(1968, Brit.); LOOKING GLASS WAR, THE(1970, Brit.); BAXTER(1973, Brit.); PINK PANTHER STRIKES AGAIN, THE(1976, Brit.)
1984
SAHARA(1984)
Paul Maxwell [Paolo Bianchini]
SUPERARGO(1968, Ital./Span.), d
Paula Maxwell
20TH CENTURY OZ(1977, Aus.)
Peter Maxwell
TOUCH AND GO(1955), d, w; BLIND SPOT(1958, Brit.), d; DESPERATE MAN, THE(1959, Brit.), d; LONG SHADOW, THE(1961, Brit.), d; SERENA(1962, Brit.), d; IMPACT(1963, Brit.), d, w; SWITCH, THE(1963, Brit.), d
Misc. Talkies
COUNTRY TOWN(1971), d; PLUNGE INTO DARKNESS(1977), d
Richard Maxwell
CHALLENGE, THE(1982), w
Robert Maxwell
SUPERMAN AND THE MOLE MEN(1951), p; GIRL IN GOLD BOOTS(1968), ph; ASTRO-ZOMBIES, THE(1969), ph; BUSHBABY, THE(1970), p, w; SONG OF THE LOON(1970), ph; UP YOUR TEDDY BEAR(1970), ph; WANDERLOVE(1970), ph; POINT OF TERROR(1971), ph; SUNDAY IN THE COUNTRY(1975, Can.), w
Roberta Maxwell
GREAT BIG THING, A(1968, U.S./Can.); RICH KIDS(1979); CHANGELING, THE(1980, Can.); POPEYE(1980)
Roger Maxwell
SAVE A LITTLE SUNSHINE(1938, Brit.); HA' PENNY BREEZE(1950, Brit.); NIGHT WAS OUR FRIEND(1951, Brit.); COLONEL MARCH INVESTIGATES(1952,Brit.); TREASURE HUNT(1952, Brit.); DEADLY NIGHTSHADE(1953, Brit.); GLAD TIDINGS(1953, Brit.); STEEL KEY, THE(1953, Brit.); JOHN WESLEY(1954, Brit.); KEEP IT CLEAN(1956, Brit.); DOCTOR ZHIVAGO(1965)
Ron Maxwell
NIGHT THE LIGHTS WENT OUT IN GEORGIA, THE(1981)
Ronald F. Maxwell
LITTLE DARLINGS(1980), d; NIGHT THE LIGHTS WENT OUT IN GEORGIA, THE(1981), d
1984
KIDCO(1984), d
Ronald Maxwell
CHRISTINE KEELER AFFAIR, THE(1964, Brit.), w
Roy Maxwell
WHISPERERS, THE(1967, Brit.)
Sharon Maxwell
PUMPKIN EATER, THE(1964, Brit.)
Stacey Maxwell
PAJAMA PARTY(1964); EIGHT ON THE LAM(1967); YOUNG RUNAWAYS, THE(1968)
Thad Maxwell
BOXCAR BERTHA(1972), m
Tony Maxwell
DEVIL AT FOUR O'CLOCK, THE(1961); DIME WITH A HALO(1963)
W. B. Maxwell
Silents
RAGGED MESSENGER, THE(1917, Brit.), w; MRS. THOMPSON(1919, Brit.), w
William Babington Maxwell
MADONNA OF THE STREETS(1930), w
Silents
GILDED HIGHWAY, THE(1926), w
William Maxwell
1984
PLOUGHMAN'S LUNCH, THE(1984, Brit.)
Theresa Maxwell-Conover
AGE OF INNOCENCE(1934)
Peter Maxwell-Davies
1984
FOREVER YOUNG(1984, Brit.), m
Ada May
DANCE, GIRL, DANCE(1933)
Alexander May
DREAM TOWN(1973, Ger.); PEDESTRIAN, THE(1974, Ger.)
Alice May
Silents
CURSE OF DRINK, THE(1922); MISSING MILLIONS(1922); WIDE-OPEN TOWN, A(1922); CRITICAL AGE, THE(1923); RAGGED EDGE, THE(1923)
Misc. Silents
BITTER TRUTH(1917)
Alyce May
BAD AND THE BEAUTIFUL, THE(1952)

Angela May
Misc. Talkies
BLACKJACK(1978)

Ann May
Silents
PARIS GREEN(1920); AMATEUR DEVIL, AN(1921); FOG, THE(1923)
Misc. Silents
MARRIAGE FOR CONVENIENCE(1919); HALF BREED, THE(1922); VERMILION PENCIL, THE(1922); O.U. WEST(1925)

Anthony May
CROMWELL(1970, Brit.); NO BLADE OF GRASS(1970, Brit.); TRIPLE ECHO, THE(1973, Brit.); MC VICAR(1982, Brit.)

April May
1984
HOLLYWOOD HIGH PART II(1984)

Benjamin May
KILL OR BE KILLED(1967, Ital.)

Bert May
THIN MAN GOES HOME, THE(1944); STRIP, THE(1951); BAND WAGON, THE(1953); CALIFORNIA SUITE(1978)

Betty May
NIGHT NURSE(1931)
Silents
EAST SIDE–WEST SIDE(1923)
Misc. Silents
FLAMING FURY(1926)

Beverly May
SO FINE(1981)

Beverly W. May
1984
FIRSTBORN(1984)

Bill May
TRAVELING SALESLADY, THE(1935)

Billy May
SUN VALLEY SERENADE(1941); NIGHTMARE(1956); FUZZY PINK NIGHTGOWN, THE(1957), m; SERGEANTS 3(1962), m; JOHNNY COOL(1963), m; TONY ROME(1967), m, md; SECRET LIFE OF AN AMERICAN WIFE, THE(1968), m; FRONT PAGE, THE(1974), m; PENNIES FROM HEAVEN(1981), m

Bob May
HARDLY WORKING(1981)

Brian May
TRUE STORY OF ESKIMO NELL, THE(1975, Aus.), m; MAD MAX(1979, Aus.), m; PATRICK(1979, Aus.), m; THIRST(1979, Aus.), m; HARLEQUIN(1980, Aus.), m; DAY AFTER HALLOWEEN, THE(1981, Aus.), m; GALLIPOLI(1981, Aus.), m; ROAD GAMES(1981, Aus.), m; ROAD WARRIOR, THE(1982, Aus.), m; ESCAPE 2000(1983, Aus.), m; KILLING OF ANGEL STREET, THE(1983, Aus.), m
1984
CLOAK AND DAGGER(1984), m; TREASURE OF THE YANKEE ZEPHYR(1984), m

Bunny May
WIND OF CHANGE, THE(1961, Brit.); ATCH ME A SPY(1971, Brit./Fr.)

C. May
UTOPIA(1952, Fr./Ital.)

Cecilia May
TOGETHER(1956, Brit.)

Claude May
GENERALS WITHOUT BUTTONS(1938, Fr.)

Clement May
RANDOM HARVEST(1942)

Curt May
BLOW OUT(1981)

Curtis May
LOOKS AND SMILES(1982, Brit.)

Cynthia May
DOWNHILL RACER(1969), cos

Daniel L. May
TENDER MERCIES(1982), set d

David May
JACK SLADE(1953)

Deborah May
1984
WOMAN IN RED, THE(1984)

Dick May
PLEASURE PLANTATION(1970), set d; DIMBOOLA(1979, Aus.)

Donald May
WRONG MAN, THE(1956); CROWDED SKY, THE(1960); KISSES FOR MY PRESIDENT(1964); TIGER WALKS, A(1964); FOLLOW ME, BOYS!(1966)

Doris May
Silents
JAILBIRD, THE(1920); BRONZE BELL, THE(1921); PECK'S BAD BOY(1921); ROOKIE'S RETURN, THE(1921); GAY AND DEVILISH(1922); COMMON LAW, THE(1923)
Misc. Silents
WHAT'S YOUR HUSBAND DOING?(1919); 23 ½ HOURS ON LEAVE(1919); MARY'S ANKLE(1920); EDEN AND RETURN(1921); FOOLISH AGE(1921); FOOLISH MATRONS, THE(1921); BOY CRAZY(1922); UNDERSTUDY, THE(1922); UP AND AT 'EM(1922); GUNFIGHTER, THE(1923); TEA–WITH A KICK(1923); CONDUCTOR 1492(1924); FAITHFUL WIVES(1926)

Doris May [Lee]
Misc. Silents
LET'S BE FASHIONABLE(1920)

Edith May
GODLESS GIRL, THE(1929)

Elaine May
ENTER LAUGHING(1967); LUV(1967); NEW LEAF, A(1971), a, d, w; HEARTBREAK KID, THE(1972), d; MIKEY AND NICKY(1976), d&w; CALIFORNIA SUITE(1978); HEAVEN CAN WAIT(1978), w; TOOTSIE(1982), w

Erna May
MOON OVER THE ALLEY(1980, Brit.)

Hans May
VIENNA, CITY OF SONGS(1931, Ger.), m; EVERYTHING IN LIFE(1936, Brit.), m; GIVE HER A RING(1936, Brit.), m/l Clifford Grey; SOUTHERN ROSES(1936, Brit.), m; STARS LOOK DOWN, THE(1940, Brit.), m; THUNDER ROCK(1944, Brit.), m; MURDER IN REVERSE(1946, Brit.), m; WALTZ TIME(1946, Brit.), a, m; WOMAN TO WOMAN(1946, Brit.), md; BRIGHTON ROCK(1947, Brit.), m; DUAL ALIBI(1947, Brit.), m; FAME IS THE SPUR(1947, Brit.), md; GHOSTS OF BERKELEY SQUARE(1947, Brit.), m; GREEN FINGERS(1947), m; UNEASY TERMS(1948, Brit.), m, md; MY BROTHER JONATHAN(1949, Brit.), m, md; GUILT IS MY SHADOW(1950, Brit.), m; LAUGHING LADY, THE(1950, Brit.), m, md; MRS. FITZHERBERT(1950, Brit.), md; NO ROOM AT THE INN(1950, Brit.), m, md; TALE OF FIVE WOMEN, A(1951, Brit.), m; FRIGHTENED BRIDE, THE(1952, Brit.), m; I'LL GET YOU(1953, Brit.), m; NEVER LET ME GO(1953, U.S./Brit.), m&md; SHOOT FIRST(1953, Brit.), m; SHADOW OF THE EAGLE(1955, Brit.), m&md; GYPSY AND THE GENTLEMAN, THE(1958, Brit.), m&md

Harry May
DETROIT 9000(1973), ph; ROOMMATES, THE(1973), ph; FRIDAY FOSTER(1975), ph; J.D.'S REVENGE(1976), ph

Helen May
Misc. Silents
SILENT WITNESS, THE(1917)

Ida May
UNION PACIFIC(1939)

Jack May
GIVE ME THE STARS(1944, Brit.); BRIEF ENCOUNTER(1945, Brit.); NO ROOM AT THE INN(1950, Brit.); HORSE'S MOUTH, THE(1953, Brit.); TIME GENTLEMEN PLEASE!(1953, Brit.); INNOCENTS IN PARIS(1955, Brit.); IT'S A GREAT DAY(1956, Brit.); CAT GIRL(1957); SILENT ENEMY, THE(1959, Brit.); PRIZE OF ARMS, A(1962, Brit.); THERE WAS A CROOKED MAN(1962, Brit.); TRAITORS, THE(1963, Brit.); FUNNY THING HAPPENED ON THE WAY TO THE FORUM, A(1966); SOLO FOR SPARROW(1966, Brit.); HOW I WON THE WAR(1967, Brit.); TWIST OF SAND, A(1968, Brit.); GOODBYE MR. CHIPS(1969, U.S./Brit.); NIGHT AFTER NIGHT AFTER NIGHT(1970, Brit.); TROG(1970, Brit.); MAN WHO WOULD BE KING, THE(1975, Brit.); SEVEN-PER-CENT SOLUTION, THE(1977, Brit.); RETURN OF THE SOLDIER, THE(1983, Brit.)
1984
BOUNTY, THE(1984)
Misc. Talkies
BIG ZAPPER(1974)

Jacqueline May
NEW KIND OF LOVE, A(1963)

James May
KEY, THE(1934); LIMEHOUSE BLUES(1934); BONNIE SCOTLAND(1935); FEATHER IN HER HAT, A(1935); WHITE ANGEL, THE(1936)

Jay May
SCHIZOID(1980); KING OF THE MOUNTAIN(1981)

Jerry L. May
NARCOTICS STORY, THE(1958), ph

Joe May
MUSIC IN THE AIR(1934), d; TWO HEARTS IN WALTZ TIME(1934, Brit.), d; NO MONKEY BUSINESS(1935, Brit.), w; CONFESSION(1937), d; HOUSE OF FEAR, THE(1939), d; SOCIETY SMUGGLERS(1939), d; HOUSE OF THE SEVEN GABLES, THE(1940), d; INVISIBLE MAN RETURNS, THE(1940), d, w; YOU'RE NOT SO TOUGH(1940), d; HIT THE ROAD(1941), d; INVISIBLE WOMAN, THE(1941), w; STRANGE DEATH OF ADOLF HITLER, THE(1943), w; JOHNNY DOESN'T LIVE HERE ANY MORE(1944), d; UNCERTAIN GLORY(1944), w; BUCCANEER'S GIRL(1950), w
Misc. Silents
HILDE WARREN AND DEATH(1916, Ger.), d; GREATEST TRUTH, THE(1922, Ger.), d; MYSTERIES OF INDIA(1922, Ger.), d; TRAGEDY OF LOVE(1923, Ger.), d; HOMECOMING(1929, Ger.), d

Julie May
HOT MILLIONS(1968, Brit.); POOR COW(1968, Brit.); WORK IS A FOUR LETTER WORD(1968, Brit.); SCHOOL FOR SEX(1969, Brit.)

Karl May
AMONG VULTURES(1964, Ger./Ital./Fr./Yugo.), w; APACHE GOLD(1965, Ger.), w; FRONTIER HELLCAT(1966, Fr./Ital./Ger./Yugo.), w; FLAMING FRONTIER(1968, Ger./Yugo.), w; OLD SHATTERHAND(1968, Ger./Yugo./Fr./Ital.), w

Karl Friedrich May
DESPERADO TRAIL, THE(1965, Ger./Yugo.), w; TREASURE OF SILVER LAKE(1965, Fr./Ger./Yugo.), w; LAST OF THE RENEGADES(1966, Fr./Ital./Ger./Yugo.), w; RAMPAGE AT APACHE WELLS(1966, Ger./Yugo.), w

Lenora May
PROMISES IN THE DARK(1979); WHEN A STRANGER CALLS(1979)

Lola May
Silents
CIVILIZATION(1916)
Misc. Silents
BEGGAR OF CAWNPORE, THE(1916); HEART OF NORA FLYNN, THE(1916); HONOR'S ALTAR(1916)

Marc May
WRONG MAN, THE(1956); ODDS AGAINST TOMORROW(1959)

Margery Land May
Silents
DESTINY'S ISLE(1922), w

Mark May
1984
IRRECONCILABLE DIFFERENCES(1984)

Martha May
TEXICAN, THE(1966, U.S./Span.)

Martin May
DAS BOOT(1982)

Marty May
SALUTE FOR THREE(1943)

Mathilda May
1984
DREAM ONE(1984, Brit./Fr.)

Mavis May
WORDS AND MUSIC(1929)
Melinda May
COP-OUT(1967, Brit.); HOT MILLIONS(1968, Brit.)
Mia May
Misc. Silents
HILDE WARREN AND DEATH(1916, Ger.); MOVING IMAGE, THE(1920, Ger.);
MYSTERIES OF INDIA(1922, Ger.); TRAGEDY OF LOVE(1923, Ger.)
Michael P. May
UNCOMMON VALOR(1983)
Michaela May
AMERICAN SUCCESS COMPANY, THE(1980)
Mildred May
Misc. Silents
COURAGE OF SILENCE, THE(1917)
Natalie May
PARASITE(1982)
Neola May
Silents
CAPTAIN OF THE GRAY HORSE TROOP, THE(1917)
Pamela May
BRIDE OF THE LAKE(1934, Brit.)
Pat May
STRAWBERRY STATEMENT, THE(1970)
Patsy May
GREAT STAGECOACH ROBBERY(1945)
Paul May [Ostrmayer]
SCOTLAND YARD HUNTS DR. MABUSE(1963, Ger.), d
Peter May
TASTE THE BLOOD OF DRACULA(1970, Brit.); SUBURBAN WIVES(1973, Brit.)
Ralph May
KID FROM CANADA, THE(1957, Brit.), p; ROCKETS IN THE DUNES(1960, Brit.), p
Rex May
FOUR GIRLS IN TOWN(1956)
Ricky May
1984
BROTHERS(1984, Aus.)
Rita May
GAMEKEEPER, THE(1980, Brit.); LOOKS AND SMILES(1982, Brit.)
Robert May
PATSY, THE(1964)
S. May
Silents
OLD CURIOSITY SHOP, THE(1913, Brit.)
Tom May
PURSUIT OF D.B. COOPER, THE(1981)
Wilfred May
Misc. Silents
SUBSTITUTE WIFE, THE(1925), d
Winston May
LITTLE SEX, A(1982)
1984
GHOSTBUSTERS(1984)
Yolande May
Silents
HOUSE OF TEMPERLEY, THE(1913, Brit.)
Kyako Maya
GLOWING AUTUMN(1981, Jap.)
Vladimir Mayakovsky
Misc. Silents
SHACKLED BY FILM(1918, USSR)
Herschal Mayall
Silents
BATTLE OF GETTYSBURG(1914); TYPHOON, THE(1914); WRATH OF THE GODS,
THE or THE DESTRUCTION OF SAKURA JIMA(1914); FORBIDDEN ADVENTURE,
THE(1915); CIVILIZATION(1916)
Misc. Silents
MAN FROM OREGON, THE(1915); ON THE NIGHT STAGE(1915); TOAST OF
DEATH, THE(1915); SORROWS OF LOVE, THE(1916); CLEOPATRA(1917); ROSE OF
BLOOD, THE(1917); SOME BOY(1917); HONOR'S CROSS(1918); MADAME DUBAR-
RY(1918); WEDLOCK(1918); SCUTTLERS, THE(1920)
Herschel Mayall
ROYAL FAMILY OF BROADWAY, THE(1930); BIG TOWN(1932)
Silents
ARYAN, THE(1916); TALE OF TWO CITIES, A(1917); MONEY CORRAL, THE(1919);
BEAUTIFUL GAMBLER, THE(1921); BLUSHING BRIDE, THE(1921); QUEEN OF
SHEBA, THE(1921); ARABIAN LOVE(1922); OATH-BOUND(1922); SMILES ARE
TRUMPS(1922); THIRTY DAYS(1922); YELLOW STAIN, THE(1922); ISLE OF LOST
SHIPS, THE(1923); MONEY! MONEY! MONEY!(1923); ALIMONY(1924)
Misc. Silents
HEART OF RACHAEL, THE(1918); ONE WOMAN, THE(1918); WINGS OF THE
MORNING, THE(1919); COAST OF OPPORTUNITY, THE(1920); CALVERT'S VAL-
LEY(1922); EXTRA! EXTRA!(1922); ITCHING PALMS(1923)
Herschell Mayall
HIS WOMAN(1931)
Silents
CARMEN OF THE KLONDIKE(1918); KISMET(1920)
Hershall Mayall
Silents
MAN IN THE OPEN, A(1919)
Hershell Mayall
FAST AND LOOSE(1930); HOTEL VARIETY(1933); WAR IS A RACKET(1934)
Hirshel Mayall
GREAT POWER, THE(1929)
J. Hershel Mayall
DANGER AHEAD(1935)
John Mayall
SGT. PEPPER'S LONELY HEARTS CLUB BAND(1978)

Rik Mayall
EYE OF THE NEEDLE(1981); SHOCK TREATMENT(1981)
Miko Mayama
WALK, DON'T RUN(1966); IMPASSE(1969); HAWAIIANS, THE(1970); THAT MAN
BOLT(1973)
Mayana
KARATE, THE HAND OF DEATH(1961)
Antonio Mayans
SAUL AND DAVID(1968, Ital./Span.); TOWN CALLED HELL, A(1971, Span./Brit.);
FROM HELL TO VICTORY(1979, Fr./Ital./Span.)
Greta Mayaro
MURDER AT 3 A.M.(1953, Brit.)
Toshiro Mayazumi
EARLY AUTUMN(1962, Jap.), m
Christiane Maybach
$(DOLLARS) (1971); THOUSAND EYES OF DR. MABUSE, THE(1960, Fr./Ital./Ger.);
HEAD, THE(1961, Ger.); STUDY IN TERROR, A(1966, Brit./Ger.); THAT MAN IN
ISTANBUL(1966, Fr./Ital./Span.); FOX AND HIS FRIENDS(1976, Ger.); JUST A
GIGOLO(1979, Ger.)
Laon Maybanke
NIGHT WATCH(1973, Brit.)
Christina Maybeck
Misc. Talkies
NAUGHTY NYMPHS(1974)
Katharina Mayberg
ETERNAL LOVE(1960, Ger.)
Katherina Mayberg
THEY WERE SO YOUNG(1955)
Lynn Mayberry
RIDE 'EM COWGIRL(1939)
Mary Mayberry
GODLESS GIRL, THE(1929)
Silents
LAW OF THE MOUNTED(1928); MANHATTAN COWBOY(1928); HEADIN' WEST-
WARD(1929)
Misc. Silents
LAW'S LASH, THE(1928); TEXAS TOMMY(1928)
Russ Mayberry
JESUS TRIP, THE(1971), d; UNIDENTIFIED FLYING ODDBALL, THE(1979, Brit.),
d
Jackie Mayble
EMPEROR JONES, THE(1933)
Platon Mayboroda
TRAIN GOES TO KIEV, THE(1961, USSR), m
Jenny Maybrook
TWO-MINUTE WARNING(1976)
Pepsi Maycock
REVENGE OF THE PINK PANTHER(1978)
Peter Maycock
GUY CALLED CAESAR, A(1962, Brit.)
Roger Maycock
SCALPS(1983)
Sabina Maydelle
MUSIC LOVERS, THE(1971, Brit.)
Clyde W. Maye
J.W. COOP(1971)
Donald Maye
CONTENDER, THE(1944)
Frank Maye
MAGNIFICENT OBSESSION(1935)
Hazel Maye
Misc. Silents
HEART OF A TEXAN, THE(1922); TABLE TOP RANCH(1922)
Jimesy Maye
Misc. Silents
NINE-TENTHS OF THE LAW(1918)
Jimsy Maye
Misc. Silents
TWO KINDS OF LOVE(1920)
Paul Maye
DIE MANNER UM LUCIE(1931), m
Eddie Mayehoff
THAT'S MY BOY(1951); STOOGE, THE(1952); OFF LIMITS(1953); ARTISTS AND
MODELS(1955); HOW TO MURDER YOUR WIFE(1965); LUV(1967)
Anne Mayen
RULES OF THE GAME, THE(1939, Fr.)
Harry Mayen
ENOUGH ROPE(1966, Fr./Ital./Ger.)
Jose Mayens
GUNFIGHTERS OF CASA GRANDE(1965, U.S./Span.)
Mayer
INVESTIGATION OF A CITIZEN ABOVE SUSPICION(1970, Ital.), cos
Adalyn Mayer
Misc. Silents
NO MAN'S LAW(1925)
Alexander A. Mayer
RAIDERS, THE(1964), art d; NOBODY'S PERFECT(1968), art d; NEWMAN'S
LAW(1974), art d
Arthur Mayer
LOWER DEPTHS, THE(1937, Fr.), p; LIFE BEGINS TOMORROW(1952, Fr.), p;
SPICE OF LIFE(1954, Fr.), p; HIGH HELL(1958), p; REDS(1981)
Augustin Mayer
HORROR OF PARTY BEACH, THE(1964)
Carl Mayer
FOUR DEVILS(1929), w; ARIANE(1931, Ger.), w; DREAMING LIPS(1937, Brit.), w
Silents
CABINET OF DR. CALIGARI, THE(1921, Ger.), w; LAST LAUGH, THE(1924,
Ger.), w; SUNRISE–A SONG OF TWO HUMANS(1927), w; TARTUFFE(1927, Ger.), w

Charles Mayer
ROOTIN' TOOTIN' RHYTHM(1937)
Edwin Justis Mayer
ROYAL SCANDAL, A(1945), w
Edwin Justus Mayer
SAL OF SINGAPORE(1929), titles; UNHOLY NIGHT, THE(1929), w; IN GAY MA-DRID(1930), w; LADY OF SCANDAL, THE(1930), w; NOT SO DUMB(1930), w; OUR BLUSHING BRIDES(1930), w; REDEMPTION(1930), w; ROMANCE(1930), w; NEV-ER THE TWAIN SHALL MEET(1931), w; PHANTOM OF PARIS, THE(1931), w; MERRILY WE GO TO HELL(1932), w; WILD GIRL(1932), w; TONIGHT IS OURS(1933), w; AFFAIRS OF CELLINI, THE(1934), w; HERE IS MY HEART(1934), w; I AM SUZANNE(1934), w; THIRTY-DAY PRINCESS(1934), w; PETER IBBET-SON(1935), w; SO RED THE ROSE(1935), w; DESIRE(1936), w; GIVE US THIS NIGHT(1936), w; BUCCANEER, THE(1938), w; EXILE EXPRESS(1939), w; GONE WITH THE WIND(1939), w; MIDNIGHT(1939), w; THEY MET IN BOMBAY(1941), w; UNDERGROUND(1941), w; TO BE OR NOT TO BE(1942), w; MASQUERADE IN MEXICO(1945), w; BUCCANEER, THE(1958), w; TO BE OR NOT TO BE(1983), w
Silents
HUSBANDS FOR RENT(1927), w; MAN-MADE WOMEN(1928), t; WHIP WOMAN, THE(1928), t; NED MCCOBB'S DAUGHTER(1929), t
Gabriele Mayer
PLANET OF THE VAMPIRES(1965, U.S./Ital./Span.), cos
Gerald Mayer
DIAL 1119(1950), d; INSIDE STRAIGHT(1951), d; SELLOUT, THE(1951), d; HOLI-DAY FOR SINNERS(1952), d; BRIGHT ROAD(1953), d; MARAUDERS, THE(1955), d; DIAMOND SAFARI(1958), p&d
Hans Mayer
MAGNIFICENT ONE, THE(1974, Fr./Ital.)
Jean Mayer
LE PLAISIR(1954, Fr.)
Jerry Mayer
GREAT GATSBY, THE(1974); BRUBAKER(1980); SIMON(1980)
John Mayer
DANGER ROUTE(1968, Brit.), m
Joseph Mayer
Silents
FALSE BRANDS(1922), ph
Justin Mayer
BLUSHING BRIDES(1930), w
Ken Mayer
AMBUSH AT CIMARRON PASS(1958); CLOWN AND THE KID, THE(1961); FRON-TIER UPRISING(1961); GUN FIGHT(1961); JACK THE GIANT KILLER(1962); BLACK GOLD(1963); SPENCER'S MOUNTAIN(1963); NEW INTERNS, THE(1964); ONE WAY WAHINI(1965); BONNIE AND CLYDE(1967); LITTLE BIG MAN(1970)
Kenneth Mayer
FBI STORY, THE(1959); MIRACLE OF THE HILLS, THE(1959)
Kenneth N. Mayer
TIGHT SPOT(1955)
Laura Walker Mayer
DOCTOR MONICA(1934), w
Louis B. Mayer
Silents
ETERNAL STRUGGLE, THE(1923), p; HE WHO GETS SLAPPED(1924), p
Michael Mayer
KILLER FORCE(1975, Switz./Ireland); KILL AND KILL AGAIN(1981)
Murray Mayer
BLACK ROOM, THE(1935), cos
Otto Mayer
RIDING TORNADO, THE(1932), ed; BEYOND THE LAW(1934), ed; STRAIGHTA-WAY(1934), ed; GIRLS' SCHOOL(1938), ed
Ray Mayer
CALL IT LUCK(1934); GAY BRIDE, THE(1934); JEALOUSY(1934); YOUNG AND BEAUTIFUL(1934); ANOTHER FACE(1935), w; ARIZONIAN, THE(1935); HOT TIP(1935); POWDERSMOKE RANGE(1935); RETURN OF PETER GRIMM, THE(1935); SEVEN KEYS TO BALDPATE(1935); TO BEAT THE BAND(1935); VILLAGE TA-LE(1935); FARMER IN THE DELL, THE(1936); FOLLOW THE FLEET(1936); HIS FAMILY TREE(1936); I MARRIED A DOCTOR(1936); LAST OUTLAW, THE(1936); M'LISS(1936); SPECIAL INVESTIGATOR(1936); HIDEAWAY(1936); MAKE WAY FOR TOMORROW(1937); MEET THE MISSUS(1937); RACING LADY(1937); SWING IT SAILOR(1937); TOP OF THE TOWN(1937); WE WHO ARE ABOUT TO DIE(1937); GARDEN OF THE MOON(1938); PRISON NURSE(1938); VIVACIOUS LADY(1938); KING OF CHINATOWN(1939); OKLAHOMA KID, THE(1939); SWEET AND LOW-DOWN(1944); SNAFU(1945); HIGH WALL, THE(1947); MR. SOFT TOUCH(1949); STALAG 17(1953), set d; REAR WINDOW(1954), set d
Renee Mayer
Misc. Silents
BACHELOR HUSBAND, THE(1920 Brit.)
Richard Mayer
NO ROOM FOR THE GROOM(1952); THERE'S ALWAYS TOMORROW(1956)
Scott Mayer
1984
SAVAGE STREETS(1984)
Tony Mayer
1984
CORRUPT(1984, Ital.)
Torben Mayer
SUNNY(1941); JACK LONDON(1943)
Wayne Mayer
LAST SUMMER(1969)
William Mayer
ETERNAL SUMMER(1961)
Yolanda Mayer
HARRY AND WALTER GO TO NEW YORK(1976)
Mayer of Rome
PRIEST'S WIFE, THE(1971, Ital./Fr.), cos
Konrad Mayerhoff
TOMORROW IS MY TURN(1962, Fr./Ital./Ger.)

Val Mayerick
DEMON LOVER, THE(1977)
Billy Mayerl
WITHOUT YOU(1934, Brit.); LOST CHORD, THE(1937, Brit.); WE'LL SMILE AGAIN(1942, Brit.)
Vojtova Mayerova
ECSTACY OF YOUNG LOVE(1936, Czech.)
Addison Mayers
OPERATION CAMEL(1961, Den.)
Dennis Mayers
SUMARINE X-1(1969, Brit.)
Sidney H. Mayers
CROSSROADS OF PASSION(1951, Fr.), titles
Paul Mayersberg
MAN WHO FELL TO EARTH, THE(1976, Brit.), w; DISAPPEARANCE, THE(1981, Brit./Can.), w; EUREKA(1983, Brit.), w; MERRY CHRISTMAS MR. LAWREN-CE(1983, Jap./Brit.), w
Arthur Mayes
DESPERATE SEARCH(1952), w
Craig Mayes
SCREAMS OF A WINTER NIGHT(1979), ed
Norman Mayes
YOU CAN'T FOOL YOUR WIFE(1940); FOUR JACKS AND A JILL(1941); REPENT AT LEISURE(1941); SAINT IN PALM SPRINGS, THE(1941); MAYOR OF 44TH STREET, THE(1942); GHOST SHIP, THE(1943); GOVERNMENT GIRL(1943); I WALKED WITH A ZOMBIE(1943); LADIES' DAY(1943); FALCON OUT WEST, THE(1944); HEAVENLY DAYS(1944)
Richard Mayes
1984
TOP SECRET!(1984)
Wendell Mayes
ENEMY BELOW, THE(1957), w; SPIRIT OF ST. LOUIS, THE(1957), w; WAY TO THE GOLD, THE(1957), w; FROM HELL TO TEXAS(1958), w; HUNTERS, THE(1958), w; ANATOMY OF A MURDER(1959), w; HANGING TREE, THE(1959), w; NORTH TO ALASKA(1960), w; ADVISE AND CONSENT(1962), w; IN HARM'S WAY(1965), w; VON RYAN'S EXPRESS(1965), w; HOTEL(1967), p, w; STALKING MOON, THE(1969), w; POSEIDON ADVENTURE, THE(1972), w; REVENGERS, THE(1972, U.S./Mex.), w; BANK SHOT(1974), w; DEATH WISH(1974), w; GO TELL THE SPAR-TANS(1978), w; LOVE AND BULLETS(1979, Brit.), w; MONSIGNOR(1982), w
Irena Mayeska
DRYLANDERS(1963, Can.); INCREDIBLE JOURNEY, THE(1963)
Irene Mayeska
PARTNERS(1976, Can.)
Mitzi Mayfair
FOUR JILLS IN A JEEP(1944)
Curtis Mayfield
SUPERFLY(1972), m; CLAUDINE(1974), m; LET'S DO IT AGAIN(1975), m; SPAR-KLE(1976), m; PIECE OF THE ACTION, A(1977), m; SHORT EYES(1977), a, m; SGT. PEPPER'S LONELY HEARTS CLUB BAND(1978)
Dora Mayfield
LIMEHOUSE BLUES(1934); LANDSLIDE(1937, Brit.)
Julian Mayfield
VIRGIN ISLAND(1960, Brit.); UPTIGHT(1968), a, w; LONG NIGHT, THE(1976), w
Leland Mayforth
YOUNG DON'T CRY, THE(1957)
Mary Mayfren
HOUSE OF UNREST, THE(1931, Brit.); FORTUNATE FOOL, THE(1933, Brit.)
Misc. Silents
GATES OF DUTY(1919, Brit.)
Jack Mayhall
1984
BODY DOUBLE(1984)
Ernest "Skillet" Mayhand
HANDLE WITH CARE(1964)
Siegfried Mayhardt
FUNERAL FOR AN ASSASSIN(1977)
Joyce Mayhead
GYPSY GIRL(1966, Brit.)
Arthur Mayhew
Silents
LITTLE DOOR INTO THE WORLD, THE(1923, Brit.)
Peter Mayhew
COLDITZ STORY, THE(1955, Brit.), ed; FIGHTING WILDCATS, THE(1957, Brit.), ed; THUNDER OVER TANGIER(1957, Brit.), ed; HAUNTED STRANGLER, THE(1958, Brit.), ed; FIRST MAN INTO SPACE(1959, Brit.), ed; CORRIDORS OF BLOOD(1962, Brit.), ed; MILLION DOLLAR MANHUNT(1962, Brit.), ed; STAR WARS(1977); TER-ROR(1979, Brit.); EMPIRE STRIKES BACK, THE(1980); RETURN OF THE JEDI(1983)
Ruth Mayhew
DISHONORED(1931)
Tony Maylam
BOBBY DEERFIELD(1977), ph; BURNING, THE(1981), d, w
1984
RIDDLE OF THE SANDS, THE(1984, Brit.), d, w
Misc. Talkies
SINS OF DORIAN GRAY(1982), d
Maylia
SINGAPORE(1947); TO THE ENDS OF THE EARTH(1948); BOSTON BLACKIE'S CHINESE VENTURE(1949); CHINATOWN AT MIDNIGHT(1949); CALL ME MIS-TER(1951)
Ken Maymard
TRAILING TROUBLE(1937)
Victor Maymudes
LAST MOVIE, THE(1971)
Anna Maynard
Silents
MERRY WIDOW, THE(1925)
Antoinette Maynard
KILL, THE(1968); PRECIOUS JEWELS(1969)

Misc. Talkies
WEEKEND LOVER(1969)
Audrey Maynard
OUR NEIGHBORS–THE CARTERS(1939); THOSE WERE THE DAYS(1940); WOMEN WITHOUT NAMES(1940)
B.W. Maynard
Misc. Silents
DETERMINATION(1920)
Biff Maynard
MACHISMO–40 GRAVES FOR 40 GUNS(1970)
1984
SURF II(1984)
Bill Maynard
ALF 'N' FAMILY(1968, Brit.); CARRY ON HENRY VIII(1970, Brit.); CARRY ON LOVING(1970, Brit.); ONE MORE TIME(1970, Brit.); CONFESSIONS OF A WINDOW CLEANER(1974, Brit.); CONFESSIONS OF A POP PERFORMER(1975, Brit.); ROBIN AND MARIAN(1976, Brit.); CONFESSIONS FROM A HOLIDAY CAMP(1977, Brit.); ALL THINGS BRIGHT AND BEAUTIFUL(1979, Brit.); DANGEROUS DAVIES–THE LAST DETECTIVE(1981, Brit.)
1984
PLAGUE DOGS, THE(1984, U.S./Brit.)
Billy Maynard
ADOLF HITLER–MY PART IN HIS DOWNFALL(1973, Brit.)
Charles Maynard
MERRY-GO-ROUND OF 1938(1937), ed; ROAD BACK,THE(1937), ed; STRANGE FACES(1938), ed; WIVES UNDER SUSPICION(1938), ed; FORGOTTEN WOMAN, THE(1939), ed; HERO FOR A DAY(1939), ed; DESTINATION UNKNOWN(1942), ed; HI, BUDDY(1943), ed; HOW'S ABOUT IT?(1943), ed; MOONLIGHT IN VERMONT(1943), ed; SING A JINGLE(1943), ed; TENTING TONIGHT ON THE OLD CAMP GROUND(1943), ed; WHEN JOHNNY COMES MARCHING HOME(1943), ed; CHIP OFF THE OLD BLOCK(1944), ed; COBRA WOMAN(1944), ed; MERRY MONAHANS, THE(1944), ed; MURDER IN THE BLUE ROOM(1944), ed; NIGHT CLUB GIRL(1944), ed; SAN DIEGO, I LOVE YOU(1944), ed
Charley Maynard
ALL BY MYSELF(1943), ed
Clair Maynard
DISORDERLY CONDUCT(1932)
Claire Maynard
GOOD SPORT(1931); OVER THE HILL(1931)
Earl Maynard
MELINDA(1972); TRUCK TURNER(1974); MANDINGO(1975); DEEP, THE(1977); CIRCLE OF IRON(1979, Brit.); NUDE BOMB, THE(1980); SWORD AND THE SORCERER, THE(1982)
George Maynard
RADIO CAB MURDER(1954, Brit.), p; WHERE THERE'S A WILL(1955, Brit.), p; HOME AND AWAY(1956, Brit.), p; JOHNNY, YOU'RE WANTED(1956, Brit.), p; ROGUE'S YARN(1956, Brit.), p; SPIN A DARK WEB(1956, Brit.), p; COSMIC MONSTERS(1958, Brit.), p; FERRY TO HONG KONG(1959, Brit.), p; MISSILE FROM HELL(1960, Brit.), p; INFORMATION RECEIVED(1962, Brit.), p; PRIZE OF ARMS, A(1962, Brit.), p; MATTER OF CHOICE, A(1963, Brit.), p
Gitta Maynard
WORLD'S GREATEST SINNER, THE(1962)
Harry Maynard
Silents
SPEED CRAZED(1926)
John Maynard
SKIN DEEP(1978, New Zealand), p
1984
VIGIL(1984, New Zealand), p
Judi Maynard
WICKED LADY, THE(1983, Brit.)
Ken Maynard
SENOR AMERICANO(1929), a, p; WAGON MASTER, THE(1929), a, P; FIGHTING LEGION, THE(1930), a, p; MOUNTAIN JUSTICE(1930), a, p; PARADE OF THE WEST(1930), a, p; SONG OF THE CABELLERO(1930), a, p; SONS OF THE SADDLE(1930); ALIAS THE BAD MAN(1931); ARIZONA TERROR(1931); BRANDED MEN(1931); FIGHTING THRU(1931); RANGE LAW(1931); TWO GUN MAN, THE(1931); BETWEEN FIGHTING MEN(1932); DYNAMITE RANCH(1932); HELL FIRE AUSTIN(1932); POCATELLO KID(1932); SUNSET TRAIL(1932); TEXAS GUN FIGHTER(1932); TOMBSTONE CANYON(1932); WHISTLIN' DAN(1932); COME ON TARZAN(1933); DRUM TAPS(1933); FARGO EXPRESS(1933); KING OF THE ARENA(1933), a, p; LONE AVENGER, THE(1933); PHANTOM THUNDERBOLT, THE(1933); STRAWBERRY ROAN(1933), a, p; FIDDLIN' BUCKAROO, THE(1934), a, p&d; GUN JUSTICE(1934), a, p; HONOR OF THE RANGE(1934), a, p; SMOKING GUNS(1934), a, p, w; TRAIL DRIVE, THE(1934), p; WHEELS OF DESTINY(1934), a, p; IN OLD SANTA FE(1935); WESTERN COURAGE(1935); WESTERN FRONTIER(1935), a, w; AVENGING WATERS(1936); CATTLE THIEF, THE(1936); FUGITIVE SHERIFF, THE(1936); HEIR TO TROUBLE(1936), a, w; HEROES OF THE RANGE(1936); LAWLESS RIDERS(1936); BOOTS OF DESTINY(1937); SIX SHOOTIN' SHERIFF(1938); WHIRLWIND HORSEMAN(1938); FLAMING LEAD(1939); DEATH RIDES THE RANGE(1940); LIGHTNING STRIKES WEST(1940); PHANTOM RANCHER(1940); BLAZING GUNS(1943); LAW RIDES AGAIN, THE(1943); WILD HORSE STAMPEDE(1943); ARIZONA WHIRLWIND(1944); DEATH VALLEY RANGERS(1944); WESTWARD BOUND(1944); WHITE STALLION(1947); BUCK AND THE PREACHER(1972); BIG FOOT(1973)
Silents
JANICE MEREDITH(1924); HAUNTED RANGE, THE(1926); UNKNOWN CAVALIER, THE(1926); SOMEWHERE IN SONORA(1927); LAWLESS LEGION, THE(1929); ROYAL RIDER, THE(1929)
Misc. Silents
$50,000 Reward(1924); DEMON RIDER, THE(1925); FIGHTING COURAGE(1925); NORTH STAR(1925); SENOR DAREDEVIL(1926); DEVIL'S SADDLE, THE(1927); GUN GOSPEL(1927); LAND BEYOND THE LAW, THE(1927); OVERLAND STAGE, THE(1927); RED RAIDERS, THE(1927); CANYON OF ADVENTURE, THE(1928); CODE OF THE SCARLET, THE(1928); GLORIOUS TRAIL, THE(1928); PHANTOM CITY, THE(1928); UPLAND RIDER, THE(1928); WAGON SHOW, THE(1928); CALIFORNIA MAIL, THE(1929); CHEYENNE(1929); LUCKY LARKIN(1930)

Kermit Maynard
DYNAMITE RANCH(1932); DRUM TAPS(1933); OUTLAW JUSTICE(1933); 42ND STREET(1933); CODE OF THE MOUNTED(1935); FIGHTING TROOPER, THE(1935); HIS FIGHTING BLOOD(1935); NORTHERN FRONTIER(1935); RED BLOOD OF COURAGE(1935); TRAILS OF THE WILD(1935); PHANTOM PATROL(1936); SONG OF THE TRAIL(1936); TIMBER WAR(1936); WILDCAT TROOPER(1936); FIGHTING TEXAN(1937); GALLOPING DYNAMITE(1937); ROARING SIX GUNS(1937); ROUGH RIDIN' RHYTHM(1937); WHISTLING BULLETS(1937); WILD HORSE ROUND-UP(1937); LAW WEST OF TOMBSTONE, THE(1938); WESTERN JAMBOREE(1938); CODE OF THE CACTUS(1939); COLORADO SUNSET(1939); NIGHT RIDERS, THE(1939); CHIP OF THE FLYING U(1940); HEROES OF THE SADDLE(1940); LAW AND ORDER(1940); NORTHWEST MOUNTED POLICE(1940); PONY POST(1940); RAGTIME COWBOY JOE(1940); RANGE BUSTERS, THE(1940); RETURN OF FRANK JAMES, THE(1940); RIDERS OF PASCO BASIN(1940); SHOWDOWN, THE(1940); WEST OF CARSON CITY(1940); BILLY THE KID(1941); BOSS OF BULLION CITY(1941); BURY ME NOT ON THE LONE PRAIRIE(1941); MAN FROM MONTANA(1941); ROYAL MOUNTED PATROL, THE(1941); SIERRA SUE(1941); STICK TO YOUR GUNS(1941); TRAIL OF THE SILVER SPURS(1941); WYOMING WILDCAT(1941); ARIZONA STAGECOACH(1942); DOWN RIO GRANDE WAY(1942); FIGHTING BILL FARGO(1942); HOME IN WYOMIN'(1942); JESSE JAMES, JR.(1942); LAW AND ORDER(1942); LONE PRAIRIE, THE(1942); MISSOURI OUTLAW, A(1942); MYSTERIOUS RIDER, THE(1942); OMAHA TRAIL, THE(1942); PRAIRIE PALS(1942); RIDERS OF THE WEST(1942); ROCK RIVER RENEGADES(1942); SABOTEUR(1942); STAGECOACH BUCKAROO(1942); TRAIL RIDERS(1942); BEYOND THE LAST FRONTIER(1943); FRONTIER BADMEN(1943); SANTA FE SCOUTS(1943); SILVER SPURS(1943); STRANGER FROM PECOS, THE(1943); TWO FISTED JUSTICE(1943); WESTERN CYCLONE(1943); BLAZING FRONTIER(1944); BRAND OF THE DEVIL(1944); DEATH RIDES THE PLAINS(1944); DEVIL RIDERS(1944); DRIFTER, THE(1944); FRONTIER OUTLAWS(1944); GUNSMOKE MESA(1944); RAIDERS OF RED GAP(1944); RAIDERS OF THE BORDER(1944); TEXAS KID, THE(1944); THUNDERING GUN SLINGERS(1944); WILD HORSE PHANTOM(1944); CHINA SKY(1945); ENEMY OF THE LAW(1945); FIGHTING BILL CARSON(1945); FLAMING BULLETS(1945); MARKED FOR MURDER(1945); PRAIRIE RUSTLERS(1945); STAGECOACH OUTLAWS(1945); THEY WERE EXPENDABLE(1945); AMBUSH TRAIL(1946); PRAIRIE BADMEN(1946); RUSTLER'S ROUNDUP(1946); STARS OVER TEXAS(1946); TERRORS ON HORSEBACK(1946); TUMBLEWEED TRAIL(1946); UNDER ARIZONA SKIES(1946); RETURN OF THE LASH(1947); RIDIN' DOWN THE TRAIL(1947); FRONTIER REVENGE(1948); FURY AT FURNACE CREEK(1948); GALLANT LEGION, THE(1948); NORTHWEST STAMPEDE(1948); PALEFACE, THE(1948); SOUTHERN YANKEE, A(1948); LUST FOR GOLD(1949); MASSACRE RIVER(1949); RANGE LAND(1949); RIDERS IN THE SKY(1949); LAW OF THE PANHANDLE(1950); SAVAGE HORDE, THE(1950); SHORT GRASS(1950); SILVER RAIDERS(1950); TRAIL OF ROBIN HOOD(1950); FORT DODGE STAMPEDE(1951); GOLDEN GIRL(1951); IN OLD AMARILLO(1951); THREE DESPERATE MEN(1951); BLACK LASH, THE(1952); FARMER TAKES A WIFE, THE(1953); LAW AND ORDER(1953); PACK TRAIN(1953); FLESH AND THE SPUR(1957); OKLAHOMAN, THE(1957); ONCE UPON A HORSE(1958); WESTBOUND(1959); NOOSE FOR A GUNMAN(1960); NORTH TO ALASKA(1960)
Misc. Talkies
VALLEY OF TERROR(1937); ALONG THE SUNDOWN TRAIL(1942); BLOCKED TRAIL, THE(1943); FUGITIVE OF THE PLAINS(1943); GALLOPING THUNDER(1946); FRONTIER FIGHTERS(1947)
Kermit "Tex" Maynard
WILDERNESS MAIL(1935)
Key Maynard
TRAIL DRIVE, THE(1934)
Mary Maynard
RETURN OF THE LASH(1947)
Mimi Maynard
HAWMPS!(1976)
Nan Maynard
THIS IS MY STREET(1964, Brit.), w
Patricia Maynard
NIGHT TRAIN TO PARIS(1964, Brit.)
Raymond Maynard
RICHARD(1972), set d
Rod Maynard
PEER GYNT(1965)
Ruth Maynard
NIGHT OF THE JUGGLER(1980)
Ted Maynard
FRIENDS OF EDDIE COYLE, THE(1973)
Tex Maynard
Misc. Silents
GUN-HAND GARRISON(1927); PRINCE OF THE PLAINS(1927); RIDIN' LUCK(1927); WANDERER OF THE WEST(1927); WILD BORN(1927); DRIFTING KID, THE(1928)
Arthur Mayne
RADIO PIRATES(1935, Brit.)
Arthur J. Mayne
Silents
KNAVE OF HEARTS, THE(1919, Brit.)
Belinda Mayne
KRULL(1983)
1984
DON'T OPEN TILL CHRISTMAS(1984, Brit.); LASSITER(1984)
C. Ferdy Mayne
MAGIC CHRISTIAN, THE(1970, Brit.)
Charles J.L. Mayne
Misc. Silents
MIRACLE BABY, THE(1923)
Clarice Mayne
EDUCATED EVANS(1936, Brit.)
Deirdre Mayne
DATE WITH DISASTER(1957, Brit.); THERE'S ALWAYS A THURSDAY(1957, Brit.)
Derek B. Mayne
LAST CURTAIN, THE(1937, Brit.), w

Eric Mayne

EAST LYNNE(1931); RACKETY RAX(1932); DEATH FROM A DISTANCE(1936); ONE RAINY AFTERNOON(1936); STORY OF LOUIS PASTEUR, THE(1936); TICKET TO PARADISE(1936); THERE'S THAT WOMAN AGAIN(1938); LADY LUCK(1946)

Silents

COTTON KING, THE(1915); NEW YORK PEACOCK, THE(1917); OTHER MEN'S DAUGHTERS(1918); PEG OF THE PIRATES(1918); OAKDALE AFFAIR, THE(1919); CONQUERING POWER, THE(1921); SILVER CAR, THE(1921); DOCTOR JACK(1922); SUZANNA(1922); MY AMERICAN WIFE(1923); GOLDFISH, THE(1924); NEVER SAY DIE(1924); EAGLE, THE(1925); BLACK BIRD, THE(1926); DRIVEN FROM HOME(1927); MARRIED ALIVE(1927)

Misc. Silents

BELOVED VAGABOND, THE(1912); THOU SHALT NOT STEAL(1917); WIFE NUMBER TWO(1917); GIRL AND THE JUDGE, THE(1918); HELP! HELP! POLICE!(1919); SCAR, THE(1919); SHOULD A HUSBAND FORGIVE?(1919); LITTLE MISS HAWKSHAW(1921); CAMEO KIRBY(1923); PRINCE OF A KING, A(1923); ACCUSED(1925); BARRIERS BURNED AWAY(1925); CYCLONE CAVALIER(1925); TOO MUCH YOUTH(1925); BEYOND THE TRAIL(1926); HEARTS AND SPANGLES(1926); MONEY TO BURN(1926); CANYON OF ADVENTURE, THE(1928)

Ferdi Mayne

WALTZ TIME(1946, Brit.)

Ferdinand Mayne

BLACK STALLION RETURNS, THE(1983)

Ferdinand [Ferdy] Mayne

FRIGHTMARE(1983); YELLOWBEARD(1983)

1984

CONAN THE DESTROYER(1984); SECRET DIARY OF SIGMUND FREUD, THE(1984)

Ferdy Mayne

OLD MOTHER RILEY OVERSEAS(1943, Brit.); MEET SEXTON BLAKE(1944, Brit.); ECHO MURDERS, THE(1945, Brit.); VOTE FOR HUGGETT(1948, Brit.); CELIA(1949, Brit.); HUGGETTS ABROAD, THE(1949, Brit.); TEMPTRESS, THE(1949, Brit.); PRELUDE TO FAME(1950, Brit.); ENCORE(1951, Brit.); HOTEL SAHARA(1951, Brit.); MADE IN HEAVEN(1952, Brit.); BLUE PARROT, THE(1953, Brit.); BROKEN HORSESHOE, THE(1953, Brit.); CAPTAIN'S PARADISE, THE(1953, Brit.); DESPERATE MOMENT(1953, Brit.); MARILYN(1953, Brit.); PARIS EXPRESS, THE(1953, Brit.); WHITE FIRE(1953, Brit.); BEAUTIFUL STRANGER(1954, Brit.); FIRE OVER AFRICA(1954, Brit.); YOU KNOW WHAT SAILORS ARE(1954, Brit.); DEADLY GAME, THE(1955, Brit.); DIVIDED HEART, THE(1955, Brit.); GENTLEMEN MARRY BRUNETTES(1955); STORM OVER THE NILE(1955, Brit.); FIND THE LADY(1956, Brit.); NARROWING CIRCLE, THE(1956, Brit.); ABANDON SHIP!(1957, Brit.); BABY AND THE BATTLESHIP, THE(1957, Brit.); BIG CHANCE, THE(1957, Brit.); THREE SUNDAYS TO LIVE(1957, Brit.); VALUE FOR MONEY(1957, Brit.); WOMAN OF MYSTERY, A(1957, Brit.); YOU PAY YOUR MONEY(1957, Brit.); BLUE MURDER AT ST. TRINIAN'S(1958, Brit.); SAFECRACKER, THE(1958, Brit.); BEN HUR(1959); DEADLY RECORD(1959, Brit.); END OF THE LINE, THE(1959, Brit.); THIRD MAN ON THE MOUNTAIN(1959); CROSSROADS TO CRIME(1960, Brit.); NEXT TO NO TIME(1960, Brit.); OUR MAN IN HAVANA(1960, Brit.); SPIDER'S WEB, THE(1960, Brit.); TOMMY THE TOREADOR(1960, Brit.); GREEN HELMET, THE(1961, Brit.); HIGHWAY TO BATTLE(1961, Brit.); PASSWORD IS COURAGE, THE(1962, Brit.); PRIVATE POTTER(1962, Brit./E. Ger.); THREE SPARE WIVES(1962, Brit.); OPERATION CROSSBOW(1965, U.S./Ital.); THOSE MAGNIFICENT MEN IN THEIR FLYING MACHINES; OR HOW I FLEW FROM LONDON TO PARIS IN 25 HOURS AND 11 MINUTES(1965, Brit.); COUNTERFEIT CONSTABLE, THE(1966, Fr.); PROMISE HER ANYTHING(1966, Brit.); BOBO, THE(1967, Brit.); FEARLESS VAMPIRE KILLERS, OR PARDON ME BUT YOUR TEETH ARE IN MY NECK, THE(1967); GATES TO PARADISE(1968, Brit./Ger.); WHERE EAGLES DARE(1968, Brit.); LIMBO LINE, THE(1969, Brit.); ADVENTURERS, THE(1970); VAMPIRE LOVERS, THE(1970, Brit.); VON RICHTHOFEN AND BROWN(1970); WALKING STICK, THE(1970, Brit.); EAGLE IN A CAGE(1971, U.S./Yugo.); WHEN EIGHT BELLS TOLL(1971, Brit.); INNOCENT BYSTANDERS(1973, Brit.); BARRY LYNDON(1975, Brit.); REVENGE OF THE PINK PANTHER(1978); FORMULA, THE(1980); HAWK THE SLAYER(1980, Brit.)

Misc. Talkies

AU PAIR GIRLS(1973)

Herbert Mayne

Silents

IN THE DAYS OF SAINT PATRICK(1920, Brit.)

Jack Mayne

MELODY CLUB(1949, Brit.)

Margo Mayne

SPACEFLIGHT IC-1(1965, Brit.)

Martina Mayne

I'M A STRANGER(1952, Brit.)

Mildred Mayne

TAKE ME OVER(1963, Brit.); PARTY'S OVER, THE(1966, Brit.)

Murray Mayne

TEENAGE BAD GIRL(1959, Brit.)

Tony Mayne

MUTATIONS, THE(1974, Brit.)

Mayne-Lynton

ON THE BEACH(1959)

Laurence Maynell

CROWN VS STEVENS(1936), w

Juliette Maynie

TROJAN HORSE, THE(1962, Fr./Ital.)

Juliette Mayniel

COUSINS, THE(1959, Fr.); HORROR CHAMBER OF DR. FAUSTUS, THE(1962, Fr./Ital.); LANDRU(1963, Fr./Ital); OPHELIA(1964, Fr.); LISTEN, LET'S MAKE LOVE(1969, Fr./Ital.)

Asa Maynor

CHICAGO CONFIDENTIAL(1957); HONG KONG CONFIDENTIAL(1958); HEY BOY! HEY GIRL!(1959); UNDER THE YUM-YUM TREE(1963); LOVED ONE, THE(1965); PROMISE HER ANYTHING(1966, Brit.); CONQUEST OF THE PLANET OF THE APES(1972)

Virginia Maynor

MAN BEAST(1956)

Mayo

LAND OF THE PHARAOHS(1955), cos; HIROSHIMA, MON AMOUR(1959, Fr./Jap.), prod d; CHEATERS, THE(1961, Fr.), cos

Alfredo Mayo

GIRL FROM VALLADOLIO(1958, Span.); LEGIONS OF THE NILE(1960, Ital.); TEACHER AND THE MIRACLE, THE(1961, Ital./Span.); COMMANDO(1962, Ital., Span., Bel., Ger.); 55 DAYS AT PEKING(1963); REVOLT OF THE MERCENARIES(1964, Ital./Span.); HUNT, THE(1967, Span.); MISSION BLOODY MARY(1967, Fr./Ital./Span.); MADIGAN'S MILLIONS(1970, Span./Ital)

Archie Mayo

MY MAN(1928), d; ON TRIAL(1928), d; STATE STREET SADIE(1928), d; IS EVERYBODY HAPPY?(1929), d; SONNY BOY(1929), d; COURAGE(1930), d; DOORWAY TO HELL(1930), d; OH! SAILOR, BEHAVE!(1930), d; VENGEANCE(1930), d; WIDE OPEN(1930), d; BOUGHT(1931), d; ILLICIT(1931), d; SVENGALI(1931), d; EXPERT, THE(1932), d; NIGHT AFTER NIGHT(1932), d; STREET OF WOMEN(1932), d; TWO AGAINST THE WORLD(1932), d; UNDER EIGHTEEN(1932), d; CONVENTION CITY(1933), d; EVER IN MY HEART(1933), d; LIFE OF JIMMY DOLAN, THE(1933), d; MAYOR OF HELL, THE(1933), d; DESIRABLE(1934), d; GAMBLING LADY(1934), d; MAN WITH TWO FACES, THE(1934), d; BORDERTOWN(1935), d; GO INTO YOUR DANCE(1935), d; GIVE ME YOUR HEART(1936), d; PETRIFIED FOREST, THE(1936), d; BLACK LEGION, THE(1937), d; CALL IT A DAY(1937), d; IT'S LOVE I'M AFTER(1937), d; ADVENTURES OF MARCO POLO, THE(1938), d; YOUTH TAKES A FLING(1938), d; THEY SHALL HAVE MUSIC(1939), d; FOUR SONS(1940), d; HOUSE ACROSS THE BAY, THE(1940), d; CHARLEY'S AUNT(1941), d; CONFIRM OR DENY(1941), d; GREAT AMERICAN BROADCAST, THE(1941), d; MOONTIDE(1942), d; ORCHESTRA WIVES(1942), d; CRASH DIVE(1943), d; SWEET AND LOWDOWN(1944), d; ANGEL ON MY SHOULDER(1946), d; NIGHT IN CASABLANCA, A(1946), d; BEAST OF BUDAPEST, THE(1958), p

Silents

JOHNNY GET YOUR HAIR CUT(1927), d; CRIMSON CITY, THE(1928), d

Misc. Silents

CHRISTINE OF THE BIG TOPS(1926), d; MONEY TALKS(1926), d; UNKNOWN TREASURES(1926), d; DEARIE(1927), d; QUARANTINED RIVALS(1927), d

Archie L. Mayo

SACRED FLAME, THE(1929), d; SAP, THE(1929), d; CASE OF THE LUCKY LEGS, THE(1935), d; I MARRIED A DOCTOR(1936), d

Silents

SLIGHTLY USED(1927), d

Misc. Silents

COLLEGE WIDOW, THE(1927), d; BEWARE OF MARRIED MEN(1928), d

Ben Mayo

LINCOLN CONSPIRACY, THE(1977)

Bob Mayo

SGT. PEPPER'S LONELY HEARTS CLUB BAND(1978)

Bobby Mayo

SAILOR BEWARE(1951)

Christine Mayo

Silents

AMATEUR DEVIL, AN(1921); DON'T MARRY FOR MONEY(1923); SHOCK, THE(1923)

Misc. Silents

SPELL OF THE YUKON, THE(1916); SUPREME SACRIFICE, THE(1916); TWO MEN AND A WOMAN(1917); WHO'S YOUR NEIGHBOR?(1917); HOUSE OF MIRTH, THE(1918); SUCCESSFUL ADVENTURE, THE(1918); FAIR AND WARMER(1919); LITTLE INTRUDER, THE(1919); DUDS(1920); PALACE OF THE DARKENED WINDOWS, THE(1920); WHEN WE WERE TWENTY-ONE(1921); UNDERSTUDY, THE(1922)

Donald Mayo

QUEEN OF BROADWAY(1942); VALLEY OF VENGEANCE(1944)

Eddie Mayo

SAILOR BEWARE(1951)

Edna Mayo

Misc. Silents

ARISTOCRACY(1914); KEY TO YESTERDAY, THE(1914); QUEST OF THE SACRED GEM, THE(1914); BLINDNESS OF VIRTUE, THE(1915); GRAUSTARK(1915); CHAPERON, THE(1916); MISLEADING LADY, THE(1916); RETURN OF EVE, THE(1916); SALVATION JOAN(1916); HEARTS OF LOVE(1918)

Eleanor R. Mayo

TARNISHED(1950), w

Frank Mayo

DOUGH BOYS(1930); ALIAS THE BAD MAN(1931); CHINATOWN AFTER DARK(1931); RANGE LAW(1931); HELL'S HEADQUARTERS(1932); LAST RIDE, THE(1932); MAGNIFICENT OBSESSION(1935); MURDER MAN(1935); NO MORE LADIES(1935); ONE HOUR LATE(1935); TALE OF TWO CITIES, A(1935); BURNING GOLD(1936); DESERT GOLD(1936); HOLLYWOOD BOULEVARD(1936); LOVE ON THE RUN(1936); SAN FRANCISCO(1936); SHOW BOAT(1936); STORY OF LOUIS PASTEUR, THE(1936); TOO MANY PARENTS(1936); LIFE OF EMILE ZOLA, THE(1937); PERFECT SPECIMEN, THE(1937); PHANTOM OF SANTA FE(1937); I AM THE LAW(1938); PENITENTIARY(1938); CODE OF THE SECRET SERVICE(1939); CONFESSIONS OF A NAZI SPY(1939); DARK VICTORY(1939); EACH DAWN I DIE(1939); GOING PLACES(1939); KID FROM KOKOMO, THE(1939); KID NIGHTINGALE(1939); NANCY DREW AND THE HIDDEN STAIRCASE(1939); NAUGHTY BUT NICE(1939); OKLAHOMA FRONTIER(1939); OKLAHOMA KID, THE(1939); SECRET SERVICE OF THE AIR(1939); SMASHING THE MONEY RING(1939); THEY MADE ME A CRIMINAL(1939); TORCHY PLAYS WITH DYNAMITE(1939); WOMEN IN THE WIND(1939); BRITISH INTELLIGENCE(1940); CASTLE ON THE HUDSON(1940); CHILD IS BORN, A(1940); FIGHTING 69TH, THE(1940); FLOWING GOLD(1940); INVISIBLE STRIPES(1940); KNUTE ROCKNE–ALL AMERICAN(1940); MAN WHO TALKED TOO MUCH, THE(1940); MURDER IN THE AIR(1940); SANTA FE TRAIL(1940); THEY DRIVE BY NIGHT(1940); 'TIL WE MEET AGAIN(1940); TORRID ZONE(1940); BRIDE CAME C.O.D., THE(1941); BULLETS FOR O'HARA(1941); KNOCKOUT(1941); MANPOWER(1941); ONE FOOT IN HEAVEN(1941); SHE COULDN'T SAY NO(1941); STRAWBERRY BLONDE, THE(1941); WAGONS ROLL AT NIGHT, THE(1941); ACROSS THE PACIFIC(1942); GENTLEMAN JIM(1942); GORILLA MAN(1942); JUKE GIRL(1942); KING'S ROW(1942); LADY GANGSTER(1942); MALE ANIMAL, THE(1942); MAN WHO CAME TO DINNER, THE(1942); SECRET ENEMIES(1942); THEY DIED WITH THEIR BOOTS ON(1942); MURDER ON THE WATERFRONT(1943); MYSTERIOUS DOCTOR, THE(1943); OLD ACQUAINTANCE(1943); PRINCESS O'ROURKE(1943); THANK YOUR LUCKY STARS(1943); CRIME BY NIGHT(1944); LAKE PLACID SERENADE(1944); LAST RIDE, THE(1944); MADEMOISELLE FIFI(1944); MUSIC IN MANHATTAN(1944); STEP LIVELY(1944); HAVING WONDERFUL CRIME(1945); STATE FAIR(1945); STRANGE MR. GREGORY, THE(1945); DEVIL'S MASK, THE(1946); MIGHTY MCGURK, THE(1946); POST-

MAN ALWAYS RINGS TWICE, THE(1946); HER HUSBAND'S AFFAIRS(1947); VARIETY GIRL(1947); EASTER PARADE(1948); HOMECOMING(1948); SMART WOMAN(1948); SAMSON AND DELILAH(1949); SLIGHTLY FRENCH(1949); UNDER-COVER MAN, THE(1949)
Silents
SOLD AT AUCTION(1917); APPEARANCE OF EVIL(1918); JOURNEY'S END(1918); AMAZING WIFE, THE(1919); RED LANE, THE(1920); BLAZING TRAIL, THE(1921); DR. JIM(1921); SHARK MASTER, THE(1921); ACROSS THE DEAD-LINE(1922); AFRAID TO FIGHT(1922); ALTAR STAIRS, THE(1922); OUT OF THE SILENT NORTH(1922); TRACKED TO EARTH(1922); WOLF LAW(1922); SIX DAYS(1923); SOULS FOR SALE(1923); IS LOVE EVERYTHING?(1924); IF I MARRY AGAIN(1925); NECESSARY EVIL, THE(1925); PASSIONATE YOUTH(1925)
Misc. Silents
BRONZE BRIDE, THE(1917); CHECKMATE, THE(1917); EASY MONEY(1917); GLO-RY(1917); SUNNY JANE(1917); POWER AND THE GLORY, THE(1918); PURPLE LILY, THE(1918); SOUL WITHOUT WINDOWS, A(1918); TINSEL(1918); WHIMS OF SOCIETY, THE(1918); WITCH WOMAN, THE(1918); BLUFFER, THE(1919); BRUTE BREAKER, THE(1919); CROOK OF DREAMS(1919); LASCA(1919); LITTLE BROTHER OF THE RICH, A(1919); LOVE DEFENDER, THE(1919); MARY REGAN(1919); MORAL DEADLINE, THE(1919); ROUGHNECK, THE(1919); BURNT WINGS(1920); GIRL IN NUMBER 29, THE(1920); HITCHIN' POSTS(1920); HONOR BOUND(1920); MARRIAGE PIT, THE(1920); PEDDLER OF LIES, THE(1920); THRU THE EYES OF MEN(1920); COLORADO(1921); FIGHTING LOVER, THE(1921); GO STRAIGHT(1921); MAGNIFICENT BRUTE, THE(1921); TIGER TRUE(1921); CAUGHT BLUFFING(1922); FLAMING HOUR, THE(1922); MAN WHO MARRIED HIS OWN WIFE, THE(1922); BOLTED DOOR, THE(1923); FIRST DEGREE, THE(1923); PLUNDERER, THE(1924); PRICE SHE PAID, THE(1924); SHADOW OF THE EAST, THE(1924); TRIFLERS, THE(1924); WILD ORANGES(1924); WOMAN ON THE JURY, THE(1924); BARRIERS BURNED AWAY(1925); UNKNOWN LOVER, THE(1925); WOMEN AND GOLD(1925); LEW TYLER'S WIVES(1926); THEN CAME THE WOMAN(1926)

James Mayo
HAMMERHEAD(1968), w
Jennifer Mayo
SUMMERSPELL(1983)
1984
SCARRED(1984)
Maren Mayo
REG'LAR FELLERS(1941)
Margaret Mayo
TWIN BEDS(1929), w; POLLY OF THE CIRCUS(1932), w; LIFE OF THE PAR-TY(1934, Brit.), w; TWIN BEDS(1942), w
Silents
BABY MINE(1917), w; POLLY OF THE CIRCUS(1917), w; TWIN BEDS(1920), w; MARRIAGE OF WILLIAM ASHE, THE(1921), w; BABY MINE(1928), w
Melvin Mayo
Misc. Silents
CONVICT KING, THE(1915); SAVED FROM THE HAREM(1915); EMBODIED THOUGHT, THE(1916); SOLDIER'S SONS(1916); MENTIONED IN CONFIDEN-CE(1917)
Raymond Mayo
1984
KILLERS, THE(1984)
Stella Mayo
Misc. Silents
REGENERATION(1923)
Susana Mayo
NO EXIT(1962, U.S./Arg.)
Tobar Mayo
SCHIZOID(1980)
Misc. Talkies
ABAR-THE FIRST BLACK SUPERMAN(1977); BIG TIME(1977)
Virginia Mayo
JACK LONDON(1943); PRINCESS AND THE PIRATE, THE(1944); SEVEN DAYS ASHORE(1944); UP IN ARMS(1944); BEST YEARS OF OUR LIVES, THE(1946); KID FROM BROOKLYN(1946); OUT OF THE BLUE(1947); SECRET LIFE OF WALTER MITTY, THE(1947); SMART GIRLS DON'T TALK(1948); SONG IS BORN, A(1948); ALWAYS LEAVE THEM LAUGHING(1949); COLORADO TERRITORY(1949); FLAXY MARTIN(1949); GIRL FROM JONES BEACH, THE(1949); RED LIGHT(1949); WHITE HEAT(1949); BACKFIRE(1950); FLAME AND THE ARROW, THE(1950); WEST POINT STORY, THE(1950); ALONG THE GREAT DIVIDE(1951); CAPTAIN HORATIO HORN-BLOWER(1951, Brit.); PAINTING THE CLOUDS WITH SUNSHINE(1951); STAR-LIFT(1951); IRON MISTRESS, THE(1952); SHE'S WORKING HER WAY THROUGH COLLEGE(1952); DEVIL'S CANYON(1953); SHE'S BACK ON BROADWAY(1953); SOUTH SEA WOMAN(1953); KING RICHARD AND THE CRUSADERS(1954); SIL-VER CHALICE, THE(1954); PEARL OF THE SOUTH PACIFIC(1955); CONGO CROSS-ING(1956); GREAT DAY IN THE MORNING(1956); PROUD ONES, THE(1956); BIG LAND, THE(1957); STORY OF MANKIND, THE(1957); TALL STRANGER, THE(1957); FORT DOBBS(1958); WESTBOUND(1959); JET OVER THE ATLANTIC(1960); RE-VOLT OF THE MERCENARIES(1964, Ital./Span.); YOUNG FURY(1965); CASTLE OF EVIL(1967); FORT UTAH(1967); HAUNTED(1976); WON TON TON, THE DOG WHO SAVED HOLLYWOOD(1976); FRENCH QUARTER(1978)
Virginie Mayo
WONDER MAN(1945)
Whitman Mayo
BLACK KLANSMAN, THE(1966); MAIN EVENT, THE(1979); D.C. CAB(1983)
Karen Mayo-Chandler
1984
BEVERLY HILLS COP(1984)
Peter Mayock
ULYSSES(1967, U.S./Brit.); WEDDING NIGHT(1970, Ireland)
Al Mayoff
HIGH(1968, Can.)
Steven Mayoff
HAPPY BIRTHDAY TO ME(1981)
Joaquin Mayol
VIRIDIANA(1962, Mex./Span.)
Bob Mayon
ELECTRA GLIDE IN BLUE(1973)

Charles Mayon
DIXIE(1943); DUFFY'S TAVERN(1945); BLUE DAHLIA, THE(1946); WELL-GROOMED BRIDE, THE(1946); TROUBLE WITH WOMEN, THE(1947)
Florence Mayon
Silents
DOWN TO EARTH(1917); SHOCKING NIGHT, A(1921)
Misc. Silents
BRINGING HOME FATHER(1917)
George Mayon
LADY IN THE DARK(1944); COURT-MARTIAL OF BILLY MITCHELL, THE(1955); HELL BOUND(1957)
Helen Mayon
VIOLENT SATURDAY(1955); BUS STOP(1956); HILDA CRANE(1956); THREE BRAVE MEN(1957)
Frank Mayor
MEET JOHN DOE(1941)
Robert Mayor
HORROR CASTLE(1965, Ital.)
Stefano Mayore
ROMA(1972, Ital./Fr.)
France Mayotte
HAIR(1979)
Roy Maypole
SNIPER, THE(1952)
Judith Mayre
WOMAN TIMES SEVEN(1967, U.S./Fr./Ital.)
Norman Mayreis
GATHERING OF EAGLES, A(1963), cos
Franz Mayrhofer
TRAPP FAMILY, THE(1961, Ger.), makeup
Lothar Mayring
VIENNESE NIGHTS(1930); WHITE DEMON, THE(1932, Ger.), w; INVISIBLE OPPO-NENT(1933, Ger.), w
Lothar M. Mayring
GIRL FROM THE MARSH CROFT, THE(1935, Ger.), w
Mayris Chaney and Her Dance Trio
HI' YA, SAILOR(1943)
The Mayris Chaney Dancers
WEEKEND PASS(1944)
Melanie Mayron
HARRY AND TONTO(1974); CARWASH(1976); GABLE AND LOMBARD(1976); YOU LIGHT UP MY LIFE(1977); GIRLFRIENDS(1978); GREAT SMOKEY ROADBLOCK, THE(1978); HEARTBEEPS(1981); MISSING(1982)
Belli Mays
BOY! WHAT A GIRL(1947)
Bill Mays
THIS STUFF'LL KILL YA!(1971)
Herschell Mays
PSYCHO FROM TEXAS(1982)
Peter Mays
BABY MAKER, THE(1970)
Rod Mays
1984
POWER, THE(1984)
William Mays
BORN YESTERDAY(1951)
Albert Maysles
SIX IN PARIS(1968, Fr.), ph
Tom Mayton
UNTIL THEY SAIL(1957)
Christie Mayuga
Misc. Talkies
EBONY, IVORY AND JADE(1977)
Mayura
CHINESE DEN, THE(1940, Brit.); MURDER ON APPROVAL(1956, Brit.)
Tashiro Mayuzumi
KREMLIN LETTER, THE(1970), m, md
Toshio Mayuzumi
ENJO(1959, Jap.), m
Toshiro Mayuzumi
OHAYO(1962, Jap.), m; WEIRD LOVE MAKERS, THE(1963, Jap.), m; WHEN A WOMAN ASCENDS THE STAIRS(1963, Jap.), m; INSECT WOMAN, THE(1964, Jap.), m; UNHOLY DESIRE(1964, Jap.), m; TWILIGHT PATH(1965, Jap.), m; BIBLE.-..IN THE BEGINNING, THE(1966), m; LONGING FOR LOVE(1966, Jap.), m; REFLEC-TIONS IN A GOLDEN EYE(1967), m; GOODBYE, MOSCOW(1968, Jap.), m; TUNNEL TO THE SUN(1968, Jap.), m; GIRL I ABANDONED, THE(1970, Jap.), m; KURAGEJI-MA-LEGENDS FROM A SOUTHERN ISLAND(1970, Jap.), m
Roxanne Mayweather
1984
CRIMES OF PASSION(1984)
Ed Maywood
WHY RUSSIANS ARE REVOLTING(1970)
Albert Mazaleyrat
PLEASURES AND VICES(1962, Fr.), p
Richard Mazar
UNCIVILISED(1937, Aus.)
Emile Mazaud
CARNIVAL(1953, Fr.), w
Elizabeth Mazel
REACHING OUT(1983), m
Adel Mazen
EMMA MAE(1976), art d; PENITENTIARY(1979), art d
Glen Mazen
DOUBLES(1978)
Arnie Mazer
TAPS(1981)
Bill Mazer
RAGING BULL(1980); EYEWITNESS(1981)

Georgia Mazetti
TIGER ROSE(1930)
Tom Mazetti
THEY GOT ME COVERED(1943)
Vic Mazetti
THEY GOT ME COVERED(1943)
Marius Mazhanian
Misc. Talkies
MELON AFFAIR, THE(1979)
Ahmed Mazhar
CAIRO(1963)
Edna Mazia
1984
DRIFTING(1984, Israel), w
Franchette Mazin
NOUS IRONS A PARIS(1949, Fr.), ed; MONTE CARLO BABY(1953, Fr.), ed; SELLERS OF GIRLS(1967, Fr.), ed
Stan Mazin
HISTORY OF THE WORLD, PART 1(1981)
Walter Mazlow
SLENDER THREAD, THE(1965)
Melonie Mazman
VOICES(1979)
Anthony Mazola
GREAT CARUSO, THE(1951)
Eugene Mazola
WAIT 'TIL THE SUN SHINES, NELLIE(1952)
Frank Mazolla
FISH THAT SAVED PITTSBURGH, THE(1979), ed
S. Mazovetskaya
LADY WITH THE DOG, THE(1962, USSR)
Mary Mazstead
GREAT MUPPET CAPER, THE(1981)
Merrill M. Mazuer
WRONG IS RIGHT(1982)
Alfred Mazure
SECRETS OF SEX(1970, Brit.), w
Mike Mazurki
BELLE OF THE NINETIES(1934); SHANGHAI GESTURE, THE(1941); DR. RENAULT'S SECRET(1942); GENTLEMAN JIM(1942); BEHIND THE RISING SUN(1943); BOMBER'S MOON(1943); HENRY ALDRICH HAUNTS A HOUSE(1943); IT AIN'T HAY(1943); MISSION TO MOSCOW(1943); SWING FEVER(1943); THANK YOUR LUCKY STARS(1943); CANTERVILLE GHOST, THE(1944); LOST ANGEL(1944); MISSING JUROR, THE(1944); PRINCESS AND THE PIRATE, THE(1944); SHINE ON, HARVEST MOON(1944); SUMMER STORM(1944); THIN MAN GOES HOME, THE(1944); ABBOTT AND COSTELLO IN HOLLYWOOD(1945); DAKOTA(1945); DICK TRACY(1945); HORN BLOWS AT MIDNIGHT, THE(1945); MURDER, MY SWEET(1945); NOB HILL(1945); SPANISH MAIN, THE(1945); FRENCH KEY, THE(1946); LIVE WIRES(1946); MYSTERIOUS INTRUDER(1946); KILLER DILL(1947); NIGHTMARE ALLEY(1947); SINBAD THE SAILOR(1947); UNCONQUERED(1947); I WALK ALONE(1948); NOOSE HANGS HIGH, THE(1948); RELENTLESS(1948); ABANDONED(1949); COME TO THE STABLE(1949); DEVIL'S HENCHMEN, THE(1949); NEPTUNE'S DAUGHTER(1949); ROPE OF SAND(1949); SAMSON AND DELILAH(1949); DARK CITY(1950); HE'S A COCKEYED WONDER(1950); NIGHT AND THE CITY(1950, Brit.); CRIMINAL LAWYER(1951); LIGHT TOUCH, THE(1951); MY FAVORITE SPY(1951); PIER 23(1951); TEN TALL MEN(1951); EGYPTIAN. THE(1954); BLOOD ALLEY(1955); DAVY CROCKETT, KING OF THE WILD FRONTIER(1955); KISMET(1955); NEW ORLEANS UNCENSORED(1955); NEW YORK CONFIDENTIAL(1955); AROUND THE WORLD IN 80 DAYS(1956); COMANCHE(1956); MAN IN THE VAULT(1956); HELL SHIP MUTINY(1957); MAN WHO DIED TWICE, THE(1958); SOME LIKE IT HOT(1959); FACTS OF LIFE, THE(1960); ERRAND BOY, THE(1961); POCKETFUL OF MIRACLES(1961); FIVE WEEKS IN A BALLOON(1962); SWINGIN' ALONG(1962); ZOTZ!(1962); DONOVAN'S REEF(1963); FOUR FOR TEXAS(1963); IT'S A MAD, MAD, MAD, MAD WORLD(1963); CHEYENNE AUTUMN(1964); DISORDERLY ORDERLY, THE(1964); REQUIEM FOR A GUNFIGHTER(1965); SEVEN WOMEN(1966); ADVENTURES OF BULLWHIP GRIFFIN, THE(1967); WILD McCULLOCHS, THE(1975); CHALLENGE TO BE FREE(1976); WON TON TON, THE DOG WHO SAVED HOLLYWOOD(1976); ONE MAN JURY(1978); MAN WITH BOGART'S FACE, THE(1980)
Joseph Mazurkiewicz
ON THE YARD(1978)
I. Mazurova
WELCOME KOSTYA!(1965, USSR)
Ye. Mazurova
WHEN THE TREES WERE TALL(1965, USSR)
Betsy Mazursky
TEMPEST(1982)
1984
MOSCOW ON THE HUDSON(1984)
Jill Mazursky
WILLIE AND PHIL(1980)
Meg Mazursky
ALEX IN WONDERLAND(1970)
Paul Mazursky
FEAR AND DESIRE(1953); BLACKBOARD JUNGLE, THE(1955); DEATHWATCH(1966); I LOVE YOU, ALICE B. TOKLAS!(1968), w; BOB AND CAROL AND TED AND ALICE(1969), d, w; ALEX IN WONDERLAND(1970), a, d, w; BLUME IN LOVE(1973), a, p,d&w; HARRY AND TONTO(1974), p&d; w; NEXT STOP, GREENWICH VILLAGE(1976), p, d&w; STAR IS BORN, A(1976); UNMARRIED WOMAN, AN(1978), a, p, d&w; MAN, A WOMAN, AND A BANK, A(1979, Can.); WILLIE AND PHIL(1980), p, d&w; HISTORY OF THE WORLD, PART 1(1981); TEMPEST(1982), a, p&d, w
1984
MOSCOW ON THE HUDSON(1984), a, p&d, w
George Mazyrack
TRIAL OF LEE HARVEY OSWALD, THE(1964)
Antonio Mazza
MADE IN ITALY(1967, Fr./Ital.)

Marc Mazza
JOY HOUSE(1964, Fr.); RIDER ON THE RAIN(1970, Fr./Ital.); POPSY POP(1971, Fr.); BLOOD IN THE STREETS(1975, Ital./Fr.)
Mario Mazza
RING AROUND THE CLOCK(1953, Ital.)
Rosy Mazzacurati
LA NOTTE(1961, Fr./Ital.)
Tony Mazzadra
TRICK BABY(1973)
Anna Mazzananio
FRANKENSTEIN-ITALIAN STYLE(1977, Ital.)
Maria Mazzanti
LA DOLCE VITA(1961, Ital./Fr.)
Piero Mazzarella
VIOLENT FOUR, THE(1968, Ital.)
A. Mazzei
I BECAME A CRIMINAL(1947), art d
Andrew Mazzei
MADONNA OF THE SEVEN MOONS(1945, Brit.), art d; UPTURNED GLASS, THE(1947, Brit.), art d; JUST WILLIAM'S LUCK(1948, Brit.), art d; SMUGGLERS, THE(1948, Brit.), art d; THIS WAS A WOMAN(1949, Brit.), art d
Anthony Mazzei
NAUGHTY ARLETTE(1951, Brit.), art d
Francesco Mazzei
WHITE, RED, YELLOW, PINK(1966, Ital.), p; CHASTITY BELT, THE(1968, Ital.), p; LOVE FACTORY(1969, Ital.), p
Lorenza Mazzetti
TOGETHER(1956, Brit.), d
Gilberto Mazzi
GRAND PRIX(1966)
Dave Mazzie
FACES(1968)
Dominick Mazzie
WALKING TALL(1973); S.O.B.(1981)
Piero Mazzinghi
NIGHT PORTER, THE(1974, Ital./U.S.)
Nino Mazziotti
BARBER OF SEVILLE, THE(1947, Ital.)
Carl Mazzocone
JAWS 3-D(1983)
Al Mazzola
FOLIES DERGERE(1935)
Eugene Mazzola
BUTCHER BAKER(NIGHTMARE MAKER)* (1982), p; PRODIGAL, THE(1955); FOUR GIRLS IN TOWN(1956); TEN COMMANDMENTS, THE(1956); WALK THE PROUD LAND(1956)
Francisco Mazzola
DEMON SEED(1977), ed
Frank Mazzola
REBEL WITHOUT A CAUSE(1955); WAY TO THE GOLD, THE(1957); STILETTO(1969), ed; MACHO CALLAHAN(1970), ed; HIRED HAND, THE(1971), ed; SECOND COMING OF SUZANNE, THE(1974), ed
Leonard A. Mazzola
RAGE(1972), set d; DEATH VALLEY(1982), set d
Richard Mazzola
JOYRIDE(1977)
Saveria Mazzola
GODFATHER, THE, PART II(1974)
Dario Mazzoli
MASOCH(1980, Ital.); STORY WITHOUT WORDS(1981, Ital.)
Carlo Mazzone
TIMES GONE BY(1953, Ital.); AMERICAN WIFE, AN(1965, Ital.); RUN FOR YOUR WIFE(1966, Fr./Ital.)
Franca Mazzone
IT HAPPENED IN ROME(1959, Ital.)
The Mazzone-Abbott Dancers
IT'S A GREAT FEELING(1949)
Carlo Mazzoni
WHITE SHEIK, THE(1956, Ital.)
Adrianna Mazzotti
FATHER'S DILEMMA(1952, Ital.)
Pascal Mazzotti
VERY CURIOUS GIRL, A(1970, Fr.)
Giuseppe Mazzuca
GOODNIGHT, LADIES AND GENTLEMEN(1977, Ital.), m
Joseph Mazzuca
HOUSE OF STRANGERS(1949)
Misc. Talkies
SISTERS OF DEATH(1976), d
Mario Mazzucchelli
LADY OF MONZA, THE(1970, Ital.), w
Anthony T. Mazzucchi
1984
BLAME IT ON THE NIGHT(1984)
Peppino Mazzulo
MAGIC WORLD OF TOPO GIGIO, THE(1961, Ital.)
Fausta Mazzunchelli
STRANGER ON THE PROWL(1953, Ital.)
Ephraim Mbhele
ZULU(1964, Brit.)
Bingo Mbonjeni
FOREVER YOUNG, FOREVER FREE(1976, South Afr.)
Letta Mbulu
WARM DECEMBER, A(1973, Brit.)
Jack McAdam
NEPTUNE FACTOR, THE(1973, Can.), prod d; WELCOME TO BLOOD CITY(1977, Brit./Can.), prod d

John McAdam
EXCUSE MY GLOVE(1936, Brit.)
Michael R. McAdam
JET PILOT(1957), ed; BACKTRACK(1969), ed
Paul McAdam
LITTLE CONVICT, THE(1980, Aus.), anim
Ann McAdams
DON'T LOOK IN THE BASEMENT(1973)
Misc. Talkies
CREATURE OF DESTRUCTION(1967)
Bob McAdams
1984
BLOOD SIMPLE(1984)
Cynthia McAdams
LILITH(1964); ME AND MY BROTHER(1969); LAST MOVIE, THE(1971)
Jack McAdams
HOMER(1970), prod d
James McAdams
THIS SAVAGE LAND(1969), p
James B. McAdams
TOWN THAT DREADED SUNDOWN, THE(1977)
Phoebe McAdams
7254(1971)
Helene McAdoo
CEILNG ZERO(1935)
Mary McAdoo
BIGGER THAN LIFE(1956); RACK, THE(1956)
Tom McAdoo
SHANE(1953), ed; COURT JESTER, THE(1956), ph; THAT CERTAIN FEE-LING(1956), ed; SHORT CUT TO HELL(1957), ed; MISSOURI TRAVELER, THE(1958), ed; SPANISH AFFAIR(1958, Span.), ed; YOUNG LAND, THE(1959), ed; CROWDED SKY, THE(1960), ed; GUNS OF THE TIMBERLAND(1960), ed; PLUNDERERS, THE(1960), ed; RIGHT APPROACH, THE(1961), ed; BOYS' NIGHT OUT(1962), ed; LAD: A DOG(1962), ed; LOVE IS A BALL(1963), ed; WHEELER DEALERS, THE(1963), ed; AMERICANIZATION OF EMILY, THE(1964), ed
Hailey McAfee
1984
MICKI AND MAUDE(1984)
Harry McAfee
SAN FRANCISCO(1936), art d; THEY GAVE HIM A GUN(1937), art d; DANCING CO-ED(1939), art d; THESE GLAMOUR GIRLS(1939), art d; SHIP AHOY(1942), art d; NOTHING BUT TROUBLE(1944), art d; THREE MEN IN WHITE(1944), art d; WITHOUT LOVE(1945), art d; HOODLUM SAINT, THE(1946), art d; BRIDE GOES WILD, THE(1948), art d
Henry McAfee
PERSONAL PROPERTY(1937), art d; MEN OF BOYS TOWN(1941), art d
Mara McAfee
KISS ME DEADLY(1955); LAS VEGAS SHAKEDOWN(1955); MAN WITH THE GUN(1955); HE LAUGHED LAST(1956); PAL JOEY(1957)
Harry McAffee
FAITHFUL IN MY FASHION(1946), art d; BRIDE GOES WILD, THE(1948), art d
Des McAleer
1984
ANNE DEVLIN(1984, Ireland); FOUR DAYS IN JULY(1984)
Don McAline
BLUE SKIES AGAIN(1983), ph
Patrick McAlinney
HORSE'S MOUTH, THE(1953, Brit.); TIME GENTLEMEN PLEASE!(1953, Brit.); TONIGHT'S THE NIGHT(1954, Brit.); NIGHT TO REMEMBER, A(1958, Brit.); SHAKE HANDS WITH THE DEVIL(1959, Ireland); TARNISHED HEROES(1961, Brit.); ALIVE AND KICKING(1962, Brit.); GENTLE TERROR, THE(1962, Brit.); RETURN OF A STRANGER(1962, Brit.); SHE DIDN'T SAY NO!(1962, Brit.); TERROR FROM UNDER THE HOUSE(1971, Brit.)
David McAlister
DECLINE AND FALL... OF A BIRD WATCHER(1969, Brit.)
Jennifer McAlister
SERIAL(1980)
Mary McAlister
ON THE LEVEL(1930)
Michael McAlister
1984
STARMAN(1984), spec eff
Michael J. McAlister
FRATERNITY ROW(1977)
Kathleen Rowe McAllen
FEAR NO EVIL(1981)
Patrick McAlliney
POT CARRIERS, THE(1962, Brit.)
Bill McAllister
FUNNY MONEY(1983, Brit.)
1984
SUPERGIRL(1984)
Chip McAllister
1984
WEEKEND PASS(1984)
David McAllister
BROTHERS, THE(1948, Brit.)
Ed McAllister
LONG NIGHT, THE(1976), ed
Gilbert McAllister
COMIN' THRU' THE RYE(1947, Brit.), w
Helen McAllister
UP IN ARMS(1944); WONDER MAN(1945)
James McAllister
PETE 'N' TILLIE(1972)
Jennifer McAllister
RESURRECTION(1980)
Misc. Talkies
KID FROM NOT SO BIG, THE(1978)

Jessie McAllister
GLAMOUR(1934)
Lon McAllister
SOULS AT SEA(1937); STELLA DALLAS(1937)
Mary McAllister
MADAME SATAN(1930)
Silents
ON TRIAL(1917); ASHES OF VENGEANCE(1923); MEASURE OF A MAN, THE(1924); ONE MINUTE TO PLAY(1926); WANING SEX, THE(1926); MIDNIGHT WATCH, THE(1927); SINGED(1927); INTO NO MAN'S LAND(1928)
Misc. Silents
KILL-JOY, THE(1917); PANTS(1917); SADIE GOES TO HEAVEN(1917); YOUNG MOTHER HUBBARD(1917); HALF A CHANCE(1920); BOOMERANG, THE(1925); RED RIDER, THE(1925); ROARING ADVENTURE, A(1925); MAN IN THE SHADOW, THE(1926); SAP, THE(1926); FIRE AND STEEL(1927); DEVIL'S SKIPPER, THE(1928); LOVES OF AN ACTRESS(1928); WICKEDNESS PREFERRED(1928)
Mary V. McAllister
Misc. Silents
LITTLE SHOES(1917)
Patrick McAllister
BLACK CAESAR(1973)
Paul McAllister
NOAH'S ARK(1928); EVANGELINE(1929); CASE OF SERGEANT GRISCHA, THE(1930); BEAU IDEAL(1931); INSPIRATION(1931); JUDGE PRIEST(1934); MARY OF SCOTLAND(1936); DOCTOR TAKES A WIFE(1940)
Silents
SCALES OF JUSTICE, THE(1914); STOLEN VOICE(1915), w; TRILBY(1915); JAMESTOWN(1923); WINNING OF BARBARA WORTH, THE(1926); SHE'S A SHEIK(1927); EVANGELINE(1929)
Misc. Silents
MAN WHO FOUND HIMSELF, THE(1915); MONEY MASTER, THE(1915); VIA WIRELESS(1915); HIS BROTHER'S WIFE(1916); ONE HOUR(1917), d; WHIP, THE(1917); COLUMBUS(1923)
Petra McAllister
SCARLET EMPRESS, THE(1934)
Shawn McAllister
ABSENCE OF MALICE(1981); FUNHOUSE, THE(1981)
Ward McAllister
Silents
GENERAL JOHN REGAN(1921, Brit.); REPENTANCE(1922, Brit.); TRAPPED BY THE MORMONS(1922, Brit.)
Misc. Silents
WOMAN OF NO IMPORTANCE, A(1921, Brit.); WHILE LONDON SLEEPS(1922, Brit.)
Michael McAloney
DESPERATE CHARACTERS(1971)
Donald McAlpin
Silents
ROSITA(1923)
Edith McAlpin
Silents
RISE OF JENNIE CUSHING, THE(1917); SPREADING DAWN, THE(1917); JOAN OF PLATTSBURG(1918)
Hal McAlpin
DESTINATION 60,000(1957), ph; PAWNEE(1957), ph; UNDERSEA GIRL(1957), ph; WHEN HELL BROKE LOOSE(1958), ph; SERGEANT WAS A LADY, THE(1961), ph; MERMAIDS OF TIBURON, THE(1962), ph
Hal A. McAlpin
SULLIVAN'S EMPIRE(1967), ph
Don McAlpine
ADVENTURES OF BARRY McKENZIE(1972, Austral.), ph; BARRY MC KENZIE HOLDS HIS OWN(1975, Aus.), ph; DON'S PARTY(1976, Aus.), ph; GETTING OF WISDOM, THE(1977, Aus.), ph; MONEY MOVERS(1978, Aus.), ph; ODD ANGRY SHOT, THE(1979, Aus.), ph; PATRICK(1979, Aus.), ph; BREAKER MORANT(1980, Aus.), ph; CLUB, THE(1980, Aus.), ph; EARTHLING, THE(1980), ph; MY BRILLIANT CAREER(1980, Aus.), ph; DON'T CRY, IT'S ONLY THUNDER(1982), ph; NOW AND FOREVER(1983, Aus.), ph; PUBERTY BLUES(1983, Aus.), ph
1984
HARRY AND SON(1984), ph; MOSCOW ON THE HUDSON(1984), ph
Donald McAlpine
TEMPEST(1982), ph
Jane McAlpine
Silents
WINNING STROKE, THE(1919)
Misc. Silents
CIRCUMSTANTIAL EVIDENCE(1920); SCRAP OF PAPER, THE(1920); WALL STREET MYSTERY, THE(1920)
Ray McAnally
SHAKE HANDS WITH THE DEVIL(1959, Ireland); NAKED EDGE, THE(1961); BILLY BUDD(1962); DESERT PATROL(1962, Brit.); MURDER IN EDEN(1962, Brit.); SHE DIDN'T SAY NO!(1962, Brit.); HE WHO RIDES A TIGER(1966, Brit.); LOOKING GLASS WAR, THE(1970, Brit.); FEAR IS THE KEY(1973)
1984
CAL(1984, Ireland)
Kenneth McAndish
KID FROM BOOKLYN, THE(1946)
Margaret McAndrew
NAKED CITY, THE(1948)
Marianne McAndrew
HELLO, DOLLY!(1969); CHANDLER(1971); SEVEN MINUTES, THE(1971); BAT PEOPLE, THE(1974)
Pat McAndrew
THUNDER IN DIXIE(1965)
Robert McAndrew
MEDIUM COOL(1969)
William G. McAndrew
THAT CHAMPIONSHIP SEASON(1982)

John McAndrews
Silents
RAGGED MESSENGER, THE(1917, Brit.); HANGING JUDGE, THE(1918, Brit.); NATURE OF THE BEAST, THE(1919, Brit.); ALF'S BUTTON(1920, Brit.); TEMPORARY VAGABOND, A(1920, Brit.); SISTER TO ASSIST 'ER, A(1922, Brit.); PIPES OF PAN, THE(1923, Brit.)
Misc. Silents
HIS DEAREST POSSESSION(1919, Brit.); WHITE HOPE, THE(1922, Brit.)

Jac McAnelley
BIG BAD MAMA(1974), cos

Jac McAnelly
YOUR THREE MINUTES ARE UP(1973), cos; CRAZY MAMA(1975), cos; HOSPITAL MASSACRE(1982), prod d

Joe McAnelly
LADY IN RED, THE(1979), prod d

Pat McAneny
WAY WE LIVE NOW, THE(1970)

Anne McAnn
GIRL IN GOLD BOOTS(1968)

George Burr McAnnan
WHITE ZOMBIE(1932); HE STAYED FOR BREAKFAST(1940)

Kip McArdle
HONEYMOON KILLERS, THE(1969)

Nancy McArdle
WHAT'S UP, DOC?(1972), cos; ANNIE HALL(1977), cos; OH, GOD!(1977), cos; DIE LAUGHING(1980), cos
1984
CLOAK AND DAGGER(1984), cos

Macs McAree
TOYS ARE NOT FOR CHILDREN(1972), w

Don McArt
JOURNEY TO FREEDOM(1957); BIG DADDY(1969)

Cynthia McArthur
TERROR IN THE JUNGLE(1968)

Fiona McArthur
WICKED LADY, THE(1983, Brit.)

Harold McArthur
SONG OF THE SARONG(1945), art d

Hugh McArthur
ROSE BOWL(1936); LITTLE ACCIDENT(1939); PANAMA PATROL(1939); STORY OF VERNON AND IRENE CASTLE, THE(1939); OH JOHNNY, HOW YOU CAN LOVE!(1940)

Kimberly McArthur
EASY MONEY(1983)

Molly McArthur
JAMAICA INN(1939, Brit.), cos; BLAST OF SILENCE(1961)

Wilson McArthur
YELLOW STOCKINGS(1930, Brit.), w

Braun McAsh
1984
POLICE ACADEMY(1984)

Clyde McAtee
LADY LUCK(1946)
Silents
KID, THE(1921); GOLD RUSH, THE(1925)
Misc. Silents
PERCY(1925)

Leon McAuliffe
RIDERS OF THE NORTHWEST MOUNTED(1943)

Alex McAvoy
BROTHERLY LOVE(1970, Brit.); PINK FLOYD–THE WALL(1982, Brit.)

Charles McAvoy
THOSE WHO DANCE(1930); BOWERY, THE(1933); SONS OF THE DESERT(1933); JEALOUSY(1934); MISS FANE'S BABY IS STOLEN(1934); MURDER AT THE VANITIES(1934); SHOOT THE WORKS(1934); WHARF ANGEL(1934); SINGING COWBOY, THE(1936); STRIKE ME PINK(1936); WEDDING PRESENT(1936); MAID OF SALEM(1937); KING OF ALCATRAZ(1938); KING OF THE TURF(1939); RULERS OF THE SEA(1939); I WANT A DIVORCE(1940); HONKY TONK(1941); INTERNATIONAL LADY(1941); MAD DOCTOR, THE(1941); MEET JOHN DOE(1941); PUBLIC ENEMIES(1941); MY FAVORITE BLONDE(1942); GYPSY WILDCAT(1944); SHINE ON, HARVEST MOON(1944); SALOME, WHERE SHE DANCED(1945); STRANGE HOLIDAY(1945); SUDAN(1945); DARK MIRROR, THE(1946); SEA OF GRASS, THE(1947); RETURN OF THE BADMEN(1948); VELVET TOUCH, THE(1948); TAKE ONE FALSE STEP(1949); SIDE STREET(1950); IT GROWS ON TREES(1952)

Charley McAvoy
CARRIE(1952)

May McAvoy
JAZZ SINGER, THE(1927); CAUGHT IN THE FOG(1928); LION AND THE MOUSE, THE(1928); TERROR, THE(1928); NO DEFENSE(1929); STOLEN KISSES(1929); THIRD FINGER, LEFT HAND(1940); TWO GIRLS ON BROADWAY(1940); RINGSIDE MAISIE(1941); LUXURY LINER(1948); MYSTERY STREET(1950); EXECUTIVE SUITE(1954); GUN GLORY(1957)
Silents
PERFECT LADY, A(1918); WAY OF A WOMAN(1919); MAN AND HIS WOMAN(1920); MORALS(1921); PRIVATE SCANDAL, A(1921); HOMESPUN VAMP, A(1922); KICK IN(1922); ONLY 38(1923); BEDROOM WINDOW, THE(1924); ENCHANTED COTTAGE, THE(1924); MARRIED FLIRTS(1924); BEN-HUR(1925); LADY WINDERMERE'S FAN(1925); TOP OF NEW YORK, THE(1925); IF I WERE SINGLE(1927); IRISH HEARTS(1927); MATINEE LADIES(1927); SLIGHTLY USED(1927)
Misc. Silents
MY HUSBAND'S OTHER WIFE(1919); DEVIL'S GARDEN, THE(1920); FORBIDDEN VALLEY(1920); HOUSE OF THE TOLLING BELLS, THE(1920); TRUTH ABOUT HUSBANDS, THE(1920); EVERYTHING FOR SALE(1921); SENTIMENTAL TOMMY(1921); VIRGINIA COURTSHIP, A(1921); CLARENCE(1922); THROUGH A GLASS WINDOW(1922); GRUMPY(1923); HER REPUTATION(1923); TARNISH(1924); THREE WOMEN(1924); WEST OF THE WATER TOWER(1924); MAD WHIRL, THE(1925); TESSIE(1925); FIRE BRIGADE, THE(1926); MY OLD DUTCH(1926); PASSIONATE QUEST, THE(1926); ROAD TO GLORY, THE(1926); SAVAGE, THE(1926); RENO DIVORCE, A(1927); LITTLE SNOB, THE(1928); NO DEFENSE(1929)

Charles McBain
WHERE THERE'S A WILL(1937, Brit.)

Diane McBain
ICE PALACE(1960); CLAUDELLE INGLISH(1961); PARRISH(1961); BLACK GOLD(1963); CARETAKERS, THE(1963); MARY, MARY(1963); DISTANT TRUMPET, A(1964); SPINOUT(1966); KARATE KILLERS, THE(1967); THUNDER ALLEY(1967); MARYJANE(1968); MINI-SKIRT MOB, THE(1968); FIVE THE HARD WAY(1969); I SAILED TO TAHITI WITH AN ALL GIRL CREW(1969); DELTA FACTOR, THE(1970); WICKED, WICKED(1973); MONSTER(1979)
Misc. Talkies
SAVAGE SEASON(1970); DEATHHEAD VIRGIN, THE(1974)

Ed McBain
COP HATER(1958), w; MUGGER, THE(1958), w; WITHOUT APPARENT MOTIVE(1972, Fr.), w

Ed [Evan Hunter] McBain
FUZZ(1972), w

Ed McBain [Evan Hunter]
PUSHER, THE(1960), w; HIGH AND LOW(1963, Jap.), w; EVERY LITTLE CROOK AND NANNY(1972), w; BLOOD RELATIVES(1978, Fr./Can.), w

Roberta McBain
1984
ORDEAL BY INNOCENCE(1984, Brit.)

Mickey McBan
FATHER AND SON(1929)
Silents
POOR MEN'S WIVES(1923); HOT WATER(1924); SPLENDID ROAD, THE(1925); UNHOLY THREE, THE(1925); RETURN OF PETER GRIMM, THE(1926); WAY OF ALL FLESH, THE(1927); WHAT EVERY GIRL SHOULD KNOW(1927)
Misc. Silents
TEMPLE OF VENUS, THE(1923); SOMEBODY'S MOTHER(1926); SORRELL AND SON(1927); WHEN A DOG LOVES(1927)

Barbara McBane
ONE FROM THE HEART(1982)

Maria McBane
FIREBALL 590(1966)

Roy McBane
EMIL(1938, Brit.)

Don McBrearty
1984
AMERICAN NIGHTMARE(1984), d
Misc. Talkies
AMERICAN NIGHTMARE(1981, Can.), d

John McBrearty
TAPS(1981)

Anthony McBride
VICTORS, THE(1963)

Carl McBride
SMILING IRISH EYES(1929), ch

Cecilia McBride
SHEILA LEVINE IS DEAD AND LIVING IN NEW YORK(1975)

Donald McBride
HIS WOMAN(1931); ANNABEL TAKES A TOUR(1938); FLYING IRISHMAN, THE(1939); FOOTLIGHT FEVER(1941); DOLL FACE(1945); PENTHOUSE RHYTHM(1945); HOLIDAY RHYTHM(1950)
Misc. Silents
FETTERED WOMAN, THE(1917)

Elizabeth McBride
TENDER MERCIES(1982), cos

Fern McBride
DAVID HOLZMAN'S DIARY(1968)

Franklin McBride
GODLESS GIRL, THE(1929), ph

Harlee McBride
HOUSE CALLS(1978)

Ian McBride
WHY SHOOT THE TEACHER(1977, Can.), ed; SIEGE(1983, Can.), ed
1984
AMERICAN NIGHTMARE(1984), ed

James McBride
Misc. Talkies
MY GIRLFRIEND'S WEDDING(1969), d

Jeri McBride
STAR TREK: THE MOTION PICTURE(1979)

Jim McBride
DAVID HOLZMAN'S DIARY(1968), p,d,w&ed; HOT TIMES(1974), d&w; LAST EMBRACE(1979); BREATHLESS(1983), d, w
Misc. Talkies
GLEN AND RANDA(1971), d

Joe McBride
CANNONBALL(1976, U.S./Hong Kong); HOLLYWOOD BOULEVARD(1976)

John McBride
HORSE'S MOUTH, THE(1953, Brit.)

Joseph McBride
BLOOD AND GUTS(1978, Can.), w; ROCK 'N' ROLL HIGH SCHOOL(1979), w

Lillian McBride
REVENGE OF THE CHEERLEADERS(1976)

Lilyan McBride
GOODBYE, NORMA JEAN(1976); VIGILANTE FORCE(1976); VAN, THE(1977)

Major McBride
SECOND HONEYMOON(1937); TELEVISION SPY(1939); RAGE IN HEAVEN(1941)

Mark McBride
BEYOND THE FOG(1981, Brit.)

Patricia McBride
MIDSUMMER NIGHT'S DREAM, A(1966)

Patsy McBride
GENTLE PEOPLE AND THE QUIET LAND, THE(1972)

Robert McBride
GARDEN OF EDEN(1954), m

Sally McBride
HAPPY DAYS ARE HERE AGAIN(1936, Brit.)
Tom McBride
FRIDAY THE 13TH PART II(1981)
1984
FRIDAY THE 13TH-THE FINAL CHAPTER(1984)
Rod McBrien
LINE, THE(1982), m
Durga McBroom
FLASHDANCE(1983)
Marcia McBroom
COME BACK CHARLESTON BLUE(1972); LEGEND OF NIGGER CHARLEY, THE(1972); JESUS CHRIST, SUPERSTAR(1973); WILLIE DYNAMITE(1973)
1984
NEW YORK NIGHTS(1984)
John McBurnie
OUTLAWS OF SANTA FE(1944), ph; OUT OF THE STORM(1948), ph
Sean McCaan
ATLANTIC CITY(1981, U.S./Can.)
Alan McCabe
ESCAPE BY NIGHT(1965, Brit.), ph
Betty McCabe
MOONLIGHT IN VERMONT(1943)
Bill McCabe
HUNCH, THE(1967, Brit.)
Don McCabe
STAR IS BORN, A(1954)
Eben McCabe
1984
ALLEY CAT(1984)
Evelyn McCabe
SONG FOR TOMORROW, A(1948, Brit.)
Frank McCabe
RAMPARTS WE WATCH, THE(1940)
Gene McCabe
Misc. Talkies
FOLLOW ME(1969), d
Harry McCabe
Silents
NO-GUN MAN, THE(1924)
Misc. Silents
WESTERN THOROUGHBRED, A(1922)
James McCabe
Misc. Silents
SPENDER OR THE FORTUNES OF PETER, THE(1915)
Joe McCabe
MISS SADIE THOMPSON(1953)
Leo McCabe
HOUSE OF ROTHSCHILD, THE(1934); INFORMER, THE(1935); BELOVED ENEMY(1936); POLO JOE(1936); LITTLE MISS MOLLY(1940); QUARE FELLOW, THE(1962, Brit.); OF HUMAN BONDAGE(1964, Brit.); BLUES FOR LOVERS(1966, Brit.)
May McCabe
Silents
JUNGLE, THE(1914)
Norm McCabe
BUGS BUNNY'S THIRD MOVIE-1001 RABBIT TALES(1982), anim
Sandra McCabe
DOGS(1976); ROSE, THE(1979); HONKY TONK FREEWAY(1981)
Stephen McCabe
MY DINNER WITH ANDRE(1981), art d
1984
MIXED BLOOD(1984), art d
Tony McCabe
SOMETHING WEIRD(1967)
Vanessa McCabe
1984
ALLEY CAT(1984)
James McCaedell
ROAD WARRIOR, THE(1982, Aus.)
John McCafferty
YOU AND ME(1938); CARIBBEAN MYSTERY, THE(1945), ed; MOLLY AND ME(1945), ed; JOHNNY COMES FLYING HOME(1946), ed; PONY SOLDIER(1952), ed; LILIES OF THE FIELD(1963), ed
Sally McCaffery
ACCEPTABLE LEVELS(1983, Brit.)
Charles McCaffrey
Misc. Silents
JESUS OF NAZARETH(1928)
Fred McCaffrey
TRACK OF THE MOONBEAST(1976)
Pat McCaffria
POLICE DOG STORY, THE(1961)
Pat McCaffrie
ALL HANDS ON DECK(1961); CINCINNATI KID, THE(1965); TROUBLE WITH ANGELS, THE(1966); GUIDE FOR THE MARRIED MAN, A(1967)
Robert McCahon
RUNNING WILD(1973), p,d&w
Misc. Talkies
DELIVER US FROM EVIL(1975), d
Sandon McCail
PLAINSONG(1982)
Frances Lee McCain
HONKY TONK FREEWAY(1981); TEX(1982)
1984
FOOTLOOSE(1984); GREMLINS(1984)
Francis Lee McCain
REAL LIFE(1979)

Lee McCain
LAUGHING POLICEMAN, THE(1973)
Teddy McCain
COOL WORLD, THE(1963)
Bud McCaleister
THAT OTHER WOMAN(1942)
George McCalister
LOVE AND THE MIDNIGHT AUTO SUPPLY(1978)
Angelita McCall
DISTANT DRUMS(1951)
C. W. McCall
CONVOY(1978), w
Carmen J. McCall
FINAL CUT, THE(1980, Aus.)
Castle McCall
RENDEZVOUS 24(1946)
Darrell McCall
WHAT AM I BID?(1967)
Enid McCall
FOLLY TO BE WISE(1953); CONSTANT HUSBAND, THE(1955, Brit.)
George McCall
STREET CORNER(1948), p
Jack McCall
WHAT AM I BID?(1967)
James McCall
WORLD ACCORDING TO GARP, The(1982)
Joan McCall
ACT OF VENGEANCE(1974); GRIZZLY(1976)
June McCall
TWO TICKETS TO BROADWAY(1951); RACERS, THE(1955); NEVER SAY GOOD-BYE(1956); TATTERED DRESS, THE(1957); MOVIE MOVIE(1978)
Mary McCall
IT'S TOUGH TO BE FAMOUS(1932), w; SCARLET DAWN(1932), w
Mary McCall, Jr.
STREET OF WOMEN(1932), w; BABBITT(1934), w; DESIRABLE(1934), w; MIDSUMMER'S NIGHT'S DREAM, A(1935), w; SECRET BRIDE, THE(1935), w; WOMAN IN RED, THE(1935), w; I PROMISE TO PAY(1937), w; WOMEN OF GLAMOUR(1937), w; BREAKING THE ICE(1938), w; MR. BELVEDERE GOES TO COLLEGE(1949), w; RIDE THE MAN DOWN(1952), w
Mary C. McCall, Jr.
MORGAN'S MARAUDERS(1929), w; DR. SOCRATES(1935), w; CRAIG'S WIFE(1936), w; IT'S ALL YOURS(1937), w; MAISIE(1939), w; CONGO MAISIE(1940), w; GOLD RUSH MAISIE(1940), w; KATHLEEN(1941), w; MAISIE WAS A LADY(1941), w; RINGSIDE MAISIE(1941), w; MAISIE GETS HER MAN(1942), w; ON THE SUNNY SIDE(1942), w; DU BARRY WAS A LADY(1943), w; SWING SHIFT MAISIE(1943), w; MAISIE GOES TO RENO(1944), w; SULLIVANS, THE(1944), w; KEEP YOUR POWDER DRY(1945), w; DANCING IN THE DARK(1949), w; THUNDERBIRDS(1952), w; SLIM CARTER(1957), w; JUKE BOX RHYTHM(1959), w
Mitzi McCall
YOU'RE NEVER TOO YOUNG(1955); CRY BABY KILLER, THE(1958); MACHINE GUN KELLY(1958); WAR OF THE SATELLITES(1958)
Philip McCall
RING OF BRIGHT WATER(1969, Brit.)
Tim McCall
ONE FLEW OVER THE CUCKOO'S NEST(1975)
William McCall
LONESOME TRAIL, THE(1930); TRAILING TROUBLE(1930); UNDER TEXAS SKIES(1931); DESERT MESA(1935); LAST OF THE CLINTONS, THE(1935); LAWLESS BORDER(1935); ACES WILD(1937); MOONLIGHT ON THE RANGE(1937); HEROES OF THE ALAMO(1938)
Misc. Talkies
OUTLAWS OF THE RANGE(1936)
Silents
IT CAN BE DONE(1921); WHERE MEN ARE MEN(1921); ANGEL OF CROOKED STREET, THE(1922); BACK TRAIL, THE(1924); DARING CHANCES(1924)
Misc. Silents
ACROSS THE BORDER(1922); FIGHTING GUIDE, THE(1922)
Yvonne McCall
GUESS WHAT WE LEARNED IN SCHOOL TODAY?(1970)
Anthony McCall-Hudson
LORD OF THE FLIES(1963, Brit.)
Irish McCalla
SHE DEMONS(1958); BEAT GENERATION, THE(1959); FIVE GATES TO HELL(1959); FIVE BOLD WOMEN(1960); HANDS OF A STRANGER(1962)
Vernon McCalla
DUKE IS THE TOPS, THE(1938); REFORM SCHOOL(1939)
Misc. Talkies
GUN MOLL(1938); MR. SMITH GOES GHOST(1940)
Charles McCallam
SUNSTRUCK(1973, Aus.)
Vernon McCallan
AM I GUILTY?(1940)
Jean McCallen
GIRL IN THE RED VELVET SWING, THE(1955)
Dave McCalley
ON THE YARD(1978)
James McCallian
KISS ME DEADLY(1955)
Clement McCallin
STOLEN LIFE(1939, Brit.); QUEEN OF SPADES(1948, Brit.); EDWARD, MY SON(1949, U.S./Brit.); ROSSITER CASE, THE(1950, Brit.); LADY WITH A LAMP, THE(1951, Brit.); CRY, THE BELOVED COUNTRY(1952, Brit.); MURDER IN THE CATHEDRAL(1952, Brit.); STORY OF ROBIN HOOD, THE(1952, Brit.); FOLLY TO BE WISE(1953); SHOOT FIRST(1953, Brit.); HAPPY DEATHDAY(1969, Brit.)
James McCallion
BOY SLAVES(1938); CODE OF THE STREETS(1939); MAN WHO DARED, THE(1939); PRIDE OF THE BLUEGRASS(1939); PLAYGIRL(1954); VERA CRUZ(1954); ILLEGAL(1955); TRIBUTE TO A BADMAN(1956); NORTH BY NORTHWEST(1959); PT 109(1963); STRANGE BEDFELLOWS(1965); GUNFIGHT IN ABILENE(1967); COOGAN'S BLUFF(1968); COCKEYED COWBOYS OF CALICO COUNTY, THE(1970);

HOW DO I LOVE THEE?(1970); SKIN GAME(1971)

Jimmy McCallion
I AM NOT AFRAID(1939)

Bud [Lon] McCallister
OVER MY DEAD BODY(1942); QUIET PLEASE, MURDER(1942)

Lon McCallister
THAT CERTAIN AGE(1938); BABES IN ARMS(1939); DANGEROUSLY THEY LIVE(1942); GENTLEMAN JIM(1942); STAGE DOOR CANTEEN(1943); HOME IN INDIANA(1944); RED HOUSE, THE(1947); SCUDDA-HOO! SCUDDA-HAY!(1948); BIG CAT, THE(1949); STORY OF SEABISCUIT, THE(1949); BOY FROM INDIANA(1950); YANK IN KOREA, A(1951); MONTANA TERRITORY(1952); COMBAT SQUAD(1953)

Pvt. Lon McCallister
WINGED VICTORY(1944)

Lynn McCallon
DIFFERENT STORY, A(1978), ed

Charles McCallum
LITTLE AUSTRALIANS(1940, Aus.); LONG JOHN SILVER(1954, Aus.); SQUEEZE A FLOWER(1970, Aus.); DEVIL'S PLAYGROUND, THE(1976, Aus.); NEXT OF KIN(1983, Aus.)

David McCallum
HELL DRIVERS(1958, Brit.); NIGHT AMBUSH(1958, Brit.); NIGHT TO REMEMBER, A(1958, Brit.); ROBBERY UNDER ARMS(1958, Brit.); SECRET PLACE, THE(1958, Brit.); VIOLENT PLAYGROUND(1958, Brit.); LONG AND THE SHORT AND THE TALL, THE(1961, Brit.); FREUD(1962); GREAT ESCAPE, THE(1963); JUNGLE STREET GIRLS(1963, Brit.); GREATEST STORY EVER TOLD, THE(1965); AROUND THE WORLD UNDER THE SEA(1966); ONE OF OUR SPIES IS MISSING(1966); ONE SPY TOO MANY(1966); SPY IN THE GREEN HAT, THE(1966); SPY WITH MY FACE, THE(1966); TO TRAP A SPY(1966); KARATE KILLERS, THE(1967); THREE BITES OF THE APPLE(1967); HELICOPTER SPIES, THE(1968); SOL MADRID(1968); MOSQUITO SQUADRON(1970, Brit.); DOGS(1976); KINGFISH CAPER, THE(1976, South Africa); KING SOLOMON'S TREASURE(1978, Can.); WATCHER IN THE WOODS, THE(1980, Brit.)
Misc. Talkies
CORVINI INHERITANCE(1984, Brit.)

David McCallum, Sr.
LAST HOLIDAY(1950, Brit.); PRELUDE TO FAME(1950, Brit.)

Jason McCallum
VALACHI PAPERS, THE(1972, Ital./Fr.)

Joanna McCallum
NICKEL QUEEN, THE(1971, Aus.); HOPSCOTCH(1980)

John McCallum
HELD FOR RANSOM(1938); BUSH CHRISTMAS(1947, Brit.); LOVES OF JOANNA GODDEN, THE(1947, Brit.); ROOT OF ALL EVIL, THE(1947, Brit.); CALENDAR, THE(1948, Brit.); LETTER FROM AN UNKNOWN WOMAN(1948); BOY, A GIRL AND A BIKE, A(1949 Brit.); IT ALWAYS RAINS ON SUNDAY(1949, Brit.); MIRANDA(1949, Brit.); FIVE ANGLES ON MURDER(1950, Brit.); TRAVELLER'S JOY(1951, Brit.); FOUR AGAINST FATE(1952, Brit.); MAGIC BOX, THE(1952, Brit.); VALLEY OF EAGLES(1952, Brit.); LONG MEMORY, THE(1953, Brit.); MELBA(1953, Brit.); TRENT'S LAST CASE(1953, Brit.); DEVIL ON HORSEBACK(1954, Brit.); TROUBLE IN THE GLEN(1954, Brit.); LADY GODIVA RIDES AGAIN(1955, Brit.); PORT OF ESCAPE(1955, Brit.); THREE IN ONE(1956, Aus.); SMILEY(1957, Brit.); NICKEL QUEEN, THE(1971, Aus.), p&d, w
Silents
TAILOR MADE MAN, A(1922)

Neil McCallum
ON THE RUN(1958, Brit.); DEVIL'S DISCIPLE, THE(1959); FOUR DESPERATE MEN(1960, Brit.); FOXHOLE IN CAIRO(1960, Brit.); JET STORM(1961, Brit.); LISA(1962, Brit.); NIGHT WITHOUT PITY(1962, Brit.); WAR LOVER, THE(1962, U.S./Brit.); EYES OF ANNIE JONES, THE(1963, Brit.), p; WALK A TIGHTROPE(1964, U.S./Brit.), a, w; DR. TERROR'S HOUSE OF HORRORS(1965, Brit.); HILL, THE(1965, Brit.); WOMAN WHO WOULDN'T DIE, THE(1965, Brit.), a, p; LOST CONTINENT, THE(1968, Brit.); THUNDERBIRDS ARE GO(1968, Brit.); MOON ZERO TWO(1970, Brit.); QUEST FOR LOVE(1971, Brit.)

Nicholas McCallum
2,000 WEEKS(1970, Aus.)

Nick McCallum
1984
RAZORBACK(1984, Aus.), art d

Paul McCallum
DEATH WISH II(1982); 10 TO MIDNIGHT(1983)

Macon McCalman
CONCORDE, THE–AIRPORT '79; SMOKEY AND THE BANDIT(1977); COMES A HORSEMAN(1978); CARBON COPY(1981); DEAD AND BURIED(1981); ROLLOVER(1981); HONKYTONK MAN(1982); TIMERIDER(1983)
1984
FLESHBURN(1984)

Mercedes McCambridge
CONCORDE, THE–AIRPORT '79(; ALL THE KING'S MEN(1949); INSIDE STRAIGHT(1951); LIGHTNING STRIKES TWICE(1951); SCARF, THE(1951); JOHNNY GUITAR(1954); GIANT(1956); FAREWELL TO ARMS, A(1957); TOUCH OF EVIL(1958); SUDDENLY, LAST SUMMER(1959, Brit.); CIMARRON(1960); ANGEL BABY(1961); RUN HOME SLOW(1965); COUNTERFEIT KILLER, THE(1968); JUSTINE(1969, Ital./Span.); LIKE A CROW ON A JUNE BUG(1972); EXORCIST, THE(1973); THIEVES(1977); ECHOES(1983)
Misc. Talkies
99 WOMEN(1969, Brit./Span./Ger./Ital.); LAST GENERATION, THE(1971)

Shane McCamey
1984
ICE PIRATES, THE(1984)

Barbara Hawks McCampbell
RIO BRAVO(1959), w

Jean McCampbell
DESPERATE WOMEN, THE(?)

Sean McCan
DURING ONE NIGHT(1962, Brit.)

Jack McCanaghy
SHINE ON, HARVEST MOON(1944), set d

James McCandlas
Misc. Silents
CHARMER, THE(1917)

Kathleen McCandless
SYNANON(1965), cos

Michael McCane
CRACKING UP(1977)

Bill McCann
TERROR EYES(1981)

Charles McCann
BOY NAMED CHARLIE BROWN, A(1969), ed; SNOOPY, COME HOME(1972), ed
Silents
TIGER WOMAN, THE(1917)

Chuck McCann
HEART IS A LONELY HUNTER, THE(1968); PROJECTIONIST, THE(1970); JENNIFER ON MY MIND(1971); WORLD OF HANS CHRISTIAN ANDERSEN, THE(1971, Jap.), a, d&w; PLAY IT AS IT LAYS(1972); HERBIE RIDES AGAIN(1974); SILENT MOVIE(1976); SURVIVAL(1976); RACE FOR YOUR LIFE, CHARLIE BROWN(1977), ed; FOUL PLAY(1978); THEY WENT THAT-A-WAY AND THAT-A-WAY(1978); C.H.O.M.P.S.(1979); LUNCH WAGON(1981); COMEBACK TRAIL, THE(1982)
1984
ROSEBUD BEACH HOTEL(1984)

Dan McCann
KENNY AND CO.(1976)

DeWitt McCann
GHOST OF ZORRO(1959), ed

Donal McCann
FIGHTING PRINCE OF DONEGAL, THE(1966, Brit.); SINFUL DAVEY(1969, Brit.); POITIN(1979, Irish)
1984
REFLECTIONS(1984, Brit.)
Misc. Talkies
PHILADELPHIA HERE I COME(1975); HARD WAY, THE(1980, Brit.)

Donald McCann
1984
CAL(1984, Ireland)

Doreen McCann
TWO GIRLS AND A SAILOR(1944); PHANTOM SPEAKS, THE(1945); FROM THIS DAY FORWARD(1946); SISTER KENNY(1946); GUILT OF JANET AMES, THE(1947); MOONRISE(1948); MARY RYAN, DETECTIVE(1949); LOVE IS BETTER THAN EVER(1952)

Eoin McCann
LONG SHOT(1981, Brit.), w

Frances McCann
CREATION OF THE HUMANOIDS(1962)

Henry McCann
PAL JOEY(1957); HOT ROD GANG(1958); NO TIME FOR SERGEANTS(1958); GHOST OF DRAGSTRIP HOLLOW(1959); SUBMARINE SEAHAWK(1959)

John McCann
SCARFACE(1983)

Laura McCann
RETURN TO PEYTON PLACE(1961)

Linda McCann
TOY, THE(1982)

Patrick McCann
MAN AT THE TOP(1973, Brit.)

Sean McCann
QUIET DAY IN BELFAST, A(1974, Can.); SUDDEN FURY(1975, Can.); FAR SHORE, THE(1976, Can.); UNCANNY, THE(1977, Brit./Can.); THREE CARD MONTE(1978, Can.); NOTHING PERSONAL(1980, Can.); DEATH HUNT(1981); SILENCE OF THE NORTH(1981, Can.); TULIPS(1981, Can); HANK WILLIAMS: THE SHOW HE NEVER GAVE(1982, Can.); TITLE SHOT(1982, Can.)

Ted McCann
Misc. Silents
SKYWAYMAN, THE(1920)

William McCann
DOUGHGIRLS, THE(1944), ph; LIFE WITH FATHER(1947), spec eff

Celia McCanon
SINGING VAGABOND, THE(1935)

Mickey McCardell
TASK FORCE(1949)

Roy L. McCardell
Silents
FOOL THERE WAS, A(1915), w; QUESTION, THE(1916), w

Donald McCardle
Silents
GAY CORINTHIAN, THE(1924); NELL GWYNNE(1926, Brit.); MUMSIE(1927, Brit.)
Misc. Silents
BONDMAN, THE(1929, Brit.)

Jim McCardle
FLASHDANCE(1983)

Marie McCardle
GEORGE WHITE'S SCANDALS(1945)

Mickey McCardle
SPIRIT OF WEST POINT, THE(1947); FIGHTER SQUADRON(1948); FATHER WAS A FULLBACK(1949); FRANCIS(1949); SCENE OF THE CRIME(1949); FATHER OF THE BRIDE(1950); PEGGY(1950)

Michele McCarel
LOCAL HERO(1983, Brit.)

Leo McCarey
SOPHOMORE, THE(1929), d; LET'S GO NATIVE(1930), p&d; PART TIME WIFE(1930), d, w; RED HOT RHYTHM(1930), d, w; WILD COMPANY(1930), d; INDISCREET(1931), d; KID FROM SPAIN, THE(1932), d; DUCK SOUP(1933), d; BELLE OF THE NINETIES(1934), d; SIX OF A KIND(1934), d; RUGGLES OF RED GAP(1935), d; MILKY WAY, THE(1936), d; AWFUL TRUTH, THE(1937), p&d; MAKE WAY FOR TOMORROW(1937), a, p&d; COWBOY AND THE LADY, THE(1938), w; LOVE AFFAIR(1939), p&d, w; MY FAVORITE WIFE(1940), p, w; ONCE UPON A HONEYMOON(1942), p&d, w; GOING MY WAY(1944), p&d, w; BELLS OF ST. MARY'S, THE(1945), p&d, w; GOOD SAM(1948), p&d, w; MY SON, JOHN(1952), p&d, w; AFFAIR TO REMEMBER, AN(1957), d, w; RALLY 'ROUND THE FLAG, BOYS!(1958),

p&d, w; SATAN NEVER SLEEPS(1962), p&d, w; MOVE OVER, DARLING(1963), w
Misc. Silents
SOCIETY SECRETS(1921), d
Ray McCarey
HOT TIP(1935), d; MILLIONS IN THE AIR(1935), d; MYSTERY MAN, THE(1935), d;
SUNSET RANGE(1935), d; THREE CHEERS FOR LOVE(1936), d; LET'S MAKE A
MILLION(1937), d; DEVIL'S PARTY, THE(1938), d; GOODBYE BROADWAY(1938),
d; TORCHY RUNS FOR MAYOR(1939), d; LITTLE ORVIE(1940), d; MILLIONAIRES
IN PRISON(1940), d; YOU CAN'T FOOL YOUR WIFE(1940), d, w; ACCENT ON
LOVE(1941), d; CADET GIRL(1941), d; COWBOY AND THE BLONDE, THE(1941), d;
MURDER AMONG FRIENDS(1941), d; PERFECT SNOB, THE(1941), d; GENTLE-
MAN AT HEART, A(1942), d; IT HAPPENED IN FLATBUSH(1942), d; THAT OTHER
WOMAN(1942), d; SO THIS IS WASHINGTON(1943), d; ATLANTIC CITY(1944), d;
FALCON OUT WEST, THE(1944), d; PASSPORT TO DESTINY(1944), d; FALCON'S
ALIBI, THE(1946), d; STRANGE TRIANGLE(1946), d; GAY INTRUDERS, THE(1948),
d, w
Raymond McCarey
PACK UP YOUR TROUBLES(1932), d; GIRL O' MY DREAMS(1935), d
Raymond B. McCarey
LIFE BEGINS WITH LOVE(1937), d; LOVE IN A BUNGALOW(1937), d; OH DOC-
TOR(1937), d; OUTSIDE THESE WALLS(1939), d
Marian McCargo
UNDEFEATED, THE(1969); DOCTORS' WIVES(1971)
Marion McCargo
FALLING IN LOVE AGAIN(1980)
Frank McCarral
GUNS OF THE LAW(1944)
Fred McCarran
GOODBYE GIRL, THE(1977)
Fred McCarren
XANADU(1980); BOOGENS, THE(1982); NATIONAL LAMPOON'S CLASS REUN-
ION(1982); STAR CHAMBER, THE(1983)
Frank McCarrol
SHERIFF OF LAS VEGAS(1944)
Frank McCarroll
TOMBSTONE TERROR(1935); SONG OF THE TRAIL(1936); TRAITOR, THE(1936);
TREACHERY RIDES THE RANGE(1936); WEST OF NEVADA(1936); GUNS OF THE
PECOS(1937); LAND BEYOND THE LAW(1937); LAW FOR TOMBSTONE(1937);
PRAIRIE THUNDER(1937); OUTLAWS OF THE PRAIRIE(1938); COME ON RANG-
ERS(1939); DESPERATE TRAILS(1939); ROUGH RIDERS' ROUNDUP(1939); SOUTH-
WARD HO!(1939); LAW AND ORDER(1940); PONY POST(1940); RAGTIME COWBOY
JOE(1940); SON OF ROARING DAN(1940); THREE MEN FROM TEXAS(1940);
DRIFTIN' KID, THE(1941); PRAIRIE PIONEERS(1941); TUMBLEDOWN RANCH IN
ARIZONA(1941); UNDERGROUND RUSTLERS(1941); WRANGLER'S ROOST(1941);
DOWN RIO GRANDE WAY(1942); HEART OF THE GOLDEN WEST(1942); MISSOURI
OUTLAW, A(1942); PIRATES OF THE PRAIRIE(1942); PRAIRIE PALS(1942); RIDING
THE WIND(1942); CALLING WILD BILL ELLIOTT(1943); FUGITIVE FROM SONO-
RA(1943); LAND OF HUNTED MEN(1943); MAN FROM THUNDER RIVER,
THE(1943); OVERLAND MAIL ROBBERY(1943); RAIDERS OF SUNSET PASS(1943);
ROBIN HOOD OF THE RANGE(1943); SAGEBRUSH LAW(1943); WAGON TRACKS
WEST(1943); WESTERN CYCLONE(1943); FIREBRANDS OF ARIZONA(1944); FUZZY
SETTLES DOWN(1944); HIDDEN VALLEY OUTLAWS(1944); OUTLAWS OF SANTA
FE(1944); RUSTLER'S HIDEOUT(1944); SHINE ON, HARVEST MOON(1944); SILVER
CITY KID(1944); SONG OF NEVADA(1944); TUCSON RAIDERS(1944); WILD HORSE
PHANTOM(1944); ALONG CAME JONES(1945); CORPUS CHRISTI BANDITS(1945);
HIS BROTHER'S GHOST(1945); LOST TRAIL, THE(1945); SHADOWS OF
DEATH(1945); CONQUEST OF CHEYENNE(1946); GUNMAN'S CODE(1946); SHE-
RIFF OF REDWOOD VALLEY(1946); ADVENTURES OF DON COYOTE(1947); BUF-
FALO BILL RIDES AGAIN(1947); TWILIGHT ON THE RIO GRANDE(1947);
BUCKAROO FROM POWDER RIVER(1948); OUTLAW BRAND(1948); SILVER RIV-
ER(1948); BRAND OF FEAR(1949); CHALLENGE OF THE RANGE(1949); RENE-
GADES OF THE SAGE(1949); COW TOWN(1950); DALLAS(1950); FENCE
RIDERS(1950); GUNSLINGERS(1950); OVER THE BORDER(1950); WEST OF WYOM-
ING(1950); CAPTIVE OF BILLY THE KID(1952)
Misc. Talkies
BLAZING GUNS(1935)
Bob McCarron
JUST OUT OF REACH(1979, Aus.), spec eff; ROAD WARRIOR, THE(1982, Aus.),
makeup
Patricia McCarron
GOOD DIE YOUNG, THE(1954, Brit.); SLEEPING TIGER, THE(1954, Brit.); EYES OF
ANNIE JONES, THE(1963, Brit.)
Charles McCarry
WRONG IS RIGHT(1982), w
Mollie McCart
TEEN-AGE CRIME WAVE(1955); DAUGHTER OF DR. JEKYLL(1957); DINO(1957)
Molly McCart
KISS BEFORE DYING, A(1956)
John McCarten
SILKEN AFFAIR, THE(1957, Brit.), w
Nancy McCarter
RUN FOR YOUR WIFE(1966, Fr./Ital.)
Scott McCarter
RATTLERS(1976)
Avis McCarthur
LORD SHANGO(1975)
Andrew McCarthy
CLASS(1983)
Ann McCarthy
TRUCK TURNER(1974), cos; CORNBREAD, EARL AND ME(1975), cos; ULTIMATE
WARRIOR, THE(1975), cos; FUTUREWORLD(1976), cos
Annette McCarthy
SECOND THOUGHTS(1983)
Barnetta McCarthy
1984
AGAINST ALL ODDS(1984)
Barry McCarthy
BROTHERS AND SISTERS(1980, Brit.)

Booger McCarthy
LAW OF THE BADLANDS(1950)
Charlie McCarthy
YOU CAN'T CHEAT AN HONEST MAN(1939); LOOK WHO'S LAUGHING(1941);
STAGE DOOR CANTEEN(1943); SONG OF THE OPEN ROAD(1944); WARRIORS,
THE(1979)
Clem McCarthy
BLACK GOLD(1947)
Denis McCarthy
DON'T SAY DIE(1950, Brit.)
Dennis McCarthy
ENCHANTMENT(1948); INVISIBLE BOY, THE(1957); MONSTER THAT CHAL-
LENGED THE WORLD, THE(1957); SCOTLAND YARD DRAGNET(1957, Brit.);
WHEN HELL BROKE LOOSE(1958); OFF THE WALL(1983), m
Dermot McCarthy
Silents
IN THE DAYS OF SAINT PATRICK(1920, Brit.)
Earl McCarthy
WORDS AND MUSIC(1929); ALL-AMERICAN, THE(1932); CHEATING BLON-
DES(1933); SUCKER MONEY(1933)
Silents
RED LIPS(1928)
Frank McCarthy
DECISION BEFORE DAWN(1951), p; SAILOR OF THE KING(1953, Brit.), p; GUIDE
FOR THE MARRIED MAN, A(1967), p; PATTON(1970), p; MAC ARTHUR(1977), p;
CUTTER AND BONE(1981); PENNIES FROM HEAVEN(1981); ZOOT SUIT(1981);
DEAD MEN DON'T WEAR PLAID(1982); MAN WITH TWO BRAINS, THE(1983);
REACHING OUT(1983); STING II, THE(1983)
Gene McCarthy
LAST TIME I SAW ARCHIE, THE(1961)
Gerald McCarthy
Silents
AMATEUR GENTLEMAN, THE(1920, Brit.); OLD COUNTRY, THE(1921, Brit.)
Misc. Silents
DR. WAKE'S PATIENT(1916, Brit.); FAIR IMPOSTER, A(1916, Brit.); BLACK TULIP,
THE(1921, Brit.); MARRIED LIFE(1921, Brit.); HARBOUR LIGHTS, THE(1923, Brit.)
Glen McCarthy
SUNSET PASS(1946); TRAIL STREET(1947)
Glenn H. McCarthy
FIVE BOLD WOMEN(1960), p
Helena McCarthy
WICKED LADY, THE(1983, Brit.)
Henry McCarthy
SENOR AMERICANO(1929), w; SONG OF LOVE, THE(1929), w; NUMBERED
MEN(1930), w; SUNNY(1930), w; BRIGHT LIGHTS(1931), w; GOING WILD(1931), w;
MAD PARADE, THE(1931), w; PART-TIME WIFE(1961, Brit.); ROMAN SPRING OF
MRS. STONE, THE(1961, U.S./Brit.); DOUBLE, THE(1963, Brit); FRENCH DRESS-
ING(1964, Brit.)
Silents
MASKED AVENGER, THE(1922), w; NIGHT SHIP, THE(1925), d&w; LODGE IN
THE WILDERNESS, THE(1926), d
Misc. Silents
TRAPPED IN THE AIR(1922), d; FLASHING FANGS(1926), d; PHANTOM OF THE
FOREST, THE(1926), d
J. P. McCarthy
HEADIN' NORTH(1930), d&w; CAVALIER OF THE WEST(1931), d, w; GOD'S
COUNTRY AND THE MAN(1931), p&d; RIDER OF THE PLAINS(1931), d; SHIPS OF
HATE(1931), d; SUNRISE TRAIL(1931), d; FORTY-NINERS, THE(1932), d; FIGHT-
ING CHAMP(1933), d; LUCKY LARRIGAN(1933), d; RETURN OF CASEY JO-
NES(1933), d, w; MARKED TRAILS(1944), d, w
Misc. Talkies
RIDIN' FOOL, THE(1931), d; WESTERN CODE(1932), d; TRAILING NORTH(1933),
d
Silents
FLIRTING WITH FATE(1916); KID BOOTS(1926), w
Jim McCarthy
1984
UNDER THE VOLCANO(1984)
John K. McCarthy
HANDLE WITH CARE(1964), p,d,&w; PARDON MY BRUSH(1964), p,d&w; HELL'S
CHOSEN FEW(1968), w
John McCarthy
PAD, THE(AND HOW TO USE IT)* (1966, Brit.), set d; BEYOND THE ROCK-
IES(1932), w; CONSPIRACY(1939), w; UNDER ARIZONA SKIES(1946), w; I SHOT
JESSE JAMES(1949), set d; ELECTRONIC MONSTER. THE(1960, Brit.); SNAKE
WOMAN, THE(1961, Brit.); ROAD TO HONG KONG, THE(1962, U.S./Brit.); DR.
STRANGELOVE: OR HOW I LEARNED TO STOP WORRYING AND LOVE THE
BOMB(1964); FATHER GOOSE(1964), set d; KILLERS, THE(1964), set d; KITTEN
WITH A WHIP(1964), set d; LIVELY SET, THE(1964), set d; MC HALE'S NAVY(1964),
set d; NIGHT WALKER, THE(1964), set d; RAIDERS, THE(1964), set d; SEND ME NO
FLOWERS(1964), set d; TAGGART(1964), set d; DARK INTRUDER(1965), set d; I
SAW WHAT YOU DID(1965), set d; LOVE AND KISSES(1965), set d; MC HALE'S
NAVY JOINS THE AIR FORCE(1965), set d; MIRAGE(1965), set d; SHENAN-
DOAH(1965), set d; STRANGE BEDFELLOWS(1965), set d; SWORD OF ALI BABA,
THE(1965), set d; THAT FUNNY FEELING(1965), set d; VERY SPECIAL FAVOR,
A(1965), set d; WAR LORD, THE(1965), set d; WILD SEED(1965), set d; GAM-
BIT(1966), set d; GHOST AND MR. CHICKEN, THE(1966), set d; GUNPOINT(1966),
set d; INCIDENT AT PHANTOM HILL(1966), set d; LET'S KILL UNCLE(1966), set d;
MADAME X(1966), set d; MOMENT TO MOMENT(1966), set d; MUNSTER, GO
HOME!(1966), set d; PLAINSMAN, THE(1966), set d; RARE BREED, THE(1966), set d;
TEXAS ACROSS THE RIVER(1966), set d; TOBRUK(1966), set d; COUNTER-
POINT(1967), set d; GAMES(1967), set d; GUNFIGHT IN ABILENE(1967), set d;
KING'S PIRATE(1967), set d; PERILS OF PAULINE, THE(1967), set d; RELUCTANT
ASTRONAUT, THE(1967), set d; RIDE TO HANGMAN'S TREE, THE(1967), set d;
ROUGH NIGHT IN JERICHO(1967), set d; SULLIVAN'S EMPIRE(1967), set d; TAM-
MY AND THE MILLIONAIRE(1967), set d; VALLEY OF MYSTERY(1967), set d;
YOUNG WARRIORS, THE(1967), set d; COOGAN'S BLUFF(1968), set d; COUNTER-
FEIT KILLER, THE(1968), set d; DID YOU HEAR THE ONE ABOUT THE TRAVEL-
ING SALESLADY?(1968), set d; DON'T JUST STAND THERE(1968), set d; HELL
WITH HEROES, THE(1968), set d; HELLFIGHTERS(1968), set d; IN ENEMY COUN-

TRY(1968), set d; JIGSAW(1968), set d; JOURNEY TO SHILOH(1968), set d; LOVELY WAY TO DIE, A(1968), set d; MADIGAN(1968), set d; NOBODY'S PERFECT(1968), set d; PINK JUNGLE, THE(1968), set d; P.J.(1968), set d; SECRET WAR OF HARRY FRIGG, THE(1968), set d; SERGEANT RYKER(1968), set d; SHAKIEST GUN IN THE WEST, THE(1968), set d; THREE GUNS FOR TEXAS(1968), set d; WHAT'S SO BAD ABOUT FEELING GOOD?(1968), set d; CHANGE OF HABIT(1969), set d; COLOSSUS: THE FORBIN PROJECT(1969), set d; DEATH OF A GUNFIGHTER(1969), set d; EYE OF THE CAT(1969), set d; HOUSE OF CARDS(1969), set d; LOST MAN, THE(1969), set d; LOVE GOD?, THE(1969), set d; MAN CALLED GANNON, A(1969), set d; TELL THEM WILLIE BOY IS HERE(1969), set d; THIS SAVAGE LAND(1969), set d; WINNING(1969), set d; COMPANY OF KILLERS(1970), set d; STORY OF A WO- MAN(1970, U.S./Ital.), set d; SHOOT OUT(1971), set d; SLAUGHTERHOUSE-FI- VE(1972), set d; ULZANA'S RAID(1972), set d; DRUM(1976), set d; CAR, THE(1977), set d

John McCarthy, Jr.
DAKOTA(1945), set d; IN OLD SACRAMENTO(1946), set d; MURDER IN THE MUSIC HALL(1946), set d; MYSTERIOUS MR. VALENTINE, THE(1946), set d; NIGHT TRAIN TO MEMPHIS(1946), set d; ONE EXCITING WEEK(1946), set d; PLAINSMAN AND THE LADY(1946), set d; RED RIVER RENEGADES(1946), set d; RENDEZVOUS WITH ANNIE(1946), set d; SANTA FE SURPRISE(1946), set d; SHE- RIFF OF REDWOOD VALLEY(1946), set d; STAGECOACH TO DENVER(1946), set d; SUN VALLEY CYCLONE(1946), set d; UNDER NEVADA SKIES(1946), set d; BLACK- MAIL(1947), set d; NORTHWEST OUTPOST(1947), set d; ON THE OLD SPANISH TRAIL(1947), set d; OREGON TRAIL SCOUTS(1947), set d; PILGRIM LADY, THE(1947), set d; THAT'S MY MAN(1947), set d; TRESPASSER, THE(1947), set d; UNDER COLORADO SKIES(1947), set d; WEB OF DANGER, THE(1947), set d; WYOMING(1947), set d; ANGEL ON THE AMAZON(1948), set d; MACBETH(1948), set d; MOONRISE(1948), set d; NIGHT TIME IN NEVADA(1948), set d; OKLAHOMA BADLANDS(1948), set d; OLD LOS ANGELES(1948), set d; OUT OF THE STORM(1948), set d; SECRET SERVICE INVESTIGATOR(1948), set d; SLIPPY MCGEE(1948), set d; SONS OF ADVENTURE(1948), set d; SUNDOWN IN SANTA FE(1948), set d; TIMBER TRAIL, THE(1948), set d; UNDER CALIFORNIA STARS(1948), set d; NAVAJO TRAIL RAIDERS(1949), set d; OUTCASTS OF THE TRAIL(1949), set d; POST OFFICE INVESTIGATOR(1949), set d; PRINCE OF THE PLAINS(1949), set d; RED MENACE, THE(1949), set d; SAN ANTONE AM- BUSH(1949), set d; SHERIFF OF WICHITA(1949), set d; SOUTH OF RIO(1949), set d; STREETS OF SAN FRANCISCO(1949), set d; TOO LATE FOR TEARS(1949), set d; WYOMING BANDIT, THE(1949), set d; HOUSE BY THE RIVER(1950), set d; RIO GRANDE(1950), set d; SURRENDER(1950), set d; TRAIL OF ROBIN HOOD(1950), set d; DESPERADOES OUTPOST(1952), set d; MONTANA BELLE(1952), set d; OLD OKLAHOMA PLAINS(1952), set d; QUIET MAN, THE(1952), set d; RIDE THE MAN DOWN(1952), set d; SOUTH PACIFIC TRAIL(1952), set d; THUNDERBIRDS(1952), set d; THUNDERING CARAVANS(1952), set d; TOUGHEST MAN IN ARIZONA(1952), set d; TROPICAL HEAT WAVE(1952), set d; WAC FROM WALLA WALLA, THE(1952), set d; WILD BLUE YONDER, THE(1952), set d; WOMAN IN THE DARK(1952), set d; WOMAN OF THE NORTH COUNTRY(1952), set d; CITY THAT NEVER SLEEPS(1953), set d; SUN SHINES BRIGHT, THE(1953), set d; JOHNNY GUITAR(1954), prod d; JUBILEE TRAIL(1954), set d; TIMBERJACK(1955), set d; MAVERICK QUEEN, THE(1956), set d; CROOKED CIRCLE, THE(1958), set d; MAN WHO DIED TWICE, THE(1958), set d; NOTORIOUS MR. MONKS(1958), set d; GHOST OF ZORRO(1959), set d

John P. McCarthy
LAND OF MISSING MEN, THE(1930), d, w; OKLAHOMA CYCLONE(1930), d, w; AT THE RIDGE(1931), d; MOTHER AND SON(1931), d; CRASHING BROAD- WAY(1933), d; LAWLESS BORDER(1935), d; SONG OF THE GRINGO(1936), d, w; RAIDERS OF THE BORDER(1944), d; CISCO KID RETURNS, THE(1945), d
Misc. Talkies
NEVADA BUCKAROO, THE(1931), d; LAW OF THE 45'S(1935), d; LION MAN, THE(1936), d
Silents
OUT OF THE DUST(1920), d&w; SHADOWS OF CONSCIENCE(1921), d, w; VAN- ISHING HOOFS(1926), d; DEVIL'S MASTERPIECE, THE(1927), d; LOVELORN, THE(1927), d; ETERNAL WOMAN, THE(1929), d
Misc. Silents
BRAND OF COWARDICE(1925), d; PALS(1925), d; BORDER WHIRLWIND, THE(1926), d; BECKY(1927), d; HIS FOREIGN WIFE(1927), d; DIAMOND HAND- CUFFS(1928), d

Johnny McCarthy
DAWN OVER IRELAND(1938, Irish)

Joseph McCarthy
FOX MOVIETONE FOLLIES OF 1930(1930), m
Silents
IRENE(1926), m

Julia McCarthy
CONFESSIONAL, THE(1977, Brit.)

Julianna McCarthy
SEED OF INNOCENCE(1980); LAST AMERICAN VIRGIN, THE(1982)

Justin Huntly McCarthy
VAGABOND KING, THE(1930), w; IF I WERE KING(1938), w; FIGHTING O'- FLYNN, THE(1949), w; VAGABOND KING, THE(1956), w

Kevin McCarthy
DEATH OF A SALESMAN(1952); DRIVE A CROOKED ROAD(1954); GAMBLER FROM NATCHEZ, THE(1954); ANNAPOLIS STORY, AN(1955); STRANGER ON HORSEBACK(1955); INVASION OF THE BODY SNATCHERS(1956); NIGHT- MARE(1956); DIAMOND SAFARI(1958); MISFITS, THE(1961); FORTY POUNDS OF TROUBLE(1962); GATHERING OF EAGLES, A(1963); PRIZE, THE(1963); AFFAIR OF THE SKIN, AN(1964); BEST MAN, THE(1964); MIRAGE(1965); BIG HAND FOR THE LITTLE LADY, A(1966); HOTEL(1967); HELL WITH HEROES, THE(1968); IF HE HOLLERS, LET HIM GO(1968); REVENGE AT EL PASO(1968, Ital.); ACE HIGH(1969, Ital.); KANSAS CITY BOMBER(1972); RICHARD(1972); ALIEN THUNDER(1975, US/Can.); BUFFALO BILL AND THE INDIANS, OR SITTING BULL'S HISTORY LESSON(1976); THREE SISTERS, THE(1977); INVASION OF THE BODY SNATCH- ERS(1978); PIRANHA(1978); HERO AT LARGE(1980); THOSE LIPS, THOSE EYES(1980); HOWLING, THE(1981); MY TUTOR(1983); TWILIGHT ZONE–THE MOV- IE(1983)
Misc. Talkies
ORDER TO KILL(1974)

Sgt. Kevin McCarthy
WINGED VICTORY(1944)

Kristi McCarthy
FOUR SEASONS, THE(1981)

L. J. McCarthy
Silents
BREWSTER'S MILLIONS(1921)

Leo J. McCarthy
RODEO RHYTHM(1941), p, w; DEVIL BAT'S DAUGHTER, THE(1946), w

Leo McCarthy
STRANGLER OF THE SWAMP(1945), w

Lillah McCarthy
Silents
MR. WU(1919, Brit.)

Lilyan McCarthy
Silents
REAL ADVENTURE, THE(1922)

Lin McCarthy
YELLOWNECK(1955); D.I., THE(1957); FACE OF A FUGITIVE(1959)

Mary C. McCarthy
IRISH LUCK(1939), w

Mary E. McCarthy
WOMAN UNAFRAID(1934), w; THEODORA GOES WILD(1936), w

Mary McCarthy
SLIGHTLY MARRIED(1933), w; KEEP SMILING(1938); CHASING TROUBLE(1940), w; SISTER KENNY(1946), w; PETTY GIRL, THE(1950), w; GROUP, THE(1966), w

Matt McCarthy
Misc. Talkies
ZOO ROBBERY(1973, Brit.), d

Michael McCarthy
GIRL ON THE CANAL, THE(1947, Brit.), w; ASSASSIN FOR HIRE(1951, Brit.), d; MYSTERY JUNCTION(1951, Brit.), d&w; NO HIGHWAY IN THE SKY(1951, Brit.); CROW HOLLOW(1952, Brit.), d; STRANGER IN BETWEEN, THE(1952, Brit.), w; FORCES' SWEETHEART(1953, Brit.); SHADOW OF A MAN(1955, Brit.), d, w; AC- CURSED, THE(1958, Brit.), d&w; IT'S NEVER TOO LATE(1958, Brit.), d; OPERATION AMSTERDAM(1960, Brit.), d, w; JOHN OF THE FAIR(1962, Brit.), d&w
Misc. Talkies
BEHIND THE HEADLINES(1953)

Miles McCarthy
Silents
GREEN FLAME, THE(1920); DOLLAR DEVILS(1923); ABRAHAM LINCOLN(1924); OH, YOU TONY!(1924)

Molly McCarthy
GREAT ST. LOUIS BANK ROBBERY, THE(1959)
1984
FLAMINGO KID, THE(1984)

Myles McCarthy
Silents
SMILES ARE TRUMPS(1922); HEART OF A COWARD, THE(1926)
Misc. Silents
FEAR NOT(1917); FALSE CODE, THE(1919); TRICKS(1925)

Neil McCarthy
SANDS OF THE DESERT(1960, Brit.); OFFBEAT(1961, Brit.); CONCRETE JUNGLE, THE(1962, Brit.); POT CARRIERS, THE(1962, Brit.); ZULU(1964, Brit.); TWO LEFT FEET(1965, Brit.); SOLO FOR SPARROW(1966, Brit.); WHERE EAGLES DARE(1968, Brit.); PUBLIC EYE, THE(1972, Brit.); DIRTY KNIGHT'S WORK(1976, Brit.); OPERA- TION DAYBREAK(1976, U.S./Brit./Czech.); CLASH OF THE TITANS(1981); MON- STER CLUB, THE(1981, Brit.); TIME BANDITS(1981, Brit.)
Misc. Talkies
YOUNG DETECTIVE, THE(1964, Brit.)

Nobu McCarthy
GEISHA BOY, THE(1958); HUNTERS, THE(1958); FIVE GATES TO HELL(1959); TOKYO AFTER DARK(1959); WAKE ME WHEN IT'S OVER(1960); WALK LIKE A DRAGON(1960); TWO LOVES(1961); LOVE WITH THE PROPER STRANGER(1963)

Patti McCarthy
DEVIL RIDERS(1944); FUZZY SETTLES DOWN(1944)

Peter McCarthy
1984
REPO MAN(1984), p

Priceless McCarthy
PINK PANTHER STRIKES AGAIN, THE(1976, Brit.)

Red McCarthy
ICE-CAPADES(1941); MURDER IN THE MUSIC HALL(1946)

Richard McCarthy
NO DRUMS, NO BUGLES(1971), ph

Robert McCarthy
REMARKABLE MR. KIPPS(1942, Brit.); FRANKENSTEIN MEETS THE SPACE MONSTER(1965), p

Rod McCarthy
ICE-CAPADES REVUE(1942)

Terence McCarthy
THIS STUFF'LL KILL YA!(1971)

Thomas McCarthy
DOC SAVAGE... THE MAN OF BRONZE(1975), ed

Thomas J. McCarthy
JOY IN THE MORNING(1965), ed; POWER, THE(1968), ed

Todd McCarthy
CANNONBALL(1976, U.S./Hong Kong); HOLLYWOOD BOULEVARD(1976); GRAND THEFT AUTO(1977)

Tom McCarthy
BLOW OUT(1981); UNCLE SCAM(1981)

Vicki McCarthy
1984
STREETS OF FIRE(1984)

Winnie McCarthy
TO BE OR NOT TO BE(1983)

Sean McCartin
NATIONAL LAMPOON'S ANIMAL HOUSE(1978)

Andrew McCartney
1984
PHILADELPHIA EXPERIMENT, THE(1984)
Joseph P. McCartney
SUPER COPS, THE(1974)
Linda McCartney
1984
GIVE MY REGARDS TO BROAD STREET(1984, Brit.)
Paul McCartney
HARD DAY'S NIGHT, A(1964, Brit.), a, m; HELP!(1965, Brit.); FAMILY WAY,
THE(1966, Brit.), m
1984
GIVE MY REGARDS TO BROAD STREET(1984, Brit.), a, w, m
Charley McCarty
Misc. Talkies
JUST BE THERE(1977)
Christopher McCarty
SPLIT IMAGE(1982)
Henry McCarty
CARNATION KID(1929), w; BLAZE O' GLORY(1930), w; TOP SPEED(1930), w; MEN
OF AMERICA(1933), w; RIGHT TO ROMANCE(1933), w; GREAT GUY(1936), w; 23 ½
HOURS LEAVE(1937), w
Silents
HIS MASTER'S VOICE(1925), w; ONE OF THE BRAVEST(1925), w
Misc. Silents
BLAZING ARROWS(1922), d; SILVER SPURS(1922), d; PART TIME WIFE,
THE(1925), d; SHATTERED LIVES(1925), d; SILENT PAL(1925), d
Mary McCarty
REBECCA OF SUNNYBROOK FARM(1938); HIGH SCHOOL(1940); ICE-CAPADES
REVUE(1942); YOUNGEST PROFESSION, THE(1943); IN THE MEANTIME, DAR-
LING(1944); SULLIVANS, THE(1944); TELL IT TO A STAR(1945); FRENCH LINE,
THE(1954); PILLOW TALK(1959); BABES IN TOYLAND(1961); MY SIX LOVES(1963);
SOMEBODY KILLED HER HUSBAND(1978)
Mary-Jane McCarty
PARADISE(1982), cos
Patti McCarty
PRAIRIE STRANGER(1941); SHE KNEW ALL THE ANSWERS(1941); UNDER
AGE(1941); YOU'LL NEVER GET RICH(1941); FIGHTING VALLEY(1943); ISLE OF
FORGOTTEN SINS(1943); BLUEBEARD(1944); GANGSTERS OF THE FRON-
TIER(1944); GUNSMOKE MESA(1944); RUSTLER'S HIDEOUT(1944); OUTLAW OF
THE PLAINS(1946); TERRORS ON HORSEBACK(1946)
Patty McCarty
WAKE ISLAND(1942); OVERLAND RIDERS(1946)
Richard McCarty
Misc. Talkies
OLE REX(1961)
Robert J. McCarty
FOREPLAY(1975), d
Robert McCarty
LIGHT FANTASTIC(1964), d, w; I COULD NEVER HAVE SEX WITH ANY MAN
WHO HAS SO LITTLE REGARD FOR MY HUSBAND(1973), d
Walter G. McCarty
Misc. Talkies
JIGGS AND MAGGIE IN JACKPOT JITTERS(1949)
Patrick McCarville
NED KELLY(1970, Brit.)
Rod McCary
CHRISTINE JORGENSEN STORY, THE(1970); NO DRUMS, NO BUGLES(1971);
HERBIE RIDES AGAIN(1974); CHEAPER TO KEEP HER(1980); WHOLLY MO-
SES(1980)
Molly McCash
WINTER CARNIVAL(1939)
Susan McCash
WINTER CARNIVAL(1939)
Neal McCaskill
THERE'S NO BUSINESS LIKE SHOW BUSINESS(1954)
Patricia McCaskill
MONKEY HUSTLE, THE(1976)
Roddy McCaskill
SITTING PRETTY(1948); CHEAPER BY THE DOZEN(1950); BELLES ON THEIR
TOES(1952)
William McCather
SET-UP, THE(1949)
Charles McCaughan
JANE AUSTEN IN MANHATTAN(1980); HEAT AND DUST(1983, Brit.)
1984
BOSTONIANS, THE(1984)
Neil McCaul
PIRATES OF PENZANCE, THE(1983)
Charles McCauley
BLACULA(1972)
Daniel McCauley
HAWAIIANS, THE(1970), set d
David McCauley
Silents
LIFE WITHOUT SOUL(1916)
Donald McCauley
Misc. Talkies
APOCALYPSE 3:16(1964)
Glenn McCauley
STEREO(1969, Can.)
Hugh J. McCauley
Silents
GREED(1925)
John McCauley
RATTLERS(1976), p&d
Misc. Talkies
RATTLERS(1976), d

Mailie McCauley
HAWAIIANS, THE(1970)
Mathew McCauley
SUDDEN FURY(1975, Can.), m
Matthew McCauley
GET BACK(1973, Can.), m; CITY ON FIRE(1979 Can.), m; MIDDLE AGE CRA-
ZY(1980, Can.), m
Nancy McCauley
VAN NUYS BLVD.(1979); GALAXINA(1980)
Peter McCauley
1984
PALLET ON THE FLOOR(1984, New Zealand)
Tim McCauley
LOVE(1982, Can.), m; SCREWBALLS(1983), m
Tom McCauley
SPEEDWAY(1968)
Wilbur McCauley
OUTLAW EXPRESS(1938); DESPERATE TRAILS(1939)
William McCauley
NEPTUNE FACTOR, THE(1973, Can.), m; IT SEEMED LIKE A GOOD IDEA AT THE
TIME(1975, Can.), m; CITY ON FIRE(1979 Can.), m
Richard McCauly
TOWER OF LONDON(1962)
James McCausland
MAD MAX(1979, Aus.), w
Ron McCavour
SPLIT, THE(1968)
Peggy McCay
CASE AGAINST BROOKLYN, THE(1958); UNCLE VANYA(1958); LAD: A
DOG(1962); FBI CODE 98(1964); PROMISES IN THE DARK(1979); AMY(1981); BUS-
TIN' LOOSE(1981); SECOND THOUGHTS(1983)
Misc. Talkies
FROM THE DESK OF MARGARET TYDING(1958)
Winsor McCay
Misc. Silents
SINKING OF THE LUSITANIA, THE(1918), d
David McCharen
POPEYE(1980); PANDEMONIUM(1982)
Margaret McChrystal
ROBERTA(1935)
Pat McChrystle
NAKED ANGELS(1969)
Billy McClain
MIGHTY BARNUM, THE(1934); VIRGINIA JUDGE, THE(1935); DIMPLES(1936);
ANGELS WITH DIRTY FACES(1938); KENTUCKY(1938); TOY WIFE, THE(1938);
ESPIONAGE AGENT(1939)
Dr. Billie McClain
NAGANA(1933)
Edward Lee McClain
SKIN GAME(1971)
Hal McClain
GONE IN 60 SECONDS(1974)
Joedda McClain
HUNGRY WIVES(1973)
John McClain
TURNABOUT(1940), w; LADY BE GOOD(1941), w; CAIRO(1942), w
Lee McClain
DEEP, THE(1977)
Nadra McClain
WORLD IS JUST A 'B' MOVIE, THE(1971)
William McClain
GONE WITH THE WIND(1939)
Rue McClanahan
GRASS EATER, THE(1961); WALK THE ANGRY BEACH(1961); ROTTEN APPLE,
THE(1963); PEOPLE NEXT DOOR, THE(1970); PURSUIT OF HAPPINESS, THE(1971);
SOME OF MY BEST FRIENDS ARE...(1971); THEY MIGHT BE GIANTS(1971)
Michael McClanathan
ALICE'S RESTAURANT(1969); SKY PIRATE, THE(1970); PANIC IN NEEDLE
PARK(1971)
Mike McClanathan
JENNIFER ON MY MIND(1971)
Ian McClaren
LES MISERABLES(1935)
John McClaren
CHANCE MEETING(1954, Brit.); FOLLOW THE BOYS(1963)
Kevin McClarnon
HEAVEN'S GATE(1980); AUTHOR! AUTHOR!(1982)
Clyde McClary
FIGHTING COWBOY(1933); CIRCLE CANYON(1934); LIGHTNING RANGE(1934);
RIDING SPEED(1934); CHEYENNE TORNADO(1935); RIDERS OF THE ROCK-
IES(1937); TRUSTED OUTLAW, THE(1937); CODE OF THE CACTUS(1939)
Misc. Talkies
WHIRLWIND RIDER, THE(1935)
Coleen McClathchey
WRITTEN ON THE WIND(1956)
Bert McClay
LADIES OF WASHINGTON(1944)
Barry McClean
DURING ONE NIGHT(1962, Brit.)
Grace McClean
Silents
BLIND HUSBANDS(1919)
John McClean
ESCAPE 2000(1983, Aus.), ph
Malcolm McClean
LIVE WIRES(1946)
Gudrun McCleary
OPEN SEASON(1974, U.S./Span.)

Ernest McClure
  BLOW OUT(1981)
Ernest M. McClure
  BEING THERE(1979)
Frank McClure
  WEEKEND AT THE WALDORF(1945); WOMAN IN THE WINDOW, THE(1945); TILL THE CLOUDS ROLL BY(1946)
Greg McClure
  IRON MAJOR, THE(1943); GREAT JOHN L. THE(1945); BURY ME DEAD(1947); LULU BELLE(1948); DALTON GANG, THE(1949); GOLDEN STALLION, THE(1949); JOE PALOOKA IN THE BIG FIGHT(1949); SKY LINER(1949); THUNDER IN THE PINES(1949); BREAKTHROUGH(1950); EMERGENCY WEDDING(1950); JOE PALOOKA IN THE SQUARED CIRCLE(1950); ROARING CITY(1951); STOP THAT CAB(1951)
Jack McClure
  FRIENDLY PERSUASION(1956); DADDY-O(1959)
John McClure
  BILLY JACK(1971)
Laura McClure
Silents
  BALLET GIRL, THE(1916)
Linda McClure
  SMOKEY AND THE BANDIT(1977); CANNONBALL RUN, THE(1981)
M'liss McClure
  FATHER'S WILD GAME(1950); OPERATION HAYLIFT(1950); FATHER TAKES THE AIR(1951); INSURANCE INVESTIGATOR(1951); WHITE GODDESS(1953)
Marc McClure
  FREAKY FRIDAY(1976); I WANNA HOLD YOUR HAND(1978); SUPERMAN(1978); SUPERMAN II(1980); USED CARS(1980); DEAD KIDS(1981 Aus./New Zealand); PANDEMONIUM(1982); SUPERMAN III(1983)
1984
  SUPERGIRL(1984)
Michael McClure
  BEYOND THE LAW(1968); MAIDSTONE(1970); HIRED HAND, THE(1971)
Norma McClure
  MACK, THE(1973)
Rev. A. W. McClure
Silents
  INTOLERANCE(1916)
Sylvia McClure
  YOUNG MR. LINCOLN(1939)
Thomas McClure
  HOSPITAL MASSACRE(1982)
Tommy McClure
1984
  SONGWRITER(1984)
Victor McClure
  THEY MET IN THE DARK(1945, Brit.), w
Warren McClure
Misc. Talkies
  RIM OF HELL(1970)
Bob McClurg
  TUNNELVISION(1976); CHEECH AND CHONG'S NEXT MOVIE(1980)
Edie McClurg
  CRACKING UP(1977); CHEECH AND CHONG'S NEXT MOVIE(1980); EATING RAOUL(1982); PANDEMONIUM(1982); MR. MOM(1983)
1984
  CHEECH AND CHONG'S THE CORSICAN BROTHERS(1984)
"Kansas City" Bob McClurg
  CRACKING UP(1977)
Bill McCluskey
  MANGANINNIE(1982, Aus.)
Jack McCluskey
  STALLION CANYON(1949), ph
Joyce McCluskey
  OUTRAGE(1950); BLUEPRINT FOR MURDER, A(1953); NIGHT HOLDS TERROR, THE(1955)
Maureen McCluskey
  ONCE IS NOT ENOUGH(1975)
Roger McCluskey
  WINNING(1969)
Mike McClusky
  10 VIOLENT WOMEN(1982), prod d
Frank McClynn
  HUCKLEBERRY FINN(1931)
Billy McColl
  MUSIC MACHINE, THE(1979, Brit.)
1984
  ORDEAL BY INNOCENCE(1984, Brit.)
Iain McColl
1984
  COMFORT AND JOY(1984, Brit.)
Kirk McColl
  FORTUNE AND MEN'S EYES(1971, U.S./Can.); WHY ROCK THE BOAT?(1974, Can.); RABID(1976, Can.)
Stewart McColl
  RANGLE RIVER(1939, Aus.)
Donald McCollan
Misc. Silents
  KNIGHTS OF THE SQUARE TABLE(1917)
Milton McCollin
  SWEET SUZY(1973)
Misc. Talkies
  BLACKSNAKE(1973)
Bud McCollister
  HENRY ALDRICH FOR PRESIDENT(1941)
Paul McCollough
  HUNGRY WIVES(1973); THE CRAZIES(1973), w; MIDNIGHT(1983), ph, ed

Philo McCollough
  TARZAN THE FEARLESS(1933); STAMPEDE(1949); DAWN AT SOCORRO(1954)
Ralph McCollough
  PARADISE EXPRESS(1937)
Barry McCollum
  HI DIDDLE DIDDLE(1943)
Donald McCollum
Misc. Silents
  UNBLAZED TRAIL(1923)
Hallie McCollum
  ULTIMATE THRILL, THE(1974)
Warren McCollum
  REEFER MADNESS(1936); BOY'S REFORMATORY(1939); OKLAHOMA TERROR(1939); SKY MURDER(1940)
Warren W. McCollum
  SONG OF SCHEHERAZADE(1947)
Carrol McComas
Silents
  JACK STRAW(1920)
Misc. Silents
  WHEN LOVE IS KING(1916)
Carroll McComas
  JAMAICA RUN(1953); CHICAGO SYNDICATE(1955); FIVE AGAINST THE HOUSE(1955)
J. L. McComas
Silents
  NIGHT LIFE IN HOLLYWOOD(1922)
Kendall McComas
  SPIDER, THE(1931); MAN'S CASTLE, A(1933)
Teri McComas
  WILD PARTY, THE(1975), stunts
David McComb
  DON'T GO IN THE HOUSE(1980)
Alec McCombie
  KONA COAST(1968), ed
J. A. S. McCombie
  TREASURE OF JAMAICA REEF, THE(1976), p
Katie McCombs
1984
  MRS. SOFFEL(1984)
Jack McConaghty
  DANGER SIGNAL(1945), set d
Jack McConaghy
  OBJECTIVE, BURMA!(1945), set d; SAN ANTONIO(1945), set d; ALWAYS TOGETHER(1947), set d; CRY WOLF(1947), set d; PURSUED(1947), set d; WHIPLASH(1948), set d
J.W. McConaughy
  PICCADILLY(1932, Brit.), ed
Michael McConkey
  LAST REMAKE OF BEAU GESTE, THE(1977)
Brian McConnachie
  CADDY SHACK(1980); STRANGE BREW(1983)
Craig McConnel
  WHO?(1975, Brit./Ger.)
Bill McConnell
  MARRIAGE OF A YOUNG STOCKBROKER, THE(1971); SIMON, KING OF THE WITCHES(1971); DRIVER, THE(1978)
Dwight McConnell
  FOOLS' PARADE(1971)
Edward McConnell
  BIG CATCH, THE(1968, Brit.), p
Fred McConnell
  LONE RIDER FIGHTS BACK, THE(1941), w; SWAMP WOMAN(1941), w
Gertrude McConnell
Misc. Silents
  WHITE PANTHER, THE(1924)
Gladys McConnell
  PERFECT CRIME, THE(1928); PARADE OF THE WEST(1930)
Silents
  THREE'S A CROWD(1927); BULLET MARK, THE(1928); CHASER, THE(1928)
Misc. Silents
  FLYING HORSEMAN, THE(1926); MARRIAGE(1927); RIDING TO FAME(1927); CODE OF THE SCARLET, THE(1928); GLORIOUS TRAIL, THE(1928); CHEYENNE(1929); WOMAN WHO WAS FORGOTTEN, THE(1930)
Gordon McConnell
  WHEN THIEF MEETS THIEF(1937, Brit.), w
Guy W. McConnell
Misc. Silents
  PENNY PHILANTHROPIST, THE(1917), d
J. Parker McConnell
Misc. Silents
  SMILING ALL THE WAY(1921)
Judith McConnell
  HOW TO SEDUCE A WOMAN(1974); THIRSTY DEAD, THE(1975)
Judy McConnell
  DOLL SQUAD, THE(1973)
Keith McConnell
  KIND LADY(1951); BORDER SADDLEMATES(1952); FIVE FINGERS(1952); PLYMOUTH ADVENTURE(1952); CADDY, THE(1953); KISS ME DEADLY(1955); SCARLET COAT, THE(1955); JET PILOT(1957); MIDNIGHT LACE(1960); MUTINY ON THE BOUNTY(1962); MORITURI(1965); FIGHTING PRINCE OF DONEGAL, THE(1966, Brit.); VULTURE, THE(1967, U.S./Brit./Can.); BREAKHEART PASS(1976); TIME AFTER TIME(1979, Brit.)
Misc. Talkies
  GOSH(1974)
Ken McConnell
  REVENGE OF THE NINJA(1983)

Lulu McConnell
LADY LUCK(1936); STAGE STRUCK(1936)
M. G. McConnell
MEN AGAINST THE SKY(1940)
Marilyn McConnell
MARKED FOR MURDER(1945)
Millie McConnell
Misc. Silents
FOOLS AND THEIR MONEY(1919); ONE OF THE FINEST(1919)
Mollie McConnell
Silents
SHOULD A WIFE FORGIVE?(1915); JOY AND THE DRAGON(1916); DANGEROUS
TO MEN(1920); NURSE MARJORIE(1920); RED HOT DOLLARS(1920); BLACK
BEAUTY(1921)
Misc. Silents
PAY DIRT(1916); BAB THE FIXER(1917); BETTY BE GOOD(1917); CHECKMATE,
THE(1917); GIRL ANGLE, THE(1917); HIS OLD-FASHIONED DAD(1917); MARTIN-
ACHE MARRIAGE, THE(1917); UNDERSTUDY, THE(1917); WILDCAT, THE(1917);
HIS OFFICIAL FIANCEE(1919); ROPED(1919)
Molly McConnell
Misc. Silents
SET FREE(1918); CHEATING HERSELF(1919)
Parker McConnell
Silents
BREWSTER'S MILLIONS(1921); BEAUTIFUL AND DAMNED, THE(1922)
Paul McConnell
STERILE CUCKOO, THE(1969)
Richard McConnell
TOMORROW(1972)
Hilton McConnico
COCKTAIL MOLOTOV(1980, Fr.), art d; HORSE OF PRIDE(1980, Fr.), art d; DI-
VA(1982, Fr.), art d; CONFIDENTIALLY YOURS(1983, Fr.), prod d; MOON IN THE
GUTTER, THE(1983, Fr./Ital.), prod d
1984
UNTIL SEPTEMBER(1984), prod d
Rhys McConnochie
WILD DUCK, THE(1983, Aus.)
Vincent McConnor
JIGSAW(1949), w
Bernard McConville
CANNONBALL EXPRESS(1932), w; KING OF THE PECOS(1936), w; LONELY
TRAIL, THE(1936), w; RIDE, RANGER, RIDE(1936), w; DEATH IN THE SKY(1937),
w; GHOST TOWN GOLD(1937), w; HEART OF THE ROCKIES(1937), w; OLD COR-
RAL, THE(1937), w; PUBLIC COWBOY NO. 1(1937), w; RIDERS OF THE WHISTLING
SKULL(1937), w; TRAPPED BY G-MEN(1937), w; BORDER G-MAN(1938), w; CALL
THE MESQUITEERS(1938), w; MAN FROM MUSIC MOUNTAIN(1938), w; OLD
BARN DANCE, THE(1938), w; OVERLAND STAGE RAIDERS(1938), w; RIDERS OF
THE BLACK HILLS(1938), w; ARIZONA LEGION(1939), w; RACKETEERS OF THE
RANGE(1939), w; TIMBER STAMPEDE(1939), w; CHEROKEE STRIP(1940), w;
PRAIRIE LAW(1940), w; RANGER AND THE LADY, THE(1940), w; WAGON
TRAIN(1940), w; OUTLAWS OF THE DESERT(1941), w; SADDLEMATES(1941), w;
RIDING THE WIND(1942), w; CHEYENNE ROUNDUP(1943), w; FIGHTING FRON-
TIER(1943), w; HOME ON THE RANGE(1946), w
Silents
GRETCHEN, THE GREENHORN(1916), w; LITTLE SCHOOL MA'AM, THE(1916),
w; ALI BABA AND THE FORTY THIEVES(1918), w; HOODLUM THE(1919), w;
NINETEEN AND PHYLLIS(1920), w; CONNECTICUT YANKEE AT KING AR-
THUR'S COURT, A(1921), w; DOUBLING FOR ROMEO(1921), w; LITTLE LORD
FAUNTLEROY(1921), w; OLD SWIMMIN' HOLE, THE(1921), w; SHAME(1921), w;
CRINOLINE AND ROMANCE(1923), w; EXTRA GIRL, THE(1923), w; STEPPING
FAST(1923), w; LAW FORBIDS, THE(1924), w; ROSE OF PARIS, THE(1924), w;
VOLCANO(1926), w; TEXAS STEER, A(1927), w; VAMPING VENUS(1928), w
John McCook
MY BLOOD RUNS COLD(1965)
Arthur McCool
BETRAYAL, THE(1948)
Bob McCord
THAT WONDERFUL URGE(1948); I'LL GET BY(1950); QUEEN BEE(1955)
Cal McCord
TOO YOUNG TO LOVE(1960, Brit.); NEVER TAKE CANDY FROM A STRAN-
GER(1961, Brit.); V.I.P.s, THE(1963, Brit.); I'VE GOTTA HORSE(1965, Brit.); ISADO-
RA(1968, Brit.); ADDING MACHINE, THE(1969)
Evan McCord
PORTRAIT OF A MOBSTER(1961); CRITIC'S CHOICE(1963); PT 109(1963)
Harold McCord
JAZZ SINGER, THE(1927), ed; NOAH'S ARK(1928), w, ed; SINGING FOOL,
THE(1928), ed
Silents
ONE WEEK OF LOVE(1922), ed; DON JUAN(1926), ed
Harold J. McCord
LION AND THE MOUSE, THE(1928), ed
Kent McCord
JIGSAW(1968); CONQUEST OF THE EARTH(1980); AIRPLANE II: THE SE-
QUEL(1982)
Mrs. Lewis McCord
Silents
VIRGINIAN, THE(1914); ARMSTRONG'S WIFE(1915); CHIMMIE FADDEN(1915);
CHIMMIE FADDEN OUT WEST(1915); KINDLING(1915); MARRIAGE OF KITTY,
THE(1915); SECRET ORCHARD(1915); WARRENS OF VIRGINIA, THE(1915); WILD
GOOSE CHASE, THE(1915); RACE, THE(1916); ON RECORD(1917); THOSE WITHOUT
SIN(1917)
Robert McCord
YOU WERE MEANT FOR ME(1948); VALLEY OF THE DOLLS(1967)
Steve McCord
TWO VOICES(1966), m
T. D. McCord
DAWN TRAIL, THE(1931), ph
Silents
SO BIG(1924), ph; DESERT FLOWER, THE(1925), ph; PACE THAT THRILLS,
THE(1925), ph; SALLY(1925), ph; IRENE(1926), ph

Ted D. McCord
LONE RIDER, THE(1930), ph; DESERT VENGEANCE(1931), ph
Ted McCord
SENOR AMERICANO(1929), ph; WAGON MASTER, THE(1929), ph; FIGHTING
LEGION, THE(1930), ph; MEN WITHOUT LAW(1930), ph; MOUNTAIN JUS-
TICE(1930), ph; PARADE OF THE WEST(1930), ph; SHADOW RANCH(1930), ph;
SONG OF THE CABELLERO(1930), ph; SONS OF THE SADDLE(1930), ph; SUN-
DOWN TRAIL(1931), ph; BEYOND THE ROCKIES(1932), ph; BIG STAMPEDE,
THE(1932), ph; CARNIVAL BOAT(1932), ph; FREIGHTERS OF DESTINY(1932), ph;
GHOST VALLEY(1932), ph; HELL FIRE AUSTIN(1932), ph; RIDE HIM, COW-
BOY(1932), ph; SADDLE BUSTER, THE(1932), ph; TOMBSTONE CANYON(1932), ph;
FARGO EXPRESS(1933), ph; KING OF THE ARENA(1933), ph; MAN FROM MON-
TEREY, THE(1933), ph; SOMEWHERE IN SONORA(1933), ph; STRAWBERRY
ROAN(1933), ph; TELEGRAPH TRAIL, THE(1933), ph; FIDDLIN' BUCKAROO,
THE(1934), ph; FUGITIVE ROAD(1934), ph; GUN JUSTICE(1934), ph; HONOR OF
THE RANGE(1934), ph; ROCKY RHODES(1934), ph; SMOKING GUNS(1934), ph;
TRAIL DRIVE, THE(1934), ph; WHEELS OF DESTINY(1934), ph; WHEN A MAN
SEES RED(1934), ph; RAINMAKERS, THE(1935), ph; STONE OF SILVER
CREEK(1935), ph; FEUD OF THE WEST(1936), ph; TRAILIN' WEST(1936), ph; BLAZ-
ING SIXES(1937), ph; CALIFORNIA MAIL, THE(1937), ph; DEVIL'S SADDLE LE-
GION, THE(1937), ph; EMPTY HOLSTERS(1937), ph; FUGITIVE IN THE
SKY(1937), ph; GUNS OF THE PECOS(1937), ph; LAND BEYOND THE LAW(1937),
ph; PRAIRIE THUNDER(1937), ed; DAREDEVIL DRIVERS(1938), ph; SERGEANT
MURPHY(1938), ph; CODE OF THE SECRET SERVICE(1939), ph; COWBOY QUAR-
TERBACK(1939), ph; PRIDE OF THE BLUEGRASS(1939), ph; PRIVATE DETEC-
TIVE(1939), ph; SECRET SERVICE OF THE AIR(1939), ph; CALLING ALL
HUSBANDS(1940), ph; FATHER IS A PRINCE(1940), ph; LADIES MUST LIVE(1940),
ph; MURDER IN THE AIR(1940), ph; BULLETS FOR O'HARA(1941), ph; CASE OF
THE BLACK PARROT, THE(1941), ph; HIGHWAY WEST(1941), ph; INTERNATION-
AL SQUADRON(1941), ph; KNOCKOUT(1941), ph; NINE LIVES ARE NOT
ENOUGH(1941), ph; SHE COULDN'T SAY NO(1941), ph; SINGAPORE WO-
MAN(1941), ph; BULLET SCARS(1942), ph; I WAS FRAMED(1942), ph; MURDER IN
THE BIG HOUSE(1942), ph; WILD BILL HICKOK RIDES(1942), ph; ACTION IN THE
NORTH ATLANTIC(1943), ph; DEEP VALLEY(1947), ph; THAT WAY WITH WOM-
EN(1947), ph; JOHNNY BELINDA(1948), ph; JUNE BRIDE(1948), ph; SMART GIRLS
DON'T TALK(1948), ph; TREASURE OF THE SIERRA MADRE, THE(1948), ph;
FLAMINGO ROAD(1949), ph; LADY TAKES A SAILOR, THE(1949), ph; BREAKING
POINT, THE(1950), ph; DAMNED DON'T CRY, THE(1950), ph; ROCKY MOUN-
TAIN(1950), ph; YOUNG MAN WITH A HORN(1950), ph; FORCE OF ARMS(1951),
ph; GOODBYE, MY FANCY(1951), ph; I'LL SEE YOU IN MY DREAMS(1951), ph;
STARLIFT(1951), ph; CATTLE TOWN(1952), ph; OPERATION SECRET(1952), ph;
STOP, YOU'RE KILLING ME(1952), ph; THIS WOMAN IS DANGEROUS(1952), ph;
SOUTH SEA WOMAN(1953), ph; EAST OF EDEN(1955), ph; I DIED A THOUSAND
TIMES(1955), ph; YOUNG AT HEART(1955), ph; BURNING HILLS, THE(1956), ph;
GIRL HE LEFT BEHIND, THE(1956), ph; PROUD REBEL, THE(1958), ph; HANGING
TREE, THE(1959), ph; HELEN MORGAN STORY, THE(1959), ph; ADVENTURES OF
HUCKLEBERRY FINN, THE(1960), ph; PRIVATE PROPERTY(1960), ph; HERO'S
ISLAND(1962), ph; TWO FOR THE SEESAW(1962), ph; WAR HUNT(1962), ph;
SOUND OF MUSIC, THE(1965), ph; FINE MADNESS, A(1966), ph
Silents
ROYAL RIDER, THE(1929), ph
Theodore McCord
FALSE FACES(1932), ph
Vera McCord
Misc. Silents
GOOD-BAD WIFE, THE(1921), d
Yvonne McCord
1984
CRIMES OF PASSION(1984)
Don McCorkindale
EXCUSE MY GLOVE(1936, Brit.); WE'RE GOING TO BE RICH(1938, Brit.); CARRY
ON CABBIE(1963, Brit.); KILLER FORCE(1975, Switz./Ireland)
Donald McCorkindale
NAVY HEROES(1959, Brit.)
Kevin McCorkle
STROKER ACE(1983)
Muriel McCormac
DYNAMITE(1930)
Silents
POOR MEN'S WIVES(1923); SKYROCKET, THE(1926); SPARROWS(1926); KING OF
KINGS, THE(1927)
Theresa McCormac
NORAH O'NEALE(1934, Brit.)
Barney McCormack
Misc. Talkies
TRAIL BLAZERS(1953)
Bartlett McCormack
HALF-NAKED TRUTH, THE(1932), w
Colin McCormack
DEATHLINE(1973, Brit.)
Edward McCormack
TAKE HER BY SURPRISE(1967, Can.)
Frank McCormack
BROTHERS(1930); CASE OF SERGEANT GRISCHA, THE(1930); BEAU
IDEAL(1931); FIGHTING TEXAN(1937)
Misc. Silents
CASE OF BECKY, THE(1921)
Frank M. McCormack
PHANTOM OF THE OPERA, THE(1929), w
H.M. McCormack
PART-TIME WIFE(1961, Brit.), w
Hugh McCormack
NIX ON DAMES(1929); WALL STREET(1929)
John McCormack
SONG O' MY HEART(1930); WINGS OF THE MORNING(1937, Brit.)
1984
SUBURBIA(1984)

John T. McCormack
PERILS OF PAULINE, THE(1967), art d; RIDE TO HANGMAN'S TREE, THE(1967), art d; SSSSSSSS(1973), art d; WILLIE DYNAMITE(1973), art d

Kathleen McCormack
THOSE WERE THE DAYS(1940)

M. M. McCormack
BATTLEAXE, THE(1962, Brit.), w; GENTLE TERROR, THE(1962, Brit.), w; LAMP IN ASSASSIN MEWS, THE(1962, Brit.), w; WHAT EVERY WOMAN WANTS(1962, Brit.), w

Marjorie McCormack
TAKE HER BY SURPRISE(1967, Can.)

Meredith McCormack
MAN FROM MUSIC MOUNTAIN(1938)

Merrill McCormack
CORNERED(1932); TOMBSTONE CANYON(1932); DEADWOOD PASS(1933); MAN OF THE FOREST(1933); LIGHTNING RANGE(1934); FIGHTING TROOPER, THE(1935); GALLANT DEFENDER(1935); LAWLESS BORDER(1935); COME ON, COWBOYS(1937); EMPTY HOLSTERS(1937); GUNS IN THE DARK(1937); PHANTOM OF SANTA FE(1937); RANGE DEFENDERS(1937); TWO-FISTED SHERIFF(1937); DANGER VALLEY(1938); GHOST TOWN RIDERS(1938); OUTLAWS OF SONORA(1938); PRAIRIE MOON(1938); IN OLD CALIENTE(1939); KANSAS TERRORS, THE(1939); LONE STAR PIONEERS(1939); MEXICALI ROSE(1939); RIDE 'EM COWGIRL(1939); HIDDEN GOLD(1940); MELODY RANCH(1940); PRAIRIE SCHOONERS(1940); DESERT BANDIT(1941); IN OLD CHEYENNE(1941); LONE RIDER FIGHTS BACK, THE(1941); SON OF DAVY CROCKETT, THE(1941); FIGHTING BILL FARGO(1942); IN OLD CALIFORNIA(1942); PIRATES OF THE PRAIRIE(1942); SOMBRERO KID, THE(1942); SOUTH OF SANTA FE(1942); STARDUST ON THE SAGE(1942); KANSAN, THE(1943); LOST CANYON(1943); ROBIN HOOD OF THE RANGE(1943); SILVER CITY RAIDERS(1943); RAIDERS OF RED GAP(1944); GUN TOWN(1946); GALLANT LEGION, THE(1948); GUN LAW JUSTICE(1949); LIGHTNING GUNS(1950); OUTLAW GOLD(1950); WHISTLING HILLS(1951); MAN FROM BLACK HILLS, THE(1952)

Pat McCormack
AROUND THE TOWN(1938, Brit.); PHYNX, THE(1970)

Patrick McCormack
MONOLITH MONSTERS, THE(1957), ed; DAMN CITIZEN(1958), ed; LAST OF THE FAST GUNS, THE(1958), ed; MONEY, WOMEN AND GUNS(1958), ed; DAYS OF WINE AND ROSES(1962), ed; EXPERIMENT IN TERROR(1962), ed

Patty McCormack
BAD SEED, THE(1956); ALL MINE TO GIVE(1957); KATHY O'(1958); SNOW QUEEN, THE(1959, USSR); ADVENTURES OF HUCKLEBERRY FINN, THE(1960); EXPLOSIVE GENERATION, THE(1961); JACKTOWN(1962); BORN WILD(1968); MARYJANE(1968); MINI-SKIRT MOB, THE(1968); YOUNG RUNAWAYS, THE(1968); BUG(1975)

Sheila McCormack
GOOD DIE YOUNG, THE(1954, Brit.)

Tim McCormack
GAL YOUNG UN(1979)

William McCormack
SANTA FE(1951)

William M. McCormack
COWBOY COUNSELOR(1933)

Al McCormick
Misc. Silents
WESTERN FEUDS(1924)

Alyce McCormick
RENO(1930)

Bill McCormick
TRAIL OF THE LONESOME PINE, THE(1936); RIDERS OF THE FRONTIER(1939)

Charles McCormick
TRAIN RIDE TO HOLLYWOOD(1975)

Ed McCormick
PUBLIC ENEMY, THE(1931), ed

F.J. McCormick
PLOUGH AND THE STARS, THE(1936); HUNGRY HILL(1947, Brit.); ODD MAN OUT(1947, Brit.)

Gilmer McCormick
SLAUGHTERHOUSE-FIVE(1972); SQUARES(1972); GODSPELL(1973); STARTING OVER(1979)
1984
SILENT NIGHT, DEADLY NIGHT(1984)

Gina McCormick
JOHNNY VIK(1973)

Ian McCormick
GENTLE TOUCH, THE(1956, Brit.), w

Joe McCormick
ON THE BEACH(1959)

John McCormick
FOOTLIGHTS AND FOOLS(1929), p; SMILING IRISH EYES(1929), p; VICTIM(1961, Brit.), w; SEVEN WOMEN(1966), w; WALK IN THE SHADOW(1966, Brit.), w
Silents
ELLA CINDERS(1926), p; IRENE(1926), p; IT MUST BE LOVE(1926), p; LILAC TIME(1928), p

John T. McCormick
HAVE ROCRET, WILL TRAVEL(1959), art d

Karen McCormick
POPEYE(1980)

Kelly McCormick
EXPERIMENT IN TERROR(1962)

Langdon McCormick
STORM, THE(1930), w; SMILIN' THROUGH(1932), w
Silents
STORM, THE(1922), w

Larry McCormick
LOVE GOD?, THE(1969)

Marlene McCormick
1984
KILLPOINT(1984)

Mary McCormick
PADDY, THE NEXT BEST THING(1933)

Maureen McCormick
PONY EXPRESS RIDER(1976); MOONSHINE COUNTY EXPRESS(1977); SKATETOWN, U.S.A.(1979); TAKE DOWN(1979); IDOLMAKER, THE(1980); TEXAS LIGHTNING(1981)

Megan McCormick
Misc. Talkies
COMING APART(1969)

Merrill McCormick
ROMANCE OF THE RIO GRANDE(1929); NEAR THE RAINBOW'S END(1930); SPOILERS, THE(1930); FIGHTING CARAVANS(1931); WHISTLIN' DAN(1932); DUDE BANDIT, THE(1933); KING OF THE ARENA(1933); WHEELS OF DESTINY(1934); NEW ADVENTURES OF TARZAN(1935); PRISONER OF SHARK ISLAND, THE(1936); WESTERNER, THE(1936); WINDS OF THE WASTELAND(1936); FORLORN RIVER(1937); GOD'S COUNTRY AND THE MAN(1937); OLD CORRAL, THE(1937); ONE MAN JUSTICE(1937); WE'RE IN THE LEGION NOW(1937); TARZAN AND THE GREEN GODDESS(1938); MUTINY IN THE BIG HOUSE(1939); OVERLAND MAIL(1939); SINGING COWGIRL, THE(1939); STAGECOACH(1939); WATER RUSTLERS(1939); SILVER BULLET, THE(1942); SCREAM IN THE NIGHT(1943); ARCTIC FURY(1949)
Silents
ROBIN HOOD(1922); RIDERS OF THE RIO GRANDE(1929)
Misc. Silents
GOOD MEN AND BAD(1923), a, d; FLASHING STEEDS(1925)

Michael McCormick
RETURN OF THE JEDI(1983)

Myron McCormick
WINTERSET(1936); ONE THIRD OF A NATION(1939); CHINA GIRL(1942); JIGSAW(1949); JOLSON SINGS AGAIN(1949); NOT AS A STRANGER(1955); THREE FOR THE SHOW(1955); NO TIME FOR SERGEANTS(1958); MAN WHO UNDERSTOOD WOMEN, THE(1959); HUSTLER, THE(1961); PUBLIC AFFAIR, A(1962)

Parker McCormick
FAN, THE(1981)

Pat McCormick
OH DAD, POOR DAD, MAMA'S HUNG YOU IN THE CLOSET AND I'M FEELIN' SO SAD(1967), w; BUFFALO BILL AND THE INDIANS, OR SITTING BULL'S HISTORY LESSON(1976); SHAGGY D.A., THE(1976); SMOKEY AND THE BANDIT(1977); WEDDING, A(1978); HOT STUFF(1979); SCAVENGER HUNT(1979); GONG SHOW MOVIE, THE(1980); SMOKEY AND THE BANDIT II(1980); HISTORY OF THE WORLD, PART 1(1981); UNDER THE RAINBOW(1981), a, w; SMOKEY AND THE BANDIT-PART 3(1983)

Red McCormick
MAGNIFICENT SEVEN RIDE, THE(1972), art d

Steve McCormick
IT HAPPENED TO JANE(1959)

Susan McCormick
THIEF(1981)

Thomas Patrick McCormick
EMERGENCY WEDDING(1950)

W.M. McCormick
REBELLION(1938)

William McCormick
SCENE OF THE CRIME(1949); DREAM WIFE(1953); SALOME(1953)
Silents
ABRAHAM LINCOLN(1924)

William Merrill McCormick
TUNDRA(1936); DODGE CITY(1939); FIGHTING STALLION, THE(1950)
Silents
APACHE RAIDER, THE(1928)
Misc. Silents
SON OF THE DESERT, A(1928), a, d

William [Merrill] McCormick
THEY WERE EXPENDABLE(1945)

John McCorry
INTRUDER, THE(1955, Brit.), cos; SWORD OF SHERWOOD FOREST(1961, Brit.), cos; TOM JONES(1963, Brit.), cos; HIGH WIND IN JAMAICA, A(1965), cos; KHARTOUM(1966, Brit.), cos

Terence McCorry
FRIDAY THE 13TH PART III(1982)
1984
ALPHABET CITY(1984), art d

Tom McCorry
HERBIE GOES TO MONTE CARLO(1977)

Rufus McCosh
Silents
MAN CRAZY(1927), t; SMILE, BROTHER, SMILE(1927), t; HEART OF A FOLLIES GIRL, THE(1928), t; NIGHT WATCH, THE(1928), t

Jack McCoskey
HINDU, THE(1953, Brit.), ph

Barry McCourmick
TEARS FOR SIMON(1957, Brit.)

Malachy McCourt
MOLLY MAGUIRES, THE(1970); BRINK'S JOB, THE(1978); Q(1982)

Margaret McCourt
JOHNNY ON THE RUN(1953, Brit.); TWICE UPON A TIME(1953, Brit.); TROUBLE IN THE GLEN(1954, Brit.)

Marguerite McCourt
TOMORROW AT TEN(1964, Brit.)

Alec McCowan
CRUEL SEA, THE(1953)

George McCowan
FROGS(1972), d; INBREAKER, THE(1974, Can.), d
Misc. Talkies
WINTER COMES EARLY(1972), d

Helen McCowan
WONDER MAN(1945)

Alec McCowen
DEEP BLUE SEA, THE(1955, Brit.); GOOD COMPANIONS, THE(1957, Brit.); THIRD KEY, THE(1957, Brit.); TIME WITHOUT PITY(1957, Brit.); DOCTOR'S DILEMMA, THE(1958, Brit.); NIGHT TO REMEMBER, A(1958, Brit.); ONE THAT GOT AWAY, THE(1958, Brit.); SILENT ENEMY, THE(1959, Brit.); MIDSUMMERS NIGHT'S DREAM, A(1961, Czech); LONELINESS OF THE LONG DISTANCE RUNNER, THE(1962, Brit.); IN THE COOL OF THE DAY(1963); DEVIL'S OWN, THE(1967, Brit.); HAWAIIANS, THE(1970); FRENZY(1972, Brit.); TRAVELS WITH MY AUNT(1972, Brit.); STEVIE(1978, Brit.); HANOVER STREET(1979, Brit.); NEVER SAY NEVER AGAIN(1983)

Alex McCowen
DIVIDED HEART, THE(1955, Brit.); TOWN ON TRIAL(1957, Brit.)

Tiec McCowen
DEEP BLUE SEA, THE(1955, Brit.)

Tom McCowen
CASE OF THE 44'S, THE(1964 Brit./Den.), d&w

Frank McCown
BULLFIGHTERS, THE(1945)

Malla McCown
COAL MINER'S DAUGHTER(1980)

Pamela McCown
COAL MINER'S DAUGHTER(1980)

Al McCoy
BOWERY, THE(1933)

Arch McCoy
HERE COME THE TIGERS(1978), w

Austin McCoy
DECOY(1946)
Misc. Talkies
SUN TAN RANCH(1948)

Breege McCoy
SOD SISTERS(1969)

Candy McCoy
OTHER SIDE OF THE MOUNTAIN, THE(1975)

David McCoy
BIONIC BOY, THE(1977, Hong Kong/Phil.)

Denys McCoy
LAST REBEL, THE(1971), d

Earl McCoy
ICE STATION ZEBRA(1968), spec eff; MOONSHINE WAR, THE(1970), spec eff; ZABRISKIE POINT(1970), spec eff

Evelyn McCoy
Silents
STING OF THE LASH(1921)
Misc. Silents
WHAT A WIFE LEARNED(1923)

Frances McCoy
SOUP TO NUTS(1930); WILD COMPANY(1930)

Frank McCoy
TEN COMMANDMENTS, THE(1956), makeup; PORGY AND BESS(1959), makeup; UNFORGIVEN, THE(1960), makeup; JACK THE GIANT KILLER(1962), art d; TARAS BULBA(1962), makeup; THREE STOOGES IN ORBIT, THE(1962), makeup; KITTEN WITH A WHIP(1964), makeup; PARIS WHEN IT SIZZLES(1964), makeup; MADE IN PARIS(1966), makeup; WAY WEST, THE(1967), makeup; PAINT YOUR WAGON(1969), makeup; THEY SHOOT HORSES, DON'T THEY?(1969), makeup; MAC ARTHUR(1977), makeup

Gertrude McCoy
Silents
HOUSE OF THE LOST CORD, THE(1915); JUNE FRIDAY(1915); DANGER MARK, THE(1918); ANGEL ESQUIRE(1919, Brit.); AUCTION MART, THE(1920, Brit.); HEARTSTRINGS(1923, Brit.); MIRIAM ROZELLA(1924, Brit.); NETS OF DESTINY(1924, Brit.); NELSON(1926, Brit.)
Misc. Silents
FRIEND WILSON'S DAUGHTER(1915); GREATER THAN ART(1915); PLOUGHSHARE, THE(1915); THROUGH TURBULENT WATERS(1915); ISLE OF LOVE, THE(1916); LASH OF DESTINY, THE(1916); MADAME SHERRY(1917); SILENT WITNESS, THE(1917); TO HIM THAT HATH(1918); CASTLE OF DREAMS(1919, Brit.); USURPER, THE(1919, Brit.); BURNT IN(1920, Brit.); CHRISTIE JOHNSTONE(1921, Brit.); GOLDEN DAWN, THE(1921, Brit.); WAS SHE GUILTY?(1922, Brit.); ROYAL DIVORCE, A(1923, Brit.); TEMPTATION OF CARLTON EARLYE, THE(1923, Brit.); CHAPPY - THAT'S ALL(1924, Brit.); DIAMOND MAN, THE(1924, Brit.)

Harry McCoy
MIDNIGHT DADDIES(1929), w; CALL IT LUCK(1934), w
Silents
TILLIE'S PUNCTURED ROMANCE(1914); FAIR ENOUGH(1918); HEADS UP(1925); CHASER, THE(1928), w
Misc. Silents
HOOSIER ROMANCE, A(1918)

Herschel McCoy
DREAM WIFE(1953), cos; LATIN LOVERS(1953), cos; PRODIGAL, THE(1955), cos

Hershel McCoy
JULIUS CAESAR(1953), cos

Homer McCoy
GIT!(1965), w

Horace McCoy
ISLAND OF LOST MEN(1939), w

Horace McCoy
HER RESALE VALUE(1933), w; HOLD THE PRESS(1933), w; SOLDIERS OF THE STORM(1933), w; FURY OF THE JUNGLE(1934), w; SPEED WINGS(1934), w; FATAL LADY(1936), w; GREAT GUY(1936), w; PAROLE(1936), w; POSTAL INSPECTOR(1936), w; TRAIL OF THE LONESOME PINE, THE(1936), w; DANGEROUS TO KNOW(1938), w; HUNTED MEN(1938), w; KING OF THE NEWSBOYS(1938), w; PERSONS IN HIDING(1939), w; TELEVISION SPY(1939), w; UNDERCOVER DOCTOR(1939), w; PAROLE FIXER(1940), w; QUEEN OF THE MOB(1940), w; TEXAS RANGERS RIDE AGAIN(1940), w; WOMEN WITHOUT NAMES(1940), w; TEXAS(1941), w; WILD GEESE CALLING(1941), w; GENTLEMAN JIM(1942), w; VALLEY OF THE SUN(1942), w; APPOINTMENT IN BERLIN(1943), w; FLIGHT FOR FREEDOM(1943), w; THERE'S SOMETHING ABOUT A SOLDIER(1943), w; FABULOUS TEXAN, THE(1947), w; FIREBALL, THE(1950), w; KISS TOMORROW GOODBYE(1950), w; BRONCO BUSTER(1952), w; LUSTY MEN, THE(1952), w; MONTANA

BELLE(1952), w; TURNING POINT, THE(1952), w; WORLD IN HIS ARMS, THE(1952), w; BAD FOR EACH OTHER(1954), w; DANGEROUS MISSION(1954), w; EL ALAMEIN(1954), w; RAGE AT DAWN(1955), w; ROAD TO DENVER, THE(1955), w; TEXAS LADY(1955), w; THEY SHOOT HORSES, DON'T THEY?(1969), w

J.L. McCoy
STAR TREK II: THE WRATH OF KHAN(1982), makeup

Jim McCoy
MAC ARTHUR(1977), makeup

Kay McCoy
COME ON, MARINES(1934); TOMBSTONE TERROR(1935); OUR RELATIONS(1936)

Kid McCoy
Silents
APRIL SHOWERS(1923)

Robert McCoy
PIECES OF DREAMS(1970)

Ruby McCoy
BROADWAY(1929)

Sid McCoy
COLOSSUS: THE FORBIN PROJECT(1969); MEDIUM COOL(1969)

Col. T. J. McCoy
Silents
COVERED WAGON, THE(1923), adv

Tim McCoy
ONE WAY TRAIL, THE(1931); CORNERED(1932); DARING DANGER(1932); END OF THE TRAIL(1932); FIGHTING FOOL, THE(1932); FIGHTING MARSHAL, THE(1932); RIDING TORNADO, THE(1932); SHOTGUN PASS(1932); TEXAS CYCLONE(1932); TWO-FISTED LAW(1932); HOLD THE PRESS(1933); POLICE CAR 17(1933); RUSTY RIDES ALONE(1933); BEYOND THE LAW(1934); HELL BENT FOR LOVE(1934); MAN'S GAME, A(1934); SPEED WINGS(1934); STRAIGHTAWAY(1934); VOICE IN THE NIGHT(1934); FIGHTING SHADOWS(1935); JUSTICE OF THE RANGE(1935); LAW BEYOND THE RANGE(1935); OUTLAW DEPUTY, THE(1935); REVENGE RIDER, THE(1935); ACES AND EIGHTS(1936); BORDER CABALLERO(1936); GHOST PATROL(1936); LIGHTNING BILL CARSON(1936); LION'S DEN, THE(1936); MAN FROM GUN TOWN, THE(1936); PRESCOTT KID, THE(1936); ROARIN' GUNS(1936); TRAITOR, THE(1936); WESTERNER, THE(1936); CODE OF THE RANGERS(1938); PHANTOM RANGER(1938); TWO-GUN JUSTICE(1938); WEST OF RAINBOW'S END(1938); CODE OF THE CACTUS(1939); FIGHTING RENEGADE(1939); OUTLAW'S PARADISE(1939); TEXAS WILDCATS(1939); TRIGGER FINGERS ½(1939); ARIZONA GANGBUSTERS(1940); FRONTIER CRUSADER(1940); GUN CODE(1940); STRAIGHT SHOOTER(1940); ARIZONA BOUND(1941); FORBIDDEN TRAILS(1941); GUN MAN FROM BODIE, THE(1941); OUTLAWS OF THE RIO GRANDE(1941); RIDERS OF BLACK MOUNTAIN(1941); TEXAS MARSHAL, THE(1941); BELOW THE BORDER(1942); DOWN TEXAS WAY(1942); GHOST TOWN LAW(1942); RIDERS OF THE WEST(1942); WEST OF THE LAW(1942); REQUIEM FOR A GUNFIGHTER(1965)
Misc. Talkies
FIGHTING FOR JUSTICE(1932); WESTERN CODE(1932); MAN OF ACTION(1933); SILENT MEN(1933); WHIRLWIND, THE(1933); BULLDOG COURAGE(1935); RIDING WILD(1935); SQUARE SHOOTER(1935); LIGHTNING CARSON RIDES AGAIN(1938); SIX-GUN TRAIL(1938); TEXAS RENEGADES(1940)
Silents
WAR PAINT(1926); CALIFORNIA(1927); FOREIGN DEVILS(1927); ADVENTURER, THE(1928); LAW OF THE RANGE, THE(1928); DESERT RIDER, THE(1929); MORGAN'S LAST RAID(1929); OVERLAND TELEGRAPH, THE(1929); SIOUX BLOOD(1929)
Misc. Silents
FRONTIERSMAN, THE(1927); SPOILERS OF THE WEST(1927); WINNERS OF THE WILDERNESS(1927); BEYOND THE SIERRAS(1928); BUSHRANGER, THE(1928); RIDERS OF THE DARK(1928); WYOMING(1928)

Col. Tim McCoy
AROUND THE WORLD IN 80 DAYS(1956); RUN OF THE ARROW(1957)

Tony McCoy
BRIDE OF THE MONSTER(1955); NAKED GUN, THE(1956)

Van McCoy
SEXTETTE(1978)

Vivian McCoy
GEORGE WHITE'S SCANDALS(1945)

Walter McCoy
WICHITA(1955)

Wayne McCoy
MAYOR OF 44TH STREET, THE(1942); MEXICAN SPITFIRE AT SEA(1942); LADIES' DAY(1943); TYCOON(1947)

William McCoy
Silents
BAB'S CANDIDATE(1920), ph; IF WOMEN ONLY KNEW(1921), ph

William M. McCoy
Silents
HEARTS OF MEN(1919), w

Esther McCracken
POISON PEN(1941, Brit.), w; QUIET WEDDING(1941, Brit.), w; RANDOLPH FAMILY, THE(1945, Brit.), w; QUIET WEEKEND(1948, Brit.), w; WEAKER SEX, THE(1949, Brit.), w; HAPPY IS THE BRIDE(1958, Brit.), w

Harold McCracken
Misc. Silents
HEART OF ALASKA(1924), d

Jeff McCracken
ONE MAN JURY(1978)

Jenny McCracken
NIGHT DIGGER, THE(1971, Brit.)

Joan McCracken
HOLLYWOOD CANTEEN(1944); GOOD NEWS(1947)

Melinda McCracken
HIGH(1968, Can.)

Michael McCracken
PSYCHO II(1983), makeup; TWILIGHT ZONE–THE MOVIE(1983), makeup

Ona McCracken
1984
COMFORT AND JOY(1984, Brit.)

R. C. McCracken
VICKI(1953)
Richard McCracken
RAMPARTS WE WATCH, THE(1940)
Robert C. McCracken
FIGHTING MAD(1948)
Rowland McCracken
IT HAPPENED ON 5TH AVENUE(1947)
Ann McCrae
PARDNERS(1956)
Margie McCrae
WINTER OF OUR DREAMS(1982, Aus.)
Jeff McCraken
RUNNING BRAVE(1983, Can.)
Paul McCrane
FAME(1980)
1984
HOTEL NEW HAMPSHIRE, THE(1984); PURPLE HEARTS(1984)
Chuck McCrann
BLOODEATERS(1980), p,d&w, ed
Charles McCrary
9/30/55(1977)
Kent McCray
1984
SAM'S SON(1984), p
Ann McCrea
DEADLINE–U.S.A.(1952); SWEETHEARTS ON PARADE(1953); RIVER OF NO RETURN(1954); KISS THEM FOR ME(1957); WILL SUCCESS SPOIL ROCK HUNTER?(1957); CHINA DOLL(1958); LADIES MAN, THE(1961); GIRLS! GIRLS! GIRLS!(1962); WAR WAGON, THE(1967); WELCOME TO HARD TIMES(1967)
Anne McCrea
ABOUT MRS. LESLIE(1954)
Dusty Iron Wing McCrea
WINDWALKER(1980)
Jody McCrea
FIRST TEXAN, THE(1956); NAKED GUN, THE(1956); GUNSIGHT RIDGE(1957); MONSTER THAT CHALLENGED THE WORLD, THE(1957); TROOPER HOOK(1957); LAFAYETTE ESCADRILLE(1958); RESTLESS YEARS, THE(1958); ALL HANDS ON DECK(1961); FORCE OF IMPULSE(1961); BROKEN LAND, THE(1962); BEACH PARTY(1963); OPERATION BIKINI(1963); YOUNG GUNS OF TEXAS(1963); BIKINI BEACH(1964); LAW OF THE LAWLESS(1964); MUSCLE BEACH PARTY(1964); PAJAMA PARTY(1964); BEACH BLANKET BINGO(1965); HOW TO STUFF A WILD BIKINI(1965); YOUNG FURY(1965); GIRLS FROM THUNDER STRIP, THE(1966); GLORY STOMPERS, THE(1967); CRY BLOOD, APACHE(1970), a, p
Joel McCrea
JAZZ AGE, THE(1929); DYNAMITE(1930); LIGHTNIN'(1930); SILVER HORDE, THE(1930); THIRTEENTH CHAIR, THE(1930); BORN TO LOVE(1931); COMMON LAW, THE(1931); GIRLS ABOUT TOWN(1931); KEPT HUSBANDS(1931); ONCE A SINNER(1931); BIRD OF PARADISE(1932); BUSINESS AND PLEASURE(1932); LOST SQUADRON, THE(1932); MOST DANGEROUS GAME, THE(1932); ROCKABYE(1932); SPORT PARADE, THE(1932); BED OF ROSES(1933); CHANCE AT HEAVEN(1933); ONE MAN'S JOURNEY(1933); SCARLET RIVER(1933); SILVER CORD(1933); GAMBLING LADY(1934); HALF A SINNER(1934); RICHEST GIRL IN THE WORLD, THE(1934); BARBARY COAST(1935); OUR LITTLE GIRL(1935); PRIVATE WORLDS(1935); SPLENDOR(1935); WOMAN WANTED(1935); ADVENTURE IN MANHATTAN(1936); BANJO ON MY KNEE(1936); COME AND GET IT(1936); THESE THREE(1936); TWO IN A CROWD(1936); DEAD END(1937); INTERNES CAN'T TAKE MONEY(1937); WELLS FARGO(1937); WOMAN CHASES MAN(1937); THREE BLIND MICE(1938); YOUTH TAKES A FLING(1938); ESPIONAGE AGENT(1939); THEY SHALL HAVE MUSIC(1939); UNION PACIFIC(1939); FOREIGN CORRESPONDENT(1940); HE MARRIED HIS WIFE(1940); PRIMROSE PATH(1940); REACHING FOR THE SUN(1941); SULLIVAN'S TRAVELS(1941); GREAT MAN'S LADY, THE(1942); PALM BEACH STORY, THE(1942); MORE THE MERRIER, THE(1943); BUFFALO BILL(1944); GREAT MOMENT, THE(1944); UNSEEN, THE(1945); VIRGINIAN, THE(1946); RAMROD(1947); FOUR FACES WEST(1948); COLORADO TERRITORY(1949); SOUTH OF ST. LOUIS(1949); FRENCHIE(1950); OUTRIDERS, THE(1950); SADDLE TRAMP(1950); STARS IN MY CROWN(1950); CATTLE DRIVE(1951); HOLLYWOOD STORY(1951); SAN FRANCISCO STORY, THE(1952); LONE HAND, THE(1953); SHOOT FIRST(1953, Brit.); BLACK HORSE CANYON(1954); BORDER RIVER(1954); STRANGER ON HORSEBACK(1955); WICHITA(1955); FIRST TEXAN, THE(1956); GUNSIGHT RIDGE(1957); OKLAHOMAN, THE(1957); TALL STRANGER, THE(1957); TROOPER HOOK(1957); CATTLE EMPIRE(1958); FORT MASSACRE(1958); GUNFIGHT AT DODGE CITY, THE(1959); RIDE THE HIGH COUNTRY(1962); CRY BLOOD, APACHE(1970); MUSTANG COUNTRY(1976)
Misc. Talkies
OUTRIDERS, THE(1950)
Joel Dee McCrea [Jody McCrea]
FREE GRASS(1969)
Moe McCrea
Misc. Silents
CIRCUS CYCLONE, THE(1925)
Peter L. McCrea
WINDWALKER(1980), ed; HARRY'S WAR(1981), ed
Tom McCreadie
ALWAYS ANOTHER DAWN(1948, Aus.), p, d
Jim McCreading
REACHING OUT(1983), ed
Tom O. McCreadle
INTO THE STRAIGHT(1950, Aus.), p&d
Ed McCready
HEAVEN WITH A GUN(1969); SSSSSSSS(1973); SUPERDAD(1974); NORTH AVENUE IRREGULARS, THE(1979); MAN WITH BOGART'S FACE, THE(1980); PARTNERS(1982)
Glenn McCreedy
DEATH VALLEY(1982)
Joey McCreery
Silents
REPUTATION(1921)

Maxine McCrey
INCIDENT, THE(1967)
Harry McCrillis
STRIKE UP THE BAND(1940)
Alex McCrindle
I BELIEVE IN YOU(1953, Brit.); TROUBLE IN THE GLEN(1954, Brit.); WEE GEORDIE(1956, Brit.); DEPTH CHARGE(1960, Brit.); PRIVATE LIFE OF SHERLOCK HOLMES, THE(1970, Brit.); STAR WARS(1977); EYE OF THE NEEDLE(1981)
Alexander McCrindle
I'LL NEVER FORGET YOU(1951)
Howard McCrorey
TRAIL STREET(1947); RETURN OF THE BADMEN(1948)
Michael McCroskey
CAR, THE(1977), ed
Patrick McCrossan
MY HANDS ARE CLAY(1948, Irish), p
William McCrow
KES(1970, Brit.), art d; FAMILY LIFE(1971, Brit.), art d; FOURTEEN, THE(1973, Brit.), art d; OPERATION DAYBREAK(1976, U.S./Brit./Czech.), art d; THIRD WALKER, THE(1978, Can.), art d
Margaret McCrystal
DANTE'S INFERNO(1935)
Russ McCubbin
WACO(1966); CAIN'S WAY(1969); HIGH PLAINS DRIFTER(1973); SANTEE(1973); SUDDEN IMPACT(1983)
Matthew McCue
THEM!(1954)
Bill McCuffie
DALEKS–INVASION EARTH 2155 A.D.(1966, Brit.), m
Jack McCullagh
NIKKI, WILD DOG OF THE NORTH(1961, U.S./Can.), set d; DRYLANDERS(1963, Can.), art d
Kathy McCullen
KING OF THE MOUNTAIN(1981)
Arnold McCuller
AMERICAN HOT WAX(1978)
Carson McCullers
MEMBER OF THE WEDDING, THE(1952), w; INDISCRETION OF AN AMERICAN WIFE(1954, U.S./Ital.), w; REFLECTIONS IN A GOLDEN EYE(1967), w; HEART IS A LONELY HUNTER, THE(1968), w
Ann McCulley
NINE TO FIVE(1980), set d; STAR 80(1983), set d
1984
PURPLE RAIN(1984), set d
Anne D. McCulley
AIRPLANE!(1980), set d
David McCulley
GREY FOX, THE(1983, Can.)
Johnston McCulley
OUTLAW DEPUTY, THE(1935), w; BOLD CABALLERO(1936), w; RED ROPE, THE(1937), w; ROOTIN' TOOTIN' RHYTHM(1937), w; TRUSTED OUTLAW, THE(1937), w; ROSE OF THE RIO GRANDE(1938), w; MARK OF ZORRO, THE(1940), w; DOOMED CARAVAN(1941), w; OUTLAWS OF STAMPEDE PASS(1943), w; RAIDERS OF THE BORDER(1944), w; SOUTH OF THE RIO GRANDE(1945), w; MARK OF THE RENEGADE(1951), w; SIGN OF ZORRO, THE(1960), w
Silents
MARK OF ZORRO(1920), w; RIDE FOR YOUR LIFE(1924), w; ICE FLOOD, THE(1926), w
May McCulley
Silents
GILDED DREAM, THE(1920)
Sandra Walker McCulley
DARK, THE(1979)
W. T. McCulley
Silents
SHOOTIN' FOR LOVE(1923); SAWDUST TRAIL(1924)
Andrew McCulloch
DAVID COPPERFIELD(1970, Brit.); KIDNAPPED(1971, Brit.); LAST VALLEY, THE(1971, Brit.); MACBETH(1971, Brit.); LAND THAT TIME FORGOT, THE(1975, Brit.); NOTHING BUT THE NIGHT(1975, Brit.); PRIEST OF LOVE(1981, Brit.)
Ian McCulloch
IT!(1967, Brit.); CROMWELL(1970, Brit.); GHOUL, THE(1975, Brit.); ZOMBIE(1980, Ital.); ALIEN CONTAMINATION(1982, Ital.); DR. BUTCHER, M.D.(1982, Ital.); MOONLIGHTING(1982, Brit.)
Misc. Talkies
ALIEN CONTAMINATION(1981)
Jack McCulloch
EAGLE HAS LANDED, THE(1976, Brit.)
Jim McCullough, Jr.
CREATURE FROM BLACK LAKE, THE(1976), w; CHARGE OF THE MODEL-T'S(1979)
Linda Briggs McCulloch
1984
HOT DOG...THE MOVIE(1984)
Patricia McCulloch
TRIAL OF BILLY JACK, THE(1974)
Robin McCulloch
HOG WILD(1980, Can.)
Ralph McCullogh
Silents
MAN OF NERVE, A(1925)
Andrew McCullouch
CRY OF THE BANSHEE(1970, Brit.)
Billy McCullough
SWEETHEARTS(1938)
Carolyn McCullough
MAIDSTONE(1970)

Donald McCullough
DREAMING(1944, Brit.)
Jim McCullough
TEENAGE MONSTER(1958); SHEPHERD OF THE HILLS, THE(1964), p; LOVE BUG, THE(1968); CREATURE FROM BLACK LAKE, THE(1976), p; CHARGE OF THE MODEL-T'S(1979), p,d&w
Kimberly McCullough
1984
BREAKIN' 2: ELECTRIC BOOGALOO(1984)
Patrick McCullough
MAGIC(1978)
Philo McCullough
CHARLATAN, THE(1929); LEATHERNECK, THE(1929); MILLION DOLLAR COLLAR, THE(1929); SPURS(1930); BRANDED(1931); DEFENDERS OF THE LAW(1931); SKY SPIDER, THE(1931); SOUTH OF THE RIO GRANDE(1932); SUNSET TRAIL(1932); DELUGE(1933); LAUGHING AT LIFE(1933); SONS OF THE DESERT(1933); INSIDE INFORMATION(1934); THUNDER OVER TEXAS(1934); WHEELS OF DESTINY(1934); ANNIE OAKLEY(1935); STRANDED(1935); GUN SMOKE(1936); KLONDIKE ANNIE(1936); LAWLESS NINETIES, THE(1936); RIFF-RAFF(1936); CAPTAINS COURAGEOUS(1937); ON SUCH A NIGHT(1937); TEXAS TRAIL(1937); BORN TO FIGHT(1938); ON THE GREAT WHITE TRAIL(1938); FRONTIER MARSHAL(1939); LET FREEDOM RING(1939); LOVE CRAZY(1941); FOLLOW THE BOYS(1944); HAIL THE CONQUERING HERO(1944); DECEPTION(1946); JANIE GETS MARRIED(1946); STOLEN LIFE, A(1946); LIFE WITH FATHER(1947); MY WILD IRISH ROSE(1947); NORA PRENTISS(1947); POSSESSED(1947); THAT WAY WITH WOMEN(1947); SMART GIRLS DON'T TALK(1948); FOUNTAINHEAD, THE(1949); JOHN LOVES MARY(1949); NIGHT UNTO NIGHT(1949); SAMSON AND DELILAH(1949); FATHER OF THE BRIDE(1950); MONTANA(1950); MRS. O'MALLEY AND MR. MALONE(1950); LULLABY OF BROADWAY, THE(1951); SUGARFOOT(1951); HORIZONS WEST(1952); TREASURE OF LOST CANYON, THE(1952); REDHEAD FROM WYOMING, THE(1953); LADY GODIVA(1955); CHEYENNE AUTUMN(1964); GREAT BANK ROBBERY, THE(1969); THEY SHOOT HORSES, DON'T THEY?(1969)
Misc. Talkies
SWANEE RIVER(1931); WHITE RENEGADE(1931); CACTUS KID, THE(1934); OUTLAWS' HIGHWAY(1934); WEST ON PARADE(1934); CAPTURED IN CHINATOWN(1935); RIDIN' THRU(1935); TWISTED RAILS(1935)
Silents
GIRL WHO WOULDN'T QUIT, THE(1918); QUICKSANDS(1918); CHILD OF M'SIEU(1919); JOHNNY-ON-THE-SPOT(1919); BLUSHING BRIDE, THE(1921); LAMPLIGHTER, THE(1921); MAID OF THE WEST(1921), d; RIGHT THAT FAILED, THE(1922); SEEING'S BELIEVING(1922); STRANGER'S BANQUET(1922); WEST OF CHICAGO(1922); YESTERDAY'S WIFE(1923); DAUGHTERS OF TODAY(1924); HOOK AND LADDER(1924); JUDGMENT OF THE STORM(1924); LADIES TO BOARD(1924); RACING FOR LIFE(1924); BLUE BLOOD(1925); DICK TURPIN(1925); ARIZONA SWEEPSTAKES(1926); LADIES AT PLAY(1926); EASY PICKINGS(1927); SILVER VALLEY(1927); SMILE, BROTHER, SMILE(1927); WE'RE ALL GAMBLERS(1927); WOMAN WHO DID NOT CARE, THE(1927); APACHE, THE(1928); CLEARING THE TRAIL(1928); NIGHT FLYER, THE(1928); POWER OF THE PRESS, THE(1928); WARMING UP(1928)
Misc. Silents
CAPTAIN KIDDO(1917); MARTINACHE MARRIAGE, THE(1917); SECRET OF BLACK MOUNTAIN, THE(1917); TEARS AND SMILES(1917); DAUGHTER ANGELE(1918); LEGION OF DEATH, THE(1918); MODERN LOVE(1918); RICH MAN'S DAUGHTER, A(1918); HAPPY THOUGH MARRIED(1919); MARKET OF SOULS, THE(1919); FLAME OF YOUTH(1920); IN THE HEART OF A FOOL(1920); LITTLE GREY MOUSE, THE(1920); UNTAMED, THE(1920); WORLD OF FOLLY, A(1920); PARTNERS OF FATE(1921); PRIMAL LAW, THE(1921); CALVERT'S VALLEY(1922); DANGEROUS ADVENTURE, A(1922); HEROES OF THE STREET(1922); MARRIED FLAPPER, THE(1922); MORE TO BE PITIED THAN SCORNED(1922); STRANGE IDOLS(1922); FIRST DEGREE, THE(1923); FORGIVE AND FORGET(1923); TRILBY(1923); DANGEROUS BLONDE, THE(1924); MANSION OF ACHING HEARTS, THE(1925); BAR-C MYSTERY, THE(1926); CHIP OF THE FLYING U(1926); MISMATES(1926); SAVAGE, THE(1926); FIRE AND STEEL(1927); WE'RE ALL GAMBLERS(1927); PAINTED POST(1928); SOUTH OF PANAMA(1928); UNTAMED JUSTICE(1929)
Ralph McCullough
MANHATTAN MELODRAMA(1934); COWBOY STAR, THE(1936); MORE THAN A SECRETARY(1936); RETURN OF SOPHIE LANG, THE(1936); WEDDING PRESENT(1936); CODE OF THE RANGE(1937); LIVE, LOVE AND LEARN(1937); MEN WITH WINGS(1938); WHO KILLED GAIL PRESTON?(1938); YOU CAN'T TAKE IT WITH YOU(1938); PIONEERS OF THE FRONTIER(1940); WOMEN WITHOUT NAMES(1940); JOAN OF OZARK(1942)
Silents
SWAMP, THE(1921); ANGEL OF CROOKED STREET, THE(1922); DON'T GET PERSONAL(1922); HIGH AND HANDSOME(1925); PASSIONATE YOUTH(1925)
Misc. Silents
HOMER COMES HOME(1920); BLOODHOUND, THE(1925); GALLOPING VENGENCE(1925); NO MAN'S LAW(1925); SPEED WILD(1925); STOLEN RANCH, THE(1926)
Ralph Fee McCullough
Misc. Silents
ACROSS THE DIVIDE(1921)
Ricky McCullough
ONE GOOD TURN(1955, Brit.)
Robin McCullough
BY DESIGN(1982)
Rusty McCullough
QUEEN OF BROADWAY(1942), w
Susan McCullough
NIGHT OF THE STRANGLER(1975)
Bartley McCullum
Misc. Silents
DOLLARS AND THE WOMAN(1916)
H. H. McCullum
Silents
KEEP MOVING(1915)

Nancy McCullum
FALCON AND THE CO-EDS, THE(1943)
Warren McCullum
GREAT COMMANDMENT, THE(1941)
Frank McCully
GET OUTTA TOWN(1960)
Johnston McCully
DON RICARDO RETURNS(1946), w
Robert J. McCully
THE CRAZIES(1973)
Bee McCune
LEMON DROP KID, THE(1934)
Grant McCune
STAR WARS(1977), ph
Jean McCune
LEMON DROP KID, THE(1934)
Anna Marie McCurdy
CROWNING EXPERIENCE, THE(1960)
George McCurdy
CROWNING EXPERIENCE, THE(1960)
Stephen McCurdy
MIDDLE AGE SPREAD(1979, New Zealand), m
John McCurry
LAST MILE, THE(1959); PAWNBROKER, THE(1965); GAMERA THE INVINCIBLE(1966, Jap.); LANDLORD, THE(1970); WHERE'S POPPA?(1970); THEY MIGHT BE GIANTS(1971); BADGE 373(1973); BINGO LONG TRAVELING ALL-STARS AND MOTOR KINGS, THE(1976); FAST BREAK(1979); JAWS OF SATAN(1980); ATLANTIC CITY(1981, U.S./Can.); WOLFEN(1981); TRADING PLACES(1983)
1984
ALPHABET CITY(1984); VAMPING(1984)
Samuel J. McCurry
ACROSS THE RIVER(1965)
Mary McCusker
CRACKING UP(1977); JEKYLL AND HYDE...TOGETHER AGAIN(1982); LOVE CHILD(1982)
Mary McCuster
TUNNELVISION(1976)
John Dale McCutchan
EVEL KNIEVEL(1971)
Beryl McCutcheon
MARRIAGE IS A PRIVATE AFFAIR(1944); HOODLUM SAINT, THE(1946); TILL THE CLOUDS ROLL BY(1946); HOW TO MARRY A MILLIONAIRE(1953)
Bill McCutcheon
SANTA CLAUS CONQUERS THE MARTIANS zero(1964); VIVA MAX!(1969); W. W. AND THE DIXIE DANCEKINGS(1975); HOT STUFF(1979); DEADHEAD MILES(1982)
George Barr McCutcheon
ROYAL ROMANCE, A(1930), w; BREWSTER'S MILLIONS(1935, Brit.), w; BREWSTER'S MILLIONS(1945), w; THREE ON A SPREE(1961, Brit.), w
Silents
BREWSTER'S MILLIONS(1914), w; CIRCUS MAN, THE(1914), w; BREWSTER'S MILLIONS(1921), w; PRISONER, THE(1923), w; BEVERLY OF GRAUSTARK(1926), w; MISS BREWSTER'S MILLIONS(1926), w
Hugh McCutcheon
PIT OF DARKNESS(1961, Brit.), w
John L. McCutcheon
Misc. Silents
MAN AND WIFE(1923), d; LAW AND THE LADY, THE(1924), d
Ross McCutcheon
Silents
EARLY TO WED(1926)
Wallace McCutcheon
Misc. Silents
FLOOR BELOW, THE(1918); THIEF, THE(1920)
William McCutcheon
STOOLIE, THE(1972)
Gillian McCutchon
DREAM MAKER, THE(1963, Brit.)
Valla Rae McDade
DARK, THE(1979)
Barry McDaniel
YOUNG LORD, THE(1970, Ger.)
Donna McDaniel
FRIGHTMARE(1983)
1984
ANGEL(1984); HOLLYWOOD HOT TUBS(1984)
Earl McDaniel
PHANTOM PLANET, THE(1961)
Etta McDaniel
VIRGINIA JUDGE, THE(1935); DEVIL IS A SISSY, THE(1936); LAWLESS NINETIES, THE(1936); LONELY TRAIL, THE(1936); MAGNIFICENT BRUTE, THE(1936); PRISONER OF SHARK ISLAND, THE(1936); THE INVISIBLE RAY(1936); EVER SINCE EVE(1937); GLORY TRAIL, THE(1937); GO-GETTER, THE(1937); LIVING ON LOVE(1937); LOVE IS NEWS(1937); MILE A MINUTE LOVE(1937); ON SUCH A NIGHT(1937); STELLA DALLAS(1937); SWEETHEART OF THE NAVY(1937); THAT CERTAIN WOMAN(1937); KEEP SMILING(1938); THREE LOVES HAS NANCY(1938); SERGEANT MADDEN(1939); TOM SAWYER, DETECTIVE(1939); CAROLINA MOON(1940); CHARTER PILOT(1940); FARMER'S DAUGHTER, THE(1940); GIVE US WINGS(1940); HOUSE ACROSS THE BAY, THE(1940); HOUSE OF THE SEVEN GABLES, THE(1940); SPORTING BLOOD(1940); LIFE WITH HENRY(1941); PITTSBURGH KID, THE(1941); THIEVES FALL OUT(1941); YOU'RE IN THE ARMY NOW(1941); AMERICAN EMPIRE(1942); GREAT MAN'S LADY, THE(1942); MONKEY(1942); FALSE FACES(1943); JOHNNY DOUGHBOY(1943); SON OF DRACULA(1943); THEY CAME TO BLOW UP AMERICA(1943); THEY GOT ME COVERED(1943); THIN MAN GOES HOME, THE(1944); WHAT A MAN!(1944); INCENDIARY BLONDE(1945)
George McDaniel
LEGACY(1976)
1984
LAST STARFIGHTER, THE(1984); THIS IS SPINAL TAP(1984)

Misc. Silents
HELL'S CRATER(1918); MAN FROM FUNERAL RANGE, THE(1918); UNCLAIMED GOODS(1918); IRON HEART, THE(1920); SHEPHERD OF THE HILLS, THE(1920); WHAT WOULD YOU DO?(1920); SILENT YEARS(1921); BAREFOOT BOY, THE(1923)

George A. McDaniel
Misc. Silents
SHE DEVIL, THE(1918)

Hattie McDaniel
BLONDE VENUS(1932); HELLO SISTER!(1933); I'M NO ANGEL(1933); STORY OF TEMPLE DRAKE, THE(1933); IMITATION OF LIFE(1934); JUDGE PRIEST(1934); OPERATOR 13(1934); ALICE ADAMS(1935); ANOTHER FACE(1935); CHINA SEAS(1935); HARMONY LANE(1935); LITTLE COLONEL, THE(1935); LITTLE MEN(1935); LOST IN THE STRATOSPHERE(1935); MURDER BY TELEVISION(1935); MUSIC IS MAGIC(1935); TRAVELING SALESLADY, THE(1935); BRIDE WALKS OUT, THE(1936); CAN THIS BE DIXIE?(1936); FIRST BABY(1936); GENTLE JULIA(1936); HEARTS DIVIDED(1936); HIGH TENSION(1936); LIBELED LADY(1936); NEXT TIME WE LOVE(1936); POSTAL INSPECTOR(1936); SHOW BOAT(1936); STAR FOR A NIGHT(1936); VALIANT IS THE WORD FOR CARRIE(1936); WE'RE ONLY HUMAN(1936); CRIME NOBOBY SAW, THE(1937); DON'T TELL THE WIFE(1937); NOTHING SACRED(1937); OVER THE GOAL(1937); RACING LADY(1937); SARATOGA(1937); TRUE CONFESSION(1937); 45 FATHERS(1937); BATTLE OF BROADWAY(1938); CAREFREE(1938); MAD MISS MANTON, THE(1938); QUICK MONEY(1938); SHINING HOUR, THE(1938); SHOPWORN ANGEL(1938); VIVACIOUS LADY(1938); EVERYBODY'S BABY(1939); GONE WITH THE WIND(1939); ZENOBIA(1939); MARYLAND(1940); AFFECTIONATELY YOURS(1941); GREAT LIE, THE(1941); GEORGE WASHINGTON SLEPT HERE(1942); IN THIS OUR LIFE(1942); MALE ANIMAL, THE(1942); THEY DIED WITH THEIR BOOTS ON(1942); JOHNNY COME LATELY(1943); THANK YOUR LUCKY STARS(1943); HI BEAUTIFUL(1944); JANIE(1944); SINCE YOU WENT AWAY(1944); 3 IS A FAMILY(1944); JANIE GETS MARRIED(1946); MARGIE(1946); NEVER SAY GOODBYE(1946); SONG OF THE SOUTH(1946); FAMILY HONEYMOON(1948); FLAME, THE(1948); MICKEY(1948)
Misc. Talkies
GOLD WEST, THE(1932)

Sam McDaniel
WITHOUT RESERVATIONS(1946); FREE SOUL, A(1931); PUBLIC ENEMY, THE(1931); GRAND HOTEL(1932); MOVIE CRAZY(1932); FOOTLIGHT PARADE(1933); LADY KILLER(1933); BELLE OF THE NINETIES(1934); EVELYN PRENTICE(1934); FASHIONS OF 1934(1934); HERE COMES THE NAVY(1934); LEMON DROP KID, THE(1934); MANHATTAN MELODRAMA(1934); OPERATOR 13(1934); TWENTY MILLION SWEETHEARTS(1934); WAGON WHEELS(1934); GEORGE WHITE'S 1935 SCANDALS(1935); LADY TUBBS(1935); UNWELCOME STRANGER(1935); WE'RE IN THE MONEY(1935); GORGEOUS HUSSY, THE(1936); HEARTS DIVIDED(1936); LOVE LETTERS OF A STAR(1936); POLO JOE(1936); RHYTHM ON THE RANGE(1936); CAPTAINS COURAGEOUS(1937); DARK MANHATTAN(1937); GIT ALONG, LITTLE DOGIES(1937); GO-GETTER, THE(1937); SINGING MARINE, THE(1937); JEZEBEL(1938); SERGEANT MURPHY(1938); STABLEMATES(1938); THREE LOVES HAS NANCY(1938); WOMEN ARE LIKE THAT(1938); FORGOTTEN WOMAN, THE(1939); GAMBLING SHIP(1939); GOOD GIRLS GO TO PARIS(1939); PRIDE OF THE BLUEGRASS(1939); SWEEPSTAKES WINNER(1939); THEY MADE ME A CRIMINAL(1939); UNION PACIFIC(1939); AM I GUILTY?(1940); CALLING ALL HUSBANDS(1940); HOWARDS OF VIRGINIA, THE(1940); MAN WHO TALKED TOO MUCH, THE(1940); TOO MANY HUSBANDS(1940); BAD MEN OF MISSOURI(1941); BROADWAY LIMITED(1941); GREAT AMERICAN BROADCAST, THE(1941); GREAT LIE, THE(1941); LOUISIANA PURCHASE(1941); NEW YORK TOWN(1941); SOUTH OF PANAMA(1941); VIRGINIA(1941); YOU BELONG TO ME(1941); ALL THROUGH THE NIGHT(1942); I WAS FRAMED(1942); IN THIS OUR LIFE(1942); MOKEY(1942); SILVER QUEEN(1942); THEY DIED WITH THEIR BOOTS ON(1942); TRAITOR WITHIN, THE(1942); DIXIE DUGAN(1943); GANGWAY FOR TOMORROW(1943); GHOST AND THE GUEST(1943); IRON MAJOR, THE(1943); SON OF DRACULA(1943); DOUBLE INDEMNITY(1944); EXPERIMENT PERILOUS(1944); HOME IN INDIANA(1944); MARRIAGE IS A PRIVATE AFFAIR(1944); THREE MEN IN WHITE(1944); WHEN STRANGERS MARRY(1944); COLONEL EFFINGHAM'S RAID(1945); GUY, A GAL AND A PAL, A(1945); LADY ON A TRAIN(1945); NAUGHTY NINETIES, THE(1945); SHE WOULDN'T SAY YES(1945); CENTENNIAL SUMMER(1946); DO YOU LOVE ME?(1946); JOE PALOOKA, CHAMP(1946); MY REPUTATION(1946); NEVER SAY GOODBYE(1946); EGG AND I, THE(1947); FOXES OF HARROW, THE(1947); HIGH BARBAREE(1947); I WONDER WHO'S KISSING HER NOW(1947); SECRET LIFE OF WALTER MITTY, THE(1947); HEART OF VIRGINIA(1948); RACE STREET(1948); SECRET SERVICE INVESTIGATOR(1948); FLAMINGO ROAD(1949); MA AND PA KETTLE(1949); FILE ON THELMA JORDAN, THE(1950); GIRLS' SCHOOL(1950); SOMETHING FOR THE BIRDS(1952); LION IS IN THE STREETS, A(1953); PRESIDENT'S LADY, THE(1953); GOOD MORNING, MISS DOVE(1955); MAN CALLED PETER, THE(1955); PARTY GIRL(1958); ICE PALACE(1960)
Misc. Talkies
BARGAIN WITH BULLETS(1937)

Sam "Deacon" McDaniel
ONCE IN A LIFETIME(1932); THREE LITTLE SISTERS(1944)

Samuel R. McDaniel
RENDEZVOUS(1935); STORMY(1935); STRANDED(1935)

Susan McDaniel
SILKWOOD(1983)

Earl McDaniels
HOT ROD GANG(1958)

Etta McDaniels
SMOKING GUNS(1934); HEARTS IN BONDAGE(1936); CRIME AFLOAT(1937)

Gene McDaniels
RING-A-DING RHYTHM(1962, Brit. 73m Amicus/COL bw (G.B: IT'S TRAD, DAD!); YOUNG SWINGERS, THE(1963)

George A. McDaniels
Misc. Silents
DOOR BETWEEN, THE(1917)

George McDaniels
Silents
SCRAPPER, THE(1922)
Misc. Silents
LOST MONEY(1919); PRETTY SMOOTH(1919); WOMAN UNDER COVER, THE(1919); TWO KINDS OF LOVE(1920)

Hattie McDaniels
GOLDEN WEST, THE(1932)

Sam McDaniels
OLD-FASHIONED WAY, THE(1934); CRACK-UP(1946)

John McDarby
TREASURE HUNT(1952, Brit.); YOU CAN'T BEAT THE IRISH(1952, Brit.)

Bob McDarra
OUTBACK(1971, Aus.)

Robert McDarra
27A(1974, Aus.)

Finlay McDermid
BOUNTY HUNTER, THE(1954), w

Marc McDermontt
Misc. Silents
BUCHANAN'S WIFE(1918)

Maureen McDermot
NOTORIOUS GENTLEMAN(1945, Brit.)

Betty McDermott
UNDER CAPRICORN(1949)

Brian McDermott
MR. PERRIN AND MR. TRAILL(1948, Brit.); PAYROLL(1962, Brit.); FIVE TO ONE(1963, Brit.); SINISTER MAN, THE(1965, Brit.); PRIEST OF LOVE(1981, Brit.); CROSSTALK(1982, Aus.)

Chris McDermott
PRIVATE SCHOOL(1983)

Edward McDermott
MAYBE IT'S LOVE(1930), ed; NIGHT NURSE(1931), ed; OTHER MEN'S WOMEN(1931), ed
Silents
PENROD AND SAM(1923), ed; DARING YOUTH(1924), ed; JOANNA(1925), ed; THANKS FOR THE BUGGY RIDE(1928), ed

Garry McDermott
LADY VANISHES, THE(1980, Brit.)

Hugh McDermott
CAPTAIN'S TABLE, THE(1936, Brit.); DAVID LIVINGSTONE(1936, Brit.); WELL DONE, HENRY(1936, Brit.); DIVORCE OF LADY X. THE(1938, Brit.); WIFE OF GENERAL LING, THE(1938, Brit.); SAINT IN LONDON, THE(1939, Brit.); WHERE'S THAT FIRE?(1939, Brit.); FOR FREEDOM(1940, Brit.); NEUTRAL PORT(1941, Brit.); SPRING MEETING(1941, Brit.); PIMPERNEL SMITH(1942, Brit.); YOUNG MR. PITT, THE(1942, Brit.); SEVENTH VEIL, THE(1946, Brit.); THIS MAN IS MINE(1946 Brit.); NO ORCHIDS FOR MISS BLANDISH(1948, Brit.); HUGGETTS ABROAD, THE(1949, Brit.); GOOD TIME GIRL(1950, Brit.); FOUR DAYS(1951, Brit.); LILLI MARLENE(1951, Brit.); SCHOOL FOR BRIDES(1952, Brit.); TRENT'S LAST CASE(1953, Brit.); WEDDING OF LILLI MARLENE, THE(1953, Brit.); DEVIL GIRL FROM MARS(1954, Brit.); FIRE OVER AFRICA(1954, Brit.); JOHNNY ON THE SPOT(1954, Brit.); LOVE LOTTERY, THE(1954, Brit.); NIGHT PEOPLE(1954); AS LONG AS THEY'RE HAPPY(1957, Brit.); YOU PAY YOUR MONEY(1957, Brit.); MAN WHO WOULDN'T TALK, THE(1958, Brit.); FIRST MEN IN THE MOON(1964, Brit.); GUNS IN THE HEATHER(1968, Brit.); ADDING MACHINE, THE(1969); FILE OF THE GOLDEN GOOSE, THE(1969, Brit.); GAMES, THE(1970); CAPTAIN APACHE(1971, Brit.); LAWMAN(1971); CHATO'S LAND(1972)

Jack McDermott
FINAL COUNTDOWN, THE(1980); ABSENCE OF MALICE(1981); FUNHOUSE, THE(1981); HARDLY WORKING(1981); SUPER FUZZ(1981)
Silents
IN THE DAYS OF SAINT PATRICK(1920, Brit.)

John McDermott
COHENS AND KELLYS IN SCOTLAND, THE(1930), a, w; COLLEGE RHYTHM(1934), w; THREE WISE FOOLS(1946), w
Silents
PATSY(1921), d&w; SKY PILOT, THE(1921), w; SPIDER AND THE ROSE, THE(1923), d; THREE WISE FOOLS(1923), w; ROLLING HOME(1926), w; EVENING CLOTHES(1927), w; SHE'S A SHEIK(1927), w; FIFTY-FIFTY GIRL, THE(1928), w; FLYING ROMEOS(1928), w
Misc. Silents
CHALICE OF SORROW, THE(1916); HER TEMPORARY HUSBAND(1923), d; MARY OF THE MOVIES(1923), d; MANHATTAN MADNESS(1925), d; WHERE THE WORST BEGINS(1925), d; LOVE THIEF, THE(1926), d

John W. McDermott
FAST WORKERS(1933), w

Keith McDermott
TOURIST TRAP, THE(1979); WITHOUT A TRACE(1983)

Loretta McDermott
Silents
LONG LIVE THE KING(1923)

Marc McDermott
Silents
KATHLEEN MAVOURNEEN(1919); AMAZING LOVERS(1921)
Misc. Silents
GIRL OF TODAY, THE(1918); SPANISH JADE(1922, Brit.)

Michael McDermott
STARTING OVER(1979)

Mickey McDermott
OPERATION BIKINI(1963)

Mo McDermott
1984
BIGGER SPLASH, A(1984)

Pat McDermott
FRENCH CONNECTION, THE(1971)

Patrick McDermott
JOE(1970)

Robert McDermott
WHO DONE IT?(1956, Brit.)

Rory McDermott
DARK ROAD, THE(1948, Brit.); MY SISTER AND I(1948, Brit.); SPARE THE ROD(1961, Brit.)

Russell McDermott
Misc. Silents
SADIE GOES TO HEAVEN(1917)

Terry McDermott
DIMBOOLA(1979, Aus.)
Misc. Talkies
COUNTRY TOWN(1971)
Tom McDermott
1984
OVER THE BROOKLYN BRIDGE(1984)
Jeffrey McDevitt
WHEN TIME RAN OUT(1980)
Ruth McDevitt
GUY WHO CAME BACK, THE(1951); PARENT TRAP, THE(1961); BOYS' NIGHT OUT(1962); BIRDS, THE(1963); LOVE IS A BALL(1963); DEAR HEART(1964); SHAKIEST GUN IN THE WEST, THE(1968); ANGEL IN MY POCKET(1969); CHANGE OF HABIT(1969); LOVE GOD?, THE(1969); WAR BETWEEN MEN AND WOMEN, THE(1972); HOMEBODIES(1974); MIXED COMPANY(1974)
Ian McDiarmid
AWAKENING, THE(1980); DRAGONSLAYER(1981); RICHARD'S THINGS(1981, Brit.); GORKY PARK(1983); RETURN OF THE JEDI(1983)
Fern McDill
TERROR OF TINY TOWN, THE(1938)
Mafra McDonagh
RISING OF THE MOON, THE(1957, Ireland)
Archer McDonald
SCANDAL AT SCOURIE(1953)
Arnold McDonald
JACK LONDON(1943), cos
Audrey McDonald
LA DOLCE VITA(1961, Ital./Fr.)
Belle McDonald
TERROR EYES(1981)
Beth McDonald
BELL JAR, THE(1979)
Beulah McDonald
LAST OUTPOST, THE(1935); TWO FOR TONIGHT(1935)
Bob McDonald
PSYCHOTRONIC MAN, THE(1980)
C. E. McDonald
Silents
INCORRIGIBLE DUKANE, THE(1915)
Cathy McDonald
BLACK TORMENT, THE(1965, Brit.)
Charles McDonald
Silents
SALVATION NELL(1921); LOYAL LIVES(1923)
Christopher McDonald
HEARSE, THE(1980); GREASE 2(1982)
1984
BLACK ROOM, THE(1984); BREAKIN'(1984); CHATTANOOGA CHOO CHOO(1984); WHERE THE BOYS ARE '84(1984)
Colt McDonald
DARING DANGER(1932), w
Country Joe McDonald
MORE AMERICAN GRAFFITI(1979)
Dan McDonald
CLASS OF '44(1973)
Daniel McDonald
1984
WHERE THE BOYS ARE '84(1984)
Dave McDonald
DAD AND DAVE COME TO TOWN(1938, Aus.)
David McDonald
STORY OF VERNON AND IRENE CASTLE, THE(1939); ONE BRIEF SUMMER(1971, Brit.), ph; HARDER THEY COME, THE(1973, Jamaica), ph; HORROR HOSPITAL(1973, Brit.), ph; SMILE ORANGE(1976, Jamaican), ph
Dawn McDonald
HALF A SIXPENCE(1967, Brit.)
Donald McDonald
BRASS LEGEND, THE(1956); GREAT DAY IN THE MORNING(1956)
1984
CONSTANCE(1984, New Zealand)
Misc. Silents
STRING BEANS(1918); YELLOW TYPHOON, THE(1920); BOOTLEGGER'S DAUGHTER, THE(1922)
Earl McDonald
CARNIVAL LADY(1933)
Edmund McDonald
BRIGHAM YOUNG–FRONTIERSMAN(1940); THEY MADE ME A KILLER(1946)
Edward J. McDonald
ESCAPE FROM ALCATRAZ(1979), set d
Frances McDonald
SHOTGUN(1955)
Silents
OUTLAWS OF RED RIVER(1927)
Francis McDonald
UNDER TWO FLAGS(1936); CARNATION KID(1929); GIRL OVERBOARD(1929); BURNING UP(1930); DANGEROUS PARADISE(1930); MOROCCO(1930); RUNAWAY BRIDE(1930); SAFETY IN NUMBERS(1930); GANG BUSTER, THE(1931); LAWYER'S SECRET, THE(1931); RULING VOICE, THE(1931); DEVIL IS DRIVING, THE(1932); HIDDEN VALLEY(1932); HONOR OF THE MOUNTED(1932); LAST MILE, THE(1932); TEXAS BUDDIES(1932); TRAILING THE KILLER(1932); WOMAN FROM MONTE CARLO, THE(1932); WORLD AND THE FLESH, THE(1932); BROADWAY BAD(1933); EVELYN PRENTICE(1934); GAY BRIDE, THE(1934); GIRL IN DANGER(1934); LINEUP, THE(1934); OPERATOR 13(1934); STRAIGHTAWAY(1934); SUCCESSFUL FAILURE, A(1934); TRUMPET BLOWS, THE(1934); VIVA VILLA!(1934); VOICE IN THE NIGHT(1934); CHEYENNE TORNADO(1935); LADIES CRAVE EXCITEMENT(1935); MISSISSIPPI(1935); RED MORNING(1935); STAR OF MIDNIGHT(1935); BIG BROWN EYES(1936); MUMMY'S BOYS(1936); PRISONER OF SHARK ISLAND, THE(1936); ROBIN HOOD OF EL DORADO(1936); BORN RECKLESS(1937); DEVIL'S PLAYGROUND(1937); LAST TRAIN FROM MADRID, THE(1937); LOVE UNDER FIRE(1937); PAROLE RACKET(1937); PLAINSMAN,

THE(1937); BUCCANEER, THE(1938); IF I WERE KING(1938); BAD LANDS(1939); BEAU GESTE(1939); IDIOT'S DELIGHT(1939); LIGHT THAT FAILED, THE(1939); RANGE WAR(1939); UNION PACIFIC(1939); DEVIL'S PIPELINE, THE(1940); GREEN HELL(1940); LONE WOLF KEEPS A DATE, THE(1940); NORTHWEST MOUNTED POLICE(1940); ONE NIGHT IN THE TROPICS(1940); SEA HAWK, THE(1940); STRANGE CARGO(1940); WYOMING(1940); KID FROM KANSAS, THE(1940); MEN OF THE TIMBERLAND(1941); SEA WOLF, THE(1941); GIRL FROM ALASKA(1942); VALLEY OF THE SUN(1942); BAR 20(1943); BUCKSKIN FRONTIER(1943); KANSAN, THE(1943); RHYTHM OF THE ISLANDS(1943); CHEYENNE WILDCAT(1944); LUMBERJACK(1944); MYSTERY MAN(1944); TEXAS MASQUERADE(1944); 'TILL WE MEET AGAIN(1944); BAD MEN OF THE BORDER(1945); CORPUS CHRISTI BANDITS(1945); GREAT STAGECOACH ROBBERY(1945); SOUTH OF THE RIO GRANDE(1945); STRANGE CONFESSION(1945); CANYON PASSAGE(1946); DEVIL'S PLAYGROUND, THE(1946); DUEL IN THE SUN(1946); INVISIBLE INFORMER(1946); MAGNIFICENT DOLL(1946); MY PAL TRIGGER(1946); NIGHT IN PARADISE, A(1946); NIGHT TRAIN TO MEMPHIS(1946); ROLL ON TEXAS MOON(1946); TANGIER(1946); THE CATMAN OF PARIS(1946); BRUTE FORCE(1947); DANGEROUS VENTURE(1947); PERILS OF PAULINE, THE(1947); SADDLE PALS(1947); SPOILERS OF THE NORTH(1947); UNCONQUERED(1947); ACT OF MURDER, AN(1948); BOLD FRONTIERSMAN, THE(1948); DEAD DON'T DREAM, THE(1948); PANHANDLE(1948); SON OF GOD'S COUNTRY(1948); THREE MUSKETEERS, THE(1948); APACHE CHIEF(1949); BROTHERS IN THE SADDLE(1949); DAUGHTER OF THE JUNGLE(1949); GAL WHO TOOK THE WEST, THE(1949); LADY GAMBLES, THE(1949); POWDER RIVER RUSTLERS(1949); RIM OF THE CANYON(1949); ROSE OF THE YUKON(1949); RUSTLERS(1949); SON OF A BAD MAN(1949); CALIFORNIA PASSAGE(1950); KIM(1950); GENE AUTRY AND THE MOUNTIES(1951); RED MOUNTAIN(1951); SANTA FE(1951); DESERT PASSAGE(1952); FORT OSAGE(1952); RANCHO NOTORIOUS(1952); STRANGER WORE A GUN, THE(1953); THREE HOURS TO KILL(1954); TEN WANTED MEN(1955); DIG THAT URANIUM(1956); RAW EDGE(1956); THUNDER OVER ARIZONA(1956); LAST STAGECOACH WEST, THE(1957); BIG FISHERMAN, THE(1959); GREAT RACE, THE(1965)
Misc. Talkies
MARRIAGE BARGAIN, THE(1935)
Silents
ANSWER, THE(1918); I LOVE YOU(1918); REAL FOLKS(1918); SOUTH SEA LOVE(1923); ARIZONA EXPRESS, THE(1924); EAST OF BROADWAY(1924); ANYTHING ONCE(1925); NORTHERN CODE(1925); BATTLING BUTLER(1926); DESERT'S TOLL, THE(1926); PUPPETS(1926); TEMPTRESS, THE(1926); YANKEE SENOR, THE(1926); NOTORIOUS LADY, THE(1927); DRAGNET, THE(1928); GIRL IN EVERY PORT, A(1928)
Misc. Silents
BLACK ORCHIDS(1917); GHOST FLOWER, THE(1918); GUN WOMAN, THE(1918); HAND AT THE WINDOW, THE(1918); PAINTED LILY, THE(1918); TONY AMERICA(1918); FINAL CLOSEUP, THE(1919); PRETTY SMOOTH(1919); PRUDENCE ON BROADWAY(1919); TOTON(1919); CONFESSION, THE(1920); KENTUCKY COLONEL, THE(1920); CALL OF THE NORTH, THE(1921); HEARTS AND MASKS(1921); PUPPETS OF FATE(1921); CAPTAIN FLY-BY-NIGHT(1922); TROOPER O'NEIL(1922); BUSTER, THE(1923); GOING UP(1923); MY LADY OF WHIMS(1925); VALLEY OF HELL, THE(1927); WRECK, THE(1927)
Francis J. McDonald
TERROR TRAIL(1933); PALEFACE, THE(1948); SAMSON AND DELILAH(1949); BANDITS OF CORSICA, THE(1953); TEN COMMANDMENTS, THE(1956); DUEL AT APACHE WELLS(1957); PAWNEE(1957); FORT MASSACRE(1958)
Silents
NOMADS OF THE NORTH(1920)
Misc. Silents
HIS DEBT(1919)
Frank McDonald
BROADWAY HOSTESS(1935), d; CEILNG ZERO(1935); BOULDER DAM(1936), d; ISLE OF FURY(1936), d; LOVE BEGINS AT TWENTY(1936), d; MURDER BY AN ARISTOCRAT(1936), d; MURDER OF DR. HARRIGAN, THE(1936), d; TREACHERY RIDES THE RANGE(1936), d; ADVENTUROUS BLONDE(1937), d; DANCE, CHARLIE, DANCE(1937), d; FLY-AWAY BABY(1937), d; HER HUSBAND'S SECRETARY(1937), d; MIDNIGHT COURT(1937), d; SMART BLONDE(1937), d; BLONDES AT WORK(1938), d; FLIRTING WITH FATE(1938), d; FRESHMAN YEAR(1938), d; OVER THE WALL(1938), d; RECKLESS LIVING(1938), d; DEATH GOES NORTH(1939), d; FIRST OFFENDERS(1939), d; JEEPERS CREEPERS(1939), d; THEY ASKED FOR IT(1939), d; CAROLINA MOON(1940), d; FORGOTTEN GIRLS(1940), w; GAUCHO SERENADE(1940), d; GRAND OLE OPRY(1940), d; IN OLD MISSOURI(1940), d; RANCHO GRANDE(1940), d; RIDE, TENDERFOOT, RIDE(1940), d; VILLAGE BARN DANCE(1940), d; ARKANSAS JUDGE(1941), d; COUNTRY FAIR(1941), d; FLYING BLIND(1941), d; NO HANDS ON THE CLOCK(1941), d; TUXEDO JUNCTION(1941), d; UNDER FIESTA STARS(1941), d; MOUNTAIN RHYTHM(1942), d; SHEPHERD OF THE OZARKS(1942), d; TRAITOR WITHIN, THE(1942), d; WILDCAT(1942), d; WRECKING CREW(1942), d; ALASKA HIGHWAY(1943), d; HIGH EXPLOSIVE(1943), d; HOOSIER HOLIDAY(1943), d; O, MY DARLING CLEMENTINE(1943), d; SUBMARINE ALERT(1943), d; SWING YOUR PARTNER(1943), d; GAMBLER'S CHOICE(1944), d; LIGHTS OF OLD SANTA FE(1944), d; ONE BODY TOO MANY(1944), d; SING, NEIGHBOR, SING(1944), d; TAKE IT BIG(1944), d; TIMBER QUEEN(1944), d; ALONG THE NAVAJO TRAIL(1945), d; BELLS OF ROSARITA(1945), d; CHICAGO KID, THE(1945), d; MAN FROM OKLAHOMA, THE(1945), d; SCARED STIFF(1945), d; SUNSET IN EL DORADO(1945), d; TELL IT TO A STAR(1945), d; MY PAL TRIGGER(1946), d; NOTORIOUS(1946); RAINBOW OVER TEXAS(1946), d; SIOUX CITY SUE(1946), d; SONG OF ARIZONA(1946), d; UNDER NEVADA SKIES(1946), d; HIT PARADE OF 1947(1947), p&d; LINDA BE GOOD(1947), d; TWILIGHT ON THE RIO GRANDE(1947), d; WHEN A GIRL'S BEAUTIFUL(1947), d; FRENCH LEAVE(1948), d; GUN SMUGGLERS(1948), d; MR. RECKLESS(1948), d; THIRTEEN LEAD SOLDIERS(1948), d; BIG SOMBRERO(1949), d; RINGSIDE(1949), d; CALL OF THE KLONDIKE(1950), d; SNOW DOG(1950), d; FATHER TAKES THE AIR(1951), d; SIERRA PASSAGE(1951), d; TEXANS NEVER CRY(1951), d; YELLOW FIN(1951), d; YUKON MANHUNT(1951), d; NORTHWEST TERRITORY(1952), d; SEA TIGER(1952), d; YUKON GOLD(1952), d; SON OF BELLE STARR(1953), d; SECURITY RISK(1954), w; THUNDER PASS(1954), d; BIG TIP OFF, THE(1955), d; TREASURE OF RUBY HILLS(1955), d; PURPLE GANG, THE(1960), d; RAYMIE(1960), d; UNDERWATER CITY, THE(1962), d; GUNFIGHT AT COMANCHE CREEK(1964), d; MARA OF THE WILDERNESS(1966), d; GREAT TRAIN ROBBERY, THE(1979, Brit.); SCALPS(1983)

Misc. Talkies
BULLDOG DRUMMOND STRIKES BACK(1947), d; GHOST OF CROSSBONES CANYON, THE(1952), d; YELLOW HAIRED KID, THE(1952), d; SECRET OF OUT- LAW FLATS(1953), d; SIX-GUN DECISION(1953), d; MARSHALS IN DIS- GUISE(1954), d; OUTLAW'S SON(1954), d; TROUBLE ON THE TRAIL(1954), d
Misc. Silents
DEVIL AT HIS ELBOW, THE(1916)
Fred McDonald
SQUATTER'S DAUGHTER(1933, Aus.); GRANDAD RUDD(1935, Aus.)
Garry McDonald
STONE(1974, Aus.); PICNIC AT HANGING ROCK(1975, Aus.); PICTURE SHOW MAN, THE(1980, Aus.); PIRATE MOVIE, THE(1982, Aus.)
1984
SECOND TIME LUCKY(1984, Aus./New Zealand), m
George McDonald
SHINE ON, HARVEST MOON(1944); CHILD OF DIVORCE(1946); EGG AND I, THE(1947); FOUR FACES WEST(1948); LEAVE IT TO HENRY(1949); MA AND PA KETTLE(1949); TRAVELING SALESWOMAN(1950); IT'S A BIG COUNTRY(1951); TOO YOUNG TO KISS(1951)
Gordon McDonald
THIRTY SECONDS OVER TOKYO(1944)
Grace McDonald
DANCING ON A DIME(1940); BEHIND THE EIGHT BALL(1942); GIVE OUT, SISTERS(1942); STRICTLY IN THE GROOVE(1942); WHAT'S COOKIN'?(1942); AL- WAYS A BRIDESMAID(1943); FLESH AND FANTASY(1943); GALS, INCORPORAT- ED(1943); GET GOING(1943); GUNG HO!(1943); HOW'S ABOUT IT?(1943); IT AIN'T HAY(1943); MUG TOWN(1943); SHE'S FOR ME(1943); DESTINY(1944); FOLLOW THE BOYS(1944); HAT CHECK HONEY(1944); MURDER IN THE BLUE ROOM(1944); MY GAL LOVES MUSIC(1944); HONEYMOON AHEAD(1945); SEE MY LAWYER(1945)
Gregory McDonald
1984
FLETCH(1984), w
Hattie McDonald
REUNION(1936)
Hazel Christie McDonald
Silents
AFTER THE SHOW(1921), w
Helen McDonald
Misc. Silents
RECKLESS WIVES(1921)
Hoima McDonald
OLD DRACULA(1975, Brit.)
Ian McDonald
SECRETS OF THE WASTELANDS(1941); SWAMP WOMAN(1941); RAMROD(1947); PORT SAID(1948); SHAGGY(1948); SPEED TO SPARE(1948)
J. Farrell McDonald
RIVER'S END(1931); SPIRIT OF NOTRE DAME, THE(1931); PHANTOM EXPRESS, THE(1932); SUBMARINE PATROL(1938); RIDERS OF THE TIMBERLINE(1941); BEAUTIFUL BLONDE FROM BASHFUL BEND, THE(1949)
Misc. Silents
GERALD CRANSTON'S LADY(1924); PAID TO LOVE(1927); RICH BUT HO- NEST(1927)
Jack McDonald
GIRL IN THE SHOW, THE(1929); SHOW BOAT(1929); SHIP FROM SHANGHAI, THE(1930)
Silents
SPOILERS, THE(1914); LAST OF THE MOHICANS, THE(1920); BAIT, THE(1921); BIG PUNCH, THE(1921); SINGING RIVER(1921); CALIFORNIA ROMANCE, A(1922); AGAINST ALL ODDS(1924); CHAMPION OF LOST CAUSES(1925); GREED(1925); LORNA DOONE(1927); 13 WASHINGTON SQUARE(1928)
Misc. Silents
HIS MAJESTY BUNKER BEAN(1918); GREAT REDEEMER, THE(1920); WESTERN SPEED(1922); CIRCUS COWBOY, THE(1924); FLAME OF THE YUKON, THE(1926)
Jack "Sockeye" McDonald
ALIAS THE CHAMP(1949)
Jesse McDonald
PUTNEY SWOPE(1969)
Jim McDonald
NAKED WORLD OF HARRISON MARKS, THE(1967, Brit.), w
Joe McDonald
INVITATION TO A GUNFIGHTER(1964), ph
John McDonald
COME BACK BABY(1968)
Joseph McDonald
ROMANCE OF THE RIO GRANDE(1941)
Kate McDonald
IMPROPER CHANNELS(1981, Can.)
Ken McDonald
CORNERED(1945); SWORD OF MONTE CRISTO, THE(1951)
Kenneth McDonald
GOOD DAME(1934); BEFORE I HANG(1940); ISLAND OF DOOMED MEN(1940); PRAIRIE PIONEERS(1941); BACK TO BATAAN(1945); CROSSFIRE(1947); RETURN OF THE BADMEN(1948); ARCTIC FLIGHT(1952); PHANTOM OF THE JUNGLE(1955)
Silents
DYNAMITE DAN(1924); IN HIGH GEAR(1924); PRIDE OF SUNSHINE AL- LEY(1924); LAW OF THE SNOW COUNTRY, THE(1926); AVENGING FANGS(1927)
Misc. Silents
SLOW AS LIGHTING(1923); WHAT LOVE WILL DO(1923); LOST TRIBE, THE(1924), d; SOUTH OF THE EQUATOR(1924); YANKEE SPEED(1924); BATTLER, THE(1925); COAST PATROL, THE(1925); DANGER ZONE, THE(1925); HE WHO LAUGHS LAST(1925); JUST PLAIN FOLKS(1925); MAKERS OF MEN(1925); SPEED DEMON, THE(1925); ROARING ROAD(1926); SHADOWS OF CHINATOWN(1926); SUNSHINE OF PARADISE ALLEY(1926); LITTLE BUCKAROO, THE(1928)
Kim McDonald
Misc. Talkies
JOHNSTOWN MONSTER, THE(1971)
Len McDonald
FAR COUNTRY, THE(1955)

Lisa McDonald
RIGHT HAND OF THE DEVIL, THE(1963)
Lorena McDonald
HIDE IN PLAIN SIGHT(1980)
Mac McDonald
1984
ELECTRIC DREAMS(1984)
Marie McDonald
IT STARTED WITH EVE(1941); LUCKY JORDAN(1942); PARDON MY SA- RONG(1942); RIDING HIGH(1943); SCREAM IN THE DARK, A(1943); TOR- NADO(1943); GUEST IN THE HOUSE(1944); I LOVE A SOLDIER(1944); OUR HEARTS WERE YOUNG AND GAY(1944); STANDING ROOM ONLY(1944); GETTING GER- TIE'S GARTER(1945); IT'S A PLEASURE(1945); LIVING IN A BIG WAY(1947); TELL IT TO THE JUDGE(1949); HIT PARADE OF 1951(1950); ONCE A THIEF(1950); GEISHA BOY, THE(1958); PROMISES, PROMISES(1963)
Mark McDonald
ON THE BUSES(1972, Brit.), ph; KADOYNG(1974, Brit.), ph
Martin McDonald
Misc. Talkies
ELECTRIC CHAIR, THE(1977)
Mary Ann McDonald
LOVE AT FIRST SIGHT(1977, Can.)
Mary Monica McDonald
BEAUTIFUL BLONDE FROM BASHFUL BEND, THE(1949)
Norman McDonald
Misc. Silents
GREAT GAY ROAD, THE(1920, Brit.), d
Pat McDonald
NO. 96(1974, Aus.)
Patricia McDonald
LITTLE AUSTRALIANS(1940, Aus.)
Patty McDonald
X-15(1961)
Philip McDonald
WHISPERING GHOSTS(1942), w; NORA PRENTISS(1947), w
Ray McDonald
BABES ON BROADWAY(1941); DOWN IN SAN DIEGO(1941); LIFE BEGINS FOR ANDY HARDY(1941); BORN TO SING(1942); PRESENTING LILY MARS(1943); TILL THE CLOUDS ROLL BY(1946); GOOD NEWS(1947); WHIPLASH(1948); FLAME OF YOUTH(1949); SHAMROCK HILL(1949); THERE'S A GIRL IN MY HEART(1949); ALL ASHORE(1953); BOOK OF NUMBERS(1973)
Robert J. McDonald
ADVENTURES OF MARTIN EDEN, THE(1942)
Ronald McDonald
JEDDA, THE UNCIVILIZED(1956, Aus.), art d
Rory McDonald
11 HARROWHOUSE(1974, Brit.)
Rufus L. McDonald
HERE COME THE GIRLS(1953)
Sam McDonald
RICH ARE ALWAYS WITH US, THE(1932)
Sandy McDonald
DUTCHMAN(1966, Brit.)
Sherwood McDonald
Silents
SOLD AT AUCTION(1917), d
Misc. Silents
LITTLE MISS GROWN-UP(1918), d; MISS MISCHIEF MAKER(1918), d; NO CHIL- DREN WANTED(1918), d
Shirley McDonald
CROSSROADS(1942)
Susan McDonald
CANNONBALL RUN, THE(1981); KING OF THE MOUNTAIN(1981)
Tanny McDonald
HERCULES IN NEW YORK(1970)
Tom McDonald
1001 ARABIAN NIGHTS(1959), d; MR. MAGOO'S HOLIDAY FESTIVAL(1970), anim
Tommy McDonald
DESTRUCTORS, THE(1968)
Treat McDonald
1984
MAKING THE GRADE(1984)
Wallace McDonald
MADAME SATAN(1930); ROGUE SONG, THE(1930); ARM OF THE LAW(1932); DARING DANGER(1932); HEARTS IN BONDAGE(1936), w; VENUS MAKES TROU- BLE(1937), p; FACE BEHIND THE MASK, THE(1941), p; LUCKY LEGS(1942), p; SHE'S A SOLDIER TOO(1944), p; EVE KNEW HER APPLES(1945), p; AMBUSH AT TOMAHAWK GAP(1953), p
Misc. Silents
PRINCESS' NECKLACE, THE(1917); CUPID FORECLOSES(1919); GIRL NAMED MARY, A(1920); HEIR-LOONS(1925); LADY, THE(1925); HELL'S 400(1926); RED SIGNALS(1927); TROPICAL NIGHTS(1928)
Watkins McDonald
SWEET KITTY BELLAIRS(1930), ph
Wilfred McDonald
Misc. Silents
SON OF ERIN, A(1916)
William McDonald
TERROR EYES(1981)
Silents
TWINKLETOES(1926)
William Colt McDonald
OVERLAND STAGE RAIDERS(1938), w
William H. McDonald
POSTMAN ALWAYS RINGS TWICE, THE(1981)
Fergus McDonell
WAY AHEAD, THE(1945, Brit.), ed; GUEST, THE(1963, Brit.), ed; NIGHT MUST FALL(1964, Brit.), ed; NOTHING BUT THE BEST(1964, Brit.), ed; WHAT'S NEW, PUSSYCAT?(1965, U.S./Fr.), ed; KHARTOUM(1966, Brit.), ed; CHARLIE BUB- BLES(1968, Brit.), ed; HERE WE GO ROUND THE MULBERRY BUSH(1968, Brit.), ed;

ONLY WHEN I LARF(1968, Brit.), ed; SPRING AND PORT WINE(1970, Brit.), ed; STATUE, THE(1971, Brit.), ed; UNMAN, WITTERING AND ZIGO(1971, Brit.), ed; GUMSHOE(1972, Brit.), ed
Col. G.L. McDonell
ILLUSION(1929); PRINCE OF DIAMONDS(1930)
Gordon McDonell
THEY WON'T BELIEVE ME(1947), w; STEP DOWN TO TERROR(1958), w; EXECUTIONER, THE(1970, Brit.), w
Margaret McDonell
TICKET OF LEAVE(1936, Brit.), w
Fergus McDonnel
ON APPROVAL(1944, Brit.), ed; PRIVATE INFORMATION(1952, Brit.), d
Arch McDonnell
ONE PLUS ONE(1961, Can.); LUCK OF GINGER COFFEY, THE(1964, U.S./Can.); HOMER(1970)
Babe McDonnell
Misc. Talkies
NOT TONIGHT HENRY(1961)
Claude McDonnell
CHINESE BUNGALOW, THE(1930, Brit.), ph
Silents
EASY VIRTUE(1927, Brit.), ph; WHEN BOYS LEAVE HOME(1928, Brit.), ph
Craig McDonnell
1984
HOLLYWOOD HOT TUBS(1984), w
Ed T. McDonnell
OUTLAWS IS COMING, THE(1965)
Fergus McDonnell
JOHNNY IN THE CLOUDS(1945, Brit.), ed; ODD MAN OUT(1947, Brit.), ed; HIDEOUT(1948, Brit.), d; PRELUDE TO FAME(1950, Brit.), d; SOME PEOPLE(1964, Brit.), ed; FOUR IN THE MORNING(1965, Brit.), ed; ALFRED THE GREAT(1969, Brit.), ed
Col. G. L. McDonnell
DR. JEKYLL AND MR. HYDE(1932)
Silents
WHITE BLACK SHEEP, THE(1926)
Gordon McDonnell
HIS LORDSHIP GOES TO PRESS(1939, Brit.), w; SHADOW OF A DOUBT(1943), w
Jeanne McDonnell
LIANNA(1983), art d
Jo McDonnell
ISLAND CLAWS(1981)
Margaret McDonnell
BORROW A MILLION(1934, Brit.), w; SECRET VOICE, THE(1936, Brit.), w; HIS LORDSHIP GOES TO PRESS(1939, Brit.), w
Mary McDonnell
1984
GARBO TALKS(1984)
Renee McDonnell
DEAD AND BURIED(1981)
Terrence McDonnell
MISSION GALACTICA: THE CYLON ATTACK(1979), w
Betty McDonough
SENORITA FROM THE WEST(1945); MA AND PA KETTLE AT HOME(1954)
Britt McDonough
1984
ALIEN FACTOR, THE(1984), ph
Edwin J. McDonough
IT'S MY TURN(1980)
Edwin McDonough
HANKY-PANKY(1982)
Eileen McDonough
HOW TO SEDUCE A WOMAN(1974)
Joe A. McDonough
PIRATES OF THE SKIES(1939), d
Mary McDonough
MORTUARY(1983)
Tom McDonough
HOUSE ON TELEGRAPH HILL(1951); CITY OF BAD MEN(1953); WOMAN THEY ALMOST LYNCHED, THE(1953); GOSPEL ROAD, THE(1973), ph
Frances McDormand
1984
BLOOD SIMPLE(1984)
Dolores McDougal
LIGHT FANTASTIC(1964)
Sandy McDougal
SEZ O'REILLY TO MACNAB(1938, Brit.)
Donald McDougall
HOT CARS(1956), d
Gordon McDougall
NED KELLY(1970, Brit.); NO. 96(1974, Aus.); KILLING OF ANGEL STREET, THE(1983, Aus.)
Ranald McDougall
SUBTERRANEANS, THE(1960), d
Rex McDougall
Misc. Silents
PLEASE HELP EMILY(1917); DAUGHTER OF THE OLD SOUTH, A(1918); MY WIFE(1918); BARGAIN, THE(1921, Brit.); HOUND OF THE BASKERVILLES, THE(1921, Brit.); GIPSY CAVALIER, A(1922, Brit.); KNIGHT ERRANT, THE(1922, Brit.)
John McDouglas [Giuseppe Addobbati]
NIGHTMARE CASTLE(1966, Ital.)
Roddy McDowald
DIRTY MARY, CRAZY LARRY(1974)
Betty McDowall
PICKUP ALLEY(1957, Brit.); DIAMOND SAFARI(1958); JACK THE RIPPER(1959, Brit.); TIME LOCK(1959, Brit.); DEAD LUCKY(1960, Brit.); SPARE THE ROD(1961, Brit.); ECHO OF DIANA(1963, Brit.); FIRST MEN IN THE MOON(1964, Brit.); TOMORROW AT TEN(1964, Brit.); LIQUIDATOR, THE(1966, Brit.)

Claire McDowall
YOUNG DESIRE(1930); MIRACLES FOR SALE(1939)
Roddy McDowall
I SEE ICE(1938); JOHN HALIFAX–GENTLEMAN(1938, Brit.); MURDER IN THE FAMILY(1938, Brit.); SCRUFFY(1938, Brit.); YELLOW SANDS(1938, Brit.); DEAD MAN'S SHOES(1939, Brit.); MURDER WILL OUT(1939, Brit.); OUTSIDER, THE(1940, Brit.); SALOON BAR(1940, Brit.); CONFIRM OR DENY(1941); HOW GREEN WAS MY VALLEY(1941); MAN HUNT(1941); POISON PEN(1941, Brit.); THIS ENGLAND(1941, Brit.); YOU WILL REMEMBER(1941, Brit.); ON THE SUNNY SIDE(1942); PIED PIPER, THE(1942); SON OF FURY(1942); LASSIE, COME HOME(1943); MY FRIEND FLICKA(1943); KEYS OF THE KINGDOM, THE(1944); WHITE CLIFFS OF DOVER, THE(1944); MOLLY AND ME(1945); THUNDERHEAD-SON OF FLICKA(1945); HOLIDAY IN MEXICO(1946); KIDNAPPED(1948); MACBETH(1948); ROCKY(1948); BLACK MIDNIGHT(1949); TUNA CLIPPER(1949); BIG TIMBER(1950); EVERYBODY'S DANCIN'(1950); KILLER SHARK(1950); STEEL FIST, THE(1952); MIDNIGHT LACE(1960); SUBTERRANEANS, THE(1960); LONGEST DAY, THE(1962); CLEOPATRA(1963); SHOCK TREATMENT(1964); GREATEST STORY EVER TOLD, THE(1965); INSIDE DAISY CLOVER(1965); LOVED ONE, THE(1965); THAT DARN CAT(1965); THIRD DAY, THE(1965); DEFECTOR, THE(1966, Ger./Fr.); LORD LOVE A DUCK(1966); ADVENTURES OF BULLWHIP GRIFFIN, THE(1967); COOL ONES THE(1967); IT!(1967, Brit.); FIVE CARD STUD(1968); PLANET OF THE APES(1968); ANGEL, ANGEL, DOWN WE GO(1969); HELLO DOWN THERE(1969); MIDAS RUN(1969); BEDKNOBS AND BROOMSTICKS(1971); ESCAPE FROM THE PLANET OF THE APES(1971); PRETTY MAIDS ALL IN A ROW(1971); CONQUEST OF THE PLANET OF THE APES(1972, Brit.), d; DEVIL'S WIDOW, THE(1972, Brit.), d; LIFE AND TIMES OF JUDGE ROY BEAN, THE(1972); POSEIDON ADVENTURE, THE(1972); ARNOLD(1973); BATTLE FOR THE PLANET OF THE APES(1973); LEGEND OF HELL HOUSE, THE(1973, Brit.); FUNNY LADY(1975); EMBRYO(1976); MEAN JOHNNY BARROWS(1976); SIXTH AND MAIN(1977); CAT FROM OUTER SPACE, THE(1978); LASERBLAST(1978); RABBIT TEST(1978); CIRCLE OF IRON(1979, Brit.); NUTCRACKER FANTASY(1979); SCAVENGER HUNT(1979); CHARLIE CHAN AND THE CURSE OF THE DRAGON QUEEN(1981); CLASS OF 1984(1982, Can.); EVIL UNDER THE SUN(1982, Brit.)
Misc. Talkies
CRICKET OF THE HEARTH, THE(1968)
Virginia McDowall
MAN HUNT(1941); THIS ABOVE ALL(1942); NATIONAL VELVET(1944); FAN, THE(1949)
Winefried McDowall
KIDNAPPED(1948)
Allen McDowell
GEORGE WASHINGTON CARVER(1940), p
Betty McDowell
ALWAYS ANOTHER DAWN(1948, Aus.); JACKPOT(1960, Brit.); SHE DIDN'T SAY NO!(1962, Brit.); BLUES FOR LOVERS(1966, Brit.)
Buddy McDowell
SQUARE DANCE JUBILEE(1949)
Claire McDowell
MARRIAGE BY CONTRACT(1928); FOUR DEVILS(1929); BIG HOUSE, THE(1930); BROTHERS(1930); MOTHERS CRY(1930); REDEMPTION(1930); SECOND FLOOR MYSTERY, THE(1930); WILD COMPANY(1930); AMERICAN TRAGEDY, AN(1931); MANHATTAN PARADE(1931); CORNERED(1932); PHANTOM EXPRESS, THE(1932); REBECCA OF SUNNYBROOK FARM(1932); STRANGE LOVE OF MOLLY LOUVAIN, THE(1932); BY APPOINTMENT ONLY(1933); CENTRAL AIRPORT(1933); PADDY, THE NEXT BEST THING(1933); WILD BOYS OF THE ROAD(1933); WORKING MAN, THE(1933); IMITATION OF LIFE(1934); IT HAPPENED ONE NIGHT(1934); JOURNAL OF A CRIME(1934); TWO HEADS ON A PILLOW(1934); MURDER BY TELEVISION(1935); AUGUST WEEK-END(1936, Brit.); SMALL TOWN GIRL(1936); HIGH, WIDE AND HANDSOME(1937); TWO-FISTED SHERIFF(1937); THREE COMRADES(1938); IDIOT'S DELIGHT(1939); STAND UP AND FIGHT(1939); THUNDER AFLOAT(1939); LADY SCARFACE(1941); REAP THE WILD WIND(1942); BLACK MARKET RUSTLERS(1943); YOUNGEST PROFESSION, THE(1943); ARE THESE OUR PARENTS?(1944); ADVENTURE(1945)
Misc. Talkies
AFRICAN INCIDENT(1934)
Silents
MAN ABOVE THE LAW(1918); FOLLIES GIRL, THE(1919); JACK KNIFE MAN, THE(1920); MARK OF ZORRO(1920); MIDSUMMER MADNESS(1920); SOMETHING TO THINK ABOUT(1920); CHICKENS(1921); PRISONERS OF LOVE(1921); WEALTH(1921); WHAT EVERY WOMAN KNOWS(1921); LYING TRUTH, THE(1922); NICE PEOPLE(1922); PENROD(1922); RAGGED HEIRESS, THE(1922); ASHES OF VENGEANCE(1923); CIRCUS DAYS(1923); ENEMIES OF CHILDREN(1923); JUDGMENT OF THE STORM(1924); BEN-HUR(1925); BIG PARADE, THE(1925); ONE OF THE BRAVEST(1925); RECKLESS SEX, THE(1925); TOWER OF LIES, THE(1925); AUCTIONEER, THE(1927); CHEATERS(1927); LITTLE JOURNEY, A(1927); SHIELD OF HONOR, THE(1927); TAXI DANCER, THE(1927); TILLIE THE TOILER(1927); DON'T MARRY(1928); TRAGEDY OF YOUTH, THE(1928); SILKS AND SADDLES(1929)
Misc. Silents
MIXED BLOOD(1916); STRANGER FROM SOMEWHERE, A(1916); BRONZE BRIDE, THE(1917); FIGHTING BACK(1917); GATES OF DOOM(1917); RIGHT TO BE HAPPY, THE(1917); SHIP OF DOOM, THE(1917); CAPTAIN OF HIS SOUL(1918); RETURN OF MARY, THE(1918); FEUD, THE(1919); HEART O' THE HILLS(1919); BLIND YOUTH(1920); THRU THE EYES OF MEN(1920); WOMAN IN THE SUITCASE, THE(1920); HEART'S HAVEN(1922); IN THE NAME OF THE LAW(1922); WESTBOUND LIMITED, THE(1923); FIGHT FOR HONOR, A(1924); LEAVE IT TO GERRY(1924); THOSE WHO DARE(1924); WAKING UP THE TOWN(1925); DIXIE MERCHANT, THE(1926); UNKNOWN SOLDIER, THE(1926); ALMOST HUMAN(1927); BLACK DIAMOND EXPRESS, THE(1927); WHEN DREAMS COME TRUE(1929)
Fred McDowell
BLOOD ALLEY(1955), ed; SLIM CARTER(1957), ed
J. N. McDowell
Silents
CUPID BY PROXY(1918)
J.B. McDowell
Misc. Silents
LOVES AND ADVENTURES IN THE LIFE OF SHAKESPEARE(1914, Brit.), d

John Herbert McDowell
MURDER A LA MOD(1968), m; WEDDING PARTY, THE(1969), m
Malcolm McDowell
IF ...(1968, Brit.); POOR COW(1968, Brit.); FIGURES IN A LANDSCAPE(1970, Brit.); CLOCKWORK ORANGE, A(1971, Brit.); LONG AGO, TOMORROW(1971, Brit.); O LUCKY MAN!(1973, Brit.); ROYAL FLASH(1975, Brit.); VOYAGE OF THE DAMNED(1976, Brit.); ACES HIGH(1977, Brit.); PASSAGE, THE(1979, Brit.); TIME AFTER TIME(1979, Brit.); BRITTANIA HOSPITAL(1982, Brit.); CAT PEOPLE(1982); BLUE THUNDER(1983); CROSS CREEK(1983); GET CRAZY(1983)
Melbourne McDowell
Silents
KING SPRUCE(1920); NOMADS OF THE NORTH(1920)
Misc. Silents
BOND OF FEAR, THE(1917); FLAME OF THE YUKON, THE(1917); HELL HATH NO FURY(1917); THEY'RE OFF(1917); CLAWS OF THE HUN, THE(1918); COALS OF FIRE(1918); THOSE WHO PAY(1918); TYRANT FEAR(1918); WOLVES OF THE RAIL(1918); BOOMERANG, THE(1919); EVE IN EXILE(1919); LAMB AND THE LION, THE(1919); MODERN HUSBANDS(1919); SOLDIERS OF FORTUNE(1919); GIFT SUPREME, THE(1920); IRON HEART, THE(1920); NOBODY'S GIRL(1920)
Melvin McDowell
Misc. Silents
WINNING WALLOP, THE(1926)
Nelson McDowell
WELCOME DANGER(1929); LAW OF THE RIO GRANDE(1931); TEXAS RANGER, THE(1931); LAW AND ORDER(1932); MASON OF THE MOUNTED(1932); SCARLET BRAND(1932); COME ON TARZAN(1933); OLIVER TWIST(1933); PHANTOM THUNDERBOLT, THE(1933); RUSTLERS' ROUNDUP(1933); FEROCIOUS PAL(1934); FIGHTING HERO(1934); HONOR OF THE RANGE(1934); WHEELS OF DESTINY(1934); DAWN RIDER(1935); FIGHTING TROOPER, THE(1935); HANDS ACROSS THE TABLE(1935); POWDERSMOKE RANGE(1935); WESTERN FRONTIER(1935); WILDERNESS MAIL(1935); FAST BULLETS(1936); FEUD OF THE WEST(1936); GIRL OF THE OZARKS(1936); GUN SMOKE(1936); LUCKY TERROR(1936); RIDE, RANGER, RIDE(1936); WHITE ANGEL, THE(1936); DESERT PHANTOM(1937); HEART OF THE ROCKIES(1937); TOAST OF NEW YORK, THE(1937); SANTA FE STAMPEDE(1938); MAN FROM TEXAS, THE(1939); RIDERS OF THE FRONTIER(1939); ROLL, WAGONS, ROLL(1939); CHAD HANNA(1940); HOUSE OF THE SEVEN GABLES, THE(1940); PIONEER DAYS(1940); RETURN OF FRANK JAMES, THE(1940); RIDERS FROM NOWHERE(1940); WESTBOUND STAGE(1940); LONE TEXAS RANGER(1945)
Misc. Talkies
RAWHIDE MAIL(1934); TERROR OF THE PLAINS(1934); BORN TO BATTLE(1935); TEXAS JACK(1935); SANTA FE RIDES(1937)
Silents
LAST OF THE MOHICANS, THE(1920); RIDERS OF THE DAWN(1920); HOME STUFF(1921); SHADOWS OF CONSCIENCE(1921); SILENT CALL, THE(1921); OLIVER TWIST(1922); GIRL OF THE GOLDEN WEST, THE(1923); SCARAMOUCHE(1923); GALLOPING GALLAGHER(1924); RAINBOW RANGERS(1924); ON THE GO(1925); LIGHTNING REPORTER(1926); VALLEY OF BRAVERY, THE(1926); WHISPERING SMITH(1926); CODE OF THE RANGE(1927); GREAT MAIL ROBBERY, THE(1927); HEART TROUBLE(1928); KIT CARSON(1928); GRIT WINS(1929); WILD BLOOD(1929)
Misc. Silents
BLOOD TEST(1923); STREAK OF LUCK, A(1925); BLIND TRAIL(1926); BORDER BLACKBIRDS(1927); HANDS OFF(1927); LITTLE SHEPHERD OF KINGDOM COME, THE(1928)
Paul McDowell
SAVAGE MESSIAH(1972, Brit.); THIRTY NINE STEPS, THE(1978, Brit.); ROUGH CUT(1980, Brit.)
Roddy McDowell
JUST WILLIAM(1939, Brit.)
Violet McDowell
TOY WIFE, THE(1938)
Violett McDowell
WATCH ON THE RHINE(1943)
Ewen McDuff
I ONLY ASKED!(1958, Brit.)
James McDuff
Misc. Silents
FLESH AND SPIRIT(1922)
Tyler McDuff
EGYPTIAN. THE(1954); FURY AT SHOWDOWN(1957)
W. S. McDunnough
THIS IS MY AFFAIR(1937)
Silents
AFRAID TO FIGHT(1922)
James McEachin
IF HE HOLLERS, LET HIM GO(1968); LAWYER, THE(1969); UNDEFEATED, THE(1969); PLAY MISTY FOR ME(1971); BUCK AND THE PREACHER(1972); FUZZ(1972); GROUNDSTAR CONSPIRACY, THE(1972, Can.); CHRISTINA(1974, Can.); SUDDEN IMPACT(1983)
1984
2010(1984)
Jim McEachin
UPTIGHT(1968)
Laurie McEathron
MY BODYGUARD(1980)
Gordon McEdward
Silents
SILENT COMMAND, THE(1923)
Blake McEdwards
LUCKY LEGS(1942)
Jack McEdwards
WORDS AND MUSIC(1929), w, w
Thomas McElarney
RAMPARTS WE WATCH, THE(1940)
Kenneth McEldownery
RIVER, THE(1951), p
Gay McEldowney
GREATEST SHOW ON EARTH, THE(1952)

Ellen McElduff
IMPOSTORS(1979); YOU BETTER WATCH OUT(1980)
Billy McElhaney
1984
COMFORT AND JOY(1984, Brit.)
Tom McElhany
SIDE STREET(1950)
David McElhatton
1984
THIEF OF HEARTS(1984)
James McElhern
Silents
FRESHIE, THE(1922); YELLOW STAIN, THE(1922); PREPARED TO DIE(1923); PASSIONATE YOUTH(1925)
Misc. Silents
FLYIN' THRU(1925)
Ina McElhinney
ACCEPTABLE LEVELS(1983, Brit.)
Harry McElhone
THIS WAS PARIS(1942, Brit.)
Joyce McElrath
Misc. Talkies
BEALE STREET MAMA(1946)
Bob McElroy
CODE OF THE SADDLE(1947); PRAIRIE EXPRESS(1947); GUN TALK(1948)
Hal McElroy
PICNIC AT HANGING ROCK(1975, Aus.), p; BLUE FIN(1978, Aus.), p; LAST WAVE, THE(1978, Aus.), p
1984
RAZORBACK(1984, Aus.), p
Howard McElroy
CARS THAT ATE PARIS, THE(1974, Aus,), p
Jack McElroy
RUN FOR THE HILLS(1953); HOLLYWOOD OR BUST(1956)
James McElroy
LAST WAVE, THE(1978, Aus.), p; YEAR OF LIVING DANGEROUSLY, THE(1982, Aus.), p
1984
MELVIN, SON OF ALVIN(1984, Aus.), p
Jim McElroy
CARS THAT ATE PARIS, THE(1974, Aus.), p; PICNIC AT HANGING ROCK(1975, Aus.), p
Leo McElroy
REAL LIFE(1979)
Florence McEnany
SLIGHTLY TERRIFIC(1944), w
Maurice McEndree
SHADOWS(1960), p, ed; 1,000 SHAPES OF A FEMALE(1963), ed; DEVIL'S ANGELS(1967); FACES(1968), p, ed; SELF-PORTRAIT(1973, U.S./Chile), d
John McEnery
OTHELLO(1965, Brit.); ROMEO AND JULIET(1968, Brit./Ital.); BARTLEBY(1970, Brit.); LADY IN THE CAR WITH GLASSES AND A GUN, THE(1970, U.S./Fr.); NICHOLAS AND ALEXANDRA(1971, Brit.); LITTLE MALCOLM(1974, Brit.); GALILEO(1975, Brit.); LAND THAT TIME FORGOT, THE(1975, Brit.); DUELLISTS, THE(1977, Brit.); SCHIZO(1977, Brit.)
Misc. Talkies
ONE RUSSIAN SUMMER(1973)
Peter McEnery
TUNES OF GLORY(1960, Brit.); VICTIM(1961, Brit.); MOON-SPINNERS, THE(1964); FIGHTING PRINCE OF DONEGAL, THE(1966, Brit.); GAME IS OVER, THE(1967, Fr.); NEGATIVES(1968, Brit.); BETTER A WIDOW(1969, Ital.); ADVENTURES OF GERARD, THE(1970, Brit.); ENTERTAINING MR. SLOANE(1970, Brit.); TALES THAT WITNESS MADNESS(1973, Brit.); CAT AND THE CANARY, THE(1979, Brit.)
Jaime McEnnan
1984
MICKI AND MAUDE(1984)
Annie McEnroe
HAND, THE(1981); BATTLETRUCK(1982); SURVIVORS, THE(1983)
1984
PURPLE HEARTS(1984)
Misc. Talkies
RUNNING SCARED(1980)
John McEnroe
PLAYERS(1979)
Robert C. McEnroe
MR. BELVEDERE RINGS THE BELL(1951), w
Mark McEntee
MONKEY GRIP(1983, Aus.)
Sean McEuan
SET, THE(1970, Aus.)
Sean McEuen
STORK(1971, Aus.)
William E. McEuen
JERK, THE(1979), p; DEAD MEN DON'T WEAR PLAID(1982), p; MAN WITH TWO BRAINS, THE(1983), p. David V. Picker
Walter McEvan
Silents
ASHAMED OF PARENTS(1921)
Bernard McEveety
RIDE BEYOND VENGEANCE(1966), d; BROTHERHOOD OF SATAN, THE(1971), d; NAPOLEON AND SAMANTHA(1972), d; ONE LITTLE INDIAN(1973), d; BEARS AND I, THE(1974), d
Misc. Silents
BACK TO LIBERTY(1927), d; BROADWAY DRIFTER, THE(1927), d; HIS RISE TO FAME(1927), d; WINNING OAR, THE(1927), d; INSPIRATION(1928), d; STRONGER WILL, THE(1928), d
Bernard F. McEveety
Misc. Silents
CLEAN-UP, THE(1929), d

Joe McEveety
HOT LEAD AND COLD FEET(1978), w
Joe L. McEveety
NO DEPOSIT, NO RETURN(1976), w
Joseph L. McEveety
COMPUTER WORE TENNIS SHOES, THE(1970), w; BAREFOOT EXECUTIVE, THE(1971), w; SUPERDAD(1974), w; STRONGEST MAN IN THE WORLD, THE(1975), w
Joseph McEveety
NOW YOU SEE HIM, NOW YOU DON'T(1972), w
Vincent McEveety
FIRECREEK(1968), d; THIS SAVAGE LAND(1969), d; $1,000,000 DUCK(1971), d; BISCUIT EATER, THE(1972), d; CHARLEY AND THE ANGEL(1973), d; CASTAWAY COWBOY, THE(1974), d; SUPERDAD(1974), d; STRONGEST MAN IN THE WORLD, THE(1975), d; GUS(1976), d; TREASURE OF MATECUMBE(1976), d; HERBIE GOES TO MONTE CARLO(1977), d; APPLE DUMPLING GANG RIDES AGAIN, THE(1979), d; HERBIE GOES BANANAS(1980), d; WATCHER IN THE WOODS, THE(1980, Brit.), d; AMY(1981), d
Verda McEvers
Silents
DUPE, THE(1916)
Bernard F. McEvetty
Misc. Silents
MONTMARTE ROSE(1929), d
Burton McEvilly
Silents
JANICE MEREDITH(1924)
Annemarie McEvoy
1984
CHILDREN OF THE CORN(1984)
Carol McEvoy
TOWERING INFERNO, THE(1974)
Charles McEvoy
SALLY IN OUR ALLEY(1931, Brit.), w; LEMON DROP KID, THE(1934)
Misc. Silents
MAN IN THE SHADOWS, THE(1915, Brit.), d
Earl McEvoy
CARGO TO CAPETOWN(1950), d; KILLER THAT STALKED NEW YORK, THE(1950), d; BAREFOOT MAILMAN, THE(1951), d
Fred McEvoy
THANK YOUR LUCKY STARS(1943)
J. P. McEvoy
SHOW GIRL(1928), w; GLORIFYING THE AMERICAN GIRL(1930), w; SHOW GIRL IN HOLLYWOOD(1930), w; ARE YOU LISTENING?(1932), w; WOMAN ACCUSED(1933), w; IT'S A GIFT(1934), w; LEMON DROP KID, THE(1934), w; MANY HAPPY RETURNS(1934), w; READY FOR LOVE(1934), w; YOU'RE TELLING ME(1934), w; LOVE IN BLOOM(1935), w; COLLEGE HOLIDAY(1936), w; JUST AROUND THE CORNER(1938), w
John McEvoy
ROB ROY, THE HIGHLAND ROGUE(1954, Brit.)
Joseph P. McEvoy
DIXIE DUGAN(1943), w
Joseph Patrick McEvoy
Silents
IT'S THE OLD ARMY GAME(1926), w; POTTERS, THE(1927), w
May McEvoy
WINGS OF EAGLES, THE(1957)
Rennie McEvoy
HOLLOW TRIUMPH(1948); LET'S MAKE IT LEGAL(1951)
Renny McEvoy
I WANTED WINGS(1941); STORY OF DR. WASSELL, THE(1944); WING AND A PRAYER(1944); MISS SUSIE SLAGLE'S(1945); SENORITA FROM THE WEST(1945); FROM THIS DAY FORWARD(1946); TRAPPED(1949); COUNTY FAIR(1950); CRY DANGER(1951); HE RAN ALL THE WAY(1951); HOME TOWN STORY(1951); RED SNOW(1952); NO ESCAPE(1953); BIGGER THAN LIFE(1956); STAR IN THE DUST(1956); DESK SET(1957); OH, MEN! OH, WOMEN!(1957); ROCKABILLY BABY(1957); GUN STREET(1962); INCIDENT IN AN ALLEY(1962)
Tom McEvoy
Silents
FIRE AND SWORD(1914)
Colin McEwan
1984
MELVIN, SON OF ALVIN(1984, Aus.)
Geraldine McEwan
BEWARE OF CHILDREN(1961, Brit.); DANCE OF DEATH, THE(1971, Brit.); BAWDY ADVENTURES OF TOM JONES, THE(1976, Brit.); LITTLEST HORSE THIEVES, THE(1977)
Ian McEwan
1984
PLOUGHMAN'S LUNCH, THE(1984, Brit.), w
Rod McEwan
SHAPE OF THINGS TO COME, THE(1979, Can.)
Brian McEwen
RETURN TO PARADISE(1953)
Geraldine McEwen
THERE WAS A YOUNG LADY(1953, Brit.)
Mike McEwen
LONG WEEKEND(1978, Aus.)
Tom McEwen
SILENCE OF THE NORTH(1981, Can.)
Walter McEwen
Silents
SHOULD A WIFE WORK?(1922)
Misc. Silents
BANDBOX, THE(1919); HER LORD AND MASTER(1921)
Malcolm "Mr. Jetsam" McFachern
WE'LL SMILE AGAIN(1942, Brit.)

Cheryl McFadden
1984
MUPPETS TAKE MANHATTAN, THE(1984)
Cyra McFadden
SERIAL(1980), w
Elizabeth McFadden
DOUBLE DOOR(1934), w
Hamilton McFadden
ARE YOU THERE?(1930), d; OH, FOR A MAN!(1930), p, d; BLACK CAMEL, THE(1931), d; MAN WHO DARED, THE(1933), d; AS HUSBANDS GO(1934), d; ESCAPE BY NIGHT(1937), d; SEA RACKETEERS(1937), d; CHICKEN WAGON FAMILY(1939); RELUCTANT DRAGON, THE(1941); YOUNG AMERICA(1942)
Ira McFadden
Silents
TESTING BLOCK, THE(1920); BRIDE OF THE STORM(1926)
Ivar McFadden
FRISCO KID(1935); YOUNG MR. LINCOLN(1939)
Ivor McFadden
RIFF-RAFF(1936)
Silents
WOLVERINE, THE(1921)
Misc. Silents
BIG TIMBER(1924); FANGS OF FATE(1925)
Patricia McFadden
TREE GROWS IN BROOKLYN, A(1945)
Patrick McFadden
1984
CHOOSE ME(1984)
Robert McFadden
TO THE SHORES OF HELL(1966), w
Tom McFadden
HOT SPUR(1968); THEY SHOOT HORSES, DON'T THEY?(1969); VALDEZ IS COMING(1971); BLACK SUNDAY(1977); PROPHECY(1979); LOVE AND MONEY(1982); WRONG IS RIGHT(1982)
Tomm Lee McFadden
BABY BLUE MARINE(1976)
Virginia McFadden
LOCKED DOOR, THE(1929)
Ed McFadyen
HUMONGOUS(1982, Can.)
John McFadyen
BLOOD AND GUTS(1978, Can.)
Bruce McFarlan
GANGSTER STORY(1959)
Amanda McFarland
UNFINISHED BUSINESS(1941)
Byron McFarland
TWILIGHT ZONE–THE MOVIE(1983)
Craig McFarland
Misc. Talkies
FERN, THE RED DEER(1977, Brit.)
Frank McFarland
UP IN CENTRAL PARK(1948); LADY GAMBLES, THE(1949); FEDERAL AGENT AT LARGE(1950); MA AND PA KETTLE AT THE FAIR(1952)
Gary McFarland
EYE OF THE DEVIL(1967, Brit.), m; WHO KILLED MARY WHAT'SER NAME?(1971), m
George "Spanky" McFarland
MISS FANE'S BABY IS STOLEN(1934); O'SHAUGHNESSY'S BOY(1935)
Lowell McFarland
MAN WHO WOULD NOT DIE, THE(1975), ph
Mike McFarland
PINK MOTEL(1983), d
Olive McFarland
FRIGHTENED CITY, THE(1961, Brit.); ALIVE AND KICKING(1962, Brit.)
Packy McFarland
LADY LIBERTY(1972, Ital./Fr.)
Spanky McFarland
HERE COMES THE BAND(1935); TRAIL OF THE LONESOME PINE, THE(1936); GENERAL SPANKY(1937); WOMAN IN THE WINDOW, THE(1945); MOONRUNNERS(1975)
"Spanky" McFarland
KENTUCKY KERNELS(1935); JOHNNY DOUGHBOY(1943)
Victoria McFarland
BLUE COLLAR(1978)
Andrew McFarlane
BREAK OF DAY(1977, Aus.)
Bruce McFarlane
SAY ONE FOR ME(1959)
George McFarlane
RICH MAN'S FOLLY(1931); UNION DEPOT(1932)
John McFarlane
Silents
BREWSTER'S MILLIONS(1921)
Louella McFarlane
STOP THAT CAB(1951), w
Spanky McFarlane
DAY OF RECKONING(1933)
Tricia McFarlin
GREAT MUPPET CAPER, THE(1981)
Bruce McFee
1984
POLICE ACADEMY(1984)
Malcolm McFee
OH! WHAT A LOVELY WAR(1969, Brit.)
Mary McFerren
HARDCORE(1979)

Toshiro Mcfune
1941(1979)
William McGaha
SPEED LOVERS(1968), a, p&d, w
Misc. Talkies
J.C.(1972), a, d
Bill McGann
Silents
WEDDING MARCH, THE(1927), ph
Celia McGann
MANIAC(1934)
William McGann
I LIKE YOUR NERVE(1931), d; HER NIGHT OUT(1932, Brit.), d; ILLEGAL(1932, Brit.), d; MURDER ON THE SECOND FLOOR(1932, Brit.), d; MAN OF IRON(1935), d; MAYBE IT'S LOVE(1935), d; BRIDES ARE LIKE THAT(1936), d; FRESHMAN LOVE(1936), d; HOT MONEY(1936), d; POLO JOE(1936), d; TIMES SQUARE PLAYBOY(1936), d; TWO AGAINST THE WORLD(1936), d; ALCATRAZ ISLAND(1937), d; MARRY THE GIRL(1937), d; PENROD AND SAM(1937), d; SH! THE OCTOPUS(1937), d; GIRLS ON PROBATION(1938), d; PENROD AND HIS TWIN BROTHER(1938), d; WHEN WERE YOU BORN?(1938), d; BLACKWELL'S ISLAND(1939), d; EVERYBODY'S HOBBY(1939), d; PRIDE OF THE BLUEGRASS(1939), d; SWEEPSTAKES WINNER(1939), d; DR. CHRISTIAN MEETS THE WOMEN(1940), d; WOLF OF NEW YORK(1940), d; HIGHWAY WEST(1941), d; PARSON OF PANAMINT, THE(1941), d; SHOT IN THE DARK, THE(1941), d; WE GO FAST(1941), d; AMERICAN EMPIRE(1942), d; IN OLD CALIFORNIA(1942), d; TOMBSTONE, THE TOWN TOO TOUGH TO DIE(1942), d; FRONTIER BADMEN(1943), d; CONSPIRATORS, THE(1944), spec eff; NEVER SAY GOODBYE(1946), spec eff; NOBODY LIVES FOREVER(1946), spec eff; STOLEN LIFE, A(1946), spec eff; ALWAYS TOGETHER(1947), spec eff; CRY WOLF(1947), spec eff; POSSESSED(1947), spec eff; PURSUED(1947), spec eff; THAT HAGEN GIRL(1947), spec eff; THAT WAY WITH WOMEN(1947), spec eff; UNFAITHFUL, THE(1947), spec eff; JOHNNY BELINDA(1948), spec eff; JUNE BRIDE(1948), spec eff; KEY LARGO(1948), spec eff; SILVER RIVER(1948), spec eff; TREASURE OF THE SIERRA MADRE, THE(1948), spec eff; WALLFLOWER(1948), spec eff; WHIPLASH(1948), spec eff; FOUNTAINHEAD, THE(1949), spec eff; GIRL FROM JONES BEACH, THE(1949), spec eff; IT'S A GREAT FEELING(1949), spec eff; JOHN LOVES MARY(1949), spec eff; CHAIN LIGHTNING(1950), spec eff
Silents
HEARTS OF MEN(1919), ph; MARK OF ZORRO(1920), ph; MOLLYCODDLE, THE(1920), ph; WHEN THE CLOUDS ROLL BY(1920), ph; NUT, THE(1921), ph; THREE AGES, THE(1923), ph
William H. McGann
NIGHT AT THE RITZ, A(1935), d
Blanche McGarity
Misc. Silents
LOVE'S REDEMPTION(1921)
Gene McGarr
1984
2010(1984)
Everett McGarrity
HALLELUJAH(1929)
Garry McGarry
Silents
PRINCE IN A PAWNSHOP, A(1916); FALSE FACES(1919)
Parnell McGarry
BEDAZZLED(1967, Brit.)
Vera McGarry
Silents
CALL OF THE NORTH, THE(1914)
Jed McGarvey
SHADOWS(1960)
Dick McGarvin
CONCORDE, THE–AIRPORT '79(; SMILE(1975); ROLLERCOASTER(1977)
W. F. McGaugh
NEW ADVENTURES OF TARZAN(1935), d
Wilbur McGaugh
MAN TRAILER, THE(1934), ph
Silents
PEACEFUL PETERS(1922); AT DEVIL'S GORGE(1923); BRANDED A BANDIT(1924); RIDIN' MAD(1924); OFFICER JIM(1926), d; SKY SKIDDER, THE(1929)
Misc. Silents
BROKEN SPUR, THE(1921); CUPID'S BRAND(1921); DEVIL DOG DAWSON(1921); ONE EIGHTH APACHE(1922); CACTUS CURE, THE(1925); FUGITIVE, THE(1925); WHISTLING JIM(1925), d; THREE PALS(1926), d
Bobby McGaughey
1984
SOLDIER'S STORY, A(1984)
Patrick McGaughy
1984
RACING WITH THE MOON(1984), a, stunts
Oliver McGauley
CAPTAIN LIGHTFOOT(1955)
Darren McGavin
KISS AND TELL(1945); SHE WOULDN'T SAY YES(1945); SONG TO REMEMBER, A(1945); FEAR(1946); QUEEN FOR A DAY(1951); COURT-MARTIAL OF BILLY MITCHELL, THE(1955); MAN WITH THE GOLDEN ARM, THE(1955); SUMMERTIME(1955); BEAU JAMES(1957); DELICATE DELINQUENT, THE(1957); CASE AGAINST BROOKLYN, THE(1958); BULLET FOR A BADMAN(1964); GREAT SIOUX MASSACRE, THE(1965); RIDE THE HIGH WIND(1967, South Africa); MISSION MARS(1968); TRIBES(1970); MRS. POLLIFAX-SPY(1971); HAPPY MOTHER'S DAY... LOVE, GEORGE(1973), p&d; NO DEPOSIT, NO RETURN(1976); AIRPORT '77(1977); HOT LEAD AND COLD FEET(1978); ZERO TO SIXTY(1978); HANGAR 18(1980); FIREBIRD 2015 AD(1981); CHRISTMAS STORY, A(1983)
1984
NATURAL, THE(1984)
Misc. Talkies
"B"...MUST DIE(1973); CRACKLE OF DEATH(1974); PETTY STORY, THE(1974)

Graem McGavin
MY TUTOR(1983)
1984
ANGEL(1984); WEEKEND PASS(1984)
Nancy McGavin
KILL, THE(1968)
Bill McGaw
SKY RIDERS(1976, U.S./Gr.), w
William C. McGaw
TO PLEASE A LADY(1950)
Alice McGeachy
COAL MINER'S DAUGHTER(1980)
Stanley McGeagh
OH! WHAT A LOVELY WAR(1969, Brit.); LAND THAT TIME FORGOT, THE(1975, Brit.)
Bill McGee
FREE, WHITE AND 21(1963); HIGH YELLOW(1965); RUBY(1977), ed
Brownie McGee
JERK, THE(1979)
Clarence McGee, Jr.
1984
KARATE KID, THE(1984)
Florence McGee
EMPIRE OF THE ANTS(1977); SUPER FUZZ(1981)
1984
WHERE THE BOYS ARE '84(1984)
Frank McGee
RED HOT TIRES(1935), ed; TRAILIN' WEST(1936), ed; TREACHERY RIDES THE RANGE(1936), ed; INTERNATIONAL SQUADRON(1941), ed; LOVE AND LEARN(1947), ed
Gordon McGee
MASON OF THE MOUNTED(1932)
Silents
STORM, THE(1922)
Col. Gordon McGee
MONKEY'S PAW, THE(1933)
Henry McGee
PANIC IN THE PARLOUR(1957, Brit.); ITALIAN JOB, THE(1969, Brit.); CARRY ON EMANUELLE(1978, Brit.); REVENGE OF THE PINK PANTHER(1978)
Jackie McGee
FOREIGN CORRESPONDENT(1940)
Jerry McGee
Misc. Talkies
BLOODRAGE(1979)
Mark McGee
1984
TANK(1984)
Mark Thomas McGee
EQUINOX(1970), d&w
Mary McGee
SWEET TRASH(1970)
Pat McGee
SHADOW OF THE THIN MAN(1941); IT'S A BIKINI WORLD(1967)
Pat R. McGee
BORDER BANDITS(1946)
Patrick McGee
DIE, MONSTER, DIE(1965, Brit.); BIRTHDAY PARTY, THE(1968, Brit.)
Roger McGee
UNTIL THEY SAIL(1957); ANGELS WITH DIRTY FACES(1938); ESCAPE, THE(1939); STOP, LOOK, AND LOVE(1939); JANIE(1944); STREET WITH NO NAME, THE(1948); MOTHER IS A FRESHMAN(1949); AS YOU WERE(1951); HALLS OF MONTEZUMA(1951); ABOVE AND BEYOND(1953); DOWN AMONG THE SHELTERING PALMS(1953); FORBIDDEN PLANET(1956); TEAHOUSE OF THE AUGUST MOON, THE(1956)
Scott McGee
Silents
SHOOTIN' IRONS(1927)
Vic McGee
SINISTER URGE, THE(1961); WIZARD OF MARS(1964); DR. TERROR'S GALLERY OF HORRORS(1967); HELL'S CHOSEN FEW(1968)
Vonetta McGee
LOST MAN, THE(1969); KREMLIN LETTER, THE(1970); HAMMER(1972); MELINDA(1972); DETROIT 9000(1973); SHAFT IN AFRICA(1973); THOMASINE AND BUSHROD(1974); EIGER SANCTION, THE(1975); BROTHERS(1977)
1984
REPO MAN(1984)
Misc. Talkies
BIG BUST-OUT, THE(1973)
Vonette McGee
BLACULA(1972)
Dennis McGeehan
NIGHTBEAST(1982)
Pat McGeehan
DARK PAST, THE(1948); SON OF THE RENEGADE(1953); CHALLENGE THE WILD(1954)
William O. McGeehan
Silents
QUARTERBACK, THE(1926), w
Gloria McGehee
CHILD IS WAITING, A(1963)
Debbit McGellin
HAPPY BIRTHDAY TO ME(1981)
Bill McGhee
QUADROON(1972); DRIVE-IN(1976)
Gloria McGhee
BOSS, THE(1956); SIERRA STRANGER(1957)
John Ray McGhee
MR. BILLION(1977)

Johnny Ray McGhee
STUDENT TEACHERS, THE(1973); WHITE LINE FEVER(1975, Can.)
Michael McGhee
BROOD, THE(1979, Can.)
William Bill McGhee
DON'T LOOK IN THE BASEMENT(1973)
Ed McGibbon
NEPTUNE FACTOR, THE(1973, Can.)
Paul McGibboney
Misc. Talkies
CAFE FLESH(1982)
Donald McGibney
Silents
WOMAN WISE(1928), w
Michael McGifford
THEY ALL LAUGHED(1981)
McGill
FIRST BABY(1936), ph
Angus McGill
PRESS FOR TIME(1966, Brit.), w
Barney McGill
HOME TOWNERS, THE(1928), ph; NOAH'S ARK(1928), ph; STATE STREET SA-
DIE(1928), ph; TERROR, THE(1928), ph; CONQUEST(1929), ph; EVIDENCE(1929),
ph; SKIN DEEP(1929), ph; MAMMY(1930), ph; CISCO KID(1931), ph; MAD GENIUS,
THE(1931), ph; SVENGALI(1931), ph; ALIAS THE DOCTOR(1932), ph; BEAUTY AND
THE BOSS(1932), ph; CABIN IN THE COTTON(1932), ph; MISS PINKERTON(1932),
ph; MOUTHPIECE, THE(1932), ph; WEEK-END MARRIAGE(1932), ph; BOWERY,
THE(1933), ph; BROADWAY THROUGH A KEYHOLE(1933), ph; BUREAU OF MISS-
ING PERSONS(1933), ph; EMPLOYEE'S ENTRANCE(1933), ph; KEYHOLE,
THE(1933), ph; 20,000 YEARS IN SING SING(1933), ph; BORN TO BE BAD(1934), ph;
I BELIEVED IN YOU(1934), ph; LAST GENTLEMAN, THE(1934), ph; MURDER IN
TRINIDAD(1934), ph; PRESIDENT VANISHES, THE(1934), ph; CHARLIE CHAN IN
SHANGHAI(1935), ph; FOLIES DERGERE(1935), ph; REDHEADS ON
PARADE(1935), ph; COUNTRY BEYOND, THE(1936), ph; EVERYBODY'S OLD
MAN(1936), ph; HIGH TENSION(1936), ph; MY MARRIAGE(1936), ph; SONG AND
DANCE MAN, THE(1936), ph; THANK YOU, JEEVES(1936), ph; CRACK-UP,
THE(1937), ph; LANCER SPY(1937), ph; LAUGHING AT TROUBLE(1937), ph; MID-
NIGHT TAXI(1937), ph; NANCY STEELE IS MISSING(1937), ph; OFF TO THE
RACES(1937), ph; SHE HAD TO EAT(1937), ph; BATTLE OF BROADWAY(1938), ph;
SHARPSHOOTERS(1938), ph; CISCO KID AND THE LADY, THE(1939), ph; GIRLS
UNDER TWENTY-ONE(1940), ph; LONE WOLF KEEPS A DATE, THE(1940), ph;
PHANTOM SUBMARINE, THE(1941), ph
Silents
KEEP SMILING(1925), ph; WHAT PRICE GLORY(1926), ph; CASEY AT THE
BAT(1927), ph; HUSBANDS FOR RENT(1927), ph; JAWS OF STEEL(1927), ph; CRIM-
SON CITY, THE(1928), ph
Barney "Chick" McGill
DOORWAY TO HELL(1930), ph; NIGHT NURSE(1931), ph; OTHER MEN'S WOM-
EN(1931), ph; HARD TO HANDLE(1933), ph; MAYOR OF HELL, THE(1933), ph
Bernard McGill
DESERT SONG, THE(1929), ph; STARK MAD(1929), ph
Billy McGill
GAME OF DEATH, THE(1979)
Bruce McGill
CITIZENS BAND(1977); NATIONAL LAMPOON'S ANIMAL HOUSE(1978); HAND,
THE(1981); BALLAD OF GREGORIO CORTEZ, THE(1983); SILKWOOD(1983); TOUGH
ENOUGH(1983)
Carole McGill
1984
CITY GIRL, THE(1984)
Chick McGill
AVIATOR, THE(1929), ph; THREE FACES EAST(1930), ph; MY PAST(1931), ph
Chris McGill
FATTY FINN(1980, Aus.), w
Don McGill
WE'VE NEVER BEEN LICKED(1943); FOLLOW THE BOYS(1944); LADIES COURA-
GEOUS(1944); BRUTE FORCE(1947); DOUBLE LIFE, A(1947)
Dook McGill
CALIFORNIA(1946)
Eddie McGill
STOLEN HARMONY(1935)
Everett McGill
YANKS(1979); BRUBAKER(1980); UNION CITY(1980); QUEST FOR FIRE(1982,
Fr./Can.)
1984
DUNE(1984)
Gordon McGill
Misc. Talkies
UP YOUR ALLEY(1975)
Ida McGill
SON OF DR. JEKYLL, THE(1951)
Lawrence McGill
Silents
GREYHOUND, THE(1914), d; SEALED VALLEY, THE(1915), d; CRIME AND PUN-
ISHMENT(1917), d
Misc. Silents
ANGEL FACTORY, THE(1917), d; FIRST LAW, THE(1918), d; GIRL FROM
BOHEMIA, THE(1918), d; WOMAN'S EXPERIENCE, A(1918)
Lawrence B. McGill
Silents
HOW MOLLY MADE GOOD(1915), d
Misc. Silents
ARIZONA(1913), d
Lawrence D. McGill
Misc. Silents
WOMAN'S LAW, THE(1916), d
Marcus McGill
IT'S A BET(1935, Brit.), w

Marguerite McGill
SOUTH OF CALIENTE(1951)
Maureen McGill
I'M GOING TO GET YOU ... ELLIOT BOY(1971, Can.)
Moyna McGill
PRIVATE ANGELO(1949, Brit.); LES MISERABLES(1952)
Silents
MIRIAM ROZELLA(1924, Brit.)
Misc. Silents
GARRYOWEN(1920, Brit.); NOTHING ELSE MATTERS(1920, Brit.); SHOULD A
DOCTOR TELL?(1923, Brit.)
Myron McGill
COACH(1978)
Ronald McGill
JULIUS CAESAR(1970, Brit.)
Howard McGillian
1984
WHERE THE BOYS ARE '84(1984)
Woody McGillicuddy
UNASHAMED(1938)
Judith McGilligan
STOP THE WORLD–I WANT TO GET OFF(1966, Brit.)
Kelly McGillis
REUBEN, REUBEN(1983)
David McGillivray
FRIGHTMARE(1974, Brit.), w; HOUSE OF WHIPCORD(1974, Brit.), a, w; SATAN'S
SLAVE(1976, Brit.), w; CONFESSIONAL, THE(1977, Brit.), w; SCHIZO(1977, Brit.), w;
TERROR(1979, Brit.), w
Greg McGillivray
SKY RIDERS(1976, U.S./Gr.), ph
Ian Warner McGilvray
JOHNNY IN THE CLOUDS(1945, Brit.)
David McGinley
TAPS(1981)
Ted McGinley
YOUNG DOCTORS IN LOVE(1982)
1984
REVENGE OF THE NERDS(1984)
Jim McGinn
ULTIMATE THRILL, THE(1974), w
1984
NADIA(1984, U.S./Yugo.), w
Russ McGinn
SLAUGHTER'S BIG RIP-OFF(1973)
1984
FOOTLOOSE(1984)
Walter McGinn
PARALLAX VIEW, THE(1974); FAREWELL, MY LOVELY(1975); THREE DAYS OF
THE CONDOR(1975); BOBBY DEERFIELD(1977)
Carol McGinnis
NASHVILLE(1975); COMMITMENT, THE(1976); GABLE AND LOMBARD(1976);
SKATEBOARD(1978)
Charlotte McGinnis
HARDCORE(1979)
Don McGinnis
HELL'S BLOODY DEVILS(1970), m
Helen McGinnis
Silents
CHILDREN OF THE NIGHT(1921)
Joel McGinnis
FACES IN THE FOG(1944); BEDSIDE MANNER(1945); WOMAN IN THE WINDOW,
THE(1945); MOONRISE(1948)
Kathi McGinnis
NEW YORK, NEW YORK(1977)
Mary Lou McGinnis
Misc. Talkies
FOLLOW ME(1969)
Niall McGinnis
CRIMSON CIRCLE, THE(1936, Brit.); DEBT OF HONOR(1936, Brit.); LAST ADVEN-
TURERS, THE(1937, Brit); STRANGLER, THE(1941, Brit.); AVENGERS, THE(1942,
Brit.); CAPTAIN BOYCOTT(1947, Brit.); HAMLET(1948, Brit.); YOU CAN'T BEAT THE
IRISH(1952, Brit.); NUN'S STORY, THE(1959); DEVIL'S AGENT, THE(1962, Brit.);
FACE IN THE RAIN, A(1963); PLAYBOY OF THE WESTERN WORLD, THE(1963,
Ireland)
Scott McGinnis
JOYSTICKS(1983); WACKO(1983)
1984
MAKING THE GRADE(1984); RACING WITH THE MOON(1984); STAR TREK III:
THE SEARCH FOR SPOCK(1984)
Terry McGinnis
JIGGS AND MAGGIE OUT WEST(1950)
Tom McGinnis
CARNIVAL OF SOULS(1962)
Vera McGinnis
SECRET MENACE(1931)
Silents
OUT OF LUCK(1919)
Joel McGinns
I RING DOORBELLS(1946)
McGinty
BRIDE OF THE LAKE(1934, Brit.)
E. B. McGinty
MAN FROM TEXAS, THE(1948), w
Maura McGiveney
W.I.A.(WOUNDED IN ACTION)*1/2 (1966); NORTH BY NORTHWEST(1959); TWIST
AROUND THE CLOCK(1961); ONCE YOU KISS A STRANGER(1969)
Owen McGiveney
IF WINTER COMES(1947); SHOW BOAT(1951); PAT AND MIKE(1952); PLYMOUTH
ADVENTURE(1952); SCARAMOUCHE(1952); BAND WAGON, THE(1953); MAZE,
THE(1953); SCANDAL AT SCOURIE(1953); TITANIC(1953); KING'S THIEF,

THE(1955); SCARLET COAT, THE(1955); LES GIRLS(1957); RAINTREE COUNTY(1957); IN THE MONEY(1958); SNOW WHITE AND THE THREE STOOGES(1961); MY FAIR LADY(1964); 36 HOURS(1965)

Maura McGiveny
DO NOT DISTURB(1965)

John McGiver
LOVE IN THE AFTERNOON(1957); I MARRIED A WOMAN(1958); ONCE UPON A HORSE(1958); GAZEBO, THE(1959); BACHELOR IN PARADISE(1961); BREAKFAST AT TIFFANY'S(1961); LOVE IN A GOLDFISH BOWL(1961); MANCHURIAN CANDIDATE, THE(1962); MR. HOBBS TAKES A VACATION(1962); PERIOD OF ADJUSTMENT(1962); WHO'S GOT THE ACTION?(1962); JOHNNY COOL(1963); MY SIX LOVES(1963); TAKE HER, SHE'S MINE(1963); WHO'S MINDING THE STORE?(1963); GLOBAL AFFAIR, A(1964); MAN'S FAVORITE SPORT[?](1964); MARRIAGE ON THE ROCKS(1965); GLASS BOTTOM BOAT, THE(1966); MADE IN PARIS(1966); FITZWILLY(1967); SPIRIT IS WILLING, THE(1967); MIDNIGHT COWBOY(1969); LAWMAN(1971); ARNOLD(1973); MAME(1974); APPLE DUMPLING GANG, THE(1975)

Cecil McGivern
GREAT EXPECTATIONS(1946, Brit.), w; BLANCHE FURY(1948, Brit.), w

Michael McGivern
DEMON LOVER, THE(1977)

William McGivern
CAPER OF THE GOLDEN BULLS, THE(1967), w

William P. McGivern
BIG HEAT, THE(1953), w; ROGUE COP(1954), w; SHIELD FOR MURDER(1954), w; HELL ON FRISCO BAY(1956), w; ODDS AGAINST TOMORROW(1959), w; I SAW WHAT YOU DID(1965), w; WRECKING CREW, THE(1968), w; BRANNIGAN(1975, Brit.), w; NIGHT OF THE JUGGLER(1980), w

Owen McGivney
BRIGADOON(1954); HONG KONG CONFIDENTIAL(1958)

Ian McGlashan
THREE NUTS IN SEARCH OF A BOLT(1964), p, w

Norman McGlen
ON HER MAJESTY'S SECRET SERVICE(1969, Brit.)

Shawn McGlory
ROUGHSHOD(1949)

Frank McGlyn
Misc. Silents
TEST, THE(1915); TRUTH ABOUT HELEN, THE(1915), d; WAY BACK, THE(1915)

Frank McGlynn
GOOD NEWS(1930); MIN AND BILL(1930); RIDERS OF THE PURPLE SAGE(1931); SECRET SIX, THE(1931); CHARLIE CHAN'S GREATEST CASE(1933); EMPLOYEE'S ENTRANCE(1933); UNKNOWN VALLEY(1933); ARE WE CIVILIZED?(1934); GOIN' TO TOWN(1935); THESE THREE(1936); WELLS FARGO(1937); GIRL OF THE GOLDEN WEST, THE(1938); THIRD FINGER, LEFT HAND(1940); GIRL, A GUY AND A GOB, A(1941); MARRY THE BOSS' DAUGHTER(1941); THREE GIRLS ABOUT TOWN(1941); IN OLD CALIFORNIA(1942); ROGUES GALLERY(1945); HOLLYWOOD BARN DANCE(1947)
Silents
ARGYLE CASE, THE(1917); POOR LITTLE RICH GIRL, A(1917)
Misc. Silents
FAITH AND FORTUNE(1915), d; ACCIDENTAL HONEYMOON, THE(1918); GIRL OF THE GYPSY CAMP, THE(1925)

Frank McGlynn, Jr.
FACE IN THE SKY(1933); MAN OF THE FOREST(1933); OPERATOR 13(1934); DR. SOCRATES(1935); HOPALONG CASSIDY(1935); IT'S A SMALL WORLD(1935); KENTUCKY KERNELS(1935); LAWLESS RANGE(1935); PUBLIC HERO NO. 1(1935); BAR 20 RIDES AGAIN(1936); TROUBLE FOR TWO(1936); WESTWARD HO(1936); KENTUCKY MOONSHINE(1938); MARIE ANTOINETTE(1938); MR. MOTO'S GAMBLE(1938); OF HUMAN HEARTS(1938); SHOPWORN ANGEL(1938); TRAIL STREET(1947)
Silents
AMERICA(1924); JUDGMENT OF THE HILLS(1927)

Frank McGlynn, Sr.
JAZZ CINDERELLA(1930); LADY AND GENT(1932); FRISCO JENNY(1933); NO MAN OF HER OWN(1933); LITTLE MISS MARKER(1934); MASSACRE(1934); MIGHTY BARNUM, THE(1934); SEARCH FOR BEAUTY(1934); CAPTAIN BLOOD(1935); FOLIES DERGERE(1935); IT'S A SMALL WORLD(1935); LITTLEST REBEL, THE(1935); LOST IN THE STRATOSPHERE(1935); OUTLAWED GUNS(1935); CAREER WOMAN(1936); FOR THE SERVICE(1936); HEARTS IN BONDAGE(1936); KING OF THE ROYAL MOUNTED(1936); LAST OF THE MOHICANS, THE(1936); PAROLE(1936); PRISONER OF SHARK ISLAND, THE(1936); TRAIL OF THE LONESOME PINE, THE(1936); NORTH OF NOME(1937); PLAINSMAN, THE(1937); SARATOGA(1937); SILENT BARRIERS(1937, Brit.); SING AND BE HAPPY(1937); WESTERN GOLD(1937); SUDDEN BILL DORN(1938); HONEYMOON'S OVER, THE(1939); LOVE AFFAIR(1939); BOOM TOWN(1940); HI-YO SILVER(1940); MAD EMPRESS, THE(1940); DELINQUENT DAUGHTERS(1944)

Franklyn McGlynn
Silents
ROUGH AND READY(1918)

L.P. McGlynn
1984
FALLING IN LOVE(1984)

Dick McGoldrick
DOZENS, THE(1981); VERDICT, THE(1982)

Richard McGonagle
TATTOO(1981); MAN, WOMAN AND CHILD(1983)

Al McGoohan
1984
DON'T OPEN TILL CHRISTMAS(1984, Brit.), w

Catherine McGoohan
1984
SAVAGE STREETS(1984)

Patrick McGoohan
DAM BUSTERS, THE(1955, Brit.); I AM A CAMERA(1955, Brit.); PASSAGE HOME(1955, Brit.); ZARAK(1956, Brit.); HIGH TIDE AT NOON(1957, Brit.); GYPSY AND THE GENTLEMAN, THE(1958, Brit.); HELL DRIVERS(1958, Brit.); ELEPHANT GUN(1959, Brit.); ALL NIGHT LONG(1961, Brit.); QUARE FELLOW, THE(1962, Brit.); THREE LIVES OF THOMASINA, THE(1963, U.S./Brit.); TWO LIVING, ONE DEAD(1964, Brit./Swed.); WALK IN THE SHADOW(1966, Brit.); ICE STATION ZEBRA(1968); MOONSHINE WAR, THE(1970); MARY, QUEEN OF SCOTS(1971, Brit.);

CATCH MY SOUL(1974), d; DR. SYN, ALIAS THE SCARECROW(1975); GENIUS, THE(1976, Ital./Fr./Ger.); SILVER STREAK(1976); BRASS TARGET(1978); ESCAPE FROM ALCATRAZ(1979); SCANNERS(1981, Can.)
1984
KINGS AND DESPERATE MEN(1984, Brit.)
Misc. Talkies
HARD WAY, THE(1980, Brit.)

Dorin McGough
Misc. Talkies
GIRLS OF 42ND STREET(1974)

Gloria McGough
MYSTERY LAKE(1953)

Philip McGough
1984
FOREVER YOUNG(1984, Brit.)

Ricky McGough
THESE WILDER YEARS(1956)

Capt. Vincent McGovern
BATTLE TAXI(1955)

Dennis McGovern
EXPOSED(1983)

Don Charles McGovern
1984
STAR TREK III: THE SEARCH FOR SPOCK(1984)

Don McGovern
WRONG MAN, THE(1956); LADY SINGS THE BLUES(1972); ICEMAN COMETH, THE(1973); LAST DETAIL, THE(1973); GOIN' SOUTH(1978)

Elizabeth McGovern
ORDINARY PEOPLE(1980); RAGTIME(1981); LOVESICK(1983)
1984
ONCE UPON A TIME IN AMERICA(1984); RACING WITH THE MOON(1984)

Elmer McGovern
NO FUNNY BUSINESS(1934, Brit.), ed

James McGovern
FRAULEIN(1958), w

John McGovern
NIGHT UNTO NIGHT(1949); ROOM FOR ONE MORE(1952); VIOLATORS, THE(1957); PARRISH(1961); SPLENDOR IN THE GRASS(1961)

Johnny McGovern
TUMBLEWEED TRAIL(1946); TEA FOR TWO(1950); WHEN I GROW UP(1951)

Mark McGovern
WITHOUT A TRACE(1983)

Maureen McGovern
AIRPLANE!(1980)

Michael McGovern
RIDE THE HIGH WIND(1967, South Africa); CAPTAIN NEMO AND THE UNDERWATER CITY(1969, Brit.); MOSQUITO SQUADRON(1970, Brit.); GOLD(1974, Brit.)

Roger McGovern
THERE'S ALWAYS VANILLA(1972)

Sen. George McGovern
CANDIDATE, THE(1972)

Tarrance McGovern
THX 1138(1971)

Terry McGovern
CANDIDATE, THE(1972); AMERICAN GRAFFITI(1973); AMERICATHON(1979)

Tommy McGovern
NO WAY BACK(1949, Brit.)

Will McGow
1984
KINGS AND DESPERATE MEN(1984, Brit.), prod d&cos

Alice McGowan
Silents
JUDITH OF THE CUMBERLANDS(1916), w

Anthony McGowan
GOODBYE COLUMBUS(1969)

D. and S. McGowan
NIGHT TRAIN TO MEMPHIS(1946), w

Dale McGowan
WHY SHOOT THE TEACHER(1977, Can.)

Darrell McGowan
TRESPASSER, THE(1947), w

Dorell McGowan
IN OLD MONTEREY(1939), w; FRIENDLY NEIGHBORS(1940), w; TIGER WOMAN, THE(1945), p

Dorothy McGowan
GHOST TALKS, THE(1929); SHE GETS HER MAN(1935)

Dorrall McGowan
SHEPHERD OF THE OZARKS(1942), w

Dorrel McGowan
BILL CRACKS DOWN(1937), w

Dorrell McGowan
COMIN' ROUND THE MOUNTAIN(1936), w; GUNS AND GUITARS(1936), w; KING OF THE PECOS(1936), w; LADY LUCK(1936), w; RED RIVER VALLEY(1936), w; RIDE, RANGER, RIDE(1936), w; SEA SPOILERS, THE(1936), w; SINGING COWBOY, THE(1936), w; BIG SHOW, THE(1937), w; GIT ALONG, LITTLE DOGIES(1937), w; MAN BETRAYED, A(1937), w; SEA RACKETEERS(1937), w; YODELIN' KID FROM PINE RIDGE(1937), w; COME ON, LEATHERNECKS(1938), w; DOWN IN ARKANSAW(1938), w; HOLLYWOOD STADIUM MYSTERY(1938), w; LADIES IN DISTRESS(1938), w; UNDER WESTERN STARS(1938), w; JEEPERS CREEPERS(1939), w; MISSING EVIDENCE(1939), w; MY WIFE'S RELATIVES(1939), w; ROVIN' TUMBLEWEEDS(1939), w; SMASHING THE SPY RING(1939), w; SOUTH OF THE BORDER(1939), w; TROUBLE IN SUNDOWN(1939), w; GRAND OLE OPRY(1940), w; IN OLD MISSOURI(1940), w; VILLAGE BARN DANCE(1940), w; ARKANSAS JUDGE(1941), w; COUNTRY FAIR(1941), w; DOWN MEXICO WAY(1941), w; MOUNTAIN MOONLIGHT(1941), w; TUXEDO JUNCTION(1941), w; HI, NEIGHBOR(1942), w; MOUNTAIN RHYTHM(1942), w; OLD HOMESTEAD, THE(1942), w; STARDUST ON THE SAGE(1942), w; O, MY DARLING CLEMENTINE(1943), w; BIG BONANZA, THE(1944), w; SAN FERNANDO VALLEY(1944), w; SING, NEIGHBOR, SING(1944), w; DON'T FENCE ME IN(1945), w; INNER CIRCLE, THE(1946), w; NIGHT TRAIN TO MEMPHIS(1946), p; VALLEY OF THE ZOM-

BIES(1946), p&w; SADDLE PALS(1947), w; TWILIGHT ON THE RIO GRANDE(1947), w; SHOWDOWN, THE(1950), d&w; SINGING GUNS(1950), w; TOKYO FILE 212(1951), p, d&w; DEVIL'S PARTNER, THE(1958), w; LITTLEST HOBO, THE(1958), w; SNOWFIRE(1958), p,d&w; BASHFUL ELEPHANT, THE(1962, Aust.), p,d&w; ICE HOUSE, THE(1969), p

George McGowan
MAGNIFICENT SEVEN RIDE, THE(1972), d; SHADOW OF THE HAWK(1976, Can.), d; SHAPE OF THINGS TO COME, THE(1979, Can.), d

J. P. McGowan
SENOR AMERICANO(1929); CANYON HAWKS(1930), d; CANYON OF MISSING MEN, THE(1930), d; CODE OF HONOR(1930), d; COVERED WAGON TRAILS(1930), a, d; NEAR THE RAINBOW'S END(1930), d; CYCLONE KID(1931), d; HEADIN' FOR TROUBLE(1931), d; RIDERS OF THE NORTH(1931), d; SON OF THE PLAINS(1931); UNDER TEXAS SKIES(1931), d; HUMAN TARGETS(1932), d; MAN FROM NEW MEXICO, THE(1932), d; SCARLET BRAND(1932), d; SHOTGUN PASS(1932), d; DEADWOOD PASS(1933), d; DRUM TAPS(1933), d, w; SOMEWHERE IN SONORA(1933); WAR OF THE RANGE(1933), d; WHEN A MAN RIDES ALONE(1933), d; EVELYN PRENTICE(1934); NO MORE WOMEN(1934); WAGON WHEELS(1934); BORDER BRIGANDS(1935); GOIN' TO TOWN(1935); MISSISSIPPI(1935); PRISONER OF SHARK ISLAND, THE(1936); RIDE 'EM COWBOY(1936); SECRET PATROL(1936), a, w; SILVER SPURS(1936); STAMPEDE(1936); THREE MESQUITEERS, THE(1936); EMPTY HOLSTERS(1937); FURY AND THE WOMAN(1937); HEART OF THE ROCKIES(1937); HIT THE SADDLE(1937); PRAIRIE THUNDER(1937); ROARING SIX GUNS(1937); ROUGH RIDIN' RHYTHM(1937), a, d; SLAVE SHIP(1937); WESTBOUND LIMITED(1937); WHAT PRICE VENGEANCE?(1937), w; HUNTED MEN(1938); WHERE THE WEST BEGINS(1938), d
Misc. Talkies
BEYOND THE LAW(1930), d; QUICK TRIGGER LEE(1931), d; LAWLESS VALLEY(1932), d; MARK OF THE SPUR(1932), d; TANGLED FORTUNES(1932), d; LONE BANDIT, THE(1934), d; OUTLAW TAMER, THE(1934), d; SILENT CODE, THE(1935)
Silents
FROM THE MANGER TO THE CROSS(1913); JUDITH OF THE CUMBERLANDS(1916), d; HILLS OF MISSING MEN(1922), a, d&w; ONE MILLION IN JEWELS(1923), a, d&w; STORMY SEAS(1923), a, d; BAFFLED(1924), d; WESTERN VENGEANCE(1924), d; BARRIERS OF THE LAW(1925), a, d; OUTWITTED(1925), a, d&w; AFLAME IN THE SKY(1927), d; LOST LIMITED, THE(1927), d; OUTLAW DOG, THE(1927), d; ARIZONA DAYS(1928), a, d; DEVIL DOGS(1928); LAW OF THE MOUNTED(1928), a, d; MANHATTAN COWBOY(1928), d; OLD CODE, THE(1928); ON THE DIVIDE(1928), a, d; WEST OF SANTA FE(1928), d; DEVIL'S TOWER(1929), a, d, w; FIGHTING TERROR, THE(1929), d; HEADIN' WESTWARD(1929), a, d; INVADERS, THE(1929), a, d; LAST ROUNDUP, THE(1929), a, d; LAWLESS LEGION, THE(1929); LONE HORSEMAN, THE(1929), a, d; OKLAHOMA KID, THE(1929), a, p&d; PHANTOM RIDER, THE(1929), a, d; PLUNGING HOOFS(1929); RIDERS OF THE RIO GRANDE(1929), d; HUNTED MEN(1930), d; OKLAHOMA SHERIFF, THE(1930), d; RECKLESS CHANCES(5 reels), a, d&w
Misc. Silents
DIAMOND RUNNERS, THE(1916), d; MANAGER OF THE B&A, THE(1916), d; MEDICINE BEND(1916), a, d; WHISPERING SMITH(1916), a, d; BELOW THE DEAD LINE(1921), d; CROOK'S ROMANCE, A(1921); DISCONTENTED WIVES(1921), a, d; MOONSHINE MENACE, THE(1921), d; RUSE OF THE RATTLER, THE(1921), a, d; TIGER TRUE(1921), d; CALIBRE 45(1924), d; COURAGE(1924), d; CROSSED TRAILS(1924), d; DESPERATE ADVENTURE, A(1924), d; TWO FISTED TENDERFOOT, A(1924), d; WHIPPING BOSS, THE(1924), a, d; BLOOD AND STEEL(1925), d; BORDER INTRIGUE(1925), d; COLD NERVE(1925), d; CRACK O'DAWN(1925); DUPED(1925), a, d; FEAR FIGHTER, THE(1925); FIGHTING SHERIFF, THE(1925), d; GAMBLING FOOL, THE(1925), d; MAKERS OF MEN(1925); PEGGY OF THE SECRET SERVICE(1925), d; TRAIN WRECKERS, THE(1925), d; WEBS OF STEEL(1925), d; ACE OF CLUBS, THE(1926), d; BURIED GOLD(1926), d; CROSSED SIGNALS(1926), d; CYCLONE BOB(1926), d; DANGER QUEST(1926); DESPERATE CHANCE(1926), d; FIGHTING LUCK(1926), d; IRON FIST(1926), d; LOST EXPRESS, THE(1926), d; LOST TRAIL, THE(1926), d; MISTAKEN ORDERS(1926), d; MORAN OF THE MOUNTED(1926); OPEN SWITCH, THE(1926), d; PATENT LEATHER PUG, THE(1926), d; PERIL OF THE RAIL(1926), d; RED BLOOD(1926), d; RIDING FOR LIFE(1926), d; RIDING ROMANCE(1926), d; ROAD AGENT(1926), d; SILVER FINGERS(1926), d; UNSEEN ENEMIES(1926), d; ARIZONA NIGHTS(1927); RED RAIDERS, THE(1927); RED SIGNALS(1927); SLAVER, THE(1927); TARZAN AND THE GOLDEN LION(1927), d; THUNDERBOLT'S TRACKS(1927), d; WHEN A DOG LOVES(1927), d; BLACK ACE, THE(1928); CODE OF THE SCARLET, THE(1928); DUGAN OF THE DUGOUTS(1928); LIGHTNIN' SHOT(1928), a, d; MYSTERY VALLEY(1928), d; PAINTED TRAIL(1928), d; SILENT TRAIL(1928), d; TEXAS TOMMY(1928), d; TRAIL RIDERS(1928), d; TRAILIN' BACK(1928), d; TWO OUTLAWS, THE(1928); BAD MEN'S MONEY(1929), a, d; BELOW THE DEADLINE(1929), d; CAPTAIN COWBOY(1929), d; CODE OF THE WEST(1929), d; COWBOY AND THE OUTLAW, THE(1929), d; MAN FROM NEVADA, THE(1929), d; 'NEATH WESTERN SKIES(1929), a, d; PIONEERS OF THE WEST(1929), a, d; RIDERS OF THE STORM(1929), d; BREEZY BILL(1930), d; CALL OF THE DESERT(1930), d; CANYON OF MISSING MEN, THE(1930), d; COVERED WAGON TRAILS(1930), d; MAN FROM NOWHERE, THE(1930), d; O'MALLEY RIDES ALONE(1930), d; PARTING OF THE TRAILS(1930), d

Jack McGowan
SITTING PRETTY(1933), w; BROADWAY MELODY OF 1936(1935), w; BORN TO DANCE(1936), w; BROADWAY MELODY OF '38(1937), w; BABES IN ARMS(1939), w; BROADWAY MELODY OF 1940(1940), w; LITTLE NELLIE KELLY(1940), w; LADY BE GOOD(1941), w; FOR ME AND MY GAL(1942), w; PANAMA HATTIE(1942), w; DU BARRY WAS A LADY(1943), w; GIRL CRAZY(1943), w; BROADWAY RHYTHM(1944), w; ZIEGFELD FOLLIES(1945), w; DERANGED(1974, Can.), ph; MARDI GRAS MASSACRE(1978), ph; BLOOD WATERS OF DOCTOR Z(1982), ph
Misc. Silents
FLOWER OF THE DUSK(1918); NOTHING BUT LIES(1920)

Jewel McGowan
TEN CENTS A DANCE(1945)

John McGowan
NOTHING BUT THE TRUTH(1929), w; HEADS UP(1930), w; HOLD EVERYTHING(1930), w; GIRL CRAZY(1932), w; STORK CLUB, THE(1945), w; IT HAPPENED IN BROOKLYN(1947), w; WHEN THE BOYS MEET THE GIRLS(1965), w
Misc. Silents
GOLD CURE, THE(1919)

John Wesley McGowan
Silents
EXCESS BAGGAGE(1928), w

Kenneth McGowan
MAN HUNT(1941), p

Laurel McGowan
MONKEY GRIP(1983, Aus.)

Mary McGowan
LITTLE AUSTRALIANS(1940, Aus.)

Melody McGowan
SNOWFIRE(1958)

Michael McGowan
PARADES(1972); LINE, THE(1982)

Molly McGowan
SNOWFIRE(1958)
Silents
LOVE CHARM, THE(1921)

Oliver McGowan
JOKER IS WILD, THE(1957); SCREAMING MIMI(1958); STAGECOACH(1966); BANNING(1967)

Robert McGowan
FRONTIER JUSTICE(1936), d; BRINGING UP BABY(1938), w; HAUNTED HOUSE, THE(1940), d; TOMBOY(1940), d; OLD SWIMMIN' HOLE, THE(1941), d
Silents
TWIN BEDS(1920), w
Misc. Silents
DIAMOND BANDIT, THE(1924)

Robert A. McGowan
GAS HOUSE KIDS GO WEST(1947), w

Robert F. McGowan
TOO MANY PARENTS(1936), d; SONS OF THE LEGION(1938), w; WHO KILLED "DOC" ROBBIN?(1948), p

Stewart E. McGowan
TIGER WOMAN, THE(1945), p

Stuart McGowan
COMIN' ROUND THE MOUNTAIN(1936), w; GUNS AND GUITARS(1936), w; KING OF THE PECOS(1936), w; LADY LUCK(1936), w; RED RIVER VALLEY(1936), w; RIDE, RANGER, RIDE(1936), w; SEA SPOILERS, THE(1936), w; SINGING COWBOY, THE(1936), w; BIG SHOW, THE(1937), w; BILL CRACKS DOWN(1937), w; GIT ALONG, LITTLE DOGIES(1937), w; MAN BETRAYED, A(1937), w; SEA RACKETEERS(1937), w; YODELIN' KID FROM PINE RIDGE(1937), w; COME ON, LEATHERNECKS(1938), w; DOWN IN ARKANSAW(1938), w; HOLLYWOOD STADIUM MYSTERY(1938), w; LADIES IN DISTRESS(1938), w; UNDER WESTERN STARS(1938), w; IN OLD MONTEREY(1939), w; JEEPERS CREEPERS(1939), w; MISSING EVIDENCE(1939), w; MY WIFE'S RELATIVES(1939), w; ROVIN' TUMBLEWEEDS(1939), w; SOUTH OF THE BORDER(1939), w; TROUBLE IN SUNDOWN(1939), w; FRIENDLY NEIGHBORS(1940), w; GRAND OLE OPRY(1940), w; IN OLD MISSOURI(1940), w; VILLAGE BARN DANCE(1940), w; ARKANSAS JUDGE(1941), w; COUNTRY FAIR(1941), w; DOWN MEXICO WAY(1941), w; MOUNTAIN MOONLIGHT(1941), w; TUXEDO JUNCTION(1941), w; HI, NEIGHBOR(1942), w; MOUNTAIN RHYTHM(1942), w; OLD HOMESTEAD, THE(1942), w; SHEPHERD OF THE OZARKS(1942), w; STARDUST ON THE SAGE(1942), w; O, MY DARLING CLEMENTINE(1943), w; BIG BONANZA, THE(1944), w; SAN FERNANDO VALLEY(1944), w; SING, NEIGHBOR, SING(1944), w; DON'T FENCE ME IN(1945), w; NIGHT TRAIN TO MEMPHIS(1946), p; VALLEY OF THE ZOMBIES(1946), p&w; HELLFIRE(1949), d&w; SHOWDOWN, THE(1950), d&w; SINGING GUNS(1950), w; TOKYO FILE 212(1951), d&w; SNOWFIRE(1958), p,d&w

Stuart E. McGowan
SMASHING THE SPY RING(1939), w; INNER CIRCLE, THE(1946), w; SADDLE PALS(1947), w; TRESPASSER, THE(1947), w; TWILIGHT ON THE RIO GRANDE(1947), w; BASHFUL ELEPHANT, THE(1962, Aust.), p,d&w; ICE HOUSE, THE(1969), d; BILLION DOLLAR HOBO, THE(1977), d, w; THEY WENT THAT-A-WAY AND THAT-A-WAY(1978), d

T. J. McGowan
MAN WITH MY FACE, THE(1951), w

Tom McGowan
MANHUNT IN THE JUNGLE(1958), d; ARISTOCATS, THE(1970), w; REUBEN, REUBEN(1983)
Misc. Talkies
CATACLYSM(1980), d

McGowan and Mack
LAKE PLACID SERENADE(1944)

John McGowans
BATTLE BEYOND THE STARS(1980)

Alec McGowen
1984
FOREVER YOUNG(1984, Brit.)

Dorell McGowen
BARNYARD FOLLIES(1940), w; HOOSIER HOLIDAY(1943), w

Dorrell Stuart McGowen
SWING YOUR PARTNER(1943), w

J.P. McGowen
BAR 20 RIDES AGAIN(1936); GUNS AND GUITARS(1936)

R.B. McGowen, Jr.
QUADROON(1972), p

Stuart McGowen
BARNYARD FOLLIES(1940), w; HOOSIER HOLIDAY(1943), w

Billy McGown
MIRACLE KID(1942)

Elaine McGown
TERMS OF ENDEARMENT(1983)

Jack McGowran
GENTLE GUNMAN, THE(1952, Brit.); NO RESTING PLACE(1952, Brit.); QUIET MAN, THE(1952); TITFIELD THUNDERBOLT, THE(1953, Brit.); JACQUELINE(1956, Brit.); STOWAWAY GIRL(1957, Brit.); BEHEMOTH, THE SEA MONSTER(1959, Brit.); CEREMONY, THE(1963, U.S./Span.)

Rodney McGrader
SPOOK WHO SAT BY THE DOOR, THE(1973)

Michael McGrady
1984
   BEAR, THE(1984)
Basil McGrail
   WHERE THERE'S A WILL(1937, Brit.); FLYING FIFTY-FIVE(1939, Brit.)
Walter McGrail
   BLOCKADE(1929); RIVER OF ROMANCE(1929); VEILED WOMAN, THE(1929); ANYBODY'S WAR(1930); LAST OF THE DUANES(1930); LONE STAR RANGER, THE(1930); MEN WITHOUT WOMEN(1930); PART TIME WIFE(1930); PAY OFF, THE(1930); SOLDIERS AND WOMEN(1930); WOMEN EVERYWHERE(1930); MURDER BY THE CLOCK(1931); NIGHT NURSE(1931); RIVER'S END(1931); SEAS BENEATH, THE(1931); EXPOSED(1932); MC KENNA OF THE MOUNTED(1932); NIGHT BEAT(1932); UNDER EIGHTEEN(1932); UNION DEPOT(1932); POLICE CALL(1933); ROBBERS' ROOST(1933); SING SINNER, SING(1933); STATE TROOPER(1933); DEMON FOR TROUBLE, A(1934); LEMON DROP KID, THE(1934); MEN OF THE NIGHT(1934); WORLD MOVES ON, THE(1934); SPECIAL AGENT K-7(1937); HELD FOR RANSOM(1938); ON THE GREAT WHITE TRAIL(1938); WEST OF RAINBOW'S END(1938); CALLING ALL MARINES(1939); CODE OF THE FEARLESS(1939); IN OLD MONTANA(1939); STAGECOACH(1939); GRAPES OF WRATH(1940); MY LITTLE CHICKADEE(1940); LAST OF THE DUANES(1941); BILLY THE KID TRAPPED(1942); RIDERS OF THE WEST(1942); DOUBLE LIFE, A(1947); LIFE OF HER OWN, A(1950); HERE COMES THE GROOM(1951)
Silents
   LIGHTS OF NEW YORK, THE(1916); ADVENTURE SHOP, THE(1918); EVERYBODY'S GIRL(1918); DARLING MINE(1920); GREATER THAN FAME(1920); BREAKING POINT, THE(1921); HER MAD BARGAIN(1921); INVISIBLE FEAR, THE(1921); PLAYTHINGS OF DESTINY(1921); CRADLE, THE(1922); KENTUCKY DERBY, THE(1922); SUZANNA(1922); ELEVENTH HOUR, THE(1923); IS DIVORCE A FAILURE?(1923); NOBODY'S MONEY(1923); IS LOVE EVERYTHING?(1924); ADVENTURE(1925); CHAMPION OF LOST CAUSES(1925); TOP OF NEW YORK, THE(1925); ACROSS THE PACIFIC(1926); 'MARRIAGE LICENSE?'(1926); AMERICAN BEAUTY(1927); MAN CRAZY(1927); HEY RUBE!(1928); MIDNIGHT MADNESS(1928); OLD CODE, THE(1928); PLAY GIRL, THE(1928); STOP THAT MAN(1928)
Misc. Silents
   DOLLAR AND THE LAW, THE(1916); INDISCRETION(1917); BUSINESS OF LIFE, THE(1918); FIND THE WOMAN(1918); MISS AMBITION(1918); SONG OF THE SOUL, THE(1918); TO THE HIGHEST BIDDER(1918); TRIUMPH OF THE WEAK, THE(1918); COUNTRY COUSIN, THE(1919); GIRL PROBLEM, THE(1919); BEWARE OF THE BRIDE(1920); BLIND YOUTH(1920); INVISIBLE DIVORCE, THE(1920); LIFE'S TWIST(1920); YOSEMITE TRAIL, THE(1922); BAD MAN, THE(1923); LIGHTS OUT(1923); WHERE THE NORTH BEGINS(1923); GERALD CRANSTON'S LADY(1924); SON OF THE SAHARA, A(1924); UNGUARDED WOMEN(1924); HAVOC(1925); SON OF HIS FATHER, A(1925); TEASER, THE(1925); WHEN THE DOOR OPENED(1925); COMBAT, THE(1926); FORBIDDEN WATERS(1926); PRISONERS OF THE STORM(1926); CONFESSIONS OF A WIFE(1928)
Walter McGrall
   SHADOW STRIKES, THE(1937)
Al McGranary
   RIOT IN JUVENILE PRISON(1959); SUNRISE AT CAMPOBELLO(1960)
T.J. McGrane
Misc. Silents
   TOO MANY CROOKS(1919)
Derek McGrath
   LAST DETAIL, THE(1973); MR. MOM(1983)
Doug McGrath
   GOIN' DOWN THE ROAD(1970, Can.); WEDDING IN WHITE(1972, Can.); HARD PART BEGINS, THE(1973, Can.); ESCAPE ARTIST, THE(1982); PORKY'S(1982); TWILIGHT ZONE–THE MOVIE(1983)
Douglas McGrath
   RUSSIAN ROULETTE(1975); GAUNTLET, THE(1977); BRONCO BILLY(1980)
Ed McGrath
   THUNDER IN CAROLINA(1960)
Frank McGrath
   VOGUES OF 1938(1937); RIDERS OF THE PURPLE SAGE(1941); SUNDOWN JIM(1942); OX-BOW INCIDENT, THE(1943); THEY WERE EXPENDABLE(1945); SOUTHERN YANKEE, A(1948); SHE WORE A YELLOW RIBBON(1949); MILKMAN, THE(1950); RIDE, VAQUERO!(1953); SEARCHERS, THE(1956); HELL BOUND(1957); TIN STAR, THE(1957); SWORD OF ALI BABA, THE(1965); GUNFIGHT IN ABILENE(1967); LAST CHALLENGE, THE(1967); RELUCTANT ASTRONAUT, THE(1967); TAMMY AND THE MILLIONAIRE(1967); WAR WAGON, THE(1967); SHAKIEST GUN IN THE WEST, THE(1968)
George McGrath
   ONE MORE TIME(1970, Brit.)
Graham McGrath
   KRULL(1983)
Harold McGrath
   RIGHT TO THE HEART(1942), w
Silents
   CARPET FROM BAGDAD, THE(1915), w; GOOSE GIRL, THE(1915), w; PUPPET CROWN, THE(1915), w; MOLLYCODDLE, THE(1920), w
Jack McGrath
   TO PLEASE A LADY(1950)
James McGrath
   SECRETS OF CHINATOWN(1935); SECRET PATROL(1936); STAMPEDE(1936); FURY AND THE WOMAN(1937); WOMAN AGAINST THE WORLD(1938); DEATH GOES NORTH(1939)
Joe McGrath
   RISING DAMP(1980, Brit.), d
John McGrath
   BILLION DOLLAR BRAIN(1967, Brit.), w; BOFORS GUN, THE(1968, Brit.), w; VIRGIN SOLDIERS, THE(1970, Brit.), w; RECKONING, THE(1971, Brit.), w
Silents
   GOLD RUSH, THE(1925)
Joseph McGrath
   CASINO ROYALE(1967, Brit.), d; BLISS OF MRS. BLOSSOM, THE(1968, Brit.), d; 30 IS A DANGEROUS AGE, CYNTHIA(1968, Brit.), d, w; MAGIC CHRISTIAN, THE(1970, Brit.), d, w; DIGBY, THE BIGGEST DOG IN THE WORLD(1974, Brit.), d; GREAT MCGONAGALL, THE(1975, Brit.), d, w

Judy McGrath
   AGE OF CONSENT(1969, Austral.)
Larry McGrath
   ARIZONA KID, THE(1930); SMART MONEY(1931); PICTURE BRIDES(1934); TWENTY MILLION SWEETHEARTS(1934); DR. SOCRATES(1935); STARS OVER BROADWAY(1935); DANGEROUS(1936); MILKY WAY, THE(1936); PERFECT SPECIMEN, THE(1937); FIFTH AVENUE GIRL(1939); GOLDEN BOY(1939); I STOLE A MILLION(1939); THUNDER AFLOAT(1939); PRIMROSE PATH(1940); MEET JOHN DOE(1941); MOON OVER MIAMI(1941); BROADWAY(1942); MIRACLE KID(1942); SIN TOWN(1942); WILSON(1944); RENEGADES OF THE RIO GRANDE(1945); THOSE ENDEARING YOUNG CHARMS(1945); DEADLINE AT DAWN(1946); TRAIL STREET(1947); RETURN OF THE BADMEN(1948); WHIPLASH(1948); WHITE HEAT(1949); DALLAS(1950); JACKIE ROBINSON STORY, THE(1950); KANSAS RAIDERS(1950); MILKMAN, THE(1950); FLAMING FEATHER(1951); SAILOR BEWARE(1951)
Silents
   KNOCKOUT REILLY(1927)
Leueen McGrath
   MOZART(1940, Brit.); SILK STOCKINGS(1957), w
Lulu McGrath
Misc. Silents
   WONDERS OF THE SEA(1922)
Maggie McGrath
   INTENT TO KILL(1958, Brit.); V.I.P.s, THE(1963, Brit.); GREAT ST. TRINIAN'S TRAIN ROBBERY, THE(1966, Brit.); HOSTILE WITNESS(1968, Brit.); FRAULEIN DOKTOR(1969, Ital./Yugo.); ALL THE WAY UP(1970, Brit.)
Margaret McGrath
   SCHWEIK'S NEW ADVENTURES(1943, Brit.); HER MAN GILBEY(1949, Brit.); BODY SAID NO!, THE(1950, Brit.); 23 PACES TO BAKER STREET(1956); NOWHERE TO GO(1959, Brit.); SEANCE ON A WET AFTERNOON(1964 Brit.)
Pat McGrath
   SOMEWHERE ON LEAVE(1942, Brit.); HALF-WAY HOUSE, THE(1945, Brit.); VARIETY JUBILEE(1945, Brit.); ODD MAN OUT(1947, Brit.); CUP-TIE HONEYMOON(1948, Brit.); GHOST SHIP(1953, Brit.); RADIO CAB MURDER(1954, Brit.), a, d&w; DEADLIEST SIN, THE(1956, Brit.)
Paul McGrath
   PAROLE FIXER(1940); THIS THING CALLED LOVE(1940); WILDCAT BUS(1940); DEAD MEN TELL(1941); MARRY THE BOSS' DAUGHTER(1941); WE GO FAST(1941); NO TIME FOR LOVE(1943); FACE IN THE CROWD, A(1957); ADVISE AND CONSENT(1962); PENDULUM(1969)
Richard McGrath
   I'D RATHER BE RICH(1964)
Thomas McGrath
Silents
   SENTIMENTAL LADY, THE(1915)
Thomas J. McGrath
   DEADLY HERO(1976), p
Tom McGrath
Misc. Silents
   CHAIN INVISIBLE, THE(1916)
William McGrath
   SECRETS OF WU SIN(1932), w; LADIES THEY TALK ABOUT(1933), w

Bill McGraw
   COPPER SKY(1957); BLOOD ARROW(1958)
Charles McGraw
   UNDYING MONSTER, THE(1942); DESTROYER(1943); MAD GHOUL, THE(1943); MOON IS DOWN, THE(1943); THEY CAME TO BLOW UP AMERICA(1943); IMPOSTER, THE(1944); KILLERS, THE(1946); BIG FIX, THE(1947); BRUTE FORCE(1947); FARMER'S DAUGHTER, THE(1947); GANGSTER, THE(1947); LONG NIGHT, THE(1947); ON THE OLD SPANISH TRAIL(1947); ROSES ARE RED(1947); T-MEN(1947); BERLIN EXPRESS(1948); BLOOD ON THE MOON(1948); HAZARD(1948); HUNTED, THE(1948); BLACK BOOK, THE(1949); BORDER INCIDENT(1949); ONCE MORE, MY DARLING(1949); STORY OF MOLLY X, THE(1949); THREAT, THE(1949); ARMORED CAR ROBBERY(1950); DOUBLE CROSSBONES(1950); I WAS A SHOPLIFTER(1950); MA AND PA KETTLE GO TO TOWN(1950); SIDE STREET(1950); HIS KIND OF WOMAN(1951); ROADBLOCK(1951); NARROW MARGIN, THE(1952); ONE MINUTE TO ZERO(1952); THUNDER OVER THE PLAINS(1953); WAR PAINT(1953); BRIDGES AT TOKO-RI, THE(1954); LOOPHOLE(1954); AWAY ALL BOATS(1956); CRUEL TOWER, THE(1956); TOWARD THE UNKNOWN(1956); JOE BUTTERFLY(1957); JOE DAKOTA(1957); SLAUGHTER ON TENTH AVENUE(1957); DEFIANT ONES, THE(1958); SADDLE THE WIND(1958); TWILIGHT FOR THE GODS(1958); MAN IN THE NET, THE(1959); WONDERFUL COUNTRY, THE(1959); CIMARRON(1960); SPARTACUS(1960); HORIZONTAL LIEUTENANT, THE(1962); BIRDS, THE(1963); IT'S A MAD, MAD, MAD WORLD(1963); BUSYBODY(1967); IN COLD BLOOD(1967); PENDULUM(1969); TELL THEM WILLIE BOY IS HERE(1969); CHANDLER(1971); JOHNNY GOT HIS GUN(1971); BOY AND HIS DOG, A(1975); KILLER INSIDE ME, THE(1976); TWILIGHT'S LAST GLEAMING(1977, U.S./Ger.)
Frank McGraw
   RED BADGE OF COURAGE, THE(1951)
Hugh McGraw
   FUNNYMAN(1967), p; LONG RIDERS, THE(1980)
John J. McGraw
Misc. Silents
   ONE TOUCH OF NATURE(1917)
William McGraw
   CATTLE EMPIRE(1958)
Joe McGray
Silents
   PENROD AND SAM(1923)
P.S. McGreeney
Misc. Silents
   GERM, THE(1923), d
Annie McGreevey
   BELOW THE BELT(1980)
John McGreevey
   HOT ROD GIRL(1956), w; DEATH IN SMALL DOSES(1957), w; BEAST OF BUDAPEST, THE(1958), w; CAST A LONG SHADOW(1959), w; NIGHT CROSSING(1982), w

Michael McGreevey
DAY OF THE OUTLAW(1959); WAY WEST, THE(1967); DEATH OF A GUNFIGHT-ER(1969); COMPUTER WORE TENNIS SHOES, THE(1970); NOW YOU SEE HIM, NOW YOU DON'T(1972); SNOWBALL EXPRESS(1972); STRONGEST MAN IN THE WORLD, THE(1975); SHAGGY D.A., THE(1976)

Mike McGreevey
CHARTROOSE CABOOSE(1960); CLOWN AND THE KID, THE(1961); IMPOSSIBLE YEARS, THE(1968)

John McGreevy
HELLO DOWN THERE(1969), w

Mike McGreevy
MAN IN THE NET, THE(1959)

Molly McGreevy
SHOOT IT: BLACK, SHOOT IT: BLUE(1974)

Oliver McGreevy
STRANGE AFFECTION(1959, Brit.); CHRISTMAS TREE, THE(1966, Brit.)

Angela Punch McGregor
ISLAND, THE(1980); SURVIVOR(1980, Aus.); WE OF THE NEVER NEVER(1983, Aus.)

Barry McGregor
SKID KIDS(1953, Brit.)

Charles McGregor
ACROSS 110TH STREET(1972); SUPERFLY(1972); THREE THE HARD WAY(1974); AARON LOVES ANGELA(1975); TAKE A HARD RIDE(1975, U.S./Ital.)

Craig McGregor
LIBIDO(1973, Aus.), w

Eduardo McGregor
1984
DEMONS IN THE GARDEN(1984, Span.)

Gordon McGregor
Misc. Silents
RICH GIRL, POOR GIRL(1921); RUSE OF THE RATTLER, THE(1921)

Hector McGregor
LOVE AT SEA(1936, Brit.); HUNGRY HILL(1947, Brit.)

Johnnie McGregor
MYSTERY AT THE BURLESQUE(1950, Brit.)

Julie McGregor
PALM BEACH(1979, Aus.)

Kathleen McGregor
MOUNTAIN MEN, THE(1980), cos

Malcolm McGregor
WHISPERING WINDS(1929); MURDER WILL OUT(1930); CAR 99(1935)
Silents
PRISONER OF ZENDA, THE(1922); ALL THE BROTHERS WERE VALIANT(1923); NOISE IN NEWBORO, A(1923); SOCIAL CODE, THE(1923); BEDROOM WINDOW, THE(1924); HOUSE OF YOUTH, THE(1924); FLAMING WATERS(1925); LADY OF THE NIGHT(1925); OVERLAND LIMITED, THE(1925); IT MUST BE LOVE(1926); KID SISTER, THE(1927); LADYBIRD, THE(1927); MATINEE LADIES(1927); FREEDOM OF THE PRESS(1928); LINGERIE(1928); STORMY WATERS(1928)
Misc. Silents
BROKEN CHAINS(1922); DANCER OF THE NILE, THE(1923); UNTAMEABLE, THE(1923); YOU CAN'T GET AWAY WITH IT(1923); ALIAS MARY FLYNN(1925); CIRCLE, THE(1925); GIRL OF GOLD, THE(1925); HAPPY WARRIOR, THE(1925); HEADLINES(1925); INFATUATION(1925); SMOULDERING FIRES(1925); VANISH-ING AMERICAN, THE(1925); DON JUAN'S THREE NIGHTS(1926); GAY DECEIVER, THE(1926); MONEY TO BURN(1926); GIRL FROM GAY PAREE, THE(1927); MILLION BID, A(1927); PRICE OF HONOR, THE(1927); WRECK, THE(1927); BUCK PRIVA-TES(1928); PORT OF MISSING GIRLS, THE(1928); TROPICAL NIGHTS(1928)

Malcom McGregor
GIRL ON THE BARGE, THE(1929)

Sandy McGregor
PETERSEN(1974, Aus.); HIGH ROLLING(1977, Aus.)

Scott McGregor
SHADOW OF FEAR(1956, Brit.), art d; HORROR OF FRANKENSTEIN, THE(1970, Brit.), art d

Sean McGregor
DEVIL TIMES FIVE(1974), d
Misc. Talkies
CAMPER JOHN(1973), d; NIGHTMARE COUNTY(1977), d

Tali McGregor
1984
GREYSTOKE: THE LEGEND OF TARZAN, LORD OF THE APES(1984)

Kate McGregor-Stewart
TATTOO(1981); MIDSUMMER NIGHT'S SEX COMEDY, A(1982); WORLD ACCORD-ING TO GARP, The(1982)

Brian McGrellis
DOUBLE, THE(1963, Brit)

Rod McGrew
CARWASH(1976)

Skeets McGrew
DOUBLES(1978), ed

Sidney McGrey
ARROWSMITH(1931)

Bobby McGriff
LAST PICTURE SHOW, THE(1971)

William McGrow
SQUEEZE, THE(1977, Brit.), art d

Thomas McGuane
SPORTING CLUB, THE(1971), w; RANCHO DELUXE(1975), w; 92 IN THE SHA-DE(1975, U.S./Brit.), d&w; MISSOURI BREAKS, THE(1976), w; TOM HORN(1980), w

Bill McGuffie
IT TAKES A THIEF(1960, Brit.), a, m; TOO HOT TO HANDLE(1961, Brit.); UN-STOPPABLE MAN, THE(1961, Brit.), m; DURING ONE NIGHT(1962, Brit.), m; COME-DY MAN, THE(1964), m; LEATHER BOYS, THE(1965, Brit.), m; CORRUPTION(1968, Brit.), m

Mary-Beth McGuffin
LIFE AND TIMES OF CHESTER-ANGUS RAMSGOOD, THE(1971, Can.)

Penny McGuiggan
KENTUCKY JUBILEE(1951); TAKE CARE OF MY LITTLE GIRL(1951)

James K. McGuiness
THREE SISTERS, THE(1930), w; MEN ON CALL(1931), w; COCKTAIL HOUR(1933), w

James Kevin McGuiness
WHEN STRANGERS MARRY(1933), w; I TAKE THIS WOMAN(1940), w

Joe McGuinn
MARSHAL OF MESA CITY, THE(1939); DARK COMMAND, THE(1940); PIONEERS OF THE WEST(1940); RIDE, TENDERFOOT, RIDE(1940); WAGONS WEST-WARD(1940); BACK IN THE SADDLE(1941); MEET JOHN DOE(1941); OFFICER AND THE LADY, THE(1941); SECRETS OF THE LONE WOLF(1941); THUNDER OVER THE PRAIRIE(1941); CYCLONE KID, THE(1942); DEVIL'S TRAIL, THE(1942); GLASS KEY, THE(1942); RIDERS OF THE NORTHLAND(1942); SHUT MY BIG MOUTH(1942); SUNDOWN KID, THE(1942); TALK OF THE TOWN(1942); WIFE TAKES A FLYER, THE(1942); ONE DANGEROUS NIGHT(1943); CHEROKEE FLASH, THE(1945); SUNSET IN EL DORADO(1945); MARRYING KIND, THE(1952); SOUTH PACIFIC TRAIL(1952); HANNAH LEE(1953); JACK MCCALL, DESPERADO(1953); CHICAGO CONFIDENTIAL(1957); 10 NORTH FREDERICK(1958); GAMBLER WORE A GUN, THE(1961); WILD WESTERNERS, THE(1962)

John McGuinn
PALS OF THE SILVER SAGE(1940)

Joseph McGuinn
THREE BRAVE MEN(1957); SHOWDOWN AT BOOT HILL(1958); STORY ON PAGE ONE, THE(1959)

Joseph F. McGuinn
PRINCE OF PIRATES(1953)

Roger McGuinn
RENALDO AND CLARA(1978)

Carola McGuinness
BODY HEAT(1981)

J. K. McGuinness
WEST OF BROADWAY(1931), w; ATTORNEY FOR THE DEFENSE(1932), w; HELL DIVERS(1932), w; THIS SPORTING AGE(1932), w

J. Kevin McGuinness
TARZAN AND HIS MATE(1934), w

James K. McGuinness
SOLITAIRE MAN, THE(1933), w; WEST POINT OF THE AIR(1935), w; LORD JEFF(1938), w
Silents
SLAVES OF BEAUTY(1927), t; GIRL IN EVERY PORT, A(1928), w; CAPTAIN LASH(1929), ed

James Kevin McGuinness
BLACK WATCH, THE(1929), w; SALUTE(1929), w; MEN WITHOUT WOMEN(1930), w; CHINA SEAS(1935), w; NIGHT AT THE OPERA, A(1935), w; MADAME X(1937), p; ARSENE LUPIN RETURNS(1938), w; FLORIAN(1940), w; MEN OF BOYS TOWN(1941), w; RIO GRANDE(1950), w
Silents
WOMAN WISE(1928), w; STRONG BOY(1929), w

Mr. McGuinness
Silents
IN THE DAYS OF SAINT PATRICK(1920, Brit.), w

Al McGuire
1984
GIRLS NIGHT OUT(1984)

Alison McGuire
1984
GIVE MY REGARDS TO BROAD STREET(1984, Brit.)

Anne Tucker McGuire
STRANGERS ON A HONEYMOON(1937, Brit.)

Annie McGuire
ROSE, THE(1979); SMALL CIRCLE OF FRIENDS, A(1980); TOY, THE(1982)

Barry McGuire
STREET OF SINNERS(1957); WEREWOLVES ON WHEELS(1971)

Betty McGuire
UP IN SMOKE(1978); HEROES(1977); COMA(1978); HOMETOWN U.S.A.(1979)

Biff McGuire
YOU'RE IN THE NAVY NOW(1951); PHENIX CITY STORY, THE(1955); STATION SIX-SAHARA(1964, Brit./Ger.); HEART IS A LONELY HUNTER, THE(1968); THOMAS CROWN AFFAIR, THE(1968); SERPICO(1973); WEREWOLF OF WASHING-TON(1973); MIDWAY(1976); LAST WORD, THE(1979); FIREBIRD 2015 AD(1981), w

Billy McGuire
THUNDER BIRDS(1942)

Dennis McGuire
SHOOT IT: BLACK, SHOOT IT: BLUE(1974), w, d

Derek McGuire
HERO(1982, Brit.)

Don McGuire
GOD IS MY CO-PILOT(1945); PILLOW TO POST(1945); PRIDE OF THE MARI-NES(1945); SAN ANTONIO(1945); TOO YOUNG TO KNOW(1945); HUMORE-SQUE(1946); MAN I LOVE, THE(1946); SHADOW OF A WOMAN(1946); ALWAYS TOGETHER(1947); LOVE AND LEARN(1947); MY WILD IRISH ROSE(1947); NORA PRENTISS(1947); POSSESSED(1947); THAT WAY WITH WOMEN(1947); FULLER BRUSH MAN(1948); I SURRENDER DEAR(1948); WALLFLOWER(1948); WHI-PLASH(1948); BOSTON BLACKIE'S CHINESE VENTURE(1949); THREAT, THE(1949); ARMORED CAR ROBBERY(1950); DIAL 1119(1950), w; DOUBLE DEAL(1950), w; JOE PALOOKA MEETS HUMPHREY(1950); SIDESHOW(1950); DOU-BLE DYNAMITE(1951); THREE GUYS NAMED MIKE(1951); BACK AT THE FRONT(1952), w; MEET DANNY WILSON(1952), w; WALKING MY BABY BACK HOME(1953), w; THREE RING CIRCUS(1954), w; JOHNNY CONCHO(1956), d, w; DELICATE DELINQUENT, THE(1957), a, d&w; FEAR STRIKES OUT(1957); HEAR ME GOOD(1957), p,d&w; TALL STRANGER, THE(1957); SUPPOSE THEY GAVE A WAR AND NOBODY CAME?(1970), w; TOOTSIE(1982), w

Dorothy McGuire
CLAUDIA(1943); ENCHANTED COTTAGE, THE(1945); TREE GROWS IN BROOK-LYN, A(1945); CLAUDIA AND DAVID(1946); SPIRAL STAIRCASE, THE(1946); TILL THE END OF TIME(1946); GENTLEMAN'S AGREEMENT(1947); MISTER 880(1950); MOTHER DIDN'T TELL ME(1950); CALLAWAY WENT THATAWAY(1951); I WANT YOU(1951); INVITATION(1952); MAKE HASTE TO LIVE(1954); THREE COINS IN THE FOUNTAIN(1954); TRIAL(1955); FRIENDLY PERSUASION(1956); OLD YELL-

ER(1957); REMARKABLE MR. PENNYPACKER, THE(1959); SUMMER PLACE, A(1959); THIS EARTH IS MINE(1959); DARK AT THE TOP OF THE STAIRS, THE(1960); SWISS FAMILY ROBINSON(1960); SUSAN SLADE(1961); SUMMER MAGIC(1963); GREATEST STORY EVER TOLD, THE(1965); FLIGHT OF THE DOVES(1971); JONATHAN LIVINGSTON SEAGULL(1973)

Duke McGuire
1984
NATURAL, THE(1984)

Florence McGuire
Silents
COST, THE(1920)

George McGuire
AIR STRIKE(1955), ed; GIRL FROM SCOTLAND YARD, THE(1937), ed; MIND YOUR OWN BUSINESS(1937), ed; DEERSLAYER(1943), ed; DETOUR(1945), ed; FOG ISLAND(1945), ed; DANNY BOY(1946), ed; DEATH VALLEY(1946), ed; DON RICARDO RETURNS(1946), ed; I RING DOORBELLS(1946), ed; BELLS OF SAN FERNANDO(1947), ed; SCARED TO DEATH(1947), ed; ENCHANTED VALLEY, THE(1948), ed; TEXAN MEETS CALAMITY JANE, THE(1950), ed
Silents
DIVORCE(1923); DESERT FLOWER, THE(1925), ed; LOST WORLD, THE(1925), ed; SALLY(1925), ed; FREEDOM OF THE PRESS(1928), ed; JAZZLAND(1928), ed; NIGHT WATCH, THE(1928), ed

Gerard McGuire
KITTY AND THE BAGMAN(1983, Aus.)

Harp McGuire
ON THE BEACH(1959); CAGE OF EVIL(1960); WALKING TARGET, THE(1960); INCIDENT IN AN ALLEY(1962)

Holden McGuire
MOTHER'S DAY(1980)

Hugh McGuire
ONCE UPON A TIME(1944)

Ida McGuire
BOOMERANG(1947); MIRACLE ON 34TH STREET, THE(1947)

James F. McGuire
THEY CALL ME MISTER TIBBS(1970), prod d; ORGANIZATION, THE(1971), prod d

James McGuire
Misc. Talkies
TUCK EVERLASTING(1981)

James P. McGuire
CALL NORTHSIDE 777(1948), w

John H. McGuire
DANTE'S INFERNO(1935)

John McGuire
STEAMBOAT ROUND THE BEND(1935); THIS IS THE LIFE(1935); YOUR UNCLE DUDLEY(1935); CHARLIE CHAN AT THE CIRCUS(1936); END OF THE TRAIL(1936); HUMAN CARGO(1936); PRISONER OF SHARK ISLAND, THE(1936); WANTED: JANE TURNER(1936); STRANGER ON THE THIRD FLOOR(1940); STREET OF MEMORIES(1940); WOMEN WITHOUT NAMES(1940); INVISIBLE GHOST, THE(1941); MAYOR OF 44TH STREET, THE(1942); MEXICAN SPITFIRE SEES A GHOST(1942); SHADOW OF A DOUBT(1943); BELLS OF SAN ANGELO(1947); FIGHTER SQUADRON(1948); HE WALKED BY NIGHT(1948); RIVER LADY(1948); STRAWBERRY ROAN, THE(1948); LADY TAKES A SAILOR, THE(1949); SANDS OF IWO JIMA(1949); SKY LINER(1949); TASK FORCE(1949); WHITE HEAT(1949); FEDERAL AGENT AT LARGE(1950); MILITARY ACADEMY WITH THAT TENTH AVENUE GANG(1950); TO PLEASE A LADY(1950); WHERE THE SIDEWALK ENDS(1950); CALL ME MISTER(1951); FIRST LEGION, THE(1951); FORCE OF ARMS(1951); STRIP, THE(1951); TANKS ARE COMING, THE(1951); YOU'RE IN THE NAVY NOW(1951)
Misc. Talkies
OUTLAW RULE(1935)

Kathryn McGuire
LONG, LONG TRAIL, THE(1929); LOST ZEPPELIN(1930)
Silents
SILENT CALL, THE(1921); NAVIGATOR, THE(1924); SHERLOCK, JR.(1924); EASY GOING GORDON(1925); LILAC TIME(1928)
Misc. Silents
PLAYING WITH FIRE(1921); FLAME OF LIFE, THE(1923); LOVE PIRATE, THE(1923); PRINTER'S DEVIL, THE(1923); SHRIEK OF ARABY, THE(1923); WOMAN OF BRONZE, THE(1923); PHANTOM JUSTICE(1924); DASHING THRU(1925); TEARING THROUGH(1925); TWO-FISTED JONES(1925); BUFFALO BILL ON THE U.P. TRAIL(1926); DAVY CROCKETT AT THE FALL OF THE ALAMO(1926); MIDNIGHT FACES(1926); SOMEBODY'S MOTHER(1926); STACKED CARDS(1926); THRILL HUNTER, THE(1926); GIRL IN THE PULLMAN, THE(1927); NAUGHTY BUT NICE(1927); BIG DIAMOND ROBBERY, THE(1929); BORDER WILDCAT, THE(1929); SYNTHETIC SIN(1929)

Kathy McGuire
1984
BAY BOY(1984, Can.)

Laurence McGuire
Misc. Silents
HEARTS OF THE WOODS(1921)

Lawrence McGuire
ATLANTIC CITY(1981, U.S./Can.)

Linda McGuire
SHOOT IT: BLACK, SHOOT IT: BLUE(1974)

Mac McGuire
REUBEN, REUBEN(1983)

Maeve McGuire
FOR LOVE OF IVY(1968); LAST SUMMER(1969)

Marcy McGuire
SEVEN DAYS LEAVE(1942); AROUND THE WORLD(1943); HIGHER AND HIGHER(1943); SEVEN DAYS ASHORE(1944); SING YOUR WAY HOME(1945); DING DONG WILLIAMS(1946); IT HAPPENED IN BROOKLYN(1947); YOU GOTTA STAY HAPPY(1948); JUMPING JACKS(1952); SUMMER MAGIC(1963)

Marion McGuire
FOLLIES GIRL(1943); CAPTAIN TUGBOAT ANNIE(1945)

Michael McGuire
DANNY BOY(1946); GOLDEN GLOVES STORY, THE(1950); INTRUDER, THE(1955, Brit.); WHERE'S POPPA?(1970); THEY MIGHT BE GIANTS(1971); BLADE(1973); HARD TIMES(1975); REPORT TO THE COMMISSIONER(1975); JEKYLL AND HYDE...TOGETHER AGAIN(1982); PARTNERS(1982)

Mickey McGuire [Mickey Rooney]
HIGH SPEED(1932); OFFICER 13(1933); ONCE UPON A TIME(1944); FOR THE LOVE OF RUSTY(1947); FORCE OF EVIL(1948); MY DOG RUSTY(1948); RUSTY LEADS THE WAY(1948); SUN COMES UP, THE(1949)

Mitchell McGuire
OH! CALCUTTA!(1972)

Neil McGuire
UNKNOWN GUEST, THE(1943), art d

Paul McGuire
DAMNED DON'T CRY, THE(1950); RAIDERS OF TOMAHAWK CREEK(1950); BONANZA TOWN(1951); I WAS A COMMUNIST FOR THE F.B.I.(1951); PEOPLE AGAINST O'HARA, THE(1951); SIERRA PASSAGE(1951); YUKON MANHUNT(1951); MARA MARU(1952); SEA TIGER(1952); WILD BLUE YONDER, THE(1952); SKY COMMANDO(1953); SON OF BELLE STARR(1953); THUNDER PASS(1954); BIG BLUFF, THE(1955); INTERRUPTED MELODY(1955); LOVE ME OR LEAVE ME(1955); ONE DESIRE(1955); SEMINOLE UPRISING(1955); SPOILERS, THE(1955); REPRISAL(1956); SECRET OF TREASURE MOUNTAIN(1956); BAND OF ANGELS(1957); PURPLE GANG, THE(1960)

Phyllis McGuire
COME BLOW YOUR HORN(1963)

Richard McGuire
1984
JUNGLE WARRIORS(1984, U.S./Ger./Mex.), art d

Stephen McGuire
Misc. Talkies
EVERYDAY(1976)

Tom McGuire
LIGHTS OF NEW YORK(1928); VOICE OF THE CITY(1929); POLITICS(1931); BY WHOSE HAND?(1932); HEARTS OF HUMANITY(1932); NO GREATER LOVE(1932); MAMA LOVES PAPA(1933); SHE DONE HIM WRONG(1933); UPPER WORLD(1934); CHARLIE CHAN AT THE OPERA(1936); SAN FRANCISCO(1936); SHE'S DANGEROUS(1937); MEET JOHN DOE(1941); MAJOR AND THE MINOR, THE(1942); HAIL THE CONQUERING HERO(1944); NIGHT AND DAY(1946); T-MEN(1947); MAD WEDNESDAY(1950)
Silents
STRANGER THAN FICTION(1921); AFRAID TO FIGHT(1922); FRONT PAGE STORY, A(1922); APRIL SHOWERS(1923); SCARLET CAR, THE(1923); DARK STAIRWAYS(1924); HER MAN(1924); RECKLESS AGE, THE(1924); BETTER 'OLE, THE(1926); BABE COMES HOME(1927); STEAMBOAT BILL, JR.(1928)
Misc. Silents
R.S.V.P.(1921); MILLION TO BURN, A(1923); FIGHTING FATE(1925); MISSING LINK, THE(1927)

Tucker McGuire
CLOTHES AND THE WOMAN(1937, Brit.); CLIMBING HIGH(1938, Brit.); SHIPYARD SALLY(1940, Brit.); TERROR HOUSE(1942, Brit.); KING OF THE UNDERWORLD(1952, Brit.); PROJECT M7(1953, Brit.); NIGHT TO REMEMBER, A(1958, Brit.); SHERIFF OF FRACTURED JAW, THE(1958, Brit.); REVOLUTIONARY, THE(1970, Brit.)
Misc. Talkies
MURDER AT SCOTLAND YARD(1952)

William Anthony McGuire
WHOOPEE(1930), w; DON'T BET ON WOMEN(1931), w; SIX CYLINDER LOVE(1931), w; DISORDERLY CONDUCT(1932), w; KID FROM SPAIN, THE(1932), w; OKAY AMERICA(1932), w; SHE WANTED A MILLIONAIRE(1932), w; KING FOR A NIGHT(1933), w; KISS BEFORE THE MIRROR, THE(1933), w; OUT ALL NIGHT(1933), w; ROMAN SCANDALS(1933), w; EMBARRASSING MOMENTS(1934), w; I BELIEVED IN YOU(1934), w; LET'S BE RITZY(1934), w; LITTLE MAN, WHAT NOW?(1934), w; MONEY MEANS NOTHING(1934), w; GREAT ZIEGFELD, THE(1936), w; ROSALIE(1937), p, w; GIRL OF THE GOLDEN WEST, THE(1938), p; HONEYMOON'S OVER, THE(1939), w; LILLIAN RUSSELL(1940), w; ZIEGFELD GIRL(1941), w
Silents
TANGLED FATES(1916), w; KID BOOTS(1926), w; TIN GODS(1926), w; TWELVE MILES OUT(1927), w

Sheila McGuire-Taylor
TIM(1981, Aus.)

Charles McGuirk
HOT FOR PARIS(1930), w
Silents
PAIR OF SIXES, A(1918), w

Charles J. McGuirk
HARMONY AT HOME(1930), w
Silents
EFFICIENCY EDGAR'S COURTSHIP(1917), w

Robert McGunigle
LADY BE GOOD(1941), w

Bob McGurk
JANIE(1944)

Frank McGurran
I AM THE CHEESE(1983)

Gary McGurrin
SIX PACK(1982)

Christopher McHale
SEDUCTION OF JOE TYNAN, THE(1979)

Dick McHale
THEY SAVED HITLER'S BRAIN(1964)

James McHale
KELLY'S HEROES(1970, U.S./Yugo.)

Michael McHale
THREAT, THE(1949); STORM WARNING(1950); MOB, THE(1951); STOP THAT CAB(1951); DUFFY OF SAN QUENTIN(1954); ENEMY BELOW, THE(1957)

Kathy McHaley
DIXIE DYNAMITE(1976)

Scotty McHarg
MY HEART GOES CRAZY(1953, Brit.)
Lindsay McHarrie
TWO KINDS OF WOMEN(1932)
Stephen McHattie
PEOPLE NEXT DOOR, THE(1970); ULTIMATE WARRIOR, THE(1975); MOVING VIOLATION(1976); GRAY LADY DOWN(1978); TOMORROW NEVER COMES(1978, Brit./Can.); DEATH VALLEY(1982)
Steve McHattie
VON RICHTHOFEN AND BROWN(1970)
Bob McHeady
CANNIBAL GIRLS(1973)
Robert McHeady
FOXY LADY(1971, Can.); DERANGED(1974, Can.)
Curtin McHenry
Silents
GREAT K & A TRAIN ROBBERY, THE(1926)
Don McHenry
THREE DAYS OF THE CONDOR(1975)
Marjorie McHenry
QUACKSER FORTUNE HAS A COUSIN IN THE BRONX(1970)
Mike McHenry
SUMMER SCHOOL TEACHERS(1977)
Charles McHugh
SMILING IRISH EYES(1929)
Silents
FAME AND FORTUNE(1918); SHOCKING NIGHT, A(1921); BEAUTIFUL AND DAMNED, THE(1922); EAGLE'S FEATHER, THE(1923); GIRL OF THE GOLDEN WEST, THE(1923); SMILIN' AT TROUBLE(1925); WANING SEX, THE(1926); FINNEGAN'S BALL(1927); PRINCESS FROM HOBOKEN, THE(1927); PHANTOM OF THE RANGE(1928)
Misc. Silents
GOAT, THE(1918); QUITTER, THE(1929)
Charles P. McHugh
Silents
DOWN TO EARTH(1917)
Charlie McHugh
Silents
NAN OF MUSIC MOUNTAIN(1917)
David McHugh
NOBODY'S PERFEKT(1981), m
1984
MOSCOW ON THE HUDSON(1984), m
Florence McHugh
ROMANY LOVE(1931, Brit.)
Frank McHugh
COLLEGE LOVERS(1930); DAWN PATROL, THE(1930); TOP SPEED(1930); WIDOW FROM CHICAGO, THE(1930); BAD COMPANY(1931); BRIGHT LIGHTS(1931); CORSAIR(1931); FRONT PAGE, THE(1931); GOING WILD(1931); KISS ME AGAIN(1931); MEN OF THE SKY(1931); MILLIE(1931); TRAVELING HUSBANDS(1931); UP FOR MURDER(1931); CROWD ROARS, THE(1932); DARK HORSE, THE(1932); HIGH PRESSURE(1932); LIFE BEGINS(1932); ONE WAY PASSAGE(1932); STRANGE LOVE OF MOLLY LOUVAIN, THE(1932); UNION DEPOT(1932); CONVENTION CITY(1933); ELMER THE GREAT(1933); EX-LADY(1933); FOOTLIGHT PARADE(1933); GRAND SLAM(1933); HAVANA WIDOWS(1933); HOLD ME TIGHT(1933); HOUSE ON 56TH STREET, THE(1933); LILLY TURNER(1933); MYSTERY OF THE WAX MUSEUM, THE(1933); PARACHUTE JUMPER(1933); PRIVATE JONES(1933); PROFESSIONAL SWEETHEART(1933); SON OF A SAILOR(1933); TELEGRAPH TRAIL, THE(1933); TOMORROW AT SEVEN(1933); FASHIONS OF 1934(1934); HAPPINESS AHEAD(1934); HEAT LIGHTNING(1934); HERE COMES THE NAVY(1934); LET'S BE RITZY(1934); MERRY WIVES OF RENO, THE(1934); RETURN OF THE TERROR(1934); SIX-DAY BIKE RIDER(1934); SMARTY(1934); DEVIL DOGS OF THE AIR(1935); GOLD DIGGERS OF 1935(1935); IRISH IN US, THE(1935); MAYBE IT'S LOVE(1935); MIDSUMMER'S NIGHT'S DREAM, A(1935); PAGE MISS GLORY(1935); STARS OVER BROADWAY(1935); THREE KIDS AND A QUEEN(1935); BULLETS OR BALLOTS(1936); FRESHMAN LOVE(1936); MOONLIGHT MURDER(1936); SNOWED UNDER(1936); STAGE STRUCK(1936); THREE MEN ON A HORSE(1936); EVER SINCE EVE(1937); MARRY THE GIRL(1937); MR. DODD TAKES THE AIR(1937); SUBMARINE D-1(1937); BOY MEETS GIRL(1938); FOUR DAUGHTERS(1938); HE COULDN'T SAY NO(1938); LITTLE MISS THOROUGHBRED(1938); SWING YOUR LADY(1938); VALLEY OF THE GIANTS(1938); DAUGHTERS COURAGEOUS(1939); DODGE CITY(1939); DUST BE MY DESTINY(1939); FOUR WIVES(1939); INDIANAPOLIS SPEEDWAY(1939); ON YOUR TOES(1939); ROARING TWENTIES, THE(1939); WINGS OF THE NAVY(1939); FIGHTING 69TH, THE(1940); I LOVE YOU AGAIN(1940); 'TIL WE MEET AGAIN(1940); VIRGINIA CITY(1940); BACK STREET(1941); CITY, FOR CONQUEST(1941); FOUR MOTHERS(1941); MANPOWER(1941); ALL THROUGH THE NIGHT(1942); HER CARDBOARD LOVER(1942); BOWERY TO BROADWAY(1944); GOING MY WAY(1944); MARINE RAIDERS(1944); MEDAL FOR BENNY, A(1945); STATE FAIR(1945); HOODLUM SAINT, THE(1946); LITTLE MISS BIG(1946); RUNAROUND, THE(1946); EASY COME, EASY GO(1947); VELVET TOUCH, THE(1948); MIGHTY JOE YOUNG(1949); MISS GRANT TAKES RICHMOND(1949); PAID IN FULL(1950); TOUGHER THEY COME, THE(1950); MY SON, JOHN(1952); PACE THAT THRILLS, THE(1952); IT HAPPENS EVERY THURSDAY(1953); LION IS IN THE STREETS, A(1953); THERE'S NO BUSINESS LIKE SHOW BUSINESS(1954); LAST HURRAH, THE(1958); CAREER(1959); SAY ONE FOR ME(1959); TIGER WALKS, A(1964); EASY COME, EASY GO(1967)
Jack McHugh
CHINATOWN NIGHTS(1929); MAN WITH TWO FACES, THE(1934); IRISH IN US, THE(1935); SPECIAL AGENT(1935); SIX-GUN RHYTHM(1939)
Jimmy McHugh
BREEZING HOME(1937), m; HELEN MORGAN STORY, THE(1959)
John McIndoe
I'LL WALK BESIDE YOU(1943, Brit.); I'LL TURN TO YOU(1946, Brit.)
Kathryn "Kitty" McHugh
HOLLYWOOD BOULEVARD(1936)
Kittie McHugh
BLONDE TROUBLE(1937)

Kitty McHugh
HOT TIP(1935); SUNSET RANGE(1935); LONGEST NIGHT, THE(1936); WOMEN ARE TROUBLE(1936); MAKE WAY FOR TOMORROW(1937); OH DOCTOR(1937); ON AGAIN-OFF AGAIN(1937); LETTER OF INTRODUCTION(1938); MEN WITH WINGS(1938); MY OLD KENTUCKY HOME(1938); BROADWAY SERENADE(1939); DISPUTED PASSAGE(1939); WHEN TOMORROW COMES(1939); GRAPES OF WRATH(1940); HOUSE ACROSS THE BAY, THE(1940); MA, HE'S MAKING EYES AT ME(1940); SECRET EVIDENCE(1941); MAGNIFICENT DOPE, THE(1942); MORE THE MERRIER, THE(1943); SCREAM IN THE DARK, A(1943); SLEEPY LAGOON(1943); STREET WITH NO NAME, THE(1948); TENSION(1949); JENNIFER(1953)
Martin J. McHugh
RISING OF THE MOON, THE(1957, Ireland), w
Matt McHugh
TRUE TO LIFE(1943); UNCLE HARRY(1945); STREET SCENE(1931); AFRAID TO TALK(1932); FREAKS(1932); LOVE IS A RACKET(1932); PURCHASE PRICE, THE(1932); TAXI!(1932); TWO SECONDS(1932); WOMAN FROM MONTE CARLO, THE(1932); DANCING LADY(1933); DEVIL'S BROTHER, THE(1933); HARD TO HANDLE(1933); HYPNOTIZED(1933); MAD GAME, THE(1933); MAN WHO DARED, THE(1933); NIGHT OF TERROR(1933); PRIZEFIGHTER AND THE LADY, THE(1933); CAT'S PAW, THE(1934); FUGITIVE LADY(1934); JUDGE PRIEST(1934); LAST TRAIL, THE(1934); SHE LOVES ME NOT(1934); BARBARY COAST(1935); DIAMOND JIM(1935); ENTER MADAME(1935); GLASS KEY, THE(1935); LADIES CRAVE EXCITEMENT(1935); LOST IN THE STRATOSPHERE(1935); MR. DYNAMITE(1935); MURDER ON A HONEYMOON(1935); WINGS IN THE DARK(1935); ANYTHING GOES(1936); COUNTRY BEYOND, THE(1936); GENTLEMAN FROM LOUISIANA(1936); IF YOU COULD ONLY COOK(1936); IT HAD TO HAPPEN(1936); TWO IN A CROWD(1936); MAN WHO CRIED WOLF, THE(1937); MANNEQUIN(1937); NAVY BLUE AND GOLD(1937); EXPOSED(1938); HOLIDAY(1938); MAD MISS MANTON, THE(1938); MY LUCKY STAR(1938); NO TIME TO MARRY(1938); PROFESSOR BEWARE(1938); THREE LOVES HAS NANCY(1938); TROPIC HOLIDAY(1938); YOU AND ME(1938); ESCAPE, THE(1939); FEDERAL MAN-HUNT(1939); JONES FAMILY IN HOLLYWOOD, THE(1939); MR. SMITH GOES TO WASHINGTON(1939); $1,000 A TOUCHDOWN(1939); HEROES OF THE SADDLE(1940); I TAKE THIS WOMAN(1940); LOVE, HONOR AND OH, BABY(1940); OH JOHNNY, HOW YOU CAN LOVE!(1940); RANGERS OF FORTUNE(1940); SAILOR'S LADY(1940); THEY DRIVE BY NIGHT(1940); YESTERDAY'S HEROES(1940); DEVIL AND MISS JONES, THE(1941); FOR BEAUTY'S SAKE(1941); MARRY THE BOSS' DAUGHTER(1941); PERFECT SNOB, THE(1941); UNFINISHED BUSINESS(1941); WEST POINT WIDOW(1941); WILD MAN OF BORNEO, THE(1941); GENTLEMAN AT HEART, A(1942); GIRL TROUBLE(1942); IT HAPPENED IN FLATBUSH(1942); LADY BODYGUARD(1942); MAN IN THE TRUNK, THE(1942); PRIDE OF THE YANKEES, THE(1942); QUIET PLEASE, MURDER(1942); STAR SPANGLED RHYTHM(1942); TOO MANY WOMEN(1942); FLIGHT FOR FREEDOM(1943); RIDING HIGH(1943); SO THIS IS WASHINGTON(1943); THANK YOUR LUCKY STARS(1943); WEST SIDE KID(1943); WHISPERING FOOTSTEPS(1943); AND THE ANGELS SING(1944); HOME IN INDIANA(1944); LADIES COURAGEOUS(1944); MARK OF THE WHISTLER, THE(1944); MR. SKEFFINGTON(1944); MY BUDDY(1944); SAN DIEGO, I LOVE YOU(1944); SECRET COMMAND(1944); UP IN ARMS(1944); WING AND A PRAYER(1944); BELLS OF ST. MARY'S, THE(1945); DUFFY'S TAVERN(1945); INCENDIARY BLONDE(1945); LADY ON A TRAIN(1945); SALOME, WHERE SHE DANCED(1945); BLUE DAHLIA, THE(1946); DARK CORNER, THE(1946); DEADLINE FOR MURDER(1946); HOW DO YOU DO?(1946); NOCTURNE(1946); OUR HEARTS WERE GROWING UP(1946); STRANGE LOVE OF MARTHA IVERS, THE(1946); VACATION IN RENO(1946); EASY COME, EASY GO(1947); MY FAVORITE BRUNETTE(1947); NORA PRENTISS(1947); SONG OF THE THIN MAN(1947); TROUBLE WITH WOMEN, THE(1947); DON'T TRUST YOUR HUSBAND(1948); GIVE MY REGARDS TO BROADWAY(1948); SCUDDA-HOO! SCUDDA-HAY!(1948); DUKE OF CHICAGO(1949); BODYHOLD(1950); KISS TOMORROW GOODBYE(1950); RETURN OF THE FRONTIERSMAN(1950); TALES OF ROBIN HOOD(1951)
Matthew McHugh
THEY WON'T BELIEVE ME(1947)
Thomas McHugh
SEA GYPSIES, THE(1978), ph
Vincent McHugh
WHAT'S SO BAD ABOUT FEELING GOOD?(1968), w
William McIllwain
Silents
ABRAHAM LINCOLN(1924); PASSIONATE YOUTH(1925)
Misc. Silents
RECKLESS COURAGE(1925)
David McIllwraith
HAPPY BIRTHDAY, GEMINI(1980)
Danny McIlravey
CHANGE OF MIND(1969); MY SIDE OF THE MOUNTAIN(1969)
Misc. Talkies
PINOCCHIO'S GREATEST ADVENTURE(1974)
Terry McIlvain
STREAMERS(1983)
Jane S. McIlvaine
IT HAPPENS EVERY THURSDAY(1953), w
Red McIlvaine
1984
OH GOD! YOU DEVIL(1984)
Bob McIlwain
GOOD DISSONANCE LIKE A MAN, A(1977)
Ron McIlwain
DETROIT 9000(1973); MIXED COMPANY(1974)
Kenneth McIlwaine
RAGGEDY ANN AND ANDY(1977), ed
David McIlwraith
OUTRAGEOUS!(1977, Can.)
Venora McIndoe
IT STARTED IN PARADISE(1952, Brit.)
Bernie McInerney
KING OF THE GYPSIES(1978); TRADING PLACES(1983)
Frances McInerney
MIRACLES FOR SALE(1939)

Joseph McInerney
  MIRACLE ON 34TH STREET, THE(1947)
Linda McInerney
Misc. Talkies
  CHERRY HILL HIGH(1977)
Bernie McInerny
  SO FINE(1981)
Frances McInnerney
  HOODLUM SAINT, THE(1946)
Angus McInnes
  SUPERMAN II(1980); DIRTY TRICKS(1981, Can.)
Pamela McInnes
  MURDERS IN THE RUE MORGUE(1971)
Colin McInnese
  DON'T GO IN THE HOUSE(1980)
Angus McInnis
  STAR WARS(1977)
Harl McInroy
Silents
  ANGEL CHILD(1918), w
Alistair Mcintire
  DAY AT THE BEACH, A(1970), ed
James McIntire
  DEATH HUNT(1981)
John McIntire
  ACT OF MURDER, AN(1948); BLACK BART(1948); CALL NORTHSIDE 777(1948); COMMAND DECISION(1948); RIVER LADY(1948); STREET WITH NO NAME, THE(1948); DOWN TO THE SEA IN SHIPS(1949); FRANCIS(1949); JOHNNY STOOL PIGEON(1949); RED CANYON(1949); SCENE OF THE CRIME(1949); TOP O' THE MORNING(1949); AMBUSH(1950); ASPHALT JUNGLE, THE(1950); NO SAD SONGS FOR ME(1950); SADDLE TRAMP(1950); SHADOW ON THE WALL(1950); WALK SOFTLY, STRANGER(1950); WINCHESTER '73(1950); RAGING TIDE, THE(1951); THAT'S MY BOY(1951); UNDER THE GUN(1951); WESTWARD THE WOMEN(1951); YOU'RE IN THE NAVY NOW(1951); GLORY ALLEY(1952); HORIZONS WEST(1952); LAWLESS BREED, THE(1952); SALLY AND SAINT ANNE(1952); LION IS IN THE STREETS, A(1953); MISSISSIPPI GAMBLER, THE(1953); PRESIDENT'S LADY, THE(1953); WAR ARROW(1953); APACHE(1954); FOUR GUNS TO THE BORDER(1954); YELLOW MOUNTAIN, THE(1954); FAR COUNTRY, THE(1955); KENTUCKIAN, THE(1955); PHENIX CITY STORY, THE(1955); SCARLET COAT, THE(1955); SPOILERS, THE(1955); STRANGER ON HORSEBACK(1955); AWAY ALL BOATS(1956); BACKLASH(1956); I'VE LIVED BEFORE(1956); WORLD IN MY CORNER(1956); TIN STAR, THE(1957); LIGHT IN THE FOREST, THE(1958); MARK OF THE HAWK, THE(1958); SING, BOY, SING(1958); GUNFIGHT AT DODGE CITY, THE(1959); ELMER GANTRY(1960); FLAMING STAR(1960); PSYCHO(1960); SEVEN WAYS FROM SUNDOWN(1960); WHO WAS THAT LADY?(1960); SUMMER AND SMOKE(1961); TWO RODE TOGETHER(1961); ROUGH NIGHT IN JERICHO(1967); HERBIE RIDES AGAIN(1974); ROOSTER COGBURN(1975); RESCUERS, THE(1977); FOX AND THE HOUND, THE(1981); HONKYTONK MAN(1982)
1984
  CLOAK AND DAGGER(1984)
Pegi McIntire
  SMALL TOWN GIRL(1953)
Stanley McIntire
  TWO(1975)
Tim McIntire
  SHENANDOAH(1965); FOLLOW ME, BOYS!(1966); STERILE CUCKOO, THE(1969); 1,000 PLANE RAID, THE(1969); JEREMIAH JOHNSON(1972), m; KID BLUE(1973), m; ALOHA, BOBBY AND ROSE(1975); BOY AND HIS DOG, A(1975); WIN, PLACE, OR STEAL(1975), m; GUMBALL RALLY, THE(1976); KILLER INSIDE ME, THE(1976), m; AMERICAN HOT WAX(1978); BRUBAKER(1980); FAST-WALKING(1982)
1984
  SACRED GROUND(1984)
Alex McIntosh
  WE SHALL SEE(1964, Brit.)
Angus McIntosh
  DOCTOR FAUSTUS(1967, Brit.)
Blanche McIntosh
Silents
  MOLLY BAWN(1916, Brit.), w; ALF'S BUTTON(1920, Brit.), w; ANNA THE ADVENTURESS(1920, Brit.), w; ONCE ABOARD THE LUGGER(1920, Brit.), w; MR. JUSTICE RAFFLES(1921, Brit.), w
Burr McIntosh
  FANCY BAGGAGE(1929); LAST WARNING, THE(1929); SKINNER STEPS OUT(1929); ROGUE SONG, THE(1930); COMMAND PERFORMANCE(1931); PRIVATE SCANDAL, A(1932); HALLELUJAH, I'M A BUM(1933); SWEETHEART OF SIGMA CHI(1933); RICHEST GIRL IN THE WORLD, THE(1934)
Silents
  WAY DOWN EAST(1920); EXCITERS, THE(1923); ON THE BANKS OF THE WABASH(1923); AVERAGE WOMAN, THE(1924); LEND ME YOUR HUSBAND(1924); SPITFIRE, THE(1924); ENEMIES OF YOUTH(1925); LIGHTNING REPORTER(1925); WILDERNESS WOMAN, THE(1926); HAZARDOUS VALLEY(1927); TAXI! TAXI!(1927); YANKEE CLIPPER, THE(1927); ADORABLE CHEAT, THE(1928); LILAC TIME(1928); RACKET, THE(1928)
Misc. Silents
  IN MIZZOURA(1914); MY PARTNER(1916); CYNTHIA-OF-THE-MINUTE(1920); DRIVEN(1923); CAMILLE OF THE BARBARY COAST(1925); PEARL OF LOVE, THE(1925); BUCKAROO KID(1926); FIRE AND STEEL(1927); HERO FOR A NIGHT, A(1927); ONCE AND FOREVER(1927); ACROSS THE ATLANTIC(1928); SAILORS' WIVES(1928); THAT CERTAIN THING(1928)
David McIntosh
  DOCTOR FAUSTUS(1967, Brit.)
Don McIntosh
  VELVET TRAP, THE(1966), ph
Duncan McIntosh
  INCUBUS, THE(1982, Can.)
Effi McIntosh
  HOLIDAYS WITH PAY(1948, Brit.)

Ellen McIntosh
  GIRL ON APPROVAL(1962, Brit.); STOLEN HOURS(1963); DOWNFALL(1964, Brit.); SILENT PLAYGROUND, THE(1964, Brit.); 20,000 POUNDS KISS, THE(1964, Brit.); WALK IN THE SHADOW(1966, Brit.); SKY BIKE, THE(1967, Brit.)
George McIntosh
Silents
  DEVIL'S CHAPLAIN(1929)
Heather McIntosh
  DR. FRANKENSTEIN ON CAMPUS(1970, Can.), cos
J.T. McIntosh
  SATELLITE IN THE SKY(1956), w
Morris McIntosh
  GIRL ON THE BARGE, THE(1929)
Robert McIntosh
1984
  PLOUGHMAN'S LUNCH, THE(1984, Brit.)
Tom McIntosh
  LEARNING TREE, THE(1969), md; BUS IS COMING, THE(1971), m; SLITHER(1973), m; HERO AIN'T NOTHIN' BUT A SANDWICH, A(1977), m
Valerie McIntosh
1984
  WEEKEND PASS(1984)
Alastair McIntyre
  SATURDAY NIGHT OUT(1964, Brit.), ed; STATION SIX-SAHARA(1964, Brit./Ger.), ed; BLACK TORMENT, THE(1965, Brit.), ed; REPULSION(1965, Brit.), ed; FEARLESS VAMPIRE KILLERS, OR PARDON ME BUT YOUR TEETH ARE IN MY NECK, THE(1967), ed; TWIST OF SAND, A(1968, Brit.), ed; MY SIDE OF THE MOUNTAIN(1969), ed; MACBETH(1971, Brit.), ed; TESS(1980, Fr./Brit.), ed
Andrew J. McIntyre
  FLAREUP(1969), ph
Arlene McIntyre
  MAN, WOMAN AND CHILD(1983)
Christine McIntyre
  RANGER'S ROUNDUP, THE(1938); FORBIDDEN TRAILS(1941); GUN MAN FROM BODIE, THE(1941); CINDERELLA SWINGS IT(1942); MAN FROM HEADQUARTERS(1942); ROCK RIVER RENEGADES(1942); STRANGER FROM PECOS, THE(1943); LOUISIANA HAYRIDE(1944); PARTNERS OF THE TRAIL(1944); FRONTIER FEUD(1945); GENTLEMAN FROM TEXAS(1946); LAND OF THE LAWLESS(1947); NEWS HOUNDS(1947); GUN TALK(1948); COLORADO AMBUSH(1951); GASOLINE ALLEY(1951); MODERN MARRIAGE, A(1962)
Misc. Talkies
  WEST OF THE RIO GRANDE(1944); VALLEY OF FEAR(1947); WANTED DEAD OR ALIVE(1951)
Clare McIntyre
  KRULL(1983); PIRATES OF PENZANCE, THE(1983)
Duncan McIntyre
  I KNOW WHERE I'M GOING(1947, Brit.); SAN DEMETRIO, LONDON(1947, Brit.); PICCADILLY INCIDENT(1948, Brit.); TROUBLE IN THE GLEN(1954, Brit.); STRONG-ROOM(1962, Brit.)
Eileen McIntyre
  ONLY THING YOU KNOW, THE(1971, Can.)
Frank McIntyre
Misc. Silents
  TRAVELING SALESMAN, THE(1916); TOO FAT TO FIGHT(1918)
Hal McIntyre
  SUN VALLEY SERENADE(1941)
Heather McIntyre
  HOME AND AWAY(1956, Brit.), w
Hugh McIntyre
  ONLY THING YOU KNOW, THE(1971, Can.)
James McIntyre
  GONE IN 60 SECONDS(1974)
Joann McIntyre
  CURTAINS(1983, Can.)
Lani McIntyre
  PARADISE ISLE(1937), m
Leila McIntyre
  ON THE LEVEL(1930); DOCTOR MONICA(1934); MARRIAGE ON APPROVAL(1934); MURDER IN THE FLEET(1935); MISTER CINDERELLA(1936); PRISONER OF SHARK ISLAND, THE(1936); LIVE, LOVE AND LEARN(1937); PICK A STAR(1937); PLAINSMAN, THE(1937); HOUSEKEEPER'S DAUGHTER(1939); WOMEN, THE(1939); THIRD FINGER, LEFT HAND(1940); WOMEN WITHOUT NAMES(1940); CRASH DIVE(1943); WINTERTIME(1943); CAPTAIN EDDIE(1945); FALLEN ANGEL(1945); NOB HILL(1945); HOODLUM SAINT, THE(1946)
Lyle McIntyre
  IT AIN'T EASY(1972), ed
Molly McIntyre
Misc. Silents
  HER GREAT HOUR(1916)
Paddy McIntyre
  SUMMER HOLIDAY(1963, Brit.); HALF A SIXPENCE(1967, Brit.); SONG OF NORWAY(1970)
Peggy McIntyre
  LOVES OF EDGAR ALLAN POE, THE(1942); SYNCOPATION(1942); I REMEMBER MAMA(1948); EL PASO(1949)
Richard McIntyre
Misc. Talkies
  BULLET FOR BILLY THE KID(1963)
Stephen McIntyre
  MONKEY GRIP(1983, Aus.), m
Tim McIntyre
  BOY AND HIS DOG, A(1975), m; CHOIRBOYS, THE(1977)
Tom McIntyre
  SEABO(1978), w; LADY GREY(1980), w; LIVING LEGEND(1980), w
1984
  ROTWEILER: DOGS OF HELL(1984), w
William McIntyre
  MURDER IS NEWS(1939)

Marianne McIsaac
IN PRAISE OF OLDER WOMEN(1978, Can.); SUZANNE(1980, Can.); IMPROPER CHANNELS(1981, Can.)

George McIver
FOUR BOYS AND A GUN(1957)

Ray McIver
FARMER, THE(1977)

Susan McIver
SHAMPOO(1975); SMOKEY AND THE BANDIT(1977)
Misc. Talkies
GIRLS FOR RENT(1974)

Betty McIvor
GOLD DIGGERS OF 1937(1936)

Mary McIvor
Silents
GAMBLING IN SOULS(1919)
Misc. Silents
PADDY O'HARA(1917); SQUARE DEAL MAN, THE(1917); SUDDEN GENTLEMAN, THE(1917); IN HIS BROTHER'S PLACE(1919); BURNING TRAIL, THE(1925)

Alexander McKaig
RAFTER ROMANCE(1934), p

David McKail
LIFE AT THE TOP(1965, Brit.)

Alden McKay
NOBODY'S PERFEKT(1981)

Allison McKay
DOCTOR, YOU'VE GOT TO BE KIDDING(1967); PUFNSTUF(1970); FRASIER, THE SENSUOUS LION(1973); SUPERDAD(1974)

Ann McKay
Misc. Silents
GOLD AND GRIT(1925); ROARIN' BRONCS(1927)

Anthony McKay
HANKY-PANKY(1982)

Barry McKay
BORN FOR GLORY(1935, Brit.)

Belva McKay
Silents
COMING AN' GOING(1926); EARLY TO WED(1926)

Brian McKay
STARLIFT(1951); MC CABE AND MRS. MILLER(1971), w

Claude McKay
BIG FELLA(1937, Brit.), w

Craig McKay
THIEVES(1977), ed; MELVIN AND HOWARD(1980), ed; REDS(1981), ed
1984
SWING SHIFT(1984), ed

Da Nang McKay
1984
TEACHERS(1984)

Doreen McKay
HIGGINS FAMILY, THE(1938); PALS OF THE SADDLE(1938); ETERNALLY YOURS(1939); NIGHT RIDERS, THE(1939)

Doug McKay
WHEN TOMORROW DIES(1966, Can.), ph; MADELEINE IS(1971, Can.), ph; VISITOR, THE(1973, Can.), ph; SALLY FIELDGOOD & CO.(1975, Can.), ph; KEEPER, THE(1976, Can.), ph
1984
BIG MEAT EATER(1984, Can.), ph

Elizabeth McKay
UNSUITABLE JOB FOR A WOMAN, AN(1982, Brit.), w

Fay McKay
GALAXY EXPRESS(1982, Jap.)

Gardner McKay
RAINTREE COUNTY(1957); PLEASURE SEEKERS, THE(1964); I SAILED TO TAHITI WITH AN ALL GIRL CREW(1969)

George McKay
TAKE A CHANCE(1933); AFTER THE DANCE(1935); CASE OF THE MISSING MAN, THE(1935); ONE-WAY TICKET(1935); PUBLIC MENACE(1935); SHE COULDN'T TAKE IT(1935); SUPERSPEED(1935); TOO TOUGH TO KILL(1935); UNKNOWN WOMAN(1935); AND SO THEY WERE MARRIED(1936); BLACKMAILER(1936); COME CLOSER, FOLKS(1936); COUNTERFEIT(1936); DON'T GAMBLE WITH LOVE(1936); END OF THE TRAIL(1936); FINAL HOUR, THE(1936); KILLER AT LARGE(1936); LONE WOLF RETURNS, THE(1936); PRIDE OF THE MARINES(1936); SHAKEDOWN(1936); TWO-FISTED GENTLEMAN(1936); YOU MAY BE NEXT(1936); COUNTERFEIT LADY(1937); DEVIL'S PLAYGROUND(1937); FIGHT TO THE FINISH, A(1937); FRAME-UP THE(1937); GIRLS CAN PLAY(1937); IT'S ALL YOURS(1937); MURDER IN GREENWICH VILLAGE(1937); RACKETEERS IN EXILE(1937); WOMAN IN DISTRESS(1937); CONVICTED(1938); DUKE OF WEST POINT, THE(1938); HIGHWAY PATROL(1938); ILLEGAL TRAFFIC(1938); LITTLE MISS ROUGHNECK(1938); SQUADRON OF HONOR(1938); THERE'S ALWAYS A WOMAN(1938); BABES IN ARMS(1939); BIG GUY, THE(1939); KING OF THE TURF(1939); MANHATTAN SHAKEDOWN(1939); MR. SMITH GOES TO WASHINGTON(1939); NEWSBOY'S HOME(1939); SPECIAL INSPECTOR(1939); $1,000 A TOUCHDOWN(1939); FARMER'S DAUGHTER, THE(1940); ISLAND OF DOOMED MEN(1940); NIGHT AT EARL CARROLL'S, A(1940); CAUGHT IN THE DRAFT(1941); FACE BEHIND THE MASK, THE(1941); HONOLULU LU(1941); PLAYMATES(1941); RICHEST MAN IN TOWN(1941); STORK PAYS OFF, THE(1941); ALIAS BOSTON BLACKIE(1942); BOOGIE MAN WILL GET YOU, THE(1942); CANAL ZONE(1942); HARVARD, HERE I COME(1942); LUCKY LEGS(1942); PARDON MY STRIPES(1942); SABOTAGE SQUAD(1942); SWEETHEART OF THE FLEET(1942); THEY ALL KISSED THE BRIDE(1942); UNDERGROUND AGENT(1942); AFTER MIDNIGHT WITH BOSTON BLACKIE(1943); IS EVERYBODY HAPPY?(1943); MURDER IN TIMES SQUARE(1943); SHE HAS WHAT IT TAKES(1943); TWO SENORITAS FROM CHICAGO(1943); AND THE ANGELS SING(1944); BEAUTIFUL BUT BROKE(1944); GOING MY WAY(1944); JAM SESSION(1944); KLONDIKE KATE(1944); LOUISIANA HAYRIDE(1944); ONE MYSTERIOUS NIGHT(1944); RETURN OF THE VAMPIRE, THE(1944); UP IN ARMS(1944); DANCING IN MANHATTAN(1945); DUFFY'S TAVERN(1945); MURDER, HE SAYS(1945); NOB HILL(1945); ROAD TO UTOPIA(1945); TEN CENTS A DANCE(1945)

Ian McKay
ROBIN AND MARIAN(1976, Brit.), stunts

James McKay
MARIANNE(1929), ed; THEY LEARNED ABOUT WOMEN(1930), ed; GOOD SAM(1948), ed; BLACK MAGIC(1949), ed
Silents
QUEEN'S EVIDENCE(1919, Brit.), d; MERRY-GO-ROUND(1923), ed; SOUL MATES(1925), ed; ZANDER THE GREAT(1925), ed; ONE HOUR OF LOVE(1927), ed
Misc. Silents
MIDNIGHT GAMBOLS(1919, Brit.), d

James C. McKay
Silents
COLLEGE DAYS(1926), ed; CHEATERS(1927), ed; PRINCESS FROM HOBOKEN, THE(1927), ed
Misc. Silents
SOULS FOR SABLES(1925), d; FOOLS OF FASHION(1926), d; BROKEN GATE, THE(1927), d; LIGHTING(1927), d

Jerry McKay
ON THE RIGHT TRACK(1981)

Jim McKay
WORLD'S GREATEST ATHLETE, THE(1973); RUNNING(1979, Can.)

Joanne McKay
JOY(1983, Fr./Can.)

Jock McKay
BLUE SMOKE(1935, Brit.); ROLLING HOME(1935, Brit.); KING OF HEARTS(1936, Brit.); MUSEUM MYSTERY(1937, Brit.); SILENT BARRIERS(1937, Brit.); FLESH AND BLOOD(1951, Brit.); TROUBLE IN THE GLEN(1954, Brit.); IT'S A WONDERFUL WORLD(1956, Brit.); LET'S BE HAPPY(1957, Brit.)

John McKay
DEAD ONE, THE(1961); ROCKET ATTACK, U.S.A.(1961)

Josie McKay
INN OF THE DAMNED(1974, Aus.)

Kathleen McKay
CHAMELEON(1978); ROAD WARRIOR, THE(1982, Aus.)

Kerry McKay
STARSTRUCK(1982, Aus.)

Michael McKay
ONE PLUS ONE(1969, Brit.)

Mike McKay
MAKER OF MEN(1931)

Nancy McKay
HOSPITAL, THE(1971)

Neil McKay
LIEUTENANT DARING, RN(1935, Brit.)

Norman McKay
KISS OF DEATH(1947); CALL NORTHSIDE 777(1948); FROGMEN, THE(1951); YOU'RE IN THE NAVY NOW(1951); NIAGARA(1953)

Norris McKay
Misc. Silents
GOLDEN DREAMS(1922)

Patti McKay
ABBOTT AND COSTELLO MEET DR. JEKYLL AND MR. HYDE(1954)

Percival McKay
TALK OF THE DEVIL(1937, Brit.), md

Percy McKay
GIRL IN DISTRESS(1941, Brit.), md

Peter McKay
UNSUITABLE JOB FOR A WOMAN, AN(1982, Brit.), p

Ronnie McKay
COUNTRYMAN(1982, Jamaica)

Scott McKay
GUEST IN THE HOUSE(1944); THIRTY SECONDS OVER TOKYO(1944); KISS AND TELL(1945); DUEL IN THE SUN(1946); GENIE, THE(1953, Brit.); FRONT, THE(1976); BELL JAR, THE(1979); YOU BETTER WATCH OUT(1980)

Scotty McKay
BLACK CAT, THE(1966)

Scutter McKay
PUFNSTUF(1970)

Sheila McKay
HOT CAR GIRL(1958)

Stanley McKay
GOOD SAM(1948)

Violet McKay
CHEYENNE KID, THE(1930)

Wanda McKay
$1,000 A TOUCHDOWN(1939); DANCING ON A DIME(1940); FARMER'S DAUGHTER, THE(1940); THOSE WERE THE DAYS(1940); LADY EVE, THE(1941); LAS VEGAS NIGHTS(1941); LIFE WITH HENRY(1941); PIONEERS, THE(1941); ROYAL MOUNTED PATROL, THE(1941); TWILIGHT ON THE TRAIL(1941); VIRGINIA(1941); BOWERY AT MIDNIGHT(1942); LAW AND ORDER(1942); ONE THRILLING NIGHT(1942); ROLLING DOWN THE GREAT DIVIDE(1942); BLACK RAVEN, THE(1943); CORREGIDOR(1943); DANGER! WOMEN AT WORK(1943); DEERSLAYER(1943); SMART GUY(1943); BELLE OF THE YUKON(1944); LEAVE IT TO THE IRISH(1944); MONSTER MAKER, THE(1944); VOODOO MAN(1944); WHAT A MAN!(1944); HOLLYWOOD AND VINE(1945); SENSATION HUNTERS(1945); THERE GOES KELLY(1945); KILROY WAS HERE(1947); BECAUSE OF EVE(1948); JIGGS AND MAGGIE IN SOCIETY(1948); JINX MONEY(1948); JUNGLE GODDESS(1948); MYSTERY OF THE GOLDEN EYE, THE(1948); STAGE STRUCK(1948); WOMAN OF DISTINCTION, A(1950); ROARING CITY(1951); MERRY WIDOW, THE(1952)
Misc. Talkies
TEXAS JUSTICE(1942)

Fred McKaye
GUN JUSTICE(1934); HONOR OF THE RANGE(1934); SMOKING GUNS(1934); WHEELS OF DESTINY(1934); OVER THE GOAL(1937)

Patti McKaye
MY FAVORITE SPY(1951)

Patty McKaye
ROAD TO BALI(1952)

Don McKayle
JAZZ SINGER, THE(1980), ch
Donald McKayle
GREAT WHITE HOPE, THE(1970), ch
Lafe McKea
COVERED WAGON TRAILS(1940)
Michael McKeag
HIGH FURY(1947, Brit.); VICE VERSA(1948, Brit.); OUTSIDER, THE(1949, Brit.); SLASHER, THE(1953, Brit.); LAST MAN TO HANG, THE(1956, Brit.)
Donald C. McKean
DELINQUENT DAUGHTERS(1944), p; ROGUES GALLERY(1945), p; GINGER(1947), w
Michael McKean
1941(1979); USED CARS(1980); YOUNG DOCTORS IN LOVE(1982)
1984
THIS IS SPINAL TAP(1984), a, w, m, m/l
Capt. Duncan McKechnie
I KNOW WHERE I'M GOING(1947, Brit.)
Cromwell McKechnie
HERE IS MY HEART(1934)
Donna McKechnie
LITTLE PRINCE, THE(1974, Brit.)
James McKechnie
COLONEL BLIMP(1945, Brit.); CAESAR AND CLEOPATRA(1946, Brit.); GIRL ON THE CANAL, THE(1947, Brit.); SAN DEMETRIO, LONDON(1947, Brit.); YEARS BETWEEN, THE(1947, Brit.); BOND STREET(1948, Brit.); SCOTT OF THE ANTARCTIC(1949, Brit.); MADELEINE(1950, Brit.)
Bob McKee
HAPPY DAYS(1930)
Bob Reel McKee
DANTE'S INFERNO(1935)
Donald McKee
WHISTLE AT EATON FALLS(1951); GODDESS, THE(1958)
Frank McKee
HAPPY DAYS(1930)
Georgette McKee
RAMPARTS WE WATCH, THE(1940)
Grace McKee
INGAGI(1931), ed
Harry McKee
WINTER MEETING(1948)
J.P. McKee
Misc. Silents
CYCLONE JONES(1923)
Jack McKee
GANG WAR(1928)
John McKee
HOUSE ON 92ND STREET, THE(1945); CHALLENGE OF THE RANGE(1949); FATHER WAS A FULLBACK(1949); IT HAPPENS EVERY SPRING(1949); SCENE OF THE CRIME(1949); TWELVE O'CLOCK HIGH(1949); MILKMAN, THE(1950); PEGGY(1950); RADAR SECRET SERVICE(1950); WHEN WILLIE COMES MARCHING HOME(1950); ANGELS IN THE OUTFIELD(1951); CALL ME MISTER(1951); TOO YOUNG TO KISS(1951); MONKEY BUSINESS(1952); MY WIFE'S BEST FRIEND(1952); PRIDE OF ST. LOUIS, THE(1952); ABOVE AND BEYOND(1953); BIG LEAGUER(1953); CLOWN, THE(1953); DANGEROUS WHEN WET(1953); GIRL WHO HAD EVERYTHING, THE(1953); KID FROM LEFT FIELD, THE(1953); THUNDER OVER THE PLAINS(1953); EXECUTIVE SUITE(1954); JOHNNY DARK(1954); ILLEGAL(1955); WRONG MAN, THE(1956); BIG COUNTRY, THE(1958); PORK CHOP HILL(1959); GALLANT HOURS, THE(1960); CAPE FEAR(1962); THAT TOUCH OF MINK(1962); GATHERING OF EAGLES, A(1963); SHOWDOWN(1963); CHEYENNE AUTUMN(1964); HALLELUJAH TRAIL, THE(1965); DIMENSION 5(1966); PROFESSIONALS, THE(1966); MONTE WALSH(1970); RIO LOBO(1970); ULZANA'S RAID(1972); BEST FRIENDS(1975); MAC ARTHUR(1977); TOUGH ENOUGH(1983)
John R. McKee
LOADED PISTOLS(1948); RIM OF THE CANYON(1949); INDIAN TERRITORY(1950); MULE TRAIN(1950); GENE AUTRY AND THE MOUNTIES(1951); SILVER CANYON(1951); TEXANS NEVER CRY(1951); VENGEANCE VALLEY(1951); STRATEGIC AIR COMMAND(1955); MOVIE MOVIE(1978); 1941(1979)
Kathrine McKee
QUADROON(1972)
L. McKee
Misc. Silents
SILENT RIDER, THE(1918)
L.S. McKee
Misc. Silents
CHARGE IT TO ME(1919); LONE HAND WILSON(1920), d
Lafayette McKee
INSIDE THE LAW(1942)
Silents
LONE WAGON, THE(1924)
Misc. Silents
FIFTH MAN, THE(1914); BLOOD TEST(1923); MILE A MINUTE MORGAN(1924)
Lafayette [Lafe] McKee
MAN FROM MONTEREY, THE(1933)
Lafe McKee
CODE OF HONOR(1930); LONESOME TRAIL, THE(1930); MEN WITHOUT LAW(1930); NEAR THE RAINBOW'S END(1930); SHADOW RANCH(1930); UNDER MONTANA SKIES(1930); UTAH KID, THE(1930); CYCLONE KID(1931); GRIEF STREET(1931); HURRICANE HORSEMAN(1931); NECK AND NECK(1931); PARTNERS OF THE TRAIL(1931); RANGE LAW(1931); RED FORK RANGE(1931); TWO GUN MAN, THE(1931); BATTLING BUCKAROO(1932); BIG STAMPEDE, THE(1932); BOILING POINT, THE(1932); DYNAMITE RANCH(1932); END OF THE TRAIL(1932); FIGHTING MARSHAL, THE(1932); GAY BUCKAROO, THE(1932); GOLD(1932); HELL FIRE AUSTIN(1932); HELLO TROUBLE(1932); KLONDIKE(1932); MAN FROM NEW MEXICO, THE(1932); RIDIN' FOR JUSTICE(1932); RIDING TORNADO, THE(1932); SECRETS OF WU SIN(1932); SPIRIT OF THE WEST(1932); TOMBSTONE CANYON(1932); WITHOUT HONORS(1932); YOUNG BLOOD(1932); CROSSFIRE(1933); DEADWOOD PASS(1933); DUDE BANDIT, THE(1933); FIGHTING CHAMP(1933); FIGHTING TEXANS(1933); GALLOPING ROMEO(1933); JAWS OF JUSTICE(1933); KING OF THE ARENA(1933); MY MOTHER(1933); RIDERS OF DESTINY(1933);

TELEGRAPH TRAIL, THE(1933); TERROR TRAIL(1933); UNDER SECRET ORDERS(1933); WAR OF THE RANGE(1933); BLUE STEEL(1934); CITY PARK(1934); DEMON FOR TROUBLE, A(1934); DUDE RANGER, THE(1934); FRONTIER DAYS(1934); GUN JUSTICE(1934); HELL BENT FOR LOVE(1934); HONOR OF THE RANGE(1934); LIGHTNING RANGE(1934); MAN FROM UTAH, THE(1934); QUITTERS, THE(1934); RIDING SPEED(1934); STRAIGHTAWAY(1934); TRAIL DRIVE, THE(1934); WEST OF THE DIVIDE(1934); CHEYENNE TORNADO(1935); COWBOY AND THE BANDIT, THE(1935); COYOTE TRAILS(1935); DESERT TRAIL(1935); FIGHTING TROOPER, THE(1935); GHOST RIDER, THE(1935); IVORY-HANDLED GUN(1935); KEEPER OF THE BEES(1935); KID COURAGEOUS(1935); LAST OF THE CLINTONS, THE(1935); NORTHERN FRONTIER(1935); PORT OF LOST DREAMS(1935); RAINBOW VALLEY(1935); REVENGE RIDER, THE(1935); WESTERN JUSTICE(1935); WHAT PRICE CRIME?(1935); FRONTIER JUSTICE(1936); FUGITIVE SHERIFF, THE(1936); GUN SMOKE(1936); HEIR TO TROUBLE(1936); HEROES OF THE RANGE(1936); KID RANGER, THE(1936); LAST OF THE WARRENS, THE(1936); LIGHTNING BILL CARSON(1936); MEN OF THE PLAINS(1936); MYSTERIOUS AVENGER, THE(1936); SWIFTY(1936); THUNDERBOLT(1936); WESTERNER, THE(1936); FIGHTING DEPUTY, THE(1937); IDAHO KID, THE(1937); LAW OF THE RANGER(1937); LOST RANCH(1937); MELODY OF THE PLAINS(1937); MYSTERY OF THE HOODED HORSEMEN, THE(1937); MYSTERY RANGE(1937); NORTH OF THE RIO GRANDE(1937); RANGERS STEP IN, THE(1937); RECKLESS RANGER(1937); SANTA FE BOUND(1937); SINGING OUTLAW(1937); BROTHERS OF THE WEST(1938); FEUD OF THE TRAIL(1938); I'M FROM THE CITY(1938); ORPHAN OF THE PECOS(1938); RAWHIDE(1938); ROLLING CARAVANS(1938); SIX SHOOTIN' SHERIFF(1938); SOUTH OF ARIZONA(1938); STAGECOACH DAYS(1938); KNIGHT OF THE PLAINS(1939); BAD MAN FROM RED BUTTE(1940); PIONEER DAYS(1940); PIONEERS OF THE FRONTIER(1940); RIDERS OF PASCO BASIN(1940); SANTA FE TRAIL(1940); SON OF ROARING DAN(1940); WHEN THE DALTONS RODE(1940); WILD HORSE VALLEY(1940); MEET JOHN DOE(1941)
Misc. Talkies
LARIATS AND SIXSHOOTERS(1931); TEXAN, THE(1932); BOSS COWBOY(1934); RAWHIDE MAIL(1934); RAWHIDE ROMANCE(1934); BIG BOY RIDES AGAIN(1935); BLAZING GUNS(1935); HAWK, THE(1935); LAW OF THE 45'S(1935); RANGE WARFARE(1935); RIDIN' THRU(1935); SILVER BULLET, THE(1935); TRAIL OF THE HAWK(1935); WOLF RIDERS(1935); SANTA FE RIDES(1937)
Silents
RAINBOW RANGERS(1924); ON THE GO(1925); CAPTAIN'S COURAGE, A(1926); WEST OF THE LAW(1926); MANHATTAN COWBOY(1928); ON THE DIVIDE(1928); AMAZING VAGABOND(1929)
Misc. Silents
BRINGIN' HOME THE BACON(1924); HUMAN TORNADO, THE(1925); BANDIT BUSTER, THE(1926); BONANZA BUCKAROO, THE(1926); ROARIN' BRONCS(1927); DESPERATE COURAGE(1928); PAINTED TRAIL(1928); RIDING RENEGADE, THE(1928); TRAIL RIDERS(1928); TRAILIN' BACK(1928); UPLAND RIDER, THE(1928); CALIFORNIA MAIL, THE(1929)
Lee McKee
ALIAS THE BAD MAN(1931)
Lefe McKee
COWBOY AND THE KID,THE(1936)
Lonette McKee
SPARKLE(1976); WHICH WAY IS UP?(1977); CUBA(1979)
1984
COTTON CLUB, THE(1984)
Maj. Johnny McKee
TWELVE O'CLOCK HIGH(1949), tech adv
Pamela McKee
YOUNG GIANTS(1983)
Pat McKee
STRAIGHT, PLACE AND SHOW(1938); GOLDEN BOY(1939); MANPOWER(1941); FOOTLIGHT SERENADE(1942); GALLANT LADY(1942); I WAKE UP SCREAMING(1942); PRISON GIRL(1942); VOODOO MAN(1944); LIKELY STORY, A(1947)
Ray McKee
Misc. Silents
LITTLE CHEVALIER, THE(1917)
Raymond McKee
FROZEN RIVER(1929); RUMBA(1935)
Silents
KIDNAPPED(1917); KATHLEEN MAVOURNEEN(1919); GIRL OF MY HEART(1920); BLIND HEARTS(1921); JOLT, THE(1921); LAMPLIGHTER, THE(1921); WING TOY(1921); BLIND BARGAIN, A(1922); DOWN TO THE SEA IN SHIPS(1923); ALONG CAME RUTH(1924); BABBITT(1924); COMPROMISE(1925); LAWFUL CHEATERS(1925); ROMANCE ROAD(1925); OH, WHAT A NIGHT!(1926); KING OF THE HERD(1927); CAMPUS KNIGHTS(1929)
Misc. Silents
SUNBEAM, THE(1916); WHEEL OF THE LAW, THE(1916); BILLY AND THE BIG STICK(1917); LADY OF THE PHOTOGRAPH, THE(1917); UNBELIEVER, THE(1918); ME AND CAPTAIN KID(1919); FLAME OF YOUTH(1920); FORTUNE TELLER, THE(1920); LITTLE WANDERER, THE(1920); LOVE'S HARVEST(1920); LOVETIME(1921); MOTHER HEART, THE(1921); THROUGH A GLASS WINDOW(1922); GIRL OF THE LIMBERLOST, A(1924); PAGAN PASSIONS(1924); SILENT ACCUSER, THE(1924); TENTH WOMAN, THE(1924); VALLEY OF HATE, THE(1924); CONTRABAND(1925); EXCLUSIVE RIGHTS(1926); SPEED LIMIT, THE(1926)
Richard McKee
FOUL PLAY(1978)
Robert McKee
Silents
KING OF KINGS, THE(1927)
Roger McKee
PEGGY(1950)
Scott McKee
MONKEY'S PAW, THE(1933)
Silents
OLIVER TWIST, JR.(1921); WING TOY(1921); ANGEL OF CROOKED STREET, THE(1922)
Tom McKee
COURT-MARTIAL OF BILLY MITCHELL, THE(1955); SEARCH FOR BRIDEY MURPHY, THE(1956); STEEL JUNGLE, THE(1956); FURY AT SHOWDOWN(1957); JAILHOUSE ROCK(1957); JEANNE EAGELS(1957); RIVER'S EDGE, THE(1957); UNDER FIRE(1957); VALERIE(1957); NO TIME FOR SERGEANTS(1958); VICE RAID(1959); THREE CAME TO KILL(1960)

Vivienne McKee
SLIPPER AND THE ROSE, THE(1976, Brit.)
Walter McKeegan
WICKED, WICKED(1973), art d
Gary McKeehan
RABID(1976, Can.); BROOD, THE(1979, Can.)
Kathy McKeel
BLACK LASH, THE(1952), w
Marie McKeen
Misc. Silents
DAUGHTER OF THE DON, THE(1917)
George McKeenan
PLAY DIRTY(1969, Brit.)
Dow McKeever
EYEWITNESS(1981)
Marlin McKeever
LOVE IN A GOLDFISH BOWL(1961); THREE STOOGES MEET HERCULES, THE(1962)
Mike McKeever
LOVE IN A GOLDFISH BOWL(1961); THREE STOOGES MEET HERCULES, THE(1962)
Dorothy McKegg
SLEEPING DOGS(1977, New Zealand); MIDDLE AGE SPREAD(1979, New Zealand)
Ian McKellan
ALFRED THE GREAT(1969, Brit.)
Ian McKellen
PROMISE, THE(1969, Brit.); THANK YOU ALL VERY MUCH(1969, Brit.); PRIEST OF LOVE(1981, Brit.); KEEP, THE(1983)
John McKellen
SON OF THE RENEGADE(1953)
Sonora McKeller
LIBERATION OF L.B. JONES, THE(1970)
Frank McKelvey
VERTIGO(1958), set d; NORTH BY NORTHWEST(1959), set d; GALLANT HOURS, THE(1960), set d
Frank R. McKelvey
HAPPIEST MILLIONAIRE, THE(1967), set d
John McKelvey
THINK DIRTY(1970, Brit.)
Allan McKelvin
Misc. Silents
ROMANCE OF ANNIE LAURIE, THE(1920, Brit.)
Frank McKelvy
RUN FOR COVER(1955), set d; SHORT CUT TO HELL(1957), set d; SPACE CHILDREN, THE(1958), set d; RAT RACE, THE(1960), set d; MISFITS, THE(1961), set d; SIGNPOST TO MURDER(1964), set d; 36 HOURS(1965), set d; TO TRAP A SPY(1966), set d; THEY SHOOT HORSES, DON'T THEY?(1969), set d; I LOVE MY WIFE(1970), set d; EARTHQUAKE(1974), set d
Frank R. McKelvy
PROUD AND THE PROFANE, THE(1956), set d; ON THE DOUBLE(1961), set d; PLEASURE OF HIS COMPANY, THE(1961), set d; ESCAPE FROM ZAHRAIN(1962), set d; GIRLS! GIRLS! GIRLS!(1962), set d; PIGEON THAT TOOK ROME, THE(1962), set d; SUMMER MAGIC(1963), set d; TIGER WALKS, A(1964), set d; FOLLOW ME, BOYS!(1966), set d; LT. ROBIN CRUSOE, U.S.N.(1966), set d; UGLY DACHSHUND, THE(1966), set d; MONKEYS, GO HOME!(1967), set d; HORSE IN THE GRAY FLANNEL SUIT, THE(1968), set d; NEVER A DULL MOMENT(1968), set d; RASCAL(1969), set d; BOATNIKS, THE(1970), set d; SCANDALOUS JOHN(1971), set d; NOW YOU SEE HIM, NOW YOU DON'T(1972), set d; SNOWBALL EXPRESS(1972), set d; GUS(1976), set d; TREASURE OF MATECUMBE(1976), Set d; RETURN FROM WITCH MOUNTAIN(1978), set d
St. Clair McKelway
MATING OF MILLIE, THE(1948), w; SLEEP, MY LOVE(1948), w; MISTER 880(1950), w
Agnes Pat McKenna
Silents
WHITE BLACK SHEEP, THE(1926), w
Andrew McKenna
GARDEN OF ALLAH, THE(1936)
Bernard McKenna
MY AIN FOLK(1974, Brit.); ODD JOB, THE(1978, Brit.), w; MONTY PYTHON'S LIFE OF BRIAN(1979, Brit.); EFFECTS(1980); YELLOWBEARD(1983), a, w
David E. McKenna
JANE AUSTEN IN MANHATTAN(1980), ed
David McKenna
TWO(1975), ed
1984
KIDCO(1984), ed
Denise McKenna
GREAT MUPPET CAPER, THE(1981); GOING BERSERK(1983)
Dudley McKenna
COURTIN' WILDCATS(1929), w
Dymphna McKenna
VON RICHTHOFEN AND BROWN(1970), cos
Flicka McKenna
LIGHT FANTASTIC(1964)
Harry McKenna
OPPOSITE SEX, THE(1956)
Harry Tom McKenna
PARTY GIRL(1958)
Joe McKenna
Misc. Talkies
LITTLE DETECTIVES, THE(1983)
Joseph McKenna
Misc. Talkies
CAMERONS, THE(1974)
Julie McKenna
GRENDEL GRENDEL GRENDEL(1981, Aus.)

Kate McKenna
BRIDE COMES HOME(1936); TOO MANY WOMEN(1942); HIGH WALL, THE(1947); MURDER IS MY BEAT(1955)
Lawrence J. McKenna
1984
BIRDY(1984)
Martha McKenna
LANCER SPY(1937), w
Marthe Cnockhaert McKenna
I WAS A SPY(1934, Brit.), w
Patrick McKenna
UP THE ACADEMY(1980)
Philip McKenna
FLOWER THIEF, THE(1962)
Richard McKenna
SAND PEBBLES, THE(1966), w
Rick McKenna
CHICAGO 70(1970)
Siobhan McKenna
HUNGRY HILL(1947, Brit.); DAUGHTER OF DARKNESS(1948, Brit.); LOST PEOPLE, THE(1950, Brit.); ADVENTURERS, THE(1951, Brit.); KING OF KINGS(1961); PLAYBOY OF THE WESTERN WORLD, THE(1963, Ireland); OF HUMAN BONDAGE(1964, Brit.); DOCTOR ZHIVAGO(1965)
1984
MEMED MY HAWK(1984, Brit.)
Misc. Talkies
PHILADELPHIA HERE I COME(1975)
T. R. McKenna
NIGHT FIGHTERS, THE(1960)
T.P. McKenna
SIEGE OF SIDNEY STREET, THE(1960, Brit.); FREEDOM TO DIE(1962, Brit.); DOWNFALL(1964, Brit.); FERRY ACROSS THE MERSEY(1964, Brit.); GIRL WITH GREEN EYES(1964, Brit.); YOUNG CASSIDY(1965, U.S./Brit.); ULYSSES(1967, U.S./Brit.); CHARGE OF THE LIGHT BRIGADE, THE(1968, Brit.); ANNE OF THE THOUSAND DAYS(1969, Brit.); PERFECT FRIDAY(1970, Brit.); BEAST IN THE CELLAR, THE(1971, Brit.); PERCY(1971, Brit.); STRAW DOGS(1971, Brit.); VILLAIN(1971, Brit.); ALL CREATURES GREAT AND SMALL(1975, Brit.); PORTRAIT OF THE ARTIST AS A YOUNG MAN, A(1979, Ireland); OUTSIDER, THE(1980); SILVER DREAM RACER(1982, Brit.)
1984
MEMED MY HAWK(1984, Brit.)
Vincent McKenna
SPECIAL INSPECTOR(1939)
Virginia McKenna
FATHER'S DOING FINE(1952, Brit.); SECOND MRS. TANQUERAY, THE(1952, Brit.); CRUEL SEA, THE(1953); HORSE'S MOUTH, THE(1953, Brit.); SIMBA(1955, Brit.); SHIP THAT DIED OF SHAME, THE(1956, Brit.); BARRETTS OF WIMPOLE STREET, THE(1957); SMALLEST SHOW ON EARTH, THE(1957, Brit.); CARVE HER NAME WITH PRIDE(1958, Brit.); TOWN LIKE ALICE, A(1958, Brit.); PASSIONATE SUMMER(1959, Brit.); WRECK OF THE MARY DEAR, THE(1959); TWO LIVING, ONE DEAD(1964, Brit./Swed.); BORN FREE(1966); RING OF BRIGHT WATER(1969, Brit.); ELEPHANT CALLED SLOWLY, AN(1970, Brit.); WATERLOO(1970, Ital./USSR); CHRISTIAN THE LION(1976, Brit.); SWALLOWS AND AMAZONS(1977, Brit.); CHOSEN, THE(1978, Brit./Ital.); DISAPPEARANCE, THE(1981, Brit./Can.)
Mary McKennedy
STOOLIE, THE(1972)
Joe McKenney
ZABRISKIE POINT(1970), makeup
Kerry McKenney
GAL YOUNG UN(1979)
Morris McKenney
DRUMS O' VOODOO(1934)
Ruth McKenney
MY SISTER EILEEN(1942), w; SAN DIEGO, I LOVE YOU(1944), w; TROUBLE WITH WOMEN, THE(1947), w; SONG OF SURRENDER(1949), w; MY SISTER EILEEN(1955), w
Michael McKennirey
DON'T LET THE ANGELS FALL(1969, Can.), ed
Dal McKennon
TOM THUMB(1958, Brit./U.S.); ONE HUNDRED AND ONE DALMATIANS(1961); TWIST AROUND THE CLOCK(1961); WOMAN HUNT(1962); HOUSE OF THE DAMNED(1963); SON OF FLUBBER(1963); WHEELER DEALERS, THE(1963); MISADVENTURES OF MERLIN JONES, THE(1964); SEVEN FACES OF DR. LAO(1964); GLORY GUYS, THE(1965); DID YOU HEAR THE ONE ABOUT THE TRAVELING SALESLADY?(1968)
Dallas McKennon
LADY AND THE TRAMP(1955); JOURNEY BACK TO OZ(1974); CAT FROM OUTER SPACE, THE(1978); HOT LEAD AND COLD FEET(1978)
1984
MYSTERY MANSION(1984)
Rodney McKennon
BROKEN LULLABY(1932)
Maxime McKenory
Misc. Talkies
ANDY WARHOL'S DRACULA(1974)
Bill McKenzie
MISTER 880(1950); MY BLUE HEAVEN(1950); WINCHESTER '73(1950); MR. SCOUTMASTER(1953); SMOKE IN THE WIND(1975)
Bleu McKenzie
PONY EXPRESS RIDER(1976)
Blue McKenzie
HITCHHIKERS, THE(1972)
Bob McKenzie
UNCLE HARRY(1945); IT'S A DEAL(1930); GOD IS MY WITNESS(1931); RIDIN' FOR JUSTICE(1932); FIDDLIN' BUCKAROO, THE(1934); GUN JUSTICE(1934); VIVA VILLA!(1934); IN PERSON(1935); POWDERSMOKE RANGE(1935); STONE OF SILVER CREEK(1935); BRIDE COMES HOME(1936); COWBOY AND THE KID,THE(1936); FEUD OF THE WEST(1936); LAWLESS RIDERS(1936); LUCKY TERROR(1936); MAN FROM GUN TOWN, THE(1936); RHYTHM ON THE RANGE(1936); SAN FRANCISCO(1936); SONG OF THE TRAIL(1936); THUNDER-

BOLT(1936); GUNSMOKE RANCH(1937); HIDEAWAY(1937); RECKLESS RANGER(1937); SINGING OUTLAW(1937); SMOKE TREE RANGE(1937); SOULS AT SEA(1937); STARS OVER ARIZONA(1937); SUNDOWN SAUNDERS(1937); WITH LOVE AND KISSES(1937); PIONEER TRAIL(1938); RED RIVER RANGE(1938); YOUNG FUGITIVES(1938); BURIED ALIVE(1939); DEATH OF A CHAMPION(1939); DESTRY RIDES AGAIN(1939); FRONTIER PONY EXPRESS(1939); DANCE, GIRL, DANCE(1940); LOVE, HONOR AND OH, BABY(1940); MY LITTLE CHICKADEE(1940); RETURN OF FRANK JAMES, THE(1940); WHEN THE DALTONS RODE(1940); CITADEL OF CRIME(1941); DEATH VALLEY OUTLAWS(1941); GIRL, A GUY AND A GOB, A(1941); SIERRA SUE(1941); IN OLD CALIFORNIA(1942); MISSOURI OUTLAW, A(1942); SOMBRERO KID, THE(1942); RED RIVER ROBIN HOOD(1943); SAGEBRUSH LAW(1943); WILD HORSE STAMPEDE(1943); JIVE JUNCTION(1944); TALL IN THE SADDLE(1944); CODE OF THE LAWLESS(1945); NIGHT AND DAY(1946); WHITE STALLION(1947); WAGON WHEELS WESTWARD(1956)
Misc. Talkies
RIDIN' ON(1936); TAKE ME BACK TO OKLAHOMA(1940)
Misc. Silents
DEVIL'S DOORYARD, THE(1923); WHERE IS THIS WEST?(1923)
Carey Lee McKenzie
MC CABE AND MRS. MILLER(1971)
Dennis McKenzie
TWO OF A KIND(1983)
Donald McKenzie
MALAGA(1962, Brit.), w
Doug McKenzie
SMASH PALACE(1982, New Zealand)
Douglas McKenzie
DRIVE, HE SAID(1971)
Ed McKenzie
DISC JOCKEY(1951)
Ella McKenzie
LAST WARNING, THE(1929); ALICE ADAMS(1935); MAN FROM GUN TOWN, THE(1936); PALM SPRINGS(1936); RIDERS OF THE DAWN(1937)
Ellis McKenzie
SYLVIA SCARLETT(1936)
Eva McKenzie
VIRTUOUS HUSBAND(1931); HOLD YOUR MAN(1933); WITH LOVE AND KISSES(1937); JUVENILE COURT(1938); PIONEER TRAIL(1938); YOU CAN'T TAKE IT WITH YOU(1938); LITTLE ACCIDENT(1939); HEAVENLY DAYS(1944)
Fay McKenzie
STUDENT TOUR(1934); FRESHMAN YEAR(1938); DISPUTED PASSAGE(1939); GUNGA DIN(1939); LITTLE ACCIDENT(1939); DEATH RIDES THE RANGE(1940); IT'S A DATE(1940); LOVE, HONOR AND OH, BABY(1940); MA, HE'S MAKING EYES AT ME(1940); WHEN THE DALTONS RODE(1940); DOWN MEXICO WAY(1941); SIERRA SUE(1941); COWBOY SERENADE(1942); HEART OF THE RIO GRANDE(1942); HOME IN WYOMIN'(1942); REMEMBER PEARL HARBOR(1942); SINGING SHERIFF, THE(1944); MURDER IN THE MUSIC HALL(1946); EXPERIMENT IN TERROR(1962); PARTY, THE(1968); S.O.B.(1981)
Misc. Talkies
BOSS COWBOY(1934); SUNDOWN TRAIL, THE(1975)
Silents
KNIGHT OF THE WEST, A(1921); ABRAHAM LINCOLN(1924); JUDGMENT OF THE STORM(1924)
George McKenzie
HE COULDN'T TAKE IT(1934), ph
Harold McKenzie
INCREDIBLE PETRIFIED WORLD, THE(1959), ed
Howard McKenzie
Silents
DOLLY'S VACATION(1918)
Ida Mae McKenzie
LEPKE(1975, U.S./Israel)
Ida McKenzie
GODLESS GIRL, THE(1929)
Silents
SHADOWS OF CONSCIENCE(1921); ABRAHAM LINCOLN(1924)
Misc. Silents
VILLAGE BLACKSMITH, THE(1922)
Jack McKenzie
PERFECT ALIBI, THE(1931, Brit.), ph; LITTLE ORPHAN ANNIE(1932), ph; MONKEY'S PAW, THE(1933), ph; GREAT GUY(1936), ph; HIDEAWAY(1937), ph; HAWAII CALLS(1938), ph; SHE'S GOT EVERYTHING(1938), ph; TIMBER(1942), ph; ADVENTURES OF A ROOKIE(1943), ph; MUG TOWN(1943), ph; MICHAEL O'HALLORAN(1948), ph; VAMPIRE, THE(1957), ph; FLAME BARRIER, THE(1958), ph; EMPIRE STRIKES BACK, THE(1980)
Silents
NIGHT SHIP, THE(1925), ph
Joyce McKenzie
TWELVE O'CLOCK HIGH(1949); MOTHER DIDN'T TELL ME(1950)
Kevin McKenzie
OLLY, OLLY, OXEN FREE(1978)
1984
BAY BOY(1984, Can.)
Liz McKenzie
GET CARTER(1971, Brit.)
Iona McKenzie
HOW TO BE VERY, VERY, POPULAR(1955)
Mary J. Todd McKenzie
HOUSE ON SKULL MOUNTAIN, THE(1974)
Melanie McKenzie
ROCKING HORSE WINNER, THE(1950, Brit.)
Michael McKenzie
LITTLE ONES, THE(1965, Brit.)
Mitzi McKenzie
1984
1984(1984, Brit.)

N'Was McKenzie
CRIME SCHOOL(1938), cos; JITTERBUGS(1943), cos
Peter McKenzie
1984
LAST HORROR FILM, THE(1984), spec eff
Randolph McKenzie
JOHN PAUL JONES(1959)
Richard McKenzie
DOC(1971); STOOLIE, THE(1972); MAN ON A SWING(1974); CORVETTE SUMMER(1978); CAN'T STOP THE MUSIC(1980), set d; MAN WITH BOGART'S FACE, THE(1980), set d; FIRST MONDAY IN OCTOBER(1981); HISTORY OF THE WORLD, PART 1(1981), set d; SOME KIND OF HERO(1982)
Rob McKenzie
GOD'S COUNTRY AND THE MAN(1937)
Robert McKenzie
SHADOW RANCH(1930); ARE THESE OUR CHILDREN?(1931); CIMARRON(1931); HALF-NAKED TRUTH, THE(1932); TILLIE AND GUS(1933); INSIDE INFORMATION(1934); MEANEST GAL IN TOWN, THE(1934); OLD-FASHIONED WAY, THE(1934); SIX OF A KIND(1934); THUNDER OVER TEXAS(1934); YOU'RE TELLING ME(1934); LIFE BEGINS AT 40(1935); MISSISSIPPI(1935); NAUGHTY MARIETTA(1935); SHOT IN THE DARK, A(1935); SOCIETY FEVER(1935); CAVALCADE OF THE WEST(1936); COMIN' ROUND THE MOUNTAIN(1936); VALLEY OF THE LAWLESS(1936); HEART OF THE WEST(1937); LUCK OF ROARING CAMP, THE(1937); RIDING ON(1937); SING, COWBOY, SING(1937); SOMETHING TO SING ABOUT(1937); WHEN YOU'RE IN LOVE(1937); HELD FOR RANSOM(1938); LAWLESS VALLEY(1938); REBELLION(1938); DREAMING OUT LOUD(1940); SAPS AT SEA(1940); TRIPLE JUSTICE(1940); SPOILERS, THE(1942); FIRST COMES COURAGE(1943); MORE THE MERRIER, THE(1943); TEXAS MASQUERADE(1944); COLORADO SERENADE(1946); DUEL IN THE SUN(1946); ROMANCE OF THE WEST(1946)
Silents
OLIVER TWIST(1916); KNIGHT OF THE WEST, A(1921), d; WESTERN DEMON, A(1922), d; COVERED TRAIL, THE(1924); ONE GLORIOUS SCRAP(1927)
Misc. Silents
FIGHTIN' DEVIL(1922), d; SHERIFF OF SUN-DOG, THE(1922); BAD MAN'S BLUFF(1926); ONE GLORIOUS SCRAP(1927); SET FREE(1927)
Rock McKenzie
BOOGEYMAN II(1983)
Sally McKenzie
WE OF THE NEVER NEVER(1983, Aus.)
Sarah McKenzie
CATHY'S CHILD(1979, Aus.)
Scott McKenzie
Misc. Talkies
GREAT LESTER BOGGS, THE(1975)
Tim McKenzie
GALLIPOLI(1981, Aus.)
Warren McKenzie
PEER GYNT(1965)
Will McKenzie
LANDLORD, THE(1970)
McKenzie Twins
Silents
JANE GOES A' WOOING(1919)
Doug McKeon
UNCLE JOE SHANNON(1978); ON GOLDEN POND(1981); NIGHT CROSSING(1982)
Keith McKeon
NIGHT CROSSING(1982)
Kevin McKeon
PINK FLOYD–THE WALL(1982, Brit.)
Thomas McKeon
MARINES COME THROUGH, THE(1943)
Allan McKeown
DOING TIME(1979, Brit.), p
Charles McKeown
MONTY PYTHON'S LIFE OF BRIAN(1979, Brit.); TIME BANDITS(1981, Brit.); MISSIONARY, THE(1982)
Douglas McKeown
DEADLY SPAWN, THE(1983), d&w
Jack McKeown
Misc. Silents
HER FATHER SAID NO(1927), d
Katie McKeown
AROUSERS, THE(1973)
Leo McKern
YESTERDAY'S ENEMY(1959, Brit.); MURDER IN THE CATHEDRAL(1952, Brit.); ALL FOR MARY(1956, Brit.); TIME WITHOUT PITY(1957, Brit.); X THE UNKNOWN(1957, Brit.); CHAIN OF EVENTS(1958, Brit.), w; TALE OF TWO CITIES, A(1958, Brit.); BEYOND THAT ROARED, THE(1959, Brit.); MOUSE THAT ROARED, THE(1959, Brit.); JAZZ BOAT(1960, Brit.); SCENT OF MYSTERY(1960); DAY THE EARTH CAUGHT FIRE, THE(1961, Brit.); I LIKE MONEY(1962, Brit.); LISA(1962, Brit.); AGENT 8 3/4(1963, Brit.); DOCTOR IN DISTRESS(1963, Brit.); JOLLY BAD FELLOW, A(1964, Brit.); KING AND COUNTRY(1964, Brit.); AMOROUS ADVENTURES OF MOLL FLANDERS, THE(1965); HELP!(1965, Brit.); MAN FOR ALL SEASONS, A(1966, Brit.); ASSIGNMENT K(1968, Brit.); HIGH COMMISSIONER, THE(1968, U.S./Brit.); SHOES OF THE FISHERMAN, THE(1968); DECLINE AND FALL... OF A BIRD WATCHER(1969, Brit.); RYAN'S DAUGHTER(1970, Brit.); MASSACRE IN ROME(1973, Ital.); ADVENTURES OF SHERLOCK HOLMES' SMARTER BROTHER, THE(1975, Brit.); OMEN, THE(1976); CANDLESHOE(1978); *BLUE LAGOON, THE(1980); FRENCH LIEUTENANT'S WOMAN, THE(1981)
Jim McKernan
GREENWICH VILLAGE STORY(1963)
Karen McKevic
BIG BIRD CAGE, THE(1972)
Cecilia McKevitt
SAINTS AND SINNERS(1949, Brit.)
Vince McKewin
1984
CRIMES OF PASSION(1984)

William McKey
Silents
MICE AND MEN(1916)
Robert McKibbon
THREE RING CIRCUS(1954)
Angos McKie
HEAVY METAL(1981, Can.), anim
Angus McKie
HEAVY METAL(1981, Can.), w
Ronald McKie
MANGO TREE, THE(1981, Aus.), w
Patricia McKiernan
DEADLY BLESSING(1981), cos
Don McKillop
AMERICAN WEREWOLF IN LONDON, AN(1981)
Donald McKillop
OTLEY(1969, Brit.)
Charlotte McKim
REFUGE(1981), p
David McKim
MAJOR AND THE MINOR, THE(1942); MY FAVORITE BLONDE(1942); SHE HAS WHAT IT TAKES(1943); FORCE OF EVIL(1948)
Harry McKim
WEST POINT WIDOW(1941); HITLER'S CHILDREN(1942); DAYS OF OLD CHEYENNE(1943); MOJAVE FIREBRAND(1944); NEVADA(1944); SWEET AND LOWDOWN(1944); WANDERER OF THE WASTELAND(1945); FIGHTER SQUADRON(1948); HALLS OF MONTEZUMA(1951)
Josephine McKim
LADY BE CAREFUL(1936); MORE THAN A SECRETARY(1936)
Peggy McKim
I REMEMBER MAMA(1948)
Robert McKim
Silents
EDGE OF THE ABYSS, THE(1915); CAPTIVE GOD, THE(1916); HELL'S HINGES(1916); PRIMAL LURE, THE(1916); DARK ROAD, THE(1917); ICED BULLET, THE(1917); LAST OF THE INGRAHAMS, THE(1917); PAWS OF THE BEAR(1917); PLAYING THE GAME(1918); WHEN DO WE EAT?(1918); DEVIL TO PAY(1920); MARK OF ZORRO(1920); OUT OF THE DUST(1920); RIDERS OF THE DAWN(1920); WHITE HANDS(1922); ALL THE BROTHERS WERE VALIANT(1923); MR. BILLINGS SPENDS HIS DIME(1923); SPIDER AND THE ROSE, THE(1923); STRANGERS OF THE NIGHT(1923); FLAMING BARRIERS(1924); GALLOPING ACE, THE(1924); RIDE FOR YOUR LIFE(1924); SPOOK RANCH(1925); BAT, THE(1926); KENTUCKY HANDICAP(1926); REGULAR SCOUT, A(1926); STRONG MAN, THE(1926); AFLAME IN THE SKY(1927); SHOW GIRL, THE(1927)
Misc. Silents
DEVIL'S DOUBLE, THE(1916); PHANTOM, THE(1916); RAIDERS, THE(1916); RETURN OF "DRAW" EGAN, THE(1916); STEPPING STONE, THE(1916); MASTER OF HIS HOME(1917); PADDY O'HARA(1917); SILENT MAN, THE(1917); SON OF HIS FATHER, THE(1917); TIME LOCKS AND DIAMONDS(1917); WEAKER SEX, THE(1917); CLAWS OF THE HUN, THE(1918); LAW OF THE NORTH, THE(1918); LOVE ME(1918); MARRIAGE RING, THE(1918); VAMP, THE(1918); BRAND, THE(1919); GREASED LIGHTING(1919); PARTNERS THREE(1919); WAGON TRACKS(1919); WESTERNERS, THE(1919); DWELLING PLACE OF LIGHT, THE(1920); MONEY CHANGERS, THE(1920); SILVER HORDE, THE(1920); CERTAIN RICH MAN, A(1921); LURE OF EGYPT, THE(1921); MAN OF THE FOREST, THE(1921); MYSTERIOUS RIDER(1921); SPENDERS, THE(1921); GRAY DAWN, THE(1922); HEART'S HAVEN(1922); MONTE CRISTO(1922); WITHOUT COMPROMISE(1922); DEAD GAME(1923); MADEMOISELLE MIDNIGHT(1924); WHEN A GIRL LOVES(1924); NORTH OF NOME(1925); DEAD LINE, THE(1926); PAY OFF, THE(1926); TEX(1926); TOUGH GUY, THE(1926); WOLF HUNTERS, THE(1926); DENVER DUDE, THE(1927)
Sam McKim
FLAMINGO ROAD(1949); THUNDERBIRDS(1952); ABOVE AND BEYOND(1953)
Sammy McKim
ANNIE OAKLEY(1935); COUNTRY GENTLEMEN(1937); GAME THAT KILLS, THE(1937); GUNSMOKE RANCH(1937); HEART OF THE ROCKIES(1937); HIT THE SADDLE(1937); TRIGGER TRIO, THE(1937); CALL THE MESQUITEERS(1938); MAMA RUNS WILD(1938); OLD BARN DANCE, THE(1938); RED RIVER RANGE(1938); NEW FRONTIER(1939); NIGHT RIDERS, THE(1939); ROVIN' TUMBLEWEEDS(1939); WESTERN CARAVANS(1939); HI-YO SILVER(1940); LADDIE(1940); LITTLE MEN(1940); ROCKY MOUNTAIN RANGERS(1940); TEXAS TERRORS(1940); FATHER'S SON(1941); PUBLIC ENEMIES(1941); WE'VE NEVER BEEN LICKED(1943); HUCKSTERS, THE(1947); I, JANE DOE(1948); YOU'RE MY EVERYTHING(1949); LONELY HEARTS BANDITS(1950)
Robert McKimson
INCREDIBLE MR. LIMPET, THE(1964), spec eff
Beth McKinley
1984
WILD LIFE, THE(1984)
Dixie McKinley
FOLIES DERGERE(1935)
Edward J. McKinley
HOW THE WEST WAS WON(1962)
J. Edward McKinley
ANGRY RED PLANET, THE(1959); WALKING TARGET, THE(1960); THUNDER OF DRUMS, A(1961); ADVISE AND CONSENT(1962); CASE OF PATTY SMITH, THE(1962); INTERNS, THE(1962); GREAT RACE, THE(1965); GHOST AND MR. CHICKEN, THE(1966); STREET IS MY BEAT, THE(1966); IMPOSSIBLE YEARS, THE(1968); PARTY, THE(1968); CHARRO(1969); FLAP(1970); HOW DO I LOVE THEE?(1970); THERE WAS A CROOKED MAN(1970); WHERE DOES IT HURT?(1972); AT LONG LAST LOVE(1975)
Jawn McKinley
STERILE CUCKOO, THE(1969)
Mary McKinley
1984
CALIFORNIA GIRLS(1984)
Narcissa McKinley
LOVE AND DEATH(1975)

Ray McKinley
MAKE BELIEVE BALLROOM(1949)
Susan McKinley
LOOKING UP(1977)
Tom McKinley
FAN, THE(1981), cos
Norman McKinnel
HER STRANGE DESIRE(1931, Brit.); HINDLE WAKES(1931, Brit.); CRIMINAL AT LARGE(1932, Brit.); OUTSIDER, THE(1933, Brit.); WHITE FACE(1933, Brit.)
Silents
FAKE, THE(1927, Brit.); WHEN BOYS LEAVE HOME(1928, Brit.)
Misc. Silents
SHULMATE, THE(1915); FOLLY OF DESIRE, THE OR THE SHULAMITE(1916); DOMBEY AND SON(1917, Brit.); HINDLE WAKES(1918, Brit.); GAMBLE IN LIVES, A(1920, Brit.); PILLARS OF SOCIETY(1920, Brit.); FANNY HAWTHORNE(1927, Brit.)
Norman McKinnell
SHERLOCK HOLMES' FATAL HOUR(1931, Brit.)
Austin McKinney
SKYDIVERS, THE(1963), ph; THRILL KILLERS, THE(1965), ed; DR. TERROR'S GALLERY OF HORRORS(1967), ph; HOUSE OF EVIL(1968, U.S./Mex.), ph; SNAKE PEOPLE, THE(1968, Mex./U.S.), ph; FREE GRASS(1969), ph; PIT STOP(1969), ph; IS THIS TRIP REALLY NECESSARY?(1970), ph; INCREDIBLE INVASION, THE(1971, Mex./U.S.), ph; LOVE BUTCHER, THE(1982), ph
Betty McKinney
CRASH DIVE(1943)
Bill McKinney
WHEN YOU COMIN' BACK, RED RYDER?(1979); SHE FREAK(1967); ROAD HUSTLERS, THE(1968); ANGEL UNCHAINED(1970); JUNIOR BONNER(1972); LIFE AND TIMES OF JUDGE ROY BEAN, THE(1972); CLEOPATRA JONES(1973); OUTFIT, THE(1973); PARALLAX VIEW, THE(1974); THUNDERBOLT AND LIGHTFOOT(1974); CANNONBALL(1976, U.S./Hong Kong); OUTLAW JOSEY WALES, THE(1976); SHOOTIST, THE(1976); FOR PETE'S SAKE(1977); GAUNTLET, THE(1977); VALENTINO(1977, Brit.); ANY WHICH WAY YOU CAN(1980); BRONCO BILLY(1980); CARNY(1980); ST. HELENS(1981); FIRST BLOOD(1982); TEX(1982); HEART LIKE A WHEEL(1983)
1984
AGAINST ALL ODDS(1984)
Billy McKinney
DELIVERANCE(1972)
Chuck McKinney
ODD ANGRY SHOT, THE(1979, Aus.); PIRATE MOVIE, THE(1982, Aus.)
Florine McKinney
CYNARA(1932); HORSE FEATHERS(1932); MIRACLE MAN, THE(1932); ONE HOUR WITH YOU(1932); BEAUTY FOR SALE(1933); DANCING LADY(1933); STUDENT TOUR(1934); CAPPY RICKS RETURNS(1935); DAVID COPPERFIELD(1935); NIGHT LIFE OF THE GODS(1935); STRANGERS ALL(1935); DIZZY DAMES(1936); MUSS 'EM UP(1936); STAR FELL FROM HEAVEN, A(1936, Brit.); BLAZING BARRIERS(1937); NIGHT AT EARL CARROLL'S, A(1940); OKLAHOMA RENEGADES(1940); PHILADELPHIA STORY, THE(1940); UNHOLY PARTNERS(1941); BROOKLYN ORCHID(1942); LITTLE JOE, THE WRANGLER(1942); PARDON MY SARONG(1942); TAKE A LETTER, DARLING(1942)
Gardland McKinney
WHERE THE RED FERN GROWS(1974)
Jennifer McKinney
RUNNING(1979, Can.); DEATH SHIP(1980, Can.); SILENCE OF THE NORTH(1981, Can.)
John McKinney
METEOR(1979); TO BE OR NOT TO BE(1983)
1984
WOMAN IN RED, THE(1984)
Kent McKinney
JENNY(1969), ed; SAVAGES(1972), ed; WILD PARTY, THE(1975), ed
Larry McKinney
HONKERS, THE(1972)
Mira McKinney
FURY(1936); BLAZING SIXES(1937); CASE OF THE STUTTERING BISHOP, THE(1937); MUSIC FOR MADAME(1937); ROAD TO RENO, THE(1938); SISTERS, THE(1938); SWEETHEARTS(1938); YOUNG FUGITIVES(1938); CAFE SOCIETY(1939); I STOLE A MILLION(1939); WHEN TOMORROW COMES(1939); ALIAS THE DEACON(1940); HOUSE OF THE SEVEN GABLES, THE(1940); NOBODY'S CHILDREN(1940); SANDY GETS HER MAN(1940); SANTA FE TRAIL(1940); SHOP AROUND THE CORNER, THE(1940); THIRD FINGER, LEFT HAND(1940); BACHELOR DADDY(1941); DANGEROUS GAME, A(1941); DOUBLE TROUBLE(1941); LIFE BEGINS FOR ANDY HARDY(1941); YOU BELONG TO ME(1941); LADY IN A JAM(1942); MADAME SPY(1942); PITTSBURGH(1942); KEEP 'EM SLUGGING(1943); MOONLIGHT IN VERMONT(1943); RHYTHM OF THE ISLANDS(1943); MUMMY'S GHOST, THE(1944); STANDING ROOM ONLY(1944); 'TILL WE MEET AGAIN(1944); FALLEN ANGEL(1945); HOLD THAT BLONDE(1945); ROUGH RIDERS OF CHEYENNE(1945); CLUNY BROWN(1946); JUNIOR PROM(1946); SHADOWS OVER CHINATOWN(1946); TALK ABOUT A LADY(1946); BEAT THE BAND(1947); T-MEN(1947); SITTING PRETTY(1948); PREJUDICE(1949); KANSAS RAIDERS(1950); WOMAN OF DISTINCTION, A(1950); GROOM WORE SPURS, THE(1951); HEART OF THE ROCKIES(1951); UNKNOWN MAN, THE(1951); RAINBOW 'ROUND MY SHOULDER(1952); LAST POSSE, THE(1953); WOMEN'S PRISON(1955)
Myra McKinney
MODERN TIMES(1936); CAPTAINS COURAGEOUS(1937); LINDA BE GOOD(1947)
Nina Mae McKinney
HALLELUJAH(1929); SAFE IN HELL(1931); KENTUCKY MINSTRELS(1934, Brit.); RECKLESS(1935); SANDERS OF THE RIVER(1935, Brit.); ON VELVET(1938, Brit.); POCOMANIA(1939); STRAIGHT TO HEAVEN(1939); DARK WATERS(1944); TOGETHER AGAIN(1944); NIGHT TRAIN TO MEMPHIS(1946); DANGER STREET(1947); PINKY(1949); COPPER CANYON(1950)
Misc. Talkies
GUN MOLL(1938); SWANEE SHOWBOAT(1939)
Odis McKinney
LUNCH WAGON(1981)
Ruth McKinney
MARGIE(1946), w; PARADES(1972)

Steve McKinney
MACHISMO–40 GRAVES FOR 40 GUNS(1970)
W.R. McKinney
1984
TEACHERS(1984), w
William McKinney
BREAKHEART PASS(1976)
George McKinnon
TROUBLE WITH WOMEN, THE(1947), set d
Jane McKinnon
1984
BAY BOY(1984, Can.)
John McKinnon
Silents
TONGUES OF MEN, THE(1916); KID, THE(1921)
Lloyd McKinnon
QUEST FOR FIRE(1982, Fr./Can.)
Mona McKinnon
TEENAGE THUNDER(1957); PLAN 9 FROM OUTER SPACE(1959)
Neil McKinnon
Misc. Silents
PHANTOM HORSEMAN, THE(1924)
Beverlee McKinsey
BRONCO BILLY(1980)
Bob McKinsey
IT'S A SMALL WORLD(1935)
Tom McKitterick
WARRIORS, THE(1979)
Minnie McKittrick
SAINTS AND SINNERS(1949, Brit.)
Adrian McKnight
1984
FEAR CITY(1984)
Ann McKnight
CIRCUS KID, THE(1928), ed; DANCE HALL(1929), ed; JAZZ AGE, THE(1929), ed; JAZZ HEAVEN(1929), ed; VERY IDEA, THE(1929), ed; HE KNEW WOMEN(1930), ed; RUNAROUND, THE(1931), ed; SMART WOMAN(1931), ed
Silents
ALEX THE GREAT(1928), ed; HEY RUBE!(1928), ed
C.A. McKnight [Rosalind Russell]
MRS. POLLIFAX-SPY(1971), w
David McKnight
J.D.'S REVENGE(1976)
Jerry McKnight
EDDIE MACON'S RUN(1983)
John McKnight
PRIVATE ANGELO(1949, Brit.)
Joy McKnight
Misc. Silents
BITTER SWEETS(1928)
Sam McKnight
SUPER SPOOK(1975)
Sandra McKnight
Misc. Talkies
HOW TO SCORE WITH GIRLS(1980)
Walter McKone
Misc. Talkies
ZOO ROBBERY(1973, Brit.)
Vivienne McKonne
BUGSY MALONE(1976, Brit.)
Rudy McKool
CHICAGO CALLING(1951)
Jim McKrell
ANNIE HALL(1977); SEMI-TOUGH(1977); HARRY'S WAR(1981); HOWLING, THE(1981); PANDEMONIUM(1982)
1984
GREMLINS(1984)
Robert McKuen
STONE COLD DEAD(1980, Can.)
Rod McKuen
ROCK, PRETTY BABY(1956); SUMMER LOVE(1958); WILD HERITAGE(1958); JOANNA(1968, Brit.), m; PRIME OF MISS JEAN BRODIE, THE(1969, Brit.), m; EMILY(1976, Brit.), m
John McKutcheon
THIEF, THE(1952)
Andrew McLachlan
FINAL OPTION, THE(1983, Brit.)
Patsy May McLachlan
1984
WARRIORS OF THE WASTELAND(1984, Ital.)
Robert McLachlan
NO ROOM AT THE INN(1950, Brit.)
Andrew McLaglen
SINCE YOU WENT AWAY(1944); PARIS UNDERGROUND(1945)
Andrew V. McLaglen
MAN IN THE VAULT(1956), d; SEVEN MEN FROM NOW(1956), p; ABDUCTORS, THE(1957), d; GUN THE MAN DOWN(1957), d; FRECKLES(1960), d; LITTLE SHE-PHERD OF KINGDOM COME(1961), d; MC LINTOCK!(1963), d; SHENAN-DOAH(1965), d; RARE BREED, THE(1966), d; MONKEYS, GO HOME!(1967), d; WAY WEST, THE(1967), d; BALLAD OF JOSIE(1968), d; BANDOLERO!(1968), d; DEVIL'S BRIGADE, THE(1968), d; UNDEFEATED, THE(1969), d; CHISUM(1970), d; FOOLS' PARADE(1971), p&d; ONE MORE TRAIN TO ROB(1971), d; SOMETHING BIG(1971), p&d; CAHILL, UNITED STATES MARSHAL(1973), d; MITCHELL(1975), d; LAST HARD MEN, THE(1976), d; BREAKTHROUGH(1978, Ger.), d; WILD GEESE, THE(1978, Brit.), d; FFOLKES(1980, Brit.), d; SEA WOLVES, THE(1981, Brit.), d
1984
SAHARA(1984), d

Arthur McLaglen
INFORMER, THE(1935)
Silents
INDIAN LOVE LYRICS, THE(1923, Brit.)
Misc. Silents
PORT OF LOST SOULS(1924, Brit.)
Cliff McLaglen
PHANTOM SHIP(1937, Brit.)
Clifford McLaglen
CALL OF THE SEA, THE(1930, Brit.); BERMONDSEY KID, THE(1933, Brit.); LATE EXTRA(1935, Brit.); LITTLE BIT OF BLUFF, A(1935, Brit.); OFF THE DOLE(1935, Brit.); PRISONER OF CORBAL(1939, Brit.)
Silents
IN THE BLOOD(1923, Brit.); FORBIDDEN CARGOES(1925, Brit.); CHINESE BUN-GALOW, THE(1926, Brit.); ALLEY CAT, THE(1929, Brit.)
Misc. Silents
WHITE SHEIK, THE(1928, Brit.)
Cyril McLaglen
BED AND BREAKFAST(1930, Brit.); SUSPENSE(1930, Brit.); DOWN RIVER(1931, Brit.); NO LADY(1931, Brit.); JOSSER JOINS THE NAVY(1932, Brit.); VERDICT OF THE SEA(1932, Brit.); FEAR SHIP, THE(1933, Brit.); MONEY FOR SPEED(1933, Brit.); ROYAL DEMAND, A(1933, Brit.); TALE OF TWO CITIES, A(1935); DAREDEVILS OF EARTH(1936, Brit.); MARY OF SCOTLAND(1936); PLOUGH AND THE STARS, THE(1936); TOILERS OF THE SEA(1936, Brit.); WHIPSAW(1936); WEE WILLIE WINKIE(1937); LONG VOYAGE HOME, THE(1940); BLACK SWAN, THE(1942); RANDOM HARVEST(1942); SON OF FURY(1942); SOLDIERS THREE(1951)
Silents
ARCADIANS, THE(1927, Brit.); LOST PATROL, THE(1929, Brit.)
Misc. Silents
JAWS OF HELL(1928, Brit.); UNDERGROUND(1928, Brit.); YOU KNOW WHAT SAILORS ARE(1928, Brit.)
Gibb McLaglen
Silents
MADAME POMPADOUR(1927, Brit.)
Kenneth McLaglen
FLAME IN THE HEATHER(1935, Brit.)
Silents
IN THE BLOOD(1923, Brit.); LAND OF HOPE AND GLORY(1927, Brit.)
Leopold McLaglen
Misc. Silents
BARS OF IRON(1920, Brit.)
Victor McLaglen
UNDER TWO FLAGS(1936); BLACK WATCH, THE(1929); COCK-EYED WORLD, THE(1929); DEVIL WITH WOMEN, A(1930); HAPPY DAYS(1930); HOT FOR PA-RIS(1930); ON THE LEVEL(1930); ANNABELLE'S AFFAIRS(1931); DIS-HONORED(1931); THREE ROGUES(1931); WICKED(1931); WOMEN OF ALL NATIONS(1931); DEVIL'S LOTTERY(1932); GAY CABALLERO, THE(1932); GUILTY AS HELL(1932); RACKETY RAX(1932); WHILE PARIS SLEEPS(1932); DICK TUR-PIN(1933, Brit.); HOT PEPPER(1933); LAUGHING AT LIFE(1933); CAPTAIN HATES THE SEA, THE(1934); LOST PATROL, THE,(1934); MURDER AT THE VANI-TIES(1934); NO MORE WOMEN(1934); WHARF ANGEL(1934); GREAT HOTEL MURDER(1935); INFORMER, THE(1935); UNDER PRESSURE(1935); KLONDIKE ANNIE(1936); MAGNIFICENT BRUTE, THE(1936); PROFESSIONAL SOLDIER(1936); NANCY STEELE IS MISSING(1937); SEA DEVILS(1937); THIS IS MY AFFAIR(1937); WEE WILLIE WINKIE(1937); BATTLE OF BROADWAY(1938); DEVIL'S PARTY, THE(1938); WE'RE GOING TO BE RICH(1938, Brit.); BIG GUY, THE(1939); CAPTAIN FURY(1939); EX-CHAMP(1939); FULL CONFESSION(1939); GUNGA DIN(1939); LET FREEDOM RING(1939); PACIFIC LINER(1939); RIO(1939); DIAMOND FRON-TIER(1940); SOUTH OF PAGO PAGO(1940); BROADWAY LIMITED(1941); CALL OUT THE MARINES(1942); CHINA GIRL(1942); POWDER TOWN(1942); FOREVER AND A DAY(1943); PRINCESS AND THE PIRATE, THE(1944); ROGER TOUHY, GANG-STER!(1944); TAMPICO(1944); LOVE, HONOR AND GOODBYE(1945); ROUGH, TOUGH AND READY(1945); WHISTLE STOP(1946); CALENDAR GIRL(1947); FOXES OF HARROW, THE(1947); MICHIGAN KID, THE(1947); FORT APACHE(1948); SHE WORE A YELLOW RIBBON(1949); RIO GRANDE(1950); QUIET MAN, THE(1952); FAIR WIND TO JAVA(1953); PRINCE VALIANT(1954); TROUBLE IN THE GLEN(1954, Brit.); BENGAZI(1955); CITY OF SHADOWS(1955); LADY GODIVA(1955); MANY RIVERS TO CROSS(1955); AROUND THE WORLD IN 80 DAYS(1956); ABDUCTORS, THE(1957); SEA FURY(1959, Brit.)
Silents
SPORT OF KINGS, THE(1921, Brit.); CRIMSON CIRCLE, THE(1922, Brit.); GLORI-OUS ADVENTURE, THE(1922, U.S./Brit.); HEARTSTRINGS(1923, Brit.); IN THE BLOOD(1923, Brit.); GAY CORINTHIAN, THE(1924); PASSIONATE ADVENTURE, THE(1924, Brit.); UNHOLY THREE, THE(1925); BEAU GESTE(1926); ISLE OF RETRI-BUTION, THE(1926); WHAT PRICE GLORY(1926); GIRL IN EVERY PORT, A(1928); CAPTAIN LASH(1929); STRONG BOY(1929)
Misc. Silents
CALL OF THE ROAD, THE(1920, Brit.); CORINTHIAN JACK(1921, Brit.); PREY OF THE DRAGON, THE(1921, Brit.); LITTLE BROTHER OF GOD(1922, Brit.); SAILOR TRAMP, A(1922, Brit.); M'LORD OF THE WHITE ROAD(1923, Brit.); ROMANY, THE(1923, Brit.); BELOVED BRUTE, THE(1924); WOMEN AND DIAMONDS(1924, Brit.); FIGHTING HEART, THE(1925); MEN OF STEEL(1926); LOVES OF CAR-MEN(1927); HANGMAN'S HOUSE(1928)
Anne McLain
EASY RIDER(1969)
Billy McLain
SARATOGA(1937); UNDERCURRENT(1946)
John McLain
WILD MAN OF BORNEO, THE(1941), w
Silents
STRONG BOY(1929), w
Karen McLain
JIM, THE WORLD'S GREATEST(1976)
Marlyn McLain
Silents
KISS FOR CINDERELLA, A(1926)
Pat McLamry
SOD SISTERS(1969)

Barton McLane
DRAEGERMAN COURAGE(1937)
Bruce McLane
DOGS OF WAR, THE(1980, Brit.)
Haley McLane
SPLIT IMAGE(1982)
Lorenzo McLane
Misc. Silents
SPIDER'S WEB, THE(1927)
Mary McLane
Silents
NIGHT SHIP, THE(1925); SPARROWS(1926)
Robert McLane
Misc. Talkies
BARBARA(1970)
Paul McLarand
SOMETHING TO SING ABOUT(1937)
Mr. McLardy
HIS MAJESTY O'KEEFE(1953)
Alice McLaren
FINGER OF GUILT(1956, Brit.), cos
Anne McLaren
THINGS TO COME(1936, Brit.)
Bruce McLaren
YOUNG RACERS, THE(1963); GRAND PRIX(1966)
Daniel McLaren
SCARECROW, THE(1982, New Zealand)
Gus Mclaren
GRENDEL GRENDEL GRENDEL(1981, Aus.), anim
Hal McLaren
VIENNESE NIGHTS(1930), ed
Hollis McLaren
SUDDEN FURY(1975, Can.); SUNDAY IN THE COUNTRY(1975, Can.); PARTNERS(1976, Can.); OUTRAGEOUS!(1977, Can.); WELCOME TO BLOOD CITY(1977, Brit./Can.); ANGRY MAN, THE(1979 Fr./Can.); LOST AND FOUND(1979); ATLANTIC CITY(1981, U.S./Can.)
Ian McLaren
YOUNG IN HEART, THE(1938)
Ivor McLaren
FALLING FOR YOU(1933, Brit.); ALONG CAME SALLY(1934, Brit.); FRIDAY THE 13TH(1934, Brit.); WOMAN IN COMMAND, THE(1934 Brit.); ME AND MARLBOROUGH(1935, Brit.); PRINCESS CHARMING(1935, Brit.); RADIO FOLLIES(1935, Brit.); GAY LOVE(1936, Brit.); BITER BIT, THE(1937, Brit.), p; WISE GUYS(1937, Brit.), p; LIGHTNING CONDUCTOR(1938, Brit.), w; WHO GOES NEXT?(1938, Brit.), p; HIGH FURY(1947, Brit.), p
Jack McLaren
ISLE OF ESCAPE(1930), w
Jean McLaren
DATE WITH JUDY, A(1948)
John McLaren
GREAT DAY(1945, Brit.); JOHNNY IN THE CLOUDS(1945, Brit.); MAN FROM MOROCCO, THE(1946, Brit.); NO ORCHIDS FOR MISS BLANDISH(1948, Brit.); POET'S PUB(1949, Brit.); KING IN NEW YORK, A(1957, Brit.); INTENT TO KILL(1958, Brit.); CHILD AND THE KILLER, THE(1959, Brit.); FIRST MAN INTO SPACE(1959, Brit.); TWO-HEADED SPY, THE(1959, Brit.); WIND OF CHANGE, THE(1961, Brit.), w
Katherine McLaren
Silents
CHILD OF M'SIEU(1919)
Misc. Silents
DADDY'S GIRL(1918)
Kay McLaren
EXCALIBUR(1981)
Mary McLaren
KEY, THE(1934); LIFE OF VERGIE WINTERS, THE(1934); HARMONY LANE(1935); LADIES CRAVE EXCITEMENT(1935); KING OF THE PECOS(1936); WESTWARD HO(1936); FARGO KID, THE(1941); MISBEHAVING HUSBANDS(1941); PRAIRIE PIONEERS(1941); FIGHTING VALLEY(1943)
Misc. Talkies
MAN'S BEST FRIEND(1935)
Misc. Silents
ROUGE AND RICHES(1920); OUTCAST(1922)
Wayne McLaren
HONKERS, THE(1972)
J. McLaren-Ross
NAKED HEART, THE(1955, Brit.), w
Paul McLarind
ROBERTA(1935)
Thomas McLarnie
Misc. Silents
BLINDNESS OF VIRTUE, THE(1915); MAN TRAIL, THE(1915)
Ed N. McLarnin
KENNEL MURDER CASE, THE(1933), ed
Jimmy McLarnin
BIG CITY(1937); JOE PALOOKA, CHAMP(1946)
Gary McLarty
WAY WEST, THE(1967); SOMETIMES A GREAT NOTION(1971); MITCHELL(1975); ROOSTER COGBURN(1975); NATIONAL LAMPOON'S ANIMAL HOUSE(1978); APPLE DUMPLING GANG RIDES AGAIN, THE(1979)
Gary R. McLarty
NATIONAL LAMPOON'S ANIMAL HOUSE(1978), stunts
James McLarty
MEATBALLS(1979, Can.); GREY FOX, THE(1983, Can.)
James E. McLarty
NONE BUT THE BRAVE(1963), a, w; SCAVENGERS, THE(1969); WEEKEND WITH THE BABYSITTER(1970), a, w; TOUCH OF SATAN, THE(1971), w
Misc. Talkies
MISSION TO DEATH(1966)

Ron McLarty
SENTINEL, THE(1977)
1984
FLAMINGO KID, THE(1984)
Murray McLauchlan
PARTNERS(1976, Can.), m
Murray McLaughlan
RIP-OFF(1971, Can.), m
Andrea McLaughlin
BURGLAR, THE(1956)
Betty McLaughlin
WHAT A LIFE(1939); FARMER'S DAUGHTER, THE(1940); NIGHT AT EARL CARROLL'S, A(1940); QUEEN OF THE MOB(1940); WAY OF ALL FLESH, THE(1940)
Bill McLaughlin
DUCHESS AND THE DIRTWATER FOX, THE(1976); S.O.B.(1981)
Bruce McLaughlin
ISLAND, THE(1980)
Emily McLaughlin
YOUNG DOCTORS IN LOVE(1982)
Gene McLaughlin
URBAN COWBOY(1980)
Gibb McLaughlin
KITTY(1929, Brit.); BRAT, THE(1930, Brit.); SCHOOL FOR SCANDAL, THE(1930, Brit.); SUCH IS THE LAW(1930, Brit.); "W" PLAN, THE(1931, Brit.); JEALOUSY(1931, Brit.); SALLY IN OUR ALLEY(1931, Brit.); THIRD TIME LUCKY(1931, Brit.); CONGRESS DANCES(1932, Ger.); FIRST MRS. FRASER, THE(1932, Brit.); LOVE CONTRACT, THE(1932, Brit.); MAGIC NIGHT(1932, Brit.); MISTRESS OF ATLANTIS, THE(1932, Ger.); MONEY MEANS NOTHING(1932, Brit.); WHERE IS THIS LADY?(1932, Brit.); BRITANNIA OF BILLINGSGATE(1933, Brit.); DICK TURPIN(1933, Brit.); HIGH FINANCE(1933, Brit.); KING OF THE RITZ(1933, Brit.); PRIVATE LIFE OF HENRY VIII, THE(1933); THIRTEENTH CANDLE, THE(1933, Brit.); WHITE FACE(1933, Brit.); CATHERINE THE GREAT(1934, Brit.); CHURCH MOUSE, THE(1934, Brit.); FRIDAY THE 13TH(1934, Brit.); LITTLE FRIEND(1934, Brit.); NO FUNNY BUSINESS(1934, Brit.); POWER(1934, Brit.); SWINGING THE LEAD(1934, Brit.); ALIAS BULLDOG DRUMMOND(1935, Brit.); DICTATOR, THE(1935, Brit./Ger.); DRAKE THE PIRATE(1935, Brit.); HYDE PARK CORNER(1935, Brit.); IRON DUKE, THE(1935, Brit.); ME AND MARLBOROUGH(1935, Brit.); OLD CURIOSITY SHOP, THE(1935, Brit.); RUNAWAY QUEEN, THE(1935, Brit.); SCANDALS OF PARIS(1935, Brit.); SCARLET PIMPERNEL, THE(1935, Brit.); ALL IN(1936, Brit.); BROKEN BLOSSOMS(1936, Brit.); IRISH FOR LUCK(1936, Brit.); WHERE THERE'S A WILL(1936, Brit); APRIL BLOSSOMS(1937, Brit.); JUGGERNAUT(1937, Brit.); YOU LIVE AND LEARN(1937, Brit.); ALMOST A GENTLEMAN(1938, Brit.); BREAK THE NEWS(1938, Brit.); HEY! HEY! U.S.A.(1938, Brit.); HOLD MY HAND(1938, Brit.); LOVES OF MADAME DUBARRY, THE(1938, Brit.); 13 MEN AND A GUN(1938, Brit.); COME ON GEORGE(1939, Brit.); CONFIDENTIAL LADY(1939, Brit.); INSPECTOR HORNLEIGH(1939, Brit.); SPY FOR A DAY(1939, Brit.); TWO'S COMPANY(1939, Brit.); THAT'S THE TICKET(1940, Brit.); COURAGEOUS MR. PENN, THE(1941, Brit.); MYSTERY OF ROOM 13(1941, Brit.); VOICE IN THE NIGHT, A(1941, Brit.); MUCH TOO SHY(1942, Brit.); YOUNG MR. PITT, THE(1942, Brit.); MY LEARNED FRIEND(1943, Brit.); GIVE US THE MOON(1944, Brit.); SPELL OF AMY NUGENT, THE(1945, Brit.); CAESAR AND CLEOPATRA(1946, Brit.); NO ORCHIDS FOR MISS BLANDISH(1948, Brit.); QUEEN OF SPADES(1948, Brit.); ONCE UPON A DREAM(1949, Brit.); BLACK ROSE, THE(1950); NIGHT AND THE CITY(1950, Brit.); I'LL NEVER FORGET YOU(1951); LAVENDER HILL MOB, THE(1951, Brit.); OLIVER TWIST(1951, Brit.); PICKWICK PAPERS, THE(1952, Brit.); PROMOTER, THE(1952, Brit.); MR. POTTS GOES TO MOSCOW(1953, Brit.); HOBSON'S CHOICE(1954, Brit.); BRAIN MACHINE, THE(1955, Brit.); DEEP BLUE SEA, THE(1955, Brit.); WICKED WIFE(1955, Brit.); MAN WHO NEVER WAS, THE(1956, Brit.); WHO DONE IT?(1956, Brit.); SEA WIFE(1957, Brit.)
Misc. Talkies
ALI BABA NIGHTS(1953)
Silents
ROAD TO LONDON, THE(1921, Brit.); POINTING FINGER, THE(1922, Brit.); LONDON(1926, Brit.); NELL GWYNNE(1926, Brit.); ONLY WAY, THE(1926, Brit.); ARCADIANS, THE(1927, Brit.); POPPIES OF FLANDERS(1927, Brit.); FARMER'S WIFE, THE(1928, Brit.); NOT QUITE A LADY(1928, Brit.); POWER OVER MEN(1929, Brit.)
Misc. Silents
GLORIOUS YOUTH(1928, Brit.); SILENT HOUSE, THE(1929, Brit.); WOMAN FROM CHINA, THE(1930, Brit.)
Gregg McLaughlin
CHARLIE, THE LONESOME COUGAR(1967), ed; KING OF THE GRIZZLIES(1970), ed; BEARS AND I, THE(1974), ed; BLACK HOLE, THE(1979), ed; AMY(1981), ed
Harry McLaughlin
Misc. Silents
HONEYMOON RANCH(1920); WEST OF THE RIO GRANDE(1921)
J. W. McLaughlin
Misc. Silents
BEYOND THE SHADOWS(1918), d; CLOSIN' IN(1918), d; HELL'S END(1918), d; MAN WHO WOKE UP, THE(1918), d
Jack McLaughlin
Misc. Silents
CLIMBER, THE(1917)
James McLaughlin
STEEL TOWN(1952); KEY MAN, THE(1957, Brit.)
Silents
REPUTATION(1921); SOUTH OF NORTHERN LIGHTS(1922)
Misc. Silents
GOD'S GOLD(1921)
James W. McLaughlin
Silents
TAR HEEL WARRIOR, THE(1917)
Jeffrey McLaughlin
NESTING, THE(1981)
John C. McLaughlin
SUMMER CAMP(1979)
John McLaughlin
Misc. Talkies
MAG WHEELS(1978)

Lee McLaughlin
SILVER STREAK(1976); CAR, THE(1977); CHEAP DETECTIVE, THE(1978)
Misc. Talkies
MELON AFFAIR, THE(1979)
Leon McLaughlin
LONG GRAY LINE, THE(1955)
Luther McLaughlin
NIGHT THE LIGHTS WENT OUT IN GEORGIA, THE(1981)
Mac McLaughlin
WILD WHEELS(1969); 1,000 PLANE RAID, THE(1969)
Margaret Ann McLaughlin
SABOTEUR(1942)
Robert H. McLaughlin
Silents
ETERNAL MAGDALENE, THE(1919), w
Sheila McLaughlin
BORN IN FLAMES(1983)
Stephen McLaughlin
CHILD'S PLAY(1972)
Suzi McLaughlin
RAGGEDY MAN(1981)
William J. McLaughlin
PIECE OF THE ACTION, A(1977), set d
William McLaughlin
ILLUSION(1929); BORDER, THE(1982)
Misc. Silents
DEVIL'S BOWL, THE(1923)
Gibb McLaughlin, Sr.
PARIS EXPRESS, THE(1953, Brit.)
Kate L. McLaurin
Silents
EYES OF JULIA DEEP, THE(1918), w
Kate McLaurin
ALWAYS GOODBYE(1931), w
Bernard McLaverty
1984
CAL(1984, Ireland), w
Michael McLaverty
KIDNAPPING OF THE PRESIDENT, THE(1980, Can.), ed
Svetlana McLe
ROYAL WEDDING(1951)
Arthur McLean
DRUMS O' VOODOO(1934)
Barbara McLean
AFFAIRS OF CELLINI, THE(1934), ed; HOUSE OF ROTHSCHILD, THE(1934), ed; CLIVE OF INDIA(1935), ed; LES MISERABLES(1935), ed; METROPOLITAN(1935), ed; COUNTRY DOCTOR, THE(1936), ed; LLOYDS OF LONDON(1936), ed; PROFESSIONAL SOLDIER(1936), ed; SING, BABY, SING(1936), ed; SINS OF MAN(1936), ed; LOVE UNDER FIRE(1937), ed; SEVENTH HEAVEN(1937), ed; ALEXANDER'S RAGTIME BAND(1938), ed; IN OLD CHICAGO(1938), ed; SUEZ(1938), ed; JESSE JAMES(1939), ed; RAINS CAME, THE(1939), ed; STANLEY AND LIVINGSTONE(1939), ed; CHAD HANNA(1940), ed; DOWN ARGENTINE WAY(1940), ed; MARYLAND(1940), ed; REMEMBER THE DAY(1941), ed; TOBACCO ROAD(1941), ed; YANK IN THE R.A.F., A(1941), ed; BLACK SWAN, THE(1942), ed; MAGNIFICENT DOPE, THE(1942), ed; RINGS ON HER FINGERS(1942), ed; HELLO, FRISCO, HELLO(1943), ed; SONG OF BERNADETTE, THE(1943), ed; WILSON(1944), ed; WINGED VICTORY(1944), ed; BELL FOR ADANO, A(1945), ed; DOLLY SISTERS, THE(1945), ed; MARGIE(1946), ed; THREE LITTLE GIRLS IN BLUE(1946), ed; CAPTAIN FROM CASTILE(1947), ed; NIGHTMARE ALLEY(1947), ed; DEEP WATERS(1948), ed; WHEN MY BABY SMILES AT ME(1948), ed; PRINCE OF FOXES(1949), ed; TWELVE O'CLOCK HIGH(1949), ed; ALL ABOUT EVE(1950), ed; GUNFIGHTER, THE(1950), ed; NO WAY OUT(1950), ed; DAVID AND BATHSHEBA(1951), ed; FOLLOW THE SUN(1951), ed; I'D CLIMB THE HIGHEST MOUNTAIN(1951), ed; PEOPLE WILL TALK(1951), ed; LURE OF THE WILDERNESS(1952), ed; O. HENRY'S FULL HOUSE(1952), ed; VIVA ZAPATA!(1952), ed; WAIT 'TIL THE SUN SHINES, NELLIE(1952), ed; DESERT RATS, THE(1953), ed; KING OF THE KHYBER RIFLES(1953), ed; NIAGARA(1953), ed; ROBE, THE(1953), ed; EGYPTIAN. THE(1954), ed; SEVEN CITIES OF GOLD(1955), p; UNTAMED(1955), ed
Barrie Angus McLean
GOLDEN APPLES OF THE SUN(1971, Can.), d, w, ed & prod d
Bill McLean
FIGHTING MAD(1948); MONEY TRAP, THE(1966); CRAZY MAMA(1975); COACH(1978); NORTH AVENUE IRREGULARS, THE(1979)
Billy McLean
MONKEY BUSINESS(1952); PAT AND MIKE(1952)
Bob McLean
TILL THE CLOUDS ROLL BY(1946); JOAN OF ARC(1948); HALLS OF MONTEZUMA(1951); WAVELENGTH(1983)
Bobby McLean
MIGHTY BARNUM, THE(1934), ed
Coll Red McLean
JAWS II(1978)
David McLean
RIGHT APPROACH, THE(1961); SILENT CALL, THE(1961); VOYAGE TO THE BOTTOM OF THE SEA(1961); X-15(1961); STRANGLER, THE(1964); NEVADA SMITH(1966); KINGDOM OF THE SPIDERS(1977); DEATHSPORT(1978)
Misc. Talkies
HUGHES AND HARLOW: ANGELS IN HELL(1978)
Diane McLean
Misc. Talkies
CHILL, THE(1981)
Dirk McLean
INCUBUS, THE(1982, Can.)
Dolly McLean
Silents
ABRAHAM LINCOLN(1924)

Don McLean
FRATERNITY ROW(1977), m
Doreen McLean
BACK STREET(1961)
Douglas McLean
SO RED THE ROSE(1935), p
Dwayne McLean
HOUSE BY THE LAKE, THE(1977, Can.), stunts; HAPPY BIRTHDAY, GEMINI(1980); INCUBUS, THE(1982, Can.), stunts; CHRISTMAS STORY, A(1983)
1984
POLICE ACADEMY(1984)
Eddie McLean
NIGHTFALL(1956)
Misc. Talkies
RIDERS OF THE PONY EXPRESS(1949)
Fred M. McLean
ONE SUNDAY AFTERNOON(1948), art d
Fred McLean
JEOPARDY(1953), set d; FOLLOW THAT DREAM(1962), set d
Grace McLean
Silents
NOBODY'S WIFE(1918)
Ian McLean
BREWSTER'S MILLIONS(1935, Brit.); MAYFAIR MELODY(1937, Brit.); QUIET PLEASE(1938, Brit.); SIMPLY TERRIFIC(1938, Brit.); TWO OF US, THE(1938, Brit.); APPOINTMENT WITH CRIME(1945, Brit.)
Jack McLean
Silents
SOCIETY SNOBS(1921); NO MOTHER TO GUIDE HER(1923)
Misc. Silents
BONDAGE OF BARBARA, THE(1919); THIN ICE(1919); PREY, THE(1920); CHARMING DECEIVER, THE(1921)
Jackie McLean
CONNECTION, THE(1962)
John McLean
TOUCH AND GO(1955), ph; DEMONSTRATOR(1971, Aus.), ph; CARS THAT ATE PARIS, THE(1974, Aus.), ph; NO. 96(1974, Aus,), ph
1984
SECOND TIME LUCKY(1984, Aus./New Zealand), ph
Mary McLean
Silents
PORTS OF CALL(1925)
May McLean
Silents
MAN WHO LAUGHS, THE(1927), w
Michael McLean
HEAVEN CAN WAIT(1943); FREEBIE AND THE BEAN(1974), ed; MR. RICCO(1975), ed
Michelle McLean
ICE CASTLES(1978)
Nick McLean
STAYING ALIVE(1983), ph; STROKER ACE(1983), ph
1984
CANNONBALL RUN II(1984), ph; CITY HEAT(1984), ph
Officer McLean
CANON CITY(1948)
Price McLean
Misc. Talkies
PHANTOM KID, THE(1983)
Stephanie McLean
Misc. Talkies
SPACE RIDERS(1984)
William McLean
FIGHTER SQUADRON(1948); I WAS A MALE WAR BRIDE(1949); STALAG 17(1953); YOUNG AT HEART(1955); OVER-EXPOSED(1956)
Janet McLeary
HONOR AMONG LOVERS(1931)
Urie McLeary
COMMAND DECISION(1948), art d
Janet McLeavy
LITTLE TOUGH GUY(1938)
Janet McLeay
CALLING ALL MARINES(1939)
Svetlana McLee
STALAG 17(1953)
Robert McLeish
GORBALS STORY, THE(1950, Brit.), d
Claire McLellan
MAHLER(1974, Brit.)
Pheona McLellan
BLUE BIRD, THE(1976); HITCH IN TIME, A(1978, Brit.)
Sarah McLellan
MAHLER(1974, Brit.)
Allan McLelland
HARRY BLACK AND THE TIGER(1958, Brit.)
Henry McLemore
MONEY FROM HOME(1953)
Victor McLemore
1984
STARMAN(1984)
Bart McLendon
MY DOG, BUDDY(1960)
Gordon McLendon
KILLER SHREWS, THE(1959)
James McLendon
EDDIE MACON'S RUN(1983), d&w
Andy McLennan
Silents
LONDON AFTER MIDNIGHT(1927)

Don McLennan
HARD KNOCKS(1980, Aus.), p&w, d
Hugh McLennan
TWO SOLITUDES(1978, Can.), d&w
Murray McLennan
FANTASIA(1940), anim
Rod McLennan
SLEEPING CITY, THE(1950); TATTOOED STRANGER, THE(1950); DEVILS OF DARKNESS, THE(1965, Brit.)
Wm. McLennan
BLACK KLANSMAN, THE(1966)
Rodney McLennon
CHARLEY'S AUNT(1930)
Anne McLeod
HIDE IN PLAIN SIGHT(1980)
Bill McLeod
MURDER WITHOUT CRIME(1951, Brit.), ph; FINAL TEST, THE(1953, Brit.), ph; GIRL ON THE PIER, THE(1953, Brit.), ph
Catherine McLeod
THIN MAN GOES HOME, THE(1944); FOREVER YOURS(1945); COURAGE OF LASSIE(1946); HARVEY GIRLS, THE(1946); I'VE ALWAYS LOVED YOU(1946); FABULOUS TEXAN, THE(1947); THAT'S MY MAN(1947); OLD LOS ANGELES(1948); SO YOUNG, SO BAD(1950); MY WIFE'S BEST FRIEND(1952); BLUEPRINT FOR MURDER, A(1953); SWORD OF VENUS(1953); OUTCAST, THE(1954); RETURN TO WARBOW(1958); SERGEANT WAS A LADY, THE(1961); TAMMY, TELL ME TRUE(1961); RIDE THE WILD SURF(1964)
Misc. Talkies
IN OLD LOS ANGELES(1948)
Catherine Frances McLeod
BLUE SIERRA(1946)
Craig McLeod
SLEEPING DOGS(1977, New Zealand), cos
Debbie McLeod
BELL JAR, THE(1979)
Don McLeod
HOWLING, THE(1981); PANDEMONIUM(1982); MAN WITH TWO BRAINS, THE(1983); TRADING PLACES(1983)
Donald McLeod
MISSING TEN DAYS(1941, Brit.)
Duncan McLeod
FINDERS KEEPERS, LOVERS WEEPERS(1968); TOMB OF THE UNDEAD(1972); LUCKY LADY(1975); VAN, THE(1977)
E. E. McLeod, Jr.
Silents
LOVES OF RICARDO, THE(1926)
Edgar McLeod
LONG RIDERS, THE(1980)
Elsie McLeod
Silents
ALADDIN'S OTHER LAMP(1917); RIGHT WAY, THE(1921)
Misc. Silents
SOMEWHERE IN GEORGIA(1916); BEAUTIFUL LIE, THE(1917)
Gavin McLeod
GENE KRUPA STORY, THE(1959); TWELVE HOURS TO KILL(1960); DEATHWATCH(1966); WOMEN OF THE PREHISTORIC PLANET(1966); KELLY'S HEROES(1970, U.S./Yugo.)
George McLeod
HE SNOOPS TO CONQUER(1944, Brit.)
Gordon McLeod
VICTORIA THE GREAT(1937, Brit.); VIRTUOUS SIN, THE(1930); CHELSEA LIFE(1933, Brit.); MIXED DOUBLES(1933, Brit.); THERE GOES THE BRIDE(1933, Brit.); BORROW A MILLION(1934, Brit.); BRIDES TO BE(1934, Brit.); CASE FOR THE CROWN, THE(1934, Brit.); DEATH AT A BROADCAST(1934, Brit.); LUCKY LOSER(1934, Brit.); PRIMROSE PATH, THE(1934, Brit.); SILENT PASSENGER, THE(1935, Brit.); CRIMSON CIRCLE, THE(1936, Brit.); NOTHING LIKE PUBLICITY(1936, Brit.); TO CATCH A THIEF(1936, Brit.); FROG, THE(1937, Brit.); MURDER ON DIAMOND ROW(1937, Brit.); TALK OF THE DEVIL(1937, Brit.); DANGEROUS MEDICINE(1938, Brit.); DOUBLE OR QUITS(1938, Brit.); I SEE ICE(1938, Brit.); RAT, THE(1938, Brit.); SIXTY GLORIOUS YEARS(1938, Brit.); THISTLEDOWN(1938, Brit.); CLOUDS OVER EUROPE(1939, Brit.); CONFIDENTIAL LADY(1939, Brit.); HOOTS MON!(1939, Brit.); SAINT IN LONDON, THE(1939, Brit.); TREACHERY ON THE HIGH SEAS(1939, Brit.); CROOKS TOUR(1940, Brit.); THAT'S THE TICKET(1940, Brit.); TWO FOR DANGER(1940, Brit.); FACING THE MUSIC(1941, Brit.); PRIME MINISTER, THE(1941, Brit.); SAINT'S VACATION, THE(1941, Brit.); BALLOON GOES UP, THE(1942, Brit.); WE'LL SMILE AGAIN(1942, Brit.); SAINT MEETS THE TIGER, THE(1943, Brit.); MEET SEXTON BLAKE(1944, Brit.); YELLOW CANARY, THE(1944, Brit.); I DIDN'T DO IT(1945, Brit.); HONEYMOON HOTEL(1946, Brit.); NIGHT BOAT TO DUBLIN(1946, Brit.); PATIENT VANISHES, THE(1947, Brit.); CORRIDOR OF MIRRORS(1948, Brit.); EASY MONEY(1948, Brit.); FLOODTIDE(1949, Brit.); CHANCE OF A LIFETIME(1950, Brit.); TWENTY QUESTIONS MURDER MYSTERY, THE(1950, Brit.); WINSLOW BOY, THE(1950); CASE FOR PC 49, A(1951, Brit.); FOUR DAYS(1951, Brit.); ONCE A SINNER(1952, Brit.); DIAMOND WIZARD, THE(1954, Brit.); TALE OF THREE WOMEN, A(1954, Brit.)
Silents
ONLY WAY, THE(1926, Brit.)
Helen McLeod
POSTMAN ALWAYS RINGS TWICE, THE(1946)
Howard McLeod
CAGE OF EVIL(1960)
Janet McLeod
ALICE ADAMS(1935)
Jenny McLeod
1984
SILENT ONE, THE(1984, New Zealand), m
Joan McLeod
GODSON, THE(1972, Ital./Fr.), d, w
John McLeod
ANOTHER TIME, ANOTHER PLACE(1983, Brit.), m

1984
ANOTHER TIME, ANOTHER PLACE(1984, Brit.), m
John P. McLeod
TYPHOON TREASURE(1939, Brit.), w
Julie McLeod
1984
POLICE ACADEMY(1984)
Kitty McLeod
ROB ROY, THE HIGHLAND ROGUE(1954, Brit.)
Marietta McLeod
ROB ROY, THE HIGHLAND ROGUE(1954, Brit.)
Mary McLeod
KEEPER OF THE FLAME(1942); LONDON BLACKOUT MURDERS(1942); BATAAN(1943); GUY NAMED JOE, A(1943); PURPLE V, THE(1943); MEET THE PEOPLE(1944); SEE HERE, PRIVATE HARGROVE(1944); GUY, A GAL AND A PAL, A(1945); HER LUCKY NIGHT(1945); KITTY(1945); STRANGE ILLUSION(1945); G.I. WAR BRIDES(1946); PIED PIPER, THE(1972, Brit.); FRENCH LIEUTENANT'S WOMAN, THE(1981); BRIMSTONE AND TREACLE(1982, Brit.); PORKY'S(1982), cos
Mary E. McLeod
CHRISTMAS STORY, A(1983), cos; PORKY'S II: THE NEXT DAY(1983), cos
Mercer McLeod
VIOLATORS, THE(1957)
Murray McLeod
ANGRY BREED, THE(1969)
Norman McLeod
FINN AND HATTIE(1931), d; MONKEY BUSINESS(1931), d; NEWLY RICH(1931), w; SKIPPY(1931), w; SOOKY(1931), w; TOUCHDOWN!(1931), w; IF I HAD A MILLION(1932), d; ALICE IN WONDERLAND(1933), d; LADY'S PROFESSION, A(1933), d; MAMA LOVES PAPA(1933), d; MANY HAPPY RETURNS(1934), d; CORONADO(1935), d; EARLY TO BED(1936), d; MIND YOUR OWN BUSINESS(1937), d; ALIAS JESSE JAMES(1959), d
Silents
NONE BUT THE BRAVE(1928), t
Norman Z. McLeod
AIR CIRCUS, THE(1928), w; ALONG CAME YOUTH(1931), d; HORSE FEATHERS(1932), d; MIRACLE MAN, THE(1932), d; IT'S A GIFT(1934), d; MELODY IN SPRING(1934), d; HERE COMES COOKIE(1935), d; REDHEADS ON PARADE(1935), d; PENNIES FROM HEAVEN(1936), d; TOPPER(1937), d; MERRILY WE LIVE(1938), d; THERE GOES MY HEART(1938), d; REMEMBER?(1939), d, w; TOPPER TAKES A TRIP(1939), d; LITTLE MEN(1940), d; LADY BE GOOD(1941), d; TRIAL OF MARY DUGAN, THE(1941), d; JACKASS MAIL(1942), d; PANAMA HATTIE(1942), d; POWERS GIRL, THE(1942), d; SWING SHIFT MAISIE(1943), d; KID FROM BOOKLYN, THE(1946), d; ROAD TO RIO(1947), d; SECRET LIFE OF WALTER MITTY, THE(1947), d; ISN'T IT ROMANTIC?(1948), d; PALEFACE, THE(1948), d; LET'S DANCE(1950), d; MY FAVORITE SPY(1951), d; NEVER WAVE AT A WAC(1952), d; CASANOVA'S BIG NIGHT(1954), d; PUBLIC PIGEON NO. 1(1957), d
Silents
PLAY GIRL, THE(1928), t
Misc. Silents
TAKING A CHANCE(1928), d
Randolph McLeod
REUNION(1932, Brit.); OUTSIDER, THE(1933, Brit.)
Misc. Silents
FOUL PLAY(1920, Brit.); LADY AUDLEY'S SECRET(1920, Brit.)
Rona McLeod
CLINIC, THE(1983, Aus.)
Sandy McLeod
LAST EMBRACE(1979)
1984
SWING SHIFT(1984); VARIETY(1984)
Shelagh McLeod
AMERICAN SUCCESS COMPANY, THE(1980)
Victor McLeod
LAW AND ORDER(1940), w; BOSS OF BULLION CITY(1941), w; BURY ME NOT ON THE LONE PRAIRIE(1941), w; HORROR ISLAND(1941), w; MUTINY IN THE ARCTIC(1941), w; GIRLS' TOWN(1942), w; RUSTLER'S ROUNDUP(1946), w; LITTLE MISS BROADWAY(1947), w; TWO BLONDES AND A REDHEAD(1947), w
Victor I. McLeod
MASKED RIDER, THE(1941), w; RAIDERS OF THE DESERT(1941), w
W. McLeod
ALIBI, THE(1943, Brit.), ph
Wayne McLeod
OUT OF THE BLUE(1982)
William McLeod
BUT NOT IN VAIN(1948, Brit.), ph; GLASS MOUNTAIN, THE(1950, Brit), ph; GUILT IS MY SHADOW(1950, Brit.), ph; NO PLACE FOR JENNIFER(1950, Brit.), ph; LAUGHTER IN PARADISE(1951, Brit.), ph; CALCULATED RISK(1963, Brit.), p; TAKE ME OVER(1963, Brit.), p
Allyn Ann McLerie
WAY WE WERE, THE(1973); REIVERS, THE(1969); THEY SHOOT HORSES, DON'T THEY?(1969); MONTE WALSH(1970); COWBOYS, THE(1972); JEREMIAH JOHNSON(1972); MAGNIFICENT SEVEN RIDE, THE(1972); CINDERELLA LIBERTY(1973); HOWZER(1973); ENTERTAINER, THE(1975); ALL THE PRESIDENT'S MEN(1976)
Allyn McLerie
WHERE'S CHARLEY?(1952, Brit.); CALAMITY JANE(1953); DESERT SONG, THE(1953); PHANTOM OF THE RUE MORGUE(1954); BATTLE FLAME(1955)
Hal McLernon
STAR WITNESS(1931), ed
Harold McLernon
FROM HEADQUARTERS(1929), ed; GENERAL CRACK(1929), ed; CHILDREN OF DREAMS(1931), ed; WOMAN FROM MONTE CARLO, THE(1932), ed; EX-LADY(1933), ed; PRIVATE DETECTIVE 62(1933), ed; DAMES(1934), ed; FOG OVER FRISCO(1934), ed; GAMBLING LADY(1934), ed; GO INTO YOUR DANCE(1935), ed; GOING HIGHBROW(1935), ed; PAYOFF, THE(1935), ed; SWEET ADELINE(1935), ed; JAILBREAK(1936), ed; KING OF HOCKEY(1936), ed; SNOWED UNDER(1936), ed; SONG OF THE SADDLE(1936), ed; CHEROKEE STRIP(1937), ed; THAT MAN'S HERE AGAIN(1937), ed; DAREDEVIL DRIVERS(1938), ed; INVISIBLE MENACE, THE(1938), ed; MR. CHUMP(1938), ed; TORCHY GETS HER MAN(1938), ed; ADVENTURES OF JANE ARDEN(1939), ed; I AM NOT AFRAID(1939), ed; MAN WHO

DARED, THE(1939), ed; PRIVATE DETECTIVE(1939), ed; TORCHY PLAYS WITH DYNAMITE(1939), ed; TUGBOAT ANNIE SAILS AGAIN(1940), ed; HERE COMES HAPPINESS(1941), ed; SHOT IN THE DARK, THE(1941), ed; DANGEROUSLY THEY LIVE(1942), ed; HIDDEN HAND, THE(1942), ed; LADY GANGSTER(1942), ed; FIND THE BLACKMAILER(1943), ed; LAST RIDE, THE(1944), ed
Silents
ANGEL OF BROADWAY, THE(1927), ed; KING OF KINGS, THE(1927), ed; HOLD 'EM YALE!(1928), ed; LET 'ER GO GALLEGHER(1928), ed; MARKED MONEY(1928), ed; MIDNIGHT MADNESS(1928), ed

Michael McLernon
LILI MARLEEN(1981, Ger.); QUERELLE(1983, Ger./Fr.)

Harold McLeron
SHE COULDN'T SAY NO(1941), ed

Ron McLewdon
LET'S ROCK(1958)

David McLey
BREAKING POINT(1976), m

Don McLiam
SLEEPER(1973)

John McLiam
DEAD TO THE WORLD(1961); MY FAIR LADY(1964); COOL HAND LUKE(1967); IN COLD BLOOD(1967); MADIGAN(1968); RIVERRUN(1968); REIVERS, THE(1969); HALLS OF ANGER(1970); MONTE WALSH(1970); R.P.M.(1970); CULPEPPER CATTLE COMPANY, THE(1972); ICEMAN COMETH, THE(1973); SHOWDOWN(1973); DOVE, THE(1974, Brit.); BITE THE BULLET(1975); LUCKY LADY(1975); RAFFERTY AND THE GOLD DUST TWINS(1975); FOOD OF THE GODS, THE(1976); MISSOURI BREAKS, THE(1976); END OF AUGUST, THE(1982); FIRST BLOOD(1982)

Shirley McLine
CURSE OF THE SWAMP CREATURE(1966)

Lloyd McLinn
MURPH THE SURF(1974)

Valerie McLintock
Silents
MOLLY BAWN(1916, Brit.)

Bronco McLoughlin
KRULL(1983)

Marion McLoughlin
GIRO CITY(1982, Brit.)

Maurice McLoughlin
JOHNNY, YOU'RE WANTED(1956, Brit.), w

Patrick McLoughlin
GYPSY GIRL(1966, Brit.), set d; DANDY IN ASPIC, A(1968, Brit.), art d; DUFFY(1968, Brit.), set d; THERE'S A GIRL IN MY SOUP(1970, Brit.), set d; UNDERCOVERS HERO(1975, Brit.), set d

R. McLoughlin
Silents
DECAMERON NIGHTS(1924, Brit.), w

Tom McLoughlin
ONE DARK NIGHT(1983), d, w

Tommy McLoughlin
BLACK HOLE, THE(1979)

Marshall McLuhan
ANNIE HALL(1977); THIRD WALKER, THE(1978, Can.)

Teri McLuhan
THIRD WALKER, THE(1978, Can.), p, d, w

Frank McLure
IN THE MEANTIME, DARLING(1944); WING AND A PRAYER(1944); NIGHT EDITOR(1946); JOLSON SINGS AGAIN(1949)

Katee McLure
ONE DARK NIGHT(1983)

Archer McMackin
Silents
ROOKIE'S RETURN, THE(1921), w

Betty McMahan
MORE THE MERRIER, THE(1943)

"Whitey" McMahan
TIME TO LOVE AND A TIME TO DIE, A(1958), spec eff

Aline McMahon
MOUTHPIECE, THE(1932); BIG HEARTED HERBERT(1934); BACK DOOR TO HEAVEN(1939)

Ben McMahon
MAN'S FAVORITE SPORT [?](1964), spec eff

Dave McMahon
STORM WARNING(1950); ROADBLOCK(1951)

David McMahon
KISS THE BLOOD OFF MY HANDS(1948); SAINTED SISTERS, THE(1948); GREAT SINNER, THE(1949); I WAS A MALE WAR BRIDE(1949); MAGNIFICENT YANKEE, THE(1950); MYSTERY STREET(1950); WHEN WILLIE COMES MARCHING HOME(1950); WHERE THE SIDEWALK ENDS(1950); I WANT YOU(1951); MOB, THE(1951); SCARF, THE(1951); EIGHT IRON MEN(1952); GLORY ALLEY(1952); SNIPER, THE(1952); SO BIG(1953); WAR OF THE WORLDS, THE(1953); I DIED A THOUSAND TIMES(1955); REBEL WITHOUT A CAUSE(1955); TOP OF THE WORLD(1955); CREATURE WALKS AMONG US, THE(1956); DANCE WITH ME, HENRY(1956); PEACEMAKER, THE(1956); OPERATION MAD BALL(1957); SPIRIT OF ST. LOUIS, THE(1957); PARTY GIRL(1958); CRIMSON KIMONO, THE(1959); ICE PALACE(1960); CASE OF PATTY SMITH, THE(1962)

Doris McMahon
MADAME SATAN(1930)

E.M. McMahon
Misc. Silents
FIFTH HORSEMAN, THE(1924), d

Ed McMahon
DEMENTIA(1955); INCIDENT, THE(1967); SLAUGHTER'S BIG RIP-OFF(1973); FUN WITH DICK AND JANE(1977); LAST REMAKE OF BEAU GESTE, THE(1977); BUTTERFLY(1982); FULL MOON HIGH(1982)

Frank McMahon
MILKMAN, THE(1950)

Gerard McMahon
DEFIANCE(1980), m

Horace McMahon
LAST GANGSTER, THE(1937); PAID TO DANCE(1937); FAST COMPANY(1938); I AM THE LAW(1938); LAUGH IT OFF(1939); THAT'S RIGHT–YOU'RE WRONG(1939); WE WHO ARE YOUNG(1940); BIRTH OF THE BLUES(1941); COME LIVE WITH ME(1941); TIMBER QUEEN(1944); FIGHTING MAD(1948); SMART WOMAN(1948); WATERFRONT AT MIDNIGHT(1948); DETECTIVE STORY(1951); ABBOTT AND COSTELLO GO TO MARS(1953); CHAMP FOR A DAY(1953); MAN IN THE DARK(1953); DUFFY OF SAN QUENTIN(1954); SUSAN SLEPT HERE(1954); BLACKBOARD JUNGLE, THE(1955); MY SISTER EILEEN(1955); BEAU JAMES(1957); DELICATE DELINQUENT, THE(1957); SWINGER, THE(1966); DETECTIVE, THE(1968)

John McMahon
TWO WORLD(1930, Brit.)

Kassid McMahon
BUBBLE, THE(1967)

Leo McMahon
MYSTERIOUS RIDER, THE(1938); JOAN OF ARC(1948); STATION WEST(1948); COLT .45(1950); DAKOTA LIL(1950); STORM OVER WYOMING(1950); GUNPLAY(1951); ESCAPE TO BURMA(1955); MADRON(1970, U.S./Israel), w

Leo J. McMahon
SILVER CITY(1951); HURRICANE SMITH(1952); SON OF PALEFACE(1952)

Louis McMahon
WILD IS MY LOVE(1963), ph; PSYCHOMANIA(1964), ph

Louis A. McMahon
Misc. Talkies
CAPTAIN CELLULOID VS THE FILM PIRATES(1974), d

Pat McMahon
LIEUTENANT WORE SKIRTS, THE(1956); ANATOMY OF A PSYCHO(1961)

Patricia McMahon
D-DAY, THE SIXTH OF JUNE(1956)

Patrick McMahon
STRANGE BREW(1983), ed

Phyllis McMahon
LEO THE LAST(1970, Brit.); 10 RILLINGTON PLACE(1971, Brit.); DEVIL WITHIN HER, THE(1976, Brit.)

Shannon McMahon
SCREWBALLS(1983)

Thomas A. McMahon
SIDEWINDER ONE(1977), w; CARAVANS(1978, U.S./Iranian), w

Whitey McMahon
WILD AND WONDERFUL(1964), spec eff; HELLFIGHTERS(1968), spec eff; COLOSSUS: THE FORBIN PROJECT(1969), spec eff

Whitney McMahon
DIAMONDS ARE FOREVER(1971, Brit.), spec eff

E. L. McManigal
WEST OF THE ROCKIES(1929), ph

E. T. McManigal
Silents
BOY RIDER, THE(1927), ph

Art McManmon
SPIRIT OF NOTRE DAME, THE(1931)

David McMann
THING, THE(1951)

Babbie McManus
LUST FOR A VAMPIRE(1971, Brit.), ch

Barney McManus
LUCK OF GINGER COFFEY, THE(1964, U.S./Can.)

Dan McManus
SO DEAR TO MY HEART(1949), anim; LADY AND THE TRAMP(1955), anim

Don McManus
1984
MRS. SOFFEL(1984)

George McManus
BRINGING UP FATHER(1946), a, w; JIGGS AND MAGGIE IN SOCIETY(1948), w; JIGGS AND MAGGIE OUT WEST(1950), a, w
Misc. Talkies
JIGGS AND MAGGIE IN COURT(1948); JIGGS AND MAGGIE IN JACKPOT JITTERS(1949)

Jim McManus
PLAYERS(1979)

Joe McManus
CYCLE SAVAGES(1969)

John McManus
FANTASIA(1940), anim, anim; PINOCCHIO(1940), anim; THREE CABALLEROS, THE(1944), anim; MAKE MINE MUSIC(1946), anim; TROUBLEMAKER, THE(1964), ed

Joseph McManus
Misc. Silents
MASTER MAN, THE(1919)

Kate McManus
ACCEPTABLE LEVELS(1983, Brit.), w, art d

Louis McManus
BOHEMIAN GIRL, THE(1936), ed

Mark McManus
NED KELLY(1970, Brit.); 2,000 WEEKS(1970, Aus.); ADAM'S WOMAN(1972, Austral.)

Michael McManus
WORLD'S GREATEST LOVER, THE(1977); POLTERGEIST(1982)

Mike McManus
MOTHER, JUGS & SPEED(1976)

Rip McManus
DOWNHILL RACER(1969)

Sharon McManus
SUMMER STORM(1944); 'TILL WE MEET AGAIN(1944); ANCHORS AWEIGH(1945); BEWITCHED(1945); BOYS' RANCH(1946); LITTLE MISTER JIM(1946); THIS TIME FOR KEEPS(1947); NO MINOR VICES(1948); PALEFACE, THE(1948); CITY ACROSS THE RIVER(1949); PREJUDICE(1949); IT'S A BIG COUNTRY(1951)

Sue McManus
TEENAGE GANG DEBS(1966)
Sally McMarrow
13 RUE MADELEINE(1946)
John McMartin
WHAT'S SO BAD ABOUT FEELING GOOD?(1968); SWEET CHARITY(1969); ALL THE PRESIDENT'S MEN(1976); THIEVES(1977); BRUBAKER(1980); PENNIES FROM HEAVEN(1981)
Lorraine McMartin
HUSBANDS(1970)
Andrew McMaster
Silents
LOST PATROL, THE(1929, Brit.)
Anew McMaster
SWORD OF SHERWOOD FOREST(1961, Brit.)
Chris McMaster
SCRUFFY(1938, Brit.)
Jack McMaster
MIDWAY(1976), spec eff
Niles McMaster
ALICE, SWEET ALICE(1978); BLOODSUCKING FREAKS(1982)
1984
WINDY CITY(1984)
Jack McMasters
EARTHQUAKE(1974), spec eff; ROOSTER COGBURN(1975), spec eff
Luke "Giant Haystacks" McMasters
1984
GIVE MY REGARDS TO BROAD STREET(1984, Brit.)
Mickey McMasters
MAN ON THE FLYING TRAPEZE, THE(1935); NOTHING SACRED(1937)
Joe McMichael
LOVE THY NEIGHBOR(1940); MELODY LANE(1941); SAN ANTONIO ROSE(1941); RIDE 'EM COWBOY(1942)
Judd McMichael
LOVE THY NEIGHBOR(1940); MELODY LANE(1941); MOONLIGHT IN HAWAII(1941); SAN ANTONIO ROSE(1941); RIDE 'EM COWBOY(1942)
Ted McMichael
LOVE THY NEIGHBOR(1940); MELODY LANE(1941); MOONLIGHT IN HAWAII(1941); SAN ANTONIO ROSE(1941); RIDE 'EM COWBOY(1942)
Mickey McMickle
SUN VALLEY SERENADE(1941)
Bill McMillan
NEW YORK, NEW YORK(1977); RESCUERS, THE(1977)
Dean McMillan
NIJINSKY(1980, Brit.)
Ian McMillan
1984
GIVE MY REGARDS TO BROAD STREET(1984, Brit.), ph
Julia McMillan
LARCENY IN HER HEART(1946); MURDER IS MY BUSINESS(1946)
Ken McMillan
GIRLFRIENDS(1978)
Kenneth McMillan
TAKING OF PELHAM ONE, TWO, THREE, THE(1974); BLOODBROTHERS(1978); OLIVER'S STORY(1978); BORDERLINE(1980); CARNY(1980); LITTLE MISS MARKER(1980); EYEWITNESS(1981); HEARTBEEPS(1981); RAGTIME(1981); TRUE CONFESSIONS(1981); WHOSE LIFE IS IT ANYWAY?(1981); CHILLY SCENES OF WINTER(1982); KILLING HOUR, THE(1982); PARTNERS(1982); BLUE SKIES AGAIN(1983)
1984
POPE OF GREENWICH VILLAGE, THE(1984); PROTOCOL(1984); RECKLESS(1984)
Lisa McMillan
EASY MONEY(1983)
Roddy McMillan
GORBALS STORY, THE(1950, Brit.); OPERATION DISASTER(1951, Brit.); HIGH AND DRY(1954, Brit.); SCOTCH ON THE ROCKS(1954, Brit.); CAT AND MOUSE(1958, Brit.); BRIDAL PATH, THE(1959, Brit.); BATTLE OF THE SEXES, THE(1960, Brit.); PRIZE OF ARMS, A(1962, Brit.); MOUSE ON THE MOON, THE(1963, Brit.); AMOROUS MR. PRAWN, THE(1965, Brit.); RING OF BRIGHT WATER(1969, Brit.); CHATO'S LAND(1972); SWEENEY 2(1978, Brit.)
Stephenie McMillan
1984
GIVE MY REGARDS TO BROAD STREET(1984, Brit.), set d
Susan O. McMillan
JAWS II(1978)
Toni McMillan
OPERATION DIAMOND(1948, Brit.); MIRANDA(1949, Brit.)
Tonie McMillan
JOSEPHINE AND MEN(1955, Brit.)
W.G. McMillan
THE CRAZIES(1973); SISTER-IN-LAW, THE(1975)
Jay McMillian
SIX PACK(1982)
Mitzi McMillin
PERSONAL BEST(1982)
William McMillin
MADE IN PARIS(1966), ed
Fraser McMinn
SON OF BILLY THE KID(1949); FAST ON THE DRAW(1950)
Teri McMinn
TEXAS CHAIN SAW MASSACRE, THE(1974)
Joan McMonagle
WITHOUT A TRACE(1983)
Patrick McMorrow
USED CARS(1980)
James McMullan
RAIDERS, THE(1964); SHENANDOAH(1965); INCREDIBLE SHRINKING WOMAN, THE(1981)

Misc. Talkies
EXTREME CLOSE-UP(1973)
Jim McMullan
HAPPIEST MILLIONAIRE, THE(1967); DOWNHILL RACER(1969); WINDSPLITTER, THE(1971)
Craig T. McMullen
ICE CASTLES(1978)
Dennis McMullen
FEAR STRIKES OUT(1957); JOKER IS WILD, THE(1957); SHORT CUT TO HELL(1957); LADY LIBERTY(1972, Ital./Fr.); FRIENDS OF EDDIE COYLE, THE(1973); WEREWOLF OF WASHINGTON(1973); MAN WHO WOULD NOT DIE, THE(1975); CHINA SYNDROME, THE(1979); WHEN A STRANGER CALLS(1979)
Doug McMullen
BACK DOOR TO HEAVEN(1939)
Ken McMullen
1984
GHOST DANCE(1984, Brit.), p,d&w
Robert McMullen
HELL'S BELLES(1969), w
Virginia McMullen
BEYOND TOMORROW(1940)
David McMullin
MAIDSTONE(1970)
Robert McMullin
SHADOW OF THE HAWK(1976, Can.), m
Roy McMullin
1984
BAY BOY(1984, Can.)
Spencer McMullin
HARRY'S WAR(1981)
Charles McMurphy
BENSON MURDER CASE, THE(1930); IF I HAD A MILLION(1932); MEN OF THE NIGHT(1934); THUNDERING HERD, THE(1934); GOIN' TO TOWN(1935); HOLD 'EM YALE(1935); STAR OF MIDNIGHT(1935); EX-MRS. BRADFORD, THE(1936); I CONQUER THE SEA(1936); MILKY WAY, THE(1936); POPPY(1936); SONG OF THE TRAIL(1936); PICK A STAR(1937); BORN TO FIGHT(1938); THERE'S THAT WOMAN AGAIN(1938); FORGOTTEN WOMAN, THE(1939); LAUGH IT OFF(1939); MY LITTLE CHICKADEE(1940); QUEEN OF THE MOB(1940); WE WHO ARE YOUNG(1940); LOVE CRAZY(1941); MAN FROM MONTANA(1941); NEVER GIVE A SUCKER AN EVEN BREAK(1941); PHANTOM SUBMARINE, THE(1941); SAN FRANCISCO DOCKS(1941); SPOILERS, THE(1942); YOU'RE TELLING ME(1942); EXPERIMENT PERILOUS(1944); LAW OF THE VALLEY(1944); SHINE ON, HARVEST MOON(1944)
Kenneth McMurphy
YOUNG GIANTS(1983)
Fred McMurray
HAPPIEST MILLIONAIRE, THE(1967)
James McMurray
WAY WE LIVE NOW, THE(1970)
Lillita McMurray [Lita Grey]
Silents
KID, THE(1921)
Richard McMurray
DAVID AND LISA(1962); SWIMMER, THE(1968); ZIGZAG(1970); 1776(1972); SO LONG, BLUE BOY(1973); RANCHO DELUXE(1975); FIRST MONDAY IN OCTOBER(1981)
Sam McMurray
FRONT, THE(1976); UNION CITY(1980); BABY, IT'S YOU(1983)
1984
C.H.U.D.(1984)
Lynn McMurrey
SWEET CHARITY(1969)
James McMurtry
DAISY MILLER(1974)
John McMurtry
POINT BLANK(1967); TOP OF THE HEAP(1972)
Larry McMurtry
HUD(1963), w; LAST PICTURE SHOW, THE(1971), w; LOVIN' MOLLY(1974), w; TERMS OF ENDEARMENT(1983), w
John McMurty
HOT SUMMER WEEK(1973, Can.)
Pam McMyler
RESTLESS ONES, THE(1965); FOR PETE'S SAKE!(1966)
Pamela McMyler
CHISUM(1970); ONE MORE TRAIN TO ROB(1971); DOGPOUND SHUFFLE(1975, Can.); STICK UP, THE(1978, Brit.); BLOOD BEACH(1981); HALLOWEEN II(1981)
Bernard McNab
IT'S NOT CRICKET(1949, Brit.), w
Jane McNab
GET HEP TO LOVE(1942)
Jean McNab
GET HEP TO LOVE(1942)
Barbara McNair
SPENCER'S MOUNTAIN(1963); IF HE HOLLERS, LET HIM GO(1968); CHANGE OF HABIT(1969); STILETTO(1969); THEY CALL ME MISTER TIBBS(1970); VENUS IN FURS(1970, Ital./Brit./Ger.); ORGANIZATION, THE(1971)
Harold McNair
ISLAND WOMEN(1958)
Sue McNair
HORROR OF THE BLOOD MONSTERS(1970, U.S./Phil.), w
Winton McNair
PAYDAY(1972)
Thomas McNallan
ONE IS A LONELY NUMBER(1972)
Maureen McNalley
SWEET HUNTERS(1969, Panama)
Pat McNalley
OLD YELLER(1957), makeup; LIGHT IN THE FOREST, THE(1958), makeup; TONKA(1958), makeup; DARBY O'GILL AND THE LITTLE PEOPLE(1959), makeup; POLLYANNA(1960), makeup; SIGN OF ZORRO, THE(1960), makeup; TOBY TYLER(1960), makeup; INCREDIBLE JOURNEY, THE(1963), makeup; SAVAGE

SAM(1963), makeup; SON OF FLUBBER(1963), makeup; SUMMER MAGIC(1963), makeup; MARY POPPINS(1964), makeup; MISADVENTURES OF MERLIN JONES, THE(1964), makeup; THOSE CALLOWAYS(1964), makeup; TIGER WALKS, A(1964), makeup; MONKEY'S UNCLE, THE(1965), makeup; UGLY DACHSHUND, THE(1966), makeup; MONKEYS, GO HOME!(1967), makeup

Dan McNally
1941(1979)

Ed McNally
MOVE OVER, DARLING(1963); CHARLY(1968)

Ed "Skipper" McNally
TIGHT SPOT(1955); CRIME OF PASSION(1957); DEADLY MANTIS, THE(1957); NEVER STEAL ANYTHING SMALL(1959); PARADISE ALLEY(1962)

Edward McNally
NAKED AND THE DEAD, THE(1958); SPACE MASTER X-7(1958); EMPEROR OF THE NORTH POLE(1973); TWO-MINUTE WARNING(1976)

Frank McNally
BRIGHTON ROCK(1947, Brit.), ed

Horace [Stephen] McNally
DR. GILLESPIE'S NEW ASSISTANT(1942); EYES IN THE NIGHT(1942); FOR ME AND MY GAL(1942); GRAND CENTRAL MURDER(1942); WAR AGAINST MRS. HADLEY, THE(1942); MAN FROM DOWN UNDER, THE(1943); AMERICAN ROMANCE, AN(1944); THIRTY SECONDS OVER TOKYO(1944); BEWITCHED(1945); DANGEROUS PARTNERS(1945); MAGNIFICENT DOLL(1946); UP GOES MAISIE(1946)

James McNally
RHYTHM OF THE RIO GRANDE(1940); FEAR STRIKES OUT(1957)

John McNally
JEALOUSY(1931, Brit.), w; ROSARY, THE(1931, Brit.), w; WICKHAM MYSTERY, THE(1931, Brit.), w; TWO HEARTS IN WALTZ TIME(1934, Brit.), w

Kevin McNally
SPY WHO LOVED ME, THE(1977, Brit.); ENIGMA(1983)

Pat McNally
CRY OF THE CITY(1948), makeup; TEN WHO DARED(1960), makeup; PARENT TRAP, THE(1961), makeup; GNOME-MOBILE, THE(1967), makeup

Raymond McNally
WEDDING PARTY, THE(1969)

Skip McNally
TIME LIMIT(1957)

Stephen McNally
KEEPER OF THE FLAME(1942); AIR RAID WARDENS(1943); HARVEY GIRLS, THE(1946); JOHNNY BELINDA(1948); ROGUES' REGIMENT(1948); CITY ACROSS THE RIVER(1949); CRISS CROSS(1949); LADY GAMBLES, THE(1949); SWORD IN THE DESERT(1949); WOMAN IN HIDING(1949); NO WAY OUT(1950); WINCHESTER '73(1950); WYOMING MAIL(1950); AIR CADET(1951); APACHE DRUMS(1951); IRON MAN, THE(1951); LADY PAYS OFF, THE(1951); RAGING TIDE, THE(1951); BATTLE ZONE(1952); BLACK CASTLE, THE(1952); DIPLOMATIC COURIER(1952); DUEL AT SILVER CREEK, THE(1952); DEVIL'S CANYON(1953); SPLIT SECOND(1953); STAND AT APACHE RIVER, THE(1953); BULLET IS WAITING, A(1954); MAKE HASTE TO LIVE(1954); MAN FROM BITTER RIDGE, THE(1955); VIOLENT SATURDAY(1955); TRIBUTE TO A BADMAN(1956); HELL'S CROSSROADS(1957); FIEND WHO WALKED THE WEST, THE(1958); HELL'S FIVE HOURS(1958); JOHNNY ROCCO(1958); HELL BENT FOR LEATHER(1960); REQUIEM FOR A GUNFIGHTER(1965); PANIC IN THE CITY(1968); ONCE YOU KISS A STRANGER(1969); BLACK GUNN(1972); HI-RIDERS(1978)

Terrence McNally
RITZ, THE(1976), w; BATTLE BEYOND THE STARS(1980); NINE TO FIVE(1980); LOOKER(1981)

Bonnie June McNamara
WOMAN REBELS, A(1936)

Brian McNamara
1984
FLAMINGO KID, THE(1984)

Cornelia McNamara
JACKSON COUNTY JAIL(1976), cos

Ed McNamara
ZIEGFELD GIRL(1941); MARGIN FOR ERROR(1943); SKY'S THE LIMIT, THE(1943); SILVER STREAK(1976); HOUSE BY THE LAKE, THE(1977, Can.); BLACK STALLION, THE(1979)

Edward McNamara
LUCKY IN LOVE(1929); GIRL OVERBOARD(1937); LEAGUE OF FRIGHTENED MEN(1937); DEVIL AND MISS JONES, THE(1941); NEW YORK TOWN(1941); STRAWBERRY BLONDE, THE(1941); CAPTAINS OF THE CLOUDS(1942); GAY SISTERS, THE(1942); MY GAL SAL(1942); JOHNNY COME LATELY(1943); THIS LAND IS MINE(1943); ARSENIC AND OLD LACE(1944)

Edward J. McNamara
I AM A FUGITIVE FROM A CHAIN GANG(1932); 20,000 YEARS IN SING SING(1933); GREAT GUY(1936); PALM BEACH STORY, THE(1942)

Hallam McNamara
Misc. Silents
GIRL FROM THE OUTSIDE, THE(1919)

J. Patrick McNamara
CLOSE ENCOUNTERS OF THE THIRD KIND(1977); FURY, THE(1978); 1941(1979)

James McNamara
YOU AND ME(1938); ICE FOLLIES OF 1939(1939); MR. SMITH GOES TO WASHINGTON(1939); STANLEY AND LIVINGSTONE(1939); UNION PACIFIC(1939); MEET JOHN DOE(1941); SIX LESSONS FROM MADAME LA ZONGA(1941); HOME IN WYOMIN'(1942)

James H. McNamara
BURIED ALIVE(1939); ONE MAN'S LAW(1940); LOVE CRAZY(1941)

Maj. James H. McNamara
LITTLE OLD NEW YORK(1940); I MARRIED AN ANGEL(1942)

James J. McNamara
HARDLY WORKING(1981), p

John McNamara
FROM HELL IT CAME(1957); SLAUGHTER ON TENTH AVENUE(1957); CRASH LANDING(1958); RETURN OF DRACULA, THE(1958); SUICIDE BATTALION(1958); WAR OF THE COLOSSAL BEAST(1958); MA BARKER'S KILLER BROOD(1960); PORTRAIT IN BLACK(1960)

Maggie McNamara
MOON IS BLUE, THE(1953); THREE COINS IN THE FOUNTAIN(1954); PRINCE OF PLAYERS(1955); CARDINAL, THE(1963)

Martin McNamara
DIRTY TRICKS(1981, Can.)

Michael McNamara
DIRTY TRICKS(1981, Can.)

Miles McNamara
WHERE THE BUFFALO ROAM(1980)
1984
PHILADELPHIA EXPERIMENT, THE(1984)

Pat McNamara
LAST WORD, THE(1979); WINDOWS(1980)
1984
CRIMES OF PASSION(1984)

Patrick McNamara
FRONT, THE(1976); OBSESSION(1976); BLOW OUT(1981)

Peter McNamara
1984
LASSITER(1984)

Richard McNamara
TERESA(1951); MAN FROM CAIRO, THE(1953); ROMAN HOLIDAY(1953); WAR AND PEACE(1956, Ital./U.S.); CAMPBELL'S KINGDOM(1957, Brit.); ATOM AGE VAMPIRE(1961, Ital.), d; QUEEN OF THE PIRATES(1961, Ital./Ger.), d; LION OF ST. MARK(1967, Ital.), d

Robert McNamara
SOL MADRID(1968); KELLY'S HEROES(1970, U.S./Yugo.)

Rosemary McNamara
PREMONITION, THE(1976)

T.J. Mcnamara
WARRIORS, THE(1979)

Ted McNamara
Silents
SHORE LEAVE(1925); WHAT PRICE GLORY(1926); GAY RETREAT, THE(1927); MONKEY TALKS, THE(1927); GATEWAY OF THE MOON, THE(1928)
Misc. Silents
CHAIN LIGHTING(1927); WHY SAILORS GO WRONG(1928)

Tom McNamara
LITTLE ORPHAN ANNIE(1932), w; CROSSFIRE(1933), w
Silents
GILDED LILY, THE(1921), t; IDOL OF THE NORTH, THE(1921), t; LITTLE ANNIE ROONEY(1925), t

Walter McNamara
SIDE STREET(1929)
Silents
TRAFFIC IN SOULS(1913), w; SHAMS OF SOCIETY(1921), w

Donald McNamee
Misc. Silents
FASHION MADNESS(1928)

Graham McNamee
GIFT OF GAB(1934); WINGS IN THE DARK(1935)

Dorothy McNames
HAPPY DAYS(1930); DON'T GET PERSONAL(1936)

Louise McNames
EVERY NIGHT AT EIGHT(1935)

Lucille McNames
DON'T GET PERSONAL(1936)

Bob McNaught
WICKED WIFE(1955, Brit.), d, w; SEA WIFE(1957, Brit.), d; STORY OF DAVID, A(1960, Brit.), d

Bruce McNaughton
LIBIDO(1973, Aus.), ph; GREAT MACARTHY, THE(1975, Aus.), ph

Charles McNaughton
THREE LIVE GHOSTS(1929); BAD ONE, THE(1930); COMMON CLAY(1930); SINGLE SIN(1931); CHARLIE CHAN'S CHANCE(1932); BIG BRAIN, THE(1933); BISHOP MISBEHAVES, THE(1933); MIDNIGHT CLUB(1933); FOUNTAIN, THE(1934); TREASURE ISLAND(1934); THREE LIVE GHOSTS(1935); LLOYDS OF LONDON(1936); SUZY(1936); BULLDOG DRUMMOND ESCAPES(1937); ADVENTURES OF ROBIN HOOD, THE(1938); BLACK SWAN, THE(1942); MY NAME IS JULIA ROSS(1945); TONIGHT AND EVERY NIGHT(1945); MOSS ROSE(1947); KISS THE BLOOD OFF MY HANDS(1948); THAT FORSYTE WOMAN(1949)
Silents
WET GOLD(1921)

Clarence McNaughton
EAST OF JAVA(1935)

Gus McNaughton
CHILDREN OF CHANCE(1930, Brit.); MURDER(1930, Brit.); HIS WIFE'S MOTHER(1932, Brit.); LAST COUPON, THE(1932, Brit.); LUCKY GIRL(1932, Brit.); MAID OF THE MOUNTAINS, THE(1932, Brit.); CHARMING DECEIVER, THE(1933, Brit.); CRIME ON THE HILL(1933, Brit.); LEAVE IT TO ME(1933, Brit.); LOVE NEST, THE(1933, Brit.); MONEY TALKS(1933, Brit.); THEIR NIGHT OUT(1933, Brit.); HAPPY(1934, Brit.); LUCK OF A SAILOR, THE(1934, Brit.); MASTER AND MAN(1934, Brit.); SPRING IN THE AIR(1934, Brit.); BARNACLE BILL(1935, Brit.); INVITATION TO THE WALTZ(1935, Brit.); JOY RIDE(1935, Brit.); MUSIC HATH CHARMS(1935, Brit.); REGAL CAVALCADE(1935, Brit.); SCANDALS OF PARIS(1935, Brit.); 39 STEPS, THE(1935, Brit.); BUSMAN'S HOLIDAY(1936, Brit.); CROUCHING BEAST, THE(1936, U. S./Brit.); HEIRLOOM MYSTERY, THE(1936, Brit.); KEEP YOUR SEATS PLEASE(1936, Brit.); NOT SO DUSTY(1936, Brit.); SOUTHERN ROSES(1936, Brit.); YOU MUST GET MARRIED(1936, Brit.); ACTION FOR SLANDER(1937, Brit.); KEEP FIT(1937, Brit.); STORM IN A TEACUP(1937, Brit.); STRANGE ADVENTURES OF MR. SMITH, THE(1937, Brit.); DIVORCE OF LADY X. THE(1938, Brit.); EASY RICHES(1938, Brit.); SMILING ALONG(1938, Brit.); SOUTH RIDING(1938, Brit.); WE'RE GOING TO BE RICH(1938, Brit.); YOU'RE THE DOCTOR(1938, Brit.); ALL AT SEA(1939, Brit.); BLIND FOLLY(1939, Brit.); CLOUDS OVER EUROPE(1939, Brit.); THERE AIN'T NO JUSTICE(1939, Brit.); TROUBLE BREWING(1939, Brit.); WHAT WOULD YOU DO, CHUMS?(1939, Brit.); GEORGE AND MARGARET(1940, Brit.); OLD BILL AND SON(1940, Brit.); SIDEWALKS OF LONDON(1940, Brit.); THAT'S THE TICKET(1940, Brit.); TWO FOR DANGER(1940, Brit.); WHO IS GUILTY?(1940, Brit.); COURAGEOUS MR. PENN, THE(1941, Brit.); FACING THE MUSIC(1941, Brit.); SOUTH AMERICAN GEORGE(1941, Brit.); LET THE PEOPLE SING(1942, Brit.);

MUCH TOO SHY(1942, Brit.); ROSE OF TRALEE(1942, Brit.); SHIPBUILDERS, THE(1943, Brit.); DEMOBBED(1944, Brit.); HERE COMES THE SUN(1945, Brit.); PLACE OF ONE'S OWN, A(1945, Brit.); TROJAN BROTHERS, THE(1946); TURNERS OF PROSPECT ROAD, THE(1947, Brit.)

Harry McNaughton
VAGABOND KING, THE(1956)
Silents
WET GOLD(1921)

Ian McNaughton
ROB ROY, THE HIGHLAND ROGUE(1954, Brit.); SILENT ENEMY, THE(1959, Brit.)

Jack McNaughton
I BECAME A CRIMINAL(1947); DULCIMER STREET(1948, Brit.); BADGER'S GREEN(1949, Brit.); CARDBOARD CAVALIER, THE(1949, Brit.); MADNESS OF THE HEART(1949, Brit.); MAN ON THE RUN(1949, Brit.); OUTSIDER, THE(1949, Brit.); NO PLACE FOR JENNIFER(1950, Brit.); SHE SHALL HAVE MURDER(1950, Brit.); TAMING OF DOROTHY, THE(1950, Brit.); CHEER THE BRAVE(1951, Brit.); GREEN GROW THE RUSHES(1951, Brit.); HOUR OF THIRTEEN, THE(1952); MAN IN THE WHITE SUIT, THE(1952); SHOOT FIRST(1953, Brit.); TRENT'S LAST CASE(1953, Brit.); CHILDREN GALORE(1954, Brit.); DETECTIVE, THE(1954, Qit.); MAN WITH A MILLION(1954, Brit.); PURPLE PLAIN, THE(1954, Brit.); YOUNG WIVES' TALE(1954, Brit.); PRIVATE'S PROGRESS(1956, Brit.); LADY OF VENGEANCE(1957, Brit); MEN OF SHERWOOD FOREST(1957, Brit.); TEARS FOR SIMON(1957, Brit.); UP THE CREEK(1958, Brit.); TREAD SOFTLY STRANGER(1959, Brit.); STRANGLERS OF BOMBAY, THE(1960, Brit.); COURT MARTIAL OF MAJOR KELLER, THE(1961, Brit.); MANIA(1961, Brit.)

R. Q. McNaughton
MANIACS ON WHEELS(1951, Brit.), d; FIEND WITHOUT A FACE(1958), ed

Tom McNaughton
Silents
TILLIE'S TOMATO SURPRISE(1915)

Charles McNaugton
GASLIGHT(1944)

Thelma McNeal
DANCE OF LIFE, THE(1929)

Howard McNear
YOU CAN'T RUN AWAY FROM IT(1956); ESCAPE FROM FORT BRAVO(1953); DRUMS ACROSS THE RIVER(1954); LONG, LONG TRAILER, THE(1954); BUNDLE OF JOY(1956); AFFAIR IN RENO(1957); PUBLIC PIGEON NO. 1(1957); BELL, BOOK AND CANDLE(1958); GOOD DAY FOR A HANGING(1958); ANATOMY OF A MURDER(1959); BIG CIRCUS, THE(1959); HELLER IN PINK TIGHTS(1960); BLUE HAWAII(1961); ERRAND BOY, THE(1961); LAST TIME I SAW ARCHIE, THE(1961); VOYAGE TO THE BOTTOM OF THE SEA(1961); BACHELOR FLAT(1962); FOLLOW THAT DREAM(1962); IRMA LA DOUCE(1963); WHEELER DEALERS, THE(1963); KISS ME, STUPID(1964); LOVE AND KISSES(1965); MY BLOOD RUNS COLD(1965); FORTUNE COOKIE, THE(1966)

Patrick McNee
CHRISTMAS CAROL, A(1951, Brit.)

Helen McNeely
BOYS IN COMPANY C, THE(1978, U.S./Hong Kong)
1984
PURPLE HEARTS(1984)

Howard McNeely
BANJO(1947); BRIGHT ROAD(1953)

Robert McNeely
CAPTAIN PIRATE(1952); BRIGHT ROAD(1953)

Mary McNeeran
WEREWOLF IN A GIRL'S DORMITORY(1961, Ital./Aust.)

Richard McNeff
SUSPENDED ALIBI(1957, Brit.); JUNGLE STREET GIRLS(1963, Brit.); MURDER CAN BE DEADLY(1963, Brit.); BRAIN, THE(1965, Ger./Brit.)

Evelyn McNeice
OF HUMAN BONDAGE(1964, Brit.)

Ian McNeice
1984
TOP SECRET!(1984)

A. McNeil
FIGHTING PLAYBOY(1937)

Allen McNeil
COQUETTE(1929), w; TAMING OF THE SHREW, THE(1929), ed; DU BARRY, WOMAN OF PASSION(1930), ed; KIKI(1931), ed; ADVICE TO THE LOVE-LORN(1933), ed; BOWERY, THE(1933), ed; BULLDOG DRUMMOND STRIKES BACK(1934), ed; HOUSE OF ROTHSCHILD, THE(1934), ed; IT HAD TO HAP-PEN(1936), ed; PRIVATE NUMBER(1936), ed; WHITE HUNTER(1936), ed; HEI-DI(1937), ed; ON THE AVENUE(1937), ed; THIS IS MY AFFAIR(1937), ed; KIDNAPPED(1938), ed; MY LUCKY STAR(1938), ed; REBECCA OF SUNNYBROOK FARM(1938), ed; GORILLA, THE(1939), ed; TAIL SPIN(1939), ed; MAN HUNT(1941), ed; RISE AND SHINE(1941), ed; TALL, DARK AND HANDSOME(1941), ed; WEEK-END IN HAVANA(1941), ed; PIED PIPER, THE(1942), ed; TO THE SHORES OF TRIPOLI(1942), ed; OX-BOW INCIDENT, THE(1943), ed; TONIGHT WE RAID CALAIS(1943), ed
Silents
MOLLY O'(1921), ed; SUZANNA(1922), ed; HOT WATER(1924), ed; FRESHMAN, THE(1925), ed; FOR HEAVEN'S SAKE(1926), ed; MY BEST GIRL(1927), w

Cerves McNeil
PUTNEY SWOPE(1969)

Claudia McNeil
LAST ANGRY MAN, THE(1959); RAISIN IN THE SUN, A(1961); THERE WAS A CROOKED MAN(1970); BLACK GIRL(1972)

Donald McNeil
ROSE BOWL(1936)

Hector McNeil
CALLING BULLDOG DRUMMOND(1951, Brit.), w

John McNeil
SEARCHING WIND, THE(1946), set d; VIRGINIAN, THE(1946), set d; WELCOME STRANGER(1947), set d

Kathryn McNeil
HOUSE ON SORORITY ROW, THE(1983)

Kathy McNeil
NOW THAT APRIL'S HERE(1958, Can.)
Misc. Talkies
BEACH HOUSE(1982)

Marguerite McNeil
MY BLOODY VALENTINE(1981, Can.)

Mary McNeil
TIGHT LITTLE ISLAND(1949, Brit.)

Norman McNeil
GIRL OF THE GOLDEN WEST(1930)

Paul McNeil
CRIMSON CULT, THE(1970, Brit.)

Peter McNeil
1984
KINGS AND DESPERATE MEN(1984, Brit.)

Ron McNeil
MAN OR GUN(1958); DADDY-O(1959)

Steve McNeil
MAN'S FAVORITE SPORT [?](1964), w

Thelma McNeil
SEVEN FOOTPRINTS TO SATAN(1929)

H. C. "Sapper" McNeile
BULLDOG DRUMMOND(1929), w; RETURN OF BULLDOG DRUMMOND, THE(1934, Brit.), w; ALIAS BULLDOG DRUMMOND(1935, Brit.), w; BULLDOG DRUMMOND ESCAPES(1937), w; ARREST BULLDOG DRUMMOND(1939, Brit.), w; DEADLIER THAN THE MALE(1967, Brit.), w
Silents
BULLDOG DRUMMOND(1923, Brit.), w; POPPIES OF FLANDERS(1927, Brit.), w

Herman Cyril McNeile
TEMPLE TOWER(1930), w

Michael McNeile
JOURNEY TOGETHER(1946, Brit.); DIAMOND SAFARI(1958)

Allen McNeill
MIGHTY BARNUM, THE(1934), ed; FOLIES DERGERE(1935), ed

Janet McNeill
CHILD IN THE HOUSE(1956, Brit.), w

Jeannie McNeill
SUPERFLY T.N.T.(1973)

Norman McNeill
Silents
OUT OF LUCK(1919)

Peter McNeill
RABID(1976, Can.)

R.W. McNeill
COCK O' THE WALK(1930), ph

Roy W. McNeill
MILLS OF THE GODS(1935), d

Tex McNeill
DON QUIXOTE(1973, Aus.)

David McNeilly
UNDER CAPRICORN(1949), ph

Frank McNellis
DYNAMITE DELANEY(1938); LOVE ISLAND(1952); TAXI(1953)

Helen McNelly
UP FROM THE DEPTHS(1979, Phil.)

Carolyn McNichol
WINNING(1969)

Jimmy McNichol
BUTCHER BAKER(NIGHTMARE MAKER) (1982); SMOKEY BITES THE DUST(1981)
Misc. Talkies
ESCAPE FROM EL DIABLO(1983, U.S./Brit./Span.)

John McNichol
PRIVATE DUTY NURSES(1972), ph; TERROR HOUSE(1972), ph

Kristy McNichol
END, THE(1978); LITTLE DARLINGS(1980); NIGHT THE LIGHTS WENT OUT IN GEORGIA, THE(1981); ONLY WHEN I LAUGH(1981); PIRATE MOVIE, THE(1982, Aus.); WHITE DOG(1982)
1984
JUST THE WAY YOU ARE(1984)

Lulu McNichol
NIGHT THE LIGHTS WENT OUT IN GEORGIA, THE(1981)

Glynis McNicoll
Misc. Talkies
ROSES BLOOM TWICE(1977)

Ian McNiece
Misc. Talkies
VOICE OVER(1983)

Kristin McNiff
1984
EXTERMINATOR 2(1984), cos

D. McNiven
UNCIVILISED(1937, Aus.)

Don McNiven
LONG JOHN SILVER(1954, Aus.)

Bill McNulty
DUNGEONS OF HARROW(1964)

Christina McNulty
Misc. Silents
LONELY TRAIL, THE(1922)

Dorothy McNulty
GOOD NEWS(1930); SEA RACKETEERS(1937)

Dorothy McNulty [Penny Singleton]
LOVE IN THE ROUGH(1930); AFTER THE THIN MAN(1936); VOGUES OF 1938(1937)

Harold McNulty
WOMAN IN THE WINDOW, THE(1945); PLACE IN THE SUN, A(1951)

John McNulty
EASY COME, EASY GO(1947), w; JACKPOT, THE(1950), w; IT'S A BIG COUN-TRY(1951), w; BIG LEAGUER(1953), w

Pat McNulty
TAMMY, TELL ME TRUE(1961)

William McNulty
Misc. Silents
UNWELCOME WIFE, THE(1915)

Patterson McNutt
CURLY TOP(1935), w; GEORGE WHITE'S 1935 SCANDALS(1935), w; SPRING TONIC(1935), w; EVERYBODY'S OLD MAN(1936), w; RETURN OF SOPHIE LANG, THE(1936), w; VACATION FROM LOVE(1938), w; COME LIVE WITH ME(1941), w; GENTLEMAN AFTER DARK, A(1942), w; JAM SESSION(1944), w; PARDON MY PAST(1945), w

William McNutt
GUN SMOKE(1931), w; HELL AND HIGH WATER(1933), w

William Slavens McNutt
MIGHTY, THE(1929), w; BURNING UP(1930), w; DANGEROUS PARADISE(1930), w; DERELICT(1930), w; LIGHT OF WESTERN STARS, THE(1930), w; TOM SA-WYER(1930), w; YOUNG EAGLES(1930), w; CONQUERING HORDE, THE(1931), w; HUCKLEBERRY FINN(1931), w; TOUCHDOWN!(1931), w; BROKEN WING, THE(1932), w; IF I HAD A MILLION(1932), w; LADY AND GENT(1932), w; NIGHT OF JUNE 13(1932), w; STRANGERS IN LOVE(1932), w; HELL AND HIGH WA-TER(1933), d; ONE SUNDAY AFTERNOON(1933), w; MRS. WIGGS OF THE CAB-BAGE PATCH(1934), w; READY FOR LOVE(1934), w; YOU BELONG TO ME(1934), w; ANNAPOLIS FAREWELL(1935), w; HOT TIP!(1935), w; LIVES OF A BENGAL LANCER(1935), w; UNMARRIED(1939), w; MRS. WIGGS OF THE CAB-BAGE PATCH(1942), w
Silents
QUARTERBACK, THE(1926), w

Maggie McOmie
THX 1138(1971)

Joe McPartland
MIND OF MR. SOAMES, THE(1970, Brit.)

John McPartland
WILD PARTY, THE(1956), w; NO DOWN PAYMENT(1957), w; NO TIME TO BE YOUNG(1957), w; STREET OF SINNERS(1957), w; LOST MISSILE, THE(1958, U.S./Can.), w; JOHNNY COOL(1963), w

Joseph McPartland
OUTSIDER, THE(1980)

Ben McPeak
ROWDYMAN, THE(1973, Can.), m

Sandy McPeak
ODE TO BILLY JOE(1976); FINAL CHAPTER–WALKING TALL zero(1977); ONION FIELD, THE(1979); OSTERMAN WEEKEND, THE(1983)

Ben McPeek
ONLY GOD KNOWS(1974, Can.), m

Quinton McPerson
FORBIDDEN MUSIC(1936, Brit.)

Cactus McPeters
HELLER IN PINK TIGHTS(1960)

Curtis McPeters
STORMY(1935)

Addie McPhail
MIDNIGHT DADDIES(1929); EXTRAVAGANCE(1930); NIGHT WORK(1930); THREE SISTERS, THE(1930); GIRLS DEMAND EXCITEMENT(1931); BORDER-TOWN(1935); WOMEN OF GLAMOUR(1937); NORTHWEST PASSAGE(1940)
Misc. Silents
ANYBODY HERE SEEN KELLY?(1928)

Angus McPhail
RETURN OF THE RAT, THE(1929, Brit.), w; TROUBLE BREWING(1939, Brit.), w; NEXT OF KIN(1942, Brit.), w; MY LEARNED FRIEND(1943, Brit.), w; SOMEWHERE IN FRANCE(1943, Brit.), w; 48 HOURS(1944, Brit.), w; IT ALWAYS RAINS ON SUNDAY(1949, Brit.), w; MAN WHO KNEW TOO MUCH, THE(1956), w

Douglas McPhail
YELLOW JACK(1938); LAST GANGSTER, THE(1937); SWEETHEARTS(1938); TEST PILOT(1938); TOY WIFE, THE(1938); BABES IN ARMS(1939); BROADWAY MELODY OF 1940(1940); LITTLE NELLIE KELLY(1940); BORN TO SING(1942)

Clyde McPhatter
MISTER ROCK AND ROLL(1957)

Quentin McPhearson
MURDER IN THE OLD RED BARN(1936, Brit.)

Duncan McPhee
BOFORS GUN, THE(1968, Brit.), cos

Hexin E. McPhee
STAR CHAMBER, THE(1983)

John McPhee
CASEY'S SHADOW(1978), w

W. L. McPheeters
Silents
ABRAHAM LINCOLN(1924)

Bruce McPherson
STONE(1974, Aus.)

Cynthia McPherson
OLIVER'S STORY(1978); WILLIE AND PHIL(1980); CLARENCE AND ANGEL(1981)

Garrett McPherson
STUNT MAN, THE(1980)

Graham McPherson
SUPERMAN(1978); SILENCE OF THE NORTH(1981, Can.)

Quinton McPherson
ANNE ONE HUNDRED(1933, Brit.); MIXED DOUBLES(1933, Brit.); GLIMPSE OF PARADISE, A(1934, Brit.); THIRD CLUE, THE(1934, Brit.); WHAT HAPPENED THEN?(1934, Brit.); MUSIC HATH CHARMS(1935, Brit.); ANNIE LAURIE(1936, Brit.); BELOVED IMPOSTER(1936, Brit.); GHOST GOES WEST, THE(1936); IF I WERE RICH(1936); KING OF THE CASTLE(1936, Brit.); REMBRANDT(1936, Brit.); THIS GREEN HELL(1936, Brit.); STORM IN A TEACUP(1937, Brit.); DANGEROUS MEDI-CINE(1938, Brit.)

Sandra McPherson
COOL WORLD, THE(1963)

Edward McPhillips
ZELIG(1983)

Arlene McQuade
GOLDBERGS, THE(1950); TOUCH OF EVIL(1958)

Billy Rae McQuade
MOTHER'S DAY(1980)

Chris McQuade
FIRM MAN, THE(1975, Aus.)

Edward McQuade
BIG SHOT, THE(1931)
Silents
DESERTED AT THE ALTAR(1922)

John McQuade
NAKED CITY, THE(1948); SERPICO(1973)

Kris McQuade
TRUE STORY OF ESKIMO NELL, THE(1975, Aus.); BUDDIES(1983, Aus.); FIGHT-ING BACK(1983, Brit.); LONELY HEARTS(1983, Aus.)
Misc. Talkies
LOVELETTERS FROM TERALBA ROAD(1977)

Mabel McQuade
Silents
IMPOSSIBLE CATHERINE(1919)

Terry McQuade
RUDE BOY(1980, Brit.)

McQuaig Twins
KENTUCKY JUBILEE(1951)

Al McQuarrie
Misc. Silents
MIDNIGHT MAN(1917); MR. DOLAN OF NEW YORK(1917)

Albert McQuarrie
Silents
ARIZONA(1918)

Frank McQuarrie
Misc. Silents
FLIRTING WITH DEATH(1917); BOSS OF THE LAZY Y, THE(1918); GIRL OF MY DREAMS, THE(1918); WOLVES OF THE BORDER(1918); UNDER SUSPICION(1919)

George McQuarrie
HOLE IN THE WALL(1929); ABRAHAM LINCOLN(1930); CALL OF THE WILD(1935); LAWLESS VALLEY(1938); LIFE RETURNS(1939)
Silents
ALL MAN(1916); SACRED SILENCE(1919)
Misc. Silents
HITTING THE TRAIL(1918)

Murdock McQuarrie
CAPTAIN OF THE GUARD(1930); NEAR THE TRAIL'S END(1931); SUNDOWN TRAIL(1931); TWO GUN MAN, THE(1931); DARING DANGER(1932); GAMBLING SEX(1932); ONE-MAN LAW(1932); CROSSFIRE(1933); PENAL CODE, THE(1933); FIGHTING HERO(1934); NEW FRONTIER, THE(1935); MODERN TIMES(1936); SONG OF THE GRINGO(1936); STORMY TRAILS(1936); SUNSET OF POWER(1936); FIGHTING TEXAN(1937); GIT ALONG, LITTLE DOGIES(1937); PINTO RUST-LERS(1937); GHOST TOWN RIDERS(1938); GUILTY TRAILS(1938); PRAIRIE JUS-TICE(1938); COLORADO SUNSET(1939); HONOR OF THE WEST(1939); DEATH RIDES THE RANGE(1940); MUMMY'S HAND, THE(1940); PINTO CANYON(1940); GHOST TOWN LAW(1942)
Misc. Talkies
LARAMIE KID, THE(1935); NORTH OF ARIZONA(1935); TONTO KID, THE(1935)
Misc. Silents
COUNT OF MONTE CRISTO, THE(1913)

Chuck McQuary
PURPLE HAZE(1982)
1984
SPLITZ(1984)

Armelia McQueen
SPARKLE(1976); QUARTET(1981, Brit./Fr.)

Butterfly McQueen
GONE WITH THE WIND(1939); AFFECTIONATELY YOURS(1941); CABIN IN THE SKY(1943); I DOOD IT(1943); FLAME OF THE BARBARY COAST(1945); MILDRED PIERCE(1945); DUEL IN THE SUN(1946); PHYNX, THE(1970); AMAZING GRA-CE(1974)
Misc. Talkies
KILLER DILLER(1948)

Chad McQueen
1984
KARATE KID, THE(1984)

Chas McQueen
1984
HADLEY'S REBELLION(1984)

Jim McQueen
MADELEINE IS(1971, Can.)

Justice McQueen
DEVIL'S BEDROOM, THE(1964)

Justus E. McQueen
BATTLE FLAME(1955)

King McQueen
Misc. Talkies
LYNCHING(1968)

Neile McQueen
BUDDY BUDDY(1981); CHU CHU AND THE PHILLY FLASH(1981)

Neile Adams McQueen
SO LONG, BLUE BOY(1973)

Simon McQueen
MANDINGO(1975); STARTING OVER(1979)

Steve McQueen
SOMEBODY UP THERE LIKES ME(1956); BLOB, THE(1958); ER LOVE A STRAN-GER(1958); GREAT ST. LOUIS BANK ROBBERY, THE(1959); NEVER SO FEW(1959); MAGNIFICENT SEVEN, THE(1960); HONEYMOON MACHINE, THE(1961); HELL IS FOR HEROES(1962); WAR LOVER, THE(1962, U.S./Brit.); GREAT ESCAPE, THE(1963); LOVE WITH THE PROPER STRANGER(1963); SOLDIER IN THE

RAIN(1963); BABY, THE RAIN MUST FALL(1965); CINCINNATI KID, THE(1965); NEVADA SMITH(1966); SAND PEBBLES, THE(1966); BULLITT(1968); THOMAS CROWN AFFAIR, THE(1968); REIVERS, THE(1969); LE MANS(1971); GETAWAY, THE(1972); JUNIOR BONNER(1972); PAPILLON(1973); TOWERING INFERNO, THE(1974); ENEMY OF THE PEOPLE, AN(1978); HUNTER, THE(1980); TOM HORN(1980)

Vernon McQueen
BIG JIM McLAIN(1952)

Edward McQueen-Mason
ALVIN RIDES AGAIN(1974, Aus.), ed; ELIZA FRASER(1976, Aus.), ed; LAST OF THE KNUCKLEMEN, THE(1981, Aus.), ed; CLINIC, THE(1983, Aus.), ed

Robert McQueeney
TIJUANA STORY, THE(1957); WORLD WAS HIS JURY, THE(1958); PORTRAIT OF A MOBSTER(1961); BRAINSTORM(1965); GLORY GUYS, THE(1965)

Ada McQuillan
Silents
WEB OF FATE(1927), w; JAZZLAND(1928), w

Terry McQuillan
LET THE BALLOON GO(1977, Aus.)

Edward McQuinn-Mason
ROAD GAMES(1981, Aus.), ed

George McQuire
Silents
PAINTED PEOPLE(1924), ed

Charles J. McQuirk
Silents
SKINNER'S DRESS SUIT(1917), w

William McQuitty
NIGHT TO REMEMBER, A(1958, Brit.), p

Jack McQuoid
1984
EVERY PICTURE TELLS A STORY(1984, Brit.)

Alan McRae
SHOOT(1976, Can.); STUDENT BODY, THE(1976); MR. PATMAN(1980, Can.); SLAYER, THE(1982)

Arthur Mcrae
MURDER AT THE BASKERVILLES(1941, Brit.), d

Bruce McRae
Silents
RING AND THE MAN, THE(1914)
Misc. Silents
VIA WIRELESS(1915); CHAIN INVISIBLE, THE(1916); GREEN SWAMP, THE(1916); HAZEL KIRKE(1916); WORLD'S A STAGE, THE(1922)

Carmen McRae
SQUARE JUNGLE, THE(1955); SUBTERRANEANS, THE(1960); HOTEL(1967)

Charles McRae
NOTHING BUT A MAN(1964)

Duncan McRae
Silents
HOUSE OF THE LOST CORD, THE(1915); JUNE FRIDAY(1915), d
Misc. Silents
GREATER THAN ART(1915); THROUGH TURBULENT WATERS(1915), a, d; FLOWER OF NO MAN'S LAND, THE(1916); LASH OF DESTINY, THE(1916); THAT SORT(1916); WOMAN'S LAW, THE(1916); MY OWN UNITED STATES(1918)

Elizabeth McRae
EVERYTHING'S DUCKY(1961); SCARECROW, THE(1982, New Zealand)

Ellen McRae [Ellen Burstyn]
GOODBYE CHARLIE(1946); FOR THOSE WHO THINK YOUNG(1964); PIT STOP(1969)

Frank McRae
DILLINGER(1973); SHAFT IN AFRICA(1973); BANK SHOT(1974); HARD TIMES(1975); PIPE DREAMS(1976); END, THE(1978); PARADISE ALLEY(1978); NORMA RAE(1979); ROCKY II(1979); 1941(1979); USED CARS(1980); CANNERY ROW(1982); 48 HOURS(1982); NATIONAL LAMPOON'S VACATION(1983)
1984
RED DAWN(1984)

Hamilton McRae
KING OF THE MOUNTAIN(1981)

Harry McRae
Silents
CRITICAL AGE, THE(1923), d

Henry McRae
RUSTLERS' ROUNDUP(1933), d; FORBIDDEN VALLEY(1938), p; DRUMS OF THE CONGO(1942), p
Misc. Silents
CORAL(1915), d; BEHIND THE LINES(1916), d; BRONZE BRIDE, THE(1917), d; MAN AND BEAST(1917), d; MONEY MADNESS(1917), d

Hilton McRae
FRENCH LIEUTENANT'S WOMAN, THE(1981); NELLY'S VERSION(1983, Brit.)
1984
GREYSTOKE: THE LEGEND OF TARZAN, LORD OF THE APES(1984)

John McRae
GOOD DIE YOUNG, THE(1954, Brit.)

Leslie McRae
FOR SINGLES ONLY(1968); GIRL IN GOLD BOOTS(1968); MONEY JUNGLE, THE(1968); HELL'S BLOODY DEVILS(1970)

Marilyn McRae
SKYDIVERS, THE(1963)

Maureen McRae
VISITING HOURS(1982, Can.); THRESHOLD(1983, Can.)

Monty McRae
SKYDIVERS, THE(1963)

Gerald McRaney
NIGHT OF BLOODY HORROR zero(1969); WOMEN AND BLOODY TERROR(1970)
1984
NEVERENDING STORY, THE(1984, Ger.)
Misc. Talkies
BRAIN MACHINE, THE(1972)

Carl McRayne
Silents
PERFECT LOVER, THE(1919)

Duncan McRea
Silents
JUNE FRIDAY(1915)

Ed McReady
APPLE DUMPLING GANG RIDES AGAIN, THE(1979)

Dexter McReynolds
Silents
STRIVING FOR FORTUNE(1926)

Reginald McReynolds
TRAP, THE(1967, Can./Brit.); WAITING FOR CAROLINE(1969, Can.)

Greig McRitchie
THIS IS NOT A TEST(1962), m

Peter McRobbie
ZELIG(1983)

Briony McRoberts
PINK PANTHER STRIKES AGAIN, THE(1976, Brit.)

Charles McShane
CRY FROM THE STREET, A(1959, Brit.)

Ian McShane
YOUNG AND WILLING(1964, Brit.); GYPSY GIRL(1966, Brit.); PLEASURE GIRLS, THE(1966, Brit.); BATTLE OF BRITAIN, THE(1969, Brit.); IF IT'S TUESDAY, THIS MUST BE BELGIUM(1969); PUSSYCAT, PUSSYCAT, I LOVE YOU(1970); VILLAIN(1971, Brit.); DEVIL'S WIDOW, THE(1972, Brit.); SITTING TARGET(1972, Brit.); LAST OF SHEILA, THE(1973); TERRORISTS, THE(1975, Brit.); JOURNEY INTO FEAR(1976, Can); BEHIND THE IRON MASK(1977); YESTERDAY'S HERO(1979, Brit.); CHEAPER TO KEEP HER(1980); EXPOSED(1983)
1984
ORDEAL BY INNOCENCE(1984, Brit.); TORCHLIGHT(1984)
Misc. Talkies
LEFT HAND OF GEMINI, THE(1972); GREAT RIVIERA BANK ROBBERY, THE(1979)

Kitty McShane
OLD MOTHER RILEY(1937, Brit.); KATHLEEN(1938, Ireland); OLD MOTHER RILEY IN PARIS(1938, Brit.); OLD MOTHER RILEY JOINS UP(1939, Brit.); OLD MOTHER RILEY MP(1939, Brit.); OLD MOTHER RILEY IN BUSINESS(1940, Brit.); OLD MOTHER RILEY IN SOCIETY(1940, Brit.), a, w; OLD MOTHER RILEY'S CIRCUS(1941, Brit.); OLD MOTHER RILEY'S GHOSTS(1941, Brit.); OLD MOTHER RILEY, DETECTIVE(1943, Brit.); OLD MOTHER RILEY OVERSEAS(1943, Brit.); OLD MOTHER RILEY AT HOME(1945, Brit.); OLD MOTHER RILEY, HEADMISTRESS(1950, Brit.); OLD MOTHER RILEY'S JUNGLE TREASURE(1951, Brit.); OLD MOTHER RILEY(1952, Brit.)

Mark McShane
SEANCE ON A WET AFTERNOON(1964 Brit.), d&w; GRASSHOPPER, THE(1970), w

Carmel McSharry
LIFE IN DANGER(1964, Brit.); LEATHER BOYS, THE(1965, Brit.); DEVIL'S OWN, THE(1967, Brit.); MAN OUTSIDE, THE(1968, Brit.)

Susan McShayne
HOPSCOTCH(1980)

Mary McSherry
SCANDAL AT SCOURIE(1953), w

Rose Marie McSherry
RUNNING BRAVE(1983, Can.), set d
1984
HIGHPOINT(1984, Can.), art d

Rosemarie McSherry
OF UNKNOWN ORIGIN(1983, Can.), art d

Clem McSpadden
J.W. COOP(1971)

Ade McSpade
SMITHEREENS(1982)

Michael McStay
PSYCHE 59(1964, Brit.); CURSE OF THE MUMMY'S TOMB, THE(1965, Brit.); ROBBERY(1967, Brit.); BATTLE BENEATH THE EARTH(1968, Brit.)

Faith McSwain
TOOLBOX MURDERS, THE(1978)

Wally McSween
CHRISTINA(1974, Can.)

Jack McSweeney
HAIL, HERO!(1969), ed; ME, NATALIE(1969), ed; ADAM AT 6 A.M.(1970), ed; EVEL KNIEVEL(1971), ed; GLORIA(1980), ed

John McSweeney
SIGNPOST TO MURDER(1964), ed; ROUNDERS, THE(1965), ed; GLASS BOTTOM BOAT, THE(1966), ed; MONEY TRAP, THE(1966), ed; DOUBLE TROUBLE(1967), ed; LIVE A LITTLE, LOVE A LITTLE(1968), ed; SOL MADRID(1968), ed; NIGHT OF THE LEPUS(1972), ed

John McSweeney, Jr.
LOVELY TO LOOK AT(1952), ed; MILLION DOLLAR MERMAID(1952), ed; DANGEROUS WHEN WET(1953), ed; LATIN LOVERS(1953), ed; DIANE(1955), ed; HIT THE DECK(1955), ed; KING'S THIEF, THE(1955), ed; GABY(1956), ed; OPPOSITE SEX, THE(1956), ed; HOUSE OF NUMBERS(1957), ed; TEN THOUSAND BEDROOMS(1957), ed; PARTY GIRL(1958), ed; SADDLE THE WIND(1958), ed; TUNNEL OF LOVE, THE(1958), ed; ASK ANY GIRL(1959), ed; IT STARTED WITH A KISS(1959), ed; MATING GAME, THE(1959), ed; ALL THE FINE YOUNG CANNIBALS(1960), ed; PLEASE DON'T EAT THE DAISIES(1960), ed; GO NAKED IN THE WORLD(1961), ed; MUTINY ON THE BOUNTY(1962), ed; TICKLISH AFFAIR, A(1963), ed; VIVA LAS VEGAS(1964), ed

Jack McSweeny
CHRISTINA(1974, Can.), ed

Alex McSweyn
RAINBOW ISLAND(1944)

Alexander McSweyn
WE WERE STRANGERS(1949)

Marie McSwigan
SNOW TREASURE(1968), w

Essie McSwine
TOP OF THE HEAP(1972)
Bud McTaggart
PAID TO DANCE(1937); SIX-GUN RHYTHM(1939); TRIGGER FINGERS ½(1939); WYOMING OUTLAW(1939); WAGON TRAIN(1940); BILLY THE KID TRAPPED(1942); LUCKY JORDAN(1942); MEET THE MOB(1942); WEST OF THE LAW(1942); AVENGING RIDER, THE(1943); FLIGHT FOR FREEDOM(1943); RED RIVER ROBIN HOOD(1943); SAGEBRUSH LAW(1943); YANKS AHOY(1943)
Malcolm McTaggart
WHO KILLED GAIL PRESTON?(1938); FULL CONFESSION(1939); I STOLE A MILLION(1939); TRIPLE JUSTICE(1940); ROBBERS OF THE RANGE(1941); FLYING TIGERS(1942); TEN GENTLEMEN FROM WEST POINT(1942); LADIES' DAY(1943); MARGIN FOR ERROR(1943); WE'VE NEVER BEEN LICKED(1943)
Malcolm "Bud" McTaggart
COME ON DANGER(1942); DEAD MAN'S GULCH(1943)
Ward McTaggart
DANGEROUS LADY(1941); SECRET EVIDENCE(1941)
Ward "Bud" McTaggart
GANGS OF SONORA(1941)
Margaret McTear
THAT SINKING FEELING(1979, Brit.)
Joe McTurk
STREET WITH NO NAME, THE(1948); LADY TAKES A SAILOR, THE(1949); MISTER 880(1950); MY SIX CONVICTS(1952); STOP, YOU'RE KILLING ME(1952); BREAKDOWN(1953); MONEY FROM HOME(1953); GUYS AND DOLLS(1955); MAN WITH THE GOLDEN ARM, THE(1955); HOUSEBOAT(1958)
Tyler McVay
LOUISIANA HUSSY(1960)
Eve McVeagh
HIGH NOON(1952); GLASS WEB, THE(1953); COBWEB, THE(1955); I'LL CRY TOMORROW(1955); TIGHT SPOT(1955); REPRISAL(1956); SIERRA STRANGER(1957); CRIME AND PUNISHMENT, U.S.A.(1959); WAY WEST, THE(1967); THREE IN THE ATTIC(1968); LIBERATION OF L.B. JONES, THE(1970); GLASS HOUSES(1972)
Pat McVeigh
NAVY BLUES(1941); SNUFFY SMITH, YARD BIRD(1942)
Pat McVeigh "McVey"
MURDER IN THE BIG HOUSE(1942)
Rosemary McVeigh
NIGHT IN HEAVEN, A(1983)
Michael McVey
TOUCH OF CLASS, A(1973, Brit.); DARK PLACES(1974, Brit.); HITCH IN TIME, A(1978, Brit.)
Misc. Talkies
SKY PIRATES(1977, Brit.)
Pat McVey
CALLING DR. GILLESPIE(1942); INVISIBLE AGENT(1942); JUKE GIRL(1942); MAN WHO CAME TO DINNER, THE(1942); MOONLIGHT IN HAVANA(1942); PIERRE OF THE PLAINS(1942); TALK OF THE TOWN(1942); THEY DIED WITH THEIR BOOTS ON(1942); TO THE SHORES OF TRIPOLI(1942); NO TIME FOR LOVE(1943); O.S.S.(1946); SHOW-OFF(1946); SWELL GUY(1946); DARK PASSAGE(1947); EASY COME, EASY GO(1947); SUDDENLY IT'S SPRING(1947); WELCOME STRANGER(1947); BIG CAPER, THE(1957)
Patrick McVey
PARTY GIRL(1958); NORTH BY NORTHWEST(1959); DETECTIVE, THE(1968); DESPERATE CHARACTERS(1971); TOP OF THE HEAP(1972); VISITORS, THE(1972); BANG THE DRUM SLOWLY(1973)
Paul McVey
JUDGE PRIEST(1934); SHE LEARNED ABOUT SAILORS(1934); STAND UP AND CHEER(1934 80m FOX bw); 365 NIGHTS IN HOLLYWOOD(1934); DANTE'S INFERNO(1935); SHOW THEM NO MERCY(1935); COUNTRY BEYOND, THE(1936); CRIME OF DR. FORBES(1936); HALF ANGEL(1936); HUMAN CARGO(1936); LADIES IN LOVE(1936); MY MARRIAGE(1936); ONE IN A MILLION(1936); PRISONER OF SHARK ISLAND, THE(1936); SING, BABY, SING(1936); STOWAWAY(1936); THANK YOU, JEEVES(1936); FAIR WARNING(1937); LOVE IS NEWS(1937); ONE MILE FROM HEAVEN(1937); SING AND BE HAPPY(1937); TIME OUT FOR ROMANCE(1937); HOLD THAT CO-ED(1938); JOSETTE(1938); MEET THE GIRLS(1938); NIGHT HAWK, THE(1938); PASSPORT HUSBAND(1938); SAFETY IN NUMBERS(1938); BURIED ALIVE(1939); DRUMS ALONG THE MOHAWK(1939); INSIDE INFORMATION(1939); PANAMA PATROL(1939); STAGECOACH(1939); LILLIAN RUSSELL(1940); PHANTOM OF CHINATOWN(1940); STRANGER ON THE THIRD FLOOR(1940); MONSTER AND THE GIRL, THE(1941); NEW YORK TOWN(1941); REMEMBER THE DAY(1941); LIVING GHOST, THE(1942); MAGNIFICENT DOPE, THE(1942); DIXIE(1943); HAPPY GO LUCKY(1943); HENRY ALDRICH HAUNTS A HOUSE(1943); IRON MAJOR, THE(1943); KEEP 'EM SLUGGING(1943); MYSTERY OF THE 13TH GUEST, THE(1943); SILVER SKATES(1943); SMART GUY(1943); LADY IN THE DARK(1944); RAINBOW ISLAND(1944); FORCE OF EVIL(1948); MA AND PA KETTLE GO TO TOWN(1950); PERFECT STRANGERS(1950); LADY PAYS OFF, THE(1951); NO ROOM FOR THE GROOM(1952); BWANA DEVIL(1953); SHANE(1953)
Tyler McVey
DAY THE EARTH STOOD STILL, THE(1951); CONFIDENCE GIRL(1952); DIPLOMATIC COURIER(1952); HORIZONS WEST(1952); O. HENRY'S FULL HOUSE(1952); ONE MINUTE TO ZERO(1952); BLUEPRINT FOR MURDER, A(1953); FROM HERE TO ETERNITY(1953); DAY OF TRIUMPH(1954); COME ON, THE(1956); TEENAGE THUNDER(1957); HOT CAR GIRL(1958); NIGHT OF THE BLOOD BEAST(1958); TERROR IN A TEXAS TOWN(1958); ATTACK OF THE GIANT LEECHES(1959); LONE TEXAN(1959); GALLANT HOURS, THE(1960); PUBLIC AFFAIR, A(1962); THAT TOUCH OF MINK(1962); BEST MAN, THE(1964); KILLERS, THE(1964); MAN'S FAVORITE SPORT[?](1964); DEAD HEAT ON A MERRY-GO-ROUND(1966); LT. ROBIN CRUSOE, U.S.N.(1966); NEVER A DULL MOMENT(1968)
John McVicar
MC VICAR(1982, Brit.), w
Sarah McVickar
Silents
TILLIE'S TOMATO SURPRISE(1915)
Julius McVicker
PHANTOM PRESIDENT, THE(1932)

Jose McVilches
COLOSSUS OF RHODES, THE(1961, Ital., Fr., Span.)
J. P. Mcvoy
ARTISTS AND MODELS ABROAD(1938), w
Ed McWade
INDIANAPOLIS SPEEDWAY(1939); NAUGHTY BUT NICE(1939)
Edward McWade
BIG CITY BLUES(1932); SIX HOURS TO LIVE(1932); TWO SECONDS(1932); EMPLOYEE'S ENTRANCE(1933); LAWYER MAN(1933); MURDERS IN THE ZOO(1933); DOCTOR MONICA(1934); I'LL TELL THE WORLD(1934); JOURNAL OF A CRIME(1934); LOST LADY, A(1934); MEANEST GAL IN TOWN, THE(1934); MURDER IN THE CLOUDS(1934); NOTORIOUS SOPHIE LANG, THE(1934); BORDERTOWN(1935); DANTE'S INFERNO(1935); DR. SOCRATES(1935); FRISCO KID(1935); GIRL FROM TENTH AVENUE, THE(1935); GOOSE AND THE GANDER, THE(1935); LIFE BEGINS AT 40(1935); MARY JANE'S PA(1935); OIL FOR THE LAMPS OF CHINA(1935); ONE EXCITING ADVENTURE(1935); RED SALUTE(1935); STRANDED(1935); BIG NOISE, THE(1936); DAN MATTHEWS(1936); DARKEST AFRICA(1936); EX-MRS. BRADFORD, THE(1936); F MAN(1936); MAN I MARRY, THE(1936); REUNION(1936); SATAN MET A LADY(1936); CASE OF THE STUTTERING BISHOP, THE(1937); GIRL WITH IDEAS, A(1937); LAUGHING AT TROUBLE(1937); LET'S GET MARRIED(1937); LOVE AND HISSES(1937); THEY WON'T FORGET(1937); WOMEN MEN MARRY, THE(1937); COMET OVER BROADWAY(1938); GARDEN OF THE MOON(1938); JEZEBEL(1938); THREE COMRADES(1938); WHITE BANNERS(1938); MAGNIFICENT FRAUD, THE(1939); OUR NEIGHBORS—THE CARTERS(1939); THEY ASKED FOR IT(1939); CHAD HANNA(1940); DISPATCH FROM REUTERS, A(1940); HOT STEEL(1940); MARGIE(1940); RETURN OF FRANK JAMES, THE(1940); MEET JOHN DOE(1941); NOTHING BUT THE TRUTH(1941); RICHEST MAN IN TOWN(1941); YOU'LL NEVER GET RICH(1941); I WAKE UP SCREAMING(1942); KEEPER OF THE FLAME(1942); LADY IN A JAM(1942); LADY IS WILLING, THE(1942); WOMAN OF THE YEAR(1942); YOU CAN'T ESCAPE FOREVER(1942); CRASH DIVE(1943); ARSENIC AND OLD LACE(1944); LOST ANGEL(1944)
Silents
UNCLE TOM'S CABIN(1914), w; STOP THIEF(1920); WING TOY(1921); STRANGER'S BANQUET(1922); TOWN SCANDAL, THE(1923); MONSTER, THE(1925)
M. McWade
Misc. Silents
PALS OF THE WEST(1922)
Margaret McWade
MR. DEEDS GOES TO TOWN(1936); POSTAL INSPECTOR(1936); THEODORA GOES WILD(1936); DANGER—LOVE AT WORK(1937); LET'S MAKE A MILLION(1937); LOST HORIZON(1937); LOVE IN A BUNGALOW(1937); WE HAVE OUR MOMENTS(1937); WINGS OVER HONOLULU(1937); FORBIDDEN VALLEY(1938); HAVING WONDERFUL TIME(1938); HOLIDAY(1938); TEXANS, THE(1938); I STOLE A MILLION(1939); WHEN TOMORROW COMES(1939); STRIKE UP THE BAND(1940); REMEDY FOR RICHES(1941); SCATTERGOOD SURVIVES A MURDER(1942); BISHOP'S WIFE, THE(1947); IT'S A JOKE, SON!(1947); IT SHOULD HAPPEN TO YOU(1954)
Silents
DARLING MINE(1920); FOOD FOR SCANDAL(1920); BLOT, THE(1921); HER MAD BARGAIN(1921); TALE OF TWO WORLDS, A(1921); ALICE ADAMS(1923); LOST WORLD, THE(1925)
Misc. Silents
GREAT VICTORY, WILSON OR THE KAISER?, THE(1918); WHY GERMANY MUST PAY(1919); CONFESSION, THE(1920); STRONGER THAN DEATH(1920); CYCLONE RIDER, THE(1924)
Marguerite McWade
PARTNERS OF THE TRAIL(1931)
Robert McWade
HOME TOWNERS, THE(1928); FEET FIRST(1930); GOOD INTENTIONS(1930); NIGHT WORK(1930); PAY OFF, THE(1930); SINS OF THE CHILDREN(1930); CIMARRON(1931); GIRLS ABOUT TOWN(1931); IT'S A WISE CHILD(1931); KEPT HUSBANDS(1931); NEW ADVENTURES OF GET-RICH-QUICK WALLINGFORD, THE(1931); SKYLINE(1931); TOO MANY COOKS(1931); BACK STREET(1932); CROWD ROARS, THE(1932); FIRST YEAR, THE(1932); GRAND HOTEL(1932); I AM A FUGITIVE FROM A CHAIN GANG(1932); LADIES OF THE JURY(1932); MADAME RACKETEER(1932); MATCH KING, THE(1932); MOVIE CRAZY(1932); ONCE IN A LIFETIME(1932); PHANTOM OF CRESTWOOD, THE(1932); CHANCE AT HEAVEN(1933); HARD TO HANDLE(1933); HEROES FOR SALE(1933); I LOVED A WOMAN(1933); KENNEL MURDER CASE, THE(1933); LADIES THEY TALK ABOUT(1933); PICK-UP(1933); PRIZEFIGHTER AND THE LADY, THE(1933); SOLITAIRE MAN, THE(1933); TUGBOAT ANNIE(1933); 42ND STREET(1933); COLLEGE RHYTHM(1934); COUNTESS OF MONTE CRISTO, THE(1934); CROSS COUNTRY CRUISE(1934); DRAGON MURDER CASE, THE(1934); FOG(1934); HOLD THAT GIRL(1934); LEMON DROP KID, THE(1934); LET'S BE RITZY(1934); MIDNIGHT ALIBI(1934); OPERATOR 13(1934); PRESIDENT VANISHES, THE(1934); THIRTY-DAY PRINCESS(1934); CAPPY RICKS RETURNS(1935); COUNTY CHAIRMAN, THE(1935); DIAMOND JIM(1935); FRISCO KID(1935); HEALER, THE(1935); HERE COMES THE BAND(1935); HIS NIGHT OUT(1935); MARY JANE'S PA(1935); NO RANSOM(1935); SOCIETY DOCTOR(1935); STRAIGHT FROM THE HEART(1935); ANYTHING GOES(1936); BUNKER BEAN(1936); EARLY TO BED(1936); FIFTEEN MAIDEN LANE(1936); HIGH TENSION(1936); MISTER CINDERELLA(1936); MOONLIGHT MURDER(1936); NEXT TIME WE LOVE(1936); OLD HUTCH(1936); CALIFORNIA STRAIGHT AHEAD(1937); GOOD OLD SOAK, THE(1937); MOUNTAIN JUSTICE(1937); ON SUCH A NIGHT(1937); THIS IS MY AFFAIR(1937); WE'RE ON THE JURY(1937); GOLD IS WHERE YOU FIND IT(1938); OF HUMAN HEARTS(1938)
Silents
NEW BROOMS(1925)
Robert McWade, Jr.
I AM THE LAW(1938)
Raymond McWalters
PAL JOEY(1957)
Raymond A. McWalters
LAST TRAIN FROM GUN HILL(1959)
W.P. McWatters
SIDE STREET(1950)
Kent McWhirter
YOUNG WARRIORS, THE(1967)

Frank McWhorter
ONE MINUTE TO ZERO(1952), ed
Mac McWhorter
TENDER IS THE NIGHT(1961)
Richard McWhorter
DOCTOR FAUSTUS(1967, Brit.), p
Willie McWhorter
GREASED LIGHTNING(1977)
Paul McWilliam
STORY OF WILL ROGERS, THE(1952)
Bill McWilliams
NORA PRENTISS(1947)
Daphene McWilliams
WIZ, THE(1978)
Glen McWilliams
FRONT PAGE, THE(1931), ph; LADY IN DISTRESS(1942, Brit.), ph
Harry McWilliams
IMPROPER CHANNELS(1981, Can.)
James McWilliams
Silents
NO. 5 JOHN STREET(1921, Brit.); OUT TO WIN(1923, Brit.)
Paul McWilliams
TASK FORCE(1949)
Paulette McWilliams
1984
BREAKIN' 2: ELECTRIC BOOGALOO(1984)
Raymond McWilliams
DAY THE FISH CAME OUT, THE(1967. Brit./Gr.)
Fraser McWinn
GAL WHO TOOK THE WEST, THE(1949)
Frank Mdhluli
NAKED PREY, THE(1966, U.S./South Africa)
Georgiy Mdivani
RED AND THE WHITE, THE(1969, Hung./USSR), w; SUNFLOWER(1970, Fr./Ital.), w
Anne Meacham
LILITH(1964); DEAR, DEAD DELILAH(1972); SEIZURE(1974); SEEDS OF EVIL(1981)
Charles Meacham
THIRTEENTH GUEST, THE(1932)
Michael Meacham
TEENAGE BAD GIRL(1959, Brit.); MIDSUMMERS NIGHT'S DREAM, A(1961, Czech); SWORD OF LANCELOT(1963, Brit.)
Michael Meachum
1984
COTTON CLUB, THE(1984), ch
Bob Mead
MEAT CLEAVER MASSACRE(1977)
Claire Mead
MEET JOHN DOE(1941)
Gregory Mead
CACTUS IN THE SNOW(1972)
J. F. Mead
MURDER(1930, Brit.), art d
Jack Mead
1984
PREPPIES(1984)
John Mead
ABDUL THE DAMNED(1935, Brit.), art d
Kent Mead
Silents
HEARTS AND FISTS(1926)
Misc. Silents
WARNING SIGNAL, THE(1926)
Kevin Mead
HOLLYWOOD HIGH(1977)
Misc. Talkies
HOLLYWOOD HIGH(1976)
Phil Mead
CHEYENNE SOCIAL CLUB, THE(1970)
1984
RED DAWN(1984)
Philip L. Mead
SHOWDOWN(1973); SECOND THOUGHTS(1983); TIMERIDER(1983)
Phillip L. Mead
GUNFIGHT, A(1971)
Robert Mead
ROMEO AND JULIET(1966, Brit.); PETER RABBIT AND TALES OF BEATRIX POTTER(1971, Brit.)
Shepherd Mead
HOW TO SUCCEED IN BUSINESS WITHOUT REALLY TRYING(1976), w
Taylor Mead
FLOWER THIEF, THE(1962); TOO YOUNG, TOO IMMORAL!(1962); HALLELUJAH THE HILLS(1963); OPEN THE DOOR AND SEE ALL THE PEOPLE(1964); ILLIAC PASSION, THE(1968); LONESOME COWBOYS(1968); MIDNIGHT COWBOY(1969); FEEDBACK(1979); UNDERGROUND U.S.A.(1980); UNION CITY(1980)
Misc. Talkies
QUEEN OF SHEBA MEETS THE ATOM MAN, THE(1963); BABO 73(1964); BRAND X(1970)
Terry Mead
MACKINTOSH & T.J.(1975), ph
Bridget Meade
RUNNERS(1983, Brit.)
Claire Meade
ROUGHLY SPEAKING(1945); NIGHT AND DAY(1946); WIFE WANTED(1946); THAT HAGEN GIRL(1947); UNFAITHFUL, THE(1947); KISS IN THE DARK, A(1949); MISS GRANT TAKES RICHMOND(1949); MOTHER IS A FRESHMAN(1949); MA AND PA KETTLE AT THE FAIR(1952); THREE SAILORS AND A GIRL(1953)

Doris Meade
SIX BRIDGES TO CROSS(1955)
Garth Meade
DOVE, THE(1974, Brit.)
Harold Meade
FACE AT THE WINDOW, THE(1932, Brit.); LORD CAMBER'S LADIES(1932, Brit.); GOOD COMPANIONS(1933, Brit.); IT ISN'T DONE(1937, Aus.); ANTS IN HIS PANTS(1940, Aus.)
Julia Meade
PILLOW TALK(1959); TAMMY, TELL ME TRUE(1961); ZOTZ!(1962)
Lawrence Meade
REEFER MADNESS(1936), w; MARINES COME THROUGH, THE(1943), w
Mary Meade
SHOW BUSINESS(1944); WONDER MAN(1945); THRILL OF BRAZIL, THE(1946); T-MEN(1947); ASSIGNED TO DANGER(1948); IN THIS CORNER(1948)
Richard Meade
JACKTOWN(1962)
Terry K. Meade
OUTSIDE MAN, THE(1973, U.S./FR.), ph
W.L. Meade
PENNY PARADISE(1938, Brit.), w
Walter Meade
HIGH COMMAND(1938, Brit.), w; ANOTHER SHORE(1948, Brit.), w; SCOTT OF THE ANTARCTIC(1949, Brit.), w; BRANDY FOR THE PARSON(1952, Brit.), w; JUDGMENT DEFERRED(1952, Brit.), w
Dan Meaden
OTHELLO(1965, Brit.); DR. JEKYLL AND SISTER HYDE(1971, Brit.); ABSOLUTION(1981, Brit.); NUTCRACKER(1982, Brit.); NEVER SAY NEVER AGAIN(1983)
Bill Meader
FOLLOW THE BOYS(1944); ISN'T IT ROMANTIC?(1948); CHICAGO DEADLINE(1949); FILE ON THELMA JORDAN, THE(1950); UNION STATION(1950); WHEN WORLDS COLLIDE(1951); CARRIE(1952); WAR OF THE WORLDS, THE(1953); LEATHER SAINT, THE(1956); LONELY MAN, THE(1957)
George Meader
COURAGEOUS DR. CHRISTIAN, THE(1940); DANCING ON A DIME(1940); EDISON, THE MAN(1940); GAMBLING ON THE HIGH SEAS(1940); I WANT A DIVORCE(1940); TUGBOAT ANNIE SAILS AGAIN(1940); TWO GIRLS ON BROADWAY(1940); BACHELOR DADDY(1941); FATHER TAKES A WIFE(1941); MAN MADE MONSTER(1941); PETTICOAT POLITICS(1941); YOU BELONG TO ME(1941); GLASS KEY, THE(1942); LET'S FACE IT(1943); MADAME CURIE(1943); SAN DIEGO, I LOVE YOU(1944); BOSTON BLACKIE BOOKED ON SUSPICION(1945); MILDRED PIERCE(1945); ROUGHLY SPEAKING(1945); SCARLET STREET(1945); SPELLBOUND(1945); TREE GROWS IN BROOKLYN, A(1945); BETTY CO-ED(1946); NIGHT AND DAY(1946); NOBODY LIVES FOREVER(1946); YOUNG WIDOW(1946); CROSSFIRE(1947); FOR THE LOVE OF RUSTY(1947); IT HAPPENED ON 5TH AVENUE(1947); KEEPER OF THE BEES(1947); LIFE WITH FATHER(1947); SMASHUP, THE STORY OF A WOMAN(1947); TOO MANY WINNERS(1947); UNSUSPECTED, THE(1947); SMUGGLERS' COVE(1948); ON THE TOWN(1949); THAT MIDNIGHT KISS(1949); CHAMPAGNE FOR CAESAR(1950); EMERGENCY WEDDING(1950); ENFORCER, THE(1951); GROOM WORE SPURS, THE(1951); SHE'S WORKING HER WAY THROUGH COLLEGE(1952); SHOOT-OUT AT MEDICINE BEND(1957); YOUNG LIONS, THE(1958)
George F. Meader
MONSTER AND THE GIRL, THE(1941); LUCKY JORDAN(1942)
Vaughn Meader
LEPKE(1975, U.S./Israel)
William Meader
PRACTICALLY YOURS(1944); LOST WEEKEND, THE(1945); MISS SUSIE SLAGLE'S(1945); BLUE DAHLIA, THE(1946); CROSS MY HEART(1946); O.S.S.(1946); WILD HARVEST(1947); MY OWN TRUE LOVE(1948); DARLING, HOW COULD YOU!(1951)
Bob Meading
TRAVELING SALESWOMAN(1950), makeup
Don Meadon
INFORMATION RECEIVED(1962, Brit.)
Josh Meador
ALICE IN WONDERLAND(1951), anim
Joshua Meador
SNOW WHITE AND THE SEVEN DWARFS(1937), anim; FANTASIA(1940), anim, anim, spec eff; PINOCCHIO(1940), anim; DUMBO(1940), anim; THREE CABALLEROS, THE(1944), anim; MAKE MINE MUSIC(1946), d; SO DEAR TO MY HEART(1949), anim; PETER PAN(1953), anim; 20,000 LEAGUES UNDER THE SEA(1954), spec eff; FORBIDDEN PLANET(1956), spec eff; DARBY O'GILL AND THE LITTLE PEOPLE(1959), anim
Josua L. Meador
RELUCTANT DRAGON, THE(1941), spec eff
Steve Meador
LEGEND OF THE LONE RANGER, THE(1981)
Edward Meadow
INCIDENT, THE(1967), p
Herb Meadow
SALLY AND SAINT ANNE(1952), w; MASTER OF BALLANTRAE, THE(1953, U.S./Brit.), w; REDHEAD FROM WYOMING, THE(1953), w; HIGHWAY DRAGNET(1954), w; COUNT THREE AND PRAY(1955), w; LONE RANGER, THE(1955), w; STRANGER ON HORSEBACK(1955), w; EVERYTHING BUT THE TRUTH(1956), w; UNGUARDED MOMENT, THE(1956), w; MAN AFRAID(1957), w
Audrey Meadows
THAT TOUCH OF MINK(1962); TAKE HER, SHE'S MINE(1963); ROSIE!(1967)
Bunty Meadows
HAPPIDROME(1943, Brit.); HOME SWEET HOME(1945, Brit.); HONEYMOON HOTEL(1946, Brit.); SOMEWHERE IN POLITICS(1949, Brit.)
Dennis Meadows [Dennis Moore]
DAWN RIDER(1935); SAGEBRUSH TROUBADOR(1935); DESERT JUSTICE(1936); LONELY TRAIL, THE(1936); SILVER SPURS(1936); TOO MUCH BEEF(1936); VALLEY OF THE LAWLESS(1936)
Misc. Talkies
WEST ON PARADE(1934)

George Meadows
LIGHTNING FLYER(1931)
Silents
MIDNIGHT EXPRESS, THE(1924)
Hal Meadows
SHEPHERD OF THE HILLS, THE(1964)
Heidi Meadows
STAR IS BORN, A(1954)
Herb Meadows
STRANGE WOMAN, THE(1946), w
Jayne Meadows
DARK DELUSION(1947); LADY IN THE LAKE(1947); SONG OF THE THIN MAN(1947); ENCHANTMENT(1948); LUCK OF THE IRISH(1948); DAVID AND BATHSHEBA(1951); FAT MAN, THE(1951); IT HAPPENED TO JANE(1959); COLLEGE CONFIDENTIAL(1960); NORMAN...IS THAT YOU?(1976)
John Meadows
HONEYSUCKLE ROSE(1980)
Joyce Meadows
FLESH AND THE SPUR(1957); OMAR KHAYYAM(1957); BRAIN FROM THE PLANET AROUS, THE(1958); FRONTIER GUN(1958); GIRL IN LOVER'S LANE, THE(1960); WALK TALL(1960); BACK STREET(1961); I SAW WHAT YOU DID(1965); ZEBRA IN THE KITCHEN(1965); CHRISTINE JORGENSEN STORY, THE(1970)
Leslie Meadows
HALF A SIXPENCE(1967, Brit.); UP THE JUNCTION(1968, Brit.); APPLE, THE(1980 U.S./Ger.)
Margery Meadows
Misc. Silents
MISS CHARITY(1921, Brit.); ROTTERS, THE(1921, Brit.)
Marjorie Meadows
Silents
ROMANCE ROAD(1925)
Noel Meadows
JENNY LAMOUR(1948, Fr.), titles
Stanley Meadows
MUMMY, THE(1959, Brit.); PAYROLL(1962, Brit.); BLOOD BEAST FROM OUTER SPACE(1965, Brit.); ESCAPE BY NIGHT(1965, Brit.); IPCRESS FILE, THE(1965, Brit.); YOU MUST BE JOKING!(1965, Brit.); KALEIDOSCOPE(1966, Brit.); MAIN CHANCE, THE(1966, Brit.); PANIC(1966, Brit.); TERRORNAUTS, THE(1967, Brit.); FIXER, THE(1968)
Stormey Meadows
GIANT GILA MONSTER, THE(1959)
Jill Meager
NEVER SAY NEVER AGAIN(1983)
Cecilia Meagher
COVER GIRL(1944)
Edward Meagher
Silents
NIGHT CRY, THE(1926), w; OVERLAND TELEGRAPH, THE(1929), w
John Meagher
LAST WAVE, THE(1978, Aus.)
1984
FANTASY MAN(1984, Aus.), d&w
Karen Meagher
EXPERIENCE PREFERRED... BUT NOT ESSENTIAL(1983, Brit.)
Ray Meagher
ODD ANGRY SHOT, THE(1979, Aus.); CHANT OF JIMMIE BLACKSMITH, THE(1980, Aus.); FIRE IN THE STONE, THE(1983, Aus.); ON THE RUN(1983, Aus.)
Charles Meakim
MAGNIFICENT DOPE, THE(1942)
Charles Meakin
PRESIDENT VANISHES, THE(1934); WEDDING PRESENT(1936); GOVERNMENT GIRL(1943); TONIGHT AND EVERY NIGHT(1945); WOMAN IN THE WINDOW, THE(1945); JOAN OF ARC(1948); LADY FROM SHANGHAI, THE(1948)
Silents
MAID OF THE WEST(1921); PENROD(1922); MARRIAGE CLAUSE, THE(1926); LADIES AT EASE(1927)
Richard Mealand
ALWAYS LEAVE THEM LAUGHING(1949), w
Walter D. Mealand
Silents
RAINBOW PRINCESS, THE(1916)
Malcolm Mealey
SHE'S WORKING HER WAY THROUGH COLLEGE(1952)
A.R. Meals
Misc. Silents
UNKNOWN RIDER, THE(1929), d
Sylvia Meals
ROCKY II(1979)
Bobby Means
DEADWOOD'76(1965)
Grant Means
HARPOON(1948); SIXTEEN FATHOMS DEEP(1948); WAKE OF THE RED WITCH(1949)
Jeffrey Means
BLUE LAGOON, THE(1980)
Ken Means
FREEWHEELIN'(1976)
Tyann Means
MODERN ROMANCE(1981)
Attilio Meanti
WHITE SISTER(1973, Ital./Span./Fr.)
Fred Meany
UNDERGROUND(1970, Brit.)
Sean Meany
10 NORTH FREDERICK(1958)
H. Fowler Mear
BED AND BREAKFAST(1930, Brit.), w; CALL OF THE SEA, THE(1930, Brit.), w; LAST HOUR, THE(1930, Brit.), w; LORD RICHARD IN THE PANTRY(1930, Brit.), w; YOU'D BE SURPRISED!(1930, Brit.), w; ALIBI(1931, Brit.), w; BLACK COFFEE(1931, Brit.), w; DEADLOCK(1931, Brit.), w; HAPPY ENDING, THE(1931, Brit.), w; LYONS

MAIL, THE(1931, Brit.), w; SHERLOCK HOLMES' FATAL HOUR(1931, Brit.), w; SPLINTERS IN THE NAVY(1931, Brit.), w; CHINESE PUZZLE, THE(1932, Brit.), w; CONDEMNED TO DEATH(1932, Brit.), w; CROOKED LADY, THE(1932, Brit.), w; FACE AT THE WINDOW, THE(1932, Brit.), w; MARRIAGE BOND, THE(1932, Brit.), w; MISSING REMBRANDT, THE(1932, Brit.), w; MURDER AT COVENT GARDEN(1932, Brit.), w; WHEN LONDON SLEEPS(1932, Brit.), w; WORLD, THE FLESH, AND THE DEVIL, THE(1932, Brit.), w; EXCESS BAGGAGE(1933, Brit.), w; GHOST CAMERA, THE(1933, Brit.), w; HIS GRACE GIVES NOTICE(1933, Brit.), w; HOME, SWEET HOME(1933, Brit.), w; I LIVED WITH YOU(1933, Brit.), w; IRON STAIR, THE(1933, Brit.), w; MAN OUTSIDE, THE(1933, Brit.), w; ROOF, THE(1933, Brit.), w; SHOT IN THE DARK, A(1933, Brit.), w; THIS WEEK OF GRACE(1933, Brit.), w; UMBRELLA, THE(1933, Brit.), w; ADMIRAL'S SECRET, THE(1934, Brit.), w; ARE YOU A MASON?(1934, Brit.), w; BELLA DONNA(1934, Brit.), w; BLACK ABBOT, THE(1934, Brit.), w; BRIDE OF THE LAKE(1934, Brit.), w; BROKEN MELODY, THE(1934, Brit.), w; FOUR MASKED MEN(1934, Brit.), w; LASH, THE(1934, Brit.), w; LORD EDGEWARE DIES(1934, Brit.), w; MAN WHO CHANGED HIS NAME, THE(1934, Brit.), w; NIGHT CLUB QUEEN(1934, Brit.), w; POINTING FINGER, THE(1934, Brit.), w; SAY IT WITH FLOWERS(1934, Brit.), w; TANGLED EVIDENCE(1934, Brit.), w; VIRGINIA'S HUSBAND(1934, Brit.), w; WHISPERING TONGUES(1934, Brit.), w; ANYTHING MIGHT HAPPEN(1935, Brit.), w; DEPARTMENT STORE(1935, Brit.), w; FIRE HAS BEEN ARRANGED, A(1935, Brit.), w; IN A MONASTERY GARDEN(1935), w; INSIDE THE ROOM(1935, Brit.), w; PHANTOM FIEND, THE(1935, Brit.), w; PRIVATE SECRETARY, THE(1935, Brit.), w; SCROOGE(1935, Brit.), w; SHE SHALL HAVE MUSIC(1935, Brit.), w; SQUIBS(1935, Brit.), w; TRIUMPH OF SHERLOCK HOLMES, THE(1935, Brit.), w; VINTAGE WINE(1935, Brit.), w; WANDERING JEW, THE(1935, Brit.), w; WOLVES OF THE UNDERWORLD(1935, Brit.), w; ELIZA COMES TO STAY(1936, Brit.), w; IN THE SOUP(1936, Brit.), w; LAST JOURNEY, THE(1936, Brit.), w; MORALS OF MARCUS, THE(1936, Brit.), w; SHADOW, THE(1936, Brit.), w; BEAUTY AND THE BARGE(1937, Brit.), w; DEATH CROONS THE BLUES(1937, Brit.), w; JUGGERNAUT(1937, Brit.), w; LITTLE MISS SOMEBODY(1937, Brit.), w; LOST CHORD, THE(1937, Brit.), w; RIDING HIGH(1937, Brit.), w; SONG OF THE FORGE(1937, Brit.), w; TALKING FEET(1937, Brit.), w; UNDERNEATH THE ARCHES(1937, Brit.), w; VICAR OF BRAY, THE(1937, Brit.), w; HIDEOUT IN THE ALPS(1938, Brit.), w; STEPPING TOES(1938, Brit.), w; CAPTAIN MOONLIGHT(1940, Brit.), w; MURDER AT THE BASKERVILLES(1941, Brit.), w; OLD MOTHER RILEY OVERSEAS(1943, Brit.), w
Silents
VIRGINIA'S HUSBAND(1928, Brit.), w; RED PEARLS(1930, Brit.), w
Harry Fowler Mear
WOULD YOU BELIEVE IT!(1930, Brit.), w
Anne Meara
LOVERS AND OTHER STRANGERS(1970); OUT OF TOWNERS, THE(1970); IRISH WHISKEY REBELLION(1973); NASTY HABITS(1976, Brit.); BOYS FROM BRAZIL, THE(1978); FAME(1980)
Margaret Mearing
FLYING DOWN TO RIO(1933)
De Ann Mears
PETULIA(1968, U.S./Brit.); JUSTINE(1969)
Martha Mears
OUR NEIGHBORS–THE CARTERS(1939); REMEMBER THE NIGHT(1940); MY FOOLISH HEART(1949); ROADBLOCK(1951); WEEKEND WITH FATHER(1951)
Stanford Mears
SEVENTEEN(1940), w
Lazare Mearson
CARNIVAL IN FLANDERS(1936, Fr.), set d
Lyon Mearson
OUR WIFE(1941), w
Taylor Measom
PROUD AND THE PROFANE, THE(1956)
Beryl Measor
DUAL ALIBI(1947, Brit.); ODD MAN OUT(1947, Brit.); MARK OF CAIN, THE(1948, Brit.); HER MAN GILBEY(1949, Brit.); WHILE THE SUN SHINES(1950, Brit.)
Meat Loaf
ROCKY HORROR PICTURE SHOW, THE(1975, Brit.); SCAVENGER HUNT(1979); ROADIE(1980)
Barry Meaton
CAESAR AND CLEOPATRA(1946, Brit.)
George Meaton
DISCOVERIES(1939, Brit.); WHAT'S GOOD FOR THE GOOSE(1969, Brit.)
Antonio Mecacci
RED TENT, THE(1971, Ital./USSR), makeup
Pier Antonio Mecacci
WE STILL KILL THE OLD WAY(1967, Ital.), makeup; FINE PAIR, A(1969, Ital.), makeup
Piero Antonio Mecacci
LA CAGE AUX FOLLES II(1981, Ital./Fr.), makeup
Piero Mecacci
SLAVE, THE(1963, Ital.), makeup; LAST MAN ON EARTH, THE(1964, U.S./Ital.), makeup; HELLBENDERS, THE(1967, U.S./Ital./Span.), makeup; YOUNG, THE EVIL AND THE SAVAGE, THE(1968, Ital.), makeup
Gianfranco Mecacci.
SABATA(1969, Ital.), makeup
Giulio Mecale
SPY IN YOUR EYE(1966, Ital.)
Comenico Meccoli
STORMBOUND(1951, Ital.), w
George Mechan
DOWN RIO GRANDE WAY(1942), ph
Vera Mechechnie
FLAW, THE(1955, Brit.)
Julio Mechoso
NOBODY'S PERFEKT(1981)
Susan Mechsner
STRIPES(1981); CONCRETE JUNGLE, THE(1982)
Misc. Talkies
LOVELY BUT DEADLY(1983)
Mary Rider Mechtold
Silents
MOUNTAIN RAT, THE(1914), w

Herman Meckler
HAIR(1979); RAGTIME(1981)
1984
AMADEUS(1984)
Nancy Meckler
CRY OF THE BANSHEE(1970, Brit.)
Guy Mecoli
STRANGER IN HOLLYWOOD(1968)
Jody Mecurio
PILOT, THE(1979), cos
Roman Mecznarowski
ASSISTANT, THE(1982, Czech.)
Ida Meda
VIOLENT FOUR, THE(1968, Ital.)
Sylvie Meda
RETURN OF MARTIN GUERRE, THE(1983, Fr.)
Peter Medak
NEGATIVES(1968, Brit.), d; DAY IN THE DEATH OF JOE EGG, A(1972, Brit.), d; RULING CLASS, THE(1972, Brit.), d; ODD JOB, THE(1978, Brit.), d; CHANGELING, THE(1980, Can.), d; ZORRO, THE GAY BLADE(1981), d
Misc. Talkies
GHOST IN THE NOONDAY SUN(1974), d
Joe Medalis
CHICKEN CHRONICLES, THE(1977); KENTUCKY FRIED MOVIE, THE(1977); METEOR(1979); DEAD AND BURIED(1981); LOOKER(1981); PENNIES FROM HEAVEN(1981); TRUE CONFESSIONS(1981); MAKING LOVE(1982)
Joseph G. Medalis
NICKELODEON(1976); ENDANGERED SPECIES(1982)
Julie Medana
PUBERTY BLUES(1983, Aus.)
Vladimir Medar
BLOOD DEMON(1967, Ger.); FIDDLER ON THE ROOF(1971)
F. Medard
WHAT'S NEW, PUSSYCAT?(1965, U.S./Fr.)
Mimi Medard
MY SEVEN LITTLE SINS(1956, Fr./Ital.)
Cliff Medaugh
NO RETURN ADDRESS(1961); EVEL KNIEVEL(1971)
Michael G. Meday
VAN, THE(1977)
James P Medbury
COUNTRY GENTLEMEN(1937), w
John Medbury
Silents
REPORTED MISSING(1922), t
John P. Medbury
LOVE IN BLOOM(1935), w; WHAT'S BUZZIN COUSIN?(1943), w
Russell Medcraft
CAMELS ARE COMING, THE(1934, Brit.), w; SO YOU WON'T TALK?(1935, Brit.), w; FAIR EXCHANGE(1936, Brit.), w; IT'S IN THE BAG(1936, Brit.), w; SKYLARKS(1936, Brit.), w; ANGEL(1937), w
Russell G. Medcraft
WHY LEAVE HOME?(1929), w; LET'S FACE IT(1943), w
Lane Meddick
MEN ARE CHILDREN TWICE(1953, Brit.); PURPLE PLAIN, THE(1954, Brit.); RICHARD III(1956, Brit.); MIRACLE IN SOHO(1957, Brit.); NOWHERE TO GO(1959, Brit.); FOXHOLE IN CAIRO(1960, Brit.); COUNTDOWN TO DANGER(1967, Brit.)
Derek Meddings
THUNDERBIRD 6(1968, Brit.), spec eff; THUNDERBIRDS ARE GO(1968, Brit.), spec eff; Z.P.G.(1972), spec eff; LIVE AND LET DIE(1973, Brit.), spec eff; LAND THAT TIME FORGOT, THE(1975, Brit.), spec eff; SHOUT AT THE DEVIL(1976, Brit.), spec eff; ACES HIGH(1977, Brit.), spec eff; SPY WHO LOVED ME, THE(1977, Brit.), spec eff; SUPERMAN(1978), spec eff; MOONRAKER(1979, Brit.), spec eff; FOR YOUR EYES ONLY(1981), spec eff; BANZAI(1983, Fr.), spec eff; KRULL(1983), spec eff
Jonathan Meddings
KILL HER GENTLY(1958, Brit.)
Mark Meddings
KRULL(1983), spec eff
Jimmy Medearis
LONG RIDERS, THE(1980)
1984
ROMANCING THE STONE(1984)
Thomas Medearis
TAPS(1981)
Father Joseph Medeglia
GODFATHER, THE, PART II(1974)
Anisio Medeiros
BYE-BYE BRASIL(1980, Braz.), ed
Jose Medeiros
XICA(1982, Braz.), ph
1984
MEMOIRS OF PRISON(1984, Braz.), ph
Ligia Medeiros
1984
MEMOIRS OF PRISON(1984, Braz.), cos
Michael Medeiros
1984
NEW YORK NIGHTS(1984)
Antonio Medellin
MISSING(1982)
Nelly Meden
MALE AND FEMALE SINCE ADAM AND EVE(1961, Arg.); THE EAVESDROPPER(1966, U.S./Arg.)
Mederow
M(1933, Ger.)
Paul Mederow
1914(1932, Ger.)

Austin Medford
ALONG CAME SALLY(1934, Brit.), w
Don Medford
TO TRAP A SPY(1966), d; ORGANIZATION, THE(1971), d; HUNTING PARTY, THE(1977, Brit.), d
George Medford
WHEN MY BABY SMILES AT ME(1948)
Harold Medford
BERLIN EXPRESS(1948), w; DAMNED DON'T CRY, THE(1950), w; TARGET UNKNOWN(1951), w; OPERATION SECRET(1952), w; MASTER OF BALLANTRAE, THE(1953, U.S./Brit.), w; PHANTOM OF THE RUE MORGUE(1954), w; KILLER IS LOOSE, THE(1956), w; THREE MOVES TO FREEDOM(1960, Ger.), w; BRAINWASHED(1961, Ger.), w; INCIDENT IN AN ALLEY(1962), w; FATE IS THE HUNTER(1964), w; SMOKY(1966), w; CAPETOWN AFFAIR(1967, U.S./South Afr.), w
Jody Medford
1984
NIGHT SHADOWS(1984)
Judy Medford
Misc. Talkies
LITTLE MISS INNOCENCE(1973)
Kay Medford
RANDOM HARVEST(1942); PILOT NO. 5(1943); SLIGHTLY DANGEROUS(1943); SWING SHIFT MAISIE(1943); THREE HEARTS FOR JULIA(1943); LOST ANGEL(1944); MEET THE PEOPLE(1944); MRS. PARKINGTON(1944); RATIONING(1944); ADVENTURE(1945); TAP ROOTS(1948); UNDERCOVER MAN, THE(1949); GUILTY BYSTANDER(1950); SINGING IN THE DARK(1956); FACE IN THE CROWD, A(1957); JAMBOREE(1957); BUTTERFIELD 8(1960); GIRL OF THE NIGHT(1960); RAT RACE, THE(1960); TWO TICKETS TO PARIS(1962); ENSIGN PULVER(1964); FINE MADNESS, A(1966); BUSYBODY, THE(1967); FUNNY GIRL(1968); ANGEL IN MY POCKET(1969); LOLA(1971, Brit./Ital.); FIRE SALE(1977); WINDOWS(1980)
Paul Medford
BLACK JOY(1977, Brit.); YESTERDAY'S HERO(1979, Brit.)
Stafford Medhurst
TALES FROM THE CRYPT(1972, Brit.)
David Median
1984
MOSCOW ON THE HUDSON(1984)
Medians
EVERYBODY'S DANCIN'(1950)
John Medici
SAM'S SONG(1971); SERPICO(1973); LOVING COUPLES(1980)
Nona Medici
FIVE BRANDED WOMEN(1960); EVA(1962, Fr./Ital.)
Henry Medicine Hat
BILLY TWO HATS(1973, Brit.)
Ron Medico
LADY IN RED, THE(1979), ed
Saverio Lo Medico
LOST MOMENT, THE(1947)
Dennis Medieros
MISS SADIE THOMPSON(1953)
John Medillo
RETURN OF THE SECAUCUS SEVEN(1980)
Enrichetta Medin
EYE OF THE NEEDLE, THE(1965, Ital./Fr.)
Gaston Medin
SIGN OF VENUS, THE(1955, Ital.), art d; ENEMY GENERAL, THE(1960), art d
Gastone Medin
THREE STEPS NORTH(1951), art d; FATAL DESIRE(1953), art d; MONTE CARLO STORY, THE(1957, Ital.), art d; SCANDAL IN SORRENTO(1957, Ital./Fr.), art d; FAST AND SEXY(1960, Fr./Ital.), art d; TWO WOMEN(1961, Ital./Fr.), art d
Harriet Medin
SQUARES(1972); BLOOD BEACH(1981)
1984
TERMINATOR, THE(1984)
Harriette White Medin
BLOOD AND BLACK LACE(1965, Ital.)
Ofelia Medin
MUSHROOM EATER, THE(1976, Mex.)
Ben Medina
GREATEST, THE(1977, U.S./Brit.)
Hazel Medina
WATERMELON MAN(1970); LIMBO(1972)
Jesus Medina
YANCO(1964, Mex.)
Julio Medina
ZOOT SUIT(1981)
Ofelia Medina
BIG FIX, THE(1978)
Patricia Medina
DINNER AT THE RITZ(1937, Brit.); DOUBLE OR QUITS(1938, Brit.); SIMPLY TERRIFIC(1938, Brit.); AVENGERS, THE(1942, Brit.); SPITFIRE(1943, Brit.); DON'T TAKE IT TO HEART(1944, Brit.); KISS THE BRIDE GOODBYE(1944, Brit.); THEY MET IN THE DARK(1945, Brit.); HOTEL RESERVE(1946, Brit.); SECRET HEART, THE(1946); WALTZ TIME(1946, Brit.); FOXES OF HARROW, THE(1947); MOSS ROSE(1947); THREE MUSKETEERS(1948); CHILDREN OF CHANCE(1949, Brit.); FIGHTING O'FLYNN, THE(1949); FRANCIS(1949); ABBOTT AND COSTELLO IN THE FOREIGN LEGION(1950); FORTUNES OF CAPTAIN BLOOD(1950); JACKPOT, THE(1950); LADY AND THE BANDIT, THE(1951); MAGIC CARPET, THE(1951); VALENTINO(1951); ALADDIN AND HIS LAMP(1952); CAPTAIN PIRATE(1952); DESPERATE SEARCH(1952); LADY IN THE IRON MASK(1952); BOTANY BAY(1953); PLUNDER OF THE SUN(1953); SANGAREE(1953); SIREN OF BAGDAD(1953); BLACK KNIGHT, THE(1954); DRUMS OF TAHITI(1954); PHANTOM OF THE RUE MORGUE(1954); DUEL ON THE MISSISSIPPI(1955); PIRATES OF TRIPOLI(1955); BEAST OF HOLLOW MOUNTAIN(1956); MIAMI EXPOSE(1956); STRANGER AT MY DOOR(1956); URANIUM BOOM(1956); BUCKSKIN LADY, THE(1957); COUNT YOUR BLESSINGS(1959); MISSILE FROM HELL(1960, Brit.); RED CLOAK, THE(1961, Ital./Fr.); SNOW WHITE AND THE THREE STOOGES(1961); MR. ARKADIN(1962, Brit./Fr./Span.); LATITUDE ZERO(1969, U.S./Jap.)

Raphael Medina
CINDERELLA(1937, Fr.); THEY WERE FIVE(1938, Fr.)

Reinaldo Medina
FORT APACHE, THE BRONX(1981)

Reynaldo Medina
Misc. Talkies
EL SUPER(1979)

Rudolph Medina
SLAVE GIRL(1947); TYCOON(1947)

Sara Medina-Pape
1984
BLOOD SIMPLE(1984), cos

Enrico Medioli
GIRL WITH A SUITCASE(1961, Fr./Ital.), w; ROCCO AND HIS BROTHERS(1961, Fr./Ital.), w; LEOPARD, THE(1963, Ital.), w; SANDRA(1966, Ital.), w; LISTEN, LET'S MAKE LOVE(1969, Fr./Ital.), w; LUDWIG(1973, Ital./Ger./Fr.), w; CONVERSATION PIECE(1976, Ital., Fr.), w; INNOCENT, THE(1979, Ital.), w
1984
ONCE UPON A TIME IN AMERICA(1984), w

Paul Medland
BROWNING VERSION, THE(1951, Brit.)

B. Joe Medley
Misc. Talkies
STARK RAVING MAD(1983)

Bill Medley
ROCKY III(1982)

Joanne Medley
GAMES(1967)

Big Boy Medlin
ROADIE(1980), w

Victoria Medlin
VANISHING POINT(1971); GROOVE TUBE, THE(1974)

Medlock and Marlow
OLD MOTHER RILEY'S CIRCUS(1941, Brit.)

Annabel Mednick
PARTY PARTY(1983, Brit.)

Mark Medoff
WHEN YOU COMIN' BACK, RED RYDER?(1979), a, w; GOOD GUYS WEAR BLACK(1978), w

Rustum Medora
SCARAB MURDER CASE, THE(1936, Brit.)

Austin Medord
JACKALS, THE(1967, South Africa), w

Tina Medotti
Silents
RIDING WITH DEATH(1921)

Dana Medricka
WHO KILLED JESSIE?(1965, Czech.)

V. Medvedev
HAMLET(1966, USSR)

Vadim Medvedev
QUEEN OF SPADES(1961, USSR)

Yuriy Medvedev
LADY WITH THE DOG, THE(1962, USSR)

A. Medvedeva
SOUND OF LIFE, THE(1962, USSR), ed

Natalie Medvedeva
SWORD AND THE DRAGON, THE(1960, USSR)

Vadim Medvediev
TWELFTH NIGHT(1956, USSR)

V. Medvedyev
NO GREATER LOVE(1944, USSR)

Patti Medwid
STRANGE INVADERS(1983)

Michael Medwin
BLACK MEMORY(1947, Brit.); COURTNEY AFFAIR, THE(1947, Brit.); ANNA KARENINA(1948, Brit.); ANOTHER SHORE(1948, Brit.); IDEAL HUSBAND, AN(1948, Brit.); JUST WILLIAM'S LUCK(1948, Brit.); LOOK BEFORE YOU LOVE(1948, Brit.); MY SISTER AND I(1948, Brit.), a, w; NIGHT BEAT(1948, Brit.); OPERATION DIAMOND(1948, Brit.); PICCADILLY INCIDENT(1948, Brit.); QUEEN OF SPADES(1948, Brit.); WILLIAM COMES TO TOWN(1948, Brit.); BOYS IN BROWN(1949, Brit.); CHILDREN OF CHANCE(1949, Brit.), w; FOR THEM THAT TRESPASS(1949, Brit.); FORBIDDEN(1949, Brit.); GAY LADY, THE(1949, Brit.); WOMAN HATER(1949, Brit.); LADY CRAVED EXCITEMENT, THE(1950, Brit.); SHADOW OF THE PAST(1950, Brit.); SOMEONE AT THE DOOR(1950, Brit.); TRIO(1950, Brit.); FOUR IN A JEEP(1951, Switz.); LONG DARK HALL, THE(1951, Brit.); CARETAKERS DAUGHTER, THE(1952, Brit.); CURTAIN UP(1952, Brit.); HOLIDAY WEEK(1952, Brit.); MISS ROBIN HOOD(1952, Brit.); BOTH SIDES OF THE LAW(1953, Brit.); GENEVIEVE(1953, Brit.); HORSE'S MOUTH, THE(1953, Brit.); MR. POTTS GOES TO MOSCOW(1953, Brit.); SPACEWAYS(1953, Brit.); BANG! YOU'RE DEAD(1954, Brit.); GREEN SCARF, THE(1954, Brit.); MALTA STORY(1954, Brit.); DOCTOR AT SEA(1955, Brit.); INTRUDER, THE(1955, Brit.); TECKMAN MYSTERY, THE(1955, Brit); ABOVE US THE WAVES(1956, Brit.); CHARLEY MOON(1956, Brit.); HELL IN KOREA(1956, Brit.); CHECKPOINT(1957, Brit.); DOCTOR AT LARGE(1957, Brit.); DUKE WORE JEANS, THE(1958, Brit.); I ONLY ASKED!(1958, Brit.); STEEL BAYONET, THE(1958, Brit.); WIND CANNOT READ, THE(1958, Brit.); HEART OF A MAN, THE(1959, Brit.); LONGEST DAY, THE(1962); CROOKS ANONYMOUS(1963, Brit.); DREAM MAKER, THE(1963, Brit.); NIGHT MUST FALL(1964, Brit.); RATTLE OF A SIMPLE MAN(1964, Brit.); I'VE GOTTA HORSE(1965, Brit.); SANDWICH MAN, THE(1966, Brit.); 24 HOURS TO KILL(1966, Brit.); COUNTESS FROM HONG KONG, A(1967, Brit.); CHARLIE BUBBLES(1968, Brit.), p; IF ...(1968, Brit.), p; SCROOGE(1970, Brit.); SPRING AND PORT WINE(1970, Brit.), p; GUMSHOE(1972, Brit.), p; O LUCKY MAN!(1973, Brit.), a, p; LAW AND DISORDER(1974); MEMOIRS OF A SURVIVOR(1981, Brit.), p; SEA WOLVES, THE(1981, Brit.); NEVER SAY NEVER AGAIN(1983)
1984
JIGSAW MAN, THE(1984, Brit.)

Z. Medzmariashvili
FATHER OF A SOLDIER(1966, USSR), art d

Albert Mee
OLD MOTHER RILEY OVERSEAS(1943, Brit.), w

Kirk Mee
NEWMAN'S LAW(1974)

Matthew Meece
EDDIE MACON'S RUN(1983)

William Meech
Silents
INCORRIGIBLE DUKANE, THE(1915)

Graham Meech-Burkestone
Misc. Talkies
BURNOUT(1979), d

Paddy Meegan
ANGEL(1982, Irish), m

Thomas Meegan
Misc. Silents
PARDON MY FRENCH(1921)

Danny Meehan
BLAST OF SILENCE(1961); DON'T DRINK THE WATER(1969)

Elizabeth Meehan
CASE OF SERGEANT GRISCHA, THE(1930), w; BEAU IDEAL(1931), w; TRANSGRESSION(1931), w; GIRL OF THE RIO(1932), w; OLIVER TWIST(1933), w; WEST OF SINGAPORE(1933), w; HARMONY LANE(1935), w; HARVESTER, THE(1936), w; OVER SHE GOES(1937, Brit.), w; SPRING HANDICAP(1937, Brit.), w; HOUSEMASTER(1938, Brit.), w; GENTLEMAN'S GENTLEMAN, A(1939, Brit.), w; SHE COULDN'T SAY NO(1939, Brit.), w; GIRL FROM GOD'S COUNTRY(1940), w; HIDDEN MENACE, THE(1940, Brit.), w; MYSTERY OF ROOM 13(1941, Brit.), w; PARACHUTE NURSE(1942), w; HEADIN' FOR GOD'S COUNTRY(1943), w; STORM OVER LISBON(1944), w; OUT OF THIS WORLD(1945), w; NORTHWEST OUTPOST(1947), w
Silents
GREAT GATSBY, THE(1926), w; TELEPHONE GIRL, THE(1927), w; LAUGH, CLOWN, LAUGH(1928), w; RESCUE, THE(1929), w

George Meehan
GHOST TALKS, THE(1929), ph; HEART PUNCH(1932), ph; SHIP OF WANTED MEN(1933), ph; INSIDE INFORMATION(1934), ph; MOTH, THE(1934), ph; FIGHTING SHADOWS(1935), ph; JUSTICE OF THE RANGE(1935), ph; TOO TOUGH TO KILL(1935), ph; ALIBI FOR MURDER(1936), ph; DANGEROUS INTRIGUE(1936), ph; LEGION OF TERROR(1936), ph; MYSTERIOUS AVENGER, THE(1936), ph; SECRET PATROL(1936), ph; STAMPEDE(1936), ph; WESTERNER, THE(1936), ph; CODE OF THE RANGE(1937), ph; CRIMINALS OF THE AIR(1937), ph; FIGHT TO THE FINISH, A(1937), ph; PAID TO DANCE(1937), ph; PAROLE RACKET(1937), ph; TWO GUN LAW(1937), ph; CONVICTED(1938), ph; LAST WARNING, THE(1938), ph; TARZAN'S REVENGE(1938), ph; GAMBLING SHIP(1939), ph; MANHATTAN SHAKEDOWN(1939), ph; MURDER IS NEWS(1939), ph; NORTH OF THE YUKON(1939), ph; OUTPOST OF THE MOUNTIES(1939), ph; RIDERS OF BLACK RIVER(1939), ph; SPECIAL INSPECTOR(1939), ph; TAMING OF THE WEST, THE(1939), ph; BLAZING SIX SHOOTERS(1940), ph; BULLETS FOR RUSTLERS(1940), ph; GIRLS OF THE ROAD(1940), ph; MAN FROM TUMBLEWEEDS, THE(1940), ph; PIONEERS OF THE FRONTIER(1940), ph; PRAIRIE SCHOONERS(1940), ph; RETURN OF WILD BILL, THE(1940), ph; STRANGER FROM TEXAS, THE(1940), ph; TEXAS STAGECOACH(1940), ph; THUNDERING FRONTIER(1940), ph; TWO-FISTED RANGERS(1940), ph; WEST OF ABILENE(1940), ph; ACROSS THE SIERRAS(1941), ph; BEYOND THE SACRAMENTO(1941), ph; HER FIRST BEAU(1941), ph; OFFICER AND THE LADY, THE(1941), ph; OUTLAWS OF THE PANHANDLE(1941), ph; PINTO KID, THE(1941), ph; ROYAL MOUNTED PATROL, THE(1941), ph; TEXAS(1941), ph; TWO IN A TAXI(1941), ph; WILDCAT OF TUCSON(1941), ph; MAN'S WORLD, A(1942), ph; PARDON MY GUN(1942), ph; WEST OF TOMBSTONE(1942), ph; COWBOY IN THE CLOUDS(1943), ph; DESPERADOES, THE(1943), ph; THERE'S SOMETHING ABOUT A SOLDIER(1943), ph; BLACK PARACHUTE, THE(1944), ph; COWBOY CANTEEN(1944), ph; LAST HORSEMAN, THE(1944), ph; MARK OF THE WHISTLER, THE(1944), ph; MEET MISS BOBBY SOCKS(1944), ph; SUNDOWN VALLEY(1944), ph; SWING IN THE SADDLE(1944), ph; THEY LIVE IN FEAR(1944), ph; ESCAPE IN THE FOG(1945), ph; ROUGH, TOUGH AND READY(1945), ph; VOICE OF THE WHISTLER(1945), ph; YOUTH ON TRIAL(1945), ph; LAWLESS EMPIRE(1946), ph
Silents
TAILOR MADE MAN, A(1922), ph; BEN-HUR(1925), ph; HANDSOME BRUTE, THE(1925), ph; LURE OF THE WILD, THE(1925), ph; NEW CHAMPION(1925), ph; SPEED MAD(1925), ph

George Meehan, Jr.
BANDIT OF SHERWOOD FOREST, THE(1946), ph

George B. Meehan
LANDRUSH(1946), ph; SINGIN' IN THE CORN(1946), ph; KING OF THE WILD HORSES(1947), ph

George B. Meehan, Jr.
BOSTON BLACKIE BOOKED ON SUSPICION(1945), ph; BOSTON BLACKIE'S RENDEZVOUS(1945), ph; BOSTON BLACKIE AND THE LAW(1946), ph; DANGEROUS BUSINESS(1946), ph; GALLANT JOURNEY(1946), ph; PHANTOM THIEF, THE(1946), ph

J. Leo Meehan
Misc. Silents
MAGIC GARDEN, THE(1927), d; MOTHER(1927), d

Jack Meehan
Misc. Silents
COURAGEOUS COWARD, THE(1924); PASSING OF WOLF MACLEAN, THE(1924); HURRICANE HAL(1925); SON OF SONTAG, THE(1925); BROKEN LAW, THE(1926)

James Leo Meehan
Silents
JUDGMENT OF THE HILLS(1927), d; NAUGHTY NANETTE(1927), d
Misc. Silents
MICHAEL O'HALLORAN(1923), d; GIRL OF THE LIMBERLOST, A(1924), d; KEEPER OF THE BEES, THE(1925), d; LADDIE(1926), d; LITTLE YELLOW HOUSE, THE(1928), d

John Meehan
BARNUM WAS RIGHT(1929), w; GENTLEMEN OF THE PRESS(1929), w; LADY LIES, THE(1929), w; DIVORCEE, THE(1930), w; LADY'S MORALS, A(1930), w; FREE SOUL, A(1931), w; MIRACLE WOMAN, THE(1931), w; PHANTOM OF PARIS, THE(1931), w; SON OF INDIA(1931), w; STRANGERS MAY KISS(1931), w; THIS

MODERN AGE(1931), w; LETTY LYNTON(1932), w; WASHINGTON MASQUERADE(1932), w; PRIZEFIGHTER AND THE LADY, THE(1933), w; STAGE MOTHER(1933), w; WHEN LADIES MEET(1933), w; PAINTED VEIL, THE(1934), w; SADIE MCKEE(1934), w; WHAT EVERY WOMAN KNOWS(1934), w; PETER IBBETSON(1935), w; HIS BROTHER'S WIFE(1936), w; MADAME X(1937), w; BOYS TOWN(1938), w; ETERNALLY YOURS(1939), w; SEVEN SINNERS(1940), w; KISMET(1944), w; BRING ON THE GIRLS(1945), art d; VALLEY OF DECISION, THE(1945), w; BRIDE WORE BOOTS, THE(1946), art d; STRANGE LOVE OF MARTHA IVERS, THE(1946), art d; VIRGINIAN, THE(1946), art d; DREAM GIRL(1947), art d; GOLDEN EARRINGS(1947), art d; SUDDENLY IT'S SPRING(1947), art d; SEALED VERDICT(1948), art d; THREE DARING DAUGHTERS(1948), w; HEIRESS, THE(1949), art d; SUNSET BOULEVARD(1950), art d; TARZAN'S PERIL(1951), art d; MARRYING KIND, THE(1952), art d; MAN IN THE DARK(1953), art d; SALOME(1953), art d; IT SHOULD HAPPEN TO YOU(1954), art d; 20,000 LEAGUES UNDER THE SEA(1954), art d; DON QUIXOTE(1973, Aus.)

John Meehan, Jr.
LET'S TALK IT OVER(1934), w; WAKE UP AND DREAM(1934), w; I'VE BEEN AROUND(1935), w; TAKE IT FROM ME(1937, Brit.), w; WHEN THIEF MEETS THIEF(1937, Brit.), w; GLAMOUR GIRL(1938, Brit.), w; HE LOVED AN ACTRESS(1938, Brit.), w; MR. SATAN(1938, Brit.), w; RETURN OF CAROL DEANE, THE(1938, Brit.), w; THANK EVANS(1938, Brit.), w; THISTLEDOWN(1938, Brit.), w; MISSING TEN DAYS(1941, Brit.), w; DESTINATION UNKNOWN(1942), w; NAZI AGENT(1942), w; THAT MAN FROM TANGIER(1953), w

John Lee Meehan
LADY OF CHANCE, A(1928), w

Leo Meehan
Silents
MASKED AVENGER, THE(1922), w
Misc. Silents
SILVER SPURS(1922), d; TRAPPED IN THE AIR(1922), d; HARVESTER, THE(1927), d; LITTLE MICKEY GROGAN(1927), d; DEVIL'S TRADEMARK, THE(1928), d; FRECKLES(1928), d; WALLFLOWERS(1928), d

Lew Meehan
FIREBRAND JORDAN(1930); PARDON MY GUN(1930); SOUTH OF SONORA(1930); THOSE WHO DANCE(1930); TRAILS OF DANGER(1930); RANGE FEUD, THE(1931); TEXAS RANGER, THE(1931); HELL FIRE AUSTIN(1932); POCATELLO KID(1932); SUNSET TRAIL(1932); WHISTLIN' DAN(1932); LONE AVENGER, THE(1933); FIGHTING HERO(1934); FIGHTING RANGER, THE(1934); LOST JUNGLE, THE(1934); MAN TRAILER, THE(1934); WAGON WHEELS(1934); DESERT MESA(1935); DESERT TRAIL(1935); GALLANT DEFENDER(1935); STONE OF SILVER CREEK(1935); WAGON TRAIL(1935); COWBOY STAR, THE(1936); FAST BULLETS(1936); FEUD OF THE WEST(1936); FUGITIVE SHERIFF, THE(1936); LAWLESS NINETIES, THE(1936); PRESCOTT KID, THE(1936); THREE ON THE TRAIL(1936); ARIZONA GUNFIGHTER(1937); DODGE CITY TRAIL(1937); DOOMED AT SUNDOWN(1937); GUN RANGER, THE(1937); GUNS IN THE DARK(1937); LAW AND LEAD(1937); LAWMAN IS BORN, A(1937); LIGHTNIN' CRANDALL(1937); MELODY OF THE PLAINS(1937); MOONLIGHT ON THE RANGE(1937); ONE MAN JUSTICE(1937); RANGERS STEP IN, THE(1937); RED ROPE, THE(1937); RIDIN' THE LONE TRAIL(1937); SPRINGTIME IN THE ROCKIES(1937); TRAIL OF VENGEANCE(1937); TRAPPED(1937); YODELIN' KID FROM PINE RIDGE(1937); FEUD MAKER(1938); PRAIRIE MOON(1938); THUNDER IN THE DESERT(1938); WHIRLWIND HORSEMAN(1938); COWBOYS FROM TEXAS(1939); RIDERS OF BLACK RIVER(1939); LAW AND ORDER(1940); RETURN OF FRANK JAMES, THE(1940); SON OF DAVY CROCKETT, THE(1941)
Misc. Talkies
MAN TRAILER, THE(1934); RIDIN' THRU(1935)
Silents
CROSSING TRAILS(1921); ACE OF THE LAW(1924); RAINBOW RANGERS(1924); RIDGEWAY OF MONTANA(1924); WALLOPING WALLACE(1924); DESERT'S TOLL, THE(1926); HAIR TRIGGER BAXTER(1926); CODE OF THE RANGE(1927); SKY RIDER, THE(1928); GUN LAW(1929); IDAHO RED(1929); HUNTED MEN(1930)
Misc. Silents
DARING DANGER(1922); LIGHTNIN' JACK(1924); MAN FROM GOD'S COUNTRY(1924); TRAVELIN' FAST(1924); THUNDERING THROUGH(1925); WHITE THUNDER(1925); FIGHTING LUCK(1926); RED BLOOD(1926); CACTUS TRAILS(1927); KING COWBOY(1928); WHITE OUTLAW, THE(1929)

Lou Meehan
ROARIN' GUNS(1936); GUN LORDS OF STIRRUP BASIN(1937)

Thomas Meehan
ANNIE(1982), w; TO BE OR NOT TO BE(1983), w

Tony Meehan
JUST FOR FUN(1963, Brit.)

Donald Meek
HOLE IN THE WALL(1929); LOVE KISS, THE(1930); GIRL HABIT(1931); PERSONAL MAID(1931); COLLEGE COACH(1933); EVER IN MY HEART(1933); LOVE, HONOR, AND OH BABY!(1933); BEDSIDE(1934); CAPTAIN HATES THE SEA, THE(1934); HI, NELLIE!(1934); LAST GENTLEMAN, THE(1934); MERRY WIDOW, THE(1934); MRS. WIGGS OF THE CABBAGE PATCH(1934); MURDER AT THE VANITIES(1934); ACCENT ON YOUTH(1935); BABY FACE HARRINGTON(1935); BARBARY COAST(1935); BIOGRAPHY OF A BACHELOR GIRL(1935); CAPTAIN BLOOD(1935); CHINA SEAS(1935); GILDED LILY, THE(1935); HAPPINESS C.O.D.(1935); INFORMER, THE(1935); KIND LADY(1935); MARK OF THE VAMPIRE(1935); OLD MAN RHYTHM(1935); PETER IBBETSON(1935); RETURN OF PETER GRIMM, THE(1935); ROMANCE IN MANHATTAN(1935); SHE COULDN'T TAKE IT(1935); SOCIETY DOCTOR(1935); TOP HAT(1935); VILLAGE TALE(1935); WHOLE TOWN'S TALKING, THE(1935); AND SO THEY WERE MARRIED(1936); BRIDE COMES HOME(1936); EVERYBODY'S OLD MAN(1936); LOVE ON THE RUN(1936); OLD HUTCH(1936); ONE RAINY AFTERNOON(1936); PENNIES FROM HEAVEN(1936); THREE MARRIED MEN(1936); THREE WISE GUYS, THE(1936); TWO IN A CROWD(1936); ARTISTS AND MODELS(1937); BEHIND THE HEADLINES(1937); BREAKFAST FOR TWO(1937); DOUBLE WEDDING(1937); MAID OF SALEM(1937); MAKE A WISH(1937); PARNELL(1937); THREE LEGIONNAIRES, THE(1937); TOAST OF NEW YORK, THE(1937); YOU'RE A SWEETHEART(1937); ADVENTURES OF TOM SAWYER, THE(1938); DOUBLE DANGER(1938); GOODBYE BROADWAY(1938); HAVING WONDERFUL TIME(1938); HOLD THAT CO-ED(1938); LITTLE MISS BROADWAY(1938); YOU CAN'T TAKE IT WITH YOU(1938); BLONDIE TAKES A VACATION(1939); HOLLYWOOD CAVALCADE(1939); HOUSEKEEPER'S DAUGHTER(1939); JESSE JAMES(1939); NICK CARTER, MASTER DETECTIVE(1939); STAGECOACH(1939); YOUNG MR. LINCOLN(1939); DR. EHRLICH'S MAGIC BULLET(1940); GHOST COMES HOME, THE(1940); HULLABALOO(1940);

MAN FROM DAKOTA, THE(1940); MY LITTLE CHICKADEE(1940); OH JOHNNY, HOW YOU CAN LOVE!(1940); PHANTOM RAIDERS(1940); RETURN OF FRANK JAMES, THE(1940); SKY MURDER(1940); STAR DUST(1940); THIRD FINGER, LEFT HAND(1940); TURNABOUT(1940); BABES ON BROADWAY(1941); BARNACLE BILL(1941); BLONDE INSPIRATION(1941); COME LIVE WITH ME(1941); DESIGN FOR SCANDAL(1941); FEMININE TOUCH, THE(1941); RISE AND SHINE(1941); WILD MAN OF BORNEO, THE(1941); WOMAN'S FACE(1941); KEEPER OF THE FLAME(1942); MAISIE GETS HER MAN(1942); OMAHA TRAIL, THE(1942); SEVEN SWEETHEARTS(1942); TORTILLA FLAT(1942); AIR RAID WARDENS(1943); DU BARRY WAS A LADY(1943); THEY GOT ME COVERED(1943); BARBARY COAST GENT(1944); BATHING BEAUTY(1944); LOST ANGEL(1944); MAISIE GOES TO RENO(1944); RATIONING(1944); THIN MAN GOES HOME, THE(1944); TWO GIRLS AND A SAILOR(1944); COLONEL EFFINGHAM'S RAID(1945); STATE FAIR(1945); AFFAIRS OF GERALDINE(1946); BECAUSE OF HIM(1946); JANIE GETS MARRIED(1946); MAGIC TOWN(1947)
Misc. Talkies
FABULOUS JOE, THE(1946)
Misc. Silents
SIX CYLINDER LOVE(1923)

John Meek
TONIGHT WE SING(1953)

Otto Meek
Misc. Silents
FORBIDDEN GRASS(1928)

Meekah
MATTER OF WHO, A(1962, Brit.)

Colleen Meeker
1984
HOLLYWOOD HIGH PART II(1984), p, w

Collenn Meeker
MY BOYS ARE GOOD BOYS(1978), p

George Meeker
STRICTLY DISHONORABLE(1931); AFRAID TO TALK(1932); BACK STREET(1932); BLESSED EVENT(1932); EMMA(1932); FAMOUS FERGUSON CASE, THE(1932); FIREMAN, SAVE MY CHILD(1932); FIRST YEAR, THE(1932); MATCH KING, THE(1932); MISLEADING LADY, THE(1932); TESS OF THE STORM COUNTRY(1932); VANITY STREET(1932); CHANCE AT HEAVEN(1933); DOUBLE HARNESS(1933); KING FOR A NIGHT(1933); LIFE OF JIMMY DOLAN, THE(1933); NIGHT OF TERROR(1933); ONLY YESTERDAY(1933); PICK-UP(1933); SWEEPINGS(1933); WORLD CHANGES, THE(1933); AGAINST THE LAW(1934); DARK HAZARD(1934); DRAGON MURDER CASE, THE(1934); EVER SINCE EVE(1934); HI, NELLIE!(1934); HIPS, HIPS, HOORAY(1934); I BELIEVED IN YOU(1934); LITTLE MAN, WHAT NOW?(1934); MELODY IN SPRING(1934); PARIS INTERLUDE(1934); RICHEST GIRL IN THE WORLD, THE(1934); UNCERTAIN LADY(1934); BACHELOR OF ARTS(1935); DANTE'S INFERNO(1935); MURDER BY TELEVISION(1935); MURDER ON A HONEYMOON(1935); OIL FOR THE LAMPS OF CHINA(1935); RAINMAKERS, THE(1935); REMEMBER LAST NIGHT(1935); WEDDING NIGHT, THE(1935); WELCOME HOME(1935); CAREER WOMAN(1936); COUNTRY DOCTOR, THE(1936); DON'T GET PERSONAL(1936); GENTLE JULIA(1936); MR. DEEDS GOES TO TOWN(1936); TANGO(1936); WALKING ON AIR(1936); WEDDING PRESENT(1936); BEWARE OF LADIES(1937); ESCAPE BY NIGHT(1937); HISTORY IS MADE AT NIGHT(1937); MAN WHO FOUND HIMSELF, THE(1937); MUSIC FOR MADAME(1937); ON AGAIN-OFF AGAIN(1937); STELLA DALLAS(1937); WESTLAND CASE, THE(1937); DANGER ON THE AIR(1938); HAVING WONDERFUL TIME(1938); MARIE ANTOINETTE(1938); MEET THE MAYOR(1938); RECKLESS LIVING(1938); SLANDER HOUSE(1938); TARZAN'S REVENGE(1938); ALL WOMEN HAVE SECRETS(1939); EVERYTHING'S ON ICE(1939); GONE WITH THE WIND(1939); LADY AND THE MOB, THE(1939); LONG SHOT, THE(1939); NICK CARTER, MASTER DETECTIVE(1939); ROARING TWENTIES, THE(1939); ROUGH RIDERS' ROUNDUP(1939); STUNT PILOT(1939); SWANEE RIVER(1939); UNDERCOVER DOCTOR(1939); MICHAEL SHAYNE, PRIVATE DETECTIVE(1940); NIGHT AT EARL CARROLL'S, A(1940); YESTERDAY'S HEROES(1940); DIVE BOMBER(1941); HIGH SIERRA(1941); LOVE CRAZY(1941); MARRY THE BOSS' DAUGHTER(1941); MOUNTAIN MOONLIGHT(1941); SINGING HILL, THE(1941); YOU'RE IN THE ARMY NOW(1941); BUSSES ROAR(1942); CAPTAINS OF THE CLOUDS(1942); CASABLANCA(1942); GAY SISTERS(1942); LARCENY, INC.(1942); MALE ANIMAL, THE(1942); MURDER IN THE BIG HOUSE(1942); SECRET ENEMIES(1942); SPY SHIP(1942); WINGS FOR THE EAGLE(1942); YOU CAN'T ESCAPE FOREVER(1942); OX-BOW INCIDENT, THE(1943); DEAD MAN'S EYES(1944); MARRIAGE IS A PRIVATE AFFAIR(1944); PORT OF 40 THIEVES, THE(1944); SEVEN DOORS TO DEATH(1944); SILENT PARTNER(1944); SONG OF NEVADA(1944); TAKE IT BIG(1944); UP IN ARMS(1944); BIG SHOW-OFF, THE(1945); BLONDE RANSOM(1945); COME OUT FIGHTING(1945); CRIME, INC.(1945); DOCKS OF NEW YORK(1945); EADIE WAS A LADY(1945); GUY, A GAL AND A PAL, A(1945); I ACCUSE MY PARENTS(1945); MR. MUGGS RIDES AGAIN(1945); NORTHWEST TRAIL(1945); ANGEL ON MY SHOULDER(1946); BELOW THE DEADLINE(1946); BLACK MARKET BABIES(1946); HER SISTER'S SECRET(1946); HOME IN OKLAHOMA(1946); MURDER IS MY BUSINESS(1946); RED DRAGON, THE(1946); APACHE ROSE(1947); ROAD TO RIO(1947); SMASH-UP, THE STORY OF A WOMAN(1947); DENVER KID, THE(1948); DUDE GOES WEST, THE(1948); GAY RANCHERO, THE(1948); KING OF THE GAMBLERS(1948); ONE TOUCH OF VENUS(1948); SILVER TRAILS(1948); CRIME DOCTOR'S DIARY, THE(1949); OMOO OMOO, THE SHARK GOD(1949); RANGER OF CHEROKEE STRIP(1949); SKY LINER(1949); TWILIGHT IN THE SIERRAS(1950); SPOILERS OF THE PLAINS(1951); WELLS FARGO GUNMASTER(1951)
Misc. Talkies
IN PARIS, A.W.O.L.(1936)
Silents
ESCAPE, THE(1928); FOUR SONS(1928)
Misc. Silents
CHICKEN A LA KING(1928); GIRL-SHY COWBOY, THE(1928); THIEF IN THE DARK, A(1928)

Herman Meeker
TAKING OFF(1971)

Patricia Meeker
WEREWOLF IN A GIRL'S DORMITORY(1961, Ital./Aust.)

Ralph Meeker
FOUR IN A JEEP(1951, Switz.); SHADOW IN THE SKY(1951); TERESA(1951); GLORY ALLEY(1952); SOMEBODY LOVES ME(1952); CODE TWO(1953); JEOPARDY(1953); NAKED SPUR, THE(1953); BIG HOUSE, U.S.A.(1955); DESERT

SANDS(1955); KISS ME DEADLY(1955); WOMAN'S DEVOTION, A(1956); FUZZY PINK NIGHTGOWN, THE(1957); PATHS OF GLORY(1957); RUN OF THE ARROW(1957); ADA(1961); SOMETHING WILD(1961); WALL OF NOISE(1963); DIRTY DOZEN, THE(1967, Brit.); GENTLE GIANT(1967); ST. VALENTINE'S DAY MASSACRE, THE(1967); DETECTIVE, THE(1968); DEVIL'S 8, THE(1969); I WALK THE LINE(1970); ANDERSON TAPES, THE(1971); HAPPINESS CAGE, THE(1972); BRANNIGAN(1975, Brit.); FOOD OF THE GODS, THE(1976); HI-RIDERS(1978); MY BOYS ARE GOOD BOYS(1978); WINTER KILLS(1979); WITHOUT WARNING(1980)

Misc. Talkies
LOVE COMES QUIETLY(1974); JOHNNY FIRECLOUD(1975); ALPHA INCIDENT, THE(1976)

Russell Meeker
STATE OF THE UNION(1948)

Edward Meekin
DOCTOR DETROIT(1983)

Edward Meeks
DAY AND THE HOUR, THE(1963, Fr./ Ital.); STOP TRAIN 349(1964, Fr./Ital./Ger.); GALIA(1966, Fr./Ital.); SICILIAN CLAN, THE(1970, Fr.); BLUEBEARD(1972)

Misc. Talkies
SEAWOLF(1974)

Jack Meeks
NUNZIO(1978)

1984
EXTERMINATOR 2(1984)

Kate Meeks
Silents
DAVID HARUM(1915)

Somcjai Meekunsut
HOT POTATO(1976)

Jeanine Meerapfel
MALOU(1983), d&w

Ernest Meershoek
WINTER KEPT US WARM(1968, Can.), ph

Kay Meersman
YOUNG ONE, THE(1961, Mex.)

Key Meersman
ARTURO'S ISLAND(1963, Ital.)

Peter Meersman
DAY THE SKY EXPLODED, THE(1958, Fr./Ital.); NAKED MAJA, THE(1959, Ital./U.S.)

Lazare Meerson
END OF THE WORLD, THE(1930, Fr.), art d; UNDER THE ROOFS OF PARIS(1930, Fr.), art d; A NOUS LA LIBERTE(1931, Fr.), set d; MILLION, THE(1931, Fr.), art d&set d; AS YOU LIKE IT(1936, Brit.), set d; FIRE OVER ENGLAND(1937, Brit.), art d, set d; KNIGHT WITHOUT ARMOR(1937, Brit.), set d; CITADEL, THE(1938), art d; DIVORCE OF LADY X. THE(1938, Brit.), prod d; SOUTH RIDING(1938, Brit.), prod d

Armand Meffre
SHAMELESS OLD LADY, THE(1966, Fr.); BLUE COUNTRY, THE(1977, Fr.)

1984
HERE COMES SANTA CLAUS(1984)

Francis Megahy
1984
REAL LIFE(1984, Brit.), d, w

Misc. Talkies
GREAT RIVIERA BANK ROBBERY, THE(1979), d

Patrick Megehee
Misc. Silents
RANGELAND(1922)

Maria Megey
GUINGUETTE(1959, Fr.)

Robert T. Megginson
COWARDS(1970), ph, ed; NIGHTMARE(1981), ed

Luis Megino
1984
DEMONS IN THE GARDEN(1984, Span.), p, w

Meglin Glee Club
REG'LAR FELLERS(1941)

The Meglin Kiddies
ROARIN' LEAD(1937)

John Megna
TO KILL A MOCKINGBIRD(1962); HUSH... HUSH, SWEET CHARLOTTE(1964); BLINDFOLD(1966); GO TELL THE SPARTANS(1978); SMOKEY AND THE BANDIT II(1980); CANNONBALL RUN, THE(1981)

Debbie Megowan
DAYS OF WINE AND ROSES(1962)

Don Megowan
KID FROM AMARILLO, THE(1951); MOB, THE(1951); ON THE LOOSE(1951); PRINCE VALIANT(1954); DAVY CROCKETT, KING OF THE WILD FRONTIER(1955); LAWLESS STREET, A(1955); TO CATCH A THIEF(1955); CREATURE WALKS AMONG US, THE(1956); GREAT LOCOMOTIVE CHASE, THE(1956); WEREWOLF, THE(1956); DELICATE DELINQUENT, THE(1957); GUN THE MAN DOWN(1957); HELL CANYON OUTLAWS(1957); STORY OF MANKIND, THE(1957); MAN WHO DIED TWICE, THE(1958); MONEY, WOMEN AND GUNS(1958); SNOWFIRE(1958); JAYHAWKERS, THE(1959); GUNS OF THE BLACK WITCH(1961, Fr./Ital.); CREATION OF THE HUMANOIDS(1962); FOR LOVE OR MONEY(1963); TARZAN AND THE VALLEY OF GOLD(1966 U.S./Switz.); DEVIL'S BRIGADE, THE(1968); IF HE HOLLERS, LET HIM GO(1968); TRUCK TURNER(1974)

Misc. Talkies
LUST TO KILL(1960); BORDER LUST(1967)

Zane Megowan
O.S.S.(1946)

Thomas Megraine
Silents
WET GOLD(1921)

Janet Megrew
HIS LORDSHIP(1932, Brit.)

Roi Cooper Megrue
IT PAYS TO ADVERTISE(1931), w

Silents
FIGHTING ODDS(1917), w; SEVEN CHANCES(1925), w; TEA FOR THREE(1927), w

Sachiko Meguro
GOLDEN DEMON(1956, Jap.)

Yuuki Meguro
FIGHT FOR THE GLORY(1970, Jap.)

Andres Meguto
CHIMES AT MIDNIGHT(1967, Span.,Switz.)

Blanche Mehaffey
DANCING DYNAMITE(1931); DUGAN OF THE BAD LANDS(1931); IS THERE JUSTICE?(1931); MOUNTED FURY(1931); RIDERS OF THE NORTH(1931); SKY SPIDER, THE(1931); SOUL OF THE SLUMS(1931); SUNRISE TRAIL(1931); ALIAS MARY SMITH(1932); DYNAMITE DENNY(1932); SALLY OF THE SUBWAY(1932); HELD FOR RANSOM(1938)

Misc. Talkies
WHITE RENEGADE(1931); PASSPORT TO PARADISE(1932); BORDER GUNS(1934); NORTH OF ARIZONA(1935); SILENT CODE, THE(1935); WILDCAT SAUNDERS(1936); DEVIL MONSTER(1946, Brit.)

Silents
TAKE IT FROM ME(1926); FINNEGAN'S BALL(1927); PRINCESS FROM HOBOKEN, THE(1927); AIR MAIL PILOT, THE(1928)

Misc. Silents
BATTLING ORIOLES, THE(1924); WHITE SHEEP, THE(1924); WOMAN OF THE WORLD, A(1925); RUNAWAY EXPRESS, THE(1926); TEXAS STREAK, THE(1926); DENVER DUDE, THE(1927); SILENT RIDER, THE(1927); MARLIE THE KILLER(1928); SMILIN' GUNS(1929)

D. A. Mehan
DULCIMER STREET(1948, Brit.)

Dodd Mehan
NO HIGHWAY IN THE SKY(1951, Brit.)

Michael Mehas
GIRLS FROM THUNDER STRIP, THE(1966), p

Mick Mehas
GIRLS FROM THUNDER STRIP, THE(1966); HELL'S CHOSEN FEW(1968); CYCLE SAVAGES(1969)

Mehdi
CATHERINE & CO.(1976, Fr.)

Elenore Meherin
Silents
SANDY(1926), w

Phil Meheux
MUSIC MACHINE, THE(1979, Brit.), ph; SCUM(1979, Brit.), ph; FINAL CONFLICT, THE(1981), ph; LONG GOOD FRIDAY, THE(1982, Brit.), ph; BEYOND THE LIMIT(1983), ph; EXPERIENCE PREFERRED... BUT NOT ESSENTIAL(1983, Brit.), ph; FINAL OPTION, THE(1983, Brit.), ph

Philip Meheux
BLACK JOY(1977, Brit.), ph

Barbara Mehlan
TINDER BOX, THE(1968, E. Ger.)

Luana Mehlberg
IT'S A BIG COUNTRY(1951)

Margo Mehling
MAGIC SPECTACLES(1961); PAJAMA PARTY(1964)

Svend Mehling
REPTILICUS(1962, U.S./Den.), ed

Clement Mehlomakulu
DINGAKA(1965, South Africa)

Lal Chand Mehra
THIRTEENTH CHAIR, THE(1930); MONKEY'S PAW, THE(1933); STAMBOUL QUEST(1934); CHARGE OF THE LIGHT BRIGADE, THE(1936); HOUSE OF A THOUSAND CANDLES, THE(1936); LEATHERNECKS HAVE LANDED, THE(1936); THIRTEENTH CHAIR, THE(1937); WINDJAMMER(1937); GUNGA DIN(1939); ISLAND OF LOST MEN(1939); PANAMA PATROL(1939); RAINS CAME, THE(1939); MURDER OVER NEW YORK(1940); CHINA GIRL(1942); DRUMS OF FU MANCHU(1943); MASK OF DIMITRIOS, THE(1944); STANDING ROOM ONLY(1944); WHITE CLIFFS OF DOVER, THE(1944); CARIBBEAN MYSTERY, THE(1945); OUT OF THIS WORLD(1945); CALCUTTA(1947); SINGAPORE(1947); MAN-EATER OF KUMAON(1948); CALL ME MADAM(1953); KING OF THE KHYBER RIFLES(1953); ESCAPE TO BURMA(1955); HELLFIGHTERS(1968)

Pran Mehra
HOUSEHOLDER, THE(1963, US/India), ed

Alain Mehrez
LAST OF THE SECRET AGENTS?, THE(1966)

Darius Mehrjui
CYCLE, THE(1979, Iran), d, w

Helen Mehrmann
SHANNONS OF BROADWAY, THE(1929)

Shayur Mehta
HIGH ROAD TO CHINA(1983)

Tarla Mehta
HEAT AND DUST(1983, Brit.)

Yusuf Mehta
1984
MOHAN JOSHI HAAZIR HO(1984, India), w

Mehtab
TIGER AND THE FLAME, THE(1955, India)

Francesco Mei
LUNA(1979, Ital.)

Lady Tsen Mei
LETTER, THE(1929)

Misc. Silents
FOR THE FREEDOM OF THE EAST(1918)

Lasy Tsen Mei
Misc. Silents
LOTUS BLOSSOM(1921)

Ruediger Meichsner
MADDEST CAR IN THE WORLD, THE(1974, Ger.), ph

Armin Meier
MOTHER KUSTERS GOES TO HEAVEN(1976, Ger.); DESPAIR(1978, Ger.)
Eva Marie Meier
GERMANY IN AUTUMN(1978, Ger.)
John Meier
1984
STAR TREK III: THE SEARCH FOR SPOCK(1984)
John C. Meier
HERBIE GOES BANANAS(1980); OUTSIDERS, THE(1983)
Penelope Meier
FRATERNITY ROW(1977)
Susanne Meierhofer
1984
CHINESE BOXES(1984, Ger./Brit.)
Egbert Meiers
NOT RECONCILED, OR "ONLY VIOLENCE HELPS WHERE IT RULES"(1969, Ger.)
Thomas Meighan
ARGYLE CASE, THE(1929); SKYLINE(1931); YOUNG SINNERS(1931); CHEATERS AT PLAY(1932); MADISON SQUARE GARDEN(1932); PECK'S BAD BOY(1934)
Silents
ARMSTRONG'S WIFE(1915); IMMIGRANT, THE(1915); KINDLING(1915); DUPE, THE(1916); ARMS AND THE GIRL(1917); EVE'S DAUGHTER(1918); M'LISS(1918); OUT OF A CLEAR SKY(1918); MALE AND FEMALE(1919); MIRACLE MAN, THE(1919); CAPPY RICKS(1921); CITY OF SILENT MEN(1921); EASY ROAD, THE(1921); PRINCE THERE WAS, A(1921); WHITE AND UNMARRIED(1921); BACK HOME AND BROKE(1922); IF YOU BELIEVE IT, IT'S SO(1922); MAN WHO SAW TOMORROW, THE(1922); OUR LEADING CITIZEN(1922); ALASKAN, THE(1924); OLD HOME WEEK(1925); NEW KLONDIKE, THE(1926); TIN GODS(1926); BLIND ALLEYS(1927); CITY GONE WILD, THE(1927); WE'RE ALL GAMBLERS(1927); RACKET, THE(1928)
Misc. Silents
(; FIGHTING HOPE, THE(1915); CLOWN, THE(1916); COMMON GROUND(1916); HEIR TO THE HOORAH, THE(1916); PUDD'NHEAD WILSON(1916); SOWERS, THE(1916); STORM, THE(1916); TRAIL OF THE LONESOME PINE, THE(1916); HER BETTER SELF(1917); LAND OF PROMISE, THE(1917); MYSTERIOUS MISS TERRY, THE(1917); SAPHO(1917); SILENT PARTNER, THE(1917); SLAVE MARKET, THE(1917); SLEEPING FIRES(1917); FORBIDDEN CITY, THE(1918); HEART OF THE WILDS(1918); IN PURSUIT OF POLLY(1918); MADAME JEALOUSY(1918); MISSING(1918); HEART OF WETONA, THE(1919); PEG O' MY HEART(1919); PROBATION WIFE, THE(1919); THUNDERBOLT, THE(1919); CIVILIAN CLOTHES(1920); CONRAD IN QUEST OF HIS YOUTH(1920); PRINCE CHAP, THE(1920); WHY CHANGE YOUR WIFE?(1920); FRONTIER OF THE STARS, THE(1921); BACHELOR DADDY, THE(1922); MANSLAUGHTER(1922); HOMEWARD BOUND(1923); NE'ER-DO-WELL, THE(1923); WOMAN-PROOF(1923); CONFIDENCE MAN, THE(1924); PIED PIPER MALONE(1924); TONGUES OF FLAME(1924); COMING THROUGH(1925); IRISH LUCK(1925); MAN WHO FOUND HIMSELF, THE(1925); CANADIAN, THE(1926); WE'RE ALL GAMBLERS(1927); MATING CALL, THE(1928)
John Meighen
1984
HOTEL NEW HAMPSHIRE, THE(1984), art d
John Meigle
Silents
DESERTED AT THE ALTAR(1922), ph
William Meigs
GLORY GUYS, THE(1965)
William S. Meigs
GUNFIGHT AT THE O.K. CORRAL(1957)
Viktor Meihsl
FIDELIO(1961, Aust.), ph
Erik J. Meijer
1984
FOURTH MAN, THE(1984, Neth.)
Gesa Meiken
CLEOPATRA(1963)
Carol Meikle
TRUE GRIT(1969), makeup
Richard Meikle
ON THE BEACH(1959)
Linda Meiklejohn
BALLAD OF JOSIE(1968); R.P.M.(1970)
Bill Meilen
GREY FOX, THE(1983, Can.)
Henri Meilhac
Silents
SO THIS IS PARIS(1926), w
Jean-Claude Meilland
LOULOU(1980, Fr.)
John Meillon
ON THE BEACH(1959); SUNDOWNERS, THE(1960); LONG AND THE SHORT AND THE TALL, THE(1961, Brit.); OFFBEAT(1961, Brit.); WATCH IT, SAILOR!(1961, Brit.); BILLY BUDD(1962); DEATH TRAP(1962, Brit.); OPERATION SNATCH(1962, Brit.); VALIANT, THE(1962, Brit./Ital.); CAIRO(1963); RUNNING MAN, THE(1963, Brit.); GUNS AT BATASI(1964, Brit.); SQUADRON 633(1964, U.S./Brit.); 633 SQUADRON(1964); DEAD MAN'S CHEST(1965, Brit.); THEY'RE A WEIRD MOB(1966, Aus.); OUTBACK(1971, Aus.); WALKABOUT(1971, Aus./U.S.); SUNSTRUCK(1973, Aus.); CARS THAT ATE PARIS, THE(1974, Aus.); DOVE, THE(1974, Brit.); INN OF THE DAMNED(1974, Aus.); SIDECAR RACERS(1975, Aus.); RIDE A WILD PONY(1976, U.S./Aus.); PICTURE SHOW MAN, THE(1980, Aus.); HEATWAVE(1983, Aus.); WILD DUCK, THE(1983, Aus.)
1984
CAMEL BOY, THE(1984, Aus.)
John Meillon, Jr.
RIDE A WILD PONY(1976, U.S./Aus.)
Helen Meinardi
I MET HIM IN PARIS(1937), w; NEXT TIME I MARRY(1938), w
Annelise Meineche
ERIC SOYA'S "17"(1967, Den.), d

Eva Maria Meineke
DREAM TOWN(1973, Ger.)
Eva Marie Meineke
CESAR AND ROSALIE(1972, Fr.)
Eva-Maria Meineke
SOMETHING FOR EVERYONE(1970); AMERICAN SUCCESS COMPANY, THE(1980)
Eva-Marie Meineke
TO THE DEVIL A DAUGHTER(1976, Brit./Ger.)
Emilio Meiners
MANHUNT IN THE JUNGLE(1958); DAUGHTER OF THE SUN GOD(1962)
Rudolf Meinert
Misc. Silents
HOUND OF THE BASKERVILLES, THE(1914, Ger.), d
Rudolph Meinert
Misc. Silents
STRANGE CASE OF DISTRICT ATTORNEY M.(1930), d
Meinhardt
Silents
NAPOLEON(1927, Fr.), art d
Edith Meinhardt
RASPUTIN(1932, Ger.)
Misc. Silents
DIARY OF A LOST GIRL(1929, Ger.)
Bob Meinhart
SLIGHT CASE OF LARCENY, A(1953)
Frederique Meininger
COCKTAIL MOLOTOV(1980, Fr.)
Donna Jean Meinke
RODEO RHYTHM(1941)
Josef Meinrad
TRIAL, THE(1948, Aust.); ONE APRIL 2000(1952, Aust.); APRIL 1, 2000(1953, Aust.); CONGRESS DANCES(1957, Ger.); TRAPP FAMILY, THE(1961, Ger.); CARDINAL, THE(1963)
Joseph Meinrad
DON JUAN(1956, Aust.); FOREVER MY LOVE(1962)
Douglas Meins
DEAD END KIDS ON DRESS PARADE(1939); GRANDPA GOES TO TOWN(1940); MONEY TO BURN(1940)
Gus Meins
BABES IN TOYLAND(1934), d; KELLY THE SECOND(1936), d; CALIFORNIAN, THE(1937), d; HIT PARADE, THE(1937), d; NOBODY'S BABY(1937), d; HIGGINS FAMILY, THE(1938), d; HIS EXCITING NIGHT(1938), d; LADIES IN DISTRESS(1938), d; ROLL ALONG, COWBOY(1938), d; ROMANCE ON THE RUN(1938), d; COVERED TRAILER, THE(1939), d; MY WIFE'S RELATIVES(1939), d; MYSTERIOUS MISS X, THE(1939), d; SHOULD HUSBANDS WORK?(1939), d; GRANDPA GOES TO TOWN(1940), p&d; MONEY TO BURN(1940), p&d; SCATTERBRAIN(1940), p&d
Eberhard Meischner
JOURNEY TO THE LOST CITY(1960, Ger./Fr./Ital.), p
Edmund Meisel
CRIMSON CIRCLE, THE(1930, Brit.), m
Silents
BATTLESHIP POTEMKIN, THE(1925, USSR), m
Kurt Meisel
COURT CONCERT, THE(1936, Ger.); FINAL CHORD, THE(1936, Ger.); THEY WERE SO YOUNG(1955); TIME TO LOVE AND A TIME TO DIE, A(1958); CAT, THE(1959, Fr.); EMBEZZLED HEAVEN(1959,Ger.); COURT MARTIAL(1962, Ger.), d; LONGEST DAY, THE(1962); WOZZECK(1962, E. Ger.); ODESSA FILE, THE(1974, Brit./Ger.)
Myron Meisel
FINAL EXAM(1981), p
1984
OASIS, THE(1984), p, w
Norbert Meisel
Misc. Talkies
ADULTERESS, THE(1976), d; I REMEMBER LOVE(1981), d
Pancho Meisenheimer
WOMAN UNDER THE INFLUENCE, A(1974)
Edith Meiser
GLAMOUR BOY(1941); GO WEST, YOUNG LADY(1941); IT GROWS ON TREES(1952); MIDDLE OF THE NIGHT(1959)
William Meisle
END OF AUGUST, THE(1982)
Nathan Meisler
SALLAH(1965, Israel)
Frederic Meisner
SECOND WIND, A(1978, Fr.)
Guenter Meisner
INSIDE OUT(1975, Brit.); SERPENT'S EGG, THE(1977, Ger./U.S.)
Gunter Meisner
QUESTION 7(1961, U.S./Ger.); FUNERAL IN BERLIN(1966, Brit.); IS PARIS BURNING?(1966, U.S./Fr.); QUILLER MEMORANDUM, THE(1966, Brit.); BRIDGE AT REMAGEN, THE(1969); ODESSA FILE, THE(1974, Brit./Ger.); BOYS FROM BRAZIL, THE(1978); JUST A GIGOLO(1979, Ger.); AMERICAN SUCCESS COMPANY, THE(1980); NIGHT CROSSING(1982)
1984
UNDER THE VOLCANO(1984)
Gunther Meisner
ACE OF ACES(1982, Fr./Ger.)
Michael Meisner
1984
RED DAWN(1984)
Sanford Meisner
STORY ON PAGE ONE, THE(1959); TENDER IS THE NIGHT(1961); MIKEY AND NICKY(1976)
Victor Meisner
1984
RED DAWN(1984)

Alfred Meissner
BAND OF ANGELS(1957)
Emma Meissner
INTERMEZZO(1937, Swed.)
Frederic Meissner
DISORDER AND EARLY TORMENT(1977, Ger.)
Gunter Meissner
COUNTERFEIT TRAITOR, THE(1962); WILLY WONKA AND THE CHOCOLATE
FACTORY(1971)
Maria Meissner
PRIVATE LIFE OF LOUIS XIV(1936, Ger.)
Georges Meister
MISTRESS FOR THE SUMMER, A(1964, Fr./Ital.)
Gloria Meister
SORCERESS(1983)
Julian Meister
LOUISIANA TERRITORY(1953)
Kurt Meister
LOST ONE, THE(1951, Ger.)
H. Meixner
VIENNA WALTZES(1961, Aust.)
Karl Meixner
MOSCOW SHANGHAI(1936, Ger.); TESTAMENT OF DR. MABUSE, THE(1943, Ger.)
Juan Carlos Meizveiro
UNDER FIRE(1983)
Bent Mejding
REPTILICUS(1962, U.S./Den.)
Al Mejia
JIM THORPE–ALL AMERICAN(1951)
Alfonso Mejia
LOS OLVIDADOS(1950, Mex.); POR MIS PISTOLAS(1969, Mex.)
Carlos Mejia
FUN IN ACAPULCO(1963)
Griselda Mejia
SANTO CONTRA BLUE DEMON EN LA ATLANTIDA(1968, Mex.); INCREDIBLE
INVASION, THE(1971, Mex./U.S.)
Isabelle Mejias
LUCKY STAR, THE(1980, Can.); JULIE DARLING(1982, Can./Ger.)
1984
BAY BOY(1984, Can.)
Constantine Mejinsky
PARADISE POUR TOUS(1982, Fr.), art d
Damir Mejovsek
LOVES AND TIMES OF SCARAMOUCHE, THE(1976, Ital.)
Andres Mejuto
SWORD OF EL CID, THE(1965, Span./Ital.); YOUNG REBEL, THE(1969, Fr./Ital./
Span.); NUN AT THE CROSSROADS, A(1970, Ital./Span.)
Adolfas Mekas
HALLELUJAH THE HILLS(1963), d,w&ed; GUNS OF THE TREES(1964); DOUBLE-
BARRELLED DETECTIVE STORY, THE(1965), d,w&ed; WINDFLOWERS(1968), a,
d&w, m, ed
Misc. Talkies
BRIG, THE(1965), d
Jonas Mekas
GUNS OF THE TREES(1964), d,w,d&ed, ph
Misc. Talkies
BRIG, THE(1965), d
Harry Mekela
RHINO(1964)
Harry Mekels
DIAMOND SAFARI(1958)
Mel Powell and Orchestra
SONG IS BORN, A(1948)
The Mel Torme Trio
PARDON MY RHYTHM(1944)
Effie Mela
ISLAND OF LOVE(1963)
Ina Mela
CRAZY QUILT, THE(1966)
George Melachrino
WOMAN TO WOMAN(1946, Brit.), m; CODE OF SCOTLAND YARD)(1948), m;
HOUSE OF DARKNESS(1948, Brit.), a, md; NO ORCHIDS FOR MISS BLAND-
ISH(1948, Brit.), m; THINGS HAPPEN AT NIGHT(1948, Brit.), m; NOW BARABBAS
WAS A ROBBER(1949, Brit.), m; SILENT DUST(1949, Brit.), md; OLD MOTHER
RILEY(1952, Brit.), m; EIGHT O'CLOCK WALK(1954, Brit.), m; GAMMA PEOPLE,
THE(1956), m; ODONGO(1956, Brit.), m, md
Joe Melalis
CAT FROM OUTER SPACE, THE(1978)
Fred Melamed
LOVESICK(1983)
I. Melamed
OTHELLO(1960, U.S.S.R.)
Dean Meland
DOUBLES(1978)
Mark Melander
1984
STONE BOY, THE(1984)
Luciano Melani
SEVEN SEAS TO CALAIS(1963, Ital.)
Melanie
ALL THE RIGHT NOISES(1973, Brit.), m
Sy Melano
SHE'S BACK ON BROADWAY(1953)
Tina Melard
HERBIE GOES BANANAS(1980)
Mariangela Melato
LOVE AND ANARCHY(1974, Ital.); NADA GANG, THE(1974, Fr./Ital.); SWEPT
AWAY...BY AN UNUSUAL DESTINY IN THE BLUE SEA OF AUGUST(1975, Ital.);
MOSES(1976, Brit./Ital.); FLASH GORDON(1980); SO FINE(1981)

Melba
NO DRUMS, NO BUGLES(1971), cos, makeup
Martin Melcher
JULIE(1956), p; GREEN-EYED BLONDE, THE(1957), p; TUNNEL OF LOVE,
THE(1958), p; PILLOW TALK(1959), p; MIDNIGHT LACE(1960), p; LOVER COME
BACK(1961), p; JUMBO(1962), p; THAT TOUCH OF MINK(1962), p; MOVE OVER,
DARLING(1963), p; THRILL OF IT ALL, THE(1963), p; DO NOT DISTURB(1965), p;
GLASS BOTTOM BOAT, THE(1966), p; CAPRICE(1967), p; WHERE WERE YOU
WHEN THE LIGHTS WENT OUT?(1968), p; WITH SIX YOU GET EGGROLL(1968), p
Frederic Melchior
ISTANBUL(1957)
Fritz Melchior
JAZZBAND FIVE, THE(1932, Ger,)
Ib Melchior
LIVE FAST, DIE YOUNG(1958), w; WHEN HELL BROKE LOOSE(1958), w; ANGRY
RED PLANET, THE(1959), d, w; JOURNEY TO THE SEVENTH PLANET(1962,
U.S./Swed.), w; REPTILICUS(1962, U.S./Den.), w; ROBINSON CRUSOE ON
MARS(1964), w; TIME TRAVELERS, THE(1964), d&w; PLANET OF THE VAM-
PIRES(1965, U.S./Ital./Span.), w; AMBUSH BAY(1966), w; DEATH RACE 2000(1975),
w
Lauritz Melchior
THRILL OF A ROMANCE(1945); TWO SISTERS FROM BOSTON(1946); THIS TIME
FOR KEEPS(1947); LUXURY LINER(1948); STARS ARE SINGING, THE(1953)
Stephan Meldegg
BOBBY DEERFIELD(1977)
Austin Meldon
SAINTS AND SINNERS(1949, Brit.); NO RESTING PLACE(1952, Brit.); CAPTAIN
LIGHTFOOT(1955)
Dominic Meldowney
1984
LAUGHTER HOUSE(1984, Brit.), m
Max Meldrum
SCOBIE MALONE(1975, Aus.); MY BRILLIANT CAREER(1980, Aus.)
Wendel Meldrum
1984
VAMPING(1984)
Aniello Mele
BLACK MAGIC(1949)
Anielo Mele
SHOE SHINE(1947, Ital.)
Dino Mele
MYTH, THE(1965, Ital.); ONCE UPON A TIME IN THE WEST(1969, U.S./Ital.);
WITCHES, THE(1969, Fr./Ital.); ASH WEDNESDAY(1973)
Nicholas Mele
GOODBYE GIRL, THE(1977); MOMMIE DEAREST(1981); SOME KIND OF HE-
RO(1982)
1984
LONELY GUY, THE(1984); UNFAITHFULLY YOURS(1984)
Nick Mele
WHOLLY MOSES(1980)
Peter Mele
1984
FEAR CITY(1984)
Rodolfo Mele
WEDDING REHEARSAL(1932, Brit.)
Sonny Mele
MADE FOR EACH OTHER(1971), ed
Marta Melecco
EVIL EYE(1964 Ital.)
Ron Melelu
BUGSY MALONE(1976, Brit.)
Bill Melendez
BON VOYAGE, CHARLIE BROWN(AND DON'T COME BACK)*** (1980), a, p, d;
BOY NAMED CHARLIE BROWN, A(1969), a, p, d; SNOOPY, COME HOME(1972), a,
p, d; RACE FOR YOUR LIFE, CHARLIE BROWN(1977), a, p, d
Misc. Talkies
DICK DEADEYE(1977, U.S./Brit.), d
Jeronimo Mitchell Melendez
HEROINA(1965), p&d, w
Maria Melendez
MY TUTOR(1983)
Pamela Melendez
JOHNNY TIGER(1966)
Steve Melendez
BOY NAMED CHARLIE BROWN, A(1969), ed
Carl Melene
SEXTON BLAKE AND THE HOODED TERROR(1938, Brit.)
Patrice Melennec
1984
ONE DEADLY SUMMER(1984, Fr.)
Patrick Melennec
1984
LES COMPERES(1984, Fr.)
Marie Melesch
MISSION TO MOSCOW(1943); NIGHT AND DAY(1946)
Alex Melesh
YELLOW TICKET, THE(1931); GIRL WITHOUT A ROOM(1933); TWO FOR TO-
NIGHT(1935); ARTISTS AND MODELS ABROAD(1938); SWISS MISS(1938); ESPION-
AGE AGENT(1939); GOLDEN BOY(1939); ON YOUR TOES(1939); PARIS
HONEYMOON(1939); SUDDEN MONEY(1939); BEYOND TOMORROW(1940);
LUCKY PARTNERS(1940); ONCE UPON A HONEYMOON(1942); GOVERNMENT
GIRL(1943); HEAVENLY BODY, THE(1943); LADY TAKES A CHANCE, A(1943);
MISSION TO MOSCOW(1943); ONCE UPON A TIME(1944); NIGHT SONG(1947)
Silents
ADVENTURER, THE(1928)
Alexander Melesh
MANHATTAN MELODRAMA(1934); MAN WHO BROKE THE BANK AT MONTE
CARLO, THE(1935); THREE WISE GUYS, THE(1936)

Nikos Meletopoulos
1984
DREAM ONE(1984, Brit./Fr.), spec eff,
Saturno Meletti
JOAN AT THE STAKE(1954, Ital./Fr.)
Darrah Meley
ROMANTIC COMEDY(1983)
John Melfi
DONDI(1961); SEND ME NO FLOWERS(1964)
Leonard Melfi
LADY LIBERTY(1972, Ital./Fr.), w; OH! CALCUTTA!(1972), w; RENT CONTROL(1981)
Austin Melford
WARM CORNER, A(1930, Brit.); NIGHT OF THE GARTER(1933, Brit.), a, w; SOUTHERN MAID, A(1933, Brit.), w; HAPPY(1934, Brit.), w; IT'S A BOY(1934, Brit.), w; ROAD HOUSE(1934, Brit.), w; CAR OF DREAMS(1935, Brit.), d, w; HEAT WAVE(1935, Brit.), w; JACK AHOY!(1935, Brit.), w; MY SONG FOR YOU(1935, Brit.), w; OH DADDY!(1935, Brit.), d, w; PHANTOM LIGHT, THE(1935, Brit.), w; DOMMED CARGO(1936, Brit.), w; FIRST OFFENCE(1936, Brit.), w; IT'S LOVE AGAIN(1936, Brit.), w; RADIO LOVER(1936, Brit.), d; FEATHER YOUR NEST(1937, Brit.), w; GIRL IN THE TAXI(1937, Brit.), w; KEEP FIT(1937, Brit.), w; SHOW GOES ON, THE(1937, Brit.), w; YOU'RE IN THE ARMY NOW(1937, Brit.), w; EVERYTHING HAPPENS TO ME(1938, Brit.), w; I SEE ICE(1938), w; TWO OF US, THE(1938, Brit.), w; THANK EVANS(1938, Brit.), w; TWO OF US, THE(1938, Brit.), w; ANYTHING TO DECLARE?(1939, Brit.), w; GENTLEMAN'S GENTLEMAN, A(1939, Brit.), w; GOOD OLD DAYS, THE(1939, Brit.), w; HIS BROTHER'S KEEPER(1939, Brit.), w; MILL ON THE FLOSS(1939, Brit.), w; MURDER WILL OUT(1939, Brit.), w; SCHOOL FOR HUSBANDS(1939, Brit.), w; DR. O'DOWD(1940, Brit.), w; LAUGH IT OFF(1940, Brit.), w; LET GEORGE DO IT(1940, Brit.), w; OLD MOTHER RILEY IN SOCIETY(1940, Brit.), w; SPARE A COPPER(1940, Brit.), w; THREE COCKEYED SAILORS(1940, Brit.), w; HE FOUND A STAR(1941, Brit.), w; SOUTH AMERICAN GEORGE(1941, Brit.), w; TURNED OUT NICE AGAIN(1941, Brit.), w; SHIPS WITH WINGS(1942, Brit.), w; WE'LL SMILE AGAIN(1942, Brit.), w; OLD MOTHER RILEY, DETECTIVE(1943, Brit.), w; THEATRE ROYAL(1943, Brit.), w; WHEN WE ARE MARRIED(1943, Brit.), w; CHAMPAGNE CHARLIE(1944, Brit.), w; GIVE ME THE STARS(1944, Brit.), w; HEAVEN IS ROUND THE CORNER(1944, Brit.), w; DON CHICAGO(1945, Brit.), w
Silents
BATTLING BUTLER(1926), w
Frank Melford
COWBOY STAR, THE(1936), w; MICHAEL O'HALLORAN(1948), p; MASSACRE RIVER(1949), p; BOY FROM INDIANA(1950), p; FORT DEFIANCE(1951), p; ROGUE RIVER(1951), p; DIAMOND QUEEN, THE(1953), p; BLACK SCORPION, THE(1957), p
George Melford
CHARLATAN, THE(1929), d; LOVE IN THE DESERT(1929), d; SEA FURY(1929), d, w; EAST OF BORNEO(1931), d; HOMICIDE SQUAD(1931), d; VIKING, THE(1931), d; BOILING POINT, THE(1932), d; SCARLET WEEKEND, A(1932), d; COWBOY COUNSELOR(1933), d; DUDE BANDIT, THE(1933), d; ELEVENTH COMMANDMENT(1933), d; OFFICER 13(1933), d; PENAL CODE, THE(1933), d; HIRED WIFE(1934), d; EAST OF JAVA(1935), d; FRONTIER MARSHAL(1939), d; LADY'S FROM KENTUCKY, THE(1939); RULERS OF THE SEA(1939); TOO BUSY TO WORK(1939); BRIGHAM YOUNG–FRONTIERSMAN(1940); MY LITTLE CHICKADEE(1940); REMEMBER THE NIGHT(1940); SAFARI(1940); FLYING CADETS(1941); LADY EVE, THE(1941); MEET JOHN DOE(1941); ROBBERS OF THE RANGE(1941); WILD GEESE CALLING(1941); LONE STAR RANGER(1942); MY GAL SAL(1942); NAVY COMES THROUGH, THE(1942); THAT OTHER WOMAN(1942); VALLEY OF THE SUN(1942); DIXIE DUGAN(1943); GOVERNMENT GIRL(1943); DOUBLE INDEMNITY(1944); HAIL THE CONQUERING HERO(1944); MIRACLE OF MORGAN'S CREEK, THE(1944); PRACTICALLY YOURS(1944); COLONEL EFFINGHAM'S RAID(1945); DIAMOND HORSESHOE(1945); TREE GROWS IN BROOKLYN, A(1945); CALIFORNIA(1946); STRANGE TRIANGLE(1946); CALL NORTHSIDE 777(1948); CRY OF THE CITY(1948); LUCK OF THE IRISH(1948); UNFAITHFULLY YOURS(1948); STRATTON STORY, THE(1949); CARRIE(1952); BLUEPRINT FOR MURDER, A(1953); CITY OF BAD MEN(1953); PRESIDENT'S LADY, THE(1953); ROBE, THE(1953); EGYPTIAN, THE(1954); THERE'S NO BUSINESS LIKE SHOW BUSINESS(1954); WOMAN'S WORLD(1954); PRINCE OF PLAYERS(1955); TEN COMMANDMENTS, THE(1956)
Misc. Talkies
MAN OF ACTION(1933), d
Silents
CELEBRATED CASE, A(1914), d; ARMSTRONG'S WIFE(1915), d; IMMIGRANT, THE(1915), d; MARRIAGE OF KITTY, THE(1915), d; PUPPET CROWN, THE(1915), d; WOMAN, THE(1915), d; EACH PEARL A TEAR(1916), d; JOAN THE WOMAN(1916), d; RACE, THE(1916), d; TENNESSEE'S PARDNER(1916), d; BRAVEST WAY, THE(1918), d; JANE GOES A' WOOING(1919), d; ROUND UP, THE(1920), d; FAITH HEALER, THE(1921), d; SHEIK, THE(1921), d; WISE FOOL, A(1921), d; BURNING SANDS(1922), d; EBB TIDE(1922), d; MORAN OF THE LADY LETTY(1922), d; WOMAN WHO WALKED ALONE, THE(1922), d; JAVA HEAD(1923), d; SALOMY JANE(1923), d; FLAMING BARRIERS(1924), d; WHISPERING SMITH(1926), d; FREEDOM OF THE PRESS(1928), d; LINGERIE(1928), d; SINNERS IN LOVE(1928), d
Misc. Silents
BOER WAR, THE(1914), d; INVISIBLE POWER, THE(1914), d; SHANNON OF THE SIXTH(1914), d; FIGHTING HOPE, THE(1915), d; STOLEN GOODS(1915), d; UNKNOWN, THE(1915), d; YOUNG ROMANCE(1915), d; GUTTER MAGDALENE, THE(1916), d; HOUSE OF THE GOLDEN WINDOWS, THE(1916), d; TO HAVE AND TO HOLD(1916), d; VICTORY OF CONSCIENCE, THE(1916), d; YEARS OF THE LOCUST, THE(1916), d; YELLOW PAWN, THE(1916), d; COST OF HATRED, THE(1917), d; CRYSTAL GAZER, THE(1917), d; EVIL EYE, THE(1917), d; HER STRANGE WEDDING(1917), d; ON THE LEVEL(1917), d; SCHOOL FOR HUSBANDS, A(1917), d; WINNING OF SALLY TEMPLE, THE(1917), d; CITY OF DIM FACE, THE(1918), d; CRUISE OF THE MAKE-BELIEVES, THE(1918), d; HIDDEN PEARLS(1918), d; SANDY(1918), d; SOURCE, THE(1918), d; SUCH A LITTLE PIRATE(1918), d; EVERYWOMAN(1919), d; GOOD GRACIOUS ANNABELLE(1919), d; MEN, WOMEN AND MONEY(1919), d; PETTIGREW'S GIRL(1919), d; SPORTING CHANCE, A(1919), d; TOLD IN THE HILLS(1919), d; BEHOLD MY WIFE!(1920), d; JUCKLINS, THE(1920), d; SEA WOLF, THE(1920), d; GREAT IMPERSONATION, THE(1921), d; LIGHT THAT FAILED, THE(1923), d; YOU CAN'T FOOL YOUR WIFE(1923), d; DAWN OF A TOMORROW, THE(1924), d; TIGER LOVE(1924), d;

FRIENDLY ENEMIES(1925), d; SIMON THE JESTER(1925), d; TOP OF THE WORLD, THE(1925), d; WITHOUT MERCY(1925), d; FLAME OF THE YUKON, THE(1926), d; GOING CROOKED(1926), d; ROCKING MOON(1926), d; MAN'S PAST, A(1927), d; WOMAN I LOVE, THE(1929), d; POOR MILLIONAIRE, THE(1930), d
George H. Melford
LIGHT THAT FAILED, THE(1939)
Silents
NAN OF MUSIC MOUNTAIN(1917), d
Misc. Silents
CALL OF THE EAST, THE(1917), d; SUNSET TRAIL(1917), d; WILD YOUTH(1918), d
Jack Melford
SPORT OF KINGS, THE(1931, Brit.); NIGHT OF THE GARTER(1933, Brit.); BIRDS OF A FEATHER(1935, Brit.); DEPARTMENT STORE(1935, Brit.); HONEYMOON FOR THREE(1935, Brit.); LOOK UP AND LAUGH(1935, Brit.); FIND THE LADY(1936, Brit.); IF I WERE RICH(1936); LUCK OF THE TURF(1936, Brit.); RADIO LOVER(1936, Brit.); COMMAND PERFORMANCE(1937, Brit.); LET'S MAKE A NIGHT OF IT(1937, Brit.); WHEN THIEF MEETS THIEF(1937, Brit.); COMING OF AGE(1938, Brit.); HOLD MY HAND(1938, Brit.); MANY TANKS MR. ATKINS(1938, Brit.); SCRUFFY(1938, Brit.); TOO MANY HUSBANDS(1938, Brit.); ANYTHING TO DECLARE?(1939, Brit.); BRIGGS FAMILY, THE(1940, Brit.); IT'S IN THE AIR(1940, Brit.); SPARE A COPPER(1940, Brit.); SPIDER, THE(1940, Brit.); THEATRE ROYAL(1943, Brit.); NOTORIOUS GENTLEMAN(1945, Brit.); WHEN YOU COME HOME(1947, Brit.); DEVIL'S PLOT, THE(1948, Brit.); OCTOBER MAN, THE(1948, Brit.); MY BROTHER JONATHAN(1949, Brit.); WARNING TO WANTONS, A(1949, Brit.); LAUGHING LADY, THE(1950, Brit.); NO ROOM AT THE INN(1950, Brit.); UP FOR THE CUP(1950, Brit.); BACKGROUND(1953, Brit.); LADYKILLERS, THE(1956, Brit.); END OF THE LINE, THE(1959, Brit.); WEB OF SUSPICION(1959, Brit.); BLUEBEARD'S TEN HONEYMOONS(1960, Brit.); COMPELLED(1960, Brit.); FEET OF CLAY(1960, Brit.); NIGHT TRAIN FOR INVERNESS(1960, Brit.); SENTENCED FOR LIFE(1960, Brit.); FOLLOW THAT MAN(1961, Brit.); TRANSATLANTIC(1961, Brit.); GENTLE TERROR, THE(1962, Brit.); HEIGHTS OF DANGER(1962, Brit.); NIGHT TRAIN TO PARIS(1964, Brit.); SHOT IN THE DARK, A(1964); WALK A TIGHTROPE(1964, U.S./Brit.); LUST FOR A VAMPIRE(1971, Brit.)
Jill Melford
BLACKOUT(1954, Brit.); CONSTANT HUSBAND, THE(1955, Brit.); WILL ANY GENTLEMAN?(1955, Brit.); ABANDON SHIP!(1957, Brit.); OUT OF THE CLOUDS(1957, Brit.); SECOND FIDDLE(1957, Brit.); MURDER AT SITE THREE(1959, Brit.); ESCORT FOR HIRE(1960, Brit.); SERVANT, THE(1964, Brit.); BUNNY LAKE IS MISSING(1965); STITCH IN TIME, A(1967, Brit.); VENGEANCE OF SHE, THE(1968, Brit.); I WANT WHAT I WANT(1972, Brit.); GREEK TYCOON, THE(1978)
Mark Melford
WHO'S YOUR FATHER?(1935, Brit.), w
Silents
FLYING FROM JUSTICE(1915, Brit.), w
Misc. Silents
DISAPPEARANCE OF THE JUDGE, THE(1919, Brit.)
Max Melford
WORLD OWES ME A LIVING, THE(1944, Brit.); HOME SWEET HOME(1945, Brit.)
Gabriel Melgar
JAGUAR LIVES(1979)
Claudine Melgrave
MC CABE AND MRS. MILLER(1971)
Marinelli Meli
NEOPOLITAN CAROUSEL(1961, Ital.)
Joe Melia
FOLLOW A STAR(1959, Brit.); TOO MANY CROOKS(1959, Brit.); FOUR IN THE MORNING(1965, Brit.); SPYLARKS(1965, Brit.); MODESTY BLAISE(1966, Brit.); OH! WHAT A LOVELY WAR(1969, Brit.); ANTONY AND CLEOPATRA(1973, Brit.); SWEENEY(1977, Brit.); ODD JOB, THE(1978, Brit.); WILDCATS OF ST. TRINIAN'S, THE(1980, Brit.); PRIVATES ON PARADE(1982); SIGN OF FOUR, THE(1983, Brit.)
1984
PRIVATES ON PARADE(1984, Brit.)
Alois Melichar
PRIVATE LIFE OF LOUIS XIV(1936, Ger.), m; TRIAL, THE(1948, Aust.), m, md; DREADING LIPS(1958, Ger.), m
Weldon Melick
BACHELOR GIRL, THE(1929), w; ESCAPE TO PARADISE(1939), w
Andre Melies
JUDEX(1966, Fr./Ital.)
Georges Melies
Misc. Silents
CURSE OF GREED, THE(1914, Fr.), d
Donal Meligan
RYAN'S DAUGHTER(1970, Brit.)
Genia Melikova
MAYERLING(1968, Brit./Fr.)
Jules Melillo
WELCOME TO L.A.(1976), cos
John Melin
SMILES OF A SUMMER NIGHT(1957, Swed.)
Max Melin
MARK OF THE DEVIL(1970, Ger./Brit.), art d
Monique Melinand
PASSION OF SLOW FIRE, THE(1962, Fr.); MAGNIFICENT SINNER(1963, Fr.); THIEF OF PARIS, THE(1967, Fr./Ital.); LADY IN THE CAR WITH GLASSES AND A GUN, THE(1970, U.S./Fr.); MAN WITH THE TRANSPLANTED BRAIN, THE(1972, Fr./Ital./Ger.)
Ernesto Melinari
VON RYAN'S EXPRESS(1965)
Max Melinger
YOU HAVE TO RUN FAST(1961)
Jose Melis
SENIOR PROM(1958)
Giovanni Melisendi
LEOPARD, THE(1963, Ital.)
Alex Melish
BIG BROADCAST, THE(1932)

Marie Melish
  CAGED(1950)
Anna Meliskova
  SWEET LIGHT IN A DARK ROOM(1966, Czech.)
Konnell Melissos
  L'IMMORTELLE(1969, Fr./Ital./Turkey), art d
Anna Melita
  ARENA, THE(1973)
Claude Melki
  SIX IN PARIS(1968, Fr.); MAN WITH CONNECTIONS, THE(1970, Fr.)
Lucien Melki
  DANTON(1983)
Michel Melki
1984
  AMERICAN DREAMER(1984)
Gary Melkonian
  GANG THAT COULDN'T SHOOT STRAIGHT, THE(1971)
Joe Mell
  ACTORS AND SIN(1952); DEADLINE–U.S.A.(1952); PRISONER OF ZENDA, THE(1952); BIG HEAT, THE(1953); EASY TO LOVE(1953); MAGNIFICENT OBSESSION(1954); ONE DESIRE(1955); HOT ROD RUMBLE(1957); JEANNE EAGELS(1957); CITY OF FEAR(1959); PILLOW TALK(1959); MOVE OVER, DARLING(1963); POINT BLANK(1967); MURPH THE SURF(1974)
Joseph Mell
  WHEN WORLDS COLLIDE(1951); KID MONK BARONI(1952); MONKEY BUSINESS(1952); FLAME OF CALCUTTA(1953); FORTY-NINTH MAN, THE(1953); LADY WANTS MINK, THE(1953); NAKED ALIBI(1954); STAR IS BORN, A(1954); I WAS A TEENAGE WEREWOLF(1957); MURDER BY CONTRACT(1958); BACK STREET(1961); 36 HOURS(1965); LORD LOVE A DUCK(1966); SWEET CHARITY(1969); SKI BUM, THE(1971)
Marisa Mell
  5 SINNERS(1961, Ger.); ORDERED TO LOVE(1963, Ger.); FRENCH DRESSING(1964, Brit.); CASANOVA '70(1965, Ital.); CITY OF FEAR(1965, Brit.); MASQUERADE(1965, Brit.); OBJECTIVE 500 MILLION(1966, Fr.); SECRET AGENT SUPER DRAGON(1966, Fr./Ital./Ger./Monaco); ANYONE CAN PLAY(1968, Ital.); DANGER: DIABOLIK(1968, Ital./Fr.); MAHOGANY(1975); SOME LIKE IT COOL(1979, Ger./Aust./Ital./Fr.)
Randle Mell
1984
  COTTON CLUB, THE(1984)
Eloy Mella
  MIGHTY URSUS(1962, Ital./Span.), ph; INVINCIBLE GLADIATOR, THE(1963, c.u. Ital./Span.), ph; GLADIATORS 7(1964, Span./Ital.), ph; SECRET SEVEN, THE(1966, Ital./Span.), ph
Mary Lou Mellace
  B.S. I LOVE YOU(1971)
Robert Mellard
  SANTEE(1973)
Emby Mellay
  TOUCH OF SATAN, THE(1971)
Misc. Talkies
  TOUCH OF SATAN, THE(1974)
Gil Melle
  ANDROMEDA STRAIN, THE(1971), m; ORGANIZATION, THE(1971), m; SAVAGE IS LOOSE, THE(1974), m; ULTIMATE WARRIOR, THE(1975), m; EMBRYO(1976), m; SENTINEL, THE(1977), m; STARSHIP INVASIONS(1978, Can.), m; BORDERLINE(1980), m; BLOOD BEACH(1981), m; LAST CHASE, THE(1981), m
Albert Mellen
  OUTRAGE(1950)
Chase Mellen III
  STOOLIE, THE(1972), p
Leonard Mellen
  TILL THE CLOUDS ROLL BY(1946)
Ronnie Mellen
  STOOLIE, THE(1972)
Victor Melleney
  KILLER FORCE(1975, Switz./Ireland)
Max Mellenger
  PERFECT STRANGERS(1950)
Harro Meller
  GANGWAY FOR TOMORROW(1943); COUNTER-ATTACK(1945); HOUSE ON 92ND STREET, THE(1945); JEWELS OF BRANDENBURG(1947)
Harry Meller
  ROGUES' REGIMENT(1948)
Pat Meller
  THERE'S ALWAYS TOMORROW(1956)
Raquel Meller
Misc. Silents
  LES OPPRIMES(1923, Fr.); VIOLETTES IMPERIALES(1924, Fr.); LA TERRE PROMISE(1925, Fr.); CARMEN(1928, Fr.)
Robert Meller
  TOMORROW'S YOUTH(1935), w
William Meller
  ELMER AND ELSIE(1934), ph; AMBUSH(1939), ph
William C. Meller
  COLLEGE HOLIDAY(1936), ph
Oscar Melli
  SUMMERSKIN(1962, Arg.), ph
Judith Mellics
  STEPPENWOLF(1974)
Bill Mellin
  PIRANHA(1978), art d
Kerry Mellin
  PIRANHA(1978), art d
Leonard Mellin
  MRS. PARKINGTON(1944); THEY WERE EXPENDABLE(1945); HOODLUM SAINT, THE(1946)
Max Mellin
  RED-DRAGON(1967, Ital./Ger./US), art d

Robert Mellin
  SON OF A GUNFIGHTER(1966, U.S./Span.), m; THE DIRTY GAME(1966, Fr./Ital./Ger.), m
Ursula Mellin
  DEEP END(1970 Ger./U.S.)
Shirley Melline
  MY FAIR LADY(1964); LADY SINGS THE BLUES(1972)
Richard Melling
  HAMLET(1976, Brit.), ed
Fred Mellinger
  BEASTS OF BERLIN(1939)
Frederic Mellinger
  DISPATCH FROM REUTERS, A(1940)
Leonie Mellinger
  MEMOIRS OF A SURVIVOR(1981, Brit.)
1984
  GHOST DANCE(1984, Brit.); MEMED MY HAWK(1984, Brit.)
Max Mellinger
  I PASSED FOR WHITE(1960); RETURN TO PEYTON PLACE(1961); SECRET OF DEEP HARBOR(1961); WHEN THE CLOCK STRIKES(1961); INCIDENT IN AN ALLEY(1962); SAINTLY SINNERS(1962)
Michael Mellinger
  GOLDEN MASK, THE(1954, Brit.); RADIO CAB MURDER(1954, Brit.); THEY WHO DARE(1954, Brit.); THE BEACHCOMBER(1955, Brit.); STARS IN YOUR EYES(1956, Brit.); SECRET MAN, THE(1958, Brit.); THREE CROOKED MEN(1958, Brit.); MAN ON A STRING(1960); PASSWORD IS COURAGE, THE(1962, Brit.); SIEGE OF THE SAXONS(1963, Brit.); GOLDFINGER(1964, Brit.); IT HAPPENED HERE(1966, Brit.); CARRY ON, UP THE KHYBER(1968, Brit.); PUPPET ON A CHAIN(1971, Brit.); AWAKENING, THE(1980); EYE OF THE NEEDLE(1981)
1984
  UNTIL SEPTEMBER(1984)
Ronald L. Mellinger
  STRAIGHT TIME(1978)
Susan Mellinger
  ANNIE HALL(1977)
Fuller Mellish
  CRIME WITHOUT PASSION(1934)
Silents
  ESMERALDA(1915); ETERNAL CITY, THE(1915); ROYAL FAMILY, A(1915); POWER OF DECISION, THE(1917); TRAIL OF THE SHADOW, THE(1917); DIANE OF STAR HOLLOW(1921); SCARAB RING, THE(1921); SINGLE TRACK, THE(1921)
Misc. Silents
  DANCING GIRL, THE(1915); GAMBLER'S ADVOCATE(1915); MAYBLOSSOM(1917); UNFORSEEN, THE(1917); INNER VOICE, THE(1920)
Fuller Mellish, Jr.
  APPLAUSE(1929); ROADHOUSE NIGHTS(1930); SARAH AND SON(1930)
Pamela Mellish
  NIGHT GAMES(1980)
Breno Mello
  BLACK ORPHEUS(1959 Fr./Ital./Braz.)
Jay Mello
  JAWS(1975)
The Mello Men
  GLENN MILLER STORY, THE(1953); LADY AND THE TRAMP(1955)
The Mellomen
  ALICE IN WONDERLAND(1951)
The Mellomen
  SWORD IN THE STONE, THE(1963)
Al Mellon
  MOB, THE(1951)
Francis Mellon
  LADY FRANKENSTEIN(1971, Ital.), art d
John Mellon
  LONGEST DAY, THE(1962)
Lydia Mellon
  VAMPIRE, THE(1968, Mex.)
Amedeo Mellone
  CARTHAGE IN FLAMES(1961, Fr./Ital.), art d; QUEEN OF THE PIRATES(1961, Ital./Ger.), set d; VAMPIRE AND THE BALLERINA, THE(1962, Ital.), art d; CAESAR THE CONQUEROR(1963, Ital.), art d; RAGE OF THE BUCCANEERS(1963, Ital.), art d; SECRET MARK OF D'ARTAGNAN, THE(1963, Fr./Ital.), art d; RED LIPS(1964, Fr./Ital.), art d; TIGER OF THE SEVEN SEAS(1964, Fr./Ital.), art d; HERCULES AGAINST THE MOON MEN(1965, Fr./Ital.), art d; SILHOUETTES(1982), art d; NANA(1983, Ital.), prod d
Ardiata Mellonino
Silents
  HER ELEPHANT MAN(1920)
Christie Mellor
1984
  OH GOD! YOU DEVIL(1984)
Douglas Mellor
  BEAST OF YUCCA FLATS, THE(1961)
Edith Mellor
Silents
  PROFLIGATE, THE(1917, Brit.)
Misc. Silents
  BECAUSE(1921, Brit.), d
Harro Mellor
  NIGHT IN CASABLANCA, A(1946)
James Mellor
  DEPTH CHARGE(1960, Brit.), p; FLIGHT FROM SINGAPORE(1962, Brit.), p; PERSECUTION AND ASSASSINATION OF JEAN-PAUL MARAT AS PERFORMED BY THE INMATES OF THE ASYLUM OF CHARENTON UNDER THE DIRECTION OF THE MARQUIS DE SADE, THE(1967, Brit.); GREAT CATHERINE(1968, Brit.); LAST SHOT YOU HEAR, THE(1969, Brit.); OBLONG BOX, THE(1969, Brit.); NIGHT AFTER NIGHT(1970, Brit.), p; PRAISE MARX AND PASS THE AMMUNITION(1970, Brit.)

Steve Mellor
JAWS 3-D(1983)

William Mellor
ENTER MADAME(1935), ph; HOME ON THE RANGE(1935), ph; COLLEGIATE(1936), ph; SKY PARADE(1936), ph; CHAMPAGNE WALTZ(1937), ph; EXCLUSIVE(1937), ph; ROMANCE IN THE DARK(1938), ph; HOTEL IMPERIAL(1939), ph; MAGNIFICENT FRAUD, THE(1939), ph; $1,000 A TOUCHDOWN(1939), ph; GREAT McGINTY, THE(1940), ph; BIRTH OF THE BLUES(1941), ph; FLEET'S IN, THE(1942), ph; MY FAVORITE BLONDE(1942), ph; ROAD TO MOROCCO(1942), ph; DIXIE(1943), ph; ABIE'S IRISH ROSE(1946), ph; SENATOR WAS INDISCREET, THE(1947), ph; TOO LATE FOR TEARS(1949), ph; ACROSS THE WIDE MISSOURI(1951), ph; IT'S A BIG COUNTRY(1951), ph; SOLDIERS THREE(1951), ph; UNKNOWN MAN, THE(1951), ph; CARBINE WILLIAMS(1952), ph; MY MAN AND I(1952), ph; SKIRTS AHOY!(1952), ph; AFFAIRS OF DOBIE GILLIS, THE(1953), ph; BIG LEAGUER(1953), ph; GIVE A GIRL A BREAK(1953), ph; NAKED SPUR, THE(1953), ph; LAST FRONTIER, THE(1955), ph; BACK FROM ETERNITY(1956), ph; JOHNNY CONCHO(1956), ph; LOVE IN THE AFTERNOON(1957), ph; PEYTON PLACE(1957), ph

William C. Mellor
WAGON WHEELS(1934), ph; CAR 99(1935), ph; WINGS IN THE DARK(1935), ph; WITHOUT REGRET(1935), ph; POPPY(1936), ph; SON COMES HOME, A(1936), ph; WOMAN TRAP(1936), ph; MAKE WAY FOR TOMORROW(1937), ph; THRILL OF A LIFETIME(1937), ph; BULLDOG DRUMMOND IN AFRICA(1938), ph; RIDE A CROOKED MILE(1938), ph; STOLEN HEAVEN(1938), ph; DISPUTED PASSAGE(1939), ph; UNDERCOVER DOCTOR(1939), ph; COMIN' ROUND THE MOUNTAIN(1940), ph; MOON OVER BURMA(1940), ph; ROAD TO SINGAPORE(1940), ph; TYPHOON(1940), ph; LAS VEGAS NIGHTS(1941), ph; REACHING FOR THE SUN(1941), ph; COMMANDOS STRIKE AT DAWN, THE(1942), ph; GREAT MAN'S LADY, THE(1942), ph; BLAZE OF NOON(1947), ph; MAN-EATER OF KUMAON(1948), ph; TEXAS, BROOKLYN AND HEAVEN(1948), ph; LOVE HAPPY(1949), ph; PLACE IN THE SUN, A(1951), ph; WESTWARD THE WOMEN(1951), ph; ALASKA SEAS(1954), ph; BAD DAY AT BLACK ROCK(1955), ph; GIANT(1956), ph; SING, BOY, SING(1958), ph; BEST OF EVERYTHING, THE(1959), ph; COMPULSION(1959), ph; DIARY OF ANNE FRANK, THE(1959), ph; WOMAN OBSESSED(1959), ph; CRACK IN THE MIRROR(1960), ph; ONE FOOT IN HELL(1960), ph; BIG GAMBLE, THE(1961), ph; WILD IN THE COUNTRY(1961), ph; MR. HOBBS TAKES A VACATION(1962), ph; STATE FAIR(1962), ph; GREATEST STORY EVER TOLD, THE(1965), ph

Marthe Mellot
LE DENIER MILLIARDAIRE(1934, Fr.); CAGE OF NIGHTINGALES, A(1947, Fr.)

Yolande Mellot
UNFINISHED BUSINESS(1941)

Gayle Mellott
HARD GUY(1941); MANPOWER(1941); SAINT IN PALM SPRINGS, THE(1941); TOM, DICK AND HARRY(1941)

Greg Mellott
FRATERNITY ROW(1977), set d

The Mellowkings
SWEET BEAT(1962, Brit.)

Jeff Mellquist
SECRET OF NIMH, THE(1982), ph

Borje Mellvig
LOVING COUPLES(1966, Swed.)

Andree Melly
SO LITTLE TIME(1953, Brit.); SECRET TENT, THE(1956, Brit.); NOVEL AFFAIR, A(1957, Brit.); NOWHERE TO GO(1959, Brit.); BEYOND THE CURTAIN(1960, Brit.); BIG DAY, THE(1960, Brit.); BRIDES OF DRACULA, THE(1960, Brit.); HORROR OF IT ALL, THE(1964, Brit.)

George Melly
SMASHING TIME(1967 Brit.), w; TAKE A GIRL LIKE YOU(1970, Brit,), w

Oscar Melly
ALIAS BIG SHOT(1962, Argen.), ph

Larry "Bud" Melman [DeForest]
FIRST TIME, THE(1983)

Umberto Melnati
TOO BAD SHE'S BAD(1954, Ital.); GOLDEN ARROW, THE(1964, Ital.)

Daniel Melnick
STRAW DOGS(1971, Brit.), p; FIRST FAMILY(1980), p; MAKING LOVE(1982), p

Joshua Melnick
QUEST FOR FIRE(1982, Fr./Can.)

Mark Melnick
UNCOMMON VALOR(1983), ed

Benjamin Melniker
SWAMP THING(1982), p

Alexander Melnikov
BALTIC DEPUTY(1937, USSR)

Ye. Melnikova
DESTINY OF A MAN(1961, USSR); HOME FOR TANYA, A(1961, USSR); WHEN THE TREES WERE TALL(1965, USSR); MEET ME IN MOSCOW(1966, USSR)

Tom Melody
2000 YEARS LATER(1969)

Tony Melody
STICK UP, THE(1978, Brit.); YANKS(1979)

Henri Melon
1984
SUGAR CANE ALLEY(1984, Fr.)

Jayne Melon
EVEL KNIEVEL(1971)

Michael Melon
TWO OF A KIND(1983)

Hal Melone
DOUBLE LIFE, A(1947); YOU GOTTA STAY HAPPY(1948)

William Brown Meloney
BELOVED ENEMY(1936), w; CLAUDIA AND DAVID(1946), w; SECRET HEART, THE(1946), w

"Little" Freddie Meloni
HONEYMOON DEFERRED(1951, Brit.)

Erkki Meloski
MAKE LIKE A THIEF(1966, Fin.), m

Eva Melova
MRS. FITZHERBERT(1950, Brit.), cos

Robin Meloy
HOUSE ON SORORITY ROW, THE(1983)

Frank Melrose
Silents
EUGENE ARAM(1914, Brit.)

Frank Melroyd
KISS ME, SERGEANT(1930, Brit.); NOT SO QUIET ON THE WESTERN FRONT(1930, Brit.); WHY SAILORS LEAVE HOME(1930, Brit.)

Christian Melsen
LAFAYETTE(1963, Fr.); LOVE ON A PILLOW(1963, Fr./Ital.); WOMEN AND WAR(1965, Fr.); WEEKEND AT DUNKIRK(1966, Fr./Ital.)

Charlie Melson
FLIRTING WITH FATE(1938), w; GLADIATOR, THE(1938), w

John Melson
BATTLE OF THE BULGE(1965), w; SAVAGE PAMPAS(1967, Span./Arg.), w; CAULDRON OF BLOOD(1971, Span.), w; LOVE AND BULLETS(1979, Brit.), w

Ira Meltcher
ISLAND OF THE DOOMED(1968, Span./Ger.), w

Ann Melton
TWO TICKETS TO BROADWAY(1951)

Arthur Melton
GIRL IS MINE, THE(1950, Brit.)

Barry Melton
GAS-S-S-S!(1970), m

Barry "the Fish" Melton
MORE AMERICAN GRAFFITI(1979)

Carolyn Melton
THUNDER IN CAROLINA(1960)

Frank Melton
ACE OF ACES(1933); STATE FAIR(1933); DAVID HARUM(1934); HANDY ANDY(1934); JUDGE PRIEST(1934); STAND UP AND CHEER(1934 80m FOX bw); WHITE PARADE, THE(1934); WORLD MOVES ON, THE(1934); 365 NIGHTS IN HOLLYWOOD(1934); BACHELOR OF ARTS(1935); COUNTY CHAIRMAN, THE(1935); DARING YOUNG MAN, THE(1935); FARMER TAKES A WIFE, THE(1935); WELCOME HOME(1935); $10 RAISE(1935); AUGUST WEEK-END(1936, Brit.); RETURN OF JIMMY VALENTINE, THE(1936); THEY MET IN A TAXI(1936); TRAITOR, THE(1936); AFFAIRS OF CAPPY RICKS(1937); DAMAGED GOODS(1937); GLORY TRAIL, THE(1937); OUTCAST(1937); TOO MANY WIVES(1937); TROUBLE AT MIDNIGHT(1937); WILD AND WOOLLY(1937); WINGS OVER HONOLULU(1937); BUCCANEER, THE(1938); FRESHMAN YEAR(1938); RIDERS OF THE BLACK HILLS(1938); CAT AND THE CANARY, THE(1939); NIGHT OF NIGHTS, THE(1939); YOU CAN'T CHEAT AN HONEST MAN(1939); FIGHTING 69TH, THE(1940); RETURN OF FRANK JAMES, THE(1940); SECOND CHORUS(1940); POT O' GOLD(1941); STRAWBERRY BLONDE, THE(1941); TANKS A MILLION(1941); THEY MEET AGAIN(1941); LOVES OF EDGAR ALLAN POE, THE(1942); WRECKING CREW(1942); CHATTERBOX(1943); MAN WHO WALKED ALONE, THE(1945); WOMAN IN THE WINDOW, THE(1945); WONDER MAN(1945); DO YOU LOVE ME?(1946); DAREDEVILS OF THE CLOUDS(1948)
Misc. Talkies
SILKS AND SADDLES(1938)

Gregory Melton
1984
CRIMES OF PASSION(1984), set d

James Melton
STARS OVER BROADWAY(1935); SING ME A LOVE SONG(1936); MELODY FOR TWO(1937); ZIEGFELD FOLLIES(1945); RESCUERS, THE(1977), ed; FOX AND THE HOUND, THE(1981), ed

Ray Melton
THUNDER IN CAROLINA(1960)

Sid Melton
JOHNNY DOESN'T LIVE HERE ANY MORE(1944); GEORGE WHITE'S SCANDALS(1945); CLOSE-UP(1948); KNOCK ON ANY DOOR(1949); ON THE TOWN(1949); TOUGH ASSIGNMENT(1949); WHITE HEAT(1949); EVERYBODY'S DANCIN'(1950); HI-JACKED(1950); HOLIDAY RHYTHM(1950); MOTOR PATROL(1950); RADAR SECRET SERVICE(1950); RETURN OF JESSE JAMES, THE(1950); WESTERN PACIFIC AGENT(1950); FINGERPRINTS DON'T LIE(1951); LEAVE IT TO THE MARINES(1951); LEMON DROP KID, THE(1951); LOST CONTINENT(1951); MASK OF THE DRAGON(1951); SAVAGE DRUMS(1951); STEEL HELMET, THE(1951); STOP THAT CAB(1951); THREE DESPERATE MEN(1951); SKY HIGH(1952); TENDER HEARTS(1955); EDGE OF HELL(1956); BEAU JAMES(1957); JOKER IS WILD, THE(1957); UNDER FIRE(1957); THUNDERING JETS(1958); ALIAS JESSE JAMES(1959); LONE TEXAN(1959); ATOMIC SUBMARINE, THE(1960); RISE AND FALL OF LEGS DIAMOND, THE(1960); IT TAKES ALL KINDS(1969, U.S./Aus.); LADY SINGS THE BLUES(1972); HIT(1973); SHEILA LEVINE IS DEAD AND LIVING IN NEW YORK(1975); SIX PACK ANNIE(1975)
Misc. Talkies
GAME SHOW MODELS(1977)

Sidney Melton
SHADOW OF THE THIN MAN(1941); BLONDIE GOES TO COLLEGE(1942); DR. BROADWAY(1942); GIRLS IN CHAINS(1943); MUG TOWN(1943); SUSPENSE(1946); GANGSTER, THE(1947); KILROY WAS HERE(1947); TREASURE OF MONTE CRISTO(1949); GARMENT JUNGLE, THE(1957)

Troy Melton
DAVY CROCKETT AND THE RIVER PIRATES(1956); FIREBRAND, THE(1962); DAY MARS INVADED EARTH, THE(1963); YOUNG GUNS OF TEXAS(1963); CYBORG 2087(1966); I WANNA HOLD YOUR HAND(1978)

Jim Meltor
ROBIN HOOD(1973), ed

Lewis Meltzer
GOLDEN BOY(1939), w; THOSE HIGH GREY WALLS(1939), w; LADY IN QUESTION, THE(1940), w; TEXAS(1941), w; FIRST COMES COURAGE(1943), w; ONCE UPON A TIME(1944), w; LADIES' MAN(1947), w; MAN-EATER OF KUMAON(1948), w; TEXAS, BROOKLYN AND HEAVEN(1948), w; LADY GAMBLES, THE(1949), w; COMMANCHE TERRITORY(1950), w; ALONG THE GREAT DIVIDE(1951), w; DESERT LEGION(1953), w; JAZZ SINGER, THE(1953), w; SHARK RIVER(1953), w; MAN WITH THE GOLDEN ARM, THE(1955), w; NEW ORLEANS UNCENSORED(1955), w;

AUTUMN LEAVES(1956), w; BROTHERS RICO, THE(1957), w; HIGH SCHOOL CONFIDENTIAL(1958), w

Louis Meltzer
BEAT GENERATION, THE(1959), w

Robert Meltzer
JOURNEY INTO FEAR(1942)
1984
MAKING THE GRADE(1984)

S. Lewis Meltzer
NEW YORK TOWN(1941), w; TUTTLES OF TAHITI(1942), w

Jean-Louis Melun
MAIS OU ET DONC ORNICAR(1979, Fr.), ph

Gino Melvazzi
X Y & ZEE(1972, Brit.)

Alan Melville
CASTLE IN THE AIR(1952, Brit.), w; FOUR AGAINST FATE(1952, Brit.), w; HOT ICE(1952, Brit.), w; SIMON AND LAURA(1956, Brit.), w; AS LONG AS THEY'RE HAPPY(1957, Brit.), w

Colette Melville
FLAMINGO AFFAIR, THE(1948, Brit.); NAUGHTY ARLETTE(1951, Brit.)

Emilie Melville
ILLUSION(1929)

Esme Melville
DIMBOOLA(1979, Aus.)

Frederick Melville
Silents
REBECCA THE JEWESS(1913, Brit.), w

George D. Melville
Misc. Silents
LIGHT OF HAPPINESS, THE(1916); WOMAN IN 47, THE(1916)

Herman Melville
MOBY DICK(1930), w; LAST OF THE PAGANS(1936), w; OMOO OMOO, THE SHARK GOD(1949), w; MOBY DICK(1956, Brit.), w; ENCHANTED ISLAND(1958), w; BILLY BUDD(1962), w; BARTLEBY(1970, Brit.), w
Silents
SEA BEAST, THE(1926), w

Jean-Pierre Melville
ORPHEUS(1950, Fr.); LES ENFANTS TERRIBLES(1952, Fr.), p&d, w; BREATH-LESS(1959, Fr.); FINGERMAN, THE(1963, Fr.), d&w; LANDRU(1963, Fr./Ital); DOULOS-THE FINGER MAN(1964, Fr./Ital.), d&w; L'ARMEE DES OMBRES(1969, Fr./Ital.), d&w; GODSON, THE(1972, Ital./Fr.), d, w; COP, A(1973, Fr.), d, w; DIRTY MONEY(1977, Fr.), d&w

Jose Melville
Misc. Silents
PATH OF DARKNESS, THE(1916); ROADSIDE IMPRESARIO, A(1917)

Josie Melville
Silents
TREASURE ISLAND(1920)

June Melville
PARACHUTE NURSE(1942)

Ken Melville
TWICE UPON A TIME(1983), m

Kenneth Melville
TWICE UPON A TIME(1953, Brit.)

Miranda Melville
BROTHERS AND SISTERS(1980, Brit.), art d

Olive Melville
JUBILEE WINDOW(1935, Brit.); STOKER, THE(1935, Brit.); HOWARD CASE, THE(1936, Brit.); IN THE SOUP(1936, Brit.)

Pauline Melville
FAR FROM THE MADDING CROWD(1967, Brit.); ULYSSES(1967, U.S./Brit.); BRITTANIA HOSPITAL(1982, Brit.)
1984
SCRUBBERS(1984, Brit.)

Rosa Melville
Silents
MAN'S LAW AND GOD'S(1922)

Sam Melville
HOUR OF THE GUN(1967); THOMAS CROWN AFFAIR, THE(1968); BIG WEDNES-DAY(1978)

Walter Melville
Silents
REBECCA THE JEWESS(1913, Brit.), w; GIRL WHO TOOK THE WRONG TURN-ING, THE(1915, Brit.), w; SHOPSOILED GIRL, THE(1915, Brit.), w

Wilbert Melville
Misc. Silents
SAVED FROM THE HAREM(1915), d; TERRIBLE ONE, THE(1915), d; SOLDIER'S SONS(1916), d

Winifred Melville
BLACK MEMORY(1947, Brit.); GREED OF WILLIAM HART, THE(1948, Brit.)

Allan Melvin
WITH SIX YOU GET EGGROLL(1968)

Donnie Melvin
LADYBUG, LADYBUG(1963); TRUMAN CAPOTE'S TRILOGY(1969)

G. S. Melvin
VARIETY PARADE(1936, Brit.)

Michael Melvin
MOTEL HELL(1980)

Murray Melvin
PETTICOAT PIRATES(1961, Brit.); RISK, THE(1961, Brit.); CONCRETE JUNGLE, THE(1962, Brit.); DAMN THE DEFIANT!(1962, Brit.); TASTE OF HONEY, A(1962, Brit.); CEREMONY, THE(1963, U.S./Span.); SPARROWS CAN'T SING(1963, Brit.); ALFIE(1966, Brit.); KALEIDOSCOPE(1966, Brit.); SOLO FOR SPARROW(1966, Brit.); SMASHING TIME(1967 Brit.); FIXER, THE(1968); START THE REVOLUTION WITH-OUT ME(1970); BOY FRIEND, THE(1971, Brit.); DAY IN THE DEATH OF JOE EGG, A(1972, Brit.); GAWAIN AND THE GREEN KNIGHT(1973, Brit.); GHOST STORY(1974, Brit.); BARRY LYNDON(1975, Brit.); BAWDY ADVENTURES OF TOM JONES, THE(1976, Brit.); SHOUT AT THE DEVIL(1976, Brit.); GULLIVER'S TRAVELS(1977, Brit., Bel.); CROSSED SWORDS(1978); STORIES FROM A FLYING TRUNK(1979, Brit.); NUTCRACKER(1982, Brit.)

1984
SACRED HEARTS(1984, Brit.)
Misc. Talkies
DEVILS, THE(1971)

Ruby Melvin
HAUNTING OF M, THE(1979)

Susan Melvin
LADYBUG, LADYBUG(1963)

Michael Melvion
KING OF THE MOUNTAIN(1981), m

Michael Melvoin
ASHANTI(1979), m

Glenn Melvyn
GREAT GAME, THE(1953, Brit.); LOVE MATCH, THE(1955, Brit.), a, w; RAMSBOT-TOM RIDES AGAIN(1956, Brit.), a, w

Glynn Melvyn
OVER THE ODDS(1961, Brit.)

Jacques Mely
SHOOT THE PIANO PLAYER(1962, Fr.), art d

V. Melyedyev
LAD FROM OUR TOWN(1941, USSR)

Julian Melzack
ANGELA(1977, Can.), p; TOMORROW NEVER COMES(1978, Brit./Can.), p

B.F. Melzer
JOE PALOOKA IN THE SQUARED CIRCLE(1950), w

Eberhard Melzer
1984
LOOSE CONNECTIONS(1984, Brit.)

Lewis Melzer
DESTROYER(1943), w

Margarete Melzer
M(1933, Ger.)

Members of the International Brigade
MAN'S HOPE(1947, Span.)

Members of the Oakland Hell's Angels
HELL'S ANGELS '69(1969)

Tito Memminger
FORTY POUNDS OF TROUBLE(1962)

George Memmoli
MEAN STREETS(1973); PHANTOM OF THE PARADISE(1974); HUSTLE(1975); HOT POTATO(1976); ROCKY(1976); ST. IVES(1976); FARMER, THE(1977); NEW YORK, NEW YORK(1977); WORLD'S GREATEST LOVER, THE(1977); BLUE COLLAR(1978); HOT TOMORROWS(1978); LUNCH WAGON(1981)

Milda Memonas
BLAST OF SILENCE(1961)

E. Memtchenko
NO GREATER LOVE(1944, USSR)

The Kings Men
IT HAPPENED ON 5TH AVENUE(1947)

Men of the Japan Karate Association
KARATE, THE HAND OF DEATH(1961)

Men of the U.S. Marine Corps
D.I., THE(1957)

James Mena
MAYOR OF 44TH STREET, THE(1942)

Salvador Lozano Mena
LITTLE ANGEL(1961, Mex.), art d; YOUNG AND EVIL(1962, Mex.), art d

Roger Menache
MR. MOM(1983)

Sam Menacker
ABBOTT AND COSTELLO IN THE FOREIGN LEGION(1950)

Sammy Menacker
ALIAS THE CHAMP(1949); MIGHTY JOE YOUNG(1949); BODYHOLD(1950)

I. Menaker
MORNING STAR(1962, USSR), w

Paul Menant
AMOUR, AMOUR(1937, Fr.)

Connie Menard
TWILIGHT ON THE RIO GRANDE(1947)

Jim Menard
WILD RIVER(1960)

Ray Menard
GIRL IN TROUBLE(1963); SOME OF MY BEST FRIENDS ARE...(1971), art d

Tiana Menard
MISSION TO MOSCOW(1943)

Tina Menard
CHEYENNE TORNADO(1935); TRAITOR, THE(1936); DAUGHTER OF SHANG-HAI(1937); LONG VOYAGE HOME, THE(1940); NOTORIOUS(1946); CASBAH(1948); WE WERE STRANGERS(1949); CAGED(1950); SURRENDER(1950); WHERE DAN-GER LIVES(1950); SALOME(1953); SECOND CHANCE(1953); JUBILEE TRAIL(1954); GREEN FIRE(1955); GIANT(1956); ESCAPE FROM RED ROCK(1958); MAN OF THE WEST(1958); DIME WITH A HALO(1963); SPLIT, THE(1968); CALIFORNIA SUI-TE(1978); STRAIGHT TIME(1978); HARD COUNTRY(1981)
Misc. Talkies
LOSER'S END(1934)

Wilmon Menard
6000 ENEMIES(1939), w

Milton Menasco
Silents
NOTORIOUS MISS LISLE, THE(1920), art d; GIRL OF THE GOLDEN WEST, THE(1923), art d; HUNTRESS, THE(1923), art d; ISLE OF LOST SHIPS, THE(1923), set d; LOVE'S WILDERNESS(1924), art d; PAINTED PEOPLE(1924), art d; SO BIG(1924), art d; AS MAN DESIRES(1925), art d; IF I MARRY AGAIN(1925), art d; KNOCKOUT, THE(1925), art d; LOST WORLD, THE(1925), set d; NECESSARY EVIL, THE(1925), art d; UNGUARDED HOUR, THE(1925), art d; PUPPETS(1926), art d; LORNA DOONE(1927), set d & cos

Michael Menaugh
DOCTOR FAUSTUS(1967, Brit.)

1984
BLAME IT ON RIO(1984)
George Mence
RHYTHM IN THE CLOUDS(1937), w
Carmen Menchaca
THAT MAN IN ISTANBUL(1966, Fr./Ital./Span.), makeup
Joseph Menchen
Misc. Silents
MIRACLE, THE(1912, Aust.), d
Hy Mencher
SO FINE(1981)
Ron Menchine
SEDUCTION OF JOE TYNAN, THE(1979)
Mirella Mencio
DILLINGER IS DEAD(1969, Ital.), ed
Robin Mencken
1984
THIS IS SPINAL TAP(1984)
Enrico Menczer
HERCULES' PILLS(1960, Ital.), ph; THE DIRTY GAME(1966, Fr./Ital./Ger.), ph; DEAD ARE ALIVE, THE(1972, Yugo./Ger./Ital.), ph; CHOSEN, THE(1978, Brit./Ital.), ph
Erico Menczer
CRAZY DESIRE(1964, Ital.), ph; FASCIST, THE(1965, Ital.), ph; HOURS OF LOVE, THE(1965, Ital.), ph; LITTLE NUNS, THE(1965, Ital.), ph; HIRED KILLER, THE(1967, Fr./Ital.), ph; OPERATION ST. PETER'S(1968, Ital.), ph; MACHINE GUN McCAIN(1970, Ital.), ph; CAT O'NINE TAILS(1971, Ital./Ger./Fr.), ph
Daniel Mendaille
TESTAMENT OF DR. MABUSE, THE(1943, Ger.); LOLA MONTES(1955, Fr./Ger.); MODIGLIANI OF MONTPARNASSE(1961, Fr./Ital.)
Danielle Mendaille
STOLEN LIFE(1939, Brit.)
Robert Mendel
DEMENTED(1980)
Stephen Mendel
TOMORROW NEVER COMES(1978, Brit./Can.); FIRE AND ICE(1983)
Mendel's Female Sextette
HONEYMOON HOTEL(1946, Brit.)
Art Mendelli
WORLD'S GREATEST LOVER, THE(1977)
Jack Mendelsohn
YELLOW SUBMARINE(1958, Brit.), w
Anthony Mendelson
IT ALWAYS RAINS ON SUNDAY(1949, Brit.), cos; SCOTT OF THE ANTARCTIC(1949, Brit.), cos; CHASE A CROOKED SHADOW(1958, Brit.), cos; MAN IN THE MOON(1961, Brit.), cos; BILLY BUDD(1962), cos; MAGUS, THE(1968, Brit.), cos; JANE EYRE(1971, Brit.), cos; BRIDGE TOO FAR, A(1977, Brit.), cos; GULLIVER'S TRAVELS(1977, Brit., Bel.), cos; ROUGH CUT(1980, Brit.), cos
Herbert E. Mendelson
AMBUSH AT CIMARRON PASS(1958), p
Lee Mendelson
BON VOYAGE, CHARLIE BROWN(AND DON'T COME BACK)*** (1980), p; BOY NAMED CHARLIE BROWN, A(1969), p; SNOOPY, COME HOME(1972), p; RACE FOR YOUR LIFE, CHARLIE BROWN(1977), p
Linda Mendelson
BOY NAMED CHARLIE BROWN, A(1969); SNOOPY, COME HOME(1972)
Mendelssohn
L'AGE D'OR(1979, Fr.), m
Eleanora Mendelssohn
BLACK HAND, THE(1950)
Felix Mendelssohn
SCARLET EMPRESS, THE(1934), m; MIDSUMMER'S NIGHT'S DREAM, A(1935), m; PROUD VALLEY, THE(1941, Brit.), m; I'VE ALWAYS LOVED YOU(1946), m; MIDSUMMER NIGHT'S DREAM, A(1966), m; MIDSUMMER NIGHT'S SEX COMEDY, A(1982), m
George Mendeluk
MERRY WIVES OF TOBIAS ROUKE, THE(1972, Can.), w; KIDNAPPING OF THE PRESIDENT, THE(1980, Can.), p, d; STONE COLD DEAD(1980, Can.), p, d&w
David Mendenhall
SPACE RAIDERS(1983)
James Mendenhall
PENNIES FROM HEAVEN(1981)
William Mendenhall
RUBY(1977), ph
George Mender
SMILING GHOST, THE(1941)
John Menderson
COP-OUT(1967, Brit.)
Dolores Mendes
Silents
GOLD RUSH, THE(1925)
Hercules Mendes
RACE STREET(1948)
John Prince Mendes
THIS IS THE ARMY(1943)
Lothar Mendes
DANGEROUS CURVES(1929), d; ILLUSION(1929), d; MARRIAGE PLAYGROUND, THE(1929), d; LADIES' MAN(1931), a, d; PERSONAL MAID(1931), p; IF I HAD A MILLION(1932), d; PAYMENT DEFERRED(1932), d; STRANGERS IN LOVE(1932), d; LUXURY LINER(1933), d; POWER(1934, Brit.), d; MAN WHO COULD WORK MIRACLES, THE(1937, Brit.), d; MOONLIGHT SONATA(1938, Brit.), p&d; INTERNATIONAL SQUADRON(1941), d; FLIGHT FOR FREEDOM(1943), d; TAMPICO(1944), d; WALLS CAME TUMBLING DOWN, THE(1946), d
Silents
NIGHT OF MYSTERY, A(1928), d; FOUR FEATHERS(1929), d
Misc. Silents
PRINCE OF TEMPTERS, THE(1926), d; ADVENTURE MAD(1928, Ger.), d

Maxwell Mendes
DR. HECKYL AND MR. HYPE(1980), prod d
Alan Mendez
ACTORS AND SIN(1952)
Bernard Mendez
DRACULA AND SON(1976, Fr.)
Fernando Mendez
LEGEND OF A BANDIT, THE(1945, Mex.), d; BLACK PIT OF DOCTOR M(1958, Mex.), d; VAMPIRE'S COFFIN, THE(1958, Mex.), d; LIVING COFFIN, THE(1965, Mex.), d; RAGE(1966, U.S./Mex.), w; VAMPIRE, THE(1968, Mex.), d
Guillermo Mendez
KID RODELO(1966, U.S./Span.); CHRISTMAS KID, THE(1968, U.S., Span.); MERCENARY, THE(1970, Ital./Span.)
Hector Mendez
GAMES MEN PLAY, THE(1968, Arg.)
Hercules Mendez
PASSPORT TO SUEZ(1943); NIGHT SONG(1947)
Jola Mendez
Silents
CHICAGO AFTER MIDNIGHT(1928)
Misc. Silents
NOT FOR PUBLICATION(1927); HEADIN' FOR DANGER(1928)
Jose Mendez
VAMPIRES, THE(1969, Mex.), art d
Julie Mendez
MAKE MINE A DOUBLE(1962, Brit.); DEVILS OF DARKNESS, THE(1965, Brit.); PANIC(1966, Brit.); TRAITOR'S GATE(1966, Brit./Ger.); DUFFY(1968, Brit.)
Lucila Mendez
CONVENTION GIRL(1935)
Lucilla Mendez
Silents
HOUSE OF YOUTH, THE(1924)
Misc. Silents
CONEY ISLAND(1928)
Richard Mendez
SCARFACE(1983)
Mary Mendham
GROOVE TUBE, THE(1974)
Members of the Mendi Tribes
SANDERS OF THE RIVER(1935, Brit.)
Charles Mendick
EGYPT BY THREE(1953)
Stephen Mendillo
ROLLERCOASTER(1977); SLAP SHOT(1977); KING OF THE GYPSIES(1978); LIANA(1983)
1984
TEACHERS(1984)
Steve Mendillo
WITHOUT A TRACE(1983)
Sergio Mendizabal
SAVAGE GUNS, THE(1962, U.S./Span.); VIRIDIANA(1962, Mex./Span.); TRISTANA(1970, Span./Ital./Fr.)
Sir Charles Mendl
NOTORIOUS(1946); IVY(1947)
Anthony Mendleson
PASSPORT TO PIMLICO(1949, Brit.), cos; RUN FOR YOUR MONEY, A(1950, Brit.), cos; MAN IN THE WHITE SUIT, THE(1952), cos; SECRET PEOPLE(1952, Brit.), cos; TITFIELD THUNDERBOLT, THE(1953, Brit.), cos; SQUARE RING, THE(1955, Brit.), cos; GENTLE TOUCH, THE(1956, Brit.), cos; SHIP THAT DIED OF SHAME, THE(1956, Brit.), cos; WHO DONE IT?(1956, Brit.), Cos; OUT OF THE CLOUDS(1957, Brit.), cos; MOUSE THAT ROARED, THE(1959, Brit.), cos; GUNS OF DARKNESS(1962, Brit.), cos; I LIKE MONEY(1962, Brit.), cos; ROAD TO HONG KONG, THE(1962, U.S./Brit.), cos; MIND BENDERS, THE(1963, Brit.), cos; MOUSE ON THE MOON, THE(1963, Brit.), cos; LONG SHIPS, THE(1964, Brit./Yugo.), cos; MOON-SPINNERS, THE(1964), cos; THUNDERBALL(1965, Brit.), cos; YELLOW ROLLS-ROYCE, THE(1965, Brit.), cos; MATTER OF INNOCENCE, A(1968, Brit.), cos; OH! WHAT A LOVELY WAR(1969, Brit.), cos; DAVID COPPERFIELD(1970, Brit.), cos; MACBETH(1971, Brit.), cos; YOUNG WINSTON(1972, Brit.), cos; BLACK WINDMILL, THE(1974, Brit.), cos; PERSECUTION(1974, Brit.), cos; 11 HARROWHOUSE(1974, Brit.), cos; MR. QUILP(1975, Brit.), cos; ONE OF OUR DINOSAURS IS MISSING(1975, Brit.), cos; INCREDIBLE SARAH, THE(1976, Brit.), cos; BOYS FROM BRAZIL, THE(1978), cos; GREAT TRAIN ROBBERY, THE(1979, Brit.), cos; DRAGONSLAYER(1981), cos; KEEP, THE(1983), cos
Hugh Anthony Mendleson
FIGHTING PRINCE OF DONEGAL, THE(1966, Brit.), cos
Ana F. Mendonca
MARGIN, THE,(1969, Braz.)
Mauro Mendonca
DONA FLOR AND HER TWO HUSHANDS(1977, Braz.)
Albert Mendoza
OPEN SEASON(1974, U.S./Span.)
Ana Maria Mendoza
UP THE MACGREGORS(1967, Ital./Span.)
Antonio Mendoza
EASY RIDER(1969)
Carlos Diaz Mendoza
THUNDERSTORM(1956)
David Mendoza
YOUNG MAN OF MANHATTAN(1930), md; PUBLIC ENEMY, THE(1931), md
Silents
PASSION(1920, Ger.), m; BEN-HUR(1925), m; BIG PARADE, THE(1925), m; MERRY WIDOW, THE(1925), m; TRAIL OF '98, THE(1929), m
George Mendoza
CLEARING THE RANGE(1931); CONQUERING HORDE, THE(1931); SPIRIT OF THE WEST(1932); PAN-AMERICANA(1945); THRILL OF BRAZIL, THE(1946); MEXICAN HAYRIDE(1948)
Harry Mendoza
SPIRITUALIST, THE(1948); THREE LITTLE WORDS(1950); PAINTING THE CLOUDS WITH SUNSHINE(1951); GOLDEN BLADE, THE(1953); STRANGER WORE A GUN, THE(1953)

Henry B. Mendoza
GUNFIGHT AT THE O.K. CORRAL(1957)
Jaime Mendoza
QUICK AND THE DEAD, THE(1963), m; FEMALE BUNCH, THE(1969), m; TEARS
OF HAPPINESS(1974), m
Joe Mendoza
SECRET CAVE, THE(1953, Brit.), w
Jorge Mendoza
PLAYERS(1979)
Jose Mendoza
TROPIC HOLIDAY(1938)
Margarito Mendoza
SCANDALOUS JOHN(1971)
Peter Mendoza
OVERNIGHT(1933, Brit.), m
Quiel Mendoza
MAD DOCTOR OF BLOOD ISLAND, THE(1969, Phil./U.S.); CURSE OF THE
VAMPIRES(1970, Phil., U.S.)
Sydney Mendoza
RIDER IN THE NIGHT, THE(1968, South Africa), art d
Victor Mendoza
BLACK PIRATES, THE(1954, Mex.); WONDERFUL COUNTRY, THE(1959)
Victor Manuel Mendoza
LOS OLVIDADOS(1950, Mex.); GARDEN OF EVIL(1954); COWBOY(1958)
Jaime Mendoza-Nava
GRASS EATER, THE(1961), m; FALLGUY(1962), m; HANDLE WITH CARE(1964),
md; NO MAN'S LAND(1964), m, md; SHELL SHOCK(1964), m, art d; HOSTAGE,
THE(1966), m, md; MARINE BATTLEGROUND(1966, U.S/S.K.), m; TALISMAN,
THE(1966), m; WITCHMAKER, THE(1969), m; HARD ROAD, THE(1970), m; SAV-
AGE WILD, THE(1970), m; WILD SCENE, THE(1970), m; BOOTLEGGERS(1974), m;
CREATURE FROM BLACK LAKE, THE(1976), m; GRAYEAGLE(1977), m; TOWN
THAT DREADED SUNDOWN, THE(1977), m; BOYS IN COMPANY C, THE(1978,
U.S./Hong Kong), m; NORSEMAN, THE(1978), m; WISHBONE CUTTER(1978), m;
EVICTORS, THE(1979), m; VAMPIRE HOOKERS, THE(1979, Phil.), m; PSYCHO
FROM TEXAS(1982), m; MAUSOLEUM(1983), m
Jamie Mendoza-Nava
BROTHERHOOD OF SATAN, THE(1971), m; LEGEND OF BOGGY CREEK,
THE(1973), m
Jaimie Mendoza-Nova
FEVER HEAT(1968), m
William Mendrek
13 RUE MADELEINE(1946); AT WAR WITH THE ARMY(1950)
Mary Mendum
NIGHT THEY ROBBED BIG BERTHA'S, THE(1975)
Carlos Mendy
NARCO MEN, THE(1969, Span./Ital.)
Sam Menecker
WRESTLER, THE(1974)
Erico Meneczer
OF WAYWARD LOVE(1964, Ital./Ger.), ph
Francis Menedez
SLUMBER PARTY MASSACRE, THE(1982)
Moises Menedez
RETURN OF THE SEVEN(1966, Span.)
Wilbur Menefee
CORPSE CAME C.O.D., THE(, set d; SHE WOULDN'T SAY YES(1945), set d;
FRAMED(1947), set d; IT HAD TO BE YOU(1947), set d; SPORT OF KINGS(1947), set
d; SWORDSMAN, THE(1947), set d; LADY FROM SHANGHAI, THE(1948), set d;
LOVES OF CARMEN, THE(1948), set d; MAN FROM COLORADO, THE(1948), set d;
RETURN OF OCTOBER, THE(1948), set d
John Menegold
RENT CONTROL(1981), w
Renato Menegotto
QUIET PLACE IN THE COUNTRY, A(1970, Ital./Fr.)
Margaret Menegoz
AVIATOR'S WIFE, THE(1981, Fr.), p; DANTON(1983), p; PAULINE AT THE
BEACH(1983, Fr.), p
1984
FULL MOON IN PARIS(1984, Fr.), p; SWANN IN LOVE(1984, Fr.Ger.), p
Angel Menendez
FACE OF TERROR(1964, Span.); NARCO MEN, THE(1969, Span./Ital.)
Juan Jose Menendez
LAZARILLO(1963, Span.); RUNNING MAN, THE(1963, Brit.); TRISTANA(1970,
Span./Ital./Fr.)
Bob Meneray
GROUNDSTAR CONSPIRACY, THE(1972, Can.)
Robert Meneray
SHOOT(1976, Can.)
Roberto Menescal
BYE-BYE BRASIL(1980, Braz.), m; XICA(1982, Braz.), m
Raquel Meneses
MIRAGE(1972, Peru)
Henri Menessier
LOVE IN MOROCCO(1933, Fr.), art d
Silents
RECOIL, THE(1924), art d
Barnard Menez
DON'T CRY WITH YOUR MOUTH FULL(1974, Fr.)
Bernard Menez
DAY FOR NIGHT(1973, Fr.)
Gloria Menezes
GIVEN WORD, THE(1964, Braz.)
Tan Yan Meng
SAINT JACK(1979)
Ho Meng-hau
FLYING GUILLOTINE, THE(1975, Chi.), d
John Mengatti
T.A.G.: THE ASSASSINATION GAME(1982)

1984
MEATBALLS PART II(1984)
Jean-Paul Mengeon
WE ARE ALL NAKED(1970, Can./Fr.), m
V. Menger
INSPECTOR GENERAL, THE(1937, Czech.), w
W. H. Menger
BLINDFOLD(1966), w
Chris Menges
KES(1970, Brit.), ph; BLACK BEAUTY(1971, Brit./Ger./Span.), ph; GUMSHOE(1972,
Brit.), ph; BLACK JACK(1979, Brit.), ph; BABYLON(1980, Brit.), ph; ANGEL(1982,
Irish), ph; BATTLETRUCK(1982), ph; LOOKS AND SMILES(1982, Brit.), ph;
BLOODY KIDS(1983, Brit.), ph; LOCAL HERO(1983, Brit.), ph
1984
COMFORT AND JOY(1984, Brit.), ph; KILLING FIELDS, THE(1984, Brit.), ph;
WINTER FLIGHT(1984, Brit.), ph
Joyce Menges
GNOME-MOBILE, THE(1967); NOW YOU SEE HIM, NOW YOU DON'T(1972)
Scott L. Menges
THX 1138(1971)
Jenner Menghi
CURSE OF THE BLOOD GHOULS(1969, Ital.), ed
Alkex Menglet
CLINIC, THE(1983, Aus.)
Mario Mengoli
ANGELO IN THE CROWD(1952, Ital.), ed
Alfio Meniconi
NAKED MAJA, THE(1959, Ital./U.S.), makeup; GRAND PRIX(1966), makeup
Furio Meniconi
GOLIATH AND THE BARBARIANS(1960, Ital.); DAVID AND GOLIATH(1961, Ital.);
TARTARS, THE(1962, Ital./Yugo.); CLEOPATRA(1963); GIANT OF METROPOLIS,
THE(1963, Ital.); SEVEN TASKS OF ALI BABA, THE(1963, Ital.); GOLD FOR THE
CAESARS(1964); SNOW DEVILS, THE(1965, Ital.); SEVEN REVENGES, THE(1967,
Ital.); KILL THEM ALL AND COME BACK ALONE(1970, Ital./Span.); DON'T TURN
THE OTHER CHEEK(1974, Ital./Ger./Span.)
Mario Meniconi
FOR A FEW DOLLARS MORE(1967, Ital./Ger./Span.); LISTEN, LET'S MAKE
LOVE(1969, Fr./Ital.)
Nello Meniconi
WHITE VOICES(1965, Fr./Ital.), p
Giulia Menin
QUIET PLACE IN THE COUNTRY, A(1970, Ital./Fr.)
Adolph Menjou
BACHELOR'S AFFAIRS(1932); FAREWELL TO ARMS, A(1932)
Adolphe Menjou
FASHIONS IN LOVE(1929); L'ENIGMATIQUE MONSIEUR PARKES(1930);
MOROCCO(1930); NEW MOON(1930); EASIEST WAY, THE(1931); FRIENDS AND
LOVERS(1931); FRONT PAGE, THE(1931); GREAT LOVER, THE(1931); MEN CALL IT
LOVE(1931); PARISIAN, THE(1931, Fr.); BLAME THE WOMAN(1932, Brit.); FORBID-
DEN(1932); NIGHT CLUB LADY(1932); PRESTIGE(1932); CIRCUS QUEEN MURDER,
THE(1933); CONVENTION CITY(1933); MORNING GLORY(1933); WIVES BEWA-
RE(1933, Brit.); WORST WOMAN IN PARIS(1933); EASY TO LOVE(1934); GREAT
FLIRTATION, THE(1934); HUMAN SIDE, THE(1934); JOURNAL OF A CRIME(1934);
LITTLE MISS MARKER(1934); MIGHTY BARNUM, THE(1934); TRUMPET BLOWS,
THE(1934); BROADWAY GONDOLIER(1935); GOLD DIGGERS OF 1935(1935); MILKY
WAY, THE(1936); ONE IN A MILLION(1936); SING, BABY, SING(1936); WIVES
NEVER KNOW(1936); CAFE METROPOLE(1937); STAGE DOOR(1937); STAR IS
BORN, A(1937); 100 MEN AND A GIRL(1937); GOLDWYN FOLLIES, THE(1938);
LETTER OF INTRODUCTION(1938); THANKS FOR EVERYTHING(1938); GOLDEN
BOY(1939); HOUSEKEEPER'S DAUGHTER(1939); KING OF THE TURF(1939);
THAT'S RIGHT-YOU'RE WRONG(1939); BILL OF DIVORCEMENT(1940); TURN-
ABOUT(1940); FATHER TAKES A WIFE(1941); ROAD SHOW(1941); ROXIE
HART(1942); SYNCOPATION(1942); YOU WERE NEVER LOVELIER(1942); HI DID-
DLE DIDDLE(1943); SWEET ROSIE O'GRADY(1943); STEP LIVELY(1944); MAN
ALIVE(1945); BACHELOR'S DAUGHTERS, THE(1946); HEARTBEAT(1946); MR. DIS-
TRICT ATTORNEY(1946); HUCKSTERS, THE(1947); I'LL BE YOURS(1947); STATE
OF THE UNION(1948); DANCING IN THE DARK(1949); MY DREAM IS YOURS(1949);
TO PLEASE A LADY(1950); ACROSS THE WIDE MISSOURI(1951); TALL TARGET,
THE(1951); SNIPER, THE(1952); MAN ON A TIGHTROPE(1953); TIMBERJACK(1955);
AMBASSADOR'S DAUGHTER, THE(1956); BUNDLE OF JOY(1956); FUZZY PINK
NIGHTGOWN, THE(1957); PATHS OF GLORY(1957); I MARRIED A WOMAN(1958);
POLLYANNA(1960)
Silents
HABIT OF HAPPINESS, THE(1916); KISS, THE(1916); MANHATTAN MAD-
NESS(1916); NEARLY A KING(1916); COURAGE(1921); FAITH HEALER, THE(1921);
QUEENIE(1921); SHEIK, THE(1921); THREE MUSKETEERS(1921); ARABIAN
LOVE(1922); SINGED WINGS(1922); RUPERT OF HENTZAU(1923); WOMAN OF
PARIS, A(1923); BROADWAY AFTER DARK(1924); FORBIDDEN PARADISE(1924);
MARRIAGE CIRCLE, THE(1924); OPEN ALL NIGHT(1924); ARE PARENTS PEO-
PLE?(1925); KISS IN THE DARK, A(1925); ACE OF CADS, THE(1926); GRAND
DUCHESS AND THE WAITER, THE(1926); SOCIAL CELEBRITY, A(1926); SORROWS
OF SATAN(1926); EVENING CLOTHES(1927); NIGHT OF MYSTERY, A(1928)
Misc. Silents
MOTH, THE(1917); ETERNAL FLAME, THE(1922); BELLA DONNA(1923);
WORLD'S APPLAUSE, THE(1923); BROKEN BARRIERS(1924); FAST SET,
THE(1924); FOR SALE(1924); MARRIAGE CHEAT, THE(1924); SHADOWS OF PA-
RIS(1924); SINNERS IN SILK(1924); KING ON MAIN STREET, THE(1925); LOST - A
WIFE(1925); SWAN, THE(1925); BLONDE OR BRUNETTE(1927); GENTLEMAN OF
PARIS, A(1927); SERENADE(1927); SERVICE FOR LADIES(1927); HIS PRIVATE
LIFE(1928); HIS TIGER LADY(1928); MARQUIS PREFERRED(1929)
Henry Menjou
SPECIAL AGENT K-7(1937)
Rolf Menke
RIVER CHANGES, THE(1956)
Sally Joe Menke
1984
COLD FEET(1984), ed

Helen Menken
STAGE DOOR CANTEEN(1943)
Marie Menken
CHELSEA GIRLS, THE(1967)
Robin Menken
FOOLS(1970); STRAWBERRY STATEMENT, THE(1970)
1984
BODY ROCK(1984)
Shep Menken
FOURTEEN HOURS(1951); JUGGLER, THE(1953); REMAINS TO BE SEEN(1953); BENGAL BRIGADE(1954); KILLERS FROM SPACE(1954); BENNY GOODMAN STORY, THE(1956); MAN FROM BUTTON WILLOW, THE(1965); PHANTOM TOLLBOOTH, THE(1970)
Shepard Menken
RED MENACE, THE(1949); GREAT CARUSO, THE(1951); HAREM GIRL(1952); MERRY WIDOW, THE(1952); CAPTAIN JOHN SMITH AND POCAHONTAS(1953); MAN IN THE DARK(1953); TANGIER INCIDENT(1953); DEMETRIUS AND THE GLADIATORS(1954)
Shepherd Menken
SWORD IN THE DESERT(1949)
Robin Menker
THANK GOD IT'S FRIDAY(1978)
Michael Menne
HOMER(1970), ed
Abdullah Mennebhi
SAADIA(1953)
Lee Menning
CHEAP DETECTIVE, THE(1978)
Rene Mennotier
PASSION(1983, Fr./Switz.)
Margaret Menogoz
LE BEAU MARIAGE(1982, Fr.), p
Sonja O. Menor
SEED OF INNOCENCE(1980)
Gian-Carlo Menotti
MEDIUM, THE(1951), d&w, m
Joseph Menou
JOHNNY FRENCHMAN(1946, Brit.)
A.N.K. Mensah
1984
WHITE ELEPHANT(1984, Brit.)
Laszlo Mensaros
LOVE(1972, Hung.)
1984
BRADY'S ESCAPE(1984, U.S./Hung.)
Bill Mensch
DELIRIUM(1979), ph
Josef Menschik
HIPPODROME(1961, Aust./Ger.)
Herbert Mensching
PEDESTRIAN, THE(1974, Ger.)
Iris Menshell
BIG CHASE, THE(1954)
N. Menshikova
DAY THE WAR ENDED, THE(1961, USSR)
Nina Menshikova
SONS AND MOTHERS(1967, USSR)
Vladimir Menshov
MOSCOW DOES NOT BELIEVE IN TEARS(1980, USSR), d
Vladimir Mensik
LEMONADE JOE(1966, Czech.); LOVES OF A BLONDE(1966, Czech.); 90 DEGREES IN THE SHADE(1966, Czech./Brit.); HAPPY END(1968, Czech.); MARKETA LAZAROVA(1968, Czech.); MURDER CZECH STYLE(1968, Czech.); WHAT WOULD YOU SAY TO SOME SPINACH(1976, Czech.)
Mark Menson
WILD RIVER(1960)
Irfan Mensur
DAY THAT SHOOK THE WORLD, THE(1977, Yugo./Czech.)
Narcisco Ibanez Menta
MASTER OF HORROR(1965, Arg.); GAMES MEN PLAY, THE(1968, Arg.); I HATE MY BODY(1975, Span./Switz.); SAGA OF DRACULA, THE(1975, Span.)
Martin Rodriguez Mentasti
END OF INNOCENCE(1960, Arg.), w
Dale Menten
IT AIN'T EASY(1972), m; LIFEGUARD(1976), m
Lola Mentes
GAY SENORITA, THE(1945)
Michel Mention
MAD BOMBER, THE(1973), m
Alla Mentone
HANDS ACROSS THE TABLE(1935)
Yehudi Menuhin
STAGE DOOR CANTEEN(1943); MAGIC BOW, THE(1947, Brit.)
Said Menyalshchikov
MOSCOW DOES NOT BELIEVE IN TEARS(1980, USSR), art d
Ken Menyard
DARK, THE(1979)
Elly Menz
ALSINO AND THE CONDOR(1983, Nicaragua), art d
Don Menza
MAN WHO LOVED WOMEN, THE(1983)
Franz Menzel
NOT RECONCILED, OR "ONLY VIOLENCE HELPS WHERE IT RULES"(1969, Ger.)
Gerhard Menzel
BARCAROLE(1935, Ger.), w; LA HABANERA(1937, Ger.), w; KING IN SHADOW(1961, Ger.), w
Jiri Menzel
CLOSELY WATCHED TRAINS(1967, Czech.), a, d, w; CAPRICIOUS SUMMER(1968, Czech.), a, d&w

Mike Menzel
WAVELENGTH(1983), spec eff
Paul Menzel
FM(1978); TERMS OF ENDEARMENT(1983)
Sharon Menzel
1984
PARIS, TEXAS(1984, Ger./Fr.)
Ursula Menzel
LIVE A LITTLE, LOVE A LITTLE(1968)
Ernest Menzer
BAND OF OUTSIDERS(1966, Fr.); MADE IN U.S.A.(1966, Fr.); WEEKEND(1968, Fr./Ital.)
Russell C. Menzer
WHEN TIME RAN OUT(1980), art d
Archie Menzies
UNDER YOUR HAT(1940, Brit.), w
Hamish Menzies
DANCING WITH CRIME(1947, Brit.); OPERATION DIAMOND(1948, Brit.); MAN'S AFFAIR, A(1949, Brit.)
Heather Menzies
SOUND OF MUSIC, THE(1965); HAWAII(1966); HOW SWEET IT IS(1968); HAIL, HERO!(1969); OUTSIDE IN(1972); SSSSSSSS(1973); PIRANHA(1978); ENDANGERED SPECIES(1982)
Ina Menzies
HAUNTING OF M, THE(1979)
James Menzies
WHITE CLIFFS OF DOVER, THE(1944); FATHER'S LITTLE DIVIDEND(1951)
Jim Menzies
JANIE(1944)
Mary Menzies
HALF-BREED, THE(1952); PIT AND THE PENDULUM, THE(1961)
Thomas Menzies
FATHER'S LITTLE DIVIDEND(1951)
Tommie Menzies
ANGELS ALLEY(1948); GUY WHO CAME BACK, THE(1951)
Tommie Mann Menzies
MISTER 880(1950)
William C. Menzies
CHANDU THE MAGICIAN(1932), d; I LOVED YOU WEDNESDAY(1933), d
William Cameron Menzies
ALIBI(1929), art d; BULLDOG DRUMMOND(1929), art d; CONDEMNED(1929), set d; LADY OF THE PAVEMENTS(1929), set d; LOCKED DOOR, THE(1929), art d&set d; TAMING OF THE SHREW, THE(1929), art d; ABRAHAM LINCOLN(1930), set d; BAD ONE, THE(1930), art d; BE YOURSELF(1930), set d; DU BARRY, WOMAN OF PASSION(1930), art d; LOTTERY BRIDE, THE(1930), prod d & art d; ONE ROMANTIC NIGHT(1930), set d; PUTTIN' ON THE RITZ(1930), art d; RAFFLES(1930), art d; ALWAYS GOODBYE(1931), d; SPIDER, THE(1931), d; ALMOST MARRIED(1932), d; ALICE IN WONDERLAND(1933), w; CAVALCADE(1933), spec eff; WHARF ANGEL(1934), d; THINGS TO COME(1936, Brit.), d; GONE WITH THE WIND(1939), d, prod d; MADE FOR EACH OTHER(1939), prod d; OUR TOWN(1940), prod d; THIEF OF BAGHDAD, THE(1940, Brit.), d; DEVIL AND MISS JONES, THE(1941), prod d; FOREIGN AGENT(1942), set d; KING'S ROW(1942), prod d; PRIDE OF THE YANKEES, THE(1942), prod d; FOR WHOM THE BELL TOLLS(1943), prod d; MR. LUCKY(1943), prod d; NORTH STAR, THE(1943), p; ADDRESS UNKNOWN(1944), d; GREEN COCKATOO, THE(1947, Brit.), d; IVY(1947), p; BLACK BOOK, THE(1949), p; DRUMS IN THE DEEP SOUTH(1951), art d, d; WHIP HAND, THE(1951), d, prod d; INVADERS FROM MARS(1953), d, w, prod d; MAZE, THE(1953), d, prod d
Silents
KINDRED OF THE DUST(1922), art d; ROSITA(1923), art d; THIEF OF BAGDAD, THE(1924), art d; COBRA(1925), set d; EAGLE, THE(1925), art d; BAT, THE(1926), art d; SON OF THE SHEIK(1926), art d; BELOVED ROGUE, THE(1927), art d; AWAKENING, THE(1928), art d; SADIE THOMPSON(1928), art d; TEMPEST(1928), art d; RESCUE, THE(1929), art d
David Meo
MARYJANE(1968)
Paul Meoe
TANGA-TIKA(1953)
Peggy Meon
TRUE CONFESSION(1937)
Viv Mephan
MAD MAX(1979, Aus.), makeup
Vivien Mephan
MAN FROM SNOWY RIVER, THE(1983, Aus.), makeup
Jacqueline Meppiel
LONG ABSENCE, THE(1962, Fr./Ital.), ed; WISE GUYS(1969, Fr./Ital.), ed
Juliano Mer
1984
LITTLE DRUMMER GIRL, THE(1984)
Edith Mera
DRAGNET NIGHT(1931, Fr.)
Mary Merach
COWBOY AND THE KID,THE(1936)
Luc Meranda
TORSO(1974, Ital.)
Doro Merande
STATE FAIR(1933); STAR MAKER, THE(1939); OUR TOWN(1940); COVER-UP(1949); MR. BELVEDERE RINGS THE BELL(1951); WHISTLE AT EATON FALLS(1951); MAN WITH THE GOLDEN ARM, THE(1955); SEVEN YEAR ITCH, THE(1955); GAZEBO, THE(1959); REMARKABLE MR. PENNYPACKER, THE(1959); CARDINAL, THE(1963); KISS ME, STUPID(1964); RUSSIANS ARE COMING, THE RUSSIANS ARE COMING, THE(1966); HURRY SUNDOWN(1967); SKIDOO(1968); CHANGE OF HABIT(1969); MAKING IT(1971); FRONT PAGE, THE(1974)
Charles Merangel
LA BONNE SOUPE(1964, Fr./Ital.), set d; WHAT'S NEW, PUSSYCAT?(1965, U.S./Fr.), set d; CLOPORTES(1966, Fr., Ital.), cos; MADEMOISELLE(1966, Fr./Brit.), set d; CASTLE KEEP(1969), set d; PROMISE AT DAWN(1970, U.S./Fr.), set d; SICILIAN CLAN, THE(1970, Fr.), set d

Jean Meranton
CHILDREN OF CHAOS(1950, Fr.)
A.U. Meray
NATIVE SON(1951, U.S., Arg.), ph
Tibor Meray
CATCH ME A SPY(1971, Brit./Fr.), w
Antonio Merayo
DOLORES(1949, Span.), ph; MAN AND THE BEAST, THE(1951, Arg.), ph
Raul Meraz
INVISIBLE MAN, THE(1958, Mex.)
G.R. Mercader
FURY BELOW(1938), p, w
Maria Mercader
KING'S JESTER, THE(1947, Ital.); DISILLUSION(1949, Ital.); HEART AND SOUL(1950, Ital.)
Martha Mercadier
WICKED GO TO HELL, THE(1961, Fr.)
Marthe Mercadier
ACT OF LOVE(1953); MAEDCHEN IN UNIFORM(1965, Ger./Fr.); ONCE IN PARIS(1978)
Hector Mercado
CROSS AND THE SWITCHBLADE, THE(1970); HAIR(1979)
Hector Jaime Mercado
SLOW DANCING IN THE BIG CITY(1978)
Nereida Mercado
LAST FIGHT, THE(1983)
Mercador
STRYKER(1983, Phil.), makeup
V. Mercantan
FLESH AND THE WOMAN(1954, Fr./Ital.), ed
Arthur Mercante
REQUIEM FOR A HEAVYWEIGHT(1962)
Mercanton
ULTIMATUM(1940, Fr.), ph
Isabelle Mercanton
SPERMULA(1976, Fr.)
Jacques Mercanton
PORTRAIT OF A WOMAN(1946, Fr.), ph; MR. HULOT'S HOLIDAY(1954, Fr.), ph; PROSTITUTION(1965, Fr.), ph; SELLERS OF GIRLS(1967, Fr.), ph
Jean Mercanton
HEART OF A NATION, THE(1943, Fr.); JOUR DE FETE(1952, Fr.), ph
Louis Mercanton
BRAT, THE(1930, Brit.), d; MYSTERY OF THE PINK VILLA, THE(1930, Fr.), w; MAN OF MAYFAIR(1931, Brit.), d; THESE CHARMING PEOPLE(1931, Brit.), d; COGNASSE(1932, Fr.), d
Silents
QUEEN ELIZABETH(1912, Fr.), p, d
Misc. Silents
JEANNE DORE(1916, Fr.), d; LE LOTUS D'OR(1916, Fr.), d; SUZANNE(1916, Fr.), d; LA P'TITE DU SIXIEME(1917, Fr.), d; LE TABLIER BLANC(1917, Fr.), d; MERES FRANCAISES(1917, Fr.), d; MIDINETTE(1917 Fr.), d; OH! CE BAISER(1917, Fr.), d; BOUCLETTE(1918, Fr.), d; LE TORRENT(1918, Fr.), d; UN ROMAN D'AMOUR ET D'AVENTURES(1918, Fr.), d; L'APPEL DU SANG(1920, Fr.), d; GYPSY PASSION(1922, Fr.), d; L'HOMME MERVEILLEUX(1922, Fr.), d; PHROSO(1922, Fr.), d; POSSESSION(1922, Brit.), d; AUX JARDINS DE MURCIE(1923, Fr.), d; LA VOYANTE(1923, Fr.), d; SARATI-LE-TERRIBLE(1923, Fr.), d; LES DEUX GOSSES(1924, Fr.), d; CINDERS(1926, Brit.), d; MONTE CARLO(1926, d; CROQUETTE(1927, Fr.), d; VENUS(1929, Fr.), d
Roger Spiri Mercanton
MARIUS(1933, Fr.), ed
Victoria Mercanton
AND GOD CREATED WOMAN(1957, Fr.), ed; NIGHT HEAVEN FELL, THE(1958, Fr.), ed; BLOOD AND ROSES(1961, Fr./Ital.), ed; LES LIAISONS DANGEREUSES(1961, Fr./Ital.), ed; LOVE ON A PILLOW(1963, Fr./Ital.), ed; NUTTY, NAUGHTY CHATEAU(1964, Fr./Ital.), ed; HAIL MAFIA(1965, Fr./Ital.), ed; VICE AND VIRTUE(1965, Fr./Ital.), ed; GAME IS OVER, THE(1967, Fr.), ed; WOMAN TIMES SEVEN(1967, U.S./Fr./Ital.), ed; BARBARELLA(1968, Fr./Ital.), ed; HOA-BINH(1971, Fr.), ed; SOMEONE BEHIND THE DOOR(1971, Fr./Brit.), ed
Adriano Mercantoni
TRINITY IS STILL MY NAME(1971, Ital.)
Mercedes
SUSPENSE(1946)
Maria Mercedes
OLD MOTHER RILEY'S JUNGLE TREASURE(1951, Brit.); WICKED WIFE(1955, Brit.); OPERATION CONSPIRACY(1957, Brit.); MY SON, THE VAMPIRE(1963, Brit.); PATRICK(1979, Aus.)
Tom Mercein
DISC JOCKEY(1951)
Alan Mercer
COOL WORLD, THE(1963)
Beryl Mercer
MOTHER'S BOY(1929); THREE LIVE GHOSTS(1929); ALL QUIET ON THE WESTERN FRONT(1930); COMMON CLAY(1930); DUMBBELLS IN ERMINE(1930); IN GAY MADRID(1930); MATRIMONIAL BED, THE(1930); OUTWARD BOUND(1930); SEVEN DAYS LEAVE(1930); ARE THESE OUR CHILDREN?(1931); EAST LYNNE(1931); INSPIRATION(1931); MAN IN POSSESSION, THE(1931); MERELY MARY ANN(1931); MIRACLE WOMAN, THE(1931); PUBLIC ENEMY(1931); SKY SPIDER, THE(1931); DEVIL'S LOTTERY(1932); FORGOTTEN WOMEN(1932); LENA RIVERS(1932); LOVERS COURAGEOUS(1932); MIDNIGHT MORALS(1932); NO GREATER LOVE(1932); SIX HOURS TO LIVE(1932); SMILIN' THROUGH(1932); UNHOLY LOVE(1932); YOUNG AMERICA(1932); BERKELEY SQUARE(1933); BLIND ADVENTURE(1933); BROKEN DREAMS(1933); CAVALCADE(1933); HER SPLENDID FOLLY(1933); SUPERNATURAL(1933); CHANGE OF HEART(1934); LITTLE MINISTER, THE(1934); RICHEST GIRL IN THE WORLD, THE(1934); AGE OF INDISCRETION(1935); JANE EYRE(1935); MAGNIFICENT OBSESSION(1935); THREE LIVE GHOSTS(1935); FORBIDDEN HEAVEN(1936); HITCH HIKE LADY(1936); MY MARRIAGE(1936); CALL IT A DAY(1937); NIGHT MUST FALL(1937); HOUND OF THE BASKERVILLES, THE(1939); LITTLE PRINCESS, THE(1939); STORY OF ALEXANDER GRAHAM BELL, THE(1939); WOMAN IS THE JUDGE, A(1939)

Silents
FINAL CURTAIN, THE(1916)
Bud Mercer
FOOTLIGHT SERENADE(1942)
Charles E. Mercer
SINS OF RACHEL CADE, THE(1960), w
Curt Mercer
THREE NUTS IN SEARCH OF A BOLT(1964)
David Mercer
MORGAN!(1966, Brit.), w; 90 DEGREES IN THE SHADE(1966, Czech./Brit.), w; FAMILY LIFE(1971, Brit.), w; DOLL'S HOUSE, A(1973, Brit.), w; PROVIDENCE(1977, Fr.), w
Diane Mercer
AMIN-THE RISE AND FALL(1982, Kenya)
Frances Mercer
ANNABEL TAKES A TOUR(1938); BLIND ALIBI(1938); CRIME RING(1938); MAD MISS MANTON, THE(1938); SMASHING THE RACKETS(1938); VIVACIOUS LADY(1938); BEAUTY FOR THE ASKING(1939); SOCIETY LAWYER(1939); STORY OF VERNON AND IRENE CASTLE, THE(1939); PICCADILLY INCIDENT(1948, Brit.); PARDNERS(1956); THERE'S ALWAYS TOMORROW(1956); YOUNG AND DANGEROUS(1957); RISE AND FALL OF LEGS DIAMOND, THE(1960); GATHERING OF EAGLES, A(1963)
Fred Mercer
FIVE LITTLE PEPPERS IN TROUBLE(1940)
Freddie Mercer
GREAT GILDERSLEEVE, THE(1942); LOVES OF EDGAR ALLAN POE, THE(1942); MAJOR AND THE MINOR, THE(1942); ON THE SUNNY SIDE(1942); SHADOWS ON THE SAGE(1942); GILDERSLEEVE ON BROADWAY(1943); GILDERSLEEVE'S BAD DAY(1943); GILDERSLEEVE'S GHOST(1944); MY GAL LOVES MUSIC(1944)
Glenn Mercer
SMITHEREENS(1982), m
Jack Mercer
MR. BUG GOES TO TOWN(1941)
Jane Mercer
STREET SCENE(1931); NAUGHTY MARIETTA(1935)
Silents
MAN AND MAID(1925)
Misc. Silents
CHAPTER IN HER LIFE, A(1923)
Jim Mercer
FOOTLIGHT SERENADE(1942)
Johnny Mercer
OLD MAN RHYTHM(1935); TO BEAT THE BAND(1935); SECOND CHORUS(1940), Hunter; DANGEROUS WHEN WET(1953), m; TOP BANANA(1954), w; DARLING LILI(1970), m
Joseph Mercer
WEREWOLF IN A GIRL'S DORMITORY(1961, Ital./Aust.)
Mabel Mercer
TROPICAL TROUBLE(1936, Brit.); EVERYTHING IS RHYTHM(1940, Brit.); SAND CASTLE, THE(1961)
Mae Mercer
TWO ARE GUILTY(1964, Fr.); HELL WITH HEROES, THE(1968); BEGUILED, THE(1971); DIRTY HARRY(1971); FROGS(1972); PRETTY BABY(1978)
Marian Mercer
JOHN AND MARY(1969); SAMMY STOPS THE WORLD zero(1978); NINE TO FIVE(1980); OH GOD! BOOK II(1980)
Marilyn Mercer
GUNS OF HATE(1948); THEY LIVE BY NIGHT(1949); MILKMAN, THE(1950); HARD, FAST, AND BEAUTIFUL(1951)
Ray Mercer
NEW ADVENTURES OF TARZAN(1935), spec eff; REVOLT OF THE ZOMBIES(1936), spec eff; JOHNNY DOESN'T LIVE HERE ANY MORE(1944), spec eff; DOCKS OF NEW YORK(1945), spec eff; MR. MUGGS RIDES AGAIN(1945), spec eff; STRANGE HOLIDAY(1945), spec eff; SUSPENSE(1946), spec eff; TREASURE OF MONTE CRISTO(1949), spec eff; STEEL HELMET, THE(1951), spec eff; SUPERMAN AND THE MOLE MEN(1951), spec eff; NO HOLDS BARRED(1952), spec eff; LOOSE IN LONDON(1953), spec eff; HIGH SOCIETY(1955), spec eff; CRASHING LAS VEGAS(1956), spec eff; SPY CHASERS(1956), spec eff; MASTER OF THE WORLD(1961), spec eff
Renee Mercer
THAT FORSYTE WOMAN(1949)
Suzanne Mercer
I AM A GROUPIE(1970, Brit.), w
Tony Mercer
DREAM MAKER, THE(1963, Brit.)
William Mercer
VELVET TOUCH, THE(1948), w; DIRT GANG, THE(1972), w
The Mercer Bros.
CASA MANANA(1951)
Paul Mercey
TIME BOMB(1961, Fr./Ital.); YOUNG WORLD, A(1966, Fr./Ital.); HIT(1973)
Michael Merchan
MAN FRIDAY(1975, Brit.), spec eff
Cathie Merchant
THAT TOUCH OF MINK(1962)
Cathy Merchant
HAUNTED PALACE, THE(1963)
Ismail Merchant
HOUSEHOLDER, THE(1963, US/India), p; SHAKESPEARE WALLAH(1966, India), p; GURU, THE(1969, U.S./India), a, p; BOMBAY TALKIE(1970, India), p; SAVAGES(1972), p; WILD PARTY, THE(1975), p; ROSELAND(1977), p; EUROPEANS, THE(1979, Brit.), p; HULLABALOO OVER GEORGIE AND BONNIE'S PICTURES(1979), p; JANE AUSTEN IN MANHATTAN(1980), p; QUARTET(1981, Brit./Fr.), p; HEAT AND DUST(1983, Brit.), p
1984
BOSTONIANS, THE(1984), p
Vivien Merchant
ALFIE(1966, Brit.); ACCIDENT(1967, Brit.); ALFRED THE GREAT(1969, Brit.); FRENZY(1972, Brit.); HOMECOMING, THE(1973); OFFENSE, THE(1973, Brit.); UNDER MILK WOOD(1973, Brit.); MAIDS, THE(1975, Brit.)

Victor Mercieca
PULP(1972, Brit.)

Ann Mercier
LE BEAU MARIAGE(1982, Fr.)

Chantal Mercier
SMALL CHANGE(1976, Fr.)

Duane Mercier
BOYS IN COMPANY C, THE(1978, U.S./Hong Kong)

Louis Mercier
UNDER TWO FLAGS(1936); TIGER ROSE(1930); QUICK MILLIONS(1931); RIP TIDE(1934); NAUGHTY MARIETTA(1935); GARDEN OF ALLAH, THE(1936); ROAD TO GLORY, THE(1936); ROSE MARIE(1936); CAFE METROPOLE(1937); CHARLIE CHAN AT MONTE CARLO(1937); I'LL TAKE ROMANCE(1937); THAT GIRL FROM PARIS(1937); ARTISTS AND MODELS ABROAD(1938); JEZEBEL(1938); BULLDOG DRUMMOND'S BRIDE(1939); CHARLIE CHAN IN THE CITY OF DARKNESS(1939); EVERYTHING HAPPENS AT NIGHT(1939); ARISE, MY LOVE(1940); THIS WOMAN IS MINE(1941); CASABLANCA(1942); LADY HAS PLANS, THE(1942); REUNION IN FRANCE(1942); SAHARA(1943); SONG OF BERNADETTE, THE(1943); CONSPIRA-TORS, THE(1944); MASK OF DIMITRIOS, THE(1944); PASSAGE TO MARSEIL-LE(1944); TO HAVE AND HAVE NOT(1944); CORNERED(1945); JOHNNY ANGEL(1945); PRISON SHIP(1945); SARATOGA TRUNK(1945); MY DARLING CLE-MENTINE(1946); SO DARK THE NIGHT(1946); TARZAN AND THE LEOPARD WOMAN(1946); HIGH CONQUEST(1947); JEWELS OF BRANDENBURG(1947); I, JANE DOE(1948); WHEN WILLIE COMES MARCHING HOME(1950); SHOW BOAT(1951); LYDIA BAILEY(1952); WHAT PRICE GLORY?(1952); FRENCH LINE, THE(1954); TO CATCH A THIEF(1955); UNTAMED(1955); WE'RE NO ANGELS(1955); ATTACK!(1956); MAN WHO KNEW TOO MUCH, THE(1956); AFFAIR TO REMEM-BER, AN(1957); WILL SUCCESS SPOIL ROCK HUNTER?(1957); WRECK OF THE MARY DEAR, THE(1959); DEVIL AT FOUR O'CLOCK, THE(1961); TENDER IS THE NIGHT(1961); WILD AND WONDERFUL(1964); ART OF LOVE, THE(1965); DARLING LILI(1970); OTHER SIDE OF MIDNIGHT, THE(1977)

Louis G. Mercier
PIRATES OF TRIPOLI(1955)

Louise Mercier
JUMP INTO HELL(1955)

Michele Mercier
GIVE ME MY CHANCE(1958, Fr.); GOODBYE AGAIN(1961); WONDERS OF ALAD-DIN, THE(1961, Fr./Ital.); SHOOT THE PIANO PLAYER(1962, Fr.); FURY AT SMUGGLERS BAY(1963, Brit.); TWO ARE GUILTY(1964, Fr.); CASANOVA '70(1965, Ital.); HIGH INFIDELITY(1965, Fr./Ital.); SYMPHONY FOR A MASSACRE(1965, Fr./Ital.); OPIATE '67(1967, Fr./Ital.); OLDEST PROFESSION, THE(1968, Fr./Ital./ Ger.); LADY HAMILTON(1969, Ger./Ital./Fr.); YOU CAN'T WIN 'EM ALL(1970, Brit.); CALL OF THE WILD(1972, Ger./ Span./Ital./Fr.); WEB OF THE SPIDER(1972, Ital./Fr./Ger.)

Michelle Mercier
NIGHTS OF LUCRETIA BORGIA, THE(1960, Ital.); GLOBAL AFFAIR, A(1964)

Patrice Mercier
1984
SUNDAY IN THE COUNTRY, A(1984, Fr.), prod d

Valerie Mercier
1984
L'ARGENT(1984, Fr./Switz.)

Wallace Merck
STROKER ACE(1983)
1984
TANK(1984)

Melina Mercouri
GYPSY AND THE GENTLEMAN, THE(1958, Brit.); NEVER ON SUNDAY(1960, Gr.); WHERE THE HOT WIND BLOWS(1960, Fr., Ital.); PHAEDRA(1962, U.S./Gr./Fr.); VICTORS, THE(1963); TOPKAPI(1964); MAN COULD GET KILLED, A(1966); 10:30 P.M. SUMMER(1966, U.S./Span.); UNINHIBITED, THE(1968, Fr./Ital./Span.); GAILY, GAILY(1969); PROMISE AT DAWN(1970, U.S./Fr.); ONCE IS NOT ENOUGH(1975); NASTY HABITS(1976, Brit.); DREAM OF PASSION, A(1978, Gr.)

Jean Mercure
BALLERINA(1950, Fr.); SWORD AND THE ROSE, THE(1953); RED AND THE BLACK, THE(1954, Fr./Ital.); DANGEROUS EXILE(1958, Brit.); DOUBLE DECEP-TION(1963, Fr.)

Monique Mercure
TAKE IT ALL(1966, Can.); DON'T LET THE ANGELS FALL(1969, Can.); WAITING FOR CAROLINE(1969, Can.); LOVE IN A FOUR LETTER WORLD(1970, Can.); MY UNCLE ANTOINE(1971, Can.); THIRD WALKER, THE(1978, Can.); QUINTET(1979); STONE COLD DEAD(1980, Can.); ODYSSEY OF THE PACIFIC(1983, Can./Fr.)

Angelo Mercuriali
LA BOHEME(1965, Ital.)

Gus Mercurio
ELIZA FRASER(1976, Aus.); HIGH ROLLING(1977, Aus.); RAW DEAL(1977, Aus.); BLUE LAGOON, THE(1980); DEAD MAN'S FLOAT(1980, Aus.); ESCAPE 2000(1983, Aus.); MAN FROM SNOWY RIVER, THE(1983, Aus.)

Micole Mercurio
FLASHDANCE(1983)

March Mercury
SPRING BREAK(1983), stunts

Carla Mercy
DRAGSTRIP GIRL(1957)

Pierre Mere
LOVE AT NIGHT(1961, Fr.), d&w; PALACE OF NUDES(1961, Fr./Ital.), d

Maria Mereader
HELLO, ELEPHANT(1954, Ital.)

Andrew Meredith
MAN WHO HAD POWER OVER WOMEN, THE(1970, Brit.), w

Billy Meredith
Misc. Silents
BALL OF FORTUNE, THE(1926, Brit.)

Bob Meredith
GREAT MIKE, THE(1944); I'LL BE SEEING YOU(1944); OVER 21(1945); ROUGH, TOUGH AND READY(1945)

Burgess Meredith
THAT UNCERTAIN FEELING(1941); WINTERSET(1936); THERE GOES THE GROOM(1937); SPRING MADNESS(1938); IDIOT'S DELIGHT(1939); OF MICE AND MEN(1939); CASTLE ON THE HUDSON(1940); SECOND CHORUS(1940); SAN FRAN-CISCO DOCKS(1941); TOM, DICK AND HARRY(1941); STREET OF CHANCE(1942); STORY OF G.I. JOE, THE(1945); DIARY OF A CHAMBERMAID(1946), a, p, w; MAGNIFICENT DOLL(1946); MINE OWN EXECUTIONER(1948, Brit.); ON OUR MERRY WAY(1948); JIGSAW(1949); MAN ON THE EIFFEL TOWER, THE(1949), a, d; GAY ADVENTURE, THE(1953, Brit.); JOE BUTTERFLY(1957); ADVISE AND CON-SENT(1962); CARDINAL, THE(1963); KIDNAPPERS, THE(1964, U.S./Phil.); IN HARM'S WAY(1965); BATMAN(1966); BIG HAND FOR THE LITTLE LADY, A(1966); CRAZY QUILT, THE(1966); MADAME X(1966); HURRY SUNDOWN(1967); SKI-DOO(1968); STAY AWAY, JOE(1968); TORTURE GARDEN(1968, Brit.); HARD CON-TRACT(1969); MACKENNA'S GOLD(1969); REIVERS, THE(1969); THERE WAS A CROOKED MAN(1970); CLAY PIGEON(1971); SUCH GOOD FRIENDS(1971); BEWARE! THE BLOB(1972); FAN'S NOTES, A(1972, Can.); MAN, THE(1972); GOLDEN NEEDLES(1974); DAY OF THE LOCUST, THE(1975); HINDENBURG, THE(1975); 92 IN THE SHADE(1975, U.S./Brit.); BURNT OFFERINGS(1976); ROCKY(1976); GOLD-EN RENDEZVOUS(1977); GREAT BANK HOAX, THE(1977); SENTINEL, THE(1977); FOUL PLAY(1978); MAGIC(1978); MANITOU, THE(1978); ROCKY II(1979); FINAL ASSIGNMENT(1980, Can.); WHEN TIME RAN OUT(1980); CLASH OF THE TI-TANS(1981); LAST CHASE, THE(1981); TRUE CONFESSIONS(1981); ROCKY III(1982); TWILIGHT ZONE–THE MOVIE(1983)
Misc. Talkies
YIN AND YANG OF DR. GO, THE(1972), d; "B"...MUST DIE(1973)

Charles Meredith
DAISY KENYON(1947); DREAM GIRL(1947); ALL MY SONS(1948); FOR THE LOVE OF MARY(1948); FOREIGN AFFAIR, A(1948); HE WALKED BY NIGHT(1948); HOMECOMING(1948); MIRACLE OF THE BELLS, THE(1948); BOY WITH THE GREEN HAIR, THE(1949); FRANCIS(1949); LADY TAKES A SAILOR, THE(1949); LUCKY STIFF, THE(1949); SAMSON AND DELILAH(1949); STREETS OF SAN FRANCISCO(1949); THEY LIVE BY NIGHT(1949); TOKYO JOE(1949); CAGED(1950); COUNTERSPY MEETS SCOTLAND YARD(1950); KISS TOMORROW GOOD-BYE(1950); MALAYA(1950); PERFECT STRANGERS(1950); SUN SETS AT DAWN, THE(1950); AL JENNINGS OF OKLAHOMA(1951); ALONG THE GREAT DIVI-DE(1951); SANTA FE(1951); STRANGERS ON A TRAIN(1951); SUBMARINE COM-MAND(1951); BIG TREES, THE(1952); CATTLE TOWN(1952); LOAN SHARK(1952); ROOM FOR ONE MORE(1952); SO THIS IS LOVE(1953); THEM!(1954); LONE RANGER, THE(1955); GIANT(1956); CHICAGO CONFIDENTIAL(1957); TOP SECRET AFFAIR(1957); OCEAN'S ELEVEN(1960); TWELVE HOURS TO KILL(1960); DEAD RINGER(1964); INCREDIBLE MR. LIMPET, THE(1964); QUICK GUN, THE(1964)
Silents
POOR RELATIONS(1919); JUDY OF ROGUES' HARBOUR(1920); LITTLE 'FRAID LADY, THE(1920); BEAUTIFUL LIAR, THE(1921); BEYOND(1921); CRADLE, THE(1922); IN HOLLYWOOD WITH POTASH AND PERLMUTTER(1924)
Misc. Silents
LUCK IN PAWN(1919); OTHER HALF, THE(1919); FAMILY HONOR, THE(1920); PERFECT WOMAN, THE(1920); ROMANTIC ADVENTURESS, A(1920); SIMPLE SOULS(1920); 13TH COMMANDMENT, THE(1920); CAVE GIRL, THE(1921); THAT SOMETHING(1921); WOMAN, WAKE UP!(1922)

Cheerio Meredith
FAT MAN, THE(1951); I'LL CRY TOMORROW(1955); CASE AGAINST BROOKLYN, THE(1958); I MARRIED A WOMAN(1958); LEGEND OF TOM DOOLEY, THE(1959); THREE STOOGES IN ORBIT, THE(1962); WONDERFUL WORLD OF THE BROTH-ERS ERIMM, THE(1962); SEX AND THE SINGLE GIRL(1964)

Dana Meredith [Dana Medricka]
VOYAGE TO THE END OF THE UNIVERSE(1963, Czech.)

Frank Meredith
MEN OF THE NIGHT(1934); IT HAD TO HAPPEN(1936); PENITENTIARY(1938); THEY MADE ME A CRIMINAL(1939); HOLD THAT WOMAN(1940); MEET JOHN DOE(1941); DICK TRACY(1945); DEADLINE AT DAWN(1946); JOHNNY COMES FLYING HOME(1946); CHICKEN EVERY SUNDAY(1948); EAST SIDE, WEST SI-DE(1949)

Iris Meredith
HAT CHECK GIRL(1932); COWBOY STAR, THE(1936); GAMBLING TERROR, THE(1937); LAWMAN IS BORN, A(1937); MYSTERY OF THE HOODED HORSEMEN, THE(1937); RIO GRANDE RANGER(1937); TRAIL OF VENGEANCE(1937); CALL OF THE ROCKIES(1938); CATTLE RAIDERS(1938); COLORADO TRAIL(1938); I AM THE LAW(1938); LAW OF THE PLAINS(1938); OUTLAWS OF THE PRAIRIE(1938); SOUTH OF ARIZONA(1938); WEST OF CHEYENNE(1938); WEST OF SANTA FE(1938); MAN FROM SUNDOWN, THE(1939); MURDER IS NEWS(1939); OUTPOST OF THE MOUN-TIES(1939); RIDERS OF BLACK RIVER(1939); SPOILERS OF THE RANGE(1939); TAMING OF THE WEST, THE(1939); TEXAS STAMPEDE(1939); THOSE HIGH GREY WALLS(1939); THUNDERING WEST, THE(1939); WESTERN CARAVANS(1939); BLAZING SIX SHOOTERS(1940); MAN FROM TUMBLEWEEDS, THE(1940); RE-TURN OF WILD BILL, THE(1940); TEXAS STAGECOACH(1940); THUNDERING FRONTIER(1940); TWO-FISTED RANGERS(1940); CAUGHT IN THE ACT(1941); LOUISIANA PURCHASE(1941); SON OF DAVY CROCKETT, THE(1941); RANGERS TAKE OVER, THE(1942); KID RIDES AGAIN, THE(1943)

Jack Meredith
Silents
MAN HATER, THE(1917)
Misc. Silents
GOLDEN ROSARY, THE(1917); POPPY(1917); SLOTH(1917); FROZEN WARNING, THE(1918)

Jane Meredith
BEHIND GREEN LIGHTS(1935)
Silents
PURSUING VENGEANCE, THE(1916)

Janice Meredith
Silents
JANICE MEREDITH(1924), w

Jay Meredith
SEEDS OF FREEDOM(1943, USSR)

Jill Meredith
SONG IS BORN, A(1948)

Jill Mai Meredith
COOL MIKADO, THE(1963, Brit.); CARRY ON SPYING(1964, Brit.); CURSE OF THE MUMMY'S TOMB, THE(1965, Brit.); LEATHER BOYS, THE(1965, Brit.); YOU MUST BE JOKING!(1965, Brit.)

Jo Anne Meredith
DIRT GANG, THE(1972); DON IS DEAD, THE(1973); HOW TO SEDUCE A WO-MAN(1974); LAST PORNO FLICK, THE(1974); J.D.'S REVENGE(1976)

1984
INVISIBLE STRANGLER(1984)
Joan Meredith
Silents
BLUE BLOOD(1925); FIGHTING BOOB, THE(1926); KING OF THE SADDLE(1926)
Misc. Silents
PERFECT CLOWN, THE(1925)
JoAnne Meredith
PEACE FOR A GUNFIGHTER(1967)
Misc. Talkies
PSYCHO LOVER(1969, Brit.)
John Meredith
STORY OF VERNON AND IRENE CASTLE, THE(1939); FOREIGN CORRESPOND-ENT(1940); CHARLEY'S AUNT(1941); INTERNATIONAL SQUADRON(1941); PARIS CALLING(1941); YANK IN THE R.A.F., A(1941); TEN GENTLEMEN FROM WEST POINT(1942); JANE EYRE(1944); NONE BUT THE LONELY HEART(1944); DEVO-TION(1946); GHOST OF HIDDEN VALLEY(1946); EXILE, THE(1947); TWO BLONDES AND A REDHEAD(1947)
Judi Meredith
JACK THE GIANT KILLER(1962); RAIDERS, THE(1964); DARK INTRUDER(1965); QUEEN OF BLOOD(1966); SOMETHING BIG(1971)
Judith Meredith
NIGHT WALKER, THE(1964)
Judy Meredith
MONEY, WOMEN AND GUNS(1958); SUMMER LOVE(1958); WILD HERITA-GE(1958)
Lee Meredith
PRODUCERS, THE(1967); HELLO DOWN THERE(1969); WELCOME TO THE CLUB(1971); STOOLIE, THE(1972); HAIL(1973); SUNSHINE BOYS, THE(1975)
Lois Meredith
CONQUEST(1937)
Silents
CONSPIRACY, THE(1914); DAN(1914); SEATS OF THE MIGHTY, THE(1914); WOM-AN, THE(1915); SOLD AT AUCTION(1917); ON THE QUIET(1918)
Misc. Silents
ANTIQUE DEALER, THE(1915); ENEMY TO SOCIETY, AN(1915); GREATER WILL, THE(1915); HELP WANTED(1915); MY BEST GIRL(1915); PRECIOUS PACKET, THE(1916); SPELLBOUND(1916); IN THE HANDS OF THE LAW(1917); OVER THE TOP(1918); LE SECRET DE ROSETTE LAMBERT(1920, Fr.); HEADLESS HORSE-MAN, THE(1922)
Lu Ann Meredith
KISS AND MAKE UP(1934); SPORTING LOVE(1936, Brit.)
Lu Anne Meredith
BALL AT SAVOY(1936, Brit.)
Lu Annie Meredith
YOUNG AND BEAUTIFUL(1934)
Luanne Meredith
SING AS YOU SWING(1937, Brit.)
Lucille Meredith
BANNING(1967); WAR BETWEEN MEN AND WOMEN, THE(1972); MIDNIGHT MAN, THE(1974)
Madeleine Meredith
Misc. Silents
SILVER BRIDGE, THE(1920, Brit.)
Madge Meredith
CHILD OF DIVORCE(1946); FALCON'S ADVENTURE, THE(1946); TRAIL STREET(1947); TO HELL AND BACK(1955); GUNS OF FORT PETTICOAT, THE(1957)
Melba Meredith
CRISIS(1950); LATIN LOVERS(1953)
Penny Meredith
FLESH AND BLOOD SHOW, THE(1974, Brit.)
Ralph Meredith
FOLLOW THE BOYS(1944)
Robert Meredith
WILD HORSE PHANTOM(1944)
Roy Meredith
SCARLET PIMPERNEL, THE(1935, Brit.)
Ruth Meredith
OLD MOTHER RILEY OVERSEAS(1943, Brit.)
Stanley Meredith
SALT OF THE EARTH(1954), ph
Susan Meredith
HOW SWEET IT IS(1968)
Meredith Neal and the Boot Heel Boys
TIGER BY THE TAIL(1970)
Iris Meredity
FIRST OFFENDERS(1939)
John Meredity
IMMORTAL SERGEANT, THE(1943)
Olga Merediz
1984
BROTHER FROM ANOTHER PLANET, THE(1984)
Madge Meredtith
TUMBLEWEED(1953)
Bess Meredyth
WONDER OF WOMEN(1929), w; BLUSHING BRIDES(1930), w; CHASING RAIN-BOWS(1930), w; IN GAY MADRID(1930), w; OUR BLUSHING BRIDES(1930), w; ROMANCE(1930), w; SEA BAT, THE(1930), w; CUBAN LOVE SONG,THE(1931), w; LAUGHING SINNERS(1931), w; PHANTOM OF PARIS, THE(1931), w; PRODIGAL, THE(1931), w; WEST OF BROADWAY(1931), w; STRANGE INTERLUDE(1932), w; LOOKING FORWARD(1933), w; AFFAIRS OF CELLINI, THE(1934), w; MIGHTY BARNUM, THE(1934), w; FOLIES DERGERE(1935), w; IRON DUKE, THE(1935, Brit.), w; METROPOLITAN(1935), w; CHARLIE CHAN AT THE OPERA(1936), w; HALF ANGEL(1936), w; GREAT HOSPITAL MYSTERY, THE(1937), w; MARK OF ZORRO, THE(1940), w; THAT NIGHT IN RIO(1941), w; UNSUSPECTED, THE(1947), w
Silents
RED, RED HEART, THE(1918), w; FIGHTING BREED, THE(1921), w; DANGEROUS AGE, THE(1922), w; ONE CLEAR CALL(1922), w; SONG OF LIFE, THE(1922), w; STRANGERS OF THE NIGHT(1923), w; BEN-HUR(1925), w; DON JUAN(1926), w;

SEA BEAST, THE(1926), w; IRISH HEARTS(1927), w; MYSTERIOUS LADY, THE(1928), w; SCARLET LADY, THE(1928), w; WOMAN OF AFFAIRS, A(1928), w
Misc. Silents
SPANISH JADE, THE(1915); GIRL FROM NOWHERE, THE(1919), d
Bernard Merefield
MAN OF AFFAIRS(1937, Brit.)
Dimitri Merejkowski
PATRIOT, THE(1928), w
Claude Merelle
Misc. Silents
LE ROI DE CAMARGUE(1921, Fr.); DIAMANT NOIR(1922, Fr.); NOTRE DAME D'AMOUR(1922, Fr.); MILADY(1923, Fr.)
Luc Merenda
LE MANS(1971)
Misc. Talkies
THEY CALLED HIM AMEN(1972)
Luke Merenda
RED SUN(1972, Fr./Ital./Span.)
Pam Merenda
FIEND(
Victor Merenda
PARDON MY FRENCH(1951, U.S./Fr.)
John Merensky
LOVE STORY(1970)
Violet Meresereau
Misc. Silents
HONOR OF MARY BLAKE, THE(1916)
Bernard Meresfield
STRANGE BOARDERS(1938, Brit.)
Carla Merey
GREEN-EYED BLONDE, THE(1957)
Isabelle Mergault
DIVA(1982, Fr.)
Olivier Mergault
MOON IN THE GUTTER, THE(1983, Fr./Ital.), w
Charles Mergendahl
BRAMBLE BUSH, THE(1960), w
Marie Mergey
GREEN MARE, THE(1961, Fr./Ital.); STORY OF THE COUNT OF MONTE CRISTO, THE(1962, Fr./Ital.); DAY AND THE HOUR, THE(1963, Fr./ Ital.); LA GUERRE EST FINIE(1967, Fr./Swed.)
Brad Merhege
SANTEE(1973)
Youssef Merhi
MEGAFORCE(1982)
B.J. Merholz
DRIVE, HE SAID(1971); SHOOTING, THE(1971); GOIN' SOUTH(1978)
Ronald Merians
1984
TEACHERS(1984)
Doris Merick
BIG NOISE, THE(1944)
Marti Mericka
ONE POTATO, TWO POTATO(1964)
Bill Merickel
WILD PARTY, THE(1975)
Tommie Merickel
WILD PARTY, THE(1975)
Iris Meridith
CONVICTED WOMAN(1940)
Jane Meridith
LOVE CAPTIVE, THE(1934)
Augusta Merighi
ROSE TATTOO, THE(1955); CATERED AFFAIR, THE(1956); ER LOVE A STRAN-GER(1958); THIS EARTH IS MINE(1959)
Maria Meriko
LADY IN THE CAR WITH GLASSES AND A GUN, THE(1970, U.S./Fr.)
Ann Meril
MORE THAN A SECRETARY(1936)
Macha Meril
ANATOMY OF A MARRIAGE(MY DAYS WITH JEAN-MARC AND MY NIGHTS WITH FRANCOISE)**1/2 (1964 Fr.); LOVE ON A PILLOW(1963, Fr./Ital.); WHO'S BEEN SLEEPING IN MY BED?(1963); MARRIED WOMAN, THE(1965, Fr.); DEFEC-TOR, THE(1966, Ger./Fr.); RAMPAGE AT APACHE WELLS(1966, Ger./Yugo.); DON'T PLAY WITH MARTIANS(1967, Fr.); BELLE DE JOUR(1968, Fr.); DEEP RED(1976, Ital.); CHINESE ROULETTE(1977, Ger.); BEAU PERE(1981, Fr.); BOLERO(1982, Fr.); COUSINS IN LOVE(1982)
Tony Merill
CLOWN, THE(1953)
Prosper Merimee
CARMEN(1931, Brit.), w; CARMEN(1946, Ital.), w; LOVES OF CARMEN, THE(1948), w; CARMEN(1949, Span.), w; VENDETTA(1950), w; GOLDEN COACH, THE(1953, Fr./Ital.), w; TAMANGO(1959, Fr.), w; DEVIL MADE A WOMAN, THE(1962, Span.), w; CARMEN, BABY(1967, Yugo./Ger.), w
1984
FIRST NAME: CARMEN(1984, Fr.), w
Silents
CARMEN(1915), w
Gregory Merims
PEKING EXPRESS(1951)
Al Merin
LINEUP, THE(1958)
Eda Reis Merin
NO WAY OUT(1950); I CAN GET IT FOR YOU WHOLESALE(1951); DON'T BOTHER TO KNOCK(1952)
Eda Reiss Merin
KNOCK ON ANY DOOR(1949); LADY GAMBLES, THE(1949); WHERE THE SIDE-WALK ENDS(1950); LILI(1953); WHAT'S SO BAD ABOUT FEELING GOOD?(1968); HESTER STREET(1975); TO BE OR NOT TO BE(1983)

1984
GHOSTBUSTERS(1984)
Eda Reys Merin
TONIGHT WE SING(1953)
Angel Merino
EXTERMINATING ANGEL, THE(1967, Mex.)
Francisco Merino
1984
DEMONS IN THE GARDEN(1984, Span.)
Jose Luis Merino
SANTO CONTRA EL DOCTOR MUERTE(1974, Span./Mex.), w
Manuel Merino
TEACHER AND THE MIRACLE, THE(1961, Ital./Span.), ph; GUNFIGHTERS OF
CASA GRANDE(1965, U.S./Span.), ph; KID RODELO(1966, U.S./Span.), ph; HOUSE
OF 1,000 DOLLS(1967, Ger./Span./Brit.), ph; BLOOD OF FU MANCHU, THE(1968,
Brit.), ph; CASTLE OF FU MANCHU, THE(1968, Ger./Span./Ital./Brit.), ph;
EVE(1968, Brit./Span.), ph; MISSION STARDUST(1968, Ital./Span./Ger.), ph; RIO
70(1970, U.S./Ger./Span.), ph
Rick Merino
NORSEMAN, THE(1978)
Victor Merinow
GIRL IN ROOM 13(1961, U.S./Braz.)
Pipo Merisi
CATHERINE & CO.(1976, Fr.)
Pippo Merisi
CESAR AND ROSALIE(1972, Fr.)
Michele Meritz
COUSINS, THE(1959, Fr.); WAR OF THE BUTTONS(1963 Fr.)
Michelle Meritz
LE BEAU SERGE(1959, Fr.)
Bernard Merivale
FLYING FOOL, THE(1931, Brit.), w; WHEN LONDON SLEEPS(1932, Brit.), w; ALL
IN(1936, Brit.), w; DOMMED CARGO(1936, Brit.), w; FOOTSTEPS IN THE
DARK(1941), w
Silents
KILTIES THREE(1918, Brit.), w
John Merivale
INVISIBLE MAN, THE(1933); PURSUIT OF THE GRAF SPEE(1957, Brit.); NIGHT
TO REMEMBER, A(1958, Brit.); CALTIKI, THE IMMORTAL MONSTER(1959, Ital.);
CIRCUS OF HORRORS(1960, Brit.); HOUSE OF MYSTERY(1961, Brit.); LIST OF
ADRIAN MESSENGER, THE(1963); KING RAT(1965); ARABESQUE(1966)
Philip Merivale
GIVE US THIS NIGHT(1936); LADY FOR A NIGHT(1941); MR. AND MRS.
SMITH(1941); RAGE IN HEAVEN(1941); CROSSROADS(1942); PACIFIC BLACK-
OUT(1942); THIS LAND IS MINE(1943); HANGMEN ALSO DIE(1943); HER
FIRST MATE(1933); MEN ARE SUCH FOOLS(1933); MIDNIGHT MARY(1933); REUN-
TURE(1945); TONIGHT AND EVERY NIGHT(1945); SISTER KENNY(1946); STRAN-
GER THE(1946)
Misc. Silents
WHISPERING SHADOWS(1922)
Phillip Merivale
MIDNIGHT ANGEL(1941); HOUR BEFORE THE DAWN, THE(1944)
Lee Meriwether
4D MAN(1959); BATMAN(1966); NAMU, THE KILLER WHALE(1966); LEGEND OF
LYLAH CLARE, THE(1968); ANGEL IN MY POCKET(1969); UNDEFEATED,
THE(1969); BROTHERS O'TOOLE, THE(1973)
Steve Merjanian
MUSCLE BEACH PARTY(1964)
Neil Merk
SATAN'S BED(1965)
Ron Merk
PINOCCHIO(1969, E. Ger.), p, d, w
Misc. Talkies
PINOCCHIO'S STORYBOOK ADVENTURES(1979), d
John Merkel
VIVA VILLA!(1934)
Una Merkel
ABRAHAM LINCOLN(1930); BAT WHISPERS, THE(1930); EYES OF THE WORLD,
THE(1930); BARGAIN, THE(1931); COMMAND PERFORMANCE(1931); DADDY
LONG LEGS(1931); DON'T BET ON WOMEN(1931); MALTESE FALCON, THE(1931);
PRIVATE LIVES(1931); SECRET WITNESS, THE(1931); SIX CYLINDER LOVE(1931);
WICKED(1931); HUDDLE(1932); IMPATIENT MAIDEN(1932); MAN WANTED(1932);
RED HEADED WOMAN(1932); SHE WANTED A MILLIONAIRE(1932); THEY CALL
IT SIN(1932); BEAUTY FOR SALE(1933); BOMBSHELL(1933); BROADWAY TO
HOLLYWOOD(1933); CLEAR ALL WIRES(1933); DAY OF RECKONING(1933); HER
FIRST MATE(1933); MEN ARE SUCH FOOLS(1933); MIDNIGHT MARY(1933); REUN-
ION IN VIENNA(1933); SECRET OF MADAME BLANCHE, THE(1933); WHISTLING
IN THE DARK(1933); 42ND STREET(1933); BULLDOG DRUMMOND STRIKES
BACK(1934); CAT'S PAW, THE(1934); EVELYN PRENTICE(1934); HAVE A
HEART(1934); MERRY WIDOW, THE(1934); MURDER IN THE PRIVATE CAR(1934);
PARIS INTERLUDE(1934); THIS SIDE OF HEAVEN(1934); WOMEN IN HIS LIFE,
THE(1934); BABY FACE HARRINGTON(1935); BIOGRAPHY OF A BACHELOR
GIRL(1935); BROADWAY MELODY OF 1936(1935); IT'S IN THE AIR(1935); MURDER
IN THE FLEET(1935); NIGHT IS YOUNG, THE(1935); ONE NEW YORK NIGHT(1935);
BORN TO DANCE(1936); RIFF-RAFF(1936); SPEED(1936); WE WENT TO COL-
LEGE(1936); CHECKERS(1937); DON'T TELL THE WIFE(1937); GOOD OLD SOAR,
THE(1937); SARATOGA(1937); TRUE CONFESSION(1937); DESTRY RIDES
AGAIN(1939); FOUR GIRLS IN WHITE(1939); ON BORROWED TIME(1939); SOME
LIKE IT HOT(1939); BANK DICK, THE(1940); COMIN' ROUND THE MOUN-
TAIN(1940); SANDY GETS HER MAN(1940); CRACKED NUTS(1941); DOUBLE
DATE(1941); ROAD TO ZANZIBAR(1941); MAD DOCTOR OF MARKET STREET,
THE(1942); TWIN BEDS(1942); THIS IS THE ARMY(1943); SWEETHEARTS OF THE
U.S.A.(1944); IT'S A JOKE, SON!(1947); BRIDE GOES WILD, THE(1948); MAN FROM
TEXAS, THE(1948); EMERGENCY WEDDING(1950); KILL THE UMPIRE(1950); MY
BLUE HEAVEN(1950); GOLDEN GIRL(1951); MILLIONAIRE FOR CHRISTY, A(1951);
RICH, YOUNG AND PRETTY(1951); MERRY WIDOW, THE(1952); WITH A SONG IN
MY HEART(1952); I LOVE MELVIN(1953); KENTUCKIAN, THE(1955); BUNDLE OF
JOY(1956); KETTLES IN THE OZARKS, THE(1956); FUZZY PINK NIGHTGOWN,
THE(1957); GIRL MOST LIKELY, THE(1957); MATING GAME, THE(1959); PARENT
TRAP, THE(1961); SUMMER AND SMOKE(1961); SUMMER MAGIC(1963); TIGER

WALKS, A(1964); SPINOUT(1966)
Silents
WAY DOWN EAST(1920)
Misc. Silents
FIFTH HORSEMAN, THE(1924)
Philip Merker
ILLIAC PASSION, THE(1968)
Vasili Merkureyev
MOSCOW–CASSIOPEIA(1974, USSR)
Vasili Merkuriev
TWELFTH NIGHT(1956, USSR)
Victor Merkuriev
ROAD HOME, THE(1947, USSR)
Vasiliy Merkuryev
SUMMER TO REMEMBER, A(1961, USSR); SONG OVER MOSCOW(1964, USSR)
Vasily Merkuryev
CRANES ARE FLYING, THE(1960, USSR)
John Merkyl
MERRY WIDOW, THE(1934); THEY ALL KISSED THE BRIDE(1942); PEARL OF
DEATH, THE(1944)
Silents
BREAKING POINT, THE(1924); CAPTAIN JANUARY(1924); UNHOLY THREE,
THE(1925)
Misc. Silents
BURDEN OF PROOF, THE(1918); MAN'S WORLD, A(1918)
Wilmuth Merkyl
Misc. Silents
GRETNA GREEN(1915); VICTORY OF VIRTUE, THE(1915); FORTUNATE YOUTH,
THE(1916); HERE SURRENDER(1916); SOUL MARKET, THE(1916); FEDORA(1918);
SUSPICION(1918)
Tony Merl
UNDER TWO FLAGS(1936)
O. Merlatti
Silents
ARSENAL(1929, USSR)
Frank Merle
TERROR-CREATURES FROM THE GRAVE(1967, U.S./Ital.), p
Robert Merle
WEEKEND AT DUNKIRK(1966, Fr./Ital.), w; DAY OF THE DOLPHIN, THE(1973),
w; MALEVIL(1981, Fr./Ger.), w
Tony Merle
O.S.S.(1946)
Zofia Merle
GUESTS ARE COMING(1965, Pol.)
Merle Travis and His Bronco Busters
CYCLONE FURY(1951)
Adalberto Maria Merli
WOMAN WITH RED BOOTS, THE(1977, Fr./Span.)
Francesco Merli
BLOODY PIT OF HORROR, THE(1965, Ital.), p
Franco Merli
ARABIAN NIGHTS(1980, Ital./Fr.)
Maurizio Merli
COVERT ACTION(1980, Ital.); PRIEST OF LOVE(1981, Brit.)
Mike Merli
Misc. Talkies
BRUTAL JUSTICE(1978)
Claude Merlin
BAROCCO(1976, Fr.), ed
Claudine Merlin
MURIEL(1963, Fr./Ital.), ed; LA GRANDE BOUFFE(1973, Fr.), ed; GET OUT YOUR
HANDKERCHIEFS(1978, Fr.), ed; BRONTE SISTERS, THE(1979, Fr.), ed; BEAU
PERE(1981, Fr.), ed
1984
MY BEST FRIEND'S GIRL(1984, Fr.), ed
Frank Merlin
WORDS AND MUSIC(1929), ch, ch
Jan Merlin
ILLEGAL(1955); RUNNING WILD(1955); SIX BRIDGES TO CROSS(1955); DAY OF
FURY, A(1956); PEACEMAKER, THE(1956); SCREAMING EAGLES(1956); STRANGE
ADVENTURE, A(1956); WOMAN AND THE HUNTER, THE(1957); COLE YOUNGER,
GUNFIGHTER(1958); HELL BENT FOR LEATHER(1960); GUNFIGHT AT COMAN-
CHE CREEK(1964); GUNS OF DIABLO(1964); ST. VALENTINE'S DAY MASSACRE,
THE(1967); STRATEGY OF TERROR(1969); TAKE THE MONEY AND RUN(1969);
TWILIGHT PEOPLE(1972, Phil.); SLAMS, THE(1973); HINDENBURG, THE(1975)
Joanna Merlin
WEDDINGS AND BABIES(1960); FAME(1980); LOVE CHILD(1982); SOUP FOR
ONE(1982); BABY, IT'S YOU(1983)
1984
KILLING FIELDS, THE(1984, Brit.)
Joanne Merlin
TEN COMMANDMENTS, THE(1956)
Milton Merlin
HENRY GOES ARIZONA(1939), w; KID FROM TEXAS, THE(1939), w
Monica Merlin
REPULSION(1965, Brit.)
Paul Merlin
Misc. Talkies
RATS(1984)
Serge Merlin
TUSK(1980, Fr.); DANTON(1983)
1984
LOVE IN GERMANY, A(1984, Fr./Ger.)
Virginie Merlin
ZAZIE(1961, Fr.)
Marisa Merlini
BREAD, LOVE AND DREAMS(1953, Ital.); FRISKY(1955, Ital.); WORLD IN MY
POCKET, THE(1962, Fr./Ital./Ger.); ENGAGEMENT ITALIANO(1966, Fr./Ital.); COR-
RUPT ONES, THE(1967, Ger.); OPIATE '67(1967, Fr./Ital.); MOTIVE WAS JEALOUSY,
THE(1970 Ital./Span.); PIZZA TRIANGLE, THE(1970, Ital./Span.)

Gene Merlino
YOUNG GIRLS OF ROCHEFORT, THE(1968, Fr.)

Anthony Merlo
Silents
ETERNAL SIN, THE(1917); JUST SYLVIA(1918)
Misc. Silents
BLACK BUTTERFLY, THE(1916); NARROW PATH, THE(1916); CROSS BEARER, THE(1918); SEA WAIF, THE(1918); SOUL OF BUDDHA, THE(1918); TINSEL(1918)

Ismael Merlo
HUNT, THE(1967, Span.)

Tony Merlo
LOVE ME TONIGHT(1932); MAN'S CASTLE, A(1933); SHOOT THE WORKS(1934); ENTER MADAME(1935); HOLD'EM YALE(1935); SECRET OF THE CHATEAU(1935); DESIRE(1936); LADIES IN LOVE(1936); LONE WOLF RETURNS, THE(1936); CHAMPAGNE WALTZ(1937); ARTISTS AND MODELS ABROAD(1938); IN NAME ONLY(1939); TILL THE CLOUDS ROLL BY(1946)

Joy Merlyn
GET CARTER(1971, Brit.)

Dan Merman
MARY BURNS, FUGITIVE(1935)

Ethel Merman
FOLLOW THE LEADER(1930); KID MILLIONS(1934); WE'RE NOT DRESSING(1934); BIG BROADCAST OF 1936, THE(1935); ANYTHING GOES(1936); STRIKE ME PINK(1936); ALEXANDER'S RAGTIME BAND(1938); HAPPY LANDING(1938); STRAIGHT, PLACE AND SHOW(1938); STAGE DOOR CANTEEN(1943); CALL ME MADAM(1953); THERE'S NO BUSINESS LIKE SHOW BUSINESS(1954); IT'S A MAD, MAD, MAD, MAD WORLD(1963); ART OF LOVE, THE(1965); JOURNEY BACK TO OZ(1974); WON TON TON, THE DOG WHO SAVED HOLLYWOOD(1976); AIRPLANE!(1980)

Merminod
THREEPENNY OPERA, THE(1931, Ger./U.S.); TESTAMENT OF DR. MABUSE, THE(1943, Ger.)

Billy Mernit
TIMES SQUARE(1980)

Edith Mero
ARTHUR(1931, Fr.)

A.A. Merola
UNDER MY SKIN(1950)

Augusta Merola
GHOSTS, ITALIAN STYLE(1969, Ital./Fr.)

Enzo Merolle
SIEGE OF SYRACUSE(1962, Fr./Ital.), p; PONTIUS PILATE(1967, Fr./Ital.), p

George Merolle
WANDERERS, THE(1979)

Nicole Merouze
FIVE WILD GIRLS(1966, Fr.)

Pierre Merovee
FORBIDDEN GAMES(1953, Fr.)

Mary Merrall
MEN OF STEEL(1932, Brit.); DR. O'DOWD(1940, Brit.); YOU WILL REMEMBER(1941, Brit.); SQUADRON LEADER X(1943, Brit.); LOVE ON THE DOLE(1945, Brit.); DEAD OF NIGHT(1946, Brit.); THIS MAN IS MINE(1946 Brit.); I BECAME A CRIMINAL(1947); NICHOLAS NICKLEBY(1947, Brit.); THREE WEIRD SISTERS, THE(1948, Brit.); BADGER'S GREEN(1949, Brit.); FOR THEM THAT TRESPASS(1949, Brit.); PINK STRING AND SEALING WAX(1950, Brit.); TRIO(1950, Brit.); ENCORE(1951, Brit.); OBSESSED(1951, Brit.); JUDGMENT DEFERRED(1952, Brit.); PICKWICK PAPERS, THE(1952, Brit.); TONIGHT AT 8:30(1953, Brit.); DESTINATION MILAN(1954, Brit.); DUEL IN THE JUNGLE(1954, Brit.); GREEN BUDDHA, THE(1954, Brit.); LAST MOMENT, THE(1954, Brit.); WEAK AND THE WICKED, THE(1954, Brit.); IT'S GREAT TO BE YOUNG(1956, Brit.); CAMPBELL'S KINGDOM(1957, Brit.); RX MURDER(1958, Brit.); SPARE THE ROD(1961, Brit.); BITTER HARVEST(1963, Brit.); AMOROUS ADVENTURES OF MOLL FLANDERS, THE(1965); WHO KILLED THE CAT?(1966, Brit.)
Silents
FATAL FINGERS(1916. Brit.)

Carol Merrell
THIS STUFF'LL KILL YA!(1971)

Dick Merrell
ONE SUMMER LOVE(1976), set d

Richard Merrell
RACHEL, RACHEL(1968), set d; EFFECT OF GAMMA RAYS ON MAN-IN-THE-MOON MARIGOLDS, THE(1972), set d

Mel Merrells
DAYS OF HEAVEN(1978), spec eff

Janine Merrey
BETRAYAL(1939, Fr.)

Charlotte Merriam
BROADWAY HOOFER, THE(1929); PLEASURE CRAZED(1929); QUEEN OF THE NIGHTCLUBS(1929); DUMBBELLS IN ERMINE(1930); SECOND CHOICE(1930); THIRD ALARM, THE(1930); NIGHT NURSE(1931); SMART MONEY(1931); CROWD ROARS, THE(1932); MAN WANTED(1932); TENDERFOOT, THE(1932); WINNER TAKE ALL(1932); ALIMONY MADNESS(1933); AVENGER, THE(1933); THREE-CORNERED MOON(1933); DANCING MAN(1934); DAMAGED LIVES(1937)
Silents
NTH COMMANDMENT, THE(1923); PAINTED PEOPLE(1924); SO BIG(1924); ONE PUNCH O'DAY(1926)
Misc. Silents
BREATHLESS MOMENT, THE(1924); CAPTAIN BLOOD(1924); CODE OF THE WILDERNESS(1924); STELLE OF THE ROYAL MOUNTED(1925); WHEN WINTER WENT(1925)

Eleanor Merriam
T.R. BASKIN(1971)

Steve Merrich
THIS MAN CAN'T DIE(1970, Ital.)

Bob Merrick
REDHEAD FROM WYOMING, THE(1953)

David Merrick
CHILD'S PLAY(1972), p; SEMI-TOUGH(1977), p; ROUGH CUT(1980, Brit.), p

Doris Merrick
GIRL TROUBLE(1942); TIME TO KILL(1942); HEAVEN CAN WAIT(1943); IN THE MEANTIME, DARLING(1944); LADIES OF WASHINGTON(1944); HIT THE HAY(1945); SENSATION HUNTERS(1945); THIS LOVE OF OURS(1945); CHILD OF DIVORCE(1946); PILGRIM LADY, THE(1947); COUNTERFEITERS, THE(1948); FIGHTING STALLION, THE(1950); UNTAMED WOMEN(1952); NEANDERTHAL MAN, THE(1953); INTERRUPTED MELODY(1955)

Frederick Merrick
SPY OF NAPOLEON(1939, Brit.), w

George Merrick
THUNDER OVER TEXAS(1934), ed; CYCLONE OF THE SADDLE(1935), w; SECRETS OF A MODEL(1940), ed; HARD GUY(1941), p; SWAMP WOMAN(1941), p; TODAY I HANG(1942), d; SUBMARINE BASE(1943), w; DELINQUENT DAUGHTERS(1944), ed; SHAKE HANDS WITH MURDER(1944), ed; YOUTH AFLAME(1945), ed; BRIDE AND THE BEAST, THE(1958), ed; SPRING AFFAIR(1960), ed

George M. Merrick
FIGHTING CABALLERO(1935), w; PALS OF THE RANGE(1935), p, w; ROUGH RIDING RANGER(1935), p, w; CITY OF MISSING GIRLS(1941), p; DAWN EXPRESS, THE(1942), p; YANK IN LIBYA, A(1942), p; TIGER FANGS(1943), ed; SWEETHEARTS OF THE U.S.A.(1944), ed
Misc. Talkies
SECRETS OF HOLLYWOOD(1933), d
Silents
KING TUT-ANKH-AMEN'S EIGHTH WIFE(1923), w; TERROR OF BAR X, THE(1927), w

George W. Merrick
MISS V FROM MOSCOW(1942), p

Ian Merrick
BLACK PANTHER, THE(1977, Brit.), p&d

Jack Merrick
KNOCKOUT(1941)

John Merrick
JOE PALOOKA IN THE SQUARED CIRCLE(1950); PREHISTORIC WOMEN(1950); SCARF, THE(1951); LAS VEGAS STORY, THE(1952); KILLERS FROM SPACE(1954); EMERGENCY HOSPITAL(1956); HOT CARS(1956); YAQUI DRUMS(1956); ESCAPE FROM SAN QUENTIN(1957); FIVE STEPS TO DANGER(1957); RIDE OUT FOR REVENGE(1957); AMBUSH AT CIMARRON PASS(1958); SEVEN GUNS TO MESA(1958); TOUGHEST GUN IN TOMBSTONE(1958); ALLIGATOR PEOPLE, THE(1959); ARSON FOR HIRE(1959); THIRTEEN FIGHTING MEN(1960)

Laurence Merrick
GUESS WHAT HAPPENED TO COUNT DRACULA(1970), d&w

Lawrence Merrick
BLACK ANGELS, THE(1970), d,w&ph

Leonard Merrick
MAGNIFICENT LIE(1931), w
Silents
IMPOSTER, THE(1918), w; WORLDLINGS, THE(1920, Brit.), w; DARLING OF THE RICH, THE(1923), w

Lynn Merrick
'TIL WE MEET AGAIN(1940); APACHE KID, THE(1941); DEATH VALLEY OUTLAWS(1941); DESERT BANDIT(1941); GAY VAGABOND, THE(1941); KANSAS CYCLONE(1941); SIS HOPKINS(1941); TWO GUN SHERIFF(1941); ARIZONA TERRORS(1942); CYCLONE KID, THE(1942); JESSE JAMES, JR.(1942); MISSOURI OUTLAW, A(1942); MOUNTAIN RHYTHM(1942); OUTLAWS OF PINE RIDGE(1942); SOMBRERO KID, THE(1942); STAGECOACH EXPRESS(1942); CARSON CITY CYCLONE(1943); CRIME DOCTOR'S STRANGEST CASE(1943); DANGEROUS BLONDES(1943); DAYS OF OLD CHEYENNE(1943); DEAD MAN'S GULCH(1943); DOUGHBOYS IN IRELAND(1943); FUGITIVE FROM SONORA(1943); IS EVERYBODY HAPPY?(1943); SWING OUT THE BLUES(1943); YOUTH ON PARADE(1943); MEET MISS BOBBY SOCKS(1944); NINE GIRLS(1944); STARS ON PARADE(1944); BLONDE FROM BROOKLYN(1945); BOSTON BLACKIE BOOKED ON SUSPICION(1945); GUY, A GAL AND A PAL, A(1945); VOICE OF THE WHISTLER(1945); CLOSE CALL FOR BOSTON BLACKIE, A(1946); DANGEROUS BUSINESS(1946); DOWN TO EARTH(1947); I LOVE TROUBLE(1947); ESCAPE FROM TERROR(1960)

Mahlon Merrick
GIRL FROM MONTEREY, THE(1943), md; SENSATIONS OF 1945(1944), md; MISS MINK OF 1949(1949), m; LAWLESS, THE(1950), m; PASSAGE WEST(1951), m; RED PLANET MARS(1952), m

Marilyn Merrick
DR. CHRISTIAN MEETS THE WOMEN(1940)

Marilyn [Lynn] Merrick
FLIGHT ANGELS(1940); RAGTIME COWBOY JOE(1940)

Philip Merrick
MY MAN GODFREY(1936)

Robert Merrick
NIGHTHAWKS(1978, Brit.)

Simon Merrick
NO BLADE OF GRASS(1970, Brit.)

William Merrick
Misc. Silents
UGLY DUCKLING, THE(1920, Brit.)

Merriel Abbott & Her Abbott Dancers
SWING FEVER(1943)

Merriel Abbott Dancers
MAN ABOUT TOWN(1939); BUCK BENNY RIDES AGAIN(1940); LOVE THY NEIGHBOR(1940)

Dick Merrifield
HELLCATS, THE(1968); SHEBA BABY(1975)

Richard Merrifield
FIVE THE HARD WAY(1969)

Tom Merrifield
HALF A SIXPENCE(1967, Brit.); YOUNG GIRLS OF ROCHEFORT, THE(1968, Fr.)

Mal Merrihue
TASK FORCE(1949)

Mal Merrihugh
LADIES' DAY(1943); PASSPORT TO SUEZ(1943)

John Merril
EXILES, THE(1966), ph

Ann Merrill
THEY MET IN A TAXI(1936)
Anthony Merrill
MANDARIN MYSTERY, THE(1937); SCENE OF THE CRIME(1949)
Barbara D. Merrill
WHATEVER HAPPENED TO BABY JANE?(1962)
Blanche Merrill
Silents
BLUEBEARD'S SEVEN WIVES(1926), w
Bob Merrill
SENORITA FROM THE WEST(1945); FUNNY GIRL(1968), w; W.C. FIELDS AND ME(1976), w
Carol Merrill
MY FAIR LADY(1964); GNOME-MOBILE, THE(1967)
Catherine Merrill
IN THE COUNTRY(1967); EDGE, THE(1968)
Concordia Merrill
Silents
LOST CHORD, THE(1917, Brit.); AVE MARIA(1918, Brit.)
Misc. Silents
MY SWEETHEART(1918, Brit.); SMART SET, A(1919, Brit.)
Dick Merrill
ATLANTIC FLIGHT(1937)
Dina Merrill
DESK SET(1957); NICE LITTLE BANK THAT SHOULD BE ROBBED, A(1958); DON'T GIVE UP THE SHIP(1959); OPERATION PETTICOAT(1959); BUTTERFIELD 8(1960); SUNDOWNERS, THE(1960); TWENTY PLUS TWO(1961); YOUNG SAVAGES, THE(1961); COURTSHIP OF EDDY'S FATHER, THE(1963); I'LL TAKE SWEDEN(1965); RUNNING WILD(1973); MEAL, THE(1975); GREATEST, THE(1977, U.S./Brit.); WEDDING, A(1978); JUST TELL ME WHAT YOU WANT(1980)
Misc. Talkies
CATCH ME IF YOU CAN(1959); DEADLY ENCOUNTER(1979)
Frank Merrill
WHITE GORILLA(1947)
Silents
LITTLE WILD GIRL, THE(1928)
Misc. Silents
BATTLING MASON(1924); FIGHTING HEART, A(1924); RECKLESS SPEED(1924); DASHING THRU(1925); GENTLEMAN ROUGHNECK, A(1925); SAVAGES OF THE SEA(1925); SHACKLED LIGHTING(1925); SPEED MADNESS(1925); CUPID'S KNOCKOUT(1926); FIGHTING DOCTOR, THE(1926); HOLLYWOOD REPORTER, THE(1926); UNKNOWN DANGERS(1926)
Gail Merrill
NIGHT IN HEAVEN, A(1983)
Gary Merrill
SLATTERY'S HURRICANE(1949); TWELVE O'CLOCK HIGH(1949); MOTHER DIDN'T TELL ME(1950); WHERE THE SIDEWALK ENDS(1950); DECISION BEFORE DAWN(1951); FROGMEN, THE(1951); ANOTHER MAN'S POISON(1951, Brit.); GIRL IN WHITE, THE(1952); NIGHT WITHOUT SLEEP(1952); PHONE CALL FROM A STRANGER(1952); BLUEPRINT FOR MURDER, A(1953); BLACK DAKOTAS, THE(1954); HUMAN JUNGLE, THE(1954); WITNESS TO MURDER(1954); BERMUDA AFFAIR(1956, Brit.); NAVY WIFE(1956); CRASH LANDING(1958); MISSOURI TRAVELER, THE(1958); WONDERFUL COUNTRY, THE(1959); GREAT IMPOSTOR, THE(1960); SAVAGE EYE, THE(1960); MYSTERIOUS ISLAND(1961, U.S./Brit.); PLEASURE OF HIS COMPANY, THE(1961); GIRL NAMED TAMIRO, A(1962); WOMAN WHO WOULDN'T DIE, THE(1965, Brit.); AROUND THE WORLD UNDER THE SEA(1966); CAST A GIANT SHADOW(1966); DESTINATION INNER SPACE(1966); RIDE BEYOND VENGEANCE(1966); CLAMBAKE(1967); INCIDENT, THE(1967); LAST CHALLENGE, THE(1967); POWER, THE(1968); SECRET OF THE SACRED FOREST, THE(1970); HUCKLEBERRY FINN(1974); THIEVES(1977)
Cpl. Gary Merrill
WINGED VICTORY(1944)
James Merrill
SOUTH OF SONORA(1930)
Joan Merrill
TIME OUT FOR RHYTHM(1941); ICELAND(1942); MAYOR OF 44TH STREET, THE(1942)
Joe J. Merrill
BIG CARNIVAL, THE(1951)
Keith Merrill
THREE WARRIORS(1977), d; TAKE DOWN(1979), p&d, w; WINDWALKER(1980), d; HARRY'S WAR(1981), p, d&w
Larry Merrill
GIRLS ON THE BEACH(1965); HAPPIEST MILLIONAIRE, THE(1967)
Lew Merrill
KIT CARSON(1940)
Lou Merrill
TROPIC FURY(1939); NORTHWEST MOUNTED POLICE(1940); NEW WINE(1941); PASSPORT TO SUEZ(1943); CHARGE OF THE LANCERS(1953); HINDU, THE(1953, Brit.); DUEL ON THE MISSISSIPPI(1955); DEVIL AT FOUR O'CLOCK, THE(1961)
Louis Merrill
LADY FROM SHANGHAI, THE(1948); FORT TI(1953); CROOKED WEB, THE(1955)
Louis D. Merrill
IRON GLOVE, THE(1954); GIANT CLAW, THE(1957)
Martha Merrill
HERE COMES THE NAVY(1934); ST. LOUIS KID(1934); DEVIL DOGS OF THE AIR(1935); G-MEN(1935); LIVING ON VELVET(1935); SHIPMATES FOREVER(1935)
Mary Merrill
PATTERNS(1956), cos; LOVELY WAY TO DIE, A(1968), cos
Norman Merrill
HALLOWEEN III: SEASON OF THE WITCH(1982)
Paul D. Merrill
BIG CARNIVAL, THE(1951)
Peter Merrill
LORDS OF DISCIPLINE, THE(1983)
Robert Merrill
AARON SLICK FROM PUNKIN CRICK(1952)

Sarah Merrill
PEER GYNT(1965)
Sherry Merrill
PAYMENT ON DEMAND(1951)
Stuart Merrill
HOOKED GENERATION, THE(1969)
Sunnie Merrill
TRADING PLACES(1983)
Toni Merrill
CRIME AND PUNISHMENT, U.S.A.(1959)
Tony Merrill
TWO LATINS FROM MANHATTAN(1941); GIRL FROM JONES BEACH, THE(1949); MY FRIEND IRMA(1949); SET-UP, THE(1949); FILE ON THELMA JORDAN, THE(1950); MAGNIFICENT YANKEE, THE(1950); NARROW MARGIN, THE(1952); DONOVAN'S BRAIN(1953); SHE COULDN'T SAY NO(1954); RAINMAKER, THE(1956); GUNFIGHT AT THE O.K. CORRAL(1957); CAT ON A HOT TIN ROOF(1958); HOT SPELL(1958)
Wally Merrill
SAGEBRUSH POLITICS(1930)
Silents
DOWN UPON THE SUWANNEE RIVER(1925)
Walter Merrill
OFFICE WIFE, THE(1930); LIGHTNING FLYER(1931); PARLOR, BEDROOM AND BATH(1931); WANTED BY THE POLICE(1938); FOR LOVE OR MONEY(1939); GOOD GIRLS GO TO PARIS(1939); HE STAYED FOR BREAKFAST(1940); FACE BEHIND THE MASK, THE(1941); SLEEPYTIME GAL(1942); THEY ALL KISSED THE BRIDE(1942); SOUTHERN YANKEE, A(1948); SEPTEMBER AFFAIR(1950); SERGEANTS 3(1962)
Misc. Silents
WHILE LONDON SLEEPS(1926); BELOW THE DEADLINE(1929)
Walter A. Merrill
VAMPIRE, THE(1957)
Walter Anthony Merrill
JUSTICE TAKES A HOLIDAY(1933), w; I AM THE LAW(1938); OBLIGING YOUNG LADY(1941); TWO-FACED WOMAN(1941); I WALK ALONE(1948)
Warren Merrill
GETTING STRAIGHT(1970)
Winston Merrill
TWO(1975)
John D. Merriman
HIS AND HERS(1961, Brit.), p
Nan Merriman
MAYTIME(1937)
Paul Merriman
FOOLS' PARADE(1971)
Clive Merrison
HENRY VIII AND HIS SIX WIVES(1972, Brit.); VICTORY(1981); FIREFOX(1982); SIGN OF FOUR, THE(1983, Brit.)
George Merrit
HORROR OF DRACULA, THE(1958, Brit.)
Abraham Merritt
DEVIL DOLL, THE(1936), w
Alan Merritt
DAUGHTER OF THE TONG(1939), w
Arnold Merritt
UNFORGIVEN, THE(1960); GIDGET GOES HAWAIIAN(1961); THIRTEEN WEST STREET(1962)
Bruce Merritt
ABIE'S IRISH ROSE(1946)
Dorothy Merritt
UP IN ARMS(1944)
Gene Merritt
GOING MY WAY(1944), set d
George Merritt
"W" PLAN, THE(1931, Brit.); BRACELETS(1931, Brit.); DREYFUS CASE, THE(1931, Brit.); GENTLEMAN OF PARIS, A(1931); BLIND SPOT(1932, Brit.); CRIME ON THE HILL(1933, Brit.); FIRE RAISERS, THE(1933, Brit.); F.P. 1(1933, Brit.); GHOST CAMERA, THE(1933, Brit.); GOING STRAIGHT(1933, Brit.); MR. QUINCEY OF MONTE CARLO(1933, Brit.); WHITE FACE(1933, Brit.); I WAS A SPY(1934, Brit.); NINE FORTY-FIVE(1934, Brit.); NO ESCAPE(1934, Brit.); POWER(1934, Brit.); SILVER SPOON, THE(1934, Brit.); BORN FOR GLORY(1935, Brit.); CRIME UNLIMITED(1935, Brit.); DRAKE THE PIRATE(1935, Brit.); LINE ENGAGED(1935, Brit.); ME AND MARLBOROUGH(1935, Brit.); MY SONG FOR YOU(1935, Brit.); PHANTOM FIEND, THE(1935, Brit.); TEN MINUTE ALIBI(1935, Brit.); DAREDEVILS OF EARTH(1936, Brit.); EDUCATED EVANS(1936, Brit.); EVERYTHING IS THUNDER(1936, Brit.); LOVE AT SEA(1936, Brit.); MAN BEHIND THE MASK, THE(1936, Brit.); MR. COHEN TAKES A WALK(1936, Brit.); PRISON BREAKER(1936, Brit.); REMBRANDT(1936, Brit.); TICKET OF LEAVE(1936, Brit.); COMPULSORY WIFE, THE(1937, Brit.); DOCTOR SYN(1937, Brit.); VICAR OF BRAY, THE(1937, Brit.); VULTURE, THE(1937, Brit.); EMIL(1938, Brit.); NO PARKING(1938, Brit.); RAT, THE(1938, Brit.); RETURN OF THE SCARLET PIMPERNEL(1938, Brit.); THEY DRIVE BY NIGHT(1938, Brit.); WIFE OF GENERAL LING, THE(1938, Brit.); YOUNG AND INNOCENT(1938, Brit.); ALL AT SEA(1939, Brit.); CLOUDS OVER EUROPE(1939, Brit.); PHANTOM STRIKES, THE(1939, Brit.); SPY OF NAPOLEON(1939, Brit.); WANTED BY SCOTLAND YARD(1939, Brit.); CASE OF THE FRIGHTENED LADY, THE(1940. Brit.); GAS-BAGS(1940, Brit.); SECRET FOUR, THE(1940, Brit.); SPARE A COPPER(1940, Brit.); THEY CAME BY NIGHT(1940, Brit.); TWO FOR DANGER(1940, Brit.); HE FOUND A STAR(1941, Brit.); MYSTERY OF ROOM 13(1941, Brit.); PROUD VALLEY, THE(1941, Brit.); BACK ROOM BOY(1942, Brit.); LADY IN DISTRESS(1942, Brit.); LET THE PEOPLE SING(1942, Brit.); MAXWELL ARCHER, DETECTIVE(1942, Brit.); SHIPS WITH WINGS(1942, Brit.); WE'LL SMILE AGAIN(1942, Brit.); WINGS AND THE WOMAN(1942, Brit.); WOMEN AREN'T ANGELS(1942, Brit.); ADVENTURE IN BLACKMAIL(1943, Brit.); ALIBI, THE(1943, Brit.); ESCAPE TO DANGER(1943, Brit.); I'LL WALK BESIDE YOU(1943, Brit.); CANTERBURY TALE, A(1944, Brit.); DE-MOBBED(1944, Brit.); DON'T TAKE IT TO HEART(1944, Brit.); GIVE ME THE STARS(1944, Brit.); UNDERGROUND GUERRILLAS(1944, Brit.); DON CHICA-GO(1945, Brit.); FOR YOU ALONE(1945, Brit.); HOME SWEET HOME(1945, Brit.); I'LL BE YOUR SWEETHEART(1945, Brit.); VARIETY JUBILEE(1945, Brit.); VOICE WITHIN, THE(1945, Brit.); I'LL TURN TO YOU(1946, Brit.); UPTURNED GLASS, THE(1947, Brit.); DAUGHTER OF DARKNESS(1948, Brit.); HATTER'S CASTLE(1948, Brit.);

LOVE IN WAITING(1948, Brit.); QUIET WEEKEND(1948, Brit.); SMUGGLERS, THE(1948, Brit.); DARK SECRET(1949, Brit.); MARRY ME!(1949, Brit.); MY BROTHER'S KEEPER(1949, Brit.); QUARTET(1949, Brit.); WATERLOO ROAD(1949, Brit.); GOOD TIME GIRL(1950, Brit.); SOMETHING IN THE CITY(1950, Brit.); POOL OF LONDON(1951, Brit.); NOOSE FOR A LADY(1953, Brit.); SMALL TOWN STORY(1953, Brit.); END OF THE ROAD, THE(1954, Brit.); GREEN SCARF, THE(1954, Brit.); NIGHT OF THE FULL MOON, THE(1954, Brit.); ENEMY FROM SPACE(1957, Brit.); TREAD SOFTLY STRANGER(1959, Brit.); STOP ME BEFORE I KILL!(1961, Brit.); WHAT EVERY WOMAN WANTS(1962, Brit.); CROMWELL(1970, Brit.); I, MONSTER(1971, Brit.); GAWAIN AND THE GREEN KNIGHT(1973, Brit.)

Joe Merritt
HOT BLOOD(1956)
John Merritt
ANGEL WHO PAWNED HER HARP, THE(1956, Brit.), ed; YOUNG SWINGERS, THE(1963); ZARDOZ(1974, Brit), ed; EXCALIBUR(1981), ed
Juanita Merritt
STRIPES(1981)
Margaret Merritt
UP THE MACGREGORS(1967, Ital./Span.)
Mary Merritt
SCOTT OF THE ANTARCTIC(1949, Brit.); NAUGHTY ARLETTE(1951, Brit.)
Max Merritt
PATRICIA GETS HER MAN(1937, Brit.), w
Ray Merritt
HARD ROAD, THE(1970)
Sterling Merritt
SHEPHERD OF THE HILLS, THE(1964), art d; PLASTIC DOME OF NORMA JEAN, THE(1966), set d
Steve Merritt
1984
GIMME AN 'F'(1984), ch
Sybil Merritt
ONCE UPON A TIME(1944); STORY OF DR. WASSELL, THE(1944); SONG TO REMEMBER, A(1945); DANNY BOY(1946); EASY TO WED(1946); SMOKY MOUNTAIN MELODY(1949); VICIOUS YEARS, THE(1950); JAPANESE WAR BRIDE(1952)
Theresa Merritt
WIZ, THE(1978); THEY MIGHT BE GIANTS(1971); GOODBYE GIRL, THE(1977); GREAT SANTINI, THE(1979); BEST LITTLE WHOREHOUSE IN TEXAS, THE(1982)
Bernard Merrivale
CONDEMNED TO DEATH(1932, Brit.), w
Nicholas Merriwether
EEGAH!(1962), w
Nicholas Merriwether [Arch Hall, Sr.]
EEGAH!(1962), p&d; WILD GUITAR(1962), p, w; NASTY RABBIT, THE(1964), p; DEADWOOD'76(1965), p
Jane Merrow
WOMAN WHO WOULDN'T DIE, THE(1965, Brit.); GIRL GETTERS, THE(1966, Brit.); ASSIGNMENT K(1968, Brit.); LION IN WINTER, THE(1968, Brit.); HANDS OF THE RIPPER(1971, Brit.); ISLAND OF THE BURNING DAMNED(1971, Brit.); ADAM'S WOMAN(1972, Austral.); DIAGNOSIS: MURDER(1974, Brit.)
Misc. Talkies
TIME FOR LOVE, A(1974)
William Merrow
EYE OF THE NEEDLE(1981)
Arlette Merry
LA FERME DU PENDU(1946, Fr.)
Carla Merry
BAND OF ANGELS(1957)
Se Merry
1984
PIGS(1984, Ireland), ed
The Merry Macs
SAN ANTONIO ROSE(1941); MR. MUSIC(1950)
Mathea Merryfield
SHE SHALL HAVE MUSIC(1935, Brit.)
Mary Mersch
EMPTY SADDLES(1937)
Silents
ONE OF MANY(1917)
Misc. Silents
COMMON GROUND(1916); MOTHER'S SECRET, A(1918); RAINBOW TRAIL, THE(1918); RIDERS OF THE PURPLE SAGE(1918); WHO KILLED WALTON?(1918); TOP OF THE WORLD, THE(1925)
May Mersch
Misc. Silents
WHISPERED NAME, THE(1924)
Anne-Marie Mersen
FRENCH CANCAN(1956, Fr.); SELLERS OF GIRLS(1967, Fr.)
Claire Mersereau
Misc. Silents
RIGHT OFF THE BAT(1915); BLACK IS WHITE(1920)
Jack Mersereau
TEXAS TRAIL(1937), w; HIDDEN GOLD(1940), w
Violet Mersereau
Silents
NERO(1922, U.S./Ital.); LUCK(1923); HER OWN FREE WILL(1924); LEND ME YOUR HUSBAND(1924)
Misc. Silents
SPITFIRE, THE(1914); AVALANCHE, THE(1915); WOLF OF DEBT, THE(1915); BROKEN FETTERS(1916); GREAT PROBLEM, THE(1916); NARROW PATH, THE(1916); PATH OF HAPPINESS, THE(1916); BOY GIRL, THE(1917); LITTLE MISS NOBODY(1917); LITTLE TERROR, THE(1917); RAGGEDY QUEEN, THE(1917); SUSAN'S GENTLEMAN(1917); GIRL BY THE ROADSIDE, THE(1918); MORGAN'S RAIDERS(1918); TOGETHER(1918); NATURE GIRL, THE(1919); FINDERS KEEPERS(1921); OUT OF THE DEPTHS(1921); THUNDERCLAP(1921); SHEPHERD KING, THE(1923); WIVES OF THE PROPHET, THE(1926)
Robert Mersey
PIE IN THE SKY(1964), m, md

Kres Mersky
PEACE KILLERS, THE(1971); UNHOLY ROLLERS(1972); WON TON TON, THE DOG WHO SAVED HOLLYWOOD(1976); RICH AND FAMOUS(1981)
1984
REVENGE OF THE NERDS(1984)
Billy Merson
RIDING HIGH(1937, Brit.); SHOW GOES ON, THE(1937, Brit.); CHIPS(1938. Brit.); SCRUFFY(1938, Brit.)
Misc. Silents
BILLY'S SPANISH LOVE SPASM(1915, Brit.); MAN IN POSSESSION, THE(1915, Brit.); ONLY MAN, THE(1915, Brit.); PERILS OF PORK PIE, THE(1916, Brit.); TALE OF A SHIRT(1916, Brit.)
Marc Merson
HEART IS A LONELY HUNTER, THE(1968), p; LEADBELLY(1976), p
Susan Merson
TIMES SQUARE(1980); TOOTSIE(1982)
Jack Merta
BILLY JACK GOES TO WASHINGTON(1977), ph
Ed Mertens
1984
SUBURBIA(1984)
Mary Mertens
Misc. Talkies
ALIEN FACTOR, THE(1978)
Patricia Mertens
LITTLE SEX, A(1982)
John Mertin
GIRL ON THE SPOT(1946)
Atle Merton
PASSIONATE DEMONS, THE(1962, Norway)
Collette Merton
GODLESS GIRL, THE(1929)
Silents
WHY BE GOOD?(1929)
Ivy Merton
HELL FIRE AUSTIN(1932)
John Merton
SONS OF THE DESERT(1933); HOPALONG CASSIDY(1935); ACES AND EIGHTS(1936); BAR 20 RIDES AGAIN(1936); CALL OF THE PRAIRIE(1936); CROOKED TRAIL, THE(1936); EAGLE'S BROOD, THE(1936); LIGHTNING BILL CARSON(1936); LION'S DEN, THE(1936); THREE MESQUITEERS, THE(1936); WILDCAT TROOPER(1936); ARIZONA GUNFIGHTER(1937); BLAZING SIXES(1937); CRUSADE AGAINST RACKETS(1937); DRUMS OF DESTINY(1937); FEDERAL BULLETS(1937); FIREFLY, THE(1937); GALLOPING DYNAMITE(1937); GUN RANGER, THE(1937); GUNSMOKE RANCH(1937); HEADLINE CRASHER(1937); LAW OF THE RANGER(1937); RANGE DEFENDERS(1937); RANGERS STEP IN, THE(1937); ROARING SIX GUNS(1937); TENDERFOOT GOES WEST, A(1937); WILD HORSE ROUND-UP(1937); COLORADO KID(1938); FEMALE FUGITIVE(1938); FURY BELOW(1938); GANG BULLETS(1938); GUNSMOKE TRAIL(1938); LAND OF FIGHTING MEN(1938); LAW COMMANDS, THE(1938); PHANTOM RANGER(1938); SHOPWORN ANGEL(1938); WHERE THE BUFFALO ROAM(1938); WOLVES OF THE SEA(1938); CODE OF THE FEARLESS(1939); FLAMING LEAD(1939); IN OLD MONTANA(1939); KNIGHT OF THE PLAINS(1939); LADY'S FROM KENTUCKY, THE(1939); RENEGADE TRAIL(1939); ROUGH RIDERS' ROUNDUP(1939); THREE TEXAS STEERS(1939); TWO-GUN TROUBADOR(1939); UNION PACIFIC(1939); BILLY THE KID IN TEXAS(1940); COVERED WAGON DAYS(1940); DARK COMMAND, THE(1940); FRONTIER CRUSADER(1940); HI-YO SILVER(1940); LONE STAR RAIDERS(1940); MELODY RANCH(1940); NORTHWEST PASSAGE(1940); PALS OF THE SILVER SAGE(1940); RAINBOW OVER THE RANGE(1940); RETURN OF WILD BILL, THE(1940); TRAIL BLAZERS, THE(1940); GREAT COMMANDMENT, THE(1941); GUN MAN FROM BODIE, THE(1941); SOUTH OF TAHITI(1941); TWO GUN SHERIFF(1941); UNDER FIESTA STARS(1941); HITLER'S CHILDREN(1942); INVISIBLE AGENT(1942); LAW AND ORDER(1942); LONE PRAIRIE, THE(1942); MISSOURI OUTLAW, A(1942); MYSTERIOUS RIDER, THE(1942); PRAIRIE PALS(1942); SHERIFF OF SAGE VALLEY(1942); BLACK MARKET RUSTLERS(1943); COWBOY COMMANDOS(1943); DESTROYER(1943); DRUMS OF FU MANCHU(1943); FIGHTING VALLEY(1943); KID RIDES AGAIN, THE(1943); LAND OF HUNTED MEN(1943); LAW RIDES AGAIN, THE(1943); SAGEBRUSH LAW(1943); DEVIL RIDERS(1944); FUZZY SETTLES DOWN(1944); GENTLE ANNIE(1944); GHOST GUNS(1944); GIRL RUSH(1944); KISMET(1944); LAND OF THE OUTLAWS(1944); MYSTERY MAN(1944); RUSTLER'S HIDEOUT(1944); TEXAS MASQUERADE(1944); VALLEY OF VENGEANCE(1944); ALONG CAME JONES(1945); BANDITS OF THE BADLANDS(1945); CHEROKEE FLASH, THE(1945); FLAME OF THE WEST(1945); OREGON TRAIL(1945); BORDER BANDITS(1946); DESERT HORSEMAN, THE(1946); GILDA(1946); NIGHT IN PARADISE, A(1946); CHEYENNE TAKES OVER(1947); I WONDER WHO'S KISSING HER NOW(1947); RAIDERS OF THE SOUTH(1947); UNCONQUERED(1947); MYSTERY OF THE GOLDEN EYE, THE(1948); SOUTHERN YANKEE, A(1948); OUTLAW COUNTRY(1949); RIDERS OF THE DUSK(1949); SAMSON AND DELILAH(1949); THIEVES' HIGHWAY(1949); ARIZONA TERRITORY(1950); BANDIT QUEEN(1950); BORDER RANGERS(1950); I SHOT BILLY THE KID(1950); WEST OF WYOMING(1950); SILVER CANYON(1951); BLUE CANADIAN ROCKIES(1952); GREATEST SHOW ON EARTH, THE(1952); OLD WEST, THE(1952); TRAIL GUIDE(1952); SON OF SINBAD(1955); FRONTIER GAMBLER(1956); TEN COMMANDMENTS, THE(1956)
Misc. Talkies
VALLEY OF TERROR(1937); IN OLD MONTANA(1939); BILLY THE KID OUTLAWED(1940); BILLY THE KID'S SMOKING GUNS(1942); BOOT HILL BANDITS(1942); SHADOWS ON THE RANGE(1946)
Silents
IT'S THE OLD ARMY GAME(1926)
Paul Merton
LAMP STILL BURNS, THE(1943, Brit.); VOICE WITHIN, THE(1945, Brit.)
Roger Merton
DOWN THE WYOMING TRAIL(1939), w; ROLL, WAGONS, ROLL(1939), w; GOLDEN TRAIL, THE(1940), w; RAINBOW OVER THE RANGE(1940), w; KING OF THE STALLIONS(1942), w; QUEEN OF THE AMAZONS(1947), w
Zienia Merton
HELP!(1965, Brit.); CHAIRMAN, THE(1969); ADVENTURERS, THE(1970)

Vera Mertskaya
NO GREATER LOVE(1944, USSR)
Connie Mertyn
DAD AND DAVE COME TO TOWN(1938, Aus.)
Arthur Mertz
BOOTS! BOOTS!(1934, Brit.), w; OFF THE DOLE(1935, Brit.), d, w; DODGING THE DOLE(1936, Brit.), w; PENNY POOL, THE(1937, Brit.), w; CALLING ALL CROOKS(1938, Brit.), w; SOMEWHERE IN ENGLAND(1940, Brit.), w; SOMEWHERE IN POLITICS(1949, Brit.), w
Paul Mertz
HATS OFF(1937, md; COWBOY BLUES(1946), md; I SURRENDER DEAR(1948), md; STRAWBERRY ROAN, THE(1948), m; HOLIDAY IN HAVANA(1949), md; APACHE COUNTRY(1952), m; SOUND OFF(1952), m; CALYPSO HEAT WAVE(1957), m
Renzo Merusi
UNA SIGNORA DELL'OVEST(1942, Ital); MATA HARI'S DAUGHTER(1954, Fr./Ital), d, w
Gaston Mervale
Misc. Silents
STUBBORNESS OF GERALDINE, THE(1915), d
Anne Mervis
SANDY THE SEAL(1969, Brit.)
William Mervyn
LOVES OF JOANNA GODDEN, THE(1947, Brit.); MARK OF CAIN, THE(1948, Brit.); STOP PRESS GIRL(1949, Brit.); IF THIS BE SIN(1950, Brit.); FUSS OVER FEATHERS(1954, Brit.); THIRD KEY, THE(1957, Brit.); CARVE HER NAME WITH PRIDE(1958, Brit.); CIRCUS OF HORRORS(1960, Brit.); INVASION QUARTET(1961, Brit.); UPSTAIRS AND DOWNSTAIRS(1961, Brit.); MURDER AHOY(1964, Brit.); TAMAHINE(1964, Brit.); OPERATION CROSSBOW(1965, U.S./Ital.); UP JUMPED A SWAGMAN(1965, Brit.); DEADLIER THAN THE MALE(1967, Brit.); FOLLOW THAT CAMEL(1967, Brit.); JOKERS, THE(1967, Brit.); HAMMERHEAD(1968); HOT MILLIONS(1968, Brit.); SALT & PEPPER(1968, Brit.); CARRY ON HENRY VIII(1970, Brit.); INCENSE FOR THE DAMNED(1970, Brit.); RAILWAY CHILDREN, THE(1971, Brit.); RULING CLASS, THE(1972, Brit.); CHARLEY-ONE-EYE(1973, Brit.); BAWDY ADVENTURES OF TOM JONES, THE(1976, Brit.)
Bannister Merwin
Silents
FIRM OF GIRDLESTONE, THE(1915, Brit.), w; ALTAR CHAINS(1916, Brit.), d&w; GREATEST WISH IN THE WORLD, THE(1918, Brit.), w; HER HERITAGE(1919, Brit.), d; LONDON PRIDE(1920, Brit.), w; PURSUIT OF PAMELA, THE(1920, Brit.), w; TRUE TILDA(1920, Brit.), w; LOVE AT THE WHEEL(1921, Brit.), d
Misc. Silents
ROGUE IN LOVE, A(1916, Brit.), d; SILVER GREYHOUND, THE(1919, Brit.), d; LADDIE(1920, Brit.), d
Sam Merwin, Jr.
MANHUNT IN THE JUNGLE(1958), w
Samuel Merwin
Silents
CROOKED STREETS(1920), w; HUSH MONEY(1921), w; JAZZLAND(1928), w
J. Miles Merwyn
IRISH AND PROUD OF IT(1938, Ireland)
Arlette Mery
ETERNAL HUSBAND, THE(1946, Fr.)
Laurence Mery
JOKER, THE(1961, Fr.), ed; CARTOUCHE(1962, Fr./Ital.), ed; ROAD TO SHAME, THE(1962, Fr.), ed; THAT MAN FROM RIO(1964, Fr./Ital.), ed
Viviane Mery
LETTERS FROM MY WINDMILL(1955, Fr.); MY BABY IS BLACK!(1965, Fr.)
Laurence Mery-Clark
RED MONARCH(1983, Brit.), ed
1984
SECRET PLACES(1984, Brit.), ed
Macha Meryl
ADORABLE LIAR(1962, Fr.)
Randi Meryl
SURVIVAL RUN(1980)
Karl-Heinz Merz
WAR AND PEACE(1983, Ger.)
Paul Merzbach
INVITATION TO THE WALTZ(1935, Brit.), d, w; MIMI(1935, Brit.), w; HAIL AND FAREWELL(1936, Brit.), p, w; STAR FELL FROM HEAVEN, A(1936, Brit.), d; GIRL THIEF, THE(1938), d; IT HAPPENED TO ONE MAN(1941, Brit.), w
Carl Merznicht
COURT CONCERT, THE(1936, Ger.)
Eddie Mesa
RAIDERS OF LEYTE GULF(1963 U.S./Phil.)
Eloy Mesa
WHO SAYS I CAN'T RIDE A RAINBOW!(1971)
Gilbert Mesa
WAY OUT(1966)
Ramon D. Mesa
BRAVE BULLS, THE(1951)
J.J. Mescal
HIS FIRST COMMAND(1929), ph
John Mescal
RED HOT RHYTHM(1930), ph; NEW MORALS FOR OLD(1932), ph; HAPPY LANDING(1938), ph; ANDY HARDY'S DOUBLE LIFE(1942), ph
The Mescalero Apache Horn Dancers
TIGER BY THE TAIL(1970)
John Mescall
HIGH VOLTAGE(1929), ph; LEATHERNECK, THE(1929), ph; SHADY LADY, THE(1929), ph; BIG MONEY(1930), ph; NIGHT WORK(1930), ph; SIN TAKES A HOLIDAY(1930), ph; AMBASSADOR BILL(1931), ph; BORN TO LOVE(1931), ph; EASIEST WAY, THE(1931), ph; ALMOST MARRIED(1932), ph; SKYLINE(1931), ph; INVISIBLE MAN, THE(1933), spec eff; RETURN OF CASEY JONES(1933), ph; AFFAIRS OF A GENTLEMAN(1934), ph; BLACK CAT, THE(1934), ph; BY CANDLELIGHT(1934), ph; ONE MORE RIVER(1934), ph; BRIDE OF FRANKENSTEIN, THE(1935), ph; I'VE BEEN AROUND(1935), ph; MAGNIFICENT OBSESSION(1935), ph; SMART GIRL(1935), ph; FOLLOW YOUR HEART(1936), ph; SHOW BOAT(1936), ph; MAKE A WISH(1937), ph; JOSETTE(1938), ph; MY LUCKY STAR(1938), ph; WHEN TOMORROW COMES(1939), ph; HER FIRST ROMANCE(1940), ph; KIT CAR-

SON(1940), ph; SOUTH OF PAGO PAGO(1940), ph; HENRY ALDRICH FOR PRESIDENT(1941), ph; NEW WINE(1941), ph; NIGHT OF JANUARY 16TH(1941), ph; NIGHT IN NEW ORLEANS, A(1942), ph; SWEATER GIRL(1942), ph; TAKE A LETTER, DARLING(1942), ph; THREE RUSSIAN GIRLS(1943), ph; DARK WATERS(1944), ph; BEDSIDE MANNER(1945), ph; DAVY CROCKETT, INDIAN SCOUT(1950), ph; DESPERADOES ARE IN TOWN, THE(1956), ph; NOT OF THIS EARTH(1957), ph; QUIET GUN, THE(1957), ph
Silents
SIX DAYS(1923), ph; SOULS FOR SALE(1923), ph; HIS HOUR(1924), ph; BELOW THE LINE(1925), ph; OH, WHAT A NURSE!(1926), ph; SO THIS IS PARIS(1926), ph; SOCIAL HIGHWAYMAN, THE(1926), ph; YANKEE CLIPPER, THE(1927), ph; LEOPARD LADY, THE(1928), ph; MAN-MADE WOMEN(1928), ph; WALKING BACK(1928), ph
John J. Mescall
SAL OF SINGAPORE(1929), ph; SOPHOMORE, THE(1929), ph; POOR RICH, THE(1934), ph; NIGHT LIFE OF THE GODS(1935), ph; ROAD BACK,THE(1937), ph; YOUTH RUNS WILD(1944), ph
Silents
ALL'S FAIR IN LOVE(1921), ph; FROM THE GROUND UP(1921), ph; WALL FLOWER, THE(1922), ph; WATCH YOUR STEP(1922), ph; GIMMIE(1923), ph; RENO(1923), ph; LOVE TOY, THE(1926), ph
Italo Mescati
CANNIBALS, THE(1970, Ital.), w
Dario Meschi
THIEF OF PARIS, THE(1967, Fr./Ital.)
Susan Meschner
1984
COTTON CLUB, THE(1984)
Jacques Mesereau
THOUSANDS CHEER(1943), set d; WHITE CLIFFS OF DOVER, THE(1944), set d
Albert J. Meserow
GREAT GOD GOLD(1935), w
Giulia Meserve
NUDE ODYSSEY(1962, Fr./Ital.)
Daniel Mesguich
LOVE ON THE RUN(1980, Fr.); BEAUTIFUL PRISONER, THE(1983, Fr.)
Daniel Mesguish
QUARTET(1981, Brit./Fr.)
Michael Meshekoff
MAN FROM GALVESTON, THE(1964), p
Natalia Meshkova
RED TENT, THE(1971, Ital./USSR), cos
The Meshpoka
TRADER HORNEE(1970)
Ajsa Mesic
WARRIORS FIVE(1962)
Ester Mesina
NIGHT OF THE ZOMBIES(1983, Span./Ital.)
Vern Mesita
LUM AND ABNER ABROAD(1956)
Dmitriy Meskhiyev
LADY WITH THE DOG, THE(1962, USSR), ph
Jack Meskill
FOX MOVIETONE FOLLIES OF 1930(1930), m
Katherine Meskill
HOLLYWOOD STORY(1951); HOUSE ON TELEGRAPH HILL(1951); UNKNOWN MAN, THE(1951); DIARY OF A MAD HOUSEWIFE(1970)
Aaron Meskin
FLYING MATCHMAKER, THE(1970, Israel)
Aharon Meskin
TWO KOUNEY LEMELS(1966, Israel)
Jack Meskin
TWONKY, THE(1953), m
Noelle Mesny
LA NUIT DE VARENNES(1983, Fr./Ital.)
Ivan Mesquita
1984
GABRIELA(1984, Braz.)
Jaime Messang
STRANGE HOLIDAY(1969, Aus.)
Messaoud
GOLDEN MASK, THE(1954, Brit.)
Souad Messaoudi
RAIDERS OF THE LOST ARK(1981)
Aline Messe
LA NUIT DE VARENNES(1983, Fr./Ital.)
Oliver Messel
PRIVATE LIFE OF DON JUAN, THE(1934, Brit.), cos; SCARLET PIMPERNEL, THE(1935, Brit.), cos; ROMEO AND JULIET(1936), set d, cos; THIEF OF BAGHDAD, THE(1940, Brit.), cos; CAESAR AND CLEOPATRA(1946, Brit.), cos; SUDDENLY, LAST SUMMER(1959, Brit.), prod d, cos
Rudolph Messel
Misc. Talkies
BLOW BUGLES BLOW(1936), d
Hannes Messemer
DEVIL STRIKES AT NIGHT, THE(1959, Ger.); GLASS TOWER, THE(1959, Ger.); SINS OF ROSE BERND, THE(1959, Ger.); BABETTE GOES TO WAR(1960, Fr.); GENERALE DELLA ROVERE(1960, Ital./Fr.); GREAT ESCAPE, THE(1963); DEFECTOR, THE(1966, Ger./Fr.); IS PARIS BURNING?(1966, U.S./Fr.); UNWILLING AGENT(1968, Ger.); ODESSA FILE, THE(1974, Brit./Ger.)
Buddy Messenger
THREE WISE GUYS, THE(1936)
Silents
FLIRT, THE(1922); FRONT PAGE STORY, A(1922); SHADOWS(1922)
Misc. Silents
UNDRESSED(1928)
Charlie Messenger
UNDER THE RAINBOW(1981); FRIDAY THE 13TH PART III(1982); SWORD AND THE SORCERER, THE(1982)

Dorothy Messenger
Silents
SINS OF ROZANNE(1920)
Gertrude Messenger
SINISTER HANDS(1932)
Marie Messenger
Silents
RIDERS OF THE DAWN(1920); WHEN SECONDS COUNT(1927)
Maurice Messenger
TREACHERY ON THE HIGH SEAS(1939, Brit.), w
Melvin Messenger
Silents
HOODLUM THE(1919)
Art Blakey's Jazz Messengers
LES LIAISONS DANGEREUSES(1961, Fr./Ital.), m
Peter Messer
CREEPSHOW(1982)
Gian Messeri
DEAD OF SUMMER(1970 Ital./Fr.), ed
Don Messick
HEY THERE, IT'S YOGI BEAR(1964); MAN CALLED FLINTSTONE, THE(1966); CHARLOTTE'S WEB(1973)
Wendy Messier
P.O.W., THE(1973)
Anthony Messina
HISTORY OF THE WORLD, PART 1(1981)
Chick Messina
DANGEROUS ASSIGNMENT(1950, Brit.), w
Dolores Messina
BABY, IT'S YOU(1983)
Emilio Messina
SUPERARGO VERSUS DIABOLICUS(1966, Ital./Span.); WEB OF VIOLENCE(1966, Ital./Span.); ORCA(1977), stunts
Louis Messina
FM(1978)
Michele Messina
MONSIGNOR(1982)
Miss Messina
SHADOW OF MIKE EMERALD, THE(1935, Brit.)
Phillip Frank Messina
BRAINSTORM(1983), w
Roberto Messina
POPEYE(1980)
1984
JUNGLE WARRIORS(1984, U.S./Ger./Mex.), stunts
Terri Messina
HOW SWEET IT IS(1968); SINGLE ROOM FURNISHED(1968); BLOOD AND LACE(1971)
Monique Messine
MY LIFE TO LIVE(1963, Fr.); VICE AND VIRTUE(1965, Fr./Ital.)
Bud Messinger
CRIME BY NIGHT(1944)
Buddy Messinger
LADY OF CHANCE, A(1928); GODLESS GIRL, THE(1929); CHEER UP AND SMILE(1930); COLLEGE HOLIDAY(1936); OUR RELATIONS(1936); WINGS OVER HONOLULU(1937); SHINING HOUR, THE(1938); TEST PILOT(1938); IDIOT'S DELIGHT(1939); HOLD BACK THE DAWN(1941); MEXICAN SPITFIRE'S BABY(1941); HENRY ALDRICH GETS GLAMOUR(1942); STORY OF DR. WASSELL, THE(1944)
Silents
JACK AND THE BEANSTALK(1917); ALI BABA AND THE FORTY THIEVES(1918); ABYSMAL BRUTE, THE(1923); PENROD AND SAM(1923)
Misc. Silents
TRIFLING WITH HONOR(1923)
Gertie Messinger
RAMPANT AGE, THE(1930)
Gertrude Messinger
JAZZ AGE, THE(1929); TWO WEEKS OFF(1929); HIDDEN VALLEY(1932); MADAME RACKETEER(1932); RIDERS OF THE DESERT(1932); HE LEARNED ABOUT WOMEN(1933); WOMAN ACCUSED(1933); ANNE OF GREEN GABLES(1934); LOVE PAST THIRTY(1934); MELODY TRAIL(1935); RIDER OF THE LAW, THE(1935); ROARING ROADS(1935); RUSTLER'S PARADISE(1935); WAGON TRAIL(1935); RETURN OF JIMMY VALENTINE, THE(1936); ROSE BOWL(1936); ACES WILD(1937); KING OF GAMBLERS(1937); FEUD OF THE RANGE(1939); OUR LEADING CITIZEN(1939); GAMBLING DAUGHTERS(1941); MIRACLE KID(1942); JOE PALOOKA IN THE COUNTERPUNCH(1949); SAMSON AND DELILAH(1949); SUNSET BOULEVARD(1950); GREATEST SHOW ON EARTH, THE(1952); REDHEAD FROM MANHATTAN(1954)
Misc. Talkies
LAWLESS VALLEY(1932); ADVENTUROUS KNIGHTS(1935); FIGHTING PILOT, THE(1935); SOCIAL ERROR(1935); BLAZING JUSTICE(1936)
Silents
ALI BABA AND THE FORTY THIEVES(1918); RIP VAN WINKLE(1921); PENROD AND SAM(1923)
Misc. Silents
ALADDIN AND THE WONDERFUL LAMP(1917)
Jack Messinger
WINTER KEPT US WARM(1968, Can.); CRIMES OF THE FUTURE(1969, Can.); STEREO(1969, Can.); RABID(1976, Can.); DEAD ZONE, THE(1983); THRESHOLD(1983, Can.)
M. Messinger
DYBBUK THE(1938, Pol.)
Marie Messinger
Silents
ALI BABA AND THE FORTY THIEVES(1918)
Herve Messir
PLAYTIME(1963, Fr.), p
Eric Messiter
GIRL IN THE PAINTING, THE(1948, Brit.); KIND HEARTS AND CORONETS(1949, Brit.); MY BROTHER JONATHAN(1949, Brit.); ONCE UPON A DREAM(1949, Brit.); MUDLARK, THE(1950, Brit.); WHILE THE SUN SHINES(1950, Brit.)

Ian Messiter
MR. DRAKE'S DUCK(1951, Brit.), d&w
Albert Messmer
DAISY MILLER(1974)
Dottie Messmer
SOMETHING TO SING ABOUT(1937)
Herbert Messmore
Silents
POLLY OF THE CIRCUS(1917), art d
Amidou Ben Messoud
TO BE A CROOK(1967, Fr.)
Harry Mestayer
LOCKED DOOR, THE(1929)
Silents
ATOM, THE(1918); ACQUITTAL, THE(1923)
Misc. Silents
HOUSE OF A THOUSAND CANDLES, THE(1915); I'M GLAD MY BOY GREW TO BE A SOLDIER(1915); MILLIONAIRE BABY, THE(1915); STOP THIEF(1915); HIGH TIDE(1918); FALSE GODS(1919); WIFE OR COUNTRY(1919)
Jacob Mestel
WANDERING JEW, THE(1933), a, w; VILNA LEGEND, A(1949, U.S./Pol.), a, w
Misc. Talkies
ABRAHAM OUR PATRIARCH(1933)
Armand Mestral
NAPOLEON(1955, Fr.); GERVAISE(1956, Fr.); MORGAN THE PIRATE(1961, Fr./Ital.); WHITE SLAVE SHIP(1962, Fr./Ital.); SOFT SKIN ON BLACK SILK(1964, Fr./Span.); HIGHWAY PICKUP(1965, Fr./Ital.); LOST COMMAND, THE(1966); SEA PIRATE, THE(1967, Fr./Span./Ital.); VISCOUNT, THE(1967, Fr./Span./Ital./Ger.); THAT RIVIERA TOUCH(1968, Brit.); THEY CAME TO ROB LAS VEGAS(1969, Fr./Ital./Span./Ger.)
Patrice Mestral
STORY OF ADELE H., THE(1975, Fr.), md
Gloria Mestre
FOXHOLE IN CAIRO(1960, Brit.); INTERVAL(1973, Mex./U.S.)
Jeanine Mestre
DON'T OPEN THE WINDOW(1974, Ital.); JETLAG(1981, U.S./Span.)
Buddy Meswinger
HOT STUFF(1929)
Antal Meszaros
FATHER(1967, Hung.)
Marta Meszaros
ANNA(1981, Fr./Hung.), d, w
1984
DIARY FOR MY CHILDREN(1984, Hung.), d&w
Jacques Metadier
CANDLELIGHT IN ALGERIA(1944, Brit.)
Grace Metalious
PEYTON PLACE(1957), w; RETURN TO PEYTON PLACE(1961), w
Budimir Metalnikov
HOME FOR TANYA, A(1961, USSR), w; SILENCE OF DR. EVANS, THE(1973, USSR), d&w
Sombat Metanee
S.T.A.B.(1976, Hong Kong/Thailand)
Bradley Metcalfe, Jr.
KING OF THE PECOS(1936)
George Metaxa
SECRETS OF A SECRETARY(1931); SWING TIME(1936); HI DIDDLE DIDDLE(1943); WEST SIDE KID(1943); SCOTLAND YARD INVESTIGATOR(1945, Brit.)
Georges Metaxa
DOCTOR TAKES A WIFE(1940); PARIS CALLING(1941); SUBMARINE BASE(1943); MASK OF DIMITRIOS, THE(1944)
Arthur Metcalf
Silents
DEAD MAN'S CURVE(1928)
Misc. Silents
PANTS(1917)
Bradley Metcalf
BAREFOOT BOY(1938)
Burt Metcalf
DIAMONDS ARE FOREVER(1971, Brit.)
Earl Metcalf
Silents
NATION'S PERIL, THE(1915); NEW TEACHER, THE(1922); SKID PROOF(1923); LONE WAGON, THE(1924); ATTA BOY!(1926); LOVE'S BLINDNESS(1926); MIDNIGHT MESSAGE, THE(1926); PARTNERS AGAIN(1926); KING OF KINGS, THE(1927); NIGHT LIFE(1927)
Misc. Silents
WHILE JUSTICE WAITS(1922); COURAGEOUS COWARD, THE(1924); VALLEY OF HATE, THE(1924); SHIP OF SOULS(1925)
Edward Metcalf
ANIMAL CRACKERS(1930)
Hugh Metcalf
Silents
HOUSE OF YOUTH, THE(1924); HEROIC LOVER, THE(1929)
James Metcalf
LIFE WITH FATHER(1947)
Ken Metcalf
TNT JACKSON(1975), a, w
1984
CAGED FURY(1984, Phil.)
Misc. Talkies
BEAST OF THE YELLOW NIGHT(1971, U.S./Phil.); SAVAGE!(1973)
Mark Metcalf
JULIA(1977); NATIONAL LAMPOON'S ANIMAL HOUSE(1978); WHERE THE BUFFALO ROAM(1980); CHILLY SCENES OF WINTER(1982), a, p; FINAL TERROR, THE(1983)
1984
ALMOST YOU(1984); OASIS, THE(1984)

Misc. Talkies
CAMPSITE MASSACRE(1981)
Nondas Metcalf
SUSPICION(1941)
Tim Metcalf
1984
REVENGE OF THE NERDS(1984), w
Adrian Metcalfe
GAMES, THE(1970)
Arthur Metcalfe
SEVEN DAYS LEAVE(1930); MR. WHAT'S-HIS-NAME(1935, Brit.); BELLES OF ST. CLEMENTS, THE(1936, Brit.)
Silents
SHORE LEAVE(1925)
Misc. Silents
GOLDEN IDIOT, THE(1917); IF WINTER COMES(1923)
Blanche Metcalfe
ALF'S CARPET(1929, Brit.), w; KISSING CUP'S RACE(1930, Brit.), w
Bob Metcalfe
DESERTERS(1983, Can.)
1984
RUNAWAY(1984)
Bradley Metcalfe
MILLIONAIRE KID(1936); TOO MANY PARENTS(1936); WESTWARD HO(1936); TRUE CONFESSION(1937); GANGSTER'S BOY(1938)
Burt Metcalfe
GIDGET(1959); CANADIANS, THE(1961, Brit.)
Charles Metcalfe
LET THE BALLOON GO(1977, Aus.)
Charlie Metcalfe
CARS THAT ATE PARIS, THE(1974, Aus,)
Earl Metcalfe
Silents
WHILE NEW YORK SLEEPS(1920); WHAT WOMEN WILL DO(1921); GREAT NIGHT, THE(1922); SURGING SEAS(1924); NOTORIOUS LADY, THE(1927); AIR MAIL PILOT, THE(1928)
Misc. Silents
GAMBLERS, THE(1914); CIPHER KEY, THE(1915); DESTINY'S SKEIN(1915); PATH TO THE RAINBOW, THE(1915); REGENERATING LOVE, THE(1915); RINGTAILED RHINOCEROS, THE(1915); ROMANCE OF THE NAVY, A(1915); IGNORANCE(1916); RACE SUICIDE(1916); BATTLER, THE(1919); COAX ME(1919); POISON PEN, THE(1919); WOMAN OF LIES(1919); CHAMBER OF MYSTERY, THE(1920); FACE AT YOUR WINDOW(1920); GARTER GIRL, THE(1920); EDEN AND RETURN(1921); MOTHER ETERNAL(1921); BACK TO YELLOW JACKET(1922); IGNORANCE(1922); SILENT ACCUSER, THE(1924); SILK STOCKING SAL(1924); CALL OF THE KLONDIKE, THE(1926); REMEMBER(1926); SIN CARGO(1926); DARING DEEDS(1927)
Earle Metcalfe
Misc. Silents
HER GOOD NAME(1917)
Ernest Metcalfe
NEUTRAL PORT(1941, Brit.); WE'LL SMILE AGAIN(1942, Brit.); OLD MOTHER RILEY, DETECTIVE(1943, Brit.); SILK NOOSE, THE(1950, Brit.); OBSESSED(1951, Brit.)
Ernie Metcalfe
GALLOPING MAJOR, THE(1951, Brit.)
Hugh Metcalfe
Misc. Silents
KINGDOM OF HUMAN HEARTS, THE(1921)
Isabelle Metcalfe
OH! WHAT A LOVELY WAR(1969, Brit.)
James Metcalfe
SWEET ROSIE O'GRADY(1943); CENTENNIAL SUMMER(1946); WALLS OF JERICHO(1948)
John Metcalfe
HORROR PLANET(1982, Brit.), ph; REMEMBRANCE(1982, Brit.), ph; XTRO(1983, Brit.), ph
Ken Metcalfe
TWILIGHT PEOPLE(1972, Phil.); WOMAN HUNT, THE(1975, U.S./Phil.); BOYS IN COMPANY C, THE(1978, U.S./Hong Kong); DYNAMITE JOHNSON(1978, Phil.), a, w; FIRECRACKER(1981), a, w; DON'T CRY, IT'S ONLY THUNDER(1982); ENTER THE NINJA(1982); STRYKER(1983, Phil.)
Robert Metcalfe
FIRST BLOOD(1982)
Jacques Metchen
AMBASSADOR'S DAUGHTER, THE(1956), md
Amar Metchiek
OLIVE TREES OF JUSTICE, THE(1967, Fr.)
John Metcalfe
SPACED OUT(1981, Brit.), ph
Jacques Metehen
NIGHT HEAVEN FELL, THE(1958, Fr.), md; LOVE AND THE FRENCHWOMAN(1961, Fr.), m; LA BONNE SOUPE(1964, Fr./Ital.), md; FRIEND OF THE FAMILY(1965, Fr./Ital.), md; IMPOSSIBLE ON SATURDAY(1966, Fr./Israel), md
Seryozha Metelitsyn
SUMMER TO REMEMBER, A(1961, USSR)
Elena Metelkina
CHEREZ TERNII K SVEZDAM(1981 USSR)
Harry V. Meter
Silents
CABARET GIRL, THE(1919)
George Metesky
CHICAGO 70(1970)
Saul Meth
SUCH GOOD FRIENDS(1971), makeup; POSSESSION OF JOEL DELANEY, THE(1972), makeup
Misc. Talkies
NIGHT TO DISMEMBER, A(1983)

Finn Methling
STRANGER KNOCKS, A(1963, Den.), w
Svend Methling
Misc. Silents
ONCE UPON A TIME(1922, Den.)
Sven Methling, Jr.
OPERATION CAMEL(1961, Den.), d
Mayo Methot
CORSAIR(1931); AFRAID TO TALK(1932); NIGHT CLUB LADY(1932); VANITY STREET(1932); VIRTUE(1932); COUNSELLOR-AT-LAW(1933); LILLY TURNER(1933); MIND READER, THE(1933); GOODBYE LOVE(1934); HAROLD TEEN(1934); JIMMY THE GENT(1934); REGISTERED NURSE(1934); SIDE STREETS(1934); CASE OF THE CURIOUS BRIDE, THE(1935); DR. SOCRATES(1935); MILLS OF THE GODS(1935); WE'RE IN THE MONEY(1935); CASE AGAINST MRS. AMES, THE(1936); MR. DEEDS GOES TO TOWN(1936); MARKED WOMAN(1937); SISTERS, THE(1938); WOMEN IN PRISON(1938); SHOULD A GIRL MARRY?(1939); UNEXPECTED FATHER(1939); WOMAN IS THE JUDGE, A(1939); BROTHER RAT AND A BABY(1940)
Misc. Talkies
NUMBERED WOMAN(1938)
George Metkovich
THREE LITTLE WORDS(1950); WINNING TEAM, THE(1952)
Tom Metletti
SHE KNEW ALL THE ANSWERS(1941)
Leo V. Metranga
TANK COMMANDOS(1959)
Art Metrano
THEY SHOOT HORSES, DON'T THEY?(1969); HEARTBREAK KID, THE(1972); THEY ONLY KILL THEIR MASTERS(1972); ALL-AMERICAN BOY, THE(1973); SLAUGHTER'S BIG RIP-OFF(1973); DIRTY O'NEIL(1974); MATILDA(1978); SEVEN(1979); CHEAPER TO KEEP HER(1980); HOW TO BEAT THE HIGH COST OF LIVING(1980); GOING APE!(1981); HISTORY OF THE WORLD, PART 1(1981); BREATHLESS(1983)
1984
TEACHERS(1984)
Misc. Talkies
WARHEAD(1974)
Marsha Metrinko
STAND UP AND BE COUNTED(1972)
George Metro
FOOLS' PARADE(1971)
Hugo Metsers
SPETTERS(1983, Holland)
Nancy Mette
RETURN OF THE SECAUCUS SEVEN(1980); LIANNA(1983); TERMS OF ENDEARMENT(1983)
Lynnette Mettey
SPECIAL DELIVERY(1976)
Klaus Mettig
FOREIGNER, THE(1978)
Russell Metty
THOROUGHLY MODERN MILLIE(1967), ph; WEST OF THE PECOS(1935), ph; NIGHT WAITRESS(1936), ph; ANNAPOLIS SALUTE(1937), ph; BEHIND THE HEADLINES(1937), ph; FORTY NAUGHTY GIRLS(1937), ph; THEY WANTED TO MARRY(1937), ph; YOU CAN'T BEAT LOVE(1937), ph; AFFAIRS OF ANNABEL(1938), ph; ANNABEL TAKES A TOUR(1938), ph; BRINGING UP BABY(1938), ph; MR. DOODLE KICKS OFF(1938), ph; NEXT TIME I MARRY(1938), ph; EVERYTHING'S ON ICE(1939), ph; GIRL AND THE GAMBLER, THE(1939), ph; GREAT MAN VOTES, THE(1939), ph; SPELLBINDER, THE(1939), ph; THAT'S RIGHT–YOU'RE WRONG(1939), ph; THREE SONS(1939), ph; CURTAIN CALL(1940), ph; DANCE, GIRL, DANCE(1940), ph; IRENE(1940), ph; NO, NO NANETTE(1940), ph; FOUR JACKS AND A JILL(1941), ph; GIRL, A GUY AND A GOB, A(1941), ph; SUNNY(1941), ph; WEEKEND FOR THREE(1941), ph; ARMY SURGEON(1942), ph; BIG STREET, THE(1942), ph; FALCON'S BROTHER, THE(1942), ph; HITLER'S CHILDREN(1942), ph; JOAN OF PARIS(1942), ph; MAGNIFICENT AMBERSONS, THE(1942), ph; MEXICAN SPITFIRE SEES A GHOST(1942), ph; AROUND THE WORLD(1943), ph; BEHIND THE RISING SUN(1943), ph; FOREVER AND A DAY(1943), ph; SKY'S THE LIMIT, THE(1943), ph; TENDER COMRADE(1943), ph; MASTER RACE, THE(1944), ph; MUSIC IN MANHATTAN(1944), ph; SEVEN DAYS ASHORE(1944), ph; BETRAYAL FROM THE EAST(1945), ph; IT'S IN THE BAG(1945), ph; PARDON MY PAST(1945), ph; STORY OF G.I. JOE, THE(1945), ph; BREAKFAST IN HOLLYWOOD(1946), ph; PERFECT MARRIAGE, THE(1946), ph; STRANGER THE(1946), ph; WHISTLE STOP(1946), ph; IVY(1947), ph; PRIVATE AFFAIRS OF BEL AMI, THE(1947), ph; RIDE THE PINK HORSE(1947), ph; WOMAN'S VENGEANCE, A(1947), ph; ALL MY SONS(1948), ph; ARCH OF TRIUMPH(1948), ph; KISS THE BLOOD OFF MY HANDS(1948), ph; MR. PEABODY AND THE MERMAID(1948), ph; YOU GOTTA STAY HAPPY(1948), ph; BAGDAD(1949), ph; LADY GAMBLES, THE(1949), ph; WE WERE STRANGERS(1949), ph; BUCCANEER'S GIRL(1950), ph; CURTAIN CALL AT CACTUS CREEK(1950), ph; DESERT HAWK, THE(1950), ph; PEGGY(1950), ph; SIERRA(1950), ph; WYOMING MAIL(1950), ph; FLAME OF ARABY(1951), ph; GOLDEN HORDE, THE(1951), ph; KATIE DID IT(1951), ph; LITTLE EGYPT(1951), ph; RAGING TIDE, THE(1951), ph; UP FRONT(1951), ph; AGAINST ALL FLAGS(1952), ph; BECAUSE OF YOU(1952), ph; SCARLET ANGEL(1952), ph; TREASURE OF LOST CANYON, THE(1952), ph; WORLD IN HIS ARMS, THE(1952), ph; YANKEE BUCCANEER(1952), ph; IT HAPPENS EVERY THURSDAY(1953), ph; MAN FROM THE ALAMO, THE(1953), ph; SEMINOLE(1953), ph; TAKE ME TO TOWN(1953), ph; TUMBLEWEED(1953), ph; VEILS OF BAGDAD, THE(1953), ph; FOUR GUNS TO THE BORDER(1954), ph; MAGNIFICENT OBSESSION(1954), ph; NAKED ALIBI(1954), ph; SIGN OF THE PAGAN(1954), ph; TAZA, SON OF COCHISE(1954), ph; ALL THAT HEAVEN ALLOWS(1955), ph; CRASHOUT(1955), ph; CULT OF THE COBRA(1955), ph; MAN FROM BITTER RIDGE, THE(1955), ph; MAN WITHOUT A STAR(1955), ph; CONGO CROSSING(1956), ph; MIRACLE IN THE RAIN(1956), ph; THERE'S ALWAYS TOMORROW(1956), ph; WRITTEN ON THE WIND(1956), ph; BATTLE HYMN(1957), ph; MAN AFRAID(1957), ph; MAN OF A THOUSAND FACES(1957), ph; MIDNIGHT STORY, THE(1957), ph; MISTER CORY(1957), ph; FEMALE ANIMAL, THE(1958), ph; MONSTER ON THE CAMPUS(1958), ph; STEP DOWN TO TERROR(1958), ph; THING THAT COULDN'T DIE, THE(1958), ph; TIME TO LOVE AND A TIME TO DIE, A(1958), ph; TOUCH OF EVIL(1958), ph; IMITATION OF LIFE(1959), ph; THIS EARTH IS MINE(1959), ph; MIDNIGHT LACE(1960), ph; PLATINUM HIGH SCHOOL(1960), ph; PORTRAIT IN BLACK(1960), ph; SPARTACUS(1960), ph; BY

LOVE POSSESSED(1961), ph; FLOWER DRUM SONG(1961), ph; MISFITS, THE(1961), ph; IF A MAN ANSWERS(1962), ph; INTERNS, THE(1962), ph; THAT TOUCH OF MINK(1962), ph; CAPTAIN NEWMAN, M.D.(1963), ph; TAMMY AND THE DOCTOR(1963), ph; THRILL OF IT ALL, THE(1963), ph; I'D RATHER BE RICH(1964), ph; ART OF LOVE, THE(1965), ph; BUS RILEY'S BACK IN TOWN(1965), ph; WAR LORD, THE(1965), ph; APPALOOSA, THE(1966), ph; MADAME X(1966), ph; TEXAS ACROSS THE RIVER(1966), ph; COUNTERPOINT(1967), ph; ROUGH NIGHT IN JERICHO(1967), ph; MADIGAN(1968), ph; PINK JUNGLE, THE(1968), ph; SECRET WAR OF HARRY FRIGG, THE(1968), ph; CHANGE OF HABIT(1969), ph; EYE OF THE CAT(1969), ph; HOW DO I LOVE THEE?(1970), ph; TRIBES(1970), ph; OMEGA MAN, THE(1971), ph; BEN(1972), ph

Russell L. Metty
CANCEL MY RESERVATION(1972), ph

A. Metyolkin
LAST GAME, THE(1964, USSR)

Misha Metyolkin
GIRL AND THE BUGLER, THE(1967, USSR)

Alfred Metz
GENTLE GIANT(1967)

Rex Metz
JIM, THE WORLD'S GREATEST(1976), ph

Rexford Metz
JAWS(1975), ph; GAUNTLET, THE(1977), ph; EVERY WHICH WAY BUT LOOSE(1978), ph; SERIAL(1980), ph; FORCED VENGEANCE(1982), ph

Vittorio Metz
PSYCOSISSIMO(1962, Ital.), w; LADY DOCTOR, THE(1963, Fr./Ital./Span.), w; LOVE, THE ITALIAN WAY(1964, Ital.), w; 00-2 MOST SECRET AGENTS(1965, Ital.), w; DOS COSMONAUTAS A LA FUERZA(1967, Span./*Ital.), w

Leo Metzenbauer
FIDELIO(1961, Aust.), set d

Alan Metzer
ON THE YARD(1978), ph

Erno Metzer
IT HAPPENED TOMORROW(1944), prod d; MACOMBER AFFAIR, THE(1947), art d

Michael L. Metzer
1984
UP THE CREEK(1984), p

Otto Metzetti
Misc. Talkies
NOW OR NEVER(1935)

Victor Metzetti
Silents
PUTTING IT OVER(1922); BULLDOG PLUCK(1927)

Alan Metzger
THAT'S THE WAY OF THE WORLD(1975), ph; VOICES(1979), ph; BELOW THE BELT(1980), ph

Ed Metzger
CARWASH(1976)

Radley Metzger
DARK ODYSSEY(1961), p&d, w, ed; FLESH EATERS, THE(1964), ed; CARMEN, BABY(1967, Yugo./Ger.), p&d; CAMILLE 2000(1969), p&d; LITTLE MOTHER(1973, U.S./Yugo./Ger.), a, p&d; CAT AND THE CANARY, THE(1979, Brit.), d&w

Radley H. Metzger
SOFT SKIN ON BLACK SILK(1964, Fr./Span.), d; THERESE AND ISABELLE(1968, U.S./Ger.), p&d

Prof. Metzl
RASPUTIN(1932, Ger.), m

Jim Metzler
FOUR FRIENDS(1981); TEX(1982)

Rick Metzler
BLACULA(1972)

Robert Metzler
RIDERS OF THE PURPLE SAGE(1941), w; CIRCUMSTANTIAL EVIDENCE(1945), w; UNDERCOVER WOMAN, THE(1946), w

Robert F. Metzler
DR. RENAULT'S SECRET(1942), w; SUNDOWN JIM(1942), w

Bea Metzman
Misc. Talkies
JOE AND MAXI(1980)

Dan Metzman
Misc. Talkies
JOE AND MAXI(1980)

Irving Metzman
ARTHUR(1981); FORT APACHE, THE BRONX(1981); SO FINE(1981); ANNIE(1982); SHOOT THE MOON(1982); STILL OF THE NIGHT(1982); WARGAMES(1983)
1984
FLAMINGO KID, THE(1984)

Erno Metzner
MISTRESS OF ATLANTIS, THE(1932, Ger.), prod d; FROM TOP TO BOTTOM(1933, Fr.), art d; PRINCESS CHARMING(1935, Brit.), art d; ROBBER SYMPHONY, THE(1937, Brit.), art d
Silents
ONE ARABIAN NIGHT(1921, Ger.), set d

Georgette Metzradt
WITNESS, THE(1982, Hung.)

Hans Meueller
LOVE WALTZ, THE(1930, Ger.), w

Belinda Meuldijk
SOLDIER OF ORANGE(1979, Dutch)

Lillian Meuller
SOME LIKE IT COOL(1979, Ger./Aust./Ital./Fr.)

Ray Meunich
JAWS 3-D(1983)

Claudine Meunier
YOUNG GIRLS OF ROCHEFORT, THE(1968, Fr.)

Fanny Meunier
COUSINS IN LOVE(1982)

Gilbert Meunier
LIFE UPSIDE DOWN(1965, Fr.)

Gus Meunier
STRANGE INVADERS(1983), set d

Gustave Meunier
STRANGE BREW(1983), set d

Jean-Claude Meunier
QUEST FOR FIRE(1982, Fr./Can.)

Pamela Meunier
UNMARRIED WOMAN, AN(1978)

Raymond Meunier
NIGHT WATCH, THE(1964, Fr./Ital.); SEVENTH JUROR, THE(1964, Fr.)
1984
ONE DEADLY SUMMER(1984, Fr.)

Catherine Meurisse
LA BALANCE(1983, Fr.), cos

Paul Meurisse
DIABOLIQUE(1955, Fr.); GUINGUETTE(1959, Fr.); PICNIC ON THE GRASS(1960, Fr.); GAME OF TRUTH, THE(1961, Fr.); LOVE AND THE FRENCHWOMAN(1961, Fr.); TRUTH, THE(1961, Fr./Ital.); BACK STREETS OF PARIS(1962, Fr.); L'ARMEE DES OMBRES(1969, Fr./Ital.)

Theo Meurisse
GIVE HER THE MOON(1970, Fr./Ital.), set d; TIME FOR LOVING, A(1971, Brit.), prod d; COP, A(1973, Fr.), art d; LIZA(1976, Fr./Ital.), art d; DIRTY MONEY(1977, Fr.), art d
1984
MY BEST FRIEND'S GIRL(1984, Fr.), set d

Theobald Meurisse
BEAU PERE(1981, Fr.), art d

Anne-Laure Meury
AVIATOR'S WIFE, THE(1981, Fr.)

Bob Meusel
Silents
SLIDE, KELLY, SLIDE(1927)

Irish Meusel
FAST COMPANY(1929)
Silents
SLIDE, KELLY, SLIDE(1927)

Robert W. Meusel
PRIDE OF THE YANKEES, THE(1942)

Christel Meuser
NOT RECONCILED, OR "ONLY VIOLENCE HELPS WHERE IT RULES"(1969, Ger.)

Bernard Meusnier
SUCKER, THE(1966, Fr./Ital.); SINGAPORE, SINGAPORE(1969, Fr./Ital.)

Randy Mewbourn
Misc. Talkies
POLK COUNTY POT PLANE(1977)

Anita Mey
HEIDI(1954, Switz.); HEIDI AND PETER(1955, Switz.)

Hans Mey
LILAC DOMINO, THE(1940, Brit.), m/l Charles Cuvillier

Lev Aleksandrovich Mey
TSAR'S BRIDE, THE(1966, USSR), w

Dot Meyberg
OFFICER 13(1933)

Vladimir Meybom
GROWN-UP CHILDREN(1963, USSR), ph

Harry Meyen
ALRAUNE(1952, Ger.); DEVIL'S GENERAL, THE(1957, Ger.); ORDERED TO LOVE(1963, Ger.); IS PARIS BURNING?(1966, U.S./Fr.); TRIPLE CROSS(1967, Fr./Brit.)

A.H. Meyer
TWO HEADS ON A PILLOW(1934), m

Abe Meyer
INTRUDER, THE(1932), md; SECRETS OF WU SIN(1932), md; FLAMING SIGNAL(1933), md; SHRIEK IN THE NIGHT, A(1933), md; SPHINX, THE(1933), md; STRANGE PEOPLE(1933), md; GREEN EYES(1934), md; HOUSE OF MYSTERY(1934), md; MOONSTONE, THE(1934), md; MURDER ON THE CAMPUS(1934), md; MYSTERY LINER(1934), md; PICTURE BRIDES(1934), md; RANDY RIDES ALONE(1934), md; STAR PACKER, THE(1934), md; COWBOY MILLIONAIRE(1935), m; GHOST WALKS, THE(1935), md; JANE EYRE(1935), md; MYSTERIOUS MR. WONG(1935), md; NEW ADVENTURES OF TARZAN(1935), md; SHOT IN THE DARK, A(1935), md; DEATH FROM A DISTANCE(1936), md; IN HIS STEPS(1936), md; MINE WITH THE IRON DOOR, THE(1936), md; REEFER MADNESS(1936), md; REVOLT OF THE ZOMBIES(1936), md; ROGUES' TAVERN, THE(1936), md; BANK ALARM(1937), md; COUNTY FAIR(1937), md; DRUMS OF DESTINY(1937), md; GLORY TRAIL, THE(1937), md; HOLLYWOOD COWBOY(1937), md; HOUSE OF SECRETS, THE(1937), md; SMALL TOWN BOY(1937), md; WINDJAMMER(1937), md; GANGSTER'S BOY(1938), md; HAWAII CALLS(1938), md; HAWAIIAN BUCKAROO(1938), md; I COVER CHINATOWN(1938), md; OLD LOUISIANA(1938), md; REBELLION(1938), m; TARZAN'S REVENGE(1938), m; I AM A CRIMINAL(1939), md; SHARK WOMAN, THE(1941), md

Alvin Meyer
FEVER HEAT(1968)

Andrew Meyer
SKY PIRATE, THE(1970), p,d&w, ed; NIGHT OF THE COBRA WOMAN(1974, U.S./Phil.), d, w; TIDAL WAVE(1975, U.S./Jap.), d

Anthony Meyer
HAMLET(1976, Brit.)

Armando Meyer
EXTERMINATING ANGEL, THE(1967, Mex.), makeup; NAZARIN(1968, Mex.), makeup

Art Meyer
MR. WONG, DETECTIVE(1938), md

Bernie Meyer
FINE MADNESS, A(1966)

Carl Meyer
Misc. Silents
PRESIDENT, THE(1918, Den.)

Clara Meyer
STEREO(1969, Can.)
Claude Meyer
1984
CHEECH AND CHONG'S THE CORSICAN BROTHERS(1984)
Cleve Meyer
Silents
CODE OF THE RANGE(1927), w
David Meyer
HAMLET(1976, Brit.); THIRD WALKER, THE(1978, Can.); DRAUGHTSMAN'S CON-TRACT, THE(1983, Brit.); OCTOPUSSY(1983, Brit.); PARSIFAL(1983, Fr.)
1984
MIDSUMMER NIGHT'S DREAM, A(1984, Brit./Span.)
Dorothy Meyer
GREATEST, THE(1977, U.S./Brit.); H.O.T.S.(1979); ROLLER BOOGIE(1979); WHOSE LIFE IS IT ANYWAY?(1981)
E. E. Meyer
MOTOR PSYCHO(1965)
Edwin Justus Meyer
TILL WE MEET AGAIN(1936), w
Elizabeth Meyer
SEVEN AGAINST THE SUN(1968, South Africa)
Emile Meyer
PANIC IN THE STREETS(1950); BIG NIGHT, THE(1951); CATTLE QUEEN(1951); GUY WHO CAME BACK, THE(1951); MOB, THE(1951); PEOPLE AGAINST O'HARA, THE(1951); BLOODHOUNDS OF BROADWAY(1952); CARBINE WILLIAMS(1952); HURRICANE SMITH(1952); WE'RE NOT MARRIED(1952); WILD NORTH, THE(1952); FARMER TAKES A WIFE, THE(1953); SHANE(1953); DRUMS ACROSS THE RIVER(1954); HUMAN JUNGLE, THE(1954); RIOT IN CELL BLOCK 11(1954); SHIELD FOR MURDER(1954); SILVER LODE(1954); BLACKBOARD JUNGLE, THE(1955); GIRL IN THE RED VELVET SWING, THE(1955); MAN WITH THE GOLDEN ARM, THE(1955); MAN WITH THE GUN(1955); STRANGER ON HORSEBACK(1955); TALL MEN, THE(1955); WHITE FEATHER(1955); MAVERICK QUEEN, THE(1956); RAW EDGE(1956); BABY FACE NELSON(1957); BADLANDS OF MONTANA(1957); DELICATE DELINQUENT, THE(1957); GUN THE MAN DOWN(1957); PATHS OF GLORY(1957); SWEET SMELL OF SUCCESS(1957); CASE AGAINST BROOKLYN, THE(1958); FIEND WHO WALKED THE WEST, THE(1958); GOOD DAY FOR A HANGING(1958); LINEUP, THE(1958); REVOLT IN THE BIG HOUSE(1958); KING OF THE WILD STALLIONS(1959); GIRL IN LOVER'S LANE, THE(1960); THREAT, THE(1960); YOUNG JESSE JAMES(1960); MOVE OVER, DAR-LING(1963); TAGGART(1964); YOUNG DILLINGER(1965); HOSTILE GUNS(1967); TIME FOR KILLING, A(1967); OUTFIT, THE(1973); MACON COUNTY LINE(1974)
Eve Meyer
DESPERATE WOMEN, THE(?); OPERATION DAMES(1959)
Frank Meyer
UNSTRAP ME(1968); SKY PIRATE, THE(1970)
Fred S. Meyer
FIGHTING YOUTH(1935), p; DANGEROUS WATERS(1936), p
Frederich Meyer
AS THE SEA RAGES(1960 Ger.), m
Friedric Meyer
DISORDER AND EARLY TORMENT(1977, Ger.), m
Friedrich Meyer
TIN DRUM, THE(1979, Ger./Fr./Yugo./Pol.), m
George Meyer
CANDIDATE, THE(1972); AMERICAN GRAFFITI(1973)
George R. Meyer
Silents
LAW OF THE LAWLESS, THE(1923), ph
Greta Meyer
ROYAL BOX, THE(1930); TONIGHT OR NEVER(1931); FLESH(1932); MAN FROM YESTERDAY, THE(1932); MATCH KING, THE(1932); JENNIE GERHARDT(1933); MEET THE BARON(1933); NUISANCE, THE(1933); LET'S FALL IN LOVE(1934); LINEUP, THE(1934); MIGHTY BARNUM, THE(1934); SERVANTS' ENTRANCE(1934); BIOGRAPHY OF A BACHELOR GIRL(1935); FORSAKING ALL OTHERS(1935); FOUR HOURS TO KILL(1935); LADDIE(1935); MR. DYNAMITE(1935); NAUGHTY MARIETTA(1935); PUBLIC HERO NO. 1(1935); RETURN OF PETER GRIMM, THE(1935); STRANGE WIVES(1935); DIMPLES(1936); GORGEOUS HUSSY, THE(1936); LIBELED LADY(1936); SPENDTHRIFT(1936); SUZY(1936); WIFE VER-SUS SECRETARY(1936); BILL CRACKS DOWN(1937); DAMAGED GOODS(1937); I'LL TAKE ROMANCE(1937); LANCER SPY(1937); NIGHT OF MYSTERY(1937); PRE-SCRIPTION FOR ROMANCE(1937); THIN ICE(1937); WHEN LOVE IS YOUNG(1937); GREAT WALTZ, THE(1938); PARADISE FOR THREE(1938); PATIENT IN ROOM 18, THE(1938); THREE LOVES HAS NANCY(1938); TORCHY GETS HER MAN(1938); NO PLACE TO GO(1939); WHEN TOMORROW COMES(1939); FOUR SONS(1940); MAN I MARRIED, THE(1940); COME LIVE WITH ME(1941); MILLION DOLLAR BA-BY(1941); FRIENDLY ENEMIES(1942); THEY GOT ME COVERED(1943)
Hans Meyer
WOODEN HORSE, THE(1951); LAST ADVENTURE, THE(1968, Fr./Ital.); PIERROT LE FOU(1968, Fr./Ital.); DON'T LOOK NOW(1969, Brit./Fr.); EROTIQUE(1969, Fr.); CANNON FOR CORDOBA(1970); BARRY LYNDON(1975, Brit.)
1984
RIDDLE OF THE SANDS, THE(1984, Brit.)
Herb Meyer
PASSION HOLIDAY(1963), p; HONEYMOON OF HORROR(1964), p
Hyman Meyer
SATURDAY NIGHT KID, THE(1929); JUDGE PRIEST(1934)
Irwin Meyer
PASSION HOLIDAY(1963), p; HONEYMOON OF HORROR(1964), d
James Meyer
1984
NATURAL, THE(1984)
Jay Meyer
KING OF THE MOUNTAIN(1981)
Jean Meyer
WOULD-BE GENTLEMAN, THE(1960, Fr.), a, d; MARRIAGE OF FIGARO, THE(1963, Fr.), a, d; SUCKER, THE(1966, Fr./Ital.)

Jenny Meyer
MY WAY(1974, South Africa)
Misc. Talkies
SUPER-JOCKS, THE(1980)
Johannes Meyer
BLONDE NIGHTINGALE(1931, Ger.), d; DREAM OF SCHONBRUNN(1933, Aus.), d; INHERITANCE IN PRETORIA(1936, Ger.), d; HAGBARD AND SIGNE(1968, Den./Iceland/Swed.)
Misc. Silents
MASTER OF THE HOUSE(1925, Den.)
John Meyer
SANTA FE TRAIL(1940)
1984
NOT FOR PUBLICATION(1984), w, m
Julius L. Meyer
1984
RED DAWN(1984)
Leo B. Meyer
FORCE OF IMPULSE(1961), art d
Linda Meyer
LADYBUG, LADYBUG(1963)
Marc E. Meyer, Jr.
NUDE BOMB, THE(1980), set d
Marco Meyer
WILD RIDERS(1971), ed
Michael Meyer
DOLL'S HOUSE, A(1973, Brit.), w
Mike Meyer
MR. BUG GOES TO TOWN(1941), a, w
Mimi Meyer
SWAMP THING(1982)
Muffie Meyer
LORDS OF FLATBUSH, THE(1974), ed
Nicholas Meyer
INVASION OF THE BEE GIRLS(1973), w; SEVEN-PER-CENT SOLUTION, THE(1977, Brit.), w; TIME AFTER TIME(1979, Brit.), d&w; STAR TREK II: THE WRATH OF KHAN(1982), d
Orville Meyer
HUCKLEBERRY FINN(1974)
Otto Meyer
ONE WAY TRAIL, THE(1931), ed; CORNERED(1932), ed; DARING DANGER(1932), ed; END OF THE TRAIL(1932), ed; FIGHTING FOOL, THE(1932), ed; FIGHTING MARSHAL, THE(1932), ed; TEXAS CYCLONE(1932), ed; TWO-FISTED LAW(1932), ed; HOLD THE PRESS(1933), ed; POLICE CAR 17(1933), ed; RUSTY RIDES ALO-NE(1933), ed; BEFORE MIDNIGHT(1934), ed; GIRL IN DANGER(1934), ed; HELL BENT FOR LOVE(1934), ed; AFTER THE DANCE(1935), ed; BEST MAN WINS, THE(1935), ed; ESCAPE FROM DEVIL'S ISLAND(1935), ed; IN SPITE OF DAN-GER(1935), ed; SUPERSPEED(1935), ed; WHITE LIES(1935), ed; ADVENTURE IN MANHATTAN(1936), ed; HELL-SHIP MORGAN(1936), ed; MEET NERO WOL-FE(1936), ed; ROAMING LADY(1936), ed; THEODORA GOES WILD(1936), ed; COUN-SEL FOR CRIME(1937), ed; FRAME-UP THE(1937), ed; I'LL TAKE ROMANCE(1937), ed; RACKETEERS IN EXILE(1937), ed; WOMEN OF GLA-MOUR(1937), ed; ADVENTURE IN SAHARA(1938), ed; HOLIDAY(1938), ed; LONE WOLF IN PARIS, THE(1938), ed; NO TIME TO MARRY(1938), ed; BLIND AL-LEY(1939), ed; BLONDIE BRINGS UP BABY(1939), ed; GOLDEN BOY(1939), ed; LADY AND THE MOB, THE(1939), ed; LONE WOLF SPY HUNT, THE(1939), ed; TAMING OF THE WEST, THE(1939), ed; ARIZONA(1940), ed; MUSIC IN MY HEART(1940), ed; TOO MANY HUSBANDS(1940), ed; PENNY SERENADE(1941), ed; YOU'LL NEVER GET RICH(1941), ed; BLONDIE GOES TO COLLEGE(1942), ed; TALK OF THE TOWN(1942), ed; HEAT'S ON, THE(1943), ed; MORE THE MERRIER, THE(1943), ed; MY KINGDOM FOR A COOK(1943), ed; SOMETHING TO SHOUT ABOUT(1943), ed; BLACK PARACHUTE, THE(1944), ed; EVER SINCE VENUS(1944), ed; LOUISIANA HAYRIDE(1944), ed; NINE GIRLS(1944), ed; TOGETHER AGAIN(1944), ed; GUY, A GAL AND A PAL, A(1945), ed; OVER 21(1945), ed; FACE TO FACE(1952), ed; TAHITIAN, THE(1956), ed; SEVEN DARING GIRLS(1962, Ger.), d
Ray Meyer
COMET OVER BROADWAY(1938)
Richard Meyer
HAPPY ANNIVERSARY(1959), ed; CAPONE(1975), ed; NIGHT OF THE AS-KARI(1978, Ger./South African), ed
Richard C. Meyer
SEVEN ANGRY MEN(1955), ed; CRIME IN THE STREETS(1956), ed; WILD PARTY, THE(1956), ed; HOT ROD RUMBLE(1957), ed; MEN IN WAR(1957), ed; MOTORCY-CLE GANG(1957), ed; REFORM SCHOOL GIRL(1957), ed; UNDERSEA GIRL(1957), ed; ANNA LUCASTA(1958), ed; GOD'S LITTLE ACRE(1958), ed; ALASKA PASS-AGE(1959), ed; RETURN OF THE FLY(1959), ed; SAD HORSE, THE(1959), ed; YOUNG JESSE JAMES(1960), ed; PYRO(1964, U.S./Span.), p; THREE IN THE AT-TIC(1968), ed; BUTCH CASSIDY AND THE SUNDANCE KID(1969), ed; WIN-NING(1969), ed; NATIONAL LAMPOON'S CLASS REUNION(1982), ed; SILENT RAGE(1982), ed
Roberto Meyer
BRUTE, THE(1952, Mex.); CRIMINAL LIFE OF ARCHIBALDO DE LA CRUZ, THE(1962, Mex.); LITTLE RED RIDING HOOD AND HER FRIENDS(1964, Mex.)
Roland Meyer
MOONSHINE COUNTY EXPRESS(1977)
Russ Meyer
DESPERATE WOMEN, THE(?), ph; ROOGIE'S BUMP(1954); FANNY HILL: ME-MOIRS OF A WOMAN OF PLEASURE zero(1965), d; MOTOR PSYCHO(1965), p&d, w, ph; ROPE OF FLESH(1965), p, d; GOOD MORNING... AND GOODBYE(1967), p&d, w, ph; FINDERS KEEPERS, LOVERS WEEPERS(1968), p&d, w, ph, ed; SEVEN MINUTES, THE(1971), p&d, w; SWEET SUZY(1973), p&d, w
Misc. Talkies
BLACKSNAKE(1973), d
Sam Meyer
STORM OVER TIBET(1952), w
Stanley Meyer
FIGHTING YOUTH(1935), w; DRAGNET(1954), p

Tony Meyer
THIRD WALKER, THE(1978, Can.); VENOM(1982, Brit.); DRAUGHTSMAN'S CONTRACT, THE(1983, Brit.); OCTOPUSSY(1983, Brit.)

Torben Meyer
LAST WARNING, THE(1929); BEHIND THE MAKEUP(1930); JUST LIKE HEAVEN(1930); LUMMOX(1930); MAMBA(1930); BIG CITY BLUES(1932); BROKEN LULLABY(1932); CRIME OF THE CENTURY, THE(1933); MANDALAY(1934); MUSIC IN THE AIR(1934); PURSUED(1934); WORLD MOVES ON, THE(1934); BLACK ROOM, THE(1935); EAST OF JAVA(1935); ENTER MADAME(1935); FRONT PAGE WOMAN(1935); MAN WHO BROKE THE BANK AT MONTE CARLO, THE(1935); MARK OF THE VAMPIRE(1935); ROBERTA(1935); SPLENDOR(1935); TO BEAT THE BAND(1935); TWO FOR TONIGHT(1935); IT HAD TO HAPPEN(1936); KING OF BURLESQUE(1936); PICCADILLY JIM(1936); TILL WE MEET AGAIN(1936); WEDDING PRESENT(1936); EMPEROR'S CANDLESTICKS, THE(1937); ESPIONAGE(1937); FIGHT FOR YOUR LADY(1937); KING AND THE CHORUS GIRL, THE(1937); PRESCRIPTION FOR ROMANCE(1937); PRISONER OF ZENDA, THE(1937); SHALL WE DANCE(1937); THIN ICE(1937); TOVARICH(1937); BULLDOG DRUMMOND'S PERIL(1938); FIRST 100 YEARS, THE(1938); ROMANCE IN THE DARK(1938); EVERYTHING HAPPENS AT NIGHT(1939); ISLAND OF LOST MEN(1939); TOPPER TAKES A TRIP(1939); CHRISTMAS IN JULY(1940); DR. EHRLICH'S MAGIC BULLET(1940); FOUR SONS(1940); NO, NO NANETTE(1940); WAY OF ALL FLESH, THE(1940); LADY EVE, THE(1941); SULLIVAN'S TRAVELS(1941); BERLIN CORRESPONDENT(1942); CASABLANCA(1942); PALM BEACH STORY, THE(1942); EDGE OF DARKNESS(1943); FRANKENSTEIN MEETS THE WOLF MAN(1943); THEY CAME TO BLOW UP AMERICA(1943); GREAT MOMENT, THE(1944); GREENWICH VILLAGE(1944); HAIL THE CONQUERING HERO(1944); MIRACLE OF MORGAN'S CREEK, THE(1944); ONCE UPON A TIME(1944); PURPLE HEART, THE(1944); HOTEL BERLIN(1945); ROYAL SCANDAL, A(1945); KID FROM BOOKLYN, THE(1946); MIGHTY MCGURK, THE(1946); EXILE, THE(1947); VARIETY GIRL(1947); JULIA MISBEHAVES(1948); LETTER FROM AN UNKNOWN WOMAN(1948); SEALED VERDICT(1948); UNFAITHFULLY YOURS(1948); BEAUTIFUL BLONDE FROM BASHFUL BEND, THE(1949); HOLD THAT BABY!(1949); MAD WEDNESDAY(1950); COME FILL THE CUP(1951); MY FAVORITE SPY(1951); CALL ME MADAM(1953); HOUDINI(1953); STORY OF THREE LOVES, THE(1953); DEEP IN MY HEART(1954); LIVING IT UP(1954); WE'RE NO ANGELS(1955); FLY, THE(1958); MATCHMAKER, THE(1958); THIS EARTH IS MINE(1959); JUDGMENT AT NUREMBERG(1961)
Silents
MAN WHO LAUGHS, THE(1927); JAZZ MAD(1928)

Torgen Meyer
CROSSROADS(1942)

William Meyer
WILD RIDE, THE(1960), ed

Mimi Meyer-Craven
1984
NIGHTMARE ON ELM STREET, A(1984)

Wilhelm Meyer-Foerster
STUDENT PRINCE, THE(1954), w

Hans Meyer-Hanno
GIRL FROM THE MARSH CROFT, THE(1935, Ger.)

Wilhelm Meyer-Ottens
DAY WILL COME, A(1960, Ger.)

Hugo Meyer-Welfing
DON JUAN(1956, Aust.)

Richard Meyerhoff
GODDESS, THE(1958), set d

V. Meyerhold
Misc. Silents
PICTURE OF DORIAN GRAY, THE(1915, USSR)

Vsevold Meyerhold
Misc. Silents
STRONG MAN, THE(1917, USSR)

Vsevolod Meyerhold
Misc. Silents
PICTURE OF DORIAN GRAY, THE(1915, USSR), d; STRONG MAN, THE(1917, USSR), d; WHITE EAGLE, THE(1928, USSR)

Hubert V. Meyerinck
EMPRESS AND I, THE(1933, Ger.)

Victoria Meyerink
BRAINSTORM(1965); SPEEDWAY(1968)

Victoria Paige Meyerink
NIGHT OF THE GRIZZLY, THE(1966); YOUNG WARRIORS(1983), p

Ralph Meyerling, Jr.
1984
ICE PIRATES, THE(1984)

Abe Meyers
MARINES ARE HERE, THE(1938), md; SALESLADY(1938), m

Alvin Meyers
TENNESSEE JOHNSON(1942), w

Andy Meyers
CURSE OF THE VOODOO(1965, Brit.)

Ari Meyers
AUTHOR! AUTHOR!(1982)

Bambi Meyers
WHAT'S THE MATTER WITH HELEN?(1971)

Barbara Meyers
NIGHT OF EVIL(1962)

Bess Meyers
TORCHY PLAYS WITH DYNAMITE(1939); MEET JOHN DOE(1941)

Billie Meyers
ONE DARK NIGHT(1939), w

Brent Meyers
1984
POLICE ACADEMY(1984)

Carmel Meyers
CAREERS(1929)

Daniel Meyers
UNDERCOVER MAN, THE(1949)

Dave Meyers
THX 1138(1971), ph

David Meyers
FIREFOX(1982)

Douglas Meyers
ONE NIGHT WITH YOU(1948, Brit), ed; AGITATOR, THE(1949), ed

Ernie Meyers
ATTACK OF THE KILLER TOMATOES(1978)

Fred Meyers
GUN RIDERS, THE(1969); HORROR OF THE BLOOD MONSTERS(1970, U.S./Phil.)

Fredricka Meyers
THIRSTY DEAD, THE(1975)

Greta Meyers
SMART GIRL(1935)

Harry Meyers
CONVICTED(1931); RAINBOW OVER BROADWAY(1933); DAMAGED LIVES(1937)
Silents
EARL OF PAWTUCKET, THE(1915), d&w

Henry Meyers
DESTRY RIDES AGAIN(1939), w

Irv Meyers
1984
IRRECONCILABLE DIFFERENCES(1984)

Jennifer Meyers
SLUMBER PARTY MASSACRE, THE(1982)

Lanny Meyers
FIRST TIME, THE(1983), m

Larry Meyers
BATTLE BEYOND THE STARS(1980)

Larry John Meyers
FLASHDANCE(1983)

Marilyn Meyers
VERY NATURAL THING, A(1974); EYES OF LAURA MARS(1978)

Martin Meyers
INCIDENT, THE(1967)

Michael Meyers
FORT APACHE(1948), cos; SHE WORE A YELLOW RIBBON(1949), cos; GOODBYE COLUMBUS(1969)

Mike Meyers
VOODOO HEARTBEAT(1972)

Mugsy Meyers
LOVE IS NEWS(1937)

Nancy Meyers
PRIVATE BENJAMIN(1980), p, w
1984
IRRECONCILABLE DIFFERENCES(1984), w; PROTOCOL(1984), w

Nicholas Meyers
BEEN DOWN SO LONG IT LOOKS LIKE UP TO ME(1977), ed

Otto Meyers
Misc. Silents
SUNDOWN SLIM(1920)

Paul Meyers
SUNNY SKIES(1930), ph

Pauline Meyers
TAKE A GIANT STEP(1959)

Ross Meyers
Misc. Talkies
SWINGING COEDS, THE(1976), d

Roxanne Meyers
WHAT'S THE MATTER WITH HELEN?(1971)

Rusty Meyers
1984
INITIATION, THE(1984)

Ruth Meyers
KITCHEN, THE(1961, Brit.); SMASHING TIME(1967 Brit.), cos
1984
WOMAN IN RED, THE(1984), cos

Sheila Meyers
ROYAL WEDDING(1951); ROAD TO HONG KONG, THE(1962, U.S./Brit.), ch

Sidney Meyers
EDGE OF THE CITY(1957), ed; SLAVES(1969), ed

Stan Meyers
INVISIBLE STRIPES(1940)

Stanley Meyers
KING, QUEEN, KNAVE(1972, Ger./U.S.), m; APPRENTICESHIP OF DUDDY KRAVITZ, THE(1974, Can.), m; ROAD MOVIE(1974), m; INCUBUS, THE(1982, Can.), m

Stephan B. Meyers
TAKE THIS JOB AND SHOVE IT(1981)

Ted Meyers
LOVE MACHINE, THE,(1971)

W. Ray Meyers
Silents
HUNCHBACK OF NOTRE DAME, THE(1923)

Willie Meyers
DAY OF THE DOLPHIN, THE(1973)

Zion Meyers
MAN ABOUT TOWN(1939), w

Meyers Sisters
FROZEN JUSTICE(1929)

Annie Meyers-Shyer
1984
IRRECONCILABLE DIFFERENCES(1984)

Jean Meyet
MY UNCLE(1958, Fr.)

Walter Meyjes
WESTMINSTER PASSION PLAY–BEHOLD THE MAN, THE(1951, Brit), w

Evelyn Meyka
1984
LOVE IN GERMANY, A(1984, Fr./Ger.)

Fintan Meyler
ZERO HOUR!(1957); SHOWDOWN AT BOOT HILL(1958)
Robert Meyn
LAST BRIDGE, THE(1957, Aust.); COURT MARTIAL(1962, Ger.); DEVIL IN SILK(1968, Ger.)
Lawrence Meynall
SHADOW MAN(1953, Brit.), w
Kermit Meynard
SHERIFF OF SAGE VALLEY(1942)
Laurence Meynell
HOUSE IN MARSH ROAD, THE(1960, Brit.), w; PRICE OF SILENCE, THE(1960, Brit.), w; GREAT ARMORED CAR SWINDLE, THE(1964), w
Lawrence Meynell
UMBRELLA, THE(1933, Brit.), w; BREAKING POINT, THE(1961, Brit.), w
Gerald Meynier
ROMEO AND JULIET(1968, Ital./Span.)
Geronimo Meynier
GREAT WAR, THE(1961, Fr., Ital.); LOVE AT TWENTY(1963, Fr./Ital./Jap./Pol./Ger.); FRIENDS FOR LIFE(1964, Ital.)
Robert Meyr
REST IS SILENCE, THE(1960, Ger.)
Jacques Meyran
ANTOINE ET ANTOINETTE(1947 Fr.)
Mary Ellen Meyran
MILDRED PIERCE(1945)
Pierre Meyrat
MISTRESS FOR THE SUMMER, A(1964, Fr./Ital.), p
Gustav Meyrink
GOLEM(1980, Pol.), w
Silents
GOLEM: HOW HE CAME INTO THE WORLD, THE(1920, Ger.), w
Michelle Meyrink
OUTSIDERS, THE(1983); VALLEY GIRL(1983)
1984
JOY OF SEX(1984); REVENGE OF THE NERDS(1984)
Inge Meysel
ROSES FOR THE PROSECUTOR(1961, Ger.)
Jose Meza
BRAVE BULLS, THE(1951)
Lee Meza
LIFE AND TIMES OF JUDGE ROY BEAN, THE(1972)
Thamila Mezbah
LE BEAU MARIAGE(1982, Fr.)
Lajos Mezei
WITNESS, THE(1982, Hung.)
S. Mezhinsky
CONCENTRATION CAMP(1939, USSR)
Sergei Mezhinsky
1812(1944, USSR)
Almos Mezo
WEB OF FEAR(1966, Fr./Span.), p
A. Mezzei
MAGIC BOW, THE(1947, Brit.), art d
Lucca Mezzofanti
TRAIL OF THE PINK PANTHER, THE(1982)
Vittorio Mezzogiorno
CAFE EXPRESS(1980, Ital.); DESIRE, THE INTERIOR LIFE(1980, Ital./Ger.); THREE BROTHERS(1982, Ital.); MOON IN THE GUTTER, THE(1983, Fr./Ital.)
Miki Mfir
JESUS(1979)
Alexander Mgebrov
IVAN THE TERRIBLE(Part I, 1947, USSR)
Mia Mia
Misc. Silents
GREATEST TRUTH, THE(1922, Ger.)
Rosa Mia
NO MAN IS AN ISLAND(1962)
Richard Miabaum
PARATROOPER(1954, Brit.), w
Pia Miacco
1984
HARDBODIES(1984)
Louis Miaille
SEVEN CAPITAL SINS(1962, Fr./Ital.), ph
Buntaro Miake
MYSTERIOUS SATELLITE, THE(1956, Jap.)
Roberto Miali
DAVID AND GOLIATH(1961, Ital.)
Erzsebet Mialkovszky
FATHER(1967, Hung.), cos
Miami
GREEN SLIME, THE(1969), cos
Andrea Miano
PIRATE OF THE BLACK HAWK, THE(1961, Fr./Ital.)
Robert Miano
BADGE 373(1973); KISS ME GOODBYE(1982); VICE SQUAD(1982)
1984
FEAR CITY(1984); FIRESTARTER(1984)
Ching Miao
LAST WOMAN OF SHANG, THE(1964, Hong Kong); LOVE ETERNE, THE(1964, Hong Kong); GRAND SUBSTITUTION, THE(1965, Hong Kong); LADY GENERAL, THE(1965, Hong Kong); MERMAID, THE(1966, Hong Kong); VERMILION DOOR(1969, Hong Kong); SACRED KNIVES OF VENGEANCE, THE(1974, Hong Kong)
Nora Miao
RETURN OF THE DRAGON(1974, Chin.)
Nicholas Miaskovsky
IRON CURTAIN, THE(1948), m

Milo Mica
I EVEN MET HAPPY GYPSIES(1968, Yugo.), ed
Paul Micale
NEW KIND OF LOVE, A(1963); I'D RATHER BE RICH(1964); DREAMS OF GLASS(1969); MARLOWE(1969); LADY SINGS THE BLUES(1972)
Paul J. Micale
ROCKY II(1979)
Renato Micali
RING AROUND THE CLOCK(1953, Ital.)
Franco Micalizzi
THEY CALL ME TRINITY(1971, Ital.), m; BATTLE OF THE AMAZONS(1973, Ital./Span.), m
1984
LAST HUNTER, THE(1984, Ital.), m
Adriano Micantoni
MINOTAUR, THE(1961, Ital.)
Franco Miccolizzi
CRIME AT PORTA ROMANA(1980, Ital.), m
Raffaela Miceli
ROVER, THE(1967, Ital.)
Chris Micelli
1984
NINJA III–THE DOMINATION(1984)
Alexis Micha
LA VIE DE CHATEAU(1967, Fr.)
Bill Michael
FARMER'S OTHER DAUGHTER, THE(1965)
Boris Michael
1984
DADDY'S DEADLY DARLING(1984), set d
Carole Michael
WHITE HUNTER(1965)
David Michael
WARKILL(1968, U.S./Phil.)
Eduard Ben Michael
FAITHFUL CITY(1952, Israel), m
Frank Michael
CHARLIE CHAN AND THE CURSE OF THE DRAGON QUEEN(1981)
George Michael
WHITE HUNTER(1965), a, p,d&w
Gertrude Michael
MASK OF FU MANCHU, THE(1932); UNASHAMED(1932); WAYWARD(1932); ANN VICKERS(1933); BEDTIME STORY, A(1933); CRADLE SONG(1933); I'M NO ANGEL(1933); NIGHT OF TERROR(1933); SAILOR BE GOOD(1933); BOLERO(1934); CLEOPATRA(1934); GEORGE WHITE'S SCANDALS(1934); HOLD THAT GIRL(1934); I BELIEVED IN YOU(1934); MENACE(1934); MURDER AT THE VANITIES(1934); MURDER ON THE BLACKBOARD(1934); NOTORIOUS SOPHIE LANG, THE(1934); SEARCH FOR BEAUTY(1934); WITCHING HOUR, THE(1934); FATHER BROWN, DETECTIVE(1935); FOUR HOURS TO KILL(1935); IT HAPPENED IN NEW YORK(1935); LAST OUTPOST, THE(1935); FORGOTTEN FACES(1936); MAKE WAY FOR A LADY(1936); RETURN OF SOPHIE LANG, THE(1936); SECOND WIFE(1936); TILL WE MEET AGAIN(1936); WOMAN TRAP(1936); MR. DODD TAKES THE AIR(1937); SOPHIE LANG GOES WEST(1937); HIDDEN POWER(1939); JUST LIKE A WOMAN(1939, Brit.); FARMER'S DAUGHTER, THE(1940); HIDDEN MENACE, THE(1940, Brit.); I CAN'T GIVE YOU ANYTHING BUT LOVE, BABY(1940); PAROLE FIXER(1940); SLIGHTLY TEMPTED(1940); PRISONER OF JAPAN(1942); BEHIND PRISON WALLS(1943); WHERE ARE YOUR CHILDREN?(1943); WOMEN IN BONDAGE(1943); FACES IN THE FOG(1944); ALLOTMENT WIVES, INC.(1945); THREE'S A CROWD(1945); CLUB HAVANA(1946); THAT WONDERFUL URGE(1948); FLAMINGO ROAD(1949); CAGED(1950); DARLING, HOW COULD YOU!(1951); BUGLES IN THE AFTERNOON(1952); NO ESCAPE(1953); WOMEN'S PRISON(1955); TWIST ALL NIGHT(1961); OUTSIDER, THE(1962)
Harry Michael
CATHY'S CHILD(1979, Aus.)
Jay Michael
1984
FEAR CITY(1984)
Jean Michael
NATIVE SON(1951, U.S., Arg.)
Jeff Michael
MIGHTY MOUSE IN THE GREAT SPACE CHASE(1983), m
John Michael
MAGNIFICENT DOLL(1946)
Joy Michael
WIND CANNOT READ, THE(1958, Brit.); HOMEWORK(1982)
1984
JOHNNY DANGEROUSLY(1984)
June Michael
WHITE HUNTER(1965)
Kathleen Michael
HIDEOUT(1948, Brit.); WEAK AND THE WICKED, THE(1954, Brit.)
Manny Michael
YOU CAN'T WIN 'EM ALL(1970, Brit.)
Mary Michael
VIOLATORS, THE(1957); IN LIKE FLINT(1967); HOW SWEET IT IS(1968)
Paul Michael
HOUSE OF DARK SHADOWS(1970); PENNIES FROM HEAVEN(1981)
Peter Michael
WITHOUT RESERVATIONS(1946); EDGE OF DARKNESS(1943); KEEP 'EM SLUGGING(1943); MISSION TO MOSCOW(1943); OVERLAND MAIL ROBBERY(1943); THEY CAME TO BLOW UP AMERICA(1943); CAPTAIN EDDIE(1945); NOB HILL(1945); CLOAK AND DAGGER(1946); O.S.S.(1946); PRETENDER, THE(1947); YANKEE FAKIR(1947); SEARCH FOR DANGER(1949); MYSTERY SUBMARINE(1950); OPERATION SECRET(1952)
Pierre Michael
LOVE AND THE FRENCHWOMAN(1961, Fr.)
Ralph Michael
FALSE EVIDENCE(1937, Brit.); JOHN HALIFAX–GENTLEMAN(1938, Brit.); GIRL WHO FORGOT, THE(1939, Brit.); FRONT LINE KIDS(1942, Brit.); GERT AND DAISY CLEAN UP(1942, Brit.); WOMEN AREN'T ANGELS(1942, Brit.); FOR THOSE IN

PERIL(1944, Brit.); THEY CAME TO A CITY(1944, Brit.); DEAD OF NIGHT(1946, Brit.); JOHNNY FRENCHMAN(1946, Brit.); SAN DEMETRIO, LONDON(1947, Brit.); SONG FOR TOMORROW, A(1948, Brit.); HASTY HEART, THE(1949); ASTONISHED HEART, THE(1950, Brit.); BREAKING THE SOUND BARRIER(1952); BLONDE BAIT(1956, U.S./Brit.); ABANDON SHIP(1957, Brit.); NIGHT TO REMEMBER, A(1958, Brit.); DATE AT MIDNIGHT(1960, Brit.); TASTE OF MONEY, A(1960, Brit.); COURT MARTIAL OF MAJOR KELLER, THE(1961, Brit.); VALIANT, THE(1962, Brit./Ital.); CHILDREN OF THE DAMNED(1963, Brit.); PRIVATE POTTER(1963, Brit.); JOLLY BAD FELLOW, A(1964, Brit.); MURDER MOST FOUL(1964, Brit.); HEROES OF TELEMARK, THE(1965, Brit.); GRAND PRIX(1966); HE WHO RIDES A TIGER(1966, Brit.); KHARTOUM(1966, Brit.); ASSASSINATION BUREAU, THE(1969, Brit.); HOUSE OF CARDS(1969); COUNT OF MONTE CRISTO(1976, Brit.)

Ryan Michael
LADY CHATTERLEY'S LOVER(1981, Fr./Brit.)

Sabina Michael
RADIO ON(1980, Brit./Ger.)

Steve Michael
SELF-PORTRAIT(1973, U.S./Chile), ed

Tony Michael
PARDNERS(1956)

William Michael
1984
DADDY'S DEADLY DARLING(1984)

Michael-Marie
TROUBLE WITH ANGELS, THE(1966)

Michaela
LAST VALLEY, THE(1971, Brit.)

Gayenne Michaeldze
STOLEN LIFE(1939, Brit.)

Cliff Michaelevski
JESUS CHRIST, SUPERSTAR(1973)

James Michaelford
HOT LEAD AND COLD FEET(1978)

Elisheva Michaeli
TWO KOUNEY LEMELS(1966, Israel); SIMCHON FAMILY, THE(1969, Israel); FLYING MATCHMAKER, THE(1970, Israel)

Don Michaelian
SNIPER, THE(1952); ESCAPE FROM ALCATRAZ(1979)

Michael Michaelian
HELL'S ANGELS '69(1969)

George Michaelides
GLORY BRIGADE, THE(1953); DREAM OF KINGS, A(1969)

V. G. Michaelides
MADALENA(1965, Gr.), p

V. Michaelides
APOLLO GOES ON HOLIDAY(1968, Ger./Swed.), p

Viktor G. Michaelides
RED LANTERNS(1965, Gr.), p; FEAR, THE(1967, Gr.), p; LOVE CYCLES(1969, Gr.), p; SISTERS, THE(1969, Gr.), p

Dario Michaelis
DEVIL'S COMMANDMENT, THE(1956, Ital.); NANA(1957, Fr./Ital.); DAY THE SKY EXPLODED, THE(1958, Fr./Ital.); HOUSE OF INTRIGUE, THE(1959, Ital.); GUNMEN OF THE RIO GRANDE(1965, Fr./Ital./Span.); TRAMPLERS, THE(1966, Ital.); MISSION BLOODY MARY(1967, Fr./Ital./Span.)

Bert Michaels
GYPSY(1962); INCIDENT IN AN ALLEY(1962); SATURDAY NIGHT FEVER(1977)

Beverly Michaels
EAST SIDE, WEST SIDE(1949); THREE LITTLE WORDS(1950); GIRL ON THE BRIDGE, THE(1951); PICKUP(1951); WICKED WOMAN(1953); BETRAYED WOMEN(1955); CRASHOUT(1955); BLONDE BAIT(1956, U.S./Brit.); BABYLON(1980, Brit.)

Brock Michaels
NEW YORK, NEW YORK(1977)

Burt Michaels
WEST SIDE STORY(1961)

Christy Michaels
SOMEWHERE IN TIME(1980)

Corrine Michaels
Misc. Talkies
LABORATORY(1980)

Dan Michaels
BLACK KING(1932); VICTIMS OF PERSECUTION(1933)

Dave Michaels
SHARKY'S MACHINE(1982)

David E. Michaels
Misc. Talkies
EVERYDAY(1976)

Delana Michaels
HARD COUNTRY(1981)
1984
2010(1984)

Dolores Michaels
FRENCH LINE, THE(1954); SON OF SINBAD(1955); APRIL LOVE(1957); TIME LIMIT(1957); WAYWARD BUS, THE(1957); FIEND WHO WALKED THE WEST, THE(1958); FRAULEIN(1958); FIVE GATES TO HELL(1959); WARLOCK(1959); ONE FOOT IN HELL(1960); BATTLE AT BLOODY BEACH(1961)

Drew Michaels
BOYS IN COMPANY C, THE(1978, U.S./Hong Kong)

Edward Michaels
HOUSE ON 92ND STREET, THE(1945)

Gary Michaels
FRANCHETTE; LES INTRIGUES(1969)

Greg Michaels
LOGAN'S RUN(1976)
Misc. Talkies
JUPITER MENACE, THE(1982)

J. Michaels
UNION CITY(1980), ed

Jamie Michaels
WANDERLOVE(1970)

Jerome Michaels
TWO OF A KIND(1983)
1984
JOHNNY DANGEROUSLY(1984)

Joel B. Michaels
TRIBUTE(1980, Can.), p; PEACE KILLERS, THE(1971), p, w; BITTERSWEET LOVE(1976), p; SILENT PARTNER, THE(1979, Can.), p; CHANGELING, THE(1980, Can.), p; AMATEUR, THE(1982), p
1984
PHILADELPHIA EXPERIMENT, THE(1984), p

John Michaels
BRIDE FOR SALE(1949); MILITARY ACADEMY WITH THAT TENTH AVENUE GANG(1950)
1984
SPLATTER UNIVERSITY(1984), a, p, w

Johnny Michaels
DEERSLAYER(1943); JIVE JUNCTION(1944); NO MAN OF HER OWN(1950)

Jordon Michaels
Misc. Talkies
LIFE POD(1980)

Joshua Michaels
LITTLE SEX, A(1982)

Kay Michaels
DR. GOLDFOOT AND THE BIKINI MACHINE(1965); DIMENSION 5(1966)

Keith Michaels
GRAND THEFT AUTO(1977), art d

Lorne Michaels
1984
NOTHING LASTS FOREVER(1984), p

Matt Michaels
SUMMER CAMP(1979)

Melissa Michaels
SQUEEZE PLAY(1981)

Michele Michaels
SLUMBER PARTY MASSACRE, THE(1982)

Mickey S. Michaels
AIRPORT '77(1977), set d; HOUSE CALLS(1978), set d; RAISE THE TITANIC(1980, Brit.), set d

Nicola Michaels
POWER AND THE PRIZE, THE(1956)

Noreen Michaels
FARMER TAKES A WIFE, THE(1953)

Norene Michaels
FLAME OF ARABY(1951)

Pat Michaels
SANTA FE UPRISING(1946); TRUE STORY OF LYNN STUART, THE(1958), w

Patrice Michaels
INCREDIBLY STRANGE CREATURES WHO STOPPED LIVING AND BECAME CRAZY MIXED-UP ZOMBIES, THE(1965)

Peter Michaels
SCREAMING EAGLES(1956)

Richard Michaels
TURN ON TO LOVE(1969); HOW COME NOBODY'S ON OUR SIDE?(1975), d; BLUE SKIES AGAIN(1983), d

Robert O. Michaels
1984
BLAME IT ON THE NIGHT(1984)

Shermaine Michaels
1984
ELECTRIC DREAMS(1984); NO SMALL AFFAIR(1984)

Sidney Michaels
KEY WITNESS(1960), w; NIGHT THEY RAIDED MINSKY'S, THE(1968), W

Steve Michaels
STUDENT BODY, THE(1976), m; RACQUET(1979), w; OH, HEAVENLY DOG!(1980); TERROR TRAIN(1980, Can.); GAS(1981, Can.)

Sue Michaels
HUNGRY WIVES(1973)

Toby Michaels
LOVE IN A GOLDFISH BOWL(1961)

Tony Michaels
BIG COMBO, THE(1955)

Victoria Michaels
SOMEWHERE IN TIME(1980)

Wayne Michaels
OCTOPUSSY(1983, Brit.), stunts

Yvonne Michaels
GET CARTER(1971, Brit.)

Kari Michaelsen
SATURDAY THE 14TH(1981)

Allen Michaelson
SILVER CHALICE, THE(1954)

Beverly Michaelson
FIVE LITTLE PEPPERS IN TROUBLE(1940)

Christian Michaelson
1984
MIDSUMMER NIGHT'S DREAM, A(1984, Brit./Span.)

Don Michaelson
RESURRECTION(1980)

Esther Michaelson
TAKE ME OUT TO THE BALL GAME(1949)

Jonathon Michaelson
DON'T LET THE ANGELS FALL(1969, Can.)

Ky Michaelson
PURPLE HAZE(1982)

Rainy Michaelyan
SKY PIRATE, THE(1970)

E.V. Michajlova
WATERLOO(1970, Ital./USSR), ed
Ray Michal
GREY FOX, THE(1983, Can.)
Robert Michal
APRIL 1, 2000(1953, Aust.)
Richard Michalak
1984
TAIL OF THE TIGER(1984, Aus.), ph
Boleslaw Michalek
DANTON(1983), w
1984
LOVE IN GERMANY, A(1984, Fr./Ger.), w
Michal Michalesko
CATSKILL HONEYMOON(1950)
Misc. Talkies
POWER OF LIFE, THE(1938); GOD, MAN AND DEVIL(1949)
Panos Michalopoulos
IPHIGENIA(1977, Gr.)
B. Michalski
PORTRAIT OF LENIN(1967, Pol./USSR)
George Michalski
1984
ON THE LINE(1984, Span.), m
Kazol Michalski
SPY WHO LOVED ME, THE(1977, Brit.)
Cherie Michan
WRONG IS RIGHT(1982)
Catherine Michard
PLEASURES AND VICES(1962, Fr.)
Peter Michas
CHARLIE CHAN AND THE CURSE OF THE DRAGON QUEEN(1981)
Andre Michaud
A NOUS LA LIBERTE(1931, Fr.)
Claude Michaud
RED(1970, Can.); GUNS(1980, Fr.), ph
Frederique Michaud
MYSTERIOUS ISLAND OF CAPTAIN NEMO, THE(1973, Fr./Ital. 87m Span./
Cameroon), ed
Jean Michaud
GIGOT(1962); GRAND PRIX(1966); JE T'AIME, JE T'AIME(1972, Fr./Swed.)
Oscar Michbeaux
BETRAYAL, THE(1948), p,d&w
Elder Micheaux
Misc. Talkies
WE'VE GOT THE DEVIL ON THE RUN(1934)
Oscar Micheaux
EXILE, THE(1931), d&w; TEMPTATION(1936), d; UNDERWORLD(1937), d
Misc. Talkies
DAUGHTER OF THE CONGO, A(1930), d; EASY STREET(1930), d; TEN MINUTES
TO LIVE(1932), d; VEILED ARISTOCRATS(1932), d; TEN MINUTES TO KILL(1933),
d; HARLEM AFTER MIDNIGHT(1934), d; GOD'S STEPCHILDREN(1937), d;
SWING(1938), d; THIRTY YEARS LATER(1938), d; LYING LIPS(1939), d
Misc. Silents
GUNSAULUS MYSTERY, THE(1921), d; MILLIONARE, THE(1927), d; THIRTY
YEARS LATER(1928), d
Michel
OUTRAGEOUS!(1977, Can.)
Albert Michel
DEVIL IN THE FLESH, THE(1949, Fr.); LES BELLES-DE-NUIT(1952, Fr.); HUNCH-
BACK OF NOTRE DAME, THE(1957, Fr.); GATES OF PARIS(1958, Fr./Ital.); BIG
CHIEF, THE(1960, Fr.); COUNTERFEITERS OF PARIS, THE(1962, Fr., Ital.); SLEEP-
ING CAR MURDER THE(1966, Fr.); TWO FOR THE ROAD(1967, Brit.); LEATHER
AND NYLON(1969, Fr./Ital.); LA NUIT DE VARENNES(1983, Fr./Ital.)
Andre Michel
YOUR SHADOW IS MINE(1963, Fr./Ital.), d, w
Clara Michel
LETTERS FROM MY WINDMILL(1955, Fr.)
Donna Michel
Misc. Talkies
PLAYMATES(1971)
Elmo Michel
QUEEN'S SWORDSMEN, THE(1963, Mex.)
Frannie Michel
DIARY OF A MAD HOUSEWIFE(1970)
Gaby Michel
DO NOT THROW CUSHIONS INTO THE RING(1970)
Germaine Michel
ROTHSCHILD(1938, Fr.); BIG CHIEF, THE(1960, Fr.)
Gigi Michel
MY FAIR LADY(1964); SILENCERS, THE(1966)
Georges-Michel Michel
MODIGLIANI OF MONTPARNASSE(1961, Fr./Ital.), w
Jacques Max Michel
THIS MAN IN PARIS(1939, Brit.)
Jean-Claude Michel
STORY OF THE COUNT OF MONTE CRISTO, THE(1962, Fr./Ital.)
Keith Michel
ALL NIGHT LONG(1961, Brit.); CROSS CREEK(1983)
Kim G. Michel
JOYSTICKS(1983)
Laura Lee Michel
PAID IN FULL(1950)
Lora Lee Michel
GOOD SAM(1948); KISS THE BLOOD OFF MY HANDS(1948); LADY AT MID-
NIGHT(1948); SNAKE PIT, THE(1948); MIGHTY JOE YOUNG(1949); MR. SOFT
TOUCH(1949); STATE DEPARTMENT–FILE 649(1949); TOKYO JOE(1949); BE-
TWEEN MIDNIGHT AND DAWN(1950); IT'S A SMALL WORLD(1950)

Marc Michel
LOLA(1961, Fr./Ital.); BEBO'S GIRL(1964, Ital.); NIGHT WATCH, THE(1964, Fr./
Ital.); UMBRELLAS OF CHERBOURG, THE(1964, Fr./Ger.); SIX DAYS A WEEK(1966,
Fr./Ital./Span.); SINGAPORE, SINGAPORE(1969, Fr./Ital.)
Silents
ITALIAN STRAW HAT, AN(1927, Fr.), w
Max Michel
LUCREZIA BORGIA(1937, Fr.)
Odile Michel
PEPPERMINT SODA(1979, Fr.)
Thomas Michel
PARIS WHEN IT SIZZLES(1964)
Marcella Michelangeli
PADRE PADRONE(1977, Ital.)
H. Michelaska
YOUNG GIRLS OF WILKO, THE(1979, Pol./Fr.)
Janee Michele
CLARENCE, THE CROSS-EYED LION(1965)
June Michele
OCEAN'S ELEVEN(1960)
Beatriz Michelena
Silents
SALOMY JANE(1914)
Misc. Silents
MRS. WIGGS OF THE CABBAGE PATCH(1914); LILY OF POVERTY FLAT,
THE(1915); MIGNON(1915); UNWRITTEN LAW, THE(1916); WOMAN WHO DARED,
THE(1916); HEART OF JUANITA(1919); JUST SQAW(1919); PRICE WOMAN PAYS,
THE(1919); FLAME OF HELLGATE, THE(1920)
Teresa Michelena
Silents
UNCLE TOM'S CABIN(1914)
Vera Michelena
Silents
DEVIL'S PLAYGROUND, THE(1918)
Misc. Silents
DRIFTWOOD(1916)
Michael Michelet
VOICE IN THE WIND(1944), m; CHASE, THE(1946), m
Michel Michelet
END OF THE WORLD, THE(1930, Fr.), m; PERSONAL COLUMN(1939, Fr.), m;
LURED(1947), m; SIREN OF ATLANTIS(1948), m; MAN ON THE EIFFEL TOWER,
THE(1949), m; OUTPOST IN MOROCCO(1949), m; M(1951), m; TARZAN'S PE-
RIL(1951), m; FORT ALGIERS(1953), m; JOURNEY, THE(1959, U.S./Aust.), m; GOD-
DESS OF LOVE, THE(1960, Ital./Fr.), m; JOURNEY TO THE LOST CITY(1960,
Ger./Fr./Ital.), m; DESERT WARRIOR(1961 Ital./Span.), m; CAPTAIN SIND-
BAD(1963), m; GIRL FROM HONG KONG(1966, Ger.), m
Claudio Micheli
VERY HANDY MAN, A(1966, Fr./Ital.)
Dario Micheli
MARRIAGE–ITALIAN STYLE(1964, Fr./Ital.), set d; TENTH VICTIM, THE(1965,
Fr./Ital.), set d; GIRL AND THE GENERAL, THE(1967, Fr./Ital.), set d; ROVER,
THE(1967, Ital.), set d; SEVEN GOLDEN MEN(1969, Fr./Ital./Span.), set d; DUCK,
YOU SUCKER!(1972, Ital.), set d
Elio Micheli
DESERTER, THE(1971 Ital./Yugo.), cos; MAN CALLED SLEDGE, A(1971, Ital.), cos
Maurizio Micheli
ALLEGRO NON TROPPO(1977, Ital.)
Ornella Micheli
MARCO POLO(1962, Fr./Ital.), ed; SAMSON AND THE SEVEN MIRACLES OF THE
WORLD(1963, Fr./Ital.), ed; WITCH'S CURSE, THE(1963, Ital.), ed; 00-2 MOST SE-
CRET AGENTS(1965, Ital.), ed; HILLS RUN RED, THE(1967, Ital.), ed; BRUTE AND
THE BEAST, THE(1968, Ital.), ed
1984
BURIED ALIVE(1984, Ital.), ed
Andre Michelin
ALPHAVILLE, A STRANGE CASE OF LEMMY CAUTION(1965, Fr.), p
Micheline
GOOD NEIGHBOR SAM(1964), cos; HOW TO SUCCEED IN BUSINESS WITHOUT
REALLY TRYING(1976), cos
Luciano Michelini
SCREAMERS(1978, Ital.), m
Tina Michelino
CHLOE IN THE AFTERNOON(1972, Fr.)
Dario Michell
EMPTY CANVAS, THE(1964, Fr./Ital.), set d
Helena Michell
MOMENTS(1974, Brit.)
Howard Michell
HIGH WALL, THE(1947)
Keith Michell
TRUE AS A TURTLE(1957, Brit.); DANGEROUS EXILE(1958, Brit.); HELLFIRE
CLUB, THE(1963, Brit.); SEVEN SEAS TO CALAIS(1963, Brit.); PRUDENCE AND THE
PILL(1968, Brit.); HOUSE OF CARDS(1969); EXECUTIONER, THE(1970, Brit.);
HENRY VIII AND HIS SIX WIVES(1972, Brit.); MOMENTS(1974, Brit.); GRENDEL
GRENDEL GRENDEL(1981, Aus.)
Ornella Michell
GRIM REAPER, THE(1981, Ital.), ed
Paul Michell
MOMENTS(1974, Brit.)
Ann Michelle
HAUNTED(1976); FRENCH QUARTER(1978)
Misc. Talkies
MISTRESS PAMELA(1974)
Anne Michelle
VIRGIN WITCH, THE(1973, Brit.); HOUSE OF WHIPCORD(1974, Brit.)
Charlotte Michelle
KILL OR BE KILLED(1980)

Donna Michelle
 GOODBYE CHARLIE(1964); BEACH BLANKET BINGO(1965); MICKEY ONE(1965); AGENT FOR H.A.R.M.(1966); ONE SPY TOO MANY(1966); SPY WITH MY FACE, THE(1966); PLAYMATES(1969, Fr./Ital.); COMPANY OF KILLERS(1970)
Jane Michelle
 SCREAM BLACULA SCREAM(1973)
Janee Michelle
 LOVE-INS, THE(1967); RED, WHITE AND BLACK, THE(1970); MEPHISTO WALTZ, THE(1971); HOUSE ON SKULL MOUNTAIN, THE(1974)
Patricia Michelle
Misc. Talkies
 CHEERING SECTION(1977)
Roni Michelle
 DOCTOR DETROIT(1983)
Vicki Michelle
 VIRGIN WITCH, THE(1973, Brit.); ALFIE DARLING(1975, Brit.); GREEK TYCOON, THE(1978)
Cliff Michelmore
 JOLLY BAD FELLOW, A(1964, Brit.)
Diego Michelotti
 SON OF THE RED CORSAIR(1963, Ital.)
Ed Michelotti
1984
 KILLPOINT(1984)
Seren Michelotti
 LOVES OF THREE QUEENS, THE(1954, Ital./Fr.)
Jerry Michelsen
 MY PAL, WOLF(1944)
Alfredo Michelson
 FIREFOX(1982)
Annette Michelson
 JOURNEYS FROM BERLIN–1971(1980)
Charles Michelson
Silents
 ACCORDING TO THE CODE(1916), w
Ed Michelson
 ADIOS GRINGO(1967, Ital./Fr./Span.), cos
Esther Michelson
 MC FADDEN'S FLATS(1935); WINGS IN THE DARK(1935); GREAT DICTATOR, THE(1940); I TAKE THIS WOMAN(1940); LADY EVE, THE(1941); PALM BEACH STORY, THE(1942); WE WERE DANCING(1942); ANCHORS AWEIGH(1945); I WOULDN'T BE IN YOUR SHOES(1948); EXECUTIVE SUITE(1954)
Ethel Michelson
 DOZENS, THE(1981); DEADLY SPAWN, THE(1983)
Harold Michelson
 PRETTY POISON(1968), art d; 1,000 PLANE RAID, THE(1969), art d; CATCH-22(1970), art d; JOHNNY GOT HIS GUN(1971), prod d; PORTNOY'S COMPLAINT(1972), art d; OUTSIDE MAN, THE(1973, U.S./FR.), prod d; MAME(1974), art d; STAR TREK: THE MOTION PICTURE(1979), prod d, art d; CAN'T STOP THE MUSIC(1980), art d; HISTORY OF THE WORLD, PART 1(1981), prod d; MOMMIE DEAREST(1981), art d; TERMS OF ENDEARMENT(1983), art d
Henry Michelson
 TWO PEOPLE(1973), art d
Leo Michelson
 GRAND THEFT AUTO(1977)
Marion Michelson
Silents
 EAGLE'S MATE, THE(1914), w
Richard Michelson
 LOUISA(1950); DAVID AND BATHSHEBA(1951)
Carlo Micheluzzi
 LADY IS FICKLE, THE(1948, Ital.)
Mafalda Micheluzzi
 LA TRAVIATA(1968, Ital.)
Nino Micheluzzi
 SCHOOLGIRL DIARY(1947, Ital.)
Gerald Michenaud
 NAKED KISS, THE(1964); BIG HAND FOR THE LITTLE LADY, A(1966); BUCKSKIN(1968); IN ENEMY COUNTRY(1968)
Dave Michener
 ARISTOCATS, THE(1970), anim
David Michener
 RESCUORS, THE(1977), w; FOX AND THE HOUND, THE(1981), w
James Michener
 UNTIL THEY SAIL(1957), w; RETURN TO PARADISE(1953), w; BRIDGES AT TOKO-RI, THE(1954), w; MEN OF THE FIGHTING LADY(1954), w; SAYONARA(1957), w; SOUTH PACIFIC(1958), w; DONOVAN'S REEF(1963), w; HAWAII(1966), w; HAWAIIANS, THE(1970), w; CARAVANS(1978, U.S./Iranian), w
Ennio Michettoni
 PRISONER OF THE IRON MASK(1962, Fr./Ital.), set d; SHOOT LOUD, LOUDER... I DON'T UNDERSTAND(1966, Ital.), set d; FIVE MAN ARMY, THE(1970, Ital.), set d
Maria Michi
 OPEN CITY(1946, Ital.); PAISAN(1948, Ital.); LADY OF MONZA, THE(1970, Ital.); REDNECK(1975, Ital./Span.)
Brian Michie
 LET'S MAKE A NIGHT OF IT(1937, Brit.)
Bryan Michie
 MAGNET, THE(1950, Brit.)
Byron Michie
 TOKYO FILE 212(1951)
Judy Michie
 PRETTY MAIDS ALL IN A ROW(1971)
Lorraine Michie
Misc. Talkies
 TROUBLE AT MELODY MESA(1949)
Ennio Michittoni
1984
 BURIED ALIVE(1984, Ital.), set d

Keith Michl
 CANNONBALL(1976, U.S./Hong Kong); HOMETOWN U.S.A.(1979), art d; ROLLER BOOGIE(1979), art d; HEARSE, THE(1980), art d
Michael E. Michlet
 HAIRY APE, THE(1944), m
Barry Michlin
 WILD GYPSIES(1969); TUNNELVISION(1976); CHEAP DETECTIVE, THE(1978)
Larry Michlin
 CHAPTER TWO(1979)
Anamarie Michnevich
1984
 RECKLESS(1984), art d
Pat Michon
 I PASSED FOR WHITE(1960)
Patricia Michon
 GREATEST SHOW ON EARTH, THE(1952)
Terry Michos
 WARRIORS, THE(1979)
Misc. Talkies
 GREAT SKYCOPTER RESCUE, THE(1982)
Frederique Michot
1984
 MY BEST FRIEND'S GIRL(1984, Fr.)
Ennio Michtettoni
 WHITE SISTER(1973, Ital./Span./Fr.), set d
Rose Michtom
 FORTUNE, THE(1975); IN GOD WE TRUST(1980)
A. Michurin
Misc. Silents
 SYMPHONY OF LOVE AND DEATH(1914, USSR); WANDERER BEYOND THE GRAVE(1915, USSR)
G. Michurin
 SECRET BRIGADE, THE(1951 USSR)
Misc. Silents
 CITIES AND YEARS(1931, USSR)
Gennadi Michurin
Misc. Silents
 DECEMBRISTS(1927, USSR)
Gregory Michurin
 ROAD HOME, THE(1947, USSR)
M. Michurin
 CAPTAIN GRANT'S CHILDREN(1939, USSR)
Milan Micic
 CROOKED ROAD, THE; DESPERADO TRAIL, THE(1965, Ger./Yugo.)
Constantin Mick
 WHITE DEMON, THE(1932, Ger.), ed
Mick the Miller
 WILD BOY(1934, Brit.)
Simon Mickael
1984
 MY NEW PARTNER(1984, Fr.), w
Jennifer K. Mickel
 BREAKING AWAY(1979)
Jerry Mickelsen
 EMERGENCY WEDDING(1950); HAPPY YEARS, THE(1950); LORNA DOONE(1951); CELL 2455, DEATH ROW(1955)
Jerry Mickelson
 NORTH STAR, THE(1943)
Richard Mickelson
 RECKLESS MOMENTS, THE(1949)
Robert Mickelson
1984
 HARD CHOICES(1984), p, d&w
Mickey
 FLOWER THIEF, THE(1962)
Arline Mickey
Misc. Silents
 PRINCE OF HIS RACE, THE(1926); CHILDREN OF FATE(1928)
Jarred Mickey
 SAM'S SONG(1971)
Ronne Mickey
 LOVE CHILD(1982)
Karen Mickievic
 I LOVE YOU, ALICE B. TOKLAS!(1968)
Witold Mickiewicz
 IDENTIFICATION MARKS: NONE(1969, Pol.), ph
Eric Micklewood
 SALUTE JOHN CITIZEN(1942, Brit.); LAMP STILL BURNS, THE(1943, Brit.); NINE MEN(1943, Brit.); UNDERGROUND GUERRILLAS(1944, Brit.); MONKEY'S PAW, THE(1948, Brit.); THINGS HAPPEN AT NIGHT(1948, Brit.); SOULS IN CONFLICT(1955, Brit.); NOTORIOUS LANDLADY, THE(1962); VON RYAN'S EXPRESS(1965)
Erick Micklewood
 36 HOURS(1965)
William Mickley
 RAGGEDY ANN AND ANDY(1977), art d
E.B. Mickus
 GREAT BIG WORLD AND LITTLE CHILDREN, THE(1962, Pol.)
Eveline Micone
 EVEL KNIEVEL(1971)
Miki Micovic
 FRAULEIN DOKTOR(1969, Ital./Yugo.)
Nick Micskey
 THEY ALL LAUGHED(1981)
Buddy Micucci
 PATERNITY(1981)
Massimo Mida
 BEHIND CLOSED SHUTTERS(1952, Ital.), w; HOUSE OF INTRIGUE, THE(1959, Ital.), w; LOVE IN 4 DIMENSIONS(1965 Fr./Ital.), d&w; LOVE FACTORY(1969, Ital.), d

Harry Middlebrooks
GOLD GUITAR, THE(1966), m
Wilfred R. Middlebrooks
NEW YORK, NEW YORK(1977)
Cary Middlecoff
BELLBOY, THE(1960)
Dr. Cary Middlecoff
FOLLOW THE SUN(1951)
Ken Middleham
PHASE IV(1974), ph
Ken Middleman
DARWIN ADVENTURE, THE(1972, Brit.), ph
Robert Middlemas
NAVY BLUE AND GOLD(1937)
Frank Middlemass
FRANKENSTEIN MUST BE DESTROYED!(1969, Brit.); OTLEY(1969, Brit.); SAY
HELLO TO YESTERDAY(1971, Brit.); BARRY LYNDON(1975, Brit.); ISLAND,
THE(1980)
Robert Middlemass
VALIANT, THE(1929), w; AFTER THE DANCE(1935); AIR HAWKS(1935); ATLAN-
TIC ADVENTURE(1935); AWAKENING OF JIM BURKE(1935); GRAND EXIT(1935);
ONE-WAY TICKET(1935); PUBLIC MENACE(1935); SHE COULDN'T TAKE IT(1935);
SUPERSPEED(1935); TOO TOUGH TO KILL(1935); UNKNOWN WOMAN(1935); CAIN
AND MABEL(1936); CASE OF THE VELVET CLAWS, THE(1936); F MAN(1936);
GRAND JURY(1936); LONE WOLF RETURNS, THE(1936); MUSS 'EM UP(1936);
NOBODY'S FOOL(1936); SON COMES HOME, A(1936); TWO AGAINST THE
WORLD(1936); YOU MAY BE NEXT(1936); DAY AT THE RACES, A(1937); GENERAL
SPANKY(1937); GUNS OF THE PECOS(1937); HATS OFF(1937); HIDEAWAY
GIRL(1937); MEET THE BOY FRIEND(1937); TRAPPED(1937); ARSENE LUPIN
RETURNS(1938); BLONDES AT WORK(1938); HIGHWAY PATROL(1938); I AM THE
LAW(1938); I STAND ACCUSED(1938); KENTUCKY(1938); MAD MISS MANTON,
THE(1938); SPAWN OF THE NORTH(1938); WHILE NEW YORK SLEEPS(1938);
BLACKMAIL(1939); BLONDIE BRINGS UP BABY(1939); COAST GUARD(1939);
HOTEL IMPERIAL(1939); IDIOT'S DELIGHT(1939); INDIANAPOLIS SPEED-
WAY(1939); MAGNIFICENT FRAUD, THE(1939); MAISIE(1939); STAND UP AND
FIGHT(1939); STANLEY AND LIVINGSTONE(1939); CAPTAIN IS A LADY,
THE(1940); LITTLE OLD NEW YORK(1940); POP ALWAYS PAYS(1940); SAINT
TAKES OVER, THE(1940); SLIGHTLY HONORABLE(1940); LADY SCARFACE(1941);
NO HANDS ON THE CLOCK(1941); ROAD TO ZANZIBAR(1941); THEY MET IN
ARGENTINA(1941); DARING YOUNG MAN, THE(1942); KLONDIKE FURY(1942);
TORPEDO BOAT(1942); BLACK RAVEN, THE(1943); BOMBARDIER(1943); PAYOFF,
THE(1943); TRUCK BUSTERS(1943); LADY IN THE DEATH HOUSE(1944); MY
BUDDY(1944); WILSON(1944); MASQUERADE IN MEXICO(1945); SPORTING
CHANCE, A(1945); SUSPENSE(1946)
Silents
OTHER MEN'S DAUGHTERS(1918)
Misc. Silents
WINCHESTER WOMAN, THE(1919)
Robert M. Middlemass
MAN WHO WOULDN'T TALK, THE(1940), w
Middlesex Cricket Club
SMALL TOWN STORY(1953, Brit.)
Burr Middleton
GOODBYE, NORMA JEAN(1976)
C.H. Middleton
BAND WAGGON(1940, Brit.)
Charles Middleton
WELCOME DANGER(1929); EAST IS WEST(1930); WAY OUT WEST(1930); CAUGHT
PLASTERED(1931); DANGEROUS AFFAIR, A(1931); MANHATTAN PARADE(1931);
MIRACLE WOMAN, THE(1931); SAFE IN HELL(1931); SHIPS OF HATE(1931); SOB
SISTER(1931); HATCHET MAN, THE(1932); HELL'S HIGHWAY(1932); HIGH PRES-
SURE(1932); HOUSE DIVIDED, A(1932); I AM A FUGITIVE FROM A CHAIN
GANG(1932); MYSTERY RANCH(1932); PACK UP YOUR TROUBLES(1932); PHAN-
TOM PRESIDENT, THE(1932); ROCKABYE(1932); SIGN OF THE CROSS, THE(1932);
SILVER DOLLAR(1932); STRANGE LOVE OF MOLLY LOUVAIN, THE(1932); BIG
EXECUTIVE(1933); BOWERY, THE(1933); DESTINATION UNKNOWN(1933); DIS-
GRACED(1933); DR. BULL(1933); PICK-UP(1933); SUNSET PASS(1933); THIS DAY
AND AGE(1933); TOMORROW AT SEVEN(1933); DAVID HARUM(1934); MASSAC-
RE(1934); MRS. WIGGS OF THE CABBAGE PATCH(1934); MYSTIC HOUR,
THE(1934); NANA(1934); WHEN STRANGERS MEET(1934); COUNTY CHAIRMAN,
THE(1935); FRISCO KID(1935); HOPALONG CASSIDY(1935); PARTY WIRE(1935);
RECKLESS(1935); SPECIAL AGENT(1935); CAREER WOMAN(1936); FLASH GOR-
DON(1936); JAILBREAK(1936); RAMONA(1936); ROAD GANG(1936); SHOW
BOAT(1936); SON COMES HOME, A(1936); SONG OF THE SADDLE(1936); TRAIL OF
THE LONESOME PINE, THE(1936); WEDDING PRESENT(1936); EMPTY SAD-
DLES(1937); GOOD EARTH, THE(1937); HOLLYWOOD COWBOY(1937); LAST TRAIN
FROM MADRID, THE(1937); SLAVE SHIP(1937); SOULS AT SEA(1937); TWO GUN
LAW(1937); WE'RE ON THE JURY(1937); JEZEBEL(1938); KENTUCKY(1938);
STRANGE FACES(1938); BLACKMAIL(1939); CAPTAIN FURY(1939); COWBOYS
FROM TEXAS(1939); FLYING DEUCES, THE(1939); JESSE JAMES(1939); OK-
LAHOMA KID, THE(1939); STRANGE CASE OF DR. MEADE(1939); THOU SHALT
NOT KILL(1939); WAY DOWN SOUTH(1939); WYOMING OUTLAW(1939); $1,000 A
TOUCHDOWN(1939); ABE LINCOLN IN ILLINOIS(1940); BRIGHAM YOUNG–FRON-
TIERSMAN(1940); CHAD HANNA(1940); CHARLIE CHAN'S MURDER CRUI-
SE(1940); ISLAND OF DOOMED MEN(1940); RANGERS OF FORTUNE(1940); SANTA
FE TRAIL(1940); SHOOTING HIGH(1940); VIRGINIA CITY(1940); BELLE
STARR(1941); JUNGLE MAN(1941); SHEPHERD OF THE HILLS, THE(1941); WEST-
ERN UNION(1941); WILD GEESE CALLING(1941); BREACH OF PROMISE(1942,
Brit.); MEN OF SAN QUENTIN(1942); MYSTERY OF MARIE ROGET, THE(1942);
BLACK RAVEN, THE(1943); HANGMEN ALSO DIE(1943); TWO WEEKS TO LI-
VE(1943); KISMET(1944); NORTHWEST TRAIL(1945); OUR VINES HAVE TENDER
GRAPES(1945); STRANGLER OF THE SWAMP(1945); TOWN WENT WILD,
THE(1945); HOW DO YOU DO?(1946); KILLERS, THE(1946); SPOOK BUSTERS(1946);
PRETENDER, THE(1947); ROAD TO RIO(1947); SEA OF GRASS, THE(1947); WEL-
COME STRANGER(1947); WYOMING(1947); FEUDIN', FUSSIN' AND A-FIGHT-
IN'(1948); MR. BLANDINGS BUILDS HIS DREAM HOUSE(1948); STATION
WEST(1948); LAST BANDIT, THE(1949)
Misc. Talkies
SQUARE SHOOTER(1935)

Silents
FAR CALL, THE(1929)
Misc. Silents
WITS VS. WITS(1920)
Charles Middleton, Sr.
YODELIN' KID FROM PINE RIDGE(1937)
Charles B. Middleton
BELLAMY TRIAL, THE(1929); BEAU BANDIT(1930); AMERICAN TRAGEDY,
AN(1931); PALMY DAYS(1931); TOO BUSY TO WORK(1932); WHITE WOMAN(1933);
LAST ROUND-UP, THE(1934); LONE COWBOY(1934); MURDER AT THE VANI-
TIES(1934); ST. LOUIS KID, THE(1934); BEHOLD MY WIFE(1935); IN SPITE OF
DANGER(1935); RED MORNING(1935); STEAMBOAT ROUND THE BEND(1935);
SUNSET OF POWER(1936); GRAPES OF WRATH(1940); WILD BILL HICKOK
RIDES(1942); UNCONQUERED(1947)
Charles D. Middleton
WHOM THE GODS DESTROY(1934)
Edgar Middleton
CAPTIVATION(1931, Brit), w
Edgar C. Middleton
RETURN OF THE RAT, THE(1929, Brit.), w; HER STRANGE DESIRE(1931, Brit.), w
Edgar G. Middleton
TIN GODS(1932, Brit.), w
Edward Middleton
SOMEONE(1968), w
Edwin Middleton
Silents
RIP VAN WINKLE(1914), w
Misc. Silents
WILDFIRE(1915), d; HAUNTED MANOR, THE(1916), d; ISLE OF LOVE, THE(1916),
d
Ethel Styles Middleton
Silents
JUDGMENT OF THE STORM(1924), w
Fay Middleton
OLIVER TWIST(1951, Brit.)
Fran Middleton
MARTIN(1979)
Francine Middleton
JOE(1970)
Misc. Talkies
SWEET SAVIOR(1971)
Gabrielle Middleton
TWO FOR THE ROAD(1967, Brit.)
George Middleton
SEVEN FACES(1929), p; BIG POND, THE(1930), w; CRAZY THAT WAY(1930), p;
DOUBLE CROSS ROADS(1930), d; ONCE A SINNER(1931), w
Silents
SOUL OF BROADWAY, THE(1915); ADAM AND EVA(1923), w
Misc. Silents
FLAME OF HELLGATE, THE(1920), d
George E. Middleton
Misc. Silents
WOMAN WHO DARED, THE(1916), d; HEART OF JUANITA(1919), d; JUST
SQAW(1919), d
Guy Middleton
JIMMY BOY(1935, Brit.); TRUST THE NAVY(1935, Brit.); TWO HEARTS IN
HARMONY(1935, Brit.); FAME(1936, Brit.); GAY ADVENTURE, THE(1936, Brit.);
MYSTERIOUS MR. DAVIS, THE(1936, Brit.); UNDER PROOF(1936, Brit.); KEEP
FIT(1937, Brit.); TAKE A CHANCE(1937, Brit.); TWO WHO DARED(1937, Brit.);
BREAK THE NEWS(1938, Brit.); FRENCH WITHOUT TEARS(1939, Brit.); GOODBYE
MR. CHIPS(1939, Brit.); FOR FREEDOM(1940, Brit.); SUICIDE SQUADRON(1942,
Brit.); TALK ABOUT JACQUELINE(1942, Brit.); CHAMPAGNE CHARLIE(1944, Brit.);
ADVENTURE FOR TWO(1945, Brit.); HALF-WAY HOUSE, THE(1945, Brit.); NOTORI-
OUS GENTLEMAN(1945, Brit.); NIGHT BOAT TO DUBLIN(1946, Brit.); BAD SIS-
TER(1947, Brit.); MAN ABOUT THE HOUSE, A(1947, Brit.); CAPTIVE HEART,
THE(1948, Brit.); ONE NIGHT WITH YOU(1948, Brit); FACTS OF LOVE(1949, Brit.);
HER MAN GILBEY(1949, Brit.); MARRY ME!(1949, Brit.); ONCE UPON A
DREAM(1949, Brit.); SNOWBOUND(1949, Brit.); HAPPIEST DAYS OF YOUR LI-
FE(1950, Brit.); NO PLACE FOR JENNIFER(1950, Brit.); LAUGHTER IN PARADIS-
E(1951, Brit.); THIRD VISITOR, THE(1951, Brit.); NEVER LOOK BACK(1952, Brit.);
ALBERT, R.N.(1953, Brit.); FAKE, THE(1953, Brit.); BELLES OF ST. TRINIAN'S,
THE(1954, Brit.); FIRE OVER AFRICA(1954, Brit.); FRONT PAGE STORY(1954, Brit.);
FUSS OVER FEATHERS(1954, Brit.); HARASSED HERO, THE(1954, Brit.); MAKE ME
AN OFFER(1954, Brit.); YOUNG WIVES' TALE(1954, Brit.); GENTLEMEN MARRY
BRUNETTES(1955); SEA SHALL NOT HAVE THEM, THE(1955, Brit.); YANK IN
ERMINE, A(1955, Brit.); NOW AND FOREVER(1956, Brit.); ALIVE ON SATUR-
DAY(1957, Brit.); BREAK IN THE CIRCLE, THE(1957, Brit.); DOCTOR AT LAR-
GE(1957, Brit.); LET'S BE HAPPY(1957, Brit.); LIGHT FINGERS(1957, Brit.);
PASSIONATE SUMMER(1959, Brit.); ESCORT FOR HIRE(1960, Brit.); FUR COLLAR,
THE(1962, Brit.); WALTZ OF THE TOREADORS(1962, Brit.); WHAT EVERY WOMAN
WANTS(1962, Brit.); OH! WHAT A LOVELY WAR(1969, Brit.); MAGIC CHRISTIAN,
THE(1970, Brit.)
Ivan L. Middleton
CAT BALLOU(1965)
James Middleton
MICKEY ONE(1965); SYNANON(1965)
James W. Middleton
SHEPHERD OF THE HILLS, THE(1964)
Joseph Middleton
JUST BEFORE DAWN(1980), w
Josephine Middleton
ADVENTURE FOR TWO(1945, Brit.); LADY SURRENDERS, A(1947, Brit.); FIVE
ANGLES ON MURDER(1950, Brit.); BROWNING VERSION, THE(1951, Brit.); SHAD-
OW OF FEAR(1956, Brit.); LIBEL(1959, Brit.)
Malcolm Middleton
VALENTINO(1977, Brit.), art d; HANOVER STREET(1979, Brit.), art d; OUT-
LAND(1981), art d; SENDER, THE(1982, Brit.), prod d; SILVER DREAM RACER(1982,
Brit.), art d

1984
RAZOR'S EDGE, THE(1984), art d; SHEENA(1984), art d
Noele Middleton
CIRCLE, THE(1959, Brit.)
Noelle Middleton
COURT MARTIAL(1954, Brit.); GOLDEN MASK, THE(1954, Brit.); TONIGHT'S THE NIGHT(1954, Brit.); YANK IN ERMINE, A(1955, Brit.); YOU CAN'T ESCAPE(1955, Brit.); IRON PETTICOAT, THE(1956, Brit.); JOHN AND JULIE(1957, Brit.); THREE MEN IN A BOAT(1958, Brit.); QUESTION OF SUSPENSE, A(1961, Brit.)
Peter Middleton
JUBILEE(1978, Brit.), ph
1984
MIDSUMMER NIGHT'S DREAM, A(1984, Brit./Span.), ph
Rev. Dr. Pierce Middleton
ALICE'S RESTAURANT(1969)
Ray Middleton
YOU AND ME(1938); GANGS OF CHICAGO(1940); LADY FOR A NIGHT(1941); LADY FROM LOUISIANA(1941); MERCY ISLAND(1941); GIRL FROM ALASKA(1942); HURRICANE SMITH(1942); I DREAM OF JEANIE(1952); SWEETHEARTS ON PARADE(1953); JUBILEE TRAIL(1954); I COVER THE UNDERWORLD(1955); ROAD TO DENVER, THE(1955); 1776(1972)
Robert Middleton
SILVER CHALICE, THE(1954); BIG COMBO, THE(1955); DESPERATE HOURS, THE(1955); TRIAL(1955); COURT JESTER, THE(1956); FRIENDLY PERSUASION(1956); LOVE ME TENDER(1956); PROUD ONES, THE(1956); RED SUNDOWN(1956); LONELY MAN, THE(1957); TARNISHED ANGELS, THE(1957); DAY OF THE BAD MAN(1958); LAW AND JAKE WADE, THE(1958); NO PLACE TO LAND(1958); CAREER(1959); DON'T GIVE UP THE SHIP(1959); GREAT IMPOSTOR, THE(1960); HELL BENT FOR LEATHER(1960); GOLD OF THE SEVEN SAINTS(1961); CATTLE KING(1963); FOR THOSE WHO THINK YOUNG(1964); BIG HAND FOR THE LITTLE LADY, A(1966); COMPANY OF KILLERS(1970); WHICH WAY TO THE FRONT?(1970); HARRAD EXPERIMENT, THE(1973); LINCOLN CONSPIRACY, THE(1977); CLARENCE AND ANGEL(1981)
Stewart Middleton
SPACEFLIGHT IC-1(1965, Brit.)
Stuart Middleton
FRANKENSTEIN CREATED WOMAN(1965, Brit.)
Tom Middleton
GREAT HOPE, THE(1954, Ital.); VIOLATORS, THE(1957); OCEAN'S ELEVEN(1960); DEVIL AT FOUR O'CLOCK, THE(1961); TWIST AROUND THE CLOCK(1961); SAND PEBBLES, THE(1966)
Silents
OLD MAID'S BABY, THE(1919), ph
Tony Middleton
YOU'VE GOT TO WALK IT LIKE YOU TALK IT OR YOU'LL LOSE THAT BEAT(1971)
Wallace Middleton
AMERICAN TRAGEDY, AN(1931)
Kofi Middleton-Mends
HAMILE(1965, Ghana)
Edward Middletown
DRIFTER(1975), w
Miles Middough
FREE, WHITE AND 21(1963)
Robin Mide
Misc. Talkies
THREE LIVES(1971)
Walter Midgeley
MY AIN FOLK(1944, Brit.)
Fannie Midgely
Silents
ALWAYS AUDACIOUS(1920)
Fanny Midgely
AMERICAN TRAGEDY, AN(1931)
Florence Midgely
Silents
EYES OF THE HEART(1920)
Alain Midgette
BEFORE THE REVOLUTION(1964, Ital.)
Alan Midgette
7254(1971)
Allen Midgette
WIND FROM THE EAST(1970, Fr./Ital./Ger.)
DAllas Midgette
WRONG MAN, THE(1956)
Dick Midgley
SABOTEUR(1942)
Dorese Midgley
SLIGHTLY SCANDALOUS(1946)
Fannie Midgley
Silents
DON'T CALL ME LITTLE GIRL(1921); PATSY(1921); STEPHEN STEPS OUT(1923); HAIR TRIGGER BAXTER(1926)
Misc. Silents
SOMEWHERE IN FRANCE(1916); GOAT, THE(1918); HEART OF YOUTH, THE(1920); BLUE BLAZES(1922); WHEN LOVE COMES(1922); THREE WISE CROOKS(1925); COWBOY CAVALIER, THE(1928)
Fanny Midgley
Silents
DESPOILER, THE(1915); ITALIAN, THE(1915); APOSTLE OF VENGEANCE, THE(1916); CIVILIZATION(1916); JIM GRIMSBY'S BOY(1916); ALL SOULS EVE(1921); GREED(1925); ACE OF ACTION(1926); FIGHTING CHEAT, THE(1926); NAUGHTY BABY(1929)
Misc. Silents
MAN FROM OREGON, THE(1915); LOTTERY MAN, THE(1919); THROUGH A GLASS WINDOW(1922); SOME PUN'KINS(1925); DANGEROUS DUB, THE(1926); FLYING BUCKAROO, THE(1928)

Florence Midgley
PAINTED FACES(1929)
Silents
PARTNERS OF THE TIDE(1921); MEMORY LANE(1926); SADIE THOMPSON(1928)
Richard Midgley
KISS OF DEATH(1947)
Massimo Midi
WHITE, RED, YELLOW, PINK(1966, Ital.), d
lp: Dale Midkiff
Misc. Talkies
NIGHTMARE WEEKEND(
Deborah Midkiff
Misc. Talkies
NIGHTMARE WEEKEND(
Bette Midler
HAWAII(1966); DIVINE MR. J., THE(1974); ROSE, THE(1979); JINXED!(1982)
Midori
DONOVAN'S REEF(1963); BOATNIKS, THE(1970); HANGUP(1974)
Mako Midori
SPOILS OF THE NIGHT(1969, Jap.)
Miko Mayama Midori
WAR WAGON, THE(1967)
Saul Midwall
FRANKENSTEIN MEETS THE SPACE MONSTER(1965), ph
The Midwesterners
SECOND GREATEST SEX, THE(1955)
Mary Midwinter
CAESAR AND CLEOPATRA(1946, Brit.); WARNING TO WANTONS, A(1949, Brit.)
Ken Midwood
FLOATING DUTCHMAN, THE(1953, Brit.)
Kenneth Midwood
Misc. Talkies
BEGGING THE RING(1979, Brit.)
Claus Miedel
CANARIS(1955, Ger.)
George Miedeske
RETURN TO PARADISE(1953)
Francis Miege
PICNIC ON THE GRASS(1960, Fr.)
Armand Miehe
PEOPLE MEET AND SWEET MUSIC FILLS THE HEART(1969, Den./Swed.)
Louis Miehe-Renard
OPERATION CAMEL(1961, Den.); COUNTERFEIT TRAITOR, THE(1962)
Eduoard Mielche
GERTRUD(1966, Den.)
Donald Miele
BRIGHT VICTORY(1951)
Terry Miele
SWINGIN' ALONG(1962)
Sandy Mielke
HOT STUFF(1979); FUNHOUSE, THE(1981); SMOKEY AND THE BANDIT–PART 3(1983)
Stanley Mieloch
SKATETOWN, U.S.A.(1979)
Jo Mielzinger
PICNIC(1955), prod d
Felipe Mier
LOS PLATILLOS VOLADORES(1955, Mex.), p
Hans Mierendorff
BECAUSE I LOVED YOU(1930, Ger.)
Vivian Miessen
GULLIVER'S TRAVELS(1977, Brit., Bel.), anim
Anne Marie Mieville
EVERY MAN FOR HIMSELF(1980, Fr.), w, ed
1984
FIRST NAME: CARMEN(1984, Fr.), w
Toshiro Mifune
SAMURAI(PART III) (1967, Jap.); SECRET SCROLLS(PART I) (1968, Jap.); DRUNKEN ANGEL(1948, Jap.); RASHOMON(1951, Jap.); SAMURAI(1955, Jap.); SEVEN SAMURAI, THE(1956, Jap.); HIDDEN FORTRESS, THE(1959, Jap.); RICKSHAW MAN, THE(1960, Jap.); I BOMBED PEARL HARBOR(1961, Jap.); IMPORTANT MAN, THE(1961, Mex.); MAN AGAINST MAN(1961, Jap.); THRONE OF BLOOD(1961, Jap.); YOJIMBO(1961, Jap.); LOWER DEPTHS, THE(1962, Jap.); SANJURO(1962, Jap.); TATSU(1962, Jap.); CHUSHINGURA(1963, Jap.); HIGH AND LOW(1963, Jap.); IDIOT, THE(1963, Jap.); STRAY DOG(1963, Jap.); YOUTH AND HIS AMULET, THE(1963, Jap.); LEGACY OF THE 500,000, THE(1964, Jap.), a, d; LIFE OF OHARU(1964, Jap.); SAGA OF THE VAGABONDS(1964, Jap.); SCANDAL(1964, Jap.); JUDO SAGA(1965, Jap.); LOST WORLD OF SINBAD, THE(1965, Jap.); SAMURAI ASSASSIN(1965, Jap.); FORT GRAVEYARD(1966, Jap.); GAMBLING SAMURAI, THE(1966, Jap.); GRAND PRIX(1966); RED BEARD(1966, Jap.); RISE AGAINST THE SWORD(1966, Jap.); I LIVE IN FEAR(1967, Jap.); MAD ATLANTIC, THE(1967, Jap.); REBELLION(1967, Jap.); SWORD OF DOOM, THE(1967, Jap.); EMPEROR AND A GENERAL, THE(1968, Jap.); HELL IN THE PACIFIC(1968); TUNNEL TO THE SUN(1968, Jap.), a, p; WHIRLWIND(1968, Jap.); DAREDEVIL IN THE CASTLE(1969, Jap.); DAY THE SUN ROSE, THE(1969, Jap.); MAN IN THE STORM, THE(1969, Jap.); UNDER THE BANNER OF SAMURAI(1969, Jap.); ZATOICHI MEETS YOJIMBO(1970, Jap.); BAND OF ASSASSINS(1971, Jap.); RED LION(1971, Jap.), a, p; RED SUN(1972, Fr./Ital./Span.); PAPER TIGER(1975, Brit.); MIDWAY(1976); WINTER KILLS(1979); INCHON(1981); BUSHIDO BLADE, THE(1982 Brit./U.S.); CHALLENGE, THE(1982)
Yannis Migadis
OEDIPUS THE KING(1968, Brit.), art d
Rosario Migale
GOSPEL ACCORDING TO ST. MATTHEW, THE(1966, Fr., Ital.)
Julia Migenes-Johnson
1984
BIZET'S CARMEN(1984, Fr./Ital.)
Bennie Miggins
Silents
NET, THE(1923), ph

Jerry Miggins
ONCE YOU KISS A STRANGER(1969), set d
Philip Verrill Mighels
Silents
IF ONLY JIM(1921), w
Mary Might
CHELSEA GIRLS, THE(1967)
The Mighty Diamonds
ROCKERS(1980)
Alan Migicovsky
THEY CAME FROM WITHIN(1976, Can.)
Allan Migicovsky
APPRENTICESHIP OF DUDDY KRAVITZ, THE(1974, Can.)
M. Miglau
YOLANTA(1964, USSR)
Brunella Migliaccio
TREE OF WOODEN CLOGS, THE(1979, Ital.)
Dirce Migliaccio
TRAIN ROBBERY CONFIDENTIAL(1965, Braz.)
Flavio Migliaccio
EARTH ENTRANCED(1970, Braz.)
Adriano Amidei Migliano
GIRL WHO COULDN'T SAY NO, THE(1969, Ital.); TIN GIRL, THE(1970, Ital.)
Adelqui Migliar
Silents
AS GOD MADE HER(1920, Brit.); FATE'S PLAYTHING(1920, Brit.); JOHN HERIOT'S WIFE(1920, Brit.); OTHER PERSON, THE(1921, Brit.)
Misc. Silents
IN THE NIGHT(1920, Brit.); LITTLE HOUR OF PETER WELLS, THE(1920, Brit.); BLOOD MONEY(1921, Brit.); CIRCUS JIM(1921, Brit.)
Anna Migliarese
CURTAINS(1983, Can.)
Armando Migliari
LITTLE MARTYR, THE(1947, Ital.); ANGELINA(1948, Ital.); HEART AND SOUL(1950, Ital.); LITTLE WORLD OF DON CAMILLO, THE(1953, Fr./Ital.)
Gianni Migliavacca
TRAGEDY OF A RIDICULOUS MAN, THE(1982, Ital.)
Gabriel Migliori
GIRL IN ROOM 13(1961, U.S./Braz.), m; GIVEN WORD, THE(1964, Braz.), m
Ralph Migliori
CHARLOTTE'S WEB(1973), ph
Romano Migliorini
BLOODY PIT OF HORROR, THE(1965, Ital.), w; KILL BABY KILL(1966, Ital.), w; BANDIDOS(1967, Ital.), w; TERROR-CREATURES FROM THE GRAVE(1967, U.S./Ital.), w
Armando Migliri
DESTINY(1938)
Annibale Migliucci
CATHY'S CHILD(1979, Aus.)
Marie-France Mignal
FIVE WILD GIRLS(1966, Fr.); WEEKEND AT DUNKIRK(1966, Fr./Ital.); LES CREATURES(1969, Fr./Swed.)
Caroline Mignini
IF EVER I SEE YOU AGAIN(1978)
Jeannette Mignola
LIAR'S DICE(1980)
Mignonne
Misc. Silents
SUNDOWN SLIM(1920)
Pierre Mignot
CORDELIA(1980, Fr., Can.), ph; COME BACK TO THE 5 & DIME, JIMMY DEAN, JIMMY DEAN(1982), ph; STREAMERS(1983), ph
1984
SECRET HONOR(1984), ph
Miguel
MADE IN U.S.A.(1966, Fr.)
Monica Miguel
UNDER FIRE(1983)
V. Migulko
MOTHER AND DAUGHTER(1965, USSR), art d
Efigenio Miha
LIFE STUDY(1973)
George Mihaita
FANTASTIC COMEDY, A(1975, Rum.)
Joanna Mihalakis
1984
SPLATTER UNIVERSITY(1984)
Mihalesco
ACCUSED–STAND UP(1930, Fr.)
Alexandre Mihalesco
MARIUS(1933, Fr.)
Mike Mihalich
NEW YEAR'S EVIL(1980)
Athena Mihalidou
SERENITY(1962)
George Mihalka
MY BLOODY VALENTINE(1981, Can.), d; PICK-UP SUMMER(1981), d
Andras Mihaly
LOVE(1972, Hung.), m
Tatsuya Mihashi
TATSU(1962, Jap.); WAYSIDE PEBBLE, THE(1962, Jap.); WISER AGE(1962, Jap.); CHUSHINGURA(1963, Jap.); HIGH AND LOW(1963, Jap.); SNOW IN THE SOUTH SEAS(1963, Jap.); CHALLENGE TO LIVE(1964, Jap.); HUMAN VAPOR, THE(1964, Jap.); LEGACY OF THE 500,000, THE(1964, Jap.); NONE BUT THE BRAVE(1965, U.S./Jap.); TIGER FLIGHT(1965, Jap.); OUTPOST OF HELL(1966, Jap.); WHAT'S UP, TIGER LILY?(1966); HARP OF BURMA(1967, Jap.); KOJIRO(1967, Jap.); MAD ATLANTIC, THE(1967, Jap.); THIN LINE, THE(1967, Jap.); TORA! TORA! TORA!(1970, U.S./Jap.)

Keitaro Miho
BEAUTIFUL SWINDLERS, THE(1967, Fr./Ital./Jap./Neth.), m
Ludmila Mikael
SERGEANT, THE(1968); VOYAGE OF SILENCE(1968, Fr.)
Mikaela
GRINGO(1963, Span./Ital.)
Misc. Talkies
THREE SWORDS OF ZORRO, THE(1960)
A. Mikahilov
DEVOTION(1955, USSR)
Franco Mikalizzi
VISITOR, THE(1980, Ital./U.S.), m, md
Go Mikami
DAWN(1979, Aus.)
Kan Mikami
MERRY CHRISTMAS MR. LAWRENCE(1983, Jap./Brit.)
Shin-ichiro Mikami
YOUTH IN FURY(1961, Jap.); TWILIGHT PATH(1965, Jap.)
Sumire Mikasa
WAY OUT, WAY IN(1970, Jap.)
Chocho Mikayo
VENGEANCE IS MINE(1980, Jap.)
Mike
SERGEANT MIKE(1945)
Silents
SAWDUST(1923); FRESHMAN, THE(1925)
Louise Mike
CLARENCE AND ANGEL(1981)
Mike B the Flea
1984
SUBURBIA(1984)
The Mike Curb Congregation
MAGIC OF LASSIE, THE(1978)
Mike Riley and Band
SLEEPY LAGOON(1943)
Mike Riley's Orchestra
KID DYNAMITE(1943)
Joseph Mikel
SOD SISTERS(1969)
Eugene Mikeler
LADY, LET'S DANCE(1944)
George Mikell
KILL HER GENTLY(1958, Brit.); ONE THAT GOT AWAY, THE(1958, Brit.); BEYOND THE CURTAIN(1960, Brit.); JACKPOT(1960, Brit.); CIRCLE OF DECEPTON(1961, Brit.); GUNS OF NAVARONE, THE(1961); HIGHWAY TO BATTLE(1961, Brit.); DESERT PATROL(1962, Brit.); PASSWORD IS COURAGE, THE(1962, Brit.); PRIMITIVES, THE(1962, Brit.); GREAT ESCAPE, THE(1963); MYSTERY SUBMARINE(1963, Brit.); OPERATION BULLSHINE(1963, Brit.); VICTORS, THE(1963); OPERATION CROSSBOW(1965, U.S./Ital.); SPY WHO CAME IN FROM THE COLD, THE(1965, Brit.); WHERE THE SPIES ARE(1965, Brit.); DATELINE DIAMONDS(1966, Brit.); DOUBLE MAN, THE(1967); ATTACK ON THE IRON COAST(1968, U.S./Brit.); JOURNEY TO THE FAR SIDE OF THE SUN(1969, Brit.); ZEPPELIN(1971, Brit.); YOUNG WINSTON(1972, Brit.); SCORPIO(1973); TAMARIND SEED, THE(1974, Brit.); SWEENEY 2(1978, Brit.); SEA WOLVES, THE(1981, Brit.); VICTORY(1981)
Gene Mikels
GIRL IN GOLD BOOTS(1968), makeup
Jason Mikels
MAKING LOVE(1982)
Robert Mikels
MAKING LOVE(1982)
Ted Mikels
HOSTAGE, THE(1966), ph; CATALINA CAPER, THE(1967), ph; ASTRO-ZOMBIES, THE(1969), w
Ted V. Mikels
DAY OF THE NIGHTMARE(1965), ph; BLACK KLANSMAN, THE(1966), p,d&ed; GIRL IN GOLD BOOTS(1968), p&d; ASTRO-ZOMBIES, THE(1969), p&d; CORPSE GRINDERS, THE(1972), p&d, ed; BLOOD ORGY OF THE SHE-DEVILS(1973), p; DOLL SQUAD, THE(1973), p&d; WORM EATERS, THE(1981), p; 10 VIOLENT WOMEN(1982), a, p&d, w, ed
Misc. Talkies
STRIKE ME DEADLY(1963), d; ALEX JOSEPH & HIS WIVES(1978), d; CRUISE MISSILE(1978), p
George Mikes
TALE OF THREE WOMEN, A(1954, Brit.), w
Gita Mikes
YOUNG LORD, THE(1970, Ger.)
Alexander Mikhailov
CHEREZ TERNII K SVEZDAM(1981 USSR)
Maxim Mikhailov
IVAN THE TERRIBLE(Part I, 1947, USSR)
Mikhail Mikhailov
CLOWN AND THE KIDS, THE(1968, U.S./Bulgaria); PEACH THIEF, THE(1969, Bulgaria)
V. Mikhailov
Silents
EARTH(1930, USSR)
Nikita Mikhalkov
MEET ME IN MOSCOW(1966, USSR); RED AND THE WHITE, THE(1969, Hung./USSR); RED TENT, THE(1971, Ital./USSR)
Andrei Mikhalkov-Konchalovsky
UNCLE VANYA(1972, USSR), d&w
Andrei Mikhalkov-Kontchalovsky
ANDREI ROUBLOV(1973, USSR), w
B. Mikhaylov
HAMLET(1966, USSR), spec eff
Grigoriy Mikhaylov
OPTIMISTIC TRAGEDY, THE(1964, USSR); ITALIANO BRAVA GENTE(1965, Ital./USSR)

P. Mikhaylov
RESURRECTION(1963, USSR)
O. Mikhaylova
WAR AND PEACE(1968, USSR)
Grigoriy Mikhaytov
HUNTING IN SIBERIA(1962, USSR)
Andre Mikhelson
GAMBLER AND THE LADY, THE(1952, Brit.); DESPERATE MOMENT(1953, Brit.); STAR OF MY NIGHT(1954, Brit.); DIVIDED HEART, THE(1955, Brit.); I AM A CAMERA(1955, Brit.); TO PARIS WITH LOVE(1955, Brit.); FINGER OF GUILT(1956, Brit.); LOSER TAKES ALL(1956, Brit.); BREAK IN THE CIRCLE, THE(1957, Brit.); DANGEROUS EXILE(1958, Brit.); DIPLOMATIC CORPSE, THE(1958, Brit.); INN OF THE SIXTH HAPPINESS, THE(1958); CHILDREN OF THE DAMNED(1963, Brit.)
Boris Mikhin
Misc. Silents
TSAR NIKOLAI II(1917, USSR), d
Solomon Mikhoels
Misc. Silents
JEWISH LUCK(1925, USSR)
George Miki
GO FOR BROKE(1951)
Minoru Miki
KARATE, THE HAND OF DEATH(1961), m, md
Norihei Miki
CHUSHINGURA(1963, Jap.); MY HOBO(1963, Jap.); HOTSPRINGS HOLIDAY(1970, Jap.); SONG FROM MY HEART, THE(1970, Jap.); DEMON POND(1980, Jap.)
1984
BALLAD OF NARAYAMA, THE(1984, Jap.)
Shinsuke Mikimoto
JUDO SHOWDOWN(1966, Jap.)
Mikk Mikiver
DEAD MOUNTAINEER HOTEL, THE(1979, USSR)
Emjor Mikkelsen
FROZEN JUSTICE(1929), w
Laila Mikkelsen
CHILDREN OF GOD'S EARTH(1983, Norwegian), d&w
A. Miklashevskaya
Misc. Silents
MISS PEASANT(1916, USSR)
Michael Mikler
WESTWORLD(1973)
Michael T. Mikler
GUNFIGHT AT COMANCHE CREEK(1964); WAR PARTY(1965); THUNDER ALLEY(1967); ICE STATION ZEBRA(1968)
Mike Mikler
PAT GARRETT AND BILLY THE KID(1973)
Gyorgy Miklosy
DIALOGUE(1967, Hung.)
Krystina Mikolajewska
WINDOWS OF TIME, THE(1969, Hung.)
Krystyna Mikolajewska
RED AND THE WHITE, THE(1969, Hung./USSR)
Adam Mikolajewski
FIRST START(1953, Pol.)
Ivan Mikolaychuk
SHADOWS OF FORGOTTEN ANCESTORS(1967, USSR)
Klaus Mikoleit
1984
WOMAN IN FLAMES, A(1984, Ger.)
Marthe Mikon
DON GIOVANNI(1979, Fr./Ital./Ger.), cos
Mikro [C.H. Kalin]
RIDER IN THE NIGHT, THE(1968, South Africa), w
Joe Miksak
SNIPER, THE(1952); CANDIDATE, THE(1972)
Joseph Miksak
PAL JOEY(1957); RIVERRUN(1968); AMERICAN GRAFFITI(1973)
Jurgen Miksch
HANSEL AND GRETEL(1965, Ger.)
Stanislaw Mikula
INN OF THE SIXTH HAPPINESS, THE(1958)
Nevenka Mikulic
TEMPEST(1958, Ital./Yugo./Fr.)
Mark Mikulski
STUCK ON YOU(1983)
1984
C.H.U.D.(1984); STUCK ON YOU(1984)
Stanislaw Mikulski
FIRST START(1953, Pol.); EVE WANTS TO SLEEP(1961, Pol.); KANAL(1961, Pol.)
Rentaro Mikuni
SAMURAI(1955, Jap.); HAHAKIRI(1963, Jap.); KWAIDAN(1965, Jap.); HARP OF BURMA(1967, Jap.); DUEL AT EZO(1970, Jap.); KURAGEJIMA-LEGENDS FROM A SOUTHERN ISLAND(1970, Jap.); BAND OF ASSASSINS(1971, Jap.); VENGEANCE IS MINE(1980, Jap.)
Katsutoshi Mikuriya
TO KILL OR TO DIE(1973, Ital.)
John Mikus
1941(1979), w
Bela Mila
IT HAPPENED IN PARIS(1935, Brit.); AVENGING HAND, THE(1936, Brit.); BALL AT SAVOY(1936, Brit.); BELOVED IMPOSTER(1936, Brit.); WAKE UP FAMOUS(1937, Brit.)
Miguel Mila
MAN WHO KILLED BILLY THE KID, THE(1967, Span./Ital.), ph
Miguel F. Mila
MURIETA(1965, Span.), ph; FLAME OVER VIETNAM(1967, Span./Ger.), ph; FEW BULLETS MORE, A(1968, Ital./Span.), ph

Nebiha Ben Milad
1984
SMURFS AND THE MAGIC FLUTE, THE(1984, Fr./Belg.), ed
James Milady
Silents
AMERICA(1924)
Misc. Silents
GIRL FROM PORCUPINE, THE(1921)
Milan
CHILDRENS GAMES(1969), m
Art Milan
MAN WHO CHEATED HIMSELF, THE(1951)
Frank Milan
BANK ALARM(1937); GOLD RACKET, THE(1937); HOLLYWOOD COWBOY(1937); JOY OF LIVING(1938); PALS OF THE SADDLE(1938); ROLL ALONG, COWBOY(1938); AND ONE WAS BEAUTIFUL(1940); KITTY FOYLE(1940); RANGERS OF FORTUNE(1940); KING'S ROW(1942)
George Milan
FORTY-NINTH MAN, THE(1953); WAR OF THE COLOSSAL BEAST(1958); CREATION OF THE HUMANOIDS(1962); I'D RATHER BE RICH(1964)
Joe Milan
ESCAPE TO BURMA(1955)
Lita Milan
DESERT SANDS(1955); TOUGHEST MAN ALIVE(1955); VIOLENT MEN, THE(1955); GUN BROTHERS(1956); BAYOU(1957); NAKED IN THE SUN(1957); RIDE BACK, THE(1957); ER LOVE A STRANGER(1958); GIRLS ON THE LOOSE(1958); LEFT-HANDED GUN, THE(1958); I, MOBSTER(1959)
Vincent Duke Milana
SECOND THOUGHTS(1983)
Vincent Milana
NICKELODEON(1976)
Amille Milane
Silents
LOVES OF RICARDO, THE(1926)
J.J. Milane
WOMEN AND BLOODY TERROR(1970), w
Chef Milani
WITHOUT RESERVATIONS(1946); GOVERNMENT GIRL(1943); SEVENTH VICTIM, THE(1943); FALCON OUT WEST, THE(1944); MRS. PARKINGTON(1944); NONE BUT THE LONELY HEART(1944); SHOW BUSINESS(1944); WHAT A BLONDE(1945); CRACK-UP(1946)
Chef Joseph Milani
HOLLYWOOD CANTEEN(1944); TO HAVE AND HAVE NOT(1944); ADVENTURE(1945)
Federica Milani
MAGIC WORLD OF TOPO GIGIO, THE(1961, Ital.)
Francisco Milani
EARTH ENTRANCED(1970, Braz.)
Joseph Milani
BELL FOR ADANO, A(1945)
Mario Milani
MAGIC WORLD OF TOPO GIGIO, THE(1961, Ital.), set d
Alyssa Milano
1984
OLD ENOUGH(1984)
Mario Milano
SPECTRE OF EDGAR ALLAN POE, THE(1974); BEYOND EVIL(1980)
Nino Milano
ANGELO IN THE CROWD(1952, Ital.)
Rosa Milano
FOLIES DERGERE(1935)
Ivan Milanov
WATERLOO(1970, Ital./USSR)
Mila Milanovic
THREE(1967, Yugo.), ed
Adolph Milar
BULLDOG DRUMMOND(1929); ISLE OF ESCAPE(1930); MEDICINE MAN, THE(1930); RAIN OR SHINE(1930); HONEYMOON LANE(1931); SAVAGE GIRL, THE(1932); GREAT IMPERSONATION, THE(1935); SUDDEN BILL DORN(1938); EVERYTHING HAPPENS AT NIGHT(1939); IDIOT'S DELIGHT(1939); MAN HUNT(1941); PARIS CALLING(1941); SO ENDS OUR NIGHT(1941); DANGEROUSLY THEY LIVE(1942); LADY HAS PLANS, THE(1942); REUNION IN FRANCE(1942)
Silents
MICHIGAN KID, THE(1928)
Misc. Silents
ROAD OF AMBITION, THE(1920); MY FRIEND, THE DEVIL(1922); MARRIAGE IN TRANSIT(1925)
Hermina Milar
FOREIGN CORRESPONDENT(1940)
Bob Milasch
$1,000 A TOUCHDOWN(1939)
Silents
ABRAHAM LINCOLN(1924)
R. E. Milasch
EXCLUSIVE(1937)
Robert Milasch
LION AND THE LAMB(1931); ISLAND OF LOST SOULS(1933); LADY'S FROM KENTUCKY, THE(1939)
Silents
BLACK BEAUTY(1921)
Misc. Silents
GRINNING GUNS(1927)
Bob Milash
DANGEROUS NAN McGREW(1930); TEXAS BAD MAN(1932)
Robert Milash
Misc. Silents
FOURTEENTH MAN, THE(1920)

Robert E. Milash
MAN IN THE IRON MASK, THE(1939)
Tamara Milashkina
QUEEN OF SPADES(1961, USSR)
Vladan Milasinovic
DEAD ARE ALIVE, THE(1972, Yugo./Ger./Ital.)
Diana Milay
STREET OF SINNERS(1957)
Axel Milberg
FRIENDS AND HUSBANDS(1983, Ger.)
David Milbern
SORCERESS(1983)
Olive Milbourne
HER PANELLED DOOR(1951, Brit.); CONTRABAND SPAIN(1955, Brit.); ONE WAY
OUT(1955, Brit.); HAPPY IS THE BRIDE(1958, Brit.); INBETWEEN AGE, THE(1958,
Brit.)
A. Milbret
YOLANTA(1964, USSR)
Les Milbrook
BRIGHTON STRANGLER, THE(1945), ed; RACHEL AND THE STRANGER(1948),
ed
Christopher Milburn
1984
ANOTHER COUNTRY(1984, Brit.)
Derek Milburn
IT HAPPENED HERE(1966, Brit.)
Ellsworth Milburn
FUNNYMAN(1967)
Mary Milburn
PARACHUTE NURSE(1942)
Mollie Hartley Milburn
TO PARIS WITH LOVE(1955, Brit.)
Russ Milburn
DARK SIDE OF TOMORROW, THE(1970)
Tony Milch
HEY THERE, IT'S YOGI BEAR(1964), ed
Arnon Milchan
BLACK JOY(1977, Brit.), p; KING OF COMEDY, THE(1983), p; SPACEHUNTER:
ADVENTURES IN THE FORBIDDEN ZONE(1983), art d
1984
ONCE UPON A TIME IN AMERICA(1984), a, p
L. Milchin
DAY THE EARTH FROZE, THE(1959, Fin./USSR), art d
Max Milder
PRIME MINISTER, THE(1941, Brit.), p; THIS WAS PARIS(1942, Brit.), p; DARK
TOWER, THE(1943, Brit.), p; NIGHT INVADER, THE(1943, Brit), p
Mildred
Silents
DADDY(1923)
Sara Mildred
SWEET SURRENDER(1935)
Michelle Mildwater
FLASH GORDON(1980)
Michael Mileham
FALLING IN LOVE AGAIN(1980), ph
Lucio Milena
GAMES MEN PLAY, THE(1968, Arg.), m
Annie Miler
WILD CHILD, THE(1970, Fr.)
Claude Miler
TWO OR THREE THINGS I KNOW ABOUT HER(1970, Fr.); TWO ENGLISH
GIRLS(1972, Fr.), p
J. Clarkson Miler
Silents
SINNERS IN LOVE(1928), w
Mildred Miler
MERRY WIVES OF WINDSOR, THE(1966, Aust.)
Nathan Miler
WILD CHILD, THE(1970, Fr.)
John Milerta
Silents
NIGHT FLYER, THE(1928)
Ann Miles
RIVALS(1972)
Art Miles
WITHOUT RESERVATIONS(1946); MAN WHO BROKE THE BANK AT MONTE
CARLO, THE(1935); OUR RELATIONS(1936); FIGHTING TEXAN(1937); ROAMING
COWBOY, THE(1937); SWEETHEART OF THE NAVY(1937); BLACKMAIL(1939);
GORILLA, THE(1939); HE STAYED FOR BREAKFAST(1940); MARKED MEN(1940);
BARNACLE BILL(1941); HONKY TONK(1941); RETURN OF DANIEL BOONE,
THE(1941); SAN FRANCISCO DOCKS(1941); ARABIAN NIGHTS(1942); JOHNNY
EAGER(1942); MY FAVORITE BLONDE(1942); SIN TOWN(1942); SPOILERS,
THE(1942); DU BARRY WAS A LADY(1943); CRAZY KNIGHTS(1944); GENTLE
ANNIE(1944); LOUISIANA HAYRIDE(1944); PRINCESS AND THE PIRATE,
THE(1944); PARIS UNDERGROUND(1945); SUDAN(1945); NIGHT IN PARADISE,
A(1946); DESPERATE(1947); COLT .45(1950); PERFECT STRANGERS(1950)
Arthur K. Miles
DAKOTA(1945)
Arthur Miles
LONG VOYAGE HOME, THE(1940); THAT NIGHT WITH YOU(1945); SPOOK
BUSTERS(1946); FEUDIN', FUSSIN' AND A-FIGHTIN'(1948); WHITE HEAT(1949)
Bernard Miles
LOVE TEST, THE(1935, Brit.); MIDNIGHT AT THE WAX MUSEUM(1936, Brit.);
TWELVE GOOD MEN(1936, Brit.); CITADEL, THE(1938); 13 MEN AND A GUN(1938,
Brit.); CHALLENGE, THE(1939, Brit.); REBEL SON, THE ½(1939, Brit.); U-BOAT
29(1939, Brit.); LION HAS WINGS, THE(1940, Brit.); PASTOR HALL(1940, Brit.);
COMMON TOUCH, THE(1941, Brit.); QUIET WEDDING(1941, Brit.); VOICE IN THE
NIGHT, A(1941, Brit.); AVENGERS, THE(1942, Brit.); BIG BLOCKADE, THE(1942,
Brit.); GOOSE STEPS OUT, THE(1942, Brit.), w; IN WHICH WE SERVE(1942, Brit.);
ONE OF OUR AIRCRAFT IS MISSING(1942, Brit.); THIS WAS PARIS(1942, Brit.);

SPITFIRE(1943, Brit.); THUNDER ROCK(1944, Brit.), w; CARNIVAL(1946, Brit.);
GREAT EXPECTATIONS(1946, Brit.); FAME IS THE SPUR(1947, Brit.); NICHOLAS
NICKLEBY(1947, Brit.); TAWNY PIPIT(1947, Brit.), a, p, d&w; OUTSIDER,
THE(1949, Brit.), a, w; CHANCE OF A LIFETIME(1950, Brit.), a, p, d, w; MAGIC
BOX, THE(1952, Brit.); NEVER LET ME GO(1953, U.S./Brit.); MAN WHO KNEW TOO
MUCH, THE(1956); MOBY DICK(1956, Brit.); TIGER IN THE SMOKE(1956, Brit.);
ZARAK(1956, Brit.); SAINT JOAN(1957); SHE PLAYED WITH FIRE(1957, Brit.);
SMALLEST SHOW ON EARTH, THE(1957, Brit.); TOM THUMB(1958, Brit./U.S.);
SAPPHIRE(1959, Brit.); HEAVENS ABOVE!(1963, Brit.); LOCK UP YOUR DAUGH-
TERS(1969, Brit.), w; RUN WILD, RUN FREE(1969, Brit.)
Betty Miles
DRIFTIN' KID, THE(1941); RETURN OF DANIEL BOONE, THE(1941); RIDING THE
CHEROKEE TRAIL(1941); RIDING THE SUNSET TRAIL(1941); WANDERERS OF
THE WEST(1941); LONE STAR LAW MEN(1942); LAW RIDES AGAIN, THE(1943);
WILD HORSE STAMPEDE(1943); GANGSTERS OF THE FRONTIER(1944); LAW OF
THE SADDLE(1944); SONORA STAGECOACH(1944); WESTWARD BOUND(1944)
Bob Miles
LAST ROUND-UP, THE(1934)
Buster Miles
NO OTHER WOMAN(1933); LAURA(1944)
Carlotte Miles
WATERFRONT LADY(1935)
Carlton Miles
LADIES THEY TALK ABOUT(1933), w; LADY GANGSTER(1942), w
Christopher Miles
UP JUMPED A SWAGMAN(1965, Brit.), d; VIRGIN AND THE GYPSY, THE(1970,
Brit.), d; TIME FOR LOVING, A(1971, Brit.), d; MAIDS, THE(1975, Brit.), d, w; THAT
LUCKY TOUCH(1975, Brit.), d; PRIEST OF LOVE(1981, Brit.), p, d
Chuck Miles
TEENAGE ZOMBIES(1960)
Connel Miles
YOUNG GIRLS OF ROCHEFORT, THE(1968, Fr.); MAN OF LA MANCHA(1972)
George Miles
AMAZING GRACE(1974); EDUCATION OF SONNY CARSON, THE(1974)
George Lee Miles
TAKING OF PELHAM ONE, TWO, THREE, THE(1974); WARRIORS, THE(1979)
Harold Miles
BIG TRAIL, THE(1930), art d; SNOW WHITE AND THE SEVEN DWARFS(1937), art
d
Silents
QUEEN KELLY(1929), art d
Helen Miles
Silents
JANE EYRE(1921)
Jack Miles
THREES, MENAGE A TROIS(1968), ed, art d
Jennings Miles
WINCHESTER '73(1950); MAN FROM BITTER RIDGE, THE(1955)
Joanna Miles
WAY WE LIVE NOW, THE(1970); BUG(1975); ULTIMATE WARRIOR, THE(1975);
FRIDAY THE 13TH... THE ORPHAN(1979); CROSS CREEK(1983)
Misc. Talkies
ORPHAN, THE(1979)
John Miles
WING AND A PRAYER(1944); GOD IS MY CO-PILOT(1945); PRIDE OF THE
MARINES(1945); JANIE GETS MARRIED(1946); NIGHT AND DAY(1946); FABU-
LOUS TEXAN, THE(1947); GUNFIGHTERS, THE(1947); MOTHER IS A FRESH-
MAN(1949); TATTOOED STRANGER, THE(1950)
Johnny Miles
PILLOW TO POST(1945); SAN ANTONIO(1945); TOO YOUNG TO KNOW(1945)
Joyce Miles
SHADOWS(1960)
Keith Miles
SQUEEZE, THE(1977, Brit.)
Kelley Miles
SKYJACKED(1972)
Kelly Miles
STONE KILLER, THE(1973)
Kevin Miles
CARS THAT ATE PARIS, THE(1974, Aus,); END PLAY(1975, Aus.)
Misc. Talkies
SPIRAL BUREAU, THE(1974)
Lillian Miles
MAN AGAINST WOMAN(1932); MOONLIGHT AND PRETZELS(1933); GAY DIVOR-
CEE, THE(1934); CODE OF THE MOUNTED(1935); GET THAT MAN(1935); OLD
HOMESTEAD, THE(1935); DIZZY DAMES(1936); REEFER MADNESS(1936)
Misc. Talkies
CALLING ALL CARS(1935)
Luther Miles
Silents
RANK OUTSIDER(1920, Brit.); PLACE OF HONOUR, THE(1921, Brit.)
Mary Miles
Misc. Silents
BACHELOR'S WIFE, A(1919)
Meg Miles
ANDERSON TAPES, THE(1971)
Michael Miles
GET ON WITH IT(1963, Brit.)
Mike Miles
RAGING BULL(1980)
Miriam Miles
Silents
IN THE BALANCE(1917); FORTUNE'S CHILD(1919)
Misc. Silents
GRELL MYSTERY, THE(1917); MOTHER'S SIN, A(1918)
Norbert Miles
DARK MIRROR, THE(1946), makeup; WALK A CROOKED MILE(1948), makeup;
VENDETTA(1950), makeup

Pamela Miles
UNDER MILK WOOD(1973, Brit.)
1984
FOREVER YOUNG(1984, Brit.)
Peter Miles
JUST WILLIAM(1939, Brit.); MURDER WILL OUT(1939, Brit.); PASSAGE TO MARSEILLE(1944); THIS LOVE OF OURS(1945); HEAVEN ONLY KNOWS(1947); ENCHANTMENT(1948); FAMILY HONEYMOON(1948); RED PONY, THE(1949); RO-SEANNA McCOY(1949); SONG OF SURRENDER(1949); SPECIAL AGENT(1949); CALIFORNIA PASSAGE(1950); GOOD HUMOR MAN, THE(1950); TRIGGER, JR.(1950); AT SWORD'S POINT(1951); QUO VADIS(1951)
Ray Miles
SWORD OF EL CID, THE(1965, Span./Ital.)
Richard Miles
THEY SAVED HITLER'S BRAIN(1964), w; THAT COLD DAY IN THE PARK(1969, U.S./Can.), w
Robert Miles
LOUISA(1950); YOUNG FURY(1965)
Robert J. Miles
PONY EXPRESS(1953)
Robert J. Miles, Jr.
DIRTY HARRY(1971)
Rosaland Miles
SHAFT'S BIG SCORE(1972)
Rosalind Miles
BLACK SIX, THE(1974)
Misc. Talkies
GIRLS FOR RENT(1974); MANHANDLERS, THE(1975)
Ruth Miles
HERE COME THE WAVES(1944); RAZOR'S EDGE, THE(1946)
Sally Miles
PRIVATE'S PROGRESS(1956, Brit.)
Sarah Miles
TERM OF TRIAL(1962, Brit.); CEREMONY, THE(1963, U.S./Span.); SERVANT, THE(1964, Brit.); THOSE MAGNIFICENT MEN IN THEIR FLYING MACHINES; OR HOW I FLEW FROM LONDON TO PARIS IN 25 HOURS AND 11 MINUTES(1965, Brit.); BLOW-UP(1966, Brit.); TIME LOST AND TIME REMEMBERED(1966, Brit.); RYAN'S DAUGHTER(1970, Brit.); LADY CAROLINE LAMB(1972, Brit./Ital.); HIREL-ING, THE(1973, Brit.); MAN WHO LOVED CAT DANCING, THE(1973); GREAT EXPECTATIONS(1975, Brit.); SAILOR WHO FELL FROM GRACE WITH THE SEA, THE(1976, Brit.); BIG SLEEP, THE½(1978, Brit.); PRIEST OF LOVE(1981, Brit.); VENOM(1982, Brit.); STAYING ALIVE(1983)
1984
ORDEAL BY INNOCENCE(1984, Brit.)
Sarah M. Miles
GOING BERSERK(1983)
1984
GIMME AN 'F'(1984)
Sherry Miles
PHYNX, THE(1970); MAKING IT(1971); TODD KILLINGS, THE(1971); VELVET VAMPIRE, THE(1971); YOUR THREE MINUTES ARE UP(1973); HARRAD SUMMER, THE(1974); PACK, THE(1977)
Misc. Talkies
CALLIOPE(1971)
Sylvia Miles
MURDER, INC.(1960); PARRISH(1961); PIE IN THE SKY(1964); PSY-CHOMANIA(1964); MIDNIGHT COWBOY(1969); LAST MOVIE, THE(1971); WHO KILLED MARY WHAT'SER NAME?(1971); FAREWELL, MY LOVELY(1975); 92 IN THE SHADE(1975, U.S./Brit.); GREAT SCOUT AND CATHOUSE THURSDAY, THE(1976); SENTINEL, THE(1977); ZERO TO SIXTY(1978); FUNHOUSE, THE(1981); EVIL UNDER THE SUN(1982, Brit.)
Misc. Talkies
HEAT(1972); SHALIMAR(1978, India)
T. Stephen Miles
YELLOWBEARD(1983), cos
Terry Miles
LITTLE BIG MAN(1970), makeup
Vera Miles
WHEN WILLIE COMES MARCHING HOME(1950); TWO TICKETS TO BROAD-WAY(1951); FOR MEN ONLY(1952); ROSE BOWL STORY, THE(1952); CHARGE AT FEATHER RIVER, THE(1953); SO BIG(1953); PRIDE OF THE BLUE GRASS(1954); TARZAN'S HIDDEN JUNGLE(1955); WICHITA(1955); AUTUMN LEAVES(1956); SEARCHERS, THE(1956); WRONG MAN, THE(1956); 23 PACES TO BAKER STREET(1956); BEAU JAMES(1957); BEYOND THIS PLACE(1959, Brit.); FBI STORY, THE(1959); FIVE BRANDED WOMEN(1960); PSYCHO(1960); TOUCH OF LARCENY, A(1960, Brit.); BACK STREET(1961); MAN WHO SHOT LIBERTY VALANCE, THE(1962); THOSE CALLOWAYS(1964); TIGER WALKS, A(1964); FOLLOW ME, BOYS!(1966); ONE OF OUR SPIES IS MISSING(1966); GENTLE GIANT(1967); SPIRIT IS WILLING, THE(1967); HELLFIGHTERS(1968); KONA COAST(1968); MISSION BATANGAS(1968); SERGEANT RYKER(1968); IT TAKES ALL KINDS(1969, U.S./Aus.); WILD COUNTRY, THE(1971); MOLLY AND LAWLESS JOHN(1972); ONE LITTLE INDIAN(1973); CASTAWAY COWBOY, THE(1974); RUN FOR THE RO-SES(1978); BRAINWAVES(1983); PSYCHO II(1983)
1984
INITIATION, THE(1984)
Misc. Talkies
LAST GENERATION, THE(1971); THOROUGHBREDS, THE(1977)
Vickie Miles
SCUM OF THE EARTH(1963)
Walter Miles
PSYCHIC KILLER(1975)
Walter O. Miles
MAC ARTHUR(1977); SUMMER SCHOOL TEACHERS(1977)
William Miles
HEADLEYS AT HOME, THE(1939), w
Wynn Miles
PASSION HOLIDAY(1963), d

Johanna Mileschikowsky
SPRING BREAK(1983)
Hank Milestone
FROM HELL TO VICTORY(1979, Fr./Ital./Span.), d
Lewis Milestone
NEW YORK NIGHTS(1929), d; ALL QUIET ON THE WESTERN FRONT(1930), d, w; FRONT PAGE, THE(1931), d; RAIN(1932), d; HALLELUJAH, I'M A BUM(1933), p&d; CAPTAIN HATES THE SEA, THE(1934), d; PARIS IN SPRING(1935), d; ANYTHING GOES(1936), d; GENERAL DIED AT DAWN, THE(1936), a, d; NIGHT OF NIGHTS, THE(1939), d; OF MICE AND MEN(1939), p&d; LUCKY PARTNERS(1940), d; MY LIFE WITH CAROLINE(1941), p&d; EDGE OF DARKNESS(1943), d; NORTH STAR, THE(1943), d; PURPLE HEART, THE(1944), d; WALK IN THE SUN, A(1945), p&d; STRANGE LOVE OF MARTHA IVERS, THE(1946), d; ARCH OF TRIUMPH(1948), d, w; NO MINOR VICES(1948), p&d; OCEAN BREAKERS(1949, Swed.), p&d; RED PONY, THE(1949), p&d; HALLS OF MONTEZUMA(1951), d; KANGAROO(1952), d; LES MISERABLES(1952), d; MELBA(1953, Brit.), d; THEY WHO DARE(1954, Brit.), d; PORK CHOP HILL(1959), d; OCEAN'S ELEVEN(1960), p&d; MUTINY ON THE BOUNTY(1962), d
Silents
CAVEMAN, THE(1926), d; NEW KLONDIKE, THE(1926), d; KID BROTHER, THE(1927), d; RACKET, THE(1928), d
Misc. Silents
SEVEN SINNERS(1925), d; TWO ARABIAN KNIGHTS(1927), d; GARDEN OF EDEN, THE(1928), d; BETRAYAL(1929), d
Nick J. Mileti
STREAMERS(1983), p
Octhvian Miletich
LUM AND ABNER ABROAD(1956), ph
Arthur Milett
Misc. Silents
BARE-FISTED GALLAGHER(1919)
Jerry Miley
TAXI 13(1928); MEXICALI ROSE(1929); SKY DEVILS(1932); PARIS IN SPRING(1935); CHARLIE CHAN'S SECRET(1936); LIVE, LOVE AND LEARN(1937); NIGHTMARE ALLEY(1947); FURY AT FURNACE CREEK(1948); EVERYBODY DOES IT(1949); LES MISERABLES(1952)
Silents
BROKEN HEARTS OF HOLLYWOOD(1926); WILD OATS LANE(1926); EASY PICKINGS(1927); JOY GIRL, THE(1927); PAJAMAS(1927); SALLY OF THE SCAN-DALS(1928)
Misc. Silents
BRED IN OLD KENTUCKY(1926)
Keith Miley
1984
REPO MAN(1984)
Bliss Milford
Misc. Silents
BELOVED VAGABOND, THE(1912); CLOSING NET, THE(1915); HOUSE OF MIR-RORS, THE(1916)
Gene Milford
FLIGHT(1929), ed; LADIES MUST PLAY(1930), ed; VENGEANCE(1930), ed; FLOOD, THE(1931), ed; LION AND THE LAMB(1931), ed; MAKER OF MEN(1931), ed; MEN ARE LIKE THAT(1931), ed; PLATINUM BLONDE(1931), ed; SHANGHAIED LOVE(1931), ed; TEXAS RANGER, THE(1931), ed; HELLO TROUBLE(1932), ed; MC KENNA OF THE MOUNTED(1932), ed; THRILL HUNTER, THE(1933), ed; LET'S FALL IN LOVE(1934), ed; MAN TRAILER, THE(1934), ed; NINTH GUEST, THE(1934), ed; ONE NIGHT OF LOVE(1934), ed; SISTERS UNDER THE SKIN(1934), ed; FIGHTING SHADOWS(1935), ed; GRAND EXIT(1935), ed; LET'S LIVE TO-NIGHT(1935), ed; LOVE ME FOREVER(1935), ed; PUBLIC MENACE(1935), ed; TOO TOUGH TO KILL(1935), ed; AND SO THEY WERE MARRIED(1936), ed; FORBID-DEN PARADISE(1936), ed; MUSIC GOES ROUND, THE(1936), ed; SHAKEDOWN(1936), ed; THEY MET IN A TAXI(1936), ed; IT CAN'T LAST FOREVER(1937), ed; LEAGUE OF FRIGHTENED MEN(1937), ed; LOST HORIZON(1937), ed; SOMETHING TO SING ABOUT(1937), ed; SWING IT SAILOR(1937), ed; WHEN YOU'RE IN LOVE(1937), ed; MR. BOGGS STEPS OUT(1938), ed; OVERLAND EXPRESS, THE(1938), ed; TAR-ZAN'S REVENGE(1938), ed; COAST GUARD(1939), ed; FRONTIER PONY EX-PRESS(1939), ed; I WAS A CONVICT(1939), ed; THOSE HIGH GREY WALLS(1939), ed; BLONDIE PLAYS CUPID(1940), ed; MILITARY ACADEMY(1940), ed; CONFESSIONS OF BOSTON BLACKIE(1941), ed; STORK PAYS OFF, THE(1941), ed; TILLIE THE TOILER(1941), ed; HIGHER AND HIGHER(1943), ed; FALCON IN HOLLYWOOD, THE(1944), ed; STEP LIVELY(1944), ed; CHINA SKY(1945), ed; HAV-ING WONDERFUL CRIME(1945), ed; ON THE WATERFRONT(1954), ed, art d; MAN WITH THE GUN(1955), ed; BABY DOLL(1956), ed; PUSHER, THE(1960), p, d; FORCE OF IMPULSE(1961), ed; SPLENDOR IN THE GRASS(1961), ed; TARAS BULBA(1962), ed; RAMPAGE(1963), ed; NEW INTERNS, THE(1964), ed; WILD AND WONDERFUL(1964), ed; STRANGE BEDFELLOWS(1965), ed; THAT FUNNY FEEL-ING(1965), ed; CHASE, THE(1966), ed; INCIDENT AT PHANTOM HILL(1966), ed; TEXAS ACROSS THE RIVER(1966), ed; VALLEY OF MYSTERY(1967), ed; WAIT UNTIL DARK(1967), ed; COUNTDOWN(1968), ed; GREAT BANK ROBBERY, THE(1969), ed; THERE WAS A CROOKED MAN(1970), ed; KLANSMAN, THE(1974), ed; W(1974), ed; COUNT OF MONTE CRISTO(1976, Brit.), ed
Silents
LADIES AT EASE(1927), ed; FREE LIPS(1928), ed; MASKED ANGEL(1928), ed
John Milford
PERSUADER, THE(1957); FACE OF A FUGITIVE(1959); GUNFIGHT AT COMAN-CHE CREEK(1964); ZEBRA IN THE KITCHEN(1965); FOR PETE'S SAKE!(1966); LAST CHALLENGE, THE(1967); JONI(1980)
Kim Milford
CIAO MANHATTAN(1973), m; BLOODBROTHERS(1978); CORVETTE SUM-MER(1978); LASERBLAST(1978)
Mary Beth Milford
Silents
AFTER DARK(1924); ARE PARENTS PEOPLE?(1925)
Misc. Silents
TURNED UP(1924); BLOODHOUND, THE(1925); GALLOPING VENGENCE(1925); ONCE IN A LIFETIME(1925); THAT MAN JACK!(1925)
Mary Milford
MILLIONAIRE PLAYBOY(1940)

Penelope Milford
MAN ON A SWING(1974); COMING HOME(1978); LAST WORD, THE(1979); ENDLESS LOVE(1981); TAKE THIS JOB AND SHOVE IT(1981); GOLDEN SEAL, THE(1983)

Penny Milford
MAIDSTONE(1970); VALENTINO(1977, Brit.)

Michael Milgram
TWILIGHT ZONE-THE MOVIE(1983)

Lynn Milgrim
TELL ME THAT YOU LOVE ME, JUNIE MOON(1970)

Michael Milgrom
SPECTRE OF EDGAR ALLAN POE, THE(1974), art d

Guy Milham
Misc. Silents
FULL HOUSE, A(1920)

Darius Milhaud
ENTENTE CORDIALE(1939, Fr.), m; RASPUTIN(1939, Fr.), m; MAN'S HOPE(1947, Span.), m; PRIVATE AFFAIRS OF BEL AMI, THE(1947), m; DREAMS THAT MONEY CAN BUY(1948), m; LIFE BEGINS TOMORROW(1952, Fr.), m

David Milhaud
1984
TO CATCH A COP(1984, Fr.), w

Bertram Milhauser
SHERLOCK HOLMES(1932), w; EVER IN MY HEART(1933), w; LIFE OF JIMMY DOLAN, THE(1933), w; JIMMY THE GENT(1934), w; GARDEN MURDER CASE, THE(1936), w; MAGNIFICENT BRUTE, THE(1936), w; EBB TIDE(1937), w; UNDER COVER OF NIGHT(1937), w; SUSPECT, THE(1944), w; WEB, THE(1947), w
Silents
FORTY WINKS(1925), w

Anne Milhench
Misc. Talkies
BLOOD DEBTS(1983)

James Milhollan
NO TIME FOR SERGEANTS(1958)

Charles Bruce Milholland
TWENTIETH CENTURY(1934), w

John Milholland
SUBMARINE PATROL(1938), w

Richard Milholland
LOOKER(1981); VICE SQUAD(1982)

James Milhollin
BON VOYAGE(1962); GET YOURSELF A COLLEGE GIRL(1964); COOL ONES THE(1967); NEVER A DULL MOMENT(1968)

John Milian
LINEUP, THE(1934)

Thomas Milian
BOCCACCIO '70(1962/Ital./Fr.); MAGNIFICENT BANDITS, THE(1969, Ital./Span.); IDENTIFICATION OF A WOMAN(1983, Ital.)

Tomas Milian
BELL' ANTONIO(1962, Ital.); LA NOTTE BRAVA(1962, Fr./Ital.); DISORDER(1964, Fr./Ital.); AGONY AND THE ECSTASY, THE(1965); TIME OF INDIFFERENCE(1965, Fr./Ital.); DEATH SENTENCE(1967, Ital.); DJANGO KILL(1967, Ital./Span.); FACE TO FACE(1967, Ital.); BIG GUNDOWN, THE(1968, Ital.); UGLY ONES, THE(1968, Ital./Span.); VIOLENT FOUR, THE(1968, Ital.); FINE PAIR, A(1969, Ital.); CANNIBALS, THE(1970, Ital.); COMPANEROS(1970 Ital./Span./Ger.); LAST MOVIE, THE(1971); RIPPED-OFF(1971, Ital.); ALMOST HUMAN(1974,Ital.); SONNY AND JED(1974, Ital.); LUNA(1979, Ital.); WINTER KILLS(1979); CRIME AT PORTA ROMANA(1980, Ital.); MONSIGNOR(1982)
Misc. Talkies
BRUTAL JUSTICE(1978); BLOOD AND GUNS(1979, Ital.)

Tomas Milian, Jr.
NIJINSKY(1980, Brit.)

Frantisek Milic
KRAKATIT(1948, Czech.), w

Rudolf Milic
DEATH IS CALLED ENGELCHEN(1963, Czech.), ph; DEVIL'S TRAP, THE(1964, Czech.), ph

Djordje Milicevic
VICTORY(1981), w

Ognjen Milicevic
HOROSCOPE(1950, Yugo.), ph

Andy Miligan
BLOOD(1974, Brit.), d&w

Catherine Milinaire
DOLL, THE(1962, Fr.)

Gilles Milinaire
LAST DAYS OF MAN ON EARTH, THE(1975, Brit.)

Sing Milintrasai
SHADOW OF EVIL(1967, Fr./Ital.)

Lou Milione
TAPS(1981)

Frank Miliott
NIGHT AND DAY(1946)

Carl Militaire
HIT AND RUN(1957)

Rick Militi
METALSTORM: THE DESTRUCTION OF JARED-SYN(1983)

John Milius
DEVIL'S 8, THE(1969), w; EVEL KNIEVEL(1971), w; JEREMIAH JOHNSON(1972), w; LIFE AND TIMES OF JUDGE ROY BEAN, THE(1972), w; DILLINGER(1973), d&w; MAGNUM FORCE(1973), w; WIND AND THE LION, THE(1975), d&w; BIG WEDNESDAY(1978), d, w; APOCALYPSE NOW(1979), w; CONAN THE BARBARIAN(1982), d, w; DEADHEAD MILES(1982); UNCOMMON VALOR(1983), p
1984
RED DAWN(1984), d, w

D. Miliutenko
SECRET MISSION(1949, USSR)

Dragan Milivojevic
NINTH CIRCLE, THE(1961, Yugo.)

John Miljan
HOME TOWNERS, THE(1928); LAND OF THE SILVER FOX(1928); TENDERLOIN(1928); TERROR, THE(1928); WOMEN THEY TALK ABOUT(1928); DESERT SONG, THE(1929); DEVIL MAY CARE(1929); FASHIONS IN LOVE(1929); HARD-BOILED ROSE(1929); INNOCENTS OF PARIS(1929); QUEEN OF THE NIGHT-CLUBS(1929); STARK MAD(1929); TIMES SQUARE(1929); UNHOLY NIGHT, THE(1929); UNTAMED(1929); VOICE OF THE CITY(1929); BLUSHING BRIDES(1930); FREE AND EASY(1930); OUR BLUSHING BRIDES(1930); PAID(1930); REMOTE CONTROL(1930); SEA BAT, THE(1930); SHOW GIRL IN HOLLYWOOD(1930); UNHOLY THREE, THE(1930); WOMAN RACKET, THE(1930); GENTLEMAN'S FATE(1931); INSPIRATION(1931); IRON MAN, THE(1931); POLITICS(1931); POSSESSED(1931); SECRET SIX, THE(1931); SON OF INDIA(1931); SUSAN LENOX-HER FALL AND RISE(1931); ARE YOU LISTENING?(1932); ARSENE LUPIN(1932); BEAST OF THE CITY, THE(1932); EMMA(1932); FLESH(1932); HELL DIVERS(1932); KID FROM SPAIN, THE(1932); NIGHT COURT(1932); PROSPERITY(1932); RICH ARE ALWAYS WITH US, THE(1932); UNASHAMED(1932); WET PARADE, THE(1932); BLIND ADVENTURE(1933); KING FOR A NIGHT(1933); MAD GAME, THE(1933); MADE ON BROADWAY(1933); NUISANCE, THE(1933); SIN OF NORA MORAN(1933); WAY TO LOVE, THE(1933); WHAT! NO BEER?(1933); WHISTLING IN THE DARK(1933); BELLE OF THE NINETIES(1934); MADAME SPY(1934); POOR RICH, THE(1934); TWIN HUSBANDS(1934); UNKNOWN BLONDE(1934); WHIRLPOOL(1934); YOUNG AND BEAUTIFUL(1934); CHARLIE CHAN IN PARIS(1935); GHOST WALKS, THE(1935); MISSISSIPPI(1935); THREE KIDS AND A QUEEN(1935); TOMORROW'S YOUTH(1935); UNDER THE PAMPAS MOON(1935); ARIZONA MAHONEY(1936); GENTLEMAN FROM LOUISIANA(1936); MURDER AT GLEN ATHOL(1936); PRIVATE NUMBER(1936); SUTTER'S GOLD(1936); NORTH OF NOME(1937); PLAINSMAN, THE(1937); BORDER G-MAN(1938); IF I WERE KING(1938); MAN-PROOF(1938); OF HUMAN HEARTS(1938); RIDE A CROOKED MILE(1938); FAST AND FURIOUS(1939); JUAREZ(1939); OKLAHOMA KID, THE(1939); PARDON OUR NERVE(1939); TORCHY RUNS FOR MAYOR(1939); EMERGENCY SQUAD(1940); NEW MOON(1940); QUEEN OF THE MOB(1940); TEXAS RANGERS RIDE AGAIN(1940); WOMEN WITHOUT NAMES(1940); YOUNG BILL HICKOK(1940); COWBOY AND THE BLONDE, THE(1941); DEADLY GAME, THE(1941); DOUBLE CROSS(1941); FORCED LANDING(1941); OBLIGING YOUNG LADY(1941); RIOT SQUAD(1941); SCATTERGOOD SURVIVES A MURDER(1942); TRUE TO THE ARMY(1942); BOMBARDIER(1943); BOSS OF BIG TOWN(1943); FALLEN SPARROW, THE(1943); IRON MAJOR, THE(1943); SUBMARINE ALERT(1943); BRIDE BY MISTAKE(1944); MERRY MONAHANS, THE(1944); BACK TO BATAAN(1945); I ACCUSE MY PARENTS(1945); IT'S IN THE BAG(1945); WILDFIRE(1945); KILLERS, THE(1946); LAST CROOKED MILE, THE(1946); WHITE TIE AND TAILS(1946); QUEEN OF THE AMAZONS(1947); SINBAD THE SAILOR(1947); THAT'S MY MAN(1947); UNCONQUERED(1947); FLAME, THE(1948); PERILOUS WATERS(1948); ADVENTURE IN BALTIMORE(1949); MRS. MIKE(1949); SAMSON AND DELILAH(1949); STAMPEDE(1949); MULE TRAIN(1950); M(1951); BONZO GOES TO COLLEGE(1952); SAVAGE, THE(1953); PIRATES OF TRIPOLI(1955); RUN FOR COVER(1955); TEN COMMANDMENTS, THE(1956); WILD DAKOTAS, THE(1956); APACHE WARRIOR(1957); LONE RANGER AND THE LOST CITY OF GOLD, THE(1958)
Misc. Talkies
CRIMINAL INVESTIGATOR(1942); IN SELF DEFENSE(1947)
Silents
ON THE STROKE OF THREE(1924); ROMANCE RANCH(1924); FLAMING WATERS(1925); OVERLAND LIMITED, THE(1925); PHANTOM OF THE OPERA, THE(1925); UNCHASTENED WOMAN(1925); ALMOST A LADY(1926); AMATEUR GENTLEMAN, THE(1926); CLOWN, THE(1927); HUSBANDS FOR RENT(1927); LADYBIRD, THE(1927); OLD SAN FRANCISCO(1927); ROUGH HOUSE ROSIE(1927); SAILOR IZZY MURPHY(1927); SAILOR'S SWEETHEART, A(1927); SILVER SLAVE, THE(1927); STRANDED(1927); WHAT HAPPENED TO FATHER(1927); WOLF'S CLOTHING(1927); YANKEE CLIPPER, THE(1927); CRIMSON CITY, THE(1928); LADY BE GOOD(1928); ETERNAL WOMAN, THE(1929)
Misc. Silents
EMPTY HEARTS(1924); LONE CHANCE, THE(1924); LOVE LETTERS(1924); SILENT SANDERSON(1925); WRECKAGE(1925); DEVIL'S CIRCUS, THE(1926); RACE WILD(1926); UNKNOWN TREASURES(1926); FINAL EXTRA, THE(1927); PAYING THE PRICE(1927); QUARANTINED RIVALS(1927); SLAVER, THE(1927)

Howard Milkin
TREE, THE(1969), ed

Edward K. Milkis
SILVER STREAK(1976), p; FOUL PLAY(1978), p

Edward Milkis
BEST LITTLE WHOREHOUSE IN TEXAS, THE(1982), p

Mariya Milkova
GORDEYEV FAMILY, THE(1961, U.S.S.R.)

Edith Mill
HOUSE OF LIFE(1953, Ger.); LOVE FEAST, THE(1966, Ger.)

Ramsey Mill
ESPIONAGE(1937)

Robert Mill
I'LL NEVER FORGET WHAT'S 'IS NAME(1967, Brit.); MAROC 7(1967, Brit.); LADY CAROLINE LAMB(1972, Brit./Ital.); SCHIZO(1977, Brit.)

Robert R. Mill
PURPLE V, THE(1943), w

Helena Millais
Misc. Silents
MEG OF THE SLUMS(1916, Brit.)

Hugh Millais
MC CABE AND MRS. MILLER(1971); IMAGES(1972, Ireland); DOGS OF WAR, THE(1980, Brit.); WICKED LADY, THE(1983, Brit.)

Ivy Millais
Misc. Silents
BOTTLE, THE(1915, Brit.)

Warren Millais
Misc. Talkies
HER SECRET(1933), d

Herman Millakowsky
WOMEN IN BONDAGE(1943), p; FACES IN THE FOG(1944), p; MURDER IN THE MUSIC HALL(1946), p

Antonio Millan
BOLDEST JOB IN THE WEST, THE(1971, Ital.), ph
Art Millan
MOB, THE(1951); VIOLENT YEARS, THE(1956); BATTLE HYMN(1957)
Joy Millan
GIVE US THE MOON(1944, Brit.)
Julie Millan
TIME GENTLEMEN PLEASE!(1953, Brit.)
Lynn Millan
CANON CITY(1948); INCIDENT(1948); SET-UP, THE(1949); SIDE STREET(1950)
Lynne Millan
ONE DESIRE(1955); WOMEN'S PRISON(1955)
Robyn Millan
WITCHMAKER, THE(1969); WHO IS HARRY KELLERMAN AND WHY IS HE SAYING THOSE TERRIBLE THINGS ABOUT ME?(1971)
Tony Millan
PIRATES OF PENZANCE, THE(1983)
Victor Millan
RING, THE(1952); THUNDERBIRDS(1952); ELEPHANT WALK(1954); APACHE AMBUSH(1955); BATTLE FLAME(1955); GIANT(1956); WALK THE PROUD LAND(1956); ESCAPE FROM SAN QUENTIN(1957); RIDE BACK, THE(1957); TERROR IN A TEXAS TOWN(1958); TOUCH OF EVIL(1958); FBI STORY, THE(1959); PINK JUNGLE, THE(1968); DOC SAVAGE... THE MAN OF BRONZE(1975); BOULEVARD NIGHTS(1979); SCARFACE(1983)
Misc. Talkies
EYES OF THE JUNGLE(1953)
Gloria Milland
GOLIATH AGAINST THE GIANTS(1963, Ital./Span.); REBEL GLADIATORS, THE(1963, Ital.); ATLAS AGAINST THE CZAR(1964, Ital.); GOLDEN ARROW, THE(1964, Ital.); HATE FOR HATE(1967, Ital.); MAN WHO KILLED BILLY THE KID, THE(1967, Span./Ital.); FEW BULLETS MORE, A(1968, Ital./Span.)
Misc. Talkies
THREE SWORDS OF ZORRO, THE(1960)
Oscar Milland
REWARD, THE(1965), w
Ray Milland
FLYING SCOTSMAN, THE(1929, Brit.); INFORMER, THE(1929, Brit.); LADY FROM THE SEA, THE(1929, Brit.); PLAYTHING, THE(1929, Brit.); PASSION FLOWER(1930); WAY FOR A SAILOR(1930); AMBASSADOR BILL(1931); BACHELOR FATHER(1931); BLONDE CRAZY(1931); BOUGHT(1931); JUST A GIGOLO(1931); STRANGERS MAY KISS(1931); MAN WHO PLAYED GOD, THE(1932); PAYMENT DEFERRED(1932); PICCADILLY(1932, Brit.); POLLY OF THE CIRCUS(1932); THIS IS THE LIFE(1933, Brit.); BOLERO(1934); CHARLIE CHAN IN LONDON(1934); MANY HAPPY RETURNS(1934); MENACE(1934); MYSTERY OF MR. X, THE(1934); ORDERS IS ORDERS(1934, Brit.); WE'RE NOT DRESSING(1934); ALIAS MARY DOW(1935); FOUR HOURS TO KILL(1935); GILDED LILY, THE(1935); GLASS KEY, THE(1935); ONE HOUR LATE(1935); BIG BROADCAST OF 1937, THE(1936); JUNGLE PRINCESS, THE(1936); NEXT TIME WE LOVE(1936); RETURN OF SOPHIE LANG, THE(1936); BULLDOG DRUMMOND ESCAPES(1937); EASY LIVING(1937); EBB TIDE(1937); THREE SMART GIRLS(1937); WINGS OVER HONOLULU(1937); WISE GIRL(1937); HER JUNGLE LOVE(1938); MEN WITH WINGS(1938); SAY IT IN FRENCH(1938); TROPIC HOLIDAY(1938); BEAU GESTE(1939); EVERYTHING HAPPENS AT NIGHT(1939); FRENCH WITHOUT TEARS(1939, Brit.); HOTEL IMPERIAL(1939); ARISE, MY LOVE(1940); DOCTOR TAKES A WIFE(1940); IRENE(1940); UNTAMED(1940); I WANTED WINGS(1941); SKYLARK(1941); ARE HUSBANDS NECESSARY?(1942); LADY HAS PLANS, THE(1942); MAJOR AND THE MINOR, THE(1942); REAP THE WILD WIND(1942); STAR SPANGLED RHYTHM(1942); CRYSTAL BALL, THE(1943); FOREVER AND A DAY(1943); LADY IN THE DARK(1944); 'TILL WE MEET AGAIN(1944); UNINVITED, THE(1944); KITTY(1945); LOST WEEKEND, THE(1945); MINISTRY OF FEAR(1945); CALIFORNIA(1946); WELL-GROOMED BRIDE, THE(1946); GOLDEN EARRINGS(1947); IMPERFECT LADY, THE(1947); TROUBLE WITH WOMEN, THE(1947); VARIETY GIRL(1947); BIG CLOCK, THE(1948); MISS TATLOCK'S MILLIONS(1948); SEALED VERDICT(1948); SO EVIL MY LOVE(1948, Brit.); ALIAS NICK BEAL(1949); IT HAPPENS EVERY SPRING(1949); COPPER CANYON(1950); LIFE OF HER OWN, A(1950); WOMAN OF DISTINCTION, A(1950); CIRCLE OF DANGER(1951, Brit.); CLOSE TO MY HEART(1951); NIGHT INTO MORNING(1951); RHUBARB(1951); BUGLES IN THE AFTERNOON(1952); SOMETHING TO LIVE FOR(1952); THIEF, THE(1952); JAMAICA RUN(1953); LET'S DO IT AGAIN(1953); DIAL M FOR MURDER(1954); GIRL IN THE RED VELVET SWING, THE(1955); MAN ALONE, A(1955), a, d; LISBON(1956), a, p&d; HIGH FLIGHT(1957, Brit.); RIVER'S EDGE, THE(1957); THREE BRAVE MEN(1957); SAFECRACKER, THE(1958, Brit.), a, d; PANIC IN YEAR ZERO!(1962), a, d; PREMATURE BURIAL, THE(1962); "X"-THE MAN WITH THE X-RAY EYES(1963); QUICK, LET'S GET MARRIED(1965); HOSTILE WITNESS(1968, Brit.), a, d; COMPANY OF KILLERS(1970); LOVE STORY(1970); BIG GAME, THE(1972); EMBASSY(1972, Brit.); FROGS(1972); THING WITH TWO HEADS, THE(1972); TERROR IN THE WAX MUSEUM(1973); GOLD(1974, Brit.); ESCAPE TO WITCH MOUNTAIN(1975); LAST TYCOON, THE(1976); SWISS CONSPIRACY, THE(1976, U.S./Ger.); ACES HIGH(1977, Brit.); SLAVERS(1977, Ger.); UNCANNY, THE(1977, Brit./Can.); BLACKOUT(1978, Fr./Can.); OLIVER'S STORY(1978); ATTIC, THE(1979); BATTLESTAR GALACTICA(1979); GAME FOR VULTURES, A(1980, Brit.); SURVIVAL RUN(1980)
Misc. Talkies
CONFESSION, THE(1964); OIL(1977, Ital.)
Adelqui Millar
Silents
LAUGHTER AND TEARS(1921, Brit.), a, w; PAGES OF LIFE(1922, Brit.), d&w; ARAB, THE(1924); APACHE, THE(1925, Brit.), a, p, d; LONDON(1926, Brit.); LIFE(1928, Brit.), a, p&d; INSEPARABLES, THE(1929, Brit.), d, p, w
Misc. Silents
I'PAGLIACCI(1923, Brit.); MOON OF ISRAEL(1927, Aust.)
Adolf Millar
SONS OF STEEL(1935)
Adolph Millar
Silents
LOVE'S WILDERNESS(1924); GATEWAY OF THE MOON, THE(1928)
Elda Millar [Hedda Hopper]
Misc. Silents
FOOD GAMBLERS, THE(1917); HER EXCELLENCY, THE GOVERNOR(1917)

Bill Millar
METAMORPHOSES(1978), ph
Gavin Millar
WEATHER IN THE STREETS, THE(1983, Brit.), d
1984
SECRETS(1984, Brit.), d
H.E. Millar, Sr.
ICE STATION ZEBRA(1968), spec eff
Henry Millar
TWILIGHT'S LAST GLEAMING(1977, U.S./Ger.), spec eff; NATIONAL LAMPOON'S ANIMAL HOUSE(1978), spec eff; LAST WORD, THE(1979), spec eff; HYSTERICAL(1983), spec eff
1984
2010(1984), spec eff
Henry Millar, Jr.
1,000 PLANE RAID, THE(1969), spec eff; TOO LATE THE HERO(1970), spec eff; CHINA SYNDROME, THE(1979), spec eff
John Millar
HIDE AND SEEK(1964, Brit.)
Lee Millar
NOBODY'S CHILDREN(1940); LADY AND THE TRAMP(1955)
Marjie Millar
MONEY FROM HOME(1953); ABOUT MRS. LESLIE(1954)
Norma Millar
MIKADO, THE(1967, Brit.)
Peter Millar
TOMORROW AT TEN(1964, Brit.), w
Ronald Millar
WE DIVE AT DAWN(1943, Brit.); FRIEDA(1947, Brit.), w; SO EVIL MY LOVE(1948, Brit.), w; MINIVER STORY, THE(1950, Brit./U.S.), w; UNKNOWN MAN, THE(1951), w; SCARAMOUCHE(1952), w; TRAIN OF EVENTS(1952, Brit.), w; NEVER LET ME GO(1953, U.S./Brit.), w; BETRAYED(1954), w
Stuart Millar
YOUNG STRANGER, THE(1957), p; STAGE STRUCK(1958), p; YOUNG DOCTORS, THE(1961), p; I COULD GO ON SINGING(1963), p; BEST MAN, THE(1964), p; PAPER LION(1968), p; LITTLE BIG MAN(1970), p; WHEN THE LEGENDS DIE(1972), p, d; ROOSTER COGBURN(1975), d
Wilson Millar
FOLIES DERGERE(1935); WHEN YOU'RE IN LOVE(1937); DESERT HAWK, THE(1950); APRIL IN PARIS(1953)
Susan Millar-Smith
LAST RHINO, THE(1961, Brit.)
Ed Millard
BRIDE OF VENGEANCE(1949)
Evelyn Millard
Misc. Silents
CHAINS OF BONDAGE(1916, Brit.)
Harry Millard
LAST MILE, THE(1959); THUNDER IN DIXIE(1965)
Helen Millard
THEIR OWN DESIRE(1929); THIRTEENTH CHAIR, THE(1930); UNFINISHED BUSINESS(1941)
Helene Millard
DIVORCEE, THE(1930); LAWFUL LARCENY(1930); PAY OFF, THE(1930); DOCTORS' WIVES(1931); DON'T BET ON WOMEN(1931); SUSAN LENOX-HER FALL AND RISE(1931); BY WHOSE HAND?(1932); LADY WITH A PAST(1932); FOURTH HORSEMAN, THE(1933); DESIRABLE(1934); BREAK OF HEARTS(1935); MARIE ANTOINETTE(1938); BISCUIT EATER, THE(1940); LADY WITH RED HAIR(1940); MEN AGAINST THE SKY(1940); SPORTING BLOOD(1940); NOTHING BUT THE TRUTH(1941); WE WERE DANCING(1942); CLOWN, THE(1953); REMAINS TO BE SEEN(1953)
Jill Millard
SECRETS OF A WINDMILL GIRL(1966, Brit.)
John Millard
MEMBER OF THE JURY(1937, Brit.), w
Joseph Millard
THEY CAME FROM BEYOND SPACE(1967, Brit.), w
Oscar E. Millard
UNCENSORED(1944, Brit.), w
Oscar Millard
COME TO THE STABLE(1949), w; FROGMEN, THE(1951), w; NO HIGHWAY IN THE SKY(1951, Brit.), w; ANGEL FACE(1953), w; SECOND CHANCE(1953), w; CONQUEROR, THE(1956), w; SONG WITHOUT END(1960), w; DEAD RINGER(1964), w; JOURNEY INTO DARKNESS(1968, Brit.), w; SALZBURG CONNECTION, THE(1972), w
S. S. Millard
Silents
IS YOUR DAUGHTER SAFE?(1927), p
Harry F. Millarde
Misc. Silents
LITTLE MISS NOBODY(1917), d
Harry Millarde
Silents
CELEBRATED CASE, A(1914); ELUSIVE ISABEL(1916); GAMBLING IN SOULS(1919), d; SACRED SILENCE(1919), d; OVER THE HILL TO THE POORHOUSE(1920), d; ON ZE BOULEVARD(1927), d; TAXI DANCER, THE(1927), d
Misc. Silents
DON CAESAR DE BAZAN(1915); LOTUS WOMAN, THE(1916), a, d; EVERY GIRL'S DREAM(1917), d; MISS U.S.A.(1917), d; UNKNOWN 274(1917), d; BLUE-EYED MARY(1918), d; BONNIE ANNIE LAURIE(1918), d; CAMOUFLAGE KISS, A(1918), d; CAUGHT IN THE ACT(1918), d; HEART OF ROMANCE, THE(1918), d; MISS INNOCENCE(1918), d; GIRL WITH NO REGRETS, THE(1919), d; LOVE THAT DARES, THE(1919), d; ROSE OF THE WEST(1919), d; WHEN FATE DECIDES(1919), d; WHITE MOLL, THE(1920), d; PERJURY(1921), d; MY FRIEND, THE DEVIL(1922), d; TOWN THAT FORGOT GOD, THE(1922), d; GOVERNOR'S LADY, THE(1923), d; FOOL, THE(1925), d
June Millarde
ONCE UPON A TIME(1944)

Diana Millay
TARZAN AND THE GREAT RIVER(1967, U.S./Switz.); NIGHT OF DARK SHADOWS(1971)
Robert Millay
GIANT SPIDER INVASION, THE(1975), spec eff
Elizabeth Millberg
DECISION BEFORE DAWN(1951)
David Millbern
SLUMBER PARTY MASSACRE, THE(1982)
Misc. Talkies
SORCERESS(1983)
Les Millbrook
BANDIT RANGER(1942), ed; FIGHTING FRONTIER(1943), ed; GILDERSLEEVE ON BROADWAY(1943), ed; GILDERSLEEVE'S BAD DAY(1943), ed; BRIDE BY MISTAKE(1944), ed; GILDERSLEEVE'S GHOST(1944), ed; NIGHT OF ADVENTURE, A(1944), ed; JOHNNY ANGEL(1945), ed; BAMBOO BLONDE, THE(1946), ed; DING DONG WILLIAMS(1946), ed; VACATION IN RENO(1946), ed; BANJO(1947), ed; BORN TO KILL(1947), ed; INDIAN AGENT(1948), ed; JUDGE STEPS OUT, THE(1949), ed; MASKED RAIDERS(1949), ed; MYSTERIOUS DESPERADO, THE(1949), ed; STAGECOACH KID(1949), ed
Jacqueline Mille
MALE HUNT(1965, Fr./Ital.)
William C. Mille
Misc. Silents
LOCKED DOORS(1925), d
Al Millen
THERE AIN'T NO JUSTICE(1939, Brit.); CONVOY(1940); SALOON BAR(1940, Brit.); IT ALWAYS RAINS ON SUNDAY(1949, Brit.)
Frances Millen
MARIE ANTOINETTE(1938); SHOPWORN ANGEL(1938)
James Knox Millen
HEALER, THE(1935), w
A. Michael Miller
PHYNX, THE(1970)
Adolph Miller
BOLERO(1934)
Al Miller
FIREFOX(1982), spec eff
Alan Miller
APPALOOSA, THE(1966), p; YOUNG GIANTS(1983)
Albert Miller
OPERATION MANHUNT(1954)
Albert G. Miller
SPIDER'S WEB, THE(1960, Brit.), w
Alice D. G. Miller
BRIDGE OF SAN LUIS REY, THE(1929), w; DISGRACED(1933), w; KEYHOLE, THE(1933), w; GIRL ON THE FRONT PAGE, THE(1936), w; ON BORROWED TIME(1939), w; TANGIER(1946), w
Silents
RED LIGHTS(1923), w; SLAVE OF DESIRE(1923), w; LADY OF THE NIGHT(1925), w; PRETTY LADIES(1925), w; EXQUISITE SINNER, THE(1926), w; ALTARS OF DESIRE(1927), w; FOUR WALLS(1928), w; MAN-MADE WOMEN(1928), w; TWO LOVERS(1928), w
Alice Duer Miller
HONEY(1930), w; MANSLAUGHTER(1930), w; PRINCESS AND THE PLUMBER, THE(1930), w; COME OUT OF THE PANTRY(1935, Brit.), w; ROBERTA(1935), w; COLLEGIATE(1936), w; ROSE MARIE(1936), w; SOAK THE RICH(1936); WIFE VERSUS SECRETARY(1936), w; AND ONE WAS BEAUTIFUL(1940), w; IRENE(1940), w; FOREVER AND A DAY(1943), w; WHITE CLIFFS OF DOVER, THE(1944), w; SPRING IN PARK LANE(1949, Brit.), w; LOVELY TO LOOK AT(1952), w
Silents
CHARM SCHOOL, THE(1921), w; ARE PARENTS PEOPLE?(1925), w
Allan Miller
BABY BLUE MARINE(1976); BOUND FOR GLORY(1976); TWO-MINUTE WARNING(1976); FUN WITH DICK AND JANE(1977); MAC ARTHUR(1977); CHAMP, THE(1979); CRUISING(1980)
1984
STAR TREK III: THE SEARCH FOR SPOCK(1984)
Allen C. Miller
DOCTOR X(1932), w
Andrea Miller
1984
GREYSTOKE: THE LEGEND OF TARZAN, LORD OF THE APES(1984)
Ann Miller
LIFE OF THE PARTY, THE(1937); NEW FACES OF 1937(1937); STAGE DOOR(1937); HAVING WONDERFUL TIME(1938); RADIO CITY REVELS(1938); ROOM SERVICE(1938); TARNISHED ANGEL(1938); YOU CAN'T TAKE IT WITH YOU(1938); HIT PARADE OF 1941(1940); MELODY RANCH(1940); TOO MANY GIRLS(1940); GO WEST, YOUNG LADY(1941); TIME OUT FOR RHYTHM(1941); PRIORITIES ON PARADE(1942); TRUE TO THE ARMY(1942); REVEILLE WITH BEVERLY(1943); WHAT'S BUZZIN COUSIN?(1943); CAROLINA BLUES(1944); HEY, ROOKIE(1944); JAM SESSION(1944); EADIE WAS A LADY(1945); EVE KNEW HER APPLES(1945); THRILL OF BRAZIL, THE(1946); EASTER PARADE(1948); KISSING BANDIT, THE(1948); ON THE TOWN(1949); WATCH THE BIRDIE(1950); TEXAS CARNIVAL(1951); TWO TICKETS TO BROADWAY(1951); LOVELY TO LOOK AT(1952); KISS ME KATE(1953); SMALL TOWN GIRL(1953); DEEP IN MY HEART(1954); HIT THE DECK(1955); GREAT AMERICAN PASTIME, THE(1956); OPPOSITE SEX, THE(1956); WON TON TON, THE DOG WHO SAVED HOLLYWOOD(1976)
Annette Miller
TERROR EYES(1981)
Annie Miller
TWO ENGLISH GIRLS(1972, Fr.); GREEN ROOM, THE(1979, Fr.)
Arlen Miller
1984
RACING WITH THE MOON(1984)
Arlin Miller
1984
IRRECONCILABLE DIFFERENCES(1984)

Arnie Miller
SCREWBALLS(1983)
Arnold Miller
SECRETS OF A WINDMILL GIRL(1966, Brit.), p, d&w; BLOOD BEAST TERROR, THE(1967, Brit.), p
Misc. Talkies
UNDER THE TABLE YOU MUST GO(1969), d
Arnold Louis Miller
SKIN GAME, THE(1965, Brit.), p, d; CONQUEROR WORM, THE(1968, Brit.), p; TOUCH OF THE OTHER, A(1970, Brit.), p, d
Art Miller
FATHER'S SON(1931), ph; BREACH OF PROMISE(1942, Brit.), ph
Arthur Miller
BELLAMY TRIAL, THE(1929), ph; BIG NEWS(1929), ph; FLYING FOOL(1929), ph; HIS FIRST COMMAND(1929), ph; OH, YEAH!(1929), ph; SAILORS' HOLIDAY(1929), ph; SPIELER, THE(1929), ph; STRANGE CARGO(1929), ph; LADY OF SCANDAL, THE(1930), ph; OFFICER O'BRIEN(1930), ph; SEE AMERICA THIRST(1930), ph; TRUTH ABOUT YOUTH, THE(1930), ph; BAD COMPANY(1931), ph; BIG SHOT, THE(1931), ph; ME AND MY GAL(1932), ph; OKAY AMERICA(1932), ph; PANAMA FLO(1932), ph; YOUNG BRIDE(1932), ph; HOLD ME TIGHT(1933), ph; MAD GAME, THE(1933), ph; MAN WHO DARED, THE(1933), ph; MY WEAKNESS(1933), ph; SAILOR'S LUCK(1933), ph; THEIR NIGHT OUT(1933, Brit.), W; BOTTOMS UP(1934), ph; BRIGHT EYES(1934), ph; EVER SINCE EVE(1934), ph; HANDY ANDY(1934), ph; LAST TRAIL, THE(1934), ph; LOVE TIME(1934), ph; WHITE PARADE, THE(1934), ph; BLACK SHEEP(1935), ph; IT'S A SMALL WORLD(1935), ph; LITTLE COLONEL, THE(1935), ph; PADDY O'DAY(1935), ph; WELCOME HOME(1935), ph; PIGSKIN PARADE(1936), ph; STOWAWAY(1936), ph; THIRTY SIX HOURS TO KILL(1936), ph; WHITE FANG(1936), ph; HEIDI(1937), ph; WEE WILLIE WINKIE(1937), ph; BARONESS AND THE BUTLER, THE(1938), ph; JUST AROUND THE CORNER(1938), ph; LITTLE MISS BROADWAY(1938), ph; REBECCA OF SUNNYBROOK FARM(1938), ph; SUBMARINE PATROL(1938), ph; HERE I AM A STRANGER(1939), ph; LITTLE PRINCESS, THE(1939), ph; RAINS CAME, THE(1939), ph; SUSANNAH OF THE MOUNTIES(1939), ph; YOUNG MR. LINCOLN(1939), ph,Bert Glennon; BLUE BIRD, THE(1940), ph; BRIGHAM YOUNG—FRONTIERSMAN(1940), ph; JOHNNY APOLLO(1940), ph; MARK OF ZORRO, THE(1940), ph; ON THEIR OWN(1940), ph; HOW GREEN WAS MY VALLEY(1941), ph; MAN HUNT(1941), ph; MEN IN HER LIFE, THE(1941), ph; ICELAND(1942), ph; SON OF FURY(1942), ph; THIS ABOVE ALL(1942), ph; IMMORTAL SERGEANT, THE(1943), ph; MOON IS DOWN, THE(1943), ph; OX-BOW INCIDENT, THE(1943), ph; SONG OF BERNADETTE, THE(1943), ph; KEYS OF THE KINGDOM, THE(1944), ph; PURPLE HEART, THE(1944), ph; ROYAL SCANDAL, A(1945), ph; ANNA AND THE KING OF SIAM(1946), ph; DRAGONWYCH(1946), ph; RAZOR'S EDGE, THE(1946), ph; GENTLEMAN'S AGREEMENT(1947), ph; ALL MY SONS(1948), w; LETTER TO THREE WIVES, A(1948), ph; WALLS OF JERICHO(1948), ph; WHIRLPOOL(1949), ph; GUNFIGHTER, THE(1950), ph; PROWLER, THE(1951), ph; DEATH OF A SALESMAN(1952), w; MISFITS, THE(1961), w; VIEW FROM THE BRIDGE, A(1962, Fr./Ital.), w; ENEMY OF THE PEOPLE, AN(1978), w
Silents
ARMS AND THE WOMAN(1916), ph; NEW YORK(1916), ph; NARROW PATH, THE(1918), ph; NAULAHKA, THE(1918), ph; AVALANCHE, THE(1919), ph; COUNTERFEIT(1919), ph; ON WITH THE DANCE(1920), ph; KICK IN(1922), ph; TO HAVE AND TO HOLD(1922), ph; CYTHEREA(1924), ph; IN HOLLYWOOD WITH POTASH AND PERLMUTTER(1924), ph; COMING OF AMOS, THE(1925), ph; VOLGA BOATMAN, THE(1926), ph; ANGEL OF BROADWAY, THE(1927), ph; NOBODY'S WIDOW(1927), ph; VANITY(1927), ph; ANNAPOLIS(1928), ph; HOLD 'EM YALE!(1928), ph
Arthur Miller [British]
MARRY THE GIRL(1935, Brit.), w
Arthur C. Miller
TOBACCO ROAD(1941), ph
Ashley Miller
Silents
KING'S GAME, THE(1916), d, w; QUEST OF LIFE, THE(1916), d; INFIDELITY(1917), d
Misc. Silents
AFFAIR OF THREE NATIONS, AN(1915), d; HOUSE OF FEAR, THE(1915), d; MENACE OF THE MUTE, THE(1915), d; OUT OF THE RUINS(1915), d; WITH BRIDGES BURNED(1915), d; WORKING OF A MIRACLE, THE(1915), d; MARRIAGE SPECULATION, THE(1917), d; MORAL CODE, THE(1917), d; PRINCESS OF PARK ROW, THE(1917), d
Barbara Ann Miller
GOING IN STYLE(1979)
Barry Miller
LEPKE(1975, U.S./Israel); SATURDAY NIGHT FEVER(1977); VOICES(1979); FAME(1980); CHOSEN, THE(1982)
Ben Miller
WILD COUNTRY, THE(1971)
Beth Miller
1984
GIMME AN 'F'(1984)
Betty Miller
1984
POPE OF GREENWICH VILLAGE, THE(1984)
Beverly Miller
BEAST OF BLOOD(1970, U.S./Phil.), a, w
Big Miller
1984
BIG MEAT EATER(1984, Can.)
Bill Miller
SINGING BLACKSMITH(1938), ph; WHEN THE LEGENDS DIE(1972), makeup; LONG GOODBYE, THE(1973), makeup
Misc. Silents
FIGHTING RANGER, THE(1922); GUILTY(1922)
Ranger Bill Miller
Silents
WEB OF THE LAW, THE(1923)
Misc. Silents
PAIR OF HELLIONS, A(1924); HEARTBOUND(1925)

Billie Miller
SCENT OF MYSTERY(1960)
Billy Miller
MOLE PEOPLE, THE(1956); RESTLESS BREED, THE(1957); RUN OF THE AR-ROW(1957)
Blaine Miller
CANAL ZONE(1942), w
Bob Miller
SHOCK WAVES(1977)
Bodil Miller
SCARLET ANGEL(1952); MA AND PA KETTLE ON VACATION(1953); REP-TILICUS(1962, U.S./Den.)
Brian Miller
SUBURBAN WIVES(1973, Brit.)
Burton Miller
KITTEN WITH A WHIP(1964), cos; COUNTERPOINT(1967), cos; SULLIVAN'S EM-PIRE(1967), cos; VALLEY OF MYSTERY(1967), cos; COMPANY OF KILLERS(1970), cos; EARTHQUAKE(1974), cos; FRONT PAGE, THE(1974), cos; SWASHBUCK-LER(1976), cos; AIRPORT '77(1977), cos; HOUSE CALLS(1978), cos; NUDE BOMB, THE(1980), cos; STING II, THE(1983), cos
Buzz Miller
PAJAMA GAME, THE(1957)
Cameron Miller
PORTRAIT OF CLARE(1951, Brit.)
Carl Miller
HONOR OF THE FAMILY(1931); TRAVELING HUSBANDS(1931); RENEGADES OF THE WEST(1932); PHANTOM BROADCAST, THE(1933); EMBARRASSING MO-MENTS(1934); LIFE BEGINS AT 40(1935); NO RANSOM(1935)
Silents
KID, THE(1921); JEALOUS HUSBANDS(1923); WOMAN OF PARIS, A(1923); RE-DEEMING SIN, THE(1925); GREAT K & A TRAIN ROBBERY, THE(1926); POWER OF THE WEAK, THE(1926); MAKING THE VARSITY(1928)
Misc. Silents
MARY REGAN(1919); CINDERELLA OF THE HILLS(1921); PARISH PRIEST, THE(1921); CONDEMNED(1923); TRAPPED(1925); WALL STREET WHIZ, THE(1925); WE MODERNS(1925); CANYON OF LIGHT, THE(1926); GOOD AS GOLD(1927); WHISPERING SAGE(1927); WHY SAILORS GO WRONG(1928)
Carlton Miller
Misc. Silents
BRIDE'S PLAY, THE(1922)
Carol Miller
RENEGADE GIRLS(1974)
Carrie Miller
LAST TYCOON, THE(1976)
Charles Miller
CIRCUS KID, THE(1928); GIVE AND TARE(1929); NIGHT OF NIGHTS, THE(1939); TOWER OF LONDON(1939); KITTY FOYLE(1940); PHANTOM OF CHINA-TOWN(1940); CAUGHT IN THE ACT(1941); GAMBLING DAUGHTERS(1941); SWAMP WATER(1941); JOAN OF OZARK(1942); PHANTOM PLAINSMEN, THE(1942); RAID-ERS OF THE RANGE(1942); SOUTH OF SANTA FE(1942); THEY ALL KISSED THE BRIDE(1942); BLACK HILLS EXPRESS(1943); DAYS OF OLD CHEYENNE(1943); JACK LONDON(1943); RAIDERS OF SUNSET PASS(1943); THUNDERING TRAILS(1943); WAGON TRACKS WEST(1943); BENEATH WESTERN SKIES(1944); HIDDEN VALLEY OUTLAWS(1944); HOUSE OF FRANKENSTEIN(1944); OH, WHAT A NIGHT(1944); PRIDE OF THE PLAINS(1944); WILSON(1944); DALTONS RIDE AGAIN, THE(1945); HONEYMOON AHEAD(1945); GUNMAN'S CODE(1946); NIGHT AND DAY(1946); RENDEZVOUS 24(1946); RUSTLER'S ROUNDUP(1946); I'LL BE YOURS(1947); CALL NORTHSIDE 777(1948); HOMECOMING(1948); MEXICAN HAY-RIDE(1948); MIRACLE OF THE BELLS, THE(1948); UP IN CENTRAL PARK(1948)
1984
RACING WITH THE MOON(1984)
Silents
CORNER IN COLLEENS, A(1916), d; HOME(1916), d; MARKET OF VAIN DESIRE, THE(1916), d; DARK ROAD, THE(1917), d; HATER OF MEN(1917), d; LITTLE BROTH-ER, THE(1917), d; FAIR PRETENDER, THE(1918), d
Misc. Silents
BAWBS O' BLUE RIDGE(1916), d; PAYMENT, THE(1916); PLAIN JANE(1916), d; FLAME OF THE YUKON, THE(1917), d; PRINCESS OF THE DARK, A(1917), d; SAWDUST RING, THE(1917), d; SECRET OF THE STORM COUNTRY, THE(1917), d, d; WEE LADY BETTY(1917), d; WILD WINSHIP'S WIDOW(1917), d; AT THE MERCY OF MEN(1918), d; BY RIGHT OF PURCHASE(1918), d; GHOSTS OF YESTER-DAY(1918), d; GREAT VICTORY, WILSON OR THE KAISER?, THE(1918), d; SER-VICE STAR, THE(1918), d; DANGEROUS AFFAIR, A(1919), d; LOVE, HONOR AND ?(1919), d; WHY GERMANY MUST PAY(1919), d; HIGH SPEED(1920), d; LAW OF THE YUKON, THE(1920), d; MAN SHE BROUGHT BACK, THE(1922), d; SHIP OF SOULS(1925), d; ROAD TO RUIN, THE(1928)
Charles B. V. Miller
LAWLESS BREED, THE(1952)
Charles F. Miller
Misc. Silents
POLLY ANN(1917), d
Charlotte Miller
SAILOR'S LUCK(1933), w
Cheryl Miller
CLARENCE, THE CROSS-EYED LION(1965); MONKEY'S UNCLE, THE(1965); DOCTOR DEATH: SEEKER OF SOULS(1973); GUARDIAN OF THE WILDER-NESS(1977)
Chris Miller
GUNSLINGER(1956); VALLEY OF THE REDWOODS(1960); NATIONAL LAM-POON'S ANIMAL HOUSE(1978), w
Christian Miller
NATIONAL LAMPOON'S ANIMAL HOUSE(1978)
Clarence Miller
NAME FOR EVIL, A(1970)
Clarkson Miller
Silents
SCARLET ROAD, THE(1916), d

Claude Miller
WILD CHILD, THE(1970, Fr.); BEST WAY, THE(1978, Fr.), d, w; LIKE A TURTLE ON ITS BACK(1981, Fr.), a, w; INQUISITOR, THE(1982, Fr.), d, w
1984
HEAT OF DESIRE(1984, Fr.), w
Cloryce Miller
TOUGH ENOUGH(1983)
Colin Miller
KISS FOR CORLISS, A(1949), p
Colleen Miller
LAS VEGAS STORY, THE(1952); MAN CRAZY(1953); FOUR GUNS TO THE BORDER(1954); PLAYGIRL(1954); PURPLE MASK, THE(1955); RAWHIDE YEARS, THE(1956); HOT SUMMER NIGHT(1957); MAN IN THE SHADOW(1957); NIGHT RUNNER, THE(1957); STEP DOWN TO TERROR(1958); GUNFIGHT AT COMANCHE CREEK(1964)
Count Prince Miller
PROSTITUTE(1980, Brit.)
Court Miller
1984
GARBO TALKS(1984)
D'Arcy Miller
REAP THE WILD WIND(1942)
Dan Miller
MEN OF SAN QUENTIN(1942), ed; GAY PURR-EE(1962), ph
Dan T. Miller
SCREAMERS(1978, Ital.), d
Daphne Miller
NEXT OF KIN(1983, Aus.)
Dave Miller
ROCK BABY, ROCK IT(1957)
David Miller
GLAMOUR(1931, Brit.); MANY WATERS(1931, Brit.); OUT OF THE BLUE(1931, Brit.); VERDICT OF THE SEA(1932, Brit.); SLEEPLESS NIGHTS(1933, Brit.); BILLY THE KID(1941), d; FLYING TIGERS(1942), d; SUNDAY PUNCH(1942), d; LOVE HAPPY(1949), d; TOP O' THE MORNING(1949), d; DRAGON OF PENDRAGON CASTLE, THE(1950, Brit.); OUR VERY OWN(1950), d; SATURDAY'S HERO(1951), d; SUDDEN FEAR(1952), d; MEET MR. LUCIFER(1953, Brit.); BEAUTIFUL STRAN-GER(1954, Brit.), d, w; CHIEF CRAZY HORSE(1955); DIANE(1955), d; OPPOSITE SEX, THE(1956), d; STORY OF ESTHER COSTELLO, THE(1957, Brit.), p, d; HAPPY ANNIVERSARY(1959), d; MIDNIGHT LACE(1960), d; BACK STREET(1961), d; LONELY ARE THE BRAVE(1962), d; CAPTAIN NEWMAN, M.D.(1963), d; CHEYENNE AUTUMN(1964); HAMMERHEAD(1968), d; HAIL, HERO!(1969), d; EX-ECUTIVE ACTION(1973), d; BITTERSWEET LOVE(1976), d; ATTACK OF THE KILL-ER TOMATOES(1978)
1984
NIGHTMARE ON ELM STREET, A(1984), makeup
David B. Miller
1984
NIGHT OF THE COMET(1984), makeup
David H. Miller
TOMAHAWK(1951)
David Humphreys Miller
STAGECOACH(1966)
Dean Miller
BECAUSE YOU'RE MINE(1952); EVERYTHING I HAVE IS YOURS(1952); SKIRTS AHOY!(1952); DREAM WIFE(1953); GIRL WHO HAD EVERYTHING, THE(1953); SMALL TOWN GIRL(1953); LORDS OF DISCIPLINE, THE(1983)
Dean R. Miller
MY BODYGUARD(1980); LOSIN' IT(1983)
1984
JOHNNY DANGEROUSLY(1984)
Deborah Miller
CAT ON A HOT TIN ROOF(1958)
Dennis Miller
SOLDIER'S TALE, THE(1964, Brit.), p, ph; IT TAKES ALL KINDS(1969, U.S./Aus.); STORK(1971, Aus.); GREAT MACARTHY, THE(1975, Aus.); ELIZA FRASER(1976, Aus.); STIR(1980, Aus.); STONE COLD DEAD(1980, Can.), ph; HOODWINK(1981, Aus.); LAST OF THE KNUCKLEMEN, THE(1981, Aus.); STARSTRUCK(1982, Aus.); BUD-DIES(1983, Aus.); HEATWAVE(1983, Aus.)
Dennis "Denny" Miller
TARZAN, THE APE MAN(1959)
Denny Miller
SOME CAME RUNNING(1959); LOVE IN A GOLDFISH BOWL(1961); DOOMSDAY MACHINE(1967); PARTY, THE(1968); MAKING IT(1971); BUCK AND THE PREACH-ER(1972); GRAVY TRAIN, THE(1974); ISLAND AT THE TOP OF THE WORLD, THE(1974); NORSEMAN, THE(1978); CABOBLANCO(1981)
Derek Miller
THAT SINKING FEELING(1979, Brit.)
Dian K. Miller
DARK END OF THE STREET, THE(1981), p
Diana Miller
Silents
EVERY MAN'S WIFE(1925); KISS BARRIER, THE(1925); RAINBOW TRAIL, THE(1925)
Misc. Silents
CURLYTOP(1924); FLAMES OF DESIRE(1924); HONOR AMONG MEN(1924); HUNTED WOMAN, THE(1925); COWBOY AND THE COUNTESS, THE(1926)
Diane Miller
THIS LOVE OF OURS(1945)
Misc. Talkies
CLOSET CASANOVA, THE(1979); ONE PAGE OF LOVE(1979)
Dick Miller
NIGHT WAITRESS(1936); APACHE WOMAN(1955); CARNIVAL ROCK(1957); NOT OF THIS EARTH(1957); ROCK ALL NIGHT(1957); SORORITY GIRL(1957); UNDEAD, THE(1957); WAR OF THE SATELLITES(1958); BUCKET OF BLOOD, A(1959); LITTLE SHOP OF HORRORS(1961); WILD, WILD WINTER(1966); TIME FOR KILLING, A(1967); TRIP, THE(1967); WILD RACERS, THE(1968); EXECUTIVE ACTION(1973); STUDENT TEACHERS, THE(1973); NIGHT CALL NURSES(1974); TRUCK TUR-NER(1974); CRAZY MAMA(1975); DARKTOWN STRUTTERS(1975); TNT JACK-SON(1975), w; WHITE LINE FEVER(1975, Can.); CANNONBALL(1976, U.S./Hong

Kong); HOLLYWOOD BOULEVARD(1976); MOVING VIOLATION(1976); MR. BILLION(1977); NEW YORK, NEW YORK(1977); SUMMER SCHOOL TEACHERS(1977); I WANNA HOLD YOUR HAND(1978); PIRANHA(1978); STARHOPS(1978); LADY IN RED, THE(1979); ROCK 'N' ROLL HIGH SCHOOL(1979); DR. HECKYL AND MR. HYPE(1980); USED CARS(1980); HEARTBEEPS(1981); HOWLING, THE(1981); VORTEX(1982); WHITE DOG(1982); GET CRAZY(1983); HEART LIKE A WHEEL(1983); SPACE RAIDERS(1983); TWILIGHT ZONE–THE MOVIE(1983)
1984
GREMLINS(1984); LIES(1984, Brit.); TERMINATOR, THE(1984)
Misc. Talkies
CANDY STRIPE NURSES(1974)
Don Miller
SPIRIT OF NOTRE DAME, THE(1931)
Doreen Miller
MADE FOR EACH OTHER(1971)
Doris Miller
PRETENDER, THE(1947), w
Misc. Silents
MAN SHE BROUGHT BACK, THE(1922)
Drew Miller
LIKELY STORY, A(1947); RIFFRAFF(1947); WOMAN ON THE BEACH, THE(1947)
Drifting Johnny Miller
COUNTRY MUSIC HOLIDAY(1958)
Drout Miller
RECESS(1967)
Dusty Miller
SWEENEY(1977, Brit.), ph; SWEENEY 2(1978, Brit.), ph
1984
BLOODBATH AT THE HOUSE OF DEATH(1984, Brit.), ph
Dutch Miller
LADY LIBERTY(1972, Ital./Fr.)
1984
ONCE UPON A TIME IN AMERICA(1984)
Misc. Talkies
AWOL(1973)
E.D. Miller
CHAPTER TWO(1979); PRINCE OF THE CITY(1981)
Ebb Miller
1984
FIRST TURN-ON!, THE(1984)
Ed Miller
MONKEY'S PAW, THE(1933); HOLD THAT WOMAN(1940)
Eddie Miller
PETE KELLY'S BLUES(1955)
Edwin Miller
MERCY PLANE(1940); LUCKY JORDAN(1942); TRUE TO THE ARMY(1942); DUEL IN THE JUNGLE(1954, Brit.), ph
Ella Miller
Silents
NORTH OF 36(1924)
Mrs. Elvira Miller
COOL ONES THE(1967)
Elwyn Miller
TWO(1975)
Emmett Miller
YES SIR, MR. BONES(1951)
Ernest Miller
MARRIAGE BY CONTRACT(1928), ph; MISTER ANTONIO(1929), ph; MOLLY AND ME(1929), ph; LOVE TRADER(1930), ph; TROOPERS THREE(1930), ph; CLEARING THE RANGE(1931), ph; EX-FLAME(1931), ph; MAD PARADE, THE(1931), ph; WILD HORSE(1931), ph; HONOR OF THE PRESS(1932), ph; PRIVATE SCANDAL, A(1932), ph; ALIMONY MADNESS(1933), ph; HER RESALE VALUE(1933), ph; REVENGE AT MONTE CARLO(1933), ph; CRIMSON ROMANCE(1934), ph; HOLLYWOOD MYSTERY(1934), ph; CONFIDENTIAL(1935), ph; HARMONY LANE(1935), ph; HEADLINE WOMAN, THE(1935), ph; IN OLD SANTA FE(1935), ph; LADIES CRAVE EXCITEMENT(1935), ph; MELODY TRAIL(1935), ph; SAGEBRUSH TROUBADOR(1935), ph; STREAMLINE EXPRESS(1935), ph; TUMBLING TUMBLEWEEDS(1935), ph; WATERFRONT LADY(1935), ph; $1,000 A MINUTE(1935), ph; DANCING FEET(1936), ph; GENTLEMAN FROM LOUISIANA(1936), ph; GIRL FROM MANDALAY(1936), ph; GUNS AND GUITARS(1936), ph; HEARTS IN BONDAGE(1936), ph; HITCH HIKE LADY(1936), ph; HOUSE OF A THOUSAND CANDLES, THE(1936), ph; LEATHERNECKS HAVE LANDED, THE(1936), ph; LEAVENWORTH CASE, THE(1936), ph; NAVY BORN(1936), ph; PRESIDENT'S MYSTERY, THE(1936), ph; SITTING ON THE MOON(1936), ph; TICKET TO PARADISE(1936), ph; AFFAIRS OF CAPPY RICKS(1937), ph; ALL OVER TOWN(1937), ph; COME ON, COWBOYS(1937), ph; COUNTRY GENTLEMEN(1937), ph; EXILED TO SHANGHAI(1937), ph; HAPPY-GO-LUCKY(1937), ph; HIT PARADE, THE(1937), ph; JOIN THE MARINES(1937), ph; MAN BETRAYED, A(1937), ph; MEET THE BOY FRIEND(1937), ph; RHYTHM IN THE CLOUDS(1937), ph; SEA RACKETEERS(1937), ph; SPRINGTIME IN THE ROCKIES(1937), ph; TRIGGER TRIO, THE(1937), ph; TWO WISE MAIDS(1937), ph; WRONG ROAD, THE(1937), ph; ARMY GIRL(1938), ph; ARSON GANG BUSTERS(1938), ph; BILLY THE KID RETURNS(1938), ph; CALL OF THE YUKON(1938), ph; COME ON, LEATHERNECKS(1938), ph; DOWN IN ARKANSAW(1938), ph; GANGS OF NEW YORK(1938), ph; HOLLYWOOD STADIUM MYSTERY(1938), ph; MAMA RUNS WILD(1938), ph; OLD BARN DANCE, THE(1938), ph; PRISON NURSE(1938), ph; PURPLE VIGILANTES, THE(1938), ph; ROMANCE ON THE RUN(1938), ph; STORM OVER BENGAL(1938), ph; TENTH AVENUE KID(1938), ph; CALLING ALL MARINES(1939), ph; COWBOYS FROM TEXAS(1939), ph; FEDERAL MAN-HUNT(1939), ph; FLIGHT AT MIDNIGHT(1939), ph; IN OLD MONTEREY(1939), ph; JEEPERS CREEPERS(1939), ph; KANSAS TERRORS, THE(1939), ph; MOUNTAIN RHYTHM(1939), ph; MYSTERIOUS MISS X, THE(1939), ph; ORPHANS OF THE STREET(1939), ph; SHE MARRIED A COP(1939), ph; STREET OF MISSING MEN(1939), ph; THREE TEXAS STEERS(1939), ph; WOMAN DOCTOR(1939), ph; ZERO HOUR, THE(1939), ph; BARNYARD FOLLIES(1940), ph; BOWERY BOY(1940), ph; CROOKED ROAD, THE(1940), ph; FORGOTTEN GIRLS(1940), ph; FRIENDLY NEIGHBORS(1940), ph; GHOST VALLEY RAIDERS(1940), ph; GIRL FROM HAVANA(1940), ph; IN OLD MISSOURI(1940), ph; MEET THE MISSUS(1940), ph; MELODY AND MOONLIGHT(1940), ph; MONEY TO BURN(1940), ph; SCATTERBRAIN(1940), ph; SING, DANCE, PLENTY HOT(1940), ph; VILLAGE BARN DANCE(1940), ph; WAGONS WESTWARD(1940), ph; ANGELS

WITH BROKEN WINGS(1941), ph; ARKANSAS JUDGE(1941), ph; BACK IN THE SADDLE(1941), ph; CITADEL OF CRIME(1941), ph; COUNTRY FAIR(1941), ph; DOCTORS DON'T TELL(1941), ph; PRAIRIE PIONEERS(1941), ph; PUBLIC ENEMIES(1941), ph; ROOKIES ON PARADE(1941), ph; SAILORS ON LEAVE(1941), ph; TUXEDO JUNCTION(1941), ph; WEST OF CIMARRON(1941), ph; ARIZONA TERRORS(1942), ph; HI, NEIGHBOR(1942), ph; HOME IN WYOMIN'(1942), ph; HURRICANE SMITH(1942), ph; JOAN OF OZARK(1942), ph; MOUNTAIN RHYTHM(1942), ph; OLD HOMESTEAD, THE(1942), ph; RAIDERS OF THE RANGE(1942), ph; REMEMBER PEARL HARBOR(1942), ph; SHEPHERD OF THE OZARKS(1942), ph; SUNDOWN KID, THE(1942), ph; TRAGEDY AT MIDNIGHT, A(1942), ph; YOKEL BOY(1942), ph; BLACK HILLS EXPRESS(1943), ph; CALLING WILD BILL ELLIOTT(1943), ph; CHANCE OF A LIFETIME, THE(1943), ph; CHATTERBOX(1943), ph; DEAD MAN'S GULCH(1943), ph; DEATH VALLEY MANHUNT(1943), ph; PURPLE V, THE(1943), ph; RIDERS OF THE RIO GRANDE(1943), ph; SECRETS OF THE UNDERGROUND(1943), ph; SHANTYTOWN(1943), ph; THUMBS UP(1943), ph; YOUTH ON PARADE(1943), ph; BENEATH WESTERN SKIES(1944), ph; CALIFORNIA JOE(1944), ph; MOJAVE FIREBRAND(1944), ph; BELLS OF ROSARITA(1945), ph; IDENTITY UNKNOWN(1945), ph; ROAD TO ALCATRAZ(1945), ph; SCOTLAND YARD INVESTIGATOR(1945, Brit.), ph; TELL IT TO A STAR(1945), ph; TIGER WOMAN, THE(1945), ph; HER ADVENTUROUS NIGHT(1946), ph; STARS OVER TEXAS(1946), ph; TUMBLEWEED TRAIL(1946), ph; CHEYENNE TAKES OVER(1947), ph; FIGHTING VIGILANTES, THE(1947), ph; GHOST TOWN RENEGADES(1947), ph; RETURN OF THE LASH(1947), ph; SHADOW VALLEY(1947), ph; UNTAMED FURY(1947), ph; BOLD FRONTIERSMAN, THE(1948), ph; DEAD MAN'S GOLD(1948), ph; HAWK OF POWDER RIVER, THE(1948), ph; MARK OF THE LASH(1948), ph; RETURN OF WILDFIRE, THE(1948), ph; VALIANT HOMBRE, THE(1948), ph; DEATH VALLEY GUNFIGHTER(1949), ph; FRONTIER INVESTIGATOR(1949), ph; GAY AMIGO, THE(1949), ph; I SHOT JESSE JAMES(1949), ph; LAW OF THE GOLDEN WEST(1949), ph; OUTLAW COUNTRY(1949), ph; RED DESERT(1949), ph; RIMFIRE(1949), ph; RINGSIDE(1949), ph; SHEP COMES HOME(1949), ph; SON OF A BADMAN(1949), ph; SON OF BILLY THE KID(1949), ph; COLORADO RANGER(1950), ph; CROOKED RIVER(1950), ph; FAST ON THE DRAW(1950), ph; HOSTILE COUNTRY(1950), ph; I SHOT BILLY THE KID(1950), ph; KING OF THE BULLWHIP(1950), ph; MARSHAL OF HELDORADO(1950), ph; RADAR SECRET SERVICE(1950), ph; TRAIN TO TOMBSTONE(1950), ph; WEST OF THE BRAZOS(1950), ph; LONGHORN, THE(1951), ph; NEVADA BADMEN(1951), ph; STAGE TO BLUE RIVER(1951), ph; TEXAS LAWMEN(1951), ph; THUNDERING TRAIL, THE(1951), ph; VANISHING OUTPOST, THE(1951), ph; WHISTLING HILLS(1951), ph; BATTLE ZONE(1952), ph; BLACK LASH, THE(1952), ph; DEAD MAN'S TRAIL(1952), ph; FARGO(1952), ph; KANSAS TERRITORY(1952), ph; LAWLESS COWBOYS(1952), ph; MAN FROM BLACK HILLS, THE(1952), ph; MAVERICK, THE(1952), ph; NIGHT RAIDERS(1952), ph; NO HOLDS BARRED(1952), ph; TEXAS CITY(1952), ph; WACO(1952), ph; HOMESTEADERS, THE(1953), ph; MARKSMAN, THE(1953), ph; REBEL CITY(1953), ph; STAR OF TEXAS(1953), ph; TOPEKA(1953), ph; VIGILANTE TERROR(1953), ph; BITTER CREEK(1954), ph; FORTYNINERS, THE(1954), ph
Silents
BEATING THE GAME(1921), ph; MADE IN HEAVEN(1921), ph; ALIAS THE NIGHT WIND(1923), ph; ON PROBATION(1924), ph; POISON(1924), ph; SURGING SEAS(1924), ph; FAIR PLAY(1925), ph; WAS IT BIGAMY?(1925), ph; DUDE COWBOY, THE(1926), ph; HAIR TRIGGER BAXTER(1926), ph; JAZZ GIRL, THE(1926), ph; VALLEY OF BRAVERY, THE(1926), ph; BULLDOG PLUCK(1927), ph; DRIVEN FROM HOME(1927), ph; EAGER LIPS(1927), ph; LADIES AT EASE(1927), ph; LADYBIRD, THE(1927), ph; RAGTIME(1927), ph; TERROR OF BAR X, THE(1927), ph; ALBANY NIGHT BOAT, THE(1928), ph; GRAIN OF DUST, THE(1928), ph; NIGHT FLYER, THE(1928), ph; ON TO RENO(1928), ph; SCARLET DOVE, THE(1928), ph; STORMY WATERS(1928), ph; TOILERS, THE(1928), ph; DEVIL'S APPLE TREE(1929), ph; JOY STREET(1929), ph
Ernest W. Miller
GRAND CANYON(1949), ph; SQUARE DANCE JUBILEE(1949), ph; BANDIT QUEEN(1950), ph; BORDER RANGERS(1950), ph; GUNFIRE(1950), ph; MOTOR PATROL(1950), ph; WESTERN PACIFIC AGENT(1950), ph; LITTLE BIG HORN(1951), ph; STEEL HELMET, THE(1951), ph; HELLGATE(1952), ph
Ernie Miller
LAUGHING AT LIFE(1933), ph; BEHIND GREEN LIGHTS(1935), ph; LITTLE MEN(1935), ph; MARINES ARE COMING, THE(1935), ph; ONE FRIGHTENED NIGHT(1935), ph; PIONEER JUSTICE(1947), ph; BLACK HILLS(1948), ph; CHECK YOUR GUNS(1948), ph; ENCHANTED VALLEY, THE(1948), ph; TIOGA KID, THE(1948), ph; WESTWARD TRAIL, THE(1948), ph; SKIPALONG ROSENBLOOM(1951), ph
Ethel Miller
Silents
BROADWAY AFTER DARK(1924)
Eve Miller
I WONDER WHO'S KISSING HER NOW(1947); BUCKAROO FROM POWDER RIVER(1948); INNER SANCTUM(1948); ARCTIC FURY(1949); NEVER FEAR(1950); VICIOUS YEARS, THE(1950); PIER 23(1951); BIG TREES, THE(1952); SHE'S WORKING HER WAY THROUGH COLLEGE(1952); STORY OF WILL ROGERS, THE(1952); WINNING TEAM, THE(1952); APRIL IN PARIS(1953); KANSAS PACIFIC(1953); THERE'S NO BUSINESS LIKE SHOW BUSINESS(1954); BIG BLUFF, THE(1955)
Evelyn Miller
SHE GETS HER MAN(1935)
F.E. Miller
BRONZE BUCKAROO, THE(1939); HARLEM RIDES THE RANGE(1939); YES SIR, MR. BONES(1951)
Misc. Talkies
COME ON, COWBOY!(1948); SHE'S TOO MEAN TO ME(1948)
F. E. [Flournoy E.] Miller
MR. WASHINGTON GOES TO TOWN(1941)
Flourney E. Miller
HARLEM ON THE PRAIRIE(1938); STORMY WEATHER(1943)
Frances Miller
Silents
ADVENTURES OF CAROL, THE(1917)
Francis Miller
INQUEST(1939, Brit.), w; DESIGN FOR MURDER(1940, Brit.), w; MYSTERIOUS MR. NICHOLSON, THE(1947, Brit.), w; BAIT(1950, Brit.), w; STARS IN YOUR EYES(1956, Brit.), w

Frank Miller
LOVE LIES(1931, Brit.), w; OUT OF THE BLUE(1931, Brit.), w; SHADOWS(1931, Brit.), w; LET ME EXPLAIN, DEAR(1932), d&w; LUCKY GIRL(1932, Brit.), d&w; MAID OF THE MOUNTAINS, THE(1932, Brit.), w; VERDICT OF THE SEA(1932, Brit.), d, w; LEAVE IT TO ME(1933, Brit.), w; LETTING IN THE SUNSHINE(1933, Brit.), w; LOVE NEST, THE(1933, Brit.), w; MONEY TALKS(1933, Brit.), w; SOUTHERN MAID, A(1933, Brit.), w; MISTER CINDERS(1934, Brit.), w; MY SONG GOES ROUND THE WORLD(1934, Brit.), w; THOSE WERE THE DAYS(1934, Brit.), w; DANDY DICK(1935, Brit.), w; HONEYMOON FOR THREE(1935, Brit.), w; IT'S A BET(1935, Brit.), w; ANNIE LAURIE(1936, Brit.), w; BED AND BREAKFAST(1936, Brit.), a, w; LIVING DEAD, THE(1936, Brit.), w; SHE KNEW WHAT SHE WANTED(1936, Brit.), w; GIRL THIEF, THE(1938), w; HANGING TREE, THE(1959), set d; 2001: A SPACE ODYSSEY(1968, U.S./Brit.)
Silents
FANCY DRESS(1919, Brit.); MARCH HARE, THE(1919, Brit.), d&w; JOYOUS ADVENTURES OF ARISTIDE PUJOL, THE(1920, Brit.), d&w; KIPPS(1921, Brit.), w; LOVE AT THE WHEEL(1921, Brit.), w; FALSE EVIDENCE(1922, Brit.), w; MARRIED TO A MORMAN(1922, Brit.), w; TRAPPED BY THE MORMONS(1922, Brit.), w; ALLEY OF GOLDEN HEARTS, THE(1924, Brit.), w; MR. NOBODY(1927, Brit.), d&w
Misc. Silents
CUPID IN CLOVER(1929, Brit.), d

Frank M. Miller
SERGEANT RUTLEDGE(1960), set d

Franklin Miller
MISS JESSICA IS PREGNANT(1970), p, w, ed

Franz Miller
SNOW WHITE(1965, Ger.), m

Fred Miller
GAMBLING(1934); SOPHIE LANG GOES WEST(1937); SERGEANT MURPHY(1938); HER HUSBAND'S AFFAIRS(1947); DOCKS OF NEW ORLEANS(1948)
Silents
ALIAS JULIUS CAESAR(1922); SISTERS(1922)

Fred J. Miller
NO ROOM FOR THE GROOM(1952)

Gail Miller
FEVER HEAT(1968)

Gene Miller
COP HATER(1958)

Geoffrey Miller
WAY OUT, THE(1956, Brit.), ed

George Miller
PARDON US(1931); PACK UP YOUR TROUBLES(1932); DEVIL'S BROTHER, THE(1933); MAD MAX(1979, Aus.), d, w; ROAD WARRIOR, THE(1982, Aus.), d, w; DRAUGHTSMAN'S CONTRACT, THE(1983, Brit.); MAN FROM SNOWY RIVER, THE(1983, Aus.), d; TWILIGHT ZONE–THE MOVIE(1983), d

George A. Miller
Misc. Silents
PARTING OF THE TRAILS(1930)

Getti Miller
SHAME, SHAME, EVERYBODY KNOWS HER NAME(1969)

Gilbert Miller
FIREBIRD, THE(1934), p; LADY IS WILLING, THE(1934, Brit.), d; LADIES IN RETIREMENT(1941), p

Glenda Miller
LORDS OF FLATBUSH, THE(1974), art d

Glenn Miller
SUN VALLEY SERENADE(1941); ORCHESTRA WIVES(1942)

Grant Miller
JOHNNY IN THE CLOUDS(1945, Brit.)

Gunnar Miller
ODESSA FILE, THE(1974, Brit./Ger.)

H.C. Miller
ALL THE KING'S MEN(1949)

Hal Miller
YOUNG FRANKENSTEIN(1974), spec eff; DISTANCE(1975)

Harlan Miller
SINCE YOU WENT AWAY(1944); OBJECTIVE, BURMA!(1945); NIGHT IN PARADISE, A(1946)

Harley Miller
FLIGHT FOR FREEDOM(1943), set d; SEVENTH VICTIM, THE(1943), set d; MARINE RAIDERS(1944), set d; NONE BUT THE LONELY HEART(1944), set d; ENCHANTED COTTAGE, THE(1945), set d; LOCKET, THE(1946), set d; SISTER KENNY(1946), set d; MR. BLANDINGS BUILDS HIS DREAM HOUSE(1948), set d; DANGEROUS PROFESSION, A(1949), set d; EASY LIVING(1949), set d; WINDOW, THE(1949), set d; WOMAN'S SECRET, A(1949), set d; DOUBLE DYNAMITE(1951), set d; ON DANGEROUS GROUND(1951), set d; TWO TICKETS TO BROADWAY(1951), set d; JET PILOT(1957), set d

Harold Miller
CEILNG ZERO(1935); HANDS ACROSS THE TABLE(1935); MUSIC FOR MADAME(1937); THREE LOVES HAS NANCY(1938); IN NAME ONLY(1939); LOVE AFFAIR(1939); KEEPER OF THE FLAME(1942); GOVERNMENT GIRL(1943); MILDRED PIERCE(1945); POSTMAN ALWAYS RINGS TWICE, THE(1946); UNDERCURRENT(1946); DUCHESS OF IDAHO, THE(1950); PLACE IN THE SUN, A(1951); BAD AND THE BEAUTIFUL, THE(1952); SOMETHING TO LIVE FOR(1952); THREE SAILORS AND A GIRL(1953); BEST THINGS IN LIFE ARE FREE, THE(1956); WARRIORS, THE(1979)
Silents
HER FIVE-FOOT HIGHNESS(1920); KISSED(1922); TIPPED OFF(1923); OUT OF THE PAST(1927)
Misc. Silents
PRINCESS OF BROADWAY, THE(1927)

Harold A. Miller
DANTE'S INFERNO(1935)
Misc. Silents
PEDDLER OF LIES, THE(1920)

Harold W. Miller
SIX BRIDGES TO CROSS(1955)

Harry Miller
SQUADRON LEADER X(1943, Brit.), spec eff

Harry B. Miller III
1984
WEEKEND PASS(1984), ed

Harry Eldon Miller
FUZZ(1972)

Harvey Miller
PRIVATE   BENJAMIN(1980), p, w;   JEKYLL   AND   HYDE...TOGETHER AGAIN(1982), w
1984
CANNONBALL RUN II(1984), w; PROTOCOL(1984), w

Heather Miller
NEVER NEVER LAND(1982)

Heidi Miller
1984
FIRST TURN-ON!, THE(1984)

Helen Topping Miller
LOVER COME BACK(1931), w

Helene Miller
LADIES OF THE JURY(1932)

Henry Miller
HUSTLE(1975), spec eff; REDS(1981)

Henry Miller, Jr.
YOUNG FRANKENSTEIN(1974), spec eff
Silents
WORLD'S CHAMPION, THE(1922)
Misc. Silents
DESPERATE HERO, THE(1920)

Henry Russell Miller
Silents
FRUITS OF DESIRE, THE(1916), w

Herb Miller
SPOTLIGHT SCANDALS(1943)

Herman Miller
VIOLENT ONES, THE(1967), w; COOGAN'S BLUFF(1968), w

Hope Miller
CRY MURDER(1936); BWANA DEVIL(1953)

Howard Miller
JAMBOREE(1957); BIG BEAT, THE(1958); SENIOR PROM(1958)

Hugh Miller
VICTORIA THE GREAT(1937, Brit.); GREEN PACK, THE(1934, Brit.); DIVINE SPARK, THE(1935, Brit./Ital.); HELL'S CARGO(1935, Brit.); BULLDOG DRUMMOND AT BAY(1937, Brit.); DOMINANT SEX, THE(1937, Brit.); SPRING HANDICAP(1937, Brit.); VICAR OF BRAY, THE(1937, Brit.); LOVES OF MADAME DUBARRY, THE(1938, Brit.); RAT, THE(1938, Brit.); RETURN OF THE SCARLET PIMPERNEL(1938, Brit.); I'LL WALK BESIDE YOU(1943, Brit.); MY SISTER AND I(1948, Brit.); WOMAN IN THE HALL, THE(1949, Brit.); DYNAMITERS, THE(1956, Brit.); SHADOW OF FEAR(1956, Brit.); BEHIND THE MASK(1958, Brit.); LAWRENCE OF ARABIA(1962, Brit.)
Silents
IN HIS GRIP(1921, Brit.); PUPPET MAN, THE(1921, Brit.); PRUDES FALL, THE(1924, Brit.); BLIND ALLEYS(1927)
Misc. Silents
BONNIE PRINCE CHARLIE(1923, Brit.); CLAUDE DUVAL(1924, Brit.); VENETIAN LOVERS(1925, Brit.); CITY OF TEMPTATION(1929, Brit.)

Hymie Miller
MIDNIGHT MADONNA(1937)

Ian Miller
BLACKMAIL(1939); WIZARDS(1977), prod d

Ira Miller
JACKSON COUNTY JAIL(1976); TUNNELVISION(1976); LOOSE SHOES(1980), a, d, w; HISTORY OF THE WORLD, PART 1(1981)

Irene Miller
Silents
JO THE CROSSING SWEEPER(1918, Brit.), w; ON LEAVE(1918, Brit.), w; EDGE O'BEYOND(1919, Brit.), w; HER LONELY SOLDIER(1919, Brit.), w

Ivan Miller
DR. SOCRATES(1935); MARY BURNS, FUGITIVE(1935); BULLDOG EDITION(1936); CHARLIE CHAN'S SECRET(1936); NOBODY'S FOOL(1936); COUNTRY GENTLEMEN(1937); FIGHT TO THE FINISH, A(1937); HIGH, WIDE AND HANDSOME(1937); LAST GANGSTER, THE(1937); LET'S MAKE A MILLION(1937); WINGS OVER HONOLULU(1937); CALL OF THE YUKON(1938); DOWN IN ARKANSAW(1938); HUNTED MEN(1938); I AM THE LAW(1938); LITTLE MISS ROUGHNECK(1938); MAN FROM MUSIC MOUNTAIN(1938); OLD BARN DANCE, THE(1938); SQUADRON OF HONOR(1938); COWBOYS FROM TEXAS(1939); FORGED PASSPORT(1939); FRONTIER VENGEANCE(1939); GERONIMO(1939); TELEVISION SPY(1939); WALL STREET COWBOY(1939); MAN WITH NINE LIVES, THE(1940); NOBODY'S CHILDREN(1940); TWENTY MULE TEAM(1940); DEVIL PAYS OFF, THE(1941); JESSE JAMES AT BAY(1941); LADY FOR A NIGHT(1941); MAN MADE MONSTER(1941); UNDER FIESTA STARS(1941); EYES IN THE NIGHT(1942); WAKE ISLAND(1942); YOUTH ON PARADE(1943); ROGER TOUHY, GANGSTER!(1944)

Ivan "Dusty" Miller
MEN WITHOUT NAMES(1935); HUMAN CARGO(1936); SERGEANT MADDEN(1939); MY SON IS GUILTY(1940)

J. Clarkson Miller
Silents
WISE HUSBANDS(, w; MISS CRUSOE(1919), w; IDLE HANDS(1921), w; IDOL OF THE NORTH, THE(1921), w; SUCH A LITTLE QUEEN(1921), w; BACK HOME AND BROKE(1922), w; IT'S THE OLD ARMY GAME(1926), w; LET'S GET MARRIED(1926), w; SO'S YOUR OLD MAN(1926), w; POTTERS, THE(1927), w; PROTECTION(1929), w

J. P. Miller
RABBIT TRAP, THE(1959), w; YOUNG SAVAGES, THE(1961), w; DAYS OF WINE AND ROSES(1962), w; BEHOLD A PALE HORSE(1964), w; PEOPLE NEXT DOOR, THE(1970), w

Jack Miller
PARK ROW(1952), cos; RAT FINK(1965), d&w; ROAD TO SALINA(1971, Fr./Ital.), w

Jack E. Miller
CRY DANGER(1951), cos
Jacob Miller
ROCKERS(1980)
Jacqueline Miller
HEAVENLY BODY, THE(1943); MODEL SHOP, THE(1969)
James Miller
NASHVILLE REBEL(1966), ed
Jan Miller
UP TO HIS NECK(1954, Brit.); YOU KNOW WHAT SAILORS ARE(1954, Brit.);
SECRET, THE(1955, Brit.); RAISING A RIOT(1957, Brit.)
Jane Miller
Misc. Silents
HIGH STAKES(1918); FORFEIT, THE(1919); UNBROKEN PROMISE, THE(1919);
HUSBAND HUNTER, THE(1920)
Janette Miller
FIRST TRAVELING SALESLADY, THE(1956)
Janice Miller
BORN LOSERS(1967)
Jason Miller
EXORCIST, THE(1973); NICKEL RIDE, THE(1974); NINTH CONFIGURATION,
THE(1980); MONSIGNOR(1982); THAT CHAMPIONSHIP SEASON(1982), d&w
1984
TOY SOLDIERS(1984)
Misc. Talkies
TOY SOLDIERS(1983)
Jean DuPont Miller
CANAL ZONE(1942), w
Jeanette Miller
THAT CERTAIN FEELING(1956); VAGABOND KING, THE(1956)
Jeff Miller
DEAD AND BURIED(1981), w
Jessie Miller
Misc. Silents
HIS WIFE'S GOOD NAME(1916)
Jim Miller
DESIRABLE(1934)
Jimmy Miller
HOOK, LINE AND SINKER(1969)
Joan Miller
TAKE IT FROM ME(1937, Brit.); CRY OF THE CITY(1948); ONE TOUCH OF
VENUS(1948); CRISS CROSS(1949); GREAT SINNER, THE(1949); WOMAN IN THE
HALL, THE(1949, Brit.); CAGED(1950); JACKPOT, THE(1950); SOMETHING FOR
THE BIRDS(1952); STORY OF THREE LOVES, THE(1953); BLONDE SINNER(1956,
Brit.); OVER-EXPOSED(1956); FIRE DOWN BELOW(1957, U.S./Brit.); MENACE IN
THE NIGHT(1958, Brit.); TOO YOUNG TO LOVE(1960, Brit.); HEAVENS ABO-
VE!(1963, Brit.); NO TREE IN THE STREET(1964, Brit.)
Jody Miller
SWINGIN' SUMMER, A(1965)
1984
NIGHT PATROL(1984)
Joe Miller
KES(1970, Brit.)
Silents
PARTNERS OF THE TIDE(1921)
Joel Miller
JOE HILL(1971, Swed./U.S.); PARASITE(1982)
John Miller
VANDERGILT DIAMOND MYSTERY, THE(1936); JURY'S SECRET, THE(1938);
YOUNG AND INNOCENT(1938, Brit.); FLYING FIFTY-FIVE(1939, Brit.); HERITAGE
OF THE DESERT(1939); JOHNNY COME LATELY(1943); MY SISTER AND I(1948,
Brit.); OCTOBER MAN, THE(1948, Brit.); SHOWTIME(1948, Brit.); MEN, THE(1950);
SHAKEDOWN(1950); VALLEY OF FIRE(1951); SHANE(1953); SECRET, THE(1955,
Brit.); GIRL IN THE PICTURE, THE(1956, Brit.); DOUBLE, THE(1963, Brit); 20,000
POUNDS KISS, THE(1964, Brit.); HAPPY AS THE GRASS WAS GREEN(1973); YOU
LIGHT UP MY LIFE(1977); HAZEL'S PEOPLE(1978)
Silents
MARCH HARE, THE(1919, Brit.)
John P. Miller
FANTASIA(1940), art d; PINOCCHIO(1940), art d; DUMBO(1941), art d
John Skins Miller
MILKMAN, THE(1950); SUNSET BOULEVARD(1950)
John "Skins" Miller
TIME OF YOUR LIFE, THE(1948); SAN FRANCISCO(1936); DEVIL'S SADDLE
LEGION, THE(1937); DOUBLE WEDDING(1937); INTERNES CAN'T TAKE MO-
NEY(1937); SARATOGA(1937); WE WHO ARE ABOUT TO DIE(1937); EVERY DAY'S
A HOLIDAY(1938); SWING YOUR LADY(1938); TORCHY PLAYS WITH DYNAMI-
TE(1939); FARMER'S DAUGHTER(1939); KING OF THE LUMBERJACKS(1940);
MURDER IN THE AIR(1940); QUEEN OF THE MOB(1940); TEXAS RANGERS RIDE
AGAIN(1940); SUN VALLEY SERENADE(1941); TOBACCO ROAD(1941); MY GAL
SAL(1942); DIXIE(1943); OUR HEARTS WERE GROWING UP(1946); I WONDER
WHO'S KISSING HER NOW(1947); PERILS OF PAULINE, THE(1947); ROAD TO
RIO(1947); WELCOME STRANGER(1947); PALEFACE, THE(1948); CRISS
CROSS(1949); ROSEANNA McCOY(1949); SAMSON AND DELILAH(1949); SORROW-
FUL JONES(1949); TOP O' THE MORNING(1949); WABASH AVENUE(1950); NIGHT
INTO MORNING(1951); RAGING TIDE, THE(1951); SCANDAL SHEET(1952)
Johnny "Skins" Miller
MERRY WIDOW, THE(1934); SOMETHING TO SING ABOUT(1937)
Jon Miller
SHEILA LEVINE IS DEAD AND LIVING IN NEW YORK(1975)
Jonathan Miller
ONE WAY PENDULUM(1965, Brit.); TAKE A GIRL LIKE YOU(1970, Brit,), d
Jonty Miller
VIRGIN SOLDIERS, THE(1970, Brit.)
Joseph Miller
LOOKIN' TO GET OUT(1982)
Josephine Miller
TOWN LIKE ALICE, A(1958, Brit.)

Joshua Miller
HALLOWEEN III: SEASON OF THE WITCH(1982)
Joyce Miller
SONG OF BERNADETTE, THE(1943); SOUTH OF DIXIE(1944)
Joyce Ann Miller
CANDIDATE, THE(1964), w
Judy Miller
Misc. Talkies
BEAUTY AND THE BODY(1963)
Karen Miller
SEA GULL, THE(1968); RACE WITH THE DEVIL(1975)
Karl Miller
GOVERNMENT GIRL(1943); THEY WERE EXPENDABLE(1945); DOBERMAN
GANG, THE(1972), animal; THEY ONLY KILL THEIR MASTERS(1972), animal
Karl Lewis Miller
WHITE DOG(1982)
Kathleen Miller
FRANCHETTE; LES INTRIGUES(1969); LAST DETAIL, THE(1973); SHAM-
POO(1975); FIGHTING MAD(1976); STAY HUNGRY(1976)
Ken Miller
DINO(1957); I WAS A TEENAGE WEREWOLF(1957); ROCKABILLY BABY(1957);
ATTACK OF THE PUPPET PEOPLE(1958); BUCCANEER, THE(1958); GOING
STEADY(1958); TOUCH OF EVIL(1958); BATTLE CRY(1959); CHECKERED FLAG,
THE(1963), art d
Kenny Miller
THIS REBEL BREED(1960); LITTLE SHEPHERD OF KINGDOM COME(1961); NUN
AND THE SERGEANT, THE(1962); GALLANT ONE, THE(1964, U.S./Peru); SURF
PARTY(1964); LITTLE LAURA AND BIG JOHN(1973)
Misc. Talkies
BLOODSTALKERS(1976)
Kim Miller
NIJINSKY(1980, Brit.)
Kimberly Ann Miller
1984
BREAKIN' 2: ELECTRIC BOOGALOO(1984)
Kristine Miller
SUSPENSE(1946); DESERT FURY(1947); TROUBLE WITH WOMEN, THE(1947); I
WALK ALONE(1948); JUNGLE PATROL(1948); SORRY, WRONG NUMBER(1948);
TOO LATE FOR TEARS(1949); HIGH LONESOME(1950); PAID IN FULL(1950);
SHADOW ON THE WALL(1950); YOUNG DANIEL BOONE(1950); STEEL FIST,
THE(1952); TROPICAL HEAT WAVE(1952); BLADES OF THE MUSKETEERS(1953);
FLIGHT NURSE(1953); FROM HERE TO ETERNITY(1953); GERALDINE(1953);
HELL'S OUTPOST(1955); THUNDER OVER ARIZONA(1956); DOMINO KID(1957);
PERSUADER, THE(1957)
Misc. Talkies
SECRET OF OUTLAW FLATS(1953)
Lainie Miller
GRADUATE, THE(1967)
Larry Miller
TAKE DOWN(1979)
Lawrence Miller
KING OF COMEDY, THE(1983), art d
1984
FLAMINGO KID, THE(1984), prod d
Lee Miller
BLOOD OF A POET, THE(1930, Fr.); JOAN OF ARC(1948); DETECTIVE STO-
RY(1951); PLACE IN THE SUN, A(1951); RHUBARB(1951); PLEASE MURDER
ME(1956)
Len Miller
GLORY STOMPERS, THE(1967), ed; MAN CALLED DAGGER, A(1967), ed; JAWS
OF SATAN(1980), ed
Lenard Miller
1984
HOT AND DEADLY(1984)
Misc. Talkies
MYSTERY IN SWING(1940); PROFESSOR CREEPS(1942)
Lenore Miller
MY FAIR LADY(1964)
Lester Miller
STAKEOUT ON DOPE STREET(1958); ROUSTABOUT(1964)
Linda Miller
KING KONG ESCAPES(1968, Jap.); GREEN SLIME, THE(1969); ONE SUMMER
LOVE(1976); ALICE, SWEET ALICE(1978); UNMARRIED WOMAN, AN(1978); SE-
CRET OF NIMH, THE(1982), anim
Linda G. Miller
NIGHT OF THE JUGGLER(1980); LITTLE SEX, A(1982)
Lindy Miller
VILLAIN(1971, Brit.)
Lorraine Miller
BALL OF FIRE(1941); STAR SPANGLED RHYTHM(1942); BEYOND THE LAST
FRONTIER(1943); CRYSTAL BALL, THE(1943); HI DIDDLE DIDDLE(1943); RIDERS
OF THE RIO GRANDE(1943); RIDING HIGH(1943); UP IN ARMS(1944); BORDER
BADMEN(1945); FIGHTING BILL CARSON(1945); FRONTIER FUGITIVES(1945);
MEN IN HER DIARY(1945); THREE IN THE SADDLE(1945); AMBUSH TRAIL(1946);
BIG SLEEP, THE(1946); RENDEZVOUS 24(1946); WHITE GORILLA(1947); IT'S A
SMALL WORLD(1950); RAPTURE(1950, Ital.)
Misc. Talkies
LONESOME TRAIL(1945)
Louise Miller
HUNTED MEN(1938)
Lu Miller
EASY LIVING(1937)
M.B. Miller
HAVE A NICE WEEKEND(1975); SEDUCTION OF JOE TYNAN, THE(1979)
Magda Miller
LET'S BE HAPPY(1957, Brit.); TOWN ON TRIAL(1957, Brit.); SECRET MAN,
THE(1958, Brit.); HOUSE OF FRIGHT(1961)

Maggie Miller
1984
PHAR LAP(1984, Aus.)

Mandy Miller
CRASH OF SILENCE(1952, Brit.); MAN IN THE WHITE SUIT, THE(1952); BACK-GROUND(1953, Brit.); ADVENTURE IN THE HOPFIELDS(1954, Brit.); DANCE LITTLE LADY(1954, Brit.); SECRET, THE(1955, Brit.); CHILD IN THE HOUSE(1956, Brit.); RAISING A RIOT(1957, Brit.); SNORKEL, THE(1958, Brit.)

Marcus Miller
1984
CHOOSE ME(1984), m/l "Choose Me," Luther Vandross

Marian Miller
JUST BEFORE DAWN(1946)

Marilyn Miller
SALLY(1929); SUNNY(1930); HER MAJESTY LOVE(1931); FRATERNITY ROW(1977)

Marion Miller
KID DYNAMITE(1943)

Marjie Miller
WHEN GANGLAND STRIKES(1956)

Mark Miller
HOOK, THE(1962); YOUNGBLOOD HAWKE(1964); GINGER IN THE MORNING(1973); MR. SYCAMORE(1975); DIXIE DYNAMITE(1976); SAVANNAH SMILES(1983), a, w

Martin Miller
ADVENTURES OF TARTU(1943, Brit.); SQUADRON LEADER X(1943, Brit.); FRENZY(1946, Brit.); HOTEL RESERVE(1946, Brit.); NIGHT BOAT TO DUBLIN(1946, Brit.); WOMAN TO WOMAN(1946, Brit.); GHOSTS OF BERKELEY SQUARE(1947, Brit.); BLIND GODDESS, THE(1948, Brit.); BONNIE PRINCE CHARLIE(1948, Brit.); COUNTER BLAST(1948, Brit.); DEVIL'S PLOT, THE(1948, Brit.); MINE OWN EXECUTIONER(1948, Brit.); HER MAN GILBEY(1949, Brit.); HUGGETTS ABROAD, THE(1949, Brit.); I WAS A MALE WAR BRIDE(1949); MAN ON THE RUN(1949, Brit.); THIRD MAN, THE(1950, Brit.); ENCORE(1951, Brit.); WHERE'S CHARLEY?(1952, Brit.); GENIE, THE(1953, Brit.); TWICE UPON A TIME(1953, Brit.); FRONT PAGE STORY(1954, Brit.); MAD ABOUT MEN(1954, Brit.); YOU KNOW WHAT SAILORS ARE(1954, Brit.); MAN OF THE MOMENT(1955, Brit.); WOMAN FOR JOE, THE(1955, Brit.); CASH ON DELIVERY(1956, Brit.); CHILD IN THE HOUSE(1956, Brit.); GAMMA PEOPLE, THE(1956); BABY AND THE BATTLESHIP, THE(1957, Brit.); MARK OF THE PHOENIX(1958, Brit.); BEASTS OF MARSEILLES, THE(1959, Brit.); EXPRESSO BONGO(1959, Brit.); LIBEL(1959, Brit.); EXODUS(1960); PEEPING TOM(1960, Brit.); PORTRAIT OF A SINNER(1961, Brit.); PHANTOM OF THE OPERA, THE(1962, Brit.); CHILDREN OF THE DAMNED(1963, Brit.); V.I.P.s, THE(1963, Brit.); 55 DAYS AT PEKING(1963); PINK PANTHER, THE(1964); UP JUMPED A SWAGMAN(1965, Brit.); YELLOW ROLLS-ROYCE, THE(1965, Brit.); INCIDENT AT MIDNIGHT(1966, Brit.); VIOLENT MOMENT(1966, Brit.)

Marvin Miller
CORPSE CAME C.O.D., THE(; WITHOUT RESERVATIONS(1946); BLOOD ON THE SUN(1945); JOHNNY ANGEL(1945); DEADLINE AT DAWN(1946); NIGHT IN PARA-DISE, A(1946); PHANTOM THIEF, THE(1946); BRASHER DOUBLOON, THE(1947); DEAD RECKONING(1947); INTRIGUE(1947); GOLDEN HORDE, THE(1951); HONG KONG(1951); PEKING EXPRESS(1951); PRINCE WHO WAS A THIEF, THE(1951); SMUGGLER'S ISLAND(1951); RED PLANET MARS(1952); OFF LIMITS(1953); JIVARO(1954); SHANGHAI STORY, THE(1954); KING DINO-SAUR(1955); STORY OF MANKIND, THE(1957); SENIOR PROM(1958); DAY THE EARTH FROZE, THE(1959, Fin./USSR); PANDA AND THE MAGIC SERPENT(1961, Jap.); WHEN THE GIRLS TAKE OVER(1962); SATURDAY NIGHT IN APPLE VALLEY(1965); HELL ON WHEELS(1967); IS THIS TRIP REALLY NECES-SARY?(1970); M(1970); MAN AND BOY(1972), p; WHERE DOES IT HURT?(1972); FANTASTIC PLANET(1973, Fr./Czech.); NAKED APE, THE(1973); HOW TO SEDUCE A WOMAN(1974); TIDAL WAVE(1975, U.S./Jap.)
1984
SWING SHIFT(1984)
Misc. Talkies
BLOOD OF THE IRON MAIDEN(1969)

Mary Louise Miller
Silents
NIGHT CRY, THE(1926); SPARROWS(1926); THIRD DEGREE, THE(1926); JAWS OF STEEL(1927)
Misc. Silents
BANDIT'S BABY, THE(1925)

Max Miller
GOOD COMPANIONS(1933, Brit.); HELL AND HIGH WATER(1933), w; I COVER THE WATERFRONT(1933), w; FRIDAY THE 13TH(1934, Brit.); THINGS ARE LOOK-ING UP(1934, Brit.); GET OFF MY FOOT(1935, Brit.); PRINCESS CHARMING(1935, Brit.); EDUCATED EVANS(1936, Brit.); DON'T GET ME WRONG(1937, Brit.); TAKE IT FROM ME(1937, Brit.); EVERYTHING HAPPENS TO ME(1938, Brit.); THANK EVANS(1938, Brit.); GOOD OLD DAYS, THE(1939, Brit.); HOOTS MON!(1939, Brit.); ASKING FOR TROUBLE(1942, Brit.); SECRET OF DEEP HARBOR(1961), w

Maxine Miller
RIP-OFF(1971, Can.); OUTRAGEOUS!(1977, Can.)

Melissa Miller
OH GOD! BOOK II(1980), w

Merle Miller
RAINS OF RANCHIPUR, THE(1955), w; KINGS GO FORTH(1958), w; TANK FORCE(1958, Brit.), w
Misc. Talkies
CAREER BED(1972)

Michael Miller
IRON MAJOR, THE(1943); ADVENTURES OF MARK TWAIN, THE(1944); PRACTI-CALLY YOURS(1944); INVISIBLE BOY, THE(1957); MEN IN WAR(1957); WOMEN OF PITCAIRN ISLAND, THE(1957); ROOMMATES(1962, Brit.); EYE OF THE DE-VIL(1967, Brit.); CHARGE OF THE LIGHT BRIGADE, THE(1968, Brit.); ANDERSON TAPES, THE(1971); DOC SAVAGE... THE MAN OF BRONZE(1975); SWITCHBLADE SISTERS(1975); THREE DAYS OF THE CONDOR(1975); FRONT, THE(1976); JACK-SON COUNTY JAIL(1976), d; SUMMER SCHOOL TEACHERS(1977); RICH KIDS(1979); SATURDAY THE 14TH(1981); NATIONAL LAMPOON'S CLASS REUN-ION(1982), d; SILENT RAGE(1982), d; SPACE RAIDERS(1983)
1984
HARDBODIES(1984)

Misc. Talkies
STREET GIRLS(1975), d; OUTSIDE CHANCE(1978), d

Michael B. Miller
ONE SUMMER LOVE(1976)

Michael R. Miller
MARRIAGE, A(1983), ed

Mike Miller
UNHOLY ROLLERS(1972); THIEVES(1977), m; I, THE JURY(1982)

Mindi Miller
1984
BODY DOUBLE(1984); SACRED GROUND(1984)

Mirta Miller
DRACULA'S GREAT LOVE(1972, Span.); BATTLE OF THE AMAZONS(1973, Ital./Span.); SANTO CONTRA EL DOCTOR MUERTE(1974, Span./Mex.)
1984
BOLERO(1984)

Mirtha Miller
NO EXIT(1962, U.S./Arg.)

Mitch Miller
SENIOR PROM(1958); LONGEST DAY, THE(1962), md

Mollie Miller
LOUISIANA(1947)

Morris Miller
DEEP SIX, THE(1958); STAKEOUT ON DOPE STREET(1958)

Murray Miller
Silents
WESTERN DEMON, A(1922)

Nancy Miller
STORY OF MANKIND, THE(1957)

Nat Miller
SECRET TENT, THE(1956, Brit.), p

Nolan Miller
HARLOW(1965), cos; HOW TO COMMIT MARRIAGE(1969), cos; MR. MOM(1983), cos

Norma Miller
SPARKLE(1976)

Pae Miller
SHENANDOAH(1965)

Pamela Miller
TWO HUNDRED MOTELS(1971, Brit.); PARADISE ALLEY(1978)
Misc. Talkies
KITTY CAN'T HELP IT(1975); CARHOPS(1980)

Pat Miller
BIG HEAT, THE(1953); WORLD IN MY CORNER(1956); I WAS A TEENAGE FRANKENSTEIN(1958); MAN IN THE NET, THE(1959); CAGE OF EVIL(1960)

Patricia Miller
SEALED VERDICT(1948); FATHER OF THE BRIDE(1950); LOVE NEST(1951)

Patrick Miller
MISTER 880(1950); FROM HERE TO ETERNITY(1953); DRIVE A CROOKED ROAD(1954); MA AND PA KETTLE AT HOME(1954); PHFFFT!(1954); TIGHT SPOT(1955); SING, BOY, SING(1958)

Patsy Ruth Miller
MARRIAGE BY CONTRACT(1928); AVIATOR, THE(1929); FALL OF EVE, THE(1929); HOTTENTOT, THE(1929); SAP, THE(1929); SO LONG LETTY(1929); TWIN BEDS(1929); WHISPERING WINDS(1929); LAST OF THE LONE WOLF(1930); WIDE OPEN(1930); LONELY WIVES(1931); NIGHT BEAT(1932); QUEBEC(1951)
Silents
SHEIK, THE(1921); HANDLE WITH CARE(1922); WATCH YOUR STEP(1922); HUNCHBACK OF NOTRE DAME, THE(1923); SOULS FOR SALE(1923); BREAKING POINT, THE(1924); DAUGHTERS OF TODAY(1924); GIRL ON THE STAIRS, THE(1924); ROSE OF THE WORLD(1925); SINGER JIM MCKEE(1924); BROKEN HEARTS OF HOLLYWOOD(1926); FIGHTING EDGE(1926); KING OF THE TURF, THE(1926); OH, WHAT A NURSE!(1926); PRIVATE IZZY MURPHY(1926); SO THIS IS PARIS(1926); WHITE BLACK SHEEP(1926); PAINTING THE TOWN(1927); WHAT EVERY GIRL SHOULD KNOW(1927); WOLF'S CLOTHING(1927); BEAUTI-FUL BUT DUMB(1928); GATE CRASHER, THE(1928); TRAGEDY OF YOUTH, THE(1928)
Misc. Silents
FIGHTING STREAK, THE(1922); FOR BIG STAKES(1922); FORTUNE'S MASK(1922); REMEMBRANCE(1922); TRIMMED(1922); WHERE IS MY WANDER-ING BOY TONIGHT?(1922); DRIVIN' FOOL, THE(1923); GIRL I LOVED(1923); BREATH OF A SCANDAL, THE(1924); FOOLS IN THE DARK(1924); GIRLS MEN FORGET(1924); MY MAN(1924); SELF-MADE FAILURE, A(1924); THOSE WHO JUDGE(1924); WISE VIRGIN, THE(1924); YANKEE CONSUL, THE(1924); BACK TO LIFE(1925); HEAD WINDS(1925); HER HUSBAND'S SECRET(1925); HOGAN'S AL-LEY(1925); LORRAINE OF THE LIONS(1925); RED HOT TIRES(1925); FIGHTING EDGE, THE(1926); HELL-BENT FOR HEAVEN(1926); WHY GIRLS GO BACK HO-ME(1926); FIRST AUTO, THE(1927); HERO FOR A NIGHT, A(1927); ONCE AND FOREVER(1927); SHANGHAIED(1927); SOUTH SEA LOVE(1927); HOT HEELS(1928); MARRIAGE BY CONRACT(1928); RED RIDERS OF CANADA(1928); TROPICAL NIGHTS(1928); WE AMERICANS(1928)

Paul Miller
NIGHTMARE CASTLE(1966, Ital.); PONTIUS PILATE(1967, Fr./Ital.)

Pearl Miller
PLACE IN THE SUN, A(1951)

Peck Miller
Misc. Silents
SKY-EYE(1920)

Peggy Miller
EXPERIMENT PERILOUS(1944); SENTIMENTAL JOURNEY(1946); PUR-SUED(1947); DIARY OF A HIGH SCHOOL BRIDE(1959)

Peter Miller
BLACKBOARD JUNGLE, THE(1955); REBEL WITHOUT A CAUSE(1955); CRIME IN THE STREETS(1956); FORBIDDEN PLANET(1956); STRANGE ADVENTURE, A(1956); TEA AND SYMPATHY(1956); DELINQUENTS, THE(1957); IRON SHERIFF, THE(1957); HANDLE WITH CARE(1958); DR. BLOOD'S COFFIN(1961), w; MARINES, LET'S GO(1961); MARY HAD A LITTLE(1961, Brit.), w; THREE ON A SPREE(1961, Brit.), w; MAN IN THE DARK(1963, Brit.), w; FOOLS' PARADE(1971); DIAGNOSIS: MURDER(1974, Brit.), p; IN-LAWS, THE(1979)

Philip Miller
DRACULA A.D. 1972(1972, Brit.); HOW TO BEAT THE HIGH COST OF LIVING(1980)
Pip Miller
RETURN OF THE JEDI(1983)
Pola Miller
RICH AND FAMOUS(1981)
Quentin Miller
SNAKE PEOPLE, THE(1968, Mex./U.S.)
R.G. Miller
FIRST BLOOD(1982)
Ralph Miller
MISSION MARS(1968)
Ray Miller
BOWERY AT MIDNIGHT(1942); TOMORROW WE LIVE(1942); BACKGROUND TO DANGER(1943); HI'YA, CHUM(1943); KID DYNAMITE(1943)
Richard Miller
GUNSLINGER(1956); IT CONQUERED THE WORLD(1956); NAKED PARADISE(1957); CAPTURE THAT CAPSULE(1961); "X"-THE MAN WITH THE X-RAY EYES(1963); GIRLS ON THE BEACH(1965); WHICH WAY TO THE FRONT?(1970), w; YOUNG NURSES, THE(1973); 1941(1979)
Misc. Talkies
SPY SQUAD(1962)
Richard "Dick" Miller
OKLAHOMA WOMAN, THE(1956); PREMATURE BURIAL, THE(1962); TERROR, THE(1963)
Richard Drout Miller
SPECIAL DELIVERY(1976)
Lt. Col. Robert Miller
STORY OF G.I. JOE, THE(1945), tech adv
Robert Miller
LILITH(1964); FOR LOVE OF IVY(1968); INCREDIBLE TWO-HEADED TRANSPLANT, THE(1971)
Robert Alan Miller
WESTWARD TRAIL, THE(1948), w
Robert Ellis Miller
ANY WEDNESDAY(1966), d; HEART IS A LONELY HUNTER, THE(1968), d; SWEET NOVEMBER(1968), d; BUTTERCUP CHAIN, THE(1971, Brit.), d; GIRL FROM PETROVKA, THE(1974), d; BALTIMORE BULLET, THE(1980), d; REUBEN, REUBEN(1983), d
Robert Wiley Miller
DEATH IN SMALL DOSES(1957), m
Robin Miller
PSYCHOMANIA(1964), w
Roger Miller
ROBIN HOOD(1973)
Roland F. Miller
1984
COUNTRY(1984)
Rolf Miller
MC HALE'S NAVY JOINS THE AIR FORCE(1965), makeup; SHENANDOAH(1965), makeup; WILD, WILD WINTER(1966), makeup; PAPER MOON(1973), makeup
Roma Miller
CAESAR AND CLEOPATRA(1946, Brit.); TOO YOUNG TO LOVE(1960, Brit.)
Ron Miller
BEATNIKS, THE(1960), p; SON OF FLUBBER(1963), p; SUMMER MAGIC(1963), p; LIVELY SET, THE(1964); MISADVENTURES OF MERLIN JONES, THE(1964), p; MONKEY'S UNCLE, THE(1965), p; THAT DARN CAT(1965), p; LT. ROBIN CRUSOE, U.S.N.(1966), p; MONKEYS, GO HOME!(1967), p; GUNS IN THE HEATHER(1968, Brit.), p; NEVER A DULL MOMENT(1968), p; RIDE A NORTHBOUND HORSE(1969), p; BOATNIKS, THE(1970), p; WILD COUNTRY, THE(1971), p; NOW YOU SEE HIM, NOW YOU DON'T(1972), p; SNOWBALL EXPRESS(1972), p; CASTAWAY COWBOY, THE(1974), p; FREAKY FRIDAY(1976), p; GUS(1976), p; NO DEPOSIT, NO RETURN(1976), p; HERBIE GOES TO MONTE CARLO(1977), p; LITTLEST HORSE THIEVES, THE(1977), p; PETE'S DRAGON(1977), p; CANDLESHOE(1978), p; CAT FROM OUTER SPACE, THE(1978), p; HOT LEAD AND COLD FEET(1978), p; RETURN FROM WITCH MOUNTAIN(1978), p; APPLE DUMPLING GANG RIDES AGAIN, THE(1979), p; BLACK HOLE, THE(1979), p; NORTH AVENUE IRREGULARS, THE(1979), p; UNIDENTIFIED FLYING ODDBALL, THE(1979, Brit.), p; HERBIE GOES BANANAS(1980), p; LAST FLIGHT OF NOAH'S ARK, THE(1980), p; MIDNIGHT MADNESS(1980), p; WATCHER IN THE WOODS, THE(1980, Brit.), p
Ronald Miller
ROSE MARIE(1954), w
Rosalie Miller
THEY ALL KISSED THE BRIDE(1942)
Rosemary Miller
LIFE IN EMERGENCY WARD 10(1959, Brit.); CONRACK(1974)
Roy Miller
AUNT CLARA(1954, Brit.), w
Ruby Miller
SORRELL AND SON(1934, Brit.); DICTATOR, THE(1935, Brit./Ger.); RIGHT AGE TO MARRY, THE(1935, Brit.); GAY OLD DOG(1936, Brit.); NOTHING LIKE PUBLICITY(1936, Brit.); DOUBLE EXPOSURES(1937, Brit.); COMING OF AGE(1938, Brit.); SHADOWED EYES(1939, Brit.); LAW AND DISORDER(1940, Brit.); FACING THE MUSIC(1941, Brit.); HUNDRED POUND WINDOW, THE(1943, Brit.); TWILIGHT HOUR(1944, Brit.); ANNA KARENINA(1948, Brit.)
Silents
EDGE O'BEYOND(1919, Brit.); MYSTERY OF MR. BERNARD BROWN(1921, Brit.); ALIMONY(1924); LAND OF HOPE AND GLORY(1927, Brit.)
Misc. Silents
IN ANOTHER GIRL'S SHOES(1917, Brit.); LITTLE WOMEN(1917, Brit.); GAMBLERS ALL(1919, Brit.); MYSTERY ROAD, THE(1921, Brit.); INFAMOUS LADY, THE(1928, Brit.)
Ruth Miller
COME BACK TO THE 5 & DIME, JIMMY DEAN, JIMMY DEAN(1982)
1984
HARD CHOICES(1984)
Silents
AFFAIRS OF ANATOL, THE(1921)

Sarah Miller
WRESTLER, THE(1974)
Scott Miller
RUN LIKE A THIEF(1968, Span.); PLAY DIRTY(1969, Brit.); OPEN SEASON(1974, U.S./Span.)
Selwyn Emerson Miller
JEKYLL AND HYDE...TOGETHER AGAIN(1982)
Seton I. Miller
AIR CIRCUS, THE(1928), w; DAWN PATROL, THE(1930), w; HARMONY AT HOME(1930), w; LONE STAR RANGER, THE(1930), w; TODAY(1930), w; CRIMINAL CODE(1931), w; CROWD ROARS, THE(1932), w; HOT SATURDAY(1932), w; IF I HAD A MILLION(1932), w; LAST MILE, THE(1932), w; ONCE IN A LIFETIME(1932), w; SCARFACE(1932), w; EAGLE AND THE HAWK, THE(1933), w; GAMBLING SHIP(1933), w; MASTER OF MEN(1933), w; MIDNIGHT CLUB(1933), w; MURDERS IN THE ZOO(1933), w; CHARLIE CHAN'S COURAGE(1934), w; MURDER IN TRINIDAD(1934), w; ST. LOUIS KID, THE(1934), w; FRISCO KID(1935), w; G-MEN(1935), w; IT HAPPENED IN NEW YORK(1935), w; MURDER ON A HONEYMOON(1935), w; BULLETS OR BALLOTS(1936), w; LEATHERNECKS HAVE LANDED, THE(1936), w; TWO IN THE DARK(1936), w; KID GALAHAD(1937), w; MARKED WOMAN(1937), w; ADVENTURES OF ROBIN HOOD, THE(1938), w; DAWN PATROL, THE(1938), w; PENITENTIARY(1938), w; VALLEY OF THE GIANTS(1938), w; CASTLE ON THE HUDSON(1940), w; SEA HAWK, THE(1940), w; HERE COMES MR. JORDAN(1941), w; THIS WOMAN IS MINE(1941), w; BLACK SWAN, THE(1942), w; MY GAL SAL(1942), w; MINISTRY OF FEAR(1945), p, w; BRIDE WORE BOOTS, THE(1946), p; CALIFORNIA(1946), p; TWO YEARS BEFORE THE MAST(1946), p, w; CALCUTTA(1947), p, w; SINGAPORE(1947), w; FIGHTER SQUADRON(1948), p, w; CONVICTED(1950), w; MAN WHO CHEATED HIMSELF, THE(1951), w; QUEEN FOR A DAY(1951), w; MISSISSIPPI GAMBLER, THE(1953), w; BENGAL BRIGADE(1954), w; SHANGHAI STORY, THE(1954), w; ISTANBUL(1957), w; LAST MILE, THE(1959), w; CONFESSIONS OF AN OPIUM EATER(1962), w; PETE'S DRAGON(1977), w
Silents
GIRL IN EVERY PORT, A(1928), w; FAR CALL, THE(1929), w
Sharon Miller
GUARDIAN OF THE WILDERNESS(1977), ed; TRUE CONFESSIONS(1981)
Sharron Miller
LITTLE SEX, A(1982)
Misc. Talkies
ALIEN ZONE(1978), d
Sheila Miller
TOUCH OF THE OTHER, A(1970, Brit.), p
Sherie Miller
Misc. Talkies
GOIN' ALL THE WAY(1982)
Shorty Miller
MOONLIGHT ON THE RANGE(1937); TROUBLE IN TEXAS(1937)
Sid Miller
MARY STEVENS, M.D.(1933); FOR PETE'S SAKE(1977)
Sidney Miller
THREE ON A MATCH(1932); MAYOR OF HELL, THE(1933); BAND PLAYS ON, THE(1934); BIG SHAKEDOWN, THE(1934); HI, NELLIE!(1934); RAFTER ROMANCE(1934); WHEN STRANGERS MEET(1934); DINKY(1935); ONE HOUR LATE(1935); LITTLE RED SCHOOLHOUSE(1936); PICCADILLY JIM(1936); BOYS TOWN(1938); CIPHER BUREAU(1938); RECKLESS LIVING(1938); ANDY HARDY GETS SPRING FEVER(1939); STREETS OF NEW YORK(1939); WHAT A LIFE(1939); 20,000 MEN A YEAR(1939); GOLDEN GLOVES(1940); STRIKE UP THE BAND(1940); CITY, FOR CONQUEST(1941); LIFE BEGINS FOR ANDY HARDY(1941); MEN OF BOYS TOWN(1941); ALIAS BOSTON BLACKIE(1942); GET HEP TO LOVE(1942); MADAME SPY(1942); GIRL CRAZY(1943); HERE COMES KELLY(1943); MOONLIGHT IN VERMONT(1943); BABES ON SWING STREET(1944); HI, GOOD-LOOKIN'(1944); HOT RHYTHM(1944); ON STAGE EVERYBODY(1945); PATRICK THE GREAT(1945); PENTHOUSE RHYTHM(1945), m; SHE GETS HER MAN(1945); THERE GOES KELLY(1945); LUCKY STIFF, THE(1949); SNIPER, THE(1952); WALKING MY BABY BACK HOME(1953); THIRTY FOOT BRIDE OF CANDY ROCK, THE(1959), d; EXPERIMENT IN TERROR(1962); GET YOURSELF A COLLEGE GIRL(1964), d; TAMMY AND THE MILLIONAIRE(1967), d; WHICH WAY TO THE FRONT?(1970); EVERYTHING YOU ALWAYS WANTED TO KNOW ABOUT SEX, BUT WE'RE AFRAID TO ASK(1972); WORLD'S GREATEST LOVER, THE(1977); STAR 80(1983)
Sigmund Miller
PORTRAIT IN SMOKE(1957, Brit.), w; JET STORM(1961, Brit.), w
Skins Miller
GIFT OF GAB(1934); STAND UP AND CHEER(1934 80m FOX bw); MEN OF SAN QUENTIN(1942)
"Snuffy" Miller
HONEYMOON OF HORROR(1964)
Sonny Miller
MURDER IN REVERSE(1946, Brit.)
Stanley Miller
SON OF A STRANGER(1957, Brit.), w; SYMPTOMS(1976, Brit.), w
Stephan E. Miller
GREY FOX, THE(1983, Can.)
Stephanie Miller
HOG WILD(1980, Can.); HAPPY BIRTHDAY TO ME(1981)
Stephen Miller
HOG WILD(1980, Can.), w; MY BLOODY VALENTINE(1981, Can.), p; FUNERAL HOME(1982, Can.)
1984
RUNAWAY(1984)
Stephen E. Miller
1984
ICEMAN(1984)
Steve Miller
ROAR(1981)
Steve "Monk" Miller
TOUGH ENOUGH(1983)
Steven K. Miller
1984
IRRECONCILABLE DIFFERENCES(1984)

Stuart Miller
BIRDMAN OF ALCATRAZ(1962), p
Sue Miller
FINAL TERROR, THE(1983), cos
Susan Miller
MIRACLE ON MAIN STREET, A(1940); NEVER GIVE A SUCKER AN EVEN BREAK(1941); SWING IT SOLDIER(1941); YOU'RE TELLING ME(1942); DON'T TRUST YOUR HUSBAND(1948); SLEEPER(1973)
T.W. Miller
ON THE RIGHT TRACK(1981)
Tallulah Miller
HANDS OF ORLAC, THE(1964, Brit./Fr.); HANDS OF THE RIPPER(1971, Brit.)
Terry Miller
1984
HARRY AND SON(1984)
Tex Miller
DESERT MESA(1935)
Thomas L. Miller
SILVER STREAK(1976), p; FOUL PLAY(1978), p
Thomas Miller
EXILES, THE(1966), ed; YEAR OF THE HORSE, THE(1966), w; BEST LITTLE WHOREHOUSE IN TEXAS, THE(1982), p
Todd Miller
GIRL MOST LIKELY, THE(1957)
Tom Miller
OLD-FASHIONED WAY, THE(1934)
Tom Miller, Jr.
TWIST ALL NIGHT(1961), makeup
Tony Miller
ATTACK OF THE CRAB MONSTERS(1957); T-BIRD GANG(1959), a, w; RETURN TO PEYTON PLACE(1961); S.O.B.(1981)
1984
LIES(1984, Brit.)
Tuesday Miller
O LUCKY MAN!(1973, Brit.)
Valerie Miller
RIDE THE HIGH WIND(1967, South Africa)
Vernal Miller
ON THE RIVERA(1951)
Vicki Miller
CRAZY QUILT, THE(1966)
Victor Miller
SEVENTEEN(1940), ph; FRIDAY THE 13TH(1980), w; FRIDAY THE 13TH PART II(1981), w; FRIDAY THE 13TH PART III(1982), w; STRANGER IS WATCHING, A(1982), w
1984
FRIDAY THE 13TH-THE FINAL CHAPTER(1984), w
Virgil Miller
GANG WAR(1928), ph; PHANTOM OF THE OPERA, THE(1929), ph; DRIFT FENCE(1936), ph; COURAGE OF THE WEST(1937), ph; DANGER–LOVE AT WORK(1937), ph; FIND THE WITNESS(1937), ph; SINGING OUTLAW(1937), ph; THANK YOU, MR. MOTO(1937), ph; MR. MOTO TAKES A CHANCE(1938), ph; MYSTERIOUS MR. MOTO(1938), ph; TIME OUT FOR MURDER(1938), ph; WALKING DOWN BROADWAY(1938), ph; CHARLIE CHAN AT TREASURE ISLAND(1939), ph; CHARLIE CHAN IN RENO(1939), ph; CHARLIE CHAN IN THE CITY OF DARKNESS(1939), ph; CHASING DANGER(1939), ph; HONEYMOON'S OVER, THE(1939), ph; INSIDE STORY(1939), ph; MR. MOTO'S LAST WARNING(1939), ph; CHARLIE CHAN AT THE WAX MUSEUM(1940), ph; CHARLIE CHAN IN PANAMA(1940), ph; CHARLIE CHAN'S MURDER CRUISE(1940), ph; MAN WHO WOULDN'T TALK, THE(1940), ph; MANHATTAN HEARTBEAT(1940), ph; MURDER OVER NEW YORK(1940), ph; PIER 13(1940), ph; JENNIE(1941), ph; MAN AT LARGE(1941), ph; PRIVATE NURSE(1941), ph; RIDE, KELLY, RIDE(1941), ph; SCOTLAND YARD(1941), ph; SMALL TOWN DEB(1941), ph; BERLIN CORRESPONDENT(1942), ph; CASTLE IN THE DESERT(1942), ph; DR. RENAULT'S SECRET(1942), ph; RIGHT TO THE HEART(1942), ph; WHO IS HOPE SCHUYLER?(1942), ph; CALLING DR. DEATH(1943), ph; MUMMY'S CURSE, THE(1944), ph; PEARL OF DEATH, THE(1944), ph; WEIRD WOMAN(1944), ph; FALCON IN SAN FRANCISCO, THE(1945), ph; HOUSE OF FEAR, THE(1945), ph; WOMAN IN GREEN, THE(1945), ph; BIG FIX, THE(1947), ph; MICHIGAN KID, THE(1947), ph; RED STALLION, THE(1947), ph; VIGILANTES RETURN, THE(1947), ph; STREET CORNER(1948), ph; MURDER WITHOUT TEARS(1953), ph; MISS ROBIN CRUSOE(1954), ph; I KILLED WILD BILL HICKOK(1956), ph
Silents
PINK TIGHTS(1920), ph; CHEATED HEARTS(1921), ph; RIDIN' WILD(1922), ph; SCRAPPER, THE(1922), ph; TRAP, THE(1922), ph; KINDLED COURAGE(1923), ph; NOBODY'S BRIDE(1923), ph; OUT OF LUCK(1923), ph; SCARLET CAR, THE(1923), ph; SHOOTIN' FOR LOVE(1923), ph; HOOK AND LADDER(1924), ph; RIDE FOR YOUR LIFE(1924), ph; SAWDUST TRAIL(1924), ph; HURRICANE KID, THE(1925), ph; LET 'ER BUCK(1925), ph; PHANTOM OF THE OPERA, THE(1925), ph; BROKEN HEARTS OF HOLLYWOOD(1926), ph; PRIVATE IZZY MURPHY(1926), ph; GAY OLD BIRD, THE(1927), ph; IRISH HEARTS(1927), ph; ALEX THE GREAT(1928), ph; CAPTAIN CARELESS(1928), ph; STOCKS AND BLONDES(1928), ph; YOUNG WHIRLWIND(1928), ph; AMAZING VAGABOND(1929), ph; LITTLE SAVAGE, THE(1929), ph; PALS OF THE PRAIRIE(1929), ph
Virgil E. Miller
NAVAJO(1952), ph; CRAZYLEGS, ALL AMERICAN(1953), ph; UNCHAINED(1955), ph
W. Chrystie Miller
Silents
JUDITH OF BETHULIA(1914)
Wade Miller
GUILTY BYSTANDER(1950), w; KITTEN WITH A WHIP(1964), w
Walter Miller
ROGUE OF THE RIO GRANDE(1930); ROUGH WATERS(1930); UTAH KID, THE(1930); HURRICANE HORSEMAN(1931); MANHATTAN PARADE(1931); SKY RAIDERS(1931); STREET SCENE(1931); BLESSED EVENT(1932); FACE ON THE BARROOM FLOOR, THE(1932); FAMOUS FERGUSON CASE, THE(1932); GHOST CITY(1932); HEART PUNCH(1932); RIDIN' FOR JUSTICE(1932); THREE WISE GIRLS(1932); PARACHUTE JUMPER(1933); SON OF A SAILOR(1933); GUN JUSTICE(1934); ROCKY RHODES(1934); SMOKING GUNS(1934); FIGHTING TROOPER,

THE(1935); IVORY-HANDLED GUN(1935); LIVING ON VELVET(1935); MAGNIFICENT OBSESSION(1935); RAVEN, THE(1935); STORMY(1935); CHINA CLIPPER(1936); DESERT GOLD(1936); FUGITIVE SHERIFF, THE(1936); GHOST PATROL(1936); NIGHT CARGO(1936); NIGHT WAITRESS(1936); PAROLE(1936); WITHOUT ORDERS(1936); BORDER CAFE(1937); BOSS OF LONELY VALLEY(1937); DANGER PATROL(1937); DRAEGERMAN COURAGE(1937); FLIGHT FROM GLORY(1937); HEART OF THE WEST(1937); LAST GANGSTER, THE(1937); MAN WHO CRIED WOLF, THE(1937); MIDNIGHT COURT(1937); RANGER COURAGE(1937); SATURDAY'S HEROES(1937); SINGING MARINE, THE(1937); SLIM(1937); SUBMARINE D-1(1937); BLIND ALIBI(1938); COME ON, LEATHERNECKS(1938); CRIME RING(1938); DOWN IN ARKANSAW(1938); INTERNATIONAL SETTLEMENT(1938); KENTUCKY(1938); LAWLESS VALLEY(1938); SERGEANT MURPHY(1938); SMASHING THE RACKETS(1938); TOO HOT TO HANDLE(1938); WILD HORSE RODEO(1938); EACH DAWN I DIE(1939); HOME ON THE PRAIRIE(1939); WINGS OF THE NAVY(1939); BULLET CODE(1940); CASTLE ON THE HUDSON(1940); CHARLIE CHAN'S MURDER CRUISE(1940); GAUCHO SERENADE(1940); GRANDPA GOES TO TOWN(1940); GRAPES OF WRATH(1940); ISLAND OF DOOMED MEN(1940); JOHNNY APOLLO(1940); SAINT'S DOUBLE TROUBLE, THE(1940); THREE CHEERS FOR THE IRISH(1940); 'TIL WE MEET AGAIN(1940); VIRGINIA CITY(1940); SABOTEUR(1942)
Misc. Talkies
HELL'S VALLEY(1931); SWANEE RIVER(1931); VALLEY OF WANTED MEN(1935)
Silents
TIE THAT BINDS, THE(1923); PLAYTHINGS OF DESIRE(1924); MANHATTAN KNIGHTS(1928)
Misc. Silents
FAMILY STAIN, THE(1915); HUMAN ORCHID, THE(1916); MARBLE HEART, THE(1916); SPIDER AND THE FLY, THE(1916); WIFE'S SACRIFICE, A(1916); DRAFT 258(1917); MOTHER'S ORDEAL, A(1917); TANGLED LIVES(1917); WITH NEATNESS AND DISPATCH(1918); GIRL AT BAY, A(1919); INVISIBLE DIVORCE, THE(1920); RETURN OF TARZAN, THE(1920); WAY WOMEN LOVE, THE(1920); LUXURY(1921); SHADOW, THE(1921); BOOTLEGGERS, THE(1922); TILL WE MEET AGAIN(1922); UNCONQUERED WOMAN(1922); WOMAN WHO BELIEVED, THE(1922); MEN, WOMEN AND MONEY(1924); SKY RAIDER, THE(1925); FIGHTING MARINE, THE(1926); UNFAIR SEX, THE(1926); HAWK OF THE HILLS(1929)
Walter C. Miller
Misc. Silents
MISS ROBINSON CRUSOE(1917); SLACKER, THE(1917)
Walter Chrystie Miller
Misc. Silents
LORD CHUMLEY(1914)
Walter Elias Miller
SON OF FLUBBER(1963)
Warren Miller
COOL WORLD, THE(1963), w; WAY WE LIVE NOW, THE(1970), w; RENEGADE GIRLS(1974); CRAZY MAMA(1975); OTHER SIDE OF THE MOUNTAIN, THE(1975); TWO-MINUTE WARNING(1976)
1984
HARD TO HOLD(1984)
Wendy Miller
1984
ELECTRIC DREAMS(1984)
William Miller
WORDS AND MUSIC(1929); MOONLIGHT AND PRETZELS(1933), ph; SWEET SURRENDER(1935), ph; TANGO BAR(1935), ph; GREEN FIELDS(1937), ph; ONE THIRD OF A NATION(1939), ph; CARNEGIE HALL(1947), ph; CLOSE-UP(1948), ph; SLEEPING CITY, THE(1950), ph
Silents
JOY GIRL, THE(1927), ph; ONE SPLENDID HOUR(1929), ph
William E. Miller
ENLIGHTEN THY DAUGHTER(1934), ph
William J. Miller
DYNAMITE DELANEY(1938), ph; LOST BOUNDARIES(1949), ph; TERESA(1951), ph
Silents
DREAM MELODY, THE(1929), ph
Wilson Miller
HAREM GIRL(1952)
Winkie Miller
GOING HOME(1971)
Winston Miller
GONE WITH THE WIND(1939), w; CAROLINA MOON(1940), w; RIDE, TENDERFOOT, RIDE(1940), w; MEDICO OF PAINTED SPRINGS, THE(1941), w; PRAIRIE STRANGER(1941), w; ROYAL MOUNTED PATROL, THE(1941), w; MAN FROM CHEYENNE(1942), w; GOOD MORNING, JUDGE(1943), w; SONG OF TEXAS(1943), w; DOUBLE EXPOSURE(1944), w; HOME IN INDIANA(1944), w; ONE BODY TOO MANY(1944), w; FOLLOW THAT WOMAN(1945), w; MY DARLING CLEMENTINE(1946), w; THEY MADE ME A KILLER(1946), w; DANGER STREET(1947), w; FURY AT FURNACE CREEK(1948), w; RELENTLESS(1948), w; STATION WEST(1948), w; ROCKY MOUNTAIN(1950), w; TRIPOLI(1950), w; HONG KONG(1951), w; LAST OUTPOST, THE(1951), w; BLAZING FOREST, THE(1952), w; CARSON CITY(1952), w; VANQUISHED, THE(1953), w; BOUNTY HUNTER, THE(1954), w; BOY FROM OKLAHOMA, THE(1954), w; JIVARO(1954), w; FAR HORIZONS, THE(1955), w; LUCY GALLANT(1955), w; RUN FOR COVER(1955), w; TENSION AT TABLE ROCK(1956), w; APRIL LOVE(1957), w; ESCAPADE IN JAPAN(1957), w; MARDI GRAS(1958), w; HOUND-DOG MAN(1959), w; PRIVATE'S AFFAIR, A(1959), w
Silents
LITTLE CHURCH AROUND THE CORNER(1923); IRON HORSE, THE(1924); MAN AND MAID(1925); STELLA DALLAS(1925)
Miller Brothers and Lola
HI-DE-HO(1947)
Nancy Miller-Corwin
WEREWOLF OF WASHINGTON(1973), art d
Susan Miller-Kovens
1984
MUPPETS TAKE MANHATTAN, THE(1984)

Don Miller-Robinson
MONKEY GRIP(1983, Aus.)

John Millerburg
YOU LIGHT UP MY LIFE(1977)

John Millerta
Silents
GOLD RUSH, THE(1925); UNHOLY THREE, THE(1925)

Arthur Millet
COUNTY FAIR, THE(1932); HIDDEN VALLEY(1932); HONOR OF THE MOUNTED(1932); WIDOW IN SCARLET(1932); STOLEN HARMONY(1935); GREAT O'MALLEY, THE(1937)
Silents
WOLF'S CLOTHING(1927)

Christiane Millet
BIRD WATCH, THE(1983, Fr.)

Creusa Millet
WILD PACK, THE(1972)

Nefti Millet
CHANGE OF HABIT(1969)

Mallory Millet-Jones
Misc. Talkies
THREE LIVES(1971)

Carl Milletaire
DOUBLE LIFE, A(1947); KISS OF DEATH(1947); NAKED CITY, THE(1948); BLACK HAND, THE(1950); SPY HUNT(1950); 711 OCEAN DRIVE(1950); FATHER TAKES THE AIR(1951); GREAT CARUSO, THE(1951); BAL TABARIN(1952); SINGIN' IN THE RAIN(1952); YOUNG MAN WITH IDEAS(1952); HOT NEWS(1953); SIREN OF BAGDAD(1953); ADVENTURES OF HAJJI BABA(1954); KNOCK ON WOOD(1954); FIGHTING CHANCE, THE(1955); NEW YORK CONFIDENTIAL(1955); PURPLE MASK, THE(1955); WILD PARTY, THE(1956); JAILHOUSE ROCK(1957); SHADOW ON THE WINDOW, THE(1957); INSIDE THE MAFIA(1959); NORTH BY NORTHWEST(1959); TRAP, THE(1959); MUSIC BOX KID, THE(1960); DANGEROUS CHARTER(1962)

A. N. Millett
Silents
ALIAS MARY BROWN(1918)

Arthur Millett
NO LIVING WITNESS(1932); WESTERN LIMITED(1932); MISSISSIPPI(1935); FUGITIVE SHERIFF, THE(1936); LION'S DEN, THE(1936); WINDS OF THE WASTELAND(1936)
Silents
KING SPRUCE(1920); BROKEN DOLL, A(1921); GAY AND DEVILISH(1922); TRACKED TO EARTH(1922); AMERICAN MANNERS(1924); CRIMSON RUNNER, THE(1925); SHOOTIN' IRONS(1927)
Misc. Silents
HUMANIZING MR. WINSBY(1916); HIDDEN SPRING, THE(1917); SHIP OF DOOM, THE(1917); GOOD LOSER, THE(1918); SEA PANTHER, THE(1918); STATION CONTENT(1918); DRAG HARLAN(1920); HEARTS UP!(1920)

Arthur N. Millett
Misc. Silents
LAND JUST OVER YONDER, THE(1916)

Arthur Millette
BITTER TEA OF GENERAL YEN, THE(1933)

Irvine H. Millgate
BLOB, THE(1958), w

Bertram Millhauser
CONSPIRACY(1930), p; LADY REFUSES, THE(1931), p; SMART WOMAN(1931), p; THREE WHO LOVED(1931), p; STORM AT DAYBREAK(1933), w; COLLEGE SCANDAL(1935), w; CRIME NOBOBY SAW, THE(1937), w; SCANDAL STREET(1938), w; NICK CARTER, MASTER DETECTIVE(1939), w; THEY MADE ME A CRIMINAL(1939), w; 6000 ENEMIES(1939), w; ANGEL FROM TEXAS, AN(1940), w; RIVER'S END(1940), w; BIG SHOT, THE(1942), w; PIERRE OF THE PLAINS(1942), w; SWEATER GIRL(1942), w; PURPLE V, THE(1943), w; SHERLOCK HOLMES FACES DEATH(1943), w; SHERLOCK HOLMES IN WASHINGTON(1943), w; ENTER ARSENE LUPIN(1944), w; INVISIBLE MAN'S REVENGE(1944), w; PEARL OF DEATH, THE(1944), w; SHERLOCK HOLMES AND THE SPIDER WOMAN(1944), w; PATRICK THE GREAT(1945), w; WOMAN IN GREEN, THE(1945), w; WHITE TIE AND TAILS(1946), w; WALK A CROOKED MILE(1948), w; TOKYO JOE(1949), w; PAY OR DIE(1960), w
Silents
CODE OF THE SEA(1924), w; LEOPARD LADY, THE(1928), p; GIRLS GONE WILD(1929), w

Bertrand Millhauser
TEXANS, THE(1938), w

Bruce Millholland
SO FINE(1981)

Ray Millholland
GIRL FROM GOD'S COUNTRY(1940), w

James Millhollin
EVERYTHING'S DUCKY(1961); GYPSY(1962); ZOTZ!(1962); UNDER THE YUM-YUM TREE(1963); FINE MADNESS, A(1966); GHOST AND MR. CHICKEN, THE(1966); HOW TO FRAME A FIGG(1971); STUDENT TEACHERS, THE(1973)

Jody Millhouse
JOURNEY TO THE CENTER OF TIME(1967)

Robert Milli
SEDUCERS, THE(1962); CURSE OF THE LIVING CORPSE, THE(1964); HAMLET(1964); KLUTE(1971)

Andra Millian
STACY'S KNIGHTS(1983)

Art Millian
MAN BEHIND THE GUN, THE(1952)

Les Millibrook
GUN SMUGGLERS(1948), ed

Steve Millicamp
MAD MAX(1979, Aus.)

Fred Millican
STRATTON STORY, THE(1949); WINNING TEAM, THE(1952)

James Millican
ADVENTURES OF GALLANT BESS(1948); I AM THE LAW(1938); WHO KILLED GAIL PRESTON?(1938); YOU CAN'T TAKE IT WITH YOU(1938); MR. SMITH GOES TO WASHINGTON(1939); SOCIETY LAWYER(1939); BARNACLE BILL(1941); DOWN IN SAN DIEGO(1941); I WANTED WINGS(1941); LOVE CRAZY(1941); MEET JOHN DOE(1941); YOU'LL NEVER GET RICH(1941); GLASS KEY, THE(1942); MAN'S WORLD, A(1942); MY FAVORITE BLONDE(1942); NAZI AGENT(1942); REMARKABLE ANDREW, THE(1942); STAR SPANGLED RHYTHM(1942); TAKE A LETTER, DARLING(1942); TRAMP, TRAMP, TRAMP(1942); WIFE TAKES A FLYER, THE(1942); AIR FORCE(1943); GUY NAMED JOE, A(1943); NORTHERN PURSUIT(1943); SO PROUDLY WE HAIL(1943); THOUSANDS CHEER(1943); I LOVE A SOLDIER(1944); PRACTICALLY YOURS(1944); STORY OF DR. WASSELL, THE(1944); AFFAIRS OF SUSAN(1945); INCENDIARY BLONDE(1945); LOVE LETTERS(1945); TOKYO ROSE(1945); BLUE DAHLIA, THE(1946); BRIDE WORE BOOTS, THE(1946); OUR HEARTS WERE GROWING UP(1946); RENDEZVOUS WITH ANNIE(1946); TO EACH HIS OWN(1946); WELL-GROOMED BRIDE, THE(1946); STEPCHILD(1947); TENDER YEARS, THE(1947); TROUBLE WITH WOMEN, THE(1947); COMMAND DECISION(1948); DISASTER(1948); HAZARD(1948); IN THIS CORNER(1948); LAST OF THE WILD HORSES(1948); LET'S LIVE AGAIN(1948); MAN FROM COLORADO, THE(1948); MR. RECKLESS(1948); RETURN OF WILDFIRE, THE(1948); ROGUES' REGIMENT(1948); DALTON GANG, THE(1949); FIGHTING MAN OF THE PLAINS(1949); GAL WHO TOOK THE WEST, THE(1949); GRAND CANYON(1949); RIMFIRE(1949); BEYOND THE PURPLE HILLS(1950); CONVICTED(1950); DEVIL'S DOORWAY(1950); EVERYBODY'S DANCIN'(1950); GREAT MISSOURI RAID, THE(1950); GUNFIGHTER, THE(1950); MILITARY ACADEMY WITH THAT TENTH AVENUE GANG(1950); MISTER 880(1950); WINCHESTER '73(1950); AL JENNINGS OF OKLAHOMA(1951); CAVALRY SCOUT(1951); FOURTEEN HOURS(1951); I WAS A COMMUNIST FOR THE F.B.I.(1951); MISSING WOMEN(1951); RAWHIDE(1951); WARPATH(1951); BUGLES IN THE AFTERNOON(1952); CARSON CITY(1952); DIPLOMATIC COURIER(1952); HIGH NOON(1952); SCANDAL SHEET(1952); SPRINGFIELD RIFLE(1952); WINNING TEAM, THE(1952); COW COUNTRY(1953); CRAZYLEGS, ALL AMERICAN(1953); GUN BELT(1953); LION IS IN THE STREETS, A(1953); SILVER WHIP, THE(1953); STRANGER WORE A GUN, THE(1953); TORPEDO ALLEY(1953); DAWN AT SOCORRO(1954); JUBILEE TRAIL(1954); LONG WAIT, THE(1954); OUTCAST, THE(1954); RIDING SHOTGUN(1954); BIG TIP OFF, THE(1955); CHIEF CRAZY HORSE(1955); I DIED A THOUSAND TIMES(1955); LAS VEGAS SHAKEDOWN(1955); MAN FROM LARAMIE, THE(1955); STRATEGIC AIR COMMAND(1955); TOP GUN(1955); VANISHING AMERICAN, THE(1955); RED SUNDOWN(1956)

James A. Millican
SPOILERS OF THE NORTH(1947)

Jane Millican
GIRL IN THE FLAT, THE(1934, Brit.); NIGHT OF THE PARTY, THE(1934, Brit.); CRIME UNLIMITED(1935, Brit.); JURY'S EVIDENCE(1936, Brit.); COLONEL BLIMP(1945, Brit.)

Jim Millican
LONE WOLF SPY HUNT, THE(1939)

Jim [James] Millican
ONLY ANGELS HAVE WINGS(1939)

June Millican
BROWN WALLET, THE(1936, Brit.)

Stephen Millichamp
ROAD GAMES(1981, Aus.)

Roy Millichip
TIME LOST AND TIME REMEMBERED(1966, Brit.), p; SMASHING TIME(1967 Brit.), p; NICE GIRL LIKE ME, A(1969, Brit.), p

Andy Milligan
NAKED WITCH, THE(1964), d, ph; GHASTLY ONES, THE(1968), d, w, ph; BLOODTHIRSTY BUTCHERS(1970), d, w, ph; TORTURE DUNGEON(1970), d, w, ph; GURU, THE MAD MONK(1971), p&d, w, ph; MAN WITH TWO HEADS, THE(1972), d&w, ph; RATS ARE COMING! THE WEREWOLVES ARE HERE!, THE(1972), d,w&ph; LEGACY OF BLOOD(1978), p,d,w,ph&ed
Misc. Talkies
BODY BENEATH, THE(1970), d; GIRLS OF 42ND STREET(1974), d; LEGACY OF HORROR(1978), d

Bill Milligan
LIGHTNING GUNS(1950), w

James Milligan
SUDDENLY IT'S SPRING(1947)

Maura Milligan
ODD MAN OUT(1947, Brit.)

Min Milligan
ODD MAN OUT(1947, Brit.)

Primrose Milligan
SLEEPING CAR TO TRIESTE(1949, Brit.)

Spencer Milligan
SLEEPER(1973)

Spike Milligan
PENNY POINTS TO PARADISE(1951, Brit.); DOWN AMONG THE Z MEN(1952, Brit.); INVASION QUARTET(1961, Brit.); RISK, THE(1961, Brit.); WATCH YOUR STERN(1961, Brit.); WHAT A WHOPPER(1961, Brit.); POSTMAN'S KNOCK(1962, Brit.), a, w; BED SITTING ROOM, THE(1969, Brit.), a, w; MAGIC CHRISTIAN, THE(1970, Brit.); MAGNIFICENT SEVEN DEADLY SINS, THE(1971, Brit.), a, w; ADVENTURES OF BARRY McKENZIE(1972, Austral.); ALICE'S ADVENTURES IN WONDERLAND(1972, Brit.); RENTADICK(1972, Brit.); ADOLF HITLER–MY PART IN HIS DOWNFALL(1973, Brit.); DIGBY, THE BIGGEST DOG IN THE WORLD(1974, Brit.); THREE MUSKETEERS, THE(1974, Panama); GREAT MCGONAGALL, THE(1975, Brit.), a, w; LAST REMAKE OF BEAU GESTE, THE(1977); MONTY PYTHON'S LIFE OF BRIAN(1979, Brit.); HOUND OF THE BASKERVILLES, THE(1980, Brit.); HISTORY OF THE WORLD, PART 1(1981); YELLOWBEARD(1983)

Stuart Milligan
OUTLAND(1981); LORDS OF DISCIPLINE, THE(1983)

W. J. Milligan, Jr.
MAN WITH THE GOLDEN GUN, THE(1974, Brit.), stunts

Wayne Milligan
TENDER MERCIES(1982)

Billy Milliken
DRIVE-IN(1976)

Sue Milliken
ODD ANGRY SHOT, THE(1979, Aus.), p; FIGHTING BACK(1983, Brit.), p

David Millin
DIAMOND SAFARI(1958), ph; CAPETOWN AFFAIR(1967, U.S./South Afr.), ph; RIDE THE HIGH WIND(1967, South Africa), d; SEVEN AGAINST THE SUN(1968, South Africa), p, d; KILLER FORCE(1975, Switz./Ireland), ph

Gloria Mills
 ANGEL IN MY POCKET(1969); SWEET CHARITY(1969)
Gordon Mills
 VAGABOND KING, THE(1956); DANIEL BOONE, TRAIL BLAZER(1957); DEVIL'S HAIRPIN, THE(1957); KRONOS(1957)
Grace Mills
 HARVEY(1950); WHERE THE SIDEWALK ENDS(1950); VENGEANCE VALLEY(1951); RUNNING WILD(1955)
Guy Mills
 THEY CAN'T HANG ME(1955, Brit.); HORROR OF DRACULA, THE(1958, Brit.)
Hank Mills
 COTTONPICKIN' CHICKENPICKERS(1967)
Hayley Mills
 TIGER BAY(1959, Brit.); POLLYANNA(1960); PARENT TRAP, THE(1961); WHISTLE DOWN THE WIND(1961, Brit.); IN SEARCH OF THE CASTAWAYS(1962, Brit.); SUMMER MAGIC(1963); CHALK GARDEN, THE(1964, Brit.); MOON-SPINNERS, THE(1964); THAT DARN CAT(1965); TRUTH ABOUT SPRING, THE(1965, Brit.); DAYDREAMER, THE(1966); FAMILY WAY, THE(1966, Brit.); GYPSY GIRL(1966, Brit.); TROUBLE WITH ANGELS, THE(1966); AFRICA–TEXAS STYLE!(1967 U.S./Brit.); MATTER OF INNOCENCE, A(1968, Brit.); TWISTED NERVE(1969, Brit.); TAKE A GIRL LIKE YOU(1970, Brit.); ENDLESS NIGHT(1971, Brit.); CRY OF THE PENGUINS(1972, Brit.); DEADLY STRANGERS(1974, Brit.); KINGFISH CAPER, THE(1976, South Africa); WHAT CHANGED CHARLEY FARTHING?(1976, Brit.)
Hazel Mills
Silents
 FIGHTING TERROR, THE(1929); LAST ROUNDUP, THE(1929)
Henry Mills
 BULLDOG DRUMMOND COMES BACK(1937), ph
Herb Mills
1984
 SIGNAL 7(1984)
Hugh Mills
 BELOVED VAGABOND, THE(1936, Brit.), w; MAN IN THE MIRROR, THE(1936, Brit.), w; PERSONAL PROPERTY(1937), w; TURNED OUT NICE AGAIN(1941, Brit.), w; BLANCHE FURY(1948, Brit.), w; BLACKMAILED(1951, Brit.), w; SO LONG AT THE FAIR(1951, Brit.), w; LOVERS, HAPPY LOVERS!(1955, Brit.), w; NAKED HEART, THE(1955, Brit.), w; PRUDENCE AND THE PILL(1968, Brit.), w
Jack Mills
 TROUBLE WITH GIRLS(AND HOW TO GET INTO IT), THE*1/2 (1969), set d; RETURN OF THE LASH(1947), art d; STAGECOACH KID(1949), set d; ROADBLOCK(1951), set d; CLASH BY NIGHT(1952), set d; LUSTY MEN, THE(1952), set d; ANGEL FACE(1953), set d; WHILE THE CITY SLEEPS(1956), set d; THUNDER OF DRUMS, A(1961), set d; WEEKEND WITH LULU, A(1961, Brit.), ph; HOW THE WEST WAS WON(1962), set d; DRUMS OF AFRICA(1963), set d; SIEGE OF THE SAXONS(1963, Brit.), ph; GET YOURSELF A COLLEGE GIRL(1964), set d; GUNS OF DIABLO(1964), set d; CLARENCE, THE CROSS-EYED LION(1965), set d; ONCE A THIEF(1965), set d; ROUNDERS, THE(1965), set d; ZEBRA IN THE KITCHEN(1965), set d; ONE OF OUR SPIES IS MISSING(1966), set d; SEVEN WOMEN(1966), set d; ICE STATION ZEBRA(1968), set d; CAPTAIN NEMO AND THE UNDERWATER CITY(1969, Brit.), sp eff; GYPSY MOTHS, THE(1969), set d; SCROOGE(1970, Brit.), spec eff; TWINS OF EVIL(1971, Brit.), spec eff
Jackie Mills
 WINDSPLITTER, THE(1971), m
James Mills
 CLOUDBURST(1952, Brit.); DEATH OF AN ANGEL(1952, Brit.); PANIC IN NEEDLE PARK(1971), w; REPORT TO THE COMMISSIONER(1975), w
1984
 DARK ENEMY(1984, Brit.)
Jed Mills
 NEW YEAR'S EVIL(1980)
Jerry Mills
 ROGUES' REGIMENT(1948); HELL'S BLOODY DEVILS(1970)
Jim Mills
 SWARM, THE(1978)
Joanna Mills
 LOVE MERCHANT, THE(1966)
Misc. Talkies
 AROUSED(1968)
Joe Mills
 TWO-FISTED JUSTICE(1931); OLD-FASHIONED WAY, THE(1934)
Joey R. Mills
 EYES OF LAURA MARS(1978)
John Mills
 HELL, HEAVEN OR HOBOKEN(1958, Brit.); MIDSHIPMAID GOB(1932, Brit.); BRITANNIA OF BILLINGSGATE(1933, Brit.); GHOST CAMERA, THE(1933, Brit.); POLITICAL PARTY, A(1933, Brit.); BLIND JUSTICE(1934, Brit.); DOCTOR'S ORDERS(1934, Brit.); LASH, THE(1934, Brit.); RIVER WOLVES, THE(1934, Brit.); THOSE WERE THE DAYS(1934, Brit.); BORN FOR GLORY(1935, Brit.); CAR OF DREAMS(1935, Brit.); CHARING CROSS ROAD(1935, Brit.); REGAL CAVALCADE(1935, Brit.); FIRST OFFENCE(1936, Brit.); LADY JANE GREY(1936, Brit.); YOU'RE IN THE ARMY NOW(1937, Brit.); GOODBYE MR. CHIPS(1939, Brit.); OLD BILL AND SON(1940, Brit.); BLACK SHEEP OF WHITEHALL, THE(1941, Brit.); BOMBSIGHT STOLEN(1941, Brit.); BIG BLOCKADE, THE(1942, Brit.); IN WHICH WE SERVE(1942, Brit.); YOUNG MR. PITT, THE(1942, Brit.); WE DIVE AT DAWN(1943, Brit.); SECRET MISSION(1944, Brit.), spec eff; THIS HAPPY BREED(1944, Brit.); JOHNNY IN THE CLOUDS(1945, Brit.); GREAT EXPECTATIONS(1946, Brit.); GREEN COCKATOO, THE(1947, Brit.); SO WELL REMEMBERED(1947, Brit.); OCTOBER MAN, THE(1948, Brit.); HISTORY OF MR. POLLY, THE(1949, Brit.), a, p; SCOTT OF THE ANTARCTIC(1949, Brit.); WATERLOO ROAD(1949, Brit.); ROCKING HORSE WINNER, THE(1950, Brit.), a, p; OPERATION DISASTER(1951, Brit.); GENTLE GUNMAN, THE(1952, Brit.); LONG MEMORY, THE(1953, Brit.); MR. DENNING DRIVES NORTH(1953, Brit.); HOBSON'S CHOICE(1954, Brit.); COLDITZ STORY, THE(1955, Brit.); END OF THE AFFAIR, THE(1955, Brit.); ESCAPADE(1955, Brit.); ABOVE US THE WAVES(1956, Brit.); AROUND THE WORLD IN 80 DAYS(1956); IT'S GREAT TO BE YOUNG(1956, Brit.); WAR AND PEACE(1956, Ital./U.S.); BABY AND THE BATTLESHIP, THE(1957, Brit.); TOWN ON TRIAL(1957, Brit.); DESERT ATTACK(1958, Brit.); DUNKIRK(1958, Brit.); CIRCLE, THE(1959, Brit.); TIGER BAY(1959, Brit.); SWISS FAMILY ROBINSON(1960); TUNES OF GLORY(1960, Brit.); FLAME IN THE STREETS(1961, Brit.); SEASON OF PASSION(1961, Aus./Brit.); SINGER NOT THE SONG, THE(1961, Brit.); TIARA TAHITI(1962, Brit.); VALIANT,

THE(1962, Brit./Ital.); CHALK GARDEN, THE(1964, Brit.); KING RAT(1965); OPERATION CROSSBOW(1965, U.S./Ital.); TRUTH ABOUT SPRING, THE(1965, Brit.); FAMILY WAY, THE(1966, Brit.); GYPSY GIRL(1966, Brit.), d; WRONG BOX, THE(1966, Brit.); AFRICA–TEXAS STYLE!(1967 U.S./Brit.); CHUKA(1967); BLACK VEIL FOR LISA, A(1969 Ital./Ger.); LADY HAMILTON(1969, Ger./Ital./Fr.); OH! WHAT A LOVELY WAR(1969, Brit.); RUN WILD, RUN FREE(1969, Brit.); RYAN'S DAUGHTER(1970, Brit.); DULCIMA(1971, Brit.); LADY CAROLINE LAMB(1972, Brit./Ital.); YOUNG WINSTON(1972, Brit.); OKLAHOMA CRUDE(1973); HUMAN FACTOR, THE(1975); DIRTY KNIGHT'S WORK(1976, Brit.); BIG SLEEP, THE½(1978, Brit.); THIRTY NINE STEPS, THE(1978, Brit.); QUATERMASS CONCLUSION(1980, Brit.); ZULU DAWN(1980, Brit.); GANDHI(1982)
1984
 SAHARA(1984)
Johnny Mills
 THIEF OF BAGHDAD, THE(1940, Brit.), spec eff
Joseph Mills
Silents
 ABRAHAM LINCOLN(1924)
Judy Mills
 CLAUDINE(1974)
Juliet Mills
 IN WHICH WE SERVE(1942, Brit.); SO WELL REMEMBERED(1947, Brit.); OCTOBER MAN, THE(1948, Brit.); HISTORY OF MR. POLLY, THE(1949, Brit.); TWICE AROUND THE DAFFODILS(1962, Brit.); CARRY ON JACK(1963, Brit.); NO, MY DARLING DAUGHTER(1964, Brit.); NURSE ON WHEELS(1964, Brit.); RARE BREED, THE(1966); OH! WHAT A LOVELY WAR(1969, Brit.); AVANTI!(1972); JONATHAN LIVINGSTON SEAGULL(1973); BEYOND THE DOOR(1975, Ital./U.S.)
Karen Mills
 NEW YEAR'S EVIL(1980)
Kim Mills
 UNHOLY FOUR, THE(1954, Brit.); FOR YOUR EYES ONLY(1981)
Larry L. Mills
 SMALL TOWN IN TEXAS, A(1976), ed
M. Mills
Silents
 QUEEN MOTHER, THE(1916, Brit.)
Malan Mills
 MARRYING KIND, THE(1952)
Marilyn Mills
Silents
 WESTERN DEMON, A(1922)
Misc. Silents
 COME ON COWBOYS!(1924); HORSE SENSE(1924); TWO FISTED JUSTICE(1924); CACTUS CURE, THE(1925); MY PAL(1925); TRICKS(1925); WHERE ROMANCE RIDES(1925); THREE PALS(1926); LOVE OF PAQUITA, THE(1927)
Marion Mills
 WORDS AND MUSIC(1929); PAPERBACK HERO(1973, Can.), cos
Mervyn Mills
 LONG HAUL, THE(1957, Brit.), w
Michael Mills
 BEAST OF BUDAPEST, THE(1958)
Mort Mills
 AFFAIR IN TRINIDAD(1952); NO HOLDS BARRED(1952); FARMER TAKES A WIFE, THE(1953); HANNAH LEE(1953); TEXAS BAD MAN(1953); CRY VENGEANCE(1954); DRIVE A CROOKED ROAD(1954); PUSHOVER(1954); DESERT SANDS(1955); DIAL RED O(1955); JUPITER'S DARLING(1955); MARAUDERS, THE(1955); TO HELL AND BACK(1955); TRIAL(1955); CRASHING LAS VEGAS(1956); DAVY CROCKETT AND THE RIVER PIRATES(1956); HARDER THEY FALL, THE(1956); IRON SHERIFF, THE(1957); MAN IN THE SHADOW(1957); SHADOW ON THE WINDOW, THE(1957); RIDE A CROOKED TRAIL(1958); TOUCH OF EVIL(1958); PSYCHO(1960); TWENTY PLUS TWO(1961); GUNFIGHT AT COMANCHE CREEK(1964); QUICK GUN, THE(1964); OUTLAWS IS COMING, THE(1965); BLINDFOLD(1966); TORN CURTAIN(1966); NAME OF THE GAME IS KILL, THE(1968); STRATEGY OF TERROR(1969); SOLDIER BLUE(1970)
Mrs. Clifford Mills
 NORTH SEA PATROL(1939, Brit.), w
Noel Mills
 MADAME CURIE(1943)
Paul Mills
 OPERATION SNATCH(1962, Brit.), w; PERMISSION TO KILL(1975, U.S./Aust.), p
Peggy Mills
Misc. Silents
 SHATTERED IDYLL, A(1916, Brit.)
Penny Anne Mills
 THIRTEEN FRIGHTENED GIRLS(1963)
Peter Mills
 JOURNEY AHEAD(1947, Brit.), p&d
Pierre Mills
 FRENZY(1946, Brit.), w; HOUSE OF MYSTERY(1961, Brit.), w
Rebecca Ortega Mills
 METAMORPHOSES(1978), prod d
Reginald Mills
 STAIRWAY TO HEAVEN(1946, Brit.), ed; BLACK NARCISSUS(1947, Brit.), ed; RED SHOES, THE(1948, Brit.), ed; TALES OF HOFFMANN, THE(1951, Brit.), ed; WHERE'S CHARLEY?(1952, Brit.), ed; WILD HEART, THE(1952, Brit.), ed; SLEEPING TIGER, THE(1954, Brit.), ed; OH ROSALINDA(1956, Brit.), ed; PURSUIT OF THE GRAF SPEE(1957, Brit.), ed; SPANISH GARDENER, THE(1957, Span.), ed; WINDOM'S WAY(1958, Brit.), ed; PASSIONATE SUMMER(1959, Brit.), ed; CHANCE MEETING(1960, Brit.), ed; CIRCUS OF HORRORS(1960, Brit.), ed; CONCRETE JUNGLE, THE(1962, Brit.), ed; KING AND COUNTRY(1964, Brit.), ed; SERVANT, THE(1964, Brit.), ed; THESE ARE THE DAMNED(1965, Brit.), ed; ULYSSES(1967, U.S./Brit.), ed; ROMEO AND JULIET(1968, Brit./Ital.), ed; RING OF BRIGHT WATER(1969, Brit.), ed; DANCE OF DEATH, THE(1971, Brit.), ed; PETER RABBIT AND TALES OF BEATRIX POTTER(1971, Brit.), d
Richard Mills
 TIME LOST AND TIME REMEMBERED(1966, Brit.), makeup; DOUBLE MAN, THE(1967), makeup; I'LL NEVER FORGET WHAT'S 'IS NAME(1967, Brit.), makeup; SMASHING TIME(1967 Brit.), makeup; VILLA RIDES(1968), makeup; HANNIBAL BROOKS(1969, Brit.), makeup; LAWMAN(1971), makeup; NIGHT COMERS, THE(1971, Brit.), makeup; WHEN DINOSAURS RULED THE EARTH(1971, Brit.),

makeup; SCORPIO(1973), makeup; NASTY HABITS(1976, Brit.), makeup; SKY RIDERS(1976, U.S./Gr.), makeup; MERRY CHRISTMAS MR. LAWRENCE(1983, Jap./Brit.)

Riley Mills
I DRINK YOUR BLOOD(1971)

Robyn Mills
MURPH THE SURF(1974)

Royce Mills
SUNDAY BLOODY SUNDAY(1971, Brit.); UP POMPEII(1971, Brit.); HISTORY OF THE WORLD, PART 1(1981)

Sally Mills
UNDERWORLD U.S.A.(1961); NAKED KISS, THE(1964)

Shirley Mills
TRUE TO LIFE(1943); UNDER-PUP, THE(1939); DIAMOND FRONTIER(1940); FIVE LITTLE PEPPERS IN TROUBLE(1940); GRAPES OF WRATH(1940); YOUNG PEOPLE(1940); HENRY ALDRICH GETS GLAMOUR(1942); MISS ANNIE ROONEY(1942); REVEILLE WITH BEVERLY(1943); SHADOW OF A DOUBT(1943); NINE GIRLS(1944); NONE SHALL ESCAPE(1944); PATRICK THE GREAT(1945); BETTY CO-ED(1946); OLD-FASHIONED GIRL, AN(1948); MODEL AND THE MARRIAGE BROKER, THE(1951)

Shirley O. Mills
IT'S A SMALL WORLD(1950)

Thomas Mills
LES MISERABLES(1935); GOLD IS WHERE YOU FIND IT(1938); WE ARE NOT ALONE(1939)
Silents
KISS BARRIER, THE(1925); GILDED HIGHWAY, THE(1926)
Misc. Silents
MAN WHO COULD'T BEAT GOD, THE(1915); NAN WHO COULDN'T BEAT GOD, THE(1915); SALLY IN A HURRY(1917)

Thomas R. Mills
GREAT IMPERSONATION, THE(1935); IT'S LOVE I'M AFTER(1937)
Silents
AMERICAN LIVE WIRE, AN(1918), d; ARIZONA ROMEO, THE(1925)
Misc. Silents
DAWN OF FREEDOM, THE(1916); DOLLAR AND THE LAW, THE(1916); DEFEAT OF THE CITY, THE(1917), d; DUPLICITY OF HARGRAVES, THE(1917), d; NIGHT IN NEW ARABIA, A(1917), d; RENAISSANCE AT CHARLEROI, THE(1917), d; MOTHER'S SIN, A(1918), d; GIRL WOMAN, THE(1919), d; DUDS(1920), d; INVISIBLE DIVORCE, THE(1920), d; STAR DUST TRAIL, THE(1924)

Tom Mills
Misc. Silents
GIRL IN HIS HOUSE, THE(1918), d; SEAL OF SILENCE, THE(1918), d; GIRL AT BAY, A(1919), d; UNKNOWN QUANTITY, THE(1919), d

Tom R. Mills
Misc. Silents
THIN ICE(1919), d

Walter Mills
HIGH COUNTRY, THE(1981, Can.)

Warren Mills
DELINQUENT DAUGHTERS(1944); DOUGHGIRLS, THE(1944); WHEN THE LIGHTS GO ON AGAIN(1944); GIRL OF THE LIMBERLOST, THE(1945); FREDDIE STEPS OUT(1946); HIGH SCHOOL HERO(1946); JUNIOR PROM(1946); MAN WHO DARED, THE(1946); MARGIE(1946); OUT OF THE DEPTHS(1946); SARGE GOES TO COLLEGE(1947); VACATION DAYS(1947); CAMPUS SLEUTH(1948); SMART POLITICS(1948); PURPLE HEART DIARY(1951)

The Mills Brothers
BROADWAY GONDOLIER(1935); CHATTERBOX(1943); HE'S MY GUY(1943); REVEILLE WITH BEVERLY(1943); RHYTHM PARADE(1943); COWBOY CANTEEN(1944); WHEN YOU'RE SMILING(1950)
Misc. Talkies
FIGHT NEVER ENDS, THE(1947)

Ingrid Mills "Miss South Africa"
YANKEE PASHA(1954)

John Mills-Cockell
TERROR TRAIN(1980, Can.), m

Charles Millsfield
SPOOK BUSTERS(1946)

Dan Millstein
GIRL HUNTERS, THE(1963, Brit.), cos

Jack Millstein
HUCKLEBERRY FINN(1974)

I.S. Millutin
HEROES OF THE SEA(1941), m

Millwall Football Club
SMALL TOWN STORY(1953, Brit.)

Dawson Millward
Silents
ELEVENTH COMMANDMENT, THE(1924, Brit.); KING OF THE CASTLE(1925, Brit.); ONE COLUMBO NIGHT(1926, Brit.)
Misc. Silents
SKIN GAME, THE(1920, Brit.); RECOIL, THE(1922, Brit.)

Milly
CONFORMIST, THE(1971, Ital., Fr)

Georgiy Millyar
DAY THE EARTH FROZE, THE(1959, Fin./USSR); HUNTING IN SIBERIA(1962, USSR); NIGHT BEFORE CHRISTMAS, A(1963, USSR); MAGIC WEAVER, THE(1965, USSR); JACK FROST(1966, USSR); WAR AND PEACE(1968, USSR)

A. A. Milne
PERFECT ALIBI, THE(1931, Brit.), w; MICHAEL AND MARY(1932, Brit.), w; WHERE SINNERS MEET(1934), w; FOUR DAYS WONDER(1936), w

Alexis Milne
DAUGHTER OF DARKNESS(1948, Brit.); NOOSE FOR A LADY(1953, Brit.)

Bernardette Milne
COVER GIRL KILLER(1960, Brit.)

Bettine Milne
STATUE, THE(1971, Brit.)

Billy Milne
SMALL TOWN STORY(1953, Brit.)

Chris Milne
DAY AFTER HALLOWEEN, THE(1981, Aus.)

Eithne Milne
SUMMER HOLIDAY(1963, Brit.)

Elizabeth Leigh Milne
VISITING HOURS(1982, Can.)

Ella Milne
GREEN SCARF, THE(1954, Brit.)
Misc. Silents
SILVER LINING, THE(1919, Brit.)

Lennox Milne
BROTHERLY LOVE(1970, Brit.)

Mary Milne
REACHING OUT(1983)

Minnie Milne
Silents
MISCHIEF MAKER, THE(1916)

Peter Milne
COME ACROSS(1929), w; CONVENTION CITY(1933), w; FROM HEADQUARTERS(1933), w; KENNEL MURDER CASE, THE(1933), w; REGISTERED NURSE(1934), w; RETURN OF THE TERROR(1934), w; GOLD DIGGERS OF 1935(1935), w; MARY JANE'S PA(1935), w; MISS PACIFIC FLEET(1935), w; WOMAN IN RED, THE(1935), w; COLLEEN(1936), w; MURDER OF DR. HARRIGAN, THE(1936), w; POLO JOE(1936), w; WALKING DEAD, THE(1936), w; GOD'S COUNTRY AND THE WOMAN(1937), w; SAN QUENTIN(1937), w; HOUSE OF FEAR, THE(1939), w; MR. MOTO IN DANGER ISLAND(1939), w; PRIVATE AFFAIRS(1940), w; RANCHO GRANDE(1940), w; THEY MEET AGAIN(1941), w; WHITE SAVAGE(1943), w; LADY, LET'S DANCE(1944), w; STEP LIVELY(1944), w; GOD IS MY CO-PILOT(1945), w; VERDICT, THE(1946), w; HIGH TIDE(1947), w; MY WILD IRISH ROSE(1947), w; APRIL SHOWERS(1948), w; DAUGHTER OF ROSIE O'GRADY, THE(1950), w; PAINTING THE CLOUDS WITH SUNSHINE(1951), w; ABOUT FACE(1952), w; SHE'S WORKING HER WAY THROUGH COLLEGE(1952), w; GERALDINE(1953), w; GLORY(1955), w
Silents
WHAT FOOLS MEN ARE(1922), w; GREAT MAIL ROBBERY, THE(1927), w; HOME STRUCK(1927), w; HOOK AND LADDER NO. 9(1927), w; SILVER SLAVE, THE(1927), w; HEAD OF THE FAMILY, THE(1928), w; MATINEE IDOL, THE(1928), w; MICHIGAN KID, THE(1928), w; NAME THE WOMAN(1928), d&w; NOTHING TO WEAR(1928), w; WAY OF THE STRONG, THE(1928), w; OBJECT–ALIMONY(1929), w

Roma Milne
TROJAN BROTHERS, THE(1946); FAHRENHEIT 451(1966, Brit.)

Anthony Milner
SUPERMAN II(1980)

Dan Milner
DANCING MAN(1934), ed; WHAT'S YOUR RACKET?(1934), ed; DANGER AHEAD(1935), ed; BARS OF HATE(1936), ed; LEAVENWORTH CASE, THE(1936), ed; PUT ON THE SPOT(1936), ed; RETURN OF JIMMY VALENTINE, THE(1936), ed; RIO GRANDE ROMANCE(1936), ed; ROGUES' TAVERN, THE(1936), ed; BANK ALARM(1937), ed; HOUSE OF SECRETS, THE(1937), ed; ISLAND CAPTIVES(1937), ph; RED LIGHTS AHEAD(1937), ed; SON OF INGAGI(1940), ed; BABY FACE MORGAN(1942), ed; HOUSE OF ERRORS(1942), ed; TOMORROW WE LIVE(1942), ed; CROSS OF LORRAINE, THE(1943), ed; HITLER'S MADMAN(1943), ed; OH, WHAT A NIGHT(1944), ed; FASHION MODEL(1945), ed; FLAME OF THE WEST(1945), ed; FRONTIER FEUD(1945), ed; WOMEN IN THE NIGHT(1948), ed; NAKED DAWN, THE(1955), ed; PHANTOM FROM 10,000 LEAGUES, THE(1956), p, d, ed; FROM HELL IT CAME(1957), d
Misc. Talkies
LAST ASSIGNMENT, THE(1936), d

Daniel Milner
KELLY OF THE SECRET SERVICE(1936), ed; PRISON SHADOWS(1936), ed

Danny Milner
LOST TRAIL, THE(1945), ed

J. Milner
FROM HELL IT CAME(1957), w

Jack Milner
PHANTOM FROM 10,000 LEAGUES, THE(1956), p, ed; FROM HELL IT CAME(1957), p, ed

Jessamine Milner
UP THE SANDBOX(1972); TRAIN RIDE TO HOLLYWOOD(1975)

Martin Milner
LIFE WITH FATHER(1947); SANDS OF IWO JIMA(1949); LOUISA(1950); OUR VERY OWN(1950); FIGHTING COAST GUARD(1951); HALLS OF MONTEZUMA(1951); I WANT YOU(1951); OPERATION PACIFIC(1951); BATTLE ZONE(1952); BELLES ON THEIR TOES(1952); CAPTIVE CITY(1952); LAST OF THE COMANCHES(1952); MY WIFE'S BEST FRIEND(1952); SPRINGFIELD RIFLE(1952); DESTINATION GOBI(1953); FRANCIS IN THE NAVY(1955); LONG GRAY LINE, THE(1955); MISTER ROBERTS(1955); PETE KELLY'S BLUES(1955); ON THE THRESHOLD OF SPACE(1956); PILLARS OF THE SKY(1956); SCREAMING EAGLES(1956); GUNFIGHT AT THE O.K. CORRAL(1957); MAN AFRAID(1957); SWEET SMELL OF SUCCESS(1957); MARJORIE MORNINGSTAR(1958); TOO MUCH, TOO SOON(1958); COMPULSION(1959); THIRTEEN GHOSTS(1960); PRIVATE LIVES OF ADAM AND EVE, THE(1961); ZEBRA IN THE KITCHEN(1965); SULLIVAN'S EMPIRE(1967); VALLEY OF THE DOLLS(1967); THREE GUNS FOR TEXAS(1968); SKI FEVER(1969, U.S./Aust./Czech.)

Martine Milner
TARAS BULBA(1962)

Marty Milner
SEX KITTENS GO TO COLLEGE(1960)

Max Milner
FLYING FORTRESS(1942, Brit.), p; PETERVILLE DIAMOND, THE(1942, Brit.), p

Nehema Milner
BIG SWITCH, THE(1970, Brit.), ed

Patricia Milner
THOMASINE AND BUSHROD(1974)

Roger Milner
QUEEN'S GUARDS, THE(1963, Brit.), w
Victor Milner
WILD PARTY, THE(1929), ph; SINS OF THE FATHERS(1928), ph; CHARMING SINNERS(1929), ph; LOVE PARADE, THE(1929), ph; MARRIAGE PLAYGROUND, THE(1929), ph; RIVER OF ROMANCE(1929), ph; STUDIO MURDER MYSTERY, THE(1929), ph; WOLF OF WALL STREET, THE(1929), ph; LET'S GO NATIVE(1930), ph; MONTE CARLO(1930), ph; TEXAN, THE(1930), ph; TRUE TO THE NAVY(1930), ph; DAUGHTER OF THE DRAGON(1931), ph; I TAKE THIS WOMAN(1931), ph; KICK IN(1931), ph; LADIES' MAN(1931), ph; MAN OF THE WORLD(1931), ph; NO LIMIT(1931), ph; BROKEN LULLABY(1932), ph; LOVE ME TONIGHT(1932), ph; ONE HOUR WITH YOU(1932), ph; THIS IS THE NIGHT(1932), ph; TROUBLE IN PARADISE(1932), ph; UNDER-COVER MAN(1932), ph; DESIGN FOR LIVING(1933), ph; LUXURY LINER(1933), ph; ONE SUNDAY AFTERNOON(1933), ph; SONG OF SONGS(1933), ph; ALL OF ME(1934), ph; CLEOPATRA(1934), ph; WHARF ANGEL(1934), ph; CRUSADES, THE(1935), ph; GILDED LILY, THE(1935), ph; SO RED THE ROSE(1935), ph; DESIRE(1936), ph; GENERAL DIED AT DAWN, THE(1936), ph; GIVE US THIS NIGHT(1936), ph; TILL WE MEET AGAIN(1936), ph; ARTISTS AND MODELS(1937), ph; BULLDOG DRUMMOND ESCAPES(1937), ph; HIGH, WIDE AND HANDSOME(1937), ph; PLAINSMAN, THE(1937), ph; BUCCANEER, THE(1938), ph; COLLEGE SWING(1938), ph; GIVE ME A SAILOR(1938), ph; HUNTED MEN(1938), ph; SAY IT IN FRENCH(1938), ph; TOUCHDOWN, ARMY(1938), ph; GREAT VICTOR HERBERT, THE(1939), ph; OUR LEADING CITIZEN(1939), ph; UNION PACIFIC(1939), ph; WHAT A LIFE(1939), ph; CHRISTMAS IN JULY(1940), ph; NORTHWEST MOUNTED POLICE(1940), ph; THOSE WERE THE DAYS(1940), ph; LADY EVE, THE(1941), ph; MAN WHO LOST HIMSELF, THE(1941), ph; MONSTER AND THE GIRL, THE(1941), ph; MY LIFE WITH CAROLINE(1941), ph; PALM BEACH STORY, THE(1942), ph; REAP THE WILD WIND(1942), ph; HOSTAGES(1943), ph; PRINCESS AND THE PIRATE, THE(1944), ph; STORY OF DR. WASSELL, THE(1944), ph; WONDER MAN(1945), ph; STRANGE LOVE OF MARTHA IVERS, THE(1946), ph; OTHER LOVE, THE(1947), ph; UNFAITHFULLY YOURS(1948), ph; YOU WERE MEANT FOR ME(1948), ph; DARK CITY(1950), ph; FURIES, THE(1950), ph; SEPTEMBER AFFAIR(1950), ph; MY FAVORITE SPY(1951), ph; CARRIE(1952), ph; JEOPARDY(1953), ph
Silents
CABARET GIRL, THE(1919), ph; OUT OF THE DUST(1920), ph; LIVE WIRES(1921), ph; SHADOWS OF CONSCIENCE(1921), ph; KENTUCKY DERBY, THE(1922), ph; LAVENDER BATH LADY, THE(1922), ph; LOVE LETTER, THE(1923), ph; TOWN SCANDAL, THE(1923), ph; ON THE STROKE OF THREE(1924), ph; EAST OF SUEZ(1925), ph; LEARNING TO LOVE(1925), ph; CAT'S PAJAMAS, THE(1926), ph; KID BOOTS(1926), ph; CHILDREN OF DIVORCE(1927), ph; ROLLED STOCKINGS(1927), ph; WAY OF ALL FLESH, THE(1927), ph; HALF A BRIDE(1928), ph; THREE SINNERS(1928), ph
W. Milner
KEY, THE(1958, Brit.), makeup
Alex Milner-Gardner
HEIGHTS OF DANGER(1962, Brit.), ed
Dan Milnere
SPEED LIMITED(1940), ed
Bernadette Milnes
DYNAMITERS, THE(1956, Brit.); GUTTER GIRLS(1964, Brit.); MAN WHO COULDN'T WALK, THE(1964, Brit.); ELEPHANT MAN, THE(1980, Brit.)
Victor Milnor
GREAT MOMENT, THE(1944), ph
Bella Milo
LAST WALTZ, THE(1936, Brit.)
George Milo
PHANTOM SPEAKS, THE(1945), set d; TRAIL OF KIT CARSON(1945), set d; MYSTERIOUS MR. VALENTINE, THE(1946), set d; ONE EXCITING WEEK(1946), set d; PLAINSMAN AND THE LADY(1946), set d; RENDEZVOUS WITH ANNIE(1946), set d; HARD BOILED MAHONEY(1947), set d; OREGON TRAIL SCOUTS(1947), set d; ANGEL ON THE AMAZON(1948), set d; OUT OF THE STORM(1948), set d; RENEGADES OF SONORA(1948), set d; UNDER CALIFORNIA STARS(1948), set d; MONTANA BELLE(1952), set d; WOMAN IN THE DARK(1952), set d; SUN SHINES BRIGHT, THE(1953), set d; JUBILEE TRAIL(1954), set d; TIMBERJACK(1955), set d; PSYCHO(1960), set d; JUDGMENT AT NUREMBERG(1961), set d; LONELY ARE THE BRAVE(1962), set d; PRESSURE POINT(1962), set d; THAT TOUCH OF MINK(1962), set d; BIRDS, THE(1963), set d; FATHER GOOSE(1964), set d; MARNIE(1964), set d; I SAW WHAT YOU DID(1965), set d; TORN CURTAIN(1966), set d; COUNTERPOINT(1967), set d; DON'T JUST STAND THERE(1968), set d; HELL WITH HEROES, THE(1968), set d; MAN CALLED GANNON, A(1969), set d; WINNING(1969), set d; SKULLDUGGERY(1970), set d; HIGH PLAINS DRIFTER(1973), set d; SHOWDOWN(1973), set d
Jacqueline Milo
NIGHT AND DAY(1946)
Jana Milo
CAT FROM OUTER SPACE, THE(1978)
Jean-Roger Milo
MOON IN THE GUTTER, THE(1983, Fr./Ital.)
1984
SUNDAY IN THE COUNTRY, A(1984, Fr.)
Mila Milo
50,000 B.C.(BEFORE CLOTHING)* (1963)
Miliza Milo
VERTIGO(1958)
Rafi Milo
JESUS(1979)
Ruth Milo
Silents
GOLD RUSH, THE(1925)
Sandra Milo
MIRROR HAS TWO FACES, THE(1959, Fr.); GENERALE DELLA ROVERE(1960, Ital./Fr.); HEROD THE GREAT(1960, Ital.); GREEN MARE, THE(1961, Fr./Ital.); LOST SOULS(1961, Ital.); 8 ½(1963, Ital.); JULIET OF THE SPIRITS(1965, Fr./Ital./W.Ger.); LOVE A LA CARTE(1965, Ital.); MALE COMPANION(1965, Fr./Ital.); WHITE VOICES(1965, Fr./Ital.); LA VISITA(1966, Ital./Fr.); WEEKEND, ITALIAN STYLE(1967, Fr./Ital./Span.); BANG BANG KID, THE(1968 U.S./Span./Ital.)

Sandro Milo
TOTO IN THE MOON(1957, Ital./Span.)
Milo Twins
I'M FROM ARKANSAS(1944)
The Milo Twins
SING, NEIGHBOR, SING(1944); MARKED FOR MURDER(1945)
Cosimo Milone
THREE BROTHERS(1982, Ital.)
Luciana Milone
HORROR CASTLE(1965, Ital.)
Milos Milos
INCUBUS(1966); RUSSIANS ARE COMING, THE RUSSIANS ARE COMING, THE(1966)
Ana Milosavljevic
INNOCENCE UNPROTECTED(1971, Yugo.)
Pera Milosavljevic
INNOCENCE UNPROTECTED(1971, Yugo.)
Dara Milosevic
25TH HOUR, THE(1967, Fr./Ital./Yugo.)
Milovan and Serena
VAMPIRE CIRCUS(1972, Brit.)
Sandra Milovanoff
Misc. Silents
LES MISERABLES(1927, Fr.)
Aleksandar Milovic
WHITE WARRIOR, THE(1961, Ital./Yugo.), art d
Sandra Milowanoff
Misc. Silents
NENE(1924, Fr.); PECHEUR D'ISLANDE(1924, Fr.); LE FANTOME DU MOULIN ROUGE(1925, Fr.); MAUPRAT(1926, Fr.); LA PROIE DU VENT(1927, Fr.)
Abe Milrad
CONCORDE, THE–AIRPORT '79(, spec eff,
Josh Milrad
BEASTMASTER, THE(1982)
Austin Milroy
Silents
REBECCA THE JEWESS(1913, Brit.)
Dido Milroy
DON'T SAY DIE(1950, Brit.), w
Jack Milroy
BLESS 'EM ALL(1949, Brit.)
Vivian Milroy
DON'T SAY DIE(1950, Brit.), p, d, w; CROW HOLLOW(1952, Brit.), w
Frank Mils
SULLIVAN'S TRAVELS(1941)
Stanislaw Milski
ASHES AND DIAMONDS(1961, Pol.); EVE WANTS TO SLEEP(1961, Pol.); PARTINGS(1962, Pol.)
Doug Milsome
1984
WILD HORSES(1984, New Zealand), ph
Victor C. Milt
PREMONITION, THE(1976), ph
Milt Britton and His Band
RIDING HIGH(1943)
The Milt Herth Trio
JUKE BOX JENNY(1942)
John Miltern
SOCIAL REGISTER(1934); DARK ANGEL, THE(1935); DIAMOND JIM(1935); MAN WHO BROKE THE BANK AT MONTE CARLO, THE(1935); EVERYBODY'S OLD MAN(1936); GIVE US THIS NIGHT(1936); MURDER ON A BRIDLE PATH(1936); PAROLE(1936); RING AROUND THE MOON(1936); SINS OF MAN(1936); LOST HORIZON(1937)
Misc. Talkies
AFRICAN INCIDENT(1934)
Silents
NEW YORK(1916); INNOCENT(1918); ON WITH THE DANCE(1920); KENTUCKIANS, THE(1921); KICK IN(1922); MAN WHO SAW TOMORROW, THE(1922); FINE MANNERS(1926)
Misc. Silents
HER FINAL RECKONING(1918); LET'S GET A DIVORCE(1918); BROTH FOR SUPPER(1919); PROFITEERS, THE(1919); EXPERIENCE(1921); LOVE'S BOOMERANG(1922); MANSLAUGHTER(1922); NE'ER-DO-WELL, THE(1923); COMING THROUGH(1925)
John Milterne
Misc. Silents
THREE LIVE GHOSTS(1922, Brit.)
A.R. Milton
BUFFALO GUN(1961), p, w
Arthur Milton
Silents
NEW CLOWN, THE(1916, Brit.)
Beaufoy Milton
LOVE AT SEA(1936, Brit.), w; YOU'RE THE DOCTOR(1938, Brit.), w; MUTINY OF THE ELSINORE, THE(1939, Brit.), w; CONQUEROR WORM, THE(1968, Brit.)
Beth Milton
AIR MAIL(1932)
Bill Milton
MEAN DOG BLUES(1978), cos
Billy Milton
YOUNG WOODLEY(1930, Brit.); GREAT GAY ROAD, THE(1931, Brit.); MAN FROM CHICAGO, THE(1931, Brit.); THREE MEN IN A BOAT(1933, Brit.); ALONG CAME SALLY(1934, Brit.); MUSIC HATH CHARMS(1935, Brit.); KING OF THE CASTLE(1936, Brit.); NO ESCAPE(1936, Brit.); SOMEONE AT THE DOOR(1936, Brit.); STAR FELL FROM HEAVEN, A(1936, Brit.); AREN'T MEN BEASTS?(1937, Brit.); DOMINANT SEX, THE(1937, Brit.); LAST CHANCE, THE(1937, Brit.); SATURDAY NIGHT REVUE(1937, Brit.); SPRING HANDICAP(1937, Brit.); WEEKEND MILLIONAIRE(1937, Brit.); OH BOY!(1938, Brit.); YES, MADAM?(1938, Brit.); KEY MAN, THE(1957, Brit.); HEAVENS ABOVE!(1963, Brit.); SET-UP, THE(1963, Brit.); WHO WAS MADDOX?(1964, Brit.); DIE, MONSTER, DIE(1965, Brit.); SECOND BEST

SECRET AGENT IN THE WHOLE WIDE WORLD, THE(1965, Brit.); HOT MIL-
LIONS(1968, Brit.); MRS. BROWN, YOU'VE GOT A LOVELY DAUGHTER(1968, Brit.)
Misc. Talkies
    ALONG CAME SALLY(1933)
Dave Milton
    I ESCAPED FROM THE GESTAPO(1943), art d; MYSTERY OF THE 13TH GUEST,
THE(1943), art d; NEARLY EIGHTEEN(1943), art d; SARONG GIRL(1943), art d;
SULTAN'S DAUGHTER, THE(1943), art d; UNKNOWN GUEST, THE(1943), art d;
CHINESE CAT, THE(1944), art d; VOODOO MAN(1944), art d; ALLOTMENT WIVES,
INC.(1945), art d; DIVORCE(1945), ed; JADE MASK, THE(1945), art d; SCARLET
CLUE, THE(1945), art d; THERE GOES KELLY(1945), art d; DARK ALIBI(1946), art
d; FEAR(1946), art d; LIVE WIRES(1946), art d; RED DRAGON, THE(1946), art d;
SHADOW RETURNS, THE(1946), art d; SHADOWS OVER CHINATOWN(1946), art d;
WIFE WANTED(1946), art d; BOWERY BUCKAROOS(1947), art d; FALL GUY(1947),
art d; HARD BOILED MAHONEY(1947), art d; NEWS HOUNDS(1947), art d; SARGE
GOES TO COLLEGE(1947), art d; VACATION DAYS(1947), art d; ANGELS AL-
LEY(1948), art d; FIGHTING MAD(1948), art d; FRENCH LEAVE(1948), art d; I
WOULDN'T BE IN YOUR SHOES(1948), art d; INCIDENT(1948), art d; JIGGS AND
MAGGIE IN SOCIETY(1948), art d; JOE PALOOKA IN WINNER TAKE ALL(1948),
art d; KIDNAPPED(1948), art d; MYSTERY OF THE GOLDEN EYE, THE(1948), art
d; PANHANDLE(1948), art d; RETURN OF WILDFIRE, THE(1948), set d; ROCK-
Y(1948), art d; STAGE STRUCK(1948), art d; ANGELS IN DISGUISE(1949), art d;
BLACK MIDNIGHT(1949), art d; FIGHTING FOOLS(1949), art d; FORGOTTEN
WOMEN(1949), art d; HENRY, THE RAINMAKER(1949), art d; JOE PALOOKA IN
THE BIG FIGHT(1949), art d; LAWTON STORY, THE(1949), art d; TRAIL OF THE
YUKON(1949), art d; TUNA CLIPPER(1949), art d; WOLF HUNTERS, THE(1949), art
d; FATHER MAKES GOOD(1950), art d; HOT ROD(1950), art d; JIGGS AND MAGGIE
OUT WEST(1950), art d; JOE PALOOKA MEETS HUMPHREY(1950), ed; KILLER
SHARK(1950), art d; LOST VOLCANO, THE(1950), art d; OUTLAW GOLD(1950), art
d; OUTLAWS OF TEXAS(1950), art d; SIDESHOW(1950), art d; SILVER RAI-
DERS(1950), art d; SQUARE DANCE KATY(1950), art d; GHOST CHASERS(1951), art
d; I WAS AN AMERICAN SPY(1951), art d; LET'S GO NAVY(1951), art d; LION
HUNTERS, THE(1951), art d; NAVY BOUND(1951), art d; NEVADA BADMEN(1951),
art d; YELLOW FIN(1951), art d; BOMBA AND THE JUNGLE GIRL(1952), art d;
FEUDIN' FOOLS(1952), art d; NORTHWEST TERRITORY(1952), art d; MEXICAN
MANHUNT(1953), art d; YOUNG GUNS, THE(1956), art d; HELL CANYON OUT-
LAWS(1957), art d; OKLAHOMAN, THE(1957), art d; ROLLERCOASTER(1977)
David Milton
    DOUBLE TROUBLE(1941), art d; LET'S GET TOUGH(1942), art d; 'NEATH BROOK-
LYN BRIDGE(1942), art d; SMART ALECKS(1942), art d; GHOSTS ON THE LOO-
SE(1943), art d; KID DYNAMITE(1943), art d; REVENGE OF THE
ZOMBIES(1943), art d; LEAVE IT TO THE IRISH(1944), art d; WHAT A MAN!(1944),
art d; COME OUT FIGHTING(1945), art d; DOCKS OF NEW YORK(1945), art d; MR.
MUGGS RIDES AGAIN(1945), art d; MISSING LADY, THE(1946), art d; MR.
HEX(1946), art d; TRAP, THE(1947), art d; JINX MONEY(1948), art d; SHANGHAI
CHEST, THE(1948), art d; SMUGGLERS' COVE(1948), art d; HOLD THAT BA-
BY!(1949), art d; JOE PALOOKA IN THE COUNTERPUNCH(1949), art d; MASTER
MINDS(1949), art d; MISSISSIPPI RHYTHM(1949), art d; SKY DRAGON(1949), art d;
FATHER'S WILD GAME(1950), art d; LUCKY LOSERS(1950), art d; SHORT
GRASS(1950), art d; SNOW DOG(1950), art d; SOUTHSIDE 1-1000(1950), art d; TEX-
AN MEETS CALAMITY JANE, THE(1950), art d; TRIPLE TROUBLE(1950), art d;
CRAZY OVER HORSES(1951), art d; DISC JOCKEY(1951), art d; FLIGHT TO
MARS(1951), art d; LONGHORN, THE(1951), art d; MONTANA DESPERADO(1951),
art d; RHYTHM INN(1951), art d; SIERRA PASSAGE(1951), art d; YUKON MAN-
HUNT(1951), art d; FARGO(1952), art d; FLAT TOP(1952), art d; FORT OSAGE(1952),
art d; HIAWATHA(1952), art d; KANSAS TERRITORY(1952), art d; MAVERICK,
THE(1952), art d; NO HOLDS BARRED(1952), art d; SEA TIGER(1952), art d; STEEL
FIST, THE(1952), art d; YUKON GOLD(1952), art d; CLIPPED WINGS(1953), art d;
FANGS OF THE ARCTIC(1953), art d; FORT VENGEANCE(1953), art d; HOME-
STEADERS, THE(1953), art d; HOT NEWS(1953), art d; JACK SLADE(1953), art d;
JALOPY(1953), art d; KANSAS PACIFIC(1953), art d; LOOSE IN LONDON(1953), art
d; MARKSMAN, THE(1953), art d; MAZE, THE(1953), art d; MURDER WITHOUT
TEARS(1953), art d; NORTHERN PATROL(1953), art d; PRIVATE EYES(1953), art d;
REBEL CITY(1953), art d; ROAR OF THE CROWD(1953), art d; ROYAL AFRICAN
RIFLES, THE(1953), art d; SAFARI DRUMS(1953), art d; SON OF BELLE
STARR(1953), art d; TANGIER INCIDENT(1953), art d; TORPEDO ALLEY(1953), art
d; WHITE LIGHTNING(1953), art d; BOWERY BOYS MEET THE MONSTERS,
THE(1954), art d; GOLDEN IDOL, THE(1954), art d; HIGHWAY DRAGNET(1954), art
d; JUNGLE GENTS(1954), art d; KILLER LEOPARD(1954), art d; LOOPHOLE(1954),
art d; PARIS PLAYBOYS(1954), art d; RIOT IN CELL BLOCK 11(1954), art d;
BOWERY TO BAGDAD(1955), art d; HIGH SOCIETY(1955), art d; JAIL BUS-
TERS(1955), art d; LORD OF THE JUNGLE(1955), art d; SEVEN ANGRY MEN(1955),
art d; WICHITA(1955), art d; CRASHING LAS VEGAS(1956), art d; DIG THAT
URANIUM(1956), art d; FIGHTING TROUBLE(1956), art d; HOT SHOTS(1956), art d;
SPY CHASERS(1956), art d; THREE FOR JAMIE DAWN(1956), art d; BABY FACE
NELSON(1957), art d; DINO(1957), art d; DISEMBODIED, THE(1957), art d; FOOT-
STEPS IN THE NIGHT(1957), art d; GUN BATTLE AT MONTEREY(1957), art d;
HOLD THAT HYPNOTIST(1957), art d; LAST OF THE BADMEN(1957), art d; LOOK-
ING FOR DANGER(1957), art d; PORTLAND EXPOSE(1957), art d; SABU AND THE
MAGIC RING(1957), art d; SPOOK CHASERS(1957), art d; TALL STRANGER,
THE(1957), art d; UP IN SMOKE(1957), art d; HELL'S FIVE HOURS(1958), art d;
HOUSE ON HAUNTED HILL(1958), art d; IN THE MONEY(1958), art d; JOHNNY
ROCCO(1958), art d; JOY RIDE(1958), art d; MAN FROM GOD'S COUNTRY(1958), art
d; QUANTRILL'S RAIDERS(1958), art d; QUEEN OF OUTER SPACE(1958), art d;
RAWHIDE TRAIL, THE(1958), art d; REVOLT IN THE BIG HOUSE(1958), art d;
UNWED MOTHER(1958), art d; BAT, THE(1959), art d; KING OF THE WILD
STALLIONS(1959), art d; REBEL SET, THE(1959), art d; PLUNDERERS, THE(1960),
art d; PURPLE GANG, THE(1960), art d; GEORGE RAFT STORY, THE(1961), art d;
KING OF THE ROARING TWENTIES–THE STORY OF ARNOLD ROTHSTEIN(1961),
    art d; TWENTY PLUS TWO(1961), art d; MODERN MARRIAGE, A(1962), art d
David Scott Milton
    BORN TO WIN(1971), w
Elvin Milton
Misc. Silents
    OUR MUTUAL FRIEND(1921, Swed.)
Ernest Milton
    SCARLET PIMPERNEL, THE(1935, Brit.); IT'S LOVE AGAIN(1936, Brit.); SOME-
WHERE IN FRANCE(1943, Brit.); FIDDLERS THREE(1944, Brit.); ALICE IN WON-
DERLAND(1951, Fr.); CAT GIRL(1957)

Fred Milton
Silents
    KINGDOM OF LOVE, THE(1918)
George Milton
    ROLLING DOWN THE GREAT DIVIDE(1942), w; WILD HORSE PHANTOM(1944),
w; BORDER BADMEN(1945), w; HIS BROTHER'S GHOST(1945), w; TERRORS ON
HORSEBACK(1946), w
Gerald Milton
    CHINA GATE(1957); DEVIL'S HAIRPIN, THE(1957); FORTY GUNS(1957); QUIET
GUN, THE(1957); RESTLESS BREED, THE(1957); UNKNOWN TERROR, THE(1957);
BEAST OF BUDAPEST, THE(1958); MAN WHO DIED TWICE, THE(1958); TOUGH-
EST GUN IN TOMBSTONE(1958); COUNTERPLOT(1959); UNDERWORLD
U.S.A.(1961); NAKED KISS, THE(1964)
Misc. Talkies
    LUST TO KILL(1960)
Gilbert Milton
    PAPER MOON(1973); SHOOT IT: BLACK, SHOOT IT: BLUE(1974)
H. A. Milton
    TOMB OF THE UNDEAD(1972), p; PIRANHA II: THE SPAWNING(1981, Neth.), w
Harry Milton
    KING OF THE RITZ(1933, Brit.); KING'S CUP, THE(1933, Brit.); ADVENTURE
LIMITED(1934, Brit.); FOLIES DERGERE(1935); CLOWN MUST LAUGH, A(1936,
Brit.); HAPPY DAYS ARE HERE AGAIN(1936, Brit.)
Inger Milton
    DUEL OF THE TITANS(1963, Ital.); DISORDER(1964, Fr./Ital.)
Ivy Milton
    I KNOW WHERE I'M GOING(1947, Brit.)
Jack Milton
    PLEASE STAND BY(1972), p,d&w
Joanna Milton
    PLEASE STAND BY(1972), p,d&w
John Milton
    UNHOLY QUEST, THE(1934, Brit.)
Josh Milton
    GOVERNMENT GIRL(1943)
Julie Milton
    RHYTHM PARADE(1943); RUN FOR YOUR MONEY, A(1950, Brit.); HAPPINESS OF
THREE WOMEN, THE(1954, Brit.); THIRD KEY, THE(1957, Brit.); MIX ME A
PERSON(1962, Brit.)
Marjorie Milton
Silents
    IN SEARCH OF A SINNER(1920)
Maud Milton
Silents
    DAMAGED GOODS(1915)
Misc. Silents
    OLD WOOD CARVER, THE(1913, Brit.)
Maude Milton
Misc. Silents
    MESSAGE FROM MARS, A(1921)
Mayrick Milton
Silents
    HIS HOUSE IN ORDER(1928, Brit.), p
Meyrick Milton
Silents
    AULD ROBIN GRAY(1917, Brit.), d; PROFLIGATE, THE(1917, Brit.), d&w; RED
POTTAGE(1918, Brit.), d; IMPOSSIBLE WOMAN, THE(1919, Brit.), d; LA POU-
PEE(1920, Brit.), d&w; ADVENTURES OF CAPTAIN KETTLE, THE(1922, Brit.), d
Misc. Silents
    AULD ROBIN GRAY(1917, Brit.), d; MY SWEETHEART(1918, Brit.), d
Paul Milton
    SEARCH FOR BEAUTY(1934), w
Rob Milton
    SPY IN THE SKY(1958)
Robert Milton
    CHARMING SINNERS(1929), d; DUMMY, THE(1929), d; BEHIND THE MA-
KEUP(1930), d; OUTWARD BOUND(1930), d; SIN TAKES A HOLIDAY(1930), w;
DEVOTION(1931), d; HUSBAND'S HOLIDAY(1931), d; LADY REFUSES, THE(1931),
w; WESTWARD PASSAGE(1932), d; STRANGE EVIDENCE(1933, Brit.), d; BELLA
DONNA(1934, Brit.), d; LUCK OF A SAILOR, THE(1934, Brit.), d; LAS VEGAS STORY,
THE(1952)
Simon Milton
    ESCAPE FROM THE SEA(1968, Brit.)
Zachary Milton
    DALTON THAT GOT AWAY(1960)
Milton DeLugg and His Swing Wing
    IT'S GREAT TO BE YOUNG(1946)
Milton Douglas Orchestra
    GIGOLETTE(1935)
Milton Fox the Penguin
    QUICK, BEFORE IT MELTS(1964)
Douglas Milvain
    WICKED LADY, THE(1983, Brit.)
Paul Milvy
    HI, MOM!(1970)
Dawson Milward
Silents
    ALTAR CHAINS(1916, Brit.); GENERAL POST(1920, Brit.)
Jo Milward
    DEVIL IS DRIVING, THE(1937), w
Joe Milware
    GUILTY GENERATION, THE(1931), w
A. Milyukhin
    OPTIMISTIC TRAGEDY, THE(1964, USSR)
D. Milyutenko
    MY NAME IS IVAN(1963, USSR)
Dieter Milz
    FITZCARRALDO(1982)

Ilhan Mimaroglu
  FELLINI SATYRICON(1969, Fr./Ital.), m
Aiko Mimaso
  NAKED GENERAL, THE(1964, Jap.)
Aiko Mimasu
  I BOMBED PEARL HARBOR(1961, Jap.); WISER AGE(1962, Jap.); YEARNING(1964, Jap.)
Paul-Robert Mimet
  TRIAL OF JOAN OF ARC(1965, Fr.)
Yvette Mimeux
  PLATINUM HIGH SCHOOL(1960)
Serdjo Mimica
  EVENT, AN(1970, Yugo.)
Vatroslav Mimica
  SULEIMAN THE CONQUEROR(1963, Ital.), p&d, w; KAYA, I'LL KILL YOU(1969, Yugo./Fr.), d, w; EVENT, AN(1970, Yugo.), d, w
Amparo Mimieux
  JACKSON COUNTY JAIL(1976)
Rene Mimieux
  FOLIES DERGERE(1935); PARIS UNDERGROUND(1945); NIGHT AND DAY(1946)
Yvette Mimieux
  TOYS IN THE ATTIC(1963); TIME MACHINE, THE(1960; Brit./U.S.); WHERE THE BOYS ARE(1960); DIAMOND HEAD(1962); FOUR HORSEMEN OF THE APOCALYPSE, THE(1962); LIGHT IN THE PIAZZA(1962); WONDERFUL WORLD OF THE BROTHERS ERIMM, THE(1962); LOOKING FOR LOVE(1964); JOY IN THE MORNING(1965); REWARD, THE(1965); CAPER OF THE GOLDEN BULLS, THE(1967); MONKEYS, GO HOME!(1967); THREE IN THE ATTIC(1968); DELTA FACTOR, THE(1970); SKYJACKED(1972); NEPTUNE FACTOR, THE(1973, Can.); JACKSON COUNTY JAIL(1976); JOURNEY INTO FEAR(1976, Can); BLACK HOLE, THE(1979)
Misc. Talkies
  NIGHT OF THE ASSASSIN, THE(1972); OUTSIDE CHANCE(1978); CIRCLE OF POWER(1984)
Mimile
  YO YO(1967, Fr.)
Yoshio Mimiya
  LONGING FOR LOVE(1966, Jap.), ph
Norma Mimos
  FOR LOVE AND MONEY(1967)
Bill Mims
  I KILLED WILD BILL HICKOK(1956); WALK TALL(1960); BAMBOO SAUCER, THE(1968)
Mavis Mims
  PINOCCHIO IN OUTER SPACE(1965, U.S./Bel.)
William Mims
  BATTLE AT BLOODY BEACH(1961); CHILDREN'S HOUR, THE(1961); SANCTUARY(1961); WILD IN THE COUNTRY(1961); LONELY ARE THE BRAVE(1962); DAY MARS INVADED EARTH, THE(1963); GUNFIGHT IN ABILENE(1967); HOT RODS TO HELL(1967); PAINT YOUR WAGON(1969); BALLAD OF CABLE HOGUE, THE(1970); FLAP(1970); TRAVELING EXECUTIONER, THE(1970); JOHNNY GOT HIS GUN(1971); PICKUP ON 101(1972)
Shintaro Mimura
  RABBLE, THE(1965, Jap.), w
Aung Min
  INN OF THE SIXTH HAPPINESS, THE(1958)
Mina E. Mina
  HEAD ON(1981, Can.)
Mina Mina
  BY DESIGN(1982)
Nika Mina
  MUSTANG COUNTRY(1976)
Tsutomu Minagami
  BANISHED(1978, Jap.), w
Hiroshi Minami
  TOPSY-TURVY JOURNEY(1970, Jap.)
Komei Minami
Misc. Silents
  SOULS ON THE ROAD(1921, Jap.)
Michio Minami
  ROAD TO ETERNITY(1962, Jap.)
Mie Minami
  LIVE YOUR OWN WAY(1970, Jap.)
Roger Minami
  ANNIE(1982); SPRING BREAK(1983), a, ch
Setsuko Minami
  FRIENDLY KILLER, THE(1970, Jap.)
Takao Minami
  KARATE, THE HAND OF DEATH(1961)
Yoshie Minami
  IKIRU(1960, Jap.); FACE OF ANOTHER, THE(1967, Jap.)
Yoko Minamida
  PORTRAIT OF CHIEKO(1968, Jap.)
Michael Minard
1984
  PERFECT STRANGERS(1984), m/1; SPECIAL EFFECTS(1984), m
Tina Minard
  CAPTAIN BLOOD(1935)
Nico Minardos
  GLORY BRIGADE, THE(1953); DESERT SANDS(1955); GHOST DIVER(1957); ISTANBUL(1957); UNDER FIRE(1957); HOLIDAY FOR LOVERS(1959); TWELVE HOURS TO KILL(1960); IT HAPPENED IN ATHENS(1962); SAMAR(1962); DARING GAME(1968); DAY OF THE EVIL GUN(1968); ASSAULT ON AGATHON(1976, Brit./Gr.), a, p
Nicos Minardos
  CANNON FOR CORDOBA(1970)
Steve Minasian
1984
  DON'T OPEN TILL CHRISTMAS(1984, Brit.), p

George Minassian
  NEGATIVES(1968, Brit.), ph
O. Minassian
  COLOR OF POMEGRANATES, THE(1980, Armenian)
Christian Minazzoli
  YOUR TURN, DARLING(1963, Fr.)
Daniele Minazzoli
  FIRST TIME, THE(1978, Fr.)
Wieslaw Mincer
  EVE WANTS TO SLEEP(1961, Pol.), p
Richard Minchenberg
  WOLFEN(1981)
1984
  IRRECONCILABLE DIFFERENCES(1984)
E. Minchenok
  SLEEPING BEAUTY, THE(1966, USSR)
Devon Minchin
  MONEY MOVERS(1978, Aus.), d&w
Mark Minchinton
  CLINIC, THE(1983, Aus.)
Nikolay Minchurm
Misc. Silents
  TRANSPORT OF FIRE(1931, USSR)
Pable Mincie
  LAST BRIDGE, THE(1957, Aust.)
Esther Minciotti
  HOUSE OF STRANGERS(1949); SHOCKPROOF(1949); UNDERCOVER MAN, THE(1949); STRICTLY DISHONORABLE(1951); MARTY(1955); FULL OF LIFE(1956); WRONG MAN, THE(1956)
Silvio Minciotti
  UNDERCOVER MAN, THE(1949); DEPORTED(1950); STRICTLY DISHONORABLE(1951); UP FRONT(1951); CLASH BY NIGHT(1952); FRANCIS COVERS THE BIG TOWN(1953); KISS ME DEADLY(1955); FULL OF LIFE(1956); SERENADE(1956); WRONG MAN, THE(1956)
The Mindbenders
  TO SIR, WITH LOVE(1967, Brit.)
David Mindel
1984
  REAL LIFE(1984, Brit.), m
Ben Mindenburg
  SAMURAI(1945), p, w
Y. Mindler
Misc. Silents
  SIMPLE TAILOR, THE(1934, USSR)
Frederick Arthur Mindlin
Silents
  OUT OF THE WEST(1926), w; TOM AND HIS PALS(1926), w
Hiroko Mine
  MAN IN THE MOONLIGHT MASK, THE(1958, Jap.)
Kazuko Mine
  VIOLATED PARADISE(1963, Ital./Jap.)
Shigeyoshi Mine
  GATE OF FLESH(1964, Jap.), ph
Roy Minear
  WORLD OWES ME A LIVING, THE(1944, Brit.)
Charlotte Mineau
Silents
  CAROLYN OF THE CORNERS(1919); LOVE IS AN AWFUL THING(1922); EXTRA GIRL, THE(1923); SPARROWS(1926)
Misc. Silents
  ROSEMARY CLIMBS THE HEIGHTS(1918)
Ryunosuke Minegishi
  GATEWAY TO GLORY(1970, Jap.)
Vincente Minelli
  PANAMA HATTIE(1942), ch; HOME FROM THE HILL(1960), d
Michael Mineo
  LIFE WITH FATHER(1947); DINO(1957)
Ralph Mineo
  LIFE WITH FATHER(1947)
Sal Mineo
  PRIVATE WAR OF MAJOR BENSON, THE(1955); REBEL WITHOUT A CAUSE(1955); SIX BRIDGES TO CROSS(1955); CRIME IN THE STREETS(1956); GIANT(1956); ROCK, PRETTY BABY(1956); SOMEBODY UP THERE LIKES ME(1956); DINO(1957); YOUNG DON'T CRY, THE(1957); TONKA(1958); GENE KRUPA STORY, THE(1959); PRIVATE'S AFFAIR, A(1959); EXODUS(1960); ESCAPE FROM ZAHRAIN(1962); LONGEST DAY, THE(1962); CHEYENNE AUTUMN(1964); GREATEST STORY EVER TOLD, THE(1965); WHO KILLED TEDDY BEAR?(1965); KRAKATOA, EAST OF JAVA(1969); 80 STEPS TO JONAH(1969); ESCAPE FROM THE PLANET OF THE APES(1971)
Misc. Talkies
  LEFT-HANDED(1972)
Allen Miner
  BLACK PIRATES, THE(1954, Mex.), d; GHOST TOWN(1956), d
Allen H. Miner
  BLACK PATCH(1957), p&d; RIDE BACK, THE(1957), d; CHUBASCO(1968), d&w
Grant Miner
1984
  SUBURBIA(1984)
Jack Miner
  BIG TOWN(1932), ed
Jan Miner
  SWIMMER, THE(1968); LENNY(1974); WILLIE AND PHIL(1980); ENDLESS LOVE(1981)
Marylu Miner
  NEW KIND OF LOVE, A(1963)
Michael Miner
1984
  SCARRED(1984), ph

Stephen Miner
HERE COME THE TIGERS(1978), p, ed
Steve Miner
FRIDAY THE 13TH PART II(1981), p, d; FRIDAY THE 13TH PART III(1982), a, d
Worthington Miner
AFTER TONIGHT(1933), w; HAT, COAT AND GLOVE(1934), d; LET'S TRY AGAIN(1934), d, w; THEY MIGHT BE GIANTS(1971)
Angela Minervini
LA VISITA(1966, Ital./Fr.); STRANGER IN TOWN, A(1968, U.S./Ital.)
Gianni Minervini
LITTLE NUNS, THE(1965, Ital.), prod d
Stephen Mines
MR. HOBBS TAKES A VACATION(1962)
Bernard Minetti
KARAMAZOV(1931, Ger.); DER FREISCHUTZ(1970, Ger.)
Bernhard Minetti
BERLIN ALEXANDERPLATZ(1933, Ger.); LEFT-HANDED WOMAN, THE(1980, Ger.)
Maria Minetti
HATE SHIP, THE(1930, Brit.)
Misc. Silents
HIS OTHER WIFE(1921, Brit.)
Borrah Minevitch
RASCALS(1938); TRAMP, TRAMP, TRAMP(1942)
Minevitch Gang
RASCALS(1938)
Sally Minford
OTHER SIDE OF THE UNDERNEATH, THE(1972, Brit.), m
Chao Ming
GRAND SUBSTITUTION, THE(1965, Hong Kong); LADY GENERAL, THE(1965, Hong Kong); VERMILION DOOR(1969, Hong Kong)
Kao Ming
DRAGON INN(1968, Chi.)
Moy Ming
TIME OF YOUR LIFE, THE(1948); BITTER TEA OF GENERAL YEN, THE(1933); PORT OF SEVEN SEAS(1938); KEYS OF THE KINGDOM, THE(1944); STORY OF DR. WASSELL, THE(1944); PRISON SHIP(1945); CALCUTTA(1947); SECRET LIFE OF WALTER MITTY, THE(1947); SAIGON(1948); LEFT HAND OF GOD, THE(1955)
Ruey Ming
VERMILION DOOR(1969, Hong Kong)
Sung Ming
BRUCE LEE–TRUE STORY(1976, Chi.), ed
Yah Ming
OUTPOST IN MALAYA(1952, Brit.); SECOND FIDDLE(1957, Brit.)
Yu Ming
NIGHT IN HONG KONG, A(1961, Jap.); STAR OF HONG KONG(1962, Jap.); HONOLULU-TOKYO-HONG KONG(1963, Hong Kong/Jap.)
Lo Ming-yau
Misc. Silents
SONG OF CHINA(1936, Chi.), d
Dick Mingalone
RAGGEDY ANN AND ANDY(1977), ph
Pierre Mingand
ABUSED CONFIDENCE(1938, Fr. ABUS DE CONFIANCE)
David Mingay
OTHER SIDE OF THE UNDERNEATH, THE(1972, Brit.), ed; RUDE BOY(1980, Brit.), p&d, w, ed
1984
BIGGER SPLASH, A(1984), w, ed
Don Mingaye
YESTERDAY'S ENEMY(1959, Brit.), art d; NEVER TAKE CANDY FROM A STRANGER(1961, Brit.), art d; SHADOW OF THE CAT, THE(1961, Brit.), art d; WATCH IT, SAILOR!(1961, Brit.), art d; CASH ON DEMAND(1962, Brit.), art d; NIGHT CREATURES(1962, Brit.), art d; PHANTOM OF THE OPERA, THE(1962, Brit.), art d; PIRATES OF BLOOD RIVER, THE(1962, Brit.), art d; KISS OF EVIL(1963, Brit.), art d; NIGHTMARE(1963, Brit.), art d; PARANOIAC(1963, Brit.), art d; CRIMSON BLADE, THE(1964, Brit.), art d; DEVIL-SHIP PIRATES, THE(1964, Brit.), art d; EVIL OF FRANKENSTEIN, THE(1964, Brit.), art d; GORGON, THE(1964, Brit.), art d; RUNAWAY, THE(1964, Brit.), art d; FRANKENSTEIN CREATED WOMAN(1965, Brit.), art d; SHE(1965, Brit.), art d; THESE ARE THE DAMNED(1965, Brit.), art d; DRACULA–PRINCE OF DARKNESS(1966, Brit.), art d; PLAGUE OF THE ZOMBIES, THE(1966, Brit.), art d; RASPUTIN–THE MAD MONK(1966, Brit.), art d; REPTILE, THE(1966, Brit.), art d; DEVIL'S OWN, THE(1967, Brit.), art d; MUMMY'S SHROUD, THE(1967, Brit.), art d; THEY CAME FROM BEYOND SPACE(1967, Brit.), art d; DANGER ROUTE(1968, Brit.), art d; SALT & PEPPER(1968, Brit.), art d; TORTURE GARDEN(1968, Brit.), art d; MIND OF MR. SOAMES, THE(1970, Brit.), art d; SCREAM AND SCREAM AGAIN(1970, Brit.), art d; LUST FOR A VAMPIRE(1971, Brit.), art d; DRACULA A.D. 1972(1972, Brit.), prod d
Gekidan Mingei
CHILDREN OF HIROSHIMA(1952, Jap.), p
Mingenne
Silents
KICK BACK, THE(1922)
Fulvio Mingozzi
BLACK BELLY OF THE TARANTULA, THE(1972, Ital.); SUSPIRIA(1977, Ital.)
Gianfranco Mingozzi
SARDINIA: RANSOM(1968, Ital.), d, w
Margarita Minguillon
ROBIN AND MARIAN(1976, Brit.)
Charles Mingus
ALL NIGHT LONG(1961, Brit.)
Charlie Mingus
SHADOWS(1960), m
Maria Minh
POSTMAN GOES TO WAR, THE(1968, Fr.)
Lillian Miniati
ISLAND OF LOVE(1963)

Val Minifie
MOMENTS(1974, Brit.)
Valerie Minifie
PIRATES OF PENZANCE, THE(1983)
Sergei Minin
Misc. Silents
MITYA(1927, USSR); BLUE EXPRESS(1929, USSR); NEURASTHENIA(1929, USSR); TWO DAYS(1929, USSR)
V. Minin
SANDU FOLLOWS THE SUN(1965, USSR)
Misc. Talkies
BRAINWASH(1982, Brit.)
Alik Miniovich
WELCOME KOSTYA!(1965, USSR)
Minipiano Ensemble of Juveniles
TALKING FEET(1937, Brit.)
Jean Minisini
FANTOMAS(1966, Fr./Ital.)
George Ministeri
TERROR OF TINY TOWN, THE(1938)
Joe Minitello
WINTER MEETING(1948)
Harold Minjer
WOMAN IN THE WINDOW, THE(1945)
Harold Minjir
BELOVED BACHELOR, THE(1931); DAUGHTER OF THE DRAGON(1931); IT'S TOUGH TO BE FAMOUS(1932); JEWEL ROBBERY(1932); LOVE AFFAIR(1932); NIGHT MAYOR, THE(1932); SUCCESSFUL CALAMITY, A(1932); TOMORROW AND TOMORROW(1932); DEATH KISS, THE(1933); KING'S VACATION, THE(1933); NO MORE ORCHIDS(1933); WORKING MAN, THE(1933); FOG OVER FRISCO(1934); SENSATION HUNTERS(1934); SERVANTS' ENTRANCE(1934); HANDS ACROSS THE TABLE(1935); IT'S A SMALL WORLD(1935); MAN WHO BROKE THE BANK AT MONTE CARLO, THE(1935); NIGHT ALARM(1935); SMART GIRL(1935); TWO FOR TONIGHT(1935); DOUGHNUTS AND SOCIETY(1936); WIFE VERSUS SECRETARY(1936); DR. RHYTHM(1938); I STOLE A MILLION(1939); MIRACLES FOR SALE(1939); SERGEANT MADDEN(1939); EDISON, THE MAN(1940); GREAT COMMANDMENT, THE(1941); WHEN LADIES MEET(1941); LUCKY JORDAN(1942); WE WERE DANCING(1942); JACK LONDON(1943); GEORGE WHITE'S SCANDALS(1945)
David Mink
MODEL SHOP, THE(1969)
Werner Mink
FRIENDS AND HUSBANDS(1983, Ger.), art d
Jan Simon Minkema
1984
QUESTION OF SILENCE(1984, Neth.)
Bill Minkin
WHO'S THAT KNOCKING AT MY DOOR?(1968); TAXI DRIVER(1976); KING OF COMEDY, THE(1983)
Barbara Minkus
WHAT'S SO BAD ABOUT FEELING GOOD?(1968); LADY SINGS THE BLUES(1972)
Hannelore Minkus
GERMAN SISTERS, THE(1982, Ger.)
Ludwig Minkus
DON QUIXOTE(1973, Aus.), m
Haunani Minn
YOUNG DOCTORS IN LOVE(1982); MAN WITH TWO BRAINS, THE(1983); SECOND THOUGHTS(1983)
Minnehaha
Silents
FOUR HORSEMEN OF THE APOCALYPSE, THE(1921)
Liza Minnelli
CHARLIE BUBBLES(1968, Brit.); STERILE CUCKOO, THE(1969); TELL ME THAT YOU LOVE ME, JUNIE MOON(1970); CABARET(1972); JOURNEY BACK TO OZ(1974); LUCKY LADY(1975); MATTER OF TIME, A(1976, Ital./U.S.); SILENT MOVIE(1976); NEW YORK, NEW YORK(1977); ARTHUR(1981); KING OF COMEDY, THE(1983)
1984
MUPPETS TAKE MANHATTAN, THE(1984)
Vincente Minnelli
TWO WEEKS IN ANOTHER TOWN(1962), d; ARTISTS AND MODELS(1937), ch; CABIN IN THE SKY(1943), d; I DOOD IT(1943), d; MEET ME IN ST. LOUIS(1944), d; CLOCK, THE(1945), d; YOLANDA AND THE THIEF(1945), d; ZIEGFELD FOLLIES(1945), d; UNDERCURRENT(1946), d; PIRATE, THE(1948), d; MADAME BOVARY(1949), d; FATHER OF THE BRIDE(1950), d; AMERICAN IN PARIS, AN(1951), d; BAD AND THE BEAUTIFUL, THE(1952), d; BAND WAGON, THE(1953), d; STORY OF THREE LOVES, THE(1953), d; BRIGADOON(1954), d; LONG, LONG TRAILER, THE(1954), d; COBWEB, THE(1955), d; KISMET(1955), d; LUST FOR LIFE(1956), d; TEA AND SYMPATHY(1956), d; DESIGNING WOMAN(1957), d; GIGI(1958), d; RELUCTANT DEBUTANTE, THE(1958), d; SOME CAME RUNNING(1959), d; BELLS ARE RINGING(1960), d; FOUR HORSEMEN OF THE APOCALYPSE, THE(1962), d; COURTSHIP OF EDDY'S FATHER, THE(1963), d; GOODBYE CHARLIE(1964), d; SANDPIPER, THE(1965), d; ON A CLEAR DAY YOU CAN SEE FOREVER(1970), d; MATTER OF TIME, A(1976, Ital./U.S.), d
Vincento Minnelli
FATHER'S LITTLE DIVIDEND(1951), d
Kathryn Minner
ANGEL IN MY POCKET(1969)
R.J. Minney
CLIVE OF INDIA(1935), w; MADONNA OF THE SEVEN MOONS(1945, Brit.), p; PLACE OF ONE'S OWN, A(1945, Brit.), p; RANDOLPH FAMILY, THE(1945, Brit.), w; WICKED LADY, THE(1946, Brit.), p; MAGIC BOW, THE(1947, Brit.), p; IDOL OF PARIS(1948, Brit.), p; FINAL TEST, THE(1953, Brit.), p; TIME GENTLEMEN PLEASE!(1953, Brit.), w; CARVE HER NAME WITH PRIDE(1958, Brit.), w
Emmi Minnich
GREAT WALTZ, THE(1972), cos; PERMISSION TO KILL(1975, U.S./Aust.), cos
Indian Minnie
Silents
SUZANNA(1922)

Minnie the Mermaid
Misc. Talkies
LOW BLOW, THE(1970)
Lee Minoff
YELLOW SUBMARINE(1958, Brit.), w
Terrence P. Minogue
ROAR(1981), m
S. Minoi
MAN COULD GET KILLED, A(1966)
Gino Minopoli
SHOOT LOUD, LOUDER... I DON'T UNDERSTAND(1966, Ital.)
Bob Minor
COFFY(1973); SCREAM BLACULA SCREAM(1973); FOXY DROWN(1974); HARD TIMES(1975); ROLLERBALL(1975); DEEP, THE(1977), a, stunts; MR. BILLION(1977); DRIVER, THE(1978); NORMA RAE(1979); SKATETOWN, U.S.A.(1979); FORCED VENGEANCE(1982); WHITE DOG(1982)
Misc. Talkies
CARNAL MADNESS(1975)
Charles Minor
SILVER FLEET, THE(1945, Brit.); CAESAR AND CLEOPATRA(1946, Brit.)
Frank Minor
OUR DAILY BREAD(1934)
Michael Minor
GUESS WHAT HAPPENED TO COUNT DRACULA(1970), art d; STAR TREK II: THE WRATH OF KHAN(1982), art d
Mike Minor
SQUARES(1972), art d
Nora Minor
QUESTION 7(1961, U.S./Ger.); SHOEMAKER AND THE ELVES, THE(1967, Ger.)
Robert Minor
SOUL OF NIGGER CHARLEY, THE(1973)
Timothy Minor
WITHOUT A TRACE(1983)
Neshida Minoru
SHANGHAI EXPRESS(1932)
Dominique Minot
CHARADE(1963)
Alex Minotis
NOTORIOUS(1946)
Alexis Minotis
CHASE, THE(1946); SIREN OF ATLANTIS(1948); PANIC IN THE STREETS(1950); LAND OF THE PHARAOHS(1955); BOY ON A DOLPHIN(1957)
Jingo Minoura
RASHOMON(1951, Jap.), p
Dimko Minov
WITH LOVE AND TENDERNESS(1978, Bulgaria), ph
Bob Minoz
BODY AND SOUL(1981), ch
Tadeusz Mins
IDENTIFICATION MARKS: NONE(1969, Pol.)
Darrell Minshall
Misc. Talkies
TWO CATCH TWO(1979)
John Minshull
THREE RING CIRCUS(1954)
Albert Minsky
TIME OF THE WOLVES(1970, Fr.)
Howard G. Minsky
LOVE STORY(1970), p
Howard Minsky
JORY(1972), p
Sam Minsky
1984
ADVENTURES OF BUCKAROO BANZAI: ACROSS THE 8TH DIMENSION, THE(1984)
Susan Minsky
LOVE IN A TAXI(1980), m
Jack Minster
Misc. Silents
DICKY MONTEITH(1922, Brit.)
The Minstrels
DARKTOWN STRUTTERS(1975)
Minta
JAWS OF THE JUNGLE(1936)
Frederica Minte
LOOKING UP(1977)
Fred Minter
YOURS FOR THE ASKING(1936)
George Minter
CHRISTMAS CAROL, A(1951, Brit.), p; OLD MOTHER RILEY'S JUNGLE TREASURE(1951, Brit.), p; PICKWICK PAPERS, THE(1952, Brit.), p; DANCE LITTLE LADY(1954, Brit.), p; ADVENTURES OF SADIE, THE(1955, Brit.), p; SVENGALI(1955, Brit.), p; CARRY ON ADMIRAL(1957, Brit.), p; NOT WANTED ON VOYAGE(1957, Brit.), p; BEYOND THIS PLACE(1959, Brit.), p; TREAD SOFTLY STRANGER(1959, Brit.), w; PORTRAIT OF A SINNER(1961, Brit.), p
Harold Minter
NEW ADVENTURES OF TARZAN(1935), ed; BILL AND COO(1947), ed; DENVER KID, THE(1948), ed; DESPERADOES OF DODGE CITY(1948), ed; MARSHAL OF AMARILLO(1948), ed; SONS OF ADVENTURE(1948), ed; ALIAS THE CHAMP(1949), ed; DAUGHTER OF THE JUNGLE(1949), ed; POST OFFICE INVESTIGATOR(1949), ed; SOUTH OF RIO(1949), ed; WYOMING BANDIT, THE(1949), ed; BELLE OF OLD MEXICO(1950), ed; OLD FRONTIER, THE(1950), ed; PRISONERS IN PETTICOATS(1950), ed; REDWOOD FOREST TRAIL(1950), ed; TRIAL WITHOUT JURY(1950), ed; UNDER MEXICALI STARS(1950), ed; WOMAN FROM HEADQUARTERS(1950), ed; DESERT OF LOST MEN(1951), ed; INSURANCE INVESTIGATOR(1951), ed; MISSING WOMEN(1951), ed; PRIDE OF MARYLAND(1951), ed; SOUTH OF CALIENTE(1951), ed; THUNDER IN GOD'S COUNTRY(1951), ed; BORDER SADDLEMATES(1952), ed; LAST MUSKETEER, THE(1952), ed; PALS OF THE GOLDEN WEST(1952), ed; SOUTH PACIFIC TRAIL(1952), ed; THUNDERING CARAVANS(1952), ed; TROPICAL HEAT WA-

VE(1952), ed; WILD HORSE AMBUSH(1952), ed; DOWN LAREDO WAY(1953), ed; OLD OVERLAND TRAIL(1953), ed; RED RIVER SHORE(1953), ed; SAVAGE FRONTIER(1953), ed; PHANTOM STALLION, THE(1954), ed; GHOST OF ZORRO(1959), ed
Harold R. Minter
MARSHAL OF CRIPPLE CREEK, THE(1947), ed; OREGON TRAIL SCOUTS(1947), ed
Mary Miles Minter
Silents
STORK'S NEST, THE(1915); DIMPLES(1916); EYES OF JULIA DEEP, THE(1918); AMAZING IMPOSTER, THE(1919); ANNE OF GREEN GABLES(1919); CUMBERLAND ROMANCE, A(1920); EYES OF THE HEART(1920); JENNY BE GOOD(1920); JUDY OF ROGUES' HARBOUR(1920); NURSE MARJORIE(1920); ALL SOULS EVE(1921); DON'T CALL ME LITTLE GIRL(1921); HER WINNING WAY(1921); LITTLE CLOWN, THE(1921); SOUTH OF SUVA(1922); TILLIE(1922)
Misc. Silents
ALWAYS IN THE WAY(1915); BARBARA FRIETCHIE(1915); FAIRY AND THE WAIF, THE(1915); DREAM OR TWO AGO, A(1916); DULCIE'S ADVENTURE(1916); FAITH(1916); LOVELY MARY(1916); ROSE OF THE ALLEY(1916); YOUTH'S ENDEARING CHARM(1916); ANNIE-FOR-SPITE(1917); CHARITY CASTLE(1917); ENVIRONMENT(1917); GENTLE INTRUDER, THE(1917); HER COUNTRY'S CALL(1917); INNOCENCE OF LIZETTE, THE(1917); MATE OF THE SALLY ANN, THE(1917); MELISSA OF THE HILLS(1917); PEGGY LEADS THE WAY(1917); PERIWINKLE(1917); BEAUTY AND THE ROGUE(1918); BIT OF JADE, A(1918); GHOST OF ROSY TAYLOR, THE(1918); POWERS THAT PREY(1918); ROSEMARY CLIMBS THE HEIGHTS(1918); SOCIAL BRIARS(1918); INTRUSION OF ISABEL, THE(1919); WIVES AND OTHER WIVES(1919); YVONNE FROM PARIS(1919); SWEET LAVANDER(1920); MOONLIGHT AND HONEYSUCKLE(1921); COWBOY AND THE LADY, THE(1922); HEART SPECIALIST, THE(1922); DRUMS OF FATE(1923); TRAIL OF THE LONESOME, THE(1923)
Pat Minter
TENDER MERCIES(1982)
Michael J. Minth
DOG'S BEST FRIEND, A(1960), ed
Dorothy Minto
CHILDREN OF CHANCE(1930, Brit.); RAISE THE ROOF(1930); INSIDE THE ROOM(1935, Brit.)
Silents
ONCE UPON A TIME(1918, Brit.); GAME OF LIFE, THE(1922, Brit.)
Misc. Silents
I WILL(1919, Brit.); LITTLE BIT OF FLUFF, A(1919, Brit.); GLAD EYE, THE(1920, Brit.)
W. E. Minto
CALYPSO(1959, Fr./It.)
Faith Minton
WANDERERS, THE(1979); SMOKEY AND THE BANDIT–PART 3(1983)
Fred Minton
APOLOGY FOR MURDER(1945), w
John Minton
1984
MICKI AND MAUDE(1984)
Mary Minton
WHITE CORRIDORS(1952, Brit.)
Robert Minton
BARGAIN, THE(1931), d
Roy Minton
SCUM(1979, Brit.), w
1984
SCRUBBERS(1984, Brit.), w
Connie Mintoya
THREE DARING DAUGHTERS(1948)
K. Mints
TIGER GIRL(1955, USSR), w
Peter Mints
LORDS OF FLATBUSH, THE(1974)
Rose Mints
Misc. Silents
WAY WOMEN LOVE, THE(1920)
David Minty
INTERNECINE PROJECT, THE(1974, Brit.), art d
Emil Minty
ROAD WARRIOR, THE(1982, Aus.)
Muriel Minty
PRICE OF THINGS, THE(1930, Brit.)
C. B. Mintz
Silents
OPEN YOUR EYES(1919), w
Eli Mintz
GOLDBERGS, THE(1950); PROUD REBEL, THE(1958); MURDER, INC.(1960); WON TON TON, THE DOG WHO SAVED HOLLYWOOD(1976); BOARDWALK(1979); STARDUST MEMORIES(1980)
Fred Mintz
SPEEDTRAP(1978), p, w
Jack Mintz
BREAKFAST FOR TWO(1937), w
Melanie Mintz
STUCK ON YOU(1983), w
1984
STUCK ON YOU(1984), w
Murray Mintz
CARDIAC ARREST(1980), d&w
Robert Mintz
ENLIGHTEN THY DAUGHTER(1934), p; FOURTEEN, THE(1973, Brit.), p
Sam Mintz
KIBITZER, THE(1929), w; ONLY SAPS WORK(1930), w; SANTA FE TRAIL, THE(1930), p, w; TOM SAWYER(1930), w; FINN AND HATTIE(1931), w; SKIPPY(1931), w; SOOKY(1931), w; HANDLE WITH CARE(1932), w; MAKE ME A STAR(1932), w; BEST OF ENEMIES(1933), w; DARING DAUGHTERS(1933), w; MAN HUNT(1933), w; NO MARRIAGE TIES(1933), w; ANNE OF GREEN GABLES(1934), w; GALLANT LADY(1934), w; GLIMPSE OF PARADISE, A(1934, Brit.), w; RAFTER ROMANCE(1934), w; HERE COMES COOKIE(1935), w; ROBERTA(1935), w; CHAT-

TERBOX(1936), w; FARMER IN THE DELL, THE(1936), w; CRACK-UP, THE(1937), w; MUSIC MAN(1948), w
Silents
EASY MONEY(1925), w; POTTERS, THE(1927), w; SHOOTIN' IRONS(1927), w; AVALANCHE(1928), w; WARMING UP(1928), w; STAIRS OF SAND(1929), w
Sheila Mintz
NAKED KISS, THE(1964)
Sidney Mintz
CRAZY OVER HORSES(1951), cos; IN THE MONEY(1958), cos
Ulpio Minucci
DAY THAT SHOOK THE WORLD, THE(1977, Yugo./Czech.), md
Baldo Minuti
WONDER MAN(1945); BLACK HAND, THE(1950)
Alexander Minz
TURNING POINT, THE(1977), a, ch
Gustave Minzenty
ROYAL DEMAND, A(1933, Brit.), d
H. Minzloff
PILLARS OF SOCIETY(1936, Ger.), set d
Sergio Mione
RAIDERS OF THE LOST ARK(1981)
Fabrizio Mioni
BLUE ANGEL, THE(1959); HERCULES(1959, Ital.); GET YOURSELF A COLLEGE GIRL(1964); GIRL HAPPY(1965); SPY WITH MY FACE, THE(1966); VENETIAN AFFAIR, THE(1967); PINK JUNGLE, THE(1968); SECRET WAR OF HARRY FRIGG, THE(1968)
Miou-Miou
GOING PLACES(1974, Fr.); GENIUS, THE(1976, Ital./Fr./Ger.); JONAH–WHO WILL BE 25 IN THE YEAR 2000(1976, Switz.); ENTRE NOUS(1983, Fr.)
1984
DOG DAY(1984, Fr.)
Jean-Pierre Miquel
Z(1969, Fr./Algeria)
David Mir
CAVALIER, THE(1928); ESCAPADE(1932); ARTISTS AND MODELS ABROAD(1938)
Silents
HIS HOUR(1924); MAN AND MAID(1925); SLIGHTLY USED(1927); MATINEE IDOL, THE(1928)
Brigitte Mira
FEAR EATS THE SOUL(1974, Ger.); EVERY MAN FOR HIMSELF AND GOD AGAINST ALL(1975, Ger.); MOTHER KUSTERS GOES TO HEAVEN(1976, Ger.); CHINESE ROULETTE(1977, Ger.); LILI MARLEEN(1981, Ger.); KAMIKAZE '89(1983, Ger.)
Irene Miracle
MIDNIGHT EXPRESS(1978, Brit.); INFERNO(1980, Ital.)
Jay Miracle
LULU(1978), ed
Silas Miracle
Misc. Silents
STARK LOVE(1927)
I. Miraeva
MAN WHO BROKE THE BANK AT MONTE CARLO, THE(1935)
Emil P. Miragala
BLOOD FEAST(1976, Ital.), d
Emilio P. Miraglia
NIGHT EVELYN CAME OUT OF THE GRAVE, THE(1973, Ital.), d, w
Shinobu Miraki
DODESKA-DEN(1970, Jap.), art d
Yoshiro Miraki
DODESKA-DEN(1970, Jap.), art d
Manuel Miranada
VENGEANCE IS MINE(1969, Ital./Span.)
Miranda
ROPE OF SAND(1949)
Aldo Miranda
ROMEO AND JULIET(1968, Brit./Ital.)
Aurora Miranda
BRAZIL(1944); PHANTOM LADY(1944); THREE CABALLEROS, THE(1944); TELL IT TO A STAR(1945)
C. Miranda
POCKET MONEY(1972)
Carlos Miranda
ASSASSINATION OF TROTSKY, THE(1972 Fr./Ital.); HAMLET(1976, Brit.), m
1984
MIDSUMMER NIGHT'S DREAM, A(1984, Brit./Span.), m
Carmen Miranda
DOWN ARGENTINE WAY(1940); THAT NIGHT IN RIO(1941); WEEKEND IN HAVANA(1941); SPRINGTIME IN THE ROCKIES(1942); GANG'S ALL HERE, THE(1943); FOUR JILLS IN A JEEP(1944); GREENWICH VILLAGE(1944); SOMETHING FOR THE BOYS(1944); DOLL FACE(1945); IF I'M LUCKY(1946); COPACABANA(1947); DATE WITH JUDY, A(1948); NANCY GOES TO RIO(1950); SCARED STIFF(1953)
Claudio Miranda
RED SKY AT MORNING(1971)
Evan Hollister Miranda
1984
UNFAITHFULLY YOURS(1984)
Isa Miranda
DEFEAT OF HANNIBAL, THE(1937, Ital.); HOTEL IMPERIAL(1939); ADVENTURE IN DIAMONDS(1940); MY WIDOW AND I(1950, Ital.); WALLS OF MALAPAGA, THE(1950, Fr./Ital.); SEVEN DEADLY SINS, THE(1953, Fr./Ital.); LA RONDE(1954, Fr.); RASPOUTINE(1954, Fr.); SUMMERTIME(1955); ROMMEL'S TREASURE(1962, Ital.); DOG EAT DOG(1963, U.S./Ger./Ital.); EMPTY CANVAS, THE(1964, Fr./Ital.); YELLOW ROLLS-ROYCE, THE(1965, Brit.); YOUNG WORLD, A(1966, Fr./Ital.); GREAT BRITISH TRAIN ROBBERY, THE(1967, Ger.); HELL IS EMPTY(1967, Brit./Ital); CAROLINE CHERIE(1968, Fr.); SHOES OF THE FISHERMAN, THE(1968); SHE AND HE(1969, Ital.); DORIAN GRAY(1970, Ital./Brit./Ger./Liechtenstein); NIGHT PORTER, THE(1974, Ital./U.S.)

Misc. Talkies
DO YOU KNOW THIS VOICE?(1964)
John Miranda
BLOODTHIRSTY BUTCHERS(1970); SEED OF INNOCENCE(1980)
Manuel Miranda
SIX DAYS A WEEK(1966, Fr./Ital./Span.); BULLET FOR SANDOVAL, A(1970, Ital./Span.)
Mark Miranda
MADAME X(1966); SULLIVAN'S EMPIRE(1967)
Misc. Talkies
NEEKA(1968)
Rosita Miranda
SUMMERSKIN(1962, Arg.)
Soledad Miranda
MIGHTY URSUS(1962, Ital./Span.); PYRO(1964, U.S./Span.); SOUND OF HORROR(1966, Span.); YOUNG REBEL, THE(1969, Fr./Ital./Span.); 100 RIFLES(1969); COUNT DRACULA(1971, Sp., Ital., Ger., Brit.)
Steve Miranda
LITTLE BIG MAN(1970)
Susana Miranda
FLAP(1970)
Tom Miranda
MAMBA(1930), w
Silents
ANCIENT MARINER, THE(1925), t; AMATEUR GENTLEMAN, THE(1926), t, ed; JAZZLAND(1928), t; RACKET, THE(1928), ed
Misc. Silents
HEARTS OF YOUTH(1921), d
Yves Mirande
MATRIMONIAL BED, THE(1930), w; IT HAPPENED IN PARIS(1935, Brit.), w; MAN OF THE MOMENT(1935, Brit.), w; MR. WHAT'S-HIS-NAME(1935, Brit.), w; CAFE DE PARIS(1938, Fr.), d&w; UN CARNET DE BAL(1938, Fr.), w; KISSES FOR BREAKFAST(1941), w; MOULIN ROUGE(1944, Fr.), d&w
Silents
EVENING CLOTHES(1927), w
Rinaldo Mirannalti
NIGHT OF THE SHOOTING STARS, THE(1982, Ital.)
Francois Mirante
CLOPORTES(1966, Fr., Ital.); RISE OF LOUIS XIV, THE(1970, Fr.)
Letty Mirasol
BIG DOLL HOUSE, THE(1971); TWILIGHT PEOPLE(1972, Phil.)
Pierre Mirat
LONG ABSENCE, THE(1962, Fr./Ital.); HOT HOURS(1963, Fr.); TWO ARE GUILTY(1964, Fr.); GREED IN THE SUN(1965, Fr./ Ital.); IS PARIS BURNING?(1966, U.S./Fr.)
Reinaldo Miravalle
ALSINO AND THE CONDOR(1983, Nicaragua)
Octave Mirbeau
DIARY OF A CHAMBERMAID(1964, Fr./Ital.), w
Nicole Mirel
GREEN MARE, THE(1961, Fr./Ital.); MARTIAN IN PARIS, A(1961, Fr.); SEVEN CAPITAL SINS(1962, Fr./Ital.)
Henry Mirelez
WITHOUT RESERVATIONS(1946); THEY WERE EXPENDABLE(1945); KISSING BANDIT, THE(1948); FANCY PANTS(1950); KIM(1950); MY FAVORITE SPY(1951)
Tony Mirelez
MY FAVORITE SPY(1951)
1984
TERMINATOR, THE(1984)
Leon Mirell
THAT COLD DAY IN THE PARK(1969, U.S./Can.), p; STACEY!(1973), p, w
Greg Mires
1984
ADVENTURES OF BUCKAROO BANZAI: ACROSS THE 8TH DIMENSION, THE(1984)
Matthew Mires
1984
ADVENTURES OF BUCKAROO BANZAI: ACROSS THE 8TH DIMENSION, THE(1984)
Talat Mirfenderski
CYCLE, THE(1979, Iran), ed
Miodrag Miric
1984
SECRET DIARY OF SIGMUND FREUD, THE(1984), art d
Voja Miric
FRONTIER HELLCAT(1966, Fr./Ital./Ger./Yugo.); THREE(1967, Yugo.); FLAMING FRONTIER(1968, Ger./Yugo.)
Antonia Mirio
FELLINI SATYRICON(1969, Fr./Ital.)
Sharon Miripolsky
HAIR(1979)
Walter M. Mirisch
FORT OSAGE(1952), p; FORT MASSACRE(1958), p; MAN OF THE WEST(1958), p; GUNFIGHT AT DODGE CITY, THE(1959), p
Walter Mirisch
TOYS IN THE ATTIC(1963), p; FALL GUY(1947), p; I WOULDN'T BE IN YOUR SHOES(1948), p; BOMBA ON PANTHER ISLAND(1949), p; BOMBA THE JUNGLE BOY(1949), p; BOMBA AND THE HIDDEN CITY(1950), p; COUNTY FAIR(1950), p; LOST VOLCANO, THE(1950), p; CAVALRY SCOUT(1951), p; ELEPHANT STAMPEDE(1951), p; FLIGHT TO MARS(1951), p; LION HUNTERS, THE(1951), p; AFRICAN TREASURE(1952), p; BOMBA AND THE JUNGLE GIRL(1952), p; FLAT TOP(1952), p; HIAWATHA(1952), p; RODEO(1952), p; WILD STALLION(1952), p; ANNAPOLIS STORY, AN(1955), p; WARRIORS, THE(1955), p; WICHITA(1955), p; FIRST TEXAN, THE(1956), p; OKLAHOMAN, THE(1957), p; TALL STRANGER, THE(1957), p; CAST A LONG SHADOW(1959), p; MAN IN THE NET, THE(1959), p; BY LOVE POSSESSED(1961), p; TWO FOR THE SEESAW(1962), p; HAWAII(1966), p; FITZWILLY(1967), p; IN THE HEAT OF THE NIGHT(1967), p; SOME KIND OF A NUT(1969), p; HAWAIIANS, THE(1970), p; ORGANIZATION, THE(1971), p; SCORPIO(1973), p; MR. MAJESTYK(1974), p; SPIKES GANG, THE(1974), p; MIDWAY(1976), p; GRAY LADY DOWN(1978), p; SAME TIME, NEXT YEAR(1978), p; DRACULA(1979), p;

Mistinquett
Misc. Silents
FLEUR DE PARIS(1916, Fr.)
George Mistral
DEVIL MADE A WOMAN, THE(1962, Span.)
Jorge Mistral
MAD QUEEN, THE(1950, Span.); BOY ON A DOLPHIN(1957); LOVE ON THE RIVIERA(1964, Fr./Ital.); GUNFIGHTERS OF CASA GRANDE(1965, U.S./Span.); SCHEHERAZADE(1965, Fr./Ital./Span.)
Ivan Mistrik
SWEET LIGHT IN A DARK ROOM(1966, Czech.); MAN WHO LIES, THE(1970, Czech./Fr.); ASSISTANT, THE(1982, Czech.)
Fali Mistry
GUIDE, THE(1965, U.S./India), ph
Misty
FLY NOW, PAY LATER(1969)
Misty Mountain Boys
NASHVILLE(1975)
Marco Misul
AMARCORD(1974, Ital.)
Hachiro Misumi
HOTSPRINGS HOLIDAY(1970, Jap.)
Kenji Misumi
BUDDHA(1965, Jap.), d; SHOWDOWN FOR ZATOICHI(1968, Jap.), d; DEVIL'S TEMPLE(1969, Jap.), d; MAGOICHI SAGA, THE(1970, Jap.), d; ZATOICHI CHALLENGED(1970, Jap.), d
Michael D. Misuraca
LOOKIN' TO GET OUT(1982)
Gita Misurova
SHOP ON MAIN STREET, THE(1966, Czech.)
Awatea Mita
1984
UTU(1984, New Zealand)
Edo Mita
HELL AND HIGH WATER(1954); PRISONER OF WAR(1954); CRIMSON KIMONO, THE(1959)
Merata Mita
1984
UTU(1984, New Zealand)
Tokiko Mita
BUDDHA(1965, Jap.)
Yoshiko Mita
FINAL WAR, THE(1960, Jap.)
Akio Mitamura
WIND AND THE LION, THE(1975); 1941(1979); CONAN THE BARBARIAN(1982)
1984
INDIANA JONES AND THE TEMPLE OF DOOM(1984)
Gen. Mitamura
BUDDHA(1965, Jap.)
Kunihiko Mitamura
ALMOST TRANSPARENT BLUE(1980, Jap.)
Noburo Mitani
MESSAGE FROM SPACE(1978, Jap.)
Sachiko Mitani
TOKYO STORY(1972, Jap.)
Mitch
DUSTY AND SWEETS McGEE(1971)
Mitch Ayres and His Orchestra
SWINGTIME JOHNNY(1944)
Mitch Ayres Orchestra
MOONLIGHT AND CACTUS(1944)
Bob Mitchel
JOHNNY ROCCO(1958)
Charlotte Mitchel
DENTIST IN THE CHAIR(1960, Brit.)
Gavin Mitchel
CHRISTMAS STORY, A(1983), art d
George Mitchel
DEVIL'S PLAYGROUND, THE(1946), set d
Les Mitchel
OUTLAW'S SON(1957)
Linda Mitchel
MY BREAKFAST WITH BLASSIE(1983), m
Madelon Mitchel
CORKY OF GASOLINE ALLEY(1951); GASOLINE ALLEY(1951); I'VE LIVED BEFORE(1956)
Mary Mitchel
GIRLS ON THE BEACH(1965)
Steve Mitchel
HIT AND RUN(1957)
Mitchell
OLD MOTHER RILEY AT HOME(1945, Brit.), w
Aaron Mitchell
Silents
DINTY(1920)
Adrian Mitchell
PERSECUTION AND ASSASSINATION OF JEAN-PAUL MARAT AS PERFORMED BY THE INMATES OF THE ASYLUM OF CHARENTON UNDER THE DIRECTION OF THE MARQUIS DE SADE, THE(1967, Brit.), w; MAN FRIDAY(1975, Brit.), w
Allan Mitchell
MC VICAR(1982, Brit.); FINAL OPTION, THE(1983, Brit.)
1984
PLOUGHMAN'S LUNCH, THE(1984, Brit.)
Andrew Mitchell
UP JUMPED A SWAGMAN(1965, Brit.), p; PLEASE SIR(1971, Brit.), p
Ann Mitchell
LADY CHATTERLEY'S LOVER(1981, Fr./Brit.)

Arthur Mitchell
MIDSUMMER NIGHT'S DREAM, A(1966); DAY THE FISH CAME OUT, THE(1967. Brit./Gr.), a, ch
1984
COTTON CLUB, THE(1984), ch
Barbara Mitchell
INN FOR TROUBLE(1960, Brit.)
Barry Mitchell
HELLDORADO(1946); SINBAD THE SAILOR(1947); TEMPEST(1982)
1984
ALPHABET CITY(1984)
Basil John Mitchell
PERFECT WOMAN, THE(1950, Brit.), w
Belle Mitchell
I LOVE THAT MAN(1933); STAMBOUL QUEST(1934); VIVA VILLA!(1934); RENDEZVOUS(1935); LEAVENWORTH CASE, THE(1936); SAN FRANCISCO(1936); FIREFLY, THE(1937); MAYTIME(1937); ANGELS WITH DIRTY FACES(1938); MARK OF ZORRO, THE(1940); ROAD TO SINGAPORE(1940); SOUTH OF TAHITI(1941); SABOTEUR(1942); PHANTOM OF THE OPERA(1943); SONG OF BERNADETTE, THE(1943); COBRA WOMAN(1944); MEET ME IN ST. LOUIS(1944); SHERLOCK HOLMES AND THE SPIDER WOMAN(1944); CORNERED(1945); SUDAN(1945); THAT NIGHT WITH YOU(1945); BEAST WITH FIVE FINGERS, THE(1946); FREDDIE STEPS OUT(1946); HIGH SCHOOL HERO(1946); JUNIOR PROM(1946); DESIRE ME(1947); UNCONQUERED(1947); VACATION DAYS(1947); PRINCE OF THIEVES, THE(1948); SWORD OF THE AVENGER(1948); THAT LADY IN ERMINE(1948); VICIOUS CIRCLE, THE(1948); PREJUDICE(1949); GHOST CHASERS(1951); MASK OF THE AVENGER(1951); VIVA ZAPATA!(1952); PASSION(1954); FIRST TRAVELING SALESLADY, THE(1956); LUST FOR LIFE(1956); LONE RANGER AND THE LOST CITY OF GOLD, THE(1958); MAJORITY OF ONE, A(1961); WAR LORD, THE(1965); HIGH PLAINS DRIFTER(1973); SOYLENT GREEN(1973)
Silents
FLYING ROMEOS(1928)
Beth Mitchell
Misc. Silents
FIGHTING STRAIN, THE(1923)
Beverlee Mitchell
SONG OF SCHEHERAZADE(1947)
Beverly Mitchell
FRONTIER BADMEN(1943)
Bill Mitchell
BURN WITCH BURN(1962); TWO AND TWO MAKE SIX(1962, Brit.); FINDERS KEEPERS(1966, Brit.); ACT OF THE HEART(1970, Can.)
Billy Mitchell
BANK DICK, THE(1940); BRIDE WORE CRUTCHES, THE(1940); MISBEHAVING HUSBANDS(1941); MY LIFE WITH CAROLINE(1941); SAN FRANCISCO DOCKS(1941); IN THIS OUR LIFE(1942); MR. CELEBRITY(1942); FALLEN SPARROW, THE(1943); HOME IN INDIANA(1944)
Billy J. Mitchell
CARRY ON ENGLAND(1976, Brit.); RAGTIME(1981); LONELY LADY, THE(1983); NEVER SAY NEVER AGAIN(1983)
1984
TOP SECRET!(1984)
Bruce Mitchell
LONESOME TRAIL, THE(1930), d; TRAPPED(1931), d; HOUSE OF MYSTERY(1934); ST. LOUIS KID, THE(1934); ALIBI IKE(1935); CASE OF THE CURIOUS BRIDE, THE(1935); FOUR HOURS TO KILL(1935); G-MEN(1935); CASE AGAINST MRS. AMES, THE(1936); GREAT GUY(1936); HALF ANGEL(1936); MILKY WAY, THE(1936); SAN FRANCISCO(1936); UNDER YOUR SPELL(1936); EMPEROR'S CANDLESTICKS, THE(1937); FIGHTING TEXAN(1937); HIGH HAT(1937); LOVE IS NEWS(1937); OH, SUSANNA(1937); PAID TO DANCE(1937); PARADISE EXPRESS(1937); WHISTLING BULLETS(1937); WITH LOVE AND KISSES(1937); AMAZING DR. CLITTERHOUSE, THE(1938); I COVER CHINATOWN(1938); MYSTERIOUS RIDER, THE(1938); PRIDE OF THE WEST(1938); PROFESSOR BEWARE(1938); SWEETHEARTS(1938); YOU CAN'T TAKE IT WITH YOU(1938); GOLDEN BOY(1939); ISLAND OF LOST MEN(1939); LET FREEDOM RING(1939); RIDERS OF THE FRONTIER(1939); SILVER ON THE SAGE(1939); STORY OF VERNON AND IRENE CASTLE, THE(1939); EDISON, THE MAN(1940); STAGE TO CHINO(1940); SUNSET MURDER CASE(1941)
Misc. Talkies
FORTY-FIVE CALIBRE ECHO(1932), d; RAWHIDE TERROR, THE(1934), d
Silents
AIR HAWK, THE(1924), d; ANOTHER MAN'S WIFE(1924), d, w; DYNAMITE DAN(1924), d&w; SKY-HIGH SAUNDERS(1927), d&w; AIR PATROL, THE(1928), d; SKY SKIDDER, THE(1929), d
Misc. Silents
STRANGER OF THE HILLS, THE(1922), d; HELLION, THE(1924), d; LOVE'S WHIRLPOOL(1924), d; CLOUD RIDER, THE(1925), d; FLYIN' THRU(1925), d; SAVAGES OF THE SEA(1925), d; SPEED MADNESS(1925), d; TRICKS(1925), d; CUPID'S KNOCKOUT(1926), d; HOLLYWOOD REPORTER, THE(1926), d; THREE MILES UP(1927), d; CLOUD DODGER, THE(1928), d; LAST LAP(1928), d; PHANTOM FLYER, THE(1928), d; SPEED CLASSIC, THE(1928), d; WON IN THE CLOUDS(1928), d
Cameron Mitchell
ADVENTURES OF GALLANT BESS(1948); LETTER FOR EVIE, A(1945); THEY WERE EXPENDABLE(1945); WHAT NEXT, CORPORAL HARGROVE?(1945); MIGHTY MCGURK, THE(1946); CASS TIMBERLANE(1947); HIGH BARBAREE(1947); COMMAND DECISION(1948); HOMECOMING(1948); LEATHER GLOVES(1948); FLIGHT TO MARS(1951); MAN IN THE SADDLE(1951); SELLOUT, THE(1951); SMUGGLER'S GOLD(1951); DEATH OF A SALESMAN(1952); JAPANESE WAR BRIDE(1952); LES MISERABLES(1952); OKINAWA(1952); OUTCASTS OF POKER FLAT, THE(1952); PONY SOLDIER(1952); HOW TO MARRY A MILLIONAIRE(1953); MAN ON A TIGHTROPE(1953); POWDER RIVER(1953); ROBE, THE(1953); DESIREE(1954); GARDEN OF EVIL(1954); GORILLA AT LARGE(1954); HELL AND HIGH WATER(1954); HOUSE OF BAMBOO(1955); LOVE ME OR LEAVE ME(1955); STRANGE LADY IN TOWN(1955); TALL MEN, THE(1955); VIEW FROM POMPEY'S HEAD, THE(1955); CAROUSEL(1956); TENSION AT TABLE ROCK(1956); ALL MINE TO GIVE(1957); ESCAPADE IN JAPAN(1957); MONKEY ON MY BACK(1957); NO DOWN PAYMENT(1957); FACE OF FIRE(1959, U.S./Brit.); INSIDE THE MAFIA(1959); PIER 5, HAVANA(1959); AS THE SEA RAGES(1960 Ger.); THREE CAME TO KILL(1960); UNSTOPPABLE MAN, THE(1961, Brit.); DULCINEA(1962, Span.); LAST OF THE VIKINGS, THE(1962, Fr./Ital.); CAESAR THE CON-

QUEROR(1963, Ital.); DOG EAT DOG(1963, U.S./Ger./Ital.); ERIK THE CON-
QUEROR(1963, Fr./Ital.); BLOOD AND BLACK LACE(1965, Ital.); MINNESOTA
CLAY(1966, Ital./Fr./Span.); RIDE IN THE WHIRLWIND(1966); HOMBRE(1967);
KNIVES OF THE AVENGER(1967, Ital.); TREASURE OF MAKUBA, THE(1967,
U.S./Span.); ISLAND OF THE DOOMED(1968, Span./Ger.); NIGHTMARE IN
WAX(1969); REBEL ROUSERS(1970); BIG GAME, THE(1972); BUCK AND THE
PREACHER(1972); SLAUGHTER(1972); KLANSMAN, THE(1974); MIDNIGHT MAN,
THE(1974); POLITICAL ASYLUM(1975, Mex./Guatemalan); HAUNTS(1977); SLAV-
ERS(1977, Ger.); VIVA KNIEVEL!(1977); SCREAMERS(1978, Ital.); SWARM,
THE(1978); TOOLBOX MURDERS, THE(1978); SUPERSONIC MAN(1979, Span.);
SILENT SCREAM(1980); WITHOUT WARNING(1980); DEMON, THE(1981, S. Africa);
TEXAS LIGHTNING(1981); KILL SQUAD(1982); MY FAVORITE YEAR(1982); RAW
FORCE(1982); GUNS AND THE FURY, THE(1983)
1984
KILLPOINT(1984)
Misc. Talkies
VENGEANCE OF VIRGO(1972); FRANKENSTEIN'S ISLAND(1982)
Camille Mitchell
Misc. Talkies
LABORATORY(1980)
Carlyle Mitchell
MAN CALLED PETER, THE(1955); EDDY DUCHIN STORY, THE(1956); ON THE
THRESHOLD OF SPACE(1956); THERE'S ALWAYS TOMORROW(1956); URANIUM
BOOM(1956); ABDUCTORS, THE(1957); BLOOD OF DRACULA(1957); JEANNE EA-
GELS(1957); GOING STEADY(1958); LITTLEST HOBO, THE(1958); BATTLE OF THE
CORAL SEA(1959); PRIVATE'S AFFAIR, A(1959); TOKYO AFTER DARK(1959)
Carolyn Mitchell
CRY BABY KILLER, THE(1958); DRAGSTRIP RIOT(1958)
Channing Mitchell
TEXAS LIGHTNING(1981)
Charles Mitchell
BIG FIX, THE(1947); HEARTACHES(1947); LOUISIANA(1947); PHILO VANCE'S
GAMBLE(1947); TOO MANY WINNERS(1947); ENTER INSPECTOR DUVAL(1961,
Brit.)
Misc. Silents
WOMAN'S POWER, A(1916)
Charlotte Mitchell
LAUGHTER IN PARADISE(1951, Brit.); NAUGHTY ARLETTE(1951, Brit.); CUR-
TAIN UP(1952, Brit.); MAN IN THE WHITE SUIT, THE(1952); GREAT GILBERT AND
SULLIVAN, THE(1953, Brit.); LADY GODIVA RIDES AGAIN(1955, Brit.); TEARS FOR
SIMON(1957, Brit.); VILLAGE OF THE DAMNED(1960, Brit.); NEARLY A NASTY
ACCIDENT(1962, Brit.); GET ON WITH IT(1963, Brit.); BLOOD ON SATAN'S CLAW,
THE(1970, Brit.); JIM, THE WORLD'S GREATEST(1976); FRENCH LIEUTENANT'S
WOMAN, THE(1981)
Chip Mitchell
1984
BROTHER FROM ANOTHER PLANET, THE(1984)
Christopher Mitchell
HERE WE GO ROUND THE MULBERRY BUSH(1968, Brit.); THIS, THAT AND THE
OTHER(1970, Brit.)
Chuck Mitchell
PENITENTIARY(1979); DON'T ANSWER THE PHONE(1980); HEARSE, THE(1980);
BOXOFFICE(1982); PORKY'S(1982); FRIGHTMARE(1983)
Misc. Talkies
GOODBYE CRUEL WORLD(1983)
Claude H. Mitchell
Misc. Silents
SEEING IT THROUGH(1920), d
Cordelia Mitchell
WOMEN IN A DRESSING GOWN(1957, Brit.)
Craig Mitchell
JIM, THE WORLD'S GREATEST(1976), d&w, ph, ed
Dale Mitchell
KID FROM CLEVELAND, THE(1949)
Dallas Mitchell
MADIGAN(1968)
David Mitchell
RICH KIDS(1979), art d; ONE-TRICK PONY(1980), prod d; MY DINNER WITH
ANDRE(1981), prod d
1984
RENO AND THE DOC(1984, Can.), a, p
Delores Mitchell
GET HEP TO LOVE(1942)
Dobson Mitchell
Silents
CONSPIRACY, THE(1914)
Dodson Mitchell
ROAD TO PARADISE(1930), w
Silents
ARE YOU A MASON?(1915)
Don Mitchell
JOHNNY DARK(1954); SHEPHERD OF THE HILLS, THE(1964), cos; THUMB
TRIPPING(1972), w; SCREAM BLACULA SCREAM(1973)
Donald Mitchell
DOCTOR, YOU'VE GOT TO BE KIDDING(1967); JIGSAW(1968)
Donna Mitchell
HAPPY HOOKER, THE(1975); BELL JAR, THE(1979); FAN, THE(1981)
Doug Mitchell
TEENAGE GANG DEBS(1966)
Douglas Mitchell
CHALLENGE FOR ROBIN HOOD, A(1968, Brit.); CRIMSON CULT, THE(1970, Brit.)
Dr. G. Clay Mitchell
CHOSEN SURVIVORS(1974 U.S.-Mex.), spec eff
Duke Mitchell
BELA LUGOSI MEETS A BROOKLYN GORILLA(1952); CRIME IN THE
STREETS(1956)
Dusty Mitchell
KING KONG(1933)

Earl Mitchell
SPEED DEVILS(1935)
Earle Mitchell
Silents
PRAISE AGENT, THE(1919), w; WIDE-OPEN TOWN, A(1922), w
Eddy Mitchell
COUP DE TORCHON(1981, Fr.)
Edmund Mitchell
Misc. Silents
LONE STAR RUSH, THE(1915), d
Ella Mitchell
LORD SHANGO(1975)
Misc. Talkies
SCALP MERCHANT, THE(1977); LAST REUNION(1978); CAPTIVE(1980); CATA-
CLYSM(1980)
Elisa Mitchell [Elissa Picelli]
KNIVES OF THE AVENGER(1967, Ital.)
Eric Mitchell
FOREIGNER, THE(1978), a, w; UNDERGROUND U.S.A.(1980), a, p, d&w; PERMA-
NENT VACATION(1982)
Ewing Mitchell
TRIPOLI(1950); LAST OUTPOST, THE(1951); BLAZING FOREST, THE(1952);
SPRINGFIELD RIFLE(1952); ABOVE AND BEYOND(1953); WINNING OF THE
WEST(1953); BLACK HORSE CANYON(1954); COURT-MARTIAL OF BILLY MITCH-
ELL, THE(1955); MAN WITHOUT A STAR(1955); BAND OF ANGELS(1957)
Florence Mitchell
VIEW FROM POMPEY'S HEAD, THE(1955)
Frances Marion Mitchell
Silents
GIRL OF MY HEART(1920), w
Frank Mitchell
SHE LEARNED ABOUT SAILORS(1934); STAND UP AND CHEER(1934 80m FOX
bw); 365 NIGHTS IN HOLLYWOOD(1934); MUSIC IS MAGIC(1935); SPRING TO-
NIC(1935); SINGING KID, THE(1936); SONS O' GUNS(1936); LITTLE AC-
CIDENT(1939); TROPIC FURY(1939); DANGER ON WHEELS(1940); DOUBLE
ALIBI(1940); LEATHER-PUSHERS, THE(1940); MA, HE'S MAKING EYES AT
ME(1940); RHYTHM OF THE RIO GRANDE(1940); WEST OF CARSON CITY(1940);
CAUGHT IN THE DRAFT(1941); LUCKY DEVILS(1941); SIX LESSONS FROM
MADAME LA ZONGA(1941); WHERE DID YOU GET THAT GIRL?(1941); DEVIL'S
TRAIL, THE(1942); LONE STAR VIGILANTES, THE(1942); FLESH AND FAN-
TASY(1943); FOLLOW THE BAND(1943); GHOST CATCHERS(1944); THAT'S MY
BABY(1944); COLONEL EFFINGHAM'S RAID(1945); GEORGE WHITE'S SCAN-
DALS(1945); LUCK OF THE IRISH(1948); NEPTUNE'S DAUGHTER(1949); MY SIX
CONVICTS(1952); SCARAMOUCHE(1952); OUR MISS BROOKS(1956); OVER-EX-
POSED(1956); SOME CAME RUNNING(1959); ADVANCE TO THE REAR(1964); COAL
MINER'S DAUGHTER(1980)
Misc. Talkies
ROARING FRONTIERS(1941); BULLETS FOR BANDITS(1942); NORTH OF THE
ROCKIES(1942); PRAIRIE GUNSMOKE(1942); VENGEANCE OF THE WEST(1942)
Frank "Billy" Mitchell
LOVE THAT BRUTE(1950)
Frank F. Mitchell
MONEY FROM HOME(1953)
Gavin Mitchell
SILENCE OF THE NORTH(1981, Can.), art d; IF YOU COULD SEE WHAT I
HEAR(1982), art d; SPASMS(1983, Can.), art d
Geneva Mitchell
BACK PAY(1930); HER WEDDING NIGHT(1930); SAFETY IN NUMBERS(1930);
SON OF THE GODS(1930); BIG GAMBLE, THE(1931); MILLIE(1931); SINGLE
SIN(1931); DISORDERLY CONDUCT(1932); FALSE FACES(1932); GET THAT
GIRL(1932); NIGHT WORLD(1932); HE LEARNED ABOUT WOMEN(1933); MAN OF
SENTIMENT, A(1933); MORNING GLORY(1933); ONLY YESTERDAY(1933); WORLD
GONE MAD, THE(1933); ABOVE THE CLOUDS(1934); BORN TO BE BAD(1934); I AM
SUZANNE(1934); SPRINGTIME FOR HENRY(1934); THIS SIDE OF HEAVEN(1934);
AIR HAWKS(1935); BEHIND THE EVIDENCE(1935); DEATH FLIES EAST(1935);
FIGHTING SHADOWS(1935); GIRL FRIEND, THE(1935); NIGHT LIFE OF THE
GODS(1935); PARTY WIRE(1935); SHE MARRIED HER BOSS(1935); WESTERN
COURAGE(1935); CATTLE THIEF, THE(1936); CRIME PATROL, THE(1936); LAW-
LESS RIDERS(1936)
Genevieve Mitchell
GOOD SPORT(1931)
George Mitchell
3:10 TO YUMA(1957); VIRGINIA(1941); CAPTAIN EDDIE(1945); UNEXPECTED
GUEST(1946), set d; NAKED ALIBI(1954), m; PHENIX CITY STORY, THE(1955);
WILD AND THE INNOCENT, THE(1959); FALLGUY(1962), w; KID GALAHAD(1962);
THIRD OF A MAN(1962), makeup; TWILIGHT OF HONOR(1963); UNSINKABLE
MOLLY BROWN, THE(1964); NEVADA SMITH(1966); RIDE IN THE WHIRL-
WIND(1966); FLIM-FLAM MAN, THE(1967); LEARNING TREE, THE(1969); AN-
DROMEDA STRAIN, THE(1971); TWO-LANE BLACKTOP(1971)
Geraldine Mitchell
DEVIL'S ROCK(1938, Brit.)
Gerry Mitchell
CAPTAIN HORATIO HORNBLOWER(1951, Brit.), p
Gordon Mitchell
CENTURION, THE(1962, Fr./Ital.); GIANT OF METROPOLIS, THE(1963, Ital.);
INVASION 1700(1965, Fr./Ital./Yugo.); REVENGE OF THE GLADIATORS(1965, Ital.);
SEVEN SLAVES AGAINST THE WORLD(1965, Ital.); BEYOND THE LAW(1967, Ital.);
KILL OR BE KILLED(1967, Ital.); REFLECTIONS IN A GOLDEN EYE(1967); FELLINI
SATYRICON(1969, Fr./Ital.); TO KILL OR TO DIE(1973, Ital.); DRUMMER OF
VENGEANCE(1974, Brit.); STAR PILOT(1977, Ital.)
1984
RUSH(1984, Ital.)
Misc. Talkies
LYNCHING(1968); BIG BUST-OUT, THE(1973); SEVEN TIMES SEVEN(1973, Ital.);
SLAUGHTERDAY(1981)
Grant Mitchell
CORPSE CAME C.O.D., THE(; MAN TO MAN(1931); STAR WITNESS(1931); BIG
CITY BLUES(1932); FAMOUS FERGUSON CASE, THE(1932); IF I HAD A MIL-
LION(1932); SUCCESSFUL CALAMITY, A(1932); THREE ON A MATCH(1932); WEEK-
END MARRIAGE(1932); CENTRAL AIRPORT(1933); CONVENTION CITY(1933);

DANCING LADY(1933); DINNER AT EIGHT(1933); HE LEARNED ABOUT WOMEN(1933); HEROES FOR SALE(1933); I LOVE THAT MAN(1933); KING FOR A NIGHT(1933); LILLY TURNER(1933); NO MAN OF HER OWN(1933); OUR BETTERS(1933); SATURDAY'S MILLIONS(1933); STRANGER'S RETURN(1933); TOMORROW AT SEVEN(1933); WILD BOYS OF THE ROAD(1933); 20,000 YEARS IN SING SING(1933); CASE OF THE HOWLING DOG, THE(1934); CAT'S PAW, THE(1934); POOR RICH, THE(1934); SHADOWS OF SING SING(1934); SHOW-OFF, THE(1934); TWENTY MILLION SWEETHEARTS(1934); WE'RE RICH AGAIN(1934); 365 NIGHTS IN HOLLYWOOD(1934); BROADWAY GONDOLIER(1935); GOLD DIGGERS OF 1935(1935); GRIDIRON FLASH(1935); IN PERSON(1935); IT'S IN THE AIR(1935); MEN WITHOUT NAMES(1935); MIDSUMMER'S NIGHT'S DREAM, A(1935); ONE EXCITING ADVENTURE(1935); ONE MORE SPRING(1935); SECRET BRIDE, THE(1935); SEVEN KEYS TO BALDPATE(1935); STRAIGHT FROM THE HEART(1935); TRAVELING SALESLADY, THE(1935); DEVIL IS A SISSY, THE(1936); EX-MRS. BRADFORD, THE(1936); GARDEN MURDER CASE, THE(1936); HER MASTER'S VOICE(1936); MOONLIGHT MURDER(1936); MY AMERICAN WIFE(1936); NEXT TIME WE LOVE(1936); PAROLE(1936); PICCADILLY JIM(1936); HOLLYWOOD HOTEL(1937); LADY BEHAVE(1937); LAST GANGSTER, THE(1937); LIFE OF EMILE ZOLA, THE(1937); MUSIC FOR MADAME(1937); PECK'S BAD BOY WITH THE CIRCUS(1938); REFORMATORY(1938); THAT CERTAIN AGE(1938); WOMEN ARE LIKE THAT(1938); YOUTH TAKES A FLING(1938); HEADLEYS AT HOME, THE(1939); HELL'S KITCHEN(1939); JUAREZ(1939); MR. SMITH GOES TO WASHINGTON(1939); ON BORROWED TIME(1939); SECRET OF DR. KILDARE, THE(1939); 6000 ENEMIES(1939); BRIDE WORE CRUTCHES, THE(1940); CASTLE ON THE HUDSON(1940); EDISON, THE MAN(1940); FATHER IS A PRINCE(1940); GRAPES OF WRATH(1940); IT ALL CAME TRUE(1940); MY LOVE CAME BACK(1940); NEW MOON(1940); WE WHO ARE YOUNG(1940); FEMININE TOUCH, THE(1941); FOOTSTEPS IN THE DARK(1941); GREAT LIE, THE(1941); NOTHING BUT THE TRUTH(1941); ONE FOOT IN HEAVEN(1941); PENALTY, THE(1941); SKYLARK(1941); TOBACCO ROAD(1941); CAIRO(1942); GAY SISTERS, THE(1942); LARCENY, INC.(1942); MAN WHO CAME TO DINNER, THE(1942); MEET THE STEWARTS(1942); MY SISTER EILEEN(1942); ORCHESTRA WIVES(1942); ALL BY MYSELF(1943); AMAZING MRS. HOLLIDAY(1943); DIXIE(1943); AND NOW TOMORROW(1944); ARSENIC AND OLD LACE(1944); IMPATIENT YEARS, THE(1944); LAURA(1944); SEE HERE, PRIVATE HARGROVE(1944); STEP LIVELY(1944); WHEN THE LIGHTS GO ON AGAIN(1944); BEDSIDE MANNER(1945); BRING ON THE GIRLS(1945); CONFLICT(1945); CRIME, INC.(1945); GUEST WIFE(1945); MEDAL FOR BENNY, A(1945); WONDER MAN(1945); EASY TO WED(1946); LEAVE HER TO HEAVEN(1946); BLONDIE'S ANNIVERSARY(1947); BLONDIE'S HOLIDAY(1947); HONEYMOON(1947); IT HAPPENED ON 5TH AVENUE(1947); WHO KILLED "DOC" ROBBIN?(1948)
Misc. Silents
  RADIO-MANIA(1923)
Guy Mitchell
  THOSE REDHEADS FROM SEATTLE(1953); RED GARTERS(1954); WILD WESTERNERS, THE(1962)
Gwen Mitchell
  CHOSEN SURVIVORS(1974 U.S.-Mex.)
Misc. Talkies
  BOOTS TURNER(1973)
Gwenn Mitchell
  RECESS(1967); SHAFT(1971)
Misc. Talkies
  BROTHER ON THE RUN(1973)
H. Bruce Mitchell
  BAR 20 JUSTICE(1938)
Hamilton Mitchell
  CADDY SHACK(1980); GOING APE!(1981)
Helen Mitchell
  UNMASKED(1929)
Herb Mitchell
1984
  BREAKIN' 2: ELECTRIC BOOGALOO(1984); SAM'S SON(1984)
Horace Mitchell
  LOST BOUNDARIES(1949)
Howard Mitchell
  COLLEGE HOLIDAY(1936); HOTEL HAYWIRE(1937); MAKE WAY FOR TOMORROW(1937); WILD MONEY(1937); COMET OVER BROADWAY(1938); HUNTED MEN(1938); PRISON FARM(1938); IRISH LUCK(1939); LUCKY NIGHT(1939); OF MICE AND MEN(1939); SOCIETY LAWYER(1939); TOM SAWYER, DETECTIVE(1939); I LOVE YOU AGAIN(1940); QUEEN OF THE MOB(1940); WYOMING(1940); HONKY TONK(1941); MAD DOCTOR, THE(1941); SKYLARK(1941); HEART OF THE RIO GRANDE(1942); PALM BEACH STORY, THE(1942); AIR RAID WARDENS(1943); HEAVENLY BODY, THE(1943); KEEP 'EM SLUGGING(1943); MISSION TO MOSCOW(1943); SEVENTH VICTIM, THE(1943); THANK YOUR LUCKY STARS(1943); GYPSY WILDCAT(1944); NOTHING BUT TROUBLE(1944); STANDING ROOM ONLY(1944); COLORADO PIONEERS(1945); SCARLET STREET(1945); SHE GETS HER MAN(1945); THOROUGHBREDS(1945); COCKEYED MIRACLE, THE(1946); GIRL ON THE SPOT(1946); NOTORIOUS(1946); POSTMAN ALWAYS RINGS TWICE, THE(1946); TILL THE CLOUDS ROLL BY(1946); DOUBLE LIFE, A(1947); EGG AND I, THE(1947); GOLDEN EARRINGS(1947); HIGH BARBAREE(1947); IT HAPPENED ON 5TH AVENUE(1947); KILLER AT LARGE(1947); SEA OF GRASS, THE(1947); SENATOR WAS INDISCREET, THE(1947); FLAME, THE(1948); HAZARD(1948); I, JANE DOE(1948); SOUTHERN YANKEE, A(1948); WHIPLASH(1948); FOLLOW ME QUIETLY(1949); HOUSE OF STRANGERS(1949); NO WAY OUT(1950); UNION STATION(1950); ENFORCER, THE(1951); CARRIE(1952); NARROW MARGIN, THE(1952)
Silents
  FAITH(1920), d; JAZZ GIRL, THE(1926), d; BOWERY CINDERELLA(1927)
Misc. Silents
  SNARES OF PARIS(1919), d; LOVE'S HARVEST(1920), d; LONE CHANCE, THE(1924), d; ROAD TO BROADWAY, THE(1926), d; BREED OF COURAGE(1927), d; HIDDEN ACES(1927), d
Howard H. Mitchell
  SWEET ADELINE(1935)
Howard M. Mitchell
  THRILL OF A LIFETIME(1937)
Silents
  TRAFFIC COP, THE(1916), a, d; SPLENDID SIN, THE(1919), d; LAMPLIGHTER, THE(1921), d; QUEENIE(1921), d; WING TOY(1921), d; GREAT NIGHT, THE(1922),

d; ROMANCE RANCH(1924), d
Misc. Silents
  BETRAYED!(1916), d; PETTICOATS AND POLITICS(1918), d; GIRL IN BOHEMIA, A(1919), d; LAW THAT DIVIDES, THE(1919), d; BEWARE OF THE BRIDE(1920), d; BLACK SHADOWS(1920), d; FLAME OF YOUTH(1920), d; HUSBAND HUNTER, THE(1920), d; MOLLY AND I(1920), d; TATTLERS, THE(1920), d; CINDERELLA OF THE HILLS(1921), d; EVER SINCE EVE(1921), d; LOVETIME(1921), d; MOTHER HEART, THE(1921), d; CRUSADER, THE(1922), d; WINNING WITH WITS(1922), d; FORGIVE AND FORGET(1923), d; MAN'S SIZE(1923), d
Irving Mitchell
  MANSLAUGHTER(1930); ALL-AMERICAN CO-ED(1941); GANG'S ALL HERE(1941); SECRETS OF THE LONE WOLF(1941); BLACK DRAGONS(1942); FRECKLES COMES HOME(1942); MADAME SPY(1942); MAN FROM HEADQUARTERS(1942); MEET THE MOB(1942); POLICE BULLETS(1942); JEANNE EAGELS(1957)
Jackie Mitchell
  SWEET CHARITY(1969)
James Mitchell
  BORDER INCIDENT(1949); COLORADO TERRITORY(1949); HOUSE ACROSS THE STREET, THE(1949); DEVIL'S DOORWAY(1950); STARS IN MY CROWN(1950); TOAST OF NEW ORLEANS, THE(1950); BAND WAGON, THE(1953); DEEP IN MY HEART(1954); OKLAHOMA(1955); PRODIGAL, THE(1955); PEACEMAKER, THE(1956); ACT OF THE HEART(1970, Can.), ed; LAST GRENADE, THE(1970, Brit.), w; SLOGAN(1970, Fr.); BIG BIRD CAGE, THE(1972), ed; INNOCENT BYSTANDERS(1973, Brit.), w; SPOOK WHO SAT BY THE DOOR, THE(1973); BUSTING(1974), ed; OUR TIME(1974), ed; CALLAN(1975, Brit.), w; PEEPER(1975), ed; FUTUREWORLD(1976), ed; DAY OF THE ANIMALS(1977), ed; TURNING POINT, THE(1977); CAPRICORN ONE(1978), ed; HANOVER STREET(1979, Brit.), ed; GONG SHOW MOVIE, THE(1980), ed
1984
  2010(1984), ed
James D. Mitchell
  LOLLIPOP COVER, THE(1965), ed
Jan Mitchell
  INSIDE AMY(1975)
Jennifer Mitchell
  LET'S MAKE UP(1955, Brit.)
Jeronimo Mitchell
  WAGES OF FEAR, THE(1955, Fr./Ital.)
Jerry Mitchell
  SECRET OF THE PURPLE REEF, THE(1960)
Jim Mitchell
  PHANTOM OF THE OPERA(1943); WHITE SAVAGE(1943); WIND AND THE LION, THE(1975); STAR CHAMBER, THE(1983), ed
Jo Mitchell
  DREAMS THAT MONEY CAN BUY(1948)
Joan Mitchell
  SHOPWORN ANGEL(1938)
Jodi Mitchell
  CONVICT STAGE(1965)
Joni Mitchell
  LOVE(1982, Can.), w
Joe Mitchell
1984
  RIVER RAT, THE(1984), set d
John Mitchell
  NAVAJO(1952); BOTTOMS UP(1960, Brit.); SING AND SWING(1964, Brit.); GROUNDSTAR CONSPIRACY, THE(1972, Can.); UNHOLY ROLLERS(1972)
Johnny Mitchell
  TWO SENORITAS FROM CHICAGO(1943); COVER GIRL(1944); HOLLYWOOD CANTEEN(1944); PILLOW TO POST(1945); CINDERELLA JONES(1946)
Joni Mitchell
  RENALDO AND CLARA(1978)
Joseph Mitchell
  REASON TO LIVE, A REASON TO DIE, A(1974, Ital./Fr./Ger./Span.)
Silents
  OUR HOSPITALITY(1923), w&t; THREE AGES, THE(1923), w; NAVIGATOR, THE(1924), w&t; SHERLOCK, JR.(1924), w; REGULAR FELLOW, A(1925), w; SEVEN CHANCES(1925), w; RAGTIME(1927), w
Julian Mitchell
  SCHWEIK'S NEW ADVENTURES(1943, Brit.); JOHN WESLEY(1954, Brit.); ARABESQUE(1966), w; WEATHER IN THE STREETS, THE(1983, Brit.), w
1984
  ANOTHER COUNTRY(1984, Brit.), w
Julien Mitchell
  EDUCATED EVANS(1936, Brit.); LAST JOURNEY, THE(1936, Brit.); DOUBLE EXPOSURES(1937, Brit.); FROG, THE(1937, Brit.); MR. SMITH CARRIES ON(1937, Brit.); DRUMS(1938, Brit.); QUIET PLEASE(1938, Brit.); IT'S IN THE AIR(1940, Brit.); SEA HAWK, THE(1940); VIGIL IN THE NIGHT(1940); GOOSE STEPS OUT, THE(1942, Brit.); RHYTHM SERENADE(1943, Brit.); ECHO MURDERS, THE(1945, Brit.); BEDELIA(1946, Brit.); HOTEL RESERVE(1946, Brit.); BONNIE PRINCE CHARLIE(1948, Brit.); BOY, A GIRL AND A BIKE, A(1949 Brit.); CHANCE OF A LIFETIME(1950, Brit.); MAGNET, THE(1950, Brit.); GALLOPING MAJOR, THE(1951, Brit.); HOBSON'S CHOICE(1954, Brit.)
June Mitchell
  DEAD ON COURSE(1952, Brit.); NEVER LOOK BACK(1952, Brit.); D-DAY, THE SIXTH OF JUNE(1956)
1984
  BOSTONIANS, THE(1984)
Keith Mitchell
  GYPSY AND THE GENTLEMAN, THE(1958, Brit.); JIM, THE WORLD'S GREATEST(1976); FOX AND THE HOUND, THE(1981)
Ken Mitchell
  HOUNDS... OF NOTRE DAME, THE(1980, Can.), w
Knolly Mitchell
  BLACK KING(1932)
Lane Mitchell
  TOGETHER BROTHERS(1974)

Langdon Mitchell
BECKY SHARP(1935), w
Silents
NEW YORK IDEA, THE(1920), w
Larry Mitchell
NIGHT MOVES(1975)
Laurie Mitchell
FIGHTING TROUBLE(1956); GIRLS IN PRISON(1956); CALYPSO JOE(1957); GARMENT JUNGLE, THE(1957); OKLAHOMAN, THE(1957); ATTACK OF THE PUPPET PEOPLE(1958); FEMALE ANIMAL, THE(1958); QUEEN OF OUTER SPACE(1958); MISSILE TO THE MOON(1959); THAT TOUCH OF MINK(1962); NEW KIND OF LOVE, A(1963); LORD LOVE A DUCK(1966); RUNAWAY GIRL(1966)
Leigh Mitchell
GRAND THEFT AUTO(1977), makeup; SUMMER SCHOOL TEACHERS(1977), makeup
Misc. Talkies
SCREAM BLOODY MURDER(1973)
Leona Mitchell
YES, GIORGIO(1982)
Leslie Mitchell
SKY'S THE LIMIT, THE(1937, Brit.); GENEVIEVE(1953, Brit.); LADY GODIVA RIDES AGAIN(1955, Brit.); WICKED WIFE(1955, Brit.); HEART OF A MAN, THE(1959, Brit.)
Lex Mitchell
STONE(1974, Aus.)
Lisa Mitchell
TEN COMMANDMENTS, THE(1956); SNOW WHITE AND THE THREE STOOGES(1961)
Madelon Mitchell
TWO DOLLAR BETTOR(1951); NEVER WAVE AT A WAC(1952)
Malcolm Mitchell
THAT KIND OF GIRL(1963, Brit.), m, md; GUTTER GIRLS(1964, Brit.), m&md
Margaret Mitchell
GONE WITH THE WIND(1939), w
Marilyn Mitchell
TERROR-CREATURES FROM THE GRAVE(1967, U.S./Ital.)
Mary Mitchell
WARNING TO WANTONS, A(1949, Brit.), w; TWIST AROUND THE CLOCK(1961); PANIC IN YEAR ZERO!(1962); DEMENTIA 13(1963); SWINGIN' SUMMER, A(1965); SPIDER BABY(1968); TAKING OFF(1971)
Misc. Talkies
PELVIS(1977)
Maurice Pete Mitchell
CHAMP, THE(1979)
Mellan Mitchell
PRIEST OF LOVE(1981, Brit.)
1984
INDIANA JONES AND THE TEMPLE OF DOOM(1984); PASSAGE TO INDIA, A(1984, Brit.)
Michael Mitchell
DAFFY DUCK'S MOVIE: FANTASTIC ISLAND(1983), prod d
Mike Mitchell
SECRET AGENT SUPER DRAGON(1966, Fr./Ital./Ger./Monaco), w
Millard Mitchell
SECRETS OF A SECRETARY(1931); DYNAMITE DELANEY(1938); MR. AND MRS. NORTH(1941); GET HEP TO LOVE(1942); GRAND CENTRAL MURDER(1942); MAYOR OF 44TH STREET, THE(1942); SLIGHTLY DANGEROUS(1943); SWELL GUY(1946); DOUBLE LIFE, A(1947); KISS OF DEATH(1947); FOREIGN AFFAIR, A(1948); EVERYBODY DOES IT(1949); THIEVES' HIGHWAY(1949); TWELVE O'CLOCK HIGH(1949); CONVICTED(1950); GUNFIGHTER, THE(1950); MISTER 880(1950); WINCHESTER '73(1950); STRICTLY DISHONORABLE(1951); YOU'RE IN THE NAVY NOW(1951); MY SIX CONVICTS(1952); SINGIN' IN THE RAIN(1952); HERE COME THE GIRLS(1953); NAKED SPUR, THE(1953)
Nancy Mitchell
BRIDAL PATH, THE(1959, Brit.)
Naylon Mitchell
1984
DELIVERY BOYS(1984)
Norma Mitchell
WHY LEAVE HOME?(1929), w; WOMAN ACCUSED(1933); LET'S FACE IT(1943), w
Norman Mitchell
UP TO HIS NECK(1954, Brit.); LAND OF FURY(1955 Brit.); POLICE DOG(1955, Brit.); KID FOR TWO FARTHINGS, A(1956, Brit.); THREE SUNDAYS TO LIVE(1957, Brit.); MAN WHO WOULDN'T TALK, THE(1958, Brit.); PRICE OF SILENCE, THE(1960, Brit.); CARRY ON SPYING(1964, Brit.); GUTTER GIRLS(1964, Brit.); LITTLE ONES, THE(1965, Brit.); GREAT ST. TRINIAN'S TRAIN ROBBERY, THE(1966, Brit.); HALF A SIXPENCE(1967, Brit.); CHALLENGE FOR ROBIN HOOD, A(1968, Brit.); OLIVER!(1968, Brit.); TWO A PENNY(1968, Brit.); TWO GENTLEMEN SHARING(1969, Brit.); ONE MORE TIME(1970, Brit.); LADY CAROLINE LAMB(1972, Brit./Ital.); AND NOW THE SCREAMING STARTS(1973, Brit.); PINK PANTHER STRIKES AGAIN, THE(1976, Brit.); MOON OVER THE ALLEY(1980, Brit.)
Norval Mitchell
DELINQUENT DAUGHTERS(1944); ONCE UPON A TIME(1944); ROGUES GALLERY(1945); TWO TICKETS TO BROADWAY(1951)
Oswald Mitchell
SUCH IS THE LAW(1930, Brit.), p; DANNY BOY(1934, Brit.), p&d, w; COCK O' THE NORTH(1935, Brit.), p&w, d; VARIETY(1935, Brit.), w; KING OF HEARTS(1936, Brit.), p,d&w; SHIPMATES O' MINE(1936, Brit.), d, w; VARIETY PARADE(1936, Brit.), d; OLD MOTHER RILEY(1937, Brit.), d, w; ALMOST A GENTLEMAN(1938, Brit.), d, w; LILY OF LAGUNA(1938, Brit.), d, w; LITTLE DOLLY DAYDREAM(1938, Brit.), d&w; NIGHT JOURNEY(1938, Brit.), d; OLD MOTHER RILEY IN PARIS(1938, Brit.), p&d; ROSE OF TRALEE(1938, Ireland), d&w; JAILBIRDS(1939, Brit.), d; MUSIC HALL PARADE(1939, Brit.), p&d, w; OLD MOTHER RILEY MP(1939, Brit.), d, w; PACK UP YOUR TROUBLES(1940, Brit.), d; SAILOR'S DON'T CARE(1940, Brit.), d, w; BOB'S YOUR UNCLE(1941, Brit.), d, w; DANNY BOY(1941, Brit.), d, w; ASKING FOR TROUBLE(1942, Brit.), d, w; ROSE OF TRALEE(1942, Brit.), w; DUMMY TALKS, THE(1943, Brit.), d; OLD MOTHER RILEY OVERSEAS(1943, Brit.), p&d; OLD MOTHER RILEY AT HOME(1945, Brit.), d; LOYAL HEART(1946, Brit.), d; BLACK MEMORY(1947, Brit.), d; MYSTERIOUS MR. NICHOLSON, THE(1947, Brit.), d, w; GREED OF WILLIAM HART, THE(1948, Brit.), d; HOUSE OF DARKNESS(1948,

Brit.), d; NO ORCHIDS FOR MISS BLANDISH(1948, Brit.), p; MAN FROM YESTERDAY, THE(1949, Brit.), d; TEMPTRESS, THE(1949, Brit.), d
Pamela Mitchell
1984
PRODIGAL, THE(1984)
Pat Mitchell
PERFECT STRANGERS(1950); GUY WHO CAME BACK, THE(1951); WELL, THE(1951); NORTHWEST TERRITORY(1952)
Patric Mitchell
HARRIET CRAIG(1950); SOMETHING TO LIVE FOR(1952)
Patsy Mitchell
BELOVED BRAT(1938)
Paula Mitchell
POINT OF TERROR(1971); GOODBYE, NORMA JEAN(1976)
Philip Mitchell
MISFITS, THE(1961)
Pinkie Mitchell
THIS IS THE ARMY(1943)
Price Mitchell
MYSTERIOUS RIDER, THE(1938)
Ray Mitchell
MEN, THE(1950)
Red Mitchell
SUBTERRANEANS, THE(1960)
"Red" Mitchell
I WANT TO LIVE!(1958)
Reha Mitchell
HIGH WALL, THE(1947)
Rhea Mitchell
ONE HOUR LATE(1935); SAN FRANCISCO(1936); TEXAS RANGERS, THE(1936); MRS. PARKINGTON(1944); HOODLUM SAINT, THE(1946); STATE OF THE UNION(1948); IT'S A BIG COUNTRY(1951); TEXAS CARNIVAL(1951); UNKNOWN MAN, THE(1951)
Silents
OVERALLS(1916); MONEY CORRAL, THE(1919); OTHER KIND OF LOVE, THE(1924)
Misc. Silents
BRINK, THE(1915); ON THE NIGHT STAGE(1915); BECKONING FLAME, THE(1916); D'ARTAGNAN(1916); DON QUIXOTE(1916); MAN FROM MANHATTAN, THE(1916); OVERCOAT, THE(1916); PHILIP HOLDEN - WASTER(1916); SABLE BLESSING, THE(1916); SEQUEL TO THE DIAMOND FROM THE SKY(1916); FATE AND THE CHILD(1917); GILDED YOUTH, A(1917); GYPSY'S TRUST, THE(1917); WHITHER THOU GOEST(1917); BLINDNESS OF DIVORCE, THE(1918); BOSTON BLACKIE'S LITTLE PAL(1918); GHOST OF THE RANCHO, THE(1918); GOAT, THE(1918); HONOR'S CROSS(1918); SOCIAL AMBITION(1918); UNEXPECTED PLACES(1918); DEVIL'S CLAIM, THE(1920); SCOFFER, THE(1920); INNOCENT CHEAT, THE(1921); RIDIN' ROMEO, A(1921); MODERN YOUTH(1926); DANGER PATROL(1928)
Capt. S.G. Mitchell, USN
TASK FORCE(1949), tech adv
Sanford Mitchell
HAREM BUNCH; OR WAR AND PIECE, THE(1969); SCAVENGERS, THE(1969); CORPSE GRINDERS, THE(1972)
Sasha Mitchell
MISSIONARY, THE(1982)
Sharon Mitchell
MANIAC(1980)
Sherry Mitchell
CHANGES(1969); EXPLOSION(1969, Can.)
Shirley Mitchell
JAMBOREE(1944); GAY LADY, THE(1949, Brit.); MR. LORD SAYS NO(1952, Brit.); CLOWN, THE(1953); DESK SET(1957); SPRING REUNION(1957); MY BLOOD RUNS COLD(1965)
Sidney Mitchell
SONG OF KENTUCKY(1929), w; THEY HAD TO SEE PARIS(1929), m; DANCING FEET(1936), m
Spring Mitchell
LOAN SHARK(1952)
Stephen Mitchell
LAST HOLIDAY(1950, Brit.), p; WALK EAST ON BEACON(1952); MR. DENNING DRIVES NORTH(1953, Brit.), p
Steve Mitchell
OTHER WOMAN, THE(1954); BIG COMBO, THE(1955); IT'S ALWAYS FAIR WEATHER(1955); TENDER HEARTS(1955); SEVEN MEN FROM NOW(1956); CHINA DOLL(1958); TERROR IN A TEXAS TOWN(1958); SUBMARINE SEAHAWK(1959); MOST DANGEROUS MAN ALIVE, THE(1961); GATHERING OF EAGLES, A(1963); OPERATION BIKINI(1963); ONCE A THIEF(1965); NEVADA SMITH(1966); YOUNG RUNAWAYS, THE(1968)
Misc. Talkies
PSYCHO SISTERS(1972)
Stuart Mitchell
OPERATION CONSPIRACY(1957, Brit.)
Susan Mitchell
1984
DELIVERY BOYS(1984)
Misc. Silents
PRINCESS' NECKLACE, THE(1917)
Tammy Mitchell
INDEPENDENCE DAY(1976)
Ted Mitchell
FREE, WHITE AND 21(1963)
Terence Mitchell
TOP OF THE FORM(1953, Brit.)
Terry Mitchell
HOUSE OF WAX(1953)
Thomas Mitchell
LITTLE ACCIDENT(1930), w; ALL OF ME(1934), w; ADVENTURE IN MANHATTAN(1936); CRAIG'S WIFE(1936); THEODORA GOES WILD(1936); HURRICANE, THE(1937); I PROMISE TO PAY(1937); LIFE BEGINS WITH LOVE(1937), w; LOST HORIZON(1937); MAKE WAY FOR TOMORROW(1937); MAN OF THE PEOPLE(1937);

WHEN YOU'RE IN LOVE(1937); LOVE, HONOR AND BEHAVE(1938); TRADE WINDS(1938); GONE WITH THE WIND(1939); HUNCHBACK OF NOTRE DAME, THE(1939); LITTLE ACCIDENT(1939), w; MR. SMITH GOES TO WASHINGTON(1939); ONLY ANGELS HAVE WINGS(1939); STAGECOACH(1939); ANGELS OVER BROADWAY(1940); LONG VOYAGE HOME, THE(1940); OUR TOWN(1940); SWISS FAMILY ROBINSON(1940); THREE CHEERS FOR THE IRISH(1940); FLIGHT FROM DESTINY(1941); OUT OF THE FOG(1941); BLACK SWAN, THE(1942); JOAN OF PARIS(1942); MOONTIDE(1942); SONG OF THE ISLANDS(1942); TALES OF MANHATTAN(1942); THIS ABOVE ALL(1942); BATAAN(1943); IMMORTAL SERGEANT, THE(1943); OUTLAW, THE(1943); BUFFALO BILL(1944); CASANOVA BROWN(1944), w; DARK WATERS(1944); KEYS OF THE KINGDOM, THE(1944); SULLIVANS, THE(1944); ADVENTURE(1945); CAPTAIN EDDIE(1945); WITHIN THESE WALLS(1945); DARK MIRROR, THE(1946); IT'S A WONDERFUL LIFE(1946); THREE WISE FOOLS(1946); HIGH BARBAREE(1947); ROMANCE OF ROSY RIDGE, THE(1947); SILVER RIVER(1948); ALIAS NICK BEAL(1949); BIG WHEEL, THE(1949); JOURNEY INTO LIGHT(1951); HIGH NOON(1952); DESTRY(1954); SECRET OF THE INCAS(1954); WHILE THE CITY SLEEPS(1956); HANDLE WITH CARE(1958); TOO YOUNG TO LOVE(1960, Brit.); BY LOVE POSSESSED(1961); POCKETFUL OF MIRACLES(1961)

Tony Mitchell
SOME OF MY BEST FRIENDS ARE...(1971), ph; HIT AND RUN(1982), ph

Ty Mitchell
FOG, THE(1980); HALLOWEEN II(1981)

V.F. Mitchell
VISITOR, THE(1973, Can.)

Valerie Mitchell
STROKER ACE(1983)

Vic Mitchell
Misc. Talkies
RATS(1984)

W. O. Mitchell
WHO HAS SEEN THE WIND(1980, Can.), w

Warren Mitchell
PASSING STRANGER, THE(1954, Brit.); STOWAWAY GIRL(1957, Brit.); ALL AT SEA(1958, Brit.); CRAWLING EYE, THE(1958, Brit.); GIRLS AT SEA(1958, Brit.); MAN WITH A GUN(1958, Brit.); THREE CROOKED MEN(1958, Brit.); BOY WHO STOLE A MILLION, THE(1960, Brit.); HELL IS A CITY(1960, Brit.); SURPRISE PACKAGE(1960); TOMMY THE TOREADOR(1960, Brit.); CURSE OF THE WEREWOLF, THE(1961); ROMAN SPRING OF MRS. STONE, THE(1961, U.S./Brit.); TWO-WAY STRETCH(1961, Brit.); MAIN ATTRACTION, THE(1962, Brit.); OPERATION SNATCH(1962, Brit.); POSTMAN'S KNOCK(1962, Brit.); VILLAGE OF DAUGHTERS(1962, Brit.); CALCULATED RISK(1963, Brit.); SMALL WORLD OF SAMMY LEE, THE(1963, Brit.); CARRY ON CLEO(1964, Brit.); SEVENTY DEADLY PILLS(1964, Brit.); SICILIANS, THE(1964, Brit.); UNEARTHLY STRANGER, THE(1964, Brit.); WHERE HAS POOR MICKEY GONE?(1964, Brit.); WHY BOTHER TO KNOCK(1964, Brit.); BLOOD BEAST FROM OUTER SPACE(1965, Brit.); HELP!(1965, Brit.); SAN FERRY ANN(1965, Brit.); SPY WHO CAME IN FROM THE COLD, THE(1965, Brit.); SPYLARKS(1965, Brit.); ARRIVEDERCI, BABY!(1966, Brit.); INCIDENT AT MIDNIGHT(1966, Brit.); PROMISE HER ANYTHING(1966, Brit.); SANDWICH MAN, THE(1966, Brit.); JOKERS, THE(1967, Brit.); ALF 'N' FAMILY(1968, Brit.); DIAMONDS FOR BREAKFAST(1968, Brit.); ASSASSINATION BUREAU, THE(1969, Brit.); BEST HOUSE IN LONDON, THE(1969, Brit.); ALL THE WAY UP(1970, Brit.); MOON ZERO TWO(1970, Brit.); INNOCENT BYSTANDERS(1973, Brit.); WHAT CHANGED CHARLEY FARTHING?(1976, Brit.); JABBERWOCKY(1977, Brit.); STAND UP VIRGIN SOLDIERS(1977, Brit.); MEETINGS WITH REMARKABLE MEN(1979, Brit.); NORMAN LOVES ROSE(1982, Aus.)
1984
PLAGUE DOGS, THE(1984, U.S./Brit.)
Misc. Talkies
ALF GARNETT SAGA, THE(1972)

Watarina Mitchell
Misc. Silents
DEVIL'S PIT, THE(1930)

William Mitchell
MAN IN THE MIDDLE(1964, U.S./Brit.)

Yvette Mitchell
Silents
PETAL ON THE CURRENT, THE(1919); INFERIOR SEX, THE(1920); KINGFISHER'S ROOST, THE(1922)
Misc. Silents
FLOWER OF DOOM, THE(1917); LAST OF HIS PEOPLE, THE(1919)

Yvonne Mitchell
GENGHIS KHAN(U.S./Brit./Ger./Yugo); QUEEN OF SPADES(1948, Brit.); CHILDREN OF CHANCE(1949, Brit.); TURN THE KEY SOFTLY(1954, Brit.); DIVIDED HEART, THE(1955, Brit.); ESCAPADE(1955, Brit.); BLONDE SINNER(1956, Brit.); WOMEN IN A DRESSING GOWN(1957, Brit.); PASSIONATE SUMMER(1959, Brit.); SAPPHIRE(1959, Brit.); TIGER BAY(1959, Brit.); CONSPIRACY OF HEARTS(1960, Brit.); MAN WITH THE GREEN CARNATION, THE(1960, Brit.); MAIN ATTRACTION, THE(1962, Brit.); JOHNNY NOBODY(1965, Brit.); CRUCIBLE OF HORROR(1971, Brit.); DEMONS OF THE MIND(1972, Brit.); GREAT WALTZ, THE(1972); INCREDIBLE SARAH, THE(1976, Brit.); WIDOWS' NEST(1977, U.S./Span.)

The Mitchell Boy's Choir
JOHNNY ROCCO(1958)

Ilan Mitchell-Smith
1984
WILD LIFE, THE(1984)

Ilan M. Mitchell-Smith
DANIEL(1983)

Bob Mitchum
BAR 20(1943); BEYOND THE LAST FRONTIER(1943); DANCING MASTERS, THE(1943); DOUGHBOYS IN IRELAND(1943); FALSE COLORS(1943); FOLLOW THE BAND(1943); GUNG HO!(1943); HOPPY SERVES A WRIT(1943); HUMAN COMEDY, THE(1943); LONE STAR TRAIL, THE(1943)

Bob [Robert] Mitchum
COLT COMRADES(1943); RIDERS OF THE DEADLINE(1943); WE'VE NEVER BEEN LICKED(1943); MR. WINKLE GOES TO WAR(1944)

Chris Mitchum
YOUNG BILLY YOUNG(1969); RIO LOBO(1970); BIG JAKE(1971); BIG FOOT(1973); CAULDRON OF DEATH, THE(1979, Ital.); DAY TIME ENDED, THE(1980, Span.)

Misc. Talkies
TO LOVE, PERHAPS TO DIE(1975)

Christopher Mitchum
CHISUM(1970); SUPPOSE THEY GAVE A WAR AND NOBODY CAME?(1970); SUMMERTIME KILLER(1973); ONCE(1974); LAST HARD MEN, THE(1976); ONE MAN JURY(1978); STINGRAY(1978); TUSK(1980, Fr.)
1984
EXECUTIONER PART II, THE(1984)

Cindy Mitchum
CHANGES(1969)

Jack Mitchum
PRAIRIE, THE(1948)

James Mitchum
LAST TIME I SAW ARCHIE, THE(1961); YOUNG GUNS OF TEXAS(1963); RIDE THE WILD SURF(1964); IN HARM'S WAY(1965); AMBUSH BAY(1966); MONEY TRAP, THE(1966, Ital.); TRAMPLERS, THE(1966, Ital.); INVINCIBLE SIX, THE(1970, U.S./Iran); MOONRUNNERS(1975)
Misc. Talkies
MASSACRE AT GRAND CANYON(1965)

Jim Mitchum
THUNDER ROAD(1958); BEAT GENERATION, THE(1959); GIRLS' TOWN(1959); VICTORS, THE(1963); LAST MOVIE, THE(1971); TWO-LANE BLACKTOP(1971); TRACKDOWN(1976); MANIAC!(1977); BLACKOUT(1978, Fr./Can.); MONSTER(1979)
Misc. Talkies
MONSTROID(1980)

John Mitchum
KNOCK ON ANY DOOR(1949); IN A LONELY PLACE(1950); DEVIL'S SLEEP, THE(1951); STALAG 17(1953); MAN IS ARMED, THE(1956); FIVE STEPS TO DANGER(1957); UP IN SMOKE(1957); COLE YOUNGER, GUNFIGHTER(1958); IN THE MONEY(1958); JOHNNY ROCCO(1958); SERGEANT WAS A LADY, THE(1961); HITLER(1962); CATTLE KING(1963); MY FAIR LADY(1964); EL DORADO(1967); WAY WEST, THE(1967); BANDOLERO!(1968); PAINT YOUR WAGON(1969); CHISUM(1970); CHANDLER(1971); DIRTY HARRY(1971); ONE MORE TRAIN TO ROB(1971); BIG FOOT(1973); HIGH PLAINS DRIFTER(1973); BREAKHEART PASS(1976); ENFORCER, THE(1976); PIPE DREAMS(1976); TELEFON(1977)

Julie Mitchum
KILLER DILL(1947); HIGH AND THE MIGHTY, THE(1954); EDGE OF HELL(1956); HIT AND RUN(1957); HOUSE ON HAUNTED HILL(1958)

Robert Mitchum
CORVETTE K-225(1943); LEATHER BURNERS, THE(1943); MINESWEEPER(1943); GIRL RUSH(1944); JOHNNY DOESN'T LIVE HERE ANY MORE(1944); NEVADA(1944); THIRTY SECONDS OVER TOKYO(1944); WHEN STRANGERS MARRY(1944); STORY OF G.I. JOE, THE(1945); WEST OF THE PECOS(1945); LOCKET, THE(1946); TILL THE END OF TIME(1946); UNDERCURRENT(1946); CROSSFIRE(1947); DESIRE ME(1947); OUT OF THE PAST(1947); PURSUED(1947); BLOOD ON THE MOON(1948); RACHEL AND THE STRANGER(1948); BIG STEAL, THE(1949); HOLIDAY AFFAIR(1949); RED PONY, THE(1949); WHERE DANGER LIVES(1950); HIS KIND OF WOMAN(1951); MY FORBIDDEN PAST(1951); RACKET, THE(1951); LUSTY MEN, THE(1952); MACAO(1952); ONE MINUTE TO ZERO(1952); ANGEL FACE(1953); SECOND CHANCE(1953); WHITE WITCH DOCTOR(1953); RIVER OF NO RETURN(1954); SHE COULDN'T SAY NO(1954); TRACK OF THE CAT(1954); MAN WITH THE GUN(1955); NIGHT OF THE HUNTER, THE(1955); NOT AS A STRANGER(1955); BANDIDO(1956); FOREIGN INTRIGUE(1956); ENEMY BELOW, THE(1957); FIRE DOWN BELOW(1957, U.S./Brit.); HEAVEN KNOWS, MR. ALLISON(1957); HUNTERS, THE(1958); THUNDER ROAD(1958), a, p, w; ANGRY HILLS, THE(1959, Brit.); WONDERFUL COUNTRY, THE(1959); GRASS IS GREENER, THE(1960); HOME FROM THE HILL(1960); NIGHT FIGHTERS, THE(1960); SUNDOWNERS, THE(1960); LAST TIME I SAW ARCHIE, THE(1961); CAPE FEAR(1962); LONGEST DAY, THE(1962); TWO FOR THE SEESAW(1962); LIST OF ADRIAN MESSENGER, THE(1963); RAMPAGE(1963); MAN IN THE MIDDLE(1964, U.S./Brit.); WHAT A WAY TO GO(1964); MISTER MOSES(1965); EL DORADO(1967); WAY WEST, THE(1967); ANZIO(1968, Ital.); FIVE CARD STUD(1968); SECRET CEREMONY(1968, Brit.); VILLA RIDES(1968); GOOD GUYS AND THE BAD GUYS, THE(1969); YOUNG BILLY YOUNG(1969); RYAN'S DAUGHTER(1970, Brit.); GOING HOME(1971); WRATH OF GOD, THE(1972); FRIENDS OF EDDIE COYLE, THE(1973); FAREWELL, MY LOVELY(1975); YAKUZA, THE(1975, U.S./Jap.); LAST TYCOON, THE(1976); MIDWAY(1976); AMSTERDAM KILL, THE(1978, Hong Kong); BIG SLEEP, THE½(1978, Brit.); BREAKTHROUGH(1978, Ger.); MATILDA(1978); AGENCY(1981, Can.); THAT CHAMPIONSHIP SEASON(1982)
1984
AMBASSADOR, THE(1984)

Trina Mitchum
MECHANIC, THE(1972)

Alex Miteff
REQUIEM FOR A HEAVYWEIGHT(1962)

Nancy Mitford
LITTLE HUT, THE(1957), w; COUNT YOUR BLESSINGS(1959), w

Rupert Mitford
SKY RAIDERS, THE(1938, Brit.)

Howard M. Mithcell
Misc. Silents
LITTLE WANDERER, THE(1920), d

Felicity Mithen
1984
UP THE CREEK(1984)

Marta Mithovitch
NUREMBERG(1961)

Georg Mitic
FRONTIER HELLCAT(1966, Fr./Ital./Ger./Yugo.)

Gojko Mitic
SIGNALS-AN ADVENTURE IN SPACE(1970, E. Ger./Pol.)

Edo Mito
SOUTH SEA WOMAN(1953); TOKYO AFTER DARK(1959)

Mitsuko Mito
SAMURAI(PART II)** (1967, Jap.); UGETSU(1954, Jap.); SAMURAI(1955, Jap.); GOLDEN DEMON(1956, Jap.)

John Mitory
VON RYAN'S EXPRESS(1965)

Henry Mitowa
HOUSE WHERE EVIL DWELLS, THE(1982)
Ajay Mitra
APARAJITO(1959, India)
Manoj Mitra
1984
HOME AND THE WORLD, THE(1984, India)
Narendara Nath Mitra
BIG CITY, THE(1963, India), w
Subrata Mitra
PATHER PANCHALI(1958, India), ph; WORLD OF APU, THE(1960, India), ph; GODDESS, THE(1962, India), ph; BIG CITY, THE(1963, India), ph; HOUSEHOLDER, THE(1963, US/India), ph; MUSIC ROOM, THE(1963, India), ph; KANCHENJUNG-HA(1966, India), ph; SHAKESPEARE WALLAH(1966, India), ph; GURU, THE(1969, U.S./India), ph; BOMBAY TALKIE(1970, India), ph
Subroto Mitra
APARAJITO(1959, India), ph
Tiberio Mitri
FAREWELL TO ARMS, A(1957); BEN HUR(1959); FIVE BRANDED WOMEN(1960); GREAT WAR, THE(1961, Fr., Ital.); BEST OF ENEMIES, THE(1962); DAMON AND PYTHIAS(1962); WASTREL, THE(1963, Ital.); HILLS RUN RED, THE(1967, Ital.); DANGER: DIABOLIK(1968, Ital./Fr.); TOYS ARE NOT FOR CHILDREN(1972)
Priamus Mitromaras
ISLAND OF LOVE(1963)
Roberto Mitrotti
1984
SECRET DIARY OF SIGMUND FREUD, THE(1984), w
Misc. Talkies
LITTLE GIRL, BIG TEASE(1977), d
Zita Mitrovic
WITNESS OUT OF HELL(1967, Ger./Yugo.), d
Marta Mitrovich
WHEN STRANGERS MARRY(1944); DARK MIRROR, THE(1946); HIGH WALL, THE(1947); UNFAITHFUL, THE(1947); GOOD SAM(1948); I, JANE DOE(1948); ONCE A THIEF(1950); PRISONERS IN PETTICOATS(1950); CHAIN OF CIRCUMSTANCE(1951); TITANIC(1953)
Martha Mitrovich
THREE HUSBANDS(1950)
Marta Mitrovitch
LADY WITHOUT PASSPORT, A(1950)
Ira Mitskik
MOTHER AND DAUGHTER(1965, USSR)
D.J. Mitsoras
Silents
ROSE OF PARIS, THE(1924)
Misc. Silents
RACING LUCK(1924)
Mitsou
MAIDSTONE(1970)
Alou Mitsou
MID-DAY MISTRESS(1968)
Mitsouko
SWEET ECSTASY(1962, Fr.); MISSION BLOODY MARY(1967, Fr./Ital./Span.)
Maryse Guy Mitsouko
THUNDERBALL(1965, Brit.)
Ken Mitsuda
BALLAD OF NARAYAMA(1961, Jap.); GREAT WALL, THE(1965, Jap.); RED BEARD(1966, Jap.); BEAUTIFUL SWINDLERS, THE(1967, Fr./Ital./Jap./Neth.); I LIVE IN FEAR(1967, Jap.); SANSHO THE BAILIFF(1969, Jap.)
Koji Mitsui
HUMAN CONDITION, THE(1959, Jap.); LOWER DEPTHS, THE(1962, Jap.); HIGH AND LOW(1963, Jap.); WOMAN IN THE DUNES(1964, Jap.); RED BEARD(1966, Jap.); EMPEROR AND A GENERAL, THE(1968, Jap.); FLOATING WEEDS(1970, Jap.)
Alexander Mitta
GIRL AND THE BUGLER, THE(1967, USSR), d
Mina Mittelman
PRETTY BABY(1978), cos
Hubert Mittendorf
HOT MONEY GIRL(1962, Brit./Ger.)
Rapindranath Mitter
ROMAN HOLIDAY(1953)
Gertraud Mittermayr
HEIDI(1968, Aust.); UNCLE TOM'S CABIN(1969, Fr./Ital./Ger./Yugo.)
Toni Mitterwurzer
MAGIC FACE, THE(1951, Aust.); NO TIME FOR FLOWERS(1952)
Vittorio Mittini
ANGELINA(1948, Ital.)
Ben Mittleman
MAKING LOVE(1982)
Gizella Mittleman
LOOKING UP(1977)
Mina Mittleman
BEN(1972), cos; 9/30/55(1977), cos
Leo Mittler
HONEYMOON FOR THREE(1935, Brit.), d; CHEER UP!(1936, Brit.), d; LAST WALTZ, THE(1936, Brit.), d; SONG OF RUSSIA(1943), w
Wolf Mittler
OPERATION GANYMED(1977, Ger.)
Tara Mitton
SLOW DANCING IN THE BIG CITY(1978)
Nomi Mitty
CARNY(1980); I OUGHT TO BE IN PICTURES(1982)
Vera Miturich
MY NAME IS IVAN(1963, USSR)
Jill Mitwell
LEAP OF FAITH(1931, Brit.), art d
G. Mityakov
WAR AND PEACE(1968, USSR)

Mitzi
FLIPPER(1963)
Dean Edward Mitzner
1941(1979), prod d; LOOKER(1981), prod d; NATIONAL LAMPOON'S CLASS REUNION(1982), prod d; TRON(1982), prod d; MAN, WOMAN AND CHILD(1983), prod d; NIGHTMARES(1983), prod d
Dean Mitzner
BIG WEDNESDAY(1978), art d; NINE TO FIVE(1980), prod d
Mitzou
LOVE AND PAIN AND THE WHOLE DAMN THING(1973), cos
K. Miuffko
THEY WANTED PEACE(1940, USSR)
Michei Miura
STOPOVER TOKYO(1957)
S. Mivashita
ANATAHAN(1953, Jap.)
Reiji Miwa
SAMURAI ASSASSIN(1965, Jap.), p
Art Mix [Victor Adamson, Denver Dixon, George Kesterson]
WEST OF THE ROCKIES(1929); LONESOME TRAIL, THE(1930); MEN WITHOUT LAW(1930); SAGEBRUSH POLITICS(1930); FIGHTING THRU(1931); CORNERED(1932); RIDING TORNADO, THE(1932); YOUNG BLOOD(1932); DUDE BANDIT, THE(1933); STRAWBERRY ROAN(1933); FIGHTING RANGER, THE(1934); HONOR OF THE RANGE(1934); KID MILLIONS(1934); KING OF THE WILD HORSES, THE(1934); SAGEBRUSH TRAIL(1934); TRAIL DRIVE, THE(1934); WAY OF THE WEST, THE(1934); COWBOY AND THE BANDIT, THE(1935); CYCLONE OF THE SADDLE(1935); GHOST RIDER, THE(1935); PALS OF THE RANGE(1935); POWDERSMOKE RANGE(1935); WESTERN FRONTIER(1935); END OF THE TRAIL(1936); FUGITIVE SHERIFF, THE(1936); HEIR TO TROUBLE(1936); LUCKY TERROR(1936); PRESCOTT KID, THE(1936); SWIFTY(1936); WINDS OF THE WASTELAND(1936); YELLOW DUST(1936); DODGE CITY TRAIL(1937); EMPTY HOLSTERS(1937); OLD WYOMING TRAIL, THE(1937); ONE MAN JUSTICE(1937); PRAIRIE THUNDER(1937); RIO GRANDE RANGER(1937); SINGING OUTLAW(1937); TRAPPED(1937); TWO-FISTED SHERIFF(1937); TWO GUN LAW(1937); WESTBOUND MAIL(1937); YODELIN' KID FROM PINE RIDGE(1937); CALL OF THE ROCKIES(1938); CATTLE RAIDERS(1938); LAW OF THE PLAINS(1938); OUTLAWS OF THE PRAIRIE(1938); SERGEANT MURPHY(1938); SOUTH OF ARIZONA(1938); WEST OF CHEYENNE(1938); LET FREEDOM RING(1939); MAISIE(1939); RIO GRANDE(1939); ROVIN' TUMBLEWEEDS(1939); SPOILERS OF THE RANGE(1939); TAMING OF THE WEST, THE(1939); THUNDERING WEST, THE(1939); MELODY RANCH(1940); STRANGER FROM TEXAS, THE(1940); WESTERNER, THE(1940); NEVADA CITY(1941); NORTH FROM LONE STAR(1941); DOWN RIO GRANDE WAY(1942); IN OLD CALIFORNIA(1942); OVERLAND STAGECOACH(1942); PARDON MY GUN(1942); RIDIN' DOWN THE CANYON(1942); SHUT MY BIG MOUTH(1942); HAIL TO THE RANGERS(1943); OUTLAWS OF STAMPEDE PASS(1943); SILVER CITY RAIDERS(1943); THUNDERING TRAILS(1943); MYSTERY MAN(1944); ROARING WESTWARD(1949)
Misc. Talkies
LARIATS AND SIXSHOOTERS(1931); PUEBLO TERROR(1931); LAWLESS VALLEY(1932); RAWHIDE TERROR, THE(1934); FIVE BAD MEN(1935)
Misc. Silents
ACE OF CACTUS RANGE(1924); RIDER OF MYSTERY RANCH(1924); ROMANCE OF THE WASTELAND(1924); SOUTH OF SANTA FE(1924); TERROR OF PUEBLO, THE(1924); DESERT VULTURES(1930)
Ruth Mix
RED FORK RANGE(1931); FIGHTING PIONEERS(1935); RIDING AVENGER, THE(1936)
Misc. Talkies
GUNFIRE(1935); SADDLE ACES(1935); TONTO KID, THE(1935)
Silents
FOUR SONS(1928)
Misc. Silents
TEX(1926); THAT GIRL OKLAHOMA(1926); LITTLE BOSS, THE(1927)
Tom Mix
DESTRY RIDES AGAIN(1932); MY PAL, THE KING(1932); RIDER OF DEATH VALLEY(1932); TEXAS BAD MAN(1932); FLAMING GUNS(1933); FOURTH HORSEMAN, THE(1933); HIDDEN GOLD(1933); RUSTLERS' ROUNDUP(1933); TERROR TRAIL(1933)
Silents
FAME AND FORTUNE(1918); CYCLONE, THE(1920); NIGHT HORSEMAN, THE(1921); QUEEN OF SHEBA(1921), d; CHASING THE MOON(1922), a, w; DO AND DARE(1922); JUST TONY(1922); SKY HIGH(1922); NORTH OF HUDSON BAY(1923); ROMANCE LAND(1923); STEPPING FAST(1923); LADIES TO BOARD(1924); OH, YOU TONY!(1924); DICK TURPIN(1925); LUCKY HORSESHOE, THE(1925); RAINBOW TRAIL, THE(1925); RIDERS OF THE PURPLE SAGE(1925); GREAT K & A TRAIN ROBBERY, THE(1926); NO MAN'S GOLD(1926); TONY RUNS WILD(1926); YANKEE SENOR, THE(1926); ARIZONA WILDCAT(1927); BRONCHO TWISTER(1927); CIRCUS ACE, THE(1927); LAST TRAIL, THE(1927); OUTLAWS OF RED RIVER(1927); SILVER VALLEY(1927); TUMBLING RIVER(1927); DAREDEVIL'S REWARD(1928); OUTLAWED(1929)
Misc. Silents
CHIP OF THE FLYING U(1914); DURAND OF THE BAD LANDS(1917); HEART OF TEXAS RYAN, THE(1917); ACE HIGH(1918); CUPID'S ROUND-UP(1918); MR. LOGAN, USA(1918); SIX-SHOOTER ANDY(1918); WESTERN BLOOD(1918); COMING OF THE LAW, THE(1919); FEUD, THE(1919); FIGHTING FOR GOLD(1919); HELL ROARIN' REFORM(1919); ROUGH RIDING ROMANCE(1919); SPEED MANIAC, THE(1919); TREAT 'EM ROUGH(1919); WILDERNESS TRAIL, THE(1919); DAREDEVIL, THE(1920), a, d; DESERT LOVE(1920); PRAIRIE TRAILS(1920); TERROR, THE(1920); TEXAN, THE(1920); THREE GOLD COINS(1920); UNTAMED(1920); AFTER YOUR OWN HEART(1921); BIG TOWN ROUND-UP(1921); HANDS OFF(1921); RIDIN' ROMEO, A(1921); ROAD DEMON, THE(1921); ROUGH DIAMOND, THE(1921); TRAILIN'(1921); ARABIA(1922); CATCH MY SMOKE(1922); FIGHTING STREAK, THE(1922); FOR BIG STAKES(1922); UP AND GOING(1922); EYES OF THE FOREST(1923); LONE STAR RANGER, THE(1923); MILE-A-MINUTE ROMEO(1923); SOFT BOILED(1923); THREE JUMPS AHEAD(1923); DEADWOOD COACH, THE(1924); FOREMAN OF BAR Z RANCH, THE(1924); GOLDEN THOUGHT, A(1924); HEART BUSTER, THE(1924); LAST OF THE DUANES, THE(1924); PALS IN BLUE(1924); STAGE COACH DRIVER(1924); TEETH(1924); TROUBLE SHOOTER, THE(1924); BEST BAD MAN, THE(1925); CHILD OF THE PRAIRIE, A(1925), a, d; DANGER RIDER(1925); EVERLASTING WHISPER, THE(1925); LAW AND THE

OUTLAW(1925); CANYON OF LIGHT, THE(1926); HARD BOILED(1926); MY OWN PAL(1926); HELLO CHEYENE(1928); HORSEMAN OF THE PLAINS, A(1928); KING COWBOY(1928); PAINTED POST(1928); SON OF THE GOLDEN WEST(1928); BIG DIAMOND ROBBERY, THE(1929); DRIFTER, THE(1929)

Alan Mixon
FIREBALL JUNGLE(1968)

Miya
CHARLIE CHAN AND THE CURSE OF THE DRAGON QUEEN(1981)

Jo Anne Miya
CONFESSIONS OF AN OPIUM EATER(1962)

Joanna Miya
WEST SIDE STORY(1961)

Kaoru Miya
HOUSE OF STRANGE LOVES, THE(1969, Jap.)

Hiroshi Miyagawa
SPACE CRUISER(1977 Jap.), m

Ichirota Miyagawa
1984
FAMILY GAME, THE(1984, Jap.)

Kazuo Miyagawa
RASHOMON(1951, Jap.), ph; UGETSU(1954, Jap.), ph; ENJO(1959, Jap.), ph; ODD OBSESSION(1961, Jap.), ph; YOJIMBO(1961, Jap.), ph; DEVIL'S TEMPLE(1969, Jap.), ph; SANSHO THE BAILIFF(1969, Jap.), ph; FLOATING WEEDS(1970, Jap.), ph; MAGOICHI SAGA, THE(1970, Jap.), ph; ZATOICHI MEETS YOJIMBO(1970, Jap.), ph; BANISHED(1978, Jap.), ph; GEISHA, A(1978, Jap.), ph; KAGEMUSHA(1980, Jap.), ph

Yasushi Miyagawa
LAS VEGAS FREE-FOR-ALL(1968, Jap.), m

Seiji Miyaguchi
SEVEN SAMURAI, THE(1956, Jap.); HUMAN CONDITION, THE(1959, Jap.); IKIRU(1960, Jap.); BALLAD OF NARAYAMA(1961, Jap.); SAMURAI FROM NOWHERE(1964, Jap.); TWIN SISTERS OF KYOTO(1964, Jap.); EMPEROR AND A GENERAL, THE(1968, Jap.); CHALLENGE, THE(1982)

Shizue Miyaguchi
YOUTH AND HIS AMULET, THE(1963, Jap.), w

Toshio Miyajima
HAHAKIRI(1963, Jap.), ph

Yoshio Miyajima
HUMAN CONDITION, THE(1959, Jap.), ph; ROAD TO ETERNITY(1962, Jap.), ph; KWAIDAN(1965, Jap.), ph; LOVE UNDER THE CRUCIFIX(1965, Jap.), ph; LIVE YOUR OWN WAY(1970, Jap.), ph; SOLDIER'S PRAYER, A(1970, Jap.), ph

Bontaro Miyake
TORA! TORA! TORA!(1970, U.S./Jap.)

Kuniko Miyake
ESCAPADE IN JAPAN(1957); OHAYO(1962, Jap.); TEA AND RICE(1964, Jap.); TOKYO STORY(1972, Jap.)

S. Miyaki
INHERITANCE, THE(1964, Jap.), ed

Chocho Miyako
TOPSY-TURVY JOURNEY(1970, Jap.); TORA-SAN PART 2(1970, Jap.); YOSAKOI JOURNEY(1970, Jap.)

Harumi Miyako
TOPSY-TURVY JOURNEY(1970, Jap.)

Nobori Miyakuni
MANSTER, THE(1962, Jap.), art d

Shinataro Miyamoto
MAGIC BOY(1960, Jap.), ed

Shintaro Miyamoto
PANDA AND THE MAGIC SERPENT(1961, Jap.), ed

Teru Miyamoto
MUDDY RIVER(1982, Jap.), w

Tomiko Miyao
ONIMASA(1983, Jap.), w

M. Miyata
ANATAHAN(1953, Jap.), ed

Mitsuji Miyata
UGETSU(1954, Jap.), ed; SANSHO THE BAILIFF(1969, Jap.), ed

Mitsuzo Miyata
GEISHA, A(1978, Jap.), ed

Kunio Miyauchi
HUMAN VAPOR, THE(1964, Jap.), m

Shohei Miyauchi
ZATOICHI(1968, Jap.), staging

Akira Miyazaki
TORA-SAN PART 2(1970, Jap.), w

Arline Miyazaki
1984
RHINESTONE(1984)

Dansho Miyazaki
TEAHOUSE OF THE AUGUST MOON, THE(1956)

Jun Miyazaki
GOLDEN DEMON(1956, Jap.)

Lani Miyazaki
FOR LOVE OF IVY(1968); ORGANIZATION, THE(1971)

Kim Miyori
ZOOT SUIT(1981)

Eiko Miyoshi
SAMURAI(1955, Jap.); HIDDEN FORTRESS, THE(1959, Jap.); LOWER DEPTHS, THE(1962, Jap.); IDIOT, THE(1963, Jap.); PRODIGAL SON, THE(1964, Jap.); I LIVE IN FEAR(1967, Jap.)

Juro Miyoshi
SAGA OF THE VAGABONDS(1964, Jap.), w

Shoraku Miyoshi
CHUSHINGURA(1963, Jap.), w

Maria Mizar
ROMANCE OF A HORSE THIEF(1971)

Buddy Mize
THAT TENNESSEE BEAT(1966)

Sgt. Kenneth W. Mize, USMC
BACK TO BATAAN(1945)

Fonce Mizell
HELL UP IN HARLEM(1973), m

Thomas Mizer
FOREIGN CORRESPONDENT(1940)

Tom Mizer
MAN I MARRIED, THE(1940)

Steve Mizerak
BALTIMORE BULLET, THE(1980)

V. Mizin
FATHER OF A SOLDIER(1966, USSR); SONS AND MOTHERS(1967, USSR)

Harry Mizler
EXCUSE MY GLOVE(1936, Brit.)

Alfred Mizner
BLOODHOUNDS OF BROADWAY(1952); O. HENRY'S FULL HOUSE(1952)

Wilson Mizner
IT'S A DEAL(1930), w; DARK HORSE, THE(1932), w; ONE WAY PASSAGE(1932), a, w; WINNER TAKE ALL(1932), w; FRISCO JENNY(1933), w; HARD TO HANDLE(1933), w; HEROES FOR SALE(1933), w; LITTLE GIANT, THE(1933), w; MIND READER, THE(1933), w; STRICTLY PERSONAL(1933), w; 20,000 YEARS IN SING SING(1933), w
Silents
GREYHOUND, THE(1914), w

Kenji Mizoguchi
UGETSU(1954, Jap.), d; LIFE OF OHARU(1964, Jap.), d, w; SANSHO THE BAILIFF(1969, Jap.), d; GEISHA, A(1978, Jap.), d
Misc. Silents
RESURRECTION OF LOVE(1922, Jap.), d; AMONG THE RUINS(1923, Jap.), d; BLOOD AND SOUL(1923, Jap.), d; DREAMS OF YOUTH(1923, Jap.), d; FOGGY HARBOR(1923, Jap.), d; NATIVE COUNTRY(1923, Jap.), d; NIGHT(1923, Jap.), d; CHRONICLE OF THE MAY RAIN(1924, Jap.), d; DEATH AT DAWN(1924, Jap.), d; WOMAN OF PLEASURE(1924, Jap.), d; WOMEN ARE STRONG(1924, Jap.), d; MAN, THE(1925, Jap.), d; SMILING EARTH, THE(1925, Jap.), d; CHILDREN OF THE SEA(1926, Jap.), d; PAPER DOLL'S WHISPER OF SPRING, A(1926, Jap.), d; PASSION OF A WOMAN TEACHER, THE(1926, Jap.), d; METROPOLITAN SYMPHONY(1929, Jap.), d; TOKYO MARCH(1929, Jap.), d

Anna Mizrahi
RIOT ON SUNSET STRIP(1967)

Freddy Mizrahi
SCAVENGERS, THE(1969)

Hy Mizrahi
ANIMALS, THE(1971), w

Isaac Mizrahi
FAME(1980)

Moshe Mizrahi
SOPHIE'S WAYS(1970, Fr.), d, w; MADAME ROSA(1977, Fr.), d, w; I SENT A LETTER TO MY LOVE(1981, Fr.), d, w; LA VIE CONTINUE(1982, Fr.), d, w
Misc. Talkies
RACHEL'S MAN(1974), d

Simon Mizrahi
CLEOPATRA(1963)

Stephanie Mizrahi
PRETTY MAIDS ALL IN A ROW(1971)

Kyoko Mizuki
PERFORMERS, THE(1970, Jap.)

Reiko Mizuki
SONG FROM MY HEART, THE(1970, Jap.)

Ryoko Mizuki
TOKYO STORY(1972, Jap.)

Yoko Mizuki
ANGRY ISLAND(1960, Jap.), w; NAKED GENERAL, THE(1964, Jap.), w; KWAIDAN(1965, Jap.), w

Kosaku Mizuno
SONG FROM MY HEART, THE(1970, Jap.)

Kumi Mizuno
WESTWARD DESPERADO(1961, Jap.); TILL TOMORROW COMES(1962, Jap.); CHUSHINGURA(1963, Jap.); OPERATION X(1963, Jap.); ATTACK OF THE MUSHROOM PEOPLE(1964, Jap.); FRANKENSTEIN CONQUERS THE WORLD(1964, Jap./US); GORATH(1964, Jap.); OPERATION ENEMY FORT(1964, Jap.); LOST WORLD OF SINBAD, THE(1965, Jap.); WHITE ROSE OF HONG KONG(1965, Jap.); GAMBLING SAMURAI, THE(1966, Jap.); GODZILLA VERSUS THE SEA MONSTER(1966, Jap.); WHAT'S UP, TIGER LILY?(1966); WHIRLWIND(1968, Jap.); MONSTER ZERO(1970, Jap.); WAR OF THE GARGANTUAS, THE(1970, Jap.)

Kiyomi Mizunoya
I LIVE IN FEAR(1967, Jap.)

Irene Mizushima
WALK, DON'T RUN(1966)

Hiroshi Mizutani
BRIDGE TO THE SUN(1961), art d; LIFE OF OHARU(1964, Jap.), art d

Yutaka Mizutani
MAN WHO STOLE THE SUN, THE(1980, Jap.)

Vic Mizzy
NIGHT WALKER, THE(1964), m; VERY SPECIAL FAVOR, A(1965), m; GHOST AND MR. CHICKEN, THE(1966), m; BUSYBODY, THE(1967), m; CAPER OF THE GOLDEN BULLS, THE(1967), m; DON'T MAKE WAVES(1967), m; PERILS OF PAULINE, THE(1967), m; RELUCTANT ASTRONAUT, THE(1967), m; SPIRIT IS WILLING, THE(1967), m, md; DID YOU HEAR THE ONE ABOUT THE TRAVELING SALESLADY?(1968), m; SHAKIEST GUN IN THE WEST, THE(1968), m; LOVE GOD?, THE(1969), m; HOW TO FRAME A FIGG(1971), m

Otto Mjaanes
MOVING FINGER, THE(1963)

L. Mkhitaryants
SONG OF THE FOREST(1963, USSR), ed

Kyra Mladeck
SERPENT'S EGG, THE(1977, Ger./U.S.)

Milada Mladova
NIGHT AND DAY(1946); ESCAPE ME NEVER(1947); SIREN OF ATLANTIS(1948); PRINCE WHO WAS A THIEF, THE(1951); SON OF ALI BABA(1952)

Arthur Mlodnicki
ASHES AND DIAMONDS(1961, Pol.)
Artur Mlodnicki
LOTNA(1966, Pol.)
Arlene Mlodzik
STEREO(1969, Can.)
Ron Mlodzik
RABID(1976, Can.)
Ronald Mlodzik
CRIMES OF THE FUTURE(1969, Can.); STEREO(1969, Can.); THEY CAME FROM WITHIN(1976, Can.)
David Mlotok
P.O.W., THE(1973), p
Mme. Derivaz
THIRD MAN ON THE MOUNTAIN(1959), ch
G. Mnatsakanova
SONG OVER MOSCOW(1964, USSR)
John MNcIntine
WORLD IN HIS ARMS, THE(1952)
Genevieve Mnich
MOTHER AND THE WHORE, THE(1973, Fr.)
1984
SUNDAY IN THE COUNTRY, A(1984, Fr.)
David Mnkwanazi
PENNYWHISTLE BLUES, THE(1952, South Africa)
A. Mnouchkine
LAW IS THE LAW, THE(1959, Fr.), p
Alexandre Mnouchkine
EAGLE WITH TWO HEADS(1948, Fr.), p; LUCRECE BORGIA(1953, Ital./Fr.), p; MY SON, THE HERO(1963, Ital./Fr.), p; THAT MAN FROM RIO(1964, Fr./Ital.), p; UP TO HIS EARS(1966, Fr./Ital.), p; LIVE FOR LIFE(1967, Fr./Ital.), p; LES GAULOISES BLEUES(1969, Fr.), p; LIFE LOVE DEATH(1969, Fr./Ital.), p; LOVE IS A FUNNY THING(1971, Fr./Ital.), p; CROOK, THE(1971, Fr.), p; MAGNIFICENT ONE, THE(1974, Fr./Ital.), p; ANOTHER MAN, ANOTHER CHANCE(1977 Fr./US), p; DEAR DETECTIVE(1978, Fr.), p; ANGRY MAN, THE(1979 Fr./Can.), p; INCORRIGIBLE(1980, Fr.), p; INQUISITOR, THE(1982, Fr.), p; LA BALANCE(1983, Fr.), p
Ariane Mnouchkine
THAT MAN FROM RIO(1964, Fr./Ital.), w
Rex Moad
PANIC IN THE STREETS(1950)
Moana
HOLIDAY RHYTHM(1950)
Tawera Moanna
INVADERS, THE,(1941)
Owen Moase
OUTBACK(1971, Aus.)
Robyn Moase
JOURNEY AMONG WOMEN(1977, Aus.)
Abbas Moayeri
SIAVASH IN PERSEPOLIS(1966, Iran); MEETINGS WITH REMARKABLE MEN(1979, Brit.)
Noah Moazezi
1984
ONCE UPON A TIME IN AMERICA(1984)
Henk Mobenberg
SPY WHO CAME IN FROM THE COLD, THE(1965, Brit.)
Vilhelm Moberg
EMIGRANTS, THE(1972, Swed.), w; NEW LAND, THE(1973, Swed.), w
Duke Moberly
MY THIRD WIFE GEORGE(1968)
Luke Moberly
LITTLE LAURA AND BIG JOHN(1973), d&w
Robert Moberly
WOLFEN(1981)
Rolf Mobius
U-47 LT. COMMANDER PRIEN(1967, Ger.)
Claresie Mobley
1984
PARIS, TEXAS(1984, Ger./Fr.)
Freeman Mobley
9/30/55(1977)
James Mobley
SELF-PORTRAIT(1973, U.S./Chile), d
Jerry Mobley
THIRTEEN FIGHTING MEN(1960); WORLD'S GREATEST SINNER, THE(1962)
Mary Ann Mobley
GET YOURSELF A COLLEGE GIRL(1964); GIRL HAPPY(1965); HARUM SCARUM(1965); YOUNG DILLINGER(1965); THREE ON A COUCH(1966); KING'S PIRATE(1967); FOR SINGLES ONLY(1968)
Roger Mobley
DOG'S BEST FRIEND, A(1960); BOY WHO CAUGHT A CROOK(1961); COMANCHEROS, THE(1961); SILENT CALL, THE(1961); JACK THE GIANT KILLER(1962); DIME WITH A HALO(1963); EMIL AND THE DETECTIVES(1964); APPLE DUMPLING GANG RIDES AGAIN, THE(1979)
G. Mocchia
TWELVE-HANDED MEN OF MARS, THE(1964, Ital./Span.), d&w
Giuseppe Moccia
LITTLE NUNS, THE(1965, Ital.), w
Jodi Moccia
THOSE LIPS, THOSE EYES(1980)
Frank Moceri
CANDIDATE, THE(1964), w
Tad Mochinaga
DAYDREAMER, THE(1966), ph
Tamekichi Mochizuki
SANSHO THE BAILIFF(1969, Jap.), m
Yuko Mochizuki
BALLAD OF NARAYAMA(1961, Jap.); DIFFERENT SONS(1962, Jap.); EARLY AUTUMN(1962, Jap.); TEA AND RICE(1964, Jap.); RED LION(1971, Jap.)

Peter Mochrie
WINTER OF OUR DREAMS(1982, Aus.)
Joan Mocine
DEAD PEOPLE(1974), art d; FRENCH POSTCARDS(1979), cos
Alice Mock
WONDER MAN(1945); I WONDER WHO'S KISSING HER NOW(1947)
Christopher Mock
MISTER BROWN(1972)
Joachim Mock
RETURN OF DR. MABUSE, THE(1961, Ger./Fr./Ital.); ORDERED TO LOVE(1963, Ger.); U-47 LT. COMMANDER PRIEN(1967, Ger.)
Laurie Mock
WAR PARTY(1965); HOT RODS TO HELL(1967); RIOT ON SUNSET STRIP(1967)
Robert Lynn Mock
UP THE ACADEMY(1980)
Wild Bill Mock
TWO-MINUTE WARNING(1976)
Mercedes Mockaitis
NIGHT IN PARADISE, A(1946)
Wayne Mockett
GREAT WALL OF CHINA, THE(1970, Brit.)
Denise Mockler
NO BLADE OF GRASS(1970, Brit.)
Robert D. Mockler
SEARCH, THE(1948), tech adv
Cyril Mockridge
LITTLEST REBEL, THE(1935), md; DAY-TIME WIFE(1939), md; STANLEY AND LIVINGSTONE(1939), m; GREAT PROFILE, THE(1940), m; LADIES OF WASHINGTON(1944), m; CLAUDIA AND DAVID(1946), m; CLUNY BROWN(1946), m; DARK CORNER, THE(1946), m; WAKE UP AND DREAM(1946), m; MIRACLE ON 34TH STREET, THE(1947), m; NIGHTMARE ALLEY(1947), m; DEEP WATERS(1948), m; GREEN GRASS OF WYOMING(1948), m; ROAD HOUSE(1948), m; SCUDDA-HOO! SCUDDA-HAY!(1948), m; BEAUTIFUL BLONDE FROM BASHFUL BEND, THE(1949), m; COME TO THE STABLE(1949), m; FATHER WAS A FULLBACK(1949), m; I WAS A MALE WAR BRIDE(1949), m; CHEAPER BY THE DOZEN(1950), m; LOVE THAT BRUTE(1950), m; MOTHER DIDN'T TELL ME(1950), m; STELLA(1950), m; AS YOUNG AS YOU FEEL(1951), m; LOVE NEST(1951), m; YOU'RE IN THE NAVY NOW(1951), m; BELLES ON THEIR TOES(1952), m; DEADLINE–U.S.A.(1952), m; NIGHT WITHOUT SLEEP(1952), m; FARMER TAKES A WIFE, THE(1953), m; HOW TO MARRY A MILLIONAIRE(1953), md; MR. SCOUTMASTER(1953), m; I MARRIED A WOMAN(1958), m; THUNDER IN THE SUN(1959), m; DONOVAN'S REEF(1963), m
Cyril J. Mockridge
JUDGE PRIEST(1934), m; ADVENTURES OF SHERLOCK HOLMES, THE(1939), md; EVERYTHING HAPPENS AT NIGHT(1939), md; HOUND OF THE BASKERVILLES, THE(1939), md; JOHNNY APOLLO(1940), md; LUCKY CISCO KID(1940), md; MANHATTAN HEARTBEAT(1940), md; PIER 13(1940), md; COWBOY AND THE BLONDE, THE(1941), md; GOLDEN HOOFS(1941), md; LAST OF THE DUANES(1941), md; VERY YOUNG LADY, A(1941), md; I WAKE UP SCREAMING(1942), m, md; MAN IN THE TRUNK, THE(1942), m; MANILA CALLING(1942), md; MOONTIDE(1942), md; OVER MY DEAD BODY(1942), m; RINGS ON HER FINGERS(1942), md; THAT OTHER WOMAN(1942), md; YOUNG AMERICA(1942), md; HAPPY LAND(1943), m; HE HIRED THE BOSS(1943), md; MEANEST MAN IN THE WORLD, THE(1943), m; OX-BOW INCIDENT, THE(1943), m; TONIGHT WE RAID CALAIS(1943), m; BIG NOISE, THE(1944), m; EVE OF ST. MARK, THE(1944), m; SULLIVANS, THE(1944), m; CAPTAIN EDDIE(1945), m; COLONEL EFFINGHAM'S RAID(1945), m; MOLLY AND ME(1945), m; THUNDERHEAD-SON OF FLICK-A(1945), m; MY DARLING CLEMENTINE(1946), m; SENTIMENTAL JOURNEY(1946), m; LATE GEORGE APLEY, THE(1947), m; LUCK OF THE IRISH(1948), m; THAT WONDERFUL URGE(1948), m; WALLS OF JERICHO(1948), m; AMERICAN GUERRILLA IN THE PHILIPPINES, AN(1950), m; TICKET TO TOMAHAWK(1950), m; WHERE THE SIDEWALK ENDS(1950), m; ELOPEMENT(1951), m; FOLLOW THE SUN(1951), m; FROGMEN, THE(1951), m; HALF ANGEL(1951), m; LET'S MAKE IT LEGAL(1951), m; MODEL AND THE MARRIAGE BROKER, THE(1951), m; MR. BELVEDERE RINGS THE BELL(1951), m; DREAMBOAT(1952), m; WE'RE NOT MARRIED(1952), m; GIRL NEXT DOOR, THE(1953), m; NIGHT PEOPLE(1954), m; RIVER OF NO RETURN(1954), m; WOMAN'S WORLD(1954), m; HOW TO BE VERY, VERY, POPULAR(1955), m; MANY RIVERS TO CROSS(1955), m, md; BUS STOP(1956), m; LIEUTENANT WORE SKIRTS, THE(1956), m; SOLID GOLD CADILLAC, THE(1956), m; APRIL LOVE(1957), md; DESK SET(1957), m; OH, MEN! OH, WOMEN!(1957), m; WILL SUCCESS SPOIL ROCK HUNTER?(1957), m; GIFT OF LOVE, THE(1958), m; RALLY 'ROUND THE FLAG, BOYS!(1958), m; HOUND-DOG MAN(1959), m; PRIVATE'S AFFAIR, A(1959), m; FLAMING STAR(1960), m; TALL STORY(1960), m; WAKE ME WHEN IT'S OVER(1960), m; ALL HANDS ON DECK(1961), m
Cyril K. Mockridge
RETURN OF THE CISCO KID(1939), md
Norton Mockridge
TEACHER'S PET(1958)
Anthony Mockus
FINNEY(1969)
Tony Mockus
F.I.S.T.(1978)
Jean-Pierre Mocky
THANK HEAVEN FOR SMALL FAVORS(1965, Fr.), d, w; SOLO(1970, Fr.), a, d, w
Daniel Mocquay
YOUNG GIRLS OF ROCHEFORT, THE(1968, Fr.)
Carlos Moctezuma
REBELLION OF THE HANGED, THE(1954, Mex.)
Carlos Lopez Moctezuma
EMPTY STAR, THE(1962, Mex.); VIVA MARIA(1965, Fr./Ital.); NIGHT OF THE BLOODY APES(1968, Mex.); CURSE OF THE CRYING WOMAN, THE(1969, Mex.)
Juan Lopez Moctezuma
DR. TARR'S TORTURE DUNGEON(1972, Mex.), d; MARY, MARY, BLOODY MARY(1975, U.S./Mex.), d
Ugo Moctezuma
1984
UNDER THE VOLCANO(1984)

Philippe Modave
OUTSIDER, THE(1980), p
Jayne Modean
SPRING BREAK(1983)
Dick Moder
Misc. Talkies
LASSIE, THE VOYAGER(1966), d
Jane Moder
UP IN SMOKE(1978)
Modern Film Effects
THREE WOMEN(1977), spec eff
The Modern Folk Quartet
PALM SPRINGS WEEKEND(1963)
The Modern Jazz Quartet
MAIDSTONE(1970), m
Modernaires
WHEN YOU'RE SMILING(1950)
The Modernaires
SUN VALLEY SERENADE(1941); ORCHESTRA WIVES(1942); DON CHICAGO(1945, Brit.); WALKING MY BABY BACK HOME(1953)
The Modernaires with Paula Kelly
GLENN MILLER STORY, THE(1953)
Bob Modes
BOXCAR BERTHA(1972), cos
Modesta
NAKED EARTH, THE(1958, Brit.)
Modesto
FORTUNE AND MEN'S EYES(1971, U.S./Can.)
Sam Modesto
1984
BURIED ALIVE(1984, Ital.)
Sohrab Modi
TIGER AND THE FLAME, THE(1955, India)
Sohrab M. Modi
TIGER AND THE FLAME, THE(1955, India), p&d
Patrick Modiano
LACOMBE, LUCIEN(1974), w
Rene Modiano
STORY OF THE COUNT OF MONTE CRISTO, THE(1962, Fr./Ital.), p
Antonio Modica
JESSE AND LESTER, TWO BROTHERS IN A PLACE CALLED TRINITY(1972, Ital.), ph
Robert Modica
RAIN PEOPLE, THE(1969); LOVE STORY(1970)
Francesca Modigliani
WHITE SISTER(1973, Ital./Span./Fr.)
Matthew Modine
BABY, IT'S YOU(1983); PRIVATE SCHOOL(1983); STREAMERS(1983)
1984
BIRDY(1984); HOTEL NEW HAMPSHIRE, THE(1984); MRS. SOFFEL(1984)
Iolanda Modio
MADE IN ITALY(1967, Fr./Ital.); STRANGER IN TOWN, A(1968, U.S./Ital.)
Jolanda Modio
FACE TO FACE(1967, Ital.)
Yolanda Modio
CASANOVA '70(1965, Ital.)
Bloke Modisane
GUNS AT BATASI(1964, Brit.); DARK OF THE SUN(1968, Brit.)
Albert Modley
BOB'S YOUR UNCLE(1941, Brit.); UP FOR THE CUP(1950, Brit.); TAKE ME TO PARIS(1951, Brit.)
Elmer Modlin
ROSEMARY'S BABY(1968); LOVE AND PAIN AND THE WHOLE DAMN THING(1973)
Margaret Modlin
LOVE AND PAIN AND THE WHOLE DAMN THING(1973); MARCH OR DIE(1977, Brit.)
P. Modnikov
DAY THE EARTH FROZE, THE(1959, Fin./USSR)
Michel Modo
LE GENDARME ET LES EXTRATERRESTRES(1978, Fr.)
Mike Modor
SUMMER LOVERS(1982), p
Gaston Modot
UNDER THE ROOFS OF PARIS(1930, Fr.); THREEPENNY OPERA, THE(1931, Ger./U.S.); PEPE LE MOKO(1937, Fr.); GRAND ILLUSION(1938, Fr.); LA MARSEILLAISE(1938, Fr.); DEVIL IS AN EMPRESS, THE(1939, Fr.); END OF A DAY, THE(1939, Fr.); ESCAPE FROM YESTERDAY(1939, Fr.); RULES OF THE GAME, THE(1939, Fr.); CHILDREN OF PARADISE(1945, Fr.); ANTOINE ET ANTOINETTE(1947 Fr.); MAN ABOUT TOWN(1947, Fr.); PORTRAIT OF INNOCENCE(1948, Fr.), w; PASSION FOR LIFE(1951, Fr.); BEAUTY AND THE DEVIL(1952, Fr./Ital.); CASQUE D'OR(1956, Fr.); FRENCH CANCAN(1956, Fr.); PARIS DOES STRANGE THINGS(1957, Fr./Ital.); LOVERS, THE(1959, Fr.); DEVIL AND THE TEN COMMANDMENTS, THE(1962, Fr.); LIARS, THE(1964, Fr.); L'AGE D'OR(1979, Fr.)
Misc. Silents
LA ZOME DE LA MORT(1917, Fr.); LA FETE ESPAGNOLE(1919, Fr.); LA SULTANE DE L'AMOUR(1919, Fr.); FIEVRE(1921, Fr.); LE SANG D'ALLAH(1922, Fr.); NENE(1924, Fr.); CARMEN(1928, Fr.); MONTE-CRISTO(1929, Fr.); SHIP OF LOST MEN, THE(1929, Ger.)
Tina Modotti
Misc. Silents
TIGER'S COAT, THE(1920)
Urszula Modrzynska
KNIGHTS OF THE TEUTONIC ORDER, THE(1962, Pol.)
Domenico Modugno
RED CLOAK, THE(1961, Ital./Fr.); LOVE A LA CARTE(1965, Ital.); THREE BITES OF THE APPLE(1967); SCIENTIFIC CARDPLAYER, THE(1972, Ital.)

Enrica Maria Modugno
NIGHT OF THE SHOOTING STARS, THE(1982, Ital.)
Lucia Modugno
GENERALE DELLA ROVERE(1960, Ital./Fr.); EVIL EYE(1964 Ital.); MY NAME IS PECOS(1966, Ital.); PRIMITIVE LOVE(1966, Ital.); NAVAJO JOE(1967, Ital./Span.); DANGER: DIABOLIK(1968, Ital./Fr.)
Luia Modugno
OPIATE '67(1967, Fr./Ital.)
Paolo Modugno
DEAD OF SUMMER(1970 Ital./Fr.)
Prince Modupe
SUNDOWN(1941); NABONGA(1944)
Alice Moe
GIRL IN THE SHOW, THE(1929); VOICE OF THE CITY(1929); CAUGHT SHORT(1930); LILIES OF THE FIELD(1930)
Marilyn Moe
GHOST OF DRAGSTRIP HOLLOW(1959); HUSTLE(1975); I WANNA HOLD YOUR HAND(1978)
Torgils Moe
CHILDREN OF GOD'S EARTH(1983, Norwegian)
Moebius [Jean Giraud]
LES MAITRES DU TEMPS(1982, Fr./Switz./Ger.), w
Rolf Moebius
THOUSAND EYES OF DR. MABUSE, THE(1960, Fr./Ital./Ger.); HEIDI(1968, Aust.)
Hans Moebus
CRASH DIVE(1943); THIS LAND IS MINE(1943); CORNERED(1945); CENTENNIAL SUMMER(1946); O.S.S.(1946); MEXICAN HAYRIDE(1948); UNION STATION(1950); PLACE IN THE SUN, A(1951)
Robert Moechel
LIFE BEGINS AT 17(1958)
Titus Moede
WORLD'S GREATEST SINNER, THE(1962); SKYDIVERS, THE(1963); INCREDIBLY STRANGE CREATURES WHO STOPPED LIVING AND BECAME CRAZY MIXED-UP ZOMBIES, THE(1965); THRILL KILLERS, THE(1965); RAT PFINK AND BOO BOO(1966)
Kansas Moehring
SERGEANT MURPHY(1938); DOWN TEXAS WAY(1942); MAN FROM THE RIO GRANDE, THE(1943); OUTLAWS OF STAMPEDE PASS(1943); WILD HORSE RUSTLERS(1943); LAND OF THE OUTLAWS(1944); FRONTIER AGENT(1948); COLT .45(1950)
Silents
OUT OF LUCK(1923); SHOOTIN' FOR LOVE(1923)
"Kansas" Moehring
CARIBOO TRAIL, THE(1950)
Ann Marie Moelders
ONCE IS NOT ENOUGH(1975)
Doug Moeller
BLUE SKIES AGAIN(1983)
Felix Moeller
GERMAN SISTERS, THE(1982, Ger.)
Gunnar Moeller
DANCING HEART, THE(1959, Ger.)
J. David Moeller
1984
NOT FOR PUBLICATION(1984)
Philip Moeller
AGE OF INNOCENCE(1934), d
Phillip Moeller
BREAK OF HEARTS(1935), d
Donna Moen
PURPLE HAZE(1982)
Merete Moen
CHILDREN OF GOD'S EARTH(1983, Norwegian)
Jerzy Moes
LOTNA(1966, Pol.); PORTRAIT OF LENIN(1967, Pol./USSR)
Nicholas Moes
PERSECUTION AND ASSASSINATION OF JEAN-PAUL MARAT AS PERFORMED BY THE INMATES OF THE ASYLUM OF CHARENTON UNDER THE DIRECTION OF THE MARQUIS DE SADE, THE(1967, Brit.)
Claude Moesching
TENANT, THE(1976, Fr.), art d
Edmund Moeschke
GERMANY, YEAR ZERO(1949, Ger.)
Terry Moesker
YELLOW SUBMARINE(1958, Brit.), animation
David Moessinger
DADDY-O(1959), w; CAPER OF THE GOLDEN BULLS, THE(1967), w; NUMBER ONE(1969), w
Emil Mofal
AFTER YOU, COMRADE(1967, S. Afr.)
Graham Mofatt
STORMY WEATHER(1935, Brit.)
Paolo Moffa
LAST DAYS OF POMPEII, THE(1960, Ital.), p; REVOLT OF THE SLAVES, THE(1961, Ital./Span./Ger.), p; SEVEN SEAS TO CALAIS(1963, Ital.), p; GOLIATH AND THE VAMPIRES(1964, Ital.), p
Charles Moffat
SALT TO THE DEVIL(1949, Brit.)
Donald Moffat
R.P.M.(1970); GREAT NORTHFIELD, MINNESOTA RAID, THE(1972); SHOWDOWN(1973); EARTHQUAKE(1974); TERMINAL MAN, THE(1974); PROMISES IN THE DARK(1979); WINTER KILLS(1979); HEALTH(1980); ON THE NICKEL(1980); POPEYE(1980); LAND OF NO RETURN, THE(1981); THING, THE(1982); RIGHT STUFF(1983)
Misc. Talkies
WHITE LIONS(1981)
Geraldine Moffat
MAN WHO HAD POWER OVER WOMEN, THE(1970, Brit.); GET CARTER(1971, Brit.)

Graham Moffat
OKAY FOR SOUND(1937, Brit.)
Silents
BUNTY PULLS THE STRINGS(1921), w
Ivan Moffat
BHOWANI JUNCTION(1956), w; D-DAY, THE SIXTH OF JUNE(1956), w;
GIANT(1956), w; BOY ON A DOLPHIN(1957), w; WAYWARD BUS, THE(1957), w;
THEY CAME TO CORDURA(1959), w; TENDER IS THE NIGHT(1961), w; HEROES
OF TELEMARK, THE(1965, Brit.), w; HITLER: THE LAST TEN DAYS(1973, Brit./
Ital.), w; BLACK SUNDAY(1977), w
Kitty Moffat
BEAST WITHIN, THE(1982)
Margaret Moffat
LEAVE IT TO SMITH(1934); RINGSIDE MAISIE(1941); I MARRIED AN AN-
GEL(1942); MY GAL SAL(1942); SABOTEUR(1942)
Tony Moffat-Lynch
DR. FRANKENSTEIN ON CAMPUS(1970, Can.)
Donald Moffat
RACHEL, RACHEL(1968); TRIAL OF THE CATONSVILLE NINE, THE(1972)
Graham Moffatt
CHARLEY'S(BIG-HEARTED) AUNT*1/2 (1940); WHERE THERE'S A WILL(1936,
Brit.); DOCTOR SYN(1937, Brit.); GANGWAY(1937, Brit.); OH, MR. PORTER!(1937,
Brit.); WHERE THERE'S A WILL(1937, Brit.); WINDBAG THE SAILOR(1937, Brit.);
CONVICT 99(1938, Brit.); OLD BONES OF THE RIVER(1938, Brit.); TO THE VIC-
TOR(1938, Brit.); ASK A POLICEMAN(1939, Brit.); CHEER BOYS CHEER(1939, Brit.);
WHERE'S THAT FIRE?(1939, Brit.); HI, GANG!(1941, Brit.); I THANK YOU(1941,
Brit.); BACK ROOM BOY(1942, Brit.); TIME FLIES(1944, Brit.); WELCOME, MR.
WASHINGTON(1944, Brit.); RANDOLPH FAMILY, THE(1945, Brit.); I KNOW
WHERE I'M GOING(1947, Brit.); WOMAN HATER(1949, Brit.); DRAGON OF PEN-
DRAGON CASTLE, THE(1950, Brit.); SECOND MATE, THE(1950, Brit.); INN FOR
TROUBLE(1960, Brit.); MY SON, THE VAMPIRE(1963, Brit.)
Mrs. Graham Moffatt
ROLLING HOME(1935, Brit.)
John Moffatt
LOSER TAKES ALL(1956, Brit.); SILENT ENEMY, THE(1959, Brit.); TOM JO-
NES(1963, Brit.); JULIUS CAESAR(1970, Brit.); LADY CAROLINE LAMB(1972,
Brit./Ital.); MURDER ON THE ORIENT EXPRESS(1974, Brit.); BRITTANIA HOSPI-
TAL(1982, Brit.)
Katy Moffatt
BILLY JACK(1971)
Margaret Moffatt
END OF THE ROAD, THE(1936, Brit.); KEEP YOUR SEATS PLEASE(1936, Brit.);
TROOPSHIP(1938, Brit.); U-BOAT 29(1939, Brit.)
Mark Moffatt
STARSTRUCK(1982, Aus.), md
Richard Moffatt
OUTRAGEOUS!(1977, Can.)
Tom Moffatt
PARDON MY PAST(1945)
Sharyn Moffet
BODY SNATCHER, THE(1945)
Barbara Moffett
RED RIVER ROBIN HOOD(1943)
Frances Moffett
SECRET CALL, THE(1931); WORKING GIRLS(1931); DANCERS IN THE
DARK(1932); SINNERS IN THE SUN(1932)
Francis Moffett
NO ONE MAN(1932)
Gregory Moffett
LET'S DANCE(1950); SADDLE TRAMP(1950); ROBOT MONSTER(1953)
John C. Moffett
RHYTHM ON THE RANGE(1936), w; TROPIC HOLIDAY(1938), w
Maxwell Moffett
HEAD ON(1981, Can.)
Sharyn Moffett
MY PAL, WOLF(1944); FALCON IN SAN FRANCISCO, THE(1945); BOY, A GIRL,
AND A DOG, A(1946); CHILD OF DIVORCE(1946); LOCKET, THE(1946); BANJO(1947);
MR. BLANDINGS BUILDS HIS DREAM HOUSE(1948); RUSTY LEADS THE
WAY(1948); JUDGE STEPS OUT, THE(1949); HER FIRST ROMANCE(1951)
Jeff Moffit
ALWAYS IN TROUBLE(1938), w
Jefferson Moffit
BONNIE SCOTLAND(1935), w
Peggy Moffit
SENIOR PROM(1958)
Elliott Moffitt
ABBY(1974)
Jack Moffitt
CENTRAL AIRPORT(1933), w; MELODY RANCH(1940), w; MAN BETRAYED,
A(1941), w; PASSAGE TO MARSEILLE(1944), w; MURDER, HE SAYS(1945), w
Jeff Moffitt
KELLY THE SECOND(1936), w
Jefferson Moffitt
Silents
OTHER KIND OF LOVE, THE(1924), w; SWORD OF VALOR, THE(1924), w; GOOD-
BYE KISS, THE(1928), w
John C. Moffitt
MURDER WITH PICTURES(1936), w; DOUBLE OR NOTHING(1937), w; EXCLU-
SIVE(1937), w; MOUNTAIN MUSIC(1937), w; NIGHT KEY(1937), w; RIDE A
CROOKED MILE(1938), w; I'M FROM MISSOURI(1939), w; OUR LEADING CITI-
ZEN(1939), w; ST. LOUIS BLUES(1939), w; STORY OF WILL ROGERS, THE(1952), w
Peggy Moffitt
YOU'RE NEVER TOO YOUNG(1955); BATTLE CRY(1959); GIRLS' TOWN(1959);
BLOW-UP(1966, Brit.)
Joe Reb Moffley
CHOSEN SURVIVORS(1974 U.S.-Mex.), w
Anna Moffo
LA TRAVIATA(1968, Ital.); ADVENTURERS, THE(1970); WEEKEND MURDERS,
THE(1972, Ital.)

Georgio Moffo
FRANCHETTE; LES INTRIGUES(1969)
Jack Mofitt
RAMROD(1947), w
Albert Mog
SONG OF LIFE, THE(1931, Ger.)
Aribert Mog
TRUNKS OF MR. O.F., THE(1932, Ger.); ECSTASY(1940, Czech.)
Ingo Mogendorf
DARLING LILI(1970); MC KENZIE BREAK, THE(1970); MURPHY'S WAR(1971,
Brit.)
Jesse Mogensen
CLINIC, THE(1983, Aus.)
Nann Mogg
CREEPSHOW(1982)
Flavio Mogherini
AIDA(1954, Ital.), set d; WOMAN OF THE RIVER(1954, Fr./Ital.), art d; ULYS-
SES(1955, Ital.), art d; WOMAN OF ROME(1956, Ital.), art d; GIRL WITH A SUIT-
CASE(1961, Fr./Ital.), art d; THIEF OF BAGHDAD, THE(1961, Ital./Fr.), art d;
WONDERS OF ALADDIN, THE(1961, Fr./Ital.), art d; LA VIACCIA(1962, Fr./Ital.),
art d; FAMILY DIARY(1963 Ital.), art d; GOLDEN ARROW, THE(1964, Ital.), art d;
DANGER: DIABOLIK(1968, Ital./Fr.), art d; DROP DEAD, MY LOVE(1968, Italy), art
d; LADY OF MONZA, THE(1970, Ital.), art d; MACHINE GUN McCAIN(1970, Ital.), art
d
Moglia
GREAT WHITE, THE(1982, Ital.), ph
Lev Mogliov
VILNA LEGEND, A(1949, U.S./Pol.)
Myron Mogul, IV
FLY NOW, PAY LATER(1969)
Leonard Moguy
AFFAIR LAFONT, THE(1939, Fr.), d
Leonid Moguy
TWO WOMEN(1940, Fr.), d
Leonide Moguy
CONFLICT(1939, Fr.), d; PARIS AFTER DARK(1943), d; ACTION IN ARABIA(1944),
d; THREE HOURS(1944, Fr.), d; WHISTLE STOP(1946), d; DIARY OF A BAD
GIRL(1958, Fr.), d; GIVE ME MY CHANCE(1958, Fr.), d, w
Ulrich Moh
UNDER TEN FLAGS(1960, U.S./Ital.), w
K.K. Mohajan
Misc. Talkies
KING MONSTER(1977)
Firooz Bahjat Mohamadi
CARAVANS(1978, U.S./Iranian)
Mena Mohamed
TEN COMMANDMENTS, THE(1956)
Chulam Mohammed
MATTER OF WHO, A(1962, Brit.)
Earle Mohan
Silents
LOVE MAKES 'EM WILD(1927)
Pankaj Mohan
GANDHI(1982)
Sheri Mohan
NINE HOURS TO RAMA(1963, U.S./Brit.)
Ursula Mohan
TELL ME LIES(1968, Brit.)
Frazier Mohawk
"EQUUS"(1977)
Vic Mohica
SHOWDOWN(1973)
Victor Mohica
DON'T ANSWER THE PHONE(1980); FINAL COUNTDOWN, THE(1980)
Misc. Talkies
JOHNNY FIRECLOUD(1975)
Orv Mohler
INVASION OF THE SAUCER MEN(1957)
Tom Mohler
STUDENT TEACHERS, THE(1973)
Jimmy Mohley
RIDING SHOTGUN(1954)
Carl Mohner
RIFIFI(1956, Fr.); LAST BRIDGE, THE(1957, Aust.); BEHIND THE MASK(1958,
Brit.); CAMP ON BLOOD ISLAND, THE(1958, Brit.); PASSIONATE SUMMER(1959,
Brit.); IT TAKES A THIEF(1960, Brit.); SINK THE BISMARCK!(1960, Brit.); KITCHEN,
THE(1961, Brit.); FALL OF ROME, THE(1963, Ital.); CAVE OF THE LIVING
DEAD(1966, Yugo./Ger.); MOONWOLF(1966, Fin./Ger.); CARMEN, BABY(1967,
Yugo./Ger.); HELL IS EMPTY(1967, Brit./Ital); ASSIGNMENT K(1968, Brit.); LAST
MERCENARY, THE(1969, Ital./Span./Ger.); CALLAN(1975, Brit.); LA BABY SIT-
TER(1975, Fr./Ital./Gen.); WOMAN AT HER WINDOW, A(1978, Fr./Ital./Ger.)
Gernot Mohner
LUDWIG(1973, Ital./Ger./Fr.)
N. Mohoff
MAN WHO BROKE THE BANK AT MONTE CARLO, THE(1935)
Egon Mohr
HOT MONEY GIRL(1962, Brit./Ger.)
Gerald Mohr
CHARLIE CHAN AT TREASURE ISLAND(1939); LOVE AFFAIR(1939); PANAMA
PATROL(1939); SEA HAWK, THE(1940); MONSTER AND THE GIRL, THE(1941);
RELUCTANT DRAGON, THE(1941); WE GO FAST(1941); LADY HAS PLANS,
THE(1942); WOMAN OF THE YEAR(1942); DESERT SONG, THE(1943); KING OF THE
COWBOYS(1943); LADY OF BURLESQUE(1943); MURDER IN TIMES SQUARE(1943);
ONE DANGEROUS NIGHT(1943); DANGEROUS BUSINESS(1946); GILDA(1946);
GUY COULD CHANGE, A(1946); INVISIBLE INFORMER(1946); MAGNIFICENT
ROGUE, THE(1946); NOTORIOUS LONE WOLF, THE(1946); PASSKEY TO DAN-
GER(1946); THE CATMAN OF PARIS(1946); TRUTH ABOUT MURDER, THE(1946);
YOUNG WIDOW(1946); HEAVEN ONLY KNOWS(1947); LONE WOLF IN LON-
DON(1947); LONE WOLF IN MEXICO, THE(1947); EMPEROR WALTZ, THE(1948);
TWO GUYS FROM TEXAS(1948); BLONDE BANDIT, THE(1950); HUNT THE MAN

DOWN(1950); UNDERCOVER GIRL(1950); DETECTIVE STORY(1951); SIROC-CO(1951); TEN TALL MEN(1951); DUEL AT SILVER CREEK, THE(1952); INVASION U.S.A.(1952); RING, THE(1952); SNIPER, THE(1952); SON OF ALI BABA(1952); DRAGONFLY SQUADRON(1953); EDDIE CANTOR STORY, THE(1953); MONEY FROM HOME(1953); RAIDERS OF THE SEVEN SEAS(1953); REDHEAD FROM MANHATTAN(1954); BUCKSKIN LADY, THE(1957); GUNS, GIRLS AND GANG-STERS(1958); MY WORLD DIES SCREAMING(1958); ANGRY RED PLANET, THE(1959); DATE WITH DEATH, A(1959); THIS REBEL BREED(1960); FUNNY GIRL(1968)

Hal Mohr
JAZZ SINGER, THE(1927), ph; NOAH'S ARK(1928), ph; TENDERLOIN(1928), ph; BROADWAY(1929), ph; LAST PERFORMANCE, THE(1929), ph; LAST WARNING, THE(1929), ph;SHANGHAI LADY(1929), ph; CAT CREEPS, THE(1930), ph; COHENS AND KELLYS IN AFRICA, THE(1930), ph; FREE LOVE(1930), ph; OUTWARD BOUND(1930), ph; BIG GAMBLE, THE(1931), ph; COMMON LAW, THE(1931), ph; DEVOTION(1931), ph; FRONT PAGE, THE(1931), ph; WOMAN OF EXPERIENCE, A(1931), ph; FIRST YEAR, THE(1932), ph; LADY WITH A PAST(1932), ph; TESS OF THE STORM COUNTRY(1932), ph; WEEK-ENDS ONLY(1932), ph; WOMAN COM-MANDS, A(1932), ph; DEVIL'S IN LOVE, THE(1933), ph; I LOVED YOU WEDNES-DAY(1933), ph; STATE FAIR(1933), ph; WARRIOR'S HUSBAND, THE(1933), ph; WORST WOMAN IN PARIS(1933), ph; AS HUSBANDS GO(1934), ph; CAROLI-NA(1934), ph; CHANGE OF HEART(1934), ph; CHARLIE CHAN'S COURAGE(1934), ph; DAVID HARUM(1934), ph; SERVANTS' ENTRANCE(1934), ph; CAPTAIN BLOOD(1935), ph; COUNTY CHAIRMAN, THE(1935), ph; MIDSUMMER'S NIGHT'S DREAM, A(1935), ph; UNDER PRESSURE(1935), ph; BULLETS OR BALLOTS(1936), ph; GREEN PASTURES(1936), ph; LADIES IN LOVE(1936), ph; WALKING DEAD, THE(1936), ph; WHEN LOVE IS YOUNG(1937), ph; I MET MY LOVE AGAIN(1938), ph; BACK DOOR TO HEAVEN(1939), ph; DESTRY RIDES AGAIN(1939), ph; RIO(1939), ph; UNDER-PUP, THE(1939), ph; WHEN THE DALTONS RODE(1940), ph; CHEERS FOR MISS BISHOP(1941), ph; INTERNATIONAL LADY(1941), ph; POT O' GOLD(1941), ph; LADY IN A JAM(1942), ph; TWIN BEDS(1942), ph; PHANTOM OF THE OPERA(1943), ph; TOP MAN(1943), ph; WATCH ON THE RHINE(1943), ph; CLIMAX, THE(1944), ph; ENTER ARSENE LUPIN(1944), ph; IMPATIENT YEARS, THE(1944), ph; LADIES COURAGEOUS(1944), ph; MY GAL LOVES MUSIC(1944), ph; SAN DIEGO, I LOVE YOU(1944), ph; THIS IS THE LIFE(1944), ph; HER LUCKY NIGHT(1945), ph; SALOME, WHERE SHE DANCED(1945), ph; SHADY LADY(1945), ph; BECAUSE OF HIM(1946), ph; NIGHT IN PARADISE, A(1946), ph; I'LL BE YOURS(1947), ph; LOST MOMENT, THE(1947), ph; PIRATES OF MONTEREY(1947), ph; SONG OF SCHEHERAZADE(1947), ph; ACT OF MURDER, AN(1948), ph; ANOTH-ER PART OF THE FOREST(1948), ph; JOHNNY HOLIDAY(1949), ph; WOMAN ON THE RUN(1950), ph; BIG NIGHT, THE(1951), ph; SECOND WOMAN, THE(1951), ph; FOUR POSTER, THE(1952), ph; MEMBER OF THE WEDDING, THE(1952), ph; RANCHO NOTORIOUS(1952), ph; WILD ONE, THE(1953), ph; BOSS, THE(1956), ph; BABY FACE NELSON(1957), ph; GUN RUNNERS, THE(1958), ph; LINEUP, THE(1958), ph; LAST VOYAGE, THE(1960), ph; UNDERWORLD U.S.A.(1961), ph; CREATION OF THE HUMANOIDS(1962), ph; MAN FROM THE DINERS' CLUB, THE(1963), ph; BAMBOO SAUCER, THE(1968), ph
Silents
WATCH HIM STEP(1922), ph; LITTLE ANNIE ROONEY(1925), ph; MONSTER, THE(1925), ph; WOMAN WHO SINNED, A(1925), ph; MARRIAGE CLAUSE, THE(1926), ph;SPARROWS(1926), ph; THIRD DEGREE, THE(1926), ph; GIRL FROM CHICAGO, THE(1927), ph; OLD SAN FRANCISCO(1927), ph; SLIGHTLY USED(1927), ph; WEDDING MARCH, THE(1927), ph

Jack Mohr
STAGECOACH(1939)

Ruth Mohr
STOP TRAIN 349(1964, Fr./Ital./Ger.), makeup

F. Jo Mohrbach
FOUL PLAY(1978)

Margot Mohrbutter
PHONY AMERICAN, THE(1964, Ger.), ed

Hans Mohrhard
DECISION BEFORE DAWN(1951)

Kikue Mohri
GATE OF HELL(1954, Jap.)

Werner Mohring
NAKED AMONG THE WOLVES(1967, Ger.)

Ursula Mohrle
SINAI COMMANDOS: THE STORY OF THE SIX DAY WAR(1968, Israel/Ger.), ed; THAT WOMAN(1968, Ger.), ed

John Mohrlein
ON THE RIGHT TRACK(1981)

Zia Mohyeddin
LAWRENCE OF ARABIA(1962, Brit.); BEHOLD A PALE HORSE(1964); BOY TEN FEET TALL, A(1965, Brit.); KHARTOUM(1966, Brit.); DEADLIER THAN THE MA-LE(1967, Brit.); SAILOR FROM GIBRALTAR, THE(1967, Brit.); THEY CAME FROM BEYOND SPACE(1967, Brit.); WORK IS A FOUR LETTER WORD(1968, Brit.); BOMBAY TALKIE(1970, India); ASHANTI(1979)

Tonino Moi
SUPERSONIC MAN(1979, Span.), p, w

Lee Moichu
OPERATION BOTTLENECK(1961)

Lila Moinar [Lily Molnar]
PANDORA AND THE FLYING DUTCHMAN(1951, Brit.)

Michele Moinet
TWO TICKETS TO PARIS(1962)

John Angelo Moio
WHAT'S UP, DOC?(1972)

John Moio
CHANGES(1969); NIGHT MOVES(1975); CAR, THE(1977); PRISONER OF ZENDA, THE(1979); WHERE THE BUFFALO ROAM(1980)

Johnny Moio
METEOR(1979)

Bruce Moir
HOLIDAY'S END(1937, Brit.)

Gunner Moir
THIRD TIME LUCKY(1931, Brit.); MR. WHAT'S-HIS-NAME(1935, Brit.); EXCUSE MY GLOVE(1936, Brit.); PHANTOM SHIP(1937, Brit.)

Richard Moir
27A(1974, Aus.), ed; IN SEARCH OF ANNA(1978, Aus.); ODD ANGRY SHOT, THE(1979, Aus.); CHAIN REACTION(1980, Aus.); HEATWAVE(1983, Aus.)
Misc. Talkies
SWEET DREAMERS(1981); PLAINS OF HEAVEN, THE(1982)

Elizabeth Moisant
MEDIUM COOL(1969)

Maurice Moiseiwitsch
SLEEPING TIGER, THE(1954, Brit.), w

Pamela Moiseiwitsch
CRY OF THE BANSHEE(1970, Brit.)

Tanya Moiseiwitsch
OEDIPUS REX(1957, Can.), set d

Nuala Moiselle
NEVER PUT IT IN WRITING(1964)

Maurice Moisiewitsch
MEET MR. PENNY(1938, Brit.), w; FLAMINGO AFFAIR, THE(1948, Brit.), w

Alexander Moissi
ROYAL BOX, THE(1930)

Bettina Moissi
LONG IS THE ROAD(1948, Ger.)

Jyotirendera Moitra
HOUSEHOLDER, THE(1963, US/India), m

King Mojave
MANHATTAN MELODRAMA(1934); TREASURE ISLAND(1934); TWENTIETH CENTURY(1934); MUTINY ON THE BOUNTY(1935); RIFF-RAFF(1936); SWORN ENEMY(1936); PUBLIC COWBOY NO. 1(1937); CITY GIRL(1938); THREE GUYS NAMED MIKE(1951); HURRICANE SMITH(1952); PAT AND MIKE(1952); DESK SET(1957)

Olga D. Mojean
Misc. Silents
FIRE CAT, THE(1921)

Don Jose Mojica
ONE MAD KISS(1930)

Jose Mojica
QUANDO EL AMOR RIE(1933)

Victor Mojica
BOY WHO STOLE A MILLION, THE(1960, Brit.); HARBOR LIGHTS(1963)

The Mojos
SEASIDE SWINGERS(1965, Brit.)

Michele Mok
DR. NO(1962, Brit.); ROAD TO HONG KONG, THE(1962, U.S./Brit.)

Zaeks Mokae
COMEDIANS, THE(1967)

Zakes Mokae
ISLAND, THE(1980)

Moti Mokan
1984
INDIANA JONES AND THE TEMPLE OF DOOM(1984)

Fay Mokotow
DIMBOOLA(1979, Aus.)

Akom Mokranond
SHADOW OF EVIL(1967, Fr./Ital.)

Misha Mokrinsky
ADVENTURE IN ODESSA(1954, USSR)

Fatima Moktari
OLIVE TREES OF JUSTICE, THE(1967, Fr.)

Steam-boat Mokuahi
BEACHHEAD(1954)

Peter Moland
PEDESTRIAN, THE(1974, Ger.); WHY DOES HERR R. RUN AMOK?(1977, Ger.); OUR HITLER, A FILM FROM GERMANY(1980, Ger.)

Arne Molander
Misc. Silents
RICHTOFEN(1932, Ger.)

Gustaf Molander
SWEDENHIELMS(1935, Swed.), d; ON THE SUNNYSIDE(1936, Swed.), d; INTER-MEZZO(1937, Swed.), d, w; DOLLAR(1938, Swed.), d, w; WOMAN'S FACE, A(1939, Swed.), d; ONLY ONE NIGHT(1942, Swed.), d; AFFAIRS OF A MODEL(1952, Swed.), d

Gustav Molander
INTERMEZZO: A LOVE STORY(1939), w; HONEYSUCKLE ROSE(1980), w
Misc. Silents
DOCTOR'S WOMEN, THE(1929, Ger.), d

Jan Molander
TORMENT(1947, Swed.)

Karin Molander
Misc. Silents
LOVE AND JOURNALISM(1916, Swed.); EROTIKON(1920, Swed.)

Elivira Molano
SALT OF THE EARTH(1954)

Jacques Molant
GOLDEN MISTRESS, THE(1954)

Molasses
MISSISSIPPI(1935)

Molasses and January
HIT PARADE, THE(1937)

Boris Molchanov
WAR AND PEACE(1968, USSR)

K. Molchanov
HOUSE ON THE FRONT LINE, THE(1963, USSR), m

Boris Molcianov
WATERLOO(1970, Ital./USSR)

Olaf Moldander
APPASSIONATA(1946, Swed.), d&w

"Moldau"
VOICE IN THE WIND(1944), m

Lillian Molderi
THREE OUTLAWS, THE(1956)

Jeff Moldovan
SPRING BREAK(1983), stunts
Max Moldrun
AGE OF CONSENT(1969, Austral.)
Rita Mole
L'AVVENTURA(1960, Ital.)
John Molecey
FRIEDA(1947, Brit.)
Onno Molenkamp
LIFT, THE(1983, Neth.)
1984
QUESTION OF SILENCE(1984, Neth.)
Helaine Moler
ARTISTS AND MODELS ABROAD(1938); SAY IT IN FRENCH(1938); TEXANS, THE(1938); YOU AND ME(1938); LADY'S FROM KENTUCKY, THE(1939); ZAZA(1939)
Ron Moler
SUNSET COVE(1978), ed
Jean Molier
NIGHTS OF CABIRIA(1957, Ital.)
Moliere
WOULD-BE GENTLEMAN, THE(1960, Fr.), d
Lillian Molieri
PRINCESS AND THE PIRATE, THE(1944); PEOPLE ARE FUNNY(1945); SOUTH OF THE RIO GRANDE(1945); TARZAN AND THE LEOPARD WOMAN(1946); FOREVER AMBER(1947); LOST MOMENT, THE(1947); HOLIDAY IN HAVANA(1949); NEPTUNE'S DAUGHTER(1949); MY FAVORITE SPY(1951); SOUTH OF CALIENTE(1951); HORIZONS WEST(1952); RING, THE(1952); GREEN FIRE(1955); HELL'S ISLAND(1955); CREATURE WALKS AMONG US, THE(1956); SERENADE(1956)
Bud Molin
FOREVER DARLING(1956), ed; GLOBAL AFFAIR, A(1964), ed; HOW SWEET IT IS(1968), ed; VIVA MAX!(1969), ed; HALLS OF ANGER(1970), ed; LAST ESCAPE, THE(1970, Brit.), ed; THEY CALL ME MISTER TIBBS(1970), ed; WHERE'S POPPA?(1970), ed; OH, GOD!(1977), ed; ONE AND ONLY, THE(1978), ed; BLOODLINE(1979), ed; JERK, THE(1979), ed; UP THE ACADEMY(1980), ed; DEAD MEN DON'T WEAR PLAID(1982), ed; MAN WITH TWO BRAINS, THE(1983), ed
1984
ALL OF ME(1984), ed
Henry Molin
FIRST TIME, THE(1969), ed
Alfred Molina
RAIDERS OF THE LOST ARK(1981)
1984
NUMBER ONE(1984, Brit.)
Angela Molina
THAT OBSCURE OBJECT OF DESIRE(1977, Fr./Span.); SABINA, THE(1979, Span./Swed.); EYES, THE MOUTH, THE(1982, Ital./Fr.)
1984
DEMONS IN THE GARDEN(1984, Span.); IT'S NEVER TOO LATE(1984, Span.)
Antonio Molina
WEREWOLF VS. THE VAMPIRE WOMAN, THE(1970, Span./Ger.), spec eff; GRAVEYARD OF HORROR(1971, Span.), spec eff; LIGHT AT THE EDGE OF THE WORLD, THE(1971, U.S./Span./Lichtenstein), spec eff; TAKE A HARD RIDE(1975, U.S./Ital.), spec eff
Aurora Molina
NAZARIN(1968, Mex.)
Carlos Molina
MEET DANNY WILSON(1952); WITH A SONG IN MY HEART(1952)
Carmen Molina
THREE CABALLEROS, THE(1944); SONG OF MEXICO(1945)
Jacinto Molina
ASSIGNMENT TERROR(1970, Ger./Span./Ital.), w; WEREWOLF VS. THE VAMPIRE WOMAN, THE(1970, Span./Ger.), w; DR. JEKYLL AND THE WOLFMAN(1971, Span.), w; DRACULA'S GREAT LOVE(1972, Span.), w; HUNCHBACK OF THE MORGUE, THE(1972, Span.), w; CURSE OF THE DEVIL(1973, Span./Mex.), w; HOUSE OF PSYCHOTIC WOMEN, THE(1973, Span.), w
Jacinto Molina [Paul Naschy]
FRANKENSTEIN'S BLOODY TERROR(1968, Span.), w
Joe Molina
EBB TIDE(1937); COMANCHE STATION(1960)
Julio Molina
SON OF A GUNFIGHTER(1966, U.S./Span.), art d; SOUND OF HORROR(1966, Span.), set d; CUSTER OF THE WEST(1968, U.S./Span.), art d; KRAKATOA, EAST OF JAVA(1969), art d; TOWN CALLED HELL, A(1971, Span./Brit.), art d; TAKE A HARD RIDE(1975, U.S./Ital.), art d
Ray Molina
VOODOO HEARTBEAT(1972), a, p
Ray Molina, Jr.
VOODOO HEARTBEAT(1972)
Rodriguez Molina
SARUMBA(1950)
Timmy Molina
STRANGERS WHEN WE MEET(1960)
Tony Molina
PYRO(1964, U.S./Span.), spec eff; FINGER ON THE TRIGGER(1965, US/Span.), spec eff; TEXICAN, THE(1966, U.S./Span.), spec eff
Vidal Molina
SEA PIRATE, THE(1967, Fr./Span./Ital.); YOUNG REBEL, THE(1969, Fr./Ital./Span.); MYSTERIOUS ISLAND OF CAPTAIN NEMO, THE(1973, Fr./Ital. 87m Span./Cameroon)
Julius Molinar, Jr.
Misc. Silents
LAST MOMENT, THE(1928)
Richard Molinare
JESUS CHRIST, SUPERSTAR(1973)
Ann Molinari
TWO WEEKS IN ANOTHER TOWN(1962)
Antoimette Molinari
1941(1979)

Ernesto Molinari
PAL JOEY(1957)
Franco Molinari
JOE HILL(1971, Swed./U.S.)
Al Molinaro
FREAKY FRIDAY(1976)
Edouard Molinaro
BACK TO THE WALL(1959, Fr.), d; PASSION OF SLOW FIRE, THE(1962, Fr.), d; ROAD TO SHAME, THE(1962, Fr.), d; SEVEN CAPITAL SINS(1962, Fr./Ital.), d; SEASON FOR LOVE, THE(1963, Fr.); MISTRESS FOR THE SUMMER, A(1964, Fr./Ital.), d, w; MALE HUNT(1965, Fr./Ital.), d; RAVISHING IDIOT, A(1966, Ital./Fr.), d, w; TO COMMIT A MURDER(1970, Fr./Ital./Ger.), w; DRACULA AND SON(1976, Fr.), d, w; LA CAGE AUX FOLLES(1979, Fr./Ital.), d, w; SUNDAY LOVERS(1980, Ital./Fr.), d; LA CAGE AUX FOLLES II(1981, Ital./Fr.), d
1984
JUST THE WAY YOU ARE(1984), d
Joe Molinas
TORRID ZONE(1940)
Richard Molinas
IT'S IN THE BAG(1943, Brit.); GIRL IN THE PAINTING, THE(1948, Brit.); SHOWTIME(1948, Brit.); CHILDREN OF CHANCE(1949, Brit.); SNOWBOUND(1949, Brit.); GREAT MANHUNT, THE(1951, Brit.); TAKE ME TO PARIS(1951, Brit.); BRANDY FOR THE PARSON(1952, Brit.); MOULIN ROUGE(1952); DAY TO REMEMBER, A(1953, Brit.); GAY ADVENTURE, THE(1953, Brit.); SWORD AND THE ROSE, THE(1953); DIVIDED HEART, THE(1955, Brit.); PORT AFRIQUE(1956, Brit.); LET'S BE HAPPY(1957, Brit.); PICKUP ALLEY(1957, Brit.); SPANISH GARDENER, THE(1957, Span.); FEMALE FIENDS(1958, Brit.); SALVAGE GANG, THE(1958, Brit.); WHOLE TRUTH, THE(1958, Brit.)
Cheryl Molineaux
EIGHT O'CLOCK WALK(1954, Brit.)
Constance Molineux
Silents
SENATOR, THE(1915)
Corniglion Molinier
BIZARRE BIZARRE(1939, Fr.), p
E.C. Molinier
REBEL SON, THE ½(1939, Brit.), p
Anthony Molino
TEXICAN, THE(1966, U.S./Span.)
Antonio Molino
TRAPPED IN TANGIERS(1960, Ital./Span.); INVINCIBLE GLADIATOR, THE(1963, c.u. Ital./Span.); LAZARILLO(1963, Span.); GLADIATORS 7(1964, Span./Ital.); KILL THEM ALL AND COME BACK ALONE(1970, Ital./Span.)
Julio Molino
BAD MAN'S RIVER(1972, Span.), art d; SPIKES GANG, THE(1974), art d
Vidal Molino
FIVE GIANTS FROM TEXAS(1966, Ital./Span.)
Jean-Paul Molinot
BEHOLD A PALE HORSE(1964)
J. Molinski
NO WAY TO TREAT A LADY(1968)
Allan J. Moll
WILD IN THE STREETS(1968)
Elick Moll
WAKE UP AND DREAM(1946), w; YOU WERE MEANT FOR ME(1948), w; HOUSE ON TELEGRAPH HILL(1951), w; NIGHT WITHOUT SLEEP(1952), w; STORM CENTER(1956), w; SPRING REUNION(1957), w
George B. Moll
PEER GYNT(1965)
Georgia Moll
DEFEND MY LOVE(1956, Ital.); COSSACKS, THE(1960, It.); THIEF OF BAGHDAD, THE(1961, Ital./Fr.); WHITE WARRIOR, THE(1961, Ital./Yugo.); ISLAND OF LOVE(1963); SULEIMAN THE CONQUEROR(1963, Ital.); DARK PURPOSE(1964); LIPSTICK(1965, Fr./Ital.); REQUIEM FOR A SECRET AGENT(1966, Ital.); BLONDE FROM PEKING, THE(1968, Fr.); ITALIAN SECRET SERVICE(1968, Ital.)
Misc. Talkies
BEYOND CONTROL(1971)
Giorgia Moll
QUIET AMERICAN, THE(1958); CONTEMPT(1963, Fr./Ital.); DEVIL IN LOVE, THE(1968, Ital.)
Mariquita Moll
MANCHURIAN CANDIDATE, THE(1962)
Peter Moll
LOVE IS A WOMAN(1967, Brit.), art d
Richard Moll
AMERICAN POP(1981); CAVEMAN(1981); HARD COUNTRY(1981); SWORD AND THE SORCERER, THE(1982); METALSTORM: THE DESTRUCTION OF JARED-SYN(1983)
William Moll
ON THE LEVEL(1930), set d
Jose Luis Martinez Molla
BULLET FOR SANDOVAL, A(1970, Ital./Span.), w
Richard Mollainas
CANDLELIGHT IN ALGERIA(1944, Brit.)
Henry M. Mollandin
FOX MOVIETONE FOLLIES(1929)
Jean-Gabriel Molle
CATHERINE & CO.(1976, Fr.)
William Mollenheimer
Silents
GREED(1925)
Edward C. Moller
CHARLIE, THE LONESOME COUGAR(1967)
Edward Fleming Moller
8 ½(1963, Ital.)
Gunnar Moller
S.O.S. PACIFIC(1960, Brit.)

Josef Moller
HAGBARD AND SIGNE(1968, Den./Iceland/Swed.), spec eff
Kai Moller
WHILE THE ATTORNEY IS ASLEEP(1945, Den.), m
Andre Molles
MOST WANTED MAN, THE(1962, Fr./Ital.), set d
Mario Molli
FRANKENSTEIN-ITALIAN STYLE(1977, Ital.), prod d
Henry Mollicone
PREMONITION, THE(1976), m
Fred Mollin
SPRING FEVER(1983, Can.), m
Dolly Mollinger
THE BEACHCOMBER(1938, Brit.)
Clifford Mollison
ALMOST A HONEYMOON(1930, Brit.); LUCKY NUMBER, THE(1933, Brit.); MEET MY SISTER(1933, Brit.); SOUTHERN MAID, A(1933, Brit.); FREEDOM OF THE SEAS(1934, Brit.); LUCK OF A SAILOR, THE(1934, Brit.); MISTER CINDERS(1934, Brit.); RADIO FOLLIES(1935, Brit.); REGAL CAVALCADE(1935, Brit.); GIVE HER A RING(1936, Brit.); BLIND FOLLY(1939, Brit.); CHRISTMAS CAROL, A(1951, Brit.); BABY AND THE BATTLESHIP, THE(1957, Brit.); MARY HAD A LITTLE(1961, Brit.); V.I.P.s, THE(1963, Brit.); OH! WHAT A LOVELY WAR(1969, Brit.)
Fiona Mollison
SWEENEY 2(1978, Brit.)
Henry Mollison
KNOWING MEN(1930, Brit.); THIRD TIME LUCKY(1931, Brit.); FACE AT THE WINDOW, THE(1932, Brit.); LETTING IN THE SUNSHINE(1933, Brit.); OUT OF THE PAST(1933, Brit.); MISTER CINDERS(1934, Brit.); DRAKE THE PIRATE(1935, Brit.); GREAT IMPERSONATION, THE(1935); HELL'S CARGO(1935, Brit.); MANHATTAN MOON(1935); REGAL CAVALCADE(1935, Brit.); SOME DAY(1935, Brit.); DEVIL'S SQUADRON(1936); LONE WOLF RETURNS, THE(1936); MUSIC GOES ROUND, THE(1936); SECRET PATROL(1936); SHAKEDOWN(1936); THEY MET IN A TAXI(1936); TRAPPED BY TELEVISION(1936); BRIDE FOR HENRY, A(1937); COUNTERFEIT LADY(1937); FIND THE WITNESS(1937); WINDMILL, THE(1937, Brit.); HUNGRY HILL(1947, Brit.); LOVES OF JOANNA GODDEN, THE(1947, Brit.); TIGHT LITTLE ISLAND(1949, Brit.); WHAT THE BUTLER SAW(1950, Brit.); CHELSEA STORY(1951, Brit.); MAN IN THE WHITE SUIT, THE(1952); FRONT PAGE STORY(1954, Brit.)
Jean Mollner
TAMMY AND THE DOCTOR(1963), makeup
Andrew Mollo
IT HAPPENED HERE(1966, Brit.), a, p,d&w, art d; WINSTANLEY(1979, Brit.), d&w, art d; XTRO(1983, Brit.), art d
1984
GREYSTOKE: THE LEGEND OF TARZAN, LORD OF THE APES(1984), set d
Carmen Mollo
WINSTANLEY(1979, Brit.), cos
Cumersindo Mollo
COBRA, THE(1968), w
Gumersindo Mollo
GOD FORGIVES–I DON'T!(1969, Ital./Span.), w
John Mollo
STAR WARS(1977), cos; ALIEN(1979), cos; EMPIRE STRIKES BACK, THE(1980), cos; OUTLAND(1981), cos; GANDHI(1982), cos; LORDS OF DISCIPLINE, THE(1983), cos
1984
GREYSTOKE: THE LEGEND OF TARZAN, LORD OF THE APES(1984), cos
Jose Luis Martinez Mollo
VENGEANCE IS MINE(1969, Ital./Span.), w; FROM HELL TO VICTORY(1979, Fr./Ital./Span.), w
Yolande Mollot
TURNABOUT(1940); LIFE BEGINS FOR ANDY HARDY(1941); UNDER AGE(1941)
Yollande Mollot
DARK STREETS OF CAIRO(1940)
Catherine Molloy
MONGREL(1982)
1984
SONGWRITER(1984)
Dearbhla Molloy
PADDY(1970, Irish); EDUCATING RITA(1983)
John Molloy
CONCRETE JUNGLE, THE(1962, Brit.); ULYSSES(1967, U.S./Brit.); BROTHERLY LOVE(1970, Brit.); PADDY(1970, Irish); FLIGHT OF THE DOVES(1971)
Joyce Molloy
Misc. Talkies
SATAN'S CHILDREN(1975)
Michael Molloy
KIDNAPPING OF THE PRESIDENT, THE(1980, Can.), ph
Mike Molloy
MAD DOG MORGAN(1976,Aus.), ph; SUMMERFIELD(1977, Aus.), ph; SHOUT, THE(1978, Brit.), ph; HUMAN FACTOR, THE(1979, Brit.), ph; SHOCK TREATMENT(1981), ph; RETURN OF CAPTAIN INVINCIBLE, THE(1983, Aus./U.S.), ph
William Molloy
JACKSON COUNTY JAIL(1976)
Michael Molly
STARDUST MEMORIES(1980), art d; STILL OF THE NIGHT(1982), art d
1984
MOSCOW ON THE HUDSON(1984), art d
David Molna
SECRET OF NIMH, THE(1982), anim
Ferenc Molnar
HIS GLORIOUS NIGHT(1929), w; PRISONERS(1929), w; LILIOM(1930), w; ONE ROMANTIC NIGHT(1930), w; GUARDSMAN, THE(1931), w; NO GREATER GLORY(1934), w; GOOD FAIRY, THE(1935), w; LILIOM(1935, Fr.), w; BRIDE WORE RED, THE(1937), w; CHOCOLATE SOLDIER, THE(1941), w; TALES OF MANHATTAN(1942), w; BLONDE FEVER(1944), w; I'LL BE YOURS(1947), w; CAROUSEL(1956), w; SWAN, THE(1956), w; BREATH OF SCANDAL, A(1960), w; ONE, TWO, THREE(1961), w; BOYS OF PAUL STREET, THE(1969, Hung./US), w; ONE-TRICK

PONY(1980), w
Istvan Molnar
1984
BRADY'S ESCAPE(1984, U.S./Hung.)
Ivan Molnar
INTERNATIONAL SQUADRON(1941)
Jules Molnar
MASK OF DIMITRIOS, THE(1944)
Julius Molnar
OVER THE HILL(1931); NO GREATER GLORY(1934)
Julius Molnar, Jr.
Silents
MAN WHO LAUGHS, THE(1927)
Misc. Silents
DAUGHTERS OF DESIRE(1929)
Lilli Molnar
UP FOR THE CUP(1950, Brit.)
Lily Molnar
LONG DARK HALL, THE(1951, Brit.)
Stanko Molnar
PADRE PADRONE(1977, Ital.)
Tibor Molnar
DIALOGUE(1967, Hung.); RED AND THE WHITE, THE(1969, Hung./USSR); ROUND UP, THE(1969, Hung.); FORBIDDEN RELATIONS(1983, Hung.)
Walter Molnar
TO HAVE AND HAVE NOT(1944)
Lilly Molner
NO ORCHIDS FOR MISS BLANDISH(1948, Brit.)
Shirley Molohon
DOWN TO EARTH(1947)
Michael Mololey
GAS(1981, Can.)
Darren Moloney
DIRTY HARRY(1971)
Jim Moloney
MISTER ROBERTS(1955); SEMINOLE UPRISING(1955); FIENDISH PLOT OF DR. FU MANCHU, THE(1980), w
John A. Moloney
DOCTOR DETROIT(1983)
Robert Moloney
SEVEN MINUTES, THE(1971)
Sean Moloney
TELEFON(1977)
Ambrogio Molteni
DAVID AND GOLIATH(1961, Ital.), w; TARTARS, THE(1962, Ital./Yugo.), w; GIANT OF METROPOLIS, THE(1963, Ital.), w; SEVEN TASKS OF ALI BABA, THE(1963, Ital.), w
P. Molteni
1984
CAGED WOMEN(1984, Ital./Fr.), w
Sonia Molteni
TENTACLES(1977, Ital.), w; TAKE ALL OF ME(1978, Ital.), w
Grynet Molvig
MY FATHER'S MISTRESS(1970, Swed.); TIME IN THE SUN, A(1970, Swed.)
Patrick J. Molyneaux
ANGELS IN THE OUTFIELD(1951)
Ray Molyneaux
HAIL, HERO!(1969), set d; SAVE THE TIGER(1973), set d; BUSTING(1974), set d; TRAIN RIDE TO HOLLYWOOD(1975), set d; CARNY(1980), set d; TOUCHED BY LOVE(1980), set d
Raymond Molyneaux
CAREY TREATMENT, THE(1972), set d; JEREMIAH JOHNSON(1972), set d; HOMEBODIES(1974), set d; KLANSMAN, THE(1974), set d; ROCKY(1976), set d
William Molyneaux
HAPPINESS CAGE, THE(1972), art d
Eileen Molyneux
Misc. Silents
KEY OF THE WORLD, THE(1918, Brit.)
William Molyneux
BEEN DOWN SO LONG IT LOOKS LIKE UP TO ME(1977), art d
Arturo S. Mom
COCK O' THE WALK(1930), w
A. Mombelli
WAR AND PEACE(1968, USSR)
Fleur Mombelli
MORE THAN A MIRACLE(1967, Ital./Fr.)
Henry Momberg
LIFE IN EMERGENCY WARD 10(1959, Brit.)
Hilary Momberger
SNOOPY, COME HOME(1972)
James Momel
MS. 45(1981), ph; MADMAN(1982), ph
Harald Momm
IS PARIS BURNING?(1966, U.S./Fr.)
Alessandro Momo
MALICIOUS(1974, Ital.)
Allessandro Momo
SCENT OF A WOMAN(1976, Ital.)
Arnaldo Momo
QUIET PLACE IN THE COUNTRY, A(1970, Ital./Fr.)
Joseph Momo
AFRICAN, THE(1983, Fr.)
1984
LE CRABE TAMBOUR(1984, Fr.)
Sara Momo
QUIET PLACE IN THE COUNTRY, A(1970, Ital./Fr.)
Kaori Momoi
KAGEMUSHA(1980, Jap.)

Mayumi Momose
MY GEISHA(1962)
Glen Momott
WOLF DOG(1958, Can.)
Jose Maria Mompin
UNINHIBITED, THE(1968, Fr./Ital./Span.)
Pierre Momtizel
ANTOINE ET ANTOINETTE(1947 Fr.), ph
Mona
CAIRO(1963)
Ed Mona
LIFE STUDY(1973)
Eugene Mona
1984
SUGAR CANE ALLEY(1984, Fr.)
Madeleine Mona
LADY GODIVA RIDES AGAIN(1955, Brit.)
Mona the Woolly Monkey
ROBINSON CRUSOE ON MARS(1964)
Anthony Monaco
VOYAGE TO THE BOTTOM OF THE SEA(1961); WIN, PLACE, OR STEAL(1975), w
Di Ann Monaco
VAN NUYS BLVD.(1979)
James V. Monaco
FOX MOVIETONE FOLLIES OF 1930(1930), m
Jimmie Monaco
GOOD INTENTIONS(1930), m/l "Slave to Love," Cliff Friend
Ralph Monaco
KING OF COMEDY, THE(1983)
Lionel Monagas
Misc. Talkies
BRAND OF CAIN, THE(1935); KEEP PUNCHING(1939)
Misc. Silents
MILLIONARE, THE(1927)
Anne Monaghan
MARK, THE(1961, Brit.)
Jay Monaghan
BAD MEN OF TOMBSTONE(1949), w
John Monaghan
RECKLESS MOMENTS, THE(1949); MY SIX CONVICTS(1952)
John P. Monaghan
UPTURNED GLASS, THE(1947, Brit.), w; LADY POSSESSED(1952)
Patrick Monaghan
1984
PALLET ON THE FLOOR(1984, New Zealand), ed
Sharon Monaghan
RECKLESS MOMENTS, THE(1949)
Brent Monahan
SPASMS(1983, Can.), w
Dan Monahan
ONLY WHEN I LAUGH(1981); PORKY'S(1982); PORKY'S II: THE NEXT DAY(1983)
1984
UP THE CREEK(1984)
David Monahan
PHANTOM TOLLBOOTH, THE(1970), d
Dick Monahan
THUNDERING JETS(1958); LONE TEXAN(1959)
Captain Idris B. Monahan
GALLANT HOURS, THE(1960), tech adv
Joe Monahan
JUMBO(1962)
Joseph Monahan
Silents
SILVER WINGS(1922)
Mary Monahan
NIGHT TO REMEMBER, A(1958, Brit.)
Richard Monahan
BREAKTHROUGH(1950); DANGER ZONE(1951); G.I. JANE(1951); LET'S GO NAVY(1951); PIER 23(1951); STEEL HELMET, THE(1951); UNTAMED WOMEN(1952); WOMAN OBSESSED(1959)
Steve Monahan
SKATEBOARD(1978)
Stevie Monahan
FREEWHEELIN'(1976)
Tom Monahan
ANOTHER TIME, ANOTHER PLACE(1958), art d
Vladimir Monakhov
DESTINY OF A MAN(1961, USSR), ph; OPTIMISTIC TRAGEDY, THE(1964, USSR), ph; PORTRAIT OF LENIN(1967, Pol./USSR)
Gisella Monaldi
UNDER THE SUN OF ROME(1949, Ital.)
Annie Monange
THAT OBSCURE OBJECT OF DESIRE(1977, Fr./Span.)
Steve Monarque
1984
NO SMALL AFFAIR(1984); SIXTEEN CANDLES(1984)
Paul Monash
OPERATION MANHUNT(1954), w; BAILOUT AT 43,000(1957), w; GUN RUNNERS, THE(1958), w; SAFECRACKER, THE(1958, Brit.), w; SING, BOY, SING(1958), w; SCARFACE MOB, THE(1962), w; DEADFALL(1968, Brit.), p; BUTCH CASSIDY AND THE SUNDANCE KID(1969), p; SLAUGHTERHOUSE-FIVE(1972), p; FRIENDS OF EDDIE COYLE, THE(1973), p, w; FRONT PAGE, THE(1974), p; CARRIE(1976), p
Nate Monaster
SAD SACK, THE(1957), w; THAT TOUCH OF MINK(1962), w; CALL ME BWANA(1963, Brit.), w; VERY SPECIAL FAVOR, A(1965), w; HOW TO SAVE A MARRIAGE—AND RUIN YOUR LIFE(1968), w
Boris Monastirsky
RAINBOW, THE(1944, USSR), ph

Boris Monastrisky
TARAS FAMILY, THE(1946, USSR), ph
Borys Monastyrski
LAST STOP, THE(1949, Pol.), ph
Boris Monastyrskiy
DAY THE WAR ENDED, THE(1961, USSR), ph
Maria Monay
FLESH AND THE SPUR(1957); TANK COMMANDOS(1959)
Georges Monca
Misc. Silents
BLESSURE D'AMOUR(1916, Fr.), d; L'ANNIVERSAIRE(1916, Fr.), d; BONHOMME DE NEIGE(1917, Fr.), d; LA PROIE(1917, Fr.), d; LE CHANSON DU FEU(1917, Fr.), d; LA BONNE HOTESE(1918, Fr.), d; LA ROUTE DE DEVOIR(1918, Fr.), d; LORSQU'UNE FEMME VENT(1919, Fr.), d; MADAME ET SON FILLEUL(1919, Fr.), d; CHOUQUETTE ET SON AS(1920, Fr.), d; LES FEMMES COLLANTES(1920, Fr.), d; PRINCE EMBETE(1920, Fr.), d; SI JAMAIS JE TE PINCE(1920, Fr.), d; CHANTELOUVE(1921, Fr.), d; LE MEURTIER DE THEODORE(1921, Fr.), d; ROMAINE KALBRIS(1921, Fr.), d; LE SANG DES FINOEL(1922, Fr.), d; L'ENGRENAGE(1923, Fr.), d; ALTEMER LE CYNIQUE(1924, Fr.), d; LA DOUBLE EXISTENCE DE LORD SAMSEY(1924, Fr.), d; L'IRONIE DU SORT(1924, Fr.), d; AUTOUR D'UN BERCEAU(1925, Fr.), d; SANS FAMILLE(1925, Fr.), d; LE CHEMINEAU(1926, Fr.), d; MISS HELYETT(1927, Fr.), d; LES FOURCHAMBAULT(1929, Fr.), d
Santiago Moncada
DRUMS OF TABU, THE(1967, Ital./Span.), w; HATCHET FOR A HONEYMOON(1969, Span./Ital.), w; NARCO MEN, THE(1969, Span./Ital.), p, w; CORRUPTION OF CHRIS MILLER, THE(1979, Span.), w
Diana Moncardo
ADVENTURES OF MARCO POLO, THE(1938)
Francoise Moncey
LIFE UPSIDE DOWN(1965, Fr.)
Peter Monch
JOURNEY TO THE SEVENTH PLANET(1962, U.S./Swed.)
Francisco Moncion
MIDSUMMER NIGHT'S DREAM, A(1966)
Sidney Monckton
ON VELVET(1938, Brit.); MILL ON THE FLOSS(1939, Brit.); SHADOWED EYES(1939, Brit.); MYSTERY JUNCTION(1951, Brit.); JOHN WESLEY(1954, Brit.)
Sydney Monckton
SOUTHERN MAID, A(1933, Brit.); GLIMPSE OF PARADISE, A(1934, Brit.); TALKING FEET(1937, Brit.); WOMEN AREN'T ANGELS(1942, Brit.); HOUSE OF DARKNESS(1948, Brit.); MY BROTHER JONATHAN(1949, Brit.); SILK NOOSE, THE(1950, Brit.); OBSESSED(1951, Brit.)
Felix Monclova
HEROINA(1965)
Pierre Moncorber
CONFESSION, THE(1970, Fr.)
Pierre Moncorbier
FRENCH CANCAN(1956, Fr.); LOVERS ON A TIGHTROPE(1962, Fr.); FIRE WITHIN, THE(1964, Fr./Ital.); UP FROM THE BEACH(1965)
Jean [Gabin] Moncorge
MAGNIFICENT TRAMP, THE(1962, Fr./Ital.), w
Edward Moncrief
Silents
WESTERN HEARTS(1921)
Mark Moncro
BABYLON(1980, Brit.)
Joseph Moncure
JEALOUSY(1934), w
Steven Mond
1941(1979)
Dick Monda
MISTER CORY(1957)
Richard Monda
EDDIE CANTOR STORY, THE(1953); MIDNIGHT STORY, THE(1957)
Giaci Mondaini
I'LL GIVE A MILLION(1938), w
Joel Mondeaux
MARRIED TOO YOUNG(1962)
Anthony Mondell
NIGHT OF THE GRIZZLY, THE(1966), set d; MODEL SHOP, THE(1969), set d; CANCEL MY RESERVATION(1972), set d; TERMS OF ENDEARMENT(1983), set d
Tony Mondell
OTHER SIDE OF MIDNIGHT, THE(1977), set d
Rino Mondellini
ADVENTURES OF ARSENE LUPIN(1956, Fr./Ital.), art d; TRAPEZE(1956), art d; QUIET AMERICAN, THE(1958), art d; FANNY(1961), art d; FRANTIC(1961, Fr.), art d; RIFF RAFF GIRLS(1962, Fr./Ital.), art d; IN THE FRENCH STYLE(1963, U.S./Fr.), art d; NIGHT ENCOUNTER(1963, Fr./Ital.), set d; LIARS, THE(1964, Fr.), set d; NIGHT WATCH, THE(1964, Fr./Ital.), set d; TWO ARE GUILTY(1964, Fr.), art d; MY WIFE'S HUSBAND(1965, Fr./Ital.), art d; SLEEPING CAR MURDER THE(1966, Fr.), art d; TWO WEEKS IN SEPTEMBER(1967, Fr./Brit.), art d; CHAMPAGNE MURDERS, THE(1968, Fr.), art d
Anthony Mondello
MAN AND BOY(1972), set d; ENEMY OF THE PEOPLE, AN(1978), set d
Antony Mondello
HISTORY OF THE WORLD, PART 1(1981), set d
Luigi Mondello
LAST OF THE VIKINGS, THE(1962, Fr./Ital.), p, w; HERCULES AGAINST THE MOON MEN(1965, Fr./Ital.), p
Bruno Monden
HEAD, THE(1961, Ger.), art d; WOZZECK(1962, E. Ger.), set d; RESTLESS NIGHT, THE(1964, Ger.), set d
B. Mondi
BRIDEGROOM FOR TWO(1932, Brit.), ph
Bruno Mondi
CASINO DE PARIS(1957, Fr./Ger.), ph; STORY OF VICKIE, THE(1958, Aust.), ph; EMBEZZLED HEAVEN(1959,Ger.), ph; HOUSE OF THE THREE GIRLS, THE(1961, Aust.), ph; FOREVER MY LOVE(1962), ph; WOZZECK(1962, E. Ger.), ph; MAN WHO WALKED THROUGH THE WALL, THE(1964, Ger.), ph

Raquel Mondin
FAME(1980)
Sandro Mondini
WILD, WILD PLANET, THE(1967, Ital.)
Mondo
SHANKS(1974)
Peggy Mondo
MUSIC MAN, THE(1962); WHO'S MINDING THE STORE?(1963); PATSY, THE(1964); DON'T WORRY, WE'LL THINK OF A TITLE(1966); ANGEL IN MY POCKET(1969); HARDLY WORKING(1981)
Luciano Mondolfo
GIRL WHO COULDN'T SAY NO, THE(1969, Ital.)
Jorge Mondragon
INVISIBLE MAN, THE(1958, Mex.); FRANKENSTEIN, THE VAMPIRE AND CO.(1961, Mex.); DOCTOR OF DOOM(1962, Mex.); SANTO EN EL MUSEO DE CERA(1963, Mex.); SPIRITISM(1965, Mex.); CURSE OF THE DOLL PEOPLE, THE(1968, Mex.)
Andrew Mondshein
1984
GARBO TALKS(1984), ed
Pierre Mondy
FOLIES BERGERE(1958, Fr.); AUSTERLITZ(1960, Fr./Ital./Yugo.); LOVE AND THE FRENCHWOMAN(1961, Fr.); STORY OF THE COUNT OF MONTE CRISTO, THE(1962, Fr./Ital.); LADY DOCTOR, THE(1963, Fr./Ital./Span.); SLEEPING CAR MURDER THE(1966, Fr.); WEEKEND AT DUNKIRK(1966, Fr./Ital.); NIGHT OF THE GENERALS, THE(1967, Brit./Fr.); GIFT, THE(1983, Fr./Ital.)
Silvia Monelli
YESTERDAY, TODAY, AND TOMORROW(1964, Ital./Fr.)
Ivy Mones
AUDREY ROSE(1977)
Paul Mones
1984
STREETS OF FIRE(1984)
Andrea Monet
BE MY GUEST(1965, Brit.)
Charles Monet
MURDER AT THE GALLOP(1963, Brit.), cos
Mona Monet
DEAD END(1937)
Monica Monet
Misc. Talkies
SPASMO(1976)
Robert Monet
THUNDER BAY(1953)
Moneta
HONEYMOON DEFERRED(1951, Brit.)
Adriana Moneta
LA DOLCE VITA(1961, Ital./Fr.)
Luigi Moneta
ROMAN HOLIDAY(1953)
Renzo Moneta
DEAF SMITH AND JOHNNY EARS(1973, Ital.)
Tulio Moneta
Misc. Talkies
THREE BULLETS FOR A LONG GUN(1973)
Bruce Monette
HUMANOIDS FROM THE DEEP(1980)
Richard Monette
NOTHING PERSONAL(1980, Can.)
1984
ICEMAN(1984)
Michael Monetti
1984
OLD ENOUGH(1984)
G.B. Zoot Money
PIRATES OF PENZANCE, THE(1983)
Susan Money
1984
C.H.U.D.(1984), cos
Zoot Money
POPDOWN(1968, Brit.)
1984
SCANDALOUS(1984); SUPERGIRL(1984)
Mike Monezzi
1984
ONCE UPON A TIME IN AMERICA(1984)
Carol Monferdini
BELL JAR, THE(1979)
John Monfort
SHAME OF THE SABINE WOMEN, THE(1962, Mex.)
Michel Monfort
FIVE WILD GIRLS(1966, Fr.)
Silvia Monfort
RIFF RAFF GIRLS(1962, Fr./Ital.)
Sylvia Monfort
EAGLE WITH TWO HEADS(1948, Fr.); ANGELS OF THE STREETS(1950, Fr.); CASE OF DR. LAURENT(1958, Fr.)
William Mong
LET US LIVE(1939); RIDIN' ON A RAINBOW(1941)
William V. Mong
HAUNTED HOUSE, THE(1928); NOAH'S ARK(1928); HOUSE OF HORROR(1929); SEVEN FOOTPRINTS TO SATAN(1929); SHOULD A GIRL MARRY?(1929); BIG TRAIL, THE(1930); DARKENED SKIES(1930); DOUBLE CROSS ROADS(1930); GIRL SAID NO, THE(1930); IN GAY MADRID(1930); MURDER ON THE ROOF(1930); BAD COMPANY(1931); DANGEROUS AFFAIR, A(1931); FLOOD, THE(1931); GUN SMOKE(1931); ARM OF THE LAW(1932); BY WHOSE HAND?(1932); CROSS-EXAMINATION(1932); DYNAMITE DENNY(1932); FIGHTING FOOL, THE(1932); IF I HAD A MILLION(1932); SIGN OF THE CROSS, THE(1932); STRANGE ADVENTURE(1932); WIDOW IN SCARLET(1932); ELEVENTH COMMANDMENT(1933); FOOTLIGHT PARADE(1933); HER FORGOTTEN PAST(1933); I LOVED A WOMAN(1933); MAYOR

OF HELL, THE(1933); NARROW CORNER, THE(1933); NO MORE ORCHIDS(1933); VAMPIRE BAT, THE(1933); WOMEN WON'T TELL(1933); DARK HAZARD(1934); MASSACRE(1934); TREASURE ISLAND(1934); COUNTY CHAIRMAN, THE(1935); HOOSIER SCHOOLMASTER(1935); LAST DAYS OF POMPEII, THE(1935); RENDEZVOUS(1935); SWEET ADELINE(1935); TOGETHER WE LIVE(1935); WHISPERING SMITH SPEAKS(1935); DANCING PIRATE(1936); DARK HOUR, THE(1936); LAST OF THE MOHICANS, THE(1936); STAND-IN(1937); PAINTED DESERT, THE(1938)
Silents
AMATEUR ADVENTURESS, THE(1919); FOLLIES GIRL, THE(1919); CHORUS GIRL'S ROMANCE, A(1920); CONNECTICUT YANKEE AT KING ARTHUR'S COURT, A(1921); PLAYTHINGS OF DESTINY(1921); SHAME(1921); TEN DOLLAR RAISE, THE(1921); SHATTERED IDOLS(1922), a, w; ALL THE BROTHERS WERE VALIANT(1923); PENROD AND SAM(1923); OH, DOCTOR(1924); WELCOME STRANGER(1924); OFF THE HIGHWAY(1925); OLD SOAK, THE(1926); SILENT LOVER, THE(1926); STRONG MAN, THE(1926); WHAT PRICE GLORY(1926); ALIAS THE LONE WOLF(1927); CLOWN, THE(1927); TAXI! TAXI!(1927); NO BABIES WANTED(1928); RANSOM(1928); TELLING THE WORLD(1928)
Misc. Silents
YELLOW TRAFFIC, THE(1914); HEART'S CRUCIBLE, A(1916); HER BITTER CUP(1916); IRON HAND, THE(1916); SHOES(1916); FANATICS(1917); GIRL AND THE CRISIS, THE(1917), a, d; WILD SUMAC(1917), d; HOPPER, THE(1918); MAN WHO WOKE UP, THE(1918); PAINTED LILY, THE(1918); LOVE'S PRISONER(1919); BURNING DAYLIGHT(1920); TURNING POINT, THE(1920); PILGRIMS OF THE NIGHT(1921); WINDING TRAIL, THE(1921); ARCTIC ADVENTURE(1922); MONTE CRISTO(1922); WOMAN HE LOVED, THE(1922); WANDERING DAUGHTERS(1923); THY NAME IS WOMAN(1924); WHAT SHALL I DO?(1924); WHY MEN LEAVE HOME(1924); ALIAS MARY FLYNN(1925); SHADOW ON THE WALL, THE(1925); SPEED(1925); UNWRITTEN LAW, THE(1925); FIFTH AVENUE(1926); PRICE OF HONOR, THE(1927); BROKEN MASK, THE(1928); CODE OF THE AIR(1928); DEVIL'S TRADEMARK, THE(1928); WHITE FLAME(1928); SEVEN FOOTPRINTS TO SATAN(1929)
Chris Monger
Misc. Talkies
VOICE OVER(1983), d
Lorenzo Mongiardino
BROTHER SUN, SISTER MOON(1973, Brit./Ital.), prod d
1984
BEYOND GOOD AND EVIL(1984, Ital./Fr./Ger.), art d
Renzo Mongiardino
ROMEO AND JULIET(1968, Brit./Ital.), prod d
Mongo Santmaria and His Band
MADE IN PARIS(1966)
Vincent Mongol
CHAINED HEAT(1983 U.S./Ger.), w
Jerzy Moniak
MAN OF MARBLE(1979, Pol.)
Monica
TILLIE THE TOILER(1941), cos
Corbett Monica
GRASSHOPPER, THE(1970)
1984
BROADWAY DANNY ROSE(1984)
Elisabeth Monica
TRADER HORNEE(1970)
M. Monicelli
SOHO CONSPIRACY(1951, Brit.), w
Mario Monicelli
RETURN OF THE BLACK EAGLE(1949, Ital.), w; FATAL DESIRE(1953), w; APPOINTMENT FOR MURDER(1954, Ital.), w; DONATELLA(1956, Ital.), d, w; BIG DEAL ON MADONNA STREET, THE(1960), d, w; UNFAITHFULS, THE(1960, Ital.), d, w; GREAT WAR, THE(1961, Fr., Ital.), d, w; PASSIONATE THIEF, THE(1963, Ital.), d, w; ORGANIZER, THE(1964, Fr./Ital./Yugo.), d, w; CASANOVA '70(1965, Ital.), d, w; HIGH INFIDELITY(1965, Fr./Ital.), d; GIRL WITH A PISTOL, THE(1968, Ital.), d; QUEENS, THE(1968, Ital./Fr.), d; LADY LIBERTY(1972, Ital./Fr.), d, w; GOODNIGHT, LADIES AND GENTLEMEN(1977, Ital.), d&w; VIVA ITALIA(1978, Ital.), d; LOVERS AND LIARS(1981, Ital.), d, w
1984
CRACKERS(1984), w
S. Monicelli
SOHO CONSPIRACY(1951, Brit.), w
Aurelio Lopez Monis
FICKLE FINGER OF FATE, THE(1967, Span./U.S.), w
Piyamatr Monjakul
1 2 3 MONSTER EXPRESS(1977, Thai.)
Alan Monk
LA TRAVIATA(1982)
Alice Monk
MRS. MINIVER(1942)
Angela Monk
SKID KIDS(1953, Brit.)
Conrad Monk
TRYGON FACTOR, THE(1969, Brit.)
Egon Monk
GREAT BRITISH TRAIN ROBBERY, THE(1967, Ger.), p
Isabell Monk
WORLD ACCORDING TO GARP, The(1982)
1984
SWING SHIFT(1984)
Isabelle Monk
LOVESICK(1983)
Jacko the Monk
Silents
TRAVELIN' ON(1922)
John Monk, Jr.
BROTHER RAT(1938), w; SO THIS IS LOVE(1953), w
Julius Monk
GIRL OF THE NIGHT(1960)

Laury Monk
DIRTY HARRY(1971)

Marilyn Monk
GENTLEMAN'S AGREEMENT(1947)

Mike Monk
FRONT PAGE WOMAN(1935)

Paddy Monk
RIVERRUN(1968), ed

Thomas Monk
PETER IBBETSON(1935); COURAGE OF THE WEST(1937)

Thorner Monk
THIRTY-DAY PRINCESS(1934)

Tom Monk
GOIN' TO TOWN(1935)

Paul Monka
SPIDER BABY(1968), p

James the Monkey
Silents
TILLIE'S TOMATO SURPRISE(1915)

Bob Monkhouse
SECRET PEOPLE(1952, Brit.); CARRY ON SERGEANT(1959, Brit.); DENTIST IN THE CHAIR(1960, Brit.), a, w; WEEKEND WITH LULU, A(1961, Brit.); GET ON WITH IT(1963, Brit.), a, w; MAID FOR MURDER(1963, Brit.); BLISS OF MRS. BLOSSOM, THE(1968, Brit.); THUNDERBIRDS ARE GO(1968, Brit.)

Jo Monkhouse
JENIFER HALE(1937, Brit.); MR. SMITH CARRIES ON(1937, Brit.)

Joe Monkhouse
SUMMER LIGHTNING(1933, Brit.); FORBIDDEN MUSIC(1936, Brit.)

Francis Monkman
LONG GOOD FRIDAY, THE(1982, Brit.), m

Noel Monkman
TYPHOON TREASURE(1939, Brit.), d, w; KING OF THE CORAL SEA(1956, Aus.), d

Phyllis Monkman
BLACKMAIL(1929, Brit.); KING OF PARIS, THE(1934, Brit.); EVERYTHING HAP-PENS TO ME(1938, Brit.); GOOD OLD DAYS, THE(1939, Brit.); YOUNG MAN'S FANCY(1943, Brit.); UNCENSORED(1944, Brit.); CARNIVAL(1946, Brit.); DIAMOND CITY(1949, Brit.)
Silents
HER HERITAGE(1919, Brit.)

Bill Monks
VICTOR/VICTORIA(1982)
1984
SUCCESS IS THE BEST REVENGE(1984, Brit.)

Elsie Monks
SING ALONG WITH ME(1952, Brit.)

James Monks
HOW GREEN WAS MY VALLEY(1941); MAN WHO WOULD NOT DIE, THE(1975)

Jimmy Monks
JOAN OF PARIS(1942)

John Monks, Jr.
BROTHER RAT AND A BABY(1940), w; STRIKE UP THE BAND(1940), w; HOUSE ON 92ND STREET, THE(1945), w; 13 RUE MADELEINE(1946), w; WILD HAR-VEST(1947), w; KNOCK ON ANY DOOR(1949), w; DIAL 1119(1950), w; WEST POINT STORY, THE(1950), w; PEOPLE AGAINST O'HARA, THE(1951), w; ABOUT FA-CE(1952), w; WHERE'S CHARLEY?(1952, Brit.), w; NO MAN IS AN ISLAND(1962), d&w, p; PARADISE ALLEY(1978)

Mary Monks
CHRISTINA(1974, Can.)

Yvonne Monlaur
BRIDES OF DRACULA, THE(1960, Brit.); CIRCUS OF HORRORS(1960, Brit.); INN FOR TROUBLE(1960, Brit.); TERROR OF THE TONGS, THE(1961, Brit.); TIME TO REMEMBER(1962, Brit.); SKY ABOVE HEAVEN(1964, Fr./Ital.); NIGHT OF LUST(1965, Fr.)

Eva Monley
COME SPY WITH ME(1967), prod d

Hubert Monloup
LE BONHEUR(1966, Fr.), art d; SHAMELESS OLD LADY, THE(1966, Fr.), art d

Egil Monn-Iversen
PASSIONATE DEMONS, THE(1962, Norway), m; SNOW TREASURE(1968), m

Gabriel Monnet
MOON IN THE GUTTER, THE(1983, Fr./Ital.)

Jacques Monnet
BLACK AND WHITE IN COLOR(1976, Fr.)

Martin Monney
CONVICTED WOMAN(1940), w

Antoine Monnier
DEVIL PROBABLY, THE(1977, FR.)

Jackie Monnier
DAVID GOLDER(1932, Fr.)
Misc. Silents
LE TORNOI(1928, Fr.); LE BLED(1929, Fr.)

Valentine Monnier
1984
AFTER THE FALL OF NEW YORK(1984, Ital./Fr.)

Nicole Monnin
PARDON MY FRENCH(1951, U.S./Fr.)

Marguerite Monnot
TEMPTATION(1962, Fr.), m; IRMA LA DOUCE(1963), m

Maurice Monnoyer
FOUR NIGHTS OF A DREAMER(1972, Fr.)

Jacque Monod
GAME IS OVER, THE(1967, Fr.)

Jacques Monod
FOUR HUNDRED BLOWS, THE(1959); PASSION OF SLOW FIRE, THE(1962, Fr.); SEVEN CAPITAL SINS(1962, Fr./Ital.); THERESE(1963, Fr.); DON'T TEMPT THE DEVIL(1964, Fr./Ital.); SEVENTH JUROR, THE(1964, Fr.); SKY ABOVE HEA-VEN(1964, Fr./Ital.); TWO ARE GUILTY(1964, Fr.); ENOUGH ROPE(1966, Fr./Ital./Ger.); MADEMOISELLE(1966, Fr./Brit.); MARCO THE MAGNIFICENT(1966, Ital./Fr./Yugo./Egypt/Afghanistan); RAVISHING IDIOT, A(1966, Ital./Fr.); STRANGER, THE(1967, Algeria/Fr./Ital.); DIRTY HEROES(1971, Ital./Fr./Ger.); TWO MEN IN TOWN(1973, Fr.); RE: LUCKY LUCIANO(1974, Fr./Ital.); TENANT, THE(1976, Fr.)

Jacques-Louis Monod
THIS SPORTING LIFE(1963, Brit.), md

Roland Monod
MAN ESCAPED, A(1957, Fr.); LA GUERRE EST FINIE(1967, Fr./Swed.); GIRL FROM LORRAINE, A(1982, Fr./Switz.)

Lionel Monogas
DRUMS O' VOODOO(1934); STRAIGHT TO HEAVEN(1939)

John Monoghan
BIGGER THAN LIFE(1956)

Richard Monoham
FBI GIRL(1951)

Richard Monohan
FIXED BAYONETS(1951); LEAVE IT TO THE MARINES(1951); STARLIFT(1951); DEADLINE–U.S.A.(1952); DOWN AMONG THE SHELTERING PALMS(1953); WHITE DOG(1982)

Tom Monohan
CIRCLE OF DECEPTON(1961, Brit.), p

Marcia Monolescue
Misc. Talkies
SUPERSONIC SAUCER(1956, Brit.)

Lili Monori
WITNESS, THE(1982, Hung.); FORBIDDEN RELATIONS(1983, Hung.)

Lawrence Monoson
LAST AMERICAN VIRGIN, THE(1982)
1984
FRIDAY THE 13TH–THE FINAL CHAPTER(1984)

Andres Monreal
LOST COMMAND, THE(1966); DESPERATE ONES, THE(1968 U.S./Span.); VILLA RIDES(1968); LOVE AND PAIN AND THE WHOLE DAMN THING(1973)

Cinzia Monreale
1984
BURIED ALIVE(1984, Ital.)

Matt Monro
Misc. Talkies
SATAN'S HARVEST(1970)

Robert Monro
FRENCH MISTRESS(1960, Brit.), w

Al Monroe
LAST MOVIE, THE(1971)

Armand Monroe
GAS(1981, Can.)

Baby Monroe
GLOBAL AFFAIR, A(1964)

Beulah Monroe
RENO(1930)

Bill Monroe
SECOND FIDDLE TO A STEEL GUITAR(1965)

Buck Monroe
DEADLINE(1948)

Craddock C. Monroe
MR. PEEK-A-BOO(1951, Fr.)

Dale Monroe
MONEY JUNGLE, THE(1968)

Del Monroe
WALKING TALL(1973)

Delbert Monroe
VOYAGE TO THE BOTTOM OF THE SEA(1961)

Doreen Monroe
BULLDOG DRUMMOND STRIKES BACK(1934); FOREVER AND A DAY(1943)

Earl Monroe
LOVE IN A TAXI(1980)

Ellen Hope Monroe
RIDE BACK, THE(1957)

Jarion Monroe
ORGANIZATION, THE(1971); CRAZY WORLD OF JULIUS VROODER, THE(1974)

Len Monroe
STOP TRAIN 349(1964, Fr./Ital./Ger.)

Louise Monroe
Misc. Talkies
ALIEN CONTAMINATION(1981)

Marilyn Monroe
DANGEROUS YEARS(1947); LADIES OF THE CHORUS(1948); SCUDDA-HOO! SCUDDA-HAY!(1948); LOVE HAPPY(1949); ALL ABOUT EVE(1950); ASPHALT JUN-GLE, THE(1950); FIREBALL, THE(1950); RIGHT CROSS(1950); TICKET TO TOMA-HAWK(1950); AS YOUNG AS YOU FEEL(1951); HOME TOWN STORY(1951); LET'S MAKE IT LEGAL(1951); LOVE NEST(1951); CLASH BY NIGHT(1952); DON'T BOTH-ER TO KNOCK(1952); MONKEY BUSINESS(1952); O. HENRY'S FULL HOUSE(1952); WE'RE NOT MARRIED(1952); GENTLEMEN PREFER BLONDES(1953); HOW TO MARRY A MILLIONAIRE(1953); NIAGARA(1953); RIVER OF NO RETURN(1954); THERE'S NO BUSINESS LIKE SHOW BUSINESS(1954); SEVEN YEAR ITCH, THE(1955); BUS STOP(1956); PRINCE AND THE SHOWGIRL, THE(1957, Brit.); SOME LIKE IT HOT(1959); LET'S MAKE LOVE(1960); MISFITS, THE(1961)

Michael Monroe
TEA AND SYMPATHY(1956); INSIDE THE MAFIA(1959)

Millie Monroe
Misc. Talkies
MR. SMITH GOES GHOST(1940)

Neville Monroe
CALL ME BWANA(1963, Brit.)

Patricia Monroe
MR. DEEDS GOES TO TOWN(1936)

Peter Monroe
ALONE IN THE DARK(1982), art d

Robert Monroe
CROOKED WAY, THE(1949), w

Rudolph Monroe
RAISIN IN THE SUN, A(1961)

Thomas Monroe
BALL OF FIRE(1941), w; AFFAIRS OF SUSAN(1945), w; SONG IS BORN, A(1948), w

Tom Monroe
POWDER RIVER RUSTLERS(1949); BORDER RANGERS(1950); BORDER TREAS-URE(1950); CARIBOO TRAIL, THE(1950); RUSTLERS ON HORSEBACK(1950); TWO LOST WORLDS(1950); HALF-BREED, THE(1952); HOODLUM EMPIRE(1952); HORI-ZONS WEST(1952); ROSE OF CIMARRON(1952); EL PASO STAMPEDE(1953); HOME-STEADERS, THE(1953); COMMAND, THE(1954); FAR HORIZONS, THE(1955); JUPITER'S DARLING(1955); SON OF SINBAD(1955); GIANT(1956); SHOOT-OUT AT MEDICINE BEND(1957); WAR DRUMS(1957); RIO BRAVO(1959); WEST-BOUND(1959); MARLOWE(1969)

Tommy Monroe
DARK CORNER, THE(1946); I SHOT BILLY THE KID(1950)

Vaughn Monroe
SINGING GUNS(1950); TOUGHEST MAN IN ARIZONA(1952)

Jake Monroy
Misc. Talkies
LAST TANGO IN ACAPULCO, THE(1975)

Manuel Monroy
REDEEMER, THE(1965, Span.)

Nicholas Monsarrat
CRUEL SEA, THE(1953), w; SHIP THAT DIED OF SHAME, THE(1956, Brit.), w; STORY OF ESTHER COSTELLO, THE(1957, Brit.), w; SOMETHING TO HIDE(1972, Brit.), d&w

Sam Monsarrat
BIRD OF PARADISE(1951)

R. Monsatirsky
HEROES ARE MADE(1944, USSR), ph

Monsigny
RULES OF THE GAME, THE(1939, Fr.), m

Jean Monsigny
LES CARABINIERS(1968, Fr./Ital.)
1984
TO CATCH A COP(1984, Fr.), ph

Arch Monson
TANGA-TIKA(1953), p

Carl Monson
LEGACY OF BLOOD(1973), p&d
Misc. Talkies
PLEASE DON'T EAT MY MOTHER(1972), d; YOUNG AND WILD(1975)

Lex Monson
NUN AT THE CROSSROADS, A(1970, Ital./Span.); VALDEZ IS COMING(1971); TATTOO(1981)

Ted Monson
SWEET CHARITY(1969)

C. Monsoor
MONKEY'S PAW, THE(1933)

Nira Monsour
PROPER TIME, THE(1959)

Nyra Monsour
SARACEN BLADE, THE(1954); AMERICANO, THE(1955)

Robert Mont
WARM IN THE BUD(1970)

Norman Mont-Eton
STRIPES(1981)

Carlotta Monta
IN OLD CALIFORNIA(1929)

Janet Monta
ALL THE WAY UP(1970, Brit.)

Joseph Montabo
SO FINE(1981)

Maurice Montabre
ROMAN HOLIDAY(1953)

Luisa Montagmana
VOYAGE, THE(1974, Ital.), w

Luisa Montagnana
FINE PAIR, A(1969, Ital.), w

Maria Luisa Montagnana
FRANKENSTEIN-ITALIAN STYLE(1977, Ital.), w

Nerina Montagnana
PRIEST'S WIFE, THE(1971, Ital./Fr.)

Nerina Montagnani
SERAFINO(1970, Fr./Ital.); CRIME AT PORTA ROMANA(1980, Ital.)

Renzo Montagnani
WHEN WOMEN HAD TAILS(1970, Ital.); ADVENTURES OF RABBI JACOB, THE(1973, Fr.); MASSACRE IN ROME(1973, Ital.); GIFT, THE(1983, Fr./Ital.)
1984
JOKE OF DESTINY LYING IN WAIT AROUND THE CORNER LIKE A STREET-BANDIT, A(1984, Ital.)

Edward Montagne
THEY WENT THAT-A-WAY AND THAT-A-WAY(1978), d
Silents
RECKLESS YOUTH(1922), w

Edward J. Montagne
IT CAN BE DONE(1929), w; LOVE TRAP, THE(1929), w; PROJECT X(1949), d; TATTOOED STRANGER, THE(1950), d; MC HALE'S NAVY(1964), p&d; MC HALE'S NAVY JOINS THE AIR FORCE(1965), p&d; GHOST AND MR. CHICKEN, THE(1966), p; RELUCTANT ASTRONAUT, THE(1967), p&d; P.J.(1968), p, w; SHAKIEST GUN IN THE WEST, THE(1968), p; LOVE GOD?, THE(1969), p; HOW TO FRAME A FIGG(1971), p, w
Silents
WHEELS OF JUSTICE(1915), w; APARTMENT 29(1917), w; DAUGHTER PAYS, THE(1920), w; AFTER MIDNIGHT(1921), w; MAN'S HOME, A(1921), w; WIDE-OPEN TOWN, A(1922), w; COMMON LAW, THE(1923), w; RUPERT OF HENTZAU(1923), w; PAINTED PEOPLE(1924), w; STORM DAUGHTER, THE(1924), w; LOVE ME AND THE WORLD IS MINE(1928), w; RED LIPS(1928), w

Edward R. Montagne
Silents
OUT YONDER(1920), w

Marie Montagne
FOUR BOYS AND A GUN(1957), ed

Guy Montagni
1984
AMERICAN DREAMER(1984)

E. Montagnini
PEDDLIN' IN SOCIETY(1949, Ital.), m

Carolyn Montagu
WHERE'S JACK?(1969, Brit.)

Elizabeth Montagu
VILLAGE, THE(1953, Brit./Switz.), w

Ewen Montagu
MAN WHO NEVER WAS, THE(1956, Brit.), a, w

Ivor Montagu
KING OF THE RITZ(1933, Brit.), w; MY OLD DUTCH(1934, Brit.), p; 39 STEPS, THE(1935, Brit.), p; PASSING OF THE THIRD FLOOR BACK, THE(1936, Brit.), p; SECRET AGENT, THE(1936, Brit.), p; SABOTAGE(1937, Brit.), p; SCOTT OF THE ANTARCTIC(1949, Brit.), w; LAST MAN TO HANG, THE(1956, Brit.), w
Silents
LODGER, THE(1926, Brit.), t, ed; EASY VIRTUE(1927, Brit.), ed; WHEN BOYS LEAVE HOME(1928, Brit.), ed

Max Montagu
LIARS, THE(1964, Fr.), w

Edward J. Montague
ANGEL IN MY POCKET(1969), p

Fred Montague
Silents
CALL OF THE NORTH, THE(1914); CIRCUS MAN, THE(1914); MAN FROM HOME, THE(1914); MASTER MIND, THE(1914); READY MONEY(1914); SQUAW MAN, THE(1914); WHERE THE TRAIL DIVIDES(1914); HIS ROBE OF HONOR(1918); ROUGH LOVER, THE(1918); ALL WRONG(1919)
Misc. Silents
WHAT'S HIS NAME?(1914); REED CASE, THE(1917); FAST COMPANY(1918); HIS DEBT(1919)

Frederick Montague
Misc. Silents
CONSCIENCE OF JOHN DAVID, THE(1916); HIDDEN LAW, THE(1916); GOD'S CRUCIBLE(1917)

John Montague
Silents
BIG TOWN IDEAS(1921), w; CHILDREN OF THE NIGHT(1921), w; GET YOUR MAN(1921), w; MAID OF THE WEST(1921), w

Kieran Montague
ASCENDANCY(1983, Brit.)

Lee Montague
MOULIN ROUGE(1952); SILENT ENEMY, THE(1959, Brit.); ANOTHER SKY(1960 Brit.); CHANCE MEETING(1960, Brit.); FOXHOLE IN CAIRO(1960, Brit.); SAVAGE INNOCENTS, THE(1960, Brit.); MAN AT THE CARLTON TOWER(1961, Brit.); SE-CRET PARTNER, THE(1961, Brit.); SINGER NOT THE SONG, THE(1961, Brit.); BILLY BUDD(1962); OPERATION SNATCH(1962, Brit.); FIVE TO ONE(1963, Brit.); SECRET OF BLOOD ISLAND, THE(1965, Brit.); YOU MUST BE JOKING!(1965, Brit.); DEAD-LIER THAN THE MALE(1967, Brit.); HOW I WON THE WAR(1967, Brit.); HIGH COMMISSIONER, THE(1968, U.S./Brit.); EAGLE IN A CAGE(1971, U.S./Yugo.); BROTHER SUN, SISTER MOON(1973, Brit./Ital.); MAHLER(1974, Brit.); BRASS TARGET(1978); LEGACY, THE(1979, Brit.); SILVER DREAM RACER(1982, Brit.); RED MONARCH(1983, Brit.)

Margaret Prescott Montague
Silents
LINDA(1929), w

Monte Montague
LONESOME TRAIL, THE(1930); TRIGGER TRICKS(1930); COME ON DAN-GER!(1932); IMPATIENT MAIDEN(1932); ROCKY RHODES(1934); AFFAIR OF SU-SAN(1935); OUTLAWED GUNS(1935); REMEMBER LAST NIGHT(1935); SHE GETS HER MAN(1935); STORMY(1935); SHOW BOAT(1936); SONG OF THE SADDLE(1936); TREACHERY RIDES THE RANGE(1936); GIT ALONG, LITTLE DOGIES(1937); GUNS OF THE PECOS(1937); PHANTOM OF SANTA FE(1937); LAW WEST OF TOMB-STONE, THE(1938); PALS OF THE SADDLE(1938); RENEGADE RANGER(1938); RIDERS OF THE BLACK HILLS(1938); ROLL ALONG, COWBOY(1938); ALLEGHE-NY UPRISING(1939); RACKETEERS OF THE RANGE(1939); ROOKIE COP, THE(1939); TIMBER STAMPEDE(1939); TROUBLE IN SUNDOWN(1939); LEGION OF THE LAWLESS(1940); PRAIRIE LAW(1940); VIRGINIA CITY(1940); WAGON TRAIN(1940); YOUNG BILL HICKOK(1940); ALONG THE RIO GRANDE(1941); APACHE KID, THE(1941); BARNACLE BILL(1941); CYCLONE ON HORSEBACK(1941); HONKY TONK(1941); SINGING HILL, THE(1941); THUNDER-ING HOOFS(1941); CYCLONE KID, THE(1942); NAVY COMES THROUGH, THE(1942); PHANTOM PLAINSMEN, THE(1942); RAIDERS OF THE RANGE(1942); STARDUST ON THE SAGE(1942); WESTWARD HO(1942); FIGHTING FRON-TIER(1943); VIGILANTES RETURN, THE(1947); FEUDIN', FUSSIN' AND A-FIGH-TIN'(1948); MOONRISE(1948); STATION WEST(1948); BROTHERS IN THE SADDLE(1949); RUSTLERS(1949); SAVAGE HORDE, THE(1950); VENGEANCE VAL-LEY(1951); HORIZONS WEST(1952); LAST MUSKETEER, THE(1952); THUNDER OVER THE PLAINS(1953)
Misc. Talkies
QUICK TRIGGER LEE(1931)
Silents
PEACEFUL PETERS(1922); WESTERN DEMON, A(1922); HEY! HEY! COW-BOY(1927); SOMEWHERE IN SONORA(1927); AIR PATROL, THE(1928); CLEARING THE TRAIL(1928); GATE CRASHER, THE(1928); SLIM FINGERS(1929)
Misc. Silents
DEFYING THE LAW(1922); SECRET OF THE PUEBLO, THE(1923)

Monte Montague, Jr.
Misc. Silents
RAMBLING RANGER, THE(1927)

Monty Montague
COURTIN' WILDCATS(1929); LITTLE TOUGH GUY(1938); ARIZONA LEGION(1939)
Silents
EYES OF THE UNDERWORLD(1929); KING OF THE RODEO(1929)
Misc. Silents
THREE BUCKAROOS, THE(1922); ONE MAN TRAIL(1926); DANGER RIDER, THE(1928); WOLVES OF THE CITY(1929)

Sara Montague
1984
TOP SECRET!(1984)
The Honorable Mrs. Montague
Silents
GREAT LOVE, THE(1918)
William Montague
BLOOD AND SAND(1941)
F. E. Montague-Thacker
Silents
DIAMOND NECKLACE, THE(1921, Brit.)
Bettina Montahners
LOOKING ON THE BRIGHT SIDE(1932, Brit.); WISHBONE, THE(1933, Brit.)
Edward J. Montaigne
SHOW BOAT(1929), ed; MAN WITH MY FACE, THE(1951), d
Lawrence Montaigne
DAMON AND PYTHIAS(1962); GREAT ESCAPE, THE(1963); PILLAR OF FIRE, THE(1963, Israel); SYNANON(1965); TOBRUK(1966); POWER, THE(1968); ESCAPE TO WITCH MOUNTAIN(1975); FRAMED(1975); DEADLY BLESSING(1981)
Misc. Talkies
PSYCHO LOVER(1969, Brit.)
Monique Montaigne
SINGING NUN, THE(1966)
Sandra Montaigu
1984
LOVE ON THE GROUND(1984,Fr.)
Josef Montaigue
RANGE WAR(1939), w
Gina Montaine
Misc. Talkies
COME ONE, COME ALL(1970)
Jean Claude Montalbam
THAT OBSCURE OBJECT OF DESIRE(1977, Fr./Span.)
Carlos Montalban
MESSAGE TO GARCIA, A(1936); WHEN YOU'RE IN LOVE(1937); CROWDED PARADISE(1956); HARDER THEY FALL, THE(1956); MYSTERIANS, THE(1959, Jap.), p; PEPE(1960); LOVE HAS MANY FACES(1965); OUT OF TOWNERS, THE(1970); BANANAS(1971)
Jean Claude Montalban
1984
UNTIL SEPTEMBER(1984)
Jean-Claude Montalban
1984
AMERICAN DREAMER(1984)
Jess Montalban
MORO WITCH DOCTOR(1964, U.S./Phil.); WALLS OF HELL, THE(1964, U.S./Phil.)
Ricardo Montalban
FIESTA(1947); KISSING BANDIT, THE(1948); ON AN ISLAND WITH YOU(1948); BATTLEGROUND(1949); BORDER INCIDENT(1949); NEPTUNE'S DAUGHTER(1949); MYSTERY STREET(1950); RIGHT CROSS(1950); TWO WEEKS WITH LOVE(1950); MARK OF THE RENEGADE(1951); MY MAN AND I(1952); LATIN LOVERS(1953); SOMBRERO(1953); SARACEN BLADE, THE(1954); LIFE IN THE BALANCE, A(1955); QUEEN OF BABYLON, THE(1956, Ital.); THREE FOR JAMIE DAWN(1956); UNTOUCHED(1956); SAYONARA(1957); LET NO MAN WRITE MY EPITAPH(1960); DESERT WARRIOR(1961 Ital./Span.); ADVENTURES OF A YOUNG MAN(1962); RELUCTANT SAINT, THE(1962, U.S./Ital.); LOVE IS A BALL(1963); RAGE OF THE BUCCANEERS(1963, Ital.); CHEYENNE AUTUMN(1964); MADAME X(1966); MONEY TRAP, THE(1966); SINGING NUN, THE(1966); BLUE(1968); SOL MADRID(1968); SWEET CHARITY(1969); DESERTER, THE(1971 Ital./Yugo.); ESCAPE FROM THE PLANET OF THE APES(1971); CONQUEST OF THE PLANET OF THE APES(1972); JOE PANTHER(1976); WON TON TON, THE DOG WHO SAVED HOLLYWOOD(1976); STAR TREK II: THE WRATH OF KHAN(1982)
1984
CANNONBALL RUN II(1984)
Misc. Talkies
KINO, THE PADRE ON HORSEBACK(1977)
Riccardo Montalban
ACROSS THE WIDE MISSOURI(1951)
Richardo Montalban
TRAIN ROBBERS, THE(1973)
Misc. Talkies
SCORPIO SCARAB, THE(1972)
Renato Montalbano
GOLDEN ARROW, THE(1964, Ital.); MANDRAGOLA(1966 Fr./Ital.); SECRET SEVEN, THE(1966, Ital./Span.); HAWKS AND THE SPARROWS, THE(1967, Ital.); LIGHTNING BOLT(1967, Ital./Sp.); WILD, WILD PLANET, THE(1967, Ital.); SWEET BODY OF DEBORAH, THE(1969, Ital./Fr.)
Carlos Montalbo
IN-LAWS, THE(1979)
Giuliano Montaldo
DUEL OF CHAMPIONS(1964 Ital./Span.), w; GRAND SLAM(1968, Ital., Span., Ger.), d; MACHINE GUN McCAIN(1970, Ital.), d, w; SACCO AND VANZETTI(1971, Ital./Fr.), d, w
Giuliano Montalo
GIORDANO BRUNO(1973, Ital.), d, w
Irene Montalto
GOLD OF NAPLES(1957, Ital.)
Celia Montalvan
TONI(1968, Fr.)
Francisco Montalvo
CEREMONY, THE(1963, U.S./Span.)
Mike Montalvo
FUNHOUSE, THE(1981)
Bull Montana
TIGER ROSE(1930); DESERT GUNS(1936); BIG CITY(1937); WHEN'S YOUR BIRTHDAY?(1937)
Silents
DOWN TO EARTH(1917); IN AGAIN-OUT AGAIN(1917); WILD AND WOOLLY(1917); FAIR ENOUGH(1918); IN BAD(1918); EASY TO MAKE MONEY(1919); IN FOR THIRTY DAYS(1919); TREASURE ISLAND(1920); CRAZY TO MARRY(1921);

FOUR HORSEMEN OF THE APOCALYPSE, THE(1921); ONE WILD WEEK(1921); GAY AND DEVILISH(1922); HELD TO ANSWER(1923); JEALOUS HUSBANDS(1923); PAINTED PEOPLE(1924); BASHFUL BUCCANEER(1925); DICK TURPIN(1925); LOST WORLD, THE(1925); SKYROCKET, THE(1926); SON OF THE SHEIK(1926)
Misc. Silents
HE COMES UP SMILING(1918); THREE MUST-GET-THERES, THE(1922); BREAKING INTO SOCIETY(1923); GOLD HUNTERS, THE(1925)
Curley Montana
Misc. Talkies
MY NAME IS LEGEND(1975)
Hombre Montana
NO HOLDS BARRED(1952)
L. Montana
Misc. Talkies
BLOOD SONG(1982)
Lenny Montana
GODFATHER, THE(1972); FINGERS(1978); MATILDA(1978); THEY WENT THAT-A-WAY AND THAT-A-WAY(1978); JERK, THE(1979); SEVEN(1979); BIG BRAWL, THE(1980); DEFIANCE(1980); EVILSPEAK(1982); PANDEMONIUM(1982)
Linda Montana
PENNIES FROM HEAVEN(1981)
Louise Montana
CHEYENNE AUTUMN(1964)
Monte Montana
MAN FROM FRISCO(1944)
Montie Montana
CIRCLE OF DEATH(1935); GUN SMOKE(1936), p; RIDERS OF THE DEADLINE(1943); DOWN DAKOTA WAY(1949); ARIZONA BUSHWHACKERS(1968)
Monty Montana
MAN WHO SHOT LIBERTY VALANCE, THE(1962); HUD(1963)
Patsy Montana
COLORADO SUNSET(1939)
Sergio Montanara
BLOOD IN THE STREETS(1975, Ital./Fr.), ed
Montanari
RED SHEIK, THE(1963, Ital.), w
Mario Montanari
CONFESSIONS OF A POLICE CAPTAIN(1971, Ital.), p
Sergio Montanari
CLIMAX, THE(1967, Fr., Ital.), ed; QUEENS, THE(1968, Ital./Fr.), ed; WILD EYE, THE(1968, Ital.), ed; GOD FORGIVES–I DON'T(1969, Ital./Span.), ed; CERTAIN, VERY CERTAIN, AS A MATTER OF FACT... PROBABLE(1970, Ital.), ed; FIVE MAN ARMY, THE(1970, Ital.), ed; LADY OF MONZA, THE(1970, Ital.), ed; MAN WHO CAME FOR COFFEE, THE(1970, Ital.), ed; SERAFINO(1970, Fr./Ital.), ed; ALFREDO, ALFREDO(1973, Ital.), ed; WHITE SISTER(1973, Ital./Span./Fr.), ed; MALICIOUS(1974, Ital.), ed; MIDNIGHT PLEASURES(1975, Ital.), ed; ERNESTO(1979, Ital.), ed; STARCRASH(1979), ed; I HATE BLONDES(1981, Ital.), ed; HERCULES(1983), ed
Lazaros Montanaris
RAPE, THE(1965, Gr.), w
Yves Montand
GATES OF THE NIGHT(1950, Fr.); RED, INN, THE(1954, Fr.); NAPOLEON(1955, Fr.); WAGES OF FEAR, THE(1955, Fr./Ital.); LET'S MAKE LOVE(1960); WHERE THE HOT WIND BLOWS(1960, Fr., Ital.); GOODBYE AGAIN(1961); SANCTUARY(1961); MY GEISHA(1962); GRAND PRIX(1966); IS PARIS BURNING?(1966, U.S./Fr.); SLEEPING CAR MURDER THE(1966, Fr.); LA GUERRE EST FINIE(1967, Fr./Swed.); LIVE FOR LIFE(1967, Fr./Ital.); ONE NIGHT... A TRAIN(1968, Fr./Bel.); DEVIL BY THE TAIL, THE(1969, Fr./Ital.); Z(1969, Fr./Algeria); CONFESSION, THE(1970, Fr.); MISTER FREEDOM(1970, Fr.); ON A CLEAR DAY YOU CAN SEE FOREVER(1970); DELUSIONS OF GRANDEUR(1971 Fr.); CESAR AND ROSALIE(1972, Fr.); STATE OF SIEGE(1973, Fr./U.S./Ital./Ger.); TOUT VA BIEN(1973, Fr.); SAVAGE, THE(1975, Fr.); POLICE PYTHON 357(1976, Fr.); WOMANLIGHT(1979, Fr./Ger./Ital.); CASE AGAINST FERRO, THE(1980, Fr.); CLAIR DE FEMME(1980,Fr.); CHOICE OF ARMS(1983, Fr.)
Indro Montanelli
GENERALE DELLA ROVERE(1960, Ital./Fr.), w
Ana Maria Montaner
HYPNOSIS(1966, Ger./Sp./Ital.)
Rock Montanio
Misc. Talkies
WHERE'S WILLIE?(1978)
Adrian Montano
PRIEST OF LOVE(1981, Brit.)
Dedi Montano
SCHOOLGIRL DIARY(1947, Ital.)
Georges Montant
IS PARIS BURNING?(1966, U.S./Fr.); MORE(1969, Luxembourg)
Paolo Montarsolo
BARBER OF SEVILLE, THE(1973, Ger./Fr.)
Ashley Montaru
ELEPHANT MAN, THE(1980, Brit.), w
Michele Montau
DEVIL AT FOUR O'CLOCK, THE(1961); HELL IS FOR HEROES(1962); MADE IN PARIS(1966); REFLECTION OF FEAR, A(1973)
Haoui Montaug
VORTEX(1982)
Max Montavon
DOLL, THE(1962, Fr.); PLEASE, NOT NOW!(1963, Fr./Ital.); TIGHT SKIRTS, LOOSE PLEASURES(1966, Fr.); WE ARE ALL NAKED(1970, Can./Fr.)
Jean Montazel
CINDERELLA(1937, Fr.), w
Pierre Montazel
IT HAPPENED AT THE INN(1945, Fr.), ph; OBSESSION(1954, Fr./Ital.), ph; NAPOLEON(1955, Fr.), ph; ROYAL AFFAIRS IN VERSAILLES(1957, Fr.), ph; FOLIES BERGERE(1958, Fr.), ph; CAT, THE(1959, Fr.), ph; GUINGUETTE(1959, Fr.), ph; RIFF RAFF GIRLS(1962, Fr./Ital.), ph
The Montclairs
FEELIN' GOOD(1966)

Alberto Monte
THIRD VOICE, THE(1960); WALK TALL(1960)
Eric Monte
COOLEY HIGH(1975), w
Joe Monte
STING II, THE(1983)
Lola Monte
RHYTHM OF THE SADDLE(1938)
Marlo Monte
Misc. Talkies
WELCOME HOME, BROTHER CHARLES(1975)
Paul Monte
THRILL OF BRAZIL, THE(1946); WE WERE STRANGERS(1949)
Toti Cal Monte
ANONYMOUS VENETIAN, THE(1971)
Barbara Monte-Britton
ECHOES(1983)
Zoe Monteanu
MR. H. C. ANDERSEN(1950, Brit.)
Lewis Montefiore
GRIM REAPER, THE(1981, Ital.), w
Luca Montefiore
UNHOLY FOUR, THE(1969, Ital.)
Luigi Montefiori
FELLINI SATYRICON(1969, Fr./Ital.)
1984
WARRIORS OF THE WASTELAND(1984, Ital.)
Beatriz Monteil
PSYCH-OUT(1968); EASY RIDER(1969); CACTUS IN THE SNOW(1972)
Genevieve Monteil
MAN WITH CONNECTIONS, THE(1970, Fr.), makeup
Lisa Monteil
NAKED PARADISE(1957)
Maria Monteil
CLOAK AND DAGGER(1946)
Hubert Monteilhet
RETURN FROM THE ASHES(1965, U.S./Brit.), w
Hurbert Monteilhet
DOCTEUR POPAUL(1972, Fr.), w
Johnny Monteilhet
SMUGGLERS, THE(1969, Fr.)
Johnny Monteiro
LOST BATTALION(1961, U.S./Phil.); BACK DOOR TO HELL(1964); KIDNAPPERS, THE(1964, U.S./Phil.); CURSE OF THE VAMPIRES(1970, Phil., U.S.)
Carmen Montejo
VAMPIRE, THE(1968, Mex.)
Blanche Montel
Misc. Silents
LA BELLE NIVERNAISE(1923, Fr.)
Michele Montel
CLAIRE'S KNEE(1971, Fr.)
Lisa Monteleone
MS. 45(1981), makeup
Sandra Monteleoni
IDENTIFICATION OF A WOMAN(1983, Ital.)
Lisa Montell
ESCAPE TO BURMA(1955); JUMP INTO HELL(1955); PEARL OF THE SOUTH PACIFIC(1955); GABY(1956); WILD DAKOTAS, THE(1956); WORLD WITHOUT END(1956); TEN THOUSAND BEDROOMS(1957); TOMAHAWK TRAIL(1957); LONE RANGER AND THE LOST CITY OF GOLD, THE(1958); SHE-GODS OF SHARK REEF(1958); LONG ROPE, THE(1961); DAUGHTER OF THE SUN GOD(1962); FIREBRAND, THE(1962)
Victor Montell
STRANGER KNOCKS, A(1963, Den.)
Nestor Montemar
LOLLIPOP(1966, Braz.)
Ricardo Montemayor
EDDIE MACON'S RUN(1983)
Davide Montemuri
LAST YEAR AT MARIENBAD(1962, Fr./Ital.); TORPEDO BAY(1964, Ital./Fr.)
A. C. Montenaro
CARWASH(1976), set d; OVER THE EDGE(1979), set d
1984
LOVELINES(1984), set d
Anthony C. Montenaro
EMPIRE OF THE ANTS(1977), set d; SMOKEY AND THE BANDIT(1977), set d
Tony Montenaro
SLAUGHTER'S BIG RIP-OFF(1973), set d; BAKER'S HAWK(1976), set d; C.H.O.M.P.S.(1979), set d
Conchita Montenegro
CISCO KID(1931); NEVER THE TWAIN SHALL MEET(1931); STRANGERS MAY KISS(1931); GAY CABALLERO, THE(1932); LAUGHING AT LIFE(1933); HANDY ANDY(1934); HELL IN THE HEAVENS(1934); ETERNAL MELODIES(1948, Ital.)
Hugo Montenegro
AMBUSHERS, THE(1967), m; HURRY SUNDOWN(1967), m; LADY IN CEMENT(1968), m, md; WRECKING CREW, THE(1968), m, md; CHARRO(1969), m; UNDEFEATED, THE(1969), m, md; VIVA MAX!(1969), m; TOOMORROW(1970, Brit.), m; FARMER, THE(1977), m
Mario Montenegro
BRIDES OF BLOOD(1968, US/Phil.); PASSIONATE STRANGERS, THE(1968, Phil.)
Rudolph Monter
VOICE IN THE WIND(1944), p
J. Monteran
Silents
OLDEST LAW, THE(1918), ph
Jacques Monteran
Silents
NEIGHBORS(1918), ph; GOOD-BYE, BILL(1919), ph

Carlotta Monterey
Silents
COST, THE(1920)
Elsa Montero
DEATH OF A BUREAUCRAT(1979, Cuba)
Germaine Montero
LOVERS, HAPPY LOVERS!(1955, Brit.); ANY NUMBER CAN WIN(1963 Fr.); GAME IS OVER, THE(1967, Fr.)
Robert Montero
SLASHER, THE(1975), d, w
Roberto B. Montero
MONSTER OF THE ISLAND(1953, Ital.), d, w
Zully Montero
Misc. Talkies
EL SUPER(1979)
Princess of Monteroduni
LA DOLCE VITA(1961, Ital./Fr.)
Rosenda Monteros
WHITE ORCHID, THE(1954); WOMAN'S DEVOTION, A(1956); VILLA!(1958); MAGNIFICENT SEVEN, THE(1960); TIARA TAHITI(1962, Brit.); MIGHTY JUNGLE, THE(1965, U.S./Mex.); SHE(1965, Brit.); SAVAGE PAMPAS(1967, Span./Arg.); EVE(1968, Brit./Span.); NAZARIN(1968, Mex.); CAULDRON OF BLOOD(1971, Span.)
Conchita Montes
55 DAYS AT PEKING(1963)
Elba Montes
1984
CRACKERS(1984)
Elisa Montes
AVENGER, THE(1966, Ital.); RETURN OF THE SEVEN(1966, Span.); COBRA, THE(1968); ISLAND OF THE DOOMED(1968, Span./Ger.); RIO 70(1970, U.S./Ger./Span.); CAPTAIN APACHE(1971, Brit.)
Felipe Montes
LOVE IN MOROCCO(1933, Fr.)
Fernando Montes
DIABOLICAL DR. Z, THE(1966 Span./Fr.)
Lola Montes
LADY AND THE MONSTER, THE(1944)
Enrico Montesano
I HATE BLONDES(1981, Ital.)
Sam Montesano
GAS(1981, Can.)
Ofelia Montesco
EXTERMINATING ANGEL, THE(1967, Mex.)
Leonida Montesi
WHITE NIGHTS(1961, Ital./Fr.)
Jacques Monteux
ENTER INSPECTOR DUVAL(1961, Brit.), w
Liliane Montevecchi
MOONFLEET(1955); MEET ME IN LAS VEGAS(1956); LIVING IDOL, THE(1957); SAD SACK, THE(1957); KING CREOLE(1958); ME AND THE COLONEL(1958); YOUNG LIONS, THE(1958)
Lillane Montevecchi
GLASS SLIPPER, THE(1955)
Maurizio Monteverde
LA TRAVIATA(1968, Ital.), prod d
Monteverdi
LES GAULOISES BLEUES(1969, Fr.), m
Claudio Monteve Monteverdi
SUMMERSKIN(1962, Arg.), m
Claudio Monteverdi
MOUCHETTE(1970, Fr.), m
Germana Monteverdi
VACATION, THE(1971, Ital.)
Conchita Montez
NIGHT HAIR CHILD(1971, Brit.)
Eva Montez
BLOOD DRINKERS, THE(1966, U.S./Phil.)
Louis Montez
CROSSROADS(1942)
Margareta Montez
HEAT LIGHTNING(1934)
Maria Montez
BOSS OF BULLION CITY(1941); INVISIBLE WOMAN, THE(1941); LUCKY DEVILS(1941); MOONLIGHT IN HAWAII(1941); RAIDERS OF THE DESERT(1941); SOUTH OF TAHITI(1941); THAT NIGHT IN RIO(1941); ARABIAN NIGHTS(1942); BOMBAY CLIPPER(1942); MYSTERY OF MARIE ROGET, THE(1942); WHITE SAVAGE(1943); ALI BABA AND THE FORTY THIEVES(1944); BOWERY TO BROADWAY(1944); COBRA WOMAN(1944); FOLLOW THE BOYS(1944); GYPSY WILDCAT(1944); SUDAN(1945); TANGIER(1946); EXILE, THE(1947); PIRATES OF MONTEREY(1947); SIREN OF ATLANTIS(1948); THIEF OF VENICE, THE(1952); VALDEZ IS COMING(1971)
Mario Montez
CHELSEA GIRLS, THE(1967); LUPE(1967)
Richard Montez
GIRL HUNTERS, THE(1963, Brit.); MAROC 7(1967, Brit.); DON'T RAISE THE BRIDGE, LOWER THE RIVER(1968, Brit.); 11 HARROWHOUSE(1974, Brit.)
Magdalena Montezuma
1984
WOMAN IN FLAMES, A(1984, Ger.)
M. J. Montfaion
MAN WHO LOVED WOMEN, THE(1977, Fr.)
Ivy Montford
Silents
BLIND BOY, THE(1917, Brit.)
Misc. Silents
FALSE WIRELESS, THE(1914, Brit.); IN THE GRIP OF SPIES(1914, Brit.); MYSTERY OF THE OLD MILL, THE(1914, Brit.); STOLEN MASTERPIECE, THE(1914, Brit.); AT THE TORRENT'S MERCY(1915, Brit.); CLUE OF THE CIGAR BAND, THE(1915, Brit.)

Sylvia Montfort
LOVE AND THE FRENCHWOMAN(1961, Fr.)

Baby Peggy Montgomery
Silents
FAMILY SECRET, THE(1924)
Misc. Silents
DARLING OF NEW YORK, THE(1923)

Barbara Montgomery
1984
MOSCOW ON THE HUDSON(1984)

Belinda Montgomery
TODD KILLINGS, THE(1971); BREAKING POINT(1976); BLACKOUT(1978, Fr./ Can.)
1984
SILENT MADNESS(1984)
Misc. Talkies
NIGHTKILLERS(1983); TELL ME THAT YOU LOVE ME(1983)

Belinda J. Montgomery
OTHER SIDE OF THE MOUNTAIN, THE(1975); OTHER SIDE OF THE MOUNTAIN-PART 2, THE(1978); STONE COLD DEAD(1980, Can.)

Betty Montgomery
MODERN LOVE(1929)

Bob Montgomery
TRANSATLANTIC(1931); GAMBLING LADY(1934); SPECIAL AGENT(1935); STARS OVER BROADWAY(1935)

Bruce Montgomery
DOCTOR IN THE HOUSE(1954, Brit.), m; LITTLE KIDNAPPERS, THE(1954, Brit.), m; DOCTOR AT SEA(1955, Brit.), m; ESCAPADE(1955, Brit.), m; EYEWITNESS(1956, Brit.), m; CHECKPOINT(1957, Brit.), m; DOCTOR AT LARGE(1957, Brit.), m; RAISING A RIOT(1957, Brit.), m; DUKE WORE JEANS, THE(1958, Brit.), m; TRUTH ABOUT WOMEN, THE(1958, Brit.), m; CARRY ON NURSE(1959, Brit.), m; CARRY ON SERGEANT(1959, Brit.), m; HOME IS THE HERO(1959, Ireland), m; CARRY ON CONSTABLE(1960, Brit.), m; DOCTOR IN LOVE(1960, Brit.), m; PLEASE TURN OVER(1960, Brit.), m; TOO YOUNG TO LOVE(1960, Brit.), m; BEWARE OF CHILDREN(1961, Brit.), m; CARRY ON REGARDLESS(1961, Brit.), m; WATCH YOUR STERN(1961, Brit.), m; CARRY ON CRUISING(1962, Brit.), m; CARRY ON TEACHER(1962, Brit.), m; CIRCUS FRIENDS(1962, Brit.), m; ROOMMATES(1962, Brit.), w, m; TWICE AROUND THE DAFFODILS(1962, Brit.), m; BRIDES OF FU MANCHU, THE(1966, Brit.), m

Bryan Montgomery
BADLANDS(1974)

Candy Montgomery
TOP BANANA(1954)

Daryl Montgomery
HUNGRY WIVES(1973)

Doreen Montgomery
LASSIE FROM LANCASHIRE(1938, Brit.), w; MEET MR. PENNY(1938, Brit.), w; DEAD MEN TELL NO TALES(1939, Brit.), w; JUST WILLIAM(1939, Brit.), w; BULLDOG SEES IT THROUGH(1940, Brit.), w; CASTLE OF CRIMES(1940, Brit.), w; FLYING SQUAD, THE(1940, Brit.), w; SECOND MR. BUSH(1940, Brit.), w; HOUSE OF MYSTERY(1941, Brit.), w; MYSTERY OF ROOM 13(1941, Brit.), w; POISON PEN(1941, Brit.), w; MAN IN GREY, THE(1943, Brit.), w; THIS MAN IS MINE(1946 Brit.), w; LADY SURRENDERS, A(1947, Brit.), w; WHILE I LIVE(1947, Brit.), w; MAN OF EVIL(1948, Brit.), w; GENIE, THE(1953, Brit.), w; DANCE LITTLE LADY(1954, Brit.), w; DESTINATION MILAN(1954, Brit.), w; FOREVER MY HEART(1954, Brit.), w; SCARLET WEB, THE(1954, Brit.), w; ONE JUMP AHEAD(1955, Brit.), w; SHADOW OF THE EAGLE(1955, Brit.), w; TIME TO KILL, A(1955, Brit.), w; YOU CAN'T ESCAPE(1955, Brit.), w; NARROWING CIRCLE, THE(1956, Brit.), w; MURDER REPORTED(1958, Brit.), w

Douglass Montgomery
LITTLE WOMEN(1933); EIGHT GIRLS IN A BOAT(1934); GIFT OF GAB(1934); LITTLE MAN, WHAT NOW?(1934); MUSIC IN THE AIR(1934); HARMONY LANE(1935); LADY TUBBS(1935); MYSTERY OF EDWIN DROOD, THE(1935); EVERYTHING IS THUNDER(1936, Brit.); TROPICAL TROUBLE(1936, Brit.); COUNSEL FOR CRIME(1937); LIFE BEGINS WITH LOVE(1937); CAT AND THE CANARY, THE(1939); JOHNNY IN THE CLOUDS(1945, Brit.); WOMAN TO WOMAN(1946, Brit.); FORBIDDEN(1949, Brit.)

Earl Montgomery
NAVY BORN(1936); DETECTIVE, THE(1968); HEAVEN CAN WAIT(1978); ROCKY II(1979); SEED OF INNOCENCE(1980)

Ed Montgomery
I WANT TO LIVE!(1958), w; SPRING FEVER(1983, Can.)

Edna Montgomery
ORPHAN OF THE WILDERNESS(1937, Aus.)

Edward Poor Montgomery
DOUBLE HARNESS(1933), w

Elizabeth Montgomery
COURT-MARTIAL OF BILLY MITCHELL, THE(1955); JOHNNY COOL(1963); WHO'S BEEN SLEEPING IN MY BED?(1963)

Elliott Montgomery
CHINATOWN(1974)

Florence Montgomery
1984
MISUNDERSTOOD(1984), w

Frank Montgomery
WAY OUT WEST(1937)
Silents
BRAND OF COWARDICE, THE(1916); MAN FROM BEYOND, THE(1922); SAINTED DEVIL, A(1924); MAD DANCER(1925); ALOMA OF THE SOUTH SEAS(1926); SO'S YOUR OLD MAN(1926)
Misc. Silents
AWAKENING OF HELENA RICHIE, THE(1916); MAGDALENE OF THE HILLS, A(1917)

Frank R. Montgomery
Silents
CARDIGAN(1922)

Gary Montgomery
BLACK SHIELD OF FALWORTH, THE(1954)

George Montgomery
CISCO KID AND THE LADY, THE(1939); CHARTER PILOT(1940); STAR DUST(1940); YOUNG PEOPLE(1940); ACCENT ON LOVE(1941); CADET GIRL(1941); COWBOY AND THE BLONDE, THE(1941); JENNIE(1941); LAST OF THE DUANES(1941); RIDERS OF THE PURPLE SAGE(1941); BOOGIE MAN WILL GET YOU, THE(1942), set d; CHINA GIRL(1942); ORCHESTRA WIVES(1942); ROXIE HART(1942); TEN GENTLEMEN FROM WEST POINT(1942); UNDERGROUND AGENT(1942), set d; BOMBER'S MOON(1943); CONEY ISLAND(1943); RACKET MAN, THE(1944), set d; TAHITI NIGHTS(1945), set d; CRIME DOCTOR'S MAN HUNT(1946), set d; DEVIL'S MASK, THE(1946), set d; NAVAJO KID, THE(1946), art d; PHANTOM THIEF, THE(1946), set d; SING WHILE YOU DANCE(1946), set d; SIX GUN MAN(1946), art d; THREE LITTLE GIRLS IN BLUE(1946); BELLE STARR'S DAUGHTER(1947); BRASHER DOUBLOON, THE(1947); GUILT OF JANET AMES, THE(1947), set d; GIRL FROM MANHATTAN(1948); LULU BELLE(1948); STRAWBERRY ROAN, THE(1948), set d; WEST OF SONORA(1948), set d; CRIME DOCTOR'S DIARY, THE(1949), set d; SOUTH OF DEATH VALLEY(1949), set d; DAKOTA LIL(1950); DAVY CROCKETT, INDIAN SCOUT(1950); IROQUOIS TRAIL, THE(1950); TRAVELING SALESWOMAN(1950), set d; INDIAN UPRISING(1951); SWORD OF MONTE CRISTO, THE(1951); TEXAS RANGERS, THE(1951); CRIPPLE CREEK(1952); PATHFINDER, THE(1952); FORT TI(1953); GUN BELT(1953); JACK MCCALL, DESPERADO(1953); BATTLE OF ROGUE RIVER(1954); LONE GUN, THE(1954); MASTERSON OF KANSAS(1954); ROBBER'S ROOST(1955); SEMINOLE UPRISING(1955); CANYON RIVER(1956); HUK(1956); BLACK PATCH(1957); GUN DUEL IN DURANGO(1957); LAST OF THE BADMEN(1957); PAWNEE(1957); STREET OF SINNERS(1957); BADMAN'S COUNTRY(1958); MAN FROM GOD'S COUNTRY(1958); TOUGHEST GUN IN TOMBSTONE(1958); KING OF THE WILD STALLIONS(1959); WATUSI(1959); STEEL CLAW, THE(1961), a, p&d; SAMAR(1962), a, p&d, w; BATTLE OF THE BULGE(1965); HALLUCINATION GENERATION(1966); HOSTILE GUNS(1967); WARKILL(1968, U.S./Phil.); DAREDEVIL, THE(1971)
Misc. Talkies
NEW DAY AT SUNDOWN(1957); GUERILLAS IN PINK LACE(1964), d; STRANGERS AT SUNRISE(1969); SATAN'S HARVEST(1970), d; RIDE THE TIGER(1971), d; LEO CHRONICLES, THE(1972)

Glenn Montgomery
1984
BEAR, THE(1984)

Goodee Montgomery
LIGHTNIN'(1930); UP THE RIVER(1930); CHARLIE CHAN CARRIES ON(1931); TRANSATLANTIC(1931); LET'S TALK IT OVER(1934); STOLEN SWEETS(1934); STOLEN HARMONY(1935); BEWARE OF LADIES(1937); MOUNTAIN MUSIC(1937)

Gray Montgomery
HUCKLEBERRY FINN(1974)

Jack Montgomery
OUTLAW DEPUTY, THE(1935); OUTLAWED GUNS(1935); TEXAS RANGERS, THE(1936); COURAGE OF THE WEST(1937); GAMBLING TERROR, THE(1937); SINGING OUTLAW(1937); BORDER WOLVES(1938); LAST STAND, THE(1938); RED RIVER RANGE(1938); WESTERN TRAILS(1938); DARK COMMAND, THE(1940); GHOST VALLEY RAIDERS(1940); SON OF ROARING DAN(1940); DESERT BANDIT(1941); WESTWARD HO(1942); RED RIVER ROBIN HOOD(1943); WAGON TRACKS WEST(1943); GUNMAN'S CODE(1946); PURSUED(1947); RUN FOR COVER(1955); GUN GLORY(1957)

James Montgomery
AVIATOR, THE(1929), w; NOTHING BUT THE TRUTH(1929), w; NOTHING BUT THE TRUTH(1941), w; RIDING HIGH(1943), w
Silents
READY MONEY(1914), w; NOT MY SISTER(1916), w; NOTHING BUT THE TRUTH(1920), w; IRENE(1926), w

James H. Montgomery
IRENE(1940), w

Jay Montgomery
BLACK GUNN(1972)

Jim Montgomery
MIDDLE AGE CRAZY(1980, Can.)

Julie Montgomery
1984
GIRLS NIGHT OUT(1984); REVENGE OF THE NERDS(1984); UP THE CREEK(1984)

Karen Montgomery
COAST TO COAST(1980); WILLIE AND PHIL(1980)

L.M. Montgomery
ANNE OF GREEN GABLES(1934), w; ANNE OF WINDY POPLARS(1940), w
Silents
ANNE OF GREEN GABLES(1919), w

Lee Montgomery
BURNT OFFERINGS(1976); SPLIT IMAGE(1982)

Lee H. Montgomery
PETE 'N' TILLIE(1972); SAVAGE IS LOOSE, THE(1974); BAKER'S HAWK(1976)

Lee Harcourt Montgomery
$1,000,000 DUCK(1971); BEN(1972)
1984
NIGHT SHADOWS(1984)

Lionel Montgomery
CONCERNING MR. MARTIN(1937, Brit.)

Lou Montgomery
TAKING TIGER MOUNTAIN(1983, U.S./Welsh)

Mabel Montgomery
Misc. Silents
FATHER AND SON(1916)

Marjorie Montgomery
FRESHMAN YEAR(1938)

Mark Montgomery
1776(1972)

Marshall Montgomery
HOTEL VARIETY(1933)

Martha Montgomery
WONDER MAN(1945); INNER CIRCLE, THE(1946); KID FROM BOOKLYN, THE(1946); POSSESSED(1947); SECRET LIFE OF WALTER MITTY, THE(1947); ONE TOUCH OF VENUS(1948); SONG IS BORN, A(1948)

Michael Montgomery
Misc. Talkies
JUST BE THERE(1977)
Monty Montgomery
LOVELESS, THE(1982), d&w
Peggy Montgomery
EIGHT GIRLS IN A BOAT(1934); HAVING WONDERFUL TIME(1938)
Silents
RAINBOW RANGERS(1924); LOOKING FOR TROUBLE(1926); SENSATION SEEK-ERS(1927); SONORA KID, THE(1927); SPLITTING THE BREEZE(1927); ARIZONA DAYS(1928); ON THE DIVIDE(1928); WEST OF SANTA FE(1928)
Misc. Silents
FIGHTING COURAGE(1925); SPEED DEMON, THE(1925); ACE OF CLUBS, THE(1926); DANGEROUS DUB, THE(1926); FIGHTING FAILURE, THE(1926); FOR-EST HAVOC(1926); HOLLYWOOD REPORTER, THE(1926); PRISONERS OF THE STORM(1926); DESERT OF THE LOST, THE(1927); TWO-GUN OF THE TUM-BLEWEED(1927); SADDLE MATES(1928); SILENT TRAIL(1928); BAD MEN'S MONEY(1929); FIGHTERS OF THE SADDLE(1929)
Phil Montgomery
SWARM, THE(1978)
Philip Montgomery
WHITE BUFFALO, THE(1977)
R. Montgomery
CHAMBER OF HORRORS(1941, Brit.)
Ralph Montgomery
SALUTE FOR THREE(1943); RIDE THE PINK HORSE(1947); SMASH-UP, THE STORY OF A WOMAN(1947); WEB, THE(1947); HAZARD(1948); HOMECO-MING(1948); NOOSE HANGS HIGH, THE(1948); SOUTHERN YANKEE, A(1948); CHICAGO DEADLINE(1949); DEAR WIFE(1949); EAST SIDE, WEST SIDE(1949); SCENE OF THE CRIME(1949); MILKMAN, THE(1950); MYSTERY STREET(1950); PEGGY(1950); SIDE STREET(1950); SUNSET BOULEVARD(1950); UNION STA-TION(1950); DETECTIVE STORY(1951); MY FAVORITE SPY(1951); ON MOONLIGHT BAY(1951); RACKET, THE(1951); IT GROWS ON TREES(1952); TURNING POINT, THE(1952); FARMER TAKES A WIFE, THE(1953); WAR OF THE WORLDS, THE(1953); JOHNNY DARK(1954); GIRL RUSH, THE(1955); LEATHER SAINT, THE(1956); FEAR STRIKES OUT(1957); JOKER IS WILD, THE(1957); 27TH DAY, THE(1957); DON'T KNOCK THE TWIST(1962); WHO'S GOT THE ACTION?(1962); WATERMELON MAN(1970); SSSSSSSS(1973); BEST FRIENDS(1975); WHICH WAY IS UP?(1977)
Ray Montgomery
MAYBE IT'S LOVE(1930); GAY SISTERS, THE(1942); HARD WAY, THE(1942); LARCENY, INC.(1942); MALE ANIMAL, THE(1942); ACTION IN THE NORTH ATLANTIC(1943); AIR FORCE(1943); THAT HAGEN GIRL(1947); UNFAITHFUL, THE(1947); UNSUSPECTED, THE(1947); JOHNNY BELINDA(1948); JUNE BRI-DE(1948); ONE SUNDAY AFTERNOON(1948); WHIPLASH(1948); HOUSE ACROSS THE STREET, THE(1949); JOHN LOVES MARY(1949); LADY TAKES A SAILOR, THE(1949); TASK FORCE(1949); WHITE HEAT(1949); LOVE NEST(1951); MR. BEL-VEDERE RINGS THE BELL(1951); PEOPLE WILL TALK(1951); STARLIFT(1951); BUGLES IN THE AFTERNOON(1952); LAS VEGAS STORY, THE(1952); MONKEY BUSINESS(1952); ONE MINUTE TO ZERO(1952); BANDITS OF THE WEST(1953); DOWN AMONG THE SHELTERING PALMS(1953); GENTLEMEN PREFER BLONDES(1953); PICKUP ON SOUTH STREET(1953); SABRE JET(1953); WHITE GODDESS(1953); PHANTOM OF THE JUNGLE(1955); THUNDER OVER SANGO-LAND(1955); BOMBERS B-52(1957); KISS THEM FOR ME(1957); PEYTON PLA-CE(1957); THREE BRAVE MEN(1957); PRIVATE'S AFFAIR, A(1959); GATHERING OF EAGLES, A(1963); SILENCERS, THE(1966); GUIDE FOR THE MARRIED MAN, A(1967); MADIGAN(1968)
Misc. Talkies
EYES OF THE JUNGLE(1953)
Raymond Montgomery
TOMAHAWK(1951); COLUMN SOUTH(1953)
Red Montgomery
ROCK YOU SINNERS(1957, Brit.)
Reggie Montgomery
THEIR OWN DESIRE(1929), m
Robert Montgomery
YELLOW JACK(1938); THEIR OWN DESIRE(1929); THREE LIVE GHOSTS(1929); UNTAMED(1929); BIG HOUSE, THE(1930); BLUSHING BRIDES(1930); DIVORCEE, THE(1930); FREE AND EASY(1930); LOVE IN THE ROUGH(1930); OUR BLUSHING BRIDES(1930); SINS OF THE CHILDREN(1930); WAR NURSE(1930); EASIEST WAY, THE(1931); INSPIRATION(1931); MAN IN POSSESSION, THE(1931); PRIVATE LIVES(1931); SHIPMATES(1931); STRANGERS MAY KISS(1931); BLONDIE OF THE FOLLIES(1932); BUT THE FLESH IS WEAK(1932); FAITHLESS(1932); LETTY LYN-TON(1932); LOVERS COURAGEOUS(1932); ANOTHER LANGUAGE(1933); HELL BELOW(1933); MADE ON BROADWAY(1933); NIGHT FLIGHT(1933); WHEN LADIES MEET(1933); FUGITIVE LOVERS(1934); HIDE-OUT(1934); MYSTERY OF MR. X, THE(1934); RIP TIDE(1934); BIOGRAPHY OF A BACHELOR GIRL(1935); FORSAK-ING ALL OTHERS(1935); NO MORE LADIES(1935); VANESSA, HER LOVE STO-RY(1935); PETTICOAT FEVER(1936); PICCADILLY JIM(1936); TROUBLE FOR TWO(1936); EVER SINCE EVE(1937); LAST OF MRS. CHEYNEY, THE(1937); LIVE, LOVE AND LEARN(1937); NIGHT MUST FALL(1937); FIRST 100 YEARS, THE(1938); THREE LOVES HAS NANCY(1938); FAST AND LOOSE(1939); BUSMAN'S HONEY-MOON(1940, Brit.); EARL OF CHICAGO(1940); HERE COMES MR. JOR-DAN(1941); MR. AND MRS. SMITH(1941); RAGE IN HEAVEN(1941); UNFINISHED BUSINESS(1941); THEY WERE EXPENDABLE(1945), a, d; LADY IN THE LA-KE(1947), a, d; RIDE THE PINK HORSE(1947), a, d; JUNE BRIDE(1948); SAXON CHARM, THE(1948); ONCE MORE, MY DARLING(1949), a, d; EYE WITNESS(1950, Brit.), a, d; GALLANT HOURS, THE(1960), a, p&d
Robert Montgomery, Jr.
PRIVATE'S AFFAIR, A(1959); SAY ONE FOR ME(1959); COLLEGE CONFIDEN-TIAL(1960); GALLANT HOURS, THE(1960); TWELVE TO THE MOON(1960)
Rutherford Montgomery
MUSTANG(1959), w
Tanis Montgomery
TODD KILLINGS, THE(1971)
Thomas Montgomery
KING KONG VERSUS GODZILLA(1963, Jap.), d

Wes Montgomery
MAIDSTONE(1970), m
Christopher Month
SANTA CLAUS CONQUERS THE MARTIANS(1964)
Joel Montheilet
GATES OF PARIS(1958, Fr./Ital.)
Marcelle Monthil
CHILDREN OF PARADISE(1945, Fr.)
Aldo Monti
VENGEANCE OF THE VAMPIRE WOMEN, THE(1969, Mex.)
Angela Monti
TURKISH CUCUMBER, THE(1963, Ger.)
Carlotta Monti
KING KONG(1933); TARZAN THE FEARLESS(1933); MAN ON THE FLYING TRAPEZE, THE(1935); NIGHT CARGO(1936); NEVER GIVE A SUCKER AN EVEN BREAK(1941); HE WALKED BY NIGHT(1948); CRISIS(1950); TO PLEASE A LA-DY(1950); W.C. FIELDS AND ME(1976), w
Charlotte [Carlotta] Monti
DEADWOOD PASS(1933)
Christine [Carlotta] Monti
CAVALIER OF THE WEST(1931)
Harry Monti
HELLZAPOPPIN'(1941)
Maria Monti
DUCK, YOU SUCKER!(1972, Ital.); NEST OF VIPERS(1979, Ital.)
Maura Monti
RAGE(1966, U.S./Mex.); SANTO CONTRA LA INVASION DE LOS MAR-CIANOS(1966, Mex.); VAMPIRES, THE(1969, Mex.); INCREDIBLE INVASION, THE(1971, Mex./U.S.)
Milli Monti
GIRL FROM SCOTLAND YARD, THE(1937); ON SUCH A NIGHT(1937); BLACK SABBATH(1963, Ital.)
Milly Monti
GIDGET GOES TO ROME(1963)
Mimi Monti
DARLING LILI(1970)
Minny Monti
LE PETIT THEATRE DE JEAN RENOIR(1974, Fr.)
Mirello Monti
TO LIVE IN PEACE(1947, Ital.)
Silvia Monti
BRAIN, THE(1969, Fr./US); FRAULEIN DOKTOR(1969, Ital./Yugo.); LADY CARO-LINE LAMB(1972, Brit./Ital.); SICILIAN CONNECTION, THE(1977)
Pierrette Monticelli
CONFIDENTIALLY YOURS(1983, Fr.)
Sara Montiel
MAD QUEEN, THE(1950, Span.)
Sarita Montiel
VERA CRUZ(1954); SERENADE(1956); RUN OF THE ARROW(1957); DEVIL MADE A WOMAN, THE(1962, Span.)
Phyllis Montifiere
23 PACES TO BAKER STREET(1956)
Frank Montiforte
1984
WILD LIFE, THE(1984)
Mario Montilles
STATE OF SIEGE(1973, Fr./U.S./Ital./Ger.)
Brizio Montinaro
PIZZA TRIANGLE, THE(1970, Ital./Span.); ANONYMOUS VENETIAN, THE(1971); TRENCHCOAT(1983)
Luigi Montini
ROME WANTS ANOTHER CAESAR(1974, Ital.)
Janella Montis
ISLAND OF PROCIDA, THE(1952, Ital.)
Ovidi Montllor
SABINA, THE(1979, Span./Swed.); NEST, THE(1982, Span.)
Felipe Montojo
ILLUSION TRAVELS BY STREETCAR, THE(1977, Mex.)
Vince Monton
TRESPASSERS, THE(1976, Aus.), ph; NORMAN LOVES ROSE(1982, Aus.), ph
Vincent Monton
TRUE STORY OF ESKIMO NELL, THE(1975, Aus.), ph; FANTASM(1976, Aus.), ph; RAW DEAL(1977, Aus.), ph; LONG WEEKEND(1978, Aus.), ph; NEWSFRONT(1978, Aus.), ph; THIRST(1979, Aus.), ph; DAY AFTER HALLOWEEN, THE(1981, Aus.), ph; ROAD GAMES(1981, Aus.), ph; CROSSTALK(1982, Aus.), ph; HEATWAVE(1983, Aus.), ph
Rita Montone
CHILDREN, THE(1980); MANIAC(1980)
Max Montor
STREET SCENE(1931)
Silents
KING OF KINGS, THE(1927)
Alfredo Montori
GUNS OF THE BLACK WITCH(1961, Fr./Ital.), set d; REBEL GLADIATORS, THE(1963, Ital.), art d; SON OF THE RED CORSAIR(1963, Ital.), art d
Edward Montoro
LOSERS, THE(1968), p&d
Edward E. Montoro
DAY OF THE ANIMALS(1977), p, w
Edward L. Montoro
DARK, THE(1979), p
Jorge Montoro
MANHUNT IN THE JUNGLE(1958); GALLANT ONE, THE(1964, U.S./Peru); LAST MOVIE, THE(1971)
Muriel Montosse
QUARTET(1981, Brit./Fr.)
Caroll Montour
Misc. Talkies
HALFWAY TO HELL(1957)

Mario Montouri
BREATH OF SCANDAL, A(1960), ph
Aline Montovani
TEN DAYS' WONDER(1972, Fr.)
Alex Montoya
RAINBOW ISLAND(1944); BEAUTY AND THE BANDIT(1946); THRILL OF BRAZIL, THE(1946); FIESTA(1947); INTRIGUE(1947); LAST ROUND-UP, THE(1947); TWILIGHT ON THE RIO GRANDE(1947); WEST TO GLORY(1947); MEXICAN HAYRIDE(1948); DAUGHTER OF THE JUNGLE(1949); SQUARE DANCE JUBILEE(1949); TOO LATE FOR TEARS(1949); CRISIS(1950); DALLAS(1950); CALIFORNIA CONQUEST(1952); GOLDEN HAWK, THE(1952); MACAO(1952); VOODOO TIGER(1952); WILD HORSE AMBUSH(1952); CONQUEST OF COCHISE(1953); ESCAPE FROM FORT BRAVO(1953); JEOPARDY(1953); SON OF BELLE STARR(1953); PASSION(1954); THREE YOUNG TEXANS(1954); APACHE AMBUSH(1955); ESCAPE TO BURMA(1955); HELL'S ISLAND(1955); STAGECOACH TO FURY(1956); WAR DRUMS(1957); TOUGHEST GUN IN TOMBSTONE(1958); GHOST OF ZORRO(1959); DANGEROUS CHARTER(1962); ISLAND OF THE BLUE DOLPHINS(1964); FLIGHT OF THE PHOENIX, THE(1965); APPALOOSA, THE(1966); KING'S PIRATE(1967); DARING GAME(1968)
Alex P. Montoya
HURRICANE ISLAND(1951)
Alicia Montoya
VAMPIRE, THE(1968, Mex.)
Connie Montoya
CRISIS(1950)
Ed Montoya
BLACKMAIL(1939)
Elena Montoya
UP THE MACGREGORS(1967, Ital./Span.)
Julia Montoya
MEXICAN HAYRIDE(1948); MY FRIEND IRMA GOES WEST(1950); ONE WAY STREET(1950); LOST IN ALASKA(1952); RING, THE(1952); VIVA ZAPATA!(1952); GREAT SIOUX UPRISING, THE(1953); THEY RODE WEST(1954); FAR HORIZONS, THE(1955); HELL'S ISLAND(1955); RAW EDGE(1956); GIRL MOST LIKELY, THE(1957)
Louis Montoya
NIGHT IN PARADISE, A(1946)
R. Montoyo
POCKET MONEY(1972)
The Montparnasse Ballet
JACK THE RIPPER(1959, Brit.)
Victor Montreal
FIVE GIANTS FROM TEXAS(1966, Ital./Span.), ph
Beni Montresor
DAY THE SKY EXPLODED, THE(1958, Fr./Ital.), art d; PILGRIMAGE(1972), d, w
Dave Montresor
ASSIGNMENT OUTER SPACE(1960, Ital.)
Belle Montrose
ABSENT-MINDED PROFESSOR, THE(1961); SON OF FLUBBER(1963)
David Montrose
PHANTOM VALLEY(1948), set d; RACING LUCK(1948), set d; WHIRLWIND RAIDERS(1948), set d
Helen Montrose
Silents
OUT OF A CLEAR SKY(1918)
Misc. Silents
DEATH DANCE, THE(1918)
Helene Montrose
Silents
COUNTERFEIT(1919)
Misc. Silents
BUCKING THE TIGER(1921)
Lonna Montrose
1984
CITY HEAT(1984); RHINESTONE(1984)
Vivian Montrose
Silents
OUT OF LUCK(1919)
Kent Montroy
MURDER, INC.(1960)
Susan Monts
PROWLER, THE(1981); SILHOUETTES(1982)
Roger Montsoret
TWO OR THREE THINGS I KNOW ABOUT HER(1970, Fr.)
Christine Montt
FIFTY FATHOMS DEEP(1931)
Carlo Montuori
TO LIVE IN PEACE(1947, Ital.), ph; BICYCLE THIEF, THE(1949, Ital.), ph; CHILDREN OF CHANCE(1949, Brit.), ph; BULLET FOR STEFANO(1950, Ital.), ph; CHILDREN OF CHANCE(1950, Ital.), ph; DIFFICULT YEARS(1950, Ital.), ph; WHITE LINE, THE(1952, Ital.), ph; HIS LAST TWELVE HOURS(1953, Ital.), ph; TIMES GONE BY(1953, Ital.), ph; FRISKY(1955, Ital.), ph; SIGN OF VENUS, THE(1955, Ital.), ph
Mario Montuori
HEART AND SOUL(1950, Ital.), ph; QUEEN OF SHEBA(1953, Ital.), ph; PRISONER OF THE VOLGA(1960, Fr./Ital.), ph; GOLIATH AND THE DRAGON(1961, Ital./Fr.), ph; SODOM AND GOMORRAH(1962, U.S./Fr./Ital.), ph; LOVE AT TWENTY(1963, Fr./Ital./Jap./Pol./Ger.), ph; KISS THE OTHER SHEIK(1968, Fr./Ital.), ph; THREE NIGHTS OF LOVE(1969, Ital.), ph; YEAR ONE(1974, Ital.), ph; AGE OF THE MEDICI, THE(1979, Ital.), ph
Irene Montwill
JUMP INTO HELL(1955)
Monty
HIDDEN ROOM, THE(1949, Brit.)
Hal Monty
BLESS 'EM ALL(1949, Brit.), a, w; SKIMPY IN THE NAVY(1949, Brit.), a, w
Harry Monty
RIDE 'EM COWBOY(1942); GEORGE WHITE'S SCANDALS(1945); CRACK-UP(1946); THREE RING CIRCUS(1954); COURT JESTER, THE(1956); HOMETOWN U.S.A.(1979)

Ole Monty
ERIC SOYA'S "17"(1967, Den.)
Piero Monviso
ATOM AGE VAMPIRE(1961, Ital.), w
Sarah Monzani
SENDER, THE(1982, Brit.), makeup
Hank Monzello
KING'S PIRATE(1967)
Henry Monzello
JULIA MISBEHAVES(1948)
San Moo
EXIT THE DRAGON, ENTER THE TIGER(1977, Hong Kong)
Bernard Moody
SLEEPING DOGS(1977, New Zealand)
Bill Moody
BABYLON(1980, Brit.)
Charles Moody
OPERATION BIKINI(1963), spec eff
David Moody
UPTIGHT(1968); CANDIDATE, THE(1972); LAUGHING POLICEMAN, THE(1973); STEELYARD BLUES(1973); STONE KILLER, THE(1973); COAST TO COAST(1980)
Don Moody
1984
HARRY AND SON(1984)
Dorothy Moody
Misc. Silents
CHANNINGS, THE(1920, Brit.); LADDIE(1920, Brit.); SWORD OF FATE, THE(1921, Brit.)
Doug Moody
1984
DUBEAT-E-O(1984), md
Elizabeth Moody
SCARECROW, THE(1982, New Zealand)
Gary Moody
1984
CLOAK AND DAGGER(1984)
H.G. Moody
Misc. Silents
FLAMES OF PASSION(1923), d; POWER DIVINE, THE(1923), d; RANGE PATROL, THE(1923), d; SCARS OF HATE(1923), d; VOW OF VENGEANCE, THE(1923), d; BEATEN(1924), d
Harry Moody
Silents
HAUNTED RANGE, THE(1926); UNDER FIRE(1926)
Misc. Silents
LONE HAND WILSON(1920), d; CRASHING COURAGE(1923), d; FRAME UP, THE(1923), d
James Moody
NAVY LARK, THE(1959, Brit.), m
Jeanne Moody
THREE ON A SPREE(1961, Brit.); MATTER OF CHOICE, A(1963, Brit.); STRICTLY FOR THE BIRDS(1963, Brit.); LONG SHIPS, THE(1964, Brit./Yugo.)
Jim Moody
FAME(1980); DEATH VENGEANCE(1982); PERSONAL BEST(1982); BAD BOYS(1983); D.C. CAB(1983)
King Moody
TEENAGERS FROM OUTER SPACE(1959); NUN AND THE SERGEANT, THE(1962); ROTTEN APPLE, THE(1963); GLASS CAGE, THE(1964); ANY WEDNESDAY(1966); DESTRUCTORS, THE(1968); SWEET NOVEMBER(1968); STRAWBERRY STATEMENT, THE(1970); GET TO KNOW YOUR RABBIT(1972)
Laurence Moody
WHAT BECAME OF JACK AND JILL?(1972, Brit.), w
Leonard Moody
HIS BROTHER'S WIFE(1936)
Lynn Moody
SCREAM BLACULA SCREAM(1973)
Lynne Moody
LAS VEGAS LADY(1976); EVIL, THE(1978); SOME KIND OF HERO(1982); WHITE DOG(1982)
Michael Moody
STORM BOY(1976, Aus.)
Patrick Moody
END, THE(1978); SMOKEY AND THE BANDIT II(1980)
Phil Moody
THREE NUTS IN SEARCH OF A BOLT(1964), m
Ralph Moody
MAN-EATER OF KUMAON(1948); SQUARE DANCE JUBILEE(1949); BIG CARNIVAL, THE(1951); RED MOUNTAIN(1951); STRANGERS ON A TRAIN(1951); AFFAIR IN TRINIDAD(1952); CARRIE(1952); ROAD TO BALI(1952); TALK ABOUT A STRANGER(1952); COLUMN SOUTH(1953); PICKUP ON SOUTH STREET(1953); SALOME(1953); SEMINOLE(1953); TUMBLEWEED(1953); FAR HORIZONS, THE(1955); I DIED A THOUSAND TIMES(1955); MANY RIVERS TO CROSS(1955); RAGE AT DAWN(1955); STRANGE LADY IN TOWN(1955); LAST HUNT, THE(1956); REPRISAL(1956); STEEL JUNGLE, THE(1956); TOWARD THE UNKNOWN(1956); MONSTER THAT CHALLENGED THE WORLD, THE(1957); PAWNEE(1957); GOING STEADY(1958); LONE RANGER AND THE LOST CITY OF GOLD, THE(1958); LEGEND OF TOM DOOLEY, THE(1959); STORY OF RUTH, THE(1960); HOMICIDAL(1961); OUTSIDER, THE(1962); CHASE, THE(1966); WILD COUNTRY, THE(1971), w
Ron Moody
FOLLOW A STAR(1959, Brit.); MAKE MINE MINK(1960, Brit.); FIVE GOLDEN HOURS(1961, Brit.); MOUSE ON THE MOON, THE(1963, Brit.); PAIR OF BRIEFS, A(1963, Brit.); SUMMER HOLIDAY(1963, Brit.); LADIES WHO DO(1964, Brit.); MURDER MOST FOUL(1964, Brit.); SAN FERRY ANN(1965, Brit.); SEASIDE SWINGERS(1965, Brit.); SANDWICH MAN, THE(1966, Brit.); OLIVER!(1968, Brit.); DAVID COPPERFIELD(1970, Brit.); TWELVE CHAIRS, THE(1970); FLIGHT OF THE DOVES(1971, Brit.); DOGPOUND SHUFFLE(1975, Can.); DOMINIQUE(1978, Brit.); UNIDENTIFIED FLYING ODDBALL, THE(1979, Brit.); WRONG IS RIGHT(1982)
1984
WHERE IS PARSIFAL?(1984, Brit.)

Misc. Talkies
LEGEND OF THE WEREWOLF(1974)
Ruth Moody
KID MILLIONS(1934)
Sephton Moody, Jr.
PENITENTIARY II(1982)
Titus Moody
HELL'S CHOSEN FEW(1968)
Misc. Talkies
LAST OF THE AMERICAN HOBOES, THE(1974), d
William Vaughn Moody
GREAT DIVIDE, THE(1930), w; WOMAN HUNGRY(1931), w
De Sacia Mooers
ARIZONA KID, THE(1930)
Silents
AVERAGE WOMAN, THE(1924); IT IS THE LAW(1924); ANY WOMAN(1925); JUST OFF BROADWAY(1929)
Misc. Silents
BLONDE VAMPIRE, THE(1922); CHALLENGE, THE(1922); BACK TO LIBER-TY(1927)
Heinz Moog
TRIAL, THE(1948, Aust.); MAGIC FACE, THE(1951, Aust.); APRIL 1, 2000(1953, Aust.); HIPPODROME(1961, Aust./Ger.); SECRET WAYS, THE(1961); SENSO(1968, Ital.); LUDWIG(1973, Ital./Ger./Fr.)
Philipp Moog
1984
LITTLE DRUMMER GIRL, THE(1984)
Beverly Mook
MA AND PA KETTLE GO TO TOWN(1950); MA AND PA KETTLE AT THE FAIR(1952); MA AND PA KETTLE ON VACATION(1953); MA AND PA KETTLE AT WAIKIKI(1955)
Don Moomaw
ALL-AMERICAN, THE(1953); SOULS IN CONFLICT(1955, Brit.)
Lewis H. Moomaw
Misc. Silents
DECEIVER, THE(1920), d; GOLDEN TRAIL, THE(1920), d; CHECHAHCOS, THE(1924), d; UNDER THE ROUGE(1925), d; FLAMES(1926), d
Andy Moon
CAIN'S WAY(1969)
Arthur Moon
Misc. Silents
WITHOUT HONOR(1918)
Autumn Moon
MUSTANG(1959)
David Moon
TROUBLEMAKER, THE(1964), art d
Donna Moon [Donna Drew]
Misc. Silents
FLAME OF YOUTH, THE(1917)
Elina Moon
Misc. Talkies
NAUGHTY NYMPHS(1974)
Elvin Moon
AT LONG LAST LOVE(1975)
Ena Moon
TO BE A LADY(1934, Brit.); RIVER HOUSE MYSTERY, THE(1935, Brit.)
Frank Moon
JOE(1970)
1984
STRANGERS KISS(1984)
George Moon
LIGHTNING CONDUCTOR(1938, Brit.); ME AND MY PAL(1939, Brit.); TIME FLIES(1944, Brit.); WHAT DO WE DO NOW?(1945, Brit.); IT'S A WONDERFUL WORLD(1956, Brit.); ALLIGATOR NAMED DAISY, AN(1957, Brit.); DAVY(1958, Brit.); BREATH OF LIFE(1962, Brit.); GUY CALLED CAESAR, A(1962, Brit.); MATTER OF CHOICE, A(1963, Brit.); DIE, MONSTER, DIE(1965, Brit.); PROMISE HER ANY-THING(1966, Brit.); HALF A SIXPENCE(1967, Brit.)
Georgina Moon
MIND BENDERS, THE(1963, Brit.); FRAGMENT OF FEAR(1971, Brit.)
H. Franco Moon
SAVAGE SISTERS(1974), w
Jodi Moon
HUNTER, THE(1980)
Keith Moon
TWO HUNDRED MOTELS(1971, Brit.); SON OF DRACULA(1974, Brit.); STAR-DUST(1974, Brit.); THAT'LL BE THE DAY(1974, Brit.); TOMMY(1975, Brit.), a, a, w, m; SEXTETTE(1978)
Lee Sue Moon
MARCO THE MAGNIFICENT(1966, Ital./Fr./Yugo./Egypt/Afghanistan)
Lorna Moon
MIN AND BILL(1930), w
Silents
AFFAIRS OF ANATOL, THE(1921), w; DON'T TELL EVERYTHING(1921), w; LOVE(1927), w; MR. WU(1927), w
Lynne Sue Moon
THIRTEEN FRIGHTENED GIRLS(1963); 55 DAYS AT PEKING(1963); TO SIR, WITH LOVE(1967, Brit.)
Sun Myung Moon
INCHON(1981), tech adv
Toni Moon
SMOKEY AND THE BANDIT–PART 3(1983)
Valerie Moon
ONE OF OUR AIRCRAFT IS MISSING(1942, Brit.)
Wally Moon
MARINE BATTLEGROUND(1966, U.S/S.K.), art d; ASTRO-ZOMBIES, THE(1969), a, art d
Moonbeam
CHEYENNE AUTUMN(1964)

Q. Moonblood
FIRST BLOOD(1982), w
Moondog
CHAPPAQUA(1967)
Art Mooney
OPPOSITE SEX, THE(1956)
Debra Mooney
CHAPTER TWO(1979); TOOTSIE(1982)
Gary Mooney
OF STARS AND MEN(1961), anim d; MOUSE AND HIS CHILD, THE(1977), anim
Gavin Mooney
NINE TO FIVE(1980)
Gavin H. Mooney
1984
SAM'S SON(1984)
Hal Mooney
RAID ON ROMMEL(1971), m; SHOWDOWN(1973), md
Jim Mooney
MC KENZIE BREAK, THE(1970)
John Mooney
FRENCH LINE, THE(1954); JUBILEE TRAIL(1954); 27TH DAY, THE(1957)
Larry Mooney
STORY OF ROBIN HOOD, THE(1952, Brit.)
Laura Mooney
TWILIGHT ZONE–THE MOVIE(1983)
Lawrence Mooney
DEVIL'S BEDROOM, THE(1964)
Margaret Mooney
Silents
INTOLERANCE(1916)
Martin Mooney
SPECIAL AGENT(1935), p, w; BULLETS OR BALLOTS(1936), w; EXCLUSIVE STO-RY(1936), w; MISSING GIRLS(1936), w; YOU CAN'T BUY LUCK(1937), w; SQUA-DRON OF HONOR(1938), w; INSIDE INFORMATION(1939), w; MUTINY IN THE BIG HOUSE(1939), w; UNDERCOVER AGENT(1939), w; GAMBLING ON THE HIGH SEAS(1940), w; MILLIONAIRES IN PRISON(1940), w; BLONDE COMET(1941), w; EMERGENCY LANDING(1941), w; FEDERAL FUGITIVES(1941), w; PAPER BUL-LETS(1941), w; BROADWAY BIG SHOT(1942), w; FOREIGN AGENT(1942), p, w; MEN OF SAN QUENTIN(1942), p, w; MR. CELEBRITY(1942), p, w; MR. WISE GUY(1942), w; PANTHER'S CLAW, THE(1942), w; DANGER! WOMEN AT WORK(1943), w; HARVEST MELODY(1943), w; GREAT MIKE, THE(1944), w; MIN-STREL MAN(1944), w; MONSTER MAKER, THE(1944), w; SHAKE HANDS WITH MURDER(1944), w; WATERFRONT(1944), w; CRIME, INC.(1945), p, w; DANGER-OUS INTRUDER(1945), p; MISSING CORPSE, THE(1945), p; PHANTOM OF 42ND STREET, THE(1945), p; CRIMINAL COURT(1946), p; DANNY BOY(1946), p; I RING DOORBELLS(1946), p; IN FAST COMPANY(1946), w; SAN QUENTIN(1946), p; DEVIL SHIP(1947), p; WOMAN FROM TANGIER, THE(1948), p; DAUGHTER OF THE WEST(1949), p
Maureen Mooney
FRENCH CONNECTION, THE(1971)
Michael M. Mooney
HINDENBURG, THE(1975), w
Paul Mooney
WHICH WAY IS UP?(1977); BUDDY HOLLY STORY, THE(1978); BUSTIN' LOO-SE(1981)
Ria Mooney
THIS OTHER EDEN(1959, Brit.)
Robert Mooney
YOU CAN'T FOOL AN IRISHMAN(1950, Ireland); DATE WITH DISASTER(1957, Brit.); PROFESSOR TIM(1957, Ireland)
Rosalind Mooney
Silents
SEVEN CHANCES(1925)
Sean Mooney
CAPTAIN LIGHTFOOT(1955)
Shane Mooney
WHICH WAY IS UP?(1977)
Tex Mooney
JUNGLE JIM(1948)
Thomas Mooney
CROSS AND THE SWITCHBLADE, THE(1970); GREAT WALDO PEPPER, THE(1975), stunts
William H. Mooney
EFFECTS(1980), d & w
William Mooney
1984
FLASH OF GREEN, A(1984)
Yvonne Mooney
WHICH WAY IS UP?(1977)
The Moonglows
ROCK, ROCK, ROCK!(1956); MISTER ROCK AND ROLL(1957)
Steve Mooni
SCAVENGERS, THE(1969), cos
Hank Moonjean
HOOPER(1978), p; SMOKEY AND THE BANDIT II(1980), p; INCREDIBLE SHRINKING WOMAN, THE(1981), p; PATERNITY(1981), p; SHARKY'S MA-CHINE(1982), p; STROKER ACE(1983), p
Susan Moonsie
1984
PURPLE RAIN(1984)
Tanya Moontaro
MARVIN AND TIGE(1983), set d
Bill Moor
IT AIN'T EASY(1972); KRAMER VS. KRAMER(1979); SEDUCTION OF JOE TYNAN, THE(1979); LOVE IN A TAXI(1980); HANKY-PANKY(1982)
Cherie Moor
CHROME AND HOT LEATHER(1971)

Deacon Moor
FIRST TRAVELING SALESLADY, THE(1956)

Michael Moor
OCTOPUSSY(1983, Brit.)

Mill Moor
LEGEND OF NIGGER CHARLEY, THE(1972)

Robert Moor
LA VIE DE CHATEAU(1967, Fr.)

Gaybe Mooradian
TEENAGE MONSTER(1958)

Judy Mooradian
STATE OF THINGS, THE(1983)

Michael Moorcock
LAND THAT TIME FORGOT, THE(1975, Brit.), w; LAST DAYS OF MAN ON EARTH, THE(1975, Brit.), w

Judy Moorcraft
SPHINX(1981), cos

Judy Moorcroft
UNMAN, WITTERING AND ZIGO(1971, Brit.), cos; CROSSED SWORDS(1978), cos; WHO IS KILLING THE GREAT CHEFS OF EUROPE?(1978, US/Ger.), cos; MURDER BY DECREE(1979, Brit.), cos; SILVER DREAM RACER(1982, Brit.), cos; YENTL(1983), cos
1984
KILLING FIELDS, THE(1984, Brit.), cos; PASSAGE TO INDIA, A(1984, Brit.), cos

Dave Moordigian
48 HOURS(1982)

Ada May Moore
POPPY(1936)

Adrienne Moore
PATTERNS(1956)

Alan Moore
TWILIGHT'S LAST GLEAMING(1977, U.S./Ger.)

Alice Moore
BABES IN TOYLAND(1934); PICK A STAR(1937); WOMAN AGAINST THE WORLD(1938)

Alvy Moore
OKINAWA(1952); YOU FOR ME(1952); CHINA VENTURE(1953); DESTINATION GOBI(1953); GENTLEMEN PREFER BLONDES(1953); GLORY BRIGADE, THE(1953); WAR OF THE WORLDS, THE(1953); WILD ONE, THE(1953); RETURN FROM THE SEA(1954); RIOT IN CELL BLOCK 11(1954); SECRET OF THE INCAS(1954); SUSAN SLEPT HERE(1954); THERE'S NO BUSINESS LIKE SHOW BUSINESS(1954); AN-NAPOLIS STORY, AN(1955); FIVE AGAINST THE HOUSE(1955); SCREAMING EAGLES(1956); DESIGNING WOMAN(1957); PERSUADER, THE(1957); PERFECT FURLOUGH, THE(1958); EVERYTHING'S DUCKY(1961); TWIST AROUND THE CLOCK(1961); WACKIEST SHIP IN THE ARMY, THE(1961); FOR LOVE OR MONEY(1963); MOVE OVER, DARLING(1963); DEVIL'S BEDROOM, THE(1964), a, assoc p; THREE NUTS IN SEARCH OF A BOLT(1964); LOVE AND KISSES(1965); ONE WAY WAHINI(1965); VERY SPECIAL FAVOR, A(1965); GNOME-MOBILE, THE(1967); WITCHMAKER, THE(1969); BROTHERHOOD OF SATAN, THE(1971), a, p; LATE LIZ, THE(1971); BOY AND HIS DOG, A(1975), a, p; DR. MINX(1975); SPECIALIST, THE(1975); MORTUARY(1983)
1984
THEY'RE PLAYING WITH FIRE(1984)
Misc. Talkies
SPECIALIST, THE(1975)

Andy Moore
KILL SQUAD(1982), makeup

Anne Moore
CAESAR AND CLEOPATRA(1946, Brit.)

Archie Moore
ADVENTURES OF HUCKLEBERRY FINN, THE(1960); CARPETBAGGERS, THE(1964); FORTUNE COOKIE, THE(1966); OUTFIT, THE(1973); BREAKHEART PASS(1976)

Arnie Moore
MAN WHO LOVED WOMEN, THE(1983)
1984
FRIDAY THE 13TH–THE FINAL CHAPTER(1984); GREMLINS(1984); HAMBONE AND HILLIE(1984); TORCHLIGHT(1984)

Audrey Moore
DESIRE IN THE DUST(1960)

Barbara Moore
DEADWOOD'76(1965)

Ben Moore
MOONSHINE MOUNTAIN(1964); TWO THOUSAND MANIACS!(1964); SHE FREAK(1967)

Bennie Moore
HEROES(1977); SHARKY'S MACHINE(1982); TOUGH ENOUGH(1983)

Benny Moore
UNDER FIRE(1983)

Bert Moore
Silents
WHAT FOOLS MEN(1925), ed

Betty Moore
Silents
HEROIC LOVER, THE(1929), w

Bill Moore
MUTINY ON THE BLACKHAWK(1939)

Bob Moore
MELODY TIME(1948), w; LOVE IS A CAROUSEL(1970)

Bobby Moore
VICTORY(1981)

Brad Moore
LOVED ONE, THE(1965); SAILOR FROM GIBRALTAR, THE(1967, Brit.)

Brenda Moore
Misc. Silents
SOLOMON IN SOCIETY(1922)

Brian Moore
LUCK OF GINGER COFFEY, THE(1964, U.S./Can.), w; TORN CURTAIN(1966), w; BLUE FIN(1978, Aus.)

Burton Moore
MARINE BATTLEGROUND(1966, U.S/S.K.), w

Cameron Moore
TOWN LIKE ALICE, A(1958, Brit.)

Candy Moore
TOMBOY AND THE CHAMP(1961); NIGHT OF THE GRIZZLY, THE(1966); LUNCH WAGON(1981)

Carl Deacon Moore
LAWLESS CODE(1949)

Carl Moore
GIANT(1956)

Carlisle Moore
MADE FOR EACH OTHER(1939)

Carlyle Moore
WHAT A MAN(1930); TRANSATLANTIC MERRY-GO-ROUND(1934); SLIM(1937); ANGELS WITH DIRTY FACES(1938); OUTLAW EXPRESS(1938); OVERLAND EX-PRESS, THE(1938); WESTERN TRAILS(1938)
Silents
STOP THIEF(1920), w

Carlyle Moore, Jr.
CEILNG ZERO(1935); HIGH SCHOOL GIRL(1935); SHIPMATES FOREVER(1935); TOGETHER WE LIVE(1935); BENGAL TIGER(1936); BULLETS OR BALLOTS(1936); CASE OF THE BLACK CAT, THE(1936); CHARGE OF THE LIGHT BRIGADE, THE(1936); CHINA CLIPPER(1936); GIVE ME YOUR HEART(1936); GOLDEN AR-ROW, THE(1936); ROAD GANG(1936); TRAILIN' WEST(1936); TREACHERY RIDES THE RANGE(1936); TWO AGAINST THE WORLD(1936); DEVIL'S SADDLE LEGION, THE(1937); FUGITIVE IN THE SKY(1937); GO-GETTER, THE(1937); KID GALA-HAD(1937); MIDNIGHT COURT(1937); PUBLIC WEDDING(1937); READY, WILLING AND ABLE(1937); DELINQUENT PARENTS(1938); ARIZONA LEGION(1939); SE-CRET SERVICE OF THE AIR(1939); WINGS OF THE NAVY(1939); CHILD IS BORN, A(1940); KNUTE ROCKNE–ALL AMERICAN(1940); MURDER IN THE AIR(1940)

Carroll Moore
SEND ME NO FLOWERS(1964), w; THAT FUNNY FEELING(1965), w

Charles Moore
TRUE TO LIFE(1943); HIS FIRST COMMAND(1929); TRIAL OF MARY DUGAN, THE(1929); EXILE, THE(1931); I'LL FIX IT(1934); FRONT PAGE WOMAN(1935); INTERNES CAN'T TAKE MONEY(1937); ADVENTURE IN SAHARA(1938); DR. RHYTHM(1938); MR. SMITH GOES TO WASHINGTON(1939); ONLY ANGELS HAVE WINGS(1939); SOUTHWARD HO!(1939); GREAT McGINTY, THE(1940); MARY-LAND(1940); QUEEN OF THE MOB(1940); HIT THE ROAD(1941); KANSAS CY-CLONE(1941); PETTICOAT POLITICS(1941); SULLIVAN'S TRAVELS(1941); I MARRIED A WITCH(1942); RINGS ON HER FINGERS(1942); STRICTLY IN THE GROOVE(1942); SON OF DRACULA(1943); HAIL THE CONQUERING HERO(1944); PIN UP GIRL(1944); COLONEL EFFINGHAM'S RAID(1945); TWO-LANE BLACK-TOP(1971)
Silents
NINETY AND NINE, THE(1922)

Charles B. Moore
PALM BEACH STORY, THE(1942)

Charles R. Moore
MANHATTAN MELODRAMA(1934); IT'S A SMALL WORLD(1935); PAGE MISS GLORY(1935); RECKLESS(1935); SARATOGA(1937); PROFESSOR BEWARE(1938); DESERT BANDIT(1941); LITTLE FOXES, THE(1941); VIRGINIA(1941); LADY BODY-GUARD(1942); MY FAVORITE BLONDE(1942); THIS GUN FOR HIRE(1942); DIX-IE(1943); HAPPY GO LUCKY(1943); RIDING HIGH(1943); OUT OF THIS WORLD(1945); MAD WEDNESDAY(1950)

Charlie Moore
WITHOUT RESERVATIONS(1946)

Charlotte Moore
RICH AND FAMOUS(1981)

Christopher Michael Moore
1984
CITY HEAT(1984)

Clayton Moore
GO CHASE YOURSELF(1938); SERGEANT MADDEN(1939); KIT CARSON(1940); SON OF MONTE CRISTO(1940); INTERNATIONAL LADY(1941); TUXEDO JUNC-TION(1941); BLACK DRAGONS(1942); OUTLAWS OF PINE RIDGE(1942); BACHE-LOR'S DAUGHTERS, THE(1946); CYCLOTRODE X(1946); ALONG THE OREGON TRAIL(1947); MARSHAL OF AMARILLO(1948); COWBOY AND THE INDIANS, THE(1949); FAR FRONTIER, THE(1949); FRONTIER INVESTIGATOR(1949); GAY AMIGO, THE(1949); MASKED RAIDERS(1949); RIDERS OF THE WHISTLING PINES(1949); SHERIFF OF WICHITA(1949); SONS OF NEW MEXICO(1949); SOUTH OF DEATH VALLEY(1949); BANDITS OF EL DORADO(1951); CYCLONE FU-RY(1951); BARBED WIRE(1952); BUFFALO BILL IN TOMAHAWK TER-RITORY(1952); CAPTIVE OF BILLY THE KID(1952); DESERT PASSAGE(1952); HAWK OF WILD RIVER, THE(1952); MONTANA TERRITORY(1952); MUTINY(1952); NIGHT STAGE TO GALVESTON(1952); BANDITS OF CORSICA, THE(1953); DOWN LAREDO WAY(1953); KANSAS PACIFIC(1953); BLACK DAKOTAS, THE(1954); LONE RANGER, THE(1955); LONE RANGER AND THE LOST CITY OF GOLD, THE(1958); GHOST OF ZORRO(1959)

Cleo Moore
DYNAMITE PASS(1950); GAMBLING HOUSE(1950); HUNT THE MAN DOWN(1950); RIO GRANDE PATROL(1950); ON DANGEROUS GROUND(1951); PACE THAT THRILLS, THE(1952); STRANGE FASCINATION(1952); ONE GIRL'S CONFESSION(1953); THY NEIGHBOR'S WIFE(1953); BAIT(1954); OTHER WOMAN, THE(1954); HOLD BACK TOMORROW(1955); WOMEN'S PRISON(1955); OVER-EX-POSED(1956); HIT AND RUN(1957)

Cleve Moore
FOOTLIGHTS AND FOOLS(1929)
Silents
IT MUST BE LOVE(1926); STOLEN BRIDE, THE(1927); LILAC TIME(1928)

Clifford Moore
RENDEZVOUS 24(1946)

Coleen Moore
Silents
DESERT FLOWER, THE(1925)

Colleen Moore
FOOTLIGHTS AND FOOLS(1929); SMILING IRISH EYES(1929); POWER AND THE GLORY, THE(1933); SCARLET LETTER, THE(1934); SOCIAL REGISTER(1934); SUC-CESS AT ANY PRICE(1934)

Silents

CYCLONE, THE(1920); DINTY(1920); SKY PILOT, THE(1921); COME ON OVER(1922); NINETY AND NINE, THE(1922); WALL FLOWER, THE(1922); APRIL SHOWERS(1923); HUNTRESS, THE(1923); NTH COMMANDMENT, THE(1923); SLIPPY MCGEE(1923); PAINTED PEOPLE(1924); SO BIG(1924); SALLY(1925); ELLA CINDERS(1926); IRENE(1926); IT MUST BE LOVE(1926); TWINKLETOES(1926); LILAC TIME(1928); OH, KAY(1928); WHY BE GOOD?(1929)

Misc. Silents

HANDS UP(1917); OLD FASHIONED YOUNG MAN, AN(1917); SAVAGE, THE(1917); HOOSIER ROMANCE, A(1918); BUSHER, THE(1919); COMMON PROPERTY(1919); EGG CRATE WALLOP, THE(1919); LITTLE ORPHANT ANNIE(1919); MAN IN THE MOONLIGHT, THE(1919); WILDERNESS TRAIL, THE(1919); DEVIL'S CLAIM, THE(1920); SO LONG LETTY(1920); WHEN DAWN CAME(1920); HIS NIBS(1921); LOTUS EATER, THE(1921); AFFINITIES(1922); BROKEN CHAINS(1922); FORSAKING ALL OTHERS(1922); BROKEN HEARTS OF BROADWAY, THE(1923); FLAMING YOUTH(1923); LOOK YOUR BEST(1923); FLIRTING WITH LOVE(1924); PERFECT FLAPPER, THE(1924); THROUGH THE DARK(1924); WE MODERNS(1925); HER WILD OAT(1927); NAUGHTY BUT NICE(1927); ORCHIDS AND ERMINE(1927); HAPPINESS AHEAD(1928); SYNTHETIC SIN(1929)

Constance Moore

PRESCRIPTION FOR ROMANCE(1937); BORDER WOLVES(1938); CRIME OF DR. HALLET(1938); FRESHMAN YEAR(1938); LAST STAND, THE(1938); LETTER OF INTRODUCTION(1938); MISSING GUEST, THE(1938); PRISON BREAK(1938); RECKLESS LIVING(1938); STATE POLICE(1938); SWING THAT CHEER(1938); WIVES UNDER SUSPICION(1938); CHARLIE MC CARTHY, DETECTIVE(1939); EX-CHAMP(1939); HAWAIIAN NIGHTS(1939); LAUGH IT OFF(1939); MUTINY ON THE BLACKHAWK(1939); WHEN TOMORROW COMES(1939); YOU CAN'T CHEAT AN HONEST MAN(1939); ARGENTINE NIGHTS(1940); FRAMED(1940); I'M NOBODY'S SWEETHEART NOW(1940); LA CONGA NIGHTS(1940); MA, HE'S MAKING EYES AT ME(1940); BUY ME THAT TOWN(1941); I WANTED WINGS(1941); LAS VEGAS NIGHTS(1941); TAKE A LETTER, DARLING(1942); ATLANTIC CITY(1944); SHOW BUSINESS(1944); DELIGHTFULLY DANGEROUS(1945); EARL CARROLL'S VANITIES(1945); MEXICANA(1945); EARL CARROLL SKETCHBOOK(1946); IN OLD SACRAMENTO(1946); HIT PARADE OF 1947(1947)

Dan Moore

ILLEGAL ENTRY(1949), w

Daniel K. Moore

1984

FOOTLOOSE(1984); HOT DOG...THE MOVIE(1984)

Daniel Moore

LAST OF THE MOHICANS, THE(1936), w; STORM, THE(1938), w; FLIGHT AT MIDNIGHT(1939), w

Daphne Moore

FOREVER AND A DAY(1943); MR. LUCKY(1943); HARVEY GIRLS, THE(1946); SISTER KENNY(1946)

Dede Moore

FRENCH LINE, THE(1954); SON OF SINBAD(1955)

Dejah Moore

PAPER MOON(1973); DRIVE-IN(1976)

Del Moore

ERRAND BOY, THE(1961); LAST TIME I SAW ARCHIE, THE(1961); IT'S ONLY MONEY(1962); STAGECOACH TO DANCER'S PARK(1962); NUTTY PROFESSOR, THE(1963); DISORDERLY ORDERLY, THE(1964); PATSY, THE(1964); MOVIE STAR, AMERICAN STYLE, OR, LSD I HATE YOU!(1966); BIG MOUTH, THE(1967); CATALINA CAPER, THE(1967)

Demi Moore

PARASITE(1982)

1984

BLAME IT ON RIO(1984); NO SMALL AFFAIR(1984)

Misc. Talkies

CHOICES(1981)

Dennie Moore

MEET NERO WOLFE(1936); SYLVIA SCARLETT(1936); ANGEL(1937); PERFECT SPECIMEN, THE(1937); SUBMARINE D-1(1937); BOY MEETS GIRL(1938); COWBOY FROM BROOKLYN(1938); FOUR'S A CROWD(1938); MYSTERY HOUSE(1938); SECRETS OF AN ACTRESS(1938); ADVENTURES OF JANE ARDEN(1939); BACHELOR MOTHER(1939); ETERNALLY YOURS(1939); I'M FROM MISSOURI(1939); NO PLACE TO GO(1939); THESE GLAMOUR GIRLS(1939); WOMEN, THE(1939); SATURDAY'S CHILDREN(1940); WOMEN IN WAR(1940); DIVE BOMBER(1941); SUNSET MURDER CASE(1941); ANNA LUCASTA(1949); MODEL AND THE MARRIAGE BROKER, THE(1951)

Dennis Moore

SAGEBRUSH TROUBADOR(1935); CHINA CLIPPER(1936); DOWN THE STRETCH(1936); HERE COMES CARTER(1936); SING ME A LOVE SONG(1936); MOUNTAIN JUSTICE(1937); READY, WILLING AND ABLE(1937); SAN QUENTIN(1937); SMART BLONDE(1937); REBELLIOUS DAUGHTERS(1938); ACROSS THE PLAINS(1939); DANGER FLIGHT(1939); GIRL FROM RIO, THE(1939); IRISH LUCK(1939); MUTINY IN THE BIG HOUSE(1939); OVERLAND MAIL(1939); TRIGGER SMITH(1939); WILD HORSE CANYON(1939); EAST SIDE KIDS(1940); FUGITIVE FROM A PRISON CAMP(1940); RAINBOW OVER THE RANGE(1940); ROCKY MOUNTAIN RANGERS(1940); ARIZONA BOUND(1941); BILLY THE KID IN SANTA FE(1941); CYCLONE ON HORSEBACK(1941); ELLERY QUEEN AND THE MURDER RING(1941); FLYING WILD(1941); LONE RIDER FIGHTS BACK, THE(1941); PALS OF THE PECOS(1941); PIRATES ON HORSEBACK(1941); ROAR OF THE PRESS(1941); SPOOKS RUN WILD(1941); BANDIT RANGER(1942); BELOW THE BORDER(1942); DAWN ON THE GREAT DIVIDE(1942); LONE RIDER AND THE BANDIT, THE(1942); LONE RIDER IN CHEYENNE, THE(1942); RAIDERS OF THE RANGE(1942); RIDERS OF THE WEST(1942); ROLLING DOWN THE GREAT DIVIDE(1942); TEXAS MAN HUNT(1942); ARIZONA TRAIL(1943); BLACK MARKET RUSTLERS(1943); COWBOY COMMANDOS(1943); DESTROYER(1943); FRONTIER LAW(1943); HITLER'S MADMAN(1943); LAND OF HUNTED MEN(1943); TENTING TONIGHT ON THE OLD CAMP GROUND(1943); FOLLOW THE BOYS(1944); IMPOSTER, THE(1944); LADIES COURAGEOUS(1944); LADY IN THE DARK(1944); MR. WINKLE GOES TO WAR(1944); MUMMY'S CURSE, THE(1944); OKLAHOMA RAIDERS(1944); SEE HERE, PRIVATE HARGROVE(1944); TWILIGHT ON THE PRAIRIE(1944); WEEKEND PASS(1944); CRIME DOCTOR'S COURAGE, THE(1945); FRONTIER FEUD(1945); COLORADO SERENADE(1946); DRIFTIN' RIVER(1946); RAINBOW OVER THE ROCKIES(1947); FRONTIER AGENT(1948); GAY RANCHERO, THE(1948); RANGE RENEGADES(1948); TIOGA KID, THE(1948); ACROSS THE RIO GRANDE(1949); NAVAJO TRAIL RAIDERS(1949); RIDERS IN THE SKY(1949); ROARING WESTWARD(1949); ARIZONA TERRITORY(1950); COLORADO RANGER(1950); CROOKED RIVER(1950); FAST ON THE DRAW(1950); FEDERAL MAN(1950); GUNSLINGERS(1950); HOSTILE COUNTRY(1950); HOT ROD(1950); I KILLED GERONIMO(1950); KING OF THE BULLWHIP(1950); MARSHAL OF HELDORADO(1950); SILVER RAIDERS(1950); WEST OF THE BRAZOS(1950); WEST OF WYOMING(1950); ABILENE TRAIL(1951); FORT DEFIANCE(1951); I WAS AN AMERICAN SPY(1951); CANYON AMBUSH(1952); LUSTY MEN, THE(1952); MONTANA BELLE(1952); I DIED A THOUSAND TIMES(1955); ONE DESIRE(1955); SQUARE JUNGLE, THE(1955); HOT SHOTS(1956); TRIBUTE TO A BADMAN(1956); CHICAGO CONFIDENTIAL(1957); GUNFIGHT AT THE O.K. CORRAL(1957); UTAH BLAINE(1957)

Misc. Talkies

BORDER ROUNDUP(1942); OUTLAWS OF BOULDER PASS(1942); TEXAS JUSTICE(1942); BULLETS AND SADDLES(1943); SONG OF THE RANGE(1944); WEST OF THE RIO GRANDE(1944); SPRINGTIME IN TEXAS(1945); HAUNTED TRAILS(1949); BLAZING BULLETS(1951); GUNS ALONG THE BORDER(1952)

Diane Moore

WHO KILLED TEDDY BEAR?(1965); GUESS WHAT WE LEARNED IN SCHOOL TODAY?(1970); UNCLE SCAM(1981)

Dick Moore

KILLER SHARK(1950); EIGHT IRON MEN(1952); MEMBER OF THE WEDDING, THE(1952)

Dickie Moore

PASSION FLOWER(1930); SON OF THE GODS(1930); ALOHA(1931); HUSBAND'S HOLIDAY(1931); MANHATTAN PARADE(1931); SEED(1931); SQUAW MAN, THE(1931); STAR WITNESS(1931); THREE WHO LOVED(1931); BLONDE VENUS(1932); DEVIL IS DRIVING, THE(1932); DISORDERLY CONDUCT(1932); EXPERT, THE(1932); MILLION DOLLAR LEGS(1932); NO GREATER LOVE(1932); SO BIG(1932); UNION DEPOT(1932); WINNER TAKE ALL(1932); DECEPTION(1933); GABRIEL OVER THE WHITE HOUSE(1933); MAN'S CASTLE, A(1933); OBEY THE LAW(1933); OLIVER TWIST(1933); RACING STRAIN(1933); GALLANT LADY(1934); HUMAN SIDE, THE(1934); IN LOVE WITH LIFE(1934); THIS SIDE OF HEAVEN(1934); UPPER WORLD(1934); LITTLE MEN(1935); PETER IBBETSON(1935); SO RED THE ROSE(1935); SWELL-HEAD(1935); TOMORROW'S YOUTH(1935); WORLD ACCUSES(1935); LITTLE RED SCHOOLHOUSE(1936); PENTHOUSE PARTY(1936); STORY OF LOUIS PASTEUR, THE(1936); TIMOTHY'S QUEST(1936); BRIDE WORE RED, THE(1937); LIFE OF EMILE ZOLA, THE(1937); ARKANSAS TRAVELER, THE(1938); GLADIATOR, THE(1938); LOVE, HONOR AND BEHAVE(1938); MY BILL(1938); HIDDEN POWER(1939); UNDER-PUP, THE(1939); DISPATCH FROM REUTERS, A(1940); GREAT MR. NOBODY, THE(1941); SERGEANT YORK(1941); ADVENTURES OF MARTIN EDEN, THE(1942); MISS ANNIE ROONEY(1942); THIS GUN FOR HIRE(1942); HAPPY LAND(1943); HEAVEN CAN WAIT(1943); SONG OF BERNADETTE, THE(1943); EVE OF ST. MARK(1944); JIVE JUNCTION(1944); SWEET AND LOWDOWN(1944); YOUTH RUNS WILD(1944); DANGEROUS YEARS(1947); OUT OF THE PAST(1947); BEHIND LOCKED DOORS(1948); SIXTEEN FATHOMS DEEP(1948); BAD BOY(1949); TUNA CLIPPER(1949)

Silents

OBJECT–ALIMONY(1929)

Dom Moore

SHOES OF THE FISHERMAN, THE(1968)

Doreen Moore

RETURN FROM THE ASHES(1965, U.S./Brit.)

Doris Langley Moore

FREUD(1962), cos

Dorothy Moore

BIG SHOT, THE(1937); BLONDIE(1938); GIRLS' SCHOOL(1938); HAVING WONDERFUL TIME(1938); QUICK MONEY(1938); VIVACIOUS LADY(1938); BLONDIE MEETS THE BOSS(1939); FREE, BLONDE AND 21(1940); GIRL IN 313(1940); I'M NOBODY'S SWEETHEART NOW(1940); WHEN THE DALTONS RODE(1940); BROADWAY(1942); SCATTERGOOD RIDES HIGH(1942); LADIES COURAGEOUS(1944)

Misc. Talkies

RAPE KILLER, THE(1976)

Dudley Moore

WRONG BOX, THE(1966, Brit.); BEDAZZLED(1967, Brit.), a, w, m; INADMISSIBLE EVIDENCE(1968, Brit.), m; 30 IS A DANGEROUS AGE, CYNTHIA(1968, Brit.), a, w, m; BED SITTING ROOM, THE(1969, Brit.); STAIRCASE(1969 U.S./Brit./Fr.), m; THOSE DARING YOUNG MEN IN THEIR JAUNTY JALOPIES(1969, Fr./Brit./ Ital.); ALICE'S ADVENTURES IN WONDERLAND(1972, Brit.); FOUL PLAY(1978); 10(1979); HOUND OF THE BASKERVILLES, THE(1980, Brit.), a, w, m; WHOLLY MOSES(1980); ARTHUR(1981); SIX WEEKS(1982), a, m; LOVESICK(1983); ROMANTIC COMEDY(1983)

1984

BEST DEFENSE(1984); MICKI AND MAUDE(1984); UNFAITHFULLY YOURS(1984)

Duke Moore

PLAN 9 FROM OUTER SPACE(1959)

Ed Moore

ONLY WHEN I LAUGH(1981)

Misc. Talkies

INTERPLAY(1970)

Edwina Moore

SHOOT THE MOON(1982)

Eileen Moore

WALTZ TIME(1946, Brit.); MR. LORD SAYS NO(1952, Brit.); GIRL ON THE PIER, THE(1953, Brit.); GOOD BEGINNING, THE(1953, Brit.); MR. DENNING DRIVES NORTH(1953, Brit.); INSPECTOR CALLS, AN(1954, Brit.); GREEN MAN, THE(1957, Brit.); MEN OF SHERWOOD FOREST(1957, Brit.); TOWN LIKE ALICE, A(1958, Brit.); DEVIL'S BAIT(1959, Brit.); CRY WOLF(1968, Brit.)

Silents

AUTOCRAT, THE(1919, Brit.)

Eira Moore

Misc. Talkies

VOICE OVER(1983)

Eleanor Moore

ROBE, THE(1953); LOVE IS A MANY-SPLENDORED THING(1955)

Ellen Moore

NEW ORLEANS AFTER DARK(1958)

Elsie Moore
WICKHAM MYSTERY, THE(1931, Brit.); LUCKY SWEEP, A(1932, Brit.)
Emily Moore
THAT SUMMER(1979, Brit.)
Emmett Moore
SWEET INNISCARRA(1934, Brit.), p,d&w
Erin O'Brien Moore
DANGEROUS CORNER(1935); RING AROUND THE MOON(1936); LONG GRAY LINE, THE(1955)
Ernie Moore
STROKER ACE(1983)
Eugene Moore
Silents
MODERN MONTE CRISTO, A(1917), d
Misc. Silents
JOSEPH IN THE LAND OF EGYPT(1914), d; WORLD AND THE WOMAN, THE(1916), d; GIRL WHO WON OUT, THE(1917), d; IMAGE MAKER, THE(1917), d
Eulabelle Moore
HORROR OF PARTY BEACH, THE(1964)
Eunice Moore
SCARLET EMPRESS, THE(1934)
Silents
CAROLYN OF THE CORNERS(1919); SOUL OF YOUTH, THE(1920)
Eunice Vin Moore
Misc. Silents
BEAUTY PRIZE, THE(1924)
Eva Moore
ALMOST A DIVORCE(1931, Brit.); BROWN SUGAR(1931, Brit.); OTHER WOMAN, THE(1931, Brit.); BUT THE FLESH IS WEAK(1932, Brit.); OLD DARK HOUSE, THE(1932); BLIND JUSTICE(1934, Brit.); CUP OF KINDNESS, A(1934, Brit.); I WAS A SPY(1934, Brit.); LEAVE IT TO SMITH(1934); LITTLE STRANGER(1934, Brit.); POWER(1934, Brit.); SONG YOU GAVE ME, THE(1934, Brit.); ANNIE, LEAVE THE ROOM(1935, Brit.); VINTAGE WINE(1935, Brit.); OLD IRON(1938, Brit.); SCOTLAND YARD INVESTIGATOR(1945, Brit.); BANDIT OF SHERWOOD FOREST, THE(1946); OF HUMAN BONDAGE(1946)
Silents
CRIMSON CIRCLE, THE(1922, Brit.); FLAMES OF PASSION(1922, Brit.)
Misc. Silents
LAW DIVINE, THE(1920, Brit.); CHU CHIN CHOW(1923, Brit.)
Evelyn Moore
WEAKER SEX, THE(1949, Brit.); BEDAZZLED(1967, Brit.); VERDICT, THE(1982)
Fay Moore
FLIGHT TO HONG KONG(1956), cos
Fiona Moore
CATCH ME A SPY(1971, Brit./Fr.)
Florence Moore
Silents
BROADWAY AFTER DARK(1924)
Frank Moore
BADGER'S GREEN(1934, Brit.); FAR SHORE, THE(1976, Can.); RABID(1976, Can.); SUPREME KID, THE(1976, Can.); THIRD WALKER, THE(1978, Can.); STONE COLD DEAD(1980, Can.)
1984
KINGS AND DESPERATE MEN(1984, Brit.)
Silents
PATCHWORK GIRL OF OZ, THE(1914)
Misc. Silents
HIS MAJESTY, THE SCARECROW OF OZ(1914)
Fred Moore
SNOW WHITE AND THE SEVEN DWARFS(1937), anim; FANTASIA(1940), anim; PINOCCHIO(1940), anim d; DUMBO(1941), anim d; RELUCTANT DRAGON, THE(1941), anim; THREE CABALLEROS, THE(1944), anim; MAKE MINE MUSIC(1946), anim; FUN AND FANCY FREE(1947), anim d; CINDERELLA(1950), anim; ALICE IN WONDERLAND(1951), anim; PETER PAN(1953), anim
Freddie Moore
PARASITE(1982)
Frederick Moore
MAN WHO WASN'T THERE, THE(1983), ph
Misc. Silents
CYCLONE BLISS(1921); STAMPEDE, THE(1921); THEY'RE OFF(1922)
Gar Moore
TO LIVE IN PEACE(1947, Ital.); PAISAN(1948, Ital.); ABBOTT AND COSTELLO MEET THE KILLER, BORIS KARLOFF(1949); ILLEGAL ENTRY(1949); JOHNNY STOOL PIGEON(1949); VICIOUS YEARS, THE(1950); WHIPPED, THE(1950); GIRL IN WHITE, THE(1952); CURSE OF THE FACELESS MAN(1958)
Garry Moore
IT HAPPENED TO JANE(1959)
Gates Moore
1984
SONGWRITER(1984)
Gavin Moore
KING RICHARD AND THE CRUSADERS(1954)
Gene Moore
CARNIVAL OF SOULS(1962), m
George Moore
HELD FOR RANSOM(1938); ESTHER WATERS(1948, Brit.), w; HELLIONS, THE(1962, Brit.); DINGAKA(1965, South Africa); KIMBERLEY JIM(1965, South Africa)
Gerald Moore
FRONT LINE KIDS(1942, Brit.); HE SNOOPS TO CONQUER(1944, Brit.); GAY INTRUDERS, THE(1946, Brit.); GREEN FINGERS(1947)
Silents
AUCTION MART, THE(1920, Brit.)
Gladys Moore
Misc. Silents
TRICKS(1925)
Glenna Moore
MAIDSTONE(1970)

Gloria Moore
EGG AND I, THE(1947); MA AND PA KETTLE(1949); DEEP IN MY HEART(1954)
Gloria Penny Moore
YOU'RE NEVER TOO YOUNG(1955)
Grace Moore
LADY'S MORALS, A(1930); NEW MOON(1930); ONE NIGHT OF LOVE(1934); LOVE ME FOREVER(1935); KING STEPS OUT, THE(1936); I'LL TAKE ROMANCE(1937); WHEN YOU'RE IN LOVE(1937); LOUISE(1940, Fr.); SO THIS IS LOVE(1953), w
Granville Moore
FAMOUS FERGUSON CASE, THE(1932), w
Lt. H.C. Moore
SEA DEVILS(1937), tech adv
Hal J. Moore
BOOTS MALONE(1952)
Harley Moore
Silents
RACING FOR LIFE(1924)
Harry Moore
DANCING WITH CRIME(1947, Brit.), art d; JUST WILLIAM'S LUCK(1948, Brit.), art d; NO ORCHIDS FOR MISS BLANDISH(1948, Brit.), art d; THINGS HAPPEN AT NIGHT(1948, Brit.), art d; ROOM AT THE TOP(1959, Brit.)
Harry T. Moore
PRIEST OF LOVE(1981, Brit.), w
Henrietta Moore
DAY MARS INVADED EARTH, THE(1963)
Hilda Moore
JEALOUSY(1929); LAW AND LAWLESS(1932)
Silents
PALAIS DE DANSE(1928, Brit.)
Misc. Silents
BROKEN MELODY, THE(1916, Brit.); SECOND MRS. TANQUERAY, THE(1916, Brit.); WHOSO IS WITHOUT SIN(1916, Brit.); JUSTICE(1917, Brit.)
Ida Moore
GHOST THAT WALKS ALONE, THE(1944); HI BEAUTIFUL(1944); ONCE UPON A TIME(1944); RECKLESS AGE(1944); RIDERS OF THE SANTA FE(1944); SHE'S A SOLDIER TOO(1944); EADIE WAS A LADY(1945); EASY TO LOOK AT(1945); GIRLS OF THE BIG HOUSE(1945); HER LUCKY NIGHT(1945); I'LL TELL THE WORLD(1945); ROUGH, TOUGH AND READY(1945); SHE WOULDN'T SAY YES(1945); CROSS MY HEART(1946); DARK MIRROR, THE(1946); FROM THIS DAY FORWARD(1946); SHOW-OFF, THE(1946); TO EACH HIS OWN(1946); DREAM GIRL(1947); EASY COME, EASY GO(1947); EGG AND I, THE(1947); HIGH BARBAREE(1947); IT'S A JOKE, SON!(1947); GOOD SAM(1948); JOHNNY BELINDA(1948); MANHATTAN ANGEL(1948); MONEY MADNESS(1948); RETURN OF THE BADMEN(1948); RUSTY LEADS THE WAY(1948); DEAR WIFE(1949); HOLD THAT BABY!(1949); LEAVE IT TO HENRY(1949); MA AND PA KETTLE(1949); ROPE OF SAND(1949); ROSEANNA McCOY(1949); SUN COMES UP, THE(1949); BACKFIRE(1950); FANCY PANTS(1950); HARVEY(1950); LET'S DANCE(1950); MOTHER DIDN'T TELL ME(1950); MR. MUSIC(1950); PAID IN FULL(1950); COMIN' ROUND THE MOUNTAIN(1951); DOUBLE DYNAMITE(1951); HONEYCHILE(1951); LEAVE IT TO THE MARINES(1951); LEMON DROP KID, THE(1951); SHOW BOAT(1951); RAINBOW 'ROUND MY SHOULDER(1952); SCANDAL SHEET(1952); SOMETHING TO LIVE FOR(1952); SCANDAL AT SCOURIE(1953); COUNTRY GIRL, THE(1954); LONG, LONG TRAILER, THE(1954); MA AND PA KETTLE AT WAIKIKI(1955); DESK SET(1957); ROCK-A-BYE BABY(1958)
Silents
MERRY WIDOW, THE(1925)
Iris Moore
LOVE ON THE RUN(1936)
Ivanna Moore
REVENGE OF THE CHEERLEADERS(1976)
Jack Moore
THUNDER TRAIL(1937); TEXANS, THE(1938); WHEN WERE YOU BORN?(1938); KEEPER OF THE FLAME(1942), set d; TALK ABOUT A STRANGER(1952)
Jack D. Moore
UNDERCURRENT(1946), set d; HUCKSTERS, THE(1947), set d; B. F.'S DAUGHTER(1948), set d; JULIA MISBEHAVES(1948), set d; KISSING BANDIT, THE(1948), set d; LITTLE WOMEN(1949), set d; ON THE TOWN(1949), set d; TENSION(1949), set d; THAT FORSYTE WOMAN(1949), set d; ASPHALT JUNGLE, THE(1950), set d; PAGAN LOVE SONG(1950), set d; LOVELY TO LOOK AT(1952), set d; LAST TIME I SAW PARIS, THE(1954), set d; TENDER TRAP, THE(1955), set d; SWEET CHARITY(1969), set d
Jacqueline Moore
LOVE, HONOR AND GOODBYE(1945)
Silents
DAMAGED GOODS(1915)
Jamal Moore
HAMMER(1972)
James Moore
FANTASIA(1940), anim; SECRET SEVEN, THE(1940), d; THUNDER OVER THE PLAINS(1953), ed; BOY FROM OKLAHOMA, THE(1954), ed; PHANTOM OF THE RUE MORGUE(1954), ed; RIVER CHANGES, THE(1956), ed; SINISTER URGE, THE(1961); LOSERS, THE(1970), ed
James C. Moore
TANKS ARE COMING, THE(1951), ed; THIS WOMAN IS DANGEROUS(1952), ed
Jan Moore
FORTY ACRE FEUD(1965)
Jay Moore
KING OF THE GYPSIES(1978), art d; WANDERERS, THE(1979), art d; ROLLOVER(1981), prod d; SURVIVORS, THE(1983), art d
Jill Esmond Moore
CHINESE BUNGALOW, THE(1930, Brit.); ETERNAL FEMININE, THE(1931, Brit.)
Jimmy Moore
CHRISTINE KEELER AFFAIR, THE(1964, Brit.); PEOPLE MEET AND SWEET MUSIC FILLS THE HEART(1969, Den./Swed.)
Jo-Anne Moore
GETTING OF WISDOM, THE(1977, Aus.); MONEY MOVERS(1978, Aus.)
Joanna Moore
SLIM CARTER(1957); APPOINTMENT WITH A SHADOW(1958); FLOOD TIDE(1958); MONSTER ON THE CAMPUS(1958); RIDE A CROOKED TRAIL(1958); TOUCH OF EVIL(1958); LAST ANGRY MAN, THE(1959); FOLLOW THAT

DREAM(1962); WALK ON THE WILD SIDE(1962); SON OF FLUBBER(1963); MAN FROM GALVESTON, THE(1964); COUNTDOWN(1968); NEVER A DULL MOMENT(1968); HINDENBURG, THE(1975)
Misc. Talkies
APPOINTMENT WITH A SHADOW(1957); J.C.(1972)

Joe Moore
1984
PHILADELPHIA EXPERIMENT, THE(1984)
Silents
FALSE BRANDS(1922); WOLF PACK(1922); GOAT GETTER(1925)
Misc. Silents
LOVE'S BATTLE(1920); WHITE RIDER, THE(1920); ARREST NORMA MACGREGOR(1921); JUDGEMENT(1922); UP IN THE AIR ABOUT MARY(1922)

John Moore
HIDDEN HOMICIDE(1959, Brit.); EL CID(1961, U.S./Ital.), art d&cos; 55 DAYS AT PEKING(1963), prod d, set d, cos; FALL OF THE ROMAN EMPIRE, THE(1964), prod d, set d; ACT OF MURDER(1965, Brit.); FROZEN DEAD, THE(1967, Brit.); DON'T RAISE THE BRIDGE, LOWER THE RIVER(1968, Brit.); CAPTAIN NEMO AND THE UNDERWATER CITY(1969, Brit.); DEVIL WITHIN HER, THE(1976, Brit.); MATTER OF TIME, A(1976, Ital./U.S.), prod d
1984
GHOSTBUSTERS(1984), art d
Misc. Talkies
MYRTE AND THE DEMONS(1948)

John J. Moore
SOPHIE'S CHOICE(1982), art d

John Jay Moore
JUST TELL ME WHAT YOU WANT(1980), art d

John M. Moore
SENTENCED FOR LIFE(1960, Brit.)

John R. Moore
DANGEROUS CHARTER(1962), p

Jonathan Moore
1776(1972); RAISE THE TITANIC(1980, Brit.); SMALL CIRCLE OF FRIENDS, A(1980); HOSPITAL MASSACRE(1982)
1984
AMADEUS(1984)

Joyce Moore
SPECKLED BAND, THE(1931, Brit.)
Misc. Silents
BEULAH(1915); GENTLEMAN OF QUALITY, A(1919)

Juanita Moore
PINKY(1949); AFFAIR IN TRINIDAD(1952); LYDIA BAILEY(1952); SKIRTS AHOY!(1952); WITNESS TO MURDER(1954); LORD OF THE JUNGLE(1955); QUEEN BEE(1955); WOMEN'S PRISON(1955); GIRL CAN'T HELP IT, THE(1956); OPPOSITE SEX, THE(1956); RANSOM(1956); BAND OF ANGELS(1957); GREEN-EYED BLONDE, THE(1957); IMITATION OF LIFE(1959); TAMMY, TELL ME TRUE(1961); WALK ON THE WILD SIDE(1962); PAPA'S DELICATE CONDITION(1963); SINGING NUN, THE(1966); ROSIE!(1967); UPTIGHT(1968); SKIN GAME(1971); MACK, THE(1973); ABBY(1974); THOMASINE AND BUSHROD(1974); PATERNITY(1981)
Misc. Talkies
FOX STYLE(1973); JOEY(1977)

Karen Moore
DESPERATE WOMEN, THE(?)

Katherine Leslie Moore
PENNIES FROM HEAVEN(1936), w

Katherine Moore
Misc. Talkies
DIRTY GERTY FROM HARLEM, USA(1946)

Katherine Perry Moore
WEDDING PRESENT(1936)

Kathryn Moore
WOMAN OF DISTINCTION, A(1950)

Kay Moore
ROCK BABY, ROCK IT(1957)

Kaycee Moore
1984
BLESS THEIR LITTLE HEARTS(1984)

Keith Moore
MIRACLE WORKER, THE(1962)

Kenny Moore
PERSONAL BEST(1982)

Kevan Moore
LIFE AND TIMES OF CHESTER-ANGUS RAMSGOOD, THE(1971, Can.)

Kevin Moore
HERE COME THE TIGERS(1978)

Kieron Moore
MAN ABOUT THE HOUSE, A(1947, Brit.); ANNA KARENINA(1948, Brit.); MINE OWN EXECUTIONER(1948, Brit.); SAINTS AND SINNERS(1949, Brit.); DAVID AND BATHSHEBA(1951); HONEYMOON DEFERRED(1951, Brit.); TEN TALL MEN(1951); RECOIL(1953); WOMAN IN HIDING(1953, Brit.); FUSS OVER FEATHERS(1954, Brit.); GREEN SCARF, THE(1954, Brit.); NAKED HEART, THE(1955, Brit.); SATELLITE IN THE SKY(1956); THREE SUNDAYS TO LIVE(1957, Brit.); KEY, THE(1958, Brit.); STEEL BAYONET, THE(1958, Brit.); ANGRY HILLS, THE(1959, Brit.); DARBY O'GILL AND THE LITTLE PEOPLE(1959); NAVY HEROES(1959, Brit.); DAY THEY ROBBED THE BANK OF ENGLAND, THE(1960, Brit.); SIEGE OF SIDNEY STREET, THE(1960, Brit.); DR. BLOOD'S COFFIN(1961); LEAGUE OF GENTLEMEN, THE(1961, Brit.); I THANK A FOOL(1962, Brit.); MAIN ATTRACTION, THE(1962, Brit.); 300 SPARTANS, THE(1962); DAY OF THE TRIFFIDS, THE(1963); HIDE AND SEEK(1964, Brit.); MODEL MURDER CASE, THE(1964, Brit.); THIN RED LINE, THE(1964); CRACK IN THE WORLD(1965); ARABESQUE(1966); SON OF A GUNFIGHTER(1966, U.S./Span.); CUSTER OF THE WEST(1968, U.S., Span.); RUN LIKE A THIEF(1968, Span.)
Misc. Talkies
BIKINI PARADISE(1967)

Larry Moore
SAMURAI(1945)

Laurens Moore
1984
FIRESTARTER(1984)

Lee Gordon Moore
NICKELODEON(1976)

Lee M. Moore
KING OF THE TURF(1939)

Lee Moore
INVITATION TO HAPPINESS(1939); HIT THE ROAD(1941); BROADWAY(1942); GREAT MAN'S LADY, THE(1942); THERE IS NO 13(1977); NIGHT OF THE ZOMBIES(1981)

Lela Moore
NIGHT AT EARL CARROLL'S, A(1940)

Lillian Moore
DEVIL'S BROTHER, THE(1933); SHE MARRIED HER BOSS(1935)

Linda Moore
Silents
UNINVITED GUEST, THE(1923, Brit.)

Lisa Moore
FOR LOVE OF IVY(1968); DREAM OF KINGS, A(1969); HIT MAN(1972); SLAUGHTER'S BIG RIP-OFF(1973); ACT OF VENGEANCE(1974); HARRAD SUMMER, THE(1974)

Louis Moore
BOY FRIEND(1939), w

Lucia Moore
Silents
CAPRICE OF THE MOUNTAINS(1916)
Misc. Silents
HER DOUBLE LIFE(1916); COURAGE OF THE COMMONPLACE(1917); 39 EAST(1920)

Lyford Moore
HOW TO BE VERY, VERY, POPULAR(1955), w

Lynn Moore
SQUAD CAR(1961)

M. Moore
Silents
KING OF KINGS, THE(1927)

Mandy Moore
POWERFORCE(1983)

Marcela Moore
EXPOSED(1983)

Marcia Moore
Silents
SECOND IN COMMAND, THE(1915)

Margaret Moore
PANIC IN THE PARLOUR(1957, Brit.); DR. TERROR'S GALLERY OF HORRORS(1967)

Margo Moore
HOUND-DOG MAN(1959); WAKE ME WHEN IT'S OVER(1960); GEORGE RAFT STORY, THE(1961); BACHELOR FLAT(1962)

Marion Moore
Misc. Silents
SQUARE JOE(1921)

Marjorie Moore
WINE, WOMEN, AND SONG(1934)

Martin Moore
GROUNDSTAR CONSPIRACY, THE(1972, Can.)

Mary Moore
ARABIAN NIGHTS(1942); UP IN ARMS(1944); WONDER MAN(1945); LOVER COME BACK(1946); SONG OF SCHEHERAZADE(1947)
Misc. Silents
DAVID GARRICK(1913, Brit.); MISS DECEPTION(1917)

Mary Tyler Moore
THOROUGHLY MODERN MILLIE(1967); X-15(1961); DON'T JUST STAND THERE(1968); WHAT'S SO BAD ABOUT FEELING GOOD?(1968); CHANGE OF HABIT(1969); ORDINARY PEOPLE(1980); SIX WEEKS(1982)

Matt Moore
COQUETTE(1929); SIDE STREET(1929); SQUEALER, THE(1930); CONSOLATION MARRIAGE(1931); FRONT PAGE, THE(1931); PENROD AND SAM(1931); COCK OF THE AIR(1932); LITTLE ORPHAN ANNIE(1932); PRIDE OF THE LEGION, THE(1932); RAIN(1932); DELUGE(1933); ALL MEN ARE ENEMIES(1934); SUCH WOMEN ARE DANGEROUS(1934); ABSOLUTE QUIET(1936); ANYTHING GOES(1936); RANGE WAR(1939); SANTA FE MARSHAL(1940); MY LIFE WITH CAROLINE(1941); TRIAL OF MARY DUGAN, THE(1941); UNEXPECTED UNCLE(1941); MAYOR OF 44TH STREET, THE(1942); MOKEY(1942); MY FAVORITE SPY(1942); HAPPY LAND(1943); WILSON(1944); SHE WENT TO THE RACES(1945); SPELLBOUND(1945); HOODLUM SAINT, THE(1946); GOOD SAM(1948); JOAN OF ARC(1948); NEPTUNE'S DAUGHTER(1949); THAT FORSYTE WOMAN(1949); BIG HANGOVER, THE(1950); MALAYA(1950); MYSTERY STREET(1950); GREAT CARUSO, THE(1951); LAW AND THE LADY, THE(1951); MR. IMPERIUM(1951); NIGHT INTO MORNING(1951); THREE GUYS NAMED MIKE(1951); TOO YOUNG TO KISS(1951); INVITATION(1952); PLYMOUTH ADVENTURE(1952); LATIN LOVERS(1953); SCANDAL AT SCOURIE(1953); EXECUTIVE SUITE(1954); LAST TIME I SAW PARIS, THE(1954); SEVEN BRIDES FOR SEVEN BROTHERS(1954); KING'S THIEF, THE(1955); THESE WILDER YEARS(1956); AFFAIR TO REMEMBER, AN(1957); I BURY THE LIVING(1958); BIRDS AND THE BEES, THE(1965)
Misc. Talkies
CALL OF THE WEST(1930)
Silents
TRAFFIC IN SOULS(1913); 20,000 LEAGUES UNDER THE SEA(1916); PRIDE OF THE CLAN, THE(1917); GETTING MARY MARRIED(1919); SAHARA(1919); HAIRPINS(1920); WHISPERS(1920); MAN'S HOME, A(1921); STRAIGHT IS THE WAY(1921); JILT, THE(1922); SISTERS(1922); STORM, THE(1922); STRANGERS OF THE NIGHT(1923); ANOTHER MAN'S WIFE(1924); BREAKING POINT, THE(1924); LOST LADY, A(1924); NARROW STREET(1924); NO MORE WOMEN(1924); UNHOLY THREE, THE(1925); CAVEMAN, THE(1926); EARLY TO WED(1926); FIRST YEAR, THE(1926); HIS JAZZ BRIDE(1926); SUMMER BACHELORS(1926); MARRIED ALIVE(1927); TILLIE THE TOILER(1927); PHYLLIS OF THE FOLLIES(1928)
Misc. Silents
RUNAWAY ROMANY(1917); HEART OF THE WILDS(1918); BONDAGE OF BARBARA, THE(1919); DARK STAR(1919); FORBIDDEN FIRE(1919); GLORIOUS LADY, THE(1919); REGULAR GIRL, A(1919); UNPARDONABLE SIN, THE(1919); UNWRITTEN CODE, THE(1919); WILD GOOSE CHASE(1919); DON'T EVER MAR-

RY(1920); LOVE MADNESS(1920); MIRACLE OF MANHATTAN, THE(1921); PAS-
SIONATE PILGRIM, THE(1921); BACK PAY(1922); MINNIE(1922); DRIFTING(1923);
WHITE TIGER(1923); FOOLS IN THE DARK(1924); SELF-MADE FAILURE, A(1924);
WISE VIRGIN, THE(1924); GROUNDS FOR DIVORCE(1925); HIS MAJESTY BUNK-
ER BEAN(1925); HOW BAXTER BUTTED IN(1925); THREE WEEKS IN PARIS(1925);
WAY OF A GIRL, THE(1925); WHERE THE WORST BEGINS(1925); DI-
PLOMACY(1926); MYSTERY CLUB, THE(1926); BEWARE OF BLONDES(1928); DRY
MARTINI(1928)

Maureen Moore
LITTLE MISS MOLLY(1940); LIFE IS A CIRCUS(1962, Brit.); GOODBYE GIRL,
THE(1977)

Mavor Moore
CITY ON FIRE(1979 Can.); DIRTY TRICKS(1981, Can.); FISH HAWK(1981, Can.);
SCANNERS(1981, Can.); THRESHOLD(1983, Can.)

McElbert Moore
EVER SINCE VENUS(1944), w; OLD-FASHIONED GIRL, AN(1948), w; SHAMROCK
HILL(1949), w

Melba Moore
SIDELONG GLANCES OF A PIGEON KICKER, THE(1970); LOST IN THE
STARS(1974); HAIR(1979)

Melvin H. Moore
MYSTERY STREET(1950)

Michael Moore
WE'VE NEVER BEEN LICKED(1943); STRANGER AT MY DOOR(1950, Brit.);
CHELSEA STORY(1951, Brit.); SILVER CITY(1951); ATOMIC CITY, THE(1952);
JAMAICA RUN(1953); LITTLE BOY LOST(1953); PONY EXPRESS(1953); SABRE
JET(1953); STALAG 17(1953); DESPERATE HOURS, THE(1955); BOOBY TRAP(1957,
Brit.); UNDERCOVER GIRL(1957, Brit.); HAND, THE(1960, Brit.); EYE FOR AN EYE,
AN(1966), d; PARADISE, HAWAIIAN STYLE(1966), d; FASTEST GUITAR ALIVE,
THE(1967), d; KILL A DRAGON(1967), d; BUCKSKIN(1968), d
1984
HOT DOG...THE MOVIE(1984)

Mickey Moore
Silents
POLLY OF THE STORM COUNTRY(1920); SOMETHING TO THINK ABOUT(1920);
ALL SOULS EVE(1921); EXIT THE VAMP(1921); MASK, THE(1921); SHAME(1921);
IMPOSSIBLE MRS. BELLEW, THE(1922); ABRAHAM LINCOLN(1924); CY-
THEREA(1924); LADY FROM HELL, THE(1926); NO MAN'S GOLD(1926)
Misc. Silents
TRUXTON KING(1923)

Micki Moore
DERANGED(1974, Can.)

Mike Moore
KNIVES OF THE AVENGER(1967, Ital.)

Millie Moore
GREAT TEXAS DYNAMITE CHASE, THE(1976), ed; JOE PANTHER(1976), ed; GO
TELL THE SPARTANS(1978), ed; STARSHIP INVASIONS(1978, Can.), ed; THOSE
LIPS, THOSE EYES(1980), ed; HALLOWEEN III: SEASON OF THE WITCH(1982), ed

Milton Moore
Silents
DON'T GET PERSONAL(1922), ph; DAUGHTERS OF TODAY(1924), ph; HE WHO
GETS SLAPPED(1924), ph; GOOSE WOMAN, THE(1925), ph; PASSIONATE
YOUTH(1925), ph; STELLA MARIS(1925), ph; COLLEGE DAYS(1926), ph; JOS-
SELYN'S WIFE(1926), ph; REDHEADS PREFERRED(1926), ph; ONE HOUR OF
LOVE(1927), ph; OUT OF THE PAST(1927), ph; WEB OF FATE(1927), ph

Monette Moore
YES SIR, MR. BONES(1951)

Muriel Moore
1984
BEAR, THE(1984)

Nam Moore
1984
MISSING IN ACTION(1984)

Nancy Moore
LUSTY MEN, THE(1952); SON OF SINBAD(1955)

Neal Moore
9/30/55(1977)

Nicholas Moore
IT HAPPENED HERE(1966, Brit.)

Nora Moore
Silents
KING'S GAME, THE(1916)

Norma Moore
FEAR STRIKES OUT(1957); UNWED MOTHER(1958); SCUM OF THE EARTH(1976)

Olga Moore
YOU CAN'T BEAT LOVE(1937), w

Owen Moore
HIGH VOLTAGE(1929); SIDE STREET(1929); EXTRAVAGANCE(1930); OUTSIDE
THE LAW(1930); WHAT A WIDOW(1930); HUSH MONEY(1931); AS YOU DESIRE
ME(1932); MAN OF SENTIMENT, A(1933); SHE DONE HIM WRONG(1933); STAR IS
BORN, A(1937)
Silents
BATTLE OF THE SEXES, THE(1914); ESCAPE, THE(1914); HOME SWEET HO-
ME(1914); CINDERELLA(1915); JORDAN IS A HARD ROAD(1915); MADCAP BET-
TY(1915); MISTRESS NELL(1915); NEARLY A LADY(1915); PRETTY MRS.
SMITH(1915); KISS, THE(1916); LOVE IS AN AWFUL THING(1922); REPORTED
MISSING(1922), a, w; SILENT PARTNER, THE(1923); EAST OF BROADWAY(1924);
TORMENT(1924); BLACK BIRD, THE(1926); ROAD TO MANDALAY, THE(1926);
SKYROCKET, THE(1926); HUSBANDS FOR RENT(1927); RED MILL, THE(1927);
TAXI DANCER, THE(1927); TEA FOR THREE(1927); ACTRESS, THE(1928)
Misc. Silents
CAPRICE(1913); AFTERMATH(1914); HELP WANTED(1915); TWAS EVER
THUS(1915); BETTY OF GRAYSTONE(1916); CONEY ISLAND PRINCESS, A(1916);
LITTLE MEENA'S ROMANCE(1916); ROLLING STONES(1916); SUSAN ROCKS THE
BOAT(1916); UNDER COVER(1916); GIRL LIKE THAT, A(1917); LITTLE BOY SCOUT,
THE(1917); CRIMSON GARDENIA, THE(1919); DESPERATE HERO, THE(1920);
PICCADILLY JIM(1920); POOR SIMP, THE(1920); SOONER OR LATER(1920); CHICK-
EN IN THE CASE, THE(1921); DIVORCE OF CONVENIENCE, A(1921); OH, MABEL
BEHAVE(1922); HER TEMPORARY HUSBAND(1923); MODERN MATRIMO-
NY(1923); THUNDERGATE(1923); CAMILLE OF THE BARBARY COAST(1925);

CODE OF THE WEST(1925); GO STRAIGHT(1925); PARASITE, THE(1925); FALSE
PRIDE(1926); MARRIED?(1926); MONEY TALKS(1926); BECKY(1927); WOMEN
LOVE DIAMONDS(1927); STOLEN LOVE(1928)

Pat Moore
GODLESS GIRL, THE(1929); CRUSADES, THE(1935); WHERE THE BULLETS
FLY(1966, Brit.), spec eff; THOSE FANTASTIC FLYING FOOLS(1967, Brit), spec eff;
LONG DAY'S DYING, THE(1968, Brit.), spec eff; ITALIAN JOB, THE(1969, Brit.), spec
eff; LAST GRENADE, THE(1970, Brit.), spec eff; LAST VALLEY, THE(1971, Brit.),
spec eff; RAILWAY CHILDREN, THE(1971, Brit.), spec eff; INNOCENT BYSTAND-
ERS(1973, Brit.), spec eff
Silents
SAHARA(1919); QUEEN OF SHEBA, THE(1921); IMPOSSIBLE MRS. BELLEW,
THE(1922); NEW TEACHER, THE(1922); STEPHEN STEPS OUT(1923); TOP OF NEW
YORK, THE(1925); APRIL FOOL(1926)
Misc. Silents
YOUNG RAHAH, THE(1922); OLD SWEETHEART OF MINE, AN(1923); LOVER OF
CAMILLE, THE(1924)

Patricia Moore
Misc. Talkies
YOUNG MAN'S BRIDE, THE(1968)

Patrick Moore
RESTLESS ONES, THE(1965)
1984
OXFORD BLUES(1984), ed

Patti Moore
SHADOW OF THE THIN MAN(1941); WHEN THE BOYS MEET THE GIRLS(1965)

Patty Moore
HER HIGHNESS AND THE BELLBOY(1945)

Paul Moore
SILENT WITNESS, THE(1962)

Paulina Moore
COLORADO(1940)

Pauline Moore
FRANKENSTEIN(1931); WAGON WHEELS(1934); BORN RECKLESS(1937);
CHARLIE CHAN AT THE OLYMPICS(1937); HEIDI(1937); LOVE IS NEWS(1937);
WILD AND WOOLLY(1937); ARIZONA WILDCAT(1938); FIVE OF A KIND(1938);
PASSPORT HUSBAND(1938); THREE BLIND MICE(1938); CHARLIE CHAN AT
TREASURE ISLAND(1939); CHARLIE CHAN IN RENO(1939); DAYS OF JESSE
JAMES(1939); THREE MUSKETEERS, THE(1939); YOUNG MR. LINCOLN(1939);
CARSON CITY KID(1940); TRAIL BLAZERS, THE(1940); YOUNG BUFFALO
BILL(1940); ARKANSAS JUDGE(1941); DOUBLE CROSS(1941); SPOILERS OF THE
FOREST(1957); LITTLEST HOBO, THE(1958)

Percy Moore
Misc. Silents
SHOCK PUNCH, THE(1925)

Peter Moore
INVADERS, THE,(1941)

Phil Moore
SOME OF MY BEST FRIENDS ARE...(1971), m

Randy Moore
JUST BEFORE DAWN(1980), art d; T.A.G.: THE ASSASSINATION GAME(1982), art
d; ONE DARK NIGHT(1983), art d
1984
SUBURBIA(1984), art d

Ray C. Moore
SEPIA CINDERELLA(1947)

Ray Moore
TEST PILOT(1938), ph

Red Moore
THEY'RE A WEIRD MOB(1966, Aus.)

Renato Moore
PROPHECY(1979)

Rex Moore
MURDER WITH PICTURES(1936); THEODORA GOES WILD(1936); WEDDING
PRESENT(1936); EASY LIVING(1937); BLONDIE PLAYS CUPID(1940); MY FAVOR-
ITE BLONDE(1942); SHANE(1953)

Rica Owen Moore
DOCTOR, YOU'VE GOT TO BE KIDDING(1967)

Richard Moore
OPERATION CIA(1965), ph; WILD ANGELS, THE(1966), ph; DEVIL'S AN-
GELS(1967), ph; MARYJANE(1968), ph; SALLY'S HOUNDS(1968); SCALPHUNT-
ERS, THE(1968), ph; WILD IN THE STREETS(1968), ph; CHANGES(1969), ph;
REIVERS, THE(1969), ph; WINNING(1969), ph; WUSA(1970), ph; LONG AGO, TO-
MORROW(1971, Brit.); SOMETIMES A GREAT NOTION(1971), ph; LIFE AND TIMES
OF JUDGE ROY BEAN, THE(1972), ph; OFFENSE, THE(1973, Brit.); STONE KILLER,
THE(1973), ph; CIRCLE OF IRON(1979, Brit.), d; HOPSCOTCH(1980); ANNIE(1982),
ph

Robert Moore
LANDSLIDE(1937, Brit.); GREEN FINGERS(1947); UNEASY TERMS(1948, Brit.);
GLORY AT SEA(1952, Brit.); SCOTLAND YARD INSPECTOR(1952, Brit.); WALLET,
THE(1952, Brit.); FORCES' SWEETHEART(1953, Brit.); GHOST SHIP(1953, Brit.);
LADYKILLERS, THE(1956, Brit.); BLOOD OF DRACULA(1957), ed; HIDE AND
SEEK(1964, Brit.); JIG SAW(1965, Brit.); WHAT'S SO BAD ABOUT FEELING
GOOD?(1968); TELL ME THAT YOU LOVE ME, JUNIE MOON(1970); MURDER BY
DEATH(1976), d; CHEAP DETECTIVE, THE(1978), d; CHAPTER TWO(1979), d; END-
LESS LOVE(1981)

Robin Moore
GREEN BERETS, THE(1968), w; FRENCH CONNECTION, THE(1971), w; HAPPY
HOOKER, THE(1975), w; INCHON(1981), w

Robyn Moore
DOT AND THE BUNNY(1983, Aus.)
1984
CAMEL BOY, THE(1984, Aus.)

Roger Moore
DOUBLE WEDDING(1937); FIRST 100 YEARS, THE(1938); OF HUMAN
HEARTS(1938); THUNDER AFLOAT(1939); SHADOW OF THE THIN MAN(1941);
NAZI AGENT(1942); PANAMA HATTIE(1942); GIRL CRAZY(1943); MEET THE
PEOPLE(1944); VACATION FROM MARRIAGE(1945, Brit.); FULLER BRUSH
MAN(1948); HOMECOMING(1948); LUXURY LINER(1948); PICCADILLY IN-
CIDENT(1948, Brit.); SHOWTIME(1948, Brit.); SOUTHERN YANKEE, A(1948); STATE

OF THE UNION(1948); EAST SIDE, WEST SIDE(1949); FRANCIS(1949); GAL WHO TOOK THE WEST, THE(1949); GAY LADY, THE(1949, Brit.); PAPER ORCHID(1949, Brit.); WHIRLPOOL(1949); DUCHESS OF IDAHO, THE(1950); FATHER OF THE BRIDE(1950); KEY TO THE CITY(1950); AS YOUNG AS YOU FEEL(1951); IT'S A BIG COUNTRY(1951); LET'S MAKE IT LEGAL(1951); STRIP, THE(1951); TOO YOUNG TO KISS(1951); MEET ME AT THE FAIR(1952); MONKEY BUSINESS(1952); STARS AND STRIPES FOREVER(1952); CLOWN, THE(1953); DANGEROUS WHEN WET(1953); PICKUP ON SOUTH STREET(1953); SCANDAL AT SCOURIE(1953); LAST TIME I SAW PARIS, THE(1954); DIANE(1955); INTERRUPTED MELODY(1955); KING'S THIEF, THE(1955); MIRACLE, THE(1959); SINS OF RACHEL CADE, THE(1960); GOLD OF THE SEVEN SAINTS(1961); CROSSPLOT(1969, Brit.); MAN WHO HAUNTED HIMSELF, THE(1970, Brit.); LIVE AND LET DIE(1973, Brit.), a, stunts; GOLD(1974, Brit.); MAN WITH THE GOLDEN GUN, THE(1974, Brit.); THAT LUCKY TOUCH(1975, Brit.); SHOUT AT THE DEVIL(1976, Brit.); STREET PEOPLE(1976, U.S./Ital.); SPY WHO LOVED ME, THE(1977, Brit.); WILD GEESE, THE(1978, Brit.); ESCAPE TO ATHENA(1979, Brit.); MOONRAKER(1979, Brit.); FFOLKES(1980, Brit.); CANNONBALL RUN, THE(1981); FOR YOUR EYES ONLY(1981); SEA WOLVES, THE(1981, Brit.); CURSE OF THE PINK PANTHER(1983); OCTOPUSSY(1983, Brit.)
1984
NAKED FACE, THE(1984)
Misc. Talkies
MISSION: MONTE CARLO(1981, Brit.)
Rowland Moore
Misc. Silents
VICE AND VIRTUE; OR, THE TEMPTERS OF LONDON(1915, Brit.)
Roy Moore
HIDDEN GOLD(1933); BLACK CHRISTMAS(1974, Can.), w
Rudy Ray Moore
DOLEMITE(1975), a, p, set d; HUMAN TORNADO, THE(1976), a, p; MONKEY HUSTLE, THE(1976); PETEY WHEATSTRAW(1978)
Misc. Talkies
DISCO GODFATHER(1979)
Ruth Moore
CITIZEN SAINT(1947); DEEP WATERS(1948), w
Sabrina Lee Moore
WORLD ACCORDING TO GARP, The(1982)
Sally Moore
TOYS ARE NOT FOR CHILDREN(1972)
Sam Moore
BRIDE, THE(1973), ed
Samuel Taylor Moore
DEAD MARCH, THE(1937), w
Scott Moore
STRUGGLE, THE(1931); HOUSE ON 92ND STREET, THE(1945)
Sharon Moore
1984
WOMAN IN RED, THE(1984)
Sherry Moore
HARRY AND WALTER GO TO NEW YORK(1976)
Sidney Moore
GANGSTER, THE(1947), set d
Smoky [Dennis] Moore
OVERLAND STAGECOACH(1942)
Stanley Moore
SQUEEZE A FLOWER(1970, Aus.), ed
Misc. Talkies
CONDEMNED MEN(1940); UP JUMPED THE DEVIL(1941); DREAMER, THE(1947); COME ON, COWBOY!(1948); SHE'S TOO MEAN TO ME(1948)
Stella Moore
ONCE A LADY(1931)
Stephen Moore
MIDSUMMERS NIGHT'S DREAM, A(1961, Czech); LAST SHOT YOU HEAR, THE(1969, Brit.); ROUGH CUT(1980, Brit.)
1984
LAUGHTER HOUSE(1984, Brit.); WHERE THE BOYS ARE '84(1984)
Sue Moore
AFTER THE THIN MAN(1936); GOLD IS WHERE YOU FIND IT(1938); SWING YOUR LADY(1938); MORTAL STORM, THE(1940); CHEERS FOR MISS BISHOP(1941); HENRY ALDRICH PLAYS CUPID(1944); ADVENTURE(1945); PILLOW TO POST(1945); RECKLESS MOMENTS, THE(1949)
Susanna Moore
SHAMPOO(1975); DEAD KIDS(1981 Aus./New Zealand), prod d, set d; STRANGE INVADERS(1983), prod d, cos
Sybil Moore
Misc. Silents
RICHTOFEN(1932, Ger.)
Syd Moore
DESERT FURY(1947), set d; WHERE THERE'S LIFE(1947), set d
Sydney Moore
PARIS UNDERGROUND(1945), set d
Ted Moore
COCKLESHELL HEROES, THE(1955), ph; PRIZE OF GOLD, A(1955), ph; GAMMA PEOPLE, THE(1956), ph; ODONGO(1956, Brit.), ph; ZARAK(1956, Brit.), ph; HIGH FLIGHT(1957, Brit.), ph; HOW TO MURDER A RICH UNCLE(1957, Brit.), ph; PICKUP ALLEY(1957, Brit.), ph; MAN INSIDE, THE(1958, Brit.), ph; TANK FORCE(1958, Brit.), ph; BANDIT OF ZHOBE, THE(1959), ph; IDOL ON PARADE(1959, Brit.), ph; IN THE NICK(1960, Brit.), ph; KILLERS OF KILIMANJARO(1960, Brit.), ph; LET'S GET MARRIED(1960, Brit.), ph; MAN WITH THE GREEN CARNATION, THE(1960, Brit.), ph; DR. NO(1962, Brit.), ph; HELLIONS, THE(1962, Brit.), ph; MIX ME A PERSON(1962, Brit.), ph; CALL ME BWANA(1963, Brit.), ph; DAY OF THE TRIFFIDS, THE(1963), ph; FROM RUSSIA WITH LOVE(1963, Brit.), ph; NINE HOURS TO RAMA(1963, U.S./Brit.), ph; GOLDFINGER(1964, Brit.), ph; AMOROUS ADVENTURES OF MOLL FLANDERS, THE(1965), ph; JOHNNY NOBODY(1965, Brit.), ph; THUNDERBALL(1965, Brit.), ph; MAN FOR ALL SEASONS, A(1966, Brit.), ph; LAST SAFARI, THE(1967, Brit.), ph; PRUDENCE AND THE PILL(1968, Brit.), ph; SHALAKO(1968, Brit.), ph; PRIME OF MISS JEAN BRODIE, THE(1969, Brit.), ph; BROTHERLY LOVE(1970, Brit.), ph; DIAMONDS ARE FOREVER(1971, Brit.), ph; LIVE AND LET DIE(1973, Brit.), ph; GOLDEN VOYAGE OF SINBAD, THE(1974, Brit.), ph; MAN WITH THE GOLDEN GUN, THE(1974, Brit.), ph; PSYCHOMANIA(1974, Brit.), ph; ORCA(1977), ph; SINBAD AND THE EYE OF THE TIGER(1977, U.S./Brit.), ph;

CLASH OF THE TITANS(1981), ph; PRIEST OF LOVE(1981, Brit.), ph
Tedde Moore
SECOND WIND(1976, Can.); CHRISTMAS STORY, A(1983)
Teddi Moore
MURDER BY DECREE(1979, Brit.)
Teddy Moore
RIP-OFF(1971, Can.)
Terrence Moore
Silents
TEN COMMANDMENTS, THE(1923)
Terry Jean Moore
LOVE CHILD(1982)
Terry Moore
TRUE TO LIFE(1943); GASLIGHT(1944); SINCE YOU WENT AWAY(1944); SWEET AND LOWDOWN(1944); SHADOWED(1946); RETURN OF OCTOBER, THE(1948); SUMMER HOLIDAY(1948); MIGHTY JOE YOUNG(1949); GAMBLING HOUSE(1950); GREAT RUPERT, THE(1950); HE'S A COCKEYED WONDER(1950); BAREFOOT MAILMAN, THE(1951); SUNNY SIDE OF THE STREET(1951); TWO OF A KIND(1951); COME BACK LITTLE SHEBA(1952); BENEATH THE 12-MILE REEF(1953); KING OF THE KHYBER RIFLES(1953); MAN ON A TIGHTROPE(1953); DADDY LONG LEGS(1955); SHACK OUT ON 101(1955); BETWEEN HEAVEN AND HELL(1956); POSTMARK FOR DANGER(1956, Brit.); BERNARDINE(1957); PEYTON PLACE(1957); CAST A LONG SHADOW(1959); PRIVATE'S AFFAIR, A(1959); PLATINUM HIGH SCHOOL(1960); WHY MUST I DIE?(1960); BLACK SPURS(1965); CITY OF FEAR(1965, Brit.); TOWN TAMER(1965); WACO(1966); MAN CALLED DAGGER, A(1967); DAREDEVIL, THE(1971); DOUBLE EXPOSURE(1982)
Thomas Moore
LITTLE COLONEL, THE(1935), m; BLACK KNIGHT, THE(1954); DOG DAY AFTERNOON(1975), w; GREAT WHITE, THE(1982, Ital.)
1984
WARRIORS OF THE WASTELAND(1984, Ital.)
Silents
KATHLEEN MAVOURNEEN(1919), w
Tim Moore
BOY! WHAT A GIRL(1947)
Misc. Silents
HIS GREAT CHANCE(1923)
Tina Moore
GAL YOUNG UN(1979)
Tom Moore
SIDE STREET(1929); COSTELLO CASE, THE(1930); WOMAN RACKET, THE(1930); LAST PARADE, THE(1931); CANNONBALL EXPRESS(1932); MEN ARE SUCH FOOLS(1933); NEIGHBORS' WIVES(1933); BOMBAY MAIL(1934); DARK ANGEL, THE(1935); PAROLE(1936); REUNION(1936); TROUBLE FOR TWO(1936); TEN LAPS TO GO(1938); BEHIND GREEN LIGHTS(1946); MOSS ROSE(1947); MOTHER WORE TIGHTS(1947); SHOCKING MISS PILGRIM, THE(1947); CRY OF THE CITY(1948); ROAD HOUSE(1948); SCUDDA-HOO! SCUDDA-HAY!(1948); WALLS OF JERICHO(1948); FIGHTING O'FLYNN, THE(1949); REDHEAD AND THE COWBOY, THE(1950); TURNING POINT, THE(1952); NATCHEZ TRACE(1960); KARATE, THE HAND OF DEATH(1961); MARK OF THE WITCH(1970), p, d; RETURN TO BOGGY CREEK(1977), d
Silents
FAIR PRETENDER, THE(1918); JUST FOR TONIGHT(1918); GO WEST, YOUNG MAN(1919); STOP THIEF(1920); BEATING THE GAME(1921); FROM THE GROUND UP(1921); MADE IN HEAVEN(1921); OVER THE BORDER(1922); ADVENTURE(1925); ON THIN ICE(1925); PRETTY LADIES(1925); GOOD AND NAUGHTY(1926); KISS FOR CINDERELLA, A(1926); SYNCOPATING SUE(1926)
Misc. Silents
SECRET ROOM, THE(1915), a, d; DOLLARS AND THE WOMAN(1916); BROWN IN HARVARD(1917); JAGUAR'S CLAWS(1917); LESSON, THE(1917); LITTLE MISS OPTIMIST(1917); PRIMROSE RING, THE(1917); CINDERELLA MAN, THE(1918); DANGER GAME, THE(1918); DODGING A MILLION(1918); FLOOR BELOW, THE(1918); KINGDOM OF YOUTH, THE(1918); THIRTY A WEEK(1918); CITY OF COMRADES, THE(1919); HEARTSEASE(1919); LORD AND LADY ALGY(1919); MAN AND HIS MONEY, A(1919); ONE OF THE FINEST(1919); TOBY'S BOW(1919); DUDS(1920); GAY LORD QUEX, THE(1920); GREAT ACCIDENT, THE(1920); OFFICER 666(1920); HOLD YOUR HORSES(1921); COWBOY AND THE LADY, THE(1922); MR. BARNES OF NEW YORK(1922); PAWNED(1922); BIG BROTHER(1923); HARBOUR LIGHTS, THE(1923, Brit.); MARRIAGE MORALS(1923); ROUGED LIPS(1923); DANGEROUS MONEY(1924); MANHANDLED(1924); ONE NIGHT IN ROME(1924); TROUBLE WITH WIVES, THE(1925); UNDER THE ROUGE(1925); CLINGING VINE, THE(1926); SONG AND DANCE MAN, THE(1926); CABARET(1927); LOVE THRILL, THE(1927); SIREN, THE(1927); WISE WIFE, THE(1927); ANYBODY HERE SEEN KELLY?(1928); HIS LAST HAUL(1928); YELLOWBACK, THE(1929)
Tommie Moore
BAND OF ANGELS(1957); GREEN-EYED BLONDE, THE(1957)
Misc. Talkies
BROKEN STRINGS(1940); MYSTERY IN SWING(1940)
Unice Vin Moore
Silents
LITTLE EVA ASCENDS(1922)
Misc. Silents
TRIP TO PARADISE, A(1921)
Unity Moore
Silents
JO THE CROSSING SWEEPER(1918, Brit.)
Vernetties Moore
BETRAYAL, THE(1948)
Victor Moore
TRUE TO LIFE(1943); DANGEROUS NAN McGREW(1930); HEADS UP(1930); GIFT OF GAB(1934); ROMANCE IN THE RAIN(1934); GOLD DIGGERS OF 1937(1936); SWING TIME(1936); LIFE OF THE PARTY, THE(1937); MAKE WAY FOR TOMORROW(1937); MEET THE MISSUS(1937); WE'RE ON THE JURY(1937); RADIO CITY REVELS(1938); SHE'S GOT EVERYTHING(1938); THIS MARRIAGE BUSINESS(1938); LOUISIANA PURCHASE(1941); STAR SPANGLED RHYTHM(1942); HEAT'S ON, THE(1943); RIDING HIGH(1943); THIS IS THE ARMY(1943); CAROLINA BLUES(1944); DUFFY'S TAVERN(1945); IT'S IN THE BAG(1945); ZIEGFELD FOLLIES(1945); IT HAPPENED ON 5TH AVENUE(1947); ON OUR MERRY WAY(1948); KISS IN THE DARK, A(1949); WE'RE NOT MARRIED(1952); SEVEN YEAR ITCH, THE(1955)

Silents
CHIMMIE FADDEN(1915); CHIMMIE FADDEN OUT WEST(1915); SNOBS(1915); RACE, THE(1916)
Misc. Silents
CLOWN, THE(1916)
Victoria Moore
Silents
POLICE PATROL, THE(1925), w
Vin Moore
COHENS AND KELLYS IN AFRICA, THE(1930), d, w; SEE AMERICA THIRST(1930), w; EX-BAD BOY(1931), d; MANY A SLIP(1931), d; VIRTUOUS HUSBAND(1931), d; RACING YOUTH(1932), d; LOVE PAST THIRTY(1934), p; FLIRTING WITH DANGER(1935), d; CHEERS OF THE CROWD(1936), d; KILLERS OF THE WILD(1940), d; COVER GIRL(1944)
Misc. Talkies
TOPA TOPA(1938), d
Silents
LAZY LIGHTNING(1926); PAINTING THE TOWN(1927), w; BEAUTY AND BULLETS(1928), w; GATE CRASHER, THE(1928), w; KID'S CLEVER, THE(1929), w
Viola Moore
LOVE ON THE RUN(1936); WE ARE NOT ALONE(1939); I MARRIED A WITCH(1942); THUNDER BIRDS(1942); HOUR BEFORE THE DAWN, THE(1944)
W. Eugene Moore
Silents
OVAL DIAMOND, THE(1916), d
Misc. Silents
MILL ON THE FLOSS, THE(1915), a, d; HER FATHER'S GOLD(1916), d; WOMAN IN POLITICS, THE(1916), d; CANDY GIRL, THE(1917), d; CAPTAIN KIDDO(1917), d; POTS AND PANS PEGGIE(1917), d; WHEN BABY FORGOT(1917), d; SUE OF THE SOUTH(1919), d
Wilfred G. Moore
SKY PARADE(1936), w
Wilfred Moore
LAST SAFARI, THE(1967, Brit.)
William Moore [Peter Potter]
RED SALUTE(1935)
William I. Moore
1984
PHILADELPHIA EXPERIMENT, THE(1984), w
William Moore
NAUGHTY MARIETTA(1935); ROSE BOWL(1936); HOLY TERROR, THE(1937); LOVE TAKES FLIGHT(1937); INTERNATIONAL CRIME(1938); MR. BOGGS STEPS OUT(1938); FIVE DAYS FROM HOME(1978), w; BLACK JACK(1979, Brit.)
William M. Moore
JET PILOT(1957), ed
Olive Moorefield
UNCLE TOM'S CABIN(1969, Fr./Ital./Ger./Yugo.)
Agnes Moorehead
CITIZEN KANE(1941); BIG STREET, THE(1942); JOURNEY INTO FEAR(1942); MAGNIFICENT AMBERSONS, THE(1942); GOVERNMENT GIRL(1943); YOUNGEST PROFESSION, THE(1943); DRAGON SEED(1944); JANE EYRE(1944); MRS. PARKINGTON(1944); SEVENTH CROSS, THE(1944); SINCE YOU WENT AWAY(1944); TOMORROW THE WORLD(1944); HER HIGHNESS AND THE BELLBOY(1945); KEEP YOUR POWDER DRY(1945); OUR VINES HAVE TENDER GRAPES(1945); DARK PASSAGE(1947); LOST MOMENT, THE(1947); JOHNNY BELINDA(1948); STATION WEST(1948); SUMMER HOLIDAY(1948); WOMAN IN WHITE, THE(1948); GREAT SINNER, THE(1949); STRATTON STORY, THE(1949); WITHOUT HONOR(1949); CAGED(1950); ADVENTURES OF CAPTAIN FABIAN(1951); BLUE VEIL, THE(1951); FOURTEEN HOURS(1951); SHOW BOAT(1951); BLAZING FOREST, THE(1952); CAPTAIN BLACK JACK(1952, U.S./Fr.); MAIN STREET TO BROADWAY(1953); SCANDAL AT SCOURIE(1953); STORY OF THREE LOVES, THE(1953); THOSE REDHEADS FROM SEATTLE(1953); MAGNIFICENT OBSESSION(1954); ALL THAT HEAVEN ALLOWS(1955); LEFT HAND OF GOD, THE(1955); UNTAMED(1955); CONQUEROR, THE(1956); OPPOSITE SEX, THE(1956); PARDNERS(1956); REVOLT OF MAMIE STOVER, THE(1956); SWAN, THE(1956); JEANNE EAGELS(1957); RAINTREE COUNTY(1957); STORY OF MANKIND, THE(1957); TRUE STORY OF JESSE JAMES, THE(1957); TEMPEST(1958, Ital./Yugo./Fr.); BAT, THE(1959); NIGHT OF THE QUARTER MOON(1959); POLLYANNA(1960); BACHELOR IN PARADISE(1961); TWENTY PLUS TWO(1961); HOW THE WEST WAS WON(1962); JESSICA(1962, U.S./Ital./Fr.); WHO'S MINDING THE STORE?(1963); HUSH... HUSH, SWEET CHARLOTTE(1964); SINGING NUN, THE(1966); WHAT'S THE MATTER WITH HELEN?(1971); DEAR, DEAD DELILAH(1972); CHARLOTTE'S WEB(1973)
Alan Moorehead
THUNDER IN THE EAST(1953), w
Brian Moorehead
FUSS OVER FEATHERS(1954, Brit.)
Jean Moorehead
VIOLENT YEARS, THE(1956); AMAZING COLOSSAL MAN, THE(1957)
Natalie Moorehead
RUNAWAY BRIDE(1930); SHADOW OF THE LAW(1930); SECRET SINNERS(1933)
Bert Moorehouse
DELIGHTFUL HOGUE(1929); PAY OFF, THE(1930); SMARTY(1934); RENDEZVOUS(1935); LAKE PLACID SERENADE(1944); LADY ON A TRAIN(1945); SHADY LADY(1945); IT'S A WONDERFUL LIFE(1946); NOCTURNE(1946); UNDERCURRENT(1946); BIG CLOCK, THE(1948); GOOD SAM(1948); I WALK ALONE(1948); SOUTHERN YANKEE, A(1948); DANGEROUS MISSION(1954)
Silents
HEY RUBE!(1928)
Misc. Silents
ROUGH RIDIN' RED(1928)
Clarence Moorehouse
CIRCUS KID, THE(1928); SO THIS IS AFRICA(1933)
De Sacia Moores
Silents
BY WHOSE HAND?(1927)
Frank Moorey
LADY CHATTERLEY'S LOVER(1981, Fr./Brit.)

Agnes Moorhead
MEET ME IN LAS VEGAS(1956)
Brian Moorhead
NORMAN CONQUEST(1953, Brit.)
Jean Moorhead
FRENCH LINE, THE(1954); LONG GRAY LINE, THE(1955); MOTORCYCLE GANG(1957); ATTACK OF THE PUPPET PEOPLE(1958); GUNMEN FROM LAREDO(1959); ATOMIC SUBMARINE, THE(1960)
Natalie Moorhead
GIRL FROM HAVANA, THE(1929); THRU DIFFERENT EYES(1929); UNHOLY NIGHT, THE(1929); BENSON MURDER CASE, THE(1930); FURIES, THE(1930); HOOK, LINE AND SINKER(1930); HOT CURVES(1930); LADIES MUST PLAY(1930); MANSLAUGHTER(1930); OFFICE WIFE, THE(1930); SPRING IS HERE(1930); CAPTAIN THUNDER(1931); DANCE, FOOLS, DANCE(1931); DECEIVER, THE(1931); DIVORCE AMONG FRIENDS(1931); ILLICIT(1931); MAKER OF MEN(1931); MORALS FOR WOMEN(1931); MY PAST(1931); PARLOR, BEDROOM AND BATH(1931); PHANTOM OF PARIS, THE(1931); STRICTLY DISHONORABLE(1931); WOMEN MEN MARRY(1931); CROSS-EXAMINATION(1932); DISCARDED LOVERS(1932); FIGHTING GENTLEMAN, THE(1932); KING MURDER, THE(1932); LOVE BOUND(1932); MENACE, THE(1932); STOKER, THE(1932); THREE WISE GIRLS(1932); BIG CHANCE, THE(1933); CORRUPTION(1933); DANCE MALL HOSTESS(1933); FORGOTTEN(1933); GIGOLETTES OF PARIS(1933); MIND READER, THE(1933); ONLY YESTERDAY(1933); PRIVATE DETECTIVE 62(1933); CURTAIN AT EIGHT(1934); DANCING MAN(1934); FIFTEEN WIVES(1934); LONG LOST FATHER(1934); THIN MAN, THE(1934); CURTAIN FALLS, THE(1935); ADVENTUROUS BLONDE(1937); KING OF GAMBLERS(1937); BELOVED BRAT(1938); HEART OF ARIZONA(1938); LETTER OF INTRODUCTION(1938); LADY OF THE TROPICS(1939); WHEN TOMORROW COMES(1939); WOMEN, THE(1939); ALL THIS AND HEAVEN TOO(1940); FLIGHT ANGELS(1940); I TAKE THIS WOMAN(1940); I WANT A DIVORCE(1940); MARGIE(1940)
Bert Moorhouse
MAN WITH TWO FACES, THE(1934); UPPER WORLD(1934); LOVE BEFORE BREAKFAST(1936); ROSE BOWL(1936); WHIPSAW(1936); HIDEAWAY GIRL(1937); DANCING CO-ED(1939); IN NAME ONLY(1939); MY FAVORITE WIFE(1940); MONSTER AND THE GIRL, THE(1941); JOAN OF OZARK(1942); AIR RAID WARDENS(1943); GOVERNMENT GIRL(1943); FALCON IN HOLLYWOOD, THE(1944); HEAVENLY DAYS(1944); MUSIC IN MANHATTAN(1944); MY PAL, WOLF(1944); NEVADA(1944); SHOW BUSINESS(1944); LADY LUCK(1946); NIGHT AND DAY(1946); SMOOTH AS SILK(1946); WHITE TIE AND TAILS(1946); LADY IN THE LAKE(1947); HE WALKED BY NIGHT(1948); HOMECOMING(1948); STATE OF THE UNION(1948); UP IN CENTRAL PARK(1948); SAMSON AND DELILAH(1949); GAMBLING HOUSE(1950); SECRET FURY, THE(1950); SUNSET BOULEVARD(1950); BIG CARNIVAL, THE(1951); I WAS A COMMUNIST FOR THE F.B.I.(1951); DESTINATION GOBI(1953); DREAM WIFE(1953); CRIME WAVE(1954)
Leslie Moorhouse
WALK THE ANGRY BEACH(1961)
Jane Moorland [Mrs. C.P. Williams]
ROYAL DEMAND, A(1933, Brit.), w
Eliza Moorman
1984
TORCHLIGHT(1984), w
Elizabeth Moorman
ELIZA'S HOROSCOPE(1975, Can.)
George Moorman
EXPERIMENT IN TERROR(1962); ZOTZ!(1962)
Trudy Moors
DAYLIGHT ROBBERY(1964, Brit.)
George Moorse
ZERO IN THE UNIVERSE(1966), a, d, w, ed
Chester Moorten
Silents
TWO FLAMING YOUTHS(1927)
Teddy Moorwood
MY SON, MY SON!(1940)
Ed Moose
PALM SPRINGS(1936)
William Moose
RED RUNS THE RIVER(1963)
Vahan Moosekian
VICE SQUAD(1982)
Daniel Moossmann
TESTAMENT OF ORPHEUS, THE(1962, Fr.)
Ursula Moot [Mood]
NEW LIFE STYLE, THE(1970, Ger.)
Margaret Mooth
WHITE SISTER, THE(1933), ed
Donna Cregan Moots
MA AND PA KETTLE AT HOME(1954)
Avram Mor
SINAI COMMANDOS: THE STORY OF THE SIX DAY WAR(1968, Israel/Ger.)
Tikva Mor
TRUNK TO CAIRO(1966, Israel/Ger.); SIMCHON FAMILY, THE(1969, Israel)
Brad Mora
MONKEY BUSINESS(1952); RETURN OF THE TEXAN(1952); FARMER TAKES A WIFE, THE(1953); VANQUISHED, THE(1953)
Bradley Mora
ANNIE GET YOUR GUN(1950); CAUSE FOR ALARM(1951)
Camilla Mora
STATE OF THINGS, THE(1983)
Carmen Mora
NAKED MAJA, THE(1959, Ital./U.S.)
Danny Mora
MR. MOM(1983)
1984
OH GOD! YOU DEVIL(1984)
Gerda Mora
STAGE DOOR(1937)

Jane Mora
VAMPYR(1932, Fr./Ger.)
Katherine Mora
STRANGER AT MY DOOR(1950, Brit.)
Marlo Mora
GLORY BRIGADE, THE(1953), ed
Nick Mora
SERENADE(1956)
Norma Mora
LOS ASTRONAUTAS(1960, Mex.); SANTO EN EL MUSEO DE CERA(1963, Mex.)
Philippe Mora
MAD DOG MORGAN(1976,Aus.), d&w; RETURN OF CAPTAIN INVINCIBLE, THE(1983, Aus./U.S.), d
1984
BREED APART, A(1984), d
Phillipe Mora
BEAST WITHIN, THE(1982), d
Tiriel Mora
1984
STRIKEBOUND(1984, Aus.)
Tony Mora
WHERE DOES IT HURT?(1972), ed
Renato Morado
1984
MISSING IN ACTION(1984)
Tom N. Moraham
JAMAICA INN(1939, Brit.), set d
Morahan
MAGNET, THE(1950, Brit.), art d
Christopher Morahan
DIAMONDS FOR BREAKFAST(1968, Brit.), d; ALL NEAT IN BLACK STOCKINGS(1969, Brit.), d
James Morahan
MIND BENDERS, THE(1963, Brit.), art d
Jim Morahan
FRIEDA(1947, Brit.), art d; GIRL ON THE CANAL, THE(1947, Brit.), art d; SARABAND(1949, Brit.), art d; SCOTT OF THE ANTARCTIC(1949, Brit.), art d; TIGHT LITTLE ISLAND(1949, Brit.), art d; POOL OF LONDON(1951, Brit.), art d; GENTLE GUNMAN, THE(1952, Brit.), art d; HIS EXCELLENCY(1952, Brit.), art d; MAN IN THE WHITE SUIT, THE(1952), art d; TRAIN OF EVENTS(1952, Brit.), art d; LEASE OF LIFE(1954, Brit.), art d; WEST OF ZANZIBAR(1954, Brit.), art d; NIGHT MY NUMBER CAME UP, THE(1955, Brit.), art d; SQUARE RING, THE(1955, Brit.), art d; LADYKILLERS, THE(1956, Brit.), art d; WHO DONE IT?(1956, Brit.), art d; DECISION AGAINST TIME(1957, Brit.), art d; OUT OF THE CLOUDS(1957, Brit.), art d; SHIRALEE, THE(1957, Brit.), art d; DUNKIRK(1958, Brit.), art d; IT TAKES A THIEF(1960, Brit.), art d; LONG AND THE SHORT AND THE TALL, THE(1961, Brit.), art d; MARY HAD A LITTLE(1961, Brit.), art d; SEASON OF PASSION(1961, Aus./Brit.), art d; THOSE MAGNIFICENT MEN IN THEIR FLYING MACHINES; OR HOW I FLEWFROM LONDON TO PARIS IN 25 HOURS AND 11 MINUTES(1965, Brit.), art d; DUTCHMAN(1966, Brit.), art d; BATTLE BENEATH THE EARTH(1968, Brit.), art d; CONQUEROR WORM, THE(1968, Brit.), art d
Thomas Morahan
TREASURE ISLAND(1950, Brit.), prod d
Thomas H. Morahan
SO EVIL MY LOVE(1948, Brit.), art d
Tom Morahan
BLACK SHEEP OF WHITEHALL, THE(1941 Brit.), art d; NEXT OF KIN(1942, Brit.), art d; SOMEWHERE IN FRANCE(1943, Brit.), art d; ON APPROVAL(1944, Brit.), art d; 48 HOURS(1944, Brit.), art d; PARADINE CASE, THE(1947), art d; MR. PERRIN AND MR. TRAILL(1948, Brit.), art d; UNDER CAPRICORN(1949), art d; WHILE THE SUN SHINES(1950, Brit.), art d; RAINBOW JACKET, THE(1954, Brit.), art d; NIGHT MY NUMBER CAME UP, THE(1955, Brit.), p; THIRD KEY, THE(1957, Brit.), p; SHAKE HANDS WITH THE DEVIL(1959, Ireland), prod d; IT TAKES A THIEF(1960, Brit.), art d; SATAN NEVER SLEEPS(1962), prod d; THIRD SECRET, THE(1964, Brit.), prod d; THOSE MAGNIFICENT MEN IN THEIR FLYING MACHINES; OR HOW I FLEWFROM LONDON TO PARIS IN 25 HOURS AND 11 MINUTES(1965, Brit.), prod d; PLAY DIRTY(1969, Brit.), art d
Lyle Moraine
CHINA CLIPPER(1936); SING ME A LOVE SONG(1936); CONFESSION(1937); FEDERAL BULLETS(1937); MIDNIGHT COURT(1937); PORT OF MISSING GIRLS(1938); DIVE BOMBER(1941); CHICAGO DEADLINE(1949); SON OF PALEFACE(1952); SHEILA LEVINE IS DEAD AND LIVING IN NEW YORK(1975)
Lyle L. Moraine
MY FAVORITE SPY(1951)
T. Morakis
ASTERO(1960, Gr.), m
Takis Morakis
AUNT FROM CHICAGO(1960, Gr.), m
Angelica Morales
VIRGIN SACRIFICE(1959)
Antonia Morales
GOLDEN EARRINGS(1947)
Antonio Morales
DREAM GIRL(1947)
Carmen Morales
LONG VOYAGE HOME, THE(1940); PRIMROSE PATH(1940); AFFECTIONATELY YOURS(1941); TWO LATINS FROM MANHATTAN(1941); LADIES' DAY(1943); THEY LIVE BY NIGHT(1949)
David Morales
SECOND CHANCE(1953)
Delfino Morales
BRAVE BULLS, THE(1951)
Esai Morales
BAD BOYS(1983)
Esy Morales
CRISS CROSS(1949)
Francisco Morales
1984
SECRET PLACES(1984, Brit.)

Frank Morales
CROSSROADS(1942)
Hector Morales
FROM NOON TO THREE(1976); ONE ON ONE(1977); HERBIE GOES BANANAS(1980); LOSIN' IT(1983)
Hector M. Morales
SHOOT THE MOON(1982)
Hilda Morales
TURNING POINT, THE(1977)
Jacob Morales
BANANAS(1971)
Jacobo Morales
UP THE SANDBOX(1972)
James Morales
MOONSHINE COUNTY EXPRESS(1977)
Joe T. Morales
SALT OF THE EARTH(1954)
Jose Morales
VALDEZ IS COMING(1971)
Jose Luis Morales
WEREWOLF VS. THE VAMPIRE WOMAN, THE(1970, Span./Ger.), makeup
Leslie Morales
1984
MAKING THE GRADE(1984), set d
Mario Morales
LAST DAYS OF POMPEII, THE(1960, Ital.); PLANET OF THE VAMPIRES(1965, U.S./Ital./Span.)
Miguel Morales
SCARAB(1982, U.S./Span.), m
Patricia A. Morales
WALK PROUD(1979)
Santos Morales
MINNIE AND MOSKOWITZ(1971); SUNSHINE BOYS, THE(1975); FUN WITH DICK AND JANE(1977); THIEVES(1977); BOYS IN COMPANY C, THE(1978, U.S./Hong Kong); DEFIANCE(1980); FORT APACHE, THE BRONX(1981); CANNERY ROW(1982); I OUGHT TO BE IN PICTURES(1982); LOSIN' IT(1983); MAX DUGAN RETURNS(1983); ROMANTIC COMEDY(1983); SCARFACE(1983)
1984
LONELY GUY, THE(1984)
Sylvia Morales
SERPENTS OF THE PIRATE MOON, THE(1973)
Jacques Morali
CAN'T STOP THE MUSIC(1980), p, m
Ernesto Moralli
ST. VALENTINE'S DAY MASSACRE, THE(1967)
Alberto Moran
TOY WIFE, THE(1938)
Anita Moran
LOVE IS A CAROUSEL(1970)
Anthony Moran
PROUD AND THE PROFANE, THE(1956)
Betty Moran
ALL WOMEN HAVE SECRETS(1939); FRONTIER VENGEANCE(1939); RANGE WAR(1939); SEVENTEEN(1940)
Charles Moran
EXPOSED(1947), w
Christopher Moran
DAVID COPPERFIELD(1970, Brit.); UNMAN, WITTERING AND ZIGO(1971, Brit.)
Daisy Moran
BETTY CO-ED(1946)
Dolores Moran
WITHOUT RESERVATIONS(1946); YANKEE DOODLE DANDY(1942); OLD ACQUAINTANCE(1943); HOLLYWOOD CANTEEN(1944); TO HAVE AND HAVE NOT(1944); HORN BLOWS AT MIDNIGHT, THE(1945); TOO YOUNG TO KNOW(1945); MAN I LOVE, THE(1946); CHRISTMAS EVE(1947); JOHNNY ONE-EYE(1950); COUNT THE HOURS(1953); SILVER LODE(1954)
E. Edwin Moran
POWERS GIRL, THE(1942), w; TWIN BEDS(1942), w; WINTERTIME(1943), w; EVE KNEW HER APPLES(1945), w; HOLD THAT BLONDE(1945), w
Eddie Moran
TWO FISTED(1935), w; TOPPER(1937), w; MERRILY WE LIVE(1938), w; THERE GOES MY HEART(1938), w; TOPPER TAKES A TRIP(1939), w; MAN WHO LOST HIMSELF, THE(1941), w; WONDER MAN(1945), w; TREASURE ISLAND(1950, Brit.)
Edward Moran
Silents
GAY RETREAT, THE(1927), w
Erin Moran
HOW SWEET IT IS(1968); 80 STEPS TO JONAH(1969); WATERMELON MAN(1970); GALAXY OF TERROR(1981)
Misc. Talkies
MAGIC PONY(1979)
Everett Moran
Misc. Silents
WHISPERING WOMEN(1921)
Francesco Moran
FOUR MEN AND A PRAYER(1938)
Francisco Moran
BEASTS OF BERLIN(1939); KING OF KINGS(1961); CASTILIAN, THE(1963, Span./U.S.); PYRO(1964, U.S./Span.)
Frank Moran
ME AND MY GAL(1932); BOWERY, THE(1933); GAMBLING SHIP(1933); SAILOR'S LUCK(1933); SHE DONE HIM WRONG(1933); CHANGE OF HEART(1934); JUDGE PRIEST(1934); NO MORE WOMEN(1934); WORLD MOVES ON, THE(1934); DANTE'S INFERNO(1935); DON'T BET ON BLONDES(1935); INFORMER, THE(1935); PUBLIC HERO NO. 1(1935); STARS OVER BROADWAY(1935); SWELL-HEAD(1935); WE'RE IN THE MONEY(1935); FOLLOW THE FLEET(1936); IT HAD TO HAPPEN(1936); MODERN TIMES(1936); SYLVIA SCARLETT(1936); ANGEL'S HOLIDAY(1937); SHALL WE DANCE(1937); THIS IS MY AFFAIR(1937); JOY OF LIVING(1938); EAST SIDE OF HEAVEN(1939); LADY'S FROM KENTUCKY, THE(1939); TORCHY PLAYS WITH DYNAMITE(1939); CHRISTMAS IN JULY(1940); DATE WITH THE FALCON,

A(1941); FEDERAL FUGITIVES(1941); HIGH SIERRA(1941); KNOCKOUT(1941); LADY EVE, THE(1941); MEET JOHN DOE(1941); PENNY SERENADE(1941); SULLIVAN'S TRAVELS(1941); CORPSE VANISHES, THE(1942); MAN WHO CAME TO DINNER, THE(1942); PALM BEACH STORY, THE(1942); STAR SPANGLED RHYTHM(1942); GHOSTS ON THE LOOSE(1943); NO TIME FOR LOVE(1943); SALUTE FOR THREE(1943); GREAT MOMENT, THE(1944); HAIL THE CONQUERING HERO(1944); I LOVE A SOLDIER(1944); MAN FROM FRISCO(1944); MAN IN HALF-MOON STREET, THE(1944); MIRACLE OF MORGAN'S CREEK, THE(1944); PRINCESS AND THE PIRATE, THE(1944); RETURN OF THE APE MAN(1944); PARDON MY PAST(1945); ROAD TO UTOPIA(1945); CRACK-UP(1946); KID FROM BROOKLYN, THE(1946); WILD HARVEST(1947); ON OUR MERRY WAY(1948); UNFAITHFULLY YOURS(1948); FIGHTING FOOLS(1949); LADY GAMBLES, THE(1949); MAD WEDNESDAY(1950); IRON MAN, THE(1951); SQUARE JUNGLE, THE(1955)
Misc. Talkies
SIX GUN JUSTICE(1935)
Frank Moran [Francisco Moran]
DRUMS OF TABU, THE(1967, Ital./Span.)
Frank C. Moran
GREAT McGINTY, THE(1940); DOUBLE CROSS(1941)
George Moran
WHY BRING THAT UP?(1929); ANYBODY'S WAR(1930); HYPNOTIZED(1933); BANK DICK, THE(1940); MY LITTLE CHICKADEE(1940)
Gussie Moran
PAT AND MIKE(1952)
Jackie Moran
AND SO THEY WERE MARRIED(1936); ANY MAN'S WIFE(1936); VALIANT IS THE WORD FOR CARRIE(1936); MICHAEL O'HALLORAN(1937); OUTCAST(1937); ADVENTURES OF TOM SAWYER, THE(1938); ARSON GANG BUSTERS(1938); MAD ABOUT MUSIC(1938); MOTHER CAREY'S CHICKENS(1938); EVERYBODY'S HOBBY(1939); GONE WITH THE WIND(1939); SPIRIT OF CULVER, THE(1939); ANNE OF WINDY POPLARS(1940); HAUNTED HOUSE, THE(1940); TOMBOY(1940); GANG'S ALL HERE(1941); LET'S GO COLLEGIATE(1941); OLD SWIMMIN' HOLE, THE(1941); HENRY ALDRICH HAUNTS A HOUSE(1943); NOBODY'S DARLING(1943); ANDY HARDY'S BLONDE TROUBLE(1944); JANIE(1944); SINCE YOU WENT AWAY(1944); SONG OF THE OPEN ROAD(1944); THREE LITTLE SISTERS(1944); LET'S GO STEADY(1945); THERE GOES KELLY(1945); BETTY CO-ED(1946); FREDDIE STEPS OUT(1946); HIGH SCHOOL HERO(1946); JUNIOR PROM(1946)
Jim Moran
SPECTER OF THE ROSE(1946); MASK, THE(1961, Can.)
Misc. Talkies
IS THERE SEX AFTER DEATH(1971)
John E. Moran
GOOD MORNING... AND GOODBYE(1967), w
Joseph Moran
PROUD AND THE PROFANE, THE(1956)
Kelly Moran
HAZING, THE(1978); YOUNG DOCTORS IN LOVE(1982)
Laurie Moran
CHAIN REACTION(1980, Aus.)
Lee Moran
SHOW GIRL(1928); TAXI 13(1928); AVIATOR, THE(1929); DANCE HALL(1929); GLAD RAG DOLL, THE(1929); GOLD DIGGERS OF BROADWAY(1929); MADONNA OF AVENUE A(1929); NO DEFENSE(1929); ON WITH THE SHOW(1929); GOLDEN DAWN(1930); HIDE-OUT, THE(1930); PARDON MY GUN(1930); SWEET MAMA(1930); OTHER MEN'S WOMEN(1931); FIGHTING GENTLEMAN, THE(1932); HAT CHECK GIRL(1932); STOWAWAY(1932); UPTOWN NEW YORK(1932); DEATH KISS, THE(1933); ELEVENTH COMMANDMENT(1933); FOOTLIGHT PARADE(1933); GOLDIE GETS ALONG(1933); GRAND SLAM(1933); HIGH GEAR(1933); RACETRACK(1933); SITTING PRETTY(1933); JIMMY THE GENT(1934); STREAMLINE EXPRESS(1935); DAN MATTHEWS(1936)
Misc. Talkies
SISTER TO JUDAS(1933)
Silents
ONCE A PLUMBER(1920), a, d; SHOCKING NIGHT, A(1921), a, d; DARING YOUTH(1924); GAMBLING WIVES(1924); AFTER BUSINESS HOURS(1925); JIMMIE'S MILLIONS(1925); LITTLE IRISH GIRL, THE(1926); SYNCOPATING SUE(1926); TAKE IT FROM ME(1926); IRRESISTIBLE LOVER, THE(1927); WOLF'S CLOTHING(1927); ACTRESS, THE(1928); OUTCAST(1928); RACKET, THE(1928); THANKS FOR THE BUGGY RIDE(1928)
Misc. Silents
MRS. PLUM'S PUDDING(1915); EVERYTHING BUT THE TRUTH(1920), a, d; FIXED BY GEORGE(1920), a, d; LA LA LUCILLE(1920); TOMBOY(1924); TESSIE(1925); WHERE WAS I?(1925); ROSE OF KILDARE, THE(1927); LADIES OF THE NIGHT CLUB(1928); LOOK OUT GIRL, THE(1928); WOMAN AGAINST THE WORLD, A(1928); NO DEFENSE(1929)
Liza Moran
IF EVER I SEE YOU AGAIN(1978)
Lois Moran
BEHIND THAT CURTAIN(1929); MAKING THE GRADE(1929); SONG OF KENTUCKY(1929); WORDS AND MUSIC(1929); DANCERS, THE(1930); MAMMY(1930); NOT DAMAGED(1930); MEN IN HER LIFE(1931); SPIDER, THE(1931); TRANSATLANTIC(1931); UNDER SUSPICION(1931); WEST OF BROADWAY(1931); ALICE IN THE CITIES(1974, W. Ger.)
Silents
STELLA DALLAS(1925); JUST SUPPOSE(1926); RECKLESS LADY, THE(1926); ROAD TO MANDALAY, THE(1926); IRRESISTIBLE LOVER, THE(1927); DON'T MARRY(1928); SHARP SHOOTERS(1928); JOY STREET(1929)
Misc. Silents
LA GALERIE DES MONSTRES(1924, Fr.); LATE MATTHEW PASCAL, THE(1925, Fr.); GOD GAVE ME TWENTY CENTS(1926); PADLOCKED(1926); PRINCE OF TEMPTERS, THE(1926); MUSIC MASTER, THE(1927); PUBLICITY MADNESS(1927); WHIRLPOOL OF YOUTH, THE(1927); BLINDFOLD(1928); LOVE HUNGRY(1928); TRUE HEAVEN(1929)
M.D. Moran
Misc. Silents
WASTED YEARS, THE(1916)
Malcolm Moran
PLAY MISTY FOR ME(1971)

Manolo Moran
MANOLETE(1950, Span.); OPERATION DELILAH(1966, U.S./Span.); FLAME OVER VIETNAM(1967, Span./Ger.)
Michael Moran
KNIGHTRIDERS(1981)
Michael P. Moran
SCARFACE(1983); SURVIVORS, THE(1983)
Mike Moran
TIME BANDITS(1981, Brit.), m; MISSIONARY, THE(1982), m
1984
BLOODBATH AT THE HOUSE OF DEATH(1984, Brit.), m
Millie Moran
MURDER IN MISSISSIPPI(1965)
Monica Moran
TAKE HER, SHE'S MINE(1963)
Neil Moran
ANGEL UNCHAINED(1970)
Misc. Silents
FOR THE FREEDOM OF THE WORLD(1917); MISFIT EARL, A(1919); SPEEDY MEADE(1919)
Paddy Moran
ON THE BEACH(1959)
Pat Moran
ARTISTS AND MODELS(1937); SOMETHING TO SING ABOUT(1937); VARIETY GIRL(1947); TROUBLE MAKERS(1948); MY FAVORITE SPY(1951); HOUSEBOAT(1958); MOVE OVER, DARLING(1963); MY SIX LOVES(1963); UNSINKABLE MOLLY BROWN, THE(1964)
Patricia Moran
EXTERMINATING ANGEL, THE(1967, Mex.)
Patsy Moran
GOLDEN TRAIL, THE(1940); SAPS AT SEA(1940); FOREIGN AGENT(1942); 'NEATH BROOKLYN BRIDGE(1942); MR. MUGGS STEPS OUT(1943); THIS IS THE ARMY(1943); MEET THE PEOPLE(1944); MILLION DOLLAR KID(1944); COME OUT FIGHTING(1945); DOCKS OF NEW YORK(1945); HOMICIDE FOR THREE(1948); SONG OF THE DRIFTER(1948); BRIDE FOR SALE(1949)
Peggy Moran
BOY MEETS GIRL(1938); GIRLS' SCHOOL(1938); RHYTHM OF THE SADDLE(1938); SISTERS, THE(1938); BIG GUY, THE(1939); LITTLE ACCIDENT(1939); NINOTCHKA(1939); ALIAS THE DEACON(1940); ARGENTINE NIGHTS(1940); DANGER ON WHEELS(1940); HOT STEEL(1940); I CAN'T GIVE YOU ANYTHING BUT LOVE, BABY(1940); MUMMY'S HAND, THE(1940); OH JOHNNY, HOW YOU CAN LOVE!(1940); ONE NIGHT IN THE TROPICS(1940); SLIGHTLY TEMPTED(1940); SPRING PARADE(1940); TRAIL OF THE VIGILANTES(1940); WEST OF CARSON CITY(1940); DOUBLE DATE(1941); FLYING CADETS(1941); HELLO SUCKER(1941); HORROR ISLAND(1941); DRUMS OF THE CONGO(1942); SEVEN SWEETHEARTS(1942); THERE'S ONE BORN EVERY MINUTE(1942); TREAT EM' ROUGH(1942); KING OF THE COWBOYS(1943)
Percy Moran
Silents
LONDON'S ENEMIES(1916, Brit.), a, d; JACK, SAM AND PETE(1919, Brit.); FIELD OF HONOR, THE(1922, Brit.), a, d; LIEUTENANT DARING RN AND THE WATER RATS(1924, Brit.), a, d, w
Misc. Silents
AT THE TORRENT'S MERCY(1915, Brit.); HOW MEN LOVE WOMEN(1915, Brit.), a, d; LONDON NIGHTHAWKS(1915, Brit.), a, d; NURSE AND MARTYR(1915, Brit.), a, d; PARTED BY THE SWORD(1915, Brit.), a, d; REDEMPTION OF HIS NAME, THE(1918, Brit.), d
Polly Moran
SO THIS IS COLLEGE(1929); UNHOLY NIGHT, THE(1929); CAUGHT SHORT(1930); CHASING RAINBOWS(1930); GIRL SAID NO, THE(1930); HOT FOR PARIS(1930); PAID(1930); REMOTE CONTROL(1930); THOSE THREE FRENCH GIRLS(1930); WAY FOR A SAILOR(1930); WAY OUT WEST(1930); GUILTY HANDS(1931); IT'S A WISE CHILD(1931); POLITICS(1931); REDUCING(1931); PASSIONATE PLUMBER(1932); PROSPERITY(1932); ALICE IN WONDERLAND(1933); DOWN TO THEIR LAST YACHT(1934); HOLLYWOOD PARTY(1934); TWO WISE MAIDS(1937); LADIES IN DISTRESS(1938); RED RIVER RANGE(1938); AMBUSH(1939); MEET THE MISSUS(1940); TOM BROWN'S SCHOOL DAYS(1940); PETTICOAT POLITICS(1941); ADAM'S RIB(1949); RED LIGHT(1949); YELLOW CAB MAN, THE(1950)
Silents
AFFAIRS OF ANATOL, THE(1921); LUCK(1923); SCARLET LETTER, THE(1926); CALLAHANS AND THE MURPHYS, THE(1927); ENEMY, THE(1927); LONDON AFTER MIDNIGHT(1927); DIVINE WOMAN, THE(1928); SHADOWS OF THE NIGHT(1928); SHOW PEOPLE(1928); TELLING THE WORLD(1928); WHILE THE CITY SLEEPS(1928); HONEYMOON(1929)
Misc. Silents
SKIRTS(1921); BEYOND THE SIERRAS(1928); BRINGING UP FATHER(1928); CHINA BOUND(1929)
Priscilla Moran
HOLD'EM NAVY!(1937); I MET HIM IN PARIS(1937)
Silents
NO BABIES WANTED(1928)
Tim Moran
SAME TIME, NEXT YEAR(1978), spec eff
Tom Moran
Misc. Silents
CRUISKEEN LAWN(1922, Brit.)
Tony Moran
HALLOWEEN(1978); HALLOWEEN II(1981)
William Moran
OUT OF SINGAPORE(1932); LATE GEORGE APLEY, THE(1947)
Silents
GREEN FLAME, THE(1920); ABRAHAM LINCOLN(1924)
Misc. Silents
BLOOD TEST(1923)
William H. Moran
SECRET SERVICE OF THE AIR(1939), w
Moran & Mack
Misc. Talkies
ANYBODY'S WAR(1930)

Nonna Mordyukova
HOME FOR TANYA, A(1961, USSR); MARRIAGE OF BALZAMINOV, THE(1966, USSR); WAR AND PEACE(1968, USSR)

Camilla More
1984
FRIDAY THE 13TH–THE FINAL CHAPTER(1984)

Carey More
1984
FRIDAY THE 13TH–THE FINAL CHAPTER(1984)

J. Neil More
SAFE AFFAIR, A(1931, Brit.); GHOST GOES WEST, THE(1936); MEN OF YESTER-DAY(1936, Brit.); NO ESCAPE(1936, Brit.); GABLES MYSTERY, THE(1938, Brit.)

Julian More
EXPRESSO BONGO(1959, Brit.), w; VALLEY OF GWANGI, THE(1969), w; IN-CENSE FOR THE DAMNED(1970, Brit.), w; CATAMOUNT KILLING, THE(1975, Ger.), w; CHANEL SOLITAIRE(1981), w

Kenneth More
LOOK UP AND LAUGH(1935, Brit.); SCHOOL FOR SECRETS(1946, Brit.); MAN ON THE RUN(1949, Brit.); NOW BARABBAS WAS A ROBBER(1949, Brit.); SCOTT OF THE ANTARCTIC(1949, Brit.); STOP PRESS GIRL(1949, Brit.); CHANCE OF A LIFETI-ME(1950, Brit.); CLOUDED YELLOW, THE(1950, Brit.); NO HIGHWAY IN THE SKY(1951, Brit.); OPERATION DISASTER(1951, Brit.); BRANDY FOR THE PAR-SON(1952, Brit.); FRANCHISE AFFAIR, THE(1952, Brit.); ISLAND RESCUE(1952, Brit.); GENEVIEVE(1953, Brit.); NEVER LET ME GO(1953, U.S./Brit.); YELLOW BALLOON, THE(1953, Brit.); DOCTOR IN THE HOUSE(1954, Brit.); ADVENTURES OF SADIE, THE(1955, Brit.); DEEP BLUE SEA, THE(1955, Brit.); ADMIRABLE CRICHTON, THE(1957, Brit.); RAISING A RIOT(1957, Brit.); REACH FOR THE SKY(1957, Brit.); NIGHT TO REMEMBER, A(1958, Brit.); SHERIFF OF FRACTURED JAW, THE(1958, Brit.); FLAME OVER INDIA(1960, Brit.); SINK THE BISMARCK!(1960, Brit.); THIRTY NINE STEPS, THE(1960, Brit.); LOSS OF INNOCENCE(1961, Brit.); MAN IN THE MOON(1961, Brit.); LONGEST DAY, THE(1962); WE JOINED THE NAVY(1962, Brit.); COMEDY MAN, THE(1964); SOME PEOPLE(1964, Brit.); DARK OF THE SUN(1968, Brit.); BATTLE OF BRITAIN, THE(1969, Brit.); FRAULEIN DOKTOR(1969, Ital./Yugo.); OH! WHAT A LOVELY WAR(1969, Brit.); SCROOGE(1970, Brit.); SLIPPER AND THE ROSE, THE(1976, Brit.); LEOPARD IN THE SNOW(1979, Brit./Can.); UNIDENTIFIED FLYING ODDBALL, THE(1979, Brit.)

Neil More
TICKET OF LEAVE(1936, Brit.)

Stella More
UNFAITHFUL(1931)

Unity More
Silents
QUEEN'S EVIDENCE(1919, Brit.)
Misc. Silents
THUNDERCLOUD, THE(1919, Brit.); WOMEN WHO WIN(1919, Brit.)

Theo Moreas
NIGHT AMBUSH(1958, Brit.)

Moreau
SECOND BUREAU(1936, Fr.); INNOCENTS IN PARIS(1955, Brit.)

Emile Moreau
MADAME(1963, Fr./Ital./Span.), w

Florence Moreau
1984
LES COMPERES(1984, Fr.)

Harry Moreau
STAR TREK: THE MOTION PICTURE(1979), spec eff

Jacqueline Moreau
UMBRELLAS OF CHERBOURG, THE(1964, Fr./Ger.), cos; UP TO HIS EARS(1966, Fr./Ital.), cos; YOUNG GIRLS OF ROCHEFORT, THE(1968, Fr.), cos; HORSEMEN, THE(1971), cos; JUDGE AND THE ASSASSIN, THE(1979, Fr.), cos

Jean Luc Moreau
WAGNER(1983, Brit./Hung./Aust.)

Jean-Jacques Moreau
HERBIE GOES TO MONTE CARLO(1977); DIVA(1982, Fr.)

Jeanne Moreau
SECRETS D'ALCOVE(1954, Fr./Ital.); DOCTORS, THE(1956, Fr.); JULIETTA(1957, Fr.); DEMONIAQUE(1958, Fr.); BACK TO THE WALL(1959, Fr.); FOUR HUNDRED BLOWS, THE(1959, Fr.); FIVE BRANDED WOMEN(1960); LOVERS, THE(1959, Fr.); FRANTIC(1961, Fr.); LA NOTTE(1961, Fr./Ital.); LES LIAISONS DAN-GEREUSES(1961, Fr./Ital.); WOMAN IS A WOMAN, A(1961, Fr./Ital.); EVA(1962, Fr./Ital.); JULES AND JIM(1962, Fr.); TRIAL, THE(1963, Fr./Ital./Ger.); VICTORS, THE(1963); BAY OF ANGELS(1964, Fr.); DIARY OF A CHAMBERMAID(1964, Fr./Ital.); FIRE WITHIN, THE(1964, Fr./Ital.); MODERATO CANTABILE(1964, Fr./Ital.); BANANA PEEL(1965, Fr.); MATA HARI(1965, Fr./Ital.); TRAIN, THE(1965, Fr./Ital./U.S.); VIVA MARIA(1965, Fr./Ital.); YELLOW ROLLS-ROYCE, THE(1965, Brit.); MADEMOISELLE(1966, Fr./Brit.); CHIMES AT MIDNIGHT(1967, Span.,Switz.); SAIL-OR FROM GIBRALTAR, THE(1967, Brit.); BRIDE WORE BLACK, THE(1968, Fr./Ital.); GREAT CATHERINE(1968, Brit.); OLDEST PROFESSION, THE(1968, Fr./Ital./Ger.); IMMORTAL STORY, THE(1969, Fr.); ALEX IN WONDERLAND(1970); MONTE WALSH(1970); NATHALIE GRANGER(1972, Fr.); GOING PLACES(1974, Fr.); JE T'AIME(1974, Can.); HU-MAN(1975, Fr.); LAST TYCOON, THE(1976); LUMIERE(1976, Fr.), a, d&w; MR. KLEIN(1976, Fr.); ADOLESCENT, THE(1978, Fr./W.Ger.), d&w; TROUT, THE(1982, Fr.); QUERELLE(1983, Ger./Fr.)
1984
HEAT OF DESIRE(1984, Fr.)

Madame Moreau
Misc. Silents
BEHOLD THE MAN(1921, US/Fr.)

Marie Moreau
WONDER BAR(1934)

Monsieur Moreau
Misc. Silents
BEHOLD THE MAN(1921, US/Fr.)

Philippe Moreau
GIRL WITH THE GOLDEN EYES, THE(1962, Fr.)

the Moreau Choir of Notre Dame
KNUTE ROCKNE–ALL AMERICAN(1940)

Eric Morecambe
SPYLARKS(1965, Brit.); MAGNIFICENT TWO, THE(1967, Brit.); THAT RIVIERA TOUCH(1968, Brit.)

Dale Moreda
HOW TO SUCCEED IN BUSINESS WITHOUT REALLY TRYING(1976), ch

Maxfield Moree
Silents
KEEP MOVING(1915)

Sam Moree
Misc. Talkies
GOD'S BLOODY ACRE(1975)

Deborah Morehart
1984
INITIATION, THE(1984)

Dick Morehead
UNDERCOVER MAN(1936); ROARING SIX GUNS(1937)

Bert Morehouse
YOU SAID A MOUTHFUL(1932); GOIN' TO TOWN(1935); SUNSET IN EL DORA-DO(1945)

Clarence Morehouse
MR. WASHINGTON GOES TO TOWN(1941)

Ed Morehouse
PAWNBROKER, THE(1965)

Gordon Morehouse
TATTERED DRESS, THE(1957)

Ward Morehouse
GENTLEMEN OF THE PRESS(1929), w; BIG CITY BLUES(1932), w; CENTRAL PARK(1932), w; IT HAPPENED IN NEW YORK(1935), w

Mario Moreira
COUNTRY DOCTOR, THE(1963, Portuguese), ph

Takis Morekis
GIRL OF THE MOUNTAINS(1958, Gr.), m

Dene Morel
Misc. Silents
SPY OF MME. POMPADOUR(1929, Ger.)

Genevieve Morel
KNOCK(1955, Fr.); MAXIME(1962, Fr.)

Genvieve Morel
LOVE AT NIGHT(1961, Fr.)

Jacques Morel
PARIS DOES STRANGE THINGS(1957, Fr./Ital.); ROYAL AFFAIRS IN VER-SAILLES(1957, Fr.); FOLIES BERGERE(1958, Fr.); MAIDEN, THE(1961, Fr.); MAN FROM COCODY(1966, Fr/Ital.)

Jean Morel
CAGE OF NIGHTINGALES, A(1947, Fr.); WOMAN OF SIN(1961, Fr.)

Karl Morel
SCHOOL FOR SECRETS(1946, Brit.)

Max Morel
1984
ONE DEADLY SUMMER(1984, Fr.)

Michael Morel
FRENCH LEAVE(1937, Brit.); CANDLELIGHT IN ALGERIA(1944, Brit.)

Natasha Morel
ADVENTURE IN ODESSA(1954, USSR)

Alexander Moreland
HER FIRST ROMANCE(1940)

Andria Moreland
LET'S FACE IT(1943)

Beatrice Moreland
Silents
SCALES OF JUSTICE, THE(1914)

Betsy Jones Moreland
GARMENT JUNGLE, THE(1957); STRANGERS WHEN WE MEET(1960)

Betty Jones Moreland
DAY OF THE OUTLAW(1959)

Carolyn Moreland
TOWN THAT DREADED SUNDOWN, THE(1977)

Craig Moreland
DANGEROUS MISSION(1954)

Deborah Moreland
1984
LIES(1984, Brit.), art d

Gloria Moreland
HERE COME THE JETS(1959); REBEL SET, THE(1959); PHANTOM PLANET, THE(1961)

Mantan Moreland
SHALL WE DANCE(1937); SPIRIT OF YOUTH(1937); HARLEM ON THE PRAI-RIE(1938); NEXT TIME I MARRY(1938); THERE'S THAT WOMAN AGAIN(1938); FRONTIER SCOUT(1939); IRISH LUCK(1939); ONE DARK NIGHT(1939); RIDERS OF THE FRONTIER(1939); TELL NO TALES(1939); CHASING TROUBLE(1940); DRUMS OF THE DESERT(1940); LAUGHING AT DANGER(1940); MILLIONAIRE PLAY-BOY(1940); ON THE SPOT(1940); STAR DUST(1940); UP IN THE AIR(1940); CRACKED NUTS(1941); DRESSED TO KILL(1941); ELLERY QUEEN'S PENTHOUSE MYS-TERY(1941); FOUR JACKS AND A JILL(1941); GANG'S ALL HERE(1941); HELLO SUCKER(1941); KING OF THE ZOMBIES(1941); LET'S GO COLLEGIATE(1941); MR. WASHINGTON GOES TO TOWN(1941); SIGN OF THE WOLF(1941); YOU'RE OUT OF LUCK(1941); ANDY HARDY'S DOUBLE LIFE(1942); EYES IN THE NIGHT(1942); FOOTLIGHT SERENADE(1942); FRECKLES COMES HOME(1942); GIRL TROU-BLE(1942); LAW OF THE JUNGLE(1942); MEXICAN SPITFIRE SEES A GHOST(1942); PALM BEACH STORY, THE(1942); PHANTOM KILLER(1942); STRANGE CASE OF DR. RX, THE(1942); TARZAN'S NEW YORK ADVENTURE(1942); TREAT EM' ROUGH(1942); CABIN IN THE SKY(1943); HI' YA, SAILOR(1943); HIT THE ICE(1943); MELODY PARADE(1943); REVENGE OF THE ZOMBIES(1943); SARONG GIRL(1943); SHE'S FOR ME(1943); SLIGHTLY DANGEROUS(1943); SWING FEVER(1943); WE'VE NEVER BEEN LICKED(1943); YOU'RE A LUCKY FELLOW, MR. SMITH(1943); BOWERY TO BROADWAY(1944); CHARLIE CHAN IN BLACK MAGIC(1944); CHARLIE CHAN IN THE SECRET SERVICE(1944); CHINESE CAT, THE(1944); CHIP OFF THE OLD BLOCK(1944); MOON OVER LAS VEGAS(1944); PIN UP GIRL(1944); SEE HERE, PRIVATE HARGROVE(1944); SOUTH OF DIXIE(1944); THIS IS THE LIFE(1944); CAPTAIN TUGBOAT ANNIE(1945); JADE MASK, THE(1945); SCARLET

CLUE, THE(1945); SHANGHAI COBRA, THE(1945); SHE WOULDN'T SAY YES(1945); SPIDER, THE(1945); DARK ALIBI(1946); SHADOWS OVER CHINATOWN(1946); CHINESE RING, THE(1947); TRAP, THE(1947); DOCKS OF NEW ORLEANS(1948); FEATHERED SERPENT, THE(1948); MYSTERY OF THE GOLDEN EYE, THE(1948); SHANGHAI CHEST, THE(1948); SKY DRAGON(1949); PATSY, THE(1964); ENTER LAUGHING(1967); SPIDER BABY(1968); WATERMELON MAN(1970); YOUNG NURSES, THE(1973)
Misc. Talkies
GUN MOLL(1938); TWO-GUN MAN FROM HARLEM(1938); WHILE THOUSANDS CHEER(1940); PROFESSOR CREEPS(1942); COSMO JONES, CRIME SMASHER(1943); TALL, TAN AND TERRIFIC(1946); JUKE JOINT(1947)

Marcella Moreland
AM I GUILTY?(1940); MOKEY(1942)
Robert H. Moreland
FOUR FACES WEST(1948), spec eff
Robert Moreland
MR. ACE(1946), spec eff; OTHER LOVE, THE(1947), spec eff
Sherry Moreland
ROCKETSHIP X-M(1950); FURY OF THE CONGO(1951); STOP, YOU'RE KILLING ME(1952); PYRO(1964, U.S./Span.); GIT!(1965); NIGHT IN HEAVEN, A(1983)
Wes Moreland [Forrest Westmoreland]
DEVIL'S MISTRESS, THE(1968), p
Andre Morell
MANY TANKS MR. ATKINS(1938, Brit.); 13 MEN AND A GUN(1938, Brit.); THREE SILENT MEN(1940, Brit.); MISSING TEN DAYS(1941, Brit.); UNPUBLISHED STORY(1942, Brit.); AGAINST THE WIND(1948, Brit.); CLOUDED YELLOW, THE(1950, Brit.); MADELEINE(1950, Brit.); NO PLACE FOR JENNIFER(1950, Brit.); SEVEN DAYS TO NOON(1950, Brit.); STAGE FRIGHT(1950, Brit.); TRIO(1950, Brit.); FLESH AND BLOOD(1951, Brit.); HIGH TREASON(1951, Brit.); SO LONG AT THE FAIR(1951, Brit.); FRIGHTENED BRIDE, THE(1952, Brit.); STOLEN FACE(1952, Brit.); HIS MAJESTY O'KEEFE(1953); BLACK KNIGHT, THE(1954); SECRET, THE(1955, Brit.); SUMMERTIME(1955); THEY CAN'T HANG ME(1955, Brit.); THREE CASES OF MURDER(1955, Brit.); BLACK TENT, THE(1956, Brit.); MAN WHO NEVER WAS, THE(1956, Brit.); ZARAK(1956, Brit.); BABY AND THE BATTLESHIP, THE(1957, Brit.); BRIDGE ON THE RIVER KWAI, THE(1957); PICKUP ALLEY(1957, Brit.); CAMP ON BLOOD ISLAND, THE(1958, Brit.); DIAMOND SAFARI(1958); PARIS HOLIDAY(1958); BEHEMOTH, THE SEA MONSTER(1959, Brit.); BEN HUR(1959); HOUND OF THE BASKERVILLES, THE(1959, Brit.); SHADOW OF THE CAT, THE(1961, Brit.); TROUBLE IN THE SKY(1961, Brit.); CASH ON DEMAND(1962, Brit.); MOON-SPINNERS, THE(1964); WOMAN OF STRAW(1964, Brit.); SHE(1965, Brit.); PLAGUE OF THE ZOMBIES, THE(1966, Brit.); MUMMY'S SHROUD, THE(1967, Brit.); VENGEANCE OF SHE, THE(1968, Brit.); JULIUS CAESAR(1970, Brit.); 10 RILLINGTON PLACE(1971, Brit.); POPE JOAN(1972, Brit.); BARRY LYNDON(1975, Brit.); MOHAMMAD, MESSENGER OF GOD(1976, Lebanon/Brit.); SLIPPER AND THE ROSE, THE(1976, Brit.); GREAT TRAIN ROBBERY, THE(1979, Brit.)
Ann Morell
EVERYTHING'S DUCKY(1961); JOHN GOLDFARB, PLEASE COME HOME(1964); RED LINE 7000(1965); TICKLE ME(1965); BOXCAR BERTHA(1972)
George Morell
CRASHING BROADWAY(1933); ROUGH RIDING RANGER(1935); SHOT IN THE DARK, A(1935); VALLEY OF THE LAWLESS(1936); OH, SUSANNA(1937); KNIGHT OF THE PLAINS(1939); HIS BROTHER'S GHOST(1945)
Henry Morell
DANGEROUS CARGO(1939, Brit.)
Linda Morell
HARDCORE(1979)
Melissa Morell
KRAMER VS. KRAMER(1979)
Parker Morell
DIAMOND JIM(1935), w
Pat Morell
THUMBELINA(1970)
Penny Morell
STITCH IN TIME, A(1967, Brit.)
Russell Morell
NIGHT OF THE LEPUS(1972)
Morell Trio
SAN FERNANDO VALLEY(1944)
Tony Morella
GIANT(1956)
Donald Morelli
Silents
KEEP SMILING(1925)
Ernesto Morelli
FOR WHOM THE BELL TOLLS(1943); ABBOTT AND COSTELLO IN THE FOREIGN LEGION(1950); MYSTERY STREET(1950); UNDER MY SKIN(1950); PEOPLE AGAINST O'HARA, THE(1951); STORY OF THREE LOVES, THE(1953); TWIST AROUND THE CLOCK(1961); CHAMP, THE(1979)
Frank Morelli
WIZARD OF GORE, THE(1970), makeup
Guiseppe Morelli
THIS WINE OF LOVE(1948, Ital.), md
Luciano Morelli
LUCIANO(1963, Ital.)
Manlio Morelli
CENTURION, THE(1962, Fr./Ital.), p
Michael Morelli
10 NORTH FREDERICK(1958)
Mike Morelli
TENSION(1949)
Mirella Morelli
RAILROAD MAN, THE(1965, Ital.), cos
R. Morelli
FURY OF HERCULES, THE(1961, Ital.), spec eff
Rina Morelli
ADVENTURE OF SALVATOR ROSA, AN(1940, Ital.); FEDORA(1946, Ital.); RETURN OF THE BLACK EAGLE(1949, Ital.); STRANGE DECEPTION(1953, Ital.); TIMES GONE BY(1953, Ital.); CENTO ANNI D'AMORE(1954, Ital.); BELL' ANTONIO(1962, Ital.); CRIME DOES NOT PAY(1962, Fr.); LA VIACCIA(1962, Fr./Ital.); LEOPARD, THE(1963, Ital.); SENSO(1968, Ital.); DRAMA OF THE RICH(1975, Ital./Fr.); INNO-

CENT, THE(1979, Ital.)
Toni Morelli
DICK BARTON STRIKES BACK(1949, Brit.)
Dedena Morello
IT HAPPENED IN CANADA(1962, Can.)
Joe Morello
SASQUATCH(1978)
John Morello
JUST BEFORE DAWN(1980), makeup
Angela Morely
SLIPPER AND THE ROSE, THE(1976, Brit.), md
Jay A. Morely, Jr.
INCREDIBLE SHRINKING MAN, THE(1957), cos
Karen Morely
HIGH STAKES(1931)
Ruth Morely
DIARY OF A MAD HOUSEWIFE(1970), cos
Jose Moren
DON'T TURN THE OTHER CHEEK(1974, Ital./Ger./Span.)
Erna Morena
Misc. Silents
MYSTERIES OF INDIA(1922, Ger.)
Gerardo Morena
UNDER FIRE(1983)
Joseph Morena
CALIFORNIA SUITE(1978)
Mona Morena
SECRET OF THE SACRED FOREST, THE(1970); TWILIGHT PEOPLE(1972, Phil.)
Ruben Morena
WHY ROCK THE BOAT?(1974, Can.)
Gary Morenmo
1984
UP THE CREEK(1984), set d
Alejandro Moreno
SMOKEY AND THE BANDIT–PART 3(1983)
Ana Moreno
HEAT(1970, Arg.)
Anthony Moreno
1984
KILLPOINT(1984)
Antonio Moreno
MIDNIGHT TAXI, THE(1928); CAREERS(1929); ROMANCE OF THE RIO GRANDE(1929); ONE MAD KISS(1930); ROUGH ROMANCE(1930); SANTA(1932, Mex.), d; SENORA CASADA NECEISITA MARIDO(1935); STORM OVER THE ANDES(1935); BOHEMIAN GIRL, THE(1936); ROSE OF THE RIO GRANDE(1938); AMBUSH(1939); SEVEN SINNERS(1940); KID FROM KANSAS, THE(1941); THEY MET IN ARGENTINA(1941); TWO LATINS FROM MANHATTAN(1941); UNDERCOVER MAN(1942); VALLEY OF THE SUN(1942); TAMPICO(1944); SPANISH MAIN, THE(1945); NOTORIOUS(1946); CAPTAIN FROM CASTILE(1947); LUST FOR GOLD(1949); CRISIS(1950); DALLAS(1950); SADDLE TRAMP(1950); MARK OF THE RENEGADE(1951); UNTAMED FRONTIER(1952); THUNDER BAY(1953); WINGS OF THE HAWK(1953); CREATURE FROM THE BLACK LAGOON(1954); SASKATCHEWAN(1954); SEARCHERS, THE(1956)
Misc. Talkies
CATCH ME IF YOU CAN(1959)
Silents
ISLAND OF REGENERATION, THE(1915); ON HER WEDDING NIGHT(1915); PRICE FOR FOLLY, A(1915); KENNEDY SQUARE(1916); ALADDIN FROM BROADWAY(1917); BY RIGHT OF POSSESSION(1917); CAPTAIN OF THE GRAY HORSE TROOP, THE(1917); MONEY MAGIC(1917); NAULAHKA, THE(1918); SECRET OF THE HILLS, THE(1921); EXCITERS, THE(1923); MY AMERICAN WIFE(1923); BLUFF(1924); FLAMING BARRIERS(1924); LEARNING TO LOVE(1925); ONE YEAR TO LIVE(1925); BEVERLY OF GRAUSTARK(1926); LOVE'S BLINDNESS(1926); MARE NOSTRUM(1926); TEMPTRESS, THE(1926); IT(1927); MADAME POMPADOUR(1927, Brit.); ADORATION(1928); NAMELESS MEN(1928); WHIP WOMAN, THE(1928); AIR LEGION, THE(1929)
Misc. Silents
DUST OF EGYPT, THE(1915); DEVIL'S PRIZE, THE(1916); ROSE OF THE SOUTH(1916); SUPREME TEMPTATION, THE(1916); TARANTULA, THE(1916); WINIFRED THE SHOP GIRL(1916); ANGEL FACTORY, THE(1917); HER RIGHT TO LIVE(1917); MAGNIFICENT MEDDLER, THE(1917); MARK OF CAIN, THE(1917); SON OF THE HILLS, A(1917); FIRST LAW, THE(1918); GUILTY CONSCIENCE, A(1921); THREE SEVENS(1921); LOOK YOUR BEST(1923); LOST AND FOUND ON A SOUTH SEA ISLAND(1923); SPANISH DANCER, THE(1923); TRAIL OF THE LONESOME, THE(1923); BORDER LEGION, THE(1924); STORY WITHOUT A NAME, THE(1924); TIGER LOVE(1924); HER HUSBAND'S SECRET(1925); FLAMING FOREST, THE(1926); COME TO MY HOUSE(1927); VENUS OF VENICE(1927); SYNTHETIC SIN(1929)
B. Moreno
HAMLET(1966, USSR)
Belita Moreno
THREE WOMEN(1977); WEDDING, A(1978); PERFECT COUPLE, A(1979); MOMMIE DEAREST(1981); JEKYLL AND HYDE...TOGETHER AGAIN(1982)
1984
OH GOD! YOU DEVIL(1984); SWING SHIFT(1984)
Carmen Moreno
DEAL OF THE CENTURY(1983)
Catalina Moreno
MURIETA(1965, Span.), cos
Christina Moreno
INTERVAL(1973, Mex./U.S.); CHOSEN SURVIVORS(1974 U.S.-Mex.)
Dargio Moreno
NATHALIE, AGENT SECRET(1960, Fr.)
Dario Moreno
WAGES OF FEAR, THE(1955, Fr./Ital.); COME DANCE WITH ME(1960, Fr.); FEMALE, THE(1960, Fr.); REVOLT OF THE SLAVES, THE(1961, Ital./Span./Ger.); CANDIDE(1962, Fr.); HOTEL PARADISO(1966, U.S./Brit.); LA PRISONNIERE(1969, Fr./Ital.)

Misc. Talkies
ATOMIC AGENT(1959, Fr.)
David Moreno
SEVEN GUNS FOR THE MACGREGORS(1968, Ital./Span.), w
Edna Moreno
ON THE RIGHT TRACK(1981)
Eduard Moreno
TOAST OF NEW ORLEANS, THE(1950)
Felix Moreno
DALTON THAT GOT AWAY(1960)
Frank S. Moreno
SWEET SURRENDER(1935)
Gary Moreno
THINGS ARE TOUGH ALL OVER(1982), set d; SLEEPER(1973), set d; KING OF THE MOUNTAIN(1981), set d
1984
OH GOD! YOU DEVIL(1984), set d
Hector Moreno
CAVEMAN(1981)
Hilda Moreno
OLD SPANISH CUSTOM, AN(1936, Brit.); MY BROTHER, THE OUTLAW(1951); JET OVER THE ATLANTIC(1960)
Inez Moreno
MASTER OF HORROR(1965, Arg.)
John Moreno
FOR YOUR EYES ONLY(1981)
1984
RAZOR'S EDGE, THE(1984)
John J. Moreno
Silents
ADVENTUROUS SOUL, THE(1927), w
Jorge Moreno
ONE-EYED JACKS(1961); WHEN THE CLOCK STRIKES(1961); YOUNG FURY(1965); I LOVE YOU, ALICE B. TOKLAS!(1968); BREAKOUT(1975); KING KONG(1976); WORLD'S GREATEST LOVER, THE(1977); HERBIE GOES BANANAS(1980)
1984
EL NORTE(1984)
Jose Moreno
KINGS OF THE SUN(1963)
Jose Elias Moreno
LITTLE RED RIDING HOOD AND THE MONSTERS(1965, Mex.); RAGE(1966, U.S./Mex.); TOM THUMB(1967, Mex.); NIGHT OF THE BLOODY APES(1968, Mex.); SURVIVE!(1977, Mex.)
Jose Lopez Moreno
FICKLE FINGER OF FATE, THE(1967, Span./U.S.), p
Joseph Elias Moreno
SANTA CLAUS(1960, Mex.)
Liza Moreno
CRY OF BATTLE(1963); RAIDERS OF LEYTE GULF(1963 U.S./Phil.)
Louis Moreno
HICKEY AND BOGGS(1972)
Margarite Moreno
CARMEN(1946, Ital.)
Marguerite Moreno
COGNASSE(1932, Fr.); LES MISERABLES(1936, Fr.); AMPHYTRYON(1937, Ger.); PEARLS OF THE CROWN(1938, Fr.); STORY OF A CHEAT, THE(1938, Fr.); LES JEUX SONT FAITS(1947, Fr.); IDIOT, THE(1948, Fr.); LOVE STORY(1949, Fr.)
Mario Moreno
TRAPPED IN TANGIERS(1960, Ital./Span.)
Mario f Moreno
NIGHT HEAVEN FELL, THE(1958, Fr.)
Paco Moreno
I MET HIM IN PARIS(1937); ARTISTS AND MODELS ABROAD(1938); I WANT A DIVORCE(1940); BLOOD AND SAND(1941); LAW OF THE TROPICS(1941); SIX LESSONS FROM MADAME LA ZONGA(1941); TOO MANY BLONDES(1941)
Ric Moreno
FOG, THE(1980)
1984
STREETS OF FIRE(1984)
Rita Moreno
PAGAN LOVE SONG(1950); TOAST OF NEW ORLEANS, THE(1950); CATTLE TOWN(1952); FABULOUS SENORITA, THE(1952); RING, THE(1952); SINGIN' IN THE RAIN(1952); FORT VENGEANCE(1953); LATIN LOVERS(1953); MA AND PA KETTLE ON VACATION(1953); EL ALAMEIN(1954); GARDEN OF EVIL(1954); JIVARO(1954); YELLOW TOMAHAWK, THE(1954); SEVEN CITIES OF GOLD(1955); UNTAMED(1955); KING AND I, THE(1956); LIEUTENANT WORE SKIRTS, THE(1956); VAGABOND KING, THE(1956); DEERSLAYER, THE(1957); THIS REBEL BREED(1960); SUMMER AND SMOKE(1961); WEST SIDE STORY(1961); SAMAR(1962); CRY OF BATTLE(1963); MARLOWE(1969); NIGHT OF THE FOLLOWING DAY, THE(1969, Brit.); POPI(1969); CARNAL KNOWLEDGE(1971); RITZ, THE(1976); BOSS'S SON, THE(1978); HAPPY BIRTHDAY, GEMINI(1980); FOUR SEASONS, THE(1981)
Robert Moreno
LOVE AND KISSES(1965), ph; SAM WHISKEY(1969), ph; SMITH(1969), ph; SKULLDUGGERY(1970), ph
Rosita Moreno
HER WEDDING NIGHT(1930); SANTA FE TRAIL, THE(1930); STAMBOUL(1931, Brit.); IO ... TU ... Y ... ELLA(1933); WALLS OF GOLD(1933); LADIES SHOULD LISTEN(1934); TWO AND ONE TWO(1934); SCOUNDREL, THE(1935); TANGO BAR(1935); TE QUIERO CON LOCURA(1935); HOUSE OF A THOUSAND CANDLES, THE(1936); MEDAL FOR BENNY, A(1945); ONE-EYED JACKS(1961), tech adv
Rosita [Rita] Moreno
SO YOUNG, SO BAD(1950)
Ruben Moreno
THIRD VOICE, THE(1960); MADAME X(1966); EL DORADO(1967); SULLIVAN'S EMPIRE(1967); LITTLE BIG MAN(1970); RESURRECTION OF ZACHARY WHEELER, THE(1971); COFFY(1973); HERBIE GOES BANANAS(1980)

Sebastian Moreno
CARMEN(1983, Span.)
Victoria Moreno
LAST MOMENT, THE(1966)
Leon Morenzie
GOLDEN APPLES OF THE SUN(1971, Can.)
G. H. Moresby-White
FRIDAY THE 13TH(1934, Brit.), w; HEIRLOOM MYSTERY, THE(1936, Brit.), w; BOMBS OVER LONDON(1937, Brit.), w; TAKE A CHANCE(1937, Brit.), w
George Moresby-White
NO SMOKING(1955, Brit.), w
Giulio Moreschi
WHITE SHEIK, THE(1956, Ital.)
Robert Moresco
WINTER KILLS(1979)
Costante Moret
FITZCARRALDO(1982)
Gina Moret
NIGHT OF THE BLOODY APES(1968, Mex.)
Paul Moret [Pablo Moret]
HEAT(1970, Arg.)
Ivor Moreton
EVERYTHING IS RHYTHM(1940, Brit.)
Kevin Moreton
ALL THINGS BRIGHT AND BEAUTIFUL(1979, Brit.)
Robert Moreton
ONE WILD OAT(1951, Brit.); TIME OF HIS LIFE, THE(1955, Brit.); TONS OF TROUBLE(1956, Brit.)
Moretti
SNOW DEVILS, THE(1965, Ital.), w
Assemblyman Robert Moretti
CANDIDATE, THE(1972)
Marino Moretti
CENTO ANNI D'AMORE(1954, Ital.), w
Nadir Moretti
JULIET OF THE SPIRITS(1965, Fr./Ital./W.Ger.)
Nanni Moretti
PADRE PADRONE(1977, Ital.)
Raoul Moretti
COGNASSE(1932, Fr.), m
Renato Moretti
CONQUERED CITY(1966, Ital.); SANDRA(1966, Ital.); WILD, WILD PLANET, THE(1967, Ital.), w; WAR BETWEEN THE PLANETS(1971, Ital.), w
Rino Moretti
HEART AND SOUL(1950, Ital.)
Sandro Moretti
SWORD OF EL CID, THE(1965, Span./Ital.); LOVE AND MARRIAGE(1966, Ital.)
Ugo Moretti
RUN WITH THE DEVIL(1963, Fr./Ital.), w
Francois Moreuil
BREATHLESS(1959, Fr.); PLAYTIME(1963, Fr.), d, w
Jean-Pierre Moreux
CATHERINE & CO.(1976, Fr.)
A. Morewski
DYBBUK THE(1938, Pol.)
Bill Morey
SOME KIND OF HERO(1982); BRAINSTORM(1983)
1984
SWORDKILL(1984)
Edward Morey, Jr.
KILLER LEOPARD(1954), d; CONFESSIONS OF AN OPIUM EATER(1962), prod d
Elaine Morey
BUCK PRIVATES(1941); KEEP 'EM FLYING(1941); LAW OF THE RANGE(1941); MOONLIGHT IN HAWAII(1941); BROADWAY(1942); PARDON MY SARONG(1942); WILD HORSE PHANTOM(1944)
Hal Morey
FLIGHT FROM VIENNA(1956, Brit.), ph; ROGUE'S YARN(1956, Brit.), ph; FIGHTING MAD(1957, Brit.), ph; ROCK YOU SINNERS(1957, Brit.), ph
Harry Morey
Silents
ALL MAN(1918); DESIRED WOMAN, THE(1918); KING OF DIAMONDS, THE(1918); OTHER MAN, THE(1918); ALOMA OF THE SOUTH SEAS(1926)
Misc. Silents
FOR A WOMAN'S FAIR NAME(1916); LAW DECIDES, THE(1916); HER SECRET(1917); QUESTION, THE(1917); RICHARD THE BRAZEN(1917); WHO GOES THERE?(1917); WITHIN THE LAW(1917); BACHELOR'S CHILDREN, A(1918); GAME WITH FATE, A(1918); GREEN GOD, THE(1918); HIS OWN PEOPLE(1918); TANGLED LIVES(1918); BEYOND THE RAINBOW(1922); HEART OF A SIREN(1925); TWIN FLAPPERS(1927)
Harry T. Morey
RETURN OF SHERLOCK HOLMES(1936)
Misc. Talkies
SHADOW LAUGHS(1933)
Silents
PRICE FOR FOLLY, A(1915); MAN'S HOME, A(1921); CURSE OF DRINK, THE(1922); CAPTAIN JANUARY(1924); ROUGHNECK, THE(1924); ADVENTUROUS SEX, THE(1925)
Misc. Silents
MILLION BID, A(1914); MY OFFICIAL WIFE(1914); CROOKY(1915); MAKING OVER OF GEOFFREY MANNING, THE(1915); SALVATION JOAN(1916); WHOM THE GODS DESTROY(1916); COURAGE OF SILENCE, THE(1917); GOLDEN GOAL, THE(1918); HOARDED ASSETS(1918); BEATING THE ODDS(1919); BEAUTY PROOF(1919); FIGHTING DESTINY(1919); GAMBLERS, THE(1919); IN HONOR'S WEB(1919); MAN WHO WON, THE(1919); SHADOWS OF THE PAST(1919); SILENT STRENGTH(1919); BIRTH OF A SOUL(1920); DARKEST HOUR, THE(1920); FLAMING CLUE, THE(1920); GAUNTLET, THE(1920); SEA RIDER, THE(1920); WILDNESS OF YOUTH(1922); EMPTY CRADLE, THE(1923); GREEN GODDESS, THE(1923); WHERE THE PAVEMENT ENDS(1923); PAINTED LADY, THE(1924); HEADLINES(1925)

Jack Morey
NIGHT OF EVIL(1962); COTTONPICKIN' CHICKENPICKERS(1967); ROAD HUSTLERS, THE(1968)

Larry Morey
SNOW WHITE AND THE SEVEN DWARFS(1937), d, m; BAMBI(1942), w

Lee Morey
1984
FLAMINGO KID, THE(1984)

Walt Morey
GENTLE GIANT(1967), w

William Morey
PRIME CUT(1972)

Gilbert Morfau
UTOPIA(1952, Fr./Ital.)

Costas Morfis
IT'S A BIG COUNTRY(1951); GLORY BRIGADE, THE(1953)

George Morfogen
WHAT'S UP, DOC?(1972); THIEF WHO CAME TO DINNER, THE(1973); DAISY MILLER(1974); THOSE LIPS, THOSE EYES(1980); TIMES SQUARE(1980); THEY ALL LAUGHED(1981), a, p
1984
HEARTBREAKERS(1984)

Sam Morford
STREET MUSIC(1982)

Thomas Morga
MOVIE MOVIE(1978)

Tom Morga
1984
STAR TREK III: THE SEARCH FOR SPOCK(1984)

Florenzio Morgado
ELEPHANT MAN, THE(1980, Brit.)

Ainsworth Morgan
MAN OF TWO WORLDS(1934), w; DOG OF FLANDERS, A(1935), w; GORGEOUS HUSSY, THE(1936), w; ESPIONAGE(1937), w; SOUTH OF TAHITI(1941), w

Al Morgan
SINGING KID, THE(1936); GREAT MAN, THE(1957), w

Alexandra Morgan
FIRST NUDIE MUSICAL, THE(1976)

Andre Morgan
S.T.A.B.(1976, Hong Kong/Thailand), w; AMSTERDAM KILL, THE(1978, Hong Kong), p; NIGHT GAMES(1980), p

Andrew Morgan
BOYS IN COMPANY C, THE(1978, U.S./Hong Kong), p

Anita Morgan
RAGE(1966, U.S./Mex.)

Ann Morgan
Silents
QUEEN KELLY(1929)

Barry Morgan
ALL NIGHT LONG(1961, Brit.)

Beatrice Morgan
Silents
CRADLE BUSTER, THE(1922)
Misc. Silents
GREAT RUBY, THE(1915)

Ben Morgan
NOTHING SACRED(1937)

Bill Morgan
ROOM AT THE TOP(1959, Brit.); ON HER MAJESTY'S SECRET SERVICE(1969, Brit.); SHOOT(1976, Can.), makeup

Bob Morgan
DAKOTA LIL(1950); SEALED CARGO(1951); WILD BLUE YONDER, THE(1952); SHOTGUN(1955); YOU'RE NEVER TOO YOUNG(1955); BOSS, THE(1956); BIG COUNTRY, THE(1958); SPARTACUS(1960); MAN WHO SHOT LIBERTY VALANCE, THE(1962); CULPEPPER CATTLE COMPANY, THE(1972)

Boyd Morgan
LUCKY CISCO KID(1940); GUN BELT(1953); THUNDER OVER THE PLAINS(1953); WINNING OF THE WEST(1953); FIVE GUNS TO TOMBSTONE(1961)

Boyd "Red" Morgan
ROSE BOWL(1936); DESERT OF LOST MEN(1951); SILVER CITY(1951); SNAKE RIVER DESPERADOES(1951); CATTLE TOWN(1952); LAST MUSKETEER, THE(1952); ROUGH, TOUGH WEST, THE(1952); SMOKY CANYON(1952); SOUND OFF(1952); THUNDERING CARAVANS(1952); GREAT SIOUX UPRISING, THE(1953); NEBRASKAN, THE(1953); COMMAND, THE(1954); RIDING SHOTGUN(1954); ROBBER'S ROOST(1955); TEN WANTED MEN(1955); VIOLENT SATURDAY(1955); D-DAY, THE SIXTH OF JUNE(1956); KETTLES ON OLD MACDONALD'S FARM, THE(1957); PILLOW TALK(1959); RIDE LONESOME(1959); GUNFIGHTERS OF ABILENE(1960); SPARTACUS(1960); GAMBLER WORE A GUN, THE(1961); HOW THE WEST WAS WON(1962); ROBIN AND THE SEVEN HOODS(1964); FIVE CARD STUD(1968); RIO LOBO(1970); DIRTY HARRY(1971); ONE LITTLE INDIAN(1973); SANTEE(1973); SOUL OF NIGGER CHARLEY, THE(1973)
Misc. Talkies
LAST MUSKETEER, THE(1952)

Bruce Morgan
MYSTERY SUBMARINE(1950)

Bryon Morgan
IT'S IN THE AIR(1935), w
Silents
RACING HEARTS(1923), w

Buck Morgan
DEMON FOR TROUBLE, A(1934)

Byron Morgan
WAY OUT WEST(1930), w; FIVE STAR FINAL(1931), w; RULING VOICE, THE(1931), d; FAST LIFE(1932), w; FLYING DEVILS(1933), w; SONS OF THE DESERT(1933), w; BAND PLAYS ON, THE(1934), w; COME ON, MARINES(1934), w; HELL IN THE HEAVENS(1934), w; SKY PARADE(1936), w; HIGH FLYERS(1937), w; BURN 'EM UP O'CONNER(1939), w; DANGER FLIGHT(1939), w; KID FROM TEXAS, THE(1939), w; WINGS FOR THE EAGLE(1942), w; GALLANT JOURNEY(1946), a, w; HUCKSTERS, THE(1947)

Silents
ROARING ROAD, THE(1919), w; EXCUSE MY DUST(1920), w; WHAT'S YOUR HURRY?(1920), w; TOO MUCH SPEED(1921), w; ACROSS THE CONTINENT(1922), w; SKID PROOF(1923), w; CODE OF THE SEA(1924), w; FLAMING BARRIERS(1924), w; AIR MAIL, THE(1925), w; PACE THAT THRILLS, THE(1925), w; ONE MINUTE TO PLAY(1926), w; CALIFORNIA OR BUST(1927), w; FAIR CO-ED, THE(1927), w; RACING ROMEO(1927), w; SMART SET, THE(1928), w; THANKS FOR THE BUGGY RIDE(1928), w; THUNDER(1929), w

Casey Morgan
LEPKE(1975, U.S./Israel)

Chad Morgan
DIMBOOLA(1979, Aus.); NEWSFRONT(1979, Aus.)

Charles Morgan
FOUNTAIN, THE(1934), w; SHADOW VALLEY(1947); TRAIN OF EVENTS(1952, Brit.); HELL IS A CITY(1960, Brit.); DAY THE EARTH CAUGHT FIRE, THE(1961, Brit.); CASH ON DEMAND(1962, Brit.); RETURN OF THE SOLDIER, THE(1983, Brit.)

Charlotte Morgan
Misc. Silents
SILVER FINGERS(1926)

Chesty Morgan
Misc. Talkies
DEADLY WEAPONS(1974); DOUBLE AGENT 73(1974)

Cindy Morgan
CADDY SHACK(1980); TRON(1982)

Clarence Morgan
Silents
JOYOUS TROUBLEMAKERS, THE(1920)

Clark Morgan
MEET JOHN DOE(1941); FOR LOVE OF IVY(1968)

Claude Morgan
WHITE ZOMBIE(1932)

Claudia Morgan
ONCE IN A LIFETIME(1932); VANITY STREET(1932); THAT'S MY STORY(1937); STAND UP AND FIGHT(1939)

Cleo Morgan
CUBAN PETE(1946); TWO SMART PEOPLE(1946)

Clive Morgan
MYSTERY OF MR. X, THE(1934); LIVES OF A BENGAL LANCER(1935); PETER IBBETSON(1935); WITHOUT REGRET(1935); DRACULA'S DAUGHTER(1936); NEXT TIME WE LOVE(1936); MAID OF SALEM(1937); BOOLOO(1938); YOU CAN'T TAKE IT WITH YOU(1938); GUNGA DIN(1939); IN NAME ONLY(1939); MY FAVORITE WIFE(1940); RAGE IN HEAVEN(1941); JOURNEY FOR MARGARET(1942); RINGS ON HER FINGERS(1942); SON OF FURY(1942); UNDYING MONSTER, THE(1942); GOVERNMENT GIRL(1943); MISSION TO MOSCOW(1943); LODGER, THE(1944); MAN IN HALF-MOON STREET, THE(1944); MINISTRY OF FEAR(1945); CLUNY BROWN(1946); UNDERCURRENT(1946); IVY(1947); JOAN OF ARC(1948); SOLDIERS THREE(1951); DREAMBOAT(1952); MILLION DOLLAR MERMAID(1952); YOUNG BESS(1953); ABBOTT AND COSTELLO MEET DR. JEKYLL AND MR. HYDE(1954); BLACK SLEEP, THE(1956); YOUNG LIONS, THE(1958); NOTORIOUS LANDLADY, THE(1962)

Corney Morgan
DAMIEN-OMEN II(1978); PSYCHOTRONIC MAN, THE(1980)

Dan Morgan
CHARLY(1968); PRETTY POISON(1968); GANG THAT COULDN'T SHOOT STRAIGHT, THE(1971)

Danny Morgan
THUNDER TRAIL(1937); LADY IN RED, THE(1979), cos

Dave Morgan
1984
OH GOD! YOU DEVIL(1984)

David Morgan
1984
BRADY'S ESCAPE(1984, U.S./Hung.)

Debbi Morgan
MONKEY HUSTLE, THE(1976)

Debbie Morgan
MANDINGO(1975)

Del Morgan
Misc. Talkies
OUTLAWS' HIGHWAY(1934)

Dennis Morgan
PICCADILLY JIM(1936); SUZY(1936); MEN WITH WINGS(1938); NO PLACE TO GO(1939); RETURN OF DR. X, THE(1939); WATERFRONT(1939); FIGHTING 69TH, THE(1940); FLIGHT ANGELS(1940); KITTY FOYLE(1940); RIVER'S END(1940); TEAR GAS SQUAD(1940); THREE CHEERS FOR THE IRISH(1940); AFFECTIONATELY YOURS(1941); BAD MEN OF MISSOURI(1941); KISSES FOR BREAKFAST(1941); CAPTAINS OF THE CLOUDS(1942); HARD WAY, THE(1942); IN THIS OUR LIFE(1942); WINGS FOR THE EAGLE(1942); DESERT SONG, THE(1943); THANK YOUR LUCKY STARS(1943); HOLLYWOOD CANTEEN(1944); SHINE ON, HARVEST MOON(1944); VERY THOUGHT OF YOU, THE(1944); CHRISTMAS IN CONNECTICUT(1945); GOD IS MY CO-PILOT(1945); ONE MORE TOMORROW(1946); TIME, THE PLACE AND THE GIRL, THE(1946); CHEYENNE(1947); MY WILD IRISH ROSE(1947); ONE SUNDAY AFTERNOON(1948); TO THE VICTOR(1948); TWO GUYS FROM TEXAS(1948); IT'S A GREAT FEELING(1949); LADY TAKES A SAILOR, THE(1949); PERFECT STRANGERS(1950); PRETTY BABY(1950); PAINTING THE CLOUDS WITH SUNSHINE(1951); RATON PASS(1951); CATTLE TOWN(1952); THIS WOMAN IS DANGEROUS(1952); GUN THAT WON THE WEST, THE(1955); PEARL OF THE SOUTH PACIFIC(1955); URANIUM BOOM(1956); WON TON TON, THE DOG WHO SAVED HOLLYWOOD(1976)
Misc. Talkies
ROGUE'S GALLERY(1968)

Devi "Debbie" Morgan
TAXI DRIVER(1976)

Diana Morgan
SHIPS WITH WINGS(1942, Brit.), w; FIDDLERS THREE(1944, Brit.), w; 48 HOURS(1944, Brit.), w; HALF-WAY HOUSE, THE(1945, Brit.), w; POET'S PUB(1949, Brit.), w; DANCE HALL(1950, Brit.), w; PINK STRING AND SEALING WAX(1950, Brit.), w; RUN FOR YOUR MONEY, A(1950, Brit.), w; LET'S BE HAPPY(1957, Brit.), w; HAND IN HAND(1960, Brit.), w

Dick Morgan
HORROR OF DRACULA, THE(1958, Brit.)
Dickson Morgan
EMBARRASSING MOMENTS(1934), w
Don Morgan
HONKY TONK FREEWAY(1981)
Donald Morgan
MEDIUM, THE(1951); SANTEE(1973), ph; HYSTERICAL(1983), ph
Donald H. Morgan
PIECE OF THE ACTION, A(1977), ph
Donald M. Morgan
LET'S DO IT AGAIN(1975), ph; SHEILA LEVINE IS DEAD AND LIVING IN NEW YORK(1975), ph; ONE ON ONE(1977), ph; I WANNA HOLD YOUR HAND(1978), ph; SKATETOWN, U.S.A.(1979), ph; USED CARS(1980), ph; CHRISTINE(1983), ph
1984
MEATBALLS PART II(1984), ph; STARMAN(1984), ph
Donald R. Morgan
OFF THE WALL(1983), ph
Ed Morgan
YOU LIGHT UP MY LIFE(1977)
Eddie Morgan
I LIVE FOR LOVE(1935)
Edward Morgan
BLONDE CRAZY(1931); SIDE SHOW(1931); BY APPOINTMENT ONLY(1933)
Edwin T. Morgan
IF EVER I SEE YOU AGAIN(1978)
Elemore Morgan
DESIRE IN THE DUST(1960)
Elliot Morgan
ROMANCE OF ROSY RIDGE, THE(1947), set d
Emily Morgan
FRENCH LIEUTENANT'S WOMAN, THE(1981)
Erskine Morgan
1984
BIRDY(1984)
Eula Morgan
GREAT AMERICAN BROADCAST, THE(1941); MRS. MINIVER(1942); SECRETS OF THE UNDERGROUND(1943); SONG OF BERNADETTE, THE(1943); ANGEL COMES TO BROOKLYN, AN(1945); LEAVE IT TO BLONDIE(1945); GALLANT JOURNEY(1946); NIGHT IN PARADISE, A(1946); MOTHER WORE TIGHTS(1947); IRON CURTAIN, THE(1948); LOVES OF CARMEN, THE(1948); MADAME BOVARY(1949); OH, YOU BEAUTIFUL DOLL(1949)
Felicite Morgan
BOOGEYMAN II(1983)
Francine Morgan
MISSIONARY, THE(1982); WICKED LADY, THE(1983, Brit.)
Francis [Frank] Morgan
Misc. Silents
DARING OF DIANA, THE(1916)
Frank Morgan
DANGEROUS NAN McGREW(1930); FAST AND LOOSE(1930); LAUGHTER(1930); QUEEN HIGH(1930); BILLION DOLLAR SCANDAL(1932); HALF-NAKED TRUTH, THE(1932); SECRETS OF THE FRENCH POLICE(1932); BEST OF ENEMIES(1933); BOMBSHELL(1933); BROADWAY TO HOLLYWOOD(1933); HALLELUJAH, I'M A BUM(1933); KISS BEFORE THE MIRROR, THE(1933); LUXURY LINER(1933); NUISANCE, THE(1933); REUNION IN VIENNA(1933); WHEN LADIES MEET(1933); AFFAIRS OF CELLINI, THE(1934); CAT AND THE FIDDLE(1934); LOST LADY, A(1934); MIGHTY BARNUM, THE(1934); SISTERS UNDER THE SKIN(1934); SUCCESS AT ANY PRICE(1934); BY YOUR LEAVE(1935); ENCHANTED APRIL(1935); ESCAPADE(1935); GOOD FAIRY, THE(1935); I LIVE MY LIFE(1935); LAZYBONES(1935, Brit.); NAUGHTY MARIETTA(1935); PERFECT GENTLEMAN, THE(1935); DANCING PIRATE(1936); DIMPLES(1936); GREAT ZIEGFELD, THE(1936); PICCADILLY JIM(1936); TROUBLE FOR TWO(1936); BEG, BORROW OR STEAL(1937); EMPEROR'S CANDLESTICKS, THE(1937); LAST OF MRS. CHEYNEY, THE(1937); ROSALIE(1937); SARATOGA(1937); BATTLE OF BROADWAY(1938); CROWD ROARS, THE(1938); PARADISE FOR THREE(1938); PORT OF SEVEN SEAS(1938); SWEETHEARTS(1938); BALALAIKA(1939); BROADWAY SERENADE(1939); HENRY GOES ARIZONA(1939); WIZARD OF OZ, THE(1939); BOOM TOWN(1940); BROADWAY MELODY OF 1940(1940); GHOST COMES HOME, THE(1940); HULLABALOO(1940); MORTAL STORM, THE(1940); SHOP AROUND THE CORNER, THE(1940); HONKY TONK(1941); KEEPING COMPANY(1941); VANISHING VIRGINIAN, THE(1941); WASHINGTON MELODRAMA(1941); WILD MAN OF BORNEO, THE(1941); TORTILLA FLAT(1942); WHITE CARGO(1942); HUMAN COMEDY, THE(1943); STRANGER IN TOWN, A(1943); THOUSANDS CHEER(1943); CASANOVA BROWN(1944); WHITE CLIFFS OF DOVER, THE(1944); YOLANDA AND THE THIEF(1945); BLUE SIERRA(1946); COCKEYED MIRACLE, THE(1946); COURAGE OF LASSIE(1946); LADY LUCK(1946); GREEN DOLPHIN STREET(1947); SUMMER HOLIDAY(1948); THREE MUSKETEERS, THE(1948); ANY NUMBER CAN PLAY(1949); GREAT SINNER, THE(1949); STRATTON STORY, THE(1949); KEY TO THE CITY(1950)
Misc. Talkies
GREAT MORGAN, THE(1946)
Silents
BABY MINE(1917); MODERN CINDERELLA, A(1917); KNIFE, THE(1918)
Misc. Silents
CHILD OF THE WILD, A(1917); GIRL PHILIPPA, THE(1917); LIGHT IN DARKNESS(1917); RAFFLES, THE AMATEUR CRACKSMAN(1917); WHO'S YOUR NEIGHBOR?(1917); AT THE MERCY OF MEN(1918); GOLDEN SHOWER, THE(1919); GRAY TOWERS MYSTERY, THE(1919); CROWED HOUR, THE(1925); MAN WHO FOUND HIMSELF, THE(1925); SCARLET SAINT(1925)
Fred Morgan
Silents
EAST LYNNE(1913, Brit.); FLYING FROM JUSTICE(1915, Brit.); GRIT OF A JEW, THE(1917, Brit.); PRIDE OF THE FANCY, THE(1920, Brit.)
Misc. Silents
(; HARBOUR LIGHTS, THE(1914, Brit.); REVOLUTIONIST, THE(1914, Brit.); MAN IN MOTLEY, THE(1916, Brit.); BEETLE, THE(1919, Brit.); FETTERED(1919, Brit.); LAND OF MYSTERY, THE(1920, Brit.); TROUSERS(1920, Brit.)

G. B. Morgan
LIVE AGAIN(1936, Brit.), p
Garfield Morgan
PRIVATE POOLEY(1962, Brit./E. Ger.); ON THE RUN(1967, Brit.); OUR MOTHER'S HOUSE(1967, Brit.); PERFECT FRIDAY(1970, Brit.); CATCH ME A SPY(1971, Brit./Fr.); HENRY VIII AND HIS SIX WIVES(1972, Brit.); DIGBY, THE BIGGEST DOG IN THE WORLD(1974, Brit.); ODESSA FILE, THE(1974, Brit./Ger.)
Gary Morgan
WAIT UNTIL DARK(1967); PEACE KILLERS, THE(1971); FUZZ(1972); STUDENT TEACHERS, THE(1973); NIGHT GOD SCREAMED, THE(1975); LOGAN'S RUN(1976); PETE'S DRAGON(1977); SUMMER SCHOOL TEACHERS(1977); NORTH AVENUE IRREGULARS, THE(1979); FINAL COUNTDOWN, THE(1980)
1984
LOVELINES(1984)
Gene Morgan
ROGUE OF THE RIO GRANDE(1930); ANYBODY'S BLONDE(1931); NECK AND NECK(1931); PARDON US(1931); BLONDE VENUS(1932); NIGHT WORLD(1932); PACK UP YOUR TROUBLES(1932); TANGLED DESTINIES(1932); ELMER THE GREAT(1933); JENNIE GERHARDT(1933); SONG OF THE EAGLE(1933); ALIBI IKE(1935); DR. SOCRATES(1935); G-MEN(1935); MEN OF THE HOUR(1935); PUBLIC MENACE(1935); SHE COULDN'T TAKE IT(1935); WE'RE IN THE MONEY(1935); WINGS IN THE DARK(1935); ALIBI FOR MURDER(1936); AND SO THEY WERE MARRIED(1936); COME CLOSER, FOLKS(1936); COUNTERFEIT(1936); DANGEROUS INTRIGUE(1936); DEVIL'S SQUADRON(1936); END OF THE TRAIL(1936); IF YOU COULD ONLY COOK(1936); LADY FROM NOWHERE(1936); MEET NERO WOLFE(1936); MR. DEEDS GOES TO TOWN(1936); MUSIC GOES ROUND, THE(1936); SHAKEDOWN(1936); TWO-FISTED GENTLEMAN(1936); YOU MAY BE NEXT(1936); ALL-AMERICAN SWEETHEART(1937); COUNSEL FOR CRIME(1937); COUNTERFEIT LADY(1937); DEVIL'S PLAYGROUND(1937); GIRLS CAN PLAY(1937); MAKE WAY FOR TOMORROW(1937); MURDER IN GREENWICH VILLAGE(1937); PAROLE RACKET(1937); SPEED TO SPARE(1937); VENUS MAKES TROUBLE(1937); WHEN YOU'RE IN LOVE(1937); WOMAN IN DISTRESS(1937); EXTORTION(1938); MAIN EVENT, THE(1938); START CHEERING(1938); THERE'S ALWAYS A WOMAN(1938); WHEN G-MEN STEP IN(1938); WHO KILLED GAIL PRESTON?(1938); YOU CAN'T TAKE IT WITH YOU(1938); FEDERAL MAN-HUNT(1939); HOMICIDE BUREAU(1939); MR. SMITH GOES TO WASHINGTON(1939); ST. LOUIS BLUES(1939); BLONDIE ON A BUDGET(1940); GAUCHO SERENADE(1940); GIRL FROM GOD'S COUNTRY(1940); PRIMROSE PATH(1940); SAPS AT SEA(1940); SON OF THE NAVY(1940); TOMBOY(1940); MEET JOHN DOE(1941); SONG IS BORN, A(1948)
George Morgan
AVENGER, THE(1931), w; CYCLONE KID(1931), w; HEADIN' FOR TROUBLE(1931), w; HUMAN TARGETS(1932), w; HER FORGOTTEN PAST(1933), w; BADGE OF HONOR(1934), w; FIGHTING ROOKIE, THE(1934), w; RESCUE SQUAD(1935), w; DESERT HORSEMAN, THE(1946); NASTY RABBIT, THE(1964); CHAFED ELBOWS(1967); PUTNEY SWOPE(1969); GREASER'S PALACE(1972)
Silents
MERCHANT OF VENICE, THE(1916, Brit.); TANGLED FATES(1916); SOULS FOR SALE(1923); ONE GLORIOUS SCRAP(1927), w; KING OF THE RODEO(1929), w; PLUNGING HOOFS(1929), w; WILD BLOOD(1929), w
Misc. Silents
HER HOUR(1917); CROSS BEARER, THE(1918)
George J. Morgan
THRILL KILLERS, THE(1965), a, p
Georgia Morgan
10 VIOLENT WOMEN(1982)
Gladys Morgan
WILD AFFAIR, THE(1966, Brit.)
Glenn Morgan
Misc. Talkies
INCOMING FRESHMEN(1979), d
Guy Morgan
ANNA KARENINA(1948, Brit.), w; CAPTIVE HEART, THE(1948, Brit.), w; COUNTER BLAST(1948, Brit.), w; DEVIL'S PLOT, THE(1948, Brit.), w; NIGHT BEAT(1948, Brit.), w; HELL IS SOLD OUT(1951, Brit.), w; HER PANELLED DOOR(1951, Brit.), w; NEVER LOOK BACK(1952, Brit.), w; ALBERT, R.N.(1953, Brit.), w; GIRL ON THE PIER, THE(1953, Brit.), w; LOVE IN PAWN(1953, Brit.), w; DEATH OF MICHAEL TURBIN, THE(1954, Brit.), w; EIGHT O'CLOCK WALK(1954, Brit.), w; FRONT PAGE STORY(1954, Brit.), w; RED DRESS, THE(1954, Brit.), w; MAN IN THE ROAD, THE(1957, Brit.), w
H.A. Morgan
BEGGARS OF LIFE(1928); ROGUE SONG, THE(1930)
Harry Morgan
HORN BLOWS AT MIDNIGHT, THE(1945); BACKLASH(1956); STAR IN THE DUST(1956); INHERIT THE WIND(1960); HOW THE WEST WAS WON(1962); JOHN GOLDFARB, PLEASE COME HOME(1964); FRANKIE AND JOHNNY(1966); WHAT DID YOU DO IN THE WAR, DADDY?(1966); FLIM-FLAM MAN, THE(1967); SUPPORT YOUR LOCAL SHERIFF(1969); VIVA MAX!(1969); BAREFOOT EXECUTIVE, THE(1971); SCANDALOUS JOHN(1971); SUPPORT YOUR LOCAL GUNFIGHTER(1971); SNOWBALL EXPRESS(1972); CHARLEY AND THE ANGEL(1973); APPLE DUMPLING GANG, THE(1975); SHOOTIST, THE(1976); CAT FROM OUTER SPACE, THE(1978); APPLE DUMPLING GANG RIDES AGAIN, THE(1979)
Harry Hayes Morgan
MY NAME IS JULIA ROSS(1945); PARIS UNDERGROUND(1945)
Harry Hays Morgan
STANDING ROOM ONLY(1944); ABIE'S IRISH ROSE(1946); AVALANCHE(1946); DO YOU LOVE ME?(1946); NEVER SAY GOODBYE(1946); DOUBLE LIFE, A(1947); IT HAD TO BE YOU(1947); IVY(1947); NIGHTMARE ALLEY(1947); JOAN OF ARC(1948); LULU BELLE(1948)
Helen Morgan
APPLAUSE(1929); SHOW BOAT(1929); GLORIFYING THE AMERICAN GIRL(1930); ROADHOUSE NIGHTS(1930); MARIE GALANTE(1934); YOU BELONG TO ME(1934); GO INTO YOUR DANCE(1935); SWEET MUSIC(1935); FRANKIE AND JOHNNY(1936); SHOW BOAT(1936); SLAVERS(1977, Ger.)
Henry Morgan
LOVES OF EDGAR ALLAN POE, THE(1942); OMAHA TRAIL(1942); CRASH DIVE(1943); HAPPY LAND(1943); EVE OF ST. MARK, THE(1944); GENTLE ANNIE(1944); BELL FOR ADANO, A(1945); DRAGONWYCH(1946); FROM THIS DAY FORWARD(1946); IT SHOULDN'T HAPPEN TO A DOG(1946); SOMEWHERE IN THE NIGHT(1946); GANGSTER, THE(1947); ALL MY SONS(1948); BIG CLOCK, THE(1948); SAXON CHARM, THE(1948); SO THIS IS NEW YORK(1948); DOWN TO THE SEA IN

SHIPS(1949); HOLIDAY AFFAIR(1949); DARK CITY(1950); SHOWDOWN, THE(1950); APPOINTMENT WITH DANGER(1951); BELLE LE GRAND(1951); BLUE VEIL, THE(1951); HIGHWAYMAN, THE(1951); APACHE WAR SMOKE(1952); BEND OF THE RIVER(1952); HIGH NOON(1952); SCANDAL SHEET(1952); WHAT PRICE GLORY?(1952); ARENA(1953); CHAMP FOR A DAY(1953); ABOUT MRS. LESLIE(1954); FORTYNINERS, THE(1954); STRATEGIC AIR COMMAND(1955); IT HAPPENED TO JANE(1959); CIMARRON(1960); MURDER, INC.(1960)

Henry [Harry] Morgan
ORCHESTRA WIVES(1942); TO THE SHORES OF TRIPOLI(1942); OX-BOW INCIDENT, THE(1943); ROGER TOUHY, GANGSTER!(1944); WING AND A PRAYER(1944); STATE FAIR(1945); JOHNNY COMES FLYING HOME(1946); MOONRISE(1948); RACE STREET(1948); SILVER RIVER(1948); YELLOW SKY(1948); MADAME BOVARY(1949); RED LIGHT(1949); STRANGE BARGAIN(1949); OUTSIDE THE WALL(1950); WELL, THE(1951); WHEN I GROW UP(1951); BOOTS MALONE(1952); MY SIX CONVICTS(1952); STOP, YOU'RE KILLING ME(1952); TOUGHEST MAN IN ARIZONA(1952); GLENN MILLER STORY, THE(1953); THUNDER BAY(1953); TORCH SONG(1953); PRISONER OF WAR(1954); FAR COUNTRY, THE(1955); NOT AS A STRANGER(1955); TEAHOUSE OF THE AUGUST MOON, THE(1956); UNDER FIRE(1957); IT STARTED WITH A KISS(1959); MOUNTAIN ROAD, THE(1960)

Horace Morgan
Silents
THREE AGES, THE(1923); SHERLOCK, JR.(1924)
Misc. Silents
BORDER LEGION, THE(1919)

Ida Morgan
STAKEOUT ON DOPE STREET(1958)

Ira Morgan
GREAT GABBO, THE(1929), ph; UNHOLY NIGHT, THE(1929), ph; BROTHERS(1930), ph; CHASING RAINBOWS(1930), ph; GIRL SAID NO, THE(1930), ph; SEA BAT, THE(1930), ph; SHIP FROM SHANGHAI, THE(1930), ph; SINNER'S HOLIDAY(1930), ph; CAPTAIN APPLEJACK(1931), ph; MAN TO MAN(1931), ph; HOTEL CONTINENTAL(1932), ph; LENA RIVERS(1932), ph; MANHATTAN TOWER(1932), ph; UNWRITTEN LAW, THE(1932), ph; WASHINGTON MERRY-GO-ROUND(1932), ph; SIN OF NORA MORAN(1933), ph; SING SINNER, SING(1933), ph; SON OF A SAILOR(1933), ph; VAMPIRE BAT, THE(1933), ph; WORLD GONE MAD, THE(1933), ph; CURTAIN AT EIGHT(1934), ph; FRIENDS OF MR. SWEENEY(1934), ph; GIRL OF THE LIMBERLOST(1934), ph; JIMMY THE GENT(1934), ph; RED HEAD(1934), ph; UNKNOWN BLONDE(1934), ph; VERY HONORABLE GUY, A(1934), ph; GIRL O' MY DREAMS(1935), ph; LOST IN THE STRATOSPHERE(1935), ph; I'D GIVE MY LIFE(1936), ph; MODERN TIMES(1936), ph; ALONG CAME LOVE(1937), ph; DAMAGED GOODS(1937), ph; GIRL OVERBOARD(1937), ph; GIRL SAID NO, THE(1937), ph; THREE LEGIONNAIRES(1937), ph; WALLABY JIM OF THE ISLANDS(1937), ph; WESTLAND CASE, THE(1937), ph; BLACK DOLL, THE(1938), ph; ON THE GREAT WHITE TRAIL(1938), ph; BORDER BUCKAROOS(1943), ph; DANGER! WOMEN AT WORK(1943), ph; FIGHTING VALLEY(1943), ph; GIRLS IN CHAINS(1943), ph; ISLE OF FORGOTTEN SINS(1943), ph; PAYOFF, THE(1943), ph; TIGER FANGS(1943), ph; WEST OF TEXAS(1943), ph; WHERE ARE YOUR CHILDREN?(1943), ph; BOWERY CHAMPS(1944), ph; CHARLIE CHAN IN THE SECRET SERVICE(1944), ph; CHINESE CAT, THE(1944), ph; DELINQUENT DAUGHTERS(1944), ph; DETECTIVE KITTY O'DAY(1944), ph; GUNSMOKE MESA(1944), ph; HOT RHYTHM(1944), ph; JIVE JUNCTION(1944), ph; JOHNNY DOESN'T LIVE HERE ANY MORE(1944), ph; LEAVE IT TO THE IRISH(1944), ph; SWEETHEARTS OF THE U.S.A.(1944), ph; TRAIL OF TERROR(1944), ph; WHEN STRANGERS MARRY(1944), ph; WHEN THE LIGHTS GO ON AGAIN(1944), ph; COME OUT FIGHTING(1945), ph; DOCKS OF NEW YORK(1945), ph; FOG ISLAND(1945), ph; HOLLYWOOD AND VINE(1945), ph; MR. MUGGS RIDES AGAIN(1945), ph; ROGUES GALLERY(1945), ph; SENSATION HUNTERS(1945), ph; STRANGE MR. GREGORY, THE(1945), ph; FREDDIE STEPS OUT(1946), ph; HIGH SCHOOL HERO(1946), ph; JUNIOR PROM(1946), ph; VACATION DAYS(1947), ph; CYCLOPS(1957), ph
Silents
POOR RELATIONS(1919), ph; WHEN KNIGHTHOOD WAS IN FLOWER(1922), ph; ENEMIES OF WOMEN, THE(1923), ph; TELL IT TO THE MARINES(1926), ph; CALLAHANS AND THE MURPHYS, THE(1927), ph; LITTLE JOURNEY, A(1927), ph; TAXI DANCER, THE(1927), ph; TWELVE MILES OUT(1927), ph; EXCESS BAGGAGE(1928), ph; RED MARK, THE(1928), ph; WEST POINT(1928), ph; DUKE STEPS OUT, THE(1929), ph; FLYING FEET, THE(1929), ph

Ira H. Morgan
I ESCAPED FROM THE GESTAPO(1943), ph; GLAMOUR GIRL(1947), ph; LAST OF THE REDMEN(1947), ph; LITTLE MISS BROADWAY(1947), ph; TWO BLONDES AND A REDHEAD(1947), ph; MANHATTAN ANGEL(1948), ph; MARY LOU(1948), ph; RACING LUCK(1948), ph; WEST OF SONORA(1948), ph; BARBARY PIRATE(1949), ph; BLAZING TRAIL, THE(1949), ph; LOST TRIBE, THE(1949), ph; MUTINEERS, THE(1949), ph; CAPTIVE GIRL(1950), ph; CHAIN GANG(1950), ph; PYGMY ISLAND(1950), ph; REVENUE AGENT(1950), ph; STATE PENITENTIARY(1950), ph; TYRANT OF THE SEA(1950), ph; FURY OF THE CONGO(1951), ph; DEVIL GODDESS(1955), ph
Silents
JACK KNIFE MAN, THE(1920), ph; ENCHANTMENT(1921), ph; JANICE MEREDITH(1924), ph; NEVER THE TWAIN SHALL MEET(1925), ph; PRETTY LADIES(1925), ph; BARRIER, THE(1926), ph; BROWN OF HARVARD(1926), ph

Ira J. Morgan
WHISTLIN' DAN(1932), ph

Ira L. Morgan
CORREGIDOR(1943), ph

Ira S. Morgan
MARK OF THE GORILLA(1950), ph

J. Lee Morgan
1984
BOSTONIANS, THE(1984)

Jackie Morgan
BAREFOOT BOY(1938)
Silents
ARIZONA SWEEPSTAKES(1926)

Jane Morgan
OUR MISS BROOKS(1956)

Janet Morgan
COWBOY AND THE BANDIT, THE(1935)
Misc. Talkies
OUTLAW TAMER, THE(1934)

Jaye P. Morgan
ALL-AMERICAN BOY, THE(1973); GONG SHOW MOVIE, THE(1980); LOOSE SHOES(1980)
1984
NIGHT PATROL(1984)

Jeanne Morgan
WHOOPEE(1930)
Silents
SORROWS OF SATAN(1926); GREAT MAIL ROBBERY, THE(1927)
Misc. Silents
BREED OF COURAGE(1927); SLINGSHOT KID, THE(1927)

Jeff Morgan
TERROR ON TOUR(1980)

Jenny Morgan
BLACK DIAMONDS(1932, Brit.); OH! WHAT A LOVELY WAR(1969, Brit.)

Jim Morgan
QUEEN FOR A DAY(1951); CUP FEVER(1965, Brit.)

Joan Morgan
HER REPUTATION(1931, Brit.); THIS WAS A WOMAN(1949, Brit.), w
Silents
IRON JUSTICE(1915, Brit.); ROAD TO LONDON, THE(1921, Brit.); CRIMSON CIRCLE, THE(1922, Brit.); FIRES OF INNOCENCE(1922, Brit.); SHADOW OF EGYPT, THE(1924, Brit.); WOMAN TEMPTED, THE(1928, Brit.); LADY NOGGS-PEERESS(1929, Brit.)
Misc. Silents
LIGHT(1915, Brit.); WORLD'S DESIRE, THE(1915, Brit.); HER GREATEST PERFORMANCE(1916, Brit.); CHILDREN OF GIBEON, THE(1920, Brit.); SCARLET WOOING, THE(1920, Brit.); TWO LITTLE WOODEN SHOES(1920, Brit.); LOWLAND CINDERELLA, A(1921, Brit.); DICKY MONTEITH(1922, Brit.); LILAC SUNBONNET, THE(1922, Brit.); TRUANTS, THE(1922, Brit.); NEGLECTED WOMEN(1924, Brit.); WINDOW IN PICCADILLY, A(1928, Brit.); THREE MEN IN A CART(1929, Brit.)

Joanna Morgan
REUBEN, REUBEN(1983)

John Morgan
BLACK DIAMONDS(1932, Brit.); BIG FIX, THE(1947); DOUBLE LIFE, A(1947); FIGHTER SQUADRON(1948); INTRUDER IN THE DUST(1949); LADY TAKES A SAILOR, THE(1949); GREAT JEWEL ROBBER, THE(1950); OUTRAGE(1950); BANNERLINE(1951); HE RAN ALL THE WAY(1951); ON THE LOOSE(1951); JET PILOT(1957); ON THE BEACH(1959); CAYMAN TRIANGLE, THE(1977)

Mrs. John Morgan
BLACK DIAMONDS(1932, Brit.)

K. Morgan
Silents
BETTER 'OLE, THE(1926)

Kate Morgan
MADAME RACKETEER(1932)

Kenneth Morgan
FRENCH WITHOUT TEARS(1939, Brit.); PAPER ORCHID(1949, Brit.)

Kewpie Morgan
AVIATOR, THE(1929); SPIELER, THE(1929); SQUARE SHOULDERS(1929); OTHER MEN'S WOMEN(1931); BABES IN TOYLAND(1934)
Silents
ATTA BOY!(1926); FINNEGAN'S BALL(1927); SPUDS(1927)
Misc. Silents
FLYING LUCK(1927)

Lee Morgan
CHEYENNE TAKES OVER(1947); FIGHTING VIGILANTES, THE(1947); RETURN OF THE LASH(1947); SHADOW VALLEY(1947); STAGE TO MESA CITY(1947); BLACK HILLS(1948); FRONTIER REVENGE(1948); WESTWARD TRAIL, THE(1948); ROLL, THUNDER, ROLL(1949); RAIDERS OF TOMAHAWK CREEK(1950); RIDIN' THE OUTLAW TRAIL(1951); VANISHING OUTPOST, THE(1951); MAN BEHIND THE GUN, THE(1952); DANIEL BOONE, TRAIL BLAZER(1957); SUN ALSO RISES, THE(1957); LAST OF THE FAST GUNS, THE(1958); SIERRA BARON(1958); VILLA!(1958); LAST REBEL, THE(1961, Mex.); WEIRD ONES, THE(1962); DUNGEONS OF HARROW(1964); NO MAN'S LAND(1964)
Misc. Talkies
RIO GRANDE(1949); BORDER FENCE(1951)
Misc. Silents
LA LA LUCILLE(1920), d

Leone Morgan
Silents
BAB'S BURGLAR(1917)

Leonora Morgan
Silents
BAB'S DIARY(1917)

Leota Morgan
Silents
STREETS OF NEW YORK, THE(1922), w; GAMBLING WIVES(1924), w; LIGHT IN THE WINDOW, THE(1927), w

Luce Morgan
WOMAN INSIDE, THE(1981)

Maitzi Morgan
MOUSE AND HIS CHILD, THE(1977)

Margaret Morgan
FUGITIVE LADY(1934); AND SO THEY WERE MARRIED(1936)

Marilyn Morgan [Marian Marsh]
HELL'S ANGELS(1930); WHOOPEE(1930)

Marion Morgan
GOIN' TO TOWN(1935), w; KLONDIKE ANNIE(1936), w

Marjorie Morgan
MARIE-ANN(1978, Can.), w

Marvin Morgan
1984
TEACHERS(1984)

Max Morgan
MAN FROM BUTTON WILLOW, THE(1965), ph
Maxine Morgan "Miss Australia"
YANKEE PASHA(1954)
Melissa Morgan
NASTY RABBIT, THE(1964); DEADWOOD'76(1965)
Michael Morgan
GUN THAT WON THE WEST, THE(1955); HOMEWORK(1982)
1984
VAMPING(1984), set d
Michael P. Morgan
SQUEEZE PLAY(1981)
Michele Morgan
PORT OF SHADOWS(1938, Fr.); HEART OF PARIS(1939, Fr.); JOAN OF PA-
RIS(1942); HEART OF A NATION, THE(1943, Fr.); HIGHER AND HIGHER(1943);
TWO TICKETS TO LONDON(1943); PASSAGE TO MARSEILLE(1944); CHASE,
THE(1946); STORMY WATERS(1946, Fr.); SYMPHONIE PASTORALE(1948, Fr.);
FALLEN IDOL, THE(1949, Brit.); FABIOLA(1951, Ital.); DAUGHTERS OF DES-
TINY(1954, Fr./Ital.); OBSESSION(1954, Fr./Ital.); NAKED HEART, THE(1955, Brit.);
NAPOLEON(1955, Fr.); GRAND MANEUVER, THE(1956, Fr.); VINTAGE, THE(1957);
MIRROR HAS TWO FACES, THE(1959, Fr.); CRIME DOES NOT PAY(1962, Fr.);
MAXIME(1962, Fr.); LANDRU(1963, Fr./Ital); THREE FACES OF SIN(1963, Fr./Ital.);
LOVE ON THE RIVIERA(1964, Fr./Ital.); LOST COMMAND, THE(1966); WEB OF
FEAR(1966, Fr./Span.); BENJAMIN(1968, Fr.); CAT AND MOUSE(1978, Fr.)
Michelle Morgan
IF PARIS WERE TOLD TO US(1956, Fr.)
Mike Morgan
HORSE'S MOUTH, THE(1958, Brit.)
Nancy Morgan
FRATERNITY ROW(1977); GRAND THEFT AUTO(1977); AMERICATHON(1979);
POLYESTER(1981)
1984
HAMBONE AND HILLIE(1984)
Norri Morgan
OUTLAND(1981)
Olive Morgan
WHEN YOU'RE IN LOVE(1937)
Paddy Morgan
MEN ARE NOT GODS(1937, Brit.)
Patsy Morgan
COWBOY FROM SUNDOWN(1940)
Patti Morgan
HERE COMES TROUBLE(1948); IDOL OF PARIS(1948, Brit.); STOP PRESS
GIRL(1949, Brit.); PERFECT WOMAN, THE(1950, Brit.); BOOBY TRAP(1957, Brit.);
THEM NICE AMERICANS(1958, Brit.)
Paul Morgan
VIENNA, CITY OF SONGS(1931, Ger.); RENDEZ-VOUS(1932, Ger.)
Misc. Silents
GOLDEN SEA, THE(1919, Ger.); SPIDERS, THE(1919, Ger.)
Paula Morgan
DAVID AND BATHSHEBA(1951)
Pauline Chew Morgan
MISTER BROWN(1972)
Percy Morgan
Misc. Silents
HIDDEN HAND, THE(1916, Brit.)
Phalba Morgan
Silents
GIRL IN EVERY PORT, A(1928)
Philippa Morgan
TOWN LIKE ALICE, A(1958, Brit.)
Priscilla Morgan
SEPARATE TABLES(1958); OPERATION SNAFU(1965, Brit.); IDOL, THE(1966, Brit.)
Ralph Morgan
HONOR AMONG LOVERS(1931); CHARLIE CHAN'S CHANCE(1932); CHEATERS
AT PLAY(1932); DANCE TEAM(1932); DEVIL'S LOTTERY(1932); DISORDERLY
CONDUCT(1932); RASPUTIN AND THE EMPRESS(1932); SON-DAUGHTER,
THE(1932); STRANGE INTERLUDE(1932); DR. BULL(1933); HUMANITY(1933); KEN-
NEL MURDER CASE, THE(1933); MAD GAME, THE(1933); TRICK FOR TRICK(1933); WALLS
OF GOLD(1933); GIRL OF THE LIMBERLOST(1934); HELL IN THE HEAVENS(1934);
LAST GENTLEMAN, THE(1934); NO GREATER GLORY(1934); ORIENT EX-
PRESS(1934); SHE WAS A LADY(1934); STAND UP AND CHEER(1934 80m FOX bw);
THEIR BIG MOMENT(1934); TRANSATLANTIC MERRY-GO-ROUND(1934); CALM
YOURSELF(1935); CONDEMNED TO LIVE(1935); I'VE BEEN AROUND(1935); LIT-
TLE MEN(1935); MAGNIFICENT OBSESSION(1935); STAR OF MIDNIGHT(1935);
UNWELCOME STRANGER(1935); ANTHONY ADVERSE(1936); EX-MRS. BRAD-
FORD, THE(1936); HUMAN CARGO(1936); LITTLE MISS NOBODY(1936); MUSS 'EM
UP(1936); SPEED(1936); YELLOWSTONE(1936); CRACK-UP, THE(1937); EXCLU-
SIVE(1937); GENERAL SPANKY(1937); LIFE OF EMILE ZOLA, THE(1937); MAN IN
BLUE, THE(1937); MANNEQUIN(1937); OUTER GATE, THE(1937); THAT'S MY
STORY(1937); WELLS FARGO(1937); ARMY GIRL(1938); BAREFOOT BOY(1938);
LOVE IS A HEADACHE(1938); MOTHER CAREY'S CHICKENS(1938); OUT WEST
WITH THE HARDYS(1938); SHADOWS OVER SHANGHAI(1938); WIVES UNDER
SUSPICION(1938); FAST AND LOOSE(1939); GERONIMO(1939); LONE WOLF SPY
HUNT, THE(1939); MAN OF CONQUEST(1939); ORPHANS OF THE STREET(1939);
SMUGGLED CARGO(1939); TRAPPED IN THE SKY(1939); WAY DOWN
SOUTH(1939); FORTY LITTLE MOTHERS(1940); I'M STILL ALIVE(1940); ADVEN-
TURE IN WASHINGTON(1941); MAD DOCTOR, THE(1941); CLOSE CALL FOR
ELLERY QUEEN, A(1942); GENTLEMAN AFTER DARK, A(1942); KLONDIKE
FURY(1942); NIGHT MONSTER(1942); TRAITOR WITHIN, THE(1942); HITLER'S
MADMAN(1943); JACK LONDON(1943); STAGE DOOR CANTEEN(1943); ENEMY OF
WOMEN(1944); IMPOSTER, THE(1944); MONSTER MAKER, THE(1944); TROCADE-
RO(1944); WEIRD WOMAN(1944); HOLLYWOOD AND VINE(1945); THIS LOVE OF
OURS(1945); BLACK MARKET BABIES(1946); MR. DISTRICT ATTORNEY(1946);
LAST ROUND-UP, THE(1947); SONG OF THE THIN MAN(1947); CREEPER,
THE(1948); SLEEP, MY LOVE(1948); SWORD OF THE AVENGER(1948); BLUE
GRASS OF KENTUCKY(1950); HEART OF THE ROCKIES(1951); GOLD FEVER(1952)

Misc. Talkies
BEHIND PRISON BARS(1937)
Misc. Silents
MADAME X(1916); PENNY PHILANTHROPIST, THE(1917); MAN WHO FOUND
HIMSELF, THE(1925)
Ray Morgan
TWO GALS AND A GUY(1951); WHITE LINE, THE(1952, Ital.)
Raymond L. Morgan
OLD WEST, THE(1952); HIDDEN GUNS(1956)
Read Morgan
ASK ANY GIRL(1959); BEACH GIRLS AND THE MONSTER, THE(1965); BLACK
SPURS(1965); DEADWOOD'76(1965); EASY COME, EASY GO(1967); FORT
UTAH(1967); HOSTILE GUNS(1967); MARLOWE(1969); KELLY'S HEROES(1970,
U.S./Yugo.); NEW CENTURIONS, THE(1972); YOUR THREE MINUTES ARE
UP(1973); SHANKS(1974); BREAKHEART PASS(1976); CANNONBALL(1976, U.S./
Hong Kong); HARRY AND WALTER GO TO NEW YORK(1976); CAR, THE(1977);
BETSY, THE(1978); I WANNA HOLD YOUR HAND(1978); METEOR(1979); TIME
AFTER TIME(1979, Brit.)
1984
ADVENTURES OF BUCKAROO BANZAI: ACROSS THE 8TH DIMENSION,
THE(1984)
Red Morgan
DALTON GIRLS, THE(1957); GUN DUEL IN DURANGO(1957); HELL BOUND(1957);
WAR DRUMS(1957); DATE WITH DEATH, A(1959); AMAZING TRANSPARENT
MAN, THE(1960); BEYOND THE TIME BARRIER(1960); ARIZONA RAIDERS(1965);
BOUNTY KILLER, THE(1965); REQUIEM FOR A GUNFIGHTER(1965); SONS OF
KATIE ELDER, THE(1965); WACO(1966); WAR WAGON, THE(1967); STALKING
MOON, THE(1969); TRUE GRIT(1969); CHEYENNE SOCIAL CLUB, THE(1970); WILD
ROVERS(1971); DEADLY TRACKERS(1973); DILLINGER(1973)
Reuven Morgan
EVERY BASTARD A KING(1968, Israel)
Ric Morgan
1984
SWORD OF THE VALIANT(1984, Brit.)
Richard Morgan
1984
PHAR LAP(1984, Aus.)
Riley Morgan
SEVEN ALONE(1975)
Rion Morgan
INCHON(1981)
Robbi Morgan
WHAT'S THE MATTER WITH HELEN?(1971); FRIDAY THE 13TH(1980)
Robert Morgan
13 RUE MADELEINE(1946); DEATH OF A SCOUNDREL(1956); ALVAREZ KEL-
LY(1966); MACHO CALLAHAN(1970); SWASHBUCKLER(1976)
Robin Morgan
CITIZEN SAINT(1947)
Robyn Morgan
ME, NATALIE(1969)
Russ Morgan
SARGE GOES TO COLLEGE(1947); DISC JOCKEY(1951), a, m, md; GREAT MAN,
THE(1957); MISTER CORY(1957)
Sandra Morgan
IN NAME ONLY(1939); NINOTCHKA(1939); CROSSROADS(1942); FLESH AND
FANTASY(1943); GIRL CRAZY(1943); YOUNGEST PROFESSION, THE(1943); WEEK-
END AT THE WALDORF(1945); NOTORIOUS(1946); LADY IN THE LAKE(1947)
Sean Morgan
WHAT'S UP, DOC?(1972)
Sharon Morgan
GIRO CITY(1982, Brit.)
Sheila Morgan
I MET A MURDERER(1939, Brit.)
Shelley Taylor Morgan
SWORD AND THE SORCERER, THE(1982); MY TUTOR(1983)
Sherill Morgan
DEVIL IN LOVE, THE(1968, Ital.)
Sidney Morgan
CONTRABAND LOVE(1931, Brit.), p&d, w; HER REPUTATION(1931, Brit.), p,d&w;
CHELSEA LIFE(1933, Brit.), p&d, w; MIXED DOUBLES(1933, Brit.), d; FACES(1934,
Brit.), d; ALMOST A GENTLEMAN(1938, Brit.), p, w; LILY OF LAGUNA(1938,
Brit.), p; HONEYMOON MERRY-GO-ROUND(1939, Brit.), p
Silents
IRON JUSTICE(1915, Brit.), d&w; AULD LANG SYNE(1917, Brit.), d&w; BID FOR
FORTUNE, A(1917, Brit.), d&w; DEMOCRACY(1918, Brit.), d&w; AFTER MANY
DAYS(1919, Brit.), d&w, w; MAN'S SHADOW, A(1920, Brit.), d&w; FIRES OF INNO-
CENCE(1922, Brit.), d&w; MIRIAM ROZELLA(1924, Brit.), d&w; SHADOW OF
EGYPT, THE(1924, Brit.), d&w; WOMAN TEMPTED, THE(1928, Brit.), w; LADY
NOGGS-PEERESS(1929, Brit.), d&w
Misc. Silents
BRASS BOTTLE, THE(1914, Brit.), d; ESTHER REDEEMED(1915, Brit.), d;
LIGHT(1915, Brit.), d; WORLD'S DESIRE, THE(1915, Brit.), d; CHARLATAN,
THE(1916, Brit.), d; STOLEN SACRIFICE, THE(1916, Brit.), d; TEMPTATION'S
HOUR(1916, Brit.), d; WHAT'S BRED...COMES OUT IN THE FLESH(1916, Brit.), d;
DERELICTS(1917, Brit.), d; DRINK(1917, Brit.), d; BECAUSE(1918, Brit.), d; SWEET
AND TWENTY(1919, Brit.), d; BLACK SHEEP, THE(1920, Brit.), d; BY BERWIN
BANKS(1920, Brit.), d; CHILDREN OF GIBEON, THE(1920, Brit.), d; LITTLE DOR-
RIT(1920, Brit.), d; SCARLET WOOING, THE(1920, Brit.), d; TWO LITTLE WOODEN
SHOES(1920, Brit.), d; WOMAN OF THE IRON BRACELETS, THE(1920, Brit.), d;
LOWLAND CINDERELLA, A(1921, Brit.), d; MAYOR OF CASTERBRIDGE,
THE(1921, Brit.), d; MOTH AND RUST(1921, Brit.), d; LILAC SUNBONNET,
THE(1922, Brit.), d; WOMAN WHO OBEYED, THE(1923, Brit.), d; THOROUGHBRED,
THE(1928, Brit.), d; WINDOW IN PICCADILLY, A(1928, Brit.), d
Sondra Morgan
POSTMAN ALWAYS RINGS TWICE, THE(1946)
Stacey Morgan
CRIMSON KIMONO, THE(1959); LIST OF ADRIAN MESSENGER, THE(1963)

Stacy Morgan
AMAZING TRANSPARENT MAN, THE(1960)
Stafford Morgan
TARGETS(1968); RUN, ANGEL, RUN(1969); CLEOPATRA JONES(1973); STUNT MAN, THE(1980); FOREST, THE(1983)
Misc. Talkies
ALPHA INCIDENT, THE(1976); CAPTURE OF BIGFOOT, THE(1979)
Stanley Morgan
CLUE OF THE SILVER KEY, THE(1961, Brit.); KONGA(1961, Brit.); HAIR OF THE DOG(1962, Brit.); L-SHAPED ROOM, THE(1962, Brit.); DOOMSDAY AT ELEVEN(1963 Brit.); NIGHT TRAIN TO PARIS(1964, Brit.); SEANCE ON A WET AFTERNOON(1964 Brit.); RETURN OF MR. MOTO, THE(1965, Brit.); SHARE OUT, THE(1966, Brit.); CLUE OF THE TWISTED CANDLE(1968, Brit.)
Susan Morgan
EIGER SANCTION, THE(1975)
Sydney Morgan
DARK RED ROSES(1930, Brit.); JUNO AND THE PAYCOCK(1930, Brit.); IN-QUEST(1931, Brit.); MINSTREL BOY, THE(1937, Brit.), p&d
Silents
ALL MEN ARE LIARS(1919, Brit.), d&w
Tanya Morgan
TARGETS(1968)
Terence Morgan
HAMLET(1948, Brit.); SHADOW OF THE PAST(1950, Brit.); CAPTAIN HORATIO HORNBLOWER(1951, Brit.); ENCORE(1951, Brit.); CRASH OF SILENCE(1952, Brit.); IT STARTED IN PARADISE(1952, Brit.); BOTH SIDES OF THE LAW(1953, Brit.); STEEL KEY, THE(1953, Brit.); ALWAYS A BRIDE(1954, Brit.); DANCE LITTLE LADY(1954, Brit.); FORBIDDEN CARGO(1954, Brit.); LOVES OF THREE QUEENS, THE(1954, Ital./Fr.); TURN THE KEY SOFTLY(1954, Brit.); SVENGALI(1955, Brit.); THEY CAN'T HANG ME(1955, Brit.); IT'S A WONDERFUL WORLD(1956, Brit.); MARCH HARE, THE(1956, Brit.); STRANGE AFFECTION(1959, Brit.); TREAD SOFT-LY STRANGER(1959, Brit.); PICCADILLY THIRD STOP(1960, Brit.); SHAKEDOWN, THE(1960, Brit.); CURSE OF THE MUMMY'S TOMB, THE(1965, Brit.); CASINO ROYALE(1967, Brit.), set d; PENTHOUSE, THE(1967, Brit.); SEA PIRATE, THE(1967, Fr./Span./Ital.)
Misc. Talkies
MISSION OF THE SEA HAWK(1962, Brit.)
Terence Morgan II
CARRY ON TEACHER(1962, Brit.), set d; DAMN THE DEFIANT!(1962, Brit.), set d; SWORD OF LANCELOT(1963, Brit.), cos; RETURN FROM THE ASHES(1965, U.S./Brit.), set d; SEBASTIAN(1968, Brit.), set d; LAST GRENADE, THE(1970, Brit.), set d; LOOT(1971, Brit.), set d
Terence Morgan III
INSPECTOR CLOUSEAU(1968, Brit.), set d
Terrence Morgan
SUNDOWNERS, THE(1960), set d
Thelma Morgan
Silents
ANY WOMAN(1925)
Tom Morgan
Misc. Silents
FEET OF CLAY(1917)
Tracey Morgan
SCANDAL INCORPORATED(1956)
Tracy Morgan
PLAY IT AS IT LAYS(1972)
Verne Morgan
LIMPING MAN, THE(1953, Brit.); UGLY DUCKLING, THE(1959, Brit.); MAN AT THE TOP(1973, Brit.)
Victoria Morgan
1984
LOVE STREAMS(1984)
Vince Morgan, Jr.
PUTNEY SWOPE(1969)
Wallace Morgan
WOMEN GO ON FOREVER(1931)
Wendy Morgan
YANKS(1979); MIRROR CRACK'D, THE(1980, Brit.)
Wesley Morgan
LONE HAND, THE(1953)
Will Morgan
LET'S GET MARRIED(1937); I AM THE LAW(1938); OLD LOUISIANA(1938); DARK VICTORY(1939); MILLION DOLLAR BABY(1941); NAVY BLUES(1941); ACROSS THE PACIFIC(1942); MALE ANIMAL, THE(1942)
William Morgan
FOUNTAIN, THE(1934), ed; OF HUMAN BONDAGE(1934), ed; THIS MAN IS MINE(1934), ed; I DREAM TOO MUCH(1935), ed; JALNA(1935), ed; MURDER ON A HONEYMOON(1935), ed; VILLAGE TALE(1935), ed; DON'T TURN'EM LOOSE(1936), ed; M'LISS(1936), ed; WITNESS CHAIR, THE(1936), ed; AFFAIRS OF CAPPY RICKS(1937), ed; JIM HANVEY, DETECTIVE(1937), ed; LADY BEHAVE!(1937), ed; MEET THE BOY FRIEND(1937), ed; NAVY BLUE AND GOLD(1937); SEA RACK-ETEERS(1937), ed; THAT GIRL FROM PARIS(1937), ed; WRONG ROAD, THE(1937), ed; ARMY GIRL(1938), ed; BORN TO BE WILD(1938), ed; DOWN IN ARKAN-SAW(1938), ed; GANGS OF NEW YORK(1938), ed; HE LOVED AN ACTRESS(1938, Brit.), ed; INVISIBLE ENEMY(1938), ed; PRISON NURSE(1938), ed; STORM OVER BENGAL(1938), ed; TENTH AVENUE KID(1938), ed; FLIGHT AT MIDNIGHT(1939), ed; MAIN STREET LAWYER(1939), ed; MICKEY, THE KID(1939), ed; SABOTA-GE(1939), ed; SHOULD HUSBANDS WORK?(1939), ed; ZERO HOUR, THE(1939), ed; BOWERY BOY(1940), d; DARK COMMAND, THE(1940), ed; GIRL FROM GOD'S COUNTRY(1940), ed; GIRL FROM HAVANA(1940), ed; MONEY TO BURN(1940), ed; THREE FACES WEST(1940), ed; GAY VAGABOND, THE(1941), d; MERCY IS-LAND(1941), d; MR. DISTRICT ATTORNEY(1941), d; SIERRA SUE(1941), d; SUNSET IN WYOMING(1941), d; BELLS OF CAPISTRANO(1942), d; COWBOY SERENA-DE(1942), d; HEART OF THE RIO GRANDE(1942), d; HOME IN WYOMIN'(1942), d; STARDUST ON THE SAGE(1942), d; HEADIN' FOR GOD'S COUNTRY(1943), d; SECRETS OF THE UNDERGROUND(1943), d; FUN AND FANCY FREE(1947), d; PORTRAIT OF JENNIE(1949), ed; MYSTERY LAKE(1953), ed

William Morgan, Jr.
BIRCH INTERVAL(1976)
William H. Morgan
SPITFIRE(1934), ed
William M. Morgan
GUEST WIFE(1945), ed; IT'S IN THE BAG(1945), ed; SONG OF THE SOUTH(1946), ed; TARANTULA(1955), ed; THERE'S ALWAYS TOMORROW(1956), ed
Zelma Morgan
Misc. Silents
YANKEE DOODLE, JR.(1922)
Morgan-Jones
1984
LE CRABE TAMBOUR(1984, Fr.)
Max Morgan-Witts
VOYAGE OF THE DAMNED(1976, Brit.), w
Teresa Morgano
"RENT-A-GIRL"(1965)
Grethe Morgensen
VENOM(1968, Den.)
Janusz Morgenstern
JOVITA(1970, Pol.), d
Ladislaus Morgenstern
TRIAL, THE(1948, Aust.)
John Morghen
CANNIBALS IN THE STREETS(1982, Ital./Span.)
Piero Morgia
ACCATTONE!(1961, Ital.); LA CAGE AUX FOLLES II(1981, Ital./Fr.)
Steven Morgoshes
SMALL CIRCLE OF FRIENDS, A(1980), md
Joe Morhaim
DOC SAVAGE... THE MAN OF BRONZE(1975), w
Joseph Morhaim
HAPPY ROAD, THE(1957), w
Rex Morhan
WHAT DID YOU DO IN THE WAR, DADDY?(1966)
Marcel Morhange
Silents
SERPENT, THE(1916)
Hans von Morhart
LANCER SPY(1937)
Joseph Morheim
EGYPT BY THREE(1953), w
Lewis Morheim
DANGER ZONE(1951), w
Lou Morheim
FOR MEN ONLY(1952), w; BEAST FROM 20,000 FATHOMS, THE(1953), w; EGYPT BY THREE(1953), w; RUMBLE ON THE DOCKS(1956), w; TIJUANA STORY, THE(1957), w; LAST BLITZKRIEG, THE(1958), w; JUKE BOX RHYTHM(1959), w; HUNTING PARTY, THE(1977, Brit.), p, w
Louis Morheim
SMART WOMAN(1948), w; MA AND PA KETTLE(1949), w; PIER 23(1951), w; ROARING CITY(1951), w; SMUGGLER'S ISLAND(1951), w; BIG LEAGUER(1953), w
Claudia Mori
ROCCO AND HIS BROTHERS(1961, Fr./Ital.); SODOM AND GOMORRAH(1962, U.S./Fr./Ital.); OF WAYWARD LOVE(1964, Ital./Ger.); BLOODLINE(1979)
Hideo Mori
TOKYO JOE(1949)
Isao Mori
HARBOR LIGHT YOKOHAMA(1970, Jap.), w
Ivao Mori
MADAME BUTTERFLY(1955 Ital./Jap.), p
Jeanne Mori
NIGHT SHIFT(1982)
1984
PROTOCOL(1984); STAR TREK III: THE SEARCH FOR SPOCK(1984)
Kazunari Mori
MONSTERS FROM THE UNKNOWN PLANET(1975, Jap.)
Kikue Mori
UGETSU(1954, Jap.); LIFE OF OHARU(1964, Jap.); SANSHO THE BAILIFF(1969, Jap.)
Kuroudo Mori
MUDDY RIVER(1982, Jap.), m
Masayuki Mori
RASHOMON(1951, Jap.); UGETSU(1954, Jap.); IDIOT, THE(1963, Jap.); WHEN A WOMAN ASCENDS THE STAIRS(1963, Jap.); ALONE ON THE PACIFIC(1964, Jap.); CHALLENGE TO LIVE(1964, Jap.); SUN ABOVE, DEATH BELOW(1969, Jap.); THROUGH DAYS AND MONTHS(1969 Jap.); GATEWAY TO GLORY(1970, Jap.)
Michic Mori
EAST CHINA SEA(1969, Jap.)
Mitsuhiro Mori
TOKYO STORY(1972, Jap.)
Mitsuko Mori
TWO IN THE SHADOW(1968, Jap.)
Ogai Mori
SANSHO THE BAILIFF(1969, Jap.), w
Paola Mori
CROSSED SWORDS(1954); MR. ARKADIN(1962, Brit./Fr./Span.)
Paula Mori
LUXURY GIRLS(1953, Ital.)
Renato Mori
SWORD OF THE CONQUEROR(1962, Ital.); I HATE BLONDES(1981, Ital.)
Shinichi Mori
PERFORMERS, THE(1970, Jap.)
Torau Mori
CRIMSON KIMONO, THE(1959)
Toschia Mori
SECRETS OF WU SIN(1932)

Toshi Mori
ROAR OF THE DRAGON(1932)

Toshia Mori
HATCHET MAN, THE(1932); BITTER TEA OF GENERAL YEN, THE(1933); BLONDIE JOHNSON(1933); FURY OF THE JUNGLE(1934); CHINATOWN SQUAD(1935)

Toshie Mori
CHARLIE CHAN ON BROADWAY(1937)

Yasuji Mori
PANDA AND THE MAGIC SERPENT(1961, Jap.), anim

Alberto Moriani
YOR, THE HUNTER FROM THE FUTURE(1983, Ital.), ed
1984
HUNTERS OF THE GOLDEN COBRA, THE(1984, Ital.), ed; LAST HUNTER, THE(1984, Ital.), ed

Evelyn Moriarity
SUSPENSE(1946); RECKLESS MOMENTS, THE(1949)

J. Pat Moriarity
FIRST COMES COURAGE(1943); NORTHERN PURSUIT(1943); LATE GEORGE APLEY, THE(1947)

P. H. Moriarity
BLOODY KIDS(1983, Brit.)

Pat Moriarity
MASQUERADE(1929); WAY FOR A SAILOR(1930); UP POPS THE DEVIL(1931); ME AND MY GAL(1932); MANHATTAN MELODRAMA(1934); MYSTERY OF MR. X, THE(1934); GOD'S COUNTRY AND THE WOMAN(1937); MUTINY IN THE BIG HOUSE(1939); RAGE IN HEAVEN(1941); KING'S ROW(1942); AMBUSH(1950)

Patrick Moriarity
GLASS KEY, THE(1935); STRANDED(1935); MESSAGE TO GARCIA, A(1936); UNION PACIFIC(1939); SON OF DRACULA(1943)

Cathy Moriarty
RAGING BULL(1980); NEIGHBORS(1981)

D.A. Moriarty
DAWN OVER IRELAND(1938, Irish), w

Don Moriarty
ZORRO, THE GAY BLADE(1981), w

Evelyn Moriarty
MOVIE MOVIE(1978)

James Moriarty
NIGHT OF THE JUGGLER(1980)

Jan Moriarty
NEW KIND OF LOVE, A(1963)

Michael Moriarty
GLORY BOY(1971); HICKEY AND BOGGS(1972); BANG THE DRUM SLOWLY(1973); LAST DETAIL, THE(1973); SHOOT IT: BLACK, SHOOT IT: BLUE(1974); REPORT TO THE COMMISSIONER(1975); WHO'LL STOP THE RAIN?(1978); Q(1982)
Misc. Talkies
REBORN(1978)

P. H. Moriarty
OUTLAND(1981); LONG GOOD FRIDAY, THE(1982, Brit.); JAWS 3-D(1983)
1984
NUMBER ONE(1984, Brit.); SLAYGROUND(1984, Brit.)

Pat Moriarty
HIS FAMILY TREE(1936); PLOUGH AND THE STARS, THE(1936); PLAINSMAN, THE(1937); DEVIL AND MISS JONES, THE(1941); VALLEY OF THE SUN(1942); LOST WEEKEND, THE(1945)

Patrick Moriarty
MC FADDEN'S FLATS(1935); ARIZONA(1940); TEXAS(1941)

Paul Moriarty
PROSTITUTE(1980, Brit.)

Annik Morice
FRENCH CANCAN(1956, Fr.); LA COLLECTIONNEUSE(1971, Fr.)

Norma Moriceau
NEWSFRONT(1979, Aus.), cos; ROAD WARRIOR, THE(1982, Aus.), cos; NATE AND HAYES(1983, U.S./New Zealand), cos

Dave Morick
EARTHQUAKE(1974); W(1974); NORTH AVENUE IRREGULARS, THE(1979); S.O.B.(1981)
1984
SAM'S SON(1984)

David Morick
PSYCH-OUT(1968); GLASS HOUSES(1972); HOUSE CALLS(1978)

Ennio Moricone
GOOD, THE BAD, AND THE UGLY, THE(1967, Ital./Span.), m

Vito Moriconi
MARRIAGE–ITALIAN STYLE(1964, Fr./Ital.)

Roger Moride
GOLDEN APPLES OF THE SUN(1971, Can.), ph

T. Morides
MADALENA(1965, Gr.)

Ruby Morie
JOAN OF OZARK(1942)

Albert Moriene
ESPIONAGE(1937)

Philippe Morier-Genoud
WOMAN NEXT DOOR, THE(1981, Fr.); CONFIDENTIALLY YOURS(1983, Fr.)

Francesca Moriggi
TREE OF WOODEN CLOGS, THE(1979, Ital.)

Franco Morigi
EVIL EYE(1964 Ital.)

Kyoko Morii
FOR LOVE OF IVY(1968)

Hiro Morikawa
MEMORY OF US(1974), ph; SILENCE(1974), ph

Shin Morikawa
MAN FROM THE EAST, THE(1961, Jap.); TORA-SAN PART 2(1970, Jap.)

Tokihisa Morikawa
LIVE YOUR OWN WAY(1970, Jap.), d

Albert Morin
TWO WEEKS IN ANOTHER TOWN(1962); CAFE METROPOLE(1937); I MET HIM IN PARIS(1937); EVERYBODY'S HOBBY(1939); GONE WITH THE WIND(1939); OUTPOST OF THE MOUNTIES(1939); WINGS OF THE NAVY(1939); DRUMS OF THE DESERT(1940); OUTLAWS OF THE DESERT(1941); CASABLANCA(1942); DESERT SONG, THE(1943); DO YOU LOVE ME?(1946); LUCK OF THE IRISH(1948); STRANGE GAMBLE(1948); THREE MUSKETEERS, THE(1948); HOUSE OF STRANGERS(1949); DAKOTA LIL(1950); FORTUNES OF CAPTAIN BLOOD(1950); GUNFIGHTER, THE(1950); SIDE STREET(1950); ON THE RIVERA(1950); TOO YOUNG TO KISS(1951); LYDIA BAILEY(1952); MAN BEHIND THE GUN, THE(1952)

Alberto Morin
MAYTIME(1937); THIN ICE(1937); GIRL OF THE GOLDEN WEST, THE(1938); SUEZ(1938); ANOTHER THIN MAN(1939); SECRET SERVICE OF THE AIR(1939); CHARLIE CHAN IN PANAMA(1940); BLOOD AND SAND(1941); THAT NIGHT IN RIO(1941); INVISIBLE AGENT(1942); FOR WHOM THE BELL TOLLS(1943); TWILIGHT ON THE RIO GRANDE(1947); ANGEL ON THE AMAZON(1948); KEY LARGO(1948); KISSING BANDIT, THE(1948); ABBOTT AND COSTELLO IN THE FOREIGN LEGION(1950); RIO GRANDE(1950); TRIPOLI(1950); UNDER MEXICALI STARS(1950); WHEN WILLIE COMES MARCHING HOME(1950); MARK OF THE RENEGADE(1951); MY FAVORITE SPY(1951); FIVE FINGERS(1952); HORIZONS WEST(1952); GLORY BRIGADE, THE(1953); KING OF THE KHYBER RIFLES(1953); MEXICAN MANHUNT(1953); STORY OF THREE LOVES, THE(1953); TITANIC(1953); THREE COINS IN THE FOUNTAIN(1954); GREEN FIRE(1955); JUMP INTO HELL(1955); JUPITER'S DARLING(1955); MY SISTER EILEEN(1955); TO CATCH A THIEF(1955); UNTAMED(1955); PILLARS OF THE SKY(1956); AFFAIR TO REMEMBER, AN(1957); WILL SUCCESS SPOIL ROCK HUNTER?(1957); WINGS OF EAGLES, THE(1957); YOUNG LIONS, THE(1958); THIS EARTH IS MINE(1959); IT'S ONLY MONEY(1962); FOR LOVE OR MONEY(1963); FUN IN ACAPULCO(1963); FOR THOSE WHO THINK YOUNG(1964); HELLFIGHTERS(1968); DREAM OF KINGS, A(1969); CHEYENNE SOCIAL CLUB, THE(1970); TWO MULES FOR SISTER SARA(1970); MEPHISTO WALTZ, THE(1971); DOC SAVAGE... THE MAN OF BRONZE(1975)

Carolyn Morin
ROBIN AND THE SEVEN HOODS(1964)

Claudia Morin
LIFE LOVE DEATH(1969, Fr./Ital.)

Jacques Morin
FOUR BAGS FULL(1957, Fr./Ital.)

Nicole Morin
GOIN' DOWN THE ROAD(1970, Can.); FOXY LADY(1971, Can.)

Roland Morin
BEAST OF YUCCA FLATS, THE(1961), p

Ione Morino
SINGING TAXI DRIVER(1953, Ital.)

Ken-Ichiro Morioka
MESSAGE FROM SPACE(1978, Jap.), m

Julio Moriones
ROMAN HOLIDAY(1953)

Katina Morisani
GARDEN OF THE FINZI-CONTINIS, THE(1976, Ital./Ger.)

Max Morise
CRIME OF MONSIEUR LANGE, THE(1936, Fr.)

Hisaya Morishige
DIPLOMAT'S MANSION, THE(1961, Jap.); LIFE OF A COUNTRY DOCTOR(1961, Jap.); EARLY AUTUMN(1962, Jap.); WAYSIDE PEBBLE, THE(1962, Jap.); MADAME AKI(1963, Jap.); SNOW IN THE SOUTH SEAS(1963, Jap.); THIS MADDING CROWD(1964, Jap.); WE WILL REMEMBER(1966, Jap.)

Aki Morishima
NAKED YOUTH(1961, Jap.)

Kuni Morishima
NAVY WIFE(1956)

Guido Morisi
LITTLE MARTYR, THE(1947, Ital.)

Patricia Morison
I'M FROM MISSOURI(1939); MAGNIFICENT FRAUD, THE(1939); PERSONS IN HIDING(1939); RANGERS OF FORTUNE(1940); UNTAMED(1940); ONE NIGHT IN LISBON(1941); ROMANCE OF THE RIO GRANDE(1941); ROUNDUP, THE(1941); ARE HUSBANDS NECESSARY?(1942); BEYOND THE BLUE HORIZON(1942); NIGHT IN NEW ORLEANS, A(1942); CALLING DR. DEATH(1943); FALLEN SPARROW, THE(1943); HITLER'S MADMAN(1943); SILVER SKATES(1943); SONG OF BERNADETTE, THE(1943); WHERE ARE YOUR CHILDREN?(1943); LADY ON A TRAIN(1945); WITHOUT LOVE(1945); DANGER WOMAN(1946); DRESSED TO KILL(1946); QUEEN OF THE AMAZONS(1947); SONG OF THE THIN MAN(1947); TARZAN AND THE HUNTRESS(1947); PRINCE OF THIEVES, THE(1948); RETURN OF WILDFIRE, THE(1948); SOFIA(1948); WALLS OF JERICHO(1948); SONG WITHOUT END(1960); WON TON TON, THE DOG WHO SAVED HOLLYWOOD(1976)

Ann Moriss
OPPOSITE SEX, THE(1956)

Brigitte Morissan
TESTAMENT OF ORPHEUS, THE(1962, Fr.)

Morita
BARBARIAN AND THE GEISHA, THE(1958)

[Noriyuki] Pat Morita
1984
SLAPSTICK OF ANOTHER KIND(1984)

Fujio Morita
MAJIN(1968, Jap.), ph; TENCHU!(1970, Jap.), ph; ONIMASA(1983, Jap.), ph

Gohei Morita
PERFORMERS, THE(1970, Jap.), art d

Kensaku Morita
FIGHT FOR THE GLORY(1970, Jap.); TOPSY-TURVY JOURNEY(1970, Jap.); YOSA-KOI JOURNEY(1970, Jap.); WAR OF THE PLANETS(1977, Jap.)

Mika Morita
NEXT TIME WE LOVE(1936)

Mike Morita
HELL AND HIGH WATER(1933); NAGANA(1933); DEATH FLIES EAST(1935); NORTH OF NOME(1937)

Miki Morita
SHANGHAI EXPRESS(1932); FRONT PAGE WOMAN(1935); GRAND EXIT(1935); I LIVE FOR LOVE(1935); OIL FOR THE LAMPS OF CHINA(1935); DANGEROUS(1936); DARK HOUR, THE(1936); ISLE OF FURY(1936); IT COULDN'T HAVE HAPPENED–BUT IT DID(1936); KELLY OF THE SECRET SERVICE(1936); SPENDTHRIFT(1936); WALKING DEAD, THE(1936); AWFUL TRUTH, THE(1937); BORDER PHANTOM(1937); GOOD EARTH, THE(1937); SHE ASKED FOR IT(1937); SINGING MARINE, THE(1937); WOMEN OF GLAMOUR(1937); HOUSE ACROSS THE BAY, THE(1940); TURNABOUT(1940)

Miyako Morita
THREE WEEKS OF LOVE(1965)

Noriyuki "Pat" Morita
1984
KARATE KID, THE(1984)

Pat Morita
THOROUGHLY MODERN MILLIE(1967); SHAKIEST GUN IN THE WEST, THE(1968); CANCEL MY RESERVATION(1972); EVERY LITTLE CROOK AND NANNY(1972); WHERE DOES IT HURT?(1972); MIDWAY(1976); WHEN TIME RAN OUT(1980); FULL MOON HIGH(1982); JIMMY THE KID(1982); SAVANNAH SMILES(1983)
1984
NIGHT PATROL(1984)

Toshiko Morita
GOODBYE, MOSCOW(1968, Jap.)

Yoshimitsu Morita
1984
FAMILY GAME, THE(1984, Jap.), d&w

Shiro Moritani
TIDAL WAVE(1975, U.S./Jap.), d

David Moritz
JOE HILL(1971, Swed./U.S.)

Dorothea Moritz
1984
LOVE IN GERMANY, A(1984, Fr./Ger.)

Henry K. Moritz
CIGARETTE GIRL(1947), w; WHEN A GIRL'S BEAUTIFUL(1947), w

Henry Moritz
SHANTYTOWN(1943), w; THUMBS UP(1943), w

Louisa Moritz
UP IN SMOKE(1978); MAN FROM O.R.G.Y., THE(1970); DEATH RACE 2000(1975); ONE FLEW OVER THE CUCKOO'S NEST(1975); CANNONBALL(1976, U.S./Hong Kong); CUBA(1979); NEW YEAR'S EVIL(1980); LUNCH WAGON(1981); TRUE CONFESSIONS(1981); LAST AMERICAN VIRGIN, THE(1982); CHAINED HEAT(1983 U.S./Ger.)
1984
JUNGLE WARRIORS(1984, U.S./Ger./Mex.)

Louise Moritz
NORTH AVENUE IRREGULARS, THE(1979); UNDER THE RAINBOW(1981)

Stefan Moritz
ANOTHER DAWN(1937)

Stephen Moritz
CHARGE OF THE LIGHT BRIGADE, THE(1936)

Ulla Moritz
EMBEZZLED HEAVEN(1959,Ger.); JOURNEY TO THE SEVENTH PLANET(1962, U.S./Swed.)

Henning Moritzen
CRAZY PARADISE(1965, Den.); CRIES AND WHISPERS(1972, Swed.)

Rollin Moriyama
PENNY SERENADE(1941); HALLS OF MONTEZUMA(1951); PEKING EXPRESS(1951); SOUTH SEA WOMAN(1953); HELL AND HIGH WATER(1954); PRISONER OF WAR(1954); SNOW CREATURE, THE,(1954); HOUSE OF BAMBOO(1955); NAVY WIFE(1956); 20 MILLION MILES TO EARTH(1957); CRIMSON KIMONO, THE(1959); MORITURI(1965); WALK, DON'T RUN(1966); FOUL PLAY(1978); HONKY TONK FREEWAY(1981)

Sam Morje
Silents
JUDITH OF THE CUMBERLANDS(1916)

Lucilla Morlacchi
LEOPARD, THE(1963, Ital.)

Giselle Morlais
LOOK BEFORE YOU LOVE(1948, Brit.)

Giselle Morlaix
TURNERS OF PROSPECT ROAD, THE(1947, Brit.)

Craig Morland
OPERATION SECRET(1952)

Nigel Morland
MRS. PYM OF SCOTLAND YARD(1939, Brit.), w

Sherry Morland
WHEN THE REDSKINS RODE(1951)

Mary Morlass
THIS IS NOT A TEST(1962)

Gaby Morlay
ACCUSED–STAND UP(1930, Fr.); ARIANE, RUSSIAN MAID(1932, Fr.); ENTENTE CORDIALE(1939, Fr.); LIVING CORPSE, THE(1940, Fr.); BLUE VEIL, THE(1947, Fr.); ANNA(1951, Ital.); FATHER'S DILEMMA(1952, Ital.); SIMPLE CASE OF MONEY, A(1952, Fr.); LE PLAISIR(1954, Fr.); ROYAL AFFAIRS IN VERSAILLES(1957, Fr.)
Misc. Silents
L'AGONIE DES AIGLES(1921, Fr.); JIM LA HOULETTE, ROI DES VOLEURS(1926, Fr.); LES NOUVEAUX MESSIEURS(1929, Fr.)

Jay Morlay
Misc. Silents
WOMAN UNTAMED, THE(1920)

Jane Morlet
VOYAGE TO AMERICA(1952, Fr.)

Angela Morley
WATERSHIP DOWN(1978, Brit.), m

Annabel Morley
OUTCAST OF THE ISLANDS(1952, Brit.)

Bob Morley
UPTIGHT(1968), makeup

Carol Morley
NEW LEAF, A(1971)

Christopher Morley
KITTY FOYLE(1940), w; YOU WILL REMEMBER(1941, Brit.), w; FREEBIE AND THE BEAN(1974)
1984
LOVE STREAMS(1984)

David Morley
BARRY LYNDON(1975, Brit.)

Donald Morley
MAN WITHOUT A BODY, THE(1957, Brit.); MIX ME A PERSON(1962, Brit.); WE SHALL SEE(1964, Brit.); HAVING A WILD WEEKEND(1965, Brit.); TERROR FROM UNDER THE HOUSE(1971, Brit.)

Elaine Morley
CRACKED NUTS(1941); DOUBLE DATE(1941); HELLO SUCKER(1941); MOB TOWN(1941); SING ANOTHER CHORUS(1941); TOO MANY BLONDES(1941); YOU'RE TELLING ME(1942)

Eric Morley
DANGEROUS YOUTH(1958, Brit.)

Fay Morley
RIVER OF NO RETURN(1954); DIANE(1955); ONE DESIRE(1955)

Gaby Morley
MONSIEUR(1964, Fr.)

James B. Morley
CHANCE AT HEAVEN(1933), ed; BACHELOR BAIT(1934), ed; CHANGE OF HEART(1934), ed; MEANEST GAL IN TOWN, THE(1934), ed; STINGAREE(1934), ed; GATEWAY(1938), ed; THREE BLIND MICE(1938), ed

James Morley
WHISPERING WINDS(1929), ed; LADIES IN LOVE(1930), ed; STRANGER IN TOWN(1932), ed; CENTRAL AIRPORT(1933), ed; FRISCO JENNY(1933), ed; LILLY TURNER(1933), ed; PROFESSIONAL SWEETHEART(1933), ed; RAFTER ROMANCE(1934), ed; KENTUCKY KERNELS(1935), ed; LADDIE(1935), ed; POWDERSMOKE RANGE(1935), ed; YELLOW DUST(1936), ed; RACING LADY(1937), ed; SMALL TOWN BOY(1937), ed

Jay Morley
NEAR THE TRAIL'S END(1931); DARK CITY(1950); SUNSET BOULEVARD(1950); ENFORCER, THE(1951); PLACE IN THE SUN, A(1951); TARANTULA(1955), cos
Silents
ALIEN ENEMY, AN(1918); GREEN FLAME, THE(1920); OUT OF LUCK(1923); PAYING THE LIMIT(1924); DRIFTIN' SANDS(1928); MAN IN THE ROUGH(1928); AMAZING VAGABOND(1929)
Misc. Silents
CONVICT KING, THE(1915); RED VIRGIN, THE(1915); FIGHTING COLLEEN, A(1919); TRAILIN'(1921); MAN WHO WAITED, THE(1922); BEHIND TWO GUNS(1924); GETTING HER MAN(1924); THREE DAYS TO LIVE(1924); WATERFRONT WOLVES(1924); SITTING BULL AT THE "SPIRIT LAKE MASSACRE"(1927); TRAIL OF COURAGE, THE(1928); COME AND GET IT(1929)

Jay Morley, Jr.
MAN FROM BITTER RIDGE, THE(1955), cos; SIX BRIDGES TO CROSS(1955), cos; FRANCIS IN THE HAUNTED HOUSE(1956), cos; KETTLES IN THE OZARKS, THE(1956), cos; RED SUNDOWN(1956), cos; THERE'S ALWAYS TOMORROW(1956), cos; UNGUARDED MOMENT, THE(1956), cos; WRITTEN ON THE WIND(1956), cos

John Morley
THAT'S MY WIFE(1933, Brit.); TOO MANY WIVES(1937); BORN YESTERDAY(1951); ABDUCTORS, THE(1957); CHICAGO CONFIDENTIAL(1957); FLOOD TIDE(1958); WHEN HELL BROKE LOOSE(1958); FIVE GATES TO HELL(1959); THAT TOUCH OF MINK(1962); CHILD IS WAITING, A(1963); FOR LOVE OR MONEY(1963); LOCK UP YOUR DAUGHTERS(1969, Brit.); WHERE'S JACK?(1969, Brit.); IMAGES(1972, Ireland)

John W. Morley
OPERATION PETTICOAT(1959)

Karen Morley
DAYBREAK(1931); INSPIRATION(1931); MATA HARI(1931); NEVER THE TWAIN SHALL MEET(1931); POLITICS(1931); SIN OF MADELON CLAUDET, THE(1931); STRANGERS MAY KISS(1931); ARE YOU LISTENING?(1932); ARSENE LUPIN(1932); FLESH(1932); MAN ABOUT TOWN(1932); MASK OF FU MANCHU, THE(1932); PHANTOM OF CRESTWOOD, THE(1932); SCARFACE(1932); WASHINGTON MASQUERADE(1932); DINNER AT EIGHT(1933); GABRIEL OVER THE WHITE HOUSE(1933); CRIME DOCTOR, THE(1934); OUR DAILY BREAD(1934); STRAIGHT IS THE WAY(1934); WEDNESDAY'S CHILD(1934); BLACK FURY(1935); HEALER, THE(1935); LITTLEST REBEL, THE(1935); THUNDER IN THE NIGHT(1935); $10 RAISE(1935); BELOVED ENEMY(1936); DEVIL'S SQUADRON(1936); GIRL FROM SCOTLAND YARD, THE(1937); LAST TRAIN FROM MADRID, THE(1937); ON SUCH A NIGHT(1937); OUTCAST(1937); KENTUCKY(1938); PRIDE AND PREJUDICE(1940); JEALOUSY(1945); UNKNOWN, THE(1946); FRAMED(1947); 13TH HOUR, THE(1947); SAMSON AND DELILAH(1949); M(1951); BORN TO THE SADDLE(1953)

Kay Morley
PRINCESS AND THE PIRATE, THE(1944); SHOW BUSINESS(1944); UP IN ARMS(1944); YOUTH AFLAME(1945); BETTY CO-ED(1946); CODE OF THE SADDLE(1947); SIX GUN SERENADE(1947); CAMPUS HONEYMOON(1948); OUTLAW BRAND(1948); SECRET BEYOND THE DOOR, THE(1948); TRAIL'S END(1949); SEALED CARGO(1951)

Lee Morley
HITCHHIKERS, THE(1972)

Malcolm Morley
DERELICT, THE(1937, Brit.); INQUEST(1939, Brit.)

Rita Morley
FLESH EATERS, THE(1964)

Robert Morley
GENGHIS KHAN(U.S./Brit./Ger./Yugo); MARIE ANTOINETTE(1938); RETURN TO YESTERDAY(1940, Brit.), w; MAJOR BARBARA(1941, Brit.); YOU WILL REMEMBER(1941, Brit.); BIG BLOCKADE, THE(1942, Brit.); THIS WAS PARIS(1942, Brit.); YOUNG MR. PITT, THE(1942, Brit.); SOMEWHERE IN FRANCE(1943, Brit.); YANK IN LONDON, A(1946, Brit.); GHOSTS OF BERKELEY SQUARE(1947, Brit.); EDWARD, MY SON(1949, U.S./Brit.), w; HOUR OF GLORY(1949, Brit.); AFRICAN QUEEN, THE(1951, U.S./Brit.); CURTAIN UP(1952, Brit.); OUTCAST OF THE ISLANDS(1952, Brit.); BEAT THE DEVIL(1953); FINAL TEST, THE(1953, Brit.); GREAT GILBERT AND SULLIVAN, THE(1953, Brit.); MELBA(1953, Brit.); BEAU BRUMMELL(1954);

GOOD DIE YOUNG, THE(1954, Brit.); RAINBOW JACKET, THE(1954, Brit.); QUENTIN DURWARD(1955); AROUND THE WORLD IN 80 DAYS(1956); LOSER TAKES ALL(1956, Brit.); DOCTOR'S DILEMMA, THE(1958, Brit.); LAW AND DISORDER(1958, Brit.); SHERIFF OF FRACTURED JAW, THE(1958, Brit.); JOURNEY, THE(1959, U.S./Aust.); LIBEL(1959, Brit.); BATTLE OF THE SEXES, THE(1960, Brit.); OSCAR WILDE(1960, Brit.); BOYS, THE(1962, Brit.); GO TO BLAZES(1962, Brit.); ROAD TO HONG KONG, THE(1962, U.S./Brit.); STORY OF JOSEPH AND HIS BRETHREN THE(1962, Ital.); WONDERFUL TO BE YOUNG!(1962, Brit.); AGENT 8 3/4(1963, Brit.); MURDER AT THE GALLOP(1963, Brit.); NINE HOURS TO RAMA(1963, U.S./Brit.); OLD DARK HOUSE, THE(1963, Brit.); TAKE HER, SHE'S MINE(1963); LADIES WHO DO(1964, Brit.); OF HUMAN BONDAGE(1964, Brit.); TOPKAPI(1964); LIFE AT THE TOP(1965, Brit.); LOVED ONE, THE(1965); THOSE MAGNIFICENT MEN IN THEIR FLYING MACHINES; OR HOW I FLEW FROM LONDON TO PARIS IN 25 HOURS AND 11 MINUTES(1965, Brit.); ALPHABET MURDERS, THE(1966); FINDERS KEEPERS(1966, Brit.); HOTEL PARADISO(1966, U.S./Brit.); STUDY IN TERROR, A(1966, Brit./Ger.); WAY...WAY OUT(1966); TENDER SCOUNDREL(1967, Fr./Ital.); WOMAN TIMES SEVEN(1967, U.S./Fr./Ital.); HOT MILLIONS(1968, Brit.); SINFUL DAVEY(1969, Brit.); SOME GIRLS DO(1969, Brit.); TRYGON FACTOR, THE(1969, Brit.); CROMWELL(1970, Brit.); DOCTOR IN TROUBLE(1970, Brit.); SONG OF NORWAY(1970); LOLA(1971, Brit./Ital.); WHEN EIGHT BELLS TOLL(1971, Brit.); THEATRE OF BLOOD(1973, Brit.); GREAT EXPECTATIONS(1975, Brit.); BLUE BIRD, THE(1976); HUGO THE HIPPO(1976, Hung./U.S.); WHO IS KILLING THE GREAT CHEFS OF EUROPE?(1978, US/Ger.); HUMAN FACTOR, THE(1979, Brit.); SCAVENGER HUNT(1979); OH, HEAVENLY DOG!(1980); GREAT MUPPET CAPER, THE(1981); LOOPHOLE(1981, Brit.); HIGH ROAD TO CHINA(1983)
1984
SECOND TIME LUCKY(1984, Aus./New Zealand)
Misc. Talkies
DEADLY GAMES(1982)
Royston Morley
ATTEMPT TO KILL(1961, Brit.), d
Ruth Morley
ER LOVE A STRANGER(1958), cos; HUSTLER, THE(1961), cos; YOUNG DOCTORS, THE(1961), cos; CONNECTION, THE(1962), cos; MIRACLE WORKER, THE(1962), cos; LILITH(1964), cos; THOUSAND CLOWNS, A(1965), cos, makeup; HOT ROCK, THE(1972), cos; TO FIND A MAN(1972), cos; MAN ON A SWING(1974), cos; FRONT, THE(1976), cos; ONE SUMMER LOVE(1976), cos; TAXI DRIVER(1976), cos; ANNIE HALL(1977), cos; BRINK'S JOB, THE(1978), cos; SLOW DANCING IN THE BIG CITY(1978), cos; KRAMER VS. KRAMER(1979), cos; LITTLE MISS MARKER(1980), cos; CHOSEN, THE(1982), cos; HAMMETT(1982), cos; I OUGHT TO BE IN PICTURES(1982), cos; ONE FROM THE HEART(1982), cos; TOOTSIE(1982), cos
1984
ULTIMATE SOLUTION OF GRACE QUIGLEY, THE(1984), cos
Steven Morley
SPY WITH A COLD NOSE, THE(1966, Brit.)
William Morley
HELL IS FOR HEROES(1962), makeup
Karen Morly
CUBAN LOVE SONG,THE(1931)
Tony Mormann
Silents
JUSTICE OF THE FAR NORTH(1925), ph
David Morne
MADELEINE(1950, Brit.)
Maryland Morne
LAST OF THE LONE WOLF(1930)
Silents
KINDRED OF THE DUST(1922)
Stanley [Dennis Morgan] Morner
I CONQUER THE SEA(1936); SUZY(1936); MAMA STEPS OUT(1937); NAVY BLUE AND GOLD(1937); SONG OF THE CITY(1937)
George Moro
THAT NIGHT WITH YOU(1945), ch
Il Moro
FELLINI SATYRICON(1969, Fr./Ital.)
Nick Moro
YOU CAN'T HAVE EVERYTHING(1937); FARMER'S DAUGHTER, THE(1940); LAS VEGAS NIGHTS(1941); ARIZONA ROUNDUP(1942); SLIGHTLY SCANDALOUS(1946)
Russ Moro
IS PARIS BURNING?(1966, U.S./Fr.)
Francois Moro-Giafferi
LA FEMME INFIDELE(1969, Fr./Ital.)
The Moroccans
ALWAYS LEAVE THEM LAUGHING(1949)
Morocco
PROJECTIONIST, THE(1970)
Miss Morocco
GREAT ZIEGFELD, THE(1936)
Giorgio Moroder
MIDNIGHT EXPRESS(1978, Brit.), m; AMERICAN GIGOLO(1980), m; FOXES(1980), m; CAT PEOPLE(1982), m; D.C. CAB(1983), m
1984
ELECTRIC DREAMS(1984), a, m; NEVERENDING STORY, THE(1984, Ger.), m
Giorgio Morodor
SCARFACE(1983), m
Madeline Moroff
WILLIE AND PHIL(1980); FAN, THE(1981)
Mike Moroff
GOING BERSERK(1983); SCARFACE(1983)
Fabrizio Moroni
HOURS OF LOVE, THE(1965, Ital.); KILL OR BE KILLED(1967, Ital.); MADE IN ITALY(1967, Fr./Ital.)
Gianfranco Moroni
1984
LAST HUNTER, THE(1984, Ital.)

Milt Moroni
LAW OF THE TIMBER(1941)
Primo Moroni
SODOM AND GOMORRAH(1962, U.S./Fr./Ital.)
Rosina Moroni
HAWKS AND THE SPARROWS, THE(1967, Ital.)
John A. Morosco
SHADOW OF THE LAW(1930), w
Oliver Morosco
SO LONG LETTY(1929), w
Silents
PRETTY MRS. SMITH(1915), w
Victor Morosco
LADY SINGS THE BLUES(1972)
Walt Morosco
STAMBOUL(1931, Brit.), p
Walter Morosco
PRISONERS(1929), p; SATURDAY'S CHILDREN(1929), p; LILIES OF THE FIELD(1930), p; MAMMY(1930), p; MAN OF MAYFAIR(1931, Brit.), p; THESE CHARMING PEOPLE(1931, Brit.), p; ARENT WE ALL?(1932, Brit.), p; EBB TIDE(1932, Brit.), p; LILY CHRISTINE(1932, Brit.), p; WOMEN WHO PLAY(1932, Brit.), p; CHARLIE CHAN AT THE WAX MUSEUM(1940), p; GAY CABALLERO, THE(1940), p; ACCENT ON LOVE(1941), p; COWBOY AND THE BLONDE, THE(1941), p; DEAD MEN TELL(1941), p; GOLDEN HOOFS(1941), p; MOON OVER HER SHOULDER(1941), p; MURDER AMONG FRIENDS(1941), p; PERFECT SNOB, THE(1941), p; CAREFUL, SOFT SHOULDERS(1942), p; GENTLEMAN AT HEART, A(1942), p; IT HAPPENED IN FLATBUSH(1942), p; MAD MARTINDALES, THE(1942), p; MAN IN THE TRUNK, THE(1942), p; OVER MY DEAD BODY(1942), p; THAT OTHER WOMAN(1942), p; DIXIE DUGAN(1943), p; SUNDAY DINNER FOR A SOLDIER(1944), p; WING AND A PRAYER(1944), p; MARGIE(1946), p; SENTIMENTAL JOURNEY(1946), p; WAKE UP AND DREAM(1946), p; GIVE MY REGARDS TO BROADWAY(1948), p; SCUDDA-HOO! SCUDDA-HAY!(1948), p; MOTHER IS A FRESHMAN(1949), p
Silents
HIS JAZZ BRIDE(1926), w
Misc. Silents
SILKEN SHACKLES(1926), d
John A. Moroso
Silents
CITY OF SILENT MEN(1921), w
John Moroso
Silents
JIMMIE'S MILLIONS(1925), w
Alexander Morosov
SON OF THE REGIMENT(1948, USSR)
Jerome Moross
NOBODY LIVES FOREVER(1946), m; CLOSE-UP(1948), m; WHEN I GROW UP(1951), m; CAPTIVE CITY(1952), m; SHARKFIGHTERS, THE(1956), m; BIG COUNTRY, THE(1958), m; PROUD REBEL, THE(1958), m; JAYHAWKERS, THE(1959), m; ADVENTURES OF HUCKLEBERRY FINN, THE(1960), m; MOUNTAIN ROAD, THE(1960), m; FIVE FINGER EXERCISE(1962), m; CARDINAL, THE(1963), m; WAR LORD, THE(1965), m; RACHEL, RACHEL(1968), m, md; HAIL, HERO!(1969), m; VALLEY OF GWANGI, THE(1969), m
Carlos Moroyoqui
SHARK(1970, U.S./Mex.), m
"Big" Ben Moroz
JOE PALOOKA IN WINNER TAKE ALL(1948)
Anotoli Morozov
Misc. Silents
STEPAN KHALTURIN(1925, USSR)
Igor Morozov
DAY THE EARTH FROZE, THE(1959, Fin./USSR), m
Keijiro Morozumi
SOLDIER'S PRAYER, A(1970, Jap.)
Tony Morphett
LAST WAVE, THE(1978, Aus.), w
Coral Morphew
MOUSE ON THE MOON, THE(1963, Brit.); SEASIDE SWINGERS(1965, Brit.)
Lewis H. Morphy
SON OF PALEFACE(1952)
Lewis Morphy
YOU CAN'T CHEAT AN HONEST MAN(1939)
Irene Morra
SUNNY SIDE UP(1929), ed; HARMONY AT HOME(1930), ed; HIGH SOCIETY BLUES(1930), ed; JUST IMAGINE(1930), ed; CONNECTICUT YANKEE, A(1931), ed; DELICIOUS(1931), ed; CHEATERS AT PLAY(1932), ed; ADORABLE(1933), ed; MY WEAKNESS(1933), ed; HERE'S TO ROMANCE(1935), ed; LITTLE COLONEL, THE(1935), ed; LITTLEST REBEL, THE(1935), ed; PIGSKIN PARADE(1936), ed; WHITE FANG(1936), ed; ALI BABA GOES TO TOWN(1937), ed; CAFE METROPOLE(1937), ed; LOVE IS NEWS(1937), ed; THANK YOU, MR. MOTO(1937), ed; CHANGE OF HEART(1938), ed; KENTUCKY(1938), ed; KENTUCKY MOONSHINE(1938), ed; STRAIGHT, PLACE AND SHOW(1938), ed; EAST SIDE OF HEAVEN(1939), ed; THAT'S RIGHT–YOU'RE WRONG(1939), ed; IF I HAD MY WAY(1940), ed; YOU'LL FIND OUT(1940), ed; CAUGHT IN THE DRAFT(1941), ed; PLAYMATES(1941), ed; MAYOR OF 44TH STREET, THE(1942), ed; ROAD TO MOROCCO(1942), ed; THANK YOUR LUCKY STARS(1943), ed; SHINE ON, HARVEST MOON(1944), ed; HORN BLOWS AT MIDNIGHT, THE(1945), ed; SAN ANTONIO(1945), ed; TIME, THE PLACE AND THE GIRL, THE(1946), ed; TWO GUYS FROM TEXAS(1948), ed; IT'S A GREAT FEELING(1949), ed; JOHN LOVES MARY(1949), ed; LOOK FOR THE SILVER LINING(1949), ed; STORY OF SEABISCUIT, THE(1949), ed; TEA FOR TWO(1950), ed; LULLABY OF BROADWAY, THE(1951), ed; PAINTING THE CLOUDS WITH SUNSHINE(1951), ed; APRIL IN PARIS(1953), ed; BY THE LIGHT OF THE SILVERY MOON(1953), ed; CALAMITY JANE(1953), ed; COMMAND, THE(1954), ed; KING RICHARD AND THE CRUSADERS(1954), ed; GLORY(1955), ed; JUMP INTO HELL(1955), ed; TALL MAN RIDING(1955), ed; GIRL HE LEFT BEHIND, THE(1956), ed; CRY BABY KILLER, THE(1958), ed; HOT CAR GIRL(1958), ed; TEENAGE CAVEMAN(1958), ed; WAR OF THE SATELLITES(1958), ed

Silents
MY BOY(1922), ed; OLIVER TWIST(1922), ed; TROUBLE(1922), ed; CIRCUS DAYS(1923), ed; DADDY(1923), ed; ONE OF THE BRAVEST(1925), ed; RAG MAN, THE(1925), ed; NEWS PARADE, THE(1928), ed; PREP AND PEP(1928), ed

Mario Morra
BATTLE OF ALGIERS, THE(1967, Ital./Alger.), ed; SEVEN GUNS FOR THE MACGREGORS(1968, Ital./Span.), ed; BETTER A WIDOW(1969, Ital.), ed; SONS OF SATAN(1969, Ital./Fr./Ger.), ed; BURN(1970), ed; DEATH TOOK PLACE LAST NIGHT(1970, Ital./Ger.), ed; WOMAN ON FIRE, A(1970, Ital.), ed; BLACK BELLY OF THE TARANTULA, THE(1972, Ital.), ed; DEAF SMITH AND JOHNNY EARS(1973, Ital.), ed; THREE TOUGH GUYS(1974, U.S./Ital.), ed; BREAD AND CHOCOLATE(1978, Ital.), ed

Pia Morra
SHOOT LOUD, LOUDER... I DON'T UNDERSTAND(1966, Ital.)

Adrian Morrall
BITTERSWEET LOVE(1976), w

John Morre
13 RUE MADELEINE(1946)

Ted Morre
JAZZ BOAT(1960, Brit.), ph

Marcel Morreau
JOUR DE FETE(1952, Fr.), ed

Andre Morrel
JUDITH(1965)

Alys Morrell
Misc. Silents
RECKLESS RIDING BILL(1924)

Andre Morrell
GOLDEN LINK, THE(1954, Brit.); DARK OF THE SUN(1968, Brit.)

Ann Morrell
PHYNX, THE(1970)

Chris Morrell
NIGHT OF THE LEPUS(1972)

David Morrell
HELL IN KOREA(1956, Brit.); SIMON AND LAURA(1956, Brit.); ADVENTURES OF HAL 5, THE(1958, Brit.); FIRST BLOOD(1982), w

Diandra Morrell
CHINA SYNDROME, THE(1979)

George Morrell
THEY WON'T BELIEVE ME(1947); VIRGINIAN, THE(1929); DUDE BANDIT, THE(1933); LUCKY TEXAN, THE(1934); CIRCLE OF DEATH(1935); FIGHTING CABALLERO(1935); FIGHTING TROOPER, THE(1935); PALS OF THE RANGE(1935); TOMBSTONE TERROR(1935); TUMBLING TUMBLEWEEDS(1935); WILD MUSTANG(1935); GUNS AND GUITARS(1936); RED RIVER VALLEY(1936); STORMY TRAILS(1936); THUNDERBOLT(1936); TIMBER WAR(1936); UNDERCOVER MAN(1936); BAR Z BAD MEN(1937); BOOTS OF DESTINY(1937); COME ON, COWBOYS(1937); GAMBLING TERROR, THE(1937); GIT ALONG, LITTLE DOGIES(1937); GUN RANGER, THE(1937); HIT THE SADDLE(1937); IDAHO KID, THE(1937); MELODY OF THE PLAINS(1937); MOONLIGHT ON THE RANGE(1937); RANGE DEFENDERS(1937); ROGUE OF THE RANGE(1937); ROUNDUP TIME IN TEXAS(1937); TROUBLE IN TEXAS(1937); TRUSTED OUTLAW, THE(1937); TWO-FISTED SHERIFF(1937); TWO GUN LAW(1937); YODELIN' KID FROM PINE RIDGE(1937); FRONTIERSMAN, THE(1938); GHOST TOWN RIDERS(1938); GUNSMOKE TRAIL(1938); HEROES OF THE ALAMO(1938); OUTLAWS OF THE PRAIRIE(1938); PHANTOM RANGER(1938); PRIDE OF THE WEST(1938); SOUTH OF ARIZONA(1938); OUTLAW'S PARADISE(1939); RIO GRANDE(1939); SILVER ON THE SAGE(1939); TAMING OF THE WEST, THE(1939); TEXAS WILDCATS(1939); PHANTOM RANCHER(1940); PRAIRIE SCHOONERS(1940); TEXAS STAGECOACH(1940); THREE MEN FROM TEXAS(1940); KID'S LAST RIDE, THE(1941); PRAIRIE STRANGER(1941); ROYAL MOUNTED PATROL, THE(1941); DAWN ON THE GREAT DIVIDE(1942); PARDON MY GUN(1942); PIRATES OF THE PRAIRIE(1942); RIDERS OF THE WEST(1942); WEST OF TOMBSTONE(1942); CATTLE STAMPEDE(1943); FALSE COLORS(1943); LOST CANYON(1943); SILVER CITY RAIDERS(1943); STRANGER FROM PECOS, THE(1943); GHOST GUNS(1944); LAND OF THE OUTLAWS(1944); LAW MEN(1944); LAW OF THE VALLEY(1944); MARKED TRAILS(1944); MYSTERY MAN(1944); RAIDERS OF RED GAP(1944); RANGE LAW(1944); TEXAS MASQUERADE(1944); WHISPERING SKULL, THE(1944); COLORADO PIONEERS(1945); LOST TRAIL, THE(1945); PRAIRIE RUSTLERS(1945); SALOME, WHERE SHE DANCED(1945); GENTLEMEN WITH GUNS(1946); GHOST OF HIDDEN VALLEY(1946); GUN TOWN(1946); RUSTLER'S ROUNDUP(1946); RAIDERS OF THE SOUTH(1947); PRAIRIE, THE(1948); GUN LAW JUSTICE(1949); MULE TRAIN(1950)
Misc. Talkies
BUZZY RIDES THE RANGE(1940); BUZZY AND THE PHANTOM PINTO(1941)
Misc. Silents
HEART OF THE NORTH, THE(1921)

Henry Morrell
UNPUBLISHED STORY(1942, Brit.); RANDOLPH FAMILY, THE(1945, Brit.); MAN FROM MOROCCO, THE(1946, Brit.); TAKE MY LIFE(1948, Brit.)

Mihaly Morrell
ADRIFT(1971, Czech.), ed

Penny Morrell
LUCKY JIM(1957, Brit.); BULLDOG BREED, THE(1960, Brit.); MAKE MINE MINK(1960, Brit.); TOO HOT TO HANDLE(1961, Brit.); MATTER OF CHOICE, A(1963, Brit.); EARLY BIRD, THE(1965, Brit.); WILD AFFAIR, THE(1966, Brit.)

Stanley Morrell
EXILE, THE(1931); I AM A CAMERA(1955, Brit.)

Stephen Morrell
VAN NUYS BLVD.(1979); WALK PROUD(1979); SHOOT THE MOON(1982)

Giuseppe Morresi
LA BOHEME(1965, Ital.)

Ennio Morricane
DEATH RIDES A HORSE(1969, Ital.), m; DOWN THE ANCIENT STAIRCASE(1975, Ital.), m

Ennio Morricione
BUTTERFLY(1982), m

Ennio Morricone
CRAZY DESIRE(1964, Ital.), m; EIGHTEEN IN THE SUN(1964, Ital.), m; FISTFUL OF DOLLARS, A(1964, Ital./Ger./Span.), m; TWELVE-HANDED MEN OF MARS, THE(1964, Ital./Span.), m; FASCIST, THE(1965, Ital.), m; LITTLE NUNS, THE(1965,

Ital.), m, md; NIGHTMARE CASTLE(1966, Ital.), m; PISTOL FOR RINGO, A(1966, Ital./Span.), m; BATTLE OF ALGIERS, THE(1967, Ital./Alger.), m; FOR A FEW DOLLARS MORE(1967, Ital./Ger./Span.), m; GIRL AND THE GENERAL, THE(1967, Fr./Ital.), m; HAWKS AND THE SPARROWS, THE(1967, Ital.), m; MATCHLESS(1967, Ital.), m; NAVAJO JOE(1967, Ital./Span.), m; OPERATION KID BROTHER(1967, Ital.), m; ROVER, THE(1967, Ital.), m; UP THE MACGREGORS(1967, Ital./Span.), m; WAKE UP AND DIE(1967, Ital.), m; BIG GUNDOWN, THE(1968, Ital.), m; CHINA IS NEAR(1968, Ital.), m; DANGER: DIABOLIK(1968, Ital./Fr.), m; FIST IN HIS POCKET(1968, Ital.), m; GALILEO(1968, Ital./Bul.), m; GRAND SLAM(1968, Ital., Span., Ger.), m; GUNS FOR SAN SEBASTIAN(1968, U.S./Fr./Mex./Ital.), m; SEVEN GUNS FOR THE MACGREGORS(1968, Ital./Span.), m; ARABELLA(1969, U.S./Ital.), m; FINE PAIR, A(1969, Ital.), m; FRAULEIN DOKTOR(1969, Ital./Yugo.), m; LISTEN, LET'S MAKE LOVE(1969, Fr./Ital.), m; ONCE UPON A TIME IN THE WEST(1969, U.S./Ital.), m&md; SHE AND HE(1969, Ital.), m; TEOREMA(1969, Ital.), m; THANK YOU, AUNT(1969, Ital.), m; BIRD WITH THE CRYSTAL PLUMAGE, THE(1970, Ital./Ger.), m; BURN(1970), m; CANNIBALS, THE(1970, Ital.), m; COMPANEROS(1970 Ital./Span./Ger.), m; FIVE MAN ARMY, THE(1970, Ital.), m; HORNET'S NEST(1970), m, md; INVESTIGATION OF A CITIZEN ABOVE SUSPICION(1970, Ital.), m; LADY OF MONZA, THE(1970, Ital.), m; MACHINE GUN McCAIN(1970, Ital.), m; MERCENARY, THE(1970, Ital.), m; QUIET PLACE IN THE COUNTRY, A(1970, Ital./Fr.), m; SICILIAN CLAN, THE(1970, Fr.), m; TWO MULES FOR SISTER SARA(1970), m; WHEN WOMEN HAD TAILS(1970, Ital.), m; CAT O'NINE TAILS(1971, Ital./Ger./Fr.), m; DIRTY HEROES(1971, Ital./Fr./Ger.), m; RED TENT, THE(1971, Ital./USSR), m; SACCO AND VANZETTI(1971, Ital./Fr.), m; THAT SPLENDID NOVEMBER(1971, Ital./Fr.), m; BLACK BELLY OF THE TARANTULA, THE(1972, Ital.), m; BLUEBEARD(1972), m; BURGLARS, THE(1972), m; DUCK, YOU SUCKER!(1972, Ital.), m; FOUR FLIES ON GREY VELVET(1972, Ital.), m; WITHOUT APPARENT MOTIVE(1972, Fr.), m; FRENCH CONSPIRACY, THE(1973, Fr.), m; GIORDANO BRUNO(1973, Ital.), m; MASSACRE IN ROME(1973, Ital.), m; SERPENT, THE(1973, Fr./Ital./Ger.), m; 'TIS A PITY SHE'S A WHORE(1973, Ital.), m; ALMOST HUMAN(1974,Ital.), m; FAMILY, THE(1974, Fr./Ital.), m; LAST DAYS OF MUSSOLINI(1974, Ital.), m; MASTER TOUCH, THE(1974, Ital./Ger.), m; MY NAME IS NOBODY(1974, Ital./Fr.), m; SONNY AND JED(1974, Ital.), m; TEMPTER, THE(1974, Ital./Brit.), m; BLOOD IN THE STREETS(1975, Ital./Fr.), m; DEVIL IS A WOMAN, THE(1975, Brit./Ital.), m; DRAMA OF THE RICH(1975, Ital./Fr.), m; HUMAN FACTOR, THE(1975), m; DESERT OF THE TARTARS, THE(1976 Fr./Ital./Iranian), m; GENIUS, THE(1976, Ital./Fr./Ger.), m; MOSES(1976, Brit./Ital.), m; 1900(1976, Ital.), m; EXORCIST II: THE HERETIC(1977), m; LA GRANDE BOURGEOISE(1977, Ital.), m; LEONOR(1977, Fr./Span./Ital.), m; ORCA(1977), m, md; CHOSEN, THE(1978, Brit./Ital.), m; DAYS OF HEAVEN(1978), m; INHERITANCE, THE(1978, Ital.), m; TEMPTER, THE(1978, Ital.), m; BLOODLINE(1979), m; DIVINE NYMPH, THE(1979, Ital.), m; HUMANOID, THE(1979, Ital.), m; LA CAGE AUX FOLLES(1979, Fr./Ital.), m; ARABIAN NIGHTS(1980, Ital./Fr.), m; ISLAND, THE(1980), m; WINDOWS(1980), m; LA CAGE AUX FOLLES II(1981, Ital./Fr.), m; LOVERS AND LIARS(1981, Ital.), m; SO FINE(1981), m; THING, THE(1982), m; TRAGEDY OF A RIDICULOUS MAN, THE(1982, Ital.), m; WHITE DOG(1982), m; NANA(1983, Ital.), m; TIME TO DIE, A(1983), m; TREASURE OF THE FOUR CROWNS(1983, Span./U.S.), m
1984
CORRUPT(1984, Ital.), m; HUNDRA(1984, Ital.), m; ONCE UPON A TIME IN AMERICA(1984), m; SAHARA(1984), m

Ronald Hugh Morrieson
SCARECROW, THE(1982, New Zealand), w
1984
PALLET ON THE FLOOR(1984, New Zealand), w

John Arthur Morril
BROTHERHOOD OF SATAN, THE(1971), ph

Chris Morrill
1984
POWER, THE(1984)

John Morrill
HELL SQUAD(1958), ph; HIDEOUS SUN DEMON, THE(1959), ph; GRASS EATER, THE(1961), ph; ONE WAY WAHINI(1965), ph; MR. SYCAMORE(1975), ph; BROTHERS(1977), ph; KINGDOM OF THE SPIDERS(1977), ph; DARK, THE(1979), ph

John A. Morrill
STEEL ARENA(1973), ph; TRUCK STOP WOMEN(1974), ph; DAY TIME ENDED, THE(1980, Span.), ph

John Arthur Morrill
QUICK AND THE DEAD, THE(1963), ph; WITCHMAKER, THE(1969), ph; BOY AND HIS DOG, A(1975), ph

Priscilla Morrill
BREEZY(1973)

Richard Morrill
CAPTAIN MILKSHAKE(1970)

Adrian Morris
AGE FOR LOVE, THE(1931); ME AND MY GAL(1932); BUREAU OF MISSING PERSONS(1933); LITTLE GIANT, THE(1933); MAYOR OF HELL, THE(1933); TRICK FOR TRICK(1933); WILD BOYS OF THE ROAD(1933); BIG SHAKEDOWN, THE(1934); LET'S BE RITZY(1934); PURSUIT OF HAPPINESS, THE(1934); DR. SOCRATES(1935); FRONT PAGE WOMAN(1935); G-MEN(1935); ONE FRIGHTENED NIGHT(1935); POWDERSMOKE RANGE(1935); STRANDED(1935); MY AMERICAN WIFE(1936); PETRIFIED FOREST, THE(1936); POPPY(1936); ROSE BOWL(1936); HER HUSBAND LIES(1937); THERE GOES THE GROOM(1937); WOMAN I LOVE, THE(1937); ANGELS WITH DIRTY FACES(1938); EVERY DAY'S A HOLIDAY(1938); IF I WERE KING(1938); MR. MOTO'S GAMBLE(1938); YOU AND ME(1938); GONE WITH THE WIND(1939); RETURN OF THE CISCO KID(1939); ROSE OF WASHINGTON SQUARE(1939); WALL STREET COWBOY(1939); $1,000 A TOUCHDOWN(1939); 6000 ENEMIES(1939); FLORIAN(1940); GRAPES OF WRATH(1940); LUCKY CISCO KID(1940); RETURN OF FRANK JAMES, THE(1940)

Aileen Morris
JOAN OF OZARK(1942)

Amarilla Morris
TOO MANY GIRLS(1940); FOUR JACKS AND A JILL(1941); YANK IN LIBYA, A(1942)

Andy Morris
Silents
GALLOPING GALLAGHER(1924)

Anita Morris
HAPPY HOOKER, THE(1975)
1984
HOTEL NEW HAMPSHIRE, THE(1984)
Misc. Talkies
BROAD COALITION, THE(1972); WHAT DO I TELL THE BOYS AT THE STATION(1972)
Ann Morris
LOOSE ENDS(1975), art d
Anne Morris
1984
HOLLYWOOD HIGH PART II(1984)
Anthony Morris
EMILY(1976, Brit.), w
Artro Morris
STRANGE AFFAIR, THE(1968, Brit.); PRAISE MARX AND PASS THE AMMUNITION(1970, Brit.); TERROR FROM UNDER THE HOUSE(1971, Brit.); THIRTY NINE STEPS, THE(1978, Brit.)
Aubrey Morris
QUARE FELLOW, THE(1962, Brit.); GREAT ST. TRINIAN'S TRAIN ROBBERY, THE(1966, Brit.); UP THE JUNCTION(1968, Brit.); IF IT'S TUESDAY, THIS MUST BE BELGIUM(1969); CLOCKWORK ORANGE, A(1971, Brit.); BLOOD FROM THE MUMMY'S TOMB(1972, Brit.); WICKER MAN, THE(1974, Brit.); LOVE AND DEATH(1975)
1984
OXFORD BLUES(1984)
Barbara Morris
WILD AND THE INNOCENT, THE(1959)
Barboura Morris
ROCK ALL NIGHT(1957); TEENAGE DOLL(1957); MACHINE GUN KELLY(1958); BUCKET OF BLOOD, A(1959); WASP WOMAN, THE(1959); ATLAS(1960); HAUNTED PALACE, THE(1963); ST. VALENTINE'S DAY MASSACRE, THE(1967); TRIP, THE(1967); DUNWICH HORROR, THE(1970)
Bea Morris
SEVEN ALONE(1975); PONY EXPRESS RIDER(1976)
Beth Morris
TALES THAT WITNESS MADNESS(1973, Brit.); THAT'LL BE THE DAY(1974, Brit.)
Bill Morris
MR. MAJESTYK(1974)
Bob Morris
GREEN SLIME, THE(1969)
Brian Morris
THAT'LL BE THE DAY(1974, Brit.), art d; FLAME(1975, Brit.), art d; FULL CIRCLE(1977, Brit./Can.), art d; YANKS(1979), prod d; PINK FLOYD–THE WALL(1982, Brit.), prod d; QUEST FOR FIRE(1982, Fr./Can.), prod d; HUNGER, THE(1983), prod d
1984
ANOTHER COUNTRY(1984, Brit.), prod d
Carol Morris
GIRL OF THE LIMBERLOST, THE(1945); BORN TO BE LOVED(1959); PARADISE ALLEY(1962)
Carole Morris
RETURN OF THE JEDI(1983)
Carolyn Morris
NIGHT THEY RAIDED MINSKY'S, THE(1968)
Charles Morris
CLEOPATRA(1934); WE'RE NOT DRESSING(1934); MAN ON THE FLYING TRAPEZE, THE(1935); ONE HOUR LATE(1935); TWO FOR TONIGHT(1935); WINGS IN THE DARK(1935)
Chester Morris
ALIBI(1929); FAST LIFE(1929); WOMAN TRAP(1929); BAT WHISPERS, THE(1930); BIG HOUSE, THE(1930); CASE OF SERGEANT GRISCHA, THE(1930); DIVORCEE, THE(1930); PLAYING AROUND(1930); SECOND CHOICE(1930); SHE COULDN'T SAY NO(1930); CORSAIR(1931); COCK OF THE AIR(1932); MIRACLE MAN, THE(1932); SINNERS IN THE SUN(1932); BLONDIE JOHNSON(1933); GOLDEN HARVEST(1933); INFERNAL MACHINE(1933); KING FOR A NIGHT(1933); TOMORROW AT SEVEN(1933); EMBARRASSING MOMENTS(1934); GAY BRIDE, THE(1934); GIFT OF GAB(1934); LET'S TALK IT OVER(1934); I'VE BEEN AROUND(1935); PRINCESS O'HARA(1935); PUBLIC HERO NO. 1(1935); PURSUIT(1935); SOCIETY DOCTOR(1935); COUNTERFEIT(1936); FRANKIE AND JOHNNY(1936); MOONLIGHT MURDER(1936); THEY MET IN A TAXI(1936); THREE GODFATHERS(1936); DEVIL'S PLAYGROUND(1937); FLIGHT FROM GLORY(1937); I PROMISE TO PAY(1937); LAW OF THE UNDERWORLD(1938); SKY GIANT(1938); SMASHING THE RACKETS(1938); BLIND ALLEY(1939); FIVE CAME BACK(1939); PACIFIC LINER(1939); THUNDER AFLOAT(1939); GIRL FROM GOD'S COUNTRY(1940); MARINES FLY HIGH, THE(1940); WAGONS WESTWARD(1940); CONFESSIONS OF BOSTON BLACKIE(1941); MEET BOSTON BLACKIE(1941); NO HANDS ON THE CLOCK(1941); ALIAS BOSTON BLACKIE(1942); BOSTON BLACKIE GOES HOLLYWOOD(1942); BREACH OF PROMISE(1942, Brit.); CANAL ZONE(1942); I LIVE ON DANGER(1942); WRECKING CREW(1942); AERIAL GUNNER(1943); AFTER MIDNIGHT WITH BOSTON BLACKIE(1943); CHANCE OF A LIFETIME, THE(1943); HIGH EXPLOSIVE(1943); TORNADO(1943); DOUBLE EXPOSURE(1944); GAMBLER'S CHOICE(1944); ONE MYSTERIOUS NIGHT(1944); SECRET COMMAND(1944); BOSTON BLACKIE BOOKED ON SUSPICION(1945); BOSTON BLACKIE'S RENDEZVOUS(1945); ROUGH, TOUGH AND READY(1945); BOSTON BLACKIE AND THE LAW(1946); CLOSE CALL FOR BOSTON BLACKIE, A(1946); ONE WAY TO LOVE(1946); PHANTOM THIEF, THE(1946); TRAPPED BY BOSTON BLACKIE(1948); BOSTON BLACKIE'S CHINESE VENTURE(1949); UNCHAINED(1955); SHE-CREATURE, THE(1956); GREAT WHITE HOPE, THE(1970)
Misc. Talkies
BLIND SPOT(1947)
Silents
LOYAL LIVES(1923)
Chester Morris, Jr.
RED HEADED WOMAN(1932)
Christina Morris
WAVELENGTH(1983)
Clifford Morris
REBEL WITHOUT A CAUSE(1955)

Colin Morris
RELUCTANT HEROES(1951, Brit.), a, w; SILKEN AFFAIR, THE(1957, Brit.)
Corbet Morris
MOON'S OUR HOME, THE(1936); THEODORA GOES WILD(1936); GREAT GARRICK, THE(1937); MAKING THE HEADLINES(1938); MARIE ANTOINETTE(1938); TARZAN'S REVENGE(1938); WESTERNER, THE(1940); MONSTER AND THE GIRL, THE(1941)
Corbett Morris
I'D GIVE MY LIFE(1936); FIREFLY, THE(1937); NOW, VOYAGER(1942)
Cullen Morris
SING AND BE HAPPY(1937)
Dave Morris
JUNO AND THE PAYCOCK(1930, Brit.); STORY OF ALEXANDER GRAHAM BELL, THE(1939); YOUNG MR. LINCOLN(1939); SWAMP WATER(1941); SITTING PRETTY(1948); UNFAITHFULLY YOURS(1948); WHEN MY BABY SMILES AT ME(1948)
Misc. Talkies
BEWARE OF BACHELORS(1928)
Misc. Silents
REJUVINATION OF AUNT MARY, THE(1914); DIVORCONS(1915)
David Morris
GAMBLING(1934); THESE THIRTY YEARS(1934); OF HUMAN BONDAGE(1964, Brit.)
David Burton Morris
LOOSE ENDS(1975), d, w; PURPLE HAZE(1982), d, w
Desmond Morris
NAKED APE, THE(1973), w
Dick Morris
WE'VE NEVER BEEN LICKED(1943)
Donald R. Morris
ALL HANDS ON DECK(1961), w
Dorothy Morris
BABES ON BROADWAY(1941); DESIGN FOR SCANDAL(1941); DOWN IN SAN DIEGO(1941); SEVEN SWEETHEARTS(1942); SOMEWHERE I'LL FIND YOU(1942); THIS TIME FOR KEEPS(1942); WAR AGAINST MRS. HADLEY, THE(1942); BATAAN(1943); CRY HAVOC(1943); HUMAN COMEDY, THE(1943); SOMEONE TO REMEMBER(1943); YOUNG IDEAS(1943); YOUNGEST PROFESSION, THE(1943); NONE SHALL ESCAPE(1944); RATIONING(1944); OUR VINES HAVE TENDER GRAPES(1945); CLUB HAVANA(1946); LITTLE MISS BIG(1946); MACABRE(1958); SECONDS(1966)
Dorothy Ruth Morris
MAIN STREET AFTER DARK(1944); THIRTY SECONDS OVER TOKYO(1944)
Earl J. Morris
SON OF INGAGI(1940)
Edmund Morris
SAVAGE GUNS, THE(1962, U.S./Span.), w; WALK ON THE WILD SIDE(1962), w; PROJECT X(1968), w
Edna Morris
CURE FOR LOVE, THE(1950, Brit.); ANOTHER MAN'S POISON(1952, Brit.); TWILIGHT WOMEN(1953, Brit.); TOUCH OF THE SUN, A(1956, Brit.); GYPSY AND THE GENTLEMAN, THE(1958, Brit.); SONS AND LOVERS(1960, Brit.); SATURDAY NIGHT AND SUNDAY MORNING(1961, Brit.); OPERATION SNAFU(1965, Brit.); IDOL, THE(1966, Brit.)
Edward Morris
Silents
PLOW GIRL, THE(1916), w
Edward Bateman Morris
WIDE OPEN(1930), w
Edwin Bateman Morris
Silents
NARROW STREET, THE(1924), w
Eric Morris
MA BARKER'S KILLER BROOD(1960); STRATEGY OF TERROR(1969); BATTLE BEYOND THE STARS(1980); WAVELENGTH(1983)
Ernest Morris
OPERATION MURDER(1957, Brit.), d; SON OF A STRANGER(1957, Brit.), d; THREE SUNDAYS TO LIVE(1957, Brit.), d; WOMAN OF MYSTERY, A(1957, Brit.), d; BETRAYAL, THE(1958, Brit.), d; ON THE RUN(1958, Brit.), d; THREE CROOKED MEN(1958, Brit.), d; NIGHT TRAIN FOR INVERNESS(1960, Brit.), d; COURT MARTIAL OF MAJOR KELLER, THE(1961, Brit.), d; HIGHWAY TO BATTLE(1961, Brit.), d; STRIP TEASE MURDER(1961, Brit.), d; TARNISHED HEROES(1961, Brit.), d; TRANSATLANTIC(1961, Brit.), d; SPANISH SWORD, THE(1962, Brit.), d; TELLTALE HEART, THE(1962, Brit.), d; THREE SPARE WIVES(1962, Brit.), d; WHAT EVERY WOMAN WANTS(1962, Brit.), d; ECHO OF DIANA(1963, Brit.), d; SHADOW OF FEAR(1963, Brit.), d; SICILIANS, THE(1964, Brit.), d; RETURN OF MR. MOTO, THE(1965, Brit.), d
Misc. Talkies
NIGHT CARGOES(1963), d
Errol Morris
Misc. Talkies
VERNON, FLORIDA(1982), d
Flora Morris
Misc. Silents
KISSING CUP(1913, Brit.); HEART OF MIDLOTHIAN, THE(1914, Brit.); AFTER DARK(1915, Brit.); MYSTERIES OF LONDON, THE(1915, Brit.); WHOSO IS WITHOUT SIN(1916, Brit.)
Frances Morris
CAT'S PAW, THE(1934); STAND UP AND CHEER(1934 80m FOX bw); HOLLYWOOD BOULEVARD(1936); MORE THAN A SECRETARY(1936); PALM SPRINGS(1936); ROSE BOWL(1936); WEDDING PRESENT(1936); EASY LIVING(1937); EXCLUSIVE(1937); HOLLYWOOD HOTEL(1937); INTERNES CAN'T TAKE MONEY(1937); SINGING MARINE, THE(1937); COCOANUT GROVE(1938); KING OF THE NEWSBOYS(1938); PROFESSOR BEWARE(1938); SISTERS, THE(1938); FORGOTTEN WOMAN, THE(1939); I STOLE A MILLION(1939); OUR LEADING CITIZEN(1939); OUR NEIGHBORS–THE CARTERS(1939); HOUSE ACROSS THE BAY, THE(1940); I WANT A DIVORCE(1940); SAILOR'S LADY(1940); SANDY GETS HER MAN(1940); CAUGHT IN THE DRAFT(1941); LIFE BEGINS FOR ANDY HARDY(1941); NEVER GIVE A SUCKER AN EVEN BREAK(1941); NEW YORK TOWN(1941); LADY BODYGUARD(1942); LADY IS WILLING, THE(1942); OVER MY DEAD BODY(1942); STRICTLY IN THE GROOVE(1942); SO PROUDLY WE HAIL(1943); WOMAN OF THE TOWN, THE(1943); CASANOVA BROWN(1944); COV-

ER GIRL(1944); FOUR JILLS IN A JEEP(1944); LUMBERJACK(1944); STORY OF DR. WASSELL, THE(1944); CONFLICT(1945); DUFFY'S TAVERN(1945); WOMAN IN THE WINDOW, THE(1945); CENTENNIAL SUMMER(1946); ONE MORE TOMORROW(1946); MILLERSON CASE, THE(1947); SMASH-UP, THE STORY OF A WOMAN(1947); SUDDENLY IT'S SPRING(1947); UNFAITHFUL, THE(1947); WILD HARVEST(1947); BIG CLOCK, THE(1948); JOAN OF ARC(1948); NIGHT HAS A THOUSAND EYES(1948); FLAXY MARTIN(1949); HOLIDAY AFFAIR(1949); MRS. MIKE(1949); BETWEEN MIDNIGHT AND DAWN(1950); CAGED(1950); EDGE OF DOOM(1950); THIS SIDE OF THE LAW(1950); CAPTIVE CITY(1952); CARRIE(1952); MIRACLE OF OUR LADY OF FATIMA, THE(1952); MY SON, JOHN(1952); MISS SADIE THOMPSON(1953); CRIME AGAINST JOE(1956); FURY AT SHOWDOWN(1957); GUN FOR A COWARD(1957); WILD IS THE WIND(1957); PORTRAIT OF A MOBSTER(1961)
Misc. Talkies
RIDIN' FOOL, THE(1931); BOSS COWBOY(1934); RAWHIDE TERROR, THE(1934)

Francis Morris
THIS GUN FOR HIRE(1942); SUMMER STORM(1944); NEVER WAVE AT A WAC(1952); WOMEN'S PRISON(1955); SHOOT-OUT AT MEDICINE BEND(1957)

Frank Morris
DIAMOND HEAD(1962); HOMETOWN U.S.A.(1979), ed; BLUE THUNDER(1983), ed
Misc. Silents
GIFT O' GAB(1917)

Garrett Morris
WHERE'S POPPA?(1970); ANDERSON TAPES, THE(1971); COOLEY HIGH(1975); CARWASH(1976); HOW TO BEAT THE HIGH COST OF LIVING(1980)
1984
CENSUS TAKER, THE(1984)

Garry Morris
YAKUZA, THE(1975, U.S./Jap.), makeup

Gary Morris
GIRLS! GIRLS! GIRLS!(1962), makeup; WIVES AND LOVERS(1963), makeup; IN COLD BLOOD(1967), makeup; WAY WEST, THE(1967); PLAZA SUITE(1971), makeup

Geoffrey Morris
ONCE UPON A DREAM(1949, Brit.); RIDE THE HIGH WIND(1967, South Africa); JOANNA(1968, Brit.); ONE MORE TIME(1970, Brit.)

George Morris
BLACK MARKET BABIES(1946), w

Gertrude Maesmore Morris
MAN IN GREY, THE(1943, Brit.)

Glenn Morris
HOLD THAT CO-ED(1938); TARZAN'S REVENGE(1938)

Gloria Morris
RODEO RHYTHM(1941)

Glyn Morris
FOX, THE(1967)

Gordon Morris
SIX HOURS TO LIVE(1932), w; IMPORTANT WITNESS, THE(1933), w; CROSS STREETS(1934), w; UNDER THE PAMPAS MOON(1935), w
Silents
JACK O'HEARTS(1926), w

Gouverneur Morris
ANYBODY'S WOMAN(1930), w; MAN WHO PLAYED GOD, THE(1932), w; EAST OF JAVA(1935), w; RED MORNING(1935), w; JUNGLE PRINCESS, THE(1936), w
Silents
PENALTY, THE(1920), w; ACE OF HEARTS, THE(1921), w; TALE OF TWO WORLDS, A(1921), w; WILD GOOSE, THE(1921), w

Greg Morris
LIVELY SET, THE(1964); NEW INTERNS, THE(1964); SWORD OF ALI BABA, THE(1965); COUNTDOWN AT KUSINI(1976, Nigerian); S.T.A.B.(1976, Hong Kong/Thailand)

Gussie Morris
TO HAVE AND HAVE NOT(1944)

Harriet Morris
Silents
DANCER'S PERIL, THE(1917), w

Harry Morris
PIRATE MOVIE, THE(1982, Aus.)

Haviland Morris
1984
RECKLESS(1984); SIXTEEN CANDLES(1984)

Henry Morris
FOURTH HORSEMAN, THE(1933)

Herschel Morris
PAPER MOON(1973)

Hope Morris
UNSTRAP ME(1968), a, cos

Howard Morris
BOYS' NIGHT OUT(1962); FORTY POUNDS OF TROUBLE(1962); NUTTY PROFESSOR, THE(1963); FLUFFY(1965); WAY...WAY OUT(1966); WHO'S MINDING THE MINT?(1967), d; WITH SIX YOU GET EGGROLL(1968), d; DON'T DRINK THE WATER(1969), a, d; MR. MAGOO'S HOLIDAY FESTIVAL(1970), d; HIGH ANXIETY(1977), d; GOIN' COCONUTS(1978), d; HISTORY OF THE WORLD, PART 1(1981)
1984
SPLASH(1984)
Misc. Talkies
ALICE OF WONDERLAND IN PARIS(1966)

Irene Morris
MY WILD IRISH ROSE(1947), ed; DAUGHTER OF ROSIE O'GRADY, THE(1950), ed

J. Morris
STRICTLY MODERN(1930), w

Jack Morris
MELODY OF MY HEART(1936, Brit.); SONG OF THE FORGE(1937, Brit.); GREEN SLIME, THE(1969)

Jackie Morris
KING, MURRAY(1969)

James Morris
TARGETS(1968); LOST AND FOUND(1979)

Jan Morris [Jan Cmiral]
VOYAGE TO THE END OF THE UNIVERSE(1963, Czech.)

Jane Morris
RED RUNS THE RIVER(1963), cos

Jeff Morris
BONNIE PARKER STORY, THE(1958); LEGEND OF TOM DOOLEY, THE(1959); KELLY'S HEROES(1970, U.S./Yugo.); PAYDAY(1972); GAUNTLET, THE(1977); GOIN' SOUTH(1978); BORDER, THE(1982)

Jeffery Morris
PARATROOP COMMAND(1959)

Jeffrey Morris
LONG ROPE, THE(1961); KID GALAHAD(1962); 36 HOURS(1965)

Joanna Morris
NOTHING BUT THE BEST(1964, Brit.)

John Morris
TALK OF THE DEVIL(1937, Brit.), ed; GENTLEMAN FROM ARIZONA, THE(1940); FOUR IN THE MORNING(1965, Brit.), p; WRONG BOX, THE(1966, Brit.); PRODUCERS, THE(1967), m, md; GAMBLERS, THE(1969), m; ITALIAN JOB, THE(1969, Brit.); TWELVE CHAIRS, THE(1970), m, md; BANK SHOT(1974), m; BLAZING SADDLES(1974), m; INN OF THE DAMNED(1974, Aus.); YOUNG FRANKENSTEIN(1974), m&md; ADVENTURES OF SHERLOCK HOLMES' SMARTER BROTHER, THE(1975, Brit.), m; SILENT MOVIE(1976), m; HIGH ANXIETY(1977), m; LAST REMAKE OF BEAU GESTE, THE(1977), m; WORLD'S GREATEST LOVER, THE(1977), m; IN-LAWS, THE(1979), m; ELEPHANT MAN, THE(1980, Brit.), m; IN GOD WE TRUST(1980), m; GALLIPOLI(1981, Aus.); HISTORY OF THE WORLD, PART 1(1981), m; TABLE FOR FIVE(1983), m; TO BE OR NOT TO BE(1983), m; YELLOWBEARD(1983), m
1984
JOHNNY DANGEROUSLY(1984), m; SLAYGROUND(1984, Brit.), spec eff; WOMAN IN RED, THE(1984), m

John David Morris
ROCKY III(1982)

Johnnie Morris
BEGGARS OF LIFE(1928); INNOCENTS OF PARIS(1929); ONCE IN A LIFETIME(1932); TWO IN A CROWD(1936); BAREFOOT BOY(1938); SONS OF THE LEGION(1938); STABLEMATES(1938); GOLDEN GLOVES(1940); LI'L ABNER(1940); BALL OF FIRE(1941)
Silents
FIFTY-FIFTY GIRL, THE(1928); STREET OF SIN, THE(1928)

Johnny Morris
SQUARE SHOULDERS(1929); THANKS FOR THE MEMORY(1938); HONEYMOON IN BALI(1939); NEWSBOY'S HOME(1939); STAR MAKER, THE(1939); $1,000 A TOUCHDOWN(1939); SECRET CAVE, THE(1953, Brit.)
Silents
LOVE AND LEARN(1928)

Joni Beth Morris
UNDERWORLD U.S.A.(1961)

Joni Morris
WALK ON THE WILD SIDE(1962)

Judy Morris
THREE TO GO(1971, Aus.); LIBIDO(1973, Aus.); GREAT MACARTHY, THE(1975, Aus.); SCOBIE MALONE(1975, Aus.); TRESPASSERS, THE(1976, Aus.); IN SEARCH OF ANNA(1978, Aus.); PICTURE SHOW MAN, THE(1980, Aus.); PLUMBER, THE(1980, Aus.)
1984
PHAR LAP(1984, Aus.); RAZORBACK(1984, Aus.)
Misc. Talkies
MAMA'S GONE A-HUNTING(1976); CASS(1977)

Kay Morris
PAROLE(1936), w

Keith Morris
SPY WHO LOVED ME, THE(1977, Brit.)

Kirk Morris
WITCH'S CURSE, THE(1963, Ital.); ATLAS AGAINST THE CZAR(1964, Ital.); HERCULES, SAMSON & ULYSSES(1964, Ital.); STAR PILOT(1977, Ital.)
Misc. Talkies
SAMSON AND THE SEA BEAST(1960); HERCULES IN VALE OF WOE(1962)

Kyle Morris
WINTER KILLS(1979)

Lamar Morris
SECOND FIDDLE TO A STEEL GUITAR(1965)

Lana Morris
AMAZING MR. BEECHAM, THE(1949, Brit.); GAY LADY, THE(1949, Brit.); SPRING IN PARK LANE(1949, Brit.); WEAKER SEX, THE(1949, Brit.); FIVE ANGLES ON MURDER(1950, Brit.); GUILT IS MY SHADOW(1950, Brit.); IT'S HARD TO BE GOOD(1950, Brit.); TRIO(1950, Brit.); OPERATION DISASTER(1951, Brit.); RELUCTANT WIDOW, THE(1951, Brit.); TALE OF FIVE WOMEN, A(1951, Brit.); GOOD BEGINNING, THE(1953, Brit.); STRAW MAN, THE(1953, Brit.); BLACK 13(1954, Brit.); PARATROOPER(1954, Brit.); RADIO CAB MURDER(1954, Brit.); MAN OF THE MOMENT(1955, Brit.); TROUBLE IN STORE(1955, Brit.); HOME AND AWAY(1956, Brit.); MOMENT OF INDISCRETION(1958, Brit.); ROOM 43(1959, Brit.); OCTOBER MOTH(1960, Brit.); JET STORM(1961, Brit.); NO TREE IN THE STREET(1964, Brit.); I START COUNTING(1970, Brit.)

Lenny Morris
MAIDSTONE(1970)

Leonard Morris
REUNION(1932, Brit.); HEARTS OF HUMANITY(1936, Brit.); WHAT WOULD YOU DO, CHUMS?(1939, Brit.); DULCIMER STREET(1948, Brit.); MUDLARK, THE(1950, Brit.); SING ALONG WITH ME(1952, Brit.)

Leslie Morris
ROCKY III(1982)
1984
TERMINATOR, THE(1984)

Leslie P. Morris
1984
RHINESTONE(1984)

Libby Morris
THREE ON A SPREE(1961, Brit.); TIARA TAHITI(1962, Brit.); PROMISE HER ANYTHING(1966, Brit.); PLANK, THE(1967, Brit.); TWO FOR THE ROAD(1967, Brit.); ADDING MACHINE, THE(1969)

Lily Morris
  THOSE WERE THE DAYS(1934, Brit.); RADIO FOLLIES(1935, Brit.); VARIETY(1935, Brit.); I THANK YOU(1941, Brit.)

Liz Morris
  JAWS 3-D(1983)

Margaret Morris
  SINGLE-HANDED SANDERS(1932); GAMBLING LADY(1934); PERSONALITY KID, THE(1934); BRIDE WALKS OUT, THE(1936); DESERT GUNS(1936); PLOUGH AND THE STARS, THE(1936); TOAST OF NEW YORK, THE(1937)
  Silents
  TOWN SCANDAL, THE(1923); GALLOPING ACE, THE(1924); WOMANHANDLED(1925); THAT'S MY BABY(1926); AVENGING SHADOW, THE(1928)
  Misc. Silents
  HORSESHOE LUCK(1924); YOUTH'S GAMBLE(1925); BORN TO THE WEST(1926); MAGIC GARDEN, THE(1927); MOULDERS OF MEN(1927); WOMAN I LOVE, THE(1929)

Margaret Ann Morris
  I WALK THE LINE(1970)

Margery Morris
  BEDTIME STORY(1938, Brit.)

Marianne Morris
  VAMPYRES, DAUGHTERS OF DRACULA(1977, Brit.)

Martha Morris
  FREAKS(1932)

Mary Morris
  VICTORIA THE GREAT(1937, Brit.); DOUBLE DOOR(1934); PRISON WITHOUT BARS(1939, Brit.); U-BOAT 29(1939, Brit.); THIEF OF BAGHDAD, THE(1940, Brit.); MAJOR BARBARA(1941, Brit.); PIMPERNEL SMITH(1942, Brit.); UNDERGROUND GUERRILLAS(1944, Brit.); MAN FROM MOROCCO, THE(1946, Brit.); AGITATOR, THE(1949); HIGH TREASON(1951, Brit.); TRAIN OF EVENTS(1952, Brit.)

Mrs. Masemore Morris
  BALLOON GOES UP, THE(1942, Brit.)

Megan Morris
  TERMS OF ENDEARMENT(1983)

Mercury Morris
  BLACK SIX, THE(1974)

Michael Morris
  CHRISTMAS IN JULY(1940); MICHAEL SHAYNE, PRIVATE DETECTIVE(1940); PIER 13(1940); BLOOD AND SAND(1941); RAGS TO RICHES(1941); FLY BY NIGHT(1942); FOR LOVE OR MONEY(1963), w; MAID FOR MURDER(1963, Brit.), makeup; WILD AND WONDERFUL(1964), w; 20,000 POUNDS KISS, THE(1964, Brit.), makeup; RICOCHET(1966, Brit.), makeup; SOLO FOR SPARROW(1966, Brit.), makeup; UNCLE, THE(1966, Brit.), makeup; MAGUS, THE(1968, Brit.), makeup; VENGEANCE OF SHE, THE(1968, Brit.), makeup; OTLEY(1969, Brit.), makeup; THREE INTO TWO WON'T GO(1969, Brit.), makeup

Michael [Adrian] Morris
  WILD GEESE CALLING(1941)

Michael Adrian Morris
  PENNY SERENADE(1941)

Mike Morris
  PRIEST OF LOVE(1981, Brit.)

Mildred Morris
  GEORGE WHITE'S 1935 SCANDALS(1935); BALL OF FIRE(1941)
  Misc. Silents
  FOUNDLING, THE(1916)

Muriel Morris
  COVER GIRL(1944); TEN CENTS A DANCE(1945)

Nan Morris
  SECRET INVASION, THE(1964); GIRLS ON THE BEACH(1965); TARGET: HARRY(1980)

Norman Morris
  WRONG BOX, THE(1966, Brit.)

Oswald Morris
  WIZ, THE(1978), ph; CAPTAIN BOYCOTT(1947, Brit.), ph; FOOLS RUSH IN(1949, Brit.), ph; ONE WOMAN'S STORY(1949, Brit.), ph; CAIRO ROAD(1950, Brit.), ph; ADVENTURERS, THE(1951, Brit.), ph; CIRCLE OF DANGER(1951, Brit.), ph; MOULIN ROUGE(1952), ph; PROMOTER, THE(1952, Brit.), ph; BEAT THE DEVIL(1953), ph; SO LITTLE TIME(1953, Brit.), ph; BEAU BRUMMELL(1954), ph; GOLDEN MASK, THE(1954, Brit.), ph; LOVERS, HAPPY LOVERS!(1955, Brit.), ph; MAN WHO NEVER WAS, THE(1956, Brit.), ph; MOBY DICK(1956), ph; FAREWELL TO ARMS, A(1957), ph; HEAVEN KNOWS, MR. ALLISON(1957), ph; KEY, THE(1958, Brit.), ph; ROOTS OF HEAVEN, THE(1958), ph; LOOK BACK IN ANGER(1959), ph; ENTERTAINER, THE(1960, Brit.), ph; OUR MAN IN HAVANA(1960, Brit.), ph; GUNS OF NAVARONE, THE(1961), ph; LOLITA(1962), ph; SATAN NEVER SLEEPS(1962), ph; TERM OF TRIAL(1962, Brit.), ph; CEREMONY, THE(1963, U.S./Span.), ph; COME FLY WITH ME(1963), ph; OF HUMAN BONDAGE(1964, Brit.), ph; PUMPKIN EATER, THE(1964, Brit.), ph; BATTLE OF THE VILLA FIORITA, THE(1965, Brit.), ph; HILL, THE(1965, Brit.), ph; LIFE AT THE TOP(1965, Brit.), ph; MISTER MOSES(1965), ph; SPY WHO CAME IN FROM THE COLD, THE(1965, Brit.), ph; STOP THE WORLD–I WANT TO GET OFF(1966, Brit.), ph; TAMING OF THE SHREW, THE(1967, U.S./Ital.), ph; GREAT CATHERINE(1968, Brit.), ph; OLIVER!(1968, Brit.), ph; WINTER'S TALE, THE(1968, Brit.), ph; GOODBYE MR. CHIPS(1969, U.S./Brit.), ph; SCROOGE(1970, Brit.), ph; FIDDLER ON THE ROOF(1971), ph; FRAGMENT OF FEAR(1971, Brit.), ph; LADY CAROLINE LAMB(1972, Brit./Ital.), ph; SLEUTH(1972, Brit.), ph; MACKINTOSH MAN, THE(1973, Brit.), ph; MAN WITH THE GOLDEN GUN, THE(1974, Brit.), ph; ODESSA FILE, THE(1974, Brit./Ger.), ph; MAN WHO WOULD BE KING, THE(1975, Brit.), ph; "EQUUS"(1977), ph; SEVEN-PER-CENT SOLUTION, THE(1977, Brit.), ph; JUST TELL ME WHAT YOU WANT(1980), ph; GREAT MUPPET CAPER, THE(1981), ph; DARK CRYSTAL, THE(1982, Brit.), ph

Pamela Morris
  EXPRESSO BONGO(1959, Brit.)

Patricia Morris
  LATE LIZ, THE(1971), cos; HIGH ANXIETY(1977), cos

Paul Morris
  RED RUNS THE RIVER(1963)

Paula Morris
  GARDEN OF EDEN(1954); NO MORE EXCUSES(1968)

Percy Morris
  GLASS KEY, THE(1935)

Phil Morris
  1984
  STAR TREK III: THE SEARCH FOR SPOCK(1984)

Philip Morris
  MADAME SPY(1934); HOME ON THE RANGE(1935); SEVEN KEYS TO BALDPATE(1935); SHOW THEM NO MERCY(1935); MESSAGE TO GARCIA, A(1936); NEXT TIME WE LOVE(1936); HIGH, WIDE AND HANDSOME(1937); STAGE DOOR(1937); SUPER SLEUTH(1937); TEXANS, THE(1938); BLACKMAIL(1939); LET US LIVE(1939); THUNDER AFLOAT(1939); BRIGHAM YOUNG–FRONTIERSMAN(1940); DANCE, GIRL, DANCE(1940); STAR DUST(1940); MAGNIFICENT AMBERSONS, THE(1942); NEVADA(1944); DOLL FACE(1945); JOHNNY ANGEL(1945); WEST OF THE PECOS(1945); CLUNY BROWN(1946); CRACK-UP(1946); DEADLINE AT DAWN(1946); DO YOU LOVE ME?(1946); CROSSFIRE(1947); VOICE OF THE TURTLE, THE(1947); LADY FROM SHANGHAI, THE(1948); WHIRLWIND RAIDERS(1948); HOLIDAY AFFAIR(1949)

Phillip Morris
  DESERT GOLD(1936); DON'T TURN'EM LOOSE(1936); GO CHASE YOURSELF(1938); I WAKE UP SCREAMING(1942); ROXIE HART(1942); TWO O'CLOCK COURAGE(1945); HOME SWEET HOMICIDE(1946); HIGH BARBAREE(1947); OUT OF THE PAST(1947); BUCKAROO FROM POWDER RIVER(1948); FIGHTING FATHER DUNNE(1948); HOLLOW TRIUMPH(1948); KNOCK ON ANY DOOR(1949); FLYING SAUCER, THE(1950)

Phyllis Morris
  GIRL IN THE CROWD, THE(1934, Brit.); LIFE OF THE PARTY(1934, Brit.); NON-STOP NEW YORK(1937, Brit.); NIGHT JOURNEY(1938, Brit.); PRISON WITHOUT BARS(1939, Brit.); FUGITIVE, THE(1940, Brit.); ADVENTURES OF TARTU(1943, Brit.); COLONEL BLIMP(1945, Brit.); IF WINTER COMES(1947); SILVER DARLINGS, THE(1947, Brit.); JULIA MISBEHAVES(1948); MY OWN TRUE LOVE(1948); EVERYBODY DOES IT(1949); SECRET OF ST. IVES, THE(1949); THREE CAME HOME(1950); KIND LADY(1951); SON OF DR. JEKYLL, THE(1951); CRASH OF SILENCE(1952, Brit.); MR. POTTS GOES TO MOSCOW(1953, Brit.); EMBEZZLER, THE(1954, Brit.)

Ramsey Morris
  Silents
  TIGRESS, THE(1914), w; NINETY AND NINE, THE(1922), w

Ray Morris
  Silents
  GOLD RUSH, THE(1925)

Rebecca Morris
  ONE IS A LONELY NUMBER(1972), w

Reg Morris
  MURDER ON APPROVAL(1956, Brit.); BLACK CHRISTMAS(1974, Can.), ph; MURDER BY DECREE(1979, Brit.), ph

Reggie Morris
  Silents
  LOVE SWINDLE(1918)

Reginald Morris
  DRYLANDERS(1963, Can.), ph; KING OF THE GRIZZLIES(1970), ph; FOOD OF THE GODS, THE(1976, Can.), ph; SECOND WIND(1976, Can.), ph; SHADOW OF THE HAWK(1976, Can.), ph; EMPIRE OF THE ANTS(1977), ph; MARIE-ANN(1978, Can.), ph; SHAPE OF THINGS TO COME, THE(1979, Can.), ph; MIDDLE AGE CRAZY(1980, Can.), ph; BELLS(1981, Can.), ph; LOVE(1982, Can.), ph
  Silents
  REGULAR FELLOW, A(1925), w; HANDS UP(1926), w; WET PAINT(1926), w; CASEY AT THE BAT(1927), w; LADIES MUST DRESS(1927), w
  Misc. Silents
  WHEN WINTER WENT(1925), d

Reginald H. Morris
  TRIBUTE(1980, Can.), ph; WELCOME TO BLOOD CITY(1977, Brit./Can.), ph; PHOBIA(1980, Can.), ph; PORKY'S(1982), ph; CHRISTMAS STORY, A(1983), ph; PORKY'S II: THE NEXT DAY(1983), ph

Richard Morris
  THOROUGHLY MODERN MILLIE(1967), w; FINDERS KEEPERS(1951), w; PRINCE WHO WAS A THIEF, THE(1951); MA AND PA KETTLE AT THE FAIR(1952), w; TAKE ME TO TOWN(1953), w; INTRUDER, THE(1955, Brit.); IF A MAN ANSWERS(1962), w; UNSINKABLE MOLLY BROWN, THE(1964), w; CHANGE OF HABIT(1969), w
  Silents
  MARRIAGE OF KITTY, THE(1915); SEA LION, THE(1921); THIRD ALARM, THE(1922); MAILMAN, THE(1923)
  Misc. Silents
  LION AND THE MOUSE, THE(1914); JUNGLE LOVERS, THE(1915); BARRIERS OF SOCIETY(1916); BLACK FRIDAY(1916); DEVIL'S BOND WOMAN, THE(1916); MIRACLE OF LOVE, A(1916); UNATTAINABLE, THE(1916); YOKE OF GOLD, A(1916); HOBBS IN A HURRY(1918)

Robert Morris
  FRANKENSTEIN CREATED WOMAN(1965, Brit.); FIVE MILLION YEARS TO EARTH(1968, Brit.)

Roland Morris
  I WANT YOU(1951)

Rolland Morris
  PAID IN FULL(1950); AS YOU WERE(1951); ON MOONLIGHT BAY(1951); STRANGERS ON A TRAIN(1951); SHE'S WORKING HER WAY THROUGH COLLEGE(1952)

Sara Morris
  1984
  SIGNAL 7(1984)

Stephen Morris
  NORTH OF THE RIO GRANDE(1937); EAGLE ROCK(1964, Brit.)

Stephen Morris [Morris Ankrum]
  HOPALONG CASSIDY RETURNS(1936); TRAIL DUST(1936); BORDERLAND(1937)

Suzanne Morris
  Silents
  HER LONELY SOLDIER(1919, Brit.); HUNTINGTOWER(1927, Brit.)

Tim Morris
  RED RUNS THE RIVER(1963), art d

Tom Morris
  UNMAN, WITTERING AND ZIGO(1971, Brit.)

James Morrison
Silents
CHRISTIAN, THE(1914); BATTLE CRY OF PEACE, THE(1915); WHEELS OF JUSTICE(1915); BABBLING TONGUES(1917); ONE LAW FOR BOTH(1917); TALE OF TWO CITIES, A(1917); MISS DULCIE FROM DIXIE(1919); SACRED SILENCE(1919); BLACK BEAUTY(1921); DANGEROUS AGE, THE(1922); HANDLE WITH CARE(1922); ONLY A SHOP GIRL(1922); SHATTERED IDOLS(1922); HELD TO ANSWER(1923); NTH COMMANDMENT, THE(1923); ON THE BANKS OF THE WABASH(1923); PRIDE OF THE FORCE, THE(1925)
Misc. Silents
PAWNS OF MARS(1915); ALIBI, THE(1916); DAWN OF FREEDOM, THE(1916); HERO OF SUBMARINE D-2, THE(1916); PHANTOM FORTUNES, THE(1916); REDEMPTION OF DAVE DARCEY, THE(1916); SEX LURE, THE(1916); TWO MEN AND A WOMAN(1917); HOW COULD YOU, CAROLINE?(1918); LIFE OR HONOR?(1918); MORAL SUICIDE(1918); OVER THE TOP(1918); LOVE WITHOUT QUESTION(1920); MIDNIGHT BRIDE, THE(1920); DANGER AHEAD(1921); SOWING THE WIND(1921); WHEN WE WERE TWENTY-ONE(1921); YANKEE GO-GETTER, A(1921); LITTLE MINISTER, THE(1922); LITTLE GIRL NEXT DOOR, THE(1923); MAN NEXT DOOR, THE(1923); CAPTAIN BLOOD(1924); WINE OF YOUTH(1924); DON'T(1925); IMPOSTER, THE(1926); SEVENTH BANDIT, THE(1926); TWIN FLAPPERS(1927)

Jane Morrison
DOWN AMONG THE Z MEN(1952, Brit.)

Janet Morrison
GIVE ME THE STARS(1944, Brit.); OLD MOTHER RILEY AT HOME(1945, Brit.); STRAWBERRY ROAN(1945, Brit.); I'LL TURN TO YOU(1946, Brit.); MY BROTHER JONATHAN(1949, Brit.)

Jean Morrison
TEENAGE ZOMBIES(1960), makeup

Jim Morrison
MACHINE GUN McCAIN(1970, Ital.)

Joe Morrison
OLD-FASHIONED WAY, THE(1934); FOUR HOURS TO KILL(1935); HOME ON THE RANGE(1935); LOVE IN BLOOM(1935); ONE HOUR LATE(1935); IT'S A GREAT LIFE(1936); SAFE AT HOME(1962); CHECKERED FLAG, THE(1963); RACING FEVER(1964); STING OF DEATH(1966)

John Morrison
BEAST OF YUCCA FLATS, THE(1961); NIGHT TRAIN TO MUNDO FINE(1966)

Jon Morrison
THAT SUMMER(1979, Brit.); FINAL OPTION, THE(1983, Brit.)
1984
SLAYGROUND(1984, Brit.)

Lee Morrison
Silents
MADAME SPY(1918), w

Lew Morrison
Silents
JAILBIRD, THE(1920)

Lou Morrison
FROZEN JUSTICE(1929)

Louis Morrison
Silents
ON RECORD(1917); BREAD(1918); FLATTERY(1925); RESCUE, THE(1929)
Misc. Silents
COLLEGE ORPHAN, THE(1915); UNEXPECTED PLACES(1918); PRODIGAL LIAR, THE(1919)

Margaret Morrison
REVERSE BE MY LOT, THE(1938, Brit.), w

Mary Morrison
KISS OF DEATH(1947)

Morris Morrison
1984
GOODBYE PEOPLE, THE(1984)

Murdo Morrison
I KNOW WHERE I'M GOING(1947, Brit.); SILVER DARLINGS, THE(1947, Brit.)

Palmer Morrison
Silents
IS YOUR DAUGHTER SAFE?(1927)
Misc. Silents
SCAR HANAN(1925)

Patty Morrison
RACING FEVER(1964)

Pete Morrison
COURTIN' WILDCATS(1929); BEYOND THE RIO GRANDE(1930); PHANTOM OF THE DESERT(1930); RIDIN' LAW(1930); SPURS(1930); TRAILS OF DANGER(1930); TRIGGER TRICKS(1930); WESTWARD BOUND(1931); RIDER OF DEATH VALLEY(1932); RIDERS OF THE GOLDEN GULCH(1932); DUDE BANDIT, THE(1933)
Silents
CROSSING TRAILS(1921); RAINBOW RANGERS(1924); BUCKING THE TRUTH(1926)
Misc. Silents
CACTUS CRANDALL(1918); KEITH OF THE BORDER(1918); LOVE'S PAY DAY(1918); HEADIN' NORTH(1921); BETTER MAN WINS, THE(1922); DARING DANGER(1922); DUTY FIRST(1922); WEST VS. EAST(1922); MAKING GOOD(1923); SMILIN' ON(1923); WESTERN BLOOD(1923); BLACK GOLD(1924); BUCKIN' THE WEST(1924); FALSE TRAILS(1924); PIONEER'S GOLD(1924); POT LUCK PARDS(1924); ALWAYS RIDIN' TO WIN(1925); COWBOY GRIT(1925); GHOST RIDER, THE(1925); MYSTERY OF THE LOST RANCH, THE(1925); ONE SHOT RANGER(1925); RANGE BUZZARDS(1925); ROPIN' RIDIN' FOOL, A(1925); SANTA FE PETE(1925); STAMPEDE THUNDER(1925); TRIPLE ACTION(1925); WEST OF ARIZONA(1925); BLUE BLAZES(1926); CHASING TROUBLE(1926); DESPERATE GAME, THE(1926); ESCAPE, THE(1926); THREE OUTCASTS, THE(1929)

Peter Morrison
CHINATOWN NIGHTS(1929); TRAILING TROUBLE(1930)
Misc. Silents
EMPTY SADDLE, THE(1925)

Priestley Morrison
Silents
ADVENTURE SHOP, THE(1918)

Misc. Silents
GIRL WOMAN, THE(1919)

Mrs. Priestly Morrison
SLEEPING CITY, THE(1950)
Silents
PRAISE AGENT, THE(1919)

Quinn Morrison
HOOKED GENERATION, THE(1969), w

Robert E. Morrison
MAN IN THE VAULT(1956), p; SEVEN MEN FROM NOW(1956), p; GUN THE MAN DOWN(1957), p; ESCORT WEST(1959), p

Robert L. Morrison
JOE PANTHER(1976), ph

Ruth Attaway Morrison
HOSPITAL, THE(1971)

Ruth Morrison
DRUMS O' VOODOO(1934)

Sammy Morrison
SPOOKS RUN WILD(1941); CLANCY STREET BOYS(1943)

Shelley Morrison
CASTLE OF EVIL(1967); DIVORCE AMERICAN STYLE(1967); HOW TO SAVE A MARRIAGE–AND RUIN YOUR LIFE(1968); THREE GUNS FOR TEXAS(1968); MAN AND BOY(1972); STAND UP AND BE COUNTED(1972); BREEZY(1973); DEVIL TIMES FIVE(1974); MAX DUGAN RETURNS(1983)

Shelly Morrison
MACKENNA'S GOLD(1969)

Steven Morrison
LAST HOUSE ON DEAD END STREET(1977)
Misc. Talkies
FUN HOUSE, THE(1977)

Sunshine Morrison
Silents
PENROD(1922)

Sunshine Sammy Morrison
THAT GANG OF MINE(1940); IN THIS OUR LIFE(1942)

"Sunshine Sammy" Morrison
FLYING WILD(1941); LET'S GET TOUGH(1942); MR. WISE GUY(1942); 'NEATH BROOKLYN BRIDGE(1942); SMART ALECKS(1942); GHOSTS ON THE LOOSE(1943); KID DYNAMITE(1943); FOLLOW THE LEADER(1944)

"Sunshine" Sammy Morrison
PRIDE OF THE BOWERY(1941)

T. J. Morrison
NEUTRAL PORT(1941, Brit.), w; MR. PERRIN AND MR. TRAILL(1948, Brit.), w; NIGHT BEAT(1948, Brit.), w; QUIET WEEKEND(1948, Brit.), w; STOP PRESS GIRL(1949, Brit.), w; DUEL IN THE JUNGLE(1954, Brit.), w; GOOD COMPANIONS, THE(1957, Brit.), w; DESERT ATTACK(1958, Brit.), w; GIRLS AT SEA(1958, Brit.), w; PETTICOAT PIRATES(1961, Brit.), w; POT CARRIERS, THE(1962, Brit.), w; SHE DIDN'T SAY NO!(1962, Brit.), w; CROOKS IN CLOISTERS(1964, Brit.), w

Tom Morrison
MARINE BATTLEGROUND(1966, U.S/S.K.), w; HOW TO BEAT THE HIGH COST OF LIVING(1980)

Van Morrison
SLIPSTREAM(1974, Can.), m

Vera Morrison
PASSPORT TO HELL(1932)

Walter Morrison
WELL, THE(1951)

Ann Morriss
CHASER, THE(1938); SPRING MADNESS(1938); HONOLULU(1939); SOCIETY LAWYER(1939); WITHIN THE LAW(1939); WOMEN, THE(1939); AND ONE WAS BEAUTIFUL(1940); BROADWAY MELODY OF 1940(1940); DR. KILDARE'S CRISIS(1940); HULLABALOO(1940); THIRD FINGER, LEFT HAND(1940); BLOSSOMS IN THE DUST(1941); LIFE BEGINS FOR ANDY HARDY(1941); PUSHOVER(1954); GREAT AMERICAN PASTIME, THE(1956); PROUD AND THE PROFANE, THE(1956); ONE FOOT IN HELL(1960)

Frank Morriss
CHARLEY VARRICK(1973), ed; MIDNIGHT MAN, THE(1974), ed; FIRST LOVE(1977), ed; I WANNA HOLD YOUR HAND(1978), ed; YOUNGBLOOD(1978), ed; EARTHLING, THE(1980), ed; INSIDE MOVES(1980), ed; WHOSE LIFE IS IT ANYWAY?(1981), ed
1984
ROMANCING THE STONE(1984), ed

Frank E. Morriss
ODE TO BILLY JOE(1976), ed

Tom Morriss
Silents
SQUIBS(1921, Brit.)

Tex Morrissay
DOUBLE OR NOTHING(1937)

Betty Morrissey
HONOR AMONG LOVERS(1931)
Silents
WOMAN OF PARIS, A(1923); GOLD RUSH, THE(1925); CIRCUS, THE(1928)
Misc. Silents
DESERT DEMON, THE(1925)

Eamon Morrissey
GUNS IN THE HEATHER(1968, Brit.)

Ed Morrissey
Misc. Silents
HOUSE BUILT UPON SAND, THE(1917), d

Edward Morrissey
Misc. Silents
STAGE STRUCK(1917), d

John F. Morrissey
GIRL IN THE SHOW, THE(1929)

Sister Marguerite Morrissey
THE RUNNER STUMBLES(1979)

Nani Morrissey
MERMAIDS OF TIBURON, THE(1962)
Neil Morrissey
1984
BOUNTY, THE(1984)
Paul Morrissey
MIDNIGHT COWBOY(1969); L'AMOUR(1973), p, d&w; HOUND OF THE BASKER-VILLES, THE(1980, Brit.), d, w; RICH AND FAMOUS(1981); FORTY DEUCE(1982), d
1984
MIXED BLOOD(1984), d, w
Misc. Talkies
HEAT(1972), d; ANDY WARHOL'S DRACULA(1974), d; ANDY WARHOL'S FRAN-KENSTEIN(1974), d
Thomas Morrissey
Misc. Silents
HEART OF NEW YORK, THE(1916)
Doug Morrisson
TIME AFTER TIME(1979, Brit.)
Renata Morroni
MOSES AND AARON(1975, Ger./Fr./Ital.), cos
Boris Morros
ACCUSING FINGER, THE(1936), md; BIG BROWN EYES(1936), md; COLLEGE HOLIDAY(1936), md; EASY TO TAKE(1936), md; GENERAL DIED AT DAWN, THE(1936), md; JUNGLE PRINCESS, THE(1936), md; MOON'S OUR HOME, THE(1936), md; MY AMERICAN WIFE(1936), md; PALM SPRINGS(1936), md; POP-PY(1936), md; RHYTHM ON THE RANGE(1936), md; SPENDTHRIFT(1936), m; TEX-AS RANGERS, THE(1936), md; TRAIL OF THE LONESOME PINE, THE(1936), md; ALONG CAME LOVE(1937), md; ANGEL(1937), md; BARRIER, THE(1937), md; BIG BROADCAST OF 1938, THE(1937), md; BLONDE TROUBLE(1937), m; CLAREN-CE(1937), md; DAUGHTER OF SHANGHAI(1937), md; DOUBLE OR NO-THING(1937), md; EASY LIVING(1937), m, md; FORLORN RIVER(1937), m; GREAT GAMBINI, THE(1937), md; HIDEAWAY GIRL(1937), md; HIGH, WIDE AND HAND-SOME(1937), md; HOLD'EM NAVY!(1937), md; I MET HIM IN PARIS(1937), md; INTERNES CAN'T TAKE MONEY(1937), md; KING OF GAMBLERS(1937), md; LAST TRAIN FROM MADRID, THE(1937), md; MAID OF SALEM(1937), md; MAKE WAY FOR TOMORROW(1937), md; MOUNTAIN MUSIC(1937), md; NIGHT OF MYS-TERY(1937), md; PARTNERS IN CRIME(1937), m; PLAINSMAN, THE(1937), md; SHE ASKED FOR IT(1937), md; SOULS AT SEA(1937), md; SWING HIGH, SWING LOW(1937), md; THIS WAY PLEASE(1937), md; THRILL OF A LIFETIME(1937), md; THUNDER TRAIL(1937), m; TRUE CONFESSION(1937), md; TURN OFF THE MOON(1937), md; VOGUES OF 1938(1937), md; WAIKIKI WEDDING(1937), md; WELLS FARGO(1937), md; WILD MONEY(1937), md; ARKANSAS TRAVELER, THE(1938), md; ARTISTS AND MODELS ABROAD(1938), md; BLOCKADE(1938), md; BULLDOG DRUMMOND IN AFRICA(1938), m; COLLEGE SWING(1938), md; GIVE ME A SAILOR(1938), md; HUNTED MEN(1938), m; IF I WERE KING(1938), md; ILLEGAL TRAFFIC(1938), md; KING OF ALCATRAZ(1938), m; MYSTERIOUS RIDER, THE(1938), md; PRISON FARM(1938), md; ROMANCE IN THE DARK(1938), md; SAY IT IN FRENCH(1938), md; SING YOU SINNERS(1938), md; SONS OF THE LEGION(1938), md; THANKS FOR THE MEMORY(1938), md; TIP-OFF GIRLS(1938), m; TOUCHDOWN, ARMY(1938), md; YOU AND ME(1938), m, md; CAFE SOCIE-TY(1939), md; DISBARRED(1939), md; FLYING DEUCES, THE(1939), p; ISLAND OF LOST MEN(1939), md; KING OF CHINATOWN(1939), md; NEVER SAY DIE(1939), md; PERSONS IN HIDING(1939), md; STAGECOACH(1939), md; TELEVISION SPY(1939), m; UNMARRIED(1939), md; EMERGENCY SQUAD(1940), m; PAROLE FIXER(1940), m; TEXAS RANGERS RIDE AGAIN(1940), md; TALES OF MANHAT-TAN(1942), p; CARNEGIE HALL(1947), p; TALE OF FIVE WOMEN, A(1951, Brit.), p; MAN ON A STRING(1960), w
Borris Morros
ROSE BOWL(1936), md; SILVER ON THE SAGE(1939), md
Beverly Jo Morrow
10 NORTH FREDERICK(1958)
Bill Morrow
TALES OF MANHATTAN(1942), w
Brad Morrow
HONEYCHILE(1951); WILD NORTH, THE(1952); BETWEEN HEAVEN AND HELL(1956); I'VE LIVED BEFORE(1956); TOY TIGER(1956); VAMPIRE, THE(1957); SON OF FLUBBER(1963)
Byron Morrow
OPERATION DAMES(1959); WAKE ME WHEN IT'S OVER(1960); PANIC IN YEAR ZERO!(1962); BLACK ZOO(1963); CAPTAIN NEWMAN, M.D.(1963); POLICE NUR-SE(1963); STRANGLER, THE(1964); 40 GUNS TO APACHE PASS(1967); MARYJA-NE(1968); COLOSSUS: THE FORBIN PROJECT(1969); JOHNNY GOT HIS GUN(1971); SPOOK WHO SAT BY THE DOOR, THE(1973); STONE KILLER, THE(1973); SIDE-WINDER ONE(1977); BORN AGAIN(1978); HOW TO BEAT THE HIGH COST OF LIVING(1980)
Charles G. Morrow
OKAY BILL(1971), m
Cloyce Morrow
JONI(1980); RICH AND FAMOUS(1981)
"Cousin" Bruce Morrow
STIGMA(1972)
David Morrow
LIVING BETWEEN TWO WORLDS(1963)
Doretta Morrow
BECAUSE YOU'RE MINE(1952)
Doug Morrow
ALONG CAME JONES(1945)
Douglas Morrow
MAISIE GOES TO RENO(1944); MARRIAGE IS A PRIVATE AFFAIR(1944); LADY LUCK(1946); STRATTON STORY, THE(1949), w; JIM THORPE–ALL AMERI-CAN(1951), w; TROUBLE ALONG THE WAY(1953), w; BEYOND A REASONABLE DOUBT(1956), w; MAURIE(1973), p, w
Ed Morrow
SINK THE BISMARCK!(1960, Brit.)
Frank Morrow
Misc. Silents
LET HIM BUCK(1924), d; RECKLESS RIDING BILL(1924), d

Guernsey Morrow
DUKE IS THE TOPS, THE(1938); ONE DARK NIGHT(1939); TAKE MY LIFE(1942)
Gurnsey Morrow
AM I GUILTY?(1940)
H. Morrow
GUNMEN OF THE RIO GRANDE(1965, Fr./Ital./Span.)
Honore Morrow
OF HUMAN HEARTS(1938), w; SEVEN ALONE(1975), w
Jackie Morrow
LITTLE MISS NOBODY(1936); FIRST LADY(1937); PENROD AND SAM(1937); PENROD AND HIS TWIN BROTHER(1938); PENROD'S DOUBLE TROUBLE(1938); EVERYBODY'S HOBBY(1939)
Jane Morrow
Silents
FLORIDA ENCHANTMENT, A(1914)
Jeff Morrow
FLIGHT TO TANGIER(1953); ROBE, THE(1953); SIEGE AT RED RIVER, THE(1954); SIGN OF THE PAGAN(1954); TANGANYIKA(1954); CAPTAIN LIGHTFOOT(1955); THIS ISLAND EARTH(1955); CREATURE WALKS AMONG US, THE(1956); FIRST TEXAN, THE(1956); PARDNERS(1956); WORLD IN MY CORNER(1956); COPPER SKY(1957); GIANT CLAW, THE(1957); HOUR OF DECISION(1957, Brit.); KRO-NOS(1957); FIVE BOLD WOMEN(1960); STORY OF RUTH, THE(1960); HARBOR LIGHTS(1963); OCTAMAN(1971); LEGACY OF BLOOD(1973)
Jo Morrow
GIDGET(1959); JUKE BOX RHYTHM(1959); LEGEND OF TOM DOOLEY, THE(1959); OUR MAN IN HAVANA(1960, Brit.); THIRTEEN GHOSTS(1960); THREE WORLDS OF GULLIVER, THE(1960, Brit.); BRUSHFIRE(1962); SUNDAY IN NEW YORK(1963); HE RIDES TALL(1964); DOCTOR DEATH: SEEKER OF SOULS(1973); TERMINAL ISLAND(1973)
Katherine Morrow
SPANISH CAPE MYSTERY(1935)
Maxwell Morrow
NIGHT THE LIGHTS WENT OUT IN GEORGIA, THE(1981)
Neyle Morrow
GUY NAMED JOE, A(1943); ANNA AND THE KING OF SIAM(1946); DANGEROUS VENTURE(1947); PIRATES OF MONTEREY(1947); SPOILERS OF THE NORTH(1947); BIG SOMBRERO, THE(1949); RANGER OF CHEROKEE STRIP(1949); CRISIS(1950); HARBOR OF MISSING MEN(1950); MARK OF THE GORILLA(1950); ON THE ISLE OF SAMOA(1950); WHEN YOU'RE SMILING(1950); FIXED BAYONETS(1951); LET'S GO NAVY(1951); STEEL HELMET, THE(1951); PARK ROW(1952); RAIDERS, THE(1952); GOLDTOWN GHOST RIDERS(1953); VALLEY OF THE HEADHUN-TERS(1953); HELL AND HIGH WATER(1954); ESCAPE TO BURMA(1955); HOUSE OF BAMBOO(1955); WHITE SQUAW, THE(1956); CHINA GATE(1957); FORTY GUNS(1957); RUN OF THE ARROW(1957); UNDER FIRE(1957); CRIMSON KIMONO, THE(1959); VERBOTEN!(1959); UNDERWORLD U.S.A.(1961); SHOCK COR-RIDOR(1963); NAKED KISS, THE(1964); WHITE DOG(1982)
Noyle Morrow
MAN-EATER OF KUMAON(1948)
Pat Morrow
MA AND PA KETTLE AT HOME(1954); KETTLES IN THE OZARKS, THE(1956); WRONG MAN, THE(1956); KETTLES ON OLD MACDONALD'S FARM, THE(1957)
Patricia Morrow
SURF PARTY(1964)
Pete Morrow
DOCTORS' WIVES(1971), tech adv
Randi Morrow
RAW WEEKEND(1964)
Scotty Morrow
BETWEEN HEAVEN AND HELL(1956); PEYTON PLACE(1957); TOUGHEST GUN IN TOMBSTONE(1958); COSMIC MAN, THE(1959)
Susan Morrow
CORKY OF GASOLINE ALLEY(1951); GASOLINE ALLEY(1951); ON THE LOO-SE(1951); BLAZING FOREST, THE(1952); CAT WOMEN OF THE MOON(1953); MAN OF CONFLICT(1953); PROBLEM GIRLS(1953); SAVAGE, THE(1953); BATTLE FLAME(1955); MACABRE(1958)
Tracey "Ice-T" Morrow
1984
BREAKIN'(1984); BREAKIN' 2: ELECTRIC BOOGALOO(1984)
Vic Morrow
BLACKBOARD JUNGLE, THE(1955); TRIBUTE TO A BADMAN(1956); MEN IN WAR(1957); GOD'S LITTLE ACRE(1958); HELL'S FIVE HOURS(1958); KING CREOLE(1958); CIMARRON(1960); PORTRAIT OF A MOBSTER(1961); POSSE FROM HELL(1961); DEATHWATCH(1966), p, d, w; MAN CALLED SLEDGE, A(1971, Ital.), d, w; DIRTY MARY, CRAZY LARRY(1974); TAKE, THE(1974); LA BABY SIT-TER(1975, Fr./Ital./Ger.); BAD NEWS BEARS, THE(1976); TREASURE OF MATE-CUMBE(1976); FUNERAL FOR AN ASSASSIN(1977); MESSAGE FROM SPACE(1978, Jap.); EVICTORS, THE(1979); HUMANOIDS FROM THE DEEP(1980); TARGET: HARRY(1980); GREAT WHITE, THE(1982, Ital.); TWILIGHT ZONE–THE MO-VIE(1983); 1990: THE BRONX WARRIORS(1983, Ital.)
William Morrow
BUCK BENNY RIDES AGAIN(1940), w; LOVE THY NEIGHBOR(1940), w; ROAD TO BALI(1952), w
1984
AGAINST ALL ODDS(1984), w
V. Morrozi
DR. BUTCHER, M.D.(1982, Ital.), art d
Barry Morse
GOOSE STEPS OUT, THE(1942, Brit.); DUMMY TALKS, THE(1943, Brit.); WHEN WE ARE MARRIED(1943, Brit.); THUNDER ROCK(1944, Brit.); LATE AT NIGHT(1946, Brit.); THIS MAN IS MINE(1946 Brit.); DAUGHTER OF DARKNESS(1948, Brit.); MRS. FITZHERBERT(1950, Brit.); NO TRACE(1950, Brit.); KINGS OF THE SUN(1963); JUSTINE(1969); PUZZLE OF A DOWNFALL CHILD(1970); ASYLUM(1972, Brit.); RUNNING SCARED(1972, Brit.); LOVE AT FIRST SIGHT(1977, Can.); WELCOME TO BLOOD CITY(1977, Brit./Can.); POWER PLAY(1978, Brit./Can.); ONE MAN(1979, Can.); SHAPE OF THINGS TO COME, THE(1979, Can.); CHANGELING, THE(1980, Can.); HOUNDS... OF NOTRE DAME, THE(1980, Can.); KLONDIKE FEVER(1980); BELLS(1981, Can.); FUNERAL HOME(1982, Can.)
Misc. Talkies
TELEPHONE BOOK, THE(1971)

Brewster Morse
PERFECT SPECIMEN, THE(1937), w
Carleton E. Morse
I LOVE A MYSTERY(1945), w; UNKNOWN, THE(1946), w
Carlton E. Morse
DEVIL'S MASK, THE(1946), w
David Morse
INSIDE MOVES(1980); MAX DUGAN RETURNS(1983)
Ella Mae Morse
REVEILLE WITH BEVERLY(1943); SKY'S THE LIMIT, THE(1943); GHOST CATCHERS(1944); SOUTH OF DIXIE(1944); HOW DO YOU DO?(1946)
Freeman Morse
SKY COMMANDO(1953); VANQUISHED, THE(1953); BATTLE OF ROGUE RIVER(1954); PROUD AND THE PROFANE, THE(1956); WOMAN OBSESSED(1959); STATE FAIR(1962)
Grace Morse
Silents
HAIRPINS(1920); OLD FASHIONED BOY, AN(1920); SINS OF ROZANNE(1920); SOUL OF YOUTH, THE(1920); CHARM SCHOOL, THE(1921); HER WINNING WAY(1921); PLAYTHINGS OF DESTINY(1921); SEEING'S BELIEVING(1922); SCARLET LILY, THE(1923)
Misc. Silents
BURGLAR-PROOF(1920); LET'S BE FASHIONABLE(1920); MARCH HARE, THE(1921)
Hamilton Morse
Silents
INVISIBLE FEAR, THE(1921)
Hayward Morse
AGENCY(1981, Can.)
Helen Morse
PETERSEN(1974, Aus.); STONE(1974, Aus.); PICNIC AT HANGING ROCK(1975, Aus.); CADDIE(1976, Aus.); AGATHA(1979, Brit.)
Heyward Morse
DEVIL'S WIDOW, THE(1972, Brit.)
Hollingsworth Morse
PUFNSTUF(1970), d; DAUGHTERS OF SATAN(1972), d
Misc. Talkies
BEYOND THE MOON(1964), d
John Morse
Misc. Silents
TRAIL OF THE LAW(1924)
John P. Morse
Silents
DANGEROUS TO MEN(1920)
Karen Morse
1984
VAMPING(1984), prod d
Karl Morse
Silents
UNDERWORLD(1927)
Lawrence Morse
OCTAMAN(1971), w
Myrtle Morse
Silents
HALDANE OF THE SECRET SERVICE(1923)
Misc. Silents
STEALERS, THE(1920)
N. Brewster Morse
EYES OF THE WORLD, THE(1930), w; HELL HARBOR(1930), w; SAVAGE GIRL, THE(1932), w; BREAKING THE ICE(1938), w; LADY WITH RED HAIR(1940), w
Perry Morse
HEART OF NEW YORK(1932), ed
Ray Morse
JOURNEY TOGETHER(1946, Brit.), spec eff
Robert Morse
PROUD AND THE PROFANE, THE(1956); MATCHMAKER, THE(1958); CARDINAL, THE(1963); HONEYMOON HOTEL(1964); QUICK, BEFORE IT MELTS(1964); LOVED ONE, THE(1965); GUIDE FOR THE MARRIED MAN, A(1967); OH DAD, POOR DAD, MAMA'S HUNG YOU IN THE CLOSET AND I'M FEELIN' SO SAD(1967); WHERE WERE YOU WHEN THE LIGHTS WENT OUT?(1968); BOATNIKS, THE(1970); HOW TO SUCCEED IN BUSINESS WITHOUT REALLY TRYING(1976)
Robin Morse
HANNAH LEE(1953); STALAG 17(1953); FAST AND THE FURIOUS, THE(1954); MARTY(1955); BOSS, THE(1956); HE LAUGHED LAST(1956); PAL JOEY(1957); ROCK ALL NIGHT(1957); SABU AND THE MAGIC RING(1957); TRUE GRIT(1969)
Ronald Morse
THAT CERTAIN SOMETHING(1941, Aus.)
Susan E. Morse
MANHATTAN(1979), ed; STARDUST MEMORIES(1980), ed; ARTHUR(1981), ed; MIDSUMMER NIGHT'S SEX COMEDY, A(1982), ed; ZELIG(1983), ed
1984
BROADWAY DANNY ROSE(1984), ed
T.O. Morse
BIG BLUFF, THE(1955), ed
Terrell Morse
TULSA(1949), ed
Silents
FRENCH DRESSING(1927), ed; HEAD MAN, THE(1928), ed; WHIP WOMAN, THE(1928), ed
Terrell O. Morse
UNKNOWN WORLD(1951), d, ed
Terrill Morse
NUMBERED MEN(1930), ed; MISBEHAVING LADIES(1931), ed; RIGHT OF WAY, THE(1931), ed; TWO SECONDS(1932), ed
Terry Morse
GIRL IN THE GLASS CAGE, THE(1929), ed; DRAGON MURDER CASE, THE(1934), ed; HAROLD TEEN(1934), ed; I SELL ANYTHING(1934), ed; MASSACRE(1934), ed; PERSONALITY KID, THE(1934), ed; CASE OF THE CURIOUS BRIDE, THE(1935), ed; FRONT PAGE WOMAN(1935), ed; I AM A THIEF(1935), ed; I LIVE FOR LOVE(1935), ed; MAN OF IRON(1935), ed; WOMAN IN RED, THE(1935), ed; BIG NOISE,

THE(1936), ed; LOVE BEGINS AT TWENTY(1936), ed; SING ME A LOVE SONG(1936), ed; MEN IN EXILE(1937), ed; PERFECT SPECIMEN, THE(1937), ed; STOLEN HOLIDAY(1937), ed; TALENT SCOUT(1937), ed; CRIME SCHOOL(1938), ed; ADVENTURES OF JANE ARDEN(1939), d; NO PLACE TO GO(1939), d; ON TRIAL(1939), d; SMASHING THE MONEY RING(1939), d; WATERFRONT(1939), d; BRITISH INTELLIGENCE(1940), d; FUGITIVE FROM JUSTICE, A(1940), d; TEAR GAS SQUAD(1940), d; THREE SONS O'GUNS(1941), ed; MURDER IN THE BIG HOUSE(1942), ed; OLD ACQUAINTANCE(1943), ed; FOG ISLAND(1945), d; DANGEROUS MONEY(1946), d; DANNY BOY(1946), d; SHADOWS OVER CHINATOWN(1946), d; BELLS OF SAN FERNANDO(1947), d; JOURNEY INTO LIGHT(1951), ed; JAPANESE WAR BRIDE(1952), ed; RUBY GENTRY(1952), ed; THIEF OF VENICE, THE(1952), ed; MOONLIGHTER, THE(1953), ed; CURUCU, BEAST OF THE AMAZON(1956), ed; GODZILLA, RING OF THE MONSTERS(1956, Jap.), d, ed; LOVE SLAVES OF THE AMAZONS(1957), ed; SPACE CHILDREN, THE(1958), ed; HANGMAN, THE(1959), ed; YOUNG CAPTIVES, THE(1959), ed; BLUEPRINT FOR ROBBERY(1961), ed; LIST OF ADRIAN MESSENGER, THE(1963), ed
Silents
WHY BE GOOD?(1929), ed
Terry O. Morse
DON RICARDO RETURNS(1946), d; LOVE IN A GOLDFISH BOWL(1961), ed; ROBINSON CRUSOE ON MARS(1964), ed; TAFFY AND THE JUNGLE HUNTER(1965), d; YOUNG DILLINGER(1965), ed; WHAT AM I BID?(1967), ed; PANIC IN THE CITY(1968), ed; GIRL WHO KNEW TOO MUCH, THE(1969), ed; TIGER BY THE TAIL(1970), ed
William Morse
Silents
SONG OF THE WAGE SLAVE, THE(1915)
Misc. Silents
OCEAN WAIF, THE(1916); EMPRESS, THE(1917)
William A. Morse
Silents
SHOOTING OF DAN MCGREW, THE(1915)
Misc. Silents
HER OWN WAY(1915)
Fred Morsell
Q(1982)
H. Tudor Morsell
Misc. Silents
GRANDEE'S RING, THE(1915)
Fulvio Morsella
FOR A FEW DOLLARS MORE(1967, Ital./Ger./Span.), w; ONCE UPON A TIME IN THE WEST(1969, U.S./Ital.), p; DUCK, YOU SUCKER!(1972, Ital.), p; GENIUS, THE(1976, Ital./Fr./Ger.), p, w
Soheir Morshedy
SIGNALS-AN ADVENTURE IN SPACE(1970, E. Ger./Pol.)
Glenn Morshower
DRIVE-IN(1976); DEAD AND BURIED(1981)
1984
PHILADELPHIA EXPERIMENT, THE(1984)
M. Morskaya
Misc. Silents
WOMAN OF TOMORROW(1914, USSR)
Ellay Mort
LADY IN THE LAKE(1947)
Patricia Mort
ATTEMPT TO KILL(1961, Brit.); TIME TO REMEMBER(1962, Brit.); THAT KIND OF GIRL(1963, Brit.)
Ray Mort
PINK FLOYD–THE WALL(1982, Brit.)
Louis Mortelle
Misc. Silents
COURAGE AND THE MAN(1915)
Clare Mortensen
BLONDE PICKUP(1955)
Elisabeth Mortensen
JULIA(1977); MARCH OR DIE(1977, Brit.); JOY(1983, Fr./Can.)
John Mortensen
PRETTY POISON(1968), set d; KLUTE(1971), set d
Noreen Mortensen
MRS. O'MALLEY AND MR. MALONE(1950); TWO TICKETS TO BROADWAY(1951)
Mary Morter
WHY ROCK THE BOAT?(1974, Can.); LITTLE GIRL WHO LIVES DOWN THE LANE, THE(1977, Can.)
Jean Mortier
FRENCH CANCAN(1956, Fr.)
Frank Mortiforte
PAJAMA PARTY(1964)
Charles Mortimar
SOMETIMES GOOD(1934, Brit.)
Caroline Mortimer
SATURDAY NIGHT OUT(1964, Brit.); PLACE FOR LOVERS, A(1969, Ital./Fr.); MC KENZIE BREAK, THE(1970); HIRELING, THE(1973, Brit.); JUGGERNAUT(1974, Brit.)
Chapman Mortimer
REFLECTIONS IN A GOLDEN EYE(1967), w
Charles Mortimer
WATCH BEVERLY(1932, Brit.); BOOMERANG(1934, Brit.); RETURN OF BULLDOG DRUMMOND, THE(1934, Brit.); THINGS ARE LOOKING UP(1934, Brit.); YOU MADE ME LOVE YOU(1934, Brit.); BIRDS OF A FEATHER(1935, Brit.); OLD ROSES(1935, Brit.); PRICE OF A SONG, THE(1935, Brit.); SMALL MAN, THE(1935, Brit.); TRIUMPH OF SHERLOCK HOLMES, THE(1935, Brit.); LIVING DANGEROUSLY(1936, Brit.); SOMEONE AT THE DOOR(1936, Brit.); AREN'T MEN BEASTS?(1937, Brit.); PHANTOM SHIP(1937, Brit.); DEAD MEN ARE DANGEROUS(1939, Brit.); POISON PEN(1941, Brit.); THEATRE ROYAL(1943, Brit.); WHEN WE ARE MARRIED(1943, Brit.); WAY OUT, THE(1956, Brit.)
Charles G. Mortimer, Jr.
FROM THE MIXED-UP FILES OF MRS. BASIL E. FRANKWEILER(1973), p

Ed Mortimer
KID MILLIONS(1934); PRESIDENT VANISHES, THE(1934); GIVE ME YOUR HEART(1936); POLO JOE(1936); IT'S LOVE I'M AFTER(1937); AMAZING DR. CLITTERHOUSE, THE(1938); THAT CERTAIN AGE(1938); VIVACIOUS LADY(1938); PAROLE FIXER(1940); HONOLULU LU(1941); THOUSANDS CHEER(1943); HEAVENLY DAYS(1944); TWO GIRLS AND A SAILOR(1944)

Edmund Mortimer
YOURS FOR THE ASKING(1936)
Silents
AS YE SOW(1914); COMMON LAW, THE(1916); ALIAS JIMMY VALENTINE(1920), d; EXILES, THE(1923), d; RAILROADED(1923), d; AGAINST ALL ODDS(1924), d; ARIZONA ROMEO, THE(1925), d, w; GOLD AND THE GIRL(1925), d
Misc. Silents
ROAD THROUGH THE DARK, THE(1918), d; SAVAGE WOMAN, THE(1918), d; COUNTY FAIR, THE(1920), d; HUSHED HOUR, THE(1920), d; MISFIT WIFE, THE(1920), d; BROAD ROAD, THE(1923), d; DESERT OUTLAW, THE(1924), d; MAN'S MATE, A(1924), d; STAR DUST TRAIL, THE(1924), d; THAT FRENCH LADY(1924), d; WOLF MAN, THE(1924), d; MAN FROM RED GULCH, THE(1925), d; PRAIRIE PIRATE, THE(1925), d; SCANDAL PROOF(1925), d; SATAN TOWN(1926), d; WOMAN'S WAY, A(1928), d

Edward Mortimer
FRISCO KID(1935); UNDER YOUR SPELL(1936); AWFUL TRUTH, THE(1937); DEVIL BAT, THE(1941)
Silents
NEPTUNE'S DAUGHTER(1914)

Eve Mortimer
WILLIAM COMES TO TOWN(1948, Brit.)

Frank Mortimer
HOT CURVES(1930), w

Glenys Mortimer
ROOM FOR TWO(1940, Brit.)

Henry Mortimer
Silents
PURSUING VENGEANCE, THE(1916)
Misc. Silents
HER GREAT PRICE(1916); THEIR COMPACT(1917); ROAD CALLED STRAIGHT, THE(1919); FEAR MARKET, THE(1920); HIS WIFE'S FRIEND(1920)

Ian Mortimer
PIRATE MOVIE, THE(1982, Aus.)

Jane Mortimer
Misc. Silents
CONFLICT, THE(1916)

Joan Mortimer
HENRY ALDRICH HAUNTS A HOUSE(1943); HENRY ALDRICH, BOY SCOUT(1944); HENRY ALDRICH'S LITTLE SECRET(1944)

John Mortimer
BRIDE OF THE LAKE(1934, Brit.); INNOCENTS, THE(1961, U.S./Brit.), w; GUNS OF DARKNESS(1962, Brit.), w; LUNCH HOUR(1962, Brit.), p, w; TRIAL AND ERROR(1962, Brit.), w; RUNNING MAN, THE(1963, Brit.), w; BUNNY LAKE IS MISSING(1965), w; FLEA IN HER EAR, A(1968, Fr.), w; JOHN AND MARY(1969), w

Johnnie Mortimer
NO SEX PLEASE–WE'RE BRITISH(1979, Brit.), w

Lee Mortimer
NEW YORK CONFIDENTIAL(1955), w; CHICAGO CONFIDENTIAL(1957), w

Lillian Mortimer
Silents
NO MOTHER TO GUIDE HER(1923), w

Louise Bates Mortimer
Misc. Silents
WIFE'S ROMANCE, A(1923)

Malcolm Mortimer
Misc. Silents
QUICKSANDS OF LIFE(1915, Brit.)

Penelope Mortimer
PUMPKIN EATER, THE(1964, Brit.), w; BUNNY LAKE IS MISSING(1965), w

Tricia Mortimer
FRIGHTMARE(1974, Brit.)

Trisha Mortimer
PERFECT FRIDAY(1970, Brit.); SCHIZO(1977, Brit.)

William Mortimer
Misc. Silents
SUPREME PASSION, THE(1921)

Snow Mortimer
Silents
WHEN KNIGHTHOOD WAS IN FLOWER(1922)

Louisa Mortiz
SIX PACK ANNIE(1975)

Doris Mortlock
MELODY OF MY HEART(1936, Brit.)

Rodolfo Mortola
MAFIA, THE(1972, Arg.), w

Morton
OPEN ROAD, THE(1940, Fr.)

Anthony Morton
OH! WHAT A LOVELY WAR(1969, Brit.)

Arthur Morton
FIT FOR A KING(1937), m; PICK A STAR(1937), m, md; RIDING ON AIR(1937), m; TURNABOUT(1940), m; WALKING HILLS, THE(1949), m; FATHER IS A BACHELOR(1950), m; ROGUES OF SHERWOOD FOREST(1950), m; HARLEM GLOBETROTTERS, THE(1951), m; NEVER TRUST A GAMBLER(1951), m; PUSHOVER(1954), m; MAN FROM LARAMIE, THE(1955), md; HE LAUGHED LAST(1956), m; COWBOY(1958), md; CRY FOR HAPPY(1961), md; SWINGIN' ALONG(1962), m; CRITIC'S CHOICE(1963), md

Bill Morton
HOUNDS... OF NOTRE DAME, THE(1980, Can.)

Caroline Morton
YOICKS!(1932, Brit.)

Cavendish Morton
Misc. Silents
BROKEN MELODY, THE(1916, Brit.), d

Charles Morton
CHRISTINA(1929); FOUR DEVILS(1929); AMOS 'N' ANDY(1930); CAMEO KIRBY(1930); CAUGHT SHORT(1930); DAWN TRAIL, THE(1931); ARMS AND THE MAN(1932, Brit.); LAST RIDE, THE(1932); GOLDIE GETS ALONG(1933); MAN FROM MUSIC MOUNTAIN(1943); CHEYENNE WILDCAT(1944); FIREBRANDS OF ARIZONA(1944); HIDDEN VALLEY OUTLAWS(1944); LUMBERJACK(1944); OUTLAWS OF SANTA FE(1944); TRAIL TO GUNSIGHT(1944); ALONG CAME JONES(1945); SUDAN(1945); PLAINSMAN AND THE LADY(1946); WYOMING(1947); RIVER LADY(1948); SURRENDER(1950); SON OF PALEFACE(1952); AT GUNPOINT(1955); SHOTGUN(1955); WESTBOUND(1959); MAN WHO SHOT LIBERTY VALANCE, THE(1962); SEX AND THE SINGLE GIRL(1964)
Silents
FOUR SONS(1928); NONE BUT THE BRAVE(1928); NEW YEAR'S EVE(1929)
Misc. Silents
COLLEEN(1927); RICH BUT HONEST(1927); WOLF FANGS(1927)

Charlton Morton
UNCENSORED(1944, Brit.)

Clive Morton
LAST COUPON, THE(1932, Brit.); FRIDAY THE 13TH(1934, Brit.); MAN WHO LIVED AGAIN, THE(1936, Brit.); DEAD MEN TELL NO TALES(1939, Brit.); HERE COME THE HUGGETTS(1948, Brit.); JASSY(1948, Brit.); MINE OWN EXECUTIONER(1948, Brit.); VOTE FOR HUGGETT(1948, Brit.); KIND HEARTS AND CORONETS(1949, Brit.); QUARTET(1949, Brit.); SCOTT OF THE ANTARCTIC(1949, Brit.); THIS WAS A WOMAN(1949, Brit.); RUN FOR YOUR MONEY, A(1950, Brit.); TRIO(1950, Brit.); WHILE THE SUN SHINES(1950, Brit.); LAVENDER HILL MOB, THE(1951, Brit.); CASTLE IN THE AIR(1952, Brit.); HIS EXCELLENCY(1952, Brit.); NIGHT WITHOUT STARS(1953, Brit.); COURT MARTIAL(1954, Brit.); HARASSED HERO, THE(1954, Brit.); TURN THE KEY SOFTLY(1954, Brit.); RICHARD III(1956, Brit.); ABANDON SHIP(1957, Brit.); AFTER THE BALL(1957, Brit.); BEYOND MOMBASA(1957); LUCKY JIM(1957, Brit.); DUKE WORE JEANS, THE(1958, Brit.); MOONRAKER, THE(1958, Brit.); SAFECRACKER, THE(1958, Brit.); NAVY LARK, THE(1959, Brit.); ORDERS ARE ORDERS(1959, Brit.); SHAKE HANDS WITH THE DEVIL(1959, Ireland); NEXT TO NO TIME(1960, Brit.); CLUE OF THE NEW PIN, THE(1961, Brit.); PURE HELL OF ST. TRINIAN'S, THE(1961, Brit.); I THANK A FOOL(1962, Brit.); MATTER OF WHO, A(1962, Brit.); MAKE MINE A MILLION(1965, Brit.); ALPHABET MURDERS, THE(1966); COP-OUT(1967, Brit.); GOODBYE MR. CHIPS(1969, U.S./Brit.); LOCK UP YOUR DAUGHTERS(1969, Brit.); JANE EYRE(1971, Brit.); ZEPPELIN(1971, Brit.); YOUNG WINSTON(1972, Brit.); 11 HARROWHOUSE(1974, Brit.)
Misc. Talkies
ALL HALLOWE'EN(1952)

Cyril Morton
Misc. Silents
GREAT POISON MYSTERY, THE(1914, Brit.); STRANGE CASE OF PHILIP KENT, THE(1916, Brit.)

Danny Morton
CRIME, INC.(1945); CRIMSON CANARY(1945); GUNMAN'S CODE(1946); SMOOTH AS SILK(1946); EYES OF TEXAS(1948); MONEY MADNESS(1948); DESTINATION BIG HOUSE(1950)

David Morton
BILLY IN THE LOWLANDS(1979)

Dean Morton
DAKOTA KID, THE(1951)

Derek Morton
1984
WILD HORSES(1984, New Zealand), d

Doris Morton
FOLIES DERGERE(1935)

Edna Morton
Misc. Silents
BURDEN OF RACE, THE(1921); SECRET SORROW(1921); SIMP, THE(1921); CALL OF HIS PEOPLE, THE(1922); EASY MONEY(1922); SPITFIRE(1922)

Elizabeth Morton
LORDS OF DISCIPLINE, THE(1983)

Esther Morton
RUNAWAY BRIDE(1930)

Frederick Morton
TRUMAN CAPOTE'S TRILOGY(1969)

Fredricka Morton
FRENCH LIEUTENANT'S WOMAN, THE(1981)

Gabrielle Morton
Silents
POWER OVER MEN(1929, Brit.)

Gary Morton
LENNY(1974)

Gene Morton
SIN'S PAYDAY(1932), w

Gregory Morton
VAGABOND KING, THE(1956); FIEND WHO WALKED THE WEST, THE(1958); FLIGHT THAT DISAPPEARED, THE(1961); INTERNS, THE(1962); BYE BYE BIRDIE(1963); JOHNNY COOL(1963); NEW INTERNS, THE(1964); SYNANON(1965); COUNTERPOINT(1967); DESTRUCTORS, THE(1968); PANIC IN THE CITY(1968); MEPHISTO WALTZ, THE(1971)
Misc. Talkies
ADULTERESS, THE(1976)

Guy Morton
SECRETS OF CHINATOWN(1935), w

Howard Morton
LIFE AND TIMES OF JUDGE ROY BEAN, THE(1972); MECHANIC, THE(1972); SCORPIO(1973); RHINOCEROS(1974)

Hugh Morton
DEADLOCK(1943, Brit.); PORTRAIT OF CLARE(1951, Brit.); BELLE OF NEW YORK, THE(1952), w; DECAMERON NIGHTS(1953, Brit.); FLOATING DUTCHMAN, THE(1953, Brit.); GAY ADVENTURE, THE(1953, Brit.); MR. DENNING DRIVES NORTH(1953, Brit.); DIAMOND WIZARD, THE(1954, Brit.); FAMILY AFFAIR(1954, Brit.); TERROR SHIP(1954, Brit.); LYONS IN PARIS, THE(1955, Brit.); MAN OF THE MOMENT(1955, Brit.); WHERE THERE'S A WILL(1955, Brit.); ROGUE'S YARN(1956, Brit.); TEARS FOR SIMON(1957, Brit.); BACHELOR OF HEARTS(1958, Brit.); THREE

Humphrey Morton *(continued)*
ON A SPREE(1961, Brit.); PAYROLL(1962, Brit.); MASTER SPY(1964, Brit.); FIVE MILLION YEARS TO EARTH(1968, Brit.); DARWIN ADVENTURE, THE(1972, Brit.); STUD, THE(1979, Brit.)
1984
OXFORD BLUES(1984)

Humphrey Morton
SWORD OF HONOUR(1938, Brit.); SING ALONG WITH ME(1952, Brit.); EIGHT O'CLOCK WALK(1954, Brit.); LADY OF VENGEANCE(1957, Brit)

J. B. Morton
BOYS WILL BE BOYS(1936, Brit.), w; TWO'S COMPANY(1939, Brit.), w

J.C. Morton
FRISCO KID(1935)

Jack Morton
Misc. Talkies
CALLING ALL CARS(1935)

James C. Morton
FOLLOW THE LEADER(1930); PACK UP YOUR TROUBLES(1932); DEVIL'S BROTHER, THE(1933); OPERATOR 13(1934); YOU'RE TELLING ME(1934); NAUGHTY MARIETTA(1935); BOHEMIAN GIRL, THE(1936); IT HAD TO HAPPEN(1936); OUR RELATIONS(1936); PICK A STAR(1937); PUBLIC COWBOY NO. 1(1937); RHYTHM IN THE CLOUDS(1937); TWO WISE MAIDS(1937); WAY OUT WEST(1937); EVERY DAY'S A HOLIDAY(1938); INTERNATIONAL SETTLEMENT(1938); MAMA RUNS WILD(1938); MIRACLES FOR SALE(1939); TELL NO TALES(1939); YOU CAN'T CHEAT AN HONEST MAN(1939); COURAGEOUS DR. CHRISTIAN, THE(1940); EARL OF PUDDLESTONE(1940); MY LITTLE CHICKADEE(1940); LADY FROM LOUISIANA(1941); PUBLIC ENEMIES(1941); WILD GEESE CALLING(1941); JOHNNY EAGER(1942); LUCKY LEGS(1942); STREET OF CHANCE(1942); TO THE SHORES OF TRIPOLI(1942); YOKEL BOY(1942)

James Morton
HOUSE OF MYSTERY(1934); TWO IN A CROWD(1936); STABLEMATES(1938); TOPPER TAKES A TRIP(1939); WHEN TOMORROW COMES(1939); DANGER ON WHEELS(1940); RETURN OF FRANK JAMES, THE(1940); WHEN THE DALTONS RODE(1940); LUCKY DEVILS(1941); BOOGIE MAN WILL GET YOU, THE(1942); IN OLD CALIFORNIA(1942); LAUGH YOUR BLUES AWAY(1943)

Joe Morton
BETWEEN THE LINES(1977); ...AND JUSTICE FOR ALL(1979)
1984
BROTHER FROM ANOTHER PLANET, THE(1984)

John Morton
TWO-GUN JUSTICE(1938); PANIC IN YEAR ZERO!(1962), w; CUBA(1979); EMPIRE STRIKES BACK, THE(1980); FLASH GORDON(1980); SUPERMAN II(1980)

Judee Morton
EXPLOSIVE GENERATION, THE(1961); EXPERIMENT IN TERROR(1962); ZOTZ!(1962); SLIME PEOPLE, THE(1963)

Julian Morton
WOLFMAN(1979)

Karen Morton
HISTORY OF THE WORLD, PART 1(1981)

Leon Morton
FROM TOP TO BOTTOM(1933, Fr.)

Margaret Morton
THEY WERE EXPENDABLE(1945)

Marjorie Morton
Silents
UNHOLY THREE, THE(1925)

Maureen Morton
NOTHING VENTURE(1948, Brit.)

May Morton
Silents
EAST LYNNE(1913, Brit.)

Michael Morton
WOMAN TO WOMAN(1929), w; ALIBI(1931, Brit.), w; YELLOW TICKET, THE(1931), w; WOMAN TO WOMAN(1946, Brit.), w
Silents
IMPOSTER, THE(1918), w; ON WITH THE DANCE(1920), w; DARLING OF THE RICH, THE(1923), w; NIGHT WATCH, THE(1928), w

Mickey Morton
HEAD ON(1971); FUN WITH DICK AND JANE(1977); NORTH AVENUE IRREGULARS, THE(1979); FIRE AND ICE(1983)
1984
SAM'S SON(1984)

Nigel Morton
HOUR BEFORE THE DAWN, THE(1944)

Pat Morton
LOVE RACE, THE(1931, Brit.), d
Misc. Silents
THREE MEN IN A CART(1929, Brit.)

Paul Morton
TIME FLIES(1944, Brit.)

Phil Morton
MONSTER A GO-GO(1965)

Terry Morse, Jr.
RETURN OF A MAN CALLED HORSE, THE(1976), p; SKY RIDERS(1976, U.S./Gr.), p; BIG BRAWL, THE(1980), p

Rob Morton
LADIES AND GENTLEMEN, THE FABULOUS STAINS(1982), w
1984
SWING SHIFT(1984), w

Robert "Tex" Morton
STIR(1980, Aus.)

Roseanna Morton
I WANNA HOLD YOUR HAND(1978), cos

Roy Morton
PSYCHO A GO-GO!(1965); FUZZ(1972)

Tex Morton
WE OF THE NEVER NEVER(1983, Aus.)

Tom Morton
MAIN STREET TO BROADWAY(1953); STARS ARE SINGING, THE(1953)

Tommy Morton
WAIT 'TIL THE SUN SHINES, NELLIE(1952)

Vincent Morton
1984
TREASURE OF THE YANKEE ZEPHYR(1984), ph

Walter Morton
Silents
WISHING RING, THE(1914)
Misc. Silents
CHOCOLATE SOLDIER, THE(1915), d

Will Morton
1984
FLESHBURN(1984)

William Morton
OTHELLO(1955, U.S./Fr./Ital.), ed

Morton Gould and His Orchestra
DELIGHTFULLY DANGEROUS(1945)

Myrette Moruen
CONSTANT HUSBAND, THE(1955, Brit.)

William Morum
OBSESSED(1951, Brit.), w

Franco Moruzzi
WITCHES, THE(1969, Fr./Ital.)

Myrette Morven
IRELAND'S BORDER LINE(1939, Ireland); UNDER YOUR HAT(1940, Brit.); DULCIMER STREET(1948, Brit.); MELODY IN THE DARK(1948, Brit.); HIGH JINKS IN SOCIETY(1949, Brit.); HAPPIEST DAYS OF YOUR LIFE(1950, Brit.); OLD MOTHER RILEY, HEADMISTRESS(1950, Brit.); FOUR AGAINST FATE(1952, Brit.); FOLLY TO BE WISE(1953, Brit.); TWICE UPON A TIME(1953, Brit.); LADY GODIVA RIDES AGAIN(1955, Brit.); LADY IS A SQUARE, THE(1959, Brit.); TEENAGE BAD GIRL(1959, Brit.); TWO-WAY STRETCH(1961, Brit.)

Philippe Mory
FRUIT IS RIPE, THE(1961, Fr./Ital.)

Gilbert Moryn
ROYAL AFFAIRS IN VERSAILLES(1957, Fr.)

Peter Mosbacher
DIABOLICALLY YOURS(1968, Fr.)

Bernd Mosblech
WAR AND PEACE(1983, Ger.), ph

Bianca Mosca
FRIEDA(1947, Brit.), cos

Joe Mosca
DIRT GANG, THE(1972)

Pippo Mosca
ORGANIZER, THE(1964, Fr./Ital./Yugo.)

Tom Mosca
TERROR IN THE JUNGLE(1968), ed

George Moscaidis
TEMPEST(1982)

Elizabetta Moscatelli
FELLINI SATYRICON(1969, Fr./Ital.)

Italo Moscati
NIGHT PORTER, THE(1974, Ital./U.S.), w
1984
BEYOND GOOD AND EVIL(1984, Ital./Fr./Ger.), w

Mike Moschella
HOW TO COMMIT MARRIAGE(1969), makeup; STERILE CUCKOO, THE(1969), makeup; SPECIAL DELIVERY(1976), makeup

Mark Anthony Moschello
FLASHDANCE(1983)

Gaston Moschin
DROP THEM OR I'LL SHOOT(1969, Fr./Ger./Span.); GODFATHER, THE, PART II(1974)
Misc. Talkies
SEVEN TIMES SEVEN(1973, Ital.)

Gastone Moschin
FIASCO IN MILAN(1963, Fr./Ital.); OF WAYWARD LOVE(1964, Ital./Ger.); LOVE IN 4 DIMENSIONS(1965 Fr./Ital.); LA VISITA(1966, Ital./Fr.); SPY IN YOUR EYE(1966, Ital.); BIRDS, THE BEES AND THE ITALIANS, THE(1967); ITALIAN SECRET SERVICE(1968, Ital.); OLDEST PROFESSION, THE(1968, Fr./Ital./Ger.); QUEENS, THE(1968, Ital./Fr.); SEVEN GOLDEN MEN(1969, Fr./Ital./Span.); CONFORMIST, THE(1971, Ital., Fr); WEEKEND MURDERS, THE(1972, Ital.); MR. SUPERINVISIBLE(1974, Ital./Span./Ger.); WOMAN AT HER WINDOW, A(1978, Fr./Ital./Ger.); WIFEMISTRESS(1979, Ital.); LION OF THE DESERT(1981, Libya/Brit.)
1984
JOKE OF DESTINY LYING IN WAIT AROUND THE CORNER LIKE A STREET-BANDIT, A(1984, Ital.)

Romano Moschini
SACCO AND VANZETTI(1971, Ital./Fr.)

Maisie Mosco
MUMSY, NANNY, SONNY, AND GIRLY(1970, Brit.), w

David Moscoe
BLACK SIX, THE(1974), m

Arie Moscona
DIAMONDS(1975, U.S./Israel)

Nicola Moscona
GREAT CARUSO, THE(1951)

Louis Mosconi
OPERATION PACIFIC(1951)

Willie Mosconi
HUSTLER, THE(1961), a, tech adv; BALTIMORE BULLET, THE(1980)

George Moscov
CHAINED FOR LIFE(1950), p

George V. Moscov
WHEN STRANGERS MARRY(1944), w

Anne Marie Moscovenko
CASTLE KEEP(1969)

Maurice Moscovich
WINTERSET(1936); LANCER SPY(1937); GATEWAY(1938); SUEZ(1938); EVERY-THING HAPPENS AT NIGHT(1939); IN NAME ONLY(1939); LOVE AFFAIR(1939); SUSANNAH OF THE MOUNTIES(1939); GREAT DICTATOR, THE(1940); GREAT COMMANDMENT, THE(1941)

Maurice Moscovitch
MAKE WAY FOR TOMORROW(1937); SOUTH TO KARANGA(1940)

David Moscovitz
SPEED LOVERS(1968), ed

Maurice Moscovitz
RIO(1939)

Bob Moscow
MOONLIGHTING WIVES(1966), p

James Moscrip
BIG GAME, THE(1936)

Erik Moseholm
WEEKEND(1964, Den.), m

Pamela Moseiwitsch
MIND OF MR. SOAMES, THE(1970, Brit.)

Tad Mosel
ALL THE WAY HOME(1963), w; DEAR HEART(1964), w; UP THE DOWN STAIR-CASE(1967), w

Alice Moseley
Silents
FLYING FROM JUSTICE(1915, Brit.)

Brian Moseley
CHARLIE BUBBLES(1968, Brit.)

Dana Moseley
DEAD OF SUMMER(1970 Ital./Fr.), w

Irwin W. Moseley
EVEL KNIEVEL(1971)

Jerry Moseley
BLOOD TIDE(1982), m; FRIGHTMARE(1983), m

Ben Moselle
SET-UP, THE(1949); FEDERAL MAN(1950)

Kenneth Mosely
GIVE ME THE STARS(1944, Brit.)

Dana Moser
1984
FLASH OF GREEN, A(1984), cos

Earl Moser
STICK TO YOUR GUNS(1941), ed

Edda Moser
DON GIOVANNI(1979, Fr./Ital./Ger.)

George Moser
PIRATES OF CAPRI, THE(1949), w

Hans Moser
MONEY ON THE STREET(1930, Aust.); HIS MAJESTY, KING BALLYHOO(1931, Ger.); BURG THEATRE(1936, Ger.); GREAT MANHUNT, THE(1951, Brit.); ONE APRIL 2000(1952, Aust.); APRIL 1, 2000(1953, Aust.); CONGRESS DANCES(1957, Ger.); DIE FLEDERMAUS(1964, Aust.)

Heidi Moser
JACK OF DIAMONDS(1967, U.S./Ger.), makeup

James E. Moser
WINGS OF THE HAWK(1953), w

Margot Moser
THERE GOES THE BRIDE(1980, Brit.)

Rochell Moser
CANNONBALL RUN, THE(1981), set d

Sonia Moser
LEGEND OF THE LOST(1957, U.S./Panama/Ital.); QUIET AMERICAN, THE(1958)

Van Moser
PRIVATE SECRETARY, THE(1935, Brit.), w

Albert Moses
MAN WHO WOULD BE KING, THE(1975, Brit.); SPY WHO LOVED ME, THE(1977, Brit.); CARRY ON EMANUELLE(1978, Brit.); OCTOPUSSY(1983, Brit.)
1984
LITTLE DRUMMER GIRL, THE(1984); SCANDALOUS(1984)

Andrew Moses
MURDER ON THE CAMPUS(1934), w

Bill Moses
NIGHT THEY ROBBED BIG BERTHA'S, THE(1975); RETURN TO MACON COUN-TY(1975); FARMER, THE(1977)

Charles A. Moses
FRANKENSTEIN 1970(1958), w

David Moses
FLAREUP(1969); DARING DOBERMANS, THE(1973); ROOMMATES, THE(1973)

Ethel Moses
TEMPTATION(1936); UNDERWORLD(1937)
Misc. Talkies
GOD'S STEPCHILDREN(1937); BIRTHRIGHT(1939)

Gilbert Moses
FISH THAT SAVED PITTSBURGH, THE(1979), d

Harry Moses
VAN, THE(1977); OTHER SIDE OF THE MOUNTAIN–PART 2, THE(1978)
Misc. Talkies
SWEATER GIRLS(1978)

Jonathon David Moses
SCARED TO DEATH(1981)

Lucia Lynn Moses
Misc. Silents
SCAR OF SHAME, THE(1927)

Marian Moses
DEAD HEAT ON A MERRY-GO-ROUND(1966); BUONA SERA, MRS. CAMP-BELL(1968, Ital.)

Nancy Moses
PHANTOM OF THE PARADISE(1974)

Maj. Raymond G. Moses
Silents
WEST POINT(1928), a, adv

Richard Moses
ON THE RIGHT TRACK(1981), w

Rick Moses
AVALANCHE(1978)

Sam Moses
NOTHING PERSONAL(1980, Can.)
1984
GHOSTBUSTERS(1984); MOSCOW ON THE HUDSON(1984)

Senta Moses
THINGS ARE TOUGH ALL OVER(1982); D.C. CAB(1983)

Stefen Moses
I LOVE YOU, I KILL YOU(1972, Ger.)

Tom Moses
YOUR THREE MINUTES ARE UP(1973)

Gilbert Moses III
WILLIE DYNAMITE(1973), d

Jeroma Moshan
FIVE FINGERS(1952)

Yehuda Ben Moshe
DREAM NO MORE(1950, Palestine)

Grete Mosheim
CAR OF DREAMS(1935, Brit.)

Mike Moshella
PRIVATE NAVY OF SGT. O'FARRELL, THE(1968), makeup

Grete Moshelm
DREYFUS CASE, THE(1940, Ger.)

Bill Mosher
GUNFIGHT, A(1971), ed

Bob Mosher
PRIVATE WAR OF MAJOR BENSON, THE(1955), w; MUNSTER, GO HOME(1966), p, w

Clara Mosher
Silents
JUDITH OF THE CUMBERLANDS(1916)

Sasha Moshovets
WELCOME KOSTYA!(1965, USSR)

Marian Mosick
JIVARO(1954)

Enid Mosier
LADY POSSESSED(1952)

Odeardo Mosini
LAST CHANCE, THE(1945, Switz.)

Ivan Mosjoukine
Misc. Silents
L'ANGOISSANTE AVENTURE(1920, Fr.); L'ENFANT DU CARNAVAL(1921, Fr.), d; LE BRASIER ARDENT(1923, Fr.), a, d; KEAN(1924, Fr.); LE LION DES MO-GOLS(1924, Fr.); LES OMBRES QUI PASSANT(1924, Fr.); LATE MATTHEW PASCAL, THE(1925, Fr.); MICHEL STROGOFF(1926, Fr.); CASANOVA(1927, Fr.)

Ivan Mosjukine
Misc. Silents
SURRENDER(1927)

Bernice Mosk
SUNSET BOULEVARD(1950); BUCCANEER, THE(1958), w

Tony Moskal
SHOCK WAVES(1977)

Andrei Moskin
Misc. Silents
KATKA'S REINETTE APPLES(1926, USSR), d

George Moskov
JOHNNY DOESN'T LIVE HERE ANY MORE(1944), art d; HEADING FOR HEAV-EN(1947), p; CHAMPAGNE FOR CAESAR(1950), p; THREE BLONDES IN HIS LIFE(1961), p, w; MARRIED TOO YOUNG(1962), d

Alla Moskova
Silents
KING OF KINGS, THE(1927)

Milord Moskovitch
DR. COPPELIUS(1968, U.S./Span.)

Edward L. Moskowitz
WRONG IS RIGHT(1982)

Gene Moskowitz
DESTRUCTORS, THE(1974, Brit.)

Jennie Moskowitz
MOTHER'S BOY(1929)

Joel Moskowitz
FIRST TIME, THE(1978, Fr.)

Minnow Moskowitz
TAKE THE MONEY AND RUN(1969)

Andrei Moskvin
IVAN THE TERRIBLE(Part I, 1947, USSR), ph

Andrey Moskvin
DON QUIXOTE(1961, USSR), ph; LADY WITH THE DOG, THE(1962, USSR), ph

I. Moskvin
Misc. Silents
STATION MASTER, THE(1928, USSR)

Ivan Moskvin
Misc. Silents
POLIKUSHKA(1919, USSR); STATION MASTER, THE(1928, USSR), d; RANKS AND PEOPLE(1929, USSR)

Brian Mosley
SPRING AND PORT WINE(1970, Brit.)

Bryan Mosley
KIND OF LOVING, A(1962, Brit.); UP JUMPED A SWAGMAN(1965, Brit.); WHERE THE BULLETS FLY(1966, Brit.); FAR FROM THE MADDING CROWD(1967, Brit.); GET CARTER(1971, Brit.)

Irvin Mosley
LIVING BETWEEN TWO WORLDS(1963); KILLERS, THE(1964)
Kevin T. Mosley
1984
SOLDIER'S STORY, A(1984)
Leonard Mosley
THEY CAN'T HANG ME(1955, Brit.), w; FOXHOLE IN CAIRO(1960, Brit.), w
Lucky Mosley
OTHER SIDE OF BONNIE AND CLYDE, THE(1968); URBAN COWBOY(1980); DEADLY BLESSING(1981)
Millidge Mosley
ENDLESS LOVE(1981)
Moe Mosley
1984
NINJA III–THE DOMINATION(1984)
Nicholas Mosley
ACCIDENT(1967, Brit.), a, w; ASSASSINATION OF TROTSKY, THE(1972 Fr./Ital.), w
Nicolas Mosley
IMPOSSIBLE OBJECT(1973, Fr.), w
Robert E. Mosley
STAY HUNGRY(1976)
Roger E. Mosley
HIT MAN(1972); NEW CENTURIONS, THE(1972); MACK, THE(1973); SWEET JESUS, PREACHER MAN(1973); MC Q(1974); DARKTOWN STRUTTERS(1975); LEADBELLY(1976); RIVER NIGER, THE(1976); GREATEST, THE(1977, U.S./Brit.); SEMI-TOUGH(1977)
Misc. Talkies
BIG TIME(1977); GET DOWN AND BOOGIE(1977)
Roger Mosley
STEEL(1980)
Misc. Talkies
WHITE LIONS(1981)
Carol Mosner
1984
BODY ROCK(1984)
Marianne Mosner
SEVENTH VICTIM, THE(1943)
Marie Mosquini
Silents
GOOD AND NAUGHTY(1926); SEVENTH HEAVEN(1927)
Misc. Silents
2 GIRLS WANTED(1927)
Carlos Mosquiz
TREASURE OF PANCHO VILLA, THE(1955)
Aaron Moss
1984
MISSION, THE(1984)
Antonia Moss
PRIME OF MISS JEAN BRODIE, THE(1969, Brit.)
Arnold Moss
TEMPTATION(1946); LOVES OF CARMEN, THE(1948); BLACK BOOK, THE(1949); BORDER INCIDENT(1949); KIM(1950); MASK OF THE AVENGER(1951); MY FAVORITE SPY(1951); QUEBEC(1951); VIVA ZAPATA!(1952); SALOME(1953); BENGAL BRIGADE(1954); CASANOVA'S BIG NIGHT(1954); HELL'S ISLAND(1955); JUMP INTO HELL(1955); 27TH DAY, THE(1957); FOOL KILLER, THE(1965); GAMBIT(1966); CAPER OF THE GOLDEN BULLS, THE(1967)
Basil Moss
HOBSON'S CHOICE(1931, Brit.); ONE BRIEF SUMMER(1971, Brit.)
Bertha Moss
INVASION OF THE VAMPIRES, THE(1961, Mex.); EXTERMINATING ANGEL, THE(1967, Mex.)
Bill Moss
ROUGHLY SPEAKING(1945); YOUNG WIDOW(1946)
Carlton Moss
Misc. Silents
HOUSE ON CEDAR HILL, THE(1926), d
Carol Moss
ROCK, ROCK, ROCK!(1956)
Charles Moss
DIRTY LITTLE BILLY(1972), w
Charles B. Moss, Jr.
LET'S SCARE JESSICA TO DEATH(1971), p; STIGMA(1972), p
Charlie Moss
LITTLE FUGITIVE, THE(1953)
Clive Moss
OLIVER!(1968, Brit.); SCROOGE(1970, Brit.)
D'Alan Moss
STREET MUSIC(1982)
Delbert Moss
NEW HOUSE ON THE LEFT, THE(1978, Brit.)
Misc. Talkies
LAST STOP ON THE NIGHT TRAIN(1976)
Diane Moss
MY BODY HUNGERS(1967)
Don Moss
DEATH WISH II(1982)
Dorothy Moss
TOWN LIKE ALICE, A(1958, Brit.)
Ellen Moss
WHERE ANGELS GO...TROUBLE FOLLOWS(1968); PAPILLON(1973)
Elmer Moss
BECAUSE OF EVE(1948), ph
Ezekiel Moss
DEATH WISH II(1982)
Frank Moss
SANGAREE(1953), w; APACHE TERRITORY(1958), w

Frank L. Moss
WHIP HAND, THE(1951), w; CARIBBEAN(1952), w; VANQUISHED, THE(1953), w
Freddy Moss
MY BODYGUARD(1980)
Gene Moss
SALZBURG CONNECTION, THE(1972); NUTCRACKER FANTASY(1979)
Maj.Geoffrey Moss
Silents
ISN'T LIFE WONDERFUL(1924), w
George Moss
Silents
AS YE SOW(1914); FRUITS OF DESIRE, THE(1916); LES MISERABLES(1918)
Misc. Silents
DAUGHTER OF FRANCE, A(1918)
Gerald Moss
APPOINTMENT WITH CRIME(1945, Brit.), ph; MRS. FITZHERBERT(1950, Brit.), ph; LITTLE BIG SHOT(1952, Brit.), ph; DESPERATE MAN, THE(1959, Brit.), ph; INVASION QUARTET(1961, Brit.), ph; POSTMAN'S KNOCK(1962, Brit.), ph; 1,000 CONVICTS AND A WOMAN(1971, Brit.), ph; VIRGIN WITCH, THE(1973, Brit.), ph
Gerald D. Moss
FRENZY(1946, Brit.), ph; LISBON STORY, THE(1946, Brit.), ph
Gerry Moss
SKIMPY IN THE NAVY(1949, Brit.), ph
Griffiths Moss
WOMAN TO WOMAN(1946, Brit.); LAUGHING LADY, THE(1950, Brit.)
Herbert Moss
GENTLE RAIN, THE(1966, Braz.)
Herbert J. Moss
WHISTLE AT EATON FALLS(1951)
Howard S. Moss
Misc. Silents
DREAM DOLL, THE(1917), d
Jack Moss
BISCUIT EATER, THE(1940), p; MONSTER AND THE GIRL, THE(1941), p; SHEPHERD OF THE HILLS, THE(1941), p; JOURNEY INTO FEAR(1942); MAGNIFICENT AMBERSONS, THE(1942), ed; MR. WINKLE GOES TO WAR(1944), p; SNAFU(1945), p&d
James Moss
MAN-EATER OF KUMAON(1948)
James E. Moss
SOMETHING TO LIVE FOR(1952)
Jennifer Moss
SING AND SWING(1964, Brit.)
Jenny Moss
OTHER SIDE OF THE UNDERNEATH, THE(1972, Brit.)
Jimmie Moss
INSIDE JOB(1946); BORDER SADDLEMATES(1952); LES MISERABLES(1952)
Jimmy Moss
THEY LIVE BY NIGHT(1949); DAMNED DON'T CRY, THE(1950); DAVY CROCKETT, INDIAN SCOUT(1950); GIRL ON THE BRIDGE, THE(1951); JIM THORPE–ALL AMERICAN(1951); DREAM WIFE(1953); MR. SCOUTMASTER(1953)
John Moss
JOAN OF ARC(1948)
Kathi Moss
KING OF THE GYPSIES(1978)
Lou Moss
UNWED MOTHER(1958), ed; BLOOD AND BLACK LACE(1965, Ital.), p
Maitland Moss
FURY AT SMUGGLERS BAY(1963, Brit.)
Paul Moss
MY DREAM IS YOURS(1949), w; BLACK WINDMILL, THE(1974, Brit.)
Paul Finder Moss
TWENTY MILLION SWEETHEARTS(1934), w; DETECTIVE, THE(1954, Qit.), p
Peter Moss
1984
FLASHPOINT(1984), ph
Rick Moss
WHO SAYS I CAN'T RIDE A RAINBOW!(1971)
Robert Moss
SECRET DOOR, THE(1964), ph
Rod Moss
SADIST, THE(1963), md
Rodney Moss
LONG GOODBYE, THE(1973)
S. Moss
SUBWAY RIDERS(1981)
Sandra Moss
ALL THE WAY UP(1970, Brit.), cos
Sandy Moss
GOODBYE GEMINI(1970, Brit.), cos; I START COUNTING(1970, Brit.), cos; SAY HELLO TO YESTERDAY(1971, Brit.), cos; GOLDEN LADY, THE(1979, Brit.), cos
Stewart Moss
IN HARM'S WAY(1965); PENDULUM(1969); ZIGZAG(1970); FUZZ(1972); DOCTOR DEATH: SEEKER OF SOULS(1973); BAT PEOPLE, THE(1974); LAST MARRIED COUPLE IN AMERICA, THE(1980); RAISE THE TITANIC(1980, Brit.)
Stewart B. Moss
PARISIAN, THE(1931, Fr.), ed
Stirling Moss
RACE FOR LIFE, A(1955, Brit.)
Stuart Moss
CHUBASCO(1968)
Thomas Moss
FINAL RECKONING, THE(1932, Brit.); GAME OF CHANCE, A(1932, Brit.); THOROUGHBRED(1932, Brit.)
Toni Moss
FIVE THE HARD WAY(1969)
Trude Moss
M(1933, Ger.)

Valerie Moss
SLEEPING CAR TO TRIESTE(1949, Brit.)
W. Stanley Moss
NIGHT AMBUSH(1958, Brit.), w
Warwick Moss
1984
PHAR LAP(1984, Aus.)
William Moss
CANTERVILLE GHOST, THE(1944); BRING ON THE GIRLS(1945); LET'S GO STEADY(1945); BADMAN'S TERRITORY(1946); FEAR(1946); BIG CAT, THE(1949), p
Moss the Dog
SHEEPDOG OF THE HILLS(1941, Brit.)
Karin Mossberg
UNINHIBITED, THE(1968, Fr./Ital./Span.); BIG CUBE, THE(1969)
Yigal Mossinson
KAZABLAN(1974, Israel), w
Robin Mossley
DESERTERS(1983, Can.)
George Mossman
DR. TERROR'S HOUSE OF HORRORS(1965, Brit.)
James Mossman
MASQUERADE(1965, Brit.)
John Mossman
HORROR OF DRACULA, THE(1958, Brit.)
Stuart Mossman
LONG RIDERS, THE(1980)
Joseph Mosso
1984
NATURAL, THE(1984)
Donny Most
CRAZY MAMA(1975); LEO AND LOREE(1980)
Karla Most
HALLELUJAH TRAIL, THE(1965); NOT WITH MY WIFE, YOU DON'T!(1966); WHAT DID YOU DO IN THE WAR, DADDY?(1966)
Mostefa
LA BALANCE(1983, Fr.)
Josh Mostel
GOING HOME(1971); KING OF MARVIN GARDENS, THE(1972); SOPHIE'S CHOICE(1982); STAR 80(1983)
1984
ALMOST YOU(1984); BROTHER FROM ANOTHER PLANET, THE(1984); WINDY CITY(1984)
Joshua Mostel
JESUS CHRIST, SUPERSTAR(1973); HARRY AND TONTO(1974)
Zero Mostel
DU BARRY WAS A LADY(1943); PANIC IN THE STREETS(1950); ENFORCER, THE(1951); GUY WHO CAME BACK, THE(1951); MODEL AND THE MARRIAGE BROKER, THE(1951); MR. BELVEDERE RINGS THE BELL(1951); SIROCCO(1951); FUNNY THING HAPPENED ON THE WAY TO THE FORUM, A(1966); PRODUCERS, THE(1967); GREAT CATHERINE(1968, Brit.); GREAT BANK ROBBERY, THE(1969); ANGEL LEVINE, THE(1970); HOT ROCK, THE(1972); MARCO(1973); ONCE UPON A SCOUNDREL(1973); RHINOCEROS(1974); FOREPLAY(1975); FRONT, THE(1976); JOURNEY INTO FEAR(1976, Can); MASTERMIND(1977); WATERSHIP DOWN(1978, Brit.)
Murray Mosten
MEAN STREETS(1973); FINGERS(1978)
Dean Moster
FIRE DOWN BELOW(1957, U.S./Brit.)
Franz Mosthav
GREAT BRITISH TRAIN ROBBERY, THE(1967, Ger.)
Rames Mostoller
SANTA CLAUS CONQUERS THE MARTIANS(1964), cos
Ramse Mostoller
HOUSE OF DARK SHADOWS(1970), cos
Murray Moston
ALICE DOESN'T LIVE HERE ANYMORE(1975); HAPPY HOOKER, THE(1975); THAT'S THE WAY OF THE WORLD(1975); FRONT, THE(1976); TAXI DRIVER(1976); NEW YORK, NEW YORK(1977); SATURDAY NIGHT FEVER(1977); EXPOSED(1983)
Leo Mostovoy
CASABLANCA(1942); ROAD TO MOROCCO(1942); MADAME CURIE(1943); IRISH EYES ARE SMILING(1944); TWO GIRLS AND A SAILOR(1944); WHITE CLIFFS OF DOVER, THE(1944); I LOVE A MYSTERY(1945); TWO SMART PEOPLE(1946); WHERE THERE'S LIFE(1947); LET'S LIVE A LITTLE(1948); LETTER FROM AN UNKNOWN WOMAN(1948); FIVE FINGERS(1952); WORLD IN HIS ARMS, THE(1952); GENTLEMEN PREFER BLONDES(1953); GLENN MILLER STORY, THE(1953); STORY OF THREE LOVES, THE(1953); TONIGHT WE SING(1953); SERENADE(1956)
Leonide Mostovoy
SINCE YOU WENT AWAY(1944)
Hallen Mostyn
Silents
ETERNAL TEMPTRESS, THE(1917)
Roman Moszkowicz
1984
ELEMENT OF CRIME, THE(1984, Den.)
Felipe Mota
BRAVE BULLS, THE(1951)
Luis Mota
XICA(1982, Braz.)
Flora Motaung
DINGAKA(1965, South Africa)
Etta Moten
FLYING DOWN TO RIO(1933); GOLD DIGGERS OF 1933(1933)
The Mothers of Invention
TWO HUNDRED MOTELS(1971, Brit.)
Daisy Lee Mothershed
WHO KILLED AUNT MAGGIE?(1940); RAGS TO RICHES(1941)

Daisy Mothershed
LITTLE ORVIE(1940); ATLANTIC CITY(1944)
Phil Motherwell
PURE S(1976, Aus.); DIMBOOLA(1979, Aus.); MAD MAX(1979, Aus.); STIR(1980, Aus.); MONKEY GRIP(1983, Aus.)
Paul Motian
PUNISHMENT PARK(1971), m
Motley
I MARRIED AN ANGEL(1942), art d, cos; OKLAHOMA(1955), cos; INNOCENTS, THE(1961, U.S./Brit.), cos; LONG DAY'S JOURNEY INTO NIGHT(1962), cos; PUMP-KIN EATER, THE(1964, Brit.), cos; SPY WHO CAME IN FROM THE COLD, THE(1965, Brit.), cos; STUDY IN TERROR, A(1966, Brit./Ger.), cos
Eva Motley
1984
SCRUBBERS(1984, Brit.)
Willard Motley
KNOCK ON ANY DOOR(1949), w; LET NO MAN WRITE MY EPITAPH(1960), w
Mori Moto
WALK, DON'T RUN(1966)
Mr. Moto
MASK OF THE DRAGON(1951)
Shojiro Motoki
SEVEN SAMURAI, THE(1956, Jap.), p
Sojiro Motoki
DRUNKEN ANGEL(1948, Jap.), p; THRONE OF BLOOD(1961, Jap.), p; LOWER DEPTHS, THE(1962, Jap.), p; STRAY DOG(1963, Jap.), p; I LIVE IN FEAR(1967, Jap.), p; TUNNEL TO THE SUN(1968, Jap.), w
Hidemi Motomochi
GIRARA(1967, Jap.), w
Akuko Motoyama
FIGHT FOR THE GLORY(1970, Jap.)
Daisei Motoyama
JUDO SHOWDOWN(1966, Jap.), w
Guy Motschen
MOULIN ROUGE(1952)
John Motson
YESTERDAY'S HERO(1979, Brit.)
Abney Mott
HOW TO MARRY A MILLIONAIRE(1953)
Alma Mott
GEORGE WHITE'S SCANDALS(1934)
Bess Mott
1984
TERMINATOR, THE(1984)
Caroline Mott
JUST LIKE A WOMAN(1967, Brit.), cos
Charles Mott
MISTER BROWN(1972)
Joe Mott
LASSIE FROM LANCASHIRE(1938, Brit.); SMILING ALONG(1938, Brit.); WE'RE GOING TO BE RICH(1938, Brit.); ME AND MY PAL(1939, Brit.); FUGITIVE, THE(1940, Brit.)
John Mott
LILIES OF THE FIELD(1934, Brit.)
Joshua Mott
1984
BREAKIN' 2: ELECTRIC BOOGALOO(1984)
Nancy Mott
ONE DARK NIGHT(1983)
1984
FEAR CITY(1984)
Valentine Mott
Silents
GOD'S OUTLAW(1919)
Zeze Motta
XICA(1982, Braz.)
Pierre Motte
JE T'AIME, JE T'AIME(1972, Fr./Swed.)
Alain Mottet
FIRE WITHIN, THE(1964, Fr./Ital.); HO(1968, Fr.)
Antoine John Mottet
1984
EXECUTIONER PART II, THE(1984)
Jean Mottet
ROAD TO SHAME, THE(1962, Fr.), p
Fil Mottola
SLEEPING BEAUTY(1959), art d; SWORD IN THE STONE, THE(1963), art d
Raffaele Mottola
AVANTI!(1972)
Tony Mottola
VIOLATED(1953), M
Anna Mottram
XTRO(1983, Brit.)
R.H. Mottram
Silents
ROSES OF PICARDY(1927, Brit.), w
Judy Motulsky
SLITHIS(1978)
Ilya Motyleff
CANTOR'S SON, THE(1937), d
Bill Motzig
JUST OUT OF REACH(1979, Aus.), m
William Motzing
NEWSFRONT(1979, Aus.), m; RETURN OF CAPTAIN INVINCIBLE, THE(1983, Aus./U.S.), m
Elizabeth Motzkin
CIRCLE OF IRON(1979, Brit.)

Jaroslav Moucka
DEVIL'S TRAP, THE(1964, Czech.)
Marthe Moudiki-Moreau
DIVA(1982, Fr.)
Bohumil Moudry
DIAMONDS OF THE NIGHT(1968, Czech.)
Andre Mouezy-Eon
MATRIMONIAL BED, THE(1930), w; AMERICAN LOVE(1932, Fr.), w; KISSES FOR BREAKFAST(1941), w; SCARLET STREET(1945), w; ARMY GAME, THE(1963, Fr.), w
Rene Moulaert
CASINO DE PARIS(1957, Fr./Ger.), set d & cos; NO TIME FOR ECSTASY(1963, Fr.), art d; SHADOW OF EVIL(1967, Fr./Ital.), art d
Ali Moulaheene
OLIVE TREES OF JUSTICE, THE(1967, Fr.)
Frank Moulan
GIRL SAID NO, THE(1937)
Rosita Moulan
CREATURES THE WORLD FORGOT(1971, Brit.)
Eric Moulard
GET OUT YOUR HANDKERCHIEFS(1978, Fr.), art d; INQUISITOR, THE(1982, Fr.), art d; JOY(1983, Fr./Can.), art d; LA BALANCE(1983, Fr.), art d
Jean Moulart
COUNTERFEITERS OF PARIS, THE(1962, Fr., Ital.)
Prentiss Moulden
NURSE SHERRI(1978)
Helen Moulder
PICTURES(1982, New Zealand)
John Moulder-Brown
NIGHT TRAIN FOR INVERNESS(1960, Brit.); MISSING NOTE, THE(1961, Brit.); 55 DAYS AT PEKING(1963); TWO LIVING, ONE DEAD(1964, Brit./Swed.); RUNAWAY RAILWAY(1965, Brit.); UNCLE, THE(1966, Brit.); CALAMITY THE COW(1967, Brit.); BOYS OF PAUL STREET, THE(1969, Hung./US); DEEP END(1970 Ger./U.S.); KING, QUEEN, KNAVE(1972, Ger./U.S.); VAMPIRE CIRCUS(1972, Brit.); GRASS IS SINGING, THE(1982, Brit./Swed.)
1984
KILLING HEAT(1984)
Carlton Moulette
TOGETHER FOR DAYS(1972), art d
Jacques Moulieres
LOVER'S NET(1957, Fr.)
Charles Moulin
BAKER'S WIFE, THE(1940, Fr.); THEY ARE NOT ANGELS(1948, Fr.); CONFESSION, THE(1970, Fr.)
Jean-Pierre Moulin
LA VIE DE CHATEAU(1967, Fr.); GREEN ROOM, THE(1979, Fr.)
Jean-Paul Moulinot
DEVIL AND THE TEN COMMANDMENTS, THE(1962, Fr.); FIRE WITHIN, THE(1964, Fr./Ital.); LOST COMMAND, THE(1966); YOU ONLY LIVE ONCE(1969, Fr.)
Charles Moulins
BERNADETTE OF LOURDES(1962, Fr.)
Rene Moullaert
JOUR DE FETE(1952, Fr.), art d
Luc Moullet
SMUGGLERS, THE(1969, Fr.), a, p,d&w
Mouloudji
LES JEUX SONT FAITS(1947, Fr.); THEY ARE NOT ANGELS(1948, Fr.); SECRETS D'ALCOVE(1954, Fr./Ital.)
Marcel Mouloudji
GENERALS WITHOUT BUTTONS(1938, Fr.); THEY MET ON SKIS(1940, Fr.); STRANGERS IN THE HOUSE(1949, Fr.)
Buck Moulton
GHOST VALLEY(1932); TEXAS BAD MAN(1932); FIGHTING CODE, THE(1934); KID RANGER, THE(1936); EMPTY SADDLES(1937); RAGTIME COWBOY JOE(1940); WESTERNER, THE(1940); TWO GUN SHERIFF(1941); DEVIL'S TRAIL, THE(1942)
Silents
MAN OF NERVE, A(1925)
Edwin Moulton
Silents
GRIT WINS(1929)
Herbert Moulton
IF I HAD A MILLION(1932); I'LL GIVE MY LIFE(1959), w
Suzanne Moulton
WALK EAST ON BEACON(1952)
Zita Moulton
EXPERT, THE(1932); SINNERS IN THE SUN(1932); TENDERFOOT, THE(1932); EMPLOYEE'S ENTRANCE(1933); AWFUL TRUTH, THE(1937)
Silents
MODERN MARRIAGE(1923)
Fred Moultrie
BRIGHT ROAD(1953)
Freddie Moultrie
I DREAM OF JEANIE(1952); GENTLEMEN PREFER BLONDES(1953)
James Moultrie
TARZAN'S PERIL(1951); BRIGHT ROAD(1953)
Jimmie Moultrie
GENTLEMEN PREFER BLONDES(1953)
Bill Mounce
HONEYSUCKLE ROSE(1980)
Lily Mounet
FRIEND WILL COME TONIGHT, A(1948, Fr.)
Colin Mounier
GERMANY IN AUTUMN(1978, Ger.), ph; DIE HAMBURGER KRANKHEIT(1979, Ger.), ph
Louis Mounier
LONGEST DAY, THE(1962)
Carey Mount
STARK FEAR(1963)

David Mount
DRAGONSLAYER(1981)
Peggy Mount
EMBEZZLER, THE(1954, Brit.); DRY ROT(1956, Brit.); PANIC IN THE PARLOUR(1957, Brit.); YOUR PAST IS SHOWING(1958, Brit.); INN FOR TROUBLE(1960, Brit.); LADIES WHO DO(1964, Brit.); ONE WAY PENDULUM(1965, Brit.); FINDERS KEEPERS(1966, Brit.); HOTEL PARADISO(1966, U.S./Brit.); OLIVER!(1968, Brit.)
Charles Mountain
DAMIEN–OMEN II(1978)
Terence Mountain
MACBETH(1971, Brit.); WICKED LADY, THE(1983, Brit.)
1984
LASSITER(1984)
Terry Mountain
ON HER MAJESTY'S SECRET SERVICE(1969, Brit.)
Diane Mountford
REMARKABLE MR. PENNYPACKER, THE(1959)
Eunice Mountjoy
LADY CHATTERLEY'S LOVER(1981, Fr./Brit.), ed
George Mouque
CHILDREN OF PARADISE(1945, Fr.), m
Gilberto Moura
PIXOTE(1981, Braz.)
Sarky Mouradian
TEARS OF HAPPINESS(1974), d&w
Edgard L. Mourino
WORLD ACCORDING TO GARP, The(1982)
Edgard Mourino
1984
EXTERMINATOR 2(1984)
Eric Mourino
FORT APACHE, THE BRONX(1981)
Erick Mourino
1984
BEAT STREET(1984)
Renier Mourino
1984
BEAT STREET(1984)
Albert Mourlan
Misc. Silents
GULLIVER IN LILLIPUT(1923, Fr.), d
Jany Mourney
AND GOD CREATED WOMAN(1957, Fr.)
Alain Moury
SWEET SKIN(1965, Fr./Ital.), w; THANK HEAVEN FOR SMALL FAVORS(1965, Fr.), w; SOLO(1970, Fr.), w
Nicos Mousoullis
TEMPEST(1982)
Abdel Salam Moussa
OMAR KHAYYAM(1957)
Ibrahim Moussa
1984
GABRIELA(1984, Braz.), p
Katherine Mousseau
RED(1970, Can.)
Mrs. Moussel
Silents
WOMAN AND WINE(1915)
Jean Mousselle
MR. HULOT'S HOLIDAY(1954, Fr.), ph
Moussorgsky-Pushkin
BORIS GODUNOV(1959, USSR), w
George Moussou
ASSAULT ON AGATHON(1976, Brit./Gr.)
Rita Moussouri
ISLAND OF LOVE(1963)
Jean Moussy
YOU ONLY LIVE ONCE(1969, Fr.)
Marcel Moussy
FOUR HUNDRED BLOWS, THE(1959), w; SHOOT THE PIANO PLAYER(1962, Fr.), w; IS PARIS BURNING?(1966, U.S./Fr.), w; LA PRISONNIERE(1969, Fr./Ital.), w
Moustache
PARIS BLUES(1961); IN THE FRENCH STYLE(1963, U.S./Fr.); CIRCUS WORLD(1964); HOW TO STEAL A MILLION(1966); FLEA IN HER EAR, A(1968, Fr.); MAYERLING(1968, Brit./Fr.); SILVER BEARS(1978)
Francois Moustache
LOVE IN THE AFTERNOON(1957)
Almira Moustafa
QUEEN OF THE AMAZONS(1947)
Amira Moustafa
DANGEROUS MONEY(1946)
Athanassia Moustaka
ASTERO(1960, Gr.)
Sotiris Moustakas
ZORBA THE GREEK(1964, U.S./Gr.)
Georges Moustaki
MAN WITH CONNECTIONS, THE(1970, Fr.), m; SOLO(1970, Fr.), m; VERY CURIOUS GIRL, A(1970, Fr.), m
Clara Moustawcesky
LUDWIG(1973, Ital./Ger./Fr.)
Moustique
CHAPPAQUA(1967)
Jean-Pierre Moutier
SEVENTH JUROR, THE(1964, Fr.)
George Moutsios
300 SPARTANS, THE(1962)

G. V. Mouzalevsky
DIARY OF A REVOLUTIONIST(1932, USSR)
Dunja Movar
HAMLET(1962, Ger.)
Andre Movell
WRONG BOX, THE(1966, Brit.)
Lisbeth Movin
DAY OF WRATH(1948, Den.); HAGBARD AND SIGNE(1968, Den./Iceland/Swed.)
Movita
CAPTAIN CALAMITY(1936); PARADISE ISLE(1937); ROSE OF THE RIO GRANDE(1938); GIRL FROM RIO, THE(1939); WOLF CALL(1939); TOWER OF TERROR, THE(1942, Brit.); WILD HORSE AMBUSH(1952); DREAM WIFE(1953); APACHE AMBUSH(1955)
A. Movzon
SECRET BRIGADE, THE(1951 USSR), w
Don Mow
OFFICE PICNIC, THE(1974, Aus.), m
Cassandra Mowan
SALT & PEPPER(1968, Brit.)
David Mowat
LOCAL HERO(1983, Brit.)
1984
ANOTHER TIME, ANOTHER PLACE(1984, Brit.)
Farley Mowat
NEVER CRY WOLF(1983), w
Alan Mowbray
THAT UNCERTAIN FEELING(1941); ALEXANDER HAMILTON(1931); GOD'S GIFT TO WOMEN(1931); GUILTY HANDS(1931); HONOR OF THE FAMILY(1931); LEFTOVER LADIES(1931); MAN IN POSSESSION, THE(1931); HOTEL CONTINENTAL(1932); JEWEL ROBBERY(1932); LOVERS COURAGEOUS(1932); MAN ABOUT TOWN(1932); MAN CALLED BACK, THE(1932); MAN FROM YESTERDAY, THE(1932); NICE WOMAN(1932); PHANTOM PRESIDENT, THE(1932); SHERLOCK HOLMES(1932); SILENT WITNESS, THE(1932); TWO AGAINST THE WORLD(1932); WINNER TAKE ALL(1932); WORLD AND THE FLESH, THE(1932); BERKELEY SQUARE(1933); MIDNIGHT CLUB(1933); OUR BETTERS(1933); PEG O' MY HEART(1933); ROMAN SCANDALS(1933); STUDY IN SCARLET, A(1933); VOLTAIRE(1933); WORLD CHANGES, THE(1933); CHARLIE CHAN IN LONDON(1934); CHEATERS(1934); EMBARRASSING MOMENTS(1934); GIRL FROM MISSOURI, THE(1934); HOUSE OF ROTHSCHILD, THE(1934); LITTLE MAN, WHAT NOW?(1934); LONG LOST FATHER(1934); ONE MORE RIVER(1934); WHERE SINNERS MEET(1934); BECKY SHARP(1935); IN PERSON(1935); LADY TUBBS(1935); NIGHT LIFE OF THE GODS(1935); SHE COULDN'T TAKE IT(1935); CASE AGAINST MRS. AMES, THE(1936); DESIRE(1936); FATAL LADY(1936); FOUR DAYS WONDER(1936); GIVE US THIS NIGHT(1936); LADIES IN LOVE(1936); MARY OF SCOTLAND(1936); MUSS 'EM UP(1936); MY MAN GODFREY(1936); RAINBOW ON THE RIVER(1936); ROSE MARIE(1936); AS GOOD AS MARRIED(1937); HOLLYWOOD HOTEL(1937); KING AND THE CHORUS GIRL, THE(1937); MARRY THE GIRL(1937); MUSIC FOR MADAME(1937); ON SUCH A NIGHT(1937); ON THE AVENUE(1937); STANDIN(1937); TOPPER(1937); VOGUES OF 1938(1937); MERRILY WE LIVE(1938); THERE GOES MY HEART(1938); NEVER SAY DIE(1939); TOPPER TAKES A TRIP(1939); WAY DOWN SOUTH(1939); BOYS FROM SYRACUSE(1940); CURTAIN CALL(1940); LLANO KID, THE(1940); MUSIC IN MY HEART(1940); QUARTERBACK, THE(1940); SCATTERBRAIN(1940); VILLAIN STILL PURSUED HER, THE(1940); COWBOY AND THE BLONDE, THE(1941); FOOTLIGHT FEVER(1941); ICE-CAPADES(1941); MOON OVER HER SHOULDER(1941); PERFECT SNOB, THE(1941); THAT HAMILTON WOMAN(1941); DEVIL WITH HITLER, THE(1942); I WAKE UP SCREAMING(1942); ISLE OF MISSING MEN(1942); MAD MARTINDALES, THE(1942); PANAMA HATTIE(1942); POWERS GIRL, THE(1942); WE WERE DANCING(1942); YANK AT ETON, A(1942); YOKEL BOY(1942); HIS BUTLER'S SISTER(1943); HOLY MATRIMONY(1943); SLIGHTLY DANGEROUS(1943); SO THIS IS WASHINGTON(1943); STAGE DOOR CANTEEN(1943); DOUGHGIRLS, THE(1944); EVER SINCE VENUS(1944); MY GAL LOVES MUSIC(1944); BRING ON THE GIRLS(1945); EARL CARROLL'S VANITIES(1945); MEN IN HER DIARY(1945); PHANTOM OF 42ND STREET, THE(1945); SUNBONNET SUE(1945); TELL IT TO A STAR(1945); WHERE DO WE GO FROM HERE?(1945); IDEA GIRL(1946); MY DARLING CLEMENTINE(1946); TERROR BY NIGHT(1946); CAPTAIN FROM CASTILE(1947); LURED(1947); MAIN STREET KID, THE(1947); MERTON OF THE MOVIES(1947); PILGRIM LADY, THE(1947); DON'T TRUST YOUR HUSBAND(1948); EVERY GIRL SHOULD BE MARRIED(1948); MY DEAR SECRETARY(1948); PRINCE OF THIEVES, THE(1948); ABBOTT AND COSTELLO MEET THE KILLER, BORIS KARLOFF(1949); LONE WOLF AND HIS LADY, THE(1949); LOVABLE CHEAT, THE(1949); YOU'RE MY EVERYTHING(1949); JACKPOT, THE(1950); WAGONMASTER(1950); CROSSWINDS(1951); LADY AND THE BANDIT, THE(1951); ANDROCLES AND THE LION(1952); BLACKBEARD THE PIRATE(1952); JUST ACROSS THE STREET(1952); MA AND PA KETTLE AT HOME(1954); STEEL CAGE, THE(1954); KING'S THIEF, THE(1955); AROUND THE WORLD IN 80 DAYS(1956); KING AND I, THE(1956); MAN WHO KNEW TOO MUCH, THE(1956); MAJORITY OF ONE, A(1961)
Misc. Talkies
HER SECRET(1933); DEVIL CHECKS UP(1944)
Daphne Mowbray
CALLBOX MYSTERY, THE(1932, Brit.)
David Mowbray
HANGMAN WAITS, THE(1947, Brit.)
Harry Mowbray
Silents
SHOULD A WIFE WORK?(1922)
Henry Mowbray
FIFTY FATHOMS DEEP(1931); MYSTERY OF MR. X, THE(1934); PURSUIT OF HAPPINESS, THE(1934); MURDER BY TELEVISION(1935); RENDEZVOUS(1935); LEATHERNECKS HAVE LANDED, THE(1936); SOULS AT SEA(1937); CLAUDIA AND DAVID(1946); LOCKET, THE(1946)
Myrette Mowen
OUTPOST IN MALAYA(1952, Brit.)
Jack Mower
CHEYENNE KID, THE(1930); RIDIN' LAW(1930); LAW AND LAWLESS(1932); LONE TRAIL, THE(1932); MIDNIGHT PATROL, THE(1932); PHANTOM EXPRESS, THE(1932); COME ON TARZAN(1933); KING OF THE ARENA(1933); SITTING PRETTY(1933); FIDDLIN' BUCKAROO, THE(1934); MARY BURNS, FUGITIVE(1935); NAUGHTY MARIETTA(1935); RED SALUTE(1935); REVENGE RIDER, THE(1935); SPECIAL AGENT(1935); HOLLYWOOD BOULEVARD(1936); NEXT TIME WE LO-

VE(1936); PUBLIC ENEMY'S WIFE(1936); CHEROKEE STRIP(1937); DEVIL'S SADDLE LEGION, THE(1937); EVER SINCE EVE(1937); FIRST LADY(1937); GREAT O'MALLEY, THE(1937); HOLLYWOOD HOTEL(1937); IT'S LOVE I'M AFTER(1937); LOVE IS ON THE AIR(1937); MARKED WOMAN(1937); MISSING WITNESSES(1937); PHANTOM OF SANTA FE(1937); PRAIRIE THUNDER(1937); SAN QUENTIN(1937); ANGELS WITH DIRTY FACES(1938); COMET OVER BROADWAY(1938); COWBOY FROM BROOKLYN(1938); CRIME SCHOOL(1938); HARD TO GET(1938); INVISIBLE MENACE, THE(1938); MYSTERY HOUSE(1938); PATIENT IN ROOM 18, THE(1938); PENROD AND HIS TWIN BROTHER(1938); SISTERS(1938); SKULL AND CROWN(1938); TARZAN AND THE GREEN GODDESS(1938); TORCHY BLANE IN PANAMA(1938); CODE OF THE SECRET SERVICE(1939); CONFESSIONS OF A NAZI SPY(1939); DARK VICTORY(1939); EVERYBODY'S HOBBY(1939); KID FROM KOKOMO, THE(1939); KING OF THE UNDERWORLD(1939); NAUGHTY BUT NICE(1939); OKLAHOMA KID, THE(1939); ON TRIAL(1939); PRIVATE DETECTIVE(1939); RETURN OF DR. X, THE(1939); SECRET SERVICE OF THE AIR(1939); SMASHING THE MONEY RING(1939); TORCHY PLAYS WITH DYNAMITE(1939); WOMEN IN THE WIND(1939); ALWAYS A BRIDE(1940); BRITISH INTELLIGENCE(1940); CASTLE ON THE HUDSON(1940); FIGHTING 69TH, THE(1940); INVISIBLE STRIPES(1940); KING OF THE LUMBERJACKS(1940); MURDER IN THE AIR(1940); MY LOVE CAME BACK(1940); SANTA FE TRAIL(1940); THEY DRIVE BY NIGHT(1940); 'TIL WE MEET AGAIN(1940); TORRID ZONE(1940); TUGBOAT ANNIE SAILS AGAIN(1940); BRIDE CAME C.O.D., THE(1941); BULLETS FOR O'HARA(1941); MALTESE FALCON, THE(1941); MEET JOHN DOE(1941); OUT OF THE FOG(1941); STRAWBERRY BLONDE, THE(1941); WAGONS ROLL AT NIGHT, THE(1941); ACROSS THE PACIFIC(1942); DANGEROUSLY THEY LIVE(1942); GAY SISTERS, THE(1942); GEORGE WASHINGTON SLEPT HERE(1942); KING'S ROW(1942); LADY GANGSTER(1942); MAGNIFICENT DOPE, THE(1942); MAN WHO CAME TO DINNER, THE(1942); MURDER IN THE BIG HOUSE(1942); SECRET ENEMIES(1942); SPY SHIP(1942); THEY DIED WITH THEIR BOOTS ON(1942); MYSTERIOUS DOCTOR, THE(1943); OLD ACQUAINTANCE(1943); PRINCESS O'ROURKE(1943); THANK YOUR LUCKY STARS(1943); WATCH ON THE RHINE(1943); CRIME BY NIGHT(1944); DESTINATION TOKYO(1944); DOUGHGIRLS, THE(1944); LAST RIDE, THE(1944); MAKE YOUR OWN BED(1944); WING AND A PRAYER(1944); CHRISTMAS IN CONNECTICUT(1945); CONFLICT(1945); SAN ANTONIO(1945); THEY WERE EXPENDABLE(1945); JANIE GETS MARRIED(1946); MAN I LOVE, THE(1946); NIGHT AND DAY(1946); SHADOWS OVER CHINATOWN(1946); STOLEN LIFE, A(1946); CHEYENNE(1947); CRY WOLF(1947); DEEP VALLEY(1947); NORA PRENTISS(1947); POSSESSED(1947); THAT HAGEN GIRL(1947); THAT WAY WITH WOMEN(1947); UNFAITHFUL, THE(1947); FIGHTING MAD(1948); JUNE BRIDE(1948); SMART GIRLS DON'T TALK(1948); SMART WOMAN(1948); FIGHTING FOOLS(1949); JOHN LOVES MARY(1949); KISS IN THE DARK, A(1949); NIGHT UNTO NIGHT(1949); COUNTY FAIR(1950); MONTANA(1950); ON MOONLIGHT BAY(1951); SPRINGFIELD RIFLE(1952); HOUSE OF WAX(1953); LONG GRAY LINE, THE(1955); SEVEN CITIES OF GOLD(1955); NO TIME FOR SERGEANTS(1958)
Misc. Talkies
TEXAN, THE(1932)
Silents
ANN'S FINISH(1918); FAIR ENOUGH(1918); ISLAND OF INTRIGUE, THE(1919); MOLLY OF THE FOLLIES(1919); BEAUTIFUL GAMBLER, THE(1921); RIDING WITH DEATH(1921); ROWDY, THE(1921); CRIMSON CHALLENGE, THE(1922); SATURDAY NIGHT(1922); PURE GRIT(1923); SHOCK, THE(1923); PRETTY CLOTHES(1927); AIR PATROL(1928); SINNER'S PARADE(1928); ANNE AGAINST THE WORLD(1929)
Misc. Silents
MISS JACKIE OF THE NAVY(1916); BUTTERFLY GIRL, THE(1917); DEVIL'S ASSISTANT, THE(1917); GIRL WHO COULDN'T GROW UP, THE(1917); LUST OF THE AGES, THE(1917); MISS JACKIE OF THE ARMY(1917); IMPOSSIBLE SUSAN(1918); JILTED JANET(1918); MANTLE OF CHARITY, THE(1918); MOLLY, GO GET 'EM(1918); MONEY ISN'T EVERYTHING(1918); PRIMITIVE WOMAN, THE(1918); SQUARE DEAL, A(1918); MILLIONAIRE PIRATE, THE(1919); SOME BRIDE(1919); BELOVED CHEATER, THE(1920); BUBBLES(1920); LIFE(1920); COTTON AND CATTLE(1921); COWBOY ACE, A(1921); DANGER AHEAD(1921); FLOWING GOLD(1921); OUT OF THE CLOUDS(1921); RANGE PIRATE, THE(1921); RUSTLERS OF THE NIGHT(1921); SHORT SKIRTS(1921); TRAIL TO RED DOG, THE(1921); GOLDEN GALLOWS, THE(1922); WHEN HUSBANDS DECEIVE(1922); LAST HOUR, THE(1923); ROBES OF SIN(1924); RATTLER, THE(1925); FALSE FRIENDS(1926); GHETTO SHAMROCK, THE(1926); HER OWN STORY(1926); MELODIES(1926); SKY HIGH CORRAL(1926); SHIPS OF THE NIGHT(1928); WOMAN WHO WAS FORGOTTEN, THE(1930)
L.J. Mower
POLTERGEIST(1982), cos
Lilian Mower
LOVE WALTZ, THE(1930, Ger.)
Patrick Mower
DEVIL'S BRIDE, THE(1968, Brit.); CRY OF THE BANSHEE(1970, Brit.); INCENSE FOR THE DAMNED(1970, Brit.); BLACK BEAUTY(1971, Brit./Ger./Span.); CATCH ME A SPY(1971, Brit./Fr.); PERCY(1971, Brit.); CHARLEY-ONE-EYE(1973, Brit.); SCHOOL FOR UNCLAIMED GIRLS(1973, Brit.); CARRY ON ENGLAND(1976, Brit.)
Misc. Talkies
HELL HOUSE GIRLS(1975, Brit.); CZECH MATE(1984, Brit.)
Helen Mowery
AVALANCHE(1946); MYSTERIOUS INTRUDER(1946); KEY WITNESS(1947); RANGE BEYOND THE BLUE(1947); TAP ROOTS(1948); WOMEN IN THE NIGHT(1948); JOLSON SINGS AGAIN(1949); KNOCK ON ANY DOOR(1949); ACROSS THE BADLANDS(1950); ALL ABOUT EVE(1950); CAGED(1950); NO MAN OF HER OWN(1950); QUEEN FOR A DAY(1951); KID FROM BROKEN GUN, THE(1952)
Misc. Talkies
FIGHTING FRONTIERSMAN, THE(1946)
William Byron Mowery
HEART OF THE NORTH(1938), w
Pat Mowry
MISSILE TO THE MOON(1959)
Patricia Mowry
JEANNE EAGELS(1957)
Hugh Moxey
MEET SIMON CHERRY(1949, Brit.); FOUR AGAINST FATE(1952, Brit.); FRANCHISE AFFAIR, THE(1952, Brit.); SPACEWAYS(1953, Brit.); FUSS OVER FEATHERS(1954, Brit.); GOOD DIE YOUNG, THE(1954, Brit.); HARASSED HERO, THE(1954, Brit.); JOSEPHINE AND MEN(1955, Brit.); NIGHT MY NUMBER CAME UP, THE(1955, Brit.); NOT WANTED ON VOYAGE(1957, Brit.); TIME WITHOUT

PITY(1957, Brit.); YOU PAY YOUR MONEY(1957, Brit.); SILENT ENEMY, THE(1959, Brit.); SNAKE WOMAN, THE(1961, Brit.); MILLION DOLLAR MANHUNT(1962, Brit.); CRY OF THE PENGUINS(1972, Brit.); HENNESSY(1975, Brit.); FINAL CONFLICT, THE(1981)

John Moxey
FOXHOLE IN CAIRO(1960, Brit.), d; HORROR HOTEL(1960, Brit.), d; DEATH TRAP(1962, Brit.), d; DOWNFALL(1964, Brit.), d; FACE OF A STRANGER(1964, Brit.), d; RICOCHET(1966, Brit.), d; STRANGLER'S WEB(1966, Brit.), d; PSYCHO-CIRCUS(1967, Brit.), d

John "Llewelyn" Moxey
20,000 POUNDS KISS, THE(1964, Brit.), d

Jon Moxley
SILENT WITNESS, THE(1962)

Tim Moxon
DR. NO(1962, Brit.); COME SPY WITH ME(1967)

Jieno Moxzer
I WALKED WITH A ZOMBIE(1943)

Wood Moy
CHAN IS MISSING(1982)

Angela Moya
ZOOT SUIT(1981)

Antoinette Moya
VERY HAPPY ALEXANDER(1969, Fr.)

Bobby Moya
TROPIC HOLIDAY(1938)

Robert Moya
LAW WEST OF TOMBSTONE, THE(1938)

Stella Moya
STORMY WEATHER(1935, Brit.); EAST MEETS WEST(1936, Brit.); SCARAB MURDER CASE, THE(1936, Brit.); UNDERNEATH THE ARCHES(1937, Brit.)

Edith Moyal
TARGET: HARRY(1980), set d

Jimmy Moyce
OPENING NIGHT(1977)

Norma Moye
JACKSON COUNTY JAIL(1976)

Judi Moyens
HOUND OF THE BASKERVILLES, THE(1959, Brit.)

Charles Moyer
WE'RE IN THE LEGION NOW(1937)

Fifi Moyer
TRENCHCOAT(1983)

Larry Moyer
MOVING FINGER, THE(1963), p&d, w, ed; GREASER'S PALACE(1972)

Megan Moyer
YOUNG GIANTS(1983), p

Michael Moyer
CALL ME BWANA(1963, Brit.)

Ray Moyer
YOU CAN'T CHEAT AN HONEST MAN(1939); HERE COME THE WAVES(1944), set d; LADY IN THE DARK(1944), set d; STANDING ROOM ONLY(1944), set d; 'TILL WE MEET AGAIN(1944), set d; LOVE LETTERS(1945), set d; CALIFORNIA(1946), set d; NIGHT HAS A THOUSAND EYES(1948), set d; SEALED VERDICT(1948), set d; SAMSON AND DELILAH(1949), set d; SUNSET BOULEVARD(1950), set d; UNION STATION(1950), set d; BIG CARNIVAL, THE(1951), set d; GREATEST SHOW ON EARTH, THE(1952), set d; JUST FOR YOU(1952), set d; HOUDINI(1953), set d; SAVAGE, THE(1953), set d; RED GARTERS(1954), set d; SABRINA(1954), set d; TEN COMMANDMENTS, THE(1956), set d; FUNNY FACE(1957), set d; LOVE IN A GOLDFISH BOWL(1961), set d; POCKETFUL OF MIRACLES(1961), set d; CLEOPATRA(1963), set d; DISORDERLY ORDERLY, THE(1964), set d; GOOD NEIGHBOR SAM(1964), set d; PATSY, THE(1964), set d; GLORY GUYS, THE(1965), set d; SONS OF KATIE ELDER, THE(1965), set d; PARADISE, HAWAIIAN STYLE(1966), set d; PICTURE MOMMY DEAD(1966), set d; RED TOMAHAWK(1967), set d; WAR WAGON, THE(1967), set d; GREEN BERETS, THE(1968), set d; ODD COUPLE, THE(1968), set d; UPTIGHT(1968), set d; WILL PENNY(1968), set d; TRUE GRIT(1969), set d; CATCH-22(1970), set d; LAWMAN(1971), set d; DEADLY TRACKERS(1973); PAT GARRETT AND BILLY THE KID(1973), set d

Raymond Moyer
LET'S FACE IT(1943), set d; BIG JAKE(1971), set d

T. Moyer
YOUNG GIANTS(1983), w

Tawny Moyer
CALIFORNIA SUITE(1978); HALLOWEEN II(1981); LOOKER(1981)

Tom Moyer
YOUNG GIANTS(1983), p

Ray Moyers
EL DORADO(1967), set d

Patricia Moyes
SCHOOL FOR SCOUNDRELS(1960, Brit.), w

Catherine Moylan
LOVE IN THE ROUGH(1930); OUR BLUSHING BRIDES(1930)

Alain Moyle
RUBBER GUN, THE(1977, Can.)

Alan Moyle
TIMES SQUARE(1980), d

Allan Bozo Moyle
MONTREAL MAIN(1974, Can.), p

Allan Moyle
MOURNING SUIT, THE(1975, Can.); RABID(1976, Can.); OUTRAGEOUS!(1977, Can.); RUBBER GUN, THE(1977, Can.), d; TIMES SQUARE(1980), w

Dan Moyles
Misc. Silents
OFFICER 666(1914); WHO'S WHO IN SOCIETY(1915)

Jack Moyles
LINEUP, THE(1958)

Charles J. Le Moyne
Misc. Silents
DESERT DRIVEN(1923)

Charles Le Moyne
Misc. Silents
FREEZE OUT, THE(1921)

F. Moyne
FREUD(1962)

Imogene Moynihan
DEATM GOES TO SCHOOL(1953, Brit.)

Maura Moynihan
1984
BOSTONIANS, THE(1984)

Tim Moynihan
MAYBE IT'S LOVE(1930)

L. C. Moyzisch
FIVE FINGERS(1952), w

Mari Carmen Moza
CONFESSIONS OF AMANS, THE(1977)

Sandra Mozaro
MUSHROOM EATER, THE(1976, Mex.)

Alex Mozart
SQUEEZE A FLOWER(1970, Aus.)

George Mozart
INDISCRETIONS OF EVE(1932, Brit.); PUBLIC LIFE OF HENRY THE NINTH, THE(1934, Brit.); BANK MESSENGER MYSTERY, THE(1936, Brit.); CAFE MASCOT(1936, Brit.); FULL SPEED AHEAD(1936, Brit.); STRANGE CARGO(1936, Brit.); TWO ON A DOORSTEP(1936, Brit.); DR. SIN FANG(1937, Brit.); PHANTOM SHIP(1937, Brit.); PYGMALION(1938, Brit.); SONG OF FREEDOM(1938, Brit.)

Wolfgang Amadeus Mozart
INVITATION TO THE WALTZ(1935, Brit.), m; LA MARSEILLAISE(1938, Fr.), m; RULES OF THE GAME, THE(1939, Fr.), m; KIND HEARTS AND CORONETS(1949, Brit.), m; VOICE IN YOUR HEART, A(1952, Ital.), m; DON GIOVANNI(1955, Brit.), w; DON JUAN(1956, Aust.), w; INTERLUDE(1957), m; MAN ESCAPED, A(1957, Fr.), m; LIFE AND LOVES OF MOZART, THE(1959, Ger.), m; WOMAN OF STRAW(1964, Brit.), m; GOSPEL ACCORDING TO ST. MATTHEW, THE(1966, Fr., Ital.), m; LE BONHEUR(1966, Fr.), m; WEEKEND(1968, Fr./Ital.), m; TEOREMA(1968, Ital.), m; TROPICS(1969, Ital.), m; FIVE EASY PIECES(1970), m; MARRIAGE OF FIGARO, THE(1970, Ger.), w, m; MY FATHER'S MISTRESS(1970, Swed.), m; SUNDAY BLOODY SUNDAY(1971, Brit.), m; I LOVE YOU, I KILL YOU(1972, Ger.), m; FACE TO FACE(1976, Swed.), m; DON GIOVANNI(1979, Fr./Ital./Ger.), w; HOPSCOTCH(1980), m
1984
AMADEUS(1984), m

Don Mozee
WORLD'S GREATEST SINNER, THE(1962)

Aldo Mozele
BEN HUR(1959)

Al Mozell
ROBBY(1968), ph; PRINCE AND THE PAUPER, THE(1969), ph

Maurice B. Mozelle
TOO MANY WINNERS(1947)

Ivan Mozhukhin
Misc. Silents
DEFENCE OF SEVASTOPOL(1911, USSR); CHRISTMAS EVE(1913, USSR); DRUNKENNESS AND ITS CONSEQUENCES(1913, USSR); TERRIBLE REVENGE, A(1913, USSR); CHRYSANTHEMUMS(1914, USSR); LIFE IN DEATH(1914, USSR); WOMAN OF TOMORROW(1914, USSR); FLOOD(1915, USSR); NATASHA ROSTOVA(1915, USSR); NIKOLAI STAVROGIN(1915, USSR); RUSLAN I LUDMILA(1915, USSR); QUEEN OF SPADES, THE(1916, USSR); WOMAN WITH A DAGGER(1916, USSR); ANDREI KOZHUKHOV(1917, USSR); PUBLIC PROSECUTOR(1917, USSR); SATAN TRIUMPHANT(1917, USSR); FATHER SERGIUS(1918, USSR); QUEEN'S SECRET, THE(1919, USSR)

Guate Mozin
FIGHTING PIONEERS(1935)

Umberto Mozzato
Silents
CABIRIA(1914, Ital.)

Madala Mphahlele
Misc. Talkies
BLACK TRASH(1978)

Mpigano
TOTO AND THE POACHERS(1958, Brit.)

Sophie MqCina
DINGAKA(1965, South Africa)

Moheddine Mrad
1984
MISUNDERSTOOD(1984)

Ivo Mrazek
JOURNEY TO THE BEGINNING OF TIME(1966, Czech), art d

J. Mrazek-Horicky
MOST BEAUTIFUL AGE, THE(1970, Czech.)

Eva Mrazova
SWEET LIGHT IN A DARK ROOM(1966, Czech.)

Ladislav Mrkvicka
SWEET LIGHT IN A DARK ROOM(1966, Czech.)

Zdzislaw Mrozewski
PARTINGS(1962, Pol.); MEPHISTO(1981, Ger.)

Zofia Mrozowska
CONSTANT FACTOR, THE(1980, Pol.); CONTRACT, THE(1982, Pol.)

Gunther Mruwka
I AIM AT THE STARS(1960)

Chu Mu
LADY GENERAL, THE(1965, Hong Kong); SHEPHERD GIRL, THE(1965, Hong Kong)

Weng Mu-lan
MAGNIFICENT CONCUBINE, THE(1964, Hong Kong)

Kung Mu-To
TRIPLE IRONS(1973, Hong Kong), ph

Mubarak
TIGER AND THE FLAME, THE(1955, India)

Antar Mubarak
CARWASH(1976)
Nasir Ibn Mubarak
ISLAND OF ALLAH(1956)
Micheline Muc
RISE OF LOUIS XIV, THE(1970, Fr.)
David Mucci
PROM NIGHT(1980)
Edulilo Mucci
Silents
ROMOLA(1925)
Jiri Mucha
90 DEGREES IN THE SHADE(1966, Czech./Brit.), w
Craig Muckler
MICROWAVE MASSACRE(1983), p, w
J. Muclinger
BORDER STREET(1950, Pol.)
Peter Muctarlane
F.P. 1(1933, Brit.), w
Betty Mudge
HOLLYWOOD BARN DANCE(1947)
Eva Mudge
NIGHT SONG(1947)
Doris Mudie
TWELVE CHAIRS, THE(1970), d&w
Leonard Mudie
MUMMY, THE(1932); VOLTAIRE(1933); CLEOPATRA(1934); HOUSE OF ROTH-
SCHILD, THE(1934); JIMMY THE GENT(1934); MANDALAY(1934); MYSTERY OF
MR. X, THE(1934); PAINTED VEIL, THE(1934); VIVA VILLA!(1934); BECKY
SHARP(1935); CAPTAIN BLOOD(1935); CLIVE OF INDIA(1935); FEATHER IN HER
HAT, A(1935); GREAT IMPERSONATION, THE(1935); MAGNIFICENT OBSES-
SION(1935); RENDEZVOUS(1935); TOP HAT(1935); ANTHONY ADVERSE(1936); HIS
BROTHER'S WIFE(1936); LLOYDS OF LONDON(1936); MARY OF SCOTLAND(1936);
STORY OF LOUIS PASTEUR, THE(1936); SYLVIA SCARLETT(1936); ANOTHER
DAWN(1937); KING AND THE CHORUS GIRL, THE(1937); LANCER SPY(1937);
LEAGUE OF FRIGHTENED MEN(1937); LONDON BY NIGHT(1937); LOST HORI-
ZON(1937); SHALL WE DANCE(1937); THEY WON'T FORGET(1937); ADVENTURES
OF ROBIN HOOD, THE(1938); JURY'S SECRET, THE(1938); KIDNAPPED(1938);
LETTER OF INTRODUCTION(1938); MAD MISS MANTON, THE(1938); SUEZ(1938);
WHEN WERE YOU BORN?(1938); ARREST BULLDOG DRUMMOND(1939, Brit.);
DARK VICTORY(1939); MAN ABOUT TOWN(1939); STORY OF VERNON AND
IRENE CASTLE, THE(1939); TROPIC FURY(1939); BRITISH INTELLIGENCE(1940);
CHARLIE CHAN'S MURDER CRUISE(1940); CONGO MAISIE(1940); DEVIL'S IS-
LAND(1940); DISPATCH FROM REUTERS, A(1940); EARL OF CHICAGO, THE(1940);
FOREIGN CORRESPONDENT(1940); HE STAYED FOR BREAKFAST(1940); LET-
TER, THE(1940); SEA HAWK, THE(1940); SOUTH OF SUEZ(1940); WATERLOO
BRIDGE(1940); YOU'LL FIND OUT(1940); NURSE'S SECRET, THE(1941); SCOTLAND
YARD(1941); SHINING VICTORY(1941); SKYLARK(1941); BERLIN CORRESPOND-
ENT(1942); RANDOM HARVEST(1942); APPOINTMENT IN BERLIN(1943); DRAGON
SEED(1944); MY NAME IS JULIA ROSS(1945); DIVORCE(1945); SCARLET CLUE,
THE(1945); DON'T GAMBLE WITH STRANGERS(1946); LOCKET, THE(1946); ES-
CAPE ME NEVER(1947); PRIVATE AFFAIRS OF BEL AMI, THE(1947); SONG OF MY
HEART(1947); CHECKERED COAT, THE(1948); ELEPHANT STAMPEDE(1951); LOR-
NA DOONE(1951); SON OF DR. JEKYLL, THE(1951); SWORD OF MONTE CRISTO,
THE(1951); WHEN WORLDS COLLIDE(1951); AFRICAN TREASURE(1952); BOMBA
AND THE JUNGLE GIRL(1952); MAGNETIC MONSTER, THE(1953); SAFARI
DRUMS(1953); GOLDEN IDOL, THE(1954); KILLER LEOPARD(1954); KING RICH-
ARD AND THE CRUSADERS(1954); LORD OF THE JUNGLE(1955); AUTUMN
LEAVES(1956); STORY OF MANKIND, THE(1957); BIG FISHERMAN, THE(1959);
TIMBUKTU(1959)
Misc. Silents
MESSAGE FROM MARS, A(1921); THROUGH THE STORM(1922)
Malcolm Mudie
WICKED LADY, THE(1983, Brit.)
Janie Mudrick
VAN, THE(1977)
Brian Muehl
GREAT MUPPET CAPER, THE(1981); DARK CRYSTAL, THE(1982, Brit.)
1984
MUPPETS TAKE MANHATTAN, THE(1984)
George Muehlen-Schute
MASTER OF THE WORLD(1935, Ger.), w
Verne Muehlstedt
WHEN THE LEGENDS DIE(1972)
Alfred Mueller
SIGNALS-AN ADVENTURE IN SPACE(1970, E. Ger./Pol.)
Charles Mueller
JOHNNY O'CLOCK(1947)
Cookie Mueller
FEMALE TROUBLE(1975); UNDERGROUND U.S.A.(1980); POLYESTER(1981);
SUBWAY RIDERS(1981); SMITHEREENS(1982)
1984
VARIETY(1984)
Elisabeth Mueller
POWER AND THE PRIZE, THE(1956); ANGRY HILLS, THE(1959, Brit.)
Elizabeth Mueller
CONFESS DR. CORDA(1960, Ger.)
Floyd Mueller
Silents
SIGN OF THE ROSE, THE(1922), art d
Fritz Mueller
LAST REBEL, THE(1971), ed
Gordon Mueller
TROIKA(1969), d
Hans Mueller
TEMPEST(1932, Ger.), w; WHITE HORSE INN, THE(1959, Ger.), w
Helen Mueller
COVER GIRL(1944)

Henry Mueller II
BLACK LIKE ME(1964), ph
Jack Mueller
LAST PICTURE SHOW, THE(1971)
Lillian Mueller
Misc. Silents
HEART OF EZRA GREER, THE(1917)
Lilo Mueller
INHERITANCE IN PRETORIA(1936, Ger.)
Merrill Mueller
SEVEN DAYS TO NOON(1950, Brit.)
Paul Mueller
NANA(1983, Ital.)
Renate Mueller
PRIVATE LIFE OF LOUIS XIV(1936, Ger.)
Richard Mueller
MAN WHO KNEW TOO MUCH, THE(1956), ph
Robbie Mueller
KINGS OF THE ROAD(1976, Ger.), ph
Robby Mueller
WILD DUCK, THE(1977, Ger./Aust.), ph
1984
CLASS ENEMY(1984, Ger.), ph
Torunn Mueller
CHILDREN OF GOD'S EARTH(1983, Norwegian), art d & cos
Walter Mueller
WHITE HORSE INN, THE(1959, Ger.)
William Mueller
THEM!(1954), spec eff
Armin Mueller-Stahl
NAKED AMONG THE WOLVES(1967, Ger.); LOLA(1982, Ger.); VERONIKA
VOSS(1982, Ger.)
1984
LOVE IN GERMANY, A(1984, Fr./Ger.)
Marianne Muellerleile
1984
TERMINATOR, THE(1984)
Marianne Muellerlemle
GOING BERSERK(1983)
Marianne Muellerliele
1984
REVENGE OF THE NERDS(1984)
Richard Muench
PATTON(1970)
Thomas Muenster
ENCOUNTERS IN SALZBURG(1964, Ger.), w
Michael Muenzer
CARMEN, BABY(1967, Yugo./Ger.)
Joachim Dieter Mues
CIRCLE OF DECEIT(1982, Fr./Ger.)
Joachim Dietmar Mues
ODESSA FILE, THE(1974, Brit./Ger.)
Lola Muethel
FROM THE LIFE OF THE MARIONETTES(1980, Ger.)
Muffey
INCREDIBLE JOURNEY, THE(1963)
Ann Muffly
FLASHDANCE(1983)
Anne Muffly
HUNGRY WIVES(1973)
Oscar Mugge
HEADING FOR HEAVEN(1947), w
Vera Mugge
TERROR OF DR. MABUSE, THE(1965, Ger.), cos; FROZEN ALIVE(1966, Brit./Ger.),
cos
Malcolm Muggeridge
I'M ALL RIGHT, JACK(1959, Brit.); HEAVENS ABOVE!(1963, Brit.); HEROS-
TRATUS(1968, Brit.)
Dan Muggia
HANNAH K.(1983, Fr.)
Don Angelo Muggia
1984
SAHARA(1984)
Kenneth Muggleston
WATERLOO(1970, Ital./USSR), set d
Ken Mugglestone
OLIVER!(1968, Brit.), set d
Amanda Muggleton
THIRST(1979, Aus.)
Marie Muggley
Silents
GOLD RUSH, THE(1925)
Francis Mugham
FLASH GORDON(1980)
Jack Muhall
Misc. Silents
WHOM THE GODS WOULD DESTROY(1919)
Herbert Muhammad
GREATEST, THE(1977, U.S./Brit.), w
W. Youngblood Muhammad
GREATEST, THE(1977, U.S./Brit.)
Donald F. Muhich
BOB AND CAROL AND TED AND ALICE(1969); BLUME IN LOVE(1973)
Donald Muhich
WILLIE AND PHIL(1980)
Edward Muhl
IF A MAN ANSWERS(1962), p; LOST MAN, THE(1969), p

Amalia Muhlach
CURSE OF THE VAMPIRES(1970, Phil., U.S.), p
Markus Muhleisen
LEFT-HANDED WOMAN, THE(1980, Ger.)
Augustus Muir
PHANTOM SUBMARINE, THE(1941), w
Barrie Muir
MANGANINNIE(1982, Aus.)
Christopher Muir
LIBIDO(1973, Aus.), p
Darren Muir
1984
IMPULSE(1984)
David Muir
JOANNA(1968, Brit.), ph; SEPARATION(1968, Brit.), ph; MUMSY, NANNY, SON-NY, AND GIRLY(1970, Brit.), ph; MY LOVER, MY SON(1970, Brit.), ph; LUST FOR A VAMPIRE(1971, Brit.), ph; AND NOW FOR SOMETHING COMPLETELY DIFFER-ENT(1972, Brit.), ph; NEITHER THE SEA NOR THE SAND(1974, Brit.), ph
Douglas Muir
CHRISTMAS CAROL, A(1951, Brit.); BREAKING THE SOUND BARRIER(1952); IT STARTED IN PARADISE(1952, Brit.); MURDER ON THE CAMPUS(1963, Brit.); DOUBLE MAN, THE(1967)
Esther Muir
DANGEROUS AFFAIR, A(1931); BOWERY, THE(1933); HELL AND HIGH WA-TER(1933); I LOVE THAT MAN(1933); SAILOR'S LUCK(1933); SO THIS IS AFRICA(1933); SWEEPINGS(1933); PARTY'S OVER, THE(1934); PICTURE BRI-DES(1934); UNKNOWN BLONDE(1934); WINE, WOMEN, AND SONG(1934); GILDED LILY, THE(1935); PUBLIC STENOGRAPHER(1935); RACING LUCK(1935); FU-RY(1936); GREAT ZIEGFELD, THE(1936); DAY AT THE RACES, A(1937); HIGH HAT(1937); I'LL TAKE ROMANCE(1937); ON AGAIN–OFF AGAIN(1937); UNDER SUSPICION(1937); BATTLE OF BROADWAY(1938); CITY GIRL(1938); LAW WEST OF TOMBSTONE, THE(1938); ROMANCE IN THE DARK(1938); THREE COM-RADES(1938); TOY WIFE, THE(1938); WESTERN JAMBOREE(1938); GIRL AND THE GAMBLER, THE(1939); STORY OF VERNON AND IRENE CASTLE, THE(1939); HONKY TONK(1941); MISBEHAVING HUSBANDS(1941); SUNSET MURDER CA-SE(1941); MAYOR OF 44TH STREET, THE(1942); X MARKS THE SPOT(1942)
Misc. Talkies
STOLEN PARADISE(1941)
Florabel Muir
FIGHTING YOUTH(1935), w
Frank Muir
CLOUDED CRYSTAL, THE(1948, Brit.); BACHELOR IN PARIS(1953, Brit.), w; LOVE IN PAWN(1953, Brit.), w; INNOCENTS IN PARIS(1955, Brit.); BOTTOMS UP(1960, Brit.), w
Gavin Muir
CHARLIE CHAN AT THE RACE TRACK(1936); HALF ANGEL(1936); LLOYDS OF LONDON(1936); MARY OF SCOTLAND(1936); FAIR WARNING(1937); HOLY TER-ROR, THE(1937); WEE WILLIE WINKIE(1937); TARZAN FINDS A SON!(1939); ONE NIGHT IN LISBON(1941); YANK IN THE R.A.F., A(1941); CAPTAINS OF THE CLOUDS(1942); DANGEROUSLY THEY LIVE(1942); EAGLE SQUADRON(1942); HI-TLER'S CHILDREN(1942); NIGHTMARE(1942); PASSPORT TO SUEZ(1943); SHER-LOCK HOLMES FACES DEATH(1943); SHERLOCK HOLMES IN WASHINGTON(1943); MASTER RACE, THE(1944); MERRY MONAHANS, THE(1944); PASSPORT TO DESTINY(1944); WHITE CLIFFS OF DOVER, THE(1944); HOUSE OF FEAR, THE(1945); PATRICK THE GREAT(1945); SALOME, WHERE SHE DAN-CED(1945); TONIGHT AND EVERY NIGHT(1945); CALIFORNIA(1946); O.S.S.(1946); TEMPTATION(1946); CALCUTTA(1947); IMPERFECT LADY, THE(1947); IVY(1947); UNCONQUERED(1947); PRINCE OF THIEVES, THE(1948); CHICAGO DEAD-LINE(1949); ROGUES OF SHERWOOD FOREST(1950); ABBOTT AND COSTELLO MEET THE INVISIBLE MAN(1951); SON OF DR. JEKYLL, THE(1951); THUNDER ON THE HILL(1951); KING OF THE KHYBER RIFLES(1953); ESCAPE TO BURMA(1955); SEA CHASE, THE(1955); ABDUCTORS, THE(1957); JOHNNY TROUBLE(1957); IS-LAND OF LOST WOMEN(1959); NIGHT TIDE(1963)
Georgette Muir
FINGERS(1978)
Graeme Muir
MEET ME AT DAWN(1947, Brit.); SHOWTIME(1948, Brit.)
Helen Muir
Silents
MISTRESS OF SHENSTONE, THE(1921)
Ian Muir
TIME BANDITS(1981, Brit.)
Janie Muir
1984
GHOST DANCE(1984, Brit.), m
Jean Muir
SON OF A SAILOR(1933); WORLD CHANGES, THE(1933); AS THE EARTH TURNS(1934); BEDSIDE(1934); DESIRABLE(1934); DOCTOR MONICA(1934); GEN-TLEMEN ARE BORN(1934); MODERN HERO, A(1934); MIDSUMMER'S NIGHT'S DREAM, A(1935); OIL FOR THE LAMPS OF CHINA(1935); ORCHIDS TO YOU(1935); WHITE COCKATOO(1935); FAITHFUL(1936, Brit.); WHITE FANG(1936); DANCE, CHARLIE, DANCE(1937); DRAEGERMAN COURAGE(1937); FUGITIVE IN THE SKY(1937); HER HUSBAND'S SECRETARY(1937); ONCE A DOCTOR(1937); OUT-CASTS OF POKER FLAT, THE(1937); WHITE BONDAGE(1937); JANE STEPS OUT(1938, Brit.); AND ONE WAS BEAUTIFUL(1940); LONE WOLF MEETS A LADY, THE(1940); CONSTANT NYMPH, THE(1943); NORTHWEST STAMPEDE(1948), w; UGLY DUCKLING, THE(1959); STRIP TEASE MURDER(1961, Brit.); BETRAY-AL(1983, Brit.), cos
Stella Muir
Silents
LASS O' THE LOOMS, A(1919, Brit.)
Misc. Silents
CALL OF THE SEA, THE(1919); HEART OF A ROSE, THE(1919, Brit.)
Alba Mujica
PUT UP OR SHUT UP(1968, Arg.)
Barbara Mujica
END OF INNOCENCE(1960, Arg.)

Chow Muk-leung
1984
AH YING(1984, Hong Kong), ed
Violet Mukabuerza
MAN OF AFRICA(1956, Brit.)
Marcus Mukai
WHEN TIME RAN OUT(1980)
Anatoliy Mukasey
UNCOMMON THIEF, AN(1967, USSR), ph
Suprova Mukerjee
RIVER, THE(1951)
Shapan Mukerji
WORLD OF APU, THE(1960, India)
Arun Mukherjee
KANCHENJUNGHA(1966, India)
Madhabi Mukherjee
BIG CITY, THE(1963, India)
Prabhatkumar Mukherjee
GODDESS, THE(1962, India), w
Purnendu Mukherjee
GODDESS, THE(1962, India)
Sita Mukherji
TWO DAUGHTERS(1963, India)
Ashok Mukhey
1984
ALLEY CAT(1984)
A. Mukhin
JACK FROST(1966, USSR)
S. Mukhin
MAGIC VOYAGE OF SINBAD, THE(1962, USSR), spec eff; MY NAME IS IVAN(1963, USSR), spec eff
Pratap Mukhopdhya
MUSIC ROOM, THE(1963, India)
Janash Muknerii
RIVER, THE(1961, India)
Hiroshi Mukouyama
MOTHRA(1962, Jap.), spec eff
Hiroshi Mukoyama
GODZILLA, RING OF THE MONSTERS(1956, Jap.), spec eff; GIGANTIS(1959, Jap./U.S.), spec eff
Domagoj Mukusic
HIGH ROAD TO CHINA(1983)
Tom Mula
STONY ISLAND(1978)
Gabriella Mulachie
DIARY OF A SCHIZOPHRENIC GIRL(1970, Ital.)
Jack Mulcahy
PORKY'S(1982); PORKY'S II: THE NEXT DAY(1983)
John Mulcahy
BLOODY KIDS(1983, Brit.)
Maurice Mulcahy
SHOWDOWN AT BOOT HILL(1958), set d
Russell Mulcahy
1984
RAZORBACK(1984, Aus.), d
Sean Mulcahy
QUIET DAY IN BELFAST, A(1974, Can.)
Terence Mulcahy
1984
NO SMALL AFFAIR(1984), w
William Mulcany
STALAG 17(1953)
G. H. Mulcaster
INQUEST(1931, Brit.); PURSE STRINGS(1933, Brit.); RIVER HOUSE MYSTERY, THE(1935, Brit.); FIVE POUND MAN, THE(1937, Brit.); OLD MOTHER RILEY(1937, Brit.); SECOND BUREAU(1937, Brit.); LILY OF LAGUNA(1938, Brit.); LITTLE DOLLY DAYDREAM(1938, Brit.); LION HAS WINGS, THE(1940, Brit.); NIGHT TRAIN(1940, Brit.); PACK UP YOUR TROUBLES(1940, Brit.); SAILOR'S DON'T CARE(1940, Brit.); LET THE PEOPLE SING(1942, Brit.); DUMMY TALKS, THE(1943, Brit.); MY LEARNED FRIEND(1943, Brit.); FOR YOU ALONE(1945, Brit.); HONEYMOON HOTEL(1946, Brit.); PATIENT VANISHES, THE(1947, Brit.); BONNIE PRINCE CHARLIE(1948, Brit.); SPRING IN PARK LANE(1949, Brit.); UNDER CA-PRICORN(1949); IF THIS BE SIN(1950, Brit.); CONTRABAND SPAIN(1955, Brit.); DOWNFALL(1964, Brit.)
Silents
PIPES OF PAN, THE(1923, Brit.); GIRL OF LONDON, A(1925, Brit.)
Misc. Silents
WILD HEATHER(1921, Brit.); MIST IN THE VALLEY(1923, Brit.); SQUIRE OF LONG HADLEY, THE(1925, Brit.); WAY OF A WOMAN, THE(1925, Brit.); SAC-RIFICE(1929, Brit.)
George Mulcaster
NAKED HEART, THE(1955, Brit.)
George [G.H.] Mulcaster
LADY OF VENGEANCE(1957, Brit)
Michael Mulcaster
GLORY AT SEA(1952, Brit.); HAMMER THE TOFF(1952, Brit.); PAUL TEMPLE RETURNS(1952, Brit.); LARGE ROPE, THE(1953, Brit.); SEA DEVILS(1953); DEVIL'S HARBOR(1954, Brit.); NAKED HEART, THE(1955, Brit.); CURSE OF FRANKEN-STEIN, THE(1957, Brit.); HOUND OF THE BASKERVILLES, THE(1959, Brit.); MANIA(1961, Brit.); JOHN OF THE FAIR(1962, Brit.); PIRATES OF BLOOD RIVER, THE(1962, Brit.)
Jim Mulcay
VARIETY GIRL(1947)
Mildred Mulcay
VARIETY GIRL(1947)
The Mulcays
NIGHT CLUB GIRL(1944)

Walt Mulconery
PERSONAL BEST(1982), ed; FLASHDANCE(1983), ed
1984
KARATE KID, THE(1984), ed
Diana Muldaur
SWIMMER, THE(1968); LAWYER, THE(1969); NUMBER ONE(1969); ONE MORE TRAIN TO ROB(1971); OTHER, THE(1972); CHOSEN SURVIVORS(1974 U.S.-Mex.); MC Q(1974)
Misc. Talkies
BEYOND REASON(1977)
Stephanie Muldenhall
MELODY(1971, Brit.)
Cor Mulder
MEMENTO MEI(1963)
Ed Mulder
HELL'S ANGELS '69(1969)
Eddie Mulder
GRAND THEFT AUTO(1977)
Carol Muldoon
THERE'S ALWAYS VANILLA(1972), cos
John J. Muldoon
SIX BRIDGES TO CROSS(1955)
Kitty Muldoon
FOUR GIRLS IN TOWN(1956); STARTING OVER(1979); WILLIE AND PHIL(1980); TWO OF A KIND(1983)
Michael Muldoon
GREAT TRAIN ROBBERY, THE(1979, Brit.); EXCALIBUR(1981)
Dominic Muldowney
BETRAYAL(1983, Brit.), m
1984
LOOSE CONNECTIONS(1984, Brit.), m; PLOUGHMAN'S LUNCH, THE(1984, Brit.), m; 1984(1984, Brit.), m
Fracesco Mule
DR. GOLDFOOT AND THE GIRL BOMBS(1966, Ital.)
Francesco Mule
IT HAPPENED IN ROME(1959, Ital.); PSYCOSISSIMO(1962, Ital.); WHITE VOICES(1965, Fr./Ital.); MAIDEN FOR A PRINCE, A(1967, Fr./Ital.); BIGGEST BUNDLE OF THEM ALL, THE(1968); CHASTITY BELT, THE(1968, Ital.); DROP DEAD, MY LOVE(1968, Italy); HOUSE OF CARDS(1969); SECRET OF SANTA VITTORIA, THE(1969); STORY OF A WOMAN(1970, U.S./Ital.); WHEN WOMEN HAD TAILS(1970, Ital.)
Gary Mule Deer
UP IN SMOKE(1978); ANNIE HALL(1977); SKATETOWN, U.S.A.(1979)
Paddy Mulelly
HIS MAJESTY O'KEEFE(1953)
Many Mules
STAGECOACH(1939)
Many Muleson
CHEYENNE AUTUMN(1964)
Clarence Mulford
BAR 20 RIDES AGAIN(1936), w
Clarence E. Mulford
HOPALONG CASSIDY(1935), w; CALL OF THE PRAIRIE(1936), w; EAGLE'S BROOD, THE(1936), w; HOPALONG CASSIDY RETURNS(1936), w; TRAIL DUST(1936), w; BORDERLAND(1937), w; HEART OF THE WEST(1937), w; HILLS OF OLD WYOMING(1937), w; HOPALONG RIDES AGAIN(1937), w; NORTH OF THE RIO GRANDE(1937), w; TEXAS TRAIL(1937), w; BAR 20 JUSTICE(1938), w; CASSIDY OF BAR 20(1938), w; FRONTIERSMAN, THE(1938), w; HEART OF ARIZONA(1938), w; PARTNERS OF THE PLAINS(1938), w; PRIDE OF THE WEST(1938), w; SUNSET TRAIL(1938), w; LAW OF THE PAMPAS(1939), w; RANGE WAR(1939), w; RENEGADE TRAIL(1939), w; SILVER ON THE SAGE(1939), w; SANTA FE MARSHAL(1940), w; SHOWDOWN, THE(1940), w; STAGECOACH WAR(1940), w; THREE MEN FROM TEXAS(1940), w; BORDER VIGILANTES(1941), w; IN OLD COLORADO(1941), w; OUTLAWS OF THE DESERT(1941), w; SECRETS OF THE WASTELANDS(1941), w; STICK TO YOUR GUNS(1941), w; TWILIGHT ON THE TRAIL(1941), w; WIDE OPEN TOWN(1941), w; UNDERCOVER MAN(1942), w; BORDER PATROL(1943), w; FALSE COLORS(1943), w; HOPPY SERVES A WRIT(1943), w; LOST CANYON(1943), w; TEXAS MASQUERADE(1944), w; DEVIL'S PLAYGROUND, THE(1946), w; FOOL'S GOLD(1946), w; MARAUDERS, THE(1947), w; DEAD DON'T DREAM, THE(1948), w; SILENT CONFLICT(1948), w
Clarence Edward Mulford
THREE ON THE TRAIL(1936), w
Lou Mulford
SKATETOWN, U.S.A.(1979); HISTORY OF THE WORLD, PART 1(1981)
Kate Mulgrew
STRANGER IS WATCHING, A(1982)
Evelyn Mulhall
CONFESSION(1937); PERFECT SPECIMEN, THE(1937); INDIANAPOLIS SPEEDWAY(1939); RINGS ON HER FINGERS(1942); IN THE MEANTIME, DARLING(1944); DO YOU LOVE ME?(1946)
Jack Mulhall
DARK STREETS(1929); TWIN BEDS(1929); TWO WEEKS OFF(1929); FALL GUY, THE(1930); FOR THE LOVE O'LIL(1930); GOLDEN CALF, THE(1930); IN THE NEXT ROOM(1930); MURDER WILL OUT(1930); ROAD TO PARADISE(1930); SECOND CHOICE(1930); SHOW GIRL IN HOLLYWOOD(1930); LOVER COME BACK(1931); REACHING FOR THE MOON(1931); HELL'S HEADQUARTERS(1932); LOVE BOUND(1932); MURDER AT DAWN(1932); NIGHT BEAT(1932); SALLY OF THE SUBWAY(1932); SINISTER HANDS(1932); SECRET SINNERS(1933); CLEOPATRA(1934); CURTAIN AT EIGHT(1934); EVELYN PRENTICE(1934); HUMAN SIDE, THE(1934); IT'S A GIFT(1934); NOTORIOUS SOPHIE LANG, THE(1934); OLD-FASHIONED WAY, THE(1934); WHOM THE GODS DESTROY(1934); CHINATOWN SQUAD(1935); GEORGE WHITE'S 1935 SCANDALS(1935); HEADLINE WOMAN, THE(1935); HIS NIGHT OUT(1935); INFORMER, THE(1935); LOVE IN BLOOM(1935); MEN WITHOUT NAMES(1935); MISSISSIPPI(1935); ONE HOUR LATE(1935); PAGE MISS GLORY(1935); PARIS IN SPRING(1935); PEOPLE WILL TALK(1935); RECKLESS(1935); ROARING ROADS(1935); STRAIGHT FROM THE HEART(1935); SWEET ADELINE(1935); TWO FOR TONIGHT(1935); WHAT PRICE CRIME?(1935); WOMAN IN RED, THE(1935); BELOVED ENEMY(1936); CHARLIE CHAN AT THE RACE TRACK(1936); FACE IN THE FOG, A(1936); HOLLYWOOD BOULEVARD(1936); KELLY OF THE SECRET SERVICE(1936); KLONDIKE ANNIE(1936); LIBELED

LADY(1936); MURDER WITH PICTURES(1936); ONE RAINY AFTERNOON(1936); PREVIEW MURDER MYSTERY(1936); ROGUES' TAVERN, THE(1936); SHOW BOAT(1936); THIRTEEN HOURS BY AIR(1936); UNDER YOUR SPELL(1936); WEDDING PRESENT(1936); WIFE VERSUS SECRETARY(1936); AMATEUR CROOK(1937); DANGEROUS HOLIDAY(1937); INTERNES CAN'T TAKE MONEY(1937); LOVE IS NEWS(1937); MUSIC FOR MADAME(1937); SATURDAY'S HEROES(1937); SECRET VALLEY(1937); TOAST OF NEW YORK, THE(1937); WINGS OVER HONOLULU(1937); 100 MEN AND A GIRL(1937); CHASER, THE(1938); CRIME RING(1938); HELD FOR RANSOM(1938); OF HUMAN HEARTS(1938); OUTLAWS OF SONORA(1938); SKULL AND CROWN(1938); SPY RING, THE(1938); STORM, THE(1938); YOU AND ME(1938); FIRST LOVE(1939); HOME ON THE PRAIRIE(1939); JUDGE HARDY AND SON(1939); MADE FOR EACH OTHER(1939); OUTLAW'S PARADISE(1939); 6000 ENEMIES(1939); BLACK FRIDAY(1940); I LOVE YOU AGAIN(1940); SON OF MONTE CRISTO(1940); STRANGE CARGO(1940); STRIKE UP THE BAND(1940); THIRD FINGER, LEFT HAND(1940); BOWERY BLITZKRIEG(1941); CHEERS FOR MISS BISHOP(1941); DANGEROUS LADY(1941); DESPERATE CARGO(1941); HARD GUY(1941); IN THE NAVY(1941); INTERNATIONAL LADY(1941); INVISIBLE GHOST, THE(1941); LOVE CRAZY(1941); MY LIFE WITH CAROLINE(1941); SADDLE MOUNTAIN ROUNDUP(1941); UNEXPECTED UNCLE(1941); DAWN EXPRESS, THE(1942); FOREIGN AGENT(1942); FOREST RANGERS, THE(1942); GENTLEMAN AFTER DARK, A(1942); GLASS KEY, THE(1942); HARVARD, HERE I COME(1942); I KILLED THAT MAN(1942); MAN FROM HEADQUARTERS(1942); MR. WISE GUY(1942); 'NEATH BROOKLYN BRIDGE(1942); QUEEN OF BROADWAY(1942); SIN TOWN(1942); TREAT EM' ROUGH(1942); WAKE ISLAND(1942); COWBOY IN MANHATTAN(1943); FALCON IN DANGER, THE(1943); GHOSTS ON THE LOOSE(1943); HI' YA, SAILOR(1943); KID DYNAMITE(1943); SWING SHIFT MAISIE(1943); LADY IN THE DARK(1944); MY BUDDY(1944); SOUTH OF DIXIE(1944); MAN WHO WALKED ALONE, THE(1945); PHANTOM OF 42ND STREET, THE(1945); DEADLINE FOR MURDER(1946); MONSIEUR BEAUCAIRE(1946); SEARCHING WIND, THE(1946); MY FRIEND IRMA(1949); SKY LINER(1949); YOU'RE MY EVERYTHING(1949); JUST FOR YOU(1952); UP IN SMOKE(1957); IN THE MONEY(1958); ATOMIC SUBMARINE, THE(1960)
Misc. Talkies
PASSPORT TO PARADISE(1932); FIGHTING LADY(1935); MURDER ON THE HIGH SEAS(1938)
Silents
FIGHTING FOR LOVE(1917); HIGH SPEED(1917); LOVE AFLAME(1917); FLAMES OF CHANCE, THE(1918); MADAME SPY(1918); MISS HOBBS(1920); SHOULD A WOMAN TELL?(1920); LITTLE CLOWN, THE(1921); MOLLY O'(1921); OFF-SHORE PIRATE, THE(1921); SLEEPWALKER, THE(1922); CALL OF THE WILD, THE(1923); DULCY(1923); GOLDFISH, THE(1924); JOANNA(1925); FAR CRY, THE(1926); PLEASURES OF THE RICH(1926); CRYSTAL CUP, THE(1927); MAN CRAZY(1927); SMILE, BROTHER, SMILE(1927); LADY BE GOOD(1928); NAUGHTY BABY(1929)
Misc. Silents
T.N.T(THE NAKED TRUTH) (1924); REJUVINATION OF AUNT MARY, THE(1914); PLACE BEYOND THE WINDS, THE(1916); WHIRLPOOL OF DESTINY, THE(1916); FLAME OF THE HOUR, THE(1917); HERO OF THE YOUTH, THE(1917); MIDNIGHT MAN(1917); MR. DOLAN OF NEW YORK(1917); SAINTLY SINNER, THE(1917); SIRENS OF THE SEA(1917); TERROR, THE(1917); DANGER, GO SLOW(1918); GRAND PASSION, THE(1918); WILD YOUTH(1918); CREAKING STAIRS(1919); FAVOR TO A FRIEND, A(1919); FOOLS AND THEIR MONEY(1919); MERRY-GO ROUND, THE(1919); SOLITARY SIN, THE(1919); SPITE BRIDE, THE(1919); ALL OF A SUDDEN PEGGY(1920); HOPE, THE(1920); YOU NEVER CAN TELL(1920); TWO WEEKS WITH PAY(1921); BROAD DAYLIGHT(1922); DUSK TO DAWN(1922); FORGOTTEN LAW, THE(1922); FOURTEENTH LOVER, THE(1922); HEROES OF THE STREET(1922); TURN TO THE RIGHT(1922); BAD MAN, THE(1923); DRUMS OF JEOPARDY, THE(1923); WITHIN THE LAW(1923); BREATH OF A SCANDAL, THE(1924); FOLLY OF VANITY, THE(1924); CLASSIFIED(1925); FRIENDLY ENEMIES(1925); MAD WHIRL, THE(1925); SHE WOLVES(1925); THREE KEYS(1925); WE MODERNS(1925); DIXIE MERCHANT, THE(1926); GOD GAVE ME TWENTY CENTS(1926); SUBWAY SADIE(1926); ORCHIDS AND ERMINE(1927); POOR NUT, THE(1927); SEE YOU IN JAIL(1927); BUTTER AND EGG MAN, THE(1928); WATERFRONT(1928); CHILDREN OF THE RITZ(1929)
Lucille Mulhall
Misc. Silents
CHEROKEE STRIP, THE(1925)
Lyle Mulhall
COURAGE OF LASSIE(1946)
Edward Mulhare
HILL 24 DOESN'T ANSWER(1955, Israel); SIGNPOST TO MURDER(1964); VON RYAN'S EXPRESS(1965); OUR MAN FLINT(1966); CAPRICE(1967); EYE OF THE DEVIL(1967, Brit.); MEGAFORCE(1982)
James Mulhauser
HIDDEN GOLD(1933), w; CHEATING CHEATERS(1934), w; STRANGE WIVES(1935), w; LOVE LETTERS OF A STAR(1936), w; CARNIVAL QUEEN(1937), w; LOVE IN A BUNGALOW(1937), w; PRESCRIPTION FOR ROMANCE(1937), w; 100 MEN AND A GIRL(1937), w; GLADIATOR, THE(1938), w
Scott Mulhern
LOOKER(1981)
Clara Mulholland
KATHLEEN(1938, Ireland), w
Declan Mulholland
DAMN THE DEFIANT!(1962, Brit.); MYSTERY SUBMARINE(1963, Brit.); CHARGE OF THE LIGHT BRIGADE, THE(1968, Brit.); GREAT CATHERINE(1968, Brit.); GUNS IN THE HEATHER(1968, Brit.); RULING CLASS, THE(1972, Brit.); THEATRE OF BLOOD(1973, Brit.); LAND THAT TIME FORGOT, THE(1975, Brit.); TIME BANDITS(1981, Brit.)
Deelan Mulholland
HAWK THE SLAYER(1980, Brit.)
Gordon Mulholland
LADY CRAVED EXCITEMENT, THE(1950, Brit.); TREASURE ISLAND(1950, Brit.); CHEER THE BRAVE(1951, Brit.); COAST OF SKELETONS(1965, Brit.)
Mark Mulholland
MC KENZIE BREAK, THE(1970); PADDY(1970, Irish)
Paul Mulholland
CRIMES OF THE FUTURE(1969, Can.); STEREO(1969, Can.)

James Mulhouser
  COHENS, AND KELLYS IN HOLLYWOOD, THE(1932), w
Monga Muli
  LAST RHINO, THE(1961, Brit.)
Fritz Muliar
  EMBEZZLED HEAVEN(1959,Ger.); GOOD SOLDIER SCHWEIK, THE(1963, Ger.)
Lisa Mulidore
  WICKED LADY, THE(1983, Brit.)
Chris Mulkey
  LOOSE ENDS(1975); SUNNYSIDE(1979); LONG RIDERS, THE(1980); FIRST BLOOD(1982); 48 HOURS(1982); TIMERIDER(1983)
1984
  DREAMSCAPE(1984); RUNAWAY(1984)
Misc. Talkies
  TOMCATS(1977)
Christian Mulkey, Sr.
  LOOSE ENDS(1975)
Randy Mulkey
1984
  NINJA III–THE DOMINATION(1984)
Edward Mull
  ISLAND OF THE BLUE DOLPHINS(1964), p
Martin Mull
  FM(1978); MY BODYGUARD(1980); SERIAL(1980); TAKE THIS JOB AND SHOVE IT(1981); MR. MOM(1983)
1984
  BAD MANNERS(1984)
Regis Mull
  WINTER KILLS(1979)
Don Mullahy
  SHE HAD TO SAY YES(1933), w
Don Mullally
  MYSTERY OF THE WAX MUSEUM, THE(1933), w
Silents
  DESERT FLOWER, THE(1925), w
Donn Mullally
  FLYING FONTAINES, THE(1959), w
Jode Mullally
Silents
  CIRCUS MAN, THE(1914); MAN FROM HOME, THE(1914); READY MONEY(1914); AFTER FIVE(1915)
Don Mullaly
  GIRL MISSING(1933), w; WANTED BY THE POLICE(1938), w
Jode Mullaly
Silents
  CALL OF THE NORTH, THE(1914)
Donna Mullane
  OPTIMISTS, THE(1973, Brit.)
Jack Mullaney
  KISS THEM FOR ME(1957); VINTAGE, THE(1957); YOUNG STRANGER, THE(1957); SOUTH PACIFIC(1958); ALL THE FINE YOUNG CANNIBALS(1960); ABSENT-MINDED PROFESSOR, THE(1961); HONEYMOON MACHINE, THE(1961); SEVEN DAYS IN MAY(1964); DR. GOLDFOOT AND THE BIKINI MACHINE(1965); TICKLE ME(1965); SPINOUT(1966); LITTLE BIG MAN(1970); WHEN THE LEGENDS DIE(1972); WHERE DOES IT HURT?(1972); GEORGE(1973, U.S./Switz.); LITTLE MISS MARKER(1980)
Arther Mullard
  CUCKOO PATROL(1965, Brit.)
Arthur Mullard
  OPERATION DIAMOND(1948, Brit.); SKIMPY IN THE NAVY(1949, Brit.); LAVENDER HILL MOB, THE(1951, Brit.); BANK RAIDERS, THE(1958, Brit.); MAN WHO LIKED FUNERALS, THE(1959, Brit.); BAND OF THIEVES(1962, Brit.); LONELINESS OF THE LONG DISTANCE RUNNER, THE(1962, Brit.); POSTMAN'S KNOCK(1962, Brit.); RING-A-DING RHYTHM(1962, Brit. 73m Amicus/COL bw (G.B: IT'S TRAD, DAD!); CROOKS ANONYMOUS(1963, Brit.); SPARROWS CAN'T SING(1963, Brit.); WRONG ARM OF THE LAW, THE(1963, Brit.); FATHER CAME TOO(1964, Brit.); COUNTERFEIT CONSTABLE, THE(1966, Fr.); GREAT ST. TRINIAN'S TRAIN ROBBERY, THE(1966, Brit.); MORGAN!(1966, Brit.); SMASHING TIME(1967 Brit.); CHITTY CHITTY BANG BANG(1968, Brit.); LOCK UP YOUR DAUGHTERS(1969, Brit.); SOPHIE'S PLACE(1970); VAULT OF HORROR, THE(1973, Brit.)
Greg Mullavey
  BOB AND CAROL AND TED AND ALICE(1969); MARIGOLD MAN(1970); CHRISTIAN LICORICE STORE, THE(1971); LOVE MACHINE, THE,(1971); RAID ON ROMMEL(1971); STAND UP AND BE COUNTED(1972); I DISMEMBER MAMA(1974); HINDENBURG, THE(1975)
1984
  CENSUS TAKER, THE(1984)
Misc. Talkies
  SINGLE GIRLS(1973); I'M GOING TO BE FAMOUS(1981); MY FRIENDS NEED KILLING(1984)
Gregory Mullavy
  SHAKIEST GUN IN THE WEST, THE(1968)
Barbara Mullen
  GIRL IN DISTRESS(1941, Brit.); THUNDER ROCK(1944, Brit.); WELCOME, MR. WASHINGTON(1944, Brit.); PLACE OF ONE'S OWN, A(1945, Brit.); TROJAN BROTHERS, THE(1946); CORRIDOR OF MIRRORS(1948, Brit.); MY SISTER AND I(1948, Brit.); GENTLE GUNMAN, THE(1952, Brit.); YOU CAN'T BEAT THE IRISH(1952, Brit.); SO LITTLE TIME(1953, Brit.); DEATH OF MICHAEL TURBIN, THE(1954, Brit.); DESTINATION MILAN(1954, Brit.); LAST MOMENT, THE(1954, Brit.); INNOCENT SINNERS(1958, Brit.); FOUR DESPERATE MEN(1960, Brit.); IT TAKES A THIEF(1960, Brit.); VERY EDGE, THE(1963, Brit.)
Clara Mullen
  FLIGHT OF THE DOVES(1971)
Clare Mullen
  ULYSSES(1967, U.S./Brit.); WHERE'S JACK?(1969, Brit.); BROTHERLY LOVE(1970, Brit.)
Eugene Mullen
Silents
  ROAD TO LONDON, THE(1921, Brit.), d

Gordon Mullen
Silents
  NOMADS OF THE NORTH(1920); PARTNERS OF THE TIDE(1921); THELMA(1922)
Gordon Douglas Mullen
Silents
  PARIS GREEN(1920)
Judy Mullen
  LITTLE ROMANCE, A(1979, U.S./Fr.)
Kathryn Mullen
  MUPPET MOVIE, THE(1979); EMPIRE STRIKES BACK, THE(1980); DARK CRYSTAL, THE(1982, Brit.)
1984
  MUPPETS TAKE MANHATTAN, THE(1984)
Leonard Mullen
  CHARRIOTS OF FIRE(1981, Brit.)
Paul Mullen
Silents
  HOODLUM THE(1919)
Paul E. Mullen
  MA BARKER'S KILLER BROOD(1960), art d
Sadie Mullen
Silents
  JANE EYRE(1921); MOONSHINE VALLEY(1922)
Steve Mullen
  WHITE RAT(1972), d, w
Sue Mullen
  HARRY IN YOUR POCKET(1973)
Virginia Mullen
  MOONRISE(1948); NAKED CITY, THE(1948); JOLSON SINGS AGAIN(1949); LUST FOR GOLD(1949); TOO LATE FOR TEARS(1949); MYSTERY STREET(1950); NEVER A DULL MOMENT(1950); BRIGHT VICTORY(1951); FOR MEN ONLY(1952); TREASURE OF LOST CANYON, THE(1952); DREAM WIFE(1953)
Joseph Mullendore
  NEW YORK CONFIDENTIAL(1955), m; I DEAL IN DANGER(1966), m
Nan Mulleneaux
Misc. Talkies
  MISSION HILL(1982)
Peter Mullens
  PENTHOUSE, THE(1967, Brit.), art d
Virginia Mullens
  CANON CITY(1948); WINCHESTER '73(1950)
Alfred Muller
  PRIVATE POOLEY(1962, Brit./E. Ger.); PINOCCHIO(1969, E. Ger.)
Andre Muller
  MAN WHO COULDN'T WALK, THE(1964, Brit.)
Andrea Muller
1984
  HOT MOVES(1984), ch
Arvid Muller
  WHILE THE ATTORNEY IS ASLEEP(1945, Den.), w
Barbara Muller
  WHITE LIGHTNING(1973)
Charlotte Muller
  SPESSART INN, THE(1961, Ger.), makeup
Charly Muller
  TURKISH CUCUMBER, THE(1963, Ger.)
Christiane Muller
  GOING PLACES(1974, Fr.)
Debbie Muller
  BON VOYAGE, CHARLIE BROWN(AND DON'T COME BACK)*** (1980); STRAWBERRY STATEMENT, THE(1970)
Dieter Muller
  LAST MERCENARY, THE(1969, Ital./Span./Ger.), d
Elke Muller
  DEEP END(1970 Ger./U.S.), makeup
Endre Muller
  JACK THE RIPPER(1959, Brit.); SECRET OF MONTE CRISTO, THE(1961, Brit.)
Eric Muller
  MALEVIL(1981, Fr./Ger.), makeup
1984
  SUNDAY IN THE COUNTRY, A(1984, Fr.), makeup
Ernest Muller
  5 SINNERS(1961, Ger.), p
Erno Muller
  EPILOGUE(1967, Den.)
Fritz Muller
  CHIMES AT MIDNIGHT(1967, Span.,Switz.), ed
G. Muller
  UNDERCOVER AGENT(1935, Brit.), ed
Geoffrey Muller
  DARK MAN, THE(1951, Brit.), ed; SHADOW MAN(1953, Brit.), ed; CASE OF THE RED MONKEY(1955, Brit.), ed; DEADLIEST SIN, THE(1956, Brit.), ed; FINGER OF GUILT(1956, Brit.), ed; COUNTERFEIT PLAN, THE(1957, Brit.), ed; SCOTLAND YARD DRAGNET(1957, Brit.), ed; HORRORS OF THE BLACK MUSEUM(1959, U.S./Brit.), ed; WITNESS, THE(1959, Brit.), d; ELECTRONIC MONSTER. THE(1960, Brit.), ed
H.H. Muller
  MALOU(1983)
Hans Muller
  MONTE CARLO(1930), w; BOMBARDMENT OF MONTE CARLO, THE(1931, Ger.), w; SMILING LIEUTENANT, THE(1931), w
Hans Carl Muller
Silents
  KRIEMHILD'S REVENGE(1924, Ger.); SIEGFRIED(1924, Ger.)
Harrison Muller
  MONSIGNOR(1982)
Misc. Talkies
  SHE(1983)

Harrison Muller, Jr.
LONELY LADY, THE(1983)
Heinz Muller
PINOCCHIO(1969, E. Ger.)
Herb Muller
JAWS II(1978)
Hero Muller
1984
FOURTH MAN, THE(1984, Neth.)
Jacques Muller
NIGHTS OF SHAME(1961, Fr.)
Jonas Muller
JACK OF DIAMONDS(1967, U.S./Ger.), makeup
Kathryn Muller
GREAT MUPPET CAPER, THE(1981)
Lillian Muller
DEVIL AND MAX DEVLIN, THE(1981); KING OF THE MOUNTAIN(1981)
Martin Muller
1984
CHINESE BOXES(1984, Ger./Brit.)
N. Muller
DIMKA(1964, USSR), cos
Norbert Muller
JOURNEY FOR MARGARET(1942); WHITE CLIFFS OF DOVER, THE(1944)
Oskar Muller
DIAMONDS OF THE NIGHT(1968, Czech.)
Paul Muller
BURIED ALIVE(1951, Ital.); DEAD WOMAN'S KISS, A(1951, Ital.); TWO NIGHTS WITH CLEOPATRA(1953, Ital.); FOUR WAYS OUT(1954, Ital.); HELL RAIDERS OF THE DEEP(1954, Ital.); MYSTERY OF THE BLACK JUNGLE(1955); STRANGERS, THE(1955, Ital.); DEVIL'S COMMANDMENT, THE(1956, Ital.); CHECKPOINT(1957, Brit.); NAKED MAJA, THE(1959, Ital./U.S.); SIGN OF THE GLADIATOR(1959, Fr./Ger./Ital.); ENEMY GENERAL, THE(1960); FRANCIS OF ASSISI(1961); MINOTAUR, THE(1961, Ital.); QUEEN OF THE PIRATES(1961, Ital./Ger.); IT HAPPENED IN ATHENS(1962); WASTREL, THE(1963, Ital.); GOLIATH AND THE SINS OF BABYLON(1964, Ital.); TORPEDO BAY(1964, Ital./Fr.); NARCO MEN, THE(1969, Span./Ital.); PUSSYCAT, PUSSYCAT, I LOVE YOU(1970); VENUS IN FURS(1970, Ital./Brit./Ger.); COUNT DRACULA(1971, Sp., Ital., Ger., Brit.); LADY FRANKENSTEIN(1971, Ital.); MALENKA, THE VAMPIRE(1972, Span./Ital.); TREASURE ISLAND(1972, Brit./Span./Fr./Ger.); ARENA, THE(1973)
Petra Muller
1984
LE DERNIER COMBAT(1984, Fr.)
Raidar Muller
U-47 LT. COMMANDER PRIEN(1967, Ger.)
Raymond Muller
PANIC IN THE STREETS(1950)
Renate Muller
STORM IN A WATER GLASS(1931, Aust.); MARRY ME(1932, Brit.); OFFICE GIRL, THE(1932, Brit.)
Richy Muller
KAMIKAZE '89(1983, Ger.)
Robby Muller
JONATHAN(1973, Ger.), ph; ALICE IN THE CITIES(1974, W. Ger.), ph; AMERICAN FRIEND, THE(1977, Ger.), ph; MYSTERIES(1979, Neth.), ph; SAINT JACK(1979), ph; HONEYSUCKLE ROSE(1980), ph; LEFT-HANDED WOMAN, THE(1980, Ger.), ph; THEY ALL LAUGHED(1981), ph
1984
BODY ROCK(1984), ph; PARIS, TEXAS(1984, Ger./Fr.), ph; REPO MAN(1984), ph
Robert Muller
WOMAN OF STRAW(1964, Brit.), w; BEAUTY JUNGLE, THE(1966, Brit.), w; GREAT BRITISH TRAIN ROBBERY, THE(1967, Ger.), w
Rolf Muller
BLUE ANGEL, THE(1930, Ger.)
Romeo Muller
WACKY WORLD OF MOTHER GOOSE, THE,(1967), w; MARCO(1973), a, w
Steven Muller
ADAM HAD FOUR SONS(1941); SEVENTH CROSS, THE(1944); WHITE CLIFFS OF DOVER, THE(1944)
Misc. Talkies
BOY FROM STALINGRAD, THE(1943)
Tom Muller
RACE FOR YOUR LIFE, CHARLIE BROWN(1977)
Vernique Muller
BLACK SPIDER, THE(1983, Swit.), cos
Vladimir Muller
Silents
ARSENAL(1929, USSR), art d
Vlado Muller
DEATH IS CALLED ENGELCHEN(1963, Czech.); ADRIFT(1971, Czech.)
Werner Muller
SCHLAGER-PARADE(1953)
Wolfgang Muller
ARENT WE WONDERFUL?(1959, Ger.); ROSES FOR THE PROSECUTOR(1961, Ger.); SPESSART INN, THE(1961, Ger.)
Kurt Muller-Graf
HEAD, THE(1961, Ger.)
Anna Muller-Lincke
GREAT YEARNING, THE(1930, Ger.)
Dominique Mullier
1984
L'ARGENT(1984, Fr./Switz.)
Barrett Mulligan
1984
SLAYGROUND(1984, Brit.)
Dennis Mulligan
KING OF COMEDY, THE(1983)

Gerry Mulligan
I WANT TO LIVE!(1958); BELLS ARE RINGING(1960); RAT RACE, THE(1960); SUBTERRANEANS, THE(1960); LUV(1967), m; LAST DAYS OF MAN ON EARTH, THE(1975, Brit.), m
Herb Mulligan
HOSPITAL, THE(1971), set d; MY FAVORITE YEAR(1982), set d
Herbert Mulligan
THOUSAND CLOWNS, A(1965), set d; WHERE'S POPPA?(1970), set d; THEY MIGHT BE GIANTS(1971), set d; TAXI DRIVER(1976), set d
Herbert F. Mulligan
DESPERATE CHARACTERS(1971), set d
John Joseph Mulligan
NAKED CITY, THE(1948)
Richard Mulligan
LOVE WITH THE PROPER STRANGER(1963); ONE POTATO, TWO POTATO(1964); GROUP, THE(1966); UNDEFEATED, THE(1969); LITTLE BIG MAN(1970); FROM THE MIXED-UP FILES OF MRS. BASIL E. FRANKWEILER(1973); IRISH WHISKEY REBELLION(1973); VISIT TO A CHIEF'S SON(1974); BIG BUS, THE(1976); SCAVENGER HUNT(1979); S.O.B.(1981); TRAIL OF THE PINK PANTHER(1982)
1984
MEATBALLS PART II(1984); MICKI AND MAUDE(1984); TEACHERS(1984)
Robert Mulligan
FEAR STRIKES OUT(1957), d; GREAT IMPOSTOR, THE(1960), d; RAT RACE, THE(1960), d; COME SEPTEMBER(1961), d; SPIRAL ROAD, THE(1962), d; TO KILL A MOCKINGBIRD(1962), d; LOVE WITH THE PROPER STRANGER(1963), d; BABY, THE RAIN MUST FALL(1965), d; INSIDE DAISY CLOVER(1965), p, d; UP THE DOWN STAIRCASE(1967), d; STALKING MOON, THE(1969), d; PURSUIT OF HAPPINESS, THE(1971), d; SUMMER OF '42(1971), a, d; OTHER, THE(1972), p&d; NICKEL RIDE, THE(1974), p&d; BLOODBROTHERS(1978), d; SAME TIME, NEXT YEAR(1978), d; KISS ME GOODBYE(1982), p&d
Terry Mulligan
CHRISTINA(1974, Can.)
Bill Mullikin
NEW FACES(1954); HELL IS FOR HEROES(1962)
Dan Mullin
INVISIBLE AVENGER, THE(1958)
Misc. Talkies
BOURBON ST. SHADOWS(1962)
Eugene Mullin
Silents
CHRISTIAN, THE(1914), w; MR. BARNES OF NEW YORK(1914), w; ON HER WEDDING NIGHT(1915), w; NEVER THE TWAIN SHALL MEET(1925), w
John Mullin
SECOND FIDDLE TO A STEEL GUITAR(1965), ed
Peter Mullin
THERE GOES THE BRIDE(1980, Brit.), prod d
Ralph Mullin
JUST FOR THE HELL OF IT(1968)
Virginia Mullin
NOT WANTED(1949)
Anne Mullinar
BLUE FIN(1978, Aus.)
Rod Mullinar
RAW DEAL(1977, Aus.); PATRICK(1979, Aus.); THIRST(1979, Aus.); BREAKER MORANT(1980, Aus.); DUET FOR FOUR(1982, Aus.)
Misc. Talkies
BREAKFAST IN PARIS(1981)
Rodney Mullinar
SET, THE(1970, Aus.)
Art Mulliner
FOREVER AND A DAY(1943)
Arthur Mulliner
EARL OF CHICAGO, THE(1940); ESCAPE TO GLORY(1940); MAN IN HALF-MOON STREET, THE(1944); PEARL OF DEATH, THE(1944); SECRETS OF SCOTLAND YARD(1944)
Arthur Mullinor
SUN NEVER SETS, THE(1939)
Bartlett Mullins
THREE WEIRD SISTERS, THE(1948, Brit.); HA' PENNY BREEZE(1950, Brit.); NO ROOM AT THE INN(1950, Brit.); STOLEN FACE(1952, Brit.); WILD HEART, THE(1952, Brit.); EIGHT O'CLOCK WALK(1954, Brit.); FUSS OVER FEATHERS(1954, Brit.); GREEN BUDDHA, THE(1954, Brit.); RED DRESS, THE(1954, Brit.); TRACK THE MAN DOWN(1956, Brit.); CURSE OF FRANKENSTEIN, THE(1957, Brit.); PEEPING TOM(1960, Brit.); FRANKENSTEIN CREATED WOMAN(1965, Brit.); HALF A SIXPENCE(1967, Brit.); NICE GIRL LIKE ME, A(1969, Brit.); TROG(1970, Brit.)
Bernard Mullins
1984
PLOUGHMAN'S LUNCH, THE(1984, Brit.)
David A. Mullins
STRIPES(1981)
Helen Mullins
ONE MAN(1979, Can.)
Jack Mullins
Misc. Silents
WOMAN AND OFFICER 26, THE(1920, Brit.)
Jerry Mullins
NO MINOR VICES(1948)
Michael Mullins
POM POM GIRLS, THE(1976)
Moon Mullins
SPIRIT OF NOTRE DAME, THE(1931)
Peter Mullins
MR. EMMANUEL(1945, Brit.); DEATH TRAP(1962, Brit.), art d; DOUBLE, THE(1963, Brit), art d; KING AND COUNTRY(1964, Brit.), art d; WE SHALL SEE(1964, Brit.), art d; 20,000 POUNDS KISS, THE(1964, Brit.), art d; SINISTER MAN, THE(1965, Brit.), art d; INCIDENT AT MIDNIGHT(1966, Brit.), art d; RICOCHET(1966, Brit.), art d; SHARE OUT, THE(1966, Brit.), art d; SOLO FOR SPARROW(1966, Brit.), art d; SPY WITH A COLD NOSE, THE(1966, Brit.), art d; NEVER BACK LOSERS(1967, Brit.), art d; ON THE RUN(1967, Brit.), art d; PROJECTED MAN, THE(1967, Brit.), art d; MAN OUTSIDE, THE(1968, Brit.), art d; MATTER OF INNOCENCE, A(1968, Brit.), art d;

WHERE EAGLES DARE(1968, Brit.), art d; CHAIRMAN, THE(1969), art d; LAST VALLEY, THE(1971, Brit.), art d; PUPPET ON A CHAIN(1971, Brit.), prod d; X Y & ZEE(1972, Brit.), art d; LUTHER(1974), prod d; 11 HARROWHOUSE(1974, Brit.), art d; RETURN OF THE PINK PANTHER, THE(1975, Brit.), prod d, art d; PINK PANTHER STRIKES AGAIN, THE(1976, Brit.), prod d; MEDUSA TOUCH, THE(1978, Brit.), art d; REVENGE OF THE PINK PANTHER(1978), prod d; DOGS OF WAR, THE(1980), prod d; TRAIL OF THE PINK PANTHER, THE(1982), prod d; BETTER LATE THAN NEVER(1983), prod d; CURSE OF THE PINK PANTHER(1983), prod d, set d
1984
LASSITER(1984), prod d; SCANDALOUS(1984), prod d
Edward B. Mulloy
CHECKERED FLAG, THE(1963), ed
Al Mulock
PICKUP ALLEY(1957, Brit.); DEATH OVER MY SHOULDER(1958, Brit.); HIGH HELL(1958); KILL ME TOMORROW(1958, Brit.); TARZAN'S GREATEST ADVENTURE(1959, Brit.); IN THE NICK(1960, Brit.); JAZZ BOAT(1960, Brit.); TARZAN THE MAGNIFICENT(1960, Brit.); HELLIONS, THE(1962, Brit.); CALL ME BWANA(1963, Brit.); SMALL WORLD OF SAMMY LEE, THE(1963, Brit.); DR. TERROR'S HOUSE OF HORRORS(1965, Brit.); GAME FOR THREE LOSERS(1965, Brit.); LOST COMMAND, THE(1966); HELLBENDERS, THE(1967, U.S./Ital./Span.); REFLECTIONS IN A GOLDEN EYE(1967); TREASURE OF MAKUBA, THE(1967, U.S./Span.); WITCH WITHOUT A BROOM, A(1967, U.S./Span.); BATTLE BENEATH THE EARTH(1968, Brit.)
Alfred Mulock
JOE MACBETH(1955)
Claude Mulot
BLOOD ROSE, THE(1970, Fr.), d, w
Kathleen Mulqueen
JOURNEY INTO LIGHT(1951); ACTORS AND SIN(1952); JAPANESE WAR BRIDE(1952); TEEN-AGE CRIME WAVE(1955); TEXAS LADY(1955); THESE WILDER YEARS(1956); TOUGHEST GUN IN TOMBSTONE(1958); LOVER COME BACK(1961); OUTSIDER, THE(1962); NIGHT WALKER, THE(1964)
Kathy Mulrooney
HOMETOWN U.S.A.(1979)
Mary Multari
SEVEN UPS, THE(1973)
Edward Mulvaney
MEMENTO MEI(1963)
Gino Mulvazzi
INTERLUDE(1968, Brit.)
Charles Mulvehill
POSTMAN ALWAYS RINGS TWICE, THE(1981), p
Charles B. Mulvehill
HAROLD AND MAUDE(1971), p
Chuck Mulvehill
PASSENGER, THE(1975, Ital.)
Ann Mulvey
STORK TALK(1964, Brit.)
Anne Mulvey
QUESTION OF SUSPENSE, A(1961, Brit.)
Doreen Mulvey
EVER SINCE VENUS(1944)
Paul Mulvey
LONE STAR VIGILANTES, THE(1942)
Patrick Mulvihill
TENTACLES(1977, Ital.)
William Mulvihill
SANDS OF THE KALAHARI(1965, Brit.), d&w
Diana Mumby
UP IN ARMS(1944); GEORGE WHITE'S SCANDALS(1945); KID FROM BOOKLYN, THE(1946); WINTER WONDERLAND(1947); SONG IS BORN, A(1948); G.I. JANE(1951); I CAN GET IT FOR YOU WHOLESALE(1951)
Diane Mumby
TWO GIRLS AND A SAILOR(1944); THRILL OF BRAZIL, THE(1946); SON OF SINBAD(1955); HARDER THEY FALL, THE(1956)
Cecil G. Mumford
Silents
LORNA DOONE(1927), w
Ethel Watts Mumford
Silents
STRAIGHT IS THE WAY(1921), w; AFTER BUSINESS HOURS(1925), w; WEDDING SONG, THE(1925), w
Karin Mumm
POSSESSION(1981, Fr./Ger.)
Dan Mummert
BITTER CREEK(1954)
Danny Mummert
BLONDIE(1938); BLONDIE BRINGS UP BABY(1939); BLONDIE MEETS THE BOSS(1939); BLONDIE TAKES A VACATION(1939); BLONDIE HAS SERVANT TROUBLE(1940); BLONDIE ON A BUDGET(1940); BLONDIE PLAYS CUPID(1940); BLONDIE GOES LATIN(1941); BLONDIE IN SOCIETY(1941); STORK PAYS OFF, THE(1941); THUNDER OVER THE PRAIRIE(1941); BLONDIE FOR VICTORY(1942); BLONDIE GOES TO COLLEGE(1942); BLONDIE'S BLESSED EVENT(1942); DARING YOUNG MAN, THE(1942); MEET THE STEWARTS(1942); MY SISTER EILEEN(1942); FOOTLIGHT GLAMOUR(1943); IT'S A GREAT LIFE(1943); BEAUTIFUL BUT BROKE(1944); LEAVE IT TO BLONDIE(1945); SENORITA FROM THE WEST(1945); BLONDIE KNOWS BEST(1946); IT'S A WONDERFUL LIFE(1946); BLONDIE IN THE DOUGH(1947); BLONDIE'S BIG MOMENT(1947); MAGIC TOWN(1947); BLONDIE'S REWARD(1948); BLONDIE'S SECRET(1948); BLONDIE HITS THE JACKPOT(1949); BLONDIE'S BIG DEAL(1949); BEWARE OF BLONDIE(1950); BLONDIE'S HERO(1950); HAPPY YEARS, THE(1950); MEMBER OF THE WEDDING, THE(1952); SNIPER, THE(1952)
Don Mummert
BRONCO BILLY(1980)
Browning Mummery
EVENSONG(1934, Brit.)

Ursel Mumoth
GENGHIS KHAN(U.S./Brit./Ger./Yugo)
Bill Mumy
RASCAL(1969); BLESS THE BEASTS AND CHILDREN(1971); PAPILLON(1973); TWILIGHT ZONE–THE MOVIE(1983)
Billy Mumy
TAMMY, TELL ME TRUE(1961); PALM SPRINGS WEEKEND(1963); TICKLISH AFFAIR, A(1963); DEAR BRIGETTE(1965)
Tony Munafo
VOICES(1979); JUST TELL ME WHAT YOU WANT(1980); NIGHTHAWKS(1981); PRINCE OF THE CITY(1981); AUTHOR! AUTHOR!(1982); STAYING ALIVE(1983); TWO OF A KIND(1983)
1984
RHINESTONE(1984)
Charles Munch
DEVIL'S ENVOYS, THE(1947, Fr.), md
Richard Munch
LONGEST DAY, THE(1962); YOUNG GO WILD, THE(1962, Ger.); RESTLESS NIGHT, THE(1964, Ger.); VISIT, THE(1964, Ger./Fr./Ital./U.S.); TRAIN, THE(1965, Fr./Ital./U.S.); BRIDGE AT REMAGEN, THE(1969)
William Munchow
DOCTOR DETROIT(1983)
Chris Muncke
NASTY HABITS(1976, Brit.)
Christopher Muncke
SPY WHO LOVED ME, THE(1977, Brit.); SATURN 3(1980)
1984
RAZOR'S EDGE, THE(1984)
Don Munday
REMEMBRANCE(1982, Brit.)
Helen Munday
Misc. Silents
STARK LOVE(1927)
Hilda Munday
BITER BIT, THE(1937, Brit.)
Mary Munday
GOLDEN HAWK, THE(1952); SERPENT ISLAND(1954); PRESSURE POINT(1962); HAWAIIANS, THE(1970); BREEZY(1973); MAGIC(1978); NORMA RAE(1979); FIRST MONDAY IN OCTOBER(1981); TRUE CONFESSIONS(1981)
Olivia Munday
CONFESSIONS OF A WINDOW CLEANER(1974, Brit.); DEADLY FEMALES, THE(1976, Brit.)
Michael Mundell
FAHRENHEIT 451(1966, Brit.); MAROC 7(1967, Brit.); STRAW DOGS(1971, Brit.)
Jesse Munden
LAST TIME I SAW ARCHIE, THE(1961), cos; MISFITS, THE(1961), cos
Maxwell Munden
HOUSE IN THE WOODS, THE(1957, Brit.), d&w; BANK RAIDERS, THE(1958, Brit.), d
Mario Munder
NIGHT GAMES(1980)
Robert Mundi
VISITOR, THE(1980, Ital./U.S.), w
Ed Mundin
CHANGE OF HEART(1934)
Frank Mundin
GOIN' TO TOWN(1935)
Herbert Mundin
UNDER TWO FLAGS(1936); EAST LYNNE ON THE WESTERN FRONT(1931, Brit.); ALMOST MARRIED(1932); BACHELOR'S AFFAIRS(1932); CHANDU THE MAGICIAN(1932); DEVIL'S LOTTERY(1932); LIFE BEGINS(1932); LOVE ME TONIGHT(1932); ONE WAY PASSAGE(1932); SHERLOCK HOLMES(1932); SILENT WITNESS, THE(1932); TRIAL OF VIVIENNE WARE, THE(1932); ADORABLE(1933); ARIZONA TO BROADWAY(1933); CAVALCADE(1933); DANGEROUSLY YOURS(1933); DEVIL'S IN LOVE, THE(1933); HOOPLA(1933); IT'S GREAT TO BE ALIVE(1933); PLEASURE CRUISE(1933); SHANGHAI MADNESS(1933); ALL MEN ARE ENEMIES(1934); BOTTOMS UP(1934); CALL IT LUCK(1934); EVER SINCE EVE(1934); LOVE TIME(1934); ORIENT EXPRESS(1934); SPRINGTIME FOR HENRY(1934); SUCH WOMEN ARE DANGEROUS(1934); BLACK SHEEP(1935); DAVID COPPERFIELD(1935); LADIES LOVE DANGER(1935); MUTINY ON THE BOUNTY(1935); PERFECT GENTLEMAN, THE(1935); CHAMPAGNE CHARLIE(1936); CHARLIE CHAN'S SECRET(1936); KING OF BURLESQUE(1936); MESSAGE TO GARCIA, A(1936); TARZAN ESCAPES(1936); WIDOW FROM MONTE CARLO, THE(1936); ANGEL(1937); ANOTHER DAWN(1937); YOU CAN'T BEAT LOVE(1937); ADVENTURES OF ROBIN HOOD, THE(1938); EXPOSED(1938); INVISIBLE ENEMY(1938); LORD JEFF(1938); SOCIETY LAWYER(1939)
Abe Mundon
Silents
SCANDAL(1915)
Wisner Mundus
ADORABLE JULIA(1964, Fr./Aust.), p
Mundviller
OPEN ROAD, THE(1940, Fr.), ph
Joseph-Louis Mundviller
CRIME AND PUNISHMENT(1935, Fr.), ph
Ed Mundy
BALL OF FIRE(1941); HONOLULU LU(1941); HELLO, FRISCO, HELLO(1943); WILSON(1944); GUNFIGHTER, THE(1950); ROBE, THE(1953); CAROUSEL(1956); PROUD ONES, THE(1956); GUN GLORY(1957)
Edmund Mundy
CAPTAIN FROM CASTILE(1947)
Edward Mundy
CHAD HANNA(1940); GOOD MORNING, MISS DOVE(1955); UNTAMED(1955)
Hilda Mundy
REGAL CAVALCADE(1935, Brit.); LASSIE FROM LANCASHIRE(1938, Brit.); I DIDN'T DO IT(1945, Brit.)
Meg Mundy
EYES OF LAURA MARS(1978); OLIVER'S STORY(1978); BELL JAR, THE(1979); ORDINARY PEOPLE(1980); SURVIVORS, THE(1983)

Robert Mundy
1984
CHATTANOOGA CHOO CHOO(1984), w
Talbot Mundy
BLACK WATCH, THE(1929), w; KING OF THE KHYBER RIFLES(1953), w
Ian Mune
SLEEPING DOGS(1977, New Zealand), a, w; GOODBYE PORK PIE(1981, New Zealand), w
1984
SILENT ONE, THE(1984, New Zealand), w
Misc. Talkies
LAST KIDS ON EARTH, THE(1983)
Nobuo Munekawa
GAMERA THE INVINCIBLE(1966, Jap.), ph
David Mungenast
1984
HARRY AND SON(1984)
Chris Munger
KISS OF THE TARANTULA(1975), d
Misc. Talkies
BLACK STARLET(1974), d
Marilyn Munger
WEREWOLVES ON WHEELS(1971)
Matthew Mungle
JUST BEFORE DAWN(1980), makeup; DEVONSVILLE TERROR, THE(1983), spec eff
1984
POWER, THE(1984), makeup
Alfonso Munguia
VENGEANCE OF THE VAMPIRE WOMEN, THE(1969, Mex.)
Jessica Munguia
VAMPIRES, THE(1969, Mex.)
Juan Jose Munguia
VAMPIRES, THE(1969, Mex.), ed
Muni
DIARY OF A CHAMBERMAID(1964, Fr./Ital.); BELLE DE JOUR(1968, Fr.); MILKY WAY, THE(1969, Fr./Ital.); PROMISE AT DAWN(1970, U.S./Fr.); DISCREET CHARM OF THE BOURGEOISIE, THE(1972, Fr.); THAT OBSCURE OBJECT OF DESIRE(1977, Fr./Span.)
Bella Muni
DECEIVER, THE(1931), w
Mike Muni
Misc. Talkies
CRUISIN' 57(1975)
Paul Muni
SEVEN FACES(1929); VALIANT, THE(1929); I AM A FUGITIVE FROM A CHAIN GANG(1932); SCARFACE(1932); WORLD CHANGES, THE(1933); HI, NELLIE!(1934); BLACK FURY(1935); BORDERTOWN(1935); DR. SOCRATES(1935); STORY OF LOUIS PASTEUR, THE(1936); GOOD EARTH, THE(1937); LIFE OF EMILE ZOLA, THE(1937); WOMAN I LOVE, THE(1937); JUAREZ(1939); WE ARE NOT ALONE(1939); HUDSON'S BAY(1940); COMMANDOS STRIKE AT DAWN, THE(1942); STAGE DOOR CANTEEN(1943); COUNTER-ATTACK(1945); SONG TO REMEMBER, A(1945); ANGEL ON MY SHOULDER(1946); STRANGER ON THE PROWL(1953, Ital.); LAST ANGRY MAN, THE(1959)
Charlotte Munier
FORTY LITTLE MOTHERS(1940)
Ferdinand Munier
AMBASSADOR BILL(1931); AFTER TOMORROW(1932); STEPPING SISTERS(1932); WILD GIRL(1932); BOWERY, THE(1933); PARACHUTE JUMPER(1933); QUEEN CHRISTINA(1933); WOMAN I STOLE, THE(1933); BABES IN TOYLAND(1934); BARRETTS OF WIMPOLE STREET, THE(1934); COUNT OF MONTE CRISTO, THE(1934); MERRY WIDOW, THE(1934); MUSIC IN THE AIR(1934); CHINA SEAS(1935); CLIVE OF INDIA(1935); FOLIES DERGERE(1935); GILDED LILY, THE(1935); HANDS ACROSS THE TABLE(1935); HARMONY LANE(1935); I DREAM TOO MUCH(1935); I FOUND STELLA PARISH(1935); MAN WHO BROKE THE BANK AT MONTE CARLO, THE(1935); ROBERTA(1935); STARS OVER BROADWAY(1935); STEAMBOAT ROUND THE BEND(1935); SWEET ADELINE(1935); TWO FISTED(1935); TWO SINNERS(1935); VAGABOND LADY(1935); WHOLE TOWN'S TALKING, THE(1935); BOLD CABALLERO(1936); CAN THIS BE DIXIE?(1936); HIS FAMILY TREE(1936); ONE RAINY AFTERNOON(1936); SWING TIME(1936); WHITE ANGEL, THE(1936); WHITE LEGION, THE(1936); CHAMPAGNE WALTZ(1937); CONFESSION(1937); DAMAGED GOODS(1937); HIGH HAT(1937); THAT GIRL FROM PARIS(1937); TOVARICH(1937); EVERY DAY'S A HOLIDAY(1938); THREE COMRADES(1938); ARREST BULLDOG DRUMMOND(1939, Brit.); EVERYTHING HAPPENS AT NIGHT(1939); GOING PLACES(1939); HE STAYED FOR BREAKFAST(1940); NORTHWEST PASSAGE(1940); MODEL WIFE(1941); COMMANDOS STRIKE AT DAWN, THE(1942); CROSSROADS(1942); FLIGHT LIEUTENANT(1942); I MARRIED AN ANGEL(1942); INVISIBLE AGENT(1942); CLAUDIA(1943); FLESH AND FANTASY(1943); KNICKERBOCKER HOLIDAY(1944); LAKE PLACID SERENADE(1944); HER HIGHNESS AND THE BELLBOY(1945); PILLOW TO POST(1945); ROAD TO UTOPIA(1945); WHERE DO WE GO FROM HERE?(1945); BANDIT OF SHERWOOD FOREST, THE(1946)
Andrzej Munk
EROICA(1966, Pol.), d; PASSENGER, THE(1970, Pol.), d, w
Jonathan Munk
ANNIE HALL(1977)
Kaj Munk
ORDET(1957, Den.), w
Martin Munkasci
HANSEL AND GRETEL(1954), ph
Hans Munkell
WEREWOLF VS. THE VAMPIRE WOMAN, THE(1970, Span./Ger.), w
Ariane Munker
ACE ELI AND RODGER OF THE SKIES(1973)
Diana Munks
VALUE FOR MONEY(1957, Brit.)
Molly Munks
ON APPROVAL(1944, Brit.); VACATION FROM MARRIAGE(1945, Brit.)

Brian Munn
1984
CAL(1984, Ireland)
Pep Munne
JETLAG(1981, U.S./Span.)
William Munns
PEACE KILLERS, THE(1971), spec eff; SWAMP THING(1982), makeup
Ramon Munox
GILDA(1946)
Albert Munoz
SALT OF THE EARTH(1954)
Alberto Munoz
MAN AND THE BEAST, THE(1951, Arg.), ph
Anthony Munoz
RIGHT STUFF, THE(1983)
Aurora Munoz
OF LOVE AND DESIRE(1963); TWO MULES FOR SISTER SARA(1970)
Eduardo Munoz
VIOLATED LOVE(1966, Arg.)
Evita Munoz
GIGANTES PLANETARIOS(1965, Mex.)
Gori Munoz
GAMES MEN PLAY, THE(1968, Arg.), art d
Jose Munoz
BANDIDO(1956); MASSACRE(1956)
Loli Munoz
HOUSE OF 1,000 DOLLS(1967, Ger./Span./Brit.)
Marilou Munoz
CRY OF BATTLE(1963)
Munuel Munoz
1984
ON THE LINE(1984, Span.), m
Rafael Munoz
LITTLE RED RIDING HOOD(1963, Mex.); QUEEN'S SWORDSMEN, THE(1963, Mex.); PUSS 'N' BOOTS(1964, Mex.)
Tita Munoz
MAD DOCTOR OF BLOOD ISLAND, THE(1969, Phil./U.S.)
Andrew Munro
OPERATION DAMES(1959)
Beatrice Munro
BLACK ROSES(1936, Ger.)
Bonnie Munro
MEET THE NAVY(1946, Brit.), md
C. E. Munro
Silents
QUEEN'S EVIDENCE(1919, Brit.), w
Caroline Munro
WHERE'S JACK?(1969, Brit.); ABOMINABLE DR. PHIBES, THE(1971, Brit.); DOCTOR PHIBES RISES AGAIN(1972, Brit.); DRACULA A.D. 1972(1972, Brit.); CAPTAIN KRONOS: VAMPIRE HUNTER(1974, Brit.); GOLDEN VOYAGE OF SINBAD, THE(1974, Brit.); AT THE EARTH'S CORE(1976, Brit.); DEVIL WITHIN HER, THE(1976, Brit.); SPY WHO LOVED ME, THE(1977, Brit.); STARCRASH(1979); MANIAC(1980)
1984
DON'T OPEN TILL CHRISTMAS(1984, Brit.); LAST HORROR FILM, THE(1984)
Charles Munro
RATS OF TOBRUK(1951, Aus.), p
Clark Munro
MONKEY GRIP(1983, Aus.), prod d
Cynthia Munro
WEDDING PARTY, THE(1969), ed
David Munro
THREE SISTERS(1974, Brit.)
Douglas Munro
Silents
RUPERT OF HENTZAU(1915, Brit.); ARSENE LUPIN(1916, Brit.); PRINCESS OF HAPPY CHANCE, THE(1916, Brit.); FLAMES(1917, Brit.); GREATEST WISH IN THE WORLD, THE(1918, Brit.); GARDEN OF RESURRECTION, THE(1919, Brit.); GENERAL POST(1920, Brit.); LONDON PRIDE(1920, Brit.); MIRAGE, THE(1920, Brit.); PURSUIT OF PAMELA, THE(1920, Brit.); TEMPORARY VAGABOND, A(1920, Brit.); TRUE TILDA(1920, Brit.); BIGAMIST, THE(1921, Brit.); SPORT OF KINGS, THE(1921, Brit.); FIRES OF FATE(1923, Brit.)
Misc. Silents
MIDDLEMAN, THE(1915, Brit.); MORALS OF WEYBURY, THE(1916, Brit.); UNDER SUSPICION(1916, Brit.); GOODBYE(1918, Brit.); LIFE STORY OF DAVID LLOYD GEORGE, THE(1918, Brit.); LURE OF CROONING WATER, THE(1920, Brit.); DICKY MONTEITH(1922, Brit.); GRASS ORPHAN, THE(1922, Brit.); SPORTING DOUBLE, A(1922, Brit.)
Eileen Munro
ASK BECCLES(1933, Brit.); CRIME AT BLOSSOMS, THE(1933, Brit.); PARIS PLANE(1933, Brit.); SAY IT WITH DIAMONDS(1935, Brit.); SHOW FLAT(1936, Brit.); SUICIDE LEGION(1940, Brit.)
George Munro
SENSATION(1936, Brit.), w
Gwen Munro
ORPHAN OF THE WILDERNESS(1937, Aus.); TYPHOON TREASURE(1939, Brit.)
Misc. Talkies
LET GEORGE DO IT(1938, Aus.)
Hugh Munro
FLOODTIDE(1949, Brit.); END OF THE ROAD, THE(1954, Brit.)
Ineth Munro
Misc. Silents
SUSPENCE(1919)
Iseth Munro
Misc. Silents
SPURS OF SYBIL, THE(1918)
Janet Munro
SMALL HOTEL(1957, Brit.); CRAWLING EYE, THE(1958, Brit.); YOUNG AND THE GUILTY, THE(1958, Brit.); DARBY O'GILL AND THE LITTLE PEOPLE(1959); THIRD MAN ON THE MOUNTAIN(1959); SWISS FAMILY ROBINSON(1960); TOMMY THE

TOREADOR(1960, Brit.); DAY THE EARTH CAUGHT FIRE, THE(1961, Brit.); BITTER HARVEST(1963, Brit.); DAYLIGHT ROBBERY(1964, Brit.); HIDE AND SEEK(1964, Brit.); JOLLY BAD FELLOW, A(1964, Brit.); WALK IN THE SHADOW(1966, Brit.); CRY WOLF(1968, Brit.); SEBASTIAN(1968, Brit.)

John Munro
CIRCLE OF DECEIT(1982, Fr./Ger.)

June Munro
ORPHAN OF THE WILDERNESS(1937, Aus.)

Klaus Munro
SERENADE FOR TWO SPIES(1966, Ital./Ger.), w; HOW TO SEDUCE A PLAYBOY(1968, Aust./Fr./Ital.), w

Nan Munro
HAPPIEST DAYS OF YOUR LIFE(1950, Brit.); END OF THE AFFAIR, THE(1955, Brit.); OFFBEAT(1961, Brit.); MORGAN!(1966, Brit.); JOKERS, THE(1967, Brit.); MRS. BROWN, YOU'VE GOT A LOVELY DAUGHTER(1968, Brit.); SONG OF NORWAY(1970); WALKING STICK, THE(1970, Brit.); GAMES THAT LOVERS PLAY(1971, Brit.); JANE EYRE(1971, Brit.)

Nina Munro
Misc. Silents
GOLDEN WEB, THE(1920, Brit.)

Pauline Munro
GIRL GETTERS, THE(1966, Brit.); STRANGLER'S WEB(1966, Brit.); COMMITTEE, THE(1968, Brit.); TELL ME LIES(1968, Brit.)

Pete Munro
MOONRUNNERS(1975)

Stanley Munro
TRYGON FACTOR, THE(1969, Brit.), w

Wendy Munro
WILD INNOCENCE(1937, Aus.)

Carmen Munroe
EXORCISM AT MIDNIGHT(1966, Brit. revised 1973, U.S.)

Cynthia Munroe
WEDDING PARTY, THE(1969), a, p,d&w

Doreen Munroe
FEATHER IN HER HAT, A(1935); MOSS ROSE(1947)

Hugh Munroe
DEADLIEST SIN, THE(1956, Brit.)

David Munrow
HENRY VIII AND HIS SIX WIVES(1972, Brit.), m; ZARDOZ(1974, Brit.), m

Patrice Munsel
MELBA(1953, Brit.)

David Munsell
GIDGET GOES TO ROME(1963)

Judy Munsen
BON VOYAGE, CHARLIE BROWN(AND DON'T COME BACK)*** (1980), m

Edna Munsey
Misc. Silents
PATSY(1917)

Kendall Kay Munsey
THE RUNNER STUMBLES(1979)

Jules Munshin
EASTER PARADE(1948); ON THE TOWN(1949); TAKE ME OUT TO THE BALL GAME(1949); THAT MIDNIGHT KISS(1949); MONTE CARLO BABY(1953, Fr.); SILK STOCKINGS(1957); TEN THOUSAND BEDROOMS(1957); WILD AND WONDERFUL(1964); MONKEYS, GO HOME!(1967); MASTERMIND(1977)

Audrey Munson
Misc. Silents
PURITY(1916)

Byron Munson
YOU CAN'T CHEAT AN HONEST MAN(1939); BLACK PATCH(1957), cos; SEVEN GUNS TO MESA(1958), cos
Silents
MASK, THE(1921); LEARNING TO LOVE(1925); ANNAPOLIS(1928)

Dan Munson
1984
RHINESTONE(1984)

Judy Munson
STREET MUSIC(1982), m

Laurel Munson
UNHINGED(1982)

Ona Munson
BROADMINDED(1931); FIVE STAR FINAL(1931); GOING WILD(1931); HOT HEIRESS(1931); DRAMATIC SCHOOL(1938); HIS EXCITING NIGHT(1938); BIG GUY, THE(1939); GONE WITH THE WIND(1939); LEGION OF LOST FLYERS(1939); SCANDAL SHEET(1940); WAGONS WESTWARD(1940); LADY FROM LOUISIANA(1941); SHANGHAI GESTURE, THE(1941); WILD GEESE CALLING(1941); DRUMS OF THE CONGO(1942); IDAHO(1943); CHEATERS, THE(1945); DAKOTA(1945); RED HOUSE, THE(1947)

Warren Munson
MOMMIE DEAREST(1981); SOME KIND OF HERO(1982)

Helga Munster
INDECENT(1962, Ger.)

Peter Munt
HANDS OF THE RIPPER(1971, Brit.)

Bo F. Munthe
Misc. Talkies
NINJA MISSION(1984)

Jim Muntz
SUBSTITUTION(1970)

David Munyua
LAST SAFARI, THE(1967, Brit.)

Jack Mylong Munz
OVERTURE TO GLORY(1940)

Ludek Munzar
VOYAGE TO THE END OF THE UNIVERSE(1963, Czech.)

Michael Munzer
UP FROM THE BEACH(1965)

Maxim Munzuk
DERSU UZALA(1976, Jap./USSR)

Lt. John B. Muoio, Jr., USN
HIGH BARBAREE(1947), tech adv

Gaetano Muola
LOVE ME FOREVER(1935), md

Betty Mur
HOT TIMES(1974)

Corinna Mura
CALL OUT THE MARINES(1942); CASABLANCA(1942); PRISONER OF JAPAN(1942); PASSAGE TO MARSEILLE(1944); GAY SENORITA, THE(1945); HONEYMOON(1947)

Kita Mura
Misc. Talkies
SILENT STRANGER, THE(1975)

Murad
TARZAN GOES TO INDIA(1962, U.S./Brit./Switz.)

Sergio Murad
TEARS OF HAPPINESS(1974), ed

Sirri Murad
MEDIUM COOL(1969)

Gregory Muradian
UNCLE HARRY(1945); CAPTAIN EDDIE(1945); HOUSE OF DRACULA(1945); ROUGHLY SPEAKING(1945); STRANGE CONFESSION(1945); BRIDE WORE BOOTS, THE(1946); CHILD OF DIVORCE(1946); NIGHT AND DAY(1946)

Hiroshi Murai
MY HOBO(1963, Jap.), ph; PRESSURE OF GUILT(1964, Jap.), ph; SAMURAI ASSASSIN(1965, Jap.), ph; ILLUSION OF BLOOD(1966, Jap.), ph; SWORD OF DOOM, THE(1967, Jap.), ph; EMPEROR AND A GENERAL, THE(1968, Jap.), ph; DUEL AT EZO(1970, Jap.), ph; TIDAL WAVE(1975, U.S./Jap.), ph

Kunio Murai
WAR OF THE MONSTERS(1972, Jap.)

Fujio Murakami
PERFORMERS, THE(1970, Jap.)

Fuyuki Murakami
GODZILLA, RING OF THE MONSTERS(1956, Jap.); MYSTERIANS, THE(1959, Jap.); BATTLE IN OUTER SPACE(1960)

Genzo Murakami
KOJIRO(1967, Jap.), w; DAREDEVIL IN THE CASTLE(1969, Jap.), w

James Murakami
ESCAPE ARTIST, THE(1982), art d; HAMMETT(1982), set d

James J. Murakami
WARGAMES(1983), art d
1984
BEVERLY HILLS COP(1984), art d; NATURAL, THE(1984), art d

Jim Murakami
VON RICHTHOFEN AND BROWN(1970), art d
1984
JOY OF SEX(1984), art d

Jimmy T. Murakami
BATTLE BEYOND THE STARS(1980), d

Ryu Murakami
ALMOST TRANSPARENT BLUE(1980, Jap.), d&w; ALL RIGHT, MY FRIEND(1983, Japan), d&w

Murakami-Wolf Productions
MOUSE AND HIS CHILD, THE(1977), anim

Shinobu Muraki
GOODBYE, MOSCOW(1968, Jap.), art d; PORTRAIT OF HELL(1969, Jap.), art d; SUN ABOVE, DEATH BELOW(1969, Jap.), art d; CREATURE CALLED MAN, THE(1970, Jap.), art d; MARCO(1973), art d

Yoshiro Muraki
THRONE OF BLOOD(1961, Jap.), art d; YOJIMBO(1961, Jap.), art d; LOWER DEPTHS, THE(1962, Jap.), art d; SANJURO(1962, Jap.), art d; HIGH AND LOW(1963, Jap.), art d; RED BEARD(1966, Jap.), art d; I LIVE IN FEAR(1967, Jap.), art d; REBELLION(1967, Jap.), art d; TORA! TORA! TORA!(1970, U.S./Jap.), art d; TIDAL WAVE(1975, U.S./Jap.), art d; KAGEMUSHA(1980, Jap.), art d

Dohei Muramatsu
MAGIC BOY(1960, Jap.), w

Nariko Muramatsu
MY GEISHA(1962)

Hideka Muranatsu
FACE OF ANOTHER, THE(1967, Jap.)

Lia Murano
ANGELO IN THE CROWD(1952, Ital.)

Laszlo Muranyi
AGE OF ILLUSIONS(1967, Hung.)

Akira Murao
KILL(1968, Jap.), w

Kenji Murase
1984
BALLAD OF NARAYAMA, THE(1984, Jap.)

Sachiko Murase
GATEWAY TO GLORY(1970, Jap.)

Zen Murase
TOKYO STORY(1972, Jap.)

Giro Murashami
THREE CAME HOME(1950)

Jean Murat
NIGHT IS OURS(1930, Fr.); ANNE-MARIE(1936, Fr.); CARNIVAL IN FLANDERS(1936, Fr.); SECOND BUREAU(1936, Fr.); GENERALS WITHOUT BUTTONS(1938, Fr.); ETERNAL RETURN, THE(1943, Fr.); ON THE RIVERA(1951); RICH, YOUNG AND PRETTY(1951); ALERT IN THE SOUTH(1954, Fr.); ROYAL AFFAIRS IN VERSAILLES(1957, Fr.); PARIS HOLIDAY(1958); LADY CHATTERLEY'S LOVER(1959, Fr.); RED CLOAK, THE(1961, Ital./Fr.); TIME BOMB(1961, Fr./Ital.); IT HAPPENED IN ATHENS(1962); SEVEN CAPITAL SINS(1962, Fr./Ital.)
Misc. Silents
LA GALERIE DES MONSTRES(1924, Fr.); SOUL OF FRANCE(1929, Fr.); VENUS(1929, Fr.)

Miranda Murat
ISLAND OF LOVE(1963)
Hideo Murata
TERROR BENEATH THE SEA(1966, Jap.); KAGEMUSHA(1980, Jap.)
Minoru Murata
Misc. Silents
GLOW OF LIFE, THE(1918, Jap.); SOULS ON THE ROAD(1921, Jap.), d
Takeo Murata
HALF HUMAN(1955, Jap.), w; GODZILLA, RING OF THE MONSTERS(1956, Jap.),
w; RODAN(1958, Jap.), w; GIGANTIS(1959, Jap./U.S.), w; MAN IN THE STORM,
THE(1969, Jap.), w
Lili Murati
DOCTOR ZHIVAGO(1965); NUN AT THE CROSSROADS, A(1970, Ital./Span.)
Lilly Murati
MISS PRESIDENT(1935, Hung.)
Lucien Muratore
Silents
MANON LESCAUT(1914)
A. Muratov
SHE-WOLF, THE(1963, USSR), d&w
Kira Muratov
SHE-WOLF, THE(1963, USSR), d&w
R. Muratov
FATHER OF A SOLDIER(1966, USSR)
Radner Muratov
HUNTING IN SIBERIA(1962, USSR)
S. Muratov
CONCENTRATION CAMP(1939, USSR)
V. Muraviev
IDIOT, THE(1960, USSR)
Aleksey Muravlev
MUMU(1961, USSR), m; FORTY-NINE DAYS(1964, USSR), m; HOUSE WITH AN
ATTIC, THE(1964, USSR), m
M. Muravyov
TRAIN GOES TO KIEV, THE(1961, USSR)
Irina Murawjova
MOSCOW DOES NOT BELIEVE IN TEARS(1980, USSR)
Mitsuo Murayama
FALCON FIGHTERS, THE(1970, Jap.), d; GATEWAY TO GLORY(1970, Jap.), d
Noe Murayama
PEARL OF TLAYUCAN, THE(1964, Mex.); BLUE DEMON VERSUS THE INFER-
NAL BRAINS(1967, Mex.); GUNS FOR SAN SEBASTIAN(1968, U.S./Fr./Mex./Ital.);
NAZARIN(1968, Mex.)
Shinji Murayama
SPOILS OF THE NIGHT(1969, Jap.), d
George Murcell
CAMPBELL'S KINGDOM(1957, Brit.); HIGH TIDE AT NOON(1957, Brit.); HELL
DRIVERS(1958, Brit.); DON'T PANIC CHAPS!(1959, Brit.); SEA FURY(1959, Brit.);
CROSSROADS TO CRIME(1960, Brit.); JET STORM(1961, Brit.); PURSUERS,
THE(1961, Brit.); DESERT PATROL(1962, Brit.); IN SEARCH OF THE CAS-
TAWAYS(1962, Brit.); FALL OF THE ROMAN EMPIRE, THE(1964); HEROES OF
TELEMARK, THE(1965, Brit.); KALEIDOSCOPE(1966, Brit.); FIXER, THE(1968);
ASSASSINATION BUREAU, THE(1969, Brit.); WALK WITH LOVE AND DEATH,
A(1969); HORSEMEN, THE(1971)
Karmin Murcelo
BORDERLINE(1980); STIR CRAZY(1980)
Bob Murch
1984
FLASH OF GREEN, A(1984)
Marcus Murch
GURU, THE(1969, U.S./India)
Valentina Murch
ANNA KARENINA(1948, Brit.)
Walter Murch
THX 1138(1971), w; CONVERSATION, THE(1974), ed; JULIA(1977), ed
Douglas Murchie
HUNCH, THE(1967, Brit.)
Jane Murchison
MY DOG, BUDDY(1960)
Jim Murchison
MY BLOODY VALENTINE(1981, Can.)
Felix Murcia
CARMEN(1983, Span.), set d
Philippe Murcier
YOU ONLY LIVE ONCE(1969, Fr.), ed
Vera Murco
WARRIORS FIVE(1962)
Richard Murcoch
NOT A HOPE IN HELL(1960, Brit.)
Derek Murcott
SIN YOU SINNERS(1963); KENTUCKY FRIED MOVIE, THE(1977)
Joel Murcott
MANFISH(1956), w
Dick Murdoch
WRESTLER, THE(1974)
Henry Murdoch
OVERLANDERS, THE(1946, Brit./Aus.); BITTER SPRINGS(1950, Aus.); PHANTOM
STOCKMAN, THE(1953, Aus.)
Iris Murdoch
SEVERED HEAD, A(1971, Brit.), w
Janet Murdoch
TERROR BY NIGHT(1946); SMASH-UP, THE STORY OF A WOMAN(1947); THAT
WAY WITH WOMEN(1947); KIDNAPPED(1948)
Richard Murdoch
CHARLEY'S(BIG-HEARTED) AUNT*1/2 (1940); EVERGREEN(1934, Brit.); OVER
SHE GOES(1937, Brit.); BAND WAGGON(1940, Brit.); I THANK YOU(1941, Brit.); YOU
CAN'T DO WITHOUT LOVE(1946, Brit.); IT HAPPENED IN SOHO(1948, Brit.); LILLI
MARLENE(1951, Brit.); MAGIC BOX, THE(1952, Brit.); GAY ADVENTURE, THE(1953,
Brit.); STRICTLY CONFIDENTIAL(1959, Brit.)

Ann Murdock
Silents
ROYAL FAMILY, A(1915); ENVY(1917); IMPOSTER, THE(1918)
Misc. Silents
CAPTAIN JINKS OF THE HORSE MARINES(1916); BEAUTIFUL ADVENTURE,
THE(1917); OUTCAST(1917); PLEASE HELP EMILY(1917); SEVENTH SIN,
THE(1917); WHERE LOVE IS(1917); MY WIFE(1918); RICHEST GIRL, THE(1918)
Bill Murdock
GREY FOX, THE(1983, Can.)
George Murdock
HE RIDES TALL(1964); TAGGART(1964); GUNN(1967); TODD KILLINGS,
THE(1971); MACK, THE(1973); WILLIE DYNAMITE(1973); EARTHQUAKE(1974);
HANGUP(1974); THOMASINE AND BUSHROD(1974); BREAKER! BREAKER!(1977);
THUNDER AND LIGHTNING(1977); SHOOT THE MOON(1982); SWORD AND THE
SORCERER, THE(1982)
Henry Murdock
KANGAROO(1952)
Jack Murdock
CRAZY WORLD OF JULIUS VROODER, THE(1974); NEWMAN'S LAW(1974);
MOVING VIOLATION(1976); CUTTER AND BONE(1981); HONKY TONK FREE-
WAY(1981)
Janet Murdock
VERDICT, THE(1946)
Joel Murdock
INVITATION TO MURDER(1962, Brit.), w
Kermit Murdock
IN THE HEAT OF THE NIGHT(1967); ON A CLEAR DAY YOU CAN SEE
FOREVER(1970)
Michael Murdock
OTHER SIDE OF THE MOUNTAIN, THE(1975)
Perry Murdock
COVERED WAGON TRAILS(1930); HEADIN' NORTH(1930); MAN FROM HELL'S
EDGES(1932); YOUNG BLOOD(1932); BREED OF THE BORDER(1933); CRASHING
BROADWAY(1933); GALLANT FOOL, THE(1933); DEMON FOR TROUBLE, A(1934);
KID COURAGEOUS(1935); PARADISE CANYON(1935); WESTERN JUSTICE(1935);
BORDER PHANTOM(1937); SHAKIEST GUN IN THE WEST, THE(1968), set d
Silents
CAPTAIN CARELESS(1928); AMAZING VAGABOND(1929); OKLAHOMA SHE-
RIFF, THE(1930)
Misc. Silents
LIGHTING SPEED(1928); COVERED WAGON TRAILS(1930)
Richard Murdock
GHOST TRAIN, THE(1941, Brit.); TERROR, THE(1941, Brit.)
Rod Murdock
NIGHT EVELYN CAME OUT OF THE GRAVE, THE(1973, Ital.)
Tim Murdock
THIRTY SECONDS OVER TOKYO(1944); KEEP YOUR POWDER DRY(1945);
THRILL OF A ROMANCE(1945); HOODLUM SAINT, THE(1946); PHILO VANCE
RETURNS(1947)
Dennis Muren
EQUINOX(1970), p, spec eff; CLOSE ENCOUNTERS OF THE THIRD KIND(1977),
ph; EMPIRE STRIKES BACK, THE(1980), spec eff; RETURN OF THE JEDI(1983),
spec eff
1984
INDIANA JONES AND THE TEMPLE OF DOOM(1984), spec eff
Paule Muret
EVERY MAN FOR HIMSELF(1980, Fr.)
G. Muretta
EMBALMER, THE(1966, Ital.), w
Colleen Murff
HOW TO BEAT THE HIGH COST OF LIVING(1980)
Jane Murfin
DANCE HALL(1929), w; HALF-MARRIAGE(1929), w; STREET GIRL(1929), w;
LAWFUL LARCENY(1930), w; LEATHERNECKING(1930), w; PAY OFF, THE(1930),
w; RUNAWAY BRIDE(1930), w; SEVEN KEYS TO BALDPATE(1930), w; FRIENDS
AND LOVERS(1931), w; TOO MANY COOKS(1931), w; WHITE SHOULDERS(1931),
w; ROCKABYE(1932), w; SMILIN' THROUGH(1932), w; WAY BACK HOME(1932), w;
WHAT PRICE HOLLYWOOD?(1932), w; YOUNG BRIDE(1932), w; AFTER TO-
NIGHT(1933), w; ANN VICKERS(1933), w; DOUBLE HARNESS(1933), w; OUR BET-
TERS(1933), w; SILVER CORD(1933), w; CRIME DOCTOR, THE(1934), w;
FOUNTAIN, THE(1934), w; LIFE OF VERGIE WINTERS, THE(1934), w; LITTLE
MINISTER, THE(1934), w; SPITFIRE(1934), w; THIS MAN IS MINE(1934), w;
ROBERTA(1935), w; ROMANCE IN MANHATTAN(1935), w; COME AND GET
IT(1936), w; I'LL TAKE ROMANCE(1937), w; THAT GIRL FROM PARIS(1937), w;
SHINING HOUR, THE(1938), w; STAND UP AND FIGHT(1939), w; WOMEN,
THE(1939), w; PRIDE AND PREJUDICE(1940), w; ANDY HARDY'S PRIVATE
SECRETARY(1941), w; SMILIN' THROUGH(1941), w; FLIGHT FOR FREE-
DOM(1943), w; DRAGON SEED(1944), w
Silents
RIGHT TO LIE, THE(1919), w; AMATEUR WIFE, THE(1920), w; PLAYTHINGS OF
DESTINY(1921), w; SILENT CALL, THE(1921), w; NOTORIOUS LADY, THE(1927),
w; LILAC TIME(1928), w
Misc. Silents
FLAPPER WIVES(1924), d
V. Murganov
WAR AND PEACE(1968, USSR)
Victor Murganov
WATERLOO(1970, Ital./USSR)
Stephanie Murgaski
SCREWBALLS(1983)
Henri Murger
MIMI(1935, Brit.), w; LA BOHEME(1965, Ital.), w
Sol Murgi
MEXICAN HAYRIDE(1948)
Antonella Murgia
STOP TRAIN 349(1964, Fr./Ital./Ger.); SQUEEZE, THE(1980, Ital.)
Misc. Talkies
REBORN(1978)

Pier Giuseppe Murgia
THANK YOU, AUNT(1969, Ital.), w
Tiberio Murgia
BIG DEAL ON MADONNA STREET, THE(1960); GREAT WAR, THE(1961, Fr., Ital.); DAMON AND PYTHIAS(1962); RIFF RAFF GIRLS(1962, Fr./Ital.); FIASCO IN MILAN(1963, Fr./Ital.); EVIL EYE(1964 Ital.); AFTER THE FOX(1966, U.S./Brit./Ital.); THAT MAN GEORGE!(1967, Fr./Ital./Span.); GIRL WITH A PISTOL, THE(1968, Ital.)
Lydie Murguet
ZITA(1968, Fr.)
Muriel
SEVENTH VEIL, THE(1946, Brit.), w
Emilio Gomez Muriel
LOS AUTOMATAS DE LA MUERTE(1960, Mex.), p; EMPTY STAR, THE(1962, Mex.), p&d; NEUTRON CONTRA EL DR. CARONTE(1962, Mex.), p; NEUTRON EL ENMASCARADO NEGRO(1962, Mex.), p; GIGANTES PLANETARIOS(1965, Mex.), p
Christine Murillo
POURQUOI PAS!(1979, Fr.)
Eduardo Murillo
VIVA MARIA(1965, Fr./Ital.)
Gerry Murillo
TESTAMENT(1983)
Mary Murillo
ACCUSED–STAND UP(1930, Fr.), w; PARISIAN, THE(1931, Fr.), w; MY OLD DUTCH(1934, Brit.), w
Silents
AMBITION(1916), w; EAST LYNNE(1916), w; ETERNAL SAPHO, THE(1916), w; JACK AND THE BEANSTALK(1917), w; NEW YORK PEACOCK, THE(1917), w; OUTWITTED(1917), w; AVENGING TRAIL, THE(1918), w; OTHER MAN'S WIFE, THE(1919), w; NEW YORK IDEA, THE(1920), w; SHAMS OF SOCIETY(1921), w; MOONSHINE VALLEY(1922), w; FORBIDDEN CARGOES(1925, Brit.), w
Miguel Murillo
UP IN SMOKE(1978)
Ted Murkland
OPEN SECRET(1948), w
Allan Murnane
Misc. Silents
LOTTERY MAN, THE(1916)
Allen Murnane
Misc. Silents
HAZEL KIRKE(1916)
Mary Murnane
Silents
IN THE DAYS OF SAINT PATRICK(1920, Brit.)
F. W. Murnau
FOUR DEVILS(1929), d; CITY GIRL(1930), d
Silents
NOSFERATU, THE VAMPIRE(1922, Ger.), d; LAST LAUGH, THE(1924, Ger.), d; FAUST(1926, Ger.), d; SUNRISE–A SONG OF TWO HUMANS(1927), d; TARTUFFE(1927, Ger.), d; TABU(1931), p, d, w
Misc. Silents
SATANAS(1919, Ger.), d; HEAD OF JANUS, THE(1920, Ger.), d; HUNCHBACK AND THE DANCER, THE(1920, Ger.), d; HAUNTED CASTLE, THE(1921, Ger.), d; PHANTOM, THE(1922, Ger.), d
Christopher Murney
SLAP SHOT(1977)
1984
ULTIMATE SOLUTION OF GRACE QUIGLEY, THE(1984)
Muro
LONE TRAIL, THE(1932)
Silents
PHANTOM OF THE NORTH(1929)
Marta Fernandez Muro
TO BEGIN AGAIN(1982, Span.)
Venancio Muro
AWFUL DR. ORLOFF, THE(1964, Span./Fr.)
Ferdinando Murolo
THREE BROTHERS(1982, Ital.)
Giuseppe Murolo
SILHOUETTES(1982), a, d, w
Roberto Murolo
COUNTERFEITERS, THE(1953, Ital.)
Y. Muromsky
Misc. Silents
IN THE KINGDOM OF OIL AND MILLIONS(1916, USSR)
Hideo Murota
MERRY CHRISTMAS MR. LAWRENCE(1983, Jap./Brit.)
Richard Murphett
IN SEARCH OF ANNA(1978, Aus.)
Michael Martin Murphey
HARD COUNTRY(1981), w
Michael Murphey
1984
HAMBONE AND HILLIE(1984), w
Al Murphy
GANG'S ALL HERE, THE(1943); MR. LUCKY(1943); SKY'S THE LIMIT, THE(1943); NONE BUT THE LONELY HEART(1944); CORNERED(1945); DAKOTA(1945); DUFFY'S TAVERN(1945); FLAME OF THE BARBARY COAST(1945); JOHNNY ANGEL(1945); HOODLUM SAINT, THE(1946); STRANGE LOVE OF MARTHA IVERS, THE(1946); THREE LITTLE GIRLS IN BLUE(1946); BUCK PRIVATES COME HOME(1947); LIKELY STORY, A(1947); SINBAD THE SAILOR(1947); TRAIL STREET(1947); TYCOON(1947); WILD HARVEST(1947); ALL MY SONS(1948); BOLD FRONTIERSMAN, THE(1948); RACE STREET(1948); SAXON CHARM, THE(1948); YOU GOTTA STAY HAPPY(1948); HOLIDAY AFFAIR(1949); UNDERCOVER MAN, THE(1949); HARRIET CRAIG(1950); HIT PARADE OF 1951(1950); SURRENDER(1950); WOMAN ON PIER 13, THE(1950); DOUBLE DYNAMITE(1951); I WANT YOU(1951); MEET ME AFTER THE SHOW(1951); ON DANGEROUS GROUND(1951); PEOPLE WILL TALK(1951); RACKET, THE(1951); LAS VEGAS STORY, THE(1952); ONE MINUTE TO ZERO(1952); QUIET MAN, THE(1952); JET PILOT(1957)

Alex Murphy
MADMAN(1982)
Althea Murphy
UNTAMED FURY(1947)
Andrew T Murphy
CROSS AND THE SWITCHBLADE, THE(1970)
Audie Murphy
BEYOND GLORY(1948); TEXAS, BROOKLYN AND HEAVEN(1948); BAD BOY(1949); KANSAS RAIDERS(1950); KID FROM TEXAS, THE(1950); SIERRA(1950); CIMARRON KID, THE(1951); RED BADGE OF COURAGE, THE(1951); DUEL AT SILVER CREEK, THE(1952); COLUMN SOUTH(1953); GUNSMOKE(1953); TUMBLEWEED(1953); DESTRY(1954); DRUMS ACROSS THE RIVER(1954); RIDE CLEAR OF DIABLO(1954); TO HELL AND BACK(1955), a, w; WALK THE PROUD LAND(1956); WORLD IN MY CORNER(1956); GUNS OF FORT PETTICOAT, THE(1957); JOE BUTTERFLY(1957); NIGHT PASSAGE(1957); GUN RUNNERS, THE(1958); QUIET AMERICAN, THE(1958); RIDE A CROOKED TRAIL(1958); CAST A LONG SHADOW(1959); NO NAME ON THE BULLET(1959); WILD AND THE INNOCENT, THE(1959); HELL BENT FOR LEATHER(1960); SEVEN WAYS FROM SUNDOWN(1960); UNFORGIVEN, THE(1960); BATTLE AT BLOODY BEACH(1961); POSSE FROM HELL(1961); SIX BLACK HORSES(1962); SHOWDOWN(1963); APACHE RIFLES(1964); BULLET FOR A BADMAN(1964); GUNFIGHT AT COMANCHE CREEK(1964); QUICK GUN, THE(1964); WAR IS HELL(1964); ARIZONA RAIDERS(1965); GUNPOINT(1966); TEXICAN, THE(1966, U.S./Span.); TRUNK TO CAIRO(1966, Israel/Ger.); 40 GUNS TO APACHE PASS(1967); TIME FOR DYING, A(1971), a, p
Basil Buller Murphy
ON THE BEACH(1959)
Ben Murphy
YOURS, MINE AND OURS(1968); 1,000 PLANE RAID, THE(1969); SIDECAR RACERS(1975, Aus.); TIME WALKER(1982)
Betty Murphy
URBAN COWBOY(1980)
Bill Murphy
DAWN OVER IRELAND(1938, Irish); DUFFY'S TAVERN(1945); STORY OF G.I. JOE, THE(1945); SECRETS OF A SORORITY GIRL(1946); UNCONQUERED(1947); FAMILY HONEYMOON(1948); FOREIGN AFFAIR, A(1948); JUNGLE PATROL(1948); PRAIRIE, THE(1948); DEAR WIFE(1949); I WAS A MALE WAR BRIDE(1949); IT HAPPENS EVERY SPRING(1949); SANDS OF IWO JIMA(1949); BIG HEAT, THE(1953)
Bill "Red" Murphy
NOB HILL(1945); YOUNG WIDOW(1946)
Bob Murphy
BROADWAY GONDOLIER(1935); MURDER MAN(1935); COLLEEN(1936); EASY LIVING(1937); HIDEAWAY GIRL(1937); PORTIA ON TRIAL(1937); YOU'RE A SWEETHEART(1937); GIRL OF THE GOLDEN WEST, THE(1938); SHINE ON, HARVEST MOON(1944)
Bri Murphy
TEENAGE ZOMBIES(1960)
Brian Murphy
SPARROWS CAN'T SING(1963, Brit.); BOY FRIEND, THE(1971, Brit.); RAGMAN'S DAUGHTER, THE(1974, Brit.); GEORGE AND MILDRED(1980, Brit.)
Misc. Talkies
MAN ABOUT THE HOUSE(1974, Brit.)
Brianne Murphy
FATSO(1980), ph
C.B. Murphy
Silents
ROWDY, THE(1921)
Misc. Silents
MAN TAMER, THE(1921)
Catherine Murphy
Misc. Silents
WASTED LIVES(1923); WHAT THREE MEN WANTED(1924)
Charles Murphy
STORMY(1935); NIGHT WAITRESS(1936); WESTBOUND LIMITED(1937); MIDNIGHT INTRUDER(1938); ROAD TO RENO, THE(1938); ROMANCE OF THE ROCKIES(1938); NEW FRONTIER(1939); YOU CAN'T CHEAT AN HONEST MAN(1939); TULSA KID, THE(1940); GIRL IN TROUBLE(1963); NIGHTMARE IN BLOOD(1978)
Silents
RIDERS OF THE DAWN(1920); SOULS FOR SALE(1923); ANYTHING ONCE(1925), ph
Charles A. Murphy
DAMN CITIZEN(1958); DIRTY HARRY(1971)
Charles B. Murphy
ONE NIGHT IN THE TROPICS(1940)
Silents
RED LIGHTS(1923)
Charles Thomas Murphy
NICKELODEON(1976); WHOLLY MOSES(1980); HISTORY OF THE WORLD, PART 1(1981)
Charlie Murphy
WESTLAND CASE, THE(1937); AMERICAN GRAFFITI(1973)
Christopher Murphy
GAMERA VERSUS GUIRON(1969, Jap.); VALLEY GIRL(1983)
Clarise Murphy
TYCOON(1947)
Daisy Murphy
MEN OF IRELAND(1938, Ireland)
Dara Murphy
LOVE CHILD(1982)
David Murphy
LOVING COUPLES(1980); WHOLLY MOSES(1980); JEKYLL AND HYDE...TOGETHER AGAIN(1982); MAKING LOVE(1982)
Dean Murphy
BROADWAY RHYTHM(1944)
Dennis Murphy
EYE OF THE DEVIL(1967, Brit.), w; SERGEANT, THE(1968), w; TODD KILLINGS, THE(1971), w; FRIDAY THE 13TH PART II(1981), p

Don Murphy
DRIFTIN' RIVER(1946)
Misc. Talkies
FROM THE DESK OF MARGARET TYDING(1958)
Donald Murphy
KILLER LEOPARD(1954); MASTERSON OF KANSAS(1954); LONG GRAY LINE, THE(1955); SHACK OUT ON 101(1955); ON THE THRESHOLD OF SPACE(1956); STRANGE INTRUDER(1956); FRANKENSTEIN'S DAUGHTER(1958); LORD LOVE A DUCK(1966)
Dudley Murphy
JAZZ HEAVEN(1929), w; CONFESSIONS OF A CO-ED(1931), d; SPORT PARADE, THE(1932), d; EMPEROR JONES(1933), d; NIGHT IS YOUNG, THE(1935), d; DON'T GAMBLE WITH LOVE(1936), d; MAIN STREET LAWYER(1939), d; ONE THIRD OF A NATION(1939), p&d, w
Silents
ALEX THE GREAT(1928), d&w; STOCKS AND BLONDES(1928), d&w
Misc. Silents
HIGH SPEED LEE(1923), d
E. Danny Murphy
GRADUATION DAY(1981)
Earl Murphy
SHADOW VALLEY(1947)
Ed Murphy
STARTING OVER(1979)
Eddie Murphy
48 HOURS(1982); TRADING PLACES(1983)
1984
BEST DEFENSE(1984); BEVERLY HILLS COP(1984)
Edna Murphy
MY MAN(1928); GREYHOUND LIMITED, THE(1929); KID GLOVES(1929); SAP, THE(1929); STOLEN KISSES(1929); DANCING SWEETIES(1930); LITTLE JOHNNY JONES(1930); LUMMOX(1930); SECOND CHOICE(1930); WIDE OPEN(1930); ANYBODY'S BLONDE(1931); BEHIND OFFICE DOORS(1931); FORGOTTEN WOMEN(1932); GIRL OF THE RIO(1932)
Silents
BRANDED WOMAN, THE(1920); NORTH WIND'S MALICE, THE(1920); OVER THE HILL TO THE POORHOUSE(1920); JOLT, THE(1921); LIVE WIRES(1921); GALLOPING KID, THE(1922); ORDEAL, THE(1922); PAID BACK(1922); RIDIN' WILD(1922); NOBODY'S BRIDE(1923); AFTER THE BALL(1924); DAUGHTERS OF TODAY(1924); KING OF THE WILD HORSES, THE(1924); CLOTHES MAKE THE PIRATE(1925); POLICE PATROL, THE(1925); COLLEGE DAYS(1926); OH, WHAT A NIGHT!(1926); ALL ABOARD(1927); SILVER COMES THROUGH(1927); SUNSET LEGION, THE(1928)
Misc. Silents
TO THE HIGHEST BIDDER(1918); DYNAMITE ALLEN(1921); PLAY SQUARE(1921); WHAT LOVE WILL DO(1921); CAUGHT BLUFFING(1922); EXTRA! EXTRA!(1922); MAN BETWEEN, THE(1923); ERMINE AND RHINESTONES(1925); HIS BUDDY'S WIFE(1925); LENA RIVERS(1925); LYING WIVES(1925); MAN MUST LIVE, THE(1925); WILDFIRE(1925); LITTLE GIANT, THE(1926); OBEY THE LAW(1926); WIVES AT AUCTION(1926); BLACK DIAMOND EXPRESS, THE(1927); BURNT FINGERS(1927); CRUISE OF THE HELLION, THE(1927); DEARIE(1927); HIS FOREIGN WIFE(1927); MCFADDEN FLATS(1927); MODERN DAUGHTERS(1927); ROSE OF THE BOWERY(1927); SILENT HERO, THE(1927); TARZAN AND THE GOLDEN LION(1927); VALLEY OF HELL, THE(1927); WILFUL YOUTH(1927); ACROSS THE ATLANTIC(1928); MIDNIGHT ADVENTURE, THE(1928); BACHELOR'S CLUB, THE(1929)
Edward Murphy
MAD DOCTOR OF BLOOD ISLAND, THE(1969, Phil./U.S.); RAW FORCE(1982), d&w
Eileen Murphy
SINFUL DAVEY(1969, Brit.); WALK WITH LOVE AND DEATH, A(1969)
Elizabeth Murphy
MC CABE AND MRS. MILLER(1971)
Emmett Murphy
WALK EAST ON BEACON(1952), w; CANYON CROSSROADS(1955), w; VALERIE(1957), w
F.O. Murphy
FOR FREEDOM(1940, Brit.)
Fidelma Murphy
NEVER PUT IT IN WRITING(1964); FIGHTING PRINCE OF DONEGAL, THE(1966, Brit.); SINFUL DAVEY(1969, Brit.)
Fieldma Murphy
Misc. Talkies
PHILADELPHIA HERE I COME(1975)
Frank Murphy
IN LOVE AND WAR(1958)
Fred Murphy
GIRLFRIENDS(1978), ph; LOCAL COLOR(1978), ph; SCENIC ROUTE, THE(1978), ph; IMPOSTORS(1979), ph; HEARTLAND(1980), ph; TELL ME A RIDDLE(1980), ph; Q(1982), ph; EDDIE AND THE CRUISERS(1983), ph; STATE OF THINGS, THE(1983), ph; TOUCHED(1983), ph
Gemma Murphy
1984
SCRUBBERS(1984, Brit.)
Geoff Murphy
SLEEPING DOGS(1977, New Zealand), spec eff; GOODBYE PORK PIE(1981, New Zealand), p, d, w
1984
UTU(1984, New Zealand), p, d, w
Geoffrey Murphy
WOMAN IN HIDING(1953, Brit.)
George Murphy
JEALOUSY(1934); KID MILLIONS(1934); AFTER THE DANCE(1935); I'LL LOVE YOU ALWAYS(1935); PUBLIC MENACE(1935); WOMAN TRAP(1936); BROADWAY MELODY OF '38(1937); LONDON BY NIGHT(1937); TOP OF THE TOWN(1937); WOMEN MEN MARRY, THE(1937); YOU'RE A SWEETHEART(1937); HOLD THAT CO-ED(1938); LETTER OF INTRODUCTION(1938); LITTLE MISS BROADWAY(1938); RISKY BUSINESS(1939); BROADWAY MELODY OF 1940(1940); LITTLE NELLIE KELLY(1940); PUBLIC DEB NO. 1(1940); TWO GIRLS ON BROADWAY(1940); GIRL, A GUY AND A GOB, A(1941); RINGSIDE MAISIE(1941); RISE AND SHINE(1941); TOM, DICK AND HARRY(1941); FOR ME AND MY GAL(1942); MAYOR OF 44TH STREET, THE(1942); NAVY COMES THROUGH, THE(1942); POWERS GIRL, THE(1942); BATAAN(1943); THIS IS THE ARMY(1943); BROADWAY RHYTHM(1944); SHOW BUSINESS(1944); STEP LIVELY(1944); HAVING WONDERFUL CRIME(1945); UP GOES MAISIE(1946); ARNELO AFFAIR, THE(1947); CYNTHIA(1947); BIG CITY(1948); TENTH AVENUE ANGEL(1948); BATTLEGROUND(1949); BORDER INCIDENT(1949); IT'S A BIG COUNTRY(1951); NO QUESTIONS ASKED(1951); TALK ABOUT A STRANGER(1952); WALK EAST ON BEACON(1952)
Gerard Murphy
BRINK'S JOB, THE(1978)
1984
ONCE UPON A TIME IN AMERICA(1984); POPE OF GREENWICH VILLAGE, THE(1984); SACRED HEARTS(1984, Brit.)
Gerard E. Murphy
SORCERER(1977)
Gerry Murphy
FORMULA, THE(1980)
Harold Murphy
LASSIE'S GREAT ADVENTURE(1963), spec eff
Harry Murphy
EDDIE MACON'S RUN(1983)
Horace Murphy
ALIAS JOHN LAW(1935); CROOKED TRAIL, THE(1936); EVERYMAN'S LAW(1936); FUGITIVE SHERIFF, THE(1936); LAST OF THE WARRENS, THE(1936); LUCKY TERROR(1936); MINE WITH THE IRON DOOR, THE(1936); SONG OF THE TRAIL(1936); TOO MUCH BEEF(1936); UNDERCOVER MAN(1936); VALLEY OF THE LAWLESS(1936); ANYTHING FOR A THRILL(1937); ARIZONA DAYS(1937); BAR Z BAD MEN(1937); BOOTHILL BRIGADE(1937); BORDER PHANTOM(1937); COME ON, COWBOYS(1937); COUNTY FAIR(1937); DOOMED AT SUNDOWN(1937); FRAME-UP THE(1937); GAMBLING TERROR, THE(1937); GHOST TOWN GOLD(1937); GIRL SAID NO, THE(1937); GUN LORDS OF STIRRUP BASIN(1937); GUN RANGER, THE(1937); LAWLESS LAND(1937); LIGHTNIN' CRANDALL(1937); MYSTERY OF THE HOODED HORSEMEN, THE(1937); RANGER COURAGE(1937); RED ROPE, THE(1937); RIDERS OF THE ROCKIES(1937); ROGUE OF THE RANGE(1937); SING, COWBOY, SING(1937); STARS OVER ARIZONA(1937); SUNDOWN SAUNDERS(1937); TEX RIDES WITH THE BOY SCOUTS(1937); TRAIL OF VENGEANCE(1937); TROUBLE IN TEXAS(1937); WESTERN GOLD(1937); BILLY THE KID RETURNS(1938); COLORADO KID(1938); DURANGO VALLEY RAIDERS(1938); FRONTIER TOWN(1938); PAROLED–TO DIE(1938); ROLLIN' PLAINS(1938); ROLLING CARAVANS(1938); STARLIGHT OVER TEXAS(1938); STOLEN HEAVEN(1938); STRANGER FROM ARIZONA, THE(1938); THUNDER IN THE DESERT(1938); UTAH TRAIL(1938); WHERE THE BUFFALO ROAM(1938); WIDE OPEN FACES(1938); COWBOYS FROM TEXAS(1939); DESPERATE TRAILS(1939); DOWN THE WYOMING TRAIL(1939); FIGHTING MAD(1939); OKLAHOMA FRONTIER(1939); OKLAHOMA KID, THE(1939); ROLLIN' WESTWARD(1939); ROVIN' TUMBLEWEEDS(1939); SAGA OF DEATH VALLEY(1939); SONG OF THE BUCKAROO(1939); SUNDOWN ON THE PRAIRIE(1939); BOOM TOWN(1940); GHOST VALLEY RAIDERS(1940); MELODY RANCH(1940); RANGE BUSTERS, THE(1940); ARIZONA BOUND(1941); BAD MAN OF DEADWOOD(1941); HONKY TONK(1941); FALLEN ANGEL(1945); RIDERS OF THE DAWN(1945); SCARLET STREET(1945); SONG OF OLD WYOMING(1945); CRACK-UP(1946)
Misc. Talkies
SPRINGTIME IN TEXAS(1945)
Howard Murphy
SATAN'S MISTRESS(1982)
J.J. Murphy
1984
CAL(1984, Ireland)
Jack Murphy
GODLESS GIRL, THE(1929); IT'S A GREAT LIFE(1936); MILKY WAY, THE(1936); PIGSKIN PARADE(1936); ROSE BOWL(1936); MAYTIME(1937); SHOPWORN ANGEL(1938); YOUNG DR. KILDARE(1938); UNDERCURRENT(1946)
Silents
PETER PAN(1924); STELLA DALLAS(1925); TUMBLEWEEDS(1925)
Jack F. Murphy
PICK-UP SUMMER(1981), p
June Murphy
RICOCHET(1966, Brit.); DEADLY AFFAIR, THE(1967, Brit.)
James Murphy
ANGELS FROM HELL(1968); LAST AMERICAN HERO, THE(1973)
James A. Murphy
Silents
RACING HEARTS(1923)
Jerry Murphy
KING OF COMEDY, THE(1983)
Jim Murphy
MISTER ROBERTS(1955); SONG AND THE SILENCE, THE(1969)
Jim Murphy [Carlo Rustichelli]
WHAT!(1965, Fr./Brit./Ital.), m
Jimmy Murphy
CELL 2455, DEATH ROW(1955); CRASHING LAS VEGAS(1956); HOT SHOTS(1956); HOLD THAT HYPNOTIST(1957); JEANNE EAGELS(1957); LOOKING FOR DANGER(1957); ROCKABILLY BABY(1957); SPOOK CHASERS(1957); CURSE OF THE UNDEAD(1959); LONE TEXAN(1959); PARATROOP COMMAND(1959); PLATINUM HIGH SCHOOL(1960); CALIFORNIA(1963); WALL OF NOISE(1963); SANDPIPER, THE(1965); FOLLOW ME, BOYS!(1966); OUT OF SIGHT(1966); GNOME-MOBILE, THE(1967); GOOD GUYS AND THE BAD GUYS, THE(1969)
Joan Murphy
DON'T DRINK THE WATER(1969); MIDNIGHT COWBOY(1969); LIMBO(1972)
Joe Murphy
Silents
CAT AND THE CANARY, THE(1927)
John Murphy
LAWLESS, THE(1950); NEVER TAKE NO FOR AN ANSWER(1952, Brit./Ital.); HELL'S HORIZON(1955); UNDER FIRE(1957); DIMBOOLA(1979, Aus.); OUTSIDER, THE(1980); GALLIPOLI(1981, Aus.); ROAD GAMES(1981, Aus.); LIGHT YEARS AWAY(1982, Fr./Switz.)
1984
GIVE MY REGARDS TO BROAD STREET(1984, Brit.)

John Daly Murphy
Silents
OUR MRS. McCHESNEY(1918); OH, JOHNNY(1919); ICEBOUND(1924)
Misc. Silents
GHOSTS OF YESTERDAY(1918); SECRET STRINGS(1918)
Joseph P. Murphy
KID FROM SANTA FE, THE(1940), w
Karen Murphy
1984
THIS IS SPINAL TAP(1984), p
Katherine Murphy
GAMERA VERSUS MONSTER K(1970, Jap.)
Kathleen Murphy
Silents
KNOCKNAGOW(1918, Ireland)
Misc. Silents
WHEN LOVE CAME TO GAVIN BURKE(1918); WILLY REILLY AND HIS COL-
LEEN BAWN(1918, Brit.)
Linus Murphy
GOODBYE PORK PIE(1981, New Zealand)
Lyn Murphy
PUBERTY BLUES(1983, Aus.)
Mark Murphy
JUST LIKE A WOMAN(1967, Brit.)
Martin Murphy
Misc. Talkies
BLACK ISLAND(1979, Brit.)
Silents
20,000 LEAGUES UNDER THE SEA(1916)
Marty Murphy
MR. MAGOO'S HOLIDAY FESTIVAL(1970), prod d
Mary Murphy
DARLING, HOW COULD YOU!(1951); MY FAVORITE SPY(1951); SAILOR
BEWARE(1951); WHEN WORLDS COLLIDE(1951); TURNING POINT, THE(1952);
HOUDINI(1953); MAIN STREET TO BROADWAY(1953); OFF LIMITS(1953); WILD
ONE, THE(1953); BEACHHEAD(1954); MAD MAGICIAN, THE(1954); MAKE HASTE
TO LIVE(1954); SITTING BULL(1954); DESPERATE HOURS, THE(1955); HELL'S
ISLAND(1955); MAN ALONE, A(1955); FINGER OF GUILT(1956, Brit.); MAVERICK
QUEEN, THE(1956); LIVE FAST, DIE YOUNG(1958); CRIME AND PUNISHMENT,
U.S.A.(1959); ELECTRONIC MONSTER. THE(1960, Brit.); FORTY POUNDS OF TROU-
BLE(1962); HARLOW(1965); JUNIOR BONNER(1972)
Misc. Talkies
DEADLY AUGUST(1966)
Matt Murphy
GUYS AND DOLLS(1955); HARDER THEY FALL, THE(1956); BLUES BROTHERS,
THE(1980)
Maura Murphy
LIFE OF HER OWN, A(1950); STRANGE FASCINATION(1952); YANK IN INDO-
CHINA, A(1952); MISTER ROBERTS(1955); TOWARD THE UNKNOWN(1956); DRAN-
GO(1957)
Maurice Murphy
SEAS BENEATH, THE(1931); WOMEN GO ON FOREVER(1931); DIVORCE IN THE
FAMILY(1932); FAITHLESS(1932); PILGRIMAGE(1933); FOUND ALIVE(1934); CRU-
SADES, THE(1935); CURLY TOP(1935); MAN WHO RECLAIMED HIS HEAD,
THE(1935); PRIVATE WORLDS(1935); DOWN TO THE SEA(1936); GENTLE JU-
LIA(1936); PRISONER OF SHARK ISLAND(1936); ROMEO AND JULIET(1936);
ROAD BACK,THE(1937); TOVARICH(1937); UNDER SUSPICION(1937); DELIN-
QUENT PARENTS(1938); MY BILL(1938); NURSE FROM BROOKLYN(1938); CA-
REER(1939); COVERED TRAILER, THE(1939); FORGED PASSPORT(1939); ABE
LINCOLN IN ILLINOIS(1940); WOLF OF NEW YORK(1940); RELUCTANT DRAGON,
THE(1941); TO BE OR NOT TO BE(1942); GUY NAMED JOE, A(1943); DESTINATION
TOKYO(1944); SEE HERE, PRIVATE HARGROVE(1944); FATTY FINN(1980, Aus.), d
Misc. Talkies
DOCTORS AND NURSES(1983), d
Silents
STELLA DALLAS(1925); ALIAS THE DEACON(1928); MICHIGAN KID, THE(1928)
Misc. Silents
SPIRIT OF YOUTH, THE(1929)
Maurice "Loop the Loop" Murphy
HELL'S ANGELS(1930)
Melissa Murphy
MAGNIFICENT SEVEN RIDE, THE(1972)
Michael Murphy
LOLLIPOP COVER, THE(1965), ph; DOUBLE TROUBLE(1967); COUNT-
DOWN(1968); LEGEND OF LYLAH CLARE, THE(1968); ARRANGEMENT,
THE(1969); DREAMS OF GLASS(1969), ph; THAT COLD DAY IN THE PARK(1969,
U.S./Can.); BREWSTER McCLOUD(1970); COUNT YORGA, VAMPIRE(1970); M(1970);
MC CABE AND MRS. MILLER(1971); WHAT'S UP, DOC?(1972); THIEF WHO CAME
TO DINNER, THE(1973); PHASE IV(1974); NASHVILLE(1975); FRONT, THE(1976);
GREAT BANK HOAX, THE(1977); CLASS OF MISS MAC MICHAEL, THE(1978,
Brit./U.S.); UNMARRIED WOMAN, AN(1978); MANHATTAN(1979); DEAD
KIDS(1981 Aus./New Zealand); ST. HELENS(1981), p; BEACH GIRLS(1982), ph;
YEAR OF LIVING DANGEROUSLY, THE(1982, Aus.)
1984
CLOAK AND DAGGER(1984)
Michael D. Murphy
SILENT SCREAM(1980), ph
1984
MIRRORS(1984), ph
Michael V. Murphy
1984
HARD TO HOLD(1984)
Micil Murphy
TAKE THE MONEY AND RUN(1969)
Mike Murphy
LENNY(1974); COACH(1978), ph
Morris Murphy
COLLEGE COQUETTE, THE(1929)

Pamela Murphy
ZIGZAG(1970)
Pat Murphy
BORN IN FLAMES(1983)
1984
ANNE DEVLIN(1984, Ireland), p, d&w
Patricia Murphy
OUR HEARTS WERE GROWING UP(1946)
Patrick Murphy
SCUM OF THE EARTH(1963), ed
Patrick J. Murphy
SQUARES(1972), p&d
Patrick Sean Murphy
1984
MICKI AND MAUDE(1984)
Paul Murphy
SOMETHING TO SING ABOUT(1937), art d; LAUGH YOUR BLUES AWAY(1943),
art d; GHOST THAT WALKS ALONE, THE(1944), art d; GIRL IN THE CASE(1944),
art d; JAM SESSION(1944), art d; VIKING QUEEN, THE(1967, Brit.); MC KENZIE
BREAK, THE(1970); QUACKSER FORTUNE HAS A COUSIN IN THE BRONX(1970);
UNDERGROUND(1970, Brit.); BUGSY MALONE(1976, Brit.)
Ralph Murphy
BIG SHOT, THE(1931), d; MILLIE(1931), w; WOMAN OF EXPERIENCE, A(1931), w;
PANAMA FLO(1932), d; YOUNG BRIDE(1932), w; 70,000 WITNESSES(1932), d; GIRL
WITHOUT A ROOM(1933), d; GOLDEN HARVEST(1933), d; SONG OF THE EA-
GLE(1933), d; STRICTLY PERSONAL(1933), d; GREAT FLIRTATION, THE(1934), d;
MENACE(1934), d; NOTORIOUS SOPHIE LANG, THE(1934), d; PRIVATE SCAN-
DAL(1934), d; SHE MADE HER BED(1934), d; MC FADDEN'S FLATS(1935), d; MEN
WITHOUT NAMES(1935), d; ONE HOUR LATE(1935), d; COLLEGIATE(1936), d;
FLORIDA SPECIAL(1936), d; MAN I MARRY, THE(1936), d; NIGHT CLUB SCAN-
DAL(1937), d; PARTNERS IN CRIME(1937), d; SH! THE OCTOPUS(1937), w; TOP OF
THE TOWN(1937), d; OUR NEIGHBORS-THE CARTERS(1939), d; I WANT A DI-
VORCE(1940), d; GLAMOUR BOY(1941), d; LAS VEGAS NIGHTS(1941), d; MID-
NIGHT ANGEL(1941), d; YOU'RE THE ONE(1941), d; MRS. WIGGS OF THE
CABBAGE PATCH(1942), p, d; NIGHT PLANE FROM CHUNGKING(1942), d; STAR
SPANGLED RHYTHM(1942); SALUTE FOR THREE(1943), d; RAINBOW IS-
LAND(1944), d; SUNBONNET SUE(1945), d, w; TOWN WENT WILD, THE(1945), d;
HOW DO YOU DO?(1946), d; SPIRIT OF WEST POINT, THE(1947); MICKEY(1948),
d; RED STALLION IN THE ROCKIES(1949), d; STAGE TO TUCSON(1950), d; LADY
AND THE BANDIT, THE(1951), d; NEVER TRUST A GAMBLER(1951), d; CAPTAIN
PIRATE(1952), d; LADY IN THE IRON MASK(1952), d; MYSTERY OF THE BLACK
JUNGLE(1955), d, w
Ralph M. Murphy
MAN IN HALF-MOON STREET, THE(1944), d
Ray Livingston Murphy
PRIVATE'S AFFAIR, A(1959), w
Richard Murphy
APACHE KID, THE(1941), w; BACK IN THE SADDLE(1941), w; FLYING
BLIND(1941), w; SINGING HILL, THE(1941), w; CYCLONE KID, THE(1942), w; I
LIVE ON DANGER(1942), w; JESSE JAMES, JR.(1942), w; WILDCAT(1942), w;
WRECKING CREW(1942), w; X MARKS THE SPOT(1942), w; BOOMERANG(1947),
w; CRY OF THE CITY(1948), w; DEEP WATERS(1948), w; SLATTERY'S HURRI-
CANE(1949), w; PANIC IN THE STREETS(1950), w; YOU'RE IN THE NAVY
NOW(1951), w; LES MISERABLES(1952), w; DESERT RATS, THE(1953), w; BROKEN
LANCE(1954), w; THREE STRIPES IN THE SUN(1955), d, w; COMPULSION(1959),
w; LAST ANGRY MAN, THE(1959), w; WACKIEST SHIP IN THE ARMY, THE(1961),
d, w; KIDNAPPING OF THE PRESIDENT, THE(1980, Can.), w; EYEWITNESS(1981)
Silents
ANTICS OF ANN, THE(1917), art d
Robert Murphy
TWO IN A CROWD(1936); LIFE BEGINS IN COLLEGE(1937); NANCY STEELE IS
MISSING(1937); YOU CAN'T HAVE EVERYTHING(1937); IN OLD CHICAGO(1938);
SINGER AND THE DANCER, THE(1977, Aus.), m; E.T. THE EXTRA-TERRE-
STRIAL(1982)
Rock Murphy
SUMMER LOVE(1958)
Rose Murphy
GEORGE WHITE'S SCANDALS(1945)
Rosemary Murphy
THAT NIGHT(1957); YOUNG DOCTORS, THE(1961); TO KILL A MOCKING-
BIRD(1962); ANY WEDNESDAY(1966); BEN(1972); FAN'S NOTES, A(1972, Can.);
YOU'LL LIKE MY MOTHER(1972); ACE ELI AND RODGER OF THE SKIES(1973);
FORTY CARATS(1973); WALKING TALL(1973); JULIA(1977); ATTIC, THE(1979);
HAND, THE(1981)
S. Murphy
Silents
GOLD RUSH, THE(1925)
Sam Murphy
DALTON THAT GOT AWAY(1960)
Scott Murphy
1984
BEVERLY HILLS COP(1984)
Sharon Murphy
HORROR OF PARTY BEACH, THE(1964)
Steve Murphy
Silents
JUSTICE OF THE FAR NORTH(1925); CIRCUS, THE(1928)
Stewart Murphy
HELL'S ANGELS(1930)
Stuart Murphy
PLASTIC DOME OF NORMA JEAN, THE(1966), p, ed
Thomas Murphy
COWARDS(1970); LADY LIBERTY(1972, Ital./Fr.); DOG DAY AFTERNOON(1975)
1984
CRIMES OF PASSION(1984)
Thomas J. Murphy
WRONG MAN, THE(1956)

Timothy Murphy
BUSHIDO BLADE, THE(1982 Brit./U.S.)
Timothy Patrick Murphy
1984
SAM'S SON(1984)
Toni Murphy
MATTER OF INNOCENCE, A(1968, Brit.)
Val Murphy
SOLO(1978, New Zealand/Aus.)
W. J. Murphy
MASSACRE RIVER(1949), ed
Walter Murphy
RAW FORCE(1982), m
Warren B. Murphy
EIGER SANCTION, THE(1975), w
William Murphy
SALTY O'ROURKE(1945); KISS TOMORROW GOODBYE(1950); FIGHTING COAST GUARD(1951); HOODLUM EMPIRE(1952); RED SKIES OF MONTANA(1952); FAIR WIND TO JAVA(1953); GAMBLER FROM NATCHEZ, THE(1954); THREE YOUNG TEXANS(1954), ed; SIX BRIDGES TO CROSS(1955); STRANGER ON HORSEBACK(1955), ed; RAWHIDE TRAIL, THE(1958)
William B. Murphy
ELOPEMENT(1951), ed; GUY WHO CAME BACK, THE(1951), ed; MR. BELVEDERE RINGS THE BELL(1951), ed; DEADLINE—U.S.A.(1952), ed; MONKEY BUSINESS(1952), ed; O. HENRY'S FULL HOUSE(1952), ed; MR. SCOUTMASTER(1953), ed; POWDER RIVER(1953), ed; PRESIDENT'S LADY, THE(1953), ed; KENTUCKIAN, THE(1955), ed; MOHAWK(1956), ed; APRIL LOVE(1957), ed; BACHELOR PARTY, THE(1957), ed; LONELY MAN, THE(1957), ed; KINGS GO FORTH(1958), ed; I, MOBSTER(1959), ed; 4D MAN(1959), ed; TOMBOY AND THE CHAMP(1961), ed; FOLLOW THAT DREAM(1962), ed; CARETAKERS, THE(1963), ed; JOHN GOLDFARB, PLEASE COME HOME(1964), ed; FANTASTIC VOYAGE(1966), ed; ST. VALENTINE'S DAY MASSACRE, THE(1967), ed; PINK JUNGLE, THE(1968), ed
William R. Murphy
PLACE IN THE SUN, A(1951)
William "Red" Murphy
EMERGENCY HOSPITAL(1956)
Murphy the Dog
THEY ONLY KILL THEIR MASTERS(1972)
Al Murray
CATSKILL HONEYMOON(1950)
Alena Murray
THREE FACES OF EVE, THE(1957); HUNTERS, THE(1958); BEST OF EVERYTHING, THE(1959); SAY ONE FOR ME(1959)
Anita Murray
HOT FOR PARIS(1930)
Arthur Murray
YOU CAN'T TAKE IT WITH YOU(1938); JIGGS AND MAGGIE IN SOCIETY(1948)
Barbara Murray
BADGER'S GREEN(1949, Brit.); BOYS IN BROWN(1949, Brit.); DON'T EVER LEAVE ME(1949, Brit.); PASSPORT TO PIMLICO(1949, Brit.); POET'S PUB(1949, Brit.); SARABAND(1949, Brit.); DARK MAN, THE(1951, Brit.); MYSTERY JUNCTION(1951, Brit.); TONY DRAWS A HORSE(1951, Brit.); ANOTHER MAN'S POISON(1952, Brit.); FRIGHTENED MAN, THE(1952, Brit.); HOT ICE(1952, Brit.); BOTH SIDES OF THE LAW(1953, Brit.); DEATM GOES TO SCHOOL(1953, Brit.); MEET MR. LUCIFER(1953, Brit.); TECKMAN MYSTERY, THE(1955, Brit.); CAMPBELL'S KINGDOM(1957, Brit.); DOCTOR AT LARGE(1957, Brit.); CRY FROM THE STREET, A(1959, Brit.); DOCTOR IN DISTRESS(1963, Brit.); OPERATION BULLSHINE(1963, Brit.); PUNCH AND JUDY MAN, THE(1963, Brit.); DANDY IN ASPIC, A(1968, Brit.); SOME WILL, SOME WON'T(1970, Brit.); UP POMPEII(1971, Brit.); TALES FROM THE CRYPT(1972, Brit.)
1984
POWER, THE(1984)
Beck Murray
HE WALKED BY NIGHT(1948), w
Bernard Murray
WICKER MAN, THE(1974, Brit.)
Bert Murray
PORT OF NEW YORK(1949), w
Betty Murray
KLUTE(1971)
Beverley Murray
CATHY'S CURSE(1977, Can.)
Bill Murray
MEATBALLS(1979, Can.); CADDY SHACK(1980); LOOSE SHOES(1980); WHERE THE BUFFALO ROAM(1980); STRIPES(1981); TOOTSIE(1982)
1984
GHOSTBUSTERS(1984); NOTHING LASTS FOREVER(1984); RAZOR'S EDGE, THE(1984), a, w
Misc. Talkies
SHAME OF THE JUNGLE(1980, Fr./Bel.)
Bill Phillips Murray
BUDDY HOLLY STORY, THE(1978)
Billy Murray
CORRUPTION(1968, Brit.); POOR COW(1968, Brit.); UP THE JUNCTION(1968, Brit.); MC VICAR(1982, Brit.)
Bob Murray
Silents
WARMING UP(1928)
Brendan Murray
JAWS 3-D(1983)
Brian Doyle Murray
FUZZ(1972); CADDY SHACK(1980)
Brian Murray
ANGRY SILENCE, THE(1960, Brit.); LEAGUE OF GENTLEMEN, THE(1961, Brit.); PORTRAIT OF THE ARTIST AS A YOUNG MAN, A(1979, Ireland)
Bryan-Doyle Murray
Misc. Talkies
SHAME OF THE JUNGLE(1980, Fr./Bel.)

Charles Murray
CLANCY IN WALL STREET(1930); CAUGHT CHEATING(1931); COHENS AND KELLYS IN TROUBLE, THE(1933); CIRCUS GIRL(1937); COUNTY FAIR(1937); WOMEN AREN'T ANGELS(1942, Brit.)
Misc. Talkies
TWO-FISTED STRANGER(1946)
Silents
TILLIE'S PUNCTURED ROMANCE(1914); SMALL TOWN IDOL, A(1921); LUCK(1923); PAINTED PEOPLE(1924); MY SON(1925); WIZARD OF OZ, THE(1925); IRENE(1926)
Misc. Silents
PUPPY LOVE(1919); LOVE, HONOR AND BEHAVE(1920); MARRIED LIFE(1920); EMPTY HEARTS(1924); GIRL IN THE LIMOUSINE, THE(1924); WHY WOMEN LOVE(1925); BOOB, THE(1926); SUBWAY SADIE(1926)
Charlie Murray
COHENS AND KELLYS IN AFRICA, THE(1930); COHENS AND KELLYS IN SCOTLAND, THE(1930); COHENS, AND KELLYS IN HOLLYWOOD, THE(1932); HYPNOTIZED(1933); DANGEROUS WATERS(1936); BREAKING THE ICE(1938); DOWN MEMORY LANE(1949); PAT AND MIKE(1952); HARRY AND WALTER GO TO NEW YORK(1976); MOVIE MOVIE(1978)
Misc. Talkies
AROUND THE CORNER(1930)
Silents
COHENS AND KELLYS, THE(1926); MIKE(1926); PARADISE(1926); RECKLESS LADY, THE(1926); SILENT LOVER, THE(1926); COHENS AND THE KELLYS IN PARIS, THE(1928); DO YOUR DUTY(1928); FLYING ROMEOS(1928); HEAD MAN, THE(1928); VAMPING VENUS(1928)
Misc. Silents
HOME TALENT(1921); MINE WITH THE IRON DOOR, THE(1924); HER SECOND CHANCE(1926); STEEL PREFERRED(1926); SWEET DADDIES(1926); GORILLA, THE(1927); LIFE OF RILEY, THE(1927); LOST AT THE FRONT(1927); MASKED WOMAN, THE(1927); MCFADDEN FLATS(1927); POOR NUT, THE(1927)
Chic Murray
GREGORY'S GIRL(1982, Brit.)
Misc. Talkies
NAUGHTY WIVES(1974)
Chris Murray
BLUE FIN(1978, Aus.), spec eff; MAD MAX(1979, Aus.), spec eff; STIR(1980, Aus.), spec eff; NEXT OF KIN(1983, Aus.), spec eff
Christine Murray
TRADER HORNEE(1970)
Christopher Murray
I AM THE CHEESE(1983)
David Murray
FOREVER AMBER(1947); RECOMMENDATION FOR MERCY(1975, Can.)
David Christie Murray
Silents
IN HIS GRIP(1921, Brit.), w; PENNILESS MILLIONAIRE, THE(1921, Brit.), w
Dennis Murray
ONE EXCITING WEEK(1946), w; STARS IN YOUR EYES(1956, Brit.)
Dianne T. Murray
ROLLERCOASTER(1977)
Don Murray
BUS STOP(1956); BACHELOR PARTY, THE(1957); HATFUL OF RAIN, A(1957); FROM HELL TO TEXAS(1958); SHAKE HANDS WITH THE DEVIL(1959, Ireland); THESE THOUSAND HILLS(1959); ONE FOOT IN HELL(1960); HOODLUM PRIEST, THE(1961), a, p; ADVISE AND CONSENT(1962); ESCAPE FROM EAST BERLIN(1962); ONE MAN'S WAY(1964); BABY, THE RAIN MUST FALL(1965); KID RODELO(1966, U.S./Span.); PLAINSMAN, THE(1966); SWEET LOVE, BITTER(1967); VIKING QUEEN, THE(1967, Brit.); CHILDISH THINGS(1969), a, p, w; CROSS AND THE SWITCHBLADE, THE(1970), d, w; HAPPY BIRTHDAY, WANDA JUNE(1971); CONQUEST OF THE PLANET OF THE APES(1972); DEADLY HERO(1976); CHARLIE CHAN AND THE CURSE OF THE DRAGON QUEEN(1981); ENDLESS LOVE(1981); I AM THE CHEESE(1983)
Misc. Talkies
CONFESSIONS OF TOM HARRIS(1972); COTTER(1972); CALL ME BY MY RIGHTFUL NAME(1973); DAMIEN'S ISLAND(1976), d
Donald E. Murray
WEDNESDAY CHILDREN, THE(1973)
Douglas Murray
MAN FROM TORONTO, THE(1933, Brit.), w; LIAR'S DICE(1980), ph
Silents
LESSONS IN LOVE(1921), w
Edgar Murray
NARROW MARGIN, THE(1952)
Edgar Murray, Jr.
Misc. Silents
MYSTERY OF NO. 47, THE(1917)
Elisabeth Murray
OH! WHAT A LOVELY WAR(1969, Brit.)
Elizabeth Murray
LUCKY IN LOVE(1929); BACHELOR FATHER(1931)
Elmo Murray
FIGHTING 69TH, THE(1940)
Feg Murray
THAT'S RIGHT–YOU'RE WRONG(1939)
Forbes Murray
EASY LIVING(1937); MAYTIME(1937); SARATOGA(1937); SOULS AT SEA(1937); THAT CERTAIN WOMAN(1937); THEY WON'T FORGET(1937); WRONG ROAD, THE(1937); AIR DEVILS(1938); INTERNATIONAL SETTLEMENT(1938); SAY IT IN FRENCH(1938); TEST PILOT(1938); COWBOYS FROM TEXAS(1939); FIRST OFFENDERS(1939); GOOD GIRLS GO TO PARIS(1939); LADY AND THE MOB, THE(1939); LONE WOLF SPY HUNT, THE(1939); ONLY ANGELS HAVE WINGS(1939); SMASHING THE SPY RING(1939); SPOILERS OF THE RANGE(1939); THAT'S RIGHT–YOU'RE WRONG(1939); CHUMP AT OXFORD, A(1940); EARL OF CHICAGO, THE(1940); FLIGHT COMMAND(1940); IN OLD MISSOURI(1940); ISLAND OF DOOMED MEN(1940); MEN AGAINST THE SKY(1940); MERCY PLANE(1940); NEW MOON(1940); NIGHT AT EARL CARROLL'S, A(1940); RIDE, TENDERFOOT, RIDE(1940); THIRD FINGER, LEFT HAND(1940); APACHE KID, THE(1941); MEET JOHN DOE(1941); PRAIRIE STRANGER(1941); SADDLEMATES(1941); SUN VALLEY

SERENADE(1941); COWBOY SERENADE(1942); GIRL TROUBLE(1942); I WAKE UP SCREAMING(1942); JESSE JAMES, JR.(1942); TALES OF MANHATTAN(1942); CALLING WILD BILL ELLIOTT(1943); CANYON CITY(1943); FLIGHT FOR FREEDOM(1943); HOPPY SERVES A WRIT(1943); LEATHER BURNERS, THE(1943); MISSION TO MOSCOW(1943); SWING YOUR PARTNER(1943); THEY CAME TO BLOW UP AMERICA(1943); THUNDERING TRAILS(1943); HI BEAUTIFUL(1944); HIDDEN VALLEY OUTLAWS(1944); LAURA(1944); MAN FROM FRISCO(1944); MR. WINKLE GOES TO WAR(1944); NOTHING BUT TROUBLE(1944); SHOW BUSINESS(1944); STANDING ROOM ONLY(1944); STORY OF DR. WASSELL, THE(1944); OVER 21(1945); SANTA FE SADDLEMATES(1945); THEY WERE EXPENDABLE(1945); BIG SLEEP, THE(1946); COWBOY BLUES(1946); DARK CORNER, THE(1946); FALCON'S ALIBI, THE(1946); FOOL'S GOLD(1946); GILDA(1946); HOODLUM SAINT, THE(1946); JANIE GETS MARRIED(1946); LADY LUCK(1946); PHANTOM THIEF, THE(1946); RAZOR'S EDGE, THE(1946); ROMANCE OF THE WEST(1946); SOMEWHERE IN THE NIGHT(1946); UNDERCURRENT(1946); DOWN TO EARTH(1947); HONEYMOON(1947); MY WILD IRISH ROSE(1947); WISTFUL WIDOW OF WAGON GAP, THE(1947); DEAD DON'T DREAM, THE(1948); SILENT CONFLICT(1948); SOUTHERN YANKEE, A(1948); THAT WONDERFUL URGE(1948); FATHER WAS A FULLBACK(1949); GAL WHO TOOK THE WEST, THE(1949); STORY OF SEABISCUIT, THE(1949); WOMAN'S SECRET, A(1949); NANCY GOES TO RIO(1950); SHAKEDOWN(1950); FINGERPRINTS DON'T LIE(1951); FOURTEEN HOURS(1951); HORIZONS WEST(1952); MONKEY BUSINESS(1952); PRISONER OF ZENDA, THE(1952); ROAD AGENT(1952); WE'RE NOT MARRIED(1952); DREAM WIFE(1953); YANKEE PASHA(1954); ONE DESIRE(1955); IMITATION OF LIFE(1959)

Fred Murray
SWEETHEART OF THE NAVY(1937); SCENE OF THE CRIME(1949)

Gary Murray
GHOST TOWN(1956); ESCAPE FROM RED ROCK(1958)

Gene Murray
HANG'EM HIGH(1968), cos

George Murray
FATHER TAKES A WIFE(1941); TILL THE CLOUDS ROLL BY(1946); RACE STREET(1948); LOVE AT FIRST SIGHT(1977, Can.)

Graeme Murray
FOOD OF THE GODS, THE(1976), art d; LADIES AND GENTLEMEN, THE FABULOUS STAINS(1982), art d; THING, THE(1982), set d; NEVER CRY WOLF(1983), art d
1984
ICEMAN(1984), art d

Guillermo Murray
GIGANTES PLANETARIOS(1965, Mex.)

Harry Murray
Misc. Silents
HOUSE OF SCANDAL, THE(1928)

Helen Murray
LOSERS, THE(1968)

Hugh Murray
CROSSED TRAILS(1948); FAN, THE(1949); PERFECT STRANGERS(1950); YOUNG MAN WITH A HORN(1950)

Ian Murray
THEY WERE NOT DIVIDED(1951, Brit.); VIRGIN QUEEN, THE(1955); FIRST TRAVELING SALESLADY, THE(1956)

J. Harold Murray
MARRIED IN HOLLYWOOD(1929); CAMEO KIRBY(1930); HAPPY DAYS(1930); WOMEN EVERYWHERE(1930); UNDER SUSPICION(1931)

J. K. Murray
Silents
OH, BOY!(1919)

Jack Murray
WHY LEAVE HOME?(1929), ed; DEVIL WITH WOMEN, A(1930), ed; GOOD INTENTIONS(1930), ed; LONE STAR RANGER, THE(1930), ed; PART TIME WIFE(1930), ed; SCOTLAND YARD(1930), ed; GIRLS DEMAND EXCITEMENT(1931), ed; YELLOW TICKET, THE(1931), ed; FIRST YEAR, THE(1932), ed; ME AND MY GAL(1932), ed; SILENT WITNESS, THE(1932), ed; STEPPING SISTERS(1932), ed; WILD GIRL(1932), ed; SAILOR'S LUCK(1933), ed; DAVID HARUM(1934), ed; IN OLD KENTUCKY(1935), ed; SHOW THEM NO MERCY(1935), ed; GIRLS' DORMITORY(1936), ed; POOR LITTLE RICH GIRL(1936), ed; PRISONER OF SHARK ISLAND, THE(1936), ed; REUNION(1936), ed; CHECKERS(1937), ed; DANGER–LOVE AT WORK(1937), ed; NANCY STEELE IS MISSING(1937), ed; BATTLE OF BROADWAY(1938), ed; RASCALS(1938), ed; ROAD DEMON(1938), ed; TIME OUT FOR MURDER(1938), ed; BACK DOOR TO HEAVEN(1939), ed; INSIDE STORY(1939), ed; FUGITIVE, THE(1947), ed; FORT APACHE(1948), ed; THREE GODFATHERS, THE(1948), ed; SHE WORE A YELLOW RIBBON(1949), ed; RIO GRANDE(1950), ed; WAGONMASTER(1950), ed; BIG JIM McLAIN(1952), ed; QUIET MAN, THE(1952), ed; SUN SHINES BRIGHT, THE(1953), ed; MISTER ROBERTS(1955), ed; SEARCHERS, THE(1956), ed; CHINA DOLL(1958), ed; LAST HURRAH, THE(1958), ed; HORSE SOLDIERS, THE(1959), ed; SERGEANT RUTLEDGE(1960), ed; LES LIAISONS DANGEREUSES(1961, Fr./Ital.), m; STEEL CLAW, THE(1961), m; TWO RODE TOGETHER(1961), ed; PLASTIC DOME OF NORMA JEAN, THE(1966)
Misc. Talkies
BLACK BIRD DESCENDING: TENSE ALIGNMENT(1977)

James Murray
LITTLE WILDCAT, THE(1928); SHAKEDOWN, THE(1929); SHANGHAI LADY(1929); HIDE-OUT, THE(1930); RAMPANT AGE, THE(1930); BRIGHT LIGHTS(1931); IN THE LINE OF DUTY(1931); KICK IN(1931); RECKONING, THE(1932); AIR HOSTESS(1933); BABY FACE(1933); BACHELOR MOTHER(1933); CENTRAL AIRPORT(1933); FRISCO JENNY(1933); HEROES FOR SALE(1933); HIGH GEAR(1933); NOW I'LL TELL(1934); SKULL AND CROWN(1938)
Silents
IN OLD KENTUCKY(1927); LOVELORN, THE(1927); ROUGH HOUSE ROSIE(1927), ph; BIG CITY, THE(1928); CROWD, THE(1928); THUNDER(1929)
Misc. Silents
ROSE-MARIE(1928)

James V. Murray
I COVER CHINATOWN(1938), ph

Jan Murray
WHO KILLED TEDDY BEAR?(1965); BUSYBODY, THE(1967); MAN CALLED DAGGER, A(1967); TARZAN AND THE GREAT RIVER(1967, U.S./Switz.); THUNDER ALLEY(1967); ANGRY BREED, THE(1969); WHICH WAY TO THE FRONT?(1970); DAY OF THE WOLVES(1973); HISTORY OF THE WORLD, PART 1(1981)

1984
FEAR CITY(1984)
Misc. Talkies
AQUARIAN, THE(1972)

Janet Murray
PICNIC AT HANGING ROCK(1975, Aus.)

Jean Murray
ROLL ON TEXAS MOON(1946), w

Jerry Murray
POLICE NURSE(1963); HAPPY BIRTHDAY, DAVY(1970)

Jim Murray
WALL OF NOISE(1963)

Jimmy Murray
Misc. Talkies
$20 A WEEK(1935)

John Murray
HOUSEWIFE(1934); TWENTY MILLION SWEETHEARTS(1934); TRUE CONFESSION(1937); ROOM SERVICE(1938), w; STEP LIVELY(1944), w; TARZAN'S PERIL(1951), ed; SHADOW OF FEAR(1963, Brit.); SECRET INVASION, THE(1964), art d; STARTING OVER(1979); THEY ALL LAUGHED(1981)
Misc. Talkies
WRONG MR. RIGHT, THE(1939); HOUSE RENT PARTY(1946); SHUT MY BIG MOUTH(1946)

John B. Murray
LIBIDO(1973, Aus.), p, d; LONELY HEARTS(1983, Aus.), p; WE OF THE NEVER NEVER(1983, Aus.), p

John Fenton Murray
MAN'S FAVORITE SPORT [(?)$rb (1964), w; ATOMIC KID, THE(1954), w; JAGUAR(1956), w; EVERYTHING'S DUCKY(1961), w; IT'S ONLY MONEY(1962), w; MAN FROM THE DINERS' CLUB, THE(1963), w; MC HALE'S NAVY JOINS THE AIR FORCE(1965), w; DID YOU HEAR THE ONE ABOUT THE TRAVELING SALESLADY?(1968), w; PUFNSTUF(1970), w; ARNOLD(1973), w

John T Murray
HONKY TONK(1929); SONNY BOY(1929); NIGHT WORK(1930); PERSONALITY(1930); ALEXANDER HAMILTON(1931); CHARLIE CHAN CARRIES ON(1931); YOUNG AS YOU FEEL(1931); MAN CALLED BACK, THE(1932); CHEATING CHEATERS(1934); EMBARRASSING MOMENTS(1934); LOVE BIRDS(1934); GIRL FRIEND, THE(1935); GREAT GOD GOLD(1935); LADY IN SCARLET, THE(1935); AFTER THE THIN MAN(1936); GOLDEN ARROW, THE(1936); HERE COMES CARTER(1936); I MARRIED A DOCTOR(1936); EVER SINCE EVE(1937); GIRL LOVES BOY(1937); HIGH, WIDE AND HANDSOME(1937); LOST HORIZON(1937); SWEETHEART OF THE NAVY(1937); COWBOY FROM BROOKLYN(1938); DOWN ON THE FARM(1938); GANG BULLETS(1938); HARDYS RIDE HIGH, THE(1939); QUICK MILLIONS(1939); FOREIGN CORRESPONDENT(1940); ACCENT ON LOVE(1941); SMALL TOWN DEB(1941); LAUGH YOUR BLUES AWAY(1943); REVEILLE WITH BEVERLY(1943)
Silents
JOANNA(1925); SALLY(1925); GAY OLD BIRD, THE(1927)
Misc. Silents
STOP FLIRTING(1925); FINGER PRINTS(1927)

Julia Murray
FOUR FRIENDS(1981)

Julie Christy Murray
MAUSOLEUM(1983)

K. Gordan Murray
GOLDEN GOOSE, THE(1966, E. Ger.), p

K. Gordon Murray
VAMPIRE'S COFFIN, THE(1958, Mex.), p; LITTLE ANGEL(1961, Mex.), p; LITTLE BOY BLUE(1963, Mex.), p; LITTLE RED RIDING HOOD(1963, Mex.), p; QUEEN'S SWORDSMEN, THE(1963, Mex.), p; TURKISH CUCUMBER, THE(1963, Ger.), p; LITTLE RED RIDING HOOD AND HER FRIENDS(1964, Mex.), p; PUSS 'N' BOOTS(1964, Mex.), p; LITTLE RED RIDING HOOD AND THE MONSTERS(1965, Mex.), p; LIVING COFFIN, THE(1965, Mex.), p; RUMPELSTILTSKIN(1965, Ger.), p; SHANTY TRAMP(1967), p; SAVAGES FROM HELL(1968), p

Kate Murray
UNDER YOUR SPELL(1936)

Ken Murray
HALF-MARRIAGE(1929); LEATHERNECKING(1930); CROONER(1932); LADIES OF THE JURY(1932); DISGRACED(1933); FROM HEADQUARTERS(1933); YOU'RE A SWEETHEART(1937); SWING, SISTER, SWING(1938); NIGHT AT EARL CARROLL'S, A(1940); SWING IT SOLDIER(1941); JUKE BOX JENNY(1942); BILL AND COO(1947), a, p, w; MARSHAL'S DAUGHTER, THE(1953), a, p; MAN WHO SHOT LIBERTY VALANCE, THE(1962); SON OF FLUBBER(1963); FOLLOW ME, BOYS!(1966); WAY WEST, THE(1967); POWER, THE(1968); WON TON TON, THE DOG WHO SAVED HOLLYWOOD(1976)

Kitty Murray
SHOW-OFF, THE(1946)

Larry Murray
GOSPEL ROAD, THE(1973), w

Lee Murray
KENTUCKY(1938); I STOLE A MILLION(1939); NEWSBOY'S HOME(1939); TWO GIRLS ON BROADWAY(1940); RIDE, KELLY, RIDE(1941); RIO RITA(1942); CITY ON FIRE(1979 Can.)

Leland Murray
WHAT AM I BID?(1967)

Lyn Murray
BIG NIGHT, THE(1951), m; PROWLER, THE(1951), m; SON OF PALEFACE(1952), m; GIRLS OF PLEASURE ISLAND, THE(1953), m; BRIDGES AT TOKO-RI, THE(1954), m; CASANOVA'S BIG NIGHT(1954), m; TO CATCH A THIEF(1955), m; D-DAY, THE SIXTH OF JUNE(1956), m; ON THE THRESHOLD OF SPACE(1956), m; SNOW WHITE AND THE THREE STOOGES(1961), md; ESCAPE FROM ZAHRAIN(1962), m; PERIOD OF ADJUSTMENT(1962), m; COME FLY WITH ME(1963), m; WIVES AND LOVERS(1963), m; SIGNPOST TO MURDER(1964), m; ROSIE!(1968), m; ANGEL IN MY POCKET(1969), m; STRATEGY OF TERROR(1969), m; COCK-EYED COWBOYS OF CALICO COUNTY, THE(1970), m

Lynn Murray
PROMISE HER ANYTHING(1966, Brit.), m

M. Gray Murray
Silents
LURE OF LONDON, THE(1914, Brit.); JIMMY(1916, Brit.); SOLDIER AND A MAN, A(1916, Brit.); PLACE OF HONOUR, THE(1921, Brit.); ELEVENTH HOUR, THE(1922, Brit.)
Misc. Silents
LOSS OF THE BIRKENHEAD, THE(1914, Brit.); SUICIDE CLUB, THE(1914, Brit.); FLORENCE NIGHTINGALE(1915, Brit.); HER NAMLESS CHILD(1915, Brit.); HOME(1915, Brit.); WILD OATS(1915, Brit.)

Mae Murray
PEACOCK ALLEY(1930); BACHELOR APARTMENT(1931); HIGH STAKES(1931); DICK BARTON STRIKES BACK(1949, Brit.), p; SHADOW OF THE PAST(1950, Brit.), p
Silents
PLOW GIRL, THE(1916); ON RECORD(1917); BRIDE'S AWAKENING, THE(1918); ON WITH THE DANCE(1920); GILDED LILY, THE(1921); BROADWAY ROSE(1922); PEACOCK ALLEY(1922); FRENCH DOLL, THE(1923); JAZZMANIA(1923); MARRIED FLIRTS(1924); MERRY WIDOW, THE(1925); ALTARS OF DESIRE(1927); SHOW PEOPLE(1928)
Misc. Silents
BIG SISTER, THE(1916); DREAM GIRL, THE(1916); SWEET KITTY BELLAIRS(1916); TO HAVE AND TO HOLD(1916); AT FIRST SIGHT(1917); MORMON MAID, A(1917); PRIMROSE RING, THE(1917); PRINCESS VIRTUE(1917); DANGER, GO SLOW(1918); FACE VALUE(1918); HER BODY IN BOND(1918); MODERN LOVE(1918); ABC OF LOVE, THE(1919); BIG LITTLE PERSON, THE(1919); DELICIOUS LITTLE DEVIL, THE(1919); SCARLET SHADOW, THE(1919); TWIN PAWNS, THE(1919); WHAT AM I BID?(1919); IDOLS OF CLAY(1920); RIGHT TO LOVE, THE(1920); FASCINATION(1922); FASHION ROW(1923); CIRCE THE ENCHANTRESS(1924); MADEMOISELLE MIDNIGHT(1924); MASKED BRIDE, THE(1925); VALENCIA(1926)

Malik Murray
LOVE IN A TAXI(1980)

Marion Murray
PARIS CALLING(1941); HARVARD, HERE I COME(1942); GOVERNMENT GIRL(1943); PIRATE, THE(1948)

Mary Murray
LUCKY IN LOVE(1929)

Mary Phillips Murray
KENNER(1969), p, w

Mavis Murray
BLUE DAHLIA, THE(1946); VARIETY GIRL(1947)

Max Murray
JAMAICA RUN(1953), w

Michael Murray
IPCRESS FILE, THE(1965, Brit.)
Misc. Talkies
FALLS, THE(1980, Brit.)

Myra Murray
Misc. Silents
RECKLESS WIVES(1921)

Nell Murray
1,000 SHAPES OF A FEMALE(1963)

Norbert M. Murray
OFFICER AND A GENTLEMAN, AN(1982)

Patrick Murray
CLASS OF MISS MAC MICHAEL, THE(1978, Brit./U.S.); MOON OVER THE ALLEY(1980, Brit.); CURSE OF THE PINK PANTHER(1983)

Paul Murray
MURDER WITHOUT TEARS(1953)

Pauline Murray
IT HAPPENED HERE(1966, Brit.)

Peg Murray
DETECTIVE, THE(1968); SOME OF MY BEST FRIENDS ARE...(1971); W. W. AND THE DIXIE DANCEKINGS(1975)

Peggy Murray
BAND WAGON, THE(1953); ILLIAC PASSION, THE(1968)

Pete Murray
6.5 SPECIAL(1958, Brit.); TASTE OF MONEY, A(1960, Brit.); TRANSATLANTIC(1961, Brit.); DESIGN FOR LOVING(1962, Brit.); RING-A-DING RHYTHM(1962, Brit. 73m Amicus/COL bw (G.B: IT'S TRAD, DAD!); COOL MIKADO, THE(1963, Brit.); OTLEY(1969, Brit.)

Peter Murray
TIME FLIES(1944, Brit.); CARAVAN(1946, Brit.); HUNGRY HILL(1947, Brit.); GIRL IN THE PAINTING, THE(1948, Brit.); MY BROTHER JONATHAN(1949, Brit.); NO HIGHWAY IN THE SKY(1951, Brit.); ESCORT FOR HIRE(1960, Brit.); COOL IT, CAROL!(1970, Brit.)

Rae Murray
VAGABOND KING, THE(1930)

Ralph Murray
PACIFIC BLACKOUT(1942), d

Ralph F. Murray
SWEEPSTAKES(1931), w

Raymond Murray
Misc. Silents
LITTLE GYPSY, THE(1915)

Richey Murray
VIOLENT SATURDAY(1955)

Rick Murray
RESTLESS ONES, THE(1965); CRACKING UP(1977), a, p; TENDER MERCIES(1982)

Rickey Murray
MATING GAME, THE(1959)

Rita Murray
ANGELS DIE HARD(1970)
Misc. Talkies
RUNAWAY(1971)

Roddy Murray
LOCAL HERO(1983, Brit.)

Rosaleen Murray
BLOW-UP(1966, Brit.)

Roseanna Murray
GIRL TROUBLE(1942); POWERS GIRL, THE(1942)

Roseanne Murray
CONFIRM OR DENY(1941); REMEMBER THE DAY(1941); THAT NIGHT IN RIO(1941); MAGNIFICENT DOPE, THE(1942); MOONTIDE(1942); MY GAL SAL(1942); HAPPY LAND(1943); JANE EYRE(1944); CUBAN PETE(1946); DARK HORSE, THE(1946); NIGHT IN PARADISE, A(1946); SLAVE GIRL(1947)

Roy Murray
WILD WOMEN OF WONGO, THE(1959); WRONG BOX, THE(1966, Brit.)

Lt. Col. Roy A. Murray, Jr.
STORY OF G.I. JOE, THE(1945), tech adv

Ruby Murray
IT'S GREAT TO BE YOUNG(1956, Brit.); TOUCH OF THE SUN, A(1956, Brit.)

Stephen Murray
PYGMALION(1938, Brit.); PRIME MINISTER, THE(1941, Brit.); NEXT OF KIN(1942, Brit.); UNDERGROUND GUERRILLAS(1944, Brit.); MASTER OF BANKDAM, THE(1947, Brit.); DULCIMER STREET(1948, Brit.); FOR THEM THAT TRESPASS(1949, Brit.); MY BROTHER JONATHAN(1949, Brit.); NOW BARABBAS WAS A ROBBER(1949, Brit.); SILENT DUST(1949, Brit.); MAGNET, THE(1950, Brit.); ALICE IN WONDERLAND(1951, Fr.); AFFAIR IN MONTE CARLO(1953, Brit.); FOUR SIDED TRIANGLE(1953, Brit.); END OF THE AFFAIR, THE(1955, Brit.); STRANGER'S HAND, THE(1955, Brit.); GUILTY?(1956, Brit.); AT THE STROKE OF NINE(1957, Brit.); TALE OF TWO CITIES, A(1958, Brit.); NUN'S STORY, THE(1959); MASTER SPY(1964, Brit.)

T. Henderson Murray
Misc. Silents
HATE(1917); BACK TO THE WOODS(1918)

Tessie Murray
ONLY ANGELS HAVE WINGS(1939); LOVES OF CARMEN, THE(1948)

Thelma Murray
Silents
CREATION(1922, Brit.)

Thomas Murray
SHINE ON, HARVEST MOON(1944); THIS EARTH IS MINE(1959)

Tom Murray
LADY IN THE LAKE(1947); STUCKEY'S LAST STAND(1980)
Silents
TOO MUCH BUSINESS(1922); PILGRIM, THE(1923); GOLD RUSH, THE(1925); PRIVATE IZZY MURPHY(1926); TRAMP, TRAMP, TRAMP(1926)

Vi Murray
COMING-OUT PARTY, A(, cos; NEVER LET GO(1960, Brit.), cos

Walter Murray
TOAST OF NEW YORK, THE(1937)

William Murray
STOLEN FACE(1952, Brit.); SWEET RIDE, THE(1968), w

Yvonne Murray
MELANIE(1982, Can.)

Charles Murray, Jr.
LAW RIDES AGAIN, THE(1943); ARIZONA WHIRLWIND(1944); BLOCK BUSTERS(1944); THEY WERE EXPENDABLE(1945)

Zon Murray
EL PASO KID, THE(1946); GHOST OF HIDDEN VALLEY(1946); SONG OF THE SIERRAS(1946); CODE OF THE SADDLE(1947); RAINBOW OVER THE ROCKIES(1947); WEST TO GLORY(1947); WISTFUL WIDOW OF WAGON GAP, THE(1947); BLOOD ON THE MOON(1948); CROSSED TRAILS(1948); FALSE PARADISE(1948); GUN TALK(1948); OKLAHOMA BLUES(1948); PHANTOM VALLEY(1948); GRAND CANYON(1949); GUN LAW JUSTICE(1949); SCENE OF THE CRIME(1949); SON OF A BADMAN(1949); TRAIL'S END(1949); DALLAS(1950); KID FROM TEXAS, THE(1950); OUTLAWS OF TEXAS(1950); FINGERPRINTS DON'T LIE(1951); HURRICANE ISLAND(1951); LONGHORN, THE(1951); NIGHT RIDERS OF MONTANA(1951); OKLAHOMA JUSTICE(1951); PECOS RIVER(1951); BORDER SADDLEMATES(1952); CRIPPLE CREEK(1952); DESPERADOES OUTPOST(1952); LARAMIE MOUNTAINS(1952); DOWN LAREDO WAY(1953); OLD OVERLAND TRAIL(1953); ON TOP OF OLD SMOKY(1953); POWDER RIVER(1953); PRESIDENT'S LADY, THE(1953); VIGILANTE TERROR(1953); BITTER CREEK(1954); HIGHWAY DRAGNET(1954); OUTLAW'S DAUGHTER, THE(1954); PASSION(1954); PHANTOM STALLION, THE(1954); LONE RANGER, THE(1955); LONELY MAN, THE(1957); MOTORCYCLE GANG(1957); ESCAPE FROM RED ROCK(1958); GUNSMOKE IN TUCSON(1958); REQUIEM FOR A GUNFIGHTER(1965)
Misc. Talkies
FIGHTING FRONTIERSMAN, THE(1946); TERROR TRAIL(1946); LAW COMES TO GUNSIGHT, THE(1947)

Charlie Murray, Jr.
DEATH VALLEY MANHUNT(1943); SONORA STAGECOACH(1944)

Murray the K
THAT'S THE WAY OF THE WORLD(1975); I WANNA HOLD YOUR HAND(1978)

Peter Murray-Hill
YANK AT OXFORD, A(1938); CASTLE OF CRIMES(1940, Brit.)

Roger Murray-Leach
LOCAL HERO(1983, Brit.), prod d

R. Murray-Leslie
SPELL OF AMY NUGENT, THE(1945, Brit.), p

David Murray-Smith
LEAP OF FAITH(1931, Brit.), p

Jeanne Murray-Vanderbilt
MISTER ROBERTS(1955)

Franklin Murrel
MAD EMPRESS, THE(1940)

Alys Murrell
Silents
BRANDED A BANDIT(1924); TEMPTRESS, THE(1926)
Misc. Silents
COLLEGIATE(1926)

Anna Murrell
YOU LIVE AND LEARN(1937, Brit.); MILL ON THE FLOSS(1939, Brit.)

Gavin Murrell
CLAY PIGEON(1971), m; JESSIE'S GIRLS(1976)
George Murrell
GOLD FEVER(1952)
Edward R. Murrow
AROUND THE WORLD IN 80 DAYS(1956)
Bill Murry
MAIN EVENT, THE(1979)
Bill Phillips Murry
NEW YORK, NEW YORK(1977)
Lyn Murry
HERE COME THE GIRLS(1953), m
Alexander Murski
RASPUTIN(1932, Ger.)
Alexander Mursky
Misc. Silents
UNCANNY ROOM, THE(1915, Ger.); HOUND OF THE BASKERVILLES, THE(1929, Ger.)
Cynthia Murtagh
Silents
HEAD OF THE FAMILY, THE(1922, Brit.); SKIPPER'S WOOING, THE(1922, Brit.)
Misc. Silents
WILL AND A WAY, A(1922, Brit.)
Gerry Murtagh
CLINIC, THE(1983, Aus.)
Karen Murtagh
HOFFMAN(1970, Brit.)
Kate Murtagh
FAREWELL, MY LOVELY(1975); FAMILY PLOT(1976); CAR, THE(1977); DOCTOR DETROIT(1983)
Kate Murtah
GUN FIGHT(1961)
James Murtaugh
ALL THE PRESIDENT'S MEN(1976); HOWLING, THE(1981)
Peter Murter
GOLDFINGER(1964, Brit.), art d
Florence Murth
Silents
GOLD RUSH, THE(1925)
Misc. Silents
THUNDERING HOOFS(1922)
Leo Murtin
MASQUERADE IN MEXICO(1945)
Lionel Murton
MEET THE NAVY(1946, Brit.); TROUBLE IN THE AIR(1948, Brit.); DANGEROUS ASSIGNMENT(1950, Brit.); GIRL IS MINE, THE(1950, Brit.); PICKWICK PAPERS, THE(1952, Brit.); NIGHT PEOPLE(1954); RUNAWAY BUS, THE(1954, Brit.); ADVENTURES OF SADIE, THE(1955, Brit.); CARRY ON ADMIRAL(1957, Brit.); FIRE DOWN BELOW(1957, U.S./Brit.); PICKUP ALLEY(1957, Brit.); PURSUIT OF THE GRAF SPEE(1957, Brit.); RAISING A RIOT(1957, Brit.); FURTHER UP THE CREEK!(1958, Brit.); UP THE CREEK(1958, Brit.); CAPTAIN'S TABLE, THE(1960, Brit.); FLAME OVER INDIA(1960, Brit.); MAIN ATTRACTION, THE(1962, Brit.); ON THE BEAT(1962, Brit.); SUMMER HOLIDAY(1963, Brit.); MAN IN THE MIDDLE(1964, U.S./Brit.); MAKE MINE A MILLION(1965, Brit.); TRUTH ABOUT SPRING, THE(1965, Brit.); CARRY ON COWBOY(1966, Brit.); CARNABY, M.D.(1967, Brit.); LAST SHOT YOU HEAR, THE(1969, Brit.); CANNON FOR CORDOBA(1970); REVOLUTIONARY, THE(1970, Brit.); WELCOME TO THE CLUB(1971); CONFESSIONS OF A WINDOW CLEANER(1974, Brit.); SEVEN NIGHTS IN JAPAN(1976, Brit./Fr.); TWILIGHT'S LAST GLEAMING(1977, U.S./Ger.)
Lionel Murton, U.S.N.
PETTICOAT PIRATES(1961, Brit.)
Peter Murton
MAN IN THE MOON(1961, Brit.), set d; I LIKE MONEY(1962, Brit.), art d; DR. STRANGELOVE: OR HOW I LEARNED TO STOP WORRYING AND LOVE THE BOMB(1964), art d; WOMAN OF STRAW(1964, Brit.), art d; IPCRESS FILE, THE(1965, Brit.), art d; THUNDERBALL(1965, Brit.), art d; FUNERAL IN BERLIN(1966, Brit.), art d; HALF A SIXPENCE(1967, Brit.), art d; LION IN WINTER, THE(1968, Brit.), art d; THREE INTO TWO WON'T GO(1969, Brit.), art d; POSSESSION OF JOEL DELANEY, THE(1972), prod d; RULING CLASS, THE(1972, Brit.), prod d; NIGHT WATCH(1973, Brit.), art d; BLACK WINDMILL, THE(1974, Brit.), art d; MAN WITH THE GOLDEN GUN, THE(1974, Brit.), prod d; MAN FRIDAY(1975, Brit.), prod d; EAGLE HAS LANDED, THE(1976, Brit.), prod d; DEATH ON THE NILE(1978, Brit.), prod d; DRACULA(1979), prod d; SUPERMAN II(1980), prod d; SUPERMAN III(1983), prod d
1984
SHEENA(1984), prod d
W. Murton
WE DIVE AT DAWN(1943, Brit.), art d
Walter Murton
WARM CORNER, A(1930, Brit.), art d; MAN IN GREY, THE(1943, Brit.), art d
William Murton
YANK IN LONDON, A(1946, Brit.)
Lautaro Murua
END OF INNOCENCE(1960, Arg.); ALIAS BIG SHOT(1962, Argen.), a, d; THE EAVESDROPPER(1966, U.S./Arg.); TRIUMPHS OF A MAN CALLED HORSE(1983, US/Mex.)
Robert Murvin
UNDER THE RAINBOW(1981)
I. Murzayeva
ANNA CROSS, THE(1954, USSR); NIGHT BEFORE CHRISTMAS, A(1963, USSR)
Robert Murzeau
ROYAL AFFAIR, A(1950); UTOPIA(1952, Fr./Ital.); RAVISHING IDIOT, A(1966, Ital./Fr.)
Tony Musante
ONCE A THIEF(1965); INCIDENT, THE(1967); DETECTIVE, THE(1968); BIRD WITH THE CRYSTAL PLUMAGE, THE(1970, Ital./Ger.); MERCENARY, THE(1970, Ital./Span.); ANONYMOUS VENETIAN, THE(1971); GRISSOM GANG, THE(1971); LAST RUN, THE(1971)

1984
POPE OF GREENWICH VILLAGE, THE(1984)
Hans Musaus
EVERY MAN FOR HIMSELF AND GOD AGAINST ALL(1975, Ger.)
Brent Musburger
MAIN EVENT, THE(1979)
Tom Musca
1984
REPO MAN(1984)
Clarence Muse
HEARTS IN DIXIE(1929); GUILTY?(1930); RAIN OR SHINE(1930); ROYAL ROMANCE, A(1930); DIRIGIBLE(1931); FIGHTING SHERIFF, THE(1931); HUCKLEBERRY FINN(1931); LAST PARADE, THE(1931); SAFE IN HELL(1931); SECRET SERVICE(1931); SECRET WITNESS, THE(1931); ATTORNEY FOR THE DEFENSE(1932); BIG CITY BLUES(1932) 65m WB bw; CABIN IN THE COTTON(1932); HELL'S HIGHWAY(1932); IF I HAD A MILLION(1932); IS MY FACE RED?(1932); LENA RIVERS(1932); MAN AGAINST WOMAN(1932); NIGHT WORLD(1932); PRESTIGE(1932); WASHINGTON MERRY-GO-ROUND(1932); WET PARADE, THE(1932); WHITE ZOMBIE(1932); WINNER TAKE ALL(1932); WOMAN FROM MONTE CARLO, THE(1932); FLYING DOWN TO RIO(1933); FROM HELL TO HEAVEN(1933); LAUGHTER IN HELL(1933); MIND READER, THE(1933); WRECKER, THE(1933); BLACK MOON(1934); BROADWAY BILL(1934); COUNT OF MONTE CRISTO, THE(1934); FURY OF THE JUNGLE(1934); KID MILLIONS(1934); MASSACRE(1934); PERSONALITY KID, THE(1934); ALIAS MARY DOW(1935); EAST OF JAVA(1935); HARMONY LANE(1935); O'SHAUGHNESSY'S BOY(1935); RED HOT TIRES(1935); SO RED THE ROSE(1935); DANIEL BOONE(1936); FOLLOW YOUR HEART(1936); LAUGHING IRISH EYES(1936); MUSS 'EM UP(1936); SHOW BOAT(1936); SPENDTHRIFT(1936); HIGH HAT(1937), a, m; MYSTERIOUS CROSSING(1937); SPIRIT OF YOUTH(1937); PRISON TRAIN(1938); SECRETS OF A NURSE(1938); TOY WIFE, THE(1938); WAY DOWN SOUTH(1939), a, w; CHAD HANNA(1940); MARYLAND(1940); MURDER OVER NEW YORK(1940); SPORTING BLOOD(1940); THAT GANG OF MINE(1940); ZANZIBAR(1940); ADAM HAD FOUR SONS(1941); FLAME OF NEW ORLEANS, THE(1941); GENTLEMAN FROM DIXIE(1941); INVISIBLE GHOST, THE(1941); KISSES FOR BREAKFAST(1941); LOVE CRAZY(1941); BLACK SWAN, THE(1942); SIN TOWN(1942); TALES OF MANHATTAN(1942); TALK OF THE TOWN(1942); TOUGH AS THEY COME(1942); FLESH AND FANTASY(1943); HEAVEN CAN WAIT(1943); HONEYMOON LODGE(1943); JOHNNY COME LATELY(1943); SHADOW OF A DOUBT(1943); SHERLOCK HOLMES IN WASHINGTON(1943); SKY'S THE LIMIT, THE(1943); WATCH ON THE RHINE(1943); DOUBLE INDEMNITY(1944); FOLLOW THE BOYS(1944); IN THE MEANTIME, DARLING(1944); JAM SESSION(1944); RACKET MAN, THE(1944); SAN DIEGO, I LOVE YOU(1944); THIN MAN GOES HOME, THE(1944); GOD IS MY CO-PILOT(1945); LOST WEEKEND, THE(1945); SCARLET STREET(1945); SHE WOULDN'T SAY YES(1945); WITHOUT LOVE(1945); NIGHT AND DAY(1946); TWO SMART PEOPLE(1946); LIKELY STORY, A(1947); MY FAVORITE BRUNETTE(1947); UNCONQUERED(1947); WELCOME STRANGER(1947); ACT OF MURDER, AN(1948); GREAT DAN PATCH, THE(1949); COUNTY FAIR(1950); RIDING HIGH(1950); APACHE DRUMS(1951); MY FORBIDDEN PAST(1951); CARIBBEAN(1952); LAS VEGAS STORY, THE(1952); JAMAICA RUN(1953); SUN SHINES BRIGHT, THE(1953); SHE COULDN'T SAY NO(1954); FIRST TRAVELING SALESLADY, THE(1956); PORGY AND BESS(1959); BUCK AND THE PREACHER(1972); WORLD'S GREATEST ATHLETE, THE(1973); CARWASH(1976); PASSING THROUGH(1977); BLACK STALLION, THE(1979)
Misc. Talkies
BROKEN STRINGS(1940)
Etiennette Muse
WAGES OF FEAR, THE(1955, Fr./Ital.), ed. Henri Rust; PROSTITUTION(1965, Fr.), ed
Kenneth Muse
HEY THERE, IT'S YOGI BEAR(1964), anim; MAN CALLED FLINTSTONE, THE(1966), anim
Margaret Muse
TEACHER'S PET(1958); FOR PETE'S SAKE!(1966); WAR BETWEEN MEN AND WOMEN, THE(1972)
Robert Musel
EMERGENCY SQUAD(1940), w; CIRCLE OF DECEPTON(1961, Brit.), w
The Musemorphoses
VERY NATURAL THING, A(1974), m
Wolf Muser
BARBAROSA(1982); KISS ME GOODBYE(1982); TO BE OR NOT TO BE(1983)
Lon Musgrave
Silents
PATCHWORK GIRL OF OZ, THE(1914)
Peter Musgrave
SILENT PLAYGROUND, THE(1964, Brit.), ed; TERRORNAUTS, THE(1967, Brit.), ed; THEY CAME FROM BEYOND SPACE(1967, Brit.), ed; GIRL ON A MOTORCYCLE, THE(1968, Fr./Brit.), ed; MY LOVER, MY SON(1970, Brit.), ed; VAMPIRE CIRCUS(1972, Brit.), ed
William Musgrave
Silents
MIDNIGHT PATROL, THE(1918); BEAU REVEL(1921)
Misc. Silents
SOCIETY'S DRIFTWOOD(1917)
Gertrude Musgrove
SCARLET PIMPERNEL, THE(1935, Brit.); GIRL FROM MAXIM'S, THE(1936, Brit.); REMBRANDT(1936, Brit.); MAN WHO COULD WORK MIRACLES, THE(1937, Brit.); BREAK THE NEWS(1938, Brit.); DIVORCE OF LADY X, THE(1938, Brit.); TROOPSHIP(1938, Brit.); BLIND FOLLY(1939, Brit.); FUGITIVE, THE(1940, Brit.); YOU WILL REMEMBER(1941, Brit.); LADY IN DISTRESS(1942, Brit.)
G. Musheghian
VOW, THE(1947, USSR.)
Gianni Musi
STATUE, THE(1971, Brit.)
S. Musial
PASSENGER, THE(1970, Pol.)
Al Music
1984
CALIFORNIA GIRLS(1984), a, d&w

Lorenzo Music
NICKELODEON(1976); OH, HEAVENLY DOG!(1980); TWICE UPON A TIME(1983)
Music Box Revue Chorus
Silents
BOWERY CINDERELLA(1927)
The Music Hall Boys
VARIETY HOUR(1937, Brit.)
The Music Machine
MUSIC MACHINE, THE(1979, Brit.), m
Music Maids
HIT PARADE OF 1943(1943)
The Music Maids
HOOSIER HOLIDAY(1943); JAMBOREE(1944); WAVE, A WAC AND A MARINE, A(1944)
The Musical Tornadoes
SUNDOWN ON THE PRAIRIE(1939)
Sally Musick
GIRL WHO HAD EVERYTHING, THE(1953)
Musicues
COME BACK BABY(1968), m
Maris Musik
NEW LIFE STYLE, THE(1970, Ger.), m
Sally Musik
SON OF SINBAD(1955)
Mirko Musil
DO YOU KEEP A LION AT HOME?(1966, Czech.); 90 DEGREES IN THE SHADE(1966, Czech./Brit.); FIFTH HORSEMAN IS FEAR, THE(1968, Czech.)
Robert Musil
YOUNG TORLESS(1968, Fr./Ger.), d&w
Cecil Musk
CIRCUS BOY(1947, Brit.), d, w; TRAPPED BY THE TERROR(1949, Brit.), d; BLOW YOUR OWN TRUMPET(1958, Brit.), d; EGGHEAD'S ROBOT(1970, Brit.), p; TROUBLESOME DOUBLE, THE(1971, Brit.), p
Frank Musker
WORLD IS FULL OF MARRIED MEN, THE(1980, Brit.), m
Jane Musky
1984
BLOOD SIMPLE(1984), prod d
Judge M.A. Musmanno
BLACK FURY(1935), w
Vincenzo Musolino
EVERYBODY GO HOME!(1962, Fr./Ital.)
Charles Musqued
ONE BIG AFFAIR(1952)
Carlos Musquiz
TORCH, THE(1950); CAPTAIN SCARLETT(1953); SEVEN CITIES OF GOLD(1955)
Hassan Mussali
Silents
ONE LAW FOR BOTH(1917)
Hassan Mussalli
Misc. Silents
GREATER WOMAN, THE(1917); SPLENDID SINNER, THE(1918); TRIUMPH OF VENUS, THE(1918)
M.A. Mussanno
LAST TEN DAYS, THE(1956, Ger.), w
Stub Mussellman
CORN IS GREEN, THE(1945)
M. M. Musselman
KENTUCKY MOONSHINE(1938), w; STRAIGHT, PLACE AND SHOW(1938), w; THREE MUSKETEERS, THE(1939), w; BRIDE CAME C.O.D., THE(1941), w; PLAYMATES(1941), w; GET HEP TO LOVE(1942), w; RHYTHM OF THE ISLANDS(1943), w; BATHING BEAUTY(1944), w; CAROLINA BLUES(1944), w; SHADY LADY(1945), w; TANGIER(1946), w
Morris Musselman
SHE HAD TO EAT(1937), w
Wallace Musselwhite
STRIKE UP THE BAND(1940)
Larry Musser
SILENCE OF THE NORTH(1981, Can.)
Charles Mussett
Silents
NUMBER 17(1920); STARDUST(1921); LIGHT IN THE DARK, THE(1922)
Gloria Mussetta
FALL OF THE ROMAN EMPIRE, THE(1964), cos; TRENCHCOAT(1983), cos
Piero Mussetta
LUXURY GIRLS(1953, Ital.), d
Charles Mussette
Silents
IMPOSTER, THE(1918)
Bill Mussetter
FIVE GRAVES TO CAIRO(1943)
Giambattista Mussetto
BANDIDOS(1967, Ital.), w
Barrows Mussey
MARCH ON PARIS 1914–OF GENERALOBERST ALEXANDER VON KLUCK–AND HIS MEMORY OF JESSIE HOLLADAY(1977)
Francine Mussey
Silents
NAPOLEON(1927, Fr.)
Frau Barrows Mussey
MARCH ON PARIS 1914–OF GENERALOBERST ALEXANDER VON KLUCK–AND HIS MEMORY OF JESSIE HOLLADAY(1977)
Carlo Mussi
RICE GIRL(1963, Fr./Ital.), w
Lucilla Mussini
TRIAL OF JOAN OF ARC(1965, Fr.), cos
Carlo Musso
REVOLT OF THE MERCENARIES(1964, Ital./Span.), w

Marion Musso
I'LL REMEMBER APRIL(1945)
Mike Musso
I'LL REMEMBER APRIL(1945)
Vito Musso
DISC JOCKEY(1951)
Alessandra Mussolini
WHITE SISTER(1973, Ital./Span./Fr.)
Allessandra Mussolini
SPECIAL DAY, A(1977, Ital./Can.)
Bennet Musson
Silents
WHITE OAK(1921), w
Bennett Musson
Silents
FORGIVEN, OR THE JACK O'DIAMONDS(1914), w
Bernard Musson
LOVE IN THE AFTERNOON(1957); COW AND I, THE(1961, Fr., Ital., Ger.); TOMORROW IS MY TURN(1962, Fr./Ital./Ger.); DIARY OF A CHAMBERMAID(1964, Fr./Ital.); MURDER AT 45 R.P.M.(1965, Fr.); FANTOMAS(1966, Fr./Ital.); BELLE DE JOUR(1968, Fr.); PARIS IN THE MONTH OF AUGUST(1968, Fr.); MILKY WAY, THE(1969, Fr./Ital.); DISCREET CHARM OF THE BOURGEOISIE, THE(1972, Fr.); MAGNIFICENT ONE, THE(1974, Fr./Ital.); CATHERINE & CO.(1976, Fr.); THAT OBSCURE OBJECT OF DESIRE(1977, Fr./Span.)
Modest Mussorgsky
FANTASIA(1940), w
Dayle Mustain
TUNNELVISION(1976), ed
Mustard & Gravy
LONE HAND TEXAN, THE(1947)
Mustard and Gravy
BANDITS OF EL DORADO(1951)
Anna Maria Mustari
QUEEN OF THE PIRATES(1961, Ital./Ger.)
Maria Mustari
BATTLE OF THE WORLDS(1961, Ital.)
Bert Mustin
TWILIGHT OF HONOR(1963); MISADVENTURES OF MERLIN JONES, THE(1964)
Burt Mustin
DETECTIVE STORY(1951); SELLOUT, THE(1951); JUST ACROSS THE STREET(1952); LUSTY MEN, THE(1952); TALK ABOUT A STRANGER(1952); LION IS IN THE STREETS, A(1953); MOONLIGHTER, THE(1953); ONE GIRL'S CONFESSION(1953); SILVER WHIP, THE(1953); VICKI(1953); EXECUTIVE SUITE(1954); SHE COULDN'T SAY NO(1954); SILVER LODE(1954); STORM CENTER(1956); THESE WILDER YEARS(1956); RAINTREE COUNTY(1957); RALLY 'ROUND THE FLAG, BOYS!(1958); HOME FROM THE HILL(1960); SON OF FLUBBER(1963); THRILL OF IT ALL, THE(1963); KILLERS, THE(1964); SEX AND THE SINGLE GIRL(1964); WHAT A WAY TO GO(1964); CAT BALLOU(1965); CINCINNATI KID, THE(1965); ADVENTURES OF BULLWHIP GRIFFIN, THE(1967); RELUCTANT ASTRONAUT, THE(1967); GREAT BANK ROBBERY, THE(1969); HAIL, HERO!(1969); WITCHMAKER, THE(1969); TIGER BY THE TAIL(1970); TIME FOR DYING, A(1971); TRAIN RIDE TO HOLLYWOOD(1975); BAKER'S HAWK(1976)
Carlo Musto
LA DOLCE VITA(1961, Ital./Fr.)
Michael Musto
SINGLE ROOM FURNISHED(1968), w
Antonio Musu
BATTLE OF ALGIERS, THE(1967, Ital./Alger.), p
Jone Salinas Musu
LA FUGA(1966, Ital.)
Mike Musura
NORA PRENTISS(1947)
Nicholas Musuraca
HOOK, LINE AND SINKER(1930), ph; SIN SHIP(1931), ph; SECOND WIFE(1936), ph; TWO IN THE DARK(1936), ph; BIG SHOT, THE(1937), ph; BORDER CAFE(1937), ph; CHINA PASSAGE(1937), ph; CRASHING HOLLYWOOD(1937), ph; FLIGHT FROM GLORY(1937), ph; LIVING ON LOVE(1937), ph; SATURDAY'S HEROES(1937), ph; BLIND ALIBI(1938), ph; CONDEMNED WOMEN(1938), ph; EVERYBODY'S DOING IT(1938), ph; LAW OF THE UNDERWORLD(1938), ph; MAD MISS MANTON, THE(1938), ph; NIGHT SPOT(1938), ph; QUICK MONEY(1938), ph; SKY GIANT(1938), ph; SMASHING THE RACKETS(1938), ph; TARNISHED ANGEL(1938), ph; ALLEGHENY UPRISING(1939), ph; FIVE CAME BACK(1939), ph; GOLDEN BOY(1939), ph; PACIFIC LINER(1939), ph; SORORITY HOUSE(1939), ph; THEY MADE HER A SPY(1939), ph; TWELVE CROWDED HOURS(1939), ph; BILL OF DIVORCEMENT(1940), ph; LITTLE MEN(1940), ph; PLAY GIRL(1940), ph; STRANGER ON THE THIRD FLOOR(1940), ph; SWISS FAMILY ROBINSON(1940), ph; TOM BROWN'S SCHOOL DAYS(1940), ph; GAY FALCON, THE(1941), ph; HURRY, CHARLIE, HURRY(1941), ph; LADY SCARFACE(1941), ph; OBLIGING YOUNG LADY(1941), ph; REPENT AT LEISURE(1941), ph; CALL OUT THE MARINES(1942), ph; CAT PEOPLE(1942), ph; NAVY COMES THROUGH, THE(1942), ph; PIRATES OF THE PRAIRIE(1942), ph; TUTTLES OF TAHITI(1942), ph; BOMBARDIER(1943), ph; FALLEN SPARROW, THE(1943), ph; FOREVER AND A DAY(1943), ph; GANGWAY FOR TOMORROW(1943), ph; GHOST SHIP, THE(1943), ph; SEVENTH VICTIM, THE(1943), ph; BRIDE BY MISTAKE(1944), ph; CURSE OF THE CAT PEOPLE, THE(1944), ph; FALCON IN HOLLYWOOD, THE(1944), ph; GIRL RUSH(1944), ph; MARINE RAIDERS(1944), ph; BACK TO BATAAN(1945), ph; CHINA SKY(1945), ph; BEDLAM(1946), ph; DEADLINE AT DAWN(1946), ph; LOCKET, THE(1946), ph; SPIRAL STAIRCASE, THE(1946), ph; BACHELOR AND THE BOBBY-SOXER, THE(1947), ph; OUT OF THE PAST(1947), ph; BLOOD ON THE MOON(1948), ph; MYSTERIOUS DESPERADO, THE(1949), ph; STAGECOACH KID(1949), ph; BORN TO BE BAD(1950), ph; COMPANY SHE KEEPS, THE(1950), ph; DYNAMITE PASS(1950), ph; HUNT THE MAN DOWN(1950), ph; RIDER FROM TUCSON(1950), ph; WHERE DANGER LIVES(1950), ph; WOMAN ON PIER 13, THE(1950), ph; HOT LEAD(1951), ph; ROADBLOCK(1951), ph; WHIP HAND, THE(1951), ph; CLASH BY NIGHT(1952), ph; GIRL IN EVERY PORT, A(1952), ph; TRAIL GUIDE(1952), ph; BLUE GARDENIA, THE(1953), ph; DEVIL'S CANYON(1953), ph; HITCH-HIKER, THE(1953), ph; SPLIT SECOND(1953), ph; SUSAN SLEPT HERE(1954), ph
Silents
ON THE BANKS OF THE WABASH(1923), ph; GILDED HIGHWAY, THE(1926), ph; LIGHTNING LARIATS(1927), ph

Nick Musuraca
SIDE STREET(1929), ph; HALF SHOT AT SUNRISE(1930), ph; INSIDE THE LI-NES(1930), ph; CRACKED NUTS(1931), ph; EVERYTHING'S ROSIE(1931), ph; SMART WOMAN(1931), ph; THREE WHO LOVED(1931), ph; TOO MANY COOKS(1931), ph; COME ON DANGER!(1932), ph; HAUNTED GOLD(1932), ph; MEN OF CHANCE(1932), ph; CHANCE AT HEAVEN(1933), ph; CROSSFIRE(1933), ph; FLYING DEVILS(1933), ph; SCARLET RIVER(1933), ph; SON OF THE BOR-DER(1933), ph; LONG LOST FATHER(1934), ph; MURDER ON THE BLACK-BOARD(1934), ph; RICHEST GIRL IN THE WORLD, THE(1934), ph; SING AND LIKE IT(1934), ph; WE'RE RICH AGAIN(1934), ph; WHERE SINNERS MEET(1934), ph; BY YOUR LEAVE(1935), ph; MURDER ON A HONEYMOON(1935), ph; OLD MAN RHYTHM(1935), ph; ROMANCE IN MANHATTAN(1935), ph; TO BEAT THE BAND(1935), ph; VILLAGE TALE(1935), ph; FARMER IN THE DELL, THE(1936), ph; MURDER ON A BRIDLE PATH(1936), ph; SILLY BILLIES(1936), ph; DANGER PATROL(1937), ph; TOO MANY WIVES(1937), ph; WE'RE ON THE JURY(1937), ph; I REMEMBER MAMA(1948), ph; MAN ON THE PROWL(1957), ph; STORY OF MANKIND, THE(1957), ph; TOO MUCH, TOO SOON(1958), ph
Silents
BRIDE OF THE STORM(1926), ph; BANDIT'S SON, THE(1927), ph; CYCLONE OF THE RANGE(1927), ph; SONORA KID, THE(1927), ph; SPLITTING THE BREE-ZE(1927), ph; AVENGING RIDER, THE(1928), ph; ORPHAN OF THE SAGE(1928), ph; PHANTOM OF THE RANGE(1928), ph; FRECKLED RASCAL, THE(1929), ph; GUN LAW(1929), ph; IDAHO RED(1929), ph

Gianni Glori Musy
JESSICA(1962, U.S./Ital./Fr.); FACTS OF MURDER, THE(1965, Ital.)

Gianni Musy
DUEL OF THE TITANS(1963, Ital.)

Jean Musy
WOMANLIGHT(1979, Fr./Ger./Ital.), m; CLAIR DE FEMME(1980,Fr.), m; CHANEL SOLITAIRE(1981), m; TANYA'S ISLAND(1981, Can.), m; BIRD WATCH, THE(1983, Fr.), m

Louis Musy
BARBER OF SEVILLE(1949, Fr.), a, md

Vittorio Glori Musy
LA FUGA(1966, Ital.), p

Anna Muszte
1984
BRADY'S ESCAPE(1984, U.S./Hung.)

Marjorie Ann Mutchie
FOOTLIGHT GLAMOUR(1943); IT'S A GREAT LIFE(1943); LEAVE IT TO BLON-DIE(1945)

Miles Mutchler
LOSERS, THE(1968); END OF AUGUST, THE(1982)

Lola Muthel
JUDGE AND THE SINNER, THE(1964, Ger.)

Lothar Muthel
Silents
GOLEM: HOW HE CAME INTO THE WORLD, THE(1920, Ger.)

Elizabeth Muthsam
GREAT WALTZ, THE(1972)

Ornella Muti
NEST OF VIPERS(1979, Ital.); FLASH GORDON(1980); LOVE AND MONEY(1982); GIRL FROM TRIESTE, THE(1983, Ital.); TALES OF ORDINARY MADNESS(1983, Ital.)
1984
SWANN IN LOVE(1984, Fr.Ger.)
Misc. Talkies
OASIS OF FEAR(1973)

Vivian Muti
WEDDING PARTY, THE(1969)

Belkis Mutlu
L'IMMORTELLE(1969, Fr./Ital./Turkey)

Anthony Muto
NICE LITTLE BANK THAT SHOULD BE ROBBED, A(1958), p

John Muto
STRANGE INVADERS(1983), spec eff
1984
NIGHT OF THE COMET(1984), prod d

Floyd Mutrux
MARYJANE(1968); ROSEMARY'S BABY(1968); COVER ME BABE(1970); CHRIS-TIAN LICORICE STORE, THE(1971), p, w; DUSTY AND SWEETS McGEE(1971), d&w; FREEBIE AND THE BEAN(1974), w; ALOHA, BOBBY AND ROSE(1975), d&w; AMERICAN HOT WAX(1978), d; HOLLYWOOD KNIGHTS, THE(1980), d, w

Goro Mutsu
MONSTERS FROM THE UNKNOWN PLANET(1975, Jap.)

Mutt
PEG O' MY HEART(1933); WAY TO LOVE, THE(1933)

Mutt the Horse
WILD HORSE(1931)

Ornella Mutti
LEONOR(1977, Fr./Span./Ital.)

Roger Mutton
CHARGE OF THE LIGHT BRIGADE, THE(1968, Brit.); GIRL ON A MOTORCYCLE, THE(1968, Fr./Brit.)

Franz Muxeneder
GREH(1962, Ger./Yugo.); GOOD SOLDIER SCHWEIK, THE(1963, Ger.); CRIME AND PASSION(1976, U.S., Ger.)

Zaim Muzaferija
KAYA, I'LL KILL YOU(1969, Yugo./Fr.)

Enzio Muzii
WITCHES, THE(1969, Fr./Ital.), w

R. Muzikant
SKI BATTALION(1938, USSR), d, w

Y. Muzikant
SKI BATTALION(1938, USSR), d, w

Enrico Muzio
VINTAGE WINE(1935, Brit.)

Lando Muzio
WITHOUT PITY(1949, Ital.)

Hiroshi Muzitani
PRESSURE OF GUILT(1964, Jap.), art d

Carlos Muzquiz
MY BROTHER, THE OUTLAW(1951); STRONGHOLD(1952, Mex.); LIFE IN THE BALANCE, A(1955); BLACK SCORPION, THE(1957); SUN ALSO RISES, THE(1957); SIERRA BARON(1958); TEN DAYS TO TULARA(1958); VILLA!(1958); JET OVER THE ATLANTIC(1960); LAST REBEL, THE(1961, Mex.)

Jan Muzurus
CARRY ON JACK(1963, Brit.)

Jan Muzynski
THRESHOLD(1983, Can.)

Joe Muzzuca
HELLO GOD(1951, U.S./Ital.)

Tom Mwangi
1984
SHEENA(1984)

Shane Mwigereri
1984
SHEENA(1984)

Ysmane My
KILLING GAME, THE(1968, Fr.)

A. Myagkov
MEET ME IN MOSCOW(1966, USSR), art d

Charles Myall
DIME WITH A HALO(1963), art d

Gennadiy Myasnikov
WAR AND PEACE(1968, USSR), art d

Barbara Myasnikova
DEFENSE OF VOLOTCHAYEVSK, THE(1938, USSR)

V. Myasnikova
MUMU(1961, USSR)

Walter C. Mycroft
TESHA(1929, Brit.), w; MURDER(1930, Brit.), w; YELLOW MASK, THE(1930, Brit.), w; CARMEN(1931, Brit.), w; KEEPERS OF YOUTH(1931, Brit.), w; MAN FROM CHICAGO, THE(1931, Brit.), w; POOR OLD BILL(1931, Brit.), p; TRAPPED IN A SUBMARINE(1931, Brit.), p, w; HIS WIFE'S MOTHER(1932, Brit.), p; MONEY FOR NOTHING(1932, Brit.), w; FOR THE LOVE OF MIKE(1933, Brit.), p; HAWLEY'S OF HIGH STREET(1933, Brit.), p; LOVE NEST, THE(1933, Brit.), p; POLITICAL PARTY, A(1933, Brit.), p; SLEEPLESS NIGHTS(1933, Brit.), p; SOUTHERN MAID, A(1933, Brit.), p; DOCTOR'S ORDERS(1934, Brit.), p; FREEDOM OF THE SEAS(1934, Brit.), p; GIRLS WILL BE BOYS(1934, Brit.), p; GREAT DEFENDER, THE(1934, Brit.), p; LOST IN THE LEGION(1934, Brit.), p; LUCK OF A SAILOR, THE(1934, Brit.), p; MASTER AND MAN(1934, Brit.), p; MISTER CINDERS(1934, Brit.), p; OUTCAST, THE(1934, Brit.), p; OVER THE GARDEN WALL(1934, Brit.), p; RETURN OF BULLDOG DRUM-MOND, THE(1934, Brit.), p; THOSE WERE THE DAYS(1934, Brit.), p; WARREN CASE, THE(1934, Brit.), p; WHAT HAPPENED THEN?(1934, Brit.), p; DANCE BAND(1935, Brit.), p; DANDY DICK(1935, Brit.), p; DRAKE THE PIRATE(1935, Brit.), p; HELL'S CARGO(1935, Brit.), p; HONOURS EASY(1935, Brit.), p; INVITA-TION TO THE WALTZ(1935, Brit.), p; IT'S A BET(1935, Brit.), p; MIMI(1935, Brit.), p; MUSIC HATH CHARMS(1935, Brit.), p; OLD CURIOSITY SHOP, THE(1935, Brit.), p; RADIO FOLLIES(1935, Brit.), p; REGAL CAVALCADE(1935, Brit.), p; GIVE HER A RING(1936, Brit.), p; LIVING DANGEROUSLY(1936, Brit.), p; LIVING DEAD, THE(1936, Brit.), p; RED WAGON(1936), p; SENSATION(1936, Brit.), p; SOMEONE AT THE DOOR(1936, Brit.), p; STAR FELL FROM HEAVEN, A(1936, Brit.), p; STUDENT'S ROMANCE, THE(1936, Brit.), p; APRIL BLOSSOMS(1937, Brit.), p; AREN'T MEN BEASTS?(1937, Brit.), p; DOMINANT SEX, THE(1937, Brit.), p; GLAM-OROUS NIGHT(1937, Brit.), p; HEART'S DESIRE(1937, Brit.), p; LET'S MAKE A NIGHT OF IT(1937, Brit.), p; OVER SHE GOES(1937, Brit.), p; PLEASE TEA-CHER(1937, Brit.), p; SPRING HANDICAP(1937, Brit.), p; TENTH MAN, THE(1937, Brit.), p; WEEKEND MILLIONAIRE(1937, Brit.), p; BLACK LIMELIGHT(1938, Brit.), p; HOLD MY HAND(1938, Brit.), p; HOUSEMASTER(1938, Brit.), p; JANE STEPS OUT(1938, Brit.), p; LOVES OF MADAME DUBARRY, THE(1938, Brit.), p; MARI-GOLD(1938, Brit.), p; OH BOY!(1938, Brit.), p; YELLOW SANDS(1938, Brit.), p; YES, MADAM?(1938, Brit.), p; BLACK EYES(1939, Brit.), p; DANGEROUS CARGO(1939, Brit.), p; DEAD MAN'S SHOES(1939, Brit.), p; JUST LIKE A WOMAN(1939, Brit.), p; JUST WILLIAM(1939, Brit.), p; LUCKY TO ME(1939, Brit.), p; MIDDLE WATCH, THE(1939, Brit.), p; NORTH SEA PATROL(1939, Brit.), p; SHE COULDN'T SAY NO(1939, Brit.), p; BULLDOG SEES IT THROUGH(1940, Brit.), p; CASTLE OF CRIMES(1940, Brit.), p; FLYING SQUAD, THE(1940, Brit.), p; HIDDEN MENACE, THE(1940, Brit.), p; MEIN KAMPF–MY CRIMES(1940, Brit.), p; MURDER IN THE NIGHT(1940, Brit.), p; ONE NIGHT IN PARIS(1940, Brit.), p; OUTSIDER, THE(1940, Brit.), p; BANANA RIDGE(1941, Brit.), p&d, w; FALSE RAPTURE(1941), p; FARM-ER'S WIFE, THE(1941, Brit.), p; MY WIFE'S FAMILY(1941, Brit.), p&d; PIRATES OF THE SEVEN SEAS(1941, Brit.), p; POISON PEN(1941, Brit.), p; SPRING MEE-TING(1941, Brit.), p&d, w; STRANGLER, THE(1941, Brit.), p; TERROR, THE(1941, Brit.), p; AMAZING MR. FORREST, THE(1943, Brit.), p; COMIN' THRU' THE RYE(1947, Brit.), d; WOMAN'S ANGLE, THE(1954, Brit.), p; GIRLS AT SEA(1958, Brit.), w
Silents
CHAMPAGNE(1928, Brit.), w

Walter Mycroft
ALMOST A HONEYMOON(1930, Brit.), w; DREYFUS CASE, THE(1931, Brit.), w; BRIDEGROOM FOR TWO(1932, Brit.), w; I SPY(1933, Brit.), p

The Mydolls
1984
PARIS, TEXAS(1984, Ger./Fr.)

Abe Myer
LOVE TAKES FLIGHT(1937), md

Douglas Myer
DYNAMITERS, THE(1956, Brit.), ed

Mark Myer
SAIL A CROOKED SHIP(1961)

Paul Myer
DEVIL'S ANGELS(1967)

Ray Myer
NO MAN OF HER OWN(1950), set d

Torben Myer
GIRL WHO CAME BACK, THE(1935)
Zion Myer
Silents
APRIL FOOL(1926), w
Michael Myerberg
HANSEL AND GRETEL(1954), p; PATTERNS(1956), p
Amos Myers
Silents
CONQUERING POWER, THE(1921), tech d; FOUR HORSEMEN OF THE APOCA-LYPSE, THE(1921), art d
Andy Myers
Misc. Talkies
TROUBLED WATERS(1964, Brit.)
Ann Myers
PLAYGIRLS AND THE BELLBOY, THE(1962,Ger.); GOLDEN BOX, THE(1970)
Misc. Talkies
TOY BOX, THE(1971)
Augie Myers
HONEYSUCKLE ROSE(1980)
Bess Myers
KISS IN THE DARK, A(1949)
Billie Myers
TAKE MY LIFE(1942), w
Bruce Myers
NO BLADE OF GRASS(1970, Brit.); MEETINGS WITH REMARKABLE MEN(1979, Brit.); AWAKENING, THE(1980)
Carmel Myers
BROADWAY SCANDALS(1929); CARELESS AGE(1929); GHOST TALKS, THE(1929); LADY SURRENDERS, A(1930); SHIP FROM SHANGHAI, THE(1930); CHINATOWN AFTER DARK(1931); LION AND THE LAMB(1931); MAD GENIUS, THE(1931); SVENGALI(1931); NICE WOMAN(1932); NO LIVING WITNESS(1932); PLEASU-RE(1933); COUNTESS OF MONTE CRISTO, THE(1934); LADY FOR A NIGHT(1941); GEORGE WHITE'S SCANDALS(1945); WHISTLE STOP(1946); WON TON TON, THE DOG WHO SAVED HOLLYWOOD(1976)
Silents
MATRIMANIAC, THE(1916); HAUNTED PAJAMAS(1917); ALL NIGHT(1918); BROADWAY SCANDAL(1918); GIRL IN THE DARK, THE(1918); GILDED DREAM, THE(1920); IN FOLLY'S TRAIL(1920); MAD MARRIAGE, THE(1921); DANGER POINT, THE(1922); LOVE GAMBLER, THE(1922); RENO(1923); SLAVE OF DESI-RE(1923); BABBITT(1924); BEAU BRUMMEL(1924); BROADWAY AFTER DARK(1924); BEN-HUR(1925); TELL IT TO THE MARINES(1926); GIRL FROM RIO, THE(1927); FOUR WALLS(1928)
Misc. Silents
LASH OF POWER, THE(1917); LOVE SUBLIME, A(1917); MIGHT AND THE MAN(1917); SIRENS OF THE SEA(1917); ALL NIGHT(1918); CITY OF TEARS, THE(1918); DREAM LADY, THE(1918); MARRIAGE LIE, THE(1918); MY UNMAR-RIED WIFE(1918); SOCIETY SENSATION, A(1918); WIFE HE BOUGHT, THE(1918); WINE GIRL, THE(1918); LITTLE WHITE SAVAGE, THE(1919); WHO WILL MARRY ME?(1919); BEAUTIFULLY TRIMMED(1920); CHEATED LOVE(1921); DANGEROUS MOMENT, THE(1921); DAUGHTER OF THE LAW, A(1921); KISS, THE(1921); DANC-ER OF THE NILE, THE(1923); GOOD-BY GIRLS!(1923); LAST HOUR, THE(1923); LITTLE GIRL NEXT DOOR, THE(1923); LOVE PIRATE, THE(1923); DEVIL'S CIRCUS, THE(1926); GAY DECEIVER, THE(1926); SORRELL AND SON(1927); UNDERSTAND-ING HEART, THE(1927); CERTAIN YOUNG MAN, A(1928); PROWLERS OF THE SEA(1928); RED SWORD, THE(1929)
Charles Myers
IT'S A BIG COUNTRY(1951)
Claire Myers
FINISHING SCHOOL(1934)
Cynthia Myers
MOLLY AND LAWLESS JOHN(1972)
David Myers
WELCOME TO L.A.(1976), ph; FM(1978), ph, ed; RENALDO AND CLARA(1978), ph; SAMMY STOPS THE WORLD zero(1978), ph; DIE LAUGHING(1980), ph; ROA-DIE(1980), ph; ZOOT SUIT(1981), ph; HUMAN HIGHWAY(1982), ph; DEADLY FORCE(1983), ph
Dennis Myers
MUSIC LOVERS, THE(1971, Brit.)
Dickie Myers
MADAME CURIE(1943)
Diwaldo Myers
SAVAGES FROM HELL(1968)
Doug Myers
RUNAWAY BUS, THE(1954, Brit.), ed; STORMY CROSSING(1958, Brit.), ed
Douglas Myers
PIMPERNEL SMITH(1942, Brit.), ed; SPITFIRE(1943, Brit.), ed; TAWNY PI-PIT(1947, Brit.), ed; CORRIDOR OF MIRRORS(1948, Brit.), ed; MISS PILGRIM'S PROGRESS(1950, Brit.), ed; MYSTERY AT THE BURLESQUE(1950, Brit.), ed; OB-SESSED(1951, Brit.), ed; BLOOD OF THE VAMPIRE(1958, Brit.), ed; WHO KILLED VAN LOON?(1984, Brit.), ed
Edwin Myers
Silents
PRETTY CLOTHES(1927), w
Elizabeth Myers
BLACKMAILED(1951, Brit.), w
Frank Myers
LOST, LONELY AND VICIOUS(1958), d
Fredricka Myers
PRETTY MAIDS ALL IN A ROW(1971)
Gerry Myers
JAMBOREE(1957)
Greta Myers
YOUNG AND BEAUTIFUL(1934)
Harry C. Myers
MARY STEVENS, M.D.(1933); MILKY WAY, THE(1936); SAN FRANCISCO(1936)
Silents
CONNECTICUT YANKEE AT KING ARTHUR'S COURT, A(1921)

Misc. Silents
MAN OF SHAME, THE(1915), a, d; FACE IN THE DARK, THE(1918)
Harry F. Myers
SAVAGE GIRL, THE(1932)
Harry Myers
WONDER OF WOMEN(1929); MEET THE WIFE(1931); STRANGE ADVEN-TURE(1932); IMPORTANT WITNESS, THE(1933); POLICE CALL(1933); WE LIVE AGAIN(1934); MISSISSIPPI(1935); HIS BROTHER'S WIFE(1936); HOLLYWOOD BOULEVARD(1936); VOGUES OF 1938(1937)
Misc. Talkies
POTLUCK PARDS(1934)
Silents
EARL OF PAWTUCKET, THE(1915); CONQUERED HEARTS(1918); NOTORIOUS MRS. SANDS, THE(1920); NOBODY'S FOOL(1921); BEAUTIFUL AND DAMNED, THE(1922); HANDLE WITH CARE(1922); KISSES(1922); COMMON LAW, THE(1923); STEPHEN STEPS OUT(1923); MARRIAGE CIRCLE, THE(1924); RECKLESS RO-MANCE(1924); ZANDER THE GREAT(1925); BEAUTIFUL CHEAT, THE(1926); EXIT SMILING(1926); NUT-CRACKER, THE(1926); BACHELOR'S BABY, THE(1927); CITY LIGHTS(1931)
Misc. Silents
PEACEFUL VALLEY(1920); SKY-EYE(1920); ON THE HIGH CARD(1921); R.S.V.P.(1921); WHY TRUST YOUR HUSBAND?(1921); TOP O' THE MORNING, THE(1922); TURN TO THE RIGHT(1922); WHEN THE LAD CAME HOME(1922); BRASS(1923); BRASS BOTTLE, THE(1923); MAIN STREET(1923); PRINTER'S DEVIL, THE(1923); BEHOLD THIS WOMAN(1924); DADDIES(1924); GROUNDS FOR DIVORCE(1925); SHE WOLVES(1925); UP IN MABEL'S ROOM(1926); FIRST NIGHT, THE(1927); GETTING GERTIE'S GARTER(1927); STREET OF ILLU-SION, THE(1928); MONTMARTE ROSE(1929)
Henry Myers
HER WEDDING NIGHT(1930), w; MURDER BY THE CLOCK(1931), w; MILLION DOLLAR LEGS(1932), w; DIPLOMANIACS(1933), w; BLACK ROOM, THE(1935), w; FATHER BROWN, DETECTIVE(1935), w; COLLEGE HOLIDAY(1936), w; LUCKIEST GIRL IN THE WORLD, THE(1936), w; MERRY-GO-ROUND OF 1938(1937), w; HEY, ROOKIE(1944), w; ALICE IN WONDERLAND(1951, Fr.), w
James Myers
MRS. BROWN, YOU'VE GOT A LOVELY DAUGHTER(1968, Brit.)
James E. Myers
SHAFT IN AFRICA(1973); UNCLE SCAM(1981)
James T. Myers
BURNT OFFERINGS(1976)
Janet Myers
TENTACLES(1977, Ital.)
Jerome Myers
MY BODYGUARD(1980)
Jerry Lynn Myers
I, JANE DOE(1948)
John Myers
M(1970); MUSIC LOVERS, THE(1971, Brit.)
Jordan Myers
1984
RHINESTONE(1984)
Kathleen Myers
Silents
REPUTATION(1921); BABBITT(1924); DICK TURPIN(1925); GO WEST(1925); GOAT GETTER(1925); HEADS UP(1925); SMILIN' AT TROUBLE(1925)
Misc. Silents
FLAMING HEARTS(1922); STOLEN SECRETS(1924); HIS SUPREME MO-MENT(1925); FLYING MAIL, THE(1926); KOSHER KITTY KELLY(1926); MUL-HALL'S GREAT CATCH(1926); SIR LUMBERJACK(1926); TRAFFIC COP, THE(1926); LADIES BEWARE(1927); LUCKY FOOL(1927); SHE'S MY BABY(1927); GENTLEMAN PREFFERED, A(1928)
Ken Myers
FINAL TERROR, THE(1983), spec eff; HOUSE ON SORORITY ROW, THE(1983)
Kenny Myers
METALSTORM: THE DESTRUCTION OF JARED-SYN(1983), makeup; WACK-O(1983), makeup
Kevin Myers
NORSEMAN, THE(1978)
Louis E. Myers
Silents
SHADOWS OF CONSCIENCE(1921), art d; BULLDOG COURAGE(1922), art d
Matt Myers
UNCLE SCAM(1981)
Mickey Myers
HUMAN DUPLICATORS, THE(1965), cos
Monroe Myers
PASSION HOLIDAY(1963); HONEYMOON OF HORROR(1964); MISSION MARS(1968)
Mr. Myers
Silents
GOLD RUSH, THE(1925)
Otto Myers
Misc. Silents
GAMBLING FOOL, THE(1925)
Pamela Myers
BLOODBROTHERS(1978)
1984
PROTOCOL(1984)
Paul Myers
DON GIOVANNI(1979, Fr./Ital./Ger.), md
Paulene Myers
COMIC, THE(1969); LOST MAN, THE(1969); ...TICK...TICK...TICK...(1970); LADY SINGS THE BLUES(1972); MAURIE(1973); STING, THE(1973); LOST IN THE STARS(1974)
Pauline Myers
SOMETHING OF VALUE(1957); HOW TO MAKE A MONSTER(1958); TO KILL A MOCKINGBIRD(1962); FATE IS THE HUNTER(1964); HONEYMOON HOTEL(1964); SHOCK TREATMENT(1964); WINNING(1969)

Peter Myers
COMING-OUT PARTY, A(; MEET MR. LUCIFER(1953, Brit.), w; FOR BETTER FOR WORSE(1954, Brit.), w; SQUARE RING, THE(1955, Brit.), w; BACHELOR OF HEARTS(1958, Brit.); RELUCTANT DEBUTANTE, THE(1958); SNORKEL, THE(1958, Brit.), w; EXPRESSO BONGO(1959, Brit.); DAY THEY ROBBED THE BANK OF ENGLAND, THE(1960, Brit.); GO TO BLAZES(1962, Brit.), w; SHE KNOWS Y'-KNOW(1962, Brit.), w; WONDERFUL TO BE YOUNG!(1962, Brit.), w; MYSTERY SUBMARINE(1963, Brit.); PUNCH AND JUDY MAN, THE(1963, Brit.); QUEEN'S GUARDS, THE(1963, Brit.); SUMMER HOLIDAY(1963, Brit.), w; FRENCH DRESSING(1964, Brit.), w; SWINGER'S PARADISE(1965, Brit.), w; HELLO-GOODBYE(1970); HOVERBUG(1970, Brit.); MAGIC CHRISTIAN, THE(1970, Brit.).

Roy Myers
Silents
RIDIN' WILD(1922), w

Ruth Myers
WORK IS A FOUR LETTER WORD(1968, Brit.), cos; NICE GIRL LIKE ME, A(1969, Brit.), cos; THREE INTO TWO WON'T GO(1969, Brit.), cos; TWELVE CHAIRS, THE(1970), cos; ROMANCE OF A HORSE THIEF(1971), cos; RULING CLASS, THE(1972, Brit.), cos; TOUCH OF CLASS, A(1973, Brit.), cos; ADVENTURES OF SHERLOCK HOLMES' SMARTER BROTHER, THE(1975, Brit.), cos; ROMANTIC ENGLISHWOMAN, THE(1975, Brit./Fr.), cos; WORLD'S GREATEST LOVER, THE(1977), cos; MAGIC(1978), cos; SILVER BEARS(1978), cos; ...AND JUSTICE FOR ALL(1979), cos; MAIN EVENT, THE(1979), cos; COMPETITION, THE(1980), cos; IN GOD WE TRUST(1980), cos; IT'S MY TURN(1980), cos; CANNERY ROW(1982), cos; SOMETHING WICKED THIS WAY COMES(1983), cos
1984
CRIMES OF PASSION(1984), cos; ELECTRIC DREAMS(1984), cos; TEACHERS(1984), cos

Sean Myers
BREAK OF DAY(1977, Aus.); LAST OF THE KNUCKLEMEN, THE(1981, Aus.)

Sheri Myers
REVENGE OF THE CHEERLEADERS(1976)

Sidney Myers
SAVAGE EYE, THE(1960), p,d&w

Stanley Myers
KALEIDOSCOPE(1966, Brit.), m, md; ULYSSES(1967, U.S./Brit.), m, Md; NO WAY TO TREAT A LADY(1968), m; SEPARATION(1968, Brit.), m; NIGHT OF THE FOLLOWING DAY, THE(1969, Brit.), m; OTLEY(1969, Brit.), m; TWO GENTLEMEN SHARING(1969, Brit.), m; TAKE A GIRL LIKE YOU(1970, Brit.), m; UNDERGROUND(1970, Brit.), m; WALKING STICK, THE(1970, Brit.), m; LONG AGO, TOMORROW(1971, Brit.), m; SEVERED HEAD, A(1971, Brit.), m; DEVIL'S WIDOW, THE(1972, Brit.), m; IT'S A 2"6" ABOVE THE GROUND WORLD(1972, Brit.), m; SITTING TARGET(1972, Brit.), m; X Y & ZEE(1972, Brit.), m; BLOCKHOUSE, THE(1974, Brit.), m; CARAVAN TO VACCARES(1974, Brit./Fr), m; FRIGHTMARE(1974, Brit.), m; LITTLE MALCOLM(1974, Brit.), m; CONDUCT UNBECOMING(1975, Brit.), m; WILBY CONSPIRACY, THE(1975, Brit.), m; CONFESSIONAL, THE(1977, Brit.), m; SCHIZO(1977, Brit.), m; CLASS OF MISS MAC MICHAEL, THE(1978, Brit./U.S.), m; COUP DE GRACE(1978, Ger./Fr.), m; DEER HUNTER, THE(1978), m; GREEK TYCOON, THE(1978), m; PORTRAIT OF THE ARTIST AS A YOUNG MAN, A(1979, Ireland), m; YESTERDAY'S HERO(1979, Brit.), md; WATCHER IN THE WOODS, THE(1980, Brit.), m; ABSOLUTION(1981, Brit.), m; LADY CHATTERLEY'S LOVER(1981, Fr./Brit.), m; COMEBACK, THE(1982, Brit.), m; MOONLIGHTING(1982, Brit.), m; NEXT ONE, THE(1982, U.S./Gr.), m; BEYOND THE LIMIT(1983), m; EUREKA(1983, Brit.), m
1984
BLIND DATE(1984), m; SUCCESS IS THE BEST REVENGE(1984, Brit.), m

Steve Myers
CHANGE OF SEASONS, A(1980)

Stevie Myers
ULTIMATE WARRIOR, THE(1975)
1984
WOMAN IN RED, THE(1984)

Susan Myers
CASEY'S SHADOW(1978); TRUE CONFESSIONS(1981)

Thelma Myers
IN WHICH WE SERVE(1942, Brit.), ed; NOTORIOUS GENTLEMAN(1945, Brit.), ed; ADVENTURESS, THE(1946, Brit.), ed; GREEN FOR DANGER(1946, Brit.), ed; CAPTAIN BOYCOTT(1947, Brit.), ed; DULCIMER STREET(1948, Brit.), ed; BLUE LAGOON, THE(1949, Brit.), ed; MUDLARK, THE(1950, Brit.), ed; GREAT MANHUNT, THE(1951, Brit.), ed

Thomas Myers
DRIVER, THE(1978)

Thomas R. Myers
LONG RIDERS, THE(1980)

Timothy Myers
I, THE JURY(1982)

Tommy Myers
SKIPPER SURPRISED HIS WIFE, THE(1950)

Truett Myers
ALL THE KING'S MEN(1949)

Virginia Myers
JENNIFER(1953), w
Misc. Silents
LUCKY FOOL(1927)

Willie Myers
HURRICANE(1979)

Z. Myers
LOVE THY NEIGHBOR(1940), w

Zion Myers
SIDEWALKS OF NEW YORK(1931), d; LUCKY DOG(1933), d, w, ed; OLD MAN RHYTHM(1935), p; TO BEAT THE BAND(1935), p; MAKE WAY FOR A LADY(1936), p; TWO IN THE DARK(1936), p; SMALL TOWN BOY(1937), p; SOMETHING TO SING ABOUT(1937), p; THEY WANTED TO MARRY(1937), p; BUCK BENNY RIDES AGAIN(1940), w; SKYLARK(1941), w; HERE COME THE WAVES(1944), w

Alan Myerson
FUNNYMAN(1967); STEELYARD BLUES(1973), d; PRIVATE LESSONS(1981), d

Bess Myerson
IT HAPPENED TO JANE(1959)

Jane Myerson
GANDHI(1982)

Jessica Myerson
VIVA MAX!(1969); GRASSHOPPER, THE(1970); GET TO KNOW YOUR RABBIT(1972); STEELYARD BLUES(1973)

Robert Myerson
MOTHRA(1962, Jap.), w

Bent Myggen
SMOKEY BITES THE DUST(1981), m

John Myhers
NEVER TAKE NO FOR AN ANSWER(1952, Brit./Ital.); WEDDINGS AND BABIES(1960); SATURDAY NIGHT IN APPLE VALLEY(1965), p,d&w, ed; PRIVATE NAVY OF SGT. O'FARRELL, THE(1968); WICKED DREAMS OF PAULA SCHULTZ, THE(1968); 2000 YEARS LATER(1969); WILLARD(1971); NOW YOU SEE HIM, NOW YOU DON'T(1972); SNOWBALL EXPRESS(1972); 1776(1972); WALKING TALL(1973); TRAIN RIDE TO HOLLYWOOD(1975); HOW TO SUCCEED IN BUSINESS WITHOUT REALLY TRYING(1976); SHAGGY D.A., THE(1976); BILLION DOLLAR HOBO, THE(1977); PRIZE FIGHTER, THE(1979), a, w; PRIVATE EYES, THE(1980), w; HISTORY OF THE WORLD, PART 1(1981)

Mykhaylovsky
Silents
ARSENAL(1929, USSR)

Mark Mylam
LIFE IN EMERGENCY WARD 10(1959, Brit.)

Billy Myles
SWEET BEAT(1962, Brit.)

Bruce Myles
NIGHT DIGGER, THE(1971, Brit.)

Dean Myles
GIRL MOST LIKELY, THE(1957)

Joan Myles
NOOSE HANGS HIGH, THE(1948); RACE STREET(1948)

Meg Myles
PHENIX CITY STORY, THE(1955); CALYPSO HEAT WAVE(1957); SATAN IN HIGH HEELS(1962); COOGAN'S BLUFF(1968); LOVELY WAY TO DIE, A(1968); TOUCHED(1983)

Norbert Myles
Misc. Talkies
SECRETS OF HOLLYWOOD(1933)
Silents
WALLOPING WALLACE(1924), w; UNDER FIRE(1926); STORMY WATERS(1928)
Misc. Silents
SHOULD SHE OBEY?(1917); DAUGHTER OF DAWN, THE(1920), d; SADDLE CYCLONE(1925); FAITHFUL WIVES(1926), d

Norbert A. Myles
Silents
NANCY'S BIRTHRIGHT(1916); TRUTHFUL TULLIVER(1917)
Misc. Silents
IN THE WEB OF THE GRAFTERS(1916); STAIN IN THE BLOOD, THE(1916); TRUTHFUL TULLIVER(1917)

Roland Myles
Silents
FRAILTY(1921, Brit.)
Misc. Silents
BARS OF IRON(1920, Brit.); MY LORD CONCEIT(1921, Brit.)

Terry Myles
Silents
WALLOPING WALLACE(1924)

Tiffany Myles
NIGHT IN HEAVEN, A(1983)

Jeffrey Mylett
GODSPELL(1973)

Charles Mylne
TROUBLE IN THE SKY(1961, Brit.)

Jack Mylong
FOR WHOM THE BELL TOLLS(1943)

John Mylong
CROSSROADS(1942); HOSTAGES(1943); MOON IS DOWN, THE(1943); STRANGE DEATH OF ADOLF HITLER, THE(1943); THEY CAME TO BLOW UP AMERICA(1943); EXPERIMENT PERILOUS(1944); MASK OF DIMITRIOS, THE(1944); STORY OF DR. WASSELL, THE(1944); FALCON IN SAN FRANCISCO, THE(1945); HOTEL BERLIN(1945); I'LL TELL THE WORLD(1945); MONSIEUR BEAUCAIRE(1946); SEARCHING WIND, THE(1946); UNCONQUERED(1947); OH, YOU BEAUTIFUL DOLL(1949); ANNIE GET YOUR GUN(1950); YOUNG DANIEL BOONE(1950); HIS KIND OF WOMAN(1951); SEA TIGER(1952); ROBOT MONSTER(1953); MAGNIFICENT OBSESSION(1954); CROOKED WEB, THE(1955); EDDY DUCHIN STORY, THE(1956); BEAST OF BUDAPEST, THE(1958); I, MOBSTER(1959); MERMAIDS OF TIBURON, THE(1962)

Mylos
TRAPEZE(1956)

Emile Mylos
LOVE IN THE AFTERNOON(1957)

Eddie Mynatt
Misc. Talkies
1ST NOTCH, THE(1977)

Patrick Mynhardt
HELLIONS, THE(1962, Brit.); NAKED PREY, THE(1966, U.S./South Africa); JACKALS, THE(1967, South Africa); SEVEN AGAINST THE SUN(1968, South Africa); ZULU DAWN(1980, Brit.); GRASS IS SINGING, THE(1982, Brit./Swed.)
1984
KILLING HEAT(1984)
Misc. Talkies
THREE BULLETS FOR A LONG GUN(1973)

Siegfried Mynhardt
DINGAKA(1965, South Africa)

Nina Myral
MAN STOLEN(1934, Fr.); PRIZE, THE(1952, Fr.)

Per Myrberg
SWEDISH MISTRESS, THE(1964, Swed.)

Anton Myrer
IN LOVE AND WAR(1958), w

Mlle. Myrga
Misc. Silents
JOCELYN(1922, Fr.); GENEVIEVE(1923, Fr.); LA BRIERE(1925, Fr.); JADE CASKET, THE(1929, Fr.)

Myriam
STORY OF A CHEAT, THE(1938, Fr.), ed; LES DERNIERES VACANCES(1947, Fr.), ed

Darlene Myrick
DEAD ONE, THE(1961)

Witold Myrkosz
CONSTANT FACTOR, THE(1980, Pol.)

A.S. Myron
Misc. Talkies
DEVIL ON DECK(1932)

George Myron
SILENCE OF THE NORTH(1981, Can.)

Helen A. Myron
PADDY O'DAY(1935), cos; THUNDER IN THE NIGHT(1935), cos; MY MARRIAGE(1936), cos; MR. MOTO'S GAMBLE(1938), cos; SAFETY IN NUMBERS(1938), cos; TRIP TO PARIS, A(1938), cos; MR. MOTO'S LAST WARNING(1939), cos; PACK UP YOUR TROUBLES(1939), cos; YOUNG AS YOU FEEL(1940), cos

Ron Myron
RING OF FIRE(1961)

Myron the Dog
MURDER BY DEATH(1976)

Fred Myrow
LEO THE LAST(1970, Brit.), m; STEAGLE, THE(1971), m; LOLLY-MADONNA XXX(1973), m; REFLECTION OF FEAR, A(1973), m, md; SCARECROW(1973), m; SOYLENT GREEN(1973), m; JIM, THE WORLD'S GREATEST(1976), m; KENNY AND CO.(1976), m; PHANTASM(1979), m

Fredric Myrow
ON THE NICKEL(1980), m

Josef Myrow
THREE LITTLE GIRLS IN BLUE(1946), m; BUNDLE OF JOY(1956), m

Myrte
Misc. Talkies
MYRTE AND THE DEMONS(1948)

J. Dinan Myrtetus
1984
SUBURBIA(1984)

J. Dinan Mytretus
1984
POWER, THE(1984)

Odette Myrtil
DODSWORTH(1936); GIRL FROM SCOTLAND YARD, THE(1937); SUEZ(1938); KITTY FOYLE(1940); OUT OF THE FOG(1941); I MARRIED AN ANGEL(1942); PIED PIPER, THE(1942); REUNION IN FRANCE(1942); YANKEE DOODLE DANDY(1942); FOREVER AND A DAY(1943); THOUSANDS CHEER(1943); DARK WATERS(1944); UNCERTAIN GLORY(1944); RHAPSODY IN BLUE(1945); DEVOTION(1946); FIGHTING KENTUCKIAN, THE(1949); MANHANDLED(1949), cos; 711 OCEAN DRIVE(1950), cos; HERE COMES THE GROOM(1951); STRANGERS ON A TRAIN(1951); LADY POSSESSED(1952)
Silents
SQUIBS, MP(1923, Brit.)

Fred Myrton
DEATH VALLEY MANHUNT(1943), w

Bru Mysak
SAIL A CROOKED SHIP(1961); NOTORIOUS LANDLADY, THE(1962)

Ninel Myshkova
SWORD AND THE DRAGON, THE(1960, USSR); HOUSE WITH AN ATTIC, THE(1964, USSR); MAGIC WEAVER, THE(1965, USSR)

Y. Myshkova
MAGIC VOYAGE OF SINBAD, THE(1962, USSR)

Alexandra Myskova
SWEET LIGHT IN A DARK ROOM(1966, Czech.); FIFTH HORSEMAN IS FEAR, THE(1968, Czech.)

Mila Myslikova
CAPRICIOUS SUMMER(1968, Czech.)

Mysty Shot
LADY TAKES A CHANCE, A(1943)

Tadeusz Myszorek
SARAGOSSA MANUSCRIPT, THE(1972, Pol.), art d

Shelly Dinah Myte
Misc. Talkies
SEX DU JOUR(1976)

Fred K. Myton
RETURN OF WILD BILL, THE(1940), w

Fred Kennedy Myton
Silents
GOLD MADNESS(1923), w; JEALOUS HUSBANDS(1923), w; ISLE OF RETRIBUTION, THE(1926), w

Fred Myton
GANG WAR(1928), w; ISLE OF LOST SHIPS(1929), w; KID GLOVES(1929), w; GREAT DIVIDE, THE(1930), w; OTHER TOMORROW, THE(1930), w; WHITE EAGLE(1932), w; KING OF THE WILD HORSES, THE(1934), w; BORDER PHANTOM(1937), w; DOOMED AT SUNDOWN(1937), w; GAMBLING TERROR, THE(1937), w; GUN LORDS OF STIRRUP BASIN(1937), w; MOONLIGHT ON THE RANGE(1937), w; ROAMING COWBOY, THE(1937), w; TRAIL OF VENGEANCE(1937), w; TRUSTED OUTLAW, THE(1937), w; DESERT PATROL(1938), w; GUNSMOKE TRAIL(1938), w; HARLEM ON THE PRAIRIE(1938), w; TERROR OF TINY TOWN, THE(1938), w; TWO-GUN JUSTICE(1938), w; CODE OF THE FEARLESS(1939), w; KNIGHT OF THE PLAINS(1939), w; ROLLIN' WESTWARD(1939), w; SIX-GUN RHYTHM(1939), w; PIONEERS OF THE FRONTIER(1940), w; PRAIRIE SCHOONERS(1940), w; TEXAS STAGECOACH(1940), w; TWO-FISTED RANGERS(1940), w; BILLY THE KID WANTED(1941), w; BILLY THE KID'S ROUNDUP(1941), w; GENTLEMAN FROM DIXIE(1941), w; PINTO KID, THE(1941), w;

WILDCAT OF TUCSON(1941), w; LONE PRAIRIE, THE(1942), w; MAD MONSTER, THE(1942), w; BLACK HILLS EXPRESS(1943), w; BLACK RAVEN, THE(1943), w; DEAD MEN WALK(1943), w; KID RIDES AGAIN, THE(1943), w; RIDERS OF THE NORTHWEST MOUNTED(1943), w; LAW OF THE SADDLE(1944), w; NABONGA(1944), w; THUNDERING GUN SLINGERS(1944), w; KID SISTER, THE(1945), w; PRAIRIE RUSTLERS(1945), w; SHADOWS OF DEATH(1945), w; STAGECOACH OUTLAWS(1945), w; BLONDE FOR A DAY(1946), w; GENTLEMEN WITH GUNS(1946), w; LADY CHASER(1946), w; MURDER IS MY BUSINESS(1946), w; PRAIRIE BADMEN(1946), w; THREE ON A TICKET(1947), w; TOO MANY WINNERS(1947), w; COUNTERFEITERS, THE(1948), w; MIRACULOUS JOURNEY(1948), w; HI-JACKED(1950), w; WESTERN PACIFIC AGENT(1950), w; WHISTLING HILLS(1951), w
Silents
FIGHTING FOR LOVE(1917), w; LOVE AFLAME(1917), w; ALL NIGHT(1918), w; LOVE SWINDLE(1918), w; CABARET GIRL, THE(1919), w; MAN IN THE OPEN, A(1919), w; SOUTH OF SUVA(1922), w; TORMENT(1924), w; QUEEN O' DIAMONDS(1926), w; AIR LEGION, THE(1929), w; SMOKE BELLEW(1929), w, t

Frederick Myton
Silents
LADY ROBINHOOD(1925), w

Madge Myton
Silents
NUT-CRACKER, THE(1926), w

Rudolph Myzet
MAN WHO BROKE THE BANK AT MONTE CARLO, THE(1935); IDIOT'S DELIGHT(1939); ONCE UPON A HONEYMOON(1942); THIS LAND IS MINE(1943); VOICE IN THE WIND(1944)

L. Myznikova
NIGHT BEFORE CHRISTMAS, A(1963, USSR)

Jonathan Mzamo
PENNYWHISTLE BLUES, THE(1952, South Africa)

Myriam Mziere
JONAH–WHO WILL BE 25 IN THE YEAR 2000(1976, Switz.)

N

N. H. P. Inc.
BRAINWAVES(1983), spec eff
N.C.S
I AM A GROUPIE(1970, Brit.), ed
Ynousse N'Diaye
MANDABI(1970, Fr./Senegal)
Serigne N'Diayes
MANDABI(1970, Fr./Senegal)
Paul N'Gei
IVORY HUNTER(1952, Brit.)
Jean-Francoise Eyou N'Guessan
BLACK AND WHITE IN COLOR(1976, Fr.)
Thi Loan N'Guyen
GREEN ROOM, THE(1979, Fr.)
1984
LES COMPERES(1984, Fr.), makeup
Thi-Loan N'Guyen
SMALL CHANGE(1976, Fr.), makeup
Joseph T. Naar
ALL-AMERICAN BOY, THE(1973), p; SCREAM BLACULA SCREAM(1973), p
Ken Naarden
LILITH(1964)
Naba the Gorilla
THREE TEXAS STEERS(1939)
Ronen Nabah
CIRCLE OF IRON(1979, Brit.)
Andrea Nabakowski
ALL-AROUND REDUCED PERSONALITY–OUTTAKES, THE(1978, Ger.)
I. Nabatov
VOW, THE(1947, USSR.)
Osami Nabe
HOTSPRINGS HOLIDAY(1970, Jap.); PERFORMERS, THE(1970, Jap.)
Osamu Nabeshima
1984
WARRIORS OF THE WIND(1984, Jap.), anim
Marva Nabili
SIAVASH IN PERSEPOLIS(1966, Iran)
1984
NIGHTSONGS(1984), d&w
Abed Salam Nabilsy
LITTLE MISS DEVIL(1951, Egypt)
James Benson Nablo
DRIVE A CROOKED ROAD(1954), w; BULLET FOR JOEY, A(1955), w; RAW EDGE(1956), w; CHINA DOLL(1958), w
Nadine Nabokov
AND HOPE TO DIE(1972 Fr/US)
Vladimir Nabokov
LOLITA(1962), w; KING, QUEEN, KNAVE(1972, Ger./U.S.), w; DESPAIR(1978, Ger.), w
Nabonga
NABONGA(1944)
Pricipe Nabor
BYE-BYE BRASIL(1980, Braz.)
Jim Nabors
BEST LITTLE WHOREHOUSE IN TEXAS, THE(1982); STROKER ACE(1983)
1984
CANNONBALL RUN II(1984)
Troy Nabors
PURSUIT(1975)
Anna Marie Nabuco
LOVE SLAVES OF THE AMAZONS(1957)
Anthony Nace
MURDER WITH PICTURES(1936); SON COMES HOME, A(1936); BETWEEN TWO WOMEN(1937); INTERNES CAN'T TAKE MONEY(1937); MURDER GOES TO COLLEGE(1937); RIDING ON AIR(1937); DUKE OF WEST POINT, THE(1938); I AM THE LAW(1938); SUNSET TRAIL(1938); I WANTED WINGS(1941); WAGONS ROLL AT NIGHT, THE(1941); TO THE SHORES OF TRIPOLI(1942); WAKE ISLAND(1942)
Wally Nachaby
CIRCLE OF DECEIT(1982, Fr./Ger.)
Estrongo Nachama
CABARET(1972)
Andi Nachman
UP IN SMOKE(1978)
Kurt Nachmann
CONGRESS DANCES(1957, Ger.), w; HIPPODROME(1961, Aust./Ger.), w; QUEEN OF THE PIRATES(1961, Ital./Ger.), w
Bernardo Nacilla
YEAR OF LIVING DANGEROUSLY, THE(1982, Aus.)
Giancarlo Nacinelli
TENTACLES(1977, Ital.)
Jean-Marie Nacry
JOHNNY FRENCHMAN(1946, Brit.)
Nadajan
HOUSE OF USHER(1960)
Michele Nadal
PARIS DOES STRANGE THINGS(1957, Fr./Ital.)
Michelle Nadal
FRENCH CANCAN(1956, Fr.)
Mickey Nadar
INSIDE AMY(1975)
Marta Naday
MISS PRESIDENT(1935, Hung.)

Robert Nadder
MAIN EVENT, THE(1979)
1984
MICKI AND MAUDE(1984)
Sarah Nade
ON HER BED OF ROSES(1966)
Claire Nadeau
JOY(1983, Fr./Can.)
Elayne Nadeau
MARTIN(1979)
Elianne Nadeau
PARTY, THE(1968)
Ray Nadeau
SATIN MUSHROOM, THE(1969), ph; TWO-MINUTE WARNING(1976)
Serge Nadejdine
Misc. Silents
LE CHIFFONNIER DE PARIS(1924, Fr.), d; L'HEUREUX MORT(1924, Fr.), d; LA CIBLE(1925, Fr.), d; LE NEGRE BLANC(1925, Fr.), d; NAPLES AU BAISER DE FEU(1925, Fr.), d
Nicholas Nadejin
MEN ARE NOT GODS(1937, Brit.); WINGS OF THE MORNING(1937, Brit.)
Arthur H. Nadel
MY DEAR SECRETARY(1948), ed; IMPACT(1949), ed; D.O.A.(1950), ed; JACKIE ROBINSON STORY, THE(1950), ed; CHICAGO CALLING(1951), ed; NO TIME FOR FLOWERS(1952), ed; WITHOUT WARNING(1952), ed; SABRE JET(1953), ed; VICE SQUAD(1953), ed; KISS OF FIRE(1955), ed; NO PLACE TO HIDE(1956), ed; LITTLEST HOBO, THE(1958), ed; SNOWFIRE(1958), ed; CLAMBAKE(1967), d; STRATEGY OF TERROR(1969), p; UNDERGROUND(1970, Brit.), d
Eli Nadel
Silents
WOMANHANDLED(1925)
Eliah Nadel
Silents
NET, THE(1923)
Ruth Nadel
RACING FEVER(1964)
Carol Nadell
KRAMER VS. KRAMER(1979)
Robert Nadell
APPOINTMENT WITH MURDER(1948)
Jess Nadelman
TWO-MINUTE WARNING(1976)
Mikola Nademski
Silents
EARTH(1930, USSR)
Mykola Nademsky
Silents
ARSENAL(1929, USSR)
George Nader
RUSTLERS ON HORSEBACK(1950); OVERLAND TELEGRAPH(1951); PROWLER, THE(1951); TAKE CARE OF MY LITTLE GIRL(1951); TWO TICKETS TO BROADWAY(1951); PHONE CALL FROM A STRANGER(1952); DOWN AMONG THE SHELTERING PALMS(1953); MONSOON(1953); ROBOT MONSTER(1953); SINS OF JEZEBEL(1953); CARNIVAL STORY(1954); FOUR GUNS TO THE BORDER(1954); MISS ROBIN CRUSOE(1954); LADY GODIVA(1955); SECOND GREATEST SEX, THE(1955); SIX BRIDGES TO CROSS(1955); AWAY ALL BOATS(1956); CONGO CROSSING(1956); FOUR GIRLS IN TOWN(1956); UNGUARDED MOMENT, THE(1956); JOE BUTTERFLY(1957); MAN AFRAID(1957); APPOINTMENT WITH A SHADOW(1958); FEMALE ANIMAL, THE(1958); FLOOD TIDE(1958); NOWHERE TO GO(1959, Brit.); SECRET MARK OF D'ARTAGNAN, THE(1963, Fr./Ital.); HUMAN DUPLICATORS, THE(1965); HOUSE OF 1,000 DOLLS(1967, Ger./Span./Brit.); MILLION EYES OF SU-MURU, THE(1967, Brit.); BEYOND ATLANTIS(1973, Phil.)
Misc. Talkies
ALARM ON 83RD STREET(1965); MEMORY OF LOVE(1949); APPOINTMENT WITH A SHADOW(1957)
Mike Nader
MUSCLE BEACH PARTY(1964); PAJAMA PARTY(1964); HOW TO STUFF A WILD BIKINI(1965); SERGEANT DEADHEAD(1965); SKI PARTY(1965); FIREBALL 590(1966)
Saladin Nader
EMBASSY(1972, Brit.)
Stephanie Nader
HOW TO STUFF A WILD BIKINI(1965)
Manoocher Naderi
INVINCIBLE SIX, THE(1970, U.S./Iran)
Nadya Nadezhdina
SPRINGTIME ON THE VOLGA(1961, USSR), w, ch
Ernst Nadherny
SENSO(1968, Ital.)
Aldo Nadi
TO HAVE AND HAVE NOT(1944)
Misc. Silents
LE TORNOI(1928, Fr.)
Sylva Nadina
RESURRECTION(1931)
Nadira
GURU, THE(1969, U.S./India); BOMBAY TALKIE(1970, India)
Nadiuska
GUYANA, CULT OF THE DAMNED(1980, Mex./Span./Panama); CONAN THE BARBARIAN(1982)
Nadja
UNHOLY GARDEN, THE(1931); NIGHT RIDER, THE(1932); MAD DOCTOR OF BLOOD ISLAND, THE(1969, Phil./U.S.)
Mike Nadler
BEACH BLANKET BINGO(1965)
Deborah Nadoolman
KENTUCKY FRIED MOVIE, THE(1977), cos; NATIONAL LAMPOON'S ANIMAL HOUSE(1978), cos; 1941(1979), cos; BLUES BROTHERS, THE(1980), cos; AMERICAN WEREWOLF IN LONDON, AN(1981), cos; RAIDERS OF THE LOST ARK(1981), cos; TRADING PLACES(1983), cos; TWILIGHT ZONE–THE MOVIE(1983), cos

1984
CRACKERS(1984), cos

The Nador Singers
SWEET SURRENDER(1935)

Barbara Von Nady
JOURNEY, THE(1959, U.S./Aust.)

Jester Naefe
CONGRESS DANCES(1957, Ger.)

Irwin Nafshun
BEAST OF YUCCA FLATS, THE(1961), m

Harimoran Nag
PATHER PANCHALI(1958, India)

Hidekazu Nagahara
SUN ABOVE, DEATH BELOW(1969, Jap.), w

Kafu Nagai
TWILIGHT STORY, THE(1962, Jap.), w

Kiyoako Nagai
CHALLENGE, THE(1982)

Mieko Nagai
MYSTERIOUS SATELLITE, THE(1956, Jap.)

Ralph Nagai
HALLS OF MONTEZUMA(1951)

Senchiki Nagai
COMPUTER FREE-FOR-ALL(1969, Jap.), ph

Toru Nagai
NEXT MAN, THE(1976)

Masayonshi Nagami
HENTAI(1966, Jap.)

Hiroshi Nagano
CREATURE CALLED MAN, THE(1970, Jap.), w

Juichi Nagano
SHE AND HE(1967, Jap.), ph

Tomiji Nagao
NAVY WIFE(1956)

Hiroyuki Nagaoka
TWILIGHT PATH(1965, Jap.), ph

Hiroyuko Nagaoka
FAREWELL, MY BELOVED(1969, Jap.), ph

Teruko Nagaoka
OHAYO(1962, Jap.); TOKYO STORY(1972, Jap.)

Ralph Nagara
GEISHA GIRL(1952)

Ichiro Nagashima
DEATH ON THE MOUNTAIN(1961, Jap.), p

Hidemasa Nagata
GAMERA VERSUS BARUGON(1966, Jap./U.S.), p; GAMERA VERSUS GAOS(1967, Jap.), p; GAMERA VERSUS VIRAS(1968, Jap), p; GAMERA VERSUS GUIRON(1969, Jap.), p; GAMERA VERSUS MONSTER K(1970, Jap.), p

Masaichi Nagata
GATE OF HELL(1954, Jap.), p; UGETSU(1954, Jap.), p; GOLDEN DEMON(1956, Jap.), p; MYSTERIOUS SATELLITE, THE(1956, Jap.), p; FIRES ON THE PLAIN(1962, Jap.), p; BUDDHA(1965, Jap.), p; GREAT WALL, THE(1965, Jap.), p; MAJIN(1968, Jap.), p; SANSHO THE BAILIFF(1969, Jap.), p

Yasushi Nagata
MAN IN THE MOONLIGHT MASK, THE(1958, Jap.); ILLUSION OF BLOOD(1966, Jap.); LIVE YOUR OWN WAY(1970, Jap.)

Hiroyuki Nagato
MADAME AKI(1963, Jap.); WEIRD LOVE MAKERS, THE(1963, Jap.); INSECT WOMAN, THE(1964, Jap.); TWIN SISTERS OF KYOTO(1964, Jap.); YOUNG SWORDSMAN(1964, Jap.); TWILIGHT PATH(1965, Jap.); SILENCE HAS NO WINGS(1971, Jap.); AFFAIR AT AKITSU(1980, Jap.)

Isamu Nagato
SAMURAI FROM NOWHERE(1964, Jap.); KOJIRO(1967, Jap.)

Aiko Nagayama
YOSAKOI JOURNEY(1970, Jap.)

Yasuko Nagazumi
DEADLIER THAN THE MALE(1967, Brit.)

Albert Nagel
TOWN WITHOUT PITY(1961, Ger./Switz./U.S.), makeup; SITUATION HOPELESS– BUT NOT SERIOUS(1965), makeup

Anna Nagel
KING OF HOCKEY(1936); SHOULD A GIRL MARRY?(1939)

Anne Nagel
SITTING PRETTY(1933); GEORGE WHITE'S 1935 SCANDALS(1935); BULLETS OR BALLOTS(1936); CHINA CLIPPER(1936); HERE COMES CARTER(1936); HOT MONEY(1936); LOVE BEGINS AT TWENTY(1936); POLO JOE(1936); ADVENTUROUS BLONDE(1937); BRIDE FOR HENRY, A(1937); CASE OF THE STUTTERING BISHOP, THE(1937); DEVIL'S SADDLE LEGION(1937); ESCAPE BY NIGHT(1937); FOOTLOOSE HEIRESS, THE(1937); GUNS OF THE PECOS(1937); HOOSIER SCHOOLBOY(1937); THREE LEGIONNAIRES, THE(1937); GANG BULLETS(1938); MYSTERY HOUSE(1938); SALESLADY(1938); UNDER THE BIG TOP(1938); CALL A MESSENGER(1939); CONVICT'S CODE(1939); LEGION OF LOST FLYERS(1939); UNEXPECTED FATHER(1939); ARGENTINE NIGHTS(1940); BLACK FRIDAY(1940); DIAMOND FRONTIER(1940); HOT STEEL(1940); MA, HE'S MAKING EYES AT ME(1940); MY LITTLE CHICKADEE(1940); INVISIBLE WOMAN, THE(1941); MAN MADE MONSTER(1941); MEET THE CHUMP(1941); MUTINY IN THE ARCTIC(1941); NEVER GIVE A SUCKER AN EVEN BREAK(1941); ROAD AGENT(1941); SEALED LIPS(1941); DAWN EXPRESS, THE(1942); MAD DOCTOR OF MARKET STREET, THE(1942); MAD MONSTER, THE(1942); STAGECOACH BUCKAROO(1942); WOMEN IN BONDAGE(1943); MURDER IN THE MUSIC HALL(1946); TRAFFIC IN CRIME(1946); BLONDIE'S HOLIDAY(1947); HUCKSTERS, THE(1947); SPIRIT OF WEST POINT, THE(1947); TRAP, THE(1947); EVERY GIRL SHOULD BE MARRIED(1948); FAMILY HONEYMOON(1948); HOMECOMING(1948); ONE TOUCH OF VENUS(1948); PREJUDICE(1949); STRATTON STORY, THE(1949)

Conrad Nagel
CAUGHT IN THE FOG(1928); STATE STREET SADIE(1928); TENDERLOIN(1928); TERROR, THE(1928); IDLE RICH, THE(1929); KID GLOVES(1929); REDEEMING SIN, THE(1929); SACRED FLAME, THE(1929); DIVORCEE, THE(1930); DU BARRY, WOMAN OF PASSION(1930); DYNAMITE(1930); FREE LOVE(1930); LADY SURRENDERS, A(1930); NUMBERED MEN(1930); ONE ROMANTIC NIGHT(1930); REDEMPTION(1930); SECOND WIFE(1930); SHIP FROM SHANGHAI, THE(1930); THIRTEENTH CHAIR, THE(1930); TODAY(1930); BAD SISTER(1931); EAST LYNNE(1931); PAGAN LADY(1931); RECKLESS HOUR, THE(1931); RIGHT OF WAY, THE(1931); SON OF INDIA(1931); THREE WHO LOVED(1931); DIVORCE IN THE FAMILY(1932); FAST LIFE(1932); HELL DIVERS(1932); KONGO(1932); MAN CALLED BACK, THE(1932); ANN VICKERS(1933); DANGEROUS CORNER(1935); DEATH FLIES EAST(1935); MARINES ARE COMING, THE(1935); ONE HOUR LATE(1935); ONE NEW YORK NIGHT(1935); BALL AT SAVOY(1936, Brit.); GIRL FROM MANDALAY(1936); WEDDING PRESENT(1936); YELLOW CARGO(1936); BANK ALARM(1937); GOLD RACKET, THE(1937); LOVE TAKES FLIGHT(1937), d; NAVY SPY(1937); I WANT A DIVORCE(1940); MAD EMPRESS, THE(1940); ONE MILLION B.C.(1940); ADVENTURES OF RUSTY(1945); FOREVER YOURS(1945); STAGE STRUCK(1948); VICIOUS CIRCLE, THE(1948); ALL THAT HEAVEN ALLOWS(1955); HIDDEN FEAR(1957); MAN WHO UNDERSTOOD WOMEN, THE(1959); STRANGER IN MY ARMS(1959)
Misc. Talkies
CONSTANT WOMAN, THE(1933)
Silents
MIDSUMMER MADNESS(1920); WHAT EVERY WOMAN KNOWS(1921); IMPOSSIBLE MRS. BELLEW, THE(1922); NICE PEOPLE(1922); ORDEAL, THE(1922); SATURDAY NIGHT(1922); SINGED WINGS(1922); LAWFUL LARCENY(1923); RENDEZVOUS, THE(1923); MARRIED FLIRTS(1924); REJECTED WOMAN, THE(1924); SNOB, THE(1924); TESS OF THE D'URBERVILLES(1924); PRETTY LADIES(1925); EXQUISITE SINNER, THE(1926); MEMORY LANE(1926); WANING SEX, THE(1926); GIRL FROM CHICAGO, THE(1927); IF I WERE SINGLE(1927); LONDON AFTER MIDNIGHT(1927); QUALITY STREET(1927); SLIGHTLY USED(1927); MICHIGAN KID, THE(1928); MYSTERIOUS LADY, THE(1928); RED WINE(1928); KISS, THE(1929)
Misc. Silents
LION AND THE MOUSE, THE(1919); REDHEAD(1919); FIGHTING CHANCE, THE(1920); UNSEEN FORCES(1920); FOOL'S PARADISE(1921); LOST ROMANCE, THE(1921); SACRED AND PROFANE LOVE(1921); HATE(1922); BELLA DONNA(1923); GRUMPY(1923); NAME THE MAN(1924); SINNERS IN SILK(1924); SO THIS IS MARRIAGE(1924); THREE WEEKS(1924); CHEAPER TO MARRY(1925); EXCUSE ME(1925); LIGHTS OF OLD BROADWAY(1925); ONLY THING, THE(1925); SUN-UP(1925); DANCE MADNESS(1926); THERE YOU ARE!(1926); TIN HATS(1926); HEAVEN ON EARTH(1927); DIAMOND HANDCUFFS(1928)

Don Nagel
BRIDE OF THE MONSTER(1955)

Marie-Luise Nagel
THOUSAND EYES OF DR. MABUSE, THE(1960, Fr./Ital./Ger.)

Rolf Nagel
GREAT BRITISH TRAIN ROBBERY, THE(1967, Ger.)

Ali Nagi
GUNS OF DARKNESS(1962, Brit.)

Yuri Nagibin
DERSU UZALA(1976, Jap./USSR), w

A. Nagits
SANDU FOLLOWS THE SUN(1965, USSR)

George Nagle
WHITE SHADOWS IN THE SOUTH SEAS(1928), ph

Jack Nagle
STING OF DEATH(1966); DARKER THAN AMBER(1970); HOW DO I LOVE THEE?(1970); LENNY(1974)

Linda Nagle
PIRATE MOVIE, THE(1982, Aus.)

P. Nagle
Silents
GOLD RUSH, THE(1925)

Paul Nagle
VAMPIRE'S COFFIN, THE(1958, Mex.), d; VAMPIRE, THE(1968, Mex.), d

Steve Nagle
1984
POWER, THE(1984)

Kurt Nagler
WILD REBELS, THE(1967)

Nancy Nagler
ONLY WHEN I LAUGH(1981)

Daniel Nagrin
JUST FOR YOU(1952); HIS MAJESTY O'KEEFE(1953), ch

A. Nagy
Silents
ANSWER, THE(1918), ph

Alice Nagy
SUN SHINES, THE(1939, Hung.)

Alix Nagy
SUDAN(1945)

Anna Nagy
FATHER(1967, Hung.)

Attila Nagy
ROUND UP, THE(1969, Hung.)

Bill Nagy
HELL, HEAVEN OR HOBOKEN(1958, Brit.); BRAIN MACHINE, THE(1955, Brit.); JOE MACBETH(1955, Brit.); ACROSS THE BRIDGE(1957, Brit.); HIGH TIDE AT NOON(1957, Brit.); OPERATION CONSPIRACY(1957, Brit.); MARK OF THE HAWK, THE(1958, Brit.); BOBBIKINS(1959, Brit.); FIRST MAN INTO SPACE(1959, Brit.); MOUSE THAT ROARED, THE(1959, Brit.); BOY WHO STOLE A MILLION, THE(1960, Brit.); SURPRISE PACKAGE(1960); TRANSATLANTIC(1961, Brit.); CROSSTRAP(1962, Brit.); DANGER BY MY SIDE(1962, Brit.); NIGHT OF THE PROWLER(1962, Brit.); ROAD TO HONG KONG, THE(1962, U.S./Brit.); GIRL HUNTERS, THE(1963, Brit.); GOLDFINGER(1964, Brit.); THOSE MAGNIFICENT MEN IN THEIR FLYING MACHINES; OR HOW I FLEW FROM LONDON TO PARIS IN 25 HOURS AND 11 MINUTES(1965, Brit.); WHERE THE SPIES ARE(1965, Brit.); COUNTESS FROM HONG KONG, A(1967, Brit.); BATTLE BENEATH THE EARTH(1968, Brit.); MAN OUTSIDE, THE(1968, Brit.); ADDING MACHINE, THE(1969); SUBTERFUGE(1969, US/Brit.); REVOLUTIONARY, THE(1970, Brit.); Z.P.G.(1972); SCORPIO(1973)

Bill Nagy, Jr.
NEVER TAKE CANDY FROM A STRANGER(1961, Brit.)

Istvan Nagy
DIALOGUE(1967, Hung.)

Ivan Nagy
BAD CHARLESTON CHARLIE(1973), d, w; DEADLY HERO(1976), d; TRACK-DOWN(1976), w

Judy Nagy
1984
ALL OF ME(1984)

Madeline Nagy
Misc. Silents
GOOD AND EVIL(1921)

Terez Nagy
FATHER(1967, Hung.)

William Nagy
LONG SHADOW, THE(1961, Brit.)

Gyorgy Nagyajtay
FRAULEIN DOKTOR(1969, Ital./Yugo.)

Gyula Nagymarosi
FATHER(1967, Hung.)

Nah
Silents
CHANG(1927)

Estrongo Nahama
MALOU(1983)

Stu Nahan
GUS(1976); ROCKY II(1979); PRIVATE BENJAMIN(1980); FAST TIMES AT RIDGE-MONT HIGH(1982); ROCKY III(1982)

Dennis Nahat
TURNING POINT, THE(1977), ch

Michael Nahay
Misc. Talkies
STORYVILLE(1974); THURSDAY MORNING MURDERS, THE(1976), d

Mike Nahay
MARDI GRAS MASSACRE(1978), spec eff

Zenno Nahayevsky
FIREFOX(1982)

Hugo Naheir
HIRED KILLER, THE(1967, Fr./Ital.), art d

Philippe Nahon
DOULOS–THE FINGER MAN(1964, Fr./Ital.)

Alan Nahuai
HAWAIIANS, THE(1970)

Maite Nahyr
TENANT, THE(1976, Fr.)

Bobby Naidoo
NINE HOURS TO RAMA(1963, U.S./Brit.)

Bobby R. Naidoo
CONCRETE JUNGLE, THE(1962, Brit.)

Leela Naidu
HOUSEHOLDER, THE(1963, US/India); GURU, THE(1969, U.S./India)

Apenisa Naigulevu
DOVE, THE(1974, Brit.)

Bob Naihe
REAL GLORY, THE(1939)

Joanne Nail
SWITCHBLADE SISTERS(1975); GUMBALL RALLY, THE(1976); VISITOR, THE(1980, Ital./U.S.); FULL MOON HIGH(1982)

Jerry Naill
TOMBOY AND THE CHAMP(1961)

Shirley Nails
RIDERS OF THE PURPLE SAGE(1931)

Fouad Naim
CIRCLE OF DECEIT(1982, Fr./Ger.)

Adeline Naiman
MAIDSTONE(1970)

Robert Nainby
COLONEL BLOOD(1934, Brit.); LITTLE FRIEND(1934, Brit.); MY OLD DUTCH(1934, Brit.); POWER(1934, Brit.); DANDY DICK(1935, Brit.); NO MONKEY BUSINESS(1935, Brit.); RADIO FOLLIES(1935, Brit.); REGAL CAVALCADE(1935, Brit.); ALL IN(1936, Brit.); CHICK(1936, Brit.); FORBIDDEN MUSIC(1936, Brit.); MURDER ON THE SET(1936, Brit.); STUDENT'S ROMANCE, THE(1936, Brit.); THERE WAS A YOUNG MAN(1937, Brit.); WISE GUYS(1937, Brit.); MAN WITH 100 FACES, THE(1938, Brit.); STRANGE BOARDERS(1938, Brit.); WE'RE GOING TO BE RICH(1938, Brit.); TWO'S COMPANY(1939, Brit.); LILAC DOMINO, THE(1940, Brit.); WHEN KNIGHTS WERE BOLD(1942, Brit.); UNDER SECRET ORDERS(1943, Brit.)

Robert Nainby, Sr.
PUBLIC NUISANCE NO. 1(1936, Brit.)

Phiroz Nair
KISMET(1944)

Ralph Nairn
Silents
OH, JOHNNY!(1919)

Jennifer Nairn-Smith
RICH AND FAMOUS(1981)

Richard Nairne
FIGHTING PIMPERNEL, THE(1950, Brit.); MUDLARK, THE(1950, Brit.)

Richmond Nairne
WILD HEART, THE(1952, Brit.)

Carey Nairnes
LOVELY WAY TO DIE, A(1968)

Herbert Naish
QUEEN OF THE MOB(1940); YOUNG DANIEL BOONE(1950)

J. Carroll Naish
GOOD INTENTIONS(1930); SCOTLAND YARD(1930); FINGER POINTS, THE(1931); GUN SMOKE(1931); HOMICIDE SQUAD(1931); KICK IN(1931); ROYAL BED, THE(1931); SURRENDER(1931); BEAST OF THE CITY, THE(1931); BIG CITY BLUES(1932) 65m WB bw; CROONER(1932); FAMOUS FERGUSON CASE, THE(1932); HATCHET MAN, THE(1932); IT'S TOUGH TO BE FAMOUS(1932); KID FROM SPAIN, THE(1932); MOUTHPIECE, THE(1932); NO LIVING WITNESS(1932); TIGER SHARK(1932); TWO SECONDS(1932); WEEK-END MARRIAGE(1932); ANN VICK-ERS(1933); ARIZONA TO BROADWAY(1933); AVENGER, THE(1933); BIG CHANCE, THE(1933); BLOOD MONEY(1933); CAPTURED(1933); DEVIL'S IN LOVE, THE(1933); ELMER THE GREAT(1933); FRISCO JENNY(1933); INFERNAL MACHINE(1933); MAD GAME, THE(1933); NO OTHER WOMAN(1933); PAST OF MARY HOLMES, THE(1933); WORLD GONE MAD, THE(1933); BRITISH AGENT(1934); GIRL IN DANGER(1934); HELL CAT, THE(1934); HELL IN THE HEAVENS(1934); LAST TRAIL, THE(1934); MURDER IN TRINIDAD(1934); NOTORIOUS BUT NICE(1934); ONE IS GUILTY(1934); RETURN OF THE TERROR(1934); SLEEPERS EAST(1934); UPPER WORLD(1934); WHAT'S YOUR RACKET?(1934); BLACK FURY(1935); CAP-TAIN BLOOD(1935); CONFIDENTIAL(1935); CRUSADES, THE(1935); FRONT PAGE WOMAN(1935); LITTLE BIG SHOT(1935); LIVES OF A BENGAL LANCER(1935); SPECIAL AGENT(1935); UNDER THE PAMPAS MOON(1935); ABSOLUTE QUIET(1936); ANTHONY ADVERSE(1936); CHARGE OF THE LIGHT BRIGADE, THE(1936); CHARLIE CHAN AT THE CIRCUS(1936); EXCLUSIVE STORY(1936); LEATHERNECKS HAVE LANDED, THE(1936); MOONLIGHT MURDER(1936); RAMONA(1936); RETURN OF JIMMY VALENTINE, THE(1936); ROBIN HOOD OF EL DORADO(1936); SPECIAL INVESTIGATOR(1936); TWO IN THE DARK(1936); BORDER CAFE(1937); BULLDOG DRUMMOND COMES BACK(1937); CRACK-UP, THE(1937); DAUGHTER OF SHANGHAI(1937); HIDEAWAY(1937); NIGHT CLUB SCANDAL(1937); SEA RACKETEERS(1937); SONG OF THE CITY(1937); THINK FAST, MR. MOTO(1937); THUNDER TRAIL(1937); WE WHO ARE ABOUT TO DIE(1937); BULLDOG DRUMMOND IN AFRICA(1938); HER JUNGLE LOVE(1938); HUNTED MEN(1938); ILLEGAL TRAFFIC(1938); KING OF ALCATRAZ(1938); PRIS-ON FARM(1938); TIP-OFF GIRLS(1938); BEAU GESTE(1939); HOTEL IM-PERIAL(1939); ISLAND OF LOST MEN(1939); KING OF CHINATOWN(1939); PERSONS IN HIDING(1939); UNDERCOVER DOCTOR(1939); DOWN ARGENTINE WAY(1940); GOLDEN GLOVES(1940); NIGHT AT EARL CARROLL'S, A(1940); QUEEN OF THE MOB(1940); TYPHOON(1940); ACCENT ON LOVE(1941); BIRTH OF THE BLUES(1941); BLOOD AND SAND(1941); CORSICAN BROTHERS, THE(1941); FORCED LANDING(1941); MR. DYNAMITE(1941); THAT NIGHT IN RIO(1941); DR. BROADWAY(1942); DR. RENAULT'S SECRET(1942); GENTLEMAN AT HEART, A(1942); JACKASS MAIL(1942); MAN IN THE TRUNK, THE(1942); PIED PIPER, THE(1942); SUNDAY PUNCH(1942); TALES OF MANHATTAN(1942); BEHIND THE RISING SUN(1943); CALLING DR. DEATH(1943); GOOD MORNING, JUDGE(1943); GUNG HO!(1943); HARRIGAN'S KID(1943); SAHARA(1943); DRAGON SEED(1944); ENTER ARSENE LUPIN(1944); HOUSE OF FRANKENSTEIN(1944); JUNGLE WOM-AN(1944); MONSTER MAKER, THE(1944); TWO-MAN SUBMARINE(1944); VOICE IN THE WIND(1944); WATERFRONT(1944); WHISTLER, THE(1944); GETTING GER-TIE'S GARTER(1945); MEDAL FOR BENNY, A(1945); SOUTHERNER, THE(1945); STRANGE CONFESSION(1945); BAD BASCOMB(1946); BEAST WITH FIVE FIN-GERS, THE(1946); HUMORESQUE(1946); CARNIVAL IN COSTA RICA(1947); FUGI-TIVE, THE(1947); JOAN OF ARC(1948); KISSING BANDIT, THE(1948); CANADIAN PACIFIC(1949); THAT MIDNIGHT KISS(1949); ANNIE GET YOUR GUN(1950); BLACK HAND, THE(1950); PLEASE BELIEVE ME(1950); RIO GRANDE(1950); TOAST OF NEW ORLEANS, THE(1950); ACROSS THE WIDE MISSOURI(1951); BANNERLINE(1951); MARK OF THE RENEGADE(1951); CLASH BY NIGHT(1952); DENVER AND RIO GRANDE(1952); RIDE THE MAN DOWN(1952); WOMAN OF THE NORTH COUNTRY(1952); BENEATH THE 12-MILE REEF(1953); FIGHTER AT-TACK(1953); SASKATCHEWAN(1954); SITTING BULL(1954); DESERT SANDS(1955); HIT THE DECK(1955); LAST COMMAND, THE(1955); NEW YORK CONFIDEN-TIAL(1955); RAGE AT DAWN(1955); VIOLENT SATURDAY(1955); REBEL IN TOWN(1956); YAQUI DRUMS(1956); THIS COULD BE THE NIGHT(1957); YOUNG DON'T CRY, THE(1957); FORCE OF IMPULSE(1961); BLOOD OF FRANKEN-STEIN(1970)
Misc. Talkies
SILENT MEN(1933); WHIRLWIND, THE(1933)

Betty Naismith
LONDON MELODY(1930, Brit.)

Laurence Naismith
TROUBLE IN THE AIR(1948, Brit.); BADGER'S GREEN(1949, Brit.); DARK SE-CRET(1949, Brit.); ROOM TO LET(1949, Brit.); HAPPIEST DAYS OF YOUR LIFE(1950, Brit.); CHELSEA STORY(1951, Brit.); HELL IS SOLD OUT(1951, Brit.); HIGH TREA-SON(1951, Brit.); POOL OF LONDON(1951, Brit.); HIS EXCELLENCY(1952, Brit.); KILLER WALKS, A(1952, Brit.); MR. LORD SAYS NO(1952, Brit.); TRAIN OF EVENTS(1952, Brit.); WHISPERING SMITH VERSUS SCOTLAND YARD(1952, Brit.); I BELIEVE IN YOU(1953, Brit.); LONG MEMORY, THE(1953, Brit.); LOVE IN PAWN(1953, Brit.); MOGAMBO(1953); PENNY PRINCESS(1953, Brit.); SHOOT FIRST(1953, Brit.); SLASHER, THE(1953, Brit.); BLACK KNIGHT, THE(1954); COURT MARTIAL(1954, Brit.); DAM BUSTERS, THE(1955, Brit.); FINAL COLUMN, THE(1955, Brit.); JOSEPHINE AND MEN(1955, Brit.); EXTRA DAY, THE(1956, Brit.); LUST FOR LIFE(1956); MAN WHO NEVER WAS, THE(1956, Brit.); RICHARD III(1956, Brit.); TIGER IN THE SMOKE(1956, Brit.); ABANDON SHIP(1957, Brit.); BARRETTS OF WIMPOLE STREET, THE(1957); BOY ON A DOLPHIN(1957); WEAPON, THE(1957, Brit.); GYPSY AND THE GENTLEMAN, THE(1958, Brit.); I ACCUSE(1958, Brit.); NAKED EARTH, THE(1958, Brit.); NIGHT TO REMEMBER, A(1958, Brit.); ROBBERY UNDER ARMS(1958, Brit.); TEMPEST(1958, Ital./Yugo./Fr.); GIDEON OF SCOTLAND YARD(1959, Brit.); THIRD MAN ON THE MOUNTAIN(1959, Brit.); TWO-HEADED SPY, THE(1959, Brit.); ANGRY SILENCE, THE(1960, Brit.); MAN WITH THE GREEN CARNATION, THE(1960, Brit.); SINK THE BISMARCK!(1960, Brit.); VILLAGE OF THE DAMNED(1960, Brit.); WORLD OF SUZIE WONG, THE(1960); GREYFRIARS BOBBY(1961, Brit.); SINGER NOT THE SONG, THE(1961, Brit.); CONCRETE JUN-GLE, THE(1962, Brit.); I THANK A FOOL(1962, Brit.); VALIANT, THE(1962, Brit./Ital.); WE JOINED THE NAVY(1962, Brit.); 300 SPARTANS, THE(1962); CLEOPATRA(1963); JASON AND THE ARGONAUTS(1963, Brit.); THREE LIVES OF THOMASINA, THE(1963, U.S./Brit.); GYPSY GIRL(1966, Brit.); CAMELOT(1967); DEADLIER THAN THE MALE(1967, Brit.); FITZWILLY(1967); LONG DUEL, THE(1967, Brit.); EYE OF THE CAT(1969); VALLEY OF GWANGI, THE(1969); BUSHBABY, THE(1970); SCROOGE(1970, Brit.); DIAMONDS ARE FOREVER(1971, Brit.); QUEST FOR LO-VE(1971, Brit.); YOUNG WINSTON(1972, Brit.); AMAZING MR. BLUNDEN, THE(1973, Brit.)
Misc. Talkies
MISSION: MONTE CARLO(1981, Brit.)

Paddie Naismith
IRON DUKE, THE(1935, Brit.)

Akira Naito
DEVIL'S TEMPLE(1969, Jap.), art d; SHOGUN ASSASSIN(1980, Jap.), art d; MUD-DY RIVER(1982, Jap.), art d

Takashi Naito
MERRY CHRISTMAS MR. LAWRENCE(1983, Jap./Brit.)

Taketoshi Naito
ROAD TO ETERNITY(1962, Jap.); SNOW COUNTRY(1969, Jap.); SOLDIER'S PRAYER, A(1970, Jap.)

Yoko Naito
RED BEARD(1966, Jap.); SWORD OF DOOM, THE(1967, Jap.); ONCE A RAINY DAY(1968, Jap.); OUR SILENT LOVE(1969, Jap.); PORTRAIT OF HELL(1969, Jap.)

Grete Naizler
DOLLY GETS AHEAD(1931, Ger.)

Tafic Najem
CIRCLE OF DECEIT(1982, Fr./Ger.)

Samib Mohammad Najib
JERUSALEM FILE, THE(1972, U.S./Israel)

Najila
TO BE FREE(1972)

Machiko Naka
IT STARTED IN THE ALPS(1966, Jap.); GODZILLA'S REVENGE(1969); YOUNG GUY GRADUATES(1969, Jap.); YOUNG GUY ON MT. COOK(1969, Jap.)

Jean Nakaba
PAL JOEY(1957)

Tatsuya Nakadai
ENJO(1959, Jap.); HUMAN CONDITION, THE(1959, Jap.); ODD OBSESSION(1961, Jap.); YOJIMBO(1961, Jap.); ROAD TO ETERNITY(1962, Jap.); SANJURO(1962, Jap.); HAHAKIRI(1963, Jap.); HIGH AND LOW(1963, Jap.); MADAME AKI(1963, Jap.); WHEN A WOMAN ASCENDS THE STAIRS(1963, Jap.); INHERITANCE, THE(1964, Jap.); LEGACY OF THE 500,000, THE(1964, Jap.); PRESSURE OF GUILT(1964, Jap.); WOMAN'S LIFE, A(1964, Jap.); LOVE UNDER THE CRUCIFIX(1965, Jap.); FORT GRAVEYARD(1966, Jap.); ILLUSION OF BLOOD(1966, Jap.); DAPHNE, THE(1967); FACE OF ANOTHER, THE(1967, Jap.); KOJIRO(1967, Jap.); REBELLION(1967, Jap.); SWORD OF DOOM, THE(1967, Jap.); KILL(1968, Jap.); TODAY IT'S ME...TOMORROW YOU!(1968, Ital.); GOYOKIN(1969, Jap.); PORTRAIT OF HELL(1969, Jap.); DUEL AT EZO(1970, Jap.); SCANDALOUS ADVENTURES OF BURAIKAN, THE(1970, Jap.); SOLDIER'S PRAYER, A(1970, Jap.); TENCHU!(1970, Jap.); HINOTORI(1980, Jap.); KAGEMUSHA(1980, Jap.); ONIMASA(1983, Jap.)
Misc. Talkies
TODAY WE KILL...TOMORROW WE DIE(1971)

Yasuko Nakado
NAKED GENERAL, THE(1964, Jap.)

Kenichi Nakagawa
YONGKARI MONSTER FROM THE DEEP(1967 S.K.), ph

Roger Nakagawa
ESCAPADE IN JAPAN(1957)

Yoshie Nakagawa
Misc. Silents
CRAZY PAGE, A(1926, Jap.)

Yoshihisa Nakagawa
WAY OUT, WAY IN(1970, Jap.), ph

Yuki Nakagawa
SCHOOL FOR SEX(1966, Jap.)

Sanae Nakahara
JUDO SHOWDOWN(1966, Jap.); SECRETS OF A WOMAN'S TEMPLE(1969, Jap.); PLAY IT COOL(1970, Jap.)

Ko Nakahira
WHIRLPOOL OF WOMAN(1966, Jap.), d

Minoru Nakahira
SILENCE HAS NO WINGS(1971, Jap.)

Akira Nakai
ALONE ON THE PACIFIC(1964, Jap.), p

Asaichi Nakai
SECRET SCROLLS(PART II)**1/2 (1968, Jap.), ph; THRONE OF BLOOD(1961, Jap.), ph; NAKED GENERAL, THE(1964, Jap.), ph; PRODIGAL SON, THE(1964, Jap.), ph; WOMAN'S LIFE, A(1964, Jap.), ph; RED BEARD(1966, Jap.), ph; WE WILL REMEMBER(1966, Jap.), ph; KAGEMUSHA(1980, Jap.), ph

Asakadru Nakai
DERSU UZALA(1976, Jap./USSR), ph

Asakasu Nakai
SEVEN SAMURAI, THE(1956, Jap.), ph

Asakazu Nakai
IKIRU(1960, Jap.), ph; ETERNITY OF LOVE(1961, Jap.), ph; EARLY AUTUMN(1962, Jap.), ph; BEAUTIFUL SWINDLERS, THE(1967, Fr./Ital./Jap./Neth.), ph; I LIVE IN FEAR(1967, Jap.), ph

Choichi Nakai
HIGH AND LOW(1963, Jap.), ph; IDIOT, THE(1963, Jap.), ph; DAPHNE, THE(1967), ph; NIGHT OF THE SEAGULL, THE(1970, Jap.), ph

Keisuke Nakai
LAKE, THE(1970, Jap.)

Gentaro Nakajima
MYSTERIOUS SATELLITE, THE(1956, Jap.), w

Haruo Nakajima
GODZILLA VS. THE THING(1964, Jap.); WAR OF THE MONSTERS(1972, Jap.)

Masayuki Nakajima
PLEASURES OF THE FLESH, THE(1965), p

Naruo Nakajima
SEVEN SAMURAI, THE(1956, Jap.)

Sonomi Nakajima
TATSU(1962, Jap.); THREE DOLLS FROM HONG KONG(1966, Jap.)

Teruo Nakajima
HARBOR LIGHT YOKOHAMA(1970, Jap.), ed

Toro Nakajima
MESSAGE FROM SPACE(1978, Jap.), ph

Satoru Nakakao
HAPPINESS OF US ALONE(1962, Jap.), art d

Toshi Nakaki
I WAS AN AMERICAN SPY(1951)

Chiefko Nakakita
DRUNKEN ANGEL(1948, Jap.)

Chieko Nakakita
HAPPINESS OF US ALONE(1962, Jap.); TATSU(1962, Jap.); YEARNING(1964, Jap.)

Sayuka Nakamaru
1984
BALLAD OF NARAYAMA, THE(1984, Jap.)

Tadao Nakamaru
SECRET OF THE TELEGIAN, THE(1961, Jap.); WESTWARD DESPERADO(1961, Jap.); OPERATION X(1963, Jap.); RABBLE, THE(1965, Jap.); WHAT'S UP, TIGER LILY?(1966); MAD ATLANTIC, THE(1967, Jap.); EMPEROR AND A GENERAL, THE(1968, Jap.); KILL(1968, Jap.); GIRL I ABANDONED, THE(1970, Jap.)

Nakamishi
TOWN LIKE ALICE, A(1958, Brit.)

Koji Nakamoto
HOTSPRINGS HOLIDAY(1970, Jap.)

Satoshi Nakamoura
RED SUN(1972, Fr./Ital./Span.)

Akika Nakamura
ONIMASA(1983, Jap.)

Akiko Nakamura
HARBOR LIGHT YOKOHAMA(1970, Jap.)

Atsuo Nakamura
CHALLENGE, THE(1982)

Ganemon Nakamura
KWAIDAN(1965, Jap.); UNDER THE BANNER OF SAMURAI(1969, Jap.)

Ganjiro Nakamura
ENJO(1959, Jap.); ODD OBSESSION(1961, Jap.); EARLY AUTUMN(1962, Jap.); LOWER DEPTHS, THE(1962, Jap.); ACTOR'S REVENGE, AN(1963, Jap.); WHEN A WOMAN ASCENDS THE STAIRS(1963, Jap.); PRODIGAL SON, THE(1964, Jap.); BUDDHA(1965, Jap.); GREAT WALL, THE(1965, Jap.); KWAIDAN(1965, Jap.); LOVE UNDER THE CRUCIFIX(1965, Jap.); FLOATING WEEDS(1970, Jap.)

Henry Nakamura
GO FOR BROKE(1951); WESTWARD THE WOMEN(1951); ATHENA(1954); BLOOD ALLEY(1955); UNCHAINED(1955); LAFAYETTE ESCADRILLE(1958)

Kankuro Nakamura
GAMBLING SAMURAI, THE(1966, Jap.); UNDER THE BANNER OF SAMURAI(1969, Jap.); SONG FROM MY HEART, THE(1970, Jap.)

Kanzaburo Nakamura
ILLUSION OF BLOOD(1966, Jap.); SONG FROM MY HEART, THE(1970, Jap.)

Katsuo Nakamura
KWAIDAN(1965, Jap.); PLEASURES OF THE FLESH, THE(1965); UNDER THE BANNER OF SAMURAI(1969, Jap.); MAGOICHI SAGA, THE(1970, Jap.); SONG FROM MY HEART, THE(1970, Jap.)

Kazuko Nakamura
MAGIC BOY(1960, Jap.), anim

Kichiemon Nakamura
KUROENKO(1968, Jap); DOUBLE SUICIDE(1970, Jap.); GATEWAY TO GLORY(1970, Jap.)

Kimihiko Nakamura
INSECT WOMAN, THE(1964, Jap.), art d

Kinnosuke Nakamura
DAY THE SUN ROSE, THE(1969, Jap.); GOYOKIN(1969, Jap.); PORTRAIT OF HELL(1969, Jap.); UNDER THE BANNER OF SAMURAI(1969, Jap.); MAGOICHI SAGA, THE(1970, Jap.)

Koree Nakamura
HOTSPRINGS HOLIDAY(1970, Jap.)

Masako Nakamura
AFFAIR AT AKITSU(1980, Jap.)

Meiko Nakamura
THIS MADDING CROWD(1964, Jap.)

Mitsuki Nakamura
1984
WARRIORS OF THE WIND(1984, Jap.), art d

Noboru Nakamura
TWIN SISTERS OF KYOTO(1964, Jap.), d; PORTRAIT OF CHIEKO(1968, Jap.), d, w; THROUGH DAYS AND MONTHS(1969 Jap.), d

Nobuo Nakamura
HALF HUMAN(1955, Jap.); HUMAN CONDITION, THE(1959, Jap.); IKIRU(1960, Jap.); DIPLOMAT'S MANSION, THE(1961, Jap.); LONGING FOR LOVE(1966, Jap.); I LIVE IN FEAR(1967, Jap.); EMPEROR AND A GENERAL, THE(1968, Jap.); CREATURE CALLED MAN, THE(1970, Jap.); TOKYO STORY(1972, Jap.); TIDAL WAVE(1975, U.S./Jap.)

Norboru Nakamura
SONG FROM MY HEART, THE(1970, Jap.), d, w

Sanzaemon Nakamura
SONG FROM MY HEART, THE(1970, Jap.)

Satoshi Nakamura
TOKYO FILE 212(1951); MADAME BUTTERFLY(1955 Ital./Jap.); MANSTER, THE(1962, Jap.); SPACE AMOEBA, THE(1970, Jap.); YOG-MONSTER FROM SPACE(1970, Jap.); THAT MAN BOLT(1973)

Senjaku Nakamura
SECRET SCROLLS(PART I)**1/2 (1968, Jap.); PRODIGAL SON, THE(1964, Jap.)

Shikaku Nakamura
TWILIGHT STORY, THE(1962, Jap.)

Shinichiro Nakamura
MOTHRA(1962, Jap.), w

Shizue Nakamura
NAVY WIFE(1956)

Shunichi Nakamura
TORA! TORA! TORA!(1970, U.S./Jap.)

Solly Nakamura
STOPOVER TOKYO(1957)

Tadao Nakamura
MONSTERS FROM THE UNKNOWN PLANET(1975, Jap.); TIDAL WAVE(1975, U.S./Jap.)

Takashi Nakamura
1984
WARRIORS OF THE WIND(1984, Jap.), anim

Takeo Nakamura
NUTCRACKER FANTASY(1979), d, ed
Tamao Nakamura
THREE STRIPES IN THE SUN(1955); ENJO(1959, Jap.); BUDDHA(1965, Jap.); SOLDIER'S PRAYER, A(1970, Jap.); SUMMER SOLDIERS(1972, Jap.)
Teddy Nakamura
GEISHA GIRL(1952)
Tetsu Nakamura
NIGHT IN HONG KONG, A(1961, Jap.); MOTHRA(1962, Jap.); LATITUDE ZE-RO(1969, U.S./Jap.); MARCO(1973)
Yutaka Nakamura
ZATOICHI(1968, Jap.)
Ryuzo Nakanishi
GAPPA THE TRIFIBIAN MONSTER(1967, Jap.), w; WAR OF THE PLANETS(1977, Jap.), w
Desmond Nakano
1984
BODY ROCK(1984), w
Kelly Ann Nakano
MODERN ROMANCE(1981)
Lane Nakano
GO FOR BROKE(1951); I WAS AN AMERICAN SPY(1951); PEKING EXPRESS(1951); JAPANESE WAR BRIDE(1952); DEEP IN MY HEART(1954); THREE WEEKS OF LOVE(1965)
Minoru Nakano
MESSAGE FROM SPACE(1978, Jap.), spec eff
Satoru Nakano
TWO IN THE SHADOW(1968, Jap.), art d
Shokei Nakano
GODZILLA VERSUS THE SMOG MONSTER(1972, Jap.), spec eff; WAR OF THE MONSTERS(1972, Jap.), spec eff; GODZILLA VERSUS THE COSMIC MON-STER(1974, Jap.), spec eff; WAR OF THE PLANETS(1977, Jap.), spec eff
Teruyoshi Nakano
PROPHECIES OF NOSTRADAMUS(1974, Jap.), spec eff; MONSTERS FROM THE UNKNOWN PLANET(1975, Jap.), spec eff; HINOTORI(1980, Jap.), spec eff
Mie Nakao
ZATOICHI CHALLENGED(1970, Jap.)
Shunichiro Nakao
MY GEISHA(1962), ph
Punchong Nakaraj
HOT POTATO(1976)
Tatsuji Nakashizu
GREAT WALL, THE(1965, Jap.), ed; GAMERA THE INVINCIBLE(1966, Jap.), ed
Ciyo Nakasone
CRY FOR HAPPY(1961)
Yasuko Nakata
RODAN(1958, Jap.)
Ichiro Nakatani
DANGEROUS KISS, THE(1961, Jap.); WESTWARD DESPERADO(1961, Jap.); OPER-ATION X(1963, Jap.)
Ichiro Nakaya
HAHAKIRI(1963, Jap.); SWORD OF DOOM, THE(1967, Jap.); EMPEROR AND A GENERAL, THE(1968, Jap.)
Noboru Nakaya
LONELY LANE(1963, Jap.); KWAIDAN(1965, Jap.); WHIRLPOOL OF WOMAN(1966, Jap.); TENCHU!(1970, Jap.)
Hisashi Nakayama
MOMENT OF TERROR(1969, Jap.)
Ichiro Nakayama
WESTWARD DESPERADO(1961, Jap.)
Jin Nakayama
PORTRAIT OF CHIEKO(1968, Jap.); THROUGH DAYS AND MONTHS(1969 Jap.); WHISPERING JOE(1969, Jap.); NIGHT OF THE SEAGULL, THE(1970, Jap.)
Kengo Nakayama
WAR OF THE MONSTERS(1972, Jap.)
Mari Nakayama
LATITUDE ZERO(1969, U.S./Jap.); YOUNG GUY ON MT. COOK(1969, Jap.); AL-MOST TRANSPARENT BLUE(1980, Jap.)
Yutaka Nakayama
GODZILLA VS. THE THING(1964, Jap.)
Kaizan Nakazato
SWORD OF DOOM, THE(1967, Jap.), w
Hanjiro Nakazawa
SPOILS OF THE NIGHT(1969, Jap.), ph
Tatsumi Nakazawa
1984
FAMILY GAME, THE(1984, Jap.), art d
Gloria Nakea
KONA COAST(1968)
Vladimir Nakhabtsev
UNCOMMON THIEF, AN(1967, USSR), ph
Rodion Nakhapetov
SONS AND MOTHERS(1967, USSR)
Z. Nakhashkiev
CITY OF YOUTH(1938, USSR)
Nakoma the Wonder Horse
KING OF THE STALLIONS(1942)
Tadao Nakumura
LOST WORLD OF SINBAD, THE(1965, Jap.)
David Nakuna
BEYOND THE REEF(1981)
Al Nalbandian
AMERICAN GRAFFITI(1973)
Albert Nalbandian
PAL JOEY(1957); DEAD HEAT ON A MERRY-GO-ROUND(1966)
Reggie Nalder
ADVENTURES OF CAPTAIN FABIAN(1951); MAN WHO KNEW TOO MUCH, THE(1956); CONVICTS FOUR(1962); MANCHURIAN CANDIDATE, THE(1962); SPI-RAL ROAD, THE(1962); DAY AND THE HOUR, THE(1963, Fr./ Ital.); MARK OF THE DEVIL(1970, Ger./Brit.); MARK OF THE DEVIL II(1975, Ger./Brit.); DRACULA'S

DOG(1978); SEVEN(1979); DEVIL AND MAX DEVLIN, THE(1981)
Misc. Talkies
DRACULA SUCKS(1979)
Enrico Naldi
ALONG CAME SALLY(1934, Brit.)
Marco Naldi
VERY PRIVATE AFFAIR, A(1962, Fr./Ital.)
Nita Naldi
Silents
DR. JEKYLL AND MR. HYDE(1920); ANNA ASCENDS(1922); BLOOD AND SAND(1922); MAN FROM BEYOND, THE(1922); REPORTED MISSING(1922); LAW-FUL LARCENY(1923); TEN COMMANDMENTS, THE(1923); BREAKING POINT, THE(1924); SAINTED DEVIL, A(1924); CLOTHES MAKE THE PIRATE(1925); CO-BRA(1925); PLEASURE GARDEN, THE(1925, Brit./Ger.); FEAR O' GOD(1926, Brit./Ger.)
Misc. Silents
DIVORCE OF CONVENIENCE, A(1921); LAST DOOR, THE(1921); SNITCHING HOUR, THE(1922); GLIMPSES OF THE MOON, THE(1923); YOU CAN'T FOOL YOUR WIFE(1923); DON'T CALL IT LOVE(1924); LADY WHO LIED, THE(1925); FEAR O'GOD(1926, Brit.); MIRACLE OF LIFE, THE(1926); UNFAIR SEX, THE(1926); WHAT PRICE BEAUTY(1928)
Spartaco Nale
BARABBAS(1962, Ital.); SWORD OF THE CONQUEROR(1962, Ital.); TARTARS, THE(1962, Ital./Yugo.)
Elaine Nalee
Misc. Talkies
KELLY(1981, Can.)
Steven Nalevansky
BLOOD BEACH(1981), p, w
Antun Nalis
APACHE GOLD(1965, Ger.); TREASURE OF SILVER LAKE(1965, Fr./Ger./Yugo.); KAYA, I'LL KILL YOU(1969, Yugo./Fr.)
William G. Nally
Misc. Silents
SHARK, THE(1920)
William Nally
Silents
JUST AROUND THE CORNER(1921); SALVATION NELL(1921); SHADOWS OF THE SEA(1922); SECOND FIDDLE(1923)
Misc. Silents
GREAT MEN AMONG US(1915)
Duke Nalon
ROAR OF THE CROWD(1953)
John Nalpern
IF EVER I SEE YOU AGAIN(1978)
Chungim Nam
YONGKARI MONSTER FROM THE DEEP(1967 S.K.)
Kungwon Nam
MONSTER WANGMAGWI(1967, S. K.)
Lee Tse Nam
EXIT THE DRAGON, ENTER THE TIGER(1977, Hong Kong), d
Marguerite Namara
CARMEN(1931, Brit.); THIRTY-DAY PRINCESS(1934); PETER IBBETSON(1935)
Misc. Silents
STOLEN MOMENTS(1920)
Joe Namath
NORWOOD(1970); C. C. AND COMPANY(1971); LAST REBEL, THE(1971); AVA-LANCHE EXPRESS(1979)
1984
CHATTANOOGA CHOO CHOO(1984)
Albert Namatjira
PHANTOM STOCKMAN, THE(1953, Aus.)
Ricky Namay
HELL WITH HEROES, THE(1968)
Ken Y. Namba
1984
MIKE'S MURDER(1984)
Shinji Nambara
HUMAN CONDITION, THE(1959, Jap.)
M.N. Nambiar
JUNGLE, THE(1952)
K. Nambu
Silents
THIEF OF BAGDAD, THE(1924)
Shozo Nambu
SANSHO THE BAILIFF(1969, Jap.)
Frank Namczy
SEPIA CINDERELLA(1947), art d
Art Names
GIRL IN GOLD BOOTS(1968), w; ASTRO-ZOMBIES, THE(1969), ed
Arthur A. Names
BLACK KLANSMAN, THE(1966), w
Misc. Talkies
FANGS(1974), d
The Names
TERROR ON TOUR(1980), m
Frank Namezy
MIRACLE IN HARLEM(1948), art d
L. Namgalashvili
FATHER OF A SOLDIER(1966, USSR), ph
Etsuko Nami
FIGHT FOR THE GLORY(1970, Jap.)
Tatsuo Namikawa
KARATE, THE HAND OF DEATH(1961), ph
Yoko Namikawa
FALCON FIGHTERS, THE(1970, Jap.); MAGOICHI SAGA, THE(1970, Jap.); WAY OUT, WAY IN(1970, Jap.)

Senryu Namiki
CHUSHINGURA(1963, Jap.), w
Fernando Namora
COUNTRY DOCTOR, THE(1963, Portuguese), w
Namu the Whale
NAMU, THE KILLER WHALE(1966)
L. Namuov
SANDU FOLLOWS THE SUN(1965, USSR)
Chiang Nan
SACRED KNIVES OF VENGEANCE, THE(1974, Hong Kong)
Monique Nana
FIRE WITHIN, THE(1964, Fr./Ital.), ed
Ralph Nanalei
ONE WAY WAHINI(1965)
Reiko Nanao
RED BEARD(1966, Jap.)
Herb Nanas
ROCKY II(1979)
Leo Nanas
PARADISE ALLEY(1978)
Ann Maria Nanasi
OUTLAW'S SON(1957)
Anna Marie Nanasi
REMARKABLE MR. PENNYPACKER, THE(1959)
D.R. Nanayakkara
1984
INDIANA JONES AND THE TEMPLE OF DOOM(1984)
Koji Nanbara
LOVE UNDER THE CRUCIFIX(1965, Jap.)
Shozo Nanbu
MYSTERIOUS SATELLITE, THE(1956, Jap.)
Syozo Nanbu
UGETSU(1954, Jap.)
Cortez Nance
SOPHIE'S CHOICE(1982)
Diane Nance
GREAT GATSBY, THE(1949)
Ellen Nance
LAUGHING POLICEMAN, THE(1973)
Jack Nance
FOOLS(1970); JUMP(1971); HAMMETT(1982)
1984
CITY HEAT(1984); DUNE(1984); JOHNNY DANGEROUSLY(1984)
John Nance
ERASERHEAD(1978)
Nancee
Misc. Talkies
MIDNIGHT PLOWBOY(1973)
Nandi
LAUGHING ANNE(1954, Brit./U.S.)
Vera Nandi
NEOPOLITAN CAROUSEL(1961, Ital.); GIRL WHO COULDN'T SAY NO, THE(1969, Ital.)
Tarapada Nandy
MUSIC ROOM, THE(1963, India)
N. Naneris
THANOS AND DESPINA(1970, Fr./Gr.)
Nanette
Silents
HILLS OF KENTUCKY(1927)
Nedelcho Nanev
PEACH THIEF, THE(1969, Bulgaria), art d
Kieu Nanh
YANK IN VIET-NAM, A(1964)
Nanita
SUPERBEAST(1972)
Chieko Naniwa
WOMEN IN PRISON(1957, Jap.); THRONE OF BLOOD(1961, Jap.); EARLY AUTUMN(1962, Jap.); MADAME AKI(1963, Jap.); SANSHO THE BAILIFF(1969, Jap.); SNOW COUNTRY(1969, Jap.); GEISHA, A(1978, Jap.)
Debbie Nankervis
LIBIDO(1973, Aus.)
Michael Nankin
MIDNIGHT MADNESS(1980), d&w
William Nanlan
WAR OF THE RANGE(1933)
Russ Nannarello, Jr.
RED, WHITE AND BLACK, THE(1970)
Luigi Nannerini
JOURNEY BENEATH THE DESERT(1967, Fr./Ital.), p
Hugh Nanning
HONEY POT, THE(1967, Brit.)
Armando Nannuzzi
YOUNG HUSBANDS(1958, Ital./Fr.), ph; BELL' ANTONIO(1962, Ital.), ph; LA NOTTE BRAVA(1962, Fr./Ital.), ph; MAFIOSO(1962, Ital.), ph; VISIT, THE(1964, Ger./Fr./Ital./U.S.), ph; DOLL THAT TOOK THE TOWN, THE(1965, Ital.), ph; LOVE A LA CARTE(1965, Ital.), ph; MAGNIFICENT CUCKOLD, THE(1965, Fr./Ital.), ph; LA FUGA(1966, Ital.), ph; LA VISITA(1966, Ital./Fr.), ph; SANDRA(1966, Ital.), ph; SIX DAYS A WEEK(1966, Fr./Ital./Span.), ph; HEAD OF THE FAMILY(1967, Ital./Fr.), ph; WAKE UP AND DIE(1967, Fr./Ital.), ph; WEEKEND, ITALIAN STYLE(1967, Fr./Ital./Span.), ph; ITALIAN SECRET SERVICE(1968, Ital.), ph; WATERLOO(1970, Ital./USSR), ph; THAT SPLENDID NOVEMBER(1971, Fr./Ital.), ph; DIARY OF A CLOISTERED NUN(1973, Ital./Fr./Ger.), ph; LUDWIG(1973, Ital./Ger./Fr.), ph; MY NAME IS NOBODY(1974, Ital./Fr./Ger.), ph; CHINO(1976, Ital., Span., Fr.), ph; NEST OF VIPERS(1979, Ital.), ph; LA CAGE AUX FOLLES II(1981, Ital./Fr.), ph; LA NUIT DE VARENNES(1983, Fr./Ital.), ph; NANA(1983, Ital.), ph
1984
BEYOND GOOD AND EVIL(1984, Ital./Fr./Ger.), ph; SAHARA(1984), ph

Nella Nannuzzi
MINOTAUR, THE(1961, Ital.), ed; WHITE SLAVE SHIP(1962, Fr./Ital.), ed
Frank Nanoia
LILITH(1964); MC MASTERS, THE(1970)
Milanka Nanovic
BOY CRIED MURDER, THE(1966, Ger./Brit./Yugo.), ed
Betty Nansen
Silents
SONG OF HATE, THE(1915)
Misc. Silents
ANNA KARENINA(1914); SHOULD A MOTHER TELL?(1915)
Taro Nanshu
FIGHT FOR THE GLORY(1970, Jap.)
Monik Nantel
OF UNKNOWN ORIGIN(1983, Can.)
Louis Nanten
Misc. Silents
CRIME AND THE PENALTY(1916, Brit.)
Nicole Nantheuil
MISTRESS FOR THE SUMMER, A(1964, Fr./Ital.)
Michiyo Naoki
GEISHA GIRL(1952)
Naomi
ISLAND WOMEN(1958)
Henry Nap
PARSIFAL(1983, Fr.), p
Annie Nap-Oleon
PARSIFAL(1983, Fr.), p
Alan Napier
UNTIL THEY SAIL(1957); CASTE(1930, Brit.); STAMBOUL(1931, Brit.); LOYALTIES(1934, Brit.); IN A MONASTERY GARDEN(1935); FOR VALOR(1937, Brit.); WIFE OF GENERAL LING, THE(1938, Brit.); WE ARE NOT ALONE(1939); WINGS OVER AFRICA(1939); HOUSE OF THE SEVEN GABLES, THE(1940); INVISIBLE MAN RETURNS, THE(1940); SECRET FOUR, THE(1940, Brit.); CONFIRM OR DENY(1941); CAT PEOPLE(1942); EAGLE SQUADRON(1942); RANDOM HARVEST(1942); WE WERE DANCING(1942); YANK AT ETON, A(1942); APPOINTMENT IN BERLIN(1943); LASSIE, COME HOME(1943); MADAME CURIE(1943); SONG OF BERNADETTE, THE(1943); ACTION IN ARABIA(1944); DARK WATERS(1944); HAIRY APE, THE(1944); LOST ANGEL(1944); MADEMOISELLE FIFI(1944); THIRTY SECONDS OVER TOKYO(1944); UNINVITED, THE(1944); HANGOVER SQUARE(1945); ISLE OF THE DEAD(1945); MINISTRY OF FEAR(1945); HOUSE OF HORRORS(1946); SCANDAL IN PARIS, A(1946); STRANGE WOMAN, THE(1946); THREE STRANGERS(1946); ADVENTURE ISLAND(1947); DRIFTWOOD(1947); FIESTA(1947); FOREVER AMBER(1947); HIGH CONQUEST(1947); IVY(1947); LONE WOLF IN LONDON(1947); LURED(1947); SINBAD THE SAILOR(1947); UNCONQUERED(1947); HILLS OF HOME(1948); JOAN OF ARC(1948); JOHNNY BELINDA(1948); MACBETH(1948); MY OWN TRUE LOVE(1948); CHALLENGE TO LASSIE(1949); CONNECTICUT YANKEE IN KING ARTHUR'S COURT, A(1949); CRISS CROSS(1949); MANHANDLED(1949); MASTER MINDS(1949); RED DANUBE, THE(1949); TARZAN'S MAGIC FOUNTAIN(1949); DOUBLE CROSSBONES(1950); TRIPOLI(1950); ACROSS THE WIDE MISSOURI(1951); BLUE VEIL, THE(1951); GREAT CARUSO, THE(1951); HIGHWAYMAN, THE(1951); STRANGE DOOR, THE(1951); TARZAN'S PERIL(1951); BIG JIM McLAIN(1952); JULIUS CAESAR(1953); YOUNG BESS(1953); DESIREE(1954); MOONFLEET(1955); COURT JESTER, THE(1956); MIAMI EXPOSE(1956); MOLE PEOPLE, THE(1956); ISLAND OF LOST WOMEN(1959); JOURNEY TO THE CENTER OF THE EARTH(1959); TENDER IS THE NIGHT(1961); WILD IN THE COUNTRY(1961); PREMATURE BURIAL, THE(1962); SWORD IN THE STONE, THE(1963); MARNIE(1964); MY FAIR LADY(1964); SIGNPOST TO MURDER(1964); LOVED ONE, THE(1965); 36 HOURS(1965); BATMAN(1966)
Charles Napier
MOONFIRE(1970); SEVEN MINUTES, THE(1971); CITIZENS BAND(1977); THUNDER AND LIGHTNING(1977); LAST EMBRACE(1979); BLUES BROTHERS, THE(1980); MELVIN AND HOWARD(1980); WACKO(1983)
1984
SWING SHIFT(1984)
Misc. Talkies
LOVE AND KISSES(?); IN SEARCH OF GOLDEN SKY(1984)
David Napier
BIDDY(1983, Brit.)
Diana Napier
HER FIRST AFFAIRE(1932, Brit.); WEDDING REHEARSAL(1932, Brit.); FOR LOVE OF YOU(1933, Brit.); CATHERINE THE GREAT(1934, Brit.); PRIVATE LIFE OF DON JUAN, THE(1934, Brit.); WARREN CASE, THE(1934, Brit.); MIMI(1935, Brit.); REGAL CAVALCADE(1935, Brit.); CLOWN MUST LAUGH, A(1936, Brit.); FORBIDDEN MUSIC(1936, Brit.); TROUBLE AHEAD(1936, Brit.); HEART'S DESIRE(1937, Brit.); BAIT(1950, Brit.)
Misc. Talkies
BUTTERFLY AFFAIR, THE(1934, Brit.)
Diane Napier
STRANGE EVIDENCE(1933, Brit.)
Elmer Napier
SUNDOWN RIDERS(1948)
Francis Napier
GIRL HUNTERS, THE(1963, Brit.); YANKS(1979)
Henry J. Napier
Misc. Silents
FAITHLESS SEX, THE(1922), d
Hugo Napier
NIGHT SHIFT(1982)
John Napier
FATHER GOOSE(1964); GREAT SIOUX MASSACRE, THE(1965); SLENDER THREAD, THE(1965); ROUGH NIGHT IN JERICHO(1967); GIRL WHO KNEW TOO MUCH, THE(1969); GYPSY MOTHS, THE(1969)
Marshall Napier
BEYOND REASONABLE DOUBT(1980, New Zeal.); GOODBYE PORK PIE(1981, New Zealand)
1984
PALLET ON THE FLOOR(1984, New Zealand); WILD HORSES(1984, New Zealand)

Patricia Napier
STORIES FROM A FLYING TRUNK(1979, Brit.); MOUSE AND THE WOMAN, THE(1981, Brit.); BIDDY(1983, Brit.)
Paul Napier
SECRET LIFE OF AN AMERICAN WIFE, THE(1968)
Robert Napier
WEEKEND AT DUNKIRK(1966, Fr./Ital.)
Russell Napier
END OF THE RIVER, THE(1947, Brit.); BLIND MAN'S BLUFF(1952, Brit.); DEATH OF AN ANGEL(1952, Brit.); STOLEN FACE(1952, Brit.); TERROR STREET(1953); COMPANIONS IN CRIME(1954, Brit.); FUSS OVER FEATHERS(1954, Brit.); UNHOLY FOUR, THE(1954, Brit.); BRAIN MACHINE, THE(1955, Brit.); CASE OF THE RED MONKEY(1955, Brit.); TIME TO KILL, A(1955, Brit.); GUILTY?(1956, Brit.); LAST MAN TO HANG, THE(1956, Brit.); NARROWING CIRCLE, THE(1956, Brit.); MAN IN THE ROAD, THE(1957, Brit.); SHIRALEE, THE(1957, Brit.); NIGHT TO REMEMBER, A(1958, Brit.); ROBBERY UNDER ARMS(1958, Brit.); NAVY HEROES(1959, Brit.); SON OF ROBIN HOOD(1959, Brit.); TREAD SOFTLY STRANGER(1959, Brit.); WITNESS, THE(1959, Brit.); ANGRY SILENCE, THE(1960, Brit.); FRANCIS OF ASSISI(1961); MARK, THE(1961, Brit.); DAMN THE DEFIANT!(1962, Brit.); MIX ME A PERSON(1962, Brit.); MAN IN THE MIDDLE(1964, U.S./Brit.); BLOOD BEAST TERROR, THE(1967, Brit.); IT!(1967, Brit.); HIGH COMMISSIONER, THE(1968, U.S./Brit.); TWISTED NERVE(1969, Brit.); BLACK WINDMILL, THE(1974, Brit.)
Russell L. Napier
HELL IS A CITY(1960, Brit.)
Stacia Napierkowska
Misc. Silents
L'ATLANTIDE(1921, Fr.); INCH'ALLAH(1922, Fr.)
Denise Naples
TICKET TO HEAVEN(1981)
Toni Naples
DOCTOR DETROIT(1983)
Art Napoleon
MAN ON THE PROWL(1957), p, d, w; TOO MUCH, TOO SOON(1958), d, w; RIDE THE WILD SURF(1964), p
Jo Napoleon
SHARKFIGHTERS, THE(1956), w; MAN ON THE PROWL(1957), p, w; TOO MUCH, TOO SOON(1958), w; RIDE THE WILD SURF(1964), p, w
Titus Napoleon
BLACK BIRD, THE(1975)
Napoleon the Dog
Silents
PEACOCK ALLEY(1922)
Art Napoleons
RIDE THE WILD SURF(1964), w
Anna Marie Napoles
ABSENCE OF MALICE(1981)
Ana Napoli
BLOW TO THE HEART(1983, Ital.), ed
Angelo Napoli
EVERY MAN FOR HIMSELF(1980, Fr.)
Nicholas Napoli
TRAIN GOES EAST, THE(1949, USSR), English titles
Ken Napper
JUST LIKE A WOMAN(1967, Brit.), m
Kenny Napper
ALL NIGHT LONG(1961, Brit.)
Malya Nappi
VICTORS, THE(1963); ONE MILLION YEARS B.C.(1967, Brit./U.S.)
Milo Nappi
VICTORS, THE(1963)
Nappy Lamare Dixieland Band
HOLIDAY RHYTHM(1950)
Gerard Naprous
KRULL(1983)
Hugo Napton
1984
LOVE STREAMS(1984)
Akemi Nara
EAST CHINA SEA(1969, Jap.)
Vencenzio Naranda
PEOPLE WHO OWN THE DARK(1975, Span.), w
Ivan Naranjo
WINDWALKER(1980); MAN WHO WASN'T THERE, THE(1983); WAVELENGTH(1983)
Johnny Naranjo
GODFATHER, THE, PART II(1974)
Tomoko Naraoka
BANISHED(1978, Jap.)
Ram Narayan
PRIVATE ENTERPRISE, A(1975, Brit.), m
R.K. Narayen
GUIDE, THE(1965, U.S./India), w
Jean Narboni
TWO OR THREE THINGS I KNOW ABOUT HER(1970, Fr.)
Roberta Narbonne
SEDUCED AND ABANDONED(1964, Fr./Ital.)
Leon Narby
SKIN DEEP(1978, New Zealand), ph
Thomas Narcejac
DIABOLIQUE(1955, Fr.), w; DEMONIAQUE(1958, Fr.), w; VERTIGO(1958), w; FACES IN THE DARK(1960, Brit.), w; CRIME DOES NOT PAY(1962, Fr.), w; HORROR CHAMBER OF DR. FAUSTUS, THE(1962, Fr./Ital.), w; WHERE THE TRUTH LIES(1962, Fr.), w; DOUBLE DECEPTION(1963, Fr.), w
Agnes Narcha
MASSACRE(1934)
Grazia Narcisco
PRIZE, THE(1963)

Nathaniel Narcisco
STALKING MOON, THE(1969)
Gracia Narciso
DRAGSTRIP GIRL(1957)
Grazia Narciso
MADONNA OF THE DESERT(1948); MUSIC MAN(1948); BETWEEN MIDNIGHT AND DAWN(1950); BLACK HAND, THE(1950); SEPTEMBER AFFAIR(1950); UP FRONT(1951); THREE COINS IN THE FOUNTAIN(1954); YOUNG AT HEART(1955)
Oscar Narciso
RICHARD'S THINGS(1981, Brit.)
Andre Narcisse
GOLDEN MISTRESS, THE(1954)
Joe Narcisse
BAND OF ANGELS(1957)
Joseph C. Narcisse
WHITE WITCH DOCTOR(1953)
Narcissus the Goat
SAPS AT SEA(1940)
Winnie Nard
FEAR(1946)
George Nardelli
COCKTAIL HOUR(1933); SYLVIA SCARLETT(1936); SEPTEMBER AFFAIR(1950); TO CATCH A THIEF(1955); FOUR GIRLS IN TOWN(1956); PAL JOEY(1957); LAFAYETTE ESCADRILLE(1958); NEW KIND OF LOVE, A(1963)
Aurelio Nardi
LA DOLCE VITA(1961, Ital./Fr.)
Corrado Nardi
SENSUALITA(1954, Ital.)
Dino Nardi
DEPORTED(1950); NEVER TAKE NO FOR AN ANSWER(1952, Brit./Ital.); WHEN IN ROME(1952)
Mia Nardi
ASSIGNMENT K(1968, Brit.)
Nadine Nardi
SULLIVAN'S EMPIRE(1967)
Nicoletta Nardi
FINE PAIR, A(1969, Ital.), ed
Pietro Nardi
VOICE IN YOUR HEART, A(1952, Ital.), w
Tonino Nardi
BLOW TO THE HEART(1983, Ital.), ph
Tony Nardi
GAS(1981, Can.)
Dominic Nardini
1984
RACING WITH THE MOON(1984)
Tom Nardini
CAT BALLOU(1965); WINTER A GO-GO(1965); AFRICA–TEXAS STYLE!(1967 U.S./Brit.); BORN WILD(1968); DEVIL'S 8, THE(1969); SIEGE(1983, Can.)
Di Nardo
YETI(1977, Ital.), p, w
Silvio Nardo
SUPERFLY T.N.T.(1973)
Graziella Narducci
TROUBLEMAKER, THE(1964)
Itaco Nardulli
IDENTIFICATION OF A WOMAN(1983, Ital.)
Brian Narelle
DARK STAR(1975); TWICE UPON A TIME(1983), anim d
Jindrich Narenta
SWEET LIGHT IN A DARK ROOM(1966, Czech.); TRANSPORT FROM PARADISE(1967, Czech.); MURDER CZECH STYLE(1968, Czech.)
Owen Nares
LOOSE ENDS(1930, Brit.); MIDDLE WATCH, THE(1930, Brit.); ARENT WE ALL?(1932, Brit.); FRAIL WOMEN(1932, Brit.); LOVE CONTRACT, THE(1932, Brit.); OFFICE GIRL, THE(1932, Brit.); WHERE IS THIS LADY?(1932, Brit.); WOMAN DECIDES, THE(1932, Brit.); WOMAN IN CHAINS(1932, Brit.); DISCORD(1933, Brit.); ONE PRECIOUS YEAR(1933, Brit.); THERE GOES THE BRIDE(1933, Brit.); PRIVATE LIFE OF DON JUAN, THE(1934, Brit.); REGAL CAVALCADE(1935, Brit.); HEAD OFFICE(1936, Brit.); SHOW GOES ON, THE(1937, Brit.); LOVES OF MADAME DUBARRY, THE(1938, Brit.); PRIME MINISTER, THE(1941, Brit.)
Silents
JUST A GIRL(1916, Brit.); FLAMES(1917, Brit.); LABOUR LEADER, THE(1917, Brit.); ONE SUMMER'S DAY(1917, Brit.); ONWARD CHRISTIAN SOLDIERS(1918, Brit.); EDGE O'BEYOND(1919, Brit.); ALL THE WINNERS(1920, Brit.); LAST ROSE OF SUMMER, THE(1920, Brit.); INDIAN LOVE LYRICS, THE(1923, Brit.); MIRIAM ROZELLA(1924, Brit.); SORROWS OF SATAN(1926); THIS MARRIAGE BUSINESS(1927, Brit.)
Misc. Silents
MILESTONES(1916, Brit.); SORROWS OF SATAN, THE(1917); GOD BLESS OUR RED, WHITE AND BLUE(1918, Brit.); MAN WHO WON, THE(1918, Brit.); TINKER, TAILOR, SOLDIER, SAILOR(1918, Brit.); WANTED - A WIFE(1918, Brit.); GAMBLERS ALL(1919, Brit.); TEMPORARY GENTLEMAN, A(1920, Brit.); FOR HER FATHER'S SAKE(1921, Brit.); BROWN SUGAR(1922, Brit.); FAITHFUL HEART, THE(1922, Brit.); YOUNG LOCHINVAR(1923, Brit.)
Hiro Narita
NEVER CRY WOLF(1983), ph
1984
GO TELL IT ON THE MOUNTAIN(1984), ph
Mikio Narita
SHOWDOWN FOR ZATOICHI(1968, Jap.); MESSAGE FROM SPACE(1978, Jap.)
Richard Narita
BABY BLUE MARINE(1976); MURDER BY DEATH(1976); CHEAP DETECTIVE, THE(1978); GOLDEN SEAL, THE(1983)
Takashi Narita
SEVEN SAMURAI, THE(1956, Jap.)
Dino Narizzano
CURSE OF THE LIVING CORPSE, THE(1964); WINDFLOWERS(1968); THREE DAYS OF THE CONDOR(1975)

Silvio Narizzano
DIE, DIE, MY DARLING(1965, Brit.), d; GEORGY GIRL(1966, Brit.), d; BLUE(1968), d; LOOT(1971, Brit.), d; REDNECK(1975, Ital./Span.), d; WHY SHOOT THE TEACHER(1977, Can.), d; CLASS OF MISS MAC MICHAEL, THE(1978, Brit./U.S.), d
Misc. Talkies
CHOICES(1981), d
Rob Narke
PACK, THE(1977)
Robin Narke
MITCHELL(1975)
Max Narlinski
Misc. Silents
MASTER OF LOVE, THE(1919, Ger.)
Alexander Narodetzky
1984
MOSCOW ON THE HUDSON(1984)
M. Narokov
Misc. Silents
ALARM, THE(1917, USSR); DAREDEVIL(1919, USSR), a, d
Miguel Naros
ISLAND OF THE DAMNED(1976, Span.)
Olya Narovchatova
SUN SHINES FOR ALL, THE(1961, USSR); FAREWELL, DOVES(1962, USSR)
Joseph T. Narr
BLACULA(1972), p
Andy Narrell
1984
SIGNAL 7(1984), m
Jack Narta
MOUNTAIN MOONLIGHT(1941), ph
Harry Narunsky
1984
ROSEBUD BEACH HOTEL(1984), w
Masashige Narusawa
LOVE UNDER THE CRUCIFIX(1965, Jap.), w; SPOILS OF THE NIGHT(1969, Jap.), w
Akiko Naruse
WAY OUT, WAY IN(1970, Jap.)
Mikio Naruse
WISER AGE(1962, Jap.), d; LONELY LANE(1963, Jap.), p, d; WHEN A WOMAN ASCENDS THE STAIRS(1963, Jap.), d; WOMAN'S LIFE, A(1964, Jap.), d; YEARNING(1964, Jap.), p, d; THIN LINE, THE(1967, Jap.), d; TWO IN THE SHADOW(1968, Jap.), d; MOMENT OF TERROR(1969, Jap.), d
Toichiro Narushima
TWIN SISTERS OF KYOTO(1964, Jap.), ph; SNOW COUNTRY(1969, Jap.), ph; DOUBLE SUICIDE(1970, Jap.), ph; AFFAIR AT AKITSU(1980, Jap.), ph; MERRY CHRISTMAS MR. LAWRENCE(1983, Jap./Brit.), ph
Ron Nary
ZAPPED!(1982), spec eff
Z. Naryshkina
DIMKA(1964, USSR)
Gianni Narzisi
RED SHEIK, THE(1963, Ital.), ph; LOVE FACTORY(1969, Ital.), ph
Annalisa Nasalli-Rocca
ROMANOFF AND JULIET(1961), cos; JESSICA(1962, U.S./Ital./Fr.), cos; VIVA MAX!(1969), cos
1984
SHEENA(1984), cos
Orietta Nasalli-Rocca
ROMANOFF AND JULIET(1961), cos; SHOES OF THE FISHERMAN, THE(1968), cos
Orietta Nasallirocca
LION OF THE DESERT(1981, Libya/Brit.), cos
Youn Nasarov
ANDREI ROUBLOV(1973, USSR)
Marcia Nasatir
HEART BEAT(1979)
Paul Naschy
FRANKENSTEIN'S BLOODY TERROR(1968, Span.); ASSIGNMENT TERROR(1970, Ger./Span./Ital.); DR. JEKYLL AND THE WOLFMAN(1971, Span.); DRACULA'S GREAT LOVE(1972, Span.); HUNCHBACK OF THE MORGUE, THE(1972, Span.); CURSE OF THE DEVIL(1973, Span./Mex.); HOUSE OF PSYCHOTIC WOMEN, THE zero(1973, Span.); LAS RATAS NO DUERMEN DE NOCHE(1974, Span./Fr.); PEOPLE WHO OWN THE DARK(1975, Span./U.S.); MONSTER ISLAND(1981, Span./U.S.)
Paul Naschy [Paul Nash]
WEREWOLF VS. THE VAMPIRE WOMAN, THE(1970, Span./Ger.)
Mario Nascimbene
BAREFOOT CONTESSA, THE(1954), m; CENTO ANNI D'AMORE(1954, Ital.), m; ANGELA(1955, Ital.), m; ALEXANDER THE GREAT(1956), m; CHILD IN THE HOUSE(1956, Brit.), m; FAREWELL TO ARMS, A(1957), m; THAT NIGHT!(1957), md; QUIET AMERICAN, THE(1958), m; VIKINGS, THE(1958), m; ROOM AT THE TOP(1959, Brit.), m; SCENT OF MYSTERY(1960), m; SONS AND LOVERS(1960, Brit.), m; CARTHAGE IN FLAMES(1961, Fr./Ital.), m; FRANCIS OF ASSISI(1961), m; GIRL WITH A SUITCASE(1961, Fr./Ital.), m; ROMANOFF AND JULIET(1961), m, md; VIOLENT SUMMER(1961, Fr./Ital.), m; BARABBAS(1962, Ital.), m; CONSTANTINE AND THE CROSS(1962, Ital.), m; HAPPY THIEVES, THE(1962), m; JESSICA(1962, U.S./Ital./Fr.), m; LIGHT IN THE PIAZZA(1962), m; STORY OF JOSEPH AND HIS BRETHREN THE(1962, Ital.), m; SWORDSMAN OF SIENA, THE(1962, Fr./Ital.), m; BACCHANTES, THE(1963, Fr./Ital.), m; JASON AND THE ARGONAUTS(1963, Brit.), md; VERONA TRIAL, THE(1963, Ital.), m; DISORDER(1964, Fr./Ital.), m; GOLDEN ARROW, THE(1964, Ital.), m; WHERE THE SPIES ARE(1965, Brit.), m; MONGOLS, THE(1966, Fr./Ital.), m; DOCTOR FAUSTUS(1967, Brit.), m; KISS THE GIRLS AND MAKE THEM DIE(1967, U.S./Ital.), m; ONE MILLION YEARS B.C.(1967, Brit./U.S.), m; VENGEANCE OF SHE, THE(1968, Brit.), m; STORY OF A WOMAN(1970, U.S./Ital.); CREATURES THE WORLD FORGOT(1971, Brit.), m; WHEN DINOSAURS RULED THE EARTH(1971, Brit.), m; AUGUSTINE OF HIPPO(1973, Ital.), m; YEAR ONE(1974, Ital.), m

Iris Nascimento
1984
GABRIELA(1984, Braz.)
Milton Nascimento
FITZCARRALDO(1982)
Ralph J. Nase
CALL OF THE CIRCUS(1930), m
James Nasella
O'HARA'S WIFE(1983), w
Alden Nash
WE'RE RICH AGAIN(1934), w; PASSPORT TO SUEZ(1943), w; MAN-EATER OF KUMAON(1948), w; SAINTED SISTERS, THE(1948), w; UNWED MOTHER(1958), w
Bill Nash
WE'VE NEVER BEEN LICKED(1943)
Bob Nash
MR. DOODLE KICKS OFF(1938); VIVA LAS VEGAS(1964)
Brian Nash
THRILL OF IT ALL, THE(1963)
Cecil Nash
OF HUMAN BONDAGE(1964, Brit.); WHERE'S JACK?(1969, Brit.); WEDDING NIGHT(1970, Ireland); GREAT TRAIN ROBBERY, THE(1979, Brit.)
Charles Nash
MARK, THE(1961, Brit.), makeup
Clarence Nash
RELUCTANT DRAGON, THE(1941); THREE CABALLEROS, THE(1944); FUN AND FANCY FREE(1947); GREATEST SHOW ON EARTH, THE(1952); MAN FROM BUTTON WILLOW, THE(1965)
Damien Nash
TWILIGHT TIME(1983, U.S./Yugo.)
Danny Nash
CLINIC, THE(1983, Aus.)
David Nash
MAN IN THE GLASS BOOTH, THE(1975)
Dorothy Nash
Misc. Silents
STAIN IN THE BLOOD, THE(1916)
Florence Nash
IT'S A GREAT LIFE(1936); WOMEN, THE(1939)
Silents
SPRINGTIME(1915)
Gene Nash
WHAT AM I BID?(1967), d&w
Misc. Talkies
DIABOLIC WEDDING(1972), d
George Nash
FIGHTING TEXANS(1933); FUGITIVE, THE(1933); GALLANT FOOL, THE(1933); GALLOPING ROMEO(1933); OLIVER TWIST(1933); PHANTOM BROADCAST, THE(1933); RAINBOW RANCH(1933); RANGER'S CODE, THE(1933); RETURN OF CASEY JONES(1933); BLUE STEEL(1934); MYSTERY LINER(1934); SIXTEEN FATHOMS DEEP(1934)
Misc. Talkies
MAN FROM ARIZONA, THE(1932)
Silents
JUNGLE, THE(1914); COTTON KING, THE(1915); VALLEY OF SILENT MEN, THE(1922); WHEN KNIGHTHOOD WAS IN FLOWER(1922); UNDER THE RED ROBE(1923); JANICE MEREDITH(1924); GREAT GATSBY, THE(1926)
Misc. Silents
FACE IN THE FOG, THE(1922); MAN MUST LIVE, THE(1925)
Heddle Nash
FOR YOU ALONE(1945, Brit.)
Helena Nash
FEAR NO MORE(1961); MONEY TRAP, THE(1966)
J. E. Nash
ILLUSION(1929)
Silents
OUT OF THE STORM(1920), w; TALE OF TWO WORLDS, A(1921), w; SIREN CALL, THE(1922), w; WORLD'S CHAMPION, THE(1922), w
Jacqueline Nash
LET'S MAKE MUSIC(1940)
Jacqueline Nash [Gale Sherwood]
THEY SHALL HAVE MUSIC(1939)
Joan Nash
MOONLIGHTING WIVES(1966)
John Nash
INN OF THE DAMNED(1974, Aus.); MAN FROM SNOWY RIVER, THE(1983, Aus.)
Johnny Nash
TAKE A GIANT STEP(1959); KEY WITNESS(1960)
June Nash
STRANGE CARGO(1929); THEIR OWN DESIRE(1929); DYNAMITE(1930); MADAME SATAN(1930); TWO KINDS OF WOMEN(1932)
Misc. Silents
DAUGHTERS OF DESIRE(1929)
Kate Nash
1984
KINGS AND DESPERATE MEN(1984, Brit.)
Kenneth Nash
CLEOPATRA(1963)
Marilyn Nash
MONSIEUR VERDOUX(1947); UNKNOWN WORLD(1951)
Mary Nash
UNCERTAIN LADY(1934); COLLEGE SCANDAL(1935); COME AND GET IT(1936); EASY LIVING(1937); HEIDI(1937); KING AND THE CHORUS GIRL, THE(1937); WELLS FARGO(1937); LITTLE PRINCESS, THE(1939); RAINS CAME, THE(1939); CHARLIE CHAN IN PANAMA(1940); GOLD RUSH MAISIE(1940); PHILADELPHIA STORY, THE(1940); SAILOR'S LADY(1940); MEN OF BOYS TOWN(1941); CALLING DR. GILLESPIE(1942); HUMAN COMEDY, THE(1943); COBRA WOMAN(1944); IN THE MEANTIME, DARLING(1944); LADY AND THE MONSTER, THE(1944); YOLANDA AND THE THIEF(1945); MONSIEUR BEAUCAIRE(1946); SWELL GUY(1946); TILL THE CLOUDS ROLL BY(1946)

Silents
ARMS AND THE WOMAN(1916)
Maxine Nash
STUDENT TOUR(1934)
Maybelle Nash
SAND CASTLE, THE(1961); OPEN THE DOOR AND SEE ALL THE PEOPLE(1964)
Michael Nash
LOST CONTINENT, THE(1968, Brit.), w
N. Richard Nash
NORA PRENTISS(1947), w; WELCOME STRANGER(1947), w; SAINTED SISTERS, THE(1948), w; DEAR WIFE(1949), w; FLYING MISSILE(1950), w; GOLDBERGS, THE(1950), w; VICIOUS YEARS, THE(1950), w; MARA MARU(1952), w; TOP OF THE WORLD(1955), w; HELEN OF TROY(1956, Ital), w; RAINMAKER, THE(1956), w; PORGY AND BESS(1959), w; ONE SUMMER LOVE(1976), w
Nancy Nash
PALMY DAYS(1931); KID FROM SPAIN, THE(1932)
Misc. Silents
CITY, THE(1926); LOVES OF CARMEN(1927); RICH BUT HONEST(1927); UP-STREAM(1927); BALLYHOO BUSTER, THE(1928)
Noreen Nash
GIRL CRAZY(1943); MAISIE GOES TO RENO(1944); MEET THE PEOPLE(1944); MONSIEUR BEAUCAIRE(1946); BIG FIX, THE(1947); DEVIL ON WHEELS, THE(1947); RED STALLION, THE(1947); TENDER YEARS, THE(1947); ADVENTURES OF CASANOVA(1948); ASSIGNED TO DANGER(1948); CHECKERED COAT, THE(1948); STORM OVER WYOMING(1950); ALADDIN AND HIS LAMP(1952); ROAD AGENT(1952); PHANTOM FROM SPACE(1953); GIANT(1956); LONE RANGER AND THE LOST CITY OF GOLD, THE(1958); WAKE ME WHEN IT'S OVER(1960)
Ogden Nash
FIREFLY, THE(1937), w; SHINING HOUR, THE(1938), w; FEMININE TOUCH, THE(1941), w; ONE TOUCH OF VENUS(1948), w
Patrick Nash
RETURNING, THE(1983), w
Patsy Nash
I LIVE ON DANGER(1942); MAN OF COURAGE(1943); SUBMARINE ALERT(1943)
Percy Nash
Silents
FLYING FROM JUSTICE(1915, Brit.), d; FLAG LIEUTENANT, THE(1919, Brit.), d; HER LONELY SOLDIER(1919, Brit.), d; OLD ARM CHAIR, THE(1920, Brit.), d; WON BY A HEAD(1920, Brit.), d; LIKENESS OF THE NIGHT, THE(1921, Brit.), d; SHIPS THAT PASS IN THE NIGHT(1921, Brit.), d&w
Misc. Silents
ENOCH ARDEN(1914, Brit.), d; HARBOUR LIGHTS, THE(1914, Brit.), d; COAL KING, THE(1915, Brit.), d; MASTER AND MAN(1915, Brit.), d; ROGUE'S WIFE, A(1915, Brit.), d; ROMANY RYE, THE(1915, Brit.), d; ROYAL LOVE(1915, Brit.), d; SCORPION'S STING, THE(1915, Brit.), d; TRUMPET CALL, THE(1915, Brit.), d; DISRAELI(1916, Brit.), d; KING OF THE PEOPLE, A(1917, Brit.), d; BOYS OF THE OTTER PATROL(1918, Brit.), d; WANTED - A WIFE(1918, Brit.), d; DARBY AND JOAN(1919, Brit.), d; WESTWARD HO!(1919, Brit.), d; WOMEN WHO WIN(1919, Brit.), d; HOBSON'S CHOICE(1920, Brit.), d; STORY OF THE ROSARY, THE(1920, Brit.), d; CROXLEY MASTER, THE(1921, Brit.), d; HIS OTHER WIFE(1921, Brit.), d; HOW KITCHENER WAS BETRAYED(1921, Brit.), d
Peter Nash
OF HUMAN BONDAGE(1964, Brit.)
Raymond Nash
DUFFY'S TAVERN(1945)
Robert Nash
GOLDEN GIRL(1951); MEET ME AFTER THE SHOW(1951); PAWNEE(1957); GUN FIGHT(1961); HOW THE WEST WAS WON(1962)
Roger Nash
SHEPHERD OF THE HILLS, THE(1964)
Rudy Nash
1984
PURPLE HEARTS(1984)
Simon Nash
XTRO(1983, Brit.)
1984
BREAKOUT(1984, Brit.)
Thomas Nash
Misc. Silents
UNBROKEN ROAD, THE(1915)
Suleiman Ali Nashnush
FELLINI SATYRICON(1969, Fr./Ital.)
John Nasht
CARTOUCHE(1957, Ital./US), p; DESERT DESPERADOES(1959), p; S.O.S. PACIFIC(1960, Brit.), p; HOT MONEY GIRL(1962, Brit./Ger.), p; CHRISTINE KEELER AFFAIR, THE(1964, Brit.), p
Nashulik
Misc. Silents
KIVALINA OF THE ICE LANDS(1925)
The Nashville Teens
GONKS GO BEAT(1965, Brit.)
Sait Nasifoglu
TARGET: HARRY(1980)
Maurice Nasil
EAGLE WITH TWO HEADS(1948, Fr.); BIG CHIEF, THE(1960, Fr.); COW AND I, THE(1961, Fr., Ital., Ger.); TWO ARE GUILTY(1964, Fr.); VERDICT(1975, Fr./Ital.)
Annalisa Nasilli-Rocca
TROUT, THE(1982, Fr.), cos
Brian Nasimok
GAS(1981, Can.); SPRING FEVER(1983, Can.)
Giuseppe Naso
THAT SPLENDID NOVEMBER(1971, Ital./Fr.)
Jack Nasome
LOVE NOW...PAY LATER(1966, Ital.)
George Nason
SECOND THOUGHTS(1983)
Leonard Nason
KEEP 'EM ROLLING(1934), w

Bona Nassalli-Rocca
SNOW JOB(1972), cos
James Nasser
LURED(1947), p; DON'T TRUST YOUR HUSBAND(1948), p
Ted Nasser
COVER-UP(1949), p
Henri Nassiet
FIRE IN THE STRAW(1943); THEY ARE NOT ANGELS(1948, Fr.); GYPSY FURY(1950, Fr.); MICHAEL STROGOFF(1960, Fr./Ital./Yugo.); BERNADETTE OF LOURDES(1962, Fr.); BAY OF ANGELS(1964, Fr.); THINGS OF LIFE, THE(1970, Fr./Ital./Switz.)
Fred Nassif
MADE FOR EACH OTHER(1971); SOMETHING SHORT OF PARADISE(1979)
Ali Nassirian
CYCLE, THE(1979, Iran)
K. Nassonov
BALLAD OF COSSACK GLOOTA(1938, USSR)
Edward Nassour
AFRICA SCREAMS(1949), p; BEAST OF HOLLOW MOUNTAIN, THE(1956), p, d
Tony Nassour
HELL WITH HEROES, THE(1968)
William Nassour
BEAST OF HOLLOW MOUNTAIN, THE(1956), p
Antica Nast
LIGHTNIN'(1930)
Carol Nast
BABY, IT'S YOU(1983), set d
Ilie Nastase
PLAYERS(1979)
Frank Nastasi
BIRDS DO IT(1966); NIGHT THEY ROBBED BIG BERTHA'S, THE(1975)
Patrice Nastasia
SUBSTITUTION(1970)
Arlette Nastat
PETULIA(1968, U.S./Brit.), cos
Michel Nastorg
THUNDER IN THE BLOOD(1962, Fr.)
Stella Nastou
TEMPEST(1982)
Lucien Nat
RASPUTIN(1939, Fr.); HEART OF A NATION, THE(1943, Fr.); ROOM UPSTAIRS, THE(1948, Fr.); ROYAL AFFAIRS IN VERSAILLES(1957, Fr.); WE ARE ALL MURDERERS(1957, Fr.); DIE GANS VON SEDAN(1962, Fr/Ger.); THERESE(1963, Fr.); THIS SPECIAL FRIENDSHIP(1967, Fr.)
Marie-Jose Nat
ANATOMY OF A MARRIAGE(MY DAYS WITH JEAN-MARC AND MY NIGHTS WITH FRANCOISE)**1/2 (1964 Fr.); AMELIE OR THE TIME TO LOVE(1961, Fr.); LOVE AND THE FRENCHWOMAN(1961, Fr.); TRUTH, THE(1961, Fr./Ital.); SEVEN CAPITAL SINS(1962, Fr./Ital.); EMBASSY(1972, Brit.); ANNA(1981, Fr./Hung.)
Nat Gonella and His Georgians
SING AS YOU SWING(1937, Brit.)
Nat King Cole Trio
SWING IN THE SADDLE(1944)
E. Natale
THIS WINE OF LOVE(1948, Ital.), w
Gloria Natale
SAVAGES(1972), makeup
Nazareno Natale
DEATH RIDES A HORSE(1969, Ital.); SERAFINO(1970, Fr./Ital.); LA CAGE AUX FOLLES II(1981, Ital./Fr.)
Paola Natale
YOUNG, THE EVIL AND THE SAVAGE, THE(1968, Ital.); PIZZA TRIANGLE, THE(1970, Ital./Span.); ROMA(1972, Ital./Fr.)
Roberto Natale
BLOODY PIT OF HORROR, THE(1965, Ital.), w; KILL BABY KILL(1966, Ital.), w; SEVEN REVENGES, THE(1967, Ital.), w; TERROR-CREATURES FROM THE GRAVE(1967, U.S./Ital.), w; LONG RIDE FROM HELL, A(1970, Ital.), w
Germano Natali
DEEP RED(1976, Ital.), spec eff; STARCRASH(1979), spec eff; TREASURE OF THE FOUR CROWNS(1983, Span./U.S.), spec eff
1984
WARRIORS OF THE WASTELAND(1984, Ital.), spec eff
Paola Natalie
SONS OF SATAN(1969, Ital./Fr./Ger.)
Giovanni Natalucci
1984
ONCE UPON A TIME IN AMERICA(1984), set d
Giulio Natalucci
RUTHLESS FOUR, THE(1969, Ital./Ger.), makeup; GARDEN OF THE FINZI-CONTINIS, THE(1976, Ital./Ger.), makeup
Emile Natan
CHEAT, THE(1950, Fr.), p; MICHAEL STROGOFF(1960, Fr./Ital./Yugo.), p; YOU ONLY LIVE ONCE(1969, Fr.), p
Agathe Natanson
HELLO–GOODBYE(1970); SOMEONE BEHIND THE DOOR(1971, Fr./Brit.)
Jacques Natanson
DARK EYES(1938, Fr.), w; UNDER SECRET ORDERS(1943, Brit.), w; LA RONDE(1954, Fr.), w; LE PLAISIR(1954, Fr.), w; LOLA MONTES(1955, Fr./Ger.), w
Joseph Natanson
FRANCIS OF ASSISI(1961), spec eff; MY SON, THE HERO(1963, Ital./Fr.), spec eff; CAVERN, THE(1965, Ital./Ger.), spec eff; SPIRITS OF THE DEAD(1969, Fr./Ital.), spec eff
Guido Natari
BEFORE HIM ALL ROME TREMBLED(1947, Ital.)
James Nataro
BEHIND THE MASK(1946)
Jimmy Nataro
DOUBLE OR NOTHING(1937)

Natasha
KILL, THE(1968)
Thorsten Nater
KAMIKAZE '89(1983, Ger.), ed
Alok Nath
GANDHI(1982)
Nagendra Nath
GODDESS, THE(1962, India); NINE HOURS TO RAMA(1963, U.S./Brit.)
Prem Nath
KENNER(1969)
Nathalie
JONAH–WHO WILL BE 25 IN THE YEAR 2000(1976, Switz.)
Nathan
MEET ME AT DAWN(1947, Brit.), cos
Adele Nathan
REDS(1981)
Dan Nathan
DESERT HAWK, THE(1950), ed
Emile Nathan
APRES L'AMOUR(1948, Fr.), p
George G. Nathan
Silents
$5,000,000 COUNTERFEITING PLOT, THE(1914), w
Herman Nathan
HERCULES(1983), spec eff
H. Nathan
DR. CRIPPEN(1963, Brit.), cos
Jack Nathan
SHUTTERED ROOM, THE(1968, Brit.), md
John Nathan
SUMMER SOLDIERS(1972, Jap.), a, w
L. Nathan
DR. CRIPPEN(1963, Brit.), cos
L&H Nathan, Ltd.
RICHARD III(1956, Brit.), cos
Lorna Nathan
GREAT WALTZ, THE(1972)
Mischa Nathan
LONG IS THE ROAD(1948, Ger.)
Norman Nathan
LITTLE BIG MAN(1970)
Paul Nathan
ROUSTABOUT(1964), w; OUT OF TOWNERS, THE(1970), p
Peggy Nathan
EVIL EYE(1964 Ital.)
Perry Nathan
Silents
MAN CRAZY(1927), w
Raffi Nathan
SINAI COMMANDOS: THE STORY OF THE SIX DAY WAR(1968, Israel/Ger.)
Robert Nathan
ONE MORE SPRING(1935), w; WHITE CLIFFS OF DOVER, THE(1944), w; CLOCK, THE(1945), w; WAKE UP AND DREAM(1946), w; BISHOP'S WIFE, THE(1947), w; PORTRAIT OF JENNIE(1949), w; PAGAN LOVE SONG(1950), w
S. Nathan
YIDDLE WITH HIS FIDDLE(1937, Pol.)
Stephen Nathan
1776(1972); FIRST NUDIE MUSICAL, THE(1976); YOU LIGHT UP MY LIFE(1977)
Vivian Nathan
TEACHER'S PET(1958); YOUNG SAVAGES, THE(1961); OUTSIDER, THE(1962); KLUTE(1971)
Elena Nathanael
FEAR, THE(1967, Gr.); LOVE CYCLES(1969, Gr.)
Helena Nathaneal
APOLLO GOES ON HOLIDAY(1968, Ger./Swed.)
Violet Nathaniel
BIRD OF PARADISE(1951)
Nathans Ltd.
KRULL(1983), cos
Nathans of London
CAPTAIN SINDBAD(1963), ed
Bernard Nathanson
WILD GEESE, THE(1978, Brit.)
Charles Nathanson
Silents
BROKEN HEARTS(1926)
E.M. Nathanson
DIRTY DOZEN, THE(1967$c Brit.), w
George Nathanson
NATIVE SON(1951, U.S., Arg.)
Joseph Nathanson
WITCHES, THE(1969, Fr./Ital.), spec eff
Louis Natheau
MEN OF THE NIGHT(1934); MAGNIFICENT OBSESSION(1935)
Louis Natheaux
BROADWAY BABIES(1929); MEXICALI ROSE(1929); WEARY RIVER(1929); MURDER ON THE ROOF(1930); SQUEALER, THE(1930); THIS MAD WORLD(1930); LITTLE CAESAR(1931); RECKLESS LIVING(1931); SECRET SIX, THE(1931); STREET SCENE(1931); TRANSATLANTIC(1931); SINISTER HANDS(1932); THIRTEEN WOMEN(1932); GAMBLING SHIP(1933); FIGHTING CODE, THE(1934); GAMBLING LADY(1934); GAY BRIDE, THE(1934); HIDE-OUT(1934); MISS FANE'S BABY IS STOLEN(1934); FRECKLES(1935); MISS PACIFIC FLEET(1935); SHE MARRIED HER BOSS(1935); SPECIAL AGENT(1935); CAPTAIN CALAMITY(1936); MODERN TIMES(1936); YOURS FOR THE ASKING(1936); MISSING WITNESSES(1937); MOUNTAIN MUSIC(1937); SWING HIGH, SWING LOW(1937); WILD MONEY(1937); THREE LOVES HAS NANCY(1938); UNION PACIFIC(1939); WEST POINT WIDOW(1941); CROSSROADS(1942)
Silents
SUPER-SEX, THE(1922); MAN BAIT(1926); DRESS PARADE(1927); KING OF KINGS, THE(1927); FOUR WALLS(1928); MIDNIGHT MADNESS(1928); STAND AND

DELIVER(1928); GIRLS GONE WILD(1929); NED MCCOBB'S DAUGHTER(1929); WHY BE GOOD?(1929)
Misc. Silents
TIN PAN ALLEY(1920); FIGHTING LOVE(1927); TURKISH DELIGHT(1927); STOOL PIGEON(1928); TENTH AVENUE(1928)
Giovanna Natili
TARTARS, THE(1962, Ital./Yugo.), cos
J.E. Nation
TOGETHER FOR DAYS(1972)
Oscar Nation
SLEEPING CAR TO TRIESTE(1949, Brit.); ISLAND RESCUE(1952, Brit.)
Terry Nation
WHAT A WHOPPER(1961, Brit.), w; DR. WHO AND THE DALEKS(1965, Brit.), w; DALEKS–INVASION EARTH 2155 A.D.(1966, Brit.), w; AND SOON THE DARKNESS(1970, Brit.), w
National Ballet of Senegal
SOUTHERN STAR, THE(1969, Fr./Brit.)
The National Folklore Theatre Of Haiti
GOLDEN MISTRESS, THE(1954)
National Jitterbug Champions
NAUGHTY BUT NICE(1939)
National Senegalese Dance Company
UP THE SANDBOX(1972)
National Youth Orchestra
LADY IS A SQUARE, THE(1959, Brit.)
Arthur Nations
TRIAL OF LEE HARVEY OSWALD, THE(1964)
Frances Natividad
1984
NIGHT PATROL(1984)
Kitten Natividad
MY TUTOR(1983)
1984
WILD LIFE, THE(1984)
Richard Natkin
BOYS IN COMPANY C, THE(1978, U.S./Hong Kong), w
Rick Natkin
BOYS IN COMPANY C, THE(1978, U.S./Hong Kong); NIGHT OF THE JUGGLER(1980), w
1984
PURPLE HEARTS(1984), a, w
Gilbert Natol
GAME OF TRUTH, THE(1961, Fr.), ed
Piero Natoli
LEAP INTO THE VOID(1982, Ital.), w
Ric Natoli
PERILS OF PAULINE, THE(1967); HANG YOUR HAT ON THE WIND(1969)
Denise Natot
THREE FABLES OF LOVE(1963, Fr./Ital./Span.), ed
Gilbert Natot
HORROR CHAMBER OF DR. FAUSTUS, THE(1962, Fr./Ital.), ed; NIGHT ENCOUNTER(1963, Fr./Ital.), ed; THERESE(1963, Fr.), ed; SWEET SKIN(1965, Fr./Ital.), ed; JUDEX(1966, Fr./Ital.), ed
Gull Natrop
SMILES OF A SUMMER NIGHT(1957, Swed.)
Ingrid Natrud
DOLL'S HOUSE, A(1973, Brit.)
Keiko Natsu
LAKE, THE(1970, Jap.)
Shizue Natsukawa
GOLDEN DEMON(1956, Jap.)
Misc. Silents
METROPOLITAN SYMPHONY(1929, Jap.)
Akira Natsuki
GAMERA VERSUS BARUGON(1966, Jap./U.S.)
Isao Natsuki
VIRUS(1980, Jap.); TIME SLIP(1981, Jap.)
Mari Natsuki
ONIMASA(1983, Jap.)
Yosuke Natsuki
I BOMBED PEARL HARBOR(1961, Jap.); LIFE OF A COUNTRY DOCTOR(1961, Jap.); YOJIMBO(1961, Jap.); WISER AGE(1962, Jap.); CHUSHINGURA(1963, Jap.); OPERATION X(1963, Jap.); YOUTH AND HIS AMULET, THE(1963, Jap.); BANDITS ON THE WIND(1964, Jap.); DAGORA THE SPACE MONSTER(1964, Jap.); OPERATION ENEMY FORT(1964, Jap.); GHIDRAH, THE THREE-HEADED MONSTER(1965, Jap.); TIGER FLIGHT(1965, Jap.); GAMBLING SAMURAI, THE(1966, Jap.); OUTPOST OF HELL(1966, Jap.); DAPHNE, THE(1967); EYES, THE SEA AND A BALL(1968 Jap.); SIEGE OF FORT BISMARK(1968, Jap.); WHIRLWIND(1968, Jap.); DAREDEVIL IN THE CASTLE(1969, Jap.)
Masako Natsume
ONIMASA(1983, Jap.)
1984
ANTARCTICA(1984, Jap.)
Chikako Natsumi
GIRL I ABANDONED, THE(1970, Jap.)
Isao Natsuyagi
GOYOKIN(1969, Jap.); TIDAL WAVE(1975, U.S./Jap.)
Jacques Natteau
FOUR BAGS FULL(1957, Fr./Ital.), ph; GAMBLER, THE(1958, Fr.), ph; LOVE IS MY PROFESSION(1959, Fr.), ph; NEVER ON SUNDAY(1960, Gr.), ph; GREEN MARE, THE(1961, Fr./Ital.), ph; PHAEDRA(1962, U.S./Gr./Fr.), ph; STORY OF THE COUNT OF MONTE CRISTO, THE(1962, Fr./Ital.), ph; ENOUGH ROPE(1966, Fr./Ital./Ger.), ph; BIRDS COME TO DIE IN PERU(1968, Fr.), p
Jack Natteford John Francis [Jack] Natteford
FLYING MARINE, THE(1929), w; LIGHT FINGERS(1929), w; NEW ORLEANS(1929), w; TWO MEN AND A MAID(1929), w; BORDER ROMANCE(1930), w; DARKENED SKIES(1930), w; LOST ZEPPELIN(1930), w; THIRD ALARM, THE(1930), w; THOROUGHBRED, THE(1930), w; TROOPERS THREE(1930), w; ARIZONA TERROR(1931), w; CLEARING THE RANGE(1931), w; FIGHTING THRU(1931), w; HARD HOMBRE(1931), w; TWO GUN MAN, THE(1931), w; WILD

HORSE(1931), w; FILE 113(1932), w; GOLD(1932), w; MY PAL, THE KING(1932), w; OUT OF SINGAPORE(1932), w; PRIVATE SCANDAL, A(1932), w; SPIRIT OF THE WEST(1932), w; CALIFORNIA TRAIL, THE(1933), w; COWBOY COUNSELOR(1933), w; DUDE BANDIT, THE(1933), w; HIDDEN GOLD(1933), w; HIS PRIVATE SECRETARY(1933), w; NEIGHBORS' WIVES(1933), w; DEMON FOR TROUBLE, A(1934), w; HOUSE OF DANGER(1934), w; MYSTIC HOUR, THE(1934), w; CRIMSON TRAIL, THE(1935), w; HEADLINE WOMAN, THE(1935), w; RIDER OF THE LAW, THE(1935), w; $1,000 A MINUTE(1935), w; LONELY TRAIL, THE(1936), w; MILLIONAIRE KID(1936), w; OREGON TRAIL, THE(1936), w; RETURN OF JIMMY VALENTINE, THE(1936), w; THREE MESQUITEERS, THE(1936), w; TICKET TO PARADISE(1936), w; HEART OF THE ROCKIES(1937), w; PARADISE EXPRESS(1937), w; ROARIN' LEAD(1937), w; ROOTIN' TOOTIN' RHYTHM(1937), w; YODELIN' KID FROM PINE RIDGE(1937), w; BILLY THE KID RETURNS(1938), w; GOLD MINE IN THE SKY(1938), w; HEROES OF THE HILLS(1938), w; INTERNATIONAL CRIME(1938), w; RAWHIDE(1938), w; SHINE ON, HARVEST MOON(1938), w; COLORADO SUNSET(1939), w; COME ON RANGERS(1939), w; DAYS OF JESSE JAMES(1939), w; KANSAS TERRORS, THE(1939), w; ROUGH RIDERS' ROUNDUP(1939), w; SOUTHWARD HO!(1939), w; WYOMING OUTLAW(1939), w; HEROES OF THE SADDLE(1940), w; ONE MAN'S LAW(1940), w; PIONEERS OF THE WEST(1940), w; DANGEROUS LADY(1941), w; DOUBLE TROUBLE(1941), w; LAW OF THE TIMBER(1941), w; INSIDE THE LAW(1942), w; THEY RAID BY NIGHT(1942), w; TRAIL OF KIT CARSON(1945), w; BADMAN'S TERRITORY(1946), w; RUSTLER'S ROUNDUP(1946), w; TRAIL TO SAN ANTONE(1947), w; BLACK BART(1947), w; RETURN OF THE BADMEN(1948), w; LAST BANDIT, THE(1949), w; RUSTLERS(1949), w; CATTLE DRIVE(1951), w; EAST OF SUMATRA(1953), w; BLACKJACK KETCHUM, DESPERADO(1956), w; NIGHT THE WORLD EXPLODED, THE(1957), w; KID RODELO(1966, U.S./Span.), w; RIDE TO HANGMAN'S TREE, THE(1967), w
Silents
EVERY WOMAN'S PROBLEM(1921), w; AFTER DARK(1924), w; FIGHTER'S PARADISE(1924), w; ON PROBATION(1924), w; SURGING SEAS(1924), w; FAIR PLAY(1925), w; WAS IT BIGAMY?(1925), w; LAST ALARM, THE(1926), w; BACKSTAGE(1927), w; LADYBIRD(1927), w; BEAUTIFUL BUT DUMB(1928), w; CLEARING THE TRAIL(1928), w; GUN RUNNER, THE(1928), w; LINGERIE(1928), w; MAN IN HOBBLES, THE(1928), w; NAMELESS MEN(1928), w; SCARLET DOVE, THE(1928), w
Jeff Natter
LOVESICK(1983)
Gino Nattera
HERCULES(1959, Ital.)
Nathalie Nattier
IDIOT, THE(1948, Fr.); GATES OF THE NIGHT(1950, Fr.); SECRET DOCUMENT – VIENNA(1954, Fr.); PRICE OF FLESH, THE(1962, Fr.)
Mark Natuzzi
HARDCORE(1979)
Grim Natwick
SNOW WHITE AND THE SEVEN DWARFS(1937), anim; GULLIVER'S TRAVELS(1939), anim d; RAGGEDY ANN AND ANDY(1977), anim
Mildred Natwick
LONG VOYAGE HOME, THE(1940); ENCHANTED COTTAGE, THE(1945); YOLANDA AND THE THIEF(1945); LATE GEORGE APLEY, THE(1947); WOMAN'S VENGEANCE, A(1947); KISSING BANDIT, THE(1948); THREE GODFATHERS, THE(1948); SHE WORE A YELLOW RIBBON(1949); CHEAPER BY THE DOZEN(1950); AGAINST ALL FLAGS(1952); QUIET MAN, THE(1952); TROUBLE WITH HARRY, THE(1955); COURT JESTER, THE(1956); TEENAGE REBEL(1956); TAMMY AND THE BACHELOR(1957); BAREFOOT IN THE PARK(1967); IF IT'S TUESDAY, THIS MUST BE BELGIUM(1969); MALTESE BIPPY, THE(1969); TRUMAN CAPOTE'S TRILOGY(1969); DAISY MILLER(1974); AT LONG LAST LOVE(1975); KISS ME GOODBYE(1982)
Myron Natwick
THREE DAYS OF THE CONDOR(1975); WRONG IS RIGHT(1982)
1984
ICE PIRATES, THE(1984)
Oscar Natzke
MEET THE NAVY(1946, Brit.)
Grete Natzler
VIENNA, CITY OF SONGS(1931, Ger.); KISS ME GOODBYE(1935, Brit.); LIVING DEAD, THE(1936, Brit.); STUDENT'S ROMANCE, THE(1936, Brit.)
Albert Naud
LIFE LOVE DEATH(1969, Fr./Ital.)
Jan Naud
COLD RIVER(1982)
Tom Naud
SAFE AT HOME(1962), p, w
William T. Naud
THUNDER IN DIXIE(1965), p&d; HOT ROD HULLABALOO(1966), p, d; BLACK JACK(1973), p, d, w, ed
Claude Naudes
LAFAYETTE(1963, Fr.)
Joey Naudic
1,000 SHAPES OF A FEMALE(1963); TEENAGE GANG DEBS(1966)
Jean-Francois Naudon
1984
L'ARGENT(1984, Fr./Switz.), ed
Alita Naughton
FRENCH DRESSING(1964, Brit.)
Bill Naughton
ALFIE(1966, Brit.), w; FAMILY WAY, THE(1966, Brit.), w; SPRING AND PORT WINE(1970, Brit.), w; ALFIE DARLING(1975, Brit.), d&w
Charlie Naughton
HIGHLAND FLING(1936, Brit.); OKAY FOR SOUND(1937, Brit.), a, w; WISE GUYS(1937, Brit.); ALF'S BUTTON AFLOAT(1938, Brit.); GASBAGS(1940, Brit.); LIFE IS A CIRCUS(1962, Brit.)
David Naughton
MIDNIGHT MADNESS(1980); AMERICAN WEREWOLF IN LONDON, AN(1981); SEPARATE WAYS(1981)
1984
HOT DOG...THE MOVIE(1984); NOT FOR PUBLICATION(1984)

Edmund Naughton
MC CABE AND MRS. MILLER(1971), w
Greg Naughton
SCARECROW, THE(1982, New Zealand)
1984
HEART OF THE STAG(1984, New Zealand)
Harry Naughton
HALF A SIXPENCE(1967, Brit.); HARRY AND WALTER GO TO NEW YORK(1976)
James Naughton
PAPER CHASE, THE(1973); SECOND WIND(1976, Can.); STRANGER IS WATCHING, A(1982)
Naughton & Gold
MY LUCKY STAR(1933, Brit.); COCK O' THE NORTH(1935, Brit.)
Barbara Naujok
KAMIKAZE '89(1983, Ger.), cos & makeup
Daniel Nauke
CITY NEWS(1983), spec eff
Rolf Naukhoff
MAN ON A TIGHTROPE(1953)
Charlotte Naulting
Misc. Silents
WOMEN MEN LOVE(1921)
N. Naum
MOTHER AND DAUGHTER(1965, USSR)
Natalia Naum
KIEV COMEDY, A(1963, USSR)
Charles Nauman
JOHNNY VIK(1973), p,d&w
Gunther Naumann
BLACK SUN, THE(1979, Czech.)
Horst Naumann
DOCTOR OF ST. PAUL, THE(1969, Ger.); PRIEST OF ST. PAULI, THE(1970, Ger.)
Lena Naumann
SOMEWHERE IN BERLIN(1949, E. Ger.), ed
Vladimir Naumov
PEACE TO HIM WHO ENTERS(1963, USSR), d, w
Nohili Naumu
WHITE HEAT(1934)
Allen Nause
THE RUNNER STUMBLES(1979)
Newton Naushaus
DRIVE-IN MASSACRE(1976)
Monique Naussac
SELLERS OF GIRLS(1967, Fr.), cos
Charles Nauu
MUTINY ON THE BOUNTY(1935)
Gregory Nava
CONFESSIONS OF AMANS, THE(1977), p&d, w, ph&ed; HAUNTING OF M, THE(1979), ph; END OF AUGUST, THE(1982), w
1984
EL NORTE(1984), d, w
Pablo Jorge Nava
TOM THUMB(1967, Mex.)
Navabeh
SMALL CIRCLE OF FRIENDS, A(1980)
Members of the Navajo Nation
LEGEND OF COUGAR CANYON(1974)
Deepti Naval
1984
MOHAN JOSHI HAAZIR HO(1984, India)
Tonia Navar
ROAD IS FINE, THE(1930, Fr.)
Ernest Navara [Arnost Navratil]
FABULOUS WORLD OF JULES VERNE, THE(1961, Czech.)
Marie-Therese Navaret
FIRST TASTE OF LOVE(1962, Fr.)
Roberto Navarette
STATE OF SIEGE(1973, Fr./U.S./Ital./Ger.)
Navarre
SHIPMATES O' MINE(1936, Brit.)
Armande Navarre
NATHALIE(1958, Fr.); DEVIL AND THE TEN COMMANDMENTS, THE(1962, Fr.)
Jean-Francois Navarre
1984
TO CATCH A COP(1984, Fr.), w
Louis Navarre
MAGNIFICENT ONE, THE(1974, Fr./Ital.)
Maurice Navarre
CASBAH(1948)
Amora Navarro
ONLY ANGELS HAVE WINGS(1939)
Anita Navarro
Misc. Silents
M'LISS(1915)
Ann Navarro
JACK SLADE(1953)
Anna Navarro
JUBILEE TRAIL(1954); SON OF SINBAD(1955); TOPAZ(1969, Brit.)
Aurora Navarro
DRUMS OF DESTINY(1937); COLT .45(1950)
Bob Navarro
BLUE PARROT, THE(1953, Brit.), ph
Carlos Navarro
DOCTOR CRIMEN(1953, Mex.); BRAVE ONE, THE(1956); EMPTY STAR, THE(1962, Mex.); ILLUSION TRAVELS BY STREETCAR, THE(1977, Mex.)
Catherine Navarro
HAPPY DAYS(1930)

Enrique Navarro
DRUMS OF TABU, THE(1967, Ital./Span.); UGLY ONES, THE(1968, Ital./Span.)
George Navarro
PIRATES OF MONTEREY(1947); SNOWS OF KILIMANJARO, THE(1952); HITCH-HIKER, THE(1953); JEOPARDY(1953); SECOND CHANCE(1953); JUBILEE TRAIL(1954); AMERICANO, THE(1955); LES GIRLS(1957); MARACAIBO(1958); WAR OF THE COLOSSAL BEAST(1958)
Jesus Navarro
LOS OLVIDADOS(1950, Mex.)
Joan Navarro
HAPPY DAYS(1930)
Jose Luis Navarro
SWORD OF EL CID, THE(1965, Span./Ital.), w; TREASURE OF MAKUBA, THE(1967, U.S./Span.), w; CAULDRON OF BLOOD(1971, Span.), m
Larry Navarro
DIARY OF A BACHELOR(1964)
Manuel Sanchez Navarro
BANDIDO(1956)
Mario Navarro
BLACK SCORPION, THE(1957); VILLA!(1958); GERONIMO(1962)
Maurice Navarro
NIGHTMARE ALLEY(1947)
Nicanor Navarro
RIGHT STUFF, THE(1983), set d
Nick Navarro
PAD, THE(AND HOW TO USE IT)* (1966, Brit.); MY FAIR LADY(1964)
Nieves Navarro
PISTOL FOR RINGO, A(1966, Ital./Span.); RETURN OF RINGO, THE(1966, Ital./Span.); BIG GUNDOWN, THE(1968, Ital.)
Paul Navarro
1984
GOODBYE PEOPLE, THE(1984)
Pedro Navarro
WALLS OF HELL, THE(1964, U.S./Phil.)
Ralph Navarro
BORDERTOWN(1935); GILDA(1946); PERILOUS HOLIDAY(1946)
Ramon Navarro
BIG STEAL, THE(1949)
Misc. Talkies
OUTRIDERS, THE(1950)
Robert Navarro
NO WAY BACK(1949, Brit.), ph; SHE SHALL HAVE MURDER(1950, Brit.), ph; ONE WILD OAT(1951, Brit.), ph
Ruben Navarro
FAT CITY(1972)
Tito Navarro
INCREDIBLE INVASION, THE(1971, Mex./U.S.)
Tony Navarro
WIDOWS' NEST(1977, U.S./Span.), p,d&w
Eddy Navas
WOLFEN(1981)
Jane Navello
IDOL ON PARADE(1959, Brit.)
Nigel Navers
WHO IS KILLING THE GREAT CHEFS OF EUROPE?(1978, US/Ger.)
Grant Navin
1984
TAIL OF THE TIGER(1984, Aus.)
John Navin
NATIONAL LAMPOON'S VACATION(1983)
John P. Navin, Jr.
TAPS(1981); LOSIN' IT(1983)
Albane Navizet
ROAD TO SALINA(1971, Fr./Ital.)
Mordechai Navon
TWO KOUNEY LEMELS(1966, Israel), p; FLYING MATCHMAKER, THE(1970, Israel), p
Mordechali Navon
PILLAR OF FIRE, THE(1963, Israel), p
Mordhay Navon
TEL AVIV TAXI(1957, Israel), p
Herbert Navratil
LONE CLIMBER, THE(1950, Brit./Aust.)
Karel Navratil
DIAMONDS OF THE NIGHT(1968, Czech.)
Stanislaw Navratil
LEMONADE JOE(1966, Czech.)
Vladimir Navratil
TRANSPORT FROM PARADISE(1967, Czech.)
Celly Navropoulou
AUNT FROM CHICAGO(1960, Gr.)
Igorde Navrotsky
MISSION TO MOSCOW(1943)
U.S. Navy
NOBODY'S PERFECT(1968), tech adv
Yoko Nawikawa
THOUSAND CRANES(1969, Jap.)
Tom Nawn
Silents
KEEP MOVING(1915); GENERAL, THE(1927)
Halina Nawrocka
ASHES AND DIAMONDS(1961, Pol.), ed; KANAL(1961, Pol.), ed; CAMERA BUFF(1983, Pol.), ed
Alla Naximova
Misc. Silents
REVELATION(1918); DOLL'S HOUSE, A(1922)
Frederic Nay
PRACTICALLY YOURS(1944); DREAM GIRL(1947)

Frederick Nay
WOMAN'S SECRET, A(1949)
Fredric Nay
LET'S FACE IT(1943)
Pierre Nay
LA MARSEILLAISE(1938, Fr.); RULES OF THE GAME, THE(1939, Fr.)
Alain Naya
LUDWIG(1973, Ital./Ger./Fr.)
Goro Naya
MONSTER ZERO(1970, Jap.)
Nayampalli
TIGER AND THE FLAME, THE(1955, India)
Evelyn Nayati
CRY, THE BELOVED COUNTRY(1952, Brit.)
Ludwig Naybert
COUNTERFEIT TRAITOR, THE(1962)
Jules Nayfack
TRIAL OF BILLY JACK, THE(1974), ed
Nicholas Nayfack
BORDER INCIDENT(1949), p; DEVIL'S DOORWAY(1950), p; NO QUESTIONS ASKED(1951), p; SELLOUT, THE(1951), p; VENGEANCE VALLEY(1951), p; GLORY ALLEY(1952), p; ESCAPE FROM FORT BRAVO(1953), p; ROGUE COP(1954), p; SCARLET COAT, THE(1955), p; FORBIDDEN PLANET(1956), p; POWER AND THE PRIZE, THE(1956), p; RANSOM(1956), p; GUN GLORY(1957), p; INVISIBLE BOY, THE(1957), p
Patsy Nayfack
THREE BAD SISTERS(1956)
Peter Naylis
JOURNEY TOGETHER(1946, Brit.)
Anthony Naylor
GIRL IN TROUBLE(1963), w; STARDUST(1974, Brit.)
Billy Naylor
REDUCING(1931); SPECIAL AGENT(1935)
Cal Naylor
GRAND THEFT AUTO(1977)
Jerry Naylor
GIRLS ON THE BEACH(1965)
Kathleen Naylor
MIKADO, THE(1939, Brit.)
Mary Naylor
MAN IN GREY, THE(1943, Brit.)
Mike Naylor
PLEASURE PLANTATION(1970)
Robert Naylor
ABDUL THE DAMNED(1935, Brit.); KES(1970, Brit.)
Ruth Naylor
SUNSHINE AHEAD(1936, Brit.)
Terry Naylor
PATSY, THE(1964)
Tom Naylor
JUST MY LUCK(1957, Brit.); NIGHT TO REMEMBER, A(1958, Brit.); NO SAFETY AHEAD(1959, Brit.); HORROR HOTEL(1960, Brit.); DANGER BY MY SIDE(1962, Brit.)
Toney Naylor
GARBAGE MAN, THE(1963)
Nello Nayo
ONCE BEFORE I DIE(1967, U.S./Phil.)
Harsh Nayyar
GANDHI(1982); EASY MONEY(1983)
Christine Nazareth
MODERN PROBLEMS(1981)
Christy Nazareth
GROOVE TUBE, THE(1974)
Rafael Nazario
BOOGEYMAN II(1983)
A. Nazarov
FATHER OF A SOLDIER(1966, USSR)
Anatoliy Nazarov
SONG OVER MOSCOW(1964, USSR), ph
Ivan Nazarov
NEW TEACHER, THE(1941, USSR)
Yuriy Nazarov
LAST GAME, THE(1964, USSR); ITALIANO BRAVA GENTE(1965, Ital./USSR)
Beverly Nazarow
JUKE BOX RACKET(1960); SIN YOU SINNERS(1963)
Norman Nazarr
SNIPER, THE(1952); PURPLE GANG, THE(1960)
Cliff Nazarro
ROMANCE RIDES THE RANGE(1936); SINGING BUCKAROO, THE(1937); ARTISTS AND MODELS ABROAD(1938); DESPERATE ADVENTURE, A(1938); OUTSIDE OF PARADISE(1938); STABLEMATES(1938); FORGED PASSPORT(1939); KING OF THE TURF(1939); ST. LOUIS BLUES(1939); ARISE, MY LOVE(1940); DIVE BOMBER(1941); IN OLD COLORADO(1941); MELODY FOR THREE(1941); MR. DYNAMITE(1941); ROOKIES ON PARADE(1941); SAILORS ON LEAVE(1941); WORLD PREMIERE(1941); YOU'LL NEVER GET RICH(1941); CALL OF THE CANYON(1942); HILLBILLY BLITZKRIEG(1942); PARDON MY STRIPES(1942); HEAVENLY BODY, THE(1943); RHYTHM PARADE(1943); SHANTYTOWN(1943); I'M FROM ARKANSAS(1944); SWING HOSTESS(1944); TROCADERO(1944); DING DONG WILLIAMS(1946)
Ray Nazarro
JIMMY THE GENT(1934), w; OUTLAWS OF THE ROCKIES(1945), d; DESERT HORSEMAN, THE(1946), d; LAST DAYS OF BOOT HILL(1947), d; LONE HAND TEXAN, THE(1947), d; PHANTOM VALLEY(1948), d; SIX-GUN LAW(1948), d; SONG OF IDAHO(1948), d; WEST OF SONORA(1948), d; CHALLENGE OF THE RANGE(1949), d; EL DORADO PASS(1949), d; LARAMIE(1949), d; QUICK ON THE TRIGGER(1949), d; RENEGADES OF THE SAGE(1949), d; SMOKY MOUNTAIN MELODY(1949), d; SOUTH OF DEATH VALLEY(1949), d; DAVID HARDING, COUNTERSPY(1950), d; FRONTIER OUTPOST(1950), d; OUTCAST OF BLACK MESA(1950), d; PALOMINO, THE(1950), d; STREETS OF GHOST TOWN(1950), d; TEXAS DYNAMO(1950), d; TOUGHER THEY COME, THE(1950), d; AL JENNINGS OF OKLAHOMA(1951), d; BANDITS OF EL DORADO(1951), d; BULLFIGHTER AND

THE LADY(1951), w; CYCLONE FURY(1951), d; FORT SAVAGE RAIDERS(1951), d; INDIAN UPRISING(1951), d; KID FROM AMARILLO, THE(1951), d; CRIPPLE CREEK(1952), d; JUNCTION CITY(1952), d; LARAMIE MOUNTAINS(1952), d; MONTANA TERRITORY(1952), d; ROUGH, TOUGH WEST, THE(1952), d; GUN BELT(1953), d; KANSAS PACIFIC(1953), d; BLACK DAKOTAS, THE(1954), d; LONE GUN, THE(1954), d; SOUTHWEST PASSAGE(1954), d; TOP GUN(1955), d; WHITE SQUAW, THE(1956), d; DOMINO KID(1957), d; FLAME OF STAMBOUL(1957), d; HIRED GUN, THE(1957), d; PHANTOM STAGECOACH, THE(1957), d; APACHE TERRITORY(1958), d; RETURN TO WARBOW(1958), d; DOG EAT DOG(1963, U.S./Ger./Ital.), d

Misc. Talkies
SONG OF THE PRAIRIE(1945), d; TEXAS PANHANDLE(1945), d; GALLOPING THUNDER(1946), d; GUNNING FOR VENGEANCE(1946), d; HEADING WEST(1946), d; LONE STAR MOONLIGHT(1946), d; ROARING RANGERS(1946), d; SINGING ON THE TRAIL(1946), d; TERROR TRAIL(1946), d; THAT TEXAS JAMBOREE(1946), d; THROW A SADDLE ON A STAR(1946), d; TWO-FISTED STRANGER(1946), d; LAW OF THE CANYON(1947), d; OVER THE SANTA FE TRAIL(1947), d; ROSE OF SANTA ROSA(1947), d; WEST OF DODGE CITY(1947), d; BLAZING ACROSS THE PECOS(1948), d; SINGING SPURS(1948), d; TRAIL TO LAREDO(1948), d; HOME IN SAN ANTONE(1949), d; TRAIL OF THE RUSTLERS(1950), d

Anatoliy Nazartov
SLEEPING BEAUTY, THE(1966, USSR), ph
Rene Nazelle
UNDER THE ROOFS OF PARIS(1930, Fr.), m/l Raoul Moretti
Shai Nazemi
INVINCIBLE SIX, THE(1970, U.S./Iran), a, cos
El Nazi
SANTO CONTRA LA INVASION DE LOS MARCIANOS(1966, Mex.)
Nazimova
IN OUR TIME(1944); SINCE YOU WENT AWAY(1944)
Silents
SALOME(1922); MY SON(1925); REDEEMING SIN, THE(1925)
Alla Nazimova
ESCAPE(1940); BLOOD AND SAND(1941); BRIDGE OF SAN LUIS REY, THE(1944)
Silents
EYE FOR EYE(1918); BRAT, THE(1919)
Misc. Silents
WAR BRIDES(1916); TOYS OF FATE(1918); OUT OF THE FOG(1919); RED LANTERN, THE(1919); BILLIONS(1920); HEART OF A CHILD, THE(1920); MADAME PEACOCK(1920); STRONGER THAN DEATH(1920); CAMILLE(1921); MADONNA OF THE STREETS(1924)
Phil Nazir
SOUTH SEA SINNER(1950)
Philip Nazir
UNKNOWN ISLAND(1948)
Phirose Nazir
MAN-EATER OF KUMAON(1948)
Gianni Nazisi
SUBVERSIVES, THE(1967, Ital.), ph
Salah Nazmi
CAIRO(1963)
Alla Nazomova
Silents
BRAT, THE(1919), w
M. Nazvanov
MAN OF MUSIC(1953, USSR)
Mikhail Nazvanov
HAMLET(1966, USSR)
Nikolai Nazvanov
IVAN THE TERRIBLE(Part I, 1947, USSR)
Amadeo Nazzari
FEDORA(1946, Ital.); BANDIT, THE(1949, Ital.); BRIEF RAPTURE(1952, Ital.); FAST AND SEXY(1960, Fr./Ital.)
Amedeo Nazzari
TIMES GONE BY(1953, Ital.); SENSUALITA(1954, Ital.); NIGHTS OF CABIRIA(1957, Ital.); WE ARE ALL MURDERERS(1957, Fr.); ANNA OF BROOKLYN(1958, Ital.); NAKED MAJA, THE(1959, Ital./U.S.); BEST OF ENEMIES, THE(1962); DEVIL MADE A WOMAN, THE(1962, Span.); QUEEN OF THE NILE(1964, Ital.); LITTLE NUNS, THE(1965, Ital.); POPPY IS ALSO A FLOWER, THE(1966); JOURNEY BENEATH THE DESERT(1967, Fr./Ital.), a, w; SICILIAN CLAN, THE(1970, Fr.); VALACHI PAPERS, THE(1972, Ital./Fr.); MATTER OF TIME, A(1976, Ital./U.S.)
Ray Nazzaro
COWBOY BLUES(1946), d; BUCKAROO FROM POWDER RIVER(1948), d; BLAZING TRAIL, THE(1949), d; HOEDOWN(1950), d; CHINA CORSAIR(1951), d; BANDITS OF CORSICA, THE(1953), d
Angelo Nazzo
SHAFT'S BIG SCORE(1972)
Gus NcNaughton
SEEING IS BELIEVING(1934, Brit.)
Muntu Ndebele
FOREVER YOUNG, FOREVER FREE(1976, South Afr.)
Tabara Ndiaye
CEDDO(1978, Nigeria)
Mick Ndisho
1984
SHEENA(1984)
Margarita Ndisi
1984
SHEENA(1984)
Frances Ne Moyer
Misc. Silents
LAW OF NATURE, THE(1919)
Beracha Ne'eman
MY MARGO(1969, Israel)
Bobby Ne'eman
CIRCLE OF IRON(1979, Brit.)
Itzhak Ne'eman
JESUS(1979)

Anna Neagle
VICTORIA THE GREAT(1937, Brit.); CHINESE BUNGALOW, THE(1930, Brit.); SCHOOL FOR SCANDAL, THE(1930, Brit.); SHOULD A DOCTOR TELL?(1931, Brit.); FLAG LIEUTENANT, THE(1932, Brit.); MAGIC NIGHT(1932, Brit.); BITTER SWEET(1933, Brit.); LITTLE DAMOZEL, THE(1933, Brit.); NELL GWYN(1935, Brit.); RUNAWAY QUEEN, THE(1935, Brit.); PEG OF OLD DRURY(1936, Brit.); BACKSTAGE(1937, Brit.); GIRLS IN THE STREET(1937, Brit.); GIRL IN THE STREET(1938, Brit.); SHOW GOES ON, THE(1938, Brit.); SIXTY GLORIOUS YEARS(1938, Brit.); NURSE EDITH CAVELL(1939); IRENE(1940); NO, NO NANETTE(1940); SUNNY(1941); WINGS AND THE WOMAN(1942, Brit.); FOREVER AND A DAY(1943); YELLOW CANARY, THE(1944, Brit.); YANK IN LONDON, A(1946, Brit.); COURTNEY AFFAIR, THE(1947, Brit.); PICCADILLY INCIDENT(1948, Brit.); ELIZABETH OF LADYMEAD(1949, Brit.); SPRING IN PARK LANE(1949, Brit.); LADY WITH A LAMP, THE(1951, Brit.); ODETTE(1951, Brit.); FOUR AGAINST FATE(1952, Brit.); MAYTIME IN MAYFAIR(1952, Brit.), a, p; KING'S RHAPSODY(1955, Brit.); LET'S MAKE UP(1955, Brit.); NO TIME FOR TEARS(1957, Brit.); DANGEROUS YOUTH(1958, Brit.), p; MAN WHO WOULDN'T TALK, THE(1958, Brit.); WONDERFUL THINGS!(1958, Brit.), p; HEART OF A MAN, THE(1959, Brit.), p; LADY IS A SQUARE, THE(1959, Brit.), a, p; TEENAGE BAD GIRL(1959, Brit.)
Alexander Neal
Silents
DARING YOUTH(1924), w
Arthur Neal
BARNACLE BILL(1935, Brit.)
Bob Neal
1984
TANK(1984)
Boyd Neal
PRISONER OF CORBAL(1939, Brit.), md
Chris Neal
BUDDIES(1983, Aus.), m
Christy Neal
TAKE DOWN(1979)
Misc. Talkies
MATTER OF LOVE, A(1979)
Coby Neal
13 RUE MADELEINE(1946)
Colin Neal
EAGLE ROCK(1964, Brit.)
David Neal
JULIUS CAESAR(1970, Brit.); SUPERMAN(1978); FLASH GORDON(1980)
Derek Neal
POLYESTER(1981)
Edwin Neal
TEXAS CHAIN SAW MASSACRE, THE(1974)
Ella Neal
MOON OVER BURMA(1940); ALOMA OF THE SOUTH SEAS(1941); CAUGHT IN THE DRAFT(1941); LADY EVE, THE(1941); LAS VEGAS NIGHTS(1941); SKYLARK(1941); LONE RIDER IN CHEYENNE, THE(1942); SWEATER GIRL(1942)
Erwin Neal
COVENANT WITH DEATH, A(1966); KONA COAST(1968), a, stunts
Frances Neal
LADY SCARFACE(1941); COME ON DANGER(1942); POWDER TOWN(1942)
Lex Neal
WELCOME DANGER(1929), w; FEET FIRST(1930), w; MR. WASHINGTON GOES TO TOWN(1941), w
Silents
BOY OF MINE(1923), w; FRESHMAN, THE(1925), w; BATTLING BUTLER(1926), w; KID BROTHER, THE(1927), w; SPEEDY(1928), w
Lloyd Neal
TOO YOUNG TO MARRY(1931); ELMER THE GREAT(1933); SIX-DAY BIKE RIDER(1934)
Marshall Neal, Jr.
RED RUNS THE RIVER(1963)
Mavis Neal
STUDS LONIGAN(1960); MR. SARDONICUS(1961); INTERNS, THE(1962); NOTORIOUS LANDLADY, THE(1962)
Nancy Neal
SON OF SINBAD(1955)
Pat Neal
INSPECTOR CALLS, AN(1954, Brit.)
Patricia Neal
FOUNTAINHEAD, THE(1949); HASTY HEART, THE(1949); IT'S A GREAT FEELING(1949); JOHN LOVES MARY(1949); BREAKING POINT, THE(1950); BRIGHT LEAF(1950); THREE SECRETS(1950); DAY THE EARTH STOOD STILL, THE(1951); OPERATION PACIFIC(1951); RATON PASS(1951); WEEKEND WITH FATHER(1951); DIPLOMATIC COURIER(1952); SOMETHING FOR THE BIRDS(1952); WASHINGTON STORY(1952); STRANGER FROM VENUS, THE(1954, Brit.); FACE IN THE CROWD, A(1957); BREAKFAST AT TIFFANY'S(1961); HUD(1963); PSYCHE 59(1964, Brit.); IN HARM'S WAY(1965); SUBJECT WAS ROSES, THE(1968); NIGHT DIGGER, THE(1971, Brit.); BAXTER(1973, Brit.); HAPPY MOTHER'S DAY... LOVE, GEORGE(1973); WIDOWS' NEST(1977, U.S./Span.); PASSAGE, THE(1979, Brit.); GHOST STORY(1981)
Misc. Talkies
"B"...MUST DIE(1973)
Peggy Neal
TERROR BENEATH THE SEA(1966, Jap.); GIRARA(1967, Jap.); LAS VEGAS FREE-FOR-ALL(1968, Jap.)
Rhoda Neal
SWAMP THING(1982), art d
Richard Neal
VALLEY OF MYSTERY(1967), w
Misc. Silents
LABYRINTH, THE(1915)
Roy Neal
CRY TERROR(1958)
Sally Neal
CALYPSO(1959, Fr./It.); JESUS CHRIST, SUPERSTAR(1973)

Thelma Neal
ONE MORE TIME(1970, Brit.)
Tom Neal
OUT WEST WITH THE HARDYS(1938); ANOTHER THIN MAN(1939); BURN 'EM UP O'CONNER(1939); FOUR GIRLS IN WHITE(1939); JOE AND ETHEL TURP CALL ON THE PRESIDENT(1939); STRONGER THAN DESIRE(1939); THEY ALL COME OUT(1939); WITHIN THE LAW(1939); 6000 ENEMIES(1939); ANDY HARDY MEETS DEBUTANTE(1940); COURAGEOUS DR. CHRISTIAN, THE(1940); SKY MURDER(1940); TOP SERGEANT MULLIGAN(1941); UNDER AGE(1941); BOWERY AT MIDNIGHT(1942); CHINA GIRL(1942); FLYING TIGERS(1942); MIRACLE KID(1942); ONE THRILLING NIGHT(1942); PRIDE OF THE YANKEES, THE(1942); TEN GENTLEMEN FROM WEST POINT(1942); AIR FORCE(1943); BEHIND THE RISING SUN(1943); GOOD LUCK, MR. YATES(1943); NO TIME FOR LOVE(1943); SHE HAS WHAT IT TAKES(1943); THERE'S SOMETHING ABOUT A SOLDIER(1943); KLONDIKE KATE(1944); RACKET MAN, THE(1944); TWO-MAN SUBMARINE(1944); UNWRITTEN CODE, THE(1944); CRIME, INC.(1945); DETOUR(1945); FIRST YANK INTO TOKYO(1945); THOROUGHBREDS(1945); BLONDE ALIBI(1946); BRUTE MAN, THE(1946); CLUB HAVANA(1946); BEYOND GLORY(1948); AMAZON QUEST(1949); APACHE CHIEF(1949); RED DESERT(1949); CALL OF THE KLONDIKE(1950); DALTON'S WOMEN, THE(1950); HUMPHREY TAKES A CHANCE(1950); I SHOT BILLY THE KID(1950); KING OF THE BULLWHIP(1950); RADAR SECRET SERVICE(1950); TRAIN TO TOMBSTONE(1950); DANGER ZONE(1951); FINGERPRINTS DON'T LIE(1951); G.I. JANE(1951); LET'S GO NAVY(1951); NAVY BOUND(1951); STOP THAT CAB(1951); GREAT JESSE JAMES RAID, THE(1953)
Misc. Talkies
MY DOG SHEP(1948)
Willer Neal
OLD MOTHER RILEY AT HOME(1945, Brit.); OLD MOTHER RILEY, HEADMISTRESS(1950, Brit.); OLD MOTHER RILEY'S JUNGLE TREASURE(1951, Brit.); OLD MOTHER RILEY(1952, Brit.)
Walter D. Nealand
Silents
ONE DAY(1916)
Link Neale
MEET THE DUKE(1949, Brit.), p
Nancy Neale
FACING THE MUSIC(1933, Brit.)
Ralph Neale
WAY OF YOUTH, THE(1934, Brit.), w; OLD CURIOSITY SHOP, THE(1935, Brit.), w; MURDER BY ROPE(1936, Brit.), w; WEDNESDAY'S LUCK(1936, Brit.), w; CAVALIER OF THE STREETS, THE(1937, Brit.), w; FATAL HOUR, THE(1937, Brit.), w; ALMOST A HONEYMOON(1938, Brit.), w
Edward G. Nealis
JOHNNY O'CLOCK(1947), p
Des Nealon
VON RICHTHOFEN AND BROWN(1970); OUTSIDER, THE(1980); EDUCATING RITA(1983)
1984
REFLECTIONS(1984, Brit.)
Frances Nealy
MANCHURIAN CANDIDATE, THE(1962); DARKTOWN STRUTTERS(1975); SCHIZOID(1980); MY BROTHER'S WEDDING(1983); WARGAMES(1983)
Frances E. Nealy
1984
GHOSTBUSTERS(1984)
Ron Nealy
GREASER'S PALACE(1972)
Ronald Nealy
CHAFED ELBOWS(1967)
Derek Neam
LILAC DOMINO, THE(1940, Brit.), w
Christopher Neame
NO BLADE OF GRASS(1970, Brit.); LUST FOR A VAMPIRE(1971, Brit.); DRACULA A.D. 1972(1972, Brit.); EMILY(1976, Brit.), p
Derek Neame
SPECIAL EDITION(1938, Brit.), w; HIDEOUT(1948, Brit.), w
Grace Neame
WEREWOLF IN A GIRL'S DORMITORY(1961, Ital./Aust.)
Ronald Neame
GIRLS WILL BE BOYS(1934, Brit.), ph; HAPPY(1934, Brit.), ph; DRAKE THE PIRATE(1935, Brit.), ph; HONOURS EASY(1935, Brit.), ph; INVITATION TO THE WALTZ(1935, Brit.), ph; JOY RIDE(1935, Brit.), ph; MUSIC HATH CHARMS(1935, Brit.), ph; CRIMES OF STEPHEN HAWKE, THE(1936, Brit.), ph; IMPROPER DUCHESS, THE(1936, Brit.), ph; STAR FELL FROM HEAVEN, A(1936, Brit.), ph; AGAINST THE TIDE(1937, Brit.), ph; BRIEF ECSTASY(1937, Brit.), ph; FEATHER YOUR NEST(1937, Brit.), ph; KEEP FIT(1937, Brit.), ph; WEEKEND MILLIONAIRE(1937, Brit.), ph; CRIME OF PETER FRAME, THE(1938, Brit.), ph; DANGEROUS SECRETS(1938, Brit.), ph; I SEE ICE(1938), ph; PENNY PARADISE(1938, Brit.), ph; WHO GOES NEXT?(1938, Brit.), ph; CHEER BOYS CHEER(1939, Brit.), ph; DEMON BARBER OF FLEET STREET, THE(1939, Brit.), ph; LET'S BE FAMOUS(1939, Brit.), ph; PHANTOM STRIKES, THE(1939, Brit.), ph; TROUBLE BREWING(1939, Brit.), ph; WARE CASE, THE(1939, Brit.), ph; IT'S IN THE AIR(1940, Brit.), ph; LET GEORGE DO IT(1940, Brit.), ph; RETURN TO YESTERDAY(1940, Brit.), ph; SALOON BAR(1940, Brit.), ph; SECRET FOUR, THE(1940, Brit.), ph; MAJOR BARBARA(1941, Brit.), ph; YANK IN THE R.A.F., A(1941), ph; IN WHICH WE SERVE(1942, Brit.), ph; ONE OF OUR AIRCRAFT IS MISSING(1942, Brit.), ph; YOUNG MAN'S FANCY(1943, Brit.), ph; THIS HAPPY BREED(1944, Brit.), w, ph; BLITHE SPIRIT(1945, Brit.), ph; GREAT EXPECTATIONS(1946, Brit.), p, w; TAKE MY LIFE(1948, Brit.), d; ONE WOMAN'S STORY(1949, Brit.), p; GOLDEN SALAMANDER(1950, Brit.), d, w; OLIVER TWIST(1951, Brit.), p; MAGIC BOX, THE(1952, Brit.), p; PROMOTER, THE(1952, Brit.), d; MAN WITH A MILLION(1954, Brit.), d; MAN WHO NEVER WAS, THE(1956, Brit.), d; SEVENTH SIN, THE(1957), d; HORSE'S MOUTH, THE(1958, Brit.), d; WINDOM'S WAY(1958, Brit.), d; TUNES OF GLORY(1960, Brit.), d; ESCAPE FROM ZAHRAIN(1962), p&d; I COULD GO ON SINGING(1963), d; CHALK GARDEN, THE(1964, Brit.), d; MISTER MOSES(1965), d; GAMBIT(1966), d; MAN COULD GET KILLED, A(1966), d; PRUDENCE AND THE PILL(1968, Brit.), d; PRIME OF MISS JEAN BRODIE, THE(1969, Brit.), d; SCROOGE(1970, Brit.), d; POSEIDON ADVENTURE, THE(1972), d; ODESSA FILE, THE(1974, Brit./Ger.), d; METEOR(1979), a, d; HOPSCOTCH(1980), d; FIRST MONDAY IN OCTOBER(1981), d

Ronald L. Neame
CAFE COLETTE(1937, Brit.), ph
Nestor M. Neana
THUNDERSTORM(1956)
Holly Near
ANGEL, ANGEL, DOWN WE GO(1969); MAGIC GARDEN OF STANLEY SWEETHART, THE(1970); MINNIE AND MOSKOWITZ(1971); TODD KILLINGS, THE(1971); SLAUGHTERHOUSE-FIVE(1972)
Kay Near
LOVE BUTCHER, THE(1982)
Laurel Near
ERASERHEAD(1978)
Timothy Near
CISCO PIKE(1971); BREAKFAST IN BED(1978)
Margaret Nearing
OLD MAN RHYTHM(1935); STOLEN HARMONY(1935); FAST BULLETS(1936)
Scott Nearing
REDS(1981)
Jacqueline Nearne
SCHOOL FOR DANGER(1947, Brit.)
Jack Neary
SUNSTRUCK(1973, Aus.), p
James Neary
MARINES COME THROUGH, THE(1943)
Joe Neary
Silents
ATTA BOY'S LAST RACE(1916)
Clifford Neate
NED KELLY(1970, Brit.)
Andre Neau
RETURN OF MARTIN GUERRE, THE(1983, Fr.), ph
Franco Nebbia
GARDEN OF THE FINZI-CONTINIS, THE(1976, Ital./Ger.)
Michael Nebbia
SWIMMER, THE(1968), ph; ALICE'S RESTAURANT(1969), ph; LIFE STUDY(1973), p&d, w, ph
Chris P. Nebe
HEARTBREAKER(1983), p
Fred Nebel
SHOT IN THE DARK, THE(1941), w
Frederick Nebel
SLEEPERS EAST(1934), w; SMART BLONDE(1937), w; TORCHY GETS HER MAN(1938), w; TORCHY PLAYS WITH DYNAMITE(1939), w; TORCHY RUNS FOR MAYOR(1939), w; SLEEPERS WEST(1941), w; BRIBE, THE(1949), w
Silents
ISLE OF LOST MEN(1928), w
Louis Frederick Nebel
FIFTY ROADS TO TOWN(1937), w
S. Nebenzahl
BETRAYAL(1939, Fr.), p
Seymour Nebenzahl
THREEPENNY OPERA, THE(1931, Ger./U.S.), p; MISTRESS OF ATLANTIS, THE(1932, Ger.), p; WE WHO ARE YOUNG(1940), p; GIRL FROM HONG KONG(1966, Ger.), p
Harold Nebenzal
MISS ROBIN CRUSOE(1954), w; WILBY CONSPIRACY, THE(1975, Brit.), w
1984
GABRIELA(1984, Braz.), p
Seymour Nebenzal
M(1933, Ger.), p; TOMORROW WE LIVE(1942), p; HITLER'S MADMAN(1943), p; SUMMER STORM(1944), p; CHASE, THE(1946), p; WHISTLE STOP(1946), p; HEAVEN ONLY KNOWS(1947), p; SIREN OF ATLANTIS(1948), p; M(1951), p
Laurence Neber
UNCOMMON VALOR(1983)
Pavel Necesal
ROCKET TO NOWHERE(1962, Czech.), spec eff; VOYAGE TO THE END OF THE UNIVERSE(1963, Czech.), spec eff
I. Nechanov
GORDEYEV FAMILY, THE(1961, U.S.S.R.)
G. Nechayev
RESURRECTION(1963, USSR)
V. Nechipailo
QUEEN OF SPADES(1961, USSR)
Frantisek Nechyba
DEVIL'S TRAP, THE(1964, Czech.)
Vaclav Neckar
CLOSELY WATCHED TRAINS(1967, Czech.)
Bruce Neckels
STRAWBERRY STATEMENT, THE(1970)
Leda Necova
MURDER AT THE VANITIES(1934)
Raisa Nedashkovskaya
SONG OF THE FOREST(1963, USSR); TSAR'S BRIDE, THE(1966, USSR)
Milos Nedbal
LEMONADE JOE(1966, Czech.); SWEET LIGHT IN A DARK ROOM(1966, Czech.)
Priscilla Nedd
EDDIE AND THE CRUISERS(1983), ed
1984
FLAMINGO KID, THE(1984), ed; NO SMALL AFFAIR(1984), ed
Stewart Nedd
ILLEGAL(1955)
Stuart Nedd
TONIGHT AND EVERY NIGHT(1945); GLORY BRIGADE, THE(1953)
Benny Nedell
Silents
LEAP TO FAME(1918)
Bernard J. Nedell
MONSIEUR VERDOUX(1947); ALBUQUERQUE(1948)

Bernard Nedell
RETURN OF THE RAT, THE(1929, Brit.); CALL OF THE SEA, THE(1930, Brit.); KNIGHT IN LONDON, A(1930, Brit./Ger.); MAN FROM CHICAGO, THE(1931, Brit.); SHADOWS(1931, Brit.); WHY SAPS LEAVE HOME(1932, Brit.); HER IMAGINARY LOVER(1933, Brit.); GIRL IN POSSESSION(1934, Brit.); HEAT WAVE(1935, Brit.); LAZYBONES(1935, Brit.); FIRST OFFENCE(1936, Brit.); TERROR ON TIPTOE(1936, Brit.); LIVE WIRE, THE(1937, Brit.); MAN WHO COULD WORK MIRACLES, THE(1937, Brit.); EXPOSED(1938); MR. MOTO'S GAMBLE(1938); OH BOY!(1938, Brit.); ANGELS WASH THEIR FACES(1939); FAST AND FURIOUS(1939); LUCKY NIGHT(1939); SECRET SERVICE OF THE AIR(1939); SOME LIKE IT HOT(1939); THEY ALL COME OUT(1939); THOSE HIGH GREY WALLS(1939); RANGERS OF FORTUNE(1940); SLIGHTLY HONORABLE(1940); SO YOU WON'T TALK(1940); STRANGE CARGO(1940); ZIEGFELD GIRL(1941); SHIP AHOY(1942); DESPERADOES, THE(1943); NORTHERN PURSUIT(1943); MAISIE GOES TO RENO(1944); ONE BODY TOO MANY(1944); ALLOTMENT WIVES, INC.(1945); BEHIND GREEN LIGHTS(1946); CRIME DOCTOR'S MAN HUNT(1946); LONE WOLF IN MEXICO, THE(1947); LOVES OF CARMEN, THE(1948); HELLER IN PINK TIGHTS(1960); HICKEY AND BOGGS(1972)
Misc. Silents
SILVER KING, THE(1929, Brit.)
Madlena Nedeva
LADY VANISHES, THE(1980, Brit.); TRAIL OF THE PINK PANTHER, THE(1982)
Semyon Nedhinsky
WINGS OF VICTORY(1941, USSR)
Norma Nedici
GIDGET GOES TO ROME(1963)
Michal Nedivi
CIRCLE OF IRON(1979, Brit.)
Claude Nedjar
SHAMELESS OLD LADY, THE(1966, Fr.), p; MURMUR OF THE HEART(1971, Fr./Ital./Ger.), p; MALEVIL(1981, Fr./Ger.), p
1984
DREAM ONE(1984, Brit./Fr.), p
Vladimir Nedobrovo
ONCE THERE WAS A GIRL(1945, USSR), w
V. Nedobrovo-Buzhinskaya
OPTIMISTIC TRAGEDY, THE(1964, USSR)
Antonie Nedosinska
MERRY WIVES, THE(1940, Czech.)
L. Nedovich
WAR AND PEACE(1968, USSR)
Craig Nedrow
NIGHT IN HEAVEN, A(1983)
Robin Nedwell
VAULT OF HORROR, THE(1973, Brit.); STAND UP VIRGIN SOLDIERS(1977, Brit.); SHILLINGBURY BLOWERS, THE(1980, Brit.)
Bernie Nee
COUNTRY MUSIC HOLIDAY(1958)
Louis Nee
VAMPYR(1932, Fr./Ger.), ph; LE DENIER MILLIARDAIRE(1934, Fr.), ph; LILIOM(1935, Fr.), ph; STORMY WATERS(1946, Fr.), ph; UTOPIA(1952, Fr./Ital.), ph
James Need
KISS OF EVIL(1963, Brit.), ed
Carole Needham
ROMEO AND JULIET(1966, Brit.)
Cheryl Needham
THIS IS ELVIS(1982)
Donna Sue Needham
–30–(1959)
Gordon Needham
SCOTLAND YARD DRAGNET(1957, Brit.); IDOL ON PARADE(1959, Brit.); INNOCENT MEETING(1959, Brit.); MAN ACCUSED(1959); NO SAFETY AHEAD(1959, Brit.); WOMAN'S TEMPTATION, A(1959, Brit.)
Hal Needham
MC LINTOCK!(1963); WAR WAGON, THE(1967); WAY WEST, THE(1967), stunts; DEVIL'S BRIGADE, THE(1968), stunts; HELLFIGHTERS(1968), stunts; UNDEFEATED, THE(1969), stunts; LITTLE BIG MAN(1970), stunts; ONE MORE TRAIN TO ROB(1971), a, stunts; SOMETIMES A GREAT NOTION(1971); CULPEPPER CATTLE COMPANY, THE(1972); THREE THE HARD WAY(1974), stunts; FRENCH CONNECTION 11(1975), stunts; PEEPER(1975), stunts; TAKE A HARD RIDE(1975, U.S./Ital.), stunts; W. W. AND THE DIXIE DANCEKINGS(1975), a, Stunts; JACKSON COUNTY JAIL(1976); NICKELODEON(1976); SEMI-TOUGH(1977), stunts; SMOKEY AND THE BANDIT(1977), d, w; END, THE(1978), stunts; FOUL PLAY(1978); HOOPER(1978), d; VILLAIN, THE(1979), d; SMOKEY AND THE BANDIT II(1980), d, w; CANNONBALL RUN, THE(1981), d; MEGAFORCE(1982), d, w; SMOKEY AND THE BANDIT–PART 3(1983), w; STROKER ACE(1983), d, w
1984
CANNONBALL RUN II(1984), a, d, w
J. Conrad Needham
Silents
WESTERN FIREBRANDS(1921)
Leo Needham
BATTLE TAXI(1955); LASSIE'S GREAT ADVENTURE(1963)
Sam Needham
JULIUS CAESAR(1952)
James Needham [Donald Crisp]
Silents
RAMONA(1916)
Wallace Needham-Clark
IVORY HUNTER(1952, Brit.)
William Needles
WAITING FOR CAROLINE(1969, Can.)
Caroline Needs
1984
SCRUBBERS(1984, Brit.)
James Needs
YESTERDAY'S ENEMY(1959, Brit.), ed; DR. JEKYLL AND MR. HYDE(1941), ed; BAD LORD BYRON, THE(1949, Brit.), ed; BOY, A GIRL AND A BIKE, A(1949 Brit.), ed; BLACK WIDOW(1951, Brit.), ed; WHISPERING SMITH VERSUS SCOTLAND YARD(1952, Brit.), ed; BAD BLONDE(1953, Brit.), ed; TERROR STREET(1953),

ed; PAID TO KILL(1954, Brit.), ed; SAINT'S GIRL FRIDAY, THE(1954, Brit.), ed; BLONDE BAIT(1956, U.S./Brit.), ed; THE CREEPING UNKNOWN(1956, Brit.), ed; CURSE OF FRANKENSTEIN, THE(1957, Brit.), ed; ENEMY FROM SPACE(1957, Brit.), ed; X THE UNKNOWN(1957, Brit.), ed; HORROR OF DRACULA, THE(1958, Brit.), ed; SNORKEL, THE(1958, Brit.), ed; MAN WHO COULD CHEAT DEATH, THE(1959, Brit.), ed; MUMMY, THE(1959, Brit.), ed; TEN SECONDS TO HELL(1959), ed; UGLY DUCKLING, THE(1959, Brit.), ed; HOUSE OF FRIGHT(1961, Brit.), ed; NEVER TAKE CANDY FROM A STRANGER(1961, Brit.), ed; PASSPORT TO CHINA(1961, Brit.), ed; SHADOW OF THE CAT, THE(1961, Brit.), ed; WATCH IT, SAILOR!(1961, Brit.), ed; NIGHTMARE(1963, Brit.), ed; OLD DARK HOUSE, THE(1963, Brit.), ed; PARANOIAC(1963, Brit.), ed; DEVIL-SHIP PIRATES, THE(1964, Brit.), ed; EVIL OF FRANKENSTEIN, THE(1964, Brit.), ed; GORGON, THE(1964, Brit.), ed; DIE, DIE, MY DARLING(1965, Brit.), ed; FRANKENSTEIN CREATED WOMAN(1965, Brit.), ed; HYSTERIA(1965, Brit.), ed; NANNY, THE(1965, Brit.), ed; SHE(1965, Brit.), ed; REPTILE, THE(1966, Brit.), ed; DEVIL'S OWN, THE(1967, Brit.), ed; MUMMY'S SHROUD, THE(1967, Brit.), ed; PREHISTORIC WOMEN(1967, Brit.), ed; DEVIL'S BRIDE, THE(1968, Brit.), ed; FIVE MILLION YEARS TO EARTH(1968, Brit.), ed; VENGEANCE OF SHE, THE(1968, Brit.), ed; FRANKENSTEIN MUST BE DESTROYED!(1969, Brit.), ed; SCARS OF DRACULA, THE(1970, Brit.), ed; VAMPIRE LOVERS, THE(1970, Brit.), ed; DR. JEKYLL AND SISTER HYDE(1971, Brit.), ed; DRACULA A.D. 1972(1972, Brit.), ed; CAPTAIN KRONOS: VAMPIRE HUNTER(1974, Brit.), ed; FRANKENSTEIN AND THE MONSTER FROM HELL(1974, Brit.), ed
Jim Needs
DEAD ON COURSE(1952, Brit.), ed; WOMAN IN HIDING(1953, Brit.), ed
Jimmy Needs
TO HAVE AND TO HOLD(1951, Brit.), ed; SCOTLAND YARD INSPECTOR(1952, Brit.), ed
Philip Needs
HAND IN HAND(1960, Brit.)
B.B. Neel
DEATH RACE 2000(1975), art d; HAPPY HOOKER GOES TO WASHINGTON, THE(1977), art d
Beala Neel
...ALL THE MARBLES(1981), art d
Joan Neel
PAJAMA PARTY(1964)
Phil Neel
JIM, THE WORLD'S GREATEST(1976), art d
Princess Neela
Silents
GOLD RUSH, THE(1925)
Neelak
WHITE DAWN, THE(1974)
Walter Neeland
Silents
DARK MIRROR, THE(1920); WOMAN'S MAN(1920)
Donald Neeld
THERE'S ALWAYS VANILLA(1972)
Magda Neeld
SHE SHALL HAVE MUSIC(1935, Brit.)
Ted Neeley
JESUS CHRIST, SUPERSTAR(1973); WISHBONE CUTTER(1978); HARD COUNTRY(1981)
1984
BLAME IT ON THE NIGHT(1984), m
Don Neely
TEENAGE ZOMBIES(1960)
George Neely
Silents
GOLD RUSH, THE(1925)
Michele Neely
1984
TEACHERS(1984), cos
Neil Neely
Silents
WEST POINT(1928)
Misc. Silents
WILD WEST ROMANCE(1928)
Richard Neely
DIRTY HANDS(1976, Fr./Ital./Ger.), w
William Neely
STROKER ACE(1983), w
Alfred Neeman
BEAU GESTE(1939), m
Isaac Neeman
JERUSALEM FILE, THE(1972, U.S./Israel)
Itzhak Bbi Neeman
1984
BEST DEFENSE(1984)
Robinson Neeman
SINGING VAGABOND, THE(1935)
Yitzhak Neeman
OPERATION THUNDERBOLT(1978, ISRAEL)
Audrie J. Neenan
SUDDEN IMPACT(1983)
Audry Neenan
TOWING(1978)
Preben Neergaard
EPILOGUE(1967, Den.); MAN WHO THOUGHT LIFE, THE(1969, Den.); PEOPLE MEET AND SWEET MUSIC FILLS THE HEART(1969, Den./Swed.); LURE OF THE JUNGLE, THE(1970, Den.)
Louis Neervort
KING RAT(1965)
Julie Neesam
OVERLORD(1975, Brit.)
Mary Jane Neese
WHAT'S UP FRONT(1964)

Liam Neeson
EXCALIBUR(1981); KRULL(1983)
1984
BOUNTY, THE(1984)
Ruadhan Neeson
ULYSSES(1967, U.S./Brit.)
June Neethling
KIMBERLEY JIM(1965, South Africa)
Neewa the Bear
NIKKI, WILD DOG OF THE NORTH(1961, U.S./Can.)
Bill Neff
FORCE OF EVIL(1948); MISS TATLOCK'S MILLIONS(1948); TAP ROOTS(1948); STARLIFT(1951); SABRINA(1954); EXPERIMENT IN TERROR(1962)
Carolyn Neff
SILENCERS, THE(1966)
Diane Neff
MAN CALLED DAGGER, A(1967)
Hildegard Neff
ALRAUNE(1952, Ger.); LANDRU(1963, Fr./Ital); AND SO TO BED(1965, Ger.); MOZAMBIQUE(1966, Brit.)
Hildegarde Neff
FILM WITHOUT A NAME(1950, Ger.); DECISION BEFORE DAWN(1951); DIPLOMATIC COURIER(1952); NIGHT WITHOUT SLEEP(1952); SNOWS OF KILIMANJARO, THE(1952); HENRIETTE'S HOLIDAY(1953, Fr.); MAN BETWEEN, THE(1953, Brit.); HOLIDAY FOR HENRIETTA(1955, Fr.); SVENGALI(1955, Brit.); SUBWAY IN THE SKY(1959, Brit.); PORT OF DESIRE(1960, Fr.); THREE PENNY OPERA(1963, Fr./Ger.)
Monica Neff
NIGHTBEAST(1982)
Pauline Neff
LADIES MUST PLAY(1930)
Silents
RANSON'S FOLLY(1926)
Ralph Neff
MAN WITH THE GOLDEN ARM, THE(1955); THESE WILDER YEARS(1956); LAST OF THE FAST GUNS, THE(1958); CAGE OF EVIL(1960); CASE OF PATTY SMITH, THE(1962)
Robert Neff
TOO LATE FOR TEARS(1949)
Thomas Neff
TUNDRA(1936), ed; GIRL SAID NO, THE(1937), ed; HENRY ALDRICH FOR PRESIDENT(1941), ed; CASANOVA BROWN(1944), ed; ALONG CAME JONES(1945), ed; NORTHWEST TRAIL(1945), ed; TOWN WENT WILD, THE(1945), ed; HOW DO YOU DO?(1946), ed; MAD WEDNESDAY(1950), ed; DAY OF TRIUMPH(1954), ed
Tom Neff
TRAIL OF VENGEANCE(1937), ed; MAN IN HALF-MOON STREET, THE(1944), ed; YOU CAN'T RATION LOVE(1944), ed
Vicki Neff
TENDER MERCIES(1982)
William Neff
THEY WERE EXPENDABLE(1945); FOREIGN AFFAIR, A(1948); I WAS A MALE WAR BRIDE(1949); THING, THE(1951); PHONE CALL FROM A STRANGER(1952); SPIRIT OF ST. LOUIS, THE(1957); COP HATER(1958)
Else Neft
I'LL SEE YOU IN MY DREAMS(1951); GLASS WALL, THE(1953); DEEP IN MY HEART(1954); NAKED STREET, THE(1955); NEVER SAY GOODBYE(1956)
Seyoum Nefta
BURNING AN ILLUSION(1982, Brit.), m
Mike Negal
POOR COW(1968, Brit.)
Jun Negami
GOLDEN DEMON(1956, Jap.); TEAHOUSE OF THE AUGUST MOON, THE(1956); BUDDHA(1965, Jap.)
Al Negbo
AT WAR WITH THE ARMY(1950); FIXED BAYONETS(1951)
Jim Negele
HAUNTED(1976); FRATERNITY ROW(1977)
Louis Negin
RABID(1976, Can.)
1984
HIGHPOINT(1984, Can.)
A. Negishi
ANATAHAN(1953, Jap.)
Akemi Negishi
HALF HUMAN(1955, Jap.); LOWER DEPTHS, THE(1962, Jap.); RED BEARD(1966, Jap.); I LIVE IN FEAR(1967, Jap.); MAN IN THE STORM, THE(1969, Jap.); PLAY IT COOL(1970, Jap.)
Howard Negley
DEAD MARCH, THE(1937); JUNIOR MISS(1945); DANGER WOMAN(1946); KILLERS, THE(1946); NOTORIOUS(1946); SMOKY(1946); BIG FIX, THE(1947); GENTLEMAN'S AGREEMENT(1947); RIDE THE PINK HORSE(1947); SONG OF THE THIN MAN(1947); TRAP, THE(1947); ABBOTT AND COSTELLO MEET FRANKENSTEIN(1948); ARE YOU WITH IT?(1948); CANON CITY(1948); DOCKS OF NEW ORLEANS(1948); FURY AT FURNACE CREEK(1948); RIVER LADY(1948); WHIPLASH(1948); CANADIAN PACIFIC(1949); FRANCIS(1949); GAL WHO TOOK THE WEST, THE(1949); SLATTERY'S HURRICANE(1949); WHIRLPOOL(1949); BREAKTHROUGH(1950); COLT .45(1950); LAWLESS, THE(1950); MILKMAN, THE(1950); MYSTERY SUBMARINE(1950); SUNSET BOULEVARD(1950); I WAS A COMMUNIST FOR THE F.B.I.(1951); MAN WHO CHEATED HIMSELF, THE(1951); MY FAVORITE SPY(1951); RAWHIDE(1951); ROADBLOCK(1951); SILVER CITY(1951); DEADLINE-U.S.A.(1952); GREATEST SHOW ON EARTH, THE(1952); KANSAS CITY CONFIDENTIAL(1952); LOST IN ALASKA(1952); SNIPER, THE(1952); FARMER TAKES A WIFE, THE(1953); LET'S DO IT AGAIN(1953); PRESIDENT'S LADY(1953); SAVAGE, THE(1953); SCANDAL AT SCOURIE(1953); SYSTEM, THE(1953); GUN THAT WON THE WEST, THE(1955); LUCY GALLANT(1955); EVERYTHING BUT THE TRUTH(1956); SHOOT-OUT AT MEDICINE BEND(1957); NORTH BY NORTHWEST(1959)

Howard J. Negley
TWILIGHT ON THE RIO GRANDE(1947); KING OF THE GAMBLERS(1948); WALK A CROOKED MILE(1948); LONELY HEARTS BANDITS(1950); MISSOURIANS, THE(1950); UNION STATION(1950); LADY WANTS MINK, THE(1953); SHANE(1953); MAN ALONE, A(1955)
Ward Negley
MAN FROM THE ALAMO, THE(1953)
Louis Neglia
FIST OF FEAR, TOUCH OF DEATH(1980); ONE DOWN TWO TO GO(1982)
Misc. Talkies
HARD WAY TO DIE, A(1980)
Joao Negrao
LOLLIPOP(1966, Braz.), m
Alain Negre
RETURN OF MARTIN GUERRE, THE(1983, Fr.), art d
Raymond Negre
NOUS IRONS A PARIS(1949, Fr.), art d; SELLERS OF GIRLS(1967, Fr.), art d
Jorge Negrete
DEVIL'S GODMOTHER, THE(1938, Mex.)
Rudy Negretl
NIGHTMARES(1983)
C. Negri
GAME FOR SIX LOVERS, A(1962, Fr.), ed
N. Negri
LOVE NOW...PAY LATER(1966, Ital.), p
Paul Negri
TAKE HER BY SURPRISE(1967, Can.)
Pola Negri
WAY OF LOST SOULS, THE(1929, Brit.); WOMAN HE SCORNED, THE(1930, Brit.); WOMAN COMMANDS, A(1932); MOSCOW SHANGHAI(1936, Ger.); HI DIDDLE DIDDLE(1943); MOON-SPINNERS, THE(1964)
Silents
PASSION(1920, Ger.); ONE ARABIAN NIGHT(1921, Ger.); FORBIDDEN PARADISE(1924); CHARMER, THE(1925); EAST OF SUEZ(1925); GOOD AND NAUGHTY(1926); BARBED WIRE(1927); WOMAN ON TRIAL, THE(1927); SECRET HOUR, THE(1928); THREE SINNERS(1928)
Misc. Silents
SLAVE OF PASSION, SLAVE OF VICE(1914, USSR); GYPSY BLOOD(1921, Ger.); LAST PAYMENT(1921, Ger.); SUMURUN(1921, Ger.); VENDETTA(1921, Ger.); DEVIL'S PAWN, THE(1922, Ger.); RED PEACOCK, THE(1922, Ger.); BELLA DONNA(1923); CHEAT, THE(1923); SPANISH DANCER, THE(1923); LILY OF THE DUST(1924); MEN(1924); SHADOWS OF PARIS(1924); FLOWER OF NIGHT(1925); WOMAN OF THE WORLD, A(1925); CROWN OF LIES, THE(1926); HOTEL IMPERIAL(1927); LOVES OF AN ACTRESS(1928); WOMAN FROM MOSCOW, THE(1928)
Sandro Negri
MAGIC WORLD OF TOPO GIGIO, THE(1961, Ital.), cos
Daniel Negrin
ALL WOMAN(1967)
Owen Negrin
PASSION HOLIDAY(1963)
Sol Negrin
PARADES(1972), ph; AMAZING GRACE(1974), ph; LINE, THE(1982), ph
Del Negro
IS PARIS BURNING?(1966, U.S./Fr.); WHO?(1975, Brit./Ger.); AGUIRRE, THE WRATH OF GOD(1977, W. Ger.)
Giorgio Negro
LA NOTTE(1961, Fr./Ital.)
Lobo Negro
BEAST OF HOLLOW MOUNTAIN, THE(1956)
Albert Negron
1984
ERENDIRA(1984, Mex./Fr./Ger.), cos
Roberto Rivera Negron
HARBOR LIGHTS(1963)
Taylor Negron
FAST TIMES AT RIDGEMONT HIGH(1982); YOUNG DOCTORS IN LOVE(1982); EASY MONEY(1983)
Jean Negroni
IS PARIS BURNING?(1966, U.S./Fr.)
Dusty Negulesco
JESSICA(1962, U.S./Ital./Fr.), cos
Jean Negulesco
EXPENSIVE HUSBANDS(1937), w; FIGHT FOR YOUR LADY(1937), w; BELOVED BRAT(1938), w; SWISS MISS(1938), w; RIO(1939), w; SINGAPORE WOMAN(1941), d; CONSPIRATORS, THE(1944), d; MASK OF DIMITRIOS, THE(1944), d; HUMORESQUE(1946), d; NOBODY LIVES FOREVER(1946), d; THREE STRANGERS(1946), d; DEEP VALLEY(1947), d; JOHNNY BELINDA(1948), d; ROAD HOUSE(1948), d; AFFAIRS OF ADELAIDE(1949, U. S./Brit.), d; MUDLARK, THE(1950, Brit.), d; THREE CAME HOME(1950), d; UNDER MY SKIN(1950), d; TAKE CARE OF MY LITTLE GIRL(1951), d; LURE OF THE WILDERNESS(1952), d; LYDIA BAILEY(1952), d; O. HENRY'S FULL HOUSE(1952), d; PHONE CALL FROM A STRANGER(1952), d; HOW TO MARRY A MILLIONAIRE(1953), d; SCANDAL AT SCOURIE(1953), d; TITANIC(1953), d; THREE COINS IN THE FOUNTAIN(1954), d; WOMAN'S WORLD(1954), d; DADDY LONG LEGS(1955), d; BOY ON A DOLPHIN(1957), d; CERTAIN SMILE, A(1958), d; GIFT OF LOVE, THE(1958), d; BEST OF EVERYTHING, THE(1959), d; COUNT YOUR BLESSINGS(1959), d; JESSICA(1962, U.S./Ital./Fr.), p, d; PLEASURE SEEKERS, THE(1964), d; HELLO-GOODBYE(1970), d; INVINCIBLE SIX, THE(1970, U.S./Iran), d
O. Negus-Fancey
SHAMUS(1959, Brit.), p; PRIMITIVES, THE(1962, Brit.), p; LITTLE OF WHAT YOU FANCY, A(1968, Brit.), p; GAMES THAT LOVERS PLAY(1971, Brit.), p
Don Nehan
OPERATION X(1951, Brit.)
Carola Neher
THREEPENNY OPERA, THE(1931, Ger./U.S.)
Jean Neher
MODERN MARRIAGE, A(1962)

Jeanne Neher
INVISIBLE AVENGER, THE(1958)
Misc. Talkies
BOURBON ST. SHADOWS(1962)
Hermann Nehlsen
THERE IS STILL ROOM IN HELL(1963, Ger.)
Andreas Nehring
PINOCCHIO(1969, E. Ger.)
David Neibel
CHROME AND HOT LEATHER(1971), w
Alice Neice
Misc. Silents
HUMANIZING MR. WINSBY(1916)
Hazel Neice
Misc. Silents
EMBODIED THOUGHT, THE(1916)
Ernst Neicher
NUMBER SEVENTEEN(1928, Brit./Ger.)
Charles Neider
ONE-EYED JACKS(1961), w
John Neiderhauser
RIOT(1969)
Elke Neidhart
TRUE STORY OF ESKIMO NELL, THE(1975, Aus.); INSIDE LOOKING OUT(1977, Aus.)
Elkey Neidhart
LIBIDO(1973, Aus.)
William J. Neidig
Silents
TRACKED TO EARTH(1922), w
William Wesley Neighbors, Jr.
1984
BEAR, THE(1984)
Sigrid Neiiendam
DAY OF WRATH(1948, Den.)
Neil
ESCAPE TO BURMA(1955); FRASIER, THE SENSUOUS LION(1973)
Bill Neil
TAXI(1953)
Bob Neil
LOGAN'S RUN(1976)
Elissa Neil
DEADLY SPAWN, THE(1983)
Gloria Neil
BEACH GIRLS AND THE MONSTER, THE(1965); KARATE KILLERS, THE(1967)
Hildegard Neil
MAN WHO HAUNTED HIMSELF, THE(1970, Brit.); ANTONY AND CLEOPATRA(1973, Brit.); ENGLANO MADE ME(1973, Brit.); TOUCH OF CLASS, A(1973, Brit.); LEGACY, THE(1979, Brit.); MIRROR CRACK'D, THE(1980, Brit.)
John Neil
1984
MISSION, THE(1984)
Martin Neil
INTERNATIONAL VELVET(1978, Brit.)
Milt Neil
FANTASIA(1940), anim; DUMBO(1941), anim; RELUCTANT DRAGON, THE(1941), anim
Peter Neil
TO HAVE AND TO HOLD(1951, Brit.); SKID KIDS(1953, Brit.); DELAVINE AFFAIR, THE(1954, Brit.); MEET MR. CALLAGHAN(1954, Brit.); YELLOW ROBE, THE(1954, Brit.); SATELLITE IN THE SKY(1956); STOLEN PLANS, THE(1962, Brit.)
R.R. Neil
Silents
DOING THEIR BIT(1918)
Richard Neil
Misc. Silents
WOMAN IN WHITE, THE(1917)
Richard R. Neil
MAKE WAY FOR TOMORROW(1937)
Robert Neil
MISSOURIANS, THE(1950); I DREAM OF JEANIE(1952); THUNDERBIRDS(1952)
Roy William Neil
Misc. Silents
LOVE ME(1918), d; SAN FRANCISCO NIGHTS(1928), d
Susan Neil
KILL HER GENTLY(1958, Brit.); WOMAN EATER, THE(1959, Brit.)
Tony Neil
LITTLE MEN(1940)
William M. Neil
FROGMEN, THE(1951)
Marshall Neilan
TAXI 13(1928), d; AWFUL TRUTH, THE(1929), d; BLACK WATERS(1929), d; TANNED LEGS(1929), d; VAGABOND LOVER(1929), d; HELL'S ANGELS(1930), d, w; SWEETHEARTS ON PARADE(1930), d; LEMON DROP KID, THE(1934), d; SOCIAL REGISTER(1934), d; THIS IS THE LIFE(1935), d; SING WHILE YOU'RE ABLE(1937), d; STAR IS BORN, A(1937); SWING IT, PROFESSOR(1937), d; THANKS FOR LISTENING(1937), d
Silents
CLASSMATES(1914); COMMANDING OFFICER, THE(1915); LITTLE PAL(1915), a, w; MADAME BUTTERFLY(1915); MAY BLOSSOM(1915); RAGS(1915); MICE AND MEN(1916); REBECCA OF SUNNYBROOK FARM(1917), d; THOSE WITHOUT SIN(1917), d; AMARILLY OF CLOTHESLINE ALLEY(1918), d; M'LISS(1918), d; OUT OF A CLEAR SKY(1918), d; STELLA MARIS(1918), d; DADDY LONG LEGS(1919), a, d; DINTY(1920), d, w; IN OLD KENTUCKY(1920), d; BOB HAMPTON OF PLACER(1921), p&d; PENROD(1922), d⊃ STRANGER'S BANQUET(1922), d, w; ETERNAL THREE, THE(1923), d, w; RENDEZVOUS, THE(1923), d; SOULS FOR SALE(1923); TESS OF THE D'URBERVILLES(1924), d; GREAT LOVE, THE(1925), d, w; MIKE(1926), d, w; SKYROCKET, THE(1926), d; WILD OATS LANE(1926), d; TAKE ME HOME(1928), d

Misc. Silents
COUNTRY BOY, THE(1915); COUNTRY THAT GOD FORGOT, THE(1916), d; CYCLE OF FATE, THE(1916), d; PRINCE CHAP, THE(1916), a, d; BOTTLE IMP, THE(1917), d; FRECKLES(1917), d; GIRL AT HOME, THE(1917), d; LITTLE PRINCESS, THE(1917), d; SILENT PARTNER, THE(1917), d; TIDES OF BARNEGAT, THE(1917), d; HEART OF THE WILDS(1918), d; HIT-THE-TRAIL HOLLIDAY(1918), d; HER KINGDOM OF DREAMS(1919), d; THREE MEN AND A GIRL(1919), d; UNPARDONABLE SIN, THE(1919), d; DON'T EVER MARRY(1920), d; GO AND GET IT(1920), d; RIVER'S END, THE(1920), d; BITS OF LIFE(1921), d; LOTUS EATER, THE(1921), d; FOOLS FIRST(1922), d; MINNIE(1922), d; DOROTHY VERNON OF HADDON HALL(1924), d; SPORTING VENUS, THE(1925), d; DIPLOMACY(1926), d; EVERYBODY'S ACTING(1926), d; HER WILD OAT(1927), d; VENUS OF VENICE(1927), d; HIS LAST HAUL(1928), d; THREE-RING MARRIAGE(1928), d
Marshall Neilan, Jr.
WATCH THE BIRDIE(1950), w; RACK, THE(1956), ed; VALLEY OF THE REDWOODS(1960), ed; LITTLE SHOP OF HORRORS(1961), ed
Martin Neilan
Silents
PINK TIGHTS(1920)
Alice O' Neill
PUTTIN' ON THE RITZ(1930), cos
Angus Neill
AFTER YOU, COMRADE(1967, S. Afr.)
Bob Neill
TRON(1982)
James Neill
IDLE RICH, THE(1929); ONLY THE BRAVE(1930); SHOOTING STRAIGHT(1930); MAN TO MAN(1931)
Silents
MAN FROM HOME, THE(1914); READY MONEY(1914); ROSE OF THE RANCHO(1914); WHERE THE TRAIL DIVIDES(1914), a, d; AFTER FIVE(1915); GOOSE GIRL, THE(1915); WARRENS OF VIRGINIA, THE(1915); WOMAN, THE(1915); JOAN THE WOMAN(1916); OLIVER TWIST(1916); TENNESSEE'S PARDNER(1916); THOSE WITHOUT SIN(1917); JULES OF THE STRONG HEART(1918); SAY! YOUNG FELLOW(1918); ROMANCE AND ARABELLA(1919); STOP THIEF(1920); VOICE IN THE DARK(1921); OUR LEADING CITIZEN(1922); SATURDAY NIGHT(1922); LONELY ROAD, THE(1923); NOBODY'S MONEY(1923); SALOMY JANE(1923); SCARS OF JEALOUSY(1923); TEN COMMANDMENTS, THE(1923); ANY WOMAN(1925); CRIMSON RUNNER, THE(1925); NEW BROOMS(1925); KING OF KINGS, THE(1927)
Misc. Silents
CHEAT, THE(1915); CLUE, THE(1915), d; DREAM GIRL, THE(1916); HOUSE OF THE GOLDEN WINDOWS, THE(1916); LASH, THE(1916); THOUSAND DOLLAR HUSBAND, THE(1916); BETTY TO THE RESCUE(1917); BLACK WOLF, THE(1917); GHOST HOUSE, THE(1917); GIRL AT HOME, THE(1917); TROUBLE BUSTER, THE(1917); GIRL WHO CAME BACK, THE(1918); PETTICOAT PILOT, A(1918); SANDY(1918); WOMAN'S WEAPONS(1918); MEN, WOMEN AND MONEY(1919); PEG O' MY HEART(1919); DOUBLE-DYED DECIEVER, A(1920); PALISER CASE, THE(1920); DANGEROUS CURVE AHEAD(1921); DUSK TO DAWN(1922); THRILL CHASER, THE(1923)
Noel Neill
HENRY AND DIZZY(1942); MISS ANNIE ROONEY(1942); LADY OF BURLESQUE(1943); LET'S FACE IT(1943); SALUTE FOR THREE(1943); ARE THESE OUR PARENTS?(1944); HENRY ALDRICH'S LITTLE SECRET(1944); HERE COME THE WAVES(1944); OUR HEARTS WERE YOUNG AND GAY(1944); RAINBOW ISLAND(1944); STANDING ROOM ONLY(1944); DUFFY'S TAVERN(1945); STORK CLUB, THE(1945); BLUE DAHLIA, THE(1946); FREDDIE STEPS OUT(1946); HIGH SCHOOL HERO(1946); JUNIOR PROM(1946); WELL-GROOMED BRIDE, THE(1946); GLAMOUR GIRL(1947); SARGE GOES TO COLLEGE(1947); SMASH-UP, THE STORY OF A WOMAN(1947); VACATION DAYS(1947); ARE YOU WITH IT?(1948); BIG CLOCK, THE(1948); CAMPUS SLEUTH(1948); MUSIC MAN(1948); SMART POLITICS(1948); WHEN MY BABY SMILES AT ME(1948); FORGOTTEN WOMEN(1949); GUN RUNNER(1949); RED, HOT AND BLUE(1949); SKY DRAGON(1949); SON OF A BADMAN(1949); ABILENE TRAIL(1951); SUBMARINE COMMAND(1951); WHISTLING HILLS(1951); GREATEST SHOW ON EARTH, THE(1952); INVASION U.S.A.(1952); LAWLESS RIDER, THE(1954); SUPERMAN(1978)
Misc. Talkies
MONTANA INCIDENT(1952)
R. W. Neill
CIRCUS QUEEN MURDER, THE(1933), d
R. William Neill
WALL STREET(1929), d; COCK O' THE WALK(1930), d; JUST LIKE HEAVEN(1930), d; MELODY MAN(1930), d; FIFTY FATHOMS DEEP(1931), d; WHIRLPOOL(1934), d
Silents
KAISER'S SHADOW, THE(1918), d; IDOL OF THE NORTH, THE(1921), d; KISS BARRIER, THE(1925), d; MAN FOUR-SQUARE, A(1926), d; ARIZONA WILDCAT(1927), d; OLYMPIC HERO, THE(1928), d
Misc. Silents
GIRL GLORY, THE(1917), d; BROKEN LAWS(1924), d; BY DIVINE RIGHT(1924), d; BLACK PARADISE(1926), d; FIGHTING BUCKAROO, THE(1926), d; BEHIND CLOSED DOORS(1929), d
Richard Neill
LEATHERNECK, THE(1929); HOTEL HAYWIRE(1937); MATING SEASON, THE(1951)
Silents
BATTLE OF LIFE, THE(1916); GOD'S HALF ACRE(1916); WHISPERING SMITH(1926); KING OF KINGS, THE(1927); SOMEWHERE IN SONORA(1927)
Misc. Silents
FOOL'S REVENGE, THE(1916); WALL STREET TRAGEDY, A(1916); HIS WIFE'S FRIEND(1920); CLOUDED NAME, A(1923); FIGHTIN' COMEBACK, THE(1927); TRUNK MYSTERY, THE(1927)
Richard B. Neill
Misc. Silents
HER SECOND HUSBAND(1918)
Richard R. Neill
Silents
FIGHTING COWARD, THE(1924); TUMBLEWEEDS(1925); BULLDOG PLUCK(1927); WHERE EAST IS EAST(1929)

Misc. Silents
PLUNGER, THE(1920); GALLOPING THUNDER(1927)

Roy Neill
Silents
CORNER IN COLLEENS, A(1916)

Roy W. Neill
BLACK MOON(1934), d

Roy William Neill
AVENGER, THE(1931), d; GOOD BAD GIRL, THE(1931), d; MENACE, THE(1932), d; THAT'S MY BOY(1932), d; AS THE DEVIL COMMANDS(1933), d; ABOVE THE CLOUDS(1934), d; BLIND DATE(1934), d; FURY OF THE JUNGLE(1934), d; I'LL FIX IT(1934), d; JEALOUSY(1934), d; NINTH GUEST, THE(1934), d; BLACK ROOM, THE(1935), d; EIGHT BELLS(1935), d; LONE WOLF RETURNS, THE(1936), d; DOCTOR SYN(1937, Brit.), d; GYPSY(1937, Brit.), d; DOUBLE OR QUITS(1938, Brit.), d; EVERYTHING HAPPENS TO ME(1938, Brit.), d; MANY TANKS MR. ATKINS(1938, Brit.), d; QUIET PLEASE(1938, Brit.), d; SIMPLY TERRIFIC(1938, Brit.), d; THANK EVANS(1938, Brit.), d; VIPER, THE(1938, Brit.), d; ANYTHING TO DECLARE?(1939, Brit.), d; GENTLEMAN'S GENTLEMAN, A(1939, Brit.), d; GOOD OLD DAYS, THE(1939, Brit.), d; HIS BROTHER'S KEEPER(1939, Brit.), d, w; HOOTS MON!(1939, Brit.), d, w; MURDER WILL OUT(1939, Brit.), d, w; MADAME SPY(1942), d; SHERLOCK HOLMES AND THE SECRET WEAPON(1942), d; EYES OF THE UNDERWORLD(1943), d; FRANKENSTEIN MEETS THE WOLF MAN(1943), d; RHYTHM OF THE ISLANDS(1943), d; SHERLOCK HOLMES FACES DEATH(1943), p&d; SHERLOCK HOLMES IN WASHINGTON(1943), d; TWO TICKETS TO LONDON(1943), w; DESTINY(1944), p; GYPSY WILDCAT(1944), d; PEARL OF DEATH, THE(1944), p&d; SCARLET CLAW, THE(1944), p&d, w; SHERLOCK HOLMES AND THE SPIDER WOMAN(1944), p&d; HOUSE OF FEAR, THE(1945), p&d; PURSUIT TO ALGIERS(1945), p&d; WOMAN IN GREEN, THE(1945), p&d; BLACK ANGEL(1946), p, d; DRESSED TO KILL(1946), p, d; TERROR BY NIGHT(1946), p&d
Silents
PRICE MARK, THE(1917), d
Misc. Silents
(, d; LOVE LETTERS(1917), d; MOTHER INSTINCT, THE(1917), d; THEY'RE OFF(1917), d; FLARE-UP SAL(1918), d; GREEN EYES(1918), d; MATING OF MARCELLA, THE(1918), d; TYRANT FEAR(1918), d; VIVE LA FRANCE(1918), d; BANDBOX, THE(1919), d; CAREER OF KATHERINE BUSH, THE(1919), d; CHARGE IT TO ME(1919), d; PUPPY LOVE(1919), d; TRIXIE FROM BROADWAY(1919), d; DANGEROUS BUSINESS(1920), d; GOOD REFERENCES(1920), d; INNER VOICE, THE(1920), d; SOMETHING DIFFERENT(1920), d; WOMAN GIVES, THE(1920), d; YES OR NO?(1920), d; IRON TRAIL, THE(1921), d; WHAT'S WRONG WITH THE WOMEN?(1922), d; RADIO-MANIA(1923), d; TOILERS OF THE SEA(1923 US/Ital.), d; VANITY'S PRICE(1924), d; GREATER THAN A CROWN(1925), d; MARRIAGE IN TRANSIT(1925), d; PERCY(1925), d; CITY, THE(1926), d; COWBOY AND THE COUNTESS, THE(1926), d; MARRIAGE(1927), d; VIKING, THE(1929), d

Sam Neill
SLEEPING DOGS(1977, New Zealand); JUST OUT OF REACH(1979, Aus.); MY BRILLIANT CAREER(1980, Aus.); FINAL CONFLICT, THE(1981); POSSESSION(1981, Fr./Ger.); ENIGMA(1983)

Steve Neill
GOD TOLD ME TO(1976), spec eff; DAY TIME ENDED, THE(1980, Span.), p, w; FULL MOON HIGH(1982), makeup; Q(1982), spec eff

Harry Neill [Roger Corman]
TARGET: HARRY(1980), d

Harry Neilman
OUR RELATIONS(1936)

Agnes Neilsen
Misc. Silents
GIRL WHO DIDN'T THINK, THE(1917); INSINUATION(1922)

Claire Neilsen
WILD AFFAIR, THE(1966, Brit.)

Claus Neilsen
EPILOGUE(1967, Den.)

Einar Neilsen
DECEPTION(1946)

Eric Neilsen
I WAS A COMMUNIST FOR THE F.B.I.(1951)

Erik Neilsen
MISTER 880(1950)

Hal Neilsen
CAPTAIN MILKSHAKE(1970)

Helen Neilsen
BLACKOUT(1954, Brit.), w

Inga Neilsen
HOUSE IS NOT A HOME, A(1964); FUNNY THING HAPPENED ON THE WAY TO THE FORUM, A(1966); SILENCERS, THE(1966); IN LIKE FLINT(1967); FUNNY GIRL(1968)

Larry Neilsen
HAPPY BIRTHDAY, DAVY(1970)

Norman Neilsen
LAW RIDES, THE(1936); BOBBY DEERFIELD(1977)

Aldon Neilson
Misc. Silents
REDEMPTION OF HIS NAME, THE(1918, Brit.)

Catherine Neilson
WICKED LADY, THE(1983, Brit.)

Denise Neilson
Misc. Talkies
MOUNTAIN CHARLIE(1982)

Harry Neilson
EARTHLING, THE(1980)

Inga Neilson
EVERYTHING YOU ALWAYS WANTED TO KNOW ABOUT SEX, BUT WE'RE AFRAID TO ASK(1972)

James Neilson
NIGHT PASSAGE(1957), d; BON VOYAGE(1962), d; MOON PILOT(1962), d; SUMMER MAGIC(1963), d; MOON-SPINNERS, THE(1964), d; ADVENTURES OF BULLWHIP GRIFFIN, THE(1967), d; GENTLE GIANT(1967), d; WHERE ANGELS GO...TROUBLE FOLLOWS(1968), d; FIRST TIME, THE(1969), d; FLAREUP(1969), d; DR. SYN, ALIAS THE SCARECROW(1975), d

John Neilson
TERROR HOUSE(1972); SHARK'S TREASURE(1975)

Lester Neilson
NIGHT OF TERROR(1933), w

Major Neilson
LAMP STILL BURNS, THE(1943, Brit.), w

Marianne Neilson
FANNY AND ALEXANDER(1983, Swed./Fr./Ger.)

Nigel Neilson
INTERRUPTED JOURNEY, THE(1949, Brit.); STRANGER AT MY DOOR(1950, Brit.); STORY OF ROBIN HOOD, THE(1952, Brit.); TIME IS MY ENEMY(1957, Brit.)

Perlita Neilson
GREAT GILBERT AND SULLIVAN, THE(1953, Brit.); TROUBLE IN STORE(1955, Brit.)

Peter Neilson
DR. BLOOD'S COFFIN(1961), spec eff

Charles Neilson-Terry
LOVE LOTTERY, THE(1954, Brit.), w

Dennis Neilson-Terry
HOUSE OF THE ARROW, THE(1930, Brit.); 77 PARK LANE(1931, Brit.); MURDER AT COVENT GARDEN(1932, Brit.)
Misc. Silents
HER GREATEST PERFORMANCE(1916, Brit.); HIS LAST DEFENCE(1919, Brit.); HUNDRETH CHANCE, THE(1920, Brit.)

Phyllis Neilson-Terry
ONE FAMILY(1930, Brit.); RX MURDER(1958, Brit.); CONSPIRACY OF HEARTS(1960, Brit.)
Misc. Silents
BOADICEA(1926, Brit.)

Hal Neiman
EVER SINCE EVE(1937); FOOTLOOSE HEIRESS, THE(1937); IDOL OF THE CROWDS(1937); SAN QUENTIN(1937)

Harold Neiman
HOUDINI(1953)

Leroy Neiman
ROCKY III(1982)

Roberta Neiman
PROWLER, THE(1981), art d

Renee Neimark
ENTITY, THE(1982)

Mary Ann Neis
DIRTY HARRY(1971)

George Neise
FLIGHT LIEUTENANT(1942); THEY RAID BY NIGHT(1942); VALLEY OF HUNTED MEN(1942); AIR FORCE(1943); MAN FROM FRISCO(1944); ONCE UPON A TIME(1944); ONE SUNDAY AFTERNOON(1948); MY DREAM IS YOURS(1949); I'LL SEE YOU IN MY DREAMS(1951); SHARKFIGHTERS, THE(1956); JEANNE EAGELS(1957); PHARAOH'S CURSE(1957); TALL STRANGER, THE(1957); TOMAHAWK TRAIL(1957); NO TIME FOR SERGEANTS(1958); OUTCASTS OF THE CITY(1958); THREE STOOGES IN ORBIT, THE(1962); JOHNNY COOL(1963); GUIDE FOR THE MARRIED MAN, A(1967); DID YOU HEAR THE ONE ABOUT THE TRAVELING SALESLADY?(1968); ON A CLEAR DAY YOU CAN SEE FOREVER(1970)

George N. Neise
EXPERIMENT PERILOUS(1944); TWENTY PLUS TWO(1961); THREE STOOGES MEET HERCULES, THE(1962); BAREFOOT EXECUTIVE, THE(1971)

George W. Neise
FORT MASSACRE(1958)

Hans Neiter
M'BLIMEY(1931, Brit.), w

Alvin J. Neitz [Alan James]
CANYON HAWKS(1930), d, w; FIREBRAND JORDAN(1930), d; TRAILS OF DANGER(1930), d&w; RED FORK RANGE(1931), d, w; TEX TAKES A HOLIDAY(1932), d; OUTLAW TRAIL(1944), w
Misc. Talkies
BREED OF THE WEST(1930), d; FLYING LARIATS(1931), d; HELL'S VALLEY(1931), d; LARIATS AND SIXSHOOTERS(1931), d; PUEBLO TERROR(1931), d
Silents
GIRL WHO DARED, THE(1920), w; LONE HAND, THE(1920), w; CROSSING TRAILS(1921), w; WESTERN HEARTS(1921), w; DOWN BY THE RIO GRANDE(1924), d; FIGHTER'S PARADISE(1924), d; RECKLESS SEX, THE(1925), d; HAZARDOUS VALLEY(1927), d; SKY RIDER, THE(1928), d&w, ed
Misc. Silents
OUTLAWED(1921), d; FIREBRAND, THE(1922), d; GUN SHY(1922), d; DANGEROUS TRAILS(1923), d; WOLVES OF THE BORDER(1923), d; CALL OF THE MATE(1924), d; COWBOY AND THE FLAPPER, THE(1924), d; CRASHIN' THROUGH(1924), d; CYCLONE BUDDY(1924), d; MAN FROM GOD'S COUNTRY(1924), d; THAT WILD WEST(1924), d; VIRGIN, THE(1924), d; WHITE PANTHER, THE(1924), d; GIRL OF THE WEST(1925), d; LURE OF THE WEST(1925), d; WARRIOR GAP(1925), d; BAD MAN'S BLUFF(1926), d; BEYOND ALL ODDS(1926), d; BORN TO BATTLE(1927), d; CHEER LEADER, THE(1928), d; SILENT SENTINEL(1929), d

Pak Nejad
INVINCIBLE SIX, THE(1970, U.S./Iran), set d

Milan Nejedly
ROCKET TO NOWHERE(1962, Czech.), spec eff; VOYAGE TO THE END OF THE UNIVERSE(1963, Czech.), spec eff; FIFTH HORSEMAN IS FEAR, THE(1968, Czech.), w, art d; SIGN OF THE VIRGIN(1969, Czech.), art d; ADELE HASN'T HAD HER SUPPER YET(1978, Czech.), set d

Victoria Nekko
1984
BIRDY(1984)

A. Nekrasov
Misc. Silents
HE WHO GETS SLAPPED(1916, USSR)

E. Nekrasova
GIRL AND THE BUGLER, THE(1967, USSR)

Azriel Nekritsch
DREAM NO MORE(1950, Palestine)
Kristine Nel
AVALANCHE EXPRESS(1979)
A. Nelidov
Misc. Silents
CHILDREN – FLOWERS OF LIFE(1919, USSR)
Stacey Nelkia
HALLOWEEN III: SEASON OF THE WITCH(1982)
Stacey Nelkin
SERIAL(1980); GOING APE!(1981); GET CRAZY(1983); YELLOWBEARD(1983)
Stacy Nelkin
UP THE ACADEMY(1980)
Carlo Nell
LOLA(1961, Fr./Ital.); UPPER HAND, THE(1967, Fr./Ital./Ger.); CESAR AND ROS-ALIE(1972, Fr.); GODSON, THE(1972, Ital./Fr.); CATHERINE & CO.(1976, Fr.)
Christa Nell
PIERROT LE FOU(1968, Fr./Ital.)
Krista Nell
MILLION EYES OF SU-MURU, THE(1967, Brit.); SLASHER, THE(1975)
Little Nell
JUBILEE(1978, Brit.)
Nathalie Nell
ECHOES(1983); MAN, WOMAN AND CHILD(1983)
Marisa Nella
BLOOD WEDDING(1981, Sp.)
Karin Nellemose
Misc. Silents
MASTER OF THE HOUSE(1925, Den.)
G. Nellep
BORIS GODUNOV(1959, USSR)
Richard Neller
SHADOW OF THE PAST(1950, Brit.)
Nellie
EARLY BIRD, THE(1965, Brit.)
Kate Nelligan
ROMANTIC ENGLISHWOMAN, THE(1975, Brit./Fr.); COUNT OF MONTE CRIS-TO(1976, Brit.); DRACULA(1979); MR. PATMAN(1980, Can.); EYE OF THE NEED-LE(1981); WITHOUT A TRACE(1983)
Misc. Talkies
BETHUNE(1977)
Thomas Nello
COP HATER(1958)
Tommy Nello
CRY OF THE CITY(1948)
Richard Nellor
TRUNK, THE(1961, Brit.)
Sylvia Nells
MOZART(1940, Brit.)
Judith Nelmes
TOMORROW WE LIVE(1936, Brit.); GREAT MR. HANDEL, THE(1942, Brit.); ANNA KARENINA(1948, Brit.); LOVERS, HAPPY LOVERS!(1955, Brit.); KID FOR TWO FARTHINGS, A(1956, Brit.); HORROR OF DRACULA, THE(1958, Brit.)
Herman Nelsen
ISLAND OF THE DOOMED(1968, Span./Ger.)
Nelson
WESTERN CARAVANS(1939), d
Albert Nelson
MAN WHO FELL TO EARTH, THE(1976, Brit.)
Alberta Nelson
MUSCLE BEACH PARTY(1964); PAJAMA PARTY(1964); DR. GOLDFOOT AND THE BIKINI MACHINE(1965); HOW TO STUFF A WILD BIKINI(1965); GHOST IN THE INVISIBLE BIKINI(1966); WILD SCENE, THE(1970)
Ann Nelson
1984
MASS APPEAL(1984)
Misc. Talkies
GHOSTS THAT STILL WALK(1977)
Argyle Nelson
LADY SINGS THE BLUES(1972), ed; HIT(1973), ed; SHEILA LEVINE IS DEAD AND LIVING IN NEW YORK(1975), ed; GABLE AND LOMBARD(1976), ed; SEX-TETTE(1978), ed; NIGHT OF THE JUGGLER(1980), ed; BUDDY BUDDY(1981), ed; CHU CHU AND THE PHILLY FLASH(1981), ed; SOMETHING WICKED THIS WAY COMES(1983), ed
Argyle Nelson, Jr.
CREEPING TERROR, THE(1964), ed; GREATEST STORY EVER TOLD, THE(1965), ed; LAWYER, THE(1969), ed; LITTLE FAUSS AND BIG HALSY(1970), ed; LIFE-GUARD(1976), ed
Art J. Nelson
CREEPING TERROR, THE(1964), p&d
Arvid Nelson
WHEN HELL BROKE LOOSE(1958)
B. J. Nelson
LONE WOLF McQUADE(1983), w
Babs Nelson
MAID OF SALEM(1937)
Barrie Nelson
SHINBONE ALLEY(1971), anim
Barry Nelson
DR. KILDARE'S VICTORY(1941); SHADOW OF THE THIN MAN(1941); AFFAIRS OF MARTHA, THE(1942); EYES IN THE NIGHT(1942); JOHNNY EAGER(1942); RIO RITA(1942); YANK ON THE BURMA ROAD, A(1942); BATAAN(1943); GUY NAMED JOE, A(1943); HUMAN COMEDY, THE(1943); BEGINNING OR THE END, THE(1947); UNDERCOVER MAISIE(1947); TENTH AVENUE ANGEL(1948); MAN WITH MY FACE, THE(1951); FIRST TRAVELING SALESLADY, THE(1956); MARY, MA-RY(1963); AIRPORT(1970); PETE 'N' TILLIE(1972); SHINING, THE(1980); ISLAND CLAWS(1981)

Cpl. Barry Nelson
WINGED VICTORY(1944)
Bek Nelson
PAL JOEY(1957); BELL, BOOK AND CANDLE(1958); COWBOY(1958); CRASH LANDING(1958); LOLLIPOP COVER, THE(1965)
Bernie Nelson
1984
KILLPOINT(1984)
Bert Nelson
ROCK ALL NIGHT(1957)
Betty Nelson
GOOD TIME GIRL(1950, Brit.); DOUBLE CONFESSION(1953, Brit.)
Bill Nelson
BROADWAY(1942); WHEN THE LIGHTS GO ON AGAIN(1944); JACKPOT, THE(1950); MILKMAN, THE(1950); HIS KIND OF WOMAN(1951); 12 ANGRY MEN(1957)
Billy Nelson
LOOK UP AND LAUGH(1935, Brit.); PENNY POOL, THE(1937, Brit.); CALLING ALL CROOKS(1938, Brit.); I LIVE ON DANGER(1942); WILDCAT(1942); WRECKING CREW(1942); COWBOY IN MANHATTAN(1943); FALSE FACES(1943); HARVEST MELODY(1943); HERS TO HOLD(1943); MINESWEEPER(1943); GAMBLER'S CHOICE(1944); WATERFRONT(1944); WHEN STRANGERS MARRY(1944); DILLIN-GER(1945); HIGH POWERED(1945); HONEYMOON AHEAD(1945); SENORITA FROM THE WEST(1945); TEN CENTS A DANCE(1945); IDEA GIRL(1946); KID FROM BOOKLYN, THE(1946); SUSPENSE(1946); SEARCH FOR DANGER(1949); UNDER-COVER MAN, THE(1949); EMERGENCY WEDDING(1950); MISTER 880(1950); PRIDE OF ST. LOUIS, THE(1952); MR. SCOUTMASTER(1953); VICKI(1953); SEVEN LITTLE FOYS, THE(1955); SOMEBODY UP THERE LIKES ME(1956)
Bob Nelson
GLASS WEB, THE(1953); TARANTULA(1955); WACKY WORLD OF DR. MORGUS, THE(1962); EVEL KNIEVEL(1971), set d; FAREWELL, MY LOVELY(1975), set d; SORCERESS(1983)
Bobbie Nelson
TWO-FISTED JUSTICE(1931); BOOTHILL BRIGADE(1937)
1984
SONGWRITER(1984)
Bobby Nelson
ROARING RANCH(1930); DARING DANGER(1932); PARTNERS(1932); COWBOY COUNSELOR(1933); KING OF THE ARENA(1933); OLIVER TWIST(1933); WAY OF THE WEST, THE(1934); COWBOY AND THE BANDIT, THE(1935); CYCLONE OF THE SADDLE(1935); GHOST RIDER, THE(1935); ROUGH RIDING RANGER(1935); TEXAS TERROR(1935); THROWBACK, THE(1935); THUNDERBOLT(1936); VALLEY OF THE LAWLESS(1936); GAMBLING TERROR, THE(1937); GUN LORDS OF STIRRUP BASIN(1937); RED ROPE, THE(1937); HONEYSUCKLE ROSE(1980)
Misc. Talkies
TWO GUN CABALLERO(1931)
Silents
FIGHTING BOOB, THE(1926); BULLDOG PLUCK(1927)
Bonnie Nelson
CANNIBAL GIRLS(1973)
Britt Nelson
SCREAM OF THE BUTTERFLY(1965)
Burt Nelson
BULLWHIP(1958); SEVEN GUNS TO MESA(1958); REVOLT OF THE SLAVES, THE(1961, Ital./Span./Ger.)
Byron Nelson
FIGHTING 69TH, THE(1940); 'TILL WE MEET AGAIN(1944); ENCHANTED VAL-LEY, THE(1948), animal t; ANNE OF THE INDIES(1951); CADDY, THE(1953)
Carine Nelson
ENTENTE CORDIALE(1939, Fr.); RASPUTIN(1939, Fr.)
Carl Nelson
OUT OF THE BLUE(1982)
Carol Nelson
STAKEOUT ON DOPE STREET(1958); YOUNG CAPTIVES, THE(1959)
Charlene Nelson
1984
LAST STARFIGHTER, THE(1984)
Charles Nelson
KONGA, THE WILD STALLION(1939), ed; OUTPOST OF THE MOUNTIES(1939), ed; BABIES FOR SALE(1940), ed; BEFORE I HANG(1940), ed; BULLETS FOR RUSTLERS(1940), ed; GIRLS OF THE ROAD(1940), ed; GIRLS UNDER TWENTY-ONE(1940), ed; MAN FROM TUMBLEWEEDS, THE(1940), ed; SECRET SEVEN, THE(1940), ed; TEXAS STAGECOACH(1940), ed; TWO-FISTED RANGERS(1940), ed; WEST OF ABILENE(1940), ed; BLONDIE IN SOCIETY(1941), ed; FACE BEHIND THE MASK, THE(1941), ed; HER FIRST BEAU(1941), ed; RIDERS OF THE BAD-LANDS(1941), ed; THREE GIRLS ABOUT TOWN(1941), ed; WILDCAT OF TUC-SON(1941), ed; BLONDIE'S BLESSED EVENT(1942), ed; FLIGHT LIEUTENANT(1942), ed; NIGHT TO REMEMBER, A(1942), ed; SAHARA(1943), ed; NONE SHALL ESCAPE(1944), ed; COUNTER-ATTACK(1945), ed; KISS AND TELL(1945), ed; SONG TO REMEMBER, A(1945), ed; GILDA(1946), ed; MAN WHO DARED, THE(1946), ed; RENEGADES(1946), ed; THRILL OF BRAZIL, THE(1946), ed; GLAMOUR GIRL(1947), ed; GUILT OF JANET AMES, THE(1947), ed; LOVES OF CARMEN, THE(1948), ed; MAN FROM COLORADO, THE(1948), ed; ANNA LUCAS-TA(1949), ed; DOOLINS OF OKLAHOMA, THE(1949), ed; SONG OF INDIA(1949), ed; TELL IT TO THE JUDGE(1949), ed; KILL THE UMPIRE(1950), ed; STAGE TO TUCSON(1950), ed; WOMAN OF DISTINCTION, A(1950), ed; BORN YESTER-DAY(1951), ed; CRIMINAL LAWYER(1951), ed; MAN IN THE SADDLE(1951), ed; MOB, THE(1951), ed; TWO OF A KIND(1951), ed; ASSIGNMENT–PARIS(1952), ed; MARRYING KIND, THE(1952), ed; SOUND OFF(1952), ed; BIG HEAT, THE(1953), ed; LET'S DO IT AGAIN(1953), ed; PRISONERS OF THE CASBAH(1953), ed; BATTLE OF ROGUE RIVER(1954), ed; IT SHOULD HAPPEN TO YOU(1954), ed; PHFFFT!(1954), ed; MY SISTER EILEEN(1955), ed; PICNIC(1955), ed; THREE STRIPES IN THE SUN(1955), ed; FULL OF LIFE(1956), ed; SOLID GOLD CADILLAC, THE(1956), ed; BROTHERS RICO, THE(1957), ed; MAN WHO TURNED TO STONE, THE(1957), ed; OPERATION MAD BALL(1957), ed; UTAH BLAINE(1957), ed; BELL, BOOK AND CANDLE(1958), ed; GHOST OF THE CHINA SEA(1958), ed; GOING STEADY(1958), ed; ME AND THE COLONEL(1958), ed; RETURN TO WAR-BOW(1958), ed; IT HAPPENED TO JANE(1959), ed; LAST ANGRY MAN, THE(1959), ed; STRANGERS WHEN WE MEET(1960), ed; DEVIL AT FOUR O'CLOCK, THE(1961), ed; WACKIEST SHIP IN THE ARMY, THE(1961), ed; NOTORIOUS LANDLADY,

THE(1962), ed; UNDER THE YUM-YUM TREE(1963), ed; GOOD NEIGHBOR SAM(1964), ed; CAT BALLOU(1965), ed; SILENCERS, THE(1966), ed; ENTER LAUGHING(1967), ed; CHASTITY BELT, THE(1968, Ital.), ed

Chris Nelson
ROLLER BOOGIE(1979)

Christine Nelson
SEND ME NO FLOWERS(1964); TWO-MINUTE WARNING(1976); GREAT MUPPET CAPER, THE(1981)

Christopher Nelson
PINK MOTEL(1983)

Christopher S. Nelson
WITHOUT WARNING(1980)

Clear Nelson, Jr.
FOXES OF HARROW, THE(1947)

Connie Nelson
GUN RUNNER(1969); ANGELS DIE HARD(1970); HARD ROAD, THE(1970)

Craig Nelson
RETURN OF COUNT YORGA, THE(1971); SCREAM BLACULA SCREAM(1973)

Craig Richard Nelson
PAPER CHASE, THE(1973); THREE WOMEN(1977); WEDDING, A(1978); QUINTET(1979); MY BODYGUARD(1980); SMALL CIRCLE OF FRIENDS, A(1980)

Craig T. Nelson
...AND JUSTICE FOR ALL(1979); PRIVATE BENJAMIN(1980); STIR CRAZY(1980); POLTERGEIST(1982); ALL THE RIGHT MOVES(1983); MAN, WOMAN AND CHILD(1983); OSTERMAN WEEKEND, THE(1983); SILKWOOD(1983)
1984
KILLING FIELDS, THE(1984, Brit.)

Dam Nelson
AS THE DEVIL COMMANDS(1933), w

Dan Nelson
ENEMY BELOW, THE(1957)

Danny Nelson
GREASED LIGHTNING(1977); NIGHT THE LIGHTS WENT OUT IN GEORGIA, THE(1981); SHARKY'S MACHINE(1982)
1984
NIGHT SHADOWS(1984); TANK(1984)

Dave Nelson
THREE HATS FOR LISA(1965, Brit.)

David Nelson
UP IN SMOKE(1978); HERE COME THE NELSONS(1952); PEYTON PLACE(1957); –30–(1959); BIG CIRCUS, THE(1959); DAY OF THE OUTLAW(1959); REMARKABLE MR. PENNYPACKER, THE(1959); BIG SHOW, THE(1961)
1984
RARE BREED(1984), d
Misc. Talkies
CONFESSIONS OF TOM HARRIS(1972), d; DEATH SCREAMS(1982), d; LAST PLANE OUT(1983), d

David Lloyd Nelson
1984
SAM'S SON(1984); SPLASH(1984)

Dick Nelson
GREAT GUNS(1941); FOLLOW THE BOYS(1944); WINK OF AN EYE(1958); ONE MORE TRAIN TO ROB(1971), w

Don Nelson
GUS(1976), w; NO DEPOSIT, NO RETURN(1976), w; HERBIE GOES TO MONTE CARLO(1977), w; HOT LEAD AND COLD FEET(1978), w

Donald Nelson
HERE COME THE NELSONS(1952), w

Dusty Nelson
EFFECTS(1980), d & w

Ed Nelson
ATTACK OF THE CRAB MONSTERS(1957); CARNIVAL ROCK(1957); INVASION OF THE SAUCER MEN(1957); ROCK ALL NIGHT(1957); TEENAGE DOLL(1957); CRY BABY KILLER, THE(1958); DEVIL'S PARTNER, THE(1958); HOT CAR GIRL(1958); NIGHT OF THE BLOOD BEAST(1958); BUCKET OF BLOOD, A(1959); T-BIRD GANG(1959); YOUNG CAPTIVES, THE(1959); CODE OF SILENCE(1960); VALLEY OF THE REDWOODS(1960); SOLDIER IN THE RAIN(1963); MAN FROM GALVESTON, THE(1964); AIRPORT 1975(1974); THAT'S THE WAY OF THE WORLD(1975); MIDWAY(1976); FOR THE LOVE OF BENJI(1977); ACAPULCO GOLD(1978)
Misc. Talkies
TIME TO RUN(1974); RIDING WITH DEATH(1976)

Edgar Nelson
MISLEADING LADY, THE(1932)
Silents
WAY DOWN EAST(1920); JANICE MEREDITH(1924); WOMANHANDLED(1925)
Misc. Silents
CHICKEN IN THE CASE, THE(1921)

Edward Nelson
SWAMP WOMEN(1956)

Edwin Nelson
BAYOU(1957); HELL ON DEVIL'S ISLAND(1957); BRAIN EATERS, THE(1958), a, p; STREET OF DARKNESS(1958)

Edwin Stafford Nelson
NEW ORLEANS UNCENSORED(1955)

Erik Nelson
GREATEST SHOW ON EARTH, THE(1952); WATERMELON MAN(1970); POSEIDON ADVENTURE, THE(1972); TOWERING INFERNO, THE(1974)

Eva Nelson
CAGED(1950)

Evelyn Nelson
Silents
PEACEFUL PETERS(1922)
Misc. Silents
BROKEN SPUR, THE(1921); CYCLONE BLISS(1921); MOTION TO ADJOURN, A(1921); RECOIL(1921); CROW'S NEST, THE(1922); DESERT BRIDEGROOM, A(1922); TWO-FISTED JEFFERSON(1922); DESERT RIDER(1923); FORBIDDEN TRAIL, THE(1923)

Felix Nelson
SANGAREE(1953); LEARNING TREE, THE(1969); BALLAD OF CABLE HOGUE, THE(1970)

Florence Nelson
Silents
ANGEL ESQUIRE(1919, Brit.); ERNEST MALTRAVERS(1920, Brit.)
Misc. Silents
DISAPPEARANCE OF THE JUDGE, THE(1919, Brit.); LAMP OF DESTINY(1919, Brit.)

Frances Nelson
Silents
FAMILY CUPBOARD, THE(1915); SINS OF SOCIETY(1915); STOLEN VOICE(1915); ONE OF MANY(1917); POWER OF DECISION, THE(1917)
Misc. Silents
CONSCIENCE(1915); COURT-MARTIALED(1915); WHITE TERROR, THE(1915); ALMIGHTY DOLLAR, THE(1916); DECOY, THE(1916); HUMAN DRIFTWOOD(1916); LOVE'S CRUCIBLE(1916); REVOLT, THE(1916); WHAT HAPPENED AT 22(1916); BEAUTIFUL LIE, THE(1917); FAITHLESS SEX, THE(1922)

Frank Nelson
GIRL IN THE SHOW, THE(1929); IN OLD ARIZONA(1929); FIGHTING PARSON, THE(1933); HOLD'EM NAVY!(1937); DOWN MEMORY LANE(1949); MILKMAN, THE(1950); WHEN YOU'RE SMILING(1950); YOU NEVER CAN TELL(1951); BONZO GOES TO COLLEGE(1952); HERE COME THE NELSONS(1952); MY PAL GUS(1952); CLOWN, THE(1953); REMAINS TO BE SEEN(1953); IT SHOULD HAPPEN TO YOU(1954); KISS THEM FOR ME(1957); MOUSE AND HIS CHILD, THE(1977)
Misc. Talkies
LOONEY, LOONEY, LOONEY BUGS BUNNY MOVIE, THE(1981)
Silents
OAKDALE AFFAIR, THE(1919); MAKING A MAN(1922); GENTLEMAN OF LEISURE, A(1923); STEPHEN STEPS OUT(1923); STRANGER, THE(1924); SEA BEAST, THE(1926); GREAT MAIL ROBBERY, THE(1927)
Misc. Silents
LAST OF THE DUANES, THE(1924)

Garr Nelson
OCEAN'S ELEVEN(1960)

Gary Nelson
MOLLY AND LAWLESS JOHN(1972), d; SANTEE(1973), d; FREAKY FRIDAY(1976), d; BLACK HOLE, THE(1979), d; JIMMY THE KID(1982), d
Misc. Talkies
CRUISIN' 57(1975)

Gay Nelson
MILLIE'S DAUGHTER(1947); BLONDIE'S REWARD(1948); WHEN WORLDS COLLIDE(1951)

Gene Nelson
I WONDER WHO'S KISSING HER NOW(1947); APARTMENT FOR PEGGY(1948); WALLS OF JERICHO(1948); DAUGHTER OF ROSIE O'GRADY, THE(1950); TEA FOR TWO(1950); WEST POINT STORY, THE(1950); LULLABY OF BROADWAY, THE(1951); PAINTING THE CLOUDS WITH SUNSHINE(1951); STARLIFT(1951); SHE'S WORKING HER WAY THROUGH COLLEGE(1952); SHE'S BACK ON BROADWAY(1953); THREE SAILORS AND A GIRL(1953), a, ch; CRIME WAVE(1954); SO THIS IS PARIS(1954), a, ch; ATOMIC MAN, THE(1955, Brit.); OKLAHOMA(1955); WAY OUT, THE(1956, Brit.); PURPLE HILLS, THE(1961); 20,000 EYES(1961); HAND OF DEATH(1962), d; HOOTENANNY HOOT(1963), d; THUNDER ISLAND(1963); KISSIN' COUSINS(1964), d, w; YOUR CHEATIN' HEART(1964), d; HARUM SCARUM(1965), d; COOL ONES THE(1967), d, w; S.O.B.(1981)

George Bob Nelson
F.I.S.T.(1978), set d

George Nelson
NO, NO NANETTE(1940)

George Nelson
PORTNOY'S COMPLAINT(1972), set d; DAY OF THE DOLPHIN, THE(1973), set d

George R. Nelson
ALL FALL DOWN(1962), set d; MAGIC SWORD, THE(1962), set d; MANCHURIAN CANDIDATE, THE(1962), set d; SUNDAY IN NEW YORK(1963), set d; HONEYMOON HOTEL(1964), set d; VIVA LAS VEGAS(1964), set d; JOY IN THE MORNING(1965), set d; SKI PARTY(1965), set d; MURDERERS' ROW(1966), set d; SILENCERS, THE(1966), set d; WALK, DON'T RUN(1966), set d; GRADUATE, THE(1967), set d; WARNING SHOT(1967), set d; HOW TO SAVE A MARRIAGE–AND RUIN YOUR LIFE(1968), set d; LITTLE BIG MAN(1970), set d; MC MASTERS, THE(1970), set d; ZABRISKIE POINT(1970), set d; CARNAL KNOWLEDGE(1971), set d; GETAWAY, THE(1972), set d; GODFATHER, THE, PART II(1974), set d; APOCALYPSE NOW(1979), set d; URBAN COWBOY(1980), set d; ESCAPE ARTIST, THE(1982), set d; HAMMETT(1982), set d
1984
BIRDY(1984), set d

George Robert Nelson
ROOSTER COGBURN(1975), set d; FROM NOON TO THREE(1976), set d

Gerri Nelson
OTHER SIDE OF THE MOUNTAIN–PART 2, THE(1978)

Gloria Nelson
YOUR NUMBER'S UP(1931), art d

Gordon Nelson
KNOCK ON ANY DOOR(1949); CHAMPAGNE FOR CAESAR(1950); FOR HEAVEN'S SAKE(1950); LAWLESS, THE(1950); NO MAN OF HER OWN(1950); GROOM WORE SPURS, THE(1951); IRON MISTRESS, THE(1952); MY PAL GUS(1952); SOMETHING FOR THE BIRDS(1952); CITY OF BAD MEN(1953); FARMER TAKES A WIFE, THE(1953); MR. SCOUTMASTER(1953)

Gwen Nelson
TECKMAN MYSTERY, THE(1955, Brit); KITCHEN, THE(1961, Brit.); DON'T TALK TO STRANGE MEN(1962, Brit.); KIND OF LOVING, A(1962, Brit.); STOLEN HOURS(1963); THREE LIVES OF THOMASINA, THE(1963, U.S./Brit.); DOCTOR ZHIVAGO(1965); STAIRCASE(1969 U.S./Brit./Fr.); RECKONING, THE(1971, Brit.); SAY HELLO TO YESTERDAY(1971, Brit.); LAST REMAKE OF BEAU GESTE, THE(1977, Brit.); ALL THINGS BRIGHT AND BEAUTIFUL(1979, Brit.)

H. Lloyd Nelson
M(1970)

Harold Nelson
TWO AGAINST THE WORLD(1932); LIVING ON VELVET(1935); CHAMPAGNE WALTZ(1937); MAID OF SALEM(1937)

Misc. Silents
  SISTERS OF EVE(1928)
Harriet Nelson
  HERE COME THE NELSONS(1952)
Harry Lloyd Nelson
  COURT JESTER, THE(1956)
Haywood Nelson
  MIXED COMPANY(1974)
Helene Nelson
  SMILE(1975)
Herb Nelson
  LITTLE BIG MAN(1970)
Herbert Nelson
  NIGHT OF BLOODY HORROR zero(1969); GREAT NORTHFIELD, MINNESOTA RAID, THE(1972); WHEN THE LEGENDS DIE(1972); HINDENBURG, THE(1975)
Misc. Talkies
  WHEN THE NORTH WIND BLOWS(1974)
Hobart Nelson
  LAUGHING POLICEMAN, THE(1973)
Howard Nelson
  CARRY ON EMANUELLE(1978, Brit.); STUD, THE(1979, Brit.)
Ida Nelson
  FUNERAL HOME(1982, Can.), w
J. Nelson
Silents
  WHEN BOYS LEAVE HOME(1928, Brit.)
Jack Nelson
  REMOTE CONTROL(1930), w
Misc. Talkies
  TWO GUN CABALLERO(1931), d; BORDER GUNS(1934), d; BORDER MENACE, THE(1934), d
Silents
  WHEN DO WE EAT?(1918); CHICKENS(1921), d; ONE A MINUTE(1921), d; ROOKIE'S RETURN, THE(1921), d; WATCH HIM STEP(1922), d; AFTER A MILLION(1924), d; COVERED TRAIL, THE(1924), d; ISLE OF HOPE, THE(1925), d; DUDE COWBOY, THE(1926), d; FIGHTING BOOB, THE(1926), d&w; HAIR TRIGGER BAXTER(1926), d; VALLEY OF BRAVERY, THE(1926), d; BULLDOG PLUCK(1927), d
Misc. Silents
  FIGHTING FOR GOLD(1919); GIRL DODGER, THE(1919); HOME STRETCH, THE(1921), d; I AM GUILTY(1921), d; THRU THE FLAMES(1923), d; BATTLING MASON(1924), d; FIGHTING HEART, A(1924), d; MIDNIGHT SECRETS(1924), d; HE WHO LAUGHS LAST(1925), d; MYSTERIOUS STRANGER, THE(1925), d; PRINCE OF PEP, THE(1925), d; WALL STREET WHIZ, THE(1925), d; BEYOND THE ROCKIES(1926), d; CALL OF THE WILDERNESS, THE(1926), d; DEAD LINE, THE(1926), d; DEVIL'S GULCH, THE(1926), d; MILE-A-MINUTE MAN, THE(1926), d; MODERN YOUTH(1926), d; SUNSHINE OF PARADISE ALLEY(1926), d; FIGHTING HOMBRE, THE(1927), d; LIFE OF AN ACTRESS(1927), d; SAY IT WITH DIAMONDS(1927), d; SHAMROCK AND THE ROSE, THE(1927), d; THROUGH THICK AND THIN(1927), d
James Nelson
  LIVELY SET, THE(1964); GIRL, THE BODY, AND THE PILL, THE(1967); TARZAN AND THE GREAT RIVER(1967, U.S./Switz.), ed; BORDERLINE(1980), p
Jeff Nelson
  BEAU GESTE(1966)
Jeffrey Nelson
  RETURN OF THE SECAUCUS SEVEN(1980), a, p; LIANNA(1983), p
Jerry Nelson
  MUPPET MOVIE, THE(1979); GREAT MUPPET CAPER, THE(1981); DARK CRYSTAL, THE(1982, Brit.)
1984
  MUPPETS TAKE MANHATTAN, THE(1984)
Jessica Nelson
  JEKYLL AND HYDE...TOGETHER AGAIN(1982); PLAINSONG(1982)
John Nelson
  JANIE(1944); OPERATION SECRET(1952)
John Arthur Nelson
Silents
  NEW DISCIPLE, THE(1921), w
Judd Nelson
1984
  MAKING THE GRADE(1984)
Julia Nelson
  THREE MEN IN A BOAT(1958, Brit.); NEVER PUT IT IN WRITING(1964)
Kathleen Nelson
  GIRL WITH IDEAS, A(1937)
Kay Anne Nelson
  THERE'S A GIRL IN MY HEART(1949)
Kay Nelson
  SUNDAY DINNER FOR A SOLDIER(1944), cos; TAKE IT OR LEAVE IT(1944), cos; UP IN MABEL'S ROOM(1944), cos; DARK CORNER, THE(1946), cos; LEAVE HER TO HEAVEN(1946), cos; SENTIMENTAL JOURNEY(1946), cos; SOMEWHERE IN THE NIGHT(1946), cos; CALL NORTHSIDE 777(1948), cos; HOLLOW TRIUMPH(1948), cos; LETTER TO THREE WIVES, A(1948), cos; ROAD HOUSE(1948), cos; SITTING PRETTY(1948), cos; STREET WITH NO NAME, THE(1948), cos; WALLS OF JERICHO(1948), cos; FATHER WAS A FULLBACK(1949), cos; MOTHER IS A FRESHMAN(1949), cos; THIEVES' HIGHWAY(1949), cos; LION IS IN THE STREETS, A(1953), cos; WITNESS TO MURDER(1954), cos; VIOLENT SATURDAY(1955), cos; TALL STORY(1960), cos
Kenneth Nelson
  BOYS IN THE BAND, THE(1970); LONELY LADY, THE(1983)
Kristin Nelson
  WHAT AM I BID?(1967); STUDENT BODIES(1981), COS; BEACH GIRLS(1982), cos; MY TUTOR(1983), cos
Kristin Harmon Nelson
  LOVE AND KISSES(1965)
Lela Nelson
  PHANTOM FROM SPACE(1953)
Lindsay Nelson
  SEMI-TOUGH(1977)

Lloyd Nelson
  MAN BEAST(1956); INCREDIBLE PETRIFIED WORLD, THE(1959); CURSE OF THE STONE HAND(1965, Mex/Chile); WILD WORLD OF BATWOMAN, THE(1966); HOUSE ON SKULL MOUNTAIN, THE(1974); HERBIE GOES TO MONTE CARLO(1977); ESCAPE FROM ALCATRAZ(1979); BRONCO BILLY(1980); HONKYTONK MAN(1982); SUDDEN IMPACT(1983)
1984
  TIGHTROPE(1984)
Misc. Talkies
  BULLET FOR BILLY THE KID(1963)
Lord Nelson
  80 STEPS TO JONAH(1969)
Lori Nelson
  BEND OF THE RIVER(1952); FRANCIS GOES TO WEST POINT(1952); MA AND PA KETTLE AT THE FAIR(1952); ALL-AMERICAN, THE(1953); ALL I DESIRE(1953); TUMBLEWEED(1953); WALKING MY BABY BACK HOME(1953); DESTRY(1954); I DIED A THOUSAND TIMES(1955); MA AND PA KETTLE AT WAIKIKI(1955); REVENGE OF THE CREATURE(1955); SINCERELY YOURS(1955); UNDERWATER!(1955); DAY THE WORLD ENDED, THE(1956); HOT ROD GIRL(1956); MOHAWK(1956); PARDNERS(1956); OUTLAW'S SON(1957); UNTAMED YOUTH(1957)
Lou Nelson
  FAT SPY(1966); DETECTIVE, THE(1968)
Louise Nelson
  NOTHING BUT THE NIGHT(1975, Brit.)
MacArthur Nelson
  CONRACK(1974)
Margaret Nelson
  PICNIC AT HANGING ROCK(1975, Aus.)
Misc. Talkies
  SCALP MERCHANT, THE(1977)
Margery Nelson
  TRUE CONFESSIONS(1981)
Margie Nelson
  PEPE(1960); SILENCERS, THE(1966); MAN CALLED DAGGER, A(1967)
Margot Nelson
  HOW SWEET IT IS(1968)
Mario Nelson
  HAIR(1979)
Marjori Nelson
Silents
  SEVEN SISTERS, THE(1915)
Marjorie Nelson
  SLENDER THREAD, THE(1965)
Mark Nelson
  FRIDAY THE 13TH(1980)
Mervin Nelson
  BOYS FROM BRAZIL, THE(1978)
Mervyn Nelson
  SOME OF MY BEST FRIENDS ARE...(1971), d&w; WHO SAYS I CAN'T RIDE A RAINBOW!(1971); EDUCATION OF SONNY CARSON, THE(1974)
1984
  GARBO TALKS(1984)
Misc. Talkies
  FUN AND GAMES(1973), d
Mimi Nelson
  PORT OF CALL(1963, Swed.); DOLL, THE(1964, Swed.)
Mique Nelson
  SNOW WHITE AND THE SEVEN DWARFS(1937), anim; MAKE MINE MUSIC(1946), cons
Miriam Nelson
  PICNIC(1955), ch; HE LAUGHED LAST(1956), ch; PUBLIC PIGEON NO. 1(1957), ch; HIGH TIME(1960), ch; VISIT TO A SMALL PLANET(1960), ch; GOOD NEIGHBOR SAM(1964), ch; HONEYMOON HOTEL(1964), ch; I'D RATHER BE RICH(1964), ch; CAT BALLOU(1965), ch; I'LL TAKE SWEDEN(1965), ch; MURDERERS' ROW(1966), ch; BOB AND CAROL AND TED AND ALICE(1969), ch; CACTUS FLOWER(1969), ch; GREAT BANK ROBBERY, THE(1969), ch; BUCK ROGERS IN THE 25TH CENTURY(1979), ch
Nancy Ann Nelson
  AIRPORT(1970)
Nancy Nelson
Misc. Talkies
  JUST BE THERE(1977)
Nels Nelson
  COURT JESTER, THE(1956)
Norbert Nelson
  CURIOUS DR. HUMPP(1967, Arg.)
Norma Jean Nelson
  ALOMA OF THE SOUTH SEAS(1941)
Norma Nelson
  NORTHWEST MOUNTED POLICE(1940); SEVENTEEN(1940); TYPHOON(1940); WAY OF ALL FLESH, THE(1940)
Norman Nelson
  GROUND ZERO(1973)
Novella Nelson
  UNMARRIED WOMAN, AN(1978); SEDUCTION OF JOE TYNAN, THE(1979)
1984
  COTTON CLUB, THE(1984); FLAMINGO KID, THE(1984)
O.A. Nelson
Silents
  AS A WOMAN SOWS(1916), w
Oliver Nelson
  DEATH OF A GUNFIGHTER(1969), m; SKULLDUGGERY(1970), m; ZIGZAG(1970), m
Oscar Nelson
  CURUCU, BEAST OF THE AMAZON(1956), cos
Otto Nelson
Silents
  KNIGHT OF THE WEST, A(1921)

Misc. Silents
THOROBRED(1922)
Ozzie Nelson
SWEETHEART OF THE CAMPUS(1941); STRICTLY IN THE GROOVE(1942); PEO-PLE ARE FUNNY(1945); HERE COME THE NELSONS(1952), a, w; LOVE AND KISSES(1965), p,d&w, w; IMPOSSIBLE YEARS, THE(1968)
Paul Nelson
WHAT A WIDOW(1930), art d
Peggy Nelson
Misc. Talkies
SCORCHING FURY(1952)
Peter Nelson
PURPLE HAZE(1982); SMORGASBORD(1983), p
1984
LAST STARFIGHTER, THE(1984)
Portia Nelson
SOUND OF MUSIC, THE(1965); TROUBLE WITH ANGELS, THE(1966); DOCTOR DOLITTLE(1967); OTHER, THE(1972); CAN'T STOP THE MUSIC(1980)
Ralph Nelson
REQUIEM FOR A HEAVYWEIGHT(1962), d; LILIES OF THE FIELD(1963), a, p&d; SOLDIER IN THE RAIN(1963), d; FATE IS THE HUNTER(1964), d; FATHER GOO-SE(1964), d; ONCE A THIEF(1965), d; DUEL AT DIABLO(1966), p, d; COUNTER-POINT(1967), a, d; CHARLY(1968), p&d; SOLDIER BLUE(1970), a, d; ...TICK...TICK...TICK...(1970), p, d; FLIGHT OF THE DOVES(1971), p&d, w; WRATH OF GOD, THE(1972), a, p,d&w; WILBY CONSPIRACY, THE(1975, Brit.), d; EM-BRYO(1976), d; HERO AIN'T NOTHIN' BUT A SANDWICH, A(1977), d
Rhys Nelson
PIRATES OF PENZANCE, THE(1983)
Richard Nelson
FIEND(; FOOL AND THE PRINCESS, THE(1948, Brit.); NO ORCHIDS FOR MISS BLANDISH(1948, Brit.); PIGEON THAT TOOK ROME, THE(1962); AMAZING GRA-CE(1974), set d
Misc. Talkies
TERROR FROM THE UNKNOWN(1983)
Rick Nelson
LOVE AND KISSES(1965); DUSTY AND SWEETS McGEE(1971), m
Ricky Nelson
HERE COME THE NELSONS(1952); STORY OF THREE LOVES, THE(1953); RIO BRAVO(1959); WACKIEST SHIP IN THE ARMY, THE(1961)
Robert Nelson
MA AND PA KETTLE AT HOME(1954); FIRE DOWN BELOW(1957, U.S./Brit.); ROSEMARY'S BABY(1968), set d
Rudolf Nelson
DOLLY GETS AHEAD(1931, Ger.), m
Rudy Nelson
WAY OUT(1966), w
Ruth Nelson
NORTH STAR, THE(1943); EVE OF ST. MARK, THE(1944); KEYS OF THE KING-DOM, THE(1944); NONE SHALL ESCAPE(1944); WILSON(1944); GIRL OF THE LIMBERLOST, THE(1945); TREE GROWS IN BROOKLYN, A(1945); HUMORE-SQUE(1946); SENTIMENTAL JOURNEY(1946); TILL THE END OF TIME(1946); MOTHER WORE TIGHTS(1947); SEA OF GRASS, THE(1947); ARCH OF TRI-UMPH(1948); LATE SHOW, THE(1977); THREE WOMEN(1977); WEDDING, A(1978)
Sam Nelson
CIRCUS KID, THE(1928); RIO RITA(1929); SOLDIERS AND WOMEN(1930); MEN-ACE, THE(1932), p; CATTLE RAIDERS(1938), d; COLORADO TRAIL(1938), d; LAW OF THE PLAINS(1938), d; OUTLAWS OF THE PRAIRIE(1938), d; SOUTH OF ARIZO-NA(1938), d; WEST OF CHEYENNE(1938), d; WEST OF SANTA FE(1938), d; KONGA, THE WILD STALLION(1939), d; MAN FROM SUNDOWN, THE(1939), d; NORTH OF THE YUKON(1939), d; PARENTS ON TRIAL(1939), d; RIO GRANDE(1939), d; TEXAS STAMPEDE(1939), d; THUNDERING WEST, THE(1939), d; BULLETS FOR RUS-TLERS(1940), d; PIONEERS OF THE FRONTIER(1940), d; PRAIRIE SCHOO-NERS(1940), d; STRANGER FROM TEXAS, THE(1940), d; OUTLAWS OF THE PANHANDLE(1941), d; AVENGING RIDER, THE(1943), d; SAGEBRUSH LAW(1943), d; LADY FROM SHANGHAI, THE(1948)
Silents
BOY RIDER, THE(1927); BANTAM COWBOY, THE(1928); FANGS OF THE WILD(1928); LITTLE SAVAGE, THE(1929); ONE MAN DOG, THE(1929)
Misc. Silents
BREED OF COURAGE(1927); SWIFT SHADOW, THE(1927); CROOKS CAN'T WIN(1928); LAW OF FEAR(1928); TRACKED(1928); VAGABOND CUB, THE(1929)
Sandy Nelson
WILD ON THE BEACH(1965)
Shawn Nelson
PIRANHA(1978); YOUNG GIANTS(1983)
Sheila Nelson
MOULIN ROUGE(1952)
Shirley Nelson
WAY OUT(1966), w
Sidney Nelson
FINAL APPOINTMENT(1954, Brit.), w; STOLEN ASSIGNMENT(1955, Brit.), w; DIPLOMATIC CORPSE, THE(1958, Brit.), w; DEAD LUCKY(1960, Brit.), w
Skip Nelson
FEVER HEAT(1968)
Stan Nelson
THIN RED LINE, THE(1964)
Stella Nelson
INDISCRETIONS OF EVE(1932, Brit.)
Steve Nelson
CLONUS HORROR, THE(1979), art d
Stewart Nelson
Silents
SHORE LEAVE(1925), ph
Terry Nelson
SOUNDER, PART 2(1976), p; MISSING(1982)
Tim Nelson
ESCAPE TO BURMA(1955)

Tracy Nelson
YOURS, MINE AND OURS(1968)
Vicky Nelson
MY BODYGUARD(1980)
Willie Nelson
ELECTRIC HORSEMAN, THE(1979); HONEYSUCKLE ROSE(1980), a, m; THIEF(1981); BARBAROSA(1982)
1984
SONGWRITER(1984)
Winifred Nelson
Silents
SILENT EVIDENCE(1922, Brit.)
Anthony Nelson-Keys
DRACULA–PRINCE OF DARKNESS(1966, Brit.), p
Anthony Nelson-Keys
FIVE MILLION YEARS TO EARTH(1968, Brit.), p; NOTHING BUT THE NIGHT(1975, Brit.), p
Howard Nelson-Rubien
LEOPARD, THE(1963, Ital.)
Eva-Lisa Nelstedt
LE VIOL(1968, Fr./Swed.), cos
Malcolm Nelthorpe
RABID(1976, Can.); AGENCY(1981, Can.); GAS(1981, Can.); TULIPS(1981, Can)
Sophie Nelville
Misc. Talkies
COPTER KIDS, THE(1976, Brit.)
Nop Nem
DRAGON SKY(1964, Fr.)
E. Nemchenko
GREAT CITIZEN, THE(1939, USSR)
Jan Nemec
DIAMONDS OF THE NIGHT(1968, Czech.), d, w; MARTYRS OF LOVE(1968, Czech.), p&d, w; REPORT ON THE PARTY AND THE GUESTS, A(1968, Czech.), d, w
Jiri Nemec
REPORT ON THE PARTY AND THE GUESTS, A(1968, Czech.)
Jan Nemecek
WHO KILLED JESSIE?(1965, Czech.), ph; MURDER CZECH STYLE(1968, Czech.), ph
Jiri Nemecek
TRANSPORT FROM PARADISE(1967, Czech.)
Boris Nemechek
CLEAR SKIES(1963, USSR), art d; FORTY-NINE DAYS(1964, USSR), art d; THERE WAS AN OLD COUPLE(1967, USSR), art d; UNCOMMON THIEF, AN(1967, USSR), art d
Frantisek Nemec
TRANSPORT FROM PARADISE(1967, Czech.)
Howard Nemerov
TALL STORY(1960), w
Scott Nemes
D.C. CAB(1983); TWILIGHT ZONE–THE MOVIE(1983)
1984
MEATBALLS PART II(1984)
Marina Nemet
EVENT, AN(1970, Yugo.)
Istvan Nemeth
WITNESS, THE(1982, Hung.)
Stephen Nemeth
1984
ICEMAN(1984)
Ted Nemeth, Jr.
FINNEGANS WAKE(1965), w, ph
William L. Nemeth
JIGSAW(1949), spec eff
Attila Nemethy
BOYS OF PAUL STREET, THE(1969, Hung./US)
Ferenc Nemethy
FORBIDDEN RELATIONS(1983, Hung.)
Max Nemetz
Silents
NOSFERATU, THE VAMPIRE(1922, Ger.)
Roger Nemier
FRANTIC(1961, Fr.), w
Irene Nemirovsky
DAVID GOLDER(1932, Fr.), d&w
Irene Nemirowsky
OPERATION X(1951, Brit.), w
Michael Nemirsky
SPACEHUNTER: ADVENTURES IN THE FORBIDDEN ZONE(1983), art d
Henry Nemo
SONG OF THE THIN MAN(1947)
Konstantin Nemolyayev
GORDEYEV FAMILY, THE(1961, U.S.S.R.); HUNTING IN SIBERIA(1962, USSR); MAGIC WEAVER, THE(1965, USSR)
Hiroshi Nemoto
Misc. Silents
CRAZY PAGE, A(1926, Jap.)
Yoshiyuki Nemoto
EAST CHINA SEA(1969, Jap.)
Jean Nemours
LEGEND OF FRENCHIE KING, THE(1971, Fr./Ital./Span./Brit.), w
Maury Nemoy
LOVE MACHINE, THE,(1971), titles
Djordje Nenedovic
FRONTIER HELLCAT(1966, Fr./Ital./Ger./Yugo.)
Helmut Nentwig
JOURNEY TO THE LOST CITY(1960, Ger./Fr./Ital.), art d; TERROR OF DR. MABUSE, THE(1965, Ger.), art d; ONLY A WOMAN(1966, Ger.), art d

Chiitra Neogy
PREMONITION, THE(1976)
Chitra Neogy
TO SIR, WITH LOVE(1967, Brit.)
Debi Neogy
TWO DAUGHTERS(1963, India)
Princess Neola
LAND OF THE SILVER FOX(1928)
Silents
RED, RED HEART, THE(1918); BARRIER, THE(1926)
Lin Neong
Misc. Silents
WAR OF THE TONGS, THE(1917)
Nikis Neoyennis
ISLAND OF LOVE(1963)
Neil Nephew
MAD DOG COLL(1961); YOUNG SAVAGES, THE(1961); PANIC IN YEAR ZE-RO!(1962)
Res Paul Nephtali
SNOW(1983, Fr.)
Luis Nepomuceno
IGOROTA, THE LEGEND OF THE TREE OF LIFE(1970, Phil.), p,d&w
Lucien Nepoty
WOMAN FROM MONTE CARLO, THE(1932), w; SACRIFICE OF HONOR(1938, Fr.), w
Vincent Neptune
JOAN OF ARC(1948); RAWHIDE(1951)
Stepan Nercessian
XICA(1982, Braz.)
Ka Nerell
ONLY ONE NIGHT(1942, Swed.)
Bella Neri
SHADOWS GROW LONGER, THE(1962, Switz./Ger.)
Fabio Neri
WHITE LINE, THE(1952, Ital.)
Giulio Neri
RIGOLETTO(1949)
Monica Neri
HERCULES IN THE HAUNTED WORLD(1964, Ital.)
Rosalba Neri
ESTHER AND THE KING(1960, U.S./Ital.); RED SHEIK, THE(1963, Ital.); ARIZONA COLT(1965, It./Fr./Span.); CONQUEST OF MYCENE(1965, Ital., Fr.); WHITE VOI-CES(1965, Fr./Ital.); JOHNNY YUMA(1967, Ital.); CASTLE OF FU MANCHU, THE(1968, Ger./Span./Ital./Brit.); NO ROSES FOR OSS 117(1968, Fr.); LONG RIDE FROM HELL, A(1970, Ital.); THIS MAN CAN'T DIE(1970, Ital.); SLAUGHTER HOTEL(1971, Ital.); DRUMMER OF VENGEANCE(1974, Brit.); MANIAC MAN-SION(1978, Ital.)
Tommaso Neri
BATTLE OF ALGIERS, THE(1967, Ital./Alger.)
Mark Nerin
RUNNERS(1983, Brit.), art d
Efrain Lopez Neris
UP THE SANDBOX(1972)
Curtis Nero
KONGO(1932); SUNDOWN(1941)
Silents
WEST OF ZANZIBAR(1928)
Franco Nero
AVENGER, THE(1966, Ital.); BIBLE...IN THE BEGINNING, THE(1966); DJAN-GO(1966 Ital./Span.); TRAMPLERS, THE(1966, Ital.); CAMELOT(1967); HIRED KILL-ER, THE(1967, Fr./Ital.); WILD, WILD PLANET, THE(1967, Ital.); BRUTE AND THE BEAST, THE(1968, Ital.); DAY OF THE OWL, THE(1968, Ital./Fr.); SARDINIA: RANSOM(1968, Ital.); COMPANEROS(1970 Ital./Span./Ger.); DETECTIVE BELLI(1970, Ital.); MERCENARY, THE(1970, Ital./Span.); QUIET PLACE IN THE COUNTRY, A(1970, Ital./Fr.); TRISTANA(1970, Span./Ital./Fr.); VIRGIN AND THE GYPSY, THE(1970, Brit.); BATTLE OF THE NERETVA(1971, Yugo./Ital./Ger.); CONFESSIONS OF A POLICE CAPTAIN(1971, Ital.); VACATION, THE(1971, Ital.); POPE JOAN(1972, Brit.); DEAF SMITH AND JOHNNY EARS(1973, Ital.); DON'T TURN THE OTHER CHEEK(1974, Ital./Ger./Span.); LAST DAYS OF MUS-SOLINI(1974, Ital.); REDNECK(1975, Ital./Span.); FORCE 10 FROM NAVARONE(1978, Brit.); MAN WITH BOGART'S FACE, THE(1980); ENTER THE NINJA(1982); MEXICO IN FLAMES(1982, USSR/Mex./Ital.); KAMIKAZE '89(1983, Ger.); QUERELLE(1983, Ger./Fr.); SALAMANDER, THE(1983, U.S./Ital./Brit.); WAGNER(1983, Brit./Hung./Aust.)
Misc. Talkies
ANONYMOUS AVENGER, THE(1976, Ital.); AQUARIAN, THE(1972); EVIL FIN-GERS(1975); STREET LAW(1981)
Peter Nero
SUNDAY IN NEW YORK(1963), a, m
Toni Nero
1984
SILENT NIGHT, DEADLY NIGHT(1984)
Natalie Nerval
SPUTNIK(1960, Fr.)
Nathalie Nerval
LAW IS THE LAW, THE(1959, Fr.); SERPENT, THE(1973, Fr./Ital./Ger.)
Rick Nervick
CRY BLOOD, APACHE(1970)
Conrad A. Nervig
WIND, THE(1928), ed; DEVIL MAY CARE(1929), ed; IDLE RICH, THE(1929), ed; LADY TO LOVE, A(1930), ed; PASSION FLOWER(1930), ed; GUARDSMAN, THE(1931), ed; INSPIRATION(1931), ed; PRIVATE LIVES(1931), ed; SON OF IN-DIA(1931), ed; DOWNSTAIRS(1932), ed; KONGO(1932), ed; LETTY LYNTON(1932), ed; PARIS INTERLUDE(1934), ed; CASINO MURDER CASE, THE(1935), ed; MUR-DER IN THE FLEET(1935), ed; NIGHT IS YOUNG, THE(1935), ed; TALE OF TWO CITIES, A(1935), ed; ABSOLUTE QUIET(1936), ed; EXCLUSIVE STORY(1936), ed; HIS BROTHER'S WIFE(1936), ed; BEG, BORROW OR STEAL(1937), ed; EMPEROR'S CANDLESTICKS, THE(1937), ed; LIVE, LOVE AND LEARN(1937), ed; MAYTI-ME(1937), ed; FIRST 100 YEARS, THE(1938), ed; LOVE IS A HEADACHE(1938), ed; SPRING MADNESS(1938), ed; HENRY GOES ARIZONA(1939), ed; HONOLU-LU(1939), ed; SERGEANT MADDEN(1939), ed; 6000 ENEMIES(1939), ed; AND ONE WAS BEAUTIFUL(1940), ed; GOLDEN FLEECING, THE(1940), ed; HUL-LABALOO(1940), ed; MAN FROM DAKOTA, THE(1940), ed; NORTHWEST PAS-SAGE(1940), ed; PHANTOM RAIDERS(1940), ed; BIG STORE, THE(1941), ed; DR. KILDARE'S WEDDING DAY(1941), ed; KATHLEEN(1941), ed; GRAND CENTRAL MURDER(1942), ed; I MARRIED AN ANGEL(1942), ed; OMAHA TRAIL, THE(1942), ed; HUMAN COMEDY, THE(1943), ed; AMERICAN ROMANCE, THE(1944), ed; NOTH-ING BUT TROUBLE(1944), ed; BLUE SIERRA(1946), ed; NO LEAVE, NO LOVE(1946), ed; HIGH BARBAREE(1947), ed; HIGH WALL, THE(1947), ed; ACT OF VIOLEN-CE(1949), ed; BORDER INCIDENT(1949), ed; DEVIL'S DOORWAY(1950), ed; KING SOLOMON'S MINES(1950), ed, art d; SIDE STREET(1950), ed; TOO YOUNG TO KISS(1951), ed; VENGEANCE VALLEY(1951), ed; BAD AND THE BEAUTIFUL, THE(1952), ed; MERRY WIDOW, THE(1952), ed; AFFAIRS OF DOBIE GILLIS, THE(1953), ed; CRY OF THE HUNTED(1953), ed; GYPSY COLT(1954), ed
Silents
FAIR CO-ED, THE(1927), ed; ACTRESS, THE(1928), ed; DIVINE WOMAN, THE(1928), ed; WILD ORCHIDS(1929), ed
Conrad Nervig
WOMEN IN HIS LIFE, THE(1934), ed; WOMEN ARE TROUBLE(1936), ed; BAD MAN, THE(1941), ed; COURAGE OF LASSIE(1946), ed; DEATH OF A SCOUN-DREL(1956), ed
Conrad V. Nervig
LAST OF MRS. CHEYNEY, THE(1929), ed
Sandy Nervig
BEES, THE(1978), ed; DEMONOID(1981), ed
Jimmy Nervo
IT'S IN THE BAG(1936, Brit.); SKYLARKS(1936, Brit.); OKAY FOR SOUND(1937, Brit.), a, w; ALF'S BUTTON AFLOAT(1938, Brit.); GASBAGS(1940, Brit.); LIFE IS A CIRCUS(1962, Brit.)
Gerard Nery
FIGHTING PIMPERNEL, THE(1950, Brit.)
Gilda Nery
LOVE SLAVES OF THE AMAZONS(1957)
Jean Nery
TOO MANY CROOKS(1959, Brit.), w
Jurgen Nesbach
FANNY HILL: MEMOIRS OF A WOMAN OF PLEASURE zero(1965)
Stuart Nesbet
Misc. Talkies
TO DIE IN PARIS(1968)
E. Nesbit
RAILWAY CHILDREN, THE(1971, Brit.), d&w
Evelyn Nesbit
Silents
I WANT TO FORGET(1918)
Misc. Silents
REDEMPTION(1917); WOMAN WHO GAVE, THE(1918); FALLEN IDOL, A(1919); MY LITTLE SISTER(1919); THOU SHALT NOT(1919); WOMAN! WOMAN!(1919); HIDDEN WOMAN, THE(1922)
Lee Nesbit
1984
AMERICAN TABOO(1984), ph
Margo Nesbit
Misc. Talkies
UPS AND DOWNS(1981)
McLean Nesbit
HEAVENLY BODY, THE(1943), set d
Pinna Nesbit
Silents
FALSE FRIEND, THE(1917); PARTNERS OF THE NIGHT(1920)
Misc. Silents
LITTLE DUCHESS, THE(1917); STOLEN PARADISE, THE(1917); BROKEN TIES(1918); LET'S GET A DIVORCE(1918); MERELY PLAYERS(1918)
Carmen Nesbitt
GENTLEMEN MARRY BRUNETTES(1955)
Cathleen Nesbitt
CANARIES SOMETIMES SING(1930, Brit.); CRIMINAL AT LARGE(1932, Brit.); HEARTS OF HUMANITY(1936, Brit.); PASSING OF THE THIRD FLOOR BACK, THE(1936, Brit.); TROUBLE AHEAD(1936, Brit.); WELL DONE, HENRY(1936, Brit.); AGAINST THE TIDE(1937, Brit.); KNIGHTS FOR A DAY(1937, Brit.); LITTLE DOLLY DAYDREAM(1938, Brit.); PYGMALION(1938, Brit.); CHAMBER OF HORRORS(1941, Brit.); LAMP STILL BURNS, THE(1943, Brit.); CAESAR AND CLEOPATRA(1946, Brit.); NICHOLAS NICKLEBY(1947, Brit.); JASSY(1948, Brit.); MAN OF EVIL(1948, Brit.); AGITATOR, THE(1949); MADNESS OF THE HEART(1949, Brit.); SO LONG AT THE FAIR(1951, Brit.); KISENGA, MAN OF AFRICA(1952, Brit.); BLACK WI-DOW(1954); DESIREE(1954); THREE COINS IN THE FOUNTAIN(1954); AFFAIR TO REMEMBER, AN(1957); SEPARATE TABLES(1958); PARENT TRAP, THE(1961); PROMISE HER ANYTHING(1966, Brit.); STAIRCASE(1969 U.S./Brit./Fr.); TRYGON FACTOR, THE(1969, Brit.); VILLAIN(1971, Brit.); FRENCH CONNECTION 11(1975); FAMILY PLOT(1976); FULL CIRCLE(1977, Brit./Can.); JULIA(1977); HAUNTING OF JULIA, THE(1981, Brit./Can.); NEVER NEVER LAND(1982)
Misc. Silents
FAITHFUL HEART, THE(1922, Brit.)
Darren Nesbitt
AMOROUS ADVENTURES OF MOLL FLANDERS, THE(1965); NAKED RUNNER, THE(1967, Brit.)
Derren Nesbitt
SILENT ENEMY, THE(1959, Brit.); IN THE NICK(1960, Brit.); MAN IN THE BACK SEAT, THE(1961, Brit.); SWORD OF SHERWOOD FOREST(1961, Brit.); VICTIM(1961, Brit.); KILL OR CURE(1962, Brit.); STRONGROOM(1962, Brit.); MATTER OF CHOICE, A(1963, Brit.), w; LIFE IN DANGER(1964, Brit.); UNDERWORLD INFORMERS(1965, Brit.); BLUE MAX, THE(1966); OPERATION THIRD FORM(1966, Brit.); HIGH COM-MISSIONER, THE(1968, U.S./Brit.); WHERE EAGLES DARE(1968, Brit.); THOSE DARING YOUNG MEN IN THEIR JAUNTY JALOPIES(1969, Fr./Brit./ Ital.); BURKE AND HARE(1972, Brit.); INNOCENT BYSTANDERS(1973, Brit.); NOT NOW DAR-LING(1975, Brit.); GET CHARLIE TULLY(1976, Brit.); FUNNY MONEY(1983, Brit.); GUNS AND THE FURY, THE(1983)

Derrin Nesbitt
Misc. Talkies
SAINT AND THE BRAVE GOOSE, THE(1981, Brit.)
Derry [Derren] Nesbitt
ROOM AT THE TOP(1959, Brit.)
E. Nesbitt
Silents
ORDEAL, THE(1914), w
Frank Nesbitt
WALK A TIGHTROPE(1964, U.S./Brit.), d; DULCIMA(1971, Brit.), d&w
Harry Nesbitt
OLD SOLDIERS NEVER DIE(1931, Brit.)
John Nesbitt
KENTUCKY(1938); SULLIVANS, THE(1944)
Kathleen Nesbitt
BELOVED VAGABOND, THE(1936, Brit.)
Max Nesbitt
OLD SOLDIERS NEVER DIE(1931, Brit.)
Miriam Nesbitt
Silents
INFIDELITY(1917)
Misc. Silents
SALLY CASTLETON, SOUTHERNER(1915); WAY BACK, THE(1915); CATSPAW, THE(1916); BUILDERS OF CASTLES(1917); LAST SENTENCE, THE(1917)
Norman Nesbitt
MAN FROM FRISCO(1944); OUT OF THIS WORLD(1945); WOMAN'S SECRET, A(1949)
Paul Nesbitt
TAMMY AND THE DOCTOR(1963)
Robert Nesbitt
LET'S MAKE UP(1955, Brit.), w
Sally Nesbitt
GORGON, THE(1964, Brit.); SICILIAN CLAN, THE(1970, Fr.); CLASS OF MISS MAC MICHAEL, THE(1978, Brit./U.S.); HOPSCOTCH(1980)
Tom Nesbitt
Silents
LAST WITNESS, THE(1925, Brit.)
Vicki Nesbitt
Misc. Talkies
HANGING WOMAN, THE(1976)
John Neschling
PIXOTE(1981, Braz.), m
Avi Nesher
Misc. Talkies
SHE(1983), d
Doron Nesher
1984
LITTLE DRUMMER GIRL, THE(1984)
Lloyd Nesler
MOULIN ROUGE(1934), ed
Michael Nesmith
HEAD(1968); TIMERIDER(1983), w, m
Ottola Nesmith
BECKY SHARP(1935); FEATHER IN HER HAT, A(1935); SHE GETS HER MAN(1935); NOBODY'S BABY(1937); FOOLS FOR SCANDAL(1938); STAR MAKER, THE(1939); TELEVISION SPY(1939); HER FIRST ROMANCE(1940); LETTER, THE(1940); LILLIAN RUSSELL(1940); DEADLY GAME, THE(1941); H.M. PULHAM, ESQ.(1941); INTERNATIONAL SQUADRON(1941); THERE'S MAGIC IN MUSIC(1941); WOLF MAN, THE(1941); GREAT MAN'S LADY, THE(1942); JOURNEY FOR MARGARET(1942); MRS. MINIVER(1942); WE WERE DANCING(1942); LEOPARD MAN, THE(1943); SEVENTH VICTIM, THE(1943); CASANOVA BROWN(1944); OUR HEARTS WERE YOUNG AND GAY(1944); PRACTICALLY YOURS(1944); RETURN OF THE VAMPIRE, THE(1944); STORY OF DR. WASSELL, THE(1944); UNINVITED, THE(1944); LOVE LETTERS(1945); MINISTRY OF FEAR(1945); MOLLY AND ME(1945); MY NAME IS JULIA ROSS(1945); CLUNY BROWN(1946); DOWN TO EARTH(1947); FOREVER AMBER(1947); LATE GEORGE APLEY, THE(1947); UNCONQUERED(1947); JULIA MISBEHAVES(1948); CHICAGO DEADLINE(1949); FILE ON THELMA JORDAN, THE(1950); SUNSET BOULEVARD(1950); SON OF DR. JEKYLL, THE(1951); GREATEST SHOW ON EARTH, THE(1952); SCARAMOUCHE(1952); MAN CRAZY(1953); STORY OF THREE LOVES, THE(1953); SOMETHING OF VALUE(1957); WITNESS FOR THE PROSECUTION(1957); FROM THE TERRACE(1960); NOTORIOUS LANDLADY, THE(1962); INSIDE DAISY CLOVER(1965)
Silents
STILL WATERS(1915); BEYOND PRICE(1921); WIFE AGAINST WIFE(1921)
Tola Nesmith
WINGS IN THE DARK(1935); THREE MEN ON A HORSE(1936)
Joe Nesnow
1984
ROMANCING THE STONE(1984); THIEF OF HEARTS(1984)
Al Nesor
LI'L ABNER(1959); SANTA CLAUS CONQUERS THE MARTIANS zero(1964); NO WAY TO TREAT A LADY(1968)
1984
HARRY AND SON(1984)
Ed Ness
LITTLE MISS MARKER(1980)
Eddie Ness
ROBIN AND THE SEVEN HOODS(1964); ROSIE!(1967); DID YOU HEAR THE ONE ABOUT THE TRAVELING SALESLADY?(1968)
Edward Ness
OUTFIT, THE(1973)
Eliot Ness
SCARFACE MOB, THE(1962), w
Helen Ness
NORTHERN LIGHTS(1978)
Jon Ness
NORTHERN LIGHTS(1978)

Mark Ness
VICE SQUAD(1982)
Ole M. Ness
JAZZ HEAVEN(1929)
Silents
CHICAGO AFTER MIDNIGHT(1928); SKINNER'S BIG IDEA(1928); HARD-BOILED(1929)
Pamela Ness
1984
NINJA III-THE DOMINATION(1984)
Ray Ness
NORTHERN LIGHTS(1978)
Ula Ness
MAIDSTONE(1970)
Bruno Nessi
INVASION 1700(1965, Fr./Ital./Yugo.)
Al Nessor
ANDY(1965); HOW TO SUCCEED IN BUSINESS WITHOUT REALLY TRYING(1976); HOT STUFF(1979)
Bill Nestel
Misc. Silents
CHEYENNE TRAILS(1928); TEXAS FLASH(1928); THRILL CHASER, THE(1928); MAN FROM NOWHERE, THE(1930)
Bill Nestell
FIGHTING THRU(1931); DEADWOOD PASS(1933); ROBBERS' ROOST(1933); BOSS OF BULLION CITY(1941); BUCKSKIN FRONTIER(1943); NORTH STAR, THE(1943)
Bob Nestell
KID GALAHAD(1937)
William Nestell
NIGHT RIDERS, THE(1939); JOAN OF OZARK(1942); SOMBRERO KID, THE(1942); STAGECOACH BUCKAROO(1942); STARDUST ON THE SAGE(1942); WAGON TRACKS WEST(1943); FALCON OUT WEST, THE(1944); MAN FROM FRISCO(1944)
Bill Nestelle
FIGHTING LEGION, THE(1930)
E. Nesterov
ROAD TO LIFE(1932, USSR), m
M. Nesterova
Misc. Silents
CRIME AND PUNISHMENT(1913, USSR)
G. Nesterovskaya
MOTHER AND DAUGHTER(1965, USSR), cos
Joel Nestler
MRS. MIKE(1949)
Peter Nestler
MAGIC FOUNTAIN, THE(1961)
Patti Nestor
LOVE ME OR LEAVE ME(1955)
John Nestor [Nestor Almendros]
GUN RUNNER(1969), ph
Nestor Amaral and his Orchestra
HOLIDAY FOR LOVERS(1959)
Nestor Amaral's Samba Band
PAN-AMERICANA(1945)
Marina Nestora
PROMISE AT DAWN(1970, U.S./Fr.)
Josef Nesvadba
LOST FACE, THE(1965, Czech.), w; DEATH OF TARZAN, THE(1968, Czech), w; I KILLED EINSTEIN, GENTLEMEN(1970, Czech.), w
Neta the Dog
THREE MEN IN A BOAT(1958, Brit.)
Robin Netcher
MY WAY(1974, South Africa), md
Louis Netheaux
MADAME SATAN(1930)
David Netheim
PIED PIPER, THE(1972, Brit.)
Bish Nethercote
Misc. Talkies
VOICE OVER(1983)
Geoffrey Nethercott
ACCIDENTAL DEATH(1963, Brit.), d; WHO WAS MADDOX?(1964, Brit.), d
Miriam Byrd Nethery
NICKELODEON(1976)
Alfredo Neto
VOYAGE OF SILENCE(1968, Fr.)
Joao Neto
VOYAGE OF SILENCE(1968, Fr.)
D. Netrebin
HUNTING IN SIBERIA(1962, USSR); OPTIMISTIC TRAGEDY, THE(1964, USSR); WAR AND PEACE(1968, USSR)
Robin Netscher
DRAGON OF PENDRAGON CASTLE, THE(1950, Brit.); NO ROOM AT THE INN(1950, Brit.); INHERITANCE, THE(1951, Brit.); WATERFRONT WOMEN(1952, Brit.)
Ben Nett
WITHOUT WARNING(1980), w
Einar Nettelbladt
RAVEN'S END(1970, Swed.), art d
Douglas Netter
MR. RICCO(1975), p
William Netter
BACKGROUND TO DANGER(1943)
David Nettheim
MAKE MINE A MILLION(1965, Brit.); MASQUERADE(1965, Brit.); PROMISE, THE(1969, Brit.)
Archibald Nettlefold
WOULD YOU BELIEVE IT!(1930, Brit.), p; YOU'D BE SURPRISED!(1930, Brit.), p; PRINCE OF ARCADIA(1933, Brit.), p

Silents
DAUGHTER IN REVOLT, A(1927, Brit.), p; VIRGINIA'S HUSBAND(1928, Brit.), p

F. J. Nettlefold
Silents
HUMAN DESIRES(1924, Brit.), p; AFRAID OF LOVE(1925, Brit.), p; EVERY MOTHER'S SON(1926, Brit.), p

Archibald Nettleford
LAST HOUR, THE(1930, Brit.), p
Silents
RED PEARLS(1930, Brit.), p

John Nettles
ONE MORE TIME(1970, Brit.); RED, WHITE AND BLACK, THE(1970)

John Nettleton
MAN FOR ALL SEASONS, A(1966, Brit.); LAST SHOT YOU HEAR, THE(1969, Brit.); AND SOON THE DARKNESS(1970, Brit.); BLACK BEAUTY(1971, Brit./Ger./Span.)

Lois Nettleton
PERIOD OF ADJUSTMENT(1962); COME FLY WITH ME(1963); MAIL ORDER BRIDE(1964); VALLEY OF MYSTERY(1967); BAMBOO SAUCER, THE(1968); GOOD GUYS AND THE BAD GUYS, THE(1969); DIRTY DINGUS MAGEE(1970); SIDELONG GLANCES OF A PIGEON KICKER, THE(1970); HONKERS, THE(1972); MAN IN THE GLASS BOOTH, THE(1975); ECHOES OF A SUMMER(1976); DEADLY BLESSING(1981); BEST LITTLE WHOREHOUSE IN TEXAS, THE(1982); BUTTERFLY(1982); SOGGY BOTTOM U.S.A.(1982)

Hadrian M. Netto
TESTAMENT OF DR. MABUSE, THE(1943, Ger.)

Hadrian Maria Netto
TRUNKS OF MR. O.F., THE(1932, Ger.)

Irena Netto
PARTINGS(1962, Pol.)

M. Netto
M(1933, Ger.)

Anton Netzer
END OF THE GAME(1976, Ger./Ital.)

Toni Netzle
LILI MARLEEN(1981, Ger.)

Howard Neu
PORKY'S II: THE NEXT DAY(1983)

Ernst Neubach
MY SONG GOES ROUND THE WORLD(1934, Brit.), w; STUDENT'S ROMANCE, THE(1936, Brit.), w

Gerd Neubart
POSSESSION(1981, Fr./Ger.)

Len Neubauer
SWEET SUZY(1973), w

Leonard Neubauer
FUGITIVE FROM JUSTICE, A(1940), w; LADY WANTS MINK, THE(1953), w; RUN FOR THE HILLS(1953), w; NEW YEAR'S EVIL(1980), w

Ernst Neubeck
VIENNA, CITY OF SONGS(1931, Ger.), w

Wolf Neuber
JOURNEY, THE(1959, U.S./Aust.)

A. Neuberg
TRICK BABY(1973), w

Harold Neuberger
CURTAIN RISES, THE(1939, Fr.), titles

Carl Neubert
MASK OF DIMITRIOS, THE(1944); THE CATMAN OF PARIS(1946)

Sonia Neudorfer
LOLA(1982, Ger.)

Sonja Neudorfer
MARRIAGE OF MARIA BRAUN, THE(1979, Ger.); VERONIKA VOSS(1982, Ger.)

Eugene Neufeld
Misc. Silents
RASPUTIN(1929, Ger.)

Mace Neufeld
FRISCO KID, THE(1979), p

Max Neufeld
TEMPTATION(1935, Brit.), d&w
Misc. Silents
PRINCE AND THE DANCER(1929, Ger.), d; RASPUTIN(1929, Ger.), a, d

Sam Neufeld
REFORM GIRL(1933), d; BIG TIME OR BUST(1934), d

Samuel Neufeld
AM I GUILTY?(1940), d

Sig Neufeld
HIS FIGHTING BLOOD(1935), p; ACES AND EIGHTS(1936), p; BORDER CABALLERO(1936), p; LION'S DEN, THE(1936), p; ROARIN' GUNS(1936), p; CRASHIN' THRU DANGER(1938), p

Sig Neufeld, Jr.
GOING HOME(1971), ed

Sigmund Neufeld
CODE OF THE MOUNTED(1935), p; TRAILS OF THE WILD(1935), p; GHOST PATROL(1936), p; LIGHTNING BILL CARSON(1936), p; TIMBER WAR(1936), p; TRAITOR, THE(1936), p; ARIZONA GANGBUSTERS(1940), p; BILLY THE KID IN TEXAS(1940), p; FRONTIER CRUSADER(1940), p; GUN CODE(1940), p; HOLD THAT WOMAN(1940), p; I TAKE THIS OATH(1940), p; INVISIBLE KILLER, THE(1940), p; MARKED MEN(1940), p; MERCY PLANE(1940), p; SAGEBRUSH FAMILY TRAILS WEST, THE(1940), p; BILLY THE KID IN SANTA FE(1941), p; BILLY THE KID WANTED(1941), p; BILLY THE KID'S FIGHTING PALS(1941), p; BILLY THE KID'S RANGE WAR(1941), p; BILLY THE KID'S ROUNDUP(1941), p; LONE RIDER AMBUSHED, THE(1941), p; LONE RIDER CROSSES THE RIO, THE(1941), p; LONE RIDER FIGHTS BACK, THE(1941), p; LONE RIDER IN GHOST TOWN, THE(1941), p; OUTLAWS OF THE RIO GRANDE(1941), p; RIDERS OF BLACK MOUNTAIN(1941), p; TEXAS MARSHAL, THE(1941), p; BILLY THE KID TRAPPED(1942), p; JUNGLE SIREN(1942), p; LAW AND ORDER(1942), p; LONE RIDER AND THE BANDIT, THE(1942), p; LONE RIDER IN CHEYENNE, THE(1942), p; MAD MONSTER, THE(1942), p; MYSTERIOUS RIDER, THE(1942), p; OVERLAND STAGECOACH(1942), p; PRAIRIE PALS(1942), p; RAIDERS OF THE WEST(1942), p; ROLLING DOWN THE GREAT DIVIDE(1942), p; TEXAS MAN HUNT(1942), p; BLACK RAVEN, THE(1943), p; CATTLE STAMPEDE(1943), p; DEAD MEN WALK(1943), p;

KID RIDES AGAIN, THE(1943), p; WESTERN CYCLONE(1943), p; WILD HORSE RUSTLERS(1943), p; WOLVES OF THE RANGE(1943), p; BLAZING FRONTIER(1944), p; DEATH RIDES THE PLAINS(1944), p; DEVIL RIDERS(1944), p; DRIFTER, THE(1944), p; FRONTIER OUTLAWS(1944), p; FUZZY SETTLES DOWN(1944), p; LAW OF THE SADDLE(1944), p; MONSTER MAKER, THE(1944), p; NABONGA(1944), p; RAIDERS OF RED GAP(1944), p; RUSTLER'S HIDEOUT(1944), p; SWING HOSTESS(1944), p; THUNDERING GUN SLINGERS(1944), p; VALLEY OF VENGEANCE(1944), p; WILD HORSE PHANTOM(1944), p; APOLOGY FOR MURDER(1945), p; BORDER BADMEN(1945), p; FIGHTING BILL CARSON(1945), p; HIS BROTHER'S GHOST(1945), p; KID SISTER, THE(1945), p; LIGHTNING RAIDERS(1945), p; SHADOWS OF DEATH(1945), p; STAGECOACH OUTLAWS(1945), p; WHITE PONGO(1945), p; BLONDE FOR A DAY(1946), p; FLYING SERPENT, THE(1946), p; GAS HOUSE KIDS(1946), p; GENTLEMEN WITH GUNS(1946), p; GHOST OF HIDDEN VALLEY(1946), p; LADY CHASER(1946), p; LARCENY IN HER HEART(1946), p; MURDER IS MY BUSINESS(1946), p; OUTLAW OF THE PLAINS(1946), p; OVERLAND RIDERS(1946), p; PRAIRIE BADMEN(1946), p; TERRORS ON HORSEBACK(1946), p; THREE ON A TICKET(1947), p; MIRACULOUS JOURNEY(1948), p; MONEY MADNESS(1948), p; STATE DEPARTMENT-FILE 649(1949), p; HI-JACKED(1950), p; WESTERN PACIFIC AGENT(1950), p; FINGERPRINTS DON'T LIE(1951), p; LEAVE IT TO THE MARINES(1951), p; LOST CONTINENT(1951), p; MASK OF THE DRAGON(1951), p; THREE DESPERATE MEN(1951), p; SKY HIGH(1952), p; SINS OF JEZEBEL(1953), p; FRONTIER GAMBLER(1956), p; LAST OF THE DESPERADOES(1956), p; THREE OUTLAWS, THE(1956), p; WILD DAKOTAS, THE(1956), p

Daniel Neufield
THE LADY DRACULA(1974), m

Sigmund Neufield
RED BLOOD OF COURAGE(1935), p; SHERIFF OF SAGE VALLEY(1942), p; PRAIRIE RUSTLERS(1945), p

Alfred Neugebauer
MONEY ON THE STREET(1930, Aust.); STORM IN A WATER GLASS(1931, Aust.); OPERETTA(1949, Ger.); STORY OF VICKIE, THE(1958, Aust.)

Lacey Neuhaus
RICH KIDS(1979); JUST TELL ME WHAT YOU WANT(1980)

Richard Neuhaus
ROMAN HOLIDAY(1953)

Rodolpho Neuhaus
MONTE CASSINO(1948, Ital.)

John E. Neukum, Jr.
ONE MAN JURY(1978)

Dorothy Neuman
CARNIVAL ROCK(1957); UNDEAD, THE(1957); GHOST OF DRAGSTRIP HOLLOW(1959)

E. Jack Neuman
VENETIAN AFFAIR, THE(1967), p, w; COMPANY OF KILLERS(1970), p, w

Edna Neuman
STARK FEAR(1963)

Harry Neuman
FILE 113(1932), ph; GIRL FROM CALGARY(1932), ph; HOOSIER SCHOOLMASTER(1935), ph; DOWN TO THE SEA(1936), ph; WILD BRIAN KENT(1936), ph; I KILLED THAT MAN(1942), ph; ROAD TO HAPPINESS(1942), ph; HIGHWAYMAN, THE(1951), ph
Silents
BULLDOG COURAGE(1922), ph; BACK TRAIL, THE(1924), ph

Joan Neuman
STARDUST MEMORIES(1980)

Kurt Neuman
BIG CAGE, THE(1933), d; ALL WOMEN HAVE SECRETS(1939), d

Liese Neuman
KARAMAZOV(1931, Ger.)

Robert Neuman
Misc. Talkies
SUNDANCE CASSIDY AND BUTCH THE KID(1975)

Ruth Neuman
BASKET CASE(1982)

Sam Neuman
CAREER GIRL(1944), w; MACHINE GUN MAMA(1944), w; DIXIE JAMBOREE(1945), w; DOWN MISSOURI WAY(1946), w; FEDERAL MAN(1950), w; I KILLED GERONIMO(1950), w; HOODLUM, THE(1951), w; HITLER(1962), w

Thomas Neuman
IN THE COUNTRY(1967)

Alfred Neumann
PATRIOT, THE(1928), w; RASPUTIN(1939, Fr.), w; NONE SHALL ESCAPE(1944), w; CONFLICT(1945), w; RETURN OF MONTE CRISTO, THE(1946), w

Deborah Neumann
1984
BLOOD SIMPLE(1984)

Dorathea Neumann
HIGH WALL, THE(1947)

Dorothy Neumann
LUCK OF THE IRISH(1948); SORRY, WRONG NUMBER(1948); FOR HEAVEN'S SAKE(1950); MY BLUE HEAVEN(1950); WABASH AVENUE(1950); DAY THE EARTH STOOD STILL, THE(1951); MR. BELVEDERE RINGS THE BELL(1951); LATIN LOVERS(1953); TAKE ME TO TOWN(1953); DESIREE(1954); LONG, LONG TRAILER, THE(1954); BLACKBOARD JUNGLE, THE(1955); MAN CALLED PETER, THE(1955); OKLAHOMAN, THE(1957); SPRING REUNION(1957); TEENAGE DOLL(1957); GIGI(1958); LONELYHEARTS(1958); RISE AND FALL OF LEGS DIAMOND, THE(1960); MAN FROM THE DINERS' CLUB, THE(1963); TERROR, THE(1963); GET YOURSELF A COLLEGE GIRL(1964); I'D RATHER BE RICH(1964); VALLEY OF THE DOLLS(1967); SHAKIEST GUN IN THE WEST, THE(1968); PRIVATE PARTS(1972)

Drew Neumann
SCALPS(1983), m

Elisabeth Neumann
HOUSE ON 92ND STREET, THE(1945)

Gerda Neumann
WHILE THE ATTORNEY IS ASLEEP(1945, Den.)

Gillian Neumann
1984
BIG MEAT EATER(1984, Can.)

Gunther Neumann
M(1933, Ger.); ARENT WE WONDERFUL?(1959, Ger.), w

Hans Neumann
Misc. Silents
MIDSUMMER NIGHT'S DREAM, A(1928, Ger.), d

Harry Neumann
COURTIN' WILDCATS(1929), ph; LONG, LONG TRAIL, THE(1929), ph; CONCENTRATIN' KID, THE(1930), ph; LAND OF MISSING MEN, THE(1930), ph; MOUNTED STRANGER, THE(1930), ph; ROARING RANCH(1930), ph; SPURS(1930), ph; TRAILING TROUBLE(1930), ph; TRIGGER TRICKS(1930), ph; AT THE RIDGE(1931), ph; HARD HOMBRE(1931), ph; LASCA OF THE RIO GRANDE(1931), ph; BOILING POINT, THE(1932), ph; GAY BUCKAROO, THE(1932), ph; INTRUDER, THE(1932), ph; LOCAL BAD MAN(1932), ph; MAN'S LAND, A(1932), ph; PARISIAN ROMANCE, A(1932), ph; SPIRIT OF THE WEST(1932), ph; STOKER, THE(1932), ph; THIRTEENTH GUEST, THE(1932), ph; UNHOLY LOVE(1932), ph; VANITY FAIR(1932), ph; COWBOY COUNSELOR(1933), ph; DUDE BANDIT, THE(1933), ph; ELEVENTH COMMANDMENT(1933), ph; IRON MASTER, THE(1933), ph; OFFICER 13(1933), ph; SHRIEK IN THE NIGHT, A(1933), ph; TARZAN THE FEARLESS(1933), ph; WEST OF SINGAPORE(1933), ph; CHEATERS(1934), ph; ONCE TO EVERY BACHELOR(1934), ph; PICTURE BRIDES(1934), ph; TAKE THE STAND(1934), ph; TWO HEADS ON A PILLOW(1934), ph; WHEN STRANGERS MEET(1934), ph; CAPPY RICKS RETURNS(1935), ph; FORCED LANDING(1935), ph; FRISCO WATERFRONT(1935), ph; HEALER, THE(1935), ph; KEEPER OF THE BEES(1935), ph; MILLION DOLLAR BABY(1935), ph; MYSTERIOUS MR. WONG(1935), ph; MYSTERY MAN, THE(1935), ph; NO RANSOM(1935), ph; NUT FARM, THE(1935), ph; OLD HOMESTEAD, THE(1935), ph; SCHOOL FOR GIRLS(1935), ph; SWEEPSTAKE ANNIE(1935), ph; TWO SINNERS(1935), ph; CHEERS OF THE CROWD(1936), ph; DIZZY DAMES(1936), ph; LET'S SING AGAIN(1936), ph; PENTHOUSE PARTY(1936), ph; CALIFORNIA STRAIGHT AHEAD(1937), ph; CALIFORNIAN, THE(1937), ph; DUKE COMES BACK, THE(1937), ph; I COVER THE WAR(1937), ph; IDOL OF THE CROWDS(1937), ph; IT HAPPENED OUT WEST(1937), ph; WESTERN GOLD(1937), ph; AIR DEVILS(1938), ph; BORDER WOLVES(1938), ph; GANGSTER'S BOY(1938), ph; LAST STAND, THE(1938), ph; MR. WONG, DETECTIVE(1938), ph; OUTLAW EXPRESS(1938), ph; PRISON BREAK(1938), ph; ROLL ALONG, COWBOY(1938), ph; SPY RING, THE(1938), ph; STATE POLICE(1938), ph; WESTERN TRAILS(1938), ph; HEROES IN BLUE(1939), ph; HONOR OF THE WEST(1939), ph; IRISH LUCK(1939), ph; MR. WONG IN CHINATOWN(1939), ph; MUTINY IN THE BIG HOUSE(1939), ph; MYSTERY OF MR. WONG, THE(1939), ph; NAVY SECRETS(1939), ph; PHANTOM STAGE, THE(1939), ph; STREETS OF NEW YORK(1939), ph; APE, THE(1940), ph; CHASING TROUBLE(1940), ph; DOOMED TO DIE(1940), ph; FATAL HOUR, THE(1940), ph; HAUNTED HOUSE, THE(1940), ph; HIDDEN ENEMY(1940), ph; MIDNIGHT LIMITED(1940), ph; ON THE SPOT(1940), ph; QUEEN OF THE YUKON(1940), ph; SON OF THE NAVY(1940), ph; TOMBOY(1940), ph; APACHE KID, THE(1941), ph; ARIZONA BOUND(1941), ph; FORBIDDEN TRAILS(1941), ph; GUN MAN FROM BODIE, THE(1941), ph; NO GREATER SIN(1941), ph; OLD SWIMMIN' HOLE, THE(1941), ph; ROAR OF THE PRESS(1941), ph; UNDER FIESTA STARS(1941), ph; BELOW THE BORDER(1942), ph; DOWN TEXAS WAY(1942), ph; GHOST TOWN LAW(1942), ph; HEART OF THE RIO GRANDE(1942), ph; MAN WITH TWO LIVES, THE(1942), ph; RIDERS OF THE WEST(1942), ph; SHE'S IN THE ARMY(1942), ph; SOUTH OF SANTA FE(1942), ph; WEST OF THE LAW(1942), ph; GENTLE GANGSTER, A(1943), ph; MURDER ON THE WATERFRONT(1943), ph; SIX GUN GOSPEL(1943), ph; STRANGER FROM PECOS, THE(1943), ph; TRUCK BUSTERS(1943), ph; ARE THESE OUR PARENTS?(1944), ph; LAND OF THE OUTLAWS(1944), ph; LAW MEN(1944), ph; MARKED TRAILS(1944), ph; MARSHAL OF GUNSMOKE(1944), ph; PARTNERS OF THE TRAIL(1944), ph; RAIDERS OF THE BORDER(1944), ph; RANGE LAW(1944), ph; TEXAS KID, THE(1944), ph; ALLOTMENT WIVES, INC.(1945), ph; CAPTAIN TUGBOAT ANNIE(1945), ph; CHINA'S LITTLE DEVILS(1945), ph; CISCO KID RETURNS, THE(1945), ph; DIVORCE(1945), ph; FASHION MODEL(1945), ph; FLAME OF THE WEST(1945), ph; FOREVER YOURS(1945), ph; FRONTIER FEUD(1945), ph; G.I. HONEYMOON(1945), ph; JADE MASK, THE(1945), ph; SUNBONNET SUE(1945), ph; BELOW THE DEADLINE(1946), ph; BLACK MARKET BABIES(1946), ph; DRIFTING ALONG(1946), ph; FACE OF MARBLE, THE(1946), ph; GENTLEMAN FROM TEXAS(1946), ph; SPOOK BUSTERS(1946), ph; SWING PARADE OF 1946(1946), ph; UNDER ARIZONA SKIES(1946), ph; WEST OF THE ALAMO(1946), ph; WIFE WANTED(1946), ph; BLACK GOLD(1947), ph; FLASHING GUNS(1947), ph; RAIDERS OF THE SOUTH(1947), ph; SONG OF THE WASTELAND(1947), ph; BACK TRAIL(1948), ph; COURTIN' TROUBLE(1948), ph; CROSSED TRAILS(1948), ph; FRONTIER AGENT(1948), ph; GUN TALK(1948), ph; GUNNING FOR JUSTICE(1948), ph; HUNTED, THE(1948), ph; OKLAHOMA BLUES(1948), ph; OUTLAW BRAND(1948), ph; PANHANDLE(1948), ph; PARTNERS OF THE SUNSET(1948), ph; RANGE RENEGADES(1948), ph; RANGERS RIDE, THE(1948), ph; SILVER TRAILS(1948), ph; SONG OF THE DRIFTER(1948), ph; STAGE STRUCK(1948), ph; GUN LAW JUSTICE(1949), ph; GUN RUNNER(1949), ph; HIDDEN DANGER(1949), ph; LAW OF THE WEST(1949), ph; LAWLESS CODE(1949), ph; RANGE JUSTICE(1949), ph; RANGE LAND(1949), ph; RIDERS OF THE DUSK(1949), ph; SHADOWS OF THE WEST(1949), ph; STAMPEDE(1949), ph; TRAIL'S END(1949), ph; WEST OF EL DORADO(1949), ph; WESTERN RENEGADES(1949), ph; ARIZONA TERRITORY(1950), ph; FENCE RIDERS(1950), ph; GUNSLINGERS(1950), ph; LAW OF THE PANHANDLE(1950), ph; OVER THE BORDER(1950), ph; SHORT GRASS(1950), ph; SILVER RAIDERS(1950), ph; TWO LOST WORLDS(1950), ph.; WEST OF WYOMING(1950), ph; ACCORDING TO MRS. HOYLE(1951), ph; CAVALRY SCOUT(1951), ph; DISC JOCKEY(1951), ph; FLIGHT TO MARS(1951), ph; I WAS AN AMERICAN SPY(1951), ph; NAVY BOUND(1951), ph; AFRICAN TREASURE(1952), ph; ARMY BOUND(1952), ph; BOMBA AND THE JUNGLE GIRL(1952), ph; FLAT TOP(1952), ph; FORT OSAGE(1952), ph; HIAWATHA(1952), ph; RODEO(1952), ph; ROSE BOWL STORY, THE(1952), ph; WAGONS WEST(1952), ph; WILD STALLION(1952), ph; CLIPPED WINGS(1953), ph; COW COUNTRY(1953), ph; DRAGONFLY SQUADRON(1953), ph; FIGHTER ATTACK(1953), ph; FORT VENGEANCE(1953), ph; JALOPY(1953), ph; KANSAS PACIFIC(1953), ph; LOOSE IN LONDON(1953), ph; MAZE, THE(1953), ph; ROAR OF THE CROWD(1953), ph; SAFARI DRUMS(1953), ph; SON OF BELLE STARR(1953), ph; BOWERY BOYS MEET THE MONSTERS(1954), ph; GOLDEN IDOL, THE(1954), ph; JUNGLE GENTS(1954), ph; KILLER LEOPARD(1954), ph; PARIS PLAYBOYS(1954), ph; PRIDE OF THE BLUE GRASS(1954), ph; RETURN FROM THE SEA(1954), ph; BOWERY TO BAGDAD(1955), ph; BULLET FOR JOEY, A(1955), ph; HIGH SOCIETY(1955), ph; LORD OF THE JUNGLE(1955), ph; PHENIX CITY STORY, THE(1955), ph; CALLING HOMICIDE(1956), ph; CRASHING LAS VEGAS(1956), ph; DIG THAT URANIUM(1956), ph; FIGHTING TROUBLE(1956), ph; HOT SHOTS(1956), ph; SCREAMING EAGLES(1956), ph; SPY CHASERS(1956), ph; CHAIN OF EVIDENCE(1957), ph; DISEMBODIED, THE(1957), ph; FOOTSTEPS IN THE NIGHT(1957), ph; GUN BATTLE AT MONTEREY(1957), ph; HOLD THAT HYPNOTIST(1957), ph; LOOKING FOR DANGER(1957), ph; MY GUN IS QUICK(1957), ph; SABU AND THE MAGIC RING(1957), ph; SPOOK CHASERS(1957), ph; UP IN SMOKE(1957), ph; WOMEN OF PITCAIRN ISLAND, THE(1957), ph; COLE YOUNGER, GUNFIGHTER(1958), ph; IN THE MONEY(1958), ph; MAN FROM GOD'S COUNTRY(1958), ph

Silents
DARING CHANCES(1924), ph; RIDGEWAY OF MONTANA(1924), ph; SPOOK RANCH(1925), ph; HEY! HEY! COWBOY(1927), ph; PAINTED PONIES(1927), ph; CLEARING THE TRAIL(1928), ph; RAWHIDE KID, THE(1928), ph; FALSE FATHERS(1929), ph; KING OF THE RODEO(1929), ph; POINTS WEST(1929), ph

Henry Neumann
ACROSS THE RIO GRANDE(1949), ph

Hermann Neumann
KING OF THE ROYAL MOUNTED(1936), ph

Jacob "Jackie" Neumann
JERUSALEM FILE, THE(1972, U.S./Israel), spec eff

James Neumann
YOU'LL LIKE MY MOTHER(1972)

Jenny Neumann
LAST MARRIED COUPLE IN AMERICA, THE(1980); HELL NIGHT(1981); MISTRESS OF THE APES(1981); MY FAVORITE YEAR(1982); OFF THE WALL(1983)
Misc. Talkies
STAGEFRIGHT(1983)

Kurt Neumann
FAST COMPANIONS(1932), d; MY PAL, THE KING(1932), d; KING FOR A NIGHT(1933), d; SECRET OF THE BLUE ROOM(1933), d; HALF A SINNER(1934), d; LET'S TALK IT OVER(1934), d; WAKE UP AND DREAM(1934), d; AFFAIR OF SUSAN(1935), d; ALIAS MARY DOW(1935), d; LET'S SING AGAIN(1936), d; RAINBOW ON THE RIVER(1936), d; ESPIONAGE(1937), d; HOLD'EM NAVY!(1937), d; MAKE A WISH(1937), d; TOUCHDOWN, ARMY(1938), d; WIDE OPEN FACES(1938), d; AMBUSH(1939), d; ISLAND OF LOST MEN(1939), d; UNMARRIED(1939), d; ELLERY QUEEN. MASTER DETECTIVE(1940), d; NIGHT AT EARL CARROLL'S, A(1940), d; ABOUT FACE(1942), d; HOSTAGES(1943); UNKNOWN GUEST, THE(1943), d; YANKS AHOY(1943), d; RETURN OF THE VAMPIRE, THE(1944), w; TARZAN AND THE AMAZONS(1945), d; SUSIE STEPS OUT(1946), w; TARZAN AND THE LEOPARD WOMAN(1946), d; TARZAN AND THE HUNTRESS(1947), d; DUDE GOES WEST, THE(1948), d; BAD BOY(1949), d; BAD MEN OF TOMBSTONE(1949), d; KID FROM TEXAS, THE(1950), d; ROCKETSHIP X-M(1950), p,d&w; CATTLE DRIVE(1951), d; REUNION IN RENO(1951), d; HIAWATHA(1952), d; RING, THE(1952), d; SON OF ALI BABA(1952), d; TARZAN AND THE SHE-DEVIL(1953), d; CARNIVAL STORY(1954), d, w; THEY WERE SO YOUNG(1955), p&d, w; DESPERADOES ARE IN TOWN, THE(1956), p&d, w; MOHAWK(1956), d; APACHE WARRIOR(1957), w; DEERSLAYER, THE(1957), p&d, w; KRONOS(1957), p, d; SHE DEVIL(1957), p&d, w; CIRCUS OF LOVE(1958, Ger.), w; FLY, THE(1958), p&d; MACHETE(1958), p&d, w; COUNTERPLOT(1959), p&d; WATUSI(1959), d; ANGELS FROM HELL(1968), p

Lena Neumann
FIRST SPACESHIP ON VENUS(1960, Ger./Pol.), ed; WOZZECK(1962, E. Ger.), ed

Lisbeth Neumann
TREASURE OF SAN GENNARO(1968, Fr./Ital./Ger.), ed

Nancy Neumann
1984
JOY OF SEX(1984)

Peter Neumann
GREAT WALL OF CHINA, THE(1970, Brit.)

Robert Neumann
ABDUL THE DAMNED(1935, Brit.), w; KING IN SHADOW(1961, Ger.), w

Sam Neumann
HITLER–DEAD OR ALIVE(1942), w; BUFFALO BILL IN TOMAHAWK TERRITORY(1952), w

Ulrik Neumann
DOLL, THE(1964, Swed.), m

Elisabeth Neumann-Viertel
FREUD(1962); CABARET(1972); AMERICAN SUCCESS COMPANY, THE(1980)
1984
LITTLE DRUMMER GIRL, THE(1984)

Elizabeth Neumann-Viertel
ODESSA FILE, THE(1974, Brit./Ger.)

Ken Neumeyer
MAX DUGAN RETURNS(1983)

Helga Neuner
HOUSE OF THE THREE GIRLS, THE(1961, Aust.); IT'S HOT IN PARADISE(1962, Ger./Yugo.)

Willy Neuner
TWILIGHT'S LAST GLEAMING(1977, U.S./Ger.), spec eff

Ronald Neunreuther
FRENCH POSTCARDS(1979)

Robert Neury
THREE LITTLE GIRLS IN BLUE(1946)

Roger Neury
BULLFIGHTERS, THE(1945); IDEA GIRL(1946); NOBODY LIVES FOREVER(1946); I WALK ALONE(1948)

Alwin Neuss
Misc. Silents
HOUND OF THE BASKERVILLES, THE(1914, Ger.)

Wolfgang Neuss
CAPTAIN FROM KOEPENICK, THE(1956, Ger.); ARENT WE WONDERFUL?(1959, Ger.); ROSES FOR THE PROSECUTOR(1961, Ger.); SPESSART INN, THE(1961, Ger.); CORPSE OF BEVERLY HILLS, THE(1965, Ger.); SERENADE FOR TWO SPIES(1966, Ital./Ger.)

Peter Neusser
FOREVER MY LOVE(1962)

Gunter Neutze
GREAT BRITISH TRAIN ROBBERY, THE(1967, Ger.)

Gunther Neutze
LAST ESCAPE, THE(1970, Brit.)

Ernest Neuville
PERSONAL COLUMN(1939, Fr.), w; IT HAPPENED IN GIBRALTAR(1943, Fr.), w; LURED(1947), w

Richard Neuweiler
VIRGIN PRESIDENT, THE(1968)
Bob Neuwirth
RENALDO AND CLARA(1978)
Michele Neuy
1984
SMURFS AND THE MAGIC FLUTE, THE(1984, Fr./Belg.), ed
Vaclav Neuzil
DIVINE EMMA, THE(1983, Czech,)
Mary Nevarro
Silents
WHEN BROADWAY WAS A TRAIL(1914)
Ellen Nevdal
DIARY OF A BACHELOR(1964)
Dorian Neve
Silents
IS DIVORCE A FAILURE?(1923), w
Kim Neve
QUADROPHENIA(1979, Brit.)
Suzanne Neve
BACKFIRE!(1961, Brit.); BUNNY LAKE IS MISSING(1965); EXORCISM AT MID-
NIGHT(1966, Brit. revised 1973, U.S.); MOSQUITO SQUADRON(1970, Brit.);
SCROOGE(1970, Brit.)
Misc. Talkies
WON'T WRITE HOME, MOM–I'M DEAD(1975, Brit.)
Georges Neveaux
TAMANGO(1959, Fr.), w
Leonid Nevedomsky
BLUE BIRD, THE(1976)
Don Nevene
WHY RUSSIANS ARE REVOLTING(1970)
Norma Nevens
RHAPSODY(1954)
Paul Nevens
SHAFT(1971); ZELIG(1983)
Ernie Nevers
SPIRIT OF STANFORD, THE(1942)
Oscar Castro Neves
WILD PACK, THE(1972)
John Nevette
WOLF DOG(1958, Can.)
George Neveux
KNOCK(1955, Fr.), w
Georges Neveux
COUNT OF MONTE-CRISTO(1955, Fr., Ital.), w; CHRISTINE(1959, Fr.), w; MAG-
NIFICENT SINNER(1963, Fr.), w
Steve Nevil
COACH(1978); THOSE LIPS, THOSE EYES(1980); HOWLING, THE(1981)
Bernard Nevill
ADMIRABLE CRICHTON, THE(1957, Brit.), cos
Roy Nevill
TOMCAT, THE(1968, Brit.), ed
Ann Neville
1984
ONCE UPON A TIME IN AMERICA(1984)
Anthony Neville
MARRY ME!(1949, Brit.)
Brian Neville
GOING IN STYLE(1979)
David Neville
CONDUCT UNBECOMING(1975, Brit.)
Dean Neville
INVASION OF THE SAUCER MEN(1957)
George Neville
Silents
WAY DOWN EAST(1920); DREAM STREET(1921); ON THE BANKS OF THE
WABASH(1923)
Grace Neville
AIR HAWKS(1935), w; DANGEROUS INTRIGUE(1936), w; SHAKEDOWN(1936), w;
ALL-AMERICAN SWEETHEART(1937), w; COUNSEL FOR CRIME(1937), w; FIND
THE WITNESS(1937), w; GAME THAT KILLS, THE(1937), w; MOTOR MAD-
NESS(1937), w; LITTLE MISS ROUGHNECK(1938), w
Harry Neville
Silents
PRETENDERS, THE(1916); MAN HATER, THE(1917)
J.T. Neville
DAWN TRAIL, THE(1931), w; HEART PUNCH(1932), w
Jack Neville
SUNDOWN RIDER, THE(1933), w; TICKET TO CRIME(1934), w; IVORY-HAN-
DLED GUN(1935), w; OUTLAWED GUNS(1935), w; RIDING ON(1937), w; TOUGH TO
HANDLE(1937), w
John Neville
OSCAR WILDE(1960, Brit.); BILLY BUDD(1962); I LIKE MONEY(1962, Brit.);
UNEARTHLY STRANGER, THE(1964, Brit.); STUDY IN TERROR, A(1966, Brit./Ger.);
ADVENTURES OF GERARD, THE(1970, Brit.)
John T. Neville
LAST OF THE LONE WOLF(1930), w; HER RESALE VALUE(1933), w; RANGER'S
CODE, THE(1933), w; REVENGE AT MONTE CARLO(1933), w; BATTLE OF
GREED(1934), w; ATLANTIC ADVENTURE(1935), w; LION'S DEN, THE(1936), w,
ed; BLAZING SIXES(1937), w; COUNTY FAIR(1937), w; DRUMS OF DESTINY(1937),
w; EMPTY HOLSTERS(1937), w; GLORY TRAIL, THE(1937), w; RAW TIM-
BER(1937), w; BAREFOOT BOY(1938), w; FEMALE FUGITIVE(1938), w; GANG BUL-
LETS(1938), w; MILLION TO ONE, A(1938), w; MY OLD KENTUCKY
HOME(1938), w; OLD LOUISIANA(1938), w; REBELLION(1938), w; GIRL FROM
RIO(1939), w; STAR REPORTER(1939), w; DRUMS OF THE DESERT(1940), w;
NEVER GIVE A SUCKER AN EVEN BREAK(1941), w; SHAKE HANDS WITH
MURDER(1944), w; ROGUES GALLERY(1945), w; FLYING SERPENT, THE(1946), w

John Thomas Neville
BROTHERS(1930), w; FLOOD, THE(1931), w; HOMICIDE SQUAD(1931), w; TRAD-
ER HORN(1931), w; HER MAD NIGHT(1932), w; HONOR OF THE PRESS(1932), w;
MIDNIGHT WARNING, THE(1932), w; ALIMONY MADNESS(1933), w; BEHIND
JURY DOORS(1933, Brit.), w; JUSTICE TAKES A HOLIDAY(1933), w; MALAY
NIGHTS(1933), w; HOLLYWOOD MYSTERY(1934), w; TRAITOR, THE(1936), w;
DEVIL BAT, THE(1941), w
Silents
ENCHANTED ISLAND, THE(1927), w
Julia Neville
Silents
DIANE OF STAR HOLLOW(1921)
Margot Neville
CRAZY PEOPLE(1934, Brit.), w
Silents
SAFETY FIRST(1926, Brit.), w
Marjean Neville
HAIL THE CONQUERING HERO(1944); HOUR BEFORE THE DAWN, THE(1944);
LADY IN THE DARK(1944); PRACTICALLY YOURS(1944)
Misc. Talkies
GUNNING FOR VENGEANCE(1946)
Neville E. Neville
MAD MEN OF EUROPE(1940, Brit.), p
Paul Neville
DANNY BOY(1934, Brit.); BANK MESSENGER MYSTERY, THE(1936, Brit.); CAFE
MASCOT(1936, Brit.); FIND THE LADY(1936, Brit.); FULL SPEED AHEAD(1936,
Brit.); KING OF HEARTS(1936, Brit.); WEDNESDAY'S LUCK(1936, Brit.); PASSEN-
GER TO LONDON(1937, Brit.); TWIN FACES(1937, Brit.)
Silents
BROKEN ROMANCE, A(1929, Brit.)
Ralph Neville
NICHOLAS AND ALEXANDRA(1971, Brit.)
Robert Neville
PRESCRIPTION FOR ROMANCE(1937), w; PECK'S BAD BOY WITH THE CIR-
CUS(1938), w; BLACK CAT, THE(1941), w
Sophie Neville
SWALLOWS AND AMAZONS(1977, Brit.)
Crocker Nevin
ROLLOVER(1981)
Dr. Robert Nevin
JAWS(1975)
Robin Nevin
IRISHMAN, THE(1978, Aus.)
Robyn Nevin
LIBIDO(1973, Aus.); CADDIE(1976, Aus.); CHANT OF JIMMIE BLACKSMITH,
THE(1980, Aus.); FIGHTING BACK(1983, Brit.)
1984
CAREFUL, HE MIGHT HEAR YOU(1984, Aus.)
V. Nevinny
LAST GAME, THE(1964, USSR)
V. Nevinnyy
HOUSE ON THE FRONT LINE, THE(1963, USSR); UNCOMMON THIEF, AN(1967,
USSR)
April Nevins
SWEET CHARITY(1969)
Claudette Nevins
MASK, THE(1961, Can.); ...ALL THE MARBLES(1981)
Frank J. Nevins
ROCK ISLAND TRAIL(1950), w
Morty Nevins
TWO GALS AND A GUY(1951), m/l
Paul Nevins
MASK, THE(1961, Can.)
Jennifer Nevinson
GREYFRIARS BOBBY(1961, Brit.)
Nancy Nevinson
COMING-OUT PARTY, A(; HIGH FLIGHT(1957, Brit.); WONDERFUL
THINGS!(1958, Brit.); FOXHOLE IN CAIRO(1960, Brit.); NIGHT TRAIN FOR INVER-
NESS(1960, Brit.); DEVIL'S DAFFODIL, THE(1961, Brit./Ger.); LIGHT IN THE
PIAZZA(1962); RING OF SPIES(1964, Brit.); SPY WHO CAME IN FROM THE COLD,
THE(1965, Brit.); RICOCHET(1966, Brit.); LOVE IS A SPLENDID ILLUSION(1970,
Brit.); SYMPTOMS(1976, Brit.); GULLIVER'S TRAVELS(1977, Brit., Bel.); RAISE THE
TITANIC(1980, Brit.)
Nigel Nevinson
SILVER BEARS(1978)
Gennie Nevison
DEADLY FEMALES, THE(1976, Brit.)
Edoardo Nevola
TEACHER AND THE MIRACLE, THE(1961, Ital./Span.); INVINCIBLE GLADIA-
TOR, THE(1963, c.u. Ital./Span.); EMPTY CANVAS, THE(1964, Fr./Ital.); RAILROAD
MAN, THE(1965, Ital.)
Babette New
STOOLIE, THE(1972)
Derek New
PASSWORD IS COURAGE, THE(1962, Brit.), m
Gary T. New
EYE FOR AN EYE, AN(1981)
Janie New
SONG IS BORN, A(1948)
Jocelyn New
KING AND I, THE(1956)
Marshal New
GAL YOUNG UN(1979)
Nancy New
EUROPEANS, THE(1979, Brit.); JANE AUSTEN IN MANHATTAN(1980)
1984
BOSTONIANS, THE(1984)

Robert New
PROM NIGHT(1980), ph
The New Age
LOVE-INS, THE(1967)
New Breed
PUTNEY SWOPE(1969), cos
The New Orleans Saints
NUMBER ONE(1969)
New Society Band
MUSICAL MUTINY(1970)
New Temperance Seven
GAMES THAT LOVERS PLAY(1971, Brit.)
Kleomenes Stamatiades New World Effects
SORCERESS(1983), cos
Members of the New York City Ballet Company
MIDSUMMER NIGHT'S DREAM, A(1966)
The New York City Breakers
1984
BEAT STREET(1984)
the New York Community Choir
EDUCATION OF SONNY CARSON, THE(1974)
New York Philharmonic Quintette
CARNEGIE HALL(1947)
The New York Rock Ensemble
ZACHARIAH(1971)
Men of the New Zealand Expeditionary Force
SOLDIER, SAILOR(1944, Brit.)
Basil Newall
SCREAM OF FEAR(1961, Brit.), makeup; KILL OR CURE(1962, Brit.), makeup; MANIAC(1963, Brit.), makeup; SWINGIN' MAIDEN, THE(1963, Brit.), makeup; WOMAN OF STRAW(1964, Brit.), makeup; WHISPERERS, THE(1967, Brit.), makeup; YOU ONLY LIVE TWICE(1967, Brit.), makeup; SOME GIRLS DO(1969, Brit.), makeup; MURPHY'S WAR(1971, Brit.), makeup; O LUCKY MAN!(1973, Brit.), makeup; ZARDOZ(1974, Brit.), makeup; SUPERMAN(1978), makeup; VENOM(1982, Brit.), makeup
Guy Newall
NUMBER SEVENTEEN(1928, Brit./Ger.); ROAD TO FORTUNE, THE(1930, Brit.); BOAT FROM SHANGHAI(1931, Brit.), d, w; ETERNAL FEMININE, THE(1931, Brit.); HER STRANGE DESIRE(1931, Brit.); ROSARY, THE(1931, Brit.), d; CHINESE PUZZLE, THE(1932, Brit.), d; MARRIAGE BOND, THE(1932, Brit.); ADMIRAL'S SECRET, THE(1934, Brit.), d; GRAND FINALE(1936, Brit.); MERRY COMES TO STAY(1937, Brit.)
Silents
FANCY DRESS(1919, Brit.), a, p; GARDEN OF RESURRECTION, THE(1919, Brit.); MARCH HARE, THE(1919, Brit.), d&w; MIRAGE, THE(1920, Brit.), w; BIGAMIST, THE(1921, Brit.), a, d&w; FOX FARM(1922, Brit.), a, d&w; GHOST TRAIN, THE(1927, Brit.)
Misc. Silents
HEART OF SISTER ANN, THE(1915, Brit.); DESPERATION(1916, Brit.); MOTHER-LOVE(1916, Brit.); SMITH(1917, Brit.); COMRADESHIP(1919, Brit.); I WILL(1919, Brit.); LURE OF CROONING WATER, THE(1920, Brit.); SQUANDERED LIVES(1920, Brit.); TESTIMONY(1920, Brit.), d; BOY WOODBURN(1922, Brit.), a, d; PERSISTENT LOVERS, THE(1922, Brit.), a, d; STARLIT GARDEN, THE(1923, Brit.), a, d; WHAT THE BUTLER SAW(1924, Brit.); GHOST TRAIN, THE(1927, Brit.)
Joan Newall
LILAC DOMINO, THE(1940, Brit.)
Patrick Newall
BECKET(1964, Brit.)
Derek Newark
CITY UNDER THE SEA(1965, Brit.); LITTLE ONES, THE(1965, Brit.); BLUE MAX, THE(1966); GIRL GETTERS, THE(1966, Brit.); OH! WHAT A LOVELY WAR(1969, Brit.); DAD'S ARMY(1971, Brit.); FRAGMENT OF FEAR(1971, Brit.); OFFENSE, THE(1973, Brit.); BLACK WINDMILL, THE(1974, Brit.); LITTLEST HORSE THIEVES, THE(1977)
Milton Newberger
BELA LUGOSI MEETS A BROOKLYN GORILLA(1952)
Bill Newberry
FRANCIS IN THE NAVY(1955), art d; MAN FROM BITTER RIDGE, THE(1955), art d; EVERYTHING BUT THE TRUTH(1956), art d; PILLARS OF THE SKY(1956), art d; WALK THE PROUD LAND(1956), art d; WORLD IN MY CORNER(1956), art d; JOE DAKOTA(1957), art d; TAMMY AND THE BACHELOR(1957), art d; TATTERED DRESS, THE(1957), art d; FLOOD TIDE(1958), art d; KATHY O'(1958), art d; RIDE A CROOKED TRAIL(1958), art d
Charles Bruce Newberry
STORK TALK(1964, Brit.), p
Doyle Newberry
MADE FOR EACH OTHER(1971); HAIL(1973)
Norman Newberry
WINTER KILLS(1979), art d; GHOST STORY(1981), art d; HISTORY OF THE WORLD, PART 1(1981), art d; STAYING ALIVE(1983), art d; TABLE FOR FIVE(1983), art d
1984
RIVER, THE(1984), art d
Pip Newberry
1984
OXFORD BLUES(1984), cos
William Newberry
KELLY AND ME(1957), art d; SEVEN WAYS FROM SUNDOWN(1960), art d; MISFITS, THE(1961), art d
Kurt Newbert
HIDEOUT IN THE ALPS(1938, Brit.), ph
Bruce Newbery
DEADLIER THAN THE MALE(1967, Brit.), p
Lionel Newbold
MELODY IN THE DARK(1948, Brit.); UNEASY TERMS(1948, Brit.)
Ira Newborn
BLUES BROTHERS, THE(1980), m; ALL NIGHT LONG(1981), m
1984
SIXTEEN CANDLES(1984), m

Phineas Newborn III
1984
BREAKIN'(1984)
Gail Newbray
MEET JOHN DOE(1941)
Peter Newbrook
MELODY CLUB(1949, Brit.), ph; THIRD TIME LUCKY(1950, Brit.), ph; IN THE COOL OF THE DAY(1963, ph; THAT KIND OF GIRL(1963, Brit.), ph; GUTTER GIRLS(1964, Brit.), ph; SATURDAY NIGHT OUT(1964, Brit.), ph; BLACK TORMENT, THE(1965, Brit.), ph; GONKS GO BEAT(1965, Brit.), p; PRESS FOR TIME(1966, Brit.), p, ph; SANDWICH MAN, THE(1966, Brit.), p, ph; CORRUPTION(1968, Brit.), p, ph; INCENSE FOR THE DAMNED(1970, Brit.), p; ASPHYX, THE(1972, Brit.), d; SCHOOL FOR UNCLAIMED GIRLS(1973, Brit.), p, ph
Frank Newburg
Silents
ABRAHAM LINCOLN(1924)
Misc. Silents
WHITE SCAR, THE(1915); FRIVOLOUS WIVES(1920)
Frank H. Newburg
Misc. Silents
FUEL OF LIFE(1917)
Fred Newburg
Misc. Silents
WHEN BABY FORGOT(1917)
Larry Newburg
1984
BREAKIN'(1984)
David Newburge
FEMALE RESPONSE, THE(1972), w
Jean Newburn
TRIAL OF BILLY JACK, THE(1974)
Gayl Newbury
SHOULD A GIRL MARRY?(1939), w
John Newbury
REVENGE OF THE PINK PANTHER(1978)
Anne Newby
WHISTLE DOWN THE WIND(1961, Brit.)
Jerry Newby
ONCE UPON A COFFEE HOUSE(1965); GENTLE GIANT(1967)
Patti Newby
WORLD IS JUST A 'B' MOVIE, THE(1971)
Peter Newby
FOURTEEN, THE(1973, Brit.)
Tricia Newby
CARRY ON ENGLAND(1976, Brit.)
Valli Newby
GET ON WITH IT(1963, Brit.); GUTTER GIRLS(1964, Brit.)
James Newcom
BISHOP MISBEHAVES, THE(1933), ed; TOPPER RETURNS(1941), ed; GUEST IN THE HOUSE(1944), ed; UP IN ARMS(1944), ed; PARIS UNDERGROUND(1945), ed; YOUNG WIDOW(1946), ed; TEXAS, BROOKLYN AND HEAVEN(1948), ed; PRISONER OF WAR(1954), ed; SCENT OF MYSTERY(1960), ed
James E. Newcom
MEET THE BARON(1933), ed; WE WENT TO COLLEGE(1936), ed; NOTHING SACRED(1937), ed; PRISONER OF ZENDA, THE(1937), ed; STAR IS BORN, A(1937), ed; GONE WITH THE WIND(1939), ed; CHOCOLATE SOLDIER, THE(1941), ed; GET-AWAY, THE(1941), ed; VANISHING VIRGINIAN, THE(1941), ed; CAIRO(1942), ed; KEEPER OF THE FLAME(1942), ed; SINCE YOU WENT AWAY(1944), ed; STRANGE WOMAN, THE(1946), ed; LURED(1947), ed; WALK A CROOKED MILE(1948), ed; RED DANUBE, THE(1949), ed; KEY TO THE CITY(1950), ed; RIGHT CROSS(1950), ed; CAUSE FOR ALARM(1951), ed; GO FOR BROKE(1951), ed; LAW AND THE LADY, THE(1951), ed; WESTWARD THE WOMEN(1951), ed; SCARAMOUCHE(1952), ed; ROGUE COP(1954), ed; IMPOSSIBLE YEARS, THE(1968), ed; TORA! TORA! TORA!(1970, U.S./Jap.), ed
Herbert Newcomb
JOHNNY HOLIDAY(1949)
James Newcomb
CAPTAIN CAUTION(1940), ed
James E. Newcomb
MURDER MAN(1935), ed; TOUGH GUY(1936), ed; MADE FOR EACH OTHER(1939), ed; LADY OF BURLESQUE(1943), ed
Mary Newcomb
FRAIL WOMEN(1932, Brit.); WOMEN WHO PLAY(1932, Brit.); STRANGE EXPERIMENT(1937, Brit.)
Misc. Silents
PASSIONATE PILGRIM, THE(1921)
Warren Newcomb
WEEKEND AT THE WALDORF(1945), spec eff; FORBIDDEN PLANET(1956), spec eff
Clovissa Newcombe
DIGBY, THE BIGGEST DOG IN THE WORLD(1974, Brit.)
Grace Newcombe
ONCE MORE, WITH FEELING(1960)
Jessamine Newcombe
WE WERE DANCING(1942)
Jessica Newcombe
THIS ABOVE ALL(1942); TRAITOR WITHIN, THE(1942); WILDCAT(1942); UNINVITED, THE(1944); MINISTRY OF FEAR(1945)
John Newcombe
GOLDENGIRL(1979)
John J. Newcombe
DAMIEN–OMEN II(1978)
Les Newcombe
STIR(1980, Aus.)
Mary Newcombe
MARRIAGE BOND, THE(1932, Brit.)
Roger Newcombe
ODD ANGRY SHOT, THE(1979, Aus.)

1984
PHAR LAP(1984, Aus.)
Warren Newcombe
DR. JEKYLL AND MR. HYDE(1941), spec eff; FEMININE TOUCH, THE(1941), spec eff; SMILIN' THROUGH(1941), spec eff; TARZAN'S SECRET TREASURE(1941), spec eff; THEY MET IN BOMBAY(1941), spec eff; I MARRIED AN ANGEL(1942), spec eff; KEEPER OF THE FLAME(1942), spec eff; MRS. MINIVER(1942), spec eff; REUNION IN FRANCE(1942), spec eff; RIO RITA(1942), spec eff; TARZAN'S NEW YORK ADVENTURE(1942), spec eff; TENNESSEE JOHNSON(1942), spec eff; TORTILLA FLAT(1942), spec eff; YANK AT ETON, A(1942), spec eff; BATAAN(1943), spec eff; GUY NAMED JOE, A(1943), spec eff; LASSIE, COME HOME(1943), spec eff; MADAME CURIE(1943), spec eff; PRESENTING LILY MARS(1943), spec eff; WHISTLING IN BROOKLYN(1943), spec eff; DRAGON SEED(1944), spec eff; GASLIGHT(1944), spec eff; KISMET(1944), spec eff; MRS. PARKINGTON(1944), spec eff; NATIONAL VELVET(1944), spec eff; THIRTY SECONDS OVER TOKYO(1944), spec eff; WHITE CLIFFS OF DOVER, THE(1944), spec eff; ADVENTURE(1945), spec eff; HER HIGHNESS AND THE BELLBOY(1945), spec eff; SON OF LASSIE(1945), spec eff; VALLEY OF DECISION, THE(1945), spec eff; WHAT NEXT, CORPORAL HARGROVE?(1945), spec eff; YOLANDA AND THE THIEF(1945), spec eff; HOLIDAY IN MEXICO(1946), spec eff; HOODLUM SAINT, THE(1946), spec eff; SAILOR TAKES A WIFE, THE(1946), spec eff; TILL THE CLOUDS ROLL BY(1946), spec eff; YEARLING, THE(1946), spec eff; BEGINNING OR THE END, THE(1947), ph; CASS TIMBERLANE(1947), spec eff; GREEN DOLPHIN STREET(1947), spec eff; HIGH BARBAREE(1947), spec eff; HIGH WALL, THE(1947), spec eff; HUCKSTERS, THE(1947), spec eff; SEA OF GRASS, THE(1947), spec eff; SONG OF LOVE(1947), spec eff; B. F.'S DAUGHTER(1948), spec eff; DATE WITH JUDY, A(1948), spec eff; EASTER PARADE(1948), spec eff; HOMECOMING(1948), spec eff; JULIA MISBEHAVES(1948), spec eff; SOUTHERN YANKEE, A(1948), spec eff; THREE MUSKETEERS, THE(1948), spec eff; BRIBE, THE(1949), spec eff; GREAT SINNER, THE(1949), spec eff; LITTLE WOMEN(1949), spec eff; ON THE TOWN(1949), spec eff; STRATTON STORY, THE(1949), spec eff; TAKE ME OUT TO THE BALL GAME(1949), spec eff; CRISIS(1950), spec eff; KIM(1950), spec eff; PAGAN LOVE SONG(1950), spec eff; TO PLEASE A LADY(1950), spec eff; TWO WEEKS WITH LOVE(1950), spec eff; WATCH THE BIRDIE(1950), spec eff; AMERICAN IN PARIS, AN(1951), spec eff; PEOPLE AGAINST O'HARA, THE(1951), spec eff; ROYAL WEDDING(1951), spec eff; SHOW BOAT(1951), spec eff; STRIP, THE(1951), spec eff; TEXAS CARNIVAL(1951), spec eff; BAD AND THE BEAUTIFUL, THE(1952), spec eff; MERRY WIDOW, THE(1952), spec eff; PAT AND MIKE(1952), spec eff; PLYMOUTH ADVENTURE(1952), spec eff; PRISONER OF ZENDA, THE(1952), spec eff; SCARAMOUCHE(1952), spec eff; SINGIN' IN THE RAIN(1952), spec eff; ABOVE AND BEYOND(1953), spec eff; ACTRESS, THE(1953), spec eff; ALL THE BROTHERS WERE VALIANT(1953), spec eff; DREAM WIFE(1953), spec eff; ESCAPE FROM FORT BRAVO(1953), spec eff; JULIUS CAESAR(1953), spec eff; KISS ME KATE(1953), spec eff; LATIN LOVERS(1953), spec eff; LILI(1953), spec eff; SOMBRERO(1953), spec eff; DEEP IN MY HEART(1954), spec eff; LONG, LONG TRAILER, THE(1954), spec eff; RHAPSODY(1954), spec eff; ROSE MARIE(1954), spec eff; DIANE(1955), spec eff; GREEN FIRE(1955), spec eff; I'LL CRY TOMORROW(1955), spec eff; IT'S ALWAYS FAIR WEATHER(1955), spec eff; LOVE ME OR LEAVE ME(1955), spec eff; PRODIGAL, THE(1955), spec eff; TRIAL(1955), spec eff; MEET ME IN LAS VEGAS(1956), spec eff; OPPOSITE SEX, THE(1956), spec eff; RAINTREE COUNTY(1957), spec eff; WINGS OF EAGLES, THE(1957), spec eff
James Newdom
REBECCA(1940), ed
Julie Newdow
STUCK ON YOU(1983)
1984
STUCK ON YOU(1984)
Audrey Newell
GOOD GUYS AND THE BAD GUYS, THE(1969), cos
Bill Newell
HE STAYED FOR BREAKFAST(1940)
Carol Irene Newell
Misc. Talkies
ALPHA INCIDENT, THE(1976)
Dave Newell
MACHINE GUN KELLY(1958), makeup
David Newell
DANGEROUS CURVES(1929); DARKENED ROOMS(1929); HOLE IN THE WALL(1929); KIBITZER, THE(1929); MARRIAGE PLAYGROUND, THE(1929); JUST LIKE HEAVEN(1930); LET'S GO NATIVE(1930); MURDER ON THE ROOF(1930); RUNAWAY BRIDE(1930); FLOOD, THE(1931); TEN CENTS A DANCE(1931); WOMAN HUNGRY(1931); DIVORCE IN THE FAMILY(1932); NEW MORALS FOR OLD(1932); WOMAN COMMANDS, A(1932); HELL BELOW(1933); MADE ON BROADWAY(1933); WHITE HEAT(1934); DEVIL DOGS OF THE AIR(1935); GOOSE AND THE GANDER, THE(1935); LIVING ON VELVET(1935); RED SALUTE(1935); SWEET ADELINE(1935); EDUCATING FATHER(1936); POLO JOE(1936); ROSE BOWL(1936); ARTISTS AND MODELS(1937); HOLLYWOOD HOTEL(1937); STAR IS BORN, A(1937); WAIKIKI WEDDING(1937); MEN WITH WINGS(1938); MR. MOTO'S GAMBLE(1938); SERGEANT MURPHY(1938); THREE LOVES HAS NANCY(1938); DARK VICTORY(1939); DAY-TIME WIFE(1939); UNION PACIFIC(1939); LETTER, THE(1940); MURDER IN THE AIR(1940); TIL WE MEET AGAIN(1940); DIVE BOMBER(1941); FOOTSTEPS IN THE DARK(1941); YOU'RE IN THE ARMY NOW(1941); RINGS ON HER FINGERS(1942); WIFE TAKES A FLYER, THE(1942); GOVERNMENT GIRL(1943); REVEILLE WITH BEVERLY(1943); B. F.'S DAUGHTER(1948); HOMECOMING(1948); SOUTHERN YANKEE, A(1948); THAT WONDERFUL URGE(1948); JOLSON SINGS AGAIN(1949); MILKMAN, THE(1950); GREATEST SHOW ON EARTH, THE(1952); MY SON, JOHN(1952); EASY TO LOVE(1953); MISSISSIPPI GAMBLER, THE(1953); PRIVATE HELL 36(1954), makeup; GREAT LOCOMOTIVE CHASE, THE(1956), makeup; WESTWARD HO THE WAGONS!(1956), makeup; JOHNNY TREMAIN(1957), makeup; PHANTOM PLANET, THE(1961), makeup
Earl Newell
FANDANGO(1970)
Elsa Newell
FURY(1936); NAVY BORN(1936)
Gordon Newell
CALIFORNIAN, THE(1937), w
Jamie Newell
1984
TEACHERS(1984)

Jim Newell
TRADING PLACES(1983)
Jimmy Newell
SING WHILE YOU'RE ABLE(1937)
Joan Newell
LAST MAN TO HANG, THE(1956, Brit.); DEVIL'S PASS, THE(1957, Brit.); STOLEN HOURS(1963); SING AND SWING(1964, Brit.); JIG SAW(1965, Brit.)
Maude Woodruff Newell
Silents
IMPULSE(1922), w
Maurie Newell
Silents
DUCKS AND DRAKES(1921)
Michael Newell
ISLAND OF DESIRE(1952, Brit.)
Mike Newell
AWAKENING, THE(1980), d
Norman Newell
SAY HELLO TO YESTERDAY(1971, Brit.), m/l
Patrick Newell
NIGHT WITHOUT PITY(1962, Brit.); TRIAL AND ERROR(1962, Brit.); FATHER CAME TOO(1964, Brit.); UNEARTHLY STRANGER, THE(1964, Brit.); SEASIDE SWINGERS(1965, Brit.); ALPHABET MURDERS, THE(1966); STUDY IN TERROR, A(1966, Brit./Ger.); LONG DUEL, THE(1967, Brit.); STRANGE AFFAIR, THE(1968, Brit.); OLD DRACULA(1975, Brit.); STAND UP VIRGIN SOLDIERS(1977, Brit.); GOLDEN LADY, THE(1979, Brit.)
Misc. Talkies
GO FOR A TAKE(1972, Brit.)
Raymond Newell
MUSIC HALL(1934, Brit.); VARIETY HOUR(1937, Brit.)
Rickey Newell
I'VE GOT YOUR NUMBER(1934); JIMMY THE GENT(1934)
Scott Newell
SHARKY'S MACHINE(1982)
Wedgewood Newell
HELL BENT FOR LOVE(1934)
Wedgwood Newell
MURDER IN THE AIR(1940); MY LOVE CAME BACK(1940)
William "Billy" Newell
YELLOW JACK(1938); BULLDOG EDITION(1936); LIBELED LADY(1936); NAVY BORN(1936); RIFF-RAFF(1936); SAN FRANCISCO(1936); SITTING ON THE MOON(1936); VOICE OF BUGLE ANN(1936); WIFE VERSUS SECRETARY(1936); BEWARE OF LADIES(1937); BIG SHOW, THE(1937); BILL CRACKS DOWN(1937); DANGEROUS HOLIDAY(1937); HAPPY-GO-LUCKY(1937); LARCENY ON THE AIR(1937); MAKE WAY FOR TOMORROW(1937); MAN BETRAYED, A(1937); MANDARIN MYSTERY, THE(1937); RHYTHM IN THE CLOUDS(1937); CITY GIRL(1938); RIDE A CROOKED MILE(1938); SLANDER HOUSE(1938); THERE'S THAT WOMAN AGAIN(1938); DAY THE BOOKIES WEPT, THE(1939); GOOD GIRLS GO TO PARIS(1939); INVITATION TO HAPPINESS(1939); LITTLE ACCIDENT(1939); MR. SMITH GOES TO WASHINGTON(1939); NAUGHTY BUT NICE(1939); HOLD THAT WOMAN(1940); INVISIBLE KILLER, THE(1940); SLIGHTLY TEMPTED(1940); BRIDE CAME C.O.D., THE(1941); CAUGHT IN THE ACT(1941); CITY, FOR CONQUEST(1941); HERE COMES MR. JORDAN(1941); MANPOWER(1941); SAN ANTONIO ROSE(1941); SKYLARK(1941); STRAWBERRY BLONDE, THE(1941); THREE GIRLS ABOUT TOWN(1941); YOU BELONG TO ME(1941); FOOTLIGHT SERENADE(1942); ICE-CAPADES REVUE(1942); KEEPER OF THE FLAME(1942); LADY BODYGUARD(1942); LADY IS WILLING, THE(1942); MAJOR AND THE MINOR, THE(1942); NIGHT TO REMEMBER, A(1942); TRAGEDY AT MIDNIGHT(1942); TWO YANKS IN TRINIDAD(1942); WHO IS HOPE SCHUYLER?(1942); GOOD MORNING, JUDGE(1943); HONEYMOON LODGE(1943); OUTLAW, THE(1943); SING A JINGLE(1943); GYPSY WILDCAT(1944); IRISH EYES ARE SMILING(1944); KANSAS CITY KITTY(1944); SEE HERE, PRIVATE HARGROVE(1944); TOGETHER AGAIN(1944); HER LUCKY NIGHT(1945); HIT THE HAY(1945); HONEYMOON AHEAD(1945); MASQUERADE IN MEXICO(1945); ON STAGE EVERYBODY(1945); SHE GETS HER MAN(1945); WITHOUT LOVE(1945); WONDER MAN(1945); BOWERY BOMBSHELL(1946); DEADLINE FOR MURDER(1946); GIRL ON THE SPOT(1946); HOODLUM SAINT, THE(1946); KID FROM BROOKLYN, THE(1946); MAN WHO DARED, THE(1946); OUT OF THE DEPTHS(1946); TILL THE END OF TIME(1946); WAKE UP AND DREAM(1946); YOUNG WIDOW(1946); KEY WITNESS(1947); LADY IN THE LAKE(1947); OUT OF THE BLUE(1947); SECOND CHANCE(1947); SECRET LIFE OF WALTER MITTY, THE(1947); SENATOR WAS INDISCREET, THE(1947); SONG OF MY HEART(1947); SUDDENLY IT'S SPRING(1947); UP IN CENTRAL PARK(1948); LONE WOLF AND HIS LADY, THE(1949); TELL IT TO THE JUDGE(1949); LOUISA(1950); TO PLEASE A LADY(1950); TRAVELING SALESWOMAN(1950); WOMAN OF DISTINCTION, A(1950); BRIGHT VICTORY(1951); LADY PAYS OFF, THE(1951); MEET ME AFTER THE SHOW(1951); HERE COME THE MARINES(1952); HIGH NOON(1952); ABBOTT AND COSTELLO GO TO MARS(1953); ESCAPE FROM FORT BRAVO(1953); PHFFFT!(1954); TENNESSEE CHAMP(1954); OUR MISS BROOKS(1956); SHORT CUT TO HELL(1957); MISSOURI TRAVELER, THE(1958); LAST TRAIN FROM GUN HILL(1959); POLLYANNA(1960); WHO WAS THAT LADY?(1960); GLOBAL AFFAIR, A(1964)
Jackie Newfield
NABONGA(1944)
Joe Newfield
BILLY THE KID WANTED(1941)
Joel Newfield
THREE DESPERATE MEN(1951)
Sam Newfield
IMPORTANT WITNESS, THE(1933), d; UNDER SECRET ORDERS(1933), d; MARRYING WIDOWS(1934), d; BRANDED A COWARD(1935), d; CODE OF THE MOUNTED(1935), d; NORTHERN FRONTIER(1935), d; RACING LUCK(1935), d; TRAILS OF THE WILD(1935), d; ACES AND EIGHTS(1936), d; BORDER CABALLERO(1936), d; BURNING GOLD(1936), d; FEDERAL AGENT(1936), d; GHOST PATROL(1936), d; LIGHTNING BILL CARSON(1936), d; LION'S DEN, THE(1936), d; ROARIN' GUNS(1936), d; STORMY TRAILS(1936), d; TIMBER WAR(1936), d; TRAITOR, THE(1936), d; ARIZONA GUNFIGHTER(1937), d; BAR Z BAD MEN(1937), d; BOOTH-ILL BRIGADE(1937), d; DOOMED AT SUNDOWN(1937), d; FIGHTING DEPUTY, THE(1937), d; GAMBLING TERROR, THE(1937), d; GUN LORDS OF STIRRUP BASIN(1937), d; GUNS IN THE DARK(1937), d; LAWMAN IS BORN, A(1937), d; LIGHTNIN' CRANDALL(1937), d; MELODY OF THE PLAINS(1937), d; MOONLIGHT

ON THE RANGE(1937), d; RIDIN' THE LONE TRAIL(1937), d; ROARIN' LEAD(1937), d; TRAIL OF VENGEANCE(1937), d; CODE OF THE RANGERS(1938), d; CRASHIN' THRU DANGER(1938), d; DESERT PATROL(1938), d; DURANGO VALLEY RAIDERS(1938), d; FEUD MAKER(1938), d; GUNSMOKE TRAIL(1938), d; HARLEM ON THE PRAIRIE(1938), d; PAROLED–TO DIE(1938), d; PHANTOM RANGER(1938), d; RANGER'S ROUNDUP, THE(1938), d; SONGS AND BULLETS(1938), d; TERROR OF TINY TOWN, THE(1938), d; THUNDER IN THE DESERT(1938), d; CODE OF THE CACTUS(1939), d; FIGHTING MAD(1939), d; FIGHTING RENEGADE(1939), d; FLAMING LEAD(1939), d; FRONTIER SCOUT(1939), d; KNIGHT OF THE PLAINS(1939), d; OUTLAW'S PARADISE(1939), d; SIX-GUN RHYTHM(1939), p&d; TEXAS WILDCATS(1939), d; TRIGGER FINGERS ½(1939), d; TRIGGER PALS(1939), d; DEATH RIDES THE RANGE(1940), d; SECRETS OF A MODEL(1940), d; STRAIGHT SHOOTER(1940), d; LONE RIDER AMBUSHED, THE(1941), d; LONE RIDER CROSSES THE RIO, THE(1941), d; LONE RIDER FIGHTS BACK, THE(1941), d; LONE RIDER IN GHOST TOWN, THE(1941), d; JUNGLE SIREN(1942), d; LONE RIDER AND THE BANDIT, THE(1942), d; LONE RIDER IN CHEYENNE, THE(1942), d; MAD MONSTER, THE(1942), d; OVERLAND STAGECOACH(1942), d; QUEEN OF BROADWAY(1942), d; BLACK RAVEN, THE(1943), d; CATTLE STAMPEDE(1943), d; DANGER! WOMEN AT WORK(1943), d; DEAD MEN WALK(1943), d; HARVEST MELODY(1943), d; TIGER FANGS(1943), d; WESTERN CYCLONE(1943), d; WILD HORSE RUSTLERS(1943), d; WOLVES OF THE RANGE(1943), d; BLAZING FRONTIER(1944), d; CONTENDER, THE(1944), d; DEATH RIDES THE PLAINS(1944), d; DEVIL RIDERS(1944), d; DRIFTER, THE(1944), d; FRONTIER OUTLAWS(1944), d; FUZZY SETTLES DOWN(1944), d; MONSTER MAKER, THE(1944), d; NABONGA(1944), d; RAIDERS OF RED GAP(1944), d; RUSTLER'S HIDEOUT(1944), d; SWING HOSTESS(1944), d; THUNDERING GUN SLINGERS(1944), d; VALLEY OF VENGEANCE(1944), d; WILD HORSE PHANTOM(1944), d; APOLOGY FOR MURDER(1945), d; BORDER BADMEN(1945), d; FIGHTING BILL CARSON(1945), d; HIS BROTHER'S GHOST(1945), d; I ACCUSE MY PARENTS(1945), d; KID SISTER, THE(1945), d; LADY CONFESSES, THE(1945), d; LIGHTNING RAIDERS(1945), d; PRAIRIE RUSTLERS(1945), d; SHADOWS OF DEATH(1945), d; STAGECOACH OUTLAWS(1945), d; WHITE PONGO(1945), d; BLONDE FOR A DAY(1946), d; GAS HOUSE KIDS(1946), d; GENTLEMEN WITH GUNS(1946), d; GHOST OF HIDDEN VALLEY(1946), d; LADY CHASER(1946), d; LARCENY IN HER HEART(1946), d; MURDER IS MY BUSINESS(1946), d; OUTLAW OF THE PLAINS(1946), d; OVERLAND RIDERS(1946), d; PRAIRIE BADMEN(1946), d; QUEEN OF BURLESQUE(1946), d; TERRORS ON HORSEBACK(1946), d; THREE ON A TICKET(1947), d; HI-JACKED(1950), d; MOTOR PATROL(1950), d; RADAR SECRET SERVICE(1950), d; WESTERN PACIFIC AGENT(1950), d; FINGERPRINTS DON'T LIE(1951), d; SKIPALONG ROSENBLOOM(1951), d; THREE DESPERATE MEN(1951), d; GAMBLER AND THE LADY, THE(1952, Brit.), d, w; OUTLAW WOMEN(1952), d; SCOTLAND YARD INSPECTOR(1952, Brit.), d; THUNDER OVER SANGOLAND(1955), d; FRONTIER GAMBLER(1956), d; LAST OF THE DESPERADOES(1956), d; THREE OUTLAWS, THE(1956), d; WILD DAKOTAS, THE(1956), d; FLAMING FRONTIER(1958, Can.), p&d; WOLF DOG(1958, Can.), p&d

Misc. Talkies
AFRICAN INCIDENT(1934), d; BEGGAR'S HOLIDAY(1934), d; BULLDOG COURAGE(1935), d; UNDERCOVER MEN(1935), d; GO-GET-'EM HAINES(1936), d; LIGHTNING CARSON RIDES AGAIN(1938), d; SIX-GUN TRAIL(1938), d; BILLY THE KID OUTLAWED(1940), d; BILLY THE KID'S GUN JUSTICE(1940), d; TEXAS RENEGADES(1940), d; LONE RIDER IN FRONTIER FURY, THE(1941), d; LONE RIDER RIDES ON, THE(1941), d; ALONG THE SUNDOWN TRAIL(1942), d; BORDER ROUNDUP(1942), d; LONE RIDER IN BORDER ROUNDUP(1942), d; OUTLAWS OF BOULDER PASS(1942), d; TEXAS JUSTICE(1942), d; TUMBLEWEED TRAIL(1942), d; FUGITIVE OF THE PLAINS(1943), d; RENEGADE, THE(1943), d; OATH OF VENGEANCE(1944), d; GANGSTER'S DEN(1945), d; CODE OF THE PLAINS(1947), d; FRONTIER FIGHTERS(1947), d

Samuel Newfield
LEAVE IT TO THE MARINES(1951), d; LOST CONTINENT(1951), d; MASK OF THE DRAGON(1951), d; SKY HIGH(1952), d

Mayo Newhall
FOR WHOM THE BELL TOLLS(1943); MADEMOISELLE FIFI(1944); MEET ME IN ST. LOUIS(1944); NOTHING BUT TROUBLE(1944); NIGHT AND DAY(1946); RAZOR'S EDGE, THE(1946); THAT LADY IN ERMINE(1948); MADAME BOVARY(1949)

Guy Newhard
Silents
HIS ROBE OF HONOR(1918)

Joyce Newhard
CAGED(1950); VIOLENT SATURDAY(1955)

Robert Newhard
PARTY GIRL(1930), ph
Silents
WHEN DO WE EAT?(1918), ph; MAN IN THE OPEN, A(1919), ph; EVERYBODY'S SWEETHEART(1920), ph; MAKING THE GRADE(1921), ph; NOBODY'S KID(1921), ph; HUNGRY HEARTS(1922), ph; TRAIL OF THE AXE, THE(1922), ph; HUNCHBACK OF NOTRE DAME, THE(1923), ph; RUBBER TIRES(1927), ph

Bob Newhart
HELL IS FOR HEROES(1962); HOT MILLIONS(1968, Brit.); CATCH-22(1970); ON A CLEAR DAY YOU CAN SEE FOREVER(1970); COLD TURKEY(1971); RESCUERS, THE(1977); FIRST FAMILY(1980); LITTLE MISS MARKER(1980)

John Newhart
BUTCH CASSIDY AND THE SUNDANCE KID(1969), art d

Joyce Newhart
TITANIC(1953)

Paul Newhaus
BATTLE OF BRITAIN, THE(1969, Brit.)

David Newhouse
SAINTS AND SINNERS(1949, Brit.), ed; SILK NOOSE, THE(1950, Brit.), ed; POINT BLANK(1967), w; WHERE'S JACK?(1969, Brit.), w; BEING, THE(1983), ed

Edward Newhouse
I WANT YOU(1951), w; SHADOW IN THE SKY(1951), w

Karen Newhouse
PURSUIT OF D.B. COOPER, THE(1981)

Rafe Newhouse
POINT BLANK(1967), w; WHERE'S JACK?(1969, Brit.), w

Shelia Newhouse
Misc. Talkies
LOST(1983)

Kathleen Newick
RETURN TO PARADISE(1953)

James Newill
RENFREW OF THE ROYAL MOUNTED(1937); SOMETHING TO SING ABOUT(1937); ON THE GREAT WHITE TRAIL(1938); CRASHING THRU(1939); FIGHTING MAD(1939); DANGER AHEAD(1940); MURDER ON THE YUKON(1940); SKY BANDITS, THE(1940); YUKON FLIGHT(1940); GREAT AMERICAN BROADCAST, THE(1941); FALCON'S BROTHER, THE(1942); BOMBARDIER(1943); BRAND OF THE DEVIL(1944); SPOOK TOWN(1944)

Jim Newill
RANGERS TAKE OVER, THE(1942); BAD MEN OF THUNDER GAP(1943); BORDER BUCKAROOS(1943); FIGHTING VALLEY(1943); RETURN OF THE RANGERS, THE(1943); WEST OF TEXAS(1943); BOSS OF THE RAWHIDE(1944); GUNS OF THE LAW(1944); GUNSMOKE MESA(1944); PINTO BANDIT, THE(1944); TRAIL OF TERROR(1944)
Misc. Talkies
OUTLAW ROUNDUP(1944); THUNDERGAP OUTLAWS(1947)

Dale Newkirk
PERSONAL BEST(1982), spec eff

Loren Newkirk
JACKSON COUNTY JAIL(1976), m

Sandra Newkirk
TERMS OF ENDEARMENT(1983)

Paul E. Newlan
PRISONERS OF THE CASBAH(1953)

Paul "Tiny" Newlan
TRUE TO LIFE(1943); MILLIONS IN THE AIR(1935); LAST TRAIN FROM MADRID, THE(1937); PRESCRIPTION FOR ROMANCE(1937); COCOANUT GROVE(1938); SAY IT IN FRENCH(1938); YOU AND ME(1938); ANOTHER THIN MAN(1939); LADY'S FROM KENTUCKY, THE(1939); GHOST BREAKERS, THE(1940); RANGERS OF FORTUNE(1940); DOWN IN SAN DIEGO(1941); GAY VAGABOND, THE(1941); HOLD THAT GHOST(1941); HONKY TONK(1941); LIFE BEGINS FOR ANDY HARDY(1941); SULLIVAN'S TRAVELS(1941); DEVIL'S TRAIL, THE(1942); DOWN RIO GRANDE WAY(1942); JACKASS MAIL(1942); YOU CAN'T ESCAPE FOREVER(1942); DU BARRY WAS A LADY(1943); ADVENTURES OF MARK TWAIN, THE(1944); GIRL RUSH(1944); I'M FROM ARKANSAS(1944); LOST IN A HAREM(1944); MAN WHO WALKED ALONE, THE(1945); ROAD TO UTOPIA(1945); SHANGHAI COBRA, THE(1945); WITHIN THESE WALLS(1945); TWO SISTERS FROM BOSTON(1946); BELLS OF SAN FERNANDO(1947); HIGH BARBAREE(1947); LIKELY STORY, A(1947); MONSIEUR VERDOUX(1947); ROAD TO RIO(1947); SECRET LIFE OF WALTER MITTY, THE(1947); FORCE OF EVIL(1948); FURY AT FURNACE CREEK(1948); SOUTHERN YANKEE, A(1948); FOUNTAINHEAD, THE(1949); MISS GRANT TAKES RICHMOND(1949); NEVER A DULL MOMENT(1950); WABASH AVENUE(1950); CALLAWAY WENT THATAWAY(1951); DAVID AND BATHSHEBA(1951); MY FAVORITE SPY(1951); SUGARFOOT(1951); CAPTIVE CITY(1952); LAWLESS BREED, THE(1952); LOST IN ALASKA(1952); SOMETHING TO LIVE FOR(1952); TREASURE OF LOST CANYON, THE(1952); ABBOTT AND COSTELLO GO TO MARS(1953); DEMETRIUS AND THE GLADIATORS(1954); RIVER OF NO RETURN(1954); JUPITER'S DARLING(1955); TO CATCH A THIEF(1955); WE'RE NO ANGELS(1955); COURT JESTER, THE(1956); DAVY CROCKETT AND THE RIVER PIRATES(1956); BADLANDS OF MONTANA(1957); LONELY MAN, THE(1957); TIJUANA STORY, THE(1957); TROOPER HOOK(1957); AMERICANIZATION OF EMILY, THE(1964); SLENDER THREAD, THE(1965); THERE WAS A CROOKED MAN(1970); DRAGNET(1974)

Douglass Newland
H.M. PULHAM, ESQ.(1941); TWO-FACED WOMAN(1941); VANISHING VIRGINIAN, THE(1941); JOHNNY EAGER(1942); RIO RITA(1942); SUNDAY PUNCH(1942)

John Newland
GENTLEMAN'S AGREEMENT(1947); NORA PRENTISS(1947); T-MEN(1947); CHALLENGE, THE(1948); HOMICIDE FOR THREE(1948); LET'S LIVE A LITTLE(1948); SONS OF ADVENTURE(1948); THIRTEEN LEAD SOLDIERS(1948); THAT NIGHT(1957); VIOLATORS, THE(1957), d; SPY WITH MY FACE, THE(1966), d; MY LOVER, MY SON(1970, Brit.), d; WHO FEARS THE DEVIL(1972), d

Mary Newland
JEALOUSY(1931, Brit.); OFFICER'S MESS, THE(1931, Brit.); TO OBLIGE A LADY(1931, Brit.); ASK BECCLES(1933, Brit.); JEWEL, THE(1933, Brit.); DEATH AT A BROADCAST(1934, Brit.); EASY MONEY(1934, Brit.); PRICE OF WISDOM, THE(1935, Brit.); SILENT PASSENGER, THE(1935, Brit.); SMALL MAN, THE(1935, Brit.)

Paul Newland
COLT .45(1950); AGAINST ALL FLAGS(1952); PIRATES OF TRIPOLI(1955)

Sally Newland
FIGHTING PIMPERNEL, THE(1950, Brit.); WOMAN IN HIDING(1953, Brit.)

Tiny Newland
SWING HIGH, SWING LOW(1937)

Anthony Newlands
BEYOND THIS PLACE(1959, Brit.); ROOM AT THE TOP(1959, Brit.); FOXHOLE IN CAIRO(1960, Brit.); MAN WITH THE GREEN CARNATION, THE(1960, Brit.); FOURTH SQUARE, THE(1961, Brit.); TROUBLE IN THE SKY(1961, Brit.); 20,000 POUNDS KISS, THE(1964, Brit.); HYSTERIA(1965, Brit.); KALEIDOSCOPE(1966, Brit.); SOLO FOR SPARROW(1966, Brit.); PSYCHO-CIRCUS(1967, Brit.); MAGUS, THE(1968, Brit.); SCREAM AND SCREAM AGAIN(1970, Brit.)

Anthony Newley
VICE VERSA(1948, Brit.); VOTE FOR HUGGETT(1948, Brit.); BOY, A GIRL AND A BIKE, A(1949 Brit.); DON'T EVER LEAVE ME(1949, Brit.); OUTSIDER, THE(1949, Brit.); HIGHLY DANGEROUS(1950, Brit.); MADELEINE(1950, Brit.); LITTLE BALLERINA, THE(1951, Brit.); OLIVER TWIST(1951, Brit.); THOSE PEOPLE NEXT DOOR(1952, Brit.); TOP OF THE FORM(1953, Brit.); UP TO HIS NECK(1954, Brit.); COCKLESHELL HEROES, THE(1955); ABOVE US THE WAVES(1956, Brit.); LAST MAN TO HANG, THE(1956, Brit.); PORT AFRIQUE(1956, Brit.); FIRE DOWN BELOW(1957, U.S./Brit.); GOOD COMPANIONS, THE(1957, Brit.); HIGH FLIGHT(1957, Brit.); HOW TO MURDER A RICH UNCLE(1957, Brit.); PURSUIT OF THE GRAF SPEE(1957, Brit.); X THE UNKNOWN(1957, Brit.); MAN INSIDE, THE(1958, Brit.); TANK FORCE(1958, Brit.); BANDIT OF ZHOBE, THE(1959, Brit.); HEART OF A MAN, THE(1959, Brit.); IDOL ON PARADE(1959, Brit.); LADY IS A SQUARE, THE(1959, Brit.); NAVY HEROES(1959, Brit.); IN THE NICK(1960, Brit.); JAZZ BOAT(1960, Brit.); KILLERS OF KILIMANJARO(1960, Brit.); LET'S GET MARRIED(1960, Brit.); SMALL WORLD OF SAMMY LEE, THE(1963, Brit.); STOP THE WORLD–I WANT TO GET OFF(1966, Brit.), w; DOCTOR DOLITTLE(1967); SWEET NOVEMBER(1968); SUMMERTREE(1971), d; IT SEEMED LIKE A GOOD IDEA AT THE TIME(1975, Can.); MR. QUILP(1975, Brit.); SAMMY STOPS THE WORLD zero(1978), w

Misc. Talkies
PLAY IT COOLER(1961); CAN HIERONYMUS MERKIN EVER FORGET MERCY HUMPPE AND FIND TRUE HAPPINESS?(1969), d

Douglass Newlin
MARRIED BACHELOR(1941)

Desmond Newling
MY BROTHER JONATHAN(1949, Brit.); OUTSIDER, THE(1949, Brit.)

Alan Newman
PROMISE, THE(1979)

Albert Newman
ATLANTIC CITY(1944), m; EARL CARROLL'S VANITIES(1945), md

Alfred Newman
DEVIL TO PAY, THE(1930), m; WHOOPEE(1930), md; ARROWSMITH(1931), m; PALMY DAYS(1931), md; STREET SCENE(1931), m; TONIGHT OR NEVER(1931), m, md; UNHOLY GARDEN, THE(1931), m; COCK OF THE AIR(1932), m; KID FROM SPAIN, THE(1932), md; MR. ROBINSON CRUSOE(1932), m; NIGHT WORLD(1932), m; SKY DEVILS(1932), m, md; ADVICE TO THE LOVELORN(1933), md; BLOOD MONEY(1933), m; BOWERY, THE(1933), m; BROADWAY THROUGH A KEYHOLE(1933), md; HALLELUJAH, I'M A BUM(1933), md; MASQUERADER, THE(1933), m; ROMAN SCANDALS(1933), md; BORN TO BE BAD(1934), md; CAT'S PAW, THE(1934), md; COUNT OF MONTE CRISTO, THE(1934), m; HOUSE OF ROTHSCHILD, THE(1934), md; KID MILLIONS(1934), md; LOOKING FOR TROUBLE(1934), md; MIGHTY BARNUM, THE(1934), m; MOULIN ROUGE(1934), md; NANA(1934), m; OUR DAILY BREAD(1934), m; TRANSATLANTIC MERRY-GO-ROUND(1934), md; WE LIVE AGAIN(1934), m, md; BARBARY COAST(1935), md; BROADWAY MELODY OF 1936(1935), md; CALL OF THE WILD(1935), m; CLIVE OF INDIA(1935), m; DARK ANGEL, THE(1935), m; FOLIES DERGERE(1935), md; LES MISERABLES(1935), md; MELODY LINGERS ON, THE(1935), md; METROPOLITAN(1935), md; SPLENDOR(1935), md; WEDDING NIGHT, THE(1935), m; BELOVED ENEMY(1936), m; BORN TO DANCE(1936), md; COME AND GET IT(1936), m; DANCING PIRATE(1936), md; DODSWORTH(1936), m; GAY DESPERADO, THE(1936), md; MODERN TIMES(1936), md; ONE RAINY AFTERNOON(1936), md; RAMONA(1936), md; STRIKE ME PINK(1936), md; THESE THREE(1936), m; DEAD END(1937), m; HURRICANE, THE(1937), m; PRISONER OF ZENDA, THE(1937), m; SLAVE SHIP(1937), m; STELLA DALLAS(1937), md; WEE WILLIE WINKIE(1937), md; WHEN YOU'RE IN LOVE(1937), md; WOMAN CHASES MAN(1937), m&md; YOU ONLY LIVE ONCE(1937), m, md; 52ND STREET(1937), md; ADVENTURES OF MARCO POLO, THE(1938), md; ALEXANDER'S RAGTIME BAND(1938), md; COWBOY AND THE LADY, THE(1938), m; TRADE WINDS(1938), m&md; DRUMS ALONG THE MOHAWK(1939), m; GUNGA DIN(1939), md; HUNCHBACK OF NOTRE DAME, THE(1939), m; RAINS CAME, THE(1939), m; REAL GLORY, THE(1939), md; STAR MAKER, THE(1939), md; THEY SHALL HAVE MUSIC(1939), a, md; WUTHERING HEIGHTS(1939), md; YOUNG MR. LINCOLN(1939), m; BLUE BIRD, THE(1940), m; BRIGHAM YOUNG–FRONTIERSMAN(1940), m; BROADWAY MELODY OF 1940(1940), md; EARTHBOUND(1940), m; FOREIGN CORRESPONDENT(1940), m; GRAPES OF WRATH(1940), m; HUDSON'S BAY(1940), m; JOHNNY APOLLO(1940), m; LILLIAN RUSSELL(1940), md; LITTLE OLD NEW YORK(1940), m; MARK OF ZORRO, THE(1940), m, md; MARYLAND(1940), m, md; PUBLIC DEB No. 1(1940), md; THEY KNEW WHAT THEY WANTED(1940), m; TIN PAN ALLEY(1940), md; VIGIL IN THE NIGHT(1940), m; WESTERNER, THE(1940), m; YOUNG PEOPLE(1940), md; BALL OF FIRE(1941), m; BELLE STARR(1941), m; BLOOD AND SAND(1941), m; CHARLEY'S AUNT(1941), md; GREAT AMERICAN BROADCAST, THE(1941), md; HOW GREEN WAS MY VALLEY(1941), m; MAN HUNT(1941), m; MOON OVER MIAMI(1941), md; REMEMBER THE DAY(1941), m; THAT NIGHT IN RIO(1941), md; WEEKEND IN HAVANA(1941), md; WILD GEESE CALLING(1941), m; YANK IN THE R.A.F., A(1941), md; BLACK SWAN, THE(1942), m; CHINA GIRL(1942), m; GIRL TROUBLE(1942), m; LIFE BEGINS AT 8:30(1942), m, md; MY GAL SAL(1942), md; ORCHESTRA WIVES(1942), md; PIED PIPER, THE(1942), m; ROXIE HART(1942), m; SON OF FURY(1942), m, md; SONG OF THE ISLANDS(1942), md; SPRINGTIME IN THE ROCKIES(1942), md; TEN GENTLEMEN FROM WEST POINT(1942), m; THIS ABOVE ALL(1942), m; TO THE SHORES OF TRIPOLI(1942), m; CLAUDIA(1943), m; CONEY ISLAND(1943), md; GANG'S ALL HERE, THE(1943), md; HEAVEN CAN WAIT(1943), m; IMMORTAL SERGEANT, THE(1943), md; MOON IS DOWN, THE(1943), m; MY FRIEND FLICKA(1943), m; SONG OF BERNADETTE, THE(1943), m, md; SWEET ROSIE O'GRADY(1943), md; IRISH EYES ARE SMILING(1944), md; KEYS OF THE KINGDOM, THE(1944), m; PURPLE HEART, THE(1944), m; SULLIVANS, THE(1944), md; SUNDAY DINNER FOR A SOLDIER(1944), m; WILSON(1944), m; BELL FOR ADANO, A(1945), m; DIAMOND HORSESHOE(1945), m; DOLLY SISTERS, THE(1945), m, md; ROYAL SCANDAL, A(1945), m; STATE FAIR(1945), md; TREE GROWS IN BROOKLYN, A(1945), m; CENTENNIAL SUMMER(1946), md; DRAGONWYCH(1946), m; LEAVE HER TO HEAVEN(1946), m; MARGIE(1946), m, md; RAZOR'S EDGE, THE(1946), m; THREE LITTLE GIRLS IN BLUE(1946), md; 13 RUE MADELEINE(1946), m; BRASHER DOUBLOON, THE(1947), m; CAPTAIN FROM CASTILE(1947), m; DAISY KENYON(1947), m; FOREVER AMBER(1947), md; FOXES OF HARROW, THE(1947), md; GENTLEMAN'S AGREEMENT(1947), m; HOMESTRETCH, THE(1947), m; I WONDER WHO'S KISSING HER NOW(1947), md; LATE GEORGE APLEY, THE(1947), md; MOSS ROSE(1947), md; MOTHER WORE TIGHTS(1947), md; SHOCKING MISS PILGRIM, THE(1947), md; CALL NORTHSIDE 777(1948), m; CHICKEN EVERY SUNDAY(1948), m; CRY OF THE CITY(1948), m; FURY AT FURNACE CREEK(1948), md; IRON CURTAIN, THE(1948), md; LETTER TO THREE WIVES, A(1948), m, m, md; SITTING PRETTY(1948), m; SNAKE PIT, THE(1948), m, md; THAT LADY IN ERMINE(1948), md; UNFAITHFULLY YOURS(1948), md; WHEN MY BABY SMILES AT ME(1948), m, md; YELLOW SKY(1948), m, md; DANCING IN THE DARK(1949), md; DOWN TO THE SEA IN SHIPS(1949), m; EVERYBODY DOES IT(1949), m; FAN, THE(1949), m; MOTHER IS A FRESHMAN(1949), m; MR. BELVEDERE GOES TO COLLEGE(1949), m; OH, YOU BEAUTIFUL DOLL(1949), m; PINKY(1949), m; PRINCE OF FOXES(1949), m; THIEVES' HIGHWAY(1949), m; TWELVE O'CLOCK HIGH(1949), m; WHIRLPOOL(1949), md; YOU'RE MY EVERYTHING(1949), md; ALL ABOUT EVE(1950), m; BIG LIFT, THE(1950), m; BROKEN ARROW(1950), m; FOR HEAVEN'S SAKE(1950), m; GUNFIGHTER, THE(1950), m; MY BLUE HEAVEN(1950), md; NO WAY OUT(1950), m, md; PANIC IN THE STREETS(1950), m; TWO FLAGS WEST(1950), md; WHEN WILLIE COMES MARCHING HOME(1950), m; CALL ME MISTER(1951), md; DAVID AND BATHSHEBA(1951), m; FOURTEEN HOURS(1951), m; HALF ANGEL(1951), md; HOUSE ON TELEGRAPH HILL(1951), md; ON THE RIVERA(1951), md; PEOPLE WILL TALK(1951), md; TAKE CARE OF MY LITTLE GIRL(1951), m; KANGAROO(1952), m; O. HENRY'S FULL HOUSE(1952), m; PONY SOLDIER(1952), md; PRISONER OF ZENDA, THE(1952), m; STARS AND STRIPES FOREVER(1952), md; VIVA ZAPATA!(1952), md; WAIT TIL THE SUN SHINES, NELLIE(1952), m; WAY OF A GAUCHO(1952), md; WHAT PRICE GLORY?(1952), m; WITH A SONG IN MY HEART(1952), md; CALL ME MADAM(1953), md; DESTINATION GOBI(1953), md; HOW TO MARRY A MILLIONAIRE(1953), md; PRESIDENT'S LADY, THE(1953), m; ROBE, THE(1953), m; TONIGHT WE SING(1953), md; TREASURE OF THE GOLDEN CONDOR(1953), md; DEMETRIUS AND THE GLADIATORS(1954), md; EGYPTIAN. THE(1954), m, md; HELL AND HIGH WATER(1954), m; THERE'S NO BUSINESS LIKE SHOW BUSINESS(1954), md; DADDY LONG LEGS(1955), m; LOVE IS A MANY-SPLENDORED THING(1955), m; MAN CALLED PETER, THE(1955), m, md; SEVEN YEAR ITCH, THE(1955), m, md; ANASTASIA(1956), m; BUS STOP(1956), m; CAROUSEL(1956), md; KING AND I, THE(1956), md; APRIL LOVE(1957), md; CERTAIN SMILE, A(1958), m; SOUTH PACIFIC(1958), md; BEST OF EVERYTHING, THE(1959), m; DIARY OF ANNE FRANK, THE(1959), m; HOLIDAY FOR LOVERS(1959), m; FLOWER DRUM SONG(1961), md; PLEASURE OF HIS COMPANY, THE(1961), m, md; COUNTERFEIT TRAITOR, THE(1962), m; HOW THE WEST WAS WON(1962), m; MAN WHO SHOT LIBERTY VALANCE, THE(1962), m. Cyril J. Mockridge; STATE FAIR(1962), m; GREATEST STORY EVER TOLD, THE(1965), m; NEVADA SMITH(1966), m; FIRECREEK(1968), m; AIRPORT(1970), m

Andrea Newman
THREE INTO TWO WON'T GO(1969, Brit.), w

Angela Newman
SIEGE OF SIDNEY STREET, THE(1960, Brit.)

Anne Newman
THRILL OF IT ALL, THE(1963); BEST MAN, THE(1964); EL DORADO(1967)

Arthur Newman
GOLDWYN FOLLIES, THE(1938), md; ZULU(1964, Brit.), cos; HELP!(1965, Brit.), cos

Barry Newman
PRETTY BOY FLOYD(1960); MOVING FINGER, THE(1963); LAWYER, THE(1969); VANISHING POINT(1971); SALZBURG CONNECTION, THE(1972); FEAR IS THE KEY(1973); CITY ON FIRE(1979 Can.); AMY(1981)

Bascom Newman
1984
PLACES IN THE HEART(1984)

Bernard Newman
RAFTER ROMANCE(1934), cos; BREAK OF HEARTS(1935), cos; I DREAM TOO MUCH(1935), cos; IN PERSON(1935), cos; ROBERTA(1935), cos; STAR OF MIDNIGHT(1935), cos; TOP HAT(1935), cos; BRIDE WALKS OUT, THE(1936), cos; FOLLOW THE FLEET(1936), cos; LADY CONSENTS, THE(1936), cos; MORE THAN A SECRETARY(1936), cos; SWING TIME(1936), cos; SYLVIA SCARLETT(1936), cos; THEODORA GOES WILD(1936), cos; TWO IN THE DARK(1936), cos; WALKING ON AIR(1936), cos; WHEN YOU'RE IN LOVE(1937), cos; VIVACIOUS LADY(1938), cos; YOU CAN'T TAKE IT WITH YOU(1938), cos; TALES OF MANHATTAN(1942), cos; DECEPTION(1946), cos; DARK PASSAGE(1947), cos; ESCAPE ME NEVER(1947), cos; POSSESSED(1947), cos; WOMAN IN WHITE, THE(1948), cos; MISSILE FROM HELL(1960, Brit.), w

Bruce Newman
COAL MINER'S DAUGHTER(1980)

Charlene Newman
JACK LONDON(1943)

Charles Newman
FLIRTING WITH FATE(1938), m; ZOMBIES ON BROADWAY(1945), w

David Newman
HE WHO RIDES A TIGER(1966, Brit.), p; BONNIE AND CLYDE(1967), w; HANNIBAL BROOKS(1969, Brit.), stunts; THERE WAS A CROOKED MAN(1970), w; BAD COMPANY(1972), w; WHAT'S UP, DOC?(1972), w; SUPERMAN(1978), w; SUPERMAN II(1980), w; JINXED!(1982), w; STILL OF THE NIGHT(1982), d&w; SUPERMAN III(1983), w
1984
SHEENA(1984), w

Dean Newman
4D MAN(1959)

Denise Newman
CITY LOVERS(1982, S. African)

Dorothy Newman
HOT ROD GANG(1958); HAIL, HERO!(1969); MISSOURI BREAKS, THE(1976)

Elizabeth Newman
ETERNAL WALTZ, THE(1959, Ger.)

Emil Newman
REUNION(1936), md; BRIDE WORE CRUTCHES, THE(1940), md; CHARLIE CHAN AT THE WAX MUSEUM(1940), md; CHARTER PILOT(1940), md; DOWN ARGENTINE WAY(1940), md; GAY CABALLERO, THE(1940), md; GIRL FROM AVENUE A(1940), md; GIRL IN 313(1940), m; MICHAEL SHAYNE, PRIVATE DETECTIVE(1940), md; MURDER OVER NEW YORK(1940), md; STREET OF MEMORIES(1940), md; YESTERDAY'S HEROES(1940), md; YOUTH WILL BE SERVED(1940), md; ACCENT ON LOVE(1941), m; CADET GIRL(1941), md; CHARLIE CHAN IN RIO(1941), md; DANCE HALL(1941), md; DEAD MEN TELL(1941), md; DRESSED TO KILL(1941), md; FOR BEAUTY'S SAKE(1941), m, md; GREAT GUNS(1941), md; JENNIE(1941), m; MAN AT LARGE(1941), md; MOON OVER HER SHOULDER(1941), md; MURDER AMONG FRIENDS(1941), md; PERFECT SNOB, THE(1941), md; RIDE, KELLY, RIDE(1941), md; RIDE ON VAQUERO(1941), md; RISE AND SHINE(1941), md; ROMANCE OF THE RIO GRANDE(1941), md; SCOTLAND YARD(1941), md; SLEEPERS WEST(1941), md; SMALL TOWN DEB(1941), md; SUN VALLEY SERENADE(1941), md; TALL, DARK AND HANDSOME(1941), md; WE GO FAST(1941), md; A-HAUNTING WE WILL GO(1942), m; BERLIN CORRESPONDENT(1942), m; CAREFUL, SOFT SHOULDERS(1942), m; CASTLE IN THE DESERT(1942), m; DR. RENAULT'S SECRET(1942), m; GENTLEMAN AT HEART, A(1942), m; ICELAND(1942), md; IT HAPPENED IN FLATBUSH(1942), md; JUST OFF BROADWAY(1942), md; LITTLE TOKYO, U.S.A.(1942), md; LONE STAR RANGER(1942), md; LOVES OF EDGAR ALLAN POE, THE(1942), md; MAD MARTINDALES, THE(1942), md; MAGNIFICENT DOPE, THE(1942), md; MAN WHO WOULDN'T DIE, THE(1942), md; MANILA CALLING(1942), md; NIGHT BEFORE THE DIVORCE, THE(1942), md; ON THE SUNNY SIDE(1942), md; OVER MY DEAD BODY(1942), m; POSTMAN DIDN'T RING, THE(1942), md; QUIET PLEASE, MURDER(1942), m; RIGHT TO THE HEART(1942), md; SECRET AGENT OF JAPAN(1942), md; SUNDOWN JIM(1942), md; THRU DIFFERENT EYES(1942), md; TIME TO KILL(1942), m; UNDYING MONSTER, THE(1942), m; WHISPERING GHOSTS(1942), md; WHO IS HOPE SCHUYLER?(1942), md; BOMBER'S MOON(1943), md; CHETNIKS(1943), md; CRASH DIVE(1943), md; DANCING MASTERS, THE(1943), md; DIXIE DUGAN(1943), m; GUADALCANAL DIARY(1943), md; HAPPY LAND(1943),

md; HELLO, FRISCO, HELLO(1943), md; HOLY MATRIMONY(1943), md; JITTER-BUGS(1943), md; MARGIN FOR ERROR(1943), md; MEANEST MAN IN THE WORLD, THE(1943), md; PARIS AFTER DARK(1943), md; STORMY WEA-THER(1943), m; THEY CAME TO BLOW UP AMERICA(1943), md; TONIGHT WE RAID CALAIS(1943), m; BERMUDA MYSTERY(1944), md; BIG NOISE, THE(1944), md; BUFFALO BILL(1944), md; EVE OF ST. MARK, THE(1944), md; FOUR JILLS IN A JEEP(1944), md; GREENWICH VILLAGE(1944), md; HOME IN INDIANA(1944), md; IN THE MEANTIME, DARLING(1944), md; LADIES OF WASHINGTON(1944), md; LAURA(1944), md; LIFEBOAT(1944), md; LODGER, THE(1944), md; PIN UP GIRL(1944), md; ROGER TOUHY, GANGSTER!(1944), md; SOMETHING FOR THE BOYS(1944), md; SWEET AND LOWDOWN(1944), md; TAKE IT OR LEAVE IT(1944), md; TAMPICO(1944), md; WING AND A PRAYER(1944), md; CAPTAIN ED-DIE(1945), md; CIRCUMSTANTIAL EVIDENCE(1945), md; COLONEL EFFING-HAM'S RAID(1945), md; DOLL FACE(1945), md; DON JUAN QUILLIGAN(1945), md; FALLEN ANGEL(1945), md; HOUSE ON 92ND STREET, THE(1945), md; JUNIOR MISS(1945), md; MOLLY AND ME(1945), md; NOB HILL(1945), md; SPIDER, THE(1945), md; THUNDERHEAD-SON OF FLICKA(1945), md; WHERE DO WE GO FROM HERE?(1945), md; WITHIN THESE WALLS(1945), md; BEHIND GREEN LIGHTS(1946), md; CLUNY BROWN(1946), md; DARK CORNER, THE(1946), md; DO YOU LOVE ME?(1946), md; IF I'M LUCKY(1946), md; IT SHOULDN'T HAPPEN TO A DOG(1946), md; JOHNNY COMES FLYING HOME(1946), md; RENDEZVOUS 24(1946), md; SHOCK(1946), md; SMOKY(1946), md; SOMEWHERE IN THE NIGHT(1946), md; STRANGE TRIANGLE(1946), md; WAKE UP AND DREAM(1946), md; BISHOP'S WIFE, THE(1947), md; SECRET LIFE OF WALTER MITTY, THE(1947), md; ENCHANTMENT(1948), md; INNER SANCTUM(1948), md; JOAN OF ARC(1948), md; JUNGLE PATROL(1948), m; SONG IS BORN, A(1948), md; TEX-AS, BROOKLYN AND HEAVEN(1948), md; MY FOOLISH HEART(1949), md; RO-SEANNA McCOY(1949), md; EDGE OF DOOM(1950), md; GOLDEN GLOVES STORY, THE(1950), md; GUILTY OF TREASON(1950), m;QUICKSAND(1950), art d; WOMAN ON THE RUN(1950), md; 711 OCEAN DRIVE(1950), md; CRY DANGER(1951), m; GROOM WORE SPURS, THE(1951), md; JOURNEY INTO LIGHT(1951), md; LADY SAYS NO, THE(1951), m; BIG JIM McLAIN(1952), m; CAPTIVE CITY(1952), md; JAPANESE WAR BRIDE(1952), m; JUST FOR YOU(1952), md; RANCHO NOTORI-OUS(1952), m; SAN FRANCISCO STORY, THE(1952), m; SOMEBODY LOVES ME(1952), md; HONDO(1953), m; ISLAND IN THE SKY(1953), m; STEEL LADY, THE(1953), m; WAR PAINT(1953), md; 99 RIVER STREET(1953), m; BEACH-HEAD(1954), m; MAD MAGICIAN, THE(1954), m; RING OF FEAR(1954), m; MAN WITH THE GUN(1955), md; NAKED STREET, THE(1955), m, md; SHARKFIGHT-ERS, THE(1956), md; CHICAGO CONFIDENTIAL(1957), m; DEATH IN SMALL DOSES(1957), m; IRON SHERIFF, THE(1957), m&md; PROUD REBEL, THE(1958), md; UNWED MOTHER(1958), m; RIOT IN JUVENILE PRISON(1959), m; GREAT SIOUX MASSACRE, THE(1965), m

Erica Newman
GIRL HABIT(1931)
Ernest Newman
NEW YORK CONFIDENTIAL(1955), cos
Ethel Newman
Silents
OLD COUNTRY, THE(1921, Brit.)
Eve Newman
THE HYPNOTIC EYE(1960), m; MUSCLE BEACH PARTY(1964), ed; PAJAMA PARTY(1964), ed; BEACH BLANKET BINGO(1965), ed; DR. GOLDFOOT AND THE BIKINI MACHINE(1965), ed; HOW TO STUFF A WILD BIKINI(1965), ed; SER-GEANT DEADHEAD(1965), ed; FIREBALL 590(1966), ed; GHOST IN THE INVISI-BLE BIKINI(1966), ed; C'MON, LET'S LIVE A LITTLE(1967), ed; THREE IN THE ATTIC(1968), ed; WILD IN THE STREETS(1968), ed; ANGEL, ANGEL, DOWN WE GO(1969), ed; BLOODY MAMA(1970), ed; LITTLE CIGARS(1973), ed; OTHER SIDE OF THE MOUNTAIN, THE(1975), ed; TWO-MINUTE WARNING(1976), ed; OTHER SIDE OF THE MOUNTAIN-PART 2, THE(1978), ed; PARADISE ALLEY(1978), ed; LITTLE MISS MARKER(1980), ed
1984
NO SMALL AFFAIR(1984), ed
G.F. Newman
TAKE, THE(1974), w
1984
NUMBER ONE(1984, Brit.), w
George Newman
MIDDLE OF THE NIGHT(1959), makeup; ANNIE HALL(1977), cos
Gladys Newman
HURRY SUNDOWN(1967)
Greatrex Newman
MISTER CINDERS(1934, Brit.), w
Harry C. Newman
WASP WOMAN, THE(1959), ph
Harry Newman [Neumann]
TOUGH KID(1939), ph
Hazel Newman
Misc. Silents
BEHIND TWO GUNS(1924)
Irene Newman
VIVACIOUS LADY(1938), cos
James Newman
COOL AND THE CRAZY, THE(1958)
James E. Newman
ANNIE GET YOUR GUN(1950), ed
Jim Newman
COUNTRYMAN(1982, Jamaica)
Joan Newman
LORDS OF FLATBUSH, THE(1974); ANNIE HALL(1977)
Joe Newman
JUNGLE PATROL(1948), d; GREAT DAN PATCH, THE(1949), d
Joseph Newman
NORTHWEST RANGERS(1942), d; ABANDONED(1949), d; GUY WHO CAME BACK, THE(1951), d; LOVE NEST(1951), d; THIS ISLAND EARTH(1955), d; DEATH IN SMALL DOSES(1957), d; BIG CIRCUS, THE(1959), d; TARZAN, THE APE MAN(1959), d
Joseph M. Newman
711 OCEAN DRIVE(1950), d; LUCKY NICK CAIN(1951), d; OUTCASTS OF POKER FLAT, THE(1952), d; PONY SOLDIER(1952), d; RED SKIES OF MONTANA(1952), d; DANGEROUS CROSSING(1953), d; HUMAN JUNGLE, THE(1954), d; KISS OF FI-

RE(1955), d; FLIGHT TO HONG KONG(1956), p&d, w; FORT MASSACRE(1958), d; GUNFIGHT AT DODGE CITY, THE(1959), d; GEORGE RAFT STORY, THE(1961), d; KING OF THE ROARING TWENTIES-THE STORY OF ARNOLD ROTHSTEIN(1961), d; THUNDER OF DRUMS, A(1961), d
Misc. Talkies
LAWBREAKERS, THE(1960), d
Laraine Newman
AMERICAN HOT WAX(1978); WHOLLY MOSES(1980)
Larraine Newman
TUNNELVISION(1976)
Laura Newman
Silents
OTHER MAN'S WIFE, THE(1919)
Leslie Newman
SUPERMAN(1978), w; SUPERMAN II(1980), w; SUPERMAN III(1983), w
Lionel Newman
SON OF FRANKENSTEIN(1939), md; JOHNNY APOLLO(1940), m; BILL AND COO(1947), md; KISS OF DEATH(1947), md; NIGHTMARE ALLEY(1947), md; APARTMENT FOR PEGGY(1948), md; CRY OF THE CITY(1948), md; DEEP WA-TERS(1948), md; GIVE MY REGARDS TO BROADWAY(1948), md; GREEN GRASS OF WYOMING(1948), md; LUCK OF THE IRISH(1948), md; ROAD HOUSE(1948), md; SCUDDA-HOO! SCUDDA-HAY!(1948), md; STREET WITH NO NAME, THE(1948), md; THAT WONDERFUL URGE(1948), md; WALLS OF JERICHO(1948), md; YOU WERE MEANT FOR ME(1948), md; COME TO THE STABLE(1949), md; FATHER WAS A FULLBACK(1949), md; I WAS A MALE WAR BRIDE(1949), md; IT HAPPENS EVERY SPRING(1949), md; SLATTERY'S HURRICANE(1949), md; THIEVES' HIGH-WAY(1949), md; CHEAPER BY THE DOZEN(1950), md; I'LL GET BY(1950), md; JACKPOT, THE(1950), m; LOVE THAT BRUTE(1950), md; MISTER 880(1950), md; MOTHER DIDN'T TELL ME(1950), md; STELLA(1950), md; THREE CAME HO-ME(1950), md; TICKET TO TOMAHAWK(1950), md; WABASH AVENUE(1950), md; WHEN WILLIE COMES MARCHING HOME(1950), md; WHERE THE SIDEWALK ENDS(1950), md; AS YOUNG AS YOU FEEL(1951), md; ELOPEMENT(1951), md; FIXED BAYONETS(1951), md; FOLLOW THE SUN(1951), md; FROGMEN, THE(1951), md; GOLDEN GIRL(1951), md; GUY WHO CAME BACK, THE(1951), md; HALLS OF MONTEZUMA(1951), md; I CAN GET IT FOR YOU WHOLESALE(1951), md; I'D CLIMB THE HIGHEST MOUNTAIN(1951), md; LET'S MAKE IT LE-GAL(1951), md; LOVE NEST(1951), md; MEET ME AFTER THE SHOW(1951), md; MODEL AND THE MARRIAGE BROKER, THE(1951), md; MR. BELVEDERE RINGS THE BELL(1951), md; RAWHIDE(1951), m, md; SECRET OF CONVICT LAKE, THE(1951), md; THIRTEENTH LETTER, THE(1951), md; YOU'RE IN THE NAVY NOW(1951), md; BELLES ON THEIR TOES(1952), md; BLOODHOUNDS OF BROAD-WAY(1952), m; DEADLINE-U.S.A.(1952), md; DIPLOMATIC COURIER(1952), md; DON'T BOTHER TO KNOCK(1952), md; DREAMBOAT(1952), md; I DON'T CARE GIRL, THE(1952), md; LES MISERABLES(1952), md; LYDIA BAILEY(1952), md; MONKEY BUSINESS(1952), md; MY PAL GUS(1952), md; MY WIFE'S BEST FRIEND(1952), md; NIGHT WITHOUT SLEEP(1952), md; OUTCASTS OF POKER FLAT, THE(1952), md; PRIDE OF ST. LOUIS, THE(1952), md; RED SKIES OF MONTANA(1952), md; RETURN OF THE TEXAN(1952), md; SOMETHING FOR THE BIRDS(1952), md; WE'RE NOT MARRIED(1952), md; BLUEPRINT FOR MURDER, A(1953), md; CITY OF BAD MEN(1953), m; DANGEROUS CROSSING(1953), m; DOWN AMONG THE SHELTERING PALMS(1953), md; GENTLEMEN PREFER BLONDES(1953), md; GIRL NEXT DOOR, THE(1953), md; INFERNO(1953), md; KID FROM LEFT FIELD, THE(1953), md; MAN IN THE ATTIC(1953), md; MR. SCOUT-MASTER(1953), md; NIAGARA(1953), md; PICKUP ON SOUTH STREET(1953), md; POWDER RIVER(1953), md; SILVER WHIP, THE(1953), md; TAXI(1953), md; TITAN-IC(1953), md; VICKI(1953), md; BROKEN LANCE(1954), md; GAMBLER FROM NAT-CHEZ, THE(1954), m; GORILLA AT LARGE(1954), md; NIGHT PEOPLE(1954), md; PRINCESS OF THE NILE(1954), m; RIVER OF NO RETURN(1954), md; ROCKET MAN, THE(1954), md; SIEGE AT RED RIVER, THE(1954), m; THERE'S NO BUSINESS LIKE SHOW BUSINESS(1954), md; THREE YOUNG TEXANS(1954), md; GIRL IN THE RED VELVET SWING, THE(1955), md; GOOD MORNING, MISS DOVE(1955), md; HOUSE OF BAMBOO(1955), md; HOW TO BE VERY, VERY, POPULAR(1955), md; RACERS, THE(1955), md; RAINS OF RANCHIPUR, THE(1955), md; SEVEN CITIES OF GOLD(1955), md; SOLDIER OF FORTUNE(1955), md; VIEW FROM POMPEY'S HEAD, THE(1955), md; VIOLENT SATURDAY(1955), md; WHITE FEATHER(1955), md; BEST THINGS IN LIFE ARE FREE, THE(1956), m; D-DAY, THE SIXTH OF JUNE(1956), md; GIRL CAN'T HELP IT, THE(1956), md; HARDER THEY FALL, THE(1956), md; HILDA CRANE(1956), md; KILLER IS LOOSE, THE(1956), m; KISS BEFORE DYING, A(1956), m; LAST WAGON, THE(1956), m; LIEUTENANT WORE SKIRTS, THE(1956), md; LOVE ME TENDER(1956), m; ON THE THRESHOLD OF SPACE(1956), md; PROUD ONES, THE(1956), m; REVOLT OF MAMIE STOVER, THE(1956), md; SOLID GOLD CADILLAC, THE(1956), md; TEEN-AGE REBEL(1956), md; 23 PACES TO BAKER STREET(1956), md; AFFAIR TO REMEMBER, AN(1957), md; BERNARDINE(1957), md; DESK SET(1957), md; ENEMY BELOW, THE(1957), md; KISS THEM FOR ME(1957), m; NO DOWN PAY-MENT(1957), md; SUN ALSO RISES, THE(1957), md; TRUE STORY OF JESSE JAMES, THE(1957), md; WAY TO THE GOLD, THE(1957), md; WAYWARD BUS, THE(1957), md; WILL SUCCESS SPOIL ROCK HUNTER?(1957), md; BRAVADOS, THE(1958), m; GIFT OF LOVE, THE(1958), md; IN LOVE AND WAR(1958), md; LONG, HOT SUMMER, THE(1958), md; MARDI GRAS(1958), m, md; NICE LITTLE BANK THAT SHOULD BE ROBBED, A(1958), m; RALLY 'ROUND THE FLAG, BOYS!(1958), md; SING, BOY, SING(1958), m; YOUNG LIONS, THE(1958), md; 10 NORTH FREDERICK(1958), md; COMPULSION(1959), m; HOUND-DOG MAN(1959), md; JOURNEY TO THE CENTER OF THE EARTH(1959), md; PRIVATE'S AFFAIR, A(1959), md; REMARKABLE MR. PENNYPACKER, THE(1959), md; SAY ONE FOR ME(1959), md; SOUND AND THE FURY, THE(1959), md; WARLOCK(1959), md; WOMAN OBSESSED(1959), md; LET'S MAKE LOVE(1960), m, md; NORTH TO ALASKA(1960), m, md; WAKE ME WHEN IT'S OVER(1960), md; MOVE OVER, DARLING(1963), m; PLEASURE SEEKERS, THE(1964), m; DO NOT DISTURB(1965), m; SAND PEBBLES, THE(1966), m; DOCTOR DOLITTLE(1967), md; ST. VALEN-TINE'S DAY MASSACRE(1967), m; FLEA IN HER EAR, A(1968, Fr.), m; THE BOSTON STRANGLER, THE(1968), m; HELLO, DOLLY!(1969), m, md; GREAT WHITE HOPE, THE(1970), m; SALZBURG CONNECTION, THE(1972), m, md; WHEN THE LEGENDS DIE(1972), m; BLUE BIRD, THE(1976), m
1984
UNFAITHFULLY YOURS(1984), md
Martin Newman
SHRIKE, THE(1955)

Melissa Newman
UNDEFEATED, THE(1969); ONE DARK NIGHT(1983)
Michele Newman
SPEEDWAY(1968)
Miller Newman
BITTER TEA OF GENERAL YEN, THE(1933)
Nanette Newman
PERSONAL AFFAIR(1954, Brit.); FACES IN THE DARK(1960, Brit.); CALL ME GENIUS(1961, Brit.); HOUSE OF MYSTERY(1961, Brit.); LEAGUE OF GENTLEMEN, THE(1961, Brit.); PIT OF DARKNESS(1961, Brit.); L-SHAPED ROOM, THE(1962, Brit.); TWICE AROUND THE DAFFODILS(1962, Brit.); MURDER CAN BE DEADLY(1963, Brit.); WRONG ARM OF THE LAW, THE(1963, Brit.); OF HUMAN BONDAGE(1964, Brit.); SEANCE ON A WET AFTERNOON(1964 Brit.); WRONG BOX, THE(1966, Brit.); WHISPERERS, THE(1967, Brit.); DEADFALL(1968, Brit.); JOURNEY INTO DARKNESS(1968, Brit.); CAPTAIN NEMO AND THE UNDERWATER CITY(1969, Brit.); MADWOMAN OF CHAILLOT, THE(1969); OH! WHAT A LOVELY WAR(1969, Brit.); LONG AGO, TOMORROW(1971, Brit.); IT'S A 2"6" ABOVE THE GROUND WORLD(1972, Brit.); MAN AT THE TOP(1973, Brit.); STEPFORD WIVES, THE(1975); INTERNATIONAL VELVET(1978, Brit.)
Nell Newman
Misc. Silents
HEART OF A CHILD, THE(1920)
Pam Newman
SHARKY'S MACHINE(1982)
Paul Newman
SILVER CHALICE, THE(1954); SOMEBODY UP THERE LIKES ME(1956); UNTIL THEY SAIL(1957); CAT ON A HOT TIN ROOF(1958); LEFT-HANDED GUN, THE(1958); LONG, HOT SUMMER, THE(1958); RALLY 'ROUND THE FLAG, BOYS!(1958); HELEN MORGAN STORY, THE(1959); YOUNG PHILADELPHIANS, THE(1959); EXODUS(1960); FROM THE TERRACE(1960); HUSTLER, THE(1961); PARIS BLUES(1961); ADVENTURES OF A YOUNG MAN(1962); SWEET BIRD OF YOUTH(1962); HUD(1963); NEW KIND OF LOVE, A(1963); PRIZE, THE(1963); OUTRAGE, THE(1964); WHAT A WAY TO GO(1964); LADY L(1965, Fr./Ital.); HARPER(1966); TORN CURTAIN(1966); COOL HAND LUKE(1967); HOMBRE(1967); RACHEL, RACHEL(1968), p&d; SECRET WAR OF HARRY FRIGG, THE(1968); BUTCH CASSIDY AND THE SUNDANCE KID(1969); WINNING(1969); WUSA(1970), a, p; SOMETIMES A GREAT NOTION(1971), a, d; THEY MIGHT BE GIANTS(1971), p; EFFECT OF GAMMA RAYS ON MAN-IN-THE-MOON MARIGOLDS, THE(1972), p&d; LIFE AND TIMES OF JUDGE ROY BEAN, THE(1972); POCKET MONEY(1972); MACKINTOSH MAN, THE(1973, Brit.); STING, THE(1973); TOWERING INFERNO, THE(1974); DROWNING POOL, THE(1975); BUFFALO BILL AND THE INDIANS, OR SITTING BULL'S HISTORY LESSON(1976); SILENT MOVIE(1976); SLAP SHOT(1977); QUINTET(1979); WHEN TIME RAN OUT(1980); ABSENCE OF MALICE(1981); FORT APACHE, THE BRONX(1981); VERDICT, THE(1982)
1984
HARRY AND SON(1984), a, p, d, w
Paul Newman, Jr.
RACK, THE(1956)
Paula Newman
RED WAGON(1936), cos; WHERE THERE'S A WILL(1936, Brit), cos
Peter Newman
WE'LL SMILE AGAIN(1942, Brit.)
Peter R. Newman
YESTERDAY'S ENEMY(1959, Brit.), w
Philip Newman
WHERE HAS POOR MICKEY GONE?(1964, Brit.); POOR COW(1968, Brit.); DARWIN ADVENTURE, THE(1972, Brit.)
Phyllis Newman
PICNIC(1955); VAGABOND KING, THE(1956); LET'S ROCK(1958); NAKED WITCH, THE(1964); BYE BYE BRAVERMAN(1968); EXPLOSION(1969, Can.), makeup; MC CABE AND MRS. MILLER(1971), makeup; TO FIND A MAN(1972); MOTHER LODE(1982), makeup
Randy Newman
COLD TURKEY(1971), m; RAGTIME(1981), m
1984
NATURAL, THE(1984), m
Raoul H. Newman
CASTLE OF BLOOD(1964, Fr./Ital.)
Raoul H. Newman [Umberto Raho]
GHOST, THE(1965, Ital.)
Richard Newman
1984
FINDERS KEEPERS(1984)
Robert Newman
IDENTITY UNKNOWN(1945), w
Roger Newman
MARLOWE(1969); TOO LATE THE HERO(1970); ANNIE HALL(1977)
Sam Newman
SHANGHAI CHEST, THE(1948), w
Samuel Newman
DESPERATE WOMEN, THE(?), a, p, w; JUDGE, THE(1949), w; JUNGLE MAN-HUNT(1951), w; TARZAN'S PERIL(1951), w; JUNGLE JIM IN THE FORBIDDEN LAND(1952), w; VOODOO TIGER(1952), w; YANK IN INDO-CHINA, A(1952), w; PRINCE OF PIRATES(1953), w; SKY COMMANDO(1953), w; VALLEY OF THE HEADHUNTERS(1953), w; JESSE JAMES VERSUS THE DALTONS(1954), w; JUNGLE MAN-EATERS(1954), w; GIANT CLAW, THE(1957), w; INVISIBLE INVADERS(1959), w; WIZARD OF BAGHDAD, THE(1960), w; GROUND ZERO(1973), w
Scott Newman
TOWERING INFERNO, THE(1974); GREAT WALDO PEPPER, THE(1975); BREAKHEART PASS(1976); FRATERNITY ROW(1977)
Serge Newman
AWFUL DR. ORLOFF, THE(1964, Span./Fr.), p
Stephen D. Newman
FUNNYMAN(1967); NEXT MAN, THE(1976); SEDUCTION OF JOE TYNAN, THE(1979); HANKY-PANKY(1982); SOPHIE'S CHOICE(1982)
Susan Kendall Newman
I WANNA HOLD YOUR HAND(1978); WEDDING, A(1978)

Theodore Newman
HIDDEN EYE, THE(1945)
Thomas Newman
CAPE FEAR(1962); SATURDAY THE 14TH(1981)
1984
GRANDVIEW, U.S.A.(1984), m; RECKLESS(1984), m; REVENGE OF THE NERDS(1984), m
Tom Newman
SURFTIDE 77(1962); FORTUNE, THE(1975)
Toni Newman
MISS GRANT TAKES RICHMOND(1949); GIRLS' SCHOOL(1950)
Valerie Newman
CHARGE OF THE LIGHT BRIGADE, THE(1968, Brit.)
Vernon Newman
NAKED WITCH, THE(1964)
Walter Newman
BIG CARNIVAL, THE(1951), w; MAN WITH THE GOLDEN ARM, THE(1955), w; UNDERWATER!(1955), w; TRUE STORY OF JESSE JAMES, THE(1957), w; CRIME AND PUNISHMENT, U.S.A.(1959), w; MAGNIFICENT SEVEN, THE(1960), w; INTERNS, THE(1962), w; CAT BALLOU(1965), w; BLOODBROTHERS(1978), w; CHAMP, THE(1979), w
Misc. Silents
LONG CHANCE, THE(1915)
Widgey Newman
SISTER TO ASSIST'ER, A(1938, Brit.), p, d
Widgey R. Newman
CASTLE SINISTER(1932, Brit.), d; UNHOLY QUEST, THE(1934, Brit.), p, w; IMMORTAL GENTLEMAN(1935, Brit.), d, w; ON VELVET(1938, Brit.), p&d; MEN WITHOUT HONOUR(1939, Brit.), d, w; HENRY STEPS OUT(1940, Brit.), p&d; TWO SMART MEN(1940, Brit.), p&d
Misc. Silents
RECKLESS GAMBLE, A(1928, Brit.), d
William Newman
SQUIRM(1976); BRUBAKER(1980); POSTMAN ALWAYS RINGS TWICE, THE(1981)
Birthe Newmann
HAPPINESS CAGE, THE(1972)
Dorothy Newmann
THINGS ARE TOUGH ALL OVER(1982); SNAKE PIT, THE(1948); ANYTHING GOES(1956)
Ed Newmann
BON VOYAGE, CHARLIE BROWN(AND DON'T COME BACK)*** (1980), anim
Harry Newmann
SPY SHIP(1942), ph
Silents
ARIZONA SWEEPSTAKES(1926), ph
Elisabeth Newmann-Viertel
SECRET WAYS, THE(1961)
Julie Newmar
LI'L ABNER(1959); ROOKIE, THE(1959); MARRIAGE-GO-ROUND, THE(1960); FOR LOVE OR MONEY(1963); MACKENNA'S GOLD(1969); MALTESE BIPPY, THE(1969); UP YOUR TEDDY BEAR(1970); HYSTERICAL(1983)
Misc. Talkies
EVILS OF THE NIGHT(1983)
Tammy Newmara
DEVIL'S MESSENGER, THE(1962 U.S./Swed.)
Lucile Newmark
UNTAMED(1929), titles
Lucille Newmark
LET US BE GAY(1930), w; NOT SO DUMB(1930), titles; MISS PACIFIC FLEET(1935), w
Silents
TEA FOR THREE(1927), t; SINGLE MAN, A(1929), t; SIOUX BLOOD(1929), t
Rayner Newmark
FRENCH LIEUTENANT'S WOMAN, THE(1981)
Fred Newmayer
EASY MILLIONS(1933), d
Fred Newmeyer
IT CAN BE DONE(1929), d; MORGAN'S MARAUDERS(1929), d; RAINBOW MAN(1929), d; SAILORS' HOLIDAY(1929), d; FAST AND LOOSE(1930), d; GRAND PARADE, THE(1930), d; QUEEN HIGH(1930), d; SUBWAY EXPRESS(1931), d; DISCARDED LOVERS(1932), d; FIGHTING GENTLEMAN, THE(1932), d; THEY NEVER COME BACK(1932), d; BIG RACE, THE(1934), d; LOST IN THE LEGION(1934, Brit.), d; NO RANSOM(1935), d; SECRETS OF CHINATOWN(1935), d; GENERAL SPANKY(1937), d; RODEO RHYTHM(1941), d; SCREAM IN THE NIGHT(1943), d
Silents
SAILOR-MADE MAN, A(1921), d; DOCTOR JACK(1922), d; GRANDMA'S BOY(1922), d; SAFETY LAST(1923), d; WHY WORRY(1923), d; GIRL SHY(1924), d; HOT WATER(1924), d; FRESHMAN, THE(1925), d; QUARTERBACK, THE(1926), d; POTTERS, THE(1927), d; WARMING UP(1928), d
Misc. Silents
FOOLISH MEN AND SMART WOMEN(1924), d; PERFECT CLOWN, THE(1925), d; SEVEN KEYS TO BALDPATE(1925), d; SAVAGE, THE(1926), d; LUNATIC AT LARGE, THE(1927), d; ON YOUR TOES(1927), d; TOO MANY CROOKS(1927), d; NIGHT BIRD, THE(1928), d; THAT'S MY DADDY(1928), d
Fred Newmeyer, Jr.
MOTH, THE(1934), d
Peter Newmeyer
ADDRESS UNKNOWN(1944)
Julie Newmeyer [Newmar]
SERPENT OF THE NILE(1953); SLAVES OF BABYLON(1953); SEVEN BRIDES FOR SEVEN BROTHERS(1954)
Joseph M. Newmnan
TWENTY PLUS TWO(1961), d
John Newmuis
TAPS(1981)
Rudy Newoff
1984
COUNTRY(1984)

James Newport
HOUSE ON SKULL MOUNTAIN, THE(1974), art d; CHEECH AND CHONG'S NICE DREAMS(1981), prod d
James William Newport
HEART LIKE A WHEEL(1983), prod d
1984
MEATBALLS PART II(1984), prod d
Jim Newport
STUDENT TEACHERS, THE(1973), art d; ZERO TO SIXTY(1978), art d; OVER THE EDGE(1979), prod d
Leslie Newport
MAN WHO KNEW TOO MUCH, THE(1956)
Michael Newport
DEVIL-SHIP PIRATES, THE(1964, Brit.); LIFE AT THE TOP(1965, Brit.); NAKED RUNNER, THE(1967, Brit.); IF ...(1968, Brit.); DECLINE AND FALL... OF A BIRD WATCHER(1969, Brit.); MISCHIEF(1969, Brit.)
Alfred Newrnan
CAMELOT(1967), md
Hazard Newsberry
TILL THE CLOUDS ROLL BY(1946)
Billy Newsbury
FLESH AND BLOOD(1951, Brit.)
Toni Newsholme
JUST FOR THE HELL OF IT(1968)
J.D. Newsom
TROUBLE IN MOROCCO(1937), w; WE'RE IN THE LEGION NOW(1937), w
James E. Newsom
TORTILLA FLAT(1942), ed
Jeremy Newsom
MC CABE AND MRS. MILLER(1971)
Lee Newsom
DRIVE-IN(1976)
Robert M. Newsom
ROAD HUSTLERS, THE(1968), p
Carmen Newsome
Misc. Talkies
GOD'S STEPCHILDREN(1937); SWING(1938); BIRTHRIGHT(1939); LYING LIPS(1939)
Don Newsome
ICE STATION ZEBRA(1968); IF HE HOLLERS, LET HIM GO(1968); GAMES, THE(1970)
Donald Newsome
NEWMAN'S LAW(1974)
Gill Newsome
DISC JOCKEY(1951)
Herbert Newsome
1984
BROTHER FROM ANOTHER PLANET, THE(1984)
John Newsome
GREAT WALL OF CHINA, THE(1970, Brit.), ed
Leroy Newsome
ON THE YARD(1978)
Nora Newsome
EXILE, THE(1931)
Jeremy Newson
ROCKY HORROR PICTURE SHOW, THE(1975, Brit.); YANKS(1979); SHOCK TREATMENT(1981)
Herbert Newstead
NORMAN LOVES ROSE(1982, Aus.)
Valerie Newstead
NORMAN LOVES ROSE(1982, Aus.)
Jonathan Newth
FAR FROM THE MADDING CROWD(1967, Brit.)
1984
CHAMPIONS(1984)
Angus Newton
WEATHER IN THE STREETS, THE(1983, Brit.), ed
Bed Newton
FATTY FINN(1980, Aus.)
Charles Newton
Silents
IMMEDIATE LEE(1916); FRAME UP, THE(1917); LOADED DOOR, THE(1922); IRON HORSE, THE(1924); RIDERS OF THE PURPLE SAGE(1925); YELLOW FINGERS(1926)
Misc. Silents
LORD LOVELAND DISCOVERS AMERICA(1916); SABLE BLESSING, THE(1916); TRUE NOBILITY(1916); WOMAN'S DARING, A(1916); MY FIGHTING GENTLEMAN(1917); COLORADO(1921)
Christopher Newton
ROMEO AND JULIET(1966, Brit.)
1984
COVERGIRL(1984, Can.)
Corky Newton
ETERNAL SUMMER(1961), ch
Daphne Newton
MURDER WILL OUT(1953, Brit.); RECOIL(1953)
David Newton
KENNY AND CO.(1976)
Debbie Newton
1984
VIGIL(1984, New Zealand)
Dodo Newton
BIG TRAIL, THE(1930)
Misc. Silents
MILLION FOR MARY, A(1916)
Douglas Newton
MEN OF STEEL(1932, Brit.), w; SELF-MADE LADY(1932, Brit.), w
Silents
BRUTE, THE(1927), w

Ernest Newton
WITH A SONG IN MY HEART(1952)
Flora Newton
LIVING DANGEROUSLY(1936, Brit.), ed; JUST LIKE A WOMAN(1939, Brit.), ed; OUTSIDER, THE(1940, Brit.), ed; POISON PEN(1941, Brit.), ed; TOWER OF TERROR, THE(1942, Brit.), ed; SUSPECTED PERSON(1943, Brit.), ed; PICCADILLY INCIDENT(1948, Brit.), ed; QUIET WEEKEND(1948, Brit.), ed
Frank Newton
Silents
ROUGH AND READY(1918)
Fred W.S. Newton
DEATH VALLEY(1982)
H. B. Newton
LITTLE MISS MARKER(1980)
Jack Newton
Silents
ELUSIVE ISABEL(1916); NUMBER 17(1920)
Misc. Silents
ALMA, WHERE DO YOU LIVE?(1917); MISS DECEPTION(1917); BERLIN VIA AMERICA(1918)
James T. Newton
1984
TANK(1984)
Joan Newton
BEDLAM(1946); RIVERBOAT RHYTHM(1946)
Joel Newton
JENNIFER(1953), d
John Newton
MAN FROM THE DINERS' CLUB, THE(1963); SATAN BUG, THE(1965)
Jonathan Newton
UNHINGED(1982), m
Margit Evelyn Newton
ZOMBIE CREEPING FLESH(1981, Ital./Span.); NIGHT OF THE ZOMBIES(1983, Span./Ital.)
1984
LAST HUNTER, THE(1984, Ital.)
Marty Newton
YOU'RE NEVER TOO YOUNG(1955)
Mary Newton
SEVENTH VICTIM, THE(1943); MY BEST GAL(1944); STANDING ROOM ONLY(1944); TOMORROW THE WORLD(1944); ESCAPE IN THE FOG(1945); GIRLS OF THE BIG HOUSE(1945); CRIME DOCTOR'S MAN HUNT(1946); DOWN TO EARTH(1947); LAST DAYS OF BOOT HILL(1947); LONE HAND TEXAN, THE(1947); MARAUDERS, THE(1947); SPIRIT OF WEST POINT, THE(1947); DYNAMITE(1948); LADY FROM SHANGHAI, THE(1948); BAD MEN OF TOMBSTONE(1949); DESERT VIGILANTE(1949); BLONDIE'S HERO(1950); EMERGENCY WEDDING(1950); MY TRUE STORY(1951); JUNCTION CITY(1952); ROOM FOR ONE MORE(1952); STRANGER WORE A GUN, THE(1953); WILD ONE, THE(1953); CRIME WAVE(1954); WOMEN'S PRISON(1955); PARDNERS(1956); ZERO HOUR!(1957); TOUGHEST GUN IN TOMBSTONE(1958)
Paul Newton
DON RICARDO RETURNS(1946)
Richard Newton
LILY OF LAGUNA(1938, Brit.); DANGEROUS MISSION(1954); PLUNDER ROAD(1957); CRASH LANDING(1958); GIDGET(1959)
Rick Newton
PAJAMA PARTY(1964); GIRLS ON THE BEACH(1965)
Robert Newton
REUNION(1932, Brit.); DARK JOURNEY(1937, Brit.); FIRE OVER ENGLAND(1937, Brit.); MURDER ON DIAMOND ROW(1937, Brit.); THE BEACHCOMBER(1938, Brit.); TROOPSHIP(1938, Brit.); YELLOW SANDS(1938, Brit.); DANGEROUS CARGO(1939, Brit.); DEAD MEN ARE DANGEROUS(1939, Brit.); JAMAICA INN(1939, Brit.); BULLDOG SEES IT THROUGH(1940, Brit.); BUSMAN'S HONEYMOON(1940, Brit.); GASLIGHT(1940); TWENTY-ONE DAYS TOGETHER(1940, Brit.); MAJOR BARBARA(1941, Brit.); POISON PEN(1941, Brit.); WINGS AND THE WOMAN(1942, Brit.); THIS HAPPY BREED(1944, Brit.); HENRY V(1946, Brit.); NIGHT BOAT TO DUBLIN(1946, Brit.); GREEN COCKATOO, THE(1947, Brit.); ODD MAN OUT(1947, Brit.); HATTER'S CASTLE(1948, Brit.); KISS THE BLOOD OFF MY HANDS(1948); HIDDEN ROOM, THE(1949, Brit.); SNOWBOUND(1949, Brit.); TEMPTATION HARBOR(1949, Brit.); TREASURE ISLAND(1950, Brit.); OLIVER TWIST(1951, Brit.); SOLDIERS THREE(1951); TOM BROWN'S SCHOOLDAYS(1951, Brit.); ANDROCLES AND THE LION(1952); BLACKBEARD THE PIRATE(1952); LES MISERABLES(1952); WATERFRONT WOMEN(1952, Brit.); DESERT RATS, THE(1953); HIGH AND THE MIGHTY, THE(1954); LONG JOHN SILVER(1954, Aus.); THE BEACHCOMBER(1955, Brit.); AROUND THE WORLD IN 80 DAYS(1956)
Robin Newton
PSYCHOTRONIC MAN, THE(1980)
Sally Newton
ARMCHAIR DETECTIVE, THE(1952, Brit.); NO HAUNT FOR A GENTLEMAN(1952, Brit.); DOUBLE EXPOSURE(1954, Brit.)
Sally Anne Newton
ZARDOZ(1974, Brit.)
Stacy Newton
GETAWAY, THE(1972); PURSUIT OF D.B. COOPER, THE(1981)
Theodore Newton
YOUR NUMBER'S UP(1931); ACE OF ACES(1933); FROM HEADQUARTERS(1933); SPHINX, THE(1933); VOLTAIRE(1933); WORKING MAN, THE(1933); WORLD CHANGES, THE(1933); GAMBLING(1934); HEAT LIGHTNING(1934); LET'S TRY AGAIN(1934); MODERN HERO, A(1934); NOW I'LL TELL(1934); UPPER WORLD(1934); JALNA(1935); MISS SUSIE SLAGLE'S(1945); WHAT NEXT, CORPORAL HARGROVE?(1945); TWO YEARS BEFORE THE MAST(1946); COME ON, THE(1956); FRIENDLY PERSUASION(1956); PROUD AND THE PROFANE, THE(1956); SOMEBODY UP THERE LIKES ME(1956); SAGA OF HEMP BROWN, THE(1958); STORY ON PAGE ONE, THE(1959); DIME WITH A HALO(1963)
Wayne Newton
80 STEPS TO JONAH(1969)
Wendy Newton
SATURDAY NIGHT OUT(1964, Brit.)

Zoe Newton
I AM A CAMERA(1955, Brit.); NO LOVE FOR JUDY(1955, Brit.)
Olivia Newton-John
TOOMORROW(1970, Brit.); GREASE(1978); XANADU(1980); TWO OF A KIND(1983)
Rona Newton-John
WHERE'S JACK?(1969, Brit.); BROTHERLY LOVE(1970, Brit.); TROG(1970, Brit.)
Noel Newton-Wood
TAWNY PIPIT(1947, Brit.), m
Henry Ney
VOYAGE TO THE PLANET OF PREHISTORIC WOMEN(1966), w
Marie Ney
HOME, SWEET HOME(1933, Brit.); SCROOGE(1935, Brit.); WANDERING JEW, THE(1935, Brit.); BRIEF ECSTASY(1937, Brit.); DANGEROUS SECRETS(1938, Brit.); JAMAICA INN(1939, Brit.); UNEASY TERMS(1948, Brit.); CONSPIRATOR(1949, Brit.); SEVEN DAYS TO NOON(1950, Brit.); SHADOW OF THE PAST(1950, Brit.); LAVENDER HILL MOB, THE(1951, Brit.); NAUGHTY ARLETTE(1951, Brit.); NIGHT WAS OUR FRIEND(1951, Brit.); SIMBA(1955, Brit.); BLONDE SINNER(1956, Brit.); SURGEON'S KNIFE, THE(1957, Brit.); WEST 11(1963, Brit.); WITCHCRAFT(1964, Brit.)
Richard Ney
MRS. MINIVER(1942); WAR AGAINST MRS. HADLEY, THE(1942); IVY(1947); LATE GEORGE APLEY, THE(1947); JOAN OF ARC(1948); FAN, THE(1949); LOVABLE CHEAT, THE(1949); SECRET OF ST. IVES, THE(1949); BABES IN BAGDAD(1952); MIDNIGHT LACE(1960); PREMATURE BURIAL, THE(1962)
Marina Neyelova
AUTUMN MARATHON(1982, USSR)
Stanislav Neygauz
GARNET BRACELET, THE(1966, USSR)
Jim Neylan
NIGHT FIGHTERS, THE(1960)
Anne Neyland
HIDDEN FEAR(1957); JAILHOUSE ROCK(1957); MOTORCYCLE GANG(1957); OCEAN'S ELEVEN(1960)
James Neylin
SAINTS AND SINNERS(1949, Brit.); QUESTION OF SUSPENSE, A(1961, Brit.); SWORD OF SHERWOOD FOREST(1961, Brit.); RUNNING MAN, THE(1963, Brit.)
Michael Neyman
BAD CHARLESTON CHARLIE(1973), ph
Tom Neyman
MANOS, THE HANDS OF FATE(1966)
Yuri Neyman
LIQUID SKY(1982), ph, spec eff
Lylia Neyung
CRAZY DESIRE(1964, Ital.)
Jinpachi Nezu
ALL RIGHT, MY FRIEND(1983, Japan)
Vitezslav Nezval
ECSTASY(1940, Czech.), w
David Ng
SAINT JACK(1979), art d
Mrs. Ng
ADVENTURES OF MARCO POLO, THE(1938)
Ronald Ng
SAINT JACK(1979)
Walter Ng
PEKING EXPRESS(1951); THING, THE(1951); MACAO(1952)
Lionel Ngakane
CRY, THE BELOVED COUNTRY(1952, Brit.); DUEL IN THE JUNGLE(1954, Brit.); ODONGO(1956, Brit.); SAFARI(1956); MARK OF THE HAWK, THE(1958); ELEPHANT GUN(1959, Brit.); MURDER CAN BE DEADLY(1963, Brit.); TWO GENTLEMEN SHARING(1969, Brit.)
Reginald Ngcobo
CRY, THE BELOVED COUNTRY(1952, Brit.)
Phuong Thi Nghiep
QUIET AMERICAN, THE(1958)
Mackson Ngobeni
SAFARI 3000(1982)
Misc. Talkies
ESCAPE FROM ANGOLA(1976)
Haing S. Ngor
1984
KILLING FIELDS, THE(1984, Brit.)
Rex Ngui
1984
INDIANA JONES AND THE TEMPLE OF DOOM(1984)
Nguyen
GLADIATORS, THE(1970, Swed.)
Lilia Nguyen
DEAD OF SUMMER(1970 Ital./Fr.)
Thi Loan Nguyen
1984
L'ARGENT(1984, Fr./Switz.), makeup
Tien Ni
ONE NIGHT STAND(1976, Fr.)
Prince Nial
AGE OF CONSENT(1969, Austral.)
Ian Niall
NO RESTING PLACE(1952, Brit.), w; TIGER WALKS, A(1964), w
Issa Niang
MANDABI(1970, Fr./Senegal)
Terry Nibert
CAROLINA MOON(1940); LITTLE FOXES, THE(1941)
Sam Niblack
Silents
KIDNAPPED(1917)
Misc. Silents
DIVORCE AND THE DAUGHTER(1916); HER LIFE AND HIS(1917)
Samuel Niblack
Misc. Silents
FIVE FAULTS OF FLO, THE(1916)

A. Sloan Nibley
SPRINGTIME IN THE SIERRAS(1947), w
Aaron Nibley
OUTLAWS IS COMING, THE(1965), ed
Aloan Nibley
DOWN DAKOTA WAY(1949), w
Christopher Sloan Nibley III
GOIN' HOME(1976), ph
Sloan Nibley
BELLS OF SAN ANGELO(1947), w; ON THE OLD SPANISH TRAIL(1947), w; EYES OF TEXAS(1948), w; GAY RANCHERO, THE(1948), w; NIGHT TIME IN NEVADA(1948), w; UNDER CALIFORNIA STARS(1948), w; FAR FRONTIER, THE(1949), w; GOLDEN STALLION, THE(1949), w; SUSANNA PASS(1949), w; BELLS OF CORONADO(1950), w; SURRENDER(1950), w; TWILIGHT IN THE SIERRAS(1950), w; IN OLD AMARILLO(1951), w; SPOILERS OF THE PLAINS(1951), w; CARSON CITY(1952), w; PALS OF THE GOLDEN WEST(1952), w; SPRINGFIELD RIFLE(1952), w; THUNDER OVER ARIZONA(1956), w; HOSTILE GUNS(1967), w
Fred Niblo
FREE AND EASY(1930); REDEMPTION(1930), d; WAY OUT WEST(1930), d; BIG GAMBLE, THE(1931), d; YOUNG DONOVAN'S KID(1931), d; BLAME THE WOMAN(1932, Brit.), d; WIVES BEWARE(1933, Brit.), d; FUGITIVE LADY(1934), w; HELL'S KITCHEN(1939), w; ELLERY QUEEN. MASTER DETECTIVE(1940); I'M STILL ALIVE(1940); LIFE WITH HENRY(1941); ONCE UPON A HONEYMOON(1942)
Silents
WHEN DO WE EAT?(1918), d; HAIRPINS(1920), d; MARK OF ZORRO(1920), d; SEX(1920), d; THREE MUSKETEERS, THE(1921), d; BLOOD AND SAND(1922), d; SOULS FOR SALE(1923); STRANGERS OF THE NIGHT(1923), p&d; BEN-HUR(1925), d; TEMPTRESS, THE(1926), d; CAMILLE(1927), d; ENEMY, THE(1927), d; MYSTERIOUS LADY, THE(1928), d; TWO LOVERS(1928), d
Misc. Silents
COALS OF FIRE(1918); FUSS AND FEATHERS(1918), d; MARRIAGE RING, THE(1918), d; HAPPY THOUGH MARRIED(1919), d; HAUNTED BEDROOM, THE(1919), d; LAW OF MEN, THE(1919), d; PARTNERS THREE(1919), d; STEPPING OUT(1919), d; VIRTUOUS THIEF, THE(1919), d; WHAT EVERY WOMAN LEARNS(1919), d; DANGEROUS HOURS(1920), d; FALSE ROAD, THE(1920), d; GREATER THAN LOVE(1920), d; HER HUSBAND'S FRIEND(1920), d; SILK HOSIERY(1920), d; WOMAN IN THE SUITCASE, THE(1920), d; MOTHER O' MINE(1921), d; BOOTLEGGER'S DAUGHTER, THE(1922); ROSE O' THE SEA(1922), d; SCANDALOUS TONGUES(1922); WOMAN HE MARRIED, THE(1922), d; FAMOUS MRS. FAIR, THE(1923), d; RED LILY, THE(1924), d; THY NAME IS WOMAN(1924), d; DREAM OF LOVE(1928), d
Fred Niblo, Jr.
CRIMINAL CODE(1931), w; EX-BAD BOY(1931), w; VIRTUOUS HUSBAND(1931), w; KING OF THE JUNGLE(1933), w; AMONG THE MISSING(1934), w; HELL CAT, THE(1934), w; NAME THE WOMAN(1934), w; WHOM THE GODS DESTROY(1934), w; DEATH FLIES EAST(1935), w; ESCAPE FROM DEVIL'S ISLAND(1935), w; UNKNOWN WOMAN(1935), w; LADY FROM NOWHERE(1936), w; MAN WHO LIVED TWICE(1936), w; ROAMING LADY(1936), w; YOU MAY BE NEXT(1936), w; ALL-AMERICAN SWEETHEART(1937), w; COUNSEL FOR CRIME(1937), w; FIND THE WITNESS(1937), w; GAME THAT KILLS, THE(1937), w; MOTOR MADNESS(1937), w; CITY STREETS(1938), w; LITTLE MISS ROUGHNECK(1938), w; PENITENTIARY(1938), w; COWBOY QUARTERBACK(1939), w; NO PLACE TO GO(1939), w; ANGEL FROM TEXAS, AN(1940), w; EAST OF THE RIVER(1940), w; FIGHTING 69TH, THE(1940), w; FATHER'S SON(1941), w; NINE LIVES ARE NOT ENOUGH(1941), w; PASSAGE FROM HONG KONG(1941), w; THREE SONS O'GUNS(1941), w; WAGONS ROLL AT NIGHT, THE(1941), w; YOU CAN'T ESCAPE FOREVER(1942), w; FALCON IN DANGER, THE(1943), w; FOUR JILLS IN A JEEP(1944), w; TAMPICO(1944), w; BODYGUARD(1948), w; IN THIS CORNER(1948), w; INCIDENT(1948), w; CONVICTED(1950), w
Misc. Silents
DEVIL DANCER, THE(1927), d
Eddie Nicart
IMPASSE(1969)
Michelle Nicastro
1984
BODY ROCK(1984)
Philipe Nicaud
TONIGHT THE SKIRTS FLY(1956, Fr.)
Philippe Nicaud
BACK TO THE WALL(1959, Fr.); COME DANCE WITH ME(1960, Fr.); MAIDEN, THE(1961, Fr.); MAGNIFICENT CUCKOLD, THE(1965, Fr./Ital.); LADY IN THE CAR WITH GLASSES AND A GUN, THE(1970, U.S./Fr.); MYSTERIOUS ISLAND OF CAPTAIN NEMO, THE(1973, Fr./Ital. 87m Span./Cameroon); CHANEL SOLITAIRE(1981)
Nicco & Tanya
LET'S FACE IT(1943)
Herb Niccolls
Misc. Talkies
FORBID THEM NOT(1961)
Herbert F. Niccolls
JOURNEY TO FREEDOM(1957), w
Arthur Nicdao
STRYKER(1983, Phil.), art d
Ramon Nicdao
STRYKER(1983, Phil.), art d
1984
PURPLE HEARTS(1984), set d
Derek Nice
1984
SWORD OF THE VALIANT(1984, Brit.), prod d
George R. Nice
CHILDREN OF RAGE(1975, Brit.-Israeli), p; ECHOES(1983), p
Gary Nichamin
ELECTRA GLIDE IN BLUE(1973)
Rollie Nicheri
HAPPY BIRTHDAY TO ME(1981)
Maurizio Nichetti
ALLEGRO NON TROPPO(1977, Ital.); RATATAPLAN(1979, Ital.), a, d&w

Ave Nichi
PULP(1972, Brit.)
Carlo Nichi
CONSTANTINE AND THE CROSS(1962, Ital.)
David Nichol
VILLAGE SQUIRE, THE(1935, Brit.)
Hamish Nichol
JOURNEY TOGETHER(1946, Brit.)
Ruth Nichol
LIFE AND TIMES OF CHESTER-ANGUS RAMSGOOD, THE(1971, Can.)
Stuart Nichol
NO HIGHWAY IN THE SKY(1951, Brit.); SCOTLAND YARD INSPECTOR(1952, Brit.); WHISPERING SMITH VERSUS SCOTLAND YARD(1952, Brit.); HORNET'S NEST, THE(1955, Brit.); HIGH TIDE AT NOON(1957, Brit.); KILL ME TOMORROW(1958, Brit.); WHAT'S GOOD FOR THE GOOSE(1969, Brit.)
Tryon Nichol
JOHNNY IN THE CLOUDS(1945, Brit.)
Nicholai
FOLLOW THE BOYS(1944)
Boris Nicholai
ANTHONY ADVERSE(1936)
Nicholas
JONAH-WHO WILL BE 25 IN THE YEAR 2000(1976, Switz.)
Allan Nicholas
IT FELL FROM THE SKY(1980), w
Anna Nicholas
CUBA(1979)
Annie Nicholas
TWO WEEKS IN SEPTEMBER(1967, Fr./Brit.)
Bayard Nicholas
TIN PAN ALLEY(1940)
Bert Nicholas
RUGGED O'RIORDANS, THE(1949, Aus.), ph
Clive Nicholas
HARASSED HERO, THE(1954, Brit.), p; TIME TO KILL, A(1955, Brit.), p
Denise Nicholas
BLACULA(1972); SOUL OF NIGGER CHARLEY, THE(1973); LET'S DO IT AGAIN(1975); MR. RICCO(1975); PIECE OF THE ACTION, A(1977); CAPRICORN ONE(1978)
Eden Nicholas
ENCHANTED COTTAGE, THE(1945); FIRST YANK INTO TOKYO(1945)
Evelyn Nicholas
Misc. Silents
FORBIDDEN GRASS(1928)
Fayard Nicholas
BIG BROADCAST OF 1936, THE(1935); LIBERATION OF L.B. JONES, THE(1970)
George Nicholas
CINDERELLA(1950), anim; LADY AND THE TRAMP(1955), anim; SLEEPING BEAUTY(1959), anim; MAN CALLED FLINTSTONE, THE(1966), anim; PHANTOM TOLLBOOTH, THE(1970), anim; ANGELO MY LOVE(1983)
Harold Nicholas
BIG BROADCAST OF 1936, THE(1935); TIN PAN ALLEY(1940); CAROLINA BLUES(1944); RECKLESS AGE(1944); EMPIRE OF NIGHT, THE(1963, Fr.); UPTOWN SATURDAY NIGHT(1974)
Misc. Talkies
DISCO 9000(1977)
John Nicholas
SATAN IN HIGH HEELS(1962); DEVIL'S SISTERS, THE(1966), w
Kim Nicholas
LIMBO(1972); IMPULSE(1975)
Nellie V. Nicholas
TWO HEADS ON A PILLOW(1934)
P.J. Nicholas
1984
1984(1984, Brit.)
Paul Nicholas
CANNABIS(1970, Fr.); SEE NO EVIL(1971, Brit.); WHAT BECAME OF JACK AND JILL?(1972, Brit.); LORDS OF FLATBUSH, THE(1974), m; STARDUST(1974, Brit.); LISZTOMANIA(1975, Brit.); TOMMY(1975, Brit.); SGT. PEPPER'S LONELY HEARTS CLUB BAND(1978); YESTERDAY'S HERO(1979, Brit.); JAZZ SINGER, THE(1980); WORLD IS FULL OF MARRIED MEN, THE(1980, Brit.); CHAINED HEAT(1983 U.S./Ger.), d, w
Misc. Talkies
NUTCRACKER(1984)
Peter Nicholas
1984
MICKI AND MAUDE(1984)
Porjai Nicholas
CONFESSIONS OF A WINDOW CLEANER(1974, Brit.)
Ray Nicholas
WHEN TOMORROW COMES(1939)
Terry Nicholas
HOT LEAD AND COLD FEET(1978)
Nicholas Bros.
STORMY WEATHER(1943)
Nicholas Brothers
JEALOUSY(1934); KID MILLIONS(1934); DOWN ARGENTINE WAY(1940); GREAT AMERICAN BROADCAST, THE(1941); ORCHESTRA WIVES(1942); PIRATE, THE(1948)
Denise Nicholas-Hill
MARVIN AND TIGE(1983)
Jack Nicholaus
POLICE NURSE(1963), ph
John Nicholaus
NIGHT OF THE BLOOD BEAST(1958), ph
John Nicholaus, Jr.
THUNDERING JETS(1958), ph; TANK COMMANDOS(1959), ph; HARBOR LIGHTS(1963), ph

John M. Nicholaus, Jr.
DESERT HELL(1958), ph; AIR PATROL(1962), ph
David Nicholl
PURSUERS, THE(1961, Brit.), w
Don Nicholl
INBETWEEN AGE, THE(1958, Brit.), w; EMERGENCY(1962, Brit.), w
Gee Nicholl
INBETWEEN AGE, THE(1958, Brit.), w
Allan Nicholls
JENNIFER ON MY MIND(1971); NASHVILLE(1975); WELCOME TO L.A.(1976); SLAP SHOT(1977); WEDDING, A(1978), a, w; PERFECT COUPLE, A(1979), a, w, m; HOME FREE ALL(1983); THRESHOLD(1983, Can.)
Anthony Nicholls
HASTY HEART, THE(1949); MAN ON THE RUN(1949, Brit.); OUTSIDER, THE(1949, Brit.); DANCING YEARS, THE(1950, Brit.); LAUGHING LADY, THE(1950, Brit.); NO PLACE FOR JENNIFER(1950, Brit.); HER PANELLED DOOR(1951, Brit.); PORTRAIT OF CLARE(1951, Brit.); FRANCHISE AFFAIR, THE(1952, Brit.); HOUSE OF THE ARROW, THE(1953, Brit.); GREEN SCARF, THE(1954, Brit.); MAKE ME AN OFFER(1954, Brit.); TONIGHT'S THE NIGHT(1954, Brit.); WOMAN'S ANGLE, THE(1954, Brit.); DUNKIRK(1958, Brit.); SAFECRACKER, THE(1958, Brit.); VICTIM(1961, Brit.); BURN WITCH BURN(1962); SEVEN KEYS(1962, Brit.); PUMPKIN EATER, THE(1964, Brit.); OTHELLO(1965, Brit.); MISTER TEN PERCENT(1967, Brit.); OUR MOTHER'S HOUSE(1967, Brit.); IF ...(1968, Brit.); WALK WITH LOVE AND DEATH, A(1969); MAN WHO HAUNTED HIMSELF, THE(1970, Brit.); ONE MORE TIME(1970, Brit.); WALKING STICK, THE(1970, Brit.); O LUCKY MAN!(1973, Brit.)
Beverley Nicholls
NINE TILL SIX(1932, Brit.), w
Dandy Nicholls
CRY FROM THE STREET, A(1959, Brit.); DON'T TALK TO STRANGE MEN(1962, Brit.)
Fred Nicholls
Silents
SONNY(1922)
George Nicholls
SOLDIER AND THE LADY, THE(1937), d
Silents
FAME AND FORTUNE(1918); HEARTS OF THE WORLD(1918); BROKEN BLOSSOMS(1919); LIGHT OF VICTORY(1919); ROMANCE OF HAPPY VALLEY, A(1919)
Misc. Silents
GHOSTS(1915), d; BATTLING JANE(1918); KEYS OF THE RIGHTEOUS, THE(1918); COMING OF THE LAW, THE(1919)
George Nicholls, Jr.
SEVEN DAYS LEAVE(1930), ed; ANN VICKERS(1933), ed; MORNING GLORY(1933), ed; SILVER CORD(1933), ed; ANNE OF GREEN GABLES(1934), d; FINISHING SCHOOL(1934), d; CHASING YESTERDAY(1935), d; RETURN OF PETER GRIMM, THE(1935), d; BIG GAME, THE(1936), d; CHATTERBOX(1936), d; M'LISS(1936), d; WITNESS CHAIR, THE(1936), d; PORTIA ON TRIAL(1937), d; ARMY GIRL(1938), d; HIGH SCHOOL(1940), d; MARINES FLY HIGH, THE(1940), d
Harcourt Nicholls
WHITE FIRE(1953, Brit.)
J. Roy Hunt Nicholls, Jr.
DOUBLE HARNESS(1933), ph
Jill Nicholls
SCOTLAND YARD DRAGNET(1957, Brit.)
Joy Nicholls
SMITHY(1946, Aus.)
Kate Nicholls
PUMPKIN EATER, THE(1964, Brit.); CHRISTMAS TREE, THE(1966, Brit.)
Mark Nicholls
VIRGIN SOLDIERS, THE(1970, Brit.)
Phoebe Nicholls
ELEPHANT MAN, THE(1980, Brit.); MISSIONARY, THE(1982); PARTY PARTY(1983, Brit.)
Richard Nicholls
NO WAY TO TREAT A LADY(1968)
Robert Nicholls
MAN IN THE MIDDLE(1964, U.S./Brit.)
Sara Nicholls
PUMPKIN EATER, THE(1964, Brit.); ALL AT SEA(1970, Brit.)
Sarah Nicholls
DR. TERROR'S HOUSE OF HORRORS(1965, Brit.); OUR MOTHER'S HOUSE(1967, Brit.); WOMEN IN LOVE(1969, Brit.)
Thomas Nicholls
ROMEO AND JULIET(1954, Brit.)
Tiny Nicholls
MC KENZIE BREAK, THE(1970), cos; STRAW DOGS(1971, Brit.), cos
H. Nicholls-Bates
Silents
GREAT GAME, THE(1918, Brit.); PRIDE OF THE NORTH, THE(1920, Brit.); LONG ODDS(1922, Brit.)
Misc. Silents
RIGHT TO LIVE, THE(1921, Brit.)
Henry Nicholls-Bates
Silents
PRODIGAL SON, THE(1923, Brit.)
Allan Nichols
POPEYE(1980)
1984
HOME FREE ALL(1984)
Anne Nichols
ABIE'S IRISH ROSE(1928), w; GIVE ME A SAILOR(1938), w; ABIE'S IRISH ROSE(1946), w
Silents
HER GILDED CAGE(1922), w; JUST MARRIED(1928), w
Andrew Nichols
Misc. Talkies
CAFE FLESH(1982)

Anthony Nichols
HIGH TREASON(1951, Brit.); WEAK AND THE WICKED, THE(1954, Brit.); MAN FOR ALL SEASONS, A(1966, Brit.); BATTLE OF BRITAIN, THE(1969, Brit.); OMEN, THE(1976)

Barbara Nichols
RIVER OF NO RETURN(1954); BEYOND A REASONABLE DOUBT(1956); KING AND FOUR QUEENS, THE(1956); MANFISH(1956); MIRACLE IN THE RAIN(1956); WILD PARTY, THE(1956); PAJAMA GAME, THE(1957); PAL JOEY(1957); SWEET SMELL OF SUCCESS(1957); NAKED AND THE DEAD, THE(1958); 10 NORTH FREDERICK(1958); THAT KIND OF WOMAN(1959); WOMAN OBSESSED(1959); WHERE THE BOYS ARE(1960); WHO WAS THAT LADY?(1960); GEORGE RAFT STORY, THE(1961); HOUSE OF WOMEN(1962); SCARFACE MOB, THE(1962); DEAR HEART(1964); DISORDERLY ORDERLY, THE(1964); LOOKING FOR LOVE(1964); HUMAN DUPLICATORS, THE(1965); SWINGER, THE(1966); POWER, THE(1968); CHARLEY AND THE ANGEL(1973); WON TON TON, THE DOG WHO SAVED HOLLYWOOD(1976)

Betty Jean Nichols
WYOMING(1940)

Beverley Nichols
GLAMOUR(1931, Brit.); EVENSONG(1934, Brit.), w

Bob Nichols
DREAMBOAT(1952); HOLD THAT LINE(1952); JET JOB(1952); PRIDE OF ST. LOUIS, THE(1952); RED SKIES OF MONTANA(1952); COMMAND, THE(1954); HOLD BACK THE NIGHT(1956)

Bradley N. Nichols
STREET FIGHTER(1959), p

Brenda Nichols
FEELIN' GOOD(1966)

Buster Nichols
MAJOR AND THE MINOR, THE(1942)

C.H. Nichols
SQUARE RING, THE(1955, Brit.)

Charles Nichols
PINOCCHIO(1940), anim; ALICE IN WONDERLAND(1951), anim

Charles A. Nichols
HEY THERE, IT'S YOGI BEAR(1964), anim d; MAN CALLED FLINTSTONE, THE(1966), anim director; CHARLOTTE'S WEB(1973), d

Conrad Nichols
1984
RUSH(1984, Ital.)
Misc. Talkies
RAGE(1984)

Dandy Nichols
NICHOLAS NICKLEBY(1947, Brit.); DON'T EVER LEAVE ME(1949, Brit.); FALLEN IDOL, THE(1949, Brit.); HISTORY OF MR. POLLY, THE(1949, Brit.); NOW BARABBAS WAS A ROBBER(1949, Brit.); SCOTT OF THE ANTARCTIC(1949, Brit.); DANCE HALL(1950, Brit.); WINSLOW BOY, THE(1950); TONY DRAWS A HORSE(1951, Brit.); MR. LORD SAYS NO(1952, Brit.); PICKWICK PAPERS, THE(1952, Brit.); WHITE CORRIDORS(1952, Brit.); MEET MR. LUCIFER(1953, Brit.); TWILIGHT WOMEN(1953, Brit.); WEDDING OF LILLI MARLENE, THE(1953, Brit.); HOLLY AND THE IVY, THE(1954, Brit.); MAD ABOUT MEN(1954, Brit.); DEEP BLUE SEA, THE(1955, Brit.); WHERE THERE'S A WILL(1955, Brit.); GENTLE TOUCH, THE(1956, Brit.); NOT SO DUSTY(1956, Brit.); TEARS FOR SIMON(1957, Brit.); TIME IS MY ENEMY(1957, Brit.); TOWN ON TRIAL(1957, Brit.); VIKINGS, THE(1958); CROOKS ANONYMOUS(1963, Brit.); MY SON, THE VAMPIRE(1963, Brit.); LADIES WHO DO(1964, Brit.); ACT OF MURDER(1965, Brit.); AMOROUS ADVENTURES OF MOLL FLANDERS, THE(1965); EARLY BIRD, THE(1965, Brit.); HELP!(1965, Brit.); KNACK ... AND HOW TO GET IT, THE(1965, Brit.); LEATHER BOYS, THE(1965, Brit.); GEORGY GIRL(1966, Brit.); CARNABY, M.D.(1967, Brit.); HOW I WON THE WAR(1967, Brit.); ALF 'N' FAMILY(1968, Brit.); BIRTHDAY PARTY, THE(1968, Brit.); CARRY ON DOCTOR(1968, Brit.); BED SITTING ROOM, THE(1969, Brit.); FIRST LOVE(1970, Ger./Switz.); O LUCKY MAN!(1973, Brit.); CONFESSIONS OF A WINDOW CLEANER(1974, Brit.); BRITTANIA HOSPITAL(1982, Brit.)
1984
PLAGUE DOGS, THE(1984, U.S./Brit.)
Misc. Talkies
ALF GARNETT SAGA, THE(1972)

Dave Nichols
STRANGE SHADOWS IN AN EMPTY ROOM(1977, Can./Ital.)

David Nichols
GAS-S-S-S!(1970), art d; STUDENT NURSES, THE(1970), art d; BOXCAR BERTHA(1972), prod d; WILD PARTY, THE(1975), art d; NEW YORK, NEW YORK(1977); HARDCORE(1979); SWAMP THING(1982), art d; TESTAMENT(1983), a, prod d
1984
HEARTBREAKERS(1984), prod d

Denny Nichols
HITCHHIKERS, THE(1972)

Derek Nichols
NAKED WORLD OF HARRISON MARKS, THE(1967, Brit.)

Dudley Nichols
BORN RECKLESS(1930), w; DEVIL WITH WOMEN, A(1930), w; MEN WITHOUT WOMEN(1930), w; ON THE LEVEL(1930), w; ONE MAD KISS(1930), w; HUSH MONEY(1931), w; SEAS BENEATH, THE(1931), w; SKYLINE(1931), w; THREE ROGUES(1931), w; THIS SPORTING AGE(1932), w; HOT PEPPER(1933), w; MAN WHO DARED, THE(1933), w; PILGRIMAGE(1933), w; ROBBERS' ROOST(1933), w; CALL IT LUCK(1934), w; HOLD THAT GIRL(1934), w; JUDGE PRIEST(1934), w; LOST PATROL, THE(1934), w; WILD GOLD(1934), w; YOU CAN'T BUY EVERYTHING(1934), w; ARIZONIAN, THE(1935), w; CRUSADES, THE(1935), w; INFORMER, THE(1935), w; LIFE BEGINS AT 40(1935), w; MYSTERY WOMAN(1935), w; SHE(1935), w; STEAMBOAT ROUND THE BEND(1935), w; THREE MUSKETEERS, THE(1935), w; MARY OF SCOTLAND(1936), w; PLOUGH AND THE STARS, THE(1936), w; HURRICANE, THE(1937), w; TOAST OF NEW YORK, THE(1937), w; BRINGING UP BABY(1938), w; CAREFREE(1938), w; STAGECOACH(1939), w; LONG VOYAGE HOME, THE(1940), w; MAN HUNT(1941), w; SWAMP WATER(1941), w; AIR FORCE(1943), w; FOR WHOM THE BELL TOLLS(1943), w; GOVERNMENT GIRL(1943), p&d; THIS LAND IS MINE(1943), p, w; IT HAPPENED TOMORROW(1944), w; AND THEN THERE WERE NONE(1945), w; BELLS OF ST. MARY'S, THE(1945), w; SCARLET STREET(1945); SISTER KENNY(1946), p&d, w; FUGITIVE, THE(1947), w; MOURNING BECOMES ELECTRA(1947), p&d, w; PINKY(1949), w; RAWHIDE(1951), w; BIG SKY, THE(1952), w; RETURN OF THE TEXAN(1952), w;

PRINCE VALIANT(1954), w; RUN FOR THE SUN(1956), w; TIN STAR, THE(1957), w; HANGMAN, THE(1959), w; HELLER IN PINK TIGHTS(1960), w; TEN LITTLE INDIANS(1965, Brit.), w; STAGECOACH(1966), w

Earl Nichols
TIME AFTER TIME(1979, Brit.); EYE FOR AN EYE, AN(1981)

Eddie Nichols
INCENDIARY BLONDE(1945)

Fred Nichols
HELL, HEAVEN OR HOBOKEN(1958, Brit.)

George Nichols
SCANDAL SHEET(1931), ed
Silents
MAN'S PREROGATIVE, A(1915), d; MICKEY(1919); GREATEST QUESTION, THE(1920); JOYOUS TROUBLEMAKERS, THE(1920); NINETEEN AND PHYLLIS(1920); MOLLY O'(1921); OLIVER TWIST, JR.(1921); QUEEN OF SHEBA, THE(1921); SHAME(1921); DON'T GET PERSONAL(1922); FLIRT, THE(1922); PRIDE OF PALOMAR, THE(1922); SUZANNA(1922); COUNTRY KID, THE(1923); DON'T MARRY FOR MONEY(1923); EXTRA GIRL, THE(1923); MIRACLE MAKERS, THE(1923); DAUGHTERS OF TODAY(1924); EAST OF BROADWAY(1924); GEARED TO GO(1924); MIDNIGHT EXPRESS, THE(1924); EAGLE, THE(1925); GOOSE WOMAN, THE(1925); MERRY WIDOW, THE(1925); PROUD FLESH(1925); BROKEN HEARTS OF HOLLYWOOD(1926); MISS NOBODY(1926); ROLLING HOME(1926); SEA HORSES(1926); WEDDING MARCH, THE(1927); WHITE FLANNELS(1927); WHITE GOLD(1927)
Misc. Silents
SON OF HIS FATHER, THE(1917); BILL APPERSON'S BOY(1919); REBELLIOUS BRIDE, THE(1919); TURN IN THE ROAD, THE(1919); WHEN DOCTORS DISAGREE(1919); WOLF, THE(1919); PINTO(1920); FOX, THE(1921); LIVE AND LET LIVE(1921); GHOST PATROL, THE(1923); LET'S GO(1923); BEAUTIFUL SINNER, THE(1924); SLANDERERS, THE(1924); HIS MAJESTY BUNKER BEAN(1925); BACHELOR BRIDES(1926); SENOR DAREDEVIL(1926)

George Nichols, Jr.
INTERFERENCE(1928), ed; DANCE OF LIFE, THE(1929), ed; DUMMY, THE(1929), ed; ILLUSION(1929), ed; MIGHTY, THE(1929), ed; MYSTERIOUS DR. FU MANCHU, THE(1929), ed; DERELICT(1930), ed; DEVIL'S HOLIDAY, THE(1930), ed; FOR THE DEFENSE(1930), ed; SWEEPINGS(1933), ed; MAN OF CONQUEST(1939), d
Silents
STREET OF SIN, THE(1928), ed; WIFE SAVERS(1928), ed

Gloria Nichols
SMOKEY AND THE BANDIT-PART 3(1983)

Guy Nichols
Silents
DAVID HARUM(1915)

Hank Nichols
GALLANT ONE, THE(1964, U.S./Peru)

J.D. Nichols
GODFATHER, THE, PART II(1974)

Jack Nichols
NIGHT OF EVIL(1962)

Jay Nichols
KING IN NEW YORK, A(1957, Brit.)

Jennifer Nichols
SATURDAY NIGHT FEVER(1977), cos

Jenny Nichols
RAGTIME(1981)

John Nichols
DETROIT 9000(1973)
Misc. Silents
WIT WINS(1920)

Josephine Nichols
PETULIA(1968, U.S./Brit.); RIVERRUN(1968); HIDE IN PLAIN SIGHT(1980)

Joy Nichols
PACIFIC ADVENTURE(1947, Aus.); NOT SO DUSTY(1956, Brit.)

Kelly Nichols
TOOLBOX MURDERS, THE(1978)
1984
DELIVERY BOYS(1984)
Misc. Talkies
IN LOVE(1983)

Leo Nichols [Ennio Morricone]
HELLBENDERS, THE(1967, U.S./Ital./Span.), m; HILLS RUN RED, THE(1967, Ital.), m

Lionel Nichols
FOR LOVE AND MONEY(1967)

Lonnie Nichols
TALES OF MANHATTAN(1942)

Major Nichols
MELODY MAN(1930); GOLDEN ARROW, THE(1936); ONCE UPON A HONEYMOON(1942)

Margaret Nichols
Misc. Silents
POWER OF EVIL, THE(1916); WHEN BABY FORGOT(1917)

Marguerite Nichols
Silents
SOLD AT AUCTION(1917)
Misc. Silents
LITTLE MARY SUNSHINE(1916); MATRIMONIAL MARTYR, A(1916); PAY DIRT(1916)

Max Nichols
RAGTIME(1981)

Michelle Nichols
1984
STAR TREK III: THE SEARCH FOR SPOCK(1984)

Mike Nichols
WHO'S AFRAID OF VIRGINIA WOOLF?(1966), d; GRADUATE, THE(1967), d; CATCH-22(1970), d; CARNAL KNOWLEDGE(1971), p&d; DAY OF THE DOLPHIN, THE(1973), d; FORTUNE, THE(1975), p, d; SILKWOOD(1983), p, d

Nellie V. Nichols
PLAYING AROUND(1930); WOMEN GO ON FOREVER(1931); UNKNOWN WOM-AN(1935); MANHATTAN MERRY-GO-ROUND(1937)

Nichelle Nichols
MISTER BUDDWING(1966); DOCTOR, YOU'VE GOT TO BE KIDDING(1967); TRUCK TURNER(1974); STAR TREK: THE MOTION PICTURE(1979); STAR TREK II: THE WRATH OF KHAN(1982)

Nick Nichols
ONLY GOD KNOWS(1974, Can.)

Norma Nichols
Silents
NE'ER-DO-WELL, THE(1916)

Oscar Nichols
GATLING GUN, THE(1972), p

Patti Nichols
LOOKS AND SMILES(1982, Brit.)

Pearl Nichols
FOUR FOR THE MORGUE(1962)

Peggy Nichols
PATRICK(1979, Aus.)

Peter Nichols
HAVING A WILD WEEKEND(1965, Brit.), a, w; GEORGY GIRL(1966, Brit.), w; DAY IN THE DEATH OF JOE EGG, A(1972, Brit.), w; NATIONAL HEALTH, OR NURSE NORTON'S AFFAIR, THE(1973, Brit.), w; PRIVATES ON PARADE(1982), w
1984
PRIVATES ON PARADE(1984, Brit.), w

Phoebe Nichols
1984
ORDEAL BY INNOCENCE(1984, Brit.)

Red Nichols
DISC JOCKEY(1951); GENE KRUPA STORY, THE(1959)

Richard Nichols
ALL THIS AND HEAVEN TOO(1940); DISPATCH FROM REUTERS, A(1940); KITTY FOYLE(1940); LITTLE MEN(1940); WOMAN'S FACE(1941)

Robert Nichols
TROUBLE WITH GIRLS(AND HOW TO GET INTO IT), THE*1/2 (1969); RED BADGE OF COURAGE, THE(1951); THING, THE(1951); EIGHT IRON MEN(1952); MONKEY BUSINESS(1952); SALLY AND SAINT ANNE(1952); GENTLEMEN PREFER BLONDES(1953); JENNIFER(1953); JOHNNY DARK(1954); THIS ISLAND EARTH(1955); TIGHT SPOT(1955); GIANT(1956); NAVY WIFE(1956); BOMBERS B-52(1957); THIRTY FOOT BRIDE OF CANDY ROCK, THE(1959); CALL ME BWA-NA(1963, Brit.); FOLLOW THE BOYS(1963); VICTORS, THE(1963); WHY BOTHER TO KNOCK(1964, Brit.); AMOROUS MR. PRAWN, THE(1965, Brit.); OUT OF TOWNERS, THE(1970); THEY ONLY KILL THEIR MASTERS(1972); WICKED, WICKED(1973); DON'T GO NEAR THE WATER(1975); NIGHT THEY ROBBED BIG BERTHA'S, THE(1975); GOD TOLD ME TO(1976); REUBEN, REUBEN(1983)

Robert E. Nichols
DREAM WIFE(1953)

Sally Nichols
BLACK SPURS(1965)

Stacy Nichols
RETURN OF THE JEDI(1983)

Stephen Nichols
DIFFERENT STORY, A(1978)

Ted Nichols
MAN CALLED FLINTSTONE, THE(1966), m

Terry L. Nichols
MOVIE MOVIE(1978)

Tiny Nichols
REVENGE OF THE PINK PANTHER(1978), cos

Alexandra Nicholson
TRIAL OF BILLY JACK, THE(1974)

Arch Nicholson
BUDDIES(1983, Aus.), d

Audrey Nicholson
OPERATION CUPID(1960, Brit.); MY WIFE'S FAMILY(1962, Brit.); TRIAL AND ERROR(1962, Brit.)

Bernice Nicholson
YOU LIGHT UP MY LIFE(1977)

Bill Nicholson
DEATH VALLEY(1982), spec eff

Bruce Nicholson
EMPIRE STRIKES BACK, THE(1980), spec eff
1984
STARMAN(1984), spec eff

C.H. Nicholson
TO BE A LADY(1934, Brit.), w

Calvin Nicholson
Misc. Silents
FLAMING CRISIS, THE(1924)

Captain Nicholson
Misc. Silents
BEST MAN, THE(1917)

Carol Nicholson
ICE PALACE(1960)

Carolyn Nicholson
LOOKS AND SMILES(1982, Brit.)

Dale J. Nicholson
SUMMER PLACE, A(1959)

David Nicholson
SUDDEN FURY(1975, Can.), ed

Debbie Nicholson
ABDICATION, THE(1974, Brit.)

E. A. Nicholson
BROTHER JOHN(1971)

E. Nicholson
TWELVE TO THE MOON(1960), spec eff

Elwood J. Nicholson
PHANTOM PLANET, THE(1961), ph

Emrich Nicholson
ONE TOUCH OF VENUS(1948), art d; RIVER LADY(1948), art d; CITY ACROSS THE RIVER(1949), art d; JOHNNY STOOL PIGEON(1949), art d; MA AND PA KETTLE(1949), art d; STORY OF MOLLY X, THE(1949), art d; TAKE ONE FALSE STEP(1949), art d; DESERT HAWK, THE(1950), art d; KANSAS RAIDERS(1950), art d; KID FROM TEXAS, THE(1950), art d; SLEEPING CITY, THE(1950), art d; UNDER-COVER GIRL(1950), art d; LADY FROM TEXAS(1951), art d; MA AND PA KETTLE BACK ON THE FARM(1951), art d; PRINCE WHO WAS A THIEF, THE(1951), art d; FLESH AND FURY(1952), art d; JUST ACROSS THE STREET(1952), art d; SON OF ALI BABA(1952), art d; MAN FROM THE ALAMO, THE(1953), art d; SEMINOLE(1953), art d; VEILS OF BAGDAD, THE(1953), art d; WALKING MY BABY BACK HOME(1953), art d; MAGNIFICENT OBSESSION(1954), art d; SIGN OF THE PAGAN(1954), art d; TAZA, SON OF COCHISE(1954), art d; BATTLE HYMN(1957), art d

George Jay Nicholson
MAC ARTHUR(1977), ed; COAST TO COAST(1980), ed

George Nicholson
UNSINKABLE MOLLY BROWN, THE(1964); MAN, THE(1972), ed; WHITE LIGHT-NING(1973), ed; GOLDENGIRL(1979), ed

Gerda Nicholson
DEVIL'S PLAYGROUND, THE(1976, Aus.)

High Nicholson
Silents
TRAPPED BY THE LONDON SHARKS(1916, Brit.)

Jack Nicholson
CRY BABY KILLER, THE(1958); STUDS LONIGAN(1960); TOO SOON TO LO-VE(1960); WILD RIDE, THE(1960); LITTLE SHOP OF HORRORS(1961); BROKEN LAND, THE(1962); RAVEN, THE(1963); TERROR, THE(1963), a, p&d; THUNDER ISLAND(1963); BACK DOOR TO HELL(1964); ENSIGN PULVER(1964); FLIGHT TO FURY(1966, U.S./Phil.), a, w; RIDE IN THE WHIRLWIND(1966), a, p, w; HELL'S ANGELS ON WHEELS(1967); ST. VALENTINE'S DAY MASSACRE, THE(1967); TRIP, THE(1967), w; HEAD(1968), a, p, w; PSYCH-OUT(1968); EASY RIDER(1969); FIVE EASY PIECES(1970); ON A CLEAR DAY YOU CAN SEE FOREVER(1970); REBEL ROUSERS(1970); CARNAL KNOWLEDGE(1971); DRIVE, HE SAID(1971), p, d, w; SAFE PLACE, A(1971); SHOOTING, THE(1971), a, p; KING OF MARVIN GARDENS, THE(1972); LAST DETAIL, THE(1973); CHINATOWN(1974); FORTUNE, THE(1975); ONE FLEW OVER THE CUCKOO'S NEST(1975); PASSENGER, THE(1975, Ital.); TOMMY(1975, Brit.); LAST TYCOON, THE(1976); MISSOURI BREAKS, THE(1976); GOIN' SOUTH(1978), a, d; SHINING, THE(1980); POSTMAN ALWAYS RINGS TWICE, THE(1981); REDS(1981); BORDER, THE(1982); TERMS OF ENDEAR-MENT(1983)

James H. Nicholson
INVASION OF THE SAUCER MEN(1957), p; SHAKE, RATTLE, AND ROCK!(1957), p; HIGH SCHOOL HELLCATS(1958), p; HOW TO MAKE A MONSTER(1958), p; PARATROOP COMMAND(1959), p; MASTER OF THE WORLD(1961), p; BEACH PARTY(1963), p; OPERATION BIKINI(1963), p; BIKINI BEACH(1964), p; MUSCLE BEACH PARTY(1964), p; PAJAMA PARTY(1964), p; BEACH BLANKET BIN-GO(1965), p; DR. GOLDFOOT AND THE BIKINI MACHINE(1965), p; HOW TO STUFF A WILD BIKINI(1965), p; SERGEANT DEADHEAD(1965), p; FIREBALL 590(1966), p; GHOST IN THE INVISIBLE BIKINI(1966), p; WILD IN THE STREETS(1968), p; DE SADE(1969), p; DUNWICH HORROR, THE(1970), p; UP IN THE CELLAR(1970), p; WUTHERING HEIGHTS(1970, Brit.), p; WHO SLEW AUNTIE ROO?(1971, U.S./Brit.), p

Janie Nicholson
CURTAINS(1983, Can.)

Jeff Nicholson
THE DOUBLE McGUFFIN(1979)

Jim Nicholson
LONGEST YARD, THE(1974)

John Kenyon Nicholson
GIRL IN THE SHOW, THE(1929), w; DIAMOND HORSESHOE(1945), d&w

John Nicholson
Silents
SPENDTHRIFT, THE(1915); KIDNAPPED(1917)

John Robert Nicholson
SMOKEY AND THE BANDIT II(1980)

Joy Nicholson
WINDFLOWERS(1968)

Kenyon Nicholson
BARKER, THE(1928), w; TWO WEEKS OFF(1929), w; LAUGHING SINNERS(1931), w; SKYLINE(1931), w; WICKED(1931), w; TAXI!(1932), w; UNION DEPOT(1932), w; HOOPLA(1933), w; LADY BE CAREFUL(1936), w; THIRTEEN HOURS BY AIR(1936), w; SWING YOUR LADY(1938), w; WATERFRONT(1939), w; FLEET'S IN, THE(1942), w; SAILOR BEWARE(1951), w

Laura Nicholson
DIARY OF A HIGH SCHOOL BRIDE(1959); MUSCLE BEACH PARTY(1964); PAJA-MA PARTY(1964); DR. GOLDFOOT AND THE BIKINI MACHINE(1965)

Lesley Lynn Nicholson
PARASITE(1982), cos

Lillian Nicholson
JUAREZ(1939); MAGNIFICENT AMBERSONS, THE(1942); CLOAK AND DAG-GER(1946)
Silents
SOUTH SEA LOVE(1923)

Lisa Nicholson
YOU LIGHT UP MY LIFE(1977)

Loretta Nicholson
WAR OF THE COLOSSAL BEAST(1958); DIARY OF A HIGH SCHOOL BRIDE(1959)

Luree Nicholson
DIARY OF A HIGH SCHOOL BRIDE(1959); COMEDY OF TERRORS, THE(1964)

Lyle Nicholson
GOSPEL ROAD, THE(1973)

Marcia Nicholson
SWARM, THE(1978); WHEN TIME RAN OUT(1980); WHY WOULD I LIE(1980)

Martin Nicholson
FORBIDDEN ZONE(1980), w

Martin W. Nicholson
FORBIDDEN ZONE(1980), ed
Meredith M. Nicholson
DECKS RAN RED, THE(1958), ph; BEYOND THE TIME BARRIER(1960), ph; DEVIL'S HAND, THE(1961), ph; DANGEROUS CHARTER(1962), ph; MAN IN THE WATER, THE(1963), ph
Meredith Nicholson
HOUSE OF A THOUSAND CANDLES, THE(1936), w; FRANKENSTEIN'S DAUGHTER(1958), ph; SHE DEMONS(1958), ph; MISSILE TO THE MOON(1959), ph; AMAZING TRANSPARENT MAN, THE(1960), ph
Silents
PORT OF MISSING MEN(1914), w
Nora Nicholson
BLUE LAGOON, THE(1949, Brit.); FOOLS RUSH IN(1949, Brit.); ONCE UPON A DREAM(1949, Brit.); CROW HOLLOW(1952, Brit.); TREAD SOFTLY(1952, Brit.); HORNET'S NEST, THE(1955, Brit.); LIGHT FINGERS(1957, Brit.); RAISING A RIOT(1957, Brit.); SEA WIFE(1957, Brit.); LAW AND DISORDER(1958, Brit.); TOWN LIKE ALICE, A(1958, Brit.); CAPTAIN'S TABLE, THE(1960, Brit.); DANGEROUS AFTERNOON(1961, Brit.); UPSTAIRS AND DOWNSTAIRS(1961, Brit.); THREE LIVES OF THOMASINA, THE(1963, U.S./Brit.); DEVIL DOLL(1964, Brit.); JOEY BOY(1965, Brit.); DIAMONDS FOR BREAKFAST(1968, Brit.); SAY HELLO TO YESTERDAY(1971, Brit.)
Patita Nicholson
CIRCUS BOY(1947, Brit.), w
Paul Nicholson
NOT QUITE DECENT(1929); FOX MOVIETONE FOLLIES OF 1930(1930); MAN TO MAN(1931); NO LIMIT(1931); SILENCE(1931); SCANDAL FOR SALE(1932); TWO ALONE(1934); SECRET OF THE CHATEAU(1935)
Silents
WOMAN GOD CHANGED, THE(1921); MARRIED FLIRTS(1924); AS MAN DESIRES(1925); JOANNA(1925); JOHNSTOWN FLOOD, THE(1926); NERVOUS WRECK, THE(1926); BERTHA, THE SEWING MACHINE GIRL(1927); BRONCHO TWISTER(1927); BRUTE, THE(1927); SMART SET, THE(1928)
R.D. Nicholson
Misc. Silents
ANSWER THE CALL(1915, Brit.)
Robert Nicholson
CONFESSIONS OF A POP PERFORMER(1975, Brit.)
Sally Nicholson
FLASH GORDON(1980)
Skip Nicholson
THIS STUFF'LL KILL YA!(1971)
Stephen Nicholson
Misc. Talkies
I REMEMBER LOVE(1981)
Steve Nicholson
BIONIC BOY, THE(1977, Hong Kong/Phil.)
Tom Nicholson
DR. JEKYLL'S DUNGEON OF DEATH(1982)
David Nichtern
STUDENT TEACHERS, THE(1973), m; WHITE LINE FEVER(1975, Can.), m
Nick Niciphor
OUR WINNING SEASON(1978), w; TUSK(1980, Fr.), w
Bill Nick
FIRST MAN INTO SPACE(1959, Brit.)
Edmund Nick
COURT CONCERT, THE(1936, Ger.), m
Nick Nickeas
THIEF(1981)
Denise Nickerson
WILLY WONKA AND THE CHOCOLATE FACTORY(1971); SMILE(1975); ZERO TO SIXTY(1978)
James Nickerson
MOVIE MOVIE(1978)
Jim Nickerson
KANSAS CITY BOMBER(1972); HARD TIMES(1975); ROLLERBALL(1975); ROCKY(1976), stunts; DEEP, THE(1977), stunts; I WANNA HOLD YOUR HAND(1978); ICE CASTLES(1978); RAGING BULL(1980), stunts
Jimmy Nickerson
SLITHER(1973), stunts; HARRY AND WALTER GO TO NEW YORK(1976); TOUGH ENOUGH(1983)
Lee Nickerson
LOOKIN' TO GET OUT(1982)
Rick Nickerson
FIRST NUDIE MUSICAL, THE(1976)
Thelma Nicklaus
TAMAHINE(1964, Brit.), w
James Nickle
NORA PRENTISS(1947)
Charles Nicklin
1984
BLIND DATE(1984)
Charley Nicklin
FOG, THE(1980)
Franz Nicklisch
TEMPEST(1932, Ger.); EMIL AND THE DETECTIVES(1964)
John Nickolaus, Jr.
NO PLACE TO LAND(1958), ph; PLUNDERERS OF PAINTED FLATS(1959), ph; DAY MARS INVADED EARTH, THE(1963), ph; HOUSE OF THE DAMNED(1963), ph; THUNDER ISLAND(1963), ph; YOUNG GUNS OF TEXAS(1963), ph
Jack M. Nickolaus, Jr.
GHOST DIVER(1957), ph
John M. Nickolaus
AMBUSH AT CIMARRON PASS(1958), ph; HOT CAR GIRL(1958), ph; TERROR, THE(1963), ph; GUNS OF DIABLO(1964), ph
John M. Nickolaus, Jr.
APACHE WARRIOR(1957), ph; UNDER FIRE(1957), ph; YOUNG AND DANGEROUS(1957), ph; GANG WAR(1958), ph; SHOWDOWN AT BOOT HILL(1958), ph; FOUR FAST GUNS(1959), ph

Tom Nickols
IT'S A BIG COUNTRY(1951)
David A. Nicksay
1984
MRS. SOFFEL(1984), p
Nico
CHELSEA GIRLS, THE(1967)
Erin Nico
DREAM ON(1981), a, p
Krista Nico
SWEET SKIN(1965, Fr./Ital.)
Willard Nico
GREAT DICTATOR, THE(1940), ed; MONSIEUR VERDOUX(1947), ed
Nicodemus
DARK MANHATTAN(1937); CABIN IN THE SKY(1943); FALSE FACES(1943); HEAVENLY BODY, THE(1943)
"Nicodemus"
HOOSIER HOLIDAY(1943)
Alex Nicol
SLEEPING CITY, THE(1950); AIR CADET(1951); RAGING TIDE, THE(1951); TARGET UNKNOWN(1951); TOMAHAWK(1951); BECAUSE OF YOU(1952); MEET DANNY WILSON(1952); RED BALL EXPRESS(1952); CHAMP FOR A DAY(1953); LAW AND ORDER(1953); LONE HAND, THE(1953); REDHEAD FROM WYOMING, THE(1953); ABOUT MRS. LESLIE(1954); BLACK GLOVE(1954, Brit.); DAWN AT SOCORRO(1954); GILDED CAGE, THE(1954, Brit.); HEATWAVE(1954, Brit.); MAN FROM LARAMIE, THE(1955); SINCERELY YOURS(1955); STRATEGIC AIR COMMAND(1955); GREAT DAY IN THE MORNING(1956); STRANGER IN TOWN(1957, Brit.); SCREAMING SKULL, THE(1958), a, d; FIVE BRANDED WOMEN(1960); UNDER TEN FLAGS(1960, U.S./Ital.); LOOK IN ANY WINDOW(1961); THEN THERE WERE THREE(1961), a, p&d; EVERYBODY GO HOME!(1962, Fr./Ital.); MATTER OF WHO, A(1962, Brit.); SAVAGE GUNS, THE(1962, U.S./Span.); RUN WITH THE DEVIL(1963, Fr./Ital.); GUNFIGHTERS OF CASA GRANDE(1965, U.S./Span.); BLOODY MAMA(1970); HOMER(1970); POINT OF TERROR(1971), d; CLONES, THE(1973); NIGHT GOD SCREAMED, THE(1975)
Misc. Talkies
A(1976, U.S./Korea); WOMAN IN THE RAIN(1976)
Michael Nicola
DARKTOWN STRUTTERS(1975), cos
Seraphim Nicola
PRIVATE RIGHT, THE(1967, Brit.)
Bruno Nicolai
CHRISMAS THAT ALMOST WASN'T. THE(1966, Ital.), m, md; PISTOL FOR RINGO, A(1966, Ital./Span.), md; PLACE CALLED GLORY, A(1966, Span./Ger.), md; FOR A FEW DOLLARS MORE(1967, Ital./Ger./Span.), md; GOOD, THE BAD, AND THE UGLY, THE(1967, Ital./Span.), md; HEAD OF THE FAMILY(1967, Ital./Fr.), md; MATCHLESS(1967, Ital.), md; OPERATION KID BROTHER(1967, Ital.), m; ROVER, THE(1967, Ital.), md; STRANGER, THE(1967, Algeria/Fr./Ital.), md; GRAND SLAM(1968, Ital., Span., Ger.), md; MINUTE TO PRAY, A SECOND TO DIE, A(1968, Ital.), md; SEVEN GUNS FOR THE MACGREGORS(1968, Ital./Span.), md; FRAULEIN DOKTOR(1969, Ital./Yugo.), md; LAND RAIDERS(1969), m, md; LAST MERCENARY, THE(1969, Ital./Span./Ger.), md; LISTEN, LET'S MAKE LOVE(1969, Fr./Ital.), md; RUTHLESS FOUR, THE(1969, Ital./Ger.), md; TEOREMA(1969, Ital.), md; THANK YOU, AUNT(1969, Ital.), md; COMPANEROS(1970 Ital./Span./Ger.), m; INVESTIGATION OF A CITIZEN ABOVE SUSPICION(1970, Ital.), md; MERCENARY, THE(1970, Ital./Span.), m; SERAFINO(1970, Fr./Ital.), md; SICILIAN CLAN, THE(1970, Fr.), md; ADIOS SABATA(1971, Ital./Span.), m; COUNT DRACULA(1971, Sp., Ital., Ger., Brit.), m; DIRTY HEROES(1971, Ital./Fr./Ger.), m; NIGHT EVELYN CAME OUT OF THE GRAVE, THE(1973, Ital.), m; SERPENT, THE(1973, Fr./Ital./Ger.), md; TEN LITTLE INDIANS(1975, Ital./Fr./Span./Ger.), m; CAMMINA CAMMINA(1983, Ital.), m
Otto Nicolai
MERRY WIVES OF WINDSOR, THE(1952, Ger.), w; MERRY WIVES OF WINDSOR, THE(1966, Aust.), w, m
Renato Nicolai
WAKE UP AND DIE(1967, Fr./Ital.)
Sergio Nicolai
TEMPEST(1982); YOR, THE HUNTER FROM THE FUTURE(1983, Ital.)
Dimitris Nicolaidis
DAY THE FISH CAME OUT, THE(1967. Brit./Gr.)
Nicolaou
YOUNG WARRIORS(1983), cos
Panos Nicolaou
NUTCRACKER(1982, Brit.), p
Ted Nicolaou
DAY TIME ENDED, THE(1980, Span.), ed; YOUNG WARRIORS(1983), ed
Linette Nicolas
HEAT OF THE SUMMER(1961, Fr.), ed; HOT HOURS(1963, Fr.), ed
Paul Nicolas
JULIE DARLING(1982, Can./Ger.), d, w; NUTCRACKER(1982, Brit.)
Bruce Nicolaysen
PASSAGE, THE(1979, Brit.), w
Andre Nicole
ACCUSED–STAND UP(1930, Fr.)
Ariela Nicole
CAN SHE BAKE A CHERRY PIE?(1983)
Claude Nicole
PORT OF DESIRE(1960, Fr.), ed
Dita Nicole
FOR SINGLES ONLY(1968)
Lydia Nicole
MAX DUGAN RETURNS(1983)
Mylene Nicole [Demongeot]
IT'S A WONDERFUL WORLD(1956, Brit.)
John Nicolella
EASY MONEY(1983), p
Natasa Nicolescu
POPE JOAN(1972, Brit.)

Louis A. Nicoletti
DESERT HAWK, THE(1950)
Louis Nicoletti
VENGEANCE VALLEY(1951); MONEY FROM HOME(1953)
Susi Nicoletti
CONFESSIONS OF FELIX KRULL, THE(1957, Ger.); TURKISH CUCUMBER, THE(1963, Ger.); DIE FLEDERMAUS(1964, Aust.)
Flavio Nicolini
SAUL AND DAVID(1968, Ital./Span.), w
Michel Nicolini
BROKEN ENGLISH(1981)
Natalia Nicolini
BARBER OF SEVILLE, THE(1947, Ital.)
Roberto Nicolisi
8 ½(1963, Ital.)
Andre Nicolle
PERSONAL COLUMN(1939, Fr.); CAGE OF NIGHTINGALES, A(1947, Fr.)
Steve Nicolle
1984
TREASURE OF THE YANKEE ZEPHYR(1984)
Fiona Nicolls
WE OF THE NEVER NEVER(1983, Aus.), cos
Ted Nicoloau
TOURIST TRAP, THE(1979), ed
Daria Nicolodi
DEEP RED(1976, Ital.); SUSPIRIA(1977, Ital.), w; BEYOND THE DOOR II(1979, Ital.); INFERNO(1980, Ital.)
Robert Nicolosi
WHITE WARRIOR, THE(1961, Ital./Yugo.), m; RITA(1963, Fr./Ital.), m
Roberto Nicolosi
ESTHER AND THE KING(1960, U.S./Ital.), m; GIANT OF MARATHON, THE(1960, Ital.), m; MIGHTY CRUSADERS, THE(1961, Ital.), m; PIRATE OF THE BLACK HAWK, THE(1961, Fr./Ital.), m; LAST OF THE VIKINGS, THE(1962, Fr./Ital.), m; BLACK SABBATH(1963, Ital.), m; ERIK THE CONQUEROR(1963, Fr./Ital.), m; TORPEDO BAY(1964, Ital./Fr.), m; WAR OF THE ZOMBIES, THE(1965 Ital.), m
Faida Nicols
DIRTY HEROES(1971, Ital./Fr./Ger.)
Michelle Nicols
TARZAN'S DEADLY SILENCE(1970)
Rosemary Nicols
PLEASURE GIRLS, THE(1966, Brit.); MINI-AFFAIR, THE(1968, Brit.)
Gerda Nicolson
GALLIPOLI(1981, Aus.); CLINIC, THE(1983, Aus.); NEXT OF KIN(1983, Aus.)
Jim Nicolson
IT HAPPENED HERE(1966, Brit.), art d
Robert Nicolson
WHISPERERS, THE(1967, Brit.), d&w
Antoine Nicos
PLAYGIRLS AND THE VAMPIRE(1964, Ital.)
Barbara Nicot
FIVE MILES TO MIDNIGHT(1963, U.S./Fr./Ital.)
Claude Nicot
ADORABLE LIAR(1962, Fr.)
Antonio Nicotra
BEHIND CLOSED SHUTTERS(1952, Ital.)
Mario Nicotra
RING AROUND THE CLOCK(1953, Ital.)
Sven Nicou
NO TIME TO KILL(1963, Brit./Swed./Ger.), p
Leda Nicova
WATERLOO BRIDGE(1940); I MARRIED AN ANGEL(1942); ONCE UPON A HONEYMOON(1942)
Walter Niebuhr
Silents
MONEY HABIT, THE(1924, Brit.), d
Misc. Silents
VENETIAN LOVERS(1925, Brit.), d; CITY OF TEMPTATION(1929, Brit.), d
Nied
M(1933, Ger.)
Otto Niedermoser
APRIL 1, 2000(1953, Aust.), set d; VIENNA WALTZES(1961, Aust.), set d
Janina Niedzwiecka
EVE WANTS TO SLEEP(1961, Pol.), ed; YELLOW SLIPPERS, THE(1965, Pol.), ed; LOTNA(1966, Pol.), ed
Dagmar Niefind
CIRCLE OF DECEIT(1982, Fr./Ger.), cos
Lennie Niehaus
1984
CITY HEAT(1984), m; TIGHTROPE(1984), m
Ruth Niehaus
GREH(1962, Ger./Yugo.)
Sidney Niehoff
RAW WEEKEND(1964), d
Marshall Nielan
FACE IN THE CROWD, A(1957)
Misc. Silents
JAGUAR'S CLAWS(1917), d
Charles Nields
BACK TO BATAAN(1945), set d; FIRST YANK INTO TOKYO(1945), set d
Asta Nielsen
Misc. Silents
HAMLET(1921, Ger.); VANINA(1922, Ger.); CROWN OF THORNS(1934, Ger.)
Bente Nielsen
SNOW TREASURE(1968)
Betty Nielsen
Misc. Talkies
REFLECTIONS FROM A BRASS BED(1976)

Bob Nielsen
WHO SAYS I CAN'T RIDE A RAINBOW!(1971)
Brigit Nielsen
RHAPSODY(1954)
Christa Nielsen
DEVIL STRIKES AT NIGHT, THE(1959, Ger.)
Christiane Nielsen
INVISIBLE MAN, THE(1963, Ger.); ISLE OF SIN(1963, Ger.); MORALIST, THE(1964, Ital.)
Edith Nisted Nielsen
REPTILICUS(1962, U.S./Den.), ed
Egon C. Nielsen
ESCAPE FROM TERROR(1960), p
Erik Nielsen
I WANT YOU(1951); CARBINE WILLIAMS(1952); WAIT 'TIL THE SUN SHINES, NELLIE(1952)
Gerda Nielsen
ORDET(1957, Den.)
Gunnar Nielsen
SMILES OF A SUMMER NIGHT(1957, Swed.)
Hans Nielsen
CONFESS DR. CORDA(1960, Ger.); GIRL OF THE MOORS, THE(1961, Ger.); VOR SONNENUNTERGANG(1961, Ger); COURT MARTIAL(1962, Ger.); YOUNG GO WILD, THE(1962, Ger.); I, TOO, AM ONLY A WOMAN(1963, Ger.); SCOTLAND YARD HUNTS DR. MABUSE(1963, Ger.); JUDGE AND THE SINNER, THE(1964, Ger.); TWO IN A SLEEPING BAG(1964, Ger.); BRAIN, THE(1965, Ger./Brit.); PLACE CALLED GLORY, A(1966, Span./Ger.); MONSTER OF LONDON CITY, THE(1967, Ger.); PHANTOM OF SOHO, THE(1967, Ger.)
Henry Nielsen
ERIC SOYA'S "17"(1967, Den.)
Inga Nielsen
SILENT MOVIE(1976)
Ingvard Nielsen
DARK INTRUDER(1965)
Jakob Nielsen
HAGBARD AND SIGNE(1968, Den./Iceland/Swed.)
Jeff Nielsen
1984
DELIVERY BOYS(1984)
Jorgen Nielsen
GERTRUD(1966, Den.), p
Kay Nielsen
FANTASIA(1940), art d
Leslie Nielsen
FORBIDDEN PLANET(1956); OPPOSITE SEX, THE(1956); RANSOM(1956); VAGABOND KING, THE(1956); HOT SUMMER NIGHT(1957); TAMMY AND THE BACHELOR(1957); SHEEPMAN, THE(1958); NIGHT TRAIN TO PARIS(1964, Brit.); DARK INTRUDER(1965); HARLOW(1965); BEAU GESTE(1966); PLAINSMAN, THE(1966); COUNTERPOINT(1967); GUNFIGHT IN ABILENE(1967); RELUCTANT ASTRONAUT, THE(1967); ROSIE!(1967); DAYTON'S DEVILS(1968); CHANGE OF MIND(1969); FOUR RODE OUT(1969, US/Span.); HOW TO COMMIT MARRIAGE(1969); RESURRECTION OF ZACHARY WHEELER, THE(1971); AND MILLIONS WILL DIE(1973); PROJECT: KILL(1976); DAY OF THE ANIMALS(1977); SIXTH AND MAIN(1977); AMSTERDAM KILL, THE(1978, Hong Kong); CITY ON FIRE(1979 Can.); AIRPLANE!(1980); PROM NIGHT(1980); CREATURE WASN'T NICE,THE(1981); CREEPSHOW(1982); WRONG IS RIGHT(1982)
Misc. Talkies
GRAND JURY(1977); RIEL(1979)
Mariane Nielsen
TWO LIVING, ONE DEAD(1964, Brit./Swed.)
Mathilde Nielsen
Misc. Silents
MASTER OF THE HOUSE(1925, Den.)
Monica Nielsen
TIME IN THE SUN, A(1970, Swed.)
Patrick Nielsen
WILD REBELS, THE(1967), set d
Peggy Nielsen
DOUBLES(1978)
Peter Nielsen
FIEND WITHOUT A FACE(1958), spec eff; WILD PACK, THE(1972)
Thomas Nielsen
1984
ZAPPA(1984, Den.)
Thor Nielsen
HUNTER, THE(1980)
The Nielsen Brothers
5 SINNERS(1961, Ger.)
Bette Nielson
Misc. Talkies
THAT GIRL IS A TRAMP(1974)
Brenda Nielson
OUT OF THE BLUE(1982), w
Claire Nielson
KIDNAPPED(1971, Brit.)
Edward Nielson
THREE(1969, Brit.), ed
Erik Nielson
TERROR BENEATH THE SEA(1966, Jap.)
Glen Nielson
SATAN'S BED(1965)
Hans Nielson
TOWN WITHOUT PITY(1961, Ger./Switz./U.S.); SHERLOCK HOLMES AND THE DEADLY NECKLACE(1962, Ger.); ONLY A WOMAN(1966, Ger.)
Inga Nielson
EVEL KNIEVEL(1971)
Jim P. Nielson
TERROR IN THE JUNGLE(1968), spec eff

John Nielson
HONKY(1971)
Leslie Nielson
POSEIDON ADVENTURE, THE(1972); VIVA KNIEVEL!(1977)
Norman Nielson
UNCLE HARRY(1945)
Perlita Nielson
SHE DIDN'T SAY NO!(1962, Brit.)
Steven Nielson
MICROWAVE MASSACRE(1983), ed
Yvonne Nielson
Misc. Talkies
BLOOD THIRST(1965 Phil./U.S.)
Phyllis Nielson-Terry
LOOK BACK IN ANGER(1959)
Leon Niemczyk
KNIGHTS OF THE TEUTONIC ORDER, THE(1962, Pol.); KNIFE IN THE WATER(1963, Pol.); EROICA(1966, Pol.); SARAGOSSA MANUSCRIPT, THE(1972, Pol.)
Al Niemela
INCREDIBLE JOURNEY, THE(1963), animal sup
Joe Niemeyer
DAMSEL IN DISTRESS, A(1937); SWING, SISTER, SWING(1938)
Kai A. Niemeyer
NOT RECONCILED, OR "ONLY VIOLENCE HELPS WHERE IT RULES"(1969, Ger.)
Lisa Niemi
1984
GRANDVIEW, U.S.A.(1984), ch
Tsao Nienlung
DEADLY CHINA DOLL(1973, Hong Kong), set d
Sally Nieper
BLACK JACK(1979, Brit.), cos
Jean-Philippe Nierman
MADE IN U.S.A.(1966, Fr.)
Edouard Niermans
IT ONLY HAPPENS TO OTHERS(1971, Fr./Ital.)
Hansi Niese
STORM IN A WATER GLASS(1931, Aust.)
Gertrude Niesen
TOP OF THE TOWN(1937); START CHEERING(1938); ROOKIES ON PARADE(1941); HE'S MY GUY(1943); THIS IS THE ARMY(1943); THUMBS UP(1943); BABE RUTH STORY, THE(1948)
Hans Niesen
DEVIL IN SILK(1968, Ger.)
Sharon Niesp
POLYESTER(1981)
Carl Niessen
5 SINNERS(1961, Ger.), m
Carlos Nieto
ORLAK, THE HELL OF FRANKENSTEIN(1960, Mex.); GIGANTES PLANETARIOS(1965, Mex.)
Jose Nieto
TANGO BAR(1935); CAPTAIN BLACK JACK(1952, U.S./Fr.); CONTRABAND SPAIN(1955, Brit.); THAT LADY(1955, Brit.); ALEXANDER THE GREAT(1956); PRIDE AND THE PASSION, THE(1957); KING OF KINGS(1961); REVOLT OF THE SLAVES, THE(1961, Ital./Span./Ger.); SAVAGE GUNS, THE(1962, U.S./Span.); CEREMONY, THE(1963, U.S./Span.); 55 DAYS AT PEKING(1963); SON OF CAPTAIN BLOOD, THE(1964, U.S./Ital./Span.); DOCTOR ZHIVAGO(1965); KID RODELO(1966, U.S./Span.); CHIMES AT MIDNIGHT(1967, Span.,Switz.); FLAME OVER VIETNAM(1967, Span./Ger.); HELLBENDERS, THE(1967, U.S./Ital./Span.); SAVAGE PAMPAS(1967, Span./Arg.); YOUNG REBEL, THE(1969, Fr./Ital./Span.); SCANDALOUS JOHN(1971); RED SUN(1972, Fr./Ital./Span.)
1984
IT'S NEVER TOO LATE(1984, Span.), m
Luciel Nieto
SEVEN CITIES OF GOLD(1955)
Paco Nieto
MERCENARY, THE(1970, Ital./Span.)
Pepe Nieto
ACTION OF THE TIGER(1957); NIGHT HEAVEN FELL, THE(1958, Fr.); JOHN PAUL JONES(1959); TOMMY THE TOREADOR(1960, Brit.)
Teresa Nieto
CARMEN(1983, Span.), cos
Velma Nieto
LONE WOLF McQUADE(1983)
Alvin G. Nietz
Silents
BORDER WOMEN(1924), d
Alvin J. Nietz
Silents
BACK FIRE(1922), d&w
Jack Nietzche
CANNERY ROW(1982), m
Jack M. Nietzsche, Jr.
LOSIN' IT(1983)
Matthew Nieuwlands
GOODBYE PORK PIE(1981, New Zealand)
Alfonso Nieva
TREASURE OF MAKUBA, THE(1967, U.S./Span.), ph; WITCH WITHOUT A BROOM, A(1967, U.S./Span.), ph; GRAVEYARD OF HORROR(1971, Span.), ph
Petra Nieva
MISSION BLOODY MARY(1967, Fr./Ital./Span.), ed
Jose Antonio Nieves-Conde
SOUND OF HORROR(1966, Span.), d
Francis Niewal
HYPNOSIS(1966, Ger./Sp./Ital.), w
Bogdan Niewinowski
YELLOW SLIPPERS, THE(1965, Pol.)

Bohdan Niewinowski
FIRST START(1953, Pol.)
Gleb Nifontov
HUNTING IN SIBERIA(1962, USSR), d
Moya Nigent
Silents
OLD CURIOSITY SHOP, THE(1913, Brit.)
Sepp Nigg
WHITE HORSE INN, THE(1959, Ger.)
Josefina Niggli
SOMBRERO(1953), w
Jane Nigh
LAURA(1944); STATE FAIR(1945); DRAGONWYCH(1946); WHISTLE STOP(1946); UNCONQUERED(1947); CRY OF THE CITY(1948); GIVE MY REGARDS TO BROADWAY(1948); LEATHER GLOVES(1948); SITTING PRETTY(1948); FIGHTING MAN OF THE PLAINS(1949); RED, HOT AND BLUE(1949); ZAMBA(1949); BLUE GRASS OF KENTUCKY(1950); BORDER TREASURE(1950); CAPTAIN CAREY, U.S.A(1950); COUNTY FAIR(1950); MOTOR PATROL(1950); OPERATION HAYLIFT(1950); RIO GRANDE PATROL(1950); BLUE BLOOD(1951); DISC JOCKEY(1951); FORT OSAGE(1952); RODEO(1952); HOLD THAT HYPNOTIST(1957)
Will Nigh
Misc. Silents
BORN RICH(1924), d; FEAR-BOUND(1925), a, d
William Nigh
LORD BYRON OF BROADWAY(1930), d; TODAY(1930), d; FIGHTING THRU(1931), d; LIGHTNING FLYER(1931), d; SEA GHOST, THE(1931), d, w; SINGLE SIN(1931), d; BORDER DEVILS(1932), d; NIGHT RIDER, THE(1932), d; WITHOUT HONORS(1932), d; MEN ARE SUCH FOOLS(1933), d; CITY LIMITS(1934), d; HE COULDN'T TAKE IT(1934), d; HOUSE OF MYSTERY(1934), d; MONTE CARLO NIGHTS(1934), d; MYSTERY LINER(1934), d; ONCE TO EVERY BACHELOR(1934), d; TWO HEADS ON A PILLOW(1934), d; HEADLINE WOMAN, THE(1935), d; HIS NIGHT OUT(1935), d; MYSTERIOUS MR. WONG(1935), d; OLD HOMESTEAD, THE(1935), d; SCHOOL FOR GIRLS(1935), d; SHE GETS HER MAN(1935), d; SWEEPSTAKE ANNIE(1935), d; CRASH DONOVAN(1936), d; DIZZY DAMES(1936), d; DON'T GET PERSONAL(1936), d; PENTHOUSE PARTY(1936), d; ATLANTIC FLIGHT(1937), d; BILL CRACKS DOWN(1937), d; BOY OF THE STREETS(1937), d; BRIDE FOR HENRY, A(1937), d; HOOSIER SCHOOLBOY(1937), d; NORTH OF NOME(1937), d; THIRTEENTH MAN, THE(1937), d; FEMALE FUGITIVE(1938), d; GANGSTER'S BOY(1938), d; LAW COMMANDS, THE(1938), d; MR. WONG, DETECTIVE(1938), d; ROMANCE OF THE LIMBERLOST(1938), d; ROSE OF THE RIO GRANDE(1938), d; I AM A CRIMINAL(1939), d; MR. WONG IN CHINATOWN(1939), d; MUTINY IN THE BIG HOUSE(1939), d; MYSTERY OF MR. WONG, THE(1939), d; STREETS OF NEW YORK(1939), d; APE, THE(1940), d; DOOMED TO DIE(1940), d; FATAL HOUR, THE(1940), d; SON OF THE NAVY(1940), d; KID FROM KANSAS, THE(1941), d; MOB TOWN(1941), d; NO GREATER SIN(1941), d; SECRET EVIDENCE(1941), d; ZIS BOOM BAH(1941), d; BLACK DRAGONS(1942), d; CITY OF SILENT MEN(1942), d; COLLEGE SWEETHEARTS(1942), d; ESCAPE FROM HONG KONG(1942), d; MR. WISE GUY(1942), d; STRANGE CASE OF DR. RX, THE(1942), d; TOUGH AS THEY COME(1942), d; CORREGIDOR(1943), d; GHOST AND THE GUEST(1943), d; LADY FROM CHUNGKING(1943), d; WHERE ARE YOUR CHILDREN?(1943), d; ARE THESE OUR PARENTS?(1944), d; TROCADERO(1944), d; ALLOTMENT WIVES, INC.(1945), d; DIVORCE(1945), d; FOREVER YOURS(1945), d; BEAUTY AND THE BANDIT(1946), d; PARTNERS IN TIME(1946), d; I WOULDN'T BE IN YOUR SHOES(1948), d; STAGE STRUCK(1948), d
Misc. Talkies
GAY CAVALIER, THE(1946), d; SOUTH OF MONTEREY(1946), d; RIDING THE CALIFORNIA TRAIL(1947), d
Silents
SALOMY JANE(1914); ROYAL FAMILY, A(1915), a, d; STORK'S NEST, THE(1915), d; MY FOUR YEARS IN GERMANY(1918), d; SCHOOL DAYS(1921), d, w; NOTORIETY(1922), d&w; RAGS TO RICHES(1922), w; MR. WU(1927), d; NEST, THE(1927), d; ACROSS THE SINGAPORE(1928), d; FOUR WALLS(1928), d; LAW OF THE RANGE, THE(1928), d; THUNDER(1929), d
Misc. Silents
YELLOW STREAK, A(1915), d; CHILD OF DESTINY, THE(1916), d; DEBT OF HONOR, A(1916), d; HER DEBT OF HONOR(1916), a, d; HIS GREAT TRIUMPH(1916), a, d; KISS OF HATE, THE(1916), d; LIFE'S SHADOWS(1916), a, d; BLUE STREAK, THE(1917), a, d; SLAVE, THE(1917), d; THOU SHALT NOT STEAL(1917), d; WIFE NUMBER TWO(1917), d; BEWARE(1919), d; DEMOCRACY(1920), a, d; SKINNING SKINNERS(1921), d; SOUL OF A MAN, THE(1921), d; WHY GIRLS LEAVE HOME(1921), d; YOUR BEST FRIEND(1922), d; MARRIAGE MORALS(1923), d; FIRE BRIGADE, THE(1926), d; LITTLE GIANT, THE(1926), d; DESERT NIGHTS(1929), d
Night
MONSTER CLUB, THE(1981, Brit.)
Eugenia Night
UNTAMED FRONTIER(1952), w
The Nightcaps X-sessive
SMITHEREENS(1982)
The Nighthawks
BILLY IN THE LOWLANDS(1979), m
Benny Nightingale
TWO GENTLEMEN SHARING(1969, Brit.)
Joe Nightingale
Misc. Silents
HOBSON'S CHOICE(1920, Brit.); ROTTERS, THE(1921, Brit.); SHIRLEY(1922, Brit.)
Laura Nightingale
ANOTHER TIME, ANOTHER PLACE(1958), cos; FRIGHTENED CITY, THE(1961, Brit.), cos; KIND OF LOVING, A(1962, Brit.), cos; HELLFIRE CLUB, THE(1963, Brit.), cos; MASQUE OF THE RED DEATH, THE(1964, U.S./Brit.), cos
Lesley Nightingale
1984
SECRET PLACES(1984, Brit.)
Michael Nightingale
PARIS EXPRESS, THE(1953, Brit.); VIOLENT STRANGER(1957, Brit.); STRANGLERS OF BOMBAY, THE(1960, Brit.); ROOMMATES(1962, Brit.); CARRY ON CABBIE(1963, Brit.); SWINGIN' MAIDEN, THE(1963, Brit.); CURSE OF THE VOODOO(1965, Brit.); CLEGG(1969, Brit.); DECLINE AND FALL... OF A BIRD WATCHER(1969, Brit.); LONG AGO, TOMORROW(1971, Brit.)

Timothy Nightingale
SOME PEOPLE(1964, Brit.)
Bill Nighy
EYE OF THE NEEDLE(1981)
1984
LITTLE DRUMMER GIRL, THE(1984)
Christina Nigra
SWORD AND THE SORCERER, THE(1982); TWILIGHT ZONE–THE MOVIE(1983)
1984
CLOAK AND DAGGER(1984)
Ron Nigrini
TICKET TO HEAVEN(1981)
Antonio Lo Nigro
SHOE SHINE(1947, Ital.)
Bea Nigro
MARRIED BEFORE BREAKFAST(1937); MARIE ANTOINETTE(1938); I LOVE YOU AGAIN(1940); NEW MOON(1940); JOURNEY FOR MARGARET(1942); THOUSANDS CHEER(1943)
Pasquale Nigro
DEAF SMITH AND JOHNNY EARS(1973, Ital.), cos
Judi Nihei
CHAN IS MISSING(1982)
Julie Nihill
1984
CAREFUL, HE MIGHT HEAR YOU(1984, Aus.)
Kazui Nihonmatsu
GIRARA(1967, Jap.), d, w
Kan Nihonyanagi
TORA! TORA! TORA!(1970, U.S./Jap.)
Nan Nihonyanagi
NAKED YOUTH(1961, Jap.)
Toshie Nihonyanagi
HOUSE OF STRANGE LOVES, THE(1969, Jap.)
Bronislava Nijinska
MIDSUMMER'S NIGHT'S DREAM, A(1935), ch
Andrea Nijinsky
SONG OF SOHO(1930, Brit.)
Kyra Nijinsky
SHE DANCES ALONE(1981, Aust./U.S.)
Romola Nijinsky
NIJINSKY(1980, Brit.), w
Yukiko Nikaido
FINAL WAR, THE(1960, Jap.)
Herb "Kneecap" Nikal
1984
ICEMAN(1984)
Nikandrof
Silents
TEN DAYS THAT SHOOK THE WORLD(1927, USSR)
Nikandrov
Misc. Silents
OCTOBER(1928, USSR)
John Nikcovich
IRON MAN, THE(1951)
Hannes Nikel
DAS BOOT(1982), ed
Hans Nikel
BASHFUL ELEPHANT, THE(1962, Aust.), ph; JACK OF DIAMONDS(1967, U.S./Ger.), ed
Jeff Niki
EYES OF LAURA MARS(1978)
Terumi Niki
RED BEARD(1966, Jap.); NO GREATER LOVE THAN THIS(1969, Jap.)
Ira Nikiforova
GORDEYEV FAMILY, THE(1961, U.S.S.R.)
Lyusya Nikiforova
GORDEYEV FAMILY, THE(1961, U.S.S.R.)
V. Nikitchenko
NIGHT BEFORE CHRISTMAS, A(1963, USSR), spec eff; MAGIC WEAVER, THE(1965, USSR), spec eff
N. Nikitich
SANDU FOLLOWS THE SUN(1965, USSR)
Fyodor Nikitin
SONG OVER MOSCOW(1964, USSR); YOLANTA(1964, USSR); SONS AND MOTHERS(1967, USSR)
Misc. Silents
PARISIAN COBBLER(1928, USSR); FRAGMENT OF AN EMPIRE(1930, USSR)
G. Nikitin
PEACE TO HIM WHO ENTERS(1963, USSR)
K. Nikitin
CRANES ARE FLYING, THE(1960, USSR)
Lenya Nikitin
DIMKA(1964, USSR)
Sergei Nikitin
MOSCOW DOES NOT BELIEVE IN TEARS(1980, USSR), m
N. Nikitina
ITALIANO BRAVA GENTE(1965, Ital./USSR)
Nikolai Nikitine
THREE TALES OF CHEKHOV(1961, USSR)
Nikki
NIKKI, WILD DOG OF THE NORTH(1961, U.S./Can.)
Jan Niklas
FORMULA, THE(1980); NIGHT CROSSING(1982)
1984
LOOSE CONNECTIONS(1984, Brit.)
Niko
PARIS BLUES(1961)

Genia Nikola
RIDE A CROOKED MILE(1938); LADY HAS PLANS, THE(1942)
Dimitri Nikolaidis
GREEK TYCOON, THE(1978)
Genia Nikolajeva
SHOT AT DAWN, A(1934, Ger.)
V. Nikolayev
BORIS GODUNOV(1959, USSR), ph
Nikolayeva
ADVENTURE IN DIAMONDS(1940)
A. Nikolayeva
FAREWELL, DOVES(1962, USSR); MOTHER AND DAUGHTER(1965, USSR)
Djordje Nikolic
TWELVE CHAIRS, THE(1970), ph
Dragan Nikolic
HOROSCOPE(1950, Yugo.); ONE-EYED SOLDIERS(1967, U.S./Brit./Yugo.)
George Nikolic
1984
SECRET DIARY OF SIGMUND FREUD, THE(1984), ph
Marko Nikolic
EARLY WORKS(1970, Yugo.)
Mira Nikolic
ENGLANO MADE ME(1973, Brit.)
Yuri Nikolin
WHEN THE TREES WERE TALL(1965, USSR)
Michael Nikolinakos
300 SPARTANS, THE(1962)
Nezilavela Nikolska
MERRY WIVES, THE(1940, Czech.)
Sergey Nikonenko
GIRL AND THE BUGLER, THE(1967, USSR); WAR AND PEACE(1968, USSR); RED AND THE WHITE, THE(1969, Hung./USSR)
Erich Nikowitz
FOREVER MY LOVE(1962)
Rev. Nikula
DOVE, THE(1974, Brit.)
V. Nikulin
NINE DAYS OF ONE YEAR(1964, USSR)
Brian Niland
NED KELLY(1970, Brit.)
Bryan Niland
SIDECAR RACERS(1975, Aus.)
D'Arcy Niland
SHIRALEE, THE(1957, Brit.), w
Blair Niles
CONDEMNED(1929), w
Chuck Niles
INVISIBLE INVADERS(1959); HAND OF DEATH(1962); SKATEBOARD(1978)
Chuck G. Niles
SLAUGHTER'S BIG RIP-OFF(1973)
Denny Niles
MISTER ROBERTS(1955)
Fred A. Niles
NASHVILLE REBEL(1966), p
Jason Niles
VIOLATED(1953)
Ken Niles
HOLLYWOOD HOTEL(1937); KID COMES BACK, THE(1937); SWEEPSTAKES WINNER(1939); HARMON OF MICHIGAN(1941); INNER CIRCLE, THE(1946); OUT OF THE PAST(1947); MY FRIEND IRMA(1949); FAT MAN, THE(1951)
Kenneth Niles
YOU WERE MEANT FOR ME(1948)
Mary Ann Niles
UNSINKABLE MOLLY BROWN, THE(1964)
Polly Niles
SUPERFLY(1972)
Richard Niles
DESTINATION INNER SPACE(1966); WHAT DID YOU DO IN THE WAR, DADDY?(1966)
Wen Niles
COWBOY FROM BROOKLYN(1938)
Wendell Niles
EVER SINCE EVE(1937); MARKED WOMAN(1937); INDIANAPOLIS SPEEDWAY(1939); GAUCHO SERENADE(1940); THREE FACES WEST(1940); HARMON OF MICHIGAN(1941); PUDDIN' HEAD(1941); TRAGEDY AT MIDNIGHT, A(1942); HERE COMES ELMER(1943); SENSATIONS OF 1945(1944); SWINGIN' ON A RAINBOW(1945); MY FRIEND IRMA GOES WEST(1950); HITCH-HIKER, THE(1953); MONEY FROM HOME(1953); I DIED A THOUSAND TIMES(1955); SQUARE JUNGLE, THE(1955); BEYOND A REASONABLE DOUBT(1956); HOLLYWOOD OR BUST(1956); JET PILOT(1957)
Wendell Niles, Jr.
WHAT AM I BID?(1967), p
David Nillo
VAGABOND KING, THE(1956)
Anna Q. Nillson
VALLEY OF DECISION, THE(1945)
Carlotta Nillson
Misc. Silents
LEAH KLESCHNA(1913)
Alejandra Nilo
FICKLE FINGER OF FATE, THE(1967, Span./U.S.); TALL WOMEN, THE(1967, Aust./Ital./Span.); CHRISTMAS KID, THE(1968, U.S., Span.)
Nilo Menendez Rhumba Band
MUSIC IN MANHATTAN(1944)
Banchong Nilpet
1 2 3 MONSTER EXPRESS(1977, Thai.)
Hazel Nilsen
APACHE CHIEF(1949); SQUARE DANCE JUBILEE(1949)

Anna Q. Nilsson

BLOCKADE(1929); SCHOOL FOR GIRLS(1935); WANDERER OF THE WASTE-LAND(1935); PARADISE FOR THREE(1938); PRISON FARM(1938); PEOPLE VS. DR. KILDARE, THE(1941); RIDERS OF THE TIMBERLINE(1941); TRIAL OF MARY DUGAN, THE(1941); CROSSROADS(1942); GIRLS' TOWN(1942); GREAT MAN'S LADY, THE(1942); I LIVE ON DANGER(1942); THEY DIED WITH THEIR BOOTS ON(1942); HEADIN' FOR GOD'S COUNTRY(1943); SECRET HEART, THE(1946); CYNTHIA(1947); FARMER'S DAUGHTER, THE(1947); IT HAD TO BE YOU(1947); EVERY GIRL SHOULD BE MARRIED(1948); FIGHTING FATHER DUNNE(1948); ADAM'S RIB(1949); MALAYA(1950); SUNSET BOULEVARD(1950); LAW AND THE LADY, THE(1951); SHOW BOAT(1951); UNKNOWN MAN, THE(1951); SEVEN BRIDES FOR SEVEN BROTHERS(1954)

Silents

SCARLET ROAD, THE(1916); INFIDELITY(1917); TOLL GATE, THE(1920); WHAT WOMEN WILL DO(1921); WITHOUT LIMIT(1921); ADAM'S RIB(1923); ENEMIES OF CHILDREN(1923); INNOCENCE(1923); ISLE OF LOST SHIPS, THE(1923); SOULS FOR SALE(1923); BROADWAY AFTER DARK(1924); FLOWING GOLD(1924); INEZ FROM HOLLYWOOD(1924); PAINTED PEOPLE(1924); SIDESHOW OF LIFE, THE(1924); IF I MARRY AGAIN(1925); SPLENDID ROAD, THE(1925); MISS NOBODY(1926); BABE COMES HOME(1927); EASY PICKINGS(1927)

Misc. Silents

REGENERATION, THE(1915); HERE SURRENDER(1916); SUPREME SACRIFICE, THE(1916); INEVITABLE, THE(1917); OVER THERE(1917); SEVEN KEYS TO BALD-PATE(1917); SILENT MASTER, THE(1917); HEART OF THE SUNSET(1918); IN JUDGEMENT OF(1918); NO MAN'S LAND(1918); TRAIL TO YESTERDAY, THE(1918); VANITY POOL, THE(1918); CHEATING CHEATERS(1919); HER KINGDOM OF DREAMS(1919); LOVE BURGLAR, THE(1919); SOLDIERS OF FORTUNE(1919); SPORTING CHANCE, A(1919); VENUS IN THE EAST(1919); VERY GOOD YOUNG MAN, A(1919); WAY OF THE STRONG, THE(1919); BRUTE MASTER, THE(1920); FIGHTING CHANCE, THE(1920); FIGUREHEAD, THE(1920); IN THE HEART OF A FOOL(1920); LUCK OF THE IRISH, THE(1920); ONE HOUR BEFORE DAWN(1920); TOLL GATE, THE(1920); 13TH COMMANDMENT, THE(1920); LOTUS EATER, THE(1921); WHY GIRLS LEAVE HOME(1921); AUCTION OF SOULS(1922); PINK GODS(1922); THREE LIVE GHOSTS(1922, Brit.); HEARTS AFLAME(1923); PONJOLA(1923); RUSTLE OF SILK, THE(1923); THUNDERING DAWN(1923); BETWEEN FRIENDS(1924); FIRE PATROL, THE(1924); HALF-A-DOLLAR BILL(1924); VANITY'S PRICE(1924); ONE WAY STREET(1925); TALKER, THE(1925); TOP OF THE WORLD, THE(1925); WINDS OF CHANCE(1925); GREATER GLORY, THE(1926); HER SECOND CHANCE(1926); MIDNIGHT LOVERS(1926); TOO MUCH MONEY(1926); LONESOME LADIES(1927); MASKED WOMAN, THE(1927); SORRELL AND SON(1927); THIRTEENTH JUROR, THE(1927); WHIP, THE(1928)

Anne Q. Nilsson

WORLD CHANGES, THE(1933)

Bo Nilsson

SILENCE, THE(1964, Swed.), m; TO LOVE(1964, Swed.), m

Britt Nilsson

CATALINA CAPER, THE(1967); THING WITH TWO HEADS, THE(1972); DEAD MEN DON'T WEAR PLAID(1982)

Harry Nilsson

SKIDOO(1968), a, m; SON OF DRACULA(1974, Brit.), a, m; POPEYE(1980), m

Helena Nilsson

DEAR JOHN(1966, Swed.)

Inger Nilsson

PIPPI IN THE SOUTH SEAS(1974, Swed./Ger.); PIPPI ON THE RUN(1977)

Karin Nilsson

TOUCH, THE(1971, U.S./Swed.)

Kjell Nilsson

PIRATE MOVIE, THE(1982, Aus.); ROAD WARRIOR, THE(1982, Aus.)

Leif Nilsson

PIPPI IN THE SOUTH SEAS(1974, Swed./Ger.), set d

Leopoldo Torre Nilsson

END OF INNOCENCE(1960, Arg.), d, w; TERRACE, THE(1964, Arg.), d; THE EAVESDROPPER(1966, U.S./Arg.), d

Maj-Britt Nilsson

AFFAIRS OF A MODEL(1952, Swed.); ILLICIT INTERLUDE(1954, Swed.); MATTER OF MORALS, A(1961, U.S./Swed.); SECRETS OF WOMEN(1961, Swed.)

Nils Nilsson

INVASION OF THE ANIMAL PEOPLE(1962, U.S./Swed.), art d

Norma Jean Nilsson

SUSPENSE(1946); GANGSTER, THE(1947); ACTRESS, THE(1953); GREEN-EYED BLONDE, THE(1957)

Rob Nilsson

NORTHERN LIGHTS(1978), p,d&w, ed

1984

SIGNAL 7(1984), d&w

Tommy Nilsson

SWEDISH WEDDING NIGHT(1965, Swed.)

Torre Nilsson

THE EAVESDROPPER(1966, U.S./Arg.), w

Nilsson Sisters

HI' YA, SAILOR(1943)

Yoshiko Nilya

NAVY WIFE(1956)

Roger Nimier

TIME OUT FOR LOVE(1963, Ital./Fr.), w

Derek Nimmo

RING-A-DING RHYTHM(1962, Brit. 73m Amicus/COL bw (G.B: IT'S TRAD, DAD!); AGENT 8 3/4(1963, Brit.); BARGEE, THE(1964, Brit.); HARD DAY'S NIGHT, A(1964, Brit.); MURDER AHOY(1964, Brit.); TAMAHINE(1964, Brit.); AMOROUS MR. PRAWN, THE(1965, Brit.); COAST OF SKELETONS(1965, Brit.); JOEY BOY(1965, Brit.); GIRL GETTERS, THE(1966, Brit.); LIQUIDATOR, THE(1966, Brit.); YELLOW HAT, THE(1966, Brit.); CASINO ROYALE(1967, Brit.); MISTER TEN PERCENT(1967, Brit.); ONE OF OUR DINOSAURS IS MISSING(1975, Brit.)

Dudy Nimmo

ROBBERY UNDER ARMS(1958, Brit.)

Ian Nimmo

IN SEARCH OF ANNA(1978, Aus.)

Leonard Nimoy

QUEEN FOR A DAY(1951); RHUBARB(1951); FRANCIS GOES TO WEST POINT(1952); KID MONK BARONI(1952); OLD OVERLAND TRAIL(1953); THEM!(1954); BRAIN EATERS, THE(1958); SATAN'S SATELLITES(1958); BALCONY, THE(1963); DEATHWATCH(1966), a, p; VALLEY OF MYSTERY(1967); CATLOW(1971, Span.); INVASION OF THE BODY SNATCHERS(1978); STAR TREK: THE MOTION PICTURE(1979); STAR TREK II: THE WRATH OF KHAN(1982)

1984

STAR TREK III: THE SEARCH FOR SPOCK(1984), a, d

Brent Nimrod

FEMALE BUNCH, THE(1969), w, ed

Ernest J. Nims

BRIDGE OF SIGHS(1936), ed

Ernest Nims

FOLLOW YOUR HEART(1936), ed; BEWARE OF LADIES(1937), ed; HIT PARADE, THE(1937), ed; IT COULD HAPPEN TO YOU(1937), ed; JOIN THE MARINES(1937), ed; MANHATTAN MERRY-GO-ROUND(1937), ed; SHEIK STEPS OUT, THE(1937), ed; TWO WISE MAIDS(1937), ed; YOUTH ON PAROLE(1937), ed; DESPERATE ADVENTURE, A(1938), ed; HIGGINS FAMILY, THE(1938), ed; I STAND ACCUSED(1938), ed; KING OF THE NEWSBOYS(1938), ed; LADIES IN DISTRESS(1938), ed; NIGHT HAWK, THE(1938), ed; OUTSIDE OF PARADISE(1938), ed; CALLING ALL MARINES(1939), ed; FIGHTING THOROUGHBREDS(1939), ed; JEEPERS CREEPERS(1939), ed; MY WIFE'S RELATIVES(1939), ed; ORPHANS OF THE STREET(1939), ed; SHE MARRIED A COP(1939), ed; SMUGGLED CARGO(1939), ed; S.O.S. TIDAL WAVE(1939), ed; STREET OF MISSING MEN(1939), ed; THOU SHALT NOT KILL(1939), ed; WOMAN DOCTOR(1939), ed; CROOKED ROAD, THE(1940), ed; EARL OF PUDDLESTONE(1940), ed; FORGOTTEN GIRLS(1940), ed; IN OLD MISSOURI(1940), ed; MEET THE MISSUS(1940), ed; MELODY AND MOONLIGHT(1940), ed; SCATTERBRAIN(1940), ed; TEAR GAS SQUAD(1940), ed; WAGONS WESTWARD(1940), ed; WOLF OF NEW YORK(1940), ed; ARKANSAS JUDGE(1941), ed; BEHIND THE NEWS(1941), ed; COUNTRY FAIR(1941), ed; LADY FOR A NIGHT(1941), ed; MERCY ISLAND(1941), ed; PITTSBURGH KID, THE(1941), ed; PUDDIN' HEAD(1941), ed; RAGS TO RICHES(1941), ed; SIS HOPKINS(1941), ed; FLYING TIGERS(1942), ed; GIRL FROM ALASKA(1942), ed; SLEEPYTIME GAL(1942), ed; CHATTERBOX(1943), ed; IN OLD OKLAHOMA(1943), ed; NOBODY'S DARLING(1943), ed; SOMEONE TO REMEMBER(1943), ed; WEST SIDE KID(1943), ed; BELLE OF THE YUKON(1944), ed; CASANOVA IN BURLESQUE(1944), ed; MAN FROM FRISCO(1944), ed; IT'S A PLEASURE(1945), ed; DARK MIRROR, THE(1946), ed; STRANGER THE(1946), ed; TEMPTATION(1946); TOMORROW IS FOREVER(1946), ed

Shari Nims

EASY COME, EASY GO(1967)

Nina

MURDER AT THE CABARET(1936, Brit.)

Gia Nina

Misc. Talkies

BEWARE THE BLACK WIDOW(1968)

Gipsy Nina

TAKE OFF THAT HAT(1938, Brit.)

Rollie Nincheri

GAS(1981, Can.)

Allesandro Ninchi

BEST OF ENEMIES, THE(1962)

Annibale Ninchi

DEFEAT OF HANNIBAL, THE(1937, Ital.); LA DOLCE VITA(1961, Ital./Fr.); TIME OUT FOR LOVE(1963, Ital./Fr.); 8 ½(1963, Ital.)

Ave Ninchi

TO LIVE IN PEACE(1947, Ital.); ANGELINA(1948, Ital.); DIFFICULT YEARS(1950, Ital.); HEART AND SOUL(1950, Ital.); WALLS OF MALAPAGA, THE(1950, Fr./Ital.); TERESA(1951); DUEL WITHOUT HONOR(1953, Ital.); STRANGER ON THE PROWL(1953, Ital.); AFFAIRS OF MESSALINA, THE(1954, Ital.); NUN'S STORY, THE(1959); PURPLE NOON(1961, Fr./Ital.); SEVEN DWARFS TO THE RESCUE, THE(1965, Ital.); HOUSE OF CARDS(1969); MURMUR OF THE HEART(1971, Fr./Ital./Ger.)

Carlo Ninchi

KING'S JESTER, THE(1947, Ital.); CALL OF THE BLOOD(1948, Brit.); SPIRIT AND THE FLESH, THE(1948, Ital.); EARTH CRIES OUT, THE(1949, Ital.); BULLET FOR STEFANO(1950, Ital.); BEAUTY AND THE DEVIL(1952, Fr./Ital.); ISLAND OF PROCIDA, THE(1952, Ital.); SINGING TAXI DRIVER(1953, Ital.); AFFAIRS OF MESSALINA, THE(1954, Ital.); ANITA GARIBALDI(1954, Ital.); CENTO ANNI D'AMORE(1954, Ital.); QUEEN OF BABYLON, THE(1956, Ital.); TWO WOMEN(1961, Ital./Fr.); MOST WANTED MAN, THE(1962, Fr./Ital.); TIGER OF THE SEVEN SEAS(1964, Fr./Ital.)

Marina Ninchi

JUST BEFORE NIGHTFALL(1975, Fr./Ital.)

Bill Nind

PACIFIC RENDEZVOUS(1942); THEY WERE EXPENDABLE(1945); CALCUTTA(1947); CROSSFIRE(1947)

William Nind

SECRETS OF SCOTLAND YARD(1944)

Ting Ning

EMPRESS WU(1965, Hong Kong)

Nino Nini

OPIATE '67(1967, Fr./Ital.); DAY OF ANGER(1970, Ital./Ger.)

Nini and Partner

VARIETY PARADE(1936, Brit.)

Nino

TEOREMA(1969, Ital.), ed

The Ninos Cantores De Morelia Choral Group

BRAVADOS, THE(1958)

Roni Nins

"IMP"PROBABLE MR. WEE GEE, THE(1966)

Hubert Niogret

LIKE A TURTLE ON ITS BACK(1981, Fr.), p

Maja Nipora

VITELLONI(1956, Ital./Fr.)

Joe Nipote

1984

MEATBALLS PART II(1984); STRANGERS KISS(1984)

William D. Nipper
1984
SLAPSTICK OF ANOTHER KIND(1984), spec eff
Dora Nirva
STREET SINGER, THE(1937, Brit.), p
Paul Nirvanas
ASTERO(1960, Gr.), w
Seiji Nissamatau
ANGRY ISLAND(1960, Jap.), d
Ben Nisbet
IT'S ALL OVER TOWN(1963, Brit.), p
Carmen Nisbet
GOODBYE CHARLIE(1964)
Charles Nisbet
Misc. Talkies
GIRL WITH THE FABULOUS BOX, THE(1969), d
McLean Nisbet
MRS. PARKINGTON(1944), set d; WITHOUT LOVE(1945), set d
Stewart Nisbet
IN THE HEAT OF THE NIGHT(1967)
Stu Nisbet
YOUR THREE MINUTES ARE UP(1973)
Stuart Nisbet
THIRD OF A MAN(1962); QUICK AND THE DEAD, THE(1963); FOR PETE'S SAKE!(1966); GAMES(1967); ANGEL IN MY POCKET(1969); HOW TO FRAME A FIGG(1971); LONERS, THE(1972); SLITHER(1973); THUNDERBOLT AND LIGHTFOOT(1974)
Carmen Nisbit
WILL SUCCESS SPOIL ROCK HUNTER?(1957)
Theo Nischwitz
HIPPODROME(1961, Aust./Ger.), stunts
Homer Nish
EXILES, THE(1966)
Minoru Nisheda
FOUR FRIGHTENED PEOPLE(1934)
Minoru Nishida
TEAHOUSE OF THE AUGUST MOON, THE(1956)
Toshiyuki Nishida
MAN WHO STOLE THE SUN, THE(1980, Jap.)
Richard R. Nishigaki
MARCO(1973), ph
Rokuro Nishigaki
MAN AGAINST MAN(1961, Jap.), ph; NIGHT IN HONG KONG, A(1961, Jap.), ph; LAST WAR, THE(1962, Jap.), ph; STAR OF HONG KONG(1962, Jap.), ph; HONOLULU-TOKYO-HONG KONG(1963, Hong Kong/Jap.), ph; FORT GRAVEYARD(1966, Jap.), ph; GAMBLING SAMURAI, THE(1966, Jap.), ph; KILL(1968, Jap.), ph; MOMENT OF TERROR(1969, Jap.), ph; PROPHECIES OF NOSTRADAMUS(1974, Jap.), ph
Yoshio Nishikawa
DAREDEVIL IN THE CASTLE(1969, Jap.), m; RED LION(1971, Jap.), p
Hiroyuki Nishimo
WOMAN IN THE DUNES(1964, Jap.)
T. Nishimoto
MADAME WHITE SNAKE(1963, Hong Kong), ph; MAGNIFICENT CONCUBINE, THE(1964, Hong Kong), ph
Akira Nishimura
YOJIMBO(1961, Jap.); PRESSURE OF GUILT(1964, Jap.); UNHOLY DESIRE(1964, Jap.); WHISPERING JOE(1969, Jap.); PLAY IT COOL(1970, Jap.)
Kiyoshi Nishimura
CREATURE CALLED MAN, THE(1970, Jap.), d
Ko Nishimura
SCARLET CAMELLIA, THE(1965, Jap.)
Tommy Nishimura
WAKE ME WHEN IT'S OVER(1960)
Kazuo Nishino
SAGA OF THE VAGABONDS(1964, Jap.), p
Yoshindon Nishioka
ONIMASA(1983, Jap.), prod d
Yoshinobu Nishioka
ZATOICHI(1968, Jap.), art d; SECRETS OF A WOMAN'S TEMPLE(1969, Jap.), art d; MAGOICHI SAGA, THE(1970, Jap.), art d; TENCHU!(1970, Jap.), art d; ZATOICHI MEETS YOJIMBO(1970, Jap.), art d
Hidetako Nishiyama
KARATE, THE HAND OF DEATH(1961), ch
Masateru Nishiyama
JUDO SHOWDOWN(1966, Jap.), d
Yoshitaka Nishiyawa
MUDDY RIVER(1982, Jap.)
Yoshinobu Nishizaki
SPACE CRUISER(1977 Jap.), p&d, w
Toshiaki Nishizawa
WAR OF THE MONSTERS(1972, Jap.)
Theo Nishwitz
HEAD, THE(1961, Ger.), spec eff
Angela Nisi
SCARFACE(1983)
Stanley Niss
FBI CODE 98(1964), p, w; PENDULUM(1969), p, w
Nissa
BRINGING UP BABY(1938)
Leon Nissam
TEL AVIV TAXI(1957, Israel), ph
Aud Egede Nissen
Silents
ONE ARABIAN NIGHT(1921, Ger.)
Misc. Silents
DR. MABUSE, THE GAMBLER(1922, Ger.); PHANTOM, THE(1922, Ger.)

Brian Nissen
ADVENTURE FOR TWO(1945, Brit.); THEY WERE SISTERS(1945, Brit.); HENRY V(1946, Brit.); BADGER'S GREEN(1949, Brit.); HER MAN GILBEY(1949, Brit.); RICHARD III(1956, Brit.); PICKUP ALLEY(1957, Brit.); SECOND FIDDLE(1957, Brit.); MAN ACCUSED(1959); TOP FLOOR GIRL(1959, Brit.); NIGHT TRAIN FOR INVERNESS(1960, Brit.); FUR COLLAR, THE(1962, Brit.); MARKED ONE, THE(1963, Brit.); RING OF SPIES(1964, Brit.)
Claus Nissen
PEOPLE MEET AND SWEET MUSIC FILLS THE HEART(1969, Den./Swed.); HAPPINESS CAGE, THE(1972); Z.P.G.(1972)
Greta Nissen
AMBASSADOR BILL(1931); GOOD SPORT(1931); TRANSATLANTIC(1931); WOMEN OF ALL NATIONS(1931); YOUR NUMBER'S UP(1931); RACKETY RAX(1932); SILENT WITNESS, THE(1932); UNWRITTEN LAW, THE(1932); BEST OF ENEMIES(1933); CIRCUS QUEEN MURDER, THE(1933); LIFE IN THE RAW(1933); MELODY CRUISE(1933, Brit.); SECRET AGENT(1933, Brit.); HIRED WIFE(1934); LUCK OF A SAILOR, THE(1934, Brit.); HONOURS EASY(1935, Brit.); RED WAGON(1936); CAFE COLETTE(1937, Brit.)
Silents
IN THE NAME OF LOVE(1925)
Misc. Silents
KING ON MAIN STREET, THE(1925); LOST - A WIFE(1925); LADY OF THE HAREM, THE(1926); LOVE THIEF, THE(1926); LUCKY LADY, THE(1926); POPULAR SIN, THE(1926); WANDERER, THE(1926); BLONDE OR BRUNETTE(1927); BUTTER AND EGG MAN, THE(1928); FAZIL(1928)
Gretta Nissen
Silents
BLIND ALLEYS(1927)
Helge Nissen
Misc. Silents
LEAVES FROM SATAN'S BOOK(1921, Den.)
Juliet Nissen
1984
JIGSAW MAN, THE(1984, Brit.)
Oscar Egede Nissen
SUICIDE MISSION(1956, Brit.)
Hugh Nissenson
PILLAR OF FIRE, THE(1963, Israel), w
Oliver Nissick
TELL ME IN THE SUNLIGHT(1967)
Marjatta Nissinen
GORKY PARK(1983)
V. Nisskaya
SUMMER TO REMEMBER, A(1961, USSR), art d; DUEL, THE(1964, USSR), cos
Anna Q. Nisson
Misc. Silents
MORAL CODE, THE(1917); MAN FROM HOME, THE(1922)
Edith Nisted
SCANDAL IN DENMARK(1970, Den.), ed
Johnnie Nit
HELLO SWEETHEART(1935, Brit.); EVERYTHING IS RHYTHM(1940, Brit.)
Johnny Nit
MORALS OF MARCUS, THE(1936, Brit.)
Nita
WINE, WOMEN AND HORSES(1937)
Niko Nitai
JESUS(1979)
Hideaki Nitani
TIDAL WAVE(1975, U.S./Jap.)
Jerzy Nitecki
JOVITA(1970, Pol.), p
Donald Nithsdale
AGATHA(1979, Brit.)
Fyodor Nitkin
Misc. Silents
HOUSE IN THE SNOW-DRIFTS, THE(1928, USSR)
Anatoliy Nitochkin
SUMMER TO REMEMBER, A(1961, USSR), ph
Emile Nitrate
FLY NOW, PAY LATER(1969)
Herbert Nitsch
LONE CLIMBER, THE(1950, Brit./Aust.)
Ray Nitschke
HEAD(1968); LONGEST YARD, THE(1974)
Helen Nitsiog
1984
MISSION, THE(1984)
Aaron Nitties
NORMAN LOVES ROSE(1982, Aus.)
John Nittolo
1984
WHERE THE BOYS ARE '84(1984)
Nitty Gritty Dirt Band
FOR SINGLES ONLY(1968)
The Nitty Gritty Dirt Band
PAINT YOUR WAGON(1969)
The Nitwits
JUKE BOX RHYTHM(1959)
Jack Nitzche
EXORCIST, THE(1973), m; BLUE COLLAR(1978), m; BREATHLESS(1983), m
Jack Nitzsche
WHEN YOU COMIN' BACK, RED RYDER?(1979), m, md; VILLAGE OF THE GIANTS(1965), m, md; GREASER'S PALACE(1972), m; ONE FLEW OVER THE CUCKOO'S NEST(1975), m; HEROES(1977), m; HARDCORE(1979), m; HEART BEAT(1979), m; CRUISING(1980), m; CUTTER AND BONE(1981), m; OFFICER AND A GENTLEMAN, AN(1982), m; PERSONAL BEST(1982), m; WITHOUT A TRACE(1983), m
1984
RAZOR'S EDGE, THE(1984), m; STARMAN(1984), m; WINDY CITY(1984), m

Erich Nitzschmann
Silents
STUDENT OF PRAGUE, THE(1927, Ger.), ph
David Niven
BARBARY COAST(1935); FEATHER IN HER HAT, A(1935); MUTINY ON THE BOUNTY(1935); SPLENDOR(1935); WITHOUT REGRET(1935); BELOVED ENEMY(1936); CHARGE OF THE LIGHT BRIGADE, THE(1936); DODSWORTH(1936); PALM SPRINGS(1936); THANK YOU, JEEVES(1936); DINNER AT THE RITZ(1937, Brit.); PRISONER OF ZENDA, THE(1937); WE HAVE OUR MOMENTS(1937); BLUEBEARD'S EIGHTH WIFE(1938); DAWN PATROL, THE(1938); FOUR MEN AND A PRAYER(1938); THREE BLIND MICE(1938); BACHELOR MOTHER(1939); ETERNALLY YOURS(1939); RAFFLES(1939); REAL GLORY, THE(1939); WUTHERING HEIGHTS(1939); SPITFIRE(1943, Brit.); WAY AHEAD, THE(1945, Brit.); MAGNIFICENT DOLL(1946); PERFECT MARRIAGE, THE(1946); STAIRWAY TO HEAVEN(1946, Brit.); BISHOP'S WIFE, THE(1947); OTHER LOVE, THE(1947); BONNIE PRINCE CHARLIE(1948, Brit.); KISS FOR CORLISS, A(1949); ENCHANTMENT(1948, Brit.); FIGHTING PIMPERNEL, THE(1950, Brit.); KISS IN THE DARK, A(1949); FIGHTING PIMPERNEL, THE(1950, Brit.); TOAST OF NEW ORLEANS, THE(1950); HAPPY GO LOVELY(1951, Brit.); LADY SAYS NO, THE(1951); SOLDIERS THREE(1951); ISLAND RESCUE(1952, Brit.); MOON IS BLUE, THE(1953); COURT MARTIAL(1954, Brit.); LOVE LOTTERY, THE(1954, Brit.); TONIGHT'S THE NIGHT(1954, Brit.); KING'S THIEF, THE(1955); AROUND THE WORLD IN 80 DAYS(1956); LITTLE HUT, THE(1957); MY MAN GODFREY(1957); OH, MEN! OH, WOMEN!(1957); SILKEN AFFAIR, THE(1957, Brit.); BONJOUR TRISTESSE(1958); SEPARATE TABLES(1958); ASK ANY GIRL(1959); HAPPY ANNIVERSARY(1959); PLEASE DON'T EAT THE DAISIES(1960); GUNS OF NAVARONE, THE(1961); BEST OF ENEMIES, THE(1962); GUNS OF DARKNESS(1962, Brit.); ROAD TO HONG KONG, THE(1962, U.S./Brit.); CAPTIVE CITY, THE(1963, Ital.); 55 DAYS AT PEKING(1963); BEDTIME STORY(1964); PINK PANTHER, THE(1964); BIRDS AND THE BEES, THE(1965); LADY L(1965, Fr./Ital.); WHERE THE SPIES ARE(1965, Brit.); CONQUERED CITY(1966, Ital.); CASINO ROYALE(1967, Brit.); EYE OF THE DEVIL(1967, Brit.); IMPOSSIBLE YEARS, THE(1968); PRUDENCE AND THE PILL(1968, Brit.); BEFORE WINTER COMES(1969, Brit.); BRAIN, THE(1969, Fr./US); EXTRAORDINARY SEAMAN, THE(1969); STATUE, THE(1971, Brit.); KING, QUEEN, KNAVE(1972, Ger./U.S.); OLD DRACULA(1975, Brit.); PAPER TIGER(1975, Brit.); MURDER BY DEATH(1976); NO DEPOSIT, NO RETURN(1976); CANDLESHOE(1977); DEATH ON THE NILE(1978, Brit.); ESCAPE TO ATHENA(1979, Brit.); ROUGH CUT(1980, Brit.); SEA WOLVES, THE(1981, Brit.); TRAIL OF THE PINK PANTHER, THE(1982); BETTER LATE THAN NEVER(1983); CURSE OF THE PINK PANTHER(1983)
Misc. Talkies
NIGHTINGALE SANG IN BERKELEY SQUARE, A(1979)
David Niven, Jr.
EAGLE HAS LANDED, THE(1976, Brit.), p; ESCAPE TO ATHENA(1979, Brit.), p; MONSIGNOR(1982), p; BETTER LATE THAN NEVER(1983), p
1984
KIDCO(1984), p
Joyce Niven
LAS VEGAS STORY, THE(1952)
Kip Niven
MAGNUM FORCE(1973); EARTHQUAKE(1974); NEWMAN'S LAW(1974); HINDENBURG, THE(1975); MIDWAY(1976); SWASHBUCKLER(1976); DAMNATION ALLEY(1977); NEW YEAR'S EVIL(1980)
Susan Niven
HEART BEAT(1979)
William Niven
AMERICAN GRAFFITI(1973)
William M. Niven
WHAT'S UP, DOC?(1972)
Kemp Niver
GROOM WORE SPURS, THE(1951)
Suzanne Nivette
LOVE AND THE FRENCHWOMAN(1961, Fr.)
Suzette Nivette
RED AND THE BLACK, THE(1954, Fr./Ital.)
Matasaburo Niwa
ZATOICHI(1968, Jap.)
Charles Nix
MAGIC CHRISTMAS TREE(1964)
E.D. Nix
Misc. Silents
PASSING OF THE OKLAHOMA OUTLAWS, THE(1915)
Melvin Nix
GUY NAMED JOE, A(1943)
Ron Nix
TRIAL OF BILLY JACK, THE(1974); WHITE LINE FEVER(1975, Can.)
Rosary Nix
DIRTY LITTLE BILLY(1972)
Teresa Nix
1984
MAKING THE GRADE(1984)
Victor Nix
Misc. Silents
GREATEST SIN, THE(1922)
Nixau
1984
GODS MUST BE CRAZY, THE(1984, Botswana)
Gisela Nixdorf
RETURN OF DR. MABUSE, THE(1961, Ger./Fr./Ital.), cos
Willi Nixdorf
RETURN OF DR. MABUSE, THE(1961, Ger./Fr./Ital.), makeup; TREASURE OF SILVER LAKE(1965, Fr./Ger./Yugo.), makeup
Alan Nixon
LINDA BE GOOD(1947); OUTLAW WOMEN(1952)
Allan Nixon
MARGIN FOR ERROR(1943); SIREN OF ATLANTIS(1948); PREHISTORIC WOMEN(1950); PICKUP(1951); ROAD TO BALI(1952); MESA OF LOST WOMEN, THE(1956); APACHE WARRIOR(1957); UNTAMED MISTRESS(1960)

Allen Nixon
DRAGNET(1974)
Alonzo Nixon
Misc. Silents
LURE OF A WOMAN, THE(1921)
Arundel Nixon
THAT CERTAIN SOMETHING(1941, Aus.)
Charles Nixon
GRAND THEFT AUTO(1977), set d
Cynthia Nixon
LITTLE DARLINGS(1980); PRINCE OF THE CITY(1981); TATTOO(1981); I AM THE CHEESE(1983)
1984
AMADEUS(1984)
David Nixon
SPIDER'S WEB, THE(1960, Brit.)
Ione Nixon
RED ROCK OUTLAW(1950)
Jim Nixon
NESTING, THE(1981)
Joan Nixon
CAPTAIN JOHN SMITH AND POCAHONTAS(1953)
Leslie Nixon
JOURNEY TOGETHER(1946, Brit.)
Lester Nixon
IDOL ON PARADE(1959, Brit.); DRYLANDERS(1963, Can.)
Marian Nixon
GENERAL CRACK(1929); GERALDINE(1929); RAINBOW MAN(1929); SAY IT WITH SONGS(1929); COURAGE(1930); LASH, THE(1930); PAY OFF, THE(1930); EX-FLAME(1931); SWEEPSTAKES(1931); WOMEN GO ON FOREVER(1931); AFTER TOMORROW(1932); AMATEUR DADDY(1932); MADISON SQUARE GARDEN(1932); PRIVATE SCANDAL, A(1932); REBECCA OF SUNNYBROOK FARM(1932); TOO BUSY TO WORK(1932); WINNER TAKE ALL(1932); BEST OF ENEMIES(1933); CHANCE AT HEAVEN(1933); DR. BULL(1933); FACE IN THE SKY(1933); PILGRIMAGE(1933); LINEUP, THE(1934); ONCE TO EVERY BACHELOR(1934); STRICTLY DYNAMITE(1934); WE'RE RICH AGAIN(1934); BY YOUR LEAVE(1935); SWEEPSTAKE ANNIE(1935); TANGO(1936)
Misc. Talkies
DRAGNET, THE(1936)
Silents
COURTSHIP OF MILES STANDISH, THE(1923); JUST OFF BROADWAY(1924); WHAT HAPPENED TO JONES(1926); OUT ALL NIGHT(1927); TAXI! TAXI!(1927)
Misc. Silents
BIG DAN(1923); CUPID'S FIREMAN(1923); CIRCUS COWBOY, THE(1924); LAST OF THE DUANES, THE(1924); VAGABOND TRAIL, THE(1924); SPORTING LIFE(1925); SPANGLES(1926); CHINESE PARROT, THE(1927); HOW TO HANDLE WOMEN(1928); OUT OF THE RUINS(1928); RED SWORD, THE(1929)
Marion Nixon
IN THE HEADLINES(1929); YOUNG NOWHERES(1929); COLLEGE LOVERS(1930); SCARLET PAGES(1930); CHARLIE CHAN'S CHANCE(1932); EMBARRASSING MOMENTS(1934); CAPTAIN CALAMITY(1936)
Silents
ROSITA(1923); HURRICANE KID, THE(1925); LET 'ER BUCK(1925); RIDERS OF THE PURPLE SAGE(1925); HANDS UP(1926); ROLLING HOME(1926); AUCTIONEER, THE(1927); DOWN THE STRETCH(1927); JAZZ MAD(1928); RED LIPS(1928); SILKS AND SADDLES(1929)
Misc. Silents
DURAND OF THE BAD LANDS(1925); I'LL SHOW YOU THE TOWN(1925); SADDLE HAWK, THE(1925); WHERE WAS I?(1925); DEVIL'S ISLAND(1926); HEROES OF THE NIGHT(1927); FOURFLUSHER, THE(1928); MAN, WOMAN AND WIFE(1929)
Marni Nixon
MY FAIR LADY(1964); SOUND OF MUSIC, THE(1965)
Pat Nixon
GREAT ZIEGFELD, THE(1936)
Richard M. Nixon
RICHARD(1972)
Ruth Nixon
SILK NOOSE, THE(1950, Brit.)
Elizabeth Nizan
Misc. Silents
LA DIXIEME SYMPHONIE(1918, Fr.)
Charles Nizet
RAVAGER, THE(1970), d; THREE-WAY SPLIT(1970), d; VOODOO HEARTBEAT(1972), d&w
Misc. Talkies
HELP ME...I'M POSSESSED(1976), d
I. Nizharadze
FATHER OF A SOLDIER(1966, USSR)
Louis Nizor
INGAGI(1931)
Joyce Nizzari
HOLE IN THE HEAD, A(1959); COME BLOW YOUR HORN(1963); CANDIDATE, THE(1964); PAJAMA PARTY(1964); GREAT RACE, THE(1965)
Cesare Nizzica
MR. BILLION(1977)
Elechukwu N. Njakar
WHITE WITCH DOCTOR(1953)
Njntsky
PRINCE OF FOXES(1949)
Nkima
NEW ADVENTURES OF TARZAN(1935)
Sandy Nkomo
NAKED PREY, THE(1966, U.S./South Africa)
Noa
PACIFIC DESTINY(1956, Brit.)
Manfred Noa
Misc. Silents
SURVIVAL(1930, Ger.), d

Jessica Noad
SEASON OF PASSION(1961, Aus./Brit.); NED KELLY(1970, Brit.)
Garry Noakes
PIRATES OF PENZANCE, THE(1983)
Robert Nobaret
LA NUIT DE VARENNES(1983, Fr./Ital.)
Agnes Nobecourt
LA NUIT DE VARENNES(1983, Fr./Ital.)
Charles Nobel
MICHELLE(1970, Fr.), ed
Kara Nobel
FUNNY MONEY(1983, Brit.)
Maurice Nobel
DUMBO(1941), art d
Thom Nobel
INSIDE OUT(1975, Brit.), ed
Agnes Nobencourt
MONSIGNOR(1982)
Paul Nobert
GREAT GUNDOWN, THE(1977), p
Desiderio Nobile
ROMA RIVUOLE CESARE(; ANGELO IN THE CROWD(1952, Ital.)
Guido Nobili
TIMES GONE BY(1953, Ital.), w
Anita Noble
IN MACARTHUR PARK(1977)
Ann Noble
CORPSE GRINDERS, THE(1972)
Misc. Talkies
SINS OF RACHEL, THE(1975)
Audrey Noble
TIME GENTLEMEN PLEASE!(1953, Brit.)
Barbara Noble
WORLDS APART(1980, U.S., Israel), d
Barry Noble
RED, WHITE AND BLACK, THE(1970), a, makeup; INCREDIBLE TWO-HEADED TRANSPLANT, THE(1971), makeup
Bob Noble
CAPE FEAR(1962)
Dennis Noble
SPANISH EYES(1930, Brit.)
Eulalie Noble
ALICE'S RESTAURANT(1969)
Felix Noble
TREASURE OF MAKUBA, THE(1967, U.S./Span.)
George Noble
CONQUEST OF THE AIR(1940), ph
Gloria Noble
LATIN LOVERS(1953); SMALL TOWN GIRL(1953)
Gordon Noble
STORM BOY(1976, Aus.), animal t
Harry Noble
STEP LIVELY(1944)
Hollister Noble
DRUMS IN THE DEEP SOUTH(1951), w; MARA MARU(1952), w; MUTINY(1952), w
J.W. Noble
Misc. Silents
SATAN SANDERSON(1915), d
Jack Noble
Silents
LIGHTNING REPORTER(1926), d&w
Misc. Silents
RIGHT OF WAY, THE(1915), d; BURNING GOLD(1927), d
Jackie Noble
OBLONG BOX, THE(1969, Brit.)
James Noble
SPORTING CLUB, THE(1971); 1776(1972); WHO?(1975, Brit./Ger.); DEATH PLAY(1976); ONE SUMMER LOVE(1976); BEING THERE(1979); PROMISES IN THE DARK(1979); 10(1979); NUDE BOMB, THE(1980); AIRPLANE II: THE SEQUEL(1982)
John W. Noble
Silents
FIGHTING BOB(1915), d; ONE MILLION DOLLARS(1915), d; BRAND OF COWARDICE, THE(1916), d; POWER OF DECISION, THE(1917), d; CARDIGAN(1922), d; HIS DARKER SELF(1924), d
Misc. Silents
BETTER MAN, THE(1915), d; HIGH ROAD, THE(1915), d; ONE MILLION DOLLARS(1915), d; THREE OF US, THE(1915), d; AWAKENING OF HELENA RICHIE, THE(1916), d; MAN AND HIS SOUL(1916), d; MILLION A MINUTE, A(1916), d; ROMEO AND JULIET(1916), d; WALL BETWEEN, THE(1916), d; BEAUTIFUL LIE, THE(1917), d; CALL OF HER PEOPLE, THE(1917), d; MAGDALENE OF THE HILLS, A(1917), d; SUNSHINE ALLEY(1917), d; MY OWN UNITED STATES(1918), d; SHAME(1918), d; BIRTH OF A RACE(1919), d; GOLDEN SHOWER, THE(1919), d; GRAY TOWERS MYSTERY, THE(1919), d; FOOTLIGHTS AND SHADOWS(1920), d; SONG OF THE SOUL, THE(1920), d
Kennely Noble
THEY ALL LAUGHED(1981)
Larry Noble
RELUCTANT HEROES(1951, Brit.); NOT WANTED ON VOYAGE(1957, Brit.); FURTHER UP THE CREEK!(1958, Brit.); UP THE CREEK(1958, Brit.); NIGHT TRAIN FOR INVERNESS(1960, Brit.); MAKE MINE A DOUBLE(1962, Brit.)
Leighton Noble
GIFT OF GAB(1934); CRAZY HOUSE(1943); IT AIN'T HAY(1943); AT GUN-POINT(1955)
Martin Noble
MISSION TO MOSCOW(1943); NORTHERN PURSUIT(1943); RHAPSODY IN BLUE(1945)
Mary Noble
VIOLATED(1953)

Maurice Noble
SNOW WHITE AND THE SEVEN DWARFS(1937), anim; INCREDIBLE MR. LIMPET, THE(1964), spec eff; PHANTOM TOLLBOOTH, THE(1970), prod d; GREAT AMERICAN BUGS BUNNY-ROAD RUNNER CHASE(1979), prod d
Milton Noble
Silents
AMERICA(1924)
Nancy Lee Noble
GIRL, THE BODY, AND THE PILL, THE(1967); JUST FOR THE HELL OF IT(1968); SHE-DEVILS ON WHEELS(1968); MEDIUM COOL(1969)
Misc. Talkies
JUST FOR THE HELL OF IT(1968)
Nancy Noble
JACKSON COUNTY JAIL(1976)
Nobby Noble
LIVING FREE(1972, Brit.)
Patsy Ann Noble
SING AND SWING(1964, Brit.); LOVE IS A WOMAN(1967, Brit.)
Peter Noble
IT'S THAT MAN AGAIN(1943, Brit.); ESCAPE DANGEROUS(1947, Brit.); FUN AT ST. FANNY'S(1956, Brit.), w; STRANGE CASE OF DR. MANNING, THE(1958, Brit.); YOUR PAST IS SHOWING(1958); SING AND SWING(1964, Brit.); MAKE MINE A MILLION(1965, Brit.)
R. T. Noble
KIDNAPPED(1938)
Ray Noble
DIE MANNER UM LUCIE(1931), m; BREWSTER'S MILLIONS(1935, Brit.), m; DAMSEL IN DISTRESS, A(1937); HERE WE GO AGAIN(1942); OUT OF THIS WORLD(1945)
Robert Noble
UNDER SUSPICION(1937); ADVENTURES OF ROBIN HOOD, THE(1938); WITNESS VANISHES, THE(1939); STIR(1980, Aus.)
Roderic Noble
NICHOLAS AND ALEXANDRA(1971, Brit.)
Sharon Noble
1984
HOTEL NEW HAMPSHIRE, THE(1984)
Shaun Noble
VOICE WITHIN, THE(1945, Brit.); CAESAR AND CLEOPATRA(1946, Brit.); BLACK NARCISSUS(1947, Brit.); SONG FOR TOMORROW, A(1948, Brit.)
Terence Noble
MR. H. C. ANDERSEN(1950, Brit.)
Terry Thom Noble
BLACK JOY(1977, Brit.), ed
Thom Noble
FAHRENHEIT 451(1966, Brit.), ed; MAN WHO HAD POWER OVER WOMEN, THE(1970, Brit.), ed; AND NOW FOR SOMETHING COMPLETELY DIFFERENT(1972, Brit.), ed; STRANGE VENEGEANCE OF ROSALIE, THE(1972), ed; APPRENTICESHIP OF DUDDY KRAVITZ, THE(1974, Can.), ed; ROSEBUD(1975), ed; JOSEPH ANDREWS(1977, Brit.), ed; ALL THINGS BRIGHT AND BEAUTIFUL(1979, Brit.), ed; IMPROPER CHANNELS(1981, Can.), ed; TATTOO(1981), ed
1984
RED DAWN(1984), ed
Tom Noble
MAN OUTSIDE, THE(1968, Brit.), ed; FIRST BLOOD(1982), ed
Tommy Noble
Misc. Silents
PIT-BOY'S ROMANCE, A(1917, Brit.)
Trisha Noble
CARRY ON CAMPING(1969, Brit.); PRIVATE EYES, THE(1980)
William Noble
BEYOND THE RIO GRANDE(1930), ph; YOUNG IDEAS(1943), w; ZIEGFELD FOLLIES(1945), w; BLUE DENIM(1959), w
William Nobles
OVERLAND BOUND(1929), ph; BAR L RANCH(1930), ph; FIREBRAND JORDAN(1930), ph; PHANTOM OF THE DESERT(1930), ph; RIDIN' LAW(1930), ph; TRAILS OF DANGER(1930), ph; AIR POLICE(1931), ph; HURRICANE HORSEMAN(1931), ph; IN OLD CHEYENNE(1931), ph; LAW OF THE TONG(1931), ph; RED FORK RANGE(1931), ph; WEST OF CHEYENNE(1931), ph; WESTWARD BOUND(1931), ph; CHEYENNE CYCLONE, THE(1932), ph; DRIFTER, THE(1932), ph; SCARLET WEEKEND, A(1932), ph; SINISTER HANDS(1932), ph; OUTLAW JUSTICE(1933), ph; RACING STRAIN(1933), ph; SUCKER MONEY(1933), ph; LOST JUNGLE, THE(1934), ph; MAN FROM HELL, THE(1934), ph; BRANDED A COWARD(1935), ph; HEADLINE WOMAN, THE(1935), ph; IN OLD SANTA FE(1935), ph; LADIES CRAVE EXCITEMENT(1935), ph; LITTLE MEN(1935), ph; MARINES ARE COMING, THE(1935), ph; ONE FRIGHTENED NIGHT(1935), ph; SINGING VAGABOND, THE(1935), ph; SMOKEY SMITH(1935), ph; COMIN' ROUND THE MOUNTAIN(1936), ph; DOUGHNUTS AND SOCIETY(1936), ph; LAWLESS NINETIES, THE(1936), ph; LONELY TRAIL, THE(1936), ph; RED RIVER VALLEY(1936), ph; RETURN OF JIMMY VALENTINE, THE(1936), ph; RIDE, RANGER, RIDE(1936), ph; WINDS OF THE WASTELAND(1936), ph; BEWARE OF LADIES(1937), ph; BIG SHOW, THE(1937), ph; BILL CRACKS DOWN(1937), ph; DANGEROUS HOLIDAY(1937), ph; OH, SUSANNA(1937), ph; ROARIN' LEAD(1937), ph; ROOTIN' TOOTIN' RHYTHM(1937), ph; ROUNDUP TIME IN TEXAS(1937), ph; YODELIN' KID FROM PINE RIDGE(1937), ph; CALL THE MESQUITEERS(1938), ph; GOLD MINE IN THE SKY(1938), ph; OUTLAWS OF SONORA(1938), ph; OVERLAND STAGE RAIDERS(1938), ph; PRAIRIE MOON(1938), ph; RIDERS OF THE BLACK HILLS(1938), ph; SHINE ON, HARVEST MOON(1938), ph; WESTERN JAMBOREE(1938), ph; WILD HORSE RODEO(1938), ph; ARIZONA KID(1939), ph; COLORADO SUNSET(1939), ph; FRONTIER PONY EXPRESS(1939), ph; IN OLD CALIENTE(1939), ph; MEXICALI ROSE(1939), ph; ROVIN' TUMBLEWEEDS(1939), ph; SOUTH OF THE BORDER(1939), ph; CAROLINA MOON(1940), ph; CARSON CITY KID(1940), ph; COVERED WAGON DAYS(1940), ph; HEROES OF THE SADDLE(1940), ph; HI-YO SILVER(1940), ph; LONE STAR RAIDERS(1940), ph; RANCHO GRANDE(1940), ph; TRAIL BLAZERS, THE(1940), ph; UNDER TEXAS SKIES(1940), ph; YOUNG BILL HICKOK(1940), ph; YOUNG BUFFALO BILL(1940), ph; BAD MAN OF DEADWOOD(1941), ph; DESERT BANDIT(1941), ph; IN OLD CHEYENNE(1941), ph; JESSE JAMES AT BAY(1941), ph; KANSAS CYCLONE(1941), ph; NEVADA CITY(1941), ph; RAGS TO RICHES(1941), ph; RIDIN' ON A RAINBOW(1941), ph; SADDLEMATES(1941), ph; SHERIFF OF TOMBSTONE(1941), ph; SINGING HILL,

THE(1941), ph; TWO GUN SHERIFF(1941), ph; WYOMING WILDCAT(1941), ph; ROMANCE ON THE RANGE(1942), ph; DRUMS OF FU MANCHU(1943), ph
Silents
CHILD OF M'SIEU(1919), ph; WHITE OUTLAW, THE(1925), ph; LOOKING FOR TROUBLE(1926), ph; WESTERN WHIRLWIND, THE(1927), ph
William P. Nobles
THREE MESQUITEERS, THE(1936), ph
Noble Sissle and His Orchestra
Misc. Talkies
JUNCTION 88(1940)
Lee Noblitt
BUSTIN' LOOSE(1981)
Speck Noblitt
HOME TOWN STORY(1951)
Marlos Nobre
ANTONIO DAS MORTES(1970, Braz.), m
Ted Nobriga
HAWAII(1966)
Harold Noce
Misc. Silents
RED MAJESTY(1929), d
Luisa Dalla Noce
ALL THE OTHER GIRLS DO!(1967, Ital.)
Luisa Della Noce
JULIET OF THE SPIRITS(1965, Fr./Ital./W.Ger.); IDENTIFICATION OF A WO-MAN(1983, Ital.)
Georgio Nocell
THREE BROTHERS(1982, Ital.), p
Giorgio Nocella
IDENTIFICATION OF A WOMAN(1983, Ital.), p
Miranda Nocelli
ERNESTO(1979, Ital.)
Nino Nocellino
SOME OF MY BEST FRIENDS ARE...(1971), set d
Ray Noch
1984
TEACHERS(1984)
Francois Nocher
LOVE AND THE FRENCHWOMAN(1961, Fr.)
Edna Nochoechea
MISSING(1982)
David Nochols
CIRCLE OF TWO(1980, Can.), ed
Eric Nocowitz
MOZART STORY, THE(1948, Aust.)
Kogo Noda
EARLY AUTUMN(1962, Jap.), w; OHAYO(1962, Jap.), w; TEA AND RICE(1964, Jap.), w; FLOATING WEEDS(1970, Jap.), w; TOKYO STORY(1972, Jap.), w; LATE AUTUMN(1973, Jap.), w
Masahiro Noda
MESSAGE FROM SPACE(1978, Jap.), spec eff
Gerald Nodin
OVER THE MOON(1940, Brit.); HANGMAN'S WHARF(1950, Brit.)
Nodonk
WAJAN(1938, South Bali)
Anne-Marie Noe
OPERATION KID BROTHER(1967, Ital.)
Lynn Noe
FIRST TRAVELING SALESLADY, THE(1956)
Robert Noe
JIGSAW(1949); PROJECT X(1949)
Virginia Noe
JANIE(1944)
Andre Noel
COURIER OF LYONS(1938, Fr.)
Annie Noel
QUARTET(1981, Brit./Fr.)
Annik Noel
LOLA(1961, Fr./Ital.)
Art Noel
HILL, THE(1965, Brit.), m
Barry Noel
HOT STUFF(1979)
Bernard Noel
FIRE WITHIN, THE(1964, Fr./Ital.); CIRCLE OF LOVE(1965, Fr.); MARRIED WOMAN, THE(1965, Fr.)
Chris Noel
SOLDIER IN THE RAIN(1963); DIARY OF A BACHELOR(1964); GET YOURSELF A COLLEGE GIRL(1964); HONEYMOON HOTEL(1964); BEACH BALL(1965); GIRL HAPPY(1965); JOY IN THE MORNING(1965); WILD, WILD WINTER(1966); GLORY STOMPERS, THE(1967); FOR SINGLES ONLY(1968)
Dai Noel
YELLOW HAT, THE(1966, Brit.), w
Daniele Noel
RETURN FROM THE ASHES(1965, U.S./Brit.); BEDAZZLED(1967, Brit.); VEN-GEANCE OF SHE, THE(1968, Brit.)
Danielle Noel
MAGUS, THE(1968, Brit.)
Gaetan Noel
MAGNIFICENT ONE, THE(1974, Fr./Ital.)
Gerard Philippe Noel
Misc. Talkies
TRIUMPH OF ROBIN HOOD, THE(1960)
Hattie Noel
LITTLE ACCIDENT(1939); OUR LEADING CITIZEN(1939); I'M NOBODY'S SWEET-HEART NOW(1940); IRENE(1940); KITTY FOYLE(1940); MARRIED AND IN LO-VE(1940); RETURN OF FRANK JAMES, THE(1940); SEVENTEEN(1940); CRACKED NUTS(1941); DOUBLE DATE(1941); LADY FOR A NIGHT(1941); KING'S ROW(1942); HONEYMOON LODGE(1943)

Hubert Noel
EARRINGS OF MADAME DE..., THE(1954, Fr.); ENEMY GENERAL, THE(1960); MAGNIFICENT SINNER(1963, Fr.); SEASON FOR LOVE, THE(1963, Fr.); DEVILS OF DARKNESS, THE(1965, Brit.); TRIPLE CROSS(1967, Fr./Brit.); LITTLE GIRL WHO LIVES DOWN THE LANE, THE(1977, Can.)
1984
AMERICAN DREAMER(1984)
Jacques Noel
SWEET AND SOUR(1964, Fr./Ital.), art d
Jean-Guy Noel
TI-CUL TOUGAS(1977, Can.), d&w
Joseph Noel
SAINT JACK(1979)
Silents
OUT OF THE SILENT NORTH(1922), w
Magali Noel
RIFIFI(1956, Fr.); PARIS DOES STRANGE THINGS(1957, Fr./Ital.); MARIE OF THE ISLES(1960, Fr.); LA DOLCE VITA(1961, Ital./Fr.); ROAD TO SHAME, THE(1962, Fr.); TEMPTATION(1962, Fr.); SECRET MARK OF D'ARTAGNAN, THE(1963, Fr./Ital.); TWELVE-HANDED MEN OF MARS, THE(1964, Ital./Span.); ALL THE OTHER GIRLS DO!(1967, Ital.); FRUSTRATIONS(1967, Fr./Ital.); FELLINI SATYRICON(1969, Fr./Ital.); Z(1969, Fr./Algeria); MAN WHO HAD POWER OVER WOMEN, THE(1970, Brit.); AMARCORD(1974, Ital.); DEATH OF MARIO RICCI, THE(1983, Ital.)
Magalie Noel
GRAND MANEUVER, THE(1956, Fr.)
Nani Noel
1984
LE BAL(1984, Fr./Ital./Algeria)
Noel Noel
JESSICA(1962, U.S./Ital./Fr.)
Noelia Noel
NIGHT OF THE BLOODY APES(1968, Mex.)
Sid Noel
MODERN MARRIAGE, A(1962)
Sterling Noel
TRIPLE DECEPTION(1957, Brit.), w
Trish Noel
1984
MUPPETS TAKE MANHATTAN, THE(1984)
Wendy Noel
BRAVE DON'T CRY, THE(1952, Brit.); YOU'RE ONLY YOUNG TWICE(1952, Brit.)
Sid Noel [Noel Rideau]
WACKY WORLD OF DR. MORGUS, THE(1962)
Frank Noel, Jr.
1984
COUNTRY(1984)
Noel-Noel
CAGE OF NIGHTINGALES, A(1947, Fr.), a, w; MR. ORCHID(1948, Fr.), a, w; SPICE OF LIFE(1954, Fr.), a, w; FRENCH, THEY ARE A FUNNY RACE, THE(1956, Fr.); SPUTNIK(1960, Fr.)
Jacqueline Noelle
LADY CHATTERLEY'S LOVER(1959, Fr.); MAIDEN, THE(1961, Fr.)
1984
LES COMPERES(1984, Fr.)
Kate Noelle
JULES AND JIM(1962, Fr.)
Marianne Noelle
FAKE, THE(1953, Brit.)
Marie Noelle
LAST OF THE RENEGADES(1966, Fr./Ital./Ger./Yugo.)
Paule Noelle
LADY IN THE CAR WITH GLASSES AND A GUN, THE(1970, U.S./Fr.)
Rudolf Noelte
CASTLE, THE(1969, Ger.), d&w
Lea Noemi
SINGING BLACKSMITH(1938)
Leah Noemi
Misc. Talkies
BAR MITSVE(1935)
Sonya Noemi
CREATURE FROM THE HAUNTED SEA(1961)
Emil Nofal
KIMBERLEY JIM(1965, South Africa), p,d&w; WILD SEASON(1968, South Africa), d&w; MY WAY(1974, South Africa), p, d, w
Misc. Talkies
SUPER-JOCKS, THE(1980), d
Irene Nofles
SOUNDER, PART 2(1976)
Ed Nofziger
1001 ARABIAN NIGHTS(1959), w
Tatsuo Nogami
1984
ANTARCTICA(1984, Jap.), w
Anna Nogara
MORE THAN A MIRACLE(1967, Ital./Fr.)
Edy Nogara
COME SEPTEMBER(1961); LOVE PROBLEMS(1970, Ital.)
Henri Nogaret
MARRIED WOMAN, THE(1965, Fr.), art d
Grinsell Nogauza
PENNYWHISTLE BLUES, THE(1952, South Africa)
Yumiko Nogawa
GATE OF FLESH(1964, Jap.); PLEASURES OF THE FLESH, THE(1965)
Haruyasu Noguchi
GAPPA THE TRIFIBIAN MONSTER(1967, Jap.), d
Tasaki Noguchi
1984
ADERYN PAPUR(1984, Brit.)

Jose Noguero
LE DENIER MILLIARDAIRE(1934, Fr.); FRENCH TOUCH, THE(1954, Fr.)
Nataljia Nogulich
1984
VAMPING(1984)
Jean Nohain
PORTRAIT OF A WOMAN(1946, Fr.)
Susan Nohr
HAUNTS(1977)
Anis Nohra
STATUE, THE(1971, Brit.), p; TROJAN WOMEN, THE(1971), p; TEMPTER, THE(1974, Ital./Brit.), p
Annis Nohra
DEVIL IS A WOMAN, THE(1975, Brit./Ital.), p
Audrey Nohra
BLACK VEIL FOR LISA, A(1969 Ital./Ger.), w; DEVIL IS A WOMAN, THE(1975, Brit./Ital.), w
Ratanaporn Noi
1 2 3 MONSTER EXPRESS(1977, Thai.)
Danny Noiman
1984
AMBASSADOR, THE(1984)
Rivka Noiman
JESUS(1979)
Leo Noimi
GREEN FIELDS(1937)
Philippe Noiret
ZAZIE(1961, Fr.); CRIME DOES NOT PAY(1962, Fr.); THERESE(1963, Fr.); MONSIEUR(1964, Fr.); LADY L(1965, Fr./Ital.); LA VIE DE CHATEAU(1967, Fr.); NIGHT OF THE GENERALS, THE(1967, Brit./Fr.); OTHER ONE, THE(1967,Fr.); TENDER SCOUNDREL(1967, Fr./Ital.); WOMAN TIMES SEVEN(1967, U.S./Fr./Ital.); ASSASSINATION BUREAU, THE(1969, Brit.); JUSTINE(1969); TOPAZ(1969, Brit.); VERY HAPPY ALEXANDER(1969, Fr.); GIVE HER THE MOON(1970, Fr./Ital.); MISTER FREEDOM(1970, Fr.); MURPHY'S WAR(1971, Brit.); TIME FOR LOVING, A(1971, Brit.); FRENCH CONSPIRACY, THE(1973, Fr.); LA GRANDE BOUFFE(1973, Fr.); SERPENT, THE(1973, Fr./Ital./Ger.); DON'T TOUCH WHITE WOMEN!(1974, Fr.); DESERT OF THE TARTARS, THE(1976 Fr./Ital./Iranian); LET JOY REIGN SUPREME(1977, Fr.); PURPLE TAXI, THE(1977, Fr./Ital./Ireland); DEAR DETECTIVE(1978, Fr.); WHO IS KILLING THE GREAT CHEFS OF EUROPE?(1978, US/Ger.); WOMAN AT HER WINDOW, A(1978, Fr./Ital./Ger.); JUDGE AND THE ASSASSIN, THE(1979, Fr.); COUP DE TORCHON(1981, Fr.); NORTH STAR, THE(1982, Fr.); THREE BROTHERS(1982, Ital.); AFRICAN, THE(1983, Fr.); L'ETOILE DU NORD(1983, Fr.)
1984
MY NEW PARTNER(1984, Fr.)
Phillippe Noiret
CLOCKMAKER, THE(1976, Fr.)
Noisette
LITTLE ARK, THE(1972)
Katherine Noisette
EXILE, THE(1931)
Misc. Talkies
WAGES OF SIN, THE(1929)
Kathleen Noisette
Misc. Talkies
DAUGHTER OF THE CONGO, A(1930)
George Noisom
TELL NO TALES(1939); NAZI AGENT(1942); THIS TIME FOR KEEPS(1942); LADIES' DAY(1943); YOUNGEST PROFESSION, THE(1943); POSTMAN ALWAYS RINGS TWICE, THE(1946)
Madame Noizet
L'AGE D'OR(1979, Fr.)
George Nokes
GASLIGHT(1944); GOING MY WAY(1944); KEYS OF THE KINGDOM, THE(1944); INCENDIARY BLONDE(1945); IT'S A WONDERFUL LIFE(1946); NIGHT AND DAY(1946); SONG OF THE SOUTH(1946); FOR THE LOVE OF RUSTY(1947); NIGHT HAS A THOUSAND EYES(1948); RETURN OF THE BADMEN(1948); SHAGGY(1948); SLIPPY MCGEE(1948); STATE OF THE UNION(1948); WHIPLASH(1948); COWBOY AND THE INDIANS, THE(1949); HENRY, THE RAINMAKER(1949); YOU'RE MY EVERYTHING(1949); FATHER MAKES GOOD(1950); FATHER'S WILD GAME(1950); FATHER TAKES THE AIR(1951)
Mile Nokolic
TWELVE CHAIRS, THE(1970), art d
Andrew Nolan
THIS SPORTING LIFE(1963, Brit.)
Barry Nolan
KING KONG(1976), spec eff
1984
DUNE(1984), spec ph eff; MEATBALLS PART II(1984), spec eff
Bob Nolan
GALLANT DEFENDER(1935); OLD HOMESTEAD, THE(1935); MYSTERIOUS AVENGER, THE(1936); SONG OF THE SADDLE(1936); OLD WYOMING TRAIL, THE(1937); COLORADO TRAIL(1938); LAW OF THE PLAINS(1938); SOUTH OF ARIZONA(1938); WEST OF CHEYENNE(1938); WEST OF SANTA FE(1938); MAN FROM SUNDOWN, THE(1939); NORTH OF THE YUKON(1939), a, m; OUTPOST OF THE MOUNTIES(1939); RIDERS OF BLACK RIVER(1939); RIO GRANDE(1939); SPOILERS OF THE RANGE(1939); TEXAS STAMPEDE(1939); THUNDERING WEST, THE(1939); WESTERN CARAVANS(1939); BLAZING SIX SHOOTERS(1940); BULLETS FOR RUSTLERS(1940); DURANGO KID, THE(1940); STRANGER FROM TEXAS, THE(1940); TEXAS STAGECOACH(1940); THUNDERING FRONTIER(1940); TWO-FISTED RANGERS(1940), a, m/l; WEST OF ABILENE(1940); OUTLAWS OF THE PANHANDLE(1941); PINTO KID, THE(1941); RED RIVER VALLEY(1941); MAN FROM CHEYENNE(1942); SUNSET ON THE DESERT(1942); KING OF THE COWBOYS(1943); HELLDORADO(1946); HIT PARADE OF 1947(1947); MELODY TIME(1948)
Bruce Nolan
RIDING THE CHEROKEE TRAIL(1941)

Colleen Nolan
MARK OF CAIN, THE(1948, Brit.)
Dani Sue Nolan
SMOKY CANYON(1952); SNIPER, THE(1952)
Danie Sue Nolan
BREAKTHROUGH(1950)
Danni Nolan
BANDIT KING OF TEXAS(1949); FLAME OF YOUTH(1949)
Danni Sue Nolan
PRISONERS IN PETTICOATS(1950)
Doris Nolan
MAN I MARRY, THE(1936); AS GOOD AS MARRIED(1937); TOP OF THE TOWN(1937); HOLIDAY(1938); ONE HOUR TO LIVE(1939); IRENE(1940); MOON OVER BURMA(1940); FOLLIES GIRL(1943); ROMANTIC ENGLISHWOMAN, THE(1975, Brit./Fr.)
Dorothy Nolan
MORGAN'S MARAUDERS(1929)
Elizabeth Nolan
WHO GOES NEXT?(1938, Brit.)
Felipe Nolan
FURY IN PARADISE(1955, U.S./Mex.)
Frederick Nolan
BRASS TARGET(1978), w
Herman Nolan
FOURTH HORSEMAN, THE(1933); TRIPLE JUSTICE(1940); TWO GUN SHERIFF(1941)
James Nolan
BOY MEETS GIRL(1938); GIRLS ON PROBATION(1938); LITTLE MISS THOROUGHBRED(1938); MEN ARE SUCH FOOLS(1938); RACKET BUSTERS(1938); TORCHY BLANE IN PANAMA(1938); LADY IN THE LAKE(1947); ILLEGAL ENTRY(1949); STRATTON STORY, THE(1949); PAID IN FULL(1950); WHISTLE AT EATON FALLS(1951); BIG CAPER, THE(1957); PORTRAIT IN BLACK(1960); DIRTY HARRY(1971)
James F. Nolan
ROGUES' REGIMENT(1948)
Jeanette Nolan
MACBETH(1948); ABANDONED(1949); KIM(1950); NO SAD SONGS FOR ME(1950); SADDLE TRAMP(1950); SECRET OF CONVICT LAKE, THE(1951); HANGMAN'S KNOT(1952); HAPPY TIME, THE(1952); BIG HEAT, THE(1953); LAWLESS STREET, A(1955); EVERYTHING BUT THE TRUTH(1956); SEVENTH CAVALRY(1956); TRIBUTE TO A BADMAN(1956); APRIL LOVE(1957); GUNS OF FORT PETTICOAT, THE(1957); HALLIDAY BRAND, THE(1957); DEEP SIX, THE(1958); WILD HERITAGE(1958); GREAT IMPOSTOR, THE(1960); TWO RODE TOGETHER(1961); MAN WHO SHOT LIBERTY VALANCE, THE(1962); TWILIGHT OF HONOR(1963); MY BLOOD RUNS COLD(1965); CHAMBER OF HORRORS(1966); RELUCTANT ASTRONAUT, THE(1967); SULLIVAN'S EMPIRE(1967); NIGHTMARE HONEYMOON(1973); RESCUERS, THE(1977); AVALANCHE(1978); MANITOU, THE(1978); FOX AND THE HOUND, THE(1981); TRUE CONFESSIONS(1981)
1984
CLOAK AND DAGGER(1984)
Misc. Talkies
WINDS OF AUTUMN, THE(1976)
Jeanette C. Nolan
ISN'T IT ROMANTIC?(1948), w
Jeannette Nolan
RABBIT TRAP, THE(1959)
Jennifer F. Nolan
BREAKING AWAY(1979)
Jim Nolan
LITTLE MISS BIG(1946); DICK TRACY MEETS GRUESOME(1947); ARIZONA RANGER, THE(1948); BERLIN EXPRESS(1948); COUNTESS OF MONTE CRISTO, THE(1948); FIGHTING FATHER DUNNE(1948); GUNS OF HATE(1948); HE WALKED BY NIGHT(1948); MIRACLE OF THE BELLS, THE(1948); NIGHT TIME IN NEVADA(1948); RACE STREET(1948); SIREN OF ATLANTIS(1948); SON OF GOD'S COUNTRY(1948); ALIAS THE CHAMP(1949); BANDIT KING OF TEXAS(1949); DAUGHTER OF THE JUNGLE(1949); DEATH VALLEY GUNFIGHTER(1949); MARY RYAN, DETECTIVE(1949); THEY LIVE BY NIGHT(1949); TOO LATE FOR TEARS(1949); WAKE OF THE RED WITCH(1949); WINDOW, THE(1949); WOMAN ON PIER 13, THE(1950); DOUBLE DYNAMITE(1951); AIRPORT(1970); CHARLEY VARRICK(1973); TELEFON(1977)
Jimmy Nolan
ONE SUNDAY AFTERNOON(1948)
John Nolan
HOT ANGEL, THE(1958); -30-(1959); LAST TIME I SAW ARCHIE, THE(1961); NELSON AFFAIR, THE(1973, Brit.); TERROR(1979, Brit.); WORLD IS FULL OF MARRIED MEN, THE(1980, Brit.)
Judy Nolan
PORTRAIT OF THE ARTIST AS A YOUNG MAN, A(1979, Ireland), cos
Kathleen Nolan
LIMBO(1972); AMY(1981)
Kathy Nolan
DESPERADOES ARE IN TOWN, THE(1956); IRON SHERIFF, THE(1957); NO TIME TO BE YOUNG(1957)
Ken Nolan
MILLION DOLLAR LEGS(1939); PARIS CALLING(1941)
Kenneth Nolan
STABLEMATES(1938)
Kirrili Nolan
CADDIE(1976, Aus.)
Kirrily Nolan
SQUEEZE A FLOWER(1970, Aus.); PUBERTY BLUES(1983, Aus.)
Leary Nolan
COUNTY FAIR(1950)
Lelan Nolan
FIENDISH PLOT OF DR. FU MANCHU, THE(1980), p
Liam Nolan
Misc. Talkies
UNDER THE TABLE YOU MUST GO(1969)

Lloyd Nolan
ATLANTIC ADVENTURE(1935); G-MEN(1935); ONE-WAY TICKET(1935); SHE COULDN'T TAKE IT(1935); STOLEN HARMONY(1935); BIG BROWN EYES(1936); COUNTERFEIT(1936); DEVIL'S SQUADRON(1936); FIFTEEN MAIDEN LANE(1936); LADY OF SECRETS(1936); TEXAS RANGERS, THE(1936); YOU MAY BE NEXT(1936); EBB TIDE(1937); EXCLUSIVE(1937); INTERNES CAN'T TAKE MONEY(1937); KING OF GAMBLERS(1937); WELLS FARGO(1937); DANGEROUS TO KNOW(1938); EVERY DAY'S A HOLIDAY(1938); HUNTED MEN(1938); KING OF ALCATRAZ(1938); PRISON FARM(1938); TIP-OFF GIRLS(1938); MAGNIFICENT FRAUD, THE(1939); ST. LOUIS BLUES(1939); UNDERCOVER DOCTOR(1939); CHARTER PILOT(1940); GANGS OF CHICAGO(1940); GOLDEN FLEECING, THE(1940); HOUSE ACROSS THE BAY, THE(1940); JOHNNY APOLLO(1940); MAN I MARRIED, THE(1940); MAN WHO WOULDN'T TALK, THE(1940); MICHAEL SHAYNE, PRIVATE DETECTIVE(1940); PIER 13(1940); BEHIND THE NEWS(1941); BLUE, WHITE, AND PERFECT(1941); BLUES IN THE NIGHT(1941); BUY ME THAT TOWN(1941); DRESSED TO KILL(1941); MR. DYNAMITE(1941); SLEEPERS WEST(1941); STEEL AGAINST THE SKY(1941); APACHE TRAIL(1942); IT HAPPENED IN FLATBUSH(1942); JUST OFF BROADWAY(1942); MAN WHO WOULDN'T DIE, THE(1942); MANILA CALLING(1942); TIME TO KILL(1942); BATAAN(1943); GUADALCANAL DIARY(1943); CAPTAIN EDDIE(1945); CIRCUMSTANTIAL EVIDENCE(1945); HOUSE ON 92ND STREET, THE(1945); TREE GROWS IN BROOKLYN, A(1945); SOMEWHERE IN THE NIGHT(1946); TWO SMART PEOPLE(1946); LADY IN THE LAKE(1947); WILD HARVEST(1947); GREEN GRASS OF WYOMING(1948); STREET WITH NO NAME, THE(1948); BAD BOY(1949); EASY LIVING(1949); SUN COMES UP, THE(1949); LEMON DROP KID, THE(1951); CRAZYLEGS, ALL AMERICAN(1953); ISLAND IN THE SKY(1953); LAST HUNT, THE(1956); SANTIAGO(1956); TOWARD THE UNKNOWN(1956); ABANDON SHIP(1957, Brit.); HATFUL OF RAIN, A(1957); PEYTON PLACE(1957); GIRL OF THE NIGHT(1960); PORTRAIT IN BLACK(1960); SUSAN SLADE(1961); WE JOINED THE NAVY(1962, Brit.); GIRL HUNTERS, THE(1963, Brit.); CIRCUS WORLD(1964); NEVER TOO LATE(1965); AMERICAN DREAM, AN(1966); DOUBLE MAN, THE(1967); ICE STATION ZEBRA(1968); SERGEANT RYKER(1968); AIRPORT(1970); EARTHQUAKE(1974); MY BOYS ARE GOOD BOYS(1978); PRIVATE FILES OF J. EDGAR HOOVER, THE(1978)

Louise Nolan
OLD MOTHER RILEY, DETECTIVE(1943, Brit.); CAESAR AND CLEOPATRA(1946, Brit.)

Margaret Nolan
FERRY ACROSS THE MERSEY(1964, Brit.); HARD DAY'S NIGHT, A(1964, Brit.); SATURDAY NIGHT OUT(1964, Brit.); BEAUTY JUNGLE, THE(1966, Brit.); GREAT ST. TRINIAN'S TRAIN ROBBERY, THE(1966, Brit.); PROMISE HER ANYTHING(1966, Brit.); CONQUEROR WORM, THE(1968, Brit.); DON'T RAISE THE BRIDGE, LOWER THE RIVER(1968, Brit.); CARRY ON HENRY VIII(1970, Brit.); TOOMORROW(1970, Brit.); NO SEX PLEASE–WE'RE BRITISH(1979, Brit.)

Mary Nolan
CHARMING SINNERS(1929); SHANGHAI LADY(1929); OUTSIDE THE LAW(1930); UNDERTOW(1930); YOUNG DESIRE(1930); BIG SHOT, THE(1931); ENEMIES OF THE LAW(1931); X MARKS THE SPOT(1931); DOCKS OF SAN FRANCISCO(1932); FILE 113(1932); MIDNIGHT PATROL, THE(1932)
Silents
WEST OF ZANZIBAR(1928); SILKS AND SADDLES(1929)
Misc. Silents
FOREIGN LEGION, THE(1928); GOOD MORNING JUDGE(1928); DESERT NIGHTS(1929)

Mike Nolan
CAPTAIN LIGHTFOOT(1955)

O'Neill Nolan
EAST OF THE RIVER(1940); ALWAYS A BRIDESMAID(1943)

Robin Nolan
TEENAGE GANG DEBS(1966); SHAFT(1971)

Tom Nolan
YOUNG WARRIORS, THE(1967); CHASTITY(1969); MOONSHINE WAR, THE(1970); YANKS(1979); FAST TIMES AT RIDGEMONT HIGH(1982)
1984
UP THE CREEK(1984)

Tommy Nolan
JEANNE EAGELS(1957); KISS ME, STUPID(1964)

William F. Nolan
LOGAN'S RUN(1976), w

William Nolan
IRON MASK, THE(1929), ed; INTRUDER, THE(1962); BURNT OFFERINGS(1976), w
Silents
ROBIN HOOD(1922), ed; THIEF OF BAGDAD, THE(1924), ed; DON Q, SON OF ZORRO(1925), ed; BLACK PIRATE, THE(1926), ed; GAUCHO, THE(1928), ed

Ann Noland
EMIL AND THE DETECTIVES(1964); DIRTY HARRY(1971); BEST FRIENDS(1975)
Misc. Talkies
BEST FRIENDS(1975)

Louis Noland
WRONG BOX, THE(1966, Brit.)

Robert Noland
REVOLT OF THE ZOMBIES(1936)

Valora Noland
FIVE FINGER EXERCISE(1962); BEACH PARTY(1963); MUSCLE BEACH PARTY(1964); WAR WAGON, THE(1967); PASSIONATE STRANGERS, THE(1968, Phil.); UP YOUR TEDDY BEAR(1970)

William Noland
SLITHER(1973)

Shergei Nolbandou
FIRE OVER ENGLAND(1937, Brit.), w

Sergei Nolbandov
BELLS, THE(1931, Brit.), p; THERE AIN'T NO JUSTICE(1939, Brit.), w; SECRET FOUR, THE(1940, Brit.), w; SHIPS WITH WINGS(1942, Brit.), w; UNDERGROUND GUERRILLAS(1944, Brit.), d, w; IT STARTED IN PARADISE(1952, Brit.), p; LITTLE KIDNAPPERS, THE(1954, Brit.), p; VALUE FOR MONEY(1957, Brit.), p; BEHIND THE MASK(1958, Brit.), p; MIX ME A PERSON(1962, Brit.), p. Victor Saville; SHE DIDN'T SAY NO!(1962, Brit.), p

Werner Nold
TAKE IT ALL(1966, Can.), ed

Brett Nolen
ODD ANGRY SHOT, THE(1979, Aus.), spec eff

Joyce Nolen
SAMMY STOPS THE WORLD zero(1978)

Maria Nolgard
TOUCH, THE(1971, U.S./Swed.)

Maggie Nolin
NIGHT OF THE ZOMBIES(1981), m

Mike Nolin
NO MERCY MAN, THE(1975), w

Bonny Lee Noll
Misc. Talkies
ALL MEN ARE APES(1965)

Edmonia Nolley
ONE THIRD OF A NATION(1939)

Lance Nolley
FANTASIA(1940), art d; FUN AND FANCY FREE(1947), w

Claude Nollier
MOULIN ROUGE(1952); LES MAINS SALES(1954, Fr.); ROYAL AFFAIRS IN VERSAILLES(1957, Fr.); FORBIDDEN FRUIT(1959, Fr.); FIDELIO(1961, Aust.); LOSS OF INNOCENCE(1961, Brit.); DEVIL AND THE TEN COMMANDMENTS, THE(1962, Fr.)

Jacques Nolot
1984
ONE DEADLY SUMMER(1984, Fr.)

Charles Nolte
WAR PAINT(1953); STEEL CAGE, THE(1954); TEN SECONDS TO HELL(1959); ARMORED COMMAND(1961)

Nick Nolte
RETURN TO MACON COUNTY(1975); DEEP, THE(1977); WHO'LL STOP THE RAIN?(1978); HEART BEAT(1979); NORTH DALLAS FORTY(1979); CANNERY ROW(1982); 48 HOURS(1982); UNDER FIRE(1983)
1984
TEACHERS(1984); ULTIMATE SOLUTION OF GRACE QUIGLEY, THE(1984)

William Nolte
MAN FROM NEW MEXICO, THE(1932); SCARLET BRAND(1932); DUKE IS THE TOPS, THE(1938), d; SUNDOWN ON THE PRAIRIE(1939), w; LAND OF HUNTED MEN(1943), w; TWO FISTED JUSTICE(1943), w

William L. Nolte
GUN PLAY(1936), w; SADDLE MOUNTAIN ROUNDUP(1941), w; LAW OF THE LASH(1947), w; SQUARE DANCE JUBILEE(1949), w

Liu Nom
GOLDEN GATE GIRL(1941)

Mike Nomad
1984
SPLASH(1984), ch

The Nomads
NIKKI, WILD DOG OF THE NORTH(1961, U.S./Can.)

Ramon Nomar
NOTORIOUS(1946)

Gerald Nomes
PLEASURE PLANTATION(1970)

Geraldine Nomis
HELLO SISTER!(1933), w

Leo Nomis
HELL'S ANGELS(1930); CROWD ROARS, THE(1932); LOST SQUADRON, THE(1932)

Kozo Nomura
BATTLE IN OUTER SPACE(1960); VARAN THE UNBELIEVABLE(1962, U.S./Jap.)

Yoshitaro Nomura
SCARLET CAMELLIA, THE(1965, Jap.), d

Klaus Nomy
1984
A NOS AMOURS(1984, Fr.), m

Lucien Nonguet
Misc. Silents
LIFE AND PASSION OF CHRIST(1921, Fr.), d

Geula Noni
SALLAH(1965, Israel); IMPOSSIBLE ON SATURDAY(1966, Fr./Israel)

Roland Nonin
JOKER, THE(1961, Fr.), p; PARIS BELONGS TO US(1962, Fr.), p

Claire Nono
CUJO(1983)

Clare Nono
48 HOURS(1982); FIRE AND ICE(1983); NIGHTMARES(1983)

Yoshiyuki Noo
ALL RIGHT, MY FRIEND(1983, Japan)

Seemee Nookiguak
WHITE DAWN, THE(1974)

Princess Noola
GIRL OF THE GOLDEN WEST(1930)

Toby Noolan
NOTHING BUT TROUBLE(1944)

William Nooles
SINGING COWBOY, THE(1936), ph

J.W. Noon
GILDA(1946)

Paisley Noon
NIGHT WORLD(1932)

Noonan
ROOKIE, THE(1959), w

Barbara Noonan
PHYNX, THE(1970)

Betty Noonan
WAR OF THE WIZARDS(1983, Taiwan)

Bruce Noonan
REBEL WITHOUT A CAUSE(1955)

Christine Noonan
IF ...(1968, Brit.); OH! WHAT A LOVELY WAR(1969, Brit.); O LUCKY MAN!(1973, Brit.)

Eric Noonan
FOREVER AMBER(1947); FAN, THE(1949)

John Ford Noonan
NEXT STOP, GREENWICH VILLAGE(1976)

Pat Noonan
BRIDE OF THE LAKE(1934, Brit.); EARLY BIRD, THE(1936, Brit.); IF I WERE RICH(1936); RIVER OF UNREST(1937, Brit.); TWO WHO DARED(1937, Brit.); WINGS OF THE MORNING(1937, Brit.); KATHLEEN(1938, Ireland); MOUNTAINS O'MOURNE(1938, Brit.); MUTINY OF THE ELSINORE, THE(1939, Brit.); DR. O'-DOWD(1940, Brit.)

Patrick J. Noonan
Misc. Silents
DO UNTO OTHERS(1915, Brit.)

Sheila Noonan
INCREDIBLE PETRIFIED WORLD, THE(1959)

Steve Noonan
STACY'S KNIGHTS(1983)

Tom Noonan
DICK TRACY(1945); GEORGE WHITE'S SCANDALS(1945); BAMBOO BLONDE, THE(1946); CRACK-UP(1946); DING DONG WILLIAMS(1946); FROM THIS DAY FORWARD(1946); TRUTH ABOUT MURDER, THE(1946); BIG FIX, THE(1947); LIKE-LY STORY, A(1947); RIFFRAFF(1947); JUNGLE PATROL(1948); OPEN SE-CRET(1948); I CHEATED THE LAW(1949); I SHOT JESSE JAMES(1949); SET-UP, THE(1949); TRAPPED(1949); HOLIDAY RHYTHM(1950); RETURN OF JESSE JAMES, THE(1950); FBI GIRL(1951); GLORIA(1980); HEAVEN'S GATE(1980); WILLIE AND PHIL(1980); WOLFEN(1981); EASY MONEY(1983); EDDIE MACON'S RUN(1983)
1984
BEST DEFENSE(1984)

Tommy Noonan
ADAM'S RIB(1949); MODEL AND THE MARRIAGE BROKER, THE(1951); GENTLE-MEN PREFER BLONDES(1953); STAR IS BORN, A(1954); HOW TO BE VERY, VERY, POPULAR(1955); VIOLENT SATURDAY(1955); AMBASSADOR'S DAUGHTER, THE(1956); BEST THINGS IN LIFE ARE FREE, THE(1956); BUNDLE OF JOY(1956); GIRL MOST LIKELY, THE(1957); ROOKIE, THE(1959), a, p; SWINGIN' ALONG(1962); PROMISES, PROMISES(1963), a, p, w; THREE NUTS IN SEARCH OF A BOLT(1964), a, p, d, w; COTTONPICKIN' CHICKENPICKERS(1967)

Pat Noone
THREE NUTS IN SEARCH OF A BOLT(1964)

Peter Noone
HOLD ON(1966); MRS. BROWN, YOU'VE GOT A LOVELY DAUGHTER(1968, Brit.); SGT. PEPPER'S LONELY HEARTS CLUB BAND(1978)

Nooney Rickett Four
PAJAMA PARTY(1964); WINTER A GO-GO(1965)

Lynn Noonkester
SADIST, THE(1963), makeup

Robert Noonoo
1984
ALLEY CAT(1984)

Abdul Noor
STEEL BAYONET, THE(1958, Brit.)

Saskia Noordhoek-Hegt
Misc. Talkies
WHAT MAISIE KNEW(1976)

Nora
KILLING GAME, THE(1968, Fr.)

Nora Lou [Martin] and the Pals of the Golden West
LAUGH YOUR BLUES AWAY(1943)

Nora Lou Martin and the Pals of the Golden West
ROVIN' TUMBLEWEEDS(1939)

M.C. Norakova
Misc. Silents
BREAK-UP, THE(1930, USSR)

Cliff Norberg
ROBIN HOOD(1973), anim; FOX AND THE HOUND, THE(1981), anim

David Norberg
JUST ONCE MORE(1963, Swed.), p

Hannah Norbert
SUNDAY BLOODY SUNDAY(1971, Brit.)

Patrick Norbert
ADOPTION, THE(1978, Fr.)

Paul Norbert
BURY ME AN ANGEL(1972), p

Rezy Norbert
TRANS-EUROP-EXPRESS(1968, Fr.)

Anders Norborg
GREAT ADVENTURE, THE(1955, Swed.)

Ghita Norby
CRAZY PARADISE(1965, Den.); ERIC SOYA'S "17"(1967, Den.)

Paul Norby
GAY FALCON, THE(1941)

Clayton Norcross
Misc. Talkies
BLOWN SKY HIGH(1984)

Elaine Norcross
LAST HOUSE ON DEAD END STREET(1977)

Frank Norcross
Silents
ETERNAL SAPHO, THE(1916); FINAL CURTAIN, THE(1916); OLDEST LAW, THE(1918); OTHER MAN, THE(1918); FORTUNE'S CHILD(1919); NINETEEN AND PHYLLIS(1920); ALL DOLLED UP(1921)
Misc. Silents
ACCIDENTAL HONEYMOON, THE(1918); BLIND ADVENTURE, THE(1918); SOAP GIRL, THE(1918); BEWARE(1919); SPARK DIVINE, THE(1919); ESCAPE, THE(1926)

Van Norcross
BEHIND PRISON WALLS(1943), w; REVENGE OF THE ZOMBIES(1943), w

Eric Nord
FLOWER THIEF, THE(1962); STEEL ARENA(1973)

Eric "Big Daddy" Nord
THE HYPNOTIC EYE(1960)

Gloria Nord
PIN UP GIRL(1944)

Hilda Nord
Misc. Silents
WEB OF LIFE, THE(1917), a, d; FOR HIS SAKE(1922)

Mary Nord
Misc. Talkies
BORDER FENCE(1951)

Paul Nord
300 SPARTANS, THE(1962), tech adv

Pierre Nord
DOUBLE CRIME IN THE MAGINOT LINE(1939, Fr.), w; ALERT IN THE SOUTH(1954, Fr.), d&w Jean Devalvre; SERPENT, THE(1973, Fr./Ital./Ger.), w

Cliff Nordberg
MAKE MINE MUSIC(1946), anim; SONG OF THE SOUTH(1946), anim; MELODY TIME(1948), animators; CINDERELLA(1950), anim; ALICE IN WONDER-LAND(1951), anim; PETER PAN(1953), anim; LADY AND THE TRAMP(1955), anim; ONE HUNDRED AND ONE DALMATIANS(1961), anim; SWORD IN THE STONE, THE(1963), anim; MARY POPPINS(1964), anim

Barbara Nordella
PENNIES FROM HEAVEN(1981)

George Nordelli
Misc. Silents
WHAT PRICE LOVE(1927)

O. Nordemar
CHILDREN, THE(1949, Swed.), ph

Beate Norden
ISLE OF SIN(1963, Ger.)

Beatrix Norden
SEVEN DARING GIRLS(1962, Ger.)

Christine Norden
IDEAL HUSBAND, AN(1948, Brit.); IDOL OF PARIS(1948, Brit.); MINE OWN EXECUTIONER(1948, Brit.); NIGHT BEAT(1948, Brit.); INTERRUPTED JOURNEY, THE(1949, Brit.); SAINTS AND SINNERS(1949, Brit.); BLACK WIDOW(1951, Brit.); CASE FOR PC 49, A(1951, Brit.); RELUCTANT HEROES(1951, Brit.)

Denis Norden
BACHELOR IN PARIS(1953, Brit.), w; LOVE IN PAWN(1953, Brit.), w; BOTTOMS UP(1960, Brit.), w; BLISS OF MRS. BLOSSOM, THE(1968, Brit.), w; BUONA SERA, MRS. CAMPBELL(1968, Ital.), w; BEST HOUSE IN LONDON, THE(1969, Brit.), w; THINK DIRTY(1970, Brit.), w; STATUE, THE(1971, Brit.), w

Eric Norden
BORDER RANGERS(1950); STAGECOACH TO FURY(1956), w; APACHE WARRI-OR(1957), w; QUIET GUN, THE(1957), w; RIDE A VIOLENT MILE(1957), w; CATTLE EMPIRE(1958), w; LITTLE SAVAGE, THE(1959), w; MATTER OF MORALS, A(1961, U.S./Swed.), ed; LEGACY OF BLOOD(1973), w

Erika Norden
GOLDEN BLADE, THE(1953)

Dr. Mary Norden
EIGHT GIRLS IN A BOAT(1932, Ger.)

Maja Norden
M(1933, Ger.)

Tommy Norden
FIVE MILES TO MIDNIGHT(1963, U.S./Fr./Ital.)

Virginia Norden
Misc. Silents
COMBAT, THE(1916)

Catherina Norden-Falk
DEVIL, THE(1963)

Kell Nordenshield
ROGUES' REGIMENT(1948)

Kjell Nordenskold
SECRETS OF WOMEN(1961, Swed.)

Veronique Nordey
THANK HEAVEN FOR SMALL FAVORS(1965, Fr.)

Erik Nordgren
ILLICIT INTERLUDE(1954, Swed.), m; SMILES OF A SUMMER NIGHT(1957, Swed.), m; SEVENTH SEAL, THE(1958, Swed.), m; FACE OF FIRE(1959, U.S./Brit.), m; MAGICIAN, THE(1959, Swed.), m; WILD STRAWBERRIES(1959, Swed.), m; VIR-GIN SPRING, THE(1960, Swed.), m; SECRETS OF WOMEN(1961, Swed.), m; TWO LIVING, ONE DEAD(1964, Brit./Swed.), m; HERE'S YOUR LIFE(1968, Swed.), m; EMIGRANTS, THE(1972, Swed.), m

Karin Nordgren
NIGHT IN JUNE, A(1940, Swed.)

Arne Nordheim
ONE DAY IN THE LIFE OF IVAN DENISOVICH(1971, U.S./Brit./Norway), m

Charles Nordhoff
MUTINY ON THE BOUNTY(1935), w; HURRICANE, THE(1937), w; TUTTLES OF TAHITI(1942), w; PASSAGE TO MARSEILLE(1944), w; HIGH BARBAREE(1947), w; BOTANY BAY(1953), w; MUTINY ON THE BOUNTY(1962), w; HURRICANE(1979), w

Flo Nordhoff
PROJECTED MAN, THE(1967, Brit.), spec eff

Puppel Nordhoff
FIEND WITHOUT A FACE(1958), spec eff

Ulf Nordholm
PASSION OF ANNA, THE(1970, Swed.), spec eff

Cleo Nordi
FRENZY(1946, Brit.)

Stephen Nordi
JOURNEY INTO LIGHT(1951), w

Erika Nordin
BORDER RIVER(1954)

Ingrid Nordine
PICNIC ON THE GRASS(1960, Fr.)

Ken Nordine
FEARLESS FRANK(1967)
Louis Nordish
MORE DEADLY THAN THE MALE(1961, Brit.), m
Ernest Nordli
FANTASIA(1940), art d; DUMBO(1941), art d; GAY PURR-EE(1962), prod d
Ernie Nordli
MAN FROM BUTTON WILLOW, THE(1965), prod d
Stephanie Nordli
ISLAND OF DESIRE(1952, Brit.), w
Karine Nordman
FUNNY FACE(1957)
Marilyn Nordman
HOOKED GENERATION, THE(1969); MAFIA GIRLS, THE(1969)
Jean-Gabriel Nordmann
ZITA(1968, Fr.); CHANEL SOLITAIRE(1981)
1984
UNTIL SEPTEMBER(1984)
Eric Nordon
COPPER SKY(1957), w
Margit Nordqvist
VIBRATION(1969, Swed.), ed
Lars Nordrum
HUNGER(1968, Den./Norway/Swed.); ONE DAY IN THE LIFE OF IVAN DENISO-VICH(1971, U.S./Brit./Norway)
Nila Nordstahl
ONLY ONE NIGHT(1942, Swed.)
Clarence Nordstrom
TRIAL OF VIVIENNE WARE, THE(1932); GOLD DIGGERS OF 1933(1933); 42ND STREET(1933); WELCOME STRANGER(1947)
Misc. Silents
LIGHTS OF NEW YORK, THE(1922)
Frances Nordstrom
PLAYING AROUND(1930), w
Silents
DAME CHANCE(1926), w; JACK O'HEARTS(1926), w; ONE WOMAN TO ANOTH-ER(1927), w
Karin Nordstrom
NEW LAND, THE(1973, Swed.)
Kim Nordstrom
JAWS 3-D(1983)
Tora Nordstrom-Bonnier
NIGHT IN JUNE, A(1940, Swed.), w
Yngve Nordwall
WILD STRAWBERRIES(1959, Swed.)
Kenneth Nordyke
HAPPY DAYS(1930)
Silents
CUPID BY PROXY(1918)
Eva Noree
WILD STRAWBERRIES(1959, Swed.)
Joseph Noreiga
MURDER, MY SWEET(1945), ed
Henry Norell
ONE FOOT IN HELL(1960); UNDERWORLD U.S.A.(1961); YOUNG SAVAGES, THE(1961)
Norman Norell
THAT TOUCH OF MINK(1962), cos; WHEELER DEALERS, THE(1963), cos; SEX AND THE SINGLE GIRL(1964), cos
Irving Noren
WINNING TEAM, THE(1952)
R. P. Noren
NIGHT THE LIGHTS WENT OUT IN GEORGIA, THE(1981)
Thielly Nores
DIARY OF A CHAMBERMAID(1946), w
David Norfleet
CINDERELLA LIBERTY(1973)
Edgar Norfolk
HOTEL SPLENDIDE(1932, Brit.); ILLEGAL(1932, Brit.); INSULT(1932, Brit.); SIGN OF FOUR, THE(1932, Brit.); HIS GRACE GIVES NOTICE(1933, Brit.); BLACK ABBOT, THE(1934, Brit.); TANGLED EVIDENCE(1934, Brit.); SEXTON BLAKE AND THE MADEMOISELLE(1935, Brit.); MEN OF YESTERDAY(1936, Brit.); MINE OWN EXECUTIONER(1948, Brit.); ELIZABETH OF LADYMEAD(1949, Brit.); SILENT DUST(1949, Brit.); LAUGHING ANNE(1954, Brit./U.S.)
Per Norgaard
HAGBARD AND SIGNE(1968, Den./Iceland/Swed.), m
Bernardo Noriega
MAMBO(1955, Ital.), m
Eduard Noriega
HIGH RISK(1981)
Eduardo Noriega
RIFFRAFF(1947); TYCOON(1947); EL PASO(1949); EAGLE AND THE HAWK, THE(1950); PLUNDER OF THE SUN(1953); FAR HORIZONS, THE(1955); HELL'S ISLAND(1955); MAGNIFICENT MATADOR, THE(1955); SEVEN CITIES OF GOLD(1955); BEAST OF HOLLOW MOUNTAIN, THE(1956); SERENADE(1956); DANIEL BOONE, TRAIL BLAZER(1957); LIVING IDOL, THE(1957); SUN ALSO RISES, THE(1957); LAST OF THE FAST GUNS, THE(1958); PIER 5, HAVANA(1959); LAST REBEL, THE(1961, Mex.); GERONIMO(1962); OF LOVE AND DESIRE(1963); TARZAN AND THE VALLEY OF GOLD(1966 U.S./Switz.); IN-LAWS, THE(1979); ZORRO, THE GAY BLADE(1981)
Misc. Talkies
ROSE OF SANTA ROSA(1947)
Edwards Noriega
FURY IN PARADISE(1955, U.S./Mex.)
Joseph Noriega
HITLER'S CHILDREN(1942), ed; BEHIND THE RISING SUN(1943), ed; DAYS OF GLORY(1944), ed; FALCON IN MEXICO, THE(1944), ed; CORNERED(1945), ed; ENCHANTED COTTAGE, THE(1945), ed; GEORGE WHITE'S SCANDALS(1945), ed

Felix Noriego
BATTLE FLAME(1955); TO HELL AND BACK(1955); PILLARS OF THE SKY(1956)
Noriko
WALK, DON'T RUN(1966)
Gus Norim
NO MINOR VICES(1948), makeup; PETULIA(1968, U.S./Brit.), makeup
Bob Norin
SORCERER(1977), makeup
Gus Norin
FORCE OF EVIL(1948), makeup; CAUGHT(1949), makeup; DON'T WORRY, WE'LL THINK OF A TITLE(1966), makeup; THUNDER ALLEY(1967), makeup; MONEY JUNGLE, THE(1968), makeup; WILLARD(1971), makeup
Gustaf M. Norin
BODY AND SOUL(1947), makeup; WAR PARTY(1965), makeup; GRASSHOPPER, THE(1970), makeup
Gustaf Norin
WITNESS FOR THE PROSECUTION(1957), makeup
John Norin
SORCERER(1977), makeup
Josef Norin
SUDDEN FEAR(1952), makeup
Ursula Norkus
$100 A NIGHT(1968, Ger.), ed
Quenna Norla
OLD-FASHIONED GIRL, AN(1948)
Misha Norland
ALL NEAT IN BLACK STOCKINGS(1969, Brit.), ed; SKI BUM, THE(1971), ed
Manuel Norlega
RANCHO GRANDE(1938, Mex.)
Richard E. Norlie
1984
IMPULSE(1984)
Evy Norlund
FLYING FONTAINES, THE(1959)
Norma
GANGSTER, THE(1947), cos; GUN CRAZY(1949), cos; SOUTHSIDE 1-1000(1950), cos; INVADERS FROM MARS(1953), cos; KENTUCKIAN, THE(1955), cos; MARTY(1955), cos; WHILE THE CITY SLEEPS(1956), cos
Norma the Elephant
Silents
GREAT LOVE, THE(1925)
The Normal
CITY NEWS(1983), m
Al Norman
PARDON MY GUN(1930); 52ND STREET(1937); AROUND THE WORLD(1943); COVER GIRL(1944)
Amber Norman
Silents
DUDE COWBOY, THE(1926)
Ann Norman
BLOW-UP(1966, Brit.); MAROC 7(1967, Brit.); SEPARATION(1968, Brit.)
B. G. Norman
BIG CLOCK, THE(1948); SUNDOWN IN SANTA FE(1948); GUNFIGHTER, THE(1950); CALLAWAY WENT THATAWAY(1951); PACK TRAIN(1953)
Bart Norman
CANDLELIGHT IN ALGERIA(1944, Brit.); NO ORCHIDS FOR MISS BLAND-ISH(1948, Brit.)
Bruce Norman
MARSHAL'S DAUGHTER, THE(1953)
Bruce Gilbert Norman
RECKLESS MOMENTS, THE(1949)
C.P. Norman
BLITHE SPIRIT(1945, Brit.), art d; SILENT DUST(1949, Brit.), art d; MUDLARK, THE(1950, Brit.), art d; NIGHT AND THE CITY(1950, Brit.), art d; I'LL NEVER FORGET YOU(1951), art d; NO HIGHWAY IN THE SKY(1951, Brit.), art d; TITFIELD THUNDERBOLT, THE(1953, Brit.), art d
Charles Norman
WISE GIRL(1937), w
Eve Norman
SILENT PARTNER, THE(1979, Can.)
Frank Norman
GOVERNMENT GIRL(1943); IN THE NICK(1960, Brit.), w
Gary Norman
DON QUIXOTE(1973, Aus.)
Gene Norman
DISC JOCKEY(1951); CASEY'S SHADOW(1978)
Geoffrey Norman
PAINT YOUR WAGON(1969)
Gertrude Norman
GREENE MURDER CASE, THE(1929); IF I HAD A MILLION(1932); SIGN OF THE CROSS, THE(1932); HE LEARNED ABOUT WOMEN(1933); TRUMPET BLOWS, THE(1934)
Silents
FANCHON THE CRICKET(1915); MAY BLOSSOM(1915); PRETTY SISTER OF JOSE(1915); ADOPTED SON, THE(1917); PERSUASIVE PEGGY(1917); PARTNERS OF THE TIDE(1921); VOICE IN THE DARK(1921); KING OF KINGS, THE(1927)
Misc. Silents
ONE OF MILLIONS(1914); INNOCENT ADVENTURESS, AN(1919); WIDOW BY PROXY(1919)
Gypsy Norman
Silents
GENTLE JULIA(1923)
Hal Jon Norman
ISLAND OF THE BLUE DOLPHINS(1964); LONERS, THE(1972)
Misc. Talkies
LAST OF THE AMERICAN HOBOES, THE(1974)
Helen Norman
BROTHERLY LOVE(1970, Brit.); WICKER MAN, THE(1974, Brit.)

Henry Norman
MAN WITH THE MAGNETIC EYES, THE(1945, Brit.)
Misc. Silents
LOVE'S PILGRIMAGE TO AMERICA(1916)
Howard Norman
URBAN COWBOY(1980)
Irene Norman
Silents
OUT TO WIN(1923, Brit.)
Misc. Silents
ROMANY, THE(1923, Brit.)
J.E. Norman
TILL DEATH(1978), m
Jack Norman
BANDITS OF DARK CANYON(1947); BLACK GOLD(1947); BOWERY BUCK-
AROOS(1947); LITTLE MISS BROADWAY(1947); LULU BELLE(1948)
Jay Norman
WEST SIDE STORY(1961); KING OF THE GYPSIES(1978)
Jett Norman [Clint Walker]
JUNGLE GENTS(1954)
John Norman
HAND, THE(1960, Brit.)
Josephine Norman
Silents
RAMSHACKLE HOUSE(1924); KING OF KINGS, THE(1927); INTO NO MAN'S
LAND(1928)
Misc. Silents
FORBIDDEN WOMAN, THE(1927)
L. Norman
OLD CURIOSITY SHOP, THE(1935, Brit.), ed
Les Norman
THIS WAS PARIS(1942, Brit.), ed
Leslie Norman
MAN FROM CHICAGO, THE(1931, Brit.), ed; MIMI(1935, Brit.), ed; RED WA-
GON(1936), ed; HEART'S DESIRE(1937, Brit.), ed; TOO DANGEROUS TO LIVE(1939,
Brit.), d; OVERLANDERS, THE(1946, Brit./Aus.), ed; NICHOLAS NICKLEBY(1947,
Brit.), ed; MASSACRE HILL(1949, Brit.), p, ed; RUN FOR YOUR MONEY, A(1950,
Brit.), p, w; CRUEL SEA, THE(1953), p; WEST OF ZANZIBAR(1954, Brit.), p; NIGHT
MY NUMBER CAME UP, THE(1955, Brit.), d; SHIRALEE, THE(1957, Brit.), d, w; X
THE UNKNOWN(1957, Brit.), d; DUNKIRK(1958, Brit.), d; LONG AND THE SHORT
AND THE TALL, THE(1961, Brit.), d; SEASON OF PASSION(1961, Aus./Brit.), p&d;
SPARE THE ROD(1961, Brit.), d; MIX ME A PERSON(1962, Brit.), d
Lon Norman
STING OF DEATH(1966), m; I EAT YOUR SKIN(1971), m, md
Lowell Norman
POWER, THE(1968), spec eff
Lucille Norman
FOR ME AND MY GAL(1942); PAINTING THE CLOUDS WITH SUNSHINE(1951);
STARLIFT(1951); CARSON CITY(1952); SWEETHEARTS ON PARADE(1953)
Maidie Norman
BURNING CROSS, THE(1947); WELL, THE(1951); BRIGHT ROAD(1953); FOREVER
FEMALE(1953); TORCH SONG(1953); ABOUT MRS. LESLIE(1954); SUSAN SLEPT
HERE(1954); TARZAN'S HIDDEN JUNGLE(1955); WRITTEN ON THE WIND(1956);
WHATEVER HAPPENED TO BABY JANE?(1962); FINAL COMEDOWN, THE(1972);
LIKE A CROW ON A JUNE BUG(1972); MAURIE(1973); AIRPORT '77(1977); MOVIE
MOVIE(1978); HALLOWEEN III: SEASON OF THE WITCH(1982)
Marc Norman
OKLAHOMA CRUDE(1973), w; ZANDY'S BRIDE(1974), w; BREAKOUT(1975), w;
KILLER ELITE, THE(1975), w
Marjorie Norman
ROCKERS(1980)
Mary Norman
OUT OF TOWNERS, THE(1970)
Michel Norman
DEAR DETECTIVE(1978, Fr.)
Monty Norman
HOUSE OF FRIGHT(1961), m; DR. NO(1962, Brit.), m; CALL ME BWANA(1963,
Brit.), m
Noelle Norman
WANDERING JEW, THE(1948, Ital.); BIG CHIEF, THE(1960, Fr.)
Nora Norman
TRAVELS WITH MY AUNT(1972, Brit.)
Noralee Norman
SO BIG(1953)
Ola Norman
Silents
HIGH HEELS(1921); NEW TEACHER, THE(1922)
Olah Norman
Silents
CONFLICT, THE(1921)
Misc. Silents
BARB WIRE(1922)
Oliver Norman
WELCOME TO THE CLUB(1971); DEVIL'S WIDOW, THE(1972, Brit.)
Pamela Norman
TOUCH AND GO(1955)
Paul Norman
IS THIS TRIP REALLY NECESSARY?(1970), m; SIDELONG GLANCES OF A
PIGEON KICKER, THE(1970); GROOVE TUBE, THE(1974)
Misc. Talkies
LOVE AND KISSES(?)
Peggy Norman
ON OUR MERRY WAY(1948)
Peter Norman
STORY OF THREE LOVES, THE(1953); DESERT SANDS(1955); RACERS,
THE(1955); EDDY DUCHIN STORY, THE(1956); ISTANBUL(1957); 27TH DAY,
THE(1957)

Ralph Norman
FALLEN IDOL, THE(1949, Brit.)
Raphael Norman
UNEASY TERMS(1948, Brit.)
Rick Norman
YOUNG FRANKENSTEIN(1974)
Robert Norman
ONE WAY TICKET TO HELL(1955)
Ron Norman
TASTE OF SIN, A(1983), w
Stanley Norman
BIG GAME, THE(1972), p
Vera Norman
JUST ME(1950, Fr.)
Zack Norman
BEEN DOWN SO LONG IT LOOKS LIKE UP TO ME(1977); TRACKS(1977);
FINGERS(1978); SITTING DUCKS(1979); RAGTIME(1981)
1984
ROMANCING THE STONE(1984)
Jack Normand
CLANCY STREET BOYS(1943)
Jacques Normand
WE ARE ALL NAKED(1970, Can./Fr.)
Mabel Normand
DOWN MEMORY LANE(1949)
Silents
TILLIE'S PUNCTURED ROMANCE(1914); JOAN OF PLATTSBURG(1918); PECK'S
BAD GIRL(1918); MICKEY(1919); PEST, THE(1919); MOLLY O'(1921); WHAT HAP-
PENED TO ROSA?(1921); SUZANNA(1922); EXTRA GIRL, THE(1923)
Misc. Silents
BACK TO THE WOODS(1918); DODGING A MILLION(1918); FLOOR BELOW,
THE(1918); PERFECT 36, A(1918); VENUS MODEL, THE(1918); JINX(1919); SIS
HOPKINS(1919); UPSTAIRS(1919); WHEN DOCTORS DISAGREE(1919); PIN-
TO(1920); SLIM PRINCESS, THE(1920); HEAD OVER HEELS(1922); OH, MABEL
BEHAVE(1922)
Robert Normand
MEN IN WAR(1957)
Roger Normand
PLEASURES AND VICES(1962, Fr.), a, w
Elizabeth Norment
1984
RUNAWAY(1984); WOMAN IN RED, THE(1984)
John Normington
INADMISSIBLE EVIDENCE(1968, Brit.); MIDSUMMER NIGHT'S DREAM, A(1969,
Brit.); RECKONING, THE(1971, Brit.); STARDUST(1974, Brit.); MEDUSA TOUCH,
THE(1978, Brit.); THIRTY NINE STEPS, THE(1978, Brit.)
Rod Normond
SPARTACUS(1960)
Richard Normoyle
THREE NUTS IN SEARCH OF A BOLT(1964)
Line Noro
PEPE LE MOKO(1937, Fr.); J'ACCUSE(1939, Fr.); WELL-DIGGER'S DAUGHTER,
THE(1946, Fr.); BLIND DESIRE(1948, Fr.); SYMPHONIE PASTORALE(1948, Fr.); WE
ARE ALL MURDERERS(1957, Fr.)
Lino Noro
IT HAPPENED AT THE INN(1945, Fr.)
William Norren
1984
KARATE KID, THE(1984)
Eduardo Norriega
CAPTAIN SCARLETT(1953)
Joe Norrin
SET-UP, THE(1949), makeup
Ava Norring
SNOWS OF KILIMANJARO, THE(1952)
Aaron Norris
OCTAGON, THE(1980), stunts, ch
Bruce Norris
CLASS(1983)
Buckley Norris
MOUNTAIN MEN, THE(1980); SWORD AND THE SORCERER, THE(1982)
Buckley F. Norris
OSTERMAN WEEKEND, THE(1983)
Charles G. Norris
SEED(1931), w
Chet Norris
HANGAR 18(1980)
Chris Norris
LADY LIBERTY(1972, Ital./Fr.)
Christopher Norris
SUMMER OF '42(1971); AIRPORT 1975(1974); EAT MY DUST!(1976); TOUGH
ENOUGH(1983)
Chuck Norris
WRECKING CREW, THE(1968); STUDENT TEACHERS, THE(1973); RETURN OF
THE DRAGON(1974, Chin.); GOOD GUYS WEAR BLACK(1978); FORCE OF ONE,
A(1979); GAME OF DEATH, THE(1979); OCTAGON, THE(1980), a, ch; EYE FOR AN
EYE, AN(1981); SLAUGHTER IN SAN FRANCISCO(1981); FORCED VENGEAN-
CE(1982); SILENT RAGE(1982); LONE WOLF McQUADE(1983)
1984
MISSING IN ACTION(1984)
Diana Norris
LOUISA(1950); MRS. O'MALLEY AND MR. MALONE(1950)
Donna Norris
LOUISA(1950); MRS. O'MALLEY AND MR. MALONE(1950)
Ed Norris
THIS SIDE OF HEAVEN(1934); WAGON TRAIL(1935); INSIDE THE WALLS OF
FOLSOM PRISON(1951)

Eddie Norris
SABOTAGE SQUAD(1942); SULTAN'S DAUGHTER, THE(1943); BREAK-THROUGH(1950); I WAS A COMMUNIST FOR THE F.B.I.(1951); MURDER WITHOUT TEARS(1953)

Edward Norris
QUEEN CHRISTINA(1933); NAUGHTY MARIETTA(1935); SHOW THEM NO MERCY(1935); MAGNIFICENT BRUTE, THE(1936); BAD GUY(1937); BETWEEN TWO WOMEN(1937); MAMA STEPS OUT(1937); SONG OF THE CITY(1937); THEY WON'T FORGET(1937); BOYS TOWN(1938); ESCAPE, THE(1939); FRONTIER MARSHAL(1939); GORILLA, THE(1939); NEWSBOY'S HOME(1939); ON TRIAL(1939); TAIL SPIN(1939); LADY IN QUESTION, THE(1940); SCANDAL SHEET(1940); SKI PATROL(1940); ANGELS WITH BROKEN WINGS(1941); BACK IN THE SADDLE(1941); DOCTORS DON'T TELL(1941); HERE COMES HAPPINESS(1941); ROAD SHOW(1941); CLOSE CALL FOR ELLERY QUEEN, A(1942); GREAT IMPERSONATION, THE(1942); I LIVE ON DANGER(1942); LADY HAS PLANS, THE(1942); MAN WITH TWO LIVES, THE(1942); MYSTERY OF MARIE ROGET, THE(1942); MUG TOWN(1943); NO PLACE FOR A LADY(1943); SING A JINGLE(1943); WINGS OVER THE PACIFIC(1943); CAREER GIRL(1944); END OF THE ROAD(1944); MEN ON HER MIND(1944); NIGHT CLUB GIRL(1944); SHADOWS IN THE NIGHT(1944); SINGING SHERIFF, THE(1944); PENTHOUSE RHYTHM(1945); DECOY(1946); MURDER IN THE MUSIC HALL(1946); TRUTH ABOUT MURDER, THE(1946); HEARTACHES(1947); TRAPPED BY BOSTON BLACKIE(1948); FORGOTTEN WOMEN(1949); MYSTERIOUS DESPERADO, THE(1949); WOLF HUNTERS, THE(1949); BLAZING SUN, THE(1950); HIGHWAY 301(1950); KILLER SHARK(1950); SURRENDER(1950); MAN FROM THE ALAMO, THE(1953); KENTUCKIAN, THE(1955)

Frances Norris
Silents
THUNDER(1929)

Frank Norris
Silents
LIFE'S WHIRLPOOL(1916), w; MORAN OF THE LADY LETTY(1922), w; GREED(1925), w

George Norris
LORD SHANGO(1975), ed; FRENCH QUARTER(1978), ed
1984
EXTERMINATOR 2(1984), ed

George T. Norris
JOE(1970), ed; JUMP(1971), ed; THERE IS NO 13(1977), ed; HE KNOWS YOU'RE ALONE(1980), ed; SQUEEZE PLAY(1981), ed

Gloria Norris
HOME MOVIES(1979), w

Guy Norris
ROAD WARRIOR, THE(1982, Aus.)

Jan Norris
MIDDLE OF THE NIGHT(1959); EXPLOSIVE GENERATION, THE(1961); SPLENDOR IN THE GRASS(1961)

Jane Norris
SUMMER OF SECRETS(1976, Aus.), art d

Jay Norris
FIGHTING SEABEES, THE(1944); MY BUDDY(1944); THIRTY SECONDS OVER TOKYO(1944); WALK IN THE SUN, A(1945); WELL-GROOMED BRIDE, THE(1946); CROSSFIRE(1947); DESPERATE(1947); UNDER THE TONTO RIM(1947); WOMAN ON THE BEACH, THE(1947); FIGHTING MAD(1948); HOMECOMING(1948)

Julia Norris
STUCKEY'S LAST STAND(1980), art d

Karen Norris
SEALED CARGO(1951); BACHELOR PARTY, THE(1957); PILLOW TALK(1959); BACK STREET(1961); LOVER COME BACK(1961); PARRISH(1961); EXPERIMENT IN TERROR(1962); MANCHURIAN CANDIDATE, THE(1962); UNDERWATER CITY, THE(1962); FOR LOVE OR MONEY(1963); FITZWILLY(1967); DESTRUCTORS, THE(1968); IMPOSSIBLE YEARS(1968); SPLIT, THE(1968)

Kathleen Norris
PASSION FLOWER(1930), w; SECOND HAND WIFE(1933), d&w; WALLS OF GOLD(1933), w; CHANGE OF HEART(1934), w; NAVY WIFE(1936), w
Silents
SISTERS(1922), w; ROSE OF THE WORLD(1925), w; JOSSELYN'S WIFE(1926), w; CALLAHANS AND THE MURPHYS, THE(1927), w; MY BEST GIRL(1927), w

Ken Norris
OCTOPUSSY(1983, Brit.)

Lenard Norris
SPOOK WHO SAT BY THE DOOR, THE(1973); MAHOGANY(1975)

Lynn Norris
SMALL HOURS, THE(1962)

Mike Norris
YOUNG WARRIORS(1983)

Pat Norris
SUPPORT YOUR LOCAL GUNFIGHTER(1971), cos; ZANDY'S BRIDE(1974), cos; SUNSHINE BOYS, THE(1975), cos; SILENT MOVIE(1976), cos

Patricia Ann Norris
BALTIMORE BULLET, THE(1980), cos

Patricia Norris
GOOD GUYS AND THE BAD GUYS, THE(1969), cos; CANDIDATE, THE(1972), cos; PRIME CUT(1972), cos; SMILE(1975), cos; MISSOURI BREAKS, THE(1976), cos; CALIFORNIA SUITE(1978), cos; CAPRICORN ONE(1978), cos; DAYS OF HEAVEN(1978), cos; HEART BEAT(1979), cos; ELEPHANT MAN, THE(1980, Brit.), cos; FATSO(1980), cos; FOUR FRIENDS(1981), cos; HISTORY OF THE WORLD, PART 1(1981), cos; FRANCES(1982), cos; VICTOR/VICTORIA(1982), cos; SCARFACE(1983), cos; STAR CHAMBER, THE(1983), cos
1984
JOHNNY DANGEROUSLY(1984), cos; MICKI AND MAUDE(1984), cos; RACING WITH THE MOON(1984), cos; 2010(1984), cos

Patrick Norris
ON THE NICKEL(1980), cos

Patrticia Norris
FOUR FRIENDS(1981), cos

Patti Norris
REFLECTION OF FEAR, A(1973), cos

Patty Norris
MOVIE MOVIE(1978), cos

Peter Norris
Silents
KING OF KINGS, THE(1927)

Peter Plunkett Norris
CHRISTINA(1974, Can.)

Richard Norris
LIEUTENANT DARING, RN(1935, Brit.); CAFE MASCOT(1936, Brit.); FULL SPEED AHEAD(1936, Brit.); STRANGE CARGO(1936, Brit.); BAD BOY(1938, Brit.); NIGHT JOURNEY(1938, Brit.); ARSENAL STADIUM MYSTERY, THE(1939, Brit.); MUSIC HALL PARADE(1939, Brit.); THERE AIN'T NO JUSTICE(1939, Brit.); NEXT OF KIN(1942, Brit.); ABIE'S IRISH ROSE(1946); SEALED CARGO(1951); HARDER THEY FALL, THE(1956); JET PILOT(1957); LAST VOYAGE, THE(1960); PORTRAIT IN BLACK(1960); X-15(1961); EXPERIMENT IN TERROR(1962); MANCHURIAN CANDIDATE, THE(1962); DESTRUCTORS, THE(1968); MONEY JUNGLE, THE(1968)

Stephen Norris
PHANTOM PATROL(1936), w; RACING BLOOD(1938), w

Ted Norris
CHARLIE BUBBLES(1968, Brit.)

Terry Norris
STORK(1971, Aus.)

William Norris
LAST AFFAIR, THE(1976)
Silents
GOOD LITTLE DEVIL, A(1914); WHEN KNIGHTHOOD WAS IN FLOWER(1922); ADAM AND EVA(1923); ETERNAL THREE, THE(1923); NEVER THE TWAIN SHALL MEET(1925); JOY GIRL, THE(1927)
Misc. Silents
GO-GETTER, THE(1923); LOVE PIKER, THE(1923); MAYTIME(1923)

John Norrman
SWEDISH WEDDING NIGHT(1965, Swed.)

Joseph Norrman
SMILES OF A SUMMER NIGHT(1957, Swed.)

Suzannah Norstrand
BELIEVE IN ME(1971)

Kai Norstrom
LOVING COUPLES(1966, Swed.)

Clarence Norstrum
CROONER(1932)

Nathalie Nort
THERESE AND ISABELLE(1968, U.S./Ger.)

Alan North
SERPICO(1973); ...AND JUSTICE FOR ALL(1979); FORMULA, THE(1980)
1984
THIEF OF HEARTS(1984)

Alex North
STREETCAR NAMED DESIRE, A(1951), m; THIRTEENTH LETTER, THE(1951), m; DEATH OF A SALESMAN(1952), m; LES MISERABLES(1952), m; MEMBER OF THE WEDDING, THE(1952), m; PONY SOLDIER(1952), m; VIVA ZAPATA!(1952), m; DESIREE(1954), m; GO, MAN, GO!(1954), m&md; DADDY LONG LEGS(1955), m; I'LL CRY TOMORROW(1955), m; MAN WITH THE GUN(1955), m; RACERS, THE(1955), m; ROSE TATTOO, THE(1955), m, md; UNCHAINED(1955), m; BAD SEED, THE(1956), m; KING AND FOUR QUEENS, THE(1956), m, md; RAINMAKER, THE(1956), m; HOT SPELL(1958), m; LONG, HOT SUMMER, THE(1958), m; STAGE STRUCK(1958), m; SOUND AND THE FURY, THE(1959), m; WONDERFUL COUNTRY, THE(1959), m, md; SPARTACUS(1960), m, md; CHILDREN'S HOUR, THE(1961), m; MISFITS, THE(1961), m, md; SANCTUARY(1961), m; ALL FALL DOWN(1962), m; CLEOPATRA(1963), m; CHEYENNE AUTUMN(1964), m; OUTRAGE, THE(1964), m, md; AGONY AND THE ECSTASY, THE(1965), m; WHO'S AFRAID OF VIRGINIA WOOLF?(1966), m; DEVIL'S BRIGADE, THE(1968), m; SHOES OF THE FISHERMAN, THE(1968), m, md; DREAM OF KINGS, A(1969), m; HARD CONTRACT(1969), m; WILLARD(1971), m, md; POCKET MONEY(1972), m; ONCE UPON A SCOUNDREL(1973), m; LOST IN THE STARS(1974), md; SHANKS(1974), m; BITE THE BULLET(1975), m; JOURNEY INTO FEAR(1976, Can), m; PASSOVER PLOT, THE(1976, Israel), m; SOMEBODY KILLED HER HUSBAND(1978), m; WISE BLOOD(1979, U.S./Ger.), m; CARNY(1980), m; DRAGONSLAYER(1981), m
1984
UNDER THE VOLCANO(1984), m

Carrington North
HEADLEYS AT HOME, THE(1939), w

Clyde North
REMOTE CONTROL(1930), w

Edmund North
ONE NIGHT OF LOVE(1934), w; I DREAM TOO MUCH(1935), w; BUNKER BEAN(1936), w; MURDER ON A BRIDLE PATH(1936), w; I'M STILL ALIVE(1940), w

Edmund H. North
DISHONORED LADY(1947), w; COLORADO TERRITORY(1949), w; FLAMINGO ROAD(1949), w; IN A LONELY PLACE(1950), w; YOUNG MAN WITH A HORN(1950), w; DAY THE EARTH STOOD STILL, THE(1951), w; ONLY THE VALIANT(1951), w; OUTCASTS OF POKER FLAT, THE(1952), w; DESTRY(1954), w; FAR HORIZONS, THE(1955), w; COWBOY(1958), w; LADY TAKES A FLYER, THE(1958), w; SINK THE BISMARCK!(1960, Brit.), w; FIERCEST HEART, THE(1961), w; DAMN THE DEFIANT!(1962, Brit.), w; SUMARINE X-1(1969, Brit.), w; PATTON(1970), w; METEOR(1979), w

Edward North
PROUD ONES, THE(1956), w

Elizabeth North
Silents
AT THE STAGE DOOR(1921)

Frank North
LITTLE BALLERINA, THE(1951, Brit.), ph; ONCE A SINNER(1952, Brit.), ph; GOLD EXPRESS, THE(1955, Brit.), ph; MONSTER OF HIGHGATE PONDS, THE(1961, Brit.), ph; STOLEN PLANS, THE(1962, Brit.), ph

Harry North
THEY MET IN BOMBAY(1941)

Heather North
GIT!(1965); I LOVE MY WIFE(1970); BAREFOOT EXECUTIVE, THE(1971)
Ian North
RENT CONTROL(1981), m
Iris North
Silents
ALLEY CAT, THE(1929, Brit.), w
Jack North
REVENGE OF THE NINJA(1983)
Jay North
BIG OPERATOR, THE(1959); MIRACLE OF THE HILLS, THE(1959); PEPE(1960); ZEBRA IN THE KITCHEN(1965); MAYA(1966); TEACHER, THE(1974)
Jerry North
REVENGE OF THE NINJA(1983)
Joe North
LADIES SHOULD LISTEN(1934); SHE COULDN'T TAKE IT(1935); THANK YOU, JEEVES(1936); FIREFLY, THE(1937); LADY EVE, THE(1941); NONE BUT THE LONELY HEART(1944)
John Ringling North
GREATEST SHOW ON EARTH, THE(1952)
Joseph North
EX-FLAME(1931); PARIS IN SPRING(1935); WITHOUT REGRET(1935)
Leslie North
YOUNG GIRLS OF ROCHEFORT, THE(1968, Fr.)
Marion North
SING SING NIGHTS(1935), w
Marjorie North
BORDERTOWN(1935)
Michael North
UNSUSPECTED, THE(1947)
Michael "Ted" North
MARK OF ZORRO, THE(1940); MANILA CALLING(1942); MY GAL SAL(1942); ROXIE HART(1942); MARGIN FOR ERROR(1943); OX-BOW INCIDENT, THE(1943)
Neil North
AFFAIRS OF ADELAIDE(1949, U. S./Brit); WINSLOW BOY, THE(1950); TOM BROWN'S SCHOOLDAYS(1951, Brit.)
Noelle North
REPORT TO THE COMMISSIONER(1975); SLUMBER PARTY '57(1977); JEKYLL AND HYDE...TOGETHER AGAIN(1982)
Misc. Talkies
SWEATER GIRLS(1978)
Rex North
HEART OF A MAN, THE(1959, Brit.), w
Robert North
DAWN PATROL, THE(1930), p; GREAT DIVIDE, THE(1930), p; KISMET(1930), p; MOTHERS CRY(1930), p; NOTORIOUS AFFAIR, A(1930), p; SHOW GIRL IN HOLLYWOOD(1930), p; BRIGHT LIGHTS(1931), p; LADY BY CHOICE(1934), p; BLACK ROOM, THE(1935), p; LET'S LIVE TONIGHT(1935), p; MILLS OF THE GODS(1935), p; PARTY WIRE(1935), p; PENITENTIARY(1938), p; MAIN STREET LAWYER(1939), p; THOU SHALT NOT KILL(1939), p; CROOKED ROAD, THE(1940), p; FORGOTTEN GIRLS(1940), p; GANGS OF CHICAGO(1940), p; GIRL FROM HAVANA(1940), p; MEET THE MISSUS(1940), p; MELODY AND MOONLIGHT(1940), p; SING, DANCE, PLENTY HOT(1940), p; WOLF OF NEW YORK(1940), p; BEHIND THE NEWS(1941), p; GAY VAGABOND, THE(1941), p; ICE-CAPADES(1941), p; PETTICOAT POLITICS(1941), p; PUBLIC ENEMIES(1941), p; SIS HOPKINS(1941), p; HURRICANE SMITH(1942), p; ICE-CAPADES REVUE(1942), p; IN OLD CALIFORNIA(1942), p; TRAGEDY AT MIDNIGHT, A(1942), p; YOKEL BOY(1942), p; IN OLD OKLAHOMA(1943), p; SOMEONE TO REMEMBER(1943), p; BRAZIL(1944), p; EARL CARROLL SKETCHBOOK(1946), p; GREEN YEARS, THE(1946); SLOW DANCING IN THE BIG CITY(1978), ch
Silents
GIRL OF THE GOLDEN WEST, THE(1923), p
Robert G. North
DANGEROUS MILLIONS(1946), w; JEWELS OF BRANDENBURG(1947), w; NIGHT WIND(1948), w
Sheree North
TROUBLE WITH GIRLS(AND HOW TO GET INTO IT), THE*1/2 (1969); EXCUSE MY DUST(1951); HERE COME THE GIRLS(1953); LIVING IT UP(1954); HOW TO BE VERY, VERY, POPULAR(1955); BEST THINGS IN LIFE ARE FREE, THE(1956); LIEUTENANT WORE SKIRTS, THE(1956); NO DOWN PAYMENT(1957); WAY TO THE GOLD, THE(1957); IN LOVE AND WAR(1958); MARDI GRAS(1958); DESTINATION INNER SPACE(1966); MADIGAN(1968); GYPSY MOTHS, THE(1969); LAWMAN(1971); ORGANIZATION, THE(1971); CHARLEY VARRICK(1973); OUTFIT, THE(1973); BREAKOUT(1975); SHOOTIST, THE(1976); SURVIVAL(1976); TELEFON(1977); RABBIT TEST(1978); ONLY ONCE IN A LIFETIME(1979)
Sherle North
ANGEL COMES TO BROOKLYN, AN(1945)
Sterling North
SO DEAR TO MY HEART(1949), w; RASCAL(1969), w
Steven North
HOMER(1970), p; SHANKS(1974), p; TENDER FLESH(1976), p
Ted North
BRIDE WORE CRUTCHES, THE(1940); CHAD HANNA(1940); YESTERDAY'S HEROES(1940); YOUNG PEOPLE(1940); CHARLIE CHAN IN RIO(1941); FOR BEAUTY'S SAKE(1941); GIRL TROUBLE(1942); SYNCOPATION(1942); THUNDER BIRDS(1942); TO THE SHORES OF TRIPOLI(1942); MEN ON HER MIND(1944); DEVIL THUMBS A RIDE, THE(1947)
Tony North
KENNER(1969)
Virginia North
DEADLIER THAN THE MALE(1967, Brit.); LONG DUEL, THE(1967, Brit.); ON HER MAJESTY'S SECRET SERVICE(1969, Brit.); SOME GIRLS DO(1969, Brit.); ABOMINABLE DR. PHIBES, THE(1971, Brit.)
Wilfred North
TRIAL OF MARY DUGAN, THE(1929); DUDE WRANGLER, THE(1930); UNASHAMED(1932); WIDOW IN SCARLET(1932); MAN WHO RECLAIMED HIS HEAD, THE(1935)
Silents
BATTLE CRY OF PEACE, THE(1915), d; KID, THE(1916), d&w; ON THIN ICE(1925); CAPTAIN CARELESS(1928)

Misc. Silents
HEARTS AND THE HIGHWAY(1915), d; BLUE ENVELOPE MYSTERY, THE(1916), d; DOLLAR AND THE LAW, THE(1916), d; GREEN STOCKINGS(1916), d; HESPER OF THE MOUNTAINS(1916), d; ORDEAL OF ELIZABETH, THE(1916), d; SALVATION JOAN(1916), d; CLOVER'S REBELLION(1917), d; INDISCRETION(1917), d; KITTY MACKAY(1917), d; SALLY IN A HURRY(1917), d; OVER THE TOP(1918), d; HUMAN DESIRE, THE(1919), d; MIND THE PAINT GIRL(1919), d; UNDERCURRENT, THE(1919), d; LUCKY CARSON(1921), d; MILLIONAIRE FOR A DAY, A(1921), d; PERIL OF THE RAIL(1926)
Mrs. Wilfred North
MAN WITH TWO FACES, THE(1934); FRISCO KID(1935); LIVING ON VELVET(1935)
Wilfrid North
Silents
HUNTRESS, THE(1923)
Misc. Silents
HIS BROTHER'S KEEPER(1921), d; SON OF WALLINGFORD, THE(1921); LOVE BRAND, THE(1923); MAN'S MATE, A(1924)
Mrs. Wilfrid North
ARISE, MY LOVE(1940); MEET JOHN DOE(1941)
Wilifrid North
Misc. Silents
MRS. DANE'S DANGER(1922, Brit.), d
Zeme North
ZOTZI(1962); PALM SPRINGS WEEKEND(1963)
John Northcote
NO. 96(1974, Aus.), art d
Peter Northcote
FLAG LIEUTENANT, THE(1932, Brit.); LITTLE DAMOZEL, THE(1933, Brit.); FACES(1934, Brit.)
Sidney Northcote
Misc. Silents
KING OF CRIME, THE(1914, Brit.), d
Sydney Northcote
VERDICT OF THE SEA(1932, Brit.), d
David Northcutt
SAME TIME, NEXT YEAR(1978)
James M. Northern
RED, WHITE AND BLACK, THE(1970), p
Mary Northmore
Misc. Silents
LITTLE MISS GROWN-UP(1918)
Mildred Northmore
Silents
IS YOUR DAUGHTER SAFE?(1927)
Anton Northpole
HIGH BARBAREE(1947); SALOME(1953)
John Northpole
WHARF ANGEL(1934); ONE MILLION B.C.(1940)
Patricia Northrop
FIGHTER SQUADRON(1948); JUNE BRIDE(1948)
Harry Northrup
LAST WARNING, THE(1929); PRISONERS(1929); PARTY GIRL(1930); MEN CALL IT LOVE(1931); SQUAW MAN, THE(1931); STAND UP AND CHEER(1934 80m FOX bw); LILITH(1964); WHO'S THAT KNOCKING AT MY DOOR?(1968); ALICE DOESN'T LIVE HERE ANYMORE(1975); CITIZENS BAND(1977); TOM HORN(1980)
1984
SWING SHIFT(1984)
Silents
CHRISTIAN, THE(1914); ARIZONA(1918); POLLY OF THE STORM COUNTRY(1920); PRINCE OF AVENUE A., THE(1920); FOUR HORSEMEN OF THE APOCALYPSE, THE(1921); JAZZMANIA(1923); WOMAN OF PARIS, A(1923); UNCHASTENED WOMAN(1925); SHIELD OF HONOR, THE(1927)
Misc. Silents
TRAVELING SALESMAN, THE(1916); GREED(1917); BRUTE BREAKER, THE(1919); TWO WOMEN(1919); BLUE MOON, THE(1920); LUCK OF THE IRISH, THE(1920); FLOWER OF THE NORTH(1921); HATE(1922); SAVED BY RADIO(1922); GREATEST MENACE, THE(1923); GAMBLING FOOL, THE(1925)
Harry S. Northrup
Silents
BATTLE CRY OF PEACE, THE(1915); TRAIL OF THE SHADOW, THE(1917); AS THE SUN WENT DOWN(1919); WING TOY(1921); RACING ROMANCE(1926); WANTED–A COWARD(1927)
Misc. Silents
BEAUTIFUL LIE, THE(1917); GREATEST POWER, THE(1917); MILLIONAIRE'S DOUBLE, THE(1917); THEIR COMPACT(1917); VOICE OF CONSCIENCE, THE(1917); EYES OF MYSTERY, THE(1918); TRAIL TO YESTERDAY, THE(1918); WAY OF THE STRONG, THE(1919); WHITE CIRCLE, THE(1920); WINNING WITH WITS(1922)
Patricia Northrup
MY DREAM IS YOURS(1949)
Harry Northup
STAR SPANGLED GIRL(1971); BOXCAR BERTHA(1972); ALL-AMERICAN BOY, THE(1973); MEAN STREETS(1973); CRAZY MAMA(1975); FIGHTING MAD(1976); TAXI DRIVER(1976); NEW YORK, NEW YORK(1977); WHICH WAY IS UP?(1977); BLUE COLLAR(1978); OVER THE EDGE(1979); ROSE, THE(1979); USED CARS(1980)
1984
HARD TO HOLD(1984)
Patsy Fay Northup
HEART OF THE RIO GRANDE(1942)
The Northwesterners
DOWN THE WYOMING TRAIL(1939)
The Northwesterners [Mark and Ray Scobee]
STARLIGHT OVER TEXAS(1938)
Nadine Nortier
MOUCHETTE(1970, Fr.)
Aida Norton
Misc. Silents
LURING SHADOWS(1920)

Alex Norton
HUNCH, THE(1967, Brit.); GREGORY'S GIRL(1982, Brit.); LOCAL HERO(1983, Brit.)
1984
COMFORT AND JOY(1984, Brit.); EVERY PICTURE TELLS A STORY(1984, Brit.)
Andrew Norton
1984
PLOUGHMAN'S LUNCH, THE(1984, Brit.)
Angie Norton
SCANDAL FOR SALE(1932); ONE RAINY AFTERNOON(1936)
Arthur Norton
RAISIN IN THE SUN, A(1961), md
B. W. L. Norton
OUTLAW BLUES(1977), w; CONVOY(1978), w; MORE AMERICAN GRAFFITI(1979), d, w; LOSIN' IT(1983), w
Barbara Norton
LUCKY NIGHT(1939); CAPTAIN IS A LADY, THE(1940)
Barbra Norton
ORGY OF THE DEAD(1965)
Barry Norton
MOTHER KNOWS BEST(1928); SINS OF THE FATHERS(1928); FOUR DEVILS(1929); DISHONORED(1931); GOD IS MY WITNESS(1931); COCKTAIL HOUR(1933); LADY FOR A DAY(1933); ONLY YESTERDAY(1933); GRAND CANARY(1934); IMITATION OF LIFE(1934); NANA(1934); UNKNOWN BLONDE(1934); WORLD MOVES ON, THE(1934); STORM OVER THE ANDES(1935); CAPTAIN CALAMITY(1936); MURDER AT GLEN ATHOL(1936); I'LL TAKE ROMANCE(1937); SHE'S DANGEROUS(1937); SHOULD HUSBANDS WORK?(1939); ONE NIGHT IN THE TROPICS(1940); FOREVER AND A DAY(1943); RAZOR'S EDGE, THE(1946); MONSIEUR VERDOUX(1947); TWILIGHT ON THE RIO GRANDE(1947); CASBAH(1948); SUN COMES UP, THE(1949); WHAT PRICE GLORY?(1952); TO CATCH A THIEF(1955)
Misc. Talkies
TIMBERESQUE(1937); PAPA SOLTERO(1939); DEVIL MONSTER(1946, Brit.)
Silents
WHAT PRICE GLORY(1926); ANKLES PREFERRED(1927); SUNRISE–A SONG OF TWO HUMANS(1927); EXALTED FLAPPER, THE(1929)
Misc. Silents
LILY, THE(1926); FLEETWING(1928); LEGION OF THE CONDEMNED(1928); SINS OF THE FATHER(1928)
Beryl Norton
Silents
CREATION(1922, Brit.)
Betty Norton
JOSSER IN THE ARMY(1932, Brit.); LORD CAMBER'S LADIES(1932, Brit.); NEW HOTEL, THE(1932, Brit.); WHY SAPS LEAVE HOME(1932, Brit.); SCHOONER GANG, THE(1937, Brit.); DANCE OF DEATH, THE(1938, Brit.)
Bill Norton, Sr.
NIGHT OF THE JUGGLER(1980), w
Bill L. Norton
CISCO PIKE(1971), d&w
Britt Norton
FLYING LEATHERNECKS(1951)
Carol Norton
WANDA NEVADA(1979)
Charles Norton
GHOST SHIP, THE(1943)
Silents
FAR CALL, THE(1929)
Cliff Norton
COUNTRY MUSIC HOLIDAY(1958); IT'S A MAD, MAD, MAD, MAD WORLD(1963); KISS ME, STUPID(1964); HARLOW(1965); MC HALE'S NAVY JOINS THE AIR FORCE(1965); GHOST AND MR. CHICKEN, THE(1966); MUNSTER, GO HOME(1966); RUSSIANS ARE COMING, THE RUSSIANS ARE COMING, THE(1966); PHANTOM TOLLBOOTH, THE(1970); SUPPOSE THEY GAVE A WAR AND NOBODY CAME?(1970); FUNNY LADY(1975); WON TON TON, THE DOG WHO SAVED HOLLYWOOD(1976); MOUSE AND HIS CHILD, THE(1977)
Danny Norton
DOWN OUR ALLEY(1939, Brit.)
Dean Norton
LOVE ISLAND(1952)
Denis Val Norton
DISHONOR BRIGHT(1936, Brit.)
Dennis Val Norton
EVENSONG(1934, Brit.); BOMBS OVER LONDON(1937, Brit.)
Dennys Val Norton
IT HAPPENED IN PARIS(1935, Brit.)
Denys Val Norton
NO WAY BACK(1949, Brit.); PAUL TEMPLE'S TRIUMPH(1951, Brit.)
Edgar Norton
LOVE PARADE, THE(1929); DU BARRY, WOMAN OF PASSION(1930); EAST IS WEST(1930); LADY OF SCANDAL, THE(1930); LADY SURRENDERS, A(1930); MAN FROM BLANKLEY'S, THE(1930); MONTE CARLO(1930); ONE ROMANTIC NIGHT(1930); RUNAWAY BRIDE(1930); BACHELOR FATHER(1931); LADY REFUSES, THE(1931); MEET THE WIFE(1931); BIG BROADCAST, THE(1932); DR. JEKYLL AND MR. HYDE(1932); LOVE ME TONIGHT(1932); BIG BRAIN, THE(1933); LADY'S PROFESSION, A(1933); SING SINNER, SING(1933); IMITATION OF LIFE(1934); MILLION DOLLAR RANSOM(1934); RICHEST GIRL IN THE WORLD, THE(1934); THIRTY-DAY PRINCESS(1934); WE LIVE AGAIN(1934); EAST OF JAVA(1935); SONS OF STEEL(1935); TOP HAT(1935); WHEN A MAN'S A MAN(1935); AUGUST WEEK-END(1936, Brit.); DRACULA'S DAUGHTER(1936); GIVE ME YOUR HEART(1936); TROUBLE FOR TWO(1936); BILL CRACKS DOWN(1937); MAYTIME(1937); YOU CAN'T BUY LUCK(1937); CAPTAIN FURY(1939); SON OF FRANKENSTEIN(1939); HOUSE OF THE SEVEN GABLES, THE(1940); MAD EMPRESS, THE(1940); RINGS ON HER FINGERS(1942); HAPPY GO LUCKY(1943); ARE THESE OUR PARENTS?(1944); PRACTICALLY YOURS(1944); DOLL FACE(1945); KITTY(1945); DEVOTION(1946)
Silents
AMAZONS, THE(1917); PAIR OF CUPIDS, A(1918); LIGHT IN THE DARK, THE(1922); BROADWAY AFTER DARK(1924); LEARNING TO LOVE(1925); REGULAR FELLOW, A(1925); LADY FROM HELL, THE(1926); 'MARRIAGE LICENSE?'(1926); MAN WHO LAUGHS, THE(1927); SINGED(1927); OH, KAY(1928)

Misc. Silents
LOST - A WIFE(1925)
Edward Norton
Silents
SINGLE TRACK, THE(1921)
Eleanor E. Norton
DAY OF THE ANIMALS(1977), w
Eleanor Elias Norton
DIRTY TRICKS(1981, Can.), w
Escott Norton
1984
EXTERMINATOR 2(1984), set d
Fletcher Norton
LOCKED DOOR, THE(1929); BIG HOUSE, THE(1930); SWEETHEARTS AND WIVES(1930); SECRET SIX, THE(1931); STAR WITNESS(1931); IS MY FACE RED?(1932); PRIVATE SCANDAL, A(1932); SINISTER HANDS(1932); BOWERY, THE(1933); SUCKER MONEY(1933); WHEN YOU'RE IN LOVE(1937)
Frank Norton
KES(1970, Brit.)
Fred Norton
GOVERNMENT GIRL(1943)
Frederic Norton
CHU CHIN CHOW(1934, Brit.), w, m
Grace Norton
SPORTING BLOOD(1940), w; DEEP IN THE HEART OF TEXAS(1942), w
Grace Keel Norton
SKY SPIDER, THE(1931), w
Harold Norton
SEPIA CINDERELLA(1947)
J.O.C. Norton
AFTER THE BALL(1932, Brit.), w
Jack Norton
COCKEYED CAVALIERS(1934); DEATH OF THE DIAMOND(1934); FINISHING SCHOOL(1934); NOW I'LL TELL(1934); ALIBI IKE(1935); BROADWAY GONDOLIER(1935); DANTE'S INFERNO(1935); DON'T BET ON BLONDES(1935); DR. SOCRATES(1935); FRONT PAGE WOMAN(1935); GILDED LILY, THE(1935); GIRL FROM TENTH AVENUE, THE(1935); GOING HIGHBROW(1935); HIS NIGHT OUT(1935); MISS PACIFIC FLEET(1935); ONE HOUR LATE(1935); ONE MORE SPRING(1935); PAGE MISS GLORY(1935); RUGGLES OF RED GAP(1935); SHE GETS HER MAN(1935); SHIP CAFE(1935); STOLEN HARMONY(1935); SWEET MUSIC(1935); AFTER THE THIN MAN(1936); MOON'S OUR HOME, THE(1936); TOO MANY PARENTS(1936); DAY AT THE RACES, A(1937); GREAT GARRICK, THE(1937); MARRIED BEFORE BREAKFAST(1937); MEET THE MISSUS(1937); MY DEAR MISS ALDRICH(1937); PICK A STAR(1937); TIME OUT FOR ROMANCE(1937); ARSENE LUPIN RETURNS(1938); JEZEBEL(1938); KING OF ALCATRAZ(1938); MAN-PROOF(1938); MEET THE GIRLS(1938); STRANGE FACES(1938); THANKS FOR THE MEMORY(1938); GRAND JURY SECRETS(1939); JOE AND ETHEL TURP CALL ON THE PRESIDENT(1939); LAUGH IT OFF(1939); LONE WOLF SPY HUNT, THE(1939); ROARING TWENTIES, THE(1939); SOCIETY SMUGGLERS(1939); BANK DICK, THE(1940); FARMER'S DAUGHTER, THE(1940); GHOST BREAKERS, THE(1940); NIGHT AT EARL CARROLL'S, A(1940); OPENED BY MISTAKE(1940); DOWN IN SAN DIEGO(1941); LOUISIANA PURCHASE(1941); ROAD SHOW(1941); YOU BELONG TO ME(1941); BROOKLYN ORCHID(1942); DR. RENAULT'S SECRET(1942); FLEET'S IN, THE(1942); ICE-CAPADES REVUE(1942); LADY BODYGUARD(1942); MOONLIGHT IN HAVANA(1942); MY FAVORITE SPY(1942); PALM BEACH STORY, THE(1942); ROXIE HART(1942); SPOILERS, THE(1942); TENNESSEE JOHNSON(1942); FALCON STRIKES BACK, THE(1943); IT AIN'T HAY(1943); KANSAN, THE(1943); SO'S YOUR UNCLE(1943); THANK YOUR LUCKY STARS(1943); ALASKA(1944); AND THE ANGELS SING(1944); BIG NOISE, THE(1944); CHINESE CAT, THE(1944); COVER GIRL(1944); GHOST CATCHERS(1944); GOING MY WAY(1944); HAIL THE CONQUERING HERO(1944); HERE COME THE WAVES(1944); MAKE YOUR OWN BED(1944); MIRACLE OF MORGAN'S CREEK, THE(1944); ONCE UPON A TIME(1944); SHINE ON, HARVEST MOON(1944); STORY OF DR. WASSELL, THE(1944); CAPTAIN TUGBOAT ANNIE(1945); FASHION MODEL(1945); FLAME OF THE BARBARY COAST(1945); GUY, A GAL AND A PAL, A(1945); HER HIGHNESS AND THE BELLBOY(1945); HOLD THAT BLONDE(1945); LADY ON A TRAIN(1945); MAN ALIVE(1945); NAUGHTY NINETIES, THE(1945); SCARLET CLUE, THE(1945); STRANGE CONFESSION(1945); STRANGE MR. GREGORY, THE(1945); TWO O'CLOCK COURAGE(1945); WONDER MAN(1945); BRINGING UP FATHER(1946); HOODLUM SAINT, THE(1946); KID FROM BOOKLYN, THE(1946); LADY LUCK(1946); NOCTURNE(1946); RENDEZVOUS 24(1946); SHADOWS OVER CHINATOWN(1946); DOWN TO EARTH(1947); LINDA BE GOOD(1947); VARIETY GIRL(1947); MAD WEDNESDAY(1950)
Jan Norton
SCREAMS OF A WINTER NIGHT(1979)
Jim Norton
STRAW DOGS(1971, Brit.)
Judy Norton
HOTEL(1967)
Kay Norton
JULIA MISBEHAVES(1948); LUXURY LINER(1948); ON AN ISLAND WITH YOU(1948); OREGON TRAIL, THE(1959), ph; SECRET OF THE PURPLE REEF, THE(1960), ph; VALLEY OF THE REDWOODS(1960), ph; LONG ROPE, THE(1961), ph; MASTER OF THE WORLD(1961), ph; SILENT CALL, THE(1961), ph; BEACH PARTY(1963), ph; SURF PARTY(1964), ph
Ken Norton
MANDINGO(1975); DRUM(1976)
Kenneth Norton
TOP OF THE HEAP(1972)
Leslie Norton
WHY SAPS LEAVE HOME(1932, Brit.), ed
Margo Norton
MURDER A LA MOD(1968)
Mark Norton
JESSE JAMES MEETS FRANKENSTEIN'S DAUGHTER(1966)
Martin Norton
PUMPKIN EATER, THE(1964, Brit.)

Mary Norton
OLD MOTHER RILEY, DETECTIVE(1943, Brit.); MURDER IN REVERSE(1946, Brit.); BEDKNOBS AND BROOMSTICKS(1971), w
Misc. Silents
WALL STREET TRAGEDY, A(1916)
Miles Norton
ROSE BOWL(1936)
Ned Norton
IN OLD KENTUCKY(1935); LONE WOLF RETURNS, THE(1936)
Misc. Talkies
RACKETEER ROUND-UP(1934); GUNNERS AND GUNS(1935)
Pearlie Norton
HOUSE ACROSS THE BAY, THE(1940)
Silents
ISOBEL(1920)
Randy Norton
HONKY TONK FREEWAY(1981)
Richard Norton
ARSENAL STADIUM MYSTERY, THE(1939, Brit.), p; LADY IN DISTRESS(1942, Brit.), p; ADVENTURE IN BLACKMAIL(1943, Brit.), p; FORCE: FIVE(1981)
Silents
ALL DOLLED UP(1921)
Misc. Silents
MURDOCK TRIAL, THE(1914, Brit.); WHAT'S BRED...COMES OUT IN THE FLESH(1916, Brit.)
Roger Norton, USAF
OPERATION HAYLIFT(1950)
Rosanna Norton
PHANTOM OF THE PARADISE(1974), cos; THE LADY DRACULA(1974), cos; CARRIE(1976), cos; OUTLAW BLUES(1977), cos; AIRPLANE!(1980), cos; STUNT MAN, THE(1980), cos; TRON(1982), cos
1984
HARD TO HOLD(1984), cos
Roy Norton
Silents
PLUNDERER, THE(1915), w; MEDIATOR, THE(1916), w; MIXED FACES(1922), w
Stephen Norton
Silents
ENCHANTED ISLAND, THE(1927), ph
Steve Norton
Silents
NANCY COMES HOME(1918), ph; FOLLIES GIRL, THE(1919), ph; WOLVERINE, THE(1921), ph; ANOTHER MAN'S WIFE(1924), ph; HUSBAND HUNTERS(1927), ph
Tom Norton
STILL OF THE NIGHT(1982)
Tony Norton
TRINITY IS STILL MY NAME(1971, Ital.)
William Norton
GRASS EATER, THE(1961), p, w; ROTTEN APPLE, THE(1963), w; FARMER'S OTHER DAUGHTER, THE(1965), p, w; SCALPHUNTERS, THE(1968), w; MARIGOLD MAN(1970), p, w, ph; TRADER HORN(1973), w; WHITE LIGHTNING(1973), w; BIG BAD MAMA(1974), w; I DISMEMBER MAMA(1974), w; BRANNIGAN(1975, Brit.), w; GATOR(1976), w; MOVING VIOLATION(1976), w; SMALL TOWN IN TEXAS, A(1976), w; DAY OF THE ANIMALS(1977), w; HUNTING PARTY, THE(1977, Brit.), w
William Norton, Sr.
DIRTY TRICKS(1981, Can.), w
William A. Norton
Misc. Silents
UNPARDONABLE SIN, THE(1916)
William W. Norton
SAM WHISKEY(1969), w
James Norval
HELLIONS, THE(1962, Brit.)
Ralph Norvel
GOLD(1974, Brit.)
Mahlom Norvell
WONDER BAR(1934)
Sally Norvell
1984
PARIS, TEXAS(1984, Ger./Fr.)
Vincenzo Norvese
DUCK, YOU SUCKER!(1972, Ital.)
Herbert Norville
BUGSY MALONE(1976, Brit.); PRESSURE(1976, Brit.); CLASS OF MISS MAC MICHAEL, THE(1978, Brit./U.S.)
Norville Brothers
YOU'RE A SWEETHEART(1937)
Eva Norvind
SANTO CONTRA LA INVASION DE LOS MARCIANOS(1966, Mex.)
Red Norvo
DISC JOCKEY(1951); KINGS GO FORTH(1958); SCREAMING MIMI(1958)
Norwich Trio
VARIETY HOUR(1937, Brit.)
Natalie Norwick
23 PACES TO BAKER STREET(1956); HIDDEN FEAR(1957)
Eille Norwood
Silents
CRIMSON CIRCLE, THE(1922, Brit.)
Misc. Silents
TEMPTATION'S HOUR(1916, Brit.); HUNDRETH CHANCE, THE(1920, Brit.); TAVERN KNIGHT, THE(1920, Brit.); HOUND OF THE BASKERVILLES, THE(1921, Brit.); RECOIL, THE(1922, Brit.); SIGN OF FOUR, THE(1923, Brit.)
Ellie Norwood
Misc. Silents
CHARLATAN, THE(1916, Brit.); GENTLEMAN OF FRANCE, A(1921, Brit.); GWYNETH OF THE WELSH HILLS(1921, Brit.)

Lance Norwood
HERE COME THE TIGERS(1978)
Lily Norwood
MISSION TO MOSCOW(1943); SOMETHING TO SHOUT ABOUT(1943)
Ralph Norwood
ETERNALLY YOURS(1939); WOMAN IN THE WINDOW, THE(1945)
Robert Norwood
RAZOR'S EDGE, THE(1946)
Jack Norworth
QUEEN OF THE NIGHTCLUBS(1929); SOUTHERNER, THE(1945)
Ned Norworth
HOTEL VARIETY(1933)
Jaime Nos
1984
SKYLINE(1984, Spain)
Marian Nosek
JOAN OF THE ANGELS(1962, Pol.)
V. Nosik
SHE-WOLF, THE(1963, USSR)
B. Noskov
MUMU(1961, USSR), spec eff
Lloyd Nosler
SHAKEDOWN, THE(1929), ed; SHE GOES TO WAR(1929), ed; EYES OF THE WORLD, THE(1930), ed; HELL HARBOR(1930), ed; MAN FROM DEATH VALLEY, THE(1931), d, w; REACHING FOR THE MOON(1931), ed; GALLOPING THRU(1932), d; SINGLE-HANDED SANDERS(1932), d; BLOOD MONEY(1933), ed; SON OF THE BORDER(1933), d; DAWN RIDER(1935), d&w; EVERYBODY'S OLD MAN(1936), ed; STOWAWAY(1936), ed; HURRICANE, THE(1937), ed; SLAVE SHIP(1937), ed; POT O' GOLD(1941), ed; NAVAJO(1952), ed
Silents
BEN-HUR(1925), ed; FLESH AND THE DEVIL(1926), ed; TEMPTRESS, THE(1926), ed
Tamara Nosova
CLEAR SKIES(1963, USSR); MARRIAGE OF BALZAMINOV, THE(1966, USSR)
Donald Nosseck
FIVE MINUTES TO LIVE(1961), ed
Martin Nosseck
MOONWOLF(1966, Fin./Ger.), p, d; ONE DARK NIGHT(1983)
Max Nosseck
GIRLS UNDER TWENTY-ONE(1940), d; OVERTURE TO GLORY(1940), d; GAMBLING DAUGHTERS(1941), d; ONE DANGEROUS NIGHT(1943), w; BRIGHTON STRANGLER, THE(1945), d, w; DILLINGER(1945), d; BLACK BEAUTY(1946), d; RETURN OF RIN TIN TIN, THE(1947), d; KILL OR BE KILLED(1950), d, w; HOODLUM, THE(1951), d; KOREA PATROL(1951), d; GARDEN OF EDEN(1954), d, w; SINGING IN THE DARK(1956), d
Noel Nosseck
BEST FRIENDS(1975), p&d; LAS VEGAS LADY(1976), d; YOUNGBLOOD(1978), d; DREAMER(1979), d; KING OF THE MOUNTAIN(1981), d
Misc. Talkies
BEST FRIENDS(1975), d
Ralph Nossek
ORDERS TO KILL(1958, Brit.); ALFRED THE GREAT(1969, Brit.); CAPTAIN NEMO AND THE UNDERWATER CITY(1969, Brit.); FRAULEIN DOKTOR(1969, Ital./Yugo.)
1984
SUCCESS IS THE BEST REVENGE(1984, Brit.)
Bram Nossen
GO, MAN, GO!(1954)
Bran Nossen
Misc. Talkies
SHADOW LAUGHS(1933)
Lloyd Nossler
OUR DAILY BREAD(1934), ed
Nick Nostro
SUPERARGO VERSUS DIABOLICUS(1966, Ital./Span.), d; WEB OF VIOLENCE(1966, Ital./Span.), d
The Notables
DOWN MISSOURI WAY(1946)
The Notables Quartet
LAW AND ORDER(1940)
Guido Notari
HELEN OF TROY(1956, Ital)
Pietro Notarianni
ENGAGEMENT ITALIANO(1966, Fr./Ital.), p; SHOOT LOUD, LOUDER... I DON'T UNDERSTAND(1966, Ital.), p
Guido Notario
BALL AT THE CASTLE(1939, Ital.)
Steve "Sugarfoot" Notario
1984
BREAKIN' 2: ELECTRIC BOOGALOO(1984)
James Notaro
LADY IN THE DARK(1944); DANGER SIGNAL(1945)
Pat Noteboom
RANCHO DELUXE(1975)
Chris Noth
SMITHEREENS(1982)
Karl Noti
HIS MAJESTY, KING BALLYHOO(1931, Ger.), w; GIRL DOWNSTAIRS, THE(1938), w
Matthew Notkins
SYNANON(1965)
Karl Notl
HAPPY(1934, Brit.), w; NO MONKEY BUSINESS(1935, Brit.), w
Karoly Notl
HIPPOLYT, THE LACKEY(1932, Hung.), w
Barney Noto
Misc. Talkies
CAPTAIN CELLULOID VS THE FILM PIRATES(1974)

Ric Notoli
HELL WITH HEROES, THE(1968)
David Nott
WHAT A CRAZY WORLD(1963, Brit.)
Roger Nott
GIRO CITY(1982, Brit.)
Gunter Notthoff
APPLE, THE(1980 U.S./Ger.)
Roxanne Nouban
1984
CHEECH AND CHONG'S THE CORSICAN BROTHERS(1984)
Claude Nougaro
MARRIED WOMAN, THE(1965, Fr.), m
Nabila Nouhy
EGYPT BY THREE(1953)
Shlomo Nouman
SIMCHON FAMILY, THE(1969, Israel), p
Jacques-Louis Nounez
L'ATALANTE(1947, Fr.), p
Frazier Nounnan
Misc. Silents
KEY TO POWER, THE(1918)
Michael Nouri
FLASHDANCE(1983)
A.A. Nourie
RAMPARTS WE WATCH, THE(1940)
Helene Nourry
SICILIAN CLAN, THE(1970, Fr.), cos
Pierre Nourry
IS PARIS BURNING?(1966, U.S./Fr.), cos; FRENCH CONSPIRACY, THE(1973, Fr.), cos; VIOLETTE(1978, Fr.), cos
Allen Nourse
PUSHOVER(1954); CELL 2455, DEATH ROW(1955); PHENIX CITY STORY, THE(1955); TIGHT SPOT(1955); ODDS AGAINST TOMORROW(1959)
Dorothy Nourse
Silents
SORROWS OF SATAN(1926)
Neysa Nourse
BELOVED(1934)
Alain Noury
WANDERER, THE(1969, Fr.)
Lachi Nov
MAGICIAN OF LUBLIN, THE(1979, Israel/Ger.)
Alex Nova
Silents
MARE NOSTRUM(1926)
Cleo Nova
LOVE MERCHANT, THE(1966); TASTE OF FLESH, A(1967)
Misc. Talkies
BED OF VIOLENCE(1967)
Harry Nova
FAKE'S PROGRESS(1950, Brit.)
Hedda Nova
Silents
BAR SINISTER, THE(1917); BY THE WORLD FORGOT(1918); SPITFIRE OF SEVILLE, THE(1919); MASK, THE(1921)
Misc. Silents
CHANGING WOMAN, THE(1918); SIGN INVISIBLE, THE(1918); CALIBRE 38(1919); CRIMSON GARDENIA, THE(1919); WHAT EVERY WOMAN WANTS(1919); SHADOWS OF THE WEST(1921); GOLDEN SILENCE(1923); GOLD HUNTERS, THE(1925)
Lou Nova
THOROUGHLY MODERN MILLIE(1967); SWING FEVER(1943); JOE PALOOKA, CHAMP(1946); SOMEWHERE IN THE NIGHT(1946); CALENDAR GIRL(1947); LOVE AND LEARN(1947); COWBOY AND THE PRIZEFIGHTER(1950); WHERE THE SIDEWALK ENDS(1950); DOUBLE DYNAMITE(1951); HALF ANGEL(1951); INSIDE STRAIGHT(1951); RED BADGE OF COURAGE, THE(1951); CLIPPED WINGS(1953); SALOME(1953); PRINCE VALIANT(1954); WORLD FOR RANSOM(1954); LEATHER SAINT, THE(1956); WHAT A WAY TO GO(1964); BLACKBEARD'S GHOST(1968)
Ludmilla Nova
SLIPPER AND THE ROSE, THE(1976, Brit.)
Renza Nova
VOYAGE TO THE END OF THE UNIVERSE(1963, Czech.)
Joseph M. Novac
DESPERADO, THE(1954), ph; TWO GUNS AND A BADGE(1954), ph
Karel Novacek
FIFTH HORSEMAN IS FEAR, THE(1968, Czech.)
Edgar Novack
SNIPER, THE(1952)
Peggy Novack
OLD MOTHER RILEY IN SOCIETY(1940, Brit.); WOMEN AREN'T ANGELS(1942, Brit.)
Shelly Novack
TELL THEM WILLIE BOY IS HERE(1969); AIRPORT(1970); KANSAS CITY BOMBER(1972); VIGILANTE FORCE(1976)
Blaine Novak
THEY ALL LAUGHED(1981), a, p
1984
STRANGERS KISS(1984), a, w; UP THE CREEK(1984)
Debbie Novak
HE KNOWS YOU'RE ALONE(1980)
Eva Novak
MEDICINE MAN, THE(1930); PHANTOM OF THE DESERT(1930); APOLOGY FOR MURDER(1945); BELLS OF ST. MARY'S, THE(1945); BLACKMAIL(1947); FOUR FACES WEST(1948); I, JANE DOE(1948); HELLFIRE(1949); BLONDE BANDIT, THE(1950); SUNSET BOULEVARD(1950); TALL MAN RIDING(1955); KETTLES ON OLD MACDONALD'S FARM, THE(1957); SERGEANT RUTLEDGE(1960); MAN WHO SHOT LIBERTY VALANCE, THE(1962); WILD SEED(1965)
Silents
TESTING BLOCK, THE(1920); LAST TRAIL(1921); O'MALLEY OF THE MOUNTED(1921); TORRENT, THE(1921); CHASING THE MOON(1922); GREAT NIGHT,

THE(1922); MAKING A MAN(1922); MAN WHO SAW TOMORROW, THE(1922); SKY HIGH(1922); DOLLAR DEVILS(1923); NOISE IN NEWBORO, A(1923); TEMPTATION(1923); TIGER'S CLAW, THE(1923); LAUGHING AT DANGER(1924); LURE OF THE YUKON(1924); RACING FOR LIFE(1924); FEARLESS LOVER, THE(1925); NORTHERN CODE(1925); SALLY(1925); DIXIE FLYER, THE(1926); IRENE(1926); NO MAN'S GOLD(1926)
Misc. Silents
FEUD, THE(1919); SPEED MANIAC, THE(1919); DAREDEVIL, THE(1920); DESERT LOVE(1920); UP IN MARY'S ATTIC(1920); WANTED AT HEADQUARTERS(1920); ROUGH DIAMOND, THE(1921); SMART SEX, THE(1921); SOCIETY SECRETS(1921); TRAILIN'(1921); WOLVES OF THE NORTH(1921); BARRIERS OF FOLLY(1922); MAN FROM HELL'S RIVER, THE(1922); UP AND GOING(1922); BOSTON BLACKIE(1923); MAN LIFE PASSED BY, THE(1923); BATTLING FOOL, THE(1924); BATTLING MASON(1924); BEAUTIFUL SINNER, THE(1924); FATAL MISTAKE, THE(1924); FIGHT FOR HONOR, A(1924); LISTEN LESTER(1924); MISSING DAUGHTERS(1924); SAFE GUARDED(1924); TAINTED MONEY(1924); WOMEN FIRST(1924); MILLIONAIRE POLICEMAN, THE(1926); 30 BELOW ZERO(1926); DUTY'S REWARD(1927); RED SIGNALS(1927)
Eve Novak
TOPEKA TERROR, THE(1945); ROBIN OF TEXAS(1947); RIDE A VIOLENT MILE(1957)
George Novak
MAD MAX(1979, Aus.); PIRATE MOVIE, THE(1982, Aus.)
Harry Novak
MACHISMO–40 GRAVES FOR 40 GUNS(1970)
Istvan Novak
WITNESS, THE(1982, Hung.)
1984
BRADY'S ESCAPE(1984, U.S./Hung.)
Ivan Novak
DESPERADO TRAIL, THE(1965, Ger./Yugo.)
James Novak
ELECTRIC HORSEMAN, THE(1979)
Jane Novak
HOLLYWOOD BOULEVARD(1936); GHOST TOWN(1937); PRISON GIRL(1942); YANKS ARE COMING, THE(1942); MAN OF COURAGE(1943); DESERT FURY(1947); FILE ON THELMA JORDAN, THE(1950); FURIES, THE(1950); PAID IN FULL(1950)
Silents
SCARLET SIN, THE(1915); TARGET, THE(1916); INNOCENT SINNER, THE(1917); NINE O'CLOCK TOWN, A(1918); MONEY CORRAL, THE(1919); ISOBEL(1920); THELMA(1922); DIVORCE(1923); JEALOUS HUSBANDS(1923); LULLABY, THE(1924); PRUDES FALL, THE(1924, Brit.); LAZYBONES(1925); LURE OF THE WILD, THE(1925); FREE LIPS(1928)
Misc. Silents
LITTLE BROTHER OF THE RICH, A(1915); WHITE SCAR, THE(1915); IRON HAND, THE(1916); EYES OF THE WORLD, THE(1917); SPIRIT OF '76, THE(1917); CLAWS OF THE HUN, THE(1918); SELFISH YATES(1918); STRING BEANS(1918); TEMPLE OF DUSK, THE(1918); TIGER MAN, THE(1918); COMING OF THE LAW, THE(1919); HIS DEBT(1919); MAN'S DESIRE(1919); TREAT 'EM ROUGH(1919); WAGON TRACKS(1919); WOLF, THE(1919); BEHIND THE DOOR(1920); GOLDEN TRAIL, THE(1920); GREAT ACCIDENT, THE(1920); RIVER'S END, THE(1920); KAZAN(1921); OTHER WOMAN, THE(1921); ROADS OF DESTINY(1921); THREE WORD BRAND(1921); BELLE OF ALASKA(1922); COLLEEN OF THE PINES(1922); ROSARY, THE(1922); SNOWSHOE TRAIL, THE(1922); SOUL OF A WOMAN, THE(1922); MAN LIFE PASSED BY, THE(1923); MAN WITHOUT A HEART, THE(1924); TWO SHALL BE BORN(1924); DANGER SIGNAL, THE(1925); SHARE AND SHARE ALIKE(1925); SUBSTITUTE WIFE, THE(1925); LOST AT SEA(1926); WHISPERING CANYON(1926); CLOSED GATES(1927); WHAT PRICE LOVE(1927); REDSKIN(1929)
Jani Novak
HILDUR AND THE MAGICIAN(1969)
Jeritza Novak
TREASURE OF MONTE CRISTO(1949)
Joe Novak
FLIGHT(1929), ph; HELL FIRE AUSTIN(1932), ph; RIDE THE HIGH IRON(1956), ph
Joseph Novak
WHEN A MAN SEES RED(1934), ph; JEANNE EAGELS(1957)
June Novak
FOREIGN CORRESPONDENT(1940)
Kim Novak
PHFFFT!(1954); PUSHOVER(1954); FIVE AGAINST THE HOUSE(1955); MAN WITH THE GOLDEN ARM, THE(1955); SON OF SINBAD(1955); EDDY DUCHIN STORY, THE(1956); JEANNE EAGELS(1957); PAL JOEY(1957); BELL, BOOK AND CANDLE(1958); VERTIGO(1958); MIDDLE OF THE NIGHT(1959); PEPE(1960); STRANGERS WHEN WE MEET(1960); BOYS' NIGHT OUT(1962); NOTORIOUS LANDLADY, THE(1962), a, cos; KISS ME, STUPID(1964); OF HUMAN BONDAGE(1964, Brit.); AMOROUS ADVENTURES OF MOLL FLANDERS, THE(1965); LEGEND OF LYLAH CLARE, THE(1968); GREAT BANK ROBBERY, THE(1969); TALES THAT WITNESS MADNESS(1973, Brit.); WHITE BUFFALO, THE(1977); JUST A GIGOLO(1979, Ger.); MIRROR CRACK'D, THE(1980, Brit.)
Lenka Novak
MOONSHINE COUNTY EXPRESS(1977); COACH(1978); VAMPIRE HOOKERS, THE(1979, Phil.)
Lindsey Novak
PSYCHOTRONIC MAN, THE(1980)
Marilyn [Kim] Novak
FRENCH LINE, THE(1954)
Mel Novak
BLACK BELT JONES(1974); TRUCK TURNER(1974); ULTIMATE WARRIOR, THE(1975); GAME OF DEATH, THE(1979); FORCE: FIVE(1981)
Misc. Talkies
LOVELY BUT DEADLY(1983)
Mickell Novak
TURNABOUT(1940), w; ONE MILLION YEARS B.C.(1967, Brit./U.S.), w
Mikell Novak
ONE MILLION B.C.(1940), w
Mykola Novak
GIRL FROM POLTAVA(1937)

Patsy Novak
NIGHT PASSAGE(1957)

Peggy Novak
I ADORE YOU(1933, Brit.); SMITHY(1933, Brit.); DIPLOMATIC LOVER, THE(1934, Brit.); MUSIC HALL(1934, Brit.); OH NO DOCTOR!(1934, Brit.); COCK O' THE NORTH(1935, Brit.); FLOOD TIDE(1935, Brit.); JIMMY BOY(1935, Brit.); LITTLE BIT OF BLUFF, A(1935, Brit.); REAL BLOKE, A(1935, Brit.); SCHOOL FOR STARS(1935, Brit.); LUCK OF THE TURF(1936, Brit.); SONG OF THE ROAD(1937, Brit.); HE LOVED AN ACTRESS(1938, Brit.); SAILING ALONG(1938, Brit.); SAVE A LITTLE SUN-SHINE(1938, Brit.); SOUTH RIDING(1938, Brit.); WARE CASE, THE(1939, Brit.); HE FOUND A STAR(1941, Brit.); SOMEWHERE IN CAMP(1942, Brit.)

Virginia Novak
Silents
THELMA(1922)

Jana Novakova
LOVES OF A BLONDE(1966, Czech.); END OF AUGUST AT THE HOTEL OZONE, THE(1967, Czech.); SKI FEVER(1969, U.S./Aust./Czech.); 24-HOUR LOVER(1970, Ger.)

Mickell Noval
ROAD SHOW(1941), w

Medea Novara
MAD EMPRESS, THE(1940)

N. Novarese
BLAZING SADDLES(1974), cos

Nino Novarese
AFFAIRS OF MESSALINA, THE(1954, Ital.), p,d&w; CROSSED SWORDS(1954), cos; LOVES OF THREE QUEENS, THE(1954, Ital./Fr.), w; SHADOW OF THE EA-GLE(1955, Brit.), cos; STORY OF RUTH, THE(1960), cos; ZACHARIAH(1971), cos; TERMINAL MAN, THE(1974), cos

Vittorio Nine Novarese
FRANCIS OF ASSISI(1961), cos

Vittorio Nino Novarese
PRINCE OF FOXES(1949), cos; WILD IS THE WIND(1957), w; SAVAGE INNO-CENTS, THE(1960, Brit.), cos; SPARTACUS(1960), tech adv; CLEOPATRA(1963), cos; AGONY AND THE ECSTASY, THE(1965), cos; GREATEST STORY EVER TOLD, THE(1965), cos; WAR LORD, THE(1965), cos; KING'S PIRATE(1967), cos; CROM-WELL(1970, Brit.), cos

Tito Novaro
SOMBRERO(1953); LOS ASTRONAUTAS(1960, Mex.)

Amparo Novarro
TWO GIRLS AND A SAILOR(1944)

Estrelita Novarro
ROLLIN' WESTWARD(1939)

George Novarro
CRISIS(1950)

Nick Novarro
HOOTENANNY HOOT(1963); SCREAM OF THE BUTTERFLY(1965)

Ramon Novarro
DEVIL MAY CARE(1929); CALL OF THE FLESH(1930); IN GAY MADRID(1930); DAYBREAK(1931); MATA HARI(1931); SON OF INDIA(1931); HUDDLE(1932); SON-DAUGHTER, THE(1932); BARBARIAN, THE(1933); CAT AND THE FIDDLE(1934); LAUGHING BOY(1934); NIGHT IS YOUNG, THE(1935); SHEIK STEPS OUT, THE(1937); DESPERATE ADVENTURE, A(1938); WE WERE STRANGERS(1949); CRISIS(1950); OUTRIDERS, THE(1950); HELLER IN PINK TIGHTS(1960)
Silents
SCARAMOUCHE(1923); ARAB, THE(1924); BEN-HUR(1925); LOVER'S OATH, A(1925); ACROSS THE SINGAPORE(1928); FLYING FEET, THE(1929)
Misc. Silents
TRIFLING WOMEN(1922); WHERE THE PAVEMENT ENDS(1923); RED LILY, THE(1924); THY NAME IS WOMAN(1924); MIDSHIPMAN, THE(1925); LO-VERS?(1927); ROAD TO ROMANCE, THE(1927); STUDENT PRINCE IN OLD HEI-DELBERG, THE(1927); CERTAIN YOUNG MAN, A(1928); FORBIDDEN HOURS(1928); PAGAN, THE(1929)

Ramon Novarro, Jr.
PAGAN, THE(1929)

Fima Noveck
GENTLE RAIN, THE(1966, Braz.), ed; HALLUCINATION GENERATION(1966), ed; PILOT, THE(1979), ed; SUZANNE(1980, Can.), ed

The Novelites
I SURRENDER DEAR(1948); BELLBOY, THE(1960)

Adriana Novelli
MAMBO(1955, Ital.), ed; GREAT WAR, THE(1961, Fr., Ital.), ed; TWO WOMEN(1961, Ital./Fr.), ed; CONDEMNED OF ALTONA, THE(1963), ed; PASSIONATE THIEF, THE(1963, Ital.), ed; LOVE ON THE RIVIERA(1964, Fr./Ital.), ed; MARRIAGE–ITALIAN STYLE(1964, Fr./Ital.), ed; YESTERDAY, TODAY, AND TOMORROW(1964, Ital./Fr.), ed; BIG GUNDOWN, THE(1968, Ital.), ed; PLACE FOR LOVERS, A(1969, Ital./Fr.), ed; SUNFLOWER(1970, Fr./Ital.), ed; GARDEN OF THE FINZI-CONTINIS, THE(1976, Ital./Ger.), ed

Adrianni Novelli
KISS THE OTHER SHEIK(1968, Fr./Ital.), ed

Amedeo Novelli
FURY OF THE PAGANS(1963, Ital.)

Amleto Novelli
Silents
QUO VADIS?(1913, Ital.)

Andriana Novelli
WITCHES, THE(1969, Fr./Ital.), ed

Anthony Novelli
Misc. Silents
JULIUS CAESAR(1914, Ital.); FABIOLA(1923, Ital.)

Armando Novelli
SLAUGHTER HOTEL(1971, Ital.), p

Franco Novelli
ITALIAN JOB, THE(1969, Brit.)

Mario Novelli
FRAULEIN DOKTOR(1969, Ital./Yugo.)

Ivor Novello
RETURN OF THE RAT, THE(1929, Brit.), a, w; SYMPHONY IN TWO FLATS(1930, Brit.), a, w; ONCE A LADY(1931); BUT THE FLESH IS WEAK(1932), w; TARZAN, THE APE MAN(1932), w; I LIVED WITH YOU(1933, Brit.), a, w; SLEEPING CAR(1933, Brit.); AUTUMN CROCUS(1934, Brit.); PHANTOM FIEND, THE(1935, Brit.), a, w; GLAMOROUS NIGHT(1937, Brit.), w; RAT, THE(1938, Brit.), w; FREE AND EASY(1941), w; DANCING YEARS, THE(1950, Brit.), w, m; KING'S RHAPSO-DY(1955, Brit.), w, m
Silents
MAN WITHOUT DESIRE, THE(1923, Brit.), a, p; WHITE ROSE, THE(1923); RAT, THE(1925, Brit.), a, w; LODGER, THE(1926, Brit.); VORTEX, THE(1927, Brit.); WHEN BOYS LEAVE HOME(1928, Brit.), a, w
Misc. Silents
L'APPEL DU SANG(1920, Fr.); CARNIVAL(1921, Brit.); BOHEMIAN GIRL, THE(1922, Brit.); GYPSY PASSION(1922, Fr.); BONNIE PRINCE CHARLIE(1923, Brit.); TRIUMPH OF THE RAT, THE(1926, Brit.); CONSTANT NYMPH, THE(1928, Brit.); SOUTH SEA BUBBLE, A(1928, Brit.)

Jay Novello
FLIRTING WITH FATE(1938); TENTH AVENUE KID(1938); CALLING ALL MA-RINES(1939); BORDER LEGION, THE(1940); GIRL FROM HAVANA(1940); BAD MAN OF DEADWOOD(1941); CITADEL OF CRIME(1941); GREAT TRAIN ROBBERY, THE(1941); ROBIN HOOD OF THE PECOS(1941); SHERIFF OF TOMBSTONE(1941); SWAMP WOMAN(1941); THEY MET IN BOMBAY(1941); TWO GUN SHERIFF(1941); UNHOLY PARTNERS(1941); BELLS OF CAPISTRANO(1942); BROADWAY(1942); SLEEPYTIME GAL(1942); MAN FROM MUSIC MOUNTAIN(1943); PASSPORT TO SUEZ(1943); SLEEPY LAGOON(1943); DRAGON SEED(1944); PHANTOM LA-DY(1944); BULLFIGHTERS, THE(1945); CHICAGO KID, THE(1945); HOTEL BER-LIN(1945); RHAPSODY IN BLUE(1945); PERILOUS HOLIDAY(1946); KISS THE BLOOD OFF MY HANDS(1948); PORT SAID(1948); TELL IT TO THE JUDGE(1949); SIROCCO(1951); SMUGGLER'S ISLAND(1951); BIG SKY, THE(1952); CAPTAIN PI-RATE(1952); CATTLE TOWN(1952); IRON MISTRESS, THE(1952); MIRACLE OF OUR LADY OF FATIMA, THE(1952); OPERATION SECRET(1952); SNIPER, THE(1952); BENEATH THE 12-MILE REEF(1953); DIAMOND QUEEN(1953); HINDU, THE(1953, Brit.); MA AND PA KETTLE ON VACATION(1953); ROBE, THE(1953); CRIME WAVE(1954); GAMBLER FROM NATCHEZ, THE(1954); MAD MAGICIAN, THE(1954); BENGAZI(1955); PRODIGAL, THE(1955); SON OF SINBAD(1955); JA-GUAR(1956); LISBON(1956); PRIDE AND THE PASSION, THE(1957); PERFECT FURLOUGH, THE(1958); WONDERFUL COUNTRY, THE(1959); LOST WORLD, THE(1960); THIS REBEL BREED(1960); ATLANTIS, THE LOST CONTINENT(1961); POCKETFUL OF MIRACLES(1961); ESCAPE FROM ZAHRAIN(1962); MAN FROM THE DINERS' CLUB, THE(1963); ART OF LOVE, THE(1965); HARUM SCARUM(1965); SYLVIA(1965); VERY SPECIAL FAVOR, A(1965); WHAT DID YOU DO IN THE WAR, DADDY?(1966); CAPER OF THE GOLDEN BULLS, THE(1967); COMIC, THE(1969); DOMINO PRINCIPLE, THE(1977)

Roselle Novello
YOUNG SAVAGES, THE(1961), cos

Ugo Novello
CHINA IS NEAR(1968, Ital.), art d

Kari Noven
MC LINTOCK!(1963)

Judy Novgrad
YOU LIGHT UP MY LIFE(1977)

Judith Novgrod
NIGHTWING(1979)
Misc. Talkies
ALIEN ZONE(1978)

Angelo Novi
GOOD, THE BAD, AND THE UGLY, THE(1967, Ital./Span.)

C.M. Novi
GIVE ME YOUR HEART(1936), art d

Charles Novi
COMET OVER BROADWAY(1938), art d; CRIME SCHOOL(1938), art d; KING OF THE UNDERWORLD(1939), art d; FATHER IS A PRINCE(1940), art d; SINGAPORE WOMAN(1941), art d; UNDERGROUND(1941), art d; DESERT SONG, THE(1943), art d; FIND THE BLACKMAILER(1943), art d; MYSTERIOUS DOCTOR, THE(1943), art d; SHINE ON, HARVEST MOON(1944), art d; TO HAVE AND HAVE NOT(1944), art d

Enrique Novi
GREEN ICE(1981, Brit.)

Ken Novick
FOXES(1980)

Margot Novick
THREE TOUGH GUYS(1974, U.S./Ital.)

Jan Novicki
ANNA(1981, Fr./Hung.)

David Novik
DARK SIDE OF TOMORROW, THE(1970), p

Lou Novikoff
STRATTON STORY, THE(1949)

Nicholas Novikoff
LEFT-HANDED WOMAN, THE(1980, Ger.)

Rashel Novikoff
HARRY AND TONTO(1974); LENNY(1974); SUNSHINE BOYS, THE(1975); NEXT STOP, GREENWICH VILLAGE(1976); ANNIE HALL(1977)

A. Novikov
DESTINY OF A MAN(1961, USSR)

F.H. Novikov
Misc. Talkies
BLOOD COUPLE(1974), d

K. Novikov
MEET ME IN MOSCOW(1966, USSR)

L. Novikov
LAST GAME, THE(1964, USSR)

V. Novikov
CHILDHOOD OF MAXIM GORKY(1938, Russ.); ON HIS OWN(1939, USSR); OPTI-MISTIC TRAGEDY, THE(1964, USSR)

V.K. Novikov
ALEXANDER NEVSKY(1939)

M. Novikova
RESURRECTION(1963, USSR)

R. Novikova
GROWN-UP CHILDREN(1963, USSR), ed

Roman Novins
  I MET HIM IN PARIS(1937)

Alex Novinsky
  NOTHING SACRED(1937); SECOND HONEYMOON(1937); HAPPY LANDING(1938); THRILL OF A ROMANCE(1945)

Pierre Novion
  1984
  A NOS AMOURS(1984, Fr.)

Donald Novis
  BULLDOG DRUMMOND(1929); MONTE CARLO(1930); ONE HOUR WITH YOU(1932); SLIGHTLY TERRIFIC(1944); SWEETHEARTS OF THE U.S.A.(1944); DOWN MEMORY LANE(1949); MR. UNIVERSE(1951)

Julieta Novis
  MUSIC IN MY HEART(1940)

Nikolay Novlyanskiy
  HOME FOR TANYA, A(1961, USSR); LAST GAME, THE(1964, USSR)

Richard Novo
  UP IN SMOKE(1978)

Amadeo Novoa
  VIOLATED LOVE(1966, Arg.)

I. Novoderezhkin
  DESTINY OF A MAN(1961, USSR), art d; OPTIMISTIC TRAGEDY, THE(1964, USSR), art d; THREE SISTERS, THE(1969, USSR), art d

Novokshenov
  Silents
  STORM OVER ASIA(1929, USSR), w

Amadeo Novos
  DOLORES(1949, Span.)

I. Novoseltsev
  CITY OF YOUTH(1938, USSR)

Ivan Novoseltsev
  THIRTEEN, THE(1937, USSR)

I. Novoseltsev
  SEVEN BRAVE MEN(1936, USSR)

Lucie Novot
  NIGHTS OF PRAGUE, THE(1968, Czech.)

Jarmila Novotna
  SEARCH, THE(1948); GREAT CARUSO, THE(1951)

Jarmilla Novotna
  LAST WALTZ, THE(1936, Brit.)

J.A. Novotny
  JOURNEY TO THE BEGINNING OF TIME(1966, Czech), w

Josef Novotny
  STOLEN DIRIGIBLE, THE(1966, Czech.), ph

Vaclav Novotny
  FIREMAN'S BALL, THE(1968, Czech.)

Vladimir Novotny
  MAN FROM THE FIRST CENTURY, THE(1961, Czech.), ph; LEMONADE JOE(1966, Czech.), ph, spec eff; SHOP ON MAIN STREET, THE(1966, Czech.), ph; HAPPY END(1968, Czech.), ph; MATTER OF DAYS, A(1969, Fr./Czech.), ph; ADRIFT(1971, Czech.), ph

Vittorio Novrese
  ROSSINI(1948, Ital.), w

Lester Novros
  FANTASIA(1940), anim

Mischa Novy
  MISTER 880(1950)

Slavko Novytsky
  ACROSS THE RIVER(1965)

Christopher Nowack
  HANKY-PANKY(1982), art d

A. Nowak
  PORTRAIT OF LENIN(1967, Pol./USSR)

Amram Nowak
  KING, MURRAY(1969), a, p

Christopher Nowak
  FORT APACHE, THE BRONX(1981), art d

Jerzy Nowak
  CAMERA BUFF(1983, Pol.)

John Nowak
  SUDDEN IMPACT(1983)

Jozef Nowak
  PORTRAIT OF LENIN(1967, Pol./USSR)

L. Nowak
  JOVITA(1970, Pol.)

Leopold Nowak
  FIRST START(1953, Pol.)

Marian Nowak
  JOAN OF THE ANGELS(1962, Pol.)

Sheryl Nowak
  DO NOT THROW CUSHIONS INTO THE RING(1970)

Adam Nowakowski
  EVE WANTS TO SLEEP(1961, Pol.), art d

Helen Nowell
  Silents
  PAYING THE LIMIT(1924)

Wedgewood Nowell
  CLEOPATRA(1934); MERRY WIDOW, THE(1934); TO MARY-WITH LOVE(1936); FIRST LADY(1937); STOLEN HOLIDAY(1937); YOU CAN'T TAKE IT WITH YOU(1938); EACH DAWN I DIE(1939); HOMICIDE BUREAU(1939); CALLING PHILO VANCE(1940); DIVE BOMBER(1941); ONE DANGEROUS NIGHT(1943); THAT NAZTY NUISANCE(1943); THEY WERE EXPENDABLE(1945); WOMAN IN THE WINDOW, THE(1945)
  Silents
  ADELE(1919); LORD LOVES THE IRISH, THE(1919); MAN WHO TURNED WHITE, THE(1919); ENTER MADAME(1922); SONG OF LIFE, THE(1922); THELMA(1922); ADAM'S RIB(1923); DON'T MARRY FOR MONEY(1923); JEALOUS HUSBANDS(1923)

Misc. Silents
  DISCIPLE, THE(1915); GOLDEN CLAW, THE(1915); DESERTER, THE(1916); BLACK ORCHIDS(1917); FLOWER OF DOOM, THE(1917); HAND THAT ROCKS THE CRADLE, THE(1917); PULSE OF LIFE, THE(1917); REWARD OF THE FAITHLESS, THE(1917); KITTY KELLY, M.D.(1919); "813"(1920); BEAUTY MARKET, THE(1920); CORSICAN BROTHERS, THE(1920); DREAM CHEATER, THE(1920); ETERNAL FLAME, THE(1922)

Wedgwood Nowell
  FUGITIVE LADY(1934); GAY BRIDE, THE(1934); FOLIES DERGERE(1935); GOLD DIGGERS OF 1937(1936); PARADISE FOR THREE(1938); DARK VICTORY(1939); NAUGHTY BUT NICE(1939); MEET JOHN DOE(1941); WATCH ON THE RHINE(1943)
  Misc. Silents
  MONEY ISN'T EVERYTHING(1918)

Erwin Nowiaszack
  DANTON(1983)

Jan Nowicki
  BARRIER(1966, Pol.); GOLEM(1980, Pol.)
  1984
  DIARY FOR MY CHILDREN(1984, Hung.)

Tom Nowicki
  1984
  HARRY AND SON(1984)

Jan Nowina-Przybylski
  YIDDLE WITH HIS FIDDLE(1937, Pol.), d

Michael Nowka
  CROSS OF IRON(1977, Brit., Ger.)

Eugene Nowland
  Misc. Silents
  BIRD OF PREY, A(1916), d; FLIGHT OF THE DUCHESS, THE(1916), d; MISS DECEPTION(1917), d; PEG O' THE SEA(1917), d

Eugenie Nowland
  Misc. Silents
  THREADS OF FATE(1917), d

Ray Nowland
  1984
  CAMEL BOY, THE(1984, Aus.), anim d

Chuck Nowlin
  JONIKO AND THE KUSH TA KA(1969)

Herman Nowlin
  FLAMING FEATHER(1951); CARRIE(1952)

Philomena Nowlin
  FIVE ON THE BLACK HAND SIDE(1973)
  Misc. Talkies
  MISS MELODY JONES(1973)

James E. Nownes
  NO WAY BACK(1976), ed; PENITENTIARY II(1982), ed

Hans Nowotny
  HIPPODROME(1961, Aust./Ger.), makeup

Rita-Maria Nowotny
  GOOSE GIRL, THE(1967, Ger.)

Andre Nox
  J'ACCUSE(1939, Fr.)
  Misc. Silents
  LA MONTEE VERS L'ACROPOLE(1920, Fr.); LE PENSEUR(1920, Fr.); LA MORT DU SOLEIL(1922, Fr.)

Nellie Noxon
  Silents
  GOLD RUSH, THE(1925)

Wilfred Noy
  INTERFERENCE(1928); CARELESS AGE(1929); DOCTOR'S SECRET(1929); FLIRTING WIDOW, THE(1930); LET US BE GAY(1930); LILIES OF THE FIELD(1930); STRICTLY UNCONVENTIONAL(1930); BARTON MYSTERY, THE(1932, Brit.); EMMA(1932); FORBIDDEN(1932); BROKEN ROSARY, THE(1934, Brit.), p; WHEN LONDON SLEEPS(1934, Brit.); CITY OF BEAUTIFUL NONSENSE, THE(1935, Brit.), p; KISS ME GOODBYE(1935, Brit.); ANNIE LAURIE(1936, Brit.), p; MELODY OF MY HEART(1936, Brit.), d; WELL DONE, HENRY(1936, Brit.), d, w; SONG OF THE FORGE(1937, Brit.), p; FATHER O'FLYNN(1938, Irish), p, d
  Silents
  KING CHARLES(1913, Brit.), d; ON THE BANKS OF ALLAN WATER(1916, Brit.), d; QUEEN MOTHER, THE(1916, Brit.), d; ASTHORE(1917, Brit.), d; LOST CHORD, THE(1917, Brit.), d; AVE MARIA(1918, Brit.), d; AS HE WAS BORN(1919, Brit.), d&w; FACE AT THE WINDOW, THE(1920, Brit.), d; JANICE MEREDITH(1924); EAGER LIPS(1927), d; SPIDER WEBS(1927), d; LINDA(1929), w
  Misc. Silents
  IN SEARCH OF A HUSBAND(1915, Brit.), d; UNDER THE RED ROBE(1915, Brit.), d; VERDICT OF THE HEART, THE(1915, Brit.), d; WHEN EAST MEETS WEST(1915, Brit.), d; LITTLE BREADWINNER, THE(1916, Brit.), d; LITTLE DAMOZEL, THE(1916, Brit.), d; MASTER OF MEN, A(1917, Brit.), d; SPINNER O' DREAMS(1918, Brit.), d; WHAT WOULD A GENTLEMAN DO?(1918, Brit.), d; CASTLE OF DREAMS(1919, Brit.), d; INHERITANCE(1920, Brit.), d; MARRIAGE LINES, THE(1921, Brit.), d; LITTLE MISS NOBODY(1923, Brit.), d; ROGUES OF THE TURF(1923, Brit.), d; TEMPTATION OF CARLTON EARLYE, THE(1923, Brit.), d; LOST CHORD, THE(1925), d; MIDNIGHT GIRL, THE(1925), d; DEVIL'S CAGE, THE(1928), d; CIRCUMSTANTIAL EVIDENCE(1929), d

Wilfrey Noy
  Misc. Silents
  LOVE OF AN ACTRESS, THE(1914, Brit.), d

Wilifred Noy
  Misc. Silents
  WHEN LONDON BURNED(1915, Brit.), d

Zachi Noy
  ENTER THE NINJA(1982)
  1984
  AMBASSADOR, THE(1984)

Phillip Noyce
  NEWSFRONT(1979, Aus.), d, w; HEATWAVE(1983, Aus.), d, w

Richard Noyce
  NIGHTHAWKS(1981); ONE DOWN TWO TO GO(1982)

Alfred Noyes
LADY AND THE BANDIT, THE(1951), w
Helen Noyes
NO ROOM FOR THE GROOM(1952)
Joanna Noyes
BREAKING POINT(1976)
1984
JUST THE WAY YOU ARE(1984)
Leslei Noyes
ALF 'N' FAMILY(1968, Brit.)
Richard Noyes
JUNIOR ARMY(1943)
Skeets Noyes
ROUGH WATERS(1930); ABBOTT AND COSTELLO IN HOLLYWOOD(1945); MIGHTY MCGURK, THE(1946); HIGH WALL, THE(1947); SEA OF GRASS, THE(1947)
Ken Noyle
KARATE, THE HAND OF DEATH(1961); SAVAGE HARVEST(1981), w
Yaacov Noyman
EVERY BASTARD A KING(1968, Israel), spec eff
Yoel Noyman
TRUNK TO CAIRO(1966, Israel/Ger.)
Ad Noyons
LIFT, THE(1983, Neth.)
Kamran Nozad
1984
MISSION, THE(1984)
Al Nozaki
WHEN WORLDS COLLIDE(1951), art d; HOUDINI(1953), art d; PONY EXPRESS(1953), art d
Albert Nozaki
BIG CLOCK, THE(1948), art d; SORROWFUL JONES(1949), art d; WAR OF THE WORLDS, THE(1953), art d; LIVING IT UP(1954), art d; LOVING YOU(1957), art d
Albert Nozala
TEN COMMANDMENTS, THE(1956), art d
M. Nozawa
BALLAD OF NARAYAMA(1961, Jap.), m
Shuji Nozawa
SUPERCHICK(1973)
Beatrice Nozes
Misc. Silents
SPHINX, THE(1916)
O. Nozhkina
TRAIN GOES TO KIEV, THE(1961, USSR); MOTHER AND DAUGHTER(1965, USSR)
Bruce Nozick
WANDERERS, THE(1979)
Hitomi Nozoe
FLOATING WEEDS(1970, Jap.)
Gaston Nrun
ROTHSCHILD(1938, Fr.), ph
Winston Ntshona
WILD GEESE, THE(1978, Brit.); ASHANTI(1979); DOGS OF WAR, THE(1980, Brit.); MARIGOLDS IN AUGUST(1980, South Africa)
1984
MARIGOLDS IN AUGUST(1984, S. Africa)
Serge Nubret
MY SON, THE HERO(1963, Ital./Fr.)
Laura Nucci
WE STILL KILL THE OLD WAY(1967, Ital.); BLOW TO THE HEART(1983, Ital.)
Gisella Nuccitelli
STORY WITHOUT WORDS(1981, Ital.), ed
Nada Nuchich
LUM AND ABNER ABROAD(1956)
Bamby Nucho
CIRCLE OF DECEIT(1982, Fr./Ger.)
Simon Nuchtern
GIRL GRABBERS, THE(1968), p&d; WOMEN IN CELL BLOCK 7(1977, Ital./U.S.), ed
1984
NEW YORK NIGHTS(1984), d; SAVAGE DAWN(1984), d; SILENT MADNESS(1984), p, d
Misc. Talkies
BODYGUARD, THE(1976), d; BROAD COALITION, THE(1972), d; WHAT DO I TELL THE BOYS AT THE STATION(1972), d; NIGHTKILLERS(1983), d
Paul Nuckles
LOSERS, THE(1970); THING WITH TWO HEADS, THE(1972), stunts; MITCHELL(1975); FINAL CHAPTER–WALKING TALL zero(1977), stunt coordinator; SATURDAY NIGHT FEVER(1977), stunts; STUNTS(1977), stunts
1984
PLACES IN THE HEART(1984)
Sam Nudell
YOUR THREE MINUTES ARE UP(1973)
Ugo Nudi
APPOINTMENT FOR MURDER(1954, Ital.), ph
Nudie
REAL LIFE(1979)
Dorothy Nuebert
BANG THE DRUM SLOWLY(1973)
Massimilino Nuefeld
BALL AT THE CASTLE(1939, Ital.), d
Sigmund Nuefeld, Jr.
CONQUEST OF THE EARTH(1980), d
Fay Nuell
MARJORIE MORNINGSTAR(1958); LADIES MAN, THE(1961)
Faye Nuell
HOT BLOOD(1956)
Delmar Nuetzman
HOUSE ON 92ND STREET, THE(1945)
Bob Nugent
1984
SHEENA(1984), spec eff

Carol Nugent
SECRET COMMAND(1944); LITTLE MISTER JIM(1946); GREEN DOLPHIN STREET(1947); IT HAD TO BE YOU(1947); SEA OF GRASS, THE(1947); TRAIL OF ROBIN HOOD(1950); IT'S A BIG COUNTRY(1951); BELLES ON THEIR TOES(1952); LUSTY MEN, THE(1952); STORY OF WILL ROGERS, THE(1952); FAST COMPANY(1953); MA AND PA KETTLE AT HOME(1954); CRIMSON KIMONO, THE(1959); INSIDE THE MAFIA(1959); VICE RAID(1959)
Carole Nugent
CHEAPER BY THE DOZEN(1950); LOST, LONELY AND VICIOUS(1958)
Danny Nugent
Misc. Talkies
BEWARE THE BLACK WIDOW(1968)
Eddie Nugent
GIRL IN THE SHOW, THE(1929); VAGABOND LOVER(1929); LOOSE ANKLES(1930); BRIGHT LIGHTS(1931); GIRLS DEMAND EXCITEMENT(1931); YOUNG SINNERS(1931); BEHIND STONE WALLS(1932); CROONER(1932); BEAUTY FOR SALE(1933); MEN ARE SUCH FOOLS(1933); PAST OF MARY HOLMES, THE(1933); THIS DAY AND AGE(1933); 42ND STREET(1933); THIS SIDE OF HEAVEN(1934); FIGHTING YOUTH(1935); FORCED LANDING(1935); GIRL O' MY DREAMS(1935); KENTUCKY BLUE STREAK(1935); LOTTERY LOVER(1935); NO RANSOM(1935); OLD HOMESTEAD, THE(1935); DANCING FEET(1936); DOUGHNUTS AND SOCIETY(1936); HARVESTER, THE(1936); PIGSKIN PARADE(1936); PRISON SHADOWS(1936); PUT ON THE SPOT(1936); RIO GRANDE ROMANCE(1936); ISLAND CAPTIVES(1937); MAN BETRAYED, A(1937); SPEED TO SPARE(1937); TWO MINUTES TO PLAY(1937); MEET THE MAYOR(1938)
Misc. Talkies
SKYBOUND(1935); JUST MY LUCK(1936)
Silents
MAN IN HOBBLES, THE(1928)
Edward Nugent
BELLAMY TRIAL, THE(1929); OUR MODERN MAIDENS(1929); UNTAMED(1929); CLANCY IN WALL STREET(1930); REMOTE CONTROL(1930); WAR NURSE(1930); NIGHT NURSE(1931); SHIPMATES(1931); DANCE, GIRL, DANCE(1933); DANCE MALL HOSTESS(1933); SHE LOVES ME NOT(1934); AH, WILDERNESS!(1935); BABY FACE HARRINGTON(1935); COLLEGE SCANDAL(1935); LOST IN THE STRATOSPHERE(1935); BIG GAME, THE(1936); BUNKER BEAN(1936); MAN OF THE PEOPLE(1937)
Silents
OUR DANCING DAUGHTERS(1928); DUKE STEPS OUT, THE(1929); FLYING FEET, THE(1929); OUR MODERN MAIDENS(1929); SINGLE MAN, A(1929)
Edward J. Nugent
BOUGHT(1931); LOCAL BOY MAKES GOOD(1931); STAR WITNESS(1931); UP POPS THE DEVIL(1931); HONOR OF THE PRESS(1932)
Eliott Nugent
WIVES NEVER KNOW(1936), d
Elliot Nugent
SO THIS IS COLLEGE(1929); MOUTHPIECE, THE(1932), d; IF I WERE FREE(1933), d; AND SO THEY WERE MARRIED(1936), d; PROFESSOR BEWARE(1938), d; CAT AND THE CANARY, THE(1939), d; NEVER SAY DIE(1939), d; MALE ANIMAL, THE(1942), w; CRYSTAL BALL, THE(1943), d
Elliott Nugent
FOR THE LOVE O'LIL(1930); NAVY BLUES(1930); NOT SO DUMB(1930); ROMANCE(1930); SINS OF THE CHILDREN(1930), a, w; UNHOLY THREE, THE(1930), a, w; WISE GIRLS(1930), a, w; LAST FLIGHT, THE(1931); LOCAL BOY MAKES GOOD(1931), w; VIRTUOUS HUSBAND(1931); LIFE BEGINS(1932), d; THREE-CORNERED MOON(1933), a, d; WHISTLING IN THE DARK(1933), d&w; SHE LOVES ME NOT(1934), d; STRICTLY DYNAMITE(1934), d; TWO ALONE(1934), d; COLLEGE SCANDAL(1935), d; ENTER MADAME(1935), d; LOVE IN BLOOM(1935), d; SPLENDOR(1935), d; IT'S ALL YOURS(1937), d; THUNDER IN THE CITY(1937, Brit.); GIVE ME A SAILOR(1938), d; NOTHING BUT THE TRUTH(1941), d; MALE ANIMAL, THE(1942), d; STAGE DOOR CANTEEN(1943); UP IN ARMS(1944), d; MY FAVORITE BRUNETTE(1947), d; WELCOME STRANGER(1947), a, d; MY GIRL TISA(1948), d; GREAT GATSBY, THE(1949), d; MR. BELVEDERE GOES TO COLLEGE(1949), d; SKIPPER SURPRISED HIS WIFE, THE(1950), d; MY BROTHER, THE OUTLAW(1951), d; JUST FOR YOU(1952), d; SHE'S WORKING HER WAY THROUGH COLLEGE(1952), w; PROFESSIONALS, THE(1966), d; GREAT GATSBY, THE(1974), d
Frank Nugent
SHE WORE A YELLOW RIBBON(1949), w; TULSA(1949), w; ANGEL FACE(1953), w; THEY RODE WEST(1954), w; TALL MEN, THE(1955), w; GUNMAN'S WALK(1958), w; LAST HURRAH, THE(1958), w; TWO RODE TOGETHER(1961), w; DONOVAN'S REEF(1963), w; INCIDENT AT PHANTOM HILL(1966), w
Frank S. Nugent
FORT APACHE(1948), w; THREE GODFATHERS, THE(1948), w; TWO FLAGS WEST(1950), w; WAGONMASTER(1950), w; QUIET MAN, THE(1952), w; PARATROOPER(1954, Brit.), w; TROUBLE IN THE GLEN(1954, Brit.), w; MISTER ROBERTS(1955), w; SEARCHERS, THE(1956), w; RISING OF THE MOON, THE(1957, Ireland), w
J.C. Nugent
ALIBI(1929), w; BIG HOUSE, THE(1930); LOVE IN THE ROUGH(1930); NAVY BLUES(1930), a, w; REMOTE CONTROL(1930); SINS OF THE CHILDREN(1930), w; THEY LEARNED ABOUT WOMEN(1930); UNHOLY THREE, THE(1930), w; WISE GIRLS(1930), a, w; LOCAL BOY MAKES GOOD(1931), w; MANY A SLIP(1931); MILLIONAIRE, THE(1931); VIRTUOUS HUSBAND(1931); LOVE IN BLOOM(1935); MEN WITHOUT NAMES(1935); IT'S ALL YOURS(1937); LIFE BEGINS IN COLLEGE(1937); STAND-IN(1937); STAR IS BORN, A(1937); THIS IS MY AFFAIR(1937); GIVE ME A SAILOR(1938); MIDNIGHT INTRUDER(1938); FOLLIES GIRL(1943)
Judith Nugent
SUMMER RUN(1974)
Judy Nugent
IT HAD TO BE YOU(1947); NIGHT STAGE TO GALVESTON(1952); DOWN LAREDO WAY(1953); MA AND PA KETTLE AT HOME(1954); MAGNIFICENT OBSESSION(1954); NAVY WIFE(1956); THERE'S ALWAYS TOMORROW(1956); GIRL MOST LIKELY, THE(1957); HIGH SCHOOL CAESAR(1960)
Judy Ann Nugent
CITY ACROSS THE RIVER(1949)
Lee Nugent
UP IN ARMS(1944); LOST BOUNDARIES(1949)

Moya Nugent
Silents
AUCTION MART, THE(1920, Brit.)
Misc. Silents
LIGHTS OF HOME, THE(1920, Brit.)
Richard Nugent
SAHARA(1943); MASTER RACE, THE(1944); PEARL OF DEATH, THE(1944); STORY OF DR. WASSELL, THE(1944); OF HUMAN BONDAGE(1946)
Twana Nugent
MR. SYCAMORE(1975)
Charles Nuitter
DR. COPPELIUS(1968, U.S./Span.), d&w
Yoshio Nukano
Misc. Talkies
SILENT STRANGER, THE(1975)
Gary Nulsen
SIX WEEKS(1982)
Yoichi Numata
HAPPINESS OF US ALONE(1962, Jap.)
Numes, Jr.
BONNE CHANCE(1935, Fr.)
Ronald Numkena
PRESIDENT'S LADY, THE(1953)
Ronald Alan Numkena
NAKED JUNGLE, THE(1953)
Anthony Numkena [Earl Holliman]
PONY SOLDIER(1952); DESTINATION GOBI(1953); SECRET OF THE INCAS(1954); ESCAPE TO BURMA(1955); STRANGE LADY IN TOWN(1955); WESTWARD HO THE WAGONS!(1956)
Bob Nunes
EVERYBODY'S DANCIN'(1950), p, w
Gilberto Costa Nunes
1984
HARRY AND SON(1984)
Grafton Nunes
LOVELESS, THE(1982), p
Michel Nunes
MAYERLING(1968, Brit./Fr.)
Robert Nunes
PORT OF HELL(1955), p
Robert A. Nunes
THUNDER PASS(1954), p
Alfred Nunez
FANCY PANTS(1950)
Daniel Nunez
LEGEND OF THE LONE RANGER, THE(1981)
Miguel A. Nunez, Jr.
1984
JOY OF SEX(1984)
Pearl Nunez
O LUCKY MAN!(1973, Brit.)
Ricardo Nunez
DOLORES(1949, Span.), p
Victor Nunez
GAL YOUNG UN(1979), p,d,w&ph, ed
1984
FLASH OF GREEN, A(1984), d&w, ph, ed
Charles Nungesser
Misc. Silents
SKY RAIDER, THE(1925)
Vicki Nunis
FIREBALL JUNGLE(1968)
Margit Nunke
HIPPODROME(1961, Aust./Ger.)
Don Nunley
1984
RAW COURAGE(1984), art d
Donald Nunley
STUDENT BODIES(1981), prod d
Donald B. Nunley
EDDIE MACON'S RUN(1983)
Alice Nunn
JOHNNY GOT HIS GUN(1971); STEAGLE, THE(1971); MOMMIE DEAREST(1981)
1984
HOUSE WHERE DEATH LIVES, THE(1984)
Misc. Talkies
FANGS(1974)
Chris Nunn
RETURN OF THE JEDI(1983)
Judy Nunn
Misc. Talkies
NEWMAN SHAME, THE(1977)
Larry Nunn
HULLABALOO(1940); STRIKE UP THE BAND(1940); MEN OF BOYS TOWN(1941); BORN TO SING(1942); CAIRO(1942); MAJOR AND THE MINOR, THE(1942); NAVY WAY, THE(1944); DESPERATE(1947)
Mandy Nunn
1984
TOP SECRET!(1984)
Terri Nunn
THANK GOD IT'S FRIDAY(1978)
Trevor Nunn
HEDDA(1975, Brit.), d&w
Wayne Nunn
ONE THIRD OF A NATION(1939)
William Nunn
GROUNDSTAR CONSPIRACY, THE(1972, Can.)

Ralph Nunn-May
SONG FOR TOMORROW, A(1948, Brit.), p
Lesley Nunnerley
STRANGER'S MEETING(1957, Brit.); TALES THAT WITNESS MADNESS(1973, Brit.)
Leslie Nunnerley
PUMPKIN EATER, THE(1964, Brit.); SINISTER MAN, THE(1965, Brit.)
Bill Nunnery
HURRY UP OR I'LL BE 30(1973); PROWLER, THE(1981)
Pierre Nunzi
CHLOE IN THE AFTERNOON(1972, Fr.)
Ali Nur
YEAR OF LIVING DANGEROUSLY, THE(1982, Aus.)
Rudolf Nureyev
ROMEO AND JULIET(1966, Brit.); SWAN LAKE, THE(1967), a, ch; INVINCIBLE SIX, THE(1970, U.S./Iran), ch; DON QUIXOTE(1973, Aus.), a, d, ch; VALENTINO(1977, Brit.); EXPOSED(1983)
V. Nurganov
SOUND OF LIFE, THE(1962, USSR)
Philippe Nuridzany
LEONOR(1977, Fr./Span./Ital.), w
Michael Nurie
GOODBYE COLUMBUS(1969)
Karl Nurk
NAKED BRIGADE, THE(1965, U.S./Gr.)
Maila Nurmi
MAGIC SWORD, THE(1962)
Maila "Vampira" Nurmi
NIGHT OF THE GHOULS(1959)
Ruth Nurmi
THRILL OF A ROMANCE(1945)
Fred Nurney
FIVE GRAVES TO CAIRO(1943); THEY CAME TO BLOW UP AMERICA(1943); HITLER GANG, THE(1944); SUMMER STORM(1944); VOICE IN THE WIND(1944); ROYAL SCANDAL, A(1945); HOODLUM SAINT, THE(1946); NOTORIOUS(1946); O.S.S.(1946); SCANDAL IN PARIS, A(1946); TWO SMART PEOPLE(1946); 13 RUE MADELEINE(1946); CALCUTTA(1947); GOLDEN EARRINGS(1947); B. F.'S DAUGHTER(1948); COBRA STRIKES, THE(1948); LETTER FROM AN UNKNOWN WOMAN(1948); SAXON CHARM, THE(1948); SLEEP, MY LOVE(1948); GREAT SINNER, THE(1949); HOLD THAT BABY!(1949); ABBOTT AND COSTELLO IN THE FOREIGN LEGION(1950); MYSTERY SUBMARINE(1950); SOUTH SEA SINNER(1950); HAS ANYBODY SEEN MY GAL?(1952); ALL I DESIRE(1953); MAGNIFICENT OBSESSION(1954); THERE'S ALWAYS TOMORROW(1956)
Ahmad Nurradin
TOGETHER BROTHERS(1974)
Jim Nurtaugh
HAIL(1973)
Antoni Nurzynski
WALKOVER(1969, Pol.), ph
Mike Nusbaum
TOWING(1978)
Loredana Nuschiah
10,000 DOLLARS BLOOD MONEY(1966, Ital.)
Loredana Nusciak
FALL OF ROME, THE(1963, Ital.); GLADIATORS 7(1964, Span./Ital.); SUPERARGO VERSUS DIABOLICUS(1966, Ital./Span.)
Lorendana Nusciak
DJANGO(1966 Ital./Span.)
I. Nusinov
WELCOME KOSTYA!(1965, USSR), w
Joseph Nussbaum
SAN QUENTIN(1937), md; SECOND WOMAN, THE(1951), md
Mike Nussbaum
T.R. BASKIN(1971); HARRY AND TONTO(1974)
Morris Nussbaum
REUNION IN VIENNA(1933)
Ralph Nussbaum
FEMALE BUNCH, THE(1969), p, w
Raphael Nussbaum
INVISIBLE MAN, THE(1963, Ger.), p&d, w; SINAI COMMANDOS: THE STORY OF THE SIX DAY WAR(1968, Israel/Ger.), p&d, w; PETS(1974), p&d
Misc. Talkies
AMOROUS ADVENTURES OF DON QUIXOTE AND SANCHO PANZA, THE(1976), d
James Nusser
IT SHOULD HAPPEN TO YOU(1954); HELL CANYON OUTLAWS(1957); HAIL, HERO!(1969); CAHILL, UNITED STATES MARSHAL(1973)
Jim Nusser
ONE GIRL'S CONFESSION(1953)
Simon Nutchern
COWARDS(1970), p,d&w
Al Nuti
ON THE RIGHT TRACK(1981)
Sergio Nuti
EYES, THE MOUTH, THE(1982, Ital./Fr.), ed
George Nutkins
SPRING AND PORT WINE(1970, Brit.)
Jonathan Nutt
FFOLKES(1980, Brit.)
Frederica Nutter
MIGHTY CRUSADERS, THE(1961, Ital.), w
Mayf Nutter
STAY HUNGRY(1976)
1984
STONE BOY, THE(1984)
Nancy Nutter
DAVID AND LISA(1962)

Tarah Nutter
WITHOUT WARNING(1980); CHILLY SCENES OF WINTER(1982)
George Nutting
PRIZE FIGHTER, THE(1979)
Pete Nutton
NELLY'S VERSION(1983, Brit.), art d
France Nuyen
IN LOVE AND WAR(1958); SOUTH PACIFIC(1958); LAST TIME I SAW ARCHIE, THE(1961); DIAMOND HEAD(1962); GIRL NAMED TAMIRO, A(1962); SATAN NEVER SLEEPS(1962); MAN IN THE MIDDLE(1964, U.S./Brit.); DIMENSION 5(1966); ONE MORE TRAIN TO ROB(1971); BIG GAME, THE(1972); BATTLE FOR THE PLANET OF THE APES(1973)
Misc. Talkies
SLINGSHOT(1971)
Bruno Nuyteen
POSSESSION(1981, Fr./Ger.), ph
Bruno Nuyten
GOING PLACES(1974, Fr.), ph
Bruno Nuytten
BAROCCO(1976, Fr.), ph; BRONTE SISTERS, THE(1979, Fr.), ph; FRENCH POSTCARDS(1979), ph; BRUBAKER(1980), ph; LIKE A TURTLE ON ITS BACK(1981, Fr.), ph; INQUISITOR, THE(1982, Fr.), ph
1984
LIFE IS A BED OF ROSES(1984, Fr.), ph
Viktor Nuzhnyy
TSAR'S BRIDE, THE(1966, USSR)
Andrew R. Nuzzo
1984
PHILADELPHIA EXPERIMENT, THE(1984)
Ferruccio Nuzzo
GOSPEL ACCORDING TO ST. MATTHEW, THE(1966, Fr., Ital.)
John Nuzzo
Misc. Talkies
BOSS LADY(1982)
Wilbur Nyabongo
1984
SHEENA(1984)
Juli Nyako
FORBIDDEN RELATIONS(1983, Hung.)
Borje Nyberg
HERE'S YOUR LIFE(1968, Swed.)
Mary Ann Nyberg
STAR IS BORN, A(1954), cos
Mary Anne Nyberg
LILI(1953), cos
Peter Nyberg
IN GOD WE TRUST(1980)
Charles Nyby
DESTINATION TOKYO(1944), ed
Chris Nyby
FIGHTER SQUADRON(1948), ed; SECOND FACE, THE(1950), ed
Christian Nyby
HOLLYWOOD CANTEEN(1944), ed; TO HAVE AND HAVE NOT(1944), ed; BIG SLEEP, THE(1946), ed; CLOAK AND DAGGER(1946), ed; JANIE GETS MARRIED(1946), ed; SHADOW OF A WOMAN(1946), ed; CHEYENNE(1947), ed; PURSUED(1947), ed; MY GIRL TISA(1948), ed; ONE SUNDAY AFTERNOON(1948), ed; RED RIVER(1948), ed; SOUTHSIDE 1-1000(1950), ed; TARZAN AND THE SLAVE GIRL(1950), ed; THING, THE(1951), d; BIG SKY, THE(1952), ed; HELL ON DEVIL'S ISLAND(1957), d; OPERATION CIA(1965), d; YOUNG FURY(1965), d; FIRST TO FIGHT(1967), d
Thelma Nyby
OPERATION CIA(1965), cos
Christian I. Nyby II
MISSION GALACTICA: THE CYLON ATTACK(1979), d
Rosali Nydegger
BLACK SPIDER, THE(1983, Swit.)
Barry Nye
NIKKI, WILD DOG OF THE NORTH(1961, U.S./Can.), makeup
Ben Nye
FALLEN ANGEL(1945), makeup; LEAVE HER TO HEAVEN(1946), makeup; SENTIMENTAL JOURNEY(1946), makeup; SOMEWHERE IN THE NIGHT(1946), makeup; 13 RUE MADELEINE(1946), makeup; BRASHER DOUBLOON, THE(1947), makeup; KISS OF DEATH(1947), makeup; CALL NORTHSIDE 777(1948), makeup; CRY OF THE CITY(1948), makeup; FURY AT FURNACE CREEK(1948), makeup; IRON CURTAIN, THE(1948), makeup; LETTER TO THREE WIVES, A(1948), makeup; ROAD HOUSE(1948), makeup; SITTING PRETTY(1948), makeup; SNAKE PIT, THE(1948), makeup; STREET WITH NO NAME, THE(1948), makeup; THAT WONDERFUL URGE(1948), makeup; UNFAITHFULLY YOURS(1948), makeup; WALLS OF JERICHO(1948), makeup; HOUSE OF STRANGERS(1949), makeup; MOTHER IS A FRESHMAN(1949), makeup; THIEVES' HIGHWAY(1949), makeup; YOU'RE MY EVERYTHING(1949), makeup; PANIC IN THE STREETS(1950), makeup; WHERE THE SIDEWALK ENDS(1950), makeup; DAVID AND BATHSHEBA(1951), makeup; HOUSE ON TELEGRAPH HILL(1951), makeup; I CAN GET IT FOR YOU WHOLESALE(1951), makeup; I'D CLIMB THE HIGHEST MOUNTAIN(1951), makeup; PEOPLE WILL TALK(1951), makeup; RAWHIDE(1951), make up; THIRTEENTH LETTER, THE(1951), makeup; YOU'RE IN THE NAVY NOW(1951), makeup; DEADLINE-U.S.A.(1952), makeup; DIPLOMATIC COURIER(1952), makeup; MONKEY BUSINESS(1952), makeup; WE'RE NOT MARRIED(1952), makeup; WITH A SONG IN MY HEART(1952), makeup; DOWN AMONG THE SHELTERING PALMS(1953), makeup; NIAGARA(1953), makeup; PRESIDENT'S LADY, THE(1953), makeup; VICKI(1953), makeup; WHITE WITCH DOCTOR(1953), makeup; EGYPTIAN. THE(1954), makeup; GARDEN OF EVIL(1954), makeup; GOOD MORNING, MISS DOVE(1955), makeup; HOUSE OF BAMBOO(1955), makeup; UNTAMED(1955), makeup; MAN IN THE GREY FLANNEL SUIT, THE(1956), makeup; TEENAGE REBEL(1956), makeup; DESK SET(1957), makeup; KISS THEM FOR ME(1957), makeup; OH, MEN! OH, WOMEN!(1957), makeup; PEYTON PLACE(1957), makeup; LONG, HOT SUMMER, THE(1958), makeup; RALLY 'ROUND THE FLAG, BOYS!(1958), makeup; YOUNG LIONS, THE(1958), makeup; 10 NORTH FREDERICK(1958), makeup; STORY ON PAGE ONE, THE(1959), makeup; WARLOCK(1959), makeup; WOMAN OBSESSED(1959), makeup; LOST WORLD, THE(1960), makeup;

NORTH TO ALASKA(1960), makeup; SEVEN THIEVES(1960), makeup; WILD RIVER(1960), makeup; MARINES, LET'S GO(1961), makeup; MISTY(1961), makeup; PIRATES OF TORTUGA(1961), makeup; RETURN TO PEYTON PLACE(1961), makeup; RIGHT APPROACH, THE(1961), makeup; SANCTUARY(1961), makeup; SECOND TIME AROUND, THE(1961), makeup; TENDER IS THE NIGHT(1961), makeup; VOYAGE TO THE BOTTOM OF THE SEA(1961), makeup; WILD IN THE COUNTRY(1961), makeup; MADISON AVENUE(1962), makeup; MR. HOBBS TAKES A VACATION(1962), makeup; STATE FAIR(1962), makeup; SWINGIN' ALONG(1962), makeup; MOVE OVER, DARLING(1963), makeup; STRIPPER, THE(1963), makeup; TAKE HER, SHE'S MINE(1963), makeup; JOHN GOLDFARB, PLEASE COME HOME(1964), makeup; PLEASURE SEEKERS, THE(1964), makeup; RIO CONCHOS(1964), makeup; SHOCK TREATMENT(1964), makeup; WHAT A WAY TO GO(1964), makeup; FLIGHT OF THE PHOENIX, THE(1965), makeup; MORITURI(1965), makeup; REWARD, THE(1965), makeup; VON RYAN'S EXPRESS(1965), makeup; I DEAL IN DANGER(1966), makeup; OUR MAN FLINT(1966), makeup; SAND PEBBLES, THE(1966), makeup; SMOKY(1966), makeup; STAGECOACH(1966), makeup; WAY...-WAY OUT(1966), makeup; DOCTOR DOLITTLE(1967), makeup; FLIM-FLAM MAN, THE(1967), makeup; GUIDE FOR THE MARRIED MAN, A(1967), makeup; HOMBRE(1967), makeup; TONY ROME(1967), makeup; VALLEY OF THE DOLLS(1967), makeup; PLANET OF THE APES(1968), makeup; MARATHON MAN(1976), makeup
Bill Nye
BOILING POINT, THE(1932); DARK CORNER, THE(1946), makeup
Ben Nye, Jr.
NORWOOD(1970), makeup; SORCERER(1977), makeup; TERMS OF ENDEARMENT(1983), makeup
Ben Nye II
10(1979), makeup
Carrie Nye
GROUP, THE(1966); SEDUCTION OF JOE TYNAN, THE(1979); CREEPSHOW(1982)
Carrol Nye
Silents
FLYING FEET, THE(1929)
Carroll Nye
LAND OF THE SILVER FOX(1928); PERFECT CRIME, THE(1928); GIRL IN THE GLASS CAGE, THE(1929); LIGHT FINGERS(1929); MADAME X(1929); SQUALL, THE(1929); BISHOP MURDER CASE, THE(1930); LOTTERY BRIDE, THE(1930); SONS OF THE SADDLE(1930); HELL BENT FOR 'FRISCO(1931); LAWLESS WOMAN, THE(1931); NECK AND NECK(1931); ONE WAY TRAIL, THE(1931); TRAVELING SALESLADY, THE(1935); SING AND BE HAPPY(1937); CITY GIRL(1938); HOLD THAT CO-ED(1938); KENTUCKY MOONSHINE(1938); REBECCA OF SUNNYBROOK FARM(1938); GONE WITH THE WIND(1939); TRAIL BLAZERS, THE(1940)
Silents
BRUTE, THE(1927); GIRL FROM CHICAGO, THE(1927); SILVER SLAVE, THE(1927); WHAT EVERY GIRL SHOULD KNOW(1927); CRAIG'S WIFE(1928); JAZZLAND(1928); POWDER MY BACK(1928); WHILE THE CITY SLEEPS(1928)
Misc. Silents
CLASSIFIED(1925); EARTH WOMAN, THE(1926); HER HONOR THE GOVERNOR(1926); IMPOSTER, THE(1926); DEATH VALLEY(1927); LITTLE MICKEY GROGAN(1927); RACE FOR LIFE, A(1928); RINTY OF THE DESERT(1928); SPORTING AGE, THE(1928)
Clinton Nye
HOOKED GENERATION, THE(1969)
G. Raymond Nye
TENDERLOIN(1928); DEADLINE, THE(1932); IN OLD KENTUCKY(1935); GIT ALONG, LITTLE DOGIES(1937); CARRIE(1952)
Silents
ALI BABA AND THE FORTY THIEVES(1918); KINGDOM OF LOVE, THE(1918); JUNGLE TRAIL, THE(1919); JOYOUS TROUBLEMAKERS, THE(1920); SAND(1920); OLIVER TWIST, JR.(1921); QUEEN OF SHEBA, THE(1921); PARDON MY NERVE!(1922); SALOMY JANE(1923); FIGHTING COWARD, THE(1924); SAWDUST TRAIL(1924); LET 'ER BUCK(1925); NINE AND THREE-FIFTHS SECONDS(1925)
Misc. Silents
GIRL WITH THE CHAMPAGNE EYES, THE(1918); MOTHER, I NEED YOU(1918); UNDER THE YOKE(1918); BROKEN COMMANDMENTS(1919); LONE STAR RANGER, THE(1919); SALOME(1919); WHEN MEN DESIRE(1919); WOLVES OF THE NIGHT(1919); DRAG HARLAN(1920); SCUTTLERS, THE(1920); TO A FINISH(1921); WHILE THE DEVIL LAUGHS(1921); BOSS OF CAMP 4, THE(1922); TIGER LOVE(1924); SADDLE HAWK, THE(1925); DRIFTIN' THRU(1926)
Louis Nye
FACTS OF LIFE, THE(1960); SEX KITTENS GO TO COLLEGE(1960); LAST TIME I SAW ARCHIE, THE(1961); ZOTZ!(1962); STRIPPER, THE(1963); WHEELER DEALERS, THE(1963); WHO'S BEEN SLEEPING IN MY BED?(1963); GOOD NEIGHBOR SAM(1964); GUIDE FOR THE MARRIED MAN, A(1967); WON TON TON, THE DOG WHO SAVED HOLLYWOOD(1976); HARPER VALLEY, P.T.A.(1978); CHARGE OF THE MODEL-T'S(1979); FULL MOON HIGH(1982)
1984
CANNONBALL RUN II(1984)
Ned Nye
Misc. Silents
UNWELCOME WIFE, THE(1915)
Pat Nye
MR. PERRIN AND MR. TRAILL(1948, Brit.); ADVENTURES OF PC 49, THE(1949, Brit.); ISLAND RESCUE(1952, Brit.); MIRROR CRACK'D, THE(1980, Brit.)
Ralph Nye
DEVIL DOGS OF THE AIR(1935)
Raymond Nye
HARD HOMBRE(1931)
Maj. Walter Nye
STORY OF G.I. JOE, THE(1945), tech adv
William Nye
MAN'S LAND, A(1932); EYES IN THE NIGHT(1942)
Misc. Silents
FREE KISSES(1926), d
Paul Nygaard
1984
FOURTH MAN, THE(1984, Neth.)
Anna Nygh
SWEENEY 2(1978, Brit.)

Ian Nygren
1984
  KILLING HEAT(1984)
Jan Nygren
  MONTENEGRO(1981, Brit./Swed.)
Annika Nyhammar
  EMIGRANTS, THE(1972, Swed.)
Sirl Nyhand
  CARNY(1980)
Erik Nyhlen
  TOUCH, THE(1971, U.S./Swed.)
Z. T. Nyi
  DISPUTED PASSAGE(1939)
Emil Nyitray
  NO, NO NANETTE(1930), w; NO, NO NANETTE(1940), w; TEA FOR TWO(1950), w
Silents
  RECKLESS ROMANCE(1924), w
Sven Nykuist
  HURRICANE(1979), ph
Sven Nykvist
  LAUGHING IN THE SUNSHINE(1953, Brit./Swed.), ph; TRUE AND THE FALSE, THE(1955, Swed.), ph; NAKED NIGHT, THE(1956, Swed.), ph; VIRGIN SPRING, THE(1960, Swed.), ph; MATTER OF MORALS, A(1961, U.S./Swed.), ph; MAKE WAY FOR LILA(1962, Swed./Ger.), ph; THROUGH A GLASS DARKLY(1962, Swed.), ph; WINTER LIGHT, THE(1963, Swed.), ph; ALL THESE WOMEN(1964, Swed.), ph; GORILLA(1964, Swed.), d, ph; SILENCE, THE(1964, Swed.), ph; TO LOVE(1964, Swed.), ph; LOVING COUPLES(1966, Swed.), ph; PERSONA(1967, Swed.), ph; HOUR OF THE WOLF, THE(1968, Swed.), ph; SHAME(1968, Swed.), ph; FIRST LOVE(1970, Ger./Switz.), ph; PASSION OF ANNA, THE(1970, Swed.), ph; RITUAL, THE(1970, Swed.), ph; LAST RUN, THE(1971), ph; ONE DAY IN THE LIFE OF IVAN DENISO-VICH(1971, U.S./Brit./Norway), ph; TOUCH, THE(1971, U.S./Swed.), ph; CRIES AND WHISPERS(1972, Swed.), ph; SIDDHARTHA(1972), ph; DOVE, THE(1974, Brit.), ph; SCENES FROM A MARRIAGE(1974, Swed.), ph; BLACK MOON(1975, Fr.), ph; TERRORISTS, THE(1975, Brit.), ph; FACE TO FACE(1976, Swed.), ph; TENANT, THE(1976, Fr.), ph; SERPENT'S EGG, THE(1977, Ger./U.S.), ph; AUTUMN SONA-TA(1978, Swed.), ph; KING OF THE GYPSIES(1978), ph; PRETTY BABY(1978), ph; STARTING OVER(1979), ph; FROM THE LIFE OF THE MARIONETTES(1980, Ger.), ph; WILLIE AND PHIL(1980), ph; POSTMAN ALWAYS RINGS TWICE, THE(1981), ph; CANNERY ROW(1982), ph; FANNY AND ALEXANDER(1983, Swed./Fr./Ger.), ph; STAR 80(1983), ph
1984
  AFTER THE REHEARSAL(1984, Swed.), ph; SWANN IN LOVE(1984, Fr.Ger.), ph
Ray Nyles
  WONDER MAN(1945)
Judy Nylon
  OFFENDERS, THE(1980)
Edward Nylund
  MAN, A WOMAN AND A KILLER, A(1975)
Lena Nyman
  AUTUMN SONATA(1978, Swed.); ADVENTURES OF PICASSO, THE(1980, Swed.)
Lennart Nyman
  ADVENTURES OF PICASSO, THE(1980, Swed.)
Michael Nyman
  DRAUGHTSMAN'S CONTRACT, THE(1983, Brit.), m; NELLY'S VERSION(1983, Brit.), m
Ron Nyman
  DONOVAN'S REEF(1963); HUSTLE(1975)
Ronald Nyman
  PRIZE, THE(1963)
Russell Nype
  LOVE STORY(1970); CAN'T STOP THE MUSIC(1980)
Sarah Nyrick
  DEVIL'S EXPRESS(1975)
Inga Nyrod
  UNSTRAP ME(1968)
Linda Nystedt
  OUTSIDERS, THE(1983)
Anders Nystrom
  TORMENT(1947, Swed.); CHILDREN, THE(1949, Swed.)
Carl Nystrom
  DATE WITH A DREAM, A(1948, Brit.), w; MELODY CLUB(1949, Brit.), w; BEAUTI-FUL STRANGER(1954, Brit.), w; KEEP IT CLEAN(1956, Brit.), w
Inge Nystrom
  DUEL OF THE TITANS(1963, Ital.)
Ron Nyswaner
  SMITHEREENS(1982), w
1984
  MRS. SOFFEL(1984), w
Bruno Nytten
  BEST WAY, THE(1978, Fr.), ph
Bruce Nyznik
  WHY SHOOT THE TEACHER(1977, Can.), ed

Harry O
Silents
I WANT TO FORGET(1918), w
Barbara O'Bannon
STAKEOUT ON DOPE STREET(1958)
Dan O'Bannon
DARK STAR(1975), a, w, ed, prod d, set d, spec eff; ALIEN(1979), w; DEAD AND BURIED(1981), w; HEAVY METAL(1981, Can.), w, anim; BLUE THUNDER(1983), w
Fred O'Beck
Silents
WANTED–A COWARD(1927); OH, KAY(1928); VAMPING VENUS(1928)
Carol O'Blath
IT LIVES AGAIN(1978), ed
Mickey O'Boyle
LADY'S FROM KENTUCKY, THE(1939)
Bob O'Bradovich
FORCED ENTRY(1975), spec eff; BLOODSUCKING FREAKS(1982), makeup
Robert O'Bradovich
NO WAY TO TREAT A LADY(1968), makeup
O'Brady
MR. PEEK-A-BOO(1951, Fr.)
Frederic O'Brady
IT HAPPENED IN PARIS(1953, Fr.); NATHALIE(1958, Fr.); PICNIC ON THE GRASS(1960, Fr.); PORT OF DESIRE(1960, Fr.); LES LIAISONS DANGEREUSES(1961, Fr./Ital.); MR. ARKADIN(1962, Brit./Fr./Span.); JULIE THE REDHEAD(1963, Fr.)
Frederick O'Brady
FOREIGN INTRIGUE(1956)
Jim O'Brady
TREASURE ISLAND(1950, Brit.)
Mary O'Brady
NOTORIOUS LANDLADY, THE(1962)
Michael O'Briaan
PLAYBOY OF THE WESTERN WORLD, THE(1963, Ireland)
Michael O'Briain
HOME IS THE HERO(1959, Ireland)
Donald O'Brian
DR. BUTCHER, M.D.(1982, Ital.)
George O'Brian
GOLD RAIDERS, THE(1952)
Hugh O'Brian
BEYOND THE PURPLE HILLS(1950); NEVER FEAR(1950); ROCKETSHIP X-M(1950); BUCKAROO SHERIFF OF TEXAS(1951); CAVE OF OUTLAWS(1951); CIMARRON KID, THE(1951); FIGHTING COAST GUARD(1951); LITTLE BIG HORN(1951); ON THE LOOSE(1951); VENGEANCE VALLEY(1951); BATTLE AT APACHE PASS, THE(1952); LAWLESS BREED, THE(1952); MEET ME AT THE FAIR(1952); RAIDERS, THE(1952); RED BALL EXPRESS(1952); SALLY AND SAINT ANNE(1952); SON OF ALI BABA(1952); BACK TO GOD'S COUNTRY(1953); MAN FROM THE ALAMO, THE(1953); SEMINOLE(1953); STAND AT APACHE RIVER, THE(1953); BROKEN LANCE(1954); DRUMS ACROSS THE RIVER(1954); FIREMAN SAVE MY CHILD(1954); SASKATCHEWAN(1954); THERE'S NO BUSINESS LIKE SHOW BUSINESS(1954); TWINKLE IN GOD'S EYE, THE(1955); WHITE FEATHER(1955); BRASS LEGEND, THE(1956); FIEND WHO WALKED THE WEST, THE(1958); COME FLY WITH ME(1963); IN HARM'S WAY(1965); LOVE HAS MANY FACES(1965); TEN LITTLE INDIANS(1965, Brit.); AMBUSH BAY(1966); AFRICA–TEXAS STYLE!(1967 U.S./Brit.); STRATEGY OF TERROR(1969); KILLER FORCE(1975, Switz./Ireland); SHOOTIST, THE(1976); GAME OF DEATH, THE(1979)
Margaret O'Brian
UNFINISHED DANCE,THE(1947)
Martha O'Brian
TWO TICKETS TO BROADWAY(1951)
Melody O'Brian
SKIN GAME, THE(1965, Brit.)
Michael O'Brian
GIRL WITH GREEN EYES(1964, Brit.); NEVER PUT IT IN WRITING(1964)
Nial O'Brian
FLIGHT OF THE DOVES(1971)
Peter O'Brian
LOVE AT FIRST SIGHT(1977, Can.), p; BLOOD AND GUTS(1978, Can.), p; GREY FOX, THE(1983, Can.), p
Sheila O'Brian
NEVER TOO LATE(1965), cos
Wilber O'Brian
SAVAGE WILD, THE(1970)
Alice O'Brien
Silents
DEMOCRACY(1918, Brit.)
Misc. Silents
DRINK(1917, Brit.)
Barry O'Brien
Misc. Silents
WOLFE OR THE CONQUEST OF QUEBEC(1914)
Beatrice O'Brien
Silents
MERRY WIDOW, THE(1925)
Bernadette O'Brien
VICE SQUAD(1982), cos
1984
EYES OF FIRE(1984), cos
Bill O'Brien
TRESPASSER, THE(1929); CITY STREETS(1931); EASIEST WAY, THE(1931); HELL BOUND(1931); LADIES' MAN(1931); NO LIMIT(1931); MOVIE CRAZY(1932); PACK UP YOUR TROUBLES(1932); FOLIES DERGERE(1935); GREAT GUY(1936); SAN FRANCISCO(1936); TROUBLE FOR TWO(1936); DAMSEL IN DISTRESS, A(1937); MARGIN FOR ERROR(1943); DESTINY(1944); DARK HORSE, THE(1946); SHAKE-

DOWN(1950)
Billy O'Brien
LONE TRAIL, THE(1932); POWER AND THE GLORY, THE(1933); WEST OF THE DIVIDE(1934); TRUE CONFESSION(1937)
Brigid O'Brien
BORN AGAIN(1978)
Chris O'Brien
PRIVATE HELL 36(1954); GUN THAT WON THE WEST, THE(1955)
Chuck O'Brien
GREAT BANK ROBBERY, THE(1969)
Clay O'Brien
COWBOYS, THE(1972); CAHILL, UNITED STATES MARSHAL(1973); ONE LITTLE INDIAN(1973); APPLE DUMPLING GANG, THE(1975); MACKINTOSH & T.J.(1975)
Colleen O'Brien
ORGY OF THE DEAD(1965)
Cubby O'Brien
WESTWARD HO THE WAGONS!(1956)
Daniel J. O'Brien
Misc. Silents
LITTLE ROBINSON CRUSOE(1924)
Dave O'Brien
DEVIL AND THE DEEP(1932); HOT SATURDAY(1932); RASPUTIN AND THE EMPRESS(1932); FOOTLIGHT PARADE(1933); SITTING PRETTY(1933); 42ND STREET(1933); BRIGHT EYES(1934); GIFT OF GAB(1934); WONDER BAR(1934); NO MORE LADIES(1935); RED SALUTE(1935); SILVER STREAK, THE(1935); SWEET MUSIC(1935); WELCOME HOME(1935); WOMAN IN RED, THE(1935); REEFER MADNESS(1936); LIGHTNIN' CRANDALL(1937); WHEN YOU'RE IN LOVE(1937); BROTHERS OF THE WEST(1938); LAW OF THE TEXAN(1938); MAN'S COUNTRY(1938); STARLIGHT OVER TEXAS(1938); WHERE THE BUFFALO ROAM(1938); WHIRLWIND HORSEMAN(1938); CODE OF THE CACTUS(1939); DAUGHTER OF THE TONG(1939); FIGHTING MAD(1939); FIGHTING RENEGADE(1939); FLAMING LEAD(1939); FRONTIER SCOUT(1939); MUTINY IN THE BIG HOUSE(1939); NEW FRONTIER(1939); OUTLAW'S PARADISE(1939); ROLLIN' WESTWARD(1939); SONG OF THE BUCKAROO(1939); SUNDOWN ON THE PRAIRIE(1939); TEXAS WILDCATS(1939); TRIGGER SMITH(1939); WYOMING OUTLAW(1939); BOYS OF THE CITY(1940); COWBOY FROM SUNDOWN(1940); DANGER AHEAD(1940); EAST SIDE KIDS(1940); GUN CODE(1940); HOLD THAT WOMAN(1940); KID FROM SANTA FE, THE(1940); MURDER ON THE YUKON(1940); PHANTOM RANCHER(1940); QUEEN OF THE YUKON(1940); SKY BANDITS, THE(1940); SON OF THE NAVY(1940); THAT GANG OF MINE(1940); YUKON FLIGHT(1940); BILLY THE KID IN SANTA FE(1941); BILLY THE KID WANTED(1941); DEADLY GAME, THE(1941); DEVIL BAT, THE(1941); DOUBLE TROUBLE(1941); FORBIDDEN TRAILS(1941); MURDER BY INVITATION(1941); SPOOKS RUN WILD(1941); TEXAS MARSHAL, THE(1941); DOWN TEXAS WAY(1942); KING OF THE STALLIONS(1942); PRISONER OF JAPAN(1942); RETURN OF THE RANGERS, THE(1943); SALUTE TO THE MARINES(1943); BRAND OF THE DEVIL(1944); DEAD OR ALIVE(1944); GANGSTERS OF THE FRONTIER(1944); GUNS OF THE LAW(1944); PINTO BANDIT, THE(1944); SPOOK TOWN(1944); WHISPERING SKULL, THE(1944); ENEMY OF THE LAW(1945); FLAMING BULLETS(1945); FRONTIER FUGITIVES(1945); MARKED FOR MURDER(1945); PHANTOM OF 42ND STREET, THE(1945); TAHITI NIGHTS(1945); THREE IN THE SADDLE(1945); KISS ME KATE(1953); TENNESSEE CHAMP(1954); DESPERADOES ARE IN TOWN, THE(1956)
Misc. Talkies
BUZZY RIDES THE RANGE(1940); BUZZY AND THE PHANTOM PINTO(1941); BILLY THE KID'S SMOKING GUNS(1942); OUTLAW ROUNDUP(1944)
Dave "Tex" O'Brien
RANGERS TAKE OVER, THE(1942); SHERIFF OF SAGE VALLEY(1942); BAD MEN OF THUNDER GAP(1943); BORDER BUCKAROOS(1943); FIGHTING VALLEY(1943); WEST OF TEXAS(1943); BOSS OF THE RAWHIDE(1944); GUNSMOKE MESA(1944); TRAIL OF TERROR(1944)
Misc. Talkies
THUNDERGAP OUTLAWS(1947)
David [Dave] O'Brien
UTAH TRAIL(1938)
David O'Brien
JENNIE GERHARDT(1933); STUDENT TOUR(1934); LITTLE COLONEL, THE(1935); SHE MARRIED HER BOSS(1935); ROUGH RIDIN' RHYTHM(1937); $1,000,000 RACKET(1937); CRASHING THRU(1939); SINGING COWGIRL, THE(1939); WATER RUSTLERS(1939); FLYING WILD(1941); GUN MAN FROM BODIE, THE(1941); 'NEATH BROOKLYN BRIDGE(1942); YANKS ARE COMING, THE(1942); MAN WHO WALKED ALONE, THE(1945); KETTLES IN THE OZARKS, THE(1956)
Davie O'Brien
DRIFTING WESTWARD(1939)
Dawna O'Brien
WRONG IS RIGHT(1982)
Denise O'Brien
SONG OF NORWAY(1970)
Desmond O'Brien
IS EVERYBODY HAPPY?(1929), ed; LUCKY BOY(1929), ed; MIDSTREAM(1929), ed; SAP, THE(1929), ed; TWO MEN AND A MAID(1929), ed; EXPENSIVE WOMEN(1931), ed; MEN OF THE SKY(1931), ed
Silents
NIGHT LIFE(1927), ed; WEB OF FATE(1927), ed; BEAUTIFUL BUT DUMB(1928), ed; FLOATING COLLEGE, THE(1928), ed; MAN IN HOBBLES, THE(1928), ed
Devon O'Brien
TERMS OF ENDEARMENT(1983)
Donal O'Brien
Misc. Talkies
PLACE CALLED TRINITY, A(1975); TRINITY(1975)
Donald O'Brien
TRAIN, THE(1965, Fr./Ital./U.S.); TRIAL OF JOAN OF ARC(1965, Fr.); CLOPORTES(1966, Fr., Ital.); GRAND PRIX(1966); WEEKEND AT DUNKIRK(1966, Fr./Ital.); LA VIE DE CHATEAU(1967, Fr.); JESSE AND LESTER, TWO BROTHERS IN A PLACE CALLED TRINITY(1972, Ital.)
Eddie O'Brien
Silents
PAYING THE LIMIT(1924); PRIDE OF SUNSHINE ALLEY(1924)

Edmond O'Brien
PRISON BREAK(1938); HUNCHBACK OF NOTRE DAME, THE(1939); GIRL, A GUY AND A GOB, A(1941); OBLIGING YOUNG LADY(1941); PARACHUTE BATTALION(1941); POWDER TOWN(1942); AMAZING MRS. HOLLIDAY(1943); KILLERS, THE(1946); DOUBLE LIFE, A(1947); WEB, THE(1947); ACT OF MURDER, AN(1948); ANOTHER PART OF THE FOREST(1948); FIGHTER SQUADRON(1948); FOR THE LOVE OF MARY(1948); WHITE HEAT(1949); ADMIRAL WAS A LADY, THE(1950); BACKFIRE(1950); D.O.A.(1950); 711 OCEAN DRIVE(1950); SILVER CITY(1951); TWO OF A KIND(1951); WARPATH(1951); DENVER AND RIO GRANDE(1952); GREATEST SHOW ON EARTH, THE(1952); TURNING POINT, THE(1952); BIGAMIST,THE(1953); CHINA VENTURE(1953); COW COUNTRY(1953); HITCH-HIKER, THE(1953); JULIUS CAESAR(1953); MAN IN THE DARK(1953); BAREFOOT CONTESSA, THE(1954); SHANGHAI STORY, THE(1954); SHIELD FOR MURDER(1954), a, d; PETE KELLY'S BLUES(1955); CRY IN THE NIGHT, A(1956); D-DAY, THE SIXTH OF JUNE(1956); GIRL CAN'T HELP IT, THE(1956); RACK, THE(1956); 1984(1956, Brit.); BIG LAND, THE(1957); STOPOVER TOKYO(1957); SING, BOY, SING(1958); UP PERISCOPE(1959); GREAT IMPOSTOR, THE(1960); LAST VOYAGE, THE(1960); THIRD VOICE, THE(1960); MAN-TRAP(1961), p, d; BIRDMAN OF ALCATRAZ(1962); LONGEST DAY, THE(1962); MAN WHO SHOT LIBERTY VALANCE, THE(1962); MOON PILOT(1962); RIO CONCHOS(1964); SEVEN DAYS IN MAY(1964); SYLVIA(1965); SYNANON(1965); FANTASTIC VOYAGE(1966); VISCOUNT, THE(1967, Fr./Span./Ital./Ger.); WILD BUNCH, THE(1969); TO COMMIT A MURDER(1970, Fr./Ital./Ger.); RE: LUCKY LUCIANO(1974, Fr./Ital.); 99 AND 44/100% DEAD(1974)
Misc. Talkies
DREAM NO EVIL(1984)
Edmund O'Brien
BETWEEN MIDNIGHT AND DAWN(1950); REDHEAD AND THE COWBOY, THE(1950); WORLD WAS HIS JURY, THE(1958); LOVE GOD?, THE(1969); THEY ONLY KILL THEIR MASTERS(1972)
Edna O'Brien
GIRL WITH GREEN EYES(1964, Brit.), w; TIME LOST AND TIME REMEMBERED(1966, Brit.), w; THREE INTO TWO WON'T GO(1969, Brit.), w; X Y & ZEE(1972, Brit.), w; LOVE(1982$c Can.), w
Misc. Talkies
HARD WAY, THE(1980, Brit.)
Edward O'Brien
FLIGHT(1960); CAPTAIN MILKSHAKE(1970)
Eileen O'Brien
RUNNERS(1983, Brit.)
Eloise O'Brien
RAGTIME(1981)
Erin O'Brien
ONIONHEAD(1958); JOHN PAUL JONES(1959); IN LIKE FLINT(1967)
Eugene O'Brien
Silents
REBECCA OF SUNNYBROOK FARM(1917); LITTLE MISS HOOVER(1918); PERFECT LOVER, THE(1919); CLAY DOLLARS(1921); JOHN SMITH(1922); ONLY WOMAN, THE(1924); FINE MANNERS(1926)
Misc. Silents
(; MOONSTONE, THE(1915); CHAPERON, THE(1916); POOR LITTLE PEPPINA(1916); RETURN OF EVE, THE(1916); RISE OF SUSAN, THE(1916); SCARLET WOMAN, THE(1916); MOTH, THE(1917); POPPY(1917); BY RIGHT OF PURCHASE(1918); DELUXE ANNIE(1918); GHOSTS OF YESTERDAY(1918); HER ONLY WAY(1918); ROMANCE OF THE UNDERWORLD, A(1918); SAFETY CURTAIN, THE(1918); UNDER THE GREENWOOD TREE(1918); SEALED HEARTS(1919); BROADWAY AND HOME(1920); BROKEN MELODY, THE(1920); FIGUREHEAD, THE(1920); FOOL AND HIS MONEY, A(1920); HIS WIFE'S MONEY(1920); WONDERFUL CHANCE, THE(1920); CHIVALROUS CHARLEY(1921); GILDED LIES(1921); IS LIFE WORTH LIVING?(1921); LAST DOOR, THE(1921); WORLDS APART(1921); CHANNING OF THE NORTHWEST(1922); PROPHET'S PARADISE, THE(1922); VOICE FROM THE MINARET, THE(1923); SECRETS(1924); DANGEROUS INNOCENCE(1925); FRIVOLOUS SAL(1925); GRAUSTARK(1925); SIEGE(1925); SIMON THE JESTER(1925); SOULS FOR SABLES(1925); FLAMES(1926); ROMANTIC AGE, THE(1927); FAITHLESS LOVER(1928)
Florence O'Brien
TELL NO TALES(1939); WOMEN, THE(1939); MR. WASHINGTON GOES TO TOWN(1941); NIGHT FOR CRIME, A(1942); I WONDER WHO'S KISSING HER NOW(1947)
Misc. Talkies
DOUBLE DEAL(1939); WHILE THOUSANDS CHEER(1940); UP JUMPED THE DEVIL(1941); PROFESSOR CREEPS(1942)
Frank O'Brien
WAIT UNTIL DARK(1967); WORLD'S GREATEST LOVER, THE(1977)
Frederick O'Brien
WHITE SHADOWS IN THE SOUTH SEAS(1928), w
Gary O'Brien
BOYS OF PAUL STREET, THE(1969, Hung./US)
George O'Brien
NOAH'S ARK(1928); SALUTE(1929); LAST OF THE DUANES(1930); LONE STAR RANGER, THE(1930); ROUGH ROMANCE(1930); FAIR WARNING(1931); HOLY TERROR, A(1931); RIDERS OF THE PURPLE SAGE(1931); SEAS BENEATH, THE(1931); GAY CABALLERO, THE(1932); GOLDEN WEST, THE(1932); MYSTERY RANCH(1932); RAINBOW TRAIL(1932); LIFE IN THE RAW(1933); ROBBERS' ROOST(1933); DUDE RANGER, THE(1934); EVER SINCE EVE(1934); FRONTIER MARSHAL(1934); LAST TRAIL, THE(1934); COWBOY MILLIONAIRE(1935); HARD ROCK HARRIGAN(1935); THUNDER MOUNTAIN(1935); WHEN A MAN'S A MAN(1935); WHISPERING SMITH SPEAKS(1935); BORDER PATROLMAN, THE(1936); DANIEL BOONE(1936); O'MALLEY OF THE MOUNTED(1936); PARK AVENUE LOGGER(1937); WINDJAMMER(1937); BORDER G-MAN(1938); GUN LAW(1938); LAWLESS VALLEY(1938); PAINTED DESERT, THE(1938); RENEGADE RANGER(1938); ARIZONA LEGION(1939); FIGHTING GRINGO(1939); MARSHAL OF MESA CITY, THE(1939); RACKETEERS OF THE RANGE(1939); TIMBER STAMPEDE(1939); TROUBLE IN SUNDOWN(1939); BULLET CODE(1940); LEGION OF THE LAWLESS(1940); PRAIRIE LAW(1940); STAGE TO CHINO(1940); TRIPLE JUSTICE(1940); MY WILD IRISH ROSE(1947); FORT APACHE(1948); SHE WORE A YELLOW RIBBON(1949); CHEYENNE AUTUMN(1964)
Misc. Talkies
SMOKE LIGHTNING(1933)

Silents
WHITE HANDS(1922); IRON HORSE, THE(1924); ROUGHNECK, THE(1924); JOHNSTOWN FLOOD, THE(1926); IS ZAT SO?(1927); SUNRISE–A SONG OF TWO HUMANS(1927); SHARP SHOOTERS(1928); MASKED EMOTIONS(1929)
Misc. Silents
MAN WHO CAME BACK, THE(1924); PAINTED LADY, THE(1924); DANCERS, THE(1925); FIGHTING HEART, THE(1925); HAVOC(1925); THANK YOU(1925); BLUE EAGLE, THE(1926); FIG LEAVES(1926); RUSTLING FOR CUPID(1926); SILVER TREASURE, THE(1926); THREE BAD MEN(1926); EAST SIDE, WEST SIDE(1927); PAID TO LOVE(1927); BLINDFOLD(1928); HONOR BOUND(1928); TRUE HEAVEN(1929)
Geraldine O'Brien
SWEET CHARITY(1969)
Misc. Silents
HIS WIFE(1915); WOMAN'S FIGHT, A(1916)
Glenn O'Brien
SUBWAY RIDERS(1981)
Gregg O'Brien
SHOW THEM NO MERCY(1935)
Gypsy O'Brien
Silents
MASTER MIND, THE(1920); SALVATION NELL(1921)
Misc. Silents
YOUNG DIANA, THE(1922); SINNER OR SAINT(1923)
Henry O'Brien
PROFESSIONALS, THE(1966); LAST CHALLENGE, THE(1967); CAR, THE(1977)
Holly O'Brien
YOURS, MINE AND OURS(1968)
Hugh O'Brien
RETURN OF JESSE JAMES, THE(1950)
Jack O'Brien
Silents
FLYING TORPEDO, THE(1916), d; BAB'S DIARY(1917); ANNABEL LEE(1921); LOVE'S PENALTY(1921); IRON HORSE, THE(1924); ACTION GALORE(1925)
Misc. Silents
DAUGHTER OF THE LAW, A(1921); THUNDER ISLAND(1921); BRIDE'S PLAY, THE(1922)
James "Dave" O'Brien
MUSIC IN THE AIR(1934)
Jane O'Brien
BELOW THE BELT(1980)
Jerry O'Brien
LIGHT YEARS AWAY(1982, Fr./Switz.)
Jillian O'Brien
1984
PALLET ON THE FLOOR(1984, New Zealand)
Jimmy O'Brien
LUCK OF THE IRISH(1948); YES SIR, MR. BONES(1951)
Joan O'Brien
HANDLE WITH CARE(1958); OPERATION PETTICOAT(1959); ALAMO, THE(1960); COMANCHEROS, THE(1961); IT'S ONLY MONEY(1962); SAMAR(1962); SIX BLACK HORSES(1962); WE JOINED THE NAVY(1962, Brit.); IT HAPPENED AT THE WORLD'S FAIR(1963); GET YOURSELF A COLLEGE GIRL(1964)
Joe O'Brien
FOREIGN CORRESPONDENT(1940)
Silents
SMILIN' AT TROUBLE(1925)
Misc. Silents
CLOUD DODGER, THE(1928)
Police Chief John O'Brien
Silents
POISON(1924)
John O'Brien
SPIRIT OF NOTRE DAME, THE(1931); TOP O' THE MORNING(1949); SCROOGE(1970, Brit.)
Misc. Silents
CAPTAIN MACKLIN(1915), d
John B. O'Brien
Silents
ETERNAL GRIND, THE(1916), d; IMPOSSIBLE CATHERINE(1919), d; OUTLAW'S DAUGHTER, THE(1925), d
Misc. Silents
HER SHATTERED IDOL(1915), d; OUTCAST, THE(1915), d; SOULS TRIUMPHANT(1915), d; BIG SISTER, THE(1916), d; DESTINY'S TOY(1916), d; FOUNDLING, THE(1916), d; HULDA FROM HOLLAND(1916), d; DAUGHTER OF MARYLAND, A(1917), d; HER SISTER(1917), d; MARY LAWSON'S SECRET(1917), d; MATERNITY(1917), d; QUEEN X(1917), d; REPUTATION(1917), d; UNFORSEEN, THE(1917), d; VANITY(1917), d; GIRL AND THE JUDGE, THE(1918), d; STREET OF SEVEN STARS, THE(1918), d; BISHOP'S EMERALDS, THE(1919), d; FAMILY CLOSET, THE(1921), d; FATHER TOM(1921), d; LONELY HEART(1921), d; THOSE WHO DARE(1924), d; DARING DAYS(1925), d
Justin O'Brien
SYMPHONIE PASTORALE(1948, Fr.), titles
Kate O'Brien
THAT LADY(1955, Brit.), w
Keith O'Brien
THRILL KILLERS, THE(1965)
Kelly O'Brien
1984
FLASH OF GREEN, A(1984)
Ken O'Brien
MAKE MINE MUSIC(1946), anim; SONG OF THE SOUTH(1946), anim; FUN AND FANCY FREE(1947), anim; MELODY TIME(1948), animators; CINDERELLA(1950), anim; PETER PAN(1953), anim; LADY AND THE TRAMP(1955), anim; SLEEPING BEAUTY(1959), anim; BOY NAMED CHARLIE BROWN, A(1969), anim; STING, THE(1973); RACE FOR YOUR LIFE, CHARLIE BROWN(1977), anim
Kenneth O'Brien
SCREAM BLACULA SCREAM(1973); IDOLMAKER, THE(1980); SOME KIND OF HERO(1982)

1984
LONELY GUY, THE(1984)

Kevin O'Brien
SERIAL(1980); FRIDAY THE 13TH PART III(1982)

Kim O'Brien
HUCKLEBERRY FINN(1974); WINTER KILLS(1979)

Laurie O'Brien
TIMERIDER(1983)

Lawrence O'Brien
MY UNCLE ANTOINE(1971, Can.), art d

Liam O'Brien
CHAIN LIGHTNING(1950), w; REDHEAD AND THE COWBOY, THE(1950), w; HERE COMES THE GROOM(1951), w; DIPLOMATIC COURIER(1952), w; STARS ARE SINGING, THE(1953), w; YOUNG AT HEART(1955), w; TRAPEZE(1956), w; REMARKABLE MR. PENNYPACKER, THE(1959), w; GREAT IMPOSTOR, THE(1960), w; DEVIL AT FOUR O'CLOCK, THE(1961), w

Linda O'Brien
1984
EL NORTE(1984), m

Lois O'Brien
MISTER ROCK AND ROLL(1957)

Mare O'Brien
TAKE THIS JOB AND SHOVE IT(1981)

Margaret O'Brien
JOURNEY FOR MARGARET(1942); DR. GILLESPIE'S CRIMINAL CASE(1943); MADAME CURIE(1943); THOUSANDS CHEER(1943); CANTERVILLE GHOST, THE(1944); JANE EYRE(1944); LOST ANGEL(1944); MEET ME IN ST. LOUIS(1944); MUSIC FOR MILLIONS(1944); OUR VINES HAVE TENDER GRAPES(1945); BAD BASCOMB(1946); THREE WISE FOOLS(1946); BIG CITY(1948); TENTH AVENUE ANGEL(1948); LITTLE WOMEN(1949); SECRET GARDEN, THE(1949); HER FIRST ROMANCE(1951); GLORY(1955); HELLER IN PINK TIGHTS(1960); AMY(1981)
Misc. Talkies
ANNABELLE LEE(1972); DIABOLIC WEDDING(1972)

Maria O'Brien
TOOMORROW(1970, Brit.); WHEN DINOSAURS RULED THE EARTH(1971, Brit.); ADVENTURES OF BARRY McKENZIE(1972, Austral.); SMILE(1975); TABLE FOR FIVE(1983)
1984
PROTOCOL(1984)

Marianne O'Brien
HOLLYWOOD CANTEEN(1944); VERY THOUGHT OF YOU, THE(1944); CINDERELLA JONES(1946)

Marissa O'Brien
KILL OR BE KILLED(1950); HER FIRST ROMANCE(1951)

Mary O'Brien
SING A JINGLE(1943); SO'S YOUR UNCLE(1943); HI, GOOD-LOOKIN'(1944); MOONLIGHT AND CACTUS(1944); SUDAN(1945); HOW SWEET IT IS(1968); I SAILED TO TAHITI WITH AN ALL GIRL CREW(1969)
Silents
BATTLING BUTLER(1926); IT MUST BE LOVE(1926)

Maureen O'Brien
MAN OF EVIL(1948, Brit.)

Michael O'Brien
PROFESSOR TIM(1957, Ireland); SHE DIDN'T SAY NO!(1962, Brit.)

Michele O'Brien
NATURAL ENEMIES(1979)

Natalie O'Brien
Silents
MAN WORTH WHILE, THE(1921)

Niall O'Brien
RYAN'S DAUGHTER(1970, Brit.); OUTSIDER, THE(1980); EXCALIBUR(1981); GORKY PARK(1983)

Paddy Manning O'Brien
UNSTOPPABLE MAN, THE(1961, Brit.), w

Pat J. O'Brien
DOOMED CARAVAN(1941)

Pat O'Brien
CONSOLATION MARRIAGE(1931); FLYING HIGH(1931); FRONT PAGE, THE(1931); HONOR AMONG LOVERS(1931); PERSONAL MAID(1931); AIR MAIL(1932); AMERICAN MADNESS(1932); CASE OF CLARA DEANE, THE(1932); FINAL EDITION(1932); HELL'S HOUSE(1932); HOLLYWOOD SPEAKS(1932); SCANDAL FOR SALE(1932); STRANGE CASE OF CLARA DEANE, THE(1932); VIRTUE(1932); BOMBSHELL(1933); BUREAU OF MISSING PERSONS(1933); COLLEGE COACH(1933); DESTINATION UNKNOWN(1933); LAUGHTER IN HELL(1933); WORLD GONE MAD, THE(1933); FLAMING GOLD(1934); FLIRTATION WALK(1934); GAMBLING LADY(1934); HERE COMES THE NAVY(1934); I SELL ANYTHING(1934); I'VE GOT YOUR NUMBER(1934); PERSONALITY KID, THE(1934); TWENTY MILLION SWEETHEARTS(1934); CEILNG ZERO(1935); DEVIL DOGS OF THE AIR(1935); IN CALIENTE(1935); IRISH IN US, THE(1935); OIL FOR THE LAMPS OF CHINA(1935); OUTLAWED GUNS(1935); PAGE MISS GLORY(1935); STARS OVER BROADWAY(1935); CHINA CLIPPER(1936); I MARRIED A DOCTOR(1936); PUBLIC ENEMY'S WIFE(1936); BACK IN CIRCULATION(1937); GREAT O'MALLEY, THE(1937); SAN QUENTIN(1937); SLIM(1937); SUBMARINE D-1(1937); BAR 20 JUSTICE(1938); BOY MEETS GIRL(1938); COWBOY FROM BROOKLYN(1938); GARDEN OF THE MOON(1938); HAWAIIAN BUCKAROO(1938); PANAMINT'S BAD MAN(1938); WOMEN ARE LIKE THAT(1938); INDIANAPOLIS SPEEDWAY(1939); KID FROM KOKOMO(1939); NIGHT OF NIGHTS, THE(1939); OFF THE RECORD(1939); CASTLE ON THE HUDSON(1940); ESCAPE TO GLORY(1940); FIGHTING 69TH, THE(1940); FLOWING GOLD(1940); KNUTE ROCKNE—ALL AMERICAN(1940); SLIGHTLY HONORABLE(1940); TIL WE MEET AGAIN(1940); TORRID ZONE(1940); BURY ME NOT ON THE LONE PRAIRIE(1941); BROADWAY(1942); FLIGHT LIEUTENANT(1942); NAVY COMES THROUGH, THE(1942); TWO YANKS IN TRINIDAD(1942); BOMBARDIER(1943); HIS BUTLER'S SISTER(1943); IRON MAJOR, THE(1943); MARINE RAIDERS(1944); SECRET COMMAND(1944); HAVING WONDERFUL CRIME(1945); MAN ALIVE(1945); CRACK-UP(1946); PERILOUS HOLIDAY(1946); RIFFRAFF(1947); FIGHTING FATHER DUNNE(1948); BOY WITH THE GREEN HAIR, THE(1949); DANGEROUS PROFESSION, A(1949); FIREBALL, THE(1950); JOHNNY ONE-EYE(1950); CRIMINAL LAWYER(1951); PEOPLE AGAINST O'HARA, THE(1951); OKINAWA(1952); JUBILEE TRAIL(1954); RING OF FEAR(1954); INSIDE DETROIT(1955); KILL ME

TOMORROW(1958, Brit.); LAST HURRAH, THE(1958); SOME LIKE IT HOT(1959); TOWN TAMER(1965); PHYNX, THE(1970); BILLY JACK GOES TO WASHINGTON(1977); END, THE(1978)
Silents
FRECKLED RASCAL, THE(1929)
Misc. Silents
SHADOWS OF THE WEST(1921); FURY OF THE WILD(1929)

Patricia O'Brien
JUSTICE TAKES A HOLIDAY(1933); RIGHT TO ROMANCE(1933)

Patrick O'Brien
PERSONALS, THE(1982)

Patty O'Brien
ONE DOWN TWO TO GO(1982); VERDICT, THE(1982)

Paul O'Brien
THINGS TO COME(1936, Brit.); KNIGHT WITHOUT ARMOR(1937, Brit.)

Philip O'Brien
FFOLKES(1980, Brit.); CHARRIOTS OF FIRE(1981, Brit.)

Richard O'Brien
TIGER WALKS, A(1964); CHAMBER OF HORRORS(1966); ROUGH NIGHT IN JERICHO(1967); PIECES OF DREAMS(1970); HONKERS, THE(1972); LONERS, THE(1972); THIEF WHO CAME TO DINNER, THE(1973); ROCKY HORROR PICTURE SHOW, THE(1975, Brit.), a, w, m; SHAGGY D.A., THE(1976); PACK, THE(1977); HEAVEN CAN WAIT(1978); JUBILEE(1978, Brit.); FLASH GORDON(1980); SHOCK TREATMENT(1981), a, w, m

Robert C. O'Brien
SECRET OF NIMH, THE(1982), w

Robert O'Brien
LADY ON A TRAIN(1945), w; FANCY PANTS(1950), w; LEMON DROP KID, THE(1951), w; BELLE OF NEW YORK, THE(1952), w; BY THE LIGHT OF THE SILVERY MOON(1953), w; LUCKY ME(1954), w; SAY ONE FOR ME(1959), w

Rory O'Brien
ONE MAN'S WAY(1964); LITTLE BIG MAN(1970)

Sam O'Brien
COWBOYS, THE(1972)

Seamus O'Brien
BLOODSUCKING FREAKS(1982)

Sheila O'Brien
DAMNED DON'T CRY, THE(1950), cos; HARRIET CRAIG(1950), cos; GOODBYE, MY FANCY(1951), cos; SUDDEN FEAR(1952), cos; THIS WOMAN IS DANGEROUS(1952), cos; JOHNNY GUITAR(1954), cos; FEMALE ON THE BEACH(1955), cos

Steve O'Brien
PRIVATE NURSE(1941)

Stewart O'Brien
DEMENTIA 13(1963), ed

Stuart O'Brien
HALLIDAY BRAND, THE(1957), ed; TERROR, THE(1963), ed

Terence O'Brien
BLOCKADE(1928, Brit.); WORLD OWES ME A LIVING, THE(1944, Brit.)
Silents
MERCHANT OF VENICE, THE(1916, Brit.)

Tex O'Brien
LAW AND ORDER(1942)

Timothy O'Brien
NIGHT MUST FALL(1964, Brit.), prod d

Timothy Eric O'Brien
1984
SUBURBIA(1984)

Tom O'Brien
DANCE HALL(1929); FLYING FOOL(1929); HIS LUCKY DAY(1929); HURRICANE(1929); IT CAN BE DONE(1929); LAST WARNING, THE(1929); SMILING IRISH EYES(1929); DARKENED SKIES(1930); MOBY DICK(1930); MIDNIGHT SPECIAL(1931); NIGHT MAYOR, THE(1932); PHANTOM EXPRESS, THE(1932); UNEXPECTED FATHER(1932); LUCKY DOG(1933); PHANTOM OF SANTA FE(1937)
Misc. Talkies
CALL OF THE WEST(1930)
Silents
YOUTH TO YOUTH(1922); SCARLET CAR, THE(1923); TIPPED OFF(1923); NEVER SAY DIE(1924); BIG PARADE, THE(1925); TAKE IT FROM ME(1926); TWELVE MILES OUT(1927); PEACOCK FAN(1929)
Misc. Silents
GENTLEMAN FROM AMERICA, THE(1923); FIRE BRIGADE, THE(1926); RUNAWAY EXPRESS, THE(1926); WINNER, THE(1926); BUGLE CALL, THE(1927); FRONTIERSMAN, THE(1927); SAN FRANCISCO NIGHTS(1928); THAT'S MY DADDY(1928)

Tomy O'Brien
PURPLE HAZE(1982)

Tracy O'Brien
1984
ALLEY CAT(1984)

Vince O'Brien
ANNIE HALL(1977)

Vincent O'Brien
HOODLUM PRIEST, THE(1961); CROSS AND THE SWITCHBLADE, THE(1970)

Virginia O'Brien
HULLABALOO(1940); SKY MURDER(1940); LADY BE GOOD(1941); RINGSIDE MAISIE(1941); PANAMA HATTIE(1942); SHIP AHOY(1942); DU BARRY WAS A LADY(1943); THOUSANDS CHEER(1943); MEET THE PEOPLE(1944); TWO GIRLS AND A SAILOR(1944); HARVEY GIRLS, THE(1946); SHOW-OFF, THE(1946); TILL THE CLOUDS ROLL BY(1946); MERTON OF THE MOVIES(1947); FRANCIS IN THE NAVY(1955)
Misc. Talkies
GREAT MORGAN, THE(1946)

W.J. O'Brien
GUILTY GENERATION, THE(1931); GILDERSLEEVE'S BAD DAY(1943); EASY LIVING(1949); IMPACT(1949); SET-UP, THE(1949); ON DANGEROUS GROUND(1951)

William O'Brien
LET US BE GAY(1930); ONCE A GENTLEMAN(1930); PLAYBOY OF PARIS(1930); STRICTLY UNCONVENTIONAL(1930); BULLDOG DRUMMOND STRIKES BACK(1934); SPLENDOR(1935); TEST PILOT(1938); SMOOTH AS SILK(1946); IT HAPPENED ON 5TH AVENUE(1947)

Silents
CHEATERS(1927)
William F. O'Brien
TELEFON(1977), art d; 1941(1979), art d; CANNERY ROW(1982), art d
William H. O'Brien
SKY RAIDERS(1931); FORCE OF EVIL(1948); YOU GOTTA STAY HAPPY(1948); SON OF FLUBBER(1963)
William J. O'Brien
SHE GETS HER MAN(1945)
Willis H. O'Brien
Silents
LOST WORLD, THE(1925), spec. eff
Willis O'Brien
KING KONG(1933), spec eff; SON OF KONG(1933), spec eff; LAST DAYS OF POMPEII, THE(1935), spec eff; MIGHTY JOE YOUNG(1949), spec eff; BEAST OF HOLLOW MOUNTAIN, THE(1956), w; KING KONG VERSUS GODZILLA(1963, Jap.), w; TROG(1970, Brit.), spec eff
Erin O'Brien-Moore
HIS GREATEST GAMBLE(1934); LITTLE MEN(1935); OUR LITTLE GIRL(1935); SEVEN KEYS TO BALDPATE(1935); STREAMLINE EXPRESS(1935); EX-MRS. BRADFORD, THE(1936); LEAVENWORTH CASE, THE(1936); PLOUGH AND THE STARS, THE(1936); TWO IN THE DARK(1936); BLACK LEGION, THE(1937); GREEN LIGHT(1937); LIFE OF EMILE ZOLA, THE(1937); DESTINATION MOON(1950); FAMILY SECRET, THE(1951); SEA OF LOST SHIPS(1953); PHANTOM OF THE RUE MORGUE(1954); PEYTON PLACE(1957); HOW TO SUCCEED IN BUSINESS WITHOUT REALLY TRYING(1976)
Manning O'Brine
BREAKAWAY(1956, Brit.), w; PASSPORT TO TREASON(1956, Brit.), w; KILL ME TOMORROW(1958, Brit.), w; MURDER AT SITE THREE(1959, Brit.), w
P. Manning O'Brine
THUNDER OVER TANGIER(1957, Brit.), w
Paddy Manning O'Brine
LONG SHADOW, THE(1961, Brit.), w; BLAZE OF GLORY(1963, Brit.), w
Rory O'Brine
LONG SHADOW, THE(1961, Brit.)
Barbara O'Bryant
GOLDEN BOX, THE(1970)
Mellisa O'Bryant
HOMETOWN U.S.A.(1979)
Maggie O'Bryne
PARTY GIRL(1958)
Patsy O'Bryne
LIKELY STORY, A(1947); ROAD TO RIO(1947)
Bryan O'Byrne
ONE MAN'S WAY(1964); GUNFIGHT IN ABILENE(1967); WHO'S MINDING THE MINT?(1967); $1,000,000 DUCK(1971); CAR, THE(1977); APPLE DUMPLING GANG RIDES AGAIN, THE(1979); LOVE AT FIRST BITE(1979); HERO AT LARGE(1980); ZAPPED!(1982)
Maggie O'Byrne
BROTHERS RICO, THE(1957)
Paddy O'Byrne
1984
GODS MUST BE CRAZY, THE(1984, Botswana)
Patsy O'Byrne
NICE WOMAN(1932); DR. BULL(1933); IT'S A GIFT(1934); INDIANAPOLIS SPEEDWAY(1939); SAPS AT SEA(1940); YOU CAN'T FOOL YOUR WIFE(1940); IN THE NAVY(1941); PRIDE OF THE YANKEES, THE(1942); UNDER WESTERN SKIES(1945); SORROWFUL JONES(1949); DARLING, HOW COULD YOU!(1951); SOMETHING TO LIVE FOR(1952)
Silents
OUTCAST(1928)
Donal O'Cahil
MEN OF IRELAND(1938, Ireland), w
Donal O'Cahill
DAWN OVER IRELAND(1938, Irish), a, w
Cindy O'Callaghan
BEDKNOBS AND BROOMSTICKS(1971); HANOVER STREET(1979, Brit.)
Ed O'Callaghan
RYAN'S DAUGHTER(1970, Brit.)
Edward G. O'Callaghan
THIS ISLAND EARTH(1955), w; FLIGHT TO HONG KONG(1956), w
Liam O'Callaghan
UNDERGROUND(1970, Brit.)
Patricia O'Callaghan
THREE CAME HOME(1950); GIVE A DOG A BONE(1967, Brit.)
Richard O'Callaghan
BOFORS GUN, THE(1968, Brit.); CARRY ON LOVING(1970, Brit.); BUTLEY(1974, Brit.); GALILEO(1975, Brit.); WATERSHIP DOWN(1978, Brit.)
Fox O'Callahan
TROUBLE IN TEXAS(1937)
Kevin O'Calloghan
VICTORY(1981)
Liam O'Calloghan
EXCALIBUR(1981)
O'Camp
VIOLENT YEARS, THE(1956), p
Al O'Camp
STRANGE WORLD(1952), w
Pedro O'Campo
VOICES(1979)
Roman O'Casey
GILDED CAGE, THE(1954, Brit.)
Ronan O'Casey
SALT TO THE DEVIL(1949, Brit.); MUDLARK, THE(1950, Brit.); YOU CAN'T BEAT THE IRISH(1952, Brit.); WHITE FIRE(1953, Brit.); ESCAPE BY NIGHT(1954, Brit.); TONIGHT'S THE NIGHT(1954, Brit.); TROUBLE IN STORE(1955, Brit.); MURDER ON APPROVAL(1956, Brit.); SATELLITE IN THE SKY(1956); 1984(1956, Brit.); BITTER VICTORY(1958, Fr.); BLIND SPOT(1958, Brit.); CROSS-UP(1958); INN FOR TROUBLE(1960, Brit.); BLOW-UP(1966, Brit.)

Sean O'Casey
JUNO AND THE PAYCOCK(1930, Brit.), w; PLOUGH AND THE STARS, THE(1936), w; YOUNG CASSIDY(1965, U.S./Brit.), w
Shivaun O'Casey
YOUNG CASSIDY(1965, U.S./Brit.)
Jim O'Catty
WHIPLASH(1948)
C. R. O'Christopher
LAST CHASE, THE(1981), w
Sean O'Coisdealbha
POITIN(1979, Irish)
L.W. O'Connall
ON THE LEVEL(1930), ph
Jim O'Connaly
BLOOD BEAST FROM OUTER SPACE(1965, Brit.), w
Danny O'Connel
GOODBYE PORK PIE(1981, New Zealand)
Robert O'Connel
BANANAS(1971)
Arthur J. O'Connell
LAW OF THE JUNGLE(1942)
Arthur O'Connell
DR. KILDARE GOES HOME(1940); MURDER IN THE NIGHT(1940, Brit.); TWO GIRLS ON BROADWAY(1940); CITIZEN KANE(1941); LUCKY DEVILS(1941); BLONDIE'S BLESSED EVENT(1942); MAN FROM HEADQUARTERS(1942); YOKEL BOY(1942); COUNTESS OF MONTE CRISTO, THE(1948); FORCE OF EVIL(1948); HOMECOMING(1948); NAKED CITY, THE(1948); ONE TOUCH OF VENUS(1948); OPEN SECRET(1948); STATE OF THE UNION(1948); LOVE THAT BRUTE(1950); WHISTLE AT EATON FALLS(1951); PICNIC(1955); BUS STOP(1956); MAN IN THE GREY FLANNEL SUIT, THE(1956); PROUD ONES, THE(1956); SOLID GOLD CADILLAC, THE(1956); APRIL LOVE(1957); MONTE CARLO STORY, THE(1957, Ital.); OPERATION MAD BALL(1957); VIOLATORS, THE(1957); MAN OF THE WEST(1958); VOICE IN THE MIRROR(1958); ANATOMY OF A MURDER(1959); GIDGET(1959); HOUND-DOG MAN(1959); OPERATION PETTICOAT(1959); CIMARRON(1960); GREAT IMPOSTOR, THE(1960); MISTY(1961); POCKETFUL OF MIRACLES(1961); THUNDER OF DRUMS, A(1961); FOLLOW THAT DREAM(1962); KISSIN' COUSINS(1964); NIGHTMARE IN THE SUN(1964); SEVEN FACES OF DR. LAO(1964); YOUR CHEATIN' HEART(1964); GREAT RACE, THE(1965); MONKEY'S UNCLE, THE(1965); THIRD DAY, THE(1965); BIRDS DO IT(1966); COVENANT WITH DEATH, A(1966); FANTASTIC VOYAGE(1966); RIDE BEYOND VENGEANCE(1966); SILENCERS, THE(1966); RELUCTANT ASTRONAUT, THE(1967); IF HE HOLLERS, LET HIM GO(1968); POWER, THE(1968); DO NOT THROW CUSHIONS INTO THE RING(1970); SUPPOSE THEY GAVE A WAR AND NOBODY CAME?(1970); THERE WAS A CROOKED MAN(1970); LAST VALLEY, THE(1971, Brit.); BEN(1972); POSEIDON ADVENTURE, THE(1972); THEY ONLY KILL THEIR MASTERS(1972); WICKED, WICKED(1973); HUCKLEBERRY FINN(1974); HIDING PLACE, THE(1975)
Bob O'Connell
STRANGERS IN THE CITY(1962); MADIGAN(1968); NO WAY TO TREAT A LADY(1968); JOE(1970); LOVE STORY(1970); THUMBELINA(1970); HURRY UP OR I'LL BE 30(1973); SHORT EYES(1977); BIG FIX, THE(1978); STING II, THE(1983)
Misc. Talkies
MORALS SQUAD(1960)
Connie O'Connell
RETURN TO CAMPUS(1975)
David J. O'Connell
BACKTRACK(1969), p; MISSION GALACTICA: THE CYLON ATTACK(1979), p
Denise O'Connell
SCARECROW, THE(1982, New Zealand)
Gene O'Connell
MAD GHOUL, THE(1943)
George O'Connell
KILLERS, THE(1964), art d
Helen O'Connell
FLEET'S IN, THE(1942); I DOOD IT(1943); FABULOUS DORSEYS, THE(1947)
Hugh O'Connell
PERSONAL MAID(1931); SECRETS OF A SECRETARY(1931); SMILING LIEUTENANT, THE(1931); BROADWAY THROUGH A KEYHOLE(1933); CHEATING CHEATERS(1934); GIFT OF GAB(1934); AFFAIR OF SUSAN(1935); CHINATOWN SQUAD(1935); DIAMOND JIM(1935); GOOD FAIRY, THE(1935); IT HAPPENED IN NEW YORK(1935); MAN WHO RECLAIMED HIS HEAD, THE(1935); MANHATTAN MOON(1935); SHE GETS HER MAN(1935); STRANGE WIVES(1935); FLY-AWAY BABY(1937); FOOTLOOSE HEIRESS, THE(1937); MARRY THE GIRL(1937); PERFECT SPECIMEN, THE(1937); READY, WILLING AND ABLE(1937); THAT CERTAIN WOMAN(1937); ACCIDENTS WILL HAPPEN(1938); MYSTERY HOUSE(1938); PENROD'S DOUBLE TROUBLE(1938); SWING YOUR LADY(1938); TORCHY BLANE IN PANAMA(1938); WOMEN ARE LIKE THAT(1938); LUCKY PARTNERS(1940); MY FAVORITE WIFE(1940); MAD DOCTOR, THE(1941); MY LIFE WITH CAROLINE(1941); PUDDIN' HEAD(1941); THREE GIRLS ABOUT TOWN(1941); MOONLIGHT IN HAVANA(1942)
Jack O'Connell
GREENWICH VILLAGE STORY(1963), p,d&w
James O'Connell
NICKELODEON(1976); HERO AT LARGE(1980); DEATH HUNT(1981); POSTMAN ALWAYS RINGS TWICE, THE(1981); SHARKY'S MACHINE(1982); SECOND THOUGHTS(1983)
Jean O'Connell
JOAN OF OZARK(1942)
John O'Connell
ACE ELI AND RODGER OF THE SKIES(1973)
L. William O'Connell
BIG TIME(1929), ph; CAMEO KIRBY(1930), ph; FOX MOVIETONE FOLLIES OF 1930(1930), ph; PRINCESS AND THE PLUMBER, THE(1930), ph; RENEGADES(1930), ph; MAKER OF MEN(1931), ph; THREE GIRLS LOST(1931), ph; MENACE, THE(1932), ph; SCARFACE(1932), ph; WHITE EAGLE(1932), ph; BENGAL TIGER(1936), ph; BIG NOISE, THE(1936), ph; FORBIDDEN TRAIL(1936), ph; POLO JOE(1936), ph; ROAD GANG(1936), ph; TIMES SQUARE PLAYBOY(1936), ph; CHEROKEE STRIP(1937), ph; ONCE A DOCTOR(1937), ph; PENROD AND SAM(1937), ph; PUBLIC WEDDING(1937), ph; WEST OF SHANGHAI(1937), ph; BROADWAY MUSKETEERS(1938), ph; HEART OF THE NORTH(1938), ph; INVISIBLE MENACE, THE(1938), ph; LITTLE MISS THOROUGHBRED(1938), ph; MYSTERY

HOUSE(1938), ph; NANCY DREW–DETECTIVE(1938), ph; NANCY DREW AND THE HIDDEN STAIRCASE(1939), ph; CALLING PHILO VANCE(1940), ph; GAMBLING ON THE HIGH SEAS(1940), ph; GRANNY GET YOUR GUN(1940), ph; MONEY AND THE WOMAN(1940), ph; DANGEROUSLY THEY LIVE(1942), ph; KLONDIKE FURY(1942), ph; RUBBER RACKETEERS(1942), ph; IS EVERYBODY HAPPY?(1943), ph; DEVIL ON WHEELS, THE(1947), ph

Silents
COME ON OVER(1922), ph; APRIL FOOL(1926), ph; MONKEY TALKS, THE(1927), ph; NO BABIES WANTED(1928), ph

L.W. O'Connell
FOUR DEVILS(1929), ph; MAKING THE GRADE(1929), ph; SUCH MEN ARE DANGEROUS(1930), ph; THREE SISTERS, THE(1930), ph; WILD COMPANY(1930), ph; BORDER LAW(1931), ph; RACKETY RAX(1932), ph; BEST OF ENEMIES(1933), ph; HUMANITY(1933), ph; TRICK FOR TRICK(1933), ph; BABY, TAKE A BOW(1934), ph; CHARLIE CHAN IN LONDON(1934), ph; OLSEN'S BIG MOMENT(1934), ph; PURSUED(1934), ph; STAND UP AND CHEER(1934), ph; BACHELOR OF ARTS(1935), ph; HERE'S TO ROMANCE(1935), ph; IN OLD KENTUCKY(1935), ph; MAN OF IRON(1935), ph; MUSIC IS MAGIC(1935), ph; SPRING TONIC(1935), ph; UNDER PRESSURE(1935), ph; KING OF HOCKEY(1936), ph; TREACHERY RIDES THE RANGE(1936), ph; ALCATRAZ ISLAND(1937), ph; WHITE BONDAGE(1937), ph; WHEN WERE YOU BORN?(1938), ph; ADVENTURES OF JANE ARDEN(1939), ph; ON TRIAL(1939), ph; BLONDE FROM SINGAPORE, THE(1941), ph; MYSTERY SHIP(1941), ph; STORK PAYS OFF, THE(1941), ph; GET HEP TO LOVE(1942), ph; UNDERGROUND AGENT(1942), ph; AFTER MIDNIGHT WITH BOSTON BLACKIE(1943), ph; DOUGHBOYS IN IRELAND(1943), ph; IT'S A GREAT LIFE(1943), ph; ONE DANGEROUS NIGHT(1943), ph; PASSPORT TO SUEZ(1943), ph; TWO SENORITAS FROM CHICAGO(1943), ph; BEAUTIFUL BUT BROKE(1944), ph; CRY OF THE WEREWOLF(1944), ph; GHOST THAT WALKS ALONE, THE(1944), ph; GIRL IN THE CASE(1944), ph; HEY, ROOKIE(1944), ph; JAM SESSION(1944), ph; LOUISIANA HAYRIDE(1944), ph; MISSING JUROR, THE(1944), ph; ONE MYSTERIOUS NIGHT(1944), ph; RETURN OF THE VAMPIRE, THE(1944), ph; STARS ON PARADE(1944), ph; ADVENTURES OF RUSTY(1945), ph; CRIME DOCTOR'S COURAGE, THE(1945), ph; CRIME DOCTOR'S WARNING(1945), ph; DANCING IN MANHATTAN(1945), ph; POWER OF THE WHISTLER, THE(1945), ph; SERGEANT MIKE(1945), ph; BLONDIE'S LUCKY DAY(1946), ph; DECOY(1946), ph; DESERT HORSEMAN, THE(1946), ph; LIFE WITH BLONDIE(1946), ph; SWEETHEART OF SIGMA CHI(1946), ph; LOST HONEYMOON(1947), ph; JIGGS AND MAGGIE IN SOCIETY(1948), ph; JIGGS AND MAGGIE OUT WEST(1950), ph

Silents
MY SON(1925), ph; REDEEMING SIN, THE(1925), ph; GIRL IN EVERY PORT, A(1928), ph

Lew O'Connell
REPEAT PERFORMANCE(1947), ph

Lewis W. O'Connell
ASSIGNED TO DANGER(1948), ph

Lou O'Connell
SHE LOVED A FIREMAN(1937), ph

Margaret O'Connell
CRASHIN' THRU DANGER(1938)

Marian O'Connell
DAWN OVER IRELAND(1938, Irish)

Marion O'Connell
SINGING VAGABOND, THE(1935)

Maura O'Connell
SIEGE(1983, Can.), p, d

Maurcie O'Connell
CURSE OF THE PINK PANTHER(1983)

Maureen O'Connell
RISING OF THE MOON, THE(1957, Ireland)

Maurice O'Connell
MEDUSA TOUCH, THE(1978, Brit.)
1984
KIPPERBANG(1984, Brit.); SECRET PLACES(1984, Brit.)

Maurice O.Connell
COUNT DRACULA AND HIS VAMPIRE BRIDE(1978, Brit.)

Michael O'Connell
JAILBREAKERS, THE(1960)

Myra O'Connell
BLACK MEMORY(1947, Brit.)

Patrick O'Connell
CROMWELL(1970, Brit.); MC KENZIE BREAK, THE(1970); RAGMAN'S DAUGHTER, THE(1974, Brit.); HUMAN FACTOR, THE(1979, Brit.); RUNNERS(1983, Brit.)

Peggy O'Connell
TOO MUCH BEEF(1936)

Robert O'Connell
LONE WOLF RETURNS, THE(1936), w; ER LOVE A STRANGER(1958)

Susan O'Connell
BALLAD OF CABLE HOGUE, THE(1970); CARDIAC ARREST(1980); TELL ME A RIDDLE(1980), p
1984
MASSIVE RETALIATION(1984)

Taafe O'Connell
NEW YEAR'S EVIL(1980)

Taaffe O'Connell
CHEECH AND CHONG'S NICE DREAMS(1981); GALAXY OF TERROR(1981)

Taffy O'Connell
1984
CAGED FURY(1984, Phil.)

Thomas Edward O'Connell
FACE BEHIND THE MASK, THE(1941), w

Tim O'Connell
1984
SLAPSTICK OF ANOTHER KIND(1984), spec eff

W. O'Connell
MURDER IN TIMES SQUARE(1943), ph

W. L. O'Connell
Silents
BROKEN DOLL, A(1921), ph

Walter O'Connell
DO YOU LOVE ME?(1946)

William O'Connell
ACCIDENTS WILL HAPPEN(1938), ph; NANCY DREW, TROUBLE SHOOTER(1939), ph; FLIGHT ANGELS(1940), ph; UNTAMED WOMEN(1952), ed; 20,000 EYES(1961); WOMAN HUNT(1962); WAY...WAY OUT(1966); IT'S A BIKINI WORLD(1967); ICE STATION ZEBRA(1968); HAPPY ENDING, THE(1969); PAINT YOUR WAGON(1969); SCANDALOUS JOHN(1971); CULPEPPER CATTLE COMPANY, THE(1972); HIGH PLAINS DRIFTER(1973); BIG BAD MAMA(1974); OUTLAW JOSEY WALES, THE(1976); ANY WHICH WAY YOU CAN(1980)
Silents
ENTER MADAME(1922), ph; UNCHASTENED WOMAN(1925), ph; SLAVES OF BEAUTY(1927), ph

William O.Connell
GAMES(1967)

Bob O'Conner
SWISS MISS(1938)

Edwin O'Conner
LAST HURRAH, THE(1958), w

Elizabeth O'Conner
IRISHMAN, THE(1978, Aus.), w

Frank O'Conner
SHADOW OF THE LAW(1930); AS HUSBANDS GO(1934)

John O'Conner
1984
SAVAGE STREETS(1984), ed

Patrick O'Conner
JOAN OF ARC(1948)

Penny O'Conner
RECKLESS MOMENTS, THE(1949)

Robert Emmett O'Conner
JACKASS MAIL(1942); COURAGE OF LASSIE(1946)

Terrence O'Conner
STAR TREK: THE MOTION PICTURE(1979)

Una O'Conner
INFORMER, THE(1935); HER FIRST BEAU(1941)

William O'Conner
DRIFTER, THE(1932), d

J.P. O'Connolly
FAREWELL PERFORMANCE(1963, Brit.), p, w; TRAITORS, THE(1963, Brit.), w

James O'Connolly
EMERGENCY(1962, Brit.), w; SHADOW OF FEAR(1963, Brit.), w; VALLEY OF GWANGI, THE(1969), d

Jim O'Connolly
HI-JACKERS, THE(1963, Brit.), d&w; TRAITORS, THE(1963, Brit.), p; SMOKESCREEN(1964, Brit.), d&w; LITTLE ONES, THE(1965, Brit.), d&w; SOPHIE'S PLACE(1970), a, d&w; BEYOND THE FOG(1981, Brit.), d&w

A. J. O'Connor
Silents
GOLD RUSH, THE(1925)

A. Kendall O'Connor
DUMBO(1941), art d

Alice O'Connor
1984
PROTOCOL(1984)

April O'Connor
KILL, THE(1968)

Bill O'Connor
I BECAME A CRIMINAL(1947); NO ORCHIDS FOR MISS BLANDISH(1948, Brit.); HAPPINESS OF THREE WOMEN, THE(1954, Brit.); TOO YOUNG TO LOVE(1960, Brit.)

Billie O'Connor
MELODY FOR TWO(1937)

Blueboy O'Connor
EMPEROR JONES, THE(1933)

Bob [Mazooka] O'Connor
PACK UP YOUR TROUBLES(1932); PICK A STAR(1937)

Bob O'Connor
OUR RELATIONS(1936); RAGTIME COWBOY JOE(1940); MASKED RIDER, THE(1941); ONCE UPON A HONEYMOON(1942); SPANISH MAIN, THE(1945); RIF-FRAFF(1947)

Bud O'Connor
NAUGHTY NINETIES, THE(1945)

Candace O'Connor
SILENT PARTNER, THE(1979, Can.); BEAR ISLAND(1980, Brit.-Can.); TICKET TO HEAVEN(1981)

Carroll O'Connor
JOHNNY FRENCHMAN(1946, Brit.); BY LOVE POSSESSED(1961); FEVER IN THE BLOOD, A(1961); PARRISH(1961); LAD: A DOG(1962); LONELY ARE THE BRAVE(1962); CLEOPATRA(1963); IN HARM'S WAY(1965); HAWAII(1966); NOT WITH MY WIFE, YOU DON'T!(1966); WHAT DID YOU DO IN THE WAR, DADDY?(1966); POINT BLANK(1967); WARNING SHOT(1967); WATERHOLE NO. 3(1967); DEVIL'S BRIGADE, THE(1968); FOR LOVE OF IVY(1968); DEATH OF A GUNFIGHTER(1969); MARLOWE(1969); RIDE A NORTHBOUND HORSE(1969); KELLY'S HEROES(1970, U.S./Yugo.); DOCTORS' WIVES(1971); LAW AND DISORDER(1974)
Misc. Talkies
BELLE SOMMERS(1962)

Cavan O'Connor
RIVER OF UNREST(1937, Brit.); HONEYMOON HOTEL(1946, Brit.)

Consuela O'Connor
KISS OF DEATH(1947)

Danny O'Connor
LOCK UP YOUR DAUGHTERS(1969, Brit.)

Darren O'Connor
TO FIND A MAN(1972)

Dennis O'Connor
1984
C.H.U.D.(1984), ed

Derrick O'Connor
LAST DAYS OF MAN ON EARTH, THE(1975, Brit.); SWEENEY 2(1978, Brit.); HAWK THE SLAYER(1980, Brit.); TIME BANDITS(1981, Brit.); MISSIONARY, THE(1982); BLOODY KIDS(1983, Brit.)

Donald O'Connor
MELODY FOR TWO(1937); MEN WITH WINGS(1938); SING YOU SINNERS(1938); SONS OF THE LEGION(1938); BEAU GESTE(1939); BOY TROUBLE(1939); DEATH OF A CHAMPION(1939); MILLION DOLLAR LEGS(1939); NIGHT WORK(1939); ON YOUR TOES(1939); TOM SAWYER, DETECTIVE(1939); UNMARRIED(1939); GET HEP TO LOVE(1942); GIVE OUT, SISTERS(1942); PRIVATE BUCKAROO(1942); WHAT'S COOKIN'?(1942); IT COMES UP LOVE(1943); MR. BIG(1943); TOP MAN(1943); WHEN JOHNNY COMES MARCHING HOME(1943); BOWERY TO BROADWAY(1944); CHIP OFF THE OLD BLOCK(1944); FOLLOW THE BOYS(1944); MERRY MONAHANS, THE(1944); THIS IS THE LIFE(1944); SOMETHING IN THE WIND(1947); ARE YOU WITH IT?(1948); FEUDIN', FUSSIN' AND A-FIGHTIN'(1948); FRANCIS(1949); YES SIR, THAT'S MY BABY(1949); CURTAIN CALL AT CACTUS CREEK(1950); DOUBLE CROSSBONES(1950); MILKMAN, THE(1950); FRANCIS GOES TO THE RACES(1951); FRANCIS GOES TO WEST POINT(1952); SINGIN' IN THE RAIN(1952); CALL ME MADAM(1953); FRANCIS COVERS THE BIG TOWN(1953); I LOVE MELVIN(1953); WALKING MY BABY BACK HOME(1953); FRANCIS JOINS THE WACS(1954); THERE'S NO BUSINESS LIKE SHOW BUSINESS(1954); FRANCIS IN THE NAVY(1955); ANYTHING GOES(1956); BUSTER KEATON STORY, THE(1957); CRY FOR HAPPY(1961); WONDERS OF ALADDIN, THE(1961, Fr./Ital.); THAT FUNNY FEELING(1965); RAGTIME(1981); PANDEMONIUM(1982)

Donald O'Connor, Jr.
PATRICK THE GREAT(1945)

Doreen O'Connor
Silents
EAST LYNNE(1913, Brit.)

Edward O'Connor
LUCKY IN LOVE(1929)
Silents
KATHLEEN MAVOURNEEN(1919)
Misc. Silents
MAN WHO STOOD STILL, THE(1916); CECILIA OF THE PINK ROSES(1918)

Esther O'Connor
NO RESTING PLACE(1952, Brit.)

Flannery O'Connor
WISE BLOOD(1979, U.S./Ger.), w

Frances O'Connor
FREAKS(1932)

Frank O'Connor
YELLOW JACK(1938); LADIES' MAN(1931); HANDLE WITH CARE(1932); DEATH KISS, THE(1933); SON OF KONG(1933); TILLIE AND GUS(1933); HIDE-OUT(1934); MEN OF THE NIGHT(1934); YOU'RE TELLING ME(1934); FALSE PRETENSES(1935); GLASS KEY, THE(1935); HIS FIGHTING BLOOD(1935); MURDER MAN(1935); RENDEZVOUS(1935); RUGGLES OF RED GAP(1935); DANGEROUS(1936); GREAT GUY(1936); MURDER AT GLEN ATHOL(1936); MAYTIME(1937); NIGHT CLUB SCANDAL(1937); PICK A STAR(1937); WRONG ROAD, THE(1937); COMET OVER BROADWAY(1938); GUN LAW(1938); PURPLE VIGILANTES, THE(1938); RIDERS OF THE BLACK HILLS(1938); SMASHING THE RACKETS(1938); STRANGE FACES(1938); HONOR OF THE WEST(1939); LAUGH IT OFF(1939); LITTLE ACCIDENT(1939); NEWSBOY'S HOME(1939); OUR LEADING CITIZEN(1939); OUR NEIGHBORS–THE CARTERS(1939); PIRATES OF THE SKIES(1939); RACKETEERS OF THE RANGE(1939); SILVER ON THE SAGE(1939); STORY OF VERNON AND IRENE CASTLE, THE(1939); YOU CAN'T CHEAT AN HONEST MAN(1939); GRAPES OF WRATH(1940); INVISIBLE MAN RETURNS, THE(1940); LOVE, HONOR AND OH, BABY(1940); STRANGER ON THE THIRD FLOOR(1940); THIRD FINGER, LEFT HAND(1940); BURY ME NOT ON THE LONE PRAIRIE(1941); CAUGHT IN THE DRAFT(1941); GAY FALCON, THE(1941); I WANTED WINGS(1941); MAN MADE MONSTER(1941); MAN WHO LOST HIMSELF, THE(1941); ROAR OF THE PRESS(1941); SAINT IN PALM SPRINGS, THE(1941); SUNSET MURDER CASE(1941); WYOMING WILDCAT(1941); MAYOR OF 44TH STREET, THE(1942); MYSTERY OF MARIE ROGET, THE(1942); QUIET PLEASE, MURDER(1942); STARDUST ON THE SAGE(1942); YOU'RE TELLING ME(1942); KEEP 'EM SLUGGING(1943); PASSPORT TO SUEZ(1943); SHE HAS WHAT IT TAKES(1943); SO'S YOUR UNCLE(1943); COVER GIRL(1944); HIDDEN VALLEY OUTLAWS(1944); SCARLET CLAW, THE(1944); SILVER CITY KID(1944); UP IN ARMS(1944); YOUTH RUNS WILD(1944); I LOVE A MYSTERY(1945); LONE TEXAS RANGER(1945); PICTURE OF DORIAN GRAY, THE(1945); BOSTON BLACKIE AND THE LAW(1946); DAYS OF BUFFALO BILL(1946); SUN VALLEY CYCLONE(1946); SUNSET PASS(1946); BUFFALO BILL RIDES AGAIN(1947); DESPERATE(1947); LAST FRONTIER UPRISING(1947); SADDLE PALS(1947); SHOOT TO KILL(1947); FORCE OF EVIL(1948); LOADED PISTOLS(1948); NOOSE HANGS HIGH, THE(1948); THAT WONDERFUL URGE(1948); COUNTY FAIR(1950); MULE TRAIN(1950); SUNSET BOULEVARD(1950); TOUGHER THEY COME, THE(1950); CYCLONE FURY(1951); SANTA FE(1951); MAN OF CONFLICT(1953); PACK TRAIN(1953); GHOST OF ZORRO(1959)

Frank O'Connor
Silents
CALL OF THE CIRCUS(1930), d; MYSTIC CIRCLE MURDER(1939), d, w; ADVENTURE IN DIAMONDS(1940), w

Frank O'Connor
WRONG MAN, THE(1956), tech adv

Frank O'Connor
HOMESPUN VAMP, A(1922), d; LAWFUL CHEATERS(1925), d&w; ONE OF THE BRAVEST(1925), d; SILENT POWER, THE(1926), d; YOUR WIFE AND MINE(1927), d; MASKED ANGEL(1928), d; JUST OFF BROADWAY(1929), d; LINDA(1929), w; RISING OF THE MOON, THE(1957, Ireland), w
Misc. Silents
CRUCIBLE OF LIFE, THE(1918); LITTLE MISS NO-ACCOUNT(1918); UNWRITTEN CODE, THE(1919); BLIND LOVE, THE(1920); EVERYTHING FOR SALE(1921), d; VIRGINIA COURTSHIP, A(1921), d; GO STRAIGHT(1925), d; BLOCK SIGNAL, THE(1926), d; DEVIL'S ISLAND(1926), d; EXCLUSIVE RIGHTS(1926), d; FALSE ALARM, THE(1926), d; HEARTS AND SPANGLES(1926), d; SPANGLES(1926), d; SPEED LIMIT, THE(1926), d; COLLEEN(1927), d; HEROES OF THE NIGHT(1927), d; SINEWS OF STEEL(1927), d

Frank L.A. O'Connor
Misc. Silents
MADAME SHERRY(1917)

Gloria O'Connor
KISS OF DEATH(1947)

Glynnis O'Connor
JEREMY(1973); BABY BLUE MARINE(1976); ODE TO BILLY JOE(1976); KID VENGEANCE(1977); CALIFORNIA DREAMING(1979); THOSE LIPS, THOSE EYES(1980); MELANIE(1982, Can.); NIGHT CROSSING(1982)
1984
JOHNNY DANGEROUSLY(1984)
Misc. Talkies
WHITE LIONS(1981)

Gwen O'Connor
MOTOR PATROL(1950)

Harry O'Connor
Silents
STRANGER THAN FICTION(1921); CYCLONE OF THE RANGE(1927)
Misc. Silents
WHEN THE LAW RIDES(1928); TRAIL OF THE HORSE THIEVES, THE(1929)

Harry M. O'Connor
Misc. Silents
LONG LANE'S TURNING, THE(1919)

Hazel O'Connor
BREAKING GLASS(1980, Brit.)

Jack O'Connor
MELODY FOR TWO(1937); LADIES' DAY(1943); MILDRED PIERCE(1945)

James O'Connor
Silents
EAST LYNNE(1916)

Jim O'Connor
BERSERK(1967), d
Misc. Talkies
MISTRESS PAMELA(1974), d

Joan O'Connor
CROWNING TOUCH, THE(1959, Brit.), w; MAN WHO LIKED FUNERALS, THE(1959, Brit.), w

Joe O'Connor
IRON MAJOR, THE(1943)

John O'Connor
DOUGHGIRLS, THE(1944); LADY IN THE DARK(1944); JANIE GETS MARRIED(1946); SENATOR WAS INDISCREET, THE(1947); MILKMAN, THE(1950); MISSISSIPPI GAMBLER, THE(1953)

John O'Connor
Silents
CASSIDY(1917)

John O'Connor
TERMINAL ISLAND(1973), ed; FINAL EXAM(1981), ed

John O'Connor
Misc. Talkies
WARHEAD(1974), d

John O.Connor
FAMILY HONEYMOON(1948)

Joseph O'Connor
CROOKS IN CLOISTERS(1964, Brit.); WALK WITH LOVE AND DEATH, A(1969)

Kathleen O'Connor
Silents
FAME AND FORTUNE(1918); LIFE'S DARN FUNNY(1921); COME ON OVER(1922); DARK STAIRWAYS(1924)
Misc. Silents
ACE HIGH(1918); MR. LOGAN, USA(1918); GUN-FIGHTIN' GENTLEMAN, A(1919); BULLET-PROOF(1920); PRAIRIE TRAILS(1920); SUNSET JONES(1921); TROUPER, THE(1922); WILD BILL HICKOK(1923)

Kendall O'Connor
SNOW WHITE AND THE SEVEN DWARFS(1937), art d; FANTASIA(1940), art d; PINOCCHIO(1940), art d

Kevin O'Connor
LET'S SCARE JESSICA TO DEATH(1971); WELCOME TO THE CLUB(1971); PASSOVER PLOT, THE(1976, Israel); BRINK'S JOB, THE(1978)
1984
SPECIAL EFFECTS(1984)

L. J. O'Connor
Silents
WATCH YOUR STEP(1922); SOULS FOR SALE(1923); NIGHT SHIP, THE(1925); OUT OF THE WEST(1926); FOUR SONS(1928)

L.J. O'Connor
Misc. Silents
RARIN' TO GO(1924); GOLD AND GRIT(1925); TIP-OFF, THE(1929)

Larry O'Connor
NEVER TAKE CANDY FROM A STRANGER(1961, Brit.)

Louis O'Connor
Silents
PARTNERS OF THE NIGHT(1920)

Louis J. O'Connor
Silents
DIANE OF STAR HOLLOW(1921)
Misc. Silents
CALL OF THE HILLS, THE(1923)

Loyola O'Connor
Silents
LILY AND THE ROSE, THE(1915); SECRET ORCHARD(1915); ATTA BOY'S LAST RACE(1916); INTOLERANCE(1916); LITTLE LIAR, THE(1916); NINA, THE FLOWER GIRL(1917); TRUE HEART SUSIE(1919); EYES OF THE HEART(1920); FAITH HEALER, THE(1921)
Misc. Silents
COUNTRY BOY, THE(1915); OLD FASHIONED YOUNG MAN, AN(1917); LIFE IN THE ORANGE GROVES(1920); OLD DAD(1920)

Maggie O'Connor
THEY SHOOT HORSES, DON'T THEY?(1969), makeup
Manning O'Connor
MICHAEL SHAYNE, PRIVATE DETECTIVE(1940), w; DRESSED TO KILL(1941), w
Marilyn O'Connor
GET OUTTA TOWN(1960)
Marlyn O'Connor
1984
PLAGUE DOGS, THE(1984, U.S./Brit.), ph
Mary O'Connor
Silents
SINS OF ROZANNE(1920), w
Mary H. O'Connor
Silents
PENITENTES, THE(1915), w; HELL-TO-PAY AUSTIN(1916), w; NINA, THE FLOW-ER GIRL(1917), w
Maureen O'Connor
BOY OF THE STREETS(1937); EXPRESSO BONGO(1959, Brit.); WEREWOLF IN A GIRL'S DORMITORY(1961, Ital./Aust.)
1984
WOMAN IN RED, THE(1984)
Michael O'Connor
Silents
NO MOTHER TO GUIDE HER(1923), w
Pat O'Connor
ACE ELI AND RODGER OF THE SKIES(1973); HUCKLEBERRY FINN(1974); RETURN TO MACON COUNTY(1975)
1984
CAL(1984, Ireland), d
Patrick O'Connor
TREASURE HUNT(1952, Brit.)
Patsy O'Connor
REDHEADS ON PARADE(1935); GIRL LOVES BOY(1937); I PROMISE TO PAY(1937); SARATOGA(1937); TOO HOT TO HANDLE(1938); IT AIN'T HAY(1943); MOONLIGHT IN VERMONT(1943); YOU'RE A LUCKY FELLOW, MR. SMITH(1943); PARDON MY RHYTHM(1944); PATRICK THE GREAT(1945); QUICKSAND(1950)
Paul "Bucky" O'Connor
SPIRIT OF NOTRE DAME, THE(1931)
Peggy O'Connor
I'LL GET BY(1950); JACKPOT, THE(1950); WHERE THE SIDEWALK ENDS(1950); TAKE CARE OF MY LITTLE GIRL(1951); GARMENT JUNGLE, THE(1957)
Rita O'Connor
ENTERTAINER, THE(1975)
Robert O'Connor
DESIRE(1936); ARSENE LUPIN RETURNS(1938); CUBAN PETE(1946)
Robert E. O'Connor
BLUSHING BRIDES(1930); FRAME-UP THE(1937); PARK AVENUE LOGGER(1937); SUPER SLEUTH(1937); FUGITIVE FROM JUSTICE, A(1940)
Silents
TIN GODS(1926); FOUR WALLS(1928); FREEDOM OF THE PRESS(1928); NOOSE, THE(1928)
Robert Emmet O'Connor
BIG HOUSE, THE(1930); TAXI!(1932); FRISCO JENNY(1933); RETURN OF THE TERROR(1934); STAR OF MIDNIGHT(1935); LONE WOLF RETURNS, THE(1936); WHEN YOU'RE IN LOVE(1937)
Robert Emmett O'Connor
SINGING FOOL, THE(1928); ISLE OF LOST SHIPS(1929); SMILING IRISH EYES(1929); ALIAS FRENCH GERTIE(1930); FRAMED(1930); IN THE NEXT ROOM(1930); OUR BLUSHING BRIDES(1930); PAID(1930); SHOOTING STRAIGHT(1930); UP THE RIVER(1930); FANNY FOLEY HERSELF(1931); MAN TO MAN(1931); PUBLIC ENEMY, THE(1931); RECKLESS LIVING(1931); SINGLE SIN(1931); THREE WHO LOVED(1931); AMERICAN MADNESS(1932); ARM OF THE LAW(1932); BLONDE VENUS(1932); DARK HORSE, THE(1932); KID FROM SPAIN, THE(1932); NIGHT WORLD(1932); TWO KINDS OF WOMEN(1932); DON'T BET ON LOVE(1933); GREAT JASPER, THE(1933); LADY FOR A DAY(1933); MIDNIGHT MARY(1933); PENTHOUSE(1933); PICTURE SNATCHER(1933); BIG SHAKEDOWN, THE(1934); BOTTOMS UP(1934); LET 'EM HAVE IT(1935); MYSTERIOUS MR. WONG(1935); NIGHT AT THE OPERA, A(1935); STOLEN HARMONY(1935); WATER-FRONT LADY(1935); WHITE LIES(1935); WHOLE TOWN'S TALKING, THE(1935); IT HAD TO HAPPEN(1936); LITTLE LORD FAUNTLEROY(1936); SING ME A LOVE SONG(1936); BOY OF THE STREETS(1937); CRIME NOBOBY SAW, THE(1937); GIRL OVERBOARD(1937); STAR IS BORN, A(1937); TRAPPED BY G-MEN(1937); WAIKIKI WEDDING(1937); WE WHO ARE ABOUT TO DIE(1937); WELLS FARGO(1937); PROFESSOR BEWARE(1938); JOE AND ETHEL TURP CALL ON THE PRESI-DENT(1939); MADE FOR EACH OTHER(1939); STREETS OF NEW YORK(1939); YOU CAN'T GET AWAY WITH MURDER(1939); DANCE, GIRL, DANCE(1940); DOUBLE ALIBI(1940); HOT STEEL(1940); NO TIME FOR COMEDY(1940); ROAD TO SIN-GAPORE(1940); TIGHT SHOES(1941); TENNESSEE JOHNSON(1942); TISH(1942); AIR RAID WARDENS(1943); HUMAN COMEDY, THE(1943); SLIGHTLY DANGER-OUS(1943); WHISTLING IN BROOKLYN(1943); MEET ME IN ST. LOUIS(1944); MEET THE PEOPLE(1944); NOTHING BUT TROUBLE(1944); RATIONING(1944); THIN MAN GOES HOME, THE(1944); ABBOTT AND COSTELLO IN HOLLYWOOD(1945); THEY WERE EXPENDABLE(1945); THRILL OF A ROMANCE(1945); BOYS' RANCH(1946); EASY TO WED(1946); HARVEY GIRLS, THE(1946); HOODLUM SAINT, THE(1946); SHOW-OFF, THE(1946); TILL THE CLOUDS ROLL BY(1946); UNDERCURRENT(1946); FIESTA(1947); HIGH BARBAREE(1947); HIGH WALL, THE(1947); HUCKSTERS, THE(1947); EASTER PARADE(1948); SUNSET BOULE-VARD(1950)
Rod O'Connor
SOUTHERN YANKEE, A(1948)
Rory O'Connor
KATHLEEN(1938, Ireland)
Susan O'Connor
MAN FROM TEXAS, THE(1948)
Suzanne O'Connor
RAZOR'S EDGE, THE(1946)
Terry O'Connor
BREAKER! BREAKER!(1977)

Tim O'Connor
ACROSS 110TH STREET(1972); GROUNDSTAR CONSPIRACY, THE(1972, Can.); BLACK JACK(1973); SSSSSSSS(1973); BUCK ROGERS IN THE 25TH CENTURY(1979)
Toni O'Connor
GNOME-MOBILE, THE(1967)
Una O'Connor
CORPSE CAME C.O.D., THE(; DARK RED ROSES(1930, Brit.); MURDER(1930, Brit.); CAVALCADE(1933); HORSEPLAY(1933); INVISIBLE MAN, THE(1933); MARY STEV-ENS, M.D.(1933); PLEASURE CRUISE(1933); TIMBUCTOO(1933, Brit.); ALL MEN ARE ENEMIES(1934); BARRETTS OF WIMPOLE STREET, THE(1934); CHAI-NED(1934); ORIENT EXPRESS(1934); POOR RICH, THE(1934); STINGAREE(1934); DAVID COPPERFIELD(1935); FATHER BROWN, DETECTIVE(1935); PERFECT GEN-TLEMAN, THE(1935); THUNDER IN THE NIGHT(1935); LITTLE LORD FAUNT-LEROY(1936); LLOYDS OF LONDON(1936); PLOUGH AND THE STARS, THE(1936); ROSE MARIE(1936); SUZY(1936); CALL IT A DAY(1937); PERSONAL PROPER-TY(1937); ADVENTURES OF ROBIN HOOD, THE(1938); RETURN OF THE FROG, THE(1938, Brit.); ALL WOMEN HAVE SECRETS(1939); HIS BROTHER'S KEE-PER(1939, Brit.); WE ARE NOT ALONE(1939); HE STAYED FOR BREAKFAST(1940); IT ALL CAME TRUE(1940); LILLIAN RUSSELL(1940); SEA HAWK, THE(1940); KISSES FOR BREAKFAST(1941); STRAWBERRY BLONDE, THE(1941); THREE GIRLS ABOUT TOWN(1941); ALWAYS IN MY HEART(1942); MY FAVORITE SPY(1942); RANDOM HARVEST(1942); FOREVER AND A DAY(1943); GOVERN-MENT GIRL(1943); HOLY MATRIMONY(1943); THIS LAND IS MINE(1943); CAN-TERVILLE GHOST, THE(1944); MY PAL, WOLF(1944); BELLS OF ST. MARY'S, THE(1945); CHRISTMAS IN CONNECTICUT(1945); CHILD OF DIVORCE(1946); OF HUMAN BONDAGE(1946); RETURN OF MONTE CRISTO, THE(1946); UNEXPECTED GUEST(1946); BANJO(1947); IVY(1947); LOST HONEYMOON(1947); FIGHTING FA-THER DUNNE(1948); ADVENTURES OF DON JUAN(1949); WITNESS FOR THE PROSECUTION(1957); ALL WOMAN(1967)
William O'Connor
TEN NIGHTS IN A BARROOM(1931), d; HER SPLENDID FOLLY(1933), d
Misc. Talkies
PLAYTHINGS OF HOLLYWOOD(1931), d
William O.Connor
CHEYENNE TORNADO(1935), d
Frank O'Connors
RIDE, TENDERFOOT, RIDE(1940)
Bob O'Conor
TORTILLA FLAT(1942)
Joseph O'Conor
STRANGER AT MY DOOR(1950, Brit.); PAUL TEMPLE'S TRIUMPH(1951, Brit.); GORGO(1961, Brit.); DEVIL-SHIP PIRATES, THE(1964, Brit.); GORGON, THE(1964, Brit.); OLIVER!(1968, Brit.); ANNE OF THE THOUSAND DAYS(1969, Brit.); YELLOW DOG(1973, Brit.); BLACK WINDMILL, THE(1974, Brit.); DARK CRYSTAL, THE(1982, Brit.)
Robert O'Conor
TROPIC HOLIDAY(1938)
Peter O'Crotty
SOFIA(1948); VENDETTA(1950), w; DEADLY COMPANIONS, THE(1961); NIGHT OF THE LEPUS(1972)
O'Curran
HOLLYWOOD OR BUST(1956), ch
Charles O'Curran
MOONLIGHT AND CACTUS(1944), ch; MUSIC IN MANHATTAN(1944), ch; SENSA-TIONS OF 1945(1944), ch; SEVEN DAYS ASHORE(1944), ch; PAN-AMERICA-NA(1945), ch; BAMBOO BLONDE, THE(1946), ch; BERLIN EXPRESS(1948), ch; MIRACLE OF THE BELLS, THE(1948), ch; RACE STREET(1948), ch; GLORY AL-LEY(1952), ch; ROAD TO BALI(1952), ch; SOMEBODY LOVES ME(1952), a, ch; ARTISTS AND MODELS(1955), ch; LOVING YOU(1957), ch; SAD SACK, THE(1957), ch; KING CREOLE(1958), ch; BELLS ARE RINGING(1960), ch; G.I. BLUES(1960), ch; GIRLS! GIRLS! GIRLS!(1962), ch; FUN IN ACAPULCO(1963), ch
Margie O'Dair
1984
TIGHTROPE(1984)
Barrie O'Daniels
GIRL OF THE PORT(1930)
Kathy O'Dare
EAT MY DUST!(1976)
Peggy O'Dare
Silents
RIDERS OF MYSTERY(1925)
Misc. Silents
THREE BUCKAROOS, THE(1922); MOCCASINS(1925)
Ted O'Darsa [Dario Sabatello]
SEVEN GUNS FOR THE MACGREGORS(1968, Ital./Span.), p
Vesey O'Davern
CLIVE OF INDIA(1935)
Vesey O'Davoran
MY SON, MY SON!(1940)
Vacey O'Davoren
MR. DEEDS GOES TO TOWN(1936)
Vasey O'Davoren
SHALL WE DANCE(1937)
Vesey O'Davoren
STELLA DALLAS(1937)
Vesey O'Davoren
UNTIL THEY SAIL(1957); JIMMY THE GENT(1934); DARK ANGEL, THE(1935); FOLIES DERGERE(1935); I FOUND STELLA PARISH(1935); RIGHT TO LIVE, THE(1935); STRANDED(1935); GOLDEN ARROW, THE(1936); LADIES IN LO-VE(1936); LONE WOLF RETURNS, THE(1936); WHITE ANGEL, THE(1936); LAST OF MRS. CHEYNEY, THE(1937); LET'S GET MARRIED(1937); RAFFLES(1939); MILK-MAN, THE(1950); SON OF DR. JEKYLL, THE(1951); SCARLET COAT, THE(1955)
Misc. Silents
WINDS OF THE PAMPAS(1927)
Vessy O'Davoren
LADY OBJECTS, THE(1938)
Alan O'Day
WILD GUITAR(1962), m; SGT. PEPPER'S LONELY HEARTS CLUB BAND(1978)

Alice O'Day
CALL ME MAME(1933, Brit.); LITTLE MISS NOBODY(1933, Brit.); PHANTOM LIGHT, THE(1935, Brit.); WHO KILLED FEN MARKHAM?(1937, Brit.); SUICIDE LEGION(1940, Brit.)
Silents
MOTORING(1927, Brit.)

Anita O'Day
WOULD YOU BELIEVE IT!(1930, Brit.); GENE KRUPA STORY, THE(1959); ZIG-ZAG(1970); OUTFIT, THE(1973)

Dawn O'Day
SINS OF THE FATHERS(1928); FOUR DEVILS(1929); CITY GIRL(1930); GUN SMOKE(1931); EMMA(1932)
Silents
MOONSHINE VALLEY(1922); CALLAHANS AND THE MURPHYS, THE(1927); NIGHT LIFE(1927)

Dawn [Anne Shirley] O'Day
LILIOM(1930)

John O'Day
WIRETAPPERS(1956), w

Kerry O'Day
MY FOOLISH HEART(1949); LIFE OF HER OWN, A(1950)

Mary O'Day
Misc. Silents
FIGHTING HOMBRE, THE(1927)

Molly O'Day
SISTERS(1930); SEA DEVILS(1931); SOB SISTER(1931); GIGOLETTES OF PARIS(1933); HIRED WIFE(1934); LIFE OF VERGIE WINTERS, THE(1934); LAWLESS BORDER(1935); BARS OF HATE(1936); SKULL AND CROWN(1938)
Misc. Talkies
DEVIL ON DECK(1932); LAW OF THE 45'S(1935)
Silents
LOVELORN, THE(1927)
Misc. Silents
PATENT LEATHER KID, THE(1927); LITTLE SHEPHERD OF KINGDOM COME, THE(1928); SHEPHERD OF THE HILL, THE(1928)

Neil O'Day
CONVENTION GIRL(1935); STAGECOACH BUCKAROO(1942)

Nell O'Day
RACKETY RAX(1932); ROAD TO RUIN(1934); THIS SIDE OF HEAVEN(1934); WOMAN IN THE DARK(1934); FLIGHT ANGELS(1940); LAW AND ORDER(1940); PONY POST(1940); RAGTIME COWBOY JOE(1940); SON OF ROARING DAN(1940); ARIZONA CYCLONE(1941); BACK STREET(1941); BOSS OF BULLION CITY(1941); BURY ME NOT ON THE LONE PRAIRIE(1941); DOUBLE DATE(1941); HELLO SUCKER(1941); LAW OF THE RANGE(1941); MAN FROM MONTANA(1941); MASKED RIDER, THE(1941); NEVER GIVE A SUCKER AN EVEN BREAK(1941); RAWHIDE RANGERS(1941); SING ANOTHER CHORUS(1941); ARIZONA STAGECOACH(1942); FIGHTING BILL FARGO(1942); MYSTERY OF MARIE ROGET, THE(1942); PIRATES OF THE PRAIRIE(1942); THERE'S ONE BORN EVERY MINUTE(1942); YOU'RE TELLING ME(1942); RETURN OF THE RANGERS, THE(1943); THUNDERING TRAILS(1943); BOSS OF THE RAWHIDE(1944)
Misc. Talkies
SMOKE LIGHTNING(1933)

Peggy O'Day
Silents
TRAIL'S END(1922); ACE OF THE LAW(1924)
Misc. Silents
ANGEL CITIZENS(1922); STORM GIRL(1922); THEY'RE OFF(1922); THUNDERING HOOFS(1922); MAN GETTER, THE(1923); BATTLIN' BUCKAROO(1924); SHOOTIN' SQUARE(1924); TRAVELIN' FAST(1924); FOUR FROM NOWHERE, THE(1925); PEGGY OF THE SECRET SERVICE(1925); RED BLOOD AND BLUE(1925); RIDERS OF THE SAND STORM(1925); SPORTING WEST(1925); WHISTLING JIM(1925); CLEAN-UP MAN, THE(1928)

Dawn O'Day [Anne Shirley]
MOTHER KNOWS BEST(1928); RICH MAN'S FOLLY(1931); PURCHASE PRICE, THE(1932); SO BIG(1932); THREE ON A MATCH(1932); YOUNG AMERICA(1932); LIFE OF JIMMY DOLAN, THE(1933); FINISHING SCHOOL(1934); KEY, THE(1934); THIS SIDE OF HEAVEN(1934); SCHOOL FOR GIRLS(1935)
Silents
RIDERS OF THE PURPLE SAGE(1925)

Deirdre O'Dea
SECRETS OF A WINDMILL GIRL(1966, Brit.)

Denis O'Dea
PLOUGH AND THE STARS, THE(1936); ODD MAN OUT(1947, Brit.); BAD LORD BYRON, THE(1949, Brit.); FALLEN IDOL, THE(1949, Brit.); MARRY ME!(1949, Brit.); TREASURE ISLAND(1950, Brit.); CAPTAIN HORATIO HORNBLOWER(1951, Brit.); LONG DARK HALL, THE(1951, Brit.); NEVER TAKE NO FOR AN ANSWER(1952, Brit./Ital.); LANDFALL(1953, Brit.); MOGAMBO(1953); SEA DEVILS(1953); CAPTAIN LIGHTFOOT(1955); STORY OF ESTHER COSTELLO, THE(1957, Brit.); ESTHER AND THE KING(1960, U.S./Ital.)

Dennis O'Dea
INFORMER, THE(1935); MARK OF CAIN, THE(1948, Brit.); UNDER CAPRICORN(1949); NIAGARA(1953); DARBY O'GILL AND THE LITTLE PEOPLE(1959)

Jimmy O'Dea
JIMMY BOY(1935, Brit.); PENNY PARADISE(1938, Brit.); CHEER BOYS CHEER(1939, Brit.); IRELAND'S BORDER LINE(1939, Ireland), a, w; LET'S BE FAMOUS(1939, Brit.); DARBY O'GILL AND THE LITTLE PEOPLE(1959); JOHNNY NOBODY(1965, Brit.)

Jimmy O'Dea
Misc. Silents
CASEY'S MILLIONS(1922, Brit.); CRUISKEEN LAWN(1922, Brit.)

John O'Dea
KILLER DILL(1947), w; ADMIRAL WAS A LADY, THE(1950), w; FUGITIVE LADY(1951), w; JACK MCCALL, DESPERADO(1953), w; PRINCE OF PIRATES(1953), w; RAIDERS OF THE SEVEN SEAS(1953), w; ROBBER'S ROOST(1955), w

Joseph O'Dea
QUIET MAN, THE(1952); RISING OF THE MOON, THE(1957, Ireland)

Judith O'Dea
NIGHT OF THE LIVING DEAD(1968)

Larry O'Dea
WHY RUSSIANS ARE REVOLTING(1970)

Maureen O'Dea
BIG GAMBLE, THE(1961)

Rita O'Dea
BOYD'S SHOP(1960, Brit.); LIES MY FATHER TOLD ME(1960, Brit.)

Sunnie O'Dea
SHOW BOAT(1936); STRIKE ME PINK(1936); IN THE NAVY(1941); MODEL WIFE(1941); MOONLIGHT IN HAWAII(1941); SING ANOTHER CHORUS(1941); YOU'LL NEVER GET RICH(1941)

Bryan O'Dell
YOUNGBLOOD(1978); GETTING OVER(1981)

Carey O'Dell
ALL-AMERICAN BOY, THE(1973), art d

Cary O'Dell
NO SAD SONGS FOR ME(1950), art d; SEX AND THE SINGLE GIRL(1964), art d; HAWAIIANS, THE(1970), prod d

David O'Dell
E.T. THE EXTRA-TERRESTRIAL(1982)

Denis O'Dell
IT'S A WONDERFUL WORLD(1956, Brit.), p; TREAD SOFTLY STRANGER(1959, Brit.), p, w; PLAYBOY OF THE WESTERN WORLD, THE(1963, Ireland), p; MAGIC CHRISTIAN, THE(1970, Brit.), p; OFFENSE, THE(1973, Brit.), p; ROYAL FLASH(1975, Brit.), p; RITZ, THE(1976), p; ROBIN AND MARIAN(1976, Brit.), p

Doye O'Dell
FUGITIVE VALLEY(1941); PIONEERS, THE(1941); HELLDORADO(1946)

Doyle O'Dell
MAN FROM RAINBOW VALLEY, THE(1946); LAST FRONTIER UPRISING(1947); SON OF A BADMAN(1949); TIGHT SPOT(1955)

Etain O'Dell
MAN WHO LIKED FUNERALS, THE(1959, Brit.)

Garry O'Dell
Silents
GOING THE LIMIT(1925)
Misc. Silents
PHANTOM JUSTICE(1924); CANVAS KISSER, THE(1925); SPEED MADNESS(1925); SHOOTING STRAIGHT(1927); STRAIGHT SHOOTIN'(1927)

Georgia O'Dell
BIG RACE, THE(1934); SHE GETS HER MAN(1935); SHOW BOAT(1936); THEODORA GOES WILD(1936); WEST OF NEVADA(1936); SINGING OUTLAW(1937); GUILTY TRAILS(1938); LITTLE TOUGH GUY(1938); YOU CAN'T TAKE IT WITH YOU(1938)
Misc. Talkies
BIG CALIBRE(1935)
Silents
IS YOUR DAUGHTER SAFE?(1927)

Gerry O'Dell
Misc. Silents
IN SEARCH OF A HERO(1926)

H. O'Dell
Silents
PENNINGTON'S CHOICE(1915)

Kent O'Dell
MASTER MINDS(1949)

Larry O'Dell
Misc. Silents
PITFALLS OF PASSION(1927)

Robert O'Dell
TOM SAWYER(1930), art d

Robert O'Dell
VARAN THE UNBELIEVABLE(1962, U.S./Jap.), cos

Rosemary O'Dell
PEGGY(1950), cos; FLUFFY(1965), cos; RASCAL(1969), cos

Scott O'Dell
ISLAND OF THE BLUE DOLPHINS(1964), w

Tony O'Dell
1984
KARATE KID, THE(1984)

Florence O'Denishawn
Silents
LAWFUL LARCENY(1923); MONSIEUR BEAUCAIRE(1924)

O'Dett
CINDERELLA(1937, Fr.)

Betty O'Doan
Misc. Silents
FAR WESTERN TRAILS(1929)

W.H. O'Docharty
TERROR OF TINY TOWN, THE(1938)

Mignon O'Doherty
FAITHFUL HEART(1933, Brit.); GOOD COMPANIONS(1933, Brit.); AUTUMN CROCUS(1934, Brit.); DANDY DICK(1935, Brit.); HARD STEEL(1941, Brit.); HE FOUND A STAR(1941, Brit.); NEUTRAL PORT(1941, Brit.); LET THE PEOPLE SING(1942, Brit.); LAMP STILL BURNS, THE(1943, Brit.); MAYTIME IN MAYFAIR(1952, Brit.); WHITE CORRIDORS(1952, Brit.); GHOST SHIP(1953, Brit.); YOU LUCKY PEOPLE(1955, Brit.); WHOLE TRUTH, THE(1958, Brit.)

Bobby O'Donald
MAFIA GIRLS, THE(1969), w, m

A. C. O'Doneghue
MAN WITH 100 FACES, THE(1938, Brit.), ed

Gene O'Donell
YOU'RE OUT OF LUCK(1941)

Joe O'Donnall
BORDER FEUD(1947), w

Sylvia O'Donnel
CLASS OF MISS MAC MICHAEL, THE(1978, Brit./U.S.)

Anne O'Donnell
HUSBANDS(1970); HOMETOWN U.S.A.(1979)

Annie O'Donnell
SATURDAY THE 14TH(1981)

Cathy O'Donnell
BEST YEARS OF OUR LIVES, THE(1946); BURY ME DEAD(1947); SPIRITUALIST, THE(1948); THEY LIVE BY NIGHT(1949); MINIVER STORY, THE(1950, Brit./U.S.); SIDE STREET(1950); DETECTIVE STORY(1951); NEVER TRUST A GAMBLER(1951); EIGHT O'CLOCK WALK(1954, Brit.); LOVES OF THREE QUEENS, THE(1954, Ital./Fr.); WOMAN'S ANGLE, THE(1954, Brit.); MAD AT THE WORLD(1955); MAN FROM LARAMIE, THE(1955); DEERSLAYER, THE(1957); STORY OF MANKIND, THE(1957); MY WORLD DIES SCREAMING(1958); BEN HUR(1959)

Diane O'Donnell
SHE MAN, THE(1967)

Erin O'Donnell
INCIDENT IN AN ALLEY(1962); SAINTLY SINNERS(1962); HELL'S BLOODY DEVILS(1970)

Eugene O'Donnell
Silents
WOMAN WHO FOOLED HERSELF, THE(1922), ph

Gene O'Donnell
APE, THE(1940); I'M NOBODY'S SWEETHEART NOW(1940); LAUGHING AT DANGER(1940); DEVIL BAT, THE(1941); KEEP 'EM FLYING(1941); LET'S GO COLLEGIATE(1941); PARIS CALLING(1941); FRECKLES COMES HOME(1942); MEET THE MOB(1942); MIRACLE KID(1942); ONE THRILLING NIGHT(1942); POLICE BULLETS(1942); SABOTEUR(1942); YOU'RE TELLING ME(1942); CORVETTE K-225(1943); NEVER A DULL MOMENT(1943); NORTH STAR, THE(1943); GREAT AMERICAN PASTIME, THE(1956); GIRL IN BLACK STOCKINGS(1957); HELL BOUND(1957); THREE BRAVE MEN(1957); PRETTY BOY FLOYD(1960); DEAR BRIGETTE(1965); LAWYER, THE(1969)

George O'Donnell
Misc. Silents
MY LADY'S SLIPPER(1916)

Jack O'Donnell
SAP FROM SYRACUSE, THE(1930), w; KING FOR A NIGHT(1933), w; RACING LUCK(1935), w; SILVER STREAK, THE(1935), w; NORTH OF THE RIO GRANDE(1937), w; TEXAS TRAIL(1937), w; GENTLEMAN FROM ARIZONA, THE(1940), w; TUCSON RAIDERS(1944), w

Jacklyn O'Donnell
YOUNG JESSE JAMES(1960)

James O'Donnell
TWO-HEADED SPY, THE(1959, Brit.), w

Jean O'Donnell
FLIGHT ANGELS(1940); HOUSE ACROSS THE BAY, THE(1940); THAT NIGHT IN RIO(1941); MIRACLE ON 34TH STREET, THE(1947)

Joe O'Donnell
MOTH, THE(1934), w; PUBLIC STENOGRAPHER(1935), w; PHANTOM RANGER(1938), w; PORT OF HATE(1939), w; REFORM SCHOOL(1939), w; LONE RIDER FIGHTS BACK, THE(1941), w; LONE RIDER IN GHOST TOWN, THE(1941), w; CATTLE STAMPEDE(1943), w; WILD HORSE RUSTLERS(1943), w; WOLVES OF THE RANGE(1943), w; DEVIL RIDERS(1944), w; FRONTIER OUTLAWS(1944), w; LAND OF THE OUTLAWS(1944), w; RAIDERS OF RED GAP(1944), w; RUSTLER'S HIDEOUT(1944), w; VALLEY OF VENGEANCE(1944), w; QUARE FELLOW, THE(1962, Brit.); GIRL WITH GREEN EYES(1964, Brit.)

Joseph O'Donnell
HIS FIGHTING BLOOD(1935), w; MURDER BY TELEVISION(1935), w; TRAILS OF THE WILD(1935), w; ACES AND EIGHTS(1936), ed; BORDER CABALLERO(1936), w; GHOST PATROL(1936), w; LIGHTNING BILL CARSON(1936), d; ROARIN' GUNS(1936), w; TIMBER WAR(1936), w; TRAITOR, THE(1936), ed; WILDCAT TROOPER(1936), w; ANYTHING FOR A THRILL(1937), w; FIGHTING TEXAN(1937), w; WHISTLING BULLETS(1937), w; WILD HORSE ROUND-UP(1937), w; YOUNG DYNAMITE(1937), w; LAND OF FIGHTING MEN(1938), w; SONGS AND BULLETS(1938), w; FLAMING LEAD(1939), w; ARIZONA GANGBUSTERS(1940), w; BILLY THE KID IN TEXAS(1940), w; GUN CODE(1940), w; INVISIBLE KILLER, THE(1940), w; STRAIGHT SHOOTER(1940), w; BILLY THE KID IN SANTA FE(1941), w; RIDERS OF BLACK MOUNTAIN(1941), w; DEATH RIDES THE PLAINS(1944), w; LAW OF THE VALLEY(1944), w; RETURN OF THE LASH(1947), w; CHECK YOUR GUNS(1948), w; NEVADA BADMEN(1951), w; OKLAHOMA JUSTICE(1951), w; PRAIRIE ROUNDUP(1951), w; MAN FROM BLACK HILLS, THE(1952), w

L.W. O'Donnell
BRINGING UP FATHER(1946), ph

Maire O'Donnell
PROFESSOR TIM(1957, Ireland); HOME IS THE HERO(1959, Ireland); PADDY(1970, Irish); WEDDING NIGHT(1970, Ireland)

Marilyn O'Donnell
CLINIC, THE(1983, Aus.)

Michael Donavon O'Donnell
SATAN'S CHEERLEADERS(1977)

Michael Donovon O'Donnell
ANGELS DIE HARD(1970); HEAD ON(1971), p

Paddy O'Donnell
QUIET MAN, THE(1952)

Peggy O'Donnell
STAGE DOOR(1937)

Peter O'Donnell
MODESTY BLAISE(1966, Brit.), w; VENGEANCE OF SHE, THE(1968, Brit.), w

Spec O'Donnell
IN THE HEADLINES(1929); SOPHOMORE, THE(1929); GRAND PARADE, THE(1930); SHOW GIRL IN HOLLYWOOD(1930); BIG BROADCAST, THE(1932); HELLO TROUBLE(1932); YOUNG AMERICA(1932); ONE NIGHT OF LOVE(1934); COLLEGE HOLIDAY(1936); FRESHMAN LOVE(1936); ROSE BOWL(1936); SAN FRANCISCO(1936); BLONDE TROUBLE(1937); EVER SINCE EVE(1937); LIFE BEGINS IN COLLEGE(1937); LOVE IS ON THE AIR(1937); NIGHT CLUB SCANDAL(1937); ACCIDENTS WILL HAPPEN(1938); PATIENT IN ROOM 18, THE(1938); SWING YOUR LADY(1938); DANGEROUSLY THEY LIVE(1942); GALLANT LADY(1942); MALE ANIMAL, THE(1942); PRISON GIRL(1942); GIRL CRAZY(1943); HERS TO HOLD(1943); IT AIN'T HAY(1943); NEVER A DULL MOMENT(1943); ONCE UPON A TIME(1944); HONEYMOON AHEAD(1945); DEADLINE FOR MURDER(1946); MURDER IN THE MUSIC HALL(1946); HAS ANYBODY SEEN MY GAL?(1952)
Misc. Talkies
EXPOSURE(1932)

Silents
LITTLE ANNIE ROONEY(1925); OLD IRONSIDES(1926); PRIVATE IZZY MURPHY(1926); SPARROWS(1926); CASEY AT THE BAT(1927); WE'RE ALL GAMBLERS(1927); HOT NEWS(1928); VAMPING VENUS(1928)

"Spec" O'Donnell
Silents
COUNTRY KID, THE(1923); DEVIL'S CARGO, THE(1925)

Sylvia O'Donnell
BLACK PANTHER, THE(1977, Brit.)

Tara O'Donnell
1984
HOTEL NEW HAMPSHIRE, THE(1984)

Tommie O'Donnell
COAL MINER'S DAUGHTER(1980)

Walter D. O'Donnell
HOUSE CALLS(1978)

Walter "Spec" O'Donnell
RIDE, KELLY, RIDE(1941); SUN VALLEY SERENADE(1941); HENRY ALDRICH GETS GLAMOUR(1942)

O'Donnell and Blair
ALWAYS LEAVE THEM LAUGHING(1949)

Maurice O'Donoghue
1984
PIGS(1984, Ireland)

Michael O'Donoghue
SAVAGES(1972), w; MANHATTAN(1979)

James T. O'Donohue
SHOW GIRL(1928), w
Silents
KINDRED OF THE DUST(1922), w; WHAT PRICE GLORY(1926), w; CHEATING CHEATERS(1927), w; NOOSE, THE(1928), w; RED LIPS(1928), w

Joseph O'Donohue
CARAVAN(1946, Brit.)

Rory O'Donohue
FATTY FINN(1980, Aus.), m

Danny O'Donovan
GOLDENGIRL(1979), p; ABSOLUTION(1981, Brit.), p

Derry O'Donovan
DEMENTIA 13(1963); OF HUMAN BONDAGE(1964, Brit.)

Desmond O'Donovan
BOY AND THE BRIDGE, THE(1959, Brit.), w

Ed O'Donovan
DROWNING POOL, THE(1975), art d; HARDCORE(1979), art d

Edwin O'Donovan
ONE FLEW OVER THE CUCKOO'S NEST(1975), art d; HEAVEN CAN WAIT(1978), art d; RESURRECTION(1980), art d; HONKY TONK FREEWAY(1981), art d

Elizabeth O'Donovan
DOCTOR FAUSTUS(1967, Brit.)

Frank O'Donovan
MURDER IN EDEN(1962, Brit.); QUARE FELLOW, THE(1962, Brit.)

Fred O'Donovan
GENERAL JOHN REGAN(1933, Brit.); HOUSE OF THE SPANIARD, THE(1936, Brit.); RIVER OF UNREST(1937, Brit.); VICAR OF BRAY, THE(1937, Brit.); YOUNG AND INNOCENT(1938, Brit.); ANOTHER SHORE(1948, Brit.)

Fred O'Donovan
Silents
KNOCKNAGOW(1918, Ireland), a, d
Misc. Silents
WHEN LOVE CAME TO GAVIN BURKE(1918), d; WILLY REILLY AND HIS COLLEEN BAWN(1918, Brit.), d

Harry O'Donovan
JIMMY BOY(1935, Brit.), a, w; IRELAND'S BORDER LINE(1939, Ireland), p&d, w

Ross O'Donovan
STARSTRUCK(1982, Aus.)

Brian O'Dowd
PSYCHO II(1983), cos

Dan O'Dowd
JOURNEY TO FREEDOM(1957)

Michael O'Dowd
ER LOVE A STRANGER(1958)

Mike O'Dowd
ON THE WATERFRONT(1954); GODDESS, THE(1958); GIRL ON THE RUN(1961); WILD IS MY LOVE(1963); PSYCHOMANIA(1964); TAKE THE MONEY AND RUN(1969); BADGE 373(1973)

Larry O'Driscoll
1984
REFLECTIONS(1984, Brit.)

Martha O'Driscoll
SHE'S DANGEROUS(1937); GIRLS' SCHOOL(1938); MAD ABOUT MUSIC(1938); JUDGE HARDY AND SON(1939); SECRET OF DR. KILDARE, THE(1939); FORTY LITTLE MOTHERS(1940); LADDIE(1940); LI'L ABNER(1940); WAGON TRAIN(1940); HENRY ALDRICH FOR PRESIDENT(1941); HER FIRST BEAU(1941); LADY EVE, THE(1941); MIDNIGHT ANGEL(1941); MY HEART BELONGS TO DADDY(1942); PACIFIC BLACKOUT(1942); REAP THE WILD WIND(1942); REMARKABLE ANDREW, THE(1942); ALLERGIC TO LOVE(1943); CRAZY HOUSE(1943); FALLEN SPARROW, THE(1943); WE'VE NEVER BEEN LICKED(1943); YOUNG AND WILLING(1943); YOUTH ON PARADE(1943); FOLLOW THE BOYS(1944); GHOST CATCHERS(1944); HI BEAUTIFUL(1944); WEEKEND PASS(1944); DALTONS RIDE AGAIN, THE(1945); HER LUCKY NIGHT(1945); HERE COME THE CO-EDS(1945); HOUSE OF DRACULA(1945); SHADY LADY(1945); UNDER WESTERN SKIES(1945); BLONDE ALIBI(1946); CRIMINAL COURT(1946); DOWN MISSOURI WAY(1946); CARNEGIE HALL(1947)

William O'Driscoll
NO ROOM FOR THE GROOM(1952)

Michael O'Duffy
RISING OF THE MOON, THE(1957, Ireland); GIDEON OF SCOTLAND YARD(1959, Brit.); JOHNNY NOBODY(1965, Brit.)

Larry O'Dwyer
Misc. Talkies
DON'T OPEN THE DOOR(1974)
Michael O'Dwyer
FURY, THE(1978)
Bernadette O'Farrell
CAPTAIN BOYCOTT(1947, Brit.); HAPPIEST DAYS OF YOUR LIFE(1950, Brit.); LIFE IN HER HANDS(1951, Brit.); SCOTLAND YARD INSPECTOR(1952, Brit.); GENIE, THE(1953, Brit.); GREAT GILBERT AND SULLIVAN, THE(1953, Brit.); LADY GODIVA RIDES AGAIN(1955, Brit.); SQUARE RING, THE(1955, Brit.); BRIDAL PATH, THE(1959, Brit.)
Broderick O'Farrell
HANDCUFFED(1929); NO LIVING WITNESS(1932); NO MORE ORCHIDS(1933); JEALOUSY(1934); MARINES ARE COMING, THE(1935); SHOT IN THE DARK, A(1935); SMART GIRL(1935); WORLD ACCUSES, THE(1935); EASY MONEY(1936); IT COULDN'T HAVE HAPPENED–BUT IT DID(1936); MILKY WAY, THE(1936); NEXT TIME WE LOVE(1936); LAST GANGSTER, THE(1937); STRANGE FACES(1938); WHO KILLED GAIL PRESTON?(1938); ETERNALLY YOURS(1939); OUR LEADING CITIZEN(1939); COURAGEOUS DR. CHRISTIAN, THE(1940); STRANGER ON THE THIRD FLOOR(1940); BUY ME THAT TOWN(1941); FATHER TAKES A WIFE(1941); LOVE CRAZY(1941); GLASS KEY, THE(1942); ICE-CAPADES REVUE(1942); GILDERSLEEVE'S BAD DAY(1943); IS EVERYBODY HAPPY?(1943); SOMEONE TO REMEMBER(1943); EXPERIMENT PERILOUS(1944); LOCKET, THE(1946); NOCTURNE(1946); SECRET LIFE OF WALTER MITTY, THE(1947); HOMECOMING(1948); GIRL FROM JONES BEACH, THE(1949)
Silents
SKINNER'S DRESS SUIT(1926); WHAT HAPPENED TO JONES(1926); PRINCESS FROM HOBOKEN, THE(1927)
John O'Farrell
FROM BEYOND THE GRAVE(1974, Brit.)
Mary O'Farrell
GENERAL JOHN REGAN(1933, Brit.)
Peter O'Farrell
LADY GODIVA RIDES AGAIN(1955, Brit.); HAWK THE SLAYER(1980, Brit.)
Talbot O'Farrell
BORN LUCKY(1932, Brit.); KATHLEEN(1938, Ireland); LILY OF LAGUNA(1938, Brit.); LITTLE DOLLY DAYDREAM(1938, Brit.); ROSE OF TRALEE(1938, Ireland); ROSE OF TRALEE(1942, Brit.)
MacDara O'Fatharta
POITIN(1979, Irish)
Ric O'Feldman
FLIPPER'S NEW ADVENTURE(1964); GENTLE GIANT(1967)
Richard O'Feldman
ABSENCE OF MALICE(1981)
Rick O'Feldman
HARDLY WORKING(1981)
Dominica More O'Ferrall
PLEASE TURN OVER(1960, Brit.)
George Moore O'Ferrall
GREEN SCARF, THE(1954, Brit.), d
George More O'Ferrall
HER PANELLED DOOR(1951, Brit.), d; ANGELS ONE FIVE(1954, Brit.), d; HEART OF THE MATTER, THE(1954, Brit.), d; HOLLY AND THE IVY, THE(1954, Brit.), d; WOMAN FOR JOE, THE(1955, Brit.), d; MARCH HARE, THE(1956, Brit.), d
Oliver O'Ferrall
DRIVE, HE SAID(1971)
George Mare O'Ferrel
THREE CASES OF MURDER(1955, Brit.), d
Dennis O'Flaherty
PROPER TIME, THE(1959); LIKE FATHER LIKE SON(1961); YOUNG SINNER, THE(1965); TRIAL OF BILLY JACK, THE(1974); WHICH WAY IS UP?(1977); WALK PROUD(1979); HAMMETT(1982), w
George O'Flaherty
FIRST COMES COURAGE(1943)
Joe O'Flaherty
TUNNELVISION(1976)
Liam O'Flaherty
INFORMER, THE(1929, Brit.), w; INFORMER, THE(1935), w; DEVIL'S PLAYGROUND(1937), w; JACQUELINE(1956, Brit.), w; UPTIGHT(1968), w
Noel O'Flaherty
1984
REFLECTIONS(1984, Brit.)
Cpl. Damian O'Flynn
WINGED VICTORY(1944)
Damian O'Flynn
MARKED WOMAN(1937); GAY FALCON, THE(1941); LADY SCARFACE(1941); RAGE IN HEAVEN(1941); BROADWAY(1942); GREAT MAN'S LADY, THE(1942); POWDER TOWN(1942); WAKE ISLAND(1942); X MARKS THE SPOT(1942); FLIGHT FOR FREEDOM(1943); SARONG GIRL(1943); SO PROUDLY WE HAIL(1943); BACHELOR'S DAUGHTERS, THE(1946); CRACK-UP(1946); DEVIL ON WHEELS, THE(1947); DEVIL SHIP(1947); PHILO VANCE RETURNS(1947); SADDLE PALS(1947); WEB OF DANGER, THE(1947); DISASTER(1948); FOREIGN AFFAIR, A(1948); SNAKE PIT, THE(1948); BLACK MIDNIGHT(1949); OUTPOST IN MOROCCO(1949); RIDERS OF THE WHISTLING PINES(1949); BOMBA AND THE HIDDEN CITY(1950); GAMBLING HOUSE(1950); PIONEER MARSHAL(1950); YOUNG DANIEL BOONE(1950); FIGHTING COAST GUARD(1951); YELLOW FIN(1951); YOU'RE IN THE NAVY NOW(1951); HALF-BREED, THE(1952); HOODLUM EMPIRE(1952); PLYMOUTH ADVENTURE(1952); PRIDE OF ST. LOUIS, THE(1952); MIAMI STORY, THE(1954); TWO GUNS AND A BADGE(1954); DADDY LONG LEGS(1955); FAR COUNTRY, THE(1955); HIDDEN GUNS(1956); APACHE WARRIOR(1957); DANIEL BOONE, TRAIL BLAZER(1957); EIGHTEEN AND ANXIOUS(1957); WHY MUST I DIE?(1960); GUNFIGHT AT COMANCHE CREEK(1964)
Damien O'Flynn
HALF PAST MIDNIGHT(1948); GLENN MILLER STORY, THE(1953); D-DAY, THE SIXTH OF JUNE(1956)
Damion O'Flynn
DRANGO(1957)

Frances O'Flynn
SPIKES GANG, THE(1974)
Paddy O'Flynn
KIBITZER, THE(1929); FIGHTING RANGER, THE(1934); THIS SIDE OF HEAVEN(1934); DANTE'S INFERNO(1935); MILLIONS IN THE AIR(1935); MILKY WAY, THE(1936); MURDER WITH PICTURES(1936); NEXT TIME WE LOVE(1936); RETURN OF SOPHIE LANG, THE(1936); LOVE IS NEWS(1937); THAT CERTAIN WOMAN(1937)
Misc. Silents
FACE VALUE(1927); UNGUARDED GIRLS(1929)
Paty O'Flynn
FIGHTING GENTLEMAN, THE(1932)
Philip O'Flynn
CAPTAIN LIGHTFOOT(1955); PROFESSOR TIM(1957, Ireland); ROONEY(1958, Brit.); BROTH OF A BOY(1959, Brit.); HOME IS THE HERO(1959, Ireland); THIS OTHER EDEN(1959, Brit.); POACHER'S DAUGHTER, THE(1960, Brit.); BIG GAMBLE, THE(1961); GUY CALLED CAESAR, A(1962, Brit.); QUARE FELLOW, THE(1962, Brit.); WHAT A CARVE UP!(1962, Brit.); NEVER PUT IT IN WRITING(1964); YOUNG CASSIDY(1965, U.S./Brit.); VIKING QUEEN, THE(1967, Brit.); VIOLENT ENEMY, THE(1969, Brit.); RYAN'S DAUGHTER(1970, Brit.)
Eamonn O'Galehur
YOU CAN'T FOOL AN IRISHMAN(1950, Ireland), m
Eamonn O'Gallagher
RISING OF THE MOON, THE(1957, Ireland), m
Jimmy O'Garty
FIGHTING FOOLS(1949)
James O'Gatty
EMERGENCY WEDDING(1950); MALAYA(1950)
Jim O'Gatty
I WAS A COMMUNIST FOR THE F.B.I.(1951)
Jimmy O'Gatty
I STOLE A MILLION(1939); KING OF THE UNDERWORLD(1939); NEWSBOY'S HOME(1939); EAST OF THE RIVER(1940); KNOCKOUT(1941); NINE LIVES ARE NOT ENOUGH(1941); SAN FRANCISCO DOCKS(1941); BROADWAY(1942); LARCENY, INC.(1942); LUCKY JORDAN(1942); ONE THRILLING NIGHT(1942); JOHNNY ANGEL(1945); CRACK-UP(1946); SONG OF THE THIN MAN(1947)
Billy O'Gorman
NO RESTING PLACE(1952, Brit.)
Dave O'Gorman
VARIETY PARADE(1936, Brit.)
George O'Gorman
SMASHING TIME(1967 Brit.); CLOCKWORK ORANGE, A(1971, Brit.)
Joe O'Gorman
VARIETY PARADE(1936, Brit.)
John O'Gorman
MINE OWN EXECUTIONER(1948, Brit.), makeup; PRIDE AND THE PASSION, THE(1957), makeup; INDISCREET(1958), makeup; VIKINGS, THE(1958), makeup; ON THE BEACH(1959), makeup; GRASS IS GREENER, THE(1960), makeup; GOODBYE AGAIN(1961), makeup; DR. NO(1962, Brit.), makeup; HAIR OF THE DOG(1962, Brit.), w; LISA(1962, Brit.), makeup; SUMMER HOLIDAY(1963, Brit.), makeup; SEVENTH DAWN, THE(1964), makeup; VISIT, THE(1964, Ger./Fr./Ital./U.S.), makeup; RETURN FROM THE ASHES(1965, U.S./Brit.), makeup; YELLOW ROLLS-ROYCE, THE(1965, Brit.), makeup; PERFECT FRIDAY(1970, Brit.), makeup; THERE'S A GIRL IN MY SOUP(1970, Brit.), makeup; HANNIE CALDER(1971, Brit.), makeup
W. G. O'Gorman
ADVENTURESS, THE(1946, Brit.)
Colleen O'Grady
CANNERY ROW(1982)
Desmond O'Grady
LA DOLCE VITA(1961, Ital./Fr.)
John O'Grady
THEY'RE A WEIRD MOB(1966, Aus.), w
Lani O'Grady
MASSACRE AT CENTRAL HIGH(1976)
Lanie O'Grady
BABY BLUE MARINE(1976)
Monty O'Grady
OH, MEN! OH, WOMEN!(1957); WALK, DON'T RUN(1966)
Silents
SPARROWS(1926); CALLAHANS AND THE MURPHYS, THE(1927)
Misc. Silents
BAITED TRAP(1926)
Roban O'Grady
LET'S KILL UNCLE(1966), w
Rynagh O'Grady
STUD, THE(1979, Brit.)
Sean O'Grady
1984
SAVAGE STREETS(1984)
Tom O'Grady
STRAIGHT FROM THE HEART(1935); HUMAN CARGO(1936); TOAST OF NEW YORK, THE(1937); TEST PILOT(1938); THREE LOVES HAS NANCY(1938); PIRATES OF THE SKIES(1939); GLASS KEY, THE(1942); MY GAL SAL(1942); RINGS ON HER FINGERS(1942); SECRET AGENT OF JAPAN(1942); SOMEWHERE I'LL FIND YOU(1942); TALES OF MANHATTAN(1942)
Silents
LIGHT IN THE WINDOW, THE(1927); HARDBOILED(1929)
Tony O'Grady
SECRET MAN, THE(1958, Brit.), w; CURSE OF THE VOODOO(1965, Brit.), w
Malcolm O'Guinn
WALK IN THE SUN, A(1945)
Gerard O'Hagan
1984
CAL(1984, Ireland)
William P. O'Hagen
SOMEWHERE IN TIME(1980)
Jack O'Halloran
FAREWELL, MY LOVELY(1975); KING KONG(1976); MARCH OR DIE(1977, Brit.); SUPERMAN(1978); BALTIMORE BULLET, THE(1980); SUPERMAN II(1980)

Michael O'Halloran
BIG CATCH, THE(1968, Brit.); RING OF BRIGHT WATER(1969, Brit.)
O'Hanlon
ROOKIE, THE(1959), w
George O'Hanlon
HELL'S KITCHEN(1939); WOMEN IN THE WIND(1939); CHILD IS BORN, A(1940); FIGHTING 69TH, THE(1940); SAILOR'S LADY(1940); NAVY BLUES(1941); NEW WINE(1941); MAN FROM HEADQUARTERS(1942); CORVETTE K-225(1943); HERS TO HOLD(1943); LADIES' DAY(1943); NEARLY EIGHTEEN(1943); HEADING FOR HEAVEN(1947); HUCKSTERS, THE(1947); SPIRIT OF WEST POINT, THE(1947); ARE YOU WITH IT?(1948); COUNTERFEITERS, THE(1948); JUNE BRIDE(1948); JOE PALOOKA IN THE BIG FIGHT(1949); ZAMBA(1949); TANKS ARE COMING, THE(1951); CATTLE TOWN(1952); LION AND THE HORSE, THE(1952); PARK ROW(1952); BATTLE STATIONS(1956); KRONOS(1957); ROOKIE, THE(1959), d; FOR THOSE WHO THINK YOUNG(1964), w; I SAILED TO TAHITI WITH AN ALL GIRL CREW(1969), w; $1,000,000 DUCK(1971); NOW YOU SEE HIM, NOW YOU DON'T(1972); CHARLEY AND THE ANGEL(1973); ROCKY(1976)
George O'Hanlon, Jr.
OUR TIME(1974); EVIL, THE(1978)
James O'Hanlon
OVER MY DEAD BODY(1942), w; SAHARA(1943), w; MAISIE GOES TO RENO(1944), w; ZIEGFELD FOLLIES(1945), w; HARVEY GIRLS, THE(1946), w; THREE WISE FOOLS(1946), w; TWO SISTERS FROM BOSTON(1946), w; SONG OF THE THIN MAN(1947), w; DESTINATION MOON(1950), w; MILKMAN, THE(1950), w; SECRET FURY, THE(1950), w; MIRACLE OF OUR LADY OF FATIMA, THE(1952), w; SALLY AND SAINT ANNE(1952), w; STOP, YOU'RE KILLING ME(1952), w; CALAMITY JANE(1953), w; LUCKY ME(1954), w; JOHNNY ROCCO(1958), w; FOR THOSE WHO THINK YOUNG(1964), w; MURIETA(1965, Span.), w; REDEEMER, THE(1965, Span.), w
Silents
THREE WISE FOOLS(1923), w
Susan Pratt O'Hanlon
SURVIVAL RUN(1980)
Keiron O'Hanrahan [Moore]
VOICE WITHIN, THE(1945, Brit.)
Barry O'Hara
JOURNEY TO FREEDOM(1957); TWIST AROUND THE CLOCK(1961); CINCINNATI KID, THE(1965); FLUFFY(1965); VERY SPECIAL FAVOR, A(1965); CHUKA(1967); VALLEY OF THE DOLLS(1967); 1776(1972)
Brett O'Hara
INCREDIBLY STRANGE CREATURES WHO STOPPED LIVING AND BECAME CRAZY MIXED-UP ZOMBIES, THE(1965)
Brian O'Hara
THEY RAID BY NIGHT(1942); CALIFORNIA JOE(1944); LOUISIANA HAYRIDE(1944); BOSTON BLACKIE AND THE LAW(1946); LAST ROUND-UP, THE(1947); VOICE OF THE TURTLE, THE(1947); SET-UP, THE(1949); TREASURE OF MONTE CRISTO(1949); UNDERCOVER MAN, THE(1949); CHAMPAGNE FOR CAESAR(1950); STRANGE FASCINATION(1952); VALERIE(1957); CRIMSON KIMONO, THE(1959); STUDS LONIGAN(1960); MARRIED TOO YOUNG(1962)
Catherine O'Hara
NOTHING PERSONAL(1980, Can.)
Misc. Talkies
ROCK 'N' RULE(1983)
Charlie O'Hara
NEVER PUT IT IN WRITING(1964), stunts
Corky O'Hara
YOU BETTER WATCH OUT(1980), ed
Darlene O'Hara
TOUGH ENOUGH(1983)
David O'Hara
1984
COMFORT AND JOY(1984, Brit.)
Dorothy O'Hara
SEARCHING WIND, THE(1946), cos; CALCUTTA(1947), cos
Fiske O'Hara
PADDY, THE NEXT BEST THING(1933); CHANGE OF HEART(1934)
Frank O'Hara
1984
VAMPING(1984)
George O'Hara
NIGHT PARADE(1929, Brit.), w; SIDE STREET(1929), w; JESSE JAMES(1939); GRAPES OF WRATH(1940); COWBOY AND THE BLONDE, THE(1941); COLONEL EFFINGHAM'S RAID(1945)
Silents
QUEENIE(1921); SMALL TOWN IDOL, A(1921); SHIRLEY OF THE CIRCUS(1922); IS THAT NICE?(1926); SEA BEAST, THE(1926); CALIFORNIA OR BUST(1927); HONEYMOON(1929), w; SINGLE MAN, A(1929), w
Misc. Silents
LOVE, HONOR AND BEHAVE(1920); CROSSROADS OF NEW YORK, THE(1922); DARWIN WAS RIGHT(1924); LISTEN LESTER(1924); BIGGER THAN BARNUM'S(1926); GOING THE LIMIT(1926); TIMID TERROR, THE(1926); LADIES BEWARE(1927); YOURS TO COMMAND(1927)
Gerry O'Hara
THAT KIND OF GIRL(1963, Brit.), d; GAME FOR THREE LOSERS(1965, Brit.), d; PLEASURE GIRLS, THE(1966, Brit.), d&w; MAROC 7(1967, Brit.), d; AMSTERDAM AFFAIR, THE(1968 Brit.), d; ALL THE RIGHT NOISES(1973, Brit.), d&w; LEOPARD IN THE SNOW(1979, Brit./Can.), d
Misc. Talkies
BITCH, THE(1979), d
Helen O'Hara
THANK YOUR LUCKY STARS(1943); NOB HILL(1945); ZIEGFELD FOLLIES(1945); JOLSON STORY, THE(1946); NIGHT AND DAY(1946)
Henry O'Hara
GENTLEMAN JIM(1942)
Jack O'Hara
TOO BUSY TO WORK(1932)
James O'Hara
CHEYENNE AUTUMN(1964); MY FAIR LADY(1964); DEATH OF A GUNFIGHTER(1969)

Jamie O'Hara
GARDEN OF EDEN(1954); LIVE FAST, DIE YOUNG(1958)
Jenny O'Hara
HEART BEAT(1979); LAST MARRIED COUPLE IN AMERICA, THE(1980)
Jill O'Hara
SIDELONG GLANCES OF A PIGEON KICKER, THE(1970)
Jim O'Hara
DEADLY COMPANIONS, THE(1961); SPENCER'S MOUNTAIN(1963); RARE BREED, THE(1966)
Joan O'Hara
HOME IS THE HERO(1959, Ireland); SHE DIDN'T SAY NO!(1962, Brit.)
John O'Hara
GENERAL DIED AT DAWN, THE(1936); HE MARRIED HIS WIFE(1940), w; I WAS AN ADVENTURESS(1940), w; MOONTIDE(1942), w; JUST WILLIAM'S LUCK(1948, Brit.); ON OUR MERRY WAY(1948), w; BEST THINGS IN LIFE ARE FREE, THE(1956), w; PAL JOEY(1957), w; 10 NORTH FREDERICK(1958), w; BUTTERFIELD 8(1960), w; FROM THE TERRACE(1960), w; GET OUTTA TOWN(1960); RAGE TO LIVE, A(1965), w
Silents
FIFTY-FIFTY GIRL, THE(1928)
Kareen O'Hara
ANY GUN CAN PLAY(1968, Ital./Span.)
Kenneth O'Hara
Silents
SHAMS OF SOCIETY(1921), w
Margaret O'Hara
HUNTER, THE(1980)
Martin O'Hara
WHAT'S SO BAD ABOUT FEELING GOOD?(1968)
Mary O'Hara
MY FRIEND FLICKA(1943), w; THUNDERHEAD-SON OF FLICKA(1945), w; GREEN GRASS OF WYOMING(1948), w
Silents
LIFE'S DARN FUNNY(1921), w; PRISONER OF ZENDA, THE(1922), w; MERRY-GO-ROUND(1923), t
Maureen O'Hara
HUNCHBACK OF NOTRE DAME, THE(1939); JAMAICA INN(1939, Brit.); BILL OF DIVORCEMENT(1940); DANCE, GIRL, DANCE(1940); LITTLE MISS MOLLY(1940); HOW GREEN WAS MY VALLEY(1941); THEY MET IN ARGENTINA(1941); BLACK SWAN, THE(1942); TEN GENTLEMEN FROM WEST POINT(1942); TO THE SHORES OF TRIPOLI(1942); FALLEN SPARROW, THE(1943); IMMORTAL SERGEANT, THE(1943); THIS LAND IS MINE(1943); BUFFALO BILL(1944); SPANISH MAIN, THE(1945); DO YOU LOVE ME?(1946); SENTIMENTAL JOURNEY(1946); FOXES OF HARROW, THE(1947); HOMESTRETCH, THE(1947); MIRACLE ON 34TH STREET, THE(1947); SINBAD THE SAILOR(1947); SITTING PRETTY(1948); AFFAIRS OF ADELAIDE(1949, U. S./Brit); BAGDAD(1949); FATHER WAS A FULLBACK(1949); WOMAN'S SECRET, A(1949); COMMANCHE TERRITORY(1950); RIO GRANDE(1950); TRIPOLI(1950); AT SWORD'S POINT(1951); FLAME OF ARABY(1951); AGAINST ALL FLAGS(1952); KANGAROO(1952); QUIET MAN, THE(1952); REDHEAD FROM WYOMING, THE(1953); WAR ARROW(1953); FIRE OVER AFRICA(1954, Brit.); LADY GODIVA(1955); LONG GRAY LINE, THE(1955); MAGNIFICENT MATADOR, THE(1955); EVERYTHING BUT THE TRUTH(1956); LISBON(1956); WINGS OF EAGLES, THE(1957); OUR MAN IN HAVANA(1960, Brit.); DEADLY COMPANIONS, THE(1961); PARENT TRAP, THE(1961); MR. HOBBS TAKES A VACATION(1962); MC LINTOCK!(1963); SPENCER'S MOUNTAIN(1963); BATTLE OF THE VILLA FIORITA, THE(1965, Brit.); RARE BREED, THE(1966); HOW DO I LOVE THEE?(1970); BIG JAKE(1971)
Maureen O'Hara
Misc. Silents
LITTLE BREADWINNER, THE(1916, Brit.)
Neal O'Hara
Silents
AIN'T LOVE FUNNY?(1927), t
Paddi O'Hara
SEX AND THE SINGLE GIRL(1964)
Pat O'Hara
UNTIL THEY SAIL(1957); GREAT IMPERSONATION, THE(1935); OUTPOST OF THE MOUNTIES(1939); INTERNATIONAL SQUADRON(1941); MIRACLE OF THE HILLS, THE(1959); RETURN OF THE FLY(1959)
Patricia Quinn O'Hara
LOST BOUNDARIES(1949)
Patrick O'Hara
YOUNG FRANKENSTEIN(1974); FIRST LOVE(1977)
Peggy O'Hara
SPEED LOVERS(1968)
Quinn O'Hara
ERRAND BOY, THE(1961); GOOD NEIGHBOR SAM(1964); PATSY, THE(1964); SWINGIN' SUMMER, A(1965); GHOST IN THE INVISIBLE BIKINI(1966); IN THE YEAR 2889(1966); CRY OF THE BANSHEE(1970, Brit.)
Riggs O'Hara
VICTORS, THE(1963); BECKET(1964, Brit.); PROMISE HER ANYTHING(1966, Brit.); VIRGIN SOLDIERS, THE(1970, Brit.)
Robin O'Hara
YOU LIGHT UP MY LIFE(1977)
Sandy O'Hara
STRANGE FETISHES, THE(1967)
Shirley O'Hara
AROUND THE WORLD(1943); GHOST SHIP, THE(1943); HIGHER AND HIGHER(1943); FALCON OUT WEST, THE(1944); SEVEN DAYS ASHORE(1944); SHOW BUSINESS(1944); STEP LIVELY(1944); TARZAN AND THE AMAZONS(1945); CHASE, THE(1946); CUBAN PETE(1946); LOVER COME BACK(1946); BELLS OF SAN FERNANDO(1947); CRIME WAVE(1954); HIGH-POWERED RIFLE, THE(1960); THIRD VOICE, THE(1960); LITTLE SHEPHERD OF KINGDOM COME(1961); LOVE IN A GOLDFISH BOWL(1961); SYLVIA(1965); HOSTAGE, THE(1966); BALLAD OF JOSIE(1968); ROCKY(1976)
Shirley O'Hara
WILD PARTY, THE(1929)
Silents
BACKSTAGE(1927)

Misc. Silents
GENTLEMAN OF PARIS, A(1927)
Terrence O'Hara
SOMETHING SHORT OF PARADISE(1979)
Corky O'Hare
EXTERMINATOR, THE(1980), ed
Michael O'Hare
PROMISE, THE(1979); PURSUIT OF D.B. COOPER, THE(1981)
1984
C.H.U.D.(1984)
Caitlin O'Heaney
HE KNOWS YOU'RE ALONE(1980); WOLFEN(1981)
Eileen O'Hearn
HONOLULU LU(1941); RICHEST MAN IN TOWN(1941); THUNDER OVER THE PRAIRIE(1941); DEVIL'S TRAIL, THE(1942); PARACHUTE NURSE(1942); SUBMARINE RAIDER(1942)
Mona O'Hearn
HOMER(1970)
Patrick O'Hearn
YANK IN THE R.A.F., A(1941)
Marie O'Henry
THREE THE HARD WAY(1974); DR. BLACK AND MR. HYDE(1976)
Misc. Talkies
JOEY(1977)
Dan O'Herlihy
HUNGRY HILL(1947, Brit.); ODD MAN OUT(1947, Brit.); KIDNAPPED(1948); LARCENY(1948); MACBETH(1948); IROQUOIS TRAIL, THE(1950); AT SWORD'S POINT(1951); BLUE VEIL, THE(1951); DESERT FOX, THE(1951); HIGHWAYMAN, THE(1951); SOLDIERS THREE(1951); ACTORS AND SIN(1952); INVASION U.S.A.(1952); OPERATION SECRET(1952); SWORD OF VENUS(1953); ADVENTURES OF ROBINSON CRUSOE, THE(1954); BENGAL BRIGADE(1954); PURPLE MASK, THE(1955); VIRGIN QUEEN, THE(1955); CITY AFTER MIDNIGHT(1957, Brit.); HOME BEFORE DARK(1958); IMITATION OF LIFE(1959); YOUNG LAND, THE(1959); NIGHT FIGHTERS, THE(1960); ONE FOOT IN HELL(1960); KING OF THE ROARING TWENTIES–THE STORY OF ARNOLD ROTHSTEIN(1961); CABINET OF CALIGARI, THE(1962); FAIL SAFE(1964); BIG CUBE, THE(1969); 100 RIFLES(1969); WATERLOO(1970, Ital./USSR); CAREY TREATMENT, THE(1972); MAC ARTHUR(1977); HALLOWEEN III: SEASON OF THE WITCH(1982)
1984
LAST STARFIGHTER, THE(1984)
Daniel "Dan" O'Herlihy
TAMARIND SEED, THE(1974, Brit.)
Daniel O'Herlihy
BLACK SHIELD OF FALWORTH, THE(1954)
Gavan O'Herlihy
NEVER SAY NEVER AGAIN(1983); SUPERMAN III(1983)
Misc. Talkies
SPACE RIDERS(1984)
Michael O'Herlihy
FIGHTING PRINCE OF DONEGAL, THE(1966, Brit.), d; ONE AND ONLY GENUINE ORIGINAL FAMILY BAND, THE(1968), d; SMITH(1969), d
Brian O'Higgins
NO RESTING PLACE(1952, Brit.); TONIGHT'S THE NIGHT(1954, Brit.); RYAN'S DAUGHTER(1970, Brit.)
Harvey O'Higgins
I MARRIED A DOCTOR(1936), w
Harvey J. O'Higgins
ARGYLE CASE, THE(1929), w; MAKE YOUR OWN BED(1944), w
Silents
ARGYLE CASE, THE(1917), w; LOVE CHARM, THE(1921), w
Marcus O'Higgins
EDUCATING RITA(1983)
Gavan O'Hirlihy
WEDDING, A(1978)
Michael O'Hogan
SIGN OF FOUR, THE(1983, Brit.)
Tom O'Horgan
CHAFED ELBOWS(1967), a, m; ALEX IN WONDERLAND(1970), m; RHINOCEROS(1974), d
Carol O'Kane
GNOME-MOBILE, THE(1967)
Johnny O'Kane
OFFENDERS, THE(1980)
Alexandra O'Karma
REFUGE(1981); TERMS OF ENDEARMENT(1983)
Allan O'Keefe
WHAT'S NEXT?(1975, Brit.)
Cornelius O'Keefe
GUNPLAY(1951)
Dennis O'Keefe
CIMARRON(1931); BIG CITY BLUES(1932); CENTRAL PARK(1932); I AM A FUGITIVE FROM A CHAIN GANG(1932); MERRILY WE GO TO HELL(1932); SCARFACE(1932); TWO AGAINST THE WORLD(1932); EAGLE AND THE HAWK, THE(1933); GOLD DIGGERS OF 1933(1933); I'M NO ANGEL(1933); DEATH OF THE DIAMOND(1934); DESIRABLE(1934); FOG OVER FRISCO(1934); GIFT OF GAB(1934); GIRL FROM MISSOURI, THE(1934); HE WAS HER MAN(1934); IMITATION OF LIFE(1934); LADY BY CHOICE(1934); SMARTY(1934); TWENTY MILLION SWEETHEARTS(1934); WONDER BAR(1934); DANTE'S INFERNO(1935); MISSISSIPPI(1935); RUMBA(1935); SHIPMATES FOREVER(1935); TOP HAT(1935); AND SO THEY WERE MARRIED(1936); GREAT GUY(1936); LIBELED LADY(1936); LOVE BEFORE BREAKFAST(1936); RHYTHM ON THE RANGE(1936); SAN FRANCISCO(1936); SWING TIME(1936); THEODORA GOES WILD(1936); THIRTEEN HOURS BY AIR(1936); YOURS FOR THE ASKING(1936); EASY LIVING(1937); FIREFLY, THE(1937); MARRIED BEFORE BREAKFAST(1937); STAR IS BORN, A(1937); THREE SMART GIRLS(1937); BAD MAN OF BRIMSTONE(1938); CHASER, THE(1938); HOLD THAT KISS(1938); JOY OF LIVING(1938); VACATION FROM LOVE(1938); BURN 'EM UP O'CONNER(1939); KID FROM TEXAS, THE(1939); THAT'S RIGHT–YOU'RE WRONG(1939); UNEXPECTED FATHER(1939); ALIAS THE DEACON(1940); ARISE, MY LOVE(1940); BOWERY BOY(1940); GIRL FROM HAVANA(1940); I'M NOBODY'S SWEETHEART NOW(1940); LA CONGA NIGHTS(1940); POP ALWAYS PAYS(1940);

YOU'LL FIND OUT(1940); BROADWAY LIMITED(1941); LADY SCARFACE(1941); MR. DISTRICT ATTORNEY(1941); TOPPER RETURNS(1941); WEEKEND FOR THREE(1941); MOONLIGHT MASQUERADE(1942); GOOD MORNING, JUDGE(1943); HANGMEN ALSO DIE(1943); HI DIDDLE DIDDLE(1943); LEOPARD MAN, THE(1943); TAHITI HONEY(1943); ABROAD WITH TWO YANKS(1944); FIGHTING SEABEES, THE(1944); SENSATIONS OF 1945(1944); STORY OF DR. WASSELL, THE(1944); UP IN MABEL'S ROOM(1944); BREWSTER'S MILLIONS(1945); DOLL FACE(1945); EARL CARROLL'S VANITIES(1945); GETTING GERTIE'S GARTER(1945); HER ADVENTUROUS NIGHT(1946); MR. DISTRICT ATTORNEY(1946); DISHONORED LADY(1947); T-MEN(1947); RAW DEAL(1948); SIREN OF ATLANTIS(1948); WALK A CROOKED MILE(1948); ABANDONED(1949); COVER-UP(1949); GREAT DAN PATCH, THE(1949); COMPANY SHE KEEPS, THE(1950); EAGLE AND THE HAWK, THE(1950); WOMAN ON THE RUN(1950); FOLLOW THE SUN(1951); PASSAGE WEST(1951); EVERYTHING I HAVE IS YOURS(1952); ONE BIG AFFAIR(1952); FAKE, THE(1953, Brit.); LADY WANTS MINK, THE(1953); DIAMOND WIZARD, THE(1954, Brit.); ANGELA(1955, Ital.), a, d; CHICAGO SYNDICATE(1955); INSIDE DETROIT(1955); LAS VEGAS SHAKEDOWN(1955); DRAGON WELLS MASSACRE(1957); LADY OF VENGEANCE(1957, Brit.); SAIL INTO DANGER(1957, Brit.); ALL HANDS ON DECK(1961); NAKED FLAME, THE(1970, Can.)
Francis O'Keefe
MURDER IN EDEN(1962, Brit.)
Michael O'Keefe
GRAY LADY DOWN(1978); GREAT SANTINI, THE(1979); CADDY SHACK(1980); SPLIT IMAGE(1982); NATE AND HAYES(1983, U.S./New Zealand)
1984
FINDERS KEEPERS(1984)
Miles O'Keefe
TARZAN, THE APE MAN(1981)
Misc. Talkies
ATOR: THE FIGHTING EAGLE(1983); ATOR, THE INVINCIBLE(1984)
Paul O'Keefe
DAYDREAMER, THE(1966); CHILD'S PLAY(1972)
Ray O'Keefe
UNHOLY ROLLERS(1972)
Raymond O'Keefe
TOP OF THE HEAP(1972); DIRTY O'NEIL(1974); GIRL FROM PETROVKA, THE(1974); METEOR(1979); NINE TO FIVE(1980)
Thomas O'Keefe
Silents
CAPTAIN SWIFT(1914)
Misc. Silents
UNBROKEN ROAD, THE(1915)
Tom O'Keefe
Misc. Silents
GIRL LIKE THAT, A(1917); VANITY(1917)
Walter O'Keefe
SOPHOMORE, THE(1929); RED HOT RHYTHM(1930); PRISON SHADOWS(1936); GO CHASE YOURSELF(1938), w
Miles O'Keeffe
1984
SWORD OF THE VALIANT(1984, Brit.)
Erin O'Kelley
MRS. PARKINGTON(1944)
Aideen O'Kelly
BOYD'S SHOP(1960, Brit.); WEBSTER BOY, THE(1962, Brit.)
Billy O'Kelly
MAJOR AND THE MINOR, THE(1942)
Don O'Kelly
FRONTIER UPRISING(1961); SHOOT OUT AT BIG SAG(1962); HOSTAGE, THE(1966)
Dorothy O'Kelly
LADY IN THE DARK(1944)
Erin O'Kelly
MEET THE PEOPLE(1944); HARVEY GIRLS, THE(1946); CLOSE-UP(1948)
Fergus O'Kelly
DEAD MAN'S EVIDENCE(1962, Brit.)
Jeffrey O'Kelly
THIN RED LINE, THE(1964); TUSK(1980, Fr.), w
Michael O'Kelly
SMELL OF HONEY, A SWALLOW OF BRINE! A(1966)
Tim O'Kelly
FOR PETE'S SAKE!(1966); TARGETS(1968); GRASSHOPPER, THE(1970)
Lt. Col. William O'Kelly
SHAKE HANDS WITH THE DEVIL(1959, Ireland), tech adv
O'Klein
JOHNNY THE GIANT KILLER(1953, Fr.), anim
Liam O'Laoghaire
MEN AGAINST THE SUN(1953, Brit.)
Barbara O'Laughlin
RETURN OF THE JEDI(1983)
Bill O'Leary
WITHOUT RESERVATIONS(1946); THEY GOT ME COVERED(1943); NONE BUT THE LONELY HEART(1944); SHINE ON, HARVEST MOON(1944); KISS OF DEATH(1947)
Billy O'Leary
WISTFUL WIDOW OF WAGON GAP, THE(1947)
Carol O'Leary
I LOVE YOU, ALICE B. TOKLAS!(1968); BOB AND CAROL AND TED AND ALICE(1969); ALEX IN WONDERLAND(1970); PHANTOM OF THE PARADISE(1974)
Jack O'Leary
JACKSON COUNTY JAIL(1976); SILVER STREAK(1976); ROSE, THE(1979); BRUBAKER(1980); INSIDE MOVES(1980); ON THE NICKEL(1980); REDS(1981); DEATH VALLEY(1982)
James O'Leary
Misc. Silents
CLOTHES(1924)

John O'Leary
JULIUS CAESAR(1952); GROUP, THE(1966); HEART IS A LONELY HUNTER, THE(1968); FAREWELL, MY LOVELY(1975); ALL THE PRESIDENT'S MEN(1976); DEMON SEED(1977); HEROES(1977); MOMENT BY MOMENT(1978); ISLAND, THE(1980)
1984
LAST STARFIGHTER, THE(1984)
Kevin O'Leary
FINNEGANS WAKE(1965)
Liam O'Leary
STRANGER AT MY DOOR(1950, Brit.)
Patsy O'Leary
Silents
ISLE OF LOST MEN(1928)
Misc. Silents
GIRL-SHY COWBOY, THE(1928)
Ray O'Leary
WINDSPLITTER, THE(1971)
Thomas O'Leary
BEN HUR(1959)
William O'Leary
DOUBLE INDEMNITY(1944); LOST WEEKEND, THE(1945); VALLEY OF DECISION, THE(1945); LADY IN THE LAKE(1947); FOR HEAVEN'S SAKE(1950); IT GROWS ON TREES(1952); SOUTH SEA WOMAN(1953)
William J. O'Leary
MISTER 880(1950)
Larry O'Leno
LONERS, THE(1972)
Gearold O'Lochlain
LIES MY FATHER TOLD ME(1960, Brit.)
Allen O'Locklin
MYSTERY STREET(1950); CLOWN, THE(1953); DREAM WIFE(1953); SCANDAL INCORPORATED(1956)
Bennett O'Loghlin
SILVER DARLINGS, THE(1947, Brit.)
Gerald O'Loughlin
HATFUL OF RAIN, A(1957); COP HATER(1958); DESPERATE CHARACTERS(1971)
Gerald S. O'Loughlin
LOVERS AND LOLLIPOPS(1956); ENSIGN PULVER(1964); FINE MADNESS, A(1966); MAN CALLED ADAM, A(1966); IN COLD BLOOD(1967); ICE STATION ZEBRA(1968); RIOT(1969); ORGANIZATION, THE(1971); VALACHI PAPERS, THE(1972, Ital./Fr.); TWILIGHT'S LAST GLEAMING(1977, U.S./Ger.); FRANCES(1982)
1984
CITY HEAT(1984); CRIMES OF PASSION(1984)
Diane O'Mack
JOYRIDE(1977)
Laurence O'Madden
SILVER FLEET, THE(1945, Brit.); GUILT IS MY SHADOW(1950, Brit.); LILLI MARLENE(1951, Brit.)
Lawrence O'Madden
GOOSE STEPS OUT, THE(1942, Brit.); UNCENSORED(1944, Brit.); LISBON STORY, THE(1946, Brit.); NIGHT BOAT TO DUBLIN(1946, Brit.); SAN DEMETRIO, LONDON(1947, Brit.); SPRINGTIME(1948, Brit.); MRS. FITZHERBERT(1950, Brit.)
Isabel O'Madigan
Silents
BAB'S BURGLAR(1917); BAB'S DIARY(1917); LOVE IN A HURRY(1919)
Misc. Silents
BAB'S MATINEE IDOL(1917); MAKE-BELIEVE WIFE, THE(1918)
Princess O'Mahoney
HOOPER(1978)
Jerry O'Mahoney
DAWN OVER IRELAND(1938, Irish)
Jock O'Mahoney
BLAZING TRAIL, THE(1949); DOOLINS OF OKLAHOMA, THE(1949); RENEGADES OF THE SAGE(1949); RIM OF THE CANYON(1949); COW TOWN(1950); DAVID HARDING, COUNTERSPY(1950); FRONTIER OUTPOST(1950); HOEDOWN(1950); HORSEMEN OF THE SIERRAS(1950); KANGAROO KID, THE(1950, Aus./U.S.); LIGHTNING GUNS(1950); NEVADAN, THE(1950); TEXAS DYNAMO(1950); TEXAS RANGERS, THE(1951)
Michael O'Mahoney
ANOTHER SHORE(1948, Brit.)
Nora O'Mahoney
RALLY 'ROUND THE FLAG, BOYS!(1958); HOLIDAY FOR LOVERS(1959); REMARKABLE MR. PENNYPACKER, THE(1959)
Jock O'Mahoney [Jock Mahoney]
SANTA FE(1951)
Nora O'Mahony
DARBY O'GILL AND THE LITTLE PEOPLE(1959)
Norah O'Mahony
DAUGHTER OF DARKNESS(1948, Brit.)
Bingo O'Malley
CREEPSHOW(1982)
Charles O'Malley
SMART MONEY(1931); OFFICER 13(1933); NO MORE LADIES(1935)
Silents
IRON HORSE, THE(1924); ONLY WOMAN, THE(1924)
Misc. Silents
GUN-HAND GARRISON(1927); RIDIN' LUCK(1927)
Daragh O'Malley
1984
CAL(1984, Ireland)
David O'Malley
ADVENTURES OF FRONTIER FREMONT, THE(1976), w; GUARDIAN OF THE WILDERNESS(1977), d; BOOGENS, THE(1982), w
Eileen O'Malley
RENDEZVOUS(1935); SEVENTH VICTIM, THE(1943)
Silents
RAGGED HEIRESS, THE(1922)

Misc. Silents
CUPID'S FIREMAN(1923)
Flynn O'Malley
MELODY OF LOVE, THE(1928)
Gordon O'Malley
HONKY TONK(1941)
Grania O'Malley
HOT ROCK, THE(1972)
J. Pat O'Malley
LITTLE TOUGH GUY(1938); THUMBS UP(1943); COURAGE OF BLACK BEAUTY(1957); FOUR BOYS AND A GUN(1957); WITNESS FOR THE PROSECUTION(1957); LONG, HOT SUMMER, THE(1958); BLUEPRINT FOR ROBBERY(1961); ONE HUNDRED AND ONE DALMATIANS(1961); CABINET OF CALIGARI, THE(1962); DAYS OF WINE AND ROSES(1962); SHOTGUN WEDDING, THE(1963); SON OF FLUBBER(1963); HEY THERE, IT'S YOGI BEAR(1964); HOUSE IS NOT A HOME, A(1964); GUNN(1967); JUNGLE BOOK, THE(1967); STAR!(1968); HELLO, DOLLY!(1969); CHEYENNE SOCIAL CLUB, THE(1970); WILLARD(1971); GUMBALL RALLY, THE(1976); CHEAPER TO KEEP HER(1980)
J. Patrick O'Malley
OVER MY DEAD BODY(1942); LASSIE, COME HOME(1943)
Jack O'Malley
CONFESSIONS OF BOSTON BLACKIE(1941); MEET BOSTON BLACKIE(1941); YOU'LL NEVER GET RICH(1941)
Janice O'Malley
LAST PICTURE SHOW, THE(1971)
Janice E. O'Malley
STUDENT BODIES(1981)
John O'Malley
SPORTING CHANCE, A(1945); RUGGED O'RIORDANS, THE(1949, Aus.); KIND LADY(1951); LES MISERABLES(1952); DESERT RATS, THE(1953); JULIUS CAESAR(1953); DIANE(1955); MOONFLEET(1955); SCARLET COAT, THE(1955); COURT JESTER, THE(1956); MAN WHO KNEW TOO MUCH, THE(1956); BLACK PATCH(1957); INVISIBLE BOY, THE(1957)
John P O'Malley
COURT JESTER, THE(1956)
Kathleen O'Malley
OLD ACQUAINTANCE(1943); COVER GIRL(1944); LADY ON A TRAIN(1945); SALOME, WHERE SHE DANCED(1945); SUDAN(1945); THIS LOVE OF OURS(1945); NIGHT IN PARADISE, A(1946); DOWN TO EARTH(1947); GUILT OF JANET AMES, THE(1947); ROAD HOUSE(1948); EMERGENCY WEDDING(1950); WAGONMASTER(1950); TWO TICKETS TO BROADWAY(1951); AFFAIR IN TRINIDAD(1952); NIGHT STAGE TO GALVESTON(1952); MAGNIFICENT OBSESSION(1954); MISTER ROBERTS(1955); LINEUP, THE(1958); KILLERS, THE(1964); ROSIE!(1967); MADIGAN(1968); DIRTY HARRY(1971); MINNIE AND MOSKOWITZ(1971); CHARLEY VARRICK(1973); SHOOTIST, THE(1976); TELEFON(1977)
Kit O'Malley
Silents
IRISH DESTINY(1925, Brit.)
Leonard O'Malley
1984
EVERY PICTURE TELLS A STORY(1984, Brit.)
Lillian O'Malley
PLOUGH AND THE STARS, THE(1936); THIS LAND IS MINE(1943)
Luke J. O'Malley
FINNEGANS WAKE(1965)
Michael O'Malley
Misc. Talkies
BIG ZAPPER(1974)
Mike O'Malley
TERROR(1979, Brit.)
P.H. O'Malley
Misc. Silents
BOLD EMMETT, IRELAND'S MARTYR(1915); NAN O' THE BACKWOODS(1915)
Pat O'Malley
ALIBI(1929); MAN I LOVE, THE(1929); FALL GUY, THE(1930); MOTHERS CRY(1930); ANYBODY'S BLONDE(1931); HOMICIDE SQUAD(1931); NIGHT LIFE IN RENO(1931); SKY SPIDER, THE(1931); FIGHTING GENTLEMAN, THE(1932); FIGHTING MARSHAL, THE(1932); HIGH SPEED(1932); KLONDIKE(1932); RECKONING, THE(1932); SPEED MADNESS(1932); THOSE WE LOVE(1932); TRIAL OF VIVIENNE WARE, THE(1932); FRISCO JENNY(1933); LAUGHING AT LIFE(1933); MAN OF SENTIMENT, A(1933); MYSTERY OF THE WAX MUSEUM, THE(1933); ONE YEAR LATER(1933); PARACHUTE JUMPER(1933); PENAL CODE, THE(1933); SING SINNER, SING(1933); SUNDOWN RIDER, THE(1933); CRIME DOCTOR(1934); EVELYN PRENTICE(1934); FUGITIVE LADY(1934); GIRL IN DANGER(1934); LOVE PAST THIRTY(1934); BEHIND THE EVIDENCE(1935); CHARLIE CHAN IN SHANGHAI(1935); LADY TUBBS(1935); MAN ON THE FLYING TRAPEZE, THE(1935); MEN OF THE HOUR(1935); PADDY O'DAY(1935); PERFECT CLUE, THE(1935); PUBLIC HERO NO. 1(1935); WANDERER OF THE WASTELAND(1935); BELOVED ENEMY(1936); HEIR TO TROUBLE(1936); HOLLYWOOD BOULEVARD(1936); ROSE BOWL(1936); SAN FRANCISCO(1936); TROUBLE FOR TWO(1936); EVER SINCE EVE(1937); MUSIC FOR MADAME(1937); MYSTERIOUS CROSSING(1937); ACCIDENTS WILL HAPPEN(1938); ANGELS WITH DIRTY FACES(1938); BRINGING UP BABY(1938); DODGE CITY(1939); FRONTIER MARSHAL(1939); LIGHT THAT FAILED, THE(1939); NIGHT OF NIGHTS, THE(1939); ROARING TWENTIES, THE(1939); ROMANCE OF THE REDWOODS(1939); SECRET SERVICE OF THE AIR(1939); SMASHING THE MONEY RING(1939); STUNT PILOT(1939); WOLF CALL(1939); BANK DICK, THE(1940); CAPTAIN CAUTION(1940); CASTLE ON THE HUDSON(1940); DISPATCH FROM REUTERS, A(1940); EMERGENCY SQUAD(1940); HOUSE ACROSS THE BAY, THE(1940); INVISIBLE STRIPES(1940); LITTLE BIT OF HEAVEN, A(1940); LITTLE NELLIE KELLY(1940); REMEMBER THE NIGHT(1940); ROCKY MOUNTAIN RANGERS(1940); SAINT'S DOUBLE TROUBLE, THE(1940); SHOOTING HIGH(1940); CRACKED NUTS(1941); DOUBLE DATE(1941); KNOCKOUT(1941); LAW OF THE RANGE(1941); PALS OF THE PECOS(1941); RAGE IN HEAVEN(1941); BOMBAY CLIPPER(1942); DEEP IN THE HEART OF TEXAS(1942); GENTLEMAN JIM(1942); GLASS KEY, THE(1942); GREAT MAN'S LADY, THE(1942); LARCENY, INC.(1942); PACIFIC RENDEZVOUS(1942); QUIET PLEASE, MURDER(1942); ROXIE HART(1942); TENNESSEE JOHNSON(1942); THIS GUN FOR HIRE(1942); IRON MAJOR, THE(1943); MISSION TO MOSCOW(1943); ADVENTURES OF MARK TWAIN, THE(1944); IRISH EYES ARE SMILING(1944); SAILOR'S HOLIDAY(1944); SINGIN' IN THE CORN(1946); HARD BOILED MAHONEY(1947); 13TH

HOUR, THE(1947); MAN FROM COLORADO, THE(1948); ADVENTURES OF ICHA-BOD AND MR. TOAD(1949); BOSTON BLACKIE'S CHINESE VENTURE(1949); RECKLESS MOMENTS, THE(1949); RIDERS IN THE SKY(1949); COW TOWN(1950); MULE TRAIN(1950); ALICE IN WONDERLAND(1951); SILVER CANYON(1951); VALLEY OF FIRE(1951); WHIRLWIND(1951); KID FROM BROKEN GUN, THE(1952); OLD WEST, THE(1952); QUIET MAN, THE(1952); GIRL WHO HAD EVERYTHING, THE(1953); WILD ONE, THE(1953); REDHEAD FROM MANHATTAN(1954); STAR IS BORN, A(1954); LONG GRAY LINE, THE(1955); BLACKJACK KETCHUM, DE-SPERADO(1956); INVASION OF THE BODY SNATCHERS(1956); SKIN GAME(1971)
Misc. Talkies
RIOT SQUAD(1933); SUNDOWN RIDER(1933); WHIRLWIND, THE(1933)
Silents
GLADIOLA(1915); PICTURE OF DORIAN GRAY, THE(1916, Brit.); ADOPTED SON, THE(1917); DINTY(1920); BOB HAMPTON OF PLACER(1921); BREAKING POINT, THE(1921); TEN DOLLAR RAISE, THE(1921); LYING TRUTH, THE(1922); ETERNAL STRUGGLE, THE(1923); SLIPPY MCGEE(1923); VIRGINIAN, THE(1923); FIGHTING AMERICAN, THE(1924); FIGHTING CUB, THE(1925); PROUD FLESH(1925); WATCH YOUR WIFE(1926); BOWERY CINDERELLA(1927); CHEATERS(1927)
Misc. Silents
BLADE O' GRASS(1915); OUT OF THE RUINS(1915); SLAVEY STUDENT, THE(1915); CELESTE OF THE AMBULANCE CORPS(1916); YOUR OBEDIENT SERVANT(1917); HER BOY(1918); HIT-THE-TRAIL HOLLIDAY(1918); SHE HIRED A HUSBAND(1919); BLOOMING ANGEL, THE(1920); BREATH OF THE GODS, THE(1920); GO AND GET IT(1920); SHERRY(1920); FALSE KISSES(1921); BROTHERS UNDER THE SKIN(1922); GAME CHICKEN, THE(1922); MY WILD IRISH ROSE(1922); LAST HOUR, THE(1923); MAN FROM BRODNEY'S, THE(1923); SOULS IN BON-DAGE(1923); BEAUTY PRIZE, THE(1924); BREAD(1924); FOOLS' HIGHWAY(1924); HAPPINESS(1924); MINE WITH THE IRON DOOR, THE(1924); WORLDLY GOODS(1924); LET WOMEN ALONE(1925); TEASER, THE(1925); TOMORROW'S LOVE(1925); WHITE DESERT, THE(1925); MY OLD DUTCH(1926); SPANGLES(1926); PERCH OF THE DEVIL(1927); PLEASURE BEFORE BUSINESS(1927); ROSE OF KILDARE, THE(1927); SLAVER, THE(1927); WOMAN'S LAW(1927); HOUSE OF SCANDAL, THE(1928)
Pat O'Malley, Sr.
REG'LAR FELLERS(1941)
Patricia O'Malley
PLOUGH AND THE STARS, THE(1936)
Patrick O'Malley
PARIS CALLING(1941)
Silents
FALSE EVIDENCE(1919)
Misc. Silents
PRUSSIAN CUR, THE(1918)
Rex O'Malley
CAMILLE(1937); MIDNIGHT(1939); ZAZA(1939); THIEF, THE(1952); TAXI(1953)
Misc. Silents
SOMEBODY'S DARLING(1925, Brit.)
Russell O'Malley
UP FROM THE DEPTHS(1979, Phil.), m
Suzanne O'Malley
PRIVATE SCHOOL(1983), w
Tom O'Malley
Silents
CAPPY RICKS(1921); RAINBOW(1921); HIS DARKER SELF(1924)
Vineta O'Malley
BUSH CHRISTMAS(1983, Aus.)
Rev. William O'Malley
EXORCIST, THE(1973)
Kathleen O'Mally
SNIPER, THE(1952)
Ellen O'Mara
UP THE DOWN STAIRCASE(1967)
Kate O'Mara
CORRUPTION(1968, Brit.); GREAT CATHERINE(1968, Brit.); DESPERADOS, THE(1969, Brit.); LIMBO LINE, THE(1969, Brit.); HORROR OF FRANKENSTEIN, THE(1970, Brit.); VAMPIRE LOVERS, THE(1970, Brit.); TAMARIND SEED, THE(1974, Brit.)
Misc. Talkies
WHOSE CHILD AM I?(1976)
Terry O'Mara
UP THE SANDBOX(1972)
John O'May
STARSTRUCK(1982, Aus.)
R.L. O'Mealy
DEVIL'S ROCK(1938, Brit.)
C. Timothy O'Meara
GOING IN STYLE(1979), ed; CONAN THE BARBARIAN(1982), ed
1984
LAST STARFIGHTER, THE(1984), ed
Tim O'Meara
BIG WEDNESDAY(1978), ed
Pat O'Moore
BETWEEN TWO WORLDS(1944); HORN BLOWS AT MIDNIGHT, THE(1945); CLOAK AND DAGGER(1946); G.I. WAR BRIDES(1946); RENDEZVOUS 24(1946); EXILE, THE(1947); TWO MRS. CARROLLS, THE(1947); FIGHTING O'FLYNN, THE(1949); THREE CAME HOME(1950); SOLDIERS THREE(1951); BWANA DE-VIL(1953); DANGEROUS WHEN WET(1953); DESERT RATS, THE(1953); TITA-NIC(1953); TROOPER HOOK(1957); PROMISES, PROMISES(1963); MY FAIR LADY(1964); THREE NUTS IN SEARCH OF A BOLT(1964); WHAT A WAY TO GO(1964); RESURRECTION OF ZACHARY WHEELER, THE(1971); HOW TO SUC-CEED IN BUSINESS WITHOUT REALLY TRYING(1976)
Misc. Talkies
BULLDOG DRUMMOND AT BAY(1947); BULLDOG DRUMMOND STRIKES BACK(1947)
Patrick O'Moore
EVENSONG(1934, Brit.); KATHLEEN(1938, Ireland); SMILIN' THROUGH(1941); CAPTAINS OF THE CLOUDS(1942); DESPERATE JOURNEY(1942); SAHARA(1943); STAGE DOOR CANTEEN(1943); CONFLICT(1945); MOLLY AND ME(1945); TONIGHT AND EVERY NIGHT(1945); MOSS ROSE(1947); KIND LADY(1951); SON OF DR.

JEKYLL, THE(1951); THIRTEENTH LETTER, THE(1951); THUNDER ON THE HILL(1951); MILLION DOLLAR MERMAID(1952); NIAGARA(1953); JUNGLE GENTS(1954); KHYBER PATROL(1954); SEA CHASE, THE(1955); BLACK WHIP, THE(1956); COPPER SKY(1957); RIDE A VIOLENT MILE(1957); UNKNOWN TER-ROR, THE(1957); BLOOD ARROW(1958); CATTLE EMPIRE(1958); DESERT HELL(1958); IN THE MONEY(1958); ROOKIE, THE(1959); MECHANIC, THE(1972); FRASIER, THE SENSUOUS LION(1973); SWORD AND THE SORCERER, THE(1982)
Denny O'Morrison
TOO LATE FOR TEARS(1949)
Devin O'Morrison
GOLDEN GLOVES STORY, THE(1950)
Kenny O'Morrison
DEAR RUTH(1947); SAIGON(1948); SET-UP, THE(1949)
Kevin O'Morrison
NEVER FEAR(1950); FRIENDS OF EDDIE COYLE, THE(1973)
Brian O'Mullin
GONG SHOW MOVIE, THE(1980)
Ann O'Neal
HENRY ALDRICH GETS GLAMOUR(1942); WOMAN IN THE WINDOW, THE(1945)
Anna O'Neal
HARVEY(1950)
Anne O'Neal
SHE GETS HER MAN(1935); STRANGE WIVES(1935); POSTAL INSPECTOR(1936); MAID OF SALEM(1937); MAN WHO CRIED WOLF, THE(1937); OF HUMAN HEARTS(1938); MARGIE(1940); DESIGN FOR SCANDAL(1941); HONKY TONK(1941); MONSTER AND THE GIRL, THE(1941); SIS HOPKINS(1941); IN OLD CALIFORNIA(1942); MADAME SPY(1942); MAGNIFICENT AMBERSONS, THE(1942); SOMBRERO KID, THE(1942); FALCON AND THE CO-EDS, THE(1943); IN OLD OKLAHOMA(1943); MEXICAN SPITFIRE'S BLESSED EVENT(1943); THANK YOUR LUCKY STARS(1943); THEY GOT ME COVERED(1943); RATIONING(1944); STRANGERS IN THE NIGHT(1944); UP IN ARMS(1944); WILSON(1944); MISSING CORPSE, THE(1945); PILLOW TO POST(1945); THREE'S A CROWD(1945); LITTLE GIANT(1946); LOVER COME BACK(1946); SLIGHTLY SCANDALOUS(1946); CHEYENNE(1947); HOMESTRETCH, THE(1947); MIRACLE ON 34TH STREET, THE(1947); B. F.'S DAUGHTER(1948); BLACK BART(1948); OPEN SECRET(1948); SITTING PRETTY(1948); BRIDE FOR SALE(1949); GUN CRAZY(1949); BELLE OF OLD MEXICO(1950); NEVER A DULL MOMENT(1950); TO PLEASE A LADY(1950); TWO TICKETS TO BROADWAY(1951); WELLS FARGO GUNMASTER(1951); RUNA-WAY DAUGHTERS(1957); VAMPIRE, THE(1957)
Bill O'Neal
1984
RIVER RAT, THE(1984)
Carol O'Neal
WHEN A STRANGER CALLS(1979)
Charles O'Neal
SEVENTH VICTIM, THE(1943), w; CRY OF THE WEREWOLF(1944), w; MISSING JUROR, THE(1944), w; I LOVE A MYSTERY(1945), w; DEVIL'S MASK, THE(1946), w; UNKNOWN, THE(1946), w; SOMETHING IN THE WIND(1947), w; RETURN OF THE BADMEN(1948), w; MONTANA(1950), w; GOLDEN GIRL(1951), w; ALLIGA-TOR PEOPLE, THE(1959), w; LASSIE'S GREAT ADVENTURE(1963), w
Christopher O'Neal
1984
LOVE STREAMS(1984)
Collette O'Neal
FRANKENSTEIN MUST BE DESTROYED!(1969, Brit.)
Cynthia O'Neal
CARNAL KNOWLEDGE(1971)
Frank O'Neal
CINDERELLA LIBERTY(1973)
Frederick O'Neal
PINKY(1949); TARZAN'S PERIL(1951); SOMETHING OF VALUE(1957); ANNA LUCASTA(1958); TAKE A GIANT STEP(1959); SINS OF RACHEL CADE, THE(1960); FREE, WHITE AND 21(1963); STRATEGY OF TERROR(1969); COTTON COMES TO HARLEM(1970)
Griffin O'Neal
NICKELODEON(1976); ESCAPE ARTIST, THE(1982)
1984
HADLEY'S REBELLION(1984)
Kevin O'Neal
TROUBLE WITH GIRLS(AND HOW TO GET INTO IT), THE (1969); VILLAGE OF THE GIANTS(1965); YOUNG FURY(1965); BIG BOUNCE, THE(1969); MECHANIC, THE(1972); WHAT'S UP, DOC?(1972)
Nance O'Neal
TRANSGRESSION(1931)
Patricia O'Neal
ROSEMARY'S BABY(1968); WHAT'S UP, DOC?(1972); NICKELODEON(1976)
Patrick O'Neal
WAY WE WERE, THE(1973); BLACK SHIELD OF FALWORTH, THE(1954); MAD MAGICIAN, THE(1954); FROM THE TERRACE(1960); MATTER OF MORALS, A(1961, U.S./Swed.); CARDINAL, THE(1963); IN HARM'S WAY(1965); KING RAT(1965); ALVAREZ KELLY(1966); CHAMBER OF HORRORS(1966); FINE MADNESS, A(1966); MATCHLESS(1967, Ital.); ASSIGNMENT TO KILL(1968); SECRET LIFE OF AN AMERICAN WIFE, THE(1968); WHERE WERE YOU WHEN THE LIGHTS WENT OUT?(1968); CASTLE KEEP(1969); STILETTO(1969); EL CONDOR(1970); JOE(1970); KREMLIN LETTER, THE(1970); CORKY(1972); SILENT NIGHT, BLOODY NIGHT(1974); STEPFORD WIVES, THE(1975)
Peggy O'Neal
BOYS IN COMPANY C, THE(1978, U.S./Hong Kong)
Peter O'Neal
DR. BUTCHER, M.D.(1982, Ital.)
Robert O'Neal
TERROR STREET(1953)
Ron O'Neal
MOVE(1970); ORGANIZATION, THE(1971); SUPERFLY(1972); SUPERFLY T.N.T.(1973), a, d, w; MASTER GUNFIGHTER, THE(1975); BROTHERS(1977); FORCE OF ONE, A(1979); WHEN A STRANGER CALLS(1979); FINAL COUNTDOWN, THE(1980); ST. HELENS(1981)
1984
RED DAWN(1984)

Barry O'Neill
Silents
CLIMBERS, THE(1915), d; LIFE'S WHIRLPOOL(1916), d&w
Misc. Silents
GAMBLERS, THE(1914), d; WOLF, THE(1914), d; UNPARDONABLE SIN, THE(1916), d; WEAKNESS OF MAN, THE(1916), d; WOMAN'S WAY, A(1916), d

Betty O'Neill
Silents
JIMMY(1916, Brit.)

Cathy O'Neill
LIFE BEGINS AT 17(1958)

Chris O'Neill
UNDERGROUND(1970, Brit.)

D.J. O'Neill
SMITHEREENS(1982)

Dick O'Neill
TAKING OF PELHAM ONE, TWO, THREE, THE(1974); CAPTURE THAT CAPSULE(1961); GAMERA THE INVINCIBLE(1966, Jap.); TO THE SHORES OF HELL(1966); PRETTY POISON(1968); HAIL(1973); FRONT PAGE, THE(1974); ENTERTAINER, THE(1975); POSSE(1975); ST. IVES(1976); MAC ARTHUR(1977); HOUSE CALLS(1978); JERK, THE(1979); WOLFEN(1981)
Misc. Talkies
SPY SQUAD(1962)

Ed O'Neill
TENNESSEE JOHNSON(1942); PLACE IN THE SUN, A(1951)

Edward O'Neill
ALF'S CARPET(1929, Brit.)
Silents
HOUSE OF TEMPERLEY, THE(1913, Brit.); ALTAR CHAINS(1916, Brit.); KING'S DAUGHTER, THE(1916, Brit.); FLAMES(1917, Brit.); NELSON(1918, Brit.); HER HERITAGE(1919, Brit.); ENCHANTMENT(1920, Brit.); MIRAGE, THE(1920, Brit.); TRUE TILDA(1920, Brit.); UNREST(1920, Brit.); WORLDLINGS, THE(1920, Brit.); GENERAL JOHN REGAN(1921, Brit.); INNOCENT(1921, Brit.); DON QUIXOTE(1923, Brit.); SCANDAL, THE(1923, Brit.); NOT FOR SALE(1924, Brit.); DAUGHTER IN REVOLT, A(1927, Brit.); DAWN(1928, Brit.); BARNES MURDER CASE, THE(1930, Brit.)
Misc. Silents
I BELIEVE(1916, Brit.); MANXMAN, THE(1916, Brit.); LAUGHING CAVALIER, THE(1917, Brit.); BIG MONEY(1918, Brit.); FORTUNE AT STAKE, A(1918, Brit.); GREAT IMPOSTER, THE(1918, Brit.); TOWN OF CROOKED WAYS(1920, Brit.); DEAR FOOL, A(1921, Brit.); ONE ARABIAN NIGHT(1923, Brit.)

Eileen O'Neill
TEENAGE MILLIONAIRE(1961); KISS ME, STUPID(1964); MAN CALLED DAGGER, A(1967); LOVING(1970)

Ella O'Neill
RUSTLERS' ROUNDUP(1933), w; FLASH GORDON(1936), w

Eugene O'Neill
ANNA CHRISTIE(1930), w; STRANGE INTERLUDE(1932), w; EMPEROR JONES, THE(1933), w; AH, WILDERNESS!(1935), w; LONG VOYAGE HOME, THE(1940), w; HAIRY APE, THE(1944), w; MOURNING BECOMES ELECTRA(1947), w; SUMMER HOLIDAY(1948), w; DESIRE UNDER THE ELMS(1958), w; LONG DAY'S JOURNEY INTO NIGHT(1962), w; ICEMAN COMETH, THE(1973), w
Silents
ANNA CHRISTIE(1923), w

Faye O'Neill
Silents
LEGALLY DEAD(1923)
Misc. Silents
GIRL IN HIS ROOM, THE(1922)

Frank O'Neill
L'ENIGMATIQUE MONSIEUR PARKES(1930); ON BORROWED TIME(1939), w; GREATEST STORY EVER TOLD, THE(1965), ed
Silents
OVERLAND LIMITED, THE(1925), d

Garry O'Neill
YELLOWBEARD(1983)

Gene O'Neill
1984
C.H.U.D.(1984)

George O'Neill
ONLY YESTERDAY(1933), w; UNCERTAIN LADY(1934), w; I'D GIVE MY LIFE(1936), w; HIGH, WIDE AND HANDSOME(1937), w

Harry O'Neill
Silents
AMERICA(1924)

Henry O'Neill
YELLOW JACK(1938); FROM HEADQUARTERS(1933); HOUSE ON 56TH STREET, THE(1933); I LOVED A WOMAN(1933); KENNEL MURDER CASE, THE(1933); LADY KILLER(1933); BIG HEARTED HERBERT(1934); BIG SHAKEDOWN, THE(1934); FASHIONS OF 1934(1934); FLIRTATION WALK(1934); FOG OVER FRISCO(1934); GENTLEMEN ARE BORN(1934); I'VE GOT YOUR NUMBER(1934); JOURNAL OF A CRIME(1934); KEY, THE(1934); MADAME DU BARRY(1934); MAN WITH TWO FACES, THE(1934); MASSACRE(1934); MIDNIGHT(1934); MIDNIGHT ALIBI(1934); MURDER IN THE CLOUDS(1934); NOW I'LL TELL(1934); PERSONALITY KID, THE(1934); SIDE STREETS(1934); TWENTY MILLION SWEETHEARTS(1934); UPPER WORLD(1934); WONDER BAR(1934); ALIAS MARY DOW(1935); BLACK FURY(1935); BORDERTOWN(1935); CASE OF THE LUCKY LEGS, THE(1935); DINKY(1935); DR. SOCRATES(1935); FLORENTINE DAGGER, THE(1935); GREAT HOTEL MURDER(1935); LIVING ON VELVET(1935); MAN WHO RECLAIMED HIS HEAD, THE(1935); OIL FOR THE LAMPS OF CHINA(1935); PERSONAL MAID'S SECRET(1935); SECRET BRIDE, THE(1935); SPECIAL AGENT(1935); STRANDED(1935); SWEET MUSIC(1935); WE'RE IN THE MONEY(1935); WHILE THE PATIENT SLEPT(1935); ANTHONY ADVERSE(1936); BIG NOISE, THE(1936); BOULDER DAM(1936); BULLETS OR BALLOTS(1936); FRESHMAN LOVE(1936); GOLDEN ARROW, THE(1936); RAINBOW ON THE RIVER(1936); ROAD GANG(1936); STORY OF LOUIS PASTEUR(1936); TWO AGAINST THE WORLD(1936); WALKING DEAD, THE(1936); WHITE ANGEL, THE(1936); DRAEGERMAN COURAGE(1937); FIRST LADY(1937); GO-GETTER, THE(1937); GREAT O'MALLEY, THE(1937); GREEN LIGHT(1937); LIFE OF EMILE ZOLA, THE(1937); MARKED WOMAN(1937); MR. DODD TAKES THE AIR(1937); SINGING MARINE, THE(1937); SUBMARINE

D-1(1937); WELLS FARGO(1937); BROTHER RAT(1938); CHASER, THE(1938); GIRLS ON PROBATION(1938); GOLD IS WHERE YOU FIND IT(1938); JEZEBEL(1938); RACKET BUSTERS(1938); TORCHY BLANE IN CHINATOWN(1938); WHITE BANNERS(1938); ANGELS WASH THEIR FACES(1939); CONFESSIONS OF A NAZI SPY(1939); DODGE CITY(1939); EVERYBODY'S HOBBY(1939); FOUR WIVES(1939); I AM NOT AFRAID(1939); JUAREZ(1939); LUCKY NIGHT(1939); MAN WHO DARED, THE(1939); WINGS OF THE NAVY(1939); BROTHER RAT AND A BABY(1940); CALLING PHILO VANCE(1940); CASTLE ON THE HUDSON(1940); CHILD IS BORN, A(1940); DR. EHRLICH'S MAGIC BULLET(1940); FIGHTING 69TH, THE(1940); INVISIBLE STRIPES(1940); KNUTE ROCKNE–ALL AMERICAN(1940); MONEY AND THE WOMAN(1940); SANTA FE TRAIL(1940); THEY DRIVE BY NIGHT(1940); 'TIL WE MEET AGAIN(1940); BILLY THE KID(1941); BLOSSOMS IN THE DUST(1941); BUGLE SOUNDS, THE(1941); DOWN IN SAN DIEGO(1941); GET-AWAY, THE(1941); HONKY TONK(1941); KEEPING COMPANY(1941); MEN OF BOYS TOWN(1941); SHADOW OF THE THIN MAN(1941); TRIAL OF MARY DUGAN, THE(1941); WHISTLING IN THE DARK(1941); BORN TO SING(1942); STAND BY FOR ACTION(1942); THIS TIME FOR KEEPS(1942); TORTILLA FLAT(1942); WHITE CARGO(1942); AIR RAID WARDENS(1943); BEST FOOT FORWARD(1943); DR. GILLESPIE'S CRIMINAL CASE(1943); GIRL CRAZY(1943); GUY NAMED JOE, A(1943); HEAVENLY BODY, THE(1943); HUMAN COMEDY, THE(1943); WHISTLING IN BROOKLYN(1943); BARBARY COAST GENT(1944); LOST ANGEL(1944); NOTHING BUT TROUBLE(1944); RATIONING(1944); TWO GIRLS AND A SAILOR(1944); ANCHORS AWEIGH(1945); DANGEROUS PARTNERS(1945); KEEP YOUR POWDER DRY(1945); THIS MAN'S NAVY(1945); BAD BASCOMB(1946); GREEN YEARS, THE(1946); HOODLUM SAINT(1946); LITTLE MISTER JIM(1946); THREE WISE FOOLS(1946); VIRGINIAN, THE(1946); BEGINNING OR THE END, THE(1947); LEATHER GLOVES(1948); RETURN OF OCTOBER, THE(1948); ALIAS NICK BEAL(1949); HOLIDAY AFFAIR(1949); RECKLESS MOMENTS, THE(1949); STRANGE BARGAIN(1949); YOU'RE MY EVERYTHING(1949); CONVICTED(1950); FLYING MISSILE(1950); MILKMAN, THE(1950); NO MAN OF HER OWN(1950); FAMILY SECRET, THE(1951); PEOPLE AGAINST O'HARA, THE(1951); SECOND WOMAN, THE(1951); SCANDAL SHEET(1952); SCARLET ANGEL(1952); SUN SHINES BRIGHT, THE(1953); UNTAMED(1955); WINGS OF EAGLES, THE(1957)

Howard O'Neill
EXILED TO SHANGHAI(1937), ed; LOVE FROM A STRANGER(1937, Brit.), ed; PORTIA ON TRIAL(1937), ed; BLACKMAIL(1939), ed; SOCIETY LAWYER(1939), ed; DR. KILDARE GOES HOME(1940), ed; WE WHO ARE YOUNG(1940), ed; DOWN MEXICO WAY(1941), ed; GAY VAGABOND, THE(1941), ed; WEST OF CIMARRON(1941), ed; HI, NEIGHBOR(1942), ed; IN OLD CALIFORNIA(1942), ed; PARDON MY STRIPES(1942), ed; YOUTH ON PARADE(1943), ed

James O'Neill
SLEEPING CITY, THE(1950)
Silents
MILLION DOLLAR ROBBERY, THE(1914); KING SPRUCE(1920); RED LANE, THE(1920)
Misc. Silents
COUNT OF MONTE CRISTO, THE(1913); TEMPTATIONS OF SATAN, THE(1914); SUSAN'S GENTLEMAN(1917); MISS ARIZONA(1919)

Jean O'Neill
ROMANCE OF THE LIMBERLOST(1938)

Jennifer O'Neill
FOR LOVE OF IVY(1968); RIO LOBO(1970); SUCH GOOD FRIENDS(1971); SUMMER OF '42(1971); CAREY TREATMENT, THE(1972); GLASS HOUSES(1972); LADY ICE(1973); REINCARNATION OF PETER PROUD, THE(1975); WHIFFS(1975); CARAVANS(1978, U.S./Iranian); FORCE OF ONE, A(1979); INNOCENT, THE(1979, Ital.); PSYCHIC, THE(1979, Ital.); CLOUD DANCER(1980); SCANNERS(1981, Can.)

John O'Neill
FAREWELL, MY LOVELY(1975)

Johnny O'Neill
YOUNG JESSE JAMES(1960)

Kevin O'Neill
YOUNG CYCLE GIRLS, THE(1979)

Kitty O'Neill
ISLE OF MISSING MEN(1942)

Maggie O'Neill
DEAD TO THE WORLD(1961)

Maire O'Neill
JUNO AND THE PAYCOCK(1930, Brit.); NORAH O'NEALE(1934, Brit.); COME OUT OF THE PANTRY(1935, Brit.); FAME(1936, Brit.); PEG OF OLD DRURY(1936, Brit.); BULLDOG DRUMMOND AT BAY(1937, Brit.); GLAMOROUS NIGHT(1937, Brit.); RIVER OF UNREST(1937, Brit.); SPRING HANDICAP(1937, Brit.); MOUNTAINS O'MOURNE(1938, Brit.); OH BOY!(1938, Brit.); PENNY PARADISE(1938, Brit.); SWORD OF HONOUR(1938, Brit.); TROOPSHIP(1938, Brit.); ARSENAL STADIUM MYSTERY, THE(1939, Brit.); DR. O'DOWD(1940, Brit.); FUGITIVE, THE(1940, Brit.); LITTLE MISS MOLLY(1940); MISSING PEOPLE, THE(1940, Brit.); SIDEWALKS OF LONDON(1940, Brit.); COURAGEOUS MR. PENN, THE(1941, Brit.); YOU WILL REMEMBER(1941, Brit.); LET THE PEOPLE SING(1942, Brit.); THOSE KIDS FROM TOWN(1942, Brit.); THEATRE ROYAL(1943, Brit.); GREAT DAY(1945, Brit.); LOVE ON THE DOLE(1945, Brit.); QUERY(1945, Brit.); MURDER IN REVERSE(1946, Brit.); SEND FOR PAUL TEMPLE(1946, Brit.); PICCADILLY INCIDENT(1948, Brit.); SHOWTIME(1948, Brit.); SPRINGTIME(1948, Brit.); SAINTS AND SINNERS(1949, Brit.); STRANGER AT MY DOOR(1950, Brit.); JUDGMENT DEFERRED(1952, Brit.); TREASURE HUNT(1952, Brit.); HORSE'S MOUTH, THE(1953, Brit.); FIGHTING PRINCE OF DONEGAL, THE(1966, Brit.)

Marie O'Neill
M'BLIMEY(1931, Brit.); HILLS OF DONEGAL, THE(1947, Brit.)

Maris O'Neill
SWEET CHARITY(1969)

Mary Ellen O'Neill
PRIZE FIGHTER, THE(1979); VAN NUYS BLVD.(1979); BIG BRAWL, THE(1980); FOXES(1980); SEED OF INNOCENCE(1980); GALAXY OF TERROR(1981)

Maureen O'Neill
LADY GODIVA RIDES AGAIN(1955, Brit.)

Michael O'Neill
JOYRIDE(1977)

Nance O'Neill
OKAY AMERICA(1932)
Misc. Silents
COUNT OF MONTE CRISTO, THE(1913)

Paddie O'Neill
EARLY BIRD, THE(1965, Brit.)
Pat O'Neill
JEALOUSY(1934); GROOVE TUBE, THE(1974), anim
Patrick O'Neill
LOOKIN' TO GET OUT(1982)
Peggy O'Neill
SONG OF THE OPEN ROAD(1944); IT'S A PLEASURE(1945); HOODLUM SAINT, THE(1946); RAZOR'S EDGE, THE(1946); LET'S DANCE(1950)
Peggy O'Neill
Misc. Silents
PENNY PHILANTHROPIST, THE(1917)
Remy O'Neill
PROTECTORS, BOOK 1, THE(1981)
Robert O'Neill
ROSEANNA McCOY(1949); YOUNG MAN WITH A HORN(1950); JOE MAC-BETH(1955); SHADOW OF A MAN(1955, Brit.); MOUSE THAT ROARED, THE(1959, Brit.); SUPERMAN(1978)
Misc. Talkies
DEADLY AND THE BEAUTIFUL(1974), d
Robert Vincent O'Neill
Misc. Talkies
PSYCHO LOVER(1969, Brit.), d
Sally O'Neill
BROADWAY SCANDALS(1929); GIRL ON THE BARGE, THE(1929); HOLD EVERY-THING(1930)
Silents
BACHELOR'S PARADISE(1928); HARDBOILED(1929)
Misc. Silents
MAD HOUR(1928)
Shannon O'Neill
CREEPING TERROR, THE(1964)
Sharon O'Neill
SMASH PALACE(1982, New Zealand), m
Sheila O'Neill
SUMMER HOLIDAY(1963, Brit.); I'VE GOTTA HORSE(1965, Brit.); HALF A SIX-PENCE(1967, Brit.)
Shelly O'Neill
FAST TIMES AT RIDGEMONT HIGH(1982)
Tex O'Neill
RIDERS OF THE DESERT(1932)
Thomas F. O'Neill
SATURDAY'S MILLIONS(1933), art d
Silents
MAN WHO LAUGHS, THE(1927), art d
Tom O'Neill
PROMISE, THE(1979)
W.G. O'Neill
STOKER, THE(1935, Brit.)
William O'Neill
Misc. Silents
SUSAN'S GENTLEMAN(1917)
Colette O'Nell
SCHOOL FOR UNCLAIMED GIRLS(1973, Brit.)
Les O'Pace
HOUSE ON TELEGRAPH HILL(1951)
Leslie O'Pace
MAN OF CONFLICT(1953)
Leslie K. O'Pace
TALK ABOUT A STRANGER(1952)
Catherine O'Quinn
MAD MISS MANTON, THE(1938)
Terrance K. O'Quinn
WITHOUT A TRACE(1983)
Terry O'Quinn
HEAVEN'S GATE(1980)
1984
MRS. SOFFEL(1984); PLACES IN THE HEART(1984)
Georgia O'Ramie
Silents
$5,000,000 COUNTERFEITING PLOT, THE(1914)
Francis O'Rawe
IT ALWAYS RAINS ON SUNDAY(1949, Brit.)
Terence O'Reagan
STOLEN FACE(1952, Brit.)
Frankie O'Rear
SNOWBALL EXPRESS(1972), w
James O'Rear
BRUTE FORCE(1947); SEA OF GRASS, THE(1947); CRISS CROSS(1949); OVER-EXPOSED(1956); TEENAGE REBEL(1956); SPIRIT OF ST. LOUIS, THE(1957); STORY ON PAGE ONE, THE(1959); WHO'S BEEN SLEEPING IN MY BED?(1963); DEAR HEART(1964); MISTER BUDDWING(1966)
John O'Rear
SNOWBALL EXPRESS(1972), w
Kathy O'Rear
THANK GOD IT'S FRIDAY(1978), cos
1984
CANNONBALL RUN II(1984), cos
James O'Reare
CHINATOWN(1974); CONRACK(1974)
Robert O'Ree
RABID(1976, Can.); PHOBIA(1980, Can.); TITLE SHOT(1982, Can.)
Kathleen O'Regan
JUNO AND THE PAYCOCK(1930, Brit.); FIRES OF FATE(1932, Brit.); SHADOW BETWEEN, THE(1932, Brit.); ROSE OF TRALEE(1938, Ireland); THURSDAY'S CHILD(1943, Brit.)
Terence O'Regan
MOULIN ROUGE(1952)

Brendan O'Reilly
FLIGHT OF THE DOVES(1971)
Cyril O'Reilly
PORKY'S(1982); PORKY'S II: THE NEXT DAY(1983)
1984
PURPLE HEARTS(1984)
Erin O'Reilly
HOW SWEET IT IS(1968); LITTLE FAUSS AND BIG HALSY(1970); T.R. BAS-KIN(1971); BUSTING(1974)
James O'Reilly
CLASS(1983)
Lisa O'Reilly
PORKY'S(1982)
Mary O'Reilly
NORAH O'NEALE(1934, Brit.)
Maureen O'Reilly
FAMILY WAY, THE(1966, Brit.)
Patricia O'Reilly
PAJAMA PARTY(1964)
Rosemary O'Reilly
NEW FACES(1954)
Stephen O'Reilly
1984
PHILADELPHIA EXPERIMENT, THE(1984)
Tex O'Reilly
Misc. Silents
HONEYMOON RANCH(1920); ON THE HIGH CARD(1921); WEST OF THE RIO GRANDE(1921)
Thomas O'Reilly
SATAN'S BED(1965)
Sean O'Riada
YOUNG CASSIDY(1965, U.S./Brit.), m
Kathleen O'Rielly
SNIPER, THE(1952)
Sean O'Rinn
DRESSED TO KILL(1980)
Shaun O'Riordan
MAN WHO LIKED FUNERALS, THE(1959, Brit.); INN FOR TROUBLE(1960, Brit.)
Shawn O'Riordan
WALLET, THE(1952, Brit.)
Charles O'Roark
LISETTE(1961), ph
Charles O'Rork
YELLOWNECK(1955), ph
Charles T. O'Rork
NAKED IN THE SUN(1957), ph; TOUCH OF FLESH, THE(1960), ph
Brefni O'Rorke
GHOST OF ST. MICHAEL'S. THE(1941, Brit.); KING ARTHUR WAS A GENTLE-MAN(1942, Brit.); MISSING MILLION, THE(1942, Brit.); MUCH TOO SHY(1942, Brit.); NEXT OF KIN(1942, Brit.); UNPUBLISHED STORY(1942, Brit.); WE'LL MEET AGAIN(1942, Brit.); WINGS AND THE WOMAN(1942, Brit.); ESCAPE TO DAN-GER(1943, Brit.); FLEMISH FARM, THE(1943, Brit.); LAMP STILL BURNS, THE(1943, Brit.); IT HAPPENED ONE SUNDAY(1944, Brit.); SECRET MISSION(1944, Brit.); TWILIGHT HOUR(1944, Brit.); NOTORIOUS GENTLEMAN(1945, Brit.); THEY MET IN THE DARK(1945, Brit.); VACATION FROM MARRIAGE(1945, Brit.); VOICE WITHIN, THE(1945, Brit.); ADVENTURESS, THE(1946, Brit.); MURDER IN RE-VERSE(1946, Brit.); WALTZ TIME(1946, Brit.); PATIENT VANISHES, THE(1947, Brit.); TAWNY PIPIT(1947, Brit.); HATTER'S CASTLE(1948, Brit.)
Ed O'Ross
1984
COTTON CLUB, THE(1984); POPE OF GREENWICH VILLAGE, THE(1984)
Baby Jean O'Rourke
Misc. Silents
HUNGER OF THE BLOOD, THE(1921)
Brefni O'Rourke
SPITFIRE(1943, Brit.); DON'T TAKE IT TO HEART(1944, Brit.); QUERY(1945, Brit.); THEY WERE SISTERS(1945, Brit.); GREEN FINGERS(1947); ROOT OF ALL EVIL, THE(1947, Brit.); UPTURNED GLASS, THE(1947, Brit.)
Charles O'Rourke
VENGEANCE OF SHE, THE(1968, Brit.)
Don O'Rourke
RESTLESS ONES, THE(1965)
Frank O'Rourke
BRAVADOS, THE(1958), w; PROFESSIONALS, THE(1966), w
Heather O'Rourke
POLTERGEIST(1982)
Heidi O'Rourke
FUNNY LADY(1975)
J.A. O'Rourke
BLARNEY KISS(1933, Brit.); WHEN LONDON SLEEPS(1934, Brit.); POT LUCK(1936, Brit.); KATHLEEN(1938, Ireland)
James C. O'Rourke
SCHLOCK(1973), p
Kevin O'Rourke
TATTOO(1981)
Michael O'Rourke
BARBAROSA(1982)
P.J. O'Rourke
WHAT!(1965, Fr./Brit./Ital.), d; EASY MONEY(1983), w
Pat O'Rourke
Silents
IRISH DESTINY(1925, Brit.)
Patricia O'Rourke
JUNGLE BOOK(1942)
Tom O'Rourke
UNHOLY PARTNERS(1941)
Mickey O'Ryan
I WAS A SHOPLIFTER(1950)

Finnuala O'Shannon
PLAYBOY OF THE WESTERN WORLD, THE(1963, Ireland)

Finola O'Shannon
POACHER'S DAUGHTER, THE(1960, Brit.)

Alfred O'Shaughnessy
BRANDY FOR THE PARSON(1952, Brit.), p

Brian O'Shaughnessy
RIDE THE HIGH WIND(1967, South Africa); RIDER IN THE NIGHT, THE(1968, South Africa); SEVEN AGAINST THE SUN(1968, South Africa); CREATURES THE WORLD FORGOT(1971, Brit.); SLAVERS(1977, Ger.); ZULU DAWN(1980, Brit.)
1984
GODS MUST BE CRAZY, THE(1984, Botswana)
Misc. Talkies
STRANGERS AT SUNRISE(1969); MR. KINGSTREET'S WAR(1973)

Charles O'Shaughnessy
KITTY(1929, Brit.)
Silents
HONEYMOON AHEAD(1927, Brit.)

Dick O'Shaughnessy
KIMBERLEY JIM(1965, South Africa)

Peter O'Shaughnessy
ON THE BEACH(1959); ADAM'S WOMAN(1972, Austral.)

Brian O'Shea
MY HANDS ARE CLAY(1948, Irish)

Danny O'Shea
MANHATTAN COCKTAIL(1928); LUMMOX(1930)
Misc. Silents
HER FATHER SAID NO(1927); ON THE STROKE OF TWELVE(1927); DUGAN OF THE DUGOUTS(1928); MANHATTAN COCKTAIL(1928)

Danny O'Shea
OF HUMAN BONDAGE(1964, Brit.)

Denis O'Shea
Silents
IRISH DESTINY(1925, Brit.)

Dick O'Shea
GUNFIGHT, A(1971)

Ethel O'Shea
RECOIL(1953)

Jack O'Shea
RANGE DEFENDERS(1937); IN EARLY ARIZONA(1938); PAINTED DESERT, THE(1938); RENEGADE RANGER(1938); RIDERS OF THE BLACK HILLS(1938); COWBOYS FROM TEXAS(1939); FRONTIER PONY EXPRESS(1939); IN OLD MONTEREY(1939); SIX-GUN RHYTHM(1939); SOUTH OF THE BORDER(1939); YOUNG BUFFALO BILL(1940); DESERT BANDIT(1941); DOWN MEXICO WAY(1941); IN OLD CHEYENNE(1941); JESSE JAMES AT BAY(1941); LONE RIDER FIGHTS BACK, THE(1941); PHANTOM COWBOY, THE(1941); SINGING HILL, THE(1941); IN OLD CALIFORNIA(1942); OUTLAWS OF PINE RIDGE(1942); ROMANCE ON THE RANGE(1942); SOMBRERO KID, THE(1942); SONS OF THE PIONEERS(1942); SOUTH OF SANTA FE(1942); WESTWARD HO(1942); KING OF THE COWBOYS(1943); MAN FROM MUSIC MOUNTAIN(1943); MAN FROM THE RIO GRANDE, THE(1943); MAN FROM THUNDER RIVER, THE(1943); OVERLAND MAIL ROBBERY(1943); RAIDERS OF SAN JOAQUIN(1943); RIDERS OF THE RIO GRANDE(1943); SILVER SPURS(1943); THUNDERING TRAILS(1943); WAGON TRACKS WEST(1943); CHEYENNE WILDCAT(1944); CODE OF THE PRAIRIE(1944); FIREBRANDS OF ARIZONA(1944); MARSHAL OF RENO(1944); OUTLAWS OF SANTA FE(1944); SAN ANTONIO KID, THE(1944); SHERIFF OF SUNDOWN(1944); SONG OF NEVADA(1944); STAGECOACH TO MONTEREY(1944); YELLOW ROSE OF TEXAS, THE(1944); FRONTIER GAL(1945); GANGS OF THE WATERFRONT(1945); MARSHAL OF LAREDO(1945); ROUGH RIDERS OF CHEYENNE(1945); SANTA FE SADDLEMATES(1945); SHERIFF OF CIMARRON(1945); CARAVAN TRAIL, THE(1946); IN OLD SACRAMENTO(1946); OUTLAW OF THE PLAINS(1946); OVERLAND RIDERS(1946); PLAINSMAN AND THE LADY(1946); RIO GRANDE RAIDERS(1946); ROMANCE OF THE WEST(1946); STARS OVER TEXAS(1946); TUMBLEWEED TRAIL(1946); BOWERY BUCKAROOS(1947); FLASHING GUNS(1947); LAW OF THE LASH(1947); OREGON TRAIL SCOUTS(1947); TWILIGHT ON THE RIO GRANDE(1947); VIGILANTES OF BOOMTOWN(1947); WYOMING(1947); KING OF THE BANDITS(1948); LAST BANDIT, THE(1949); OUTLAW COUNTRY(1949); RIDE, RYDER, RIDE!(1949); ROLL, THUNDER, ROLL(1949); SHERIFF OF WICHITA(1949); SAVAGE HORDE, THE(1950); SILVER CANYON(1951); FRONTIER PHANTOM, THE(1952); PERILOUS JOURNEY, A(1953); JUBILEE TRAIL(1954); MAVERICK QUEEN, THE(1956); GHOST OF ZORRO(1959)

James O'Shea
Silents
ACQUITTED(1916); HELL-TO-PAY AUSTIN(1916)
Misc. Silents
MARRIAGE OF MOLLY-O, THE(1916); RUMMY, THE(1916)

John O'Shea
PICTURES(1982, New Zealand), p, w

Kevin O'Shea
KEYS OF THE KINGDOM, THE(1944); PURPLE HEART, THE(1944); WING AND A PRAYER(1944)

Michael O'Shea
JACK LONDON(1943); LADY OF BURLESQUE(1943); EVE OF ST. MARK, THE(1944); MAN FROM FRISCO(1944); SOMETHING FOR THE BOYS(1944); CIRCUMSTANTIAL EVIDENCE(1945); IT'S A PLEASURE(1945); MR. DISTRICT ATTORNEY(1946); LAST OF THE REDMEN(1947); VIOLENCE(1947); SMART WOMAN(1948); BIG WHEEL, THE(1949); CAPTAIN CHINA(1949); PAROLE, INC.(1949); THREAT, THE(1949); WHIPPED, THE(1950); DISC JOCKEY(1951); FIXED BAYONETS(1951); MODEL AND THE MARRIAGE BROKER, THE(1951); BLOODHOUNDS OF BROADWAY(1952); IT SHOULD HAPPEN TO YOU(1954)

Milo O'Shea
YOU CAN'T BEAT THE IRISH(1952, Brit.); THIS OTHER EDEN(1959, Brit.); MRS. GIBBONS' BOYS(1962, Brit.); CARRY ON CABBIE(1963, Brit.); NEVER PUT IT IN WRITING(1964); ULYSSES(1967, U.S./Brit.); BARBARELLA(1968, Fr./Ital.); ROMEO AND JULIET(1968, Brit./Ital.); ADDING MACHINE, THE(1969); ANGEL LEVINE, THE(1970); PADDY(1970, Irish); LOOT(1971, Brit.); SACCO AND VANZETTI(1971, Ital./Fr.); IT'S A 2"6" ABOVE THE GROUND WORLD(1972, Brit.); THEATRE OF BLOOD(1973, Brit.); DIGBY, THE BIGGEST DOG IN THE WORLD(1974, Brit.); ARABIAN ADVENTURE(1979, Brit.); IT'S NOT THE SIZE THAT COUNTS(1979, Brit.); PILOT, THE(1979); VERDICT, THE(1982)

Missy O'Shea
1984
NEW YORK NIGHTS(1984)

Oscar O'Shea
WITHOUT RESERVATIONS(1946); BIG CITY(1937); CAPTAINS COURAGEOUS(1937); DOUBLE WEDDING(1937); MANNEQUIN(1937); ROSALIE(1937); ANGELS WITH DIRTY FACES(1938); BORDER WOLVES(1938); INTERNATIONAL CRIME(1938); KING OF THE NEWSBOYS(1938); MAIN EVENT, THE(1938); MANPROOF(1938); RACKET BUSTERS(1938); REBELLIOUS DAUGHTERS(1938); SHINING HOUR, THE(1938); STABLEMATES(1938); YOU'RE ONLY YOUNG ONCE(1938); YOUTH TAKES A FLING(1938); BIG TOWN CZAR(1939); INVITATION TO HAPPINESS(1939); KING OF THE TURF(1939); LOVE AFFAIR(1939); LUCKY NIGHT(1939); MISSING EVIDENCE(1939); NIGHT OF NIGHTS, THE(1939); OF MICE AND MEN(1939); SHE MARRIED A COP(1939); S.O.S. TIDAL WAVE(1939); STAR MAKER, THE(1939); TELL NO TALES(1939); THOSE HIGH GREY WALLS(1939); UNDERCOVER AGENT(1939); ALWAYS A BRIDE(1940); PIER 13(1940); STRANGER ON THE THIRD FLOOR(1940); SUSAN AND GOD(1940); TWENTY MULE TEAM(1940); WILDCAT BUS(1940); YOU CAN'T FOOL YOUR WIFE(1940); ZANZIBAR(1940); ACCENT ON LOVE(1941); HARMON OF MICHIGAN(1941); MUTINY IN THE ARCTIC(1941); OFFICER AND THE LADY, THE(1941); PHANTOM SUBMARINE, THE(1941); RIDERS OF THE PURPLE SAGE(1941); RINGSIDE MAISIE(1941); SLEEPERS WEST(1941); BASHFUL BACHELOR, THE(1942); FLY BY NIGHT(1942); HALF WAY TO SHANGHAI(1942); HENRY ALDRICH, EDITOR(1942); I WAS FRAMED(1942); JUST OFF BROADWAY(1942); LADY BODYGUARD(1942); POSTMAN DIDN'T RING, THE(1942); SIN TOWN(1942); TORPEDO BOAT(1942); CORVETTE K-225(1943); GOOD MORNING, JUDGE(1943); HAPPY LAND(1943); THREE HEARTS FOR JULIA(1943); TWO TICKETS TO LONDON(1943); TWO WEEKS TO LIVE(1943); HER PRIMITIVE MAN(1944); HERE COME THE WAVES(1944); MUMMY'S GHOST, THE(1944); SOUTH OF DIXIE(1944); BEWITCHED(1945); SENORITA FROM THE WEST(1945); PERSONALITY KID(1946); IT HAD TO BE YOU(1947); MY WILD IRISH ROSE(1947); SPORT OF KINGS(1947); STALLION ROAD(1947); WHERE THERE'S LIFE(1947); FURY AT FURNACE CREEK(1948); ONE SUNDAY AFTERNOON(1948); DAUGHTER OF ROSIE O'GRADY, THE(1950); THY NEIGHBOR'S WIFE(1953)

Richard O'Shea
1776(1972)

Rory O'Shea
PICTURES(1982, New Zealand), ph

Shannon O'Shea
MAN FROM O.R.G.Y., THE(1970)

Sonya O'Shea
ADVENTURES OF JANE, THE(1949, Brit.); MATTER OF MURDER, A(1949, Brit.); OVER THE GARDEN WALL(1950, Brit.); TWENTY QUESTIONS MURDER MYSTERY, THE(1950, Brit.)

Ted O'Shea
SWING TIME(1936); MEN AGAINST THE SKY(1940); FOUR JACKS AND A JILL(1941); MEXICAN SPITFIRE'S BABY(1941); LADIES' DAY(1943); NOCTURNE(1946)

Tessie O'Shea
WAY AHEAD, THE(1945, Brit.); HOLIDAYS WITH PAY(1948, Brit.); SOMEWHERE IN POLITICS(1949, Brit.); MY HEART GOES CRAZY(1953, Brit.); SHIRALEE, THE(1957, Brit.); RUSSIANS ARE COMING, THE RUSSIANS ARE COMING, THE(1966); BEST HOUSE IN LONDON, THE(1969, Brit.); BEDKNOBS AND BROOMSTICKS(1971)

William O'Shea
MY FAVORITE BLONDE(1942), ed
Silents
WHITE OAK(1921), ed

Fiona O'Shiel
HARRIET CRAIG(1950); CARBINE WILLIAMS(1952)

Parra O'Siochain
TROIKA(1969)

Sam O'Steen
KISSES FOR MY PRESIDENT(1964), ed; ROBIN AND THE SEVEN HOODS(1964), ed; YOUNGBLOOD HAWKE(1964), ed; MARRIAGE ON THE ROCKS(1965), ed; NONE BUT THE BRAVE(1965, U.S./Jap.); WHO'S AFRAID OF VIRGINIA WOOLF?(1966), ed; COOL HAND LUKE(1967), ed; GRADUATE, THE(1967), ed; HOTEL(1967), ed; ROSEMARY'S BABY(1968), ed; STERILE CUCKOO, THE(1969), ed; CATCH-22(1971), ed; CARNAL KNOWLEDGE(1971), ed; PORTNOY'S COMPLAINT(1972), ed; DAY OF THE DOLPHIN, THE(1973), ed; CHINATOWN(1974), ed; SPARKLE(1976), d; STRAIGHT TIME(1978), ed; HURRICANE(1979), ed; AMITYVILLE II: THE POSSESSION(1982), ed; SILKWOOD(1983), ed

Archie O'Sullivan
RYAN'S DAUGHTER(1970, Brit.); VICTOR FRANKENSTEIN(1975, Swed./Ireland)

Arthur O'Sullivan
QUARE FELLOW, THE(1962, Brit.); MYSTERY SUBMARINE(1963, Brit.); GIRL WITH GREEN EYES(1964, Brit.); YOUNG CASSIDY(1965, U.S./Brit.); VIKING QUEEN, THE(1967, Brit.); BARRY LYNDON(1975, Brit.)

Brian O'Sullivan
DAWN OVER IRELAND(1938, Irish); MEN OF IRELAND(1938, Ireland)

Jerry O'Sullivan
SPRINGFIELD RIFLE(1952); PICKUP ON SOUTH STREET(1953); NORTH TO ALASKA(1960)

Lawrence O'Sullivan
DELICIOUS(1931)

Mairin O'Sullivan
PURPLE TAXI, THE(1977, Fr./Ital./Ireland)

Maureen O'Sullivan
JUST IMAGINE(1930); PRINCESS AND THE PLUMBER, THE(1930); SO THIS IS LONDON(1930); SONG O' MY HEART(1930); BIG SHOT, THE(1931); CONNECTICUT YANKEE, A(1931); SKYLINE(1931); FAST COMPANIONS(1932); OKAY AMERICA(1932); PAYMENT DEFERRED(1932); SILVER LINING(1932); SKYSCRAPER SOULS(1932); STRANGE INTERLUDE(1932); TARZAN, THE APE MAN(1932); BISHOP MISBEHAVES, THE(1933); COHENS AND KELLYS IN TROUBLE, THE(1933); ROBBERS' ROOST(1933); STAGE MOTHER(1933); TUGBOAT ANNIE(1933); BARRETTS OF WIMPOLE STREET, THE(1934); HIDE-OUT(1934); TARZAN AND HIS MATE(1934); THIN MAN, THE(1934); ANNA KARENINA(1935); CARDINAL RICHELIEU(1935); DAVID COPPERFIELD(1935); FLAME WITHIN, THE(1935); WEST POINT OF THE AIR(1935); WOMAN WANTED(1935); DEVIL DOLL, THE(1936); TARZAN ESCAPES(1936); VOICE OF BUGLE ANN(1936); BETWEEN TWO WOMEN(1937); DAY AT THE RACES, A(1937); EMPEROR'S CANDLESTICKS,

THE(1937); MY DEAR MISS ALDRICH(1937); CROWD ROARS, THE(1938); HOLD THAT KISS(1938); PORT OF SEVEN SEAS(1938); SPRING MADNESS(1938); YANK AT OXFORD, A(1938); LET US LIVE(1939); TARZAN FINDS A SON!(1939); PRIDE AND PREJUDICE(1940); SPORTING BLOOD(1940); MAISIE WAS A LADY(1941); TARZAN'S SECRET TREASURE(1941); TARZAN'S NEW YORK ADVENTURE(1942); BIG CLOCK, THE(1948); WHERE DANGER LIVES(1950); BONZO GOES TO COLLEGE(1952); NO RESTING PLACE(1952, Brit.); ALL I DESIRE(1953); MISSION OVER KOREA(1953); DUFFY OF SAN QUENTIN(1954); STEEL CAGE, THE(1954); TALL T, THE(1957); WILD HERITAGE(1958); NEVER TOO LATE(1965); PHYNX, THE(1970)

Michael O'Sullivan
YOU'RE A BIG BOY NOW(1966); HANG'EM HIGH(1968)
1984
NOT FOR PUBLICATION(1984), a, art d

Owen O'Sullivan
RYAN'S DAUGHTER(1970, Brit.)

Pat O'Sullivan
DUBLIN NIGHTMARE(1958, Brit.)

Richard O'Sullivan
DANCE LITTLE LADY(1954, Brit.); GREEN SCARF, THE(1954, Brit.); MAKE ME AN OFFER(1954, Brit.); SECRET, THE(1955, Brit.); STRANGER'S HAND, THE(1955, Brit.); WARRIORS, THE(1955); IT'S GREAT TO BE YOUNG(1956, Brit.); JACQUELINE(1956, Brit.); NO TIME FOR TEARS(1957, Brit.); DANGEROUS EXILE(1958, Brit.); NUN'S STORY, THE(1959); WITNESS IN THE DARK(1959, Brit.); AND WOMEN SHALL WEEP(1960, Brit.); STORY OF DAVID, A(1960, Brit.); SPARE THE ROD(1961, Brit.); CARRY ON TEACHER(1962, Brit.); WEBSTER BOY, THE(1962, Brit.); WONDERFUL TO BE YOUNG!(1962, Brit.); CLEOPATRA(1963); SEASIDE SWINGERS(1965, Brit.); SWINGER'S PARADISE(1965, Brit.); DANDY IN ASPIC, A(1968, Brit.); HORROR HOUSE(1970, Brit.)
Misc. Talkies
AU PAIR GIRLS(1973); MAN ABOUT THE HOUSE(1974, Brit.)

Robert Hugh O'Sullivan
REDEEMER, THE(1965, Span.), w

Sheila O'Sullivan
ULYSSES(1967, U.S./Brit.)

Terry O'Sullivan
WHITE HEAT(1949)

Thaddeus O'Sullivan
1984
ANNE DEVLIN(1984, Ireland), ph; PIGS(1984, Ireland), ph

William J. O'Sullivan
INNER CIRCLE, THE(1946), p; INVISIBLE INFORMER(1946), p; MAGNIFICENT ROGUE, THE(1946), p; PASSKEY TO DANGER(1946), p; BLACKMAIL(1947), p; EXPOSED(1947), p; PILGRIM LADY, THE(1947), p; TRESPASSER, THE(1947), p; HELLFIRE(1949), p; SHOWDOWN, THE(1950), p; PERILOUS JOURNEY, A(1953), p; OUTCAST, THE(1954), p; HEADLINE HUNTERS(1955), p; STRANGE ADVENTURE, A(1956), p; WHEN GANGLAND STRIKES(1956), p; TAMING SUTTON'S GAL(1957), p

Kevin O'Sullivan [Kevin J. Wilson]
1984
WILD HORSES(1984, New Zealand), w

Jeeds O'Tilbury
ONLY WAY HOME, THE(1972), w

Annette O'Toole
ENTERTAINER, THE(1975); SMILE(1975); ONE ON ONE(1977); KING OF THE GYPSIES(1978); FOOLIN' AROUND(1980); CAT PEOPLE(1982); 48 HOURS(1982); SUPERMAN III(1983)

Barney O'Toole
OUR RELATIONS(1936)

Dave O'Toole
OH, MR. PORTER!(1937, Brit.)
Silents
QUALIFIED ADVENTURER, THE(1925, Brit.)

John O'Toole
WHO KILLED MARY WHAT'SER NAME?(1971), w

Kathy O'Toole
MARIGOLD MAN(1970), art d

Ollie O'Toole
SIDE STREET(1950); OREGON TRAIL, THE(1959); NORTH TO ALASKA(1960); LITTLE SHEPHERD OF KINGDOM COME(1961); 20,000 EYES(1961); MAN'S FAVORITE SPORT(1964); ONE OF OUR SPIES IS MISSING(1966); MADIGAN(1968)

Peter O'Toole
DAY THEY ROBBED THE BANK OF ENGLAND, THE(1960, Brit.); KIDNAPPED(1960); SAVAGE INNOCENTS, THE(1960, Brit.); LAWRENCE OF ARABIA(1962, Brit.); BECKET(1964, Brit.); LORD JIM(1965, Brit.); SANDPIPER, THE(1965); WHAT'S NEW, PUSSYCAT?(1965, U.S./Fr.); BIBLE...IN THE BEGINNING, THE(1966); HOW TO STEAL A MILLION(1966); CASINO ROYALE(1967, Brit.); NIGHT OF THE GENERALS, THE(1967, Brit./Fr.); GREAT CATHERINE(1968, Brit.); LION IN WINTER, THE(1968, Brit.); GOODBYE MR. CHIPS(1969, U.S./Brit.); BROTHERLY LOVE(1970, Brit.); MURPHY'S WAR(1971, Brit.); MAN OF LA MANCHA(1972); RULING CLASS, THE(1972, Brit.); UNDER MILK WOOD(1973, Brit.); MAN FRIDAY(1975, Brit.); ROSEBUD(1975); FOXTROT(1977, Mex./Swiss); POWER PLAY(1978, Brit./Can.); STUNT MAN, THE(1980); ZULU DAWN(1980, Brit.); MY FAVORITE YEAR(1982)
1984
SUPERGIRL(1984)

Rosebud O'Toole
1,000 SHAPES OF A FEMALE(1963)

Stanley O'Toole
SQUEEZE, THE(1977, Brit.), p; BOYS FROM BRAZIL, THE(1978), p; NIJINSKY(1980, Brit.), p; SPHINX(1981), p

John O'Verlin
PLANET OF DINOSAURS(1978), m

David Oake
GLORY AT SEA(1952, Brit.); MAGIC BOX, THE(1952, Brit.)

John Oaker
Silents
JOAN THE WOMAN(1916)
Misc. Silents
MAJESTY OF THE LAW, THE(1915); CONSCIENCE OF JOHN DAVID, THE(1916); SOUL'S CYCLE, THE(1916); LORELEI OF THE SEA(1917); SNEAK, THE(1919)

Bill Oakes
GREASE(1978), md

Christopher Oakes
ARENA, THE(1973)

Harry Oakes
THUNDERBIRD 6(1968, Brit.), ph; JOURNEY TO THE FAR SIDE OF THE SUN(1969, Brit.), spec eff

Mary Oakes
VOGUES OF 1938(1937)

Phillip Oakes
PUNCH AND JUDY MAN, THE(1963, Brit.), w

Randi Oakes
ACAPULCO GOLD(1978); BATTLESTAR GALACTICA(1979)

Sue Oakes
WEST SIDE STORY(1961)

Evelyn Oakie
TOO MUCH HARMONY(1933)

Jack Oakie
WILD PARTY, THE(1929); CHINATOWN NIGHTS(1929); CLOSE HARMONY(1929); DUMMY, THE(1929); FAST COMPANY(1929); HARD TO GET(1929); MAN I LOVE, THE(1929); STREET GIRL(1929); SWEETIE(1929); HIT THE DECK(1930); LET'S GO NATIVE(1930); SAP FROM SYRACUSE, THE(1930); SEA LEGS(1930); SOCIAL LION, THE(1930); DUDE RANCH(1931); GANG BUSTER, THE(1931); JUNE MOON(1931); TOUCHDOWN!(1931); DANCERS IN THE DARK(1932); IF I HAD A MILLION(1932); MADISON SQUARE GARDEN(1932); MAKE ME A STAR(1932); MILLION DOLLAR LEGS(1932); ONCE IN A LIFETIME(1932); SKY BRIDE(1932); UPTOWN NEW YORK(1932); ALICE IN WONDERLAND(1933); COLLEGE HUMOR(1933); EAGLE AND THE HAWK, THE(1933); FROM HELL TO HEAVEN(1933); SAILOR BE GOOD(1933); SITTING PRETTY(1933); TOO MUCH HARMONY(1933); COLLEGE RHYTHM(1934); LOOKING FOR TROUBLE(1934); MURDER AT THE VANITIES(1934); SHOOT THE WORKS(1934); BIG BROADCAST OF 1936, THE(1935); CALL OF THE WILD(1935); COLLEEN(1936); COLLEGIATE(1936); FLORIDA SPECIAL(1936); KING OF BURLESQUE(1936); TEXAS RANGERS, THE(1936); CHAMPAGNE WALTZ(1937); FIGHT FOR YOUR LADY(1937); HITTING A NEW HIGH(1937); SUPER SLEUTH(1937); THAT GIRL FROM PARIS(1937); TOAST OF NEW YORK, THE(1937); AFFAIRS OF ANNABEL(1938); ANNABEL TAKES A TOUR(1938); RADIO CITY REVELS(1938); THANKS FOR EVERYTHING(1938); GREAT DICTATOR, THE(1940); LITTLE MEN(1940); TIN PAN ALLEY(1940); YOUNG PEOPLE(1940); GREAT AMERICAN BROADCAST(1941); NAVY BLUES(1941); RISE AND SHINE(1941); ICELAND(1942); SONG OF THE ISLANDS(1942); HELLO, FRISCO, HELLO(1943); SOMETHING TO SHOUT ABOUT(1943); WINTERTIME(1943); BOWERY TO BROADWAY(1944); IT HAPPENED TOMORROW(1944); MERRY MONAHANS, THE(1944); SWEET AND LOWDOWN(1944); ON STAGE EVERYBODY(1945); THAT'S THE SPIRIT(1945); DEVOTION(1946), spec eff; SHE WROTE THE BOOK(1946); NORTHWEST STAMPEDE(1948); WHEN MY BABY SMILES AT ME(1948); THIEVES' HIGHWAY(1949); LAST OF THE BUCCANEERS(1950); TOMAHAWK(1951); AROUND THE WORLD IN 80 DAYS(1956); WONDERFUL COUNTRY, THE(1959); RAT RACE, THE(1960); LOVER COME BACK(1961)
Silents
ROAD HOUSE(1928)
Misc. Silents
FLEET'S IN, THE(1928); SOMEONE TO LOVE(1928); SIN TOWN(1929)

Joe Oakie
BROADWAY BIG SHOT(1942); ONCE UPON A HORSE(1958); NORWOOD(1970)

Ben Oakland
LADY OBJECTS, THE(1938), m; GLAMOUR FOR SALE(1940), m; WHEN THE GIRLS TAKE OVER(1962), m

Dagmar Oakland
STOLEN HEAVEN(1931); STAND UP AND CHEER(1934 80m FOX bw); LEAVENWORTH CASE, THE(1936); WEDDING PRESENT(1936); YOU CAN'T TAKE IT WITH YOU(1938); MR. SKEFFINGTON(1944); THRILL OF A ROMANCE(1945); TONIGHT AND EVERY NIGHT(1945)

Ethelmary Oakland
Misc. Silents
ALWAYS IN THE WAY(1915); HEARTS OF MEN(1915); SHINE GIRL, THE(1916)

Simon Oakland
BROTHERS KARAMAZOV, THE(1958); I WANT TO LIVE!(1958); MURDER, INC.(1960); PSYCHO(1960); RISE AND FALL OF LEGS DIAMOND, THE(1960); WHO WAS THAT LADY?(1960); WEST SIDE STORY(1961); ADVENTURES OF A YOUNG MAN(1962); FOLLOW THAT DREAM(1962); THIRD OF A MAN(1962); WALL OF NOISE(1963); RAIDERS, THE(1964); READY FOR THE PEOPLE(1964); SATAN BUG, THE(1965); PLAINSMAN, THE(1966); SAND PEBBLES, THE(1966); TONY ROME(1967); BULLITT(1968); CHUBASCO(1968); ON A CLEAR DAY YOU CAN SEE FOREVER(1970); SCANDALOUS JOHN(1971); CHATO'S LAND(1972); EMPEROR OF THE NORTH POLE(1973); HAPPY MOTHER'S DAY... LOVE, GEORGE(1973); HUNTING PARTY, THE(1977, Brit.)
Misc. Talkies
SCORPIO SCARAB, THE(1972); CRACKLE OF DEATH(1974)

Vivian Oakland
IN THE HEADLINES(1929); TIME, THE PLACE AND THE GIRL, THE(1929); BACK PAY(1930); FLORODORA GIRL(1930); LADY SURRENDERS, A(1930); MATRIMONIAL BED, THE(1930); OH! SAILOR, BEHAVE!(1930); PERSONALITY(1930); AGE FOR LOVE, THE(1931); GOLD DUST GERTIE(1931); COCK OF THE AIR(1932); HOUSE DIVIDED, A(1932); ONLY YESTERDAY(1933); DEFENSE RESTS, THE(1934); MONEY MEANS NOTHING(1934); RENDEZVOUS AT MIDNIGHT(1935); BRIDE WALKS OUT, THE(1936); LADY LUCK(1936); AMATEUR CROOK(1937); DOUBLE DANGER(1938); REBELLIOUS DAUGHTERS(1938); MAN IN THE TRUNK, THE(1942); LAUGH YOUR BLUES AWAY(1943); MAN WHO WALKED ALONE, THE(1945); LOCKET, THE(1946)
Silents
RAINBOW TRAIL, THE(1925); REDHEADS PREFERRED(1926); TONY RUNS WILD(1926); WEDDING BILL$(1927); MAN IN HOBBLES, THE(1928)

Vivien Oakland
MANY A SLIP(1931); TENDERFOOT, THE(1932); NEIGHBORS' WIVES(1933); THEY JUST HAD TO GET MARRIED(1933); STAR OF MIDNIGHT(1935); CRIME AFLOAT(1937); MILE A MINUTE LOVE(1937); WAY OUT WEST(1937); SLANDER HOUSE(1938); THERE'S THAT WOMAN AGAIN(1938); ISLAND OF LOST MEN(1939); GIRL WHO DARED, THE(1944); UTAH(1945); MAGNIFICENT DOLL(1946); NIGHT AND DAY(1946); SMASH-UP, THE STORY OF A WOMAN(1947); BUNCO SQUAD(1950); SECRET FURY, THE(1950)

Barry Oakley
GREAT MACARTHY, THE(1975, Aus.), w
Florence Oakley
MOST IMMORAL LADY, A(1929)
Miss Laura Oakley
Silents
DUMB GIRL OF PORTICI(1916)
Patricia Oakley
THEY KNEW WHAT THEY WANTED(1940)
Robert Oakley
HAWAII(1966)
Roger Oakley
SLEEPING DOGS(1977, New Zealand)
Joan Oakley-Smith
CITY LOVERS(1982, S. African), m
Wheeler Oakman
LIGHTS OF NEW YORK(1928); DONOVAN AFFAIR, THE(1929); FATHER AND SON(1929); GIRL FROM WOOLWORTH'S, THE(1929); HANDCUFFED(1929); ON WITH THE SHOW(1929); SHAKEDOWN, THE(1929); SHANGHAI LADY(1929); COSTELLO CASE, THE(1930); LITTLE JOHNNY JONES(1930); ON YOUR BACK(1930); ROARING RANCH(1930); FIRST AID(1931); GOOD BAD GIRL, THE(1931); LAWLESS WOMAN, THE(1931); SKY RAIDERS(1931); BEAUTY PARLOR(1932); BOILING POINT, THE(1932); END OF THE TRAIL(1932); GORILLA SHIP, THE(1932); HEART PUNCH(1932); HONOR OF THE PRESS(1932); RIDING TORNADO, THE(1932); TEXAS CYCLONE(1932); TWO-FISTED LAW(1932); HOLD THE PRESS(1933); REVENGE AT MONTE CARLO(1933); SOLDIERS OF THE STORM(1933); SUNDOWN RIDER, THE(1933); FRONTIER DAYS(1934); LOST JUNGLE, THE(1934); MURDER IN THE CLOUDS(1934); ONE IS GUILTY(1934); OPERATOR 13(1934); ANNAPOLIS FAREWELL(1935); CODE OF THE MOUNTED(1935); G-MEN(1935); IN OLD SANTA FE(1935); MOTIVE FOR REVENGE(1935); TRAILS OF THE WILD(1935); ACES AND EIGHTS(1936); DARKEST AFRICA(1936); DEATH FROM A DISTANCE(1936); GHOST PATROL(1936); MAN FROM GUN TOWN, THE(1936); MYSTERIOUS AVENGER, THE(1936); ROARIN' GUNS(1936); SONG OF THE TRAIL(1936); TIMBER WAR(1936); BANK ALARM(1937); CRUSADE AGAINST RACKETS(1937); DEATH IN THE SKY(1937); VICE RACKET(1937); CODE OF THE RANGERS(1938); LAND OF FIGHTING MEN(1938); TEXANS, THE(1938); IN OLD MONTANA(1939); MUTINY IN THE BIG HOUSE(1939); TORTURE SHIP(1939); WOLF CALL(1939); DOUBLE TROUBLE(1941); MEDICO OF PAINTED SPRINGS, THE(1941); MEET THE MOB(1942); APE MAN, THE(1943); FIGHTING BUCKAROO(1943); GHOSTS ON THE LOOSE(1943); GIRL FROM MONTEREY, THE(1943); KID DYNAMITE(1943); BOWERY CHAMPS(1944); RIDING WEST(1944); SUNDOWN VALLEY(1944); WHAT A MAN!(1944)
Misc. Talkies
BIG FIGHT, THE(1930); DEVIL ON DECK(1932); GUILTY OR NOT GUILTY(1932); WESTERN CODE(1932); MAN OF ACTION(1933); SILENT MEN(1933); SPEED DEMON(1933); SUNDOWN RIDER(1933); UNDERCOVER MEN(1935); GAMBLING WITH SOULS(1936); DEATH IN THE AIR(1937); ROUGH RIDIN' JUSTICE(1945)
Silents
SPOILERS, THE(1914); CARPET FROM BAGDAD, THE(1915); NE'ER-DO-WELL, THE(1916); I LOVE YOU(1918); FALSE EVIDENCE(1919); MICKEY(1919); SPLENDID SIN, THE(1919); OUTSIDE THE LAW(1921); PECK'S BAD BOY(1921); SON OF THE WOLF, THE(1922); SLIPPY MCGEE(1923); PACE THAT THRILLS, THE(1925); FANGS OF JUSTICE(1926); IN BORROWED PLUMES(1926); HEY! HEY! COWBOY(1927); OUT ALL NIGHT(1927); GOOD-BYE KISS, THE(1928); MASKED ANGEL(1928); POWER OF THE PRESS, THE(1928); WHAT A NIGHT!(1928); WHILE THE CITY SLEEPS(1928); DEVIL'S CHAPLAIN(1929); MORGAN'S LAST RAID(1929)
Misc. Silents
STORY OF THE BLOOD RED ROSE, THE(1914); ROSARY, THE(1915); SWEET ALYSSUM(1915); BATTLE OF HEARTS(1916); CYCLE OF FATE, THE(1916); PRINCESS VIRTUE(1917); CLAIM, THE(1918); FACE VALUE(1918); REVENGE(1918); BACK TO GOD'S COUNTRY(1919 US/Can.); EVE IN EXILE(1919); WOMAN OF PLEASURE, A(1919); VIRGIN OF STAMBOUL, THE(1920); WHAT WOMEN LOVE(1920); PENNY OF TOP HILL TRAIL(1921); HALF BREED, THE(1922); LOVE TRAP, THE(1923); MINE TO KEEP(1923); OTHER MEN'S DAUGHTERS(1923); LILLIES OF THE STREETS(1925); HEROES OF THE NIGHT(1927); SNARL OF HATE, THE(1927); BLACK FEATHER(1928); BROKEN MASK, THE(1928); DANGER PATROL(1928); HEART OF BROADWAY, THE(1928)
Connie Oaks
DON'T GO IN THE HOUSE(1980)
Theresa Oaks
LADY FROM CHEYENNE(1941), w
Gordon Oas-Heim
NASHVILLE REBEL(1966); GREEK TYCOON, THE(1978)
Cecily Oates
MANY WATERS(1931, Brit.); GIRLS PLEASE!(1934, Brit.)
Cicely Oates
I LIVED WITH YOU(1933, Brit.); THINGS ARE LOOKING UP(1934, Brit.); BREAKERS AHEAD(1935, Brit.); MAN WHO KNEW TOO MUCH, THE(1935, Brit.); WANDERING JEW, THE(1935, Brit.)
Cicily Oates
PRICE OF WISDOM, THE(1935, Brit.)
Hubert J. Oates
PUZZLE OF A DOWNFALL CHILD(1970), set d
Hubert Oates
MAN ON A SWING(1974), set d
John W. Oates
LEGEND OF BOGGY CREEK, THE(1973)
Simon Oates
NIGHT TRAIN TO PARIS(1964, Brit.); TERRORNAUTS, THE(1967, Brit.); DOOMWATCH(1972, Brit.)
Warren Oates
UP PERISCOPE(1959); YELLOWSTONE KELLY(1959); PRIVATE PROPERTY(1960); RISE AND FALL OF LEGS DIAMOND, THE(1960); HERO'S ISLAND(1962); RIDE THE HIGH COUNTRY(1962); MAIL ORDER BRIDE(1964); MAJOR DUNDEE(1965); SHENANDOAH(1965); RETURN OF THE SEVEN(1966, Span.); IN THE HEAT OF THE NIGHT(1967); WELCOME TO HARD TIMES(1967); SPLIT, THE(1968); SMITH(1969); WILD BUNCH, THE(1969); BARQUERO(1970); SOPHIE'S PLACE(1970); THERE WAS A CROOKED MAN(1970); CHANDLER(1971); HIRED HAND, THE(1971); SHOOTING, THE(1971); TWO-LANE BLACKTOP(1971); DILLINGER(1973); KID BLUE(1973); THIEF WHO CAME TO DINNER, THE(1973); TOM SAWYER(1973); BAD-

LANDS(1974); BRING ME THE HEAD OF ALFREDO GARCIA(1974); WHITE DAWN, THE(1974); BORN TO KILL(1975); RACE WITH THE DEVIL(1975); 92 IN THE SHADE(1975, U.S./Brit.); DIXIE DYNAMITE(1976); DRUM(1976); SLEEPING DOGS(1977, New Zealand); BRINK'S JOB, THE(1978); CHINA 9, LIBERTY 37(1978, Ital.); 1941(1979); STRIPES(1981); BORDER, THE(1982); BLUE THUNDER(1983); TOUGH ENOUGH(1983)
Patti Oatman
SLIPSTREAM(1974, Can.)
Oaxchitl
COUNT YOUR BULLETS(1972)
Hideo Oba
FAREWELL, MY BELOVED(1969, Jap.), d; SNOW COUNTRY(1969, Jap.), d, w
Obago
TOTO AND THE POACHERS(1958, Brit.)
Ramon Obal, Jr.
MADAME DEATH(1968, Mex.), w
William Obanhein
ALICE'S RESTAURANT(1969)
Shuchi Obara
1984
WARRIORS OF THE WIND(1984, Jap.), anim
Jean Obe
RISE OF LOUIS XIV, THE(1970, Fr.); TALL BLOND MAN WITH ONE BLACK SHOE, THE(1973, Fr.); LACEMAKER, THE(1977, Fr.); GIRL FROM LORRAINE, A(1982, Fr./Switz.)
Sharon Obeck
RUN FOR YOUR WIFE(1966, Fr./Ital.)
Mark Obenhaus
NOMADIC LIVES(1977), d&w
Arlon Ober
INCREDIBLE MELTING MAN, THE(1978), m; EATING RAOUL(1982), m; HOSPITAL MASSACRE(1982), m; NIGHTBEAST(1982), m
1984
HOSPITAL MASSACRE(1984), m
Dillon Ober
EVERY NIGHT AT EIGHT(1935)
Gerti Ober
PILLARS OF SOCIETY(1936, Ger.)
Gertrud Ober
TRUNKS OF MR. O.F., THE(1932, Ger.)
Harry L. Ober
JENNY LAMOUR(1948, Fr.), titles
Louise Ober
RIVERRUN(1968)
Phil Ober
UNKNOWN MAN, THE(1951)
Philip Ober
MAGNIFICENT YANKEE, THE(1950); NEVER A DULL MOMENT(1950); SECRET FURY, THE(1950); COME BACK LITTLE SHEBA(1952); WASHINGTON STORY(1952); CLOWN, THE(1953); FROM HERE TO ETERNITY(1953); GIRLS OF PLEASURE ISLAND, THE(1953); SCANDAL AT SCOURIE(1953); ABOUT MRS. LESLIE(1954); BROKEN LANCE(1954); ESCAPADE IN JAPAN(1957); TAMMY AND THE BACHELOR(1957); HIGH COST OF LOVING, THE(1958); TORPEDO RUN(1958); 10 NORTH FREDERICK(1958); BELOVED INFIDEL(1959); MATING GAME, THE(1959); NORTH BY NORTHWEST(1959); ELMER GANTRY(1960); FACTS OF LIFE, THE(1960); LET NO MAN WRITE MY EPITAPH(1960); GO NAKED IN THE WORLD(1961); UGLY AMERICAN, THE(1963); BRASS BOTTLE, THE(1964); GHOST AND MR. CHICKEN, THE(1966); ASSIGNMENT TO KILL(1968)
Robert Ober
IDLE RICH, THE(1929); IN THE HEADLINES(1929); WOMAN RACKET, THE(1930), d; BIRTH OF A BABY(1938)
Silents
BIG PARADE, THE(1925); INTRODUCE ME(1925); HELD BY THE LAW(1927); KING OF KINGS, THE(1927)
Misc. Silents
MYSTIC, THE(1925); BUTTERFLIES IN THE RAIN(1926); CHECKERED FLAG, THE(1926); FOOLS OF FASHION(1926); LITTLE ADVENTURESS, THE(1927); RENO DIVORCE, A(1927); ACROSS THE ATLANTIC(1928)
Igor Oberberg
FILM WITHOUT A NAME(1950, Ger.), ph; TOXI(1952, Ger.), ph; ORDERED TO LOVE(1963, Ger.), ph
Ira Oberberg
YOUNG GO WILD, THE(1962, Ger.), ed; MAEDCHEN IN UNIFORM(1965, Ger./Fr.), ed
Casimir Oberfeld
FRIC FRAC(1939, Fr.), m
Brita Oberg
SHAME(1968, Swed.); PASSION OF ANNA, THE(1970, Swed.)
Ralph Oberg
HOUSE OF A THOUSAND CANDLES, THE(1936), art d; GUNFIRE AT INDIAN GAP(1957), art d; LAST STAGECOACH WEST, THE(1957), art d; LAWLESS EIGHTIES, THE(1957), art d; PANAMA SAL(1957), art d; TAMING SUTTON'S GAL(1957), art d; CROOKED CIRCLE, THE(1958), art d; JUVENILE JUNGLE(1958), art d; MAN OR GUN(1958), art d; MAN WHO DIED TWICE, THE(1958), art d; NOTORIOUS MR. MONKS, THE(1958), art d; YOUNG AND WILD(1958), art d
Tom Oberhaus
1984
TERMINATOR, THE(1984)
Hermann Oberlaender
MISTRESS OF ATLANTIS, THE(1932, Ger.), w
Heinrich Oberlander
INVISIBLE OPPONENT(1933, Ger.), w
Florence Oberle
Silents
ACCORDING TO THE CODE(1916); SKINNER'S DRESS SUIT(1917)
Misc. Silents
HER COUNTRY FIRST(1918); R.S.V.P.(1921); BARNSTORMER, THE(1922); SMUDGE(1922)

Roger Ocomapo
TWILIGHT PEOPLE(1972, Phil.)
Enzo Ocone
ARABIAN NIGHTS(1980, Ital./Fr.), ed
Donovan Octette
HONEYMOON HOTEL(1946, Brit.)
Gene October
JUBILEE(1978, Brit.)
Masao Oda
ANGRY ISLAND(1960, Jap.); DIPLOMAT'S MANSION, THE(1961, Jap.); TWILIGHT STORY, THE(1962, Jap.); WAYSIDE PEBBLE, THE(1962, Jap.); RIFIFI IN TOKYO(1963, Fr./Ital.)
Motoyoshi Oda
GIGANTIS(1959, Jap./U.S.), d
Tom Odachi
PUTNEY SWOPE(1969)
Miki Odagiri
IKIRU(1960, Jap.)
Georg Oddner
WEEKEND(1964, Den.), ph; FLIGHT OF THE EAGLE(1983, Swed.), w
George Oddner
NEW LAND, THE(1973, Swed.), m
Frank Oddo
1984
MISSION, THE(1984)
Jerry Oddo
COPPER SKY(1957); FROM HELL TO TEXAS(1958)
Nathaniel F. Oddo
DAMN CITIZEN(1958)
Charles Odds
DARK WATERS(1944), art d; SENSATIONS OF 1945(1944), art d
Eric Ode
SCHLAGER-PARADE(1953), d
Erik Ode
F.P. 1 DOESN'T ANSWER(1933, Ger.)
Myron Odegaard
SLAP SHOT(1977)
Cary Odell
TOYS IN THE ATTIC(1963), art d; WALKING DEAD, THE(1936), cos; THEY ALL KISSED THE BRIDE(1942), art d; COVER GIRL(1944), art d; EVER SINCE VENUS(1944), art d; IMPATIENT YEARS, THE(1944), art d; TWO-MAN SUBMARINE(1944), art d; PERSONALITY KID(1946), art d; SING WHILE YOU DANCE(1946), art d; JOHNNY O'CLOCK(1947), art d; DARK PAST, THE(1948), art d; LOVES OF CARMEN, THE(1948), art d; TO THE ENDS OF THE EARTH(1948), art d; RECKLESS MOMENTS, THE(1949), art d; SECRET OF ST. IVES, THE(1949), art d; WE WERE STRANGERS(1949), art d; HARLEM GLOBETROTTERS, THE(1951), art d; MOB, THE(1951), art d; MY TRUE STORY(1951), art d; DEATH OF A SALESMAN(1952), art d; MEMBER OF THE WEDDING, THE(1952), art d; 5,000 FINGERS OF DR. T. THE(1953), art d; CAINE MUTINY, THE(1954), art d; MAN FROM LARAMIE, THE(1955), art d; WOMEN'S PRISON(1955), art d; WYOMING RENEGADES(1955), art d; STORM CENTER(1956), art d; FLAME OF STAMBOUL(1957), art d; 20 MILLION MILES TO EARTH(1957), art d; BELL, BOOK AND CANDLE(1958), art d; COWBOY(1958), art d; SCREAMING MIMI(1958), art d; IT HAPPENED TO JANE(1959), art d; THEY CAME TO CORDURA(1959), art d; MOUNTAIN ROAD, THE(1960), art d; THIRTEEN GHOSTS(1960), art d; HOMICIDAL(1961), art d; MR. SARDONICUS(1961), art d; KID GALAHAD(1962), art d; NOTORIOUS LANDLADY, THE(1962), art d; PATSY, THE(1964), art d; SEVEN DAYS IN MAY(1964), art d; HALLELUJAH TRAIL, THE(1965), art d; HAWAII(1966), prod d; COOL HAND LUKE(1967), art d; HOTEL(1967), art d; WITH SIX YOU GET EGGROLL(1968), art d; MR. MAJESTYK(1974), art d; W(1974), art d
David Odell
DEALING: OR THE BERKELEY-TO-BOSTON FORTY-BRICK LOST-BAG BLUES(1971), w; FOREPLAY(1975), w; DARK CRYSTAL, THE(1982, Brit.), w; NATE AND HAYES(1983, U.S./New Zealand), w
1984
SUPERGIRL(1984), w
Gary Odell
FROM HERE TO ETERNITY(1953), art d; GYPSY MOTHS, THE(1969), art d; MACKENNA'S GOLD(1969), art d
George Odell
Silents
BAB'S DIARY(1917); FIGHTING ODDS(1917)
George R. Odell
Misc. Silents
WOLF AND HIS MATE, THE(1918)
J. Harold Odell
FIEND OF DOPE ISLAND(1961), p
Kent Odell
STAGECOACH(1939)
Molly Odell
FIEND OF DOPE ISLAND(1961)
Robert Odell
FIGHTING CARAVANS(1931), art d; ALICE IN WONDERLAND(1933), art d; MRS. WIGGS OF THE CABBAGE PATCH(1934), art d; NOTORIOUS SOPHIE LANG, THE(1934), art d; SIX OF A KIND(1934), art d; YOU'RE TELLING ME(1934), art d; RUGGLES OF RED GAP(1935), art d; ARIZONA MAHONEY(1936), art d; TIMOTHY'S QUEST(1936), art d; DAUGHTER OF SHANGHAI(1937), art d; HOLD'EM NAVY!(1937), art d; KING OF GAMBLERS(1937), art d; PARTNERS IN CRIME(1937), art d; TIP-OFF GIRLS(1938), art d; BEAU GESTE(1939), art d; KING OF CHINATOWN(1939), art d; LIGHT THAT FAILED, THE(1939), art d; UNMARRIED(1939), art d; MYSTERY SEA RAIDER(1940), art d; NIGHT AT EARL CARROLL'S, A(1940), art d; ROAD TO SINGAPORE(1940), art d
Rosemary Odell
PAD, THE(AND HOW TO USE IT)* (1966, Brit.), cos; BRUTE FORCE(1947), cos; WISTFUL WIDOW OF WAGON GAP, THE(1947), cos; FRANCIS(1949), cos; STORY OF MOLLY X, THE(1949), cos; YES SIR, THAT'S MY BABY(1949), cos; MILKMAN, THE(1950), cos; SLEEPING CITY, THE(1950), cos; REUNION IN RENO(1951), cos; STRANGE DOOR, THE(1951), cos; BEND OF THE RIVER(1952), cos; HAS ANYBODY SEEN MY GAL?(1952), cos; MEET ME AT THE FAIR(1952), cos; SCARLET ANGEL(1952), cos; ALL I DESIRE(1953), cos; SEMINOLE(1953), cos; THUNDER BAY(1953), cos; VEILS OF BAGDAD, THE(1953), cos; ABBOTT AND COSTELLO MEET DR. JEKYLL AND MR. HYDE(1954), cos; DESTRY(1954), cos; NAKED ALIBI(1954), cos; RIDE CLEAR OF DIABLO(1954), cos; SO THIS IS PARIS(1954), cos; TANGANYIKA(1954), cos; YANKEE PASHA(1954), cos; CHIEF CRAZY HORSE(1955), cos; FRANCIS IN THE NAVY(1955), cos; MAN WITHOUT A STAR(1955), cos; PRIVATE WAR OF MAJOR BENSON, THE(1955), cos; SQUARE JUNGLE, THE(1955), cos; BACKLASH(1956), cos; DAY OF FURY, A(1956), cos; FOUR GIRLS IN TOWN(1956), cos; OUTSIDE THE LAW(1956), cos; PILLARS OF THE SKY(1956), cos; ROCK, PRETTY BABY(1956), cos; SHOWDOWN AT ABILENE(1956), cos; TOY TIGER(1956), cos; KELLY AND ME(1957), cos; NIGHT RUNNER, THE(1957), cos; QUANTEZ(1957), cos; TAMMY, TELL ME TRUE(1961), cos; SPIRAL ROAD, THE(1962), cos; THAT TOUCH OF MINK(1962), cos; TO KILL A MOCKINGBIRD(1962), cos; CAPTAIN NEWMAN, M.D.(1963), cos; SHOWDOWN(1963), cos; TAMMY AND THE DOCTOR(1963), cos; UGLY AMERICAN, THE(1963), cos; ISLAND OF THE BLUE DOLPHINS(1964), cos; LIVELY SET, THE(1964), cos; WILD AND WONDERFUL(1964), cos; SHENANDOAH(1965), cos; APPALOOSA, THE(1966), cos; GHOST AND MR. CHICKEN, THE(1966), cos; MOMENT TO MOMENT(1966), cos; RARE BREED, THE(1966), cos; TEXAS ACROSS THE RIVER(1966), cos; RELUCTANT ASTRONAUT, THE(1967), cos; RIDE TO HANGMAN'S TREE, THE(1967), cos; ROUGH NIGHT IN JERICHO(1967), cos; NOBODY'S PERFECT(1968), cos
Valerie Odell
LEADBELLY(1976)
Fritz Odemar
HIS MAJESTY, KING BALLYHOO(1931, Ger.); 1914(1932, Ger.); M(1933, Ger.); SHOT AT DAWN, A(1934, Ger.); FILM WITHOUT A NAME(1950, Ger.)
Elisabeth Oden
DOLL, THE(1964, Swed.)
Christophe Odent
1984
A NOS AMOURS(1984, Fr.); FIRST NAME: CARMEN(1984, Fr.)
Kanahichi Odera
SANSHO THE BAILIFF(1969, Jap.), m
Citizens of Odessa
SEEDS OF FREEDOM(1943, USSR)
Silents
BATTLESHIP POTEMKIN, THE(1925, USSR)
Clifford Odets
GENERAL DIED AT DAWN, THE(1936), a, w; GOLDEN BOY(1939), w; NONE BUT THE LONELY HEART(1944), d&w; DEADLINE AT DAWN(1946), w; HUMORESQUE(1946), w; CLASH BY NIGHT(1952), w; COUNTRY GIRL, THE(1954), d&w; BIG KNIFE, THE(1955), w; SWEET SMELL OF SUCCESS(1957), w; STORY ON PAGE ONE, THE(1959), d&w; WILD IN THE COUNTRY(1961), w
Odetta
SANCTUARY(1961)
Odette
LAST TIME I SAW PARIS, THE(1954)
Mary Odette
Silents
AS GOD MADE HER(1920, Brit.); ENCHANTMENT(1920, Brit.); JOHN HERIOT'S WIFE(1920, Brit.); NO. 5 JOHN STREET(1921, Brit.); LION'S MOUSE, THE(1922, Brit.); NETS OF DESTINY(1924, Brit.); NOT FOR SALE(1924, Brit.); EMERALD OF THE EAST(1928, Brit.)
Misc. Silents
CASTLE OF DREAMS(1919, Brit.); LADY CLARE, THE(1919, Brit.); BREED OF THE TRESHAMS, THE(1920, Brit.); INHERITANCE(1920, Brit.); MR. GILFIL'S LOVE STORY(1920, Brit.); TORN SAILS(1920, Brit.); WITH ALL HER HEART(1920, Brit.); CHERRY RIPE(1921, Brit.); DOUBLE EVENT, THE(1921, Brit.); WONDERFUL YEAR, THE(1921, Brit.); HYPOCRITES, THE(1923, Brit.); DIAMOND MAN, THE(1924, Brit.); EUGENE ARAM(1924, Brit.); KEAN(1924, Fr.)
Greg Odhambo
SAVAGE HARVEST(1981)
Daniel Odier
LIGHT YEARS AWAY(1982, Fr./Switz.), w
Jane Odin
WEDDING PARTY, THE(1969)
Susan Odin
ANNIE GET YOUR GUN(1950); WILD STALLION(1952); EDDIE CANTOR STORY, THE(1953); GIRLS IN THE NIGHT(1953); SUMMER PLACE, A(1959); BECAUSE THEY'RE YOUNG(1960)
Susan Odinn
WRITTEN ON THE WIND(1956)
Bruce Odlum
SPANISH AFFAIR(1958, Span.), p
Jerome Odlum
DUST BE MY DESTINY(1939), w; EACH DAWN I DIE(1939), w; NINE LIVES ARE NOT ENOUGH(1941), w; I WAS FRAMED(1942), w; CRIME DOCTOR(1943), w; SCREAM IN THE DARK, A(1943), w; STRANGE AFFAIR(1944), w; LAST FRONTIER UPRISING(1947), w; COVER-UP(1949), w; SONG OF INDIA(1949), w; NEVER TRUST A GAMBLER(1951), w; FAST AND THE FURIOUS, THE(1954), w; HIGHWAY DRAGNET(1954), w
Laurette Odney
RETURN OF COUNT YORGA, THE(1971), ed
Franco Odoardi
SACCO AND VANZETTI(1971, Ital./Fr.)
Jack Odom
INTRUDER IN THE DUST(1949)
Ray Odom
PEACE FOR A GUNFIGHTER(1967)
Traci Odom
1984
INITIATION, THE(1984)
Johanna Odry
NOT RECONCILED, OR "ONLY VIOLENCE HELPS WHERE IT RULES"(1969, Ger.)
Stefan Odry
NOT RECONCILED, OR "ONLY VIOLENCE HELPS WHERE IT RULES"(1969, Ger.)
Paul Oduor
LION, THE(1962, Brit.)

Rita Oehmen
GO CHASE YOURSELF(1938); GUN LAW(1938)
Walter Oehmichen
SNOW WHITE(1965, Ger.), w
George Oekonomou
OEDIPUS THE KING(1968, Brit.)
Richard Oelers
MISTRESS OF THE WORLD(1959, Ital./Fr./Ger.), ph
Ken Oelofse
ELEPHANT GUN(1959, Brit.)
Vera Oelschlegel
PINOCCHIO(1969, E. Ger.)
Walter Oemichen
SNOW WHITE AND ROSE RED(1966, Ger.), w
Marie Conway Oemler
SLIPPY MCGEE(1948), w
Silents
SLIPPY MCGEE(1923), w
Christa Oenicke
PUSS 'N' BOOTS(1967, Ger.)
William L. Oereira
SINCE YOU WENT AWAY(1944), prod d
Jacques Oerlemans
MAN ESCAPED, A(1957, Fr.)
Gertrude Oertel
PARSIFAL(1983, Fr.)
Oestergard
THAT WOMAN(1968, Ger.)
R. Oesterreicher
HER MAJESTY LOVE(1931), w
Rudolf Oesterreicher
MONEY ON THE STREET(1930, Aust.), w; ONCE A LADY(1931), w
Christine Oestreicher
1984
EVERY PICTURE TELLS A STORY(1984, Brit.), p
John Oettinger
SIDELONG GLANCES OF A PIGEON KICKER, THE(1970), ed
Pralith Jngam Oeurn
FIENDISH PLOT OF DR. FU MANCHU, THE(1980)
Offbeats
DAYTONA BEACH WEEKEND(1965)
Offenbach
BARCAROLE(1935, Ger.), w
Jacques Offenbach
SYMPHONY OF LIVING(1935), m; TALES OF HOFFMANN, THE(1951, Brit.), p,d&w, m; GREAT WALTZ, THE(1972), m; LUDWIG(1973, Ital./Ger./Fr.), m
1984
HOTEL NEW HAMPSHIRE, THE(1984), m
Joseph Offenbach
GIRL OF THE MOORS, THE(1961, Ger.); YOUNG GO WILD, THE(1962, Ger.); WILLY(1963, U.S./Ger.); RESTLESS NIGHT, THE(1964, Ger.); GIRL AND THE LEGEND, THE(1966, Ger.)
Rudolf Offenbach
COLDITZ STORY, THE(1955, Brit.)
Rudolph Offenbach
LAUGHING ANNE(1954, Brit./U.S.); BAY OF SAINT MICHEL, THE(1963, Brit.)
Ted Offenbacher
WORLD FOR RANSOM(1954), set d
Ted Offenbacker
SAXON CHARM, THE(1948), set d
Fred Offenbecker
SQUARE DANCE JUBILEE(1949), set d; VANISHING OUTPOST, THE(1951), set d
T.F. Offenbecker
IVY(1947), set d; WOMAN'S VENGEANCE, A(1947), set d
Ted Offenbecker
LOVER COME BACK(1946), set d; MAGNIFICENT DOLL(1946), set d; UP IN CENTRAL PARK(1948), set d; SON OF A BADMAN(1949), set d; SON OF BILLY THE KID(1949), set d
Theodore F. Offenbecker
RIDE THE MAN DOWN(1952), set d
George Offenman, Jr.
SAN QUENTIN(1937)
Lucy Offerall
TWO HUNDRED MOTELS(1971, Brit.)
George Offerman
PERSONAL MAID(1931); CODE OF THE SECRET SERVICE(1939); HELL'S KITCH-EN(1939); JOHNNY ALLEGRO(1949); PEOPLE WILL TALK(1951); WITH A SONG IN MY HEART(1952); JOKER IS WILD, THE(1957)
George Offerman, Jr.
GIRL ON THE BARGE, THE(1929); MAYOR OF HELL, THE(1933); HOUSE OF ROTHSCHILD, THE(1934); TWENTIETH CENTURY(1934); GRAND OLD GIRL(1935); JALNA(1935); OUTLAW DEPUTY, THE(1935); CHATTERBOX(1936); FURY(1936); MEET NERO WOLFE(1936); PIGSKIN PARADE(1936); STAGE STRUCK(1936); WEDDING PRESENT(1936); LOVE IS NEWS(1937); MAKE WAY FOR TOMORROW(1937); MIDNIGHT COURT(1937); NIGHT CLUB SCANDAL(1937); OVER THE GOAL(1937); TOAST OF NEW YORK, THE(1937); WINGS OVER HONOLULU(1937); ANGELS WITH DIRTY FACES(1938); CRIME SCHOOL(1938); EXTORTION(1938); PATIENT IN ROOM 18, THE(1938); SCANDAL STREET(1938); THREE COMRADES(1938); BOY'S REFORMATORY(1939); CALL A MESSENGER(1939); FIRST OFFENDERS(1939); FRONTIER VENGEANCE(1939); WHEN TOMORROW COMES(1939); YOU CAN'T CHEAT AN HONEST MAN(1939); FOREIGN CORRESPONDENT(1940); FUGITIVE FROM A PRISON CAMP(1940); CAPTAINS OF THE CLOUDS(1942); PRIDE OF THE YANKEES, THE(1942); SABOTEUR(1942); SWEATER GIRL(1942); TOUGH AS THEY COME(1942); ACTION IN THE NORTH ATLANTIC(1943); AIR FORCE(1943); GIRL CRAZY(1943); SEE HERE, PRIVATE HARGROVE(1944); SULLIVANS, THE(1944); WALK IN THE SUN, A(1945); OUT OF THE DEPTHS(1946); HOMECOMING(1948); LETTER TO THREE WIVES, A(1948); SMART POLITICS(1948); LET'S GO NA-VY(1951); PURPLE HEART DIARY(1951); RED BADGE OF COURAGE, THE(1951)

Officers and Men of the U.S.S. Stephen Potter
DEEP SIX, THE(1958)
Hilda Offley
MIRACLE IN HARLEM(1948)
Deborah Offner
SMALL CIRCLE OF FRIENDS, A(1980); GHOST STORY(1981); SOUP FOR ONE(1982)
Mortimer Offner
LITTLE MINISTER, THE(1934), w; ALICE ADAMS(1935), w; SYLVIA SCAR-LETT(1936), w; QUALITY STREET(1937), w; SOLDIER AND THE LADY, THE(1937), w; LITTLE TOUGH GUYS IN SOCIETY(1938), w; RADIO CITY REVELS(1938), w; SAINT IN NEW YORK, THE(1938), w; FAMILY NEXT DOOR, THE(1939), w
Bert Offord
Silents
ALIAS JULIUS CAESAR(1922)
Dick Offord
NO BLADE OF GRASS(1970, Brit.)
Lenore Glen Offord
MACABRE(1958), w
Edith Offutt
Misc. Silents
YORK STATE FOLKS(1915)
L. Jerome Offutt
LILITH(1964)
W. Jerome Offutt
LILITH(1964)
N. Ofitserov
RESURRECTION(1963, USSR)
Nobuko Oganesoff
SEIZURE(1974), ed
Geunrikh Oganissian
THREE TALES OF CHEKHOV(1961, USSR), w
Genrikh Oganisyan
SPRINGTIME ON THE VOLGA(1961, USSR), d
Keiko Ogasawara
BALLAD OF NARAYAMA(1961, Jap.)
Roy Ogat
WALK, DON'T RUN(1966)
Ken Ogata
FAREWELL, MY BELOVED(1969, Jap.); UNDER THE BANNER OF SAMURAI(1969, Jap.); SONG FROM MY HEART, THE(1970, Jap.); VENGEANCE IS MINE(1980, Jap.); VIRUS(1980, Jap.)
1984
BALLAD OF NARAYAMA, THE(1984, Jap.)
Kuniko Ogata
HARBOR LIGHT YOKOHAMA(1970, Jap.)
Roy Ogata
VARAN THE UNBELIEVABLE(1962, U.S./Jap.); GREAT BANK ROBBERY, THE(1969)
Ei Ogawa
MAN AGAINST MAN(1961, Jap.), w; YOG-MONSTER FROM SPACE(1970, Jap.), w
El Ogawa
SPACE AMOEBA, THE(1970, Jap.), w
Hideo Ogawa
MAD ATLANTIC, THE(1967, Jap.), w
Hirooki Ogawa
MANSTER, THE(1962, Jap.), m; FIGHT FOR THE GLORY(1970, Jap.), m; HOT-SPRINGS HOLIDAY(1970, Jap.), m
Kazuo Ogawa
COMPUTER FREE-FOR-ALL(1969, Jap.), art d
Mayumi Ogawa
VENGEANCE IS MINE(1980, Jap.); GLOWING AUTUMN(1981, Jap.)
Noboo Ogawa
NUTCRACKER FANTASY(1979), ed
Nobuo Ogawa
MUDDY RIVER(1982, Jap.), ed
Toranosuke Ogawa
SEVEN SAMURAI, THE(1956, Jap.); IKIRU(1960, Jap.); LIFE OF OHARU(1964, Jap.); I LIVE IN FEAR(1967, Jap.)
Y. Ogawa
Misc. Silents
SLUMS OF TOKYO(1930, Jap.)
Yoshinobu Ogawa
LOST SEX(1968, Jap.)
Yukiko Ogawa
Misc. Silents
CROSSWAYS(1928, Jap.)
Amando Ogaz
LOSIN' IT(1983)
Charlton Ogburn, Jr.
MERRILL'S MARAUDERS(1962), w
C. Ogden
Silents
NON-STOP FLIGHT, THE(1926)
Charlotte Ogden
DANCE OF LIFE, THE(1929)
Daphne Ogden
SMALL TOWN DEB(1941); YOUNG AMERICA(1942)
David Ogden
SMILE ORANGE(1976, Jamaican), w
Denis Ogden
HALF-WAY HOUSE, THE(1945, Brit.), w
Donald Ogden
SMILIN' THROUGH(1932), w
Edward Ogden
EMERGENCY(1962, Brit.); DR. CRIPPEN(1963, Brit.); MARKED ONE, THE(1963, Brit.); SHADOW OF FEAR(1963, Brit.); ISLAND OF TERROR(1967, Brit.)

Gordon Ogden
NIGHT OF BLOODY HORROR zero(1969)
James Ogden
FAN, THE(1981)
Jennifer M. Ogden
1984
GARBO TALKS(1984)
Joan Ogden
RATS ARE COMING! THE WEREWOLVES ARE HERE!, THE(1972)
Kay Ogden
STUDENT BODIES(1981)
Merry Ogden
NAKED GUN, THE(1956)
Roy Ogden
LONGEST YARD, THE(1974)
Valerie Ogden
I NEVER SANG FOR MY FATHER(1970)
Viva Ogden
Silents
AT THE STAGE DOOR(1921); JOHN SMITH(1922)
Vivia Ogden
Silents
WAY DOWN EAST(1920); STARDUST(1921); TIMOTHY'S QUEST(1922); UNGUARD-ED HOUR, THE(1925)
Misc. Silents
MRS. WIGGS OF THE CABBAGE PATCH(1919); LOVEY MARY(1926)
Vivian Ogden
Silents
SOCIAL SECRETARY, THE(1916)
Misc. Silents
CHICKEN IN THE CASE, THE(1921)
Pascal Oge
MICHELLE(1970, Fr.)
Myron "Butch" Ogelsby
EVENTS(1970)
Kathrin Ogen
SUPERBUG, SUPER AGENT(1976, Ger.)
Tom Ogen
BLOB, THE(1958)
Frank Oger
1984
THREE CROWNS OF THE SAILOR(1984, Fr.)
John Oger
PROBLEM GIRLS(1953)
Klaus Ogermann
PLAYGIRLS AND THE BELLBOY, THE(1962,Ger.), m; $100 A NIGHT(1968, Ger.), m
James Ogg
DOWN AMONG THE SHELTERING PALMS(1953); I'LL CRY TOMORROW(1955); TEEN-AGE CRIME WAVE(1955); CRIME IN THE STREETS(1956)
Jimmy Ogg
REDWOOD FOREST TRAIL(1950); I WANT YOU(1951); SHE'S WORKING HER WAY THROUGH COLLEGE(1952); TREASURE OF LOST CANYON, THE(1952); THESE WILDER YEARS(1956)
Sammy Ogg
MIRACLE OF OUR LADY OF FATIMA, THE(1952); NAVAJO(1952); JACK SLA-DE(1953); KID FROM LEFT FIELD, THE(1953); MR. SCOUTMASTER(1953); PRINCE VALIANT(1954); VIOLENT SATURDAY(1955); DESK SET(1957); FRONTIER GUN(1958)
Chikage Ogi
KURAGEJIMA–LEGENDS FROM A SOUTHERN ISLAND(1970, Jap.)
Hiroko Ogi
FRIENDLY KILLER, THE(1970, Jap.)
Bulle Ogier
SOPHIE'S WAYS(1970, Fr.); DISCREET CHARM OF THE BOURGEOISIE, THE(1972, Fr.); CELINE AND JULIE GO BOATING(1974, Fr.), a, w
Pascale Ogier
1984
AVE MARIA(1984, Fr.); FULL MOON IN PARIS(1984, Fr.), a, art d, cos; GHOST DANCE(1984, Brit.)
Quentin Ogier
1984
SUNDAY IN THE COUNTRY, A(1984, Fr.)
Barbara Ogilivie
DURING ONE NIGHT(1962, Brit.)
Barbara Ogilvie
PERFECT FRIDAY(1970, Brit.)
Elizabeth Ogilvie
HIGH TIDE AT NOON(1957, Brit.), w
Jack Ogilvie
STRANGE CARGO(1929), ed; OFFICER O'BRIEN(1930), ed; PHANTOM OF PARIS, THE(1931), ed; CITY LIMITS(1934), ed; KING KELLY OF THE U.S.A(1934), ed; LOUDSPEAKER, THE(1934), ed; SHOCK(1934), ed; SUCCESSFUL FAILURE, A(1934), ed; FORCED LANDING(1935), ed; GIRL O' MY DREAMS(1935), ed; GREAT GOD GOLD(1935), ed; HEALER, THE(1935), ed; MYSTERIOUS MR. WONG(1935), ed; SPANISH CAPE MYSTERY(1935), ed; TWO SINNERS(1935), ed; WOMEN MUST DRESS(1935), ed; FORBIDDEN HEAVEN(1936), ed; KELLY THE SECOND(1936), ed; MISTER CINDERELLA(1936), ed; CONFLICT(1937), ed; FIT FOR A KING(1937), ed; RIDING ON AIR(1937), ed; WHEN'S YOUR BIRTHDAY?(1937), ed; PRISON BREAK(1938), ed; WIDE OPEN FACES(1938), ed; DRUMS OF THE DESERT(1940), ed; LAUGHING AT DANGER(1940), ed; PHANTOM OF CHINATOWN(1940), ed; UP IN THE AIR(1940), ed; GANG'S ALL HERE(1941), ed; LET'S GO COLLEGIATE(1941), ed; ROAR OF THE PRESS(1941), ed; SIGN OF THE WOLF(1941), ed; YOU'RE OUT OF LUCK(1941), ed; FRECKLES COMES HOME(1942), ed; LAW OF THE JUN-GLE(1942), ed; LIVING GHOST, THE(1942), ed; LURE OF THE ISLANDS(1942), ed; MAN FROM HEADQUARTERS(1942), ed; MEET THE MOB(1942), ed; PHANTOM KILLER(1942), ed; POLICE BULLETS(1942), ed; SHE'S IN THE ARMY(1942), ed; QUEEN OF BURLESQUE(1946), ed; HIGH LONESOME(1950), ed; SUNDOWNERS, THE(1950), ed; QUEBEC(1951), ed; ALADDIN AND HIS LAMP(1952), ed; BATTLE ZONE(1952), ed; ZOMBIES OF MORA TAU(1957), ed; CHOPPERS, THE(1961), ed

Jack W. Ogilvie
EDDY DUCHIN STORY, THE(1956), ed; HE LAUGHED LAST(1956), ed; ROCK AROUND THE CLOCK(1956), ed
Richard Ogilvie
TERROR IN THE JUNGLE(1968), w
Ian Ogilvy
SHE BEAST, THE(1966, Brit./Ital./Yugo.); COP-OUT(1967, Brit.); DAY THE FISH CAME OUT, THE(1967. Brit./Gr.); SORCERERS, THE(1967, Brit.); CONQUEROR WORM, THE(1968, Brit.); INVINCIBLE SIX, THE(1970, U.S./Iran); WATERLOO(1970, Ital./USSR); WUTHERING HEIGHTS(1970, Brit.); AND NOW THE SCREAMING STARTS(1973, Brit.); NO SEX PLEASE–WE'RE BRITISH(1979, Brit.)
Misc. Talkies
SAINT AND THE BRAVE GOOSE, THE(1981, Brit.)
Keiko Oginome
1984
ANTARCTICA(1984, Jap.)
Kathrin Oginski
MADDEST CAR IN THE WORLD, THE(1974, Ger.)
Terry Ogisu
METAMORPHOSES(1978), p
Charles Ogle
Silents
NAN OF MUSIC MOUNTAIN(1917); ON RECORD(1917); REBECCA OF SUNNY-BROOK FARM(1917); ROMANCE OF THE REDWOODS, A(1917); SECRET GAME, THE(1917); THOSE WITHOUT SIN(1917); JULES OF THE STRONG HEART(1918); M'LISS(1918); ALIAS MIKE MORAN(1919); HAWTHORNE OF THE U.S.A.(1919); JACK STRAW(1920); MIDSUMMER MADNESS(1920); TREASURE ISLAND(1920); WHAT'S YOUR HURRY?(1920); AFFAIRS OF ANATOL, THE(1921); AFTER THE SHOW(1921); BREWSTER'S MILLIONS(1921); CRAZY TO MARRY(1921); GASOLINE GUS(1921); WHAT EVERY WOMAN KNOWS(1921); WISE FOOL, A(1921); HOMES-PUN VAMP, A(1922); IF YOU BELIEVE IT, IT'S SO(1922); KICK IN(1922); NORTH OF THE RIO GRANDE(1922); OUR LEADING CITIZEN(1922); THIRTY DAYS(1922); WOMAN WHO WALKED ALONE, THE(1922); COVERED WAGON, THE(1923); GARRISON'S FINISH(1923); RUGGLES OF RED GAP(1923); SALOMY JANE(1923); SIXTY CENTS AN HOUR(1923); TEN COMMANDMENTS, THE(1923); ALASKAN, THE(1924); BEDROOM WINDOW, THE(1924); FLAMING BARRIERS(1924); MERTON OF THE MOVIES(1924); ONE MINUTE TO PLAY(1926)
Misc. Silents
GREAT PHYSICAN, THE(1913); GREEN EYE OF THE YELLOW GOD, THE(1913); UNDER SOUTHERN SKIES(1915); SUNSET TRAIL(1917); FIREFLY OF FRANCE, THE(1918); RIMROCK JONES(1918); TOO MANY MILLIONS(1918); DUB, THE(1919); VALLEY OF THE GIANTS, THE(1919); HEART OF YOUTH, THE(1920); JUCKLINS, THE(1920); YOUNG RAHAH, THE(1922); GARDEN OF WEEDS, THE(1924); TRI-UMPH(1924); CODE OF THE WEST(1925)
David Ogle
URBAN COWBOY(1980)
Maude Ogle
MIGHTY BARNUM, THE(1934)
Natalie Ogle
JOSEPH ANDREWS(1977, Brit.); STUD, THE(1979, Brit.)
Misc. Talkies
AERODROME, THE(1983, Brit.)
Pam Ogles
FOLLOW THAT DREAM(1962)
Michael Oglesbee
WOMEN AND BLOODY TERROR(1970)
Col. Oglethorpe
JOHN WESLEY(1954, Brit.)
Carlo Ogliotti
HEART AND SOUL(1950, Ital.)
Jack Oglivie
TOP SERGEANT MULLIGAN(1941), ed; MESSENGER OF PEACE(1950), ed
Jack W. Oglivie
HER SISTER'S SECRET(1946), ed
M. Ogonkov
LAST GAME, THE(1964, USSR)
Virginie Ogouz
CHANEL SOLITAIRE(1981)
Hideo Oguni
MYSTERIOUS SATELLITE, THE(1956, Jap.), w; SEVEN SAMURAI, THE(1956, Jap.), w; HIDDEN FORTRESS, THE(1959, Jap.), w; IKIRU(1960, Jap.), w; THRONE OF BLOOD(1961, Jap.), w; YOJIMBO(1961, Jap.), w; LOWER DEPTHS, THE(1962, Jap.), w; SANJURO(1962, Jap.), w; HIGH AND LOW(1963, Jap.), w; SAMURAI FROM NOWHERE(1964, Jap.), w; RED BEARD(1966, Jap.), w; I LIVE IN FEAR(1967, Jap.), w; DODESKA-DEN(1970, Jap.), w; TORA! TORA! TORA!(1970, U.S./Jap.), w
Ichiro Ogura
WAY OUT, WAY IN(1970, Jap.)
Kohei Oguri
MUDDY RIVER(1982, Jap.), d
Toranosuke Ogwawa
GODZILLA, RING OF THE MONSTERS(1956, Jap.)
John Ogwen
1984
ADERYN PAPUR(1984, Brit.)
Soon Taik Oh
MAN WITH THE GOLDEN GUN, THE(1974, Brit.)
Soon-Taik Oh
ONE MORE TRAIN TO ROB(1971)
Soon-Teck Oh
FINAL COUNTDOWN, THE(1980)
Yungil Oh
YONGKARI MONSTER FROM THE DEEP(1967 S.K.)
Oh Ogunde Dancers
OBLONG BOX, THE(1969, Brit.)
Natsuko Ohama
TITLE SHOT(1982, Can.)
Claudia Ohana
1984
ERENDIRA(1984, Mex./Fr./Ger.)

Jill Ohannison
STACY'S KNIGHTS(1983), cos
Corky Ohara
HOME MOVIES(1979), ed
Joji Ohara
WOMEN IN PRISON(1957, Jap.), ph
Kenji Ohara
Misc. Talkies
SILENT STRANGER, THE(1975)
Reiko Ohara
SPOILS OF THE NIGHT(1969, Jap.); HINOTORI(1980, Jap.)
Rene Ohashi
1984
LISTEN TO THE CITY(1984, Can.), ph
Takashi Ohashi
HIGH VELOCITY(1977), p
Manny Oheda
SUPERBEAST(1972)
Osamu Ohkawa
MARCO(1973)
Bob Ohlen
FORCE OF ARMS(1951)
Karolyne Ohler
FATHER(1967, Hung.)
Ake Ohlmarks
PIMPERNEL SVENSSON(1953, Swed.), w
Rudolf Ohlschmidt
SECRET WAYS, THE(1961), makeup; MIRACLE OF THE WHITE STAL-
LIONS(1963), makeup
Bertil Ohlsson
HUNGER(1968, Den./Norway/Swed.), p
Bror Ohlsson
OCEAN BREAKERS(1949, Swed.)
Henning Ohlsson
OCEAN BREAKERS(1949, Swed.)
Jan Ohlsson
VICTOR FRANKENSTEIN(1975, Swed./Ireland)
Marrit Ohlsson
GUILT(1967, Swed.)
Terry Ohlsson
SCOBIE MALONE(1975, Aus.), d
Gunnar Ohlund
ISLAND AT THE TOP OF THE WORLD, THE(1974)
Christer Ohman
WINTER LIGHT, THE(1963, Swed.)
Ernest Ohman
TO PLEASE A LADY(1950)
Phil Ohman
CAPTAIN CAUTION(1940), m; MILLION DOLLAR WEEKEND(1948), m
Carol Ohmart
SCARLET HOUR, THE(1956); WILD PARTY, THE(1956); HOUSE ON HAUNTED
HILL(1958); BORN RECKLESS(1959); SCAVENGERS, THE(1959, U.S./Phil.); WILD
YOUTH(1961); ONE MAN'S WAY(1964); SPIDER BABY(1968); SPECTRE OF EDGAR
ALLAN POE, THE(1974)
Misc. Talkies
CAXAMBU(1968); SPECTRE OF EDGAR ALLAN POE(1973)
Kiyoharu Ohnaka
RODAN(1958, Jap.)
Georges Ohnet
IRON MASTER, THE(1933), w
Silents
AMERICAN METHODS(1917), w
Tadashi Ohono
WOMAN IN THE DUNES(1964, Jap.), p
Catherine Ohotnikoff
CATHERINE & CO.(1976, Fr.)
Michael Ohrenbach
MURDER, MY SWEET(1945), set d
Dr. Ohrenstein
FREUD(1962)
Fred Ohringer
GURU, THE(1969, U.S./India)
Ben Ohta
FAREWELL, MY LOVELY(1975)
Bennett Ohta
MIDWAY(1976); CHARLIE CHAN AND THE CURSE OF THE DRAGON
QUEEN(1981); UNDER THE RAINBOW(1981)
Ryuzo Ohtani
BALLAD OF NARAYAMA(1961, Jap.), p
Masako Ohtsuki
BEACH RED(1967)
Shun Oide
PORTRAIT OF HELL(1969, Jap.)
Esther H. Oier
Silents
DESTRUCTION(1915)
Akira Oizumi
LIFE OF OHARU(1964, Jap.)
Hiroshi Oizumi
LIFE OF OHARU(1964, Jap.)
Patty Oja
EYES OF LAURA MARS(1978)
Arvo Ojala
OREGON TRAIL, THE(1959)
Inga Ojala
1984
WILD LIFE, THE(1984)

Manuel Ojeda
EAGLE'S WING(1979, Brit.); GREEN ICE(1981, Brit.)
1984
ROMANCING THE STONE(1984)
Silents
MAN WHO TURNED WHITE, THE(1919)
Misc. Silents
RUSTLING A BRIDE(1919)
Manuel R. Ojeda
LAST REBEL, THE(1961, Mex.), w; QUEEN'S SWORDSMEN, THE(1963, Mex.), w
Louis Ojena
ORGY OF THE DEAD(1965); MACHISMO–40 GRAVES FOR 40 GUNS(1970)
John Ojerholm
UNPUBLISHED STORY(1942, Brit.)
Ok-Ba-Ok
Misc. Silents
PRIMITIVE LOVE(1927)
Kazuhiko Okabe
PANDA AND THE MAGIC SERPENT(1961, Jap.), d, art d
Masazumi Okabe
MESSAGE FROM SPACE(1978, Jap.)
Tadashi Okabe
GODZILLA, RING OF THE MONSTERS(1956, Jap.)
Oldrich Okac
MARKETA LAZAROVA(1968, Czech.), set d
Eiji Okada
HIROSHIMA, MON AMOUR(1959, Fr./Jap.); UGLY AMERICAN, THE(1963); WOM-
AN IN THE DUNES(1964, Jap.); GHIDRAH, THE THREE-HEADED MONSTER(1965,
Jap.); JUDO SAGA(1965, Jap.); SCARLET CAMELLIA, THE(1965, Jap.); FACE OF
ANOTHER, THE(1967, Jap.); GIRARA(1967, Jap.); SHE AND HE(1967, Jap.); POR-
TRAIT OF CHIEKO(1968, Jap.); TUNNEL TO THE SUN(1968, Jap.); VIXEN(1970, Jap.);
ZATOICHI'S CONSPIRACY(1974, Jap.)
1984
ANTARCTICA(1984, Jap.)
Eric Okada
RIFIFI IN TOKYO(1963, Fr./Ital.)
Kaai Okada
RED LION(1971, Jap.)
Mariko Okada
SAMURAI(PART III)** (1967, Jap.); SECRET SCROLLS(PART I)**1/2 (1968, Jap.);
SAMURAI(1955, Jap.); WOMEN IN PRISON(1957, Jap.); TWILIGHT PATH(1965, Jap.);
ILLUSION OF BLOOD(1966, Jap.); LAKE, THE(1970, Jap.); LATE AUTUMN(1973,
Jap.); AFFAIR AT AKITSU(1980, Jap.), a, cos
Masumi Okada
LATITUDE ZERO(1969, U.S./Jap.); MARCO(1973)
Nana Okada
TIME SLIP(1981, Jap.)
Reiko Okada
KARATE, THE HAND OF DEATH(1961); THREE WEEKS OF LOVE(1965)
Shigeiu Okada
ONIMASA(1983, Jap.), p
Tokihiko Okada
Misc. Talkies
LASCIVIOUSNESS OF THE VIPER, THE(1920, Jap.); PAPER DOLL'S WHISPER OF
SPRING, A(1926, Jap.); WOMAN WHO TOUCHED THE LEGS, THE(1926, Jap.);
YOUNG MISS(1930, Jap.); CHORUS OF TOKYO(1931, Jap.)
Yu Okada
1984
FAMILY GAME, THE(1984, Jap.), p
Yuji Okada
GAPPA THE TRIFIBIAN MONSTER(1967, Jap.)
Tsuyako Okajima
HOUSE WHERE EVIL DWELLS, THE(1982)
Jojiro Okami
MYSTERIANS, THE(1959, Jap.), w
Jotaro Okami
BATTLE IN OUTER SPACE(1960), w
Ken K. Okamoto
GO FOR BROKE(1951)
Kichachi Okamoto
WARRING CLANS(1963, Jap.), d
Kido Okamoto
FOX WITH NINE TAILS, THE(1969, Jap.), w
Kihachi Okamoto
WESTWARD DESPERADO(1961, Jap.), d, w; OPERATION X(1963, Jap.), d&w;
SAMURAI ASSASSIN(1965, Jap.), d; FORT GRAVEYARD(1966, Jap.), d, w; SWORD
OF DOOM, THE(1967, Jap.), d; EMPEROR AND A GENERAL, THE(1968, Jap.), d;
KILL(1968, Jap.), d, w, ed; ZATOICHI MEETS YOJIMBO(1970, Jap.), d, w; RED
LION(1971, Jap.), d, w
Masami Okamoto
1984
BALLAD OF NARAYAMA, THE(1984, Jap.)
Arthur Okamura
FUNNYMAN(1967)
George Okamura
CRIMSON KIMONO, THE(1959)
Gerald Okamura
CHARLIE CHAN AND THE CURSE OF THE DRAGON QUEEN(1981)
Misc. Talkies
ANGEL OF H.E.A.T.(1982)
Seitaro Okamura
SONG FROM MY HEART, THE(1970, Jap.)
Norbert Okare
HUMAN FACTOR, THE(1979, Brit.)
Henry Okawa
GEISHA GIRL(1952); THREE STRIPES IN THE SUN(1955); BRIDGE ON THE
RIVER KWAI, THE(1957); WIND CANNOT READ, THE(1958, Brit.); MARINES, LET'S
GO(1961)

Hiroshi Okawa
TRAITORS(1957, Jap.), p; PANDA AND THE MAGIC SERPENT(1961, Jap.), p; GULLIVER'S TRAVELS BEYOND THE MOON(1966, Jap.), p; WORLD OF HANS CHRISTIAN ANDERSEN, THE(1971, Jap.), p

Hoirachiro Okawa
TOKYO FILE 212(1951)

Yaman Okay
1984
HORSE, THE(1984, Turk.)

Hajime Okayasu
1984
BALLAD OF NARAYAMA, THE(1984, Jap.), ed

Bob Okazaki
SECRET AGENT OF JAPAN(1942); NAVY WIFE(1956); JUNGLE HEAT(1957); HELL TO ETERNITY(1960); CRY FOR HAPPY(1961); SEVEN WOMEN FROM HELL(1961); GIRL NAMED TAMIRO, A(1962); WOMAN HUNT(1962); WALK, DON'T RUN(1966)

Hiro Okazaki
BLADE RUNNER(1982)

Jiro Okazaki
HOUSE OF STRANGE LOVES, THE(1969, Jap.)

Kozo Okazaki
MAN FROM THE EAST, THE(1961, Jap.), ph; TILL TOMORROW COMES(1962, Jap.), ph; MADAME AKI(1963, Jap.), ph; THIS MADDING CROWD(1964, Jap.), ph; RIVER OF FOREVER(1967, Jap.), ph; GOYOKIN(1969, Jap.), ph; OUR SILENT LOVE(1969, Jap.), ph; SCANDALOUS ADVENTURES OF BURAIKAN, THE(1970, Jap.), ph; BAD NEWS BEARS GO TO JAPAN, THE(1978), ph; GLOWING AUTUMN(1981, Jap.), ph; CHALLENGE, THE(1982), ph; ALL RIGHT, MY FRIEND(1983, Japan), ph

Randy Okazaki
WALK, DON'T RUN(1966)

Rob Okazaki
KARATE KILLERS, THE(1967)

Robert Okazaki
HOUSE OF BAMBOO(1955); TOKYO AFTER DARK(1959); BLADE RUNNER(1982)

Ichiro Okeda
WHITE ROSE OF HONG KONG(1965, Jap.), w

Dennis OKeefe
AFFAIRS OF SUSAN(1945)

Chukemeka Okeke
WHITE WITCH DOCTOR(1953)

Jack Okey
BROADWAY BABIES(1929), art d; NUMBERED MEN(1930), art d; SHOW GIRL IN HOLLYWOOD(1930), art d; FIVE STAR FINAL(1931), art d; HER MAJESTY LOVE(1931), art d; LAST FLIGHT, THE(1931), art d; SAFE IN HELL(1931), art d; CROWD ROARS, THE(1932), art d; DARK HORSE, THE(1932), art d; I AM A FUGITIVE FROM A CHAIN GANG(1932), art d; LOVE IS A RACKET(1932), art d; PURCHASE PRICE, THE(1932), art d; SO BIG(1932), art d; THEY CALL IT SIN(1932), art d; TIGER SHARK(1932), art d; YOU SAID A MOUTHFUL(1932), art d; COLLEGE COACH(1933), art d; EX-LADY(1933), art d; FEMALE(1933), art d; KENNEL MURDER CASE, THE(1933), art d; PARACHUTE JUMPER(1933), art d; PRIVATE DETECTIVE 62(1933), art d; WORKING MAN, THE(1933), art d; WORLD CHANGES, THE(1933), art d; 42ND STREET(1933), art d; DRAGON MURDER CASE, THE(1934), art d; FASHIONS OF 1934(1934), art d; FLIRTATION WALK(1934), art d; FOG OVER FRISCO(1934), art d; HEAT LIGHTNING(1934), art d; LOST LADY, A(1934), art d; MADAME DU BARRY(1934), art d; MERRY FRINKS, THE(1934), art d; MERRY WIVES OF RENO, THE(1934), art d; ST. LOUIS KID, THE(1934), art d; VERY HONORABLE GUY, A(1934), art d; WONDER BAR(1934), art d; BORDERTOWN(1935), art d; I AM A THIEF(1935), art d; JUNGLE BOOK(1942), set d; HIGHER AND HIGHER(1943), art d; JOHNNY COME LATELY(1943), art d; EXPERIMENT PERILOUS(1944), art d; MASTER RACE, THE(1944), art d; NONE BUT THE LONELY HEART(1944), art d; PASSPORT TO DESTINY(1944), art d; SHOW BUSINESS(1944), art d; JOHNNY ANGEL(1945), art d; CRACK-UP(1946), art d; DEADLINE AT DAWN(1946), art d; IT'S A WONDERFUL LIFE(1946), art d; SPIRAL STAIRCASE, THE(1946), art d; TILL THE END OF TIME(1946), art d; NIGHT SONG(1947), art d; OUT OF THE PAST(1947), art d; RACHEL AND THE STRANGER(1948), art d; SET-UP, THE(1949), art d; DOUBLE DEAL(1950), art d; HARD, FAST, AND BEAUTIFUL(1951), art d; RACKET, THE(1951), art d; NARROW MARGIN, THE(1952), art d; ONE MINUTE TO ZERO(1952), art d; DEVIL'S CANYON(1953), art d; SPLIT SECOND(1953), art d; GREAT DAY IN THE MORNING(1956), art d; SCREAMING EAGLES(1956), art d; RUN OF THE ARROW(1957), art d; MISSOURI TRAVELER, THE(1958), art d; YOUNG LAND, THE(1959), art d
Silents
OUTLAWS OF THE SEA(1923), d&w; IN EVERY WOMAN'S LIFE(1924), art d; INEZ FROM HOLLYWOOD(1924), set d; TORMENT(1924), set d; JUST A WOMAN(1925), art d; ONE YEAR TO LIVE(1925), art d; OLD LOVES AND NEW(1926), art d

H. Okhawa
STOPOVER TOKYO(1957)

Minoru Okhi
SHOGUN ASSASSIN(1980, Jap.)

N.P. Okhlopkov
ALEXANDER NEVSKY(1939)

Nikolai Okhlopkov
1812(1944, USSR)
Misc. Silents
DEATH BAY(1926, USSR); TRAITOR(1926, USSR); MITYA(1927, USSR), a, d; SOLD APPETITE, THE(1928, USSR), d

G. Okhrimenko
HUNTING IN SIBERIA(1962, USSR)

Masaya Oki
WAR OF THE PLANETS(1977, Jap.)

Jack Okie
LYDIA(1941), art d

Hideko Okiyama
KURAGEJIMA-LEGENDS FROM A SOUTHERN ISLAND(1970, Jap.); SONG FROM MY HEART, THE(1970, Jap.)

Oklahoma City Symphony Orchestra
STARK FEAR(1963), m

The Oklahoma Wranglers
HOEDOWN(1950)

Ruth Oklander
HOUSE OF USHER(1960)

Denjiro Okochi
SECRET SCROLLS(PART I) (1968, Jap.)

Tom Okon
IF EVER I SEE YOU AGAIN(1978)

George Okonkowsky
GIRL IN THE TAXI(1937, Brit.), w

L. Okrent
TRAIN GOES TO KIEV, THE(1961, USSR)

Guler Okten
1984
HORSE, THE(1984, Turk.)

Auhofe Okuampa
HAMILE(1965, Ghana)

Dona Jean Okubo
NAVY WIFE(1956)

Masanobu Okubo
SEVEN SAMURAI, THE(1956, Jap.)

Tomihiko Okubo
1984
WARRIORS OF THE WIND(1984, Jap.), anim

Hisashi Okuda
MAJIN(1968, Jap.), art d

Kikumaru Okuda
NONE BUT THE BRAVE(1965, U.S./Jap.), w

Otto Okuga
Silents
ON THE QUIET(1918)

Vladimir Okulich
COUNTRY BRIDE(1938, USSR), ph

Charles Okun
LOVESICK(1983), p

Milton Okun
GONE ARE THE DAYS(1963), m

Gerald Okuneff
NORMA RAE(1979)

Gerry Okuneff
TWO-MINUTE WARNING(1976)

Kazukimi Okuni
SANSHO THE BAILIFF(1969, Jap.)

Johnny Okura
MERRY CHRISTMAS MR. LAWRENCE(1983, Jap./Brit.)

Nagaharu Okuyama
WALL-EYED NIPPON(1963, Jap.), w

Reiko Okuyama
MAGIC BOY(1960, Jap.), anim

Bill Okwirry
SAVAGE HARVEST(1981)

Oky Miller and Company
DARKTOWN STRUTTERS(1975)

Robert Okzzaki
CRIMSON KIMONO, THE(1959)

Pierre Olaf
FRENCH CANCAN(1956, Fr.); WILD AND WONDERFUL(1964); ART OF LOVE, THE(1965); COUNTERFEIT CONSTABLE, THE(1966, Fr.); CAMELOT(1967); DON'T DRINK THE WATER(1969); GAMBLERS, THE(1969); LE PETIT THEATRE DE JEAN RENOIR(1974, Fr.)
1984
AMERICAN DREAMER(1984); CHEECH AND CHONG'S THE CORSICAN BROTHERS(1984)

Prince Olafami
EDUCATION OF SONNY CARSON, THE(1974)

Orest Olaff
FLOATING DUTCHMAN, THE(1953, Brit.)

Johan Olafs
WINTER LIGHT, THE(1963, Swed.)

Ruth Olafs
FROM THE LIFE OF THE MARIONETTES(1980, Ger.)

Phil "Swedish Angel" Olafsson
MIGHTY JOE YOUNG(1949)

Juan Olaguibel
CEREMONY, THE(1963, U.S./Span.); KID RODELO(1966, U.S./Span.)

Juan Olaguible
GOD FORGIVES-I DON'T!(1969, Ital./Span.)

Juan Olaguivel
AVENGERS, THE(1950); PRIDE AND THE PASSION, THE(1957); BOY WHO STOLE A MILLION, THE(1960, Brit.); SCENT OF MYSTERY(1960); HOUSE OF 1,000 DOLLS(1967, Ger./Span./Brit.)

Antonia Oland
FIVE LITTLE PEPPERS IN TROUBLE(1940)

Bill Oland
1984
SPECIAL EFFECTS(1984)

Inger-Berit Oland
EDVARD MUNCH(1976, Norway/Swed.)

Warner Oland
JAZZ SINGER, THE(1927); CHINATOWN NIGHTS(1929); MIGHTY, THE(1929); MYSTERIOUS DR. FU MANCHU, THE(1929); STUDIO MURDER MYSTERY, THE(1929); DANGEROUS PARADISE(1930); RETURN OF DR. FU MANCHU, THE(1930); VAGABOND KING, THE(1930); BIG GAMBLE, THE(1931); BLACK CAMEL, THE(1931); CHARLIE CHAN CARRIES ON(1931); DAUGHTER OF THE DRAGON(1931); DISHONORED(1931); DRUMS OF JEOPARDY(1931); CHARLIE CHAN'S CHANCE(1932); PASSPORT TO HELL(1932); SHANGHAI EXPRESS(1932); SONDAUGHTER, THE(1932); BEFORE DAWN(1933); CHARLIE CHAN'S GREATEST CASE(1933); AS HUSBANDS GO(1934); BULLDOG DRUMMOND STRIKES BACK(1934); CHARLIE CHAN IN LONDON(1934); CHARLIE CHAN'S COURAGE(1934); MANDALAY(1934); PAINTED VEIL, THE(1934); CHARLIE CHAN IN

EGYPT(1935); CHARLIE CHAN IN PARIS(1935); CHARLIE CHAN IN SHANG-HAI(1935); SHANGHAI(1935); WEREWOLF OF LONDON, THE(1935); CHARLIE CHAN AT THE CIRCUS(1936); CHARLIE CHAN AT THE OPERA(1936); CHARLIE CHAN AT THE RACE TRACK(1936); CHARLIE CHAN'S SECRET(1936); CHARLIE CHAN AT MONTE CARLO(1937); CHARLIE CHAN AT THE OLYMPICS(1937); CHARLIE CHAN ON BROADWAY(1937)

Silents

DESTRUCTION(1915); SIN(1915); ETERNAL SAPHO, THE(1916); NAULAHKA, THE(1918); AVALANCHE, THE(1919); EAST IS WEST(1922); PRIDE OF PALOMAR, THE(1922); FIGHTING AMERICAN, THE(1924); DON Q, SON OF ZORRO(1925); RIDERS OF THE PURPLE SAGE(1925); WINDING STAIR, THE(1925); DON JUAN(1926); MARRIAGE CLAUSE, THE(1926); TELL IT TO THE MARINES(1926); TWINKLETOES(1926); OLD SAN FRANCISCO(1927); SAILOR IZZY MURPHY(1927); WHAT HAPPENED TO FATHER(1927); SCARLET LADY, THE(1928); STAND AND DELIVER(1928)

Misc. Silents

LIFE OF JOHN BUNYAN-PILGRIM'S PROGRESS(1912); ETERNAL QUESTION, THE(1916); REAPERS, THE(1916); RISE OF SUSAN, THE(1916); CIGARETTE GIRL, THE(1917); CONVICT 993(1918); MYSTERIOUS CLIENT, THE(1918); YELLOW TICK-ET, THE(1918); MANDARIN'S GOLD(1919); TWIN PAWNS, THE(1919); WITNESS FOR THE DEFENSE, THE(1919); CURLYTOP(1924); FLOWER OF NIGHT(1925); INFATUATION(1925); MAN OF THE FOREST(1926); GOOD TIME CHARLEY(1927); MILLION BID, A(1927); WHEN A MAN LOVES(1927); DREAM OF LOVE(1928); WHEEL OF CHANCE(1928); FAKER, THE(1929)

Joan Olander
TWO TICKETS TO BROADWAY(1951)

Kid Olanf
I LOVE YOU, I KILL YOU(1972, Ger.), m

Susan Olar
STAYING ALIVE(1983)

Adrianna Olasio
8 ½(1963, Ital.), ed

Janos Olasz
SUN SHINES, THE(1939, Hung.)

Ponciano Olayta, Jr.
SPOOK WHO SAT BY THE DOOR, THE(1973)

Daniel Olbrychski
JOVITA(1970, Pol.); BOXER(1971, Pol.); TIN DRUM, THE(1979, Ger./Fr./Yugo./Pol.); YOUNG GIRLS OF WILKO, THE(1979, Pol./Fr.); BOLERO(1982, Fr.); TROUT, THE(1982, Fr.)
1984
LOVE IN GERMANY, A(1984, Fr./Ger.)

Daniel Olbrychsky
ROME WANTS ANOTHER CAESAR(1974, Ital.)

Antonio Perez Olca
PLANET OF THE VAMPIRES(1965, U.S./Ital./Span.), m

Andrea Olch
BY DESIGN(1982)

Elaine Olcott
PULP(1972, Brit.); DAISY MILLER(1974)

Rita Olcott
MY WILD IRISH ROSE(1947), w

Sidney Olcott
Silents
FROM THE MANGER TO THE CROSS(1913), a, d&w; MADAME BUTTER-FLY(1915), d; MOTH AND THE FLAME, THE(1915), d; SENTIMENTAL LADY, THE(1915), d; SEVEN SISTERS, THE(1915), d; INNOCENT LIE, THE(1916), d; MY LADY INCOG(1916), d; RIGHT WAY, THE(1921), d; TIMOTHY'S QUEST(1922), d; MONSIEUR BEAUCAIRE(1924), p; ONLY WOMAN, THE(1924), d; CHARMER, THE(1925), d; NOT SO LONG AGO(1925), d; AMATEUR GENTLEMAN, THE(1926), d; RANSON'S FOLLY(1926), d; WHITE BLACK SHEEP, THE(1926), d

Misc. Silents
WOLFE OR THE CONQUEST OF QUEBEC(1914), d; BOLD EMMETT, IRELAND'S MARTYR(1915), a, d; NAN O' THE BACKWOODS(1915), d; DAUGHTER OF MAC-GREGOR, A(1916), d; DIPLOMACY(1916), d; POOR LITTLE PEPPINA(1916), d; SMUGGLERS, THE(1916), d; BELGIAN, THE(1917), d; MARRIAGE FOR CONVENI-ENCE(1919), d; SCRATCH MY BACK(1920), d; GOD'S COUNTRY AND THE LAW(1921), d; PARDON MY FRENCH(1921), d; GREEN GODDESS, THE(1923), d; HUMMING BIRD, THE(1924), d; BEST PEOPLE, THE(1925), d; SALOME OF THE TENEMENTS(1925), d; CLAW, THE(1927), d

John M. Old [Mario Bava]
ROAD TO FORT ALAMO, THE(1966, Fr./Ital.), d

Mae Old Coyote
DIRTY DINGUS MAGEE(1970)

Lawrence Old Cross
MAN CALLED HORSE, A(1970)

Georg Olden
1984
BAD MANNERS(1984); JOHNNY DANGEROUSLY(1984)

John Olden
GREAT BRITISH TRAIN ROBBERY, THE(1967, Ger.), d

Ole Oldendorp
1984
1984(1984, Brit.)

Alan Oldfield
DOGS(1976), m; FOREST, THE(1983), m
1984
INVISIBLE STRANGLER(1984), m

Barney Oldfield
BLONDE COMET(1941)
Misc. Silents
FIRST AUTO, THE(1927)

Brent Oldfield
Misc. Talkies
BLINKER'S SPY-SPOTTER(1971)

Dorothy Oldfield
MR. SMITH CARRIES ON(1937, Brit.)

Eric Oldfield
Misc. Talkies
CHOPPER SQUAD(1971); ISLAND TRADER(1982)

Hilda Oldfield
Misc. Silents
HEAR THE PIPERS CALLING(1918, Brit.)

Mike Oldfield
1984
KILLING FIELDS, THE(1984, Brit.), m

Richard Oldfield
EMILY(1976, Brit.); GOLDEN LADY, THE(1979, Brit.); EMPIRE STRIKES BACK, THE(1980); FINAL CONFLICT, THE(1981); LORDS OF DISCIPLINE, THE(1983)
1984
RAZOR'S EDGE, THE(1984); SCREAM FOR HELP(1984)

Derek Oldham
BROKEN ROSARY, THE(1934, Brit.); ON THE AIR(1934, Brit.); CHARING CROSS ROAD(1935, Brit.); CITY OF BEAUTIFUL NONSENSE, THE(1935, Brit.); MELODY OF MY HEART(1936, Brit.); DANGEROUS EXILE(1958, Brit.)

Michael Oldham
LAUGHING ANNE(1954, Brit./U.S.)

Esther Oldham-Farfan
COCAINE COWBOYS(1979)

Lilian Oldland
Silents
DAUGHTER IN REVOLT, A(1927, Brit.); FURTHER ADVENTURES OF THE FLAG LIEUTENANT(1927, Brit.)

Lillian Oldland
Silents
FLAG LIEUTENANT, THE(1926, Brit.); PASSION ISLAND(1927, Brit.); VIRGINIA'S HUSBAND(1928, Brit.)
Misc. Silents
CITY OF YOUTH, THE(1928, Brit.); TROUBLESOME WIVES(1928, Brit.)

Gary Oldman
REMEMBRANCE(1982, Brit.)

Enrico Oldoini
BINGO BONGO(1983, Ital.), w

Alfred Oldridge
MIKADO, THE(1967, Brit.)

Harry Oldridge
DOUBLE LIFE, A(1947)

William Olds
GREEN BERETS, THE(1968)

Antonio Perez Olea
MURIETA(1965, Span.), m, md; REQUIEM FOR A SECRET AGENT(1966, Ital.), m; BLOOD SPATTERED BRIDE, THE(1974, Span.), p

Frank Olegario
HARRY BLACK AND THE TIGER(1958, Brit.); FLAME OVER INDIA(1960, Brit.); NINE HOURS TO RAMA(1963, U.S./Brit.); DIAMONDS ARE FOREVER(1971, Brit.)
1984
INDIANA JONES AND THE TEMPLE OF DOOM(1984)

Galina Oleinichenko
YOLANTA(1964, USSR)

P. Oleinikov
SEVEN BRAVE MEN(1936, USSR)

Jan Olejniczak
FIRST SPACESHIP ON VENUS(1960, Ger./Pol.), spec eff

Henry Olek
EVEL KNIEVEL(1971); ROLLERCOASTER(1977); DIFFERENT STORY, A(1978), w; METEOR(1979); ONLY WHEN I LAUGH(1981)
1984
ALL OF ME(1984), w

Bob Olen
HUNTERS, THE(1958)

S. Rodger Olenicoff
ICE CASTLES(1978), p

Johnny Olenn
GIRL CAN'T HELP IT, THE(1956)

Ole Olesen
PAROLED FROM THE BIG HOUSE(1938)

C. Olesenko
HAMLET(1966, USSR)

I. Olesha
CONCENTRATION CAMP(1939, USSR), w

N. Oleshchenko
HOUSE WITH AN ATTIC, THE(1964, USSR)

Keri Oleson
SWIMMER, THE(1968)

Maggie Oleson
GAILY, GAILY(1969)

Norman Olestad
WINCHESTER '73(1950)

Pat Oleszko
CRY DR. CHICAGO(1971)

A. Olevanov
QUEEN OF SPADES(1961, USSR)

Galina Oleynichenko
TSAR'S BRIDE, THE(1966, USSR)

Ken Olfson
YOU LIGHT UP MY LIFE(1977); HOUSE CALLS(1978); ONE AND ONLY, THE(1978); H.O.T.S.(1979); MR. MOM(1983)
1984
ANGEL(1984); BREAKIN' 2: ELECTRIC BOOGALOO(1984); MICKI AND MAU-DE(1984)

Mary Olga
HAPPY HOOKER, THE(1975)

Castro Olguin
TROPIC HOLIDAY(1938)

Eduardo Olguin
TROPIC HOLIDAY(1938)
Maria Olguin
TROPIC HOLIDAY(1938)
Teresa Olguin
TROPIC HOLIDAY(1938)
Jody Lee Olhava
Misc. Talkies
THREE WAY WEEKEND(1979)
Joel Oliansky
COUNTERPOINT(1967), w; TODD KILLINGS, THE(1971), w; COMPETITION, THE(1980), d&w
Lothar Olias
FREDDY UNTER FREMDEN STERNEN(1962, Ger.), m
Karla Olicova
SKELETON ON HORSEBACK(1940, Czech.)
Huguette Oligny
KAMOURASKA(1973, Can./Fr.)
Stephen Oliker
PEACE KILLERS, THE(1971), set d
Ken Olin
GHOST STORY(1981)
Lena Olin
FANNY AND ALEXANDER(1983, Swed./Fr./Ger.)
1984
AFTER THE REHEARSAL(1984, Swed.)
Stig Olin
TORMENT(1947, Swed.); ILLICIT INTERLUDE(1954, Swed.); TRUE AND THE FALSE, THE(1955, Swed.); DEVIL'S WANTON, THE(1962, Swed.); PORT OF CALL(1963, Swed.)
Alan Oliney
STAR CHAMBER, THE(1983)
1984
STAR TREK III: THE SEARCH FOR SPOCK(1984)
Allen Oliney
WHICH WAY IS UP?(1977), stunts
Ronald G. Oliney
PENNIES FROM HEAVEN(1981)
Jim Oliphant
BEAST OF YUCCA FLATS, THE(1961)
Peter Oliphant
DEADLY DUO(1962); MR. HOBBS TAKES A VACATION(1962); HOT RODS TO HELL(1967); ROOMMATES, THE(1973)
Tom Oliphant
SAN QUENTIN(1946), set d; GODDESS, THE(1958), set d
Joseph Olita
AMIN–THE RISE AND FALL(1982, Kenya)
1984
SHEENA(1984)
Esther Oliva
CUBAN REBEL GIRLS(1960)
Francisco Oliva
SCALPHUNTERS, THE(1968)
Gilda Oliva
CRUSADES, THE(1935); SEPTEMBER AFFAIR(1950); MATING SEASON, THE(1951); ROGUE COP(1954); HOUSEBOAT(1958)
Nadia Haro Oliva
EXTERMINATING ANGEL, THE(1967, Mex.)
Alfred Olivant
TO THE VICTOR(1938, Brit.), w
Silents
OWD BOB(1924, Brit.), w
Burt Olivar
NO MAN IS AN ISLAND(1962)
Carlos A. Olivari
ROMANCE ON THE HIGH SEAS(1948), w
Carlos Olivari
YOU WERE NEVER LOVELIER(1942), w
Robert Olivas
SNIPER'S RIDGE(1961), cos; TWO LITTLE BEARS, THE(1961), cos
E. E. Olive
BULLDOG DRUMMOND'S REVENGE(1937); MARYLAND(1940)
Marian Olive
NIGHT OF MAGIC, A(1944, Brit.)
Aloysio Oliveira
THREE CABALLEROS, THE(1944), ch
Jose Oliveira
THREE CABALLEROS, THE(1944); HELL'S ISLAND(1955)
Luis Oliveira
VOYAGE OF SILENCE(1968, Fr.)
Oliver
WINDOWS(1980)
Aimee Oliver
RECESS(1967)
Anita Oliver
LONELINESS OF THE LONG DISTANCE RUNNER, THE(1962, Brit.)
Anthony Oliver
MAGNET, THE(1950, Brit.); MANIACS ON WHEELS(1951, Brit.); GLORY AT SEA(1952, Brit.); MR. LORD SAYS NO(1952, Brit.); WATERFRONT WOMEN(1952, Brit.); BOTH SIDES OF THE LAW(1953, Brit.); PENNY PRINCESS(1953, Brit.); MAD ABOUT MEN(1954, Brit.); RUNAWAY BUS, THE(1954, Brit.); THEY CAN'T HANG ME(1955, Brit.); CASH ON DELIVERY(1956, Brit.); EYEWITNESS(1956, Brit.); SUICIDE MISSION(1956, Brit.); CHECKPOINT(1957, Brit.); TEARS FOR SIMON(1957, Brit.); CROSSROADS TO CRIME(1960, Brit.); ENTERTAINER, THE(1960, Brit.); TRANSATLANTIC(1961, Brit.); DAMN THE DEFIANT!(1962, Brit.); DANGER BY MY SIDE(1962, Brit.); OUT OF THE FOG(1962, Brit.)
Misc. Talkies
FOR MEMBERS ONLY(1960)

Barret Oliver
JEKYLL AND HYDE...TOGETHER AGAIN(1982); KISS ME GOODBYE(1982); UNCOMMON VALOR(1983)
1984
NEVERENDING STORY, THE(1984, Ger.)
Barrie Oliver
BIG BUSINESS(1930, Brit.)
Barry Oliver
MIDNIGHT PATROL, THE(1932)
Beverly Oliver
STREET IS MY BEAT, THE(1966)
Bill Oliver
MEET THE NAVY(1946, Brit.)
Cettina Borg Oliver
PULP(1972, Brit.)
Charles Oliver
AVENGING HAND, THE(1936, Brit.); BELOVED IMPOSTER(1936, Brit.); MIDNIGHT AT THE WAX MUSEUM(1936, Brit.); FIFTY-SHILLING BOXER(1937, Brit.); SECOND BUREAU(1937, Brit.); DRUMS(1938, Brit.); IF I WERE BOSS(1938, Brit.); LADY VANISHES, THE(1938, Brit.); MOUNTAINS O'MOURNE(1938, Brit.); SEXTON BLAKE AND THE HOODED TERROR(1938, Brit.); ASK A POLICEMAN(1939, Brit.); THIS MAN IN PARIS(1939, Brit.); WINGS OVER AFRICA(1939); CROOKS TOUR(1940, Brit.); NIGHT TRAIN(1940, Brit.); THREE SILENT MEN(1940, Brit.); UNDER YOUR HAT(1940, Brit.); MAIL TRAIN(1941, Brit.); GREEN COCKATOO, THE(1947, Brit.)
Cisco Oliver
BOYS IN COMPANY C, THE(1978, U.S./Hong Kong)
Claire Oliver
VERY CURIOUS GIRL, A(1970, Fr.)
Clarence Oliver
Misc. Silents
LAUGHING BILL HYDE(1918); SERVICE STAR, THE(1918); RACING STRAIN(1919)
Daly Stephen Oliver
SUNBURN(1979), w
Damienne Oliver
WELCOME HOME, SOLDIER BOYS(1972)
Dave Oliver
THESE GLAMOUR GIRLS(1939); MISSISSIPPI GAMBLER(1942)
David Oliver
GIRL ON THE FRONT PAGE, THE(1936); POSTAL INSPECTOR(1936); ARMORED CAR(1937); AS GOOD AS MARRIED(1937); GIRL OVERBOARD(1937); NIGHT KEY(1937); WHEN LOVE IS YOUNG(1937); YOU'RE A SWEETHEART(1937); DEVIL'S PARTY, THE(1938); EXPOSED(1938); LITTLE TOUGH GUYS IN SOCIETY(1938); NURSE FROM BROOKLYN(1938); ROAD TO RENO, THE(1938); SECRETS OF A NURSE(1938); STATE POLICE(1938); SWING THAT CHEER(1938); THAT CERTAIN AGE(1938); WIVES UNDER SUSPICION(1938); YOU CAN'T CHEAT AN HONEST MAN(1939); LITTLE BIT OF HEAVEN, A(1940); LOVE, HONOR AND OH, BABY(1940); MARGIE(1940); SUSAN AND GOD(1940); CAUGHT IN THE DRAFT(1941); FACE BEHIND THE MASK, THE(1941); LUCKY DEVILS(1941); MILLION DOLLAR BABY(1941)
Davis Oliver
CARNIVAL QUEEN(1937)
Deanna Oliver
1984
CRIMES OF PASSION(1984)
Demian Oliver
WILD GYPSIES(1969)
Don Oliver
Misc. Talkies
DYNAMITE BROTHERS, THE(1974)
Donald Oliver
WRONG BOX, THE(1966, Brit.)
Dwayne Oliver
LORD SHANGO(1975)
Ed Oliver
CASS TIMBERLANE(1947)
Eddie Oliver
EASY TO LOVE(1953)
Edna Mae Oliver
CIMARRON(1931); LITTLE MISS BROADWAY(1938); PARADISE FOR THREE(1938)
Edna May Oliver
SATURDAY NIGHT KID, THE(1929); HALF SHOT AT SUNRISE(1930); CRACKED NUTS(1931); FANNY FOLEY HERSELF(1931); LAUGH AND GET RICH(1931); NEWLY RICH(1931); CONQUERORS, THE(1932); HOLD'EM JAIL(1932); LADIES OF THE JURY(1932); PENGUIN POOL MURDER, THE(1932); ALICE IN WONDERLAND(1933); ANN VICKERS(1933); GREAT JASPER, THE(1933); IT'S GREAT TO BE ALIVE(1933); LITTLE WOMEN(1933); MEET THE BARON(1933); ONLY YESTERDAY(1933); LAST GENTLEMAN, THE(1934); MURDER ON THE BLACKBOARD(1934); POOR RICH, THE(1934); WE'RE RICH AGAIN(1934); DAVID COPPERFIELD(1935); MURDER ON A HONEYMOON(1935); NO MORE LADIES(1935); TALE OF TWO CITIES, A(1935); ROMEO AND JULIET(1936); MY DEAR MISS ALDRICH(1937); PARNELL(1937); ROSALIE(1937); DRUMS ALONG THE MOHAWK(1939); NURSE EDITH CAVELL(1939); SECOND FIDDLE(1939); STORY OF VERNON AND IRENE CASTLE, THE(1939); PRIDE AND PREJUDICE(1940); LYDIA(1941)
Silents
ICEBOUND(1924); MANHATTAN(1924); AMERICAN VENUS, THE(1926); LET'S GET MARRIED(1926)
Misc. Silents
LUCKY DEVIL(1925)
Elinor Oliver
Misc. Silents
DOLL'S HOUSE, A(1922)
Ethel Oliver
Misc. Silents
SOUL'S AWAKENING, A(1922, Brit.)

Fenwich Oliver
Silents
BURNING SANDS(1922)
Fenwick Oliver
Silents
MERRY-GO-ROUND(1923)
Gene Oliver
SULTAN'S DAUGHTER, THE(1943)
Gordon Oliver
ALCATRAZ ISLAND(1937); CASE OF THE STUTTERING BISHOP, THE(1937); DRAEGERMAN COURAGE(1937); EXPENSIVE HUSBANDS(1937); FLY-AWAY BABY(1937); FUGITIVE IN THE SKY(1937); GO-GETTER, THE(1937); ONCE A DOCTOR(1937); OVER THE GOAL(1937); SAN QUENTIN(1937); WEST OF SHANG-HAI(1937); WHITE BONDAGE(1937); YOUTH ON PAROLE(1937); BLONDIE(1938); BROTHER RAT(1938); DAREDEVIL DRIVERS(1938); JEZEBEL(1938); MARINES ARE HERE, THE(1938); THERE'S THAT WOMAN AGAIN(1938); WOMEN ARE LIKE THAT(1938); MY SON IS A CRIMINAL(1939); PRIDE OF THE NAVY(1939); RO-MANCE OF THE REDWOODS(1939); SABOTAGE(1939); WOMAN IS THE JUDGE, A(1939); SWEETHEART OF THE CAMPUS(1941); FOLLIES GIRL(1943); HEAVENLY DAYS(1944); PASSPORT TO DESTINY(1944); SEVEN DAYS ASHORE(1944); SPIRAL STAIRCASE, THE(1946); STATION WEST(1948); BORN TO BE BAD(1950); MY FORBIDDEN PAST(1951); LAS VEGAS STORY, THE(1952); CANCEL MY RESERVA-TION(1972), a, p
Greg Oliver
CARNY(1980)
Gregory J. Oliver
LINCOLN CONSPIRACY, THE(1977)
Guy Oliver
KIBITZER, THE(1929); STUDIO MURDER MYSTERY, THE(1929); WOMAN TRAP(1929); DEVIL'S HOLIDAY, THE(1930); LIGHT OF WESTERN STARS, THE(1930); ONLY THE BRAVE(1930); PLAYBOY OF PARIS(1930); BELOVED BACHELOR, THE(1931); CAUGHT(1931); DUDE RANCH(1931); GUN SMOKE(1931); HUCKLEBERRY FINN(1931); I TAKE THIS WOMAN(1931); MURDER BY THE CLOCK(1931); RICH MAN'S FOLLY(1931); SKIPPY(1931); SOOKY(1931); UP POPS THE DEVIL(1931)
Silents
CARPET FROM BAGDAD, THE(1915); EACH TO HIS KIND(1917); NAN OF MUSIC MOUNTAIN(1917); THOSE WITHOUT SIN(1917); BRAVEST WAY, THE(1918); JULES OF THE STRONG HEART(1918); M'LISS(1918); ALIAS MIKE MORAN(1919); HAW-THORNE OF THE U.S.A.(1919); MALE AND FEMALE(1919); PUTTING IT OVER(1919); ROARING ROAD, THE(1919); ALWAYS AUDACIOUS(1920); CUMBER-LAND ROMANCE, A(1920); EXCUSE MY DUST(1920); ROUND UP, THE(1920); SINS OF ROZANNE(1920); AFFAIRS OF ANATOL, THE(1921); BIG GAME(1921); CITY OF SILENT MEN(1921); PRINCE THERE WAS, A(1921); TOO MUCH SPEED(1921); WHAT EVERY WOMAN KNOWS(1921); ACROSS THE CONTINENT(1922); HOMES-PUN VAMP, A(1922); OUR LEADING CITIZEN(1922); WORLD'S CHAMPION, THE(1922); COVERED WAGON, THE(1923); MR. BILLINGS SPENDS HIS DI-ME(1923); RUGGLES OF RED GAP(1923); SIXTY CENTS AN HOUR(1923); TO THE LAST MAN(1923); BEDROOM WINDOW, THE(1924); NORTH OF 36(1924); AIR MAIL, THE(1925); OLD IRONSIDES(1926); ARIZONA BOUND(1927); NEVADA(1927); SHOO-TIN' IRONS(1927); AVALANCHE(1928); EASY COME, EASY GO(1928); HALF A BRIDE(1928); LOVE AND LEARN(1928); STAIRS OF SAND(1929); SUNSET PASS(1929)
Misc. Silents
CIRCULAR STAIRCASE, THE(1915); I'M GLAD MY BOY GREW TO BE A SOL-DIER(1915); DEVIL, THE SERVANT AND THE MAN, THE(1916); INTO THE PRIMITIVE(1916); THOU SHALT NOT COVET(1916); BOTTLE IMP, THE(1917); GOLDEN FETTER, THE(1917); SUCH A LITTLE PIRATE(1918); IT PAYS TO ADVER-TISE(1919); VENUS IN THE EAST(1919); SINS OF ST. ANTHONY, THE(1920)
H. C. Oliver
Silents
GOLD RUSH, THE(1925)
Harry Oliver
LUCKY STAR(1929), art d; SUNNY SIDE UP(1929), art d; THEY HAD TO SEE PARIS(1929), art d; LIGHTNIN'(1930), art d; LILIOM(1930), art d; SONG O' MY HEART(1930), art d; MOVIE CRAZY(1932), art d; DANCING LADY(1933), art d & set d; TILLIE AND GUS(1933), art d; WHITE WOMAN(1933), art d; CAT'S PAW, THE(1934), art d; VIVA VILLA!(1934), art d; GOOD EARTH, THE(1937), art d; MAKE A WISH(1937), art d; OF HUMAN HEARTS(1938), art d
Silents
LITTLE ANNIE ROONEY(1925), art d; SPARROWS(1926), art d; SEVENTH HEAV-EN(1927), set d
Henry Oliver
FATAL LADY(1936); PLASTIC DOME OF NORMA JEAN, THE(1966)
James Oliver
THUNDER TOWN(1946), w; HELL'S ANGELS ON WHEELS(1967); CISCO PI-KE(1971); VAN, THE(1977); MALIBU BEACH(1978)
Silents
GIRL WHO WOULDN'T QUIT, THE(1918), w
Jennie Harris Oliver
MOKEY(1942), w
Jody Oliver
1984
DELIVERY BOYS(1984)
Joe Oliver
COOL WORLD, THE(1963)
Jonathan Oliver
RETURN OF THE JEDI(1983)
Juan Louis Oliver
UNSATISFIED, THE(1964, Span.), ed
Kevin Oliver
GOIN' HOME(1976)
Kyle Oliver
HOUSE CALLS(1978)
Larry Oliver
BORN YESTERDAY(1951)
Leslie Oliver
STUDENT TEACHERS, THE(1973)

Lolly Oliver
DO NOT THROW CUSHIONS INTO THE RING(1970)
Margaret Oliver
JAZZ SINGER, THE(1927)
Michael Oliver
HELL, HEAVEN OR HOBOKEN(1958, Brit.)
Nelson Oliver
GIRL IN ROOM 13(1961, U.S./Braz.)
Pam Oliver
HOODWINK(1981, Aus.), p
Phil Oliver
WINSTANLEY(1979, Brit.)
Pita Oliver
PROM NIGHT(1980)
Pom Oliver
CATHY'S CHILD(1979, Aus.), p
Ray Oliver
PRIVATE BENJAMIN(1980)
Raymond Oliver
FORBIDDEN WORLD(1982)
Robert Oliver
HOUSE OF FREAKS(1973, Ital.), d
Rochelle Oliver
HAPPY HOOKER, THE(1975); NEXT STOP, GREENWICH VILLAGE(1976); LIAN-NA(1983)
Roland Oliver
Silents
GOOD NIGHT, PAUL(1918), w
Ruth Oliver
1984
GHOSTBUSTERS(1984)
Sherline Oliver
TALK OF HOLLYWOOD, THE(1929)
Shirling Oliver
VICTIMS OF PERSECUTION(1933)
Simon Oliver
GUY NAMED JOE, A(1943); GASLIGHT(1944)
Stephanie Oliver
YOURS, MINE AND OURS(1968)
Stephen Oliver
MOTOR PSYCHO(1965); ANGELS FROM HELL(1968); NAKED ZOO, THE(1970); WEREWOLVES ON WHEELS(1971); SAVAGE ABDUCTION(1975); VAN, THE(1977); MALIBU BEACH(1978); WAGNER(1983, Brit./Hung./Aust.)
Steve Oliver
TOM HORN(1980)
Steven Oliver
GREAT GUNDOWN, THE(1977)
Susan Oliver
GREEN-EYED BLONDE, THE(1957); GENE KRUPA STORY, THE(1959); BUTTER-FIELD 8(1960); CARETAKERS, THE(1963); DISORDERLY ORDERLY, THE(1964); GUNS OF DIABLO(1964); LOOKING FOR LOVE(1964); YOUR CHEATIN' HEART(1964); LOVE-INS, THE(1967); CHANGE OF MIND(1969); MAN CALLED GANNON, A(1969); MONITORS, THE(1969); COMPANY OF KILLERS(1970); GINGER IN THE MORNING(1973); WIDOWS' NEST(1977, U.S./Span.); MURDER BY DE-CREE(1979, Brit.); HARDLY WORKING(1981)
Sy Oliver
SHIP AHOY(1942), m
Ted Oliver
YELLOW JACK(1938); CENTRAL PARK(1932); ROBBERS' ROOST(1933); WE'RE NOT DRESSING(1934); CAR 99(1935); GOIN' TO TOWN(1935); SHE COULDN'T TAKE IT(1935); STOLEN HARMONY(1935); BORDER FLIGHT(1936); KLONDIKE AN-NIE(1936); MODERN TIMES(1936); PUBLIC ENEMY'S WIFE(1936); RETURN OF SOPHIE LANG, THE(1936); YELLOW DUST(1936); FRAME-UP THE(1937); LET'S GET MARRIED(1937); PLAINSMAN, THE(1937); SHE LOVED A FIREMAN(1937); TRAPPED(1937); GO CHASE YOURSELF(1938); MAD MISS MANTON, THE(1938); THERE'S ALWAYS A WOMAN(1938); BLACKMAIL(1939); LET US LIVE(1939); GRAPES OF WRATH(1940); MAN FROM DAKOTA, THE(1940); MORTAL STORM, THE(1940); NEW MOON(1940); NORTHWEST PASSAGE(1940); SKY MURDER(1940); SON OF MONTE CRISTO(1940); HONKY TONK(1941); OBLIGING YOUNG LA-DY(1941); WAGONS ROLL AT NIGHT, THE(1941); THERE'S ONE BORN EVERY MINUTE(1942)
Misc. Silents
FIGHTING PEACEMAKER, THE(1926)
Thelma Oliver
PAWNBROKER, THE(1965)
Tom Oliver
NICKEL QUEEN, THE(1971, Aus.); NO. 96(1974, Aus.)
Tony Oliver
IT HAPPENED HERE(1966, Brit.)
1984
ALLEY CAT(1984)
Tristan Oliver
1984
ANOTHER COUNTRY(1984, Brit.)
Vic Oliver
RHYTHM IN THE AIR(1936, Brit.); WHO'S YOUR LADY FRIEND?(1937, Brit.); AROUND THE TOWN(1938, Brit.); MEET MR. PENNY(1938, Brit.); ROOM FOR TWO(1940, Brit.); HE FOUND A STAR(1941, Brit.); HI, GANG!(1941, Brit.); GIVE US THE MOON(1944, Brit.); I'LL BE YOUR SWEETHEART(1945, Brit.)
William Elwell Oliver
Silents
FIGHTING AMERICAN, THE(1924), w
Gerald Oliver-Smith
LADY ESCAPES, THE(1937); PRIDE AND PREJUDICE(1940)
Don Olivera
FORBIDDEN WORLD(1982), spec eff
Hector Olivera
NO EXIT(1962, U.S./Arg.), p

1984
DEATHSTALKER, THE(1984), p
Mimi Olivera
MARIE ANTOINETTE(1938)
Frank Oliveras
PISTOL FOR RINGO, A(1966, Ital./Span.); SUNSCORCHED(1966, Span./Ger.); SEA
PIRATE, THE(1967, Fr./Span./Ital.); DAY THE HOTLINE GOT HOT, THE(1968,
Fr./Span.)
Joaquin Oliveras
SANDOKAN THE GREAT(1964, Fr./Ital./Span.)
Mariella Oliveri
TIN DRUM, THE(1979, Ger./Fr./Yugo./Pol.)
Richard Oliveri
1984
NATURAL, THE(1984)
Nubia Olivero
BADGE 373(1973)
Ramiro Oliveros
1984
YELLOW HAIR AND THE FORTRESS OF GOLD(1984)
Romiro Oliveros
1984
HUNDRA(1984, Ital.)
Marcello Oliveto
SWEET SKIN(1965, Fr./Ital.)
Olivette
KISS ME, SERGEANT(1930, Brit.); NOT SO QUIET ON THE WESTERN
FRONT(1930, Brit.); WHY SAILORS LEAVE HOME(1930, Brit.); WHAT A
NIGHT!(1931, Brit.); BOYS WILL BE GIRLS(1937, Brit.)
Nina Olivette
QUEEN HIGH(1930)
Marie-Claire Olivia
RED, INN, THE(1954, Fr.)
Anthony Olivier
FLASH GORDON(1980)
Claire Olivier
MR. ORCHID(1948, Fr.); LE PLAISIR(1954, Fr.)
Claude Olivier
DEAR DETECTIVE(1978, Fr.), w
Eric Olivier
SWEET AND SOUR(1964, Fr./Ital.), w; EGLANTINE(1972, Fr.), w
Harry Olivier
SCARFACE(1932), prod d
Laurence Olivier
TEMPORARY WIDOW, THE(1930, Ger./Brit.); FRIENDS AND LOVERS(1931); HER
STRANGE DESIRE(1931, Brit.); YELLOW TICKET, THE(1931); WESTWARD PAS-
SAGE(1932); PERFECT UNDERSTANDING(1933, Brit.); NO FUNNY BUSINESS(1934,
Brit.); AS YOU LIKE IT(1936, Brit.); I STAND CONDEMNED(1936, Brit.); FIRE OVER
ENGLAND(1937, Brit.); DIVORCE OF LADY X. THE(1938, Brit.); CLOUDS OVER
EUROPE(1939, Brit.); WUTHERING HEIGHTS(1939); CONQUEST OF THE AIR(1940);
PRIDE AND PREJUDICE(1940); REBECCA(1940); TWENTY-ONE DAYS TOGE-
THER(1940, Brit.); INVADERS, THE,(1941); THAT HAMILTON WOMAN(1941); THIS
HAPPY BREED(1944, Brit.); ADVENTURE FOR TWO(1945, Brit.); HENRY V(1946,
Brit.), a, p, d, w; HAMLET(1948, Brit.), a, p&d; CARRIE(1952); MAGIC BOX,
THE(1952, Brit.); BEGGAR'S OPERA, THE(1953), a, p; RICHARD III(1956, Brit.), a, p,
d, w; PRINCE AND THE SHOWGIRL, THE(1957, Brit.), a, p&d; DEVIL'S DISCIPLE,
THE(1959); ENTERTAINER, THE(1960, Brit.); SPARTACUS(1960); TERM OF
TRIAL(1962, Brit.); BUNNY LAKE IS MISSING(1965); OTHELLO(1965, Brit.); KHAR-
TOUM(1966, Brit.); ROMEO AND JULIET(1968, Brit./Ital.); SHOES OF THE FISHER-
MAN, THE(1968); BATTLE OF BRITAIN, THE(1969, Brit.); OH! WHAT A LOVELY
WAR(1969, Brit.); NICHOLAS AND ALEXANDRA(1971, Brit.); DAVID COPPER-
FIELD(1970, Brit.); DANCE OF DEATH, THE(1971, Brit.); LADY CAROLINE
LAMB(1972, Brit./Ital.); SLEUTH(1972, Brit.); THREE SISTERS(1974, Brit.), a, d;
MARATHON MAN(1976); BRIDGE TOO FAR, A(1977, Brit.); SEVEN-PER-CENT
SOLUTION, THE(1977, Brit.); UNCLE VANYA(1977, Brit.), a, d; BETSY, THE(1978);
BOYS FROM BRAZIL, THE(1978); DRACULA(1979); LITTLE ROMANCE, A(1979,
U.S./Fr.); JAZZ SINGER, THE(1980); CLASH OF THE TITANS(1981); INCHON(1981);
WAGNER(1983, Brit./Hung./Aust.)
1984
JIGSAW MAN, THE(1984, Brit.)
Sir Laurence Olivier
1984
BOUNTY, THE(1984)
Paul Olivier
UNDER THE ROOFS OF PARIS(1930, Fr.); A NOUS LA LIBERTE(1931, Fr.);
MILLION, THE(1931, Fr.); LE DENIER MILLIARDAIRE(1934, Fr.); MAN ABOUT
TOWN(1947, Fr.)
Silents
ITALIAN STRAW HAT, AN(1927, Fr.)
Tarquin Olivier
EAGLE SQUADRON(1942); TWO TICKETS TO LONDON(1943)
Louis Oliviera
WILD PACK, THE(1972), m
Amilcare Olivieri
WANDERING JEW, THE(1948, Ital.)
Dennis Olivieri
OUTSIDE IN(1972); BREEZY(1973); NAKED APE, THE(1973); PHANTOM OF THE
PARADISE(1974)
Egisto Olivieri
WANDERING JEW, THE(1948, Ital.); CARMELA(1949, Ital.); OUTCRY(1949, Ital.)
Enrico Olivieri
WOMAN OF THE RIVER(1954, Fr./Ital.); WAR AND PEACE(1956, Ital./U.S.);
BLACK SUNDAY(1961, Ital.)
Giustino Olivieri
ROMAN HOLIDAY(1953)
Carmelo Oliviero
MAFIOSO(1962, Ital.); WE STILL KILL THE OLD WAY(1967, Ital.)

Nino Oliviero
RUN FOR YOUR WIFE(1966, Fr./Ital.), m; MATTER OF TIME, A(1976, Ital./U.S.), m
Janie Olivor
SATURDAY NIGHT AT THE BATHS(1975)
Walter Olkewicz
1941(1979); JIMMY THE KID(1982)
1984
HEARTBREAKERS(1984); MAKING THE GRADE(1984)
Misc. Talkies
CIRCLE OF POWER(1984)
Judy Ollerneshaw
WHISTLE DOWN THE WIND(1961, Brit.)
Norman Ollestad
WHIPLASH(1948); KISS IN THE DARK, A(1949); CHEAPER BY THE DOZEN(1950)
Richard Olley
CARRY ON ENGLAND(1976, Brit.)
May Ollis
QUACKSER FORTUNE HAS A COUSIN IN THE BRONX(1970)
Alain Ollivier
LOVE ON THE RUN(1980, Fr.)
Norman Ollstead
HI, BUDDY(1943); VALLEY OF DECISION, THE(1945)
Marty Ollstein
PENITENTIARY(1979), ph
Olly Alston and His Band
TAKE OFF THAT HAT(1938, Brit.)
Maud Olmar
Misc. Silents
FEMALE SWINDLER, THE(1916, Brit.); GIRL WHO WRECKED HIS HOME,
THE(1916, Brit.)
Vit Olmer
MAN FROM THE FIRST CENTURY, THE(1961, Czech.); DEVIL'S TRAP, THE(1964,
Czech.); BRIDGE AT REMAGEN, THE(1969); MATTER OF DAYS, A(1969, Fr./Czech.)
Janne Olmes
FLAMING SIGNAL(1933)
Boy Olmi
DEATHSTALKER(1983, Arg./U.S.)
1984
DEATHSTALKER, THE(1984)
Corrado Olmi
EASY LIFE, THE(1963, Ital.); WAKE UP AND DIE(1967, Fr./Ital.); CAT O'NINE
TAILS(1971, Ital./Ger./Fr.)
Ermanno Olmi
SOUND OF TRUMPETS, THE(1963, Ital.), d&w; FIANCES, THE(1964, Ital.), d&w;
AND THERE CAME A MAN(1968, Ital.), d, w; TREE OF WOODEN CLOGS, THE(1979,
Ital.), d,w&ph, ed
Edward J. Olmos
VIRUS(1980, Jap.)
Edward James Olmos
WOLFEN(1981); ZOOT SUIT(1981); BLADE RUNNER(1982); BALLAD OF GRE-
GORIO CORTEZ, THE(1983), a, m
Edward Olmos
ALAMBRISTA!(1977)
Mico Olmos
TESTAMENT(1983)
Edward Olmstead
CRIME OF DR. CRESPI, THE(1936), w
Edwin Olmstead
WOMAN IN DISTRESS(1937), w
Gertrude Olmstead
LONE WOLF'S DAUGHTER, THE(1929); SONNY BOY(1929); TIME, THE PLACE
AND THE GIRL, THE(1929)
Misc. Talkies
HIT OF THE SNOW(1928)
Silents
SHADOWS OF CONSCIENCE(1921); LOADED DOOR, THE(1922); SCRAPPER,
THE(1922); BABBITT(1924); EMPTY HANDS(1924); LADIES TO BOARD(1924); LOV-
ER'S LANE(1924); COBRA(1925); PUPPETS(1926); SWEET ADELINE(1926); MR.
WU(1927); HEY RUBE!(1928); MIDNIGHT LIFE(1928); SPORTING GOODS(1928);
SWEET SIXTEEN(1928)
Misc. Silents
GEORGE(; CAMEO KIRBY(1923); MONTE CARLO(1926); BECKY(1927); BUT-
TONS(1927); CHEERFUL FRAUD, THE(1927); CHEER LEADER, THE(1928); GREEN
GRASS WIDOWS(1928)
Harry F. Olmstead
GUN LORDS OF STIRRUP BASIN(1937), w; LAWMAN IS BORN, A(1937), w;
OUTLAWS OF THE PRAIRIE(1938), w; STAGECOACH WAR(1940), w
Nelson Olmstead
DIARY OF A MADMAN(1963); BUTCH CASSIDY AND THE SUNDANCE KID(1969)
Remington Olmstead
BEN HUR(1959)
Shirley Olmstead
STARFIGHTERS, THE(1964)
Gertrude Olmsted
Silents
MONSTER, THE(1925); TORRENT, THE(1926); CALLAHANS AND THE MURPHYS,
THE(1927)
Misc. Silents
FIGHTING LOVER, THE(1921); FOX, THE(1921); CALIFORNIA STRAIGHT
AHEAD(1925); TIME, THE COMEDIAN(1925); BOOB, THE(1926); PASSION SONG,
THE(1928)
Harry F. Olmsted
ARIZONA GUNFIGHTER(1937), w; COLORADO KID(1938), w; DURANGO VAL-
LEY RAIDERS(1938), w; FEUD MAKER(1938), w; PAROLED–TO DIE(1938), w
Harry W. Olmsted
BOOTHILL BRIGADE(1937), w
Nelson Olmsted
MIDDLE OF THE NIGHT(1959); THAT TOUCH OF MINK(1962); DEAR
HEART(1964); QUICK, BEFORE IT MELTS(1964); FITZWILLY(1967)

Stanley Olmsted
Silents
MAN AND HIS WOMAN(1920), w

Nicolai Olonovski
THREE TALES OF CHEKHOV(1961, USSR), ph

Mercedes Olonso
HOUSE THAT SCREAMED, THE(1970, Span.), ed

Enrico Olorio
INDISCRETION OF AN AMERICAN WIFE(1954, U.S./Ital.)

April Olrich
BLONDE BAIT(1956, U.S./Brit.); PURSUIT OF THE GRAF SPEE(1957, Brit.); KILL ME TOMORROW(1958, Brit.); DEADLY RECORD(1959, Brit.); ROOM AT THE TOP(1959, Brit.); IT'S ALL OVER TOWN(1963, Brit.); MACBETH(1963); SKULL, THE(1965, Brit.); SPYLARKS(1965, Brit.)

Carl Olsen
LOVE MERCHANT, THE(1966)

Chic Olsen
Silents
CODE OF THE RANGE(1927)

Chris Olsen
CRASHOUT(1955); NAKED HILLS, THE(1956); TALL T, THE(1957); TARNISHED ANGELS, THE(1957); RETURN TO WARBOW(1958)

Christie Olsen
MARRYING KIND, THE(1952)

Christopher Olsen
MY PAL GUS(1952); LONG, LONG TRAILER, THE(1954); BIGGER THAN LIFE(1956); FASTEST GUN ALIVE(1956); MAN WHO KNEW TOO MUCH, THE(1956)

Christopher Robin Olsen
IRON CURTAIN, THE(1948)

Dana Olsen
GOING BERSERK(1983), w; WACKO(1983), w
1984
MAKING THE GRADE(1984)

Dennis Olsen
BREAK OF DAY(1977, Aus.)

Don Olsen
GIRL ON A CHAIN GANG(1966), w

Edwin E. Olsen
EAST OF KILIMANJARO(1962, Brit./Ital.), ph

Einar Olsen
WHILE THE ATTORNEY IS ASLEEP(1945, Den.), ph

Flemming Olsen
DOUBLE STOP(1968), ph; JESUS TRIP, THE(1971), ph; WHO FEARS THE DEVIL(1972), ph

Gary Olsen
BREAKING GLASS(1980, Brit.); OUTLAND(1981); PINK FLOYD–THE WALL(1982, Brit.); PARTY PARTY(1983, Brit.)
1984
LOOSE CONNECTIONS(1984, Brit.); WINTER FLIGHT(1984, Brit.)

Harriett Olsen
OLD ACQUAINTANCE(1943)

Harriette Olsen
THANK YOUR LUCKY STARS(1943)

Ivy Olsen
LET'S TALK ABOUT WOMEN(1964, Fr./Ital.)

Joanne Olsen
PUBERTY BLUES(1983, Aus.)

Johnny Olsen
SIN OF MONA KENT, THE(1961)

Larry Joe Olsen
ADDRESS UNKNOWN(1944); CASANOVA BROWN(1944); SERGEANT MIKE(1945)

Larry Olsen
HAPPY LAND(1943); MY PAL, WOLF(1944); DIVORCE(1945); ISN'T IT ROMANTIC?(1948); SITTING PRETTY(1948); WHO KILLED "DOC" ROBBIN?(1948); WINCHESTER '73(1950); ROOM FOR ONE MORE(1952); STORY OF THREE LOVES, THE(1953)

Merlin Olsen
UNDEFEATED, THE(1969); ONE MORE TRAIN TO ROB(1971); SOMETHING BIG(1971); MITCHELL(1975)

Merritt Olsen
CUJO(1983)

Milt Olsen
PAY OR DIE(1960), spec eff; RAYMIE(1960), spec eff; GEORGE RAFT STORY, THE(1961), spec eff; KING OF THE ROARING TWENTIES–THE STORY OF ARNOLD ROTHSTEIN(1961), spec eff; TWENTY PLUS TWO(1961), spec eff; CONFESSIONS OF AN OPIUM EATER(1962), spec eff; CONVICTS FOUR(1962), spec eff

Milton Olsen
TWICE TOLD TALES(1963), spec eff

Moroni Olsen
ANNIE OAKLEY(1935); SEVEN KEYS TO BALDPATE(1935); THREE MUSKETEERS, THE(1935); FARMER IN THE DELL, THE(1936); GRAND JURY(1936); MARY OF SCOTLAND(1936); M'LISS(1936); MUMMY'S BOYS(1936); PLOUGH AND THE STARS, THE(1936); TWO IN REVOLT(1936); WITNESS CHAIR, THE(1936); YELLOW DUST(1936); ADVENTURE'S END(1937); LIFE OF EMILE ZOLA, THE(1937); MANHATTAN MERRY-GO-ROUND(1937); SNOW WHITE AND THE SEVEN DWARFS(1937); GOLD IS WHERE YOU FIND IT(1938); KENTUCKY(1938); KIDNAPPED(1938); MARIE ANTOINETTE(1938); SUBMARINE PATROL(1938); ALLEGHENY UPRISING(1939); BARRICADE(1939); CODE OF THE SECRET SERVICE(1939); DUST BE MY DESTINY(1939); HOMICIDE BUREAU(1939); ROSE OF WASHINGTON SQUARE(1939); SUSANNAH OF THE MOUNTIES(1939); THAT'S RIGHT–YOU'RE WRONG(1939); THREE MUSKETEERS, THE(1939); BRIGHAM YOUNG–FRONTIERSMAN(1940); BROTHER RAT AND A BABY(1940); EAST OF THE RIVER(1940); IF I HAD MY WAY(1940); INVISIBLE STRIPES(1940); SANTA FE TRAIL(1940); VIRGINIA CITY(1940); DIVE BOMBER(1941); LIFE WITH HENRY(1941); ONE FOOT IN HEAVEN(1941); THREE SONS O'GUNS(1941); DANGEROUSLY THEY LIVE(1942); GLASS KEY, THE(1942); MRS. WIGGS OF THE CABBAGE PATCH(1942); MY FAVORITE SPY(1942); NAZI AGENT(1942); REUNION IN FRANCE(1942); SHIP AHOY(1942); AIR FORCE(1943); MADAME CURIE(1943); MISSION TO MOSCOW(1943); SONG OF BERNADETTE, THE(1943); WE'VE NEVER BEEN LICKED(1943); ALI BABA AND THE FORTY THIEVES(1944); BUFFALO

BILL(1944); COBRA WOMAN(1944); ROGER TOUHY, GANGSTER!(1944); THIRTY SECONDS OVER TOKYO(1944); BEHIND CITY LIGHTS(1945); DON'T FENCE ME IN(1945); PRIDE OF THE MARINES(1945); WEEKEND AT THE WALDORF(1945); BOYS' RANCH(1946); FROM THIS DAY FORWARD(1946); NIGHT IN PARADISE, A(1946); NOTORIOUS(1946); WALLS CAME TUMBLING DOWN, THE(1946); BLACK GOLD(1947); HIGH WALL, THE(1947); LIFE WITH FATHER(1947); LONG NIGHT, THE(1947); POSSESSED(1947); THAT HAGEN GIRL(1947); CALL NORTHSIDE 777(1948); COMMAND DECISION(1948); UP IN CENTRAL PARK(1948); FOUNTAINHEAD, THE(1949); SAMSON AND DELILAH(1949); TASK FORCE(1949); FATHER OF THE BRIDE(1950); AT SWORD'S POINT(1951); FATHER'S LITTLE DIVIDEND(1951); NO QUESTIONS ASKED(1951); PAYMENT ON DEMAND(1951); SUBMARINE COMMAND(1951); LONE STAR(1952); WASHINGTON STORY(1952); MARRY ME AGAIN(1953); SO THIS IS LOVE(1953); LONG, LONG TRAILER, THE(1954); SIGN OF THE PAGAN(1954)

Nancy Olsen
SMITH(1969)

Olaf Olsen
SIXTY GLORIOUS YEARS(1938, Brit.); THREE COCKEYED SAILORS(1940, Brit.); LILLI MARLENE(1951, Brit.); MAN IN THE WHITE SUIT, THE(1952); TREAD SOFTLY(1952, Brit.)

Ole Olsen
OH! SAILOR, BEHAVE!(1930); GOLD DUST GERTIE(1931); ALL OVER TOWN(1937); COUNTRY GENTLEMEN(1937); HELLZAPOPPIN'(1941); CRAZY HOUSE(1943); GHOST CATCHERS(1944); SEE MY LAWYER(1945)

Olive Olsen
SOCIAL REGISTER(1934)

Pauline Olsen
JOHNNY ON THE SPOT(1954, Brit.); STAR OF MY NIGHT(1954, Brit.)

Phil Olsen
ONE MORE TRAIN TO ROB(1971)

Ray Olsen
Silents
WINGS(1927), ph

Rolf Olsen
QUEEN OF THE PIRATES(1961, Ital./Ger.), w; 5 SINNERS(1961, Ger.); TURKISH CUCUMBER, THE(1963, Ger.), d, w; $100 A NIGHT(1968, Ger.); DOCTOR OF ST. PAUL, THE(1969, Ger.), d&w; PRIEST OF ST. PAULI, THE(1970, Ger.), d&w
Misc. Talkies
NURSES FOR SALE(1977), d

Steve Olsen
WITHIN THESE WALLS(1945); DARK CORNER, THE(1946); DRAGONWYCH(1946); HIGH BARBAREE(1947); I WONDER WHO'S KISSING HER NOW(1947); SMASH-UP, THE STORY OF A WOMAN(1947)

Theodore V. Olsen
STALKING MOON, THE(1969), w; SOLDIER BLUE(1970), w

Tillie Olsen
TELL ME A RIDDLE(1980), w

Tracy Olsen
TERRIFIED!(1963); JOHNNY RENO(1966); WACO(1966); JOURNEY TO THE CENTER OF TIME(1967); RED TOMAHAWK(1967)

William Olsen
Misc. Talkies
GETTING IT ON(1983), d

Olsen & Johnson
FIFTY MILLION FRENCHMEN(1931)

Olsen's Sea Lions
VARIETY(1935, Brit.); SHOW GOES ON, THE(1937, Brit.)

John Olscewski
SON OF FLUBBER(1963)

Alexander Olshanetsky
CANTOR'S SON, THE(1937), m; OVERTURE TO GLORY(1940), m

Iosif Olshanskiy
DAY THE WAR ENDED, THE(1961, USSR), w

Yury Olshansky
1984
MOSCOW ON THE HUDSON(1984)

Laura Olsher
MR. MAGOO'S HOLIDAY FESTIVAL(1970)

Ilya Olshvanger
THEY CALL ME ROBERT(1967, USSR), d

Brad Olson
SPRING AFFAIR(1960)

Carla Olson
MAGIC SPECTACLES(1961)

Carlene Olson
FRATERNITY ROW(1977); FRIGHTMARE(1983)

Carrie Olson
Misc. Talkies
CHERRY HILL HIGH(1977)

Christie Olson
ABOVE AND BEYOND(1953)

Christy Olson
I'LL SEE YOU IN MY DREAMS(1951)

Donald Olson
TRAIL STREET(1947)

Ellen Olson
Silents
AMATEUR WIFE, THE(1920)

Eric Olson
MIXED COMPANY(1974); VIVA KNIEVEL!(1977)

Gary Olson
BLOODY KIDS(1983, Brit.)

Gerald Olson
MOONSHINE COUNTY EXPRESS(1977), art d

Gunnar Olson
WILD STRAWBERRIES(1959, Swed.)

Ivan Olson
FAST COMPANY(1929)

Jack Olson
TIME WALKER(1982)
James Olson
SHARKFIGHTERS, THE(1956); STRANGE ONE, THE(1957); RACHEL, RACHEL(1968); MOON ZERO TWO(1970, Brit.); ANDROMEDA STRAIN, THE(1971); WILD ROVERS(1971); CRESCENDO(1972, Brit.); GROUNDSTAR CONSPIRACY, THE(1972, Can.); THREE SISTERS, THE(1977); MAFU CAGE, THE(1978); RAGTIME(1981); AMITYVILLE II: THE POSSESSION(1982)
Misc. Talkies
MANHUNT IN SPACE(1954)
James P. Olson
BAR Z BAD MEN(1937), w
John Olson
GIRL IN A MILLION, A(1946, Brit.); SMUGGLERS, THE(1948, Brit.)
Ken Olson
JAWS 3-D(1983)
Larry Olson
LONE TEXAS RANGER(1945)
Larry Joe Olson
CHANCE OF A LIFETIME, THE(1943)
Mary Olson
IT AIN'T EASY(1972), w
Milton Olson
LAST MILE, THE(1959), spec eff
Moroni Olson
WE'RE ONLY HUMAN(1936); LAST GANGSTER, THE(1937); SUNDOWN JIM(1942); MILDRED PIERCE(1945); STRANGE WOMAN, THE(1946)
Nancy Olson
CANADIAN PACIFIC(1949); MR. MUSIC(1950); SUNSET BOULEVARD(1950); UNION STATION(1950); FORCE OF ARMS(1951); SUBMARINE COMMAND(1951); BIG JIM McLAIN(1952); SO BIG(1953); BOY FROM OKLAHOMA, THE(1954); BATTLE FLAME(1955); POLLYANNA(1960); ABSENT-MINDED PROFESSOR, THE(1961); SON OF FLUBBER(1963); SNOWBALL EXPRESS(1972); AIRPORT 1975(1974); MAKING LOVE(1982)
Ole Olson
FIGHTING MAD(1939)
Olive Olson
DANCE, CHARLIE, DANCE(1937)
Pat Olson
ISLAND OF LOVE(1963)
Patricia Olson
NEW KIND OF LOVE, A(1963)
Reid Olson
MODERN PROBLEMS(1981)
Ronald B. Olson
SASQUATCH(1978), w
Rosella Olson
GUESS WHAT WE LEARNED IN SCHOOL TODAY?(1970)
Steve Olson
STATE FAIR(1945)
Stu Olson
RUBY(1977)
Terry Olson
LAST MOMENT, THE(1966)
Tracy Olson
Misc. Talkies
LAST MOMENT, THE(1976)
Frederik Olsson
PIPPI IN THE SOUTH SEAS(1974, Swed./Ger.)
Gunnar Olsson
ILLICIT INTERLUDE(1954, Swed.); SEVENTH SEAL, THE(1958, Swed.)
Marrit Olsson
FANNY AND ALEXANDER(1983, Swed./Fr./Ger.)
L. Olszewska
PASSENGER, THE(1970, Pol.)
John Olszewski
JUPITER'S DARLING(1955)
Mike Olton
SHAMPOO(1975)
Elsie Olusola
COUNTDOWN AT KUSINI(1976, Nigerian)
Alberto Olvera
1984
UNDER THE VOLCANO(1984)
Oswald Olvera
TARZAN AND THE VALLEY OF GOLD(1966 U.S./Switz.)
William Olvis
DEEP IN MY HEART(1954)
Dagmar Olwson
DOLL, THE(1964, Swed.)
The Olympic Trio
VOGUES OF 1938(1937)
Kin Omae
EAST CHINA SEA(1969, Jap.); LATITUDE ZERO(1969, U.S./Jap.)
Misc. Talkies
SILENT STRANGER, THE(1975)
Wataru Omae
YOG-MONSTER FROM SPACE(1970, Jap.)
Rico Omagap
BLOOD DRINKERS, THE(1966, U.S./Phil.), w
Maria Rosaria Omaggio
CITY OF THE WALKING DEAD(1983, Span./Ital.)
Rosemary Omaggio
Misc. Talkies
BRUTAL JUSTICE(1978)
Omar of Omaha
DID YOU HEAR THE ONE ABOUT THE TRAVELING SALESLADY?(1968), cos

Julia Trevelyan Oman
JULIUS CAESAR(1970, Brit.), prod d
Paul Oman
LADY IS WILLING, THE(1942); FRENCHMAN'S CREEK(1944); SUDDENLY IT'S SPRING(1947)
Phil Oman
DICK TRACY VS. CUEBALL(1946), m
Sam Omani
1984
SAHARA(1984)
Omar
Silents
DIAMONDS ADRIFT(1921)
Kanza Omar
TO HAVE AND HAVE NOT(1944); EASY TO WED(1946); SAIGON(1948)
Sigrunn Omark
STILL OF THE NIGHT(1982)
Mitsuyo Omata
LAKE, THE(1970, Jap.)
Gennaro Ombra
AMARCORD(1974, Ital.)
Mara Ombra
PASSIONATE THIEF, THE(1963, Ital.)
Gail Omeasoo
RUNNING BRAVE(1983, Can.)
Patrick Omeirs
MOVIE MOVIE(1978)
Judd Omen
SEEMS LIKE OLD TIMES(1980)
1984
DUNE(1984); RED DAWN(1984)
Estelle Omens
JOE(1970); EFFECT OF GAMMA RAYS ON MAN-IN-THE-MOON MARIGOLDS, THE(1972); DOG DAY AFTERNOON(1975); LOVING COUPLES(1980); STIR CRAZY(1980); DEAD AND BURIED(1981); LOOKER(1981); MR. MOM(1983)
1984
UNFAITHFULLY YOURS(1984)
Woody Omens
HISTORY OF THE WORLD, PART 1(1981), ph
Teruko Omi
THREE STRIPES IN THE SUN(1955); SANSHO THE BAILIFF(1969, Jap.)
A. Omiadze
DRAGONFLY, THE(1955 USSR)
Afemo Omilami
TRADING PLACES(1983)
Yukietsu Omiya
WAR OF THE MONSTERS(1972, Jap.)
Gail Ommerle
GOODBYE COLUMBUS(1969)
Genevieve Omni
1984
AMERICAN DREAMER(1984)
Mutia Omoolu
TRADER HORN(1931)
Seitaro Omori
HOUSE OF STRANGE LOVES, THE(1969, Jap.), m; FALCON FIGHTERS, THE(1970, Jap.), m; GATEWAY TO GLORY(1970, Jap.), m
Hiroyasu Omoto
LAST UNICORN, THE(1982), ph
Nira Omri
SHE BEAST, THE(1966, Brit./Ital./Yugo.), ed
Alba Oms
FAME(1980); WHOSE LIFE IS IT ANYWAY?(1981)
Nikolai Omtrosky
HEROES ARE MADE(1944, USSR), w, p,d&w
Fumitake Omura
MAN IN THE MOONLIGHT MASK, THE(1958, Jap.)
Kon Omura
WE WILL REMEMBER(1966, Jap.); GAMERA VERSUS GUIRON(1969, Jap.); GAMERA VERSUS MONSTER K(1970, Jap.)
Senkichi Omura
SEVEN SAMURAI, THE(1956, Jap.); KING KONG VERSUS GODZILLA(1963, Jap.)
Wataru Omura
DESTROY ALL MONSTERS(1969, Jap.)
Seitaro Omuri
PERFORMERS, THE(1970, Jap.), m
Ley On
THE BEACHCOMBER(1938, Brit.); INVADERS, THE,(1941); BLACK NARCISSUS(1947, Brit.)
Casey Onaitis
1001 ARABIAN NIGHTS(1959), anim; MR. MAGOO'S HOLIDAY FESTIVAL(1970), anim
Frank Onaitis
SHINBONE ALLEY(1971), anim
Hideo Onchi
ONCE A RAINY DAY(1968, Jap.), d
Kachain Onching
HOT POTATO(1976)
Ondine
RAW WEEKEND(1964); CHELSEA GIRLS, THE(1967); SILENT NIGHT, BLOODY NIGHT(1974)
Misc. Talkies
TELEPHONE BOOK, THE(1971); SUGAR COOKIES(1973)
Anny Ondra
BLACKMAIL(1929, Brit.)
Silents
MANXMAN, THE(1929, Brit.)
Misc. Silents
GLORIOUS YOUTH(1928, Brit.); GOD'S CLAY(1928, Brit.)

Miroslav Ondricek
  LOVES OF A BLONDE(1966, Czech.), ph; FIREMAN'S BALL, THE(1968, Czech.), ph;
  IF ...(1968, Brit.), ph; MARTYRS OF LOVE(1968, Czech.), ph; DIANE'S BODY(1969,
  Fr./Czech.), ph; INTIMATE LIGHTING(1969, Czech.), ph; TAKING OFF(1971), ph;
  SLAUGHTERHOUSE-FIVE(1972), ph; O LUCKY MAN!(1973, Brit.), ph; BLACK SUN,
  THE(1979, Czech.), ph; HAIR(1979), ph; RAGTIME(1981), ph; WORLD ACCORDING
  TO GARP, The(1982), ph; DIVINE EMMA, THE(1983, Czech,), ph; SILKWOOD(1983),
  ph
  1984
  AMADEUS(1984), ph
Zuzana Ondrouchova
  GIRL WITH THREE CAMELS, THE(1968, Czech.)
Pierre Ondry
  TOUT VA BIEN(1973, Fr.)
Mik One
  1984
  NIGHT PATROL(1984)
Lloyd One Star
  MAN CALLED HORSE, A(1970)
Ellen Oneal
  SKATEBOARD(1978)
Henry ONeill
  AMAZING DR. CLITTERHOUSE, THE(1938)
David Onell
  SPRING BREAK(1983)
Ricardo Oneto
  LA TRAVIATA(1982)
Dawn Oney
  FRENCH LINE, THE(1954); SON OF SINBAD(1955)
Dana Ong
  Silents
  LOVE AFLAME(1917)
  Misc. Silents
  FLASH OF FATE, THE(1918)
Max Ong
  THEY WERE EXPENDABLE(1945)
Betty Onge
  I DON'T CARE GIRL, THE(1952); LAS VEGAS STORY, THE(1952); ROAD TO
  BALI(1952); SON OF SINBAD(1955)
Julius Ongewe
  FIRST SPACESHIP ON VENUS(1960, Ger./Pol.)
Byron Ongley
  BREWSTER'S MILLIONS(1935, Brit.), w; BREWSTER'S MILLIONS(1945), w;
  THREE ON A SPREE(1961, Brit.), w
  Silents
  BREWSTER'S MILLIONS(1914), w; BREWSTER'S MILLIONS(1921), w; MISS
  BREWSTER'S MILLIONS(1926), w
Leo Ongley
  Silents
  TEMPTRESS, THE(1926), w
Michael Onida
  DRIFTER, THE(1966)
Rashidi Onikoyi
  KONGI'S HARVEST(1971, U.S./Nigeria)
Oliver Onions
  1984
  AFTER THE FALL OF NEW YORK(1984, Ital./Fr.), m
S.D. Onions
  CURSE OF THE WRAYDONS, THE(1946, Brit.), ph; BLACK MEMORY(1947, Brit.),
  ph; MYSTERIOUS MR. NICHOLSON, THE(1947, Brit.), ph; GREED OF WILLIAM
  HART, THE(1948, Brit.), ph; BLESS 'EM ALL(1949, Brit.), ph; MATTER OF MURDER,
  A(1949, Brit.), ph; TEMPTRESS, THE(1949, Brit.), ph; SIX MEN, THE(1951, Brit.), ph;
  KING OF THE UNDERWORLD(1952, Brit.), ph; MURDER AT 3 A.M.(1953, Brit.), ph;
  SKID KIDS(1953, Brit.), ph; DON GIOVANNI(1955, Brit.), ph; TIM DRISCOLL'S
  DONKEY(1955, Brit.), ph; STARS IN YOUR EYES(1956, Brit.), ph; DEVIL'S PASS,
  THE(1957, Brit.), ph; SENTENCED FOR LIFE(1960, Brit.), ph; NIGHT WE GOT THE
  BIRD, THE(1961, Brit.), ph; SWEET BEAT(1962, Brit.), ph; ROMEO AND JU-
  LIET(1966, Brit.), ph
Gerald Onn
  AFRICAN QUEEN, THE(1951, U.S./Brit.)
Kuroemon Ono
  SAMURAI(PART II)** (1967, Jap.)
Miyuki Ono
  TIME SLIP(1981, Jap.)
Rosemary Ono
  1984
  NINJA III—THE DOMINATION(1984)
Yasuko Ono
  LAKE, THE(1970, Jap.), w
Yoko Ono
  SATAN'S BED(1965)
Sho Onoda
  KARATE, THE HAND OF DEATH(1961)
K. Onoe
  ANATAHAN(1953, Jap.)
Kikunosuke Onoe
  KOJIRO(1967, Jap.)
Kuroemon Onoe
  SAMURAI(1955, Jap.)
Waldyr Onofre
  1984
  MEMOIRS OF PRISON(1984, Braz.)
Fabrizio Onofri
  GALILEO(1968, Ital./Bul.), w; SACCO AND VANZETTI(1971, Ital./Fr.), w; DEVIL IS
  A WOMAN, THE(1975, Brit./Ital.), w
Kozaburo Onogawa
  WAY OUT, WAY IN(1970, Jap.)

Glauco Onorato
  BLACK SABBATH(1963, Ital.); RED SHEIK, THE(1963, Ital.); SUNFLOWER(1970,
  Fr./Ital.); LA CAGE AUX FOLLES II(1981, Ital./Fr.)
Paul Onorato
  SIDECAR RACERS(1975, Aus.), ph; TIM(1981, Aus.), ph; ON THE RUN(1983, Aus.),
  ph
Virginia Onorato
  MARCO THE MAGNIFICENT(1966, Ital./Fr./Yugo./Egypt/Afghanistan)
Alex Onslow
  Misc. Silents
  FOOTLIGHTS AND SHADOWS(1920)
Kyle Onstott
  MANDINGO(1975), w; DRUM(1976), w
Santiago Ontanon
  INVINCIBLE GLADIATOR, THE(1963, c.u. Ital./Span.), art d; PLACE CALLED
  GLORY, A(1966, Span./Ger.); HOUSE OF 1,000 DOLLS(1967, Ger./Span./Brit.), art d;
  EVE(1968, Brit./Span.), art d; RUN LIKE A THIEF(1968, Span.), art d; LAST DAY OF
  THE WAR, THE(1969, U.S./Ital./Span.), set d
Ontanoni
  EL GRECO(1966, Ital., Fr.)
Bill Ontiveros
  1984
  PRODIGAL, THE(1984)
Lupe Ontiveros
  WORLD'S GREATEST LOVER, THE(1977); BIG FIX, THE(1978); CALIFORNIA
  SUITE(1978); ZOOT SUIT(1981)
  1984
  EL NORTE(1984)
Michael Ontkean
  PEACE KILLERS, THE(1971); NECROMANCY(1972); PICKUP ON 101(1972); HOT
  SUMMER WEEK(1973, Can.); SLAP SHOT(1977); VOICES(1979); WILLIE AND
  PHIL(1980); MAKING LOVE(1982)
  1984
  JUST THE WAY YOU ARE(1984)
Marda Onyx
  GABY(1956)
Narda Onyx
  HITLER(1962); JESSE JAMES MEETS FRANKENSTEIN'S DAUGHTER(1966)
Onyx Club Band
  MUSIC GOES ROUND, THE(1936)
Shoji Ooki
  WESTWARD DESPERADO(1961, Jap.)
Madeleine Oolie
  RUN, ANGEL, RUN(1969), prod d
Dity Oorthuis
  SPY IN THE SKY(1958)
Peter Oosthoek
  SPETTERS(1983, Holland)
Mitsuru Ooya
  HOTSPRINGS HOLIDAY(1970, Jap.)
Kazimierz Opalinski
  GUESTS ARE COMING(1965, Pol.); EROICA(1966, Pol.); SARAGOSSA MANUS-
  CRIPT, THE(1972, Pol.)
Marian Opania
  GOLEM(1980, Pol.); MAN OF IRON(1981, Pol.)
Danny Opatoshu
  STUDENT TEACHERS, THE(1973), w; GET CRAZY(1983), w
David O. Opatoshu
  WHO'LL STOP THE RAIN?(1978)
David Opatoshu
  NAKED CITY, THE(1948); THIEVES' HIGHWAY(1949); GOLDBERGS, THE(1950);
  CROWDED PARADISE(1956); BROTHERS KARAMAZOV, THE(1958); PARTY
  GIRL(1958); CIMARRON(1960); EXODUS(1960); BEST OF ENEMIES, THE(1962);
  GUNS OF DARKNESS(1962, Brit.); MOST WANTED MAN, THE(1962, Fr./Ital.);
  REBELS AGAINST THE LIGHT(1964); DEFECTOR, THE(1966, Ger./Fr.); ONE SPY
  TOO MANY(1966); SANDS OF BEERSHEBA(1966, U.S./Israel); TARZAN AND THE
  VALLEY OF GOLD(1966 U.S./Switz.); TORN CURTAIN(1966); ENTER LAUGH-
  ING(1967); FIXER, THE(1968); DEATH OF A GUNFIGHTER(1969); ROMANCE OF A
  HORSE THIEF(1971), a, w; AMERICATHON(1979); BEYOND EVIL(1980); IN
  SEARCH OF HISTORIC JESUS(1980); FORCED VENGEANCE(1982)
  Misc. Talkies
  DOBBIN, THE(1939)
Joseph Opatoshu
  ROMANCE OF A HORSE THIEF(1971), w
Alan Opeenheimer
  GUNN(1967)
The Open Theater of Joe Chaikin
  ZABRISKIE POINT(1970)
David Openshaw
  LONDON MELODY(1930, Brit.)
Earth Opera
  MARCH OF THE SPRING HARE(1969), m; ROOMMATES(1971), m
Sylvia Opert
  ROAD TO MOROCCO(1942); DESERT SONG, THE(1943); THANK YOUR LUCKY
  STARS(1943); DEVOTION(1946)
Shai K. Ophir
  DIAMONDS(1975, U.S./Israel); MAGICIAN OF LUBLIN, THE(1979, Israel/Ger.)
Shaike Ophir
  OPERATION THUNDERBOLT(1978, ISRAEL)
Shy Ophir
  TEL AVIV TAXI(1957, Israel)
Marcel Ophuls
  LOVE AT TWENTY(1963, Fr./Ital./Jap./Pol./Ger.), d&w; BANANA PEEL(1965, Fr.),
  d, w; EGON SCHIELE—EXCESS AND PUNISHMENT(1981, Ger.)
Max Ophuls
  MAN STOLEN(1934, Fr.), d; EXILE, THE(1947), d; LETTER FROM AN UNKNOWN
  WOMAN(1948), d; CAUGHT(1949), d; RECKLESS MOMENTS, THE(1949), d; VEN-
  DETTA(1950), d; EARRINGS OF MADAME DE..., THE(1954, Fr.), p&d, w; LA
  RONDE(1954, Fr.), d, w; LE PLAISIR(1954, Fr.), p&d, w; LOLA MONTES(1955, Fr./
  Ger.), d, w; MODIGLIANI OF MONTPARNASSE(1961, Fr./Ital.), w

Linda Opie
MUSCLE BEACH PARTY(1964); PAJAMA PARTY(1964)
George Opoka
MARK OF CAIN, THE(1948, Brit.)
Sarfo Opoku
1984
WHITE ELEPHANT(1984, Brit.)
Stefano Oppedisano
LEGIONS OF THE NILE(1960, Ital.)
Arthur Oppenheim
Silents
ETERNAL CITY, THE(1915)
David Oppenheim
SILVER SKATES(1943), m
E. Phillips Oppenheim
LION AND THE LAMB(1931), w; MIDNIGHT CLUB(1933), w; MONTE CARLO NIGHTS(1934), w; GREAT IMPERSONATION, THE(1935), w; ROMANCE AND RICHES(1937, Brit.), w; STRANGE BOARDERS(1938, Brit.), w; GREAT IMPERSONATION, THE(1942), w
Silents
FLOOR ABOVE, THE(1914), w; IN THE BALANCE(1917), w; DOUBLE LIFE OF MR. ALFRED BURTON, THE(1919, Brit.), w; ANNA THE ADVENTURESS(1920, Brit.), w; AMAZING PARTNERSHIP, THE(1921, Brit.), w; MYSTERY OF MR. BERNARD BROWN(1921, Brit.), w; FALSE EVIDENCE(1922, Brit.), w; BARNES MURDER CASE, THE(1930, Brit.), w
Jon Oppenheim
SISTER-IN-LAW, THE(1975); KING OF THE GYPSIES(1978)
Marella Oppenheim
MIRROR CRACK'D, THE(1980, Brit.)
Menashe Oppenheim
Misc. Talkies
KOL NIDRE(1939)
Sonny Oppenheim
APPRENTICESHIP OF DUDDY KRAVITZ, THE(1974, Can.)
Alan Oppenheimer
IN THE HEAT OF THE NIGHT(1967); HOW TO SAVE A MARRIAGE–AND RUIN YOUR LIFE(1968); STAR!(1968); MALTESE BIPPY, THE(1969); LITTLE BIG MAN(1970); GROUNDSTAR CONSPIRACY, THE(1972, Can.); THIEF WHO CAME TO DINNER, THE(1973); HINDENBURG, THE(1975); WIN, PLACE, OR STEAL(1975); FREAKY FRIDAY(1976); RECORD CITY(1978); PRIVATE BENJAMIN(1980)
1984
NEVERENDING STORY, THE(1984, Ger.)
Misc. Talkies
PLEASURE DOING BUSINESS, A(1979)
Edgar Oppenheimer
BLOOD ROSE, THE(1970, Fr.), p, w
Gary Oppenheimer
HEAD ON(1981, Can.), ed
George Oppenheimer
ROMAN SCANDALS(1933), w; RENDEZVOUS(1935), w; WE WENT TO COLLEGE(1936), w; DAY AT THE RACES, A(1937), w; I'LL TAKE ROMANCE(1937), w; LONDON BY NIGHT(1937), w; MARRIED BEFORE BREAKFAST(1937), w; CROWD ROARS, THE(1938), w; MAN-PROOF(1938), w; PARADISE FOR THREE(1938), w; THREE LOVES HAS NANCY(1938), w; YANK AT OXFORD, A(1938), w; BROADWAY MELODY OF 1940(1940), w; I LOVE YOU AGAIN(1940), w; FEMININE TOUCH, THE(1941), w; TWO-FACED WOMAN(1941), w; PACIFIC RENDEZVOUS(1942), w; WAR AGAINST MRS. HADLEY, THE(1942), w; YANK AT ETON, A(1942), w; SLIGHTLY DANGEROUS(1943), w; YOUNGEST PROFESSION, THE(1943), w; EASY TO WED(1946), w; UNDERCURRENT(1946), w; KILLER McCOY(1947), w; ADVENTURES OF DON JUAN(1949), w; BORN TO BE BAD(1950), w; PERFECT STRANGERS(1950), w; ANYTHING CAN HAPPEN(1952), w; DECAMERON NIGHTS(1953, Brit.), w; TONIGHT WE SING(1953), w
Hans Oppenheimer
STOP TRAIN 349(1964, Fr./Ital./Ger.), p
Peer Oppenheimer
1984
SECRET DIARY OF SIGMUND FREUD, THE(1984), p
Peer J. Oppenheimer
OPERATION CIA(1965), p, w
Peter J. Oppenheimer
NEW GIRL IN TOWN(1977), p, w
Don Opper
ANDROID(1982), a, w
Jeannine Oppewall
MY BODYGUARD(1980), set d; TENDER MERCIES(1982), art d; LOVE LETTERS(1983), art d
Yvonne Oppstedt
EMIGRANTS, THE(1972, Swed.)
Charlie Opuni
SHE DEMONS(1958)
Charles Opunui
TAHITI NIGHTS(1945)
Louis Oquendo
MAN IN THE WATER, THE(1963)
Fred Orain
CHILDREN OF PARADISE(1945, Fr.), p; JOUR DE FETE(1952, Fr.), p; VOYAGE TO AMERICA(1952, Fr.), p; MR. HULOT'S HOLIDAY(1954, Fr.), p
Robert Oram
FRATERNITY ROW(1977)
Kaz Oran
FLAME BARRIER, THE(1958)
Orange County Ramblers
SKIDOO(1968)
Alessio Orano
COUNT OF MONTE CRISTO(1976, Brit.); HOUSE OF EXORCISM, THE(1976, Ital.)
Misc. Talkies
MAY MORNING(1970)

Sandra Orans
THAT NIGHT WITH YOU(1945)
V.A. Oransky
DIARY OF A REVOLUTIONIST(1932, USSR), m
Andrew Orapeza
POINT BLANK(1967)
Jerry Orbach
COP HATER(1958); MAD DOG COLL(1961); JOHN GOLDFARB, PLEASE COME HOME(1964); GANG THAT COULDN'T SHOOT STRAIGHT, THE(1971); FAN'S NOTES, A(1972, Can.); FOREPLAY(1975); SENTINEL, THE(1977); PRINCE OF THE CITY(1981)
Misc. Talkies
UNDERGROUND ACES(1981)
Richard Orbach
JESUS CHRIST, SUPERSTAR(1973)
Judith Orban
ONE PLUS ONE(1961, Can.)
Tibor Orban
WINTER WIND(1970, Fr./Hung.)
Fred Orbing
Silents
PASSION(1920, Ger.), w
Roxanne Orbis
NEW YEAR'S EVIL(1980)
Roy Orbison
FASTEST GUITAR ALIVE, THE(1967); ROADIE(1980)
Attila Orbok
MY LIPS BETRAY(1933), w
Eric Orbom
FRANCIS GOES TO WEST POINT(1952), art d; MA AND PA KETTLE AT THE FAIR(1952), art d; MEET ME AT THE FAIR(1952), art d; GLASS WEB, THE(1953), art d; GOLDEN BLADE, THE(1953), art d; ABBOTT AND COSTELLO MEET DR. JEKYLL AND MR. HYDE(1954), art d; ALL THAT HEAVEN ALLOWS(1955), art d; CAPTAIN LIGHTFOOT(1955), art d; MA AND PA KETTLE AT WAIKIKI(1955), art d; PURPLE MASK, THE(1955), art d; RED SUNDOWN(1956), art d; THERE'S ALWAYS TOMORROW(1956), art d; GIRL IN THE KREMLIN, THE(1957), art d; GREAT MAN, THE(1957), art d; ISTANBUL(1957), art d; MAN OF A THOUSAND FACES(1957), art d; MIDNIGHT STORY, THE(1957), art d; SLIM CARTER(1957), art d; THING THAT COULDN'T DIE, THE(1958), art d; TWILIGHT FOR THE GODS(1958), art d; SPARTACUS(1960), art d
Ernie Orbom
MISTER CORY(1957), art d
Bernard Orbovich
1984
RECKLESS(1984)
Eric Orbum
CAN'T STOP THE MUSIC(1980), set d
Pierre Orcel
1984
MOSCOW ON THE HUDSON(1984)
John Orchard
GENTLE GUNMAN, THE(1952, Brit.); I BELIEVE IN YOU(1953, Brit.); GENTLE TOUCH, THE(1956, Brit.); KING RAT(1965); STRANGE BEDFELLOWS(1965); ICE STATION ZEBRA(1968); SPLIT, THE(1968); THOMAS CROWN AFFAIR, THE(1968); BEDKNOBS AND BROOMSTICKS(1971); RAID ON ROMMEL(1971); THAT MAN BOLT(1973); CAPONE(1975)
Julian Orchard
THREE ON A SPREE(1961, Brit.); KILL OR CURE(1962, Brit.); GREAT VAN ROBBERY, THE(1963, Brit.); FATHER CAME TOO(1964, Brit.); HIDE AND SEEK(1964, Brit.); SPY WITH A COLD NOSE, THE(1966, Brit.); COP-OUT(1967, Brit.); FOLLOW THAT CAMEL(1967, Brit.); HALF A SIXPENCE(1967, Brit.); CARRY ON DOCTOR(1968, Brit.); CARRY ON HENRY VIII(1970, Brit.); PERFECT FRIDAY(1970, Brit.); SLIPPER AND THE ROSE, THE(1976, Brit.); CROSSED SWORDS(1978); REVENGE OF THE PINK PANTHER(1978)
George Mitchell and His Swing Orchestra
IT'S A WONDERFUL DAY(1949, Brit.)
Orchestra and Chorus of La Scala, Milan
LA BOHEME(1965, Ital.)
the Orchestra and Chorus of the Covent Garden Opera
MELBA(1953, Brit.)
The Orchestras of Henry Busse
LADY, LET'S DANCE(1944)
Jenny Orchse
DOT AND THE BUNNY(1983, Aus.), anim
Oscar Orcini
EXECUTIVE ACTION(1973)
John Orcsik
PETERSEN(1974, Aus.)
Baroness Emma Magdalena Rosalia Maria Josepha Barbara Orczy
SCARLET PIMPERNEL, THE(1935, Brit.), w
Baroness Orczy
EMPEROR'S CANDLESTICKS, THE(1937), w; RETURN OF THE SCARLET PIMPERNEL(1938, Brit.), w; SPY OF NAPOLEON(1939, Brit.), w; FIGHTING PIMPERNEL, THE(1950, Brit.), d&w
Silents
ELUSIVE PIMPERNEL, THE(1919, Brit.), w
Emmuska Orczy
Silents
TWO LOVERS(1928), w
Murray Ord
1984
RUNAWAY(1984)
Ord Hamilton and His Band
DEATH AT A BROADCAST(1934, Brit.)
Beryl Orde
RADIO FOLLIES(1935, Brit.); SING AS YOU SWING(1937, Brit.); DUMMY TALKS, THE(1943, Brit.)

Julian Orde
HIDEOUT(1948, Brit.), w
Mary Ordette
Silents
ALL ROADS LEAD TO CALVARY(1921, Brit.); CRIMSON CIRCLE, THE(1922, Brit.);
IF YOUTH BUT KNEW(1926, Brit.)
Liane Ordeyne
GANGWAY(1937, Brit.)
Victor Ordonez
1984
ALLEY CAT(1984), p, d
Pepita Orduna
CALABUCH(1956, Span./Ital.), ed
Wyatt Ordung
COMBAT SQUAD(1953), w; DRAGON'S GOLD(1954)
Wyott Ordung
FIXED BAYONETS(1951); ROBOT MONSTER(1953), w; MONSTER FROM THE
OCEAN FLOOR, THE(1954), a, d; WALK THE DARK STREET(1956), p,d&w; FIRST
MAN INTO SPACE(1959, Brit.), w
Frederick I. Ordway III
2001: A SPACE ODYSSEY(1968, U.S./Brit.), cons
Richard Ordynski
PARIS AFTER DARK(1943); IN OUR TIME(1944)
Misc. Silents
ROSE OF BLOOD, THE(1917); 10 CONDEMNED(1932, Pol.), d
Guillermo Orea
CASTLE OF THE MONSTERS(1958, Mex.); VAMPIRE'S COFFIN, THE(1958, Mex.)
Tom Oreb
MAKE MINE MUSIC(1946), w; FUN AND FANCY FREE(1947), w; ALICE IN
WONDERLAND(1951), w
Don Oreck
TARGET ZERO(1955)
Joshua Oreck
WAVELENGTH(1983)
Francesco Orefici
AUGUSTINE OF HIPPO(1973, Ital.), p
Ron Oreiux
SKIP TRACER, THE(1979, Can.), ph
Antonio Orellana
SANTO CONTRA EL CEREBRO DIABOLICO zero(1962, Mex.), w
Carlos Orellana
SANTA(1932, Mex.); LOS PLATILLOS VOLADORES(1955, Mex.), w; CASTLE OF
THE MONSTERS(1958, Mex.), a, w; CHIQUTTO PERO PICOSO(1967, Mex.), w
Elie Oren
1984
HOTEL NEW HAMPSHIRE, THE(1984)
Riki Oren
JESUS CHRIST, SUPERSTAR(1973)
Al Orenbach
LIFE BEGINS AT 8:30(1942), set d; JITTERBUGS(1943), set d; MARGIN FOR
ERROR(1943), set d; BIG NOISE, THE(1944), set d; FOUR JILLS IN A JEEP(1944), set
d; ROGER TOUHY, GANGSTER!(1944), set d; STATE FAIR(1945), set d; TULSA(1949),
set d; D.O.A.(1950), set d; I'D CLIMB THE HIGHEST MOUNTAIN(1951), set d;
PICKUP ON SOUTH STREET(1953), set d
Alexander Orenbach
BEHIND LOCKED DOORS(1948), set d
Michael Orenbach
CRACK-UP(1946), set d; RIFFRAFF(1947), set d
Brian Orenstein
RETURN OF THE JEDI(1983)
John Oresik
TRESPASSERS, THE(1976, Aus.)
Oreste [Kirkop]
VAGABOND KING, THE(1956)
Liana Orfei
AVENGER, THE(1962, Fr./Ital.); DAMON AND PYTHIAS(1962); TARTARS,
THE(1962, Ital./Yugo.); GIANT OF METROPOLIS, THE(1963, Ital.); MILL OF THE
STONE WOMEN(1963, Fr./Ital.); RAGE OF THE BUCCANEERS(1963, Ital.); HER-
CULES, SAMSON & ULYSSES(1964, Ital.); QUEEN OF THE NILE(1964, Ital.);
CASANOVA '70(1965, Ital.); DEVIL IN LOVE, THE(1968, Ital.)
Moira Orfei
QUEEN OF THE PIRATES(1961, Ital./Ger.); MIGHTY URSUS(1962, Ital./Span.);
HERO OF BABYLON(1963, Ital.); SAMSON AND THE SLAVE QUEEN(1963, Ital.);
CASANOVA '70(1965, Ital.); HERCULES VS THE GIANT WARRIORS(1965 Fr./Ital.)
Nando Orfei
AMARCORD(1974, Ital.)
Valentino Orfeo
SACCO AND VANZETTI(1971, Ital./Fr.)
Hans Peter Orff
CIRCLE OF DECEIT(1982, Fr./Ger.)
Betty Orgar
NO RESTING PLACE(1952, Brit.), ed
Lee Orgel
MR. MAGOO'S HOLIDAY FESTIVAL(1970), p
Klaus Orgermann
BIMBO THE GREAT(1961, Ger.), m
Arnold H. Orgolini
EMBRYO(1976), p
Arnold Orgolini
METEOR(1979), p; SMORGASBORD(1983), p
Gyozo Orgon
FATHER(1967, Hung.)
Meral Orhousoy
YOL(1982, Turkey)
Leon Oriana
Misc. Talkies
DYNAMITE(1972)

Vanja Orico
VARIETY LIGHTS(1965, Ital.)
Ron Orieux
HOUNDS... OF NOTRE DAME, THE(1980, Can.), ph
Kunie Origa
GIRL I ABANDONED, THE(1970, Jap.)
The Original California Collegians
TO BEAT THE BAND(1935)
C.M. Origo
MAKE-UP(1937, Brit.), p
Junkichi Orimoto
MESSAGE FROM SPACE(1978, Jap.)
Barry Oringer
DAMON AND PYTHIAS(1962), w; SYNANON(1965), w
Maurice Orion
TRANSPORT FROM PARADISE(1967, Czech.)
Bill Orisman
TEXAN MEETS CALAMITY JANE, THE(1950)
Tony Oritz
HAREM BUNCH; OR WAR AND PIECE, THE(1969)
Jobst Oriwal
1984
HOTEL NEW HAMPSHIRE, THE(1984)
Senih Orkan
TOPKAPI(1964)
Harvey Orkin
CANDIDATE, THE(1972)
Ruth Orkin
LITTLE FUGITIVE, THE(1953), d&w, ed; LOVERS AND LOLLIPOPS(1956), p&d,
w, ed
Therese Orkin
YEAR OF THE HORSE, THE(1966), p
B. Harrison Orkow
TRUTH ABOUT YOUTH, THE(1930), w; HELL'S HOUSE(1932), w
B.H. Orkow
WINGS FOR THE EAGLE(1942), w
Ben Orkow
BOY SLAVES(1938), w
Harrison Orkow
ALASKA(1944), w
R. Harrison Orkow
ARMY WIVES(1944), w
W. Harrison Orkow
GORILLA, THE(1931), w
Nina Orla
ONE NIGHT IN THE TROPICS(1940); BUCK PRIVATES(1941); WHERE DID YOU
GET THAT GIRL?(1941)
Ressel Orla
Misc. Silents
GOLDEN SEA, THE(1919, Ger.); HALFBREED(1919, Ger.); SPIDERS, THE(1919,
Ger.)
Madge Orlamond
Silents
BLUSHING BRIDE, THE(1921)
Ruth Orlamond
Silents
JOHNNY-ON-THE-SPOT(1919)
William A. Orlamond
Silents
AWAKENING, THE(1928)
William H. Orlamond
Silents
ARABIAN LOVE(1922); ALL THE BROTHERS WERE VALIANT(1923)
William Orlamond
WIND, THE(1928); WORDS AND MUSIC(1929); HER PRIVATE AFFAIR(1930); WAY
OF ALL MEN, THE(1930); ARE THESE OUR CHILDREN?(1931); CIMARRON(1931);
ROAR OF THE DRAGON(1932); GORGEOUS HUSSY, THE(1936); SWORN ENE-
MY(1936)
Silents
BEATING THE GAME(1921); DOUBLING FOR ROMEO(1921); EAGLE'S FEATHER,
THE(1923); ETERNAL THREE, THE(1923); SLANDER THE WOMAN(1923); SLAVE
OF DESIRE(1923); SOULS FOR SALE(1923); NELLIE, THE BEAUTIFUL CLOAK
MODEL(1924); FLESH AND THE DEVIL(1926); KIKI(1926); THAT'S MY BABY(1926);
RED MILL, THE(1927); TAXI DANCER, THE(1927); TEXAS STEER, A(1927); SKIN-
NER'S BIG IDEA(1928); WHILE THE CITY SLEEPS(1928)
Misc. Silents
MADAME PEACOCK(1920); LOOK YOUR BEST(1923); LITTLE YELLOW HOUSE,
THE(1928)
Pierre Mac Orlan
ESCAPE FROM YESTERDAY(1939, Fr.), w
Felice Orlandi
KILLER'S KISS(1955); HARDER THEY FALL, THE(1956); ER LOVE A STRAN-
GER(1958); PUSHER, THE(1960); BULLITT(1968); THEY SHOOT HORSES, DON'T
THEY?(1969); CATCH-22(1970); OUTSIDE MAN, THE(1973, U.S./Fr.); HARD TI-
MES(1975); DRIVER, THE(1978); LONG RIDERS, THE(1980)
Nora Orlandi
JOHNNY YUMA(1967, Ital.), m; SWEET BODY OF DEBORAH, THE(1969, Ital./Fr.),
m; NEXT!(1971, Ital./Span.), m
Giuseppe Orlandini
OF WAYWARD LOVE(1964, Ital./Ger.), w
Leo Orlandini
Silents
QUO VADIS?(1913, Ital.)
Orlando
JUBILEE(1978, Brit.)
Antonio Orlando
1984
BASILEUS QUARTET(1984, Ital.)

Don Orlando
TWO WEEKS IN ANOTHER TOWN(1962); PALS OF THE SADDLE(1938); ROMANCE OF THE ROCKIES(1938); TORRID ZONE(1940); LAW OF THE TROPICS(1941); FIXED BAYONETS(1951); KANSAS CITY CONFIDENTIAL(1952); PARK ROW(1952); HELL AND HIGH WATER(1954); HELL'S ISLAND(1955); WALK THE DARK STREET(1956); DOMINO KID(1957); RUN OF THE ARROW(1957); 20 MILLION MILES TO EARTH(1957)
Misc. Talkies
HAWK, THE(1935); TRAIL OF THE HAWK(1935)

John Orlando
Misc. Talkies
BYE-BYE BUDDY(1929)

Orazio Orlando
BAMBOLE!(1965, Ital.); INVESTIGATION OF A CITIZEN ABOVE SUSPICION(1970, Ital.); WATERLOO(1970, Ital./USSR)

Phil Orlando
I PASSED FOR WHITE(1960), ch

Rosemary Orlando
Misc. Talkies
SATAN'S CHILDREN(1975)

Tony Orlando
STAR IS BORN, A(1976)

Will Orlean
KILLER DILL(1947)

Jenny Orleans
LIFE UPSIDE DOWN(1965, Fr.); SLEEPING CAR MURDER THE(1966, Fr.); NIGHT OF THE GENERALS, THE(1967, Brit./Fr.)

Will Orleans
HEAVEN ONLY KNOWS(1947); SINISTER JOURNEY(1948); LEAVE IT TO THE MARINES(1951); SKY HIGH(1952)

Lester Orleback
HIT THE SADDLE(1937), ed; COWBOY SERENADE(1942), ed

Les Orlebeck
PIONEERS OF THE WEST(1940), d; APACHE KID, THE(1941), ed; CITADEL OF CRIME(1941), ed; GAUCHOS OF EL DORADO(1941), d; NEVADA CITY(1941), ed; OUTLAWS OF THE CHEROKEE TRAIL(1941), d; PALS OF THE PECOS(1941), d; PRAIRIE PIONEERS(1941), d; SINGING HILL, THE(1941), ed; WEST OF CIMARRON(1941), d; SHADOWS ON THE SAGE(1942), ed; HOME IN OKLAHOMA(1946), ed; ROLL ON TEXAS MOON(1946), ed; STAGECOACH TO DENVER(1946), ed; TRAFFIC IN CRIME(1946), ed; APACHE ROSE(1947), ed; BANDITS OF DARK CANYON(1947), ed; BELLS OF SAN ANGELO(1947), ed; WILD FRONTIER, THE(1947), ed; SLIPPY MCGEE(1948), ed

Lester Orlebeck
MELODY TRAIL(1935), ed; SAGEBRUSH TROUBADOR(1935), ed; SINGING VAGABOND, THE(1935), ed; BOLD CABALLERO(1936), ed; GUNS AND GUITARS(1936), ed; KING OF THE PECOS(1936), ed; LONELY TRAIL, THE(1936), ed; SINGING COWBOY, THE(1936), ed; CIRCUS GIRL(1937), ed; COME ON, COWBOYS(1937), ed; GHOST TOWN GOLD(1937), ed; HEART OF THE ROCKIES(1937), ed; HIT PARADE, THE(1937), ed; JOIN THE MARINES(1937), ed; OLD CORRAL, THE(1937), ed; PUBLIC COWBOY NO. 1(1937), ed; RANGE DEFENDERS(1937), ed; ROUNDUP TIME IN TEXAS(1937), ed; SPRINGTIME IN THE ROCKIES(1937), ed; YODELIN' KID FROM PINE RIDGE(1937), ed; CALL THE MESQUITEERS(1938), ed; GOLD MINE IN THE SKY(1938), ed; MAN FROM MUSIC MOUNTAIN(1938), ed; OLD BARN DANCE, THE(1938), ed; PRAIRIE MOON(1938), ed; PURPLE VIGILANTES, THE(1938), ed; RHYTHM OF THE SADDLE(1938), ed; RIDERS OF THE BLACK HILLS(1938), ed; SHINE ON, HARVEST MOON(1938), ed; UNDER WESTERN STARS(1938), ed; WESTERN JAMBOREE(1938), ed; WILD HORSE RODEO(1938), ed; ARIZONA KID, THE(1939), ed; BLUE MONTANA SKIES(1939), ed; HOME ON THE PRAIRIE(1939), ed; MOUNTAIN RHYTHM(1939), ed; MYSTERIOUS MISS X, THE(1939), ed; NIGHT RIDERS, THE(1939), ed; ROUGH RIDERS' ROUND-UP(1939), ed; SAGA OF DEATH VALLEY(1939), ed; SOUTH OF THE BORDER(1939), ed; SOUTHWARD HO!(1939), ed; WALL STREET COWBOY(1939), ed; GANGS OF CHICAGO(1940), ed; GHOST VALLEY RAIDERS(1940), ed; HEROES OF THE SADDLE(1940), ed; ONE MAN'S LAW(1940), ed; RANGER AND THE LADY, THE(1940), ed; RIDE, TENDERFOOT, RIDE(1940), ed; ROCKY MOUNTAIN RANGERS(1940), ed; YOUNG BILL HICKOK(1940), ed; GREAT TRAIN ROBBERY, THE(1941), ed; SADDLEMATES(1941), d; SIERRA SUE(1941), ed; WYOMING WILDCAT(1941), ed; HEART OF THE RIO GRANDE(1942), ed; ROMANCE ON THE RANGE(1942), ed; SUNSET ON THE DESERT(1942), ed; HELLDORADO(1946), ed

Orlenev
Misc. Silents
BRAND(1915, USSR)

Pavel Orlenev
Misc. Silents
CRIME AND PUNISHMENT(1913, USSR); BRAND(1915, USSR), d; GHOSTS(1915, USSR)

Helen Orlenko
COSSACKS IN EXILE(1939, Ukrainian)

April Orlich
1984
SUPERGIRL(1984)

Jaroslav Orlicky
DO YOU KEEP A LION AT HOME?(1966, Czech.)

Y. Orlitskaya
Misc. Silents
IN THE KINGDOM OF OIL AND MILLIONS(1916, USSR)

B. Orlitsky
Misc. Silents
DAYS OF OUR LIFE(1914, USSR)

Antonio Orllana
BLUE DEMON VERSUS THE INFERNAL BRAINS(1967, Mex.), w

Harold Orlob
CITIZEN SAINT(1947), m, w

Arthur Orloff
BEAUTY ON PARADE(1950), w; BUCKAROO SHERIFF OF TEXAS(1951), w; DESPERADOES OUTPOST(1952), w; SOUTH PACIFIC TRAIL(1952), w; EL PASO STAMPEDE(1953), w; GUN BELT(1953), w; RED RIVER SHORE(1953), w; SKY COMMANDO(1953), w; HELL BOUND(1957), w; FIVE GUNS TO TOMBSTONE(1961), w

Arthur E. Orloff
CHEYENNE TAKES OVER(1947), w; LONE WOLF IN LONDON(1947), w; WILD COUNTRY(1947), w; CODE OF THE SILVER SAGE(1950), w; MISSOURIANS, THE(1950), w; THUNDER IN GOD'S COUNTRY(1951), w; LAST MUSKETEER, THE(1952), w; TRAIL GUIDE(1952), w

Count John Orloff
Misc. Silents
HANDS OF NARA, THE(1922)

Nicolas Orloff
BALLERINA(1950, Fr.)

Orest Orloff
DIVIDED HEART, THE(1955, Brit.); LOSER TAKES ALL(1956, Brit.)

Orlov
Misc. Silents
BRAND(1915, USSR)

A. Orlov
TIGER GIRL(1955, USSR); LADY WITH THE DOG, THE(1962, USSR)

D.N. Orlov
ALEXANDER NEVSKY(1939)

Ida Orlov
Misc. Silents
ATLANTIS(1913, Ger./Den.)

V. Orlov
LOSS OF FEELING(1935, USSR)

Lubov Orlova
SPRING(1948, USSR)

Lyubov Orlova
MAN OF MUSIC(1953, USSR)

N. Orlova
MOTHER AND DAUGHTER(1965, USSR), w

V. Orlova
DIMKA(1964, USSR); WHEN THE TREES WERE TALL(1965, USSR)

Vera Orlova
Misc. Silents
QUEEN OF SPADES, THE(1916, USSR); ANDREI KOZHUKHOV(1917, USSR); PUBLIC PROSECUTOR(1917, USSR); TSAR NIKOLAI II(1917, USSR); POWER OF DARKNESS, THE(1918, USSR)

Mica Orlovic
MARCO THE MAGNIFICENT(1966, Ital./Fr./Yugo./Egypt/Afghanistan)

Gil Orlovitz
OVER-EXPOSED(1956), w

D. Orlovskiy
OPTIMISTIC TRAGEDY, THE(1964, USSR)

Julius Orlovsky
ME AND MY BROTHER(1969)

Peter Orlovsky
CHAPPAQUA(1967); ME AND MY BROTHER(1969)

Edgar Orman
1984
MAKING THE GRADE(1984)

Felix Orman
Silents
GLORIOUS ADVENTURE, THE(1922, U.S./Brit.), w

Roscoe Orman
WILLIE DYNAMITE(1973)

Gary Van Ormand
RATTLERS(1976)

Robert Ormand
Misc. Silents
MARVELOUS MACISTE, THE(1918, Ital.)

Ron Ormand
MARK OF THE LASH(1948), w; RIMFIRE(1949), w; SQUARE DANCE JUBILEE(1949), p; CROOKED RIVER(1950), p; UNTAMED MISTRESS(1960), p,d&w

Eugene Ormandy
NIGHT SONG(1947)

Kenan Ormanlar
1984
HORSE, THE(1984, Turk.), ph

Charles Orme
MC GUIRE, GO HOME!(1966, Brit.), prod d

Donna Roberts Orme
MATILDA(1978), cos

Geoffrey Orme
SUNSHINE AHEAD(1936, Brit.), w; TALKING FEET(1937, Brit.), w; WHAT WOULD YOU DO, CHUMS?(1939, Brit.), w; OLD MOTHER RILEY IN BUSINESS(1940, Brit.), w; COMMON TOUCH, THE(1941, Brit.), w; OLD MOTHER RILEY'S CIRCUS(1941, Brit.), w; OLD MOTHER RILEY'S GHOSTS(1941, Brit.), w; LET THE PEOPLE SING(1942, Brit.), w; OLD MOTHER RILEY, DETECTIVE(1943, Brit.), w; THEATRE ROYAL(1943, Brit.), w; HERE COMES THE SUN(1945, Brit.), w; GRAND ESCAPADE, THE(1946, Brit.), w; FORTUNE LANE(1947, Brit.), w; WHEN YOU COME HOME(1947, Brit.), w; LAST LOAD, THE(1948, Brit.), w; NOTHING VENTURE(1948, Brit.), w; JUDGMENT DEFERRED(1952, Brit.), w; DELAYED ACTION(1954, Brit.), w; DEVIL ON HORSEBACK(1954, Brit.), w; END OF THE ROAD, THE(1954, Brit.), w; LOVE MATCH, THE(1955, Brit.), w; RAMSBOTTOM RIDES AGAIN(1956, Brit.), w; HEART WITHIN, THE(1957, Brit.), w; BOY AND THE BRIDGE, THE(1959, Brit.), w; ORDERS ARE ORDERS(1959, Brit.), w; LONG DUEL, THE(1967, Brit.), w

Kenneth Lee Orme
SPOOK WHO SAT BY THE DOOR, THE(1973)

Tom Ormeny
ONLY WHEN I LAUGH(1981)

Paolo Ormi
NEXT!(1971, Ital./Span.), md

Dave Ormond
JET PILOT(1957)

Jean Ormond
LURE, THE(1933, Brit.)

June Ormond
WHITE LIGHTNIN' ROAD(1967), p; EXOTIC ONES, THE(1968)
Linda Ormond
DEAD ONE, THE(1961)
Ron Ormond
DEAD MAN'S GOLD(1948), p; FRONTIER REVENGE(1948), p; MARK OF THE LASH(1948), p; DALTON GANG, THE(1949), p; OUTLAW COUNTRY(1949), p, w; RED DESERT(1949), p, w; RIMFIRE(1949), p; RINGSIDE(1949), p, w; SHEP COMES HOME(1949), p; SON OF A BADMAN(1949), p, w; SON OF BILLY THE KID(1949), p, w; SQUARE DANCE JUBILEE(1949), p, w; COLORADO RANGER(1950), p, w; CROOKED RIVER(1950), p, w; DALTON'S WOMEN, THE(1950), p, w; FAST ON THE DRAW(1950), p, w; HOSTILE COUNTRY(1950), p, w; KING OF THE BULLWHIP(1950), p&d; MARSHAL OF HELDORADO(1950), p, w; WEST OF THE BRAZOS(1950), p, w; KENTUCKY JUBILEE(1951), p&d, w; THUNDERING TRAIL, THE(1951), p&d; VANISHING OUTPOST, THE(1951), p&d; YES SIR, MR. BONES(1951), p,d&w; BLACK LASH, THE(1952), p&d; FRONTIER PHANTOM, THE(1952), p&d; OUTLAW WOMEN(1952), p, d; MESA OF LOST WOMEN, THE(1956), d; NAKED GUN, THE(1956), p, w; FORTY ACRE FEUD(1965), d; WHITE LIGHTNIN' ROAD(1967), p, d; EXOTIC ONES, THE(1968), a, p, d, w
Misc. Talkies
FRONTIER WOMAN(1956), d; GIRL FROM TOBACCO ROW, THE(1966), d
Tim Ormond
WHITE LIGHTNIN' ROAD(1967)
Misc. Talkies
GIRL FROM TOBACCO ROW, THE(1966)
Czeni Ormonde
1001 ARABIAN NIGHTS(1959), w
Czenzi Ormonde
STRANGERS ON A TRAIN(1951), w; STEP DOWN TO TERROR(1958), w
Eugene Ormonde
Silents
MANHATTAN MADNESS(1916); MODERN MUSKETEER, A(1917); REACHING FOR THE MOON(1917)
Misc. Silents
BELLA DONNA(1915); SLANDER(1916); CAILLAUX CASE, THE(1918); LIGHT, THE(1919)
John Ormonde
PENNY POINTS TO PARADISE(1951, Brit.), w
Sylvia Ormonde
Misc. Silents
WORLD OF TODAY, THE(1915)
David Ormont
MAN FROM PLANET X, THE(1951)
James Ormont
Silents
BAFFLED(1924), w; WESTERN VENGEANCE(1924), w; DUDE COWBOY, THE(1926), w; FIGHTING BOOB, THE(1926), w; HAIR TRIGGER BAXTER(1926), w; VALLEY OF BRAVERY, THE(1926), w; SOULS AFLAME(1928), p
Misc. Silents
MY HUSBAND'S FRIEND(1918), d
Jesse J. Ormont
Misc. Silents
SHATTERED FAITH(1923), d
Alan Ormsby
CHILDREN SHOULDN'T PLAY WITH DEAD THINGS(1972), a, w; DEATHDREAM(1972, Can.), w; DERANGED(1974, Can.), d, w; SHOCK WAVES(1977), makeup; LITTLE DRAGONS, THE(1980), w; MY BODYGUARD(1980), w; CAT PEOPLE(1982), w; PORKY'S II: THE NEXT DAY(1983), w
Anya Ormsby
CHILDREN SHOULDN'T PLAY WITH DEAD THINGS(1972); DEATHDREAM(1972, Can.)
Ian Ormsby-Knox
MOONLIGHTING(1982, Brit.)
Nicholson Ormsby-Scott
Silents
MESSAGE FROM MARS, A(1913, Brit.), p
Frank Ormston
Silents
TESS OF THE STORM COUNTRY(1922), art d; ISLE OF RETRIBUTION, THE(1926), art d
Ornadel
SUBTERFUGE(1969, US/Brit.), md
Cyril Ornadel
SOME MAY LIVE(1967, Brit.), m; SUBTERFUGE(1969, US/Brit.), m; MAN OF VIOLENCE(1970, Brit.), m; WEDDING NIGHT(1970, Ireland), m, md; CHRISTINA(1974, Can.), m; TIFFANY JONES(1976), m
Luigi Ornaghi
TREE OF WOODEN CLOGS, THE(1979, Ital.)
Cyril Ornandel
COOL IT, CAROL!(1970, Brit.), m
Barbro Hiort Af Ornas
BRINK OF LIFE(1960, Swed.); SCENES FROM A MARRIAGE(1974, Swed.)
Adolfo Ornelas
BARON OF ARIZONA, THE(1950); ELEPHANT WALK(1954)
Norman Ornellas
SERPICO(1973)
Eric Orner
FAST CHARLIE... THE MOONBEAM RIDER(1979), ed
Ota Ornest
MATTER OF DAYS, A(1969, Fr./Czech.)
Arthur Ornitz
PUSHER, THE(1960), ph; WITHOUT EACH OTHER(1962), ph; CHARLY(1968), ph; CHANGE OF MIND(1969), ph; ANDERSON TAPES, THE(1971), ph; SWEET SUZY(1973), ph; NEXT STOP, GREENWICH VILLAGE(1976), ph; OLIVER'S STORY(1978), ph; UNMARRIED WOMAN, AN(1978), ph; TATTOO(1981), ph; CHOSEN, THE(1982), ph; HANKY-PANKY(1982), ph
Arthur J. Ornitz
GODDESS, THE(1958), ph; TEENAGE MILLIONAIRE(1961), ph; YOUNG DOCTORS, THE(1961), ph; CONNECTION, THE(1962), ph; JACKTOWN(1962), ph; REQUIEM FOR A HEAVYWEIGHT(1962), ph; ACT ONE(1964), ph; WORLD OF HENRY

ORIENT, THE(1964), ph; THOUSAND CLOWNS, A(1965), ph; MIDSUMMER NIGHT'S DREAM, A(1966), ph; TIGER MAKES OUT, THE(1967), ph; ME, NATALIE(1969), ph; BOYS IN THE BAND, THE(1970), ph; HOUSE OF DARK SHADOWS(1970), ph; SOLDIER BLUE(1970), ph; MINNIE AND MOSKOWITZ(1971), ph; POSSESSION OF JOEL DELANEY, THE(1972), ph; BADGE 373(1973), ph; SERPICO(1973), ph; DEATH WISH(1974), ph; LAW AND DISORDER(1974), ph; FOREVER YOUNG, FOREVER FREE(1976, South Afr.), ph; THIEVES(1977), ph
Sam Ornitz
ONE MAN'S JOURNEY(1933), w; TWO WISE MAIDS(1937), w; THEY LIVE IN FEAR(1944), w; CHINA'S LITTLE DEVILS(1945), w
Samuel Ornitz
CHINATOWN NIGHTS(1929), w; SINS OF THE CHILDREN(1930), w; HELL'S HIGHWAY(1932), w; SECRETS OF THE FRENCH POLICE(1932), w; THIRTEEN WOMEN(1932), w; MEN OF AMERICA(1933), w; MAN WHO RECLAIMED HIS HEAD, THE(1935), w; ONE EXCITING ADVENTURE(1935), w; THREE KIDS AND A QUEEN(1935), w; FATAL LADY(1936), w; FOLLOW YOUR HEART(1936), w; DOCTOR'S DIARY, A(1937), w; HIT PARADE, THE(1937), w; IT COULD HAPPEN TO YOU(1937), w; PORTIA ON TRIAL(1937), w; ARMY GIRL(1938), w; KING OF THE NEWSBOYS(1938), w; LITTLE ORPHAN ANNIE(1938), w; MIRACLE ON MAIN STREET, A(1940), w; THREE FACES WEST(1940), w; CIRCUMSTANTIAL EVIDENCE(1945), w
Bruce Ornstein
SATURDAY NIGHT FEVER(1977)
Michael Ornstein
1984
LIES(1984, Brit.), ed
Ludwig Orny
WEREWOLF VS. THE VAMPIRE WOMAN, THE(1970, Span./Ger.), art d
A. Orochko
DAY THE EARTH FROZE, THE(1959, Fin./USSR)
Vincent Orona, Jr.
IMPORTANT MAN, THE(1961, Mex.), w
Andre Oropeza
THIRD VOICE, THE(1960)
Bertha E. Oropeza
ZOOT SUIT(1981)
Elvira Oropeza
REVENGERS, THE(1972, U.S./Mex.), makeup; SWEET SUGAR(1972)
Elvira Oropoeza
TARZAN AND THE VALLEY OF GOLD(1966 U.S./Switz.), makeup
Esteban Oropreza
OVER-UNDER, SIDEWAYS-DOWN(1977)
Henry Orosco
STRANGE VOYAGE(1945)
Mary L. Orosco
THREE RING CIRCUS(1954)
Tom Orosco
LEOPARD MAN, THE(1943)
Margherita Orowitz
WILD, WILD PLANET, THE(1967, Ital.)
Manuel Orozco
BRAVE BULLS, THE(1951)
Mary Orozco
CAROUSEL(1956)
Russell Orozco
MAN WITH TWO BRAINS, THE(1983)
Children of the Orphan's Home in Korea
BATTLE HYMN(1957)
Bob Orpin
TRACK OF THE MOONBEAST(1976), m
Aletha Orr
WARNING TO WANTONS, A(1949, Brit.); HELL IS SOLD OUT(1951, Brit.); TALE OF FIVE WOMEN, A(1951, Brit.); TRUTH ABOUT WOMEN, THE(1958, Brit.); BATTLE OF THE SEXES, THE(1960, Brit.)
Angelyn Orr
BLONDIE'S LUCKY DAY(1946)
Buxton Orr
FIEND WITHOUT A FACE(1958), m; HAUNTED STRANGLER, THE(1958, Brit.), m; FIRST MAN INTO SPACE(1959, Brit.), m; SUDDENLY, LAST SUMMER(1959, Brit.), m, md; DR. BLOOD'S COFFIN(1961), m; SNAKE WOMAN, THE(1961, Brit.), m; CORRIDORS OF BLOOD(1962, Brit.), m; EYES OF ANNIE JONES, THE(1963, Brit.), m; WALK A TIGHTROPE(1964, U.S./Brit.), m
Clifford Orr
SHOT IN THE DARK, A(1935), w
Corinne Orr
WORLD OF HANS CHRISTIAN ANDERSEN, THE(1971, Jap.)
Corrinne Orr
LIGHT FANTASTIC(1964)
David Orr
CREST OF THE WAVE(1954, Brit.); NIGHT MY NUMBER CAME UP, THE(1955, Brit.); DEPTH CHARGE(1960, Brit.)
Denis Gordon Orr
CUBA(1979), art d
Dorothy Darlene Orr
TOWN THAT DREADED SUNDOWN, THE(1977)
Forrest Orr
RAINBOW ISLAND(1944)
Gertrude Orr
MAD PARADE, THE(1931), w; SILVER LINING(1932), w; LITTLE MEN(1935), w; DOUGHNUTS AND SOCIETY(1936), w; HARVESTER, THE(1936), w; PENTHOUSE PARTY(1936), w; COUNTRY GENTLEMEN(1937), w; MANDARIN MYSTERY, THE(1937), w; CALL OF THE YUKON(1938), w; SLANDER HOUSE(1938), w
Silents
SMILIN' AT TROUBLE(1925), w; BLIND GODDESS, THE(1926), w; BERTHA, THE SEWING MACHINE GIRL(1927), w; MARRIED ALIVE(1927), w; NIGHT LIFE(1927), w; SINGED(1927), w
Howard Orr
1984
WINDY CITY(1984)

Ian Orr
THRESHOLD(1983, Can.)
Mary Orr
WALLFLOWER(1948), w; ALL ABOUT EVE(1950), w; SIDELONG GLANCES OF A PIGEON KICKER, THE(1970)
Michael Orr
EXPERIMENT PERILOUS(1944)
Owen Orr
HIRED HAND, THE(1971); LAST MOVIE, THE(1971); WEREWOLVES ON WHEELS(1971); KID BLUE(1973); GREAT GUNDOWN, THE(1977); KING OF THE MOUNTAIN(1981); TRICK OR TREATS(1982)
Owen E. Orr
1984
BEAR, THE(1984)
Pat Orr
STRATTON STORY, THE(1949); DERANGED(1974, Can.)
Simon Orr
BIG CATCH, THE(1968, Brit.)
Stanley Orr
STRANGE FACES(1938); GUY NAMED JOE, A(1943); EAST SIDE, WEST SIDE(1949); RHUBARB(1951); IT SHOULD HAPPEN TO YOU(1954)
Stanley W. Orr
WAR OF THE WORLDS, THE(1953)
William Orr
HARDYS RIDE HIGH, THE(1939); INVITATION TO HAPPINESS(1939); MY LOVE CAME BACK(1940); BIG STREET, THE(1942)
William T. Orr
MORTAL STORM, THE(1940); HONEYMOON FOR THREE(1941); NAVY BLUES(1941); THIEVES FALL OUT(1941); THREE SONS O'GUNS(1941); UNHOLY PARTNERS(1941); GAY SISTERS, THE(1942); HE HIRED THE BOSS(1943); SEX AND THE SINGLE GIRL(1964), p
Robert Orrell
WINNING TEAM, THE(1952)
Henni Orri
PUPPET ON A CHAIN(1971, Brit.)
David Orrick
BLACKJACK KETCHUM, DESPERADO(1956); RUMBLE ON THE DOCKS(1956); SPIRIT OF ST. LOUIS, THE(1957)
Orrin Tucker's Orchestra
YOU'RE THE ONE(1941)
Col. William L. Orris, USAF
MC CONNELL STORY, THE(1955), tech adv
Bob Orrison
CULPEPPER CATTLE COMPANY, THE(1972); MITCHELL(1975); SUNBURN(1979)
George Orrison
ESCAPE FROM ALCATRAZ(1979); BRONCO BILLY(1980); FIREFOX(1982); HONKYTONK MAN(1982)
1984
CITY HEAT(1984); TIGHTROPE(1984), stunts
Jack Orrison
I MARRIED A MONSTER FROM OUTER SPACE(1958); WOLF LARSEN(1958); NEVER STEAL ANYTHING SMALL(1959); SECOND TIME AROUND, THE(1961); MADISON AVENUE(1962); MOVE OVER, DARLING(1963); I'D RATHER BE RICH(1964)
Kathy Orrison
1984
RUNNING HOT(1984), set d
Michael Orrom
NO RESTING PLACE(1952, Brit.), w, ed
Orry-Kelly
MAYBE IT'S LOVE(1930), cos; I AM A FUGITIVE FROM A CHAIN GANG(1932), cos; ONE WAY PASSAGE(1932), cos; RICH ARE ALWAYS WITH US, THE(1932), cos; SCARLET DAWN(1932), cos; SILVER DOLLAR(1932), cos; SO BIG(1932), cos; TIGER SHARK(1932), cos; WINNER TAKE ALL(1932), cos; BABY FACE(1933), cos; EX-LADY(1933), cos; FEMALE(1933), cos; GOLD DIGGERS OF 1933(1933), cos; GRAND SLAM(1933), cos; HARD TO HANDLE(1933), cos; HAVANA WIDOWS(1933), cos; HOUSE ON 56TH STREET, THE(1933), cos; KENNEL MURDER CASE, THE(1933), cos; KEYHOLE, THE(1933), cos; LADIES THEY TALK ABOUT(1933), cos; LADY KILLER(1933), cos; MARY STEVENS, M.D.(1933), cos; MAYOR OF HELL, THE(1933), cos; PICTURE SNATCHER(1933), cos; VOLTAIRE(1933), cos; WORKING MAN, THE(1933), cos; 20,000 YEARS IN SING SING(1933), cos; 42ND STREET(1933), cos; DAMES(1934), cos; DOCTOR MONICA(1934), cos; EASY TO LOVE(1934), cos; FASHIONS OF 1934(1934), cos; FLIRTATION WALK(1934), cos; FOG OVER FRISCO(1934), cos; GAMBLING LADY(1934), cos; HAPPINESS AHEAD(1934), cos; HE WAS HER MAN(1934), cos; HEAT LIGHTNING(1934), cos; HERE COMES THE NAVY(1934), cos; I'VE GOT YOUR NUMBER(1934), cos; JIMMY THE GENT(1934), cos; JOURNAL OF A CRIME(1934), cos; LOST LADY, A(1934), cos; MANDALAY(1934), cos; MERRY WIVES OF RENO, THE(1934), cos; MIDNIGHT ALIBI(1934), cos; MODERN HERO, A(1934), cos; PERSONALITY KID, THE(1934), cos; REGISTERED NURSE(1934), cos; RETURN OF THE TERROR(1934), cos; SIDE STREETS(1934), cos; ST. LOUIS KID, THE(1934), cos; TWENTY MILLION SWEETHEARTS(1934), cos; UPPER WORLD(1934), cos; VERY HONORABLE GUY, A(1934), cos; WONDER BAR(1934), cos; CEILNG ZERO(1935), cos; DEVIL DOGS OF THE AIR(1935), cos; FRISCO KID(1935), cos; G-MEN(1935), cos; GIRL FROM TENTH AVENUE, THE(1935), cos; GOING HIGHBROW(1935), cos; GOOSE AND THE GANDER, THE(1935), cos; I FOUND STELLA PARISH(1935), cos; I LIVE FOR LOVE(1935), cos; IRISH IN US, THE(1935), cos; LIVING ON VELVET(1935), cos; MISS PACIFIC FLEET(1935), cos; OIL FOR THE LAMPS OF CHINA(1935), cos; PAGE MISS GLORY(1935), cos; PAY-OFF, THE(1935), cos; PERSONAL MAID'S SECRET(1935), cos; SECRET BRIDE, THE(1935), cos; SHIPMATES FOREVER(1935), cos; STARS OVER BROADWAY(1935), cos; STRANDED(1935), cos; SWEET ADELINE(1935), cos; TRAVELING SALESLADY, THE(1935), cos; WOMAN IN RED, THE(1935), cos; CHINA CLIPPER(1936), cos; COLLEEN(1936), cos; DANGEROUS(1936), cos; FRESHMAN LOVE(1936), cos; GIVE ME YOUR HEART(1936), cos; GOLDEN ARROW, THE(1936), cos; MURDER BY AN ARISTOCRAT(1936), cos; PETRIFIED FOREST, THE(1936), cos; POLO JOE(1936), cos; SATAN MET A LADY(1936), cos; SINGING KID, THE(1936), cos; SNOWED UNDER(1936), cos; STAGE STRUCK(1936), cos; WALKING DEAD, THE(1936), cos; WIDOW FROM MONTE CARLO, THE(1936), cos; ANOTHER DAWN(1937), cos; CONFESSION(1937), cos; GO-GETTER, THE(1937), cos; GREEN LIGHT(1937), cos; IT'S LOVE I'M AFTER(1937), cos; KID GALAHAD(1937),

cos; KING AND THE CHORUS GIRL, THE(1937), cos; MARKED WOMAN(1937), cos; SINGING MARINE, THE(1937), cos; STOLEN HOLIDAY(1937), cos; THAT CERTAIN WOMAN(1937), cos; COMET OVER BROADWAY(1938), cos; FOUR'S A CROWD(1938), cos; JEZEBEL(1938), cos; MY BILL(1938), cos; SECRETS OF AN ACTRESS(1938), cos; SISTERS, THE(1938), cos; WOMEN ARE LIKE THAT(1938), cos; DARK VICTORY(1939), cos; JUAREZ(1939), cos; KING OF THE UNDERWORLD(1939), cos; OKLAHOMA KID, THE(1939), cos; OLD MAID, THE(1939), cos; ON YOUR TOES(1939), cos; PRIVATE LIVES OF ELIZABETH AND ESSEX, THE(1939), cos; WINGS OF THE NAVY(1939), cos; WOMEN IN THE WIND(1939), cos; ALL THIS AND HEAVEN TOO(1940), cos; LETTER, THE(1940), cos; MY LOVE CAME BACK(1940), cos; SEA HAWK, THE(1940), cos; 'TIL WE MEET AGAIN(1940), cos; BRIDE CAME C.O.D., THE(1941), cos; GREAT LIE, THE(1941), cos; LITTLE FOXES, THE(1941), cos; MALTESE FALCON, THE(1941), cos; MILLION DOLLAR BABY(1941), cos; STRAWBERRY BLONDE, THE(1941), cos; CASABLANCA(1942), cos; IN THIS OUR LIFE(1942), cos; MAN WHO CAME TO DINNER, THE(1942), cos; MURDER IN THE BIG HOUSE(1942), cos; NOW, VOYAGER(1942), cos; OLD ACQUAINTANCE(1943), cos; THIS IS THE ARMY(1943), cos; WATCH ON THE RHINE(1943), cos; MR. SKEFFINGTON(1944), cos; CORN IS GREEN, THE(1945), cos; DOLLY SISTERS, THE(1945), cos; STOLEN LIFE, A(1946), cos; MOTHER WORE TIGHTS(1947), cos; WOMAN'S VENGEANCE, A(1947), cos; BERLIN EXPRESS(1948), cos; FAMILY HONEYMOON(1948), cos; ONE TOUCH OF VENUS(1948), cos; ROGUES' REGIMENT(1948), cos; JOHNNY STOOL PIGEON(1949), cos; LADY GAMBLES, THE(1949), cos; ONCE MORE, MY DARLING(1949), cos; TAKE ONE FALSE STEP(1949), cos; UNDERTOW(1949), cos; ONE WAY STREET(1950), cos; SOUTH SEA SINNER(1950), cos; UNDER THE GUN(1951), cos; PAT AND MIKE(1952), cos; I CONFESS(1953), cos; MY HEART GOES CRAZY(1953, Brit.), cos; STAR, THE(1953), cos; OKLAHOMA(1955), cos; LES GIRLS(1957), cos; AUNTIE MAME(1958), cos; TOO MUCH, TOO SOON(1958), cos; HANGING TREE, THE(1959), cos; SOME LIKE IT HOT(1959), cos; MAJORITY OF ONE, A(1961), cos; CHAPMAN REPORT, THE(1962), cos; FIVE FINGER EXERCISE(1962), cos; FOUR HORSEMEN OF THE APOCALYPSE, THE(1962), cos; GYPSY(1962), cos; SWEET BIRD OF YOUTH(1962), cos; TWO FOR THE SEESAW(1962), cos; IN THE COOL OF THE DAY(1963), cos; IRMA LA DOUCE(1963), cos; SUNDAY IN NEW YORK(1963), cos; WHEN TIME RAN OUT(1980), cos
Frank Orsati
JESUS TRIP, THE(1971); LENNY(1974)
Ernie Orsatti
MECHANIC, THE(1972); LAST AMERICAN HERO, THE(1973); TOWERING INFERNO, THE(1974); NIGHT MOVES(1975); SKY RIDERS(1976, U.S./Gr.); CAR, THE(1977); VIVA KNIEVEL!(1977); SWARM, THE(1978)
1984
EVIL THAT MEN DO, THE(1984), stunts
Frank Orsatti
IRISH IN US, THE(1935), w
Victor M. Orsatti
DOMINO KID(1957), p; HIRED GUN, THE(1957), p; APACHE TERRITORY(1958), p
Marina Orschel
TATTERED DRESS, THE(1957); BIMBO THE GREAT(1961, Ger.)
Moira Orsei
SCENT OF A WOMAN(1976, Ital.)
Rene Orsell
MADE FOR EACH OTHER(1939)
Ed Orshan
OUT OF IT(1969), ed; RENT CONTROL(1981), ed
Lee Orsher
WORLDS APART(1980, U.S., Israel)
Bill Orsi
1984
SIXTEEN CANDLES(1984)
Umberto Orsin
MYTH, THE(1965, Ital.)
Silvio Orsini
Misc. Silents
TOILER, THE(1932, Ital.)
Umberto Orsini
BATTLE OF THE WORLDS(1961, Ital.); LA DOLCE VITA(1961, Ital./Fr.); DON'T TEMPT THE DEVIL(1964, Fr./Ital.), a, w; SWEET SKIN(1965, Fr./Ital.); MADEMOISELLE(1966, Fr./Brit.); GIRL AND THE GENERAL, THE(1967, Fr./Ital.); SAILOR FROM GIBRALTAR, THE(1967, Brit.); CANDY(1968, Ital./Fr.); THAT WOMAN(1968, Ger.); CESAR AND ROSALIE(1972, Fr.); LUDWIG(1973, Ital./Ger./Fr.); OUTSIDE MAN, THE(1973, U.S./Fr.); FAMILY, THE(1974, Fr./Ital.); NO WAY OUT(1975, Ital./Fr.); TEMPTER, THE(1978, Ital.); WOMAN AT HER WINDOW, A(1978, Fr./Ital./Ger.); SOME LIKE IT COOL(1979, Ger./Aust./Ital./Fr.); GOODBYE EMMANUELLE(1980, Fr.)
1984
BEYOND GOOD AND EVIL(1984, Ital./Fr./Ger.)
Anna Maria Orso
BIBLE...IN THE BEGINNING, THE(1966); DAY OF ANGER(1970, Ital./Ger.)
Anna Orso
LEAP INTO THE VOID(1982, Ital.)
Luigi Orso
SUPERFLY T.N.T.(1973)
Ronald Orso
DON'T CRY, IT'S ONLY THUNDER(1982)
Erzsi Orsolya
LOVE(1972, Hung.)
Erie Orsom
LONE HAND, THE(1953), art d
Barbara Orson
Misc. Talkies
MISSION HILL(1982)
Elen Orson
COMMITMENT, THE(1976), ed
Janice Orson
COMMITMENT, THE(1976), art d
Orson Welles' Mercury Wonder Show
FOLLOW THE BOYS(1944)

Odette Orsy
FINAL CHORD, THE(1936, Ger.)
Josef Ort-Snep
MOST BEAUTIFUL AGE, THE(1970, Czech.), ph
Sergio Orta
ZIEGFELD GIRL(1941); MOONLIGHT IN HAVANA(1942); SEVEN DAYS LEAVE(1942)
Julio Ortas
ONE STEP TO HELL(1969, U.S./Ital./Span.), ph
Julio Ortaz
MYSTERIOUS ISLAND OF CAPTAIN NEMO, THE(1973, Fr./Ital. 87m Span./Cameroon), ph
Angie Ortega
HOSPITAL, THE(1971); PANIC IN NEEDLE PARK(1971)
Art Ortega
STAR PACKER, THE(1934)
Silents
AVENGING TRAIL, THE(1918)
Artie Ortega
SERGEANT MURPHY(1938); STAGECOACH(1939)
Silents
RIDING WITH DEATH(1921); FIGHTING BOOB, THE(1926)
Casimiro Ortega
Misc. Talkies
ANGRY GOD, THE(1948)
Cuauatemoc Ortega
MASSACRE(1956)
David Ortega
LOVES OF CARMEN, THE(1948)
Ernie Ortega
1984
MISSING IN ACTION(1984)
Francisco Ortega
THIRD VOICE, THE(1960); FUN IN ACAPULCO(1963)
Frankie Ortega
LONG ROPE, THE(1961), m
John Ortega
NAPOLEON AND SAMANTHA(1972)
Kenny Ortega
XANADU(1980), ch; ONE FROM THE HEART(1982), ch
Leon Ortega
GERONIMO(1962), spec eff; TWO MULES FOR SISTER SARA(1970), spec eff; LAWMAN(1971), spec eff; BUCK AND THE PREACHER(1972), spec eff; SLAUGHTER(1972), spec eff; MAGNIFICENT ONE, THE(1974, Fr./Ital.), spec eff; MAN FRIDAY(1975, Brit.), spec eff
Pablo Garcia Ortega
1984
YELLOW HAIR AND THE FORTRESS OF GOLD(1984)
Pedro Ortega
MANOLETE(1950, Span.)
Santos Ortega
FAMILY SECRET, THE(1951); CROWDED PARADISE(1956)
Sergio Ortega
JORY(1972), ed; BRING ME THE HEAD OF ALFREDO GARCIA(1974), ed
Sofia Ortega
BIRD OF PARADISE(1932)
Art Ortego
OKLAHOMA JIM(1931)
Silents
GIRL OF THE GOLDEN WEST, THE(1915)
Arthur Ortego
RANDY RIDES ALONE(1934)
Silents
AMERICAN ARISTOCRACY(1916)
Artie Ortego
GOD'S COUNTRY AND THE MAN(1931); NEAR THE TRAIL'S END(1931); SQUAW MAN, THE(1931); CORNERED(1932); GALLOPING THRU(1932); RIDING TORNADO, THE(1932); KING OF THE ARENA(1933); LUCKY TEXAN, THE(1934); MAN FROM UTAH, THE(1934); MAN TRAILER, THE(1934); 'NEATH THE ARIZONA SKIES(1934); TRAIL BEYOND, THE(1934); WEST OF THE DIVIDE(1934); WHEELS OF DESTINY(1934); DESERT TRAIL(1935); FIGHTING TROOPER(1935); LAWLESS FRONTIER, THE(1935); NORTHERN FRONTIER(1935); PALS OF THE RANGE(1935); ROUGH RIDING RANGER(1935); TOMBSTONE TERROR(1935); CROOKED TRAIL, THE(1936); GHOST PATROL(1936); HEIR TO TROUBLE(1936); KING OF THE ROYAL MOUNTED(1936); LIGHTNING BILL CARSON(1936); ROARIN' GUNS(1936); SONG OF THE TRAIL(1936); THREE ON THE TRAIL(1936); TREACHERY RIDES THE RANGE(1936); EMPTY HOLSTERS(1937); HOPALONG RIDES AGAIN(1937); LAND BEYOND THE LAW(1937); KANSAS TERRORS, THE(1939); PIONEERS OF THE WEST(1940); DAWN ON THE GREAT DIVIDE(1942); PIRATES OF THE PRAIRIE(1942); OUTLAWS OF STAMPEDE PASS(1943); SIX GUN GOSPEL(1943); STRANGER FROM PECOS, THE(1943); WESTERN CYCLONE(1943); DEVIL RIDERS(1943); TRAIL OF TERROR(1944); TRIGGER TRAIL(1944); IN OLD NEW MEXICO(1945); ROUGH RIDERS OF CHEYENNE(1945); SUDAN(1945); GENTLEMAN FROM TEXAS(1946); GUNMAN'S CODE(1946); LAWLESS BREED(1946); RUSTLER'S ROUNDUP(1946); SONG OF THE SIERRAS(1946); SUNSET PASS(1946); PRAIRIE EXPRESS(1947); RAIDERS OF THE SOUTH(1947); SIX GUN SERENADE(1947); CROSSED TRAILS(1948); GUNNING FOR JUSTICE(1948); STAMPEDE(1949); WEST OF EL DORADO(1949); COLT .45(1950); OVER THE BORDER(1950); NEVADA BADMEN(1951); SKIPALONG ROSENBLOOM(1951)
Artie Ortego [Art Ardigan]
SPURS(1930)
John Ortego
Silents
GIRL OF THE GOLDEN WEST, THE(1915)
Berta Ortegosa
END OF INNOCENCE(1960, Arg.); HAND IN THE TRAP, THE(1963, Arg./Span.)
Artie Ortejo
ESCAPE TO BURMA(1955)

Bruno Ortensi
SHOE SHINE(1947, Ital.)
Frank Orth
UNWELCOME STRANGER(1935); HOT MONEY(1936); POLO JOE(1936); TWO AGAINST THE WORLD(1936); DEVIL'S SADDLE LEGION, THE(1937); EVER SINCE EVE(1937); FOOTLOOSE HEIRESS, THE(1937); LAND BEYOND THE LAW(1937); PRAIRIE THUNDER(1937); COMET OVER BROADWAY(1938); MR. CHUMP(1938); NANCY DREW—DETECTIVE(1938); PATIENT IN ROOM 18, THE(1938); BROADWAY SERENADE(1939); BURN 'EM UP O'CONNER(1939); FAST AND FURIOUS(1939); IDIOT'S DELIGHT(1939); NANCY DREW—REPORTER(1939); NANCY DREW AND THE HIDDEN STAIRCASE(1939); SECRET OF DR. KILDARE, THE(1939); SOCIETY LAWYER(1939); STANLEY AND LIVINGSTONE(1939); TELL NO TALES(1939); YOUNG MR. LINCOLN(1939); BOOM TOWN(1940); DOCTOR TAKES A WIFE(1940); DR. KILDARE'S CRISIS(1940); DR. KILDARE'S STRANGE CASE(1940); FATHER IS A PRINCE(1940); FLORIAN(1940); HIS GIRL FRIDAY(1940); LA CONGA NIGHTS(1940); LET'S MAKE MUSIC(1940); MEXICAN SPITFIRE OUT WEST(1940); MICHAEL SHAYNE, PRIVATE DETECTIVE(1940); PIER 13(1940); 'TIL WE MEET AGAIN(1940); BLUE, WHITE, AND PERFECT(1941); COME LIVE WITH ME(1941); DR. KILDARE'S VICTORY(1941); DR. KILDARE'S WEDDING DAY(1941); GREAT AMERICAN BROADCAST, THE(1941); KISSES FOR BREAKFAST(1941); PEOPLE VS. DR. KILDARE, THE(1941); SERGEANT YORK(1941); SKYLARK(1941); STRAWBERRY BLONDE, THE(1941); DR. GILLESPIE'S NEW ASSISTANT(1942); FOOTLIGHT SERENADE(1942); I WAKE UP SCREAMING(1942); LITTLE TOKYO, U.S.A.(1942); MAGNIFICENT DOPE, THE(1942); MY GAL SAL(1942); ORCHESTRA WIVES(1942); OVER MY DEAD BODY(1942); RIGHT TO THE HEART(1942); RINGS ON HER FINGERS(1942); ROXIE HART(1942); SPRINGTIME IN THE ROCKIES(1942); TALES OF MANHATTAN(1942); THEY DIED WITH THEIR BOOTS ON(1942); TO THE SHORES OF TRIPOLI(1942); CONEY ISLAND(1943); HELLO, FRISCO, HELLO(1943); SWEET ROSIE O'GRADY(1943); BUFFALO BILL(1944); CAROLINA BLUES(1944); GREENWICH VILLAGE(1944); IMPATIENT YEARS, THE(1944); ROGER TOUHY, GANGSTER(1944); STORM OVER LISBON(1944); SUMMER STORM(1944); TALL IN THE SADDLE(1944); WILSON(1944); COLONEL EFFINGHAM'S RAID(1945); DOLL FACE(1945); DOLLY SISTERS, THE(1945); LOST WEEKEND, THE(1945); NOB HILL(1945); PILLOW TO POST(1945); SHE WENT TO THE RACES(1945); TELL IT TO A STAR(1945); WONDER MAN(1945); BLONDIE'S LUCKY DAY(1946); BRIDE WORE BOOTS, THE(1946); HOODLUM SAINT, THE(1946); IT'S GREAT TO BE YOUNG(1946); MURDER IN THE MUSIC HALL(1946); SHOW-OFF, THE(1946); STRANGE LOVE OF MARTHA IVERS, THE(1946); WAKE UP AND DREAM(1946); BORN TO SPEED(1947); GAS HOUSE KIDS IN HOLLYWOOD(1947); GUILT OF JANET AMES, THE(1947); HEARTACHES(1947); IT HAD TO BE YOU(1947); LADY IN THE LAKE(1947); MOTHER WORE TIGHTS(1947); BIG CLOCK, THE(1948); BLONDIE'S SECRET(1948); FAMILY HONEYMOON(1948); FURY AT FURNACE CREEK(1948); GIRL FROM MANHATTAN(1948); SO THIS IS NEW YORK(1948); BRIDE FOR SALE(1949); MAKE BELIEVE BALLROOM(1949); RED LIGHT(1949); CHEAPER BY THE DOZEN(1950); FATHER OF THE BRIDE(1950); GREAT RUPERT, THE(1950); PETTY GIRL, THE(1950); SOMETHING TO LIVE FOR(1952); HERE COME THE GIRLS(1953); HOUDINI(1953)
Margit Orth
INTERMEZZO(1937, Swed.)
Marian Orth
DR. CHRISTIAN MEETS THE WOMEN(1940), w
Marion Orth
MOTHER KNOWS BEST(1928), w; STREET ANGEL(1928), w; CHRISTINA(1929), w; FOUR DEVILS(1929), w; NOT QUITE DECENT(1929), w; ROMANCE OF THE RIO GRANDE(1929), w; CAMEO KIRBY(1930), w; CITY GIRL(1930), w; CRAZY THAT WAY(1930), d&w; MAN TROUBLE(1930), w; THREE SISTERS, THE(1930), w; BEAUTY PARLOR(1932), w; CHARLIE CHAN'S GREATEST CASE(1933), w; SUCCESSFUL FAILURE, A(1934), w; WELCOME HOME(1935), w; PARADISE ISLE(1937), w; ROMANCE OF THE LIMBERLOST(1938), w; SALESLADY(1938), w; UNDER THE BIG TOP(1938), w; HIDDEN ENEMY(1940), w; SON OF THE NAVY(1940), w; TOMBOY(1940), w; SING ANOTHER CHORUS(1941), w; SIX LESSONS FROM MADAME LA ZONGA(1941), w; MISSISSIPPI GAMBLER(1942), w; OH, WHAT A NIGHT(1944), w
Silents
MIDNIGHT ROMANCE, A(1919), w; DARK STAIRWAYS(1924), w; AS MAN DESIRES(1925), w; CORPORAL KATE(1926), w; BY WHOSE HAND?(1927), w; WHITE GOLD(1927), w; WOMAN WHO DID NOT CARE, THE(1927), w; SHARP SHOOTERS(1928), w
Burkhard Orthgies
ROSES FOR THE PROSECUTOR(1961, Ger.)
Ben Ortico
BLOOD DRINKERS, THE(1966, U.S./Phil.), art d
Sophia Ortiga
Misc. Silents
REVENGE(1928)
Carlos David Ortigos
SUN ALSO RISES, THE(1957)
Carlos Ortigoza
LITTLEST OUTLAW, THE(1955)
Leopoldo Ortin
LAST REBEL, THE(1961, Mex.)
Ginny Ortix
WILLIE AND PHIL(1980)
Alicia Ortiz
Misc. Silents
SOUL OF MEXICO(1932, Mex.)
Angel Ortiz
LAST DAYS OF POMPEII, THE(1960, Ital.); GOLIATH AGAINST THE GIANTS(1963, Ital./Span.); NAVAJO JOE(1967, Ital./Span.); MERCENARY, THE(1970, Ital./Span.)
Church Ortiz
DEFIANCE(1980); HERO AT LARGE(1980)
David Ortiz
BANANAS(1971)
Eddie Ortiz
FIEND OF DOPE ISLAND(1961)
Fernando Morales Ortiz
LITTLE RED RIDING HOOD(1963, Mex.), w; LITTLE RED RIDING HOOD AND THE MONSTERS(1965, Mex.), w

Ginny Ortiz
WARRIORS, THE(1979)
Israel Ortiz
TEENAGE MOTHER(1967), ed
Joe Ortiz
BLACK SHAMPOO(1976)
Jose Carlos Ortiz
PEARL OF TLAYUCAN, THE(1964, Mex.)
Juan Omar Ortiz
CAVEMAN(1981)
Juan Ortiz
UNDER THE PAMPAS MOON(1935)
Manuel Ortiz
JOE PALOOKA, CHAMP(1946); SCUM OF THE EARTH(1963), m
Matador Pepe Ortiz
LITTLEST OUTLAW, THE(1955)
Mecha Ortiz
Misc. Talkies
HOUSE OF SHADOWS(1977, Arg.)
Nina Ortiz
WE SHALL RETURN(1963)
Peter Ortiz
TWELVE O'CLOCK HIGH(1949); RIO GRANDE(1950); SPY HUNT(1950); WHEN WILLIE COMES MARCHING HOME(1950); SIROCCO(1951); JUBILEE TRAIL(1954); KING RICHARD AND THE CRUSADERS(1954); LAWLESS STREET, A(1955); SON OF SINBAD(1955); SEVENTH CAVALRY(1956); WINGS OF EAGLES, THE(1957)
Rosanna Ortiz
SAVAGE SISTERS(1974)
Rossana Ortiz
Misc. Talkies
SAVAGE!(1973)
Sammy Ortiz
HIGH RISK(1981)
Leoncid Ortiz-Gil
JONIKO AND THE KUSH TA KA(1969), ed
Leon Ortiz-Gill
BATTLESTAR GALACTICA(1979), ed
Alfred Ortlieb
Silents
SHOOTING OF DAN MCGREW, THE(1915), ph; LIFTING SHADOWS(1920), ph; MODERN SALOME, A(1920), ph; BAIT, THE(1921), ph; LOVE'S PENALTY(1921), ph; STARDUST(1921), ph; LIGHT IN THE DARK, THE(1922), ph; STREETS OF NEW YORK, THE(1922), ph; LOVER'S ISLAND(1925), ph
Riz Ortolani
EASY LIFE, THE(1963, Ital.), m; FALL OF ROME, THE(1963, Ital.), m; CASTLE OF BLOOD(1964, Fr./Ital.), m; NAKED HOURS, THE(1964, Ital.), m; SEVENTH DAWN, THE(1964), m, md; GLORY GUYS, THE(1965); m; HORROR CASTLE(1965, Ital.), m; YELLOW ROLLS-ROYCE, THE(1965, Brit.), m; MAYA(1966); m; SPY IN YOUR EYE(1966, Ital.), m; SPY WITH A COLD NOSE, THE(1966, Brit.), m, md; LIGHTNING BOLT(1967, Ital./Sp.), m; RED-DRAGON(1967, Ital./Ger./US), m, md; WOMAN TIMES SEVEN(1967, U.S./Fr./Ital.), m, md; ANZIO(1968, Ital.), m; BIGGEST BUNDLE OF THEM ALL, THE(1968), m; BLISS OF MRS. BLOSSOM, THE(1968, Brit.), m; BUONA SERA, MRS. CAMPBELL(1968, Ital.), m; CHASTITY BELT, THE(1968, Ital.), m, md; OLD SHATTERHAND(1968, Ger./Yugo./Fr./Ital.), m; SARDINIA: RANSOM(1968, Ital.), m; VIOLENT FOUR, THE(1968, Ital.), m; FIGHT FOR ROME(1969, Ger./Rum.), m; GIRL WHO COULDN'T SAY NO, THE(1969, Ital.), m; LADY HAMILTON(1969, Ger./Ital./Fr.), m; ADVENTURES OF GERARD, THE(1970, Brit.), m; DAY OF ANGER(1970, Ital./Ger.), m; MADRON(1970, U.S./Israel), m; MC KENZIE BREAK, THE(1970), m; CONFESSIONS OF A POLICE CAPTAIN(1971, Ital.), m; SAY HELLO TO YESTERDAY(1971, Brit.), m; STATUE, THE(1971, Brit.), m, md; DEAD ARE ALIVE, THE(1972, Yugo./Ger./Ital.), m; VALACHI PAPERS, THE(1972, Ital./Fr.), m; WEB OF THE SPIDER(1972, Ital./Fr./Ger.), m; REASON TO LIVE, A REASON TO DIE, A(1974, Ital./Fr./Ger./Span.), m; BEYOND THE DOOR(1975, Ital./U.S.), m; MEAN FRANK AND CRAZY TONY(1976, Ital.), m; BEHIND THE IRON MASK(1977), m; HUNTING PARTY, THE(1977, Brit.), m, md; THERE IS NO 13(1977), m; FROM HELL TO VICTORY(1979, Fr./Ital./Span.), m; SOME LIKE IT COOL(1979, Ger./Aust./Ital./Fr.), m; GIRL FROM TRIESTE, THE(1983, Ital.), m
Stefano Ortolani
MONSIGNOR(1982), art d
Harold Orton
GIRL ON APPROVAL(1962, Brit.), p; LUNCH HOUR(1962, Brit.), p; SKY BIKE, THE(1967, Brit.), p; HITCH IN TIME, A(1978, Brit.), p
J. O. C. Orton
WOMAN IN COMMAND, THE(1934 Brit.), w; NON-STOP NEW YORK(1937, Brit.), w; IT'S IN THE BLOOD(1938, Brit.), w; MANY TANKS MR. ATKINS(1938, Brit.), w; MAIL TRAIN(1941, Brit.), w
J.O.C. Orton
LEAVE IT TO SMITH(1934), w; ALIAS BULLDOG DRUMMOND(1935, Brit.), w; BORN FOR GLORY(1935, Brit.), w; JACK AHOY!(1935, Brit.), w; TURN OF THE TIDE(1935, Brit.), w; EVERYTHING IS THUNDER(1936, Brit.), w; FLYING DOCTOR, THE(1936, Aus.), w; OH, MR. PORTER!(1937, Brit.), w; TAKE IT FROM ME(1937, Brit.), w; HEY! HEY! U.S.A.(1938, Brit.), w; MR. SATAN(1938, Brit.), w; OLD BONES OF THE RIVER(1938, Brit.), w; THISTLEDOWN(1938, Brit.), w; TWO OF US, THE(1938, Brit.), w; VIPER, THE(1938, Brit.), w; FROZEN LIMITS, THE(1939, Brit.), w; INSPECTOR HORNLEIGH ON HOLIDAY(1939, Brit.), w; WHERE'S THAT FIRE?(1939, Brit.), w; BOMBSIGHT STOLEN(1941, Brit.), w; GHOST TRAIN, THE(1941, Brit.), w; HI, GANG!(1941, Brit.), w; FOR THOSE IN PERIL(1944, Brit.), w; TIME FLIES(1944, Brit.), w
Joe Orton
ENTERTAINING MR. SLOANE(1970, Brit.), w; LOOT(1971, Brit.), w; SWEET CREEK COUNTY WAR, THE(1979)
John Orton
LIMPING MAN, THE(1931, Brit.), p,d&w; OUT OF THE BLUE(1931, Brit.), d; WINDJAMMER, THE(1931, Brit.), d, w; UP TO HIS NECK(1954, Brit.), w
Misc. Silents
CELESTIAL CITY, THE(1929, Brit.), d
Peter Z. Orton
1984
NIGHT SHADOWS(1984), w

Ray Orton
PRIVATE ENTERPRISE, A(1975, Brit.), ph; WHAT'S NEXT?(1975, Brit.), ph
1984
BREAKOUT(1984, Brit.), ph
Wallace Orton
SAY IT WITH FLOWERS(1934, Brit.), w; SUNSHINE AHEAD(1936, Brit.), d; OLD MOTHER RILEY'S CIRCUS(1941, Brit.), p; ASKING FOR TROUBLE(1942, Brit.), p; SALUTE JOHN CITIZEN(1942, Brit.), p; DUMMY TALKS, THE(1943, Brit.), p; CANDLES AT NINE(1944, Brit.), p
Danda Ortone
SONS OF SATAN(1969, Ital./Fr./Ger.), cos
John Ortstadt
LOOKIN' TO GET OUT(1982)
Rita Ortway
Silents
LOVE'S OLD SWEET SONG(1917, Brit.)
Jozefa Orvos-Toth
FATHER(1967, Hung.)
George Orwell
ANIMAL FARM(1955, Brit.), w; 1984(1956, Brit.), w
1984
1984(1984, Brit.), w
Edward "Kid" Ory
BENNY GOODMAN STORY, THE(1956)
Kid Ory
NEW ORLEANS(1947)
Kasia Orzazekski
I WAS A COMMUNIST FOR THE F.B.I.(1951)
Kazi Orzazewaki
EXECUTIVE SUITE(1954)
Kasia Orzazewski
CALL NORTHSIDE 777(1948); RED DANUBE, THE(1949); THIEVES' HIGHWAY(1949); QUEEN FOR A DAY(1951); DEADLINE–U.S.A.(1952)
Al Orzechowski
SPRING FEVER(1983, Can.)
K. Orzechowski
YOUNG GIRLS OF WILKO, THE(1979, Pol./Fr.)
Richard Orzel
ME AND MY BROTHER(1969)
Arata Osada
CHILDREN OF HIROSHIMA(1952, Jap.), w
Shiro Osaka
MAN FROM THE EAST, THE(1961, Jap.); TOKYO STORY(1972, Jap.)
Kaoru Osanai
Misc. Silents
SOULS ON THE ROAD(1921, Jap.), d
Sono Osato
KISSING BANDIT, THE(1948)
Tetsuzo Osawa
MESSAGE FROM SPACE(1978, Jap.), art d
Alan Osbiston
UPTURNED GLASS, THE(1947, Brit.), ed; AGAINST THE WIND(1948, Brit.), ed; CHANCE OF A LIFETIME(1950, Brit.), d, ed; LAUGHING LADY, THE(1950, Brit.), ed; I'LL NEVER FORGET YOU(1951), ed; OPERATION DISASTER(1951, Brit.), ed; IT STARTED IN PARADISE(1952, Brit.), ed; BEAUTIFUL STRANGER(1954, Brit.), ed; INSPECTOR CALLS, AN(1954, Brit.), ed; COCKLESHELL HEROES, THE(1955), ed; END OF THE AFFAIR, THE(1955, Brit.), ed; FOOTSTEPS IN THE FOG(1955, Brit.), ed; INTRUDER, THE(1955, Brit.), ed; GAMMA PEOPLE, THE(1956), ed; ODONGO(1956, Brit.), ed; ZARAK(1956, Brit.), ed; STOWAWAY GIRL(1957, Brit.), ed; TIME WITHOUT PITY(1957, Brit.), ed; DEVIL'S DISCIPLE, THE(1959), ed; SILENT ENEMY, THE(1959, Brit.), ed; SON OF ROBIN HOOD(1959, Brit.), ed; ENTERTAINER, THE(1960, Brit.), ed; IT TAKES A THIEF(1960, Brit.), ed; TOUCH OF LARCENY, A(1960, Brit.), ed; GUNS OF NAVARONE, THE(1961), ed; ROAD TO HONG KONG, THE(1962, U.S./Brit.), ed; VICTORS, THE(1963), ed; LORD JIM(1965), ed; THE DIRTY GAME(1966, Fr./Ital./Ger.), ed; WRONG BOX, THE(1966, Brit.), ed; BILLION DOLLAR BRAIN(1967, Brit.), ed; NIGHT OF THE GENERALS, THE(1967, Brit./Fr.), ed; PLAY DIRTY(1969, Brit.), ed; THREE INTO TWO WON'T GO(1969, Brit.), ed
Max Osbiston
PHANTOM STOCKMAN, THE(1953, Aus.)
Andrew Osborn
WHO GOES NEXT?(1938, Brit.); IDOL OF PARIS(1948, Brit.); POET'S PUB(1949, Brit.); DARK INTERVAL(1950, Brit.); SHADOW OF THE PAST(1950, Brit.); HER PANELLED DOOR(1951, Brit.); LADY WITH A LAMP, THE(1951, Brit.); SECOND MRS. TANQUERAY, THE(1952, Brit.); BLOOD ORANGE(1953, Brit.); SPACEWAYS(1953, Brit.); BLACKOUT(1954, Brit.)
Bud Osborn
ACROSS THE PLAINS(1939); 'NEATH BROOKLYN BRIDGE(1942)
Daniel Osborn
SMILE(1975), m
David Osborn
MURDER SHE SAID(1961, Brit.), w; MALAGA(1962, Brit.), w; FOLLOW THE BOYS(1963), w; DEADLIER THAN THE MALE(1967, Brit.), w; MAROC 7(1967, Brit.), w; TRAP, THE(1967, Can./Brit.), w; SOME GIRLS DO(1969, Brit.), w; WHO SLEW AUNTIE ROO?(1971, U.S./Brit.), w; OPEN SEASON(1974, U.S./Span.), w
David D. Osborn
CHASE A CROOKED SHADOW(1958, Brit.), w
Judy Osborn
LADY POSSESSED(1952)
Lyn Osborn
INVASION OF THE SAUCER MEN(1957); TOP SECRET AFFAIR(1957); TOO MUCH, TOO SOON(1958); ARSON FOR HIRE(1959); COSMIC MAN, THE(1959)
Lynn Osborn
AMAZING COLOSSAL MAN, THE(1957)
Marie Osborn
HERE COME THE CO-EDS(1945)
Michael Osborn
1984
WHERE THE BOYS ARE '84(1984)

Paul Osborn

SHOULD LADIES BEHAVE?(1933), w; YOUNG IN HEART, THE(1938), w; MADAME CURIE(1943), w; YEARLING, THE(1946), w; HOMECOMING(1948), w; PORTRAIT OF JENNIE(1949), w; INVITATION(1952), w; EAST OF EDEN(1955), w; SAYONARA(1957), w; SOUTH PACIFIC(1958), w; WILD RIVER(1960), w; WORLD OF SUZIE WONG, THE(1960), w

Rupert Osborn

NIGHT CREATURES(1962, Brit.)

Ted Osborn

GIRL WITH IDEAS, A(1937); STATE POLICE(1938); CAPTAIN CAUTION(1940); CHARLIE CHAN AT THE WAX MUSEUM(1940)

Theodore Osborn

GIRL WITH IDEAS, A(1937); PRESCRIPTION FOR ROMANCE(1937); MIDNIGHT INTRUDER(1938)

Tom Osborn
Misc. Talkies

GOLD DIGGERS, THE(1984, Brit.)

Ralph Osborn III

RALLY 'ROUND THE FLAG, BOYS!(1958)

John Jay Osborn, Jr.

PAPER CHASE, THE(1973), w

Alan Osborne

GENTLE TRAP, THE(1960, Brit.), w

Baby Marie Osborne

SWING TIME(1936); FOLLOW THE BOYS(1944)
Silents

JOY AND THE DRAGON(1916); LITTLE PATRIOT, A(1917); CUPID BY PROXY(1918); DOLLY'S VACATION(1918); CHILD OF M'SIEU(1919); OLD MAID'S BABY, THE(1919)
Misc. Silents

LITTLE MARY SUNSHINE(1916)

Beverly Osborne

ONLY WAY HOME, THE(1972)

Brian Osborne

WOMEN IN LOVE(1969, Brit.); CARRY ON ENGLAND(1976, Brit.); NIGHTHAWKS(1981)

Bud Osborne

WEST OF THE ROCKIES(1929); CANYON OF MISSING MEN, THE(1930); UTAH KID, THE(1930); ONE WAY TRAIL, THE(1931); RED FORK RANGE(1931); COME ON DANGER!(1932); MC KENNA OF THE MOUNTED(1932); RIDING TORNADO, THE(1932); SUNSET TRAIL(1932); TEXAS BAD MAN(1932); DEADWOOD PASS(1933); DIAMOND TRAIL(1933); FLAMING GUNS(1933); FOURTH HORSE-MAN, THE(1933); RUSTLERS' ROUNDUP(1933); WHEN A MAN RIDES ALONE(1933); FIGHTING RANGER, THE(1934); LAST ROUND-UP, THE(1934); RIDING SPEED(1934); ROCKY RHODES(1934); CRIMSON TRAIL, THE(1935); FIGHTING SHADOWS(1935); GALLANT DEFENDER(1935); JUSTICE OF THE RANGE(1935); OUTLAW DEPUTY, THE(1935); PALS OF THE RANGE(1935); STORMY(1935); WANDERER OF THE WASTELAND(1935); FUGITIVE SHERIFF, THE(1936); GUN SMOKE(1936); HEROES OF THE RANGE(1936); MOONLIGHT ON THE PRAIRIE(1936); PRESCOTT KID, THE(1936); SONG OF THE SADDLE(1936); TRAILIN' WEST(1936); TREACHERY RIDES THE RANGE(1936); WESTERNER, THE(1936); BOOTS AND SADDLES(1937); CHEROKEE STRIP(1937); DEVIL'S SADDLE LEGION, THE(1937); GHOST TOWN GOLD(1937); GUNS OF THE PECOS(1937); HEADIN' FOR THE RIO GRANDE(1937); LAND BEYOND THE LAW(1937); LAW OF THE RANGER(1937); PINTO RUSTLERS(1937); PLAINSMAN, THE(1937); RANGER COURAGE(1937); RECKLESS RANGER(1937); WESTERN GOLD(1937); WHERE TRAILS DIVIDE(1937); YODELIN' KID FROM PINE RIDGE(1937); DANGER VALLEY(1938); IN EARLY ARIZONA(1938); JUVENILE COURT(1938); MAN'S COUNTRY(1938); MEXICALI KID, THE(1938); OVERLAND EXPRESS, THE(1938); OVERLAND STAGE RAIDERS(1938); PAINTED TRAIL, THE(1938); PRAIRIE MOON(1938); ROLL ALONG, COWBOY(1938); ROLLING CARAVANS(1938); SANTA FE STAMPEDE(1938); SIX SHOOTIN' SHERIFF(1938); UTAH TRAIL(1938); WEST OF SANTA FE(1938); COWBOYS FROM TEXAS(1939); DAYS OF JESSE JAMES(1939); DODGE CITY(1939); FRONTIER PONY EXPRESS(1939); FRONTIERS OF '49(1939); NEW FRONTIER(1939); NIGHT RIDERS, THE(1939); RACKETEERS OF THE RANGE(1939); ROVIN' TUMBLEWEEDS(1939); SUNDOWN ON THE PRAIRIE(1939); TIMBER STAMPEDE(1939); TWO-GUN TROUBADOR(1939); COWBOY FROM SUNDOWN(1940); DEATH RIDES THE RANGE(1940); GHOST VALLEY RAIDERS(1940); LAND OF THE SIX GUNS(1940); LEGION OF THE LAWLESS(1940); LONE STAR RAIDERS(1940); ONE MAN'S LAW(1940); PIONEER DAYS(1940); PRAIRIE LAW(1940); RAGTIME COWBOY JOE(1940); RANCHO GRANDE(1940); STRANGER ON THE THIRD FLOOR(1940); VIRGINIA CITY(1940); WEST OF ABILENE(1940); WEST OF PINTO BASIN(1940); WILD HORSE VALLEY(1940); BANDIT TRAIL, THE(1941); BURY ME NOT ON THE LONE PRAIRIE(1941); GANGS OF SONORA(1941); LAW OF THE RANGE(1941); MEDICO OF PAINTED SPRINGS, THE(1941); OUTLAWS OF THE CHEROKEE TRAIL(1941); OUTLAWS OF THE PANHANDLE(1941); PALS OF THE PECOS(1941); PHANTOM COWBOY, THE(1941); RETURN OF DANIEL BOONE, THE(1941); ROBBERS OF THE RANGE(1941); TWILIGHT ON THE TRAIL(1941); UNDERGROUND RUSTLERS(1941); BELOW THE BORDER(1942); CODE OF THE OUTLAW(1942); DAWN ON THE GREAT DIVIDE(1942); DEVIL'S TRAIL, THE(1942); FIGHTING BILL FARGO(1942); IN OLD CALIFORNIA(1942); RANGERS TAKE OVER, THE(1942); RIDERS OF THE WEST(1942); RIDING THE WIND(1942); SPOILERS, THE(1942); TRAIL RIDERS(1942); VALLEY OF THE SUN(1942); WEST OF THE LAW(1942); WESTWARD HO(1942); AVENGING RIDER, THE(1943); BAD MEN OF THUNDER GAP(1943); CANYON CITY(1943); CARSON CITY CYCLONE(1943); COWBOY COMMANDOS(1943); FIGHTING FRONTIER(1943); HAUNTED RANCH, THE(1943); RIDERS OF THE RIO GRANDE(1943); ROBIN HOOD OF THE RANGE(1943); SILVER SPURS(1943); SIX GUN GOSPEL(1943); STRANGER FROM PECOS, THE(1943); TENTING TONIGHT ON THE OLD CAMP GROUND(1943); CHEYENNE WILDCAT(1944); DEAD OR ALIVE(1944); DEVIL RIDERS(1944); GIRL RUSH(1944); LARAMIE TRAIL, THE(1944); LAW MEN(1944); MARKED TRAILS(1944); MARSHAL OF GUNSMOKE(1944); MOJAVE FIREBRAND(1944); OUTLAW TRAIL(1944); PRIDE OF THE PLAINS(1944); RAIDERS OF RED GAP(1944); RANGE LAW(1944); RUSTLER'S HIDEOUT(1944); SONORA STAGECOACH(1944); TEXAS KID, THE(1944); TRIGGER TRAIL(1944); VALLEY OF VENGEANCE(1944); CHEROKEE FLASH, THE(1945); FIGHTING BILL CARSON(1945); FLAME OF THE WEST(1945); FLAMING BULLETS(1945); HIS BROTHER'S GHOST(1945); IN OLD NEW MEXICO(1945); NAVAJO TRAIL, THE(1945); NORTHWEST TRAIL(1945); OREGON TRAIL(1945); PRAIRIE RUSTLERS(1945); SALOME, WHERE SHE DANCED(1945); SUNSET IN EL DORADO(1945); THREE IN THE SADDLE(1945); BORDER BANDITS(1946); CARAVAN TRAIL, THE(1946); DESERT HORSEMAN, THE(1946); LANDRUSH(1946); NAVAJO KID, THE(1946); OUTLAW OF THE PLAINS(1946); OVERLAND RIDERS(1946); RAINBOW OVER TEXAS(1946); RUSTLER'S ROUND-UP(1946); SIX GUN MAN(1946); THUNDER TOWN(1946); WILD WEST(1946); BOWERY BUCKAROOS(1947); CODE OF THE SADDLE(1947); LAST ROUND-UP, THE(1947); RETURN OF THE LASH(1947); SIX GUN SERENADE(1947); TWILIGHT ON THE RIO GRANDE(1947); WHITE STALLION(1947); BLOOD ON THE MOON(1948); COURTIN' TROUBLE(1948); COWBOY CAVALIER(1948); CROSSED TRAILS(1948); FRONTIER REVENGE(1948); GALLANT LEGION, THE(1948); GUNNING FOR JUSTICE(1948); INDIAN AGENT(1948); OUTLAW BRAND(1948); PANHANDLE(1948); PRAIRIE OUTLAWS(1948); RANGERS RIDE, THE(1948); RETURN OF THE BADMEN(1948); SILVER RIVER(1948); SILVER TRAILS(1948); SIX-GUN LAW(1948); SONG OF THE DRIFTER(1948); STATION WEST(1948); SUNDOWN RIDERS(1948); ACROSS THE RIO GRANDE(1949); GAY AMIGO, THE(1949); GUN LAW JUSTICE(1949); GUN RUNNER(1949); LAW OF THE WEST(1949); LAWLESS CODE(1949); RIDERS IN THE SKY(1949); ROARING WESTWARD(1949); SHADOWS OF THE WEST(1949); SON OF BILLY THE KID(1949); WEST OF EL DORADO(1949); ARIZONA TERRITORY(1950); BORDER OUTLAWS(1950); BORDER RANGERS(1950); COLORADO RANGER(1950); COW TOWN(1950); CROOKED RIVER(1950); DALTON'S WOMEN, THE(1950); FAST ON THE DRAW(1950); FRONTIER OUTPOST(1950); FULLER BRUSH GIRL, THE(1950); HOSTILE COUNTRY(1950); MARSHAL OF HELDORADO(1950); OUTLAW GOLD(1950); OVER THE BORDER(1950); SAVAGE HORDE, THE(1950); WEST OF THE BRAZOS(1950); WEST OF WYOMING(1950); WINCHESTER '73(1950); NEVADA BADMEN(1951); STAGE TO BLUE RIVER(1951); THUNDERING TRAIL, THE(1951); VALLEY OF FIRE(1951); VANISHING OUTPOST, THE(1951); WHIRLWIND(1951); WHISTLING HILLS(1951); BLACK LASH, THE(1952); BUGLES IN THE AFTERNOON(1952); FRONTIER PHANTOM, THE(1952); LAST OF THE COMANCHES(1952); MAN FROM BLACK HILLS, THE(1952); SO BIG(1953); LAWLESS RIDER, THE(1954); RIDING SHOTGUN(1954); BRIDE OF THE MONSTER(1955); FASTEST GUN ALIVE(1956); SOLID GOLD CADILLAC, THE(1956); TRIBUTE TO A BADMAN(1956); FLESH AND THE SPUR(1957); GUN GLORY(1957); STORM RIDER, THE(1957); ESCAPE FROM RED ROCK(1958); HANGING TREE, THE(1959)
Misc. Talkies

MARK OF THE SPUR(1932); RIDIN' THRU(1935); SONG OF THE RANGE(1944)
Silents

KNIGHT OF THE RANGE, A(1916); RAIDERS, THE(1921); STRUGGLE, THE(1921); LOSER'S END, THE(1924); ACROSS THE DEADLINE(1925); KNOCKOUT KID, THE(1925); LAW OF THE SNOW COUNTRY, THE(1926); LOOKING FOR TROUBLE(1926); KING OF THE HERD(1927); SKY-HIGH SAUNDERS(1927); LAW OF THE MOUNTED(1928); ON THE DIVIDE(1928); WEST OF SANTA FE(1928); FIGHTING TERROR, THE(1929); INVADERS, THE(1929); LARIAT KID, THE(1929); LAST ROUNDUP, THE(1929)
Misc. Silents

PRAIRIE MYSTERY, THE(1922); CYCLONE BUDDY(1924); BLIND TRAIL(1926); WITHOUT ORDERS(1926); RIDERS OF THE WEST(1927); BRONC STOMPER, THE(1928); CHEYENNE TRAILS(1928); FORBIDDEN TRAILS(1928); MYSTERY RIDER(1928); SECRETS OF THE RANGE(1928); TEXAS FLASH(1928); TEXAS TOMMY(1928); THRILL CHASER, THE(1928); WHERE THE WEST BEGINS(1928); COWBOY AND THE OUTLAW, THE(1929); FAR WESTERN TRAILS(1929); SMILING TERROR, THE(1929); CALL OF THE DESERT(1930); CANYON OF MISSING MEN, THE(1930); O'MALLEY RIDES ALONE(1930)

David Osborne

STOPOVER FOREVER(1964, Brit.), w; 2001: A SPACE ODYSSEY(1968, U.S./Brit.), spec eff

Debbie Osborne
Misc. Talkies

CINDY AND DONNA(1971); MIDNIGHT PLOWBOY(1973); MANSON MASSACRE, THE(1976)

Deborah Osborne
Misc. Talkies

TOY BOX, THE(1971)

Frances Osborne

JOE PALOOKA IN THE BIG FIGHT(1949); I, THE JURY(1953); MAN CRAZY(1953); SO BIG(1953); BEHIND THE HIGH WALL(1956); MURDER BY CONTRACT(1958); WILD WESTERNERS, THE(1962)

G.K. Osborne

LILITH(1964)

Gregory Osborne

I'M DANCING AS FAST AS I CAN(1982)

Holmes Osborne

STUDENT BODY, THE(1976)

Hubert Osborne

FOLLOW THE FLEET(1936), w; STRANGE EXPERIMENT(1937, Brit.), w; HIT THE DECK(1955), w
Silents

SHORE LEAVE(1925), w

Hugh R. Osborne
Silents

NUGGET NELL(1919), w

Jeff Osborne
Silents

ONCE A PLUMBER(1920)

Jesse Osborne

BLACK GIRL(1972), m

Jim Osborne

SUMMER'S CHILDREN(1979, Can.), w

John Osborne

LOOK BACK IN ANGER(1959), w; ENTERTAINER, THE(1960, Brit.), w; TOM JONES(1963, Brit.), w; INADMISSIBLE EVIDENCE(1968, Brit.), w; FIRST LOVE(1970, Ger./Switz.); GET CARTER(1971, Brit.); LUTHER(1974), w; ENTERTAINER, THE(1975), w; TOMORROW NEVER COMES(1978, Brit./Can.); FLASH GORDON(1980)

Judy Osborne

CHARADE(1953)

Kent Osborne

BLOOD OF DRACULA'S CASTLE(1967); CAIN'S WAY(1969), p, d; GUN RIDERS, THE(1969); WILD WHEELS(1969), d, w; HELL'S BLOODY DEVILS(1970)

Lennie "Bud" Osborne
Misc. Talkies
BALLAD OF BILLIE BLUE(1972), d; FIVE ANGRY WOMEN(1975), d

Lennie "Bud" Osborne
TEXAS CITY(1952)

Lorraine Adele Osborne
HOMETOWN U.S.A.(1979)

Lucille Osborne
CIRCUS GIRL(1937); SINGING MARINE, THE(1937)

Marie Osborne
HAVING WONDERFUL TIME(1938); MY OWN TRUE LOVE(1948)
Misc. Silents
SHADOWS AND SUNSHINE(1916); CAPTAIN KIDDO(1917); SUNSHINE AND GOLD(1917); TEARS AND SMILES(1917); TOLD AT THE TWILIGHT(1917); TWIN KIDDIES(1917); WHEN BABY FORGOT(1917); DADDY'S GIRL(1918); DAUGHTER OF THE WEST, A(1918); DOLLY DOES HER BIT(1918); MILADY O' THE BEAN STALK(1918); VOICE OF DESTINY, THE(1918); WINNING GRANDMA(1918); LITTLE DIPLOMAT, THE(1919); SAWDUST DOLL, THE(1919)

Marie Osborne
LOVE IS A FUNNY THING(1970, Fr., Ital), cos

Marjorie Osborne
Misc. Silents
BLUE MOUNTAIN MYSTERY, THE(1922)

Michael Osborne
MAN WITH THE GOLDEN GUN, THE(1974, Brit.)

Molly Osborne
ADVENTURE IN THE HOPFIELDS(1954, Brit.); DOG AND THE DIAMONDS, THE(1962, Brit.)

Nancy Osborne
I WANNA HOLD YOUR HAND(1978); HOMETOWN U.S.A.(1979)

Paul Osborne
ON BORROWED TIME(1939), w; CRY HAVOC(1943), w

Ralph Osborne
Misc. Silents
HIDDEN CODE, THE(1920)

Robert Osborne
MAN WITH BOGART'S FACE, THE(1980)

Ron Osborne
Misc. Talkies
HOW TO SCORE WITH GIRLS(1980)

Rupert Osborne
WITNESS, THE(1959, Brit.); KONGA(1961, Brit.); HELLFIRE CLUB, THE(1963, Brit.); PUMPKIN EATER, THE(1964, Brit.)

Samuel Scott Osborne
1984
RIVER, THE(1984)

Ted Osborne
JURY'S SECRET, THE(1938); ROAD TO RENO, THE(1938); BURIED ALIVE(1939); ISLE OF DESTINY(1940)

Tony Osborne
WEEKEND WITH LULU, A(1961, Brit.), m; SECRET DOOR, THE(1964), m, md; SEASIDE SWINGERS(1965, Brit.), m; BLACK GUNN(1972), m

Virgil Osborne
ROSE TATTOO, THE(1955)

Vivienne Osborne
MORGAN'S MARAUDERS(1929); BELOVED BACHELOR, THE(1931); HUSBAND'S HOLIDAY(1931); DARK HORSE, THE(1932); FAMOUS FERGUSON CASE, THE(1932); LIFE BEGINS(1932); TWO KINDS OF WOMEN(1932); TWO SECONDS(1932); WEEKEND MARRIAGE(1932); DEVIL'S IN LOVE, THE(1933); LUXURY LINER(1933); MEN ARE SUCH FOOLS(1933); PHANTOM BROADCAST, THE(1933); SAILOR BE GOOD(1933); SUPERNATURAL(1933); TOMORROW AT SEVEN(1933); NO MORE LADIES(1935); FOLLOW YOUR HEART(1936); LET'S SING AGAIN(1936); SINNER TAKE ALL(1936); WIVES NEVER KNOW(1936); CHAMPAGNE WALTZ(1937); CRIME NOBOBY SAW, THE(1937); SHE ASKED FOR IT(1937); CAPTAIN CAUTION(1940); PRIMROSE PATH(1940); SO YOU WON'T TALK(1940); I ACCUSE MY PARENTS(1945); DRAGONWYCH(1946)
Silents
IN WALKED MARY(1920); OVER THE HILL TO THE POORHOUSE(1920); RIGHT WAY, THE(1921)
Misc. Silents
LOVE'S FLAME(1920); GOOD PROVIDER, THE(1922)

Wendy Osborne
Misc. Silents
KINGDOM OF TWILIGHT, THE(1929, Brit.)

Will Osborne
SWING PARADE OF 1946(1946)

William Hamilton Osborne
Silents
RUNNING FIGHT, THE(1915), w

Zorenah Osborne
HELP!(1965, Brit.)

Brian Osbourne
UNDER MILK WOOD(1973, Brit.)

Bud Osbourne
LAW COMES TO TEXAS, THE(1939)

Lloyd Osbourne
EBB TIDE(1937), w; WRONG BOX, THE(1966, Brit.), w
Silents
INFATUATION(1915), w; MAN WHO, THE(1921), w; WHERE LIGHTS ARE LOW(1921), w; EBB TIDE(1922), w

Oscar
BIG RACE, THE(1934)

Oscar [Lou Fulton]
GUNSMOKE RANCH(1937)

Oscar the Elephant
Silents
SOUL OF THE BEAST(1923)

Henry Oscar
BRIDES TO BE(1934, Brit.); STRIKE!(1934, Brit.); CASE OF GABRIEL PERRY, THE(1935, Brit.); MAN WHO KNEW TOO MUCH, THE(1935, Brit.); ME AND MARLBOROUGH(1935, Brit.); NIGHT MAIL(1935, Brit.); SEXTON BLAKE AND THE BEARDED DOCTOR(1935, Brit.); TRANSATLANTIC TUNNEL(1935, Brit.); DISHONOR BRIGHT(1936, Brit.); DOMMED CARGO(1936, Brit.); LOVE IN EXILE(1936, Brit.); MAN BEHIND THE MASK, THE(1936, Brit.); NO ESCAPE(1936, Brit.); SENSATION(1936, Brit.); DARK JOURNEY(1937, Brit.); FIRE OVER ENGLAND(1937, Brit.); WHO KILLED JOHN SAVAGE?(1937, Brit.); BLACK LIMELIGHT(1938, Brit.); FATHER O'FLYNN(1938, Irish); RETURN OF THE SCARLET PIMPERNEL(1938, Brit.); DANGEROUS CARGO(1939, Brit.); DEAD MAN'S SHOES(1939, Brit.); FOUR FEATHERS, THE(1939, Brit.); NORTH SEA PATROL(1939, Brit.); SAINT IN LONDON, THE(1939, Brit.); SPY OF NAPOLEON(1939, Brit.); FLYING SQUAD, THE(1940, Brit.); FUGITIVE, THE(1940, Brit.); SPIES OF THE AIR(1940, Brit.); TILLY OF BLOOMSBURY(1940, Brit.); TWO FOR DANGER(1940, Brit.); ATLANTIC FERRY(1941, Brit.); COURAGEOUS MR. PENN(1941, Brit.); TERROR, THE(1941, Brit.); AVENGERS, THE(1942, Brit.); SQUADRON LEADER X(1943, Brit.); UPTURNED GLASS, THE(1947, Brit.); BONNIE PRINCE CHARLIE(1948, Brit.); GREED OF WILLIAM HART, THE(1948, Brit.); HATTER'S CASTLE(1948, Brit.); HOUSE OF DARKNESS(1948, Brit.); IDOL OF PARIS(1948, Brit.); IT HAPPENED IN SOHO(1948, Brit.); BAD LORD BYRON, THE(1949, Brit.); MAN FROM YESTERDAY, THE(1949, Brit.); BLACK ROSE, THE(1950, Brit.); MRS. FITZHERBERT(1950, Brit.); PRELUDE TO FAME(1950, Brit.); BEAU BRUMMELL(1954); DIPLOMATIC PASSPORT(1954, Brit.); IT'S A GREAT DAY(1956, Brit.); POSTMARK FOR DANGER(1956, Brit.); PRIVATE'S PROGRESS(1956, Brit.); LITTLE HUT, THE(1957); SECRET MAN, THE(1958, Brit.); SPANIARD'S CURSE, THE(1958, Brit.); BEYOND THIS PLACE(1959, Brit.); BRIDES OF DRACULA, THE(1960, Brit.); FOXHOLE IN CAIRO(1960, Brit.); OSCAR WILDE(1960, Brit.); LAWRENCE OF ARABIA(1962, Brit.); LONG SHIPS, THE(1964, Brit./Yugo.); MURDER AHOY(1964, Brit.); CITY UNDER THE SEA(1965, Brit.)

John Oscar
COURTIN' WILDCATS(1929); BRANDED(1931); MAN FROM DEATH VALLEY, THE(1931)

Oscar and Elmer
HIT PARADE, THE(1937); MEET THE BOY FRIEND(1937)

Oscar and Elmer [Ed Platt and Lou Fulton]
OLD CORRAL, THE(1937)

Oscar &Lonzo
COUNTRY BOY(1966)

Miko Oscard
BROTHERS KARAMAZOV, THE(1958); FACE OF FIRE(1959, U.S./Brit.)

Paul Oscard
ROAD TO MOROCCO(1942), ch; HAPPY GO LUCKY(1943), ch; GOIN' TO TOWN(1944), ch; SONG OF MY HEART(1947), ch

Per Oscarsson
DOLL, THE(1964, Swed.); DANDY IN ASPIC, A(1968, Brit.); HERE'S YOUR LIFE(1968, Swed.); HUNGER(1968, Den./Norway/Swed.); NIGHT VISITOR, THE(1970, Swed./U.S.); ENDLESS NIGHT(1971, Brit.); LAST VALLEY, THE(1971, Brit.); SECRETS(1971); DREAM TOWN(1973, Ger.); NEW LAND, THE(1973, Swed.); BLOCKHOUSE, THE(1974, Brit.); VICTOR FRANKENSTEIN(1975, Swed./Ireland); ADVENTURES OF PICASSO, THE(1980, Swed.); MONTENEGRO(1981, Brit./Swed.)

Gem Thorpe Osceola
JOE PANTHER(1976)

Bill Osco
1984
NIGHT PATROL(1984), p, w
Misc. Talkies
FLESH GORDON(1974), d

William Osco
BEING, THE(1983), p

Mara Oscuro
SERAFINO(1970, Fr./Ital.)

Jay Ose
FLIM-FLAM MAN, THE(1967); WATERHOLE NO. 3(1967)

Hans Oser
THREEPENNY OPERA, THE(1931, Ger./U.S.), ed; MISTRESS OF ATLANTIS, THE(1932, Ger.), ed

Jean Oser
FROM TOP TO BOTTOM(1933, Fr.), ed

John Oser
PORTRAIT OF A WOMAN(1946, Fr.), ed

Peter Oser
SEASON FOR LOVE, THE(1963, Fr.), p

Emilio Rodriguez Oses
THEY CAME TO ROB LAS VEGAS(1969, Fr./Ital./Span./Ger.), ed
1984
CONQUEST(1984, Ital./Span./Mex.), ed

Fernando Oses
SANTO CONTRA EL CEREBRO DIABOLICO zero(1962, Mex.), w; SANTO EN EL MUSEO DE CERA(1963, Mex.); BLUE DEMON VERSUS THE INFERNAL BRAINS(1967, Mex.), w; VENGEANCE OF THE VAMPIRE WOMEN, THE(1969, Mex.), a, w; SANTO CONTRA LA HIJA DE FRANKENSTEIN(1971, Mex.), w

Giorgio Osfuri
VIOLENT FOUR, THE(1968, Ital.)

Pearl Osgood
FOR LOVE OF YOU(1933, Brit.)

Shuy Osherov
NOT MINE TO LOVE(1969, Israel)

Nagisa Oshima
NAKED YOUTH(1961, Jap.), d&w; PLEASURES OF THE FLESH, THE(1965), d&w; DIARY OF A SHINJUKU BURGLAR(1969, Jap.), d, w, ed; MERRY CHRISTMAS MR. LAWRENCE(1983, Jap./Brit.), d, w

Tomoyo Oshima
MERRY CHRISTMAS MR. LAWRENCE(1983, Jap./Brit.), ed

Andris Oshin
DAY THE EARTH FROZE, THE(1959, Fin./USSR)

Julie Oshins
THIS IS THE ARMY(1943); I'LL SEE YOU IN MY DREAMS(1951)

Grace Oshita
REVENGE OF THE NINJA(1983)

Haruyoski Oshita
NONE BUT THE BRAVE(1965, U.S./Jap.), art d

Friedrich Oshsner
HERE'S YOUR LIFE(1968, Swed.)
Osibisa
SUPERFLY T.N.T.(1973), m
Maria Osiecka-Kuminek
MAN OF MARBLE(1979, Pol.), prod d
Frank Orsatti
VIVA MAX!(1969), stunts; B.S. I LOVE YOU(1971); MECHANIC, THE(1972); MID-NIGHT MAN, THE(1974); MOONSHINE COUNTY EXPRESS(1977), stunts
Stefan Osiecki
NO WAY BACK(1949, Brit.), d, w
Julian Osieki
MY WAY(1974, South Africa)
David Osieli
IVORY HUNTER(1952, Brit.); WEST OF ZANZIBAR(1954, Brit.)
Cesar Osinaga
TEXICAN, THE(1966, U.S./Span.)
Pedro Osinaga
MURIETA(1965, Span.)
G. Osipenko
DON QUIXOTE(1961, USSR)
V. Osipov
DON QUIXOTE(1961, USSR)
Valeriy Osipov
LETTER THAT WAS NEVER SENT, THE(1962, USSR), w
Lee Oskar
SGT. PEPPER'S LONELY HEARTS CLUB BAND(1978)
Michael Osler
FULL SPEED AHEAD(1939, Brit.)
William Osler
U-TURN(1973, Can.)
Misc. Talkies
GIRL IN BLUE, THE(1974)
Ahmed Osman
AWAKENING, THE(1980)
Kenneth Osman
SECOND-HAND HEARTS(1981)
Lawrence Osman
FOREIGN CORRESPONDENT(1940)
Russell Osman
VICTORY(1981)
Simon Osman
1984
LITTLE DRUMMER GIRL, THE(1984)
Cliff Osmond
IRMA LA DOUCE(1963); KISS ME, STUPID(1964); RAIDERS, THE(1964); WILD AND WONDERFUL(1964); FORTUNE COOKIE, THE(1966); THREE GUNS FOR TEX-AS(1968); DEVIL'S 8, THE(1969); SWEET SUGAR(1972); OKLAHOMA CRUDE(1973); FRONT PAGE, THE(1974); SHARK'S TREASURE(1975); JOE PANTHER(1976); GUARDIAN OF THE WILDERNESS(1977); MOUSE AND HIS CHILD, THE(1977); GREAT BRAIN, THE(1978); APPLE DUMPLING GANG RIDES AGAIN, THE(1979); NORTH AVENUE IRREGULARS, THE(1979); HANGAR 18(1980)
Misc. Talkies
IN SEARCH OF GOLDEN SKY(1984)
Donny Osmond
GOIN' COCONUTS(1978)
Felix Osmond
GAMBLER AND THE LADY, THE(1952, Brit.)
Hal Osmond
VOTE FOR HUGGETT(1948, Brit.); DIAMOND CITY(1949, Brit.); IT'S NOT CRICK-ET(1949, Brit.); MARRY ME!(1949, Brit.); MIRANDA(1949, Brit.); ONCE UPON A DREAM(1949, Brit.); EYE WITNESS(1950, Brit.); LAST HOLIDAY(1950, Brit.); HELL IS SOLD OUT(1951, Brit.); BRAVE DON'T CRY, THE(1952, Brit.); DEATH OF AN ANGEL(1952, Brit.); MR. LORD SAYS NO(1952, Brit.); SPIDER AND THE FLY, THE(1952, Brit.); STOLEN FACE(1952, Brit.); STORY OF ROBIN HOOD, THE(1952, Brit.); DOUBLE CONFESSION(1953, Brit.); LOVE IN PAWN(1953, Brit.); MR. POTTS GOES TO MOSCOW(1953, Brit.); PROJECT M7(1953, Brit.); SWORD AND THE ROSE, THE(1953); WHITE FIRE(1953, Brit.); FORBIDDEN CARGO(1954, Brit.); ROB ROY, THE HIGHLAND ROGUE(1954, Brit.); YOU KNOW WHAT SAILORS ARE(1954, Brit.); YOU CAN'T ESCAPE(1955, Brit.); CASH ON DELIVERY(1956, Brit.); IT'S A WONDER-FUL WORLD(1956, Brit.); LAST MAN TO HANG, THE(1956, Brit.); LOSER TAKES ALL(1956, Brit.); SIMON AND LAURA(1956, Brit.); DEPRAVED, THE(1957, Brit.); HIGH FLIGHT(1957, Brit.); VALUE FOR MONEY(1957, Brit.); BLOOD OF THE VAMPIRE(1958, Brit.); LINKS OF JUSTICE(1958); TRUTH ABOUT WOMEN, THE(1958, Brit.); INNOCENT MEETING(1959, Brit.); JACK THE RIPPER(1959, Brit.); NO SAFETY AHEAD(1959, Brit.); TOP FLOOR GIRL(1959, Brit.); TREAD SOFTLY STRANGER(1959, Brit.); WEB OF SUSPICION(1959, Brit.); GREAT VAN ROBBERY, THE(1963, Brit.)
Jimmy Osmond
HUGO THE HIPPO(1976, Hung./U.S.); GREAT BRAIN, THE(1978)
Ken Osmond
C'MON, LET'S LIVE A LITTLE(1967)
Kenneth Osmond
SO BIG(1953); GOOD MORNING, MISS DOVE(1955)
Lesley Osmond
WE'LL MEET AGAIN(1942, Brit.); IT'S IN THE BAG(1943, Brit.); UP WITH THE LARK(1943, Brit.); MYSTERIOUS MR. NICHOLSON, THE(1947, Brit.); WHEN YOU COME HOME(1947, Brit.); HOUSE OF DARKNESS(1948, Brit.); STORY OF SHIRLEY YORKE, THE(1948, Brit.); THIS WAS A WOMAN(1949, Brit.); STICK 'EM UP(1950, Brit.); CHELSEA STORY(1951, Brit.); DEATH IS A NUMBER(1951, Brit.)
Marian Osmond
Silents
CHINESE BUNGALOW, THE(1926, Brit.), w
Marie Osmond
HUGO THE HIPPO(1976, Hung./U.S.); GOIN' COCONUTS(1978)
Marion Osmond
CHINESE BUNGALOW, THE(1930, Brit.), w; CHINESE DEN, THE(1940, Brit.), w

Patrick Osmond
LA NUIT DE VARENNES(1983, Fr./Ital.)
V. Osmond
Silents
LITTLE LORD FAUNTLEROY(1914, Brit.)
Hal Osmonde
MURDER REPORTED(1958, Brit.)
Dick Osmun
SATIN MUSHROOM, THE(1969)
Leighton Osmun
Silents
EACH PEARL A TEAR(1916), w; EAST SIDE–WEST SIDE(1923), w
Cliff Osmund
INVASION OF THE BEE GIRLS(1973)
Hal Osmund
DOG AND THE DIAMONDS, THE(1962, Brit.)
Ken Osmund
EVERYTHING BUT THE TRUTH(1956)
Elena Osmyalovskaya
TARAS FAMILY, THE(1946, USSR)
Tony Osoba
GAME FOR VULTURES, A(1980, Brit.)
Osoka
KING OF THE KHYBER RIFLES(1953), ch
Hector Osorio
FAN, THE(1981)
Rica Osorio
LOS ASTRONAUTAS(1960, Mex.)
Jose Luis Ospira
ADVENTURERS, THE(1970)
N. J. Osrag
TOYS ARE NOT FOR CHILDREN(1972)
Luther W. Ossenbrink
NATIONAL BARN DANCE(1944)
Mark Ossepijan
THREE DAYS OF VIKTOR TSCHERNIKOFF(1968, USSR), d
Leonidas Ossetynski
GAMBLING HOUSE(1950); MAN IN THE GLASS BOOTH, THE(1975)
David Ossman
ZACHARIAH(1971), w
Adolphe Osso
ARTHUR(1931, Fr.), p
Alfonso Ossorio
MAIDSTONE(1970)
Jeff Ossuno
COPS AND ROBBERS(1973)
Viktor Ost
OCEAN BREAKERS(1949, Swed.)
F. Osten
Misc. Silents
SHIRAZ(1929), d
Frank Osten
Misc. Silents
THROW OF THE DICE(1930, Brit.), d
Lisa Osten
FOUR BOYS AND A GUN(1957)
Maria Osten-Sacken
TOXI(1952, Ger.), w
Martha Ostenso
SISTER KENNY(1946), w
Fred Oster
LAST BLITZKRIEG, THE(1958)
Jim Ostercamp
1984
COUNTRY(1984)
Jens Osterholm
COUNTERFEIT TRAITOR, THE(1962); WEEKEND(1964, Den.)
Corveth Osterhouse
IT'S ALIVE(1968)
Dave Osterhout
GAY DECEIVERS, THE(1969)
David Osterhout
CURIOUS FEMALE, THE(1969); GAS-S-S-S!(1970); VON RICHTHOFEN AND BROWN(1970); MR. SYCAMORE(1975)
David R. Osterhout
BOXCAR BERTHA(1972); MOVING VIOLATION(1976), w
Bob Osterloh
GREAT MISSOURI RAID, THE(1950); BABY FACE NELSON(1957); FORT MAS-SACRE(1958)
Robert Osterloh
DARK PAST, THE(1948); INCIDENT(1948); CITY ACROSS THE RIVER(1949); CRISS CROSS(1949); DOOLINS OF OKLAHOMA, THE(1949); GUN CRAZY(1949); I CHEAT-ED THE LAW(1949); ILLEGAL ENTRY(1949); PINKY(1949); WHITE HEAT(1949); HARBOR OF MISSING MEN(1950); LADY WITHOUT PASSPORT, A(1950); PALOMI-NO, THE(1950); SOUTHSIDE 1-1000(1950); 711 OCEAN DRIVE(1950); DAY THE EARTH STOOD STILL, THE(1951); DRUMS IN THE DEEP SOUTH(1951); FAT MAN, THE(1951); NEW MEXICO(1951); NO QUESTIONS ASKED(1951); PROWLER, THE(1951); WELL, THE(1951); MUTINY(1952); ONE MINUTE TO ZERO(1952); RED SKIES OF MONTANA(1952); RING, THE(1952); PRIVATE EYES(1953); ROYAL AFRICAN RIFLES, THE(1953); WICKED WOMAN(1953); WILD ONE, THE(1953); JOHNNY GUITAR(1954); RIOT IN CELL BLOCK 11(1954); ANNAPOLIS STORY, AN(1955); MAN WITH THE GUN(1955); SEVEN ANGRY MEN(1955); VIOLENT SATURDAY(1955); DESPERADOES ARE IN TOWN, THE(1956); HOT CARS(1956); JOHNNY CONCHO(1956); STAR IN THE DUST(1956); CASE AGAINST BROOKLYN, THE(1958); I BURY THE LIVING(1958); WARLOCK(1959); SCARFACE MOB, THE(1962); RED LINE 7000(1965); YOUNG DILLINGER(1965); ROSEMARY'S BA-BY(1968)

Shelley Osterloh
BEYOND AND BACK(1978)
Robert Osterlohk
UNDERCOVER MAN, THE(1949)
Emil Osterm
DOCTOR DEATH: SEEKER OF SOULS(1973), ph
Jack Osterman
WOLVES(1930, Brit.)
Jiri Ostermann
FIFTH HORSEMAN IS FEAR, THE(1968, Czech.)
Ralf Ostermann
TRUNKS OF MR. O.F., THE(1932, Ger.)
Tony Ostermeier
JUNKMAN, THE(1982), stunts
Bernauer Osterreicher
Silents
THREE SINNERS(1928), w
Bibi Osterwald
PARRISH(1961); WORLD OF HENRY ORIENT, THE(1964); FINE MADNESS,
A(1966); TIGER MAKES OUT, THE(1967); BANK SHOT(1974); GREAT SMOKEY
ROADBLOCK, THE(1978)
Robert Osth
DON'T GO IN THE HOUSE(1980)
Karin Maria Ostholt
INDECENT(1962, Ger.)
Roger Ostime
BLUE MAX, THE(1966)
Leslie Ostinelli
SILVER DARLINGS, THE(1947, Brit.), spec eff
Gene Ostler
HARUM SCARUM(1965), cos; ZIGZAG(1970), cos
Emil Ostlin
ONCE UPON A HONEYMOON(1942)
George Ostos
ANGEL, ANGEL, DOWN WE GO(1969)
Isabelle Ostrander
Silents
ISLAND OF INTRIGUE, THE(1919), w

Jean-Claude Ostrander
1984
JUST THE WAY YOU ARE(1984)
William Ostrander
CHRISTINE(1983); FIRE AND ICE(1983); STRYKER(1983, Phil.)
1984
MIKE'S MURDER(1984)
Nadja Ostreovska
Misc. Silents
NIGHT HAWK, THE(1921, Brit.)

Bertram M. Ostrer
GET ON WITH IT(1963, Brit.), p
Bertram Ostrer
NORMAN CONQUEST(1953, Brit.), p; GREEN SCARF, THE(1954, Brit.), p; MARCH
HARE, THE(1956, Brit.), p; SILENT ENEMY, THE(1959, Brit.), p; DENTIST IN THE
CHAIR(1960, Brit.), p; NEARLY A NASTY ACCIDENT(1962, Brit.), p; FRIENDS AND
NEIGHBORS(1963, Brit.), p, w; MYSTERY SUBMARINE(1963, Brit.), p, w; CAPTAIN
NEMO AND THE UNDERWATER CITY(1969, Brit.), p
Harry Ostrer
IDOL OF PARIS(1948, Brit.), w
Pamela Ostrer
POWER(1934, Brit.)
Muriel Ostriche
Silents
DAUGHTER OF THE SEA, A(1915); BY WHOSE HAND?(1916); KENNEDY
SQUARE(1916); MEN SHE MARRIED, THE(1916); JOURNEY'S END(1918); LEAP TO
FAME(1918)
Misc. Silents
WHEN IT STRIKES HOME(1915); BIRTH OF CHARACTER, THE(1916); SALLY IN
OUR ALLEY(1916); GOOD FOR NOTHING, THE(1917); MORAL COURAGE(1917);
PURPLE LILY, THE(1918); ROAD TO FRANCE, THE(1918); TINSEL(1918); VOLUN-
TEER, THE(1918); MORAL DEADLINE, THE(1919); SACRED FLAME, THE(1919);
SHADOW, THE(1921)
Howard Ostroff
WACKIEST WAGON TRAIN IN THE WEST, THE(1976), w
William Ostroff
LADY LIBERTY(1972, Ital./Fr.)
Ilsa Ostroffsky
PAL JOEY(1957)
Nadja Ostrovska
Misc. Silents
MYSTERY ROAD, THE(1921, Brit.)
Grisha Ostrovski
DETOUR, THE(1968, Bulgarian), d
Aleksandr Nikolayevich Ostrovskiy
MARRIAGE OF BALZAMINOV, THE(1966, USSR), w
Ben Ostrovsky
CUBAN REBEL GIRLS(1960)
L.L. Ostrow
RENDEZVOUS AT MIDNIGHT(1935), p
Lew Ostrow
Silents
REVELATION(1924), ed
Lou L. Ostrow
SECRET OF THE CHATEAU(1935), p
Lou Ostrow
LADY TUBBS(1935), p; YOUNG DR. KILDARE(1938), p; CALLING DR. KIL-
DARE(1939), p; JUDGE HARDY AND SON(1939), p; LIFE RETURNS(1939), p; WITH-
IN THE LAW(1939), p; MARRY THE BOSS' DAUGHTER(1941), p; WE GO
FAST(1941), p; ON THE SUNNY SIDE(1942), p

Steve Ostrow
SATURDAY NIGHT AT THE BATHS(1975), a, p
Peter Ostrum
WILLY WONKA AND THE CHOCOLATE FACTORY(1971)
Gus E. Ostwalt
BUT NOT IN VAIN(1948, Brit.), p
Berthe Ostyn
GREAT YEARNING, THE(1930, Ger.); BLONDE NIGHTINGALE(1931, Ger.)
Reijiro Osugi
SONG FROM MY HEART, THE(1970, Jap.)
Jun-ichi Osumi
SAMURAI FROM NOWHERE(1964, Jap.), art d; LOVE UNDER THE CRUCI-
FIX(1965, Jap.), art d
Jess Osuna
COOGAN'S BLUFF(1968); NEW LEAF, A(1971); EFFECT OF GAMMA RAYS ON
MAN-IN-THE-MOON MARIGOLDS, THE(1972); MAN WHO WOULD NOT DIE,
THE(1975); THREE DAYS OF THE CONDOR(1975); ALL THE PRESIDENT'S
MEN(1976); THIEVES(1977); KRAMER VS. KRAMER(1979); TAPS(1981)
V.I. Osvetimsky
HEROES OF THE SEA(1941)
V. Osvetsinsky
Misc. Silents
CHILDREN – FLOWERS OF LIFE(1919, USSR)
Oswald
YOU'RE A SWEETHEART(1937)
Gerd Oswald
BRASS LEGEND, THE(1956), d; KISS BEFORE DYING, A(1956), d; CRIME OF
PASSION(1957), d; FURY AT SHOWDOWN(1957), d; VALERIE(1957), d; PARIS
HOLIDAY(1958), d; SCREAMING MIMI(1958), d; THREE MOVES TO FREE-
DOM(1960, Ger.), d, w; BRAINWASHED(1960, Ger.), d; LONGEST DAY, THE(1962),
d; AGENT FOR H.A.R.M.(1966), d; 80 STEPS TO JONAH(1969), w; BUNNY O'-
HARE(1971), p&d
Marianne Oswald
LOVERS OF VERONA, THE(1951, Fr.); HUNCHBACK OF NOTRE DAME, THE(1957,
Fr.); MODIGLIANI OF MONTPARNASSE(1961, Fr./Ital.)
Richard Oswald
DAUGHTER OF EVIL(1930, Ger.), d; VIENNA, CITY OF SONGS(1931, Ger.), p&d;
TALES OF THE UNCANNY(1932, Ger.), d; 1914(1932, Ger.), d; CAPTAIN FROM
KOEPENICK(1933, Ger.), d; MY SONG GOES ROUND THE WORLD(1934, Brit.),
p&d; DREYFUS CASE, THE(1940, Ger.), p&d; ISLE OF MISSING MEN(1942), p&d;
LOVABLE CHEAT, THE(1949), p, d, w
Misc. Silents
UNCANNY ROOM, THE(1915, Ger.), d; HOUND OF THE BASKERVILLES,
THE(1917, Ger.), d; PICTURE OF DORIAN GRAY, THE(1917, Ger.), d; FIVE SINIS-
TER STORIES(1919, Ger.), d; CAGLIOSTRO(1928, Fr.), d; HOUND OF THE BASKER-
VILLES, THE(1929, Ger.), d
Robert J. Oswald
STREET OF DARKNESS(1958), ed
Ossi Oswalda
Misc. Silents
OYSTER PRINCESS, THE(1919, Ger.); SIR OR MADAM(1928, Brit.)
Maxim Oswarl
LOLA(1982, Ger.)
Sandor Oszter
FORTRESS, THE(1979, Hung.)
Hiroyuki Ota
WAYSIDE PEBBLE, THE(1962, Jap.)
Yoshiharu Ota
SAMURAI FROM NOWHERE(1964, Jap.), ph
Hideharu Otaki
GIRL I ABANDONED, THE(1970, Jap.)
Hideji Otaki
KAGEMUSHA(1980, Jap.)
Kip Otanez
TAKE DOWN(1979)
Fumio Otani
NUTCRACKER FANTASY(1979), ph
Reiko Otani
TOKYO FILE 212(1951)
Liuba Otasevic
HUNCHBACK OF ROME, THE(1963, Ital.)
M. Otava
MOST BEAUTIFUL AGE, THE(1970, Czech.)
Nobuke Otawa
SECRET SCROLLS(PART II) (1968, Jap.)
Jan Otcenasek
SWEET LIGHT IN A DARK ROOM(1966, Czech.), w; MURDER CZECH STYLE(1968,
Czech.), w
Grande Otelo
TRAIN ROBBERY CONFIDENTIAL(1965, Braz.)
Frank Oteri
FAME(1980)
Adriana Otero
MELODY OF MY HEART(1936, Brit.)
Carlos Otero
LAS RATAS NO DUERMEN DE NOCHE(1974, Span./Fr.)
Manolo Otero
ANTONY AND CLEOPATRA(1973, Brit.)
Othello [Otello Colangeli]
KNIVES OF THE AVENGER(1967, Ital.), ed
Grande Otelo
ROSE FOR EVERYONE, A(1967, Ital.); FITZCARRALDO(1982)
Frank W. Othile
99 WOUNDS(1931), w
Fred Othman
THAT'S RIGHT–YOU'RE WRONG(1939)
Mohamed Ben Othman
1984
MISUNDERSTOOD(1984)

Harry Otho
BLAZING SIXES(1937)

Henry Otho
DEVIL'S MATE(1933); HERE COMES THE NAVY(1934); KANSAS CITY PRINCESS(1934); UPPER WORLD(1934); CAPTAIN BLOOD(1935); RED SALUTE(1935); STRANDED(1935); LOVE BEGINS AT TWENTY(1936); MURDER BY AN ARISTOCRAT(1936); SONS O' GUNS(1936); TRAILIN' WEST(1936); TREACHERY RIDES THE RANGE(1936); TWO IN A CROWD(1936); DEVIL'S SADDLE LEGION, THE(1937); EMPTY HOLSTERS(1937); EVER SINCE EVE(1937); GUNS OF THE PECOS(1937); HOLY TERROR, THE(1937); LAND BEYOND THE LAW(1937); PRAIRIE THUNDER(1937); SLIM(1937); CLIPPED WINGS(1938); COMET OVER BROADWAY(1938); OVERLAND STAGE RAIDERS(1938); PRIDE OF THE WEST(1938); SERGEANT MURPHY(1938); DODGE CITY(1939); EACH DAWN I DIE(1939); MEXICALI ROSE(1939); SECRET SERVICE OF THE AIR(1939)

Julia Otho
ISN'T IT ROMANTIC?(1948)

Yvonne Othon
WEST SIDE STORY(1961)

Ben Otico
BEAST OF BLOOD(1970, U.S./Phil.), art d; CURSE OF THE VAMPIRES(1970, Phil., U.S.), set d; BIG DOLL HOUSE, THE(1971), prod d; BIG BIRD CAGE, THE(1972), art d; HOT BOX, THE(1972, U.S./Phil.), art d; WONDER WOMEN(1973, Phil.), art d; TNT JACKSON(1975), art d

Clyde Otis
OLGA'S GIRLS(1964), m

Don Otis
WHEN YOU'RE SMILING(1950)

Ed Otis
1984
KILLPOINT(1984)

Elita Proctor Otis
Silents
GREYHOUND, THE(1914)

James Otis
ONE SUMMER LOVE(1976)
Silents
CIRCUS DAYS(1923), w

Johnny Otis
JUKE BOX RHYTHM(1959)

Joyce Otis
MR. BELVEDERE GOES TO COLLEGE(1949); GIRLS' SCHOOL(1950); PEOPLE AGAINST O'HARA, THE(1951)

Leslie Otis
ANGELS DIE HARD(1970); RENEGADE GIRLS(1974)

Oleta Otis
Silents
SECRET OF THE HILLS, THE(1921); MISS NOBODY(1926)

Oscar Otis
NOOSE HANGS HIGH, THE(1948)

Ted Otis
BEST OF EVERYTHING, THE(1959); OCEAN'S ELEVEN(1960); HANDS OF A STRANGER(1962)

Nobuko Otoba
PRESSURE OF GUILT(1964, Jap.)

Wieslawa Otocka
JOAN OF THE ANGELS(1962, Pol.), ed; JOVITA(1970, Pol.), ed

Yachiyo Otori
YOUTH IN FURY(1961, Jap.)

W. OtoSuski
EVE WANTS TO SLEEP(1961, Pol.)

Nobuko Otowa
CHILDREN OF HIROSHIMA(1952, Jap.); ISLAND, THE(1962, Jap.); LAST WAR, THE(1962, Jap.); TILL TOMORROW COMES(1962, Jap.); TWILIGHT STORY, THE(1962, Jap.); YOUTH AND HIS AMULET, THE(1963, Jap.); THIS MADDING CROWD(1964, Jap.); ONIBABA(1965, Jap.); TWILIGHT PATH(1965, Jap.); RISE AGAINST THE SWORD(1966, Jap.); KUROENKO(1968, Jap); LOST SEX(1968, Jap.); ONCE A RAINY DAY(1968, Jap.); OUR SILENT LOVE(1969, Jap.); RED LION(1971, Jap.)

John Otrin
TO BE OR NOT TO BE(1983)

Fyodor Otsep
Misc. Silents
LIVING CORPSE, A(1931, USSR), d

Shiro Otsuji
BUDDHA(1965, Jap.)

Kanou Otsuka
LONGING FOR LOVE(1966, Jap.), p

Michiko Otsuka
REBELLION(1967, Jap.); LIVE YOUR OWN WAY(1970, Jap.)

Seigo Otsuka
MAGIC BOY(1960, Jap.), ph; ALAKAZAM THE GREAT!(1961, Jap.), ph

Yasuo Otsuka
PANDA AND THE MAGIC SERPENT(1961, Jap.), anim

Bob Ott
ELECTRA GLIDE IN BLUE(1973)

Capt. Jack Ott
LOVE IS A CAROUSEL(1970)

Horace Ott
GORDON'S WAR(1973), m

Johannes Ott
THOUSAND EYES OF DR. MABUSE, THE(1960, Fr./Ital./Ger.), art d; GIRL FROM HONG KONG(1966, Ger.), art d

Max Ott, Jr.
DEEP END(1970 Ger./U.S.), art d

Paul Ott
LADY GREY(1980)

Paul J. Ott
SATURDAY NIGHT AT THE BATHS(1975)

Warrene Ott
PHANTOM PLANET, THE(1961); IF A MAN ANSWERS(1962); BLACK ZOO(1963); RAT FINK(1965); UNDERTAKER AND HIS PALS, THE(1966); GUIDE FOR THE MARRIED MAN, A(1967); WHERE IT'S AT(1969); WITCHMAKER, THE(1969); INVINCIBLE SIX, THE(1970, U.S./Iran)

Roberto Ottaviano
QUO VADIS(1951)

Matteo Ottaviano [Matt Cimber]
SINGLE ROOM FURNISHED(1968), d

John Ottavino
1984
FALLING IN LOVE(1984)

James Ottaway
MAN WHO LIKED FUNERALS, THE(1959, Brit.); ROOM 43(1959, Brit.); IN THE WAKE OF A STRANGER(1960, Brit.); MAN WHO FINALLY DIED, THE(1967, Brit.); INADMISSIBLE EVIDENCE(1968, Brit.); THAT'LL BE THE DAY(1974, Brit.); ABSOLUTION(1981, Brit.)

John Otte
HARDCORE(1979)

Bengt Ottekil
TOUCH, THE(1971, U.S./Swed.), a, makeup

Alice Morten Otten
Silents
RAMONA(1916)

Marie-Louise Otten
KIMBERLEY JIM(1965, South Africa)

John Ottenberg
PAPERBACK HERO(1973, Can.)

Albert M. Ottenheimer
FRONT, THE(1976); NOCTURNA(1979)

Albert Ottenheimer
ANNIE HALL(1977)

Jack Otterman
HIT THE ROAD(1941), art d; ARABIAN NIGHTS(1942), prod d

George Otterson
EYES OF THE UNDERWORLD(1943), art d

Jack Otterson
CHANGE OF HEART(1934), set d; NOW I'LL TELL(1934), art d; DOUBTING THOMAS(1935), art d; DRESSED TO THRILL(1935), art d; ONE MORE SPRING(1935), art d; THANKS A MILLION(1935), art d; GIRL WITH IDEAS, A(1937), art d; NIGHT KEY(1937), art d; OH DOCTOR(1937), art d; PRESCRIPTION FOR ROMANCE(1937), art d; SHE'S DANGEROUS(1937), art d; THIS WAY PLEASE(1937), art d; WE HAVE OUR MOMENTS(1937), art d; YOU'RE A SWEETHEART(1937), art d; DANGER ON THE AIR(1938), art d; FRESHMAN YEAR(1938), art d; LAST WARNING, THE(1938), art d; LITTLE TOUGH GUY(1938), art d; LITTLE TOUGH GUYS IN SOCIETY(1938), art d; MIDNIGHT INTRUDER(1938), art d; NURSE FROM BROOKLYN(1938), art d; RAGE OF PARIS, THE(1938), art d; RECKLESS LIVING(1938), art d; ROAD TO RENO(1938), art d; SECRETS OF A NURSE(1938), art d; SERVICE DE LUXE(1938), art d; SINNERS IN PARADISE(1938), art d; SWING, SISTER, SWING(1938), art d; THAT CERTAIN AGE(1938), art d; WIVES UNDER SUSPICION(1938), art d; YOUTH TAKES A FLING(1938), art d; DESTRY RIDES AGAIN(1939), art d; EAST SIDE OF HEAVEN(1939), art d; FAMILY NEXT DOOR, THE(1939), art d; FIRST LOVE(1939), art d; FOR LOVE OR MONEY(1939), art d; FORGOTTEN WOMAN, THE(1939), art d; GAMBLING SHIP(1939), art d; LITTLE ACCIDENT(1939), art d; NEWSBOY'S HOME(1939), art d; SOCIETY SMUGGLERS(1939), art d; SON OF FRANKENSTEIN(1939), art d; SPIRIT OF CULVER, THE(1939), art d; SUN NEVER SETS, THE(1939), art d; TOWER OF LONDON(1939), art d; UNEXPECTED FATHER(1939), art d; YOU CAN'T CHEAT AN HONEST MAN(1939), art d; BANK DICK, THE(1940), art d; BLACK FRIDAY(1940), art d; FRAMED(1940), art d; GIVE US WINGS(1940), art d; HIRED WIFE(1940), art d; HOUSE OF THE SEVEN GABLES, THE(1940), art d; IF I HAD MY WAY(1940), art d; I'M NOBODY'S SWEETHEART NOW(1940), art d; LA CONGA NIGHTS(1940), art d; LEATHER-PUSHERS, THE(1940), art d; LITTLE BIT OF HEAVEN, A(1940), art d; MA, HE'S MAKING EYES AT ME(1940), art d; MARGIE(1940), art d; MY LITTLE CHICKADEE(1940), art d; ONE NIGHT IN THE TROPICS(1940), art d; SANDY IS A LADY(1940), art d; SEVEN SINNERS(1940), art d; TRAIL OF THE VIGILANTES(1940), art d; WHEN THE DALTONS RODE(1940), art d; YOU'RE NOT SO TOUGH(1940), art d; CRACKED NUTS(1941), art d; FLAME OF NEW ORLEANS, THE(1941), art d; FLYING CADETS(1941), art d; HELLO SUCKER(1941), art d; INVISIBLE WOMAN, THE(1941), art d; IT STARTED WITH EVE(1941), art d; LADY FROM CHEYENNE(1941), art d; MELODY LANE(1941), art d; MEN OF THE TIMBERLAND(1941), art d; MOB TOWN(1941), art d; MOONLIGHT IN HAWAII(1941), art d; NEVER GIVE A SUCKER AN EVEN BREAK(1941), art d; PARIS CALLING(1941), art d; ROAD AGENT(1941), art d; SO ENDS OUR NIGHT(1941), art d; SOUTH OF TAHITI(1941), art d; TIGHT SHOES(1941), art d; UNFINISHED BUSINESS(1941), art d; WOLF MAN, THE(1941), art d; BETWEEN US GIRLS(1942), art d; DANGER IN THE PACIFIC(1942), art d; DESTINATION UNKNOWN(1942), art d; DRUMS OF THE CONGO(1942), art d; EAGLE SQUADRON(1942), art d; ESCAPE FROM HONG KONG(1942), art d; GHOST OF FRANKENSTEIN, THE(1942), art d; GIVE OUT, SISTERS(1942), art d; GREAT IMPERSONATION, THE(1942), art d; HALF WAY TO SHANGHAI(1942), art d; INVISIBLE AGENT(1942), art d; LADY IN A JAM(1942), art d; LITTLE JOE, THE WRANGLER(1942), art d; MEN OF TEXAS(1942), art d; MISSISSIPPI GAMBLER(1942), art d; MOONLIGHT IN HAVANA(1942), art d; MUMMY'S TOMB, THE(1942), art d; MYSTERY OF MARIE ROGET, THE(1942), art d; NIGHT MONSTER(1942), art d; PARDON MY SARONG(1942), art d; PRIVATE BUCKAROO(1942), art d; RIDE 'EM COWBOY(1942), art d; SABOTEUR(1942), art d; SHERLOCK HOLMES AND THE SECRET WEAPON(1942), art d; SHERLOCK HOLMES AND THE VOICE OF TERROR(1942), art d; SILVER BULLET, THE(1942), art d; SIN TOWN(1942), art d; SPOILERS, THE(1942), art d; STRICTLY IN THE GROOVE(1942), art d; THERE'S ONE BORN EVERY MINUTE(1942), art d; TOP SERGEANT(1942), art d; TOUGH AS THEY COME(1942), art d; WHAT'S COOKIN'?(1942), art d; WHO DONE IT?(1942), art d; HI'YA, CHUM(1943), art d; IT COMES UP LOVE(1943), art d; MUG TOWN(1943), art d; OLD CHISHOLM TRAIL(1943), art d; SHERLOCK HOLMES IN WASHINGTON(1943), art d; TENTING TONIGHT ON THE OLD CAMP GROUND(1943), art d; BLACK ANGEL(1946), art d; DANGER WOMAN(1946), art d; DARK HORSE, THE(1946), art d; DRESSED TO KILL(1946), art d; GUNMAN'S CODE(1946), art d; HER ADVENTUROUS NIGHT(1946), art d; IDEA GIRL(1946), art d; INSIDE JOB(1946), art d; KILLERS, THE(1946), art d; LITTLE MISS BIG(1946), art d; LOVER COME BACK(1946), art d; RUNAROUND, THE(1946), art d; RUSTLER'S ROUNDUP(1946), art d; SHE-WOLF

OF LONDON(1946), art d; SHE WROTE THE BOOK(1946), art d; SLIGHTLY SCAN-DALOUS(1946), art d; SMOOTH AS SILK(1946), art d; STRANGE CONQUEST(1946), art d; TIME OF THEIR LIVES, THE(1946), art d; WHITE TIE AND TAILS(1946), art d; WILD BEAUTY(1946), art d; MICHIGAN KID, THE(1947), art d; PIRATES OF MONTEREY(1947), art d; SONG OF SCHEHERAZADE(1947), art d; VIGILANTES RETURN, THE(1947), art d

Rafaela Ottiano
AS YOU DESIRE ME(1932); WASHINGTON MASQUERADE(1932); BON-DAGE(1933); FEMALE(1933); SHE DONE HIM WRONG(1933); ALL MEN ARE ENEMIES(1934); GREAT EXPECTATIONS(1934); LAST GENTLEMAN, THE(1934); LOST LADY, A(1934); MANDALAY(1934); CURLY TOP(1935); ENCHANTED APRIL(1935); FLORENTINE DAGGER, THE(1935); LOTTERY LOVER(1935); ONE FRIGHTENED NIGHT(1935); REMEMBER LAST NIGHT(1935); ANTHONY AD-VERSE(1936); DEVIL DOLL, THE(1936); MAD HOLIDAY(1936); RIFF-RAFF(1936); WE'RE ONLY HUMAN(1936); LEAGUE OF FRIGHTENED MEN(1937); MAYTI-ME(1937); SEVENTH HEAVEN(1937); THAT GIRL FROM PARIS(1937); I'LL GIVE A MILLION(1938); MARIE ANTOINETTE(1938); SUEZ(1938); TOY WIFE, THE(1938); PARIS HONEYMOON(1939); LITTLE BIT OF HEAVEN, A(1940); LONG VOYAGE HOME, THE(1940); VICTORY(1940); TOPPER RETURNS(1941); ADVENTURES OF MARTIN EDEN, THE(1942); I MARRIED AN ANGEL(1942)

Rafaella Ottiano
GRAND HOTEL(1932); ANN VICKERS(1933)

Rafaelo Ottiano
CRIME AND PUNISHMENT(1935)

Ottiero Ottieri
LA NOTTE(1961, Fr./Ital.); ECLIPSE(1962, Fr./Ital.), w

Barbara Ottinger
METAMORPHOSES(1978), ed

Leonora Ottinger
Silents
GILDED LILY, THE(1921)

Oleta Ottis
Silents
TORRENT, THE(1921)

Carl Ottmar
MAN HUNT(1941); UNDERGROUND(1941)

Otto the Dog
HIGH JINKS IN SOCIETY(1949, Brit.)

Barry Otto
NORMAN LOVES ROSE(1982, Aus.)

Carl Otto
DIE FASTNACHTSBEICHTE(1962, Ger.), ed

Denise Otto
MATCHLESS(1974, Aus.)

Frank Otto
WOMAN IN THE DARK(1934); EVER SINCE EVE(1937); IDOL OF THE CROWDS(1937); KID COMES BACK, THE(1937); CRIME SCHOOL(1938); DYNAMITE DELANEY(1938); STRANGE FACES(1938); MILLION DOLLAR BABY(1941); MIRA-CLE KID(1942); BORN YESTERDAY(1951)
Misc. Silents
WHO LOVED HIM BEST?(1918)

Henry Otto
IRON MASK, THE(1929); ONE HYSTERICAL NIGHT(1930); SEA DEVILS(1931)
Silents
BIG TREMAINE(1916), d&w; ANGEL CHILD(1918), d; AMATEUR ADVENTU-RESS, THE(1919), d; ISLAND OF INTRIGUE, THE(1919), d; DANTE'S INFER-NO(1924), d; ANCIENT MARINER, THE(1925), d
Misc. Silents
HALF A ROGUE(1916), d; MAN FROM NOWHERE, THE(1916), d; MISTER 44(1916), d; RIVER OF ROMANCE, THE(1916), d; UNDINE(1916), d; BUTTERFLY GIRL, THE(1917), d; LORELEI OF THE SEA(1917), d; WILD LIFE(1918), d; FAIR AND WARMER(1919), d; GREAT ROMANCE, THE(1919), d; MICROBE, THE(1919), d; SOME BRIDE(1919), d; CHEATER, THE(1920), d; SLAVE OF VANITY, A(1920), d; WILLOW TREE, THE(1920), d; LOVEBOUND(1923), d; TEMPLE OF VENUS, THE(1923), d; FOLLY OF VANITY, THE(1924), d

Karl Otto
MARRIAGE OF FIGARO, THE(1970, Ger.)

Lisa Otto
YOUNG LORD, THE(1970, Ger.)

Paul Otto
ELISABETH OF AUSTRIA(1931, Ger.); STORM IN A WATER GLASS(1931, Aust.); BARBERINA(1932, Ger.); RASPUTIN(1932, Ger.); CAPTAIN FROM KO-EPENICK(1933, Ger.); FINAL CHORD, THE(1936, Ger.)
Misc. Silents
ASIAN SUN, THE(1921, Ger.)

Philip Otto
Misc. Talkies
DAY SANTA CLAUS CRIED, THE(1980), d

Theo Otto
FAUST(1963, Ger.), set d, cos

Ted Otton
JUST OUT OF REACH(1979, Aus.), ed

Sirkka Ottonen
RAT FINK(1965)

Wanda Ottoni
FRENCH LINE, THE(1954); GIRL IN THE KREMLIN, THE(1957)

Carl Ottosen
OPERATION CAMEL(1961, Den.); JOURNEY TO THE SEVENTH PLANET(1962, U.S./Swed.); REPTILICUS(1962, U.S./Den.); CHRISTINE KEELER AFFAIR, THE(1964, Brit.); HUNGER(1968, Den./Norway/Swed.)

Lars Henrik Ottoson
GORILLA(1964, Swed.), d, w

William J. Otts
Misc. Silents
BATTLING KING(1922)

Robert K. Ottum
STROKER ACE(1983), w

A. Dorian Otvos
MERRY-GO-ROUND OF 1938(1937), w; FLIRTING WITH FATE(1938), w

Nico Otzak
LA DOLCE VITA(1961, Ital./Fr.)

Felix Oudart
UTOPIA(1952, Fr./Ital.); BACK STREETS OF PARIS(1962, Fr.)
Misc. Silents
CRAINQUEBILLE(1922, Fr.); TIRE AU FLANC(1929, Fr.)

Pierre Oudrey
DOLL'S HOUSE, A(1973, Brit.)

Pierre Oudry
S(1974)

Jean-Rene Ouellet
JE T'AIME(1974, Can.)

Oueret
MARIUS(1933, Fr.)

Norman Ough
SCOTT OF THE ANTARCTIC(1949, Brit.), spec eff

Winifred Oughton
SUCH IS THE LAW(1930, Brit.); WOMAN DECIDES, THE(1932, Brit.); BERMOND-SEY KID, THE(1933, Brit.); CALL ME MAME(1933, Brit.); ENEMY OF THE POLI-CE(1933, Brit.); MAYFAIR GIRL(1933, Brit.); THERE GOES THE BRIDE(1933, Brit.); THIRTEENTH CANDLE, THE(1933, Brit.); GLIMPSE OF PARADISE, A(1934, Brit.); SPRING IN THE AIR(1934, Brit.); JUBILEE WINDOW(1935, Brit.); SCHOOL FOR STARS(1935, Brit.); WINDMILL, THE(1937, Brit.); SHOW GOES ON, THE(1938, Brit.); DEAD MEN ARE DANGEROUS(1939, Brit.); NIGHT TRAIN(1940, Brit.); YELLOW CANARY, THE(1944, Brit.); THEY KNEW MR. KNIGHT(1945, Brit.); CRIME DOES NOT PAY(1962, Fr.), w

Meyer Ouhayoun
LAST OUTPOST, THE(1935)

Ouida
UNDER TWO FLAGS(1936), w; DOG OF FLANDERS, A(1935), w; DOG OF FLAND-ERS, A(1959), w

Bebe Ouie
EVERY LITTLE CROOK AND NANNY(1972)

Daniele Ouimet
DAUGHTERS OF DARKNESS(1971, Bel./ Fr./ Ger./ Ital.)

Vladimir Oukhtomsky
MIDNIGHT LACE(1960)

Oulanova
ROMEO AND JULIET(1955, USSR)

Brian Oulton
COMING-OUT PARTY, A(; TOO MANY HUSBANDS(1938, Brit.); HUGGETTS ABROAD, THE(1949, Brit.); IT'S NOT CRICKET(1949, Brit.); MIRANDA(1949, Brit.); WARNING TO WANTONS, A(1949, Brit.); LAST HOLIDAY(1950, Brit.); CASTLE IN THE AIR(1952, Brit.); DOCTOR IN THE HOUSE(1954, Brit.); MAN WITH A MIL-LION(1954, Brit.); YOUNG WIVES' TALE(1954, Brit.); DEEP BLUE SEA, THE(1955, Brit.); MISS TULIP STAYS THE NIGHT(1955, Brit.); WILL ANY GENTLEMAN?(1955, Brit.); MAN WHO NEVER WAS, THE(1956, Brit.); PRIVATE'S PROGRESS(1956, Brit.); BROTHERS IN LAW(1957, Brit.); GOOD COMPANIONS, THE(1957, Brit.); LET'S BE HAPPY(1957, Brit.); TWO GROOMS FOR A BRIDE(1957); HAPPY IS THE BRIDE(1958, Brit.); SPANIARD'S CURSE, THE(1958, Brit.); CARRY ON NURSE(1959, Brit.); I'M ALL RIGHT, JACK(1959, Brit.); SILENT ENEMY, THE(1959, Brit.); BULLDOG BREED, THE(1960, Brit.); CARRY ON CONSTABLE(1960, Brit.); FRENCH MIS-TRESS(1960, Brit.); THIRTY NINE STEPS, THE(1960, Brit.); BEWARE OF CHIL-DREN(1961, Brit.); RISK, THE(1961, Brit.); DOG AND THE DIAMONDS, THE(1962, Brit.); HAIR OF THE DOG(1962, Brit.); ROOMMATES(1962, Brit.); THERE WAS A CROOKED MAN(1962, Brit.); KISS OF EVIL(1963, Brit.); SWINGIN' MAIDEN, THE(1963, Brit.); CARRY ON CLEO(1964, Brit.); DEVILS OF DARKNESS, THE(1965, Brit.); JIG SAW(1965, Brit.); SPYLARKS(1965, Brit.); THESE ARE THE DAM-NED(1965, Brit.); CRY OF THE PENGUINS(1972, Brit.); GET CHARLIE TULLY(1976, Brit.)

Eric Oulton
ROMAN HOLIDAY(1953); WAR AND PEACE(1956, Ital./U.S.)

Andre Oumansky
TRUTH, THE(1961, Fr./Ital.); SUNDAYS AND CYBELE(1962, Fr.); JOY HOUSE(1964, Fr.); LADY IN THE CAR WITH GLASSES AND A GUN, THE(1970, U.S./Fr.); DESTRUCTORS, THE(1974, Brit.)
1984
JUST THE WAY YOU ARE(1984)

Charles Fulton Oursler
SPIDER, THE(1945), w

Fulton Oursler [Anthony Abbott]
SECOND WIFE(1930), w; SPIDER, THE(1931), w; SECOND WIFE(1936), w; GREAT-EST STORY EVER TOLD, THE(1965), w

G. Oury
ANTOINE ET ANTOINETTE(1947 Fr.)

Gerard Oury
MR. PEEK-A-BOO(1951, Fr.); SEA DEVILS(1953); SWORD AND THE ROSE, THE(1953); DETECTIVE, THE(1954, Qit.); HEART OF THE MATTER, THE(1954, Brit.); LOVES OF THREE QUEENS, THE(1954, Ital./Fr.); THEY WHO DARE(1954, Brit.); WOMAN OF THE RIVER(1954, Fr./Ital.); TRIPLE DECEPTION(1957, Brit.); BACK TO THE WALL(1959, Fr.); JOURNEY, THE(1959, U.S./Aust.); MIRROR HAS TWO FACES, THE(1959, Fr.), a, w; BABETTE GOES TO WAR(1960, Fr.), w; CRIME DOES NOT PAY(1962, Fr.), d; PRIZE, THE(1963); SUCKER, THE(1966, Fr./Ital.), d, w; BRAIN, THE(1969, Fr./US), d, w; DON'T LOOK NOW(1969, Brit./Fr.), d, w; DELUSIONS OF GRANDEUR(1971 Fr.), d, w; ADVENTURES OF RABBI JACOB, THE(1973, Fr.), d, w; ACE OF ACES(1982, Fr./Ger.), d, w

Sverre Ousdal
ISLAND AT THE TOP OF THE WORLD, THE(1974)

Dina Ousley
Misc. Talkies
TRIP WITH THE TEACHER(1975)

Maria Ouspenskaya
DODSWORTH(1936); CONQUEST(1937); JUDGE HARDY AND SON(1939); LOVE AFFAIR(1939); RAINS CAME, THE(1939); BEYOND TOMORROW(1940); DANCE, GIRL, DANCE(1940); DR. EHRLICH'S MAGIC BULLET(1940); MAN I MARRIED, THE(1940); MORTAL STORM, THE(1940); WATERLOO BRIDGE(1940); SHANGHAI GESTURE, THE(1941); WOLF MAN, THE(1941); KING'S ROW(1942); MYSTERY OF MARIE ROGET, THE(1942); FRANKENSTEIN MEETS THE WOLF MAN(1943);

TARZAN AND THE AMAZONS(1945); I'VE ALWAYS LOVED YOU(1946); KISS IN THE DARK, A(1949)

Mme. Maria Ouspenskaya
WYOMING(1947)

Nick Outin
HEAVEN CAN WAIT(1978); DIE LAUGHING(1980)

Geoff Outlaw
ALICE'S RESTAURANT(1969)

Martha Outlaw
COVER GIRL(1944); SINCE YOU WENT AWAY(1944)

The Outlaws
SING AND SWING(1964, Brit.)

Robin Outterside
GOODBYE PORK PIE(1981, New Zealand), art d

Steve Ouvaroff
GREEN HELMET, THE(1961, Brit.)

Gaston Ouvrard
SUCH A GORGEOUS KID LIKE ME(1973, Fr.)

George Ovalle
1984
DELIVERY BOYS(1984)

Vyacheslav Ovchinnikov
VIOLIN AND ROLLER(1962, USSR), m; WAR AND PEACE(1968, USSR), m

Lyudmila Ovchinnikova
DAY THE WAR ENDED, THE(1961, USSR); HOME FOR TANYA, A(1961, USSR); SPRINGTIME ON THE VOLGA(1961, USSR); SUN SHINES FOR ALL, THE(1961, USSR); NINE DAYS OF ONE YEAR(1964, USSR); GIRL AND THE BUGLER, THE(1967, USSR)

Horace Ove
PRESSURE(1976, Brit.), d, w

Margalit Oved
HILL 24 DOESN'T ANSWER(1955, Israel)

Ali Oveisi
POPPY IS ALSO A FLOWER, THE(1966)

Richard Over
CITY OF FEAR(1965, Brit.), set d

Ronald LeRoy "Baby LeRoy" Overacker
TILLIE AND GUS(1933)

Neville Overall
STONE(1974, Aus.)

Roy Overbaugh
RETURN OF THE RAT, THE(1929, Brit.), ph; BISHOP MURDER CASE, THE(1930), ph; LITTLE ACCIDENT(1930), ph; OUTSIDE THE LAW(1930), ph; WHAT MEN WANT(1930), ph; WOLVES(1930, Brit.), ph; YOUNG DESIRE(1930), ph; MADAME GUILLOTINE(1931, Brit.), ph; PENROD AND SAM(1931), ph; SOLITAIRE MAN, THE(1933), ph; TOGETHER WE LIVE(1935), ph
Silents
MAN WHO MADE GOOD, THE(1917), ph; ERSTWHILE SUSAN(1919), ph; AWAY GOES PRUDENCE(1920), ph; DR. JEKYLL AND MR. HYDE(1920), ph; WHITE SISTER, THE(1923), ph; CLASSMATES(1924), ph; SHORE LEAVE(1925), ph

Robert Overbeck
WICKED DREAMS OF PAULA SCHULTZ, THE(1968), spec eff

Camilla Overbye
1984
ELEMENT OF CRIME, THE(1984, Den.)

Hal Overell
FIRST TO FIGHT(1967), set d; JIGSAW(1968), set d

William Overgard
BUSHIDO BLADE, THE(1982 Brit./U.S.), w

Wayne D. Overholser
CAST A LONG SHADOW(1959), w

Miles Overholt
Silents
MEDDLER, THE(1925), w

Robert Overholzer
HEARTLAND(1980)

Web Overlander
QUIET MAN, THE(1952); MC LINTOCK!(1963), makeup; SKIDOO(1968), makeup

Webb Overlander
MYSTERY OF THE GOLDEN EYE, THE(1948), makeup; FIGHTING KENTUCKIAN, THE(1949), makeup; SKY DRAGON(1949), makeup; TUNA CLIPPER(1949), makeup; RETURN TO PARADISE(1953); HORSE SOLDIERS, THE(1959), makeup

Anthony Overman
DEATH GAME(1977), w

Jack Overman
NEVADA(1944); FRONTIER GAL(1945); G.I. HONEYMOON(1945); HONEYMOON AHEAD(1945); I'LL TELL THE WORLD(1945); JOHNNY ANGEL(1945); JUNGLE CAPTIVE(1945); NAUGHTY NINETIES, THE(1945); DARK HORSE, THE(1946); FAITHFUL IN MY FASHION(1946); MISSING LADY, THE(1946); NIGHT IN PARADISE, A(1946); RUNAROUND, THE(1946); BRASHER DOUBLOON, THE(1947); BRUTE FORCE(1947); FALL GUY(1947); LONG NIGHT, THE(1947); T-MEN(1947); ASSIGNED TO DANGER(1948); FIGHTING MAD(1948); FORCE OF EVIL(1948); NOOSE HANGS HIGH, THE(1948); SECRET SERVICE INVESTIGATOR(1948); CHICAGO DEADLINE(1949); FLAXY MARTIN(1949); LONE WOLF AND HIS LADY, THE(1949); MISS GRANT TAKES RICHMOND(1949); ONCE MORE, MY DARLING(1949); PRISON WARDEN(1949); GOOD HUMOR MAN, THE(1950); JOHNNY ONE-EYE(1950); JET PILOT(1957)

Lynne Overman
PERFECT CRIME, THE(1928); BROADWAY BILL(1934); GREAT FLIRTATION, THE(1934); LITTLE MISS MARKER(1934); MIDNIGHT(1934); SHE LOVES ME NOT(1934); YOU BELONG TO ME(1934); ENTER MADAME(1935); MEN WITHOUT NAMES(1935); PARIS IN SPRING(1935); RUMBA(1935); TWO FOR TONIGHT(1935); COLLEGIATE(1936); JUNGLE PRINCESS, THE(1936); POPPY(1936); THREE MARRIED MEN(1936); YOURS FOR THE ASKING(1936); BIG BROADCAST OF 1938, THE(1937); BLONDE TROUBLE(1937); DON'T TELL THE WIFE(1937); HOTEL HAYWIRE(1937); MURDER GOES TO COLLEGE(1937); NIGHT CLUB SCANDAL(1937); NOBODY'S BABY(1937); PARTNERS IN CRIME(1937); TRUE CONFESSION(1937); WILD MONEY(1937); HER JUNGLE LOVE(1938); HUNTED MEN(1938); MEN WITH WINGS(1938); RIDE A CROOKED MILE(1938); SONS OF THE LEGION(1938); SPAWN OF THE NORTH(1938); DEATH OF A CHAMPION(1939); PERSONS IN HIDING(1939);

UNION PACIFIC(1939); EDISON, THE MAN(1940); NORTHWEST MOUNTED POLICE(1940); SAFARI(1940); TYPHOON(1940); ALOMA OF THE SOUTH SEAS(1941); CAUGHT IN THE DRAFT(1941); NEW YORK TOWN(1941); THERE'S MAGIC IN MUSIC(1941); FOREST RANGERS, THE(1942); REAP THE WILD WIND(1942); ROXIE HART(1942); SILVER QUEEN(1942); STAR SPANGLED RHYTHM(1942); DESERT SONG, THE(1943); DIXIE(1943)

The Overseas Press Club of America
GUILTY OF TREASON(1950), w

Brent Overstreet
Silents
LONE EAGLE, THE(1927)

Tonya Overstreet
PINKY(1949)

Bill Overton
LORD SHANGO(1975)

Evart Overton
Silents
BATTLE CRY OF PEACE, THE(1915); TWO-EDGED SWORD, THE(1916)
Misc. Silents
CROOKY(1915); ENEMY, THE(1916); HESPER OF THE MOUNTAINS(1916); MAN BEHIND THE CURTAIN, THE(1916); ORDEAL OF ELIZABETH, THE(1916); BOTTOM OF THE WELL(1917); GLORY OF YOLANDA, THE(1917); LOVE DOCTOR, THE(1917); MONEY MILL, THE(1917); SOLDIERS OF CHANCE(1917); MENACE, THE(1918)

Frank Overton
MYSTERY STREET(1950); NO WAY OUT(1950); TRUE STORY OF JESSE JAMES, THE(1957); DESIRE UNDER THE ELMS(1958); LONELYHEARTS(1958); LAST MILE, THE(1959); DARK AT THE TOP OF THE STAIRS, THE(1960); WILD RIVER(1960); CLAUDELLE INGLISH(1961); POSSE FROM HELL(1961); TO KILL A MOCKINGBIRD(1962); FAIL SAFE(1964)

Rick Overton
YOUNG DOCTORS IN LOVE(1982)
1984
BEVERLY HILLS COP(1984)

Sherrie Overton
GIRLS' SCHOOL(1938); STRIKE UP THE BAND(1940)

Toi Overton
1984
BREAKIN' 2: ELECTRIC BOOGALOO(1984)

Tom Overton
KING OF MARVIN GARDENS, THE(1972)

Zdenek Oves
CLOSELY WATCHED TRAINS(1967, Czech.), p

George Ovey
HIT THE DECK(1930); NIGHT RIDE(1930); ALICE IN WONDERLAND(1933); YOU'RE TELLING ME(1934); MURDER WITH PICTURES(1936); ROSE BOWL(1936); GIRL WITH IDEAS, A(1937); TRUE CONFESSION(1937); SWING YOUR LADY(1938); YOUNG FUGITIVES(1938); STAND UP AND FIGHT(1939); YOU CAN'T CHEAT AN HONEST MAN(1939); LIFE BEGINS FOR ANDY HARDY(1941); UNHOLY PARTNERS(1941); WAGONS ROLL AT NIGHT, THE(1941); STRATTON STORY, THE(1949); SEALED CARGO(1951)
Silents
ARIZONA SWEEPSTAKES(1926); YANKEE CLIPPER, THE(1927)
Misc. Silents
PALS IN PERIL(1927)

Ovid
METAMORPHOSES(1978), w

Yu. Ovsyannikov
WAR AND PEACE(1968, USSR)

Vlatcheslav Ovtchinnikov
ANDREI ROUBLOV(1973, USSR), m

Yoshisaburo Owa
PERFORMERS, THE(1970, Jap.)

Norman Mac Owan
VALLEY OF EAGLES(1952, Brit.)

Robert Owczarek
BILLY IN THE LOWLANDS(1979)

Baard Owe
GERTRUD(1966, Den.)

Alun Owen
MEN ARE CHILDREN TWICE(1953, Brit.); I'M ALL RIGHT, JACK(1959, Brit.); IN THE WAKE OF A STRANGER(1960, Brit.); JET STORM(1961, Brit.); CONCRETE JUNGLE, THE(1962, Brit.), w; HARD DAY'S NIGHT, A(1964, Brit.), w; SERVANT, THE(1964, Brit.)

Arthur Owen
MRS. PYM OF SCOTLAND YARD(1939, Brit.)

Arthur E. Owen
LITTLE DOLLY DAYDREAM(1938, Brit.); HUMAN MONSTER, THE(1940, Brit.); LOYAL HEART(1946, Brit.)

Beth Owen
MACBETH(1971, Brit.)

Beverley Owen
BULLET FOR A BADMAN(1964)

Bill Owen
DAYDREAK(1948, Brit.); EASY MONEY(1948, Brit.); TROUBLE IN THE AIR(1948, Brit.); DIAMOND CITY(1949, Brit.); GAY LADY, THE(1949, Brit.); GIRL WHO COULDN'T QUITE, THE(1949, Brit.); MY BROTHER'S KEEPER(1949, Brit.); WEAKER SEX, THE(1949, Brit.); HOTEL SAHARA(1951, Brit.); MANIACS ON WHEELS(1951, Brit.); STORY OF ROBIN HOOD, THE(1952, Brit.); DAY TO REMEMBER, A(1953, Brit.); THERE WAS A YOUNG LADY(1953, Brit.); RAINBOW JACKET, THE(1954, Brit.); SQUARE RING, THE(1955, Brit.); NOT SO DUSTY(1956, Brit.); SHIP THAT DIED OF SHAME, THE(1956, Brit.); CARVE HER NAME WITH PRIDE(1958, Brit.); DAVY(1958, Brit.); CARRY ON NURSE(1959, Brit.); CARRY ON SERGEANT(1959, Brit.); SHAKEDOWN, THE(1960, Brit.); CARRY ON REGARDLESS(1961, Brit.); CARRY ON CABBIE(1963, Brit.); HELLFIRE CLUB, THE(1963, Brit.); OPERATION SNAFU(1965, Brit.); SECRET OF BLOOD ISLAND, THE(1965, Brit.); FIGHTING PRINCE OF DONEGAL, THE(1966, Brit.); GEORGY GIRL(1966, Brit.); HEADLINE HUNTERS(1968, Brit.); MISCHIEF(1969, Brit.); O LUCKY MAN!(1973, Brit.); KADOYNG(1974, Brit.); IN CELEBRATION(1975, Brit.); COMEBACK, THE(1982, Brit.)

1984
LAUGHTER HOUSE(1984, Brit.)
Carroll Owen
Silents
SIGN OF THE ROSE, THE(1922), w
Capt. J.I.H. Owen
SAFECRACKER, THE(1958, Brit.), tech adv
Catherine Dale Owen
HIS GLORIOUS NIGHT(1929); BORN RECKLESS(1930); ROGUE SONG, THE(1930); STRICTLY UNCONVENTIONAL(1930); SUCH MEN ARE DANGEROUS(1930); TODAY(1930); BEHIND OFFICE DOORS(1931); DEFENDERS OF THE LAW(1931)
Cecil Owen
Silents
SPREADING DAWN, THE(1917); PAIR OF SIXES, A(1918)
Misc. Silents
GIRL BY THE ROADSIDE, THE(1918)
Christopher Owen
CONFESSIONS OF A WINDOW CLEANER(1974, Brit.)
Claire Owen
MARIE ANTOINETTE(1938); SHINING HOUR, THE(1938)
Clare Owen
ECHO OF DIANA(1963, Brit.); SHADOW OF FEAR(1963, Brit.)
Cliff Owen
PRIZE OF ARMS, A(1962, Brit.), d; WRONG ARM OF THE LAW, THE(1963, Brit.), d; MAGNIFICENT TWO, THE(1967, Brit.), d; THAT RIVIERA TOUCH(1968, Brit.), d; VENGEANCE OF SHE, THE(1968, Brit.), d; STEPTOE AND SON(1972, Brit.), d; BAWDY ADVENTURES OF TOM JONES, THE(1976, Brit.), d; GET CHARLIE TULLY(1976, Brit.), d; NO SEX PLEASE–WE'RE BRITISH(1979, Brit.), d
Colinson Owen
Silents
ZERO(1928, Brit.), w
Dan Owen
PARTNERS(1976, Can.), p, d, w
Dickie Owen
HELL IS A CITY(1960, Brit.); CONCRETE JUNGLE, THE(1962, Brit.); ZULU(1964, Brit.); CURSE OF THE MUMMY'S TOMB, THE(1965, Brit.); MUMMY'S SHROUD, THE(1967, Brit.)
Dillwyn Owen
UNDER MILK WOOD(1973, Brit.)
Don Owen
NOBODY WAVED GOODBYE(1965, Can.), p, d&w
Douglas Owen
HOSPITAL, THE(1971)
Dudley Owen
UNDER MILK WOOD(1973, Brit.)
Edgar Owen
IMMORTAL GENTLEMAN(1935, Brit.)
Frank Owen
AVENGERS, THE(1942, Brit.), w; BIG BLOCKADE, THE(1942, Brit.)
Fred Owen
DICK BARTON AT BAY(1950, Brit.)
Frederick Owen
STOP PRESS GIRL(1949, Brit.)
Garry Owen
CHILD OF MANHATTAN(1933); HOLD YOUR MAN(1933); PRIZEFIGHTER AND THE LADY, THE(1933); SON OF A SAILOR(1933); BOMBAY MAIL(1934); EVELYN PRENTICE(1934); GAY BRIDE, THE(1934); LITTLE MISS MARKER(1934); MANHATTAN MELODRAMA(1934); THIN MAN, THE(1934); CEILNG ZERO(1935); RED SALUTE(1935); SPECIAL AGENT(1935); CASE OF THE BLACK CAT, THE(1936); KING OF HOCKEY(1936); RETURN OF SOPHIE LANG, THE(1936); ROSE BOWL(1936); DEVIL'S PLAYGROUND(1937); RACKETEERS IN EXILE(1937); SAN QUENTIN(1937); TRUE CONFESSION(1937); CALL OF THE YUKON(1938); DANGEROUS TO KNOW(1938); HEART OF THE NORTH(1938); MEN WITH WINGS(1938); TEST PILOT(1938); ANGELS WASH THEIR FACES(1939); LUCKY NIGHT(1939); NAUGHTY BUT NICE(1939); CHILD IS BORN, A(1940); GRANDPA GOES TO TOWN(1940); TOO MANY HUSBANDS(1940); BLONDIE IN SOCIETY(1941); FOOTSTEPS IN THE DARK(1941); MEET JOHN DOE(1941); SAILORS ON LEAVE(1941); WAGONS ROLL AT NIGHT, THE(1941); YOU'LL NEVER GET RICH(1941); GAY SISTERS, THE(1942); LADY IN A JAM(1942); YANKEE DOODLE DANDY(1942); WATCH ON THE RHINE(1943); WHISTLING IN BROOKLYN(1943); WOMAN OF THE TOWN, THE(1943); ARSENIC AND OLD LACE(1944); NOTHING BUT TROUBLE(1944); ONCE UPON A TIME(1944); THIN MAN GOES HOME, THE(1944); FALLEN ANGEL(1945); MILDRED PIERCE(1945); PHANTOM SPEAKS, THE(1945); TIGER WOMAN, THE(1945); WITHOUT LOVE(1945); DARK MIRROR, THE(1946); HOODLUM SAINT, THE(1946); IDEA GIRL(1946); KILLERS, THE(1946); LADY CHASER(1946); NOTORIOUS(1946); OUR HEARTS WERE GROWING UP(1946); POSTMAN ALWAYS RINGS TWICE, THE(1946); SWELL GUY(1946); IT HAD TO BE YOU(1947); IT HAPPENED ON 5TH AVENUE(1947); MAGIC TOWN(1947); MY FAVORITE BRUNETTE(1947); FLAME, THE(1948); CRISS CROSS(1949); I CHEATED THE LAW(1949); TOO LATE FOR TEARS(1949); ADMIRAL WAS A LADY, THE(1950); FILE ON THELMA JORDAN, THE(1950); FLYING SAUCER, THE(1950); MILKMAN, THE(1950); TWO TICKETS TO BROADWAY(1951)
Gary Owen
HAVANA WIDOWS(1933); HOLD'EM YALE(1935); IDIOT'S DELIGHT(1939); MADE FOR EACH OTHER(1939); HIGH SIERRA(1941); NIGHT TO REMEMBER, A(1942); ANCHORS AWEIGH(1945); HONEYMOON AHEAD(1945); IT'S A WONDERFUL LIFE(1946); MISSING LADY, THE(1946); NIGHT AND DAY(1946); DEAD RECKONING(1947); CHECKERED COAT, THE(1948); KNOCK ON ANY DOOR(1949); SCANDAL SHEET(1952)
George Owen
FRENCH LEAVE(1931, Brit.); WILDCATTER, THE(1937), p; PITTSBURGH(1942), w; SOMETHING TO SHOUT ABOUT(1943), w
Gerry Owen
NO RANSOM(1935)
Gillian Owen
NO TIME FOR TEARS(1957, Brit.); PRINCE AND THE SHOWGIRL, THE(1957, Brit.); LADY MISLAID, A(1958, Brit.)

Glyn Owen
LIFE IN EMERGENCY WARD 10(1959, Brit.); INN FOR TROUBLE(1960, Brit.); ATTACK ON THE IRON COAST(1968, U.S./Brit.); ONE MORE TIME(1970, Brit.)
Granville Owen
ADVENTUROUS BLONDE(1937); DEVIL'S SADDLE LEGION, THE(1937); THAT CERTAIN WOMAN(1937); GREAT PLANE ROBBERY, THE(1940); LI'L ABNER(1940)
Gwyneth Owen
UNDER MILK WOOD(1973, Brit.)
Harold Owen
Silents
MR. WU(1919, Brit.), w; MR. WU(1927), w
Harry Owen
RETURN OF SOPHIE LANG, THE(1936)
Hughie Owen
FIGHTING GENTLEMAN, THE(1932)
Ifor Owen
UNDER MILK WOOD(1973, Brit.)
Jack Owen
HEAT'S ON, THE(1943)
Jay Owen
MEET NERO WOLFE(1936)
Jean Z. Owen
ACCORDING TO MRS. HOYLE(1951), w
John Owen
GREY FOX, THE(1983, Can.)
Joyce Owen
UPPER WORLD(1934)
Kendrick Owen
TREASURE HUNT(1952, Brit.); ROOM AT THE TOP(1959, Brit.)
Lyla Hay Owen
HARD TIMES(1975)
Mary Owen
YOU BELONG TO ME(1934)
Maureen Owen
SECRETS OF SEX(1970, Brit.), w
Meg Wynn Owen
BLUE BLOOD(1973, Brit.); UNDER MILK WOOD(1973, Brit.); DUELLISTS, THE(1977, Brit.)
Michael Owen
STELLA DALLAS(1937); DEATH VALLEY OUTLAWS(1941); GUY NAMED JOE, A(1943); SHE HAS WHAT IT TAKES(1943); SOMEONE TO REMEMBER(1943); SEE HERE, PRIVATE HARGROVE(1944); MR. MUGGS RIDES AGAIN(1945); OVER 21(1945); THOROUGHBREDS(1945); YOUTH AFLAME(1945)
Milton Owen
EVELYN PRENTICE(1934); ROSE MARIE(1936); GREAT GARRICK, THE(1937); LOST HORIZON(1937); BLONDES AT WORK(1938)
Milton A. Owen
EXILE, THE(1947)
Myrtle Owen
Misc. Silents
THIRD WOMAN, THE(1920); WHERE THE NORTH BEGINS(1923)
Nancy Lea Owen
1984
RIVER RAT, THE(1984)
Nicholas Owen
CONFESSIONS FROM A HOLIDAY CAMP(1977, Brit.)
Paul Owen
WAR IS A RACKET(1934)
Peter Owen
THREE-WAY SPLIT(1970)
Reg Owen
COMING-OUT PARTY, A(, m; MURDER REPORTED(1958, Brit.), m; PAYROLL(1962, Brit.), m, md
Reginald Owen
LETTER, THE(1929); MAN IN POSSESSION, THE(1931); PLATINUM BLONDE(1931); DOWNSTAIRS(1932); LOVERS COURAGEOUS(1932); MAN CALLED BACK, THE(1932); SHERLOCK HOLMES(1932); WOMAN COMMANDS, A(1932); BIG BRAIN, THE(1933); BISHOP MISBEHAVES, THE(1933); DOUBLE HARNESS(1933); NARROW CORNER, THE(1933); QUEEN CHRISTINA(1933); ROBBERS' ROOST(1933); STUDY IN SCARLET, A(1933), a, w; VOLTAIRE(1933); COUNTESS OF MONTE CRISTO, THE(1934); FASHIONS OF 1934(1934); HERE IS MY HEART(1934); HOUSE OF ROTHSCHILD, THE(1934); HUMAN SIDE, THE(1934); MADAME DU BARRY(1934); MANDALAY(1934); MUSIC IN THE AIR(1934); NANA(1934); OF HUMAN BONDAGE(1934); STINGAREE(1934); WHERE SINNERS MEET(1934); ANNA KARENINA(1935); CALL OF THE WILD(1935); ENCHANTED APRIL(1935); ESCAPADE(1935); GOOD FAIRY, THE(1935); TALE OF TWO CITIES, A(1935); ADVENTURE IN MANHATTAN(1936); GIRL ON THE FRONT PAGE, THE(1936); GREAT ZIEGFELD, THE(1936); LOVE ON THE RUN(1936); PETTICOAT FEVER(1936); ROSE MARIE(1936); TROUBLE FOR TWO(1936); YOURS FOR THE ASKING(1936); BRIDE WORE RED, THE(1937); CONQUEST(1937); DANGEROUS NUMBER(1937); MADAME X(1937); PERSONAL PROPERTY(1937); ROSALIE(1937); CHRISTMAS CAROL, A(1938); EVERYBODY SING(1938); GIRL DOWNSTAIRS, THE(1938); KIDNAPPED(1938); PARADISE FOR THREE(1938); STABLEMATES(1938), w; THREE LOVES HAS NANCY(1938); VACATION FROM LOVE(1938); BAD LITTLE ANGEL(1939); BRIDAL SUITE(1939); FAST AND LOOSE(1939); HOTEL IMPERIAL(1939); REAL GLORY, THE(1939); REMEMBER?(1939); EARL OF CHICAGO, THE(1940); FLORIAN(1940); GHOST COMES HOME, THE(1940); HULLABALOO(1940); BLONDE INSPIRATION(1941); CHARLEY'S AUNT(1941); FREE AND EASY(1941); LADY BE GOOD(1941); TARZAN'S SECRET TREASURE(1941); THEY MET IN BOMBAY(1941); WOMAN'S FACE(1941); CAIRO(1942); CROSSROADS(1942); I MARRIED AN ANGEL(1942); MRS. MINIVER(1942); PIERRE OF THE PLAINS(1942); RANDOM HARVEST(1942); REUNION IN FRANCE(1942); SOMEWHERE I'LL FIND YOU(1942); WE WERE DANCING(1942); WHITE CARGO(1942); WOMAN OF THE YEAR(1942); ABOVE SUSPICION(1943); ASSIGNMENT IN BRITTANY(1943); FOREVER AND A DAY(1943); MADAME CURIE(1943); SALUTE TO THE MARINES(1943); THREE HEARTS FOR JULIA(1943); CANTERVILLE GHOST, THE(1944); NATIONAL VELVET(1944); CAPTAIN KIDD(1945); KITTY(1945); PICTURE OF DORIAN GRAY, THE(1945); SHE WENT TO THE RACES(1945); VALLEY OF DECISION, THE(1945); CLUNY BROWN(1946); DIARY OF A CHAMBERMAID(1946); MONSIEUR BEAUCAIRE(1946); SAILOR

TAKES A WIFE, THE(1946); GREEN DOLPHIN STREET(1947); IF WINTER COMES(1947); IMPERFECT LADY, THE(1947); HILLS OF HOME(1948); JULIA MISBEHAVES(1948); PICCADILLY INCIDENT(1948, Brit.); PIRATE, THE(1948); THREE MUSKETEERS, THE(1948); CHALLENGE TO LASSIE(1949); SECRET GARDEN, THE(1949); GROUNDS FOR MARRIAGE(1950); KIM(1950); MINIVER STORY, THE(1950, Brit./U.S.); GREAT DIAMOND ROBBERY(1953); RED GARTERS(1954); DARBY'S RANGERS(1958); FIVE WEEKS IN A BALLOON(1962); TAMMY AND THE DOCTOR(1963); THRILL OF IT ALL, THE(1963); MARY POPPINS(1964); VOICE OF THE HURRICANE(1964); ROSIE!(1967); BEDKNOBS AND BROOMSTICKS(1971)
Silents
PLACE IN THE SUN, A(1916, Brit.)
Misc. Silents
SALLY IN OUR ALLEY(1916, Brit.); GRASS ORPHAN, THE(1922, Brit.); POSSESSION(1922, Brit.)

Rex Owen
WHEN TOMORROW DIES(1966, Can.)
Rica Owen
ALL ASHORE(1953); IRON GLOVE, THE(1954)
Richard Owen
Misc. Talkies
TIGHTROPE TO TERROR(1977, Brit.)
Rita Owen
CAUGHT IN THE DRAFT(1941)
Robert Owen
RANGER'S ROUNDUP, THE(1938)
Ron Owen
OTLEY(1969, Brit.)
Russell Owen
GHOST SHIP, THE(1943)
Ruth Bryan Owen
Silents
ONCE UPON A TIME(1922), a, d&w
Sally Owen
FLESH AND BLOOD(1951, Brit.)
Seena Owen
MARRIAGE PLAYGROUND, THE(1929); OFFICER 13(1933); RUMBA(1935), w; CLARENCE(1937), w; THIS WAY PLEASE!(1937), w; THRILL OF A LIFETIME(1937), w; ALOMA OF THE SOUTH SEAS(1941), w; GREAT MAN'S LADY, THE(1942), w; RAINBOW ISLAND(1944), w; CARNEGIE HALL(1947), w
Silents
LAMB, THE(1915); PENITENTES, THE(1915); INTOLERANCE(1916); MARTHA'S VINDICATION(1916); BRANDING BROADWAY(1918); BREED OF MEN(1919); RIDERS OF VENGEANCE(1919); CHEATER REFORMED, THE(1921); LAVENDER AND OLD LACE(1921); WOMAN GOD CHANGED, THE(1921); SISTERS(1922); RUSH HOUR, THE(1927); MAN-MADE WOMEN(1928); SINNERS IN LOVE(1928); QUEEN KELLY(1929)
Misc. Silents
WOMAN'S AWAKENING, A(1917); CITY OF COMRADES, THE(1919); FUGITIVE FROM MATRIMONY(1919); LIFE LINE, THE(1919); MAN AND HIS MONEY, A(1919); ONE OF THE FINEST(1919); SHERIFF'S SON, THE(1919); VICTORY(1919); GIFT SUPREME, THE(1920); HOUSE OF TOYS, THE(1920); PRICE OF REDEMPTION, THE(1920); SOONER OR LATER(1920); AT THE CROSSROADS(1922); BACK PAY(1922); FACE IN THE FOG, THE(1922); GO-GETTER, THE(1923); LEAVENWORTH CASE, THE(1923); UNSEEING EYES(1923); FOR WOMAN'S FAVOR(1924); I AM THE MAN(1924); NEGLECTED WOMEN(1924, Brit.); FAINT PERFUME(1925); HUNTED WOMAN, THE(1925); FLAME OF THE YUKON, THE(1926); SHIPWRECKED(1926); BLUE DANUBE, THE(1928); HIS LAST HAUL(1928)
Sion Tudor Owen
EXPERIENCE PREFERRED... BUT NOT ESSENTIAL(1983, Brit.)
Tom Owen
GOODBYE MR. CHIPS(1969, U.S./Brit.); UNMAN, WITTERING AND ZIGO(1971, Brit.)
Tony Owen
TRAVELING SALESWOMAN(1950), p; DUEL IN THE JUNGLE(1954, Brit.), p; BEYOND MOMBASA(1957), p; NORMAN LOVES ROSE(1982, Aus.)
Tudor Owen
UP IN CENTRAL PARK(1948); PORT OF NEW YORK(1949); TOP O' THE MORNING(1949); JACKPOT, THE(1950); MONTANA(1950); LORNA DOONE(1951); AGAINST ALL FLAGS(1952); BLACK CASTLE, THE(1952); DEADLINE-U.S.A.(1952); LES MISERABLES(1952); MY COUSIN RACHEL(1952); STEEL TOWN(1952); TALK ABOUT A STRANGER(1952); WHEN IN ROME(1952); BACK TO GOD'S COUNTRY(1953); DANGEROUS WHEN WET(1953); HOUDINI(1953); HOW TO MARRY A MILLIONAIRE(1953); TREASURE OF THE GOLDEN CONDOR(1953); ARROW IN THE DUST(1954); BRIGADOON(1954); YANKEE PASHA(1954); KING'S THIEF, THE(1955); SEA CHASE, THE(1955); CONGO CROSSING(1956); COURT JESTER, THE(1956); OKLAHOMA WOMAN, THE(1956); LONELY MAN, THE(1957); STORY OF MANKIND, THE(1957); JET OVER THE ATLANTIC(1960); NORTH TO ALASKA(1960); FRONTIER UPRISING(1961); MOST DANGEROUS MAN ALIVE, THE(1961); ONE HUNDRED AND ONE DALMATIANS(1961); HOW THE WEST WAS WON(1962); JACK THE GIANT KILLER(1962); NOTORIOUS LANDLADY, THE(1962)
Misc. Talkies
RETURN OF GILBERT AND SULLIVAN(1952)
Tutor Owen
Silents
BRIDE OF THE STORM(1926)
Virginia Owen
SUSPENSE(1946); RIFFRAFF(1947); THUNDER MOUNTAIN(1947)
W. Armitage Owen
SAVE A LITTLE SUNSHINE(1938, Brit.), w
Yvonne Owen
GIRL IN A MILLION, A(1946, Brit.); SEVENTH VEIL, THE(1946, Brit.); HOLIDAY CAMP(1947, Brit.); YEARS BETWEEN, THE(1947, Brit.); EASY MONEY(1948, Brit.); GIRL IN THE PAINTING, THE(1948, Brit.); MARRY ME!(1949, Brit.); MIRANDA(1949, Brit.); MY BROTHER'S KEEPER(1949, Brit.); SILENT DUST(1949, Brit.); SOMEONE AT THE DOOR(1950, Brit.); THIRD TIME LUCKY(1950, Brit.)
Zandah Owen
RUNAROUND, THE(1931), w

Bill Owen [Rowbotham]
JOHNNY IN THE CLOUDS(1945, Brit.); WHEN THE BOUGH BREAKS(1947, Brit.)
Paul Owen-Lowe
SCARECROW, THE(1982, New Zealand)
Brian Owen-Smith
LAST SAFARI, THE(1967, Brit.), cos; ROBBERY(1967, Brit.), cos
Bonnie Owens
KILLERS THREE(1968); FROM NASHVILLE WITH MUSIC(1969)
Buck Owens
FROM NASHVILLE WITH MUSIC(1969)
Carol Jean Owens
SQUIRM(1976)
Charles Owens
SITTING PRETTY(1948); YOU WERE MEANT FOR ME(1948)
Chris Owens
WACKY WORLD OF DR. MORGUS, THE(1962)
Cliff Owens
OFFBEAT(1961, Brit.), d; PINOCCHIO IN OUTER SPACE(1965, U.S./Bel.)
Doris Owens
HUCKLEBERRY FINN(1974)
F. Rufus Owens
MOTOR PSYCHO(1965); ROPE OF FLESH(1965)
Garry Owens
ZIEGFELD FOLLIES(1945); GOOD SAM(1948)
Gary Owens
LOVE BUG, THE(1968); MIDNIGHT COWBOY(1969); LOOSE SHOES(1980); HYSTERICAL(1983)
Harrison Owens
UNEASY VIRTUE(1931, Brit.), d&w; TORPEDOED!(1939), w; SUICIDE LEGION(1940, Brit.), w
Harry Owens
COCOANUT GROVE(1938)
Hugh Owens
HIDEOUT(1948, Brit.); LAUGHING LADY, THE(1950, Brit.); RULING CLASS, THE(1972, Brit.)
James Owens
HELL'S BELLES(1969)
Jay Owens
RETURN OF SOPHIE LANG, THE(1936)
John Owens
OH! WHAT A LOVELY WAR(1969, Brit.)
Laura Mish Owens
FRENCH QUARTER(1978)
LaVerne Owens
SOFT SKIN ON BLACK SILK(1964, Fr./Span.), w
Maggie Owens
DARK ODYSSEY(1961)
Marjorie Owens
CRIME OF PASSION(1957)
Mark Owens
FRIDAY THE 13TH... THE ORPHAN(1979)
Milton Owens
MY NAME IS JULIA ROSS(1945)
Nancy Lee Owens
ABBY(1974)
Pat Owens
HER MAN GILBEY(1949, Brit.); MYSTERY JUNCTION(1951, Brit.); CROW HOLLOW(1952, Brit.); UNHOLY FOUR, THE(1954, Brit.)
Pat [Patricia] Owens
WHILE THE SUN SHINES(1950, Brit.)
Patricia Owens
MISS LONDON LTD.(1943, Brit.); GIVE US THE MOON(1944, Brit.); YOU CAN'T DO WITHOUT LOVE(1946, Brit.); THINGS HAPPEN AT NIGHT(1948, Brit.); PAPER ORCHID(1949, Brit.); BAIT(1950, Brit.); HAPPIEST DAYS OF YOUR LIFE(1950, Brit.); OLD MOTHER RILEY, HEADMISTRESS(1950, Brit.); COLONEL MARCH INVESTIGATES(1952, Brit.); GHOST SHIP(1953, Brit.); HOUSE OF BLACKMAIL(1953, Brit.); GOOD DIE YOUNG, THE(1954, Brit.); TALE OF THREE WOMEN, A(1954, Brit.); WINDFALL(1955 Brit.); ALIVE ON SATURDAY(1957, Brit.); ISLAND IN THE SUN(1957); NO DOWN PAYMENT(1957); SAYONARA(1957); FLY, THE(1958); GUN RUNNERS, THE(1958); LAW AND JAKE WADE, THE(1958); FIVE GATES TO HELL(1959); THESE THOUSAND HILLS(1959); HELL TO ETERNITY(1960); SEVEN WOMEN FROM HELL(1961); X-15(1961); WALK A TIGHTROPE(1964, U.S./Brit.); BLACK SPURS(1965); DESTRUCTORS, THE(1968)
Peter Owens
TELL ME A RIDDLE(1980)
Richard Owens
VAMPIRE CIRCUS(1972, Brit.)
Suzanne Owens
MAN OUTSIDE, THE(1968, Brit.)
Virgil Owens
Silents
ABSENT(1928)
Wroe Owens
NONE BUT THE BRAVE(1963), p
Earl Owensby
CHALLENGE(1974), a, p; SEABO(1978), a, p; WOLFMAN(1979), a, p; LADY GREY(1980), p; LIVING LEGEND(1980), a, p
1984
ROTWEILER: DOGS OF HELL(1984), a, p
Misc. Talkies
BRASS RING, THE(1975); DEATH DRIVER(1977); DARK SUNDAY(1978); MANHUNTER(1983)
John Owerns
SCOTT OF THE ANTARCTIC(1949, Brit.)
John Owers
GIRL ON THE CANAL, THE(1947, Brit.); PINK STRING AND SEALING WAX(1950, Brit.)

Rita Owin
LOVE ME TONIGHT(1932); OUR LITTLE GIRL(1935); WINGS IN THE DARK(1935); MAID OF SALEM(1937); BLONDIE ON A BUDGET(1940); MEXICAN SPITFIRE OUT WEST(1940); WEST POINT WIDOW(1941)

Fred Lee Own
MOONLIGHTING(1982, Brit.)
1984
SUPERGIRL(1984)

Ina Ownbey
NIGHT WAITRESS(1936); SALOME, WHERE SHE DANCED(1945)

Phillip Ownes
SATURDAY NIGHT AT THE BATHS(1975)

David Owsley
JAWS II(1978)

Monroe Owsley
FREE LOVE(1930); HOLIDAY(1930); HONOR AMONG LOVERS(1931); INDISCREET(1931); TEN CENTS A DANCE(1931); THIS MODERN AGE(1931); CALL HER SAVAGE(1932); JAZZ BABIES(1932); UNASHAMED(1932); BRIEF MOMENT(1933); EX-LADY(1933); KEYHOLE, THE(1933); LITTLE MAN, WHAT NOW?(1934); SHE WAS A LADY(1934); SHOCK(1934); TWIN HUSBANDS(1934); WILD GOLD(1934); BEHOLD MY WIFE(1935); GOIN' TO TOWN(1935); REMEMBER LAST NIGHT(1935); RUMBA(1935); MISTER CINDERELLA(1936); PRIVATE NUMBER(1936); YELLOWSTONE(1936); HIDEAWAY GIRL(1937); HIT PARADE, THE(1937)

Martin Owusu
HAMILE(1965, Ghana)

Ben Oxenbould
FATTY FINN(1980, Aus.)

Daphne Oxenford
THAT'LL BE THE DAY(1974, Brit.); ALL CREATURES GREAT AND SMALL(1975, Brit.); SWEET WILLIAM(1980, Brit.)

John Oxenham
HEARTS IN EXILE(1929), w

Buckleigh F. Oxford
Silents
REGULAR SCOUT, A(1926), w

Buckleigh Fritz Oxford
Silents
OTHER KIND OF LOVE, THE(1924), w; LARIAT KID, THE(1929), w

Earl Oxford
RIP TIDE(1934); SADIE MCKEE(1934); THIS IS THE ARMY(1943)

John Oxford
BAIT(1950, Brit.)

Vernon Oxford
COAL MINER'S DAUGHTER(1980)

Oxford Scientific Films
HORROR PLANET(1982, Brit.), spec eff

Bill Oxley
VENGEANCE IS MINE(1948, Brit.), ph

David Oxley
YESTERDAY'S ENEMY(1959, Brit.); FIGHTING PIMPERNEL, THE(1950, Brit.); ARMCHAIR DETECTIVE, THE(1952, Brit.); SVENGALI(1955, Brit.); BLACK ICE, THE(1957, Brit.); SAINT JOAN(1957); BONJOUR TRISTESSE(1958); NIGHT AMBUSH(1958, Brit.); HOUND OF THE BASKERVILLES, THE(1959, Brit.); SEA FURY(1959, Brit.); BUNNY LAKE IS MISSING(1965); LIFE AT THE TOP(1965, Brit.); HOUSE OF THE LIVING DEAD(1973, S. Afr.)

Jill Oxley
SECRET CEREMONY(1968, Brit.), set d; CONNECTING ROOMS(1971, Brit.), set d

Roy Oxley
DULCIMER STREET(1948, Brit.), art d; PASSPORT TO PIMLICO(1949, Brit.), art d

Alice Colombo Oxman
END OF THE WORLD(in Our Usual Bed In a Night Full of Rain), THE (1978, Ital.)

Phil Oxnam
ARTHUR(1981)

Paul Oxon
SLASHER, THE(1975)

Ken Oxtoby
O LUCKY MAN!(1973, Brit.)

Haimi Oy
MAKE LIKE A THIEF(1966, Fin.), set d

B. Oya
FORTY-NINE DAYS(1964, USSR)

Ichijiro Oya
TEMPTRESS AND THE MONK, THE(1963, Jap.)

Soichi Oya
EMPEROR AND A GENERAL, THE(1968, Jap.), w

Aya Oyama
TEAHOUSE OF THE AUGUST MOON, THE(1956); CRIMSON KIMONO, THE(1959)

Kenji Oyama
Misc. Silents
CHORUS OF TOKYO(1931, Jap.)

Mas Oyama
Misc. Talkies
FIGHTING BLACK KINGS(1977)

Reiko Oyama
STOPOVER TOKYO(1957)

Ted Oyama
HERE COME THE TIGERS(1978)

David Oyang
YEAR OF LIVING DANGEROUSLY, THE(1982, Aus.)

Henry Oyasato
GO FOR BROKE(1951)

Beatrice Fung Oye
ON STAGE EVERYBODY(1945)

Henry Oyen
Silents
AVENGING TRAIL, THE(1918), w

Raoul Oyen
SNOW TREASURE(1968)

Oyo
KILLING GAME, THE(1968, Fr.)

Ben Oyserman
DREAM NO MORE(1950, Palestine), ph

Moishe Oysher
CANTOR'S SON, THE(1937); SINGING BLACKSMITH(1938); OVERTURE TO GLORY(1940); SINGING IN THE DARK(1956)

Frank Oz
MUPPET MOVIE, THE(1979); BLUES BROTHERS, THE(1980); EMPIRE STRIKES BACK, THE(1980); AMERICAN WEREWOLF IN LONDON, AN(1981); GREAT MUPPET CAPER, THE(1981), a, p; DARK CRYSTAL, THE(1982, Brit.), a, d; RETURN OF THE JEDI(1983); TRADING PLACES(1983)
1984
MUPPETS TAKE MANHATTAN, THE(1984), a, d, w

Shizu Ozaka
FIGHT FOR THE GLORY(1970, Jap.), ed

Koyo Ozaki
GOLDEN DEMON(1956, Jap.), w

Nana Ozaki
FAREWELL, MY BELOVED(1969, Jap.); FIGHT FOR THE GLORY(1970, Jap.); PERFORMERS, THE(1970, Jap.)

Christine Ozanne
DAVID COPPERFIELD(1970, Brit.)

Robert Ozanne
LOWER DEPTHS, THE(1937, Fr.); PEPE LE MOKO(1937, Fr.); THEY WERE FIVE(1938, Fr.)

Eitaro Ozawa
H-MAN, THE(1959, Jap.); HUMAN CONDITION, THE(1959, Jap.); WHEN A WOMAN ASCENDS THE STAIRS(1963, Jap.); ILLUSION OF BLOOD(1966, Jap.); DAY THE SUN ROSE, THE(1969, Jap.); MOMENT OF TERROR(1969, Jap.); VIXEN(1970, Jap.)

Sakae Ozawa
UGETSU(1954, Jap.); SCANDAL(1964, Jap.)

Shoich Ozawa
1984
BALLAD OF NARAYAMA, THE(1984, Jap.)

Shoichi Ozawa
INSECT WOMAN, THE(1964, Jap.); SCARLET CAMELLIA, THE(1965, Jap.); ONCE A RAINY DAY(1968, Jap.); GIRL I ABANDONED, THE(1970, Jap.); SCANDALOUS ADVENTURES OF BURAIKAN, THE(1970, Jap.); SILENCE HAS NO WINGS(1971, Jap.); SUMMER SOLDIERS(1972, Jap.)

Sheila Ozden
TEMPEST(1982)

Lajos Oze
ROUND UP, THE(1969, Hung.); WITNESS, THE(1982, Hung.)

A Sandy Ozeka
HOUSE OF BAMBOO(1955)

Ozenne
CHEAT, THE(1950, Fr.)

Jean Ozenne
MOULIN ROUGE(1952); BEDEVILLED(1955); PARIS DOES STRANGE THINGS(1957, Fr./Ital.); LOSS OF INNOCENCE(1961, Brit.); FIVE MILES TO MIDNIGHT(1963, U.S./Fr./Ital.); JULIE THE REDHEAD(1963, Fr.); DIARY OF A CHAMBERMAID(1964, Fr./Ital.); TWO ARE GUILTY(1964, Fr.); SECRET AGENT FIREBALL(1965, Fr./Ital.)

Fedor Ozep
TWO WHO DARED(1937, Brit.), w; BETRAYAL(1939, Fr.), d; IT HAPPENED IN GIBRALTAR(1943, Fr.), d; THREE RUSSIAN GIRLS(1943), d; WHISPERING CITY(1947, Can.), d

Fyodor Ozep
KARAMAZOV(1931, Ger.), d, w

Madeleine Ozeray
CRIME AND PUNISHMENT(1935, Fr.); LILIOM(1935, Fr.); END OF A DAY, THE(1939, Fr.)

Magdeleine Ozeray
DR. KNOCK(1936, Fr.)

Igor Ozerov
GARNET BRACELET, THE(1966, USSR)

D. Ozerova
MEET ME IN MOSCOW(1966, USSR), cos

Ali Ozgenturk
1984
HORSE, THE(1984, Turk.), d

Isil Ozgenturk
1984
HORSE, THE(1984, Turk.), w

Ozi and Glesne
MOUSE AND THE WOMAN, THE(1981, Brit.)

Ozie Walters and His Colorado Rangers
LANDRUSH(1946); PHANTOM VALLEY(1948); STREETS OF GHOST TOWN(1950)

Eren Ozker
MUPPET MOVIE, THE(1979)

Bob Ozman
ISLAND OF DR. MOREAU, THE(1977); PARTNERS(1982)
1984
ICE PIRATES, THE(1984)

Earle Ozman
NIGHT IN PARADISE, A(1946)

Hal Ozmond
BOY, A GIRL AND A BIKE, A(1949 Brit.)

Karlos Ozols
LOOSE ENDS(1975)

Yoko Ozono
LONGING FOR LOVE(1966, Jap.)

Mayumi Ozora
MADAME AKI(1963, Jap.); PRESSURE OF GUILT(1964, Jap.); RABBLE, THE(1965, Jap.); ILLUSION OF BLOOD(1966, Jap.); RISE AGAINST THE SWORD(1966, Jap.); KOJIRO(1967, Jap.); EYES, THE SEA AND A BALL(1968 Jap.); FAREWELL, MY BELOVED(1969, Jap.); OUR SILENT LOVE(1969, Jap.); THROUGH DAYS AND MONTHS(1969 Jap.); UNDER THE BANNER OF SAMURAI(1969, Jap.)

Mariano Ozores
DESERT WARRIOR(1961 Ital./Span.), w; SEVEN GOLDEN MEN(1969, Fr./Ital./Span.), w
Armand Ozory
CASTLE, THE(1969, Ger.)
Ozu
TEA AND RICE(1964, Jap.), w
Yasujiro Ozu
EARLY AUTUMN(1962, Jap.), d, w; OHAYO(1962, Jap.), d, w; TEA AND RICE(1964, Jap.), d; TWILIGHT PATH(1965, Jap.), w; FLOATING WEEDS(1970, Jap.), d, w; TOKYO STORY(1972, Jap.), d, w; LATE AUTUMN(1973, Jap.), d, w
Misc. Silents
SWORD OF PENITENCE(1927, Jap.), d; BODY BEAUTIFUL(1928, Jap.), d; COUPLE ON THE MOVE, A(1928, Jap.), d; DREAMS OF YOUTH(1928, Jap.), d; PUMPKIN(1928, Jap.), d; WIFE LOST(1928, Jap.), d; STRAIGHTFORWARD BOY, A(1929, Jap.), d; I FLUNKED, BUT...(1930, Jap.), d; INTRODUCTION TO MARRIAGE(1930, Jap.), d; LUCK TOUCHED MY LEGS(1930, Jap.), d; REVENGEFUL SPIRIT OF EROS, THE(1930, Jap.), d; THAT NIGHT'S WIFE(1930, Jap.), d; WALK CHEERFULLY(1930, Jap.), d; YOUNG MISS(1930, Jap.), d; BEAUTY'S SORROWS(1931, Jap.), d; CHORUS OF TOKYO(1931, Jap.), d; LADY AND THE BEARD, THE(1931, Jap.), d; I WAS BORN, BUT...(1932, Jap.), d; SPRING COMES WITH THE LADIES(1932, Jap.), d; UNTIL THE DAY WE MEET AGAIN(1932, Jap.), d; WHERE ARE THE DREAMS OF YOUTH?(1932, Jap.), d; PASSING FANCY(1933, Jap.), d; WOMAN OF TOKYO(1933, Jap.), d; WOMEN ON THE FIRING LINE(1933, Jap.), d; INNOCENT MAID, AN(1934, Jap.), d; MOTHER SHOULD BE LOVED, A(1934, Jap.), d; STORY OF FLOATING WEEDS, A(1934, Jap.), d; INN IN TOKYO, AN(1935, Jap.), d; COLLEGE IS A NICE PLACE(1936, Jap.), d
Jun-ichi Ozumi
HAHAKIRI(1963, Jap.), art d; TWIN SISTERS OF KYOTO(1964, Jap.), art d
Ozzie Nelson and His Orchestra
HONEYMOON LODGE(1943)
Ozzie Nelson and His Orchestra
HI, GOOD-LOOKIN'(1944); TAKE IT BIG(1944)

P

Solomon Pa
BIRD OF PARADISE(1951)
Alexander Paal
TALE OF FIVE WOMEN, A(1951, Brit.), p; CLOUDBURST(1952, Brit.), p; FOUR SIDED TRIANGLE(1953, Brit.), p; WOMAN IN HIDING(1953, Brit.), p; THREE CASES OF MURDER(1955, Brit.), p; GOLDEN HEAD, THE(1965, Hung., U.S.), p; COUNTESS DRACULA(1972, Brit.), p
Laszlo Paal
BOYS OF PAUL STREET, THE(1969, Hung./US)
Aimo Paapio
MAKE LIKE A THIEF(1966, Fin.)
Jack Paar
EASY LIVING(1949); WALK SOFTLY, STRANGER(1950); LOVE NEST(1951); DOWN AMONG THE SHELTERING PALMS(1953)
Erik Paaske
WEEKEND(1964, Den.); CRAZY PARADISE(1965, Den.)
Levan Paatashvili
STEPCHILDREN(1962, USSR), ph
Al Pabian
BON VOYAGE, CHARLIE BROWN(AND DON'T COME BACK)***(1980), anim; RACE FOR YOUR LIFE, CHARLIE BROWN(1977), anim
Pablo Ferro Films
THOMAS CROWN AFFAIR, THE(1968), spec eff
G.W. Pabst
FROM TOP TO BOTTOM(1933, Fr.), d; MODERN HERO, A(1934), d; DON QUIXOTE(1935, Fr.), d; SHANGHAI DRAMA, THE(1945, Fr.), d; TRIAL, THE(1948, Aust.), p; LAST TEN DAYS, THE(1956, Ger.), d
Silents
PANDORA'S BOX(1929, Ger.), d
Misc. Silents
SECRETS OF A SOUL(1925, Ger.), d; LOVE OF JEANNE NEY, THE(1927, Ger.), d; DIARY OF A LOST GIRL(1929, Ger.), d
Georg Wilhelm Pabst
THREEPENNY OPERA, THE(1931, Ger./U.S.), d; MISTRESS OF ATLANTIS, THE(1932, Ger.), d
Norman Pabst
CRIMINALS OF THE AIR(1937); FRONTIER UPRISING(1961)
William Pabst
KING OF MARVIN GARDENS, THE(1972); PORTNOY'S COMPLAINT(1972); GOING IN STYLE(1979)
Pacci
LAUGH PAGLIACCI(1948, Ital.)
Anna Maria Pace
HERCULES AGAINST THE SONS OF THE SUN(1964, Span./Ital.)
Auguste Pace
JE T'AIME, JE T'AIME(1972, Fr./Swed.), art d
Diane Pace
GYPSY(1962)
Gary Pace
HIDE IN PLAIN SIGHT(1980)
Gayle Pace
GUY WHO CAME BACK, THE(1951); HALF ANGEL(1951)
Jim Pace
RED, WHITE AND BLACK, THE(1970)
Judy Pace
THIRTEEN FRIGHTENED GIRLS(1963); FORTUNE COOKIE, THE(1966); THOMAS CROWN AFFAIR, THE(1968); THREE IN THE ATTIC(1968); COTTON COMES TO HARLEM(1970); UP IN THE CELLAR(1970); COOL BREEZE(1972); FROGS(1972); SLAMS, THE(1973)
Lloyd Pace
BASKET CASE(1982)
Lois Pace
HER FIRST ROMANCE(1951)
Margherita Pace
1984
ONCE UPON A TIME IN AMERICA(1984)
Owen Hith Pace
ST. IVES(1976)
Owen Pace
TOGETHER BROTHERS(1974); BROTHERS(1977)
Ralph Pace
NIGHT THE LIGHTS WENT OUT IN GEORGIA, THE(1981)
Richard Pace
I SPIT ON YOUR GRAVE(1983)
Roger Pace
WAR OF THE COLOSSAL BEAST(1958)
Thom Pace
LIFE AND TIMES OF GRIZZLY ADAMS, THE(1974), m
Tom Pace
EDEN CRIED(1967); GIRL IN GOLD BOOTS(1968); ASTRO-ZOMBIES, THE(1969)
Joseph G. Pacelli
1984
STONE BOY, THE(1984), prod d
The Pacemakers
RIDE, TENDERFOOT, RIDE(1940)
Peter Pacey
NUTCRACKER(1982, Brit.)
Steven Pacey
JULIUS CAESAR(1970, Brit.)

Janos Pach
BOYS OF PAUL STREET, THE(1969, Hung./US)
Wilhelm Pach
PINOCCHIO(1969, E. Ger.), w
Maleen Pacha
YOUNG TORLESS(1968, Fr./Ger.), art d
Pacheco
PROUD AND THE DAMNED, THE(1972)
Geneva Pacheco
SPLIT, THE(1968)
Godfrey Pacheco
THOSE DIRTY DOGS(1974, U.S./Ital./Span.), ph
Godofredo Pacheco
AWFUL DR. ORLOFF, THE(1964, Span./Fr.), ph; REVOLT OF THE MERCENARIES(1964, Ital./Span.), ph; SANTO CONTRA EL DOCTOR MUERTE(1974, Span./Mex.), ph
Gofferdo Pacheco
DULCINEA(1962, Span.), ph
Jose Emilio Pacheco
CASTLE OF PURITY(1974, Mex.), w; FOXTROT(1977, Mex./Swiss), w
Mario Pacheco
LEGIONS OF THE NILE(1960, Ital.), ph; CASTILIAN, THE(1963, Span./U.S.), ph; OPERATION DELILAH(1966, U.S./Span.), ph
Mike Pacheco
SUMMER LOVE(1958)
Rafael Pacheco
FACE TO FACE(1967, Ital.), ph; FOUR RODE OUT(1969, US/Span.), ph; ANTONY AND CLEOPATRA(1973, Brit.), ph
Richard Pacheco
Misc. Talkies
SIMPLY IRRESISTIBLE(1983)
Herb Pacheko
STONE COLD DEAD(1980, Can.)
Albinoni Pachelbel
EVERY MAN FOR HIMSELF AND GOD AGAINST ALL(1975, Ger.), m
Johann Pachelbel
TO BEGIN AGAIN(1982, Span.), m
Oscar Pacheli
PRISONER OF THE IRON MASK(1962, Fr./Ital.), makeup
Pacific Gas & Electric
TELL ME THAT YOU LOVE ME, JUNIE MOON(1970)
Pacific Palisades High School Madrigals
TROUBLE WITH GIRLS(AND HOW TO GET INTO IT), THE (1969)
Louis Pacigalupi
SONG OF BERNADETTE, THE(1943)
Raffaello Pacini
GIANT OF MARATHON, THE(1960, Ital.), w
Al Pacino
ME, NATALIE(1969); PANIC IN NEEDLE PARK(1971); GODFATHER, THE(1972); SCARECROW(1973); SERPICO(1973); GODFATHER, THE, PART II(1974); DOG DAY AFTERNOON(1975); BOBBY DEERFIELD(1977); ...AND JUSTICE FOR ALL(1979); CRUISING(1980); AUTHOR! AUTHOR!(1982); SCARFACE(1983)
Dustin Pacino, Jr.
SUMMER CAMP(1979)
Tony Pacioni
ADULTEROUS AFFAIR(1966)
Charles Lloyd Pack
HIGH TREASON(1951, Brit.); GLORY AT SEA(1952, Brit.); I'M A STRANGER(1952, Brit.); NOOSE FOR A LADY(1953, Brit.); FUSS OVER FEATHERS(1954, Brit.); RIVER BEAT(1954); CONSTANT HUSBAND, THE(1955, Brit.); ALL FOR MARY(1956, Brit.); LOSER TAKES ALL(1956, Brit.); TRACK THE MAN DOWN(1956, Brit.); ALIVE ON SATURDAY(1957, Brit.); DOCTOR AT LARGE(1957, Brit.); ENEMY FROM SPACE(1957, Brit.); FLESH IS WEAK, THE(1957, Brit.); PICKUP ALLEY(1957, Brit.); STRANGER IN TOWN(1957, Brit.); VALUE FOR MONEY(1957, Brit.); FURTHER UP THE CREEK!(1958, Brit.); HORROR OF DRACULA, THE(1958, Brit.); REVENGE OF FRANKENSTEIN, THE(1958, Brit.); SAFECRACKER, THE(1958, Brit.); THREE MEN IN A BOAT(1958, Brit.); STRANGE AFFECTION(1959, Brit.); COVER GIRL KILLER(1960, Brit.); THREE WORLDS OF GULLIVER, THE(1960, Brit.); CIRCLE OF DECEPTON(1961, Brit.); KITCHEN, THE(1961, Brit.); TERROR OF THE TONGS, THE(1961, Brit.); TROUBLE IN THE SKY(1961, Brit.); VICTIM(1961, Brit.); CORRIDORS OF BLOOD(1962, Brit.); FLAT TWO(1962, Brit.); CROOKS ANONYMOUS(1963, Brit.); SIEGE OF THE SAXONS(1963, Brit.); THIRD SECRET, THE(1964, Brit.); SEASIDE SWINGERS(1965, Brit.); REPTILE, THE(1966, Brit.); BEDAZZLED(1967, Brit.); DIAMONDS FOR BREAKFAST(1968, Brit.); IF ...(1968, Brit.); SEBASTIAN(1968, Brit.); SHUTTERED ROOM, THE(1968, Brit.); TWO A PENNY(1968, Brit.); I START COUNTING(1970, Brit.); MAN WHO HAUNTED HIMSELF, THE(1970, Brit.); SONG OF NORWAY(1970)
Gene Pack
1984
FOOTLOOSE(1984)
Roger Lloyd Pack
MAGUS, THE(1968, Brit.); FIGURES IN A LANDSCAPE(1970, Brit.); FIDDLER ON THE ROOF(1971); FRIGHT(1971, Brit.); GO-BETWEEN, THE(1971, Brit.); MEETINGS WITH REMARKABLE MEN(1979, Brit.)
1984
1984(1984, Brit.)
Clayton Packard
Silents
KING OF KINGS, THE(1927)
Frank L. Packard
MIRACLE MAN, THE(1932), w
Silents
MIRACLE MAN, THE(1919), w; SMILES ARE TRUMPS(1922), w
Frank Lucius Packard
Silents
SIN THAT WAS HIS, THE(1920), w
Frank Packard
SPECTRE OF EDGAR ALLAN POE, THE(1974)

Fred M. Packard
ROGUES OF SHERWOOD FOREST(1950), p
Ruth Packard
TURNING POINT, THE(1952); SHE COULDN'T SAY NO(1954)
Doris Packer
MEET ME AT THE FAIR(1952); BON VOYAGE(1962); MR. HOBBS TAKES A VACATION(1962); PARADISE, HAWAIIAN STYLE(1966); PERILS OF PAULINE, THE(1967); SHAMPOO(1975)
Jean Packer
PAUL TEMPLE'S TRIUMPH(1951, Brit.)
Joy Packer
ELEPHANT GUN(1959, Brit.), w
Mae Packer
ZAZA(1939)
Netta Packer
THEY WON'T BELIEVE ME(1947); CONDEMNED WOMEN(1938); ENEMY AGENT(1940); PRAIRIE SCHOONERS(1940); FATHER TAKES A WIFE(1941); REG'- LAR FELLERS(1941); RICHEST MAN IN TOWN(1941); TOM, DICK AND HAR- RY(1941); LIFE BEGINS AT 8:30(1942); SHE HAS WHAT IT TAKES(1943); DESPERATE(1947); GLAMOUR GIRL(1947); GOOD SAM(1948); SMART WO- MAN(1948); KNOCK ON ANY DOOR(1949); IT STARTED WITH A KISS(1959)
Peter Packer
COUNTRYMAN(1982, Jamaica)
Peter Packer
SEVENTH CAVALRY(1956), w
Robert Packer
FROM THE MIXED-UP FILES OF MRS. BASIL E. FRANKWEILER(1973)
Tina Packer
TWO A PENNY(1968, Brit.); PRAISE MARX AND PASS THE AMMUNITION(1970, Brit.)
Wednesday Lea Packer
MISTER BROWN(1972)
William Packer
SACCO AND VANZETTI(1971, Ital./Fr.)
Geoffrey Packett [Godofredo Pacheco]
SUPERARGO(1968, Ital./Span.), ph
Bill Packham
FORTY ACRE FEUD(1965), p&w; GOLD GUITAR, THE(1966), p, w
Norval E. Packwood
GARDEN OF EDEN(1954)
Packy the Elephant
TARZAN'S JUNGLE REBELLION(1970)
Maria Pacome
GENDARME OF ST. TROPEZ, THE(1966, Fr./Ital.); UP TO HIS EARS(1966, Fr./Ital.); WEB OF FEAR(1966, Fr./Span.); TENDER SCOUNDREL(1967, Fr./Ital.); DAY- DREAMER, THE(1975, Fr.)
Joseph Pacovsky
MY FATHER'S HOUSE(1947, Palestine)
Laszlo Pacsery
AZURE EXPRESS(1938, Hung.), w
Joanna Pacula
GORKY PARK(1983)
Johnny Paczynski
PIE IN THE SKY(1964)
Tom Padaca
SKATEBOARD(1978)
Erich Padalewski
CRIME AND PASSION(1976, U.S., Ger.)
Erich Padalewsky
SEVEN-PER-CENT SOLUTION, THE(1977, Brit.)
Alyque Padamsee
GANDHI(1982)
Wendy Padburt
CHARLIE BUBBLES(1968, Brit.)
Wendy Padbury
BLOOD ON SATAN'S CLAW, THE(1970, Brit.)
Allan L. Paddack
JAWS II(1978)
Niall Padden
PRIEST OF LOVE(1981, Brit.); BLOODY KIDS(1983, Brit.)
Sara Padden
TESS OF THE STORM COUNTRY(1932); MAD LOVE(1935); CASANOVA BROWN(1944); POSSESSED(1947); BIG JIM McLAIN(1952)
Sarah Padden
SOPHOMORE, THE(1929); WONDER OF WOMEN(1929); HIDE-OUT, THE(1930); TODAY(1930); GREAT, MEADOW, THE(1931); MATA HARI(1931); SOB SISTER(1931); YELLOW TICKET, THE(1931); BLONDIE OF THE FOLLIES(1932); CROSS-EXAMI- NATION(1932); MIDNIGHT LADY(1932); RASPUTIN AND THE EMPRESS(1932); REBECCA OF SUNNYBROOK FARM(1932); WILD GIRL(1932); YOUNG AMERI- CA(1932); ANN VICKERS(1933); FACE IN THE SKY(1933); IMPORTANT WITNESS, THE(1933); POWER AND THE GLORY, THE(1933); SIN OF NORA MORAN(1933); WOMEN WON'T TELL(1933); DAVID HARUM(1934); DEFENSE HESTS, THE(1934); HE WAS HER MAN(1934); LITTLE MAN, WHAT NOW?(1934); MAN OF TWO WORLDS(1934); MARRYING WIDOWS(1934); WHEN STRANGERS MEET(1934); DOG OF FLANDERS, A(1935); HOOSIER SCHOOLMASTER(1935); STRANDED(1935); EXILED TO SHANGHAI(1937); YOUTH ON PAROLE(1937); FORBIDDEN VAL- LEY(1938); LITTLE ORPHAN ANNIE(1938); RICH MAN, POOR GIRL(1938); RO- MANCE OF THE LIMBERLOST(1938); THREE COMRADES(1938); WOMAN AGAINST WOMAN(1938); WOMEN IN PRISON(1938); I STOLE A MILLION(1939); LET FREEDOM RING(1939); MAN OF CONQUEST(1939); OFF THE RECORD(1939); SHOULD A GIRL MARRY?(1939); ZERO HOUR, THE(1939); CHAD HANNA(1940); FORGOTTEN GIRLS(1940); LONE STAR RAIDERS(1940); SON OF THE NAVY(1940); CITY OF MISSING GIRLS(1941); CORSICAN BROTHERS, THE(1941); IN OLD COLORADO(1941); MAN WHO LOST HIMSELF, THE(1941); MURDER BY INVITA- TION(1941); OUTLAWS OF THE CHEROKEE TRAIL(1941); REG'LAR FEL- LERS(1941); TIGHT SHOES(1941); WOMAN'S FACE(1941); DEVIL'S TRAIL, THE(1942); HEART OF THE RIO GRANDE(1942); LADY IN A JAM(1942); LAW AND ORDER(1942); MAD MONSTER, THE(1942); PRIDE OF THE YANKEES, THE(1942); RIDERS OF THE WEST(1942); SNUFFY SMITH, YARD BIRD(1942); THIS GUN FOR HIRE(1942); WILD BILL HICKOK RIDES(1942); ASSIGNMENT IN BRITTANY(1943);

HANGMEN ALSO DIE(1943); JACK LONDON(1943); NORTH STAR, THE(1943); SO THIS IS WASHINGTON(1943); GHOST GUNS(1944); GIRL RUSH(1944); RANGE LAW(1944); SAN DIEGO, I LOVE YOU(1944); SUMMER STORM(1944); TRAIL TO GUNSIGHT(1944); UNCERTAIN GLORY(1944); DAKOTA(1945); HONEYMOON AHEAD(1945); IDENTITY UNKNOWN(1945); MARSHAL OF LAREDO(1945); RID- ERS OF THE DAWN(1945); SONG OF OLD WYOMING(1945); WILDFIRE(1945); ANGEL ON MY SHOULDER(1946); IDEA GIRL(1946); JOE PALOOKA, CHAMP(1946); THAT BRENNAN GIRL(1946); WILD WEST(1946); MILLERSON CASE, THE(1947); RAMROD(1947); TRAIL STREET(1947); DUDE GOES WEST, THE(1948); FIGHTING MAD(1948); FRONTIER REVENGE(1948); PRAIRIE OUTLAWS(1948); RETURN OF THE WHISTLER, THE(1948); HOMICIDE(1949); RANGE JUSTICE(1949); GUNSLIN- GERS(1950); HOUSE BY THE RIVER(1950); LIFE OF HER OWN, A(1950); MISSOURI- ANS, THE(1950); UTAH WAGON TRAIN(1951); PRINCE OF PLAYERS(1955); KETTLES IN THE OZARKS, THE(1956)
Silents
WOMAN WHO DID NOT CARE, THE(1927)
Hugh Paddick
SCHOOL FOR SCOUNDRELS(1960, Brit.); WE SHALL SEE(1964, Brit.); SAN FERRY ANN(1965, Brit.); UP POMPEII(1971, Brit.); UP THE CHASTITY BELT(1971, Brit.)
Charles Paddock
DELINQUENTS, THE(1957), ph
Charles Paddock
Silents
NINE AND THREE-FIFTHS SECONDS(1925); OLYMPIC HERO, THE(1928)
Charlie Paddock
JONIKO AND THE KUSH TA KA(1969)
Charles Paddock
Silents
CAMPUS FLIRT, THE(1926)
Jesse Paddock
JONIKO AND THE KUSH TA KA(1969)
Rose Paddon
IT HAPPENED HERE(1966, Brit.)
Paddy the Dog
LITTLE MISS MOLLY(1940)
Daphne Padel
TWENTY QUESTIONS MURDER MYSTERY, THE(1950, Brit.)
Ignace Jan Paderewski
MOONLIGHT SONATA(1938, Brit.)
Philip Padfield
CIRCLE OF DECEIT(1982, Fr./Ger.)
Jack Padgen
Silents
KING OF KINGS, THE(1927)
Bob Padget
PARTY CRASHERS, THE(1958); TANK BATTALION(1958); BIG NIGHT, THE(1960)
Lewis Padget [Henry Kuttner]
TWONKY, THE(1953), w
Billy Padgett
Misc. Talkies
PELVIS(1977)
Calvin Jackson Padgett
SECRET AGENT SUPER DRAGON(1966, Fr./Ital./Ger./Monaco), d, w
H. W. Padgett
Silents
LAST STRAW, THE(1920)
Dick Padgette
LOOKIN' TO GET OUT(1982)
Paulo Padilha
XICA(1982, Braz.)
Manuel Padilla
DIME WITH A HALO(1963); YOUNG AND THE BRAVE, THE(1963); ROBIN AND THE SEVEN HOODS(1964); BLACK SPURS(1965); SYLVIA(1965); TAFFY AND THE JUNGLE HUNTER(1965); MAN CALLED HORSE, A(1970); MORE AMERICAN GRAFFITI(1979)
Manuel Padilla, Jr.
TARZAN AND THE VALLEY OF GOLD(1966 U.S./Switz.); TARZAN AND THE GREAT RIVER(1967, U.S./Switz.); GREAT WHITE HOPE, THE(1970); TARZAN'S DEADLY SILENCE(1970); TARZAN'S JUNGLE REBELLION(1970); AMERICAN GRAFFITI(1973); SCARFACE(1983)
Margaret Padilla
FIGHTER, THE(1952)
Miguel Padilla
PASSION(1954), w
Robert Padilla
MACHISMO-40 GRAVES FOR 40 GUNS(1970); SCANDALOUS JOHN(1971); GREAT GUNDOWN, THE(1977), a, w
Roy Padilla
1984
NINJA III-THE DOMINATION(1984)
Ruben Padilla
BULLFIGHTER AND THE LADY(1951); ALAMO, THE(1960)
Padillia Sisters
PAN-AMERICANA(1945)
Aldo Padinotti
ATLAS AGAINST THE CYCLOPS(1963, Ital.)
Jack Padjan
WILD GIRL(1932); GUNSMOKE RANCH(1937)
Silents
TONY RUNS WILD(1926)
Misc. Silents
LAND OF THE LAWLESS(1927); CRASHING THROUGH(1928); FORBIDDEN GRASS(1928)
John Padjan
Silents
IRON HORSE, THE(1924)
Guglielmo Padoni
TREE OF WOODEN CLOGS, THE(1979, Ital.)

Lea Padovani
CALL OF THE BLOOD(1948, Brit.); WHITE DEVIL, THE(1948, Ital.); OUTCRY(1949, Ital.); SALT TO THE DEVIL(1949, Brit.); HONEYMOON DEFERRED(1951, Brit.); THREE STEPS NORTH(1951); CENTO ANNI D'AMORE(1954, Ital.); GRAN VARIETA(1955, Ital.); ANGELS OF DARKNESS(1956, Ital.); SCANDAL IN SORRENTO(1957, Ital./Fr.); ANATOMY OF LOVE(1959, Ital.); NAKED MAJA, THE(1959, U.S.); MODIGLIANI OF MONTPARNASSE(1961, Fr./Ital.); RELUCTANT SAINT, THE(1962, U.S./Ital.); GERMINAL(1963, Fr.); EMPTY CANVAS, THE(1964, Fr./Ital.); CANDY(1968, Ital./Fr.)
Misc. Talkies
OUR MEN IN BAGHDAD(1967, Ital.)

John Padovano
FOREIGN INTRIGUE(1956)

Padua Hill Players
THREE CABALLEROS, THE(1944)

Anna Maria Paduan
BAREFOOT CONTESSA, THE(1954)

Margaret Padula
LADY OF THE TROPICS(1939); KID DYNAMITE(1943)

Marguerita Padula
CUCKOOS, THE(1930); HIT THE DECK(1930); ROAD TO SINGAPORE(1940); GANGSTER, THE(1947)

Vincent Padula
AVENGERS, THE(1950); THREE COINS IN THE FOUNTAIN(1954); GIRL RUSH, THE(1955); SERENADE(1956); THREE OUTLAWS, THE(1956); HELL CANYON OUTLAWS(1957); ESCAPE FROM RED ROCK(1958); FLAME BARRIER, THE(1958); PIER 5, HAVANA(1959); RAYMIE(1960)

Anne Padwick
TRAITORS, THE(1963, Brit.); LITTLE ONES, THE(1965, Brit.); BLUES FOR LOVERS(1966, Brit.); MAROC 7(1967, Brit.)

Armand Paenny
LEVIATHAN(1961, Fr.), ed

Barbara Paepcke
GERMAN SISTERS, THE(1982, Ger.)

Rebecca Paepcke
GERMAN SISTERS, THE(1982, Ger.)

Darryl Paes
2001: A SPACE ODYSSEY(1968, U.S./Brit.)

Charles Paetow
PEER GYNT(1965)

Maria Pafusto
TWIST, THE(1976, Fr.), w

Albert Pagac
DESERTER AND THE NOMADS, THE(1969, Czech./Ital.)

Antone Pagan
STRIPES(1981)

Bill Pagan
INVISIBLE AGENT(1942)

Peter Pagan
OVERLANDERS, THE(1946, Brit./Aus.)

William Pagan
LUCKY CISCO KID(1940); SANTA FE MARSHAL(1940); HONKY TONK(1941); MR. CELEBRITY(1942)

Giuseppe Paganelli
MODESTY BLAISE(1966, Brit.)

Amedeo Pagani
NIGHT PORTER, THE(1974, Ital./U.S.), w

Emanuele Pagani
MAGIC WORLD OF TOPO GIGIO, THE(1961, Ital.), animation

Enrico Pagani
DREAMS IN A DRAWER(1957, Fr./Ital.)

Amadeo Paganini
ERNESTO(1979, Ital.), w

Nicolo Paganini
1984
BASILEUS QUARTET(1984, Ital.), m

Angela Pagano
SEED OF MAN, THE(1970, Ital.)

Anna Pagano
WOMAN ON FIRE, A(1970, Ital.)

Bartolomeo Pagano
Silents
CABIRIA(1914, Ital.)

Ernest B. Pagano
GREENWICH VILLAGE(1944), w

Ernest Pagano
RACETRACK(1933), w; SON OF A SAILOR(1933), w; OLD MAN RHYTHM(1935), w; DAMSEL IN DISTRESS, A(1937), w; FIGHT FOR YOUR LADY(1937), w; SHALL WE DANCE(1937), w; SUPER SLEUTH(1937), w; CAREFREE(1938), w; VIVACIOUS LADY(1938), w; FLYING IRISHMAN, THE(1939), w; FORTY LITTLE MOTHERS(1940), w; LOVE THY NEIGHBOR(1940), w; LAS VEGAS NIGHTS(1941), w; YOU'LL NEVER GET RICH(1941), w; YOU WERE NEVER LOVELIER(1942), w; FIRED WIFE(1943), w; HER PRIMITIVE MAN(1944), w; MERRY MONAHANS, THE(1944), p, w; SAN DIEGO, I LOVE YOU(1944), p, w; FRONTIER GAL(1945), p, w; THAT NIGHT WITH YOU(1945), p, w; THAT'S THE SPIRIT(1945), p, w; LOVER COME BACK(1946), p&w; SLAVE GIRL(1947), p, w
Silents
MATINEE IDOL, THE(1928), w

Ernest S. Pagano
Silents
SPITE MARRIAGE(1929), w

Ernesto Pagano
Misc. Silents
MARVELOUS MACISTE, THE(1918, Ital.)

Jo Pagano
TARNISHED ANGEL(1938), w; ALMOST A GENTLEMAN(1939), w; ROOKIE COP, THE(1939), w; LEATHER BURNERS, THE(1943), w; HOTEL BERLIN(1945), w; TOO YOUNG TO KNOW(1945), w; MAN I LOVE, THE(1946), w; THUNDER IN THE PINES(1949), w; SOUND OF FURY, THE(1950), w; MURDER WITHOUT TEARS(1953), w; SECURITY RISK(1954), w; JUNGLE MOON MEN(1955), w; YAQUI DRUMS(1956), w

Joe Pagano
THEY MADE HER A SPY(1939), w; ADVENTURES IN SILVERADO(1948), w

Marie Pagano
Silents
JOAN OF THE WOODS(1918)

Gabor Pagany
TORPEDO BAY(1964, Ital./Fr.), ph

Sophie Pagay
BECAUSE I LOVED YOU(1930, Ger.)

Leonard Pagden
Silents
AUNT RACHEL(1920, Brit.)

Addison Page
RED HEAD(1934)

Adrian Page
PIONEER JUSTICE(1947), w

Adriana Page
FORCE OF ARMS(1951)

Al Page
COURT-MARTIAL OF BILLY MITCHELL, THE(1955)

Alan Page
LONELY MAN, THE(1957)

Angel Del Page
Misc. Talkies
CONVOY BUDDIES(1977)

Anita Page
BROADWAY MELODY, THE(1929); OUR MODERN MAIDENS(1929); BLUSHING BRIDES(1930); CAUGHT SHORT(1930); FREE AND EASY(1930); LITTLE ACCIDENT(1930); NAVY BLUES(1930); OUR BLUSHING BRIDES(1930); WAR NURSE(1930); EASIEST WAY, THE(1931); GENTLEMAN'S FATE(1931); REDUCING(1931); SIDEWALKS OF NEW YORK(1931); ARE YOU LISTENING?(1932); NIGHT COURT(1932); PROSPERITY(1932); SKYSCRAPER SOULS(1932); UNDER EIGHTEEN(1932); BIG CAGE, THE(1933); I HAVE LIVED(1933); JUNGLE BRIDE(1933); SOLDIERS OF THE STORM(1933); HITCH HIKE TO HEAVEN(1936)
Silents
OUR DANCING DAUGHTERS(1928); TELLING THE WORLD(1928); WHILE THE CITY SLEEPS(1928); FLYING FEET, THE(1929); OUR MODERN MAIDENS(1929)
Misc. Silents
SPEEDWAY(1929)

Anne Page
STRANGER IN TOWN(1957, Brit.)

Anthony Page
INADMISSIBLE EVIDENCE(1968, Brit.), d; ALPHA BETA(1973, Brit.), d; FAMILY HONOR(1973); I NEVER PROMISED YOU A ROSE GARDEN(1977), d; LADY VANISHES, THE(1980, Brit.), d; ABSOLUTION(1981, Brit.), d

Antony Page
WHO KILLED MARY WHAT'SER NAME?(1971); NO PLACE TO HIDE(1975)

Arthur Page
SCARLET ANGEL(1952); WINNING TEAM, THE(1952)

Bill Page
NO HOLDS BARRED(1952)

Bob Page
IS THIS TRIP REALLY NECESSARY?(1970), m

Bradley Page
ATTORNEY FOR THE DEFENSE(1932); FINAL EDITION(1932); LOVE AFFAIR(1932); NIGHT AFTER NIGHT(1932); CHIEF, THE(1933); FROM HELL TO HEAVEN(1933); GOLDIE GETS ALONG(1933); HOLD THE PRESS(1933); LOVE IS LIKE THAT(1933); SUNDOWN RIDER, THE(1933); THIS DAY AND AGE(1933); AGAINST THE LAW(1934); CRIME OF HELEN STANLEY(1934); FIGHTING RANGER, THE(1934); GENTLEMEN ARE BORN(1934); GOOD DAME(1934); HE WAS HER MAN(1934); HELL BENT FOR LOVE(1934); MILLION DOLLAR RANSOM(1934); NAME THE WOMAN(1934); ONCE TO EVERY BACHELOR(1934); SEARCH FOR BEAUTY(1934); SHADOWS OF SING SING(1934); SIX OF A KIND(1934); TAKE THE STAND(1934); CAPPY RICKS RETURNS(1935); CHAMPAGNE FOR BREAKFAST(1935); CHINATOWN SQUAD(1935); FORCED LANDING(1935); KING SOLOMON OF BROADWAY(1935); MR. DYNAMITE(1935); NUT FARM, THE(1935); ONE HOUR LATE(1935); PUBLIC MENACE(1935); RED HOT TIRES(1935); SHADOW OF A DOUBT(1935); UNWELCOME STRANGER(1935); CHEERS OF THE CROWD(1936); PRINCESS COMES ACROSS, THE(1936); THREE OF A KIND(1936); TWO IN A CROWD(1936); WEDDING PRESENT(1936); WOMAN TRAP(1936); CRASHING HOLLYWOOD(1937); DON'T TELL THE WIFE(1937); FIFTY ROADS TO TOWN(1937); HER HUSBAND LIES(1937); HIDEAWAY(1937); MUSIC FOR MADAME(1937); OUTCASTS OF POKER FLAT, THE(1937); SUPER SLEUTH(1937); THERE GOES MY GIRL(1937); TOAST OF NEW YORK, THE(1937); TROUBLE IN MOROCCO(1937); YOU CAN'T BEAT LOVE(1937); AFFAIRS OF ANNABEL(1938); ANNABEL TAKES A TOUR(1938); CRIME RING(1938); FUGITIVES FOR A NIGHT(1938); GO CHASE YOURSELF(1938); LAW WEST OF TOMBSTONE, THE(1938); NIGHT SPOT(1938); FIXER DUGAN(1939); TWELVE CROWDED HOURS(1939); CAFE HOSTESS(1940); ENEMY AGENT(1940); GIRL FROM HAVANA(1940); BADLANDS OF DAKOTA(1941); BEYOND THE SACRAMENTO(1941); FOOTLIGHT FEVER(1941); SCATTERGOOD BAINES(1941); SCATTERGOOD MEETS BROADWAY(1941); FRECKLES COMES HOME(1942); ISLE OF MISSING MEN(1942); PRIDE OF THE ARMY(1942); SONS OF THE PIONEERS(1942); TOP SERGEANT(1942); TRAITOR WITHIN, THE(1942); FIND THE BLACKMAILER(1943); SHERLOCK HOLMES IN WASHINGTON(1943); WHAT'S BUZZIN COUSIN?(1943); CARTER CASE, THE(1947)
Misc. Talkies
I HATE WOMEN(1934); ROARING FRONTIERS(1941)

Charles Page
GLITTERBALL, THE(1977, Brit), spec eff

Chris Page
BRAVE DON'T CRY, THE(1952, Brit.)

Christopher Page
SIX MEN, THE(1951, Brit.)

David Page
SECRET MISSION(1944, Brit.)

Diane Page
1984
INITIATION, THE(1984)

Dorothy Page
KING SOLOMON OF BROADWAY(1935); MANHATTAN MOON(1935); MAMA RUNS WILD(1938); RIDE 'EM COWGIRL(1939); SINGING COWGIRL, THE(1939); WATER RUSTLERS(1939)

Eileen Page
WEDDING NIGHT(1970, Ireland); REMEMBRANCE(1982, Brit.)

Elizabeth Page
HOWARDS OF VIRGINIA, THE(1940), w

Ethel Mae Page
DATE BAIT(1960), w; HIGH SCHOOL CAESAR(1960), w

Gail Page
WHAT DO WE DO NOW?(1945, Brit.)

Gale Page
TIME OF YOUR LIFE, THE(1948); AMAZING DR. CLITTERHOUSE, THE(1938); CRIME SCHOOL(1938); FOUR DAUGHTERS(1938); HEART OF THE NORTH(1938); DAUGHTERS COURAGEOUS(1939); FOUR WIVES(1939); INDIANAPOLIS SPEEDWAY(1939); NAUGHTY BUT NICE(1939); YOU CAN'T GET AWAY WITH MURDER(1939); CHILD IS BORN, A(1940); KNUTE ROCKNE–ALL AMERICAN(1940); THEY DRIVE BY NIGHT(1940); FOUR MOTHERS(1941); ANNA LUCASTA(1949); ABOUT MRS. LESLIE(1954)

Gene Page
BREWSTER McCLOUD(1970), m; BLACULA(1972), m; FUN WITH DICK AND JANE(1977), m

Genevieve Page
FANFAN THE TULIP(1952, Fr.); FOREIGN INTRIGUE(1956); SILKEN AFFAIR, THE(1957, Brit.); MICHAEL STROGOFF(1960, Fr./Ital./Yugo.); SONG WITHOUT END(1960); TRAPPED IN TANGIERS(1960, Ital./Span.); EL CID(1961, U.S./Ital.); NUDE IN HIS POCKET(1962, Fr.); DAY AND THE HOUR, THE(1963, Fr./ Ital.); YOUNGBLOOD HAWKE(1964); GRAND PRIX(1966); TENDER SCOUNDREL(1967, Fr./Ital.); BELLE DE JOUR(1968, Fr.); MAYERLING(1968, Brit./Fr.); DECLINE AND FALL... OF A BIRD WATCHER(1969, Brit.); PRIVATE LIFE OF SHERLOCK HOLMES, THE(1970, Brit.)
Misc. Talkies
BROTHER CARL(1972)

Geraldine Page
TOYS IN THE ATTIC(1963); HONDO(1953); TAXI(1953); SUMMER AND SMOKE(1961); SWEET BIRD OF YOUTH(1962); DEAR HEART(1964); YOU'RE A BIG BOY NOW(1966); HAPPIEST MILLIONAIRE, THE(1967); MONDAY'S CHILD(1967, U.S., Arg.); TRUMAN CAPOTE'S TRILOGY(1969); WHAT EVER HAPPENED TO AUNT ALICE?(1969); BEGUILED, THE(1971); J.W. COOP(1971); PETE 'N' TILLIE(1972); HAPPY AS THE GRASS WAS GREEN(1973); DAY OF THE LOCUST, THE(1975); NASTY HABITS(1976, Brit.); RESCUERS, THE(1977); THREE SISTERS, THE(1977); HAZEL'S PEOPLE(1978); INTERIORS(1978); HARRY'S WAR(1981); HONKY TONK FREEWAY(1981); I'M DANCING AS FAST AS I CAN(1982)
1984
POPE OF GREENWICH VILLAGE, THE(1984)

Gertrude Page
PADDY, THE NEXT BEST THING(1933), w
Silents
EDGE O'BEYOND(1919, Brit.), w; PADDY, THE NEXT BEST THING(1923, Brit.), w

Grant Page
MAN FROM HONG KONG(1975); DEATHCHEATERS(1976, Aus.), a, stunts; HIGH ROLLING(1977, Aus.), stunts; LET THE BALLOON GO(1977, Aus.), stunts; MAD MAX(1979, Aus.), stunts; ODD ANGRY SHOT, THE(1979, Aus.), stunts; THIRST(1979, Aus.), stunts; ROAD GAMES(1981, Aus.)

Ilse Page
TIN DRUM, THE(1979, Ger./Fr./Yugo./Pol.)

Jackie Page
GORDON'S WAR(1973)

Jacqueline Page
1984
MUPPETS TAKE MANHATTAN, THE(1984)

James E. Page
Misc. Silents
CHARLEY'S AUNT(1925)

James Page
HE SNOOPS TO CONQUER(1944, Brit.); TREASURE HUNT(1952, Brit.)

Jimmy Page
STRANGER AT MY DOOR(1950, Brit.); DEATH WISH II(1982), m

Joanne Page
MAN-EATER OF KUMAON(1948)

Jon Page
HOLLYWOOD HIGH(1977)

Joy Ann Page
KISMET(1944)

Joy Page
CASABLANCA(1942); BULLFIGHTER AND THE LADY(1951); CONQUEST OF COCHISE(1953); FIGHTER ATTACK(1953); SHRIKE, THE(1955); TONKA(1958)

June Page
LAWLESS WOMAN, THE(1931)

Kari Page
EYES OF LAURA MARS(1978)

Katherine Page
TWILIGHT WOMEN(1953, Brit.); FINGER OF GUILT(1956, Brit.); KID FROM CANADA, THE(1957, Brit.); VIOLENT STRANGER(1957, Brit.); ROOM AT THE TOP(1959, Brit.); KNACK ... AND HOW TO GET IT, THE(1965, Brit.)

Kathleen Page
FLOATING DUTCHMAN, THE(1953, Brit.)

Keva Page
PAJAMA PARTY(1964)

Lang Page
KNICKERBOCKER HOLIDAY(1944)

Laurel Page
SIX WEEKS(1982)

Lawanda Page
ZAPPED!(1982); MAUSOLEUM(1983)

Leila Page
TILLY OF BLOOMSBURY(1931, Brit.); KING'S CUP, THE(1933, Brit.)

Leonie Page
SWEET BEAT(1962, Brit.)

Lillian Page
Silents
ALIAS MRS. JESSOP(1917)

Liza Page
UNSTOPPABLE MAN, THE(1961, Brit.)

Louis Page
SANDERS OF THE RIVER(1935, Brit.), ph; PORT OF SHADOWS(1938, Fr.), ph; LUMIERE D'ETE(1943, Fr.), ph; BELLMAN, THE(1947, Fr.), ph; MAN'S HOPE(1947, Span.), ph; WALLS OF MALAPAGA, THE(1950, Fr./Ital.), ph; LE CIEL EST A VOUS(1957, Fr.), ph; LIGHT ACROSSS THE STREET, THE(1957, Fr.), ph; PLEASE! MR. BALZAC(1957, Fr.), ph; GORILLA GREETS YOU, THE(1958, Fr.), ph; NIGHT AFFAIR(1961, Fr.), ph; COUNTERFEITERS OF PARIS, THE(1962, Fr., Ital.), ph; MAGNIFICENT TRAMP, THE(1962, Fr./Ital.), ph; MONKEY IN WINTER, A(1962, Fr.), ph; MONSIEUR(1964, Fr.), ph

Mann Page
LONESOME(1928), w; IT CAN BE DONE(1929), w; SHE HAD TO CHOOSE(1934), w; AFFAIR OF SUSAN(1935), w; CRASHING HOLLYWOOD(1937), w
Silents
ANTHING ONCE(1917), w; EASY TO GET(1920), w; BLAZING TRAIL, THE(1921), w

Marco Page
FAST COMPANY(1938), w

Maria Page
MADAME CURIE(1943)

Mario Page
LOVE SLAVES OF THE AMAZONS(1957), ph

Nicholas Page
IF ...(1968, Brit.)

Norman Page
Silents
ELUSIVE PIMPERNEL, THE(1919, Brit.); AT THE VILLA ROSE(1920, Brit.); ADVENTURES OF MR. PICKWICK, THE(1921, Brit.); OLD WIVES' TALE, THE(1921, Brit.); OUT TO WIN(1923, Brit.)
Misc. Silents
LIFE STORY OF DAVID LLOYD GEORGE, THE(1918, Brit.); CRY FOR JUSTICE, THE(1919, Brit.); BLEAK HOUSE(1920, Brit.); YELLOW CLAW, THE(1920, Brit.); DICK TURPIN'S RIDE TO YORK(1922, Brit.)

Pat Page
THIRTEEN WEST STREET(1962), cos; THREE STOOGES IN ORBIT, THE(1962), cos

Patricia Page
HAMMER THE TOFF(1952, Brit.)

Patsy Page
LILIES OF THE FIELD(1930)

Patti Page
ELMER GANTRY(1960); DONDI(1961); BOYS' NIGHT OUT(1962)

Patty Page
HALLIDAY BRAND, THE(1957), cos

Paul Page
GIRL FROM HAVANA, THE(1929); SPEAKEASY(1929); BORN RECKLESS(1930); GOLDEN CALF, THE(1930); HAPPY DAYS(1930); MEN WITHOUT WOMEN(1930); NAUGHTY FLIRT, THE(1931); PALMY DAYS(1931); WOMEN GO ON FOREVER(1931); 70,000 WITNESSES(1932); BACHELOR MOTHER(1933); BELOW THE SEA(1933); PHANTOM BROADCAST, THE(1933); PLEASURE(1933); COUNTESS OF MONTE CRISTO, THE(1934); HAVE A HEART(1934); MOTH, THE(1934); ROAD TO RUIN(1934); KENTUCKY KERNELS(1935)
Silents
PROTECTION(1929)

Peaches Page
BLONDE PICKUP(1955)

Peggy Page
MR. DEEDS GOES TO TOWN(1936)

Ray Page
CRAZY OVER HORSES(1951); ROOM FOR ONE MORE(1952); EL ALAMEIN(1954)

Rebecca Page
Misc. Talkies
DANNY(1979)

Rita Page
ARENT WE ALL?(1932, Brit.); BRIDEGROOM FOR TWO(1932, Brit.); BULLDOG DRUMMOND COMES BACK(1937); LITTLE PRINCESS, THE(1939); RAINS CAME, THE(1939); LITTLE NELLIE KELLY(1940); VIGIL IN THE NIGHT(1940); THIS ABOVE ALL(1942); UNINVITED, THE(1944)

Robert Page
DRIVE, HE SAID(1971)

Robison Page
UNDER THE GREENWOOD TREE(1930, Brit.)

Sam Page
INVISIBLE AVENGER, THE(1958)

Thomas Page
BUG(1975), w

Tilsa Page
EDWARD, MY SON(1949, U.S./Brit.)

Tony Page
PRINCE OF THE CITY(1981); Q(1982)

Veronica Page
OLIVER!(1968, Brit.)

Vicki Page
PENNY POINTS TO PARADISE(1951, Brit.)

William Page
ABANDONED(1949)

Wray Page
Silents
OUR LITTLE WIFE(1918)
Misc. Silents
MAKE-BELIEVE WIFE, THE(1918)

Page Cavanaugh Trio
BIG CITY(1948); ROMANCE ON THE HIGH SEAS(1948); LULLABY OF BROADWAY, THE(1951); FRANKENSTEIN'S DAUGHTER(1958)

The Page Cavanaugh Trio
SONG IS BORN, A(1948)
The Pageant Players
MARCH OF THE SPRING HARE(1969)
Madeline Pageau
RABID(1976, Can.)
Hayes Pagel
PHANTOM PLANET, THE(1961), m
Kathleen Pagel
UNHOLY ROLLERS(1972)
Raoul Pagel
STRANGLER OF THE SWAMP(1945), p
A.C. Pagenkoff
YOUNG SINNER, THE(1965)
Antal Pager
KIND STEPMOTHER(1936, Hung.); AZURE EXPRESS(1938, Hung.)
Eduardo Ugarte Pages
CRIMINAL LIFE OF ARCHIBALDO DE LA CRUZ, THE(1962, Mex.), w
Mario Pages
VIOLENT AND THE DAMNED, THE(1962, Braz.), ph
Paloma Pages
HOUSE THAT SCREAMED, THE(1970, Span.)
Alfred Paget
Silents
LAMB, THE(1915); MARTYRS OF THE ALAMO, THE(1915); INTOLERANCE(1916); OLD FOLKS AT HOME, THE(1916); NINA, THE FLOWER GIRL(1917)
Misc. Silents
ENOCH ARDEN(1915); BIG TIMBER(1917); WHEN A GIRL LOVES(1919)
Calvin Jackson Paget
Misc. Talkies
BATTLE OF EL ALAMEIN(1971), d
David Paget
SLEEPING PARTNERS(1930, Brit.)
Debra Paget
CRY OF THE CITY(1948); HOUSE OF STRANGERS(1949); IT HAPPENS EVERY SPRING(1949); MOTHER IS A FRESHMAN(1949); BROKEN ARROW(1950); ANNE OF THE INDIES(1951); BIRD OF PARADISE(1951); FOURTEEN HOURS(1951); BELLES ON THEIR TOES(1952); LES MISERABLES(1952); STARS AND STRIPES FOREVER(1952); DEMETRIUS AND THE GLADIATORS(1954); GAMBLER FROM NATCHEZ, THE(1954); PRINCE VALIANT(1954); PRINCESS OF THE NILE(1954); SEVEN ANGRY MEN(1955); WHITE FEATHER(1955); LAST HUNT, THE(1956); LOVE ME TENDER(1956); TEN COMMANDMENTS, THE(1956); OMAR KHAYYAM(1957); RIVER'S EDGE, THE(1957); FROM THE EARTH TO THE MOON(1958); JOURNEY TO THE LOST CITY(1960, Ger./Fr./Ital.); WHY MUST I DIE?(1960); MOST DANGEROUS MAN ALIVE, THE(1961); TALES OF TERROR(1962); CLEOPATRA'S DAUGHTER(1963, Fr., Ital.); HAUNTED PALACE, THE(1963)
Doriel Paget
Misc. Silents
SMART SET, A(1919, Brit.)
Elizabeth Paget
TELL-TALE HEART, THE(1962, Brit.)
Lady Paget
Silents
GREAT LOVE, THE(1918)
Patti Paget
LOVE MERCHANT, THE(1966)
Reginald Paget
TELL ME LIES(1968, Brit.)
Robert Paget
CHOPPERS, THE(1961); HOT ROD HULLABALOO(1966); DRUMMER OF VENGEANCE(1974, Brit.), p,d&w
Susan Paget
Misc. Talkies
TEN GLADIATORS, THE(1960); OLD TESTAMENT(1963, Ital.)
Cecily Paget-Bowman
ISN'T LIFE WONDERFUL!(1953, Brit.); MAN WHO NEVER WAS, THE(1956, Brit.); MAN WITH THE GREEN CARNATION, THE(1960, Brit.)
Cicely Paget-Bowman
CONSPIRATOR(1949, Brit.); MINIVER STORY, THE(1950, Brit./U.S.); TRYGON FACTOR, THE(1969, Brit.)
Eddie Pagett
KETTLES IN THE OZARKS, THE(1956)
Edward G. Pagett
LEATHER SAINT, THE(1956)
Gary Pagett
COME TO THE STABLE(1949); MISTER 880(1950); MY BLUE HEAVEN(1950); WEEKEND WITH FATHER(1951); MA AND PA KETTLE AT HOME(1954); PRIVATE WAR OF MAJOR BENSON, THE(1955); JEANNE EAGELS(1957); STRIPPER, THE(1963); MELINDA(1972); FOR PETE'S SAKE(1977)
Leslie Pagett
CALIFORNIA SUITE(1978)
Nicola Pagett
VIKING QUEEN, THE(1967, Brit.); ANNE OF THE THOUSAND DAYS(1969, Brit.); THERE'S A GIRL IN MY SOUP(1970, Brit.); COME BACK PETER(1971, Brit.); OPERATION DAYBREAK(1976, U.S./Brit./Czech.); OLIVER'S STORY(1978); PRIVATES ON PARADE(1982)
1984
PRIVATES ON PARADE(1984, Brit.)
Klaus Pagh
OPERATION CAMEL(1961, Den.)
Ugo Pagliai
SHADOWMAN(1974, Fr./Ital.)
Ugo Pagliani
MAGNIFICENT BANDITS, THE(1969, Ital./Span.)
Marcel Pagliero
DEDEE(1949, Fr.); DAUGHTERS OF DESTINY(1954, Fr./Ital.), d; NAKED AUTUMN(1963, Fr.); YOUR SHADOW IS MINE(1963, Fr./Ital.); HAIL MAFIA(1965, Fr./Ital.); LES GAULOISES BLEUES(1969, Fr.)

Marcello Pagliero
OPEN CITY(1946, Ital.); PAISAN(1948, Ital.), w
Michel Pagliero
LES JEUX SONT FAITS(1947, Fr.)
Lina Pagliughi
RIGOLETTO(1949)
Joe Pagliuso
REVENGE OF THE NINJA(1983)
Joseph Pagnano
JUNGLE GODDESS(1948), w
Eros Pagni
LOVE AND ANARCHY(1974, Ital.); ALL SCREWED UP(1976, Ital.); DEEP RED(1976, Ital.); VIVA ITALIA(1978, Ital.); NEST OF VIPERS(1979, Ital.)
Regis Pagniez
CHAPPAQUA(1967), art d
Sergo Pagnio
VIOLATED PARADISE(1963, Ital./Jap.), m
Ernesto Pagno
IN SEARCH OF GREGORY(1970, Brit./Ital.)
Jacqueline Pagnol
PRIZE, THE(1952, Fr.); CARNIVAL(1953, Fr.)
Marcel Pagnol
MARIUS(1933, Fr.), p, w; TOPAZE(1933), w; ANGELE(1934 Fr.), p&d; TOPAZE(1935, Fr.), w; CESAR(1936, Fr.), p,d&w; PORT OF SEVEN SEAS(1938), w; HARVEST(1939, Fr.), p,d; BAKER'S WIFE, THE(1940, Fr.), d&w; WELL-DIGGER'S DAUGHTER, THE(1946, Fr.), p,d&w; FANNY(1948, Fr.), p, w; WAYS OF LOVE(1950, Ital./Fr.), d; PRIZE, THE(1952, Fr.), p, w; CARNIVAL(1953, Fr.), p, w; LETTERS FROM MY WINDMILL(1955, Fr.), p,d&w; FANNY(1961, Fr.), w; I LIKE MONEY(1962, Brit.), w
Florent Pagny
LA BALANCE(1983, Fr.)
Louise Pago
TIM(1981, Aus.)
Thanasis Pagonis
TEMPEST(1982)
Bill Pagwell
DEAD END(1937)
Albin Pahernik
HALF A SIXPENCE(1967, Brit.); YOUNG GIRLS OF ROCHEFORT, THE(1968, Fr.); FIDDLER ON THE ROOF(1971); OH, HEAVENLY DOG!(1980)
Andreijah Pahich
DARK STAR(1975)
Ted Pahle
JAZZ AGE, THE(1929), ph; MARIUS(1933, Fr.), ph; AFFAIR LAFONT, THE(1939, Fr.), ph; CONFLICT(1939, Fr.), ph; ENTENTE CORDIALE(1939, Fr.), ph; ULTIMATUM(1940, Fr.), ph; IT HAPPENED IN GIBRALTAR(1943, Fr.), ph
Theodore J. Pahle
4D MAN(1959), ph
Victor Pahlen
PIRATES OF CAPRI, THE(1949), p; LOVES OF THREE QUEENS, THE(1954, Ital./Fr.), p
Jo Pahu
1984
SILENT ONE, THE(1984, New Zealand)
Shripad Pai
YOU PAY YOUR MONEY(1957, Brit.)
Suzee Pai
SHARKY'S MACHINE(1982)
Chou Pai-kui
DREAM OF THE RED CHAMBER, THE(1966, Chi.)
Pai-Ying
REVENGE OF THE SHOGUN WOMEN(1982, Taiwan)
Hawksha Paia
WINGS OVER THE PACIFIC(1943)
Eric Paice
MAN IN THE BACK SEAT, THE(1961, Brit.), w; LIFE IN DANGER(1964, Brit.), w
Marty Paich
HEY THERE, IT'S YOGI BEAR(1964), m; MAN CALLED FLINTSTONE, THE(1966), m; SWINGER, THE(1966), m; MODEL SHOP, THE(1969), md
1984
DUNE(1984), m
Al Paige
DAYS OF WINE AND ROSES(1962)
Ann Paige
TEARS FOR SIMON(1957, Brit.); CHINA DOLL(1958); YOUNG LIONS, THE(1958)
Anthony Paige
THEY ALL LAUGHED(1981)
Bob Paige
IT HAPPENED TO JANE(1959)
Carol Paige
YOU AND ME(1938)
David Paige
WILLIAM COMES TO TOWN(1948, Brit.); CATSKILL HONEYMOON(1950)
Dorothy Paige
CATSKILL HONEYMOON(1950)
Erik Paige
TIGHT SPOT(1955)
Grant Paige
ON THE RUN(1983, Aus.), stunts
Janice Paige
ROMANCE ON THE HIGH SEAS(1948); WELCOME TO HARD TIMES(1967)
Janis Paige
BATHING BEAUTY(1944); HOLLYWOOD CANTEEN(1944); HER KIND OF MAN(1946); OF HUMAN BONDAGE(1946); TIME, THE PLACE AND THE GIRL, THE(1946); CHEYENNE(1947); LOVE AND LEARN(1947); ONE SUNDAY AFTERNOON(1948); WALLFLOWER(1948); WINTER MEETING(1948); HOUSE ACROSS THE STREET, THE(1949); YOUNGER BROTHERS, THE(1949); THIS SIDE OF THE LAW(1950); FUGITIVE LADY(1951); MR. UNIVERSE(1951); TWO GALS AND A GUY(1951); SILK STOCKINGS(1957); PLEASE DON'T EAT THE DAISIES(1960); BACHELOR IN PARADISE(1961); CARETAKERS, THE(1963); FOLLOW THE

BOYS(1963)

Jean Paige
Silents
DESIRED WOMAN, THE(1918); KING OF DIAMONDS, THE(1918); BLACK BEAU-TY(1921)
Misc. Silents
BLIND MAN'S HOLIDAY(1917); INDIAN SUMMER OF DRY VALLEY JOHNSON, THE(1917); SKYLIGHT ROOM, THE(1917); GOLDEN GOAL, THE(1918); TANGLED LIVES(1918); BEATING THE ODDS(1919); DARING HEARTS(1919); TOO MANY CROOKS(1919); BIRTH OF A SOUL, THE(1920); DARKEST HOUR, THE(1920); FORTUNE HUNTER, THE(1920); PRODIGAL JUDGE, THE(1922); CAPTAIN BLOOD(1924)

LeRoy "Satchel" Paige
WONDERFUL COUNTRY, THE(1959)

Lillian Paige
Misc. Silents
SCARLET OATH, THE(1916); HEDDA GABLER(1917)

Mabel Paige
TRUE TO LIFE(1943); LUCKY JORDAN(1942); MY HEART BELONGS TO DAD-DY(1942); CRYSTAL BALL, THE(1943); GOOD FELLOWS, THE(1943); HAPPY GO LUCKY(1943); SOMEONE TO REMEMBER(1943); YOUNG AND WILLING(1943); NATIONAL BARN DANCE(1944); YOU CAN'T RATION LOVE(1944); DANGEROUS PARTNERS(1945); MURDER, HE SAYS(1945); OUT OF THIS WORLD(1945); SHE WOULDN'T SAY YES(1945); BEHIND GREEN LIGHTS(1946); NOCTURNE(1946); BEAT THE BAND(1947); HER HUSBAND'S AFFAIRS(1947); JOHNNY O'CLOCK(1947); CANON CITY(1948); HALF PAST MIDNIGHT(1948); HOLLOW TRI-UMPH(1948); IF YOU KNEW SUSIE(1948); JOHNNY BELINDA(1948); MATING OF MILLIE, THE(1948); ROSEANNA McCOY(1949); EDGE OF DOOM(1950); PETTY GIRL, THE(1950); SNIPER, THE(1952); HOUDINI(1953)
Misc. Silents
EIGHT BELLS(1916)

Nina Paige
TWO TICKETS TO PARIS(1962)

Paul Paige
Misc. Talkies
THREE WAY LOVE(1977)

Raymond Paige
HAWAII CALLS(1938)

Robert Paige
HIGHWAY PATROL(1938); I STAND ACCUSED(1938); LADY OBJECTS, THE(1938); LAST WARNING, THE(1938); MAIN EVENT, THE(1938); THERE'S ALWAYS A WOMAN(1938); WHEN G-MEN STEP IN(1938); WHO KILLED GAIL PRE-STON?(1938); DEATH OF A CHAMPION(1939); HOMICIDE BUREAU(1939); DANC-ING ON A DIME(1940); EMERGENCY SQUAD(1940); GOLDEN GLOVES(1940); OPENED BY MISTAKE(1940); PAROLE FIXER(1940); WOMEN WITHOUT NA-MES(1940); DON'T GET PERSONAL(1941); HELLZAPOPPIN'(1941); MELODY LA-NE(1941); MONSTER AND THE GIRL, THE(1941); SAN ANTONIO ROSE(1941); ALMOST MARRIED(1942); GET HEP TO LOVE(1942); JAIL HOUSE BLUES(1942); PARDON MY SARONG(1942); WHAT'S COOKIN'?(1942); YOU'RE TELLING ME(1942); COWBOY IN MANHATTTAN(1943); CRAZY HOUSE(1943); FIRED WI-FE(1943); FRONTIER BADMEN(1943); GET GOING(1943); HI, BUDDY(1943); HI'YA, CHUM(1943); HOW'S ABOUT IT?(1943); KEEP 'EM SLUGGING(1943); MR. BIG(1943); SON OF DRACULA(1943); FOLLOW THE BOYS(1944); HER PRIMITIVE MAN(1944); SHADY LADY(1945); TANGIER(1946); RED STALLION, THE(1947); FLAME, THE(1948); BLONDE ICE(1949); GREEN PROMISE, THE(1949), a, p; ABBOTT AND COSTELLO GO TO MARS(1953); SPLIT SECOND(1953); MARRIAGE-GO-ROUND, THE(1960); BYE BYE BIRDIE(1963); MEDIUM COOL(1969)

Ronnie Paige
SONS OF THE LEGION(1938); FISHERMAN'S WHARF(1939)

Satchel Paige
KID FROM CLEVELAND, THE(1949)

Yascha Paii
VOICE IN THE WIND(1944), md

Frank Paiker
HEY THERE, IT'S YOGI BEAR(1964), ph

Pailenberg's Bears
SENSATIONS OF 1945(1944)

Jean Paillaud
SUITOR, THE(1963, Fr.), m; YO YO(1967, Fr.), m

William Pailleton
PRISONER, THE(1955, Brit.), makeup

Laure Paillette
MADEMOISELLE(1966, Fr./Brit.); YOUNG WORLD, A(1966, Fr./Ital.); LA GUERRE EST FINIE(1967, Fr./Swed.); PLAYTIME(1973, Fr.)

Barry Pain
Silents
BLIND BARGAIN, A(1922), w

Bunty Pain
THIS'LL MAKE YOU WHISTLE(1938, Brit.)

Brian Painchaud
WHO HAS SEEN THE WIND(1980, Can.)

Nick Paindiris
WHITE RAT(1972), p, w

Cathey Paine
AVALANCHE(1978)
Misc. Talkies
IMAGE OF DEATH(1977, Brit.)

Debbie Paine
COMPUTER WORE TENNIS SHOES, THE(1970)

Harry Paine
TRADE WINDS(1938)

Jenny Paine
JOE(1970)

Richard Paine
ZAPPED!(1982)

Tom Paine
HERO(1982, Brit.), art d

Paul Paino
GOODBYE PORK PIE(1981, New Zealand)

Paint the Killer Stallion
KING OF THE STALLIONS(1942)

Austin Kelly Painter
SMOKEY AND THE BANDIT–PART 3(1983)

Charlene Painter
TO BE OR NOT TO BE(1983), ch
1984
PROTOCOL(1984), ch

Chuck Painter
WAY OUT(1966)

K. Painter
Silents
KAISER, BEAST OF BERLIN, THE(1918)

Walter Painter
SWEET CHARITY(1969)

Basil Painting
MOUSE AND THE WOMAN, THE(1981, Brit.)

B. Paipert
OUT OF TOWNERS, THE(1970)

Jim Pair
PIRANHA II: THE SPAWNING(1981, Neth.)

The Pair Extraordinaire
C'MON, LET'S LIVE A LITTLE(1967)

Father Ralph W. Pairon
AND NOW MIGUEL(1966)

Ian Paiser
LOOSE SHOES(1980), w

Sue Paishon
KONA COAST(1968)

Dina Paisner
PRETTY BOY FLOYD(1960); LILITH(1964)

Nestor Paiva
TRUE TO LIFE(1943); PRISON TRAIN(1938); RIDE A CROOKED MILE(1938); ANOTHER THIN MAN(1939); BEAU GESTE(1939); MAGNIFICENT FRAUD, THE(1939); MIDNIGHT(1939); UNION PACIFIC(1939); ARISE, MY LOVE(1940); DARK STREETS OF CAIRO(1940); HE STAYED FOR BREAKFAST(1940); MARINES FLY HIGH, THE(1940); NORTHWEST MOUNTED POLICE(1940); PRIMROSE PATH(1940); SANTA FE TRAIL(1940); SEA HAWK, THE(1940); THEY KNEW WHAT THEY WANTED(1940); HOLD BACK THE DAWN(1941); HOLD THAT GHOST(1941); KID FROM KANSAS, THE(1941); POT O' GOLD(1941); RISE AND SHINE(1941); WILD GEESE CALLING(1941); BROADWAY(1942); FLY BY NIGHT(1942); GIRL FROM ALASKA(1942); HARD WAY, THE(1942); JOHNNY EAGER(1942); LADY HAS PLANS, THE(1942); PITTSBURGH(1942); REAP THE WILD WIND(1942); ROAD TO MOROCCO(1942); SHIP AHOY(1942); TIMBER(1942); BACKGROUND TO DAN-GER(1943); CRYSTAL BALL, THE(1943); DANCING MASTERS, THE(1943); DESERT SONG, THE(1943); FALLEN SPARROW, THE(1943); RHYTHM OF THE IS-LANDS(1943); SONG OF BERNADETTE, THE(1943); TORNADO(1943); FALCON IN MEXICO, THE(1944); KISMET(1944); PURPLE HEART, THE(1944); SHINE ON, HARVEST MOON(1944); TAMPICO(1944); ALONG THE NAVAJO TRAIL(1945); COR-NERED(1945); MEDAL FOR BENNY, A(1945); NOB HILL(1945); ROAD TO UTO-PIA(1945); SALOME, WHERE SHE DANCED(1945); SENSATION HUNTERS(1945); SOUTHERNER, THE(1945); THOUSAND AND ONE NIGHTS, A(1945); BADMAN'S TERRITORY(1946); FEAR(1946); HUMORESQUE(1946); LAST CROOKED MILE, THE(1946); SUSPENSE(1946); CARNIVAL IN COSTA RICA(1947); LIKELY STORY, A(1947); LONE WOLF IN MEXICO, THE(1947); RAMROD(1947); ROAD TO RIO(1947); SHOOT TO KILL(1947); TROUBLE WITH WOMEN, THE(1947); ANGELS AL-LEY(1948); JOAN OF ARC(1948); MR. BLANDINGS BUILDS HIS DREAM HOUSE(1948); MR. RECKLESS(1948); PALEFACE(1948); ALIAS NICK BEAL(1949); BRIDE OF VENGEANCE(1949); FOLLOW ME QUIETLY(1949); INSPEC-TOR GENERAL, THE(1949); MIGHTY JOE YOUNG(1949); OH, YOU BEAUTIFUL DOLL(1949); ROPE OF SAND(1949); DESERT HAWK, THE(1950); I WAS A SHOPLIFT-ER(1950); YOUNG MAN WITH A HORN(1950); DOUBLE DYNAMITE(1951); GREAT CARUSO, THE(1951); JIM THORPE-ALL AMERICAN(1951); LADY PAYS OFF, THE(1951); MILLIONAIRE FOR CHRISTY, A(1951); MY FAVORITE SPY(1951); ON DANGEROUS GROUND(1951); FABULOUS SENORITA, THE(1952); FIVE FIN-GERS(1952); MARA MARU(1952); PHONE CALL FROM A STRANGER(1952); SOUTH PACIFIC TRAIL(1952); VIVA ZAPATA!(1952); WITH A SONG IN MY HEART(1952); BANDITS OF CORSICA, THE(1953); CALL ME MADAM(1953); KILLER APE(1953); PRISONERS OF THE CASBAH(1953); CASANOVA'S BIG NIGHT(1954); CREATURE FROM THE BLACK LAGOON(1954); DESPERADO, THE(1954); FOUR GUNS TO THE BORDER(1954); JIVARO(1954); THUNDER PASS(1954); NEW YORK CONFIDEN-TIAL(1955); REVENGE OF THE CREATURE(1955); TARANTULA(1955); COMAN-CHE(1956); HELL ON FRISCO BAY(1956); MOLE PEOPLE, THE(1956); RIDE THE HIGH IRON(1956); SCANDAL INCORPORATED(1956); WILD PARTY, THE(1956); FLAME OF STAMBOUL(1957); GUNS OF FORT PETTICOAT, THE(1957); LES GIRLS(1957); CASE AGAINST BROOKLYN, THE(1958); DEEP SIX, THE(1958); LADY TAKES A FLYER, THE(1958); OUTCASTS OF THE CITY(1958); PIER 5, HAVANA(1959); VICE RAID(1959); CAN-CAN(1960); PURPLE GANG, THE(1960); FRONTIER UPRISING(1961); FOUR HORSEMEN OF THE APOCALYPSE, THE(1962); GIRLS! GIRLS! GIRLS!(1962); THREE STOOGES IN ORBIT, THE(1962); WILD WESTERNERS, THE(1962); CALIFORNIA(1963); BALLAD OF A GUNFIGHTER(1964); THEY SAVED HITLER'S BRAIN(1964); JESSE JAMES MEETS FRANKENSTEIN'S DAUGHTER(1966); LET'S KILL UNCLE(1966); SPIRIT IS WILLING, THE(1967)

Alfred Paix
MASK OF DIMITRIOS, THE(1944); 'TILL WE MEET AGAIN(1944); SONG TO REMEMBER, A(1945); GILDA(1946); LOVES OF CARMEN, THE(1948); FOREVER FEMALE(1953); GENTLEMEN PREFER BLONDES(1953)

J. Paixio
MAN COULD GET KILLED, A(1966)

Aleka Paizi
INVESTIGATION OF A CITIZEN ABOVE SUSPICION(1970, Ital.)

Pajarito
PISTOL FOR RINGO, A(1966, Ital./Span.); RETURN OF RINGO, THE(1966, Ital./Span.)

Ivo Pajer
SOPHIE'S CHOICE(1982)
Louise Pajo
NORMAN LOVES ROSE(1982, Aus.)
Zsuzsa Pajzs
FATHER(1967, Hung.)
Pierre Pakamoff
HORSEMEN, THE(1971), stunts
Chalong Pakdivijit
S.T.A.B.(1976, Hong Kong/Thailand), p&d
Eric Pakeman
BEYOND THE CURTAIN(1960, Brit.), m
Kenneth Pakeman
OCTOBER MAN, THE(1948, Brit.), m; BOY, A GIRL AND A BIKE, A(1949 Brit.), m
Aleksandra Pakhmutova
THERE WAS AN OLD COUPLE(1967, USSR), m
Jaakko Pakkasvirta
TIME OF ROSES(1970, Fin.), w
Shahnaz Pakravan
CARAVANS(1978, U.S./Iranian)
Alan J. Pakula
TO KILL A MOCKINGBIRD(1962), p; LOVE WITH THE PROPER STRANGER(1963), p; INSIDE DAISY CLOVER(1965), p; UP THE DOWN STAIRCASE(1967), p; STALKING MOON, THE(1969), p; STERILE CUCKOO, THE(1969), p&d; KLUTE(1971), p, d; LOVE AND PAIN AND THE WHOLE DAMN THING(1973), p&d; PARALLAX VIEW, THE(1974), p&d; ALL THE PRESIDENT'S MEN(1976), d; STARTING OVER(1979), p, d; ROLLOVER(1981), d; SOPHIE'S CHOICE(1982), p, d&w
Alan Pakula
FEAR STRIKES OUT(1957), p; BABY, THE RAIN MUST FALL(1965), p; COMES A HORSEMAN(1978), d
Pal
LASSIE, COME HOME(1943)
David Pal
JACK THE GIANT KILLER(1962), spec eff
George Pal
VARIETY GIRL(1947), Puppeteer; DESTINATION MOON(1950), p; GREAT RUPERT, THE(1950), p; WHEN WORLDS COLLIDE(1951), p; HOUDINI(1953), p; NAKED JUNGLE, THE(1953), p; WAR OF THE WORLDS, THE(1953), a, p; CONQUEST OF SPACE(1955), p; TOM THUMB(1958, Brit./U.S.), p&d; TIME MACHINE, THE(1960, Brit./U.S.), p&d; ATLANTIS, THE LOST CONTINENT(1961), p&d; WONDERFUL WORLD OF THE BROTHERS ERIMM, THE(1962), p, d; SEVEN FACES OF DR. LAO(1964), p&d; POWER, THE(1968), p; DOC SAVAGE... THE MAN OF BRONZE(1975), p, w
Laszlo Pal
SCORCHY(1976), ph
Neevy Pal
1984
KILLING FIELDS, THE(1984, Brit.)
Niranjan Pal
GENTLEMAN OF PARIS, A(1931), w
Pal Ming Production
BRUCE LEE–TRUE STORY(1976, Chi.), p
Pal the Dog
Silents
IF ONLY JIM(1921); QUEENIE(1921); GOLD AND THE GIRL(1925); GAY RETREAT, THE(1927)
Pal the Horse
Silents
HURRICANE KID, THE(1925)
Cesare Palacco
BURIED ALIVE(1951, Ital.)
Joanne Palace
1984
PHILADELPHIA EXPERIMENT, THE(1984), cos
Anita Palacine
SOMEWHERE IN FRANCE(1943, Brit.)
Hotel Palacio
THIRD VOICE, THE(1960)
Jose Maria Palacio
EVERY DAY IS A HOLIDAY(1966, Span.), w
Adele Palacios
FUN IN ACAPULCO(1963)
Angel M. Gordordo Palacios
AVENGERS, THE(1950)
Begonia Palacios
MAJOR DUNDEE(1965)
Ricardo Palacios
RETURN OF THE SEVEN(1966, Span.); DESPERATE ONES, THE(1968 U.S./Span.); UGLY ONES, THE(1968, Ital./Span.); YOUNG REBEL, THE(1969, Fr./Ital./Span.); EL CONDOR(1970); HORSEMEN, THE(1971); MAN CALLED NOON, THE(1973, Brit.); SPIKES GANG, THE(1974); TAKE A HARD RIDE(1975, U.S./Ital.); WIDOWS' NEST(1977, U.S./Span.); COMIN' AT YA!(1981)
Ricardo Palacois
WIND AND THE LION, THE(1975)
Riccardo Paladini
OPIATE '67(1967, Fr./Ital.)
Roberta Paladini
INNOCENT, THE(1979, Ital.)
J.J. Paladino
SAGA OF DRACULA, THE(1975, Span.)
Fernando Palaeicini
HIGH RISK(1981)
Franco Palaggi
CON MEN, THE(1973, Ital.,Span.), p
Anoma Palalak
S.T.A.B.(1976, Hong Kong/Thailand)
Palan
SIAVASH IN PERSEPOLIS(1966, Iran), ph

Brooke Palance
FORTY CARATS(1973); EMPIRE OF THE ANTS(1977)
Cody Palance
GOD'S GUN(1977)
Holly Palance
OMEN, THE(1976); COMEBACK, THE(1982, Brit.); UNDER FIRE(1983)
Misc. Talkies
TUXEDO WARRIOR(1982)
Ivan Palance
SWORD OF THE CONQUEROR(1962, Ital.)
Jack Palance [Walter Palance]
PANIC IN THE STREETS(1950); HALLS OF MONTEZUMA(1951); SUDDEN FEAR(1952); ARROWHEAD(1953); FLIGHT TO TANGIER(1953); MAN IN THE ATTIC(1953); SECOND CHANCE(1953); SHANE(1953); SIGN OF THE PAGAN(1954); SILVER CHALICE, THE(1954); BIG KNIFE, THE(1955); I DIED A THOUSAND TIMES(1955); KISS OF FIRE(1955); ATTACK!(1956); HOUSE OF NUMBERS(1957); LONELY MAN, THE(1957); MAN INSIDE, THE(1958, Brit.); TEN SECONDS TO HELL(1959); AUSTERLITZ(1960, Fr./Ital./Yugo.); BARABBAS(1962, Ital.); SWORD OF THE CONQUEROR(1962, Ital.); WARRIORS FIVE(1962); CONTEMPT(1963, Fr./Ital.); ONCE A THIEF(1965); MONGOLS, THE(1966, Fr./Ital.); PROFESSIONALS, THE(1966); SPY IN THE GREEN HAT, THE(1966); KILL A DRAGON(1967); TORTURE GARDEN(1968, Brit.); CHE!(1969); DESPERADOS, THE(1969); JUSTINE(1969, Ital./Span.); THEY CAME TO ROB LAS VEGAS(1969, Fr./Ital./Span./Ger.); COMPANEROS(1970 Ital./Span./Ger.); MC MASTERS, THE(1970); MERCENARY, THE(1970, Ital./Span.); MONTE WALSH(1970); BIG AND THE BAD, THE(1971, Ital./Fr./Span.); HORSEMEN, THE(1971); CHATO'S LAND(1972); CON MEN, THE(1973, Ital.,Span.); OKLAHOMA CRUDE(1973); CRAZE(1974, Brit.); FOUR DEUCES, THE(1976); GREAT ADVENTURE, THE(1976, Span./Ital.); GOD'S GUN(1977); WELCOME TO BLOOD CITY(1977, Brit./Can.); ONE MAN JURY(1978); COCAINE COWBOYS(1979); SHAPE OF THINGS TO COME, THE(1979, Can.); ANGELS BRIGADE(1980); HAWK THE SLAYER(1980, Brit.); WITHOUT WARNING(1980); ALONE IN THE DARK(1982)
Misc. Talkies
MISTER SCARFACE(1977); UNKNOWN POWERS(1979); PORTRAIT OF A HITMAN(1984)
Ferenc Palancy
FORBIDDEN RELATIONS(1983, Hung.)
Inez Palang
MONSTER FROM THE OCEAN FLOOR, THE(1954)
Inez Palange
YELLOW JACK(1938); SCARFACE(1932); MEN OF AMERICA(1933); MELODY LINGERS ON, THE(1935); NIGHT AT THE OPERA, A(1935); DODSWORTH(1936); HIS BROTHER'S WIFE(1936); IT HAD TO HAPPEN(1936); LIBELED LADY(1936); WOMAN REBELS, A(1936); EBB TIDE(1937); FIREFLY, THE(1937); PORTIA ON TRIAL(1937); SONG OF THE CITY(1937); YOU CAN'T HAVE EVERYTHING(1937); FLIRTING WITH FATE(1938); KING OF THE NEWSBOYS(1938); LITTLE MISS ROUGHNECK(1938); MARIE ANTOINETTE(1938); ROAD DEMON(1938); SPEED TO BURN(1938); CHICKEN WAGON FAMILY(1939); ONLY ANGELS HAVE WINGS(1939); WINNER TAKE ALL(1939); GRAPES OF WRATH(1940); I WAS AN ADVENTURESS(1940); ON THEIR OWN(1940); ONE MILLION B.C.(1940); CAUGHT IN THE ACT(1941); ROMANCE OF THE RIO GRANDE(1941); UNDER FIESTA STARS(1941); BEYOND THE BLUE HORIZON(1942); GAY SISTERS, THE(1942); LIFE BEGINS AT 8:30(1942); OUT OF THIS WORLD(1945); MURDER IN THE MUSIC HALL(1946); HOMESTRETCH, THE(1947); UNCONQUERED(1947); LOVES OF CARMEN, THE(1948); SEPTEMBER AFFAIR(1950)
Gelsa Palao
HEY, GOOD LOOKIN'(1982)
Gerard Palaprat
TRANS-EUROP-EXPRESS(1968, Fr.)
Mimo Palarmo
SIGN OF THE GLADIATOR(1959, Fr./Ger./Ital.)
A. Palasthy
BEASTS OF BERLIN(1939)
Silents
KING OF KINGS, THE(1927); STAND AND DELIVER(1928)
Alex Palasthy
UNDER TWO FLAGS(1936); I'LL TAKE ROMANCE(1937); PRESCRIPTION FOR ROMANCE(1937)
Alexander Palasthy
LADY IN QUESTION, THE(1940)
Irene Palasty
MARRIED IN HOLLYWOOD(1929)
Palau
DR. KNOCK(1936, Fr.); CROSSROADS(1938, Fr.); RASPUTIN(1939, Fr.); ANGEL AND SINNER(1947, Fr.); CARNIVAL OF SINNERS(1947, Fr.); RAVEN, THE(1948, Fr.); LES BELLES-DE-NUIT(1952, Fr.)
Jose Gras Palau
1984
CONQUEST(1984, Ital./Span./Mex.)
Pierre Palau
DEVIL IN THE FLESH, THE(1949, Fr.); NANA(1957, Fr./Ital.); JOKER, THE(1961, Fr.); KING OF HEARTS(1967, Fr./Ital.)
Fernando Palaviccini
SURVIVE!(1977, Mex.)
Fernando Palavicini
HIGH RISK(1981)
Alfred Palca
HARLEM GLOBETROTTERS, THE(1951), w
Euzhan Palcy
1984
SUGAR CANE ALLEY(1984, Fr.), d&w
Joel Palcy
1984
SUGAR CANE ALLEY(1984, Fr.)
Norman Pale
BEACH RED(1967)
Oreste Palella
JESSICA(1962, U.S./Ital./Fr.), d; TARTARS, THE(1962, Ital./Yugo.), w; GIANT OF METROPOLIS, THE(1963, Ital.), w; SEDUCED AND ABANDONED(1964, Fr./Ital.); THE DIRTY GAME(1966, Fr./Ital./Ger.), w; SERAFINO(1970, Fr./Ital.)

Orste Palella
LIGHTNING BOLT(1967, Ital./Sp.)
Piero Palemini
BURIED ALIVE(1951, Ital.)
Cole Palen
ZELIG(1983)
Jim Palen
MISFITS, THE(1961), stunts
Richard Palenske
WICKED DIE SLOW, THE(1968)
Gina Palerme
Misc. Silents
DANGER LINE, THE(1924)
Piero Palermini
TO LIVE IN PEACE(1947, Ital.); WAR AND PEACE(1956, Ital./U.S.); FALL OF ROME, THE(1963, Ital.); QUEEN OF THE NILE(1964, Ital.)
Alfonse L. Palermo
TRUE CONFESSIONS(1981), ch
Luchiano Palermo
SACCO AND VANZETTI(1971, Ital./Fr.)
Mary Lou Palermo
CAULDRON OF BLOOD(1971, Span.)
Joe Palese
1984
FEAR CITY(1984)
R. Palester
LAST STOP, THE(1949, Pol.), m
Roman Palester
BORDER STREET(1950, Pol.), m
Joan Palethorpe
SUMMER HOLIDAY(1963, Brit.)
Doris Palette
AULD LANG SYNE(1937, Brit.)
Eugene Palette
Misc. Silents
HEIR OF THE AGES, THE(1917); FAIR AND WARMER(1919)
Max Palevsky
FUN WITH DICK AND JANE(1977), p; ISLANDS IN THE STREAM(1977), p
Frank Paley
RUMBLE ON THE DOCKS(1956), w
Grace Paley
MILESTONES(1975)
Jackie Paley
LADIES OF WASHINGTON(1944); CARIBBEAN MYSTERY, THE(1945)
Natalie Paley
SYLVIA SCARLETT(1936)
Nora Paley
SALLY'S HOUNDS(1968)
Petronia Paley
ALMOST SUMMER(1978)
Stanley Paley
ANGEL COMES TO BROOKLYN, AN(1945), w
Susan Paley
DEATH OF A CHAMPION(1939); UNTAMED(1940); LADY IN THE DARK(1944)
The Paley Brothers
SGT. PEPPER'S LONELY HEARTS CLUB BAND(1978)
Gyorgy Palffy
WITNESS, THE(1982, Hung.)
Lotta Palfi
ABOVE SUSPICION(1943); IN OUR TIME(1944); SON OF LASSIE(1945)
Lotte Palfi
UNDERGROUND(1941); MASK OF DIMITRIOS, THE(1944); WALK EAST ON BEACON(1952)
Victor Palfi
UNCLE TOM'S CABIN(1969, Fr./Ital./Ger./Yugo.), ed
May Palfrey
Misc. Silents
GREAT DAY, THE(1921, Brit.)
Yolanda Palfrey
DRAGONSLAYER(1981)
Lou Palfy
GILDA(1946)
Jeanne Pali
ISLAND RESCUE(1952, Brit.); HOUSE OF THE ARROW, THE(1953, Brit.)
Maria Teresa Paliani
ANGELA(1955, Ital.)
Jose Palido
MASSACRE(1956)
Veronica Palileo
NO MAN IS AN ISLAND(1962)
Ron Palillo
SKATETOWN, U.S.A.(1979)
Michael Palin
AND NOW FOR SOMETHING COMPLETELY DIFFERENT(1972, Brit.), a, w; MONTY PYTHON AND THE HOLY GRAIL(1975, Brit.), a, w; JABBERWOCKY(1977, Brit.); MONTY PYTHON'S LIFE OF BRIAN(1979, Brit.), a, w; TIME BANDITS(1981, Brit.), a, w; MISSIONARY, THE(1982), a, p, w; MONTY PYTHON'S THE MEANING OF LIFE(1983, Brit.), a, w
Jack Palinkas
STUNT MAN, THE(1980)
Ken Palius
GIVE'EM HELL, HARRY!(1975), ph
Amby Paliwoda
ONE HUNDRED AND ONE DALMATIANS(1961), anim; SHINBONE ALLEY(1971), anim
Anna Palk
PLAY IT COOL(1963, Brit.); EARTH DIES SCREAMING, THE(1964, Brit.); SKULL, THE(1965, Brit.); FAHRENHEIT 451(1966, Brit.); FROZEN DEAD, THE(1967, Brit.); TOMCAT, THE(1968, Brit.); NIGHT COMERS, THE(1971, Brit.); BEYOND THE FOG(1981, Brit.)

Tony Palk
PLEASURE GIRLS, THE(1966, Brit.), ed; ASSAULT(1971, Brit.), ed; TERROR FROM UNDER THE HOUSE(1971, Brit.), ed
Tom Palky
FIGHTING COWBOY(1933)
Gloria Pall
ALL ASHORE(1953); MA AND PA KETTLE ON VACATION(1953); FRENCH LINE, THE(1954); CITY OF SHADOWS(1955); SON OF SINBAD(1955); GARMENT JUNGLE, THE(1957); JAILHOUSE ROCK(1957); CRIMSON KIMONO, THE(1959)
Larry Pall
Misc. Talkies
OFF YOUR ROCKER(1980), d
Andrew Pallack
KARATE, THE HAND OF DEATH(1961), cos
Jeff Palladini
MARATHON MAN(1976)
Carmen Pallais
RIDE THE PINK HORSE(1947)
Dorita Pallais
THREE DARING DAUGHTERS(1948); KID FROM TEXAS, THE(1950); SOMBRERO(1953)
Maria Pallais
JETLAG(1981, U.S./Span.), art d
Art Pallans
DISC JOCKEY(1951)
Gregg C. Pallas
NIGHT IN CASABLANCA, A(1946), ed
Mickey Pallas
MEDIUM COOL(1969)
Aubert Pallascio
KIDNAPPING OF THE PRESIDENT, THE(1980, Can.)
Giovanni Pallavicino
WE STILL KILL THE OLD WAY(1967, Ital.)
Juan Palleja
THAT MAN IN ISTANBUL(1966, Fr./Ital./Span.), ed
Conde B. Pallen
Misc. Silents
ETERNAL LIGHT, THE(1919), d
Anita Pallenberg
BARBARELLA(1968, Fr./Ital.); CANDY(1968, Ital./Fr.); DEGREE OF MURDER, A(1969, Ger.); DILLINGER IS DEAD(1969, Ital.)
Misc. Talkies
PERFORMANCE(1970, Brit.)
Rospo Pallenberg
EXCALIBUR(1981), w
Gary Paller
FIREBIRD 2015 AD(1981), spec eff
Jack Paller
STREET IS MY BEAT, THE(1966), p
Eugene Pallette
LIGHTS OF NEW YORK(1928); CANARY MURDER CASE, THE(1929); DUMMY, THE(1929); GREENE MURDER CASE, THE(1929); KIBITZER, THE(1929); LOVE PARADE, THE(1929); STUDIO MURDER MYSTERY, THE(1929); VIRGINIAN, THE(1929); BENSON MURDER CASE, THE(1930); BORDER LEGION, THE(1930); FOLLOW THRU(1930); LET'S GO NATIVE(1930); MEN ARE LIKE THAT(1930); PLAYBOY OF PARIS(1930); POINTED HEELS(1930); SANTA FE TRAIL, THE(1930); SEA GOD, THE(1930); SEA LEGS(1930); SLIGHTLY SCARLET(1930); DUDE RANCH(1931); FIGHTING CARAVANS(1931); GIRLS ABOUT TOWN(1931); GUN SMOKE(1931); HUCKLEBERRY FINN(1931); IT PAYS TO ADVERTISE(1931); PARLOR, BEDROOM AND BATH(1931); DANCERS IN THE DARK(1932); HALF-NAKED TRUTH, THE(1932); NIGHT MAYOR, THE(1932); SHANGHAI EXPRESS(1932); STRANGERS OF THE EVENING(1932); THUNDER BELOW(1932); TOM BROWN OF CULVER(1932); WILD GIRL(1932); FROM HEADQUARTERS(1933); HELL BELOW(1933); KENNEL MURDER CASE, THE(1933); MADE ON BROADWAY(1933); MR. SKITCH(1933); SHANGHAI MADNESS(1933); STORM AT DAYBREAK(1933); CARAVAN(1934); CROSS COUNTRY CRUISE(1934); DRAGON MURDER CASE, THE(1934); FRIENDS OF MR. SWEENEY(1934); I'VE GOT YOUR NUMBER(1934); STRICTLY DYNAMITE(1934); ALL THE KING'S HORSES(1935); BABY FACE HARRINGTON(1935); BLACK SHEEP(1935); BORDERTOWN(1935); ONE EXCITING ADVENTURE(1935); STEAMBOAT ROUND THE BEND(1935); DISHONOR BRIGHT(1936, Brit.); EASY TO TAKE(1936); GHOST GOES WEST, THE(1936); GOLDEN ARROW, THE(1936); LUCKIEST GIRL IN THE WORLD, THE(1936); MY MAN GODFREY(1936); STOWAWAY(1936); CLARENCE(1937); CRIME NOBOBY SAW, THE(1937); SHE HAD TO EAT(1937); TOPPER(1937); 100 MEN AND A GIRL(1937); ADVENTURES OF ROBIN HOOD, THE(1938); THERE GOES MY HEART(1938); FIRST LOVE(1939); MR. SMITH GOES TO WASHINGTON(1939); WIFE, HUSBAND AND FRIEND(1939); HE STAYED FOR BREAKFAST(1940); IT'S A DATE(1940); LITTLE BIT OF HEAVEN, A(1940); MARK OF ZORRO, THE(1940); SANDY IS A LADY(1940); YOUNG TOM EDISON(1940); APPOINTMENT FOR LOVE(1941); BRIDE CAME C.O.D., THE(1941); LADY EVE, THE(1941); RIDE, KELLY, RIDE(1941); SWAMP WATER(1941); UNFINISHED BUSINESS(1941); WORLD PREMIERE(1941); ALMOST MARRIED(1942); ARE HUSBANDS NECESSARY?(1942); BIG STREET, THE(1942); FOREST RANGERS, THE(1942); LADY IN A JAM(1942); MALE ANIMAL, THE(1942); SILVER QUEEN(1942); TALES OF MANHATTAN(1942); GANG'S ALL HERE, THE(1943); HEAVEN CAN WAIT(1943); IT AIN'T HAY(1943); KANSAN, THE(1943); SLIGHTLY DANGEROUS(1943); HEAVENLY DAYS(1944); IN THE MEANTIME, DARLING(1944); LAKE PLACID SERENADE(1944); PIN UP GIRL(1944); SENSATIONS OF 1945(1944); STEP LIVELY(1944); CHEATERS, THE(1945); IN OLD SACRAMENTO(1946); SUSPENSE(1946)
Silents
BIRTH OF A NATION, THE(1915); GRETCHEN, THE GREENHORN(1916); HELL-TO-PAY AUSTIN(1916); INTOLERANCE(1916); EACH TO HIS KIND(1917); HIS ROBE OF HONOR(1918); TARZAN OF THE APES(1918); ALIAS JIMMY VALENTINE(1920); TWIN BEDS(1920); FINE FEATHERS(1921); THREE MUSKETEERS, THE(1921); NORTH OF HUDSON BAY(1923); TO THE LAST MAN(1923); FIGHTING EDGE(1926); WHISPERING SMITH(1926); CHICAGO(1928); GOOD-BYE KISS, THE(1928); RED MARK, THE(1928)
Misc. Silents
LONESOME CHAP, THE(1917); WORLD APART, THE(1917); BREAKERS AHEAD(1918); NO MAN'S LAND(1918); TURN OF THE CARD, THE(1918); VIVIET-

TE(1918); WORDS AND MUSIC BY...(1919); PARLOR, BEDROOM AND BATH(1920); HELL'S HOLE(1923); WANDERING HUSBANDS(1924); MANTRAP(1926); HIS PRIVATE LIFE(1928)

Gene Pallette
Silents
AMATEUR ADVENTURESS, THE(1919)

Byron Pallia
SERENITY(1962)

Ingemar Pallin
TIME OF DESIRE, THE(1957, Swed.)

Bryon Pallis
GIRL OF THE MOUNTAINS(1958, Gr.)

Viron Pallis
STEFANIA(1968, Gr.)

Walter Pallman
IRON MASK, THE(1929), spec eff

Jackie Pallo
RECKONING, THE(1971, Brit.)

Tony Pallodino
Misc. Talkies
AROUSED(1968)

Steven Pallos
CALL OF THE BLOOD(1948, Brit.), p; TWENTY QUESTIONS MURDER MYSTERY, THE(1950, Brit.), p; FAKE, THE(1953, Brit.), p; DIAMOND WIZARD, THE(1954, Brit.), p; ANGELA(1955, Ital.), p; MASTER PLAN, THE(1955, Brit.), p; SHADOW OF FEAR(1956, Brit.), p; NO ROAD BACK(1957, Brit.), p; SAIL INTO DANGER(1957, Brit.), p; FOXHOLE IN CAIRO(1960, Brit.), p; DEVIL'S DAFFODIL, THE(1961, Brit./Ger.), p; JET STORM(1961, Brit.), p; HANDS OF ORLAC, THE(1964, Brit./Fr.), p; WHERE THE SPIES ARE(1965, Brit.), p; CATCH ME A SPY(1971, Brit./Fr.), p

Albert Pallot
JULIA MISBEHAVES(1948)

Riccardo Pallotini
SNOW DEVILS, THE(1965, Ital.), ph; RINGO AND HIS GOLDEN PISTOL(1966, Ital.), ph; BLINDMAN(1972, Ital.), ph; TAKE A HARD RIDE(1975, U.S./Ital.), ph

Richard Pallotin [Riccardo Pallotini]
LADY FRANKENSTEIN(1971, Ital.), ph

Gabriella Pallotta
IL GRIDO(1962, U.S./Ital.); LA VIACCIA(1962, Fr./Ital.); PIGEON THAT TOOK ROME, THE(1962); MADAME(1963, Fr./Ital./Span.); BIBLE...IN THE BEGINNING, THE(1966); MONGOLS, THE(1966, Fr./Ital.); SAILOR FROM GIBRALTAR, THE(1967, Brit.)

Gabriella Pallotti
FAST AND SEXY(1960, Fr./Ital.)

Riccardo Pallottini
FATAL DESIRE(1953), ph; TWO NIGHTS WITH CLEOPATRA(1953, Ital.), ph; MARCO POLO(1962, Fr./Ital.), ph; SON OF SAMSON(1962, Fr./Ital./Yugo.), ph; STORY OF JOSEPH AND HIS BRETHREN THE(1962, Ital.), ph; ATLAS AGAINST THE CYCLOPS(1963, Ital.), ph; DOG EAT DOG(1963, U.S./Ger./Ital.), ph; FALL OF ROME, THE(1963, Ital.), ph; SAMSON AND THE SEVEN MIRACLES OF THE WORLD(1963, Fr./Ital.), ph; WITCH'S CURSE, THE(1963, Ital.), ph; DR. MABUSE'S RAYS OF DEATH(1964, Ger./Fr./Ital.), ph; EIGHTEEN IN THE SUN(1964, Ital.), ph; EYE OF THE NEEDLE, THE(1965, Ital./Fr.), ph; HORROR CASTLE(1965, Ital.), ph; HE WHO SHOOTS FIRST(1966, Ital.), ph; LOVE AND MARRIAGE(1966, Ital.), ph; LIGHTNING BOLT(1967, Ital./Sp.), ph; BRUTE AND THE BEAST, THE(1968, Ital.), ph; MISSION STARDUST(1968, Ital./Span./Ger.), ph; VENGEANCE(1968, Ital./Ger.), ph; WAR BETWEEN THE PLANETS(1971, Ital.), ph
1984
LAST HUNTER, THE(1984, Ital.), ph

Richard Pallton [Riccardo Pallottini]
WILD, WILD PLANET, THE(1967, Ital.), ph

Georges Pallu
GLORY OF FAITH, THE(1938, Fr.), d

Pally
CONFESSIONS OF A ROGUE(1948, Fr.)

A. Carle Palm
Silents
MONSTER, THE(1925), ed

Walter Palm
MASK OF DIMITRIOS, THE(1944)

Andrea Palma
TARZAN AND THE MERMAIDS(1948); CRIMINAL LIFE OF ARCHIBALDO DE LA CRUZ, THE(1962, Mex.)

Gene Palma
TAXI DRIVER(1976)

Joe Palma
LOUISIANA HAYRIDE(1944); TWO YEARS BEFORE THE MAST(1946); JOHNNY ALLEGRO(1949); KNOCK ON ANY DOOR(1949); UNDERCOVER MAN, THE(1949); EMERGENCY WEDDING(1950); MY SIX CONVICTS(1952); SNIPER, THE(1952); STRANGERS WHEN WE MEET(1960); NOTORIOUS LANDLADY, THE(1962); IRMA LA DOUCE(1963); GOOD NEIGHBOR SAM(1964); GREAT RACE, THE(1965)

Joseph Palma
BOSTON BLACKIE BOOKED ON SUSPICION(1945); BOSTON BLACKIE'S RENDEZVOUS(1945); GILDA(1946); NIGHT EDITOR(1946); LIKELY STORY, A(1947); LADY FROM SHANGHAI, THE(1948); RECKLESS MOMENTS, THE(1949); FULLER BRUSH GIRL, THE(1950)

Mona Palma
Silents
QUARTERBACK, THE(1926)
Misc. Silents
CANADIAN, THE(1926); CABARET(1927)

Pamela Palma
MYSTERY OF THE BLACK JUNGLE(1955)

Stella Palma
PASSION HOLIDAY(1963)

Paul Palmantola
CHARGE OF THE LANCERS(1953), art d

Mimmo Palmara
WAR AND PEACE(1956, Ital./U.S.); HERCULES(1959, Ital.); HERCULES UNCHAINED(1960, Ital./Fr.); LAST DAYS OF POMPEII, THE(1960, Ital.); COLOSSUS OF RHODES, THE(1961, Ital., Fr., Span.); SODOM AND GOMORRAH(1962, U.S./Fr./Ital.);

TROJAN HORSE, THE(1962, Fr./Ital.); GOLIATH AGAINST THE GIANTS(1963, Ital./Span.); HERCULES AND THE CAPTIVE WOMEN(1963, Fr./Ital.); GOLIATH AND THE SINS OF BABYLON(1964, Ital.); SANDOKAN THE GREAT(1964, Fr./Ital./Span.); STRANGER, THE(1967, Algeria/Fr./Ital.); DESERTER, THE(1971 Ital./Yugo.)

Martin Palmares
UNDER FIRE(1983)

Eulf Palme
COUNTERFEIT TRAITOR, THE(1962)

Ulf Palme
DREAMS(1960, Swed.); DEVIL, THE(1963); HERE'S YOUR LIFE(1968, Swed.)

Paul Palmentola
HEART PUNCH(1932), art d; HONOR OF THE PRESS(1932), art d; SWEETHEART OF THE NAVY(1937), art d; WALLABY JIM OF THE ISLANDS(1937), art d; MYSTIC CIRCLE MURDER(1939), art d; TIGER FANGS(1943), art d; DELINQUENT DAUGHTERS(1944), art d; GREAT MIKE(1944), art d; JOHNNY DOESN'T LIVE HERE ANY MORE(1944), art d; MEN ON HER MIND(1944), art d; MINSTREL MAN(1944), art d; MONSTER MAKER, THE(1944), art d; SHAKE HANDS WITH MURDER(1944), art d; WATERFRONT(1944), art d; WHEN THE LIGHTS GO ON AGAIN(1944), art d; DIXIE JAMBOREE(1945), art d; I ACCUSE MY PARENTS(1945), art d; KID SISTER, THE(1945), art d; LADY CONFESSES, THE(1945), art d; MAN WHO WALKED ALONE, THE(1945), art d; MISSING CORPSE, THE(1945), art d; PHANTOM OF 42ND STREET, THE(1945), art d; ROGUES GALLERY(1945), art d; STRANGE ILLUSION(1945), art d; FREDDIE STEPS OUT(1946), art d; GLAMOUR GIRL(1947), art d; LAST OF THE REDMEN(1947), art d; LITTLE MISS BROADWAY(1947), art d; TWO BLONDES AND A REDHEAD(1947), art d; I SURRENDER DEAR(1948), art d; JUNGLE JIM(1948), art d; MANHATTAN ANGEL(1948), art d; MARY LOU(1948), art d; PRINCE OF THIEVES, THE(1948), art d; RACING LUCK(1948), art d; BOSTON BLACKIE'S CHINESE VENTURE(1949), art d; KAZAN(1949), art d; LOST TRIBE, THE(1949), art d; MAKE BELIEVE BALLROOM(1949), art d; MUTINEERS, THE(1949), art d; CAPTIVE GIRL(1950), art d; LAST OF THE BUCCANEERS(1950), art d; MARK OF THE GORILLA(1950), art d; PYGMY ISLAND(1950), art d; REVENUE AGENT(1950), art d; STATE PENITENTIARY(1950), md; TYRANT OF THE SEA(1950), art d; FURY OF THE CONGO(1951), art d; HURRICANE ISLAND(1951), art d; JUNGLE MANHUNT(1951), art d; MAGIC CARPET, THE(1951), art d; PURPLE HEART DIARY(1951), art d; WHEN THE REDSKINS RODE(1951), art d; YANK IN KOREA, A(1951), art d; CALIFORNIA CONQUEST(1952), art d; GOLDEN HAWK, THE(1952), art d; HAREM GIRL(1952), art d; JUNGLE JIM IN THE FORBIDDEN LAND(1952), art d; LAST TRAIN FROM BOMBAY(1952), art d; PATHFINDER, THE(1952), art d; THIEF OF DAMASCUS(1952), art d; VOODOO TIGER(1952), art d; YANK IN INDO-CHINA, A(1952), art d; FLAME OF CALCUTTA(1953), art d; FORTYNINTH MAN, THE(1953), art d; JACK MCCALL, DESPERADO(1953), art d; KILLER APE(1953), art d; PRINCE OF PIRATES(1953), art d; PRISONERS OF THE CASBAH(1953), art d; SAVAGE MUTINY(1953), art d; SERPENT OF THE NILE(1953), art d; SIREN OF BAGDAD(1953), art d; SLAVES OF BABYLON(1953), art d; VALLEY OF THE HEADHUNTERS(1953), art d; JESSE JAMES VERSUS THE DALTONS(1954), art d; JUNGLE MAN-EATERS(1954), art d; MIAMI STORY, THE(1954), art d; CROOKED WEB, THE(1955), art d; DEVIL GODDESS(1955), art d; DUEL ON THE MISSISSIPPI(1955), art d; GUN THAT WON THE WEST, THE(1955), art d; INSIDE DETROIT(1955), art d; IT CAME FROM BENEATH THE SEA(1955), art d; JUNGLE MOON MEN(1955), art d; NEW ORLEANS UNCENSORED(1955), art d; PIRATES OF TRIPOLI(1955), art d; SEMINOLE UPRISING(1955), art d; TEEN-AGE CRIME WAVE(1955), art d; DON'T KNOCK THE ROCK(1956), art d; EARTH VS. THE FLYING SAUCERS(1956), art d; HOUSTON STORY, THE(1956), art d; MIAMI EXPOSE(1956), art d; ROCK AROUND THE CLOCK(1956), art d; RUMBLE ON THE DOCKS(1956), art d; URANIUM BOOM(1956), art d; WEREWOLF, THE(1956), art d; ESCAPE FROM SAN QUENTIN(1957), art d; GIANT CLAW, THE(1957), art d; MAN WHO TURNED TO STONE, THE(1957), art d; NIGHT THE WORLD EXPLODED, THE(1957), art d; TIJUANA STORY, THE(1957), art d; UTAH BLAINE(1957), art d; ZOMBIES OF MORA TAU(1957), art d; GOING STEADY(1958), art d; LIFE BEGINS AT 17(1958), art d; WORLD WAS HIS JURY, THE(1958), art d; FLYING FONTAINES, THE(1959), art d; JUKE BOX RHYTHM(1959), art d

Ada Palmer
Silents
PURSUIT OF PAMELA, THE(1920, Brit.)

Adele Palmer
MAN OF CONQUEST(1939), cos; RIO GRANDE(1939), cos; THOU SHALT NOT KILL(1939), cos; ZERO HOUR, THE(1939), cos; THREE FACES WEST(1940), cos; VILLAGE BARN DANCE(1940), cos; WAGONS WESTWARD(1940), cos; WHO KILLED AUNT MAGGIE?(1940), cos; WOMEN IN WAR(1940), cos; ICE-CAPADES(1941), cos; RAGS TO RICHES(1941), cos; ROOKIES ON PARADE(1941), cos; SAILORS ON LEAVE(1941), cos; TUXEDO JUNCTION(1941), cos.; MY BEST GAL(1944), cos; THREE LITTLE SISTERS(1944), cos; PHANTOM SPEAKS, THE(1945), cos; STEPPIN' IN SOCIETY(1945), cos; UTAH(1945), cos; MYSTERIOUS MR. VALENTINE, THE(1946), cos; OUT CALIFORNIA WAY(1946), cos; PLAINSMAN AND THE LADY(1946), cos; SIOUX CITY SUE(1946), cos; THAT BRENNAN GIRL(1946), cos; UNDERCOVER WOMAN, THE(1946), cos; NORTHWEST OUTPOST(1947), cos; PILGRIM LADY, THE(1947), cos; ROBIN OF TEXAS(1947), cos; TRAIL TO SAN ANTONE(1947), cos; TRESPASSER, THE(1947), cos; WYOMING(1947), cos; I, JANE DOE(1948), cos; MACBETH(1948), cos; MOONRISE(1948), cos; OLD LOS ANGELES(1948), cos; OUT OF THE STORM(1948), cos; SECRET SERVICE INVESTIGATOR(1948), cos; SLIPPY MCGEE(1948), cos; TRAIN TO ALCATRAZ(1948), cos; FIGHTING KENTUCKIAN, THE(1949), cos; STREETS OF SAN FRANCISCO(1949), cos; TOO LATE FOR TEARS(1949), cos; HOUSE BY THE RIVER(1950), cos; RIO GRANDE(1950), cos; SURRENDER(1950), cos; TARNISHED(1950), cos; TRAIL OF ROBIN HOOD(1950), cos; TRIAL WITHOUT JURY(1950), cos; UNMASKED(1950), cos; BELLE LE GRAND(1951), cos; MILLION DOLLAR PURSUIT(1951), cos; MISSING WOMEN(1951), cos; RODEO KING AND THE SENORITA(1951), cos; STREET BANDITS(1951), cos; HOODLUM EMPIRE(1952), cos; MONTANA BELLE(1952), cos; QUIET MAN, THE(1952), cos; SOUTH PACIFIC TRAIL(1952), cos; TROPICAL HEAT WAVE(1952), cos; WILD BLUE YONDER, THE(1952), cos; WOMAN IN THE DARK(1952), cos; WOMAN OF THE NORTH COUNTRY(1952), cos; CITY THAT NEVER SLEEPS(1953), cos; SAN ANTONE(1953), cos; SUN SHINES BRIGHT, THE(1953), cos; WOMAN THEY ALMOST LYNCHED, THE(1953), cos; JUBILEE TRAIL(1954), cos; UNTAMED HEIRESS(1954), cos; CITY OF SHADOWS(1955), cos; ETERNAL SEA, THE(1955), cos; FIGHTING CHANCE, THE(1955), cos; HEADLINE HUNTERS(1955), cos; LAST COMMAND, THE(1955), cos; MAN ALONE, A(1955), cos; NO MAN'S WOMAN(1955), cos; ROAD TO DENVER, THE(1955), cos; SANTA FE PASSAGE(1955), cos; TIMBERJACK(1955), cos; TWINKLE IN GOD'S EYE, THE(1955), cos; VANISHING AMERICAN, THE(1955), cos; COME NEXT SPRING(1956), cos; JAGUAR(1956), cos; MAVERICK QUEEN,

THE(1956), cos; STRANGE ADVENTURE, A(1956), cos; STRANGER AT MY DOOR(1956), cos; TERROR AT MIDNIGHT(1956), cos; THUNDER OVER ARIZONA(1956), cos; WHEN GANGLAND STRIKES(1956), cos; WOMAN'S DEVOTION, A(1956), cos; PEYTON PLACE(1957), cos; IN LOVE AND WAR(1958); LONG, HOT SUMMER, THE(1958), cos; BEST OF EVERYTHING, THE(1959), cos; FBI STORY, THE(1959), cos; HOUND-DOG MAN(1959), cos; SAY ONE FOR ME(1959), cos; SOUND AND THE FURY, THE(1959), cos

Andria Palmer
SNUFFY SMITH, YARD BIRD(1942)

Ann Palmer
MARS NEEDS WOMEN(1966)

Anthony Palmer
PANIC IN NEEDLE PARK(1971); RANCHO DELUXE(1975)
1984
RAW COURAGE(1984)

Arispah Palmer
I'D CLIMB THE HIGHEST MOUNTAIN(1951)

Arnold Palmer
RETURN TO CAMPUS(1975)

Art Palmer
FANTASIA(1940), anim, anim; PINOCCHIO(1940), anim; DUMBO(1941), anim

Belinda Palmer
CLAY PIGEON(1971); CHINATOWN(1974)
Misc. Talkies
NOT MY DAUGHTER(1975)

Bert Palmer
KIND OF LOVING, A(1962, Brit.); NATIONAL HEALTH, OR NURSE NORTON'S AFFAIR, THE(1973, Brit.)

Betsy Palmer
LONG GRAY LINE, THE(1955); MISTER ROBERTS(1955); QUEEN BEE(1955); TIN STAR, THE(1957); TRUE STORY OF LYNN STUART, THE(1958); IT HAPPENED TO JANE(1959); LAST ANGRY MAN, THE(1959); FRIDAY THE 13TH(1980); FRIDAY THE 13TH PART II(1981)
1984
FRIDAY THE 13TH–THE FINAL CHAPTER(1984)

Bob Palmer
ROOM AT THE TOP(1959, Brit.); THIRTEEN FIGHTING MEN(1960); YOUNG JESSE JAMES(1960)

Brett Palmer
GUARDIAN OF THE WILDERNESS(1977)

Bruce Palmer
STARK FEAR(1963)

Bud Palmer
WORLD'S GREATEST ATHLETE, THE(1973)

Byron Palmer
MAN IN THE ATTIC(1953); TONIGHT WE SING(1953); GLORY(1955); MA AND PA KETTLE AT WAIKIKI(1955); BEST THINGS IN LIFE ARE FREE, THE(1956); EMERGENCY HOSPITAL(1956)

Cap Palmer
MAKE MINE MUSIC(1946), w

Carla Palmer
DRIVE-IN(1976)

Carleton Palmer
SPEED LOVERS(1968), m

Carol Palmer
PROSTITUTE(1980, Brit.)

Charles A. Palmer
LOST BOUNDARIES(1949), w

Charles Palmer
SELLOUT, THE(1951), w; LAND UNKNOWN, THE(1957), w

Christene Palmer
MIKADO, THE(1967, Brit.)

Christy Palmer
HUNT THE MAN DOWN(1950)

Conway Palmer
STRANGE CARGO(1936, Brit.); BORN THAT WAY(1937, Brit.); STRANGERS ON A HONEYMOON(1937, Brit.); SUICIDE SQUADRON(1942, Brit.); QUIET WEEKEND(1948, Brit.)

Corliss Palmer
HONEYMOON LANE(1931)
Silents
INTO THE NIGHT(1928); NOOSE, THE(1928)
Misc. Silents
HONEYMOON HATE(1927); POLLY OF THE MOVIES(1927); RETURN OF BOSTON BLACKIE, THE(1927); GEORGE WASHINGTON COHEN(1928); SCARLET YOUTH(1928); TRIAL MARRIAGE(1928); BROADWAY FEVER(1929); SEX MADNESS(1929)

Corp. Thomas Palmer
COLONEL BLIMP(1945, Brit.)

David Palmer
THESE ARE THE DAMNED(1965, Brit.)
Misc. Talkies
RUDDIGORE(1967, Brit.)

Denys Palmer
LIFE IS A CIRCUS(1962, Brit.), ch; PREHISTORIC WOMEN(1967, Brit.), ch

Dermot Palmer
FOREVER MY HEART(1954, Brit.); PARATROOPER(1954, Brit.); FIND THE LADY(1956, Brit.), w

Dick Palmer
TROUBLE IN TEXAS(1937)

Dick Palmer
ARENA, THE(1973)

Dick Palmer [Mimmo Palmara]
SERENADE FOR TWO SPIES(1966, Ital./Ger.); LONG RIDE FROM HELL, A(1970, Ital.)

Don Palmer
QUADROON(1972), m

Donna Palmer
EYES OF LAURA MARS(1978); TRADING PLACES(1983)

E. G. Palmer
Silents
IVANHOE(1913), ph

E. H. Palmer
CHILDREN OF CHANCE(1930, Brit.), ph

Edward Palmer
HIDEOUT(1948, Brit.); ROOM AT THE TOP(1959, Brit.); DESIGN FOR LOVING(1962, Brit.); MIND BENDERS, THE(1963, Brit.); CONQUEROR WORM, THE(1968, Brit.)

Edwin Palmer
LOOK BEFORE YOU LOVE(1948, Brit.); BATTLE BEYOND THE SUN(1963), w

Effie L. Palmer
WAY BACK HOME(1932)

Elsa Palmer
MAN WHO KNEW TOO MUCH, THE(1956)

Ernest G. Palmer
Silents
PRISONERS OF LOVE(1921), ph; ALWAYS THE WOMAN(1922), ph; ONE CLEAR CALL(1922), ph; RED HOT ROMANCE(1922), ph; WANTERS, THE(1923), ph; WAGES FOR WIVES(1925), ph; EARLY TO WED(1926), ph; YELLOW FINGERS(1926), ph

Ernest Palmer
UNDER TWO FLAGS(1936), ph; RIVER, THE(1928), ph; STREET ANGEL(1928), ph; FOUR DEVILS(1929), ph; PLEASURE CRAZED(1929), ph; SUNNY SIDE UP(1929), ph; THRU DIFFERENT EYES(1929), ph; CITY GIRL(1930), ph; JUST IMAGINE(1930), ph; WOMEN EVERYWHERE(1930), ph; BROWN SUGAR(1931, Brit.), ph; CONNECTICUT YANKEE, A(1931), ph; DELICIOUS(1931), ph; GOLDIE(1931), ph; OUT OF THE BLUE(1931, Brit.), ph; SIX CYLINDER LOVE(1931), ph; BUSINESS AND PLEASURE(1932), ph; CHEATERS AT PLAY(1932), ph; DEVIL'S LOTTERY(1932), ph; DOWN TO EARTH(1932), ph; PAINTED WOMAN(1932), ph; TRIAL OF VIVIENNE WARE, THE(1932), ph; BERKELEY SQUARE(1933), ph; CAVALCADE(1933), ph; CHARLIE CHAN'S GREATEST CASE(1933), ph; HIS GRACE GIVES NOTICE(1933), ph; HOOPLA(1933), ph; PLEASURE CRUISE(1933), ph; UMBRELLA, THE(1933, Brit.), ph; CARAVAN(1934), ph; LASH, THE(1934, Brit.), ph; MUSIC IN THE AIR(1934), ph; NOW I'LL TELL(1934), ph; RIVER WOLVES, THE(1934, Brit.), ph; SLEEPERS EAST(1934), ph; STAND UP AND CHEER(1934 80m FOX bw), ph; ACE OF SPADES, THE(1935, Brit.), ph; ANYTHING MIGHT HAPPEN(1935, Brit.), ph; BIRDS OF A FEATHER(1935, Brit.), ph; CHARLIE CHAN IN PARIS(1935), ph; GREAT HOTEL MURDER(1935), ph; LAZYBONES(1935, Brit.), ph; MAN WHO BROKE THE BANK AT MONTE CARLO, THE(1935), ph; MYSTERY WOMAN(1935), ph; WAY DOWN EAST(1935), ph; WHILE PARENTS SLEEP(1935, Brit.), ph; BANJO ON MY KNEE(1936), ph; CAN THIS BE DIXIE?(1936), ph; CRIME OF DR. FORBES(1936), ph; GENTLE JULIA(1936), ph; MURDER BY ROPE(1936, Brit.), ph; MURDER ON THE SET(1936, Brit.), ph; STAR FOR A NIGHT(1936), ph; ALI BABA GOES TO TOWN(1937), ph; EDGE OF THE WORLD, THE(1937, Brit.), ph; LAST CHANCE, THE(1937, Brit.), ph; LOVE IS NEWS(1937), ph; LOVE UNDER FIRE(1937), ph; RHYTHM RACKETEER(1937, Brit.), ph; SECOND HONEYMOON(1937), ph; SLAVE SHIP(1937), ph; WHAT A MAN!(1937, Brit.), ph; BEDTIME STORY(1938, Brit.), ph; FOUR MEN AND A PRAYER(1938), ph; GANG, THE(1938, Brit.), ph; KENTUCKY(1938), ph; MURDER TOMORROW(1938, Brit.), ph; SAVE A LITTLE SUNSHINE(1938, Brit.), ph; STRAIGHT, PLACE AND SHOW(1938), ph; THREE BLIND MICE(1938), ph; FLYING FIFTY-FIVE(1939, Brit.), ph; HOLLYWOOD CAVALCADE(1939), ph; HONEYMOON MERRY-GO-ROUND(1939, Brit.), ph; IT COULD HAPPEN TO YOU(1939), ph; ME AND MY PAL(1939, Brit.), ph; NEWS IS MADE AT NIGHT(1939), ph; WIFE, HUSBAND AND FRIEND(1939), ph; 20,000 MEN A YEAR(1939), ph; CHAD HANNA(1940), ph; EVERYTHING IS RHYTHM(1940, Brit.), ph; GREAT PROFILE, THE(1940), ph; HE MARRIED HIS WIFE(1940), ph; LITTLE MISS MOLLY(1940), ph; PUBLIC DEB NO. 1(1940), ph; SAILOR'S LADY(1940), ph; SHOOTING HIGH(1940), ph; SPIDER, THE(1940, Brit.), ph; STARS LOOK DOWN, THE(1940, Brit.), ph; BELLE STARR(1941), ph; BLOOD AND SAND(1941), ph; HE FOUND A STAR(1941, Brit.), ph; TALL, DARK AND HANDSOME(1941), ph; WEEKEND IN HAVANA(1941), ph; GOOSE STEPS OUT, THE(1942, Brit.), ph; MY GAL SAL(1942), ph; NEXT OF KIN(1942, Brit.), ph; SONG OF THE ISLANDS(1942), ph; SPRINGTIME IN THE ROCKIES(1942), ph; THUNDER BIRDS(1942), ph; BELLS GO DOWN, THE(1943, Brit.), ph; CONEY ISLAND(1943), ph; SWEET ROSIE O'GRADY(1943), ph; FOR THOSE IN PERIL(1944, Brit.), ph; MY AIN FOLK(1944, Brit.), ph; PIN UP GIRL(1944), ph; SOMETHING FOR THE BOYS(1944), ph; DIAMOND HORSESHOE(1945), ph; DOLLY SISTERS, THE(1945), ph; FOR YOU ALONE(1945, Brit.), ph; QUERY(1945, Brit.), ph; CENTENNIAL SUMMER(1946), ph; LISBON STORY, THE(1946, Brit.), ph; MEET THE NAVY(1946, Brit.), ph; MURDER IN REVERSE(1946, Brit.), ph; THREE LITTLE GIRLS IN BLUE(1946), ph; TROJAN BROTHERS, THE(1946), ph; WALTZ TIME(1946, Brit.), ph; GHOSTS OF BERKELEY SQUARE(1947, Brit.), ph; GREEN FINGERS(1947), ph; I WONDER WHO'S KISSING HER NOW(1947), ph; SAN DEMETRIO, LONDON(1947, Brit.), ph; BUT NOT IN VAIN(1948, Brit.), ph; SCUDDA-HOO! SCUDDA-HAY!(1948), ph; SPRINGTIME(1948, Brit.), ph; THREE WEIRD SISTERS, THE(1948, Brit.), ph; UNEASY TERMS(1948, Brit.), ph; FACTS OF LOVE(1949, Brit.), ph; MEET THE DUKE(1949, Brit.), ph; SCHOOL FOR RANDLE(1949, Brit.), ph; SOMEWHERE IN POLITICS(1949, Brit.), ph; WHAT A CARRY ON!(1949, Brit.), ph; BAIT(1950, Brit.), ph; BROKEN ARROW(1950), ph; OVER THE GARDEN WALL(1950, Brit.), ph; STICK 'EM UP(1950, Brit.), ph; TWENTY QUESTIONS MURDER MYSTERY, THE(1950, Brit.), ph; IT'S A GRAND LIFE(1953, Brit.), ph; TAKE A POWDER(1953, Brit.), ph; HEART WITHIN, THE(1957, Brit.), ph; ZOO BABY(1957, Brit.), ph; CROWNING TOUCH, THE(1959, Brit.), ph; HIDDEN HOMICIDE(1959, Brit.), ph; WOMAN EATER, THE(1959, Brit.), ph; MILLION DOLLAR MANHUNT(1962, Brit.), ph
Silents
MIRACLE MAN, THE(1919), ph; SONG OF LIFE, THE(1922), ph; CHAMPION OF LOST CAUSES(1925), ph; 'MARRIAGE LICENSE?'(1926), ph; MARRIED ALIVE(1927), ph; SEVENTH HEAVEN(1927), ph; NO OTHER WOMAN(1928), ph

Ernie Palmer
THEM NICE AMERICANS(1958, Brit.), ph

Ethel Palmer
MR. DEEDS GOES TO TOWN(1936)

Frederick Palmer
ISLAND CAPTIVES(1937)
Silents
NEW COMMANDMENT, THE(1925), w

Gaston Palmer
SHOW GOES ON, THE(1938, Brit.); I DIDN'T DO IT(1945, Brit.); MADWOMAN OF CHAILLOT, THE(1969)

Gene Palmer
DEVIL'S CANYON(1953), ed; DANGEROUS MISSION(1954), ed; STORY OF MANKIND, THE(1957), ed; RAIDERS, THE(1964), ed; SWORD OF ALI BABA, THE(1965), ed; GUNFIGHT IN ABILENE(1967), ed; RIDE TO HANGMAN'S TREE, THE(1967), ed; LOVELY WAY TO DIE, A(1968), ed; NOBODY'S PERFECT(1968), ed; MAN CALLED GANNON, A(1969), ed; RAID ON ROMMEL(1971), ed

Genie Palmer
SOD SISTERS(1969)

Geoffrey Palmer
INCIDENT AT MIDNIGHT(1966, Brit.); O LUCKY MAN!(1973, Brit.); BEYOND THE LIMIT(1983)

Gregg Palmer
MY FRIEND IRMA GOES WEST(1950); ALL-AMERICAN, THE(1953); MAGNIFICENT OBSESSION(1954); PLAYGIRL(1954); TAZA, SON OF COCHISE(1954); TO HELL AND BACK(1955); CREATURE WALKS AMONG US, THE(1956); HILDA CRANE(1956); FOOTSTEPS IN THE NIGHT(1957); FROM HELL IT CAME(1957); REVOLT AT FORT LARAMIE(1957); ZOMBIES OF MORA TAU(1957); FEMALE ANIMAL, THE(1958); THUNDERING JETS(1958); REBEL SET, THE(1959); SAD HORSE, THE(1959); CAT BURGLAR, THE(1961); FIVE GUNS TO TOMBSTONE(1961); GUN FIGHT(1961); MOST DANGEROUS MAN ALIVE, THE(1961); FORTY POUNDS OF TROUBLE(1962); PRIZE, THE(1963); ADVANCE TO THE REAR(1964); QUICK GUN, THE(1964); SHENANDOAH(1965); RARE BREED, THE(1966); IF HE HOLLERS, LET HIM GO(1968); UNDEFEATED, THE(1969); CHISUM(1970); MC KENZIE BREAK, THE(1970); BIG JAKE(1971); SHOOTIST, THE(1976); HOT LEAD AND COLD FEET(1978); MAN WITH BOGART'S FACE, THE(1980)

H.E. Palmer
GABLES MYSTERY, THE(1931, Brit.), ph; WHY SAPS LEAVE HOME(1932, Brit.), ph; GABLES MYSTERY, THE(1938, Brit.), ph

Harold Palmer
OUR BLUSHING BRIDES(1930), ed

Henning Palmer
HAGBARD AND SIGNE(1968, Den./Iceland/Swed.)

Hilde Palmer
WE'LL SMILE AGAIN(1942, Brit.); OLD MOTHER RILEY, DETECTIVE(1943, Brit.)

Inda Palmer
Silents
NET, THE(1916)
Misc. Silents
HIS WIFE(1915); IMAGE MAKER, THE(1917); WHEN LOVE WAS BLIND(1917)

J.L. Palmer
WESTERN LIMITED(1932); SEA OF GRASS, THE(1947)

James Palmer
PLEDGEMASTERS, THE(1971)

Jasper L. Palmer
NAVAJO TRAIL, THE(1945)

Jasper Palmer
SALOME, WHERE SHE DANCED(1945); SONG OF THE SIERRAS(1946); RAINBOW OVER THE ROCKIES(1947); KING OF THE BANDITS(1948)

Joe Palmer
POOR COW(1968, Brit.)

John Palmer
CHANCE OF A LIFETIME(1950, Brit.), p; BONJOUR TRISTESSE(1958), d; CIAO MANHATTAN(1973), d&w, ph

John Palmer
LITTLE CONVICT, THE(1980, Aus.), w; DOT AND THE BUNNY(1983, Aus.), w
1984
CAMEL BOY, THE(1984, Aus.), w

Joni Palmer
COMA(1978); POSTMAN ALWAYS RINGS TWICE, THE(1981)

June Palmer
NAKED WORLD OF HARRISON MARKS, THE(1967, Brit.); GAMES THAT LOVERS PLAY(1971, Brit.)

Karen Palmer
TAMPICO(1944)

Keith Palmer
I START COUNTING(1970, Brit.), ed; DOOMWATCH(1972, Brit.), ed; S(1974), ed; NOTHING BUT THE NIGHT(1975, Brit.), ed; DEVIL WITHIN HER, THE(1976, Brit.), ed; EMILY(1976, Brit.), ed; WELCOME TO BLOOD CITY(1977, Brit./Can.), ed; QUATERMASS CONCLUSION(1980, Brit.), ed; AMIN-THE RISE AND FALL(1982, Kenya), ed; PRAYING MANTIS(1982, Brit.), ed; LONELY LADY, THE(1983), ed

Leland Palmer
ALL THAT JAZZ(1979)

Leslie Palmer
I TAKE THIS WOMAN(1931); UNFAITHFUL(1931); STRANGERS IN LOVE(1932); MISS FANE'S BABY IS STOLEN(1934)

Lili Palmer
ADORABLE JULIA(1964, Fr./Aust.)

Lilli Palmer
CRIME UNLIMITED(1935, Brit.); FIRST OFFENCE(1936, Brit.); SECRET AGENT, THE(1936, Brit.); WOLF'S CLOTHING(1936, Brit.); COMMAND PERFORMANCE(1937, Brit.); SILENT BARRIERS(1937, Brit.); WHERE THERE'S A WILL(1937, Brit.); MAN WITH 100 FACES, THE(1938, Brit.); BLIND FOLLY(1939, Brit.); SUICIDE LEGION(1940, Brit.); CHAMBER OF HORRORS(1941, Brit.); GIRL MUST LIVE, A(1941, Brit.); GENTLE SEX, THE(1943, Brit.); THUNDER ROCK(1944, Brit.); NOTORIOUS GENTLEMAN(1945, Brit.); BEWARE OF PITY(1946, Brit.); CLOAK AND DAGGER(1946); BODY AND SOUL(1947); MY GIRL TISA(1948); NO MINOR VICES(1948); HER MAN GILBEY(1949, Brit.); LONG DARK HALL, THE(1951, Brit.); FOUR POSTER, THE(1952); MAIN STREET TO BROADWAY(1953); BUT NOT FOR ME(1959); GLASS TOWER, THE(1959, Ger.); BETWEEN TIME AND ETERNITY(1960, Ger.); CONSPIRACY OF HEARTS(1960, Brit.); MRS. WARREN'S PROFESSION(1960, Ger.); LEVIATHAN(1961, Fr.); MODIGLIANI OF MONTPARNASSE(1961, Fr./Ital.); PLEASURE OF HIS COMPANY, THE(1961); COUNTERFEIT TRAITOR, THE(1962); MIDNIGHT MEETING(1962, Fr.); END OF MRS. CHENEY(1963, Ger.); MIRACLE OF THE WHITE STALLIONS(1963); TORPEDO BAY(1964, Ital./Fr.); AMOROUS ADVENTURES OF MOLL FLANDERS, THE(1965); AND SO TO BED(1965, Ger.); MAEDCHEN IN UNIFORM(1965, Ger./Fr.); OPERATION CROSSBOW(1965, U.S./Ital.); JACK OF DIAMONDS(1967, U.S./Ger.); DEVIL IN SILK(1968, Ger.); HIGH COMMISSIONER, THE(1968, U.S./Brit.); OEDIPUS THE KING(1968, Brit.); SEBASTIAN(1968, Brit.); DE SADE(1969); HARD CONTRACT(1969); HOUSE THAT SCREAMED, THE(1970, Span.); MURDERS IN THE RUE MORGUE(1971); NIGHT HAIR CHILD(1971, Brit.); BOYS FROM BRAZIL, THE(1978)

Lisa Palmer
LOVE NOW...PAY LATER(1966)

Lorna Palmer
Misc. Silents
DOUBLE ACTION DANIELS(1925)

Lou Palmer
WINNING(1969)

M.E. Palmer
AFTER OFFICE HOURS(1932, Brit.), ph

Mabelle Palmer
WINGS OVER HONOLULU(1937)

Maria Palmer
MISSION TO MOSCOW(1943); DAYS OF GLORY(1944); LADY ON A TRAIN(1945); RENDEZVOUS 24(1946); OTHER LOVE, THE(1947); WEB, THE(1947); THIRTEEN LEAD SOLDIERS(1948); SURRENDER(1950); STRICTLY DISHONORABLE(1951); BY THE LIGHT OF THE SILVERY MOON(1953); FLIGHT NURSE(1953); THREE FOR JAMIE DAWN(1956); OUTCASTS OF THE CITY(1958); EVIL OF FRANKENSTEIN, THE(1964, Brit.)

Max Palmer
SNIPER, THE(1952); INVADERS FROM MARS(1953); KILLER APE(1953); BIG BLUFF, THE(1955)

May Palmer
Silents
ONE MORE AMERICAN(1918)

Mollie Palmer
GOOD TIME GIRL(1950, Brit.); WHAT THE BUTLER SAW(1950, Brit.); TECKMAN MYSTERY, THE(1955, Brit); KID FOR TWO FARTHINGS, A(1956, Brit.)
Misc. Talkies
UNDEFEATED, THE(1951, Brit.)

Molly Palmer
MAN IN BLACK, THE(1950, Brit.)

Nancy Palmer
Misc. Silents
OUT OF THE FOG(1919)

Nora Palmer
ALIAS BIG SHOT(1962, Argen.)

Norman Palmer
TEN WHO DARED(1960), ed; SHAGGY D.A., THE(1976), ed; ST. IVES(1976); NEW YORK, NEW YORK(1977); MOMMIE DEAREST(1981)

Norman R. Palmer
LEGEND OF LOBO, THE(1962), ed; INCREDIBLE JOURNEY, THE(1963), ed; GNOME-MOBILE, THE(1967), ed; RASCAL(1969), ed; MIDNIGHT MADNESS(1980), ed

Pat Palmer
GODLESS GIRL, THE(1929)

Patricia Palmer
Silents
BY THE WORLD FORGOT(1918); MONEY CORRAL, THE(1919); SAND(1920); MR. BILLINGS SPENDS HIS DIME(1923); WEB OF THE LAW, THE(1923); KING OF KINGS, THE(1927); NAUGHTY NANETTE(1927); LITTLE SAVAGE, THE(1929)
Misc. Silents
HOME TRAIL, THE(1918); FAITH OF THE STRONG(1919); THINGS MEN DO(1921); ACROSS THE BORDER(1922); COWBOY KING, THE(1922); ROUNDING UP THE LAW(1922); PAIR OF HELLIONS, A(1924); WHO'S YOUR FRIEND(1925)

Patrick Palmer
BILLY TWO HATS(1973, Brit.), p; ...AND JUSTICE FOR ALL(1979), p; BEST FRIENDS(1982), p
1984
ICEMAN(1984), p; SOLDIER'S STORY, A(1984), p

Paul Palmer
DANTE'S INFERNO(1935); LOVE CRAZY(1941); FALLEN ANGEL(1945); OUT OF THE BLUE(1947); WALLS OF JERICHO(1948); GAL WHO TOOK THE WEST, THE(1949); MILKMAN, THE(1950)

Penelope Palmer
MALEVIL(1981, Fr./Ger.)

Peter Palmer
LI'L ABNER(1959)

Remzo Palmer
CON MEN, THE(1973, Ital.,Span.)

Reno Palmer
Misc. Talkies
STREET LAW(1981)

Renzo Palmer
BATTLE OF THE WORLDS(1961, Ital.); LA VIACCIA(1962, Fr./Ital.); VISIT, THE(1964, Ger./Fr./Ital./U.S.); FASCIST, THE(1965, Ital.); ENGAGEMENT ITALIANO(1966, Fr./Ital.); WEB OF VIOLENCE(1966, Ital./Span.); BUONA SERA, MRS. CAMPBELL(1968, Ital.); DANGER: DIABOLIK(1968, Ital./Fr.); HOUSE OF CARDS(1969); SEVEN GOLDEN MEN(1969, Fr./Ital./Span.); SPIRITS OF THE DEAD(1969, Fr./Ital.); DETECTIVE BELLI(1970, Ital.); EAGLE OVER LONDON(1973, Ital.); SALAMANDER, THE(1983, U.S./Ital./Brit.)
Misc. Talkies
ANONYMOUS AVENGER, THE(1976, Ital.)

Richard Palmer
TREASURE AT THE MILL(1957, Brit.); WHIRLPOOL(1959, Brit.); FRENCH MISTRESS(1960, Brit.); LAS RATAS NO DUERMEN DE NOCHE(1974, Span./Fr.)

Robert Palmer
THAT HAGEN GIRL(1947); LITTLE SAVAGE, THE(1959); HELLER IN PINK TIGHTS(1960); WHISTLE DOWN THE WIND(1961, Brit.); MUTINY IN OUTER SPACE(1965); DESPERATE ONES, THE(1968 U.S./Span.); SGT. PEPPER'S LONELY HEARTS CLUB BAND(1978)

Roger Palmer
ISABEL(1968, Can.), cos; DR. FRANKENSTEIN ON CAMPUS(1970, Can.), cos

Scott Palmer
92 IN THE SHADE(1975, U.S./Brit.)

Shelton Leigh Palmer
XTRO(1983, Brit.), m
Shirley Palmer
MARRIAGE BY CONTRACT(1928); LADIES MUST PLAY(1930); THIS SPORTING AGE(1932); SOMEWHERE IN SONORA(1933)
Silents
BEAUTIFUL BUT DUMB(1928); SCARLET DOVE, THE(1928); STORMY WATERS(1928); CAMPUS KNIGHTS(1929)
Misc. Silents
WINNING WALLOP, THE(1926); BURNING GOLD(1927); SITTING BULL AT THE "SPIRIT LAKE MASSACRE"(1927); YOURS TO COMMAND(1927); CHEER LEADER, THE(1928)
Sid Palmer
MUSIC HALL PARADE(1939, Brit.)
Stuart Palmer
PENGUIN POOL MURDER, THE(1932), w; MURDER ON THE BLACKBOARD(1934), w; MURDER ON A HONEYMOON(1935), w; NITWITS, THE(1935), w; ONE FRIGHTENED NIGHT(1935), w; MURDER ON A BRIDLE PATH(1936), w; PLOT THICKENS, THE(1936), w; YELLOWSTONE(1936), w; FORTY NAUGHTY GIRLS(1937), w; BULLDOG DRUMMOND'S PERIL(1938), w; HOLLYWOOD STADIUM MYSTERY(1938), w; ARREST BULLDOG DRUMMOND(1939, Brit.), w; BULLDOG DRUMMOND'S BRIDE(1939), w; DEATH OF A CHAMPION(1939), w; EMERGENCY SQUAD(1940), w; OPENED BY MISTAKE(1940), w; SEVENTEEN(1940), w; WHO KILLED AUNT MAGGIE?(1940), w; SECRETS OF THE LONE WOLF(1941), w; SMILING GHOST, THE(1941), w; FALCON'S BROTHER, THE(1942), w; HALF WAY TO SHANGHAI(1942), w; PARDON MY STRIPES(1942), w; X MARKS THE SPOT(1942), w; FALCON STRIKES BACK, THE(1943), w; MURDER IN TIMES SQUARE(1943), w; PETTICOAT LARCENY(1943), w; STEP BY STEP(1946), w; MRS. O'MALLEY AND MR. MALONE(1950), w
Syd Palmer
GANG, THE(1938, Brit.)
Ted Palmer
TRACK THE MAN DOWN(1956, Brit.)
Terry Palmer
BOMB IN THE HIGH STREET(1961, Brit.); MIND BENDERS, THE(1963, Brit.); KING AND COUNTRY(1964, Brit.)
Tex Palmer
RIDING TORNADO, THE(1932); CRASHING BROADWAY(1933); LUCKY TEXAN, THE(1934); RANDY RIDES ALONE(1934); STAR PACKER, THE(1934); WEST OF THE DIVIDE(1934); PARADISE CANYON(1935); RIDER OF THE LAW(1935); FUGITIVE SHERIFF, THE(1936); KING OF THE PECOS(1936); LAWLESS NINETIES, THE(1936); BAR Z BAD MEN(1937); GAMBLING TERROR, THE(1937); GUN LORDS OF STIRRUP BASIN(1937); GUN RANGER, THE(1937); GUNS IN THE DARK(1937); HEADIN' FOR THE RIO GRANDE(1937); LAWMAN IS BORN, A(1937); LIGHTNIN' CRANDALL(1937); MOONLIGHT ON THE RANGE(1937); MYSTERY OF THE HOODED HORSEMEN, THE(1937); RANGERS STEP IN, THE(1937); RECKLESS RANGER(1937); RIDERS OF THE ROCKIES(1937); ROGUE OF THE RANGE(1937); SING, COWBOY, SING(1937); STARS OVER ARIZONA(1937); TRAIL OF VENGEANCE(1937); TRAILING TROUBLE(1937); DANGER VALLEY(1938); DESERT PATROL(1938); FEUD MAKER(1938); IN EARLY ARIZONA(1938); OUTLAW EXPRESS(1938); PALS OF THE SADDLE(1938); PIONEER TRAIL(1938); PRAIRIE JUSTICE(1938); ROLLING CARAVANS(1938); ROMANCE OF THE ROCKIES(1938); STARLIGHT OVER TEXAS(1938); WESTERN TRAILS(1938); LONE STAR PIONEERS(1939); PHANTOM STAGE, THE(1939); KID FROM SANTA FE, THE(1940); LIGHTNING STRIKES WEST(1940); KID'S LAST RIDE, THE(1941); RAWHIDE RANGERS(1941); SADDLE MOUNTAIN ROUNDUP(1941); TONTO BASIN OUTLAWS(1941); TUMBLEDOWN RANCH IN ARIZONA(1941); UNDERGROUND RUSTLERS(1941); WRANGLER'S ROOST(1941); ARIZONA ROUNDUP(1942); FIGHTING BILL FARGO(1942); ROCK RIVER RENEGADES(1942); ROLLING DOWN THE GREAT DIVIDE(1942); TEXAS TO BATAAN(1942); THUNDER RIVER FEUD(1942); TRAIL RIDERS(1942); WESTERN MAIL(1942); WESTWARD HO(1942); HAUNTED RANCH, THE(1943); SILVER CITY RAIDERS(1943); TWO FISTED JUSTICE(1943); WILD HORSE STAMPEDE(1943); OUTLAW TRAIL(1944); RANGE LAW(1944); HAWK OF POWDER RIVER, THE(1948); TIOGA KID, THE(1948); LAW OF THE PANHANDLE(1950)
Texas Palmer
FUZZY SETTLES DOWN(1944)
Tom Palmer
TWO WEEKS IN ANOTHER TOWN(1962); GULLIVER'S TRAVELS(1939), anim d; DAYS OF WINE AND ROSES(1962); ONE MAN'S WAY(1964); GUNN(1967)
Tommy Palmer
WELCOME, MR. WASHINGTON(1944, Brit.)
Toni Palmer
TOO HOT TO HANDLE(1961, Brit.); SMALL WORLD OF SAMMY LEE, THE(1963, Brit.); STRICTLY FOR THE BIRDS(1963, Brit.); JOEY BOY(1965, Brit.); OPERATION SNAFU(1965, Brit.); YELLOW HAT, THE(1966, Brit.); COP-OUT(1967, Brit.); SMASHING TIME(1967 Brit.); FRENCH LIEUTENANT'S WOMAN, THE(1981)
Tony Palmer
TWO HUNDRED MOTELS(1971, Brit.), d&w, ph; WAGNER(1983, Brit./Hung./Aust.), d
Valentine Palmer
YELLOW HAT, THE(1966, Brit.)
Violet Palmer
Silents
NEIGHBORS(1918); ROUGH AND READY(1918); FINGER PRINTS(1923); FIGHTING BOOB, THE(1926); NIGHT LIFE(1927)
Misc. Silents
BLUE STREAK, THE(1917); SLAVE, THE(1917); LIFE OR HONOR?(1918); WOMAN ETERNAL, THE(1918); GINGER(1919); DEVOTION(1921); TANGLED TRAILS(1921)
Virginia Palmer
Misc. Silents
OUTSIDER, THE(1917)
Zoe Palmer
BLARNEY KISS(1933, Brit.)
Silents
WALLS OF PREJUDICE(1920, Brit.); OTHER PERSON, THE(1921, Brit.)
Misc. Silents
BLACK TULIP, THE(1921, Brit.); WAS SHE GUILTY?(1922, Brit.); SWEENEY TODD(1928, Brit.)

Mayta Palmera
LAW OF THE TROPICS(1941); RAIDERS OF THE DESERT(1941); SOUTH OF TAHITI(1941)
Mimi Palmeri
Silents
RAGGED EDGE, THE(1923); IT IS THE LAW(1924); SECOND YOUTH(1924)
Pieor Palmeri
DUEL OF CHAMPIONS(1964 Ital./Span.)
Daniele Palmero
MADE IN U.S.A.(1966, Fr.)
Rafael Palmero
1984
HOLY INNOCENTS, THE(1984, Span.), art d
Emma Palmese
THIS EARTH IS MINE(1959)
Aurore Palmgren
PIMPERNEL SVENSSON(1953, Swed.)
Bert Palmgren
THOSE DARING YOUNG MEN IN THEIR JAUNTY JALOPIES(1969, Fr./Brit./Ital.), ph
Bertil Palmgren
FOREIGN INTRIGUE(1956), ph
Helena Palmgren
WINTER LIGHT, THE(1963, Swed.)
Doriglia Palmi
SEVEN BEAUTIES(1976, Ital.)
Jo Palmie
MY DOG, BUDDY(1960)
Joe Palmiere
FOREPLAY(1975)
Charlie Palmieri
HEROINA(1965), m
Fulvio Palmieri
STORMBOUND(1951, Ital.), w; CONSTANTINE AND THE CROSS(1962, Ital.), w
Joe Palmieri
SCARECROW IN A GARDEN OF CUCUMBERS(1972)
Tony Palmieri
ADIOS AMIGO(1975), ph
Vice Palmieri
HOT TOMORROWS(1978)
Vince Palmieri
LONG GOODBYE, THE(1973); CALIFORNIA SPLIT(1974)
Vincent Palmieri
1984
STRANGERS KISS(1984)
Chazz Palminteri
1984
HOME FREE ALL(1984)
Conrad E. Palmisano
1984
LOVELINES(1984)
Conrad Palmisano
CONCORDE, THE–AIRPORT '79(; PIRANHA(1978), stunts; METEOR(1979); PENNIES FROM HEAVEN(1981)
N. A. Palmisano
WEREWOLVES ON WHEELS(1971)
Nick Palmisano
PIRANHA(1978); METEOR(1979)
Zoe Palmner
Misc. Silents
SERVING TWO MASTERS(1921)
Eduardo Palmos
1984
ALLEY CAT(1984), d
Dan Palmquist
CARNIVAL OF SOULS(1962), a, ed
Gunilla Palmstierna-Weiss
PERSECUTION AND ASSASSINATION OF JEAN-PAUL MARAT AS PERFORMED BY THE INMATES OF THE ASYLUM OF CHARENTON UNDER THE DIRECTION OF THE MARQUIS DE SADE, THE(1967, Brit.), cos
Nadja Palmstjerna-Weiss
1984
AFTER THE REHEARSAL(1984, Swed.)
Carlo Palmucci
LEOPARD, THE(1963, Ital.); DARLING(1965, Brit.); ROMEO AND JULIET(1968, Brit./Ital.)
Leland Palner
VALENTINO(1977, Brit.)
Sam Palo
MYSTERY STREET(1950), makeup
Rosita Palomar
FLAME OVER VIETNAM(1967, Span./Ger.); MINUTE TO PRAY, A SECOND TO DIE, A(1968, Ital.)
Martin Palomares
1984
ERENDIRA(1984, Mex./Fr./Ger.); UNDER THE VOLCANO(1984)
Ada Palombi
MORE THAN A MIRACLE(1967, Ital./Fr.), makeup
Franco Palombi
MY NAME IS PECOS(1966, Ital.), p
Ron Palombo
PUTNEY SWOPE(1969)
Carlos Palomino
DANCE OF THE DWARFS(1983, U.S., Phil.)
1984
STRANGERS KISS(1984)
Carol Palomino
SORCERESS(1983), makeup

Gabriella Palotta
ANNA OF BROOKLYN(1958, Ital.)
Pierre Palov
CHILDREN OF PARADISE(1945, Fr.)
Tom Palozola
Misc. Talkies
CALIGARI'S CURE(1983), d
Pals of the Golden West
RANCHO GRANDE(1940); STAGE TO CHINO(1940); SILVER BULLET, THE(1942)
The Pals of the Golden West
BOSS OF HANGTOWN MESA(1942)
Nani Palsa
WHITE HEAT(1934)
Tove Palsbo
JOURNEY TO THE SEVENTH PLANET(1962, U.S./Swed.), ed
Fred Palsey
SCARFACE(1932), w
Nan Palshikar
MAYA(1966)
Nana Palsikar
GURU, THE(1969, U.S./India)
Sigurdur Sverrir Palsson
OUTLAW: THE SAGE OF GISLI(1982, Iceland), ph
David Paltenghi
QUEEN OF SPADES(1948, Brit.), a, ch; SLEEPING CAR TO TRIESTE(1949, Brit.); SWORD AND THE ROSE, THE(1953), ch; BLACK KNIGHT, THE(1954), a, ch; YOU KNOW WHAT SAILORS ARE(1954, Brit.), ch; LOVE MATCH, THE(1955, Brit.), d; KEEP IT CLEAN(1956, Brit.), d; PORT AFRIQUE(1956, Brit.), ch; ORDERS ARE ORDERS(1959, Brit.), d
Lew Palter
STEAGLE, THE(1971); FIRST MONDAY IN OCTOBER(1981)
Anita Paltrinieri
END OF THE WORLD(in Our Usual Bed In a Night Full of Rain), THE (1978, Ital.)
Medusa Paltrinieri
PIRANHA II: THE SPAWNING(1981, Neth.), art d
Bruce Paltrow
LITTLE SEX, A(1982), p, d
Robert Paltz
PROJECT MOONBASE(1953)
Ivo Paluch
MARKETA LAZAROVA(1968, Czech.)
Richard Paluck
MELANIE(1982, Can.), w
Ezra Paluette
LAW FOR TOMBSTONE(1937)
Albino Palumbo
JONAH–WHO WILL BE 25 IN THE YEAR 2000(1976, Switz.)
Dennis Palumbo
MY FAVORITE YEAR(1982), w
Dolores Palumbo
NEOPOLITAN CAROUSEL(1961, Ital.); VERY HANDY MAN, A(1966, Fr./Ital.)
Vera Palumbo
LUXURY GIRLS(1953, Ital.)
Luciana Paluzzi
TANK FORCE(1958, Brit.); SEA FURY(1959, Brit.); RETURN TO PEYTON PLACE(1961); RELUCTANT SAINT, THE(1962, U.S./Ital.); MUSCLE BEACH PARTY(1964); THUNDERBALL(1965, Brit.); VICE AND VIRTUE(1965, Fr./Ital.); TO TRAP A SPY(1966); CHUKA(1967); MY WIFE'S ENEMY(1967, Ital.); ONE-EYED SOLDIERS(1967, U.S./Brit./Yugo.); VENETIAN AFFAIR, THE(1967); NO ROSES FOR OSS 117(1968, Fr.); BLACK VEIL FOR LISA, A(1969 Ital./Ger.); CAPTAIN NEMO AND THE UNDERWATER CITY(1969, Brit.); GREEN SLIME, THE(1969); COMETOGETHER(1971); BLACK GUNN(1972); ITALIAN CONNECTION, THE(1973, U.S./Ital./Ger.); KLANSMAN, THE(1974); GREEK TYCOON, THE(1978)
Misc. Talkies
99 WOMEN(1969, Brit./Span./Ger./Ital.); SOLDIER NAMED JOE, A(1970); MEAN MOTHER(1974)
Kelly Palzis
10 TO MIDNIGHT(1983)
Pam
DUSTY AND SWEETS McGEE(1971)
Giuseppi Pambieri
WOLF LARSEN(1978, Ital.)
Shashi Pameholi
NINE HOURS TO RAMA(1963, U.S./Brit.)
Carlo Pammucci
BURN(1970)
Colombo Pamolli
HELL RAIDERS OF THE DEEP(1954, Ital.)
Silvana Pampanini
ANTHONY OF PADUA(1952, Ital.); GUNS OF THE BLACK WITCH(1961, Fr./Ital.); DAY IN COURT, A(1965, Ital.)
Misc. Talkies
ORIENT EXPRESS(1952)
Lilo Pampeit
WHY DOES HERR R. RUN AMOK?(1977, Ger.)
Mirella Pamphili
JOHNNY YUMA(1967, Ital.); OPERATION KID BROTHER(1967, Ital.); PAYMENT IN BLOOD(1968, Ital.); GIRL WHO COULDN'T SAY NO, THE(1969, Ital.); PLACE FOR LOVERS, A(1969, Ital./Fr.); SWEET BODY OF DEBORAH, THE(1969, Ital./Fr.); VENUS IN FURS(1970, Ital./Brit./Ger.)
Louis Pampino
UNHOLY ROLLERS(1972)
Joaquim Pamplona
TRISTANA(1970, Span./Ital./Fr.)
Eva Pampuch
WHY DOES HERR R. RUN AMOK?(1977, Ger.)
Hermes Pan
GAY DIVORCEE, THE(1934), ch; I DREAM TOO MUCH(1935), ch; IN PERSON(1935), ch; OLD MAN RHYTHM(1935), ch; ROBERTA(1935), ch; TOP HAT(1935), ch; FOLLOW THE FLEET(1936), ch; SWING TIME(1936), ch; WOMAN REBELS, A(1936), ch; DAMSEL IN DISTRESS, A(1937), ch; SHALL WE DANCE(1937), ch; CAREFREE(1938), ch; RADIO CITY REVELS(1938), ch; STORY OF VERNON AND IRENE CASTLE, THE(1939), ch; SECOND CHORUS(1940), ch; BLOOD AND SAND(1941), ch; MOON OVER MIAMI(1941), ch; RISE AND SHINE(1941), ch; SUN VALLEY SERENADE(1941), ch; THAT NIGHT IN RIO(1941), ch; WEEKEND IN HAVANA(1941), ch; FOOTLIGHT SERENADE(1942), ch; MY GAL SAL(1942), a, ch; ROXIE HART(1942), ch; SONG OF THE ISLANDS(1942), ch; SPRINGTIME IN THE ROCKIES(1942), ch; CONEY ISLAND(1943), ch; HELLO, FRISCO, HELLO(1943), ch; SWEET ROSIE O'GRADY(1943), ch; IRISH EYES ARE SMILING(1944), ch; PIN UP GIRL(1944), a, ch; DIAMOND HORSESHOE(1945), ch; BLUE SKIES(1946), ch; I WONDER WHO'S KISSING HER NOW(1947), ch; SHOCKING MISS PILGRIM, THE(1947), ch; THAT LADY IN ERMINE(1948), ch; BARKLEYS OF BROADWAY, THE(1949), ch; LET'S DANCE(1950), ch; LIFE OF HER OWN, A(1950); THREE LITTLE WORDS(1950), ch; EXCUSE MY DUST(1951), ch; TEXAS CARNIVAL(1951), ch; LOVELY TO LOOK AT(1952), ch; KISS ME KATE(1953), a, ch; SOMBRERO(1953), ch; STUDENT PRINCE, THE(1954), ch; HIT THE DECK(1955), ch; JUPITER'S DARLING(1955), ch; MEET ME IN LAS VEGAS(1956), ch; PAL JOEY(1957), a, ch; SILK STOCKINGS(1957), ch; BLUE ANGEL, THE(1959), ch; NEVER STEAL ANYTHING SMALL(1959), ch; PORGY AND BESS(1959), ch; CAN-CAN(1960), ch; FLOWER DRUM SONG(1961), ch; PLEASURE OF HIS COMPANY, THE(1961), ch; CLEOPATRA(1963), ch; MY FAIR LADY(1964), ch; PINK PANTHER, THE(1964), ch; GREAT RACE, THE(1965), ch; FINIAN'S RAINBOW(1968), ch; DARLING LILI(1970), ch; LOST HORIZON(1973), ch
Ingrid Pan
WHITE HORSE INN, THE(1959, Ger.)
Lucien Pan
FLIGHT TO FURY(1966, U.S./Phil.)
Misc. Talkies
OMEGANS, THE(1968)
Peter Pan
DEATH WISH II(1982)
1984
PROTOCOL(1984)
Pan African People's Arkestra
PASSING THROUGH(1977), m
Pan Panagiotopoulos
OEDIPUS THE KING(1968, Brit.)
Michael Panaieff
LADY, LET'S DANCE(1944), ch; NIGHT AND DAY(1946); PRIZE, THE(1963)
Michel Panaieff
MISSION TO MOSCOW(1943); GABY(1956), ch
Ika Panajotovic
OPERATION CROSS EAGLES(1969, U.S./Yugo.), p
Juan Panalle
SPECTER OF THE ROSE(1946)
Frank Panama
ABOVE AND BEYOND(1953), w
Fred Saidy Norman Panama
STAR SPANGLED RHYTHM(1942), w
Norman Panama
MY FAVORITE BLONDE(1942), w; HAPPY GO LUCKY(1943), w; THANK YOUR LUCKY STARS(1943), w; AND THE ANGELS SING(1944), w; DUFFY'S TAVERN(1945), w; ROAD TO UTOPIA(1945), w; MONSIEUR BEAUCAIRE(1946), w; OUR HEARTS WERE GROWING UP(1946), w; IT HAD TO BE YOU(1947), w; MR. BLANDINGS BUILDS HIS DREAM HOUSE(1948), p, w; RETURN OF OCTOBER, THE(1948), w; SOUTHERN YANKEE, A(1948), w; REFORMER AND THE REDHEAD, THE(1950), p,d&w; CALLAWAY WENT THATAWAY(1951), p,d&w; STRICTLY DISHONORABLE(1951), p,d&w; ABOVE AND BEYOND(1953), p&d; KNOCK ON WOOD(1954), p,d&w; WHITE CHRISTMAS(1954), w; COURT JESTER, THE(1956), p,d&w; THAT CERTAIN FEELING(1956), p&d, w; JAYHAWKERS, THE(1959), p; LI'L ABNER(1959), p, w; TRAP, THE(1959), p, d, w; FACTS OF LIFE, THE(1960), p, w; ROAD TO HONG KONG, THE(1962, U.S./Brit.), d, w; STRANGE BEDFELLOWS(1965), w; NOT WITH MY WIFE, YOU DON'T!(1966), p&d, w; HOW TO COMMIT MARRIAGE(1969), d; MALTESE BIPPY, THE(1969), d; I WILL ...I WILL ...FOR NOW(1976), d, w
Darshana Panangala
1984
INDIANA JONES AND THE TEMPLE OF DOOM(1984)
Alessandra Panaro
ROCCO AND HIS BROTHERS(1961, Fr./Ital.); BACCHANTES, THE(1963, Fr./Ital.); SECRET MARK OF D'ARTAGNAN, THE(1963, Fr./Ital.); SON OF CAPTAIN BLOOD, THE(1964, U.S./Ital./Span.); CONQUEST OF MYCENE(1965, Ital., Fr.)
Maria Luisa Panaro
CAESAR THE CONQUEROR(1963, Ital.), cos; THIS MAN CAN'T DIE(1970, Ital.), cos
Alex Panas
SPRING BREAK(1983)
Alexander Panas
MAN IN THE WATER, THE(1963); HONEYMOON OF HORROR(1964), a, w
N. Panasyev
TRAIN GOES TO KIEV, THE(1961, USSR)
A. Panasyuk
GIRL AND THE BUGLER, THE(1967, USSR), ph
Cosmos Panayotidis
ISLAND OF LOVE(1963)
Kakia Panayotou
STEFANIA(1968, Gr.)
Roger Pancake
MACON COUNTY LINE(1974), art d; WHERE THE RED FERN GROWS(1974); SEVEN ALONE(1975); CAT FROM OUTER SPACE, THE(1978); I WANNA HOLD YOUR HAND(1978); CHINA SYNDROME, THE(1979)
Anna Maria Pancani
LE AMICHE(1962, Ital.)
Mario Navarro Panchito
BEAST OF HOLLOW MOUNTAIN, THE(1956)
Al Panci
HOTEL VARIETY(1933), art d
Silents
SUMMER BACHELORS(1926), set d

Baseo Panday
NINE HOURS TO RAMA(1963, U.S./Brit.)
Alexandra Pandev
1984
CHEECH AND CHONG'S THE CORSICAN BROTHERS(1984)
K. S. Pandey
APARAJITO(1959, India)
Arjun Pandher
1984
INDIANA JONES AND THE TEMPLE OF DOOM(1984)
Korla Pandit
SOMETHING TO LIVE FOR(1952); WHICH WAY IS UP?(1977)
Shanti Pandit
MEN AGAINST THE SUN(1953, Brit.)
Elio Pandolfi
TIMES GONE BY(1953, Ital.); SON OF THE RED CORSAIR(1963, Ital.); PRIEST OF LOVE(1981, Brit.)
Vincent Pandoliano
LIQUID SKY(1982)
Pandopoulos
SERENITY(1962)
Miriam Pandor
JUST FOR YOU(1952)
Leif Panduro
EPILOGUE(1967, Den.), w; ONLY WAY, THE(1970, Panama/Den./U.S.), w
Bob Pane
PAJAMA PARTY(1964)
Alberto Panella
POLYESTER(1981)
Alessandra Panelli
CITY OF WOMEN(1980, Ital./Fr.)
Paolo Panelli
ASSASSIN, THE(1961, Ital./Fr.); TWELVE-HANDED MEN OF MARS, THE(1964, Ital./Span.)
Rolando Panerai
LA BOHEME(1965, Ital.)
Tony Panetta
NUNZIO(1978)
Mariella Panfili
KILL BABY KILL(1966, Ital.)
Eddie Pang
HAWAIIANS, THE(1970)
Peter Pang
SAINT JACK(1979)
Franklin Pangborn
ON TRIAL(1928); LADY OF THE PAVEMENTS(1929); SAP, THE(1929); CHEER UP AND SMILE(1930); HER MAN(1930); LADY SURRENDERS, A(1930); NOT SO DUMB(1930); WOMAN OF EXPERIENCE, A(1931); DESIGN FOR LIVING(1933); FLYING DOWN TO RIO(1933); HEADLINE SHOOTER(1933); IMPORTANT WITNESS, THE(1933); INTERNATIONAL HOUSE(1933); ONLY YESTERDAY(1933); PROFESSIONAL SWEETHEART(1933); SWEEPINGS(1933); COLLEGE RHYTHM(1934); IMITATION OF LIFE(1934); KING KELLY OF THE U.S.A(1934); MANHATTAN LOVE SONG(1934); MANY HAPPY RETURNS(1934); STRICTLY DYNAMITE(1934); THAT'S GRATITUDE(1934); UNKNOWN BLONDE(1934); YOUNG AND BEAUTIFUL(1934); EIGHT BELLS(1935); HEADLINE WOMAN, THE(1935); SHE COULDN'T TAKE IT(1935); TOMORROW'S YOUTH(1935); $1,000 A MINUTE(1935); DON'T GAMBLE WITH LOVE(1936); DOUGHNUTS AND SOCIETY(1936); MR. DEEDS GOES TO TOWN(1936); MY MAN GODFREY(1936); TANGO(1936); TO MARY-WITH LOVE(1936); ALL OVER TOWN(1937); DANGEROUS HOLIDAY(1937); EASY LIVING(1937); HIGH HAT(1937); HOTEL HAYWIRE(1937); I'LL TAKE ROMANCE(1937); IT HAPPENED IN HOLLYWOOD(1937); LADY ESCAPES, THE(1937); LIFE OF THE PARTY, THE(1937); LIVING ON LOVE(1937); LOVE ON TOAST(1937); MANDARIN MYSTERY, THE(1937); SHE HAD TO EAT(1937); SHE'S DANGEROUS(1937); STAGE DOOR(1937); STAR IS BORN, A(1937); STEP LIVELY, JEEVES(1937); SWING HIGH, SWING LOW(1937); THREE SMART GIRLS(1937); THRILL OF A LIFETIME(1937); TURN OFF THE MOON(1937); WE HAVE OUR MOMENTS(1937); ALWAYS GOODBYE(1938); CAREFREE(1938); DR. RHYTHM(1938); FOUR'S A CROWD(1938); GIRL DOWNSTAIRS, THE(1938); JOY OF LIVING(1938); JUST AROUND THE CORNER(1938); MAD ABOUT MUSIC(1938); MEET THE MAYOR(1938); REBECCA OF SUNNYBROOK FARM(1938); SHE MARRIED AN ARTIST(1938); THREE BLIND MICE(1938); VIVACIOUS LADY(1938); BROADWAY SERENADE(1939); FIFTH AVENUE GIRL(1939); TOPPER TAKES A TRIP(1939); BANK DICK, THE(1940); CHRISTMAS IN JULY(1940); HIT PARADE OF 1941(1940); PUBLIC DEB NO. 1(1940); SPRING PARADE(1940); TURNABOUT(1940); VILLAIN STILL PURSUED HER, THE(1940); BACHELOR DADDY(1941); FLAME OF NEW ORLEANS, THE(1941); GIRL, A GUY AND A GOB, A(1941); NEVER GIVE A SUCKER AN EVEN BREAK(1941); OBLIGING YOUNG LADY(1941); SULLIVAN'S TRAVELS(1941); TILLIE THE TOILER(1941); WEEKEND FOR THREE(1941); WHERE DID YOU GET THAT GIRL?(1941); CALL OUT THE MARINES(1942); GEORGE WASHINGTON SLEPT HERE(1942); MOONLIGHT MASQUERADE(1942); NOW, VOYAGER(1942); PALM BEACH STORY, THE(1942); STRICTLY IN THE GROOVE(1942); WHAT'S COOKIN'?(1942); ALLERGIC TO LOVE(1943); CRAZY HOUSE(1943); HIS BUTLER'S SISTER(1943); HOLY MATRIMONY(1943); HONEYMOON LODGE(1943); NEVER A DULL MOMENT(1943); REVEILLE WITH BEVERLY(1943); STAGE DOOR CANTEEN(1943); TWO WEEKS TO LIVE(1943); GREAT MOMENT, THE(1944); HAIL THE CONQUERING HERO(1944); MY BEST GAL(1944); RECKLESS AGE(1944); HORN BLOWS AT MIDNIGHT, THE(1945); SEE MY LAWYER(1945); TELL IT TO A STAR(1945); YOU CAME ALONG(1945); LOVER COME BACK(1946); CALENDAR GIRL(1947); CARTER CASE, THE(1947); I'LL BE YOURS(1947); ROMANCE ON THE HIGH SEAS(1948); DOWN MEMORY LANE(1949); MY DREAM IS YOURS(1949); MAD WEDNESDAY(1950); OH, MEN! OH, WOMEN!(1957); STORY OF MANKIND, THE(1957)
Silents
EXIT SMILING(1926); NIGHT BRIDE, THE(1927)
Misc. Silents
CRADLE SNATCHERS, THE(1927); GIRL IN THE PULLMAN, THE(1927); MY FRIEND FROM INDIA(1927); REJUVINATION OF AUNT MARY, THE(1927); BLONDE FOR A NIGHT, A(1928)

Franklyn Pangborn
COCKEYED CAVALIERS(1934); DANGEROUS NUMBER(1937); HATS OFF(1937); HOLLYWOOD AND VINE(1945)
Andreas Pangritz
CHRONICLE OF ANNA MAGDALENA BACH(1968, Ital., Ger.)
Susan Panhaligon
PRIVATE ROAD(1971, Brit.)
Corrada Pani
LA GRANDE BOURGEOISE(1977, Ital.)
Corrado Pani
GIRL WITH A SUITCASE(1961, Fr./Ital.); ROCCO AND HIS BROTHERS(1961, Fr./Ital.); WHITE NIGHTS(1961, Ital./Fr.); CLEOPATRA'S DAUGHTER(1963, Fr., Ital.); RUN WITH THE DEVIL(1963, Fr./Ital.); DRAMA OF THE RICH(1975, Ital./Fr.)
C. Paniagua
MATHIAS SANDORF(1963, Fr.), ph
Cecilio Paniagua
REVOLT OF THE SLAVES, THE(1961, Ital./Span./Ger.), ph; COMMANDO(1962, Ital., Span., Bel., Ger.), ph; CUSTER OF THE WEST(1968, U.S., Span.), ph; DR. COPPELIUS(1968, U.S./Span.), ph; ISLAND OF THE DOOMED(1968, Span./Ger.), ph; 100 RIFLES(1969), ph; TREASURE ISLAND(1972, Brit./Span./Fr./Ger.), ph; HUNTING PARTY, THE(1977, Brit.), ph
Cecillo Paniagua
MYSTERIOUS HOUSE OF DR. C., THE(1976), ph
Igor Panich
1984
MOSCOW ON THE HUDSON(1984)
Anna Paniez
GREEN ROOM, THE(1979, Fr.)
Jean Panisse
CHARLES AND LUCIE(1982, Fr.)
Patrick Pankhurst
1984
HOUSE WHERE DEATH LIVES, THE(1984)
Stuart Pankin
SCAVENGER HUNT(1979); HANGAR 18(1980); HOLLYWOOD KNIGHTS, THE(1980); EARTHBOUND(1981)
1984
IRRECONCILABLE DIFFERENCES(1984)
Tom Panko
MUSIC MAN, THE(1962), ch; THEY SHOOT HORSES, DON'T THEY?(1969), ch
Bill Pankow
1984
BODY DOUBLE(1984), ed
John Pankow
HUNGER, THE(1983)
Patrick Pankurst
HALLOWEEN III: SEASON OF THE WITCH(1982)
Piero Panli
ROSSINI(1948, Ital.)
Tony Michael Pann
WARRIORS, THE(1979)
Tony Pann
SCARFACE(1983)
William Pannell
NORMA RAE(1979)
Frank T. Panno
1984
GRANDVIEW, U.S.A.(1984)
Nick Pannone
1984
FIRST TURN-ON!, THE(1984)
Mario Pannunzio
GREATEST LOVE, THE(1954, Ital.), w
Dimiter Panoff
FOUNTAIN OF LOVE, THE(1968, Aust.)
Katy Panos
ANNA OF RHODES(1950, Gr.)
Ketty Panou
MATCHMAKING OF ANNA, THE(1972, Gr.)
Nick Panouzis
DELIRIUM(1979)
Nikolai Panov
Misc. Silents
WOMAN WITH A DAGGER(1916, USSR); BLOOD NEED NOT BE SPILLED(1917, USSR); HER SACRIFICE(1917, USSR); POWER OF DARKNESS, THE(1918, USSR); LOCKSMITH AND CHANCELLOR(1923, USSR); TRAITOR(1926, USSR)
Valeri Panov
SLEEPING BEAUTY, THE(1966, USSR)
A. Panova
SUMMER TO REMEMBER, A(1961, USSR); RESURRECTION(1963, USSR)
Alexandra Panova
LUCKY BRIDE, THE(1948, USSR)
L. Panova
SANDU FOLLOWS THE SUN(1965, USSR)
Vera Panova
SUMMER TO REMEMBER, A(1961, USSR), w
Rose Pansano
HUCKLEBERRY FINN(1974)
Ed Pansullo
1984
REPO MAN(1984)
Eddie Pansullo
1984
SCARRED(1984)
Pansy
Silents
IS DIVORCE A FAILURE?(1923)

Pansy the Horse
TAKE IT BIG(1944)
Lou Pant
POM POM GIRLS, THE(1976)
Lloyd Pantages
DANTE'S INFERNO(1935)
Det. Pantane
LAST FIGHT, THE(1983)
Tony Pantanello
NIGHT OF THE LIVING DEAD(1968), spec eff
Nicholas Pantano
1984
BROADWAY DANNY ROSE(1984)
Rocco Pantano
1984
BROADWAY DANNY ROSE(1984)
Bruno W. Pantel
THOUSAND EYES OF DR. MABUSE, THE(1960, Fr./Ital./Ger.); SHERLOCK
HOLMES AND THE DEADLY NECKLACE(1962, Ger.)
Alexander Panteleyev
Misc. Silents
CONGESTION(1918, USSR), d; INFINITE SORROW(1922, USSR), d; MIRACLE-
MAKER(1922, USSR), d
T. Panteleyeva
MEET ME IN MOSCOW(1966, USSR), makeup
Andy Pantelidou
YANKS(1979)
Bruno W. Pantell
ESCAPE FROM EAST BERLIN(1962)
Peter Pantellic
PIRATE MOVIE, THE(1982, Aus.)
Malou Pantera
VIOLENT STRANGER(1957, Brit.); FEMALE FIENDS(1958, Brit.); HORRORS OF
THE BLACK MUSEUM(1959, U.S./Brit.); ELECTRONIC MONSTER. THE(1960, Brit.);
TRANSATLANTIC(1961, Brit.); SEPARATION(1968, Brit.)
Joe Pantoliano
IDOLMAKER, THE(1980); MONSIGNOR(1982); EDDIE AND THE CRUISERS(1983);
FINAL TERROR, THE(1983); RISKY BUSINESS(1983)
Buddy Pantsari
CAPTAIN MILKSHAKE(1970); TRADER HORNEE(1970)
Buddy Pantsary
LIMIT, THE(1972)
Pinyo Panui
1 2 3 MONSTER EXPRESS(1977, Thai.)
Ron Panvini
PEOPLE NEXT DOOR, THE(1970)
Rich Panzarella
CIRCLE OF DECEIT(1982, Fr./Ger.)
Sola Panzdrovna
Misc. Silents
CALIBRE 38(1919)
Paul Panze
WHOOPEE(1930)
Paul Panzer
THREE FACES EAST(1930); CAVALIER OF THE WEST(1931); DEFENDERS OF
THE LAW(1931); FIRST AID(1931); MONTANA KID, THE(1931); SEA DEVILS(1931);
MAN WHO PLAYED GOD, THE(1932); BEDTIME STORY, A(1933); BOLERO(1934);
CAT'S PAW, THE(1934); JOURNAL OF A CRIME(1934); LAND BEYOND THE
LAW(1937); PRAIRIE THUNDER(1937); SMART BLONDE(1937); PORT OF SEVEN
SEAS(1938); BEASTS OF BERLIN(1939); IDIOT'S DELIGHT(1939); KING OF THE
UNDERWORLD(1939); SECRET SERVICE OF THE AIR(1939); MURDER IN THE
AIR(1940); MEET JOHN DOE(1941); SHE COULDN'T SAY NO(1941); UNDER-
GROUND(1941); SHINE ON, HARVEST MOON(1944); UNCERTAIN GLORY(1944);
HOTEL BERLIN(1945); MILDRED PIERCE(1945); STOLEN LIFE, A(1946); CRY
WOLF(1947); PERILS OF PAULINE, THE(1947); STALLION ROAD(1947); KISS IN
THE DARK, A(1949); NIGHT UNTO NIGHT(1949)
Silents
LAST VOLUNTEER, THE(1914); WHEN ROME RULED(1914); ELUSIVE ISA-
BEL(1916); WHEN KNIGHTHOOD WAS IN FLOWER(1922); ENEMIES OF WOMEN,
THE(1923); JACQUELINE, OR BLAZING BARRIERS(1923); UNDER THE RED
ROBE(1923); ANCIENT MARINER, THE(1925); JOHNSTOWN FLOOD, THE(1926);
SIBERIA(1926); GIRL FROM CHICAGO, THE(1927); SALLY IN OUR ALLEY(1927);
WOLF'S CLOTHING(1927)
Misc. Silents
WHO'S YOUR BROTHER?(1919); BOOTLEGGERS, THE(1922); FOOL, THE(1925);
THUNDER MOUNTAIN(1925); RINTY OF THE DESERT(1928)
William N. Panzer
DEATH COLLECTOR(1976), p; STEEL(1980), p, w; O'HARA'S WIFE(1983), p; OST-
ERMAN WEEKEND, THE(1983), p
William Panzer
STUNTS(1977), p
Sandro Panzeri
SOUND OF TRUMPETS, THE(1963, Ital.)
Jose Panzio
ROYAL HUNT OF THE SUN, THE(1969, Brit.)
Kao Pao-shu
LOVE ETERNE, THE(1964, Hong Kong)
Gilbert Paol
TENDER IS THE NIGHT(1961)
Frank Paolasso
DOGS(1976)
Domenico Paolella
GRAN VARIETA(1955, Ital.), d, w; REBEL GLADIATORS, THE(1963, Ital.), d, w;
HATE FOR HATE(1967, Ital.), d, w; DIARY OF A CLOISTERED NUN(1973, Ital./Fr./
Ger.), d, w
Giorgio Paoletti
SACCO AND VANZETTI(1971, Ital./Fr.)

Marco Paoletti
TEACHER AND THE MIRACLE, THE(1961, Ital./Span.); LAZARILLO(1963, Span.);
SAUL AND DAVID(1968, Ital./Span.)
Roberto Paoletti
EVA(1962, Fr./Ital.)
Tonino Paoletti
MASOCH(1980, Ital.), p
Deno Paoli
SANTEE(1973), p
Gino Paoli
BEFORE THE REVOLUTION(1964, Ital.), m
Luciana Paoli
CASANOVA '70(1965, Ital.)
Raoul Paoli
SAFETY IN NUMBERS(1930)
Silents
COWARD, THE(1927); KIT CARSON(1928); NIGHT OF MYSTERY, A(1928); OLYM-
PIC HERO, THE(1928); WOMAN WISE(1928)
Germana Paolieri
DISILLUSION(1949, Ital.); MONSTER OF THE ISLAND(1953, Ital.)
Germanin Paolieri
DREAM OF BUTTERFLY, THE(1941, Ital.)
Luigi Paolillo
JOAN AT THE STAKE(1954, Ital./Fr.)
Bruno Paolinelli
ANGELS OF DARKNESS(1956, Ital.), w
Christine Paolini
HATTER'S GHOST, THE(1982, Fr.)
Paolo Paolini
AND THE SHIP SAILS ON(1983, Ital./Fr.)
Paolo
PADRE PADRONE(1977, Ital.), titles
Catherine Paolone
HEART LIKE A WHEEL(1983)
Elvira Paoloni
APE WOMAN, THE(1964, Ital.)
Omero Paoloni
UNDER THE SUN OF ROME(1949, Ital.)
Eduardo Paolozzi
TOGETHER(1956, Brit.)
Giovanni Paolucci
MONTE CASSINO(1948, Ital.), w; WASTREL, THE(1963, Ital.), d
Luciana Paoluzzi
PLEASE! MR. BALZAC(1957, Fr.); JOURNEY TO THE LOST CITY(1960, Ger./Fr./
Ital.); MAN IN A COCKED HAT(1960, Bri.)
Lucianna Paoluzzi "Paluzzi"
MY SEVEN LITTLE SINS(1956, Fr./Ital.)
Andy Pap
LAST ESCAPE, THE(1970, Brit.)
Annie Papa
MONSIGNOR(1982)
Anny Papa
END OF THE WORLD(in Our Usual Bed In a Night Full of Rain), THE (1978, Ital.)
Sal Papa
ENSIGN PULVER(1964)
Dimitri Papacostandis
SUMMER LOVERS(1982), ph
Niki Papadatou
AUNT FROM CHICAGO(1960, Gr.)
Anne Marie Papadelis
1984
BLIND DATE(1984), prod d,set d&cos
John Papadopoulos
MATCHLESS(1974, Aus.), p&d
Panos Papadopoulos
JOURNEY TO THE LOST CITY(1960, Ger./Fr./Ital.); FOR A FEW DOLLARS
MORE(1967, Ital./Ger./Span.)
Zanino Papadopoulos
NAKED BRIGADE, THE(1965, U.S./Gr.)
Maja Papadopulo
ENGLANO MADE ME(1973, Brit.)
Panos Papadopulos
FEDORA(1978, Ger./Fr.)
Olympia Papadouka
PHAEDRA(1962, U.S./Gr./Fr.); DREAM OF PASSION, A(1978, Gr.)
Spyros Papafrantzis
1984
BLIND DATE(1984)
Margarita Papageorgiou
AUNT FROM CHICAGO(1960, Gr.)
D. Papagianopoulos
LISA, TOSCA OF ATHENS(1961, Gr.); POLICEMAN OF THE 16TH PRECINCT,
THE(1963, Gr.)
Dino Papagianopoulos
YOU CAME TOO LATE(1962, Gr.)
Panos Papaioannou
DREAM OF PASSION, A(1978, Gr.)
Nicholas Papakonstantinou
300 SPARTANS, THE(1962); NAKED BRIGADE, THE(1965, U.S./Gr.)
Kostas Papakonstantinou
YOUNG APHRODITES(1966, Gr.); DAY THE FISH CAME OUT, THE(1967. Brit./Gr.)
Nicholas Papakonstantinou
GUNS OF NAVARONE, THE(1961)
Demetris Papakonstantis
HOT MONTH OF AUGUST, THE(1969, Gr.), ph; SISTERS, THE(1969, Gr.), ph
Mike Papalexis
SERENITY(1962)

Joe Papalimu
WHEN TIME RAN OUT(1980)
George Papalios
DAYS OF 36(1972, Gr.), p
P. Papaloukas
ANNA OF RHODES(1950, Gr.), w
Dimitris Papamichael
MIDWIFE, THE(1961, Greece); MADALENA(1965, Gr.); RED LANTERNS(1965, Gr.); DREAM OF PASSION, A(1978, Gr.)
Phedon Papamichael
FACES(1968), art d; RED, WHITE AND BLACK, THE(1970), art d&set d; WOMAN UNDER THE INFLUENCE, A(1974), art d; KILLING OF A CHINESE BOOKIE, THE(1976), art d
1984
LOVE STREAMS(1984), a, art d
Dimitrios Papamichail
AUNT FROM CHICAGO(1960, Gr.)
Dimitri Papamikail
NEVER ON SUNDAY(1960, Gr.)
Tatiana Papamoskou
IPHIGENIA(1977, Gr.)
Alex Papana
ABOVE SUSPICION(1943); SONG OF BERNADETTE, THE(1943); PURPLE HEART, THE(1944)
Alex Papanao
PASSAGE TO MARSEILLE(1944)
Anatoliy Papanov
SANDU FOLLOWS THE SUN(1965, USSR); UNCOMMON THIEF, AN(1967, USSR)
Miguel Paparelli
HEAT(1970, Arg.)
Irene Papas
MAN FROM CAIRO, THE(1953); TRIBUTE TO A BADMAN(1956); ATTILA(1958, Ital.); UNFAITHFULS, THE(1960, Ital.); GUNS OF NAVARONE, THE(1961); ANTIGONE(1962 Gr.); ELECTRA(1962, Gr.); MOON-SPINNERS, THE(1964); ZORBA THE GREEK(1964, U.S./Gr.); WE STILL KILL THE OLD WAY(1967, Ital.); WITNESS OUT OF HELL(1967, Ger./Yugo.); BROTHERHOOD, THE(1968); DESPERATE ONES, THE(1968 U.S./Span.); ANNE OF THE THOUSAND DAYS(1969, Brit.); DREAM OF KINGS, A(1969); N. P.(1971, Ital.); TROJAN WOMEN, THE(1971); MOHAMMAD, MESSENGER OF GOD(1976, Lebanon/Brit.); MOSES(1976, Brit./Ital.); IPHIGENIA(1977, Gr.); BLOODLINE(1979); EBOLI(1980, Ital.); LION OF THE DESERT(1981, Libya/Brit.)
1984
ERENDIRA(1984, Mex./Fr./Ger.)
Misc. Talkies
1931, ONCE UPON A TIME IN NEW YORK(1972); OASIS OF FEAR(1973)
Kostas Papas
CANNON AND THE NIGHTINGALE, THE(1969, Gr.)
Michael Papas
PRIVATE RIGHT, THE(1967, Brit.), p,d&w
George Papashvily
ANYTHING CAN HAPPEN(1952), w
Helen Papashvily
ANYTHING CAN HAPPEN(1952), w
Nico Papatakis
LES ABYSSES(1964, Fr.), p&d; THANOS AND DESPINA(1970, Fr./Gr.), d, w
Van Gelis Papathanassiou
CRIME AND PASSION(1976, U.S., Ger.), m
Vangelis Papathanassiou
CHARRIOTS OF FIRE(1981, Brit.), m
Mikhail Papava
MY NAME IS IVAN(1963, USSR), w
Robert A. Papazian
COFFY(1973), p
Lionel Pape
MAN WHO BROKE THE BANK AT MONTE CARLO, THE(1935); TWO FOR TONIGHT(1935); BELOVED ENEMY(1936); MARY OF SCOTLAND(1936); PLOUGH AND THE STARS, THE(1936); SYLVIA SCARLETT(1936); WHITE LEGION, THE(1936); WOMAN REBELS, A(1936); ANGEL(1937); BIG BROADCAST OF 1938, THE(1937); EMPEROR'S CANDLESTICKS, THE(1937); KING AND THE CHORUS GIRL, THE(1937); PRINCE AND THE PAUPER, THE(1937); SARATOGA(1937); WEE WILLIE WINKIE(1937); BOOLOO(1938); FOOLS FOR SCANDAL(1938); FOUR MEN AND A PRAYER(1938); OUTSIDE OF PARADISE(1938); YOUNG IN HEART, THE(1938); DRUMS ALONG THE MOHAWK(1939); ETERNALLY YOURS(1939); FIFTH AVENUE GIRL(1939); MIDNIGHT(1939); RAFFLES(1939); RULERS OF THE SEA(1939); ARISE, MY LOVE(1940); CONGO MAISIE(1940); HUDSON'S BAY(1940); LONG VOYAGE HOME, THE(1940); PHILADELPHIA STORY, THE(1940); TIN PAN ALLEY(1940); ZANZIBAR(1940); CHARLEY'S AUNT(1941); HOW GREEN WAS MY VALLEY(1941); SCOTLAND YARD(1941); WOMAN'S FACE(1941); ALMOST MARRIED(1942); WE WERE DANCING(1942)
Silents
EVIDENCE(1915); NEW YORK IDEA, THE(1920); NOBODY(1921)
Misc. Silents
FLAME OF PASSION, THE(1915); PEARL OF ANTILLES, THE(1915); FATAL HOUR, THE(1920)
Mal Pape
MR. BILLION(1977), cos
Mel Pape
STANLEY(1973); SMOKEY AND THE BANDIT(1977); HOT STUFF(1979); SMOKEY AND THE BANDIT–PART 3(1983)
Melvin Pape
EYES OF A STRANGER(1980)
Paul Pape
SATURDAY NIGHT FEVER(1977)
Geraldine Papel
UNDER THE RAINBOW(1981)
Tony Papenfuss
FIREFOX(1982)

Lloyd S. Papez
DARK INTRUDER(1965), art d; OUT OF SIGHT(1966), art d; CLAMBAKE(1967), art d; THREE GUNS FOR TEXAS(1968), art d; SAM WHISKEY(1969), art d; CAR, THE(1977), art d
George Papi
GRAND SLAM(1968, Ital., Span., Ger.), p
Giorgio Papi
FISTFUL OF DOLLARS, A(1964, Ital./Ger./Span.), p; SACCO AND VANZETTI(1971, Ital./Fr.), p; FAMILY, THE(1974, Fr./Ital.), p
Giuliano Papi
ATLAS AGAINST THE CYCLOPS(1963, Ital.), cos; HOURS OF LOVE, THE(1965, Ital.), cos; LITTLE NUNS, THE(1965, Ital.), cos
Krsto Papic
RAT SAVIOUR, THE(1977, Yugo.), d&w
Stephen Papich
DESIREE(1954), ch; EGYPTIAN. THE(1954), ch; RAINS OF RANCHIPUR, THE(1955), ch; UNTAMED(1955), ch
Stephen Papick
DEMETRIUS AND THE GLADIATORS(1954), ch; SILVER CHALICE, THE(1954), ch
Louise Papillon
PIRATES OF PENZANCE, THE(1983)
Nadine Papin
WHAT'S NEW, PUSSYCAT?(1965, U.S./Fr.)
Bernard Papineau
THIS MAN MUST DIE(1970, Fr./Ital.)
Gail Papineau
FANTASIA(1940), spec eff
Dannunzio Papini
AUGUSTINE OF HIPPO(1973, Ital.)
Jeanne Papir
LOVE IN THE AFTERNOON(1957)
Umberto Papiri
YOUNG, THE EVIL AND THE SAVAGE, THE(1968, Ital.)
Billy Papke
MADISON SQUARE GARDEN(1932)
Dimitrios Papmichail
ASTERO(1960, Gr.)
Papouf
BIG CHIEF, THE(1960, Fr.)
Jaroslav Papousek
LOVES OF A BLONDE(1966, Czech.), w; FIREMAN'S BALL, THE(1968, Czech.), w; INTIMATE LIGHTING(1969, Czech.), w; MOST BEAUTIFUL AGE, THE(1970, Czech.), d&w
Emerico Papp
QUEEN OF THE NILE(1964, Ital.), w
Frantisek Papp
SHOP ON MAIN STREET, THE(1966, Czech.)
Joseph Papp
PIRATES OF PENZANCE, THE(1983), p
Mihaly Papp
WINTER WIND(1970, Fr./Hung.)
Veronika Papp
ANGI VERA(1980, Hung.)
Ignazio Pappalardi
GODFATHER, THE, PART II(1974)
Michael A. Pappalardo
SILHOUETTES(1982)
Andrew Pappas
THREE TO GO(1971, Aus.)
George Pappas
JEREMY(1973), p; FAREWELL, MY LOVELY(1975), p; 92 IN THE SHADE(1975, U.S./Brit.), p; STICK UP, THE(1978, Brit.), p; FIRST DEADLY SIN, THE(1980), p
Irene Pappas
Z(1969, Fr./Algeria)
Jack Pappas
BENEATH THE 12-MILE REEF(1953)
Jim Pappas
NATURAL ENEMIES(1979)
John Pappas
SIGN OF AQUARIUS(1970), w
Nick Pappas
ROSE BOWL(1936)
Robin Pappas
SHINING, THE(1980); SUPERMAN II(1980)
Stuart H. Pappe
PRESIDENT'S ANALYST, THE(1967), ed; ALEX IN WONDERLAND(1970), ed; GUMBALL RALLY, THE(1976), ed; OLIVER'S STORY(1978), ed; UNMARRIED WOMAN, AN(1978), ed; WANDERERS, THE(1979), ed
Stuart Pappe
CARNY(1980), ed
Stan Papps
DEVIL'S WEDDING NIGHT, THE(1973, Ital.)
Chris Paps
1984
BLIND DATE(1984)
Ye. Paptsov
LAST GAME, THE(1964, USSR)
Keith Papworth
DEVIL'S DAFFODIL, THE(1961, Brit./Ger.), m
Pamela Papworth
INADMISSIBLE EVIDENCE(1968, Brit.)
Paquerette
MODIGLIANI OF MONTPARNASSE(1961, Fr./Ital.)
Mme. Paquerette
FRENCH CANCAN(1956, Fr.)
Silents
MARE NOSTRUM(1926)

Felix Paquet
CINDERELLA(1937, Fr.); JUST ME(1950, Fr.); ROYAL AFFAIR, A(1950)
Jean Paquet
CLANDESTINE(1948, Fr.), m
Paulette Paquet
LORD BYRON OF BROADWAY(1930); GOIN' TO TOWN(1935)
Letitia Paquette
LAST CHALLENGE, THE(1967)
Pauline Paquette
Silents
BLUFF(1924)
Russ Paquette
JACKTOWN(1962)
Lawrence Paquin
BOOMERANG(1947); WHISTLE AT EATON FALLS(1951)
Nicole Paquin
WOMAN IS A WOMAN, A(1961, Fr./Ital.)
Robert A. Paquin
THREE HOURS TO KILL(1954)
Gerard Paquis
SHOUT AT THE DEVIL(1976, Brit.)
Oscal L. Par
PUT UP OR SHUT UP(1968, Arg.)
Josephine Para
SEA CHASE, THE(1955)
Mario Paradetti
SEVEN TASKS OF ALI BABA, THE(1963, Ital.), ph
Anna Paradine
PARADINE CASE, THE(1947)
Jessie Paradise
TREASURE OF MAKUBA, THE(1967, U.S./Span.)
Lynda Paradise
WANDA NEVADA(1979), art d
Marjorie B. Paradise
THIS SIDE OF HEAVEN(1934), w
Michael J. Paradise [Giulio Paradisi]
VISITOR, THE(1980, Ital./U.S.), d
Phil Paradise
3 IS A FAMILY(1944), prod d
Richard Paradise
MACHISMO–40 GRAVES FOR 40 GUNS(1970)
Robin Paradise
PORKY'S II: THE NEXT DAY(1983)
Giulio Paradisi
LA DOLCE VITA(1961, Ital./Fr.); 8 ½(1963, Ital.)
Pietro Domenico Paradisi
EXTERMINATING ANGEL, THE(1967, Mex.), m
Sergei Paradjanov
COLOR OF POMEGRANATES, THE(1980, Armenian), d
Ron Parady
1984
NAKED FACE, THE(1984)
Sergey Paradzhanov
SHADOWS OF FORGOTTEN ANCESTORS(1967, USSR), d, w
John Paragon
THINGS ARE TOUGH ALL OVER(1982); EATING RAOUL(1982); PANDEMONI-UM(1982); GOING BERSERK(1983)
Brice Parain
MY LIFE TO LIVE(1963, Fr.)
Paraluman
SURRENDER–HELL!(1959); MORO WITCH DOCTOR(1964, U.S./Phil.); LOSERS, THE(1970); DAUGHTERS OF SATAN(1972)
I. Paramonov
ITALIANO BRAVA GENTE(1965, Ital./USSR)
John Paramor
PRIVATE COLLECTION(1972, Aus.)
Norrie Paramor
FRIGHTENED CITY, THE(1961, Brit.), a, m; BAND OF THIEVES(1962, Brit.); RING-A-DING RHYTHM(1962, Brit. 73m Amicus/COL bw (G.B: IT'S TRAD, DAD!), md; TWO AND TWO MAKE SIX(1962, Brit.), m; DOCTOR IN DISTRESS(1963, Brit.), m; FAST LADY, THE(1963, Brit.), m; PAIR OF BRIEFS, A(1963, Brit.), m; PLAY IT COOL(1963, Brit.), m, md; FATHER CAME TOO(1964, Brit.), m; NO, MY DARLING DAUGHTER(1964, Brit.), m; YOUNG AND WILLING(1964, Brit.), m&md; UP JUMPED A SWAGMAN(1965, Brit.), m; MY LOVER, MY SON(1970, Brit.), m, md
E. E. Paramore
BABY, TAKE A BOW(1934), w; TWENTY MULE TEAM(1940), w; CHETNIKS(1943), w
E. E. Paramore, Jr.
SANTA FE TRAIL, THE(1930), w; MYSTERY WOMAN(1935), w; PORTIA ON TRIAL(1937), w; MAN OF CONQUEST(1939), w; CROOKED ROAD, THE(1940), w
Edward E. Paramore
BORDER LEGION, THE(1930), w; OKLAHOMA KID, THE(1939), w; TOMBSTONE, THE TOWN TOO TOUGH TO DIE(1942), w
Edward E. Paramore, Jr.
SATURDAY NIGHT KID, THE(1929), w; VIRGINIAN, THE(1929), w; ONLY THE BRAVE(1930), w; FIGHTING CARAVANS(1931), w; ROCKY MOUNTAIN MYS-TERY(1935), w; THREE GODFATHERS(1936), w; TROUBLE FOR TWO(1936), w; MYSTERY SEA RAIDER(1940), w; VIRGINIAN, THE(1946), w
Edward Paramore
NIGHT PARADE(1929, Brit.), w; BITTER TEA OF GENERAL YEN, THE(1933), w; MASTER OF MEN(1933), w; THREE COMRADES(1938), w
Edward Paramore, Jr.
DANGEROUS WOMAN(1929), w; NEWLY RICH(1931), w; RICH MAN'S FOL-LY(1931), w
Edward Paramore III
WILD RIDERS(1971), p
Gil Parando
WIND AND THE LION, THE(1975), prod d

Mario Parapetti
EMBALMER, THE(1966, Ital.), ph
Michael Paras
LILITH(1964)
Peter Parasheles
RUN LIKE A THIEF(1968, Span.), ed; ROYAL HUNT OF THE SUN, THE(1969, Brit.), ed; WEREWOLVES ON WHEELS(1971), ed; THIS IS A HIJACK(1973), ed; TRICK BABY(1973), ed; HOMEBODIES(1974), ed; ULTIMATE THRILL, THE(1974), ed; NEVER CRY WOLF(1983), ed
Walter Parazaider
ELECTRA GLIDE IN BLUE(1973)
Michel Parbot
LIVE FOR LIFE(1967, Fr./Ital.)
James Milton Parcher
SUNDAY IN THE COUNTRY(1975, Can.), art d
Don Parchment
CHILDREN OF BABYLON(1980, Jamaica)
Joaquin Pardave
GUADALAJARA(1943, Mex.)
Jose Pardave
LA NAVE DE LOS MONSTRUOS(1959, Mex.)
Jose Luis Parddes
WRATH OF GOD, THE(1972)
Doc Pardee
GENTLEMAN FROM ARIZONA, THE(1940)
Ida Pardee
Silents
PLAYTHINGS OF DESIRE(1924)
Phil Pardee
CROWD ROARS, THE(1932)
Anibal Pardeiro
HEAT(1970, Arg.)
Mirabella Pardi
DESTINY(1938)
Edmund Pardo
Misc. Silents
HER SILENT SACRIFICE(1917)
Monica Pardo
Misc. Talkies
ISLAND OF LOST GIRLS(1975)
Tova Pardo
MY MARGO(1969, Israel)
David Pardoll
BORN YESTERDAY(1951)
William Pardue
MANNEQUIN(1933, Brit.); WOMAN IN COMMAND, THE(1934 Brit.)
Silents
OLD BILL THROUGH THE AGES(1924, Brit.); ONE COLUMBO NIGHT(1926, Brit.)
Michael Pare
EDDIE AND THE CRUISERS(1983)
1984
PHILADELPHIA EXPERIMENT, THE(1984); STREETS OF FIRE(1984)
Americo Paredes
BALLAD OF GREGORIO CORTEZ, THE(1983), w
Conchita Paredes
HOUSE THAT SCREAMED, THE(1970, Span.)
Daniel Paredes
CARWASH(1976), cos; AMERICATHON(1979), cos
1984
ICE PIRATES, THE(1984), cos
Danile Paredes
CAT PEOPLE(1982), cos
Jean Paredes
FANFAN THE TULIP(1952, Fr.); LES BELLES-DE-NUIT(1952, Fr.); CADET-ROUS-SELLE(1954, Fr.); MADAME DU BARRY(1954 Fr./Ital.); FRENCH CANCAN(1956, Fr.); IF PARIS WERE TOLD TO US(1956, Fr.); MICHAEL STROGOFF(1960, Fr./Ital./Yugo.); LOVE IS A BALL(1963); WHAT'S NEW, PUSSYCAT?(1965, U.S./Fr.); JOHNNY BANCO(1969, Fr./Ital./Ger.); VERY CURIOUS GIRL, A(1970, Fr.); WHO IS KILLING THE GREAT CHEFS OF EUROPE?(1978, US/Ger.)
Pierre Parel
LONG ABSENCE, THE(1962, Fr./Ital.)
Mila Parely
LILIOM(1935, Fr.); RULES OF THE GAME, THE(1939, Fr.); THEY MET ON SKIS(1940, Fr.); BEAUTY AND THE BEAST(1947, Fr.); SNOWBOUND(1949, Brit.); ANGELS OF THE STREETS(1950, Fr.); BLOOD ORANGE(1953, Brit.)
Mira Parely
LE PLAISIR(1954, Fr.)
Claude Parent
YOUNG GIRLS OF ROCHEFORT, THE(1968, Fr.)
Gail Parent
SHEILA LEVINE IS DEAD AND LIVING IN NEW YORK(1975), w; MAIN EVENT, THE(1979), w
Jacqueline Parent
MALEVIL(1981, Fr./Ger.)
Jerome Parentae
VELVET TRAP, THE(1966)
Nildo Parente
1984
MEMOIRS OF PRISON(1984, Braz.)
Franco Parenti
SHOOT LOUD, LOUDER... I DON'T UNDERSTAND(1966, Ital.)
Noel Parenti
SERGEANT WAS A LADY, THE(1961), ch; POPEYE(1980)
Alessandro Parenzo
MALICIOUS(1974, Ital.), w
Valentine Parera
TWO AND ONE TWO(1934)

Mildred Pares
HOUSE ON SKULL MOUNTAIN, THE(1974), w
Philippe Pares
MILLION, THE(1931, Fr.), m
Phillipe Pares
DRAGNET NIGHT(1931, Fr.), m
Mila Parey
SHANGHAI DRAMA, THE(1945, Fr.)
Nikolai Parfenov
SON OF THE REGIMENT(1948, USSR)
Judy Parfitt
HIDE AND SEEK(1964, Brit.); HAMLET(1969, Brit.); MIND OF MR. SOAMES, THE(1970, Brit.); GALILEO(1975, Brit.)
1984
CHAMPIONS(1984)
Woodrow Parfrey
CATTLE KING(1963); WAR LORD, THE(1965); FLIM-FLAM MAN, THE(1967); KING'S PIRATE(1967); HOW TO SAVE A MARRIAGE–AND RUIN YOUR LIFE(1968); MADIGAN(1968); PLANET OF THE APES(1968); SAM WHISKEY(1969); COLD TURKEY(1971); DIRTY HARRY(1971); CHARLEY VARRICK(1973); OKLAHOMA CRUDE(1973); PAPILLON(1973); OUTLAW JOSEY WALES, THE(1976); STAY HUNGRY(1976); SENIORS, THE(1978); BRONCO BILLY(1980); CARNY(1980); USED CARS(1980); FRANCES(1982); SEDUCTION, THE(1982)
Woody Parfrey
STING II, THE(1983)
Nikolay Parfyonov
RED AND THE WHITE, THE(1969, Hung./USSR)
Christoph Parge
GERMAN SISTERS, THE(1982, Ger.)
Edith Pargiter
SPANIARD'S CURSE, THE(1958, Brit.), w
Isobel Pargiter
DEVIL ON HORSEBACK(1954, Brit.), p
Conrad Parham
WARKILL(1968, U.S./Phil.)
Barbara Paridon
STING OF DEATH(1966)
Manoug Parikian
SONG OF NORWAY(1970)
Roberto Parilla
MONDAY'S CHILD(1967, U.S., Arg.)
Adolph Parina
Silents
FRUITS OF DESIRE, THE(1916)
Claudine Paringaux
DON'T CRY WITH YOUR MOUTH FULL(1974, Fr.)
Anatole Paris
SOMEONE BEHIND THE DOOR(1971, Fr./Brit.), makeup
Bartlett Paris
CARETAKERS, THE(1963), w
Daniele Paris
TOGETHER(1956, Brit.), m; NIGHT PORTER, THE(1974, Ital./U.S.), m
1984
BEYOND GOOD AND EVIL(1984, Ital./Fr./Ger.), m
Dany Paris
BEBO'S GIRL(1964, Ital.); EMPTY CANVAS, THE(1964, Fr./Ital.); JULIET OF THE SPIRITS(1965, Fr./Ital./W.Ger.)
Dominic Paris
1984
SPLITZ(1984), w
Domonic Paris
LAST RITES(1980), d, w, ph
1984
SPLITZ(1984), d
Freddie Paris
ODD ANGRY SHOT, THE(1979, Aus.)
George Paris
BLOOD ON THE SUN(1945); NORTHWEST OUTPOST(1947); GREAT SINNER, THE(1949); TO CATCH A THIEF(1955)
Gerry Paris
1984
TOP SECRET!(1984)
Jacques Paris
YOUR SHADOW IS MINE(1963, Fr./Ital.), art d
Jerry Paris
MY FOOLISH HEART(1949); SWORD IN THE DESERT(1949); CYRANO DE BERGERAC(1950); FLYING MISSILE(1950); OUTRAGE(1950); BRIGHT VICTORY(1951); CALL ME MISTER(1951); SUBMARINE COMMAND(1951); BONZO GOES TO COLLEGE(1952); MONKEY BUSINESS(1952); FLIGHT TO TANGIER(1953); GLASS WALL, THE(1953); SABRE JET(1953); WILD ONE, THE(1953); CAINE MUTINY, THE(1954); DRIVE A CROOKED ROAD(1954); PRISONER OF WAR(1954); GOOD MORNING, MISS DOVE(1955); HELL'S HORIZON(1955); MARTY(1955); NAKED STREET, THE(1955); UNCHAINED(1955); VIEW FROM POMPEY'S HEAD, THE(1955); D-DAY, THE SIXTH OF JUNE(1956); I'VE LIVED BEFORE(1956); NEVER SAY GOODBYE(1956); MAN ON THE PROWL(1957); ZERO HOUR!(1957); FEMALE ANIMAL, THE(1958); LADY TAKES A FLYER, THE(1958); NAKED AND THE DEAD, THE(1958); SING, BOY, SING(1958); CAREER(1959); NO NAME ON THE BULLET(1959); GREAT IMPOSTOR, THE(1960); CARETAKERS, THE(1963), w; DON'T RAISE THE BRIDGE, LOWER THE RIVER(1968, Brit.), a, d; HOW SWEET IT IS(1968), d; NEVER A DULL MOMENT(1968), a, d; VIVA MAX!(1969), d; GRASSHOPPER, THE(1970), d; STAR SPANGLED GIRL(1971), d; LEO AND LOREE(1980), a, d
John Paris
WAY OF A GAUCHO(1952); WOLF DOG(1958, Can.)
Jonni Paris
SEMINOLE UPRISING(1955); SON OF SINBAD(1955); PROUD ONES, THE(1956)
Judith Paris
SAVAGE MESSIAH(1972, Brit.)

Lucien Paris
PANIQUE(1947, Fr.)
Manuel Paris
FLYING DOWN TO RIO(1933); MAN WHO BROKE THE BANK AT MONTE CARLO, THE(1935); MESSAGE TO GARCIA, A(1936); I'LL TAKE ROMANCE(1937); WHEN YOU'RE IN LOVE(1937); ARTISTS AND MODELS ABROAD(1938); MIRACLES FOR SALE(1939); FOR WHOM THE BELL TOLLS(1943); STORM OVER LISBON(1944); MONSIEUR BEAUCAIRE(1946); PERILOUS HOLIDAY(1946); THRILL OF BRAZIL, THE(1946); CASS TIMBERLANE(1947); IVY(1947); OUT OF THE PAST(1947); ANGEL ON THE AMAZON(1948); FRENCH LEAVE(1948); JOAN OF ARC(1948); LETTER FROM AN UNKNOWN WOMAN(1948); LADY GAMBLES, THE(1949); MADAME BOVARY(1949); CRISIS(1950); HAVANA ROSE(1951); MACAO(1952); PRISONER OF ZENDA, THE(1952); SECOND CHANCE(1953); STORY OF THREE LOVES, THE(1953); JUBILEE TRAIL(1954); TO CATCH A THIEF(1955); HOT BLOOD(1956); ISTANBUL(1957); PERFECT FURLOUGH, THE(1958)
Marie-Madeleine Paris
TRIPLE CROSS(1967, Fr./Brit.), makeup; THERESE AND ISABELLE(1968, U.S./Ger.), makeup
Renee Paris
LORDS OF FLATBUSH, THE(1974); FRONT, THE(1976)
Robin Mary Paris
ANNIE HALL(1977)
Simone Paris
DIARY OF A BAD GIRL(1958, Fr.); LOVE AND THE FRENCHWOMAN(1961, Fr.); LOVE AT NIGHT(1961, Fr.); PLEASURES AND VICES(1962, Fr.); MAN AND A WOMAN, A(1966, Fr.); THERESE AND ISABELLE(1968, U.S./Ger.)
Terry Paris
BLOODY KIDS(1983, Brit.)
Titi Paris
BELOW THE BELT(1980)
William M. Paris
TROUBLE WITH GIRLS(AND HOW TO GET INTO IT), THE*1/2 (1969)
The Paris Sisters
RING-A-DING RHYTHM(1962, Brit. 73m Amicus/COL bw (G.B: IT'S TRAD, DAD!)
The Women's Team of the Paris Ski Club
THEY MET ON SKIS(1940, Fr.)
Geoffredo Parise
AGOSTINO(1962, Ital.), w; CONJUGAL BED, THE(1963, Ital.), w
Goffredo Parise
KISS THE OTHER SHEIK(1968, Fr./Ital.), w; SHE AND HE(1969, Ital.), w; NEST OF VIPERS(1979, Ital.), w
Alfred Pariser
FULL CIRCLE(1977, Brit./Can.), p; HAUNTING OF JULIA, THE(1981, Brit./Can.), p; IMPROPER CHANNELS(1981, Can.), p
Dick Parish
MAGIC CHRISTMAS TREE(1964)
Dough Parish
STATUE, THE(1971, Brit.)
George Parish
CRIME SCHOOL(1938), md
Katrina Parish
10 TO MIDNIGHT(1983)
Richard C. Parish
MAGIC CHRISTMAS TREE(1964), d
Robert Parish
Silents
CITY LIGHTS(1931)
Maria Parisi
ANGELO IN THE CROWD(1952, Ital.)
The Parisian Twisters
TWIST ALL NIGHT(1961)
Andrea Parisy
CHEATERS, THE(1961, Fr.); SWEET AND SOUR(1964, Fr./Ital.); GREED IN THE SUN(1965, Fr./ Ital.); MAYERLING(1968, Brit./Fr.); DON'T LOOK NOW(1969, Brit./Fr.); SLOGAN(1970, Fr.)
Dale Park
FIRE AND ICE(1983)
Ed Park
13TH HOUR, THE(1947)
Ernest J. Park
JOHNNY CONCHO(1956), makeup
Ernie Park
LONG ROPE, THE(1961), makeup; SNIPER'S RIDGE(1961), makeup; RIDER ON A DEAD HORSE(1962), makeup
Ida May Park
Silents
GILDED SPIDER, THE(1916), w; FLASHLIGHT, THE(1917), d&w; RESCUE, THE(1917), d&w; BREAD(1918), d&w; RISKY ROAD, THE(1918), d&w
Misc. Silents
FIRES OF REBELLION(1917), d; BROADWAY LOVE(1918), d; GRAND PASSION, THE(1918), d; MODEL'S CONFESSION(1918), d; VANITY POOL(1918), d; BONNIE MAY(1920), d; MIDLANDERS, THE(1920), d
Ida May Park [Mrs. Joseph De Grasse]
Misc. Silents
BONDAGE(1917), d
Jacqueline Park
RED, HOT AND BLUE(1949)
Lester Park
Misc. Silents
SIDEWALKS OF NEW YORK(1923), d
MacDonald Park
WINGS AND THE WOMAN(1942, Brit.)
Phil Park
MEN ARE CHILDREN TWICE(1953, Brit.), w; WARRIORS, THE(1955), w
Post Park
PIONEERS, THE(1941); EL PASO KID(1946); RIDIN' DOWN THE TRAIL(1947); HANGMAN'S KNOT(1952); GUN FURY(1953); POWDER RIVER(1953); WOMAN THEY ALMOST LYNCHED, THE(1953); TALL MEN, THE(1955)

Reg Park
HERCULES AND THE CAPTIVE WOMEN(1963, Fr./Ital.); HERCULES IN THE HAUNTED WORLD(1964, Ital.)
Misc. Talkies
HERCULES, PRISONER OF EVIL(1967)

Richard Park
TARGET ZERO(1955)

Simon Park
NUTCRACKER(1982, Brit.), m

Bo Parkam
1984
PHILADELPHIA EXPERIMENT, THE(1984)

Fred Parke
Misc. Silents
FREE KISSES(1926)

Henry C. Parke
SPEEDTRAP(1978), w

J. McDonald Parke
PENNY PRINCESS(1953, Brit.)

Lawrence Parke
WATERMELON MAN(1970)

Macdonald Parke
HELL, HEAVEN OR HOBOKEN(1958, Brit.); SHIPYARD SALLY(1940, Brit.); CANDLELIGHT IN ALGERIA(1944, Brit.); YELLOW CANARY, THE(1944, Brit.); FOOL AND THE PRINCESS, THE(1948, Brit.); NO ORCHIDS FOR MISS BLANDISH(1948, Brit.); DANGEROUS ASSIGNMENT(1950, Brit.); TALE OF FIVE WOMEN, A(1951, Brit.); BABES IN BAGDAD(1952); ISLAND OF DESIRE(1952, Brit.); PARIS EXPRESS, THE(1953, Brit.); GOOD DIE YOUNG, THE(1954, Brit.); LAST MOMENT, THE(1954, Brit.); SUMMERTIME(1955); MARCH HARE, THE(1956, Brit.); BEYOND MOMBASA(1957); JOHN PAUL JONES(1959); MOUSE THAT ROARED, THE(1959, Brit.); BATTLE OF THE SEXES, THE(1960, Brit.); NEVER TAKE CANDY FROM A STRANGER(1961, Brit.)

McDonald Parke
IS YOUR HONEYMOON REALLY NECESSARY?(1953, Brit.)

William Parke
Silents
OUT OF THE STORM(1920), d; TAILOR MADE MAN, A(1922); CLEAN UP, THE(1923), d; LEGALLY DEAD(1923), d
Misc. Silents
OTHER PEOPLE'S MONEY(1916), d; PRUDENCE THE PIRATE(1916); SHINE GIRL, THE(1916), d; CIGARETTE GIRL, THE(1917), d; CROOKED ROMANCE, A(1917), d; LAST OF THE CARNABYS, THE(1917), d; MISS NOBODY(1917), d; OVER THE HILL(1917), d; STREETS OF ILLUSION, THE(1917), d; CONVICT 993(1918), d; KEY TO POWER, THE(1918), d; YELLOW TICKET, THE(1918), d; PALISER CASE, THE(1920), d; WOMAN WHO UNDERSTOOD, A(1920), d; BEACH OF DREAMS(1921), d; MILLION TO BURN, A(1923), d

William Parke, Jr.
Silents
MORAL FIBRE(1921)
Misc. Silents
PRUDENCE THE PIRATE(1916); CANDY GIRL, THE(1917); CIGARETTE GIRL, THE(1917); CROOKED ROMANCE, A(1917); HER NEW YORK(1917); LAST OF THE CARNABYS, THE(1917); MISS NOBODY(1917); OVER THE HILL(1917); STREETS OF ILLUSION, THE(1917); GHOST IN THE GARRET, THE(1921); NOT FOR SALE(1924)

William Parke, Sr.
Silents
HUNCHBACK OF NOTRE DAME, THE(1923)
Misc. Silents
GREAT MEN AMONG US(1915), d

Cecil Parkee
WE OF THE NEVER NEVER(1983, Aus.)

A. G. Parker
Silents
ETERNAL SIN, THE(1917)

Al Parker
ROLLING IN MONEY(1934, Brit.), d

Alan Parker
MELODY(1971, Brit.), w; BUGSY MALONE(1976, Brit.), d&w; MIDNIGHT EXPRESS(1978, Brit.), d; FAME(1980), d; PINK FLOYD–THE WALL(1982, Brit.), d; SHOOT THE MOON(1982), d; JAWS 3-D(1983), m
1984
BIRDY(1984), d

Albert Parker
FOLLOW THE LEADER(1930), w; RIGHT TO LIVE, THE(1933, Brit.), d; THIRD CLUE, THE(1934, Brit.), d; LATE EXTRA(1935, Brit.), d; RIVERSIDE MURDER, THE(1935, Brit.), d; WHITE LILAC(1935, Brit.), d; BLIND MAN'S BLUFF(1936, Brit.), d; TROUBLED WATERS(1936, Brit.), d; FIVE POUND MAN, THE(1937, Brit.), p&d; STRANGE EXPERIMENT(1937, Brit.), d; THERE WAS A YOUNG MAN(1937, Brit.), p&d; CRIME OF PETER FRAME, THE(1938, Brit.), d; MURDER IN THE FAMILY(1938, Brit.), p&d
Silents
AMERICAN ARISTOCRACY(1916); IN AGAIN-OUT AGAIN(1917); MAN HATER, THE(1917), d; ANNEXING BILL(1918), d; ARIZONA(1918), d; KNICKERBOCKER BUCKAROO, THE(1919), d; BRANDED WOMAN, THE(1920), d, w; LOVE'S REDEMPTION(1921), d; SHERLOCK HOLMES(1922), d; REJECTED WOMAN, THE(1924), d; SECOND YOUTH(1924), d; BLACK PIRATE, THE(1926), d
Misc. Silents
FOOD GAMBLERS, THE(1917), d; FOR VALOUR(1917), d; HAUNTED HOUSE, THE(1917), a, d; HER EXCELLENCY, THE GOVERNOR(1917), d; FROM TWO TO SIX(1918), d; OTHER WOMAN, THE(1918), d; SECRET CODE, THE(1918), d; SHIFTING SANDS(1918), d; WAIFS(1918), d; EYES OF YOUTH(1919), d; LOVE OF SUNYA, THE(1927), d

Alex Parker
ESTHER WATERS(1948, Brit.)

Alison Parker
MIKADO, THE(1967, Brit.)

Althe Parker
LAMP STILL BURNS, THE(1943, Brit.)

Andy Parker
SHADOW VALLEY(1947)

Anthony Parker
CRAWLING EYE, THE(1958, Brit.); CAUGHT IN THE NET(1960, Brit.)

Art Parker
NORTH DALLAS FORTY(1979), set d

Arthur J. Parker
COMES A HORSEMAN(1978), set d; PRIVATE BENJAMIN(1980), set d

Arthur Jeph Parker
W.C. FIELDS AND ME(1976), set d; STAYING ALIVE(1983), set d; TABLE FOR FIVE(1983), set d
1984
NO SMALL AFFAIR(1984), set d

Arthur Parker
NORWOOD(1970), set d; OUT OF TOWNERS, THE(1970), set d; PUFNSTUF(1970), set d; SHOOTIST, THE(1976), set d; CHINA SYNDROME, THE(1979), set d

Arthur Seph Parker
WINTER KILLS(1979), set d

Austin Parker
HONOR AMONG LOVERS(1931), w; RICH ARE ALWAYS WITH US, THE(1932), w; SUCCESSFUL CALAMITY, A(1932), w; HOUSE ON 56TH STREET, THE(1933), w; SHANGHAI MADNESS(1933), w; MANDALAY(1934), w; COME OUT OF THE PANTRY(1935, Brit.), w; GIRL ON THE FRONT PAGE, THE(1936), w; LOVE IN A BUNGALOW(1937), w; SOMETHING TO SING ABOUT(1937), w; THREE SMART GIRLS(1937), w; WHEN KNIGHTS WERE BOLD(1942, Brit.), w

Barnett Parker
GENERAL DIED AT DAWN, THE(1936); LIBELED LADY(1936); MR. DEEDS GOES TO TOWN(1936); PRESIDENT'S MYSTERY, THE(1936); BROADWAY MELODY OF '38(1937); DANGEROUS NUMBER(1937); DOUBLE WEDDING(1937); EMPEROR'S CANDLESTICKS, THE(1937); ESPIONAGE(1937); LAST OF MRS. CHEYNEY, THE(1937); MARRIED BEFORE BREAKFAST(1937); NAVY BLUE AND GOLD(1937); PERSONAL PROPERTY(1937); READY, WILLING AND ABLE(1937); WAKE UP AND LIVE(1937); WE WHO ARE ABOUT TO DIE(1937); WHEN YOU'RE IN LOVE(1937); GIRL DOWNSTAIRS, THE(1938); HOLD THAT KISS(1938); LISTEN, DARLING(1938); LOVE IS A HEADACHE(1938); MARIE ANTOINETTE(1938); SALLY, IRENE AND MARY(1938); AT THE CIRCUS(1939); BABES IN ARMS(1939); HOTEL FOR WOMEN(1939); SHE MARRIED A COP(1939); HE MARRIED HIS WIFE(1940); HIT PARADE OF 1941(1940); HULLABALOO(1940); IF I HAD MY WAY(1940); LA CONGA NIGHTS(1940); LOVE THY NEIGHBOR(1940); ONE NIGHT IN THE TROPICS(1940); KISSES FOR BREAKFAST(1941); MAN BETRAYED, A(1941); NEW WINE(1941); RELUCTANT DRAGON, THE(1941); TALL, DARK AND HANDSOME(1941)

Barrett Parker
BORN TO DANCE(1936)

Ben Parker
GEORGE WASHINGTON CARVER(1940), d; GUERRILLA GIRL(1953), w; INVISIBLE AVENGER, THE(1958), d; MODERN MARRIAGE, A(1962), d; SHEPHERD OF THE HILLS, THE(1964), w, d
Misc. Talkies
BOURBON ST. SHADOWS(1962), d

Bob Parker
IT HAPPENED HERE(1966, Brit.)

Brett Parker
TROUBLE WITH GIRLS(AND HOW TO GET INTO IT), THE (1969); STAY AWAY, JOE(1968); NAKED APE, THE(1973)

Bryan Parker
DREAM MAKER, THE(1963, Brit.)

Burnett Parker
Silents
TRAFFIC COP, THE(1916)
Misc. Silents
FLIGHT OF THE DUCHESS, THE(1916)

C. Franklin Parker
AIR HAWKS(1935)

Carl Parker
JOHN AND MARY(1969)

Carol Parker
HOLD'EM NAVY!(1937); ARTISTS AND MODELS ABROAD(1938); COCOANUT GROVE(1938); DRAMATIC SCHOOL(1938); YOU AND ME(1938); DRIFTER, THE(1944)
Misc. Talkies
SCORE(1973)

Carole Parker
Misc. Talkies
INTIMATE PLAYMATES, THE(1976)

Cecelia Parker
UNKNOWN VALLEY(1933); HERE IS MY HEART(1934); THREE LIVE GHOSTS(1935); DAMAGED LIVES(1937)

Cecil Parker
CUCKOO IN THE NEST, THE(1933, Brit.); GOLDEN CAGE, THE(1933, Brit.); BLUE SQUADRON, THE(1934, Brit.); DIRTY WORK(1934, Brit.); LADY IN DANGER(1934, Brit.); LITTLE FRIEND(1934, Brit.); NINE FORTY-FIVE(1934, Brit.); SILVER SPOON, THE(1934, Brit.); CRIME UNLIMITED(1935, Brit.); FOREIGN AFFAIRES(1935, Brit.); HER LAST AFFAIRE(1935, Brit.); ME AND MARLBOROUGH(1935, Brit.); DISHONOR BRIGHT(1936, Brit.); MAN WHO LIVED AGAIN, THE(1936, Brit.); MEN OF YESTERDAY(1936, Brit.); DARK JOURNEY(1937, Brit.); STORM IN A TEACUP(1937, Brit.); CITADEL, THE(1938); HOUSEMASTER(1938, Brit.); LADY VANISHES, THE(1938, Brit.); OLD IRON(1938, Brit.); TWO OF US, THE(1938, Brit.); SHE COULDN'T SAY NO(1939, Brit.); SONS OF THE SEA(1939, Brit.); SPIDER, THE(1940, Brit.); STARS LOOK DOWN, THE(1940, Brit.); TWO FOR DANGER(1940, Brit.); UNDER YOUR HAT(1940, Brit.); SAINT'S VACATION, THE(1941, Brit.); SHIPS WITH WINGS(1942, Brit.); SUICIDE SQUADRON(1942, Brit.); CAESAR AND CLEOPATRA(1946, Brit.); CAPTAIN BOYCOTT(1947, Brit.); HUNGRY HILL(1947, Brit.); MAGIC BOW, THE(1947, Brit.); AFFAIRS OF A ROGUE(1949, Brit.); AMAZING MR. BEECHAM, THE(1949, Brit.); DEAR MR. PROHACK(1949, Brit.); UNDER CAPRICORN(1949); WEAKER SEX, THE(1949, Brit.); WOMAN IN THE HALL, THE(1949, Brit.); TONY DRAWS A HORSE(1951, Brit.); HIS EXCELLENCY(1952, Brit.); MAGIC BOX, THE(1952, Brit.); MAN IN THE WHITE SUIT, THE(1952); I BELIEVE IN YOU(1953, Brit.); ISN'T LIFE WONDERFUL!(1953, Brit.); DETECTIVE, THE(1954, Qit.); FOR BETTER FOR WORSE(1954, Brit.); CONSTANT HUSBAND, THE(1955, Brit.); COURT JESTER, THE(1956); IT'S GREAT TO BE YOUNG(1956, Brit.); LADY-

KILLERS, THE(1956, Brit.); 23 PACES TO BAKER STREET(1956); ADMIRABLE CRICHTON, THE(1957, Brit.); TRUE AS A TURTLE(1957, Brit.); HAPPY IS THE BRIDE(1958, Brit.); INDISCREET(1958); TALE OF TWO CITIES, A(1958, Brit.); NAVY LARK, THE(1959, Brit.); WRECK OF THE MARY DEAR, THE(1959); FOLLOW THAT HORSE!(1960, Brit.); FRENCH MISTRESS(1960, Brit.); SWISS FAMILY ROBINSON(1960); UNDER TEN FLAGS(1960, U.S./Ital.); PETTICOAT PIRATES(1961, Brit.); PURE HELL OF ST. TRINIAN'S, THE(1961, Brit.); MAKE MINE A DOUBLE(1962, Brit.); CARRY ON JACK(1963, Brit.); HEAVENS ABOVE!(1963, Brit.); SWINGIN' MAIDEN, THE(1963, Brit.); COMEDY MAN, THE(1964); GUNS AT BATASI(1964, Brit.); AMOROUS ADVENTURES OF MOLL FLANDERS, THE(1965); AMOROUS MR. PRAWN, THE(1965, Brit.); BRAIN, THE(1965, Ger./Brit.); LADY L(1965, Fr./Ital.); OPERATION SNAFU(1965, Brit.); MAN COULD GET KILLED, A(1966); STUDY IN TERROR, A(1966, Brit./Ger.); MAGNIFICENT TWO, THE(1967, Brit.); PSYCHO-CIRCUS(1967, Brit.); OH! WHAT A LOVELY WAR(1969, Brit.)

Cecilia Parker
MYSTERY RANCH(1932); RAINBOW TRAIL(1932); TOMBSTONE CANYON(1932); FUGITIVE, THE(1933); RAINBOW RANCH(1933); RIDERS OF DESTINY(1933); SECRET SINNERS(1933); GUN JUSTICE(1934); HONOR OF THE RANGE(1934); LOST JUNGLE, THE(1934); MAN TRAILER, THE(1934); PAINTED VEIL, THE(1934); TRAIL DRIVE, THE(1934); AH, WILDERNESS!(1935); ENTER MADAME(1935); HIGH SCHOOL GIRL(1935); NAUGHTY MARIETTA(1935); BELOW THE DEADLINE(1936); IN HIS STEPS(1936); MINE WITH THE IRON DOOR, THE(1936); OLD HUTCH(1936); FAMILY AFFAIR, A(1937); GIRL LOVES BOY(1937); HOLLYWOOD COWBOY(1937); SWEETHEART OF THE NAVY(1937); JUDGE HARDY'S CHILDREN(1938); LOVE FINDS ANDY HARDY(1938); OUT WEST WITH THE HARDYS(1938); ROLL ALONG, COWBOY(1938); YOU'RE ONLY YOUNG ONCE(1938); ANDY HARDY GETS SPRING FEVER(1939); BURN 'EM UP O'CONNER(1939); HARDYS RIDE HIGH, THE(1939); JUDGE HARDY AND SON(1939); ANDY HARDY MEETS DEBUTANTE(1940); GAMBLING DAUGHTERS(1941); ANDY HARDY'S DOUBLE LIFE(1942); COURTSHIP OF ANDY HARDY, THE(1942); GRAND CENTRAL MURDER(1942); SEVEN SWEETHEARTS(1942); ANDY HARDY COMES HOME(1958)
Misc. Talkies
MAN TRAILER, THE(1934)

Charles Parker
MAN ABOUT THE HOUSE, A(1947, Brit.), makeup; GIGI(1958), makeup; KING OF KINGS(1961), makeup; FOUR HORSEMEN OF THE APOCALYPSE, THE(1962), makeup; LAWRENCE OF ARABIA(1962, Brit.), makeup; ZULU(1964, Brit.), makeup; LORD JIM(1965, Brit.), makeup; WHAT'S NEW, PUSSYCAT?(1965, U.S./Fr.), makeup; PROMISE HER ANYTHING(1966, Brit.), makeup; VIKING QUEEN, THE(1967, Brit.), makeup; MAGUS, THE(1968, Brit.), makeup; WOMEN IN LOVE(1969, Brit.), makeup; RYAN'S DAUGHTER(1970, Brit.), makeup; MAN OF LA MANCHA(1972), makeup; RULING CLASS, THE(1972, Brit.), makeup

Charles Parker
1984
BREAKIN'(1984), w; BREAKIN' 2: ELECTRIC BOOGALOO(1984), w

Charlie Parker
MURMUR OF THE HEART(1971, Fr./Ital./Ger.), m

Chauncey G. Parker III
OF UNKNOWN ORIGIN(1983, Can.), w

Chris Parker
PERMANENT VACATION(1982)

Christopher Parker
LONELINESS OF THE LONG DISTANCE RUNNER, THE(1962, Brit.)

Clifford Parker
YELLOW CANARY, THE(1944, Brit.), m

Clifton Parker
SCHWEIK'S NEW ADVENTURES(1943, Brit.), m; VACATION FROM MARRIAGE(1945, Brit.), m; JOHNNY FRENCHMAN(1946, Brit.), m; SILVER DARLINGS, THE(1947, Brit.), m; WHEN THE BOUGH BREAKS(1947, Brit.), m; BLANCHE FURY(1948, Brit.), m; DAUGHTER OF DARKNESS(1948, Brit.), m; SMUGGLERS, THE(1948, Brit.), m; BLUE LAGOON, THE(1949, Brit.), m; DIAMOND CITY(1949, Brit.), m; MARRY ME!(1949, Brit.), m; MY BROTHER'S KEEPER(1949, Brit.), m; TREASURE ISLAND(1950, Brit.), m; STORY OF ROBIN HOOD, THE(1952, Brit.), m; DAY TO REMEMBER, A(1953, Brit.), m; SAILOR OF THE KING(1953, Brit.), m; SWORD AND THE ROSE, THE(1953, Brit.), m; HELL BELOW ZERO(1954, Brit.), m; TECKMAN MYSTERY, THE(1955, Brit.), m; GENTLE TOUCH, THE(1956, Brit.), m; BIRTHDAY PRESENT, THE(1957, Brit.), m; CAMPBELL'S KINGDOM(1957, Brit.), m; TARZAN AND THE LOST SAFARI(1957, Brit.), m; CURSE OF THE DEMON(1958), m; HARRY BLACK AND THE TIGER(1958, Brit.), m; SECRET PLACE, THE(1958, Brit.), m; HOUSE OF THE SEVEN HAWKS, THE(1959), m; SINK THE BISMARCK!(1960, Brit.), m; THIRTY NINE STEPS, THE(1960, Brit.), m; VIRGIN ISLAND(1960, Brit.), m; CIRCLE OF DECEPTON(1961, Brit.), m; SCREAM OF FEAR(1961, Brit.), m; SECRET OF MONTE CRISTO, THE(1961, Brit.), m; DAMN THE DEFIANT!(1962, Brit.), m; DESERT PATROL(1962, Brit.), m; HELLFIRE CLUB, THE(1963, Brit.), m; MYSTERY SUBMARINE(1963, Brit.), m; UNDERWORLD INFORMERS(1965, Brit.), m

Corey Parker
1984
SCREAM FOR HELP(1984)

Creston B. Parker
1984
RIVER RAT, THE(1984)

Cyril Parker
TANGIER ASSIGNMENT(1954, Brit.), p

Daniel Parker
1984
SWORD OF THE VALIANT(1984, Brit.), spec eff

David Parker
EMBASSY(1972, Brit.)

Debi Parker
UNCOMMON VALOR(1983)

Dick Parker
HATARI!(1962), spec eff; RETURN OF THE SEVEN(1966, Span.), spec eff; LONG DUEL, THE(1967, Brit.), spec eff; THOSE DARING YOUNG MEN IN THEIR JAUNTY JALOPIES(1969, Fr./Brit./ Ital.), spec eff

Dolores Parker
HOUSE OF STRANGERS(1949)

Don Parker
CHARLIE CHAN AND THE CURSE OF THE DRAGON QUEEN(1981)

Donald Parker
Silents
NORTHERN CODE(1925), ph

Dorian Leigh Parker
NAKED AUTUMN(1963, Fr.)

Dorothy Parker
LADY BE CAREFUL(1936), w; MOON'S OUR HOME, THE(1936), w; SUZY(1936), w; THREE MARRIED MEN(1936), w; STAR IS BORN, A(1937), w; SWEETHEARTS(1938), w; TRADE WINDS(1938), w; LITTLE FOXES, THE(1941), w; WEEKEND FOR THREE(1941), w; SABOTEUR(1942), w; SMASH-UP, THE STORY OF A WOMAN(1947), w; FAN, THE(1949), w; QUEEN FOR A DAY(1951), w; STAR IS BORN, A(1954), w

Earl Parker
TERROR HOUSE(1972)

Ed Parker
STAR PACKER, THE(1934); OUR RELATIONS(1936); GOD'S COUNTRY AND THE MAN(1937); RHYTHM IN THE CLOUDS(1937); INDIANAPOLIS SPEEDWAY(1939); WINGS OF THE NAVY(1939); VIRGINIA CITY(1940); THEY DIED WITH THEIR BOOTS ON(1942); CLOAK AND DAGGER(1946); SILVER RIVER(1948); FLAXY MARTIN(1949); RACKET, THE(1951); SECRET DOOR, THE(1964); DIMENSION 5(1966); MONEY JUNGLE, THE(1968); SEABO(1978); SEVEN(1979); CURSE OF THE PINK PANTHER(1983)
Misc. Talkies
KILL THE GOLDEN GOOSE(1979)

Eddie Parker
'NEATH THE ARIZONA SKIES(1934); TRAIL BEYOND, THE(1934); GHOST RIDER, THE(1935); LAWLESS FRONTIER, THE(1935); RAINBOW VALLEY(1935); WERE-WOLF OF LONDON, THE(1935); GIT ALONG, LITTLE DOGIES(1937); LAST GANGSTER, THE(1937); PROFESSOR BEWARE(1938); SPY RING, THE(1938); DESPERATE TRAILS(1939); MEXICALI ROSE(1939); SON OF FRANKENSTEIN(1939); NORTHWEST PASSAGE(1940); RAGTIME COWBOY JOE(1940); OBLIGING YOUNG LADY(1941); MUMMY'S TOMB, THE(1942); SPOILERS, THE(1942), stunts; FRANKENSTEIN MEETS THE WOLF MAN(1943), stunts; HIT THE ICE(1943); LONE STAR TRAIL, THE(1943); MUG TOWN(1943); PISTOL PACKIN' MAMA(1943); COBRA WOMAN(1944); CRIME BY NIGHT(1944); ADVENTURES OF RUSTY(1945); LOST TRAIL, THE(1945); DAYS OF BUFFALO BILL(1946); INNER CIRCLE, THE(1946); MILLERSON CASE, THE(1947); MY WILD IRISH ROSE(1947); RAIDERS OF THE SOUTH(1947); SHADOW VALLEY(1947); FIGHTING RANGER, THE(1948); HAWK OF POWDER RIVER, THE(1948); ONE TOUCH OF VENUS(1948); STRAWBERRY ROAN, THE(1948); TIOGA KID, THE(1948); LAW OF THE WEST(1949); POWDER RIVER RUSTLERS(1949); RANGE JUSTICE(1949); CONVICTED(1950); GOOD HUMOR MAN, THE(1950); LOUISA(1950); MILKMAN, THE(1950); MULE TRAIN(1950); ONE TOO MANY(1950); BIG GUSHER, THE(1951); KID FROM BROKEN GUN, THE(1952); GLASS WEB, THE(1953); WINNING OF THE WEST(1953); TARANTULA(1955); THIS ISLAND EARTH(1955); MOLE PEOPLE, THE(1956); MONSTER ON THE CAMPUS(1958); IMITATION OF LIFE(1959); SPARTACUS(1960)

Edward Parker
LUCKY TEXAN, THE(1934); COURAGEOUS AVENGER, THE(1935); GETTING STRAIGHT(1970), set d

Edwin Parker
TOO HOT TO HANDLE(1938); DANGER FLIGHT(1939); SKY MURDER(1940); 'TIL WE MEET AGAIN(1940); DAYS OF OLD CHEYENNE(1943); THUNDERING TRAILS(1943); FRONTIER FEUD(1945); ADVENTURES OF DON COYOTE(1947); I WOULDN'T BE IN YOUR SHOES(1948); WHIRLWIND RAIDERS(1948); KNOCK ON ANY DOOR(1949); AL JENNINGS OF OKLAHOMA(1951); STRANGE DOOR, THE(1951); BARBED WIRE(1952); FLESH AND FURY(1952); HAWK OF WILD RIVER, THE(1952); HORIZONS WEST(1952); MY SIX CONVICTS(1952); PAULA(1952); SCARLET ANGEL(1952); ALL ASHORE(1953); LAW AND ORDER(1953); REAR WINDOW(1954); ABBOTT AND COSTELLO MEET THE MUMMY(1955); FAR COUNTRY, THE(1955); OVER-EXPOSED(1956); STORM CENTER(1956); CURSE OF THE UNDEAD(1959); NEVER STEAL ANYTHING SMALL(1959)

Eleanor Parker
BUSSES ROAR(1942); MISSION TO MOSCOW(1943); MYSTERIOUS DOCTOR, THE(1943); BETWEEN TWO WORLDS(1944); CRIME BY NIGHT(1944); HOLLY-WOOD CANTEEN(1944); LAST RIDE, THE(1944); VERY THOUGHT OF YOU, THE(1944); PRIDE OF THE MARINES(1945); NEVER SAY GOODBYE(1946); OF HUMAN BONDAGE(1946); ESCAPE ME NEVER(1947); VOICE OF THE TURTLE, THE(1947); WOMAN IN WHITE, THE(1948); IT'S A GREAT FEELING(1949); CAGED(1950); CHAIN LIGHTNING(1950); THREE SECRETS(1950); DETECTIVE STORY(1951); MILLIONAIRE FOR CHRISTY, A(1951); VALENTINO(1951); SCARAMOUCHE(1952); ABOVE AND BEYOND(1953); ESCAPE FROM FORT BRAVO(1953); NAKED JUNGLE, THE(1953); VALLEY OF THE KINGS(1954); INTERRUPTED MELODY(1955); MAN WITH THE GOLDEN ARM, THE(1955); MANY RIVERS TO CROSS(1955); KING AND FOUR QUEENS, THE(1956); LIZZIE(1957); SEVENTH SIN, THE(1957); HOLE IN THE HEAD, A(1959); HOME FROM THE HILL(1960); RETURN TO PEYTON PLACE(1961); MADISON AVENUE(1962); PANIC BUTTON(1964); SOUND OF MUSIC, THE(1965); AMERICAN DREAM, AN(1966); OSCAR, THE(1966); TIGER AND THE PUSSYCAT, THE(1967, U.S., Ital.); WARNING SHOT(1967); EYE OF THE CAT(1969); SUNBURN(1979)
Misc. Talkies
HANS BRINKER AND THE SILVER SKATES(1969)

Ellen Parker
COP HATER(1958); LOST MISSILE, THE(1958, U.S./Can.); KRAMER VS. KRAMER(1979); NIGHT OF THE JUGGLER(1980)

Erwin Parker
GEORGE(1973, U.S./Switz.)

F. William Parker
HUNTER, THE(1980); TERMS OF ENDEARMENT(1983); YOUNG GIANTS(1983)
1984
BUDDY SYSTEM, THE(1984); MASS APPEAL(1984); REVENGE OF THE NERDS(1984)

Faith Parker
DEMENTIA(1955)

Fess Parker
NO ROOM FOR THE GROOM(1952); SPRINGFIELD RIFLE(1952); UNTAMED FRONTIER(1952); DRAGONFLY SQUADRON(1953); KID FROM LEFT FIELD, THE(1953); TAKE ME TO TOWN(1953); THUNDER OVER THE PLAINS(1953); THEM!(1954); BATTLE FLAME(1955); DAVY CROCKETT, KING OF THE WILD

FRONTIER(1955); DAVY CROCKETT AND THE RIVER PIRATES(1956); GREAT LOCOMOTIVE CHASE, THE(1956); WESTWARD HO THE WAGONS!(1956); OLD YELLER(1957); LIGHT IN THE FOREST, THE(1958); ALIAS JESSE JAMES(1959); HANGMAN, THE(1959); JAYHAWKERS, THE(1959); HELL IS FOR HEROES(1962); SMOKY(1966)

Flora Parker
Misc. Silents
YOUTH OF FORTUNE, A(1916)

Frank Parker
CONCORDE, THE–AIRPORT '79(; TRANSATLANTIC MERRY-GO-ROUND(1934); SWEET SURRENDER(1935); LITTLE ACCIDENT(1939); PAT AND MIKE(1952); FRESH FROM PARIS(1955); PARIS FOLLIES OF 1956(1955)

Franklin Parker
MILLIE(1931); HONOR OF THE PRESS(1932); TWO SECONDS(1932); BEHIND JURY DOORS(1933, Brit.); FRISCO JENNY(1933); HELL AND HIGH WATER(1933); HER RESALE VALUE(1933); PAST OF MARY HOLMES, THE(1933); SWEETHEART OF SIGMA CHI(1933); HE COULDN'T TAKE IT(1934); OPERATOR 13(1934); PICTURE BRIDES(1934); STRAIGHT FROM THE HEART(1935); WOMAN IN RED, THE(1935); F MAN(1936); FURY(1936); RETURN OF JIMMY VALENTINE, THE(1936); NIGHT CLUB SCANDAL(1937); TIME OUT FOR ROMANCE(1937); HIGGINS FAMILY, THE(1938); MEN WITH WINGS(1938); TRADE WINDS(1938); ETERNALLY YOURS(1939); INVITATION TO HAPPINESS(1939); TEXAS RANGERS RIDE AGAIN(1940); LUCKY LEGS(1942); SALUTE FOR THREE(1943); FOLLOW THE BOYS(1944); I'LL TELL THE WORLD(1945); THEY WERE EXPENDABLE(1945); BLUE DAHLIA, THE(1946); SENATOR WAS INDISCREET, THE(1947); GOOD SAM(1948); MR. BLANDINGS BUILDS HIS DREAM HOUSE(1948); ON AN ISLAND WITH YOU(1948); UNDERCOVER MAN, THE(1949); NARROW MARGIN, THE(1952)

Franklin Parker, Sr.
SPIRIT OF WEST POINT, THE(1947)

Franklin "Pinky" Parker
JACKPOT, THE(1950)

Franklyn Parker
WHEN STRANGERS MEET(1934); I'D GIVE MY LIFE(1936); SMALL TOWN GIRL(1936); I COVER THE WAR(1937); CIPHER BUREAU(1938)

Fred Parker
DUDE WRANGLER, THE(1930); HELL'S HEADQUARTERS(1932); WAY OF THE WEST, THE(1934); COWBOY AND THE BANDIT, THE(1935); TIMBER TERRORS(1935); TROUBLE IN TEXAS(1937); YOU CAN'T TAKE IT WITH YOU(1938); PALS OF THE SILVER SAGE(1940)
Misc. Talkies
GALLOPING KID, THE(1932); LONE RIDER, THE(1934); ROAMIN' WILD(1936)

Fred Parker, Jr.
INDEPENDENCE DAY(1976)

Gary Parker
COAL MINER'S DAUGHTER(1980)

George Parker
GRANDAD RUDD(1935, Aus.), w; IT HAPPENED HERE(1966, Brit.)

Gilbert Parker
Silents
WISE FOOL, A(1921), w; OVER THE BORDER(1922), w; LODGE IN THE WILDERNESS, THE(1926), w

Gloria Parker
1984
BROADWAY DANNY ROSE(1984)

Gordon Parker
Silents
GENERAL JOHN REGAN(1921, Brit.)
Misc. Silents
WHEELS OF CHANCE, THE(1922, Brit.)

Hall Parker
MAN FROM WYOMING, A(1930)

Harrell Parker, Jr.
RETURN OF THE JEDI(1983)

Howard Parker
GIRL MOST LIKELY, THE(1957)

Jack Parker
WITHOUT RESERVATIONS(1946); FOUR DEVILS(1929); BATTLE OF GALLIPOLI(1931, Brit.), ph; CARNIVAL(1931, Brit.), ph; TRAPPED IN A SUBMARINE(1931, Brit.), ph; WINDJAMMER, THE(1931, Brit.), ph; DANCE PRETTY LADY(1932, Brit.), ph; MEET MY SISTER(1933, Brit.), ph; SECRET AGENT(1933, Brit.), ph; LOST IN THE LEGION(1934, Brit.), ph; RETURN OF BULLDOG DRUMMOND, THE(1934, Brit.), ph; WARREN CASE, THE(1934, Brit.), ph; DANDY DICK(1935, Brit.), ph; ANNIE LAURIE(1936, Brit.), ph; END OF THE ROAD, THE(1936, Brit.), ph; LOVE UP THE POLE(1936, Brit.), ph; NEXT TIME WE LOVE(1936); WELL DONE, HENRY(1936, Brit.), ph; OLD MOTHER RILEY(1937, Brit.), ph; SCHOONER GANG, THE(1937, Brit.), ph; SING AS YOU SWING(1937, Brit.), ph; WANTED(1937, Brit.), ph; ROSE OF TRALEE(1942, Brit.), ph; DEAD OF NIGHT(1946, Brit.), ph; TILL THE END OF TIME(1948, Brit.), ph; CAPTIVE HEART, THE(1948, Brit.), ph; STAMPEDE(1949); MAN BEHIND THE GUN, THE(1952); SEVENTH CAVALRY(1956)

James P. Parker
1984
KILLPOINT(1984)

James Parker, Jr.
SEAS BENEATH, THE(1931), w

Jameson Parker
BELL JAR, THE(1979); SMALL CIRCLE OF FRIENDS, A(1980); WHITE DOG(1982)

Janet Lee Parker
DAVID AND LISA(1962)

Jean Parker
DIVORCE IN THE FAMILY(1932); RASPUTIN AND THE EMPRESS(1932); GABRIEL OVER THE WHITE HOUSE(1933); LADY FOR A DAY(1933); LITTLE WOMEN(1933); MADE ON BROADWAY(1933); SECRET OF MADAME BLANCHE, THE(1933); STORM AT DAYBREAK(1933); WHAT PRICE INNOCENCE?(1933); CARAVAN(1934); HAVE A HEART(1934); LAZY RIVER(1934); LIMEHOUSE BLUES(1934); OPERATOR 13(1934); SEQUOIA(1934); TWO ALONE(1934); WICKED WOMAN, A(1934); YOU CAN'T BUY EVERYTHING(1934); MURDER IN THE FLEET(1935); PRINCESS O'HARA(1935); FARMER IN THE DELL, THE(1936); GHOST GOES WEST, THE(1936); TEXAS RANGERS, THE(1936); BARRIER, THE(1937); LIFE BEGINS WITH LOVE(1937); ARKANSAS TRAVELER, THE(1938); PENITENTIARY(1938); ROMANCE OF THE LIMBERLOST(1938); FLIGHT AT MID-

NIGHT(1939); FLYING DEUCES, THE(1939); PARENTS ON TRIAL(1939); ROMANCE OF THE REDWOODS(1939); SHE MARRIED A COP(1939); ZENOBIA(1939); BEYOND TOMORROW(1940); KNIGHTS OF THE RANGE(1940); SON OF THE NAVY(1940); FLYING BLIND(1941); NO HANDS ON THE CLOCK(1941); PITTSBURGH KID, THE(1941); POWER DIVE(1941); ROAR OF THE PRESS(1941); GIRL FROM ALASKA(1942); HELLO ANNAPOLIS(1942); HI, NEIGHBOR(1942); I LIVE ON DANGER(1942); TOMORROW WE LIVE(1942); TORPEDO BOAT(1942); TRAITOR WITHIN, THE(1942); WRECKING CREW(1942); ALASKA HIGHWAY(1943); DEERSLAYER(1943); HIGH EXPLOSIVE(1943); MINESWEEPER(1943); ADVENTURES OF KITTY O'DAY(1944); BLUEBEARD(1944); DEAD MAN'S EYES(1944); DETECTIVE KITTY O'DAY(1944); LADY IN THE DEATH HOUSE(1944); NAVY WAY, THE(1944); OH, WHAT A NIGHT(1944); ONE BODY TOO MANY(1944); GUNFIGHTER, THE(1950); TOUGHEST MAN IN ARIZONA(1952); THOSE REDHEADS FROM SEATTLE(1953); BLACK TUESDAY(1955); LAWLESS STREET, A(1955); PARSON AND THE OUTLAW, THE(1957); APACHE UPRISING(1966); STIGMA(1972)
Misc. Talkies
ROLLING HOME(1948)

Jeff Parker
TWIST AROUND THE CLOCK(1961); GYPSY(1962)

Jefferson Parker
GREAT GOD GOLD(1935), w; TWO SINNERS(1935), w; FORBIDDEN HEAVEN(1936), w; HUMAN CARGO(1936), w; PEPPER(1936), w; YELLOWSTONE(1936), w; MYSTERIOUS CROSSING(1937), w; UNDER SUSPICION(1937), w; CRIME TAKES A HOLIDAY(1938), w; FLIGHT INTO NOWHERE(1938), w; MAKING THE HEADLINES(1938), w; FIVE LITTLE PEPPERS AND HOW THEY GREW(1939), w; GENTLE GANGSTER, A(1943), w

Jetsy Parker
KEEP YOUR POWDER DRY(1945); PETTY GIRL, THE(1950); ROYAL WEDDING(1951)

Jim Parker
GALLANT ONE, THE(1964, U.S./Peru)

Jim Parker
STAR SPANGLED GIRL(1971), w; SNOWBALL EXPRESS(1972), w

Joe Parker
EIGHTEEN AND ANXIOUS(1957), d; HOT ANGEL, THE(1958), d

John F. Parker
SUPERMAN(1978)

John Parker
BECAUSE OF EVE(1948); DEMENTIA(1955), p,d&w; WRONG BOX, THE(1966, Brit.); DARKER THAN AMBER(1970), m; HARD ROAD, THE(1970); CORKY(1972), m

John T. Parker
1984
MIRRORS(1984), p

Judge Parker
FARMER, THE(1977)

Judy Parker
WINTER A GO-GO(1965)

Karen Parker
FIVE FINGER EXERCISE(1962); RUMBLE FISH(1983)

Karyn Parker
1984
ANGEL(1984)

Kathleen Parker
UP THE MACGREGORS(1967, Ital./Span.); YOUNG, THE EVIL AND THE SAVAGE, THE(1968, Ital.); ROCKY(1976)

Kay Parker
Misc. Talkies
CHORUS CALL(1979)

Ken L. Parker
FRIDAY THE 13TH(1980)

Kenneth Parker
WALK, DON'T RUN(1966)

Kim Parker
UP TO HIS NECK(1954, Brit.); LAND OF FURY(1955 Brit.); STOCK CAR(1955, Brit.); FIRE MAIDENS FROM OUTER SPACE(1956, Brit.); GOOD COMPANIONS, THE(1957, Brit.); MAN WITHOUT A BODY, THE(1957, Brit.); UNDERCOVER GIRL(1957, Brit.); FIEND WITHOUT A FACE(1958); COUNT YOUR BLESSINGS(1959)

L. Parker
Silents
KID, THE(1921)

Lady Parker
Silents
AFFAIRS OF ANATOL, THE(1921)

Lara Parker
HI, MOM!(1970); NIGHT OF DARK SHADOWS(1971); SAVE THE TIGER(1973); RACE WITH THE DEVIL(1975)

Lee Parker
RUDE BOY(1980, Brit.)

Lee W. Parker
Silents
TWO FLAMING YOUTHS(1927)

Leonard Parker
NOTHING BUT A MAN(1964); LAST OF THE RED HOT LOVERS(1972)

Leslie Parker
WALLET, THE(1952, Brit.)

Lew Parker
ARE YOU WITH IT?(1948); COUNTRY MUSIC HOLIDAY(1958)

Linda Parker
STUDENT TOUR(1934); NAUGHTY MARIETTA(1935); WHEN YOU COME HOME(1947, Brit.)

Lisa Parker
SOUP FOR ONE(1982)

Lloyd "Sunshine" Parker
HEART BEAT(1979)

Lottie Blair Parker
WAY DOWN EAST(1935), w
Silents
WAY DOWN EAST(1920), w

Louis N. Parker
MONKEY'S PAW, THE(1933), w; DRAKE THE PIRATE(1935, Brit.), w; CARDINAL, THE(1936, Brit.), w

Louis Napoleon Parker
DISRAELI(1929), w

Lucy Parker
Misc. Silents
CRUCIBLE, THE(1914)

Mack Parker
MIRACLE WOMAN, THE(1931), art d

Martha Parker
IN PRAISE OF OLDER WOMEN(1978, Can.)

Mary Cecil Parker
Silents
PERSUASIVE PEGGY(1917)

Mary Parker
TALES OF THE UNCANNY(1932, Ger.); ARTISTS AND MODELS ABROAD(1938); COCOANUT GROVE(1938); HUNTED MEN(1938); CAFE SOCIETY(1939); ST. LOUIS BLUES(1939); SUDDEN MONEY(1939); LADY IN THE DARK(1944); MUSIC FOR MILLIONS(1944); DEADLY GAME, THE(1955, Brit.); YOU LUCKY PEOPLE(1955, Brit.); HOSTAGE, THE(1956, Brit.)

Max Parker
NIGHT NURSE(1931), art d; PUBLIC ENEMY, THE(1931), art d; CALL HER SAVAGE(1932), art d; CHANDU THE MAGICIAN(1932), art d; TOO BUSY TO WORK(1932), art d; POWER AND THE GLORY, THE(1933), art d; SPRINGTIME FOR HENRY(1934), set d; CHINA CLIPPER(1936), art d; COLLEEN(1936), art d; GIVE ME YOUR HEART(1936), ed, art d; SATAN MET A LADY(1936), art d; FIRST LADY(1937), art d; GREEN LIGHT(1937), art d; MARKED WOMAN(1937), art d; MARRY THE GIRL(1937), art d; MOUNTAIN JUSTICE(1937), art d; THAT CERTAIN WOMAN(1937), art d; BROTHER RAT(1938), art d; FOUR'S A CROWD(1938), art d; MEN ARE SUCH FOOLS(1938), art d; MY BILL(1938), art d; SLIGHT CASE OF MURDER, A(1938), art d; WOMEN ARE LIKE THAT(1938), art d; EACH DAWN I DIE(1939), art d; ROARING TWENTIES, THE(1939), art d; BROTHER ORCHID(1940), art d; DEVIL'S ISLAND(1940), art d; INVISIBLE STRIPES(1940), art d; IT ALL CAME TRUE(1940), art d; LADY WITH RED HAIR(1940), art d; MY LOVE CAME BACK(1940), art d; FOOTSTEPS IN THE DARK(1941), art d; MANPOWER(1941), art d; ALL THROUGH THE NIGHT(1942), art d; GEORGE WASHINGTON SLEPT HERE(1942), art d; WINGS FOR THE EAGLE(1942), art d; PRINCESS O'ROURKE(1943), art d; ARSENIC AND OLD LACE(1944), art d; CLOAK AND DAGGER(1946), art d; DEEP VALLEY(1947), art d; SECRET BEYOND THE DOOR, THE(1948), prod d
Silents
RED DICE(1926), art d; VOLGA BOATMAN, THE(1926), art d

Monica Parker
MERRY WIVES OF TOBIAS ROUKE, THE(1972, Can.); IMPROPER CHANNELS(1981, Can.)
1984
WOMAN IN RED, THE(1984)

Morton S. Parker
HELL'S HEADQUARTERS(1932), w

Murray Parker
SIN TOWN(1942); TANGIER(1946); FLYING FONTAINES, THE(1959)

Norman Parker
PRINCE OF THE CITY(1981); KILLING HOUR, THE(1982); DANIEL(1983)

Norman S. Parker
SKY PATROL(1939), w

Norton A. Parker
Misc. Silents
ROAD TO RUIN, THE(1928), d

Norton Parker
SINISTER HANDS(1932), w

Norton S. Parker
TEN NIGHTS IN A BARROOM(1931), w; TUNDRA(1936), w; COURAGE OF THE WEST(1937), w; BORDER WOLVES(1938), w; LAST STAND, THE(1938), w; OUTLAW EXPRESS(1938), w; PRISON BREAK(1938), w; WESTERN TRAILS(1938), w; STAGE TO CHINO(1940), w; THREE MEN FROM TEXAS(1940), w; YOUNG BILL HICKOK(1940), w; BANDIT TRAIL, THE(1941), w; CYCLONE ON HORSEBACK(1941), w; IN OLD COLORADO(1941), w; SIX GUN GOLD(1941), w; COME ON DANGER(1942), w; FIGHTING FRONTIER(1943), w; RIO GRANDE RAIDERS(1946), w; DEVIL'S CANYON(1953), w
Silents
LADY FROM HELL, THE(1926), w
Misc. Silents
PACE THAT KILLS, THE(1928), d

Obie Parker
MEN, THE(1950)

Patricia Ann Parker
HEX(1973)

Pauline Parker
HUMAN TARGETS(1932)

Penney Parker
DARK AT THE TOP OF THE STAIRS, THE(1960)

Penny Parker
TILL THE CLOUDS ROLL BY(1946)

Percy Parker
MARK OF THE DEVIL(1970, Ger./Brit.), w

Phyllis Parker
TWO LOST WORLDS(1950), w; STEEL FIST, THE(1952), w

Pinky Parker
LIBELED LADY(1936)

Ralph Parker
Misc. Silents
POWER DIVINE, THE(1923)

Raymond Parker
FRESHMAN YEAR(1938); HIS EXCITING NIGHT(1938); LAST WARNING, THE(1938); LETTER OF INTRODUCTION(1938); LITTLE TOUGH GUY(1938); SERVICE DE LUXE(1938); SWING THAT CHEER(1938); EAST SIDE OF HEAVEN(1939); FOR LOVE OR MONEY(1939); HOUSE OF FEAR, THE(1939); SOCIETY SMUGGLERS(1939)

Rena Parker
Silents
DANGEROUS HOUR(1923), w

Rhonda Parker
HUSBANDS(1970)

Richard M. Parker
LIGHT AT THE EDGE OF THE WORLD, THE(1971, U.S./Span./Lichtenstein), spec eff; MAN IN THE WILDERNESS(1971, U.S./Span.), spec eff; WHITE BUFFALO, THE(1977), spec eff

Richard Parker
THOSE MAGNIFICENT MEN IN THEIR FLYING MACHINES; OR HOW I FLEW FROM LONDON TO PARIS IN 25 HOURS AND 11 MINUTES(1965), spec eff; KHARTOUM(1966, Brit.), spec eff; WHERE EAGLES DARE(1968, Brit.), spec eff; SINFUL DAVEY(1969, Brit.), spec eff; HELLO–GOODBYE(1970), spec eff; YAKUZA, THE(1975, U.S./Jap.), spec eff

Robert Parker
PRIVATE SCHOOL(1983)

Roger Parker
TUNNELVISION(1976), ed; CRACKING UP(1977), ed

Ross Parker
GIRL GETTERS, THE(1966, Brit.); CHITTY CHITTY BANG BANG(1968, Brit.)

Russell Parker
EDGE, THE(1968)
Silents
KENTUCKIANS, THE(1921)

Sage Parker
1984
SONGWRITER(1984)

Sarah Jessica Parker
1984
FIRSTBORN(1984); FOOTLOOSE(1984)

Scott Parker
DIE LAUGHING(1980), w; HE KNOWS YOU'RE ALONE(1980), w

Shirley Parker
MISSION MARS(1968); MINX, THE(1969)

Sir Gilbert Parker
RIGHT OF WAY, THE(1931), w; BEHOLD MY WIFE(1935), w
Silents
SEATS OF THE MIGHTY, THE(1914), w; JORDAN IS A HARD ROAD(1915), w

Sir Lewis Parker
Silents
PIERRE OF THE PLAINS(1914), w

Stephen Parker
TEENAGE MONSTER(1958)

Steve Parker
MY GEISHA(1962), p; JOHN GOLDFARB, PLEASE COME HOME(1964), p

Stewart Parker
FUNERAL FOR AN ASSASSIN(1977)

Sunshine Parker
HOMETOWN U.S.A.(1979); CANNERY ROW(1982)
Misc. Talkies
SPITTIN' IMAGE(1983)

Suzy Parker
FUNNY FACE(1957); KISS THEM FOR ME(1957); 10 NORTH FREDERICK(1958); BEST OF EVERYTHING, THE(1959); CIRCLE OF DECEPTON(1961, Brit.); INTERNS, THE(1962); FLIGHT FROM ASHIYA(1964, U.S./Jap.); CHAMBER OF HORRORS(1966)

Talley Parker
SHEILA LEVINE IS DEAD AND LIVING IN NEW YORK(1975)

Tex Parker
TWO GUN SHERIFF(1941)

Tom Parker
Misc. Talkies
AMAZING LOVE SECRET(1975), d; KEEP IT UP, JACK!(1975), d

Col. Tom Parker
FOLLOW THAT DREAM(1962), tech adv

Ursula Parker
LIGHTNING BOLT(1967, Ital./Sp.)

Valeri Parker
WATCHED(1974)

Warren Parker
TOO SOON TO LOVE(1960); HOODLUM PRIEST, THE(1961); RETURN TO PEYTON PLACE(1961); CAREY TREATMENT, THE(1972)

Will Parker
CYNTHIA(1947)

Willard Parker
DEVIL'S SADDLE LEGION, THE(1937); LOVE IS ON THE AIR(1937); OVER THE GOAL(1937); THAT CERTAIN WOMAN(1937); ACCIDENTS WILL HAPPEN(1938); SLIGHT CASE OF MURDER, A(1938); ZERO HOUR, THE(1939); WHAT A WOMAN!(1943); FIGHTING GUARDSMAN, THE(1945); ONE WAY TO LOVE(1946); RENEGADES(1946); MATING OF MILLIE, THE(1948); RELENTLESS(1948); YOU GOTTA STAY HAPPY(1948); CALAMITY JANE AND SAM BASS(1949); SLIGHTLY FRENCH(1949); BANDIT QUEEN(1950); BODYHOLD(1950); DAVID HARDING, COUNTERSPY(1950); EMERGENCY WEDDING(1950); HUNT THE MAN DOWN(1950); SECRET FURY, THE(1950); APACHE DRUMS(1951); MY TRUE STORY(1951); CARIBBEAN(1952); GREAT JESSE JAMES RAID, THE(1953); KISS ME KATE(1953); SANGAREE(1953); VANQUISHED, THE(1953); NAKED GUN, THE(1956); LURE OF THE SWAMP(1957); LONE TEXAN(1959); HIGH-POWERED RIFLE, THE(1960); WALK TALL(1960); YOUNG JESSE JAMES(1960); AIR PATROL(1962); EARTH DIES SCREAMING, THE(1964, Brit.); WACO(1966); GREAT WALTZ, THE(1972)
Misc. Talkies
WRECK OF THE HESPERUS(1948)

William Parker
PRIVATES ON PARADE(1982)
1984
PRIVATES ON PARADE(1984, Brit.)
Silents
ANTHING ONCE(1917), w; JACK KNIFE MAN, THE(1920), w; NUT, THE(1921), w

Yvonne Parker
RIP TIDE(1934)
Cecil Parkes
HELL, HEAVEN OR HOBOKEN(1958, Brit.)
Clifford Parkes
MIKADO, THE(1967, Brit.); CHALLENGE FOR ROBIN HOOD, A(1968, Brit.), p
Clifton Parkes
WOODEN HORSE, THE(1951), m
Eddie Parkes
THRILL OF BRAZIL, THE(1946); TAKE ME OUT TO THE BALL GAME(1949); GUNFIGHTER, THE(1950); IN GOD WE TRUST(1980)
Frances Parkes
Silents
GIRL WHO STAYED AT HOME, THE(1919)
Gerald Parkes
YESTERDAY(1980, Can.)
Gerard Parkes
GREAT BIG THING, A(1968, U.S./Can.); ISABEL(1968, Can.); FIRST TIME, THE(1969); SECOND WIND(1976, Can.); WHO HAS SEEN THE WIND(1980, Can.); SPASMS(1983, Can.)
James Parkes
TWO-MINUTE WARNING(1976)
James R. Parkes
TRACKDOWN(1976)
John Parkes
PROFILE(1954, Brit.)
Michael Parkes
GRAND PRIX(1966)
Penelope Parkes
AVENGING HAND, THE(1936, Brit.); BELOVED IMPOSTER(1936, Brit.)
Tim Parkes
BLUE MAX, THE(1966)
Timothy Parkes
SUBURBAN WIVES(1973, Brit.)
Walter F. Parkes
WARGAMES(1983), w
Conrad Parkham
PROUD AND THE DAMNED, THE(1972)
Misc. Talkies
FORTRESS OF THE DEAD(1965)
Tony Parkham
POLYESTER(1981)
Forbes Parkhill
ALIAS JOHN LAW(1935), w; NO MAN'S RANGE(1935), w; LAW RIDES, THE(1936), w; STAND UP AND FIGHT(1939), w
Lance Parkhill
TEX(1982)
Leonid Parkhomenko
IDIOT, THE(1960, USSR)
Michael Parkhurst
MOONFIRE(1970), d
Pixie Parkhurst
BETWEEN HEAVEN AND HELL(1956)
Dean Parkin
WAR OF THE COLOSSAL BEAST(1958)
Duncan Parkin
CYCLOPS(1957)
Mary Parkin
Misc. Silents
PANTS(1917)
Tony Parkin
BARTLEBY(1970, Brit.)
Beaulah Parkington
MAN'S WORLD, A(1942)
Beulah Parkington
SUDDENLY IT'S SPRING(1947); KNOCK ON ANY DOOR(1949); MY BLUE HEAVEN(1950); MATING SEASON, THE(1951)
Barbara Parkins
20,000 EYES(1961); VALLEY OF THE DOLLS(1967); KREMLIN LETTER, THE(1970); MEPHISTO WALTZ, THE(1971); PUPPET ON A CHAIN(1971, Brit.); ASYLUM(1972, Brit.); DEADLY TRAP, THE(1972, Fr./Ital.); CHRISTINA(1974, Can.); SHOUT AT THE DEVIL(1976, Brit.); BEAR ISLAND(1980, Brit.-Can.)
Misc. Talkies
BREAKFAST IN PARIS(1981)
Jack Parkins
LIFE IN DANGER(1964, Brit.), p
Austin Parkinson
DEADLY FEMALES, THE(1976, Brit.), ph
Chuck Parkinson, Jr.
ROLLERBALL(1975)
Cliff Parkinson
ROUGH RIDIN' RHYTHM(1937); WHISTLING BULLETS(1937); IN OLD MEXICO(1938); RAWHIDE(1938); SIX-GUN RHYTHM(1939); LAW AND ORDER(1940); SANTA FE MARSHAL(1940); BORDER PATROL(1943); CALLING WILD BILL ELLIOTT(1943); RIDERS OF THE DEADLINE(1943); SAN ANTONIO KID, THE(1944); COLORADO PIONEERS(1945); RAMROD(1947); SUNDOWN RIDERS(1948)
Dorothy Parkinson
MANCHURIAN CANDIDATE, THE(1962), makeup; KITTEN WITH A WHIP(1964), makeup
Georgina Parkinson
ROMEO AND JULIET(1966, Brit.); MUSIC LOVERS, THE(1971, Brit.)
H. B. Parkinson
EVERYTHING OKAY(1936, Brit.), w
Silents
LEAD, KINDLY LIGHT(1918, Brit.), w; GOD IN THE GARDEN, THE(1921, Brit.), p; LOVE AT THE WHEEL(1921, Brit.), p; MARRIED TO A MORMAN(1922, Brit.), p&d; TRAPPED BY THE MORMONS(1922, Brit.), p&d; GAMBLE WITH HEARTS, A(1923, Brit.), p

H.B. Parkinson
SISTER TO ASSIST'ER, A(1930, Brit.), p
Misc. Silents
CHANNINGS, THE(1920, Brit.), d; LAW DIVINE, THE(1920, Brit.), d; BLEAK HOUSE(1922, Brit.), d
John Parkinson
MONTENEGRO(1981, Brit./Swed.)
Michael Parkinson
MADHOUSE(1974, Brit.)
Ricky Parkinson
MC VICAR(1982, Brit.)
Robin Parkinson
FAMILY WAY, THE(1966, Brit.); THEY CAME FROM BEYOND SPACE(1967, Brit.); TWISTED NERVE(1969, Brit.); THERE'S A GIRL IN MY SOUP(1970, Brit.); CATCH ME A SPY(1971, Brit./Fr.); ALFIE DARLING(1975, Brit.)
Roy Parkinson
BLUEBEARD'S TEN HONEYMOONS(1960, Brit.), p
Tom Parkinson
CRUCIBLE OF TERROR(1971, Brit.), p, w; DISCIPLE OF DEATH(1972, Brit.), p, d, w
Chuck Parkison
HONKERS, THE(1972)
Chuck Parkison, Jr.
NIGHT MOVES(1975)
Andrew Parks
STRAWBERRY STATEMENT, THE(1970); W.C. FIELDS AND ME(1976)
Andy Parks
SUMMER RUN(1974); DRIVE-IN(1976)
Misc. Talkies
SUMMER RUN(1974)
Barbara Parks
1984
CALIFORNIA GIRLS(1984)
Bert Parks
THAT'S THE WAY OF THE WORLD(1975)
Catherine Parks
LOOKER(1981); FRIDAY THE 13TH PART III(1982)
Charles Parks
ON THE NICKEL(1980); S.O.B.(1981); I OUGHT TO BE IN PICTURES(1982)
1984
CITY HEAT(1984)
Darlene Parks
HAPPY HOOKER, THE(1975)
E.L. Parks
BEHIND THAT CURTAIN(1929)
Ed Parks
UNSUSPECTED, THE(1947); HEY THERE, IT'S YOGI BEAR(1964), anim; MAN CALLED FLINTSTONE, THE(1966), anim
Eddie Parks
O, MY DARLING CLEMENTINE(1943); SPOTLIGHT SCANDALS(1943); AVALANCHE(1946); CRACK-UP(1946); CUBAN PETE(1946); PLAINSMAN AND THE LADY(1946); SING WHILE YOU DANCE(1946); DARK DELUSION(1947); DESPERATE(1947); HIGH CONQUEST(1947); KILLER AT LARGE(1947); LIKELY STORY, A(1947); MAGIC TOWN(1947); ARE YOU WITH IT?(1948); CRY OF THE CITY(1948); INNER SANCTUM(1948); LET'S LIVE A LITTLE(1948); LUCK OF THE IRISH(1948); SAINTED SISTERS, THE(1948); THAT WONDERFUL URGE(1948); SKY DRAGON(1949); FILE ON THELMA JORDAN, THE(1950); SLAUGHTER TRAIL(1951); BUSHWHACKERS, THE(1952); HOUSE OF WAX(1953); FORTY GUNS(1957)
Edward Parks
CHRISTMAS EVE(1947)
Ernie Parks
YOU'RE MY EVERYTHING(1949), makeup
Frances Parks
Silents
JACK STRAW(1920)
Fred Parks
Misc. Talkies
RIDERS OF RIO(1931)
George Parks
Silents
KING'S GAME, THE(1916)
Gordon Parks
LEARNING TREE, THE(1969), p,d&w, m; SHAFT'S BIG SCORE(1972); SUPER COPS, THE(1974), d; LEADBELLY(1976), d
Gordon Parks, Jr.
SUPERFLY(1972), d; THOMASINE AND BUSHROD(1974), d; THREE THE HARD WAY(1974), d; AARON LOVES ANGELA(1975), d
Gordon Parks, Sr.
SHAFT(1971), d; SHAFT'S BIG SCORE(1972), d, m
Hildy Parks
NIGHT HOLDS TERROR, THE(1955); FAIL SAFE(1964); GROUP, THE(1966)
J. Gower Parks
MY BROTHER JONATHAN(1949, Brit.), cos
Jackson Parks
TRAPPED(1931), w
Jean Parks
PLEASURE PLANTATION(1970)
Joan Parks
HURRY SUNDOWN(1967)
Johnson Parks
IN OLD MONTANA(1939), w
Larry Parks
HARMON OF MICHIGAN(1941); MYSTERY SHIP(1941); SING FOR YOUR SUPPER(1941); THREE GIRLS ABOUT TOWN(1941); YOU BELONG TO ME(1941); ALIAS BOSTON BLACKIE(1942); ATLANTIC CONVOY(1942); BLONDIE GOES TO COLLEGE(1942); BOOGIE MAN WILL GET YOU, THE(1942); CANAL ZONE(1942); FLIGHT LIEUTENANT(1942); HARVARD, HERE I COME(1942); HELLO ANNAPOLIS(1942); MAN'S WORLD, A(1942); SUBMARINE RAIDER(1942); THEY ALL KISSED THE BRIDE(1942); YOU WERE NEVER LOVELIER(1942); DEERSLAYER(1943); DESTROYER(1943); FIRST COMES COURAGE(1943); IS EVERY-

BODY HAPPY?(1943); POWER OF THE PRESS(1943); REVEILLE WITH BEVER-
LY(1943); BLACK PARACHUTE, THE(1944); HEY, ROOKIE(1944); RACKET MAN,
THE(1944); SHE'S A SWEETHEART(1944); STARS ON PARADE(1944); COUNTER-
ATTACK(1945); SERGEANT MIKE(1945); JOLSON STORY, THE(1946); RENE-
GADES(1946); DOWN TO EARTH(1947); HER HUSBAND'S AFFAIRS(1947);
SWORDSMAN, THE(1947); GALLANT BLADE, THE(1948); JOLSON SINGS
AGAIN(1949); EMERGENCY WEDDING(1950); LOVE IS BETTER THAN EVER(1952);
REDHEAD FROM MANHATTAN(1954); CROSS-UP(1958); FREUD(1962)

Michael Parks
BUS RILEY'S BACK IN TOWN(1965); WILD SEED(1965); BIBLE...IN THE BEGIN-
NING, THE(1966); IDOL, THE(1966, Brit.); HAPPENING, THE(1967); GET BACK(1973,
Can.); LAST HARD MEN, THE(1976); SIDEWINDER ONE(1977); BREAK-
THROUGH(1978, Ger.); LOVE AND THE MIDNIGHT AUTO SUPPLY(1978); PRIVATE
FILES OF J. EDGAR HOOVER, THE(1978); EVICTORS, THE(1979); FFOLKES(1980,
Brit.); HARD COUNTRY(1981); SAVANNAH SMILES(1983)

Nanette Parks
TIME OF YOUR LIFE, THE(1948); OVER 21(1945); SNAFU(1945); VARIETY
GIRL(1947); SPEED TO SPARE(1948)
Misc. Talkies
TEXAS PANHANDLE(1945)

Patricia Parks
NORTH STAR, THE(1943)

Post Parks
SHE WORE A YELLOW RIBBON(1949)

R. Gower Parks
MEET ME AT DAWN(1947, Brit.), cos

Ronnie Parks
JAWS 3-D(1983)

Roy Parks
RIVERRUN(1968)

Stan Parks
SCARFACE(1983), spec eff
1984
RIVER, THE(1984), spec eff

Trina Parks
DIAMONDS ARE FOREVER(1971, Brit.); DARKTOWN STRUTTERS(1975)
Misc. Talkies
MUTHERS, THE(1976); GET DOWN AND BOOGIE(1977)

Van Dyke Parks
SWAN, THE(1956); GOIN' SOUTH(1978), m
Misc. Talkies
GIFT FOR HEIDI, A(1958)

Parkyakarkus
LIFE OF THE PARTY, THE(1937); NEW FACES OF 1937(1937); SHE'S GOT
EVERYTHING(1938); EARL CARROLL'S VANITIES(1945); OUT OF THIS
WORLD(1945)

Parkyakarkus [Harry Einstein]
STRIKE ME PINK(1936); NIGHT SPOT(1938); YANK IN LIBYA, A(1942); YANKS
ARE COMING, THE(1942)

Lesie Parkyn
FATHER CAME TOO(1964, Brit.), p

Leslie Parkyn
COMING-OUT PARTY, A(, p; IT STARTED IN PARADISE(1952, Brit.), p; LITTLE
KIDNAPPERS, THE(1954, Brit.), p; WOMAN FOR JOE, THE(1955, Brit.), p; TIGER IN
THE SMOKE(1956, Brit.), p; WHITE TRAP, THE(1959, Brit.), p; CIRCUS OF HOR-
RORS(1960, Brit.), p; OCTOBER MOTH(1960, Brit.), p; SNOWBALL(1960, Brit.), p;
HOUSE OF MYSTERY(1961, Brit.), p; MAN IN THE BACK SEAT, THE(1961, Brit.), p;
SEVEN KEYS(1962, Brit.), p; BITTER HARVEST(1963, Brit.), p; CROOKS ANONY-
MOUS(1963, Brit.), p; FAST LADY, THE(1963, Brit.), p; MALPAS MYSTERY,
THE(1967, Brit.), p

Alicia Parla
Misc. Talkies
ANGRY GOD, THE(1948)

Stanley Parlam
TEN GENTLEMEN FROM WEST POINT(1942)

George Parleton
LOST CONTINENT, THE(1968, Brit.), makeup; CLOCKWORK ORANGE, A(1971,
Brit.), makeup

Dita Parlo
HONOR OF THE FAMILY(1931); COURIER OF LYONS(1938, Fr.); GRAND ILLU-
SION(1938, Fr.); ULTIMATUM(1940, Fr.); UNDER SECRET ORDERS(1943, Brit.);
L'ATALANTE(1947, Fr.)
Misc. Silents
SECRETS OF THE ORIENT(1932, Ger.)

Dito Parlo
Misc. Silents
AU BONHEUR DES DAMES(1929, Fr.)

Gianfranco Parloni
SAMSON(1961, Ital.), d, w

V. Parlov
HOUSE ON THE FRONT LINE, THE(1963, USSR)

Melvin Parlow
STARK FEAR(1963), makeup

Tula Parma
LEOPARD MAN, THE(1943)

Tony Parmalee
SHAFT'S BIG SCORE(1972), spec eff; HOUSE BY THE LAKE, THE(1977, Can.), spec
eff

William Parmalee
Silents
GOLD RUSH, THE(1925)

Quinto Parmeggiana
WEEKEND MURDERS, THE(1972, Ital.)

Bernard Parmeggiani
DOLL, THE(1962, Fr.), m

Quinto Parmeggiani
SECRET OF SANTA VITTORIA, THE(1969); CLARETTA AND BEN(1983, Ital., Fr.)

Tony Parmelee
TAXI DRIVER(1976), spec eff

Pam Parmelli
LOOKIN' TO GET OUT(1982)

Noel Parmental
BEYOND THE LAW(1968)

Noel E. Parmentel, Jr.
MAIDSTONE(1970)

Adele Parmenter
KISS TOMORROW GOODBYE(1950), cos; WAGONMASTER(1950), cos; MAN WITH
THE GOLDEN ARM, THE(1955), cos; IT HAPPENED IN ATHENS(1962), cos

Brigitte Parmentier
BELLE DE JOUR(1968, Fr.)

Richard Parmentier
PEOPLE THAT TIME FORGOT, THE(1977, Brit.); SUPERMAN II(1980); SILVER
DREAM RACER(1982, Brit.); OCTOPUSSY(1983, Brit.)

Rick Lee Parmentier
STARDUST(1974, Brit.)

Arturo Parmiani
RED DESERT(1965, Fr./Ital.)

Bertram Parnell
Misc. Silents
DOWN UNDER DONOVAN(1922, Brit.)

Clive Parnell
KIMBERLEY JIM(1965, South Africa)

Effie Parnell
THAT'S RIGHT–YOU'RE WRONG(1939); MARGIE(1940); STRANGLER OF THE
SWAMP(1945)

Emory Parnell
ANGELS WITH DIRTY FACES(1938); ARSON GANG BUSTERS(1938); CALL OF
THE YUKON(1938); DR. RHYTHM(1938); I AM THE LAW(1938); KING OF ALCA-
TRAZ(1938); MAD MISS MANTON, THE(1938); SWEETHEARTS(1938); DAY THE
BOOKIES WEPT, THE(1939); EAST SIDE OF HEAVEN(1939); HOUSE OF FEAR,
THE(1939); I STOLE A MILLION(1939); IDIOT'S DELIGHT(1939); LET FREEDOM
RING(1939); LITTLE ACCIDENT(1939); OFF THE RECORD(1939); ONE HOUR TO
LIVE(1939); PACIFIC LINER(1939); SPELLBINDER, THE(1939); ST. LOUIS
BLUES(1939); STAR MAKER, THE(1939); THEY SHALL HAVE MUSIC(1939); UNION
PACIFIC(1939); WINTER CARNIVAL(1939); YOU CAN'T GET AWAY WITH MUR-
DER(1939); BLONDIE ON A BUDGET(1940); FOREIGN CORRESPONDENT(1940);
GREAT McGINTY, THE(1940); IF I HAD MY WAY(1940); INVISIBLE STRIPES(1940);
NORTHWEST MOUNTED POLICE(1940); OUT WEST WITH THE PEPPERS(1940);
STRANGER ON THE THIRD FLOOR(1940); SUED FOR LIBEL(1940); BLONDE FROM
SINGAPORE, THE(1941); CASE OF THE BLACK PARROT, THE(1941); KISS THE
BOYS GOODBYE(1941); LADY FROM CHEYENNE(1941); LOUISIANA PUR-
CHASE(1941); MALTESE FALCON, THE(1941); MONSTER AND THE GIRL,
THE(1941); MR. AND MRS. SMITH(1941); OBLIGING YOUNG LADY(1941); SHOT IN
THE DARK, THE(1941); SO ENDS OUR NIGHT(1941); SULLIVAN'S TRAVELS(1941);
UNHOLY PARTNERS(1941); ARABIAN NIGHTS(1942); I MARRIED A WITCH(1942);
JOHNNY EAGER(1942); KING'S ROW(1942); LARCENY, INC.(1942); MAJOR AND
THE MINOR, THE(1942); ONCE UPON A HONEYMOON(1942); OVER MY DEAD
BODY(1942); REMARKABLE ANDREW, THE(1942); SABOTEUR(1942); THEY ALL
KISSED THE BRIDE(1942); WINGS FOR THE EAGLE(1942); DANCING MASTERS,
THE(1943); DU BARRY WAS A LADY(1943); GOVERNMENT GIRL(1943); HUMAN
COMEDY, THE(1943); LET'S FACE IT(1943); MISSION TO MOSCOW(1943); MR.
LUCKY(1943); OUTLAW, THE(1943); THAT NAZTY NUISANCE(1943); TWO SENORI-
TAS FROM CHICAGO(1943); UNKNOWN GUEST, THE(1943); YOUNG IDEAS(1943);
ADDRESS UNKNOWN(1944); CASANOVA BROWN(1944); FALCON IN HOLLY-
WOOD, THE(1944); FALCON IN MEXICO, THE(1944); GILDERSLEEVE'S
GHOST(1944); HEAVENLY DAYS(1944); MIRACLE OF MORGAN'S CREEK,
THE(1944); NIGHT OF ADVENTURE, A(1944); ONCE UPON A TIME(1944); SEVEN
DAYS ASHORE(1944); TALL IN THE SADDLE(1944); COLONEL EFFINGHAM'S
RAID(1945); CRIME DOCTOR'S COURAGE, THE(1945); HAVING WONDERFUL
CRIME(1945); IT'S IN THE BAG(1945); MAMA LOVES PAPA(1945); SING YOUR WAY
HOME(1945); STATE FAIR(1945); TWO O'CLOCK COURAGE(1945); WHAT A
BLONDE(1945); ABIE'S IRISH ROSE(1946); BADMAN'S TERRITORY(1946); DEAD-
LINE AT DAWN(1946); DEADLINE FOR MURDER(1946); FALCON'S ALIBI,
THE(1946); LITTLE IODINE(1946); QUEEN OF BURLESQUE(1946); SHOW-OFF,
THE(1946); STRANGE TRIANGLE(1946); CALENDAR GIRL(1947); CRIME DOC-
TOR'S GAMBLE(1947); GAS HOUSE KIDS GO WEST(1947); GUILT OF JANET AMES,
THE(1947); STORK BITES MAN(1947); VIOLENCE(1947); HERE COMES TROU-
BLE(1948); MR. BLANDINGS BUILDS HIS DREAM HOUSE(1948); SONG OF IDA-
HO(1948); STRIKE IT RICH(1948); SUMMER HOLIDAY(1948); YOU GOTTA STAY
HAPPY(1948); ALASKA PATROL(1949); BEAUTIFUL BLONDE FROM BASHFUL
BEND, THE(1949); BLONDE ICE(1949); HELLFIRE(1949); HIDEOUT(1949); MA AND
PA KETTLE(1949); MASSACRE RIVER(1949); ROSE OF THE YUKON(1949); WOM-
AN'S SECRET, A(1949); BEWARE OF BLONDIE(1950); CHAIN GANG(1950); COUNTY
FAIR(1950); KEY TO THE CITY(1950); MA AND PA KETTLE GO TO TOWN(1950);
ROCK ISLAND TRAIL(1950); TO PLEASE A LADY(1950); TRAIL OF ROBIN
HOOD(1950); UNMASKED(1950); GOLDEN GIRL(1951); HONEYCHILE(1951); LET'S
GO NAVY(1951); MA AND PA KETTLE BACK ON THE FARM(1951); MY TRUE
STORY(1951); SHOW BOAT(1951); BOOTS MALONE(1952); DREAMBOAT(1952);
FABULOUS SENORITA, THE(1952); GOBS AND GALS(1952); HAS ANYBODY SEEN
MY GAL?(1952); LAWLESS BREED, THE(1952); LOST IN ALASKA(1952); MA AND
PA KETTLE AT THE FAIR(1952); MACAO(1952); OKLAHOMA ANNIE(1952); WASH-
INGTON STORY(1952); WHEN IN ROME(1952); BAND WAGON, THE(1953); CALL
ME MADAM(1953); EASY TO LOVE(1953); FORT VENGEANCE(1953); GIRL WHO
HAD EVERYTHING, THE(1953); SAFARI DRUMS(1953); SHADOWS OF TOMB-
STONE(1953); SWEETHEARTS ON PARADE(1953); BATTLE OF ROGUE RI-
VER(1954); JUNGLE GENTS(1954); LONG, LONG TRAILER, THE(1954); MA AND PA
KETTLE AT HOME(1954); PRIDE OF THE BLUE GRASS(1954); ROCKET MAN,
THE(1954); SABRINA(1954); ARTISTS AND MODELS(1955); HOW TO BE VERY,
VERY, POPULAR(1955); LOOTERS, THE(1955); YOU'RE NEVER TOO YOUNG(1955);
PARDNERS(1956); THAT CERTAIN FEELING(1956); DELICATE DELINQUENT,
THE(1957); HOT ANGEL, THE(1958); MAN OF THE WEST(1958); NOTORIOUS MR.
MONKS, THE(1958); HOLE IN THE HEAD, A(1959); THIS EARTH IS MINE(1959);
TWO LITTLE BEARS, THE(1961); BOUNTY KILLER, THE(1965); GIT!(1965)

Iris Parnell
SHADOW OF MIKE EMERALD, THE(1935, Brit.)

Jack Parnell
MY HEART GOES CRAZY(1953, Brit.)
James Parnell
NO ROOM FOR THE GROOM(1952); YANKEE BUCCANEER(1952); WAR PAINT(1953); WHITE CHRISTMAS(1954); YELLOW MOUNTAIN, THE(1954); LOOTERS, THE(1955); SHOTGUN(1955); CRIME AGAINST JOE(1956); PARDNERS(1956); RUNNING TARGET(1956); STAR IN THE DUST(1956); OUTLAW'S SON(1957); WAR DRUMS(1957); WALKING TARGET, THE(1960); CLOWN AND THE KID, THE(1961); GUN FIGHT(1961); INCIDENT IN AN ALLEY(1962)
Jean Parnell
LAST SAFARI, THE(1967, Brit.)
Jimmie Parnell
G.I. JANE(1951)
Norma Parnell
MARK OF THE PHOENIX(1958, Brit.); EXPRESSO BONGO(1959, Brit.); NAKED FURY(1959, Brit.); PARTNER, THE(1966, Brit.)
Patrick Parnell
DUEL IN THE JUNGLE(1954, Brit.); DOUBLE, THE(1963, Brit)
R.J. Parnell
1984
THIS IS SPINAL TAP(1984)
Reg Parnell
RACE FOR LIFE, A(1955, Brit.)
Traci Parnell
FAME(1980)
Joe Parnello
CACTUS IN THE SNOW(1972), m
Larry Parnes
I'VE GOTTA HORSE(1965, Brit.), p, w
Arlene Parness
HOW SWEET IT IS(1968)
Alejandro Parodi
ALSINO AND THE CONDOR(1983, Nicaragua)
Nicoletta Parodi
LITTLE MARTYR, THE(1947, Ital.)
Cecilia Paroldi
FRIEND WILL COME TONIGHT, A(1948, Fr.)
Julienne Paroli
PERSONAL COLUMN(1939, Fr.); GAME OF LOVE, THE(1954, Fr.)
Aiace Parolin
SEDUCED AND ABANDONED(1964, Fr./Ital.), ph; MOMENT OF TRUTH, THE(1965, Ital./Span.), ph; RAILROAD MAN, THE(1965, Ital.), ph; SHOOT LOUD, LOUDER... I DON'T UNDERSTAND(1966, Ital.), ph; BIRDS, THE BEES AND THE ITALIANS, THE(1967), ph; CLIMAX, THE(1967, Fr., Ital.), ph; MINUTE TO PRAY, A SECOND TO DIE, A(1968, Ital.), ph; SEATED AT HIS RIGHT(1968, Ital.), ph; SERAFINO(1970, Fr./Ital.), ph; ALFREDO, ALFREDO(1973, Ital.), ph; STREET PEOPLE(1976, U.S./Ital.), ph
Gianfranco Parolini
FURY OF HERCULES, THE(1961, Ital.), d; GOLIATH AGAINST THE GIANTS(1963, Ital./Span.), w; BOUNTY HUNTERS, THE(1970, Ital.), w; RETURN OF SABATA(1972, Ital./Fr./Ger.), w, ed; YETI(1977, Ital.), p
Marilu Parolini
1984
LOVE ON THE GROUND(1984,Fr.), w
P. Parolini
FURY OF HERCULES, THE(1961, Ital.), w
Alexander Paromenko
WATERLOO(1970, Ital./USSR)
Catherine Parquier
MADEMOISELLE(1966, Fr./Brit.)
Anthony Parr
AGENCY(1981, Can.)
Bobby Parr
DR. JEKYLL AND SISTER HYDE(1971, Brit.); AT THE EARTH'S CORE(1976, Brit.)
Charles T. Parr
Silents
KAISER'S FINISH, THE(1918)
David Parr
PRICE OF THINGS, THE(1930, Brit.); STREET MUSIC(1982)
Gloria Parr
VIOLENT YEARS, THE(1956)
Gregory Joe Parr
OSTERMAN WEEKEND, THE(1983)
June Parr
MAGIC SPECTACLES(1961)
Katherine Parr
THIS SPORTING LIFE(1963, Brit.); OTLEY(1969, Brit.); SEVERED HEAD, A(1971, Brit.)
Larry Parr
1984
CONSTANCE(1984, New Zealand), p; PALLET ON THE FLOOR(1984, New Zealand), p
Louisa Parr
Silents
QUEEN'S EVIDENCE(1919, Brit.), w
Marc Parr
SHAPE OF THINGS TO COME, THE(1979, Can.)
Mark Parr
"EQUUS"(1977)
Pamela Parr
Misc. Silents
LILY OF KILLARNEY(1929, Brit.); LITTLE MISS LONDON(1929, Brit.)
Peggy Parr
Silents
JUST AROUND THE CORNER(1921); MAN WORTH WHILE, THE(1921); STRAIGHT IS THE WAY(1921)
Misc. Silents
DUCHESS OF DOUBT, THE(1917); SOWERS AND REAPERS(1917); LOVE WITHOUT QUESTION(1920)

Russell Parr
1984
CHOOSE ME(1984)
Sally Parr
SUN SETS AT DAWN, THE(1950)
Stephen Parr
JONI(1980)
Terry Parr
MOHAMMAD, MESSENGER OF GOD(1976, Lebanon/Brit.), art d
Thelma Parr
Silents
DEVIL'S TOWER(1929)
Tony Parr
HOMER(1970)
Harry Parr-Davies
LOOK UP AND LAUGH(1935, Brit.), m; LISBON STORY, THE(1946, Brit.), w, m
Joaquin Parra
BULLET FOR THE GENERAL, A(1967, Ital.); VALDEZ IS COMING(1971); ROBIN AND MARIAN(1976, Brit.), stunts
Josephine Parra
TARZAN AND THE SLAVE GIRL(1950); THIS EARTH IS MINE(1959)
Manuel Parra
FUGITIVE, THE(1947), set d
Victor Parra
UNTOUCHED(1956)
Vincent Parra
SOFT SKIN ON BLACK SILK(1964, Fr./Span.)
Misc. Talkies
APARTMENT ON THE THIRTEENTH FLOOR(1973)
Armando Parracino
CITY OF WOMEN(1980, Ital./Fr.)
Lynn Parraga
ABSENCE OF MALICE(1981)
Gi Parrendo
SEVENTH VOYAGE OF SINBAD, THE(1958), art d
Gil Parrendo
THREE WORLDS OF GULLIVER, THE(1960, Brit.), art d
Bruno Parreto
DONA FLOR AND HER TWO HUSHANDS(1977, Braz.), d&w
Suzanne Parrett
WHEREVER SHE GOES(1953, Aus.)
Gloria Parri
SLAVE, THE(1963, Ital.)
Geraldina Parrinello
TIMES GONE BY(1953, Ital.)
Carl Parris
SUPERMAN II(1980)
Hamilton Parris
Misc. Talkies
BIM(1976)
Pat Parris
WOLFEN(1981)
Anne Parrish
BORN TO BE BAD(1950), w
Blake Parrish
Misc. Talkies
THREE WAY WEEKEND(1979)
Bob Parrish
FORBIDDEN(1932); THRILL OF A LIFETIME(1937); MR. DOODLE KICKS OFF(1938)
Catherine Parrish
Silents
LOVE AND LEARN(1928)
Claire Parrish
MISBEHAVING HUSBANDS(1941), w
Clifford Parrish
ALL THE WAY UP(1970, Brit.)
David P. Parrish
PLEDGEMASTERS, THE(1971), p&d, ph
Dennis Parrish
WELCOME TO L.A.(1976), set d; MARCH OR DIE(1977, Brit.), set d
Edna Parrish
TAZA, SON OF COCHISE(1954)
Edward Parrish
FIVE THE HARD WAY(1969)
Enid Parrish
TWO-GUN JUSTICE(1938)
Frank Parrish
MAN CALLED FLINTSTONE, THE(1966), ph
George Parrish
EXILE EXPRESS(1939), m; HEY THERE, IT'S YOGI BEAR(1964), ph
Gigi Parrish
ROMAN SCANDALS(1933); DOWN TO THEIR LAST YACHT(1934); GIRL OF THE LIMBERLOST(1934); KISS AND MAKE UP(1934); TWENTIETH CENTURY(1934); GIRL O' MY DREAMS(1935); SYMPHONY OF LIVING(1935); AUGUST WEEKEND(1936, Brit.)
Gwendolyn Parrish
Misc. Talkies
IN THE RAPTURE(1976)
Helen Parrish
HIS FIRST COMMAND(1929); WORDS AND MUSIC(1929); BIG TRAIL, THE(1930); CIMARRON(1931); PUBLIC ENEMY, THE(1931); SEED(1931); X MARKS THE SPOT(1931); FELLER NEEDS A FRIEND(1932); FORBIDDEN(1932); DOG OF FLANDERS, A(1935); STRAIGHT FROM THE HEART(1935); MAKE WAY FOR A LADY(1936); MAYTIME(1937); LITTLE TOUGH GUY(1938); LITTLE TOUGH GUYS IN SOCIETY(1938); MAD ABOUT MUSIC(1938); FIRST LOVE(1939); THREE SMART GIRLS GROW UP(1939); WINTER CARNIVAL(1939); I'M NOBODY'S SWEETHEART NOW(1940); YOU'LL FIND OUT(1940); SIX LESSONS FROM MADAME LA ZONGA(1941); TOO MANY BLONDES(1941); WHERE DID YOU GET THAT GIRL?(1941); IN OLD CALIFORNIA(1942); SUNSET SERENADE(1942); THEY ALL KISSED THE

BRIDE(1942); TOUGH AS THEY COME(1942); X MARKS THE SPOT(1942); MYSTERY OF THE 13TH GUEST, THE(1943); STAGE DOOR CANTEEN(1943); TROUBLE MAKERS(1948); QUICK ON THE TRIGGER(1949); WOLF HUNTERS, THE(1949)

Imboden Parrish
AMERICAN TRAGEDY, AN(1931); GUN SMOKE(1931)

James Parrish
BULLDOG DRUMMOND AT BAY(1937, Brit.), w

John Parrish
UNEXPECTED GUEST(1946); HONEYMOON(1947); T-MEN(1947); DEAD DON'T DREAM, THE(1948); FOUR FACES WEST(1948); HE WALKED BY NIGHT(1948); JOAN OF ARC(1948); LET'S LIVE AGAIN(1948); THAT LADY IN ERMINE(1948); CANADIAN PACIFIC(1949); RIDERS IN THE SKY(1949); SAMSON AND DELILAH(1949); WOMAN'S SECRET, A(1949); AS YOU WERE(1951); GREATEST SHOW ON EARTH, THE(1952); WAGONS WEST(1952); JULIUS CAESAR(1953); PRISONERS OF THE CASBAH(1953); SALOME(1953); THREE SAILORS AND A GIRL(1953); TREASURE OF THE GOLDEN CONDOR(1953); BAREFOOT CONTESSA, THE(1954); KRONOS(1957)

John Parrish, Jr.
SAGINAW TRAIL(1953)

Julie Parrish
NUTTY PROFESSOR, THE(1963); WINTER A GO-GO(1965); FIREBALL 590(1966); PARADISE, HAWAIIAN STYLE(1966); DOBERMAN GANG, THE(1972)

Lane Parrish
1984
FOOTLOOSE(1984)

Laura R. Parrish
SENATOR WAS INDISCREET, THE(1947)

Lee Parrish
MIGHTY GORGA, THE(1969); WILD WHEELS(1969); CHROME AND HOT LEATHER(1971)

Leonard Parrish
PAISAN(1948, Ital.)

Leslie Parrish
GIRL IN THE RED VELVET SWING, THE(1955); HOW TO BE VERY, VERY, POPULAR(1955); LIEUTENANT WORE SKIRTS, THE(1956); LI'L ABNER(1959); PORTRAIT OF A MOBSTER(1961); MANCHURIAN CANDIDATE, THE(1962); FOR LOVE OR MONEY(1963); SEX AND THE SINGLE GIRL(1964); THREE ON A COUCH(1966); MONEY JUNGLE, THE(1968); CANDY MAN, THE(1969); DEVIL'S 8, THE(1969); GIANT SPIDER INVASION, THE(1975); CRASH(1977)
1984
INVISIBLE STRANGLER(1984)
Misc. Talkies
BROTHER, CRY FOR ME(1970)

Pat Parrish
MEET MISS BOBBY SOCKS(1944); THEY LIVE IN FEAR(1944); LET'S GO STEADY(1945); THOUSAND AND ONE NIGHTS, A(1945); ONE TOUCH OF VENUS(1948)
Misc. Talkies
BOTH BARRELS BLAZING(1945)

Randall Parrish
Silents
BOB HAMPTON OF PLACER(1921), w

Robert Parrish
MEN WITHOUT WOMEN(1930); UP THE RIVER(1930); DR. BULL(1933); JUDGE PRIEST(1934); INFORMER, THE(1935); PRISONER OF SHARK ISLAND, THE(1936); BODY AND SOUL(1947), ed; DOUBLE LIFE, A(1947), ed; NO MINOR VICES(1948), ed; CAUGHT(1949), ed; CRY DANGER(1951), d; MOB, THE(1951), d; ASSIGNMENT-PARIS(1952), d; MY PAL GUS(1952), d; SAN FRANCISCO STORY, THE(1952), d; SHOOT FIRST(1953, Brit.), d; PURPLE PLAIN, THE(1954, Brit.), d; LUCY GALLANT(1955), d; FIRE DOWN BELOW(1957, U.S./Brit.), d; SADDLE THE WIND(1958), d; WONDERFUL COUNTRY, THE(1959), d; IN THE FRENCH STYLE(1963, U.S./Fr.), p, d; UP FROM THE BEACH(1965), d; BOBO, THE(1967, Brit.), d; CASINO ROYALE(1967, Brit.), d; DUFFY(1968, Brit.), d; JOURNEY TO THE FAR SIDE OF THE SUN(1969, Brit.), d; TOWN CALLED HELL, A(1971, Span./Brit.), d; DESTRUCTORS, THE(1974, Brit.), d
Silents
FOUR SONS(1928); RILEY THE COP(1928)

Veronica Parrish
Misc. Talkies
OVERSEXED(1974)

Clive Parritt
SIMON AND LAURA(1956, Brit.)

Gil Parrondo
PRIDE AND THE PASSION, THE(1957), art d; MR. ARKADIN(1962, Brit./Fr./Span.), set d; TRUTH ABOUT SPRING, THE(1965, Brit.), art d; SOUND OF HORROR(1966, Span.), art d; SAVAGE PAMPAS(1967, Span./Arg.), art d; BATTLE OF BRITAIN, THE(1969, Brit.), art d; VALLEY OF GWANGI, THE(1969), art d; PATTON(1970), art d; CAULDRON OF BLOOD(1971, Span.), art d; HORSEMEN, THE(1971), art d; NICHOLAS AND ALEXANDRA(1971, Brit.), art d; TRAVELS WITH MY AUNT(1972, Brit.), art d; OPEN SEASON(1974, U.S./Span.), art d; ROBIN AND MARIAN(1976, Brit.), art d; MARCH OR DIE(1977, Brit.), prod d; CUBA(1979), prod d, set d; SPHINX(1981), art d; TO BEGIN AGAIN(1982, Span.), prod d, art d

Gill Parrondo
DR. COPPELIUS(1968, U.S./Span.), art d

Charles Parrott
Silents
KING OF THE WILD HORSES, THE(1924)

James Parrott
PARDON US(1931), a, d; WAY OUT WEST(1937), w; BLOCKHEADS(1938), w; SWISS MISS(1938), w

Jimmie Parrott
Silents
BIG TOWN IDEAS(1921)

Ursula Parrott
DIVORCEE, THE(1930), w; GENTLEMAN'S FATE(1931), w; LEFTOVER LADIES(1931), w; STRANGERS MAY KISS(1931), w; WOMAN ACCUSED(1933), w; BRILLIANT MARRIAGE(1936), w; NEXT TIME WE LOVE(1936), w; THERE'S ALWAYS TOMORROW(1956), w

Ursulla Parrott
LOVE AFFAIR(1932), w

Barbara Parry
WAR DRUMS(1957); FORT BOWIE(1958)

Bernard Parry
PURSE STRINGS(1933, Brit.), w

Charlotte Parry
SLEEPLESS NIGHTS(1933, Brit.); YOU MADE ME LOVE YOU(1934, Brit.); IT'S A BET(1935, Brit.); TAKE IT FROM ME(1937, Brit.); WINDMILL, THE(1937, Brit.)

Geoff Parry
MAD MAX(1979, Aus.); GALLIPOLI(1981, Aus.); CLINIC, THE(1983, Aus.)

Gordon Parry
BOND STREET(1948, Brit.), d; NOW BARABBAS WAS A ROBBER(1949, Brit.), d&w; THIRD TIME LUCKY(1950, Brit.), d; MIDNIGHT EPISODE(1951, Brit.), d; NIGHT WAS OUR FRIEND(1951, Brit.), p; TOM BROWN'S SCHOOLDAYS(1951, Brit.), d; GAY ADVENTURE, THE(1953, Brit.), d; TWILIGHT WOMEN(1953, Brit.), d; FAST AND LOOSE(1954, Brit.), d; FRONT PAGE STORY(1954, Brit.), d; INNOCENTS IN PARIS(1955, Brit.), d; YANK IN ERMINE, A(1955, Brit.), d; TOUCH OF THE SUN, A(1956, Brit.), d; PANIC IN THE PARLOUR(1957, Brit.), d; SURGEON'S KNIFE, THE(1957, Brit.), d; NAVY LARK, THE(1959, Brit.), d; TREAD SOFTLY STRANGER(1959, Brit.), d; FRIENDS AND NEIGHBORS(1963, Brit.), d

Harvey Parry
BOWERY, THE(1933); AFTER THE THIN MAN(1936); MOUNTAIN MUSIC(1937); DUKE OF CHICAGO(1949); NAVY BOUND(1951); SILVER CITY(1951); HURRICANE SMITH(1952); SPARTACUS(1960); WALKING TARGET, THE(1960); HOW THE WEST WAS WON(1962); PAINT YOUR WAGON(1969); OKLAHOMA CRUDE(1973); DRUM(1976); MAIN EVENT, THE(1979); SOME KIND OF HERO(1982)
1984
JOHNNY DANGEROUSLY(1984)
Silents
UNHOLY THREE, THE(1925)

Ivan Parry
RED RIVER(1948)

Jack Parry
ISLAND OF LOST MEN(1939)

Jean Parry
THREE MUSKETEERS, THE(1939)

Ken Parry
FRIENDS AND NEIGHBORS(1963, Brit.); JUST FOR FUN(1963, Brit.); TAMING OF THE SHREW, THE(1967, U.S./Ital.); OTLEY(1969, Brit.); SPRING AND PORT WINE(1970, Brit.); START THE REVOLUTION WITHOUT ME(1970)

Lee Parry
Misc. Silents
MONNA VANNA(1923, Ger.)

Loretta Parry
HAND IN HAND(1960, Brit.)

Michael Parry
UNCANNY, THE(1977, Brit./Can.), w

Michel Parry
XTRO(1983, Brit.), w

Natasha Parry
DANCE HALL(1950, Brit.); DARK MAN, THE(1951, Brit.); MIDNIGHT EPISODE(1951, Brit.); CROW HOLLOW(1952, Brit.); GAY ADVENTURE, THE(1953, Brit.); LOVERS, HAPPY LOVERS!(1955, Brit.); WINDOM'S WAY(1958, Brit.); MIDNIGHT LACE(1960); FOURTH SQUARE, THE(1961, Brit.); PORTRAIT OF A SINNER(1961, Brit.); MODEL MURDER CASE, THE(1964, Brit.); ROMEO AND JULIET(1968, Brit./Ital.); OH! WHAT A LOVELY WAR(1969, Brit.); MEETINGS WITH REMARKABLE MEN(1979, Brit.)

Nina Parry
FLESH AND BLOOD(1951, Brit.); DEATM GOES TO SCHOOL(1953, Brit.); TWO AND TWO MAKE SIX(1962, Brit.)

Paul Parry
SERVANTS' ENTRANCE(1934); I LOVE YOU AGAIN(1940); DESTINATION TOKYO(1944)

Richard Parry
JENIFER HALE(1937, Brit.); UNDER MILK WOOD(1973, Brit.)

Robert Parry [Lesley Selander]
TOMAHAWK TRAIL(1957), d

Ron Parry
FAREWELL PERFORMANCE(1963, Brit.)

Roy Parry
LASSIE, COME HOME(1943)

William Parry
Silents
MIRAGE, THE(1920, Brit.); INDIAN LOVE LYRICS, THE(1923, Brit.)
Misc. Silents
CIGARETTE MAKER'S ROMANCE, A(1920, Brit.)

Zale Parry
UNDERWATER WARRIOR(1958)

Rick Parse
EAGLE HAS LANDED, THE(1976, Brit.)

Nino Parsello
SAUL AND DAVID(1968, Ital./Span.)

Martha Parsey
1984
SUPERGIRL(1984); 1984(1984, Brit.)

Miles Parsey
BIDDY(1983, Brit.)

Ruby Parsley
MARRIAGE PLAYGROUND, THE(1929)

Frederick Parslow
LAST WAVE, THE(1978, Aus.)

Phil Parslow
PROFESSIONALS, THE(1966)

Philip L. Parslow
MASTER GUNFIGHTER, THE(1975), p

Ray Parslow
SOME MAY LIVE(1967, Brit.), ph; HOUSE THAT DRIPPED BLOOD, THE(1971, Brit.), ph; STRANGE VENEGEANCE OF ROSALIE, THE(1972), ph; ENGLANO MADE ME(1973, Brit.), ph; MADHOUSE(1974, Brit.), ph; WORLD IS FULL OF

MARRIED MEN, THE(1980, Brit.), ph
Bob Parson
GAS(1981, Can.)
Dete Parson
HOOKED GENERATION, THE(1969)
Jennifer Parson
COMING HOME(1978), cos
Marion Parsonnet
BEG, BORROW OR STEAL(1937), w; LIVE, LOVE AND LEARN(1937), w; THIR-TEENTH CHAIR, THE(1937), w; LOVE IS A HEADACHE(1938), w; MIRACLES FOR SALE(1939), w; THESE GLAMOUR GIRLS(1939), w; GALLANT SONS(1940), w; GOLDEN FLEECING, THE(1940), w; BLONDE INSPIRATION(1941), w; WASHING-TON MELODRAMA(1941), w; DANGEROUSLY THEY LIVE(1942), w; COVER GIRL(1944), w; I'LL BE SEEING YOU(1944), w; DANGEROUS PARTNERS(1945), w; GILDA(1946), w; MY FORBIDDEN PAST(1951), w; UNCLE VANYA(1958), p
Marlon Parsonnet
BETWEEN TWO WOMEN(1937), w
A. J. L. Parsons
MAID TO ORDER(1932), w
Agnes Parsons
Silents
RIDING WITH DEATH(1921), w; RIP VAN WINKLE(1921), w; CHAIN LIGHT-NING(1922), w; JOSSELYN'S WIFE(1926), w; JEWELS OF DESIRE(1927), w
Alan Parsons
AMERICATHON(1979), m
Alibe Parsons
GAME FOR VULTURES, A(1980, Brit.)
Allyn Parsons
NEW KIND OF LOVE, A(1963)
Barbara Parsons
EVEL KNIEVEL(1971)
Benny Parsons
STROKER ACE(1983)
C. Jack Parsons
COVER GIRL KILLER(1960, Brit.), p; DANGER TOMORROW(1960, Brit.), p; MOD-EL FOR MURDER(1960, Brit.), p; HAIR OF THE DOG(1962, Brit.), p; DOOMSDAY AT ELEVEN(1963 Brit.), p
Carola Parsons
Misc. Silents
DYNAMITE ALLEN(1921)
Cherilyn Parsons
HARDCORE(1979)
Clem Parsons
BIONIC BOY, THE(1977, Hong Kong/Phil.); NIGHT GAMES(1980)
Clive Parsons
SCUM(1979, Brit.), p; THAT SUMMER(1979, Brit.), p; BREAKING GLASS(1980, Brit.), p; BRITTANIA HOSPITAL(1982, Brit.), p; GREGORY'S GIRL(1982, Brit.), p; PARTY PARTY(1983, Brit.), p
1984
COMFORT AND JOY(1984, Brit.), p
Derek Parsons
TELL-TALE HEART, THE(1962, Brit.), ed; THIN RED LINE, THE(1964), ed; BAT-TLE OF THE BULGE(1965), ed; CRACK IN THE WORLD(1965), ed; ATTIC, THE(1979), ed
Donovan Parsons
BRAT, THE(1930, Brit.), w; EAST LYNNE ON THE WESTERN FRONT(1931, Brit.), w; F.P. 1(1933, Brit.), m
Dulcie Parsons
Silents
HER LONELY SOLDIER(1919, Brit.)
E.M. Parsons
SQUAD CAR(1961), w; READY FOR THE PEOPLE(1964), w
Edwin C. Parsons
BLAZING BARRIERS(1937), w; MARINES ARE HERE, THE(1938), w; DANGER FLIGHT(1939), w
Estelle Parsons
LADYBUG, LADYBUG(1963); BONNIE AND CLYDE(1967); RACHEL, RA-CHEL(1968); DON'T DRINK THE WATER(1969); I NEVER SANG FOR MY FA-THER(1970); I WALK THE LINE(1970); WATERMELON MAN(1970); TWO PEOPLE(1973); FOREPLAY(1975); FOR PETE'S SAKE(1977)
Geoffrey Parsons
GOOD COMPANIONS, THE(1957, Brit.), m
George Parsons
Silents
STRAIGHT IS THE WAY(1921)
Harriet Parsons
JOAN OF OZARK(1942), p; ENCHANTED COTTAGE, THE(1945), p; NIGHT SONG(1947), p; I REMEMBER MAMA(1948), p; NEVER A DULL MOMENT(1950), b; CLASH BY NIGHT(1952), p; SUSAN SLEPT HERE(1954), p
Hugh Parsons
MIDNIGHT MAN, THE(1974)
J. Palmer Parsons
Silents
WHITE GOLD(1927), w
Jack Parsons
STRANGER'S MEETING(1957, Brit.), p; GENTLE TRAP, THE(1960, Brit.), p; NIGHT WITHOUT PITY(1962, Brit.), p; EYES OF ANNIE JONES, THE(1963, Brit.), p; EARTH DIES SCREAMING, THE(1964, Brit.), p; NIGHT TRAIN TO PARIS(1964, Brit.), p; WALK A TIGHTROPE(1964, U.S./Brit.), p; WITCHCRAFT(1964, Brit.), p; CURSE OF THE FLY(1965, Brit.), p; RETURN OF MR. MOTO, THE(1965, Brit.), p; SPACEFLIGHT IC-1(1965, Brit.), p; WOMAN WHO WOULDN'T DIE, THE(1965, Brit.), p; MURDER GAME, THE(1966, Brit.), p; LAST SHOT YOU HEAR, THE(1969, Brit.), p
Jennifer Parsons
STERILE CUCKOO, THE(1969), cos
1984
BEST DEFENSE(1984), cos
John Parsons
WATCHED(1974), d&w

Johnnie Parsons
ROAR OF THE CROWD(1953)
Johnny Parsons
TO PLEASE A LADY(1950)
Julie Parsons
HOMETOWN U.S.A.(1979)
Misc. Talkies
SWEATER GIRLS(1978)
Lindsay Parsons
FRONTIER TOWN(1938), w; ALASKA(1944), p
Lindsley Parsons
MAN FROM UTAH, THE(1934), w; RANDY RIDES ALONE(1934), w; SAGEBRUSH TRAIL(1934), w; TRAIL BEYOND, THE(1934), w; DESERT TRAIL(1935), w; LAW-LESS RANGE(1935), w; PARADISE CANYON(1935), w; RAINBOW VALLEY(1935), w; OREGON TRAIL, THE(1936), w; WESTWARD HO(1936), w; HEADIN' FOR THE RIO GRANDE(1937), w; RIDERS OF THE ROCKIES(1937), w; TEX RIDES WITH THE BOY SCOUTS(1937), w; TROUBLE IN TEXAS(1937), w; PANAMINT'S BAD MAN(1938), w; ROLLIN' PLAINS(1938), w; UTAH TRAIL(1938), w; WANTED BY THE POLICE(1938), p; BOY'S REFORMATORY(1939), p; OKLAHOMA TER-ROR(1939), w, p; LAUGHING AT DANGER(1940), p; UP IN THE AIR(1940), p; ARIZONA CYCLONE(1941), w; GANG'S ALL HERE(1941), p; KING OF THE ZOM-BIES(1941), p; LET'S GO COLLEGIATE(1941), p; FRECKLES COMES HOME(1941), p; YOU'RE OUT OF LUCK(1941), p; TOP SERGEANT MULLIGAN(1941), p; LAW OF THE JUNGLE(1942), p; LURE OF THE ISLANDS(1942), p; MAN FROM HEADQUAR-TERS(1942), p; MEET THE MOB(1942), p; POLICE BULLETS(1942), p; CAMPUS RHYTHM(1943), p; MELODY PARADE(1943), p; MYSTERY OF THE 13TH GUEST, THE(1943), p; NEARLY EIGHTEEN(1943), p; REVENGE OF THE ZOMBIES(1943), p; SILVER SKATES(1943), p; WINGS OVER THE PACIFIC(1943), p; ADVENTURES OF KITTY O'DAY(1944), p; ARMY WIVES(1944), p; DETECTIVE KITTY O'DAY(1944), p; HOT RHYTHM(1944), p; LEAVE IT TO THE IRISH(1944), p; G.I. HONEY-MOON(1945), p; BELOW THE DEADLINE(1946), p; BOWERY BOMBSHELL(1946), p; FEAR(1946), p; IN FAST COMPANY(1946), p; LIVE WIRES(1946), p; SWING PARADE OF 1946(1946), p; GINGER(1947), p; LOUISIANA(1947), p; KIDNAP-PED(1948), p; ROCKY(1948), p; BLACK MIDNIGHT(1949), p; MISSISSIPPI RHYTHM(1949), p; TRAIL OF THE YUKON(1949), p; TUNA CLIPPER(1949), p; WOLF HUNTERS, THE(1949), p; BIG TIMBER(1950), p; CALL OF THE KLON-DIKE(1950), p; KILLER SHARK(1950), p; SNOW DOG(1950), p; SQUARE DANCE KATY(1950), p; CASA MANANA(1951), p; RHYTHM INN(1951), p; SIERRA PAS-SAGE(1951), p; YELLOW FIN(1951), p; YUKON MANHUNT(1951), p; ARCTIC FLIGHT(1952), p; DESERT PURSUIT(1952), p; NORTHWEST TERRITORY(1952), p; FANGS OF THE ARCTIC(1953), p; JACK SLADE(1953), p; MEXICAN MAN-HUNT(1953), p; NORTHERN PATROL(1953), p; TANGIER INCIDENT(1953), p; TOR-PEDO ALLEY(1953), p; CRY VENGEANCE(1954), p; LOOPHOLE(1954), p; FINGER MAN(1955), p; RETURN OF JACK SLADE, THE(1955), p; COME ON, THE(1956), p; CRUEL TOWER, THE(1956), p; STRANGE INTRUDER(1956), p; DRAGON WELLS MASSACRE(1957), p; PORTLAND EXPOSE(1957), p; OREGON PASSAGE(1958), p; WOLF LARSEN(1958), p; PURPLE GANG, THE(1960), p; GOOD TIMES(1967), p; BIG CUBE, THE(1969), p
Lon Parsons
FEVER HEAT(1968)
Louella O. Parsons
SUSAN SLEPT HERE(1954)
Louella Parsons
WITHOUT RESERVATIONS(1946); HOLLYWOOD HOTEL(1937); STARLIFT(1951)
Silents
ISLE OF FORGOTTEN WOMEN(1927), w; SHOW PEOPLE(1928)
M.B. Parsons
UNDER A CLOUD(1937, Brit.), w
M.J. Parsons
PASSIONATE STRANGERS, THE(1968, Phil.), p
Mary Parsons
EAST LYNNE ON THE WESTERN FRONT(1931, Brit.), w
Michael J. Parsons
HIGH VELOCITY(1977), w
Michael Parsons
CRY OF BATTLE(1963); RAIDERS OF LEYTE GULF(1963 U.S./Phil.); MORO WITCH DOCTOR(1964, U.S./Phil.); WALLS OF HELL, THE(1964, U.S./Phil.); RAVAGERS, THE(1965, U.S./Phil.); BEACH RED(1967); PASSIONATE STRANGERS, THE(1968, Phil.); SECRET OF THE SACRED FOREST, THE(1970); TOO LATE THE HERO(1970)
Milton Parsons
THEY WON'T BELIEVE ME(1947); ANOTHER THIN MAN(1939); WHEN TOMOR-ROW COMES(1939); EDISON, THE MAN(1940); SKY MURDER(1940); THIRD FIN-GER, LEFT HAND(1940); WHO KILLED AUNT MAGGIE?(1940); BEHIND THE NEWS(1941); CRACKED NUTS(1941); DEAD MEN TELL(1941); DRESSED TO KILL(1941); HOLD THAT GHOST(1941); MAN AT LARGE(1941); MURDER AMONG FRIENDS(1941); CASTLE IN THE DESERT(1942); GIRL FROM ALASKA(1942); GREAT MAN'S LADY, THE(1942); HIDDEN HAND, THE(1942); LIFE BEGINS AT 8:30(1942); MAN IN THE TRUNK, THE(1942); MY FAVORITE BLONDE(1942); OVER MY DEAD BODY(1942); REMARKABLE ANDREW, THE(1942); ROXIE HART(1942); WHISPERING GHOSTS(1942); WHO DONE IT?(1942); HOLY MATRIMONY(1943); SWEET ROSIE O'GRADY(1943); CRY OF THE WEREWOLF(1944); LOST IN A HAREM(1944); RATIONING(1944); ANCHORS AWEIGH(1945); DICK TRACY(1945); GREAT JOHN L. THE(1945); MURDER, HE SAYS(1945); BOWERY BOMB-SHELL(1946); DARK ALIBI(1946); DICK TRACY VS. CUEBALL(1946); LEAVE HER TO HEAVEN(1946); MARGIE(1946); BURY ME DEAD(1947); CALCUTTA(1947); CRIM-SON KEY, THE(1947); DICK TRACY MEETS GRUESOME(1947); GAS HOUSE KIDS IN HOLLYWOOD(1947); I WONDER WHO'S KISSING HER NOW(1947); SECRET LIFE OF WALTER MITTY, THE(1947); SENATOR WAS INDISCREET, THE(1947); THAT HAGEN GIRL(1947); SECRET SERVICE INVESTIGATOR(1948); SHANGHAI CHEST, THE(1948); SMART WOMAN(1948); WALLS OF JERICHO(1948); DANCING IN THE DARK(1949); OUTCASTS OF THE TRAIL(1949); WHITE HEAT(1949); CAP-TURE, THE(1950); JACKPOT, THE(1950); LAST OF THE COMANCHES(1952); SOME-BODY LOVES ME(1952); ROGUE COP(1954); HOW TO BE VERY, VERY, POPULAR(1955); KING'S THIEF, THE(1955); MONSTER THAT CHALLENGED THE WORLD, THE(1957); SILENT CALL, THE(1961); TWO LITTLE BEARS, THE(1961); MUSIC MAN, THE(1962); NOTORIOUS LANDLADY, THE(1962); HAUNTED PAL-ACE, THE(1963); 2000 YEARS LATER(1969)

N. Parsons
CASH ON DELIVERY(1956, Brit.)
Nancy Anne Parsons
LADY IN RED, THE(1979)
Nancy Parsons
I NEVER PROMISED YOU A ROSE GARDEN(1977); MOTEL HELL(1980); HONKY TONK FREEWAY(1981); PENNIES FROM HEAVEN(1981); PORKY'S(1982); PORKY'S II: THE NEXT DAY(1983); SUDDEN IMPACT(1983)
Ned Parsons
HEAD(1968), set d; HOW DO I LOVE THEE?(1970), set d; CLAY PIGEON(1971), art d; SUMMERTREE(1971), art d; CAPONE(1975), set d; NIGHT MOVES(1975), set d; HAWMPS!(1976), art d; WON TON TON, THE DOG WHO SAVED HOLLYWOOD(1976), set d; TILT(1979), prod d
1984
DUBEAT-E-O(1984), set d
Nicholas Parsons
MASTER OF BANKDAM, THE(1947, Brit.); EYEWITNESS(1956, Brit.); SIMON AND LAURA(1956, Brit.); BROTHERS IN LAW(1957, Brit.); THIRD KEY, THE(1957, Brit.); HAPPY IS THE BRIDE(1958, Brit.); TOO MANY CROOKS(1959, Brit.); DOCTOR IN LOVE(1960, Brit.); LET'S GET MARRIED(1960, Brit.); MAN IN A COCKED HAT(1960, Bri.); UPSTAIRS AND DOWNSTAIRS(1961, Brit.); MURDER AHOY!(1964, Brit.); SEASIDE SWINGERS(1965, Brit.); WRONG BOX, THE(1966, Brit.); DON'T RAISE THE BRIDGE, LOWER THE RIVER(1968, Brit.)
Nonny Parsons
RAINBOW ISLAND(1944)
Pamela Parsons
PROJECT: KILL(1976)
Parcy Parsons
POWER(1934, Brit.)
Patrick Parsons
RETURN OF THE FROG, THE(1938, Brit.)
Patrick Parsons [Patrick Holt]
SWORD OF HONOUR(1938, Brit.)
Patsy Lee Parsons
THEY WANTED TO MARRY(1937); MEET DR. CHRISTIAN(1939); HEROES OF THE SADDLE(1940); MELODY FOR THREE(1941); THEY MEET AGAIN(1941); YANKEE DOODLE DANDY(1942); ROUGHLY SPEAKING(1945)
Percy Parsons
VICTORIA THE GREAT(1937, Brit.); BLACKMAIL(1929, Brit.); BEYOND THE CITIES(1930, Brit.); BRAT, THE(1930, Brit.); SUSPENSE(1930, Brit.); LIMPING MAN, THE(1931, Brit.); CRIMINAL AT LARGE(1932, Brit.); HAPPY EVER AFTER(1932, Ger./Brit.); LOVE ON WHEELS(1932, Brit.); GOOD COMPANIONS(1933, Brit.); MAN FROM TORONTO, THE(1933, Brit.); SLEEPLESS NIGHTS(1933, Brit.); THIS IS THE LIFE(1933, Brit.); CAMELS ARE COMING, THE(1934, Brit.); FRIDAY THE 13TH(1934, Brit.); ORDERS IS ORDERS(1934, Brit.); STRIKE!(1934, Brit.); BIG SPLASH, THE(1935, Brit.); EVERYBODY DANCE(1936, Brit.); GAY ADVENTURE, THE(1936, Brit.); KING OF THE DAMNED(1936, Brit.); RED WAGON(1936); TWELVE GOOD MEN(1936, Brit.); NON-STOP NEW YORK(1937, Brit.); SONG OF THE ROAD(1937, Brit.); STRANGERS ON A HONEYMOON(1937, Brit.); BLONDES FOR DANGER(1938, Brit.); CITADEL, THE(1938); HI, GANG!(1941, Brit.); FLYING FORTRESS(1942, Brit.); SUICIDE SQUADRON(1942, Brit.)
Perry Parsons
WINGS AND THE WOMAN(1942, Brit.)
Ray Parsons
CHATTERBOX(1943); RUN FOR THE HILLS(1953)
Robert Parsons
HONEYMOON OF HORROR(1964)
Roger Parsons
YOU'VE GOT TO WALK IT LIKE YOU TALK IT OR YOU'LL LOSE THAT BEAT(1971)
Roney Parsons
SOMEWHERE IN ENGLAND(1940, Brit.), w; SOMEWHERE IN CAMP(1942, Brit.), w; SOMEWHERE ON LEAVE(1942, Brit.), w; DEMOBBED(1944, Brit.), w; HOME SWEET HOME(1945, Brit.), w; HONEYMOON HOTEL(1946, Brit.), w
Sue Parsons
Misc. Talkies
COUNTRY TOWN(1971)
Ted Parsons
HELL IN THE HEAVENS(1934), w; DARKEST AFRICA(1936), w
Tom Parsons
GIGOLETTES OF PARIS(1933), ed; LOST LADY, A(1934)
Virginia Parsons
1984
DUBEAT-E-O(1984), set d
William E. Parsons
Silents
INNOCENT SINNER, THE(1917); EYES OF THE HEART(1920)
Misc. Silents
TERRIBLE ONE, THE(1915)
John Parsonson
GAME FOR VULTURES, A(1980, Brit.)
Brian Part
BIRCH INTERVAL(1976); MAX DUGAN RETURNS(1983)
Paul A. Partain
TEXAS CHAIN SAW MASSACRE, THE(1974); RACE WITH THE DEVIL(1975)
Roy Partee
STRATTON STORY, THE(1949)
W.T. Partelton
QUILLER MEMORANDUM, THE(1966, Brit.), makeup
Peter Parten
AND SO TO BED(1965, Ger.); LE MANS(1971)
Eftihia Partheniadou
APOLLO GOES ON HOLIDAY(1968, Ger./Swed.)
Billy Partleton
WICKER MAN, THE(1974, Brit.), makeup
George Partleton
SHERIFF OF FRACTURED JAW, THE(1958, Brit.), makeup; LOSS OF INNOCENCE(1961, Brit.), makeup; HOT MONEY GIRL(1962, Brit./Ger.), makeup; LOLITA(1962), makeup; WAR LOVER, THE(1962, U.S./Brit.), makeup; STOLEN HOURS(1963), makeup; MASQUE OF THE RED DEATH, THE(1964, U.S./Brit.),

makeup; AMOROUS MR. PRAWN, THE(1965, Brit.), makeup; FRANKENSTEIN CREATED WOMAN(1965, Brit.), makeup; HILL, THE(1965, Brit.), makeup; OTHELLO(1965, Brit.), makeup; MUMMY'S SHROUD, THE(1967, Brit.), makeup; PENTHOUSE, THE(1967, Brit.), makeup; MAN WHO HAD POWER OVER WOMEN, THE(1970, Brit.), makeup; TAKE A GIRL LIKE YOU(1970, Brit.), makeup; GET CARTER(1971, Brit.), makeup; POPE JOAN(1972, Brit.), makeup; PULP(1972, Brit.), makeup; PERMISSION TO KILL(1975, U.S./Aust.), makeup
W. Partleton
SNOWBOUND(1949, Brit.), makeup
W.T. Partleton
JASSY(1948, Brit.), makeup; SMUGGLERS, THE(1948, Brit.), makeup; GOOD TIME GIRL(1950, Brit.), makeup; IRON PETTICOAT, THE(1956, Brit.), makeup; SWINGIN' MAIDEN, THE(1963, Brit.), makeup; YOUNG AND WILLING(1964, Brit.), makeup; KALEIDOSCOPE(1966, Brit.), makeup; INTERLUDE(1968, Brit.), makeup; LOCK UP YOUR DAUGHTERS(1969, Brit.), makeup; PERFECT FRIDAY(1970, Brit.), makeup; KIDNAPPED(1971, Brit.), makeup
William Partleton
ROOT OF ALL EVIL, THE(1947, Brit.), makeup; MAN IN THE MOON(1961, Brit.), makeup; NO LOVE FOR JOHNNIE(1961, Brit.), makeup; WALTZ OF THE TOREADORS(1962, Brit.), makeup; NO, MY DARLING DAUGHTER(1964, Brit.), makeup; THOSE MAGNIFICENT MEN IN THEIR FLYING MACHINES; OR HOW I FLEW FROM LONDON TO PARIS IN 25 HOURS AND 11 MINUTES(1965, Brit.), makeup
Cindy Partlow
NIGHT THE LIGHTS WENT OUT IN GEORGIA, THE(1981)
Elaine Partnow
TARGETS(1968); TERROR IN THE JUNGLE(1968); MARIGOLD MAN(1970); WHAT'S UP, DOC?(1972); HOWZER(1973); NICKELODEON(1976)
Dolly Parton
NINE TO FIVE(1980); BEST LITTLE WHOREHOUSE IN TEXAS, THE(1982)
1984
RHINESTONE(1984)
Frank Parton
AND NOW TOMORROW(1944), w
Reg Parton
FOUR GUNS TO THE BORDER(1954); BACKLASH(1956); APACHE TERRITORY(1958); SPARTACUS(1960); LAW OF THE LAWLESS(1964); YOUNG FURY(1965); JOHNNY RENO(1966); WACO(1966); FORT UTAH(1967); HOSTILE GUNS(1967); RED TOMAHAWK(1967); ARIZONA BUSHWHACKERS(1968); LOVE BUG, THE(1968); SPLIT, THE(1968); SLAUGHTER'S BIG RIP-OFF(1973); HERBIE GOES TO MONTE CARLO(1977)
Reggie Parton
ULTIMATE WARRIOR, THE(1975), a, stunts
Regina Parton
LOVE BUG, THE(1968); DIRTY HARRY(1971)
1984
CANNONBALL RUN II(1984)
Regis Parton
KEEP 'EM FLYING(1941); THIS ISLAND EARTH(1955); HIRED GUN, THE(1957)
Tony Parton
CALIFORNIA(1946)
Erzsi Partos
DIALOGUE(1967, Hung.)
Frank Partos
GUILTY AS HELL(1932), w; HER BODYGUARD(1933), w; HERITAGE OF THE DESERT(1933), w; GOOD DAME(1934), w; THIRTY-DAY PRINCESS(1934), w; WHARF ANGEL(1934), w; COLLEGE SCANDAL(1935), w; LAST OUTPOST, THE(1935), w; RUMBA(1935), w; WINGS IN THE DARK(1935), w; ROSE OF THE RANCHO(1936), w; GREAT GAMBINI, THE(1937), w; NIGHT OF MYSTERY(1937), w; SHE'S NO LADY(1937), w; ROMANCE IN THE DARK(1938), w; HONOLULU(1939), w; RIO(1939), w; STRANGER ON THE THIRD FLOOR(1940), w; UNINVITED, THE(1944), w; SNAKE PIT, THE(1948), w; HOUSE ON TELEGRAPH HILL(1951), w; NIGHT WITHOUT SLEEP(1952), w; PORT AFRIQUE(1956, Brit.), w
Franke Partos
CRADLE SONG(1933), w
G. Partos
MISS PRESIDENT(1935, Hung.)
Geza Partos
FATHER(1967, Hung.)
Gus Partos
CLOSE HARMONY(1929)
Silents
NIGHT WATCH, THE(1928); VAMPING VENUS(1928)
Gustav Partos
LONESOME(1928); LAST PERFORMANCE, THE(1929)
Derek Partridge
KING AND COUNTRY(1964, Brit.); VERDICT, THE(1964, Brit.); WHERE THE SPIES ARE(1965, Brit.); MURDER GAME, THE(1966, Brit.); SAVAGE HARVEST(1981); MY TUTOR(1983)
Don Partridge
POPDOWN(1968, Brit.)
Geoffrey B. Partridge
Misc. Silents
BALL OF FORTUNE, THE(1926, Brit.)
Jacob Partridge
WHITE DAWN, THE(1974)
Kimberley Partridge
BETTER LATE THAN NEVER(1983)
Michael Partridge
MEET MR. CALLAGHAN(1954, Brit.)
Norman Partridge
CURE FOR LOVE, THE(1950, Brit.)
Silents
ERNEST MALTRAVERS(1920, Brit.)
Misc. Silents
ERNEST MALTRAVERS(1920, Brit.)
Sarah Partridge
RISKY BUSINESS(1983)

Wendy Partridge
HIGH COUNTRY, THE(1981, Can.), cos
Robert Party
SERPENT, THE(1973, Fr./Ital./Ger.)
Jussi Parvianen
GORKY PARK(1983)
Ted Parvin
WILD SEED(1965), cos; MAN CALLED HORSE, A(1970), cos; RIO LOBO(1970), cos; SOLDIER BLUE(1970), cos; FLIGHT OF THE DOVES(1971), cos; CULPEPPER CATTLE COMPANY, THE(1972), cos; LAST DETAIL, THE(1973), cos
Theodore Parvin
METEOR(1979), p
Ty Parvis
SONS OF THE DESERT(1933)
Elfie Parvo
CARMEN(1946, Ital.)
Elli Parvo
KING'S JESTER, THE(1947, Ital.); OUTCRY(1949, Ital.); DISHONORED(1950, Ital.); HIS LAST TWELVE HOURS(1953, Ital.); GODDESS OF LOVE, THE(1960, Ital./Fr.)
Karl Paryla
BURG THEATRE(1936, Ger.)
Michael Paryla
HAMLET(1962, Ger.); SHADOWS GROW LONGER, THE(1962, Switz./Ger.)
Stefan Paryla
LITTLE NIGHT MUSIC, A(1977, Aust./U.S./Ger.)
Stephan Paryla
WAGNER(1983, Brit./Hung./Aust.)
de Van Parys
ADORABLE CREATURES(1956, Fr.), m
Van Parys
DRAGNET NIGHT(1931, Fr.), m; CAFE DE PARIS(1938, Fr.), m
Carlo Pas
DEAD OF SUMMER(1970 Ital./Fr.), m
Bob Pasaak
AMERICAN GRAFFITI(1973)
Tomislav Pasaric
SEVENTH CONTINENT, THE(1968, Czech./Yugo.)
Alfonsino Pasca
PAISAN(1948, Ital.)
Barry Pascal
APPRENTICESHIP OF DUDDY KRAVITZ, THE(1974, Can.)
Christine Pascal
CLOCKMAKER, THE(1976, Fr.); LET JOY REIGN SUPREME(1977, Fr.); BEST WAY, THE(1978, Fr.); JUDGE AND THE ASSASSIN, THE(1979, Fr.); YOUNG GIRLS OF WILKO, THE(1979, Pol./Fr.); ENTRE NOUS(1983, Fr.)
Earnest Pascal
FLESH AND FANTASY(1943), w
Eddie Pascal
Misc. Talkies
JEWISH KING LEAR(1935)
Ernest L. Pascal
FAIR WARNING(1931), w
Ernest Pascal
INTERFERENCE(1928), w; CHARLATAN, THE(1929), w; LAST OF THE DUANES(1930), w; WEDDING RINGS(1930), w; AGE FOR LOVE, THE(1931), w; BORN TO LOVE(1931), w; HUSBAND'S HOLIDAY(1931), w, w; KING'S VACATION, THE(1933), w; AS THE EARTH TURNS(1934), w; GRAND CANARY(1934), w; HUMAN SIDE, THE(1934), w; WHITE PARADE, THE(1934), w; HERE'S TO ROMANCE(1935), w; UNDER THE PAMPAS MOON(1935), w; LLOYDS OF LONDON(1936), w; LOVE UNDER FIRE(1937), w; WEE WILLIE WINKIE(1937), w; KIDNAPPED(1938), w; HOUND OF THE BASKERVILLES, THE(1939), w; BLUE BIRD, THE(1940), w; JACK LONDON(1943), w; DESTINY(1944), w; CANYON PASSAGE(1946), w; NIGHT IN PARADISE, A(1946), w
Silents
SENSATION SEEKERS(1927), w; MAN-MADE WOMEN(1928), w
Francoise Pascal
ONE PLUS ONE(1969, Brit.); THERE'S A GIRL IN MY SOUP(1970, Brit.); UNDERCOVERS HERO(1975, Brit.)
Gabriel Pascal
TALES OF THE UNCANNY(1932, Ger.), p; CAFE MASCOT(1936, Brit.), p; REASONABLE DOUBT(1936, Brit.), p; PYGMALION(1938, Brit.), p; MAJOR BARBARA(1941, Brit.), p, d; CAESAR AND CLEOPATRA(1946, Brit.), p&d; ANDROCLES AND THE LION(1952), p
Gisele Pascal
IF PARIS WERE TOLD TO US(1956, Fr.); ROYAL AFFAIRS IN VERSAILLES(1957, Fr.)
Gisella Pascal
1984
LES COMPERES(1984, Fr.)
Giselle Pascal
APRES L'AMOUR(1948, Fr.); NAKED WOMAN, THE(1950, Fr.); NIGHTS OF SHAME(1961, Fr.); SECRET WORLD(1969, Fr.)
Guenole Pascal
1984
A NOS AMOURS(1984, Fr.)
Henry Pascal
GAY ADVENTURE, THE(1953, Brit.)
Irving Pascal
HOLLYWOOD CAVALCADE(1939), w
J. C. Pascal
PERFECTIONIST, THE(1952, Fr.)
Jane Pascal
Misc. Silents
SERPENT'S TOOTH, THE(1917)
Jean-Claude Pascal
ALERT IN THE SOUTH(1954, Fr.); FLESH AND THE WOMAN(1954, Fr./Ital.); GUINGUETTE(1959, Fr.); POPPY IS ALSO A FLOWER, THE(1966)

Jefferson Pascal
SWORD OF LANCELOT(1963, Brit.), w; BEACH RED(1967), w; NO BLADE OF GRASS(1970, Brit.), w
Louis A. Pascal
TEMPTATION(1962, Fr.), w
Olivia Pascal
SOME LIKE IT COOL(1979, Ger./Aust./Ital./Fr.)
Misc. Talkies
C.O.D.(1983)
Peter Pascal
SULLIVAN'S EMPIRE(1967)
Rene Pascal
LE PLAISIR(1954, Fr.); FRENCH CANCAN(1956, Fr.)
Sylvia Pascal
Misc. Talkies
ALARM ON 83RD STREET(1965)
Philippine Pascale
1984
SWANN IN LOVE(1984, Fr.Ger.)
Borislav Pascan
LONG SHIPS, THE(1964, Brit./Yugo.), md
Nathalie Pascaud
MR. HULOT'S HOLIDAY(1954, Fr.)
Reginald Pasch
FREE LOVE(1930); MOTHERS CRY(1930); BROKEN LULLABY(1932); EVENINGS FOR SALE(1932); MAN FROM YESTERDAY, THE(1932); CAPTURED(1933); SILVER CORD(1933); DOCTOR MONICA(1934); MADAME SPY(1934); MAN ON A STRING(1960); QUESTION 7(1961, U.S./Ger.)
Regnald Pasch
PURSUIT OF HAPPINESS, THE(1934)
Nikos Paschalides
OEDIPUS THE KING(1968, Brit.)
Nicos Paschalidis
ISLAND OF LOVE(1963); FANTASIES(1981)
Alexandre Pasche
1984
L'ARGENT(1984, Fr./Switz.)
Susanne Paschen
ENDLESS NIGHT, THE(1963, Ger.), ed; OLDEST PROFESSION, THE(1968, Fr./Ital./Ger.), ed
A.F. Paschenko
HOUSE OF GREED(1934, USSR), m
Jupp Paschke
MAEDCHEN IN UNIFORM(1965, Ger./Fr.), makeup
Roger Paschy
1984
PERILS OF GWENDOLINE, THE(1984, Fr.)
Chris Pasco
SMASH PALACE(1982, New Zealand)
Isabelle Pasco
1984
AVE MARIA(1984, Fr.)
Richard Pasco
YESTERDAY'S ENEMY(1959, Brit.); KILL ME TOMORROW(1958, Brit.); ROOM AT THE TOP(1959, Brit.); MISFITS, THE(1961), stunts; SWORD OF SHERWOOD FOREST(1961, Brit.); SIX BLACK HORSES(1962); AGENT 8 3/4(1963, Brit.); GORGON, THE(1964, Brit.); RASPUTIN-THE MAD MONK(1966, Brit.); WATCHER IN THE WOODS, THE(1980, Brit.); WAGNER(1983, Brit./Hung./Aust.)
Donald Pascoe
RAISING A RIOT(1957, Brit.)
Alfonso Pase
DESERT WARRIOR(1961 Ital./Span.), w
Myrtle Paseler
RAMPARTS WE WATCH, THE(1940)
Tancredi Pasero
ROSSINI(1948, Ital.)
John Pasetti
RING AROUND THE CLOCK(1953, Ital.)
Reginald Pash
MURDER MAN(1935)
Kalla Pasha
SEVEN FOOTPRINTS TO SATAN(1929)
Silents
SMALL TOWN IDOL, A(1921); DICTATOR, THE(1922); THIRTY DAYS(1922); RACING HEARTS(1923); RUGGLES OF RED GAP(1923); SCARAMOUCHE(1923); HEADS UP(1925); WOLF'S CLOTHING(1927); TILLIE'S PUNCTURED ROMANCE(1928); WEST OF ZANZIBAR(1928)
Misc. Silents
BREAKING INTO SOCIETY(1923); MILLION TO BURN, A(1923); MIDNIGHT ON THE BARBARY COAST(1929)
Vera Pashennaya
IDIOT, THE(1960, USSR)
Misc. Silents
POLIKUSHKA(1919, USSR)
Pyotr Pashkevich
GORDEYEV FAMILY, THE(1961, U.S.S.R.), art d
A. Pashukhina
WHEN THE TREES WERE TALL(1965, USSR)
Jean-Pierre Pasier
GODSON, THE(1972, Ital./Fr.)
P. M. Pasinetti
LADY WITHOUT CAMELLIAS, THE(1981, Ital.), w
Frantisek Paska
FIREMAN'S BALL, THE(1968, Czech.)
Cleo Paskal
LIES MY FATHER TOLD ME(1975, Can.)
Bata Paskaljevic
FRAULEIN DOKTOR(1969, Ital./Yugo.)

Goran Paskaljevic
TWILIGHT TIME(1983, U.S./Yugo.), d, w
Stanley Pasken
WE'LL SMILE AGAIN(1942, Brit.)
Stan Paskin
HEAD OFFICE(1936, Brit.); LIVE AGAIN(1936, Brit.); JOHNNY FRENCHMAN(1946, Brit.)
Stanley Paskin
LET THE PEOPLE SING(1942, Brit.); MILLIONS LIKE US(1943, Brit.); OLD MOTH-ER RILEY, DETECTIVE(1943, Brit.); GIVE ME THE STARS(1944, Brit.)
Encarna Paso
TO BEGIN AGAIN(1982, Span.)
1984
DEMONS IN THE GARDEN(1984, Span.)
Pier Paolo Pasolini
WOMAN OF THE RIVER(1954, Fr./Ital.), w; NIGHTS OF CABIRIA(1957, Ital.), w; YOUNG HUSBANDS(1958, Ital./Fr.), w; ACCATTONE!(1961, Ital.), d&w; FROM A ROMAN BALCONY(1961, Fr./Ital.), w; BELL' ANTONIO(1962, Ital.), w; LA NOTTE BRAVA(1962, Fr./Ital.), w; MAMMA ROMA(1962, Ital.), d&w; HUNCHBACK OF ROME, THE(1963, Ital.); GOSPEL ACCORDING TO ST. MATTHEW, THE(1966, Fr., Ital.); HAWKS AND THE SPARROWS, THE(1967, Ital.), d&w; TEOREMA(1969, Ital.), d&w; WITCHES, THE(1969, Fr./Ital.), d, w; MEDEA(1971, Ital./Fr./Ger.), d&w; ARABIAN NIGHTS(1980, Ital./Fr.), d&w
Susanna Pasolini
GOSPEL ACCORDING TO ST. MATTHEW, THE(1966, Fr., Ital.); TEOREMA(1969, Ital.)
Jimmy L. Pasqual
DEVIL WOMAN(1976, Phil.), p
Pasquali
ROTHSCHILD(1938, Fr.); NOUS IRONS A PARIS(1949, Fr.); MY SEVEN LITTLE SINS(1956, Fr./Ital.); FERNANDEL THE DRESSMAKER(1957, Fr.); NUDE IN HIS POCKET(1962, Fr.)
Alberto Pasquali
Misc. Silents
PASSION OF ST. FRANCIS(1932, Ital.)
Armando Pasquali
Silents
SWORD OF VALOR, THE(1924)
Pasquall
COUNSEL FOR ROMANCE(1938, Fr.)
Ernest Pasque
Silents
FALSE FACES(1919); SAHARA(1919)
Silvia Pasquel
SANTO CONTRA BLUE DEMON EN LA ATLANTIDA(1968, Mex.)
Helen Pasquelle
RAZOR'S EDGE, THE(1946)
Margherita Pasquero
ROSE TATTOO, THE(1955)
Catherine Pasques
UNTAMED(1955)
Christian Pasques
LITTLE BOY LOST(1953); LAST TIME I SAW PARIS, THE(1954); UNTAMED(1955); YOUNG LIONS, THE(1958)
Genevieve Pasques
MILLION DOLLAR MERMAID(1952); LES GIRLS(1957)
Jean Pasquier
Misc. Silents
MENILMONTANT(1926, Fr.)
Master Franck Pasquier
LAST METRO, THE(1981, Fr.)
Benasseti Pasquino
INVINCIBLE SIX, THE(1970, U.S./Iran), spec eff
Katherine Pass
BORDERLINE(1980); CUTTER AND BONE(1981)
Leonard H. Pass
ENDLESS LOVE(1981)
Mary Kay Pass
KANSAS CITY BOMBER(1972); NURSE SHERRI(1978)
Ezio Passadore
FIST IN HIS POCKET(1968, Ital.), p
Antonio Passalia
VOYAGE OF SILENCE(1968, Fr.); WHO'S GOT THE BLACK BOX?(1970, Fr./Gr./Ital.); LE BOUCHER(1971, Fr./Ital.)
Jean Passanante
RETURN OF THE SECAUCUS SEVEN(1980); LIANNA(1983)
Mario Passante
TOO BAD SHE'S BAD(1954, Ital.); GOLD OF NAPLES(1957, Ital.); NIGHTS OF CABIRIA(1957, Ital.); BLACK SUNDAY(1961, Ital.); THIEF OF BAGHDAD, THE(1961, Ital./Fr.); SWINDLE, THE(1962, Fr./Ital.)
Art Passarella
THAT TOUCH OF MINK(1962)
Edoardo Passarelli
JOURNEY TO LOVE(1953, Ital.)
Eduardo Passarelli
OPEN CITY(1946, Ital.)
Marie Passarelli
PINK FLOYD–THE WALL(1982, Brit.)
H.B. Passat
PATRICIA GETS HER MAN(1937, Brit.)
Bernie Passeltiner
TOOTSIE(1982)
Hans Passendorf
MAKE-UP(1937, Brit.), w
Dirch Passer
CRAZY PARADISE(1965, Den.)
Dirk Passer
REPTILICUS(1962, U.S./Den.)

Ivan Passer
LOVES OF A BLONDE(1966, Czech.), w; FIREMAN'S BALL, THE(1968, Czech.), w; INTIMATE LIGHTING(1969, Czech.), d, w; BORN TO WIN(1971), d; LAW AND DISORDER(1974), d, w; CRIME AND PASSION(1976, U.S., Ger.), d; SILVER BEARS(1978), d; CUTTER AND BONE(1981), d
Ada Passeri
LA DOLCE VITA(1961, Ital./Fr.)
Marina Passerova
DIAMOND JIM(1935)
Jean Pol Passet
CITY ON FIRE(1979 Can.), ed
Renee Passeur
CARNIVAL(1953, Fr.); MALE COMPANION(1965, Fr./Ital.); SWEET SKIN(1965, Fr./Ital.); CLOPORTES(1966, Fr., Ital.)
Steve Passeur
LIFE AND LOVES OF BEETHOVEN, THE(1937, Fr.), w; ENTENTE COR-DIALE(1939, Fr.), w; J'ACCUSE(1939, Fr.), w; LOUISE(1940, Fr.), w
Lars Passgard
THROUGH A GLASS DARKLY(1962, Swed.); SWEDISH WEDDING NIGHT(1965, Swed.); TIME IN THE SUN, A(1970, Swed.)
Jack Passin
TO HAVE AND HAVE NOT(1944)
Alyce Passman
CALIFORNIA SPLIT(1974)
H. Fraser Passmore
SPORTING LOVE(1936, Brit.), p; LAST ADVENTURERS, THE(1937, Brit), p; SONG OF FREEDOM(1938, Brit.), p
Henry Passmore
FLY AWAY PETER(1948, Brit.), p; LOVE IN WAITING(1948, Brit.), p; CHILDREN GALORE(1954, Brit.), p; DELAVINE AFFAIR, THE(1954, Brit.), p; CONSCIENCE BAY(1960, Brit.), p; BOMB IN THE HIGH STREET(1961, Brit.), p; MISSING NOTE, THE(1961, Brit.), p
M. Fraser Passmore
PHANTOM SHIP(1937, Brit.), p
Michael Passmore
IT HAPPENED HERE(1966, Brit.)
John Dos Passos
DEVIL IS A WOMAN, THE(1935), w
Jose Marcio Passos
BYE-BYE BRASIL(1980, Braz.)
George Pastell
GAMBLER AND THE LADY, THE(1952, Brit.); MOULIN ROUGE(1952); GOLDEN MASK, THE(1954, Brit.); BLIND SPOT(1958, Brit.); ANGRY HILLS, THE(1959, Brit.); DEADLY RECORD(1959, Brit.); MUMMY, THE(1959, Brit.); TIGER BAY(1959, Brit.); BOTTOMS UP(1960, Brit.); MISSILE FROM HELL(1960, Brit.); SIEGE OF SIDNEY STREET, THE(1960, Brit.); STRANGLERS OF BOMBAY, THE(1960, Brit.); FRIGHT-ENED CITY, THE(1961, Brit.); KONGA(1961, Brit.); ON THE BEAT(1962, Brit.); VILLAGE OF DAUGHTERS(1962, Brit.); FROM RUSSIA WITH LOVE(1963, Brit.); IMPACT(1963, Brit.); MANIAC(1963, Brit.); MOON-SPINNERS, THE(1964); SECRET DOOR, THE(1964); CURSE OF THE MUMMY'S TOMB, THE(1965, Brit.); SECOND BEST SECRET AGENT IN THE WHOLE WIDE WORLD, THE(1965, Brit.); KHAR-TOUM(1966, Brit.); MAN COULD GET KILLED, A(1966); MC GUIRE, GO HOME!(1966, Brit.); RUN WITH THE WIND(1966, Brit.); DEADLIER THAN THE MALE(1967, Brit.); LONG DUEL, THE(1967, Brit.); MAGUS, THE(1968, Brit.); THAT RIVIERA TOUCH(1968, Brit.)
Nino Pastellides
SALT TO THE DEVIL(1949, Brit.)
Robert Pastene
BUTTERFIELD 8(1960)
Fred Pasternack
TEMPEST(1982)
Joe Pasternak
UNFINISHED DANCE,THE(1947), p
Boris Pasternak
DOCTOR ZHIVAGO(1965), w
James D. Pasternak
TELL ME THAT YOU LOVE ME, JUNIE MOON(1970)
Joe Pasternak
JOHNNY STEALS EUROPE(1932, Ger.), p; 100 MEN AND A GIRL(1937), p; MAD ABOUT MUSIC(1938), p; THAT CERTAIN AGE(1938), p; DESTRY RIDES AGAIN(1939), p; FIRST LOVE(1939), p; THREE SMART GIRLS GROW UP(1939), p; UNDER-PUP, THE(1939), p; LITTLE BIT OF HEAVEN, A(1940), p; SEVEN SIN-NERS(1940), p; SPRING PARADE(1940), p; FLAME OF NEW ORLEANS, THE(1941), p; IT STARTED WITH EVE(1941), p; NICE GIRL?(1941), p; SEVEN SWEET-HEARTS(1942), p; PRESENTING LILY MARS(1943), p; THOUSANDS CHEER(1943), p; MUSIC FOR MILLIONS(1944), p; TWO GIRLS AND A SAILOR(1944), p; ANCHORS AWEIGH(1945), p; HER HIGHNESS AND THE BELLBOY(1945), p; THRILL OF A ROMANCE(1945), p; HOLIDAY IN MEXICO(1946), p; NO LEAVE, NO LOVE(1946), p; TWO SISTERS FROM BOSTON(1946), p; BIG CITY(1948), p; DATE WITH JUDY, A(1948), p; KISSING BANDIT, THE(1948), p; LUXURY LINER(1948), p; ON AN ISLAND WITH YOU(1948), p; THREE DARING DAUGHTERS(1948), p; IN THE GOOD OLD SUMMERTIME(1949), p; THAT MIDNIGHT KISS(1949), p; DUCHESS OF IDAHO, THE(1950), p; NANCY GOES TO RIO(1950), p; SUMMER STOCK(1950), p; TOAST OF NEW ORLEANS, THE(1950), p; GREAT CARUSO, THE(1951), p; RICH, YOUNG AND PRETTY(1951), p; STRIP, THE(1951), p; BECAUSE YOU'RE MI-NE(1952), p; MERRY WIDOW, THE(1952), p; EASY TO LOVE(1953), p; LATIN LOV-ERS(1953), p; SMALL TOWN GIRL(1953), p; ATHENA(1954), p; FLAME AND THE FLESH(1954), p; STUDENT PRINCE, THE(1954), p; HIT THE DECK(1955), p; LOVE ME OR LEAVE ME(1955), p; MEET ME IN LAS VEGAS(1956), p; TEN THOUSAND BEDROOMS(1957), p; THIS COULD BE THE NIGHT(1957), p; PARTY GIRL(1958), p; ASK ANY GIRL(1959), p; PLEASE DON'T EAT THE DAISIES(1960), p; WHERE THE BOYS ARE(1960), p; HORIZONTAL LIEUTENANT, THE(1962), p; JUMBO(1962), p; COURTSHIP OF EDDY'S FATHER, THE(1963), p; TICKLISH AFFAIR, A(1963), p; LOOKING FOR LOVE(1964), p; GIRL HAPPY(1965), p; MADE IN PARIS(1966), p; SPINOUT(1966), p; SWEET RIDE, THE(1968), p
Joseph Pasternak
THREE SMART GIRLS(1937), p; YOUTH TAKES A FLING(1938), p; IT'S A DA-TE(1940), p; SONG OF RUSSIA(1943), p; THIS TIME FOR KEEPS(1947), p; SKIRTS AHOY!(1952), p; OPPOSITE SEX, THE(1956), p

Michael Pasternak
WANDERERS, THE(1979)
Georges Pastier
DEADLY TRAP, THE(1972, Fr./Ital.), ph
Joan Pastin
SON OF SINBAD(1955)
Giorgio Pastina
JOURNEY TO LOVE(1953, Ital.), d
Bob Pastine
JAMBOREE(1957)
Carol Pastinsky
SWEET SUBSTITUTE(1964, Can.)
Misc. Talkies
CARESSED(1965)
Robert Pastner
ONE DOWN TWO TO GO(1982)
Asagni V. Pastor
BLACK MAMA, WHITE MAMA(1973), ed
Isagani V. Pastor
SAVAGE SISTERS(1974), ed
Tony Pastor, Jr.
OPERATION PETTICOAT(1959)
Louis Pastore
FAMILY HONOR(1973), p, w; PREMONITION, THE(1976), w
Michael Pastore
HERE COME THE TIGERS(1978)
Piero Pastore
WAR AND PEACE(1956, Ital./U.S.); ATTILA(1958, Ital.); PRISONER OF THE IRON MASK(1962, Fr./Ital.)
Pietro Pastore
ROMAN HOLIDAY(1953)
Dan Pastorini
KILLER FISH(1979, Ital./Braz.); TRICK OR TREATS(1982)
Franco Pastorino
FRENCH CANCAN(1956, Fr.)
Malvina Pastorino
GAMES MEN PLAY, THE(1968, Arg.)
Willie Pastrano
WILD REBELS, THE(1967); HOOKED GENERATION, THE(1969); NAKED ZOO, THE zero(1970)
Giovanni Pastrone
Misc. Silents
TIGRIS(1913, Ita.), d; HAND OF THE HUN, THE(1917, Ital.), d
Giovanni Pastrone [Piero Fosco]
Silents
CABIRIA(1914, Ital.), d, w
Marina Pastukhova
LAST HILL, THE(1945, USSR)
Nikolai Pastukov
UNCLE VANYA(1972, USSR)
Franca Pasut
ACCATTONE!(1961, Ital.); LA DOLCE VITA(1961, Ital./Fr.); DUEL OF CHAMPIONS(1964 Ital./Span.)
Erzsi Paszior
ANGI VERA(1980, Hung.)
Janos Pasztor
DIALOGUE(1967, Hung.)
Pat
ALF'S CARPET(1929, Brit.)
Pat Heywood and Her Troupe
HOLIDAYS WITH PAY(1948, Brit.)
Pat Russell and the Spare Change
YOUNG GRADUATES, THE(1971)
Patachon
ALF'S CARPET(1929, Brit.)
Misc. Silents
COCTAILS(1928, Brit.)
Patachou
NAPOLEON(1955, Fr.); FRENCH CANCAN(1956, Fr.)
Michael Pataki
YOUNG LIONS, THE(1958); 10 NORTH FREDERICK(1958); EASY RIDER(1969); FIVE THE HARD WAY(1969); DIRT GANG, THE(1972); GRAVE OF THE VAMPIRE(1972); SWEET JESUS, PREACHER MAN(1973); BAT PEOPLE, THE(1974); LAST PORNO FLICK, THE(1974); MANSION OF THE DOOMED(1976), d; AIRPORT '77(1977); DRACULA'S DOG(1978); LAST WORD, THE(1979); LOVE AT FIRST BITE(1979); ONION FIELD, THE(1979); GLOVE, THE(1980); RAISE THE TITANIC(1980, Brit.); DEAD AND BURIED(1981); GRADUATION DAY(1981); SWEET SIXTEEN(1983)
Misc. Talkies
BRUTE CORPS(1972); CARNAL MADNESS(1975)
Mike Pataki
RETURN OF COUNT YORGA, THE(1971)
Veronica Pataky
MIRACLE OF THE BELLS, THE(1948)
Veronika Pataky
ARABIAN NIGHTS(1942); LOVES OF CARMEN, THE(1948); REMAINS TO BE SEEN(1953)
Enno Patalas
GERMANY IN AUTUMN(1978, Ger.)
Giuseppe Patane
LA TRAVIATA(1968, Ital.), md
Prabhakar Patankar
GANDHI(1982)
Patch
TALKING FEET(1937, Brit.)
Jeffrey Patch
SECRET OF NIMH, THE(1982), ed

Wally Patch
CHARLEY'S(BIG HEARTED) AUNT(1940); HIGH TREASON(1929, Brit.); GREAT GAME, THE(1930); KISSING CUP'S RACE(1930, Brit.); GREAT GAY ROAD, THE(1931, Brit.); NEVER TROUBLE TROUBLE(1931, Brit.); SHADOWS(1931, Brit.); SPORT OF KINGS, THE(1931, Brit.); CASTLE SINISTER(1932, Brit.); HERE'S GEORGE(1932, Brit.); BRITANNIA OF BILLINGSGATE(1933, Brit.); CRIME AT BLOSSOMS, THE(1933, Brit.); GOOD COMPANIONS(1933, Brit.); MAROONED(1933, Brit.); TIGER BAY(1933, Brit.); TROUBLE(1933, Brit.); BADGER'S GREEN(1934, Brit.); BORROW A MILLION(1934, Brit.); CHANNEL CROSSING(1934, Brit.); CRAZY PEOPLE(1934, Brit.); FRIDAY THE 13TH(1934, Brit.); GLIMPSE OF PARADISE, A(1934, Brit.); MAN I WANT, THE(1934, Brit.); MUSIC HALL(1934, Brit.); ORDERS IS ORDERS(1934, Brit.); PASSING SHADOWS(1934, Brit.); PERFECT FLAW, THE(1934, Brit.); PUBLIC LIFE OF HENRY THE NINTH, THE(1934, Brit.); SCOOP, THE(1934, Brit.); SORRELL AND SON(1934, Brit.); THOSE WERE THE DAYS(1934, Brit.); VIRGINIA'S HUSBAND(1934, Brit.); WHAT HAPPENED TO HARKNESS(1934, Brit.); DANDY DICK(1935, Brit.); DON QUIXOTE(1935, Fr.); GET OFF MY FOOT(1935, Brit.); HIS MAJESTY AND CO(1935, Brit.); HOPE OF HIS SIDE(1935, Brit.); MARRY THE GIRL(1935, Brit.); OFF THE DOLE(1935, Brit.); OLD CURIOSITY SHOP, THE(1935, Brit.); OLD FAITHFUL(1935, Brit.); ONCE IN A NEW MOON(1935, Brit.); STREET SONG(1935, Brit.); THAT'S MY UNCLE(1935, Brit.); WHILE PARENTS SLEEP(1935, Brit.); WIFE OR TWO, A(1935, Brit.); BUSMAN'S HOLIDAY(1936, Brit.), a, w; EVERYTHING OKAY(1936, Brit.); EXCUSE MY GLOVE(1936, Brit.); HAIL AND FAREWELL(1936, Brit.); INTERRUPTED HONEYMOON, THE(1936, Brit.); KING OF THE CASTLE(1936, Brit.); LIVING DEAD, THE(1936, Brit.); LUCK OF THE TURF(1936, Brit.); MURDER ON THE SET(1936, Brit.); NOT SO DUSTY(1936, Brit.), a, w; PRISON BREAKER(1936, Brit.); SCARAB MURDER CASE, THE(1936, Brit.); TICKET OF LEAVE(1936, Brit.); TOUCH OF THE MOON, A(1936, Brit.); YOU MUST GET MARRIED(1936, Brit.); CAPTAIN'S ORDERS(1937, Brit.); DOCTOR SYN(1937, Brit.); HOLIDAY'S END(1937, Brit.); MAN WHO COULD WORK MIRACLES, THE(1937, Brit.); MEN ARE NOT GODS(1937, Brit.); MISSING, BELIEVED MARRIED(1937, Brit.); NIGHT RIDE(1937, Brit.); PRICE OF FOLLY, THE(1937, Brit.); SKY'S THE LIMIT, THE(1937, Brit.); STREET SINGER, THE(1937, Brit.); ALF'S BUTTON AFLOAT(1938, Brit.); ALMOST A HONEYMOON(1938, Brit.); BANK HOLIDAY(1938, Brit.); BREAK THE NEWS(1938, Brit.); HIGH COMMAND(1938, Brit.); NIGHT ALONE(1938, Brit.); ON VELVET(1938, Brit.); PYGMALION(1938, Brit.); QUIET PLEASE(1938, Brit.); SWORD OF HONOUR(1938, Brit.); TO THE VICTOR(1938, Brit.); TROOPSHIP(1938, Brit.); 13 MEN AND A GUN(1938, Brit.); DOWN OUR ALLEY(1939, Brit.); HOME FROM HOME(1939, Brit.); INSPECTOR HORNLEIGH(1939, Brit.); INSPECTOR HORNLEIGH ON HOLIDAY(1939, Brit.); WARE CASE, THE(1939, Brit.); WHAT WOULD YOU DO, CHUMS?(1939, Brit.); BAND WAGGON(1940, Brit.); GASBAGS(1940, Brit.); HENRY STEPS OUT(1940, Brit.); LAUGH IT OFF(1940, Brit.); MYSTERIOUS MR. REEDER, THE(1940, Brit.); OLD MOTHER RILEY IN BUSINESS(1940, Brit.); PACK UP YOUR TROUBLES(1940, Brit.); RETURN TO YESTERDAY(1940, Brit.); THEY CAME BY NIGHT(1940, Brit.); TWO SMART MEN(1940, Brit.); BOB'S YOUR UNCLE(1941, Brit.); BOMBSIGHT STOLEN(1941, Brit.); COMMON TOUCH, THE(1941, Brit.); FACING THE MUSIC(1941, Brit.); GERT AND DAISY'S WEEKEND(1941, Brit.); I THANK YOU(1941, Brit.); MAIL TRAIN(1941, Brit.); NEUTRAL PORT(1941, Brit.); ONCE A CROOK(1941, Brit.); POISON PEN(1941, Brit.); QUIET WEDDING(1941, Brit.); SEVENTH SURVIVOR, THE(1941, Brit.); IN WHICH WE SERVE(1942, Brit.); LET THE PEOPLE SING(1942, Brit.); SABOTAGE AT SEA(1942, Brit.); UNPLEASANT STORY(1942, Brit.); WE'LL SMILE AGAIN(1942, Brit.); BUTLER'S DILEMMA, THE(1943, Brit.); GET CRACKING(1943, Brit.); APPOINTMENT WITH CRIME(1945, Brit.); DON CHICAGO(1945, Brit.); I DIDN'T DO IT(1945, Brit.); OLD MOTHER RILEY AT HOME(1945, Brit.); GEORGE IN CIVVY STREET(1946, Brit.); WANTED FOR MURDER(1946, Brit.); GHOSTS OF BERKELEY SQUARE(1947, Brit.); GREEN FINGERS(1947); CALLING PAUL TEMPLE(1948, Brit.); DATE WITH A DREAM, A(1948, Brit.); SHOWTIME(1948, Brit.); ADVENTURES OF JANE, THE(1949, Brit.); HISTORY OF MR. POLLY, THE(1949, Brit.); OUTSIDER, THE(1949, Brit.); TWENTY QUESTIONS MURDER MYSTERY, THE(1950, Brit.); HAMMER THE TOFF(1952, Brit.); SALUTE THE TOFF(1952, Brit.); WEDDING OF LILLI MARLENE, THE(1953, Brit.); JOSEPHINE AND MEN(1955, Brit.); WILL ANY GENTLEMAN?(1955, Brit.); NOT SO DUSTY(1956, Brit.); SUSPENDED ALIBI(1957, Brit.); STRANGE CASE OF DR. MANNING, THE(1958, Brit.); YOUR PAST IS SHOWING(1958, Brit.); I'M ALL RIGHT, JACK(1959, Brit.); IT TAKES A THIEF(1960, Brit.); MILLIONAIRESS, THE(1960, Brit.); OPERATION CUPID(1960, Brit.); NOTHING BARRED(1961, Brit.); SERENA(1962, Brit.); SPARROWS CAN'T SING(1963, Brit.); JOLLY BAD FELLOW, A(1964, Brit.); POOR COW(1968, Brit.)
Misc. Silents
RECKLESS GAMBLE, A(1928, Brit.); SHOOTING STARS(1928)
Walter Patch
ILLEGAL(1932, Brit.)
Marcus Patchet
SORCERESS(1983), spec eff,
Tom Patchett
UP THE ACADEMY(1980), w; GREAT MUPPET CAPER, THE(1981), w
1984
MUPPETS TAKE MANHATTAN, THE(1984), w
Christopher Pate
RAW DEAL(1977, Aus.); MANGO TREE, THE(1981, Aus.)
David Pate
PLAYERS(1979)
Johnny Pate
SHAFT IN AFRICA(1973), m; BUCKTOWN(1975), m; DR. BLACK AND MR. HYDE(1976), m
Katharine Pate
DURANT AFFAIR, THE(1962, Brit.)
Lee Pate
Silents
ROSE OF THE RANCHO(1914); TENNESSEE'S PARDNER(1916)
Michael Pate
RUGGED O'RIORDANS, THE(1949, Aus.); BITTER SPRINGS(1950, Aus.); STRANGE DOOR, THE(1951); TEN TALL MEN(1951); THUNDER ON THE HILL(1951); BLACK CASTLE, THE(1952); FACE TO FACE(1952); FIVE FINGERS(1952); ROGUE'S MARCH(1952); TARGET HONG KONG(1952); ALL THE BROTHERS WERE VALIANT(1953); DESERT RATS, THE(1953); ESCAPE FROM FORT BRAVO(1953), w; HONDO(1953); HOUDINI(1953); JULIUS CAESAR(1953); MAZE, THE(1953); ROYAL AFRICAN RIFLES, THE(1953); SCANDAL AT SCOURIE(1953); EL ALAMEIN(1954); KING RICHARD AND THE CRUSADERS(1954); SECRET OF THE INCAS(1954); SILVER CHALICE, THE(1954); LAWLESS STREET, A(1955); CONGO CROSSING(1956); COURT JESTER, THE(1956); KILLER IS LOOSE, THE(1956); RE-

PRISAL(1956); REVOLT OF MAMIE STOVER, THE(1956); SEVENTH CAVAL-RY(1956); OKLAHOMAN, THE(1957); SOMETHING OF VALUE(1957); TALL STRAN-GER, THE(1957); DESERT HELL(1958); HONG KONG CONFIDENTIAL(1958); CURSE OF THE UNDEAD(1959); GREEN MANSIONS(1959); WESTBOUND(1959); WALK LIKE A DRAGON(1960); CANADIANS, THE(1961, Brit.); MOST DANGEROUS MAN ALIVE, THE(1961), w; SERGEANTS 3(1962); TOWER OF LONDON(1962); BEAUTY AND THE BEAST(1963); CALIFORNIA(1963); DRUMS OF AFRICA(1963); MC LIN-TOCK!(1963); PT 109(1963); ADVANCE TO THE REAR(1964); BRAINSTORM(1965); GREAT SIOUX MASSACRE, THE(1965); MAJOR DUNDEE(1965); SINGING NUN, THE(1966); LITTLE JUNGLE BOY(1969, Aus.); MAD DOG MORGAN(1976,Aus.); MANGO TREE, THE(1981, Aus.), p, w; TIM(1981, Aus.), p,d&w; DUET FOR FOUR(1982, Aus.); RETURN OF CAPTAIN INVINCIBLE, THE(1983, Aus./U.S.); WILD DUCK, THE(1983, Aus.)

1984
CAMEL BOY, THE(1984, Aus.)

Bhasker Patel
1984
INDIANA JONES AND THE TEMPLE OF DOOM(1984)

Sharad Patel
AMIN-THE RISE AND FALL(1982, Kenya), p&d

Surya Patel
BORN FREE(1966)

George Patelis
ANDERSON TAPES, THE(1971)

Daniele Patella
ALFREDO, ALFREDO(1973, Ital.)

Fabio Patella
JOHNNY HAMLET(1972, Ital.)

Denys de la Patellière
SABRA(1970, Fr./Ital./Israel), w

A. Patenovskaya
RESURRECTION(1963, USSR), makeup

Will Patent
COWARDS(1970)

Meschino Paterlini
METEOR(1979)

Alessi Paternostro
ANGELO IN THE CROWD(1952, Ital.), w

A. B. "Banjo" Paterson
MAN FROM SNOWY RIVER, THE(1983, Aus.), w

Bill Paterson
ODD JOB, THE(1978, Brit.)
1984
COMFORT AND JOY(1984, Brit.); KILLING FIELDS, THE(1984, Brit.); PLOUGH-MAN'S LUNCH, THE(1984, Brit.)

Charlie Paterson
NIGHT IN JUNE, A(1940, Swed.)

George Paterson
COLONEL MARCH INVESTIGATES(1952,Brit.), art d

Kenneth Paterson
CRISS CROSS(1949)

Lesley Paterson
ANNE OF THE THOUSAND DAYS(1969, Brit.); PRIME OF MISS JEAN BRODIE, THE(1969, Brit.)

Neil Paterson
MAN ON A TIGHTROPE(1953), w; DEVIL ON HORSEBACK(1954, Brit.), w; LITTLE KIDNAPPERS, THE(1954, Brit.), w; WOMAN FOR JOE, THE(1955, Brit.), w; HIGH TIDE AT NOON(1957, Brit.), w; SHIRALEE, THE(1957, Brit.), w; INNOCENT SIN-NERS(1958, Brit.), w; ROOM AT THE TOP(1959, Brit.), w; SPIRAL ROAD, THE(1962), w

Oscar Paterson
13 MEN AND A GUN(1938, Brit.)

Pat Paterson
GREAT GAY ROAD, THE(1931, Brit.); OTHER WOMAN, THE(1931, Brit.); HERE'S GEORGE(1932, Brit.); LORD BABS(1932, Brit.); MURDER ON THE SECOND FLOOR(1932, Brit.); BERMONDSEY KID, THE(1933, Brit.); BITTER SWEET(1933, Brit.); HEAD OF THE FAMILY(1933, Brit.); LOVE WAGER, THE(1933, Brit.); MEDI-CINE MAN, THE(1933, Brit.); RIGHT TO LIVE, THE(1933, Brit.); BOTTOMS UP(1934); LOVE TIME(1934); CHARLIE CHAN IN EGYPT(1935); SPENDTHRIFT(1936); 52ND STREET(1937); COAL MINER'S DAUGHTER(1980)

"Pat" Paterson
CALL IT LUCK(1934); LOTTERY LOVER(1935)

Ronald Paterson
ADVENTURERS, THE(1970), cos; TOOMORROW(1970, Brit.), cos; SPY WHO LOVED ME, THE(1977, Brit.), cos

Sally Paterson
SUPREME KID, THE(1976, Can.), ed

Terry Paterson
1984
SECOND TIME LUCKY(1984, Aus./New Zealand), ed

Tony Paterson
MOUTH TO MOUTH(1978, Aus.), ed; DIMBOOLA(1979, Aus.), ed; MAD MAX(1979, Aus.), ed
1984
PHAR LAP(1984, Aus.), ed

William Paterson
DIRTY HARRY(1971); AT LONG LAST LOVE(1975)

Christian Patey
1984
L'ARGENT(1984, Fr./Switz.)

Dina Pathak
1984
MOHAN JOSHI HAAZIR HO(1984, India); PASSAGE TO INDIA, A(1984, Brit.)

Madhusdan Pathak
MAYA(1966)

Ratna Pathak
HEAT AND DUST(1983, Brit.)

Supriya Pathak
GANDHI(1982)

Vinod S. Pathak
GOLDEN MOUNTAINS(1958, Den.), p

Peter Pathenis
DAS BOOT(1982)

John Patience
PRIME MINISTER, THE(1941, Brit.)

Princess Patience
LEO THE LAST(1970, Brit.)

Alan Patillo
WALKABOUT(1971, Aus./U.S.), ed; MUSIC MACHINE, THE(1979, Brit.), ed

Mandy Patinkin
FRENCH POSTCARDS(1979); LAST EMBRACE(1979); NIGHT OF THE JUG-GLER(1980); RAGTIME(1981); DANIEL(1983); YENTL(1983)

Tony Patino
VALLEY OF MYSTERY(1967)

Danick Patisson
GIVE ME MY CHANCE(1958, Fr.)

Danik Patisson
SUN ALSO RISES, THE(1957); DIARY OF A BAD GIRL(1958, Fr.); TOO HOT TO HANDLE(1961, Brit.); DANIELLA BY NIGHT(1962, Fr/Ger.); PLEASURES AND VICES(1962, Fr.); MAEDCHEN IN UNIFORM(1965, Ger./Fr.)

Beda F. Patka
FRIDAY THE 13TH... THE ORPHAN(1979), ph

Ida Patlanski
MELODY IN THE DARK(1948, Brit.); MELODY CLUB(1949, Brit.); WARNING TO WANTONS, A(1949, Brit.); HOT ICE(1952, Brit.)

Helena Patockova
EMPEROR AND THE NIGHTINGALE, THE(1949, Czech.)

Stuart Patom
Silents
ELUSIVE ISABEL(1916), d

Alan Paton
CRY, THE BELOVED COUNTRY(1952, Brit.), p, w

Angela Paton
DIRTY HARRY(1971)

Antonio Paton
WIND AND THE LION, THE(1975), art d

Bill Paton
STORY OF VERNON AND IRENE CASTLE, THE(1939)

Carling Paton
SCRAMBLE(1970, Brit.)

Charles Paton
BLACKMAIL(1929, Brit.); FEATHER, THE(1929, Brit.); SISTER TO ASSIST'ER, A(1930, Brit.); "W" PLAN, THE(1931, Brit.); GIRL IN THE NIGHT, THE(1931, Brit.); GLAMOUR(1931, Brit.); GREAT GAY ROAD, THE(1931, Brit.); LYONS MAIL, THE(1931, Brit.); SHERLOCK HOLMES' FATAL HOUR(1931, Brit.); SPECKLED BAND, THE(1931, Brit.); WHAT A NIGHT!(1931, Brit.); BACHELOR'S BABY(1932, Brit.); JOSSER JOINS THE NAVY(1932, Brit.); MY WIFE'S FAMILY(1932, Brit.); PICCADILLY(1932, Brit.); THIRD STRING, THE(1932, Brit.); IRON STAIR, THE(1933, Brit.); LOVE NEST, THE(1933, Brit.); THIS ACTING BUSINESS(1933, Brit.); TOO MANY WIVES(1933, Brit.); FREEDOM OF THE SEAS(1934, Brit.); GIRL IN POSSES-SION(1934, Brit.); GIRLS WILL BE BOYS(1934, Brit.); SONG AT EVENTIDE(1934, Brit.); MUSIC HATH CHARMS(1935, Brit.); NO MONKEY BUSINESS(1935, Brit.); ONCE IN A NEW MOON(1935, Brit.); REGAL CAVALCADE(1935, Brit.); JURY'S EVIDENCE(1936, Brit.); REMBRANDT(1936, Brit.); VANDERGILT DIAMOND MYS-TERY, THE(1936); DOMINANT SEX, THE(1937, Brit.); LAST CHANCE, THE(1937, Brit.); MISSING, BELIEVED MARRIED(1937, Brit.); MUSEUM MYSTERY(1937, Brit.); OLD MOTHER RILEY(1937, Brit.); DOUBLE OR QUITS(1938, Brit.); SAILING ALONG(1938, Brit.); SISTER TO ASSIST'ER, A(1938, Brit.); WEDDINGS ARE WON-DERFUL(1938, Brit.); MEN WITHOUT HONOUR(1939, Brit.); PRISONER OF COR-BAL(1939, Brit.); SAINT IN LONDON, THE(1939, Brit.); WARE CASE, THE(1939, Brit.); OLD MOTHER RILEY'S GHOSTS(1941, Brit.); SOUTH AMERICAN GEORGE(1941, Brit.); PIMPERNEL SMITH(1942, Brit.); WHEN KNIGHTS WERE BOLD(1942, Brit.); YOUNG MR. PITT, THE(1942, Brit.); OLD MOTHER RILEY, DETECTIVE(1943, Brit.); GIVE US THE MOON(1944, Brit.); HE SNOOPS TO CONQUER(1944, Brit.); UNCEN-SORED(1944, Brit.); ADVENTURE FOR TWO(1945, Brit.); STRAWBERRY ROAN(1945, Brit.); CAESAR AND CLEOPATRA(1946, Brit.); WALTZ TIME(1946, Brit.); WOMAN TO WOMAN(1946, Brit.); GREEN FINGERS(1947); HOUSE OF DARKNESS(1948, Brit.); LOVE IN WAITING(1948, Brit.); MAN ON THE RUN(1949, Brit.); MIRAN-DA(1949, Brit.); ADVENTURERS, THE(1951, Brit.); PORTRAIT OF CLARE(1951, Brit.); ONCE A SINNER(1952, Brit.); MY HEART GOES CRAZY(1953, Brit.)

Staurt Paton
FIRST AID(1931), d

Stuart Paton
AIR POLICE(1931), d; CHINATOWN AFTER DARK(1931), d; HELL BENT FOR 'FRISCO(1931), d; IN OLD CHEYENNE(1931), d; IS THERE JUSTICE?(1931), d; MOUNTED FURY(1931), d; THUNDERBOLT(1936), d; CLIPPED WINGS(1938), d
Misc. Talkies
SILENT CODE, THE(1935), d
Silents
20,000 LEAGUES UNDER THE SEA(1916), d&w; GIRL IN THE DARK, THE(1918), d; DEVIL'S TRAIL, THE(1919), d; CONFLICT, THE(1921), d; DR. JIM(1921), w; TORRENT, THE(1921), d; MAN TO MAN(1922), d; WOLF LAW(1922), d; SCARLET CAR, THE(1923), d; LADY FROM HELL, THE(1926), d
Misc. Silents
CONSCIENCE(1915), d; COURT-MARTIALED(1915), d; GREAT MEN AMONG US(1915); WHITE TERROR, THE(1915), d; BELOVED JIM(1917), d; LIKE WILD-FIRE(1917), d; BORDER RAIDERS, THE(1918), d; MARRIAGE LIE, THE(1918), d; WINE GIRL, THE(1918), d; LITTLE DIPLOMAT, THE(1919), d; WANTED AT HEAD-QUARTERS(1920), d; BLACK BAG, THE(1922), d; MARRIED FLAPPER, THE(1922), d; ONE WONDERFUL NIGHT(1922), d; BAVU(1923), d; BURNING WORDS(1923), d; LOVE BRAND, THE(1923), d; NIGHT HAWK, THE(1924), d; BAITED TRAP(1926), d; FOREST HAVOC(1926), d; FRENZIED FLAMES(1926), d; WOLF HUNTERS, THE(1926), d; FANGS OF DESTINY(1927), d; FOUR-FOOTED RANGER, THE(1928), d; HOUND OF THE SILVER CREEK, THE(1928), d

Tony Paton
JEZEBEL(1938); DANGER ON WHEELS(1940); GREEN HELL(1940); TORRID ZONE(1940); SIGN OF THE WOLF(1941); BROADWAY(1942); MONSIEUR BEAU-CAIRE(1946)

Hester Paton-Brown
MAN WHO LIKED FUNERALS, THE(1959, Brit.)

James Paton-Watson
WAY WE LIVE, THE(1946, Brit.)

Raphael Patorni
CHILDREN OF PARADISE(1945, Fr.); BLIND DESIRE(1948, Fr.)

Candice Patou
LES MISERABLES(1982, Fr.)
1984
EDITH AND MARCEL(1984, Fr.)

Jean Patou
EMPTY STAR, THE(1962, Mex.), cos

Jeanne Patou
ACES HIGH(1977, Brit.)

Patrasche The Wonder Dog
DOG OF FLANDERS, A(1959)

Tito Patri
HILDUR AND THE MAGICIAN(1969)

Walter Patriarca
SAMSON AND THE SLAVE QUEEN(1963, Ital.), cos; SEVEN SLAVES AGAINST THE WORLD(1965, Ital.), cos; CANNIBALS IN THE STREETS(1982, Ital./Span.), art d; DR. BUTCHER, M.D.(1982, Ital.), w; YOR, THE HUNTER FROM THE FUTU-RE(1983, Ital.), art d

Gil Patric
MAD MONSTER, THE(1942); CHEYENNE ROUNDUP(1943); HOPPY'S HOLI-DAY(1947); ADAM'S RIB(1949)

Ann Patrice
CAPTAIN NEMO AND THE UNDERWATER CITY(1969, Brit.)

Francois Patrice
DEVIL'S DAUGHTER(1949, Fr.)

Gloria Patrice
GIRL OF THE LIMBERLOST, THE(1945)

Alain Patrick
DRUM(1976)
Misc. Talkies
PANAMA RED(1976)

Both Patrick
EXILES, THE(1966), ed

Butch Patrick
TWO LITTLE BEARS, THE(1961); HAND OF DEATH(1962); PRESSURE POINT(1962); ONE MAN'S WAY(1964); MUNSTER, GO HOME(1966); 80 STEPS TO JONAH(1969); PHANTOM TOLLBOOTH, THE(1970); WILD PACK, THE(1972)

Cynthia Patrick
FOUR GIRLS IN TOWN(1956); MOLE PEOPLE, THE(1956); WRITTEN ON THE WIND(1956)

Dave Patrick
ONE MAN(1979, Can.)

David Patrick
1984
KINGS AND DESPERATE MEN(1984, Brit.)

Dennis Patrick
TIME TRAVELERS, THE(1964); DADDY'S GONE A-HUNTING(1969); HOUSE OF DARK SHADOWS(1970); JOE(1970); TIGER BY THE TAIL(1970); DEAR, DEAD DELILAH(1972)

Diana Patrick
NIGHT DIGGER, THE(1971, Brit.)

Dorothy Patrick
UP IN ARMS(1944); BOYS' RANCH(1946); MIGHTY MCGURK, THE(1946); TILL THE CLOUDS ROLL BY(1946); HIGH WALL, THE(1947); NEW ORLEANS(1947); ALIAS A GENTLEMAN(1948); COME TO THE STABLE(1949); FOLLOW ME QUIET-LY(1949); BELLE OF OLD MEXICO(1950); BLONDE BANDIT, THE(1950); DESTINA-TION BIG HOUSE(1950); FEDERAL AGENT AT LARGE(1950); HOUSE BY THE RIVER(1950); LONELY HEARTS BANDITS(1950); TARNISHED(1950); UNDER MEX-ICALI STARS(1950); 711 OCEAN DRIVE(1950); BIG GUSHER, THE(1951); BAD AND THE BEAUTIFUL, THE(1952); DESERT PASSAGE(1952); ROAD AGENT(1952); SCARAMOUCHE(1952); SINGIN' IN THE RAIN(1952); HALF A HERO(1953); MAN OF CONFLICT(1953); SAVAGE FRONTIER(1953); TANGIER INCIDENT(1953); TORCH SONG(1953); MEN OF THE FIGHTING LADY(1954); OUTLAW STALLION, THE(1954); THUNDER PASS(1954); LAS VEGAS SHAKEDOWN(1955); VIOLENT SATURDAY(1955); PEACEMAKER, THE(1956)

Edward Patrick
REFORM SCHOOL(1939)
Silents
MAN WHO SAW TOMORROW, THE(1922); MR. BILLINGS SPENDS HIS DI-ME(1923)

Elbert Andre Patrick
TOY, THE(1982)

Elizabeth Patrick
WEREWOLF IN A GIRL'S DORMITORY(1961, Ital./Aust.)

Gail Patrick
IF I HAD A MILLION(1932); MURDERS IN THE ZOO(1933); MYSTERIOUS RIDER, THE(1933); PHANTOM BROADCAST, THE(1933); PICK-UP(1933); TO THE LAST MAN(1933); CRIME OF HELEN STANLEY(1934); DEATH TAKES A HOLIDAY(1934); MURDER AT THE VANITIES(1934); TAKE THE STAND(1934); WAGON WHEELS(1934); BIG BROADCAST OF 1936, THE(1935); DOUBTING THOMAS(1935); MISSISSIPPI(1935); NO MORE LADIES(1935); ONE HOUR LATE(1935); RUM-BA(1935); SMART GIRL(1935); TWO FISTED(1935); WANDERER OF THE WASTE-LAND(1935); EARLY TO BED(1936); LONE WOLF RETURNS, THE(1936); MURDER WITH PICTURES(1936); MY MAN GODFREY(1936); PREVIEW MURDER MYS-TERY(1936); TWO IN THE DARK(1936); WHITE HUNTER(1936); ARTISTS AND MODELS(1937); HER HUSBAND LIES(1937); JOHN MEADE'S WOMAN(1937); STAGE DOOR(1937); DANGEROUS TO KNOW(1938); KING OF ALCATRAZ(1938); MAD ABOUT MUSIC(1938); WIVES UNDER SUSPICION(1938); DISBARRED(1939); GRAND JURY SECRETS(1939); MAN OF CONQUEST(1939); RENO(1939); DOCTOR TAKES A WIFE(1940); GALLANT SONS(1940); MY FAVORITE WIFE(1940); KATH-LEEN(1941); LOVE CRAZY(1941); QUIET PLEASE, MURDER(1942); TALES OF MANHATTAN(1942); WE WERE DANCING(1942); HIT PARADE OF 1943(1943); WOMEN IN BONDAGE(1943); UP IN MABEL'S ROOM(1944); BREWSTER'S MIL-LIONS(1945); TWICE BLESSED(1945); CLAUDIA AND DAVID(1946); MADONNA'S SECRET, THE(1946); PLAINSMAN AND THE LADY(1946); RENDEZVOUS WITH ANNIE(1946); CALENDAR GIRL(1947); KING OF THE WILD HORSES(1947); INSIDE STORY, THE(1948)

George L. Patrick
LOVE NEST(1951), art d

George Patrick
FIXED BAYONETS(1951), art d; DEADLINE–U.S.A.(1952), art d; MONKEY BUSI-NESS(1952), art d; SOMETHING FOR THE BIRDS(1952), art d; PICKUP ON SOUTH STREET(1953), art d; RACERS, THE(1955), art d; WEREWOLF IN A GIRL'S DORMI-TORY(1961, Ital./Aust.), ph; JOURNEY TO SHILOH(1968), art d; BACKTRACK(1969), art d; LOVE GOD?, THE(1969), art d; COCKEYED COWBOYS OF CALICO COUNTY, THE(1970), art d

Gil Patrick
FLESH AND FANTASY(1943); BUFFALO BILL RIDES AGAIN(1947); TEXAS CARNIVAL(1951)

J. Patrick
3 IS A FAMILY(1944), prod d

Jack Patrick
FRAMED(1947), w

Jerome Patrick
Silents
DON'T CALL ME LITTLE GIRL(1921); SCHOOL DAYS(1921)
Misc. Silents
THREE MEN AND A GIRL(1919); FURNANCE, THE(1920); HER FIRST ELOPE-MENT(1920); OFFICER 666(1920); HEART LINE, THE(1921); OTHER WOMAN, THE(1921)

Joan Patrick
LOVER COME BACK(1961); ASTRO-ZOMBIES, THE(1969)

John Patrick
EDUCATING FATHER(1936), w; FIFTEEN MAIDEN LANE(1936), w; HIGH TEN-SION(1936), w; THIRTY SIX HOURS TO KILL(1936), w; BIG TOWN GIRL(1937), w; BORN RECKLESS(1937), w; DANGEROUSLY YOURS(1937), w; HOLY TERROR, THE(1937), w; MIDNIGHT TAXI(1937), w; ONE MILE FROM HEAVEN(1937), w; SING AND BE HAPPY(1937), w; TIME OUT FOR ROMANCE(1937), w; BATTLE OF BROADWAY(1938), w; FIVE OF A KIND(1938), w; INTERNATIONAL SETTLE-MENT(1938), w; MR. MOTO TAKES A CHANCE(1938), w; UP THE RIVER(1938), w; STRANGE LOVE OF MARTHA IVERS, THE(1946), w; SECOND CHANCE(1947), w; ENCHANTMENT(1948), w; HASTY HEART, THE(1949), w; PRESIDENT'S LADY, THE(1953), w; THREE COINS IN THE FOUNTAIN(1954), w; LOVE IS A MANY-SPLENDORED THING(1955), w; HIGH SOCIETY(1956), w; TEAHOUSE OF THE AUGUST MOON, THE(1956), w; DANIEL BOONE, TRAIL BLAZER(1957), w; LES GIRLS(1957), w; SPOILERS OF THE FOREST(1957); SOME CAME RUNNING(1959), w; WORLD OF SUZIE WONG, THE(1960), w; GIGOT(1962), w; MAIN ATTRACTION, THE(1962, Brit.), p; SHOES OF THE FISHERMAN, THE(1968), w
Silents
GOLDFISH, THE(1924); SHERLOCK, JR.(1924); AFTER BUSINESS HOURS(1925); WHAT FOOLS MEN(1925); CAVEMAN, THE(1926); FIRST YEAR, THE(1926); HIS JAZZ BRIDE(1926); LADIES AT PLAY(1926); SOCIAL HIGHWAYMAN, THE(1926); RUBBER TIRES(1927); STAGE KISSES(1927); SINNER'S PARADE(1928)
Misc. Silents
DARK SWAN, THE(1924); DON'T DOUBT YOUR HUSBAND(1924); DON'T(1925); MAN WITHOUT A CONSCIENCE, THE(1925); SEVEN SINNERS(1925); WHILE LONDON SLEEPS(1926); LIFE OF AN ACTRESS(1927); GOLF WIDOWS(1928)

Laurel Patrick
1984
HIGHWAY TO HELL(1984); RUNNING HOT(1984)

Lee Patrick
STRANGE CARGO(1929); BORDER CAFE(1937); CRASHING HOLLYWOOD(1937); DANGER PATROL(1937); HIDEAWAY(1937); MUSIC FOR MADAME(1937); CON-DEMNED WOMEN(1938); LAW OF THE UNDERWORLD(1938); MAID'S NIGHT OUT(1938); NIGHT SPOT(1938); SISTERS, THE(1938); FISHERMAN'S WHARF(1939); FATHER IS A PRINCE(1940); INVISIBLE STRIPES(1940); LADIES MUST LIVE(1940); MONEY AND THE WOMAN(1940); SATURDAY'S CHILDREN(1940); SOUTH OF SUEZ(1940); CITY, FOR CONQUEST(1941); FOOTSTEPS IN THE DARK(1941); HONEYMOON FOR THREE(1941); KISSES FOR BREAKFAST(1941); MALTESE FALCON, THE(1941); MILLION DOLLAR BABY(1941); NURSE'S SECRET, THE(1941); SMILING GHOST, THE(1941); DANGEROUSLY THEY LIVE(1942); GEORGE WASHINGTON SLEPT HERE(1942); IN THIS OUR LIFE(1942); NIGHT TO REMEMBER, A(1942); NOW, VOYAGER(1942); SOMEWHERE I'LL FIND YOU(1942); JITTERBUGS(1943); LARCENY WITH MUSIC(1943); NOBODY'S DARLING(1943); FACES IN THE FOG(1944); GAMBLER'S CHOICE(1944); MOON OVER LAS VE-GAS(1944); MRS. PARKINGTON(1944); KEEP YOUR POWDER DRY(1945); MILDRED PIERCE(1945); OVER 21(1945); SEE MY LAWYER(1945); STRANGE JOURNEY(1946); WAKE UP AND DREAM(1946); WALLS CAME TUMBLING DOWN, THE(1946); MOTHER WORE TIGHTS(1947); INNER SANCTUM(1948); SNAKE PIT, THE(1948); DOOLINS OF OKLAHOMA, THE(1949); CAGED(1950); FULLER BRUSH GIRL, THE(1950); LAWLESS, THE(1950); TOMORROW IS ANOTHER DAY(1951); TAKE ME TO TOWN(1953); THERE'S NO BUSINESS LIKE SHOW BUSINESS(1954); AUNTIE MAME(1958); VERTIGO(1958); PILLOW TALK(1959); VISIT TO A SMALL PLA-NET(1960); GOODBYE AGAIN(1961); SUMMER AND SMOKE(1961); GIRL NAMED TAMIRO, A(1962); WIVES AND LOVERS(1963); NEW INTERNS, THE(1964); SEVEN FACES OF DR. LAO(1964); BLACK BIRD, THE(1975)
Misc. Talkies
SINGING SPURS(1948)

Lilian Patrick
JULIE THE REDHEAD(1963, Fr.)

Liliane Patrick
JOKER, THE(1961, Fr.); LOVE AND THE FRENCHWOMAN(1961, Fr.); MAX-IME(1962, Fr.)

Loren Patrick
SHE'S DANGEROUS(1937), art d

Lory Patrick
SURF PARTY(1964); HOW TO SUCCEED IN BUSINESS WITHOUT REALLY TRYING(1976)

Marian Patrick
SWAMP COUNTRY(1966)
Mervyn Patrick
NO BLADE OF GRASS(1970, Brit.)
Mil Patrick
SCARLET ANGEL(1952); RAINTREE COUNTY(1957)
Millicent Patrick
WORLD IN HIS ARMS, THE(1952); WHITE GODDESS(1953); MAN WITHOUT A STAR(1955); THIS ISLAND EARTH(1955), mutant design; WOMEN OF PITCAIRN ISLAND, THE(1957)
Neil Patrick
Misc. Talkies
FUGITIVE KILLER(1975)
Nigel Patrick
MRS. PYM OF SCOTLAND YARD(1939, Brit.); UNEASY TERMS(1948, Brit.); JACK OF DIAMONDS, THE(1949, Brit.), a, w; SILENT DUST(1949, Brit.); SPRING IN PARK LANE(1949, Brit.); PERFECT WOMAN, THE(1950, Brit.); SILK NOOSE, THE(1950, Brit.); TRIO(1950, Brit.); BROWNING VERSION, THE(1951, Brit.); ENCORE(1951, Brit.); OPERATION DISASTER(1951, Brit.); PANDORA AND THE FLYING DUTCHMAN(1951, Brit.); BREAKING THE SOUND BARRIER(1952); PASSIONATE SENTRY, THE(1952, Brit.); PICKWICK PAPERS, THE(1952, Brit.); TONIGHT AT 8:30(1953, Brit.); FORBIDDEN CARGO(1954, Brit.); YOUNG WIVES' TALE(1954, Brit.); SEA SHALL NOT HAVE THEM, THE(1955, Brit.); WICKED WIFE(1955, Brit.); ALL FOR MARY(1956, Brit.); HOW TO MURDER A RICH UNCLE(1957, Brit.), a, d; RAINTREE COUNTY(1957); COUNT FIVE AND DIE(1958, Brit.); MAN INSIDE, THE(1958, Brit.); SAPPHIRE(1959, Brit.); MAN WITH THE GREEN CARNATION, THE(1960, Brit.); LEAGUE OF GENTLEMEN, THE(1961, Brit.); JOHNNY NOBODY(1965, Brit.), a, d; UNDERWORLD INFORMERS(1965, Brit.); BATTLE OF BRITAIN, THE(1969, Brit.); EXECUTIONER, THE(1970, Brit.); VIRGIN SOLDIERS, THE(1970, Brit.); GREAT WALTZ, THE(1972); TALES FROM THE CRYPT(1972, Brit.); MACKINTOSH MAN, THE(1973, Brit.)
Pat Patrick
SHE MARRIED HER BOSS(1935); SECRET LIFE OF WALTER MITTY, THE(1947)
Patricia Patrick
SCARLET EMPRESS, THE(1934)
Randy Patrick
CARNY(1980); HOPSCOTCH(1980); ZAPPED!(1982)
Robert Patrick
MIGHTY JUNGLE, THE(1965, U.S./Mex.), p; SWAMP COUNTRY(1966), p&d; HELL ON WHEELS(1967), p; FROM NASHVILLE WITH MUSIC(1969), p&d
Roy Patrick
ROAD TO HONG KONG, THE(1962, U.S./Brit.)
Vincent Patrick
1984
POPE OF GREENWICH VILLAGE, THE(1984), w
Vittoriano Patrick
BLACK VEIL FOR LISA, A(1969 Ital./Ger.), w
William Patrick
CLUE OF THE MISSING APE, THE(1953, Brit.)
Patrick, the Harp
JACK AND THE BEANSTALK(1952)
Susan Patricof
STILL OF THE NIGHT(1982)
Tom Patricola
FROZEN JUSTICE(1929); MARRIED IN HOLLYWOOD(1929); SOUTH SEA ROSE(1929); WORDS AND MUSIC(1929); ANYBODY'S WOMAN(1930); HAPPY DAYS(1930); ONE MAD KISS(1930); THREE SISTERS, THE(1930); CHILDREN OF DREAMS(1931); RHAPSODY IN BLUE(1945)
James Patridge
MOVE OVER, DARLING(1963)
Joe Patridge
THE HYPNOTIC EYE(1960)
Joseph Patridge
CONVICT STAGE(1965); FORT COURAGEOUS(1965)
Father Patrinakos
GLORY BRIGADE, THE(1953)
Jean Patriquin
LITTLE IODINE(1946)
Massimo Patrizi
ITALIAN SECRET SERVICE(1968, Ital.), w; PRICE OF POWER, THE(1969, Ital./Span.), w
Stefano Patrizi
CONVERSATION PIECE(1976, Ital., Fr.); CASSANDRA CROSSING, THE(1977); NEST OF VIPERS(1979, Ital.); WIFEMISTRESS(1979, Ital.); LION OF THE DESERT(1981, Libya/Brit.)
Carmelo Patrono
STRANGER IN TOWN, A(1968, U.S./Ital.), art d; BROTHER SUN, SISTER MOON(1973, Brit./Ital.), set d
Daniel Patrucci
BREAD AND CHOCOLATE(1978, Ital.), m
Pierre Patry
TROUBLE-FETE(1964, Can.), d, w
Robert Pattack
BELLS OF SAN FERNANDO(1947), ph
Jean-Marie Patte
RISE OF LOUIS XIV, THE(1970, Fr.)
H.H. Pattee
Silents
SALAMANDER, THE(1915)
Misc. Silents
MILLIONAIRE'S DOUBLE, THE(1917)
Herbert Horton Pattee
Misc. Silents
FOR THE FREEDOM OF THE EAST(1918)
Herbert Pattee
Silents
NEIGHBORS(1918); ONE MILLION IN JEWELS(1923); OUTLAWS OF THE SEA(1923)

Misc. Silents
CAMBRIC MASK, THE(1919)
Bob Patten
APARTMENT FOR PEGGY(1948); STREET WITH NO NAME, THE(1948); FATHER WAS A FULLBACK(1949); MOTHER IS A FRESHMAN(1949); MR. BELVEDERE GOES TO COLLEGE(1949); SAND(1949); AMERICAN GUERRILLA IN THE PHILIPPINES, AN(1950); WHERE THE SIDEWALK ENDS(1950); FROGMEN, THE(1951); UNCHAINED(1955)
Dorothy Patten
BOTANY BAY(1953)
Jane Patten
KITTY FOYLE(1940); LUCKY PARTNERS(1940); FOOTLIGHT FEVER(1941); MEXICAN SPITFIRE'S BABY(1941); REPENT AT LEISURE(1941); TOM, DICK AND HARRY(1941); MAYOR OF 44TH STREET, THE(1942); PARDON MY SARONG(1942)
Lewis B. Patten
RED SUNDOWN(1956), w; DEATH OF A GUNFIGHTER(1969), w; DON'T TURN THE OTHER CHEEK(1974, Ital./Ger./Span.), w
Luana Patten
LITTLE MISTER JIM(1946); SONG OF THE SOUTH(1946); FUN AND FANCY FREE(1947); MELODY TIME(1948); SO DEAR TO MY HEART(1949); ROCK, PRETTY BABY(1956); JOE DAKOTA(1957); JOHNNY TREMAIN(1957); RESTLESS YEARS, THE(1958); YOUNG CAPTIVES, THE(1959); HOME FROM THE HILL(1960); MUSIC BOX KID, THE(1960); GO NAKED IN THE WORLD(1961); LITTLE SHEPHERD OF KINGDOM COME(1961); THUNDER OF DRUMS, A(1961); SHOOT OUT AT BIG SAG(1962); FOLLOW ME, BOYS!(1966); THEY RAN FOR THEIR LIVES(1968)
Peggy Lloyd Patten
WHAT'S THE MATTER WITH HELEN?(1971)
Peggy Patten
EXPERIMENT IN TERROR(1962)
Robert Patten
WHEN MY BABY SMILES AT ME(1948); IT HAPPENS EVERY SPRING(1949); TWELVE O'CLOCK HIGH(1949); RETURN FROM THE SEA(1954); LOVE IN A GOLDFISH BOWL(1961); GUIDE FOR THE MARRIED MAN, A(1967); AIRPORT(1970); ZIGZAG(1970); WESTWORLD(1973); BLACK SUNDAY(1977); FM(1978); PERSONAL BEST(1982)
Wim Patten
LIARS, THE(1964, Fr.)
Chuck Patterson
NIGHT OF THE STRANGLER(1975); HAIR(1979)
Cjon Damitri Patterson
SEA GYPSIES, THE(1978)
Colonel Patterson
Silents
JANICE MEREDITH(1924)
David J. Patterson
HEARTACHES(1981, Can.), p; CROSS COUNTRY(1983, Can.), p
Dick Patterson
DONDI(1961); MATTER OF INNOCENCE, A(1968, Brit.); GREASE(1978); CAN'T STOP THE MUSIC(1980); GREASE 2(1982)
Don Patterson
FANTASIA(1940), anim; PINOCCHIO(1940), anim; DUMBO(1941), anim; MAKE MINE MUSIC(1946), anim
Edwina Patterson
LADY CONFESSES, THE(1945)
Elizabeth Patterson
TARNISHED LADY(1931); SOUTH SEA ROSE(1929); WORDS AND MUSIC(1929); CAT CREEPS, THE(1930); HARMONY AT HOME(1930); LONE STAR RANGER, THE(1930); DADDY LONG LEGS(1931); HEAVEN ON EARTH(1931); HUSBAND'S HOLIDAY(1931); SMILING LIEUTENANT, THE(1931); BILL OF DIVORCEMENT, A(1932); GUILTY AS HELL(1932); JAZZ BABIES(1932); LIFE BEGINS(1932); LOVE ME TONIGHT(1932); MISS PINKERTON(1932); NEW MORALS FOR OLD(1932); PLAY GIRL(1932); SO BIG(1932); THEY CALL IT SIN(1932); DINNER AT EIGHT(1933); DR. BULL(1933); EVER IN MY HEART(1933); GOLDEN HARVEST(1933); HOLD YOUR MAN(1933); INFERNAL MACHINE(1933); NO MAN OF HER OWN(1933); SECRET OF THE BLUE ROOM(1933); STORY OF TEMPLE DRAKE, THE(1933); THEY JUST HAD TO GET MARRIED(1933); HIDE-OUT(1934); CHASING YESTERDAY(1935); MEN WITHOUT NAMES(1935); SO RED THE ROSE(1935); GO WEST, YOUNG MAN(1936); HER MASTER'S VOICE(1936); OLD HUTCH(1936); RETURN OF SOPHIE LANG, THE(1936); SMALL TOWN GIRL(1936); THREE CHEERS FOR LOVE(1936); TIMOTHY'S QUEST(1936); HIGH, WIDE AND HANDSOME(1937); HOLD'EM NAVY!(1937); NIGHT CLUB SCANDAL(1937); NIGHT OF MYSTERY(1937); BLUEBEARD'S EIGHTH WIFE(1938); BULLDOG DRUMMOND'S PERIL(1938); SCANDAL STREET(1938); SING YOU SINNERS(1938); SONS OF THE LEGION(1938); BAD LITTLE ANGEL(1939); BULLDOG DRUMMOND'S BRIDE(1939); BULLDOG DRUMMOND'S SECRET POLICE(1939); CAT AND THE CANARY, THE(1939); OUR LEADING CITIZEN(1939); STORY OF ALEXANDER GRAHAM BELL, THE(1939); ADVENTURE IN DIAMONDS(1940); ANNE OF WINDY POPLARS(1940); EARTHBOUND(1940); MICHAEL SHAYNE, PRIVATE DETECTIVE(1940); REMEMBER THE NIGHT(1940); WHO KILLED AUNT MAGGIE?(1940); BELLE STARR(1941); KISS THE BOYS GOODBYE(1941); TOBACCO ROAD(1941); VANISHING VIRGINIAN, THE(1941); ALMOST MARRIED(1942); BEYOND THE BLUE HORIZON(1942); HER CARDBOARD LOVER(1942); I MARRIED A WITCH(1942); LUCKY LEGS(1942); MY SISTER EILEEN(1942); SKY'S THE LIMIT, THE(1943); FOLLOW THE BOYS(1944); HAIL THE CONQUERING HERO(1944); TOGETHER AGAIN(1944); COLONEL EFFINGHAM'S RAID(1945); LADY ON A TRAIN(1945); I'VE ALWAYS LOVED YOU(1946); SECRET HEART, THE(1946); OUT OF THE BLUE(1947); SHOCKING MISS PILGRIM, THE(1947); WELCOME STRANGER(1947); MISS TATLOCK'S MILLIONS(1948); INTRUDER IN THE DUST(1949); LITTLE WOMEN(1949); SONG OF SURRENDER(1949); BRIGHT LEAF(1950); KATIE DID IT(1951); WASHINGTON STORY(1952); LAS VEGAS SHAKEDOWN(1955); PAL JOEY(1957); OREGON TRAIL, THE(1959); TALL STORY(1960)
Silents
RETURN OF PETER GRIMM, THE(1926)
Elmer Patterson
Silents
ETERNAL SIN, THE(1917)
Frances Taylor Patterson
Silents
BROKEN HEARTS(1926), w

Garry Patterson
HOW WILLINGLY YOU SING(1975, Aus.), a, p,d&w

George Patterson
MASTER OF BANKDAM, THE(1947, Brit.), art d; MIRANDA(1949, Brit.), art d; LONG DARK HALL, THE(1951, Brit.), art d; PAUL TEMPLE RETURNS(1952, Brit.); OPERATION CUPID(1960, Brit.); I DRINK YOUR BLOOD(1971); GOD TOLD ME TO(1976)

Georgina Patterson
GUTTER GIRLS(1964, Brit.)

Gerri Patterson
SON OF SINBAD(1955)

Ginna Patterson
PLAY MISTY FOR ME(1971)

Gyr Patterson
REDEEMER, THE(1978)

Hank Patterson
ABILENE TOWN(1946); EL PASO KID, THE(1946); I RING DOORBELLS(1946); SANTA FE UPRISING(1946); WILD BEAUTY(1946); BELLS OF SAN ANGELO(1947); ROBIN OF TEXAS(1947); SPRINGTIME IN THE SIERRAS(1947); UNDER COLORADO SKIES(1947); DENVER KID, THE(1948); NIGHT TIME IN NEVADA(1948); OKLAHOMA BADLANDS(1948); RELENTLESS(1948); COWBOY AND THE INDIANS, THE(1949); RED CANYON(1949); RIDERS IN THE SKY(1949); CODE OF THE SILVER SAGE(1950); GUNFIGHTER, THE(1950); INDIAN UPRISING(1951); SILVER CITY BONANZA(1951); CALIFORNIA CONQUEST(1952); BLADES OF THE MUSKETEERS(1953); TARANTULA(1955); FIRST TRAVELING SALESLADY, THE(1956); JULIE(1956); AMAZING COLOSSAL MAN, THE(1957); STORM RIDER, THE(1957); ATTACK OF THE PUPPET PEOPLE(1958); DECKS RAN RED, THE(1958); ESCAPE FROM RED ROCK(1958); MONSTER ON THE CAMPUS(1958); SPIDER, THE(1958); TERROR IN A TEXAS TOWN(1958); LONE TEXAN(1959); GUNFIGHTERS OF ABILENE(1960)

Henri Patterson
ROOTS OF HEAVEN, THE(1958), m

Herbert Patterson
TEN GENTLEMEN FROM WEST POINT(1942); PEACEMAKER, THE(1956); VOODOO ISLAND(1957)

James Patterson
LILITH(1964); IN THE HEAT OF THE NIGHT(1967); CASTLE KEEP(1969); FABLE, A(1971); SILENT NIGHT, BLOODY NIGHT(1974)

Jamie Patterson
FAN, THE(1981)

Jay Patterson
1984
PLACES IN THE HEART(1984)

Jean Patterson
DISTANT TRUMPET(1952, Brit.); NOW AND FOREVER(1956, Brit.)

Jeanne Patterson
BOY FROM INDIANA(1950)

Jerry Patterson
INCREDIBLE TWO-HEADED TRANSPLANT, THE(1971)

Jimmy Patterson
YOUNG WARRIORS(1983)

John D. Patterson
Misc. Talkies
LEGEND OF EARL DURAND, THE(1974), d

John Patterson
YELLOW JACK(1938); BLONDE TROUBLE(1937); BORN TO THE WEST(1937); DAUGHTER OF SHANGHAI(1937); FORLORN RIVER(1937); HOTEL HAYWIRE(1937); KING OF GAMBLERS(1937); TIP-OFF GIRLS(1938); THREE CABALLEROS, THE(1944), anim

Judith Patterson
Misc. Talkies
PREMONITION(1972)

Ken Patterson
JOHNNY STOOL PIGEON(1949); LADY TAKES A SAILOR, THE(1949); SHAKEDOWN(1950); IRON MAN, THE(1951); FLESH AND FURY(1952); I'LL CRY TOMORROW(1955); SIX BRIDGES TO CROSS(1955); BABY FACE NELSON(1957); PLUNDERERS, THE(1960)

Kenneth Patterson
DECOY(1946); BRUTE FORCE(1947); ONE TOUCH OF VENUS(1948); OUTRAGE(1950); HARD, FAST, AND BEAUTIFUL(1951); LADY FROM TEXAS, THE(1951); CARRIE(1952); OPERATION SECRET(1952); THIS WOMAN IS DANGEROUS(1952); WINNING TEAM, THE(1952); PRIVATE HELL 36(1954); VIOLENT MEN, THE(1955); INVASION OF THE BODY SNATCHERS(1956); I'D RATHER BE RICH(1964); BEING THERE(1979)

Larry Patterson
OVER-UNDER, SIDEWAYS-DOWN(1977)

Lee Patterson
TERROR STREET(1953); GOOD DIE YOUNG, THE(1954, Brit.); MALTA STORY(1954, Brit.); PASSING STRANGER, THE(1954, Brit.); ABOVE US THE WAVES(1956, Brit.); DRY ROT(1956, Brit.); SPIN A DARK WEB(1956, Brit.); CHECKPOINT(1957, Brit.); COUNTERFEIT PLAN, THE(1957, Brit.); KEY MAN, THE(1957, Brit.); MAILBAG ROBBERY(1957, Brit.); REACH FOR THE SKY(1957, Brit.); STORY OF ESTHER COSTELLO, THE(1957, Brit.); CAT AND MOUSE(1958, Brit.); INBETWEEN AGE, THE(1958, Brit.); MAN WITH A GUN(1958, Brit.); SPANIARD'S CURSE, THE(1958, Brit.); DEADLY RECORD(1959, Brit.); JACK THE RIPPER(1959, Brit.); THIRD MAN ON THE MOUNTAIN(1959); TIME LOCK(1959, Brit.); WHITE TRAP, THE(1959, Brit.); OCTOBER MOTH(1960, Brit.); THREE WORLDS OF GULLIVER, THE(1960, Brit.); AIR PATROL(1962); CEREMONY, THE(1963, U.S./Span.); VALLEY OF MYSTERY(1967); CHATO'S LAND(1972); AIRPLANE II: THE SEQUEL(1982)
Misc. Talkies
BREAKOUT(1959); SEARCH FOR THE EVIL ONE(1967)

Lorna Patterson
AIRPLANE!(1980)

Mary Patterson
IT HAD TO BE YOU(1947); MC LINTOCK!(1963)

May Patterson
DISCOVERIES(1939, Brit.)

Melody Patterson
ANGRY BREED, THE(1969); CYCLE SAVAGES(1969); BLOOD AND LACE(1971); HARRAD EXPERIMENT, THE(1973)

Neva Patterson
TAXI(1953); SOLID GOLD CADILLAC, THE(1956); AFFAIR TO REMEMBER, AN(1957); DESK SET(1957); TOO MUCH, TOO SOON(1958); DAVID AND LISA(1962); SPIRAL ROAD, THE(1962); DEAR HEART(1964); COUNTERPOINT(1967); SKIN GAME(1971); ALL THE PRESIDENT'S MEN(1976); DOMINO PRINCIPLE, THE(1977); BUDDY HOLLY STORY, THE(1978); STAR 80(1983)
1984
ALL OF ME(1984)

Nita Patterson
Misc. Talkies
ELECTRIC CHAIR, THE(1977)

Norma Patterson
YOU LIVE AND LEARN(1937, Brit.), w

Ottilie Patterson
RING-A-DING RHYTHM(1962, Brit. 73m Amicus/COL bw (G.B: IT'S TRAD, DAD!)

Owen Patterson
RETURN OF CAPTAIN INVINCIBLE, THE(1983, Aus./U.S.), art d

Pat Patterson
IDIOT'S DELIGHT(1939); RUSTLERS(1949); MOONSHINE MOUNTAIN(1964); SECRETS OF A WINDMILL GIRL(1966, Brit.); HILLBILLYS IN A HAUNTED HOUSE(1967); GAS-S-S-S!(1970); TRAVELING EXECUTIONER, THE(1970); GREATEST, THE(1977, U.S./Brit.)
Misc. Talkies
ELECTRIC CHAIR, THE(1977), d

Patrick Patterson
IMPROPER CHANNELS(1981, Can.)

Patsy Patterson
RIDERS OF THE PURPLE SAGE(1941)

Patti Patterson
SHOW BOAT(1936)

Patty Patterson
HI BEAUTIFUL(1944)

Peggy Patterson
Silents
POLAR STAR, THE(1919, Brit.); HOUSE ON THE MARSH, THE(1920, Brit.); MR. JUSTICE RAFFLES(1921, Brit.); LITTLE DOOR INTO THE WORLD, THE(1923, Brit.)
Misc. Silents
HOMEMAKER, THE(1919, Brit.); HER BENNY(1920, Brit.)

Rae Patterson
VARIETY GIRL(1947); NIGHT HAS A THOUSAND EYES(1948)

Rafaelle Patterson
MAN CALLED DAGGER, A(1967), makeup; PSYCH-OUT(1968), makeup

Ray Patterson
FANTASIA(1940), anim; DUMBO(1941), anim; GAY PURR-EE(1962), anim; HEY THERE, IT'S YOGI BEAR(1964), anim

Raymond Patterson
FIRST TIME, THE(1983)

Richard L. Patterson
WILD AFFAIR, THE(1966, Brit.), p

Richard Patterson
Misc. Talkies
DAY THE EARTH GOT STONED, THE(1978), d

Rick Patterson
YOUNG GIANTS(1983), m

Robert Patterson
BRUTE FORCE(1947), w

Robert Patterson
HOW WILLINGLY YOU SING(1975, Aus.), md

Rosemary Patterson
1984
ALLEY CAT(1984)

Rudi Patterson
TWO A PENNY(1968, Brit.); ONE PLUS ONE(1969, Brit.)

Russell Patterson
BOTTOMS UP!(1934), cos; STAND UP AND CHEER(1934), art d; ARTISTS AND MODELS(1937)

Sally Patterson
KEEPER, THE(1976, Can.), ed; HANK WILLIAMS: THE SHOW HE NEVER GAVE(1982, Can.), ed

Shirley Patterson
BOSTON BLACKIE GOES HOLLYWOOD(1942); LUCKY LEGS(1942); MAN'S WORLD, A(1942); PARACHUTE NURSE(1942); RIDERS OF THE NORTHLAND(1942); SPIRIT OF STANFORD, THE(1942); THEY ALL KISSED THE BRIDE(1942); LAUGH YOUR BLUES AWAY(1943); LAW OF THE NORTHWEST(1943); MORE THE MERRIER, THE(1943); MARRIAGE IS A PRIVATE AFFAIR(1944); RIDING WEST(1944); TEXAS KID, THE(1944); KEEP YOUR POWDER DRY(1945); DRIFTIN' RIVER(1946); STARS OVER TEXAS(1946); TUMBLEWEED TRAIL(1946); BLACK HILLS(1948); SECOND CHANCE(1953); FRENCH LINE, THE(1954); REDHEAD FROM MANHATTAN(1954)
Misc. Talkies
NORTH OF THE ROCKIES(1942); RIDING THROUGH NEVADA(1942); VIGILANTES RIDE, THE(1944)

Starke Patterson
Silents
MORALS(1921)
Misc. Silents
WOLVES OF THE NORTH(1921)

Stephanie Patterson
CLASS OF MISS MAC MICHAEL, THE(1978, Brit./U.S.)

Stewart Patterson
Silents
EUGENE ARAM(1914, Brit.)

Sue Patterson
VAGABOND KING, THE(1930)

Tony Patterson
FANTASM(1976, Aus.), ed; FINAL CUT, THE(1980, Aus.), ed
Troy Patterson
UNDER FIRE(1957); ATTACK OF THE PUPPET PEOPLE(1958); SPIDER, THE(1958); TANK BATTALION(1958); SPEED CRAZY(1959); LAST REBEL, THE(1971); STATUE, THE(1971, Brit.)
Vivien Patterson
FEATHER IN HER HAT, A(1935)
Walt Patterson
WILD WEST WHOOPEE(1931)
Walter Patterson
MOUNTED STRANGER, THE(1930); FLAMING GUNS(1933); RIDE 'EM COW-GIRL(1939); TRIPLE JUSTICE(1940)
Silents
OKLAHOMA KID, THE(1929)
Warren Patterson
BOY! WHAT A GIRL(1947)
Zelda Patterson
LOVE CHILD(1982)
Ercole Patti
OF WAYWARD LOVE(1964, Ital./Ger.), w; THAT SPLENDID NOVEMBER(1971, Ital./Fr.), w
Paolo Patti
MAKE A FACE(1971)
Pino Patti
INVESTIGATION OF A CITIZEN ABOVE SUSPICION(1970, Ital.)
Yolanda Patti
CHANGE OF HEART(1934)
Patti-Chandler
SKI PARTY(1965)
Alan Pattillo
INNOCENT BYSTANDERS(1973, Brit.), ed; MAN CALLED NOON, THE(1973, Brit.), ed; OPEN SEASON(1974, U.S./Span.), ed; STRAIGHT ON TILL MORNING(1974, Brit.), ed; PAPER TIGER(1975, Brit.), ed; GAME OF DEATH, THE(1979), ed
Allan Pattillo
BOYS IN COMPANY C, THE(1978, U.S./Hong Kong), ed
Barrie Pattison
IT HAPPENED HERE(1966, Brit.)
Diantha Pattison
GIRLS' SCHOOL(1950)
Gerry Pattison
LAW OF THE WEST(1949)
Ray Pattison
WE OF THE NEVER NEVER(1983, Aus.)
Roy Pattison
BATTLE BENEATH THE EARTH(1968, Brit.); CHARGE OF THE LIGHT BRIGADE, THE(1968, Brit.)
Anna Patton
SLUMBER PARTY MASSACRE, THE(1982)
Bart Patton
BECAUSE THEY'RE YOUNG(1960); STRANGERS WHEN WE MEET(1960); GIDGET GOES HAWAIIAN(1961); ZOTZ!(1962); DEMENTIA 13(1963); BEACH BALL(1965), p; OUT OF SIGHT(1966), p; WILD, WILD WINTER(1966), p; RAIN PEOPLE, THE(1969), p
Bill Patton
STRAWBERRY ROAN(1933); WAY OF THE WEST, THE(1934); ARIZONA TRAILS(1935); COWBOY AND THE BANDIT, THE(1935); DESERT MESA(1935); GHOST RIDER, THE(1935); JUSTICE OF THE RANGE(1935); PALS OF THE RAN-GE(1935); LAW FOR TOMBSTONE(1937); LITTLE JOE, THE WRANGLER(1942); PRAIRIE PALS(1942)
Silents
BULLDOG COURAGE(1922); ACE OF THE LAW(1924); LAST CHANCE, THE(1926); UNDER FIRE(1926); BANTAM COWBOY, THE(1928); ORPHAN OF THE SAGE(1928); YOUNG WHIRLWIND(1928); FRECKLED RASCAL, THE(1929); PALS OF THE PRAIRIE(1929)
Misc. Silents
OUTLAWED(1921); TRACKS(1922); CYCLONE JONES(1923); BATTLIN' BUCK-AROO(1924); DESERT SECRET, THE(1924); FIGHTIN' THRU(1924); GAME FIGHT-ER, A(1924); LAST MAN, THE(1924); SMOKING TRAIL, THE(1924); FANGS OF FATE(1925); FIGHTIN' ODDS(1925); FLASHING STEEDS(1925); BEYOND THE TRAIL(1926); FORT FRAYNE(1926); LUCKY SPURS(1926); WESTERN TRAILS(1926)
Cheryl Patton
Misc. Talkies
FUGITIVE KILLER(1975)
F. G. Patton
Silents
PECK'S BAD GIRL(1918)
Frances Gray Patton
GOOD MORNING, MISS DOVE(1955), w
Frank Patton
SIX WEEKS(1982)
Gene Patton
MY TUTOR(1983)
George E. Patton
Misc. Silents
MOTHERHOOD; LIFE'S GREATEST MIRACLE(1928)
Gilbert Patton
Silents
TEMPORARY MARRIAGE(1923), w
John Patton
YOU LIGHT UP MY LIFE(1977), cos
Laura Patton
DARK SIDE OF TOMORROW, THE(1970)
Lucille Patton
GAMBLER, THE(1974)
Malcolm Patton
KIND OF LOVING, A(1962, Brit.)

Mark Patton
COME BACK TO THE 5 & DIME, JIMMY DEAN, JIMMY DEAN(1982)
Mary Patton
SEARCH, THE(1948); IN LOVE AND WAR(1958); DARK AT THE TOP OF THE STAIRS, THE(1960); MARRIAGE-GO-ROUND, THE(1960); PLEASE DON'T EAT THE DAISIES(1960); CASE OF PATTY SMITH, THE(1962); OUTSIDER, THE(1962); ROME ADVENTURE(1962); DISTANT TRUMPET, A(1964)
Michael Patton
RECESS(1967)
Micheline Patton
GUTTER GIRLS(1964, Brit.)
N. F. Patton
Silents
KNOCKNAGOW(1918, Ireland), w
Nick Patton
DEVIL'S EXPRESS(1975), p
Phil Patton
SNOW QUEEN, THE(1959, USSR), d
Robert Patton
RIOT IN CELL BLOCK 11(1954)
Stuart Patton
Silents
REPUTATION(1921), d; BULLET MARK, THE(1928), d
Tony Patton
TWO-GUN JUSTICE(1938); REAP THE WILD WIND(1942)
Virgina Patton
NOBODY LIVES FOREVER(1946)
Virginia Patton
OLD ACQUAINTANCE(1943); THANK YOUR LUCKY STARS(1943); HOLLYWOOD CANTEEN(1944); JANIE(1944); LAST RIDE, THE(1944); CANYON PASSAGE(1946); IT'S A WONDERFUL LIFE(1946); BURNING CROSS, THE(1947); DOUBLE LIFE, A(1947); BLACK EAGLE(1948); LUCKY STIFF, THE(1949)
Will Patton
PICTURE OF DORIAN GRAY, THE(1945)
Will Patton
KING BLANK(1983); SILKWOOD(1983)
1984
CHINESE BOXES(1984, Ger./Brit.); VARIETY(1984)
William Patton
HONOR OF THE RANGE(1934)
Silents
SAND(1920); ONE MAN DOG, THE(1929)
Misc. Silents
ALIAS PHIL KENNEDY(1922); GROWING BETTER(1923)
Patricia Patts
BON VOYAGE, CHARLIE BROWN(AND DON'T COME BACK)*** (1980)
Budge Patty
KEEP 'EM SLUGGING(1943)
Tom Patty
LEGEND OF LYLAH CLARE, THE(1968)
John Patu
POWER OF THE WHISTLER, THE(1945), art d
Daniele Patucchi
DEAF SMITH AND JOHNNY EARS(1973, Ital.), m
George Patullo
Silents
GASOLINE GUS(1921), w
Dominique Patural
SEVEN CAPITAL SINS(1962, Fr./Ital.)
Alix Paturel
TOMORROW IS MY TURN(1962, Fr./Ital./Ger.), ed
Dominique Paturel
GIRL FROM LORRAINE, A(1982, Fr./Switz.)
Peter Patzak
Misc. Talkies
SLAUGHTERDAY(1981), d; UPPERCRUST, THE(1982), d
Heinz Pauck
AFFAIRS OF JULIE, THE(1958, Ger.), w; AREN'T WE WONDERFUL?(1959, Ger.), w; SPESSART INN, THE(1961, Ger.), w; SHADOWS GROW LONGER, THE(1962, Switz./Ger.), w
Maria Paudler
Misc. Silents
MADAME WANTS NO CHILDREN(1927, Ger.)
Santini Pauiloa
WINGS OVER THE PACIFIC(1943)
Norman Pauker
LEPKE(1975, U.S./Israel)
Paul
NEW ORLEANS(1947), w; FRASIER, THE SENSUOUS LION(1973)
Adolph Paul
ONE MAD KISS(1930), w
Adreina Paul
FRAULEIN DOKTOR(1969, Ital./Yugo.)
Alexandra Paul
CHRISTINE(1983)
1984
AMERICAN NIGHTMARE(1984); JUST THE WAY YOU ARE(1984)
Andreina Paul
ROAD TO FORT ALAMO, THE(1966, Fr./Ital.)
Andrew Paul
BUGSY MALONE(1976, Brit.); PIRATES OF PENZANCE, THE(1983)
Anthony Paul
HEROSTRATUS(1968, Brit.)
B. Paul
SLEEPING CAR MURDER THE(1966, Fr.)
Betty Paul
FLESH AND BLOOD(1951, Brit.); OLIVER TWIST(1951, Brit.)

Bonnie Paul
VICKI(1953); SIDELONG GLANCES OF A PIGEON KICKER, THE(1970); FALLING IN LOVE AGAIN(1980)

Byron Paul
LT. ROBIN CRUSOE, U.S.N.(1966), d; DAY OF THE LOCUST, THE(1975)

Catherine Paul
CHILDREN OF CHANCE(1949, Brit.); ELIZABETH OF LADYMEAD(1949, Brit.); SPRING IN PARK LANE(1949, Brit.); ODETTE(1951, Brit.)

Charlotte Paul
GUERRILLA GIRL(1953)

Christina Paul
DEEP END(1970 Ger./U.S.); MACBETH(1971, Brit.); VAMPIRE CIRCUS(1972, Brit.)

Christine Paul
CONTRACT, THE(1982, Pol.)

Don Michael Paul
1984
LOVELINES(1984)

Dudley Paul
SHIPBUILDERS, THE(1943, Brit.)

Ed Paul
SECOND CHORUS(1940), md

Eddie Paul
I'M FROM ARKANSAS(1944), md
1984
ICE PIRATES, THE(1984)

Edna Paul
DIRTYMOUTH(1970), ed

Edna Ruth Paul
FEAR NO EVIL(1981), ed; EVIL DEAD, THE(1983), ed

Edward Paul
CHIEF, THE(1933), ph
Silents
SECRETS OF PARIS, THE(1922), ph; DARLING OF THE RICH, THE(1923), ph; LOYAL LIVES(1923), ph; MODERN MARRIAGE(1923), ph; DAUGHTERS WHO PAY(1925), ph; IRON MAN, THE(1925), ph

Edward Paul
FLYING DEUCES, THE(1939), md; LONG VOYAGE HOME, THE(1940), md; MISS ANNIE ROONEY(1942), md; TALES OF MANHATTAN(1942), md; HAIRY APE, THE(1944), md; UP IN MABEL'S ROOM(1944), md; FIGHTING STALLION, THE(1950), m; BAMBOO SAUCER, THE(1968), m

Elliot Paul
WOMAN'S FACE(1941), w; IT'S A PLEASURE(1945), w; NEW ORLEANS(1947), w; MY HEART GOES CRAZY(1953, Brit.), w

Elliott Paul
RHAPSODY IN BLUE(1945), w

Eugenia Paul
JIVARO(1954); BIGGER THAN LIFE(1956); APACHE WARRIOR(1957); DISEMBODIED, THE(1957); MAN ON THE PROWL(1957); GUNFIGHTERS OF ABILENE(1960); SIGN OF ZORRO, THE(1960)

Fred Paul
YELLOW STOCKINGS(1930, Brit.), w; ROMANY LOVE(1931, Brit.), d
Silents
EAST LYNNE(1913, Brit.); IN THE HANDS OF THE LONDON CROOKS(1913, Brit.); JOHN HALIFAX, GENTLEMAN(1915, Brit.); ROGUES OF LONDON(1915, Brit.); NEW CLOWN, THE(1916, Brit.), d; STILL WATERS RUN DEEP(1916, Brit.), d; HOUSE ON THE MARSH, THE(1920, Brit.), d; IF FOUR WALLS TOLD(1922, Brit.), a, d; LONG ODDS(1922, Brit.); HOTEL MOUSE, THE(1923, Brit.), d; RECOIL, THE(1924); LAST WITNESS, THE(1925, Brit.), a, d; SAFETY FIRST(1926, Brit.), d; THOU FOOL(1926, Brit.), d; BROKEN MELODY, THE(1929, Brit.), d, w
Misc. Silents
LIGHTS O' LONDON, THE(1914, Brit.); STUDY IN SCARLET, A(1914, Brit.); CINEMA GIRL'S ROMANCE, A(1915, Brit.); INFELICE(1915, Brit.), a, d; DR. WAKE'S PATIENT(1916, Brit.), d; HER GREATEST PERFORMANCE(1916, Brit.), d; LADY WINDERMERE'S FAN(1916, Brit.), d; LOVE TRAIL, THE(1916, Brit.), a, d; LYONS MAIL, THE(1916, Brit.), d; SECOND MRS. TANQUERAY, THE(1916, Brit.), d; VICAR OF WAKEFIELD, THE(1916, Brit.), d; WHOSO IS WITHOUT SIN(1916, Brit.), d; MASKS AND FACES(1917, Brit.), d; DUCHESS OF SEVEN DIALS, THE(1920, Brit.), d; LADY TETLEY'S DEGREE(1920, Brit.), d; LIGHTS OF HOME, THE(1920, Brit.), d; LITTLE WELSH GIRL, THE(1920, Brit.), d; UNCLE DICK'S DARLING(1920, Brit.), d; HOW KITCHENER WAS BETRAYED(1921, Brit.), d; BROWN SUGAR(1922, Brit.), d; CASTLES IN THE AIR(1923, Brit.), d; RIGHT TO STRIKE, THE(1923), a, d; STRAWS IN THE WIND(1924, Brit.); LUCK OF THE NAVY, THE(1927, Brit.), d

George Paul
DRIVE A CROOKED ROAD(1954); HOUSE OF USHER(1960)

Georgie Paul
DEMON SEED(1977)

Gloria Paul
SPYLARKS(1965, Brit.); GIRL GAME(1968, Braz./Fr./Ital.); DARLING LILI(1970)

Graham Paul
1984
TIGHTROPE(1984)

Haida Paul
1984
MY KIND OF TOWN(1984, Can.)

Holmes Paul
OLD MOTHER RILEY'S GHOSTS(1941, Brit.), art d; LOVE ON THE DOLE(1945, Brit.), art d

Ian Paul
1984
SILENT ONE, THE(1984, New Zealand), ph

Ike Paul
Misc. Silents
BROKEN VIOLIN, THE(1927)

Isaac Paul
RAINBOW BOYS, THE(1973, Can.)

Jackie Paul
MY GUN IS QUICK(1957)

Jeremy Paul
JOURNEY INTO MIDNIGHT(1968, Brit.), w; COUNTESS DRACULA(1972, Brit.), w; MONKEY GRIP(1983, Aus.)

John Paul
HANSEL AND GRETEL(1954), d; FLESH IS WEAK, THE(1957, Brit.); LAW AND DISORDER(1958, Brit.); MAN WHO WOULDN'T TALK, THE(1958, Brit.); STEEL BAYONET, THE(1958, Brit.); DEADLY RECORD(1959, Brit.); TIME LOCK(1959, Brit.); TAKE ME OVER(1963, Brit.); CURSE OF THE MUMMY'S TOMB, THE(1965, Brit.); VIOLENT MOMENT(1966, Brit.); BLOOD BEAST TERROR, THE(1967, Brit.); COUNTESS FROM HONG KONG, A(1967, Brit.); STRANGE AFFAIR, THE(1968, Brit.); DESPERADOS, THE(1969); CROMWELL(1970, Brit.); DOOMWATCH(1972, Brit.); EYE OF THE NEEDLE(1981)
Misc. Talkies
BREAKOUT(1959)

Johnny Paul
VANISHING OUTPOST, THE(1951)

Julia Paul
YOUNG SINNER, THE(1965)

June Paul
TWO TICKETS TO BROADWAY(1951)

Kurt Paul
SKATETOWN, U.S.A.(1979)

Lawrence G. Paul
WHICH WAY IS UP?(1977), prod d; BLADE RUNNER(1982), set d; DOCTOR DETROIT(1983), prod d

Lee Paul
BEN(1972); STING, THE(1973); ISLAND AT THE TOP OF THE WORLD, THE(1974)

Leon Paul
MEET ME AT DAWN(1947, Brit.), ch

Les Paul
SENSATIONS OF 1945(1944); SARGE GOES TO COLLEGE(1947)

Logan Paul
Silents
ISLAND OF REGENERATION, THE(1915); KENNEDY SQUARE(1916); TWO-EDGED SWORD, THE(1916); ARSENE LUPIN(1917)
Misc. Silents
PRICE OF FAME, THE(1916)

Lorraine Paul
FLASH GORDON(1980)

Michael Paul
1984
MY KIND OF TOWN(1984, Can.)

Mimi Paul
MIDSUMMER NIGHT'S DREAM, A(1966)

Morgan Paul
MURPH THE SURF(1974)

Morrison B. Paul
BIG DADDY(1969), ph

Nadeen Paul
Silents
GENTLEMAN OF LEISURE, A(1923)

Nancy Paul
1984
SHEENA(1984)

P. R. Paul
HOLLYWOOD KNIGHTS, THE(1980)

Parveen Paul
SHAKESPEARE WALLAH(1966, India); HEAT AND DUST(1983, Brit.)

Praveen Paul
HOUSEHOLDER, THE(1963, US/India); GUIDE, THE(1965, U.S./India)

R. Holmes Paul
HIGH COMMAND(1938, Brit.), art d; MURDER IN REVERSE(1946, Brit.), art d; WOMAN TO WOMAN(1946, Brit.), art d; UNEASY TERMS(1948, Brit.), art d; LAUGHING LADY, THE(1950, Brit.), art d; MRS. FITZHERBERT(1950, Brit.), art d; LILLI MARLENE(1951, Brit.), art d

Ray Paul
MOLLY AND LAWLESS JOHN(1972), set d; SIDEWINDER ONE(1977), set d

Raymond Paul
BONNIE AND CLYDE(1967), set d; EIGHT ON THE LAM(1967), set d; WICKED DREAMS OF PAULA SCHULTZ, THE(1968), set d; BABY MAKER, THE(1970), set d

Rene Paul
C-MAN(1949); ADVISE AND CONSENT(1962)

Renee Paul
BEST FRIENDS(1975)
Misc. Talkies
BEST FRIENDS(1975)

Richard Paul
EATING RAOUL(1982); MAN WHO WASN'T THERE, THE(1983)
1984
NOT FOR PUBLICATION(1984)

Rita Paul
SCHLAGER-PARADE(1953); UNDER FIRE(1957)

Rodrick Paul
PAPER CHASE, THE(1973), p

Russell Paul
ROMANCE OF THE ROCKIES(1938)

Sandy Paul
PUBERTY BLUES(1983, Aus.)

Stephen Paul
STARFIGHTERS, THE(1964), m

Steven Paul
HAPPY BIRTHDAY, WANDA JUNE(1971); FALLING IN LOVE AGAIN(1980), a, p&d, w
1984
SLAPSTICK OF ANOTHER KIND(1984), a, p,d&w

Stuart Paul
FALLING IN LOVE AGAIN(1980)

Sue Paul
ALL THAT JAZZ(1979)
Taffy Paul
LIKE FATHER LIKE SON(1961); TAMMY, TELL ME TRUE(1961)
Tony Paul
EAGLE ROCK(1964, Brit.)
Val Paul
F MAN(1936), p; MAN I MARRY, THE(1936), p; YELLOWSTONE(1936), p; MIGHTY
TREVE, THE(1937), p; MYSTERIOUS CROSSING(1937), p; RECKLESS LIV-
ING(1938), p
Silents
FAME AND FORTUNE(1918); M'LISS(1918); RED, RED HEART, THE(1918); KICK
BACK, THE(1922), d; CRASHIN' THRU(1923), d
Misc. Silents
END OF THE RAINBOW, THE(1916); GIRL OF LOST LAKE, THE(1916); IT
HAPPENED IN HONOLULU(1916); ROMANCE OF BILLY GOAT HILL, A(1916);
SECRET OF THE SWAMP, THE(1916); GOD'S CRUCIBLE(1917); LAIR OF THE WOLF,
THE(1917); SQUARE DEAL, A(1918); HOOP-LA(1919); SMILES(1919); TREAT 'EM
ROUGH(1919); HEARTS UP(1920), d; SUNDOWN SLIM(1920), d; GOOD MEN AND
TRUE(1922), d; DESERT DRIVEN(1923), d; MIRACLE BABY, THE(1923), d
Van Paul
Misc. Silents
CANYON OF THE FOOLS(1923), d
Vicky Paul
HUNGER, THE(1983), art d
Victor Paul
SCENE OF THE CRIME(1949); GAMBLING HOUSE(1950); BIG BOUNCE,
THE(1969); DIRTY HARRY(1971); WHAT'S UP, DOC?(1972); NIGHT MOVES(1975);
SWASHBUCKLER(1976), stunts; PRISONER OF ZENDA, THE(1979); JAZZ SINGER,
THE(1980)
1984
RACING WITH THE MOON(1984)
Winston R. Paul
CURIOUS FEMALE, THE(1969), w
Paul and Paulina
KID RANGER, THE(1936)
Paul Lavert and his Swinging Cavemen
50,000 B.C.(BEFORE CLOTHING) (1963)
Paul Raymond Bunnies
IT'S ALL OVER TOWN(1963, Brit.)
Paul Specht and His Orchestra
LOVE AT FIRST SIGHT(1930)
Paul Whiteman and His King's Men
THANKS A MILLION(1935)
Paul Whiteman and His Orchestra
ATLANTIC CITY(1944); RHAPSODY IN BLUE(1945)
Silents
LONDON(1926, Brit.)
Paul Whiteman and Orchestra
STRIKE UP THE BAND(1940)
Andre Paul-Antoine
RECORD 413(1936, Fr.), w
George Paulais
TESTAMENT OF DR. MABUSE, THE(1943, Ger.)
Georges Paulais
ROTHSCHILD(1938, Fr.); CAGE OF NIGHTINGALES, A(1947, Fr.)
Misc. Silents
LE DROIT A LA VIE(1917, Fr.)
Roderick Paulate
SUPERBEAST(1972)
Rodney Paulden
UNMAN, WITTERING AND ZIGO(1971, Brit.)
Andrew Paulds
ONCE MORE, WITH FEELING(1960)
Pauleon
BATTLE OF THE RAILS(1949, Fr.)
Jack Pauleson
PIRANHA(1978)
Pierre Paulet
LOVE AND THE FRENCHWOMAN(1961, Fr.); TIME BOMB(1961, Fr./Ital.)
Reine Paulet
ESCAPE FROM YESTERDAY(1939, Fr.)
Ezra Paulette
SUDDEN BILL DORN(1938); TRAIL TO GUNSIGHT(1944); TRIGGER TRAIL(1944)
Geraldine Paulette
HOUSE OF USHER(1960)
Pauley
TOPAZE(1935, Fr.); ROTHSCHILD(1938, Fr.)
Paul Pauley
LIFE AND LOVES OF BEETHOVEN, THE(1937, Fr.)
Irms Pauli
DESPERADO TRAIL, THE(1965, Ger./Yugo.), cos; INVISIBLE DR. MABUSE,
THE(1965, Ger.), cos; TREASURE OF SILVER LAKE(1965, Ger.), cos;
FRONTIER HELLCAT(1966, Fr./Ital./Yugo.), cos; LAST OF THE RENEGA-
DES(1966, Fr./Ital./Ger./Yugo.), cos; RAMPAGE AT APACHE WELLS(1966, Ger./
Yugo.), cos; BLOOD DEMON(1967, Ger.), cos; FLAMING FRONTIER(1968, Ger./
Yugo.), cos
Yamata Pauli
GENGHIS KHAN(U.S./Brit./Ger./Yugo)
Albert Paulig
Misc. Silents
PRINCE AND THE DANCER(1929, Ger.)
Oskar Paulig
PHONY AMERICAN, THE(1964, Ger.)
James Paulin
SUBSTITUTION(1970)
Scott Paulin
SERIAL(1980); CAT PEOPLE(1982); FORBIDDEN WORLD(1982); RIGHT STUFF,
THE(1983)

1984
SOLDIER'S STORY, A(1984)
Albert Pauling
Misc. Silents
HER GREATEST BLUFF(1927, Ger.)
Justo Paulino
PASSIONATE STRANGERS, THE(1968, Phil.), ph; MAD DOCTOR OF BLOOD
ISLAND, THE(1969, Phil./U.S.), ph; BEAST OF BLOOD(1970, U.S./Phil.), ph; BLACK
MAMA, WHITE MAMA(1973), ph; SAVAGE SISTERS(1974), ph
Alan Paull
SUNNY SIDE UP(1929)
H. M. Paull
Silents
NEW CLOWN, THE(1916, Brit.), w
Larry Paull
NICKEL RIDE, THE(1974), art d; W. W. AND THE DIXIE DANCEKINGS(1975),
prod d
Lawrence G. Paull
LITTLE FAUSS AND BIG HALSY(1970), art d; CHANDLER(1971), art d; HIRED
HAND, THE(1971), art d; STAR SPANGLED GIRL(1971), prod d; THEY ONLY KILL
THEIR MASTERS(1972), art d; NAKED APE, THE(1973), prod d; FM(1978), prod d;
HOW TO BEAT THE HIGH COST OF LIVING(1980), prod d; IN GOD WE
TRUST(1980), prod d
1984
ROMANCING THE STONE(1984), prod d
Lawrence Paull
LAST AMERICAN HERO, THE(1973), art d
Morgan Paull
PATTON(1970); FOOLS' PARADE(1971); CAHILL, UNITED STATES MAR-
SHAL(1973); DIRTY O'NEIL(1974); MITCHELL(1975); LAST HARD MEN, THE(1976);
TWILIGHT'S LAST GLEAMING(1977, U.S./Ger.); SWARM, THE(1978); APPLE DUM-
PLING GANG RIDES AGAIN, THE(1979); NORMA RAE(1979); FADE TO
BLACK(1980); BLADE RUNNER(1982)
1984
SURF II(1984)
Pete Paull
LET'S ROCK(1958)
Ricky G. Paull
PIRANHA II: THE SPAWNING(1981, Neth.)
Stephanie Paull
MILLION DOLLAR WEEKEND(1948)
Steve Paullada
RED, WHITE AND BLACK, THE(1970)
Frank Paulo
WOMAN FOR JOE, THE(1955, Brit.)
Harry Paulo
Silents
JOHN HALIFAX, GENTLEMAN(1915, Brit.); PUPPET MAN, THE(1921, Brit.)
Misc. Silents
STUDY IN SCARLET, A(1914, Brit.)
Kathy Paulo
Misc. Talkies
HE IS MY BROTHER(1976)
Paulot
ROOM UPSTAIRS, THE(1948, Fr.)
Valentin Paulov
SIX P.M.(1946, USSR), ph
Albert Paulsen
ALL FALL DOWN(1962); MANCHURIAN CANDIDATE, THE(1962); GUNN(1967);
CHE!(1969); MRS. POLLIFAX-SPY(1971); LAUGHING POLICEMAN, THE(1973);
NEXT MAN, THE(1976); THREE SISTERS, THE(1977); EYEWITNESS(1981)
Arno Paulsen
MURDERERS AMONG US(1948, Ger.); AFFAIR BLUM, THE(1949, Ger.); ROSE-
MARY(1960, Ger.); WOZZECK(1962, E. Ger.)
David Paulsen
KAZABLAN(1974, Israel), w; DIAMONDS(1975, U.S./Israel), w; THREE SISTERS,
THE(1977); SCHIZOID(1980), d&w; SAVAGE WEEKEND(1983), p, d&w
Harald Paulsen
DAUGHTER OF EVIL(1930, Ger.); STORM IN A WATER GLASS(1931, Aust.); TALES
OF THE UNCANNY(1932, Ger.); TRUNKS OF MR. O.F., THE(1932, Ger.); DREAMER,
THE(1936, Ger.)
Pat Paulsen
WHERE WERE YOU WHEN THE LIGHTS WENT OUT?(1968); FOREPLAY(1975);
HARPER VALLEY, P.T.A.(1978)
1984
ELLIE(1984); NIGHT PATROL(1984)
Peter Paulsen
1984
SQUIZZY TAYLOR(1984, Aus.)
Rob Paulsen
1984
BODY DOUBLE(1984)
George Paulsin
HAWAIIANS, THE(1970); SIMON, KING OF THE WITCHES(1971); BAT PEOPLE,
THE(1974)
Dan Paulson
COMES A HORSEMAN(1978), p
Pamela Paulson
ROBOT MONSTER(1953)
William Paulson
1984
BROADWAY DANNY ROSE(1984)
Siw Paulsson
DESIREE(1954)
Edward A. Paulton
Silents
NIOBE(1915), w

Edward Paulton
GET OFF MY FOOT(1935, Brit.), w
Ernest Paulton
BRIDEGROOM FOR TWO(1932, Brit.), w
Harry Paulton
Silents
NIOBE(1915), w
Andre Paulve
ETERNAL RETURN, THE(1943, Fr.), p; LUMIERE D'ETE(1943, Fr.), p; BEAUTY AND THE BEAST(1947, Fr.), p; DEVIL'S ENVOYS, THE(1947, Fr.), p; BLIND DESIRE(1948, Fr.), p; DAMNED, THE(1948, Fr.), p; RUY BLAS(1948, Fr.), p; JUST ME(1950, Fr.), p; ROYAL AFFAIR, A(1950), p; SYLVIA AND THE PHANTOM(1950, Fr.), p; PERFECTIONIST, THE(1952, Fr.), p
Edgar Pauly
M(1933, Ger.)
Rebecca Pauly
STATE OF THINGS, THE(1983)
Ursule Pauly
WILD RACERS, THE(1968)
Alfred Paumier
Silents
AMATEUR GENTLEMAN, THE(1920, Brit.)
Misc. Silents
LIFEGUARDSMAN, THE(1916, Brit.)
Claire Pauncefoot
Silents
HOUSE OF TEMPERLEY, THE(1913, Brit.)
Claire Pauncefort
Silents
GAY LORD QUEX, THE(1917, Brit.); ADAM BEDE(1918, Brit.)
George Pauncefort
LET 'EM HAVE IT(1935); HOLIDAY(1938); WOMAN'S FACE(1941)
Silents
NO TRESPASSING(1922)
Misc. Silents
HER GREAT PRICE(1916); FREE AIR(1922); THAT WOMAN(1922)
Rita Pauncefort
IT ISN'T DONE(1937, Aus.); MR. CHEDWORTH STEPS OUT(1939, Aus.); RANGLE RIVER(1939, Aus.); ON THE BEACH(1959)
Yves Pauthe
HU-MAN(1975, Fr.), p
U. Pauzer
YOLANTA(1964, USSR), cos
Marisa Pavan
WHAT PRICE GLORY?(1952); DOWN THREE DARK STREETS(1954); DRUM BEAT(1954); DIANE(1955); ROSE TATTOO, THE(1955); MAN IN THE GREY FLANNEL SUIT, THE(1956); MIDNIGHT STORY, THE(1957); JOHN PAUL JONES(1959)
Anna Pavane
PORTRAIT IN TERROR(1965)
Livio Pavanelli
Misc. Silents
UNCANNY ROOM, THE(1915, Ger.); HOUND OF THE BASKERVILLES, THE(1929, Ger.)
Luciano Pavarotti
YES, GIORGIO(1982)
Marc Pavaux
ADIEU PHILLIPINE(1962, Fr./Ital.), ed
Paul Pavaux
CLANDESTINE(1948, Fr.), p
Ed Paveitti
CAYMAN TRIANGLE, THE(1977), ph
Anika Pavel
CONFESSIONS OF A WINDOW CLEANER(1974, Brit.); SPY WHO LOVED ME, THE(1977, Brit.); GOLDEN LADY, THE(1979, Brit.)
Paul Pavel
MY LIFE TO LIVE(1963, Fr.); SLEEPING CAR MURDER THE(1966, Fr.); BRIDE WORE BLACK, THE(1968, Fr./Ital.); ZITA(1968, Fr.); MILKY WAY, THE(1969, Fr./Ital.); STOLEN KISSES(1969, Fr.)
Samy Pavel
PUSSYCAT, PUSSYCAT, I LOVE YOU!(1970)
Ted Pavelec
FIGHTING MAD(1948); JOE PALOOKA IN THE BIG FIGHT(1949); MILLION DOLLAR PURSUIT(1951)
Teddy Pavelec
HARD BOILED MAHONEY(1947); MISS SADIE THOMPSON(1953)
Vanda Pavelic
NINTH CIRCLE, THE(1961, Yugo.), cos
Harry Pavelis
TRUE CONFESSIONS(1981)
Ondrej Pavelka
NINTH HEART, THE(1980, Czech.)
Maria Pavelle
PRIME TIME, THE(1960)
Cesare Paves
LE AMICHE(1962, Ital.), w
Luigi Pavese
ETERNAL MELODIES(1948, Ital.); LOVE AND LARCENY(1963, Fr./Ital.)
Nino Pavese
VOICE IN YOUR HEART, A(1952, Ital.)
Paolo Pavesi
1900(1976, Ital.)
Anthony Pavey
BOND OF FEAR(1956, Brit.)
Lucy Pavey
FALL OF THE HOUSE OF USHER, THE(1952, Brit.)
Michael C. Pavey
OFFICER AND A GENTLEMAN, AN(1982)

Richard S. Pavey
FAME IS THE SPUR(1947, Brit.), ph; PINK STRING AND SEALING WAX(1950, Brit.), ph
Stan Pavey
DREAMING(1944, Brit.), ph; THEY CAME TO A CITY(1944, Brit.), ph; HERE COMES THE SUN(1945, Brit.), ph; DAUGHTER OF DARKNESS(1948, Brit.), ph; HIDEOUT(1948, Brit.), ph; HAPPIEST DAYS OF YOUR LIFE(1950, Brit.), ph; HAPPINESS OF THREE WOMEN, THE(1954, Brit.), ph; RUNAWAY BUS, THE(1954, Brit.), ph; GUILTY?(1956, Brit.), ph; HOUR OF DECISION(1957, Brit.), ph; MAN IN THE ROAD, THE(1957, Brit.), ph; MY SON, THE VAMPIRE(1963, Brit.), ph
Stanley Pavey
GALLOPING MAJOR, THE(1951, Brit.), ph; CURTAIN UP(1952, Brit.), ph; MR. POTTS GOES TO MOSCOW(1953, Brit.), ph; SHOOT FIRST(1953, Brit.), ph; BELLES OF ST. TRINIAN'S, THE(1954, Brit.), ph; TONIGHT'S THE NIGHT(1954, Brit.), ph; YOUR PAST IS SHOWING(1958, Brit.), ph; HOME IS THE HERO(1959, Ireland), ph; TOO MANY CROOKS(1959, Brit.), ph; MYSTERY SUBMARINE(1963, Brit.), ph; MODEL MURDER CASE, THE(1964, Brit.), ph; PROJECTED MAN, THE(1967, Brit.), ph
Terele Pavez
1984
HOLY INNOCENTS, THE(1984, Span.)
Efrat Pavi
MARTYR, THE(1976, Ger./Israel)
Frantisek Pavicek
MARKETA LAZAROVA(1968, Czech.), w
Ivan Pavicevac
DEAD ARE ALIVE, THE(1972, Yugo./Ger./Ital.)
Bozidar Pavicevic
TWILIGHT TIME(1983, U.S./Yugo.)
Marie Pavis
Silents
MRS. BLACK IS BACK(1914); ABABIAN KNIGHT, AN(1920)
Yvonne Pavis
Misc. Silents
HIGH TIDE(1918); TONY AMERICA(1918); SCARLET AND GOLD(1925)
Dennis Pavitt
EXORCISM AT MIDNIGHT(1966, Brit. revised 1973, U.S.), art d
Denyis Pavitt
MURDER REPORTED(1958, Brit.), art d
Eric Pavitt
MY FRIEND THE KING(1931, Brit.); STAMBOUL(1931, Brit.); REUNION(1932, Brit.); CHILDREN OF THE FOG(1935, Brit.); FIND THE LADY(1936, Brit.)
Owen Pavitt
VENGEANCE(1964)
N. Pavlenko
VOW, THE(1947, USSR.), w
P. Pavlenko
MAN OF MUSIC(1953, USSR), w
Pavel Pavlenko
JACK FROST(1966, USSR)
Peter Pavlenko
ALEXANDER NEVSKY(1939), w
Karel Pavlik
90 DEGREES IN THE SHADE(1966, Czech./Brit.); MATTER OF DAYS, A(1969, Fr./Czech.)
Piotr Pavlikovsky
SIGNALS-AN ADVENTURE IN SPACE(1970, E. Ger./Pol.)
Aleksandr Pavlinov
LITTLE HUMPBACKED HORSE, THE(1962, USSR)
Johanna Pavlis
1984
UNTIL SEPTEMBER(1984)
Steve Pavlisin
SILENT WITNESS, THE(1962)
Polvcarpe Pavloff
INNOCENTS IN PARIS(1955, Brit.)
Polycarpe Pavloff
ANASTASIA(1956)
D. Pavlov
VOW, THE(1947, USSR.)
P. Pavlov
Misc. Silents
SATAN TRIUMPHANT(1917, USSR)
V. Pavlov
IDIOT, THE(1960, USSR), ph
Valentine Pavlov
SYMPHONY OF LIFE(1949, USSR), ph
A. Pavlova
MUMU(1961, USSR); NINE DAYS OF ONE YEAR(1964, USSR); MEET ME IN MOSCOW(1966, USSR)
Anna Pavlova
Silents
DUMB GIRL OF PORTICI(1916)
Nadejda Pavlova
BLUE BIRD, THE(1976)
Soraya Pavlova
MOTHER AND DAUGHTER(1965, USSR)
Ye. Pavlova
GORDEYEV FAMILY, THE(1961, U.S.S.R.)
Danka Pavlovic
FRAGRANCE OF WILD FLOWERS, THE(1979, Yugo.), cos
Robert Pavlovitch
CAT PEOPLE(1982)
Janusz Pavlovski
TEST OF PILOT PIRX, THE(1978, Pol./USSR), ph
Muriel Pavlow
SING AS WE GO(1934, Brit.); LOST ON THE WESTERN FRONT(1940, Brit.); QUIET WEDDING(1941, Brit.); NIGHT BOAT TO DUBLIN(1946, Brit.); CODE OF SCOTLAND YARD(1948); IT STARTED IN PARADISE(1952, Brit.); PROJECT M7(1953, Brit.); DOCTOR IN THE HOUSE(1954, Brit.); FOREVER MY HEART(1954, Brit.); FUSS

OVER FEATHERS(1954, Brit.); MALTA STORY(1954, Brit.); EYEWITNESS(1956, Brit.); SIMON AND LAURA(1956, Brit.); TIGER IN THE SMOKE(1956, Brit.); DOCTOR AT LARGE(1957, Brit.); REACH FOR THE SKY(1957, Brit.); ROONEY(1958, Brit.); WHIRLPOOL(1959, Brit.); MURDER SHE SAID(1961, Brit.)

Tatiana Pavlowa
BLACK MAGIC(1949)

Antonina Pavlycheva
PORTRAIT OF LENIN(1967, Pol./USSR)

Corrado Pavolini
STORMBOUND(1951, Ital.), w

Giuseppe Pavoni
Silents
WHITE SISTER, THE(1923)

Pier Lidovico Pavoni
TIKO AND THE SHARK(1966, U.S./Ital./Fr.), ph

Pier Ludovico Pavoni
PHAROAH'S WOMAN, THE(1961, Ital.), ph; PLANETS AGAINST US, THE(1961, Ital./Fr.), ph; CENTURION, THE(1962, Fr./Ital.), ph; INVASION 1700(1965, Fr./Ital./Yugo.), ph; LIPSTICK(1965, Fr./Ital.), ph

Pierludovico Pavoni
CALYPSO(1959, Fr./It.), ph; BACCHANTES, THE(1963, Fr./Ital.), ph; GLADIATOR OF ROME(1963, Ital.), ph; MILL OF THE STONE WOMEN(1963, Fr./Ital.), ph; HERCULES VS THE GIANT WARRIORS(1965 Fr./Ital.), ph

Vico Pavoni
PLANETS AGAINST US, THE(1961, Ital./Fr.), p

Heidi Pawellek
SHADOWS GROW LONGER, THE(1962, Switz./Ger.)

Nick Pawl
PAY OR DIE(1960)

Lennox Pawle
MARRIED IN HOLLYWOOD(1929); SKY HAWK(1929); HOT FOR PARIS(1930); SIN OF MADELON CLAUDET, THE(1931); DAVID COPPERFIELD(1935); GAY DECEPTION, THE(1935); SYLVIA SCARLETT(1936)
Silents
ADMIRABLE CRICHTON, THE(1918, Brit.); ALL THE SAD WORLD NEEDS(1918, Brit.); GLORIOUS ADVENTURE, THE(1922, U.S./Brit.)

Anthony Pawley
ROSE BOWL(1936); AFFAIRS OF CAPPY RICKS(1937); FIREFLY, THE(1937); PARADISE EXPRESS(1937); COOL AND THE CRAZY, THE(1958)

Brian Pawley
MAN WHO LIVED AGAIN, THE(1936, Brit.)

Charles Pawley
LIKELY STORY, A(1947); WOMAN ON THE BEACH, THE(1947)

Ed Pawley
THIRTEEN WOMEN(1932); IT CAN'T LAST FOREVER(1937); EACH DAWN I DIE(1939); CITY, FOR CONQUEST(1941); TREAT EM' ROUGH(1942)

Edward J. Pawley
YOU AND ME(1938); LADY'S FROM KENTUCKY, THE(1939); TOM SAWYER, DETECTIVE(1939)

Edward Pawley
TESS OF THE STORM COUNTRY(1932); OLSEN'S BIG MOMENT(1934); TREASURE ISLAND(1934); DANTE'S INFERNO(1935); G-MEN(1935); KING SOLOMON OF BROADWAY(1935); MISSISSIPPI(1935); SINNER TAKE ALL(1936); SWORN ENEMY(1936); TOUGH GUY(1936); HOOSIER SCHOOLBOY(1937); LAST GANGSTER, THE(1937); MOUNTAIN JUSTICE(1937); ANGELS WITH DIRTY FACES(1938); DANGEROUS TO KNOW(1938); GUN LAW(1938); LITTLE TOUGH GUY(1938); PRISON BREAK(1938); ROMANCE OF THE LIMBERLOST(1938); SMASHING THE RACKETS(1938); SONS OF THE LEGION(1938); BIG GUY, THE(1939); OKLAHOMA KID, THE(1939); UNMARRIED(1939); CASTLE ON THE HUDSON(1940); FLOWING GOLD(1940); RIVER'S END(1940); TEXAS RANGERS RIDE AGAIN(1940); HIT THE ROAD(1941); HOLD THAT GHOST(1941); SAN FRANCISCO DOCKS(1941); FLIGHT LIEUTENANT(1942); ROMANCE ON THE RANGE(1942); TRUE TO THE ARMY(1942); DESPERADOES, THE(1943); EYES OF THE UNDERWORLD(1943)

Nancy Pawley
IT HAPPENED IN PARIS(1935, Brit.); FIND THE LADY(1936, Brit.); NOT SO DUSTY(1936, Brit.); OLD IRON(1938, Brit.)

Richard Pawley
MARY BURNS, FUGITIVE(1935)

William Pawley
BAD GIRL(1931); OVER THE HILL(1931); SPIDER, THE(1931); SURRENDER(1931); AFTER TOMORROW(1932); AMATEUR DADDY(1932); CARELESS LADY(1932); CENTRAL PARK(1932); CHEATERS AT PLAY(1932); I AM A FUGITIVE FROM A CHAIN GANG(1932); LETTY LYNTON(1932); SPEAK EASILY(1932); TRIAL OF VIVIENNE WARE, THE(1932); YOUNG AMERICA(1932); GABRIEL OVER THE WHITE HOUSE(1933); ROBBERS' ROOST(1933); AFFAIR OF SUSAN(1935); DARING YOUNG MAN, THE(1935); KENTUCKY KERNELS(1935); MARY BURNS, FUGITIVE(1935); STOLEN HARMONY(1935); BIG NOISE, THE(1936); BOULDER DAM(1936); BULLETS OR BALLOTS(1936); PUBLIC ENEMY'S WIFE(1936); WHIPSAW(1936); BORN RECKLESS(1937); SAN QUENTIN(1937); TRAPPED BY G-MEN(1937); WHEN YOU'RE IN LOVE(1937); ANGELS WITH DIRTY FACES(1938); CRIME TAKES A HOLIDAY(1938); INTERNATIONAL CRIME(1938); PRAIRIE MOON(1938); WHITE BANNERS(1938); DISPUTED PASSAGE(1939); PANAMA LADY(1939); ROUGH RIDERS' ROUNDUP(1939); UNION PACIFIC(1939); DOUBLE ALIBI(1940); GAMBLING ON THE HIGH SEAS(1940); GRAPES OF WRATH(1940); GREAT PROFILE, THE(1940); JOHNNY APOLLO(1940); MERCY PLANE(1940); PUBLIC DEB NO. 1(1940); QUEEN OF THE MOB(1940); RETURN OF FRANK JAMES, THE(1940); SKY BANDITS, THE(1940); WEST OF ABILENE(1940); YUKON FLIGHT(1940); GREAT AMERICAN BROADCAST, THE(1941); TIME TO KILL(1942); ROGER TOUHY, GANGSTER!(1944)

William Pawley, Jr.
CROWNING EXPERIENCE, THE(1960); VOICE OF THE HURRICANE(1964)

Danny Pawlick
1984
POLICE ACADEMY(1984)

B. Pawlik
GREAT BIG WORLD AND LITTLE CHILDREN, THE(1962, Pol.)

Bronislaw Pawlik
YELLOW SLIPPERS, THE(1965, Pol.)

Adam Pawlikowski
ASHES AND DIAMONDS(1961, Pol.); KANAL(1961, Pol.); LOTNA(1966, Pol.); SARAGOSSA MANUSCRIPT, THE(1972, Pol.)

Rebecca Pawlo
LOVING COUPLES(1966, Swed.)

Toivo Pawlo
MAGICIAN, THE(1959, Swed.); LOVING COUPLES(1966, Swed.); LOVE MATES(1967, Swed.)

Toiwo Pawlo
STORY OF A WOMAN(1970, U.S./Ital.)

Tolvo Pawlo
CRIME AND PUNISHMENT(1948, Swed.)

Irene Pawloff
NIGHT AFFAIR(1961, Fr.), cos

Vera Pawlowa
Misc. Silents
DIARY OF A LOST GIRL(1929, Ger.)

Doris Pawn
Silents
OUT OF THE STORM(1920); PENALTY, THE(1920); CHEATED HEARTS(1921); GUILE OF WOMEN(1921); MILLIONAIRE, THE(1921); SHAME(1921); WHAT HAPPENED TO ROSA?(1921); ALWAYS THE WOMAN(1922); ONE CLEAR CALL(1922); PUTTING IT OVER(1922); HERO, THE(1923)
Misc. Silents
BLUE BLOOD AND RED(1916); LITTLE EVE EDGARTON(1916); BOOK AGENT, THE(1917); HIGH FINANCE(1917); SOME BOY(1917); SPIRIT OF '76, THE(1917); CITY OF DIM FACE, THE(1918); KID IS CLEVER, THE(1918); TOBY'S BOW(1919); BELOVED CHEATER, THE(1920); FIGHTIN' MAD(1921); MIDNIGHT BELL, A(1921); BING BANG BOOM(1922); STRANGE IDOLS(1922); BUSTER, THE(1923); FOOLS AND RICHES(1923)

Pawnee Bill, Jr.
Misc. Silents
ACROSS THE PLAINS(1928); ARIZONA SPEED(1928); CHEYENNE TRAILS(1928)

Hargrave Pawson
FIRST MRS. FRASER, THE(1932, Brit.); MAN IN GREY, THE(1943, Brit.)

Katina Paxinou
FOR WHOM THE BELL TOLLS(1943); HOSTAGES(1943); MOURNING BECOMES ELECTRA(1947); PRINCE OF FOXES(1949); INHERITANCE, THE(1951, Brit.); MIRACLE, THE(1959); ROCCO AND HIS BROTHERS(1961, Fr./Ital.); MR. ARKADIN(1962, Brit./Fr./Span.); ZITA(1968, Fr.)

Katine Paxinou
CONFIDENTIAL AGENT(1945)

Eduardo Paxon
HIGH RISK(1981)

Omar Paxson
1984
LIES(1984, Brit.)

Bill Paxton
STRIPES(1981); MORTUARY(1983); TAKING TIGER MOUNTAIN(1983, U.S./Welsh), a, prod d
1984
IMPULSE(1984); STREETS OF FIRE(1984); TERMINATOR, THE(1984)

Dick Paxton
THIRD FINGER, LEFT HAND(1940); HENRY ALDRICH FOR PRESIDENT(1941); PUBLIC ENEMIES(1941); ANGELS ALLEY(1948); FIGHTER SQUADRON(1948); SMART POLITICS(1948); NO WAY OUT(1950); MASK OF THE DRAGON(1951); HOODLUM EMPIRE(1952); IRON MISTRESS, THE(1952); SKY COMMANDO(1953); HIT AND RUN(1957); LIZZIE(1957)

Glenn Paxton
WHEN THE LEGENDS DIE(1972), m

Guy Paxton
CARETAKER'S DAUGHTER, THE(1952, Brit.), w

Jay Paxton
DOBERMAN GANG, THE(1972)

John Paxton
MY PAL, WOLF(1944), w; CORNERED(1945), w; MURDER, MY SWEET(1945), w; CRACK-UP(1946), w; CROSSFIRE(1947), w; SO WELL REMEMBERED(1947, Brit.), w; ROPE OF SAND(1949), w; FOURTEEN HOURS(1951), w; WILD ONE, THE(1953), w; COBWEB, THE(1955), w; PRIZE OF GOLD, A(1955), w; HOW TO MURDER A RICH UNCLE(1957, Brit.), p, w; PICKUP ALLEY(1957, Brit.), w; ON THE BEACH(1959), w; KOTCH(1971), w

Lesley Paxton
PILGRIM, FAREWELL(1980)

Lettie Paxton
Misc. Silents
BOYS OF THE OLD BRIGADE, THE(1916, Brit.); TWO LANCASHIRE LASSES IN LONDON(1916, Brit.); MAN WHO MADE GOOD, THE(1917, Brit.)

Letty Paxton
Silents
JIMMY(1916, Brit.)

Marie Paxton
OUANGA(1936, Brit.)

Richard A. Paxton
TASK FORCE(1949)

Richard Paxton
LITTLE BIG HORN(1951); YANK IN KOREA, A(1951); HELLGATE(1952); WACO(1952)

Sidney Paxton
Silents
GIRL FROM DOWNING STREET, THE(1918, Brit.); OLD HOME WEEK(1925)

Steve Paxton
CRY DR. CHICAGO(1971)

Sydney Paxton
Silents
MAN'S SHADOW, A(1920, Brit.); BACHELORS' CLUB, THE(1921, Brit.); OLD COUNTRY, THE(1921, Brit.); PRINCE AND THE BEGGARMAID, THE(1921, Brit.); CRIMSON CIRCLE, THE(1922, Brit.); AUDACIOUS MR. SQUIRE, THE(1923, Brit.); MIRIAM ROZELLA(1924, Brit.)

Tony Paxton-

Misc. Silents
BLUFF(1921, Brit.); ROTTERS, THE(1921, Brit.); SINGLE LIFE(1921, Brit.); HYPO-CRITES, THE(1923, Brit.)

Tony Paxton
WILD PARTY, THE(1975)

"Wild" Bill Paxton
LORDS OF DISCIPLINE, THE(1983)

William Paxton
GROOVE TUBE, THE(1974)

Diana Payan
SOLUTION BY PHONE(1954, Brit.)

Ilka Payan
SCARFACE(1983)

Gilles Payant
BIG RED(1962)

Johnny Paycheck
TAKE THIS JOB AND SHOVE IT(1981)
Misc. Talkies
SWEET COUNTRY ROAD(1981)

Jean Payen
PRICE OF FLESH, THE(1962, Fr.)

Harry Payer
MONEY ON THE STREET(1930, Aust.); FIDELIO(1961, Aust.)

Ivo Payer
DAVID AND GOLIATH(1961, Ital.); CAESAR THE CONQUEROR(1963, Ital.)

Clark L. Paylow
SAVANNAH SMILES(1983), p

Clark Paylow
COWBOY COMMANDOS(1943), w; RING OF TERROR(1962), d; HEX(1973), p

David Paymer
IN-LAWS, THE(1979)
1984
BEST DEFENSE(1984); IRRECONCILABLE DIFFERENCES(1984)

Graham Payn
BOYS IN BROWN(1949, Brit.); ASTONISHED HEART, THE(1950, Brit.); JIG SAW(1965, Brit.); ITALIAN JOB, THE(1969, Brit.)

Payne
IN LIKE FLINT(1967), set d

A. W. Payne
MILL ON THE FLOSS(1939, Brit.)

Adrian Payne
1984
FANTASY MAN(1984, Aus.), m

Andrew Payne
SPACED OUT(1981, Brit.), w

Arthur Payne
TICKET OF LEAVE MAN, THE(1937, Brit.)

Arthur West Payne
BANK HOLIDAY(1938, Brit.)

Benny Payne
SUNNY SIDE OF THE STREET(1951); CRUISIN' DOWN THE RIVER(1953)

Bob Payne
LITTLE ONES, THE(1965, Brit.); MUPPET MOVIE, THE(1979); DARK CRYSTAL, THE(1982, Brit.)

Bobby Payne
BEACH PARTY(1963)

Boy Payne
GREAT MUPPET CAPER, THE(1981)

Bruce Payne
MY COUSIN RACHEL(1952); PRISONER OF ZENDA, THE(1952); LITTLE BOY LOST(1953); THUNDER IN THE EAST(1953); DRAGON'S GOLD(1954); TEXAS LA-DY(1955); PRIVATES ON PARADE(1982); KEEP, THE(1983)
1984
OXFORD BLUES(1984); PRIVATES ON PARADE(1984, Brit.)

Bunty Payne
FARMER'S WIFE, THE(1941, Brit.); STRANGLER, THE(1941, Brit.)

Cy Payne
MURDER ON THE CAMPUS(1963, Brit.), m

David Payne
GIRO CITY(1982, Brit.), p; DRAUGHTSMAN'S CONTRACT, THE(1983, Brit.), p

Don Payne
FARMER, THE(1977)
1984
POLICE ACADEMY(1984)

Douglas Payne
YOU'D BE SURPRISED!(1930, Brit.); FLAW, THE(1933, Brit.)
Silents
FLYING FROM JUSTICE(1915, Brit.); LASS O' THE LOOMS, A(1919, Brit.); WON BY A HEAD(1920, Brit.); POTTER'S CLAY(1922, Brit.), a, d; OLD BILL THROUGH THE AGES(1924, Brit.); LADY OF THE LAKE, THE(1928, Brit.); MAN WHO CHANGED HIS NAME, THE(1928, Brit.)
Misc. Silents
AVIATOR SPY, THE(1914, Brit.); FIENDS OF HELL(1914, Brit.); MYSTERY OF THE DIAMOND BELT(1914, Brit.); STOLEN MASTERPIECE, THE(1914, Brit.); AVENGING HAND, THE(1915, Brit.); FINE FEATHERS(1915, Brit.); MASTER AND MAN(1915, Brit.); SCORPION'S STING, THE(1915, Brit.); TRUMPET CALL, THE(1915, Brit.); FURTHER EXPLOITS OF SEXTON BLAKE, THE - MYSTERY OF THE S.S. OLYM-PIC, THE(1919, Brit.); HEART OF A ROSE, THE(1919, Brit.); WHAT NEXT?(1928, Brit.)

Freda Payne
BOOK OF NUMBERS(1973)

G. Payne
POCKET MONEY(1972)

Harold Payne
1984
JOY OF SEX(1984), m

Hatty Payne
Misc. Silents
KENT THE FIGHTING MAN(1916, Brit.)

Hettie Payne
Silents
PAULA(1915, Brit.)

Hetty Payne
Silents
KENT, THE FIGHTING MAN(1916, Brit.)

Jack Payne
SAY IT WITH MUSIC(1932, Brit.); JAMBOREE(1957)

James Payne
LADIES MAN, THE(1961), set d; COME BLOW YOUR HORN(1963), set d; NEW KIND OF LOVE, A(1963), set d; PAPA'S DELICATE CONDITION(1963), set d; WHO'S MINDING THE STORE?(1963), set d; STRANGLER, THE(1964), set d; HAR-LOW(1965), set d; LOVED ONE, THE(1965), set d; LAST OF THE SECRET AGENTS?, THE(1966), set d; OSCAR, THE(1966), set d; HOW SWEET IT IS(1968), set d; YOURS, MINE AND OURS(1968), set d; PIECES OF DREAMS(1970), set d; SKIN GAME(1971), set d; TODD KILLINGS, THE(1971), set d; PRIME CUT(1972), set d; BREEZY(1973), set d; SCREAM BLACULA SCREAM(1973), set d; STING, THE(1973), set d; GREAT WALDO PEPPER, THE(1975), set d; HEROES(1977), set d; SLAP SHOT(1977), set d; MAIN EVENT, THE(1979), set d; COMPETITION, THE(1980), set d; DRAGONSLAYER(1981)

James W. Payne
SOLDIER IN THE RAIN(1963), art d; HARD CONTRACT(1969), set d; SUPPOSE THEY GAVE A WAR AND NOBODY CAME?(1970), set d; LATE LIZ, THE(1971), set d; FRONT PAGE, THE(1974), set d; FAMILY PLOT(1976), set d; ROLLERCOAST-ER(1977), set d; SCOTT JOPLIN(1977), set d

Jim Payne
GET TO KNOW YOUR RABBIT(1972), set d; LOLLY-MADONNA XXX(1973), set d
1984
PRODIGAL, THE(1984), set d

Jody Payne
HONEYSUCKLE ROSE(1980)
1984
SONGWRITER(1984)

John Howard Payne
FAIR WARNING(1937)
Silents
HOME SWEET HOME(1914), w

John M. Payne
Silents
IRON JUSTICE(1915, Brit.), a, p

John Payne
TEMPORARY WIDOW, THE(1930, Ger./Brit.); DODSWORTH(1936); HATS OFF(1937); LOVE ON TOAST(1937); COLLEGE SWING(1938); GARDEN OF THE MOON(1938); INDIANAPOLIS SPEEDWAY(1939); KID NIGHTINGALE(1939); WINGS OF THE NAVY(1939); GREAT PROFILE, THE(1940); KING OF THE LUM-BERJACKS(1940); MARYLAND(1940); STAR DUST(1940); TEAR GAS SQUAD(1940); TIN PAN ALLEY(1940); GREAT AMERICAN BROADCAST, THE(1941); REMEMBER THE DAY(1941); SUN VALLEY SERENADE(1941); WEEKEND IN HAVANA(1941); FOOTLIGHT SERENADE(1942); ICELAND(1942); SPRINGTIME IN THE ROCK-IES(1942); TO THE SHORES OF TRIPOLI(1942); HELLO, FRISCO, HELLO(1943); DOLLY SISTERS, THE(1945); RAZOR'S EDGE, THE(1946); SENTIMENTAL JOUR-NEY(1946); WAKE UP AND DREAM(1946); MIRACLE ON 34TH STREET, THE(1947); LARCENY(1948); SAXON CHARM, THE(1948); CAPTAIN CHINA(1949); CROOKED WAY, THE(1949); EL PASO(1949); EAGLE AND THE HAWK, THE(1950); TRIPO-LI(1950); CROSSWINDS(1951); PASSAGE WEST(1951); BLAZING FOREST, THE(1952); CARIBBEAN(1952); KANSAS CITY CONFIDENTIAL(1952); RAIDERS OF THE SEVEN SEAS(1953); VANQUISHED, THE(1953); 99 RIVER STREET(1953); RAILS INTO LARAMIE(1954); SILVER LODE(1954); HELL'S ISLAND(1955); ROAD TO DENVER, THE(1955); SANTA FE PASSAGE(1955); TENNESSEE'S PART-NER(1955); BOSS, THE(1956); HOLD BACK THE NIGHT(1956); REBEL IN TOWN(1956); SLIGHTLY SCARLET(1956); BAILOUT AT 43,000(1957); HIDDEN FEAR(1957); RISK, THE(1961, Brit.); THEY RAN FOR THEIR LIVES(1968), a, d; SAVAGE WILD, THE(1970)

Julia Payne
MANCHURIAN CANDIDATE, THE(1962)

Julie Payne
BEST OF EVERYTHING, THE(1959); ISLAND OF THE BLUE DOLPHINS(1964); DON'T MAKE WAVES(1967); STRAWBERRY STATEMENT, THE(1970); THX 1138(1971); REAL LIFE(1979); PRIVATE SCHOOL(1983); TWICE UPON A TIME(1983)
1984
LONELY GUY, THE(1984); THIS IS SPINAL TAP(1984)

Kathy Payne
1984
TANK(1984)

Laurence Payne
TRAIN OF EVENTS(1952, Brit.); GLAD TIDINGS(1953, Brit.); CRAWLING EYE, THE(1958, Brit.); DANGEROUS EXILE(1958, Brit.); NIGHT AMBUSH(1958, Brit.); BEN HUR(1959); COURT MARTIAL OF MAJOR KELLER, THE(1961, Brit.); SINGER NOT THE SONG, THE(1961, Brit.); THIRD ALIBI, THE(1961, Brit.); CROSSTRAP(1962, Brit.); TELL-TALE HEART, THE(1962, Brit.); MYSTERY SUBMARINE(1963, Brit.); MODEL MURDER CASE, THE(1964, Brit.), w; VAMPIRE CIRCUS(1972, Brit.)

Lawrence Payne
BARABBAS(1962, Ital.)

Lola Payne
GYPSY GIRL(1966, Brit.)

Lou Payne
EVANGELINE(1929); LAWFUL LARCENY(1930); HEAVENLY DAYS(1944)
Silents
AS MAN DESIRES(1925); LAST EDITION, THE(1925); EVANGELINE(1929)

Louis Payne
INTERFERENCE(1928); BIG NEWS(1929); DUDE WRANGLER, THE(1930); PART TIME WIFE(1930); SUSAN AND GOD(1940); LOOK WHO'S LAUGHING(1941); GOV-ERNMENT GIRL(1943); SARATOGA TRUNK(1945); WOMAN IN THE WINDOW, THE(1945); JOAN OF ARC(1948); MY FORBIDDEN PAST(1951)
Silents
BLIND GODDESS, THE(1926); OUTSIDER, THE(1926); KING OF KINGS, THE(1927); VANITY(1927); YANKEE CLIPPER, THE(1927)
Misc. Silents
DUBARRY(1915); LADY WHO LIED, THE(1925); ONLY THING, THE(1925); SHAM-ROCK HANDICAP, THE(1926)

Louise Payne
WHEN TOMORROW DIES(1966, Can.)

Marjorie Payne
Misc. Silents
BEWARE OF THE LAW(1922)

Michael Payne
COVER ME BABE(1970); BLACK SAMSON(1974); TRAIN RIDE TO HOL-LYWOOD(1975)

Roy Payne
LOVE AT FIRST SIGHT(1977, Can.), m

Sally Payne
BIG SHOW, THE(1937); EXILED TO SHANGHAI(1937); HIGGINS FAMILY, THE(1938); MAN FROM MUSIC MOUNTAIN(1938); MY WIFE'S RELATIVES(1939); WHEN TOMORROW COMES(1939); I LOVE YOU AGAIN(1940); LA CONGA NIGHTS(1940); NO, NO NANETTE(1940); ONE NIGHT IN THE TROPICS(1940); WHEN THE DALTONS RODE(1940); YOUNG BILL HICKOK(1940); BAD MAN OF DEADWOOD(1941); IN OLD CHEYENNE(1941); JESSE JAMES AT BAY(1941); LADY FROM CHEYENNE(1941); NEVADA CITY(1941); PLAYMATES(1941); RED RIVER VALLEY(1941); ROBIN HOOD OF THE PECOS(1941); SHERIFF OF TOMB-STONE(1941); TUXEDO JUNCTION(1941); MAN FROM CHEYENNE(1942); MOUN-TAIN RHYTHM(1942); ROMANCE ON THE RANGE(1942)

Sharyn Payne
SMASH-UP, THE STORY OF A WOMAN(1947)

Shelby Payne
KISMET(1944); SHOW BUSINESS(1944); TWO GIRLS AND A SAILOR(1944); UP IN ARMS(1944); HAVING WONDERFUL CRIME(1945); BIG SLEEP, THE(1946); WIFE WANTED(1946)

Sidney Payne
Misc. Silents
BRAND OF LOPEZ, THE(1920); BEACH OF DREAMS(1921)

Stephen Payne
SWIFTY(1936), w

Steven Payne
FLASH GORDON(1980)

Susan Payne
HEADLINE HUNTERS(1968, Brit.); UP IN THE AIR(1969, Brit.); WALKING STICK, THE(1970, Brit.)

Thomas H. Payne
CREATURE WASN'T NICE,THE(1981), spec eff

Tiff Payne
MRS. PARKINGTON(1944)

Tom Payne
KEEP YOUR SEATS PLEASE(1936, Brit.); QUEEN OF HEARTS(1936, Brit.); SHOW GOES ON, THE(1937, Brit.); WE'RE GOING TO BE RICH(1938, Brit.); CURUCU, BEAST OF THE AMAZON(1956); LOVE SLAVES OF THE AMAZONS(1957)

William Payne
HAUNTING OF M, THE(1979)

Willy Payne
TWO GENTLEMEN SHARING(1969, Brit.)

Bob Paynter
LAWMAN(1971), ph

Elizabeth Paynter
MIKADO, THE(1939, Brit.)

Ernest Paynter
SHIPMATES(1931), w

Robert Paynter
HANNIBAL BROOKS(1969, Brit.), ph; GAMES, THE(1970), ph; NIGHT COMERS, THE(1971, Brit.), ph; CHATO'S LAND(1972), ph; MECHANIC, THE(1972), ph; SCORPIO(1973), ph; BIG SLEEP, THE½(1978, Brit.), ph; FIREPOWER(1979, Brit.), ph; SUPERMAN II(1980), ph; AMERICAN WEREWOLF IN LONDON, AN(1981), ph; FINAL CONFLICT, THE(1981), ph; CURTAINS(1983, Can.), ph; SUPERMAN III(1983), ph; TRADING PLACES(1983), ph
1984
MUPPETS TAKE MANHATTAN, THE(1984), ph; SCREAM FOR HELP(1984), ph

Tony Paynter
MRS. DANE'S DEFENCE(1933, Brit.)

Denis Payque
HIGH(1968, Can.)

Roger Payrot
RETURN OF MARTIN GUERRE, THE(1983, Fr.)

Amanda Pays
1984
OXFORD BLUES(1984)

Howard Pays
NIGHT TO REMEMBER, A(1958, Brit.); JUST JOE(1960, Brit.); URGE TO KILL(1960, Brit.); DANGEROUS AFTERNOON(1961, Brit.); TROUBLE IN THE SKY(1961, Brit.); PASSWORD IS COURAGE, THE(1962, Brit.); HEAVENS ABOVE!(1963, Brit.); JUN-GLE STREET GIRLS(1963, Brit.); TWO LEFT FEET(1965, Brit.); NEVER BACK LOSERS(1967, Brit.); ATTACK ON THE IRON COAST(1968, U.S./Brit.)

Catherine Paysan
MARRIAGE CAME TUMBLING DOWN, THE(1968, Fr.), w

Edward Paysen
SUSAN AND GOD(1940)

Blanche Payson
WICKED(1931); IMPATIENT MAIDEN(1932); SHE GETS HER MAN(1935); ALL OVER TOWN(1937); YOU CAN'T TAKE IT WITH YOU(1938); ANGELS OVER BROADWAY(1940); HONOLULU LU(1941); SALUTE FOR THREE(1943)
Silents
THREE AGES, THE(1923); OH, DOCTOR(1924); BACHELOR'S BABY, THE(1927)

Ed Payson
WYOMING OUTLAW(1939)

William Farquhar Payson
Silents
CHEATED HEARTS(1921), w

Barbara Payton
ONCE MORE, MY DARLING(1949); TRAPPED(1949); DALLAS(1950); KISS TOMOR-ROW GOODBYE(1950); BRIDE OF THE GORILLA(1951); DRUMS IN THE DEEP SOUTH(1951); ONLY THE VALIANT(1951); BAD BLONDE(1953, Brit.); FOUR SIDED TRIANGLE(1953, Brit.); GREAT JESSE JAMES RAID, THE(1953); RUN FOR THE HILLS(1953); MURDER IS MY BEAT(1955)

Claude Payton
FARGO EXPRESS(1933); BARBARY COAST(1935); ETERNALLY YOURS(1939)
Silents
MARSHAL OF MONEYMINT, THE(1922); MASKED AVENGER, THE(1922); SONG OF LIFE, THE(1922); BACK TRAIL, THE(1924); DARING CHANCES(1924); MAN FROM WYOMING, THE(1924); YELLOW BACK, THE(1926); WESTERN WHIRL-WIND, THE(1927); GATE CRASHER, THE(1928)
Misc. Silents
WOMAN THERE WAS, A(1919); DESERT'S CRUCIBLE, THE(1922); TROOPER O'NEIL(1922); TWO-FISTED JEFFERSON(1922); TEXAS TRAIL, THE(1925); SET FREE(1927)

Denis Payton
HAVING A WILD WEEKEND(1965, Brit.)

Douglas Payton
FIRE AND ICE(1983)

Ethel Payton
Silents
FIGHTING BREED, THE(1921)

Gloria Payton
Silents
WHERE LIGHTS ARE LOW(1921)
Misc. Silents
BRAND'S DAUGHTER(1917); FAITH OF THE STRONG(1919); SUNSET SPRA-GUE(1920)

Jay Payton
MACK, THE(1973)

Larry Payton
Silents
GOOSE GIRL, THE(1915)

Lawrence Payton
Silents
GREATER LAW, THE(1917)

Lew Payton
VALIANT IS THE WORD FOR CARRIE(1936); ON SUCH A NIGHT(1937); RACING LADY(1937); JEZEBEL(1938); LADY'S FROM KENTUCKY, THE(1939); LADY FOR A NIGHT(1941)

Lucy Payton
Silents
LOVE LIAR, THE(1916)
Misc. Silents
LURE OF THE MASK, THE(1915); SHADOWS AND SUNSHINE(1916); HIS OLD-FASHIONED DAD(1917); YELLOW BULLET, THE(1917)

Robert Payton
BORDER TREASURE(1950)

Stuart Payton
Misc. Silents
MAN WHO MARRIED HIS OWN WIFE, THE(1922), d

Pamela Payton-Wright
CORKY(1972); GOING IN STYLE(1979); RESURRECTION(1980); DARK END OF THE STREET, THE(1981)
Misc. Talkies
HAUNTING OF ROSALIND, THE(1973)

Charles Payzant
FANTASIA(1940), art d

Anibal Gonzalez Paz
END OF INNOCENCE(1960, Arg.), ph; VIOLATED LOVE(1966, Arg.), ph

Aviva Paz
EVERY BASTARD A KING(1968, Israel)

Jeni Paz
MANIAC(1980)

Juan Carlos Paz
END OF INNOCENCE(1960, Arg.), m

Shlomo Paz
TRUNK TO CAIRO(1966, Israel/Ger.)

Vaclav Pazdernik
JOURNEY TO THE BEGINNING OF TIME(1966, Czech), ph

Joe Pazen
SIX-GUN RHYTHM(1939)

N. Pazhitnov
RESURRECTION(1963, USSR)

Nikolai Pazhitnov
IDIOT, THE(1960, USSR)

Ferenc Pazmany
HIPPOLYT, THE LACKEY(1932, Hung.)

Felipe Pazos
OLD MAN AND THE SEA, THE(1958)

Giovanni Pazzafini
ARIZONA COLT(1965, It./Fr./Span.)

Nello Pazzafini
GOLIATH AGAINST THE GIANTS(1963, Ital./Span.); MAN COULD GET KILLED, A(1966); BIG GUNDOWN, THE(1968, Ital.); LA CAGE AUX FOLLES II(1981, Ital./Fr.)

Riccardo Pazzaglia
RED CLOAK, THE(1961, Ital./Fr.), w

Pe'a
Misc. Silents
MOANA(1926)

Dennis Peabody
BURY ME AN ANGEL(1972)

Dick Peabody
GOOD GUYS AND THE BAD GUYS, THE(1969); SUPPORT YOUR LOCAL SHE-RIFF(1969)

Dixie Peabody
BURY ME AN ANGEL(1972)

Eddie Peabody
LEMON DROP KID, THE(1934)

Jack Peabody
BIG TRAIL, THE(1930), a, w

Richard "Dick" Peabody
MACKENNA'S GOLD(1969)
Richard Peabody
MOONSHINE WAR, THE(1970)
Sandra Peabody
Misc. Talkies
TEENAGE HITCHHIKERS(1975)
Caesar Peace
ASSIGNMENT OUTER SPACE(1960, Ital.), spec eff
Moses Peace
1984
MAKING THE GRADE(1984)
Rock Peace
ATTACK OF THE KILLER TOMATOES(1978)
Steve Peace
ATTACK OF THE KILLER TOMATOES(1978), p
Vera Peace
YES, MADAM?(1938, Brit.)
Frances Peach
1984
FLAMINGO KID, THE(1984)
Jack Peach
SPITFIRE(1943, Brit.)
Jane Peach
TO SIR, WITH LOVE(1967, Brit.); OLIVER!(1968, Brit.)
Ken Peach
JESSE JAMES' WOMEN(1954), ph
Kenneth Peach
SONS OF THE DESERT(1933), ph; I REMEMBER MAMA(1948), spec eff; GIRL FROM SAN LORENZO, THE(1950), ph; GUN BROTHERS(1956), ph; FIVE STEPS TO DANGER(1957), ph; IRON SHERIFF, THE(1957), ph; CURSE OF THE FACELESS MAN(1958), ph; GUNS, GIRLS AND GANGSTERS(1958), ph; HONG KONG CONFIDENTIAL(1958), ph; LONE RANGER AND THE LOST CITY OF GOLD, THE(1958), ph; LOST MISSILE, THE(1958, U.S./Can.), ph; DOG'S BEST FRIEND, A(1960), ph; BATTLE AT BLOODY BEACH(1961), ph; SNIPER'S RIDGE(1961), ph; INCREDIBLE JOURNEY, THE(1963), ph; BLOOD ON THE ARROW(1964), ph; TIME FOR KILLING, A(1967), ph; HELL'S BELLES(1969), ph; PUFNSTUF(1970), ph
Kenneth Peach, Sr.
CHICAGO CONFIDENTIAL(1957), ph; IT! THE TERROR FROM BEYOND SPACE(1958), ph; TOUGHEST GUN IN TOMBSTONE(1958), ph; WHEN THE CLOCK STRIKES(1961), ph
L. Du Garde Peach
GREAT, MEADOW, THE(1931), w; PRINCESS CHARMING(1935, Brit.), w; FORBIDDEN MUSIC(1936, Brit.), w; HEART'S DESIRE(1937, Brit.), w; HIDEOUT IN THE ALPS(1938, Brit.), w; SPY OF NAPOLEON(1939, Brit.), w; GREAT MR. HANDEL, THE(1942, Brit.), w
L. DuGarde Peach
CHU CHIN CHOW(1934, Brit.), w; GHOUL, THE(1934, Brit.), w; PATH OF GLORY, THE(1934, Brit.), w; STRIKE!(1934, Brit.), w; CASE OF GABRIEL PERRY, THE(1935, Brit.), w; IT'S A BET(1935, Brit.), w; MUSIC HATH CHARMS(1935, Brit.), w; TRANSATLANTIC TUNNEL(1935, Brit.), w; TURN OF THE TIDE(1935, Brit.), w; DOMMED CARGO(1936, Brit.), w; MAN WHO LIVED AGAIN, THE(1936, Brit.), w; MELODY AND ROMANCE(1937, Brit.), w; GET CRACKING(1943, Brit.), w
Maggie Peach
MAIDSTONE(1970)
Mary Peach
LADY IS A SQUARE, THE(1959, Brit.); ROOM AT THE TOP(1959, Brit.); FOLLOW THAT HORSE!(1960, Brit.); NO LOVE FOR JOHNNIE(1961, Brit.); GATHERING OF EAGLES, A(1963); PAIR OF BRIEFS, A(1963, Brit.); BLUES FOR LOVERS(1966, Brit.); PROJECTED MAN, THE(1967, Brit.); SCROOGE(1970, Brit.)
Charles Peachey
TRAPPED IN A SUBMARINE(1931, Brit.)
John Peachey
Silents
CALL OF YOUTH, THE(1920, Brit.); DIAMOND NECKLACE, THE(1921, Brit.)
Capt. Leslie T. Peacock
Silents
BLACK BEAUTY(1921)
Chiara Peacock
THOSE LIPS, THOSE EYES(1980)
Daniel Peacock
DOING TIME(1979, Brit.); TRAIL OF THE PINK PANTHER, THE(1982); BLOODY KIDS(1983, Brit.); PARTY PARTY(1983, Brit.), a, w
David Peacock
SCROOGE(1970, Brit.)
John Peacock
SCHOOL FOR UNCLAIMED GIRLS(1973, Brit.), w
Keith Peacock
BANG, BANG, YOU'RE DEAD(1966); PSYCHO-CIRCUS(1967, Brit.)
Kemper Peacock
MY BODY HUNGERS(1967), ed; SHAME, SHAME, EVERYBODY KNOWS HER NAME(1969), ed
Kim Peacock
CLUE OF THE NEW PIN, THE(1929, Brit.); CROOKED BILLET, THE(1930, Brit.); WARM CORNER, A(1930, Brit.); EXPERT'S OPINION(1935, Brit.); MAD HATTERS, THE(1935, Brit.); GRAND FINALE(1936, Brit.); MIDNIGHT AT THE WAX MUSEUM(1936, Brit.), a, w; CAPTAIN'S ORDERS(1937, Brit.); DANGEROUS CARGO(1939, Brit.); FLANNELFOOT(1953, Brit.)
Silents
MY LORD THE CHAUFFEUR(1927, Brit.); MANXMAN, THE(1929, Brit.)
Misc. Silents
CLUE OF THE NEW PIN, THE(1929, Brit.)
Marjorie Peacock
CONCERNING MR. MARTIN(1937, Brit.)
Michael Peacock
STRAIGHT ON TILL MORNING(1974, Brit.), w
Trevor Peacock
WHAT A WHOPPER(1961, Brit.), w; BARBER OF STAMFORD HILL, THE(1963, Brit.); HE WHO RIDES A TIGER(1966, Brit.), w; CATCH ME A SPY(1971, Brit./Fr.); LADY CAROLINE LAMB(1972, Brit./Ital.)

Walter Peacock
NIGHT IN MONTMARTE, A(1931, Brit.), w
William Peacock
PAYROLL(1962, Brit.)
Leslie T. Peacocke
Silents
NEPTUNE'S DAUGHTER(1914), w; ANGEL CHILD(1918)
Misc. Silents
BAB THE FIXER(1917); BETTY BE GOOD(1917)
Thomas Peacocke
HOUNDS... OF NOTRE DAME, THE(1980, Can.)
1984
BAY BOY(1984, Can.)
Jennifer Peak
STAY AWAY, JOE(1968)
Barry Peake
COTTON QUEEN(1937, Brit.), w
Don Peake
MOVING VIOLATION(1976), m; BLACK OAK CONSPIRACY(1977), m; HILLS HAVE EYES, THE(1978), m; WALK PROUD(1979), m
1984
HOUSE WHERE DEATH LIVES, THE(1984), m; PREY, THE(1984), m
Lisa Peake
EXPRESSO BONGO(1959, Brit.); MATTER OF CHOICE, A(1963, Brit.)
Michael Peake
STOWAWAY GIRL(1957, Brit.); ZOO BABY(1957, Brit.); MARK OF THE PHOENIX(1958, Brit.); HIGH JUMP(1959, Brit.); MAKE MINE MINK(1960, Brit.); STRIP TEASE MURDER(1961, Brit.); BAND OF THIEVES(1962, Brit.); PIRATES OF BLOOD RIVER, THE(1962, Brit.); STRONGROOM(1962, Brit.); BAY OF SAINT MICHEL, THE(1963, Brit.); DEVIL-SHIP PIRATES, THE(1964, Brit.); GORGON, THE(1964, Brit.); SPYLARKS(1965, Brit.)
E.J. Peaker
HELLO, DOLLY!(1969); FOUR DEUCES, THE(1976); GRADUATION DAY(1981)
Norman Vincent Peale
ONE FOOT IN HEAVEN(1941), tech adv
Guilene Pean
JE T'AIME, JE T'AIME(1972, Fr./Swed.)
Peanuts
MUMMY'S GHOST, THE(1944)
Misc. Talkies
CRUISIN' 57(1975)
The Peanuts
LAS VEGAS FREE-FOR-ALL(1968, Jap.)
Peanuts the Dog
WHO'S MINDING THE MINT?(1967)
A. Leslie Pearce
FALL GUY, THE(1930), d; MEET THE WIFE(1931), d
Adele Pearce
STAGE DOOR(1937); UTAH TRAIL(1938); FULL CONFESSION(1939); GIRL FROM RIO, THE(1939); SORORITY HOUSE(1939); THREE SONS(1939); MILLIONAIRE PLAYBOY(1940); ONE CROWDED NIGHT(1940); POP ALWAYS PAYS(1940); NO GREATER SIN(1941)
Adele Pearce [Pamela Blake]
WYOMING OUTLAW(1939); MR. AND MRS. SMITH(1941)
Al Pearce
HERE COMES ELMER(1943); HITCHHIKE TO HAPPINESS(1945); ONE EXCITING WEEK(1946); MAIN STREET KID, THE(1947)
Alice Pearce
ON THE TOWN(1949); BELLE OF NEW YORK, THE(1952); HOW TO BE VERY, VERY, POPULAR(1955); OPPOSITE SEX, THE(1956); LAD: A DOG(1962); MY SIX LOVES(1963); TAMMY AND THE DOCTOR(1963); THRILL OF IT ALL, THE(1963); DEAR HEART(1964); DISORDERLY ORDERLY, THE(1964); KISS ME, STUPID(1964); BUS RILEY'S BACK IN TOWN(1965); DEAR BRIGETTE(1965); GLASS BOTTOM BOAT, THE(1966)
Ann Pearce
BAGDAD(1949); GAL WHO TOOK THE WEST, THE(1949); ONCE MORE, MY DARLING(1949); UNDERTOW(1949); DESERT HAWK, THE(1950); LOUISA(1950); MA AND PA KETTLE GO TO TOWN(1950); PEGGY(1950)
Babe Pearce
THREE LITTLE GIRLS IN BLUE(1946), ch
Bernard Pearce
KID FROM BOOKLYN, THE(1946), ch; ROAD TO RIO(1947), ch; VARIETY GIRL(1947), ch; CASBAH(1948), ch
Betty Pearce
Silents
ANSWER, THE(1918); REAL FOLKS(1918)
Damon Pearce
WIZ, THE(1978)
David Pearce
Misc. Talkies
VOICE OVER(1983)
Donn Pearce
COOL HAND LUKE(1967), a, w
George C. Pearce
AWFUL TRUTH, THE(1937); STAR MAKER, THE(1939)
Silents
COUNTRY KID, THE(1923)
George Pearce
VALIANT, THE(1929); LONE RIDER, THE(1930); PERSONALITY(1930); VENGEANCE(1930); THIS RECKLESS AGE(1932); STORY OF TEMPLE DRAKE, THE(1933); BRITISH AGENT(1934); LONE COWBOY(1934); MRS. WIGGS OF THE CABBAGE PATCH(1934); SIX OF A KIND(1934); MAN FROM GUN TOWN, THE(1936); MOON'S OUR HOME, THE(1936); SINGING COWBOY, THE(1936); WHEN YOU'RE IN LOVE(1937); I AM THE LAW(1938); YOU CAN'T TAKE IT WITH YOU(1938)
Silents
SABLE LORCHA, THE(1915); MARTHA'S VINDICATION(1916); NANCY COMES HOME(1918); REAL FOLKS(1918); DARING YOUTH(1924); NARROW STREET, THE(1924); SOCIAL HIGHWAYMAN, THE(1926); DROPKICK, THE(1927); IRRESISTIBLE LOVER, THE(1927)

Misc. Silents
GAMBLER OF THE WEST, THE(1915); CLOSIN' IN(1918); DESERT LAW(1918); EVERYWOMAN'S HUSBAND(1918); FRAMING FRAMERS(1918); MLLE PAULETTE(1918); OLD LOVES FOR NEW(1918)
Georgia Pearce [Constance Talmadge]
Silents
INTOLERANCE(1916)
Guy Pearce
WEEKEND IN HAVANA(1941), makeup; MY GAL SAL(1942), makeup; ROXIE HART(1942), makeup; TALES OF MANHATTAN(1942), makeup; OX-BOW INCIDENT, THE(1943), makeup; BIG NOISE, THE(1944), makeup; WILSON(1944), makeup; IDOL OF PARIS(1948, Brit.), makeup
Hayden Pearce
WHAT'S GOOD FOR THE GOOSE(1969, Brit.), art d; HORROR HOUSE(1970, Brit.), art d; TERROR(1979, Brit.), art d; MOUSE AND THE WOMAN, THE(1981, Brit.), p, art d; HORROR PLANET(1982, Brit.), prod d; ANOTHER TIME, ANOTHER PLACE(1983, Brit.), art d
1984
ANOTHER TIME, ANOTHER PLACE(1984, Brit.), art d; YR ALCOHOLIG LION(1984, Brit.), p, art d
Jacqueline Pearce
GYPSY GIRL(1966, Brit.); PLAGUE OF THE ZOMBIES, THE(1966, Brit.); REPTILE, THE(1966, Brit.); DON'T RAISE THE BRIDGE, LOWER THE RIVER(1968, Brit.)
Jana Pearce
DEAD TO THE WORLD(1961)
Janene Pearce
Misc. Talkies
PERILOUS JOURNEY(1983)
Jeanette Pearce
IT'S A WONDERFUL WORLD(1956, Brit.)
John B. Pearce
STUNT MAN, THE(1980)
John Pearce
COOL HAND LUKE(1967); STUDENT NURSES, THE(1970); THX 1138(1971); CULPEPPER CATTLE COMPANY, THE(1972); GREAT NORTHFIELD, MINNESOTA RAID, THE(1972); ULZANA'S RAID(1972); BILLY TWO HATS(1973, Brit.); KLANSMAN, THE(1974); 9/30/55(1977)
1984
FLESHBURN(1984)
Leslie Pearce
DELIGHTFUL HOGUE(1929), d; CAN YOU HEAR ME MOTHER?(1935, Brit.), d; STOKER, THE(1935, Brit.), d; YOU MUST GET MARRIED(1936, Brit.), d
Malcolm Pearce
BATTLE IN OUTER SPACE(1960)
Marshall Pearce
WACKY WORLD OF DR. MORGUS, THE(1962)
Mary Vivian Pearce
MONDO TRASHO(1970); FEMALE TROUBLE(1975); POLYESTER(1981)
Mathew Pearce
LOVE CHILD(1982)
May Keller Pearce
SHARKY'S MACHINE(1982)
Mervin Pearce
OTHER WOMAN, THE(1931, Brit.)
Mike Pearce
1984
SUPERGIRL(1984)
Mimi Pearce
GIRLS OF LATIN QUARTER(1960, Brit.)
Monty Pearce
SPEED TO SPARE(1948), ed; HIGH SCHOOL CAESAR(1960), m; WINGS OF CHANCE(1961, Can.), ed
Peggy Pearce
Silents
FALSE EVIDENCE(1919); SEX(1920)
Misc. Silents
FALSE AMBITION(1918); GOLDEN FLEECE, THE(1918); GOOD LOSER, THE(1918); RED-HAIRED CUPID, A(1918); ACE OF THE SADDLE(1919)
Perce Pearce
SNOW WHITE AND THE SEVEN DWARFS(1937), d; BAMBI(1942), w; SO DEAR TO MY HEART(1949), p; TREASURE ISLAND(1950, Brit.), p; STORY OF ROBIN HOOD, THE(1952, Brit.), p; SWORD AND THE ROSE, THE(1953), p; ROB ROY, THE HIGHLAND ROGUE(1954, Brit.), p
Peter Pearce
WILBY CONSPIRACY, THE(1975, Brit.)
Richard Pearce
HEARTLAND(1980), d; THRESHOLD(1983, Can.), d
1984
COUNTRY(1984), d
Sally Pearce
GENTLE TOUCH, THE(1956, Brit.)
Tim Pearce
MIX ME A PERSON(1962, Brit.)
Vera Pearce
JUST MY LUCK(1933, Brit.); THAT'S A GOOD GIRL(1933, Brit.); YES, MR. BROWN(1933, Brit.); HEAT WAVE(1935, Brit.); REGAL CAVALCADE(1935, Brit.); SO YOU WON'T TALK?(1935, Brit.); SOUTHERN ROSES(1936, Brit.); PLEASE TEACHER(1937, Brit.); WHAT A MAN!(1937, Brit.); NICHOLAS NICKLEBY(1947, Brit.); ONE WILD OAT(1951, Brit.); MEN OF SHERWOOD FOREST(1957, Brit.); NIGHT WE GOT THE BIRD, THE(1961, Brit.); NOTHING BARRED(1961, Brit.); MAKE MINE A DOUBLE(1962, Brit.)
Wynn Pearce
POCKET MONEY(1972)
Lyle Pearcy
NEW YEAR'S EVIL(1980)
Patricia Pearcy
SQUIRM(1976); GOODBYE GIRL, THE(1977)
1984
HOUSE WHERE DEATH LIVES, THE(1984)

Misc. Talkies
HOUSE WHERE DEATH LIVES, THE(1982)
Pearl
SERGEANT MIKE(1945)
Barry Pearl
GREASE(1978)
Dan Pearl
FIFTH FLOOR, THE(1980), ph
Daniel Pearl
TEXAS CHAIN SAW MASSACRE, THE(1974), ph; RETURN, THE(1980), ph; FULL MOON HIGH(1982), ph; ZAPPED!(1982), ph
Dorothy Pearl
POSTMAN ALWAYS RINGS TWICE, THE(1981), makeup; TOOTSIE(1982), makeup
Edith Cash Pearl
PURPLE HILLS, THE(1961), w
Edith Pearl
BROKEN LAND, THE(1962), w
Elna Pearl
TO SIR, WITH LOVE(1967, Brit.)
Gay Pearl
CALTIKI, THE IMMORTAL MONSTER(1959, Ital.)
Harold Pearl
DUMBO(1941), w
Herb Pearl
PSYCHIC KILLER(1975), ph
Jack Pearl
MEET THE BARON(1933); HOLLYWOOD PARTY(1934)
Jeff Pearl
TO THE SHORES OF HELL(1966)
Linda Pearl
GRAND THEFT AUTO(1977), cos; LEO AND LOREE(1980), art d; PRIVATE LESSONS(1981), art d; MY TUTOR(1983), art d; TESTAMENT(1983), art d; TIMERIDER(1983), art d; WAVELENGTH(1983), art d
Minnie Pearl
FORTY ACRE FEUD(1965); SECOND FIDDLE TO A STEEL GUITAR(1965); THAT TENNESSEE BEAT(1966)
Philip Pearl
VIRGIN SACRIFICE(1959)
Queen Pearl
Silents
RAINBOW PRINCESS, THE(1916)
Willa Pearl
PRINCE OF PEACE, THE(1951)
Princess Pearl [Pearl Vyner Brooke]
RHYTHM RACKETEER(1937, Brit.); EVERYTHING IS RHYTHM(1940, Brit.)
Pearl & Bard
Silents
TWO FLAMING YOUTHS(1927)
Cindy Pearlman
1984
HARD TO HOLD(1984)
Fred Pearlman
KELLY'S HEROES(1970, U.S./Yugo.)
Gilbert Pearlman
TOMORROW(1972), p
Joel Pearlman
NORMAN LOVES ROSE(1982, Aus.)
Lilli Pearlman
FAT SPY(1966), cos
Michael Pearlman
ONE-TRICK PONY(1980); SOUP FOR ONE(1982)
Nan Pearlman
HE KNOWS YOU'RE ALONE(1980), p
Rhea Pearlman
LOVE CHILD(1982)
Stephen Pearlman
ICEMAN COMETH, THE(1973); AUDREY ROSE(1977); ROLLERCOASTER(1977)
Emma Pearlstein
RAINBOW, THE(1944, USSR)
Philip Pearman
HE LOVED AN ACTRESS(1938, Brit.)
Dahlia Pears
Misc. Silents
FOREST KING, THE(1922)
Richard D. Pearsall
PINTO CANYON(1940), w
John Pearse
Misc. Talkies
MOVIEMAKERS(1970), d
A. Y. Pearson
Silents
POLICE PATROL, THE(1925), w
Anne Pearson
DANGEROUS AGE, A(1960, Can.)
Barry Pearson
PAPERBACK HERO(1973, Can.), w; SALLY FIELDGOOD & CO.(1975, Can.), w; PLAGUE(1978, Can.), p&w; FIREBIRD 2015 AD(1981), w
1984
ISAAC LITTLEFEATHERS(1984, Can.), p, w
Beatrice Pearson
FORCE OF EVIL(1948); LOST BOUNDARIES(1949)
Bill Pearson
RETURN OF OCTOBER, THE(1948)
Billy Pearson
BOOTS MALONE(1952); LIFE AND TIMES OF JUDGE ROY BEAN, THE(1972)
Brett Pearson
STAGECOACH(1966); THIS PROPERTY IS CONDEMNED(1966)

Bud Pearson
IF YOU KNEW SUSIE(1948), w
Carl Pearson
BLACK BEAUTY(1933), ed; OLIVER TWIST(1933), ed; CALIFORNIAN, THE(1937), ed
Charles Pearson
Misc. Silents
FLAMES OF WRATH(1923)
Drew Pearson
DAY THE EARTH STOOD STILL, THE(1951); DEAD TO THE WORLD(1961)
Durk Pearson
BRAINSTORM(1983), cons
Edith Pearson
Misc. Silents
WINDING ROAD, THE(1920); LAND OF MY FATHERS(1921, Brit.)
Eve Pearson
UP IN CENTRAL PARK(1948)
F. Pearson
ONE NIGHT WITH YOU(1948, Brit), set d
Ford Pearson
LOUISIANA(1947)
Fort Pearson
QUEEN FOR A DAY(1951)
Freda Pearson
SIEGE OF SIDNEY STREET, THE(1960, Brit.), set d; IMMORAL CHARGE(1962, Brit.), set d; FROM RUSSIA WITH LOVE(1963, Brit.), set d; GOLDFINGER(1964, Brit.), set d; WOMAN OF STRAW(1964, Brit.), set d; THUNDERBALL(1965, Brit.), set d; POPPY IS ALSO A FLOWER, THE(1966), set d; SOPHIE'S PLACE(1970), set d
Garret Pearson
BOULEVARD NIGHTS(1979)
Ge-Ge Pearson
CAMPUS RHYTHM(1943)
Gearge Pearson
Misc. Silents
WEE MACGREGOR'S SWEETHEART, THE(1922, Brit.), d
George Pearson
AULD LANG SYNE(1929, Brit.), p&d, w; JOURNEY'S END(1930), p; YELLOW STOCKINGS(1930, Brit.), p; EAST LYNNE ON THE WESTERN FRONT(1931, Brit.), d, w; THIRD STRING, THE(1932, Brit.), p, d, w; GOOD COMPANIONS(1933, Brit.), p; SHOT IN THE DARK, A(1933, Brit.), d; FOUR MASKED MEN(1934, Brit.), d; OPEN ALL NIGHT(1934, Brit.), d; POINTING FINGER, THE(1934, Brit.), d; RIVER WOLVES, THE(1934, Brit.), d; WHISPERING TONGUES(1934, Brit.), d; ACE OF SPADES, THE(1935, Brit.), d; CHECKMATE(1935, Brit.), d; GENTLEMAN'S AGREEMENT(1935, Brit.), d; JUBILEE WINDOW(1935, Brit.), d, w; ONCE A THIEF(1935, Brit.), d; SQUIBS(1935, Brit.), w; THAT'S MY UNCLE(1935, Brit.), d; MIDNIGHT AT THE WAX MUSEUM(1936, Brit.), d; MURDER BY ROPE(1936, Brit.), d; SECRET VOICE, THE(1936, Brit.), d; SHIPMATES O' MINE(1936, Brit.), w; WEDNESDAY'S LUCK(1936, Brit.), d; COMMAND PERFORMANCE(1937, Brit.), w; FATAL HOUR, THE(1937, Brit.), d; FOLLOW YOUR STAR(1938, Brit.), w; COLD JOURNEY(1975, Can.), p
Silents
JOHN HALIFAX, GENTLEMAN(1915, Brit.), d; ANGEL ESQUIRE(1919, Brit.), w; OLD CURIOSITY SHOP, THE(1921, Brit.), p; SQUIBS(1921, Brit.), d, w; SQUIBS WINS THE CALCUTTA SWEEP(1922, Brit.), d&w; SQUIBS, MP(1923, Brit.), p&d, w; SATAN'S SISTER(1925, Brit.), p, d&w; SQUIBS' HONEYMOON(1926, Brit.), d, w; HUNTINGTOWER(1927, Brit.), d; BROKEN MELODY, THE(1929, Brit.), p
Misc. Silents
STUDY IN SCARLET, A(1914, Brit.), d; CINEMA GIRL'S ROMANCE, A(1915, Brit.), d; SALLY BISHOP(1916, Brit.), d; BLINKEYES(192?), d; GARRYOWEN(1920, Brit.), d; NOTHING ELSE MATTERS(1920, Brit.), d; MARY-FIND-THE-GOLD(1921, Brit.), d; REVEILLE(1924, Brit.), d; LITTLE PEOPLE, THE(1926, Brit.), d; LOVE'S OPTION(1928, Brit.), d
Ginger Pearson
ZIEGFELD GIRL(1941)
H. P. Pearson
Silents
HIGH SPEED(1917), w
Humphrey Pearson
BROADWAY BABIES(1929), w; ON WITH THE SHOW(1929), w; BRIDE OF THE REGIMENT(1930), w; PLAYING AROUND(1930), w; SUNNY(1930), w; TOP SPEED(1930), w; BRIGHT LIGHTS(1931), w; CONSOLATION MARRIAGE(1931), w; GOING WILD(1931), w; TRAVELING HUSBANDS(1931), w; AGGIE APPLEBY, MAKER OF MEN(1933), w; FACE IN THE SKY(1933), w; MEN OF AMERICA(1933), w; ELMER AND ELSIE(1934), w; GREAT FLIRTATION, THE(1934), w; RED SALUTE(1935), w; RUGGLES OF RED GAP(1935), w; PALM SPRINGS(1936), w
J. Logan Pearson
Silents
ESCAPE, THE(1928), ed
Jesse Pearson
BYE BYE BIRDIE(1963); ADVANCE TO THE REAR(1964); NORSEMAN, THE(1978)
Jill Pearson
CHARLEY-ONE-EYE(1973, Brit.)
John Pearson
SAN FRANCISCO(1936); TALENT SCOUT(1937); PRISON TRAIN(1938); GYPSY WILDCAT(1944)
Johnny Pearson
JOKERS, THE(1967, Brit.), m
Josephine Pearson
ONE DARK NIGHT(1939)
Karen Pearson
MY SIDE OF THE MOUNTAIN(1969); "EQUUS"(1977)
Lloyd Pearson
INCIDENT IN SHANGHAI(1937, Brit.); CHALLENGE, THE(1939, Brit.); TILLY OF BLOOMSBURY(1940, Brit.); REMARKABLE MR. KIPPS(1942, Brit.); YOUNG MR. PITT, THE(1942, Brit.); MY LEARNED FRIEND(1943, Brit.); RHYTHM SERENADE(1943, Brit.); SCHWEIK'S NEW ADVENTURES(1943, Brit.); WHEN WE ARE MARRIED(1943, Brit.); TIME FLIES(1944, Brit.); UNCENSORED(1944, Brit.); WAY AHEAD, THE(1945, Brit.); MR. PERRIN AND MR. TRAILL(1948, Brit.); THREE WEIRD SISTERS, THE(1948, Brit.); AGITATOR, THE(1949); DEAR MR. PROHACK(1949, Brit.); PASSPORT TO PIMLICO(1949, Brit.); PORTRAIT OF CLARE(1951,

Brit.); HOLIDAY WEEK(1952, Brit.); PRIVATE INFORMATION(1952, Brit.); GOOD COMPANIONS, THE(1957, Brit.); ANGRY SILENCE, THE(1960, Brit.)
Lora Pearson
HAND, THE(1981)
Michael Pearson
ONE PLUS ONE(1969, Brit.), p
Molly Pearson
Misc. Silents
PASSING OF THE THIRD FLOOR BACK, THE(1918, Brit.)
Mrs. Arch Pearson
DEVIL'S BEDROOM, THE(1964)
Neil Pearson
PRIVATES ON PARADE(1982)
1984
PRIVATES ON PARADE(1984, Brit.)
Patrick Pearson
PRIVATES ON PARADE(1982)
1984
PRIVATES ON PARADE(1984, Brit.)
Peter Pearson
PAPERBACK HERO(1973, Can.), d; ONLY GOD KNOWS(1974, Can.), d; ONE MAN(1979, Can.), w
Richard Pearson
FIVE ANGLES ON MURDER(1950, Brit.); GIRL IS MINE, THE(1950, Brit.); HER PANELLED DOOR(1951, Brit.); BLUE PARROT, THE(1953, Brit.); DANGEROUS CARGO(1954, Brit.); FABIAN OF THE YARD(1954, Brit.); SVENGALI(1955, Brit.); SEA FURY(1959, Brit.); MODEL FOR MURDER(1960, Brit.); ATTEMPT TO KILL(1961, Brit.); MAN IN THE MOON(1961, Brit.); GUNS OF DARKNESS(1962, Brit.); LIFE IN DANGER(1964, Brit.); AGONY AND THE ECSTASY, THE(1965); YELLOW ROLLS-ROYCE, THE(1965, Brit.); HOW I WON THE WAR(1967, Brit.); CHARLIE BUBBLES(1968, Brit.); INSPECTOR CLOUSEAU(1968, Brit.); STRANGE AFFAIR, THE(1968, Brit.); RISE AND RISE OF MICHAEL RIMMER, THE(1970, Brit.); CATCH ME A SPY(1971, Brit./Fr.); MACBETH(1971, Brit.); SUNDAY BLOODY SUNDAY(1971, Brit.); POPE JOAN(1972, Brit.); BLUE BIRD, THE(1976); ALL THINGS BRIGHT AND BEAUTIFUL(1979, Brit.); MIRROR CRACK'D, THE(1980, Brit.); TESS(1980, Fr./Brit.)
Rodney Pearson
CLASS(1983)
Rose Pearson
SEMI-TOUGH(1977)
Sid Pearson
CREATURES THE WORLD FORGOT(1971, Brit.), spec eff
Sidney Pearson
MAN IN THE WHITE SUIT, THE(1952), spec eff
Stuart Pearson
NIGHT WON'T TALK, THE(1952, Brit.)
Syd Pearson
IN SEARCH OF THE CASTAWAYS(1962, Brit.), spec eff; GORGON, THE(1964, Brit.), spec eff; LONG SHIPS, THE(1964, Brit./Yugo.), spec eff; HEROES OF TELEMARK, THE(1965, Brit.), spec eff; SECRET OF BLOOD ISLAND, THE(1965, Brit.), spec eff
Sydney Pearson
SCOTT OF THE ANTARCTIC(1949, Brit.), spec eff; BRIDES OF DRACULA, THE(1960, Brit.), spec eff
Ted Pearson
NAVY BLUE AND GOLD(1937); TEST PILOT(1938); YOU'RE ONLY YOUNG ONCE(1938); BOY FRIEND(1939); GUY WHO CAME BACK, THE(1951); MR. BELVEDERE RINGS THE BELL(1951)
Virginia Pearson
PHANTOM OF THE OPERA, THE(1929)
Silents
STAIN, THE(1914); IMPOSSIBLE CATHERINE(1919); LOVE AUCTION, THE(1919); PHANTOM OF THE OPERA, THE(1925); RED KIMONO(1925); WIZARD OF OZ, THE(1925); ATTA BOY!(1926); TAXI MYSTERY, THE(1926); DRIVEN FROM HOME(1927); ACTRESS, THE(1928); BIG CITY, THE(1928)
Misc. Silents
AFTERMATH(1914); THOU ART THE MAN(1915); TURN OF THE ROAD, THE(1915); BLAZING LOVE(1916); DAREDEVIL KATE(1916); HUNTED WOMAN, THE(1916); HYPOCRISY(1916); THOU ART THE MAN(1916); TORTURED HEART, A(1916); VITAL QUESTION, THE(1916); WAR BRIDE'S SECRET, THE(1916); WRITING ON THE WALL, THE(1916); ALL FOR A HUSBAND(1917); BITTER TRUTH(1917); ROYAL ROMANCE(1917); SISTER AGAINST SISTER(1917); THOU SHALT NOT STEAL(1917); WHEN FALSE TONGUES SPEAK(1917); WRATH OF LOVE(1917); BUCHANAN'S WIFE(1918); DAUGHTER OF FRANCE, A(1918); FIREBRAND, THE(1918); HER PRICE(1918); LIAR, THE(1918); QUEEN OF HEARTS, THE(1918); STOLEN HONOR(1918); BISHOP'S EMERALDS, THE(1919); WILDNESS OF YOUTH(1922); PRINCE OF A KING, A(1923); WHAT PRICE BEAUTY(1928); SMILIN' GUNS(1929); DANGER MAN, THE(1930)
W.B. Pearson
Misc. Silents
HELL'S CRATER(1918), d
William Pearson
FEVER IN THE BLOOD, A(1961), w
Tom Pearsons
PLEASURE(1933), ed
Joan Peart
TELL-TALE HEART, THE(1962, Brit.)
Pauline Peart
SUBURBAN WIVES(1973, Brit.); CUBA(1979)
Pippa Pearthree
1984
MRS. SOFFEL(1984)
Hal Peary
TIGER WALKS, A(1964); CLAMBAKE(1967)
Harold Peary
COMIN' ROUND THE MOUNTAIN(1940); COUNTRY FAIR(1941); LOOK WHO'S LAUGHING(1941); GREAT GILDERSLEEVE, THE(1942); HERE WE GO AGAIN(1942); SEVEN DAYS LEAVE(1942); GILDERSLEEVE ON BROADWAY(1943); GILDERSLEEVE'S BAD DAY(1943); GILDERSLEEVE'S GHOST(1944); PORT OF HELL(1955)

Fred Pease
MURDER AT COVENT GARDEN(1932, Brit.)

Patsy Pease
HE KNOWS YOU'RE ALONE(1980); SPACE RAIDERS(1983)

Royal S. Pease
Silents
ANNAPOLIS(1928), w

Julie Peasgood
ROMANTIC ENGLISHWOMAN, THE(1975, Brit./Fr.); HOUSE OF LONG SHADOWS, THE(1983, Brit.)

Richard Peaslee
PERSECUTION AND ASSASSINATION OF JEAN-PAUL MARAT AS PERFORMED BY THE INMATES OF THE ASYLUM OF CHARENTON UNDER THE DIRECTION OF THE MARQUIS DE SADE, THE(1967, Brit.), m; TELL ME LIES(1968, Brit.), m

Colin Peasley
DON QUIXOTE(1973, Aus.)

Harold R. Peat
Silents
PRIVATE PEAT(1918)

Harold Reginald Peat
Silents
PRIVATE PEAT(1918), w

Sonia Peat
MOUTH TO MOUTH(1978, Aus.)

James Peatman
MAN CALLED DAGGER, A(1967), w

Leighton L. Peatman
GIRL IN GOLD BOOTS(1968), w

Yvonne Peattie
CONFIDENCE GIRL(1952); DANGEROUS CROSSING(1953); PRIVATE WAR OF MAJOR BENSON, THE(1955); KELLY AND ME(1957); FEMALE ANIMAL, THE(1958); MADISON AVENUE(1962); THAT TOUCH OF MINK(1962); DONOVAN'S REEF(1963); MY SIX LOVES(1963)

Stephane Peau
RETURN OF MARTIN GUERRE, THE(1983, Fr.)

William Peavy
Misc. Silents
JAN OF THE BIG SNOWS(1922)

The Pebbles
HELL'S PLAYGROUND(1967)

Steven Apostle Pec
1984
RHINESTONE(1984)

Clayton Peca
SINISTER URGE, THE(1961)

Teresa Pecanins
YELLOWBEARD(1983), set d

Max Pecas
DANIELLA BY NIGHT(1962, Fr/Ger.), d, w; SWEET ECSTASY(1962, Fr.), d, w; FIVE WILD GIRLS(1966, Fr.), d, w; HEAT OF MIDNIGHT(1966, Fr.), p&d, w
Misc. Talkies
I AM FRIGID...WHY?(1973), d

Alex Pecate
DYNAMITE JOHNSON(1978, Phil.)

Bill Pecchi
1984
FLESHBURN(1984), ph

Aldo Pecchioli
CONDEMNED OF ALTONA, THE(1963)

Angelo Peccianti
ROSE BOWL(1936)

Andrew Pece
1984
SUBURBIA(1984)

Ferd Pecenka
BOHEMIAN RAPTURE(1948, Czech), ph

Ferdinand Pecenka
EMPEROR AND THE NIGHTINGALE, THE(1949, Czech.), ph

W. Pechanz
SNOW WHITE(1965, Ger.), cos

Dina Pechellini
LITTLE MARTYR, THE(1947, Ital.)

N. Pechentsov
DESTINY OF A MAN(1961, USSR)

Kurt Pecher
LONGEST DAY, THE(1962)

Freddy Pecherelly
SUPERZAN AND THE SPACE BOY(1972, Mex.)

Bruce Pecheur
ROAD TO SALINA(1971, Fr./Ital.)

Sierra Pecheur
THREE WOMEN(1977); BELOW THE BELT(1980); BRONCO BILLY(1980); HARD COUNTRY(1981)

V. Pechnikov
HOUSE ON THE FRONT LINE, THE(1963, USSR)

Peter Pechowski
VON RICHTHOFEN AND BROWN(1970), ph

Ann B. Peck
MC LINTOCK!(1963), cos; CHEYENNE AUTUMN(1964), cos

Ann Peck
FORT APACHE(1948), cos; SHE WORE A YELLOW RIBBON(1949), cos; MOONLIGHTER, THE(1953), cos; PARIS MODEL(1953), cos; STAR, THE(1953), cos; PHENIX CITY STORY, THE(1955), cos; BACK FROM ETERNITY(1956), cos; SEARCHERS, THE(1956), cos; MISSOURI TRAVELER, THE(1958), cos; HORSE SOLDIERS, THE(1959), cos; YOUNG LAND, THE(1959), cos

Brian Peck
WHILE THE SUN SHINES(1950, Brit.); PORTRAIT OF CLARE(1951, Brit.); ECHO OF BARBARA(1961, Brit.); TARNISHED HEROES(1961, Brit.); MYSTERY SUBMARINE(1963, Brit.); SET-UP, THE(1963, Brit.); JOKERS, THE(1967, Brit.); FIVE MILLION YEARS TO EARTH(1968, Brit.); TWISTED NERVE(1969, Brit.); PERFECT FRIDAY(1970, Brit.); LAST AMERICAN VIRGIN, THE(1982)

Carey Paul Peck
ON THE BEACH(1959)

Charles Peck
DEAD END(1937); MAD ABOUT MUSIC(1938); OF HUMAN HEARTS(1938); ANDY HARDY GETS SPRING FEVER(1939); FIVE LITTLE PEPPERS AND HOW THEY GREW(1939); TOWER OF LONDON(1939); FIVE LITTLE PEPPERS AT HOME(1940); FIVE LITTLE PEPPERS IN TROUBLE(1940); OUT WEST WITH THE PEPPERS(1940); OBLIGING YOUNG LADY(1941); LOVE LAUGHS AT ANDY HARDY(1946)

Charles K. Peck, Jr.
BASKETBALL FIX, THE(1951), w; YANKEE BUCCANEER(1952), w; SEMINOLE(1953), w

Charles Motimer Peck
Silents
ARIZONA CATCLAW, THE(1919), w

Clare Peck
1984
SPLASH(1984)

Darryl Peck
LORDS OF FLATBUSH, THE(1974)

David Peck
GAL YOUNG UN(1979)

Ed Peck
ONE MAN'S WAY(1964); COUNTERPOINT(1967); GUNN(1967); RIDE TO HANGMAN'S TREE, THE(1967); BULLITT(1968); I LOVE YOU, ALICE B. TOKLAS!(1968); SHAKIEST GUN IN THE WEST, THE(1968); COMIC, THE(1969); MAN CALLED GANNON, A(1969); PRISONER OF SECOND AVENUE, THE(1975); RAFFERTY AND THE GOLD DUST TWINS(1975); ZOOT SUIT(1981); HEY, GOOD LOOKIN'(1982)

Ed V. Peck
HEAVEN CAN WAIT(1978)

Esther Peck
HOLIDAY(1938)

George Peck
DEATHTRAP(1982)
Misc. Talkies
DAWN OF THE MUMMY(1981)

George W. Peck
PECK'S BAD BOY(1934), w

George Wilbur Peck
Silents
PECK'S BAD BOY(1921), w

Gregory Peck
DAYS OF GLORY(1944); KEYS OF THE KINGDOM, THE(1944); SPELLBOUND(1945); VALLEY OF DECISION, THE(1945); DUEL IN THE SUN(1946); YEARLING, THE(1946); GENTLEMAN'S AGREEMENT(1947); MACOMBER AFFAIR, THE(1947); PARADINE CASE, THE(1947); YELLOW SKY(1948); GREAT SINNER, THE(1949); TWELVE O'CLOCK HIGH(1949); GUNFIGHTER, THE(1950); CAPTAIN HORATIO HORNBLOWER(1951, Brit.); DAVID AND BATHSHEBA(1951); ONLY THE VALIANT(1951); SNOWS OF KILIMANJARO, THE(1952); WORLD IN HIS ARMS, THE(1952); ROMAN HOLIDAY(1953); MAN WITH A MILLION(1954, Brit.); NIGHT PEOPLE(1954); PURPLE PLAIN, THE(1954, Brit.); MAN IN THE GREY FLANNEL SUIT, THE(1956); MOBY DICK(1956, Brit.); DESIGNING WOMAN(1957); BIG COUNTRY, THE(1958); BRAVADOS, THE(1958); BELOVED INFIDEL(1959); ON THE BEACH(1959); PORK CHOP HILL(1959); GUNS OF NAVARONE, THE(1961); CAPE FEAR(1962); HOW THE WEST WAS WON(1962); TO KILL A MOCKINGBIRD(1962); CAPTAIN NEWMAN, M.D.(1963); BEHOLD A PALE HORSE(1964); MIRAGE(1965); ARABESQUE(1966); CHAIRMAN, THE(1969); MACKENNA'S GOLD(1969); MAROONED(1969); STALKING MOON, THE(1969); I WALK THE LINE(1970); SHOOT OUT(1971); TRIAL OF THE CATONSVILLE NINE, THE(1972), p; BILLY TWO HATS(1973, Brit.); DOVE, THE(1974, Brit.), p; OMEN, THE(1976); MAC ARTHUR(1977); BOYS FROM BRAZIL, THE(1978); SEA WOLVES, THE(1981, Brit.)

J.B. Peck
WRECKING CREW, THE(1968)

Kimi Peck
LITTLE DARLINGS(1980), w

Lila Peck
Misc. Silents
LOVE, HATE AND A WOMAN(1921)

Linda Peck
VALLEY OF THE DOLLS(1967)

Norman Peck
HELLO SISTER(1930)

Oscar Peck
MEETINGS WITH REMARKABLE MEN(1979, Brit.)

Raymond Peck
Silents
CRITICAL AGE, THE(1923)

Robert Peck
Silents
PREP AND PEP(1928)

Rodger Peck
ACE ELI AND RODGER OF THE SKIES(1973)

Ron Peck
NIGHTHAWKS(1978, Brit.), p, d, w

Stephen Peck
WHO'S BEEN SLEEPING IN MY BED?(1963), ch

Steve Peck
LION AND THE HORSE, THE(1952); JOHNNY COOL(1963); HOUSE IS NOT A HOME, A(1964); LADY IN CEMENT(1968)

Steven Apostlee Peck
IDOLMAKER, THE(1980)

Steven Peck
MOONRISE(1948); GUN RUNNERS, THE(1958); SOME CAME RUNNING(1959); BELLS ARE RINGING(1960); FRECKLES(1960); OSCAR, THE(1966), ch; GIRL WHO KNEW TOO MUCH, THE(1969)

William Peck
UNDER AGE(1964)

Yvonne Peck
COUNTERPLOT(1959); FIEND OF DOPE ISLAND(1961)
Yair Pecker
SIMCHON FAMILY, THE(1969, Israel), p
George Peckham
DUEL AT DIABLO(1966), spec eff; MONTE WALSH(1970), spec eff
Ruth Peckham
RECOMMENDATION FOR MERCY(1975, Can.)
Sam Peckingpah
WILD BUNCH, THE(1969), w
Kristen Peckinpah
OSTERMAN WEEKEND, THE(1983)
Matthew Peckinpah
JUNIOR BONNER(1972); KILLER ELITE, THE(1975)
Sam Peckinpah
INVASION OF THE BODY SNATCHERS(1956), a, w; DEADLY COMPANIONS, THE(1961), d; RIDE THE HIGH COUNTRY(1962), d; GLORY GUYS, THE(1965), w; MAJOR DUNDEE(1965), d, w; VILLA RIDES(1968), w; WILD BUNCH, THE(1969), d; BALLAD OF CABLE HOGUE, THE(1970), p, d; STRAW DOGS(1971, Brit.), d, w; GETAWAY, THE(1972), d; JUNIOR BONNER(1972), d; PAT GARRETT AND BILLY THE KID(1973), a, d; BRING ME THE HEAD OF ALFREDO GARCIA(1974), d, w; KILLER ELITE, THE(1975), d; CROSS OF IRON(1977, Brit., Ger.), d; CHINA 9, LIBERTY 37(1978, Ital.); CONVOY(1978), d; VISITOR, THE(1980, Ital./U.S.); OSTERMAN WEEKEND, THE(1983), d
Barbara Peckinpaugh
1984
BODY DOUBLE(1984)
George Peclet
MYSTERY OF THE PINK VILLA, THE(1930, Fr.)
Georges Peclet
HELL ON EARTH(1934, Ger.); PEPE LE MOKO(1937, Fr.); GRAND ILLUSION(1938, Fr.); LA BETE HUMAINE(1938, Fr.); LA MARSEILLAISE(1938, Fr.)
Charles Pecora
MRS. PARKINGTON(1944)
John Pecora
MAN WHO BROKE THE BANK AT MONTE CARLO, THE(1935)
Anthony Pecoraro
WILD PARTY, THE(1975)
Adriana Pecorelli
LEAP INTO THE VOID(1982, Ital.)
Greg Pecque
HEARTBREAK KID, THE(1972)
Maurice Pecqueux
PASSION FOR LIFE(1951, Fr.), ph; LADIES OF THE PARK(1964, Fr.), ph
Jozsef Pecsenke
WINTER WIND(1970, Fr./Hung.); WITNESS, THE(1982, Hung.)
Sandor Pecsi
DIALOGUE(1967, Hung.); BOYS OF PAUL STREET, THE(1969, Hung./US)
Gizy Pecsy
KIND STEPMOTHER(1936, Hung.)
Angelo Pedari
SHAPE OF THINGS TO COME, THE(1979, Can.)
Maurice Pedbrey
HAPPY BIRTHDAY TO ME(1981)
Jim Peddie
LAST GUNFIGHTER, THE(1961, Can.)
Liddell Peddieson
MAN WHO KNEW TOO MUCH, THE(1956)
Donavan Pedelty
CITY OF BEAUTIFUL NONSENSE, THE(1935, Brit.), w
Donovan Pedelty
LITTLE DAMOZEL, THE(1933, Brit.), w; THAT'S A GOOD GIRL(1933, Brit.), w; SEEING IS BELIEVING(1934, Brit.), w; BREWSTER'S MILLIONS(1935, Brit.), w; FLAME IN THE HEATHER(1935, Brit.), d&w; RADIO PIRATES(1935, Brit.), w; SCHOOL FOR STARS(1935, Brit.), w; EARLY BIRD, THE(1936, Brit.), d&w; TWO ON A DOORSTEP(1936, Brit.), w; BEHIND YOUR BACK(1937, Brit.), d&w; FALSE EVIDENCE(1937, Brit.), d&w; FIRST NIGHT(1937, Brit.), d&w; LANDSLIDE(1937, Brit.), d&w; LUCK OF THE IRISH, THE(1937, Ireland), p, d&w; BEDTIME STORY(1938, Brit.), d&w; IRISH AND PROUD OF IT(1938, Ireland), d, w; MURDER TOMORROW(1938, Brit.), d&w
Elena Pedemonte
THEY CALL ME TRINITY(1971, Ital.)
David Peden
CHAMP, THE(1979)
Leif Pederen
FOR LOVE OF IVY(1968), set d
Eric Pedersen
FIGHTING COAST GUARD(1951)
Freddy Pedersen
LURE OF THE JUNGLE, THE(1970, Den.)
Katja Pedersen
EDVARD MUNCH(1976, Norway/Swed.)
Leif Pedersen
TROUBLEMAKER, THE(1964), set d; TRUMAN CAPOTE'S TRILOGY(1969), set d; MAGIC GARDEN OF STANLEY SWEETHART, THE(1970), set d; OWL AND THE PUSSYCAT, THE(1970), set d; WHO IS HARRY KELLERMAN AND WHY IS HE SAYING THOSE TERRIBLE THINGS ABOUT ME?(1971), set d
Maren Pedersen
Misc. Silents
WITCHCRAFT THROUGH THE AGES(1921, Swed.)
Rachel Pedersen
EDVARD MUNCH(1976, Norway/Swed.)
Gianna Pedersini
ROSSINI(1948, Ital.)
Carlo Pedersoli
FAREWELL TO ARMS, A(1957)
Chris Pederson
1984
NIGHT OF THE COMET(1984); SUBURBIA(1984)

Con Pederson
2001: A SPACE ODYSSEY(1968, U.S./Brit.), spec eff
Eric Pederson
SEDUCTION OF JOE TYNAN, THE(1979)
Guy Pederson
PARIS BLUES(1961)
Hal James Pederson
TROUBLE WITH GIRLS(AND HOW TO GET INTO IT), THE (1969)
Lilla Pederson
1984
BIG MEAT EATER(1984, Can.), ed
Orla Pederson
ELEPHANT MAN, THE(1980, Brit.)
1984
SUPERGIRL(1984)
Josefa Pedhlatova
END OF A PRIEST(1970, Czech.)
Tom Pedi
TAKING OF PELHAM ONE, TWO, THREE, THE(1974); CRY MURDER(1936); NATIVE LAND(1942); NAKED CITY, THE(1948); STATE OF THE UNION(1948); UP IN CENTRAL PARK(1948); CRISS CROSS(1949); SORROWFUL JONES(1949); ICEMAN COMETH, THE(1973); ST. IVES(1976); CAT FROM OUTER SPACE, THE(1978); ONE MAN JURY(1978); NORTH AVENUE IRREGULARS, THE(1979); LITTLE MISS MARKER(1980)
Tom Pedigo
TERMS OF ENDEARMENT(1983), set d
1984
STAR TREK III: THE SEARCH FOR SPOCK(1984), set d
Aldo Pedinotti
ALWAYS VICTORIOUS(1960, Ital.)
Gertrude Pedlar
FORBIDDEN(1932); READY, WILLING AND ABLE(1937)
Silents
WHITE YOUTH(1920); LAWFUL CHEATERS(1925)
Anna Pedoni
SHOE SHINE(1947, Ital.)
J. Pedotova
HEROES ARE MADE(1944, USSR)
Miguel Pedregosa
ROBIN AND MARIAN(1976, Brit.), stunts
Alberto Pedret
BANDIDO(1956); VILLA!(1958); GINA(1961, Fr./Mex.); DEATH IN THE GARDEN(1977, Fr./Mex.)
Gale Pedrick
GEORGE IN CIVVY STREET(1946, Brit.), w; MEET SIMON CHERRY(1949, Brit.), w
John Pedrick
RETURN OF THE JEDI(1983); SIGN OF FOUR, THE(1983, Brit.)
Irene Pedrini
MISSION TO MOSCOW(1943)
John Pedrini
HOUSE OF STRANGERS(1949); ICE PALACE(1960); ROBIN AND THE SEVEN HOODS(1964)
Rene Pedrini
LEOPARD MAN, THE(1943)
Antonio Pedro
1984
GABRIELA(1984, Braz.)
Ellario Pedro
EAST OF SUDAN(1964, Brit.)
Illario Pedro
FILE OF THE GOLDEN GOOSE, THE(1969, Brit.); ONE PLUS ONE(1969, Brit.); BUSHBABY, THE(1970)
The Pedrolas
JUMBO(1962)
Emilio Pedroni
TREE OF WOODEN CLOGS, THE(1979, Ital.)
Lorenzo Pedroni
TREE OF WOODEN CLOGS, THE(1979, Ital.)
Alfonso Pedrosa
DESIRE(1936)
Lawrence Williams Pedrose
Silents
WINGS OF THE STORM(1926), w
Adelina Pedroza
STORY OF RUTH, THE(1960)
Alfonso Pedroza
MEXICAN HAYRIDE(1948); WE WERE STRANGERS(1949)
Alphonso Pedroza
GAY DESPERADO, THE(1936)
Inez Pedroza
STORY OF RUTH, THE(1960); GLOBAL AFFAIR, A(1964); TICKLE ME(1965); SINGING NUN, THE(1966); R.P.M.(1970); EARTHQUAKE(1974); BUSTIN' LOOSE(1981)
Pee Wee King and His Band
ROUGH, TOUGH WEST, THE(1952)
Pee Wee King and His Golden West Cowboys
FLAME OF THE WEST(1945); RIDIN' THE OUTLAW TRAIL(1951)
John W. Peebles
DIRTY HARRY(1971)
Denys Peek
LIMBO LINE, THE(1969, Brit.); CRIMSON CULT, THE(1970, Brit.)
Kevin Peek
BATTLETRUCK(1982), m
Dave Peel
NASHVILLE(1975)
David Peel
ESCAPE TO DANGER(1943, Brit.); SQUADRON LEADER X(1943, Brit.); WE DIVE AT DAWN(1943, Brit.); THEY WHO DARE(1954, Brit.); BRIDES OF DRACULA, THE(1960, Brit.); HANDS OF ORLAC, THE(1964, Brit./Fr.); PLEASE STAND BY(1972)

Eda Peel
SPORTING LOVE(1936, Brit.)
Edward Peel
O LUCKY MAN!(1973, Brit.)
1984
LASSITER(1984)
Eileen Peel
AFTER OFFICE HOURS(1932, Brit.); FIRST MRS. FRASER, THE(1932, Brit.); HYDE PARK CORNER(1935, Brit.); HEAD OFFICE(1936, Brit.); IN WHICH WE SERVE(1942, Brit.); TALK ABOUT JACQUELINE(1942, Brit.); BAD SISTER(1947, Brit.); TEARS FOR SIMON(1957, Brit.); QUEEN'S GUARDS, THE(1963, Brit.)
Richard Peel
DESERT RATS, THE(1953); KING OF THE KHYBER RIFLES(1953); TITANIC(1953); SCARLET COAT, THE(1955); PHARAOH'S CURSE(1957); MIDNIGHT LACE(1960); NOTORIOUS LANDLADY, THE(1962); IRMA LA DOUCE(1963); LIST OF ADRIAN MESSENGER, THE(1963); MY FAIR LADY(1964); 36 HOURS(1965); ONE OF OUR SPIES IS MISSING(1966)
Spencer Peel
BON VOYAGE, CHARLIE BROWN(AND DON'T COME BACK)*** (1980), anim; SHINBONE ALLEY(1971), anim; RAGGEDY ANN AND ANDY(1977), anim
Tracy Peel
Misc. Talkies
HIJACK(1975, Brit.)
Eileen Peele
DIVORCE OF LADY X. THE(1938, Brit.)
Guy Peellaert
KILLING GAME, THE(1968, Fr.), ph
Cornelius Peeples
JULIUS CAESAR(1952)
Dennis Peeples
HARD TIMES(1975), set d; DUCHESS AND THE DIRTWATER FOX, THE(1976), set d; FUTUREWORLD(1976), set d; FIRE SALE(1977), set d; LAST WORD, THE(1979), set d; SILKWOOD(1983), set d
1984
SAM'S SON(1984), set d
Samuel A. Peeples
ADVANCE TO THE REAR(1964), w; FINAL CHAPTER–WALKING TALL ze-ro(1977), w
Richard Peer
Misc. Silents
PLOUGHSHARE, THE(1915)
Salmaan Peer
TWISTED NERVE(1969, Brit.); CRY OF THE PENGUINS(1972, Brit.); PRIVATE ENTERPRISE, A(1975, Brit.)
Salman Peer
HORSEMEN, THE(1971)
Jan Peerce
CARNEGIE HALL(1947); SOMETHING IN THE WIND(1947); GOODBYE COLUMBUS(1969)
Larry Peerce
ONE POTATO, TWO POTATO(1964), d; INCIDENT, THE(1967), d; GOODBYE COLUMBUS(1969), d; SPORTING CLUB, THE(1971), d; SEPARATE PEACE, A(1972), d; ASH WEDNESDAY(1973), d; OTHER SIDE OF THE MOUNTAIN, THE(1975), d; TWO-MINUTE WARNING(1976), d; OTHER SIDE OF THE MOUNTAIN–PART 2, THE(1978), d; BELL JAR, THE(1979), d; WHY WOULD I LIE(1980), d; LOVE CHILD(1982), d
1984
HARD TO HOLD(1984), d
Max Peerce
GOODBYE COLUMBUS(1969)
Sander Peerce
TWO-MINUTE WARNING(1976)
Georges Peerinal
SAINT JOAN(1957), ph
Donald Peers
BALLOON GOES UP, THE(1942, Brit.); SING ALONG WITH ME(1952, Brit.)
Elwyn Peers
ON THE BEACH(1959)
Joan Peers
APPLAUSE(1929); ANYBODY'S WAR(1930); RAIN OR SHINE(1930); TOL'ABLE DAVID(1930); OVER THE HILL(1931); PARLOR, BEDROOM AND BATH(1931); TIP-OFF, THE(1931)
Misc. Talkies
ANYBODY'S WAR(1930); AROUND THE CORNER(1930)
Leon Peers
MANIAC(1963, Brit.)
Lisa Peers
JOURNEY AMONG WOMEN(1977, Aus.); SOLO(1978, New Zealand/Aus.); BUD-DIES(1983, Aus.); MONKEY GRIP(1983, Aus.)
V. Peers
Misc. Silents
SHIRAZ(1929), d
Victor Peers
Misc. Silents
CARRY ON!(1927, Brit.), d; SACRIFICE(1929, Brit.), d
Bill Peet
THREE CABALLEROS, THE(1944), w; ALICE IN WONDERLAND(1951), w; PETER PAN(1953), w; ONE HUNDRED AND ONE DALMATIANS(1961), w; SWORD IN THE STONE, THE(1963), w
Graham Peet
ONE PLUS ONE(1969, Brit.)
William Peet
SONG OF THE SOUTH(1946), w; CINDERELLA(1950), w
Bob Peete
DRIVE-IN(1976), w
Barbara Peeters
GUN RUNNER(1969); DARK SIDE OF TOMORROW, THE(1970), d&w; STAR-HOPS(1978), d; HUMANOIDS FROM THE DEEP(1980), d

Misc. Talkies
JUST THE TWO OF US(1975), d
Hay Peetrie
PEG OF OLD DRURY(1936, Brit.)
Remus Peets
TWILIGHT ZONE–THE MOVIE(1983)
Dick Pefferle
JOURNEY FOR MARGARET(1942), set d; GO NAKED IN THE WORLD(1961), set d; PERIOD OF ADJUSTMENT(1962), set d; WONDERFUL WORLD OF THE BROTHERS ERIMM, THE(1962), set d; PRIZE, THE(1963), set d; SPY IN THE GREEN HAT, THE(1966), set d; KARATE KILLERS, THE(1967), set d; IF HE HOLLERS, LET HIM GO(1968), set d; WHERE WERE YOU WHEN THE LIGHTS WENT OUT?(1968), set d; MALTESE BIPPY, THE(1969), set d
Richard A. Pefferle
DATE WITH JUDY, A(1948), set d; MADAME BOVARY(1949), set d; TWO WEEKS WITH LOVE(1950), set d; MR. IMPERIUM(1951), set d
Richard Pefferle
KISMET(1944), set d; MARRIAGE IS A PRIVATE AFFAIR(1944), set d; ANCHORS AWEIGH(1945), set d; YOLANDA AND THE THIEF(1945), set d; TILL THE CLOUDS ROLL BY(1946), set d; CASS TIMBERLANE(1947), set d; ON AN ISLAND WITH YOU(1948), set d; SUMMER HOLIDAY(1948), set d; SECRET GARDEN, THE(1949), set d; MILLION DOLLAR MERMAID(1952), set d; PRISONER OF ZENDA, THE(1952), set d; SCARAMOUCHE(1952), set d; KISS ME KATE(1953), set d; MOON-FLEET(1955), set d; HIGH SOCIETY(1956), set d; MEET ME IN LAS VEGAS(1956), set d; PARTY GIRL(1958), set d; NEVER SO FEW(1959), set d
Bob Pegg
BLACK JACK(1979, Brit.), m
Vesta Pegg
Silents
CRASHIN' THRU(1923)
Vester Pegg
DAWN TRAIL, THE(1931); SO IT'S SUNDAY(1932); JUDGE PRIEST(1934); STEAM-BOAT ROUND THE BEND(1935); BORN TO THE WEST(1937); FORLORN RI-VER(1937); THUNDER TRAIL(1937); STAGECOACH(1939); COLORADO(1940); MY LITTLE CHICKADEE(1940); UNDER TEXAS SKIES(1940); SHERIFF OF TOMB-STONE(1941)
Silents
OUTCASTS OF POKER FLAT, THE(1919); RIDERS OF VENGEANCE(1919); LAST CHANCE, THE(1921); RAIDERS, THE(1921); STRUGGLE, THE(1921); KICK BACK, THE(1922); BUCKING THE TRUTH(1926); JACK O'HEARTS(1926)
Misc. Silents
BLUE BLOOD AND RED(1916); MARKED MAN, A(1917); SECRET MAN, THE(1917); BUCKING BROADWAY(1918); HELL BENT(1918); SCARLET DROP, THE(1918); THIEVES' GOLD(1918); WILD WOMEN(1918); RIDER OF THE LAW(1919); WHEN THE DESERT SMILES(1919); GALLOPING DEVILS(1920); FIGHTING STRANGER, THE(1921); LONE FIGHTER(1923); HURRICANE HORSEMAN(1925); ROUGH GO-ING(1925)
Vestor Pegg
WEST OF ABILENE(1940)
Baby Peggy
Silents
CAPTAIN JANUARY(1924); HELEN'S BABIES(1924); LAW FORBIDS, THE(1924); APRIL FOOL(1926)
Dolores Donlon Peggy
SECURITY RISK(1954)
Peggy and Peanuts
THAT'S MY BABY(1944)
Peggy and Ready
LET'S MAKE A NIGHT OF IT(1937, Brit.)
Peggy the Bear
MAN IN THE WILDERNESS(1971, U.S./Span.)
Westbrook Pegler
MADISON SQUARE GARDEN(1932)
Lorenzo Pegoraro
DOLL THAT TOOK THE TOWN, THE(1965, Ital.), p
Henry Pegueo
PICNIC(1955)
Gino Peguri
BLOODY PIT OF HORROR, THE(1965, Ital.), m; WOMAN ON FIRE, A(1970, Ital.), m; SUPERSONIC MAN(1979, Span.), m
1984
NOSTALGHIA(1984, USSR/Ital.), md
Heinz Pehlke
DIE FASTNACHTSBEICHTE(1962, Ger.), ph; FREDDY UNTER FREMDEN STERN-EN(1962, Ger.), ph; CORRUPT ONES, THE(1967, Ger.), ph; DE SADE(1969), ph
Inger Pehrsson
SCENES FROM A MARRIAGE(1974, Swed.), cos; AUTUMN SONATA(1978, Swed.), cos; MONTENEGRO(1981, Brit./Swed.), cos
1984
AFTER THE REHEARSAL(1984, Swed.), cos
Betty Ting Pei
BRUCE LEE AND I(1976, Chi.)
Ting Pei
ONE NIGHT STAND(1976, Fr.)
Cheng Pei-pei
LOVERS' ROCK(1966, Taiwan)
Giacomo Peier
BLACK SPIDER, THE(1983, Swit.), spec eff
Peignot
GERVAISE(1956, Fr.)
Jo Peignot
DEMONIAQUE(1958, Fr.)
Barbara Peil
SUMMER SCHOOL TEACHERS(1977)
Paul L. Peil
BETRAYED WOMEN(1955), w
Paul Leslie Peil
GUNSMOKE IN TUCSON(1958), w

Franco Pellerani
CONFORMIST, THE(1971, Ital., Fr)
Alex Pelletier
ADOLESCENTS, THE(1967, Can.), w; JE T'AIME(1974, Can.), w
Andrea Pelletier
MARIE-ANN(1978, Can.)
Andree Pelletier
OUTRAGEOUS!(1977, Can.); THIRD WALKER, THE(1978, Can.)
Evon Pelletier
Silents
BRIDE OF THE STORM(1926)
Gilles Pelletier
THIRTEENTH LETTER, THE(1951); I CONFESS(1953)
Jean-Claude Pelletier
JE T'AIME, JE T'AIME(1972, Fr./Swed.), m
Louis Pelletier
BIG RED(1962), w; THOSE CALLOWAYS(1964), w; FOLLOW ME, BOYS!(1966), w; HORSE IN THE GRAY FLANNEL SUIT, THE(1968), w; SMITH(1969), w
Louis Pelletier, Jr.
COWBOY FROM BROOKLYN(1938), w; TWO GUYS FROM TEXAS(1948), w
Olga Pelletier
1984
HERE COMES SANTA CLAUS(1984), cos; MY NEW PARTNER(1984, Fr.), cos
Roger Pelletier
LA GUERRE EST FINIE(1967, Fr./Swed.)
Vincent Pelletier
SECRET LIFE OF WALTER MITTY, THE(1947); SENATOR WAS INDISCREET, THE(1947)
Yvonne Pelletier
RIDERS OF THE PURPLE SAGE(1931); YOUNG SINNERS(1931)
Misc. Talkies
LIGHTNING TRIGGERS(1935)
Silents
CHILDREN OF DIVORCE(1927)
John Pelletti
OUTRAGE(1950); SOUND OF FURY, THE(1950); CHICAGO CONFIDENTIAL(1957)
Antoinette Pellevant
MARCO POLO(1962, Fr./Ital.), w
Dudley Pelley
Silents
SAWDUST TRAIL(1924), w
William Dudley Pelley
COME ACROSS(1929), w; DRAG(1929), w
Silents
LIGHT IN THE DARK, THE(1922), w; AS A MAN LIVES(1923), w; FOG, THE(1923), w; HER FATAL MILLIONS(1923), w; SHOCK, THE(1923), w; LADIES TO BOARD(1924), w; TORMENT(1924), w; LADYBIRD, THE(1927), w; SUNSET DERBY, THE(1927), w
Pellicana
LAUGHING BOY(1934)
Jose Luis Pellicena
SWORD OF EL CID, THE(1965, Span./Ital.)
Oscar Pellicer
SUNSCORCHED(1966, Span./Ger.); DAY THE HOTLINE GOT HOT, THE(1968, Fr./Span.)
Pilar Pellicer
DAY OF THE EVIL GUN(1968); NAZARIN(1968, Mex.); ZORRO, THE GAY BLADE(1981)
Pina Pellicer
MACARIO(1961, Mex.); ONE-EYED JACKS(1961)
Mark Pellicori
SPRING BREAK(1983)
Biagio Pelligra
PLUCKED(1969, Fr./Ital.)
Diana Pelligrini
STREET MUSIC(1982), ed
George Pelling
GREEN FINGERS(1947); D-DAY, THE SIXTH OF JUNE(1956); 20 MILLION MILES TO EARTH(1957); ONE HUNDRED AND ONE DALMATIANS(1961); NOTORIOUS LANDLADY, THE(1962); MY FAIR LADY(1964); BRAINSTORM(1965); KING RAT(1965)
Maurice Pelling
DESERT PATROL(1962, Brit.), art d; CLEOPATRA(1963), art d; DALEKS–INVASION EARTH 2155 A.D.(1966, Brit.), set d; JULIUS CAESAR(1970, Brit.), art d; ANTONY AND CLEOPATRA(1973, Brit.), prod d
Liliana Pellini
SKY IS RED, THE(1952, Ital.)
Daryl Pellizzer
CLINIC, THE(1983, Aus.)
Cliff Pello
FRISCO KID, THE(1979)
Gabriel Pellon
FREDDY UNTER FREMDEN STERNEN(1962, Ger.), art d; INVISIBLE DR. MABUSE, THE(1965, Ger.), art d; BLOOD DEMON(1967, Ger.), art d
Giorgio Pelloni
TROPICS(1969, Ital.), ph, ed
Raffaella Pelloni
FURY OF THE PAGANS(1963, Ital.)
Cliff Pellow
TIDAL WAVE(1975, U.S./Jap.); STAY HUNGRY(1976); WHICH WAY IS UP?(1977); WHITE BUFFALO, THE(1977); LOVE AND BULLETS(1979, Brit.); WHITE DOG(1982)
Clifford A. Pellow
COMES A HORSEMAN(1978); LITTLE DRAGONS, THE(1980)
Patricia Pellows
TERROR EYES(1981)
Anthony Pelly
I'LL NEVER FORGET YOU(1951); DREAM MAKER, THE(1963, Brit.)

Charles Pelly
Silents
MANCHESTER MAN, THE(1920, Brit.)
Claire Pelly
DRIFTER, THE(1966)
Farrell Pelly
DARBY O'GILL AND THE LITTLE PEOPLE(1959)
Ina Pelly
ONE WOMAN'S STORY(1949, Brit.)
Tony Pelly
RECOIL(1953)
Don Pelosi
HILL, THE(1965, Brit.), m
R.N. Pelot
COUNTRY BOY(1966)
Karl Heinz Pelser
FROM THE LIFE OF THE MARIONETTES(1980, Ger.)
George Pelster
GETTING OVER(1981)
Tim Pelt
CROSS AND THE SWITCHBLADE, THE(1970); COME BACK CIHARLESTON BLUE(1972); SERPICO(1973); CLAUDINE(1974)
William Pelt
CUTTER AND BONE(1981)
Willie Pelt
SERPICO(1973)
Avraham Pelta
MADRON(1970, U.S./Israel)
Kanout Peltier
VIVA MARIA(1965, Fr./Ital.), ed
Kenout Peltier
ZAZIE(1961, Fr.), ed; VERY PRIVATE AFFAIR, A(1962, Fr./Ital.), ed; MURIEL(1963, Fr./Ital.), ed; MATA HARI(1965, Fr./Ital.), ed; TASTE FOR WOMEN, A(1966, Fr./Ital.), ed; CHAPPAQUA(1967), ed; SWEET HUNTERS(1969, Panama), ed; GOING PLACES(1974, Fr.), ed; ADOPTION, THE(1978, Fr.), ed
1984
ERENDIRA(1984, Mex./Fr./Ger.), ed; LA PETIT SIRENE(1984, Fr.), ed
I. Peltier
ADVENTURE IN ODESSA(1954, USSR)
T. Peltser
TIGER GIRL(1955, USSR)
T. Pelttser
JACK FROST(1966, USSR)
Nelson Peltz
HI, MOM!(1970)
Paul Peltz
MEN, THE(1950)
Roger Peltz
LOOSE SHOES(1980)
I. Peltzer
NO GREATER LOVE(1944, USSR)
Meeno Peluce
AMITYVILLE HORROR, THE(1979)
Misc. Talkies
DON'T GO NEAR THE PARK(1981)
M. Pelufa
MESSAGE TO GARCIA, A(1936)
Ana Luisa Peluffo
SAIL INTO DANGER(1957, Brit.); INVISIBLE MAN, THE(1958, Mex.); LIVING HEAD, THE(1969, Mex.)
Stelita Peluffo
OUTLAWS OF SONORA(1938)
Manuel Pelufo
TANGO BAR(1935); WE'RE IN THE LEGION NOW(1937)
Allen Peluso
FIRST NUDIE MUSICAL, THE(1976), ed
Claudia Peluso
BRINK'S JOB, THE(1978)
Lisa Peluso
SATURDAY NIGHT FEVER(1977)
Bridgit Pelz
1984
RUSH(1984, Ital.)
Duke Pelzer
Silents
RAMSHACKLE HOUSE(1924)
Steven E. Pelzer
LOOKIN' TO GET OUT(1982)
Clifford Pember
TILLY OF BLOOMSBURY(1931, Brit.), art d
Silents
WAY DOWN EAST(1920), art d
Ron Pember
POOR COW(1968, Brit.); OH! WHAT A LOVELY WAR(1969, Brit.); SUBTERFUGE(1969, US/Brit.); JULIUS CAESAR(1970, Brit.); YOUNG WINSTON(1972, Brit.); DEATHLINE(1973, Brit.); LAND THAT TIME FORGOT, THE(1975, Brit.); GLITTERBALL, THE(1977, Brit); MURDER BY DECREE(1979, Brit.); ROUGH CUT(1980, Brit.); BULLSHOT(1983)
1984
ORDEAL BY INNOCENCE(1984, Brit.)
Roy Pember
LOCK UP YOUR DAUGHTERS(1969, Brit.)
Antonia Pemberton
1984
PASSAGE TO INDIA, A(1984, Brit.)
Brock Pemberton
STAGE DOOR CANTEEN(1943)

Frank Pemberton
MURDER ON APPROVAL(1956, Brit.); IN THE WAKE OF A STRANGER(1960, Brit.)
Henry Pemberton
Misc. Silents
WAY WOMEN LOVE, THE(1920); LUXURY(1921)
Henry W. Pemberton
Misc. Silents
DEAD ALIVE, THE(1916); I ACCUSE(1916)
Marg Pemberton
TWO TICKETS TO BROADWAY(1951)
Margaret Pemberton
WESTWARD PASSAGE(1932), cos; WHAT PRICE HOLLYWOOD?(1932), cos
Marge Pemberton
RAZOR'S EDGE, THE(1946)
N.W. Baring Pemberton
WATCH BEVERLY(1932, Brit.), w; WISHBONE, THE(1933, Brit.), w
Reece Pemberton
TIME WITHOUT PITY(1957, Brit.), prod d; GUEST, THE(1963, Brit.), art d; NOTHING BUT THE BEST(1964, Brit.), art d; ONE WAY PENDULUM(1965, Brit.), prod d; ARABESQUE(1966), art d; OUR MOTHER'S HOUSE(1967, Brit.), art d; DIAMONDS FOR BREAKFAST(1968, Brit.), prod d
Rich Pemberton
TERROR ON TOUR(1980)
Tom Pemberton
LEGEND OF NIGGER CHARLEY, THE(1972)
Noel Pemberton-Billing
HIGH TREASON(1929, Brit.), w
Georgia Pembleton
HAPPY DAYS(1930)
Pemborke
JAZZ CINDERELLA(1930), w
Clifford Pembroke
Silents
SANCTUARY(1916, Brit.); IF THOU WERT BLIND(1917, Brit.); LOVE'S OLD SWEET SONG(1917, Brit.); POWER OF RIGHT, THE(1919, Brit.); IRISH DESTINY(1925, Brit.)
Misc. Silents
FOR HER PEOPLE(1914, Brit.); SHEPHERD LASSIE OF ARGYLE, THE(1914, Brit.); THROUGH THE VALLEY OF SHADOWS(1914, Brit.)
George Pembroke
FALSE EVIDENCE(1937, Brit.); DARTS ARE TRUMPS(1938, Brit.); IRISH AND PROUD OF IT(1938, Ireland); MERELY MR. HAWKINS(1938, Brit.); BURIED ALIVE(1939); COWBOY FROM SUNDOWN(1940); FLYING WILD(1941); INVISIBLE GHOST, THE(1941); MEET JOHN DOE(1941); PAPER BULLETS(1941); SPOOKS RUN WILD(1941); BLACK DRAGONS(1942); DAWN EXPRESS, THE(1942); I KILLED THAT MAN(1942); THEY ALL KISSED THE BRIDE(1942); DRUMS OF FU MANCHU(1943); BLUEBEARD(1944); CALL NORTHSIDE 777(1948); CARBINE WILLIAMS(1952); RED SNOW(1952); GIRL RUSH, THE(1955); I'LL CRY TOMORROW(1955); FEAR STRIKES OUT(1957); HELL CANYON OUTLAWS(1957); OUTLAW'S SON(1957); SHOOT-OUT AT MEDICINE BEND(1957); SHOWDOWN AT BOOT HILL(1958)
Misc. Talkies
LAST ALARM, THE(1940)
Jerry Pembroke
Misc. Silents
CHEROKEE KID, THE(1927)
Scott Pembroke
SHOULD A GIRL MARRY?(1929), d; JAZZ CINDERELLA(1930), d; LAST DANCE, THE(1930), d; MEDICINE MAN, THE(1930), d; OKAY AMERICA(1932), w; KING FOR A NIGHT(1933), w; LAWLESS NINETIES, THE(1936), w; OREGON TRAIL, THE(1936), d; COTTON QUEEN(1937, Brit.), w; TELEPHONE OPERATOR(1938), d
Silents
LIGHT IN THE WINDOW, THE(1927), d; RAGTIME(1927), d; TERROR OF BAR X, THE(1927), d; GYPSY OF THE NORTH(1928), d; MY HOME TOWN(1928), d; SWEET SIXTEEN(1928), d
Misc. Silents
FOR LADIES ONLY(1927), d; GALLOPING THUNDER(1927), d; POLLY OF THE MOVIES(1927), d; BLACK PEARL, THE(1928), d; BRANDED MAN(1928), d; DIVINE SINNER(1928), d; LAW AND THE MAN(1928), d; SISTERS OF EVE(1928), d; BROTHERS(1929), d; SHANGHAI ROSE(1929), d; TWO SISTERS(1929), d
Stanley Pembroke
Misc. Silents
WHATEVER THE COST(1918)
Lilo Pempeit
EFFI BRIEST(1974, Ger.); IN A YEAR OF THIRTEEN MOONS(1980, Ger.); LILI MARLEEN(1981, Ger.); VERONIKA VOSS(1982, Ger.)
Howard C. Pen
1984
SWORD OF THE VALIANT(1984, Brit.), w
Janine Pen
Silents
NAPOLEON(1927, Fr.)
Albert Pena
WHEN YOU COMIN' BACK, RED RYDER?(1979)
Andrew Pena
NORTHWEST PASSAGE(1940)
Elizabeth Pena
TIMES SQUARE(1980); THEY ALL LAUGHED(1981)
Felipe Pena
SUNSCORCHED(1966, Span./Ger.)
Garcia Pena
TORCH, THE(1950)
J. Noe Pena
CARMEN(1949, Span.)
Julio Pena
STORM OVER THE ANDES(1935); ALEXANDER THE GREAT(1956); REVOLT OF THE SLAVES, THE(1961, Ital./Span./Ger.); HAPPY THIEVES, THE(1962); CASTILIAN, THE(1963, Span./U.S.); KID RODELO(1966, U.S./Span.); MINNESOTA CLAY(1966, Ital./Fr./Span.); SUNSCORCHED(1966, Span./Ger.); WEB OF VIOLENCE(1966, Ital./Span.); CHIMES AT MIDNIGHT(1967, Span.,Switz.); HELLBENDERS, THE(1967, U.S./Ital./Span.); SAVAGE PAMPAS(1967, Span./Arg.); ONE STEP TO

HELL(1969, U.S./Ital./Span.); EL CONDOR(1970); WEREWOLF VS. THE VAMPIRE WOMAN, THE(1970, Span./Ger.); RED SUN(1972, Fr./Ital./Span.); TRAVELS WITH MY AUNT(1972, Brit.)
1984
ESCAPE FROM SEGOVIA(1984, Span.), ed
Luis Pena
MAIN STREET(1956, Span.); TRAPPED IN TANGIERS(1960, Ital./Span.)
Luz Maria Pena
GREAT SCOUT AND CATHOUSE THURSDAY, THE(1976); HIGH RISK(1981)
Manuel Pena
CEREMONY, THE(1963, U.S./Span.)
Nettie Pena
HOME SWEET HOME(1981), d
Pascual G. Pena
LIFE IN THE BALANCE, A(1955)
Pascual Garcia Pena
BIG STEAL, THE(1949); BEAST OF HOLLOW MOUNTAIN, THE(1956)
Pascual Pena
SOMBRERO(1953); JIVARO(1954); BLACK SCORPION, THE(1957)
Pasqual Garcia Pena
MY MAN AND I(1952)
Pasqual Garcia Pena
CITY OF BAD MEN(1953)
Pasquel Pena
TREASURE OF PANCHO VILLA, THE(1955)
Sergio Pena
AFFAIR IN HAVANA(1957)
Louis Penafiel
MASTER OF HORROR(1965, Arg.), w
Luis Penafiel
HOUSE THAT SCREAMED, THE(1970, Span.), w; ISLAND OF THE DAMNED(1976, Span.), w
Gaby Penalba
NUN AT THE CROSSROADS, A(1970, Ital./Span.), ed
Juanita Penaloza
VALDEZ IS COMING(1971)
Juan Penas
MAN WHO WAGGED HIS TAIL, THE(1961, Ital./Span.), ed
Beverly Penberthy
I NEVER SANG FOR MY FATHER(1970)
P.L. Penbroke
Misc. Silents
GIRL WHO WON OUT, THE(1917)
Denise Pence
JESUS CHRIST, SUPERSTAR(1973)
Glen A. Pence
NIGHT OF THE ZOMBIES(1981)
George Pencheff
LEAVE IT TO ME(1937, Brit.)
Jean-Claude Penchenat
INQUISITOR, THE(1982, Fr.)
1984
LE BAL(1984, Fr./Ital./Algeria), a, w
Marius Penczner
Misc. Talkies
I WAS A ZOMBIE FOR THE F.B.I.(1982), d
Austin Pendleton
GREAT SMOKEY ROADBLOCK, THE(1978)
Gaylord Pendleton
INFORMER, THE(1935); HOMECOMING(1948)
Nat Pendleton
RULING VOICE, THE(1931)
Helen Pender
ARABIAN NIGHTS(1942); MILDRED PIERCE(1945); NEVER SAY GOODBYE(1946); NIGHT AND DAY(1946); ESCAPE ME NEVER(1947)
Tommy Pender
WATER BABIES, THE(1979, Brit.)
Penderecki
LES GAULOISES BLEUES(1969, Fr.), m
Krystof Penderecki
JE T'AIME, JE T'AIME(1972, Fr./Swed.), m
Krzysztof Penderecki
SARAGOSSA MANUSCRIPT, THE(1972, Pol.), m; SHINING, THE(1980), m
Tony Penderell
YELLOW ROBE, THE(1954, Brit.)
Les Pendergast
1984
GIVE MY REGARDS TO BROAD STREET(1984, Brit.)
Tana Pendergast
1984
GIVE MY REGARDS TO BROAD STREET(1984, Brit.)
Teddy Pendergrass
SOUP FOR ONE(1982)
Hugh Pendexter
Silents
WOLF LAW(1922), w
Ann Pendlebury
PETERSEN(1974, Aus.)
Ann Pendleton
ROOTIN' TOOTIN' RHYTHM(1937)
Austin Pendleton
PETULIA(1968, U.S./Brit.); SKIDOO(1968); CATCH-22(1970); EVERY LITTLE CROOK AND NANNY(1972); WHAT'S UP, DOC?(1972); THIEF WHO CAME TO DINNER, THE(1973); FRONT PAGE, THE(1974); MUPPET MOVIE, THE(1979); STARTING OVER(1979); FIRST FAMILY(1980); SIMON(1980)
Dave Pendleton
YOUNGBLOOD(1978)

David Pendleton
ABDUCTION(1975); MIKEY AND NICKY(1976)
Diane Pendleton
AROUND THE WORLD(1943); CAROLINA BLUES(1944)
Edna Pendleton
Silents
20,000 LEAGUES UNDER THE SEA(1916)
Eugene Pendleton
WIRETAPPERS(1956), ed; PERSUADER, THE(1957), ed; RESTLESS ONES, THE(1965), ed; FOR PETE'S SAKE!(1966), ed; TWO A PENNY(1968, Brit.), ed
Gaylord [Steve] Pendleton
SERGEANT YORK(; MANSLAUGHTER(1930); UP THE RIVER(1930); LAST PARADE, THE(1931); SEAS BENEATH, THE(1931); YOUNG SINNERS(1931); LIFE IN THE RAW(1933); UNKNOWN VALLEY(1933); WOMAN ACCUSED(1933); LOVE PAST THIRTY(1934); PLOUGH AND THE STARS, THE(1936); EXCLUSIVE(1937); HOLY TERROR, THE(1937); INTERNES CAN'T TAKE MONEY(1937); DUKE OF WEST POINT, THE(1938); I AM THE LAW(1938); RIDE A CROOKED MILE(1938); SKY GIANT(1938); DISPUTED PASSAGE(1939); WHEN TOMORROW COMES(1939); ENEMY AGENT(1940); FLIGHT COMMAND(1940); GRAPES OF WRATH(1940); I'M NOBODY'S SWEETHEART NOW(1940); KNUTE ROCKNE–ALL AMERICAN(1940); MANHATTAN HEARTBEAT(1940); ONE CROWDED NIGHT(1940); ROAD TO SINGAPORE(1940); SAILOR'S LADY(1940); THOSE WERE THE DAYS(1940); YOUNG BUFFALO BILL(1940); DIVE BOMBER(1941); KNOCKOUT(1941); MEN OF THE TIMBERLAND(1941); MILLION DOLLAR BABY(1941); NAVY BLUES(1941); TO THE SHORES OF TRIPOLI(1942); RETURN OF RIN TIN TIN, THE(1947); UNTAMED FURY(1947); WILD HARVEST(1947); BEYOND GLORY(1948); ENCHANTMENT(1948); HE WALKED BY NIGHT(1948); HIGHWAY 13(1948); ALIAS NICK BEAL(1949); ARSON, INC.(1949); BLAZING TRAIL, THE(1949); JOHNNY ALLEGRO(1949); RIDE, RYDER, RIDE!(1949); ROLL, THUNDER, ROLL!(1949); SKY DRAGON(1949); SKY LINER(1949); SONS OF NEW MEXICO(1949); GREAT MISSOURI RAID, THE(1950); GUNFIRE(1950); NO MAN OF HER OWN(1950); RIO GRANDE(1950); ROOKIE FIREMAN(1950); SUNSET IN THE WEST(1950); WHERE DANGER LIVES(1950); BUCKAROO SHERIFF OF TEXAS(1951); CHICAGO CALLING(1951); DESERT OF LOST MEN(1951); PURPLE HEART DIARY(1951); SNIPER, THE(1952); GLENN MILLER STORY, THE(1953); GREAT JESSE JAMES RAID, THE(1953); KILLERS FROM SPACE(1954); TARGET EARTH(1954); LOVING YOU(1957); NIGHT RUNNER, THE(1957); UNHOLY WIFE, THE(1957); I MARRIED A WOMAN(1958); ONCE UPON A HORSE(1958); OCEAN'S ELEVEN(1960)
Misc. Talkies
FIGHTING TO LIVE(1934); BORDER CITY RUSTLERS(1953)
Silents
SUCCESS(1923)
Gaylord Steve Pendleton
EYES OF THE UNDERWORLD(1943)
Karen Pendleton
WESTWARD HO THE WAGONS!(1956)
Lynda Pendleton
DON'T LOOK IN THE BASEMENT(1973), art d
Nat Pendleton
BIG POND, THE(1930); LAST OF THE DUANES(1930); LAUGHING LADY, THE(1930); LILIOM(1930); SEA WOLF, THE(1930); BLONDE CRAZY(1931); FAIR WARNING(1931); MANHATTAN PARADE(1931); MR. LEMON OF ORANGE(1931); SEAS BENEATH, THE(1931); SECRET WITNESS, THE(1931); SPIRIT OF NOTRE DAME, THE(1931); STAR WITNESS(1931); ATTORNEY FOR THE DEFENSE(1932); BEAST OF THE CITY, THE(1932); BY WHOSE HAND?(1932); FLESH(1932); HELL FIRE AUSTIN(1932); HORSE FEATHERS(1932); NIGHT CLUB LADY(1932); PLAY GIRL(1932); SIGN OF THE CROSS, THE(1932); TAXI!(1932); BABY FACE(1933); CHIEF, THE(1933); DECEPTION(1933), a, w; GOLDIE GETS ALONG(1933); I'M NO ANGEL(1933); LADY FOR A DAY(1933); PENTHOUSE(1933); WHISTLING IN THE DARK(1933); WHITE SISTER, THE(1933); CAT'S PAW, THE(1934); DEATH OF THE DIAMOND(1934); DEFENSE HESTS(1934); FUGITIVE LOVERS(1934); GAY BRIDE, THE(1934); GIRL FROM MISSOURI, THE(1934); LAZY RIVER(1934); MANHATTAN MELODRAMA(1934); SING AND LIKE IT(1934); STRAIGHT IS THE WAY(1934); THIN MAN, THE(1934); BABY FACE HARRINGTON(1935); CALM YOURSELF(1935); IT'S IN THE AIR(1935); MURDER IN THE FLEET(1935); RECKLESS(1935); TIMES SQUARE LADY(1935); GARDEN MURDER CASE, THE(1936); GREAT ZIEGFELD, THE(1936); LUCKIEST GIRL IN THE WORLD, THE(1936); SING ME A LOVE SONG(1936); SWORN ENEMY(1936); TRAPPED BY TELEVISION(1936); TWO IN A CROWD(1936); GANGWAY(1937, Brit.); LIFE BEGINS IN COLLEGE(1937); SONG OF THE CITY(1937); UNDER COVER OF NIGHT(1937); ARSENE LUPIN RETURNS(1938); CHASER, THE(1938); CROWD ROARS, THE(1938); FAST COMPANY(1938); MEET THE MAYOR(1938); SHOPWORN ANGEL(1938); SWING YOUR LADY(1938); YOUNG DR. KILDARE(1938); ANOTHER THIN MAN(1939); AT THE CIRCUS(1939); BURN 'EM UP O'CONNER(1939); CALLING DR. KILDARE(1939); IT'S A WONDERFUL WORLD(1939); ON BORROWED TIME(1939); SECRET OF DR. KILDARE, THE(1939); 6000 ENEMIES(1939); DR. KILDARE GOES HOME(1940); DR. KILDARE'S CRISIS(1940); DR. KILDARE'S STRANGE CASE(1940); FLIGHT COMMAND(1940); GHOST COMES HOME, THE(1940); GOLDEN FLEECING, THE(1940); NORTHWEST PASSAGE(1940); PHANTOM RAIDERS(1940); BUCK PRIVATES(1941); TOP SERGEANT MULLIGAN(1941); CALLING DR. GILLESPIE(1942); DR. GILLESPIE'S NEW ASSISTANT(1942); JAIL HOUSE BLUES(1942); MAD DOCTOR OF MARKET STREET, THE(1942); DR. GILLESPIE'S CRIMINAL CASE(1943); SWING FEVER(1943); DEATH VALLEY(1946); BUCK PRIVATES COME HOME(1947); SCARED TO DEATH(1947)
Silents
LET'S GET MARRIED(1926)
Robert B. Pendleton
SOURDOUGH(1977), p
Ross Pendleton
HOME AND AWAY(1956, Brit.)
Steve Gaylord Pendleton
TWENTIETH CENTURY(1934); GERONIMO(1939)
Wyman Pendleton
SIDELONG GLANCES OF A PIGEON KICKER, THE(1970); SEDUCTION OF JOE TYNAN, THE(1979)
Anthony Pendrell
BLUE SCAR(1949, Brit.); WHAT A CARRY ON!(1949, Brit.); SHADOW OF THE PAST(1950, Brit.); STICK 'EM UP(1950, Brit.); BLIND MAN'S BLUFF(1952, Brit.); HOT ICE(1952, Brit.); NO HAUNT FOR A GENTLEMAN(1952, Brit.); VIOLENT STRANGER(1957, Brit.); MAN WHO WOULDN'T TALK, THE(1958, Brit.); RUNAWAY,

THE(1964, Brit.)
Ernest Pendrell
VIOLATORS, THE(1957), w
Nicolette Pendrell
HE WHO RIDES A TIGER(1966, Brit.)
Tony Pendrell
HOME SWEET HOME(1945, Brit.); I'LL TURN TO YOU(1946, Brit.)
Michael Pendrey
BLADE(1973)
Dennis Pendrith
HOMER(1970)
Michael Pendry
GOD TOLD ME TO(1976)
Richard Pendry
CANNON FOR CORDOBA(1970); REVOLUTIONARY, THE(1970, Brit.)
Julian Pene, Jr.
Misc. Talkies
SKATEBOARD MADNESS(1980), d
Yves Peneau
WAR OF THE BUTTONS(1963 Fr.)
The Penegrysis Greek Folk Dance and Songs Society
BOY ON A DOLPHIN(1957)
Emma Penella
NOT ON YOUR LIFE(1965, Ital./Span.)
Erick Penet
NAKED HEARTS(1970, Fr.)
Rene Penetra
WEEKEND AT DUNKIRK(1966, Fr./Ital.)
Christopher Penfold
TAKE ME HIGH(1973, Brit.), w
Mark Penfold
SILVER BEARS(1978)
Lo Peng
FLYING GUILLOTINE, THE(1975, Chi.)
Tien Peng
DRAGON INN(1968, Chi.)
Misc. Talkies
RETURN OF 18 BRONZEMEN(1984)
Elizabeth Pengally
SHIPS WITH WINGS(1942, Brit.)
Penge Formation Dancers
MAKE MINE A MILLION(1965, Brit.)
Thaao Penghlis
SLOW DANCING IN THE BIG CITY(1978); BELL JAR, THE(1979); ALTERED STATES(1980)
Ivan Pengov
CAVE OF THE LIVING DEAD(1966, Yugo./Ger.), art d
Susan Penhaligan
CONFESSIONAL, THE(1977, Brit.)
Susan Penhaligon
UNDER MILK WOOD(1973, Brit.); LAND THAT TIME FORGOT, THE(1975, Brit.); NASTY HABITS(1976, Brit.); UNCANNY, THE(1977, Brit./Can.); LEOPARD IN THE SNOW(1979, Brit./Can.); NO SEX PLEASE–WE'RE BRITISH(1979, Brit.); PATRICK(1979, Aus.); SOLDIER OF ORANGE(1979, Dutch)
Jon Penington
HEART WITHIN, THE(1957, Brit.), p; DUBLIN NIGHTMARE(1958, Brit.), p; MAN WHO LIKED FUNERALS, THE(1959, Brit.), p; FACES IN THE DARK(1960, Brit.), p; IN THE WAKE OF A STRANGER(1960, Brit.), p; SHADOW OF THE CAT, THE(1961, Brit.), p; VALIANT, THE(1962, Brit./Ital.), p; CASE OF THE 44'S, THE(1964 Brit./Den.), p
Eric Peniston
MISSISSIPPI SUMMER(1971), p
Rainer Penkert
TOXI(1952, Ger.); REST IS SILENCE, THE(1960, Ger.); REVOLT OF THE SLAVES, THE(1961, Ital./Span./Ger.); MORITURI(1965)
Riner Penkert
LONGEST DAY, THE(1962)
Charles Penland
FAST BREAK(1979)
Michael Penland
FOREIGNER, THE(1978), ed
Tim Penland
MACKINTOSH & T.J.(1975), p
Derek Penley
ODETTE(1951, Brit.)
Derick Penley
EYE WITNESS(1950, Brit.)
Derrick Penley
SKIMPY IN THE NAVY(1949, Brit.)
Graham Penley
SHIPS WITH WINGS(1942, Brit.); CANDLELIGHT IN ALGERIA(1944, Brit.)
Lea Penman
FANCY PANTS(1950); STELLA(1950); WE'RE NO ANGELS(1955); PORTLAND EXPOSE(1957)
Patricia Penman
IN THE WAKE OF THE BOUNTY(1933, Aus.)
Alan Penn
HIGH FLIGHT(1957, Brit.); ZOO BABY(1957, Brit.)
Misc. Talkies
BEGGING THE RING(1979, Brit.)
Ann Penn
RADIO LOVER(1936, Brit.)
Arthur Penn
LEFT-HANDED GUN, THE(1958), d; MIRACLE WORKER, THE(1962), d; MICKEY ONE(1965), p&d; CHASE, THE(1966), d; BONNIE AND CLYDE(1967), d; ALICE'S RESTAURANT(1969), d, w; LITTLE BIG MAN(1970), d; NIGHT MOVES(1975), d; MISSOURI BREAKS, THE(1976), d; FOUR FRIENDS(1981), p, d, p, d

Christopher Penn
ALL THE RIGHT MOVES(1983); RUMBLE FISH(1983)
1984
FOOTLOOSE(1984); WILD LIFE, THE(1984)
Clifford Penn
FALL GUY(1947)
Dalia Penn
VILLAGE OF DAUGHTERS(1962, Brit.)
Dena Penn
DAYS OF GLORY(1944); HEAVENLY DAYS(1944)
Edith Penn
WINGS OVER HONOLULU(1937); CROSSROADS(1942)
Leo Penn
NOT WANTED(1949); UNDERCOVER MAN, THE(1949); STORY ON PAGE ONE, THE(1959); MAN CALLED ADAM, A(1966), d; SIXTH AND MAIN(1977)
1984
WILD LIFE, THE(1984)
Leonard M. Penn
RANGE LAND(1949)
Leonard Penn
BETWEEN TWO WOMEN(1937); FIREFLY, THE(1937); WOMEN MEN MARRY, THE(1937); ARSENE LUPIN RETURNS(1938); GIRL OF THE GOLDEN WEST, THE(1938); JUDGE HARDY'S CHILDREN(1938); LADIES IN DISTRESS(1938); MAN-PROOF(1938); MARIE ANTOINETTE(1938); THREE COMRADES(1938); TOY WIFE, THE(1938); YOUNG DR. KILDARE(1938); ALMOST A GENTLEMAN(1939); BACHELOR MOTHER(1939); WAY OF ALL FLESH, THE(1940); HIGH SCHOOL HERO(1946); HOPPY'S HOLIDAY(1947); I COVER BIG TOWN(1947); KILLER AT LARGE(1947); COURTIN' TROUBLE(1948); DEAD DON'T DREAM, THE(1948); OUTLAW BRAND(1948); PARTNERS OF THE SUNSET(1948); THREE MUSKETEERS, THE(1948); GIRL FROM SAN LORENZO, THE(1950); GUNFIRE(1950); LAW OF THE BADLANDS(1950); LONELY HEARTS BANDITS(1950); SILVER RAIDERS(1950); WOMAN FROM HEADQUARTERS(1950); ON THE LOOSE(1951); SIROCCO(1951); SOUTH OF CALIENTE(1951); BARBED WIRE(1952); NO HOLDS BARRED(1952); OUTLAW WOMEN(1952); THIEF OF DAMASCUS(1952); YANK IN INDO-CHINA, A(1952); FANGS OF THE ARCTIC(1953); FLAME OF CALCUTTA(1953); MURDER WITHOUT TEARS(1953); SAVAGE MUTINY(1953); KING RICHARD AND THE CRUSADERS(1954); SARACEN BLADE, THE(1954); STAR IS BORN, A(1954); TO CATCH A THIEF(1955); IN THE MONEY(1958); SPARTACUS(1960)
Misc. Talkies
STAGECOACH DRIVER(1951); WANTED DEAD OR ALIVE(1951); MARSHALS IN DISGUISE(1954)
M. O. Penn
Silents
PRINCE OF INDIA, A(1914)
Nina Penn
SPLENDOR(1935)
Peter Penn
I'LL TURN TO YOU(1946, Brit.); SPRINGTIME(1948, Brit.)
Sean Penn
TAPS(1981); FAST TIMES AT RIDGEMONT HIGH(1982); BAD BOYS(1983)
1984
CRACKERS(1984); RACING WITH THE MOON(1984)
Rosa Maria Penna
ANTONIO DAS MORTES(1970, Braz.)
Tarva Penna
RUNAWAY QUEEN, THE(1935, Brit.); PRISON BREAKER(1936, Brit.); SHOW GOES ON, THE(1938, Brit.); CHALLENGE, THE(1939, Brit.); THEY KNEW MR. KNIGHT(1945, Brit.)
Tarver Penna
AVENGING HAND, THE(1936, Brit.); MAN WITH 100 FACES, THE(1938, Brit.)
Pennachi
SEVEN HILLS OF ROME, THE(1958)
Malvina Penne
CHLOE IN THE AFTERNOON(1972, Fr.)
Raimondo Penne
SACCO AND VANZETTI(1971, Ital./Fr.)
D.A. Pennebaker
BEYOND THE LAW(1968), ph; WILD 90(1968), a, ph; MAIDSTONE(1970), ph
Judy Pennebaker
FARMER'S OTHER DAUGHTER, THE(1965)
Chuck Pennell
WHOLE SHOOTIN' MATCH, THE(1979), m
1984
LAST NIGHT AT THE ALAMO(1984), m
Dan Pennell
Silents
JAVA HEAD(1923)
Daniel Pennell
Silents
NANETTE OF THE WILDS(1916)
Misc. Silents
HIS BRIDAL NIGHT(1919)
Eagle Pennell
WHOLE SHOOTIN' MATCH, THE(1979), p, d, w, ph
1984
LAST NIGHT AT THE ALAMO(1984), a, p, d, ed
Ken Pennell
MIDWAY(1976)
Larry Pennell
FAR HORIZONS, THE(1955); HELL'S HORIZON(1955); SEVEN ANGRY MEN(1955); COURT JESTER, THE(1956); VAGABOND KING, THE(1956); DEVIL'S HAIRPIN, THE(1957); FBI STORY, THE(1959); FLAMING FRONTIER(1968, Ger./Yugo.); GREAT WHITE HOPE, THE(1970); JOURNEY THROUGH ROSEBUD(1972); REVENGERS, THE(1972, U.S./Mex.); MATILDA(1978); MAN WITH BOGART'S FACE, THE(1980); PERSONAL BEST(1982); METALSTORM: THE DESTRUCTION OF JARED-SYN(1983)
Misc. Talkies
OUR MAN IN JAMAICA(1965); BROTHER, CRY FOR ME(1970)

Nicholas Pennell
RASPUTIN–THE MAD MONK(1966, Brit.); ISADORA(1968, Brit.); ONLY WHEN I LARF(1968, Brit.); BATTLE OF BRITAIN, THE(1969, Brit.); DAVID COPPER-FIELD(1970, Brit.); CRY OF THE PENGUINS(1972, Brit.)
R. O. Pennell
ON THE LEVEL(1930)
Silents
RENDEZVOUS, THE(1923)
Richard Pennell
Silents
OLYMPIC HERO, THE(1928)
Aldo Pennelli
PAYMENT IN BLOOD(1968, Ital.), ph
Ed Penner
MAKE MINE MUSIC(1946), w
Erdman Penner
PINOCCHIO(1940), w; MELODY TIME(1948), w; ADVENTURES OF ICHABOD AND MR. TOAD(1949), w; CINDERELLA(1950), w; ALICE IN WONDERLAND(1951), w; PETER PAN(1953), w; LADY AND THE TRAMP(1955), w
H. John Penner
MISSION GALACTICA: THE CYLON ATTACK(1979), ph
J. E. Penner
UNHINGED(1982)
Joe Penner
COLLEGE RHYTHM(1934); COLLEGIATE(1936); LIFE OF THE PARTY, THE(1937); NEW FACES OF 1937(1937); GO CHASE YOURSELF(1938), a, m/l "I'm From the City," Hal Raynor; I'M FROM THE CITY(1938); MR. DOODLE KICKS OFF(1938); DAY THE BOOKIES WEPT, THE(1939); BOYS FROM SYRACUSE(1940); MILLIONAIRE PLAYBOY(1940)
Joseph Penner
DESPERATE WOMEN, THE(?)
Alan Penney
MONEY MOVERS(1978, Aus.)
Allan Penney
MATCHLESS(1974, Aus.); EARTHLING, THE(1980)
Edmund Penney
FORT YUMA(1955); UNDER FIRE(1957); BALLAD OF CABLE HOGUE, THE(1970), w
Hannibal Penney, Jr.
LOVE IN A TAXI(1980)
Jennifer Penney
ROMEO AND JULIET(1966, Brit.)
Ralph Penney
DEVIL COMMANDS, THE(1941); ROAD TO MOROCCO(1942)
J. Ronald Pennick
DRUMS ALONG THE MOHAWK(1939)
Jack Pennick [Ronald Pennick]
SERGEANT YORK(; UNDER TWO FLAGS(1936); VIRGINIAN, THE(1929); BORN RECKLESS(1930); MIN AND BILL(1930); WAY OUT WEST(1930); AIR MAIL(1932); HELL DIVERS(1932); IF I HAD A MILLION(1932); PHANTOM EXPRESS, THE(1932); RENEGADES OF THE WEST(1932); MAN OF SENTIMENT, A(1933); SKYWAY(1933); STRANGE PEOPLE(1933); TUGBOAT ANNIE(1933); NOTORIOUS SOPHIE LANG, THE(1934); WORLD MOVES ON, THE(1934); DON'T BET ON BLONDES(1935); GOIN' TO TOWN(1935); STEAMBOAT ROUND THE BEND(1935); DRIFT FENCE(1936); GREAT GUY(1936); PLOUGH AND THE STARS, THE(1936); PRISONER OF SHARK ISLAND, THE(1936); PRIVATE NUMBER(1936); ROSE MARIE(1936); DEVIL'S PLAY-GROUND(1937); DOUBLE OR NOTHING(1937); LAST GANGSTER, THE(1937); NAVY BLUE AND GOLD(1937); WEE WILLIE WINKIE(1937); ALEXANDER'S RAGTIME BAND(1938); COCOANUT GROVE(1938); KING OF THE NEWSBOYS(1938); SUBMA-RINE PATROL(1938); TIP-OFF GIRLS(1938); YOU AND ME(1938); MOUNTAIN RHYTHM(1939); SERGEANT MADDEN(1939); STAGECOACH(1939); STAR MAKER, THE(1939); UNION PACIFIC(1939); YOUNG MR. LINCOLN(1939); GRAPES OF WRATH(1940); LONG VOYAGE HOME, THE(1940); NORTHWEST MOUNTED PO-LICE(1940); WESTERNER, THE(1940); LADY FROM LOUISIANA(1941); TOBACCO ROAD(1941); WILD GEESE CALLING(1941); THEY WERE EXPENDABLE(1945); MY DARLING CLEMENTINE(1946); UNCONQUERED(1947); FORT APACHE(1948); THREE GODFATHERS, THE(1948); FIGHTING KENTUCKIAN, THE(1949); SHE WORE A YELLOW RIBBON(1949); RIO GRANDE(1950); TRIPOLI(1950); WHEN WILLIE COMES MARCHING HOME(1950); FIGHTING COAST GUARD(1951); OPER-ATION PACIFIC(1951); SEA HORNET, THE(1951); HOODLUM EMPIRE(1952); WHAT PRICE GLORY?(1952); BEAST FROM 20,000 FATHOMS, THE(1953); SUN SHINES BRIGHT, THE(1953); LAST FRONTIER, THE(1955); LONG GRAY LINE, THE(1955); MISTER ROBERTS(1955); SEARCHERS, THE(1956); WINGS OF EAGLES, THE(1957); LAST HURRAH, THE(1958); HORSE SOLDIERS, THE(1959); ALAMO, THE(1960), tech adv; SERGEANT RUTLEDGE(1960); TWO RODE TOGETHER(1961); HOW THE WEST WAS WON(1962); MAN WHO SHOT LIBERTY VALANCE, THE(1962)
Silents
BRONCHO TWISTER(1927); LONE EAGLE, THE(1927); FOUR SONS(1928); STRONG BOY(1929)
Misc. Silents
PLASTERED IN PARIS(1928)
Tom Pennick
MY BROTHER'S WEDDING(1983), ed
Jon Pennigton
AT THE STROKE OF NINE(1957, Brit.), p, w
Ann Pennington
GOLD DIGGERS OF BROADWAY(1929); IS EVERYBODY HAPPY?(1929); NIGHT PARADE(1929, Brit.); TANNED LEGS(1929); HAPPY DAYS(1930); GREAT ZIEG-FELD, THE(1936); TEXAS TERRORS(1940); UNHOLY PARTNERS(1941); CHINA GIRL(1942)
Silents
RAINBOW PRINCESS, THE(1916); ANTICS OF ANN, THE(1917); KISS IN THE DARK, A(1925); LUCKY HORSESHOE, THE(1925); MAD DANCER(1925); PRETTY LADIES(1925)
Misc. Silents
SUSIE SNOWFLAKE(1916); LITTLE BOY SCOUT, THE(1917); SUNSHINE NAN(1918); MADAME BEHAVE(1925)

Chuck Pennington
PLANET OF DINOSAURS(1978)
Earl Pennington
IN PRAISE OF OLDER WOMEN(1978, Can.); TOMORROW NEVER COMES(1978, Brit./Can.); CITY ON FIRE(1979 Can.); JACOB TWO-TWO MEETS THE HOODED FANG(1979, Can.); HAPPY BIRTHDAY TO ME(1981); OF UNKNOWN ORIGIN(1983, Can.)
Edna Pennington
Misc. Silents
SLOW AS LIGHTING(1923)
Janice Pennington
I LOVE MY WIFE(1970)
John Pennington
EXPRESSO BONGO(1959, Brit.), p
Jon Pennington
ZOO BABY(1957, Brit.), p; CROWNING TOUCH, THE(1959, Brit.), p; MOUSE THAT ROARED, THE(1959, Brit.), p; COMEDY MAN, THE(1964), p; LIQUIDATOR, THE(1966, Brit.), p; PLANK, THE(1967, Brit.), p; ALF 'N' FAMILY(1968, Brit.), p
Marla Pennington
JIM, THE WORLD'S GREATEST(1976); NATIONAL LAMPOON'S CLASS REUNION(1982)
Michael Pennington
HAMLET(1969, Brit.); RETURN OF THE JEDI(1983)
Ray Pennington
DOWN OUR ALLEY(1939, Brit.)
C. Pennington-Richards
ESTHER WATERS(1948, Brit.), ph; ALL OVER THE TOWN(1949, Brit.), ph; CHRISTMAS CAROL, A(1951, Brit.), ph; TOM BROWN'S SCHOOLDAYS(1951, Brit.), ph; PENNYWHISTLE BLUES, THE(1952, South Africa), w, ph; TREASURE HUNT(1952, Brit.), ph; ALWAYS A BRIDE(1954, Brit.), ph; AUNT CLARA(1954, Brit.), ph; STAR OF INDIA(1956, Brit.), ph; 1984(1956, Brit.), ph; IT'S NEVER TOO LATE(1958, Brit.), ph; STORMY CROSSING(1958, Brit.), d
Misc. Talkies
BLACK TIDE(1958), d
C.M. Pennington-Richards
HIDDEN ROOM, THE(1949, Brit.), ph; TARZAN AND THE LOST SAFARI(1957, Brit.), ph; INN FOR TROUBLE(1960, Brit.), d; DOUBLE BUNK(1961, Brit.), d&w; RELUCTANT SAINT, THE(1962, U.S./Ital.), ph; GET ON WITH IT(1963, Brit.), d; MYSTERY SUBMARINE(1963, Brit.), d; GUNS AT BATASI(1964, Brit.), w; LADIES WHO DO(1964, Brit.), d; CHALLENGE FOR ROBIN HOOD, A(1968, Brit.), d
G. Pennington-Richards
WOODEN HORSE, THE(1951), ph
Mario Pennisi
HAWKS AND THE SPARROWS, THE(1967, Ital.)
Chris Pennock
GREAT TEXAS DYNAMITE CHASE, THE(1976)
Christopher Pennock
NIGHT OF DARK SHADOWS(1971); SAVAGES(1972); CALIFORNIA SUITE(1978); FRANCES(1982)
Alan Penny
TIM(1981, Aus.)
Don Penny
Misc. Talkies
PICK-UP(1975)
Ed Penny
WHEN HELL BROKE LOOSE(1958)
Frank Penny
ONE NIGHT IN THE TROPICS(1940); HOLD THAT GHOST(1941); IN THE NAVY(1941); KEEP 'EM FLYING(1941); PARDON MY SARONG(1942); WHO DONE IT?(1942); IT AIN'T HAY(1943); MISSION TO MOSCOW(1943); SHE'S FOR ME(1943); KISMET(1944); LOST IN A HAREM(1944)
Hank Penny
BLAZING TRAIL, THE(1949); FRONTIER OUTPOST(1950)
Hannibal Penny
Misc. Talkies
J.C.(1972)
Joe Penny
OUR WINNING SEASON(1978); S.O.B.(1981)
Misc. Talkies
BLOODY BIRTHDAY(1980); LIFE POD(1980)
John Penny
1984
POWER, THE(1984), w
Pat Penny
FORTY THOUSAND HORSEMEN(1941, Aus.); BUSH CHRISTMAS(1947, Brit.)
Richard Penny
NO BLADE OF GRASS(1970, Brit.)
Ed Pennybacker
CHEYENNE SOCIAL CLUB, THE(1970); WRONG IS RIGHT(1982)
Dirk Peno
MACHISMO–40 GRAVES FOR 40 GUNS(1970)
Nancy Penoyer
SMALL CIRCLE OF FRIENDS, A(1980)
A. G. Penrod
Silents
MAN FROM BEYOND, THE(1922), ph
Alexander G. Penrod
Silents
DOWN TO THE SEA IN SHIPS(1923), ph
E. A. Penrod
VIKING, THE(1931), ph
Allan Penrose
Misc. Silents
DANGEROUS TRAILS(1923)
Charles Penrose
CALLING THE TUNE(1936, Brit.); CRIMES OF STEPHEN HAWKE, THE(1936, Brit.); DREAMS COME TRUE(1936, Brit.); DERELICT, THE(1937, Brit.); HUMAN MONSTER, THE(1940, Brit.); MAN WITH THE MAGNETIC EYES, THE(1945, Brit.); MIRANDA(1949, Brit.)

John Penrose
UNDERCOVER AGENT(1935, Brit.); LION HAS WINGS, THE(1940, Brit.); VOICE IN THE NIGHT, A(1941, Brit.); ADVENTURES OF TARTU(1943, Brit.); CORRIDOR OF MIRRORS(1948, Brit.); IDOL OF PARIS(1948, Brit.); ADVENTURES OF PC 49, THE(1949, Brit.); KIND HEARTS AND CORONETS(1949, Brit.); HOT ICE(1952, Brit.); SECRET PEOPLE(1952, Brit.); SHADOW MAN(1953, Brit.); WOMAN IN HIDING(1953, Brit.)
Mark Penrose
MERRY CHRISTMAS MR. LAWRENCE(1983, Jap./Brit.)
Norman Penrose
Misc. Silents
LOVERS IN ARABY(1924, Brit.)
Peter Penrose
SORRELL AND SON(1934, Brit.); LORNA DOONE(1935, Brit.); OLD CURIOSITY SHOP, THE(1935, Brit.)
Lonnie Pense
YOUNG CYCLE GIRLS, THE(1979)
Virginia Penta
STUCK ON YOU(1983)
1984
STUCK ON YOU(1984)
Pentangle
CHRISTIAN THE LION(1976, Brit.), m
Bud Pente
GHOST OF THE CHINA SEA(1958)
George Pentecost
ALL THE PRESIDENT'S MEN(1976); LAST MARRIED COUPLE IN AMERICA, THE(1980)
1984
NO SMALL AFFAIR(1984)
Hugh Pentecost
APPOINTMENT WITH A SHADOW(1958), w
Arthur Pentelow
PRIVILEGE(1967, Brit.); CHARLIE BUBBLES(1968, Brit.); GLADIATORS, THE(1970, Swed.)
Alan Pentland
CLINIC, THE(1983, Aus.)
Kate Pentzer
RESCUE SQUAD(1935)
Andre Penvern
SOMEONE BEHIND THE DOOR(1971, Fr./Brit.); TENANT, THE(1976, Fr.); MARCH OR DIE(1977, Brit.); FRENCH POSTCARDS(1979); DOGS OF WAR, THE(1980, Brit.)
1984
CHEECH AND CHONG'S THE CORSICAN BROTHERS(1984)
Duncan Penwarden
GENTLEMEN OF THE PRESS(1929); LADY LIES, THE(1929)
Misc. Silents
IMP, THE(1920)
Hazel Penwarden
MAN IN BLACK, THE(1950, Brit.)
Guardsmen Penwill
Silents
GAY CORINTHIAN, THE(1924)
Alan Penwrith
MISSING(1982)
Anthony Penya
HUMANOIDS FROM THE DEEP(1980); MEGAFORCE(1982); PORKY'S II: THE NEXT DAY(1983)
1984
WEEKEND PASS(1984)
Giacomo Penza
ROMAN HOLIDAY(1953)
Jean Penzar
MALEVIL(1981, Fr./Ger.), ph
Jean Bernard Penzer
INCORRIGIBLE(1980, Fr.), ph
Jean Penzer
JOKER, THE(1961, Fr.), ph; SEVEN CAPITAL SINS(1962, Fr./Ital.), ph; PLAYTIME(1963, Fr.), ph; TWO OF US, THE(1968, Fr.), ph; DESTROY, SHE SAID(1969, Fr.), ph; DEVIL BY THE TAIL, THE(1969, Fr./Ital.), ph; GIVE HER THE MOON(1970, Fr./Ital.), ph; WITHOUT APPARENT MOTIVE(1972, Fr.), ph; GET OUT YOUR HANDKERCHIEFS(1978, Fr.), ph; LADY OSCAR(1979, Fr./Jap.), ph; AFRICAN, THE(1983, Fr.), ph
1984
LE BON PLAISIR(1984, Fr.), ph; MY BEST FRIEND'S GIRL(1984, Fr.), ph
E. A. Penzlin
MYSTERIOUS ISLAND(1941, USSR), d
Ernest Penzoldt
DAY WILL COME, A(1960, Ger.), w
Ramon Peon
DEVIL'S GODMOTHER, THE(1938, Mex.), d
Misc. Silents
LA VIRGEN DE LA CARIDAD(1930, Cuba), d
the people of the island of Foula
EDGE OF THE WORLD, THE(1937, Brit.)
People's Defense Committee
1984
WHITE ELEPHANT(1984, Brit.)
Bob Peoples
CRAZY OVER HORSES(1951); GHOST CHASERS(1951); LET'S GO NAVY(1951); HOLD THAT LINE(1952); STEEL FIST, THE(1952); COMBAT SQUAD(1953); PRINCE OF PIRATES(1953); TALL MAN RIDING(1955)
Dave Peoples
STEEL ARENA(1973), ed
David Peoples
BLADE RUNNER(1982), w
Neva Peoples
DUKE IS THE TOPS, THE(1938)

Robert Peoples
WAKE ME WHEN IT'S OVER(1960)
Willie Pep
REQUIEM FOR A HEAVYWEIGHT(1962)
Nico Pepe
BITTER RICE(1950, Ital.); THOUSAND EYES OF DR. MABUSE, THE(1960, Fr./Ital./Ger.); MINOTAUR, THE(1961, Ital.); CHECKERBOARD(1969, Fr.)
Pepere the dog
LA BELLE AMERICAINE(1961, Fr.)
Joe Pepi
HARD ROAD, THE(1970); NOTORIOUS CLEOPATRA, THE(1970); YOUNG GRADUATES, THE(1971)
Ken Pepiot
SCARFACE(1983), spec eff
1984
RIVER, THE(1984), spec eff
Kenneth D. Pepiot
1984
BEVERLY HILLS COP(1984), spec eff
Kenneth Pepiot
CARRIE(1976), spec eff; DEATH WISH II(1982), spec eff
Pepito
ANNABEL TAKES A TOUR(1938); ARMY GIRL(1938); TROPIC HOLIDAY(1938)
Nino Pepitone
VOICE OF THE TURTLE, THE(1947); JOHN LOVES MARY(1949)
Edward H. Peple
QUEEN HIGH(1930), w; BELOVED BACHELOR, THE(1931), w; ON AGAIN–OFF AGAIN(1937), w
Edward Peple
LITTLEST REBEL, THE(1935), w
Silents
PAIR OF SIXES, A(1918), w
Martin Pepler
STONE COLD DEAD(1980, Can.), ed
Clare Peploe
ZABRISKIE POINT(1970), w; LUNA(1979, Ital.), w
Mark Peploe
LA BABY SITTER(1975, Fr./Ital./Gen.), w; PASSENGER, THE(1975, Ital.), w
George Peppard
STRANGE ONE, THE(1957); PORK CHOP HILL(1959); HOME FROM THE HILL(1960); SUBTERRANEANS, THE(1960); BREAKFAST AT TIFFANY'S(1961); HOW THE WEST WAS WON(1962); VICTORS, THE(1963); CARPETBAGGERS, THE(1964); OPERATION CROSSBOW(1965, U.S./Ital.); THIRD DAY, THE(1965); BLUE MAX, THE(1966); TOBRUK(1966); ROUGH NIGHT IN JERICHO(1967); P.J.(1968); WHAT'S SO BAD ABOUT FEELING GOOD?(1968); HOUSE OF CARDS(1969); PENDULUM(1969); CANNON FOR CORDOBA(1970); EXECUTIONER, THE(1970, Brit.); ONE MORE TRAIN TO ROB(1971); GROUNDSTAR CONSPIRACY, THE(1972, Can.); NEWMAN'S LAW(1974); DAMNATION ALLEY(1977); FIVE DAYS FROM HOME(1978), a, p&d; FROM HELL TO VICTORY(1979, Fr./Ital./Span.); BATTLE BEYOND THE STARS(1980)
1984
TREASURE OF THE YANKEE ZEPHYR(1984)
Misc. Talkies
TARGET EAGLE(1982)
Stacy Peppell
RICH KIDS(1979)
Ann Pepper
OLGA'S GIRLS(1964)
Anna Pepper
SPACED OUT(1981, Brit.), m
Art Pepper
SUBTERRANEANS, THE(1960)
Barbara Pepper
UNCLE HARRY(1945); ROMAN SCANDALS(1933); KID MILLIONS(1934); OUR DAILY BREAD(1934); DANTE'S INFERNO(1935); FORCED LANDING(1935); FRISCO WATERFRONT(1935); LET 'EM HAVE IT(1935); SAGEBRUSH TROUBADOR(1935); SINGING VAGABOND, THE(1935); WATERFRONT LADY(1935); BIG GAME, THE(1936); M'LISS(1936); MUMMY'S BOYS(1936); NIGHT WAITRESS(1936); ROGUES' TAVERN, THE(1936); SHOW BOAT(1936); WANTED: JANE TURNER(1936); WINTERSET(1936); BIG SHOT, THE(1937); FORTY NAUGHTY GIRLS(1937); MUSIC FOR MADAME(1937); OUTCASTS OF POKER FLAT, THE(1937); PORTIA ON TRIAL(1937); SEA DEVILS(1937); TAMING THE WILD(1937); TOO MANY WIVES(1937); WESTLAND CASE, THE(1937); YOU CAN'T BEAT LOVE(1937); YOU CAN'T BUY LUCK(1937); ARMY GIRL(1938); CHASER, THE(1938); HOLLYWOOD STADIUM MYSTERY(1938); LADY IN THE MORGUE(1938); SWEETHEARTS(1938); VIVACIOUS LADY(1938); WIDE OPEN FACES(1938); COLORADO SUNSET(1939); FLIGHT AT MIDNIGHT(1939); MAGNIFICENT FRAUD, THE(1939); OF MICE AND MEN(1939); OFF THE RECORD(1939); STRANGE CASE OF DR. MEADE(1939); THEY MADE ME A CRIMINAL(1939); THREE SONS(1939); CASTLE ON THE HUDSON(1940); FOREIGN CORRESPONDENT(1940); FORGOTTEN GIRLS(1940); FRAMED(1940); RETURN OF FRANK JAMES, THE(1940); SAILOR'S LADY(1940); WOMEN IN WAR(1940); MAN AT LARGE(1941); MANPOWER(1941); OUT OF THE FOG(1941); SOUTH OF TAHITI(1941); THREE SONS O'GUNS(1941); MY FAVORITE SPY(1942); ONE THRILLING NIGHT(1942); STAR SPANGLED RHYTHM(1942); GIRLS IN CHAINS(1943); LET'S FACE IT(1943); SO THIS IS WASHINGTON(1943); COVER GIRL(1944); HENRY ALDRICH PLAYS CUPID(1944); I LOVE A SOLDIER(1944); ONCE UPON A TIME(1944); SINCE YOU WENT AWAY(1944); BREWSTER'S MILLIONS(1945); MURDER, HE SAYS(1945); NAUGHTY NINETIES, THE(1945); PRISON SHIP(1945); MILLERSON CASE, THE(1947); SNAKE PIT, THE(1948); FULLER BRUSH GIRL, THE(1950); MY BLUE HEAVEN(1950); UNMASKED(1950); THUNDERBIRDS(1952); INFERNO(1953); YOUNG AT HEART(1955); D.I., THE(1957); IT'S ONLY MONEY(1962); MUSIC MAN, THE(1962); CHILD IS WAITING, A(1963); IT'S A MAD, MAD, MAD, MAD WORLD(1963); WHO'S MINDING THE STORE?(1963); KISS ME, STUPID(1964); MY FAIR LADY(1964); PATSY, THE(1964)
Misc. Talkies
TERROR TRAIL(1946)

Bob Pepper
WITHOUT RESERVATIONS(1946); THEY WON'T BELIEVE ME(1947); HIDDEN EYE, THE(1945); CRACK-UP(1946)
Buddy Pepper
GANGSTER'S BOY(1938); THAT CERTAIN AGE(1938); STREETS OF NEW YORK(1939); SEVENTEEN(1940); GOLDEN HOOFS(1941); HENRY ALDRICH FOR PRESIDENT(1941); RELUCTANT DRAGON, THE(1941); SMALL TOWN DEB(1941)
Cynthia Pepper
TAKE HER, SHE'S MINE(1963); KISSIN' COUSINS(1964)
Dan Pepper
HOLD THAT HYPNOTIST(1957), w; ENEMY GENERAL, THE(1960), w
Dave Pepper
WAY OUT WEST(1937)
David Pepper
WOMAN IN THE WINDOW, THE(1945)
Florence Pepper
DICK TRACY(1945); DEADLINE AT DAWN(1946); SUNSET PASS(1946)
Harry S. Pepper
KENTUCKY MINSTRELS(1934, Brit.), w; SUNSHINE AHEAD(1936, Brit.)
Jack Pepper
ROAD TO SINGAPORE(1940); MY FAVORITE SPY(1951); SILVER CANYON(1951); SON OF PALEFACE(1952); STOP, YOU'RE KILLING ME(1952); LUCY GALLANT(1955); SEVEN LITTLE FOYS, THE(1955); THAT CERTAIN FEELING(1956)
John Pepper
EVA(1962, Fr./Ital.); LITTLE ROMANCE, A(1979, U.S./Fr.)
Keith Pepper
SALLY FIELDGOOD & CO.(1975, Can.); KEEPER, THE(1976, Can.), art d; SHADOW OF THE HAWK(1976, Can.), art d; ANGELA(1977, Can.), art d
Martin Pepper
1984
CHEECH AND CHONG'S THE CORSICAN BROTHERS(1984)
Paul Pepper
TEENAGE ZOMBIES(1960)
Robin Pepper
OTHER SIDE OF THE MOUNTAIN, THE(1975)
Varvara Pepper
HAUNTING OF M, THE(1979)
Ethel Pepperell
Misc. Silents
MAINSPRING, THE(1917)
Paul Pepperman
PHANTASM(1979), p, spec eff; BEASTMASTER, THE(1982), p, w
The Peppermint Loungers
HEY, LET'S TWIST!(1961)
Catherine Peppers
FIGHT FOR YOUR LIFE(1977)
Hans Peppier
1914(1932, Ger.)
Peppino
ALONE IN THE STREETS(1956, Ital.)
Ethel Pepprell
Misc. Silents
LITTLE MISS GROWN-UP(1918)
Peppy & Peanuts
SWING YOUR PARTNER(1943)
Peppy the Monkey
TESS OF THE STORM COUNTRY(1932)
Arnold Crust Per Spook of Paris
FIREPOWER(1979, Brit.), ed
Lisa Pera
DO NOT DISTURB(1965); DREAM OF KINGS, A(1969); HINDENBURG, THE(1975)
Misc. Talkies
SEARCH FOR THE EVIL ONE(1967)
Marilia Pera
PIXOTE(1981, Braz.)
1984
MIXED BLOOD(1984)
Radames Pera
DREAM OF KINGS, A(1969)
1984
RED DAWN(1984)
Branko Perak
INNOCENCE UNPROTECTED(1971, Yugo.), ph
John Perak
COFFY(1973)
Nicos Perakis
TIN DRUM, THE(1979, Ger./Fr./Yugo./Pol.), prod d, art d
Juan Antonio Peral
FINGER ON THE TRIGGER(1965, US/Span.); TEXICAN, THE(1966, U.S./Span.)
Angel Peralta
THAT LADY(1955, Brit.); EVERY DAY IS A HOLIDAY(1966, Span.)
Goyo Peralta
BLOOD MONEY(1974, U.S./Hong Kong/Ital./Span.)
Lou Peralta
BLACK ANGELS, THE(1970), md
Stacey Peralta
Misc. Talkies
SKATEBOARD MADNESS(1980)
Stacy Peralta
FREEWHEELIN'(1976)
Peranio
POLYESTER(1981), set d
Ed Peranio
FEMALE TROUBLE(1975)
Vincent Peranio
PRIZE FIGHTER, THE(1979), art d; PRIVATE EYES, THE(1980), art d
Robert Perault
LAST MARRIED COUPLE IN AMERICA, THE(1980); STAR 80(1983)

1984
FRIDAY THE 13TH–THE FINAL CHAPTER(1984)

Eulogio Peraza
BANANAS(1971)

Dina Perbellini
ANNA(1951, Ital.); TIMES GONE BY(1953, Ital.); FRIENDS FOR LIFE(1964, Ital.)

Fred Perce
COURT-MARTIAL OF BILLY MITCHELL, THE(1955)

Hugh Perceval
MAN OF MAYFAIR(1931, Brit.), w; THESE CHARMING PEOPLE(1931, Brit.), w; SILENT PASSENGER, THE(1935, Brit.), p; CALLING THE TUNE(1936, Brit.), p; HOUSE OF THE SPANIARD, THE(1936, Brit.), p; BRIEF ECSTASY(1937, Brit.), p; WHAT A MAN!(1937, Brit.), p; DANGEROUS SECRETS(1938, Brit.), p; I MARRIED A SPY(1938), p, w; GARRISON FOLLIES(1940, Brit.), p; DANNY BOY(1941, Brit.), p; FRONT LINE KIDS(1942, Brit.), p; MISSING MILLION, THE(1942, Brit.), p; RINGER, THE(1953, Brit.), p; THREE CASES OF MURDER(1955, Brit.), p; RAISING A RIOT(1957, Brit.), p, w

John Perceval
RUNAWAY, THE(1964, Brit.), w

Lance Perceval
WHAT A WHOPPER(1961, Brit.)

Robert Perceval
TALE OF THREE WOMEN, A(1954, Brit.); SERENA(1962, Brit.)

Charles Percheskly
MUSIC MAN, THE(1962)

Nicolas Perchicaut
NIGHT HEAVEN FELL, THE(1958, Fr.)

Nicolas Perchicot
FLAME OVER VIETNAM(1967, Span./Ger.)

Cyril Percival
Silents
LOVE IN A WOOD(1915, Brit.); PRINCESS OF HAPPY CHANCE, THE(1916, Brit.); LONDON PRIDE(1920, Brit.); SPORT OF KINGS, THE(1921, Brit.)
Misc. Silents
TOWN OF CROOKED WAYS, THE(1920, Brit.); FOUR FEATHERS, THE(1921, Brit.); KNAVE OF DIAMONDS, THE(1921, Brit.); WOMAN WITH THE FAN, THE(1921, Brit.); WEE MACGREGOR'S SWEETHEART, THE(1922, Brit.)

David Percival
GIRL STROKE BOY(1971, Brit.), w

Elsie Percival
P.C. JOSSER(1931, Brit.)

Harold Percival
Silents
KAISER'S SHADOW, THE(1918), art d

Horace Percival
IT'S THAT MAN AGAIN(1943, Brit.); FAMILY AFFAIR(1954, Brit.); LYONS IN PARIS, THE(1955, Brit.)

Hugh Percival
JEWEL, THE(1933, Brit.), p; DEATH AT A BROADCAST(1934, Brit.), p

Kate Percival
1984
FOREVER YOUNG(1984, Brit.)

Lance Percival
YELLOW SUBMARINE(1958, Brit.); DEVIL'S DAFFODIL, THE(1961, Brit./Ger.); CARRY ON CRUISING(1962, Brit.); POSTMAN'S KNOCK(1962, Brit.); ROOMMATES(1962, Brit.); TWICE AROUND THE DAFFODILS(1962, Brit.); IT'S ALL OVER TOWN(1963, Brit.), a, w; V.I.P.s, THE(1963, Brit.); HIDE AND SEEK(1964, Brit.); BIG JOB, THE(1965, Brit.); JOEY BOY(1965, Brit.); OPERATION SNAFU(1965, Brit.); YELLOW ROLLS-ROYCE, THE(1965, Brit.); YOU MUST BE JOKING!(1965, Brit.); MRS. BROWN, YOU'VE GOT A LOVELY DAUGHTER(1968, Brit.); DARLING LILI(1970); THERE'S A GIRL IN MY SOUP(1970, Brit.); TOO LATE THE HERO(1970); UP POMPEII(1971, Brit.); OUR MISS FRED(1972, Brit.); UP THE FRONT(1972, Brit.); WEEKEND MURDERS, THE(1972, Ital.); CONFESSIONS FROM A HOLIDAY CAMP(1977, Brit.)
Misc. Talkies
BOY WITH TWO HEADS, THE(1974, Brit.)

Lucien Percival
AFTER TONIGHT(1933)

Michael Percival
PERSECUTION AND ASSASSINATION OF JEAN-PAUL MARAT AS PERFORMED BY THE INMATES OF THE ASYLUM OF CHARENTON UNDER THE DIRECTION OF THE MARQUIS DE SADE, THE(1967, Brit.); NO BLADE OF GRASS(1970, Brit.)
1984
WINTER FLIGHT(1984, Brit.)

Robert Percival
ROSSITER CASE, THE(1950, Brit.); SCARLET WEB, THE(1954, Brit.); MAN WITH THE GREEN CARNATION, THE(1960, Brit.); FRIGHTENED CITY, THE(1961, Brit.); LONELINESS OF THE LONG DISTANCE RUNNER, THE(1962, Brit.); SHARE OUT, THE(1966, Brit.)

Ted Percival
YELLOW SUBMARINE(1958, Brit.), animation

W.I. Percival
Misc. Silents
SYLVIA ON A SPREE(1918)

Walker Percival
LIGHTS OF NEW YORK(1928)

Walter C. Percival
HOMICIDE SQUAD(1931); IF I HAD A MILLION(1932); TILLIE AND GUS(1933)

Walter E. Percival
Silents
ALMOST MARRIED(1919)
Misc. Silents
CASTLES IN THE AIR(1919)

Walter Percival
LIGHTNIN'(1930); AVENGER, THE(1931); BLONDE CRAZY(1931); SMART MONEY(1931); CABIN IN THE COTTON(1932); CARNIVAL BOAT(1932); TENDERFOOT, THE(1932)
Silents
OUR MRS. McCHESNEY(1918); BIG CITY, THE(1928)

Misc. Silents
FLYING HORSEMAN, THE(1926)

Percival Mackey and His Band
THIS IS THE LIFE(1933, Brit.); DEATH AT A BROADCAST(1934, Brit.); HONEYMOON FOR THREE(1935, Brit.); MOUNTAINS O'MOURNE(1938, Brit.)

Percival Mackey and His Orchestra
SOMEWHERE ON LEAVE(1942, Brit.)

Percival Mackey's Band
GARRISON FOLLIES(1940, Brit.); FACING THE MUSIC(1941, Brit.)

Percival Mackey's Orchestra
SOMEWHERE IN ENGLAND(1940, Brit.)

Marie Percivale
Silents
JEWELS OF DESIRE(1927)

Bill Percy
HEARTS OF HUMANITY(1936, Brit.)

Billy Percy
BIRDS OF A FEATHER(1935, Brit.); SCHOONER GANG, THE(1937, Brit.); SISTER TO ASSIST'ER, A(1938, Brit.); ASKING FOR TROUBLE(1942, Brit.); RAMSBOTTOM RIDES AGAIN(1956, Brit.)

David Percy
BLACK WATCH, THE(1929); FOX MOVIETONE FOLLIES(1929); WORDS AND MUSIC(1929); MONTE CARLO(1930)

Donna Percy
YOU'RE NEVER TOO YOUNG(1955)

Edward Percy
DESIGN FOR MURDER(1940, Brit.), w; LADIES IN RETIREMENT(1941), w; CODE OF SCOTLAND YARD)(1948), w; BRIDES OF DRACULA, THE(1960, Brit.), w; MAD ROOM, THE(1969), w
Silents
IF FOUR WALLS TOLD(1922, Brit.), w

Eileen Percy
BROADWAY HOOFER, THE(1929); WICKED(1931); COHENS, AND KELLYS IN HOLLYWOOD, THE(1932)
Misc. Talkies
TEMPTATION(1930)
Silents
DOWN TO EARTH(1917); MAN FROM PAINTED POST, THE(1917); REACHING FOR THE MOON(1917); WILD AND WOOLLY(1917); BIG TOWN IDEAS(1921); BLUSHING BRIDE, THE(1921); MAID OF THE WEST(1921); WHATEVER SHE WANTS(1921); ELOPE IF YOU MUST(1922); FLIRT, THE(1922); PARDON MY NERVE!(1922); EAST SIDE–WEST SIDE(1923); PRISONER, THE(1923); YESTERDAY'S WIFE(1923); COBRA(1925); UNCHASTENED WOMAN(1925); BACKSTAGE(1927); TWELVE MILES OUT(1927); TELLING THE WORLD(1928)
Misc. Silents
EMPTY CAB, THE(1918); HITTING THE HIGH SPOTS(1918); BRASS BUTTONS(1919); DESERT GOLD(1919); GRAY HORIZON, THE(1919); IN MIZOURA(1919); ONE-THING-AT-A-TIME O'DAY(1919); SOME LIAR(1919); WHERE THE WEST BEGINS(1919); BELOVED CHEATER, THE(1920); BEWARE OF THE BRIDE(1920); HER HONOR THE MAYOR(1920); HUSBAND HUNTER, THE(1920); LAND OF JAZZ, THE(1920); LEAVE IT TO ME(1920); MAN WHO DARED, THE(1920); HICKVILLE TO BROADWAY(1921); LITTLE MISS HAWKSHAW(1921), d; TOMBOY, THE(1921); WHY TRUST YOUR HUSBAND?(1921); FAST MAIL, THE(1922); WESTERN SPEED(1922); CHILDREN OF JAZZ(1923); FOURTH MUSKETEER, THE(1923); LET'S GO(1923); WITHIN THE LAW(1923); MISSING DAUGHTERS(1924); TONGUES OF FLAME(1924); SHADOW ON THE WALL, THE(1925); UNDER THE ROUGE(1925); PHANTOM BULLET, THE(1926); RACE WILD(1926); THAT MODEL FROM PARIS(1926); BURNT FINGERS(1927)

Esme Percy
MURDER(1930, Brit.); BITTER SWEET(1933, Brit.); LUCKY NUMBER, THE(1933, Brit.); SECRET AGENT(1933, Brit.); SUMMER LIGHTNING(1933, Brit.); LORD EDGEWARE DIES(1934, Brit.); LOVE, LIFE AND LAUGHTER(1934, Brit.); INVITATION TO THE WALTZ(1935, Brit.); IT HAPPENED IN PARIS(1935, Brit.); NELL GWYN(1935, Brit.); REGAL CAVALCADE(1935, Brit.); ACCUSED(1936, Brit.); AMATEUR GENTLEMAN(1936, Brit.); FORBIDDEN MUSIC(1936, Brit.); OLD SPANISH CUSTOM, AN(1936, Brit.); FROG, THE(1937, Brit.); TWO WHO DARED(1937, Brit.); WHEN THIEF MEETS THIEF(1937, Brit.); PYGMALION(1938, Brit.); RETURN OF THE SCARLET PIMPERNEL(1938, Brit.); SONG OF FREEDOM(1938, Brit.); TORPEDOED!(1939); TWENTY-ONE DAYS TOGETHER(1940, Brit.); GIRL IN DISTRESS(1941, Brit.); YOUNG MR. PITT, THE(1942, Brit.); CAESAR AND CLEOPATRA(1946, Brit.); DEAD OF NIGHT(1946, Brit.); LISBON STORY, THE(1946, Brit.); GHOSTS OF BERKELEY SQUARE(1947, Brit.); UNFINISHED SYMPHONY, THE(1953, Aust./Brit.)

Fred Percy
Silents
BEAUTIFUL KITTY(1923, Brit.)

Graham Percy
HUGO THE HIPPO(1976, Hung./U.S.), prod d

John Percy
SPRING MEETING(1941, Brit.), w

Lee Percy
SHOGUN ASSASSIN(1980, Jap.), ed

Maria Percy
MORALIST, THE(1964, Ital.)

Neville Percy
Misc. Silents
SMART SET, A(1919, Brit.); SWINDLER, THE(1919, Brit.); HER MAJESTY(1922)

Paul Percy
LOVE IN THE DESERT(1929), w

Thelma Percy
Misc. Silents
BEGGAR PRINCE, THE(1920); STAR ROVER, THE(1920); SEVEN YEARS BAD LUCK(1921)

W.S. Percy
HIGHLAND FLING(1936, Brit.)

William Percy
WORM'S EYE VIEW(1951, Brit.)

Percy Athos Follies
LET'S MAKE A NIGHT OF IT(1937, Brit.)
Thomas Wigney Percyval
GRUMPY(1930), w
Helen Perdriere
PHANTOM OF LIBERTY, THE(1974, Fr.)
John Perdrini
JOAN OF ARC(1948)
Curtis Perdue
HOOKED GENERATION, THE(1969)
Derelys Perdue
Misc. Silents
DANGEROUS ADVENTURE, A(1922); BISHOP OF THE OZARKS, THE(1923); BLOW YOUR OWN HORN(1923); DAYTIME WIVES(1923); LAST MAN ON EARTH, THE(1924); UNTAMED YOUTH(1924); QUICK TRIGGERS(1928); SMILING TERROR, THE(1929)
Virginia Perdue
SHADOW OF A WOMAN(1946), w
Alexandre Dumas Pere
Silents
THREE MUSKETEERS, THE(1921), w
Carol Mon Pere
MOUSE AND HIS CHILD, THE(1977), w
Jan Pere
ONE NIGHT... A TRAIN(1968, Fr./Bel.)
Frank Peregini
Misc. Silents
SCAR OF SHAME, THE(1927), d
Didi Perego
EVERYBODY GO HOME!(1962, Fr./Ital.); KAPO(1964, Ital./Fr./Yugo.); LITTLE NUNS, THE(1965, Ital.); LA VISITA(1966, Ital./Fr.); SIX DAYS A WEEK(1966, Fr./Ital./Span.); APPOINTMENT, THE(1969); GIVE HER THE MOON(1970, Fr./Ital.); STORY OF A WOMAN(1970, U.S./Ital.); MAN CALLED SLEDGE, A(1971, Ital.)
Filippo Perego
WATERLOO(1970, Ital./USSR)
Maria Perego
MAGIC WORLD OF TOPO GIGIO, THE(1961, Ital.), w, animation
Walt Peregoy
SLEEPING BEAUTY(1959), art d; SWORD IN THE STONE, THE(1963), art d; SANTA AND THE THREE BEARS(1970), art d
A. Pereguda
TRAIN GOES TO KIEV, THE(1961, USSR), w
I. Peregudov
LITTLE HUMPBACKED HORSE, THE(1962, USSR)
Paulo Cesar Pereio
EARTH ENTRANCED(1970, Braz.)
Fernando Pereira
TIGER BY THE TAIL(1970)
Gerard Pereira
TENANT, THE(1976, Fr.)
Hal Pereira
ROMA RIVUOLE CESARE(, art d; AND THE ANGELS SING(1944), art d; DOUBLE INDEMNITY(1944), art d; MEDAL FOR BENNY, A(1945), art d; MINISTRY OF FEAR(1945), art d; YOU CAME ALONG(1945), art d; GOLDBERGS, THE(1950), art d; REDHEAD AND THE COWBOY, THE(1950), art d; DARLING, HOW COULD YOU!(1951), art d; DEAR BRAT(1951), art d; DETECTIVE STORY(1951), art d; HERE COMES THE GROOM(1951), art d; LEMON DROP KID, THE(1951), art d; MATING SEASON, THE(1951), art d; MY FAVORITE SPY(1951), art d; PEKING EXPRESS(1951), art d; RED MOUNTAIN(1951), art d; RHUBARB(1951), art d; SAILOR BEWARE(1951), art d; SILVER CITY(1951), art d; SUBMARINE COMMAND(1951), art d; THAT'S MY BOY(1951), art d; WHEN WORLDS COLLIDE(1951), art d; CARRIE(1952), art d; DENVER AND RIO GRANDE(1952), art d; GREATEST SHOW ON EARTH, THE(1952), art d; HURRICANE SMITH(1952), art d; JUMPING JACKS(1952), art d; JUST FOR YOU(1952), art d; MY SON, JOHN(1952), art d; ROAD TO BALI(1952), art d; SOMEBODY LOVES ME(1952), art d; SOMETHING TO LIVE FOR(1952), art d; SON OF PALEFACE(1952), art d; STOOGE, THE(1952), art d; TURNING POINT, THE(1952), art d; FLIGHT TO TANGIER(1953), art d; FOREVER FEMALE(1953), art d; GIRLS OF PLEASURE ISLAND, THE(1953), art d; HERE COME THE GIRLS(1953), art d; HOUDINI(1953), art d; JAMAICA RUN(1953), art d; LITTLE BOY LOST(1953), art d; OFF LIMITS(1953), art d; PONY EXPRESS(1953), art d; SANGAREE(1953), art d; SAVAGE, THE(1953), art d; SCARED STIFF(1953), art d; SHANE(1953), art d; STALAG 17(1953), art d; STARS ARE SINGING, THE(1953), art d; TROPIC ZONE(1953), art d; VANQUISHED, THE(1953), art d; WAR OF THE WORLDS, THE(1953), art d; BRIDGES AT TOKO-RI, THE(1954), art d; ELEPHANT WALK(1954), art d; JIVARO(1954), art d; LIVING IT UP(1954), art d; REAR WINDOW(1954), art d; RED GARTERS(1954), art d; SABRINA(1954), art d; SECRET OF THE INCAS(1954), art d; WHITE CHRISTMAS(1954), art d; DESPERATE HOURS, THE(1955), art d; FAR HORIZONS, THE(1955), art d; GIRL RUSH, THE(1955), art d; HELL'S ISLAND(1955), art d; LUCY GALLANT(1955), art d; ROSE TATTOO, THE(1955), art d; RUN FOR COVER(1955), art d; SEVEN LITTLE FOYS, THE(1955), art d; STRATEGIC AIR COMMAND(1955), art d; TROUBLE WITH HARRY, THE(1955), art d; WE'RE NO ANGELS(1955), art d; YOU'RE NEVER TOO YOUNG(1955), art d; HOLLYWOOD OR BUST(1956), art d; LEATHER SAINT, THE(1956), art d; MAN WHO KNEW TOO MUCH, THE(1956), art d; MOUNTAIN, THE(1956), art d; PARDNERS(1956), art d; PROUD AND THE PROFANE, THE(1956), art d; RAINMAKER, THE(1956), art d; SCARLET HOUR, THE(1956), art d; SEARCH FOR BRIDEY MURPHY, THE(1956), art d; TEN COMMANDMENTS, THE(1956), art d; THAT CERTAIN FEELING(1956), art d; THREE VIOLENT PEOPLE(1956), art d; VAGABOND KING, THE(1956), art d; DELICATE DELINQUENT, THE(1957), art d; DEVIL'S HAIRPIN, THE(1957), art d; FUNNY FACE(1957), art d; GUNFIGHT AT THE O.K. CORRAL(1957), art d; HEAR ME GOOD(1957), art d; JOKER IS WILD, THE(1957), art d; LONELY MAN, THE(1957), art d; LOVING YOU(1957), art d; OMAR KHAYYAM(1957), art d; SAD SACK, THE(1957), art d; SHORT CUT TO HELL(1957), art d; TIN STAR, THE(1957), art d; WILD IS THE WIND(1957), art d; DESIRE UNDER THE ELMS(1958), art d; GEISHA BOY, THE(1958), art d; HOT SPELL(1958), art d; HOUSEBOAT(1958), art d; I MARRIED A MONSTER FROM OUTER SPACE(1958), art d; KING CREOLE(1958), art d; MARACAIBO(1958), art d; MATCHMAKER, THE(1958), art d; ROCK-A-BYE BABY(1958), art d; SPACE CHILDREN, THE(1958), art d; SPANISH AFFAIR(1958, Span.), art d; ST. LOUIS BLUES(1958), art d; TEACHER'S PET(1958), art d; VERTIGO(1958), art d; ALIAS JESSE JAMES(1959), art d;

BLACK ORCHID(1959), art d; CAREER(1959), art d; DON'T GIVE UP THE SHIP(1959), art d; FIVE PENNIES, THE(1959), art d; HANGMAN, THE(1959), art d; LAST TRAIN FROM GUN HILL(1959), art d; LI'L ABNER(1959), art d; THAT KIND OF WOMAN(1959), art d; YOUNG CAPTIVES, THE(1959), art d; BELLBOY, THE(1960), art d; BREATH OF SCANDAL, A(1960), art d; CINDERFELLA(1960), art d; G.I. BLUES(1960), art d; HELLER IN PINK TIGHTS(1960), art d; IT STARTED IN NAPLES(1960), art d; RAT RACE, THE(1960), art d; VISIT TO A SMALL PLANET(1960), art d; WALK LIKE A DRAGON(1960), art d; ALL IN A NIGHT'S WORK(1961), art d; BLUEPRINT FOR ROBBERY(1961), art d; ERRAND BOY, THE(1961), art d; LADIES MAN, THE(1961), art d; LOVE IN A GOLDFISH BOWL(1961), art d; ON THE DOUBLE(1961), art d; ONE-EYED JACKS(1961), art d; PLEASURE OF HIS COMPANY, THE(1961), art d; POCKETFUL OF MIRACLES(1961), art d; SUMMER AND SMOKE(1961), art d; ESCAPE FROM ZAHRAIN(1962), art d; GIRL NAMED TAMIRO, A(1962), art d; GIRLS! GIRLS! GIRLS!(1962), art d; HATARI!(1962), art d; HELL IS FOR HEROES(1962), art d; IT'S ONLY MONEY(1962), art d; MAN WHO SHOT LIBERTY VALANCE, THE(1962), art d; MY GEISHA(1962), art d; PIGEON THAT TOOK ROME, THE(1962), art d; COME BLOW YOUR HORN(1963), art d; DONOVAN'S REEF(1963), art d; FUN IN ACAPULCO(1963), art d; HUD(1963), art d; LOVE WITH THE PROPER STRANGER(1963), art d; MC LINTOCK!(1963), art d; MY SIX LOVES(1963), art d; NEW KIND OF LOVE, A(1963), art d; NUTTY PROFESSOR, THE(1963), art d; PAPA'S DELICATE CONDITION(1963), art d; WHO'S BEEN SLEEPING IN MY BED?(1963), art d; WHO'S MINDING THE STORE?(1963), art d; WIVES AND LOVERS(1963), art d; CARPETBAGGERS, THE(1964), art d; DISORDERLY ORDERLY, THE(1964), art d; FOR THOSE WHO THINK YOUNG(1964), art d; HOUSE IS NOT A HOME, A(1964), art d; LADY IN A CAGE(1964), art d; LAW OF THE LAWLESS(1964), art d; PATSY, THE(1964), art d; ROBINSON CRUSOE ON MARS(1964), art d; ROUSTABOUT(1964), art d; STAGE TO THUNDER ROCK(1964), art d; STRANGLER, THE(1964), art d; WHERE LOVE HAS GONE(1964), art d; BLACK SPURS(1965), art d; BOEING BOEING(1965), art d; FAMILY JEWELS, THE(1965), art d; HARLOW(1965), art d; RED LINE 7000(1965), art d; SLENDER THREAD, THE(1965), art d; SONS OF KATIE ELDER, THE(1965), art d; SPY WHO CAME IN FROM THE COLD, THE(1965, Brit.), prod d; SYLVIA(1965), art d; TICKLE ME(1965), art d; TOWN TAMER(1965), art d; YOUNG FURY(1965), art d; JOHNNY RENO(1966), art d; LAST OF THE SECRET AGENTS?, THE(1966), art d; NEVADA SMITH(1966), art d; NIGHT OF THE GRIZZLY, THE(1966), art d; OSCAR, THE(1966), art d; PARADISE, HAWAIIAN STYLE(1966), art d; SWINGER, THE(1966), art d; THIS PROPERTY IS CONDEMNED(1966), art d; WACO(1966), art d; EASY COME, EASY GO(1967), art d; EL DORADO(1967), art d; FORT UTAH(1967), art d; HOSTILE GUNS(1967), art d; PRESIDENT'S ANALYST, THE(1967), art d; RED TOMAHAWK(1967), art d; SPIRIT IS WILLING, THE(1967), art d; WARNING SHOT(1967), art d; ARIZONA BUSHWHACKERS(1968), art d; NO WAY TO TREAT A LADY(1968), art d; ODD COUPLE, THE(1968), art d; WILL PENNY(1968), art d
Joan Pereira
GENTLEMAN OF PARIS, A(1931); STRANGE EXPERIMENT(1937, Brit.)
Tonico Pereira
1984
MEMOIRS OF PRISON(1984, Braz.)
W.L. Pereira
REAP THE WILD WIND(1942), spec eff
William L. Pereira
JOHNNY ANGEL(1945), p; FROM THIS DAY FORWARD(1946), p
William Pereira
NEW YORK TOWN(1941), art d
Zeni Pereira
1984
BLAME IT ON RIO(1984); GABRIELA(1984, Braz.)
Hal Pereiva
PROJECT X(1968), art d
John Perell
OTHER SIDE OF THE MOUNTAIN, THE(1975)
Sidney Perell
PROMISES, PROMISES(1963), makeup
Frank Ray Perelli
END OF THE WORLD(1977), w
Laura Perelman
PARIS INTERLUDE(1934), w; FLORIDA SPECIAL(1936), w; AMBUSH(1939), w; BOY TROUBLE(1939), w; GOLDEN FLEECING, THE(1940), w; LARCENY, INC.(1942), w
S.J. Perelman
MONKEY BUSINESS(1931), w; HOLD'EM JAIL(1932), w; HORSE FEATHERS(1932), w; SITTING PRETTY(1933), w; PARIS INTERLUDE(1934), w; FLORIDA SPECIAL(1936), w; AMBUSH(1939), w; BOY TROUBLE(1939), w; GOLDEN FLEECING, THE(1940), w; LARCENY, INC.(1942), w; ONE TOUCH OF VENUS(1948), w; AROUND THE WORLD IN 80 DAYS(1956), w
V. Perelyotov
CLEAR SKIES(1963, USSR), cos; GROWN-UP CHILDREN(1963, USSR), cos
Robert Pereno
XTRO(1983, Brit.)
1984
LITTLE DRUMMER GIRL, THE(1984)
V. Perepyolov
OPTIMISTIC TRAGEDY, THE(1964, USSR), cos
Marcel Peres
PORT OF SHADOWS(1938, Fr.); DAYBREAK(1940, Fr.); CHILDREN OF PARADISE(1945, Fr.); IT HAPPENED AT THE INN(1945, Fr.); PANIQUE(1947, Fr.); LE PLAISIR(1954, Fr.); LA PARISIENNE(1958, Fr./Ital.); HORROR CHAMBER OF DR. FAUSTUS, THE(1962, Fr./Ital.); WHERE THE TRUTH LIES(1962, Fr.); TWO ARE GUILTY(1964, Fr.); THANK HEAVEN FOR SMALL FAVORS(1965, Fr.); MILKY WAY, THE(1969, Fr./Ital.); RIDER ON THE RAIN(1970, Fr./Ital.); VERY CURIOUS GIRL, A(1970, Fr.)
Spyros Peresiadi
GIRL OF THE MOUNTAINS(1958, Gr.), w
Perestiani
Misc. Silents
GRIFFON OF AN OLD WARRIOR(1916, USSR)
I. Perestiani
THEY WANTED PEACE(1940, USSR)

Ivan Perestiani
Misc. Silents
REVOLUTIONIST(1917, USSR); EVA(1918, USSR), a, d; LOVE - HATE - DEATH(1918, USSR), a, d; MURDER OF GENERAL GRYAZNOV, THE(1921, USSR), a, d

Ivan L. Perestiany
Misc. Silents
SCANDAL?(1929, USSR), d

William Peresz
MAN CALLED FLINTSTONE, THE(1966), art d

Dino Peretti
SUNFLOWER(1970, Fr./Ital.)

Natale Peretti
GREEN TREE, THE(1965, Ital.)

Pio Peretti
LONE WOLF IN PARIS, THE(1938)

Susan Peretz
HURRY UP OR I'LL BE 30(1973); DOG DAY AFTERNOON(1975); MELVIN AND HOWARD(1980); HONKYTONK MAN(1982)
1984
OH GOD! YOU DEVIL(1984); SWING SHIFT(1984)

Vitya Perevalov
MAGIC WEAVER, THE(1965, USSR)

Ivan Perevertsev
SKY CALLS, THE(1959, USSR)

I. Pereverzev
MAGIC VOYAGE OF SINBAD, THE(1962, USSR); DREAM OF A COSSACK(1982, USSR)

Alfredo Perez
HARBOR LIGHTS(1963)

Angos Perez
LYDIA BAILEY(1952)

Barbara Perez
NO MAN IS AN ISLAND(1962)

Barbra Perez
SCARFACE(1983)

Ben Perez
HUK(1956); STEEL CLAW, THE(1961)

Bill Perez
BUGS BUNNY'S THIRD MOVIE–1001 RABBIT TALES(1982), d

Carlos Perez
RACING FEVER(1964), makeup

Francisca Perez
RACING FEVER(1964), makeup

Inez Perez
NIGHT OF THE LEPUS(1972)

Isabel Maria Perez
10:30 P.M. SUMMER(1966, U.S./Span.)

Isabelle Perez
FOND MEMORIES(1982, Can.)

Ismael Perez
BULLFIGHTER AND THE LADY(1951)

Jack Perez
1984
MISSING IN ACTION(1984)

Jeanne Perez
DEVIL IN THE FLESH, THE(1949, Fr.); LE BEAU SERGE(1959, Fr.); WHERE THE TRUTH LIES(1962, Fr.); THERESE(1963, Fr.); DIARY OF A CHAMBERMAID(1964, Fr./Ital.)

Jorge Perez
CRIMINAL LIFE OF ARCHIBALDO DE LA CRUZ, THE(1962, Mex.), m

Jose Dolores Perez
BLOOD AND SAND(1941), cos

Jose Perez
CALIFORNIA FRONTIER(1938); WE WERE STRANGERS(1949); LIFE IN THE BALANCE, A(1955); YOUNG SAVAGES, THE(1961); SHORT EYES(1977); NIGHT FLOWERS(1979); D.C. CAB(1983); STING II, THE(1983)

Lazaro Perez
FORTUNE AND MEN'S EYES(1971, U.S./Can.); GUMBALL RALLY, THE(1976)

Manny Perez
HEY, GOOD LOOKIN'(1982), anim

Manuel Perez
UNDER THE PAMPAS MOON(1935); GOLIATH AGAINST THE GIANTS(1963, Ital./Span.), p; ISLAND OF THE DAMNED(1976, Span.), p

Marcel Perez
LA BETE HUMAINE(1938, Fr.)
Silents
OUT ALL NIGHT(1927), w
Misc. Silents
WAY WOMEN LOVE, THE(1920), d; LUXURY(1921), d; BETTER MAN WINS, THE(1922), d; DUTY FIRST(1922), d; UNCONQUERED WOMAN(1922), d; WEST VS. EAST(1922), d; VULGAR YACHTSMEN, THE(1926), d

Marta Lorena Perez
ALSINO AND THE CONDOR(1983, Nicaragua)

Michel Perez
SECOND WIND, A(1978, Fr.), w

Naomi Perez
WAY OUT(1966)

Olga Perez
RIDE THE PINK HORSE(1947); CASA MANANA(1951)

Pablo Perez
HORROR EXPRESS(1972, Span./Brit.), spec eff

Paul Perez
ISLE OF LOST SHIPS(1929), w; MAN AND THE MOMENT, THE(1929), w; PRISON-ERS(1929), titles; SATURDAY'S CHILDREN(1929), w; WEARY RIVER(1929), ed; GOLDIE(1931), w; KISS ME AGAIN(1931), w; DOOMED BATTALION, THE(1932), w; HOTEL CONTINENTAL(1932), w; IT'S GREAT TO BE ALIVE(1933), w; ONE YEAR LATER(1933), w; SMOKY(1933), w; GREAT DEFENDER, THE(1934, Brit.), w; EAST OF JAVA(1935), w; RADIO FOLLIES(1935, Brit.), w; AUGUST WEEK-END(1936, Brit.), w; BRILLIANT MARRIAGE(1936), w; EASY MONEY(1936), w; LAST OF THE

MOHICANS, THE(1936), w; LITTLE RED SCHOOLHOUSE(1936), w; RING AROUND THE MOON(1936), w; APRIL BLOSSOMS(1937, Brit.), w; ONCE A DOCTOR(1937), w; ONE MAN JUSTICE(1937), w; PARADISE EXPRESS(1937), w; TWO-FISTED SHE-RIFF(1937), w; LOVES OF MADAME DUBARRY, THE(1938, Brit.), w; MISSING GUEST, THE(1938), w
Silents
FLOATING COLLEGE, THE(1928), t; GRAIN OF DUST, THE(1928), t; GUN RUN-NER, THE(1928), t; OUT WITH THE TIDE(1928), t, ed; WHY BE GOOD?(1929), t
Misc. Silents
APPLE-TREE GIRL, THE(1917)

Pepito Perez
LADY IN THE DARK(1944); MASQUERADE IN MEXICO(1945); MEDAL FOR BENNY, A(1945); GOLDEN EARRINGS(1947); ROAD TO RIO(1947); ALIAS NICK BEAL(1949); RAGING TIDE, THE(1951); HERE COME THE GIRLS(1953)

Rafael A. Perez
LITTLE RED RIDING HOOD AND HER FRIENDS(1964, Mex.), w

Ramon Chavez Perez
MASSACRE(1956)

Raul Perez
GREAT DIVIDE, THE(1930), w

Shabazz Perez
THINGS ARE TOUGH ALL OVER(1982)

Tigre Perez
BANANAS(1971)

Tony Perez
SCARFACE(1983)

Victor Perez
1984
MIKE'S MURDER(1984)

Beatriz Perez-Porro
1984
SKYLINE(1984, Spain)

Hamit Perezic
ANNIE HALL(1977)

Shaul Perezovsky
TWO KOUNEY LEMELS(1966, Israel), m

Frank Perfitt
ALF'S CARPET(1929, Brit.); YOU'D BE SURPRISED!(1930, Brit.); COM-PROMISED!(1931, Brit.); LOVE RACE, THE(1931, Brit.); NIGHT BIRDS(1931, Brit.); TONIGHT'S THE NIGHT(1932, Brit.); PRIDE OF THE FORCE, THE(1933, Brit.); FEATHER YOUR NEST(1937, Brit.)
Silents
FLYING FIFTY-FIVE, THE(1924, Brit.); SATAN'S SISTER(1925, Brit.); NEL-SON(1926, Brit.); MUMSIE(1927, Brit.); SOMEHOW GOOD(1927, Brit.); AFTER-WARDS(1928, Brit.); DAWN(1928, Brit.); RED PEARLS(1930, Brit.)

Louis Pergantes
OKAY FOR SOUND(1937, Brit.)

Louis Pergaud
GENERALS WITHOUT BUTTONS(1938, Fr.), w; WAR OF THE BUTTONS(1963 Fr.), w

James Pergola
THUNDER AND LIGHTNING(1977), ph; HOT STUFF(1979), ph; HARDLY WORK-ING(1981), ph; ISLAND CLAWS(1981), ph; NOBODY'S PERFEKT zero(1981), ph; LOVE CHILD(1982), ph; SMOKEY AND THE BANDIT–PART 3(1983), ph

Michael Pergolami
COUNTERFEIT COMMANDOS(1981, Ital.)

G. B. Pergolesi
END OF THE WORLD(in Our Usual Bed In a Night Full of Rain), THE*1/2 (1978, Ital.), m

Giovanni Battista Pergolesi
1984
AMADEUS(1984), m

Peri
HONEYMOON OF TERROR(1961), d

Enzo Peri
LAST DAYS OF MUSSOLINI(1974, Ital.), p; LILI MARLEEN(1981, Ger.), p

J. Roger Periard
RABID(1976, Can.)

Roger Periard
LOST AND FOUND(1979)
1984
HIGHPOINT(1984, Can.)

V. Periat-Petrenko
HEROES ARE MADE(1944, USSR)

Michel Pericart
PICNIC ON THE GRASS(1960, Fr.)

Donna Perich
UNMARRIED WOMAN, AN(1978)

Ugo Pericoli
EASY LIFE, THE(1963, Ital.), art d; LOVE ON THE RIVIERA(1964, Fr./Ital.), cos; OPIATE '67(1967, Fr./Ital.), art d; WATERLOO(1970, Ital./USSR), cos; NANA(1983, Ital.), cos

Etienne Perier
BRIDGE TO THE SUN(1961), d; SWORDSMAN OF SIENA, THE(1962, Fr./Ital.), d; MURDER AT 45 R.P.M.(1965, Fr.), d, w; DAY THE HOTLINE GOT HOT, THE(1968, Fr./Span.), d; WHEN EIGHT BELLS TOLL(1971, Brit.), d; ZEPPELIN(1971, Brit.), d
1984
LOUISIANE(1984, Fr./Can.), w

Francois Perier
MAN ABOUT TOWN(1947, Fr.); ORPHEUS(1950, Fr.); SYLVIA AND THE PHAN-TOM(1950, Fr.); CADET-ROUSSELLE(1954, Fr.); SECRETS D'ALCOVE(1954, Fr./Ital.); GERVAISE(1956, Fr.); NIGHTS OF CABIRIA(1957, Ital.); DEMONIAQUE(1958, Fr.); LOVE AND THE FRENCHWOMAN(1961, Fr.); LOVERS ON A TIGHTROPE(1962, Fr.); TESTAMENT OF ORPHEUS, THE(1962, Fr.); ORGANIZER, THE(1964, Fr./Ital./Yugo.); SWEET AND SOUR(1964, Fr./Ital.); LA VISITA(1966, Ital./Fr.); WEEKEND AT DUNKIRK(1966, Fr./Ital.); SHOCK TROOPS(1968, Ital./Fr.); LES GAULOISES BLEUES(1969, Fr.); Z(1969, Fr./Algeria); GODSON, THE(1972, Ital./Fr.); FRENCH CONSPIRACY, THE(1973, Fr.); STAVISKY(1974, Fr.); JUST BEFORE NIGHT-FALL(1975, Fr./Ital.); POLICE PYTHON 357(1976, Fr.); NO TIME FOR BREAK-FAST(1978, Fr.); CASE AGAINST FERRO, THE(1980, Fr.)

Francoise Perier
GIVE HER THE MOON(1970, Fr./Ital.)
Jean Perier
PASTEUR(1936, Fr.)
Jean-Pierre Perier
SLEEPING CAR MURDER THE(1966, Fr.)
John Perier
LA MARSEILLAISE(1938, Fr.), set d
Hal Periera
BIG CARNIVAL, THE(1951), art d; TO CATCH A THIEF(1955), art d
Joan Periera
SEEING IS BELIEVING(1934, Brit.)
Ute Periginelli
1984
GERMANY PALE MOTHER(1984, Ger.), ed
Frank Ray Perilli
DOBERMAN GANG, THE(1972), w; LITTLE CIGARS(1973), w; MANSION OF THE DOOMED(1976), w; DRACULA'S DOG(1978), p, w; LASERBLAST(1978), w; LAND OF NO RETURN, THE(1981), w
Ivo Perilli
ANNA(1951, Ital.), w; GREATEST LOVE, THE(1954, Ital.), w; MAMBO(1955, Ital.), w; ULYSSES(1955, Ital.), w; WAR AND PEACE(1956, Ital./U.S.), w; MILLER'S WIFE, THE(1957, Ital.), w; TEMPEST(1958, Ital./Yugo./Fr.), w; FIVE BRANDED WOMEN(1960), w; UNFAITHFULS, THE(1960, Ital.), w; BIBLE...IN THE BEGINNING, THE(1966), w; TILL MARRIAGE DO US PART(1979, Ital.), w
Brigitte Perin
JUST BEFORE NIGHTFALL(1975, Fr./Ital.)
George Perinal
DAVID GOLDER(1932, Fr.), ph; CATHERINE THE GREAT(1934, Brit.), ph; CHALLENGE, THE(1939, Brit.), ph; AFFAIRS OF ADELAIDE(1949, U. S./Brit), ph
Georges Perinal
BLOOD OF A POET, THE(1930, Fr.), ph; UNDER THE ROOFS OF PARIS(1930, Fr.), ph; A NOUS LA LIBERTE(1931, Fr.), ph; MILLION, THE(1931, Fr.), ph; PRIVATE LIFE OF HENRY VIII, THE(1933), ph; PRIVATE LIFE OF DON JUAN, THE(1934, Brit.), ph; SANDERS OF THE RIVER(1935, Brit.), ph; GIRL FROM MAXIM'S, THE(1936, Brit.), ph; REMBRANDT(1936, Brit.), ph; THINGS TO COME(1936, Brit.), ph; DARK JOURNEY(1937, Brit.), ph; MURDER ON DIAMOND ROW(1937, Brit.), ph; UNDER THE RED ROBE(1937, Brit.), ph; DRUMS(1938, Brit.), ph; FOUR FEATHERS, THE(1939, Brit.), ph; PRISON WITHOUT BARS(1939, Brit.), ph; OLD BILL AND SON(1940, Brit.), ph; THIEF OF BAGHDAD, THE(1940, Brit.), ph; SUICIDE SQUADRON(1942, Brit.), ph; SPITFIRE(1943, Brit.), ph; COLONEL BLIMP(1945, Brit.), ph; VACATION FROM MARRIAGE(1945, Brit.), ph; MAN ABOUT THE HOUSE, A(1947, Brit.), ph; IDEAL HUSBAND, AN(1948, Brit.), ph; FALLEN IDOL, THE(1949, Brit.), ph; IF THIS BE SIN(1950, Brit.), ph; MUDLARK, THE(1950, Brit.), ph; I'LL NEVER FORGET YOU(1951), ph; NO HIGHWAY IN THE SKY(1951, Brit.), ph; OPERATION X(1951, Brit.), ph; MAN WHO LOVED REDHEADS, THE(1955, Brit.), ph; THREE CASES OF MURDER(1955, Brit.), ph; WOMAN FOR JOE, THE(1955, Brit.), ph; LOSER TAKES ALL(1956, Brit.), ph; SATELLITE IN THE SKY(1956), ph; KING IN NEW YORK, A(1957, Brit.), ph; BONJOUR TRISTESSE(1958), ph; TOM THUMB(1958, Brit./U.S.), ph; DAY THEY ROBBED THE BANK OF ENGLAND, THE(1960, Brit.), ph; ONCE MORE, WITH FEELING(1960), ph; OSCAR WILDE(1960, Brit.), ph; IMMORAL CHARGE(1962, Brit.), ph
Jean Perine
LOVE AT NIGHT(1961, Fr.), w
Louis Perino
NIGHT OF EVIL(1962), w
George Periolat
Silents
EYES OF JULIA DEEP, THE(1918); AMAZING IMPOSTER, THE(1919); JUDY OF ROGUES' HARBOUR(1920); MARK OF ZORRO(1920); WEALTH(1921); BLOOD AND SAND(1922); DUST FLOWER, THE(1922); GAY AND DEVILISH(1922); SHATTERED IDOLS(1922); ROSITA(1923); SLAVE OF DESIRE(1923); TIGER'S CLAW, THE(1923); GIRL ON THE STAIRS, THE(1924); LOVER'S LANE(1924); ANY WOMAN(1925); ATTA BOY!(1926); NUT-CRACKER, THE(1926); NIGHT WATCH, THE(1928); SECRET HOUR, THE(1928); ONE SPLENDID HOUR(1929)
Misc. Silents
AND THE LAW SAYS(1916); PHILIP HOLDEN - WASTER(1916); VALLEY OF DECISION, THE(1916); ENVIRONMENT(1917); GAME OF WITS, A(1917); HER COUNTRY'S CALL(1917); MATE OF THE SALLY ANN, THE(1917); MELISSA OF THE HILLS(1917); SANDS OF SACRIFICE(1917); BEAUTY AND THE ROGUE(1918); GHOST OF ROSY TAYLOR, THE(1918); PUT UP YOUR HANDS!(1919); SPORTING CHANCE, A(1919); TIGER LILY, THE(1919); TRIXIE FROM BROADWAY(1919); WIVES AND OTHER WIVES(1919); BECKONING ROADS(1920); KISS, THE(1921); PARISIAN SCANDAL, A(1921); TWO WEEKS WITH PAY(1921); WHO AM I?(1921); FIGHTING YOUTH(1925); PHANTOM EXPRESS, THE(1925); MILE-A-MINUTE MAN, THE(1926); FANGS OF DESTINY(1927); THROUGH THICK AND THIN(1927)
Marika Perioli
MADE IN U.S.A.(1966, Fr.)
Peris
KID RODELO(1966, U.S./Span.), cos
Zoran Perisic
SUPERMAN(1978), spec eff; SUPERMAN II(1980), spec eff
Jennifer Perito
GOING BERSERK(1983)
Nick Perito
DON'T JUST STAND THERE(1968), m
Bill Periwee
CARRY ON LOVING(1970, Brit.)
Jon Periwee
CARRY ON CLEO(1964, Brit.); CARRY ON COWBOY(1966, Brit.)
Mike Perjanik
PRIVATE COLLECTION(1972, Aus.), m; NORMAN LOVES ROSE(1982, Aus.), m, md; BUSH CHRISTMAS(1983, Aus.), m
Kenneth Perkens
RIDING SHOTGUN(1954), w
Albert H. Perkin
SHE'S DANGEROUS(1937), w

Jack Perkin
RUBY(1977)
Al Perkins
RELUCTANT DRAGON, THE(1941), w
Albert R. Perkins
GIRL ON THE FRONT PAGE, THE(1936), w; MIGHTY TREVE, THE(1937), w; PRESCRIPTION FOR ROMANCE(1937), w
Alberta Perkins
DRUMS O' VOODOO(1934)
Anthony Perkins
ACTRESS, THE(1953); FRIENDLY PERSUASION(1956); FEAR STRIKES OUT(1957); LONELY MAN, THE(1957); TIN STAR, THE(1957); DESIRE UNDER THE ELMS(1958); MATCHMAKER, THE(1958); THIS ANGRY AGE(1958, Ital./Fr.); GREEN MANSIONS(1959); ON THE BEACH(1959); PSYCHO(1960); TALL STORY(1960); GOODBYE AGAIN(1961); PHAEDRA(1962, U.S./Gr./Fr.); FIVE MILES TO MIDNIGHT(1963, U.S./Fr./Ital.); TRIAL, THE(1963, Fr./Ital./Ger.); TWO ARE GUILTY(1964, Fr.); FOOL KILLER, THE(1965); IS PARIS BURNING?(1966, U.S./Fr.); RAVISHING IDIOT, A(1966, Ital./Fr.); CHAMPAGNE MURDERS, THE(1968, Fr.); PRETTY POISON(1968); CATCH-22(1970); WUSA(1970); SOMEONE BEHIND THE DOOR(1971, Fr./Brit.); LIFE AND TIMES OF JUDGE ROY BEAN, THE(1972); PLAY IT AS IT LAYS(1972); TEN DAYS' WONDER(1972, Fr.); LAST OF SHEILA, THE(1973), w; LOVIN' MOLLY(1974); MURDER ON THE ORIENT EXPRESS(1974, Brit.); MAHOGANY(1975); REMEMBER MY NAME(1978); BLACK HOLE, THE(1979); WINTER KILLS(1979); DOUBLE NEGATIVE(1980, Can.); FFOLKES(1980, Brit.); PSYCHO II(1983)
1984
CRIMES OF PASSION(1984)
Misc. Talkies
SINS OF DORIAN GRAY(1982)
April Perkins
RETURN OF THE JEDI(1983)
Bobbie Perkins
Misc. Silents
DAUGHTERS OF THE NIGHT(1924)
Carl Perkins
JAMBOREE(1957)
Caroline Anne Perkins
OLD HUTCH(1936)
Curtiss D. Perkins
FANTASIA(1940), art d
Eric Boyd Perkins
CURSE OF THE MUMMY'S TOMB, THE(1965, Brit.), ed; JULIUS CAESAR(1970, Brit.), ed; HAWK THE SLAYER(1980, Brit.), ed; MOTHER LODE(1982), ed
Frank Perkins
GLORY(1955), m; COUCH, THE(1962), m; GYPSY(1962), md; MARY, MARY(1963), m; PALM SPRINGS WEEKEND(1963), m; INCREDIBLE MR. LIMPET, THE(1964), m; READY FOR THE PEOPLE(1964), m
Gay Perkins
HOOKED GENERATION, THE(1969); DAREDEVIL, THE(1971)
Gil Perkins
KING KONG(1933); FEATHER IN HER HAT, A(1935); CAPTAINS COURAGEOUS(1937); BLACKMAIL(1939); HELLZAPOPPIN'(1941); YANK IN THE R.A.F., A(1941); JOURNEY FOR MARGARET(1942); MRS. MINIVER(1942); THEY GOT ME COVERED(1943); HEAVENLY DAYS(1944); CLOAK AND DAGGER(1946); DESIRE ME(1947); TWILIGHT ON THE RIO GRANDE(1947); THREE MUSKETEERS, THE(1948); LOST TRIBE, THE(1949); TAKE ME OUT TO THE BALL GAME(1949); FATHER OF THE BRIDE(1950); DOUBLE DYNAMITE(1951); HANS CHRISTIAN ANDERSEN(1952); STEEL FIST, THE(1952); CITY OF BAD MEN(1953); CLOWN, THE(1953); PRIVATE EYES(1953); ABBOTT AND COSTELLO MEET DR. JEKYLL AND MR. HYDE(1954); BIG CHASE, THE(1954); I DIED A THOUSAND TIMES(1955); SEA CHASE, THE(1955); BABY FACE NELSON(1957); CALYPSO HEAT WAVE(1957); SHOOT-OUT AT MEDICINE BEND(1957); HIGH SCHOOL CONFIDENTIAL(1958); SPARTACUS(1960); PORTRAIT OF A MOBSTER(1961); VALLEY OF THE DRAGONS(1961); EXPERIMENT IN TERROR(1962); BATMAN(1966); SAND PEBBLES, THE(1966); WHAT'S UP, DOC?(1972); WALKING TALL(1973), a, stunts; FRAMED(1975), stunts; PRISONER OF ZENDA, THE(1979)
Gilbert Perkins
DEMETRIUS AND THE GLADIATORS(1954); SEA CHASE, THE(1955); TEENAGE THUNDER(1957); TEENAGE MONSTER(1958)
Gilbert V. Perkins
BRAVE WARRIOR(1952)
Grace Perkins
PERSONAL MAID(1931), w; NO MORE ORCHIDS(1933), w; TORCH SINGER(1933), w; SOCIAL REGISTER(1934), w
Hayward Perkins
GETTING OVER(1981), art d
Jack Perkins
STRIKE IT RICH(1948), cos; LOVE BUG, THE(1968); MAN CALLED GANNON, A(1969); FUZZ(1972); LIMIT, THE(1972); WHAT'S UP, DOC?(1972); NICKELODEON(1976); GRAND THEFT AUTO(1977); APPLE DUMPLING GANG RIDES AGAIN, THE(1979); NORTH AVENUE IRREGULARS, THE(1979); HERBIE GOES BANANAS(1980); NIGHT SHIFT(1982)
Jean Perkins
MIDNIGHT MAN, THE(1974)
Jeffrey Perkins
BABY MAKER, THE(1970)
John Perkins
RICH AND FAMOUS(1981)
1984
FAR FROM POLAND(1984)
Julia Ellen Perkins
OLD HUTCH(1936)
Julia Perkins
LOVE IS ON THE AIR(1937)
Kenneth Perkins
RIDE HIM, COWBOY(1932), w; RELENTLESS(1948), w; SONG OF INDIA(1949), w; DESERT PURSUIT(1952), w; TUMBLEWEED(1953), w; ESCAPE TO BURMA(1955), w
Silents
ROMANCE LAND(1923), w; UNKNOWN CAVALIER, THE(1926), w

Kent Perkins
DRIVE-IN(1976); BEING, THE(1983)
1984
ADVENTURES OF BUCKAROO BANZAI: ACROSS THE 8TH DIMENSION, THE(1984); NIGHT PATROL(1984)
Larry Perkins
1,000 PLANE RAID, THE(1969); CROWD INSIDE, THE(1971, Can.); FORTUNE AND MEN'S EYES(1971, U.S./Can.)
Marion Perkins
DIFFERENT STORY, A(1978)
Millie Perkins
DIARY OF ANNE FRANK, THE(1959); WILD IN THE COUNTRY(1961); DULCINEA(1962, Span.); ENSIGN PULVER(1964); RIDE IN THE WHIRLWIND(1966); WILD IN THE STREETS(1968); SHOOTING, THE(1971); BORN TO KILL(1975); TABLE FOR FIVE(1983)
Misc. Talkies
WITCH WHO CAME FROM THE SEA, THE(1976)
Osgood Perkins
TARNISHED LADY(1931); MOTHER'S BOY(1929); SYNCOPATION(1929); SCARFACE(1932); KANSAS CITY PRINCESS(1934); MADAME DU BARRY(1934); PRESIDENT VANISHES, THE(1934); I DREAM TOO MUCH(1935); SECRET OF THE CHATEAU(1935); GOLD DIGGERS OF 1937(1936); PSYCHO II(1983)
Silents
CRADLE BUSTER, THE(1922); SECOND FIDDLE(1923); GRIT(1924); KNOCKOUT REILLY(1927)
Misc. Silents
PURITAN PASSIONS(1923); LOVE 'EM AND LEAVE 'EM(1926)
Pat Perkins
PRETTY BABY(1978)
Patricia Perkins
CAT PEOPLE(1982)
Peter Perkins
FIGHTING RANGER, THE(1948); GALLANT LEGION, THE(1948); MARSHAL OF AMARILLO(1948); GORGO(1961, Brit.)
Ray Perkins
UNDER A TEXAS MOON(1930), m; MIDDLETON FAMILY AT THE N.Y. WORLD'S FAIR(1939); JAMBOREE(1957)
Red Perkins
TWO WEEKS IN ANOTHER TOWN(1962); HOW THE WEST WAS WON(1962)
Ron Perkins
ENDLESS LOVE(1981)
Sherman Perkins
TOGETHER FOR DAYS(1972)
Sydney Perkins
PHONE CALL FROM A STRANGER(1952)
Toby Perkins
DOUBLE CROSS(1956, Brit.); DOUBLE BUNK(1961, Brit.); MAKE MINE A DOUBLE(1962, Brit.)
Trudy Perkins
HAIR(1979)
Valentine Perkins
OUR HEARTS WERE YOUNG AND GAY(1944); PRISONERS IN PETTICOATS(1950); ROCK ISLAND TRAIL(1950); ROGUES OF SHERWOOD FOREST(1950); TYRANT OF THE SEA(1950)
Vic Perkins
CANNIBALS IN THE STREETS(1982, Ital./Span.)
Voltaire Perkins
SANGAREE(1953); VANQUISHED, THE(1953); FAR HORIZONS, THE(1955); I'LL CRY TOMORROW(1955); MAN CALLED PETER, THE(1955); FOUR GIRLS IN TOWN(1956); OVER-EXPOSED(1956); SOLID GOLD CADILLAC, THE(1956); MY MAN GODFREY(1957); FRANKENSTEIN'S DAUGHTER(1958); MACABRE(1958); YOUNG LIONS, THE(1958); COMPULSION(1959); SANCTUARY(1961); GLOBAL AFFAIR, A(1964)
Von Eric Perkins
PRETTY BABY(1978)
Walter Perkins
Silents
ATOM, THE(1918); NEW DISCIPLE, THE(1921)
Misc. Silents
WEE LADY BETTY(1917)
William Perkins
MESA OF LOST WOMEN, THE(1956), p
William R. Perkins
SUBTERRANEANS, THE(1960)
Coleridge Taylor Perkinson
AMAZING GRACE(1974), m
Coleridge-Taylor Perkinson
MC MASTERS, THE(1970), m, md; TOGETHER FOR DAYS(1972), m; WARM DECEMBER, A(1973, Brit.), m; THOMASINE AND BUSHROD(1974), m
Jack Perks
Silents
DAVID AND JONATHAN(1920, Brit.)
Aino Perkskanen
SILENT PARTNER, THE(1979, Can.)
Alan Perl
TOY WIFE, THE(1938)
Arnold Perl
GOLD FOR THE CAESARS(1964), w; COTTON COMES TO HARLEM(1970), w
Linda Perl
ROCK 'N' ROLL HIGH SCHOOL(1979), set d
Lloyd Perl
Misc. Silents
TREASURE ISLAND(1917); ACE HIGH(1918)
Lothar Perl
THIS LAND IS MINE(1943), m
B. J. Perla
DANDY, THE ALL AMERICAN GIRL(1976), w

William Perlberg
KING STEPS OUT, THE(1936), p; IT'S ALL YOURS(1937), p; LADY OBJECTS, THE(1938), p; THERE'S ALWAYS A WOMAN(1938), p; GOLDEN BOY(1939), p; GOOD GIRLS GO TO PARIS(1939), p; LET US LIVE(1939), p; DOCTOR TAKES A WIFE(1940), p; THIS THING CALLED LOVE(1940), p; CHARLEY'S AUNT(1941), p; REMEMBER THE DAY(1941), p; MAGNIFICENT DOPE, THE(1942), p; TEN GENTLEMEN FROM WEST POINT(1942), p; CLAUDIA(1943), p; CONEY ISLAND(1943), p; MEANEST MAN IN THE WORLD, THE(1943), p; SONG OF BERNADETTE, THE(1943), p; SWEET ROSIE O'GRADY(1943), p; EVE OF ST. MARK, THE(1944), p; DIAMOND HORSESHOE(1945), p; JUNIOR MISS(1945), p; STATE FAIR(1945), p; WHERE DO WE GO FROM HERE?(1945), p; CLAUDIA AND DAVID(1946), p; FOREVER AMBER(1947), p; MIRACLE ON 34TH STREET, THE(1947), p; SHOCKING MISS PILGRIM, THE(1947), p; APARTMENT FOR PEGGY(1948), p; CHICKEN EVERY SUNDAY(1948), p; ESCAPE(1948, Brit.), p; AFFAIRS OF ADELAIDE(1949, U.S./Brit.), p; IT HAPPENS EVERY SPRING(1949), p; SLATTERY'S HURRICANE(1949), p; BIG LIFT, THE(1950), p; FOR HEAVEN'S SAKE(1950), p; I'LL GET BY(1950), p; WABASH AVENUE(1950), p; RHUBARB(1951), p; AARON SLICK FROM PUNKIN CRICK(1952), p; ANYTHING CAN HAPPEN(1952), p; SOMEBODY LOVES ME(1952), p; LITTLE BOY LOST(1953), p; BRIDGES AT TOKO-RI, THE(1954), p; COUNTRY GIRL, THE(1954), p; PROUD AND THE PROFANE, THE(1956), p; TIN STAR, THE(1957), p; TEACHER'S PET(1958), p; BUT NOT FOR ME(1959), p; RAT RACE, THE(1960), p; PLEASURE OF HIS COMPANY, THE(1961), p; COUNTERFEIT TRAITOR, THE(1962), p; HOOK, THE(1962), p; TWILIGHT OF HONOR(1963), p; 36 HOURS(1965), p
Rebecca Perle
1984
SAVAGE STREETS(1984); TIGHTROPE(1984)
Nadine Perles
Misc. Talkies
TEENAGE TEASERS(1982)
Charles Perley
Silents
PLAYING THE GAME(1918)
Misc. Silents
GAMBLER OF THE WEST, THE(1915); IDLE WIVES(1916); DEVIL'S PAY DAY, THE(1917); GIRL AND THE CRISIS, THE(1917); HER ONE MISTAKE(1918)
Amelio Perlini
DUCK, YOU SUCKER!(1972, Ital.)
Cindy Perlman
NIGHT IN HEAVEN, A(1983); STAYING ALIVE(1983)
1984
RHINESTONE(1984)
Milton Perlman
GODDESS, THE(1958), p
Ron Perlman
QUEST FOR FIRE(1982, Fr./Can.)
1984
ICE PIRATES, THE(1984)
Sidney Perlman
HOLLYWOOD HOTEL(1937)
Van Terrys Perlman
THAT'S MY STORY(1937), w
David M. Perlmutter
NOTHING PERSONAL(1980, Can.), p
David Perlmutter
IT SEEMED LIKE A GOOD IDEA AT THE TIME(1975, Can.), p; SUNDAY IN THE COUNTRY(1975, Can.), p
Renee Perlmutter
LOVE(1982, Can.), p
Richard Perlmutter
Misc. Talkies
BRANCHES(1971)
Bob Perlow
1984
NIGHT OF THE COMET(1984)
William Perlow, M.D.
HOSPITAL, THE(1971)
Frank Perls
LUST FOR LIFE(1956)
Michael Perlstein
DEADLY SPAWN, THE(1983), m
Don Perman
STUCK ON YOU(1983), w
1984
STUCK ON YOU(1984), w
Deborah Permenter
HALF A SIXPENCE(1967, Brit.)
David Perna
HOUR OF THE GUN(1967)
Tina Perna
TAMING OF THE SHREW, THE(1967, U.S./Ital.)
Vincent Pernaio
POLYESTER(1981), prod d
Ronald Pernee
1984
SCREAM FOR HELP(1984)
Louise Pernell
SEBASTIAN(1968, Brit.)
Andre Pernet
LOUISE(1940, Fr.)
Pierre Pernet
RISE OF LOUIS XIV, THE(1970, Fr.)
Renato Pernic
TWILIGHT TIME(1983, U.S./Yugo.), ch
Gino Pernice
ITALIANO BRAVA GENTE(1965, Ital./USSR); MINNESOTA CLAY(1966, Ital./Fr./Span.); HELLBENDERS, THE(1967, U.S./Ital./Span.)

Steve Pernie
1984
HIGHPOINT(1984, Can.)
Paul Perodi
UNDER THE PAMPAS MOON(1935)
Benito Perojo
DOLORES(1949, Span.), d; DESERT WARRIOR(1961 Ital./Span.), p; DEVIL MADE A WOMAN, THE(1962, Span.), p
Jan Perold
RIDER IN THE NIGHT, THE(1968, South Africa), d
Flying Officer Z. Peromowski
JOURNEY TOGETHER(1946, Brit.)
Denise Peron
LOVE AND DEATH(1975)
Nina Peron
VIRGIN SACRIFICE(1959)
C. Perone
MAN COULD GET KILLED, A(1966)
Kalle Peronkoski
MAKE LIKE A THIEF(1966, Fin.), ph
Denise Peronne
MY UNCLE(1958, Fr.); SUNDAYS AND CYBELE(1962, Fr.); SUITOR, THE(1963, Fr.); THANK HEAVEN FOR SMALL FAVORS(1965, Fr.); MADEMOISELLE(1966, Fr./Brit.); TWO OF US, THE(1968, Fr.)
Michael Perotta
IDOLMAKER, THE(1980)
Yuri Perov
YOLANTA(1964, USSR)
Slobodan Perovic
THREE(1967, Yugo.)
Barry Perowne
WALK A CROOKED PATH(1969, Brit.), a, w
Roberto Perpignani
BEFORE THE REVOLUTION(1964, Ital.), ed; CHINA IS NEAR(1968, Ital.), ed; LONG RIDE FROM HELL, A(1970, Ital.), ed; THAT SPLENDID NOVEMBER(1971, Ital./Fr.), ed; BLINDMAN(1972, Ital.), ed; PADRE PADRONE(1977, Ital.), ed; LEAP INTO THE VOID(1982, Ital.), ed; NIGHT OF THE SHOOTING STARS, THE(1982, Ital.), ed
Andre Perqament
ENIGMA(1983), p
Jo Perque
LIKE A TURTLE ON ITS BACK(1981, Fr.)
Harvey Perr
1984
STRANGER THAN PARADISE(1984, U.S./Ger.)
Vincent Perrania
HOUSE ON SORORITY ROW, THE(1983), art d
Charles Perrault
CINDERELLA(1950), w; LITTLE RED RIDING HOOD(1963, Mex.), w; PUSS 'N' BOOTS(1964, Mex.), w; SLEEPING BEAUTY, THE(1966, USSR), w; PUSS 'N' BOOTS(1967, Ger.), w; TOM THUMB(1967, Mex.), w; WACKY WORLD OF MOTHER GOOSE, THE,(1967), w
Georges Perrault
LOVE IN THE AFTERNOON(1957)
Gilles Perrault
SERPENT, THE(1973, Fr./Ital./Ger.), w
Louis Perrault
MR. HULOT'S HOLIDAY(1954, Fr.)
Nicole Perrault
STORK TALK(1964, Brit.)
Serge Perrault
TONIGHT WE SING(1953); FOLIES BERGERE(1958, Fr.)
Jean Perre
JE T'AIME, JE T'AIME(1972, Fr./Swed.)
Perreau
TWO GIRLS AND A SAILOR(1944)
Gerald Perreau [Peter Miles]
HI BEAUTIFUL(1944); SAN DIEGO, I LOVE YOU(1944); POSSESSED(1947); WHO KILLED "DOC" ROBBIN?(1948)
Ghislaine [Gigi] Perreau
MASTER RACE, THE(1944); YOLANDA AND THE THIEF(1945)
Gigi Perreau
MADAME CURIE(1943); DARK WATERS(1944); MR. SKEFFINGTON(1944); GOD IS MY CO-PILOT(1945); VOICE OF THE WHISTLER(1945); GREEN DOLPHIN STREET(1947); HIGH BARBAREE(1947); SONG OF LOVE(1947); ENCHANTMENT(1948); FAMILY HONEYMOON(1948); SAINTED SISTERS, THE(1948); MY FOOLISH HEART(1949); ROSEANNA McCOY(1949); SONG OF SURRENDER(1949); FOR HEAVEN'S SAKE(1950); NEVER A DULL MOMENT(1950); SHADOW ON THE WALL(1950); LADY PAYS OFF, THE(1951); REUNION IN RENO(1951); WEEKEND WITH FATHER(1951); BONZO GOES TO COLLEGE(1952); HAS ANYBODY SEEN MY GAL?(1952); DANCE WITH ME, HENRY(1956); MAN IN THE GREY FLANNEL SUIT, THE(1956); THERE'S ALWAYS TOMORROW(1956); COOL AND THE CRAZY, THE(1958); WILD HERITAGE(1958); GIRLS' TOWN(1959); LOOK IN ANY WINDOW(1961); TAMMY, TELL ME TRUE(1961); HELL ON WHEELS(1967); JOURNEY TO THE CENTER OF TIME(1967)
Misc. Talkies
ALIAS MR. TWILIGHT(1946)
Janine Perreau
SONG OF LOVE(1947); RED DANUBE, THE(1949); NEVER A DULL MOMENT(1950); REDHEAD AND THE COWBOY, THE(1950); M(1951); WEEKEND WITH FATHER(1951); THREE FOR BEDROOM C(1952); INVADERS FROM MARS(1953)
Laureen Perreau
IT HAPPENS EVERY THURSDAY(1953)
Michele Perrein
TRUTH, THE(1961, Fr./Ital.), w
Allesandro Perrella
LUDWIG(1973, Ital./Ger./Fr.)

Freddie Perren
COOLEY HIGH(1975), m; RECORD CITY(1978), m
Didier Perret
TWO OF US, THE(1968, Fr.)
Edith Perret
1984
UNTIL SEPTEMBER(1984)
Leonce Perret
ARTHUR(1931, Fr.), d
Silents
LIFTING SHADOWS(1920), d&w; MODERN SALOME, A(1920), d, w
Misc. Silents
MODERN OTHELLO, A(1917), d; SILENT MASTER, THE(1917), d; ACCIDENTAL HONEYMOON, THE(1918), d; LAFAYETTE, WE COME!(1918), d; LEST WE FORGET(1918), d; MILLION DOLLAR DOLLIES, THE(1918), d; ABC OF LOVE, THE(1919), d; THIRTEENTH CHAIR, THE(1919), d; TWIN PAWNS, THE(1919), d; UNKNOWN LOVE, THE(1919), d; EMPIRE OF DIAMONDS, THE(1920), d; L'EMPIRE DU DIAMENT(1921, Fr.), d; MONEY MANIAC, THE(1921), d; L'ECUYERE(1922, Fr.), d; KOENIGSMARK(1923, Fr.), d; MADAME SANS-GENE(1925), d; PRINTEMPS D'AMOUR(1927, Fr.), d; LA DANSEUSE ORCHIDEE(1928, Fr.), d; MODEL FROM MONTMARTE, THE(1928, Fr.), d; LA POSSESSION(1929, Fr.), d; MORGANE, THE ENCHANTRESS(1929, Fr.), d; QUAND NOUS ETIONS DEUX(1929, Fr.), d
Pierre Perret
WE'LL GROW THIN TOGETHER(1979, Fr.), m; CHARLES AND LUCIE(1982, Fr.), m
Mireille Perrey
DOCTEUR LAENNEC(1949, Fr.); HOTEL SAHARA(1951, Brit.); PRIZE, THE(1952, Fr.); EARRINGS OF MADAME DE..., THE(1954, Fr.); KNOCK(1955, Fr.); GREEN MARE, THE(1961, Fr./Ital.); UMBRELLAS OF CHERBOURG, THE(1964, Fr./Ger.)
Mirielle Perrey
HANDS OF ORLAC, THE(1964, Brit./Fr.)
John Perri
HE WALKED BY NIGHT(1948); SHE'S WORKING HER WAY THROUGH COLLEGE(1952); BABES IN TOYLAND(1961)
Marco Perri
HOLLYWOOD HIGH(1977), ed; YOUNG CYCLE GIRLS, THE(1979), ed
Mariko Perri
FLESH MERCHANT, THE(1956)
Paul Perri
HIT AND RUN(1982)
Raphael Perri
BIG GUNDOWN, THE(1968, Ital.), art d
Terri Perri
WANDERERS, THE(1979)
Ron Perriam
MYSTERY AT THE BURLESQUE(1950, Brit.)
Gregg Perrie
Misc. Talkies
SCORING(1980)
Lynne Perrie
KES(1970, Brit.)
Anna Perrier
MAN WHO LOVED WOMEN, THE(1977, Fr.)
Denise Perrier
DIAMONDS ARE FOREVER(1971, Brit.)
Jacqueline Perrier
CONJUGAL BED, THE(1963, Ital.)
Jean Perrier
END OF THE WORLD, THE(1930, Fr.), art d; ENTENTE CORDIALE(1939, Fr.); IT HAPPENED IN GIBRALTAR(1943, Fr.)
Jean-Francois Perrier
1984
LE BAL(1984, Fr./Ital./Algeria)
David Perrin
COMPANIONS IN CRIME(1954, Brit.)
Dick Perrin
HAMLET(1976, Brit.), ph
Freddie Perrin
HELL UP IN HARLEM(1973), m
Gerald Perrin
SAVAGE BRIGADE(1948, Fr.), ph
Henri Perrin
YOUR TURN, DARLING(1963, Fr.), ph
Jack Perrin
OVERLAND BOUND(1929); BEYOND THE RIO GRANDE(1930); PHANTOM OF THE DESERT(1930); RIDIN' LAW(1930); TRAILS OF DANGER(1930); KID FROM ARIZONA, THE(1931); RIDER OF THE PLAINS(1931); WILD WEST WHOOPEE(1931); DYNAMITE RANCH(1932); HELL FIRE AUSTIN(1932); LONE TRAIL, THE(1932); MOVIE CRAZY(1932); TEX TAKES A HOLIDAY(1932); ARIZONA NIGHTS(1934); DESERT JUSTICE(1936); LAST TRAIN FROM MADRID, THE(1937); LIVE, LOVE AND LEARN(1937); RECKLESS RANGER(1937); WRONG ROAD, THE(1937); PURPLE VIGILANTES, THE(1938); TEXANS, THE(1938); WESTERN JAMBOREE(1938); ETERNALLY YOURS(1939); PAL FROM TEXAS, THE(1939); STORY OF VERNON AND IRENE CASTLE, THE(1939); $1,000 A TOUCHDOWN(1939); FIGHTING 69TH, THE(1940); LAND OF THE SIX GUNS(1940); NEW MOON(1940); TEXAS RANGERS RIDE AGAIN(1940); WEST OF PINTO BASIN(1940); BROADWAY BIG SHOT(1942); DIXIE(1943); NORTH STAR, THE(1943); DUFFY'S TAVERN(1945); I WALK ALONE(1948); BANDIT QUEEN(1950); I SHOT BILLY THE KID(1950); TREASURE OF LOST CANYON, THE(1952); THEM!(1954); COURT-MARTIAL OF BILLY MITCHELL, THE(1955); TEN WANTED MEN(1955); WHEN GANGLAND STRIKES(1956); WESTBOUND(1959); SUNRISE AT CAMPOBELLO(1960)
Misc. Talkies
APACHE KID'S ESCAPE, THE(1930); LARIATS AND SIXSHOOTERS(1931); SHERIFF'S SECRET, THE(1931); FORTY-FIVE CALIBRE ECHO(1932); GIRL TROUBLE(1933); CACTUS KID, THE(1934); LOSER'S END(1934); MYSTERY RANCH(1934); RAWHIDE MAIL(1934); NORTH OF ARIZONA(1935); TEXAS JACK(1935); WOLF RIDERS(1935); GUN GRIT(1936); HAIR-TRIGGER CASEY(1936); WILDCAT SAUNDERS(1936)

Silents
BLIND HUSBANDS(1919); PINK TIGHTS(1920); PARTNERS OF THE TIDE(1921); RAGE OF PARIS, THE(1921); TORRENT, THE(1921); KNOCKOUT KID, THE(1925); GREY DEVIL, THE(1926); WEST OF THE RAINBOW'S END(1926); CODE OF THE RANGE(1927); LAFFIN' FOOL, THE(1927); HARVEST OF HATE, THE(1929); HOOF-BEATS OF VENGEANCE(1929); PLUNGING HOOFS(1929); WILD BLOOD(1929)

Misc. Silents
TOTON(1919); ADORABLE SAVAGE, THE(1920); MATCH-BREAKER, THE(1921); DANGEROUS LITTLE DEMON, THE(1922); GUTTERSNIPE, THE(1922); TROUPER, THE(1922); GOLDEN SILENCE(1923); LONE HORSEMAN, THE(1923); CRASHIN' THROUGH(1924); LIGHTNIN' JACK(1924); RIDIN' WEST(1924); SHOOTIN' SQUARE(1924); TRAVELIN' FAST(1924); VIRGINIAN OUTCAST(1924); BORDER VENGENCE(1925); CACTUS TRAILS(1925); CANYON RUSTLERS(1925); DANGEROUS FISTS(1925); DESERT MADNESS(1925); DOUBLE FISTED(1925); SILENT SHELDON(1925); STARLIGHT, THE UNTAMED(1925); WINNING A WOMAN(1925); DANGEROUS TRAFFIC(1926); HI-JACKING RUSTLERS(1926); MAN FROM OKLAHOMA, THE(1926); MIDNIGHT FACES(1926); MISTAKEN ORDERS(1926); RIDIN' GENT, A(1926); STARLIGHT'S REVENGE(1926); THUNDERBOLT STRIKES, THE(1926); FIRE AND STEEL(1927); THUNDERBOLT'S TRACKS(1927); WHERE THE NORTH HOLDS SWAY(1927); GUARDIANS OF THE WILD(1928); TWO OUTLAWS, THE(1928)

Jacques Perrin
GIRL WITH A SUITCASE(1961, Fr./Ital.); TRUTH, THE(1961, Fr./Ital.); FIRST TASTE OF LOVE(1962, Fr.); FAMILY DIARY(1963 Ital.); SLEEPING CAR MURDER THE(1966, Fr.); ALL THE OTHER GIRLS DO!(1967, Ital.); SHOCK TROOPS(1968, Ital./Fr.); YOUNG GIRLS OF ROCHEFORT, THE(1968, Fr.); Z(1969, Fr./Algeria), a, p; BLANCHE(1971, Fr.); STATE OF SIEGE(1973, Fr./U.S./Ital./Ger.), a, p; DONKEY SKIN(1975, Fr.); BLACK AND WHITE IN COLOR(1976, Fr.), p; DESERT OF THE TARTARS, THE(1976 Fr./Ital./Iranian); ADOPTION, THE(1978, Fr.)
1984
LE CRABE TAMBOUR(1984, Fr.)

Jean-Claude Perrin
DEATH OF MARIO RICCI, THE(1983, Ital.); RETURN OF MARTIN GUERRE, THE(1983, Fr.)

Marco Perrin
TWO OF US, THE(1968, Fr.); EGLANTINE(1972, Fr.); GOING PLACES(1974, Fr.); ATTENTION, THE KIDS ARE WATCHING(1978, Fr.)

Nar Perrin
DIMPLES(1936), w

Nat Perrin
DUCK SOUP(1933), w; ROMAN SCANDALS(1933), w; KID MILLIONS(1934), w; PIGSKIN PARADE(1936), w; ROSE OF THE RANCHO(1936), w; STOWAWAY(1936), w; DON'T TELL THE WIFE(1937), w; NEW FACES OF 1937(1937), w; ON AGAIN-OFF AGAIN(1937), w; GRACIE ALLEN MURDER CASE(1939), w; ALIAS THE DEACON(1940), w; HULLABALOO(1940), w; BIG STORE, THE(1941), w; HELLZAPOPPIN'(1941), w; KEEP 'EM FLYING(1941), w; WHISTLING IN DIXIE(1942), w; SWING FEVER(1943), w; WHISTLING IN BROOKLYN(1943), w; ABBOTT AND COSTELLO IN HOLLYWOOD(1945), w; MIGHTY MCGURK, THE(1946), p; SONG OF THE THIN MAN(1947), p, w; ALIAS A GENTLEMAN(1948), p; MISS GRANT TAKES RICHMOND(1949), w; TELL IT TO THE JUDGE(1949), w; EMERGENCY WEDDING(1950), p, w; PETTY GIRL, THE(1950), p, w; I'LL TAKE SWEDEN(1965), w; FRANKIE AND JOHNNY(1966), w; WICKED DREAMS OF PAULA SCHULTZ, THE(1968), w
Misc. Talkies
GREAT MORGAN, THE(1946), d

Sam Perrin
GOLDWYN FOLLIES, THE(1938), w; ARE YOU WITH IT?(1948), w

Vic Perrin
FOREVER FEMALE(1953); KLANSMAN, THE(1974); BLACK OAK CONSPIRACY(1977)

Victor Perrin
OUTRAGE(1950); DON'T BOTHER TO KNOCK(1952); SYSTEM, THE(1953); DRAGNET(1954); RIDING SHOTGUN(1954); BLACK TUESDAY(1955); BUBBLE, THE(1967)

Nat Perrine
PARDON MY SARONG(1942), w

Valerie Perrine
SLAUGHTERHOUSE-FIVE(1972); LAST AMERICAN HERO, THE(1973); LENNY(1974); W.C. FIELDS AND ME(1976); MR. BILLION(1977); SUPERMAN(1978); ELECTRIC HORSEMAN, THE(1979); MAGICIAN OF LUBLIN, THE(1979, Israel/Ger.); CAN'T STOP THE MUSIC(1980); SUPERMAN II(1980); AGENCY(1981, Can.); BORDER, THE(1982)

Leslie Perrins
HOUSE OF UNREST, THE(1931, Brit.); ROSARY, THE(1931, Brit.); SHERLOCK HOLMES' FATAL HOUR(1931, Brit.); BETRAYAL(1932, Brit.); EARLY TO BED(1933, Brit./Ger.); ROOF, THE(1933, Brit.); WHITE FACE(1933, Brit.); LASH, THE(1934, Brit.); LEAVE IT TO SMITH(1934); LORD EDGEWARE DIES(1934, Brit.); MAN WHO CHANGED HIS NAME, THE(1934, Brit.); OPEN ALL NIGHT(1934, Brit.); POINTING FINGER, THE(1934, Brit.); SONG AT EVENTIDE(1934, Brit.); WOMANHOOD(1934, Brit.); EXPERT'S OPINION(1935, Brit.); LINE ENGAGED(1935, Brit.); LUCKY DAYS(1935, Brit.); SHADOW OF MIKE EMERALD, THE(1935, Brit.); SILENT PASSENGER, THE(1935, Brit.); TRIUMPH OF SHERLOCK HOLMES, THE(1935, Brit.); VILLAGE SQUIRE, THE(1935, Brit.); WHITE LILAC(1935, Brit.); GAY LOVE(1936, Brit.); LADY JANE GREY(1936, Brit.); LIMPING MAN, THE(1936, Brit.); LIVING DEAD, THE(1936, Brit.); NO ESCAPE(1936, Brit.); RHYTHM IN THE AIR(1936, Brit.); SENSATION(1936, Brit.); SOUTHERN ROSES(1936, Brit.); SUNSHINE AHEAD(1936, Brit.); THEY DIDN'T KNOW(1936, Brit.); BULLDOG DRUMMOND AT BAY(1937, Brit.); HIGH TREASON(1937, Brit.); LOST CHORD, THE(1937, Brit.); PRICE OF FOLLY, THE(1937, Brit.); CALLING ALL CROOKS(1938, Brit.); GABLES MYSTERY, THE(1938, Brit.); HIGH COMMAND(1938, Brit.); I MARRIED A SPY(1938); NO PARKING(1938, Brit.); OLD IRON(1938, Brit.); ROMANCE A LA CARTE(1938, Brit.); ALL AT SEA(1939, Brit.); BLIND FOLLY(1939, Brit.); HIS LORDSHIP GOES TO PRESS(1939, Brit.); NORTH SEA PATROL(1939, Brit.); WANTED BY SCOTLAND YARD(1939, Brit.); CAPTAIN MOONLIGHT(1940, Brit.); WHO IS GUILTY?(1940, Brit.); MYSTERY OF ROOM 13(1941, Brit.); PRIME MINISTER, THE(1941, Brit.); WOMEN AREN'T ANGELS(1942, Brit.); AMAZING MR. FORREST, THE(1943, Brit.); SUSPECTED PERSON(1943, Brit.); HEAVEN IS ROUND THE CORNER(1944, Brit.); I'LL TURN TO YOU(1946, Brit.); TURNERS OF PROSPECT ROAD, THE(1947, Brit.); IDOL OF PARIS(1948, Brit.); MAN ON THE RUN(1949, Brit.); RUN FOR YOUR MONEY, A(1950, Brit.); MIDNIGHT EPISODE(1951, Brit.); BIG FRAME, THE(1953, Brit.); GUILTY?(1956, Brit.); HAUNTED STRANGLER, THE(1958, Brit.)

Adriana Perris
LAUGH PAGLIACCI(1948, Ital.)

Bernard Perris
DAUGHTERS OF DARKNESS(1971, Bel./ Fr./ Ger./ Ital.), cos

Ted Perritt
ENEMY BELOW, THE(1957)

Clement Perron
MY UNCLE ANTOINE(1971, Can.), w

Larry Perron
TIMBUKTU(1959); SPARTACUS(1960)

R. Perron
SNOW DEVILS, THE(1965, Ital.), set d

Marc Perrone
1984
SUNDAY IN THE COUNTRY, A(1984, Fr.), a, m

Marion Perroni
BEAT THE DEVIL(1953)

Denise Perronne
FORBIDDEN GAMES(1953, Fr.); GERVAISE(1956, Fr.)

Francois Perrot
NADA GANG, THE(1974, Fr./Ital.); DIRTY HANDS(1976, Fr/Ital./Ger.); COUP DE TORCHON(1981, Fr.); BANZAI(1983, Fr.)
1984
MY BEST FRIEND'S GIRL(1984, Fr.)

Jules Perrot
TURNING POINT, THE(1977), ch

Bill Perrott
DAKOTA LIL(1950)

Ruth Perrott
THIRTY FOOT BRIDE OF CANDY ROCK, THE(1959)

William Perrott
SON OF BILLY THE KID(1949)

Michael Perrotta
YOUR THREE MINUTES ARE UP(1973)

Mike Perrotta
WILD WHEELS(1969)

Brian Perrow
GAY DECEIVERS, THE(1969), makeup

Eugene Perrson
TRAIL STREET(1947)

Gene Perrson
PARTY CRASHERS, THE(1958)

Jorgen Perrson
ADALEN 31(1969, Swed.), ph

Perruzzi
MINOTAUR, THE(1961, Ital.), cos

Perry
MAN WHO LOVED CAT DANCING, THE(1973), w

Ann Perry
INSIDE AMY(1975)

Annette Perry
Silents
AFTER MARRIAGE(1925)

Anthony Perry
SIMBA(1955, Brit.), w; GIRL ON APPROVAL(1962, Brit.), p; IMPERSONATOR, THE(1962, Brit.), p; PARTY'S OVER, THE(1966, Brit.), p

Augusta Perry
Misc. Silents
HERITAGE(1920)

Barbara Perry
COUNSELLOR-AT-LAW(1933); Hl BEAUTIFUL(1944); ANGEL COMES TO BROOKLYN, AN(1945); I WAS A MALE WAR BRIDE(1949); SHOCK CORRIDOR(1963); NAKED KISS, THE(1964)

Ben L. Perry
BOSS, THE(1956), w; TERROR IN A TEXAS TOWN(1958), w

Ben Perry
FOLLOW THAT WOMAN(1945), w; BROTHERS RICO, THE(1957), w

Bob E. Perry
LARCENY(1948)

Bob Perry
BEHIND THE MAKEUP(1930); THOSE WHO DANCE(1930); TRAILING TROUBLE(1930); IRON MAN, THE(1931); OTHER MEN'S WOMEN(1931); POLITICS(1931); CARNIVAL BOAT(1932); FIGHTING MARSHAL, THE(1932); WINNER TAKE ALL(1932); TRIAL OF VIVIENNE WARE, THE(1932); HELL'S HIGHWAY(1932); LITTLE GIANT, THE(1933); MAYOR OF HELL, THE(1933); PICTURE SNATCHER(1933); EVELYN PRENTICE(1934); TWENTY MILLION SWEETHEARTS(1934); RENDEZVOUS(1935); GREAT O'MALLEY, THE(1937); STAGE DOOR(1937); BORN TO FIGHT(1938); JUVENILE COURT(1938); SISTERS, THE(1938); EACH DAWN I DIE(1939); FIFTH AVENUE GIRL(1939); KID FROM KOKOMO, THE(1939); SMASHING THE MONEY RING(1939); THEY MADE ME A CRIMINAL(1939); TORCHY PLAYS WITH DYNAMITE(1939); TWO THOROUGHBREDS(1939); FOUR JACKS AND A JILL(1941); MEET JOHN DOE(1941); STRAWBERRY BLONDE, THE(1941); UNFINISHED BUSINESS(1941); GREAT MAN'S LADY, THE(1942); ROXIE HART(1942); THEY DIED WITH THEIR BOOTS ON(1942); HAIRY APE, THE(1944); DILLINGER(1945); WITHIN THESE WALLS(1945); STRANGE LOVE OF MARTHA IVERS, THE(1946); EGG AND I, THE(1947); JOHNNY O'CLOCK(1947); WHIPLASH(1948); QUIET MAN, THE(1952); SECOND FIDDLE TO A STEEL GUITAR(1965)
Silents
OATH-BOUND(1922); FORTUNE HUNTER, THE(1927)

Carolyn Perry
LITTLE SEX, A(1982)

Cecil Perry
DAD AND DAVE COME TO TOWN(1938, Aus.); RANGLE RIVER(1939, Aus.)

Charles Bates Perry
SUN COMES UP, THE(1949)

Charles E. Perry
TATTERED DRESS, THE(1957)

Charles Perry
EACH DAWN I DIE(1939), w; TALK OF THE TOWN(1942); JOHNNY O'CLOCK(1947); DEAR MR. PROHACK(1949, Brit.); JOLSON SINGS AGAIN(1949); ABBOTT AND COSTELLO MEET THE INVISIBLE MAN(1951); THEY WERE NOT DIVIDED(1951, Brit.); MOULIN ROUGE(1952); SECOND MRS. TANQUERAY, THE(1952, Brit.); STORY OF ROBIN HOOD, THE(1952, Brit.); THEM!(1954); NIGHT MY NUMBER CAME UP, THE(1955, Brit.)

Charlotte Perry
GIRL IN POSSESSION(1934, Brit.)

Dan Perry
DELIRIUM(1979), ed; MALIBU HIGH(1979), ed; ECHOES(1983), ed

Dean Perry
CHEAP DETECTIVE, THE(1978)

Desdemond Perry
SACCO AND VANZETTI(1971, Ital./Fr.)

Desmond Perry
GUY CALLED CAESAR, A(1962, Brit.); ULYSSES(1967, U.S./Brit.); BROTHERLY LOVE(1970, Brit.); MC KENZIE BREAK, THE(1970); PADDY(1970, Irish); RECKONING, THE(1971, Brit.)

Don Perry
LINCOLN CONSPIRACY, THE(1977), md
1984
NIGHT OF THE COMET(1984), md

Earl Perry
KONA COAST(1968)

Edd Perry
BATTLE BEYOND THE SUN(1963)

Elaine Perry
DEADLY TRAP, THE(1972, Fr./Ital.), w

Eleanor Perry
DAVID AND LISA(1962), w; LADYBUG, LADYBUG(1963), w; SWIMMER, THE(1968), w; LAST SUMMER(1969), w; TRUMAN CAPOTE'S TRILOGY(1969), w; DIARY OF A MAD HOUSEWIFE(1970), w; LADY IN THE CAR WITH GLASSES AND A GUN, THE(1970, U.S./Fr.), w; MAN WHO LOVED CAT DANCING, THE(1973), p

Elizabeth Perry
TAPS(1981)

Felton Perry
MEDIUM COOL(1969); TROUBLE MAN(1972); MAGNUM FORCE(1973); WALKING TALL(1973); NIGHT CALL NURSES(1974); TOWERING INFERNO, THE(1974); MEAN DOG BLUES(1978)
Misc. Talkies
SUDDEN DEATH(1977)

Frank Perry
RIO RITA(1942); ISLAND WOMEN(1958), art d; DAVID AND LISA(1962), d; LADYBUG, LADYBUG(1963), p&d; SWIMMER, THE(1968), p, d; LAST SUMMER(1969), d; MY SIDE OF THE MOUNTAIN(1969); TRUMAN CAPOTE'S TRILOGY(1969), p&d; DIARY OF A MAD HOUSEWIFE(1970), p&d; DOC(1971), p&d; PLAY IT AS IT LAYS(1972), p, d; NEPTUNE FACTOR, THE(1973, Can.); MAN ON A SWING(1974), d; RANCHO DELUXE(1975), d; MOMMIE DEAREST(1981), d, w; MONSIGNOR(1982), d
Misc. Talkies
BUSH PILOT(1947); ACCIDENT(1983)

Fred C. Perry
1984
BLIND DATE(1984), w

Fred Perry
Misc. Silents
POPPY(1917)

Frederick Perry
Silents
INNOCENT(1918)
Misc. Silents
DR. RAMEAU(1915); FAMILY STAIN, THE(1915); RAFFLES, THE AMATEUR CRACKSMAN(1917)

Gene Perry
PARIS INTERLUDE(1934); WONDER BAR(1934)

George Perry
MONSTER A GO-GO(1965)

George Sessions Perry
ARKANSAS TRAVELER, THE(1938), w; SOUTHERNER, THE(1945), w

Gil Perry
SOURDOUGH(1977)

Harry Perry
HELL'S ANGELS(1930), ph; CORVETTE K-225(1943), ph
Silents
SINS OF ROZANNE(1920), ph; CAPPY RICKS(1921), ph; CITY OF SILENT MEN(1921), ph; EASY ROAD, THE(1921), ph; FAITH HEALER, THE(1921), ph; PRINCE THERE WAS, A(1921), ph; WHITE AND UNMARRIED(1921), ph; CRIMSON CHALLENGE, THE(1922), ph; IF YOU BELIEVE IT, IT'S SO(1922), ph; ORDEAL, THE(1922), ph; SHADOWS(1922), ph; APRIL SHOWERS(1923), ph; ARE YOU A FAILURE?(1923), ph; VIRGINIAN, THE(1923), ph; FIGHTING AMERICAN, THE(1924), ph; FLATTERY(1925), ph; NOW WE'RE IN THE AIR(1927), ph; WINGS(1927), ph

Hart Perry
WATCHED(1974), ph

Harvey G. Perry
MOVIE MOVIE(1978)

Harvey Perry
WINNER TAKE ALL(1932); IRISH IN US, THE(1935); WHIPLASH(1948); NEVER STEAL ANYTHING SMALL(1959)

Helen Perry
SHEEPDOG OF THE HILLS(1941, Brit.)

Howard Perry
PROLOGUE(1970, Can.)

Ida Perry
ELISABETH OF AUSTRIA(1931, Ger.); RASPUTIN(1932, Ger.)

Jack Perry
YOUNG DONOVAN'S KID(1931); STEADY COMPANY(1932); PERSONALITY KID, THE(1934); STOLEN HARMONY(1935); MILKY WAY, THE(1936); PROFESSOR BEWARE(1938); BALL OF FIRE(1941); KNOCK ON ANY DOOR(1949); SCARLET

ANGEL(1952); DIMBOOLA(1979, Aus.)

Jack Perry
DOCTOR SYN(1937, Brit), ph

Jaime Perry
FRIDAY THE 13TH PART II(1981)
1984
FRIDAY THE 13TH–THE FINAL CHAPTER(1984)

Jamie Perry
WIZ, THE(1978); WARRIORS, THE(1979)

Jean Perry
SWING TIME(1936); CAFE METROPOLE(1937); ESPIONAGE(1937); FIREFLY, THE(1937); HOLLYWOOD HOTEL(1937); ARSENE LUPIN RETURNS(1938); ARTISTS AND MODELS ABROAD(1938); SUEZ(1938)
Silents
HILLS OF MISSING MEN(1922); HEADS UP(1925); HIGH AND HANDSOME(1925)
Misc. Silents
DISCONTENTED WIVES(1921); RUSE OF THE RATTLER, THE(1921); PASSION'S PATHWAY(1924)

Jeffrey Perry
1984
OXFORD BLUES(1984)

Jeffrey S. Perry
REMEMBER MY NAME(1978); WEDDING, A(1978)

Jessie Perry
STAND UP AND CHEER(1934 80m FOX bw); FRISCO KID(1935); AND SO THEY WERE MARRIED(1936); THEODORA GOES WILD(1936); LET US LIVE(1939); TORCHY PLAYS WITH DYNAMITE(1939); SHE COULDN'T SAY NO(1941)

Jimmy Perry
DAD'S ARMY(1971, Brit.), w

Joan Perry
CASE OF THE MISSING MAN, THE(1935); GALLANT DEFENDER(1935); DANGEROUS INTRIGUE(1936); HEIR TO TROUBLE(1936); MEET NERO WOLFE(1936); MYSTERIOUS AVENGER, THE(1936); SHAKEDOWN(1936); COUNTERFEIT LADY(1937); DEVIL IS DRIVING, THE(1937); START CHEERING(1938); BLIND ALLEY(1939); GOOD GIRLS GO TO PARIS(1939); LONE WOLF STRIKES, THE(1940); BULLETS FOR O'HARA(1941); INTERNATIONAL SQUADRON(1941); MAISIE WAS A LADY(1941); NINE LIVES ARE NOT ENOUGH(1941); STRANGE ALIBI(1941)

Joe Perry
GREATEST STORY EVER TOLD, THE(1965)

John Bennett Perry
LIPSTICK(1976); LEGEND OF THE LONE RANGER, THE(1981); ONLY WHEN I LAUGH(1981)

John Perry
MAN ABOUT THE HOUSE, A(1947, Brit.), w; TREASURE HUNT(1952, Brit.), w; MAN, THE(1972), cos

Joseph Perry
DON'T JUST STAND THERE!(1968); LOVE GOD?, THE(1969); DOMINO PRINCIPLE, THE(1977)

Joyce Perry
CINCINNATI KID, THE(1965); MOSQUITO SQUADRON(1970, Brit.), w

Julyan Perry
HORRIBLE DR. HICHCOCK, THE(1964, Ital.), w

Karen Perry
1984
BROTHER FROM ANOTHER PLANET, THE(1984), cos

Katherine Perry
AIR MAIL(1932)
Misc. Silents
DIVORCE OF CONVENIENCE, A(1921); FOOLS AND RICHES(1923)

Kathryn Perry
SIDE STREET(1929); MY MAN GODFREY(1936)
Silents
LOVE IS AN AWFUL THING(1922); EARLY TO WED(1926); FIRST YEAR, THE(1926); WOMANPOWER(1926); HUSBANDS FOR RENT(1927); IS ZAT SO?(1927)
Misc. Silents
BLOOD WILL TELL(1927)

Ken Perry
CHINA DOLL(1958); PARTY GIRL(1958)

Kevin Perry
CONRACK(1974)

Dr. Leroy R. Perry, Jr.
PERSONAL BEST(1982)

Leslie Perry
HARRY'S WAR(1981)

Lester Perry
Silents
JORDAN IS A HARD ROAD(1915)

Linda Perry
SING ME A LOVE SONG(1936); TWO AGAINST THE WORLD(1936); CALIFORNIA MAIL, THE(1937); CASE OF THE STUTTERING BISHOP, THE(1937); GREAT GARRICK, THE(1937); LAND BEYOND THE LAW(1937); MR. DODD TAKES THE AIR(1937); THEY WON'T FORGET(1937)

Linette Perry
SECRET PLACE, THE(1958, Brit.), w

Loretta Perry
NO TIME FOR TEARS(1957, Brit.)

Lou Perry
NIGHT OF EVIL(1962), p, w; WHOLE SHOOTIN' MATCH, THE(1979); POLTERGEIST(1982)

Margaret Perry
NEW MORALS FOR OLD(1932); CEILNG ZERO(1935); GO WEST, YOUNG MAN(1936); CONRACK(1974)

Marguerite Perry
FRENCH WAY, THE(1952, Fr.)

Mary Perry
UNCLE VANYA(1958); ALL THE WAY HOME(1963)

Mike Perry
GOLDEN BOX, THE(1970)

Morris Perry
NOTHING BUT THE NIGHT(1975, Brit.); SWEENEY(1977, Brit.)
Nick Perry
SMITHY(1946, Aus.), p
Nora Perry
EARL OF CHICAGO, THE(1940); TRIAL OF MARY DUGAN, THE(1941)
P. Perry
Silents
JOAN THE WOMAN(1916)
Pamela Perry
SHANGRI-LA(1961)
Pascale Perry
GALLANT FOOL, THE(1933); KING OF THE ARENA(1933); FIDDLIN' BUCKAROO, THE(1934); GUN JUSTICE(1934); HONOR OF THE RANGE(1934); GUNS AND GUITARS(1936); LAWLESS RIDERS(1936); ROARIN' LEAD(1937); TRAIL BLAZERS, THE(1940); DESERT BANDIT(1941); UNDER FIESTA STARS(1941); SHADOWS ON THE SAGE(1942); SOMBRERO KID, THE(1942); THUNDER TOWN(1946); SPRING-TIME IN THE SIERRAS(1947); EYES OF TEXAS(1948); GUN RUNNER(1949)
Paschal Perry
WHERE'S JACK?(1969, Brit.)
Pasquel Perry
DAYS OF JESSE JAMES(1939); SAGA OF DEATH VALLEY(1939)
Patricia Perry
WILD RIVER(1960)
Paul Perry
LOVE IN THE DESERT(1929), ph; MIDNIGHT CLUB(1933); ROSE BOWL(1936); DESTROYER(1943)
Silents
NAN OF MUSIC MOUNTAIN(1917), ph; JANE GOES A' WOOING(1919), ph; ROUND UP, THE(1920), ph; OUTSIDE WOMAN, THE(1921), ph; OVER THE BOR-DER(1922), ph; SINGED WINGS(1922), ph; ON THE STROKE OF THREE(1924), ph; INTRODUCE ME(1925), ph; SINNERS IN LOVE(1928), ph; AIR LEGION, THE(1929), ph
Pauline Perry
Silents
KISS FOR SUSIE, A(1917)
Peter Perry
HONEYMOON OF TERROR(1961), p; MANTIS IN LACE(1968), ed; GUN RIDERS, THE(1969), ed; HORROR OF THE BLOOD MONSTERS(1970, U.S./Phil.), ed; HOLLY-WOOD HIGH(1977), p; YOUNG CYCLE GIRLS, THE(1979), p&d
Peter Perry, Jr.
FLESH MERCHANT, THE(1956), w
Phyllis Perry
STORY OF DR. WASSELL, THE(1944)
Robert E. Perry
MANHATTAN MERRY-GO-ROUND(1937); MEN WITH WINGS(1938); LONG VOY-AGE HOME, THE(1940); JACKASS MAIL(1942)
Robert Perry
BEGGARS OF LIFE(1928); MAN I LOVE, THE(1929); NOISY NEIGHBORS(1929); SKIN DEEP(1929); SEA GOD, THE(1930); LAWYER'S SECRET, THE(1931); DR. SOCRATES(1935); MURDER WITH PICTURES(1936); MY MAN GODFREY(1936); RIFF-RAFF(1936); TIMOTHY'S QUEST(1936); MURDER GOES TO COLLEGE(1937); BEAU GESTE(1939); LADY'S FROM KENTUCKY, THE(1939); NATURAL ENE-MIES(1979)
Silents
VOLCANO(1926); JAWS OF STEEL(1927); WHITE GOLD(1927)
Misc. Silents
DRESSED TO KILL(1928)
Rod Perry
BLACK GESTAPO, THE(1975); SOURDOUGH(1977), w, ph
Misc. Talkies
BLACK GODFATHER, THE(1974)
Roger Perry
FLYING FONTAINES, THE(1959); FOLLOW THE BOYS(1963); CAT, THE(1966); YOU'VE GOT TO BE SMART(1967); HEAVEN WITH A GUN(1969); COUNT YORGA, VAMPIRE(1970); RETURN OF COUNT YORGA, THE(1971); THING WITH TWO HEADS, THE(1972); ROLLER BOOGIE(1979)
Ron Perry
DEMENTIA 13(1963)
Ronald Perry
COOL WORLD, THE(1963)
Sara Perry
DAMNED DON'T CRY, THE(1950); ONE TOO MANY(1950)
Scott Perry
SILENCERS, THE(1966); GETTING STRAIGHT(1970); D.C. CAB(1983); NATIONAL LAMPOON'S VACATION(1983)
Simon Perry
ANOTHER TIME, ANOTHER PLACE(1983, Brit.), p
1984
ANOTHER TIME, ANOTHER PLACE(1984, Brit.), p; LOOSE CONNECTIONS(1984, Brit.), p; 1984(1984, Brit.), p
Stanella Perry
OH, WHAT A NIGHT(1935)
Stephen Perry
SOUND AND THE FURY, THE(1959); RAISIN IN THE SUN, A(1961); LEARNING TREE, THE(1969)
Steven Perry
MAN IN THE NET, THE(1959)
Stevie Perry
THIS REBEL BREED(1960)
Stuart Perry
O LUCKY MAN!(1973, Brit.)
Sue Carol Perry
DEADHEAD MILES(1982)
Susan Perry
JULIA MISBEHAVES(1948); KNOCK ON ANY DOOR(1949)
Terra Perry
TOUGH ENOUGH(1983)

Tileston Perry
THIS IS THE ARMY(1943)
Ty Perry
AT WAR WITH THE ARMY(1950); TWIST ALL NIGHT(1961)
Vic Perry
ATOMIC MAN, THE(1955, Brit.); MOZAMBIQUE(1966, Brit.)
Victor Perry
JULIUS CAESAR(1953); PICKUP ON SOUTH STREET(1953)
Vincent G. Perry
TATTERED DRESS, THE(1957)
Vincent Perry
GOOD MORNING, MISS DOVE(1955)
Vivian Perry
Misc. Silents
WHEN LOVE IS KING(1916)
Walter Perry
KATHLEEN MAVOURNEEN(1930); THIRD ALARM, THE(1930); THOROUGH-BRED, THE(1930); TRIGGER TRICKS(1930); TROOPERS THREE(1930); TWO GUN MAN, THE(1931); DYNAMITE DENNY(1932); SPIRIT OF THE WEST(1932); SHE COULDN'T TAKE IT(1935); LETTER OF INTRODUCTION(1938)
Silents
CORNER IN COLLEENS, A(1916); TRUTHFUL TULLIVER(1917); BY PROXY(1918); FLY GOD, THE(1918); PRISONER OF THE PINES(1918); END OF THE GAME, THE(1919); MAN WHO TURNED WHITE, THE(1919); SCRAPPER, THE(1922); SE-COND HAND ROSE(1922); SOULS FOR SALE(1923); DARK STAIRWAYS(1924); UNHOLY THREE, THE(1925); JOHNSTOWN FLOOD, THE(1926); IRISH HEARTS(1927)
Misc. Silents
LEARNIN' OF JIM BENTON, THE(1917); MLLE PAULETTE(1918); DANGEROUS WATERS(1919); FUGITIVE FROM MATRIMONY(1919); PAGAN GOD, THE(1919); PRODIGAL LIAR, THE(1919); FIRE EATER, THE(1921); GUTTERSNIPE, THE(1922); WHITE FANG(1925); WILFUL YOUTH(1927)
Wanda Perry
KID MILLIONS(1934); MURDER AT THE VANITIES(1934); ROBERTA(1935); THIN ICE(1937); GUILT OF JANET AMES, THE(1947); CALL NORTHSIDE 777(1948); JOLSON SINGS AGAIN(1949); MISS GRANT TAKES RICHMOND(1949)
William Perry
Silents
MARK OF ZORRO(1920), m
Winton Perry
CHEYENNE TORNADO(1935)
Ralph Perry-Robinson
1984
ANOTHER COUNTRY(1984, Brit.)
Clara Perryman
1984
BLACK ROOM, THE(1984)
Dian Perryman
1984
NINJA III–THE DOMINATION(1984), set d; SILENT NIGHT, DEADLY NIGHT(1984), prod d
Diane Perryman
REVENGE OF THE NINJA(1983), set d
John Perryman
ON THE NICKEL(1980)
1984
FOOTLOOSE(1984); NINJA III–THE DOMINATION(1984)
Lloyd Perryman
SOUTH OF ARIZONA(1938); RIO GRANDE(1950)
Louis Perryman
1984
LAST NIGHT AT THE ALAMO(1984)
Ronald Perryman
NONE BUT THE BRAVE(1963), ph, ed
Mandy Perryment
MUSIC MACHINE, THE(1979, Brit.)
Joseph Persaud
ADIOS SABATA(1971, Ital./Span.)
Toolsie Persaud [Tulsi Prasad]
MUMMY'S SHROUD, THE(1967, Brit.)
Maria Perschy
MAN'S FAVORITE SPORT[(?)$rb; FREUD(1962); PASSWORD IS COURAGE, THE(1962, Brit.); NO SURVIVORS, PLEASE(1963, Ger.); ORDERED TO LOVE(1963, Ger.); SQUADRON 633(1964, U.S./Brit.); 633 SQUADRON(1964); MAD EXECUTION-ERS, THE(1965, Ger.); FIVE GOLDEN DRAGONS(1967, Brit.); RIDE THE HIGH WIND(1967, South Africa); TALL WOMEN, THE(1967, Aust./Ital./Span.); WITCH WITHOUT A BROOM, A(1967, U.S./Span.); CASTLE OF FU MANCHU, THE(1968, Ger./Span./Ital./Brit.); DESPERATE ONES, THE(1968 U.S./Span.); LAST DAY OF THE WAR, THE(1969, U.S./Ital./Span.); MURDERS IN THE RUE MORGUE(1971); HUNCHBACK OF THE MORGUE, THE(1972, Span.); HOUSE OF PSYCHOTIC WOMEN, THE zero(1973, Span.); HORROR OF THE ZOMBIES(1974, Span.); PEOPLE WHO OWN THE DARK(1975, Span.)
Misc. Talkies
LEO CHRONICLES, THE(1972)
Frank Pershing
THAT OTHER WOMAN(1942); TUCSON RAIDERS(1944); STRANGE TRIAN-GLE(1946); THREE DARING DAUGHTERS(1948); IMPACT(1949); WHEN WILLIE COMES MARCHING HOME(1950); UNKNOWN MAN, THE(1951)
Maj. Frank Pershing
THEY WERE EXPENDABLE(1945)
Marcella Pershing
Misc. Silents
LOOPED FOR LIFE(1924)
Elena Persiani
TIN GIRL, THE(1970, Ital.)
Hubert Persicke
WILLY(1963, U.S./Ger.)

Benito Persico
END OF THE WORLD(in Our Usual Bed In a Night Full of Rain), THE*1/2 (1978, Ital.), cos
Rodja Persidsky
PIMPERNEL SVENSSON(1953, Swed.)
Henri Persin
LONGEST DAY, THE(1962), ph; EXTERMINATORS, THE(1965 Fr.), ph; SERGEANT, THE(1968), ph; VIVA MAX!(1969), ph; EL CONDOR(1970), ph; LEGEND OF FRENCHIE KING, THE(1971, Fr./Ital./Span./Brit.), ph
Bill Persky
SERIAL(1980), d
Lester Persky
FORTUNE AND MEN'S EYES(1971, U.S./Can.), p; "EQUUS"(1977), p; HAIR(1979), p; YANKS(1979), p
Lisa Jane Persky
GREAT SANTINI, THE(1979); LOVE IN A TAXI(1980); AMERICAN POP(1981)
1984
COTTON CLUB, THE(1984)
Lisa Persky
BREATHLESS(1983)
Marilyn Persky
FRONT, THE(1976)
Nehemiah Persoff
ON THE WATERFRONT(1954); HARDER THEY FALL, THE(1956); WILD PARTY, THE(1956); WRONG MAN, THE(1956); MEN IN WAR(1957); STREET OF SINNERS(1957); BADLANDERS, THE(1958); THIS ANGRY AGE(1958, Ital./Fr.); AL CAPONE(1959); DAY OF THE OUTLAW(1959); GREEN MANSIONS(1959); NEVER STEAL ANYTHING SMALL(1959); SOME LIKE IT HOT(1959); BIG SHOW, THE(1961); COMANCHEROS, THE(1961); HOOK, THE(1962); FATE IS THE HUNTER(1964); GLOBAL AFFAIR, A(1964); GREATEST STORY EVER TOLD, THE(1965); DAY OF THE OWL, THE(1968, Ital./Fr.); MONEY JUNGLE, THE(1968); PANIC IN THE CITY(1968); POWER, THE(1968); TOO MANY THIEVES(1968); GIRL WHO KNEW TOO MUCH, THE(1969); MAFIA(1969, Fr./Ital.); PEOPLE NEXT DOOR, THE(1970); MRS. POLLIFAX-SPY(1971); RED SKY AT MORNING(1971); PSYCHIC KILLER(1975); VOYAGE OF THE DAMNED(1976, Brit.); IN SEARCH OF HISTORIC JESUS(1980); ST. HELENS(1981); O'HARA'S WIFE(1983); YENTL(1983)
Misc. Talkies
DEADLY HARVEST(1972)
Michele Person
1984
REPO MAN(1984)
Fred Personne
EVERY MAN FOR HIMSELF(1980, Fr.)
1984
LE CRABE TAMBOUR(1984, Fr.)
Fort Bliss Personnel
TAKE THE HIGH GROUND(1953)
Ed Persons
MY SIDE OF THE MOUNTAIN(1969)
Fern Persons
GOLDEN GLOVES STORY, THE(1950); ON THE RIGHT TRACK(1981); CLASS(1983); RISKY BUSINESS(1983)
1984
GRANDVIEW, U.S.A.(1984)
Mark Persons
SILENT RUNNING(1972)
Thomas Persons
CONVICTED(1931), ed; SEA GHOST, THE(1931), ed; DRIFTER, THE(1932), ed
Tom Persons
LAWLESS WOMAN, THE(1931), ed; MIDNIGHT SPECIAL(1931), ed; SMART GIRL(1935), ed
Thomas H. Persse
Misc. Silents
HUGON THE MIGHTY(1918); UP THE ROAD WITH SALLIE(1918)
Thomas Persse
Silents
PAIR OF SILK STOCKINGS, A(1918)
Allen Persselin
HOMEWORK(1982), ed
Edvard Persson
PIMPERNEL SVENSSON(1953, Swed.)
Essy Persson
MISSION STARDUST(1968, Ital./Span./Ger.); OPERATION LOVEBIRDS(1968, Den.); THERESE AND ISABELLE(1968, U.S./Ger.); VIBRATION(1969, Swed.); CRY OF THE BANSHEE(1970, Brit.)
Eugene Persson
SWELL GUY(1946); EGG AND I, THE(1947); STRATTON STORY, THE(1949); MA AND PA KETTLE GO TO TOWN(1950); MA AND PA KETTLE AT THE FAIR(1952)
Gene Persson
MA AND PA KETTLE(1949); ON DANGEROUS GROUND(1951); EARTH VS. THE SPIDER(1958); SPIDER, THE(1958); DUTCHMAN(1966, Brit.), p
Hasse Persson
JOE HILL(1971, Swed./U.S.)
Jan Persson
OBSESSION(1968, Swed.), ed; ADVENTURES OF PICASSO, THE(1980, Swed.), ed
Jorgen Persson
ELVIRA MADIGAN(1967, Swed.), ph; JOE HILL(1971, Swed./U.S.), ph
Maria Persson
PIPPI IN THE SOUTH SEAS(1974, Swed./Ger.); PIPPI ON THE RUN(1977)
Sven Persson
RHINO(1964), ph; ONE STEP TO HELL(1969, U.S./Ital./Span.), ph
Yvonne Persson
VIBRATION(1969, Swed.)
Joseph Persuad
BURN(1970)
Margaret Pert
THAT NIGHT WITH YOU(1945)

Inge Perten
ADVENTURE FOR TWO(1945, Brit.)
Domenenico Pertica
AMARCORD(1974, Ital.)
Elfie Pertramer
MAN WHO WALKED THROUGH THE WALL, THE(1964, Ger.)
Theo Pertsinidis
FIRE IN THE STONE, THE(1983, Aus.)
Bill Pertwee
DAD'S ARMY(1971, Brit.); CONFESSIONS OF A POP PERFORMER(1975, Brit.)
Carolyn Pertwee
MOUSE ON THE MOON, THE(1963, Brit.)
John Pertwee
HELTER SKELTER(1949, Brit.)
Jon Pertwee
YANK AT OXFORD, A(1938); SECRET FOUR, THE(1940, Brit.); TROUBLE IN THE AIR(1948, Brit.); WILLIAM COMES TO TOWN(1948, Brit.); DEAR MR. PROHACK(1949, Brit.); BODY SAID NO!, THE(1950, Brit.); MISS PILGRIM'S PROGRESS(1950, Brit.); MYSTERY AT THE BURLESQUE(1950, Brit.); MR. DRAKE'S DUCK(1951, Brit.); GAY DOG, THE(1954, Brit.); WILL ANY GENTLEMAN?(1955, Brit.); YANK IN ERMINE, A(1955, Brit.); UGLY DUCKLING, THE(1959, Brit.); JUST JOE(1960, Brit.); NOT A HOPE IN HELL(1960, Brit.); NEARLY A NASTY ACCIDENT(1962, Brit.); LADIES WHO DO(1964, Brit.); I'VE GOTTA HORSE(1965, Brit.); YOU MUST BE JOKING!(1965, Brit.); CARRY ON SCREAMING(1966, Brit.); UP IN THE AIR(1969, Brit.); HOUSE THAT DRIPPED BLOOD, THE(1971, Brit.)
Michael Pertwee
MAN WITH 100 FACES, THE(1938, Brit.), w; 2,000 WOMEN(1944, Brit.), w; AGAINST THE WIND(1948, Brit.), w; TROUBLE IN THE AIR(1948, Brit.), w; INTERRUPTED JOURNEY, THE(1949, Brit.), w; SILENT DUST(1949, Brit.), w; LAUGHTER IN PARADISE(1951, Brit.), a, w; MADAME LOUISE(1951, Brit.), w; NIGHT WAS OUR FRIEND(1951, Brit.), a, w; CURTAIN UP(1952, Brit.), w; THIEF OF VENICE, THE(1952), w; MR. POTTS GOES TO MOSCOW(1953, Brit.), w; TONIGHT'S THE NIGHT(1954, Brit.), w; IT'S A GREAT DAY(1956, Brit.), w; NOW AND FOREVER(1956, Brit.), a, w; NOT WANTED ON VOYAGE(1957, Brit.), w; YOUR PAST IS SHOWING(1958, Brit.), w; LOVE SPECIALIST, THE(1959, Ital.), w; TOO MANY CROOKS(1959, Brit.), w; BOTTOMS UP(1960, Brit.), w; IT STARTED IN NAPLES(1960), w; MAKE MINE MINK(1960, Brit.), w; MOUSE ON THE MOON, THE(1963, Brit.), w; IN THE DOGHOUSE(1964, Brit.), w; LADIES WHO DO(1964, Brit.), w; CAVERN, THE(1965, Ital./Ger.), w; STRANGE BEDFELLOWS(1965), w; FINDERS KEEPERS(1966, Brit.), w; FUNNY THING HAPPENED ON THE WAY TO THE FORUM, A(1966), w; MAGNIFICENT TWO, THE(1967, Brit.), w, ed; SALT & PEPPER(1968, Brit.), w; ONE MORE TIME(1970, Brit.), w; SOME WILL, SOME WON'T(1970, Brit.), w; DON'T JUST LIE THERE, SAY SOMETHING!(1973, Brit.), w; DIGBY, THE BIGGEST DOG IN THE WORLD(1974, Brit.), w
Roland Pertwee
INTERFERENCE(1928), w; HONOR OF THE FAMILY(1931), w; I LIKE YOUR NERVE(1931), w; MONKEY BUSINESS(1931), w; ROAD TO SINGAPORE(1931), w; BLIND SPOT(1932, Brit.), w; HELP YOURSELF(1932, Brit.), w; ILLEGAL(1932, Brit.), w; MURDER ON THE SECOND FLOOR(1932, Brit.), w; CRUCIFIX, THE(1934, Brit.), w; GHOUL, THE(1934, Brit.), w; NIGHT OF THE PARTY, THE(1934, Brit.), w; HONOURS EASY(1935, Brit.), w; MAN OF THE MOMENT(1935, Brit.), w; WITHOUT REGRET(1935), w; DINNER AT THE RITZ(1937, Brit.), w; NON-STOP NEW YORK(1937, Brit.), w; YANK AT OXFORD, A(1938), w; TWO'S COMPANY(1939, Brit.), w; U-BOAT 29(1939, Brit.), w; WARE CASE, THE(1939, Brit.), w; RETURN TO YESTERDAY(1940, Brit.), w; SECRET FOUR, THE(1940, Brit.), a, w; THEY CAME BY NIGHT(1940, Brit.), w; GIRL IN DISTRESS(1941, Brit.), w; IT HAPPENED TO ONE MAN(1941, Brit.), w; PROUD VALLEY, THE(1941, Brit.), w; VOICE IN THE NIGHT, A(1941, Brit.), w; PIMPERNEL SMITH(1942, Brit.), a, w; PLAYBOY, THE(1942, Brit.), w; TALK ABOUT JACQUELINE(1942, Brit.), a, w; ADVENTURE IN BLACKMAIL(1943, Brit.), d, w; GENTLE SEX, THE(1943, Brit.), w; LAMP STILL BURNS, THE(1943, Brit.), w; NIGHT INVADER, THE(1943, Brit), w; YOUNG MAN'S FANCY(1943, Brit.), w; HALF-WAY HOUSE, THE(1945, Brit.), w; MADONNA OF THE SEVEN MOONS(1945, Brit.), w; THEY WERE SISTERS(1945, Brit.), a, w; CARAVAN(1946, Brit.), w; MAGIC BOW, THE(1947, Brit.), w; NIGHT BEAT(1948, Brit.), w; DIAMOND CITY(1949, Brit.), w; SILENT DUST(1949, Brit.), w; PINK STRING AND SEALING WAX(1950, Brit.), w; IT'S A GREAT DAY(1956, Brit.), w; NOT WANTED ON VOYAGE(1957, Brit.), w
Silents
BRIDAL CHAIR, THE(1919, Brit.), w; AUNT RACHEL(1920, Brit.), w; LAST ROSE OF SUMMER, THE(1920, Brit.), w; OUT TO WIN(1923, Brit.), w
Peru
LAST MOVIE, THE(1971), m
Luciano Perugia
WHITE VOICES(1965, Fr./Ital.), p; GIRL WHO COULDN'T SAY NO, THE(1969, Ital.), p; BROTHER SUN, SISTER MOON(1973, Brit./Ital.), p; DEAF SMITH AND JOHNNY EARS(1973, Ital.), p
Leo Perutz
Silents
BOLIBAR(1928, Brit.), w
Peruzzi
GUNS OF THE BLACK WITCH(1961, Fr./Ital.), cos
Archille Peruzzi
GOLIATH AND THE DRAGON(1961, Ital./Fr.), cos
Ditta Peruzzi
DAVID AND GOLIATH(1961, Ital.), cos
Giuseppe Peruzzi
THIS MAN CAN'T DIE(1970, Ital.), makeup
Patrick Pervion
MY SIDE OF THE MOUNTAIN(1969)
P. Pervushin
LADY WITH THE DOG, THE(1962, USSR)
Sandrine Pery
1984
EDITH AND MARCEL(1984, Fr.), ed
Notis Peryalis
ELECTRA(1962, Gr.); RED LANTERNS(1965, Gr.)
Carlo Pes
DORIAN GRAY(1970, Ital./Brit./Ger./Liechtenstein), m

Giorgio Pes
LEOPARD, THE(1963, Ital.), set d
Diego Pesaola
GIRL FROM TRIESTE, THE(1983, Ital.)
Reno Pesauri
NIGHT THEY RAIDED MINSKY'S, THE(1968)
Richard Pesavento
E.T. THE EXTRA-TERRESTRIAL(1982)
Leo Pescarolo
GIORDANO BRUNO(1973, Ital.), p
Leonardo Pescarolo
GALILEO(1968, Ital./Bul.), p
Richard Pescaud
SAY HELLO TO YESTERDAY(1971, Brit.)
Frank Pesce
ONE MAN JURY(1978); PARADISE ALLEY(1978); KILLER FISH(1979, Ital./Braz.); DEFIANCE(1980); MANIAC(1980); BIG SCORE, THE(1983); EUREKA(1983, Brit.)
1984
BEVERLY HILLS COP(1984)
Frank Pesche
FINGERS(1978)
Joey Peschl
DON'T GO IN THE HOUSE(1980)
Ildika Pesci
ASSISTANT, THE(1982, Czech.)
Joe Pesci
RAGING BULL(1980); I'M DANCING AS FAST AS I CAN(1982); DEAR MR. WONDERFUL(1983, Ger.); EASY MONEY(1983); EUREKA(1983, Brit.)
1984
ONCE UPON A TIME IN AMERICA(1984)
Joseph Pesci
DEATH COLLECTOR(1976)
Misc. Talkies
FAMILY ENFORCER(1978)
Paolo Pescini
SANDRA(1966, Ital.)
Carl Pescino
PIRATE OF THE BLACK HAWK, THE(1961, Fr./Ital.), p
Giorgio Pescino
PIRATE OF THE BLACK HAWK, THE(1961, Fr./Ital.), p
Donna Pescow
SATURDAY NIGHT FEVER(1977)
Gabriella Pescucci
DRIVER'S SEAT, THE(1975, Ital.), cos; DIVINE NYMPH, THE(1979, Ital.), cos; CITY OF WOMEN(1980, Ital./Fr.), cos; PASSION OF LOVE(1982, Ital./Fr.), cos; LA NUIT DE VARENNES(1983, Fr./Ital.), cos
1984
ONCE UPON A TIME IN AMERICA(1984), cos
Richard Pescud
INTERLUDE(1968, Brit.)
1984
OXFORD BLUES(1984); TOP SECRET!(1984)
Ladislav Pesek
MERRY WIVES, THE(1940, Czech.); TRANSPORT FROM PARADISE(1967, Czech.); ADELE HASN'T HAD HER SUPPER YET(1978, Czech.)
O. Peshkov
JACK FROST(1966, USSR)
Alexander Peskanov
HE KNOWS YOU'RE ALONE(1980), m
Mark Peskanov
HE KNOWS YOU'RE ALONE(1980), m
Ben Peskay
TOP BANANA(1954), p
Dina Peskin
FAITHFUL CITY(1952, Israel)
Ben Pesner
STARTING OVER(1979)
Leo B. Pessin
LETTER FROM AN UNKNOWN WOMAN(1948)
Leo Pessin
DAVID AND BATHSHEBA(1951)
Luiz Alberto Luciano Pessoa
MARGIN, THE,(1969, Braz.)
Louis C. Pessolano
FARMER, THE(1977)
Jean-Pierre Pessoz
MURMUR OF THE HEART(1971, Fr./Ital./Ger.)
Emilio Petacci
ANNA(1951, Ital.)
Costa Petals
LEO AND LOREE(1980), ph
Buckley Petawabano
COLD JOURNEY(1975, Can.)
Bill Petch
WINSTANLEY(1979, Brit.)
Pete Daily and His Chicagoans
YES SIR, MR. BONES(1951)
Pete the Dog
Silents
WESTERN VENGEANCE(1924)
Pete, the Dog of Flanders
SILENT CALL, THE(1961)
Ilona Petenyi
FATHER(1967, Hung.)
Katalin Petenyi
1984
REVOLT OF JOB, THE(1984, Hung./Ger.), w, ed

David Peter
I'LL TELL THE WORLD(1945)
Hans Peter
KING OF BURLESQUE(1936), art d; SECOND FIDDLE(1939), art d; PRISONER OF ZENDA, THE(1952), art d
Rene Peter
Silents
GOOD AND NAUGHTY(1926), w
Sinay Peter
HANNAH K.(1983, Fr.)
Svi Peter
1984
IMPULSE(1984)
The Peter Meremblum California Junior Symphony Orchestra
THEY SHALL HAVE MUSIC(1939)
Peter Meremblum Junior Orchestra
MEXICANA(1945)
Peter Meremblum's California Junior Symphony Orchestra
SONG OF RUSSIA(1943)
The Peter Sisters
NOUS IRONS A PARIS(1949, Fr.)
Peter the Great
Misc. Silents
WILD JUSTICE(1925); KING OF THE PACK(1926)
"Peter"
HERE COMES THE SUN(1945, Brit.)
Frantisek Peterka
LADY ON THE TRACKS, THE(1968, Czech.)
Don Peterman
WHEN A STRANGER CALLS(1979), ph; RICH AND FAMOUS(1981), ph; YOUNG DOCTORS IN LOVE(1982), ph; FLASHDANCE(1983), ph
1984
BEST DEFENSE(1984), ph; MASS APPEAL(1984), ph; SPLASH(1984), ph
Donald Peterman
KING OF THE MOUNTAIN(1981), ph; KISS ME GOODBYE(1982), ph
Joe Peterman
Silents
DOUBLE LIFE OF MR. ALFRED BURTON, THE(1919, Brit.)
Misc. Silents
LADS OF THE VILLAGE, THE(1919, Brit.)
Ilse Peternell
PRIEST OF ST. PAULI, THE(1970, Ger.)
A.D. Peters
LAST HOLIDAY(1950, Brit.), p; INSPECTOR CALLS, AN(1954, Brit.), p
Alex Peters
WAY OF A GAUCHO(1952)
Aliba Peters
COMEDIANS, THE(1967)
Aphasia Peters
1984
MICKI AND MAUDE(1984)
Audrey Peters
MIDDLE OF THE NIGHT(1959)
Barbara Peters
BURY ME AN ANGEL(1972), d&w; YOUNG NURSES, THE(1973); art d; SUMMER SCHOOL TEACHERS(1977), d&w
Barry Peters
AMSTERDAM AFFAIR, THE(1968 Brit.), ed; AT THE EARTH'S CORE(1976, Brit.), ed; PEOPLE THAT TIME FORGOT, THE(1977, Brit.), ed; ARABIAN ADVENTURE(1979, Brit.), ed; HOUSE WHERE EVIL DWELLS, THE(1982), ed
1984
SWORD OF THE VALIANT(1984, Brit.), ed
Bernadette Peters
ACE ELI AND RODGER OF THE SKIES(1973); LONGEST YARD, THE(1974); SILENT MOVIE(1976); VIGILANTE FORCE(1976); W.C. FIELDS AND ME(1976); JERK, THE(1979); HEARTBEEPS(1981); PENNIES FROM HEAVEN(1981); TULIPS(1981, Can); ANNIE(1982)
Brenda Peters
RAGMAN'S DAUGHTER, THE(1974, Brit.)
Brock Peters
CARMEN JONES(1954); PORGY AND BESS(1959); L-SHAPED ROOM, THE(1962, Brit.); TO KILL A MOCKINGBIRD(1962); HEAVENS ABOVE!(1963, Brit.); MAJOR DUNDEE(1965); PAWNBROKER, THE(1965); INCIDENT, THE(1967); DARING GAME(1968); P.J.(1968); REVENGE AT EL PASO(1968, Ital.); ACE HIGH(1969, Ital.); MC MASTERS, THE(1970); BLACK GIRL(1972); FIVE ON THE BLACK HAND SIDE(1973), p; SLAUGHTER'S BIG RIP-OFF(1973); SOYLENT GREEN(1973); LOST IN THE STARS(1974); FRAMED(1975); TWO-MINUTE WARNING(1976)
Brooke L. Peters
UNEARTHLY, THE(1957), p&d; ANATOMY OF A PSYCHO(1961), p&d
Cactus Mack Peters
SUNDOWN KID, THE(1942); SUNDOWN RIDERS(1948)
Carol Peters
GOOD MORNING... AND GOODBYE(1967)
Charles Peters
WALTZ TIME(1946, Brit.); IT'S A GRAND LIFE(1953, Brit.)
Charlie Peters
PATERNITY(1981), w; KISS ME GOODBYE(1982), w
1984
BLAME IT ON RIO(1984), w
Chris Peters
LUM AND ABNER ABROAD(1956)
Clarke Peters
MUSIC MACHINE, THE(1979, Brit.); OUTLAND(1981); SILVER DREAM RACER(1982, Brit.)
Clive Peters
NIGHTHAWKS(1978, Brit.)
Colleen Peters
MY SIX LOVES(1963)

Dave "Howdy" Peters
FORBIDDEN ISLAND(1959)
David Peters
GUADALCANAL DIARY(1943)
Deedy Peters
Misc. Talkies
HELP ME...I'M POSSESSED(1976)
Denis Peters
DUTCHMAN(1966, Brit.)
Dennis Alaba Peters
CURSE OF THE VOODOO(1965, Brit.)
Don Peters
TEN GENTLEMEN FROM WEST POINT(1942); DESTROYER(1943); INCREDIBLE MR. LIMPET, THE(1964), spec eff; BLOODY MAMA(1970), w
Donald A. Peters
GOODBYE, MY LADY(1956), art d; LAFAYETTE ESCADRILLE(1958), prod d; NAKED PREY, THE(1966, U.S./South Africa), w; BEACH RED(1967), w
Edith Peters
CARTHAGE IN FLAMES(1961, Fr./Ital.); TURKISH CUCUMBER, THE(1963, Ger.); TRAMPLERS, THE(1966, Ital.); KISS THE GIRLS AND MAKE THEM DIE(1967, U.S./Ital.)
Edythe Peters
BLOOD AND ROSES(1961, Fr./Ital.)
Erika Peters
MR. SARDONICUS(1961); HOUSE OF THE DAMNED(1963); ATOMIC BRAIN, THE(1964)
Felicitas Peters
KING, QUEEN, KNAVE(1972, Ger./U.S.)
Fred Peters
I CONQUER THE SEA(1936)
Fred W. Peters
Misc. Silents
RECLAIMED(1918)
Frederic Peters
Silents
KISMET(1920); POLLYANNA(1920)
Misc. Silents
MILLIONAIRE COWBOY, THE(1924); TARZAN AND THE GOLDEN LION(1927)
Frederick Peters
Silents
ONCE A PLUMBER(1920); SALOME(1922)
Gail Peters
WALK, DON'T RUN(1966)
Gale Peters
ROSEMARY'S BABY(1968)
George Peters
HOUSE OF SECRETS(1929), ph; CONVICT'S CODE(1930), ph
Silents
WANTED FOR MURDER(1919), ph; JACQUELINE, OR BLAZING BARRIERS(1923), ph; ADVENTUROUS SEX, THE(1925), ph; STEPPING ALONG(1926), ph; ALL ABOARD(1927), ph
George Peters
KEEP YOUR POWDER DRY(1945); OVER 21(1945); TILL THE CLOUDS ROLL BY(1946); DREAM GIRL(1947); SCARLET COAT, THE(1955); TEENAGE MOTHER(1967); FAN, THE(1981)
Gerald Peters
HICKEY AND BOGGS(1972)
Gerald S. Peters
MAC ARTHUR(1977)
Gerald Saunderson Peters
MECHANIC, THE(1972); JEKYLL AND HYDE...TOGETHER AGAIN(1982)
Gordon Peters
RUN ACROSS THE RIVER(1961); LOVELY WAY TO DIE, A(1968)
Grant Peters
LIFE BEGINS IN COLLEGE(1937)
Gunnar Peters
LILITH(1964)
Gus Peters
SAMSON AND DELILAH(1949), cos; HARD RIDE, THE(1971); J.W. COOP(1971); SUPERCHICK(1973); JACKSON COUNTY JAIL(1976); TRACKDOWN(1976)
Hans Peters
DRESSED TO THRILL(1935), art d; BANJO ON MY KNEE(1936), art d; GIRLS' DORMITORY(1936), art d; ROAD TO GLORY, THE(1936), art d; CAFE METROPOLE(1937), art d; HEIDI(1937), art d; LIFE BEGINS IN COLLEGE(1937), art d; SLAVE SHIP(1937), art d; ALWAYS GOODBYE(1938), art d; BARONESS AND THE BUTLER, THE(1938), art d; HOLD THAT CO-ED(1938), art d; REBECCA OF SUNNYBROOK FARM(1938), art d; SUBMARINE PATROL(1938), art d; HOUND OF THE BASKERVILLES, THE(1939), art d; LITTLE PRINCESS, THE(1939), art d; POT O' GOLD(1941), set d; SO THIS IS WASHINGTON(1943), art d; STAGE DOOR CANTEEN(1943), art d; TARZAN TRIUMPHS(1943), art d; TARZAN'S DESERT MYSTERY(1943), art d; MUSIC FOR MILLIONS(1944), art d; PICTURE OF DORIAN GRAY, THE(1945), art d; THRILL OF A ROMANCE(1945), art d; TWICE BLESSED(1945), art d; EASY TO WED(1946), art d; GREEN YEARS, THE(1946), art d; IF WINTER COMES(1947), art d; MUSIC FOR MILLIONS(1947), art d; ACT OF VIOLENCE(1949), art d; GREAT SINNER, THE(1949), art d; RED DANUBE, THE(1949), art d; KEY TO THE CITY(1950), art d; KIM(1950), art d; RED BADGE OF COURAGE, THE(1951), art d; STRICTLY DISHONORABLE(1951), art d; LONE STAR(1952), art d; SCARAMOUCHE(1952), art d; KNIGHTS OF THE ROUND TABLE(1953), art d; REMAINS TO BE SEEN(1953), art d; SMALL TOWN GIRL(1953), art d; ROGUE COP(1954), art d; DIANE(1955), art d; MANY RIVERS TO CROSS(1955), art d; MOONFLEET(1955), art d; HIGH SOCIETY(1956), art d; LUST FOR LIFE(1956), art d; POWER AND THE PRIZE, THE(1956), art d; SLANDER(1956), art d; MAN ON FIRE(1957), art d; TIP ON A DEAD JOCKEY(1957), art d; HIGH SCHOOL CONFIDENTIAL(1958), art d; GIRLS' TOWN(1959), art d; IT STARTED WITH A KISS(1959), art d; MIRACLE, THE(1959), art d; NEVER SO FEW(1959), art d; TARZAN, THE APE MAN(1959), art d; WRECK OF THE MARY DEAR, THE(1959), art d; PLEASE DON'T EAT THE DAISIES(1960), art d; RETURN TO PEYTON PLACE(1961), art d; HOOK, THE(1962), art d

Hattie Peters
Silents
WHITE YOUTH(1920)
Hjalmar Peters
SWEDENHIELMS(1935, Swed.); WALPURGIS NIGHT(1941, Swed.)
Hortense Peters
WIZARD OF BAGHDAD, THE(1960)
House Peters
REBEL WITHOUT A CAUSE(1955)
Silents
PRIDE OF JENNICO, THE(1914); SALOMY JANE(1914); CAPTIVE, THE(1915); GIRL OF THE GOLDEN WEST, THE(1915); WARRENS OF VIRGINIA, THE(1915); AS MEN LOVE(1917); ISOBEL(1920); INVISIBLE POWER, THE(1921); LYING LIPS(1921); RICH MEN'S WIVES(1922); STORM, THE(1922); DON'T MARRY FOR MONEY(1923); HELD TO ANSWER(1923); RAFFLES, THE AMATEUR CRACKSMAN(1925)
Misc. Silents
IN THE BISHOP'S CARRIAGE(1913); LADY OF QUALITY, A(1913); LEAH KLESCHNA(1913); PORT OF DOOM, THE(1913); MRS. WIGGS OF THE CABBAGE PATCH(1914); MIGNON(1915); STOLEN GOODS(1915); UNAFRAID, THE(1915); WINGED IDOL, THE(1915); BETWEEN MEN(1916); CLOSED ROAD, THE(1916); GREAT DIVIDE, THE(1916); HAND OF PERIL, THE(1916); RAIL RIDER, THE(1916); VELVET PAW, THE(1916); HAPPINESS OF THREE WOMEN, THE(1917); HEIR OF THE AGES, THE(1917); HIGHWAY OF HOPE, THE(1917); LONESOME CHAP, THE(1917); FORFEIT, THE(1919); THUNDERBOLTS OF FATE(1919); YOU NEVER KNOW YOUR LUCK(1919); GREAT REDEEMER, THE(1920); LEOPARD WOMAN, THE(1920); SILK HUSBANDS AND CALICO WIVES(1920); MAN FROM LOST RIVER, THE(1921); HUMAN HEARTS(1922); LOST AND FOUND ON A SOUTH SEA ISLAND(1923); TORNADO, THE(1924); COUNSEL FOR THE DEFENSE(1925); HEAD WINDS(1925); STORM BREAKER, THE(1925); COMBAT, THE(1926); PRISONERS OF THE STORM(1926); ROSE-MARIE(1928)
House Peters, Jr.
FLASH GORDON(1936); PUBLIC COWBOY NO. 1(1937); COURTIN' TROUBLE(1948); DESPERADOES OF DODGE CITY(1948); GUNNING FOR JUSTICE(1948); OKLAHOMA BADLANDS(1948); RENEGADES OF SONORA(1948); UNDER CALIFORNIA STARS(1948); GAL WHO TOOK THE WEST, THE(1949); OUTLAW COUNTRY(1949); SHERIFF OF WICHITA(1949); SON OF BILLY THE KID(1949); BORDER TREASURE(1950); COW TOWN(1950); TWILIGHT IN THE SIERRAS(1950); DAKOTA KID, THE(1951); DAY THE EARTH STOOD STILL, THE(1951); GENE AUTRY AND THE MOUNTIES(1951); LORNA DOONE(1951); RED BADGE OF COURAGE, THE(1951); SPOILERS OF THE PLAINS(1951); THREE DESPERATE MEN(1951); FARGO(1952); KANSAS CITY CONFIDENTIAL(1952); KANSAS TERRITORY(1952); LION AND THE HORSE, THE(1952); OKLAHOMA ANNIE(1952); OLD WEST, THE(1952); RED PLANET MARS(1952); WACO(1952); PORT SINISTER(1953); WINNING OF THE WEST(1953); HIGHWAY DRAGNET(1954); OVERLAND PACIFIC(1954); TARGET EARTH(1954); THUNDER OVER SANGOLAND(1955); BLACK PATCH(1957); WOMEN OF PITCAIRN ISLAND, THE(1957); MAN FROM GOD'S COUNTRY(1958); INSIDE THE MAFIA(1959); BIG NIGHT, THE(1960); TERROR AT BLACK FALLS(1962); WHO'S GOT THE ACTION?(1962); RIO CONCHOS(1964); GREAT SIOUX MASSACRE, THE(1965)
Misc. Talkies
BLAZING BULLETS(1951); MAN FROM SONORA(1951); WYOMING ROUNDUP(1952); NEW DAY AT SUNDOWN(1957)
Ina Peters
SPESSART INN, THE(1961, Ger.)
Jacki Peters
WOMAN UNDER THE INFLUENCE, A(1974)
Jane Peters
Misc. Talkies
RUNNING WITH THE DEVIL(1973)
Janice Peters
GODLESS GIRL, THE(1929)
Silents
NOOSE, THE(1928)
Jean Peters
CAPTAIN FROM CASTILE(1947); DEEP WATERS(1948); IT HAPPENS EVERY SPRING(1949); LOVE THAT BRUTE(1950); ANNE OF THE INDIES(1951); AS YOUNG AS YOU FEEL(1951); TAKE CARE OF MY LITTLE GIRL(1951); LURE OF THE WILDERNESS(1952); O. HENRY'S FULL HOUSE(1952); VIVA ZAPATA!(1952); WAIT 'TIL THE SUN SHINES, NELLIE(1952); BLUEPRINT FOR MURDER, A(1953); NIAGARA(1953); PICKUP ON SOUTH STREET(1953); VICKI(1953); APACHE(1954); BROKEN LANCE(1954); THREE COINS IN THE FOUNTAIN(1954); MAN CALLED PETER, THE(1955)
Jerry Peters
MELINDA(1972), m
Jessica Peters
YOUNG GUY ON MT. COOK(1969, Jap.)
Jo Peters
ONLY WAY HOME, THE(1972); CONFESSIONS OF A WINDOW CLEANER(1974, Brit.); TO THE DEVIL A DAUGHTER(1976, Brit./Ger.)
John Peters
WHITE ZOMBIE(1932); BEASTS OF BERLIN(1939); MYSTERY PLANE(1939); SKY PATROL(1939); ONCE UPON A HONEYMOON(1942); WIFE TAKES A FLYER, THE(1942); GOLDEN EARRINGS(1947); NORTHWEST OUTPOST(1947); ROGUES' REGIMENT(1948); TOMAHAWK(1951); CHIEF CRAZY HORSE(1955); CASTLE OF BLOOD(1964, Fr./Ital.); MAN WHO WOULD NOT DIE, THE(1975); SMALL CIRCLE OF FRIENDS, A(1980)
Silents
AMATEUR GENTLEMAN, THE(1926); DOG OF THE REGIMENT(1927); SCARLET LADY, THE(1928)
John S. Peters
DEATH IN THE SKY(1937)
Silents
ENEMY, THE(1927)
Capt. John S. Peters
Silents
RANSON'S FOLLY(1926)
Jon Peters
STAR IS BORN, A(1976), p; EYES OF LAURA MARS(1978), p; MAIN EVENT, THE(1979), p; SIX WEEKS(1982), p

Capt. John Peters
Silents
WEDDING MARCH, THE(1927)
Judy Peters
FAUST(1964)
Karl Heinz Peters
GIRL AND THE LEGEND, THE(1966, Ger.); LUDWIG(1973, Ital./Ger./Fr.)
Karsten Peters
NOT RECONCILED, OR "ONLY VIOLENCE HELPS WHERE IT RULES"(1969, Ger.); LOLA(1982, Ger.)
Katie Peters
BOOK OF NUMBERS(1973)
Kay Peters
FLAREUP(1969); SEVEN MINUTES, THE(1971); HOW TO SEDUCE A WO-MAN(1974)
Kelly Jean Peters
AMERICAN DREAM, AN(1966); ANY WEDNESDAY(1966); LITTLE BIG MAN(1970); POCKET MONEY(1972); ACE ELI AND RODGER OF THE SKIES(1973); DEADLY TRACKERS(1973); GREAT WALDO PEPPER, THE(1975)
Ken Peters
THERE'S ALWAYS VANILLA(1972); HUNGRY WIVES(1973)
Kenneth Peters
VICE SQUAD(1982), w
Krika Peters
HEROES DIE YOUNG(1960)
Lance Peters
CARRY ON EMANUELLE(1978, Brit.), w
Lauri Peters
MR. HOBBS TAKES A VACATION(1962); SUMMER HOLIDAY(1963, Brit.); FOR LOVE OF IVY(1968)
Layla Peters
TASTE OF FLESH, A(1967)
Lee Peters
SOME MAY LIVE(1967, Brit.); CONQUEROR WORM, THE(1968, Brit.)
Lorraine Peters
MORE DEADLY THAN THE MALE(1961, Brit.); WICKER MAN, THE(1974, Brit.)
Luan Peters
MAN OF VIOLENCE(1970, Brit.); LUST FOR A VAMPIRE(1971, Brit.); TWINS OF EVIL(1971, Brit.); FLESH AND BLOOD SHOW, THE(1974, Brit.); LAND OF THE MINOTAUR(1976, Gr.)
Lynn Peters
GRAVE OF THE VAMPIRE(1972)
Martha Peters
MARK OF THE WITCH(1970), w
Mary Peters
EVEL KNIEVEL(1971)
Matthew Peters
BARBER OF STAMFORD HILL, THE(1963, Brit.)
1984
SCREAM FOR HELP(1984)
Mattie Peters
Silents
EXIT THE VAMP(1921); SAWDUST(1923); SCARS OF JEALOUSY(1923); HELEN'S BABIES(1924)
Michael Peters
SCOTT JOPLIN(1977), ch
Molly Peters
THUNDERBALL(1965, Brit.); DON'T RAISE THE BRIDGE, LOWER THE RIVER(1968, Brit.)
Nicki Peters
BEAUTY JUNGLE, THE(1966, Brit.)
Page E. Peters
Silents
GOOSE GIRL, THE(1915)
Page Peters
Silents
CAPTIVE, THE(1915); WARRENS OF VIRGINIA, THE(1915)
Misc. Silents
UNAFRAID, THE(1915); HE FELL IN LOVE WITH HIS WIFE(1916); MADAME LA PRESIDENTE(1916); PASQUALE(1916)
Patricia Peters
SINCE YOU WENT AWAY(1944)
Paul Peters
ROADIE(1980), prod d; SECOND THOUGHTS(1983), prod d; STROKER ACE(1983), art d
Pauline Peters
DEADLOCK(1931, Brit.)
Silents
JOYOUS ADVENTURES OF ARISTIDE PUJOL, THE(1920, Brit.)
Misc. Silents
WHEN PARIS SLEEPS(1917, Brit.); GLAD EYE, THE(1920, Brit.); TRENT'S LAST CASE(1920, Brit.); HER PENALTY(1921, Brit.); IN FULL CRY(1921, Brit.); LOUDWATER MYSTERY, THE(1921, Brit.); MAYOR OF CASTERBRIDGE, THE(1921, Brit.); LILAC SUNBONNET, THE(1922, Brit.)
Perry Peters
OLGA'S GIRLS(1964)
Peter Peters
SING ANOTHER CHORUS(1941)
Petra Peters
TO THE DEVIL A DAUGHTER(1976, Brit./Ger.)
Ralph Peters
GREAT GAMBINI, THE(1937); ROUGH RIDIN' RHYTHM(1937); ACCIDENTS WILL HAPPEN(1938); MAN'S COUNTRY(1938); OUTLAWS OF SONORA(1938); SANTA FE STAMPEDE(1938); STRANGER FROM ARIZONA, THE(1938); WANTED BY THE POLICE(1938); WHERE THE WEST BEGINS(1938); COLORADO SUNSET(1939); FLAMING LEAD(1939); OKLAHOMA TERROR(1939); ROVIN' TUMBLEWEEDS(1939); SIX-GUN RHYTHM(1939); TOUGH KID(1939); TRIGGER FINGERS ½(1939); WYOMING OUTLAW(1939); BLONDIE ON A BUDGET(1940); DEATH RIDES THE RANGE(1940); DURANGO KID, THE(1940); GHOST VALLEY RAIDERS(1940); LADY IN QUESTION, THE(1940); LAUGHING AT DANGER(1940);

MARGIE(1940); PIONEERS OF THE FRONTIER(1940); SON OF ROARING DAN(1940); TOO MANY HUSBANDS(1940); ACROSS THE SIERRAS(1941); BALL OF FIRE(1941); BILLY THE KID'S RANGE WAR(1941); FACE BEHIND THE MASK, THE(1941); HONKY TONK(1941); LONE RIDER AMBUSHED, THE(1941); OUTLAWS OF THE RIO GRANDE(1941); RAIDERS OF THE DESERT(1941); RICHEST MAN IN TOWN(1941); RIDERS OF BLACK MOUNTAIN(1941); SUNSET IN WYOMING(1941); TEXAS(1941); TWO IN A TAXI(1941); YOU BELONG TO ME(1941); YOU'RE OUT OF LUCK(1941); I MARRIED A WITCH(1942); IN OLD CALIFORNIA(1942); JOAN OF OZARK(1942); LUCKY JORDAN(1942); MAN'S WORLD, A(1942); NIGHT TO REMEMBER, A(1942); RIDE 'EM COWBOY(1942); SHUT MY BIG MOUTH(1942); TALK OF THE TOWN(1942); THEY ALL KISSED THE BRIDE(1942); TWO YANKS IN TRINIDAD(1942); YOU WERE NEVER LOVELIER(1942); FIND THE BLACKMAILER(1943); GOOD MORNING, JUDGE(1943); IT AIN'T HAY(1943); MY KINGDOM FOR A COOK(1943); ONE DANGEROUS NIGHT(1943); CHARLIE CHAN IN BLACK MAGIC(1944); COVER GIRL(1944); GHOST CATCHERS(1944); MUSIC IN MANHATTAN(1944); ROGER TOUHY, GANGSTER!(1944); STANDING ROOM ONLY(1944); TAKE IT BIG(1944); TWILIGHT ON THE PRAIRIE(1944); HOLD THAT BLONDE(1945); HONEYMOON AHEAD(1945); LADY ON A TRAIN(1945); MURDER, HE SAYS(1945); NOB HILL(1945); ON STAGE EVERYBODY(1945); RADIO STARS ON PARADE(1945); SEE MY LAWYER(1945); CANYON PASSAGE(1946); DARK MIRROR, THE(1946); LITTLE GIANT(1946); NOBODY LIVES FOREVER(1946); DESERT FURY(1947); IT HAD TO BE YOU(1947); TRAIL TO SAN ANTONE(1947); WHERE THERE'S LIFE(1947); CREEPER, THE(1948); HAZARD(1948); ONE TOUCH OF VENUS(1948); SLEEP, MY LOVE(1948); TEXAS, BROOKLYN AND HEAVEN(1948); VALIANT HOMBRE, THE(1948); CHICAGO DEADLINE(1949); FIGHTING FOOLS(1949); SKY LINER(1949); SORROWFUL JONES(1949); TAKE ONE FALSE STEP(1949); BEYOND THE PURPLE HILLS(1950); DARK CITY(1950); EXPERIMENT ALCATRAZ(1950); FATHER OF THE BRIDE(1950); LET'S DANCE(1950); NEVER A DULL MOMENT(1950); THREE HUSBANDS(1950); WHERE THE SIDEWALK ENDS(1950); GASOLINE ALLEY(1951); MILLIONAIRE FOR CHRISTY, A(1951); RACKET, THE(1951); SLAUGHTER TRAIL(1951); SNIPER, THE(1952); GENTLEMEN PREFER BLONDES(1953); DESTRY(1954); THREE RING CIRCUS(1954); WHILE THE CITY SLEEPS(1956); BADLANDS OF MONTANA(1957)
Misc. Talkies
GUN GRIT(1936)
Raymond Peters
LOVE CHILD(1982)
Reg Peters
INADMISSIBLE EVIDENCE(1968, Brit.)
Rev. Madison C. Peters
Silents
GOVERNOR'S BOSS, THE(1915)
Rick Peters
Misc. Talkies
CONVOY BUDDIES(1977)
Robert House Peters
OVER THE BORDER(1950)
Robert House Peters, Jr.
STRATEGIC AIR COMMAND(1955)
Robert L. Peters
YOICKS!(1932, Brit.), ed
Robert Peters
RED SNOW(1952), w
Roberta Peters
TONIGHT WE SING(1953)
Ronald Peters
SING ANOTHER CHORUS(1941)
S.J. Peters
HIGH PRESSURE(1932), w
Sabine Peters
EIGHT GIRLS IN A BOAT(1932, Ger.); FOUR COMPANIONS, THE(1938, Ger.)
Sally Peters
VIOLATED(1953)
Scott Peters
AMAZING COLOSSAL MAN, THE(1957); HELL BOUND(1957); INVASION OF THE SAUCER MEN(1957); MOTORCYCLE GANG(1957); OUTLAW'S SON(1957); ATTACK OF THE PUPPET PEOPLE(1958); HOT ROD GANG(1958); SUICIDE BATTALION(1958); FBI STORY, THE(1959); SUBMARINE SEAHAWK(1959); CAPE CANAVERAL MONSTERS(1960); CANADIANS, THE(1961, Brit.); PANIC IN YEAR ZERO!(1962); GIRL HUNTERS, THE(1963, Brit.); THEY SAVED HITLER'S BRAIN(1964)
Sharon Peters
GOING BERSERK(1983)
Steve Peters
DALEKS–INVASION EARTH 2155 A.D.(1966, Brit.)
Susan Peters
MAN WHO TALKED TOO MUCH, THE(1940); MONEY AND THE WOMAN(1940); SUSAN AND GOD(1940); SCATTERGOOD PULLS THE STRINGS(1941); STRAWBERRY BLONDE, THE(1941); THREE SONS O'GUNS(1941); ANDY HARDY'S DOUBLE LIFE(1942); BIG SHOT, THE(1942); DR. GILLESPIE'S NEW ASSISTANT(1942); RANDOM HARVEST(1942); TISH(1942); ASSIGNMENT IN BRITTANY(1943); SONG OF RUSSIA(1943); YOUNG IDEAS(1943); KEEP YOUR POWDER DRY(1945); SIGN OF THE RAM, THE(1948); RUBY(1971)
Tiffany Peters
Misc. Talkies
WELCOME HOME, BROTHER CHARLES(1975)
Timothy Peters
ALFIE DARLING(1975, Brit.)
Tom Peters
FOR PETE'S SAKE!(1966); GAILY, GAILY(1969); EXECUTIVE ACTION(1973); FUN WITH DICK AND JANE(1977)
Vicki Peters
BLOOD MANIA(1971)
Vicky Peters
MITCHELL(1975)
Virginia Peters
FAST TIMES AT RIDGEMONT HIGH(1982)

Walter Peters
CHRONICLE OF ANNA MAGDALENA BACH(1968, Ital., Ger.)
Wayne Peters
STAGE TO THUNDER ROCK(1964)
Wendy Peters
SHAKEDOWN, THE(1960, Brit.)
Werner Peters
DEVIL STRIKES AT NIGHT, THE(1959, Ger.); ROSEMARY(1960, Ger.); THOUSAND EYES OF DR. MABUSE, THE(1960, Fr./Ital./Ger.); DEAD RUN(1961, Fr./Ital./Ger.); RETURN OF DR. MABUSE, THE(1961, Ger./Fr./Ital.); ROSES FOR THE PROSECUTOR(1961, Ger.); COUNTERFEIT TRAITOR, THE(1962); COURT MARTIAL(1962, Ger.); DOG EAT DOG(1963, U.S./Ger./Ital.); ENDLESS NIGHT, THE(1963, Ger.); SCOTLAND YARD HUNTS DR. MABUSE(1963, Ger.); RESTLESS NIGHT, THE(1964, Ger.); BATTLE OF THE BULGE(1965); INVISIBLE DR. MABUSE, THE(1965, Ger.); 36 HOURS(1965); FINE MADNESS, A(1966); HYPNOSIS(1966, Ger./Sp./Ital.); I DEAL IN DANGER(1966); CORRUPT ONES, THE(1967, Ger.); PHANTOM OF SOHO, THE(1967, Ger.); WITNESS OUT OF HELL(1967, Ger./Yugo.); ASSIGNMENT K(1968, Brit.); SECRET WAR OF HARRY FRIGG, THE(1968)
Misc. Talkies
BLONDE CONNECTION, THE(1975)
William F. Peters
Silents
WAY DOWN EAST(1920), m
William Frederick Peters
Silents
WHEN KNIGHTHOOD WAS IN FLOWER(1922), m; UNDER THE RED ROBE(1923), m; FOUR FEATHERS(1929), m
Willy Peters
SHAME(1968, Swed.)
Peters Sisters
LOVE AND HISSES(1937); HAPPY LANDING(1938)
The Peters Sisters
HI-DE-HO(1947)
Anne Marie Petersen
DAY OF WRATH(1948, Den.), ed
Arthur Petersen
BORN WILD(1968)
Chris Petersen
SWARM, THE(1978); LITTLE DRAGONS, THE(1980)
Colin Petersen
SMILEY(1957, Brit.); CRY FROM THE STREET, A(1959, Brit.); STRANGE AFFECTION(1959, Brit.)
David Petersen
SKIP TRACER, THE(1979, Can.)
1984
ICEMAN(1984)
Diane Petersen
SEVEN ALONE(1975)
Don Petersen
ALMOST PERFECT AFFAIR, AN(1979), w
Dorothy Petersen
CANYON PASSAGE(1946)
Elsa Petersen
HOUSE ACROSS THE BAY, THE(1940); MEET JOHN DOE(1941)
Erika Petersen
HEAVEN'S GATE(1980)
Gary Petersen
TAKE DOWN(1979)
Hans W. Petersen
CRAZY PARADISE(1965, Den.); HUNGER(1968, Den./Norway/Swed.)
Julie Petersen
SEVEN ALONE(1975)
Karen Petersen
PETERSEN(1974, Aus.)
Karin Petersen
RE: LUCKY LUCIANO(1974, Fr./Ital.)
Keith Petersen
THEY'RE A WEIRD MOB(1966, Aus.)
Kjeld Petersen
HIDDEN FEAR(1957); REPTILICUS(1962, U.S./Den.); CRAZY PARADISE(1965, Den.)
Lenka Petersen
BLACK LIKE ME(1964)
Mark Petersen
TWO ENGLISH GIRLS(1972, Fr.)
Mogens Viggo Petersen
GOLDEN MOUNTAINS(1958, Den.)
Monica Petersen
CHANGES(1969)
Pat Petersen
LITTLE DRAGONS, THE(1980); COLD RIVER(1982)
Paul Petersen
HOUSEBOAT(1958); IN THE YEAR 2889(1966); TIME FOR KILLING, A(1967)
Peter Petersen
ETERNAL MASK, THE(1937, Swiss)
Rob Petersen
1984
STRANGERS KISS(1984)
Robert Petersen
NEW YORK, NEW YORK(1977)
Scott Petersen
SEVEN ALONE(1975)
Stewart Petersen
AGAINST A CROOKED SKY(1975); SEVEN ALONE(1975); PONY EXPRESS RIDER(1976)
Suzanne Petersen
SEVEN ALONE(1975)

Teddi Petersen
VELVET VAMPIRE, THE(1971), art d
Tommy Petersen
OFFICER AND A GENTLEMAN, AN(1982)
Wolfgang Petersen
DAS BOOT(1982), w
1984
NEVERENDING STORY, THE(1984, Ger.), d, w
Dirk Petersmann
TOUCHED(1983), p
Art Peterson
STRANGE JOURNEY(1946), art d
Arthur Peterson
CALL NORTHSIDE 777(1948); RETURN TO PEYTON PLACE(1961); INVITATION TO A GUNFIGHTER(1964); TARGETS(1968); GREAT NORTHFIELD, MINNESOTA RAID, THE(1972); ROLLERCOASTER(1977)
Barbara Peterson
WAY WE WERE, THE(1973)
Barry Peterson
WARM IN THE BUD(1970)
Betty Peterson
Misc. Silents
SEVEN YEARS BAD LUCK(1921)
Bo Ivan Peterson
MONTENEGRO(1981, Brit./Swed.)
Bob Peterson
SONS OF KATIE ELDER, THE(1965), spec eff; GOOD TIMES(1967), spec eff
C. G. Peterson
Silents
EVIDENCE(1918), ph
C. Gus Peterson
Silents
I LOVE YOU(1918), ph
C. O. Peterson
Silents
REAL FOLKS(1918), ph
Caleb Peterson
TILL THE CLOUDS ROLL BY(1946); ANY NUMBER CAN PLAY(1949); SCENE OF THE CRIME(1949)
Calib Peterson
OUT OF THE PAST(1947)
Carol Peterson
I NEVER SANG FOR MY FATHER(1970)
Casandra Peterson
COAST TO COAST(1980)
Cassandra Peterson
WORKING GIRLS, THE(1973); KING OF THE MOUNTAIN(1981); JEKYLL AND HYDE...TOGETHER AGAIN(1982); STING II, THE(1983); STROKER ACE(1983)
Clifford Peterson
CHARLIE, THE LONESOME COUGAR(1967)
Craig Peterson
LIFE AND TIMES OF CHESTER-ANGUS RAMSGOOD, THE(1971, Can.)
Dan Peterson
Misc. Silents
WHISTLING JIM(1925)
Dane Peterson
GALLIPOLI(1981, Aus.)
Darryl Peterson
TAKE DOWN(1979)
David Peterson
GREY FOX, THE(1983, Can.)
Diane Peterson
HI-RIDERS(1978); MAN WITH TWO BRAINS, THE(1983)
Don Peterson
HEY THERE, IT'S YOGI BEAR(1964), anim; SHOOT IT: BLACK, SHOOT IT: BLUE(1974)
Dorothy Peterson
MOTHERS CRY(1930); BOUGHT(1931); PARTY HUSBAND(1931); PENROD AND SAM(1931); RECKLESS HOUR, THE(1931); RICH MAN'S FOLLY(1931); SKYLINE(1931); TRAVELING HUSBANDS(1931); UP FOR MURDER(1931); ATTORNEY FOR THE DEFENSE(1932); BEAST OF THE CITY, THE(1932); BUSINESS AND PLEASURE(1932); CABIN IN THE COTTON(1932); EMMA(1932); FELLER NEEDS A FRIEND(1932); FORBIDDEN(1932); LIFE BEGINS(1932); NIGHT WORLD(1932); PAYMENT DEFERRED(1932); SHE WANTED A MILLIONAIRE(1932); SO BIG(1932); THRILL OF YOUTH(1932); WAY BACK HOME(1932); BIG EXECUTIVE(1933); HOLD ME TIGHT(1933); I'M NO ANGEL(1933); MAYOR OF HELL, THE(1933); REFORM GIRL(1933); AS THE EARTH TURNS(1934); BELOVED(1934); PECK'S BAD BOY(1934); SIDE STREETS(1934); TREASURE ISLAND(1934); UNCERTAIN LADY(1934); FRECKLES(1935); LADDIE(1935); MAN OF IRON(1935); PURSUIT(1935); SOCIETY DOCTOR(1935); SWEEPSTAKE ANNIE(1935); COUNTRY DOCTOR, THE(1936); REUNION(1936); CONFESSION(1937); GIRL LOVES BOY(1937); HER HUSBAND LIES(1937); UNDER COVER OF NIGHT(1937); 52ND STREET(1937); BREAKING THE ICE(1938); GIRLS ON PROBATION(1938); HUNTED MEN(1938); DARK VICTORY(1939); FIVE LITTLE PEPPERS AND HOW THEY GREW(1939); FLYING IRISHMAN, THE(1939); SABOTAGE(1939); TWO BRIGHT BOYS(1939); FIVE LITTLE PEPPERS AT HOME(1940); FIVE LITTLE PEPPERS IN TROUBLE(1940); LILLIAN RUSSELL(1940); OUT WEST WITH THE PEPPERS(1940); TOO MANY HUSBANDS(1940); WOMEN IN WAR(1940); CHEERS FOR MISS BISHOP(1941); HENRY ALDRICH FOR PRESIDENT(1941); RIDE, KELLY, RIDE(1941); MAN IN THE TRUNK, THE(1942); SABOTEUR(1942); AIR FORCE(1943); MOON IS DOWN, THE(1943); THIS IS THE ARMY(1943); FACES IN THE FOG(1944); MR. SKEFFINGTON(1944); THIS IS THE LIFE(1944); WHEN THE LIGHTS GO ON AGAIN(1944); WOMAN IN THE WINDOW, THE(1945); SISTER KENNY(1946); THAT HAGEN GIRL(1947)
Eileen Peterson
PUTNEY SWOPE(1969)
Elmer Peterson
IT GROWS ON TREES(1952); GIRL WHO HAD EVERYTHING, THE(1953)

Elsa Peterson
MADAME SATAN(1930); EXPERT, THE(1932); GUILTY AS HELL(1932); PARIS IN SPRING(1935); GIVE ME YOUR HEART(1936); GOLDEN ARROW, THE(1936); POLO JOE(1936); CONFESSION(1937); SULLIVANS, THE(1944); IVY(1947); EMERGENCY WEDDING(1950); YOU'RE IN THE NAVY NOW(1951); FUNNY FACE(1957)

Eric Peterson
VISITOR, THE(1973, Can.)

Erika Peterson
LIFE STUDY(1973)

Ernest Peterson
Misc. Silents
PEAKS OF DESTINY(1927, Ger.)

Eugene Peterson
BREEZY(1973); MAC ARTHUR(1977); POSTMAN ALWAYS RINGS TWICE, THE(1981)

Evangeline Peterson
STATE OF SIEGE(1973, Fr./U.S./Ital./Ger.)

Floyd L. Peterson
HI, MOM!(1970)

Frances Peterson
1984
INITIATION, THE(1984)

Gail Peterson
LOVE BUTCHER, THE(1982), makeup

Gale Peterson
MOONSHINE COUNTY EXPRESS(1977), makeup

Gene Peterson
HIAWATHA(1952); WILD ONE, THE(1953)

Gerald Peterson
1984
ADVENTURES OF BUCKAROO BANZAI: ACROSS THE 8TH DIMENSION, THE(1984)

Gil Peterson
COOL ONES, THE(1967)
Misc. Talkies
BRAIN MACHINE, THE(1972)

Gus Peterson
CHARLEY'S AUNT(1930), ph; SWEETHEARTS ON PARADE(1930), ph; PAGAN LADY(1931), ph; NEW FRONTIER, THE(1935), ph; RIDER OF THE LAW, THE(1935), ph; OREGON TRAIL, THE(1936), ph; SONG OF THE GRINGO(1936), ph; ADVENTURE'S END(1937), ph; ARIZONA DAYS(1937), ph; GIT ALONG, LITTLE DOGIES(1937), ph; GUNSMOKE RANCH(1937), ph; MYSTERY OF THE HOODED HORSEMEN, THE(1937), ph; RIDERS OF THE ROCKIES(1937), ph; SING, COWBOY, SING(1937), ph; TEX RIDES WITH THE BOY SCOUTS(1937), ph; TROUBLE IN TEXAS(1937), ph; BLACK BANDIT(1938), ph; FRONTIER TOWN(1938), ph; GUILTY TRAILS(1938), ph; PRAIRIE JUSTICE(1938), ph; LADY IN THE DEATH HOUSE(1944), ph; MACHINE GUN MAMA(1944), ph
Silents
ASHES OF HOPE(1917), ph; SKY PILOT, THE(1921), ph; RECKLESS ROMANCE(1924), ph

Gustave Peterson
CAREER GIRL(1944), ph

Harry Peterson
Silents
ADVENTUROUS YOUTH(1928, Brit.)

Henry Peterson
JACK AHOY!(1935, Brit.); SEXTON BLAKE AND THE MADEMOISELLE(1935, Brit.); NORSEMAN, THE(1978), set d

Herb Peterson
I, THE JURY(1982); VERDICT, THE(1982); TRADING PLACES(1983)

Ian Peterson
UP JUMPED A SWAGMAN(1965, Brit.)

James Peterson
FIEND OF DOPE ISLAND(1961), m

Jean Peterson
INTERNES CAN'T TAKE MONEY(1937)

Jeannie Peterson
FIVE WILD GIRLS(1966, Fr.)

Jerry Peterson
Silents
JANICE MEREDITH(1924)

Johann Peterson
CARNY(1980)

John Peterson
SYNANON(1965)

Keith Peterson
NED KELLY(1970, Brit.)

Lembit Peterson
DEAD MOUNTAINEER HOTEL, THE(1979, USSR)

Lenka Peterson
PANIC IN THE STREETS(1950); TAKE CARE OF MY LITTLE GIRL(1951); PHENIX CITY STORY, THE(1955); HOMER(1970)

Lorna Peterson
HERE COME THE CO-EDS(1945)

Louis Peterson
TEMPEST(1958, Ital./Yugo./Fr.), w

Louis S. Peterson
TAKE A GIANT STEP(1959), w

Madelaine Peterson
STACEY!(1973)

Margaret Ann Peterson
ANGEL IN MY POCKET(1969); LOVE GOD?, THE(1969)

Margaret Peterson
Silents
SONG OF LOVE, THE(1923), w

Marjorie Peterson
LOVE IS A RACKET(1932); PANAMA FLO(1932); TESS OF THE STORM COUNTRY(1932)

Mark Peterson
DR. WHO AND THE DALEKS(1965, Brit.)
1984
SIXTEEN CANDLES(1984), cos

Marlies Peterson
MARK OF THE DEVIL(1970, Ger./Brit.)

Maurice Peterson
HOMEWORK(1982), w

Monica Peterson
M(1970); ANTONY AND CLEOPATRA(1973, Brit.); DARK, THE(1979)

Nan Peterson
GIRLS' TOWN(1959); HIDEOUS SUN DEMON, THE(1959); LOUISIANA HUSSY(1960); SHOTGUN WEDDING, THE(1963)

Nate Peterson
HERE COMES THE BAND(1935)

Oscar Peterson
SILENT PARTNER, THE(1979, Can.), m

Pam Peterson
PRIZE, THE(1963); SINGING NUN, THE(1966)

Pat Peterson
BOOK OF NUMBERS(1973)

Paul Peterson
HAPPIEST MILLIONAIRE, THE(1967); JOURNEY TO SHILOH(1968)
1984
PURPLE RAIN(1984)

Pete Peterson
ONE NIGHT IN LISBON(1941); SWING OUT THE BLUES(1943); THING WITH TWO HEADS, THE(1972), makeup

Peter Peterson
MIGHTY JOE YOUNG(1949), spec eff

Captain R. Peterson
IT CAME FROM BENEATH THE SEA(1955)

Ralph Peterson
THREE IN ONE(1956, Aus.), w; HOODLUM PRIEST, THE(1961)

Ralph W. Peterson
SQUARE RING, THE(1955, Brit.), w

Richard Peterson
JESUS(1979)

Rick Peterson
HORNET'S NEST(1970)

Robert A. Peterson
GARMENT JUNGLE, THE(1957), art d

Robert Peterson
YOU CAN'T RUN AWAY FROM IT(1956), art d; DANGEROUS BUSINESS(1946), art d; DEVIL'S MASK, THE(1946), art d; NIGHT EDITOR(1946), art d; PHANTOM THIEF, THE(1946), art d; DEVIL SHIP(1947), art d; JEWELS OF BRANDENBURG(1947), art d; LONE WOLF IN LONDON(1947), art d; LADIES OF THE CHORUS(1948), art d; HOLIDAY IN HAVANA(1949), art d; KNOCK ON ANY DOOR(1949), art d; TOKYO JOE(1949), art d; WALKING HILLS, THE(1949), art d; FULLER BRUSH GIRL, THE(1950), art d; IN A LONELY PLACE(1950), art d; WOMAN OF DISTINCTION, A(1950), art d; SATURDAY'S HERO(1951), art d; SIROCCO(1951), art d; SCANDAL SHEET(1952), art d; BIG HEAT, THE(1953), art d; FORT ALGIERS(1953), art d; JUGGLER, THE(1953), art d; NEBRASKAN, THE(1953), art d; HUMAN DESIRE(1954), art d; FIVE AGAINST THE HOUSE(1955), art d; LAST FRONTIER, THE(1955), art d; LONG GRAY LINE, THE(1955), art d; HOT BLOOD(1956), art d; DECISION AT SUNDOWN(1957), art d; SHADOW ON THE WINDOW, THE(1957), art d; GOOD DAY FOR A HANGING(1958), art d; GUNMAN'S WALK(1958), art d; LAST HURRAH, THE(1958), art d; EDGE OF ETERNITY(1959), art d; FACE OF A FUGITIVE(1959), art d; GENE KRUPA STORY, THE(1959), art d; RIDE LONESOME(1959), art d; SAIL A CROOKED SHIP(1961), art d; TWO RODE TOGETHER(1961), art d; UNDERWORLD U.S.A.(1961), art d; EXPERIMENT IN TERROR(1962), art d; WILD WESTERNERS, THE(1962), art d; ZOTZ!(1962), art d; GIDGET GOES TO ROME(1963), art d; I'LL TAKE SWEDEN(1965), art d; OUTLAWS IS COMING, THE(1965), art d; PRIVATE BENJAMIN(1980), spec eff

Rod Peterson
CHARTROOSE CABOOSE(1960), w; KING OF THE GRIZZLIES(1970), w

Roy Peterson
CALIFORNIA DREAMING(1979), ed

Ruth Peterson
HINDLE WAKES(1931, Brit.); CHARLIE CHAN IN PARIS(1935); GREAT HOSPITAL MYSTERY, THE(1937); JOSETTE(1938)

Sam Peterson
Misc. Silents
LET'S GO GALLAGHER(1925)

Stewart Peterson
WHERE THE RED FERN GROWS(1974)

Sven Peterson
PRIZE, THE(1963)

Teddy Peterson
FATHER TAKES A WIFE(1941)

Toddy Peterson
BABY FACE MORGAN(1942); ADVENTURES OF A ROOKIE(1943)

Vidal Peterson
SOMETHING WICKED THIS WAY COMES(1983)

Wally Peterson
CROOKED SKY, THE(1957, Brit.)

Warren Peterson
STERILE CUCKOO, THE(1969)

William L. Peterson
THIEF(1981)

Wolfgang Peterson
DAS BOOT(1982), d

Arthur Peterson, Jr.
ONE MAN'S WAY(1964)

H.G. Petersson
APACHE GOLD(1965, Ger.), w

Harald G. Petersson
YOUNG GO WILD, THE(1962, Ger.), w; DESPERADO TRAIL, THE(1965, Ger./Yugo.), w; TREASURE OF SILVER LAKE(1965, Fr./Ger./Yugo.), w; LAST OF THE RENEGADES(1966, Fr./Ital./Ger./Yugo.), w; THUNDER AT THE BORDER(1966,

Ger./Yugo.), w

M.G. Petersson
MISTRESS OF THE WORLD(1959, Ital./Fr./Ger.), w

Louise Petherbridge
PICTURES(1982, New Zealand)

Sandor Pethes
BLUE IDOL, THE(1931, Hung.); MISS PRESIDENT(1935, Hung.); SUN SHINES, THE(1939, Hung.)

Hazel Pethig
JABBERWOCKY(1977, Brit.), cos; MONTY PYTHON'S LIFE OF BRIAN(1979, Brit.), cos

Sandor Peti
BLUE IDOL, THE(1931, Hung.)

Helmut Petigk
LOLA(1982, Ger.)

Irra Petina
THERE'S MAGIC IN MUSIC(1941)

Marius Petipa
SLEEPING BEAUTY, THE(1966, USSR), ch; TURNING POINT, THE(1977), ch

Petit
RETURN OF MARTIN GUERRE, THE(1983, Fr.)

Albert Petit
RUGGLES OF RED GAP(1935); FOOLS FOR SCANDAL(1938); ONCE UPON A HONEYMOON(1942); DOLLY SISTERS, THE(1945); NIGHT AND DAY(1946); O.S.S.(1946); RAZOR'S EDGE, THE(1946); DESIRE ME(1947); THAT FORSYTE WOMAN(1949)

Christopher Petit
RADIO ON(1980, Brit./Ger.), d, w; UNSUITABLE JOB FOR A WOMAN, AN(1982, Brit.), d, w
1984
CHINESE BOXES(1984, Ger./Brit.), a, d, w; FLIGHT TO BERLIN(1984, Ger./Brit.), d, w

E. Petit
RICH ARE ALWAYS WITH US, THE(1932), w

Jean-Claude Petit
TESTAMENT OF ORPHEUS, THE(1962, Fr.); TUSK(1980, Fr.), m

Michael Petit
HUSH... HUSH, SWEET CHARLOTTE(1964); NIGHTMARE IN THE SUN(1964)

Michel Petit
MARRIAGE ON THE ROCKS(1965)

Pascale Petit
CHEATERS, THE(1961, Fr.); END OF DESIRE(1962 Fr./Ital.); MIDNIGHT FOLLY(1962, Fr.); CROSS OF THE LIVING(1963, Fr.); JULIE THE REDHEAD(1963, Fr.); RITA(1963, Fr./Ital.); MISTRESS FOR THE SUMMER, A(1964, Fr./Ital.); LAST MERCENARY, THE(1969, Ital./Span./Ger.)

Pierre Petit
RASPOUTINE(1954, Fr.), ph; MARIE OF THE ISLES(1960, Fr.), ph; DEAD RUN(1961, Fr./Ital./Ger.), ph; MAN FROM COCODY(1966, Fr/Ital.), ph; THE DIRTY GAME(1966, Fr./Ital./Ger.), ph; LADY HAMILTON(1969, Ger./Ital./Fr.), ph; BEYOND FEAR(1977, Fr.), ph

Rene Petit
ODYSSEY OF THE PACIFIC(1983, Can./Fr.), prod d

Roland Petit
HANS CHRISTIAN ANDERSEN(1952), a, ch; DADDY LONG LEGS(1955), ch; GLASS SLIPPER, THE(1955), ch; FOLIES BERGERE(1958, Fr.), ch; BLACK TIGHTS(1962, Fr.), a, ch

Valentine Petit
Misc. Silents
MODERN OTHELLO, A(1917)

Wanda Petit
Misc. Silents
BROADWAY SPORT, THE(1917); CUPID'S ROUND-UP(1918)

Wanda Petit [Hawley]
Misc. Silents
THIS IS THE LIFE(1917); HEART OF A LION, THE(1918)

D.B. Petitclerc
RED SUN(1972, Fr./Ital./Span.), w

Denne Bart Petitclerc
ISLANDS IN THE STREAM(1977), w

Petite
PLEASURE LOVERS, THE(1964, Brit.)

Laurent Petitgirard
ROSEBUD(1975), m

Enzo Petito
LOVE AND LARCENY(1963, Fr./Ital.); GOOD, THE BAD, AND THE UGLY, THE(1967, Ital./Span.)

Tony Petito
TREASURE OF THE FOUR CROWNS(1983, Span./U.S.), w

George Petitot
HIT(1973), art d; CARAVAN TO VACCARES(1974, Brit./Fr), art d

Georges Petitot
BLONDE FROM PEKING, THE(1968, Fr.), art d; MADWOMAN OF CHAILLOT, THE(1969), art d

Tony Petitto
COMIN' AT YA!(1981), w

Boris Petker
SPRING(1948, USSR)

Bernice Petkere
SABOTAGE SQUAD(1942), w

Dimiter Petkov
FITZCARRALDO(1982)

Aleksandar Petkovic
LOVE AFFAIR; OR THE CASE OF THE MISSING SWITCHBOARD OPERATOR(1968, Yugo.), ph

Frank E. Petley
Silents
POWER OF RIGHT, THE(1919, Brit.); MYSTERY OF MR. BERNARD BROWN(1921, Brit.)

Misc. Silents
GRIP OF IRON, THE(1913, Brit.); DIANA AND DESTINY(1916, Brit.); SILVER GREYHOUND, THE(1919, Brit.)

Frank Petley
NIGHT RIDE(1937, Brit.)
Silents
FALSE EVIDENCE(1922, Brit.)
Misc. Silents
BRANDED SOUL, THE(1920, Brit.); GOLDEN DAWN, THE(1921, Brit.)

Frantisek Peto
DESERTER AND THE NOMADS, THE(1969, Czech./Ital.)

Hortense Petra
GODLESS GIRL, THE(1929); WORLD WAS HIS JURY, THE(1958); JUKE BOX RHYTHM(1959); PIRATES OF TORTUGA(1961); DON'T KNOCK THE TWIST(1962); GET YOURSELF A COLLEGE GIRL(1964); KISSIN' COUSINS(1964); YOUR CHEATIN' HEART(1964); WHEN THE BOYS MEET THE GIRLS(1965); HOLD ON(1966); HOT RODS TO HELL(1967); LOVE-INS, THE(1967); RIOT ON SUNSET STRIP(1967); FOR SINGLES ONLY(1968); YOUNG RUNAWAYS, THE(1968); LONERS, THE(1972)
Silents
IS YOUR DAUGHTER SAFE?(1927)

Enzo Petracca
CAESAR THE CONQUEROR(1963, Ital.)

Joe Petracca
PROUD REBEL, THE(1958), w

Joseph Petracca
IT'S A BIG COUNTRY(1951), w; SOMETHING FOR THE BIRDS(1952), w; SEVEN CITIES OF GOLD(1955), w; PROUD ONES, THE(1956), w; JAYHAWKERS, THE(1959), w; GUNS OF THE TIMBERLAND(1960), w; RELUCTANT SAINT, THE(1962, U.S./Ital.), w

Ricardo Petraglia
1984
GABRIELA(1984, Braz.)

Harry Mark Petrakis
DREAM OF KINGS, A(1969), w

Russ Petranto
NETWORK(1976)

Gerald Petrarca
GODDESS, THE(1958)

Victor Petrashevic
MINX, THE(1969), ph; PROJECTIONIST, THE(1970), ph; RICHARD(1972), ph

Victor Petrashevich
Misc. Talkies
DEATH ON CREDIT(1976), d

Victor Petrashevitz
COMEBACK TRAIL, THE(1982), ph

Goffredo Petrassi
BITTER RICE(1950, Ital.), m; FAMILY DIARY(1963 Ital.), m

Libero Petrassi
BARBER OF SEVILLE, THE(1947, Ital.), art d

Libero Petrazzi
THIS WINE OF LOVE(1948, Ital.), w

Gio Petre
WILD STRAWBERRIES(1959, Swed.); DOLL, THE(1964, Swed.); GORILLA(1964, Swed.); LOVING COUPLES(1966, Swed.); MY FATHER'S MISTRESS(1970, Swed.)

Tony C. Petrea
CARNY(1980)

Ian Petrella
CHRISTMAS STORY, A(1983)
1984
CRIMES OF PASSION(1984)

Sandra Petrelli
HOUSE OF 1,000 DOLLS(1967, Ger./Span./Brit.)

Irina Petrescu
STEPS TO THE MOON(1963, Rum.)

Renzo Petretto
PSYCHOUT FOR MURDER(1971, Arg./Ital.)

Petri
HIROSHIMA, MON AMOUR(1959, Fr./Jap.), prod d

Elio Petri
ASSASSIN, THE(1961, Ital./Fr.), d, w; HUNCHBACK OF ROME, THE(1963, Ital.), w; HIGH INFIDELITY(1965, Fr./Ital.), d; TENTH VICTIM, THE(1965, Fr./Ital.), d, w; OPIATE '67(1967, Fr./Ital.), w; WE STILL KILL THE OLD WAY(1967, Ital.), d, w; INVESTIGATION OF A CITIZEN ABOVE SUSPICION(1970, Ital.), d, w; QUIET PLACE IN THE COUNTRY, A(1970, Ital./Fr.), d, w

Hella Petri
MONKEY IN WINTER, A(1962, Fr.); RITA(1963, Fr./Ital.); LADY L(1965, Fr./Ital.); MATA HARI(1965, Fr./Ital.); TIGHT SKIRTS, LOOSE PLEASURES(1966, Fr.); DESTRUCTORS, THE(1974, Brit.); S(1974)

Ilse Petri
GIRL FROM THE MARSH CROFT, THE(1935, Ger.); TURKISH CUCUMBER, THE(1963, Ger.)

Luciana Petri
LIGHTNING BOLT(1967, Ital./Sp.)

Mario Petri
HUNS, THE(1962, Fr./Ital.); HERCULES AND THE CAPTIVE WOMEN(1963, Fr./Ital.); SECRET MARK OF D'ARTAGNAN, THE(1963, Fr./Ital.)

Maurice Petri
FOREIGN INTRIGUE(1956), art d; OLDEST PROFESSION, THE(1968, Fr./Ital./Ger.), art d; TWO OF US, THE(1968, Fr.), art d

Walter Petri
Misc. Silents
DOES IT PAY?(1923)

Vlada Petric
TWELVE CHAIRS, THE(1970)

Andrea Petricca
LOVE AND LARCENY(1963, Fr./Ital.)

Harry Petricek
TEENAGE GANG DEBS(1966), ph; VIXENS, THE(1969), ph

Konstantin Petrichenko
MUMU(1961, USSR), ph
D. Hay Petrie
SUSPENSE(1930, Brit.); CARMEN(1931, Brit.); MANY WATERS(1931, Brit.); NIGHT BIRDS(1931, Brit.); HELP YOURSELF(1932, Brit.); LUCKY NUMBER, THE(1933, Brit.)
Daniel Petrie
BRAMBLE BUSH, THE(1960), d; RAISIN IN THE SUN, A(1961), d; MAIN ATTRACTION, THE(1962, Brit.), d; STOLEN HOURS(1963), d; IDOL, THE(1966, Brit.), d; SPY WITH A COLD NOSE, THE(1966, Brit.), d; NEPTUNE FACTOR, THE(1973, Can.), d; LIFEGUARD(1976), d; BETSY, THE(1978), d; RESURRECTION(1980), d; FORT APACHE, THE BRONX(1981), d; SIX PACK(1982), d
1984
BAY BOY(1984, Can.), d&w, ed
Misc. Talkies
BUSTER AND BILLIE(1974), d
Daniel Petrie, Jr.
1984
BEVERLY HILLS COP(1984), w
Donald Petrie
TURNING POINT, THE(1977); H.O.T.S.(1979); HEARSE, THE(1980); FORT APACHE, THE BRONX(1981)
Doris Petrie
WEDDING IN WHITE(1972, Can.); TICKET TO HEAVEN(1981)
Edna Petrie
ANGRY SILENCE, THE(1960, Brit.); THERE WAS A CROOKED MAN(1962, Brit.); MURDER AHOY(1964, Brit.)
George O. Petrie
WAVELENGTH(1983)
George Petrie
BOOMERANG(1947); FOUR DAYS LEAVE(1950, Switz.); AT SWORD'S POINT(1951); GYPSY(1962); HUD(1963); WALL OF NOISE(1963); HE RIDES TALL(1964); WHAT'S SO BAD ABOUT FEELING GOOD?(1968); TELEFON(1977); OTHER SIDE OF THE MOUNTAIN–PART 2, THE(1978)
Pfc. George Petrie
WINGED VICTORY(1944)
Gordon Petrie
PSYCHO-CIRCUS(1967, Brit.); DEATHLINE(1973, Brit.)
Hay Petrie
COUNTY FAIR(1933, Brit.); CRIME ON THE HILL(1933, Brit.); DAUGHTERS OF TODAY(1933, Brit.); MATINEE IDOL(1933, Brit.); BLIND JUSTICE(1934, Brit.); COLONEL BLOOD(1934, Brit.); PRIVATE LIFE OF DON JUAN, THE(1934, Brit.); INVITATION TO THE WALTZ(1935, Brit.); OLD CURIOSITY SHOP, THE(1935, Brit.); RUNAWAY QUEEN, THE(1935, Brit.); GHOST GOES WEST, THE(1936); HEARTS OF HUMANITY(1936, Brit.); HOUSE OF THE SPANIARD, THE(1936, Brit.); I STAND CONDEMNED(1936, Brit.); MEN OF YESTERDAY(1936, Brit.); RED WAGON(1936); FOREVER YOURS(1937, Brit.); KNIGHT WITHOUT ARMOR(1937, Brit.); I MARRIED A SPY(1938, Brit.); LAST BARRICADE, THE(1938, Brit.); LOVES OF MADAME DUBARRY, THE(1938, Brit.); SMILING ALONG(1938, Brit.); CLOUDS OVER EUROPE(1939, Brit.); INQUEST(1939, Brit.); JAMAICA INN(1939, Brit.); SPY FOR A DAY(1939, Brit.); TREACHERY ON THE HIGH SEAS(1939, Brit.); U-BOAT 29(1939, Brit.); BLACKOUT(1940, Brit.); CONQUEST OF THE AIR(1940); CONVOY(1940, Brit.); CRIMES AT THE DARK HOUSE(1940, Brit.); DESIGN FOR MURDER(1940, Brit.); PASTOR HALL(1940, Brit.); THIEF OF BAGHDAD, THE(1940, Brit.); TWENTY-ONE DAYS TOGETHER(1940, Brit.); BOMBSIGHT STOLEN(1941, Brit.); GHOST OF ST. MICHAEL'S. THE(1941, Brit.); HARD STEEL(1941, Brit.); MISSING TEN DAYS(1941, Brit.); QUIET WEDDING(1941, Brit.); TURNED OUT NICE AGAIN(1941, Brit.); VOICE IN THE NIGHT, A(1941, Brit.); GREAT MR. HANDEL, THE(1942, Brit.); ONE OF OUR AIRCRAFT IS MISSING(1942, Brit.); THIS WAS PARIS(1942, Brit.); WINGS AND THE WOMAN(1942, Brit.); BATTLE FOR MUSIC(1943, Brit.); ESCAPE TO DANGER(1943, Brit.); CANTERBURY TALE, A(1944, Brit.); KISS THE BRIDE GOODBYE(1944, Brit.); ON APPROVAL(1944, Brit.); FOR YOU ALONE(1945, Brit.); SPELL OF AMY NUGENT, THE(1945, Brit.); VOICE WITHIN, THE(1945, Brit.); GREAT EXPECTATIONS(1946, Brit.); HONEYMOON HOTEL(1946, Brit.); NIGHT BOAT TO DUBLIN(1946, Brit.); WALTZ TIME(1946, Brit.); MONKEY'S PAW, THE(1948, Brit.); QUEEN OF SPADES(1948, Brit.); RED SHOES, THE(1948, Brit.); FALLEN IDOL, THE(1949, Brit.); OUTSIDER, THE(1949, Brit.); LAUGHING LADY, THE(1950, Brit.); SILK NOOSE, THE(1950, Brit.)
Howard Petrie
FANCY PANTS(1950); ROCKY MOUNTAIN(1950); WALK SOFTLY, STRANGER(1950); CATTLE DRIVE(1951); GOLDEN HORDE, THE(1951); NO QUESTIONS ASKED(1951); BEND OF THE RIVER(1952); CARBINE WILLIAMS(1952); PONY SOLDIER(1952); RED BALL EXPRESS(1952); WILD NORTH, THE(1952); WOMAN OF THE NORTH COUNTRY(1952); FAIR WIND TO JAVA(1953); FORT TI(1953); TROUBLE ALONG THE WAY(1953); VEILS OF BAGDAD, THE(1953); BOB MATHIAS STORY, THE(1954); BORDER RIVER(1954); BOUNTY HUNTER, THE(1954); SEVEN BRIDES FOR SEVEN BROTHERS(1954); SIGN OF THE PAGAN(1954); HOW TO BE VERY, VERY, POPULAR(1955); RAGE AT DAWN(1955); RETURN OF JACK SLADE, THE(1955); TIMBERJACK(1955); JOHNNY CONCHO(1956); KISS BEFORE DYING, A(1956); MAVERICK QUEEN, THE(1956); TIN STAR, THE(1957)
Scott Petrie
BATTLE CRY(1959)
Sue Helen Petrie
RIP-OFF(1971, Can.)
Sue Petrie
SUNDAY IN THE COUNTRY(1975, Can.)
Misc. Talkies
LIONS FOR BREAKFAST(1977)
Susan Petrie
FAR SHORE, THE(1976, Can.); THEY CAME FROM WITHIN(1976, Can.)
Walter Petrie
BATTLE OF PARIS, THE(1929)
Doris Petrik
FUNERAL HOME(1982, Can.)
Erika Petrik
GOOSE GIRL, THE(1967, Ger.), ed
Didi Petrikat
ALICE IN THE CITIES(1974, W. Ger.)

Vittoriano Petrilli
UNDER TEN FLAGS(1960, U.S./Ital.), w; HUNCHBACK OF ROME, THE(1963, Ital.), w; RED SHEIK, THE(1963, Ital.), w; OPERATION CROSSBOW(1965, U.S./Ital.), w; FRAULEIN DOKTOR(1969, Ital./Yugo.), w
Vittorio Petrilli
TRAPPED IN TANGIERS(1960, Ital./Span.), w
Sammy Petrillo
BELA LUGOSI MEETS A BROOKLYN GORILLA(1952); SHANGRI-LA(1961)
Paola Petrini
WHITE SLAVE SHIP(1962, Fr./Ital.)
Anatoliy Petritskiy
WAR AND PEACE(1968, USSR), ph
Hortense Petro
TOMBSTONE TERROR(1935)
Kathleen L. Petro
1984
TANK(1984)
Antonio Petrocelli
EYES, THE MOUTH, THE(1982, Ital./Fr.)
Hamil Petrof
BEAT GENERATION, THE(1959), ch
Boris L. Petroff
RED SNOW(1952), p, d; OUTCASTS OF THE CITY(1958), p&d; SHOTGUN WEDDING, THE(1963), p&d
Boris Petroff
HATS OFF(1937), p&d; ARCTIC FURY(1949), p; TWO LOST WORLDS(1950), p
Gloria Petroff
MINSTREL MAN(1944); ARCTIC FURY(1949); TWO LOST WORLDS(1950); LORNA DOONE(1951)
Hamil Petroff
SOFIA(1948); SAMSON AND DELILAH(1949); PHFFFT!(1954); MUTINY ON THE BOUNTY(1962), ch; CALIFORNIA(1963), p&d; RUNAWAY GIRL(1966), p&d
Manuel Petroff
TEXAS CARNIVAL(1951)
Victor Petroff
HATS OFF(1937), ch
Jean-Pierre Petrolacci
FINO A FARTI MALE(1969, Fr./Ital.), w
Nick Petron
LITTLE SEX, A(1982)
Joan Petrone
ONE-EYED JACKS(1961)
Giulio Petroni
DEATH RIDES A HORSE(1969, Ital.), d, w
Misc. Talkies
BLOOD AND GUNS(1979, Ital.), d
Brigitte Petronio
CITY OF WOMEN(1980, Ital./Fr.)
Tatiana Petronio
CITY OF WOMEN(1980, Ital./Fr.)
Penny Petropulos
ACE ELI AND RODGER OF THE SKIES(1973)
Victor Petroshevic
ROUND TRIP(1967), ph
Joaquin Petrosino
DARK RIVER(1956, Arg.); PUT UP OR SHUT UP(1968, Arg.)
Vincent Petrosino
WIRE SERVICE(1942), cos
Adam Petroski
COLD RIVER(1982)
Andrey Petrov
LAST GAME, THE(1964, USSR), m; MEET ME IN MOSCOW(1966, USSR), m; PORTRAIT OF LENIN(1967, Pol./USSR); UNCOMMON THIEF, AN(1967, USSR), m
Eugene Petrov [Y. Katayev]
KEEP YOUR SEATS PLEASE(1936, Brit.), w; TAXI TO HEAVEN(1944, USSR), w
Ivan Petrov
YOLANTA(1964, USSR)
Naicho Petrov
CLOWN AND THE KIDS, THE(1968, U.S./Bulgaria)
S. Petrov
Silents
ARSENAL(1929, USSR)
Misc. Silents
JEW AT WAR, A(1931, USSR)
S.S. Petrov
HEROES OF THE SEA(1941)
Sasha Petrov
LAST GAME, THE(1964, USSR)
Valeri Petrov
WITH LOVE AND TENDERNESS(1978, Bulgaria), w
Vassily Petrov
ASSIGNMENT OUTER SPACE(1960, Ital.), w; BATTLE OF THE WORLDS(1961, Ital.), w
Vladimir Petrov
THUNDERSTORM(1934, USSR), d&w; 1812(1944, USSR), d
Misc. Silents
CHILDREN OF THE NEW DAY(1930, USSR), d
Yevgeniy Petrov
TWELVE CHAIRS, THE(1970), d&w
G. Petrova
SPRINGTIME ON THE VOLGA(1961, USSR)
Mme Petrova
Misc. Silents
BRIDGES BURNED(1917)
Mme. Petrova
Misc. Silents
BLACK BUTTERFLY, THE(1916)

Nadia Petrova
ARISE, MY LOVE(1940)
Olga Petrova
Silents
TIGRESS, THE(1914); LAW OF THE LAND, THE(1917)
Misc. Silents
HEART OF A PAINTED WOMAN, THE(1915); VAMPIRE, THE(1915); WHAT WILL PEOPLE SAY(1915); ETERNAL QUESTION, THE(1916); EXTRAVAGANCE(1916); MY MADONNA(1916); PLAYING WITH FIRE(1916); SCARLET WOMAN, THE(1916); SOUL MARKET, THE(1916); DAUGHTER OF DESTINY(1917); EXILE(1917); MORE TRUTH THAN POETRY(1917); SECRET OF EVE, THE(1917); SILENCE SELLERS, THE(1917); SOUL OF MAGDALEN, THE(1917); TO THE DEATH(1917); UNDYING FLAME, THE(1917); WAITING SOUL, THE(1917); LIFE MASK, THE(1918); LIGHT WITHIN, THE(1918); TEMPERED STEEL(1918); PANTHER WOMAN, THE(1919)
Olya Petrova
WHEN THE TREES WERE TALL(1965, USSR)
Sona Petrova
LUDWIG(1973, Ital./Ger./Fr.)
V. Petrova
JACK FROST(1966, USSR)
Aleksandar Petrovic
THREE(1967, Yugo.), d, w; I EVEN MET HAPPY GYPSIES(1968, Yugo.), d&w, m
Cedomir Petrovic
FRAGRANCE OF WILD FLOWERS, THE(1979, Yugo.)
Milo Petrovic
MONTENEGRO(1981, Brit./Swed.)
Petar Petrovic
RAMPAGE AT APACHE WELLS(1966, Ger./Yugo.)
Ivan Petrovich
DEVIL MAKES THREE, THE(1952); JOURNEY, THE(1959, U.S./Aust.); FRANTIC(1961, Fr.); FOREVER MY LOVE(1962)
Misc. Silents
AME D'ARTISTE(1925, Fr.); MAGICIAN, THE(1926); GARDEN OF ALLAH, THE(1927); MODEL FROM MONTMARTE, THE(1928, Fr.); MORGANE, THE ENCHANTRESS(1929, Fr.); SECRETS OF THE ORIENT(1932, Ger.)
Michael Petrovich
ESCAPE 2000(1983, Aus.)
Emil Petrovics
BOYS OF PAUL STREET, THE(1969, Hung./US), m
Ivan Petrovicz
MANULESCU(1933, Ger.)
Ivan Petrovitch
TRIAL, THE(1948, Aust.)
Misc. Silents
THREE PASSIONS, THE(1928, Brit.)
Michael Petrovitch
TALES THAT WITNESS MADNESS(1973, Brit.); NEITHER THE SEA NOR THE SAND(1974, Brit.); S(1974)
Nastasia Petrovna
STEPPE, THE(1963, Fr./Ital.)
Gundula Petrovska
1984
LOVE IN GERMANY, A(1984, Fr./Ger.)
Mischa Petrow
STRANGE INVADERS(1983), art d; VIGILANTE(1983), prod d
1984
EXTERMINATOR 2(1984), art d; HOME FREE ALL(1984), prod d
Marina Petrowa
5 SINNERS(1961, Ger.); I SPIT ON YOUR GRAVE(1962, Fr.)
Xenia Petrowsky
DR. COPPELIUS(1968, U.S./Span.)
Giovanni Petrucci
L'AVVENTURA(1960, Ital.); COBRA, THE(1968); DEATH RIDES A HORSE(1969, Ital.); DIRTY OUTLAWS, THE(1971, Ital.)
Luigi Petrucci
IT HAPPENED IN CANADA(1962, Can.), p,d,w&ph, ed
Rick Petrucelli
ANNIE HALL(1977); WINDOWS(1980)
Joe Petrullo
WHITE RAT(1972); ABSENCE OF MALICE(1981)
Didier Petrus
CALYPSO(1959, Fr./It.)
Yevsie Petrushansky
GIRL FEVER(1961), d
Gina Petrushka
SECRET OF THE PURPLE REEF, THE(1960)
Julian Petruzzi
TENTH AVENUE KID(1938); VERTIGO(1958)
Gedda Petry
EUROPEANS, THE(1979, Brit.)
David Petrychka
EMIL AND THE DETECTIVES(1964)
Jacek Petrycki
CAMERA BUFF(1983, Pol.), ph
Eva Marie Petryshen
WELCOME TO THE CLUB(1971)
Graham Pette
Misc. Silents
BEYOND THE SHADOWS(1918); BOSS OF THE LAZY Y, THE(1918)
Graham Pette [Pettie]
Misc. Silents
HEIRESS FOR A DAY(1918)
Arturo Petterino
JOKER IS WILD, THE(1957)
Kjell Pettersen
1984
KAMILLA(1984, Norway)

Hjordis Petterson
TRUE AND THE FALSE, THE(1955, Swed.)
Sigrid Petterson
PRIZE, THE(1963)
Birgitta Pettersson
VIRGIN SPRING, THE(1960, Swed.)
Brigitta Pettersson
MAGICIAN, THE(1959, Swed.)
Britta Pettersson
LES CREATURES(1969, Fr./Swed.)
Hjordis Pettersson
PASSION OF ANNA, THE(1970, Swed.)
Thyra Pettersson
VIBRATION(1969, Swed.)
William Pettersson
VIBRATION(1969, Swed.)
Joanna Pettet
GROUP, THE(1966); CASINO ROYALE(1967, Brit.); NIGHT OF THE GENERALS, THE(1967, Brit./Fr.); ROBBERY(1967, Brit.); BLUE(1968); BEST HOUSE IN LONDON, THE(1969, Brit.); TENDER FLESH(1976); EVIL, THE(1978); DOUBLE EXPOSURE(1982)
Giovanni Petti
ISLAND OF PROCIDA, THE(1952, Ital.)
Robyn Petti
I WANNA HOLD YOUR HAND(1978)
Vincent Petti
HONEYMOON OF HORROR(1964)
H.O. Pettibone
Misc. Silents
BEHOLD THE MAN(1921, US/Fr.)
Graham Pettie
Silents
AMATEUR DEVIL, AN(1921); ONE A MINUTE(1921)
Misc. Silents
HIS ENEMY THE LAW(1918); HONEST MAN, AN(1918); WESTERNERS, THE(1919)
Yvonne Pettie
DOWN MEMORY LANE(1949)
Brian Pettifer
IF ...(1968, Brit.); O LUCKY MAN!(1973, Brit.); BRITTANIA HOSPITAL(1982, Brit.)
1984
AMADEUS(1984)
Julian Pettifer
ROSEBUD(1975)
Oscar Pettiford
CRIMSON CANARY(1945)
Selika Pettiford
SWING OUT, SISTER(1945)
Angelique Pettijohn
Misc. Talkies
BIO-HAZARD(1984)
Daniele Pettinari
CAGLIOSTRO(1975, Ital.), d, w
Frank Pettingell
HOBSON'S CHOICE(1931, Brit.); JEALOUSY(1931, Brit.); CROOKED LADY, THE(1932, Brit.); FRAIL WOMEN(1932, Brit.); CUCKOO IN THE NEST, THE(1933, Brit.); EXCESS BAGGAGE(1933, Brit.); GOOD COMPANIONS(1933, Brit.); LUCKY NUMBER, THE(1933, Brit.); MEDICINE MAN, THE(1933, Brit.); THAT'S MY WIFE(1933, Brit.); THIS WEEK OF GRACE(1933, Brit.); KEEP IT QUIET(1934, Brit.); MY OLD DUTCH(1934, Brit.); SING AS WE GO(1934, Brit.); BIG SPLASH, THE(1935, Brit.); HOPE OF HIS SIDE(1935, Brit.); IN A MONASTERY GARDEN(1935); RIGHT AGE TO MARRY, THE(1935, Brit.); SAY IT WITH DIAMONDS(1935, Brit.); AMATEUR GENTLEMAN(1936, Brit.); EVERYTHING OKAY(1936, Brit.); FAME(1936, Brit.); LAST JOURNEY, THE(1936, Brit.); MILLIONS(1936, Brit.); RED WAGON(1936); IT'S A GRAND OLD WORLD(1937, Brit.); SPRING HANDICAP(1937, Brit.); TAKE MY TIP(1937, Brit.); SAILING ALONG(1938, Brit.); BUSMAN'S HONEYMOON(1940, Brit.); GASLIGHT(1940); RETURN TO YESTERDAY(1940, Brit.); ONCE A CROOK(1941, Brit.); PIRATES OF THE SEVEN SEAS(1941, Brit.); SEVENTH SURVIVOR, THE(1941, Brit.); THIS ENGLAND(1941, Brit.); GOOSE STEPS OUT, THE(1942, Brit.); REMARKABLE MR. KIPPS(1942, Brit.); SHIPS WITH WINGS(1942, Brit.); YOUNG MR. PITT, THE(1942, Brit.); BUTLER'S DILEMMA, THE(1943, Brit.); GET CRACKING(1943, Brit.); ESCAPE(1948, Brit.); SHOWTIME(1948, Brit.); NO ROOM AT THE INN(1950, Brit.); MAGIC BOX, THE(1952, Brit.); PROMOTER, THE(1952, Brit.); GREAT GAME, THE(1953, Brit.); MEET MR. LUCIFER(1953, Brit.); TONIGHT AT 8:30(1953, Brit.); VALUE FOR MONEY(1957, Brit.); UP THE CREEK(1958, Brit.); CORRIDORS OF BLOOD(1962, Brit.); TERM OF TRIAL(1962, Brit.); TRIAL AND ERROR(1962, Brit.); BECKET(1964, Brit.)
Deen Pettinger
EL DORADO(1967)
Gary Pettinger
48 HOURS(1982)
1984
ELECTRIC DREAMS(1984)
Peter Pettinger
AGITATOR, THE(1949), w
Frank Pettingill
CRIMSON PIRATE, THE(1952)
John Pettis
1984
BEVERLY HILLS COP(1984)
Eric Pettit
SUBMARINE D-1(1937)
Francis Ann Pettit
OUT OF THE BLUE(1982)
Harry Pettit, Jr.
TREASURE AT THE MILL(1957, Brit.)
Mr. Harry Pettit, Sr.
TREASURE AT THE MILL(1957, Brit.)

Mrs. Harry Pettit, Sr.
TREASURE AT THE MILL(1957, Brit.)
Hilary Pettit
TREASURE AT THE MILL(1957, Brit.)
Merrilyn Pettit
TREASURE AT THE MILL(1957, Brit.)
Miller Pettit
BLACK ANGELS, THE(1970); FANDANGO(1970)
Peggy Pettit
BLACK GIRL(1972), a, ch
Rosemary Pettit
FURIES, THE(1950); WALK EAST ON BEACON(1952); GIRL ON THE RUN(1961)
Suzanna Pettit
GIRLFRIENDS(1978), ed
Suzanne Pettit
TELL ME A RIDDLE(1980), ed; TESTAMENT(1983), ed; TIMERIDER(1983), ed
Wilfred H. Pettit
VOICE OF THE WHISTLER(1945), w
Wilfrid H. Pettit
SWORDSMAN, THE(1947), w
Frank Pettitt
HEART WITHIN, THE(1957, Brit.); KITCHEN, THE(1961, Brit.); SATURDAY NIGHT AND SUNDAY MORNING(1961, Brit.); VICTIM(1961, Brit.)
Jomarie Pettitt
SERGEANT WAS A LADY, THE(1961)
Wilfred H. Pettitt
THOUSAND AND ONE NIGHTS, A(1945), w; BANDIT OF SHERWOOD FOREST, THE(1946), w
Wilfred Pettitt
THEY LIVE IN FEAR(1944), w
Wilfrid H. Pettitt
NINE GIRLS(1944), w; WALLS CAME TUMBLING DOWN, THE(1946), w
Ralph Pettofrezzo
GAS(1981, Can.)
Bert Pettus
ESCAPE TO BURMA(1955), animalt
Ken Pettus
INCIDENT AT PHANTOM HILL(1966), w; LAND RAIDERS(1969), w
Claude Petty
1984
DEATHSTALKER, THE(1984)
Jack Petty
SECONDS(1966), makeup; ODD COUPLE, THE(1968), makeup; I WALK THE LINE(1970), makeup; NEW LEAF, A(1971), makeup; GETAWAY, THE(1972), makeup; TERROR ON TOUR(1980), makeup
Jerry Petty
KILLERS THREE(1968); GUN RUNNER(1969); UNHOLY ROLLERS(1972)
Karen Petty
1984
NINJA III–THE DOMINATION(1984)
Kyle Petty
STROKER ACE(1983)
Richard Petty
THUNDER IN DIXIE(1965)
Misc. Talkies
PETTY STORY, THE(1974)
Tom Petty
FM(1978)
Angelique Pettyjohn
CLAMBAKE(1967); CHILDISH THINGS(1969); CURIOUS FEMALE, THE(1969); HEAVEN WITH A GUN(1969); HELL'S BELLES(1969); TELL ME THAT YOU LOVE ME, JUNIE MOON(1970); UP YOUR TEDDY BEAR(1970)
1984
REPO MAN(1984)
Misc. Talkies
G.I. EXECUTIONER, THE(1971)
Angelique Pettyjohn [Heaven St. John]
MAD DOCTOR OF BLOOD ISLAND, THE(1969, Phil./U.S.)
A. Petukhov
SHE-WOLF, THE(1963, USSR), spec eff
House Peters, Sr.
O. HENRY'S FULL HOUSE(1952); OLD WEST, THE(1952); TREASURE OF THE GOLDEN CONDOR(1953)
Anna Petukhova
ROAD HOME, THE(1947, USSR)
Gypsy Petulengro
CARAVAN(1946, Brit.)
Johann Peturrson
PREHISTORIC WOMEN(1950)
Harriet Petworth
ROOM TO LET(1949, Brit.); WARNING TO WANTONS, A(1949, Brit.)
Malte Petzel
BATTLE OF BRITAIN, THE(1969, Brit.)
Marcel Peulade
MADLY(1970, Fr.), ed
Michel Peurilon
GOING PLACES(1974, Fr.)
Osiride Pevarelli
MINUTE TO PRAY, A SECOND TO DIE, A(1968, Ital.)
Osiride Pevarello
VACATION, THE(1971, Ital.)
1984
RUSH(1984, Ital.)
John Peverall
DEER HUNTER, THE(1978), p
R. Peverello
DOCTOR FAUSTUS(1967, Brit.)

Ralph Peverill
GRENDEL GRENDEL GRENDEL(1981, Aus.), anim
Joseph Pevney
NOCTURNE(1946); BODY AND SOUL(1947); STREET WITH NO NAME, THE(1948); THIEVES' HIGHWAY(1949); OUTSIDE THE WALL(1950); SHAKEDOWN(1950), d; UNDERCOVER GIRL(1950), d; AIR CADET(1951), d; IRON MAN, THE(1951), d; LADY FROM TEXAS, THE(1951), d; STRANGE DOOR, THE(1951), d BECAUSE OF YOU(1952), d; FLESH AND FURY(1952), d; JUST ACROSS THE STREET(1952), d; MEET DANNY WILSON(1952), d; BACK TO GOD'S COUNTRY(1953), d; DESERT LEGION(1953), d; IT HAPPENS EVERY THURSDAY(1953), d; PLAYGIRL(1954), d; THREE RING CIRCUS(1954), d; YANKEE PASHA(1954), d; FEMALE ON THE BEACH(1955), d; FOXFIRE(1955), d; SIX BRIDGES TO CROSS(1955), d; AWAY ALL BOATS(1956), d; CONGO CROSSING(1956), d; ISTANBUL(1957), d; MAN OF A THOUSAND FACES(1957), d; MIDNIGHT STORY, THE(1957), d; TAMMY AND THE BACHELOR(1957), d; TORPEDO RUN(1958), d; TWILIGHT FOR THE GODS(1958), d; CASH McCALL(1960), d; CROWDED SKY, THE(1960), d; PLUNDERERS, THE(1960), p&d; PORTRAIT OF A MOBSTER(1961), d; NIGHT OF THE GRIZZLY, THE(1966), d
Illarion Pevtsov
Misc. Silents
HE WHO GETS SLAPPED(1916, USSR); DEATH OF THE GODS(1917, USSR)
Karel Peyer
DEATH OF TARZAN, THE(1968, Czech)
Michel Peynet
LIFE UPSIDE DOWN(1965, Fr.), p
Jacques Peyrac
LA NUIT DE VARENNES(1983, Fr./Ital.)
Arlette Peyran
Misc. Silents
VISAGE D'ENFANTS(1926, Fr.)
Joseph Peyre
LOVE IN A HOT CLIMATE(1958, Fr./Span.), w. Maurice Gerry
Rober Peyrefitte
THIS SPECIAL FRIENDSHIP(1967, Fr.), w
Roger Peyrefitte
SEVEN CAPITAL SINS(1962, Fr./Ital.), w; NEST OF VIPERS(1979, Ital.), w
Michel Peyrelon
DOCTEUR POPAUL(1972, Fr.); TUSK(1980, Fr.)
Frank Peyrinaud
ONCE IN PARIS(1978)
Yves Peyrot
JONAH–WHO WILL BE 25 IN THE YEAR 2000(1976, Switz.), p; PROVIDENCE(1977, Fr.), p; GIRL FROM LORRAINE, A(1982, Fr./Switz.), p; DEATH OF MARIO RICCI, THE(1983, Ital.), p
Arnold Peyser
TROUBLE WITH GIRLS(AND HOW TO GET INTO IT), THE*1/2 (1969), w
John Peyser
UNDERSEA GIRL(1957), d; YOUNG WARRIORS, THE(1967), d; FOUR RODE OUT(1969, US/Span.), d
Misc. Talkies
CENTERFOLD GIRLS, THE(1974), d
Julian I. Peyser
HEARTACHES(1947), w
Lois Peyser
TROUBLE WITH GIRLS(AND HOW TO GET INTO IT), THE*1/2 (1969), w
Penny Peyser
ALL THE PRESIDENT'S MEN(1976); FRISCO KID, THE(1979); IN-LAWS, THE(1979)
1984
UNFAITHFULLY YOURS(1984)
Casey Peyson
PRETTY BOY FLOYD(1960); DEAD TO THE WORLD(1961)
Claude Peyton
TEX TAKES A HOLIDAY(1932); THUNDER OVER TEXAS(1934); MISS PACIFIC FLEET(1935); NIGHT AT THE OPERA, A(1935)
Silents
SOUL OF YOUTH, THE(1920); KNIGHT OF THE WEST, A(1921); DO AND DARE(1922); SKID PROOF(1923); GOLD AND THE GIRL(1925)
Misc. Silents
BELLS OF SAN JUAN(1922); CATCH MY SMOKE(1922); MEN OF ZANSIBAR, THE(1922); DESERT RIDER(1923)
Frances Peyton
Silents
DEBT OF HONOR(1922, Brit.)
Gail Peyton
NATIONAL VELVET(1944)
Lawrence Peyton
Silents
JOAN THE WOMAN(1916)
Misc. Silents
MY BEST GIRL(1915)
Pamela Peyton
THIS LOVE OF OURS(1945)
Patrick Peyton
REDEEMER, THE(1965, Span.), p
Penni Peyton
LOVE MERCHANT, THE(1966)
Robert Peyton
NIGHT STAGE TO GALVESTON(1952); RED SNOW(1952)
1984
SUBURBIA(1984)
Robert Peyton [Lee Frederick]
TOKYO FILE 212(1951)
Armando Valdez Peza
LIVING IDOL, THE(1957), cos
Alexis Pezas
PHAEDRA(1962, U.S./Gr./Fr.)
A. W. Pezet
BROADWAY BAD(1933), w

Christian Pezey
FIRST TASTE OF LOVE(1962, Fr.); SWEET ECSTASY(1962, Fr.)
Giacinta Pezzana
Misc. Silents
TERESA RAQUIN(1915, Ital.)
Lucia Pezzoli
TREE OF WOODEN CLOGS, THE(1979, Ital.)
Addie Pezzotta
KING, MURRAY(1969)
Franco Pezzullo
LAST DAY OF THE WAR, THE(1969, U.S./Ital./Span.), m
Marjorie L. Pfaelzer
3 IS A FAMILY(1944), w; TARZAN AND THE AMAZONS(1945), w
Florence Leighton Pfalzgraf
OUR LITTLE GIRL(1935), w
Frank Pfandler
TRIAL, THE(1948, Aust.)
Kenneth Pfeffer
WIRE SERVICE(1942), w
Ben Pfeifer
TERROR IN THE JUNGLE(1968)
Henri Pfeifer
STORY OF A CHEAT, THE(1938, Fr.)
Ben Pfeiffer
ROOMMATES, THE(1973)
Carolyn Pfeiffer
ROADIE(1980), p; ENDANGERED SPECIES(1982), p
1984
CHOOSE ME(1984), p
David Pfeiffer
CHINA SYNDROME, THE(1979)
Hermann Pfeiffer
FINAL CHORD, THE(1936, Ger.)
Max Pfeiffer
BOMBARDMENT OF MONTE CARLO, THE(1931, Ger.), p; BOCCACCIO(1936, Ger.),
p
Michelle Pfeiffer
HOLLYWOOD KNIGHTS, THE(1980); CHARLIE CHAN AND THE CURSE OF THE
DRAGON QUEEN(1981); GREASE 2(1982); SCARFACE(1983)
Walter Pfeil
MONSTER OF LONDON CITY, THE(1967, Ger.)
Glen Pfiefer
OUT OF THE BLUE(1982)
Michelle Pfiefer
FALLING IN LOVE AGAIN(1980)
Sonia Pfirmann
ENTRE NOUS(1983, Fr.)
Edward Pfitzenmeier
LUCKY IN LOVE(1929), ed; MOTHER'S BOY(1929), ed; SYNCOPATION(1929), ed
Gunter Pfitzmann
HELDINNEN(1962, Ger.)
Gunther Pfitzmann
BRIDGE, THE(1961, Ger.)
Hans Pfitzner
DISORDER AND EARLY TORMENT(1977, Ger.), m
Dennis Pflederer
STACY'S KNIGHTS(1983)
Mickey Pfleger
SCARLET ANGEL(1952)
Michael Pfleghar
CORPSE OF BEVERLY HILLS, THE(1965, Ger.), d, w; SERENADE FOR TWO
SPIES(1966, Ital./Ger.), d, w; HOW TO SEDUCE A PLAYBOY(1968, Aust./Fr./Ital.), d,
w
Michael Pflueger
Misc. Talkies
LEGACY(1963)
Eva Pflug
CONFESS DR. CORDA(1960, Ger.); MAN ON A STRING(1960); DEAD RUN(1961,
Fr./Ital./Ger.); GIRL FROM HONG KONG(1966, Ger.); I DEAL IN DANGER(1966)
Jo Ann Pflug
M(1970); CATLOW(1971, Span.); WHERE DOES IT HURT?(1972)
Charles Pfluger
WEDDING PARTY, THE(1969)
Helmuth Pfluger
WEDDING PARTY, THE(1969)
Andy Pforsich
BOY NAMED CHARLIE BROWN, A(1969)
Guy Pforsich
BOY NAMED CHARLIE BROWN, A(1969)
ph
LOST SQUADRON, THE(1932), ph
Robert Deane Phaar
BOOK OF NUMBERS(1973), w
Phaedra
GREAT SCOUT AND CATHOUSE THURSDAY, THE(1976)
Douglas Phair
RATS ARE COMING! THE WEREWOLVES ARE HERE!, THE(1972)
Robert Phalen
THREE DAYS OF THE CONDOR(1975); HALLOWEEN(1978); ZOOT SUIT(1981)
1984
STARMAN(1984)
Dada Phalke
Misc. Silents
HARISCHANDRA(1913, India), d
Phar Lap
WINNER'S CIRCLE, THE(1948)
Frank Phares
NEW ORLEANS AFTER DARK(1958), w; FOUR FOR THE MORGUE(1962), w

Vera Phares
GENERALS WITHOUT BUTTONS(1938, Fr.)
Richard G. Pharo
ROADRACERS, THE(1959)
Ashley Pharoah
1984
WHITE ELEPHANT(1984, Brit.), w
Frank Pharr
THEY WON'T BELIEVE ME(1947); GOLD IS WHERE YOU FIND IT(1938); SWING
YOUR LADY(1938); LADY IN QUESTION, THE(1940); JUKE GIRL(1942); DEVIL
BAT'S DAUGHTER, THE(1946); WILD WEST(1946); HIGH BARBAREE(1947); SEA OF
GRASS, THE(1947); FORCE OF EVIL(1948); SUN COMES UP, THE(1949); SUMMER
STOCK(1950); TEXAN MEETS CALAMITY JANE, THE(1950)
Isabelle Phat
TALES OF PARIS(1962, Fr./Ital.), w
Lee Phebs
WYOMING(1940)
Anne Phelan
DEVIL'S PLAYGROUND, THE(1976, Aus.)
Brian Phelan
KITCHEN, THE(1961, Brit.); CONCRETE JUNGLE, THE(1962, Brit.); DAMN THE
DEFIANT!(1962, Brit.); SERVANT, THE(1964, Brit.); SOLDIER'S TALE, THE(1964,
Brit.); FOUR IN THE MORNING(1965, Brit.); HIGH WIND IN JAMAICA, A(1965);
LEATHER BOYS, THE(1965, Brit.); ACCIDENT(1967, Brit.); LITTLE MOTHER(1973,
U.S./Yugo./Ger.), w; HONEYBABY, HONEYBABY(1974), a, w
Dorothy Phelan
1984
MRS. SOFFEL(1984)
Jim Phelan
NIGHT JOURNEY(1938, Brit.), w
1984
ALMOST YOU(1984)
Kathleen Phelan
LILITH(1964)
Martin Phelan
ELIZA FRASER(1976, Aus.); JOURNEY AMONG WOMEN(1977, Aus.)
Pat Phelan
MOONLIGHT IN VERMONT(1943); MISS SUSIE SLAGLE'S(1945); SPEED TO
SPARE(1948); TRIPLE THREAT(1948); LEAVE IT TO HENRY(1949)
Raymond A. Phelan
TOO YOUNG, TOO IMMORAL!(1962), a, p,d,w&ph, ed
Barry Phelps
GHOST SHIP(1953, Brit.)
Billy Phelps
Silents
OVER THE STICKS(1929, Brit.)
Bud Phelps
LAST WARNING, THE(1929)
Buster Phelps
FEET FIRST(1930); LEFTOVER LADIES(1931); HANDLE WITH CARE(1932); LIT-
TLE ORPHAN ANNIE(1932); SCANDAL FOR SALE(1932); THREE ON A
MATCH(1932); BROKEN DREAMS(1933); LAUGHING AT LIFE(1933); ONE MAN'S
JOURNEY(1933); SAILOR'S LUCK(1933); WORLD GONE MAD, THE(1933); NOW
AND FOREVER(1934); SERVANTS' ENTRANCE(1934); AFFAIR OF SUSAN(1935);
ANNA KARENINA(1935); LITTLE MEN(1935); STRANGE WIVES(1935); SMALL
TOWN GIRL(1936); TOO MANY PARENTS(1936); GIRL LOVES BOY(1937); LITTLE
TOUGH GUY(1938); HERO FOR A DAY(1939); HOWARDS OF VIRGINIA, THE(1940);
WAGONS ROLL AT NIGHT, THE(1941); AND THE ANGELS SING(1944); TOMOR-
ROW IS FOREVER(1946); MOTHER IS A FRESHMAN(1949)
Cooke Phelps
FORBIDDEN(1932)
Earl Phelps
GUN LAW(1938)
Eleanor Phelps
CLEOPATRA(1934); COUNT OF MONTE CRISTO, THE(1934)
George Phelps
KID FROM LEFT FIELD, THE(1953)
John Phelps
Silents
LAST ROSE OF SUMMER, THE(1920, Brit.)
Kate Phelps
SHINING, THE(1980)
Lee Phelps
THEY WON'T BELIEVE ME(1947); ANNA CHRISTIE(1930); PUTTIN' ON THE
RITZ(1930); CRIMINAL CODE(1931); FREE SOUL, A(1931); LADIES' MAN(1931);
LAUGHING SINNERS(1931); NO LIMIT(1931); PUBLIC ENEMY, THE(1931); QUICK
MILLIONS(1931); CROSS-EXAMINATION(1932); GRAND HOTEL(1932); HOLD'EM
JAIL(1932); NIGHT CLUB LADY(1932); RICH ARE ALWAYS WITH US, THE(1932);
TAXI!(1932); THIRTEEN WOMEN(1932); WESTWARD PASSAGE(1932); WINNER
TAKE ALL(1932); HEROES FOR SALE(1933); I COVER THE WATERFRONT(1933);
PAROLE GIRL(1933); SITTING PRETTY(1933); WOMAN I STOLE, THE(1933);
CHAINED(1934); FASHIONS OF 1934(1934); GIRL FROM MISSOURI, THE(1934);
HOUSEWIFE(1934); MANHATTAN MELODRAMA(1934); SADIE MCKEE(1934); SIX
OF A KIND(1934); ST. LOUIS KID, THE(1934); THIS SIDE OF HEAVEN(1934);
TRANSATLANTIC MERRY-GO-ROUND(1934); YOU'RE TELLING ME(1934); FRISCO
KID(1935); G-MEN(1935); MAN WHO RECLAIMED HIS HEAD, THE(1935); RECK-
LESS(1935); RENDEZVOUS(1935); SHE COULDN'T TAKE IT(1935); SPECIAL
AGENT(1935); WINGS IN THE DARK(1935); $1,000 A MINUTE(1935); BOSS RIDER
OF GUN CREEK(1936); GORGEOUS HUSSY, THE(1936); HUMAN CARGO(1936);
MURDER WITH PICTURES(1936); OUR RELATIONS(1936); PALM SPRINGS(1936);
RETURN OF SOPHIE LANG, THE(1936); ROSE MARIE(1936); SHOW BOAT(1936);
STRIKE ME PINK(1936); THEODORA GOES WILD(1936); TRAIL OF THE LONE-
SOME PINE, THE(1936); UNDER YOUR SPELL(1936); WE'RE ONLY HUMAN(1936);
BOSS OF LONELY VALLEY(1937); EASY LIVING(1937); HIDEAWAY GIRL(1937);
INTERNES CAN'T TAKE MONEY(1937); LAST GANGSTER, THE(1937); LEFT-
HANDED LAW(1937); NATION AFLAME(1937); NOTHING SACRED(1937); PER-
FECT SPECIMEN, THE(1937); RAW TIMBER(1937); SANDFLOW(1937); SMOKE
TREE RANGE(1937); STAR IS BORN, A(1937); SUBMARINE D-1(1937); TIME OUT
FOR ROMANCE(1937); TOUGH TO HANDLE(1937); UNDER SUSPICION(1937);
ANGELS WITH DIRTY FACES(1938); ANNABEL TAKES A TOUR(1938); CITY

Claude-Jean Philippe
CHLOE IN THE AFTERNOON(1972, Fr.)
Gerard Philippe
ROYAL AFFAIRS IN VERSAILLES(1957, Fr.)
J. Claude Philippe
NIGHT OF THE GENERALS, THE(1967, Brit./Fr.), cos
Jean Philippe
JAZZ BOAT(1960, Brit.)
Michele Philippe
NAKED WOMAN, THE(1950, Fr.); FRENCH CANCAN(1956, Fr.); VICE DOLLS(1961, Fr.); HOT HOURS(1963, Fr.)
Pierre Philippe
Misc. Silents
CATHERINE(1924, Fr.); LA FILLE DE L'EAU(1924, Fr.)
Richard Philippe
PUZZLE OF A DOWNFALL CHILD(1970), makeup
M. Philippe-Gerard
1984
LIFE IS A BED OF ROSES(1984, Fr.), m
Charles Philippi
FANTASIA(1940), art d; PINOCCHIO(1940), art d; RELUCTANT DRAGON, THE(1941), anim d
Erich Philippi
MISSING GUEST, THE(1938), w; MURDER IN THE BLUE ROOM(1944), w
Andreas Philippides
ATLAS(1960); PHAEDRA(1962, U.S./Gr./Fr.)
Art Philipps
LUCKY STAR, THE(1980, Can.), m
Alex Philips
ADVENTURES OF ROBINSON CRUSOE, THE(1954), ph; FOR THE LOVE OF MIKE(1960), ph
Barney Philips
JUDGE, THE(1949); MY SIX CONVICTS(1952)
Bertram Philips
Misc. Silents
GAYEST OF THE GAY, THE(1924, Brit.), d
Don Philips
LITTLE SEX, A(1982)
Dorothy Philips
Misc. Silents
HURRICANE'S GAL(1922)
Eddie Philips
NO WAY TO TREAT A LADY(1968)
Misc. Silents
BLACK LIGHTING(1924); FOURFLUSHER, THE(1928)
Edwin Philips
SOAK THE RICH(1936)
Geremy Philips
UGLY DUCKLING, THE(1959, Brit.)
Howard Philips
GREAT HOSPITAL MYSTERY, THE(1937)
John Philips
WELL, THE(1951)
Julie Philips
BABY, IT'S YOU(1983)
1984
LIES(1984, Brit.); RACING WITH THE MOON(1984)
Lee Philips
PEYTON PLACE(1957); MIDDLE OF THE NIGHT(1959); TESS OF THE STORM COUNTRY(1961); PSYCHOMANIA(1964); LOLLIPOP COVER, THE(1965); ON THE RIGHT TRACK(1981), d
Leslie Philips
CITADEL, THE(1938)
Lily Philips
Silents
WHITE FLOWER, THE(1923)
Mary Philips
FAREWELL TO ARMS, A(1932); WINGS OVER HONOLULU(1937); LADY IN THE DARK(1944); CAPTAIN EDDIE(1945); KISS AND TELL(1945); DEAR RUTH(1947); DEAR WIFE(1949); LIFE OF RILEY, THE(1949); DEAR BRAT(1951); I CAN GET IT FOR YOU WHOLESALE(1951); PRINCE VALIANT(1954)
Paul Philips
YOU'LL NEVER GET RICH(1941)
Ronnie Philips
HARD TIMES(1975)
Rosemary Philips
STOP THE WORLD–I WANT TO GET OFF(1966, Brit.)
Sian Philips
NIJINSKY(1980, Brit.)
Wendell Philips
SEEDS OF FREEDOM(1943, USSR)
William "Bill" Philips
HOLIDAY IN MEXICO(1946); MAN WITHOUT A STAR(1955)
Betty Philipsen
LOLA MONTES(1955, Fr./Ger.)
Preben Philipsen
I, TOO, AM ONLY A WOMAN(1963, Ger.), p; AMONG VULTURES(1964, Ger./Ital./Fr./Yugo.), p; FRONTIER HELLCAT(1966, Fr./Ital./Ger./Yugo.), p; CREATURE WITH THE BLUE HAND(1971, Ger.), p
Harriet Philipson
CRIME AND PUNISHMENT(1948, Swed.)
John Philliber
LADY TAKES A CHANCE, A(1943); DOUBLE INDEMNITY(1944); GENTLE AN-NIE(1944); IMPOSTER, THE(1944); IT HAPPENED TOMORROW(1944); LADIES OF WASHINGTON(1944); SUMMER STORM(1944); 3 IS A FAMILY(1944)
Alex Phillip
FIGHTING PLAYBOY(1937), w

Harold Phillip
BIMBO THE GREAT(1961, Ger.), d, w
Louis Phillip
WILD HEART, THE(1952, Brit.)
Andre Phillipe
BOB AND CAROL AND TED AND ALICE(1969); ALEX IN WONDERLAND(1970); BLACK BELT JONES(1974)
Erich Phillipi
SECRET OF THE BLUE ROOM(1933), w
Andre Phillippe
INVASION OF THE BEE GIRLS(1973)
Charles Phillippi
SNOW WHITE AND THE SEVEN DWARFS(1937), art d
Louis Phillippi
RIDERS TO THE STARS(1954), makeup
Patti Phillippi
MURDER IN THE MUSIC HALL(1946)
Betty Phillippsen
MONTE CARLO STORY, THE(1957, Ital.)
Aaron Phillips
TAKE ME OUT TO THE BALL GAME(1949)
Alec Phillips
WONDERFUL COUNTRY, THE(1959), ph
Silents
NERVOUS WRECK, THE(1926), ph
Alex Phillips
CARNATION KID(1929), ph; MAD EMPRESS, THE(1940), ph; PANCHO VILLA RETURNS(1950, Mex.), ph; LITTLEST OUTLAW, THE(1955), ph; LAST OF THE FAST GUNS, THE(1958), ph; SIERRA BARON(1958), ph; TEN DAYS TO TULARA(1958), ph; VILLA!(1958), ph; GERONIMO(1962), ph; SHAME OF THE SABINE WOMEN, THE(1962, Mex.), ph; LITTLE RED RIDING HOOD(1963, Mex.), ph; OF LOVE AND DESIRE(1963), ph; QUEEN'S SWORDSMEN, THE(1963, Mex.), ph; CASTLE OF PURI-TY(1974, Mex.), ph; NIGHT OF A THOUSAND CATS(1974, Mex.), ph; MAN FRI-DAY(1975, Brit.), ph
1984
BLAME IT ON THE NIGHT(1984), ph; SURF II(1984), ph; TORCHLIGHT(1984), ph
Angela Phillips
CHILLY SCENES OF WINTER(1982)
Anthony Phillips
Silents
LES MISERABLES(1918)
Anya Phillips
FOREIGNER, THE(1978)
Arlene Phillips
CAN'T STOP THE MUSIC(1980), ch; FAN, THE(1981), ch; ANNIE(1982), ch; MONTY PYTHON'S THE MEANING OF LIFE(1983, Brit.), ch
Arnold Phillips
GAMBLING DAUGHTERS(1941), w; ONE DANGEROUS NIGHT(1943), w; BLUE-BEARD(1944), w; BRIGHTON STRANGLER, THE(1945), w; JEALOUSY(1945), w; MURDER IN THE MUSIC HALL(1946), w; RETURN OF MONTE CRISTO, THE(1946), w; TIME OUT OF MIND(1947), w; KILL OR BE KILLED(1950), w; GIRL ON THE BRIDGE, THE(1951), w; PICKUP(1951), w; STORY OF THREE LOVES, THE(1953), w
Art Phillips
POSSESSION(1981, Fr./Ger.), m
Silents
SO THIS IS ARIZONA(1922)
Arthur Phillips
LIMEHOUSE BLUES(1934), w; YELLOWSTONE(1936), w; GOLDWYN FOLLIES, THE(1938), w; PLAYMATES(1941), w; STAR SPANGLED RHYTHM(1942), w; RID-ING HIGH(1943), w; RAINBOW ISLAND(1944), w; DELIGHTFULLY DAN-GEROUS(1945), w; LOVE, HONOR AND GOODBYE(1945), w; OUT OF THIS WORLD(1945), w
Misc. Silents
LIFE'S A STAGE(1929, Brit.), d; THREE MEN IN A CART(1929, Brit.), d
Augustus Phillips
Silents
JUNE FRIDAY(1915); INNOCENCE OF RUTH, THE(1916); ALADDIN'S OTHER LAMP(1917); GRIM GAME, THE(1919)
Misc. Silents
CHILD IN JUDGEMENT, A(1915); RING OF THE BORGIAS, THE(1915); TRUTH ABOUT HELEN, THE(1915); GATES OF EDEN, THE(1916); GOD'S LAW AND MAN'S(1917); LADY BARNACLE(1917); MORTAL SIN, THE(1917); THREADS OF FATE(1917); BRASS CHECK, THE(1918); DAYBREAK(1918); CHARGE IT TO ME(1919); ONE HOUR BEFORE DAWN(1920)
Austin Phillips
Silents
ONE COLUMBO NIGHT(1926, Brit.), w
Barney Phillips
EIGHT IRON MEN(1952); HAS ANYBODY SEEN MY GAL?(1952); ALL-AMERICAN, THE(1953); BLUEPRINT FOR MURDER, A(1953); DOWN AMONG THE SHELTER-ING PALMS(1953); NIGHT HOLDS TERROR, THE(1955); SQUARE JUNGLE, THE(1955); BEHIND THE HIGH WALL(1956); JULIE(1956); DRANGO(1957); I WAS A TEENAGE WEREWOLF(1957); TRUE STORY OF JESSE JAMES, THE(1957); CRY TERROR(1958); DECKS RAN RED, THE(1958); GANG WAR(1958); KATHY O'(1958); THREAT, THE(1960); SAND PEBBLES, THE(1966); THIS IS A HIJACK(1973)
Misc. Talkies
BEYOND REASON(1977)
Bernard Phillips
RUBY GENTRY(1952)
Bertram Phillips
Silents
MAN THE ARMY MADE, A(1917, Brit.), d; IT'S HAPPINESS THAT COUNTS(1918, Brit.), p&d; ALLEY OF GOLDEN HEARTS, THE(1924, Brit.), p&d
Misc. Silents
CHANCE OF A LIFETIME, THE(1916, Brit.), d; MEG O' THE WOODS(1918, Brit.), d; ROCK OF AGES(1918, Brit.), d; LITTLE CHILD SHALL LEAD THEM, A(1919, Brit.), d; TROUSERS(1920, Brit.), d; SCHOOL FOR SCANDAL, THE(1923, Brit.), d; STRAWS IN THE WIND(1924, Brit.), d

Betty Phillips
1984
RUNAWAY(1984)
Bill Phillips
SET-UP, THE(1949), makeup; THREAT, THE(1949), makeup; BREAKING POINT, THE(1950), makeup
Bob Phillips
SHOOT IT: BLACK, SHOOT IT: BLUE(1974); MEAN JOHNNY BARROWS(1976)
Bridgette Phillips
PICNIC AT HANGING ROCK(1975, Aus.)
Bunty Phillips
PERSECUTION AND ASSASSINATION OF JEAN-PAUL MARAT AS PERFORMED BY THE INMATES OF THE ASYLUM OF CHARENTON UNDER THE DIRECTION OF THE MARQUIS DE SADE, THE(1967, Brit.), makeup; THEY CAME FROM BEYOND SPACE(1967, Brit.), makeup
Carman Phillips
EASY RIDER(1969)
Carmen Phillips
PARTY GIRL(1958); ASK ANY GIRL(1959); IT STARTED WITH A KISS(1959); SOME CAME RUNNING(1959); OCEAN'S ELEVEN(1960); PLEASE DON'T EAT THE DAISIES(1960); CONVICTS FOUR(1962); RIDE THE HIGH COUNTRY(1962); DON'T WORRY, WE'LL THINK OF A TITLE(1966); GAMES(1967)
Silents
CABARET GIRL, THE(1919); MAN WHO TURNED WHITE, THE(1919); ALWAYS AUDACIOUS(1920); ALL SOULS EVE(1921); THIRTY DAYS(1922); ASHES OF VENGEANCE(1923); FIGHTING COWARD, THE(1924)
Misc. Silents
FORBIDDEN PATHS(1917); PLANTER, THE(1917); VELVET HAND, THE(1918); HOME TOWN GIRL, THE(1919); MRS. TEMPLE'S TELEGRAM(1920); GENTLEMAN FROM AMERICA, THE(1923); FAIR WEEK(1924); SIX SHOOTIN' ROMANCE, A(1926)
Charles Phillips
ROLLIN' HOME TO TEXAS(1941); RAIDERS OF THE RANGE(1942); SEVENTH VICTIM, THE(1943); STORM WARNING(1950)
Chris Phillips
STAGECOACH(1939)
Christian Phillips
SUDDEN IMPACT(1983)
Christine Phillips
EXPRESSO BONGO(1959, Brit.)
Claire Phillips
I WAS AN AMERICAN SPY(1951), w
Conrad Phillips
SONG FOR TOMORROW, A(1948, Brit.); TEMPTRESS, THE(1949, Brit.); LILLI MARLENE(1951, Brit.); IT STARTED IN PARADISE(1952, Brit.); MAN BAIT(1952, Brit.); WOMAN IN HIDING(1953, Brit.); LAST MAN TO HANG, THE(1956, Brit.); SECRET TENT, THE(1956, Brit.); ZARAK(1956, Brit.); STRANGER'S MEETING(1957, Brit.); DESPERATE MAN, THE(1959, Brit.); QUESTION OF ADULTERY, A(1959, Brit.); WHITE TRAP, THE(1959, Brit.); WITNESS IN THE DARK(1959, Brit.); SONS AND LOVERS(1960, Brit.); FOURTH SQUARE, THE(1961, Brit.); MURDER SHE SAID(1961, Brit.); SECRET PARTNER, THE(1961, Brit.); SHADOW OF THE CAT, THE(1961, Brit.); DEAD MAN'S EVIDENCE(1962, Brit.); DON'T TALK TO STRANGE MEN(1962, Brit.); DURANT AFFAIR, THE(1962, Brit.); GUY CALLED CAESAR, A(1962, Brit.); HEAVENS ABOVE!(1963, Brit.); IMPACT(1963, Brit.), a, w; SWITCH, THE(1963, Brit.); STOPOVER FOREVER(1964, Brit.); DATELINE DIAMONDS(1966, Brit.); MURDER GAME, THE(1966, Brit.); WHO KILLED THE CAT?(1966, Brit.)
David Graham Phillips
Silents
OLD WIVES FOR NEW(1918), w; COST, THE(1920), w; GRAIN OF DUST, THE(1928), w
David Phillips
PETERSEN(1974, Aus.); ELIZA FRASER(1976, Aus.)
Demetre Phillips
ZAPPED!(1982)
Don Phillips
DESPERATE JOURNEY(1942); MALE ANIMAL, THE(1942); FIGHTER SQUADRON(1948); FRIGHTENED BRIDE, THE(1952, Brit.); MELVIN AND HOWARD(1980), p
1984
WILD LIFE, THE(1984), p
Doris Phillips
SON OF THE PLAINS(1931)
Dorothea Phillips
UNDER MILK WOOD(1973, Brit.)
Dorothy Phillips
JAZZ CINDERELLA(1930); THANK YOU, JEEVES(1936); MY FAVORITE SPY(1942); MRS. PARKINGTON(1944); POSTMAN ALWAYS RINGS TWICE, THE(1946); RECKLESS MOMENTS, THE(1949); FATHER OF THE BRIDE(1950); VIOLENT SATURDAY(1955); MAN IN THE GREY FLANNEL SUIT, THE(1956); MAN WHO SHOT LIBERTY VALANCE, THE(1962)
Silents
FLASHLIGHT, THE(1917); RESCUE, THE(1917); RISKY ROAD, THE(1918); SLANDER THE WOMAN(1923); EVERY MAN'S WIFE(1925)
Misc. Silents
IF MY COUNTRY SHOULD CALL(1916); MARK OF CAIN, THE(1916); PLACE BEYOND THE WINDS, THE(1916); PRICE OF SILENCE, THE(1916); BONDAGE(1917); DOLL'S HOUSE, A(1917); FIRES OF REBELLION(1917); GIRL IN THE CHECKERED COAT, THE(1917); HELL MORGAN'S GIRL(1917); PAY ME(1917); PIPER'S PRICE, THE(1917); TRIUMPH(1917); BROADWAY LOVE(1918); GRAND PASSION, THE(1918); MORTGAGED WIFE, THE(1918); SOUL FOR SALE, A(1918); TALK OF THE TOWN(1918); DESTINY(1919); HEART OF HUMANITY, THE(1919); PAID IN ADVANCE(1919); RIGHT TO HAPPINESS, THE(1919); ONCE TO EVERY WOMAN(1920); MAN–WOMAN–MARRIAGE(1921); WORLD'S A STAGE, THE(1922); SPORTING CHANCE, THE(1925); WITHOUT MERCY(1925); BAR-C MYSTERY, THE(1926); REMEMBER(1926); BROKEN GATE, THE(1927)
Douglas Phillips
LIEUTENANT DARING, RN(1935, Brit.); MURDER AT THE CABARET(1936, Brit.)
E. Phillips
Silents
AS IN A LOOKING GLASS(1916), w

Eddie Phillips
LONESOME(1928); COLLEGE LOVE(1929); HIS LUCKY DAY(1929); SCANDAL(1929); BIG BOY(1930); CHASING RAINBOWS(1930); DANCING SWEETIES(1930); NIGHT WORLD(1932); PHANTOM EXPRESS, THE(1932); PRIVATE SCANDAL, A(1932); PROBATION(1932); RACING YOUTH(1932); SCARLET WEEKEND, A(1932); STRANGE ADVENTURE(1932); SYMPHONY OF SIX MILLION(1932); THIRTEENTH GUEST, THE(1932); HER FORGOTTEN PAST(1933); POLICE CALL(1933); PRIVATE DETECTIVE 62(1933); RACING STRAIN, THE(1933); SATURDAY'S MILLIONS(1933); MYSTIC HOUR, THE(1934); WOMAN UNAFRAID(1934); DANGER AHEAD(1935); IVORY-HANDLED GUN(1935); LIVING ON VELVET(1935); ONE HOUR LATE(1935); PORT OF LOST DREAMS(1935); THROWBACK, THE(1935); AMBUSH VALLEY(1936); NEXT TIME WE LOVE(1936); PHANTOM PATROL(1936); RING AROUND THE MOON(1936); WEDDING PRESENT(1936); WILDCAT TROOPER(1936); FEDERAL BULLETS(1937); FIREFLY, THE(1937); SMOKE TREE RANGE(1937); BORN TO FIGHT(1938); YOU'RE NOT SO TOUGH(1938); LAW OF THE TIMBER(1941); BILLY THE KID TRAPPED(1942); TEXAS MAN HUNT(1942); DEATH VALLEY MANHUNT(1943); MY LEARNED FRIEND(1943, Brit.); CHAMPAGNE CHARLIE(1944, Brit.); CYCLONE PRAIRIE RANGERS(1944); STATE OF THE UNION(1948); WHITE HEAT(1949); BUFFALO BILL IN TOMAHAWK TERRITORY(1952)
Misc. Talkies
PASSPORT TO PARADISE(1932); FIGHTING TO LIVE(1934); VENGEANCE OF RANNAH(1936)
Silents
NTH COMMANDMENT, THE(1923); ON PROBATION(1924); KING OF THE TURF, THE(1926); HONEYMOON FLATS(1928)
Misc. Silents
BEAUTY PRIZE, THE(1924); WHIPPING BOSS, THE(1924); CAPITAL PUNISHMENT(1925); PEGGY OF THE SECRET SERVICE(1925); SHATTERED LIVES(1925); SILENT PAL(1925); UNDER THE ROUGE(1925); PHANTOM OF THE FOREST, THE(1926); LITTLE FIREBRAND, THE(1927); SAVAGE PASSIONS(1927); WE AMERICANS(1928)

Edna Phillips
Silents
NOTHING BUT THE TRUTH(1920)
Edward D. Phillips
SQUEEZE PLAY(1981)
Edward Phillips
CROSSFIRE(1933)
Silents
JUST AROUND THE CORNER(1921); LOVE LIGHT, THE(1921); SCARAB RING, THE(1921); FOG, THE(1923); ON THE STROKE OF THREE(1924); APRIL FOOL(1926)

Edwin Phillips
WILD BOYS OF THE ROAD(1933)
Eleanor Phillips
ORPHANS OF THE NORTH(1940)
Eric Phillips
ADVENTURES OF PC 49, THE(1949, Brit.); LIGHT TOUCH, THE(1955, Brit.)
Erica Phillips
1984
HADLEY'S REBELLION(1984), cos
Ethel Phillips
Silents
COMMANDING OFFICER, THE(1915)
Frank Phillips
NOTORIOUS GENTLEMAN(1945, Brit.); RUNAWAY BUS, THE(1954, Brit.); DAM BUSTERS, THE(1955, Brit.); THE CREEPING UNKNOWN(1956, Brit.); I'M ALL RIGHT, JACK(1959, Brit.); RIDER ON A DEAD HORSE(1962), ph; IT HAPPENED HERE(1966, Brit.); WILD, WILD WINTER(1966), ph; ONE AND ONLY GENUINE ORIGINAL FAMILY BAND, THE(1968), ph; COMPUTER WORE TENNIS SHOES, THE(1970), ph; DARKER THAN AMBER(1970), ph; BEDKNOBS AND BROOMSTICKS(1971), ph; SCANDALOUS JOHN(1971), ph; WILD COUNTRY, THE(1971), ph; NOW YOU SEE HIM, NOW YOU DON'T(1972), ph; SNOWBALL EXPRESS(1972), ph; WORLD'S GREATEST ATHLETE, THE(1973), ph; HERBIE RIDES AGAIN(1974), ph; ISLAND AT THE TOP OF THE WORLD, THE(1974), ph; APPLE DUMPLING GANG, THE(1975), ph; ESCAPE TO WITCH MOUNTAIN(1975), ph; GUS(1976), ph; NO DEPOSIT, NO RETURN(1976), ph; SHAGGY D.A., THE(1976), ph; TREASURE OF MATECUMBE(1976), ph; PETE'S DRAGON(1977), ph; GOIN' COCONUTS(1978), ph; HOT LEAD AND COLD FEET(1978), ph; RETURN FROM WITCH MOUNTAIN(1978), ph; APPLE DUMPLING GANG RIDES AGAIN, THE(1979), ph; BLACK HOLE, THE(1979), ph; HERBIE GOES BANANAS(1980), ph; MIDNIGHT MADNESS(1980), ph
Misc. Talkies
BATTLE OF THE EAGLES(1981)
Frank V. Phillips
GOING APE!(1981), ph
Fred B. Phillips
RIDE BEYOND VENGEANCE(1966), makeup
Fred Phillips
VELVET TOUCH, THE(1948), makeup; STAMPEDE(1949), makeup; TELL IT TO THE JUDGE(1949), makeup; HOUSE OF USHER(1960), make up; MASTER OF THE WORLD(1961), makeup; MARRIED TOO YOUNG(1962), makeup; R.P.M.(1970), makeup; ONE FLEW OVER THE CUCKOO'S NEST(1975), makeup; VIVA KNIEVEL!(1977), makeup; STAR TREK: THE MOTION PICTURE(1979), makeup
Garrison Phillips
THREE DAYS OF THE CONDOR(1975)
Genevieve Phillips
ONE HOUR LATE(1935)
Gonrad Phillips
CIRCUS OF HORRORS(1960, Brit.)
Gordon Phillips
I'M AN EXPLOSIVE(1933, Brit.), d&w; DESERT JUSTICE(1936), w; LILITH(1964); VON RICHTHOFEN AND BROWN(1970)
Gregory Phillips
I COULD GO ON SINGING(1963); PUMPKIN EATER, THE(1964, Brit.); WHO KILLED THE CAT?(1966, Brit.); I START COUNTING(1970, Brit.); VIRGIN SOLDIERS, THE(1970, Brit.)

Greigh Phillips
BRAIN EATERS, THE(1958); FORBIDDEN ISLAND(1959)

Guy Phillips
Silents
SATAN'S SISTER(1925, Brit.)

H. I. Phillips
Silents
REPORTED MISSING(1922), t

H.W. Phillips
FOLLOW ME QUIETLY(1949), makeup

Hazel Phillips
SET, THE(1970, Aus.)

Helen Phillips
TWO SECONDS(1932); LET'S MAKE MUSIC(1940), w

Helena Phillips
GREENE MURDER CASE, THE(1929); LIFE BEGINS(1932); DESIGN FOR LIVING(1933); KING'S VACATION, THE(1933); VOLTAIRE(1933); KISS AND MAKE UP(1934)

Helene Phillips
REMARKABLE ANDREW, THE(1942); GOING BERSERK(1983)

Henry Albert Phillips
Silents
JUST A SONG AT TWILIGHT(1922), w

Henry Wallace Phillips
Silents
BY PROXY(1918), w

Herbert O. Phillips
ENEMY OF WOMEN(1944), w

Herbert Q. Phillips
HIT AND RUN(1957), w

Howard Phillips
SOB SISTER(1931); SPIDER, THE(1931); SURRENDER(1931); CARELESS LADY(1932); LAST MILE, THE(1932); STEPPING SISTERS(1932); TRIAL OF VIVIENNE WARE, THE(1932); FUGITIVE IN THE SKY(1937); WHITE BONDAGE(1937); GANGS OF NEW YORK(1938)

Irving Phillips
SEVEN DAYS ASHORE(1944), w; SONG OF THE OPEN ROAD(1944), w; DELIGHTFULLY DANGEROUS(1945), w; CREEPING TERROR, THE(1964), ph

Ivor Phillips
SKIN GAME, THE(1965, Brit.)

Jack Phillips
UP THE JUNCTION(1968, Brit.)
Silents
GOLD RUSH, THE(1925)

James Atlee Phillips
THUNDER ROAD(1958), w

James Phillips
STORMY(1935)

Jean Phillips
THOSE WERE THE DAYS(1940); AMONG THE LIVING(1941); LAS VEGAS NIGHTS(1941); OUTLAWS OF THE DESERT(1941); WEST POINT WIDOW(1941); DR. BROADWAY(1942); NIGHT IN NEW ORLEANS, A(1942); STAR SPANGLED RHYTHM(1942); TIMBER(1942)

Jeremy Phillips
THESE ARE THE DAMNED(1965, Brit.)

Jerry Phillips
THIS IS ELVIS(1982)

Jim Phillips
EQUINOX(1970)

Jimmie Phillips
QUEEN OF THE NIGHTCLUBS(1929)
Silents
ATTA BOY!(1926)

Jimmy Phillips
LAST STAND, THE(1938); PRAIRIE JUSTICE(1938)
Silents
SALLY OF THE SCANDALS(1928)
Misc. Silents
DESERT DUST(1927)

Joan Phillips
ROONEY(1958, Brit.)

Joanna Phillips
CHRISTIAN LICORICE STORE, THE(1971); SNOWBALL EXPRESS(1972)

Joe Phillips
AFTER THE THIN MAN(1936); RIFF-RAFF(1936); CHATTERBOX(1943); CROOKED RIVER(1950)
Silents
AUCTION BLOCK, THE(1917)

John I. Phillips
DANGER BY MY SIDE(1962, Brit.), p; NIGHT OF THE PROWLER(1962, Brit.), p; SERENA(1962, Brit.), p; ECHO OF DIANA(1963, Brit.), p; HI-JACKERS, THE(1963, Brit.), p; IMPACT(1963, Brit.), p; SHADOW OF FEAR(1963, Brit.), p; SICILIANS, THE(1964, Brit.), p; SMOKESCREEN(1964, Brit.), p

John Phillips
BLACK ANGEL(1946); HELLDORADO(1946); SO GOES MY LOVE(1946); KEY LARGO(1948); SMART WOMAN(1948); SCENE OF THE CRIME(1949); KID FROM TEXAS, THE(1950); SIDE STREET(1950); SUPERMAN AND THE MOLE MEN(1951); CONFIDENCE GIRL(1952); HOODLUM EMPIRE(1952); SKY HIGH(1952); SEMINOLE(1953); DIAL RED O(1955); WARRIORS, THE(1955); RICHARD III(1956, Brit.); SEVEN MEN FROM NOW(1956); SHE PLAYED WITH FIRE(1957, Brit.); SHIRALEE, THE(1957, Brit.); TATTERED DRESS, THE(1957); FLOODS OF FEAR(1958, Brit.); HOW TO MAKE A MONSTER(1958); I ACCUSE(1958, Brit.); JOHN PAUL JONES(1959); FOLLOW THAT HORSE!(1960, Brit.); VILLAGE OF THE DAMNED(1960, Brit.); MAN IN THE MOON(1961, Brit.); OFFBEAT(1961, Brit.); ROMAN SPRING OF MRS. STONE, THE(1961, U.S./Brit.); ROMANOFF AND JULIET(1961); PRIZE OF ARMS, A(1962, Brit.); WE JOINED THE NAVY(1962, Brit.); MOUSE ON THE MOON, THE(1963, Brit.); BECKET(1964, Brit.); BLOOD BEAST FROM OUTER SPACE(1965, Brit.), p; JOEY BOY(1965, Brit.); MUMMY'S SHROUD, THE(1967, Brit.); TORTURE GARDEN(1968, Brit.); CIAO MANHATTAN(1973), m; MAN WHO FELL TO EARTH, THE(1976, Brit.), md; ASCENDANCY(1983, Brit.)

Johnnie Phillips
JERUSALEM FILE, THE(1972, U.S./Israel)

Johnny Phillips
BASKETBALL FIX, THE(1951)

Julia Phillips
STEELYARD BLUES(1973), p; STING, THE(1973), p; TAXI DRIVER(1976), p; CLOSE ENCOUNTERS OF THE THIRD KIND(1977), p

Knox Phillips
THIS IS ELVIS(1982)

LaRae Phillips
CAPTURE THAT CAPSULE(1961)

Lawrence Phillips
1984
CITY GIRL, THE(1984)

Lee Phillips
HUNTERS, THE(1958)

Leo Phillips
TREASURE ISLAND(1950, Brit.); CRUEL SEA, THE(1953); SPACEWAYS(1953, Brit.); WEDDING IN WHITE(1972, Can.)

Leon Phillips
LUNCH WAGON(1981), w

Leslie Phillips
COMING-OUT PARTY, A(; HELL, HEAVEN OR HOBOKEN(1958, Brit.); LASSIE FROM LANCASHIRE(1938, Brit.); GALLOPING MAJOR, THE(1951, Brit.); HER PANELLED DOOR(1951, Brit.); POOL OF LONDON(1951, Brit.); BREAKING THE SOUND BARRIER(1952); TRAIN OF EVENTS(1952, Brit.); FAKE, THE(1953, Brit.); LIMPING MAN, THE(1953, Brit.); GAMMA PEOPLE, THE(1956); BARRETTS OF WIMPOLE STREET, THE(1957); BROTHERS IN LAW(1957, Brit.); HIGH FLIGHT(1957, Brit.); JUST MY LUCK(1957, Brit.); LES GIRLS(1957); SMALLEST SHOW ON EARTH, THE(1957, Brit.); VALUE FOR MONEY(1957, Brit.); ANGRY HILLS, THE(1959, Brit.); CARRY ON NURSE(1959, Brit.); MAN WHO LIKED FUNERALS, THE(1959, Brit.); NAVY LARK, THE(1959, Brit.); THIS OTHER EDEN(1959, Brit.); CARRY ON CONSTABLE(1960, Brit.); DOCTOR IN LOVE(1960, Brit.); INN FOR TROUBLE(1960, Brit.); PLEASE TURN OVER(1960, Brit.); BEWARE OF CHILDREN(1961, Brit.); WATCH YOUR STERN(1961, Brit.); WEEKEND WITH LULU, A(1961, Brit.); BIG MONEY, THE(1962, Brit.); CARRY ON TEACHER(1962, Brit.); LONGEST DAY, THE(1962); MAKE MINE A DOUBLE(1962, Brit.); ROOMMATES(1962, Brit.); CROOKS ANONYMOUS(1963, Brit.); FAST LADY, THE(1963, Brit.); FATHER CAME TOO(1964, Brit.); IN THE DOGHOUSE(1964, Brit.); YOU MUST BE JOKING!(1965, Brit.); CARNABY, M.D.(1967, Brit.); MAROC 7(1967, Brit.), a, p; DOCTOR IN TROUBLE(1970, Brit.); SOME WILL, SOME WON'T(1970, Brit.); MAGNIFICENT SEVEN DEADLY SINS, THE(1971, Brit.); DON'T JUST LIE THERE, SAY SOMETHING!(1973, Brit.); NOT NOW DARLING(1975, Brit.); SPANISH FLY(1975, Brit.)

Little Esther Phillips
1984
BLESS THEIR LITTLE HEARTS(1984), m

Lloyd Phillips
BATTLETRUCK(1982), p; NATE AND HAYES(1983, U.S./New Zealand), p, w

Mackenzie Phillips
AMERICAN GRAFFITI(1973); RAFFERTY AND THE GOLD DUST TWINS(1975); MORE AMERICAN GRAFFITI(1979); LOVE CHILD(1982)

Malcolm Phillips
BREAK OF DAY(1977, Aus.)

Marcella Phillips
TRUE TO LIFE(1943); LUCKY JORDAN(1942); STAR SPANGLED RHYTHM(1942); CRYSTAL BALL, THE(1943); FOR WHOM THE BELL TOLLS(1943); SALUTE FOR THREE(1943); STANDING ROOM ONLY(1944)

Margaret Phillips
LIFE OF HER OWN, A(1950); NUN'S STORY, THE(1959)

Marilyn Phillips
GENTLEMAN JIM(1942)

Marla Phillips
1984
BLAME IT ON THE NIGHT(1984)

Martin Phillips
LORDS OF DISCIPLINE, THE(1983)

Mary Phillips
LIFE BEGINS(1932); AS GOOD AS MARRIED(1937); BRIDE WORE RED, THE(1937); MANNEQUIN(1937); THAT CERTAIN WOMAN(1937); INCENDIARY BLONDE(1945); LEAVE HER TO HEAVEN(1946); WOMAN'S SECRET, A(1949)

Michael J. Phillips
SALOME, WHERE SHE DANCED(1945), w

Michael Phillips
ELECTRA GLIDE IN BLUE(1973); STEELYARD BLUES(1973), p; STING, THE(1973), p; TAXI DRIVER(1976), p; CLOSE ENCOUNTERS OF THE THIRD KIND(1977), p; HEARTBEEPS(1981), p; CANNERY ROW(1982), p
1984
FLAMINGO KID, THE(1984), p

Michele Phillips
SHAMPOO(1975)

Michelle Phillips
LAST MOVIE, THE(1971); DILLINGER(1973); VALENTINO(1977, Brit.); BLOODLINE(1979); MAN WITH BOGART'S FACE, THE(1980); SAVAGE HARVEST(1981)

Mickey Phillips
JUNGLE PRINCESS, THE(1936); GAY FALCON, THE(1941)

Mike Phillips
LIMBO(1972)

Minna Phillips
THREE GIRLS ABOUT TOWN(1941); MALE ANIMAL, THE(1942); MY SISTER EILEEN(1942); YANK AT ETON, A(1942); GALS, INCORPORATED(1943); HERS TO HOLD(1943); NORTH STAR, THE(1943); SHERLOCK HOLMES FACES DEATH(1943); HAT CHECK HONEY(1944); BANDIT QUEEN(1950); TRAIN TO TOMBSTONE(1950); QUEEN FOR A DAY(1951); STRANGERS ON A TRAIN(1951)

Miriam Phillips
WAY WE LIVE NOW, THE(1970); FAN, THE(1981); STREET MUSIC(1982)

Monica Phillips
LOSERS, THE(1970)

N. Watts Phillips
Silents
LIEUTENANT DARING RN AND THE WATER RATS(1924, Brit.)
Nadia Phillips
Misc. Talkies
BIBI(1977)
Nancie Phillips
LOVING(1970); ALL-AMERICAN BOY, THE(1973)
Nancy Phillips
Silents
CITY GONE WILD, THE(1927); ROLLED STOCKINGS(1927)
Neil Phillips
PRIVATES ON PARADE(1982)
Nelson Phillips
INQUEST(1931, Brit.)
Silents
KENT, THE FIGHTING MAN(1916, Brit.)
Neville Phillips
SVENGALI(1955, Brit.)
Noreen Phillips
Misc. Silents
SECRET STUDIO, THE(1927)
Norman Phillips
HOTEL IMPERIAL(1939); OUR NEIGHBORS–THE CARTERS(1939); BLONDIE IN THE DOUGH(1947); KILROY WAS HERE(1947); THAT WONDERFUL URGE(1948)
Paul Phillips
ROARING TWENTIES, THE(1939); BROTHER ORCHID(1940); DANCE, GIRL, DANCE(1940); HOUSE ACROSS THE BAY, THE(1940); MAN WHO TALKED TOO MUCH, THE(1940); MURDER IN THE AIR(1940); KNOCKOUT(1941); NINE LIVES ARE NOT ENOUGH(1941); NO GREATER SIN(1941); STRANGE ALIBI(1941); STRAWBERRY BLONDE, THE(1941); LADY HAS PLANS, THE(1942); LUCKY JORDAN(1942); SABOTEUR(1942); STREET OF CHANCE(1942); HENRY ALDRICH HAUNTS A HOUSE(1943); NO TIME FOR LOVE(1943); MURDER, MY SWEET(1945); LAST HOUSE ON DEAD END STREET(1977)
Misc. Talkies
FUN HOUSE, THE(1977)
Peggy Phillips
CRIMSON CANARY(1945), w
Penny Ann Phillips
DARK, THE(1979)
Phil Phillips
TALL STORY(1960)
Philip Phillips
HOT SHOTS(1956); TALL STRANGER, THE(1957)
R. Phillips
Silents
OLD CURIOSITY SHOP, THE(1913, Brit.)
Randy Phillips
WEREWOLF OF WASHINGTON(1973)
Redmond Phillips
NIGHT TO REMEMBER, A(1958, Brit.); LEFT, RIGHT AND CENTRE(1959); NAKED FURY(1959, Brit.); CHANCE MEETING(1960, Brit.); CONCRETE JUNGLE, THE(1962, Brit.); THERE WAS A CROOKED MAN(1962, Brit.); LOVE IS A BALL(1963); TOM JONES(1963, Brit.); GORGON, THE(1964, Brit.); PLEASURE LOVERS, THE(1964, Brit.); DEMONSTRATOR(1971, Aus.); EARTHLING, THE(1980)
1984
PHAR LAP(1984, Aus.); RAZORBACK(1984, Aus.)
Rev. Thomas N. Phillips
SOUNDER(1972)
Robert Phillips
KILLERS, THE(1964); CAT BALLOU(1965); DIMENSION 5(1966); SILENCERS, THE(1966); DIRTY DOZEN, THE(1967, Brit.); HOUR OF THE GUN(1967); MACKENNA'S GOLD(1969); DARKER THAN AMBER(1970); SLAUGHTER(1972); DETROIT 9000(1973); SLAMS, THE(1973); GRAVY TRAIN, THE(1974); ADIOS AMIGO(1975); MITCHELL(1975); KILLING OF A CHINESE BOOKIE, THE(1976); CAR, THE(1977); FINAL CHAPTER–WALKING TALL zero(1977); TELEFON(1977)
Robin Phillips
DECLINE AND FALL... OF A BIRD WATCHER(1969, Brit.); TWO GENTLEMEN SHARING(1969, Brit.); DAVID COPPERFIELD(1970, Brit.); TALES FROM THE CRYPT(1972, Brit.)
Roger Phillips
MEDIUM COOL(1969)
Ronald Phillips
IT HAPPENED HERE(1966, Brit.)
Ronnie Phillips
RETURN OF THE JEDI(1983)
Ruth Phillips
BLOB, THE(1958), w
Sarah Phillips
LOOKING UP(1977)
Shawn Phillips
RUN WITH THE WIND(1966, Brit.)
Sian Phillips
LONGEST DAY, THE(1962); BECKET(1964, Brit.); YOUNG CASSIDY(1965, U.S./Brit.); GOODBYE MR. CHIPS(1969, U.S./Brit.); MURPHY'S WAR(1971, Brit.); UNDER MILK WOOD(1973, Brit.); CLASH OF THE TITANS(1981)
1984
DUNE(1984)
Simon Phillips
SCARECROW, THE(1982, New Zealand)
Stanley Phillips
SEEDS OF FREEDOM(1943, USSR)
Stephen Phillips
PROJECTIONIST, THE(1970); EYE OF THE NEEDLE(1981)
1984
LAUGHTER HOUSE(1984, Brit.)
Stu Phillips
MAD DOG COLL(1961), m; MAN FROM THE DINERS' CLUB, THE(1963), m; RIDE THE WILD SURF(1964), m; DEAD HEAT ON A MERRY-GO-ROUND(1966), m; HELL'S ANGELS ON WHEELS(1967), m; ANGELS FROM HELL(1968), m; NAME OF

THE GAME IS KILL, THE(1968), m, md; CURIOUS FEMALE, THE(1969), m; GAY DECEIVERS, THE(1969), m; RUN, ANGEL, RUN(1969), m; 2000 YEARS LATER(1969), m, md; LOSERS, THE(1970), m; RED, WHITE AND BLACK, THE(1970), m; JUD(1971), m; SEVEN MINUTES, THE(1971), m, md; SIMON, KING OF THE WITCHES(1971), m, md; PICKUP ON 101(1972), m; HOW TO SEDUCE A WOMAN(1974), m; MACON COUNTY LINE(1974), m; MEAL, THE(1975), m; BATTLESTAR GALACTICA(1979), m; BUCK ROGERS IN THE 25TH CENTURY(1979), m; FAST CHARLIE... THE MOONBEAM RIDER(1979), m
Thalia Phillips
JOHNNY RENO(1966), cos; F.I.S.T.(1978), cos
Thom Phillips
SEMI-TOUGH(1977)
Thomas Hal Phillips
TARZAN'S FIGHT FOR LIFE(1958), w; CALIFORNIA SPLIT(1974)
Timothy Phillips
NATIONAL LAMPOON'S CLASS REUNION(1982); ANGELO MY LOVE(1983)
1984
STONE BOY, THE(1984)
Tita Phillips
MAN IN THE ATTIC(1953)
Tubby Phillips
UNDER THE GREENWOOD TREE(1930, Brit.)
Silents
POPPIES OF FLANDERS(1927, Brit.)
Misc. Silents
BELLS OF ST. MARY'S, THE(1928, Brit.)
Val Phillips
WILD WOMEN OF WONGO, THE(1959)
Van Phillips
BREAK THE NEWS(1938, Brit.), m; BIG MONEY, THE(1962, Brit.), m
W. H. Phillips
WOMAN ON PIER 13, THE(1950), makeup
Wally Phillips
TOMBOY AND THE CHAMP(1961)
Walt Phillips
KILL, THE(1968)
Wendell Phillips
KISS OF DEATH(1947); CLOSE-UP(1948); BURGLAR, THE(1956); FOOL KILLER, THE(1965)
Wendy Phillips
FRATERNITY ROW(1977); AIRPLANE II: THE SEQUEL(1982)
William [Bill] Phillips
KNOCKOUT(1941); JUKE GIRL(1942); LADY GANGSTER(1942); LARCENY, INC.(1942); MURDER IN THE BIG HOUSE(1942); FIRST COMES COURAGE(1943); SEE HERE, PRIVATE HARGROVE(1944); SWINGTIME JOHNNY(1944); THIRTY SECONDS OVER TOKYO(1944); ABBOTT AND COSTELLO IN HOLLYWOOD(1945); ANCHORS AWEIGH(1945); HIDDEN EYE, THE(1945); WHAT NEXT, CORPORAL HARGROVE?(1945); COURAGE OF LASSIE(1946); FAITHFUL IN MY FASHION(1946); HARVEY GIRLS, THE(1946); TILL THE CLOUDS ROLL BY(1946); LIVING IN A BIG WAY(1947); SEA OF GRASS, THE(1947); BLONDIE'S SECRET(1948); MAN FROM COLORADO, THE(1948); SOUTHERN YANKEE, A(1948); THREE MUSKETEERS, THE(1948); BIG JACK(1949); EASY LIVING(1949); JOHNNY ALLEGRO(1949); MARY RYAN, DETECTIVE(1949); ON THE TOWN(1949); PRISON WARDEN(1949); RED LIGHT(1949); SET-UP, THE(1949); BREAKING POINT, THE(1950), makeup; CHAIN GANG(1950); CUSTOMS AGENT(1950); FATHER OF THE BRIDE(1950); HE'S A COCKEYED WONDER(1950); REVENUE AGENT(1950); WABASH AVENUE(1950); AL JENNINGS OF OKLAHOMA(1951); CAVALRY SCOUT(1951); DETECTIVE STORY(1951); RED BADGE OF COURAGE, THE(1951); SMUGGLER'S GOLD(1951); YANK IN KOREA, A(1951); BAD AND THE BEAUTIFUL, THE(1952); BUGLES IN THE AFTERNOON(1952); HIGH NOON(1952); LOAN SHARK(1952); LOVE IS BETTER THAN EVER(1952); DEVIL'S CANYON(1953); GUN BELT(1953); LION IS IN THE STREETS, A(1953); PRIVATE EYES(1953); WICKED WOMAN(1953); LAW VS. BILLY THE KID(1954); FORT YUMA(1955); NEW YORK CONFIDENTIAL(1955); TOP GUN(1955); BROKEN STAR, THE(1956); FASTEST GUN ALIVE(1956); GHOST TOWN(1956); LAST HUNT, THE(1956); MAN IN THE GREY FLANNEL SUIT, THE(1956); NAKED GUN, THE(1956); STAGECOACH TO FURY(1956); HELLCATS OF THE NAVY(1957); REVOLT AT FORT LARAMIE(1957); SECOND FIDDLE TO A STEEL GUITAR(1965); YOURS, MINE AND OURS(1968), makeup; NIGHT THE LIGHTS WENT OUT IN GEORGIA, THE(1981); CHRISTINE(1983), w
Woolf Phillips
DIAMOND SAFARI(1958), m
Alex Phillips, Jr.
YANCO(1964, Mex.), ph; FOOL KILLER, THE(1965), ph; MONDAY'S CHILD(1967, U.S., Arg.), ph; SAM'S SONG(1971), ph; BUCK AND THE PREACHER(1972), ph; WRATH OF GOD, THE(1972), ph; SAVAGE IS LOOSE, THE(1974), ph; DEVIL'S RAIN, THE(1975, U.S./Mex.), ph; GREAT SCOUT AND CATHOUSE THURSDAY, THE(1976), ph; FOXTROT(1977, Mex./Swiss), ph; GOOD LUCK, MISS WYCKOFF(1979), ph; SUNBURN(1979), ph; FADE TO BLACK(1980), ph; SURVIVAL RUN(1980), ph; CABOBLANCO(1981), ph; DEMONOID(1981), ph; HIGH RISK(1981), ph; SORCERESS(1983), ph
Norman Phillips, Jr.
FIFTY MILLION FRENCHMEN(1931); MIDNIGHT SPECIAL(1931); SIDEWALKS OF NEW YORK(1931); LOVERS COURAGEOUS(1932); TOM BROWN OF CULVER(1932); BAND PLAYS ON, THE(1934); OFF THE RECORD(1939)
Wendell Phillips, Jr.
LILITH(1964)
Preben Phillipsen
FLAMING FRONTIER(1968, Ger./Yugo.), p
Gordon Phillott
FOOL AND THE PRINCESS, THE(1948, Brit.); BATTLE OF THE SEXES, THE(1960, Brit.); FIVE GOLDEN HOURS(1961, Brit.); MOUSE ON THE MOON, THE(1963, Brit.)
Adelaide Philpotts
YELLOW SAND(1938, Brit.), w
Ambrosine Philpotts
HAPPY GO LOVELY(1951, Brit.); FATHER'S DOING FINE(1952, Brit.); FRANCHISE AFFAIR, THE(1952, Brit.); MR. DENNING DRIVES NORTH(1953, Brit.); UP IN THE WORLD(1957, Brit.); DUKE WORE JEANS, THE(1958, Brit.); RELUCTANT DEBUTANTE, THE(1958); CARRY ON REGARDLESS(1961, Brit.); ROOMMATES(1962, Brit.); TWO AND TWO MAKE SIX(1962, Brit.); CARRY ON CABBIE(1963, Brit.);

OPERATION BULLSHINE(1963, Brit.); LIFE AT THE TOP(1965, Brit.); GET CHARLIE TULLY(1976, Brit.)

Eden Phillpotts
AMERICAN PRISONER, THE(1929 Brit.), w

Tim Philo
EVIL DEAD, THE(1983), ph

Maxime Philoe
TARZAN, THE APE MAN(1981)

Dick Philpott
BRONCO BULLFROG(1972, Brit.)

Gordon Philpott
MAKE MINE MINK(1960, Brit.)

Toby Philpott
DARK CRYSTAL, THE(1982, Brit.); RETURN OF THE JEDI(1983)

Ambrosine Philpotts
THIS MAN IS MINE(1946 Brit.); STOLEN FACE(1952, Brit.); CAPTAIN'S PARADISE, THE(1953, Brit.); TRUTH ABOUT WOMEN, THE(1958, Brit.); EXPRESSO BONGO(1959, Brit.); ROOM AT THE TOP(1959, Brit.); DOCTOR IN LOVE(1960, Brit.); BERSERK(1967); WILDCATS OF ST. TRINIAN'S, THE(1980, Brit.)

Eden Philpotts
YELLOW SANDS(1938, Brit.), w; FARMER'S WIFE, THE(1941, Brit.), w
Silents
FARMER'S WIFE, THE(1928, Brit.), w

Betty Philson
WISE GIRL(1937)

Morgan Philthorpe
Misc. Silents
WAIF, THE(1915)

Robert Phippeny
NIGHT OF THE FOLLOWING DAY, THE(1969, Brit.), w; SIMON, KING OF THE WITCHES(1971), w

Bill Phipps
FLAT TOP(1952); CAT WOMEN OF THE MOON(1953); FORT ALGIERS(1953); INVADERS FROM MARS(1953); JULIUS CAESAR(1953); NORTHERN PATROL(1953); RED RIVER SHORE(1953); SAVAGE FRONTIER(1953); JESSE JAMES VERSUS THE DALTONS(1954); SNOW CREATURE, THE,(1954); FAR HORIZONS, THE(1955); SMOKE SIGNAL(1955); VIOLENT MEN, THE(1955); BOSS, THE(1956)

Catherine Phipps
JAZZ BABIES(1932)

Charles Phipps
SECRET EVIDENCE(1941); THUNDERING HOOFS(1941); MAGNIFICENT AMBERSONS, THE(1942); RIDING THE WIND(1942)

Elissa Phipps
1984
DARK ENEMY(1984, Brit.)

John Phipps
MEET ME IN ST. LOUIS(1944); MRS. PARKINGTON(1944)

Kevin Phipps
1984
CONAN THE DESTROYER(1984), art d

Max Phipps
CARS THAT ATE PARIS, THE(1974, Aus,); THIRST(1979, Aus.); STIR(1980, Aus.); ROAD WARRIOR, THE(1982, Aus.); NATE AND HAYES(1983, U.S./New Zealand); RETURN OF CAPTAIN INVINCIBLE, THE(1983, Aus./U.S.)

Nicholas Phipps
OLD BILL AND SON(1940, Brit.); YOU WILL REMEMBER(1941, Brit.); THIS MAN IS MINE(1946 Brit.), w; YANK IN LONDON, A(1946, Brit.), w; COURTNEY AFFAIR, THE(1947, Brit.), w; PICCADILLY INCIDENT(1948, Brit.), w; AFFAIRS OF A ROGUE, THE(1949, Brit.), w; ELIZABETH OF LADYMEAD(1949, Brit.), a, w; SPRING IN PARK LANE(1949, Brit.), a, w; WOMAN HATER(1949, Brit.), w; MADELEINE(1950, Brit.), w; MAN IN THE DINGHY, THE(1951, Brit.), w; ISLAND RESCUE(1952, Brit.), w; MAYTIME IN MAYFAIR(1952, Brit.), a, w; CAPTAIN'S PARADISE, THE(1953, Brit.), a, w; I BELIEVE IN YOU(1953, Brit.), w; I'LL GET YOU(1953, Brit.), w; DOCTOR IN THE HOUSE(1954, Brit.), a, w; MAD ABOUT MEN(1954, Brit.); DOCTOR AT SEA(1955, Brit.), w; INTRUDER, THE(1955, Brit.), w; ALL FOR MARY(1956, Brit.); IRON PETTICOAT, THE(1956, Brit.); WHO DONE IT?(1956, Brit.); DOCTOR AT LARGE(1957, Brit.), a, w; OUT OF THE CLOUDS(1957, Brit.); TRUE AS A TURTLE(1957, Brit.), w; MAD LITTLE ISLAND(1958, Brit.); ORDERS TO KILL(1958, Brit.); DON'T PANIC CHAPS!(1959, Brit.); LADY IS A SQUARE, THE(1959, Brit.), w; NAVY LARK, THE(1959, Brit.); CAPTAIN'S TABLE, THE(1960, Brit.), a, w; DOCTOR IN LOVE(1960, Brit.), a, w; TOMMY THE TOREADOR(1960, Brit.), w; NO LOVE FOR JOHNNIE(1961, Brit.), w; PURE HELL OF ST. TRINIAN'S, THE(1961, Brit.); UPSTAIRS AND DOWNSTAIRS(1961, Brit.); DOCTOR IN DISTRESS(1963, Brit.), w; HEAVENS ABOVE!(1963, Brit.); PAIR OF BRIEFS, A(1963, Brit.), a, w; SUMMER HOLIDAY(1963, Brit.); YOUNG AND WILLING(1964, Brit.), w; AMOROUS MR. PRAWN, THE(1965, Brit.), w; CHARLIE BUBBLES(1968, Brit.); SOME GIRLS DO(1969, Brit.); THOSE DARING YOUNG MEN IN THEIR JAUNTY JALOPIES(1969, Fr./Brit./ Ital.); RISE AND RISE OF MICHAEL RIMMER, THE(1970, Brit.)

Sally Phipps
Silents
BERTHA, THE SEWING MACHINE GIRL(1927); LOVE MAKES 'EM WILD(1927); NEWS PARADE, THE(1928); NONE BUT THE BRAVE(1928); JOY STREET(1929)
Misc. Silents
HIGH SCHOOL HERO(1927); WHY SAILORS GO WRONG(1928)

Thomas Phipps
YANK AT ETON, A(1942), w

Tom Phipps
YOU LIVE AND LEARN(1937, Brit.), w; GLAMOUR GIRL(1938, Brit.), w; RETURN OF CAROL DEANE, THE(1938, Brit.), w; SINGING COP, THE(1938, Brit.), w; SO THIS IS LONDON(1940, Brit.), w

William Phipps
BELLE STARR'S DAUGHTER(1947); CROSSFIRE(1947); ARIZONA RANGER, THE(1948); DESPERADOES OF DODGE CITY(1948); STATION WEST(1948); TRAIN TO ALCATRAZ(1948); MAN ON THE EIFFEL TOWER, THE(1949); SCENE OF THE CRIME(1949); THEY LIVE BY NIGHT(1949); CINDERELLA(1950); RIDER FROM TUCSON(1950); VANISHING WESTERNER, THE(1950); FIVE(1951); NO QUESTIONS ASKED(1951); RED BADGE OF COURAGE, THE(1951); FORT OSAGE(1952); LOAN SHARK(1952); ROSE OF CIMARRON(1952); TWONKY, THE(1953); WAR OF THE WORLDS, THE(1953); EXECUTIVE SUITE(1954); RIOT IN CELL BLOCK 11(1954); TWO GUNS AND A BADGE(1954); INDIAN FIGHTER, THE(1955); LORD OF THE JUNGLE(1955); MAN WITHOUT A STAR(1955); FIRST TEXAN, THE(1956); LUST FOR LIFE(1956); MAN IN THE GREY FLANNEL SUIT, THE(1956); WILD PARTY, THE(1956); BADLANDS OF MONTANA(1957); BROTHERS RICO, THE(1957); KISS THEM FOR ME(1957); ESCAPE FROM RED ROCK(1958); FBI STORY, THE(1959); BLACK GOLD(1963); CAVALRY COMMAND(1963, U.S./Phil.); EVIL OF FRANKENSTEIN, THE(1964, Brit.); KIDNAPPERS, THE(1964, U.S./Phil.); INCIDENT AT PHANTOM HILL(1966); GUNFIGHT IN ABILENE(1967); VALLEY OF MYSTERY(1967)

V. Phipps-Wilson
ERASERHEAD(1978)

Nigel Phoenix
NINE HOURS TO RAMA(1963, U.S./Brit.)

Patricia Phoenix
L-SHAPED ROOM, THE(1962, Brit.)

The Phoenix Suns
MIXED COMPANY(1974)

Janos Phohaska
ADVANCE TO THE REAR(1964)

Anne Marie Photamo
WOLFEN(1981)

Clown Photographer
PREMONITION, THE(1976)

Phra Visuals
CAPTAIN MILKSHAKE(1970), spec eff

Lan Phuong
HOA-BINH(1971, Fr.)

H. Lewis Physioc
Silents
KNIFE, THE(1918), ph

Lewis Physioc
Silents
BAB'S DIARY(1917), ph

Lou Physioc
MIDNIGHT PATROL, THE(1932), ph; WESTERN LIMITED(1932), ph

Louis Physioc
CALL OF THE CIRCUS(1930), ph
Silents
PECK'S BAD GIRL(1918), ph

Louis W. Physioc
Silents
NO-GUN MAN, THE(1924), ph

Ray Physioc
Misc. Silents
SHADOW OF DOUBT, THE(1916), d; GULF BETWEEN, THE(1918), d

Wray Physioc
Misc. Silents
BLONDE VAMPIRE, THE(1922), d; LOVE NEST, THE(1922), d; MADNESS OF LOVE, THE(1922), d

Steve Phytas
ON HER MAJESTY'S SECRET SERVICE(1969, Brit.)

Al Pia
1984
FIRST TURN-ON!, THE(1984)

Albert Pia
STUCK ON YOU(1983)
1984
STUCK ON YOU(1984)

Betty Pia
1984
FIRST TURN-ON!, THE(1984)

Isabelle Pia
LOVE AT NIGHT(1961, Fr.)

Maria Pia
Misc. Talkies
LAST TANGO IN ACAPULCO, THE(1975)

Valentina Piacente
LUCIANO(1963, Ital.)

Maurizio Piacenti
LA TRAVIATA(1968, Ital.)

Donata Piacentini
NIGHT OF THE SHOOTING STARS, THE(1982, Ital.)

Franco Piacentini
NIGHT OF THE SHOOTING STARS, THE(1982, Ital.)

Giancarlo Piacentini
CHE?(1973, Ital./Fr./Ger.)

Edith Piaf
FRENCH CANCAN(1956, Fr.); ROYAL AFFAIRS IN VERSAILLES(1957, Fr.)

Maria Teresa Piaggio
SEED OF MAN, THE(1970, Ital.)

C. Piakowski
LAST STOP, THE(1949, Pol.), set d

Aldo Pial
BEN HUR(1959)

Maurice Pialat
ME(1970, Fr.), d; THIS MAN MUST DIE(1970, Fr./Ital.); LOULOU(1980, Fr.), d, w
1984
A NOS AMOURS(1984, Fr.), a, p&d, w

Carlo Della Piane
RING AROUND THE CLOCK(1953, Ital.)

Carlo Delle Piane
HEART AND SOUL(1950, Ital.); CHE?(1973, Ital./Fr./Ger.)

Emilio Delle Piane
TRINITY IS STILL MY NAME(1971, Ital.)

Lorenzo Piani
FELLINI SATYRICON(1969, Fr./Ital.); MAN CALLED SLEDGE, A(1971, Ital.)

Melanie Pianka
SOPHIE'S CHOICE(1982)

Joseph Piantadosi
SCHLOCK(1973)

Francesco Piastra
PASSION OF LOVE(1982, Ital./Fr.)
Jean Piat
WOULD-BE GENTLEMAN, THE(1960, Fr.); MARRIAGE OF FIGARO, THE(1963, Fr.); MILKY WAY, THE(1969, Fr./Ital.); RIDER ON THE RAIN(1970, Fr./Ital.)
Gregor Piatigorsky
CARNEGIE HALL(1947)
Francesco Maria Piave
LA TRAVIATA(1982), w
Francisco Maria Piave
LA TRAVIATA(1968, Ital.), w
Alice Piavetti
GIRL IN ROOM 13(1961, U.S./Braz.), cos
Astor Piazolla
BELLA DONNA(1983, Ger.), m
Antonio Piazza
DIARY OF AN ITALIAN(1972, Ital.), ph
Ben Piazza
HANGING TREE, THE(1959); DANGEROUS AGE, A(1960, Can.); NO EXIT(1962, U.S./Arg.); TELL ME THAT YOU LOVE ME, JUNIE MOON(1970); OUTSIDE MAN, THE(1973, U.S./FR.); BAD NEWS BEARS, THE(1976); I NEVER PROMISED YOU A ROSE GARDEN(1977); NIGHTWING(1979); WALTZ ACROSS TEXAS(1982)
Misc. Talkies
CANDY SNATCHERS, THE(1974)
Dario Piazza
WHERE THERE'S LIFE(1947); MY FAVORITE SPY(1951)
Fernando Piazza
BOOM!(1968); JESSE AND LESTER, TWO BROTHERS IN A PLACE CALLED TRINITY(1972, Ital.), p; SUPERFLY T.N.T.(1973)
Lida Piazza
WILL SUCCESS SPOIL ROCK HUNTER?(1957)
Zora Piazza
MONTE CASSINO(1948, Ital.); PEDDLIN' IN SOCIETY(1949, Ital.)
Achille Piazzi
HERCULES AND THE CAPTIVE WOMEN(1963, Fr./Ital.), p; HERCULES IN THE HAUNTED WORLD(1964, Ital.), p; OF WAYWARD LOVE(1964, Ital./Ger.), p
Archille Piazzi
GOLIATH AND THE DRAGON(1961, Ital./Fr.), p
Astor Piazzola
LUMIERE(1976, Fr.), m
Roberto D'Ettore Piazzoli
PIRANHA II: THE SPAWNING(1981, Neth.), ph; SILHOUETTES(1982), ph
Roberto Piazzoli
TAKE ALL OF ME(1978, Ital.), ph
Antonio Pica
FEW BULLETS MORE, A(1968, Ital./Span.); NUN AT THE CROSSROADS, A(1970, Ital./Span.); TRAVELS WITH MY AUNT(1972, Brit.); SANTO CONTRA EL DOCTOR MUERTE(1974, Span./Mex.)
Tina Pica
BREAD, LOVE AND DREAMS(1953, Ital.); MELODY OF LOVE(1954, Ital.); FRISKY(1955, Ital.); SIGN OF VENUS, THE(1955, Ital.); SCANDAL IN SORRENTO(1957, Ital./Fr.); YESTERDAY, TODAY, AND TOMORROW(1964, Ital./Fr.)
Andre Picard
Silents
KIKI(1926), w; EVENING CLOTHES(1927), w
Burt Picard
ENEMY GENERAL, THE(1960), w
Dad Picard
RIDERS OF THE DAWN(1945)
Frank Picard
THOSE LIPS, THOSE EYES(1980)
Fred A. Picard
THAT WONDERFUL URGE(1948), cos
Howard Picard
TOGETHER BROTHERS(1974)
Marcel Picard
SHADOW STRIKES, THE(1937), ph; OUTLAW'S PARADISE(1939), ph; TEXAS WILDCATS(1939), ph; GANG WAR(1940), ph; RETURN OF THE APE MAN(1944), ph
Silents
GUILE OF WOMEN(1921), ph
Cesarino Miceli Picardi
LA DOLCE VITA(1961, Ital./Fr.); 8 ½(1963, Ital.); JULIET OF THE SPIRITS(1965, Fr./Ital./W.Ger.)
Robert Picardo
HOWLING, THE(1981); GET CRAZY(1983); STAR 80(1983)
1984
OH GOD! YOU DEVIL(1984)
Lamberto Picasso
DEFEAT OF HANNIBAL, THE(1937, Ital.); CUCKOO CLOCK, THE(1938, Ital.); ROSSINI(1948, Ital.)
Pablo Picasso
LIFE BEGINS TOMORROW(1952, Fr.); TESTAMENT OF ORPHEUS, THE(1962, Fr.)
Raul Picasso
UNDER FIRE(1983)
Juliet Picaud
MOVIE STAR, AMERICAN STYLE, OR, LSD I HATE YOU!(1966)
Jean Louis Picavet
ENIGMA(1983), ph
Jean-Louis Picavet
PASSION OF SLOW FIRE, THE(1962, Fr.), ph; WE ARE ALL NAKED(1970, Can./Fr.), ph
Angel Picazo
THAT MAN IN ISTANBUL(1966, Fr./Ital./Span.); NUN AT THE CROSSROADS, A(1970, Ital./Span.)
Miguel Picazo
SPIRIT OF THE BEEHIVE, THE(1976, Span.)
B.S. Piccard
FABULOUS WORLD OF JULES VERNE, THE(1961, Czech.), ph

Alvero Piccardi
ITALIAN SECRET SERVICE(1968, Ital.)
Steven Piccaro
WOMAN HUNT(1962)
Gene Picchi
CHAMP, THE(1979)
Anita Picchiarini
1984
LE BAL(1984, Fr./Ital./Algeria)
Frank Picchioni
IT HAPPENED IN CANADA(1962, Can.)
Vladimiro Picciafuochi
MINOTAUR, THE(1961, Ital.)
Patrick Piccininni
PRIVATE LESSONS(1981)
Piero Piccioni
TEMPEST(1958, Ital./Yugo./Fr.), m; ASSASSIN, THE(1961, Ital./Fr.), m; FROM A ROMAN BALCONY(1961, Fr./Ital.), m, md; BELL' ANTONIO(1962, Ital.), m, md; LA NOTTE BRAVA(1962, Fr./Ital.), m; LA VIACCIA(1962, Fr./Ital.), m; MAFIOSO(1962, Ital.), m; CAPTIVE CITY, THE(1963, Ital.), m; DEVIL, THE(1963), m; DUEL OF THE TITANS(1963, Ital.), m; HUNCHBACK OF ROME, THE(1963, Ital.), m; RUN WITH THE DEVIL(1963, Fr./Ital.), m; SLAVE, THE(1963, Ital.), m; LOVE ON THE RIVIERA(1964, Fr./Ital.), m; LOVE A LA CARTE(1965, Ital.), m; MOMENT OF TRUTH, THE(1965, Ital./Span.), m; TENTH VICTIM, THE(1965, Fr./Ital.), m; CONQUERED CITY(1966, Ital.), m; LA FUGA(1966, Ital.), m; MAN WHO LAUGHS, THE(1966, Ital.), m; MINNESOTA CLAY(1966, Ital./Fr./Span.), m; SALVATORE GIULIANO(1966, Ital.), m; MATCHLESS(1967, Ital.), m; MORE THAN A MIRACLE(1967, Ital./Fr.), m; STRANGER, THE(1967, Algeria/Fr./Ital.), m; NO ROSES FOR OSS 117(1968, Fr.), m; CAMILLE 2000(1969), m; KENNER(1969), m; THREE NIGHTS OF LOVE(1969, Ital.), m; WITCHES, THE(1969, Fr./Ital.), m; DESERTER, THE(1971 Ital./Yugo.), m; LIGHT AT THE EDGE OF THE WORLD, THE(1971, U.S./Span./Lichtenstein), m; PUPPET ON A CHAIN(1971, Brit.), m; SCIENTIFIC CARDPLAYER, THE(1972, Ital.), m; WITCHES, THE(1969, Fr./Ital.), m; DIARY OF A CLOISTERED NUN(1973, Ital./Fr./Ger.), m; RE: LUCKY LUCIANO(1974, Fr./Ital.), m; SWEPT AWAY...BY AN UNUSUAL DESTINY IN THE BLUE SEA OF AUGUST(1975, Ital.), m; ALL SCREWED UP(1976, Ital.), m; EBOLI(1980, Ital.), m; DEATH VENGEANCE(1982), m; THREE BROTHERS(1982, Ital.), m
Michel Piccol
EYES, THE MOUTH, THE(1982, Ital./Fr.)
Peppino Piccol
SAMSON AND THE SLAVE QUEEN(1963, Ital.), set d
Henri Piccoli
PLAYTIME(1973, Fr.); DON'T TOUCH WHITE WOMEN!(1974, Fr.)
Michel Piccoli
FRENCH CANCAN(1956, Fr.); NATHALIE(1958, Fr.); GINA(1961, Fr./Mex.); CONTEMPT(1963, Fr./Ital.); DAY AND THE HOUR, THE(1963, Fr./ Ital.); FINGERMAN, THE(1963, Fr.); DIARY OF A CHAMBERMAID(1964, Fr./Ital.); DOULOS–THE FINGER MAN(1964, Fr./Ital.); LADY L(1965, Fr./Ital.); MASQUERADE(1965, Brit.); IS PARIS BURNING?(1966, U.S./Fr.); SLEEPING CAR MURDER THE(1966, Fr.); GAME IS OVER, THE(1967, Fr.); LA GUERRE EST FINIE(1967, Fr./Swed.); BELLE DE JOUR(1968, Fr.); BENJAMIN(1968, Fr.); DANGER: DIABOLIK(1968, Ital./Fr.); DE L'AMOUR(1968, Fr./Ital.); SHOCK TROOPS(1968, Ital./Fr.); YOUNG GIRLS OF ROCHEFORT, THE(1968, Fr.); DILLINGER IS DEAD(1969, Ital.); LA PRISONNIERE(1969, Fr./Ital.); LES CREATURES(1969, Fr./Swed.); MILKY WAY, THE(1969, Fr./Ital.); TOPAZ(1969, Brit.); THINGS OF LIFE, THE(1970, Fr./Ital./Switz.); DISCREET CHARM OF THE BOURGEOISIE, THE(1972, Fr.); TEN DAYS' WONDER(1972, Fr.); FRENCH CONSPIRACY, THE(1973, Fr.); LA GRANDE BOUFFE(1973, Fr.); DON'T TOUCH WHITE WOMEN!(1974, Fr.); PHANTOM OF LIBERTY, THE(1974, Fr.); LIZA(1976, Fr./Ital.); DEATH IN THE GARDEN(1977, Fr./Mex.); LEONOR(1977, Fr./Span./Ital.); ATLANTIC CITY(1981, U.S./Can.); LEAP INTO THE VOID(1982, Ital.); LA NUIT DE VARENNES(1983, Fr./Ital.); LA PASSANTE(1983, Fr./Ger.); PASSION(1983, Fr./Switz.)
1984
SUCCESS IS THE BEST REVENGE(1984, Brit.)
The Piccoli Marionette Troupe
I AM SUZANNE(1934)
Marco Piccolo
GOLIATH AND THE DRAGON(1961, Ital./Fr.), w
Ottavia Piccolo
LEOPARD, THE(1963, Ital.); SERAFINO(1970, Fr./Ital.)
Ugo Piccone
CHRONICLE OF ANNA MAGDALENA BACH(1968, Ital., Ger.), ph; SARDINIA: RANSOM(1968, Ital.), ph; MOSES AND AARON(1975, Ger./Fr./Ital.), ph
John Piccori
FALSE PRETENSES(1935); LONE WOLF RETURNS, THE(1936); MIRACLES FOR SALE(1939); COMRADE X(1940); WHISTLING IN THE DARK(1941)
Charles Picerni
FUZZ(1972); SHAMUS(1973); DEAD MEN DON'T WEAR PLAID(1982); TRON(1982)
1984
AGAINST ALL ODDS(1984)
Charles Picerni, Jr.
1984
RACING WITH THE MOON(1984); STAR TREK III: THE SEARCH FOR SPOCK(1984)
Paul Picerni
BREAKTHROUGH(1950); I'LL GET BY(1950); SADDLE TRAMP(1950); SECRET FURY, THE(1950); FORCE OF ARMS(1951); FORT WORTH(1951); I WAS A COMMUNIST FOR THE F.B.I.(1951); INSIDE THE WALLS OF FOLSOM PRISON(1951); OPERATION PACIFIC(1951); TANKS ARE COMING, THE(1951); CATTLE TOWN(1952); MARA MARU(1952); OPERATION SECRET(1952); DESERT SONG, THE(1953); HOUSE OF WAX(1953); SHE'S BACK ON BROADWAY(1953); SYSTEM, THE(1953); BOUNTY HUNTER(1954); DRIVE A CROOKED ROAD(1954); PUSHOVER(1954); RIDING SHOTGUN(1954); SHANGHAI STORY, THE(1954); BOBBY WARE IS MISSING(1955); DIAL RED O(1955); HELL'S ISLAND(1955); LORD OF THE JUNGLE(1955); TO HELL AND BACK(1955); COME ON, THE(1956); FLIGHT TO HONG KONG(1956); MIRACLE IN THE RAIN(1956); WIRETAPPERS(1956); BIG CAPER, THE(1957); BROTHERS RICO, THE(1957); OMAR KHAYYAM(1957); OPERATION MAD BALL(1957); SHADOW ON THE WINDOW, THE(1957); MAN WHO DIED TWICE, THE(1958); MARJORIE MORNINGSTAR(1958); RETURN TO WARBOW(1958); TORPEDO RUN(1958); YOUNG PHILADELPHIANS, THE(1959); STRAN-

GERS WHEN WE MEET(1960); SCARFACE MOB, THE(1962); SCALPHUNTERS, THE(1968); CHE!(1969); LAND RAIDERS(1969); AIRPORT(1970); KOTCH(1971); BEYOND THE POSEIDON ADVENTURE(1979)

Paul V. Picerni, Jr.
WARGAMES(1983)

Lou Picetti
SLEEPER(1973); MR. SYCAMORE(1975); ANNIE HALL(1977)

Louis Picetti, Jr.
FOOLS(1970)

Picha
Misc. Talkies
SHAME OF THE JUNGLE(1980, Fr./Bel.), d

Heide Picha
SERPENT'S EGG, THE(1977, Ger./U.S.)

Hermann Picha
BECAUSE I LOVED YOU(1930, Ger.); WORLD WITHOUT A MASK, THE(1934, Ger.)

Irving Pichel
THEY WON'T BELIEVE ME(1947), d; AMERICAN TRAGEDY, AN(1931); CHEAT, THE(1931); MURDER BY THE CLOCK(1931); RIGHT TO LOVE, THE(1931); ROAD TO RENO(1931); BILLION DOLLAR SCANDAL(1932); FORGOTTEN COMMANDMENTS(1932); MADAME BUTTERFLY(1932); MIRACLE MAN, THE(1932); MOST DANGEROUS GAME, THE(1932), d; PAINTED WOMAN(1932); STRANGE JUSTICE(1932); TWO KINDS OF WOMEN(1932); WESTWARD PASSAGE(1932); WILD GIRL(1932); BEFORE DAWN(1933); I'M NO ANGEL(1933); KING OF THE JUNGLE(1933); MYSTERIOUS RIDER, THE(1933); OLIVER TWIST(1933); RIGHT TO ROMANCE(1933); STORY OF TEMPLE DRAKE, THE(1933); WOMAN ACCUSED(1933); BRITISH AGENT(1934); CLEOPATRA(1934); FOG OVER FRISCO(1934); RETURN OF THE TERROR(1934); SUCH WOMEN ARE DANGEROUS(1934); I AM A THIEF(1935); SHE(1935), d; SILVER STREAK, THE(1935); SPECIAL AGENT(1935); THREE KIDS AND A QUEEN(1935); DON'T GAMBLE WITH LOVE(1936); DOWN TO THE SEA(1936); DRACULA'S DAUGHTER(1936); GENTLEMAN FROM LOUISIANA(1936), d; HEARTS IN BONDAGE(1936); HOUSE OF A THOUSAND CANDLES, THE(1936); ARMORED CAR(1937); BEWARE OF LADIES(1937), d; DUKE COMES BACK, THE(1937), d; GENERAL SPANKY(1937); HIGH, WIDE AND HANDSOME(1937); JOIN THE MARINES(1937); LARCENY ON THE AIR(1937), d; SHEIK STEPS OUT, THE(1937), d; SPECIAL AGENT K-7(1937); JEZEBEL(1938); THERE GOES MY HEART(1938); EXILE EXPRESS(1939); GAMBLING SHIP(1939); JUAREZ(1939); NEWSBOY'S HOME(1939); RIO(1939); TOPPER TAKES A TRIP(1939); TORTURE SHIP(1939); EARTHBOUND(1940), d; HUDSON'S BAY(1940), d; MAN I MARRIED, THE(1940), d; DANCE HALL(1941), d; GREAT COMMANDMENT, THE(1941), d; HOW GREEN WAS MY VALLEY(1941); SWAMP WATER(1941), d; LIFE BEGINS AT 8:30(1942), d; PIED PIPER, THE(1942), d; SECRET AGENT OF JAPAN(1942), d; HAPPY LAND(1943), d; MOON IS DOWN, THE(1943), a, d; AND NOW TOMORROW(1944), d; COLONEL EFFINGHAM'S RAID(1945), d; MEDAL FOR BENNY, A(1945), d; BRIDE WORE BOOTS, THE(1946), d; O.S.S.(1946), d; TEMPTATION(1946), d; TOMORROW IS FOREVER(1946), a, d; SOMETHING IN THE WIND(1947), d; MIRACLE OF THE BELLS, THE(1948), d; MR. PEABODY AND THE MERMAID(1948), d; SHE WORE A YELLOW RIBBON(1949); WITHOUT HONOR(1949), d; DESTINATION MOON(1950), d; GREAT RUPERT, THE(1950), d; QUICKSAND(1950), d; SANTA FE(1951), a, d; MARTIN LUTHER(1953), a, d; DAY OF TRIUMPH(1954), d

J. Pichelski
BORDER STREET(1950, Pol.)

Jerzy Pichelski
LOTNA(1966, Pol.)

Evzen Pichl
DIAMONDS OF THE NIGHT(1968, Czech.)

Anne Pichon
FAREWELL TO CINDERELLA(1937, Brit.)

Catherine Anne Pichon
GAME FOR THREE LOSERS(1965, Brit.)

Edgcumb Pichon
VIVA ZAPATA!(1952), w

Catherine Pichonnier
FINNEGANS WAKE(1965), ed

Aaron Picht
1984
STRANGER THAN PARADISE(1984, U.S./Ger.), m

Debbie Pick
Misc. Talkies
INVASION FROM INNER EARTH(1977)

Francois Pick
1984
LE BAL(1984, Fr./Ital./Algeria)

Lupu Pick
KNIGHT IN LONDON, A(1930, Brit./Ger.), d
Silents
SPIES(1929, Ger.)
Misc. Silents
NEW YEAR'S EVE(1923, Ger.), d

Pick and Pat
HIT PARADE, THE(1937)

Helena Pickard
LORD RICHARD IN THE PANTRY(1930, Brit.); SPLINTERS IN THE NAVY(1931, Brit.); MUSIC HALL(1934, Brit.); NELL GWYN(1935, Brit.); BACKSTAGE(1937, Brit.); LET GEORGE DO IT(1940, Brit.); SALOON BAR(1940, Brit.); FOREVER AND A DAY(1943); LODGER, THE(1944); TURNERS OF PROSPECT ROAD, THE(1947, Brit.); MISS PILGRIM'S PROGRESS(1950, Brit.); LADY WITH A LAMP, THE(1951, Brit.); LOVE LOTTERY, THE(1954, Brit.); DOUBLE CROSS(1956, Brit.)

John M. Pickard
ARROWHEAD(1953)

John Pickard
CITY ACROSS THE RIVER(1949); ONCE MORE, MY DARLING(1949); WAKE OF THE RED WITCH(1949); WHITE HEAT(1949); DAVID HARDING, COUNTERSPY(1950); GUNFIGHTER, THE(1950); STAGE TO TUCSON(1950); LITTLE BIG HORN(1951); OH! SUSANNA(1951); SNAKE RIVER DESPERADOES(1951); BUGLES IN THE AFTERNOON(1952); HELLGATE(1952); HOODLUM EMPIRE(1952); OPERATION SECRET(1952); RED BALL EXPRESS(1952); SNIPER, THE(1952); TRAIL GUIDE(1952); ABOVE AND BEYOND(1953); BANDITS OF CORSICA, THE(1953); FIGHTING LAWMAN, THE(1953); FLIGHT TO TANGIER(1953); STORY OF THREE

LOVES, THE(1953); ARROW IN THE DUST(1954); BITTER CREEK(1954); BLACK HORSE CANYON(1954); HUMAN DESIRE(1954); MASSACRE CANYON(1954); RETURN FROM THE SEA(1954); ROSE MARIE(1954); TWO GUNS AND A BADGE(1954); AT GUNPOINT(1955); FLAME OF THE ISLANDS(1955); I DIED A THOUSAND TIMES(1955); LONE RANGER, THE(1955); MC CONNELL STORY, THE(1955); SEMINOLE UPRISING(1955); SEVEN ANGRY MEN(1955); SHOTGUN(1955); TO HELL AND BACK(1955); BLACK WHIP, THE(1956); BROKEN STAR, THE(1956); CRIME AGAINST JOE(1956); FRIENDLY PERSUASION(1956); KENTUCKY RIFLE(1956); BADLANDS OF MONTANA(1957); COPPER SKY(1957); NIGHT RUNNER, THE(1957); OKLAHOMAN, THE(1957); OUTLAW'S SON(1957); RIDE A VIOLENT MILE(1957); WAR DRUMS(1957); DANGEROUS CHARTER(1962); GUN STREET(1962); GATHERING OF EAGLES, A(1963); GREATEST STORY EVER TOLD, THE(1965); COUNTRY BOY(1966); PANIC IN THE CITY(1968); CHARRO(1969); TRUE GRIT(1969); CHISUM(1970); ACT OF VENGEANCE(1974)

Lioni Pickard
HEART'S DESIRE(1937, Brit.), w

Marcel Pickard
HERE'S FLASH CASEY(1937), ph

Margery Pickard
SING AS WE GO(1934, Brit.); DARK JOURNEY(1937, Brit.)

Obed "Dad" Pickard
FRONTIER VENGEANCE(1939); SEA OF GRASS, THE(1947)

Sorrells Pickard
1984
HIGHWAY TO HELL(1984); RUNNING HOT(1984)

Sorrels Pickard
1984
HARDBODIES(1984)

Timothy Pickard
LEADBELLY(1976)

The Pickard Family
RAWHIDE RANGERS(1941)

Slim Pickens
ROCKY MOUNTAIN(1950); BORDER SADDLEMATES(1952); COLORADO SUNDOWN(1952); LAST MUSKETEER, THE(1952); OLD OKLAHOMA PLAINS(1952); SOUTH PACIFIC TRAIL(1952); STORY OF WILL ROGERS, THE(1952); THUNDERBIRDS(1952); DOWN LAREDO WAY(1953); IRON MOUNTAIN TRAIL(1953); OLD OVERLAND TRAIL(1953); RED RIVER SHORE(1953); SHADOWS OF TOMBSTONE(1953); SUN SHINES BRIGHT, THE(1953); BOY FROM OKLAHOMA, THE(1954); OUTCAST, THE(1954); PHANTOM STALLION, THE(1954); LAST COMMAND, THE(1955); SANTA FE PASSAGE(1955); GREAT LOCOMOTIVE CHASE, THE(1956); GUN BROTHERS(1956); STRANGER AT MY DOOR(1956); WHEN GANGLAND STRIKES(1956); GUNSIGHT RIDGE(1957); SHEEPMAN, THE(1958); TONKA(1958); ESCORT WEST(1959); CHARTROOSE CABOOSE(1960); ONE-EYED JACKS(1961); THUNDER OF DRUMS, A(1961); SAVAGE SAM(1963); DR. STRANGELOVE: OR HOW I LEARNED TO STOP WORRYING AND LOVE THE BOMB(1964); GLORY GUYS, THE(1965); IN HARM'S WAY(1965); MAJOR DUNDEE(1965); UP FROM THE BEACH(1965); EYE FOR AN EYE, AN(1966); STAGECOACH(1966); FLIM-FLAM MAN, THE(1967); ROUGH NIGHT IN JERICHO(1967); NEVER A DULL MOMENT(1968); SKIDOO(1968); WILL PENNY(1968); 80 STEPS TO JONAH(1969); BALLAD OF CABLE HOGUE, THE(1970); DESERTER, THE(1971 Ital./Yugo.); COWBOYS, THE(1972); GETAWAY, THE(1972); HONKERS, THE(1972); GINGER IN THE MORNING(1973); PAT GARRETT AND BILLY THE KID(1973); BLAZING SADDLES(1974); BOOTLEGGERS(1974); APPLE DUMPLING GANG, THE(1975); RANCHO DELUXE(1975); WHITE LINE FEVER(1975, Can.); HAWMPS!(1976); PONY EXPRESS RIDER(1976); MR. BILLION(1977); WHITE BUFFALO, THE(1977); SWARM, THE(1978); WISHBONE CUTTER(1978); BEYOND THE POSEIDON ADVENTURE(1979); SPIRIT OF THE WIND(1979); SWEET CREEK COUNTY WAR, THE(1979); 1941(1979); HONEYSUCKLE ROSE(1980); TOM HORN(1980); HOWLING, THE(1981); PINK MOTEL(1983)
Misc. Talkies
LAST MUSKETEER, THE(1952); OPERATION SNAFU(1970, Ital./Yugo.); SAVAGE SEASON(1970); J.C.(1972); LEGEND OF EARL DURAND, THE(1974); POOR PRETTY EDDIE(1975); HEARTBREAK MOTEL(1978); SMOKEY AND THE GOODTIME OUTLAWS(1978)

David V. Picker
ROYAL FLASH(1975, Brit.), p; WON TON TON, THE DOG WHO SAVED HOLLYWOOD(1976), p; OLIVER'S STORY(1978), p; ONE AND ONLY, THE(1978), p; BLOODLINE(1979), p; JERK, THE(1979), p; DEAD MEN DON'T WEAR PLAID(1982), p
1984
BEAT STREET(1984), p; GOODBYE PEOPLE, THE(1984), p

Leonard S. Picker
POWER OF THE WHISTLER, THE(1945), p; BANDIT OF SHERWOOD FOREST, THE(1946), p; MAN WHO DARED, THE(1946), p; STEPCHILD(1947), p; APACHE CHIEF(1949), p, w; OMOO OMOO, THE SHARK GOD(1949), p; TREASURE OF MONTE CRISTO(1949), p

Leonard S. Picker [Bryan Foy]
ADVENTURES OF CASANOVA(1948), p

Sidney Picker
MARSHAL OF LAREDO(1945), p; ROAD TO ALCATRAZ(1945), p; SANTA FE UPRISING(1946), p; SHERIFF OF REDWOOD VALLEY(1946), p; SUN VALLEY CYCLONE(1946), p; HOMESTEADERS OF PARADISE VALLEY(1947), p; MAIN STREET KID, THE(1947), p; MARSHAL OF CRIPPLE CREEK, THE(1947), p; OREGON TRAIL SCOUTS(1947), p; ROBIN OF TEXAS(1947), p; RUSTLERS OF DEVIL'S CANYON(1947), p; SADDLE PALS(1947), p; VIGILANTES OF BOOMTOWN(1947), p; HEART OF VIRGINIA(1948), p; LIGHTNIN' IN THE FOREST(1948), p; OUT OF THE STORM(1948), p; SECRET SERVICE INVESTIGATOR(1948), p; FLAMING FURY(1949), p; HIDEOUT(1949), p; POST OFFICE INVESTIGATOR(1949), p; STREETS OF SAN FRANCISCO(1949), p; BLONDE BANDIT, THE(1950), p; HARBOR OF MISSING MEN(1950), p; TARNISHED(1950), p; CUBAN FIREBALL(1951), p; HAVANA ROSE(1951), p; HONEYCHILE(1951), p; GOBS AND GALS(1952), p; OKLAHOMA ANNIE(1952), p; TOUGHEST MAN IN ARIZONA(1952), p; TROPICAL HEAT WAVE(1952), p; WAC FROM WALLA WALLA, THE(1952), p; GERALDINE(1953), p; UNTAMED HEIRESS(1954), p; LAY THAT RIFLE DOWN(1955), p; SANTA FE PASSAGE(1955), p; STRANGER AT MY DOOR(1956), p; WAGON WHEELS WESTWARD(1956), p; AFFAIR IN RENO(1957), p; JUVENILE JUNGLE(1958), p; YOUNG AND WILD(1958), p

Sylvia Picker
LUCKY DEVILS(1933)
June Pickerell
TEXAS MASQUERADE(1944)
Awretha Pickering
Misc. Silents
WHEN THE DESERT SMILES(1919)
Betsy Pickering
STRANGE INVADERS(1983)
Bob Pickering
1984
ELLIE(1984), m
Col. Pickering
IT HAPPENED HERE(1966, Brit.)
Don Pickering
SCARAB(1982, U.S./Span.)
Donald Pickering
CARRY ON ADMIRAL(1957, Brit.); DOCTOR AT LARGE(1957, Brit.); NOTHING BUT
THE BEST(1964, Brit.); BATTLE OF THE BULGE(1965); FAHRENHEIT 451(1966,
Brit.); CHALLENGE FOR ROBIN HOOD, A(1968, Brit.); THIRTY NINE STEPS,
THE(1978, Brit.); ZULU DAWN(1980, Brit.)
Loring Pickering
I, THE JURY(1982)
Robert Pickering
LET'S KILL UNCLE(1966); RELUCTANT ASTRONAUT, THE(1967); LADY LIBER-
TY(1972, Ital./Fr.)
Rod Pickering
GAMES, THE(1970)
Bill Pickett
Misc. Silents
CRIMSON SKULL, THE(1921); BULL DODGER, THE(1922)
Bob Pickett
CHROME AND HOT LEATHER(1971)
Bobby Pickett
STRANGE INVADERS(1983)
Cindy Pickett
NIGHT GAMES(1980); HYSTERICAL(1983)
Misc. Talkies
BRAINWASH(1982, Brit.); CIRCLE OF POWER(1984)
Elizabeth Pickett
Silents
'MARRIAGE LICENSE?'(1926), t; WINGS OF THE STORM(1926), t
George Pickett
Silents
OLD ARM CHAIR, THE(1920, Brit.), w
James Pickett
Misc. Talkies
THREE ON A MEATHOOK(1973); ZEBRA KILLER, THE(1974)
Mary Pickett
MAN ON FIRE(1957)
Robert Pickett
IT'S A BIKINI WORLD(1967); BABY MAKER, THE(1970)
Wilson Pickett
SGT. PEPPER'S LONELY HEARTS CLUB BAND(1978)
The Pickett Sisters
TAKE ME TO TOWN(1953)
Jack Pickford
GANG WAR(1928)
Silents
EAGLE'S MATE, THE(1914); HIS LAST DOLLAR(1914); HOME SWEET HO-
ME(1914); COMMANDING OFFICER, THE(1915); FANCHON THE CRICKET(1915);
PRETTY SISTER OF JOSE(1915); GREAT EXPECTATIONS(1917); JACK AND
JILL(1917); HUCK AND TOM(1918); JUST OUT OF COLLEGE(1921); LITTLE LORD
FAUNTLEROY(1921), d; GARRISON'S FINISH(1923); GOOSE WOMAN, THE(1925);
MY SON(1925); BAT, THE(1926); BROWN OF HARVARD(1926); EXIT SMILING(1926)
Misc. Silents
WILDFLOWER(1914); LOVE ROUTE, THE(1915); POOR LITTLE PEPPINA(1916);
SEVENTEEN(1916); DUMMY, THE(1917); FRECKLES(1917); GHOST HOUSE,
THE(1917); GIRL AT HOME, THE(1917); TOM SAWYER(1917); VARMINT, THE(1917);
WHAT MONEY CAN'T BUY(1917); HIS MAJESTY BUNKER BEAN(1918); MILE-A-
MINUTE KENDALL(1918); SANDY(1918); SPIRIT OF '17, THE(1918); BILL APPER-
SON'S BOY(1919); BURGLAR BY PROXY(1919); IN WRONG(1919); DOUBLE-DYED
DECIEVER, A(1920); LITTLE SHEPARD OF KINGDOM COME, THE(1920); MAN
WHO HAD EVERYTHING, THE(1920); HILL BILLY, THE(1924); WAKING UP THE
TOWN(1925)
Jimmy Pickford
INVASION OF THE SAUCER MEN(1957); SHAKE, RATTLE, AND ROCK!(1957)
Kaylan Pickford
LOVESICK(1983)
Lottie Pickford
Silents
FANCHON THE CRICKET(1915)
Misc. Silents
REWARD OF PATIENCE, THE(1916); ON THE LEVEL(1917); THEY SHALL
PAY(1921)
Mary Pickford
COQUETTE(1929); TAMING OF THE SHREW, THE(1929); KIKI(1931); SE-
CRETS(1933); GAY DESPERADO, THE(1936), p
Silents
EAGLE'S MATE, THE(1914); GOOD LITTLE DEVIL, A(1914); HEARTS
ADRIFT(1914), a, w; SUCH A LITTLE QUEEN(1914); TESS OF THE STORM COUN-
TRY(1914); CINDERELLA(1915); DAWN OF A TOMORROW, THE(1915); ESMERAL-
DA(1915); FANCHON THE CRICKET(1915); LITTLE PAL(1915); MADAME
BUTTERFLY(1915); MISTRESS NELL(1915); RAGS(1915), a, w; ETERNAL GRIND,
THE(1916); POOR LITTLE RICH GIRL(1916); PRIDE OF THE CLAN, THE(1917);
REBECCA OF SUNNYBROOK FARM(1917); ROMANCE OF THE REDWOODS,
A(1917); AMARILLY OF CLOTHESLINE ALLEY(1918); M'LISS(1918); STELLA MA-
RIS(1918); DADDY LONG LEGS(1919); HOODLUM THE(1919); POLLYANNA(1920);
SUDS(1920); LITTLE LORD FAUNTLEROY(1921); LOVE LIGHT, THE(1921); TESS OF
THE STORM COUNTRY(1922); GARRISON'S FINISH(1923), t; ROSITA(1923); LIT-

TLE ANNIE ROONEY(1925); SPARROWS(1926); MY BEST GIRL(1927); GAUCHO,
THE(1928)
Misc. Silents
CAPRICE(1913); IN THE BISHOP'S CARRIAGE(1913); BEHIND THE SCENES(1914);
FOUNDLING, THE(1916); HULDA FROM HOLLAND(1916); LESS THAN THE
DUST(1916); POOR LITTLE PEPPINA(1916); LITTLE AMERICAN, THE(1917); LIT-
TLE PRINCESS, THE(1917); HOW COULD YOU, JEAN?(1918); JOHANNA EN-
LISTS(1918); CAPTAIN KIDD, JR.(1919); HEART O' THE HILLS(1919); THROUGH
THE BACK DOOR(1921); DOROTHY VERNON OF HADDON HALL(1924)
Philippe Pickford
ORCA(1977), cos
Carolyn Pickles
AGATHA(1979, Brit.); BROTHERS AND SISTERS(1980, Brit.); MIRROR CRACK'D,
THE(1980, Brit.); TESS(1980, Fr./Brit.)
1984
CHAMPIONS(1984)
Christina Pickles
SEIZURE(1974)
Vivian Pickles
DESERT ATTACK(1958, Brit.); PLAY DIRTY(1969, Brit.); HELLO–GOODBYE(1970);
HAROLD AND MAUDE(1971); NICHOLAS AND ALEXANDRA(1971, Brit.); SUNDAY
BLOODY SUNDAY(1971, Brit.); O LUCKY MAN!(1973, Brit.); CANDLESHOE(1978);
BRITTANIA HOSPITAL(1982, Brit.)
Vivien Pickles
LOOKING GLASS WAR, THE(1970, Brit.)
Wilfred Pickles
GAY DOG, THE(1954, Brit.); IMMORAL CHARGE(1962, Brit.); BILLY LIAR(1963,
Brit.); FAMILY WAY, THE(1966, Brit.)
Leonard Pickley
FANTASIA(1940), spec eff
Carolyn Pickman
FRIENDS OF EDDIE COYLE, THE(1973)
Lyn Pickney
SEBASTIAN(1968, Brit.)
Polina Pickowska
Misc. Silents
LOVE ONE ANOTHER(1922, Den.)
Gre Pickrell
HISTORY OF THE WORLD, PART 1(1981), set d
June Pickrell
HOLD BACK THE DAWN(1941); SUDAN(1945); RACE STREET(1948)
Stacey Pickren
SUNNYSIDE(1979); BORDER, THE(1982); LOOKIN' TO GET OUT(1982)
Stacy Pickren
FLASHDANCE(1983)
Elza Pickthorne
THRESHOLD(1983, Can.)
Ronald Pickup
DAY OF THE JACKAL, THE(1973, Brit./Fr.); MAHLER(1974, Brit.); THREE SIS-
TERS(1974, Brit.); THIRTY NINE STEPS, THE(1978, Brit.); NIJINSKY(1980, Brit.);
ZULU DAWN(1980, Brit.); NEVER SAY NEVER AGAIN(1983); WAGNER(1983,
Brit./Hung./Aust.)
Michael Pickwoad
HAWK THE SLAYER(1980, Brit.), art d
1984
PLOUGHMAN'S LUNCH, THE(1984, Brit.), art d
Mike Pickwood
HOUSE OF LONG SHADOWS, THE(1983, Brit.), art d
Antonio Pico
BULLET FOR SANDOVAL, A(1970, Ital./Span.)
Marco Pico
VOYAGE OF SILENCE(1968, Fr.)
Molly Picon
LET'S MAKE A NIGHT OF IT(1937, Brit.); YIDDLE WITH HIS FIDDLE(1937, Pol.);
COME BLOW YOUR HORN(1963); FIDDLER ON THE ROOF(1971); FOR PETE'S
SAKE(1977); CANNONBALL RUN, THE(1981)
1984
CANNONBALL RUN II(1984)
Misc. Silents
MAZEL TOV(1924)
Joe Picorri
BIG BROWN EYES(1936)
John Picorri
DOWN TO THE SEA(1936); EASY LIVING(1937); EMPEROR'S CANDLESTICKS,
THE(1937); FIREFLY, THE(1937); ROSALIE(1937); SEVENTH HEAVEN(1937); BOM-
BAY CLIPPER(1942); CROSSROADS(1942)
Blanche Picot
NUDE IN HIS POCKET(1962, Fr.), makeup
Olga George Picot
TWO FOR THE ROAD(1967, Brit.)
Olga Georges Picot
GOODBYE EMMANUELLE(1980, Fr.)
Rene Picot
Misc. Silents
THUNDERING ROMANCE(1924)
Jean-Noel Picq
MOTHER AND THE WHORE, THE(1973, Fr.)
Odette Picquet
ZAZIE(1961, Fr.)
Bill Picton
MAIN ATTRACTION, THE(1962, Brit.)
Don Picton
MAN AT THE TOP(1973, Brit.), art d; TO THE DEVIL A DAUGHTER(1976,
Brit./Ger.), art d; CLASH OF THE TITANS(1981), art d
Mac Harry Picton
LOYAL HEART(1946, Brit.)
Mac Picton
BRAVE DON'T CRY, THE(1952, Brit.)

Jose Ignacio Pidal
NARCO MEN, THE(1969, Span./Ital.)
Francis Pidgeon
VALUE FOR MONEY(1957, Brit.)
Walter Pidgeon
MELODY OF LOVE, THE(1928); HER PRIVATE LIFE(1929); MOST IMMORAL
LADY, A(1929); BRIDE OF THE REGIMENT(1930); SHOW GIRL IN HOL-
LYWOOD(1930); SWEET KITTY BELLAIRS(1930); VIENNESE NIGHTS(1930); GO-
ING WILD(1931); GORILLA, THE(1931); HOT HEIRESS(1931); KISS ME AGAIN(1931);
ROCKABYE(1932); KISS BEFORE THE MIRROR, THE(1933); JOURNAL OF A
CRIME(1934); BIG BROWN EYES(1936); FATAL LADY(1936); AS GOOD AS MAR-
RIED(1937); GIRL OVERBOARD(1937); GIRL WITH IDEAS, A(1937); MY DEAR MISS
ALDRICH(1937); SARATOGA(1937); SHE'S DANGEROUS(1937); GIRL OF THE
GOLDEN WEST, THE(1938); LISTEN, DARLING(1938); MAN-PROOF(1938); SHOP-
WORN ANGEL(1938); TOO HOT TO HANDLE(1938); NICK CARTER, MASTER
DETECTIVE(1939); SOCIETY LAWYER(1939); STRONGER THAN DESIRE(1939);
6000 ENEMIES(1939); DARK COMMAND, THE(1940); FLIGHT COMMAND(1940);
HOUSE ACROSS THE BAY, THE(1940); IT'S A DATE(1940); PHANTOM RAI-
DERS(1940); SKY MURDER(1940); BLOSSOMS IN THE DUST(1941); DESIGN FOR
SCANDAL(1941); HOW GREEN WAS MY VALLEY(1941); MAN HUNT(1941); MRS.
MINIVER(1942); WHITE CARGO(1942); MADAME CURIE(1943); YOUNGEST
PROFESSION, THE(1943); MRS. PARKINGTON(1944); WEEKEND AT THE WAL-
DORF(1945); HOLIDAY IN MEXICO(1946); SECRET HEART, THE(1946); CASS
TIMBERLANE(1947); IF WINTER COMES(1947); COMMAND DECISION(1948);
JULIA MISBEHAVES(1948); RED DANUBE, THE(1949); THAT FORSYTE WO-
MAN(1949); MINIVER STORY, THE(1950, Brit./U.S.); CALLING BULLDOG DRUM-
MOND(1951, Brit.); QUO VADIS(1951); SELLOUT, THE(1951); SOLDIERS
THREE(1951); UNKNOWN MAN, THE(1951); BAD AND THE BEAUTIFUL,
THE(1952); MILLION DOLLAR MERMAID(1952); DREAM WIFE(1953); SCANDAL
AT SCOURIE(1953); DEEP IN MY HEART(1954); EXECUTIVE SUITE(1954); LAST
TIME I SAW PARIS, THE(1954); MEN OF THE FIGHTING LADY(1954); GLASS
SLIPPER, THE(1955); HIT THE DECK(1955); FORBIDDEN PLANET(1956); THESE
WILDER YEARS(1956); VOYAGE TO THE BOTTOM OF THE SEA(1961); ADVISE
AND CONSENT(1962); BIG RED(1962); TWO COLONELS, THE(1963, Ital.); WARNING
SHOT(1967); FUNNY GIRL(1968); RASCAL(1969); SKYJACKED(1972); HARRY IN
YOUR POCKET(1973); NEPTUNE FACTOR, THE(1973, Can.); TWO-MINUTE WARN-
ING(1976); WON TON TON, THE DOG WHO SAVED HOLLYWOOD(1976); SEX-
TETTE(1978)
Misc. Talkies
VOICE WITHIN, THE(1929)
Silents
'MARRIAGE LICENSE?'(1926); MISS NOBODY(1926); OLD LOVES AND
NEW(1926); OUTSIDER, THE(1926); GIRL FROM RIO, THE(1927); GATEWAY OF
THE MOON, THE(1928); WOMAN WISE(1928)
Misc. Silents
HEART OF SALOME, THE(1927); THIRTEENTH JUROR, THE(1927); CLOTHES
MAKE THE WOMAN(1928); TURN BACK THE HOURS(1928)
Walter Pidgeon, Sr.
RACK, THE(1956)
Franciszek Pieczka
JOAN OF THE ANGELS(1962, Pol.); WALKOVER(1969, Pol.); SARAGOSSA MANUS-
CRIPT, THE(1972, Pol.)
Fransiszek Pieczka
BEADS OF ONE ROSARY, THE(1982, Pol.)
Pied Pipers
I'M FROM ARKANSAS(1944)
The Pied Pipers
SHIP AHOY(1942); GALS, INCORPORATED(1943); SWEET AND LOWDOWN(1944);
MAKE MINE MUSIC(1946); HOEDOWN(1950)
The Pied Pipers and Nan Wynn
JAM SESSION(1944)
Emiliano Piedra
CHIMES AT MIDNIGHT(1967, Span.,Switz.), p; BLOOD WEDDING(1981, Sp.), p;
CARMEN(1983, Span.), p
Ernesto Piedra
TORRID ZONE(1940)
Nonnie Piefer
INTO THE STRAIGHT(1950, Aus.)
Henri Piegay
SKY ABOVE HEAVEN(1964, Fr./Ital.)
Ho Pieh
RETURN OF THE DRAGON(1974, Chin.)
Lo Pieh
BLOOD MONEY(1974, U.S./Hong Kong/Ital./Span.)
Kay Piehl
HOLD BACK TOMORROW(1955)
Vern Piehl
PURSUIT(1975), p
Misc. Talkies
EVIDENCE OF POWER(1979), d
Wolfgang Pieiss
BOYS FROM BRAZIL, THE(1978)
Don Piel
MARDI GRAS MASSACRE(1978), ph
Ed Piel
SINGING OUTLAW(1937); MILLION TO ONE, A(1938); SIX SHOOTIN' SHE-
RIFF(1938); SINGING COWGIRL, THE(1939); LEGION OF THE LAWLESS(1940)
Eddie Piel
HATCHET MAN, THE(1932)
Edward Piel
COCK O' THE WALK(1930); CLEARING THE RANGE(1931); CORNERED(1932);
GAY BUCKAROO, THE(1932); MOVIE CRAZY(1932); FOG OVER FRISCO(1934);
MYSTERIOUS MR. WONG(1935); RECKLESS(1935); WHITE LEGION, THE(1936);
OLD WYOMING TRAIL, THE(1937); RIDERS OF THE WHISTLING SKULL(1937);
GANGSTER'S BOY(1938); HEROES OF THE ALAMO(1938); YOU CAN'T TAKE IT
WITH YOU(1938); RIDERS OF PASCO BASIN(1940); SANTA FE TRAIL(1940); BLACK
DRAGONS(1942); BOMBARDIER(1943); KID RIDES AGAIN, THE(1943); HEAVENLY
DAYS(1944); PRINCESS AND THE PIRATE, THE(1944); WISTFUL WIDOW OF
WAGON GAP, THE(1947); LADY FROM SHANGHAI, THE(1948)

Silents
MAN FROM MONTANA, THE(1917); FLY GOD, THE(1918); GREATEST THING IN
LIFE, THE(1918); BROKEN BLOSSOMS(1919); GIRL WHO STAYED AT HOME,
THE(1919); DREAM STREET(1921); KILLER, THE(1921); DUST FLOWER, THE(1922);
SONG OF LIFE, THE(1922); STEPPING FAST(1923); IRON HORSE, THE(1924);
GREAT K & A TRAIN ROBBERY, THE(1926); YELLOW FINGERS(1926); KING OF
KINGS, THE(1927)
Misc. Silents
RAGGED EARL, THE(1914); JUNGLE LOVERS, THE(1915); AT PINEY RID-
GE(1916); STRONGER LOVE, THE(1916); VALIANTS OF VIRGINIA, THE(1916);
SERPENT'S TOOTH, THE(1917); WHOSE WIFE?(1917); BORROWED CLO-
THES(1918); YOU CAN'T BELIEVE EVERYTHING(1918); BOOTS(1919); DRAGON
PAINTER, THE(1919); FIGHTING CRESSY(1919); GRAY WOLF'S GHOST, THE(1919);
PEPPY POLLY(1919); SAGE BRUSH HAMLET, A(1919); HAUNTING SHA-
DOWS(1920); ROAD TO DIVORCE, THE(1920); THAT GIRL MONTANA(1921); DON'T
DOUBT YOUR WIFE(1922); PURPLE DAWN(1923); THREE JUMPS AHEAD(1923);
TEETH(1924); $50,000 Reward(1924); BLACK PARADISE(1926)
Edward Piel, Jr.
COLLEGE COQUETTE, THE(1929); COWBOY STAR, THE(1936); WHEN TOMOR-
ROW COMES(1939); CAUGHT IN THE DRAFT(1941)
Edward Piel, Sr.
IN OLD ARIZONA(1929); SHADOW OF THE LAW(1930); AVENGER, THE(1931);
TEXAS RANGER, THE(1931); WILD HORSE(1931); DESTRY RIDES AGAIN(1932);
LOCAL BAD MAN(1932); TOMBSTONE CANYON(1932); BLUE STEEL(1934); JOUR-
NAL OF A CRIME(1934); KID MILLIONS(1934); MADAME SPY(1934); MAN FROM
UTAH, THE(1934); PURSUIT OF HAPPINESS, THE(1934); HANDS ACROSS THE
TABLE(1935); MILLION DOLLAR BABY(1935); TALE OF TWO CITIES, A(1935);
SHOW BOAT(1936); SNOWED UNDER(1936); WHIPSAW(1936); YOURS FOR THE
ASKING(1936); AWFUL TRUTH, THE(1937); CAPTAINS COURAGEOUS(1937); CODE
OF THE RANGE(1937); CRUSADE AGAINST RACKETS(1937); GHOST TOWN
GOLD(1937); GUNSMOKE RANCH(1937); OH, SUSANNA!(1937); PAID TO DAN-
CE(1937); SAN QUENTIN(1937); THIS IS MY AFFAIR(1937); TOAST OF NEW YORK,
THE(1937); TRAPPED(1937); TWO-FISTED SHERIFF(1937); CATTLE RAIDERS(1938);
COLORADO TRAIL(1938); I STOLE A MILLION(1939); MAN FROM SUNDOWN,
THE(1939); NIGHT RIDERS, THE(1939); ONE HOUR TO LIVE(1939); PIRATES OF
THE SKIES(1939); RACKETEERS OF THE RANGE(1939); RIO GRANDE(1939);
SPOILERS OF THE RANGE(1939); SUNDOWN ON THE PRAIRIE(1939); THUNDER-
ING WEST, THE(1939); I TAKE THIS OATH(1940); MY SON IS GUILTY(1940); ONE
MAN'S LAW(1940); TWO GIRLS ON BROADWAY(1940); YOU'RE NOT SO
TOUGH(1940); BILLY THE KID'S FIGHTING PALS(1941); FUGITIVE VALLEY(1941);
I WANTED WINGS(1941); IN OLD CHEYENNE(1941); JESSE JAMES AT BAY(1941);
KANSAS CYCLONE(1941); LONE RIDER IN GHOST TOWN, THE(1941); LOVE
CRAZY(1941); LUCKY DEVILS(1941); MEET JOHN DOE(1941); PENNY SERENA-
DE(1941); RED RIVER VALLEY(1941); RIDERS OF BLACK MOUNTAIN(1941);
SKYLARK(1941); TEXAS MARSHAL, THE(1941); TONTO BASIN OUTLAWS(1941);
UNDERGROUND RUSTLERS(1941); CODE OF THE OUTLAW(1942); DOWN RIO
GRANDE WAY(1942); GLASS KEY, THE(1942); JUKE GIRL(1942); MAJOR AND THE
MINOR, THE(1942); MY FAVORITE BLONDE(1942); RIDERS OF THE WEST(1942);
SHUT MY BIG MOUTH(1942); SIN TOWN(1942); CANYON CITY(1943); OUTLAW,
THE(1943); ROBIN HOOD OF THE RANGE(1943); MAN FROM FRISCO(1944);
SILVER CITY KID(1944); SHADOWS OF DEATH(1945); LAST ROUND-UP,
THE(1947); SADDLE PALS(1947); WYOMING(1947); FORCE OF EVIL(1948); THREE
DARING DAUGHTERS(1948); UP IN CENTRAL PARK(1948); WALLS OF JERI-
CHO(1948); MY FOOLISH HEART(1949); RED, HOT AND BLUE(1949); SUN COMES
UP, THE(1949); KANSAS RAIDERS(1950); EXCUSE MY DUST(1951)
Silents
TUMBLING RIVER(1927); MASKED EMOTIONS(1929)
Misc. Silents
MIDNIGHT FACES(1926)
Harry Piel
JOHNNY STEALS EUROPE(1932, Ger.), a, d&w; WORLD WITHOUT A MASK,
THE(1934, Ger.), a, d; MASTER OF THE WORLD(1935, Ger.), d
Misc. Silents
HER GREATEST BLUFF(1927, Ger.), a, d
Trix Pienaar
GUEST AT STEENKAMPSKRAAL, THE(1977, South Africa)
Claude Pieplu
LOVE AND THE FRENCHWOMAN(1961, Fr.); GENDARME OF ST. TROPEZ,
THE(1966, Fr./Ital.); DEVIL BY THE TAIL, THE(1969, Fr./Ital.); LA PRISON-
NIERE(1969, Fr./Ital.); MAN WITH CONNECTIONS, THE(1970, Fr.); DISCREET
CHARM OF THE BOURGEOISIE, THE(1972, Fr.); ADVENTURES OF RABBI JACOB,
THE(1973, Fr.); PHANTOM OF LIBERTY, THE(1974, Fr.); TENANT, THE(1976, Fr.);
BEST WAY, THE(1978, Fr.)
Pierre Pierade
MAN STOLEN(1934, Fr.)
Pieral
LUCRECE BORGIA(1953, Ital./Fr.); HUNCHBACK OF NOTRE DAME, THE(1957,
Fr.); THAT OBSCURE OBJECT OF DESIRE(1977, Fr./Span.)
Pierre Pieral
ETERNAL RETURN, THE(1943, Fr.)
Paolo Pierani
DEAF SMITH AND JOHNNY EARS(1973, Ital.)
Marlise Pieratt
LONG RIDERS, THE(1980)
A. Leslie Pierce
CARNATION KID(1929), d
Arther C. Pierce
DIMENSION 5(1966), w
Arthur C. Pierce
COSMIC MAN, THE(1959), w; INVASION OF THE ANIMAL PEOPLE(1962, U.S./
Swed.), w, m; HUMAN DUPLICATORS, THE(1965), p, w; MUTINY IN OUTER
SPACE(1965), p, w; CYBORG 2087(1966), w; DESTINATION INNER SPACE(1966), w;
LAS VEGAS HILLBILLYS(1966), d; WOMEN OF THE PREHISTORIC PLANET(1966),
d&w; DESTRUCTORS, THE(1968), w
1984
INVISIBLE STRANGLER(1984), w
Arthur G. Pierce
BEYOND THE TIME BARRIER(1960), w

Arthur Pierce
COPS AND ROBBERS(1973)
Bar Pierce
EVIL DEAD, THE(1983), spec eff
Barbara Pierce
Silents
GOLD RUSH, THE(1925); SEVEN CHANCES(1925); GRAND DUCHESS AND THE WAITER, THE(1926)
Barry Pierce
MANGO TREE, THE(1981, Aus.); MANGANINNIE(1982, Aus.)
Misc. Talkies
IMAGE OF DEATH(1977, Brit.)
Betty Pierce
ALIAS FRENCH GERTIE(1930); HOTEL SAHARA(1951, Brit.), set d
Silents
GOLD RUSH, THE(1925)
Bobby Pierce
FREEWHEELIN'(1976)
Bruce B. Pierce
RING, THE(1952), ed; CLIPPED WINGS(1953), ed
Bruce Pierce
IT HAPPENS EVERY SPRING(1949), ed; RIOT IN CELL BLOCK 11(1954), ed; HAMLET(1964), ed
Charles B. Pierce
LEGEND OF BOGGY CREEK, THE(1973), p&d, ph; BOOTLEGGERS(1974), p&d; WINTERHAWK(1976), p&d, w; GRAYEAGLE(1977), a, p,d&w; TOWN THAT DREADED SUNDOWN, THE(1977), a, p&d; NORSEMAN, THE(1978), p,d&w; EVICTORS, THE(1979), p&d, w; SUDDEN IMPACT(1983), w
1984
SACRED GROUND(1984), d,w&ph
Misc. Talkies
WINDS OF AUTUMN, THE(1976), d
Charles I. Pierce
Silents
KID, THE(1921)
Charles Pierce
SKYJACKED(1972), set d; DILLINGER(1973), set d; BLACK BELT JONES(1974), set d; CASEY'S SHADOW(1978), set d; CHEAP DETECTIVE, THE(1978), set d
Charles R. Pierce
PRETTY MAIDS ALL IN A ROW(1971), set d; HEARTS OF THE WEST(1975), set d; CARNY(1980), set d
Charlotte Pierce
Silents
LAVENDER BATH LADY, THE(1922); SUPER-SEX, THE(1922); TAILOR MADE MAN, A(1922)
Misc. Silents
GAS, OIL AND WATER(1922); THRU THE FLAMES(1923); OIL AND ROMANCE(1925); QUEEN OF SPADES(1925); SKY'S THE LIMIT(1925); FIGHTING GOB, THE(1926); SHEEP TRAIL(1926)
Christopher Pierce
LADY CHATTERLEY'S LOVER(1981, Fr./Brit.), p
Chuck Pierce
EYE FOR AN EYE, AN(1966), set d; WACO(1966), set d; STERILE CUCKOO, THE(1969), set d; DIRTY DINGUS MAGEE(1970), set d; PHANTOM TOLLBOOTH, THE(1970), set d; STRAWBERRY STATEMENT, THE(1970), set d; ZIGZAG(1970), set d; BLACK EYE(1974), art d; OUR TIME(1974), set d; OUTLAW JOSEY WALES, THE(1976), set d
1984
PROTOCOL(1984), set d
Chuck Pierce, Jr.
WINTERHAWK(1976)
Curtis Pierce
Silents
DOWN TO THE SEA IN SHIPS(1923)
David Pierce
1984
TERMINATOR, THE(1984)
Don Pierce
CHRISTINE JORGENSEN STORY, THE(1970)
Douglas Pierce
JANIE(1944); LOVE IN WAITING(1948, Brit.), d; DELAVINE AFFAIR, THE(1954, Brit.), d
Silents
LIVINGSTONE(1925, Brit.)
Edgar Pierce
PHANTOM SHIP(1937, Brit.)
Edward Pierce
HOT NEWS(1936, Brit.)
Evelyn Pierce
TENDERLOIN(1928); MILLION DOLLAR COLLAR, THE(1929); ONCE A GENTLEMAN(1930); AMERICAN TRAGEDY, AN(1931); MONKEY BUSINESS(1931)
Misc. Silents
BORDER CAVALIER, THE(1927); SONIA(1928)
Frank Richardson Pierce
RENEGADES OF THE WEST(1932), w
Fred Pierce
STAR 80(1983)
George Pierce
MASQUERADE(1929); RIGHT OF WAY, THE(1931); DYNAMITE RANCH(1932); REVENGE RIDER, THE(1935); HEART OF THE ROCKIES(1937)
Silents
LITTLE SCHOOL MA'AM, THE(1916); BLACK BEAUTY(1921); WATCH YOUR STEP(1922); DO YOUR DUTY(1928)
Misc. Silents
YANKEE PRINCESS, A(1919)
Gerald A. Pierce
MY FAVORITE BLONDE(1942)

Gerald Pierce
HOUSE OF ROTHSCHILD, THE(1934); LOVE, HONOR AND OH, BABY(1940); BALL OF FIRE(1941); HERE COMES MR. JORDAN(1941); MADAME SPY(1942); MAYOR OF 44TH STREET, THE(1942); SABOTEUR(1942); STRICTLY IN THE GROOVE(1942); FLIGHT FOR FREEDOM(1943); SHE'S FOR ME(1943); MUSIC IN MANHATTAN(1944); FIRST YANK INTO TOKYO(1945); LADY FROM SHANGHAI, THE(1948); MAGNIFICENT YANKEE, THE(1950)
Glenda Pierce
NIGHT THEY ROBBED BIG BERTHA'S, THE(1975)
Grace A. Pierce
Silents
JUDITH OF BETHULIA(1914), w
Guy Pierce
HOW GREEN WAS MY VALLEY(1941), makeup; CRY OF THE BANSHEE(1970, Brit.)
Jack P. Pierce
WATERLOO BRIDGE(1931), makeup; FRANKENSTEIN(1931), makeup; MUMMY, THE(1932), makeup; OLD DARK HOUSE, THE(1932), makeup; WHITE ZOMBIE(1932), makeup; THEY JUST HAD TO GET MARRIED(1933), makeup; BLACK CAT, THE(1934), makeup; RAVEN, THE(1935), makeup; NEXT TIME WE LOVE(1936), makeup; THE INVISIBLE RAY(1936), makeup; SON OF FRANKENSTEIN(1939), makeup; TOWER OF LONDON(1939), makeup; WOLF MAN, THE(1941), makeup; HOUSE OF FRANKENSTEIN(1944), makeup; HOUSE OF HORRORS(1946), makeup; KILLERS, THE(1946), makeup; MAGNIFICENT DOLL(1946), makeup; I'LL BE YOURS(1947), makeup; MASTER MINDS(1949), makeup; DEVIL'S HAND, THE(1961), makeup; BEAUTY AND THE BEAST(1963), makeup
Jack Pierce
MASQUERADE(1929); INVISIBLE MAN, THE(1933), makeup; BRIDE OF FRANKENSTEIN, THE(1935), makeup; WEREWOLF OF LONDON, THE(1935), makeup; NIGHT KEY(1937), makeup; ROAD BACK,THE(1937), makeup; NIGHT MONSTER(1942), makeup; FRANKENSTEIN MEETS THE WOLF MAN(1943), makeup; PHANTOM OF THE OPERA(1943), makeup; MUMMY'S CURSE, THE(1944), makeup; MUMMY'S GHOST, THE(1944), makeup; JOAN OF ARC(1948), makeup; BLACK BOOK, THE(1949), makeup; CURSE OF FRANKENSTEIN, THE(1957, Brit.), makeup
Jack Pierce
DUNWICH HORROR, THE(1970)
Jake P. Pierce
CLIMAX, THE(1944), makeup
James Pierce
SUICIDE FLEET(1931); HORSE FEATHERS(1932); BELLE OF THE NINETIES(1934); GOIN' TO TOWN(1935); MURDER MAN(1935); VIRGINIA JUDGE, THE(1935); FLASH GORDON(1936); FOLLOW THE FLEET(1936); TIMBER WAR(1936); THESE GLAMOUR GIRLS(1939); STRANGE CARGO(1940); LOVE CRAZY(1941)
Silents
HER MAN(1924); JESSE JAMES(1927); WINGS(1927); LADIES OF THE MOB(1928); PHANTOM OF THE RANGE(1928)
Misc. Silents
TARZAN AND THE GOLDEN LION(1927); HER SUMMER HERO(1928)
Jay Pierce
VERY NATURAL THING, A(1974)
Jim Pierce
OUR RELATIONS(1936); GREEN LIGHT(1937); LIFE BEGINS IN COLLEGE(1937); RACKET BUSTERS(1938); DISBARRED(1939); UNION PACIFIC(1939); ARIZONA FRONTIER(1940); CHAD HANNA(1940); JOHNNY APOLLO(1940); NORTHWEST MOUNTED POLICE(1940); RAINBOW OVER THE RANGE(1940); TEXAS RANGERS RIDE AGAIN(1940); ACROSS THE SIERRAS(1941); MR. AND MRS. SMITH(1941); ROXIE HART(1942); NOCTURNE(1946); MY FAVORITE BRUNETTE(1947); MIRACLE OF THE BELLS, THE(1948); RIGHT CROSS(1950); CATTLE QUEEN(1951); FOLLOW THE SUN(1951); SHOW BOAT(1951)
Jonnie Pierce
NEPTUNE'S DAUGHTER(1949)
Judy Pierce
GOING BERSERK(1983)
Lonnie Pierce
FRENCH LINE, THE(1954); RIDING SHOTGUN(1954); MISTER ROBERTS(1955)
Lou W. Pierce
TEXAN MEETS CALAMITY JANE, THE(1950)
Louis Pierce
Silents
INNER MAN, THE(1922); STEADFAST HEART, THE(1923)
Maggie Pierce
NEVER SO FEW(1959); GO NAKED IN THE WORLD(1961); TALES OF TERROR(1962); CATTLE KING(1963); FASTEST GUITAR ALIVE, THE(1967)
Mary Pierce
YOUNG LIONS, THE(1958)
Michael Pierce
TWO TICKETS TO BROADWAY(1951); THREE SAILORS AND A GIRL(1953)
Mike Pierce
PARTY GIRL(1958)
Nat Pierce
NEW YORK, NEW YORK(1977)
Noel Pierce
UNDER PRESSURE(1935), w
Norma Pierce
IN WHICH WE SERVE(1942, Brit.)
Norman Pierce
CAN YOU HEAR ME MOTHER?(1935, Brit.); BUSMAN'S HOLIDAY(1936, Brit.); CRIMES OF STEPHEN HAWKE, THE(1936, Brit.); EVERYTHING IS THUNDER(1936, Brit.); GAY OLD DOG(1936, Brit.); THIS GREEN HELL(1936, Brit.); TO CATCH A THIEF(1936, Brit.); TICKET OF LEAVE MAN, THE(1937, Brit.); SEXTON BLAKE AND THE HOODED TERROR(1938, Brit.); SPECIAL EDITION(1938, Brit.); DEMON BARBER OF FLEET STREET, THE(1939, Brit.); FLYING FIFTY-FIVE(1939, Brit.); FOUR FEATHERS, THE(1939, Brit.); SALOON BAR(1940, Brit.); SOUTH AMERICAN GEORGE(1941, Brit.); FRONT LINE KIDS(1942, Brit.); BELLS GO DOWN, THE(1943, Brit.); UNCENSORED(1944, Brit.); UNDERGROUND GUERRILLAS(1944, Brit.); COLONEL BLIMP(1945, Brit.); GREAT DAY(1945, Brit.); MR. EMMANUEL(1945, Brit.); SEND FOR PAUL TEMPLE(1946, Brit.); FRIEDA(1947, Brit.); WILLIAM COMES TO TOWN(1948, Brit.); ELIZABETH OF LADYMEAD(1949, Brit.); MY BROTHER'S KEEPER(1949, Brit.); MAGIC BOX, THE(1952, Brit.); SWORD AND

THE ROSE, THE(1953); ANGELS ONE FIVE(1954, Brit.); PORT OF ESCAPE(1955, Brit.); IT'S GREAT TO BE YOUNG(1956, Brit.); TREAD SOFTLY STRANGER(1959, Brit.); BRIDES OF DRACULA, THE(1960, Brit.); PORTRAIT OF A SINNER(1961, Brit.)
Paul A. Pierce
LET'S DANCE(1950)
Paul Pierce
LADY IN THE DARK(1944)
Preston Pierce
YOUNG FURY(1965)
Misc. Talkies
GIRLS FOR RENT(1974); WHISKEY MOUNTAIN(1977)
Ray Pierce
WILD IS MY LOVE(1963), ed
Richard Pierce
BASKET CASE(1982)
Roger Lawrence Pierce
MALIBU BEACH(1978)
Sam Pierce
FLESH AND FURY(1952); HAS ANYBODY SEEN MY GAL?(1952); KANSAS CITY CONFIDENTIAL(1952); MEET ME AT THE FAIR(1952); NIGHT WITHOUT SLEEP(1952); PAT AND MIKE(1952); CATALINA CAPER, THE(1967), w
Misc. Talkies
BOSS COWBOY(1934)
Stack Pierce
HAMMER(1972); TROUBLE MAN(1972); TRADER HORN(1973); NEWMAN'S LAW(1974); NIGHT CALL NURSES(1974); CORNBREAD, EARL AND ME(1975); PRISONER OF SECOND AVENUE, THE(1975); PSYCHIC KILLER(1975); NO WAY BACK(1976); GREATEST, THE(1977, U.S./Brit.); VICE SQUAD(1982); WARGAMES(1983)
1984
KILLPOINT(1984)
Ted Pierce
GULLIVER'S TRAVELS(1939), w; MR. BUG GOES TO TOWN(1941), a, w
Tiana Pierce
MOTHER'S DAY(1980)
Victor Pierce
FARMER'S OTHER DAUGHTER, THE(1965), m
Warren Pierce
LULU(1978)
Webb Pierce
BUFFALO GUN(1961); SECOND FIDDLE TO A STEEL GUITAR(1965); LAST PICTURE SHOW, THE(1971), m
William A. Pierce
POWERS GIRL, THE(1942), w
William Pierce
ARMORED CAR(1937), w; NIGHT KEY(1937), w; STAR MAKER, THE(1939), w; HOLD THAT WOMAN(1940), w
John Pierce-Jones
1984
SWORD OF THE VALIANT(1984, Brit.)
Tony Pierce-Roberts
1984
KIPPERBANG(1984, Brit.), ph
Jennifer Piercey
ANOTHER TIME, ANOTHER PLACE(1983, Brit.)
1984
ANOTHER TIME, ANOTHER PLACE(1984, Brit.)
Andre Pierdel
MAGNIFICENT ONE, THE(1974, Fr./Ital.), spec eff
Antonio Pierfederici
BLACK SUNDAY(1961, Ital.); ROMEO AND JULIET(1968, Brit./Ital.)
Enrico Piergentili
VARIETY LIGHTS(1965, Ital.)
Sergia Pieri
1984
BASILEUS QUARTET(1984, Ital.)
Frances Pieriot
AFFAIRS OF SUSAN(1945)
Miriam Pieris
DRUMS(1938, Brit.)
Kurd Pieritz
INVISIBLE DR. MABUSE, THE(1965, Ger.); MONSTER OF LONDON CITY, THE(1967, Ger.)
Stephanie Pieritz
HUNTING PARTY, THE(1977, Brit.)
Frances Pierlot
CAPTAIN IS A LADY, THE(1940); THE CATMAN OF PARIS(1946); ACCUSED, THE(1949)
Francis Pierlot
NIGHT ANGEL, THE(1931); ALWAYS A BRIDE(1940); ESCAPE TO GLORY(1940); STRIKE UP THE BAND(1940); BARNACLE BILL(1941); CRACKED NUTS(1941); INTERNATIONAL LADY(1941); PUBLIC ENEMIES(1941); REMEMBER THE DAY(1941); RISE AND SHINE(1941); GENTLEMAN AT HEART, A(1942); HENRY ALDRICH, EDITOR(1942); JUST OFF BROADWAY(1942); MY HEART BELONGS TO DADDY(1942); NIGHT MONSTER(1942); YANKEE DOODLE DANDY(1942); EDGE OF DARKNESS(1943); MISSION TO MOSCOW(1943); MYSTERY BROADCAST(1943); STAGE DOOR CANTEEN(1943); YOU'RE A LUCKY FELLOW, MR. SMITH(1943); BATHING BEAUTY(1944); DOUGHGIRLS, THE(1944); UNCERTAIN GLORY(1944); VERY THOUGHT OF YOU, THE(1944); BEWITCHED(1945); GRISSLY'S MILLIONS(1945); HIDDEN EYE, THE(1945); HIT THE HAY(1945); OUR VINES HAVE TENDER GRAPES(1945); ROUGHLY SPEAKING(1945); TREE GROWS IN BROOKLYN, A(1945); YOLANDA AND THE THIEF(1945); CRIME DOCTOR'S MAN HUNT(1946); DRAGONWYCH(1946); FEAR(1946); G.I. WAR BRIDES(1946); HOW DO YOU DO?(1946); LIFE WITH BLONDIE(1946); SHOW-OFF, THE(1946); YANK IN LONDON, A(1946, Brit.); CIGARETTE GIRL(1947); LATE GEORGE APLEY, THE(1947); MOSS ROSE(1947); PHILO VANCE'S GAMBLE(1947); SECOND CHANCE(1947); SENATOR WAS INDISCREET, THE(1947); TRESPASSER, THE(1947); CHICKEN EVERY SUNDAY(1948); DATE WITH JUDY, A(1948); DUDE GOES WEST, THE(1948); I, JANE DOE(1948); LOVES OF CARMEN, THE(1948); STATE OF THE UNION(1948); THAT LADY IN ERMINE(1948); THAT WONDERFUL URGE(1948);

BAD BOY(1949); MY FRIEND IRMA(1949); TAKE ONE FALSE STEP(1949); COPPER CANYON(1950); FLAME AND THE ARROW, THE(1950); ANNE OF THE INDIES(1951); LEMON DROP KID, THE(1951); MAN WITH A CLOAK, THE(1951); SAVAGE DRUMS(1951); THAT'S MY BOY(1951); HOLD THAT LINE(1952); HOODLUM EMPIRE(1952); PRISONER OF ZENDA, THE(1952); IT HAPPENS EVERY THURSDAY(1953); ROBE, THE(1953)

Francis Pierot
TRIAL OF MARY DUGAN, THE(1941)
Lawrence Pierott
1984
BLESS THEIR LITTLE HEARTS(1984)
Mario Pierotti
HILLS RUN RED, THE(1967, Ital.), w
Piero Pierotti
PIRATE AND THE SLAVE GIRL, THE(1961, Fr./Ital.), d, w; PLANETS AGAINST US, THE(1961, Ital./Fr.), w; MARCO POLO(1962, Fr./Ital.), w; WITCH'S CURSE, THE(1963, Ital.), w; WAR OF THE ZOMBIES, THE(1965 Ital.), w
Giuseppe Pierozzi
BALL AT THE CASTLE(1939, Ital.); WHEN IN ROME(1952)
Oliver Pierpaoli
1984
KILLING FIELDS, THE(1984, Brit.)
Eric Pierpoint
1984
WINDY CITY(1984)
Laura Pierpont
COLLEEN(1936); MY BLUE HEAVEN(1950)
Guy Pierraud
LIGHT ACROSSS THE STREET, THE(1957, Fr.)
Guy Pierrault
PEEK-A-BOO(1961, Fr.)
Carlos Pierre
DEADFALL(1968, Brit.)
Edwige Pierre
DAS BOOT(1982)
Fay Pierre
PALMY DAYS(1931)
Jacques Pierre
DEADLY DECOYS, THE(1962, Fr.), w; PASSION OF SLOW FIRE, THE(1962, Fr.)
Jean-Eric Pierre
1984
MY NEW PARTNER(1984, Fr.), makeup
Lora Pierre
SEPIA CINDERELLA(1947)
Oliver Pierre
FIREFOX(1982)
Olivier Pierre
NUTCRACKER(1982, Brit.); SENDER, THE(1982, Brit.); VICTOR/VICTORIA(1982); LONELY LADY, THE(1983)
Roger Pierre
LA BELLE AMERICAINE(1961, Fr.); LOVE AND THE FRENCHWOMAN(1961, Fr.)
Pierre-Gaspard-Huit
CHRISTINE(1959, Fr.), d& w
Pierre-Louis
COW AND I, THE(1961, Fr., Ital., Ger.); LOVE AND THE FRENCHWOMAN(1961, Fr.)
Jacqueline Pierreux
TOP OF THE FORM(1953, Brit.); BLACK SABBATH(1963, Ital.); THREE PENNY OPERA(1963, Fr./Ger.)
Henry Pierrig
SCANNERS(1981, Can.), spec eff
"Pierrot"
PIERROT LE FOU(1968, Fr./Ital.)
Marguerite Pierry
COURRIER SUD(1937, Fr.); CONFLICT(1939, Fr.); WHIRLWIND OF PARIS(1946, Fr.); KNOCK(1955, Fr.); NANA(1957, Fr./Ital.)
Helen Piers
ONE WOMAN'S STORY(1949, Brit.)
Thors Piers
TWO GENTLEMEN SHARING(1969, Brit.)
Walter Piers
ROSARY, THE(1931, Brit.); WICKHAM MYSTERY, THE(1931, Brit.); THREADS(1932, Brit.)
James A. Piersall
FEAR STRIKES OUT(1957), w
Richard Piersall
RIDERS FROM NOWHERE(1940), w
Franco Piersanti
BLOW TO THE HEART(1983, Ital.), m
1984
YELLOW HAIR AND THE FORTRESS OF GOLD(1984), m
Henry Piersig
STRANGE BREW(1983), spec eff
Arthur Pierson
BACHELOR'S AFFAIRS(1932); GOLDEN WEST, THE(1932); HAT CHECK GIRL(1932); NO ONE MAN(1932); RACKETY RAX(1932); STRANGE CASE OF CLARA DEANE, THE(1932); TOMORROW AND TOMORROW(1932); AIR HOSTESS(1933); ANN CARVER'S PROFESSION(1933); DEVIL'S BROTHER, THE(1933); WAY TO LOVE, THE(1933); MURDER IN THE CLOUDS(1934); YOU BELONG TO ME(1934); SWEET SURRENDER(1935); FOLLIES GIRL(1943); DANGEROUS YEARS(1947), d; FIGHTING O'FLYNN, THE(1949), d; HOME TOWN STORY(1951), p,d&w; FOOTSTEPS IN THE FOG(1955, Brit.), w
Cal Pierson
INSIDE THE LAW(1942), ed
Carl F. Pierson
MOONSTONE, THE(1934), ed

Carl L. Pierson
MYSTERIOUS ISLAND(1929), w, ed; FLORODORA GIRL, THE(1930), ed; MONTANA MOON(1930), ed; RIDERS OF DESTINY(1933), ed; YAQUI DRUMS(1956), ed
Carl Pierson
MAN FROM HELL'S EDGES(1932), ed; RIDERS OF THE DESERT(1932), ed; GREAT JASPER, THE(1933), ed; WEST OF SINGAPORE(1933), ed; BLUE STEEL(1934), ed; GIRL OF THE LIMBERLOST(1934), ed; HOUSE OF MYSTERY(1934), ed; LUCKY TEXAN, THE(1934), ed; MAN FROM UTAH, THE(1934), ed; MANHATTAN LOVE SONG(1934), ed; MYSTERY LINER(1934), ed; 'NEATH THE ARIZONA SKIES(1934), ed; RANDY RIDES ALONE(1934), ed; STAR PACKER, THE(1934), ed; WEST OF THE DIVIDE(1934), ed; WINE, WOMEN, AND SONG(1934), ed; CAPPY RICKS RETURNS(1935), ed; DAWN RIDER(1935), ed; DESERT TRAIL(1935), ed; FLIRTING WITH DANGER(1935), ed; FRISCO WATERFRONT(1935), ed; HOOSIER SCHOOLMASTER(1935), ed; JANE EYRE(1935), ed; KEEPER OF THE BEES(1935), ed; LAWLESS FRONTIER, THE(1935), ed; LAWLESS RANGE(1935), ed; LOST IN THE STRATOSPHERE(1935), ed; MAKE A MILLION(1935), ed; MILLION DOLLAR BABY(1935), ed; MYSTERY MAN, THE(1935), ed; NEW FRONTIER, THE(1935), d; NUT FARM, THE(1935), ed; PARADISE CANYON(1935), d; RAINBOW VALLEY(1935), ed; SING SING NIGHTS(1935), ed; SINGING VAGABOND, THE(1935), d; TEXAS TERROR(1935), ed; TOMORROW'S YOUTH(1935), ed; HONEYMOON LIMITED(1936), ed; OREGON TRAIL, THE(1936), ed; RED RIVER VALLEY(1936), ed; REEFER MADNESS(1936), ed; WESTWARD HO(1936), ed; OUTER GATE, THE(1937), ed; WESTERN GOLD(1937), ed; GUILTY TRAILS(1938), ed; I COVER CHINATOWN(1938), ed; KING OF THE SIERRAS(1938), ed; PRAIRIE JUSTICE(1938), ed; WHERE THE WEST BEGINS(1938), ed; MYSTERY PLANE(1939), ed; SKY PATROL(1939), ed; STUNT PILOT(1939), ed; WOLF CALL(1939), ed; BOYS OF THE CITY(1940), ed; MAD EMPRESS, THE(1940), ed; THAT GANG OF MINE(1940), ed; ARIZONA BOUND(1941), ed; FORBIDDEN TRAILS(1941), ed; GUN MAN FROM BODIE, THE(1941), ed; REDHEAD(1941), ed; REG'LAR FELLERS(1941), ed; BELOW THE BORDER(1942), ed; BLACK DRAGONS(1942), ed; BOWERY AT MIDNIGHT(1942), ed; CITY OF SILENT MEN(1942), ed; DAWN ON THE GREAT DIVIDE(1942), ed; DOWN TEXAS WAY(1942), ed; GHOST TOWN LAW(1942), ed; MR. WISE GUY(1942), ed; 'NEATH BROOKLYN BRIDGE(1942), ed; RIDERS OF THE WEST(1942), ed; ROAD TO HAPPINESS(1942), ed; WEST OF THE LAW(1942), ed; APE MAN, THE(1943), ed; CLANCY STREET BOYS(1943), ed; GHOSTS ON THE LOOSE(1943), ed; HERE COMES KELLY(1943), ed; KID DYNAMITE(1943), ed; MR. MUGGS STEPS OUT(1943), ed; OUTLAWS OF STAMPEDE PASS(1943), ed; RHYTHM PARADE(1943), ed; SARONG GIRL(1943), ed; SIX GUN GOSPEL(1943), ed; SMART GUY(1943), ed; SPOTLIGHT SCANDALS(1943), ed; STRANGER FROM PECOS, THE(1943), ed; WINGS OVER THE PACIFIC(1943), ed; BLOCK BUSTERS(1944), ed; BLUEBEARD(1944), ed; DEATH VALLEY RANGERS(1944), ed; FOLLOW THE LEADER(1944), ed; MILLION DOLLAR KID(1944), ed; MINSTREL MAN(1944), ed; RAIDERS OF THE BORDER(1944), ed; RETURN OF THE APE MAN(1944), ed; TEXAS KID, THE(1944), ed; VOODOO MAN(1944), ed; DANGEROUS INTRUDER(1945), ed; STRANGE ILLUSION(1945), ed; WHY GIRLS LEAVE HOME(1945), ed; CLUB HAVANA(1946), ed; COURTIN' TROUBLE(1948), ed; OUTLAW BRAND(1948), ed; ROARING WESTWARD(1949), ed; BANDIT QUEEN(1950), ed; BORDER RANGERS(1950), ed; GUNFIRE(1950), ed; I SHOT BILLY THE KID(1950), ed; RADAR SECRET SERVICE(1950), ed; TRAIN TO TOMBSTONE(1950), ed; WESTERN PACIFIC AGENT(1950), ed; DANGER ZONE(1951), ed; LEAVE IT TO THE MARINES(1951), ed; LITTLE BIG HORN(1951), ed; MASK OF THE DRAGON(1951), ed; PIER 23(1951), ed; ROARING CITY(1951), ed; SAVAGE DRUMS(1951), ed; THREE DESPERATE MEN(1951), ed; SKY HIGH(1952), ed; GREAT JESSE JAMES RAID, THE(1953), ed; SINS OF JEZEBEL(1953), ed; MASSACRE(1956), ed; STAGECOACH TO FURY(1956), ed; TWO-GUN LADY(1956), ed; SHE DEVIL(1957), ed; DIAMOND SAFARI(1958), ed; LITTLE SHEPHERD OF KINGDOM COME(1961), ed; SILENT CALL, THE(1961), ed; SNIPER'S RIDGE(1961), ed; TWO LITTLE BEARS, THE(1961), ed; WOMAN HUNT(1962), ed; RAIDERS FROM BENEATH THE SEA(1964), ed; THAT TENNESSEE BEAT(1966), ed
Carol Dawn Pierson
UP IN CENTRAL PARK(1948)
Claude Pierson
WE ARE ALL NAKED(1970, Can./Fr.), p&d
Curl Pierson
HAND OF DEATH(1962), ed
Don Pierson
Misc. Silents
HEARTS OF THE WOODS(1921)
Frank Pierson
CAT BALLOU(1965), w; DOG DAY AFTERNOON(1975), w; STAR IS BORN, A(1976), d, w; KING OF THE GYPSIES(1978), d&w
Frank R. Pierson
COOL HAND LUKE(1967), w; HAPPENING, THE(1967), w; LOOKING GLASS WAR, THE(1970, Brit.), d&w; ANDERSON TAPES, THE(1971), w
Isabelle Pierson
WE ARE ALL NAKED(1970, Can./Fr.)
Jane Pierson
UNDER THE ROOFS OF PARIS(1930, Fr.); BOUDU SAVED FROM DROWNING(1967, Fr.); LA CHIENNE(1975, Fr.)
John "Red" Pierson
NIGHT AND DAY(1946)
Leo Pierson
Silents
HEARTS OF MEN(1919); POPPY GIRL'S HUSBAND, THE(1919)
Misc. Silents
T.N.T(THE NAKED TRUTH) (1924); AT PINEY RIDGE(1916); BIRTH OF PATRIOTISM, THE(1917); WIFE ON TRAIL, A(1917); '49 - '17(1917); COVE OF MISSING MEN(1918); GIRL OF MY DREAMS, THE(1918); SPREADING EVIL, THE(1919)
Logan Pierson
FIGHTING PIONEERS(1935), ed
Loretta Pierson
Misc. Talkies
BEST, THE(1979)
Louise Randall Pierson
ROUGHLY SPEAKING(1945), w
R.E. Pierson
Misc. Talkies
CLAWS(1977), d

Rex Pierson
STING II, THE(1983)
Richard Pierson
DINER(1982)
Ronda Pierson
ON THE RIGHT TRACK(1981)
Suzy Pierson
Misc. Silents
6 ½ X 11(1927, Fr.)
Ted Pierson
BASKETBALL FIX, THE(1951)
Tom Pierson
PERFECT COUPLE, A(1979); QUINTET(1979), m, md
William Pierson
STALAG 17(1953); FUN WITH DICK AND JANE(1977)
Pierval
UP FROM THE BEACH(1965)
Piestrak
TEST OF PILOT PIRX, THE(1978, Pol./USSR), w
Marek Piestrak
TEST OF PILOT PIRX, THE(1978, Pol./USSR), d
Ed Piet, Sr.
COLT .45(1950)
Walter Pietela
KNICKERBOCKER HOLIDAY(1944)
Andre Pieters
GOLDEN RENDEZVOUS(1977), p
Barbara Pieters
HOLLYWOOD BOULEVARD(1976)
John Pieters
GAL YOUNG UN(1979)
Sean Pieters
HOLLYWOOD BOULEVARD(1976)
Andre Pieterse
FOREVER YOUNG, FOREVER FREE(1976, South Afr.), p, w
Walter Pietila
RIDING HIGH(1943); ONCE UPON A TIME(1944); WONDER MAN(1945)
Walter S. Pietila
O.S.S.(1946)
Walter Pietilla
SHINE ON, HARVEST MOON(1944)
Antonio Pietrangeli
LA TERRA TREMA(1947, Ital.); IT HAPPENED IN ROME(1959, Ital.), d, w; OSSESSIONE(1959, Ital.), w; LOVE A LA CARTE(1965, Ital.), d, w; MAGNIFICENT CUCKOLD, THE(1965, Fr./Ital.), d; LA VISITA(1966, Ital./Fr.), d, w; QUEENS, THE(1968, Ital./Fr.), d
A. Pietrangelli
HONEYMOON DEFERRED(1951, Brit.), w
Leonard Pietraszak
DANTON(1983)
Leon Pietraszkiewicz
PASSENGER, THE(1970, Pol.)
Jerzy Pietraszkiewiez
FIRST START(1953, Pol.)
Donald Pietro
MRS. MIKE(1949)
Massimo Pietrobon
SODOM AND GOMORRAH(1962, U.S./Fr./Ital.)
Angela Pietropinto
NUNZIO(1978); EASY MONEY(1983); WITHOUT A TRACE(1983)
Antonia Pietrosi
FELLINI SATYRICON(1969, Fr./Ital.); SPIRITS OF THE DEAD(1969, Fr./Ital.)
Ryszard Pietruski
GUESTS ARE COMING(1965, Pol.); GOLEM(1980, Pol.)
Oskar Pietsch
INVISIBLE DR. MABUSE, THE(1965, Ger.), art d
Rod Piffath
HOT LEAD AND COLD FEET(1978), w
John Piffl
UNDERGROUND(1941); TWO SMART PEOPLE(1946)
John Piffle
FRIENDLY ENEMIES(1942); WE WERE DANCING(1942); LEOPARD MAN, THE(1943); GREAT SINNER, THE(1949)
Aldo Piga
VAMPIRE AND THE BALLERINA, THE(1962, Ital.), m; PLAYGIRLS AND THE VAMPIRE(1964, Ital.), m; TERROR-CREATURES FROM THE GRAVE(1967, U.S./Ital.), m; CURSE OF THE BLOOD GHOULS(1969, Ital.), m
Roger Pigaut
ANTOINE ET ANTOINETTE(1947 Fr.); BELLMAN, THE(1947, Fr.); LOVE STORY(1949, Fr.); COUNT OF MONTE-CRISTO(1955, Fr., Ital.); NAPOLEON(1955, Fr.); LIGHT ACROSSS THE STREET, THE(1957, Fr.); MAYERLING(1968, Brit./Fr.)
Corky Pigeon
FOREST, THE(1983)
Ginette Pigeon
TONIGHT THE SKIRTS FLY(1956, Fr.); MAEDCHEN IN UNIFORM(1965, Ger./Fr.)
Tempe Piggott
SEVEN DAYS LEAVE(1930); ONE MORE RIVER(1934); TALE OF TWO CITIES, A(1935); FOOLS FOR SCANDAL(1938)
Silents
ROAD HOUSE(1928)
Tim Piggott-Smith
CLASH OF THE TITANS(1981)
Doris Pignatelli
LA DOLCE VITA(1961, Ital./Fr.)
Rene Pigneres
GENDARME OF ST. TROPEZ, THE(1966, Fr./Ital.), p; LAST ADVENTURE, THE(1968, Fr./Ital.), p

Christine Pignet
1984
FIRST NAME: CARMEN(1984, Fr.)

Gina Pignier
LA GRANDE BOUFFE(1973, Fr.), ed

Jean Pignol
TOUT VA BIEN(1973, Fr.)

Claude Pignot
MATA HARI(1965, Fr./Ital.), art d; VOYAGE OF SILENCE(1968, Fr.), art d; FINO A FARTI MALE(1969, Fr./Ital.), art d; LES CREATURES(1969, Fr./Swed.), set d; STOLEN KISSES(1969, Fr.), art d; MISSISSIPPI MERMAID(1970, Fr./Ital.), art d; MAN WITH THE TRANSPLANTED BRAIN, THE(1972, Fr./Ital./Ger.), art d; BENVENUTA(1983, Fr.), art d

Yves Pignot
LADY IN THE CAR WITH GLASSES AND A GUN, THE(1970, U.S./Fr.); INQUISITOR, THE(1982, Fr.)

Tim Pigot-Smith
RICHARD'S THINGS(1981, Brit.)

Tempe Pigott
NIGHT WORK(1930); DEVOTION(1931); DR. JEKYLL AND MR. HYDE(1932); CAVALCADE(1933); DR. BULL(1933); IF I WERE FREE(1933); MAN OF THE FOREST(1933); OLIVER TWIST(1933); LEMON DROP KID, THE(1934); LIMEHOUSE BLUES(1934); LONG LOST FATHER(1934); OF HUMAN BONDAGE(1934); BECKY SHARP(1935); CALM YOURSELF(1935); DEVIL IS A WOMAN, THE(1935); FEATHER IN HER HAT, A(1935); I FOUND STELLA PARISH(1935); WEREWOLF OF LONDON, THE(1935); LITTLE LORD FAUNTLEROY(1936); STORY OF LOUIS PASTEUR, THE(1936); SUZY(1936); TIMOTHY'S QUEST(1936); WHITE ANGEL, THE(1936); ROAD BACK,THE(1937); ARISE, MY LOVE(1940); EARL OF CHICAGO, THE(1940); ONE FOOT IN HEAVEN(1941); NOW, VOYAGER(1942); HOUR BEFORE THE DAWN, THE(1944); JANE EYRE(1944); KITTY(1945); FOREVER AMBER(1947); FAN, THE(1949)
Silents
MASKED AVENGER, THE(1922); NARROW STREET, THE(1924); GREED(1925); BLACK PIRATE, THE(1926)

Temple Pigott
STUDY IN SCARLET, A(1933)

William Pigott
Silents
NEW DISCIPLE, THE(1921), w

Tim Pigott-Smith
SWEET WILLIAM(1980, Brit.); VICTORY(1981)

Luciano Pigozzi
SPY IN YOUR EYE(1966, Ital.); HATCHET FOR A HONEYMOON(1969, Span./Ital.); PULP(1972, Brit.)

Lida Pigurenko
LULLABY(1961, USSR)

Anita Pike
SUEZ(1938); SHINE ON, HARVEST MOON(1944)

Bernard Pike
SKULLDUGGERY(1970)

Dennis Pike
FUNERAL HOME(1982, Can.), spec eff

Don Pike
EYE FOR AN EYE, AN(1981); I, THE JURY(1982), a, stunts

Grace Pike
Silents
JENNY BE GOOD(1920); FROM THE GROUND UP(1921)
Misc. Silents
MOUNTAIN MADNESS(1920)

Hy Pike
1984
BAD MANNERS(1984)

James A. Pike
FEELIN' GOOD(1966), p,d,&ph, w

John Pike
ONE WISH TOO MANY(1956, Brit.); CAT GANG, THE(1959, Brit.); WOMAN'S TEMPTATION, A(1959, Brit.); KIDNAPPED(1960); REACH FOR GLORY(1963, Brit.); SING AND SWING(1964, Brit.); BE MY GUEST(1965, Brit.)
Misc. Talkies
YOUNG JACOBITES(1959)

Karen Pike
PHOBIA(1980, Can.)

Kelvin Pike
DRESSER, THE(1983), ph

Kevin Pike
1984
LAST STARFIGHTER, THE(1984), spec eff

Melvin Pike
DR. STRANGELOVE: OR HOW I LEARNED TO STOP WORRYING AND LOVE THE BOMB(1964), ph

Miles E. Pike
FANTASIA(1940), spec eff

Nita Pike
PALMY DAYS(1931); ESPIONAGE(1937); THEY GAVE HIM A GUN(1937); GREAT DICTATOR, THE(1940); MADAME CURIE(1943)

Peter Pike
HAND IN HAND(1960, Brit.); IT TAKES A THIEF(1960, Brit.)

Rex Pike
HOMECOMING, THE(1973), ed

Richard Pike
ADVENTURES OF KITTY O'DAY(1944), ed

Robert L. Pike
BULLITT(1968), w

Robert Pike
FROM HERE TO ETERNITY(1953)

Samuel M. Pike
WHEN'S YOUR BIRTHDAY?(1937), w

Travis Pike
FEELIN' GOOD(1966)

William Pike
Silents
CARDIGAN(1922)
Misc. Silents
UNWRITTEN LAW, THE(1916); WOMAN WHO DARED, THE(1916); WE SHOULD WORRY(1918); JUST SQAW(1919); FLAME OF HELLGATE, THE(1920)

Bohuslav Pikhart
STOLEN DIRIGIBLE, THE(1966, Czech.), ph

Mario Pilar
FIRST TASTE OF LOVE(1962, Fr.); VALACHI PAPERS, THE(1972, Ital./Fr.); VERDICT(1975, Fr./Ital.)

L. Pilarska
JOVITA(1970, Pol.)

Gert Pilary
ELISABETH OF AUSTRIA(1931, Ger.)

Robert Pilat
NIGHT AFFAIR(1961, Fr.), set d

Joseph Pilato
EFFECTS(1980)

Barbara Pilavin
VOYAGE, THE(1974, Ital.); GARDEN OF THE FINZI-CONTINIS, THE(1976, Ital./Ger.); VICE SQUAD(1982); FRIGHTMARE(1983); 10 TO MIDNIGHT(1983)

Jan Pilbeam
FOUR AGAINST FATE(1952, Brit.)

Nova Pilbeam
LITTLE FRIEND(1934, Brit.); MAN WHO KNEW TOO MUCH, THE(1935, Brit.); LADY JANE GREY(1936, Brit.); YOUNG AND INNOCENT(1938, Brit.); CHEER BOYS CHEER(1939, Brit.); PASTOR HALL(1940, Brit.); BANANA RIDGE(1941, Brit.); SPRING MEETING(1941, Brit.); NEXT OF KIN(1942, Brit.); YELLOW CANARY, THE(1944, Brit.); THIS MAN IS MINE(1946 Brit.); GREEN FINGERS(1947); COUNTER BLAST(1948, Brit.); DEVIL'S PLOT, THE(1948, Brit.); THREE WEIRD SISTERS, THE(1948, Brit.)

Richard Pilbrow
SWALLOWS AND AMAZONS(1977, Brit.), p

Harry Pilcer
CINDERELLA(1937, Fr.), ch; THANK YOUR LUCKY STARS(1943); RAZOR'S EDGE, THE(1946)

Jim Pilcher
MAJOR AND THE MINOR, THE(1942)

Roy Pilcher
Silents
SPENDTHRIFT, THE(1915)
Misc. Silents
BETRAYED!(1916)

Joe Pileggi
UNCLE SCAM(1981)

Mitch Pileggi
MONGREL(1982)
1984
ON THE LINE(1984, Span.)

Tom Pileggi
UNCLE SCAM(1981), p&d, w

Franco Pilenga
TREE OF WOODEN CLOGS, THE(1979, Ital.)

Tihomir Piletic
AS THE SEA RAGES(1960 Ger.), art d

Reggie Pilgrim
SISTER TO ASSIST'ER, A(1948, Brit.), ph

Ronnie Pilgrim
IT HAPPENED IN SOHO(1948, Brit.), ph; OPERATION DIAMOND(1948, Brit.), d, ph

Ray Pili
1984
BIRDY(1984)

Margarita Pilikhina
GORDEYEV FAMILY, THE(1961, U.S.S.R.), ph

George Pilita
PARADISE ISLE(1937)

Pilitak
WHITE DAWN, THE(1974)

Bill Pilkington
MIND OF MR. SOAMES, THE(1970, Brit.); O LUCKY MAN!(1973, Brit.)

Gordon Pilkington
MARRY ME!(1949, Brit.), ed; STORY OF ROBIN HOOD, THE(1952, Brit.), ed; LOVE IN PAWN(1953, Brit.), ed; BLACK KNIGHT, THE(1954), ed; PARATROOPER(1954, Brit.), ed; MARCH HARE, THE(1956, Brit.), ed; NO TIME FOR TEARS(1957, Brit.), ed; CAST A DARK SHADOW(1958, Brit.), ed; CHASE A CROOKED SHADOW(1958, Brit.), ed; SHAKE HANDS WITH THE DEVIL(1959, Ireland), ed; ENEMY GENERAL, THE(1960), ed; VIRGIN ISLAND(1960, Brit.), ed; CIRCLE OF DECEPTON(1961, Brit.), ed; NAKED EDGE, THE(1961), ed; PORTRAIT OF A SINNER(1961), ed; DESERT PATROL(1962, Brit.), ed; SATAN NEVER SLEEPS(1962), ed; WHAT A CARVE UP!(1962, Brit.), ed; PUNCH AND JUDY MAN, THE(1963, Brit.), ed; FLIGHT FROM ASHIYA(1964, U.S./Jap.), ed; HAVING A WILD WEEKEND(1965, Brit.), ed; SOME MAY LIVE(1967, Brit.), ed; WINTER'S TALE, THE(1968, Brit.), ed; NIGHT OF THE FOLLOWING DAY, THE(1969, Brit.), ed

Joe Pilkington
MC KENZIE BREAK, THE(1970); UNDERGROUND(1970, Brit.); LIGHT YEARS AWAY(1982, Fr./Switz.)

Roger Pilkington
GOLDEN HEAD, THE(1965, Hung., U.S.), w

Tom Pilkington
ENTER ARSENE LUPIN(1944); KISS THE BLOOD OFF MY HANDS(1948)

Paola Pilla
MARRY ME! MARRY ME!(1969, Fr.), cos

Paulo Pilla
1984
GABRIELA(1984, Braz.)

Gary Pillar
WILD SCENE, THE(1970)
Andre Pillette
GRAND PRIX(1966)
Teddy Pillette
GRAND PRIX(1966)
Clyde Pillmore
HIT THE HAY(1945)
Rod Pilloud
FRANCES(1982)
1984
PRODIGAL, THE(1984)
Ray Pillow
COUNTRY BOY(1966)
Garth Pillsbury
GOODBYE, NORMA JEAN(1976)
Helen Pillsbury
Silents
PRICE FOR FOLLY, A(1915); CHARM SCHOOL, THE(1921)
Misc. Silents
LAST DOOR, THE(1921)
Henry Pillsbury
MISTER FREEDOM(1970, Fr.)
Matthew Pillsbury
1984
LE BON PLAISIR(1984, Fr.)
Sam Pillsbury
SCARECROW, THE(1982, New Zealand), d, w
Adaya Pilo
JESUS CHRIST, SUPERSTAR(1973)
Daniel Pilon
MILKY WAY, THE(1969, Fr./Ital.); PLAY DIRTY(1969, Brit.); RED(1970, Can.); MALPERTIUS(1972, Bel./Fr.); BRANNIGAN(1975, Brit.); PLAGUE(1978, Can.); STAR-SHIP INVASIONS(1978, Can.)
Misc. Talkies
M3: THE GEMINI STRAIN(1980)
Donald Pilon
RED(1970, Can.); PYX, THE(1973, Can.); CHILD UNDER A LEAF(1975, Can.); UNCANNY, THE(1977, Brit./Can.); I MISS YOU, HUGS AND KISSES(1978, Can.); CITY ON FIRE(1979 Can.)
Roger Pilon
1984
HEY BABE!(1984, Can.), m
Tom Pilong
UNCLE SCAM(1981), w
Camillo Pilooto
GODDESS OF LOVE, THE(1960, Ital./Fr.)
Michel Pilorge
GOING PLACES(1974, Fr.)
Andre Pilot
BECAUSE I LOVED YOU(1930, Ger.)
Bernice Pilot
HEARTS IN DIXIE(1929); PUBLIC ENEMY'S WIFE(1936); BACK IN CIRCULA-TION(1937); ON SUCH A NIGHT(1937); PENROD AND SAM(1937); THAT CERTAIN WOMAN(1937); WHITE BONDAGE(1937); BELOVED BRAT(1938); MY BILL(1938); PENROD AND HIS TWIN BROTHER(1938); PENROD'S DOUBLE TROUBLE(1938); SAY IT IN FRENCH(1938); SKY GIANT(1938); NO PLACE TO GO(1939); PRIDE OF THE BLUEGRASS(1939); SWEEPSTAKES WINNER(1939); FUGITIVE FROM JUS-TICE, A(1940); SANTA FE TRAIL(1940); CITY, FOR CONQUEST(1941); FATHER'S SON(1941); SEA OF GRASS, THE(1947)
Bernie Pilot
CRIMINALS WITHIN(1941)
Camillo Pilotto
DEFEAT OF HANNIBAL, THE(1937, Ital.); FURIA(1947, Ital.); ROSSINI(1948, Ital.); BULLET FOR STEFANO(1950, Ital.); THIEF OF VENICE, THE(1952); AFFAIRS OF MESSALINA, THE(1954, Ital.); HEAD OF A TYRANT(1960, Fr./Ital.); MARCO PO-LO(1962, Fr./Ital.)
Harry Pilser
RAZOR'S EDGE, THE(1946), ch
Andre Piltant
PICNIC ON THE GRASS(1960, Fr.), set d; LAST YEAR AT MARIENBAD(1962, Fr./Ital.), set d; IMMORTAL STORY, THE(1969, Fr.), art d; MISTER FREEDOM(1970, Fr.), art d; THINGS OF LIFE, THE(1970, Fr./Ital./Switz.), art d
George Piltz
EBB TIDE(1937); RIDERS OF THE NORTHLAND(1942); DAUGHTER OF THE JUNGLE(1949)
S. Pilyavskaya
SILVER DUST(1953, USSR); HOUSE ON THE FRONT LINE, THE(1963, USSR)
Pimenoff
DARK EYES(1938, Fr.), set d
Serge Pimenoff
DIE GANS VON SEDAN(1962, Fr/Ger.), art d
Hugo Pimental
CASTILIAN, THE(1963, Span./U.S.)
Heleen Pimentel
LITTLE ARK, THE(1972)
Hugo Pimentel
PYRO(1964, U.S./Span.)
The Pimento Twins
RUMBA(1935)
Claire Pimpare
YESTERDAY(1980, Can.); TICKET TO HEAVEN(1981)
Misc. Talkies
THIS TIME FOREVER(1981)
Pims's Comedy Navy
BOB'S YOUR UNCLE(1941, Brit.)
Chris Pin-Martin
RIDE THE MAN DOWN(1952)

Abel Pina
TANGIER(1946); CASBAH(1948); SALOME(1953)
Angel Oliver Pina
GOD FORGIVES—I DON'T!(1969, Ital./Span.), m
Antonio Pina
TANGIER(1946); CASBAH(1948)
Henry Pina
TANGIER(1946); CASBAH(1948); SALOME(1953)
Jerry Pina
CASBAH(1948); SALOME(1953)
Jerry Pina, Jr.
TANGIER(1946)
Lionel Pina
LAW AND DISORDER(1974); DOG DAY AFTERNOON(1975); MARATHON MAN(1976); HERO AT LARGE(1980); FAN, THE(1981); PRINCE OF THE CITY(1981)
Lionel Pina, Jr.
WILLIE AND PHIL(1980)
The Pina Troupe
THEY KNEW WHAT THEY WANTED(1940)
Rostislav Pinaff
SPRING(1948, USSR)
The Pinafores
RIDERS OF THE WHISTLING PINES(1949)
Silvia Pinal
VIRIDIANA(1962, Mex./Span.); EXTERMINATING ANGEL, THE(1967, Mex.); GUNS FOR SAN SEBASTIAN(1968, U.S./Fr./Mex./Ital.); SHARK(1970, U.S./Mex.)
The Pinas
WHO DONE IT?(1942); LOST IN A HAREM(1944)
Mariette Pinchart
LET'S SCARE JESSICA TO DEATH(1971), cos
Ron Pinchbeck
STING OF DEATH(1966)
Edgcumb Pinchon
VIVA VILLA!(1934), w
Edgecumb Pinchon
DANIEL BOONE(1936), w
Bronson Pinchot
RISKY BUSINESS(1983)
1984
BEVERLY HILLS COP(1984); FLAMINGO KID, THE(1984)
Rosamond Pinchot
THREE MUSKETEERS, THE(1935)
Renato Pincicoli
L'AVVENTURA(1960, Ital.)
Renato Pinciroli
MORE THAN A MIRACLE(1967, Ital./Fr.); VOYAGE, THE(1974, Ital.)
Martin Pinckney
ENDLESS LOVE(1981)
Dave Pincus
THESE THIRTY YEARS(1934), d&w
Irving Pincus
TO FIND A MAN(1972), p
Wallace Pindell
OVER 21(1945)
Alex Pinder
WINTER OF OUR DREAMS(1982, Aus.)
Donna Pinder
FINAL TERROR, THE(1983)
Sian Pinder
1984
GIVE MY REGARDS TO BROAD STREET(1984, Brit.)
Bill Pine
ALASKA HIGHWAY(1943), p
Ed Pine
RECKLESS MOMENTS, THE(1949); ERRAND BOY, THE(1961), set d
F. A. E. Pine
Silents
TOM AND HIS PALS(1926), w; CYCLONE OF THE RANGE(1927), w; LIGHTNING LARIATS(1927), w; OUTLAW DOG, THE(1927), w
Frank Pine
GREAT WALDO PEPPER, THE(1975), stunts
Howard B. Pine
BAILOUT AT 43,000(1957), p
Howard Pine
CULT OF THE COBRA(1955), p; MAN FROM BITTER RIDGE, THE(1955), p; PRIVATE WAR OF MAJOR BENSON, THE(1955), p; RUNNING WILD(1955), p; NIGHTMARE(1956), p; BIG CAPER, THE(1957), p; RIDE A CROOKED TRAIL(1958), p; SPEEDTRAP(1978), p
Judy Pine
FEMALE ON THE BEACH(1955)
Larry Pine
HANKY-PANKY(1982); I, THE JURY(1982); Q(1982)
Les Pine
WILD SEED(1965), w; MAN CALLED ADAM, A(1966), w; POPI(1969), w
Lester Pine
CLAUDINE(1974), w
Phil Pine
I SHOT JESSE JAMES(1949); BLACK TUESDAY(1955)
Philip Pine
MY FOOLISH HEART(1949); WILD BLUE YONDER, THE(1952); PHANTOM FROM 10,000 LEAGUES, THE(1956); MEN IN WAR(1957); LOST MISSILE, THE(1958, U.S./Can.)
Misc. Talkies
POSSE FROM HEAVEN(1975), d; POT! PARENTS! POLICE!(1975), d
Phillip E. Pine
DEAD HEAT ON A MERRY-GO-ROUND(1966); PROJECT X(1968)
Phillip Pine
STREET WITH NO NAME, THE(1948); RED LIGHT(1949); SET-UP, THE(1949); INSURANCE INVESTIGATOR(1951); UNDER THE GUN(1951); HOODLUM EM-PIRE(1952); PRICE OF FEAR, THE(1956); DESERT HELL(1958); MURDER BY

CONTRACT(1958); BIG FISHERMAN, THE(1959); BRAINSTORM(1965); HOOK, LINE AND SINKER(1969); CAT ATE THE PARAKEET, THE(1972), a, p, d&w; GLASS HOUSES(1972)
Misc. Talkies
POT! PARENTS! POLICE!(1975); MONEY TO BURN(1981)

Robert Pine
GUNPOINT(1966); MUNSTER, GO HOME(1966); OUT OF SIGHT(1966); YOUNG WARRIORS, THE(1967); COUNTERFEIT KILLER, THE(1968); JOURNEY TO SHILOH(1968); ONE LITTLE INDIAN(1973); BEARS AND I, THE(1974); DAY OF THE LOCUST, THE(1975); EMPIRE OF THE ANTS(1977); APPLE DUMPLING GANG RIDES AGAIN, THE(1979)

Tina Pine
POPI(1969), w; CLAUDINE(1974), w; ON THE RIGHT TRACK(1981), w

Virginia Pine
DOCTOR MONICA(1934); FUGITIVE LADY(1934); WHOLE TOWN'S TALKING, THE(1935)
Misc. Talkies
HOT OFF THE PRESS(1935)

William H. Pine
FLYING BLIND(1941), p; FORCED LANDING(1941), p; NO HANDS ON THE CLOCK(1941), p; I LIVE ON DANGER(1942), p; WILDCAT(1942), p; AERIAL GUNNER(1943), p&d; TORNADO(1943), p; DOUBLE EXPOSURE(1944), p; TAKE IT BIG(1944), p; TOKYO ROSE(1945), p; FEAR IN THE NIGHT(1947), p; SEVEN WERE SAVED(1947), p, d; DYNAMITE(1948), p, d; CAPTAIN CHINA(1949), p; MANHANDLED(1949), p; EAGLE AND THE HAWK, THE(1950), p; LAWLESS, THE(1950), p; TRIPOLI(1950), p; HONG KONG(1951), p; LAST OUTPOST, THE(1951), p; BLAZING FOREST, THE(1952), p; JAMAICA RUN(1953), p; SANGAREE(1953), p; THOSE RED-HEADS FROM SEATTLE(1953), p; TROPIC ZONE(1953), p; VANQUISHED, THE(1953), p; JIVARO(1954), p; FAR HORIZONS, THE(1955), p; HELL'S ISLAND(1955), p; LUCY GALLANT(1955), p; RUN FOR COVER(1955), p

William Pine
POWER DIVE(1941), p; WRECKING CREW(1942), p; MINESWEEPER(1943), p; SUBMARINE ALERT(1943), p; DARK MOUNTAIN(1944), p; GAMBLER'S CHOICE(1944), p; NAVY WAY, THE(1944), p; ONE BODY TOO MANY(1944), p; TIMBER QUEEN(1944), p; FOLLOW THAT WOMAN(1945), p; HIGH POWERED(1945), p; SCARED STIFF(1945), p; HOT CARGO(1946), p; SWAMP FIRE(1946), p, d; THEY MADE ME A KILLER(1946), p; ADVENTURE ISLAND(1947), p; BIG TOWN(1947), p; BIG TOWN AFTER DARK(1947), p; DANGER STREET(1947), p; I COVER BIG TOWN(1947), p; JUNGLE FLIGHT(1947), p; ALBUQUERQUE(1948), p; BIG TOWN SCANDAL(1948), p; DISASTER(1948), p, d; MR. RECKLESS(1948), p; SHAGGY(1948), p; SPEED TO SPARE(1948), p; WATERFRONT AT MIDNIGHT(1948), p; EL PASO(1949), p; SPECIAL AGENT(1949), p; CROSSWINDS(1951), p; PASSAGE WEST(1951), p; CARIBBEAN(1952), p

Guy Pinecoos, Jr.
WHEN THE LEGENDS DIE(1972)

Rosa Maria Pineiro
SANTO CONTRA BLUE DEMON EN LA ATLANTIDA(1968, Mex.)

Philippe Francois Pinel
Silents
ROSITA(1923), w

Enrique Pinella
MIRAGE(1972, Peru), m

Sandrino Pinelli
CONJUGAL BED, THE(1963, Ital.)

T. Pinelli
BULLET FOR STEFANO(1950, Ital.), w

Tullio Pinelli
WITHOUT PITY(1949, Ital.), w; WAYS OF LOVE(1950, Ital./Fr.), w; LA STRADA(1956, Ital.), w; VITELLONI(1956, Ital./Fr.), w; WHITE SHEIK, THE(1956, Ital.), w; NIGHTS OF CABIRIA(1957, Ital.), w; LA DOLCE VITA(1961, Ital./Fr.), w; BOCCACCIO '70(1962/Ital./Fr.), w; SWINDLE, THE(1962, Fr./Ital.), w; STEPPE, THE(1963, Fr./Ital.), w; 8 ½(1963, Ital.), w; JULIET OF THE SPIRITS(1965, Fr./Ital./W.Ger.), w; LOVE A LA CARTE(1965, Ital.), w; THREE FACES OF A WOMAN(1965, Ital.), w; VARIETY LIGHTS(1965, Ital.), w; CLIMAX, THE(1967, Fr., Ital.), w; GALILEO(1968, Ital./Bul.), w; SERAFINO(1970, Fr./Ital.), w; ALFREDO, ALFREDO(1973, Ital.), w; DOWN THE ANCIENT STAIRCASE(1975, Ital.), w

Arthur Wing Pinero
THOSE WERE THE DAYS(1934, Brit.), w; DANDY DICK(1935, Brit.), Clifford Grey; SECOND MRS. TANQUERAY, THE(1952, Brit.), d
Silents
IRIS(1915, Brit.), w; GAY LORD QUEX, THE(1917, Brit.), w; PROFLIGATE, THE(1917, Brit.), w; ENCHANTED COTTAGE, THE(1924), w; ACTRESS, THE(1928), w; HIS HOUSE IN ORDER(1928, Brit.), w

Dadi Pinero
LOOKING UP(1977); FORT APACHE, THE BRONX(1981)
1984
BEAT STREET(1984)

Federico Pinero
HORSE IN THE GRAY FLANNEL SUIT, THE(1968)

Fred Pinero
DEVIL'S SISTERS, THE(1966); DEATH CURSE OF TARTU(1967)

Miguel Pinero
LOOKING UP(1977); SHORT EYES(1977), a, w; TIMES SQUARE(1980); FORT APACHE, THE BRONX(1981); EXPOSED(1983)
1984
ALMOST YOU(1984); ALPHABET CITY(1984)

Richie Pinero
1984
DELIVERY BOYS(1984)

Sir Arthur Wing Pinero
ENCHANTED COTTAGE, THE(1945), w
Silents
AMAZONS, THE(1917), w

Larry Pines
I WANNA HOLD YOUR HAND(1978); HULLABALOO OVER GEORGIE AND BONNIE'S PICTURES(1979, Brit.); FRANCES(1982)

Romain Pines
SUNDAYS AND CYBELE(1962, Fr.), p

Gloria A. Pineyro
HEROINA(1965), ed

Gloria Pineyro
FAT ANGELS(1980, U.S./Span.), ed

An Ping
EXIT THE DRAGON, ENTER THE TIGER(1977, Hong Kong)

Chen Ping
GOLIATHON(1979, Hong Kong)

Ho Ping
MAGNIFICENT CONCUBINE, THE(1964, Hong Kong); LADY GENERAL, THE(1965, Hong Kong)

Poing Ping
MARCO POLO(1962, Fr./Ital.)

Wang Ping
DREAM OF THE RED CHAMBER, THE(1966, Chi.), d; FIVE FINGERS OF DEATH(1973, Hong Kong); SACRED KNIVES OF VENGEANCE, THE(1974, Hong Kong)

Yeh Ping
FIGHT TO THE LAST(1938, Chi.)

Carl Pingatore
PRIME CUT(1972), ed

Mike Pingatore
FABULOUS DORSEYS, THE(1947)

Earl Pingee
ARE THESE OUR CHILDREN?(1931)

Carl Pingitore
FEMALE JUNGLE, THE(1955), ed; RAIDERS OF OLD CALIFORNIA(1957), ed; BUFFALO GUN(1961), ed; BEGUILED, THE(1971), ed; DIRTY HARRY(1971), ed; PLAY MISTY FOR ME(1971), ed; DEADLY TRACKERS(1973), ed; THAT MAN BOLT(1973), ed

Earl M. Pingree
IT HAPPENED ONE NIGHT(1934); MILKY WAY, THE(1936); MURDER WITH PICTURES(1936)

Earl Pingree
DARK STREETS(1929); HOLY TERROR, A(1931); GUILTY AS HELL(1932); MRS. WIGGS OF THE CABBAGE PATCH(1934); THROWBACK, THE(1935); COLLEGE HOLIDAY(1936); LONE WOLF RETURNS, THE(1936)

L. Pinhao
MAN COULD GET KILLED, A(1966)

David Pinheiro
1984
MEMOIRS OF PRISON(1984, Braz.)

Julie Pinheiro
SIGNS OF LIFE(1981, Ger.)

Victor Pinhiero
ALEX AND THE GYPSY(1976)

Maggie Pinhorn
MUMSY, NANNY, SONNY, AND GIRLY(1970, Brit.), art d

Aldo Pini
ANGELA(1955, Ital.); ATTILA(1958, Ital.); ANGEL WORE RED, THE(1960); SWORD OF THE CONQUEROR(1962, Ital.); CAESAR THE CONQUEROR(1963, Ital.); WASTREL, THE(1963, Ital.); HERCULES, SAMSON & ULYSSES(1964, Ital.); TORPEDO BAY(1964, Ital./Fr.); SEVEN SLAVES AGAINST THE WORLD(1965, Ital.)

Enrico Pini
TABLE FOR FIVE(1983)

E. Pinikova
Misc. Silents
JEW AT WAR, A(1931, USSR)

Luis Pinilla
1984
SUCCESS IS THE BEST REVENGE(1984, Brit.)

Jose Maria Pinillo
TEXICAN, THE(1966, U.S./Span.)

Efren C. Pinion
Misc. Talkies
BLIND RAGE(1978), d

Sid Pink
ANGRY RED PLANET, THE(1959), p, w

Sidney Pink
JOURNEY TO THE SEVENTH PLANET(1962, U.S./Swed.), p&d, w; REPTILICUS(1962, U.S./Den.), p&d, w; FINGER ON THE TRIGGER(1965, US/Span.), p&d, w; DRUMS OF TABU, THE(1967, Ital./Span.), p; FICKLE FINGER OF FATE, THE(1967, Span./U.S.), p; FLAME OVER VIETNAM(1967, Span./Ger.), p; TREASURE OF MAKUBA, THE(1967, U.S./Span.), p; WITCH WITHOUT A BROOM, A(1967, U.S./Span.), p; BANG BANG KID, THE(1968 U.S./Span./Ital.), p; MADIGAN'S MILLIONS(1970, Span./Ital), p; MAN FROM O.R.G.Y., THE(1970), p
Misc. Talkies
GIRL OF THE NILE, THE(1967, US/ Ger.), d

Sidney T. Pink
ARE WE CIVILIZED?(1934)

Sidney W. Pink
CASTILIAN, THE(1963, Span./U.S.), p, w; PYRO(1964, U.S./Span.), p, w; OPERATION DELILAH(1966, U.S./Span.), p, w; CHRISTMAS KID, THE(1968, U.S., Span.), p&d

Pink Floyd
MORE(1969, Luxembourg), ph

Craig Pinkard
WANDA NEVADA(1979)

Fred Pinkard
J.D.'S REVENGE(1976); SCOTT JOPLIN(1977)

Josef Pinkava
WISHING MACHINE(1971, Czech.), d, w

Jochen Pinkert
WHY DOES HERR R. RUN AMOK?(1977, Ger.)

Katherine Pinkerton
Silents
NANCY FROM NOWHERE(1922), w

W.W. Pinkerton
RAMPARTS WE WATCH, THE(1940)
Willis Pinkett
FOR LOVE OF IVY(1968); LANDLORD, THE(1970)
Pinkie and Pal
SOMETHING TO SING ABOUT(1937)
Tonya Pinkins
1984
BEAT STREET(1984)
Bill Pinkney
WHO KILLED MARY WHAT'SER NAME?(1971), makeup
John Pinkney
THIRST(1979, Aus.), w
Leon Pinkney
GAMBLER, THE(1974); AARON LOVES ANGELA(1975); CARWASH(1976)
Lyn Pinkney
PERSECUTION AND ASSASSINATION OF JEAN-PAUL MARAT AS PERFORMED BY THE INMATES OF THE ASYLUM OF CHARENTON UNDER THE DIRECTION OF THE MARQUIS DE SADE, THE(1967, Brit.)
Jet Pinkston
DELINQUENTS, THE(1957)
Suzanne Pinkstone
NO BLADE OF GRASS(1970, Brit.)
Lulu Pinkus
MAD MAX(1979, Aus.); THIRST(1979, Aus.); DAY AFTER HALLOWEEN, THE(1981, Aus.)
Pinky and the Killers
YOSAKOI JOURNEY(1970, Jap.)
Peggy Pinnell
1984
LAST NIGHT AT THE ALAMO(1984)
David Pinner
ROBBERY(1967, Brit.)
Dick Pinner
MOB, THE(1951); MONSTER FROM THE OCEAN FLOOR, THE(1954)
Richard Pinner
GIRL ON THE BRIDGE, THE(1951); RED SNOW(1952)
Charles A. Pinney
MOLLY AND LAWLESS JOHN(1972)
Charles Pinney
UP IN THE CELLAR(1970); COLD TURKEY(1971); BIG BAD MAMA(1974)
Clay Pinney
MAN WITH TWO BRAINS, THE(1983), spec eff
Patrick Pinney
1984
TERMINATOR, THE(1984)
Helga Pinnow
MERRY WIVES OF WINDSOR, THE(1966, Aust.), cos; AMERICAN SUCCESS COMPANY, THE(1980), cos
Suzi Pinns
JUBILEE(1978, Brit.), m
Don Pino
PUNISHMENT PARK(1971)
Dominique Pinon
DIVA(1982, Fr.); MOON IN THE GUTTER, THE(1983, Fr./Ital.); RETURN OF MARTIN GUERRE, THE(1983, Fr.)
1984
DREAM ONE(1984, Brit./Fr.); GHOST DANCE(1984, Brit.)
Giuseppe Pinori
CAGLIOSTRO(1975, Ital.), ph
1984
CORRUPT(1984, Ital.), ph
Claude Pinoteau
LOLA MONTES(1955, Fr./Ger.); CROOK, THE(1971, Fr.), w; ANGRY MAN, THE(1979 Fr./Can.), d, w; LA BOUM(1983, Fr.), d, w
Gordon Pinsent
THOMAS CROWN AFFAIR, THE(1968); COLOSSUS: THE FORBIN PROJECT(1969); CHANDLER(1971); BLACULA(1972); ROWDYMAN, THE(1973, Can.), a, w; NEWMAN'S LAW(1974); ONLY GOD KNOWS(1974, Can.); WHO HAS SEEN THE WIND(1980, Can.); SILENCE OF THE NORTH(1981, Can.)
Leah Pinsent
1984
BAY BOY(1984, Can.)
Gordon Pinset
LYDIA(1964, Can.)
David Pinski
SINGING BLACKSMITH(1938), w
Alan Pinson
FROM HERE TO ETERNITY(1953)
Allan Pinson
TIMBUKTU(1959); MR. MAJESTYK(1974)
Allen Pinson
FRENCHMAN'S CREEK(1944); PRACTICALLY YOURS(1944); MASQUERADE IN MEXICO(1945); WONDER MAN(1945); JOAN OF ARC(1948); IN A LONELY PLACE(1950); LORNA DOONE(1951); THUNDER BAY(1953); HELL ON DEVIL'S ISLAND(1957); CRIMSON KIMONO, THE(1959); ADVANCE TO THE REAR(1964); ONCE BEFORE I DIE(1967, U.S./Phil.); WRECKING CREW, THE(1968); MELINDA(1972)
David Pinson
BABES IN TOYLAND(1961)
Henriette Pinson
Silents
NAPOLEON(1927, Fr.), ed
Inga-Maria Pinson
DRIFTER(1975)
Lucille Pinson
NINOTCHKA(1939)

Guy Pintat
RISE OF LOUIS XIV, THE(1970, Fr.)
Danny Pintauro
CUJO(1983)
Gyorgy Pinter
WINTER WIND(1970, Fr./Hung.)
Harold Pinter
GUEST, THE(1963, Brit.), w; PUMPKIN EATER, THE(1964, Brit.), w; SERVANT, THE(1964, Brit.), a, w; QUILLER MEMORANDUM, THE(1966, Brit.), w; ACCIDENT(1967, Brit.), a, w; BIRTHDAY PARTY, THE(1968, Brit.), w; RISE AND RISE OF MICHAEL RIMMER, THE(1970, Brit.); GO-BETWEEN, THE(1971, Brit.), w; HOMECOMING, THE(1973), w; BUTLEY(1974, Brit.), d; LAST TYCOON, THE(1976), w; FRENCH LIEUTENANT'S WOMAN, THE(1981), w; BETRAYAL(1983, Brit.), w
Herbert Pinter
PLUMBER, THE(1980, Aus.), art d; GALLIPOLI(1981, Aus.), art d; YEAR OF LIVING DANGEROUSLY, THE(1982, Aus.), art d
Tomaslav Pinter
STEPPENWOLF(1974), ph
Tomislav Pinter
THREE(1967, Yugo.), ph; I EVEN MET HAPPY GYPSIES(1968, Yugo.), ph; GAMBLERS, THE(1969), ph; MONTENEGRO(1981, Brit./Swed.), ph; TWILIGHT TIME(1983, U.S./Yugo.), ph
Angela Pietro Pinto
SO FINE(1981)
Mercedes Pinto
EL(1955, Mex.), w
Ralph J. Pinto
JENNIFER ON MY MIND(1971)
Stanley Pinto
GUY WHO CAME BACK, THE(1951)
Ernest Pintoff
HARVEY MIDDLEMAN, FIREMAN(1965), d&w, m; GHOSTS, ITALIAN STYLE(1969, Ital./Fr.), w; BLADE(1973), d, w; JAGUAR LIVES(1979), d; LUNCH WAGON(1981), d; ST. HELENS(1981), d
Ernie Pintoff
WHO KILLED MARY WHAT'SER NAME?(1971), d
Pintudi
JEDDA, THE UNCIVILIZED(1956, Aus.)
Margo Pinvidic
CHRISTINA(1974, Can.)
Margot Pinvidic
MEATBALLS(1979, Can.)
Carla Pinza
SWEET LOVE, BITTER(1967)
Ezio Pinza
CARNEGIE HALL(1947); MR. IMPERIUM(1951); STRICTLY DISHONORABLE(1951); TONIGHT WE SING(1953)
Victor Pinzon
BOYS IN COMPANY C, THE(1978, U.S./Hong Kong)
Elith Pio
WHILE THE ATTORNEY IS ASLEEP(1945, Den.)
Misc. Silents
PRESIDENT, THE(1918, Den.)
Lionello Pio Di Savola
MADE IN ITALY(1967, Fr./Ital.)
K. Piontkovskaya
Misc. Silents
IN THE KINGDOM OF OIL AND MILLIONS(1916, USSR)
Andrew Piotrowski
RECESS(1967), w
Minerva Pious
IT'S IN THE BAG(1945); JOE MACBETH(1955); LOVE IN THE AFTERNOON(1957); PINOCCHIO IN OUTER SPACE(1965, U.S./Bel.); SUMMER WISHES, WINTER DREAMS(1973)
Antonio Piovanelli
EYES, THE MOUTH, THE(1982, Ital./Fr.); LEAP INTO THE VOID(1982, Ital.)
Nicola Piovani
N. P.(1971, Ital.), m; EYES, THE MOUTH, THE(1982, Ital./Fr.), m; LEAP INTO THE VOID(1982, Ital.), m; NIGHT OF THE SHOOTING STARS, THE(1982, Ital.), m
Nicolai Piovani
GIRL WITH THE RED HAIR, THE(1983, Neth.), m
Pina Piovani
WOMAN OF ROME(1956, Ital.)
Guido Piovene
MAMBO(1955, Ital.), w; RITA(1963, Fr./Ital.), w
Pip
FREAKS(1932)
Jacqueline Pipard
MILKY WAY, THE(1969, Fr./Ital.), makeup
Anne Piper
NICE GIRL LIKE ME, A(1969, Brit.), w; YES, GIORGIO(1982), w
Bill Piper
SHARK RIVER(1953)
Diana Piper
THREE STOOGES MEET HERCULES, THE(1962)
Evelyn Piper
BUNNY LAKE IS MISSING(1965), w; NANNY, THE(1965, Brit.), w
Fred Piper
GOOD COMPANIONS(1933, Brit.)
Frederick Piper
CROWN VS STEVENS(1936); EVERYTHING IS THUNDER(1936, Brit.); FAME(1936, Brit.); WHERE THERE'S A WILL(1936, Brit); FEATHER YOUR NEST(1937, Brit.); NON-STOP NEW YORK(1937, Brit.); OH, MR. PORTER!(1937, Brit.); SABOTAGE(1937, Brit.); TWO OF US, THE(1938, Brit.); YOUNG AND INNOCENT(1938, Brit.); JAMAICA INN(1939, Brit.); SECRET FOUR, THE(1940, Brit.); INVADERS, THE,(1941); IN WHICH WE SERVE(1942, Brit.); NINE MEN(1943, Brit.); CHAMPAGNE CHARLIE(1944, Brit.); FIDDLERS THREE(1944, Brit.); IT HAPPENED ONE SUNDAY(1944, Brit.); JOHNNY FRENCHMAN(1946, Brit.); LOVES OF JOANNA GODDEN, THE(1947, Brit.); MASTER OF BANKDAM, THE(1947, Brit.); SAN DEMETRIO, LONDON(1947, Brit.); EASY MONEY(1948, Brit.); ESCAPE(1948, Brit.); FLY AWAY

PETER(1948, Brit.); LOOK BEFORE YOU LOVE(1948, Brit.); OCTOBER MAN, THE(1948, Brit.); VOTE FOR HUGGETT(1948, Brit.); DON'T EVER LEAVE ME(1949, Brit.); IT ALWAYS RAINS ON SUNDAY(1949, Brit.); IT'S NOT CRICKET(1949, Brit.); MY BROTHER'S KEEPER(1949, Brit.); PASSPORT TO PIMLICO(1949, Brit.); BLUE LAMP, THE(1950, Brit.); HUE AND CRY(1950, Brit.); PINK STRING AND SEALING WAX(1950, Brit.); LAVENDER HILL MOB, THE(1951, Brit.); BRANDY FOR THE PARSON(1952, Brit.); STRANGER IN BETWEEN, THE(1952, Brit.); I'LL GET YOU(1953, Brit.); MURDER ON MONDAY(1953, Brit.); SLASHER, THE(1953, Brit.); FUSS OVER FEATHERS(1954, Brit.); LEASE OF LIFE(1954, Brit.); RAINBOW JACKET, THE(1954, Brit.); DOCTOR AT SEA(1955, Brit.); BIRTHDAY PRESENT, THE(1957, Brit.); DOCTOR AT LARGE(1957, Brit.); MAN IN THE ROAD, THE(1957, Brit.); NOVEL AFFAIR, A(1957, Brit.); SECOND FIDDLE(1957, Brit.); SUSPENDED ALIBI(1957, Brit.); ALL AT SEA(1958, Brit.); DUNKIRK(1958, Brit.); DAY THEY ROBBED THE BANK OF ENGLAND, THE(1960, Brit.); DEAD LUCKY(1960, Brit.); FRIGHTENED CITY, THE(1961, Brit.); MONSTER OF HIGHGATE PONDS, THE(1961, Brit.); ONLY TWO CAN PLAY(1962, Brit.); PIPER'S TUNE, THE(1962, Brit.); RETURN OF A STRANGER(1962, Brit.); WHAT A CARVE UP!(1962, Brit.); ONE WAY PENDULUM(1965, Brit.); WOMAN WHO WOULDN'T DIE, THE(1965, Brit.); RICOCHET(1966, Brit.); VIOLENT MOMENT(1966, Brit.)

Fredrick Piper
STRANGLER, THE(1941, Brit.); HE WHO RIDES A TIGER(1966, Brit.)

Hans Piper
QUESTION 7(1961, U.S./Ger.)

Jacki Piper
CARRY ON LOVING(1970, Brit.); CARRY ON UP THE JUNGLE(1970, Brit.); DOCTOR IN TROUBLE(1970, Brit.)

Kelly Piper
MANIAC(1980); VICE SQUAD(1982)

Nonnie Piper
BITTER SPRINGS(1950, Aus.)

Roberto Piperio
PAL JOEY(1957)

Giacomo Piperno
SACCO AND VANZETTI(1971, Ital./Fr.)

J. Henry Piperno
ENTER INSPECTOR DUVAL(1961, Brit.), w; AMBUSH IN LEOPARD STREET(1962, Brit.), d; BREATH OF LIFE(1962, Brit.), d&w

Hermina Pipinic
STEPPE, THE(1963, Fr./Ital.); FLAMING FRONTIER(1968, Ger./Yugo.); SEVENTH CONTINENT, THE(1968, Czech./Yugo.)

Nino Pipitone
MADAME SPY(1942); SUBMARINE RAIDER(1942); THEY GOT ME COVERED(1943); MASK OF DIMITRIOS, THE(1944); WONDER MAN(1945); MONSIEUR BEAUCAIRE(1946); ANNIE GET YOUR GUN(1950); TOAST OF NEW ORLEANS, THE(1950)

Nino Pipitone, Jr.
HEAVEN CAN WAIT(1943); SONG OF BERNADETTE, THE(1943); THEY WERE EXPENDABLE(1945)

Nino Pipitone, Sr.
SONG OF BERNADETTE, THE(1943)

Nino Pipitoni
ARCH OF TRIUMPH(1948)

Al Pipkin
JAWS 3-D(1983)

Pipo
YO YO(1967, Fr.)

Pipolo
FASCIST, THE(1965, Ital.), w; HOURS OF LOVE, THE(1965, Ital.), w; WAR ITALIAN STYLE(1967, Ital.), w; KISS THE OTHER SHEIK(1968, Fr./Ital.), w; THREE NIGHTS OF LOVE(1969, Ital.), w

Franco Castellano Pipolo
EIGHTEEN IN THE SUN(1964, Ital.), w

G. Pipolo
TWELVE-HANDED MEN OF MARS, THE(1964, Ital./Span.), d&w

Pipolo [Giuseppe Moccia]
MY WIFE'S ENEMY(1967, Ital.), w

Franco Castellano, Pipolo [Guiseppe Moccia]
CRAZY DESIRE(1964, Ital.), w

Castellano Pipolu
DR. GOLDFOOT AND THE GIRL BOMBS(1966, Ital.), w

Eulalio Gonzalez Piporro
LA NAVE DE LOS MONSTRUOS(1959, Mex.)

Pippin
Silents
EAST LYNNE(1913, Brit.)

Concha Marquez Piquer
1984
YELLOW HAIR AND THE FORTRESS OF GOLD(1984)

Francisco Piquer
SOUND OF HORROR(1966, Span.)

Odette Piquet
THIEF OF PARIS, THE(1967, Fr./Ital.); ZITA(1968, Fr.); BORSALINO(1970, Fr.)

Luigi Pirandello
AS YOU DESIRE ME(1932), w; THIS LOVE OF OURS(1945), w; TIMES GONE BY(1953, Ital.), w; VERY HANDY MAN, A(1966, Fr./Ital.), w; VOYAGE, THE(1974, Ital.), w

Pinuccio Pirazzoli
BINGO BONGO(1983, Ital.), m

Antonio J. Pires
HOUSE ON 92ND STREET, THE(1945)

Gloria Pires
1984
MEMOIRS OF PRISON(1984, Braz.)

Miriam Pires
1984
GABRIELA(1984, Braz.)

Veloso Pires
KILL OR BE KILLED(1950)

Antonio Piretti
VERY HANDY MAN, A(1966, Fr./Ital.)

Katiuscia Piretti
MAFIOSO(1962, Ital.)

Mary Pirie
LOST AND FOUND(1979); FISH HAWK(1981, Can.)

Ivan Piriev
SIX P.M.(1946, USSR), d; SYMPHONY OF LIFE(1949, USSR), d

Leo Pirinkoff
Misc. Silents
MIDNIGHT AT MAXIM'S(1915)

Ivan Piriov
COUNTRY BRIDE(1938, USSR), d

Sal Piro
FAME(1980)

A. Pirogov
BORIS GODUNOV(1959, USSR)

L. Pirogov
DUEL, THE(1964, USSR)

Vittorio Pirone
PRIVATE ANGELO(1949, Brit.), m

Simeon Pironkov
PEACH THIEF, THE(1969, Bulgaria), m

Johnnie Pironne
HIGH SCHOOL(1940)

Junior Pironne
LOTUS LADY(1930)

Johnny Pironne, Jr.
ROAD DEMON(1938)

Dusan Piros
FRAULEIN DOKTOR(1969, Ital./Yugo.), spec eff

Robert Pirosh
WINNING TICKET, THE(1935), w; DAY AT THE RACES, A(1937), w; QUARTERBACK, THE(1940), w; NIGHT OF JANUARY 16TH(1941), w; I MARRIED A WITCH(1942), w; RINGS ON HER FINGERS(1942), w; SONG OF THE ISLANDS(1942), w; UP IN ARMS(1944), w; MAN ABOUT TOWN(1947, Fr.), w; BATTLEGROUND(1949), w; GO FOR BROKE(1951), d&w; WASHINGTON STORY(1952), d&w; VALLEY OF THE KINGS(1954), d, w; GIRL RUSH, THE(1955), d, w; SPRING REUNION(1957), d, w; HELL IS FOR HEROES(1962), w; GATHERING OF EAGLES, A(1963), w; WHAT'S SO BAD ABOUT FEELING GOOD?(1968), w

R. Pirozhenko
SONG OF THE FOREST(1963, USSR)

James Pirrie
NON-STOP NEW YORK(1937, Brit.); RHYTHM RACKETEER(1937, Brit.); NIGHT ALONE(1938, Brit.); ESCAPE TO DANGER(1943, Brit.); THUNDER ROCK(1944, Brit.)

Ugo Pirro
FIVE BRANDED WOMEN(1960), w; WARRIORS FIVE(1962), w; HUNCHBACK OF ROME, THE(1963, Ital.), w; VERONA TRIAL, THE(1963, Ital.), w; NAVAJO JOE(1967, Ital./Span.), w; WAKE UP AND DIE(1967, Fr./Ital.), w; WE STILL KILL THE OLD WAY(1967, Ital.), w; DAY OF THE OWL, THE(1968, Ital./Fr.), w; SARDINIA: RANSOM(1968, Ital.), w; WILD EYE, THE(1968, Ital.), w; MAFIA(1969, Fr./Ital.), w; INVESTIGATION OF A CITIZEN ABOVE SUSPICION(1970, Ital.), w; BATTLE OF THE NERETVA(1971, Yugo./Ital./Ger.), w; GARDEN OF THE FINZI-CONTINIS, THE(1976, Ital./Ger.), w; GOODNIGHT, LADIES AND GENTLEMEN(1977, Ital.), d&w; INHERITANCE, THE(1978, Ital.), w

Joe Pirrone
Silents
WARMING UP(1928)

John Pirrone
LOVE IS ON THE AIR(1937); PENROD AND SAM(1937); PENROD AND HIS TWIN BROTHER(1938)

Johnnie Pirrone
SPEED TO BURN(1938)

Johnny Pirrone
I CONQUER THE SEA(1936)

Johnnie Pirrone, Jr.
WINNER TAKE ALL(1939)

Andrew J. Pirtle
WALKING TALL(1973)

Carla Pisacane
MORE THAN A MIRACLE(1967, Ital./Fr.)

Carlo Pisacane
BIG DEAL ON MADONNA STREET, THE(1960); FIASCO IN MILAN(1963, Fr./Ital.); LAZARILLO(1963, Span.); PASSIONATE THIEF, THE(1963, Ital.); TIGER OF THE SEVEN SEAS(1964, Fr./Ital.); DEATH RIDES A HORSE(1969, Ital.)

Frank Pisani
1984
HARD TO HOLD(1984)

Nando Pisani
KILL BABY KILL(1966, Ital.), p

Remo Pisani
NIGHT OF EVIL(1962); LAST OF THE SECRET AGENTS?, THE(1966)

Berto Pisano
KILL! KILL! KILL!(1972, Fr./Ger./Ital./Span.), m

Franco Pisano
SUPERARGO VERSUS DIABOLICUS(1966, Ital./Span.), m; WEB OF VIOLENCE(1966, Ital./Span.), m

Isabel Pisano
SAVAGE PAMPAS(1967, Span./Arg.)

Rosita Pisano
ANNA(1951, Ital.)

Vittorina Pisano
BANDITS OF ORGOSOLO(1964, Ital.)

Anna Pisarikova
MOST BEAUTIFUL AGE, THE(1970, Czech.)

Carlo Piscane
PAISAN(1948, Ital.); VERY HANDY MAN, A(1966, Fr./Ital.)

Herta Pischinger
CASTLE, THE(1969, Ger.), art d; SOMETHING FOR EVERYONE(1970), set d; CRIME AND PASSION(1976, U.S., Ger.), art d; LITTLE NIGHT MUSIC, A(1977, Aust./U.S./Ger.), art d
Hertha Pischinger
PEDESTRIAN, THE(1974, Ger.), set d
Otto Pischinger
AS THE SEA RAGES(1960 Ger.), art d; TURKISH CUCUMBER, THE(1963, Ger.), art d; CASTLE, THE(1969, Ger.), art d; SOMETHING FOR EVERYONE(1970), art d; ROMANCE OF A HORSE THIEF(1971), art d
Adriano Pischiutta
FELLINI SATYRICON(1969, Fr./Ital.), spec eff; MAN OF LA MANCHA(1972), spec eff; ROMA(1972, Ital./Fr.), spec eff
Joe Piscopo
1984
JOHNNY DANGEROUSLY(1984)
Gino Piserchio
LOVELY WAY TO DIE, A(1968)
Paul Pisget
FACE OF TERROR(1964, Span.)
Marie-France Pisier
LOVE AT TWENTY(1963, Fr./Ital./Jap./Pol./Ger.); TRANS-EUROP-EXPRESS(1968, Fr.); STOLEN KISSES(1969, Fr.); CELINE AND JULIE GO BOATING(1974, Fr.), a, w; BAROCCO(1976, Fr.); COUSIN, COUSINE(1976, Fr.); OTHER SIDE OF MIDNIGHT, THE(1977); BRONTE SISTERS, THE(1979, Fr.); FRENCH POSTCARDS(1979); LOVE ON THE RUN(1980, Fr.), a, w; CHANEL SOLITAIRE(1981)
Marie-Frances Pisier
ACE OF ACES(1982, Fr./Ger.)
Litz Pisk
ISADORA(1968, Brit.), ch
Juan Pison
LADY DOCTOR, THE(1963, Fr./Ital./Span.), ed
Ed Pisoni
ENDLESS LOVE(1981), art d
Edward Pisoni
CRUISING(1980), art d; PRINCE OF THE CITY(1981), art d; DEATHTRAP(1982), art d; VERDICT, THE(1982), prod d; KING OF COMEDY, THE(1983), art d
1984
SLAYGROUND(1984, Brit.), art d
Larry Pisoni
POPEYE(1980)
Pascal Pistacio
ENTRE NOUS(1983, Fr.)
Pistafilm
ONE PLUS ONE(1961, Can.), anim
Doris Pistek
CARMEN, BABY(1967, Yugo./Ger.)
Theo Pistek
Misc. Silents
EROTIKON(1929, Czech.)
Theodor Pistek
MERRY WIVES, THE(1940, Czech.); DEATH OF TARZAN, THE(1968, Czech), cos
1984
AMADEUS(1984), cos
Misc. Silents
SUCH IS LIFE(1929, Czech)
Carl Pistilli
1984
BROADWAY DANNY ROSE(1984)
Luigi Pistilli
FOR A FEW DOLLARS MORE(1967, Ital./Ger./Span.); GOOD, THE BAD, AND THE UGLY, THE(1967, Ital./Span.); WE STILL KILL THE OLD WAY(1967, Ital.); DEATH RIDES A HORSE(1969, Ital.); SWEET BODY OF DEBORAH, THE(1969, Ital./Fr.); DEAD OF SUMMER(1970 Ital./Fr.); LADY OF MONZA, THE(1970, Ital.); MACHINE GUN McCAIN(1970, Ital.); EAGLE OVER LONDON(1973, Ital.); TWITCH OF THE DEATH NERVE(1973, Ital.); COLD SWEAT(1974, Ital., Fr.); TORMENTED, THE(1978, Ital.)
Goffredo Pistoni
DUCK, YOU SUCKER!(1972, Ital.)
Elisabeth Pistorio
ONE SINGS, THE OTHER DOESN'T(1977, Fr.), ed
Mario Pisu
COSSACKS, THE(1960, It.); 8 ½(1963, Ital.); ORGANIZER, THE(1964, Fr./Ital./Yugo.); JULIET OF THE SPIRITS(1965, Fr./Ital./W.Ger.); MYTH, THE(1965, Ital.); JOHNNY BANCO(1969, Fr./Ital./Ger.)
Raffaele Pisu
ITALIANO BRAVA GENTE(1965, Ital./USSR); WEEKEND, ITALIAN STYLE(1967, Fr./Ital./Span.)
Aurora Pita
BIG BOODLE, THE(1957)
Robert Pitack
SUSIE STEPS OUT(1946), ph
Paol Pitagora
BLOOD IN THE STREETS(1975, Ital./Fr.)
Paola Pitagora
LA VIACCIA(1962, Fr./Ital.); FIST IN HIS POCKET(1968, Ital.); GIRL WHO COULDN'T SAY NO, THE(1969, Ital.); IN SEARCH OF GREGORY(1970, Brit./Ital.); PSYCHOUT FOR MURDER(1971, Arg./Ital.); SERPENT, THE(1973, Fr./Ital./Ger.)
Manohar Pitale
GANDHI(1982)
Gustavo Pitaluga
VIRIDIANA(1962, Mex./Span.), md
Antonio Pitanga
TROPICS(1969, Ital.)
Daniele Pitani
CALTIKI, THE IMMORTAL MONSTER(1959, Ital.); VOYAGE, THE(1974, Ital.)
Anna Pitasova
MAN FROM THE FIRST CENTURY, THE(1961, Czech.)

Veerapol Pitavan
HOT POTATO(1976)
Jack Pitcairn
JOURNEY'S END(1930)
Silents
WESTERN FIREBRANDS(1921)
George Pitcher
GLORY AT SEA(1952, Brit.), p; IT'S NEVER TOO LATE(1958, Brit.), p; LAW AND DISORDER(1958, Brit.), p; WHIRLPOOL(1959, Brit.), p; STORY OF DAVID, A(1960, Brit.), p; DAY OF THE TRIFFIDS, THE(1963), p
Julie Pitcher
STOP THE WORLD-I WANT TO GET OFF(1966, Brit.)
Dean Pitchford
1984
FOOTLOOSE(1984), w
Scott Pitcock
TAKING TIGER MOUNTAIN(1983, U.S./Welsh)
Wensley Pithey
DULCIMER STREET(1948, Brit.); MARK OF CAIN, THE(1948, Brit.); GUILT IS MY SHADOW(1950, Brit.); FATHER'S DOING FINE(1952, Brit.); SCOTLAND YARD INSPECTOR(1952, Brit.); ISN'T LIFE WONDERFUL!(1953, Brit.); TITFIELD THUNDERBOLT, THE(1953, Brit.); WOMAN'S ANGLE, THE(1954, Brit.); YOU CAN'T ESCAPE(1955, Brit.); TIGER IN THE SMOKE(1956, Brit.); DOCTOR AT LARGE(1957, Brit.); LONG HAUL, THE(1957, Brit.); MEN OF SHERWOOD FOREST(1957, Brit.); HELL DRIVERS(1958, Brit.); KILL ME TOMORROW(1958, Brit.); MAKE MINE MINK(1960, Brit.); SNOWBALL(1960, Brit.); PURE HELL OF ST. TRINIAN'S, THE(1961, Brit.); BOYS, THE(1962, Brit.); IMMORAL CHARGE(1962, Brit.); BARBER OF STAMFORD HILL, THE(1963, Brit.); KNACK ... AND HOW TO GET IT, THE(1965, Brit.); OLIVER!(1968, Brit.); OH! WHAT A LOVELY WAR(1969, Brit.)
Anthony Pitillo
TALES OF ORDINARY MADNESS(1983, Ital.)
Robert Pitkin
Misc. Talkies
STAIRWAY FOR A STAR(1947)
Waldo Pitkin
PANIC IN THE STREETS(1950)
Walter B. Pitkin
LIFE BEGINS AT 40(1935), w
Noam Pitlik
HALLELUJAH TRAIL, THE(1965); FORTUNE COOKIE, THE(1966); FITZWILLY(1967); YOUNG WARRIORS, THE(1967); BIG BOUNCE, THE(1969); DOWNHILL RACER(1969); 1,000 PLANE RAID, THE(1969); FRONT PAGE, THE(1974)
Misc. Talkies
FADE-IN(1968)
Robert Pitman
REMEMBRANCE(1982, Brit.)
Ludmilla Pitoeff
WEEKEND AT THE WALDORF(1945)
Mila Pitoeff
WHIRLWIND OF PARIS(1946, Fr.)
Sacha Pitoeff
ANASTASIA(1956); DOLL, THE(1962, Fr.); LAST YEAR AT MARIENBAD(1962, Fr./Ital.); PRIZE, THE(1963); LADY L(1965, Fr./Ital.); IS PARIS BURNING?(1966, U.S./Fr.); IMMORAL MOMENT, THE(1967, Fr.); NIGHT OF THE GENERALS, THE(1967, Brit./Fr.); CATCH ME A SPY(1971, Brit./Fr.); INFERNO(1980, Ital.)
Svetlana Pitoeff
ABUSED CONFIDENCE(1938, Fr.)
Cynthia Piton
EDDIE MACON'S RUN(1983)
Anne Pitoniak
SURVIVORS, THE(1983)
1984
OLD ENOUGH(1984)
Lou Pitoscia
1984
MRS. SOFFEL(1984)
Riccardo Pitrazzi
1984
WARRIORS OF THE WASTELAND(1984, Ital.), stunts
Felix Pitre
1984
POPE OF GREENWICH VILLAGE, THE(1984)
Gina Marie Pitrello
1984
THIS IS SPINAL TAP(1984)
Pierre Pitrou
1984
THREE CROWNS OF THE SAILOR(1984, Fr.), set d
V. Pitsek
SUN SHINES FOR ALL, THE(1961, USSR); LAST GAME, THE(1964, USSR); MAGIC WEAVER, THE(1965, USSR); FATHER OF A SOLDIER(1966, USSR)
Allen Pitt
NARCOTICS STORY, THE(1958)
Archie Pitt
SALLY IN OUR ALLEY(1931, Brit.), w; LOOKING ON THE BRIGHT SIDE(1932, Brit.), w; DANNY BOY(1934, Brit.), a, w; BARNACLE BILL(1935, Brit.), a, w; EXCUSE MY GLOVE(1936, Brit.)
Arthur Pitt
Misc. Talkies
SUNDANCE CASSIDY AND BUTCH THE KID(1975), d; CONVOY BUDDIES(1977), d
Misc. Silents
HOBSON'S CHOICE(1920, Brit.)
Bruce Pitt
PASSIONATE SUMMER(1959, Brit.)
Charles Pitt
SKATETOWN, U.S.A.(1979)
Misc. Talkies
KING FRAT(1979)

Dale Pitt
CONSPIRACY OF HEARTS(1960, Brit.), w
Ingrid Pitt
SOUND OF HORROR(1966, Span.); WHERE EAGLES DARE(1968, Brit.); VAMPIRE LOVERS, THE(1970, Brit.); HOUSE THAT DRIPPED BLOOD, THE(1971, Brit.); COUNTESS DRACULA(1972, Brit.); WICKER MAN, THE(1974, Brit.); FINAL OPTION, THE(1983, Brit.)
Misc. Talkies
OMEGANS, THE(1968)
John Pitt
PASSING STRANGER, THE(1954, Brit.)
Nini Pitt
HAUNTING OF M, THE(1979)
Norman Pitt
WHAT THE BUTLER SAW(1950, Brit.); STRICTLY CONFIDENTIAL(1959, Brit.); FRENCH DRESSING(1964, Brit.); OLIVER!(1968, Brit.); ONE MORE TIME(1970, Brit.)
Peter Pitt
DIAMOND SAFARI(1958), ed; MENACE IN THE NIGHT(1958, Brit.), ed; STRICTLY CONFIDENTIAL(1959, Brit.), ed; YOUNG, WILLING AND EAGER(1962, Brit.), ed; GREAT ARMORED CAR SWINDLE, THE(1964), ed; PLEASURE LOVERS, THE(1964, Brit.), ed; MAKE MINE A MILLION(1965, Brit.), ed; HORROR HOUSE(1970, Brit.), ed; WARM DECEMBER, A(1973, Brit.), ed
Ray Pitt
DANGEROUS SECRETS(1938, Brit.), ed; I MARRIED A SPY(1938), ed; LET'S BE FAMOUS(1939, Brit.), ed; THERE AIN'T NO JUSTICE(1939, Brit.), ed; LET GEORGE DO IT(1940, Brit.), ed; SALOON BAR(1940, Brit.), ed; SPARE A COPPER(1940, Brit.), ed; THREE COCKEYED SAILORS(1940, Brit.), ed; BLACK SHEEP OF WHITEHALL, THE(1941 Brit.), ed; PROUD VALLEY, THE(1941, Brit.), ed; NEXT OF KIN(1942, Brit.), ed; GUNMAN HAS ESCAPED, A(1948, Brit.), ed
William Pitt
CASEY'S SHADOW(1978)
Robert Pittack
PENNIES FROM HEAVEN(1936), ph; GIRL FROM SCOTLAND YARD, THE(1937), ph; MIDNIGHT MADONNA(1937), ph; MIND YOUR OWN BUSINESS(1937), ph; MEET DR. CHRISTIAN(1939), ph; KIT CARSON(1940), ph; ALL-AMERICAN CO-ED(1941), ph; TANKS A MILLION(1941), ph; BROOKLYN ORCHID(1942), ph; DEVIL WITH HITLER, THE(1942), ph; DUDES ARE PRETTY PEOPLE(1942), ph; HAY FOOT(1942), ph; THAT NAZTY NUISANCE(1943), ph; YANKS AHOY(1943), ph; GOIN' TO TOWN(1944), ph; I'M FROM ARKANSAS(1944), ph; THAT'S MY BABY(1944), ph; VAMPIRE'S GHOST, THE(1945), ph; LITTLE IODINE(1946), ph; QUEEN OF THE AMAZONS(1947), ph; MAD WEDNESDAY(1950), ph; WACO(1966), ph
Robert W. Pittack
STRANGE IMPERSONATION(1946), ph; STORK BITES MAN(1947), ph; YANKEE FAKIR(1947), ph
Bob Pittard
DEVIL AND DANIEL WEBSTER, THE(1941); HENRY ALDRICH FOR PRESIDENT(1941); LIFE BEGINS FOR ANDY HARDY(1941); MAGNIFICENT AMBERSONS, THE(1942)
Eric Pittard
GUNS(1980, Fr.), ph
Robert Pittard
ROAR OF THE PRESS(1941); ANDY HARDY'S DOUBLE LIFE(1942); KEEPER OF THE FLAME(1942)
Elsie Pittas
ELECTRA(1962, Gr.)
Mike Pittel
ADDING MACHINE, THE(1969), set d
Mel Pittenger
THOSE LIPS, THOSE EYES(1980)
Carl C. Pitti
HIGH PLAINS DRIFTER(1973)
Carl Pitti
OF MICE AND MEN(1939); BILLY THE KID(1941); BANDIT QUEEN(1950); LAWLESS BREED, THE(1952); WOMAN THEY ALMOST LYNCHED, THE(1953); TRIBUTE TO A BADMAN(1956); GUN GLORY(1957); HALLELUJAH TRAIL, THE(1965)
Giuliana Pitti
SCHOOLGIRL DIARY(1947, Ital.)
Karla Pitti
WHOSE LIFE IS IT ANYWAY?(1981)
Paola Pitti
SECRET SEVEN, THE(1966, Ital./Span.)
William Pittinger
Silents
GENERAL, THE(1927), w
Donald Pittman
EMIL(1938, Brit.)
Eliana Pittman
WILD PACK, THE(1972)
Mary Virginia Pittman
CURIOUS FEMALE, THE(1969)
Monte Pittman
ENFORCER, THE(1951); OPERATION SECRET(1952)
Montgomery Pittman
UNTAMED WOMEN(1952); COME NEXT SPRING(1956), w; SLIM CARTER(1957), w; TARZAN AND THE LOST SAFARI(1957, Brit.), w; MONEY, WOMEN AND GUNS(1958), w
Monty Pittman
G.I. JANE(1951)
Richard Pittman
SHAFT'S BIG SCORE(1972)
Thomas Pittman
APACHE TERRITORY(1958); PROUD REBEL, THE(1958)
Tom Pittman
BERNARDINE(1957); BLACK PATCH(1957); NO TIME TO BE YOUNG(1957); TRUE STORY OF JESSE JAMES, THE(1957); WAY TO THE GOLD, THE(1957); YOUNG STRANGER, THE(1957); HIGH SCHOOL BIG SHOT(1959); VERBOTEN!(1959); INVASION OF THE BEE GIRLS(1973)

Frank Pitto
BLOOD FEAST(1976, Ital.), w
Michael Pittock
WHERE THE BULLETS FLY(1966, Brit.), w
Joseph Pittoors
PROVIDENCE(1977, Fr.)
Fabio Pittorru
WEEKEND MURDERS, THE(1972, Ital.), w; LAST DAYS OF MUSSOLINI(1974, Ital.), w
Fabio Pittoru
NIGHT EVELYN CAME OUT OF THE GRAVE, THE(1973, Ital.), w
Charles Pitts
HARDLY WORKING(1981)
Charles W. Pitts
Misc. Talkies
MISS LESLIE'S DOLLS(1972)
Clay Pitts
I DRINK YOUR BLOOD(1971), m&md
Ella Pitts
Misc. Silents
LADY IN THE LIBRARY, THE(1917)
Juanita Pitts
Misc. Talkies
IT HAPPENED IN HARLEM(1945)
Randolph Pitts
1984
SCARRED(1984)
Tony Pitts
LOOKS AND SMILES(1982, Brit.)
ZaSu Pitts
SINS OF THE FATHERS(1928); ARGYLE CASE, THE(1929); DUMMY, THE(1929); HER PRIVATE LIFE(1929); LOCKED DOOR, THE(1929); OH, YEAH!(1929); PARIS(1929); SQUALL, THE(1929); THIS THING CALLED LOVE(1929); TWIN BEDS(1929); DEVIL'S HOLIDAY, THE(1930); FREE LOVE(1930); HONEY(1930); LITTLE ACCIDENT(1930); LOTTERY BRIDE, THE(1930); MONTE CARLO(1930); NO, NO NANETTE(1930); PASSION FLOWER(1930); SIN TAKES A HOLIDAY(1930); SQUEALER, THE(1930); WAR NURSE(1930); BAD SISTER(1931); BEYOND VICTORY(1931); FINN AND HATTIE(1931); GUARDSMAN, THE(1931); PENROD AND SAM(1931); RIVER'S END(1931); SECRET WITNESS, THE(1931); SEED(1931); WOMAN OF EXPERIENCE, A(1931); BACK STREET(1932); BLONDIE OF THE FOLLIES(1932); BROKEN LULLABY(1932); CROOKED CIRCLE(1932); DESTRY RIDES AGAIN(1932); IS MY FACE RED?(1932); MADISON SQUARE GARDEN(1932); MAKE ME A STAR(1932); ONCE IN A LIFETIME(1932); ROAR OF THE DRAGON(1932); SHOPWORN(1932); STEADY COMPANY(1932); STRANGERS OF THE EVENING(1932); TRIAL OF VIVIENNE WARE, THE(1932); UNEXPECTED FATHER(1932); VANISHING FRONTIER, THE(1932); WESTWARD PASSAGE(1932); AGGIE APPLEBY, MAKER OF MEN(1933); HELLO SISTER!(1933); HER FIRST MATE(1933); LOVE, HONOR, AND OH BABY!(1933); MEET THE BARON(1933); MR. SKITCH(1933); OUT ALL NIGHT(1933); PROFESSIONAL SWEETHEART(1933); THEY JUST HAD TO GET MARRIED(1933); DAMES(1934); GAY BRIDE, THE(1934); LOVE BIRDS(1934); MEANEST GAL IN TOWN, THE(1934); MRS. WIGGS OF THE CABBAGE PATCH(1934); PRIVATE SCANDAL(1934); SING AND LIKE IT(1934); THEIR BIG MOMENT(1934); THREE ON A HONEYMOON(1934); TWO ALONE(1934); AFFAIR OF SUSAN(1935); GOING HIGHBROW(1935); HOT TIP(1935); RUGGLES OF RED GAP(1935); SHE GETS HER MAN(1935); SPRING TONIC(1935); MAD HOLIDAY(1936); PLOT THICKENS, THE(1936); SING ME A LOVE SONG(1936); THIRTEEN HOURS BY AIR(1936); FORTY NAUGHTY GIRLS(1937); MERRY COMES TO STAY(1937, Brit.); WANTED(1937, Brit.); 52ND STREET(1937); ETERNALLY YOURS(1939); LADY'S FROM KENTUCKY, THE(1939); MICKEY, THE KID(1939); NAUGHTY BUT NICE(1939); NURSE EDITH CAVELL(1939); IT ALL CAME TRUE(1940); NO, NO NANETTE(1940); BROADWAY LIMITED(1941); MEXICAN SPITFIRE'S BABY(1941); WEEKEND FOR THREE(1941); BASHFUL BACHELOR, THE(1942); MEET THE MOB(1942); MEXICAN SPITFIRE AT SEA(1942); TISH(1942); LET'S FACE IT(1943); BREAKFAST IN HOLLYWOOD(1946); PERFECT MARRIAGE, THE(1946); LIFE WITH FATHER(1947); FRANCIS(1949); DENVER AND RIO GRANDE(1952); FRANCIS JOINS THE WACS(1954); THIS COULD BE THE NIGHT(1957); TEENAGE MILLIONAIRE(1961); IT'S A MAD, MAD, MAD, MAD WORLD(1963); THRILL OF IT ALL, THE(1963)
Misc. Talkies
THEIR MAD MOMENT(1931)
Silents
MODERN MUSKETEER, A(1917); REBECCA OF SUNNYBROOK FARM(1917); GOOD NIGHT, PAUL(1918); AS THE SUN WENT DOWN(1919); POOR RELATIONS(1919); PATSY(1921); YOUTH TO YOUTH(1922); POOR MEN'S WIVES(1923); SOULS FOR SALE(1923); THREE WISE FOOLS(1923); DAUGHTERS OF TO-DAY(1924); GOLDFISH, THE(1924); LEGEND OF HOLLYWOOD, THE(1924); GREAT LOVE, THE(1925); GREED(1925); LAZYBONES(1925); PRETTY LADIES(1925); WAGES FOR WIVES(1925); EARLY TO WED(1926); WHAT HAPPENED TO JONES(1926); CASEY AT THE BAT(1927); OLD SHOES(1927); WEDDING MARCH, THE(1927); WIFE SAVERS(1928); 13 WASHINGTON SQUARE(1928)
Misc. Silents
LITTLE PRINCESS, THE(1917); SOCIETY SENSATION, A(1918); BETTER TIMES(1919); OTHER HALF, THE(1919); BRIGHT SKIES(1920); HEART OF TWENTY, THE(1920); SEEING IT THROUGH(1920); FOR THE DEFENSE(1922); FAST SET, THE(1924); BUSINESS OF LOVE, THE(1925); RE-CREATION OF BRIAN KENT, THE(1925); WOMAN'S FAITH, A(1925); HER BIG NIGHT(1926); MANNEQUIN(1926); SUNNYSIDE UP(1926); BUCK PRIVATES(1928)
Werner Pittschau
GERMANY, YEAR ZERO(1949, Ger.)
Misc. Silents
PRINCE AND THE DANCER(1929, Ger.)
Terry Pittsford
MOONSHINE COUNTY EXPRESS(1977)
Patricia Pivaar
1984
BEST DEFENSE(1984)
Ben Pivar
BACHELOR GIRL, THE(1929), ed; BROADWAY SCANDALS(1929), ed; FLIGHT(1929), ed; MAN WHO LIVED TWICE(1936), p; TRAPPED BY TELEVISION(1936), p; TWO-FISTED GENTLEMAN(1936), p; MR. BOGGS STEPS OUT(1938),

p; LEGION OF LOST FLYERS(1939), p, w; MUTINY ON THE BLACKHAWK(1939), p, w; TROPIC FURY(1939), p, w; ALIAS THE DEACON(1940), p; BLACK DIAMONDS(1940), p; DANGER ON WHEELS(1940), p, w; DEVIL'S PIPELINE, THE(1940), p; DOUBLE ALIBI(1940), p; ENEMY AGENT(1940), p; FRAMED(1940), p; HOT STEEL(1940), p; LEATHER-PUSHERS, THE(1940), p; MAN FROM MONTREAL, THE(1940), p, w; MUMMY'S HAND, THE(1940), p; DANGEROUS GAME, A(1941), p; HORROR ISLAND(1941), p; KID FROM KANSAS, THE(1941), p; LUCKY DEVILS(1941), p; MEN OF THE TIMBERLAND(1941), p; MUTINY IN THE ARCTIC(1941), p; RAIDERS OF THE DESERT(1941), p; ROAD AGENT(1941), p; DANGER IN THE PACIFIC(1942), p; MUMMY'S TOMB, THE(1942), p; TIMBER(1942), p; TOP SERGEANT(1942), p; CALLING DR. DEATH(1943), p; CAPTIVE WILD WOMAN(1943), p; EYES OF THE UNDERWORLD(1943), p; MAD GHOUL, THE(1943), p; STRANGE DEATH OF ADOLF HITLER, THE(1943), p; MUMMY'S GHOST, THE(1944), p; PILLOW OF DEATH(1945), p; STRANGE CONFESSION(1945), p; BLONDE ALIBI(1946), p; BRUTE MAN, THE(1946), p; HOUSE OF HORRORS(1946), p; INSIDE JOB(1946), p; SHE-WOLF OF LONDON(1946), p; CHALLENGE, THE(1948), p; THIRTEEN LEAD SOLDIERS(1948), p; LEECH WOMAN, THE(1960), w
Silents
NAME THE WOMAN(1928), ed; NOTHING TO WEAR(1928), ed; SINNER'S PARADE(1928), ed; ETERNAL WOMAN, THE(1929), ed; OBJECT–ALIMONY(1929), ed

Maurice Pivar
BROADWAY(1929), ed; CHARLATAN, THE(1929), ed; LOVE TRAP, THE(1929), ed; PHANTOM OF THE OPERA, THE(1929), ed; SCANDAL(1929), ed; SHOW BOAT(1929), ed; TONIGHT AT TWELVE(1929), ed; BOUDOIR DIPLOMAT(1930), ed; CAT CREEPS, THE(1930), ed; FREE LOVE(1930), ed; LADY SURRENDERS, A(1930), ed; DRACULA(1931), ed; FRANKENSTEIN(1931), ed; GRAFT(1931), ed; HOMICIDE SQUAD(1931), ed; IRON MAN, THE(1931), ed; MANY A SLIP(1931), ed; RESURRECTION(1931), ed; STRICTLY DISHONORABLE(1931), ed; NIGHT WORLD(1932), ed; PRINCESS O'HARA(1935), ed; STORM OVER THE ANDES(1935), p
Silents
MERRY-GO-ROUND(1923), ed; PHANTOM OF THE OPERA, THE(1925), ed; MAN WHO LAUGHS, THE(1927), ed

Byrne Piven
DOUBLE-BARRELLED DETECTIVE STORY, THE(1965)

Vitaliy Pivnenko
FORTY-NINE DAYS(1964, USSR)

Anita Pivnick
Misc. Talkies
PRISM(1971), d

Anitra Pivnick
PRISM(1971), p, d&w, ed

Frank Pixley
Silents
PRINCE OF PILSEN, THE(1926), w

Pizani
AZAIS(1931, Fr.); MAN OF THE HOUR, THE(1940, Fr.)

Robert Pizani
CAFE DE PARIS(1938, Fr.); MAN ABOUT TOWN(1947, Fr.); DEADLIER THAN THE MALE(1957, Fr.); FERNANDEL THE DRESSMAKER(1957, Fr.); LA PARISIENNE(1958, Fr./Ital.)

Fidel Pizarro
CHIQUTTO PERO PICOSO(1967, Mex.), p

Larry Pizer
FOUR IN THE MORNING(1965, Brit.), ph; PUSSYCAT ALLEY(1965, Brit.), ph; MORGAN!(1966, Brit.), ph; PARTY'S OVER, THE(1966, Brit.), ph; OUR MOTHER'S HOUSE(1967, Brit.), ph; ISADORA(1968, Brit.), ph; ALL NEAT IN BLACK STOCKINGS(1969, Brit.), ph; OPTIMISTS, THE(1973, Brit.), ph; PHANTOM OF THE PARADISE(1974), ph; EUROPEANS, THE(1979, Brit.), ph; NIGHT FLOWERS(1979), ph; CATTLE ANNIE AND LITTLE BRITCHES(1981), ph; TIMERIDER(1983), ph
1984
ULTIMATE SOLUTION OF GRACE QUIGLEY, THE(1984), ph

Alfred Hollingsworth Pizon
Silents
AS THE SUN WENT DOWN(1919)

William M. Pizor
MURDER BY TELEVISION(1935), p

William Pizor
ARIZONA CYCLONE(1934), p

Ildebrando Pizzeti
SPIRIT AND THE FLESH, THE(1948, Ital.), m
Silents
CABIRIA(1914, Ital.), m

Ildebrando Pizzetti
DEFEAT OF HANNIBAL, THE(1937, Ital.), m

Pizzi
GIRL WHO COULDN'T SAY NO, THE(1969, Ital.), cos

Alberto Pizzi
HOUSE OF CARDS(1969), ph

Nilla Pizzi
MANDRAGOLA(1966 Fr./Ital.)

Pier Luigi Pizzi
GIANT OF MARATHON, THE(1960, Ital.), cos; CONDEMNED OF ALTONA, THE(1963), cos; DUEL OF THE TITANS(1963, Ital.), cos; WHITE VOICES(1965, Fr./Ital.), cos; AFTER THE FOX(1966, U.S./Brit./Ital.); MADE IN ITALY(1967, Fr./Ital.), cos; MAIDEN FOR A PRINCE, A(1967, Fr./Ital.); QUEENS, THE(1968, Ital./Fr.), art d; WILD EYE, THE(1968, Ital.), art d; GIRL WHO COULDN'T SAY NO, THE(1969, Ital.), art d; WITCH, THE(1969, Ital.), cos

Mario Pizzin
1984
BURIED ALIVE(1984, Ital.)

Sandra Pizzorni
LOVE NOW...PAY LATER(1966, Ital.)

Fred Pizzot
TOMB OF TORTURE(1966, Ital.)

Riccardo Pizzuti
UP THE MACGREGORS(1967, Ital./Span.); MAN FROM THE EAST, A(1974, Ital./Fr.); THREE STOOGES VS. THE WONDER WOMEN(1975, Ital./Chi.)

Richard Pizzuti
1984
RUSH(1984, Ital.)

Graham Place
MR. BUG GOES TO TOWN(1941), w; FEMALE RESPONSE, THE(1972), ed

Ken Place
MORE AMERICAN GRAFFITI(1979); RAISE THE TITANIC(1980, Brit.); BIG CHILL, THE(1983)

Lou Place
APACHE WOMAN(1955); SWAMP WOMEN(1956); DADDY-O(1959), d

Mary Kay Place
NEW YORK, NEW YORK(1977); MORE AMERICAN GRAFFITI(1979); STARTING OVER(1979); PRIVATE BENJAMIN(1980); MODERN PROBLEMS(1981); WALTZ ACROSS TEXAS(1982); BIG CHILL, THE(1983); TERMS OF ENDEARMENT(1983)

Pat Place
OFFENDERS, THE(1980)

Anna Placido
PHAROAH'S WOMAN, THE(1961, Ital.)

Michele Placido
DIVINE NYMPH, THE(1979, Ital.); ERNESTO(1979, Ital.); TILL MARRIAGE DO US PART(1979, Ital.); LEAP INTO THE VOID(1982, Ital.); THREE BROTHERS(1982, Ital.)

Werner Plack
MADAME SPY(1934)

Lori Plager
PRIVATE SCHOOL(1983)

Curtis Plagge
TIMERIDER(1983)

The Plainsmen
COWBOY BLUES(1946); SHADOW VALLEY(1947)

Rene Plaissetty
Misc. Silents
YELLOW CLAW, THE(1920, Brit.), d; BROKEN ROAD, THE(1921, Brit.), d; FOUR FEATHERS, THE(1921, Brit.), d; KNAVE OF DIAMONDS, THE(1921, Brit.), d; WOMAN WITH THE FAN, THE(1921, Brit.), d

Nick Plakias
UFO: TARGET EARTH(1974)

Vasili Plaksin
WATERLOO(1970, Ital./USSR)

Ratislav Plamenac
PERMISSION TO KILL(1975, U.S./Aust.)

Caroline Plamondon
GAS(1981, Can.)

Luc Plamondon
SUZANNE(1980, Can.), m

Tony Plana
SEED OF INNOCENCE(1980); ZOOT SUIT(1981); LOVE AND MONEY(1982); OFFICER AND A GENTLEMAN, AN(1982); NIGHTMARES(1983); VALLEY GIRL(1983)
1984
EL NORTE(1984)

Boy Planas
CAVALRY COMMAND(1963, U.S./Phil.)

Silvia Planas
DEATH OF A BUREAUCRAT(1979, Cuba)

Phyllis Planchard
HEARTACHES(1947); WESTWARD TRAIL, THE(1948); DANCING IN THE DARK(1949); ROADBLOCK(1951)

Roger Planchon
DANTON(1983); RETURN OF MARTIN GUERRE, THE(1983, Fr.)

Robert H. Planck
THREE LIVE GHOSTS(1929), ph; BAT WHISPERS, THE(1930), ph; BE YOURSELF(1930), ph

Robert Planck
REACHING FOR THE MOON(1931), ph; SECRET WITNESS, THE(1931), ph; SILVER LINING(1932), ph; BROKEN DREAMS(1933), ph; IT'S GREAT TO BE ALIVE(1933), ph; LIFE IN THE RAW(1933), ph; FRONTIER MARSHAL(1934), ph; KING KELLY OF THE U.S.A(1934), ph; MANHATTAN LOVE SONG(1934), ph; MONEY MEANS NOTHING(1934), ph; MOONSTONE, THE(1934), ph; OUR DAILY BREAD(1934), ph; JANE EYRE(1935), ph; LET 'EM HAVE IT(1935), ph; MELODY LINGERS ON, THE(1935), ph; RED SALUTE(1935), ph; RENDEZVOUS AT MIDNIGHT(1935), ph; SECRET OF THE CHATEAU(1935), ph; CAREER WOMAN(1936), ph; LAST OF THE MOHICANS, THE(1936), ph; LIFE BEGINS IN COLLEGE(1937), ph; LOVE AND HISSES(1937), ph; THAT I MAY LIVE(1937), ph; THIN ICE(1937), ph; THIS IS MY AFFAIR(1937), ph; TIME OUT FOR ROMANCE(1937), ph; WE WHO ARE ABOUT TO DIE(1937), ph; WOMAN-WISE(1937), ph; ALWAYS GOODBYE(1938), ph; DUKE OF WEST POINT, THE(1938), ph; HOLD THAT CO-ED(1938), ph; KENTUCKY MOONSHINE(1938), ph; KING OF THE TURF(1939), ph; LIFE RETURNS(1939), ph; MAN IN THE IRON MASK, THE(1939), ph; ESCAPE(1940), ph; STRANGE CARGO(1940), ph; SUSAN AND GOD(1940), ph; WHEN LADIES MEET(1941), ph; EYES IN THE NIGHT(1942), ph; HER CARDBOARD LOVER(1942), ph; REUNION IN FRANCE(1942), ph; WE WERE DANCING(1942), ph; ABOVE SUSPICION(1943), ph; GIRL CRAZY(1943), ph; HEAVENLY BODY, THE(1943), ph; CANTERVILLE GHOST, THE(1944), ph; MAISIE GOES TO RENO(1944), ph; ANCHORS AWEIGH(1945), ph; WEEKEND AT THE WALDORF(1945), ph; LOVE LAUGHS AT ANDY HARDY(1946), ph; SHOW-OFF, THE(1946), ph; UP GOES MAISIE(1946), ph; CASS TIMBERLANE(1947), ph; IT HAPPENED IN BROOKLYN(1947), ph; LUXURY LINER(1948), ph; THREE MUSKETEERS, THE(1948), ph; DOCTOR AND THE GIRL, THE(1949), ph; LITTLE WOMEN(1949), ph; MADAME BOVARY(1949), ph; PLEASE BELIEVE ME(1950), ph; SUMMER STOCK(1950), ph; RICH, YOUNG AND PRETTY(1951), ph; ROYAL WEDDING(1951), ph; TEXAS CARNIVAL(1951), ph; BELLE OF NEW YORK, THE(1952), ph; LILI(1953), ph; REMAINS TO BE SEEN(1953), ph; SCANDAL AT SCOURIE(1953), ph; TORCH SONG(1953), ph; ATHENA(1954), ph; PRISONER OF WAR(1954), ph; RHAPSODY(1954), ph; DIANE(1955), ph; KING'S THIEF, THE(1955), ph; MOONFLEET(1955), ph; GABY(1956), ph; GIRL MOST LIKELY, THE(1957), ph; JEANNE EAGELS(1957), ph; YOUNG STRANGER, THE(1957), ph

George Planco
CUTTER AND BONE(1981)

Jason Planco
1984
JOY OF SEX(1984)
Theo Plane
ROMAN SCANDALS(1933)
Frank F. [Franz] Planer
ROMA RIVUOLE CESARE(, ph; DICTATOR, THE(1935, Brit./Ger.), ph; DIVINE SPARK, THE(1935, Brit./Ital.), ph; BELOVED VAGABOND, THE(1936, Brit.), ph; ADVENTURE IN SAHARA(1938), ph; GIRLS' SCHOOL(1938), ph; HOLIDAY(1938), ph; NORTH OF SHANGHAI(1939), ph; REBEL SON, THE ½(1939, Brit.), ph; ESCAPE TO GLORY(1940), ph; GLAMOUR FOR SALE(1940), ph; FACE BEHIND THE MASK, THE(1941), ph; HONOLULU LU(1941), ph; MEET BOSTON BLACKIE(1941), ph; OUR WIFE(1941), ph; SING FOR YOUR SUPPER(1941), ph; SWEETHEART OF THE CAMPUS(1941), ph; THEY DARE NOT LOVE(1941), ph; THREE GIRLS ABOUT TOWN(1941), ph; TIME OUT FOR RHYTHM(1941), ph; ADVENTURES OF MARTIN EDEN, THE(1942), ph; CANAL ZONE(1942), ph; DARING YOUNG MAN, THE(1942), ph; FLIGHT LIEUTENANT(1942), ph; HARVARD, HERE I COME(1942), ph; SABOTAGE SQUAD(1942), ph; SPIRIT OF STANFORD, THE(1942), ph; SUBMARINE RAIDER(1942), ph; WIFE TAKES A FLYER, THE(1942), ph; APPOINTMENT IN BERLIN(1943), ph; DESTROYER(1943), ph; HEAT'S ON, THE(1943), ph; MY KINGDOM FOR A COOK(1943), ph; SOMETHING TO SHOUT ABOUT(1943), ph; ONCE UPON A TIME(1944), ph; SECRET COMMAND(1944), ph; STRANGE AFFAIR(1944), ph; I LOVE A BANDLEADER(1945), ph; LEAVE IT TO BLONDIE(1945), ph; SNAFU(1945), ph; CHASE, THE(1946), ph; HER SISTER'S SECRET(1946), ph; EXILE, THE(1947), ph; LETTER FROM AN UNKNOWN WOMAN(1948), ph; ONE TOUCH OF VENUS(1948), ph; CHAMPION(1949), ph; CRISS CROSS(1949), ph; ONCE MORE, MY DARLING(1949), ph; TAKE ONE FALSE STEP(1949), ph; CYRANO DE BERGERAC(1950), ph; THREE HUSBANDS(1950), ph; VENDETTA(1950), ph; 711 OCEAN DRIVE(1950), ph; BLUE VEIL, THE(1951), ph; DECISION BEFORE DAWN(1951), ph; SCARF, THE(1951), ph; DEATH OF A SALESMAN(1952), ph; UNFINISHED SYMPHONY, THE(1953, Aust./Brit.), ph; 5,000 FINGERS OF DR. T. THE(1953), ph; 99 RIVER STREET(1953), ph; BAD FOR EACH OTHER(1954), ph; BULLET IS WAITING, A(1954), ph; CAINE MUTINY, THE(1954), ph; LONG WAIT, THE(1954), ph; 20,000 LEAGUES UNDER THE SEA(1954), ph; LEFT HAND OF GOD, THE(1955), ph; NOT AS A STRANGER(1955), ph; MOUNTAIN, THE(1956), ph; PRIDE AND THE PASSION, THE(1957), ph; BIG COUNTRY, THE(1958), ph; STAGE STRUCK(1958), ph; NUN'S STORY, THE(1959), ph; UNFORGIVEN, THE(1960), ph; BREAKFAST AT TIFFANY'S(1961), ph; CHILDREN'S HOUR, THE(1961), ph; KING OF KINGS(1961), ph
Lillian Planer
WAVE, A WAC AND A MARINE, A(1944), w
Nigel Planer
YELLOWBEARD(1983)
Melinda Plank
GREENWICH VILLAGE STORY(1963)
Robert Plank
WOMAN'S FACE(1941), ph
Tom Plank
DESIRE ME(1947); KENTUCKY JUBILEE(1951)
Jean Plannette
WHISPERING WINDS(1929), w
Silents
RAGTIME(1927), w
J.J. Plans
ISLAND OF THE DAMNED(1976, Span.), w
Jack Plant
ULYSSES(1967, U.S./Brit.)
James Plant
OFF THE DOLE(1935, Brit.)
Jimmy Plant
DEMOBBED(1944, Brit.); SOLDIER, SAILOR(1944, Brit.)
Joe Plant
Silents
KISSING CUP'S RACE(1920, Brit.)
Mark Plant
RINGSIDE(1949)
Pamela Plant
TELL-TALE HEART, THE(1962, Brit.)
Plantation Girls
VARIETY JUBILEE(1945, Brit.)
The Plantation Singers
SHOW BOAT(1929)
Don Plante
GREEN SLIME, THE(1969)
Laura La Plante
Misc. Silents
TEASER, THE(1925)
Louis Plante
MAN, WOMAN AND CHILD(1983)
Louis R. Plante
1984
RIVER RAT, THE(1984)
Laura Planting
BON VOYAGE, CHARLIE BROWN(AND DON'T COME BACK)*** (1980)
Regis Des Plas
1984
UNTIL SEPTEMBER(1984), art d
Otto Plaschkes
GEORGY GIRL(1966, Brit.), p; BOFORS GUN, THE(1968, Brit.), p; SEPARATE PEACE, A(1972), p; SAILOR'S RETURN, THE(1978, Brit.), p; HOUND OF THE BASKERVILLES, THE(1983, Brit.), p; SIGN OF FOUR, THE(1983, Brit.), p
Jiri Plashy
EMPEROR AND THE GOLEM, THE(1955, Czech.)
Peter Plaskett
CHILDREN GALORE(1954, Brit.), w
Naomi Plaskitt
HIGHLAND FLING(1936, Brit.); WRATH OF JEALOUSY(1936, Brit.)

Alex Plasschaert
ADVENTURES OF BULLWHIP GRIFFIN, THE(1967), ch
1984
CITY HEAT(1984)
Steven Plastrik
ZELIG(1983), anim
Jiri Platcy
KRAKATIT(1948, Czech.)
Roberto Plate
1984
LOVE ON THE GROUND(1984,Fr.), set d
Carl Platen
BECAUSE I LOVED YOU(1930, Ger.)
Silents
PASSION(1920, Ger.)
Karl Platen
M(1933, Ger.); MASTER OF THE WORLD(1935, Ger.); TESTAMENT OF DR. MABUSE, THE(1943, Ger.)
Alan Plater
VIRGIN AND THE GYPSY, THE(1970, Brit.), w; JUGGERNAUT(1974, Brit.), w; ALL THINGS BRIGHT AND BEAUTIFUL(1979, Brit.), w; PRIEST OF LOVE(1981, Brit.), w
Sylvia Plath
BELL JAR, THE(1979), w
David D. Platko
STRIPES(1981)
Jonathan Platnick
LOOKING UP(1977), w
Dana Plato
RETURN TO BOGGY CREEK(1977)
James Plato
TILL THE CLOUDS ROLL BY(1946)
Tove Platon
$(DOLLARS)**1/2 (1971)
A. Platonov
THREE BROTHERS(1982, Ital.), d&w
Alma Platt
JOHNNY HOLIDAY(1949); SWEET CHARITY(1969); WINNING(1969)
Billy Platt
FACE IN THE SKY(1933); TERROR OF TINY TOWN, THE(1938)
Edward C. Platt
PRIVATE WAR OF MAJOR BENSON, THE(1955); UNGUARDED MOMENT, THE(1956); WRITTEN ON THE WIND(1956); GREAT MAN, THE(1957); TATTERED DRESS, THE(1957); DAMN CITIZEN(1958); LAST OF THE FAST GUNS, THE(1958); SUMMER LOVE(1958); CASH McCALL(1960); BULLET FOR A BADMAN(1964)
Edward C. Platt, Sr.
ROCK, PRETTY BABY(1956)
Edward Platt
ILLEGAL(1955); MC CONNELL STORY, THE(1955); REBEL WITHOUT A CAUSE(1955); SHRIKE, THE(1955); SINCERELY YOURS(1955); BACKLASH(1956); LIEUTENANT WORE SKIRTS, THE(1956); PROUD ONES, THE(1956); REPRISAL(1956); SERENADE(1956); STEEL JUNGLE, THE(1956); STORM CENTER(1956); DESIGNING WOMAN(1957); HOUSE OF NUMBERS(1957); OMAR KHAYYAM(1957); GIFT OF LOVE, THE(1958); GUNMAN'S WALK(1958); HIGH COST OF LOVING, THE(1958); OREGON PASSAGE(1958); HELEN MORGAN STORY, THE(1959); INSIDE THE MAFIA(1959); NORTH BY NORTHWEST(1959); REBEL SET, THE(1959); THEY CAME TO CORDURA(1959); POLLYANNA(1960); ATLANTIS, THE LOST CONTINENT(1961); EXPLOSIVE GENERATION, THE(1961); FIERCEST HEART, THE(1961); CAPE FEAR(1962); BLACK ZOO(1963); TICKLISH AFFAIR, A(1963); MAN FROM BUTTON WILLOW, THE(1965); SANTEE(1973), p
George Foster Platt
Silents
NET, THE(1916), d
Misc. Silents
HIS WIFE(1915), d; FIVE FAULTS OF FLO, THE(1916), d
Howard Platt
T.R. BASKIN(1971); PRIME CUT(1972); WESTWORLD(1973); NEWMAN'S LAW(1974); THREE THE HARD WAY(1974); GREAT SCOUT AND CATHOUSE THURSDAY, THE(1976)
Howard T Platt
CAT FROM OUTER SPACE, THE(1978)
Joseph B. Platt
PARADINE CASE, THE(1947), set d; PORTRAIT OF JENNIE(1949), art d
Joseph Platt
LADY OF BURLESQUE(1943), prod d
Louise Platt
I MET MY LOVE AGAIN(1938); SPAWN OF THE NORTH(1938); STAGECOACH(1939); TELL NO TALES(1939); CAPTAIN CAUTION(1940); FORGOTTEN GIRLS(1940); STREET OF CHANCE(1942)
Marc Platt
TONIGHT AND EVERY NIGHT(1945); TARS AND SPARS(1946); DOWN TO EARTH(1947); SWORDSMAN, THE(1947); WHEN A GIRL'S BEAUTIFUL(1947); SEVEN BRIDES FOR SEVEN BROTHERS(1954); OKLAHOMA(1955); THESE WILDER YEARS(1956)
Polly Platt
TARGETS(1968), w, prod d; LAST PICTURE SHOW, THE(1971), prod d; WHAT'S UP, DOC?(1972), prod d; PAPER MOON(1973), prod d; THIEF WHO CAME TO DINNER, THE(1973), prod d, art d; BAD NEWS BEARS, THE(1976), prod d; STAR IS BORN, A(1976), prod d; PRETTY BABY(1978), w; GOOD LUCK, MISS WYCKOFF(1979), w; YOUNG DOCTORS IN LOVE(1982), prod d; MAN WITH TWO BRAINS, THE(1983), prod d; TERMS OF ENDEARMENT(1983), prod d
Raymond Platt
LITTLE MALCOLM(1974, Brit.)
Ruth Platt
MURDERS IN THE RUE MORGUE(1971)
Victor Platt
HISTORY OF MR. POLLY, THE(1949, Brit.); DEADLY NIGHTSHADE(1953, Brit.); NORMAN CONQUEST(1953, Brit.); GREEN BUDDHA, THE(1954, Brit.); MOONRAKER, THE(1958, Brit.); STEEL BAYONET, THE(1958, Brit.); MAN DETAINED(1961, Brit.); PLAYBACK(1962, Brit.); TRAITORS, THE(1963, Brit.); HOT MILLIONS(1968, Brit.)

William Platt
Silents
TWO FLAMING YOUTHS(1927); TILLIE'S PUNCTURED ROMANCE(1928)
Rudolf Platte
F.P. 1 DOESN'T ANSWER(1933, Ger.); GOLD(1934, Ger.); COURT CONCERT, THE(1936, Ger.); AFFAIRS OF JULIE, THE(1958, Ger.); VERONIKA VOSS(1982, Ger.)
The Platters
GIRL CAN'T HELP IT, THE(1956); ROCK AROUND THE CLOCK(1956); CARNIVAL ROCK(1957); ROCK ALL NIGHT(1957); GIRLS' TOWN(1959)
The Platters
BITTER TEARS OF PETRA VON KANT, THE(1972, Ger.), m
Jack Platts
BROTHERS AND SISTERS(1980, Brit.)
Stanley Platts
WOMAN EATER, THE(1959, Brit.)
Barney Platts-Mills
PRIVATE ROAD(1971, Brit.), d&w; BRONCO BULLFROG(1972, Brit.), d&w
Gus Platz
Silents
REFEREE, THE(1922)
Laura Platz
SHE-DEVILS ON WHEELS(1968)
Erwin Platzer
SNOW WHITE(1965, Ger.)
Pierre Plauzales
LITTLE BOY LOST(1953)
Lucien Plauzoles
FRENCH LINE, THE(1954); SO THIS IS PARIS(1954)
A. Plavan
RESURRECTION(1963, USSR)
Gary Plaxton
ONE MAN(1979, Can.)
Marion J. Playan
LOVE BUG, THE(1968)
The Playboys
COLLEGE SWING(1938)
Ernest Player
OVER THE ODDS(1961, Brit.), w
Piano Player
NASHVILLE(1975)
Susan Player
POM POM GIRLS, THE(1976)
Wellington A. Player
Silents
RING AND THE MAN, THE(1914)
Toufic Barham Players
HAREM BUNCH; OR WAR AND PIECE, THE(1969), m
Patrick Playez
LOULOU(1980, Fr.)
Arthur Playfair
Misc. Silents
JUDGED BY APPEARANCES(1916, Brit.)
Elliot Playfair
DEPTH CHARGE(1960, Brit.)
Joan Playfair
GUEST OF HONOR(1934, Brit.); SILVER SPOON, THE(1934, Brit.)
Nigel Playfair
CRIME ON THE HILL(1933, Brit.); LITTLE STRANGER(1934, Brit.)
Misc. Silents
LADY WINDERMERE'S FAN(1916, Brit.); SUNKEN ROCKS(1919, Brit.)
Sir Nigel Playfair
PERFECT UNDERSTANDING(1933, Brit.)
Wendy Playfair
RIDE A WILD PONY(1976, U.S./Aus.)
Alice Playten
LADYBUG, LADYBUG(1963); WHO KILLED MARY WHAT'SER NAME?(1971); CALIFORNIA DREAMING(1979); HEAVY METAL(1981, Can.)
Wellington A. Playter
Silents
COUNTY CHAIRMAN, THE(1914); MRS. BLACK IS BACK(1914)
Misc. Silents
MARTA OF THE LOWLANDS(1914); WOMAN'S TRIUMPH, A(1914)
Wellington Playter
Silents
HIS LAST DOLLAR(1914); PRIDE OF JENNICO, THE(1914); PENNINGTON'S CHOICE(1915); POLLY OF THE CIRCUS(1917)
Misc. Silents
MAN FROM MEXICO, THE(1914); CORAL(1915); SOUL OF A CHILD, THE(1916); STRUGGLE EVERLASTING, THE(1918); BACK TO GOD'S COUNTRY(1919 US/Can.); FOOL'S GOLD(1919); IN SEARCH OF ARCADY(1919); WICKED DARLING, THE(1919)
Playwright
RETURN TO YESTERDAY(1940, Brit.)
Begona Plaza
48 HOURS(1982)
Plaza Tiller Girls
RAISE THE ROOF(1930)
Enzo Plazzotta
HOTEL SAHARA(1951, Brit.)
Harry Pleasant
Misc. Silents
TIES OF BLOOD(1921)
The Pleasant Valley Boys
TWO THOUSAND MANIACS!(1964)
Philip Pleasants
Misc. Talkies
NAKED RIVER(1977)

Angela Pleasence
HERE WE GO ROUND THE MULBERRY BUSH(1968, Brit.); HITLER: THE LAST TEN DAYS(1973, Brit./Ital.); FROM BEYOND THE GRAVE(1974, Brit.); SYMPTOMS(1976, Brit.); GODSEND, THE(1980, Can.)
Donald Pleasence
THE BEACHCOMBER(1955, Brit.); BLACK TENT, THE(1956, Brit.); 1984(1956, Brit.); DECISION AGAINST TIME(1957, Brit.); STOWAWAY GIRL(1957, Brit.); VALUE FOR MONEY(1957, Brit.); ALL AT SEA(1958, Brit.); HEART OF A CHILD(1958, Brit.); MAN INSIDE, THE(1958, Brit.); TALE OF TWO CITIES, A(1958, Brit.); WIND CANNOT READ, THE(1958, Brit.); LOOK BACK IN ANGER(1959); ORDERS ARE ORDERS(1959, Brit.); TWO-HEADED SPY, THE(1959, Brit.); BATTLE OF THE SEXES, THE(1960, Brit.); BIG DAY, THE(1960, Brit.); CIRCUS OF HORRORS(1960, Brit.); HELL IS A CITY(1960, Brit.); KILLERS OF KILIMANJARO(1960, Brit.); SHAKEDOWN, THE(1960, Brit.); SONS AND LOVERS(1960, Brit.); STORY OF DAVID, A(1960, Brit.); MANIA(1961, Brit.); NO LOVE FOR JOHNNIE(1961, Brit.); RISK, THE(1961, Brit.); SPARE THE ROD(1961, Brit.); WIND OF CHANGE, THE(1961, Brit.); LISA(1962, Brit.); WHAT A CARVE UP!(1962, Brit.); DR. CRIPPEN(1963, Brit.); GREAT ESCAPE, THE(1963); GUEST, THE(1963, Brit.); HANDS OF ORLAC, THE(1964, Brit./Fr.); GREATEST STORY EVER TOLD, THE(1965); HALLELUJAH TRAIL, THE(1965); CUL-DE-SAC(1966, Brit.); FANTASTIC VOYAGE(1966); EYE OF THE DEVIL(1967, Brit.); MATCHLESS(1967, Ital.); NIGHT OF THE GENERALS, THE(1967, Brit./Fr.); YOU ONLY LIVE TWICE(1967, Brit.); WILL PENNY(1968); MADWOMAN OF CHAILLOT, THE(1969); MISTER FREEDOM(1970, Fr.); SOLDIER BLUE(1970, Brit.); KIDNAPPED(1971, Brit.); OUTBACK(1971, Aus.); THX 1138(1971); HENRY VIII AND HIS SIX WIVES(1972, Brit.); JERUSALEM FILE, THE(1972, U.S./Israel); PIED PIPER, THE(1972, Brit.); WEDDING IN WHITE(1972, Can.); DEATHLINE(1973, Brit.); INNOCENT BYSTANDERS(1973, Brit.); MALACHI'S COVE(1973, Brit.); RAINBOW BOYS, THE(1973, Can.); TALES THAT WITNESS MADNESS(1973, Brit.); BLACK WINDMILL, THE(1974, Brit.); MUTATIONS, THE(1974, Brit.); BARRY MC KENZIE HOLDS HIS OWN(1975, Aus.); ESCAPE TO WITCH MOUNTAIN(1975); HEARTS OF THE WEST(1975); COUNT OF MONTE CRISTO(1976, Brit.); DEVIL WITHIN HER, THE(1976, Brit.); DIRTY KNIGHT'S WORK(1976, Brit.); EAGLE HAS LANDED, THE(1976, Brit.); JOURNEY INTO FEAR(1976, Can); LAND OF THE MINOTAUR(1976, Gr.); LAST TYCOON, THE(1976); PASSOVER PLOT, THE(1976, Israel); OH, GOD!(1977); TELEFON(1977); UNCANNY, THE(1977, Brit./Can.); BLOOD RELATIVES(1978, Fr./Can.); HALLOWEEN(1978); POWER PLAY(1978, Can.); SGT. PEPPER'S LONELY HEARTS CLUB BAND(1978); TOMORROW NEVER COMES(1978, Brit./Can.); ANGRY MAN, THE(1979 Fr./Can.); DRACULA(1979); GOOD LUCK, MISS WYCKOFF(1979); JAGUAR LIVES(1979); NIGHT CREATURE(1979); ESCAPE FROM NEW YORK(1981); HALLOWEEN II(1981); MONSTER CLUB, THE(1981, Brit.); ALONE IN THE DARK(1982); DEVONSVILLE TERROR, THE(1983)
1984
AMBASSADOR, THE(1984); BREED APART, A(1984); TREASURE OF THE YANKEE ZEPHYR(1984); WHERE IS PARSIFAL?(1984, Brit.)
Misc. Talkies
PUMA MAN, THE(1980); TREASURE OF THE AMAZON(1983)
Pat Pleasence
ROOM 43(1959, Brit.)
Alberto Plebani
NAKED MAJA, THE(1959, Ital./U.S.); MINOTAUR, THE(1961, Ital.); JULIET OF THE SPIRITS(1965, Fr./Ital./W.Ger.)
Werner Pledath
JAZZBAND FIVE, THE(1932, Ger,)
John Pleffer
SINGER AND THE DANCER, THE(1977, Aus.), w
Jack Pleis
DIARY OF A BACHELOR(1964), m
Helene Plemianikoff
POPSY POP(1971, Fr.), ed
Helen Plemianikov
PHANTOM OF LIBERTY, THE(1974, Fr.), ed
Helene Plemianikov
DON'T CRY WITH YOUR MOUTH FULL(1974, Fr.), ed
Helene Plemiannikov
FAREWELL, FRIEND(1968, Fr./Ital.), ed; SPIRITS OF THE DEAD(1969, Fr./Ital.), ed; DISCREET CHARM OF THE BOURGEOISIE, THE(1972, Fr.), ed; THAT OBSCURE OBJECT OF DESIRE(1977, Fr./Span.), ed
Helene Plemmianikov
SHOCK TREATMENT(1973, Fr.), ed
Trix Plenaar
1984
GUEST, THE(1984, Brit.)
Vadim Plenianikoy
LOVES OF THREE QUEENS, THE(1954, Ital./Fr.), w
Gianfranco Plenixio
AND THE SHIP SAILS ON(1983, Ital./Fr.), m
Gianfranco Plenizio
PIZZA TRIANGLE, THE(1970, Ital./Span.), md; TRINITY IS STILL MY NAME(1971, Ital.), md; MASOCH(1980, Ital.), m
Yvette Plenne
PEARLS OF THE CROWN(1938, Fr.)
Alec Pleon
SCHOOL FOR RANDLE(1949, Brit.); OVER THE GARDEN WALL(1950, Brit.)
Branko Plesa
SQUARE OF VIOLENCE(1963, U.S./Yugo.); ROMANCE OF A HORSE THIEF(1971)
Honoria Plesch
FAME IS THE SPUR(1947, Brit.), cos; IDOL OF PARIS(1948, Brit.), cos; SAINTS AND SINNERS(1949, Brit.), cos; YELLOW HAT, THE(1966, Brit.), d, w, cos
Honoris Plesch
THUNDER ROCK(1944, Brit.), cos
Michael Pleschkoff
Silents
EAGLE, THE(1925)
John Pleshette
PARADES(1972); HOUSE CALLS(1978); ROCKY II(1979); S.O.B.(1981)
1984
MICKI AND MAUDE(1984)

Suzanne Pleshette
GEISHA BOY, THE(1958); FORTY POUNDS OF TROUBLE(1962); ROME ADVENTURE(1962); BIRDS, THE(1963); WALL OF NOISE(1963); DISTANT TRUMPET, A(1964); FATE IS THE HUNTER(1964); YOUNGBLOOD HAWKE(1964); RAGE TO LIVE, A(1965); MISTER BUDDWING(1966); NEVADA SMITH(1966); UGLY DACHSHUND, THE(1966); ADVENTURES OF BULLWHIP GRIFFIN, THE(1967); BLACKBEARD'S GHOST(1968); POWER, THE(1968); IF IT'S TUESDAY, THIS MUST BE BELGIUM(1969); SUPPOSE THEY GAVE A WAR AND NOBODY CAME?(1970); SUPPORT YOUR LOCAL GUNFIGHTER(1971); SHAGGY D.A., THE(1976); HOT STUFF(1979); OH GOD! BOOK II(1980); TARGET: HARRY(1980)

Jiri Pleskot
FIFTH HORSEMAN IS FEAR, THE(1968, Czech.)

Henry Pless
TRUNKS OF MR. O.F., THE(1932, Ger.); TESTAMENT OF DR. MABUSE, THE(1943, Ger.)

Mimis Plessas
STEFANIA(1968, Gr.), m

Jacqueline Plessis
SEVEN DEADLY SINS, THE(1953, Fr./Ital.); NANA(1957, Fr./Ital.)

Pierre Plessis
COUSIN, COUSINE(1976, Fr.)

Tom Pletts
COAST TO COAST(1980); FOXES(1980); CANNERY ROW(1982)

Patrick Pleven
OH! CALCUTTA!(1972), p

Vera Plevnik
MONKEY GRIP(1983, Aus.)

Marita Pleyer
LOLA(1982, Ger.)

Eduardo Gonzales Pliego
SEVEN CITIES OF GOLD(1955)

Eduardo Gonzalez Pliego
PANCHO VILLA RETURNS(1950, Mex.); LAST REBEL, THE(1961, Mex.)

Eduardo Pliego
VILLA!(1958)

Walter Plimmer, Jr.
Silents
ISN'T LIFE WONDERFUL(1924)

George Plimpton
BEYOND THE LAW(1968); DETECTIVE, THE(1968); PAPER LION(1968), w; RIO LOBO(1970); IF EVER I SEE YOU AGAIN(1978); PRIVATE FILES OF J. EDGAR HOOVER, THE(1978); REDS(1981)

Harry Plimpton
Silents
JUNGLE TRAIL, THE(1919), ph; NERO(1922, U.S./Ital.), ph

Martha Plimpton
ROLLOVER(1981)
1984
RIVER RAT, THE(1984)

Shelley Plimpton
ALICE'S RESTAURANT(1969); PUTNEY SWOPE(1969)
Misc. Talkies
GLEN AND RANDA(1971)

Karl Plintzer
AFFAIR BLUM, THE(1949, Ger.), ph

Maya Plisetskaya
LITTLE HUMPBACKED HORSE, THE(1962, USSR)

George Pliz
WAKE OF THE RED WITCH(1949)

Herbert Ploberger
UNCLE TOM'S CABIN(1969, Fr./Ital./Ger./Yugo.), cos

Andrej Plocki
BEADS OF ONE ROSARY, THE(1982, Pol.), art d

Roy Plomley
DR. MORELLE–THE CASE OF THE MISSING HEIRESS(1949, Brit.), w; DOUBLE CONFESSION(1953, Brit.)

Eric Plooyer
1984
QUESTION OF SILENCE(1984, Neth.)

Edith Ploquin
THERESE AND ISABELLE(1968, U.S./Ger.)

Raoul Ploquin
COUNSEL FOR ROMANCE(1938, Fr.), d; JUPITER(1952, Fr.), p; GORILLA GREETS YOU, THE(1958, Fr.), p; MAXIME(1962, Fr.), p; LADIES OF THE PARK(1964, Fr.), p; NAKED HEARTS(1970, Fr.), p

Joe Ploski
ROSE BOWL(1936); I MET HIM IN PARIS(1937); EGG AND I, THE(1947); EXILE, THE(1947); CALL NORTHSIDE 777(1948); GREAT SINNER, THE(1949); LOVE NEST(1951); STALAG 17(1953); JUBILEE TRAIL(1954); WE'RE NO ANGELS(1955); LI'L ABNER(1959); DR. GOLDFOOT AND THE BIKINI MACHINE(1965); MC HALE'S NAVY JOINS THE AIR FORCE(1965)

Marya Ploss
GIGI(1958)

Ken Plotin
BEYOND EVIL(1980), ph

Monique Plotin
PARIS DOES STRANGE THINGS(1957, Fr./Ital.), cos

Chen Plotkin
DIAMONDS(1975, U.S./Israel)

Grisha Plotkin
FIREFOX(1982)

Marcy Plotnick
GREAT BIG THING, A(1968, U.S./Can.)

Stanley Plotnick
PILGRIM, FAREWELL(1980), p

Boleslaw Plotnicki
NAKED AMONG THE WOLVES(1967, Ger.)

N. Plotnikov
ON HIS OWN(1939, USSR); UNIVERSITY OF LIFE(1941, USSR); VOW, THE(1947, USSR.)

Nikolai Plotnikov
THREE TALES OF CHEKHOV(1961, USSR)

Nikolay Plotnikov
NINE DAYS OF ONE YEAR(1964, USSR)

Sergey Plotnikov
FAREWELL, DOVES(1962, USSR)

Francis Plottner
Silents
PENROD(1922)

Claude Plouganio
STRANDED(1965), ed

Merel Ploway
BABY, IT'S YOU(1983)

Dore Plowden
Misc. Silents
RUNAWAY, THE(1917)

Roger Plowden
FIVE FINGERS(1952)

John Plowman
ABSOLUTION(1981, Brit.)

Linda Plowman
GREEN-EYED BLONDE, THE(1957)

Melinda Plowman
MA AND PA KETTLE(1949); MY BLUE HEAVEN(1950); THREE CAME HOME(1950); CHICAGO CALLING(1951); HOME TOWN STORY(1951); CARRIE(1952); MONKEY BUSINESS(1952); PACK TRAIN(1953); WIRETAPPERS(1956); BILLY THE KID VS. DRACULA(1966)

Christopher Plowright
DOT AND THE BUNNY(1983, Aus.), ed
1984
CAMEL BOY, THE(1984, Aus.), ed

Hilda Plowright
UNTIL THEY SAIL(1957); HOLIDAY(1938); PARTNERS OF THE PLAINS(1938); YOU CAN'T TAKE IT WITH YOU(1938); CAFE SOCIETY(1939); RAFFLES(1939); TELEVISION SPY(1939); WOMEN, THE(1939); FOREIGN CORRESPONDENT(1940); KITTY FOYLE(1940); PHILADELPHIA STORY, THE(1940); SUSPICION(1941); TWO-FACED WOMAN(1941); MAGNIFICENT AMBERSONS, THE(1942); NOW, VOYAGER(1942); RANDOM HARVEST(1942); MR. LUCKY(1943); HOUR BEFORE THE DAWN, THE(1944); WILSON(1944); KITTY(1945); MINISTRY OF FEAR(1945); DEVOTION(1946); IMPERFECT LADY, THE(1947); LIFE OF HER OWN, A(1950); RHUBARB(1951); ABBOTT AND COSTELLO MEET DR. JEKYLL AND MR. HYDE(1954); SEPARATE TABLES(1958); LOVER COME BACK(1961); SUMMER MAGIC(1963); MY FAIR LADY(1964); 36 HOURS(1965)

Joan Plowright
TIME WITHOUT PITY(1957, Brit.); ENTERTAINER, THE(1960, Brit.); THREE SISTERS(1974, Brit.); "EQUUS"(1977); UNCLE VANYA(1977, Brit.); BRIMSTONE AND TREACLE(1982, Brit.); BRITTANIA HOSPITAL(1982, Brit.); WAGNER(1983, Brit./Hung./Aust.)

Bernard Pludow
CRAZY OVER HORSES(1951); MA BARKER'S KILLER BROOD(1960)

George Plues
GUNS AND GUITARS(1936); COME ON, COWBOYS(1937); HIT THE SADDLE(1937); RANGERS STEP IN, THE(1937); RECKLESS RANGER(1937); OVERLAND STAGE RAIDERS(1938); NEW FRONTIER(1939); LAW AND ORDER(1940); RAGTIME COWBOY JOE(1940); TWO GUN SHERIFF(1941); MEXICAN SPITFIRE'S BLESSED EVENT(1943); OX-BOW INCIDENT, THE(1943); TENTING TONIGHT ON THE OLD CAMP GROUND(1943); SUNSET PASS(1946); MY COUSIN RACHEL(1952)

Georges Plues
ROARIN' LEAD(1937)

Eric Pluet
MURIEL(1963, Fr./Ital.), ed; NO TIME FOR ECSTASY(1963, Fr.), ed; IMPOSSIBLE ON SATURDAY(1966, Fr./Israel), ed; LA GUERRE EST FINIE(1967, Fr./Swed.), ed

Marcelle Pluet
IMMORTAL STORY, THE(1969, Fr.), ed

Erika Pluhar
JUST A GIGOLO(1979, Ger.)

Victoria Plum
MONTY PYTHON'S THE MEANING OF LIFE(1983, Brit.)

Charles Plumb
Silents
ELLA CINDERS(1926), w

D. Hay Plumb
DEADLOCK(1931, Brit.); POWER(1934, Brit.); THINGS ARE LOOKING UP(1934, Brit.); SAILING ALONG(1938, Brit.)

Edward H. Plumb
DUMBO(1941), md; THREE CABALLEROS, THE(1944), md; PETER PAN(1953), m

Edward Plumb
BAMBI(1942), m; QUEBEC(1951), m

Elizabeth Plumb
DARK SIDE OF TOMORROW, THE(1970)
Misc. Talkies
PSYCHO LOVER(1969, Brit.); JUST THE TWO OF US(1975)

Flora Plumb
MALIBU BEACH(1978)

Hay Plumb
HOUSE OF TRENT, THE(1933, Brit.); BLUE SQUADRON, THE(1934, Brit.); CHANNEL CROSSING(1934, Brit.); GUEST OF HONOR(1934, Brit.); ORDERS IS ORDERS(1934, Brit.); WIDOW'S MIGHT(1934, Brit.); CAR OF DREAMS(1935, Brit.); SONG OF THE FORGE(1937, Brit.); STRANGE BOARDERS(1938, Brit.); FLYING FIFTY-FIVE(1939, Brit.); LET'S BE FAMOUS(1939, Brit.)
Silents
HAMLET(1913, Brit.), d
Misc. Silents
CLOISTER AND THE HEARTH, THE(1913, Brit.), a, d; DAVID GARRICK(1913, Brit.), d; DEAD HEART, THE(1914, Brit.), d; SON OF DAVID, A(1920, Brit.), d

Kenneth Plumb
COOL AND THE CRAZY, THE(1958)
Rose Plumber
DARK MOUNTAIN(1944)
Lincoln Plumer
Silents
TEN DOLLAR RAISE, THE(1921); RECKLESS ROMANCE(1924); BULLET MARK, THE(1928)
Misc. Silents
DEUCE OF SPADES, THE(1922)
Rose Plumer
INSIDE THE LAW(1942); KNOCK ON ANY DOOR(1949); UNDERCOVER MAN, THE(1949)
George Plumes
PUBLIC COWBOY NO. 1(1937)
Pat Plumet
LOVE NOW...PAY LATER(1966, Ital.)
Don Plumley
SEDUCTION OF JOE TYNAN, THE(1979); RAGTIME(1981); HANKY-PANKY(1982)
Albert Plummer
Misc. Silents
DARKNESS AND DAYLIGHT(1923), d
Amanda Plummer
CATTLE ANNIE AND LITTLE BRITCHES(1981); WORLD ACCORDING TO GARP, The(1982); DANIEL(1983)
1984
HOTEL NEW HAMPSHIRE, THE(1984)
Christopher Plummer
STAGE STRUCK(1958); WIND ACROSS THE EVERGLADES(1958); FALL OF THE ROMAN EMPIRE, THE(1964); INSIDE DAISY CLOVER(1965); SOUND OF MUSIC, THE(1965); NIGHT OF THE GENERALS, THE(1967, Brit./Fr.); TRIPLE CROSS(1967, Fr./Brit.); HIGH COMMISSIONER, THE(1968, U.S./Brit.); OEDIPUS THE KING(1968, Brit.); BATTLE OF BRITAIN, THE(1969, Brit.); LOCK UP YOUR DAUGHTERS(1969, Brit.); ROYAL HUNT OF THE SUN, THE(1969, Brit.); WATERLOO(1970, Ital./USSR); PYX, THE(1973, Can.); CONDUCT UNBECOMING(1975, Brit.); MAN WHO WOULD BE KING, THE(1975, Brit.); RETURN OF THE PINK PANTHER, THE(1975, Brit.); SPIRAL STAIRCASE, THE(1975, Brit.); ACES HIGH(1977, Brit.); DAY THAT SHOOK THE WORLD, THE(1977, Yugo./Czech.); INTERNATIONAL VELVET(1978, Brit.); HANOVER STREET(1979, Brit.); MURDER BY DECREE(1979, Brit.); SILENT PART-NER, THE(1979, Can.); STARCRASH(1979); SOMEWHERE IN TIME(1980); DISAP-PEARANCE, THE(1981, Brit./Can.); EYEWITNESS(1981); AMATEUR, THE(1982)
1984
DREAMSCAPE(1984); HIGHPOINT(1984, Can.); ORDEAL BY INNOCENCE(1984, Brit.)
Misc. Talkies
ASSIGNMENT, THE(1978); RIEL(1979)
Elmer Plummer
FANTASIA(1940), art d; DUMBO(1941), art d; MAKE MINE MUSIC(1946), art d
Lincoln Plummer
Silents
REGULAR FELLOW, A(1925); ATTA BOY!(1926); WHEN THE WIFE'S AWAY(1926); BACKSTAGE(1927); DOWN THE STRETCH(1927); ALIAS THE DEACON(1928); MASKED ANGEL(1928)
Misc. Silents
HER FACE VALUE(1921); CONFIDENCE(1922); GLORY OF CLEMENTINA, THE(1922); FOOLS' HIGHWAY(1924)
Peter Plummer
JUNKET 89(1970, Brit.), d
Rose Plummer
SHE MARRIED HER BOSS(1935); VAGABOND LADY(1935); GIT ALONG, LITTLE DOGIES(1937); ROVIN' TUMBLEWEEDS(1939); JACK LONDON(1943); TRAIL OF TERROR(1944); PHANTOM OF THE PLAINS(1945); CRACK-UP(1946); DUEL IN THE SUN(1946); POSSESSED(1947); FLAXY MARTIN(1949); SON OF PALEFACE(1952)
Misc. Talkies
BULLETS AND SADDLES(1943)
Terence Plummer
TAMARIND SEED, THE(1974, Brit.)
Terry Plummer
HEROES OF TELEMARK, THE(1965, Brit.); WHERE'S JACK?(1969, Brit.); DEATH-LINE(1973, Brit.); EAGLE HAS LANDED, THE(1976, Brit.); PINK PANTHER STRIKES AGAIN, THE(1976, Brit.)
Edward Plump
WOMAN WHO CAME BACK(1945), m
Vaudie Plunk
WALKING TALL(1973)
Gordon Plunkett
UNEASY TERMS(1948, Brit.)
Jim Plunkett
HARLOW(1965)
Oliver Plunkett
SUMMER HOLIDAY(1963, Brit.), cos
Patricia Plunkett
BOND STREET(1948, Brit.); FOR THEM THAT TRESPASS(1949, Brit.); IT ALWAYS RAINS ON SUNDAY(1949, Brit.); MURDER WITHOUT CRIME(1951, Brit.); CRASH OF SILENCE(1952, Brit.); LANDFALL(1953, Brit.); CROWDED DAY, THE(1954, Brit.); FLESH IS WEAK, THE(1957, Brit.); DUNKIRK(1958, Brit.); ESCORT FOR HIRE(1960, Brit.); IDENTITY UNKNOWN(1960, Brit.)
Paul Plunkett
BUTCH AND SUNDANCE: THE EARLY DAYS(1979)
Walter Plunkett
TWO WEEKS IN ANOTHER TOWN(1962), cos; LOVE IN THE DESERT(1929), cos; FLYING DOWN TO RIO(1933), cos; LITTLE WOMEN(1933), cos; MORNING GLO-RY(1933), cos; SON OF KONG(1933), cos; FINISHING SCHOOL(1934), cos; GAY DIVORCEE, THE(1934), cos; LITTLE MINISTER, THE(1934), cos; OF HUMAN BOND-AGE(1934), cos; SPITFIRE(1934), cos; STINGAREE(1934), cos; STRICTLY DYNA-MITE(1934), cos; WEDNESDAY'S CHILD(1934), cos; WE'RE RICH AGAIN(1934), cos; WHERE SINNERS MEET(1934), cos; ALICE ADAMS(1935), cos; INFORMER, THE(1935), cos; THREE MUSKETEERS, THE(1935), cos; TO BEAT THE BAND(1935), cos; MARY OF SCOTLAND(1936), cos; PLOUGH AND THE STARS, THE(1936), cos; WOMAN REBELS, A(1936), cos; NOTHING SACRED(1937), cos; QUALITY

STREET(1937), cos; GONE WITH THE WIND(1939), cos; STAGECOACH(1939), cos; STORY OF VERNON AND IRENE CASTLE, THE(1939), cos; VIGIL IN THE NIGHT(1940), cos; GO WEST, YOUNG LADY(1941), cos; LYDIA(1941), cos; SUN-DOWN(1941), cos; HEAT'S ON, THE(1943), cos; ALONG CAME JONES(1945), cos; SONG TO REMEMBER, A(1945), cos; DUEL IN THE SUN(1946), cos; MY BROTHER TALKS TO HORSES(1946), cos; GREEN DOLPHIN STREET(1947), cos; SEA OF GRASS, THE(1947), cos; SONG OF LOVE(1947), cos; KISSING BANDIT, THE(1948), cos; SUMMER HOLIDAY(1948), cos; THREE MUSKETEERS, THE(1948), cos; ADAM'S RIB(1949), cos; LITTLE WOMEN(1949), cos; MADAME BOVARY(1949), cos; SECRET GARDEN, THE(1949), cos; THAT FORSYTE WOMAN(1949), cos; FATHER OF THE BRIDE(1950), cos; KING SOLOMON'S MINES(1950), cos; MINIVER STORY, THE(1950, Brit./U.S.), cos; SUMMER STOCK(1950), cos; TOAST OF NEW ORLEANS, THE(1950), cos; TWO WEEKS WITH LOVE(1950), cos; MAN WITH A CLOAK, THE(1951), cos; MR. IMPERIUM(1951), cos; SHOW BOAT(1951), cos; VENGEANCE VALLEY(1951), cos; WESTWARD THE WOMEN(1951), cos; PLYMOUTH ADVEN-TURE(1952), cos; PRISONER OF ZENDA, THE(1952), cos; SINGIN' IN THE RAIN(1952), cos; ACTRESS, THE(1953), cos; KISS ME KATE(1953), cos; RIDE, VAQUERO!(1953), cos; SCANDAL AT SCOURIE(1953), cos; SEVEN BRIDES FOR SEVEN BROTHERS(1954), cos; VALLEY OF THE KINGS(1954), cos; DIANE(1955), cos; GLASS SLIPPER, THE(1955), cos; JUPITER'S DARLING(1955), cos; KING'S THIEF, THE(1955), cos; MANY RIVERS TO CROSS(1955), cos; MOONFLEET(1955), cos; SCARLET COAT, THE(1955), cos; FORBIDDEN PLANET(1956), cos; LUST FOR LIFE(1956), cos; TRIBUTE TO A BADMAN(1956), cos; GUN GLORY(1957), cos; RAIN-TREE COUNTY(1957), cos; WINGS OF EAGLES, THE(1957), cos; BROTHERS KARAMAZOV, THE(1958), cos; LAW AND JAKE WADE, THE(1958), cos; MERRY ANDREW(1958), cos; SHEEPMAN, THE(1958), cos; SOME CAME RUNNING(1959), cos; BELLS ARE RINGING(1960), cos; CIMARRON(1960), cos; HOME FROM THE HILL(1960), cos; POLLYANNA(1960), cos; POCKETFUL OF MIRACLES(1961), cos; FOUR HORSEMEN OF THE APOCALYPSE, THE(1962), cos; HOW THE WEST WAS WON(1962), cos; MARRIAGE ON THE ROCKS(1965), cos; SEVEN WOMEN(1966), cos
Silents
SINNERS IN LOVE(1928), cos
G.D. Pluzhnik
HEROES OF THE SEA(1941)
Gregory Pluzhnik
SON OF THE REGIMENT(1948, USSR)
B. Pluzhnikov
SUMMER TO REMEMBER, A(1961, USSR), spec eff; VIOLIN AND ROLLER(1962, USSR), spec eff; MEET ME IN MOSCOW(1966, USSR), spec eff
Elmer Plymmer
THREE CABALLEROS, THE(1944), w
George H. Plympton
STORMY(1935), w; BOOTHILL BRIGADE(1937), w; GAMBLING TERROR, THE(1937), w; LAWMAN IS BORN, A(1937), w; DURANGO VALLEY RAIDERS(1938), w; FEUD MAKER(1938), w; PAROLED—TO DIE(1938), w; THUNDER IN THE DES-ERT(1938), w; DAUGHTER OF THE TONG(1939), w; TEXAS WILDCATS(1939), w; OUTLAWS OF THE RIO GRANDE(1941), w; BETTY CO-ED(1946), w; LAST OF THE REDMEN(1947), w; MANHATTAN ANGEL(1948), w
Silents
ADVENTURE SHOP, THE(1918), w; HELP WANTED—MALE!(1920), w; WESTERN FATE(1924), w; BLAZING DAYS(1927), w; ONE GLORIOUS SCRAP(1927), w; HAR-VEST OF HATE, THE(1929), w
George Plympton
ONE WAY TRAIL, THE(1931), w; LOVE BOUND(1932), w; TARZAN THE FEAR-LESS(1933), w; CAVALRY(1936), w; CROOKED TRAIL, THE(1936), w; FLASH GOR-DON(1936), w; ARIZONA GUNFIGHTER(1937), w; BAR Z BAD MEN(1937), w; DOOMED AT SUNDOWN(1937), w; GUN LORDS OF STIRRUP BASIN(1937), w; GUN RANGER, THE(1937), w; IDAHO KID, THE(1937), w; RED ROPE, THE(1937), w; TRAIL OF VENGEANCE(1937), w; TRUSTED OUTLAW, THE(1937), w; PAROLED FROM THE BIG HOUSE(1938), w; RANGER'S ROUNDUP, THE(1938), w; SONGS AND BULLETS(1938), w; WHIRLWIND HORSEMAN(1938), w; MESQUITE BUCK-AROO(1939), w; SMOKY TRAILS(1939), w; TRIGGER PALS(1939), w; TRAILING DOUBLE TROUBLE(1940), w; BILLY THE KID'S FIGHTING PALS(1941), w; PRIDE OF THE BOWERY(1941), w; DEVIL GODDESS(1955), w; ZOMBIES OF MORA TAU(1957), w
Silents
BEAUTY AND BULLETS(1928), w; GRIT WINS(1929), w; HOOFBEATS OF VEN-GEANCE(1929), w
Horace G. Plympton
Silents
ASHAMED OF PARENTS(1921), d; SHOULD A WIFE WORK?(1922), d
Misc. Silents
STREAM OF LIFE, THE(1919), d; THROUGH THE STORM(1922), d
Stephan Plytas
INTERLUDE(1968, Brit.)
Steve Plytas
ROOM 43(1959, Brit.); PURSUERS, THE(1961, Brit.); HOT MONEY GIRL(1962, Brit./Ger.); LIGHT IN THE PIAZZA(1962); MOON-SPINNERS, THE(1964); SPY WHO CAME IN FROM THE COLD, THE(1965, Brit.); THOSE MAGNIFICENT MEN IN THEIR FLYING MACHINES; OR HOW I FLEW FROM LONDON TO PARIS IN 25 HOURS AND 11 MINUTES(1965, Brit.); DUFFY(1968, Brit.); OH! WHAT A LOVELY WAR(1969, Brit.); GET CHARLIE TULLY(1976, Brit.); SILVER BEARS(1978)
Michael Pniewski
1984
BEVERLY HILLS COP(1984)
Avi Pnini
1984
AMBASSADOR, THE(1984)
Hung Kam Po
MAN FROM HONG KONG(1975)
Hung Kim Po
GAME OF DEATH, THE(1979)
Iuy Ling Po
FEMALE PRINCE, THE(1966, Hong Kong)
Ivy Ling Po
LOVE ETERNE, THE(1964, Hong Kong); GRAND SUBSTITUTION, THE(1965, Hong Kong); LADY GENERAL, THE(1965, Hong Kong); MERMAID, THE(1966, Hong Kong); VERMILION DOOR(1969, Hong Kong)

Sham Chien Po
BRUCE LEE–TRUE STORY(1976, Chi.)

Henry Poach
CONNECTION, THE(1962)

Darryl Poafbybitty
TOUGH ENOUGH(1983)

Tom Poata
1984
UTU(1984, New Zealand); WILD HORSES(1984, New Zealand)

Leon Pober
RIDERS TO THE STARS(1954), m/l "Riders to the Stars," Sukman

Vladimir Pobol
THEY CALL ME ROBERT(1967, USSR)

Werner Pochat
VENGEANCE(1968, Ital./Ger.); CAT O'NINE TAILS(1971, Ital./Ger./Fr.); SONNY AND JED(1974, Ital.)

Werner Pochath
SKY RIDERS(1976, U.S./Gr.); JUST A GIGOLO(1979, Ger.); SOME LIKE IT COOL(1979, Ger./Aust./Ital./Fr.)

Esther Poche
WALK THE ANGRY BEACH(1961), ed

Alex Pochet
BEAT THE DEVIL(1953)

John Pochna
INCHON(1981)

Bernie Pock
1984
STREETS OF FIRE(1984)

T. Pockena
DREAM COME TRUE, A(1963, USSR)

Christine Pocket
SALT & PEPPER(1968, Brit.); VENGEANCE OF SHE, THE(1968, Brit.)

Graham Pocket
FULL CIRCLE(1935, Brit.)

Christine Pockett
KILLERS OF KILIMANJARO(1960, Brit.)

Pockriss
SUBJECT WAS ROSES, THE(1968), md

Lee Pockriss
SUBJECT WAS ROSES, THE(1968), m

Adrienne Pocock
IF YOU COULD SEE WHAT I HEAR(1982)

Mike Pocock
YELLOW SUBMARINE(1958, Brit.), animation

Roger Pocock
Silents
MAN IN THE OPEN, A(1919), w

Maurice Podbrey
WHY ROCK THE BOAT?(1974, Can.)

Nicholas Podbrey
1984
HOTEL NEW HAMPSHIRE, THE(1984)

A. Poddubinskiy
MOTHER AND DAUGHTER(1965, USSR)

Art Podell
1984
BLACK ROOM, THE(1984), m

Rick Podell
HERO AT LARGE(1980); LUNCH WAGON(1981)
1984
OASIS, THE(1984)

Virginia Podesser
KIDNAPPING OF THE PRESIDENT, THE(1980, Can.)

Rosanna Podesta
LUXURY GIRLS(1953, Ital.)

Rossana Podesta
ULYSSES(1955, Ital.); SANTIAGO(1956); RAW WIND IN EDEN(1958); SODOM AND GOMORRAH(1962, U.S./Fr./Ital.); TEMPTATION(1962, Fr.); ALONE AGAINST ROME(1963, Ital.); FURY OF THE PAGANS(1963, Ital.); GOLDEN ARROW, THE(1964, Ital.); NAKED HOURS, THE(1964, Ital.); HORROR CASTLE(1965, Ital.); SEVEN DWARFS TO THE RESCUE, THE(1965, Ital.); SEVEN GOLDEN MEN(1969, Fr./Ital./Span.); SUNDAY LOVERS(1980, Ital./Fr.); HERCULES(1983)

Rossanna Podesta
HELEN OF TROY(1956, Ital)

Slim Podgett
Misc. Silents
HEARTS OF THE WEST(1925)

N.A. Podgorny
HOUSE OF DEATH(1932, USSR)

Nikita Podgorny
IDIOT, THE(1960, USSR)

Col. Alois Podhajsky
MIRACLE OF THE WHITE STALLIONS(1963), w

Podobed
Misc. Silents
EXTRAORDINARY ADVENTURES OF MR. WEST IN THE LAND OF THE BOLSHEVIKS(1924, USSR)

Porfiri Podobed
Misc. Silents
DEATH RAY, THE(1925, USSR)

Earl Podolnik
NONE BUT THE BRAVE(1963), p

Richard A. Podolor
BIG FOOT(1973), m

Jean Podromides
24 HOURS IN A WOMAN'S LIFE(1968, Fr./Ger.), m

Les Podwell
NIGHT OF EVIL(1962); GAILY, GAILY(1969)

Amos Poe
FOREIGNER, THE(1978), p&d, w, ed; SUBWAY RIDERS(1981), a, P, d&w, ed; SMITHEREENS(1982)
1984
ALPHABET CITY(1984), d, w

Carey Poe
TAXI DRIVER(1976)
Misc. Talkies
YUM-YUM GIRLS(1976)

Edgar Allan Poe
MURDERS IN THE RUE MORGUE(1932), w; JAWS OF JUSTICE(1933), w; BLACK CAT, THE(1934), w; BUCKET OF BLOOD(1934, Brit.), w; BLACK CAT, THE(1941), w; FALL OF THE HOUSE OF USHER, THE(1952, Brit.), w; PHANTOM OF THE RUE MORGUE(1954), w; MANFISH(1956), w; PREMATURE BURIAL, THE(1962), w; TELL-TALE HEART, THE(1962, Brit.), w; RAVEN, THE(1963), w; MASQUE OF THE RED DEATH, THE(1964, U.S./Brit.), w; MASTER OF HORROR(1965, Arg.), w; TOMB OF LIGEIA, THE(1965, Brit.), w; SPIRITS OF THE DEAD(1969, Fr./Ital.), w; MURDERS IN THE RUE MORGUE(1971), w; DR. TARR'S TORTURE DUNGEON(1972, Mex.), w; WEB OF THE SPIDER(1972, Ital./Fr./Ger.), w; FALL OF THE HOUSE OF USHER, THE(1980), w
1984
BLACK CAT, THE(1984, Ital./Brit.), w
Silents
AVENGING CONSCIENCE, THE(1914), w; ANNABEL LEE(1921), w; STUDENT OF PRAGUE, THE(1927, Ger.), w

Edgar Allen Poe
MYSTERY OF MARIE ROGET, THE(1942), w; HOUSE OF USHER(1960), w; PIT AND THE PENDULUM, THE(1961), w; HAUNTED PALACE, THE(1963), title; BLOOD DEMON(1967, Ger.), w; OBLONG BOX, THE(1969, Brit.), w

Emily Poe
SUBWAY RIDERS(1981)

Evelyn Poe
OLD MAN RHYTHM(1935); TO BEAT THE BAND(1935)

Fernando Poe, Jr.
WALLS OF HELL, THE(1964, U.S./Phil.); RAVAGERS, THE(1965, U.S./Phil.)

Gene Allan Poe
FANTASM(1976, Aus.)

Harlan Cary Poe
STIGMA(1972); TOYS ARE NOT FOR CHILDREN(1972); DOGS OF WAR, THE(1980, Brit.)

James Poe
TOYS IN THE ATTIC(1963), w; CLOSE-UP(1948), w; WITHOUT HONOR(1949), w; PAULA(1952), w; SCANDAL SHEET(1952), w; SLIGHT CASE OF LARCENY, A(1953), w; BIG KNIFE, THE(1955), w; AROUND THE WORLD IN 80 DAYS(1956), w; ATTACK!(1956), w; CAT ON A HOT TIN ROOF(1958), w; HOT SPELL(1958), w; LAST TRAIN FROM GUN HILL(1959), w; SANCTUARY(1961), w; SUMMER AND SMOKE(1961), w; LILIES OF THE FIELD(1963), w; BEDFORD INCIDENT, THE(1965, Brit.), w; RIOT(1969), w; THEY SHOOT HORSES, DON'T THEY?(1969), w

Jeanne Poe
Silents
BULLDOG COURAGE(1922), w; PELL STREET MYSTERY, THE(1924), w

Stephen Poe
1984
MEATBALLS PART II(1984), p

Alfred Poell
DON JUAN(1956, Aust.)

Rita Poelvoorde
BOLERO(1982, Fr.)

Hans Poelzig
Silents
GOLEM: HOW HE CAME INTO THE WORLD, THE(1920, Ger.), art d

Collette Poeppel
COWBOYS, THE(1972)

Adelina Poerio
DON'T LOOK NOW(1973, Brit./Ital.)

Hans Poessenbacher
MAN WHO WALKED THROUGH THE WALL, THE(1964, Ger.)

Jack Poessiger
STUDENT BODY, THE(1976)

Mayor Poeui
TANGA-TIKA(1953)

Ion Poff
Silents
BIG TOWN IDEAS(1921)

Lon Poff
IRON MASK, THE(1929); CAUGHT(1931); MIDNIGHT WARNING, THE(1932); SO BIG(1932); TILLIE AND GUS(1933); KID MILLIONS(1934); SHE COULDN'T TAKE IT(1935); TOAST OF NEW YORK, THE(1937); TEXANS, THE(1938); I MARRIED AN ANGEL(1942); MORE THE MERRIER, THE(1943); JOAN OF ARC(1948); MADAME BOVARY(1949); FATHER'S LITTLE DIVIDEND(1951)
Silents
LAST STRAW, THE(1920); SAND(1920); NIGHT HORSEMAN, THE(1921); OLD SWIMMIN' HOLE, THE(1921); THREE MUSKETEERS, THE(1921); SUZANNA(1922); TRACKED TO EARTH(1922); DANTE'S INFERNO(1924); EXCITEMENT(1924); MAN FROM WYOMING, THE(1924); GREED(1925); MERRY WIDOW, THE(1925); 'MARRIAGE LICENSE?'(1926); MAN WHO LAUGHS, THE(1927); SILVER VALLEY(1927); TENDER HOUR, THE(1927)
Misc. Silents
BONNIE MAY(1920); GREASED LIGHTING(1928)

Gabor Pogani
HORNET'S NEST(1970), ph

Gabor Pogany
CARMELA(1949, Ital.), ph; STORMBOUND(1951, Ital.), ph; STRANGE DECEPTION(1953, Ital.), ph; TIMES GONE BY(1953, Ital.), ph; JOAN AT THE STAKE(1954, Ital./Fr.), ph; MATA HARI'S DAUGHTER(1954, Fr./Ital), ph; QUEEN OF BABYLON, THE(1956, Ital.), ph; HOUSE OF INTRIGUE, THE(1959, Ital.), ph; TRAPPED IN TANGIERS(1960, Ital./Span.), ph; TWO WOMEN(1961, Ital./Fr.), ph; IMPERIAL VENUS(1963, Ital./Fr.), ph; LADY DOCTOR, THE(1963, Fr./Ital./Span.), ph; DARK PURPOSE(1964), ph; FRIENDS FOR LIFE(1964, Ital.), ph; CAVERN, THE(1965, Ital./Ger.), ph; WAR OF THE ZOMBIES, THE(1965 Ital.), ph; MAN COULD GET KILLED,

A(1966), ph; 10:30 P.M. SUMMER(1966, U.S./Span.), ph; DOCTOR FAUSTUS(1967, Brit.), ph; THREE BITES OF THE APPLE(1967), ph; BUONA SERA, MRS. CAMPBELL(1968, Ital.), ph; ROMEO AND JULIET(1968, Ital./Span.), ph; UNINHIBITED, THE(1968, Fr./Ital./Span.), ph; THOSE DARING YOUNG MEN IN THEIR JAUNTY JALOPIES(1969, Fr./Brit./ Ital.), ph; NUN AT THE CROSSROADS, A(1970, Ital./Span.), ph; VALDEZ IS COMING(1971), ph; BLUEBEARD(1972), ph; SNOW JOB(1972), ph

Gyorgy Pogany
FORBIDDEN RELATIONS(1983, Hung.)

Karl Pogany
YOUNG WARRIORS(1983), prod d

Willie Pogany
DAMES(1934), art d

Willy Pogany
PALMY DAYS(1931), set d; TONIGHT OR NEVER(1931), art d; UNHOLY GARDEN, THE(1931), art d; MUMMY, THE(1932), art d; FASHIONS OF 1934(1934), art d; DANTE'S INFERNO(1935), set d

Alessandro Poggi
TENTACLES(1977, Ital.)

Gernando Poggi
JASON AND THE ARGONAUTS(1963, Brit.)

Grace Poggi
KID FROM SPAIN, THE(1932); ROMAN SCANDALS(1933); HEAT WAVE(1935, Brit.); MELODY LINGERS ON, THE(1935); NEVER A DULL MOMENT(1943); SNAKE PIT, THE(1948); SORRY, WRONG NUMBER(1948)

Huguette Poggi
OLIVE TREES OF JUSTICE, THE(1967, Fr.)

Igor Poggi
NEVER A DULL MOMENT(1943)

Miranda Poggi
VERY HANDY MAN, A(1966, Fr./Ital.)

Nando Poggi
FALL OF ROME, THE(1963, Ital.); MINNESOTA CLAY(1966, Ital./Fr./Span.); MYSTERY OF THUG ISLAND, THE(1966, Ital./Ger.), a, ch; JOHNNY YUMA(1967, Ital.)

Octavio Poggi
MIGHTY CRUSADERS, THE(1961, Ital.), p

Ottario Poggi
SECRET MARK OF D'ARTAGNAN, THE(1963, Fr./Ital.), p, w; TIGER OF THE SEVEN SEAS(1964, Fr./Ital.), w

Ottavio Poggi
HANNIBAL(1960, Ital.), p; QUEEN OF THE PIRATES(1961, Ital./Ger.), p; RAGE OF THE BUCCANEERS(1963, Ital.), p, w; QUEEN OF THE NILE(1964, Ital.), p, w; TIGER OF THE SEVEN SEAS(1964, Fr./Ital.), p; MYSTERY OF THUG ISLAND, THE(1966, Ital./Ger.), w; SUPERARGO VERSUS DIABOLICUS(1966, Ital./Span.), p; WEB OF VIOLENCE(1966, Ital./Span.), p, w; LION OF ST. MARK(1967, Ital.), w

Roberto Poggi
TENTACLES(1977, Ital.)

Sylvia Poggioli
VALDEZ IS COMING(1971)

Pogo
ILLUSTRATED MAN, THE(1969)

Shelley Pogoda
1984
JOHNNY DANGEROUSLY(1984); RHINESTONE(1984)

N. Pogodin
SUN SHINES FOR ALL, THE(1961, USSR)

Margareta Pogonat
POPE JOAN(1972, Brit.)

V. Pogosheva
WHEN THE TREES WERE TALL(1965, USSR), w

S. Lee Pogostin
PRESSURE POINT(1962), w; SYNANON(1965), w; HARD CONTRACT(1969), d&w; NIGHTMARE HONEYMOON(1973), w; HIGH ROAD TO CHINA(1983), w

Abigail Pogrebin
RENT CONTROL(1981)

Robin Pogrebin
RENT CONTROL(1981)

E. O. Pogson
IT ALWAYS RAINS ON SUNDAY(1949, Brit.), m

N.A. Pogson
ADVENTURES OF MARCO POLO, THE(1938), w

Charles Pogue
HOUND OF THE BASKERVILLES, THE(1983, Brit.), w; SIGN OF FOUR, THE(1983, Brit.), w

Joseph Pogue
MAN OF IRON(1935)

Ken Pogue
SILENT PARTNER, THE(1979, Can.); SUZANNE(1980, Can.); SILENCE OF THE NORTH(1981, Can.); DEAD ZONE, THE(1983); GREY FOX, THE(1983, Can.)

Kenneth Pogue
NEPTUNE FACTOR, THE(1973, Can.); SECOND WIND(1976, Can.); LOST AND FOUND(1979)
Misc. Talkies
DANGEROUS RELATIONS(1973)

Mel Pogue
FIXED BAYONETS(1951); MA AND PA KETTLE AT THE FAIR(1952); FARMER TAKES A WIFE, THE(1953)

Thomas Pogue
AFTER THE THIN MAN(1936); I MARRIED A DOCTOR(1936); LIBELED LADY(1936); LLOYDS OF LONDON(1936); LONE WOLF RETURNS, THE(1936); ROSE BOWL(1936); STAGE STRUCK(1936); IT'S LOVE I'M AFTER(1937); ONCE A DOCTOR(1937); SECOND HONEYMOON(1937); WOMEN OF GLAMOUR(1937); YOU CAN'T HAVE EVERYTHING(1937); NO PLACE TO GO(1939); FOREIGN CORRESPONDENT(1940)

Jan Pohan
LEMONADE JOE(1966, Czech.); NAKED AMONG THE WOLVES(1967, Ger.)

Maria Pohji
Misc. Talkies
PEPPER AND HIS WACKY TAXI(1972)

Dr. Max Pohl
KARAMAZOV(1931, Ger.)

Klaus Pohl
M(1933, Ger.); GIRL FROM THE MARSH CROFT, THE(1935, Ger.); MASTER OF THE WORLD(1935, Ger.); TESTAMENT OF DR. MABUSE, THE(1943, Ger.); WHITE HORSE INN, THE(1959, Ger.)
Silents
WOMAN ON THE MOON, THE(1929, Ger.)

Hansjurgen Pohland
CORPSE OF BEVERLY HILLS, THE(1965, Ger.), p, w; SERENADE FOR TWO SPIES(1966, Ital./Ger.), p

Lawrence Pohle
BIG SHOT, THE(1937), w; BREAKFAST FOR TWO(1937), w; LET'S MAKE A MILLION(1937), w

Robyn Pohle
COACH(1978)

Peter Pohlenz
NORTH STAR, THE(1943)

Eric Pohlmann
GIRL IN THE PAINTING, THE(1948, Brit.); CHILDREN OF CHANCE(1949, Brit.); BLACKOUT(1950, Brit.); CHANCE OF A LIFETIME(1950, Brit.); CLOUDED YELLOW, THE(1950, Brit.); HIGHLY DANGEROUS(1950, Brit.); THIRD MAN, THE(1950, Brit.); GREAT MANHUNT, THE(1951, Brit.); HELL IS SOLD OUT(1951, Brit.); LONG DARK HALL, THE(1951, Brit.); TRAVELLER'S JOY(1951, Brit.); GAMBLER AND THE LADY, THE(1952, Brit.); HIS EXCELLENCY(1952, Brit.); MOULIN ROUGE(1952); ASSASSIN, THE(1953, Brit.); BLOOD ORANGE(1953, Brit.); HUNDRED HOUR HUNT(1953, Brit.); MOGAMBO(1953); MONSOON(1953); PARIS EXPRESS, THE(1953, Brit.); PENNY PRINCESS(1953, Brit.); TERROR STREET(1953); BELLES OF ST. TRINIAN'S, THE(1954, Brit.); FLAME AND THE FLESH(1954); FORBIDDEN CARGO(1954, Brit.); ROB ROY, THE HIGHLAND ROGUE(1954, Brit.); THEY WHO DARE(1954, Brit.); WOMAN'S ANGLE, THE(1954, Brit.); CONSTANT HUSBAND, THE(1955, Brit.); GENTLEMEN MARRY BRUNETTES(1955); GLASS TOMB, THE(1955, Brit.); LOVERS, HAPPY LOVERS!(1955, Brit.); PRIZE OF GOLD, A(1955); QUENTIN DURWARD(1955); DYNAMITERS, THE(1956, Brit.); LUST FOR LIFE(1956); ACROSS THE BRIDGE(1957, Brit.); BREAK IN THE CIRCLE, THE(1957, Brit.); COUNTERFEIT PLAN, THE(1957, Brit.); FIRE DOWN BELOW(1957, U.S./Brit.); HIGH TERRACE(1957, Brit.); NOT WANTED ON VOYAGE(1957, Brit.); PICKUP ALLEY(1957, Brit.); REACH FOR THE SKY(1957, Brit.); TRIPLE DECEPTION(1957, Brit.); ALL AT SEA(1958, Brit.); DUKE WORE JEANS, THE(1958, Brit.); FURTHER UP THE CREEK!(1958, Brit.); I ACCUSE(1958, Brit.); MAN INSIDE, THE(1958, Brit.); MARK OF THE PHOENIX(1958, Brit.); TALE OF TWO CITIES, A(1958, Brit.); THREE CROOKED MEN(1958, Brit.); ELEPHANT GUN(1959, Brit.); EXPRESSO BONGO(1959, Brit.); HOUSE OF THE SEVEN HAWKS, THE(1959); JOHN PAUL JONES(1959); SANDS OF THE DESERT(1960, Brit.); SNOWBALL(1960, Brit.); SURPRISE PACKAGE(1960); BEWARE OF CHILDREN(1961, Brit.); CARRY ON REGARDLESS(1961, Brit.); KITCHEN, THE(1961, Brit.); PASSPORT TO CHINA(1961, Brit.); SINGER NOT THE SONG, THE(1961, Brit.); UPSTAIRS AND DOWNSTAIRS(1961, Brit.); ALIVE AND KICKING(1962, Brit.); DEVIL'S AGENT, THE(1962, Brit.); LIFE IS A CIRCUS(1962, Brit.); MRS. GIBBONS' BOYS(1962, Brit.); VILLAGE OF DAUGHTERS(1962, Brit.); AGENT 8 3/4(1963, Brit.); CAIRO(1963); FOLLOW THE BOYS(1963); SHADOW OF FEAR(1963, Brit.); 55 DAYS AT PEKING(1963); CARRY ON SPYING(1964, Brit.); MAN WHO COULDN'T WALK, THE(1964, Brit.); NIGHT TRAIN TO PARIS(1964, Brit.); SICILIANS, THE(1964, Brit.); JOEY BOY(1965, Brit.); THOSE MAGNIFICENT MEN IN THEIR FLYING MACHINES; OR HOW I FLEWFROM LONDON TO PARIS IN 25 HOURS AND 11 MINUTES(1965, Brit.); WHERE THE SPIES ARE(1965, Brit.); INSPECTOR CLOUSEAU(1968, Brit.); MINI-AFFAIR, THE(1968, Brit.); HORSEMEN, THE(1971, Brit.); DR. SYN, ALIAS THE SCARECROW(1975); RETURN OF THE PINK PANTHER, THE(1975, Brit.); TIFFANY JONES(1976)

Peter F.U. Pohlney
FIVE GRAVES TO CAIRO(1943)

Dan Poho
GUEST AT STEENKAMPSKRAAL, THE(1977, South Africa)
1984
GUEST, THE(1984, Brit.)

Poia
MAEVA(1961)

Michel Poinareff
DELUSIONS OF GRANDEUR(1971 Fr.), m; LIPSTICK(1976), m

Eugene Poinc
OLLY, OLLY, OXEN FREE(1978), w

Pierre Poincarde
MAN ON A STRING(1960), ph

Byron Poindester
PLAY IT AS IT LAYS(1972), makeup

Poindexter
RETURN FROM WITCH MOUNTAIN(1978)

Byron Poindexter
LADY IN THE DARK(1944); KITTY(1945); MISS SUSIE SLAGLE'S(1945); O.S.S.(1946); PERILS OF PAULINE, THE(1947); TROUBLE WITH WOMEN, THE(1947); JOAN OF ARC(1948); RECKLESS MOMENTS, THE(1949); ROGUES OF SHERWOOD FOREST(1950)

Ina Poindexter
GIANT(1956)

Larry Poindexter
GOING BERSERK(1983)
1984
TOY SOLDIERS(1984)

Anita Pointer
SGT. PEPPER'S LONELY HEARTS CLUB BAND(1978)

Anton Pointer
ROYAL WALTZ, THE(1936)

Guy Kingsley Pointer
CROOKED SKY, THE(1957, Brit.)

Muriel Pointer
Misc. Silents
WHERE THE RAINBOW ENDS(1921, Brit.)

Priscilla Pointer
CARRIE(1976); NICKELODEON(1976); LOOKING FOR MR. GOODBAR(1977); ONION FIELD, THE(1979); COMPETITION, THE(1980); HONEYSUCKLE ROSE(1980); MOMMIE DEAREST(1981); TWILIGHT ZONE–THE MOVIE(1983)

1984
MICKI AND MAUDE(1984)
The Pointer Sisters
CARWASH(1976)
Glen Pointing
BORN LUCKY(1932, Brit.)
Glenore Pointing
OUTSIDER, THE(1933, Brit.)
Richard Pointing
ROCKY HORROR PICTURE SHOW, THE(1975, Brit.), cos
Anton Pointner
TEMPEST(1932, Ger.)
Misc. Silents
HEADS UP, CHARLIE(1926, Ger.); THAT MURDER IN BERLIN(1929, Ger.)
Alain Poire
MIRROR HAS TWO FACES, THE(1959, Fr.), p; NIGHT ENCOUNTER(1963, Fr./Ital.), w; PARIS PICK-UP(1963, Fr./Ital.), p; TWO ARE GUILTY(1964, Fr.), P; FANTOMAS STRIKES BACK(1965, Fr./Ital.), p; GREED IN THE SUN(1965, Fr./ Ital.), p; FANTOMAS(1966, Fr./Ital.), p; MAN FROM COCODY(1966, Fr./Ital.), p; BRAIN, THE(1969, Fr./US), p; TO COMMIT A MURDER(1970, Fr./Ital./Ger.), p; TALL BLOND MAN WITH ONE BLACK SHOE, THE(1973, Fr.), p; DRACULA AND SON(1976, Fr.), p; ACE OF ACES(1982, Fr./Ger.), p; LA BOUM(1983, Fr.), p
Alaine Poire
MAN ESCAPED, A(1957, Fr.), p
Jean-Marie Poire
DRACULA AND SON(1976, Fr.), w; MEN PREFER FAT GIRLS(1981, Fr.), d, w
Leon Poirer
CALL, THE(1938, Fr.), p,d&w
Misc. Silents
L'AFFAIRE DU COURRIER DE LYON(1923, Fr.), d
Rene Poirer
SEA DEVILS(1953)
Jean Poiret
LOVE AND THE FRENCHWOMAN(1961, Fr.); TALES OF PARIS(1962, Fr./Ital.); THREE FABLES OF LOVE(1963, Fr./Ital./Span.); THANK HEAVEN FOR SMALL FAVORS(1965, Fr.); LA CAGE AUX FOLLES(1979, Fr./Ital.), w; LA CAGE AUX FOLLES II(1981, Ital./Fr.), w; LAST METRO, THE(1981, Fr.)
Poiret and Serrault
CANDIDE(1962, Fr.)
Arlette Poirier
FRENCH TOUCH, THE(1954, Fr.); MODIGLIANI OF MONTPARNASSE(1961, Fr./Ital.)
Cheryl Poirier
1984
AGAINST ALL ODDS(1984)
Harvey Poirier
ARTISTS AND MODELS(1937)
Henri Poirier
PARIS BELONGS TO US(1962, Fr.); SOLO(1970, Fr.); MURMUR OF THE HEART(1971, Fr./Ital./Ger.); GIRL FROM LORRAINE, A(1982, Fr./Switz.)
Laurent Poirier
ONE MAN(1979, Can.)
Leon Poirier
AMOUR, AMOUR(1937, Fr.), p
Misc. Silents
AMES D'ORIENT(1919, Fr.), d; LE PENSEUR(1920, Fr.), d; NARAYANA(1920, Fr.), d; L'OMBRE DECHIREE(1921, Fr.), d; JOCELYN(1922, Fr.), d; GENEVIEVE(1923, Fr.), d; LA BRIERE(1925, Fr.), d; JADE CASKET, THE(1929, Fr.), d; VERDUN, VISIONS D'HISTOIRE(1929, Fr.), d
Marie-Claude Poirier
NAKED AUTUMN(1963, Fr.)
Rene Poirier
WOMAN TO WOMAN(1946, Brit.); MOULIN ROUGE(1952); HOUSE OF THE ARROW, THE(1953, Brit.)
Gerard Poirot
SOFT SKIN, THE(1964, Fr.); LES CARABINIERS(1968, Fr./Ital.)
Jean-Baptiste Poirot
1984
LA PETIT SIRENE(1984, Fr.), art d
Poison Gardner Trio
MY BUDDY(1944)
Odile Poisson
LAST ADVENTURE, THE(1968, Fr./Ital.); LACEMAKER, THE(1977, Fr.)
Kenneth Poitevin
FRAULEIN DOKTOR(1969, Ital./Yugo.)
Robby Poitevin
TEXICAN, THE(1966, U.S./Span.), md; HIRED KILLER, THE(1967, Fr./Ital.), m
Cyril Poitier
SAVAGES FROM HELL(1968); DAREDEVIL, THE(1971)
Pamela Poitier
STIR CRAZY(1980)
Sidney Poitier
NO WAY OUT(1950); CRY, THE BELOVED COUNTRY(1952, Brit.); RED BALL EXPRESS(1952); GO, MAN, GO!(1954); BLACKBOARD JUNGLE, THE(1955); GOODBYE, MY LADY(1956); EDGE OF THE CITY(1957); SOMETHING OF VALUE(1957); DEFIANT ONES, THE(1958); MARK OF THE HAWK, THE(1958); PORGY AND BESS(1959); ALL THE YOUNG MEN(1960); VIRGIN ISLAND(1960, Brit.); PARIS BLUES(1961); RAISIN IN THE SUN, A(1961); PRESSURE POINT(1962); LILIES OF THE FIELD(1963); LONG SHIPS, THE(1964, Brit./Yugo.); BEDFORD INCIDENT, THE(1965, Brit.); GREATEST STORY EVER TOLD, THE(1965); PATCH OF BLUE, A(1965); SLENDER THREAD, THE(1965); DUEL AT DIABLO(1966); GUESS WHO'S COMING TO DINNER(1967); IN THE HEAT OF THE NIGHT(1967); TO SIR, WITH LOVE(1967, Brit.); FOR LOVE OF IVY(1968), a, w; LOST MAN, THE(1969); THEY CALL ME MISTER TIBBS(1970); BROTHER JOHN(1971); ORGANIZATION, THE(1971); BUCK AND THE PREACHER(1972), a, d; WARM DECEMBER, A(1973, Brit.), a, d; UPTOWN SATURDAY NIGHT(1974), a, d; LET'S DO IT AGAIN(1975), a, d; WILBY CONSPIRACY, THE(1975, Brit.); PIECE OF THE ACTION, A(1977), a, d; STIR CRAZY(1980), d; HANKY-PANKY(1982), d

Jean-Claude Poitras
1984
COVERGIRL(1984, Can.), cos
Lucie Poitras
WAITING FOR CAROLINE(1969, Can.)
Jacques Poitrenaud
BALLERINA(1950, Fr.), ed; TALES OF PARIS(1962, Fr./Ital.), d; SWEET SKIN(1965, Fr./Ital.), d, w; MARRIAGE CAME TUMBLING DOWN, THE(1968, Fr.), d, w
1984
SUNDAY IN THE COUNTRY, A(1984, Fr.)
Poitrenaud,Cosne
TALES OF PARIS(1962, Fr./Ital.), w
Irene Poitrowski
1984
THIEF OF HEARTS(1984)
Annette Poivre
ANTOINE ET ANTOINETTE(1947 Fr.); CONFESSIONS OF A ROGUE(1948, Fr.); TALE OF FIVE WOMEN, A(1951, Brit.); GATES OF PARIS(1958, Fr./Ital.); JOY HOUSE(1964, Fr.); WHAT'S NEW, PUSSYCAT?(1965, U.S./Fr.)
Bretislav Pojar
MIDSUMMERS NIGHT'S DREAM, A(1961, Czech), anim
Ewa Pokas
CAMERA BUFF(1983, Pol.)
David Pokitillow
SHADOWS(1960)
Eija Pokkinen
DISTANCE(1975)
N. Pokoptsev
SLEEPING BEAUTY, THE(1966, USSR), spec eff
Jaroslava Pokorna
SIGN OF THE VIRGIN(1969, Czech.)
Bohumil Pokorny
DO YOU KEEP A LION AT HOME?(1966, Czech.), set d
A. Pokorskiy
HOUSE WITH AN ATTIC, THE(1964, USSR)
Barbara Pokras
I ESCAPED FROM DEVIL'S ISLAND(1973), ed; LAST DAYS OF MAN ON EARTH, THE(1975, Brit.), ed; TNT JACKSON(1975), ed; SUMMER SCHOOL TEACHERS(1977), ed; H.O.T.S.(1979), ed; DON'T CRY, IT'S ONLY THUNDER(1982), ed
Samuel Pokrass
LIFE BEGINS IN COLLEGE(1937), w; LITTLE PRINCESS, THE(1939), m
Ana Maria Pol
HOUSE THAT SCREAMED, THE(1970, Span.)
Talitha Pol
VILLAGE OF DAUGHTERS(1962, Brit.); WE SHALL SEE(1964, Brit.); RETURN FROM THE ASHES(1965, U.S./Brit.); GIRL GETTERS, THE(1966, Brit.)
Andre Pola
CASBAH(1948); SMUGGLERS' COVE(1948); LOVABLE CHEAT, THE(1949)
Claude Pola
AVALANCHE(1978), w
Claudia Pola
MOON IN THE GUTTER, THE(1983, Fr./Ital.)
Eddie Pola
SUNSHINE AHEAD(1936, Brit.); CATCH AS CATCH CAN(1937, Brit.); HEY! HEY! U.S.A.(1938, Brit.); OUTSIDER, THE(1940, Brit.)
Hanna Pola
Misc. Talkies
NINJA MISSION(1984)
Isa Pola
UNA SIGNORA DELL'OVEST(1942, Ital); FURIA(1947, Ital); LITTLE MARTYR, THE(1947, Ital.); ANGELO IN THE CROWD(1952, Ital.); QUEEN OF SHEBA(1953, Ital.)
Fernando Sanchez Polac
SABINA, THE(1979, Span./Swed.)
Cesare Polacco
WANDERING JEW, THE(1948, Ital.)
Fernando Sanchez Polack
DRUMS OF TABU, THE(1967, Ital./Span.); HUNT, THE(1967, Span.); UGLY ONES, THE(1968, Ital./Span.)
Eva Polagova
DEATH IS CALLED ENGELCHEN(1963, Czech.)
Polaire
AMOUR, AMOUR(1937, Fr.)
Pauline Polaire
Misc. Silents
MACISTE IN HELL(1926, Ital.)
Fernando Sanches Polak
PIZZA TRIANGLE, THE(1970, Ital./Span.)
Jindrich Polak
ROCKET TO NOWHERE(1962, Czech.), d, w; VOYAGE TO THE END OF THE UNIVERSE(1963, Czech.), d, w
Chris Polakof
SATAN'S MISTRESS(1982)
James P. Polakof
MEMORY OF US(1974), p
James Polakof
SILENCE(1974), p; LOVE AND THE MIDNIGHT AUTO SUPPLY(1978), p,d&w; SATAN'S MISTRESS(1982), p, d, w
Misc. Talkies
DARK EYES(1980), d
James Polakoff
Misc. Talkies
SUNBURST(1975), d; SWIM TEAM(1979), d
Phil Polakoff
1984
SIGNAL 7(1984)
Diana Polakov
SUPERSONIC MAN(1979, Span.)

Claire Polan
FIVE THE HARD WAY(1969)
Linda Polan
AND THE SHIP SAILS ON(1983, Ital./Fr.)
Lou Polan
FOURTEEN HOURS(1951); YOU NEVER CAN TELL(1951); MURDER, INC.(1960); ACROSS THE RIVER(1965); HOSPITAL, THE(1971); SEVEN UPS, THE(1973)
Nat Polan
WHAT'S SO BAD ABOUT FEELING GOOD?(1968)
Nina Polan
SOPHIE'S CHOICE(1982)
Rui Polanah
FITZCARRALDO(1982)
Cliff Poland
MISSION MARS(1968), ph; HELLO DOWN THERE(1969), ph; STANLEY(1973), ph
Clifford Poland
FORCE OF IMPULSE(1961), ph; AROUND THE WORLD UNDER THE SEA(1966), ph; FIREBALL JUNGLE(1968), ph
Clifford H. Poland, Jr.
WILD REBELS, THE(1967), ph
John Poland
LOCAL HERO(1983, Brit.)
Joseph E. Poland
Silents
ROUGH LOVER, THE(1918), w
Joseph F. Poland
CATTLE RAIDERS(1938), w; ON THE GREAT WHITE TRAIL(1938), w; STAGE TO MESA CITY(1947), w; STAGE TO BLUE RIVER(1951), w; TEXAS BAD MAN(1953), w
Joseph Franklin Poland
SAILORS' HOLIDAY(1929), w; SOPHOMORE, THE(1929), w; SILVER SPURS(1936), w
Silents
AMATEUR WIDOW, AN(1919), w; AMAZING IMPOSTER, THE(1919), w; SPITFIRE OF SEVILLE, THE(1919), w; BLIND HEARTS(1921), w; ONE A MINUTE(1921), w; SEA LION, THE(1921), w; ELOPE IF YOU MUST(1922), w; GREAT NIGHT, THE(1922), w; MADNESS OF YOUTH(1923), w; ROMANCE LAND(1923), w; THAT'S MY BABY(1926), w; HONEYMOON FLATS(1928), w; STOP THAT MAN(1928), w; THANKS FOR THE BUGGY RIDE(1928), ed
Joseph Poland
IT CAN BE DONE(1929), w; TWO WEEKS OFF(1929), w; SAGEBRUSH TROUBA-DOR(1935), w; LAWLESS NINETIES, THE(1936), w; WINDS OF THE WAS-TELAND(1936), w; OLD CORRAL, THE(1937), w; RANGE DEFENDERS(1937), w; TRIGGER TRIO, THE(1937), w; CONQUEST OF CHEYENNE(1946), w; BLACK HILLS(1948), w; LAW OF THE PANHANDLE(1950), w; TEXAS LAWMEN(1951), w; CANYON AMBUSH(1952), w; DEAD MAN'S TRAIL(1952), w; FARGO(1952), w; TEX-AS CITY(1952), w
Silents
KNOCKOUT, THE(1925), w; UNGUARDED HOUR, THE(1925), w; COHENS AND THE KELLYS IN PARIS, THE(1928), sup
Rhondi Polango
FIRST TIME, THE(1969)
Anna Maria Polani
HERCULES AGAINST THE MOON MEN(1965, Fr./Ital.); MAIDEN FOR A PRINCE, A(1967, Fr./Ital.)
Lorne Polanski
MATTER OF INNOCENCE, A(1968, Brit.)
Roman Polanski
KNIFE IN THE WATER(1963, Pol.), d, w; REPULSION(1965, Brit.), a, d, w; CUL-DE-SAC(1966, Brit.), d, w; LOTNA(1966, Pol.); TASTE FOR WOMEN, A(1966, Fr./Ital.), w; BEAUTIFUL SWINDLERS, THE(1967, Fr./Ital./Jap./Neth.), d, w; FEARLESS VAMPIRE KILLERS, OR PARDON ME BUT YOUR TEETH ARE IN MY NECK, THE(1967), a, d, w; ROSEMARY'S BABY(1968), d&w; DAY AT THE BEACH, A(1970), p, w; MAGIC CHRISTIAN, THE(1970, Brit.); MACBETH(1971, Brit.), p, d, w; CHE?(1973, Ital./Fr./Ger.), a, d, w, ed; CHINATOWN(1974), a, d; TENANT, THE?(1976, Fr.), a, d, w; TESS(1980, Fr./Brit.), d, w
Pavla Polaskova
MARKETA LAZAROVA(1968, Czech.)
Marya Polbentseva
SONG OVER MOSCOW(1964, USSR)
Gregory Polcyn
THINGS ARE TOUGH ALL OVER(1982)
Bridget Pole
WATCHED(1974)
Colin Pole
WATCH BEVERLY(1932, Brit.)
Frances Pole
1984
ULTIMATE SOLUTION OF GRACE QUIGLEY, THE(1984)
Joseph Pole
HIGHWAY TO BATTLE(1961, Brit.), w
Basil Poledouris
TINTORERA...BLOODY WATERS(1977, Brit./Mex.), m; BIG WEDNESDAY(1978), m; BLUE LAGOON, THE(1980), m; DEFIANCE(1980), m; CONAN THE BAR-BARIAN(1982), m; SUMMER LOVERS(1982), m
1984
CONAN THE DESTROYER(1984), m; HOUSE OF GOD, THE(1984), m; MAKING THE GRADE(1984), m; PROTOCOL(1984), m; RED DAWN(1984), m
Lou Polen
SEEDS OF FREEDOM(1943, USSR)
Nat Polen
ACROSS 110TH STREET(1972)
David Poleri
PAY OR DIE(1960)
Franca Polesello
EASY LIFE, THE(1963, Ital.); MISSION BLOODY MARY(1967, Fr./Ital./Span.); NAVAJO JOE(1967, Ital./Span.); TARZANA, THE WILD GIRL(1973)
France Polesello
LOVE IN 4 DIMENSIONS(1965 Fr./Ital.)

Herbert Polesie
EAST SIDE OF HEAVEN(1939), p, w
Albert Polet
BLACK CAT, THE(1934)
Robert Poletick
1984
PREPPIES(1984)
Adelaide Poletti
Misc. Silents
FABIOLA(1923, Ital.)
Victor Poletti
AND THE SHIP SAILS ON(1983, Ital./Fr.)
Piero Poletto
MINOTAUR, THE(1961, Ital.), art d; ECLIPSE(1962, Fr./Ital.), art d; PRISONER OF THE IRON MASK(1962, Fr./Ital.), art d; GLADIATOR OF ROME(1963, Ital.), art d; GLADIATORS 7(1964, Span./Ital.), art d; RED DESERT(1965, Fr./Ital.), art d; TENTH VICTIM, THE(1965, Fr./Ital.), art d; SECRET SEVEN, THE(1966, Ital./Span.), art d; MORE THAN A MIRACLE(1967, Ital./Fr.), art d; WILD, WILD PLANET, THE(1967, Ital.), art d; CHASTITY BELT, THE(1968, Ital.), art d; PLACE FOR LOVERS, A(1969, Ital./Fr.), art d; SEVEN GOLDEN MEN(1969, Fr./Ital./Span.), art d; WITCHES, THE(1969, Fr./Ital.), art d; IN SEARCH OF GREGORY(1970, Brit./Ital.), art d; SUN-FLOWER(1970, Fr./Ital.), art d; TWELVE PLUS ONE(1970, Fr./Ital.), m; BLACK BELLY OF THE TARANTULA, THE(1972, Ital.), art d; PASSENGER, THE(1975, Ital.), art d
Pierro Poletto
GHOSTS, ITALIAN STYLE(1969, Ital./Fr.), art d
Yelena Polevetskaya
QUEEN OF SPADES(1961, USSR)
Yelena Polevitskaya
MUMU(1961, USSR)
L. Polevoy
Misc. Silents
ENGINEER PRITE'S PROJECT(1918, USSR)
Geza Polgar
WINTER WIND(1970, Fr./Hung.)
Tibor Polgar
IN PRAISE OF OLDER WOMEN(1978, Can.), a, m
Van Nest Polglase
UNTAMED(1929), art d; BED OF ROSES(1933), art d; CHANCE AT HEAVEN(1933), art d; CHRISTOPHER STRONG(1933), art d; DOUBLE HARNESS(1933), art d; EMER-GENCY CALL(1933), set d; FLYING DOWN TO RIO(1933), art d; KING KONG(1933), art d; LITTLE WOMEN(1933), art d; MELODY CRUISE(1933), art d; MORNING GLORY(1933), art d; OUR BETTERS(1933), art d; PROFESSIONAL SWEET-HEART(1933), art d; SON OF KONG(1933), art d; FINISHING SCHOOL(1934), art d; GAY DIVORCEE, THE(1934), art d; LITTLE MINISTER, THE(1934), art d; LOST PATROL, THE,(1934), art d; OF HUMAN BONDAGE(1934), art d; RAFTER RO-MANCE(1934), art d; SPITFIRE(1934), art d; THIS MAN IS MINE(1934), art d; ALICE ADAMS(1935), art d; ANNIE OAKLEY(1935), art d; BREAK OF HEARTS(1935), art d; I DREAM TOO MUCH(1935), art d; IN PERSON(1935), art d; INFORMER, THE(1935), art d; JALNA(1935), art d; OLD MAN RHYTHM(1935), art d; POWDERSMOKE RANGE(1935), art d; ROBERTA(1935), art d; ROMANCE IN MANHATTAN(1935), art d; SHE(1935), art d; STAR OF MIDNIGHT(1935), art d; TOP HAT(1935), art d; VILLAGE TALE(1935), art d; BRIDE WALKS OUT, THE(1936), art d; FOLLOW THE FLEET(1936), art d; LADY CONSENTS, THE(1936), art d; MARY OF SCOT-LAND(1936), art d; M'LISS(1936), art d; NIGHT WAITRESS(1936), art d; PLOUGH AND THE STARS, THE(1936), art d; SWING TIME(1936), art d; SYLVIA SCAR-LETT(1936), art d; BREAKFAST FOR TWO(1937), art d; DAMSEL IN DISTRESS, A(1937), art d; DON'T TELL THE WIFE(1937), art d; FIGHT FOR YOUR LADY(1937), art d; FORTY NAUGHTY GIRLS(1937), art d; HIDEAWAY(1937), art d; LIFE OF THE PARTY, THE(1937), art d; LIVING ON LOVE(1937), art d; MEET THE MISSUS(1937), art d; MUSIC FOR MADAME(1937), art d; ON AGAIN–OFF AGAIN(1937), art d; QUALITY STREET(1937), art d; SEA DEVILS(1937), art d; SHALL WE DANCE(1937), art d; STAGE DOOR(1937), art d; SUPER SLEUTH(1937), art d; THAT GIRL FROM PARIS(1937), art d; THEY WANTED TO MARRY(1937), art d; TOAST OF NEW YORK, THE(1937), art d; TOO MANY WIVES(1937), art d; WOMAN I LOVE, THE(1937), art d; BRINGING UP BABY(1938), art d; CAREFREE(1938), art d; EV-ERYBODY'S DOING IT(1938), art d; GO CHASE YOURSELF(1938), art d; HAVING WONDERFUL TIME(1938), art d; I'M FROM THE CITY(1938), art d; JOY OF LIVING(1938), art d; LAW WEST OF TOMBSTONE, THE(1938), art d; MAD MISS MANTON, THE(1938), art d; MAN TO REMEMBER, A(1938), art d; RADIO CITY REVELS(1938), art d; RENEGADE RANGER(1938), art d; ROOM SERVICE(1938), art d; SAINT IN NEW YORK, THE(1938), art d; TARNISHED ANGEL(1938), art d; VIVACIOUS LADY(1938), art d; FIFTH AVENUE GIRL(1939), art d; FIVE CAME BACK(1939), art d; GIRL FROM MEXICO, THE(1939), art d; GREAT MAN VOTES, THE(1939), art d; GUNGA DIN(1939), art d; HUNCHBACK OF NOTRE DAME, THE(1939), art d; IN NAME ONLY(1939), art d; MARSHAL OF MESA CITY, THE(1939), art d; MEXICAN SPITFIRE(1939), art d; PANAMA LADY(1939), art d; RENO(1939), art d; STORY OF VERNON AND IRENE CASTLE, THE(1939), art d; THAT'S RIGHT-YOU'RE WRONG(1939), art d; DANCE, GIRL, DANCE(1940), art d; I'M STILL ALIVE(1940), art d; KITTY FOYLE(1940), art d; LADDIE(1940), art d; LET'S MAKE MUSIC(1940), art d; LITTLE MEN(1940), art d; LUCKY PART-NERS(1940), art d; MARRIED AND IN LOVE(1940), art d; MEXICAN SPITFIRE OUT WEST(1940), art d; MILLIONAIRE PLAYBOY(1940), art d; MILLIONAIRES IN PRIS-ON(1940), art d; MY FAVORITE WIFE(1940), art d; ONE CROWDED NIGHT(1940), art d; POP ALWAYS PAYS(1940), art d; PRIMROSE PATH(1940), art d; STRANGER ON THE THIRD FLOOR(1940), art d; SUED FOR LIBEL(1940), art d; THEY KNEW WHAT THEY WANTED(1940), art d; TOM BROWN'S SCHOOL DAYS(1940), art d; TOO MANY GIRLS(1940), art d; VIGIL IN THE NIGHT(1940), art d; WAGON TRAIN(1940), art d; YOU CAN'T FOOL YOUR WIFE(1940), art d; YOU'LL FIND OUT(1940), art d; CITIZEN KANE(1941), art d; GAY FALCON, THE(1941), art d; LOOK WHO'S LAUGHING(1941), art d; MR. AND MRS. SMITH(1941), art d; SUSPI-CION(1941), art d; TOM, DICK AND HARRY(1941), art d; FALLEN SPARROW, THE(1943), prod d; WHAT A WOMAN!(1943), art d; TOGETHER AGAIN(1944), art d; KISS AND TELL(1945), art d; SHE WOULDN'T SAY YES(1945), art d; SONG TO REMEMBER, A(1945), art d; GILDA(1946), art d; THRILL OF BRAZIL, THE(1946), art d; CROOKED WAY, THE(1949), prod d; FIREBALL, THE(1950), art d; MAN WHO CHEATED HIMSELF, THE(1951), prod d; CATTLE QUEEN OF MONTANA(1954), art d; PASSION(1954), art d; SILVER LODE(1954), art d; ESCAPE TO BURMA(1955), art d; PEARL OF THE SOUTH PACIFIC(1955), art d; TENNESSEE'S PARTNER(1955), art d; SLIGHTLY SCARLET(1956), art d; RIVER'S EDGE, THE(1957), art d

Silents
  KISS IN THE DARK, A(1925), art d
Van Nest Polglasse
  WOMAN REBELS, A(1936), art d
Afro Poli
  AIDA(1954, Ital.); HERCULES(1959, Ital.); LA TRAVIATA(1968, Ital.)
Domenico Poli
  MONSIGNOR(1982)
Maurice Poli
  AVENGER, THE(1962, Fr./Ital.); LA VIACCIA(1962, Fr./Ital.); LONGEST DAY, THE(1962); SANDOKAN THE GREAT(1964, Fr./Ital./Span.); SEVEN GOLDEN MEN(1969, Fr./Ital./Span.)
Mimmi Poli
  AFTER YOU, COMRADE(1967, S. Afr.)
Mimmo Poli
  ROMAN HOLIDAY(1953); NIGHTS OF CABIRIA(1957, Ital.); MORGAN THE PIRATE(1961, Fr./Ital.); PRISONER OF THE IRON MASK(1962, Fr./Ital.); DUEL OF THE TITANS(1963, Ital.); LOVE AND LARCENY(1963, Fr./Ital.); TORPEDO BAY(1964, Ital./Fr.); HONEY POT, THE(1967, Brit.); SABATA(1969, Ital.); ROMA(1972, Ital./Fr.); LUNA(1979, Ital.)
Olivia Poli
  SOFT SKIN, THE(1964, Fr.)
Piero Poli
  NOT RECONCILED, OR "ONLY VIOLENCE HELPS WHERE IT RULES"(1969, Ger.)
Stephen Poliachik
1984
  NATURAL, THE(1984)
Alexis Poliakoff
  MADE IN U.S.A.(1966, Fr.); PIERROT LE FOU(1968, Fr./Ital.)
Stephen Poliakoff
  STRONGER THAN THE SUN(1980, Brit.), w; BLOODY KIDS(1983, Brit.), w; RUNNERS(1983, Brit.), w
Vladimir Poliakoff
  INNOCENTS IN PARIS(1955, Brit.)
A. Poliakov
  1812(1944, USSR)
Lev Poliakov
  WATERLOO(1970, Ital./USSR)
A. Polibin
  CITY OF YOUTH(1938, USSR); GREAT CITIZEN, THE(1939, USSR)
Henry Polic II
  LAST REMAKE OF BEAU GESTE, THE(1977); SCAVENGER HUNT(1979)
Sandy Policare
1984
  RHINESTONE(1984)
Polidor
  ACCATTONE!(1961, Ital.); LA DOLCE VITA(1961, Ital./Fr.); CONJUGAL BED, THE(1963, Ital.); 8 ½(1963, Ital.); SPIRITS OF THE DEAD(1969, Fr./Ital.)
Cianni Polidori
  MY NAME IS NOBODY(1974, Ital./Fr./Ger.), art d
Giani Polidori
  WAR AND PEACE(1956, Ital./U.S.), art d
Gianni Polidori
  MORGAN THE PIRATE(1961, Fr./Ital.), set d; LE AMICHE(1962, Ital.), art d; WHITE SLAVE SHIP(1962, Fr./Ital.), art d; FOUR DAYS OF NAPLES, THE(1963, US/Ital.), set d; GOLIATH AND THE VAMPIRES(1964, Ital.), art d; SHOOT LOUD, LOUDER... I DON'T UNDERSTAND(1966, Ital.), art d; ROSE FOR EVERYONE, A(1967, Ital.), art d; ROVER, THE(1967, Ital.), art d; PRIEST'S WIFE, THE(1971, Ital./Fr.), art d; LADY WITHOUT CAMELLIAS, THE(1981, Ital.), set d
Pino Polidori
  DIRTY OUTLAWS, THE(1971, Ital.)
Gian L. Polidoro
  RENT CONTROL(1981), d
Gian Luigi Polidoro
  DEVIL, THE(1963), d; AMERICAN WIFE, AN(1965, Ital.), d, w; RUN FOR YOUR WIFE(1966, Fr./Ital.), d, w; CLARETTA AND BEN(1983, Ital., Fr.), d, w
Igi Polidoro
  CONJUGAL BED, THE(1963, Ital.); MAN WITH THE BALLOONS, THE(1968, Ital./Fr.)
Richard K. Polimer
  BIG GUY, THE(1939), w; WINNER'S CIRCLE, THE(1948), p; BEHIND THE HIGH WALL(1956), w
Vladimir Polin
  STAR INSPECTOR, THE(1980, USSR), d
Joe Polina
  WHAT DID YOU DO IN THE WAR, DADDY?(1966)
David Polinger
  WHO SAYS I CAN'T RIDE A RAINBOW!(1971)
Radford Polinsky
1984
  ADVENTURES OF BUCKAROO BANZAI: ACROSS THE 8TH DIMENSION, THE(1984)
Richard Polinsky
1984
  REVENGE OF THE NERDS(1984), cos
Joel Polis
  THING, THE(1982)
1984
  BEST DEFENSE(1984)
Peter Politanoff
  T.A.G.: THE ASSASSINATION GAME(1982), prod d
Charlene Polite
  MEMORY OF US(1974)
Lena Politeo
  EVENT, AN(1970, Yugo.)
Isacco Politi
  SANDRA(1966, Ital.)

Eugene Polito
  PLUNDERERS, THE(1960), ph; PORTRAIT OF A MOBSTER(1961), ph
Gene Polito
  UP IN SMOKE(1978), ph; TWIST ALL NIGHT(1961), ph; RIDE TO HANGMAN'S TREE, THE(1967), ph; COLOSSUS: THE FORBIN PROJECT(1969), ph; PRIME CUT(1972), ph; FIVE ON THE BLACK HAND SIDE(1973), ph; WESTWORLD(1973), ph; FUTUREWORLD(1976), ph; TRACKDOWN(1976), ph
Jean Polito
  BAD NEWS BEARS GO TO JAPAN, THE(1978), ph
Jennifer Polito
  INCREDIBLE SHRINKING WOMAN, THE(1981), set d; PSYCHO II(1983), set d
1984
  SIXTEEN CANDLES(1984), set d
Jon Polito
1984
  C.H.U.D.(1984)
Lina Polito
  LOVE AND ANARCHY(1974, Ital.); ALL SCREWED UP(1976, Ital.)
Sol Polito
  SHOW GIRL(1928), ph; BROADWAY BABIES(1929), ph; ISLE OF LOST SHIPS(1929), ph; MAN AND THE MOMENT, THE(1929), ph; PARIS(1929), ph; SEVEN FOOTPRINTS TO SATAN(1929), ph; TWIN BEDS(1929), ph; GIRL OF THE GOLDEN WEST(1930), ph; MADONNA OF THE STREETS(1930), ph; NO, NO NANETTE(1930), ph; NUMBERED MEN(1930), ph; PLAYING AROUND(1930), ph; SHOW GIRL IN HOLLYWOOD(1930), ph; WIDOW FROM CHICAGO, THE(1930), ph; BIG BUSINESS GIRL(1931), ph; FIVE STAR FINAL(1931), ph; GOING WILD(1931), ph; HOT HEIRESS(1931), ph; LOCAL BOY MAKES GOOD(1931), ph; RULING VOICE, THE(1931), ph; SUICIDE FLEET(1931), ph; WOMAN HUNGRY(1931), ph; BLESSED EVENT(1932), ph; DARK HORSE, THE(1932), ph; FIREMAN, SAVE MY CHILD(1932), ph; I AM A FUGITIVE FROM A CHAIN GANG(1932), ph; IT'S TOUGH TO BE FAMOUS(1932), ph; THREE ON A MATCH(1932), ph; TWO SECONDS(1932), ph; UNION DEPOT(1932), ph; GOLD DIGGERS OF 1933(1933), ph; MIND READER, THE(1933), ph; PICTURE SNATCHER(1933), ph; WORKING MAN, THE(1933), ph; 42ND STREET(1933), ph; DARK HAZARD(1934), ph; DOCTOR MONICA(1934), ph; FLIRTATION WALK(1934), ph; HI, NELLIE!(1934), ph; MADAME DU BARRY(1934), ph; WONDER BAR(1934), ph; FRISCO KID(1935), ph; G-MEN(1935), ph; GO INTO YOUR DANCE(1935), ph; IN CALIENTE(1935), ph; SHIPMATES FOREVER(1935), ph; SWEET ADELINE(1935), ph; WOMAN IN RED, THE(1935), ph; CHARGE OF THE LIGHT BRIGADE, THE(1936), ph; PETRIFIED FOREST, THE(1936), ph; SONS O' GUNS(1936), ph; THREE MEN ON A HORSE(1936), ph; PRINCE AND THE PAUPER, THE(1937), ph; READY, WILLING AND ABLE(1937), ph; VARSITY SHOW(1937), ph; ADVENTURES OF ROBIN HOOD, THE(1938), ph; ANGELS WITH DIRTY FACES(1938), ph; BOY MEETS GIRL(1938), ph; GOLD DIGGERS IN PARIS(1938), ph; GOLD IS WHERE YOU FIND IT(1938), ph; CONFESSIONS OF A NAZI SPY(1939), ph; DODGE CITY(1939), ph; FOUR WIVES(1939), ph; ON YOUR TOES(1939), ph; PRIVATE LIVES OF ELIZABETH AND ESSEX, THE(1939), ph; YOU CAN'T GET AWAY WITH MURDER(1939), ph; SANTA FE TRAIL(1940), ph; SEA HAWK, THE(1940), ph; VIRGINIA CITY(1940), ph; CITY, FOR CONQUEST(1941), ph; SEA WOLF, THE(1941), ph; CAPTAINS OF THE CLOUDS(1942), ph; GAY SISTERS, THE(1942), ph; NOW, VOYAGER(1942), ph; OLD ACQUAINTANCE(1943), ph; THIS IS THE ARMY(1943), ph; ADVENTURES OF MARK TWAIN, THE(1944), ph; ARSENIC AND OLD LACE(1944), ph; CORN IS GREEN, THE(1945), ph; RHAPSODY IN BLUE(1945), ph; CINDERELLA JONES(1946), ph; CLOAK AND DAGGER(1946), ph; STOLEN LIFE, A(1946), ph; ESCAPE ME NEVER(1947), ph; LONG NIGHT, THE(1947), ph; VOICE OF THE TURTLE, THE(1947), ph; SORRY, WRONG NUMBER(1948), ph; ANNA LUCASTA(1949), ph
Silents
  SINS OF SOCIETY(1915), ph; RECKONING DAY, THE(1918), ph; ARE YOU LEGALLY MARRIED?(1919), ph; ALIAS JIMMY VALENTINE(1920), ph; SHOULD A WOMAN TELL?(1920), ph; LOADED DOOR, THE(1922), ph; GIRL OF THE GOLDEN WEST, THE(1923), ph; ROARING RAILS(1924), ph; CRIMSON RUNNER, THE(1925), ph; UNKNOWN CAVALIER, THE(1926), ph; SOMEWHERE IN SONORA(1927), ph; SCARLET SEAS(1929), ph
Haydee Politoff
  DON'T PLAY WITH MARTIANS(1967, Fr.); LOVE PROBLEMS(1970, Ital.); LA COLLECTIONNEUSE(1971, Fr.), a, w; CHLOE IN THE AFTERNOON(1972, Fr.); DRACULA'S GREAT LOVE(1972, Span.); HUMAN FACTOR, THE(1975)
Vassili Politselmako
  ROAD HOME, THE(1947, USSR)
Luis Politti
  NEST, THE(1982, Span.)
Steven Polivka
1984
  RAW COURAGE(1984), ed
Vic Polizos
  BRUBAKER(1980); EDDIE MACON'S RUN(1983)
1984
  C.H.U.D.(1984); MUPPETS TAKE MANHATTAN, THE(1984)
Cecilia Polizzi
  DIVINE NYMPH, THE(1979, Ital.)
Charles Polizzi
  HOODLUM SAINT, THE(1946)
Vincenzo Polizzi
  ITALIANO BRAVA GENTE(1965, Ital./USSR)
Brigid Polk
  CHELSEA GIRLS, THE(1967)
Charles Polk
  GAMBLER, THE(1974)
David Polk
  I'M DANCING AS FAST AS I CAN(1982)
Gordon Polk
  STARLIFT(1951); SUBMARINE COMMAND(1951); INHERIT THE WIND(1960)
Jeff Polk
  INDEPENDENCE DAY(1983)
Oscar Polk
  GREEN PASTURES(1936); IT'S A GREAT LIFE(1936); UNDERWORLD(1937); GONE WITH THE WIND(1939); REAP THE WILD WIND(1942); WHITE CARGO(1942); CABIN IN THE SKY(1943)

Rudolph Polk
OTHER LOVE, THE(1947), md; RAMROD(1947), md; FORCE OF EVIL(1948), md; CAUGHT(1949), md; KISS FOR CORLISS, A(1949), md

Alex Polks
1984
NIGHT PATROL(1984)

Lee Poll
SAILOR WHO FELL FROM GRACE WITH THE SEA, THE(1976, Brit.), cos; DIFFERENT STORY, A(1978), set d; CHAPTER TWO(1979), set d; FORMULA, THE(1980), set d; SEEMS LIKE OLD TIMES(1980), set d; GREASE 2(1982), set d
1984
PLACES IN THE HEART(1984), set d

Mark Poll
JAZZ SINGER, THE(1980), set d

Martin H. Poll
LOVE IS A BALL(1963), p; SYLVIA(1965), p

Martin Poll
LION IN WINTER, THE(1968, Brit.), p; MAGIC GARDEN OF STANLEY SWEE-THART, THE(1970), p; POSSESSION OF JOEL DELANEY, THE(1972), p; MAN WHO LOVED CAT DANCING, THE(1973), p; NIGHT WATCH(1973, Brit.), p; SAILOR WHO FELL FROM GRACE WITH THE SEA, THE(1976, Brit.), p; SOMEBODY KILLED HER HUSBAND(1978), p; NIGHTHAWKS(1981), p
1984
GIMME AN 'F'(1984), p

Alice Pollack
TOWN CALLED HELL, A(1971, Span./Brit.), cos

Anne Pollack
PIRANHA II: THE SPAWNING(1981, Neth.)

Aubrey Pollack
NON-STOP NEW YORK(1937, Brit.)

Barry Pollack
COOL BREEZE(1972), d&w; THIS IS A HIJACK(1973), d

Ben Pollack
DISC JOCKEY(1951); GLENN MILLER STORY, THE(1953); BENNY GOODMAN STORY, THE(1956)

Bernard Pollack
NECROMANCY(1972), cos; NETWORK(1976)

Bernie Pollack
BOBBY DEERFIELD(1977), cos; STRAIGHT TIME(1978), cos; ELECTRIC HORSE-MAN, THE(1979), cos; ORDINARY PEOPLE(1980), cos; ABSENCE OF MALICE(1981), cos; TOOTSIE(1982)
1984
NATURAL, THE(1984), cos

Deborah Pollack
1984
SIXTEEN CANDLES(1984)

Dee Pollack
BLUE VEIL, THE(1951); TAKE A GIANT STEP(1959); EMBASSY(1972, Brit.)

Eileen Pollack
Misc. Talkies
STAIRWAY FOR A STAR(1947)

Ellen Pollack
GOLDEN LINK, THE(1954, Brit.); WICKED LADY, THE(1983, Brit.)

Fernando Sanchez Pollack
CAPTAIN APACHE(1971, Brit.)

George Pollack
BROTH OF A BOY(1959, Brit.), d

Lew Pollack
YANKS ARE COMING, THE(1942), a, w; MAN OF COURAGE(1943), w

Mimi Pollack
ILLICIT INTERLUDE(1954, Swed.)

Murray Pollack
TATTERED DRESS, THE(1957)

Nancy R. Pollack
SUCH GOOD FRIENDS(1971)

Rebecca Pollack
1984
RACING WITH THE MOON(1984)

Sidney Pollack
BOBBY DEERFIELD(1977), p&d; ELECTRIC HORSEMAN, THE(1979), d

Sydney Pollack
WAY WE WERE, THE(1973), d; WAR HUNT(1962); SLENDER THREAD, THE(1965), d; THIS PROPERTY IS CONDEMNED(1966), d; SCALPHUNTERS, THE(1968), d; SWIMMER, THE(1968), d; CASTLE KEEP(1969), d; THEY SHOOT HORSES, DON'T THEY?(1969), p, d; JEREMIAH JOHNSON(1972), d; THREE DAYS OF THE CONDOR(1975), d; YAKUZA, THE(1975, U.S./Jap.), p&d; ABSENCE OF MALICE(1981), p&d; TOOTSIE(1982), a, p, d
1984
SONGWRITER(1984), p

Ulf Pollack
GOSPEL ROAD, THE(1973)

Joseph Pollak
WORLDS APART(1980, U.S., Israel)

Kay Pollak
ELVIS! ELVIS!(1977, Swed.), d, w

Mimi Pollak
NIGHT IN JUNE, A(1940, Swed.); FLIGHT OF THE EAGLE(1983, Swed.)

Mel Pollan
STAKEOUT ON DOPE STREET(1958)

Tracy Pollan
BABY, IT'S YOU(1983)

Polland
M(1933, Ger.)

Gene Pollar
Misc. Silents
RETURN OF TARZAN, THE(1920)

A. Paul Pollard
LAST TIME I SAW ARCHIE, THE(1961), spec eff; HALLELUJAH TRAIL, THE(1965), spec eff; REIVERS, THE(1969), spec eff

Alan Pollard
IN NAME ONLY(1939)

Alex Pollard
WITHOUT REGRET(1935); LITTLE LORD FAUNTLEROY(1936); OUR RELATIONS(1936); CHAMPAGNE WALTZ(1937); THREE BLIND MICE(1938); DAY-TIME WIFE(1939); KING OF CHINATOWN(1939); FLORIAN(1940); LILLIAN RUS-SELL(1940); GIRL, A GUY AND A GOB, A(1941); JOHNNY EAGER(1942); SONG OF THE ISLANDS(1942); TALES OF MANHATTAN(1942); WE WERE DANCING(1942); FOUR JILLS IN A JEEP(1944); HAVING WONDERFUL CRIME(1945); WOMAN IN THE WINDOW, THE(1945); DECEPTION(1946); EASY TO WED(1946); SECRET HEART, THE(1946)

Alexander Pollard
CROSS-EXAMINATION(1932); MONSTER MAKER, THE(1944); KID FROM BOOK-LYN, THE(1946)

Aubrey P. Pollard
GLORY BOY(1971), spec eff

Bob Pollard
VELVET TRAP, THE(1966); PEACE FOR A GUNFIGHTER(1967)

Bud Pollard
BLACK KING(1932), d; VICTIMS OF PERSECUTION(1933), a, d; DEAD MARCH, THE(1937), p&d; BEWARE(1946), d, ed; LOOK OUT SISTER(1948), d, ed
Misc. Talkies
ALICE IN WONDERLAND(1931), d; IT HAPPENED IN HARLEM(1945), d; TALL, TAN AND TERRIFIC(1946), d; BIG TIMERS(1947), d
Misc. Silents
DANGER MAN, THE(1930), d

Budd Pollard
LOVE ISLAND(1952), d

Daphne Pollard
BIG TIME(1929); SKY HAWK(1929); SOUTH SEA ROSE(1929); LOOSE ANK-LES(1930); SWING HIGH(1930); WHAT A WIDOW(1930); BRIGHT LIGHTS(1931); LADY REFUSES, THE(1931); BONNIE SCOTLAND(1935); OUR RELATIONS(1936); TILLIE THE TOILER(1941); DANCING MASTERS, THE(1943); KID DYNAMITE(1943)
Silents
SINNERS IN LOVE(1928)

E. C. Pollard
COLLISION(1932, Brit.), w

Harry A. Pollard
TONIGHT AT TWELVE(1929), p&d, w; UNDERTOW(1930), d
Silents
LOADED DOOR, THE(1922), d; OH, DOCTOR(1924), d
Misc. Silents
GIRL WHO COULDN'T GROW UP, THE(1917), d; TRIFLING WITH HONOR(1923), d; SPORTING YOUTH(1924), d; I'LL SHOW YOU THE TOWN(1925), d; POKER FACES(1926), d

Harry Pollard
SHOW BOAT(1929), d, w; PRODIGAL, THE(1931), d; SHIPMATES(1931), d; FAST LIFE(1932), d; FELLER NEEDS A FRIEND(1932), d
Silents
DAMAGED GOODS(1915), w; GIRL FROM HIS TOWN, THE(1915), d; INFATUA-TION(1915); RECKONING DAY, THE(1918), d; K–THE UNKNOWN(1924), d; RECK-LESS AGE, THE(1924), d; COHENS AND KELLYS, THE(1926), d, w
Misc. Silents
QUEST, THE(1915), a, d; DRAGON, THE(1916), d; MISS JACKIE OF THE NA-VY(1916), d; PEARL OF PARADISE, THE(1916), a, d; DEVIL'S ASSISTANT, THE(1917), d; DANGER GAME, THE(1918), d; CONFIDENCE(1922), d; TRIM-MED(1922), d; CALIFORNIA STRAIGHT AHEAD(1925), d

Hoyt J. Pollard
DELIVERANCE(1972)

Laura Pollard
Silents
KID, THE(1921)

Michael J. Pollard
ADVENTURES OF A YOUNG MAN(1962); STRIPPER, THE(1963); SUMMER MAG-IC(1963); RUSSIANS ARE COMING, THE RUSSIANS ARE COMING, THE(1966); WILD ANGELS, THE(1966); BONNIE AND CLYDE(1967); CAPRICE(1967); ENTER LAUGHING(1967); JIGSAW(1968); HANNIBAL BROOKS(1969, Brit.); LITTLE FAUSS AND BIG HALSY(1970); LEGEND OF FRENCHIE KING, THE(1971, Fr./Ital./Span./Brit.); DIRTY LITTLE BILLY(1972); SUNDAY IN THE COUNTRY(1975, Can.); BE-TWEEN THE LINES(1977); MELVIN AND HOWARD(1980)

Paul Pollard
X-15(1961), spec eff; MANCHURIAN CANDIDATE, THE(1962), spec eff; SER-GEANTS 3(1962), spec eff; SATAN BUG, THE(1965), spec eff; IS PARIS BUR-NING?(1966, U.S./Fr.), spec eff; POPPY IS ALSO A FLOWER, THE(1966), spec eff; HORNET'S NEST(1970), spec eff

Peter Pollard
SMALL CIRCLE OF FRIENDS, A(1980)

Samm Pollard
BODY AND SOUL(1981), ed

Samuel Pollard
NIGHT OF THE ZOMBIES(1981), ed

Snub Pollard
EX-FLAME(1931); MAKE ME A STAR(1932); MIDNIGHT PATROL, THE(1932); PURCHASE PRICE, THE(1932); COCKEYED CAVALIERS(1934); STINGAREE(1934); NIGHT IS YOUNG, THE(1935); BARS OF HATE(1936); CRIME PATROL, THE(1936); GENTLEMAN FROM LOUISIANA(1936); WHITE LEGION, THE(1936); ARIZONA DAYS(1937); HEADIN' FOR THE RIO GRANDE(1937); HITTIN' THE TRAIL(1937); NATION AFLAME(1937); RIDERS OF THE ROCKIES(1937); SING, COWBOY, SING(1937); SPECIAL AGENT K-7(1937); TEX RIDES WITH THE BOY SCOUTS(1937); FRONTIER TOWN(1938); ROLLIN' PLAINS(1938); STARLIGHT OVER TEXAS(1938); UTAH TRAIL(1938); WHERE THE BUFFALO ROAM(1938); HOLLYWOOD CAVAL-CADE(1939); LURE OF THE WASTELAND(1939); MESQUITE BUCKAROO(1939); SONG OF THE BUCKAROO(1939); MURDER ON THE YUKON(1940); GIRL, A GUY AND A GOB, A(1941); 'NEATH BROOKLYN BRIDGE(1942); KID DYNAMITE(1943); KID RIDES AGAIN, THE(1943); CASANOVA BROWN(1944); GYPSY WILDCAT(1944); KITTY(1945); SAN ANTONIO(1945); KID FROM BOOKLYN, THE(1946); CHEYEN-NE(1947); FRAMED(1947); MAGIC TOWN(1947); MIRACLE ON 34TH STREET, THE(1947); PERILS OF PAULINE, THE(1947); BACK TRAIL(1948); FAMILY HONEY-MOON(1948); ISN'T IT ROMANTIC?(1948); JOHNNY BELINDA(1948); LOADED PISTOLS(1948); MIRACLE OF THE BELLS, THE(1948); CROOKED WAY, THE(1949);

BOOTS MALONE(1952); CARRIE(1952); LIMELIGHT(1952); PETE KELLY'S BLUES(1955); JEANNE EAGELS(1957); MAN OF A THOUSAND FACES(1957); IN THE MONEY(1958); ROCK-A-BYE BABY(1958); WHO WAS THAT LADY?(1960); ERRAND BOY, THE(1961); ONE-EYED JACKS(1961); POCKETFUL OF MIRA-CLES(1961)
Misc. Talkies
JUST MY LUCK(1936); SANTA FE RIDES(1937)
Snubby Pollard
STUDS LONIGAN(1960)
Thommy Pollard
PENITENTIARY(1979)
Twila Pollard
Misc. Talkies
69 MINUTES(1977)
Flight Officer W. Pollard
SCHOOL FOR DANGER(1947, Brit.), ph
William Pollard
MYSTERY ON BIRD ISLAND(1954, Brit.), ph
Silents
DOING THEIR BIT(1918)
Peter Pollatschek
PINOCCHIO(1969, E. Ger.)
G. Pollatschik
HIS MAJESTY, KING BALLYHOO(1931, Ger.), ed; OUTSIDER, THE(1933, Brit.), ed
Albert Pollet
MERRY WIDOW, THE(1934); FOLIES DERGERE(1935); GILDED LILY, THE(1935); DESIRE(1936); YOURS FOR THE ASKING(1936); CAFE METROPOLE(1937); ESPION-AGE(1937); I MET HIM IN PARIS(1937); MAYTIME(1937); THIN ICE(1937); I WAKE UP SCREAMING(1942); GILDA(1946); RAZOR'S EDGE, THE(1946); CALCUTTA(1947); CASS TIMBERLANE(1947); DOUBLE LIFE, A(1947); HOMECOMING(1948); NIGHT HAS A THOUSAND EYES(1948); SUN COMES UP, THE(1949); ON THE RIVE-RA(1951); GOLDEN HAWK, THE(1952); TO CATCH A THIEF(1955)
Silents
MYSTERIOUS LADY, THE(1928)
Jean-Daniel Pollet
SIX IN PARIS(1968, Fr.), d, w
Luciano Polletin
KNIVES OF THE AVENGER(1967, Ital.)
Mario Polletin
SEVEN TASKS OF ALI BABA, THE(1963, Ital.)
Albert Pollett
ROGUES' REGIMENT(1948); FOR HEAVEN'S SAKE(1950)
Alex Pollette
FIFTEEN WIVES(1934)
Piero Polletto
L'AVVENTURA(1960, Ital.), set d
Jack Pollexfen
MR. BIG(1943), w; TREASURE OF MONTE CRISTO(1949), w; DESERT HAWK, THE(1950), w; AT SWORD'S POINT(1951), w; MAN FROM PLANET X(1951), p, w; SECRET OF CONVICT LAKE, THE(1951), w; SON OF DR. JEKYLL, THE(1951), w; CAPTIVE WOMEN(1952), p&w; LADY IN THE IRON MASK(1952), w; CAPTAIN JOHN SMITH AND POCAHONTAS(1953), p, w; NEANDERTHAL MAN, THE(1953), p, w; PORT SINISTER(1953), p, w; PROBLEM GIRLS(1953), p, w; SWORD OF VENUS(1953), p, w; CAPTAIN KIDD AND THE SLAVE GIRL(1954), w; DRA-GON'S GOLD(1954), p,d&w; RETURN TO TREASURE ISLAND(1954), p, w; SON OF SINBAD(1955), w; INDESTRUCTIBLE MAN, THE(1956), p&d; DAUGHTER OF DR. JEKYLL(1957), p, w; FIVE BOLD WOMEN(1960), w; ATOMIC BRAIN, THE(1964), p
Gerard Pollicand
VERY CURIOUS GIRL, A(1970, Fr.), ed; PLAYTIME(1973, Fr.), ed
Teno Pollick
MADAME X(1966); HINDENBURG, THE(1975)
Ferdinand Pollina
SPECTER OF THE ROSE(1946)
Francis Pollini
PRETTY MAIDS ALL IN A ROW(1971), w
Joe Pollini
JESSICA(1962, U.S./Ital./Fr.); FALL OF ROME, THE(1963, Ital.); REASON TO LIVE, A REASON TO DIE, A(1974, Ital./Fr./Ger./Span.)
Leo Pollini
ROCK AROUND THE WORLD(1957, Brit.)
Richard Pollister
PAPER LION(1968), ph
James L. Pollitt
Silents
JOHN HALIFAX, GENTLEMAN(1915, Brit.), w
Lydia Pollman
BEAUTIFUL ADVENTURE(1932, Ger.)
Lydia Pollmann
MONEY ON THE STREET(1930, Aust.)
Jackie Pollo
NOT NOW DARLING(1975, Brit.)
Aubrey Pollock
MEMBER OF THE JURY(1937, Brit.); PASSENGER TO LONDON(1937, Brit.); SAM SMALL LEAVES TOWN(1937, Brit.)
Ben Pollock
YOU WERE MEANT FOR ME(1948); I WAS A MALE WAR BRIDE(1949)
Channing Pollock
LOCKED DOOR, THE(1929), w; MIDNIGHT INTRUDER(1938), w; RED SHEIK, THE(1963, Ital.); JUDEX(1966, Fr./Ital.)
Silents
LITTLE GRAY LADY, THE(1914), w; SUCH A LITTLE QUEEN(1914), w; SECRET ORCHARD(1915), w; BY WHOSE HAND?(1916), w; FINAL CURTAIN, THE(1916), w; PRETENDERS, THE(1916), w; RED WIDOW, THE(1916), w; HIS FATHER'S SON(1917), w; PERFECT LADY, A(1918), w; SUCH A LITTLE QUEEN(1921), w; ENEMY, THE(1927), w; METROPOLIS(1927, Ger.), t
D. Pollock
CAPTAIN APACHE(1971, Brit.)

David Pollock
BAD NEWS BEARS, THE(1976); JIM, THE WORLD'S GREATEST(1976); BAD NEWS BEARS IN BREAKING TRAINING, THE(1977); BAD NEWS BEARS GO TO JAPAN, THE(1978)
Dee Pollock
BEWARE, MY LOVELY(1952); IT GROWS ON TREES(1952); OLD WEST, THE(1952); PARK ROW(1952); MR. SCOUTMASTER(1953); CAROUSEL(1956); WAYWARD BUS, THE(1957); LINEUP, THE(1958); LEGEND OF TOM DOOLEY, THE(1959); PLUNDER-ERS, THE(1960); KELLY'S HEROES(1970, U.S./Yugo.)
Eileen Pollock
1984
FOUR DAYS IN JULY(1984)
Ellen Pollock
INFORMER, THE(1929, Brit.); GENTLEMAN OF PARIS, A(1931); NIGHT BIRDS(1931, Brit.); FIRST MRS. FRASER, THE(1932, Brit.); LAST COUPON, THE(1932, Brit.); MY WIFE'S FAMILY(1932, Brit.); PICCADILLY(1932, Brit.); CHARM-ING DECEIVER, THE(1933, Brit.); CHANNEL CROSSING(1934, Brit.); MISTER CINDERS(1934, Brit.); IT'S A BET(1935, Brit.); REGAL CAVALCADE(1935, Brit.); HAPPY FAMILY, THE(1936, Brit.); MILLIONS(1936, Brit.); AREN'T MEN BEASTS?(1937, Brit.); NON-STOP NEW YORK(1937, Brit.); SPLINTERS IN THE AIR(1937, Brit.); STREET SINGER, THE(1937, Brit.); LOVES OF MADAME DUBAR-RY, THE(1938, Brit.); SONS OF THE SEA(1939, Brit.); SPARE A COPPER(1940, Brit.); KISS THE BRIDE GOODBYE(1944, Brit.); DON CHICAGO(1945, Brit.); WARNING TO WANTONS, A(1949, Brit.); SOMETHING IN THE CITY(1950, Brit.); GALLOPING MAJOR, THE(1951, Brit.); TO HAVE AND TO HOLD(1951, Brit.); FAKE, THE(1953, Brit.); TIME OF HIS LIFE, THE(1955, Brit.); NOT SO DUSTY(1956, Brit.); SCOTLAND YARD DRAGNET(1957, Brit.); LONG KNIFE, THE(1958, Brit.); SO EVIL SO YOUNG(1961, Brit.); MASTER SPY(1964, Brit.); RAPTURE(1965); FINDERS KEEP-ERS(1966, Brit.); WHO KILLED THE CAT?(1966, Brit.); HORROR HOSPITAL(1973, Brit.)
Silents
MOULIN ROUGE(1928, Brit.)
Gene Pollock
WORLD'S GREATEST SINNER, THE(1962); INCREDIBLY STRANGE CREATURES WHO STOPPED LIVING AND BECAME CRAZY MIXED-UP ZOMBIES, THE(1965), a, w; THRILL KILLERS, THE(1965), w
Misc. Talkies
DEVIL WOLF OF SHADOW MOUNTAIN, THE(1964)
George Pollock
STRANGER IN TOWN(1957, Brit.), d; ROONEY(1958, Brit.), d; DON'T PANIC CHAPS!(1959, Brit.), d; AND THE SAME TO YOU(1960, Brit.), d; MURDER SHE SAID(1961, Brit.), d; KILL OR CURE(1962, Brit.), d; VILLAGE OF DAUGHTERS(1962, Brit.), d; MURDER AT THE GALLOP(1963, Brit.), d; MURDER AHOY(1964, Brit.), d; MURDER MOST FOUL(1964, Brit.), d; TEN LITTLE INDIANS(1965, Brit.), d
Gordon Pollock
Silents
NINE AND THREE-FIFTHS SECONDS(1925), ph; QUEEN KELLY(1929), ph
Guy Cameron Pollock
TORPEDOED!(1939), w
Janet Pollock
LIFE AND TIMES OF CHESTER-ANGUS RAMSGOOD, THE(1971, Can.)
Larry Pollock
JIM, THE WORLD'S GREATEST(1976)
Leon Pollock
Silents
JACK, SAM AND PETE(1919, Brit.), p
Louis Pollock
STORK BITES MAN(1947), w; PORT SAID(1948), w; JACKIE ROBINSON STORY, THE(1950), w; GAMMA PEOPLE, THE(1956), w
Max Pollock
ON TRIAL(1928), w
Nancy R. Pollock
LAST ANGRY MAN, THE(1959); GO NAKED IN THE WORLD(1961); PAWNBR-OKER, THE(1965); DEATH PLAY(1976)
Nicholas Pollock
STRANGE AFFAIR, THE(1968, Brit.), art d
Nick Pollock
PRAISE MARX AND PASS THE AMMUNITION(1970, Brit.), art d
Robert Pollock
LOOPHOLE(1981, Brit.), w
William Pollock
SAY IT WITH MUSIC(1932, Brit.), w
Aubrey Pollok
DARK STAIRWAY, THE(1938, Brit.)
Polly Jenkins and Her Plowboys
MAN FROM MUSIC MOUNTAIN(1938)
Polly the Horse
SONG OF THE ROAD(1937, Brit.)
P. V. Polnitz
FREUD(1962)
Polo
PACIFIC DESTINY(1956, Brit.)
Eddie Polo
IT'S A DATE(1940); SON OF ROARING DAN(1940); WOLF MAN, THE(1941); DEEP IN THE HEART OF TEXAS(1942); LOOSE IN LONDON(1953), makeup
Silents
CAMPBELLS ARE COMING, THE(1915); KENTUCKY CINDERELLA, A(1917); DANGEROUS HOUR(1923); KNOCK ON THE DOOR, THE(1923); PREPARED TO DIE(1923)
Misc. Silents
BRONZE BRIDE, THE(1917); MONEY MADNESS(1917)
Eddy Polo
HONEYMOON LODGE(1943)
Malvina Polo
Silents
WOMAN OF PARIS, A(1923)
Malvine Polo
Silents
FOOLISH WIVES(1920)

Maria Polo
GUN RIDERS, THE(1969)
Mio Polo
WRONG IS RIGHT(1982)
Robert Polo
CRISIS(1950); UNDERWATER!(1955)
Barbara Polomska
EIGHTH DAY OF THE WEEK, THE(1959, Pol./Ger.); EROICA(1966, Pol.)
Vicki Polon
PLEASANTVILLE(1976), d&w; GIRLFRIENDS(1978), w
V. Polonskaya
WAR AND PEACE(1968, USSR)
Abraham Polonsky
BODY AND SOUL(1947), w; GOLDEN EARRINGS(1947), w; FORCE OF EVIL(1948),
d, w; I CAN GET IT FOR YOU WHOLESALE(1951), w; MADIGAN(1968), w; TELL
THEM WILLIE BOY IS HERE(1969), d&w; ROMANCE OF A HORSE THIEF(1971), d;
AVALANCHE EXPRESS(1979), w; MONSIGNOR(1982), w
Alan Polonsky
CHARIOTS OF FIRE(1981, Brit.)
1984
ELECTRIC DREAMS(1984)
David Polonsky
VALLEY OF VENGEANCE(1944)
Sonya Polonsky
BABY, IT'S YOU(1983), ed
Vitgold Polonsky
Misc. Silents
QUEEN OF THE SCREEN(1916, USSR)
Vitold Polonsky
Misc. Silents
NATASHA ROSTOVA(1915, USSR); SINGED WINGS(1915, USSR); SONG OF TRI-
UMPHANT LOVE(1915, USSR); LIFE FOR A LIFE, A(1916, USSR)
Anna Polony
1984
DIARY FOR MY CHILDREN(1984, Hung.)
F. Lara Polop
HUNCHBACK OF THE MORGUE, THE(1972, Span.), p
F. Laura Polop
DRACULA'S GREAT LOVE(1972, Span.), p
G. Poloskov
HOUSE ON THE FRONT LINE, THE(1963, USSR)
K. Polovikova
LULLABY(1961, USSR); WAR AND PEACE(1968, USSR)
Klavdia Polovikova
IDIOT, THE(1960, USSR)
Renato Polselli
VAMPIRE AND THE BALLERINA, THE(1962, Ital.), d, w
Pamela Polsgrove
THIS STUFF'LL KILL YA!(1971)
Galina Polskikh
MEET ME IN MOSCOW(1966, USSR); THERE WAS AN OLD COUPLE(1967, USSR)
G. Troye Polskiy
SHE-WOLF, THE(1963, USSR), d&w
Abe Polsky
GAY DECEIVERS, THE(1969), w; REBEL ROUSERS(1970), w; BABY, THE(1973), p,
w
Milton Polsky
BABY, THE(1973), p
Cecily Polsohn
DOVE, THE(1974, Brit.)
Cecily Polson
YEAR OF LIVING DANGEROUSLY, THE(1982, Aus.)
N. Poltautseva
Silents
BATTLESHIP POTEMKIN, THE(1925, USSR)
Kurt Polter
GENERALE DELLA ROVERE(1960, Ital./Fr.); THEN THERE WERE THREE(1961);
PASSIONATE THIEF, THE(1963, Ital.)
P. Poltoratski
LOSS OF FEELING(1935, USSR)
Henri Poltras
WHISPERING CITY(1947, Can.)
Sergei Poluya nov
THERE WAS AN OLD COUPLE(1967, USSR), ph
Sergey Poluyanov
CLEAR SKIES(1963, USSR), ph; RESURRECTION(1963, USSR), ph
Vanna Polverosi
BLACK VEIL FOR LISA, A(1969 Ital./Ger.)
Patrick Polvey
LOULOU(1980, Fr.)
L. Polyakov
WAR AND PEACE(1968, USSR)
Pom Pom
PETTICOAT POLITICS(1941)
Ron Pomber
CRIMSON CULT, THE(1970, Brit.)
Hope Pomerance
STOOLIE, THE(1972); THUNDER AND LIGHTNING(1977)
Alberto Pomerani
ANTHONY OF PADUA(1952, Ital.)
Vera Pomerant
NEW TEACHER, THE(1941, USSR)
N. Pomerantsev
Misc. Silents
TEARS(1914, USSR)
Earl Pomerantz
MERRY WIVES OF TOBIAS ROUKE, THE(1972, Can.)

Francis Pomerantz
Silents
FALSE FATHERS(1929)
Jeff Pomerantz
GREEK TYCOON, THE(1978); CHEECH AND CHONG'S NICE DREAMS(1981)
Misc. Talkies
NEEKA(1968)
Jeffrey David Pomerantz
SAVAGE WEEKEND(1983)
Leon Pomerantz
SUMMER HOLIDAY(1963, Brit.)
David Pomeranz
AMERICATHON(1979), m
Alan Pomeroy
SPOILERS, THE(1942), stunts; THIS IS THE ARMY(1943)
Allan Pomeroy
THIRTEEN WOMEN(1932)
Allen Pomeroy
CAIN AND MABEL(1936); HIDEAWAY GIRL(1937); SMART BLONDE(1937);
TENNESSEE JOHNSON(1942); ROAD TO UTOPIA(1945)
John Pomeroy
DANCE LITTLE LADY(1954, Brit.), ed; SVENGALI(1955, Brit.), ed; IT'S A WON-
DERFUL WORLD(1956, Brit.), ed; CARRY ON ADMIRAL(1957, Brit.), ed; DUBLIN
NIGHTMARE(1958, Brit.), d; HORROR HOTEL(1960, Brit.), ed; SHADOW OF THE
CAT, THE(1961, Brit.), ed; VALIANT, THE(1962, Brit./Ital.), ed; PRIVATE POT-
TER(1963, Brit.), ed; PLANK, THE(1967, Brit.), ed; SECRET OF NIMH, THE(1982), p,
w, anim
Julia Pomeroy
OVER THE EDGE(1979)
Lorna Pomeroy
SECRET OF NIMH, THE(1982), anim
Robert Pomeroy
STATUE, THE(1971, Brit.)
Roy J. Pomeroy
INTERFERENCE(1928), d; INSIDE THE LINES(1930), d; SHOCK(1934), d, w
Roy Pomeroy
Silents
TEN COMMANDMENTS, THE(1923), tech d; PETER PAN(1924), spec eff; OLD
IRONSIDES(1926), spec eff
Earl Pomerrantz
CANNIBAL GIRLS(1973)
Felix de Pomes
JOHN PAUL JONES(1959)
Leopold Pomes
Misc. Talkies
ANDREA(1979), d
Yvegeni Pomeschikov
COUNTRY BRIDE(1938, USSR), w
E. Pomeshchikov
TIGER GIRL(1955, USSR), w
Yevgeny Pomeshchikov
SKY CALLS, THE(1959, USSR), w
E. Pomeshnikov
BOUNTIFUL SUMMER(1951, USSR), w
Georges Pomies
Misc. Silents
TIRE AU FLANC(1929, Fr.)
Nicolo Pomilia
YETI(1977, Ital.), p
Eugene Pomischikov
SYMPHONY OF LIFE(1949, USSR), w
Eric Pommer
SIDEWALKS OF LONDON(1940, Brit.), p
Erich Pommer
BLUE ANGEL, THE(1930, Ger.), p; DAUGHTER OF EVIL(1930, Ger.), p; LOVE
WALTZ, THE(1930, Ger.), p; TEMPORARY WIDOW, THE(1930, Ger./Brit.), p; CON-
GRESS DANCES(1932, Ger.), p; HAPPY EVER AFTER(1932, Ger./Brit.), p; TEM-
PEST(1932, Ger.), p; EARLY TO BED(1933, Brit./Ger.), p; EMPRESS AND I, THE(1933,
Ger.), p; F.P. 1(1933, Brit.), p; F.P. 1 DOESN'T ANSWER(1933, Ger.), p; HEART
SONG(1933, Brit.), p; MAN STOLEN(1934, Fr.), p; MUSIC IN THE AIR(1934), p;
LILIOM(1935, Fr.), p; FIRE OVER ENGLAND(1937, Brit.), p; THE BEACHCOM-
BER(1938, Brit.), p&d; TROOPSHIP(1938, Brit.), p; JAMAICA INN(1939, Brit.), p;
DANCE, GIRL, DANCE(1940), p; THEY KNEW WHAT THEY WANTED(1940), p
Silents
CABINET OF DR. CALIGARI, THE(1921, Ger.), p; DECAMERON NIGHTS(1924,
Brit.), p; KRIEMHILD'S REVENGE(1924, Ger.), p; LAST LAUGH, THE(1924, Ger.), p;
SIEGFRIED(1924, Ger.), p; BARBED WIRE(1927), p
Otto Pommerening
MAYBE IT'S LOVE(1930)
Daniel Pommereulle
WEEKEND(1968, Fr./Ital.); LA COLLECTIONNEUSE(1971, Fr.), a, w
Felix de Pommes
SAIL INTO DANGER(1957, Brit.)
Alain Pommier
IS PARIS BURNING?(1966, U.S./Fr.)
Joe Pompa
1984
STRANGERS KISS(1984)
Robert Jose Pomper
1984
BEYOND GOOD AND EVIL(1984, Ital./Fr./Ger.), ed
Paul Pompian
CHESTY ANDERSON, U.S. NAVY(1976), p, w
Misc. Talkies
STREET GIRLS(1975)
Mireilla Pompili
SONS OF SATAN(1969, Ital./Fr./Ger.)

Pompom the Dog
NO PLACE TO HIDE(1956)
Pompie Pomposello
BADGE 373(1973)
Joe Ponazecki
WHAT'S SO BAD ABOUT FEELING GOOD?(1968); CLASS OF '44(1973); MAN ON A SWING(1974)
Connie Ponce
1984
REPO MAN(1984)
Danny Ponce
1984
OH GOD! YOU DEVIL(1984)
Manuel Barbachano Ponce
NAZARIN(1968, Mex.), p
Poncie Ponce
PORTRAIT OF A MOBSTER(1961); SPEEDWAY(1968)
Yolanda Ponce
SANTO Y BLUE DEMON CONTRA LOS MONSTRUOS(1968, Mex.); VENGEANCE OF THE VAMPIRE WOMEN, THE(1969, Mex.)
Christina Ponce-Enrile
SECRET OF THE SACRED FOREST, THE(1970)
Marcel Poncin
JOHNNY FRENCHMAN(1946, Brit.); DUAL ALIBI(1947, Brit.); BLIND GODDESS, THE(1948, Brit.); RED SHOES, THE(1948, Brit.); HUGGETTS ABROAD, THE(1949, Brit.); MADNESS OF THE HEART(1949, Brit.); ONE WOMAN'S STORY(1949, Brit.); SLEEPING CAR TO TRIESTE(1949, Brit.); GOLDEN SALAMANDER(1950, Brit.); LOST PEOPLE, THE(1950, Brit.); LILLI MARLENE(1951, Brit.); NO HIGHWAY IN THE SKY(1951, Brit.); SO LONG AT THE FAIR(1951, Brit.); JUDGMENT DEFERRED(1952, Brit.); DAY TO REMEMBER, A(1953, Brit.); MELBA(1953, Brit.); SAADIA(1953); THERE WAS A YOUNG LADY(1953, Brit.); TOP OF THE FORM(1953, Brit.); LOVE LOTTERY, THE(1954, Brit.)
Martha Poncin
HENRIETTE'S HOLIDAY(1953, Fr.), ed
Marthe Poncin
POIL DE CAROTTE(1932, Fr.), ed; THEY WERE FIVE(1938, Fr.), ed; ESCAPE FROM YESTERDAY(1939, Fr.), ed; PANIQUE(1947, Fr.), ed; HOLIDAY FOR HENRIETTA(1955, Fr.), ed
Elmer S. Pond [Elmer Clifton]
KID FROM GOWER GULCH, THE(1949), w; RED ROCK OUTLAW(1950), d&w; SILVER BANDIT, THE(1950), w
Mary Paz Pondal
LAZARILLO(1963, Span.); TRISTANA(1970, Span./Ital./Fr.)
Jack Ponder
Silents
ARIZONA DAYS(1928); LILAC TIME(1928)
Beans Ponedel
X-15(1961), makeup
Bernard Ponedel
MAN WITH THE GOLDEN ARM, THE(1955), makeup; JOHNNY CONCHO(1956), makeup; PRIDE AND THE PASSION, THE(1957), makeup; KINGS GO FORTH(1958), makeup; MANCHURIAN CANDIDATE, THE(1962), makeup
Dorothy Ponedel
Misc. Silents
GALLOPING VENGENCE(1925)
Poncie Ponee
WORLD'S GREATEST LOVER, THE(1977)
Jean Pierre Ponelle
BARBER OF SEVILLE, THE(1973, Ger./Fr.), art d
Tullio Ponelli
SWEET CHARITY(1969), w
George Ponford
BALALAIKA(1939), w
Alfred Pongratz
WHITE HORSE INN, THE(1959, Ger.); PHONY AMERICAN, THE(1964, Ger.)
Beta Ponicanova
END OF AUGUST AT THE HOTEL OZONE, THE(1967, Czech.)
Darryl Ponicsan
CINDERELLA LIBERTY(1973), w; LAST DETAIL, THE(1973), w; TAPS(1981), w
Anthony Ponizine
1984
FEAR CITY(1984)
A. Ponomarenko
WAR AND PEACE(1968, USSR)
Eugene Ponomarenko
TARAS FAMILY, THE(1946, USSR)
M. Ponomarenko
SHADOWS OF FORGOTTEN ANCESTORS(1967, USSR), ed
Vova Ponomarlov
RAINBOW, THE(1944, USSR)
Vladimir Ponomaryov
KATERINA IZMAILOVA(1969, USSR), ph
Beatrice Pons
DIARY OF A BACHELOR(1964); RACHEL, RACHEL(1968)
Isabelle Pons
MADE IN U.S.A.(1966, Fr.); WEEKEND(1968, Fr./Ital.)
Jim Pons
TWO HUNDRED MOTELS(1971, Brit.)
Lily Pons
I DREAM TOO MUCH(1935); HITTING A NEW HIGH(1937); THAT GIRL FROM PARIS(1937); CARNEGIE HALL(1947)
Lisa Pons
SECOND TIME AROUND, THE(1961); RUNAWAY GIRL(1966)
Ramon Pons
Misc. Talkies
TO LOVE, PERHAPS TO DIE(1975)
Joan Ponsford
NIGHT RIDE(1937, Brit.); REVERSE BE MY LOT, THE(1938, Brit.); SCRUFFY(1938, Brit.)

Ye. Ponsova
OVERCOAT, THE(1965, USSR)
Maria Luisa Ponte
NOT ON YOUR LIFE(1965, Ital./Span.); NEST, THE(1982, Span.)
Renato Pontecchi
DUCK, YOU SUCKER!(1972, Ital.)
G. Pontecorvo
OUTCRY(1949, Ital.)
Gillo Pontecorvo
KAPO(1964, Ital./Fr./Yugo.), d, w; BURN(1970), d, w
Gino Pontecorvo
BATTLE OF ALGIERS, THE(1967, Ital./Alger.), d, w, m
Gunilla Ponten
DEAR JOHN(1966, Swed.), cos
Robin Ponterio
TRUMAN CAPOTE'S TRILOGY(1969)
Donna Ponterotto
SERIAL(1980); GOING APE!(1981); HEY, GOOD LOOKIN'(1982)
Francois Ponthier
LAFAYETTE(1963, Fr.), w
Alex Ponti
KILLER FISH(1979, Ital./Braz.), p
Carlo Ponti
TO LIVE IN PEACE(1947, Ital.), p; CHILDREN OF CHANCE(1950, Ital.), p; ANNA(1951, Ital.), p; WHITE LINE, THE(1952, Ital.), p; FATAL DESIRE(1953), p; TWO NIGHTS WITH CLEOPATRA(1953, Ital.), p; MAMBO(1955, Ital.), p; ULYSSES(1955, Ital.), p; LA STRADA(1956, Ital.), p; GOLD OF NAPLES(1957, Ital.), p; MILLER'S WIFE, THE(1957, Ital.), p; ATTILA(1958, Ital.), p; BLACK ORCHID(1959), p; THAT KIND OF WOMAN(1959), p; BREATH OF SCANDAL, A(1960), p; HELLER IN PINK TIGHTS(1960), p; UNFAITHFULS, THE(1960, Ital.), p; LOLA(1961, Fr./Ital.), p; TWO WOMEN(1961, Ital./Fr.), p; WOMAN IS A WOMAN, A(1961, Fr./Ital.), p; BOCCACCIO '70(1962/Ital./Fr.), p; ARTURO'S ISLAND(1963, Ital.), p; CONDEMNED OF ALTONA, THE(1963), p; CONTEMPT(1963, Fr./Ital.), p; LANDRU(1963, Fr./Ital.), p; RICE GIRL(1963, Fr./Ital.), p; RITA(1963, Fr./Ital.), p; THIRD LOVER, THE(1963, Fr./Ital.), p; APE WOMAN, THE(1964, Ital.), p; EMPTY CANVAS, THE(1964, Fr./Ital.), p; MARRIAGE–ITALIAN STYLE(1964, Fr./Ital.), p; YESTERDAY, TODAY, AND TOMORROW(1964, Ital./Fr.), p; CASANOVA '70(1965, Ital.), p; DAY IN COURT, A(1965, Ital.), p; DOCTOR ZHIVAGO(1965), p; LADY L(1965, Fr./Ital.), p; OPERATION CROSSBOW(1965, U.S./Ital.), p; RAILROAD MAN, THE(1965, Ital.), p; TENTH VICTIM, THE(1965, Fr./Ital.), p; BLOW-UP(1966, Brit.), p; GIRL AND THE GENERAL, THE(1967, Fr./Ital.), p; MORE THAN A MIRACLE(1967, Ital./Fr.), p; SMASHING TIME(1967 Brit.), p; 25TH HOUR, THE(1967, Fr./Ital./Yugo.), p; DIAMONDS FOR BREAKFAST(1968, Brit.), p; FIFTH HORSEMAN IS FEAR, THE(1968, Czech.), p; KISS THE OTHER SHEIK(1968, Fr./Ital.), p; LES CARABINIERS(1968, Fr./Ital.), p; MAN WITH THE BALLOONS, THE(1968, Ital./Fr.), p; GHOSTS, ITALIAN STYLE(1969, Ital./Fr.), p; PLACE FOR LOVERS, A(1969, Ital./Fr.), p; SUNFLOWER(1970, Fr./Ital.), p; ZABRISKIE POINT(1970), p; PRIEST'S WIFE, THE(1971, Fr./Ital.), p; LADY LIBERTY(1972, Ital./Fr.), p; CHE?(1973, Ital./Fr./Ger.), p; GAWAIN AND THE GREEN KNIGHT(1973, Brit.), p; MASSACRE IN ROME(1973, Ital.), p; WHITE SISTER(1973, Ital./Span./Fr.), p; TORSO(1974, Ital.), p; VOYAGE, THE(1974, Ital.), p; LA BABY SITTER(1975, Fr./Ital./Gen.), p; PASSENGER, THE(1975, Ital.), p; VERDICT(1975, Fr./Ital.), p; CASSANDRA CROSSING, THE(1977), p; SPECIAL DAY, A(1977, Ital./Can.), p; CLARETTA AND BEN(1983, Ital., Fr.), p
Carlo Ponti, Jr.
SUNFLOWER(1970, Fr./Ital.)
Sal Ponti
DOCTOR DEATH: SEEKER OF SOULS(1973), w
Virgilio Ponti
TRAMPLERS, THE(1966, Ital.)
Pontifex
MAN COULD GET KILLED, A(1966)
Andre Pontin
ZAZIE(1961, Fr.), m
Roy Ponting
KING AND COUNTRY(1964, Brit.), cos
Julian Lee, Larry Pontius
MARCO POLO JUNIOR(1973, Aus.), m/1
Erich Ponto
FINAL CHORD, THE(1936, Ger.); FOUR COMPANIONS, THE(1938, Ger.); FILM WITHOUT A NAME(1950, Ger.); THIRD MAN, THE(1950, Brit.); GIRL AND THE LEGEND, THE(1966, Ger.)
Roland Pontoiseau
TESTAMENT OF ORPHEUS, THE(1962, Fr.), ph
Yvan Ponton
SLAP SHOT(1977)
Clara Pontoppidan
Misc. Silents
WITCHCRAFT THROUGH THE AGES(1921, Swed.); ONCE UPON A TIME(1922, Den.)
Kaete Pontow
HELP I'M INVISIBLE(1952, Ger.)
Kate Pontow
FILM WITHOUT A NAME(1950, Ger.)
Beatrice Pontrelli
UNDERWORLD U.S.A.(1961), cos
Bernice Pontrelli
PUBLIC PIGEON NO. 1(1957), cos; CRIMSON KIMONO, THE(1959), cos; VERBOTEN!(1959), cos; BIG NIGHT, THE(1960), cos
Gina Pontrelli
THREE BROTHERS(1982, Ital.)
Francoise Ponty
RISE OF LOUIS XIV, THE(1970, Fr.)
Anthony Ponzini
GRAY LADY DOWN(1978)
Antony Ponzini
OTHER SIDE OF MIDNIGHT, THE(1977); SOME KIND OF HERO(1982)
1984
FRIDAY THE 13TH–THE FINAL CHAPTER(1984); HARDBODIES(1984)

Pietro Longari Ponzoni
TRAGEDY OF A RIDICULOUS MAN, THE(1982, Ital.)
Emily Pooe
CRY, THE BELOVED COUNTRY(1952, Brit.)
Archie Pool
PRESSURE(1976, Brit.); BABYLON(1980, Brit.)
1984
SUCCESS IS THE BEST REVENGE(1984, Brit.)
John Pool
ORPHANS OF THE NORTH(1940)
Johnny Pool
SKATETOWN, U.S.A.(1979)
Muriel Pool
SNOWFIRE(1958), cos; BALLAD OF A GUNFIGHTER(1964), cos
Anthony Poole
EVIL OF FRANKENSTEIN, THE(1964, Brit.)
Arthur Poole
Silents
PHANTOM PICTURE, THE(1916, Brit.)
Misc. Silents
FEMALE SWINDLER, THE(1916, Brit.); GIRL WHO WRECKED HIS HOME, THE(1916, Brit.)
Bob Poole
DISC JOCKEY(1951)
David Poole
DANCE LITTLE LADY(1954, Brit.)
Donald Poole
JAWS(1975)
Douglas Poole
WAY OF A GAUCHO(1952)
Duane Poole
C.H.O.M.P.S.(1979), w
Gordon Poole
1984
TAIL OF THE TIGER(1984, Aus.)
Jackie Poole
DR. JEKYLL AND SISTER HYDE(1971, Brit.)
Jonathan Brooks Poole
DESTRUCTORS, THE(1974, Brit.)
John Poole
Misc. Talkies
DISCO 9000(1977)
Mabbie Poole
SAINTS AND SINNERS(1949, Brit.), w; WOMAN'S ANGLE, THE(1954, Brit.), w
Michael Poole
STOLEN PLANS, THE(1962, Brit.), d&w; INNOCENT BYSTANDERS(1973, Brit.); MACKINTOSH MAN, THE(1973, Brit.)
Richard Poole
PEACEMAKER, THE(1956), w
Robert Dale Poole
GOIN' HOME(1976)
Robert J. Poole
MACK, THE(1973), w
Roy Poole
EXPERIMENT IN TERROR(1962); UP THE DOWN STAIRCASE(1967); GAILY, GAILY(1969); SOMETIMES A GREAT NOTION(1971); 1776(1972); MANDINGO(1975); NETWORK(1976); BETSY, THE(1978); BRUBAKER(1980); END OF AUGUST, THE(1982); STRANGER IS WATCHING, A(1982)
Wakefield Poole
Misc. Talkies
BIJOU(1972), d; TAKE ONE(1977), d
John Pooley
LONG JOHN SILVER(1954, Aus.)
Olaf Pooley
HUGGETTS ABROAD, THE(1949, Brit.); HIGHLY DANGEROUS(1950, Brit.); LOST PEOPLE, THE(1950, Brit.); SHE SHALL HAVE MURDER(1950, Brit.); HELL IS SOLD OUT(1951, Brit.); GLORY AT SEA(1952, Brit.); MR. POTTS GOES TO MOSCOW(1953, Brit.); WOMAN'S ANGLE, THE(1954, Brit.); GAMMA PEOPLE, THE(1956); WINDOM'S WAY(1958, Brit.); LEFT, RIGHT AND CENTRE(1959); BATTLEAXE, THE(1962, Brit.); PASSWORD IS COURAGE, THE(1962, Brit.); ASSASSINATION BUREAU, THE(1969, Brit.); CRUCIBLE OF HORROR(1971, Brit.), a, w; GODSEND, THE(1980, Can.), w
Misc. Talkies
JOHNSTOWN MONSTER, THE(1971), d
Seyton Pooley
LAST VALLEY, THE(1971, Brit.)
Willem Poolman
CRIMES OF THE FUTURE(1969, Can.)
Narong Poomin
1 2 3 MONSTER EXPRESS(1977, Thai.), p, d, w
Vinai Poomin
1 2 3 MONSTER EXPRESS(1977, Thai.), d
Suki Poor
SKY PIRATE, THE(1970), ed
Dan Poore
BRONCO BUSTER(1952); HORIZONS WEST(1952); MAN FROM THE ALAMO, THE(1953); SEMINOLE(1953)
Richard Poore
1984
WILD HORSES(1984, New Zealand)
Robert Poore
NAME OF THE GAME IS KILL, THE(1968), p
Anthony Popafio
SANDERS OF THE RIVER(1935, Brit.)
Popcorn
1984
ALPHABET CITY(1984)

Alec Pope
GANGSTER, THE(1947)
Alex Pope
MALAYA(1950); PRISONER OF ZENDA, THE(1952); HANNAH LEE(1953); ROBE, THE(1953)
Alexander Pope
HITLER GANG, THE(1944); BURNING CROSS, THE(1947); WABASH AVENUE(1950); FBI GIRL(1951)
Anthony Pope
GALAXY EXPRESS(1982, Jap.)
Bud Pope
SAGEBRUSH TROUBADOR(1935); TUMBLING TUMBLEWEEDS(1935); LONELY TRAIL, THE(1936); RIDE, RANGER, RIDE(1936); CHEYENNE RIDES AGAIN(1937)
Silents
RANSON'S FOLLY(1926)
Cliff Pope
FREE, WHITE AND 21(1963), w
Georgette Pope
Misc. Talkies
SELF-SERVICE SCHOOLGIRLS(1976)
Gloria Pope
DOCKS OF NEW YORK(1945); IT'S IN THE BAG(1945)
Greta Pope
STRAWBERRY STATEMENT, THE(1970)
Hinton Pope
MANTIS IN LACE(1968)
John Pope
ECHOES OF SILENCE(1966)
Joseph Pope
NIGHT IN NEW ORLEANS, A(1942)
Leslie Pope
1984
ALMOST YOU(1984), set d
Marie Pope
SONG OF BERNADETTE, THE(1943)
Muriel Pope
DARK STAIRWAY, THE(1938, Brit.)
Patricia Pope
ONE MILLION B.C.(1940)
Peggy Pope
MADE FOR EACH OTHER(1971); HAIL(1973); NINE TO FIVE(1980)
1984
LAST STARFIGHTER, THE(1984)
R. W. Pope
MIGHTY MOUSE IN THE GREAT SPACE CHASE(1983), ph
Richard Downing Pope
EASY TO LOVE(1953)
Richard Pope
SWAPPERS, THE(1970, Brit.), ph
Robert Pope
CRUISING(1980)
Roland Pope
PREACHERMAN(1971), m
Ron Pope
SECOND BEST SECRET AGENT IN THE WHOLE WIDE WORLD, THE(1965, Brit.), ed; WHERE THE BULLETS FLY(1966, Brit.), ed; GULLIVER'S TRAVELS(1977, Brit., Bel.), ed
Skiles Ralph Pope
Silents
NON-STOP FLIGHT, THE(1926)
Steve Pope
BLADE RUNNER(1982)
Thomas Pope
HAMMETT(1982), w; LORDS OF DISCIPLINE, THE(1983), w
Tim Pope
DON'T LOOK IN THE BASEMENT(1973), w
Tom Pope
SHEPHERD OF THE HILLS, THE(1964); MANITOU, THE(1978), w
Pope Pius XII
EMBEZZLED HEAVEN(1959,Ger.)
Mary Ellen Popel
WOMAN'S FACE(1941); WILD WEED(1949); EXPERIMENT IN TERROR(1962)
Nina Popelikova
LOST FACE, THE(1965, Czech.); DEATH OF TARZAN, THE(1968, Czech)
Paul Popenoe
MODERN MARRIAGE, A(1962), w
Elvire Popesco
MAN OF THE HOUR, THE(1940, Fr.); BLUE VEIL, THE(1947, Fr.); PURPLE NOON(1961, Fr./Ital.)
Alexandru Popescu
STEPS TO THE MOON(1963, Rum.), spec eff
Horea Popescu
FANTASTIC COMEDY, A(1975, Rum.)
Peter Popescu
LAST WAVE, THE(1978, Aus.), w
Ion Popescu-Gopo
STEPS TO THE MOON(1963, Rum.), d&w; FANTASTIC COMEDY, A(1975, Rum.), d&w
Harald Popig
PINOCCHIO(1969, E. Ger.)
Harry M. Popkin
DUKE IS THE TOPS, THE(1938), p; ONE DARK NIGHT(1939), p; REFORM SCHOOL(1939), p; GANG WAR(1940), p; TAKE MY LIFE(1942), p&d; AND THEN THERE WERE NONE(1945), p; BIG WHEEL, THE(1949), p; WELL, THE(1951), p
Harry Popkin
CHAMPAGNE FOR CAESAR(1950), p
Leo C. Popkin
ONE DARK NIGHT(1939), d; REFORM SCHOOL(1939), d; GANG WAR(1940), d; IMPACT(1949), p; D.O.A.(1950), p

Leo G. Popkin
MY DEAR SECRETARY(1948), p
Leo Popkin
WELL, THE(1951), d
J. S. Poplin
MEAN DOG BLUES(1978), art d
Jack Poplin
MURDER BY CONTRACT(1958), art d; RISE AND FALL OF LEGS DIAMOND, THE(1960), art d; STUDS LONIGAN(1960), art d; HOODLUM PRIEST, THE(1961), art d; PORTRAIT OF A MOBSTER(1961), art d; COUCH, THE(1962), art d; LAD: A DOG(1962), art d; FAMILY JEWELS, THE(1965), art d; SLENDER THREAD, THE(1965), art d; COUNTDOWN(1968), art d; CHANGES(1969), art d; GREAT BANK ROBBERY, THE(1969), prod d; STALKING MOON, THE(1969), art d; SUPPOSE THEY GAVE A WAR AND NOBODY CAME?(1970), prod d; KOTCH(1971), art d; MRS. POLLIFAX-SPY(1971), art d; SPECIAL DELIVERY(1976), art d; GREAT SANTINI, THE(1979), prod d; CLASS(1983), art d
John S. Poplin
KLANSMAN, THE(1974), prod d
John S. Poplin, Jr.
WRATH OF GOD, THE(1972), prod d
Judith Poplinski
LOOSE ENDS(1975)
A. Popov
Misc. Silents
THREE FRIENDS AND AN INVENTION(1928, USSR)
Alexei Popov
Misc. Silents
THREE FRIENDS AND AN INVENTION(1928, USSR), d
Andrei Popov
OTHELLO(1960, U.S.S.R.)
Andrey Popov
HAMLET(1966, USSR)
G. Popov
NO GREATER LOVE(1944, USSR), m
Gavril Popov
ISLAND OF DOOM(1933, USSR), m
N. Popov
Silents
TEN DAYS THAT SHOOK THE WORLD(1927, USSR)
Misc. Silents
OCTOBER(1928, USSR)
Oleg Popov
BLUE BIRD, THE(1976)
S. Popov
THREE TALES OF CHEKHOV(1961, USSR), ed
V. Popov
Silents
BATTLESHIP POTEMKIN, THE(1925, USSR), ph; TEN DAYS THAT SHOOK THE WORLD(1927, USSR), ph
Vladimir Popov
Misc. Silents
KATORGA(1928, USSR)
A. Popova
SKY CALLS, THE(1959, USSR)
Ira Popova
MOSCOW-CASSIOPEIA(1974, USSR)
V. Popova
JACK FROST(1966, USSR)
Misc. Silents
BRAND(1915, USSR); BROKEN CHAINS(1925, USSR)
L. Popovchenko
LULLABY(1961, USSR)
Gorica Popovic
FRAGRANCE OF WILD FLOWERS, THE(1979, Yugo.)
Mavid Popovic
APACHE GOLD(1965, Ger.); FRAULEIN DOKTOR(1969, Ital./Yugo.); TWELVE CHAIRS, THE(1970)
Nikola Popovic
WHITE WARRIOR, THE(1961, Ital./Yugo.)
Vladimir Popovic
PERMISSION TO KILL(1975, U.S./Aust.)
Joe Popovich
ONE WAY TICKET TO HELL(1955)
Michael Popovich
TUNNELVISION(1976)
Lucia Popp
MERRY WIVES OF WINDSOR, THE(1966, Aust.); FIDELIO(1970, Ger.)
Peter Popp
BIG NOISE, THE(1936, Brit.); HIGHLAND FLING(1936, Brit.); TROUBLED WATERS(1936, Brit.); UNDER PROOF(1936, Brit.); LANCASHIRE LUCK(1937, Brit.); THERE WAS A YOUNG MAN(1937, Brit.); WISE GUYS(1937, Brit.)
Hans Poppe
TINDER BOX, THE(1968, E. Ger.), art d
Harry H. Poppe
THREE KIDS AND A QUEEN(1935), w; LITTLE MISS BIG(1946), w
Harry Poppe
SPEED(1936), ed
Herman Poppe
STIR CRAZY(1980)
Nils Poppe
SEVENTH SEAL, THE(1958, Swed.); DEVIL'S EYE, THE(1960, Swed.)
Marc Poppel
CHRISTINE(1983)
1984
NIGHT OF THE COMET(1984)
Marine Capt. J.R. Poppen
DIVE BOMBER(1941), tech adv

Frau Poppendick
PIED PIPER, THE(1972, Brit.)
Giorgio Poppi
TROPICS(1969, Ital.)
Jack Popplewell
TREAD SOFTLY STRANGER(1959, Brit.), w
Pops and Louie
HIT PARADE OF 1943(1943)
El Teatro Popular
STUDENT NURSES, THE(1970)
Albert Popwell
COOGAN'S BLUFF(1968); JOURNEY TO SHILOH(1968); DIRTY HARRY(1971); PEACE KILLERS, THE(1971); FUZZ(1972); GLASS HOUSES(1972); CHARLEY VARRICK(1973); CLEOPATRA JONES(1973); MAGNUM FORCE(1973); CLEOPATRA JONES AND THE CASINO OF GOLD(1975 U. S. Hong Kong); ENFORCER, THE(1976); BUDDY HOLLY STORY, THE(1978); SUDDEN IMPACT(1983)
John Popwell
FARMER, THE(1977)
Johnny Popwell
HEART IS A LONELY HUNTER, THE(1968); DELIVERANCE(1972); CHALLENGE(1974); VISITOR, THE(1980, Ital./U.S.)
Misc. Talkies
ALL THE YOUNG WIVES(1975); BRASS RING, THE(1975); NAKED RIVER(1977); MANHUNTER(1983)
Wade Popwell
BLOOD WATERS OF DOCTOR Z(1982)
Edmund Porada
O.S.S.(1946)
Darr Poran
KAREN, THE LOVEMAKER(1970)
Joanna Poraska
YOUNG GIRLS OF WILKO, THE(1979, Pol./Fr.)
Orna Porat
MARTYR, THE(1976, Ger./Israel)
Ove Porath
VIRGIN SPRING, THE(1960, Swed.)
Paul Porcasi
BROADWAY(1929); BORN RECKLESS(1930); DERELICT(1930); LADY'S MORALS, A(1930); MOROCCO(1930); MURDER ON THE ROOF(1930); THREE SISTERS, THE(1930); BOUGHT(1931); CRIMINAL CODE(1931); DOCTORS' WIVES(1931); GENTLEMAN'S FATE(1931); GOOD BAD GIRL, THE(1931); I LIKE YOUR NERVE(1931); PARTY HUSBAND(1931); SMART MONEY(1931); SVENGALI(1931); CYNARA(1932); DEVIL AND THE DEEP(1932); FAREWELL TO ARMS, A(1932); KID FROM SPAIN, THE(1932); MAN WHO PLAYED GOD, THE(1932); PAINTED WOMAN(1932); PARISIAN ROMANCE, A(1932); PASSIONATE PLUMBER(1932); RED-HAIRED ALIBI, THE(1932); STOWAWAY(1932); UNDER-COVER MAN(1932); UNDER EIGHTEEN(1932); WHILE PARIS SLEEPS(1932); WOMAN FROM MONTE CARLO, THE(1932); DEATH KISS, THE(1933); DEVIL'S MATE(1933); FLYING DOWN TO RIO(1933); FOOTLIGHT PARADE(1933); GIGOLETTES OF PARIS(1933); GRAND SLAM(1933); HELL BELOW(1933); I LOVED A WOMAN(1933); KING KONG(1933); MEN ARE SUCH FOOLS(1933); ROMAN SCANDALS(1933); SATURDAY'S MILLIONS(1933); TERROR ABOARD(1933); WHEN STRANGERS MARRY(1933); BRITISH AGENT(1934); CHAINED(1934); GAY DIVORCEE, THE(1934); GREAT FLIRTATION, THE(1934); HE COULDN'T TAKE IT(1934); IMITATION OF LIFE(1934); LOOKING FOR TROUBLE(1934); RIP TIDE(1934); TARZAN AND HIS MATE(1934); WAKE UP AND DREAM(1934); CHARLIE CHAN IN EGYPT(1935); ENTER MADAME(1935); FLORENTINE DAGGER, THE(1935); I DREAM TOO MUCH(1935); MILLION DOLLAR BABY(1935); NIGHT AT THE RITZ, A(1935); PAYOFF, THE(1935); RUMBA(1935); STARS OVER BROADWAY(1935); UNDER THE PAMPAS MOON(1935); WATERFRONT LADY(1935); CRASH DONOVAN(1936); DOWN TO THE SEA(1936); HI GAUCHO!(1936); LADY CONSENTS, THE(1936); LEATHERNECKS HAVE LANDED, THE(1936); MR. DEEDS GOES TO TOWN(1936); MUSS 'EM UP(1936); ROSE MARIE(1936); TROUBLE FOR TWO(1936); TWO IN A CROWD(1936); BRIDE WORE RED, THE(1937); CAFE METROPOLE(1937); EMPEROR'S CANDLESTICKS, THE(1937); MAYTIME(1937); SEVENTH HEAVEN(1937); BULLDOG DRUMMOND IN AFRICA(1938); CRIME SCHOOL(1938); VACATION FROM LOVE(1938); EVERYTHING HAPPENS AT NIGHT(1939); LADY OF THE TROPICS(1939); ARGENTINE NIGHTS(1940); BORDER LEGION, THE(1940); DR. KILDARE'S STRANGE CASE(1940); I WAS AN ADVENTURESS(1940); MOON OVER BURMA(1940); TORRID ZONE(1940); DOCTORS DON'T TELL(1941); RAGS TO RICHES(1941); ROAD TO ZANZIBAR(1941); TRIAL OF MARY DUGAN, THE(1941); TWO IN A TAXI(1941); CASABLANCA(1942); QUIET PLEASE, MURDER(1942); ROAD TO HAPPINESS(1942); STAR SPANGLED RHYTHM(1942); WE WERE DANCING(1942); BACKGROUND TO DANGER(1943); HI DIDDLE DIDDLE(1943); MELODY PARADE(1943); HAIL THE CONQUERING HERO(1944); HOT RHYTHM(1944); NOTHING BUT TROUBLE(1944); SWING HOSTESS(1944); I'LL REMEMBER APRIL(1945)
Marisa Porcel
ISLAND OF THE DAMNED(1976, Span.)
Claudia Porcelli
SUBWAY RIDERS(1981), makeup
Enzo Porcelli
EYES, THE MOUTH, THE(1982, Ital./Fr.), p; BLOW TO THE HEART(1983, Ital.), p
Lucille Porcett
CAPTAIN BLOOD(1935); MASQUERADE IN MEXICO(1945)
Jacqueline Porcher
TELL ME LIES(1968, Brit.)
Ruth Porcher
KIND OF LOVING, A(1962, Brit.)
Adrien Porchet
THEY MET ON SKIS(1940, Fr.), ph; PORTRAIT OF A WOMAN(1946, Fr.), ph
Tac Porchon
SHOW BOAT(1951)
Anita Poree
LIVING BETWEEN TWO WORLDS(1963); TARGETS(1968)
Didi Porego
LA NUIT DE VARENNES(1983, Fr./Ital.)
Jacqueline Porel
ANATOMY OF A MARRIAGE(MY DAYS WITH JEAN-MARC AND MY NIGHTS WITH FRANCOISE) (1964 Fr.); LOVE AND THE FRENCHWOMAN(1961, Fr.); TRUTH, THE(1961, Fr./Ital.); FIVE MILES TO MIDNIGHT(1963, U.S./Fr./Ital.); LOVE

ON A PILLOW(1963, Fr./Ital.); LADY IN THE CAR WITH GLASSES AND A GUN, THE(1970, U.S./Fr.); PROMISE AT DAWN(1970, U.S./Fr.)

Macqueline Porel
DESPERATE DECISION(1954, Fr.)

Marc Porel
SECRET WORLD(1969, Fr.); SICILIAN CLAN, THE(1970, Fr.); ROAD TO SALINA(1971, Fr./Ital.); LUDWIG(1973, Ital./Ger./Fr.); NO WAY OUT(1975, Ital./Fr.); INNOCENT, THE(1979, Ital.); PSYCHIC, THE(1979, Ital.)

Giuseppe Poreli
LOST HAPPINESS(1948, Ital.)

Giuseppe Porelli
MELODY OF LOVE(1954, Ital.); MISTRESS FOR THE SUMMER, A(1964, Fr./Ital.); GENDARME OF ST. TROPEZ, THE(1966, Fr./Ital.)

Jan Porisson
OUTLAW: THE SAGE OF GISLI(1982, Iceland), art d

Pork Chops and Kidney Stew
STREET OF DARKNESS(1958)

Mary Porke
Misc. Silents
CASTLE(1917, Brit.)

Alfredo Porras
ROYAL HUNT OF THE SUN, THE(1969, Brit.)

Jean-Luc Porraz
DIVA(1982, Fr.)

Fred Porrett
PAPER LION(1968), ph

Frank Porretta
SONG OF NORWAY(1970)

Ronit Port
RABBI AND THE SHIKSE, THE(1976, Israel)

Schoolchildren from the Port Elliot Primary School
STORM BOY(1976, Aus.)

Antonella Della Porta
WITCH'S CURSE, THE(1963, Ital.); HEAD OF THE FAMILY(1967, Ital./Fr.); ROMEO AND JULIET(1968, Ital./Span.)

Elvio Porta
CAFE EXPRESS(1980, Ital.), w

Pedro Portabella
MOMENT OF TRUTH, THE(1965, Ital./Span.), w

Louise Portal
CORDELIA(1980, Fr., Can.)

Michel Portal
LE VIOL(1968, Fr./Swed.), m; HOA-BINH(1971, Fr.), m; ADOPTION, THE(1978, Fr.), m; RETURN OF MARTIN GUERRE, THE(1983, Fr.), m

Piero Portalupe
BELLISSIMA(1952, Ital.), ph

Piero Portalupi
MONTE CASSINO(1948, Ital.), ph; LUXURY GIRLS(1953, Ital.), ph; AIDA(1954, Ital.), ph; FAREWELL TO ARMS, A(1957), ph; CARTHAGE IN FLAMES(1961, Fr./Ital.), ph; FRANCIS OF ASSISI(1961), ph; JESSICA(1962, U.S./Fr.), ph; LOVES OF SALAMMBO, THE(1962, Fr./Ital.), ph; WASTREL, THE(1963, Ital.), ph; BIGGEST BUNDLE OF THEM ALL, THE(1968), ph; HOUSE OF CARDS(1969), ph; INVINCIBLE SIX, THE(1970, U.S./Iran), ph; STORY OF A WOMAN(1970, U.S./Ital.), ph; ROMANCE OF A HORSE THIEF(1971), ph; STATUE, THE(1971, Brit.), ph

Angela Portaluri
LEGEND OF THE LOST(1957, U.S./Panama/Ital.); OPIATE '67(1967, Fr./Ital.)

Mike Portanova
DESERT HAWK, THE(1950); I'VE LIVED BEFORE(1956)

Joe Portaro
1984
THEY'RE PLAYING WITH FIRE(1984)

Piero Portawpi
NEOPOLITAN CAROUSEL(1961, Ital.), ph

Pierre Porte
MR. KLEIN(1976, Fr.), m

Robert Porte
DOCTORS, THE(1956, Fr.); TIME BOMB(1961, Fr./Ital.); SELLERS OF GIRLS(1967, Fr.)

Petula Portell
DR. JEKYLL AND SISTER HYDE(1971, Brit.)

Henny Porten
Misc. Silents
BACKSTAIRS(1921, Ger.); CROWN OF THORNS(1934, Ger.)

Lew Porten
PRAIRIE PALS(1942), m

Cam Porteous
GROUNDSTAR CONSPIRACY, THE(1972, Can.), art d

Cameron Porteous
CHRISTINA(1974, Can.), art d

Emma Porteous
ENTERTAINING MR. SLOANE(1970, Brit.), cos; QUEST FOR LOVE(1971, Brit.), cos; SITTING TARGET(1972, Brit.), cos; BRANNIGAN(1975, Brit.), cos; SKY RIDERS(1976, U.S./Gr.), cos; ISLAND OF DR. MOREAU, THE(1977), cos; FORCE 10 FROM NAVARONE(1978, Brit.), cos; DOGS OF WAR, THE(1980, Brit.), cos; WATCHER IN THE WOODS, THE(1980, Brit.), cos; CLASH OF THE TITANS(1981), cos; OCTOPUSSY(1983, Brit.), cos
1984
SUPERGIRL(1984), cos; TOP SECRET!(1984), cos; 1984(1984, Brit.), cos

Peter Porteous
PSYCHE 59(1964, Brit.); IDOL, THE(1966, Brit.); TRAITOR'S GATE(1966, Brit./Ger.); JOANNA(1968, Brit.); SHUTTERED ROOM, THE(1968, Brit.); VENOM(1982, Brit.); OCTOPUSSY(1983, Brit.)

Shane Porteous
SCOBIE MALONE(1975, Aus.)

Aloha Porter
THIRTEEN WOMEN(1932); DANTE'S INFERNO(1935)

Ann Porter
WILD RIDE, THE(1960), w

Silents
IS YOUR DAUGHTER SAFE?(1927)

Arthur Gould Porter
FRENCHMAN'S CREEK(1944); SCARLET STREET(1945); SINGAPORE(1947); HOUDINI(1953); MONEY FROM HOME(1953); THUNDER IN THE EAST(1953); GIRL RUSH, THE(1955); STRANGE BEDFELLOWS(1965)

Ashley Porter
YOUNG NURSES, THE(1973)

Beth Porter
NAKED WITCH, THE(1964); ME AND MY BROTHER(1969); GREAT GATSBY, THE(1974); LOVE AND DEATH(1975)

Bob Porter
PEGGY(1950)

Bobby Porter
BATTLE FOR THE PLANET OF THE APES(1973); DAY OF THE ANIMALS(1977); UNDER THE RAINBOW(1981)
1984
NIGHT OF THE COMET(1984); PLACES IN THE HEART(1984), a, stunts

Brereton Porter
END OF THE RIVER, THE(1947, Brit.), ed; ESTHER WATERS(1948, Brit.), ed

Caleb Porter
CLUE OF THE NEW PIN, THE(1929, Brit.)
Silents
ONE SUMMER'S DAY(1917, Brit.); ENCHANTMENT(1920, Brit.); SATAN'S SISTER(1925, Brit.)

Carol Porter
PURE S(1976, Aus.)

Cole Porter
BATTLE OF PARIS, THE(1929), m; PARIS(1929), w; FIFTY MILLION FRENCHMEN(1931), w, m; GAY DIVORCEE, THE(1934), w; TOP HAT(1935), w; ANYTHING GOES(1936), w; PANAMA HATTIE(1942), w; LET'S FACE IT(1943), w; SOMETHING FOR THE BOYS(1944), w; MEXICAN HAYRIDE(1948), w; PIRATE, THE(1948), m; KISS ME KATE(1953), w; ANYTHING GOES(1956), w; LES GIRLS(1957), m; SILK STOCKINGS(1957), m; CAN-CAN(1960), w, m; EVIL UNDER THE SUN(1982, Brit.), m; TO BEGIN AGAIN(1982, Span.), m

D. David Porter
LIANNA(1983)

David Porter
Silents
DOWN TO EARTH(1917)

Debby Porter
TWILIGHT ZONE–THE MOVIE(1983)
1984
CITY HEAT(1984)

Don Porter
SING FOR YOUR SUPPER(1941); EAGLE SQUADRON(1942); MADAME SPY(1942); NIGHT MONSTER(1942); TOP SERGEANT(1942); WHO DONE IT?(1942); EYES OF THE UNDERWORLD(1943); KEEP 'EM SLUGGING(1943); CUBAN PETE(1946); DANGER WOMAN(1946); SHE-WOLF OF LONDON(1946); WILD BEAUTY(1946); BUCK PRIVATES COME HOME(1947); MRS. O'MALLEY AND MR. MALONE(1950); RACKET, THE(1951); BECAUSE YOU'RE MINE(1952); CRIPPLE CREEK(1952); TURNING POINT, THE(1952); OUR MISS BROOKS(1956); BACHELOR IN PARADISE(1961); GIDGET GOES TO ROME(1963); YOUNGBLOOD HAWKE(1964); LIVE A LITTLE, LOVE A LITTLE(1968); CANDIDATE, THE(1972); FORTY CARATS(1973); MAME(1974); WHITE LINE FEVER(1975, Can.)
Misc. Talkies
WOMAN FOR ALL MEN, A(1975)

Donald Porter
MY FRIEND IRMA GOES WEST(1950); 711 OCEAN DRIVE(1950); SAVAGE, THE(1953)

Donna Porter
TWO OF A KIND(1983)

Dorene Porter
DEVIL'S HAIRPIN, THE(1957)

Dorothy Porter
THIS TIME FOR KEEPS(1947); CHECKERED COAT, THE(1948); THREE DARING DAUGHTERS(1948); WRITTEN ON THE WIND(1956)

Ed Porter
CHEYENNE TORNADO(1935)

Edward Porter
Silents
HER FIGHTING CHANCE(1917)

Edwin S. Porter
Silents
GOOD LITTLE DEVIL, A(1914), d, ph; HEARTS ADRIFT(1914), d; SUCH A LITTLE QUEEN(1914), d; TESS OF THE STORM COUNTRY(1914), d&w; ETERNAL CITY, THE(1915), d&w, ph; PRINCE AND THE PAUPER, THE(1915), d&w; SOLD(1915), d
Misc. Silents
COUNT OF MONTE CRISTO, THE(1913), d; IN THE BISHOP'S CARRIAGE(1913), d; CRUCIBLE, THE(1914), d; BELLA DONNA(1915), d; WHEN WE WERE TWENTY-ONE(1915), d; LYDIA GILMORE(1916), d

Eleanor H. Porter
HAS ANYBODY SEEN MY GAL?(1952), w; POLLYANNA(1960), w
Silents
POLLYANNA(1920), w

Eric Porter
FALL OF THE ROMAN EMPIRE, THE(1964); PUMPKIN EATER, THE(1964, Brit.); HEROES OF TELEMARK, THE(1965, Brit.); KALEIDOSCOPE(1966, Brit.); LOST CONTINENT, THE(1968, Brit.); HANDS OF THE RIPPER(1971, Brit.); NICHOLAS AND ALEXANDRA(1971, Brit.); ANTONY AND CLEOPATRA(1973, Brit.); DAY OF THE JACKAL, THE(1973, Brit./Fr.); HITLER: THE LAST TEN DAYS(1973, Brit./Ital.); MARCO POLO JUNIOR(1973, Aus.), p&d; CALLAN(1975, Brit.); HENNESSY(1975, Brit.); BELSTONE FOX, THE(1976, 1976); THIRTY NINE STEPS, THE(1978, Brit.)

Gene Stratton Porter
GIRL OF THE LIMBERLOST(1934), w; KEEPER OF THE BEES(1935), w; ROMANCE OF THE LIMBERLOST(1938), w; HER FIRST ROMANCE(1940), w; GIRL OF THE LIMBERLOST, THE(1945), w; KEEPER OF THE BEES(1947), w
Misc. Silents
FRECKLES(1928)

George Porter
HEART OF THE RIO GRANDE(1942)
Giora Porter
1984
BEST DEFENSE(1984), set d
Hal Porter
LIBIDO(1973, Aus.), w
Howard Porter
HAIR(1979)
Ian Porter
WINTER KEPT US WARM(1968, Can.), w
J. Robert Porter
QUEEN OF BLOOD(1966); FIRECREEK(1968); MACKENNA'S GOLD(1969)
Jake Vernon Porter
NEW YORK, NEW YORK(1977)
Jan Porter
DEMON LOVER, THE(1977)
Jean Porter
GAMBLING SEX(1932); PENAL CODE, THE(1933); INSIDE INFORMATION(1934); ONE MILLION B.C.(1940); NEVER GIVE A SUCKER AN EVEN BREAK(1941); THERE'S MAGIC IN MUSIC(1941); ABOUT FACE(1942); HEART OF THE RIO GRANDE(1942); HOME IN WYOMIN'(1942); THAT NAZTY NUISANCE(1943); YOUNGEST PROFESSION, THE(1943); ANDY HARDY'S BLONDE TROUBLE(1944); BATHING BEAUTY(1944); SAN FERNANDO VALLEY(1944); ABBOTT AND COSTELLO IN HOLLYWOOD(1945); TWICE BLESSED(1945); WHAT NEXT, CORPORAL HARGROVE?(1945); BETTY CO-ED(1946); EASY TO WED(1946); TILL THE END OF TIME(1946); LITTLE MISS BROADWAY(1947); THAT HAGEN GIRL(1947); TWO BLONDES AND A REDHEAD(1947); CRY DANGER(1951); G.I. JANE(1951); KENTUCKY JUBILEE(1951); RACING BLOOD(1954); LEFT HAND OF GOD, THE(1955)
Misc. Talkies
SWEET GENEVIEVE(1947)
Misc. Silents
BARB WIRE(1922); UNGUARDED GIRLS(1929)
Jill Porter
DEATHCHEATERS(1976, Aus.), makeup
Joan Porter
FRONT, THE(1976)
John Porter
YOU'LL NEVER GET RICH(1941)
Julio Porter
SANTO EN EL MUSEO DE CERA(1963, Mex.), w
Katherine Anne Porter
SHIP OF FOOLS(1965), w
Lange and Porter
RIDERS FROM NOWHERE(1940), md
Lawrence Porter
NORTHWEST PASSAGE(1940)
Lew Porter
HARLEM ON THE PRAIRIE(1938), md; RANGER'S ROUNDUP, THE(1938), a, md; HARLEM RIDES THE RANGE(1939), m; ARIZONA GANGBUSTERS(1940), md; BILLY THE KID IN TEXAS(1940), md; EAST SIDE KIDS(1940); GANG WAR(1940), m; LIGHTNING STRIKES WEST(1940), m; MURDER ON THE YUKON(1940), m; PHANTOM RANCHER(1940), m; THAT GANG OF MINE(1940), md; BILLY THE KID IN SANTA FE(1941), md; BILLY THE KID'S RANGE WAR(1941), m; FLYING WILD(1941), m; LONE RIDER CROSSES THE RIO, THE(1941), m; LONE RIDER IN GHOST TOWN, THE(1941), m/l Johnny Lange; PAPER BULLETS(1941), md; PRIDE OF THE BOWERY(1941), md; SPOOKS RUN WILD(1941), md; ZIS BOOM BAH(1941), md; BILLY THE KID TRAPPED(1942), md; I KILLED THAT MAN(1942), md; LET'S GET TOUGH(1942), md; LONE RIDER IN CHEYENNE, THE(1942), m; MR. WISE GUY(1942), md; ROLLING DOWN THE GREAT DIVIDE(1942), m; SHERIFF OF SAGE VALLEY(1942), m; TEXAS MAN HUNT(1942), m
Lillian Porter
GIRLS' DORMITORY(1936); ONE IN A MILLION(1936); SECOND HONEYMOON(1937); I'LL GIVE A MILLION(1938); JOSETTE(1938); THREE BLIND MICE(1938); SECOND FIDDLE(1939); STOP, LOOK, AND LOVE(1939); HIGH SCHOOL(1940); MAN I MARRIED, THE(1940); TIN PAN ALLEY(1940); YOUTH WILL BE SERVED(1940); THAT NIGHT IN RIO(1941); YANK IN THE R.A.F., A(1941); SONG OF THE ISLANDS(1942); LADIES OF WASHINGTON(1944); PIN UP GIRL(1944); DO YOU LOVE ME?(1946)
Lulu Porter
BRASS BOTTLE, THE(1964)
Mike Porter
SCUM(1979, Brit.), art d
Nancy Porter
OUT OF THIS WORLD(1945)
Nyree Dawn Porter
IDENTITY UNKNOWN(1960, Brit.); SENTENCED FOR LIFE(1960, Brit.); MAN AT THE CARLTON TOWER(1961, Brit.); PART-TIME WIFE(1961, Brit.); LIVE NOW-PAY LATER(1962, Brit.); CRACKSMAN, THE(1963, Brit.); TWO LEFT FEET(1965, Brit.); HOUSE THAT DRIPPED BLOOD, THE(1971, Brit.); JANE EYRE(1971, Brit.); FROM BEYOND THE GRAVE(1974, Brit.)
Paul Porter
MURDER, INC.(1960)
Railway Porter
RAILWAY CHILDREN, THE(1971, Brit.)
Rand Porter
Misc. Talkies
MY NAME IS LEGEND(1975)
Reed Porter
STREET OF CHANCE(1942)
Richard Lee Porter
DEADLY SPAWN, THE(1983)
Robert Porter
JESUS TRIP, THE(1971); KLANSMAN, THE(1974)
Misc. Talkies
TRIP WITH THE TEACHER(1975)
Robie Porter
THREE(1969, Brit.); CAREY TREATMENT, THE(1972)

Rose Porter
ALL OF ME(1934), w
Steven Porter
1984
ANGEL(1984)
Todd Porter
EARTHBOUND(1981)
Uriel Porter
HE FOUND A STAR(1941, Brit.); GERT AND DAISY CLEAN UP(1942, Brit.); LISBON STORY, THE(1946, Brit.); SILK NOOSE, THE(1950, Brit.); KISENGA, MAN OF AFRICA(1952, Brit.)
Valerie Porter
THREE BLONDES IN HIS LIFE(1961)
Vern Porter
SILENT WITNESS, THE(1962); MR. MAJESTYK(1974); DUCHESS AND THE DIRT-WATER FOX, THE(1976); SILKWOOD(1983)
1984
COUNTRY(1984)
Misc. Talkies
BEASTS(1983)
William Porter
HIDEOUT(1949), w
Maurice Porterat
MARRIAGE OF FIGARO, THE(1963, Fr.)
Anne Porterfield
FOXTROT(1977, Mex./Swiss)
Robert Porterfield
SERGEANT YORK(1941); YEARLING, THE(1946); THUNDER ROAD(1958)
Capt. John Porters
Silents
FOUR SONS(1928)
Alison Portes
SQUEEZE, THE(1977, Brit.)
Jacques Portet
CHEATERS, THE(1961, Fr.); LIVE FOR LIFE(1967, Fr./Ital.); TO BE A CROOK(1967, Fr.); FINO A FARTI MALE(1969, Fr./Ital.); LIFE LOVE DEATH(1969, Fr./Ital.)
Emma Porteus
PERCY(1971, Brit.), cos; LADY VANISHES, THE(1980, Brit.), cos
Rosemary Portia
SPOOKS RUN WILD(1941)
P. Portier
LOVE IN MOROCCO(1933, Fr.), ph
Adolfo Lopez Portillo
LIVING HEAD, THE(1969, Mex.), w
Adolfo Torres Portillo
LITTLE RED RIDING HOOD AND THE MONSTERS(1965, Mex.), w; TOM THUMB(1967, Mex.), w
Adolpho Portillo
SANTA CLAUS(1960, Mex.), w
Hector Portillo
LOS OLVIDADOS(1950, Mex.)
Rafael Lopez Portillo
AZTEC MUMMY, THE(1957, Mex.), d
Rafael Portillo
CURSE OF THE AZTEC MUMMY, THE(1965, Mex.), d; ROBOT VS. THE AZTEC MUMMY, THE(1965, Mex.), d
Raul Portillo
YANCO(1964, Mex.), ed
Rose Portillo
EXORCIST II: THE HERETIC(1977); WALK PROUD(1979); ZOOT SUIT(1981)
Virginia Portingale
1984
CAREFUL, HE MIGHT HEAR YOU(1984, Aus.)
Charles Portis
TRUE GRIT(1969), w; NORWOOD(1970), w; ROOSTER COGBURN(1975), w
Eric Portman
ABDUL THE DAMNED(1935, Brit.); HYDE PARK CORNER(1935, Brit.); OLD ROSES(1935, Brit.); CARDINAL, THE(1936, Brit.); CRIMES OF STEPHEN HAWKE, THE(1936, Brit.); GIRL FROM MAXIM'S, THE(1936, Brit.); HEARTS OF HUMANITY(1936, Brit.); MURDER IN THE OLD RED BARN(1936, Brit.); PRINCE AND THE PAUPER, THE(1937); SINGING MARINE, THE(1937); MOONLIGHT SONATA(1938, Brit.); INVADERS, THE,(1941); ONE OF OUR AIRCRAFT IS MISSING(1942, Brit.); ESCAPE TO DANGER(1943, Brit.); MILLIONS LIKE US(1943, Brit.); SQUADRON LEADER X(1943, Brit.); WE DIVE AT DAWN(1943, Brit.); CANTERBURY TALE, A(1944, Brit.); UNCENSORED(1944, Brit.); GREAT DAY(1945, Brit.); WANTED FOR MURDER(1946, Brit.); DEAR MURDERER(1947, Brit.); BLIND GODDESS, THE(1948, Brit.); CORRIDOR OF MIRRORS(1948, Brit.); DAYDREAK(1948, Brit.); MARK OF CAIN, THE(1948, Brit.); CAIRO ROAD(1950, Brit.); HIS EXCELLENCY(1952, Brit.); KISENGA, MAN OF AFRICA(1952, Brit.); MAGIC BOX, THE(1952, Brit.); SPIDER AND THE FLY, THE(1952, Brit.); GOLDEN MASK, THE(1954, Brit.); COLDITZ STORY, THE(1955, Brit.); DEEP BLUE SEA, THE(1955, Brit.); CHILD IN THE HOUSE(1956, Brit.); GOOD COMPANIONS, THE(1957, Brit.); NAKED EDGE, THE(1961); FREUD(1962); WEST 11(1963, Brit.); BEDFORD INCIDENT, THE(1965, Brit.); SPY WITH A COLD NOSE, THE(1966, Brit.); MAN WHO FINALLY DIED, THE(1967, Brit.); WHISPERERS, THE(1967, Brit.); ASSIGNMENT TO KILL(1968); DEADFALL(1968, Brit.)
Michael Portman
Misc. Talkies
AVALANCHE(1975, Brit.)
Rachel Portman
PRIVILEGED(1982, Brit.), m
1984
FOUR DAYS IN JULY(1984), m; REFLECTIONS(1984, Brit.), m
Charlotte Portney
FRANKENSTEIN'S DAUGHTER(1958)
Hugh Portnow
CRY OF THE BANSHEE(1970, Brit.)

Paulo Porto
ALL NUDITY SHALL BE PUNISHED(1974, Brazil), a, p
1984
MEMOIRS OF PRISON(1984, Braz.)
Frank Portos
JENNIE GERHARDT(1933), w
Penelope Portrait
FRENCH GAME, THE(1963, Fr.)
Jose Portugal
BULLFIGHTERS, THE(1945); FIESTA(1947); OUT OF THE PAST(1947)
Rene Portugal
YOUNG GIANTS(1983)
Alex Porwal
1984
ORDEAL BY INNOCENCE(1984, Brit.)
Dante Posani
LA VIACCIA(1962, Fr./Ital.); LEOPARD, THE(1963, Ital.); DARLING(1965, Brit.)
Edith Posca
Misc. Silents
NEW YEAR'S EVE(1923, Ger.)
Hanno Poschl
QUERELLE(1983, Ger./Fr.)
Jacquelyn Poseley
Misc. Talkies
HITCHHIKE TO HELL(1978)
I.M. Poselsky
Misc. Silents
SPARTAKIADA(1929, USSR), d
Yakov Poselsky
Misc. Silents
LIFE AND DEATH OF LIEUTENANT SCHMIDT(1917, USSR), d; WHEN WILL WE DEAD AWAKEN?(1918, USSR), d
Hans Posenbacher
BASHFUL ELEPHANT, THE(1962, Aust.)
Curtis Posey
DRIVE-IN(1976)
Matthew Posey
1984
PLACES IN THE HEART(1984)
Sam Posey
HEART LIKE A WHEEL(1983)
Stephen Posey
EMMA MAE(1976), ph
1984
HOUSE WHERE DEATH LIVES, THE(1984), ph; SAVAGE STREETS(1984), ph
Steve Posey
PENITENTIARY II(1982), ph; SLUMBER PARTY MASSACRE, THE(1982), ph
Steven Posey
1984
ON THE LINE(1984, Span.), ph
George Posford
MAGIC NIGHT(1932, Brit.), w; GOOD COMPANIONS(1933, Brit.), m; INVITATION TO THE WALTZ(1935, Brit.), w, m
Jean-Pierre Posier
ZAZIE(1961, Fr.)
Michele Posier
TWO FOR THE ROAD(1967, Brit.), cos
B. Poslavsky
GREAT CITIZEN, THE(1939, USSR)
Boris Poslavsky
Misc. Silents
LACE(1928, USSR)
Mieczyslaw Posmiechowicz
JOVITA(1970, Pol.), makeup
Zofia Posmysz-Piasecka
PASSENGER, THE(1970, Pol.), w
Alan H. Posner
ARGYLE SECRETS, THE(1948), p
Anita Posner
JAMBOREE(1957), ed
Bill Posner
TEEN-AGE STRANGLER(1967), d
Phil Posner
CEREMONY, THE(1963, U.S./Span.); GUNFIGHTERS OF CASA GRANDE(1965, U.S./Span.)
Rosalie Posner
LILITH(1964)
Sheryl Posner
WANDERERS, THE(1979)
Abraham Posnic
HAREM BUNCH; OR WAR AND PIECE, THE(1969), ed
Anne Pospischill
IN SEARCH OF ANNA(1978, Aus.), makeup
Michal Pospisil
STOLEN DIRIGIBLE, THE(1966, Czech.)
Vladimir Pospisil
GIRL WITH THREE CAMELS, THE(1968, Czech.); SKI FEVER(1969, U.S./Aust./Czech.)
Jerzy Possack
PASSENGER, THE(1970, Pol.), art d
Luciana Possamay
SUMMERSKIN(1962, Arg.)
Werner Possardt
GERMANY IN AUTUMN(1978, Ger.)
Hans Possenbacher
CASTLE, THE(1969, Ger.); SOMETHING FOR EVERYONE(1970)
Bud Post
Silents
M'LISS(1918)

Buddy Post
Silents
BOB HAMPTON OF PLACER(1921); OFF THE HIGHWAY(1925)
Misc. Silents
TODD OF THE TIMES(1919); MIDNIGHT FLYER, THE(1925)
Carl Post
AIN'T MISBEHAVIN'(1955)
Charles A. Post
NEAR THE RAINBOW'S END(1930), w; SUNRISE TRAIL(1931), ed; SINGLE-HANDED SANDERS(1932), w; LI'L ABNER(1940)
Silents
LOVER'S OATH, A(1925); REDHEADS PREFERRED(1926); TENDER HOUR, THE(1927); GYPSY OF THE NORTH(1928), ed; MY HOME TOWN(1928), ed
Misc. Silents
BEHOLD THIS WOMAN(1924); CROWN OF LIES, THE(1926)
Charles "Buddy" Post
Silents
OVERLAND LIMITED, THE(1925)
Misc. Silents
DEFYING THE LAW(1924)
Clayton Post
LINEUP, THE(1958)
David Post
SECRET OF CONVICT LAKE, THE(1951); ENEMY BELOW, THE(1957)
Dick Post
YOUR NUMBER'S UP(1931), ed
G. O. Post
Silents
SHIRLEY OF THE CIRCUS(1922), ph; GENTLE JULIA(1923), ph; JUST OFF BROADWAY(1924), ph; OUTSIDER, THE(1926), ph
Guy Bates Post
PRESTIGE(1932); CASE AGAINST MRS. AMES, THE(1936); FATAL LADY(1936); TILL WE MEET AGAIN(1936); TROUBLE FOR TWO(1936); BLAZING BARRIERS(1937); CHAMPAGNE WALTZ(1937); DAUGHTER OF SHANGHAI(1937); MAYTIME(1937); MARIE ANTOINETTE(1938); OF HUMAN HEARTS(1938); MAD EMPRESS, THE(1940); CROSSROADS(1942); EASY TO WED(1946); DOUBLE LIFE, A(1947)
Silents
GOLD MADNESS(1923)
Misc. Silents
MASQUERADER, THE(1922); OMAR THE TENTMAKER(1922)
John H. Post
BOY...A GIRL, A(1969), ed; WOMEN AND BLOODY TERROR(1970), ed
Mike Post
RABBIT TEST(1978), m; DEEP IN THE HEART(1983), m; RUNNING BRAVE(1983, Can.), m
1984
HADLEY'S REBELLION(1984), m; RHINESTONE(1984), m; RIVER RAT, THE(1984), m
Rollin Post
CANDIDATE, THE(1972)
Ted Post
PEACEMAKER, THE(1956), d; LEGEND OF TOM DOOLEY, THE(1959), d; HANG-'EM HIGH(1968), d; BENEATH THE PLANET OF THE APES(1970), d; BABY, THE(1973), d; HARRAD EXPERIMENT, THE(1973), d; MAGNUM FORCE(1973), d; WHIFFS(1975), d; GO TELL THE SPARTANS(1978), d; GOOD GUYS WEAR BLACK(1978), d
W. H. Post
Silents
LOVE'S WILDERNESS(1924)
Wiley Post
AIR HAWKS(1935)
William H. Post
VAGABOND KING, THE(1930), w; NEVER SAY DIE(1939), w; VAGABOND KING, THE(1956), w
Silents
NEVER SAY DIE(1924), w
William A. Post, Jr.
BABES ON BROADWAY(1941)
William Post, Jr.
BLACK CAMEL, THE(1931); SECRET SERVICE(1931); BIRTH OF A BABY(1938); MR. AND MRS. NORTH(1941); NAZI AGENT(1942); PACIFIC RENDEZVOUS(1942); SHERLOCK HOLMES AND THE SECRET WEAPON(1942); SHIP AHOY(1942); MOON IS DOWN, THE(1943); BRIDE BY MISTAKE(1944); EXPERIMENT PERILOUS(1944); ROGER TOUHY, GANGSTER!(1944); HOUSE ON 92ND STREET, THE(1945); CALL NORTHSIDE 777(1948)
Post Production Associates
ROOMMATES, THE(1973), m; STANLEY(1973), m
Adrienne Posta
TO SIR, WITH LOVE(1967, Brit.); HERE WE GO ROUND THE MULBERRY BUSH(1968, Brit.); UP THE JUNCTION(1968, Brit.); SOME GIRLS DO(1969, Brit.); ALL THE WAY UP(1970, Brit.); SPRING AND PORT WINE(1970, Brit.); PERCY(1971, Brit.); UP POMPEII(1971, Brit.); IT'S NOT THE SIZE THAT COUNTS(1979, Brit.)
Misc. Talkies
ALF GARNETT SAGA, THE(1972)
Charles Postal
UNKNOWN TERROR, THE(1957); NORTH BY NORTHWEST(1959)
Florence Postal
BIG TRAIL, THE(1930), w
Ron Postal
THOMAS CROWN AFFAIR, THE(1968), cos
Robert Postee
CLEO FROM 5 TO 7(1961, Fr.)
Adrienne Poster
NO TIME FOR TEARS(1957, Brit.)
Jean Poster
Misc. Talkies
LAST THREE(1942)

Stephen Poster
SPRING BREAK(1983), ph
Steve Poster
BLOOD BEACH(1981), ph; DEAD AND BURIED(1981), ph
Steven Poster
STRANGE BREW(1983), ph; TESTAMENT(1983), ph
Giorgio Postiglione
HURRICANE(1979), art d; CONAN THE BARBARIAN(1982), set d; AMITYVILLE 3-D(1983), art d
1984
FIRESTARTER(1984), art d
Lauren C. Postma
Misc. Talkies
HEROES THREE(1984)
P. Postnikova
FAREWELL, DOVES(1962, USSR)
Michal Postnikow
FIRST SPACESHIP ON VENUS(1960, Ger./Pol.)
Dick Poston
JESUS TRIP, THE(1971), w; LADY SINGS THE BLUES(1972)
Francesca Poston
APPLE, THE(1980 U.S./Ger.)
Pat Poston
SHE-DEVILS ON WHEELS(1968)
Thomas Poston
CITY THAT NEVER SLEEPS(1953)
Tom Poston
ZOTZ!(1962); OLD DARK HOUSE, THE(1963, Brit.); SOLDIER IN THE RAIN(1963); COLD TURKEY(1971); HAPPY HOOKER, THE(1975); RABBIT TEST(1978); UP THE ACADEMY(1980); CARBON COPY(1981)
Leo Postrel
1984
OVER THE BROOKLYN BRIDGE(1984)
Geza Poszar
1984
NADIA(1984, U.S./Yugo.)
A. Potapov
PORTRAIT OF LENIN(1967, Pol./USSR)
Alan Potashnick
KING OF COMEDY, THE(1983)
Oscar Poteker
BLONDE VENUS(1932), m
Vic Potel
FRONTIER DAYS(1934); COWBOY AND THE BANDIT, THE(1935); WHISPERING SMITH SPEAKS(1935); DOWN TO THE SEA(1936); MOONLIGHT ON THE PRAIRIE(1936); GOD'S COUNTRY AND THE WOMAN(1937); WHITE BONDAGE(1937); ON THE GREAT WHITE TRAIL(1938); SWING YOUR LADY(1938); ROVIN' TUMBLEWEEDS(1939); STRANGE CASE OF DR. MEADE(1939); CHIP OF THE FLYING U(1940); CHRISTMAS IN JULY(1940); ENEMY AGENT(1940); GIRL FROM GOD'S COUNTRY(1940); GREAT McGINTY, THE(1940); SLIGHTLY HONORABLE(1940); GIRL, A GUY AND A GOB, A(1941); NEVER GIVE A SUCKER AN EVEN BREAK(1941); EDGE OF DARKNESS(1943); MORE THE MERRIER, THE(1943); GREAT MOMENT, THE(1944); KANSAS CITY KITTY(1944); CAPTAIN TUGBOAT ANNIE(1945); STRANGE ILLUSION(1945); GLASS ALIBI, THE(1946); EGG AND I, THE(1947); MILLERSON CASE, THE(1947); SHOCKING MISS PILGRIM, THE(1947)
Misc. Talkies
BIG BOY RIDES AGAIN(1935); TWISTED RAILS(1935)
Silents
BOB HAMPTON OF PLACER(1921); STEP ON IT!(1922); PENROD AND SAM(1923)
Vice Potel
WEST OF CARSON CITY(1940)
Victor Potel
MELODY OF LOVE, THE(1928); VIRGINIAN, THE(1929); BAD ONE, THE(1930); BORDER ROMANCE(1930); DOUGH BOYS(1930); PARADISE ISLAND(1930); VIRTUOUS SIN, THE(1930); SQUAW MAN, THE(1931); TEN CENTS A DANCE(1931); MAKE ME A STAR(1932); PARTNERS(1932); PURCHASE PRICE, THE(1932); INSIDE INFORMATION(1934), a, w; BARBARY COAST(1935); GIRL FRIEND, THE(1935); LADY TUBBS(1935); LAST OF THE CLINTONS, THE(1935); MISSISSIPPI(1935); RUGGLES OF RED GAP(1935); SHE COULDN'T TAKE IT(1935); SHIPMATES FOREVER(1935); WATERFRONT LADY(1935); FURY(1936); MILKY WAY, THE(1936); O'MALLEY OF THE MOUNTED(1936); SONG OF THE SADDLE(1936); THREE GODFATHERS(1936); YELLOW DUST(1936); SMALL TOWN BOY(1937); TWO GUN LAW(1937); WESTERN GOLD(1937); GIRL OF THE GOLDEN WEST, THE(1938); HOLLYWOOD CAVALCADE(1939); LET FREEDOM RING(1939); STAND UP AND FIGHT(1939); LADY EVE, THE(1941); NOTHING BUT THE TRUTH(1941); SULLIVAN'S TRAVELS(1941); PALM BEACH STORY, THE(1942); GIRL CRAZY(1943); SKY'S THE LIMIT, THE(1943); HAIL THE CONQUERING HERO(1944); MIRACLE OF MORGAN'S CREEK, THE(1944); MEDAL FOR BENNY, A(1945); MAD WEDNESDAY(1950)
Silents
GOOD-FOR-NOTHING, THE(1914); AMATEUR ADVENTURESS, THE(1919); OUTCASTS OF POKER FLAT, THE(1919); PETAL ON THE CURRENT, THE(1919); LAVENDER AND OLD LACE(1921); ONE A MINUTE(1921); LOADED DOOR, THE(1922); TAILOR MADE MAN, A(1922); ANNA CHRISTIE(1923); RENO(1923); ALONG CAME RUTH(1924); LAW FORBIDS, THE(1924); LOST LADY, A(1924); BELOW THE LINE(1925); CARNIVAL GIRL, THE(1926); LODGE IN THE WILDERNESS, THE(1926); RACING ROMANCE(1926); ACTION CRAVER, THE(1927), d; SPECIAL DELIVERY(1927); LINGERIE(1928)
Misc. Silents
BILLIONS(1920); MARY'S ANKLE(1920); AT THE SIGN OF THE JACK O'LANTERN(1922); TEN DAYS(1925); MORGANSON'S FINISH(1926); CAPTAIN SWAGGER(1928)
Vadia Potenza
1984
STAR TREK III: THE SEARCH FOR SPOCK(1984)
Frederic Potler
MONSTER FROM THE GREEN HELL(1958)

Ladislav Potmesil
90 DEGREES IN THE SHADE(1966, Czech./Brit.); TRANSPORT FROM PARADISE(1967, Czech.); FIFTH HORSEMAN IS FEAR, THE(1968, Czech.)
Jan Potocki
SARAGOSSA MANUSCRIPT, THE(1972, Pol.), w
Zarko Potocnjak
VISITORS FROM THE GALAXY(1981, Yugo.)
Julius Potocsny
ADRIFT(1971, Czech.), p
Chaim Potok
CHOSEN, THE(1982), w
Rebecca Potok
1984
CHEECH AND CHONG'S THE CORSICAN BROTHERS(1984)
Stane Potokar
SULEIMAN THE CONQUEROR(1963, Ital.)
Oscar Potoker
FIGHTING CARAVANS(1931), m
S. Potolski
BALLAD OF COSSACK GLOOTA(1938, USSR), m
Stan Potosky
SOD SISTERS(1969), w
Micheline Potous
Misc. Silents
HEART OF SISTER ANN, THE(1915, Brit.)
Hank Pott
CRIMSON TRAIL, THE(1935)
Marty Pottenger
BORN IN FLAMES(1983)
Art Potter
NO TIME FOR LOVE(1943)
Beatrix Potter
PETER RABBIT AND TALES OF BEATRIX POTTER(1971, Brit.), w
Betty Potter
STAIRWAY TO HEAVEN(1946, Brit.)
Bill Potter
COURTIN' TROUBLE(1948); GUNNING FOR JUSTICE(1948); ACROSS THE RIO GRANDE(1949); BRAND OF FEAR(1949); HIDDEN DANGER(1949); RANGE JUSTICE(1949); WEST OF EL DORADO(1949); WESTERN RENEGADES(1949)
Bob Potter
DIRTY O'NEIL(1974)
Brian Potter
YOUR THREE MINUTES ARE UP(1973), m/l; TUNNELVISION(1976), m
Chip Potter
SSSSSSSS(1973)
Cliff Potter
MAN CALLED GANNON, A(1969)
David Potter
Silents
DIANE OF STAR HOLLOW(1921), w
Denise Potter
GREAT MUPPET CAPER, THE(1981)
Dennis Potter
PENNIES FROM HEAVEN(1981), w; BRIMSTONE AND TREACLE(1982, Brit.), w; GORKY PARK(1983), w
Diane Potter
HOT MONEY GIRL(1962, Brit./Ger.)
Garry Potter
MUSIC MAN, THE(1962)
Gillie Potter
DEATH AT A BROADCAST(1934, Brit.); RADIO FOLLIES(1935, Brit.)
H.C. Potter
TIME OF YOUR LIFE, THE(1948), d; BELOVED ENEMY(1936), d; WINGS OVER HONOLULU(1937), d; COWBOY AND THE LADY, THE(1938), d; ROMANCE IN THE DARK(1938), d; SHOPWORN ANGEL(1938), d; BLACKMAIL(1939), d; FIXER DUGAN(1939), w; STORY OF VERNON AND IRENE CASTLE, THE(1939), d; HELLZAPOPPIN'(1941), d; MR. LUCKY(1943), d; FARMER'S DAUGHTER, THE(1947), d; LIKELY STORY, A(1947), d; MR. BLANDINGS BUILDS HIS DREAM HOUSE(1948), d; YOU GOTTA STAY HAPPY(1948), d; MINIVER STORY, THE(1950, Brit./U.S.), d; THREE FOR THE SHOW(1955), d; TOP SECRET AFFAIR(1957), d
Henry Potter
CONGO MAISIE(1940), d
Herbert Potter
Silents
DESIRED WOMAN, THE(1918)
Irene Potter
GLAMOUR(1931, Brit.)
James Potter
AMAZING DOBERMANS, THE(1976), ed; TENDER FLESH(1976), ed
Jennifer Potter
1984
FLIGHT TO BERLIN(1984, Ger./Brit.), w
Jerry Potter
1984
RHINESTONE(1984)
Jessica Potter
EAT MY DUST!(1976); AMERICAN GIGOLO(1980)
Jim Potter
DANGEROUS MISSION(1954)
Joan Potter
BRAMBLE BUSH, THE(1960)
John Potter
OLIVER TWIST(1951, Brit.); THERE'S NO BUSINESS LIKE SHOW BUSINESS(1954)
Leigh Potter
THOMASINE AND BUSHROD(1974)
Luce Potter
INVADERS FROM MARS(1953)

Madeleine Potter
1984
BOSTONIANS, THE(1984)
Mark Potter
1984
BOSTONIANS, THE(1984), ed
Martin Potter
FELLINI SATYRICON(1969, Fr./Ital.); GOODBYE GEMINI(1970, Brit.); ONLY WAY, THE(1970, Panama/Den./U.S.); NICHOLAS AND ALEXANDRA(1971, Brit.); CRAZE(1974, Brit.); SATAN'S SLAVE(1976, Brit.); BIG SLEEP, THE½(1978, Brit.)
Misc. Talkies
ALL COPPERS ARE...(l972, Brit.)
Maureen Potter
RISING OF THE MOON, THE(1957, Ireland); GIDEON OF SCOTLAND YARD(1959, Brit.); ULYSSES(1967, U.S./Brit.); PORTRAIT OF THE ARTIST AS A YOUNG MAN, A(1979, Ireland)
Michael Potter
FEMALE TROUBLE(1975); PURSUIT OF D.B. COOPER, THE(1981)
Mike Potter
FLASH GORDON(1980)
Miles Potter
STONE COLD DEAD(1980, Can.)
Paul Potter
Silents
ARSENE LUPIN(1917), w; MONEY HABIT, THE(1924, Brit.), w
Peter Potter [Bill Moore]
SHIPMATES FOREVER(1935); THEY WON'T FORGET(1937); PRAIRIE MOON(1938); PRISON TRAIN(1938); ENEMY AGENT(1940); STAR SPANGLED RHYTHM(1942); I'LL TELL THE WORLD(1945); I SURRENDER DEAR(1948)
Philip Potter
MIKADO, THE(1967, Brit.)
Richard Potter
GUILTY MELODY(1936, Brit.), d
Sally Potter
Misc. Talkies
GOLD DIGGERS, THE(1984, Brit.), d
Stephen Potter
SHIPBUILDERS, THE(1943, Brit.), w; SCHOOL FOR SCOUNDRELS(1960, Brit.), w
Steve Potter
MEAL, THE(1975); JAWS II(1978), ed
Steven Potter
DEAR BRIGETTE(1965), set d; ST. VALENTINE'S DAY MASSACRE, THE(1967), set d
Tiffany Potter
DEMON SEED(1977)
Vivien Pottersman
BURNING AN ILLUSION(1982, Brit.), p
Gerald Potterton
TIKI TIKI(1971, Can.), d, w; RAINBOW BOYS, THE(1973, Can.), d&w; RAGGEDY ANN AND ANDY(1977), anim; HEAVY METAL(1981, Can.), d
Jerry Potterton
YELLOW SUBMARINE(1958, Brit.), animation
Harold Pottie
TEARS FOR SIMON(1957, Brit.), art d
Denise Pottier
TAHITIAN, THE(1956)
Richard Pottier
RECORD 413(1936, Fr.), d; LE MONDE TREMBLERA(1939, Fr.), d; CAROLINE CHERIE(1951, Fr.), d; DAVID AND GOLIATH(1961, Ital.), d
Capt. Pottinger
FOR FREEDOM(1940, Brit.)
David Pottinger
GOODBYE PORK PIE(1981, New Zealand)
Harold Pottle
WILBY CONSPIRACY, THE(1975, Brit.), prod d
Harry Pottle
COMING-OUT PARTY, A(, art d; CHANCE MEETING(1960, Brit.), art d; WALTZ OF THE TOREADORS(1962, Brit.), art d; CROOKS ANONYMOUS(1963, Brit.), art d; FATHER CAME TOO(1964, Brit.), art d; UNEARTHLY STRANGER, THE(1964, Brit.), art d; YOU ONLY LIVE TWICE(1967, Brit.), art d; CHITTY CHITTY BANG BANG(1968, Brit.), art d; ADVENTURERS, THE(1970), art d; TAMARIND SEED, THE(1974, Brit.), art d; CONFESSIONS FROM A HOLIDAY CAMP(1977, Brit.), art d; STAND UP VIRGIN SOLDIERS(1977, Brit.), prod d; UNCANNY, THE(1977, Brit./ Can.), prod d; BIG SLEEP, THE½(1978, Brit.), prod d; THIRTY NINE STEPS, THE(1978, Brit.), prod d; MURDER BY DECREE(1979), prod d; FUNNY MONEY(1983, Brit.), prod d
Annie Potts
CORVETTE SUMMER(1978); KING OF THE GYPSIES(1978); HEARTACHES(1981, Can.)
1984
CRIMES OF PASSION(1984); GHOSTBUSTERS(1984)
Cliff Potts
SOMETIMES A GREAT NOTION(1971); COUNT YOUR BULLETS(1972); GROUND-STAR CONSPIRACY, THE(1972, Can.); SILENT RUNNING(1972); SNOW JOB(1972); HANGUP(1974)
1984
SAHARA(1984)
Daniel Potts
1984
GREYSTOKE: THE LEGEND OF TARZAN, LORD OF THE APES(1984)
Nancy Potts
DEAR, DEAD DELILAH(1972), cos
Nell Potts
RACHEL, RACHEL(1968); EFFECT OF GAMMA RAYS ON MAN-IN-THE-MOON MARIGOLDS, THE(1972)
Nyanza Potts
LITTLE COLONEL, THE(1935)

Ralph B. Potts
SPECIALIST, THE(1975), w
Peter Potulski
KING OF COMEDY, THE(1983)
Ernie Potvin
SILENT SCREAM(1980)
Paul Potyen
1984
MASSIVE RETALIATION(1984), m
L. Potyomkin
JACK FROST(1966, USSR)
Henri Pouctal
Misc. Silents
ALSACE(1916, FR.), d; L'ALIBI(1917, Fr.), d; LE ROMAN D'UN SPAHI(1917, Fr.), d; L'INSTINCT(1917, Fr.), d; VOLONTE(1917, Fr.), d; LE DIEU DU HASARD(1919, Fr.), d; GIGOLETTE(1920, Fr.), d; TRAVAIL(1920, Fr.), d; LE CRIME DU BOUIF(1921, Fr.), d; LA RESURRECTION DU BOUIF(1922, Fr.), d
Eugene Pouget
Silents
MERRY WIDOW, THE(1925)
Leo Pouget
Silents
PASSION OF JOAN OF ARC, THE(1928, Fr.), m
Patrice Pouget
LIVE FOR LIFE(1967, Fr./Ital.), ph; FINO A FARTI MALE(1969, Fr./Ital.), ph; TARGET: HARRY(1980), ph
Mel Pough
CHICAGO CALLING(1951)
Denis Pouira
TIKO AND THE SHARK(1966, U.S./Ital./Fr.)
Georges Poujouly
FORBIDDEN GAMES(1953, Fr.); DIABOLIQUE(1955, Fr.); AND GOD CREATED WOMAN(1957, Fr.); FRANTIC(1961, Fr.); MISTRESS FOR THE SUMMER, A(1964, Fr./Ital.); VICE AND VIRTUE(1965, Fr./Ital.); IS PARIS BURNING?(1966, U.S./Fr.)
George Poulais
ACCUSED–STAND UP(1930, Fr.)
Dominique Poulange
TENANT, THE(1976, Fr.)
Joseph Poulard
LE BOUCHER(1971, Fr./Ital.), cos
Eliazabeth Poule
PENAL CODE, THE(1933)
Ezelle Poule
WINTER MEETING(1948); BORDER RANGERS(1950); CAGED(1950); FILE ON THELMA JORDAN, THE(1950); PERFECT STRANGERS(1950); LEAVE IT TO THE MARINES(1951); PLACE IN THE SUN, A(1951); STARLIFT(1951); ROOM FOR ONE MORE(1952); BIG HEAT, THE(1953); REDHEAD FROM MANHATTAN(1954); TWIST AROUND THE CLOCK(1961)
Francis Poulenc
ROPE(1948), m; VOYAGE TO AMERICA(1952, Fr.), m
Sylvie Poulet
WANDERER, THE(1969, Fr.), cos
Angi O. Poulis
PEOPLE AGAINST O'HARA, THE(1951)
Angi O. Poulos
THANK YOUR LUCKY STARS(1943); GIRL FROM JONES BEACH, THE(1949); SIDE STREET(1950)
Angie O. Poulos
MADAME BOVARY(1949)
Elaine Poulos
ON HER BED OF ROSES(1966)
Mitchell Poulos
JACK AND THE BEANSTALK(1970)
Karen Poulsen
Misc. Silents
ONCE UPON A TIME(1922, Den.)
Major Poulsen
OPERATION CAMEL(1961, Den.)
Patty Poulsen
AIRPORT(1970)
William A. Poulsen
ANOTHER THIN MAN(1939)
Gerry Poulson
Misc. Talkies
UNDER THE DOCTOR(1976), d
Howard Poulson
RETURN TO PARADISE(1953)
C.B. Poultney
WIFE OR TWO, A(1935, Brit.), w
A.G. Poulton
GREAT GAME, THE(1930); HINDLE WAKES(1931, Brit.); SHOULD A DOCTOR TELL?(1931, Brit.); COLLISION(1932, Brit.); LUCKY SWEEP, A(1932, Brit.)
Silents
ONE SUMMER'S DAY(1917, Brit.); BACHELORS' CLUB, THE(1921, Brit.); FLAMES OF PASSION(1922, Brit.)
Charles Poulton
FIGHTING PIMPERNEL, THE(1950, Brit.), ed
Mabel Poulton
RETURN OF THE RAT, THE(1929, Brit.); TAXI FOR TWO(1929, Brit.); CHILDREN OF CHANCE(1930, Brit.); ESCAPE(1930, Brit.); BED AND BREAKFAST(1936, Brit.); CROWN VS STEVENS(1936); TERROR ON TIPTOE(1936, Brit.)
Silents
GOD IN THE GARDEN, THE(1921, Brit.); OLD CURIOSITY SHOP, THE(1921, Brit.); DAUGHTER IN REVOLT, A(1927, Brit.); NOT QUITE A LADY(1928, Brit.); PALAIS DE DANSE(1928, Brit.); VIRGINIA'S HUSBAND(1928, Brit.); ALLEY CAT, THE(1929, Brit.)
Misc. Silents
MARY-FIND-THE-GOLD(1921, Brit.); AME D'ARTISTE(1925, Fr.); BALL OF FORTUNE, THE(1926, Brit.); GLAD EYE, THE(1927, Brit.); CONSTANT NYMPH, THE(1928, Brit.); HELLCAT, THE(1928, Brit.); TROUBLESOME WIVES(1928, Brit.);

SILENT HOUSE, THE(1929, Brit.)

R. Poulton
SPRING IN PARK LANE(1949, Brit.), ed

Ray Poulton
FLAME AND THE FLESH(1954), ed; ABANDON SHIP(1957, Brit.), ed; BLUES FOR LOVERS(1966, Brit.), ed; FORCE 10 FROM NAVARONE(1978, Brit.), ed

Raymond Poulton
EDWARD, MY SON(1949, U.S./Brit.), ed; OPERATION X(1951, Brit.), ed; HOUR OF THIRTEEN, THE(1952), ed; MAYTIME IN MAYFAIR(1952, Brit.), ed; BETRAYED(1954), ed; STORM OVER THE NILE(1955, Brit.), ed; THAT LADY(1955, Brit.), ed; INVITATION TO THE DANCE(1956), ed; PORT AFRIQUE(1956, Brit.), ed; LONG HAUL, THE(1957, Brit.), ed; GIDEON OF SCOTLAND YARD(1959, Brit.), ed; MOUSE THAT ROARED, THE(1959, Brit.), ed; TWO-HEADED SPY, THE(1959, Brit.), ed; THREE WORLDS OF GULLIVER, THE(1960, Brit.), ed; SECRET PARTNER, THE(1961, Brit.), ed; BARABBAS(1962, Ital.), ed; CAPTIVE CITY, THE(1963, Ital.), ed; JUST FOR FUN(1963, Brit.), ed; CONQUERED CITY(1966, Ital.), ed; BERSERK(1967), ed; VENGEANCE OF SHE, THE(1968, Brit.), ed; BUSHBABY, THE(1970, Brit.), ed; FRIGHT(1971, Brit.), ed; LIVE AND LET DIE(1973, Brit.), ed; MAN WITH THE GOLDEN GUN, THE(1974, Brit.), ed; BREAKTHROUGH(1978, Ger.), ed

Reginald Pound
COUNTY FAIR(1933, Brit.), w; ME AND MARLBOROUGH(1935, Brit.), w; TROUBLED WATERS(1936, Brit.), w; SHIPBUILDERS, THE(1943, Brit.), w

Toots Pound
DEADLY GAME, THE(1955, Brit.)

Virginia Pound
HOLD'EM NAVY!(1937)

C.C.H. Pounder
I'M DANCING AS FAST AS I CAN(1982)
1984
GO TELL IT ON THE MOUNTAIN(1984)

Gina Kaye Pounders
NORMA RAE(1979)

Claude Pounds
MY THIRD WIFE GEORGE(1968)

Courtice Pounds
Misc. Silents
BROKEN MELODY, THE(1916, Brit.)

Louise Pounds
Silents
FARMER'S WIFE, THE(1928, Brit.)

Toots Pounds
SVENGALI(1955, Brit.)

Henri Poupon
HARVEST(1939, Fr.); ROOM UPSTAIRS, THE(1948, Fr.); WAYS OF LOVE(1950, Ital./Fr.); PASSION FOR LIFE(1951, Fr.)

Vicki Poure
NEW KIND OF LOVE, A(1963)

Armelle Pourriche
DEAR DETECTIVE(1978, Fr.)

Mohammad Poursattar
CARAVANS(1978, U.S./Iranian)

Raymond Pousaz
GIRL FROM LORRAINE, A(1982, Fr./Switz.), p

Lena Pousette
BLOOD BEACH(1981)
1984
LONELY GUY, THE(1984)

Andre Pousse
SICILIAN CLAN, THE(1970, Fr.); COP, A(1973, Fr.); DIRTY MONEY(1977, Fr.)

Eugen Pouyet
Silents
LONE EAGLE, THE(1927)

Eugene Pouyet
Silents
HEARTS OF THE WORLD(1918); CONQUERING POWER, THE(1921); KISSES(1922)

Philippe Pouzenc
MADE IN U.S.A.(1966, Fr.)

Jean Pouzet
LE DENIER MILLIARDAIRE(1934, Fr.), ed

Phyllis Povah
WOMEN, THE(1939); LET'S FACE IT(1943); MARRYING KIND, THE(1952); PAT AND MIKE(1952); HAPPY ANNIVERSARY(1959)

Jean-Louis Poveda
HATTER'S GHOST, THE(1982, Fr.), art d

L.S. Poveda
SOFT SKIN ON BLACK SILK(1964, Fr./Span.), w

M. Povolotski
ON HIS OWN(1939, USSR)

Jason Pai Pow
Misc. Talkies
SUPER WEAPON, THE(1976)

Steve Powder
PIRANHA II: THE SPAWNING(1981, Neth.), m

Jerry Powderly
HOW WILLINGLY YOU SING(1975, Aus.)

John Powe
MEET SEXTON BLAKE(1944, Brit.); JUST WILLIAM'S LUCK(1948, Brit.); WILLIAM COMES TO TOWN(1948, Brit.); HA' PENNY BREEZE(1950, Brit.); MYSTERY AT THE BURLESQUE(1950, Brit.); MADAME LOUISE(1951, Brit.); SCARLET THREAD(1951, Brit.); HAMMER THE TOFF(1952, Brit.)

A. Van Buren Powell
Silents
MONEY MAGIC(1917), w; EVERYBODY'S GIRL(1918), w; CAPTAIN'S CAPTAIN, THE(1919), w

Ace Powell
WINTERHAWK(1976)

Addison Powell
MATING GAME, THE(1959); YOUNG DOCTORS, THE(1961); IN THE FRENCH STYLE(1963, U.S./Fr.); THOMAS CROWN AFFAIR, THE(1968); THREE DAYS OF THE CONDOR(1975); MAC ARTHUR(1977)

Misc. Talkies
CURSE OF KILIMANJARO(1978)

Alisa Powell
SATAN'S CHEERLEADERS(1977)

Amos Powell
INVASION OF THE STAR CREATURES(1962), prod d; CURSE OF THE STONE HAND(1965, Mex/Chile), w

Anthony Powell
ROYAL HUNT OF THE SUN, THE(1969, Brit.), cos; TRAVELS WITH MY AUNT(1972, Brit.), cos; PAPILLON(1973), cos; SORCERER(1977), cos; DEATH ON THE NILE(1978, Brit.), cos; TESS(1980, Fr./Brit.), cos; PRIEST OF LOVE(1981, Brit.), cos; EVIL UNDER THE SUN(1982, Brit.), cos
1984
INDIANA JONES AND THE TEMPLE OF DOOM(1984), cos

Arla Powell
BATTLE BEYOND THE SUN(1963)

Bellenden Powell
REMBRANDT(1936, Brit.); TROUBLED WATERS(1936, Brit.)

Bertha Powell
KING'S ROW(1942)

Bill Powell
DISHONORED(1931)

Buddy Powell
1984
OH GOD! YOU DEVIL(1984)

Charles Arthur Powell
PANAMINT'S BAD MAN(1938), w; HOME ON THE PRAIRIE(1939), w

Charles H. Powell
REQUIEM FOR A GUNFIGHTER(1965), ed

Cheryl Powell
Misc. Talkies
CINDY AND DONNA(1971)

Clifton Powell
1984
ALPHABET CITY(1984)

Clive Powell
CHILDREN OF THE DAMNED(1963, Brit.)

Dave Powell
JOHN WESLEY(1954, Brit.), ed

David Powell
WINTERHAWK(1976), art d
Silents
ONE OF OUR GIRLS(1914); DAWN OF A TOMORROW, THE(1915); FINE FEATHERS(1915); HER GREAT CHANCE(1918); IMPOSTER, THE(1918); COUNTERFEIT(1919); ON WITH THE DANCE(1920); APPEARANCES(1921); ANNA ASCENDS(1922); HER GILDED CAGE(1922); MISSING MILLIONS(1922); SIREN CALL, THE(1922); AVERAGE WOMAN, THE(1924); LEND ME YOUR HUSBAND(1924)
Misc. Silents
LESS THAN THE DUST(1916); BEAUTIFUL ADVENTURE, THE(1917); HER SISTER(1917); MATERNITY(1917); OUTCAST(1917); PRICE SHE PAID, THE(1917); UNFORSEEN, THE(1917); BETTER HALF, THE(1918); GIRL AND THE JUDGE, THE(1918); HER HUSBAND'S HONOR(1918); LIE, THE(1918); MAKE-BELIEVE WIFE, THE(1918); RICHEST GIRL, THE(1918); ROMANCE OF THE UNDERWORLD, A(1918); FIRING LINE, THE(1919); HIS PARISIAN WIFE(1919); TEETH OF THE TIGER, THE(1919); WOMAN UNDER OATH, THE(1919); IDOLS OF CLAY(1920); LADY ROSE'S DAUGHTER(1920); RIGHT TO LOVE, THE(1920); DANGEROUS LIES(1921, Brit.); MYSTERY ROAD, THE(1921, Brit.); PRINCESS OF NEW YORK, THE(1921 US/Brit.); LOVE'S BOOMERANG(1922); OUTCAST(1922); SPANISH JADE(1922, Brit.); FOG BOUND(1923); GLIMPSES OF THE MOON, THE(1923); GREEN GODDESS, THE(1923); MAN WITHOUT A HEART, THE(1924); TRUTH ABOUT WOMEN, THE(1924); VIRTUOUS LIARS(1924); BACK TO LIFE(1925); LOST CHORD, THE(1925)

Dawn Powell
HELLO SISTER!(1933), w; MAN OF IRON(1935), w

Denise Powell
HOTEL PARADISO(1966, U.S./Brit.)

Dick Powell
TRUE TO LIFE(1943); YOU CAN'T RUN AWAY FROM IT(1956), p&d; BIG CITY BLUES(1932); BLESSED EVENT(1932); TOO BUSY TO WORK(1932); COLLEGE COACH(1933); CONVENTION CITY(1933); FOOTLIGHT PARADE(1933); GOLD DIGGERS OF 1933(1933); KING'S VACATION, THE(1933); 42ND STREET(1933); DAMES(1934); FLIRTATION WALK(1934); HAPPINESS AHEAD(1934); TWENTY MILLION SWEETHEARTS(1934); WONDER BAR(1934); BROADWAY GONDOLIER(1935); GOLD DIGGERS OF 1935(1935); MIDSUMMER'S NIGHT'S DREAM, A(1935); PAGE MISS GLORY(1935); SHIPMATES FOREVER(1935); THANKS A MILLION(1935); COLLEEN(1936); GOLD DIGGERS OF 1937(1936); HEARTS DIVIDED(1936); STAGE STRUCK(1936); HOLLYWOOD HOTEL(1937); ON THE AVENUE(1937); SINGING MARINE, THE(1937); VARSITY SHOW(1937); COWBOY FROM BROOKLYN(1938); HARD TO GET(1938); GOING PLACES(1939); NAUGHTY BUT NICE(1939); CHRISTMAS IN JULY(1940); I WANT A DIVORCE(1940); IN THE NAVY(1941); MODEL WIFE(1941); STAR SPANGLED RHYTHM(1942); HAPPY GO LUCKY(1943); RIDING HIGH(1943); IT HAPPENED TOMORROW(1944); MEET THE PEOPLE(1944); CORNERED(1945); MURDER, MY SWEET(1945); JOHNNY O'CLOCK(1947); PITFALL(1948); ROGUES' REGIMENT(1948); STATION WEST(1948); TO THE ENDS OF THE EARTH(1948); MRS. MIKE(1949); REFORMER AND THE REDHEAD, THE(1950); RIGHT CROSS(1950); CRY DANGER(1951); TALL TARGET, THE(1951); YOU NEVER CAN TELL(1951); BAD AND THE BEAUTIFUL, THE(1952); SPLIT SECOND(1953), d; SUSAN SLEPT HERE(1954); CONQUEROR, THE(1956), p&d; ENEMY BELOW, THE(1957), p&d; HUNTERS, THE(1958), p&d

Dick Powell, Jr.
DAY OF THE LOCUST, THE(1975)

Dinnie Powell
GET CHARLIE TULLY(1976, Brit.)

Dinny Powell
CLARENCE, THE CROSS-EYED LION(1965); TOWN TAMER(1965); GREAT CATHERINE(1968, Brit.); THOSE DARING YOUNG MEN IN THEIR JAUNTY JALOPIES(1969, Fr./Brit./ Ital.); CATCH ME A SPY(1971, Brit./Fr.); 1,000 CONVICTS AND A WOMAN(1971, Brit.); MACKINTOSH MAN, THE(1973, Brit.); PINK PANTHER STRIKES AGAIN, THE(1976, Brit.); SUPERMAN II(1980)

Richard M. Powell
WILD AND WONDERFUL(1964), w

Richard Powell
STREET SCENE(1931); HUMAN SIDE, THE(1934); OPERATOR 13(1934); TREASURE ISLAND(1934); EVERY NIGHT AT EIGHT(1935); GINGER(1935); NAUGHTY MARIETTA(1935); PADDY O'DAY(1935); RENDEZVOUS(1935); WEDDING NIGHT, THE(1935); WOMAN WANTED(1935); CASE AGAINST MRS. AMES, THE(1936); GOLDEN ARROW, THE(1936); GORGEOUS HUSSY, THE(1936); HOLLYWOOD BOULEVARD(1936); IF YOU COULD ONLY COOK(1936); LOVE ON THE RUN(1936); MOON'S OUR HOME, THE(1936); WEDDING PRESENT(1936); YOURS FOR THE ASKING(1936); ANOTHER DAWN(1937); CAPTAINS COURAGEOUS(1937); CLARENCE(1937); LOVE IS NEWS(1937); MY GUN IS QUICK(1957), w; YOUNG PHILADELPHIANS, THE(1959), w; FOLLOW THAT DREAM(1962), w

Rick Powell
LOSIN' IT(1983)

Robert Powell
ITALIAN JOB, THE(1969, Brit.); SECRETS(1971); ASPHYX, THE(1972, Brit.); ASYLUM(1972, Brit.); RUNNING SCARED(1972, Brit.); MAHLER(1974, Brit.); TOMMY(1975, Brit.); THIRTY NINE STEPS, THE(1978, Brit.); HARLEQUIN(1980, Aus.); JANE AUSTEN IN MANHATTAN(1980); SURVIVOR(1980, Aus.)
1984
BEYOND GOOD AND EVIL(1984, Ital./Fr./Ger.); JIGSAW MAN, THE(1984, Brit.)

Russ Powell
DANGEROUS CURVES(1929); BIG TRAIL, THE(1930); AMBASSADOR BILL(1931); PUBLIC ENEMY, THE(1931); SIN OF MADELON CLAUDET, THE(1931); IF I HAD A MILLION(1932); ME AND MY GAL(1932); MYSTERY RANCH(1932); TAXI!(1932); KING KONG(1933); SITTING PRETTY(1933); ZOO IN BUDAPEST(1933); STAMBOUL QUEST(1934); BARBARY COAST(1935); CALL OF THE WILD(1935); I DREAM TOO MUCH(1935); MAN WHO RECLAIMED HIS HEAD, THE(1935); GIVE ME YOUR HEART(1936); SUTTER'S GOLD(1936); TRAIL OF THE LONESOME PINE, THE(1936); WEDDING PRESENT(1936); EMPEROR'S CANDLESTICKS, THE(1937); FIREFLY, THE(1937); HIT THE SADDLE(1937); MUSIC FOR MADAME(1937); PRISONER OF ZENDA, THE(1937); TOAST OF NEW YORK, THE(1937); WRONG ROAD, THE(1937); COWBOY AND THE LADY, THE(1938); IF I WERE KING(1938); EVERYTHING HAPPENS AT NIGHT(1939); FOR LOVE OR MONEY(1939); HERO FOR A DAY(1939); I STOLE A MILLION(1939); NEWSBOY'S HOME(1939); NIGHT OF NIGHTS, THE(1939); TOWER OF LONDON(1939); HOUSE OF THE SEVEN GABLES, THE(1940); RETURN OF FRANK JAMES, THE(1940); WHEN THE DALTONS RODE(1940); KING OF DODGE CITY(1941); PRAIRIE STRANGER(1941); FALLEN SPARROW, THE(1943)
Silents
SOUL OF YOUTH, THE(1920); ONE STOLEN NIGHT(1923); VAMPING VENUS(1928)
Misc. Silents
BROTHERS DIVIDED(1919); SLIM PRINCESS, THE(1920); SMOULDERING EMBERS(1920); HEAD OVER HEELS(1922)

Russell Powell
FASHIONS IN LOVE(1929); LOVE PARADE, THE(1929); AMOS 'N' ANDY(1930); GRAND PARADE, THE(1930); ARE THESE OUR CHILDREN?(1931); SIN SHIP(1931); LADY AND GENT(1932); TO THE LAST MAN(1933); MERRY WIDOW, THE(1934); WHARF ANGEL(1934); GARDEN OF ALLAH, THE(1936)
Silents
SOFT CUSHIONS(1927); GATE CRASHER, THE(1928); RILEY THE COP(1928)

Sandy Powell
THIRD STRING, THE(1932, Brit.); CAN YOU HEAR ME MOTHER?(1935, Brit.), a, w; IT'S A GRAND OLD WORLD(1937, Brit.), a, w; LEAVE IT TO ME(1937, Brit.); I'VE GOT A HORSE(1938, Brit.), a, w; ALL AT SEA(1939, Brit.); HOME FROM HOME(1939, Brit.); CUP-TIE HONEYMOON(1948, Brit.)

Scott Powell
CADDY SHACK(1980)

Sherard Powell
CASE FOR THE CROWN, THE(1934, Brit.), w; WAY OF YOUTH, THE(1934, Brit.), w; VILLAGE SQUIRE, THE(1935, Brit.), w; SHOW FLAT(1936, Brit.), w; TRAPPED BY THE TERROR(1949, Brit.), w

Shezwae Powell
1984
SUPERGIRL(1984)

Simon Powell
HARLEQUIN(1980, Aus.), d

Templar Powell
Silents
PURSUIT OF PAMELA, THE(1920, Brit.); EXPERIMENT, THE(1922, Brit.); MONSIEUR BEAUCAIRE(1924)

Vaughan Powell
KEEPERS OF YOUTH(1931, Brit.)

Villet Powell
BADGER'S GREEN(1934, Brit.), w

Violet E. Powell
Silents
JUST SUPPOSE(1926), w; WHITE BLACK SHEEP, THE(1926), w

Violet Powell
KITTY(1929, Brit.), w; PLAYTHING, THE(1929, Brit.), w; GIRL IN THE FLAT, THE(1934, Brit.), w; TO BE A LADY(1934, Brit.), w
Silents
POPPIES OF FLANDERS(1927, Brit.), w; PARADISE(1928, Brit.), w

William H. Powell
Silents
SHERLOCK HOLMES(1922); WHEN KNIGHTHOOD WAS IN FLOWER(1922); UNDER THE RED ROBE(1923); ROMOLA(1925)

William Powell
INTERFERENCE(1928); CANARY MURDER CASE, THE(1929); CHARMING SINNERS(1929); GREENE MURDER CASE, THE(1929); BEHIND THE MAKEUP(1930); BENSON MURDER CASE, THE(1930); FOR THE DEFENSE(1930); POINTED HEELS(1930); SHADOW OF THE LAW(1930); STREET OF CHANCE(1930); LADIES' MAN(1931); MAN OF THE WORLD(1931); ROAD TO SINGAPORE(1931); HIGH PRESSURE(1932); JEWEL ROBBERY(1932); ONE WAY PASSAGE(1932); DOUBLE HARNESS(1933); KENNEL MURDER CASE, THE(1933); LAWYER MAN(1933); PRIVATE DETECTIVE 62(1933); EVELYN PRENTICE(1934); FASHIONS OF 1934(1934); KEY, THE(1934); MANHATTAN MELODRAMA(1934); THIN MAN, THE(1934); ESCAPADE(1935); RECKLESS(1935); RENDEZVOUS(1935); STAR OF MIDNIGHT(1935);

AFTER THE THIN MAN(1936); EX-MRS. BRADFORD, THE(1936); GREAT ZIEGFELD, THE(1936); LIBELED LADY(1936); MY MAN GODFREY(1936); DOUBLE WEDDING(1937); EMPEROR'S CANDLESTICKS, THE(1937); LAST OF MRS. CHEYNEY, THE(1937); BARONESS AND THE BUTLER, THE(1938); ANOTHER THIN MAN(1939); I LOVE YOU AGAIN(1940); LOVE CRAZY(1941); SHADOW OF THE THIN MAN(1941); CROSSROADS(1942); HEAVENLY BODY, THE(1943); YOUNGEST PROFESSION, THE(1943); THIN MAN GOES HOME, THE(1944); ZIEGFELD FOLLIES(1945); HOODLUM SAINT, THE(1946); LIFE WITH FATHER(1947); SENATOR WAS INDISCREET, THE(1947); SONG OF THE THIN MAN(1947); MR. PEABODY AND THE MERMAID(1948); DANCING IN THE DARK(1949); TAKE ONE FALSE STEP(1949); IT'S A BIG COUNTRY(1951); TREASURE OF LOST CANYON, THE(1952); GIRL WHO HAD EVERYTHING, THE(1953); HOW TO MARRY A MILLIONAIRE(1953); MISTER ROBERTS(1955)
Silents
ALOMA OF THE SOUTH SEAS(1926); BEAU GESTE(1926); GREAT GATSBY, THE(1926); RUNAWAY, THE(1926); SEA HORSES(1926); TIN GODS(1926); NEVADA(1927); NEW YORK(1927); SHE'S A SHEIK(1927); SPECIAL DELIVERY(1927); TIME TO LOVE(1927); BEAU SABREUR(1928); DRAGNET, THE(1928); LAST COMMAND, THE(1928); PARTNERS IN CRIME(1928); FOUR FEATHERS(1929)
Misc. Silents
DANGEROUS MONEY(1924); BEAUTIFUL CITY, THE(1925); FAINT PERFUME(1925); MY LADY'S LIPS(1925); TOO MANY KISSES(1925); DESERT GOLD(1926); WHITE MICE(1926); LOVE'S GREATEST MISTAKE(1927); SENORITA(1927); FORGOTTEN FACES(1928); VANISHING PIONEER, THE(1928)

Tony Powell-Bristow
FALL OF THE HOUSE OF USHER, THE(1952, Brit.)

Russ Powells
CHAMPAGNE WALTZ(1937)

Thomas Powels
HONKYTONK MAN(1982)

[Frederick] Tyrone Power
Silents
JANICE MEREDITH(1924); REGULAR FELLOW, A(1925)
Misc. Silents
SWEET ALYSSUM(1915); TEXAS STEER, A(1915); THOU SHALT NOT COVET(1916); WHERE ARE MY CHILDREN?(1916); LORELEI OF THE SEA(1917); PLANTER, THE(1917); FOOTFALLS(1921); FURY(1922); DAY OF FAITH, THE(1923); TRUTH ABOUT WIVES, THE(1923); GREATER THAN MARRIAGE(1924); LAW AND THE LADY, THE(1924); LONE WOLF, THE(1924); STORY WITHOUT A NAME, THE(1924); OUT OF THE STORM(1926); TEST OF DONALD NORTON, THE(1926)

Anne Power
SAFARI 3000(1982)

Brenda Power
GNOME-MOBILE, THE(1967)

Cathy Power
PALM BEACH(1979, Aus.)

Chris Power
PIRATES OF PENZANCE, THE(1983)

Derry Power
NEVER PUT IT IN WRITING(1964); ULYSSES(1967, U.S./Brit.); LOCK UP YOUR DAUGHTERS(1969, Brit.); UNDERGROUND(1970, Brit.); WARLORDS OF ATLANTIS(1978, Brit.); GREAT TRAIN ROBBERY, THE(1979, Brit.); EDUCATING RITA(1983)

Douglas Power
Misc. Talkies
LISA(1977)

Ed Power
WAY WE WERE, THE(1973)

Edward Power
EMPIRE OF THE ANTS(1977)

Hartley Power
DOWN RIVER(1931, Brit.); YES, MR. BROWN(1933, Brit.); ALONG CAME SALLY(1934, Brit.); CAMELS ARE COMING, THE(1934, Brit.); EVERGREEN(1934, Brit.); FRIDAY THE 13TH(1934, Brit.); LEAVE IT TO SMITH(1934); ROAD HOUSE(1934, Brit.); JURY'S EVIDENCE(1936, Brit.); LIVING DANGEROUSLY(1936, Brit.); WHERE THERE'S A WILL(1936, Brit); RETURN OF THE FROG, THE(1938, Brit.); JUST LIKE A WOMAN(1939, Brit.); MURDER WILL OUT(1939, Brit.); RETURN TO YESTERDAY(1940, Brit.); ATLANTIC FERRY(1941, Brit.); LADY IN DISTRESS(1942, Brit.); ALIBI, THE(1943, Brit.); JOHNNY IN THE CLOUDS(1945, Brit.); DEAD OF NIGHT(1946, Brit.); GIRL IN A MILLION, A(1946, Brit.); MAN FROM MOROCCO, THE(1946, Brit.); ARMCHAIR DETECTIVE, THE(1952, Brit.); PROJECT M7(1953, Brit.); ROMAN HOLIDAY(1953); MAN WITH A MILLION(1954, Brit.); CASH ON DELIVERY(1956, Brit.); ISLAND IN THE SUN(1957)
Misc. Talkies
ALONG CAME SALLY(1933)

Jack Power
TREASURE OF MONTE CRISTO(1949)

John Power
MYSTERY OF MR. X, THE(1934); DRACULA'S DAUGHTER(1936); LOVE ON THE RUN(1936); MAID OF SALEM(1937); RAFFLES(1939); RULERS OF THE SEA(1939); ZAZA(1939); EARL OF CHICAGO, THE(1940); MRS. MINIVER(1942); LASSIE, COME HOME(1943); MAN IN HALF-MOON STREET, THE(1944); PICTURE SHOW MAN, THE(1980, Aus.), d

Lorraine Power
GOLDEN HEAD, THE(1965, Hung., U.S.)

Madge Power
Silents
INVISIBLE FEAR, THE(1921), w

Max Power
STRATEGIC AIR COMMAND(1955); SCARLET HOUR, THE(1956); GUNFIGHT AT THE O.K. CORRAL(1957); HOUSE IS NOT A HOME, A(1964)

Pamela Power
HUNGER, THE(1983), ed

Paul Power
WORDS AND MUSIC(1929); PERSONALITY KID, THE(1934); WONDER BAR(1934); DANTE'S INFERNO(1935); SHE COULDN'T TAKE IT(1935); WOMEN OF GLAMOUR(1937); I MARRIED AN ANGEL(1942); FIRST COMES COURAGE(1943); PHANTOM OF 42ND STREET, THE(1945); NOBODY LIVES FOREVER(1946); UNDER CALIFORNIA STARS(1948); MILKMAN, THE(1950); PEGGY(1950); SOMETHING FOR THE BIRDS(1952); LAST TIME I SAW PARIS, THE(1954); SILVER CHALICE,

THE(1954); WOMAN'S WORLD(1954); GIRL IN THE RED VELVET SWING, THE(1955); I DIED A THOUSAND TIMES(1955); GARMENT JUNGLE, THE(1957); 27TH DAY, THE(1957); JET ATTACK(1958); MA BARKER'S KILLER BROOD(1960); UNDERWATER CITY, THE(1962); CHEECH AND CHONG'S NEXT MOVIE(1980), anim
Misc. Silents
TRIAL MARRIAGE(1928)
Romima Power
24 HOURS IN A WOMAN'S LIFE(1968, Fr./Ger.)
Ronald Power
Silents
DOUBLE LIFE OF MR. ALFRED BURTON, THE(1919, Brit.)
Misc. Silents
ROCK OF AGES(1918, Brit.); UNCLE DICK'S DARLING(1920, Brit.)
Rose Power
RICHARD'S THINGS(1981, Brit.)
Sandra Power
NANNY, THE(1965, Brit.)
Taryn Power
COUNT OF MONTE CRISTO(1976, Brit.); SINBAD AND THE EYE OF THE TIGER(1977, U.S./Brit.); TRACKS(1977)
Tyrone Power
NORTHERN FRONTIER(1935); LLOYDS OF LONDON(1936); CAFE METROPOLE(1937); LOVE IS NEWS(1937); SECOND HONEYMOON(1937); THIN ICE(1937); ALEXANDER'S RAGTIME BAND(1938); IN OLD CHICAGO(1938); MARIE ANTOINETTE(1938); SUEZ(1938); DAY-TIME WIFE(1939); JESSE JAMES(1939); RAINS CAME, THE(1939); ROSE OF WASHINGTON SQUARE(1939); SECOND FIDDLE(1939); BRIGHAM YOUNG–FRONTIERSMAN(1940); JOHNNY APOLLO(1940); MARK OF ZORRO, THE(1940); BLOOD AND SAND(1941); YANK IN THE R.A.F., A(1941); BLACK SWAN, THE(1942); SON OF FURY(1942); THIS ABOVE ALL(1942); CRASH DIVE(1943); RAZOR'S EDGE, THE(1946); CAPTAIN FROM CASTILE(1947); NIGHTMARE ALLEY(1947); LUCK OF THE IRISH(1948); THAT WONDERFUL URGE(1948); PRINCE OF FOXES(1949); AMERICAN GUERRILLA IN THE PHILIPPINES, AN(1950); BLACK ROSE, THE(1950); I'LL NEVER FORGET YOU(1951); RAWHIDE(1951); DIPLOMATIC COURIER(1952); PONY SOLDIER(1952); KING OF THE KHYBER RIFLES(1953); MISSISSIPPI GAMBLER, THE(1953); LONG GRAY LINE, THE(1955); UNTAMED(1955); EDDY DUCHIN STORY, THE(1956); ABANDON SHIP!(1957, Brit.); RISING OF THE MOON, THE(1957, Ireland); SUN ALSO RISES, THE(1957); WITNESS FOR THE PROSECUTION(1957)
Silents
JOHN NEEDHAM'S DOUBLE(1916); GREAT SHADOW, THE(1920); DREAM STREET(1921); RED KIMONO(1925); BRIDE OF THE STORM(1926)
Misc. Silents
ARISTOCRACY(1914); EYE OF GOD, THE(1916)
Tyrone Power, Jr.
TOM BROWN OF CULVER(1932); FLIRTATION WALK(1934); GIRLS' DORMITORY(1936); LADIES IN LOVE(1936)
Tyrone Power, Sr.
BIG TRAIL, THE(1930)
Silents
HANDS ACROSS THE BORDER(1926)
Misc. Silents
DAMAGED HEARTS(1924)
Udana Power
HIGH RISK(1981)
William H. Power
Misc. Silents
WHO'S WHO IN SOCIETY(1915)
A. Powers
Silents
RIDERS OF VENGEANCE(1919), p
Alexandra Powers
1984
PRODIGAL, THE(1984)
Art Powers
FRAMED(1975), w
Barbara Powers
DARK MIRROR, THE(1946)
1984
TERMINATOR, THE(1984)
Ben Powers
THINGS ARE TOUGH ALL OVER(1982); MAN WHO LOVED WOMEN, THE(1983)
Beverly Powers
KISSIN' COUSINS(1964); MORE DEAD THAN ALIVE(1968); ANGEL IN MY POCKET(1969); J.W. COOP(1971); LIKE A CROW ON A JUNE BUG(1972); INVASION OF THE BEE GIRLS(1973)
Bill Powers
WIRETAPPERS(1956), art d
Bruce Powers
LILITH(1964); HORROR OF THE BLOOD MONSTERS(1970, U.S./Phil.)
Charles Powers
BOY SLAVES(1938)
Curtis Powers
WINDWALKER(1980)
David Powers
FIENDISH PLOT OF DR. FU MANCHU, THE(1980)
Derek Powers
FUNHOUSE, THE(1981), p
Dick Powers
OUTLAW'S DAUGHTER, THE(1954)
Douglas Powers
Misc. Talkies
AXE(1977)
Francis Powers
FROM HEADQUARTERS(1929), w; MADONNA OF AVENUE A(1929), w; ONE RAINY AFTERNOON(1936)
Silents
LITTLE GRAY LADY, THE(1914), d; RING AND THE MAN, THE(1914), d; OUT OF THE DUST(1920); SHADOWS OF CONSCIENCE(1921), w; PLAYING IT WILD(1923); ABRAHAM LINCOLN(1924); IRON HORSE, THE(1924)

Hunt Powers
ASSASSINATION OF TROTSKY, THE(1972 Fr./Ital.)
Misc. Talkies
DEAD MEN DON'T MAKE SHADOWS(1970); THAT CURSED WINTER'S DAY, DJANGO & SARTANA TO THE LAST SHOT(1970)
Jack Powers
LONG ROPE, THE(1961)
Jill Powers
Misc. Talkies
MASSACRE AT GRAND CANYON(1965)
John Powers
GREAT IMPERSONATION, THE(1935); MUTINY ON THE BOUNTY(1935); HILLS OF OLD WYOMING(1937); RUSTLER'S VALLEY(1937); WE ARE NOT ALONE(1939); RAMROD(1947); THAT'S THE WAY OF THE WORLD(1975); LAST OF THE KNUCKLEMEN, THE(1981, Aus.), w
Silents
ADAM AND EVA(1923)
Col. John "Shorty" Powers
WAY...WAY OUT(1966)
John R. Powers
POWERS GIRL, THE(1942), w
Johnny Powers
TWILIGHT ON THE TRAIL(1941)
Jon Powers
DAY THE EARTH FROZE, THE(1959, Fin./USSR)
Jule Powers
Silents
SILVER LINING, THE(1921)
Len Powers
Silents
KNIGHT OF THE WEST, A(1921), ph
Lena Powers
SWEET SURRENDER(1935)
Leona Powers
DEEP WATERS(1948); VALLEY OF THE DOLLS(1967)
Lucille Powers
MAN TO MAN(1931); TWO GUN MAN, THE(1931); AMATEUR DADDY(1932); PRIVATE SCANDAL, A(1932); TEXAS BAD MAN(1932); MYSTIC HOUR, THE(1934)
Misc. Silents
THREE WEEK-ENDS(1928); MARQUIS PREFERRED(1929)
Mala Powers
TOUGH AS THEY COME(1942); CYRANO DE BERGERAC(1950); EDGE OF DOOM(1950); OUTRAGE(1950); ROSE OF CIMARRON(1952); CITY BENEATH THE SEA(1953); CITY THAT NEVER SLEEPS(1953); GERALDINE(1953); YELLOW MOUNTAIN, THE(1954); BENGAZI(1955); RAGE AT DAWN(1955); DEATH IN SMALL DOSES(1957); MAN ON THE PROWL(1957); STORM RIDER, THE(1957); TAMMY AND THE BACHELOR(1957); UNKNOWN TERROR, THE(1957); COLOSSUS OF NEW YORK, THE(1958); SIERRA BARON(1958); FEAR NO MORE(1961); FLIGHT OF THE LOST BALLOON(1961); DOOMSDAY MACHINE(1967); DADDY'S GONE A-HUNTING(1969)
Marie Powers
MEDIUM, THE(1951)
Maurine Powers
Silents
NOTORIETY(1922)
Misc. Silents
BEWARE(1919); DEMOCRACY(1920); WHY GIRLS LEAVE HOME(1921); FREE KISSES(1926)
Michelle Powers
ELECTRA GLIDE IN BLUE(1973)
Mr. Powers
Misc. Silents
BETTER MAN, THE(1914), d
Nick Powers
LOVE AND MONEY(1982)
P. A. Powers
LOVE KISS, THE(1930), p
Silents
KICK BACK, THE(1922), p; WEDDING MARCH, THE(1927), p
Pamela Powers
DUELLISTS, THE(1977, Brit.), ed
Pat Powers
MY BODY HUNGERS(1967)
Paul Powers
EASY TO LOOK AT(1945)
Ray Powers
OPENING NIGHT(1977)
Richard Powers [Tom Keene]
JUNGLE WOMAN(1944); LIGHTS OF OLD SANTA FE(1944); NAVY WAY, THE(1944); PORT OF 40 THIEVES, THE(1944); UP IN ARMS(1944); DANGEROUS INTRUDER(1945); GIRLS OF THE BIG HOUSE(1945); SERGEANT MIKE(1945); SAN QUENTIN(1946); CROSSFIRE(1947); DICK TRACY'S DILEMMA(1947); SEVEN KEYS TO BALDPATE(1947); THUNDER MOUNTAIN(1947); UNDER THE TONTO RIM(1947); WILD HORSE MESA(1947); BLOOD ON THE MOON(1948); INDIAN AGENT(1948); RETURN OF THE BADMEN(1948); WESTERN HERITAGE(1948); STORM OVER WYOMING(1950); TEXANS NEVER CRY(1951); RED PLANET MARS(1952); DIG THAT URANIUM(1956)
Stefanie Powers
EXPERIMENT IN TERROR(1962); IF A MAN ANSWERS(1962); INTERNS, THE(1962); MC LINTOCK!(1963); PALM SPRINGS WEEKEND(1963); NEW INTERNS, THE(1964); DIE, DIE, MY DARLING(1965, Brit.); LOVE HAS MANY FACES(1965); YOUNG SINNER, THE(1965); STAGECOACH(1966); WARNING SHOT(1967); CRESCENDO(1972, Brit.); MAGNIFICENT SEVEN RIDE, THE(1972); HERBIE RIDES AGAIN(1974); IT SEEMED LIKE A GOOD IDEA AT THE TIME(1975, Can.); ESCAPE TO ATHENA(1979, Brit.)
1984
INVISIBLE STRANGLER(1984)
Misc. Talkies
MANHUNT IN SPACE(1954); GONE WITH THE WEST(1976)

Stephanie Powers
TAMMY, TELL ME TRUE(1961); BOATNIKS, THE(1970)
Stephen Powers
SWARM, THE(1978)
Steve Powers
TRUE CONFESSIONS(1981)
1984
HOME FREE ALL(1984)
Terri Powers
1,000 SHAPES OF A FEMALE(1963)
Tom Powers
THEY WON'T BELIEVE ME(1947); TIME OF YOUR LIFE, THE(1948); DOUBLE INDEMNITY(1944); PRACTICALLY YOURS(1944); CHICAGO KID, THE(1945); PHANTOM SPEAKS, THE(1945); BLUE DAHLIA, THE(1946); HER ADVENTUROUS NIGHT(1946); LAST CROOKED MILE, THE(1946); TWO YEARS BEFORE THE MAST(1946); ANGEL AND THE BADMAN(1947); FARMER'S DAUGHTER, THE(1947); FOR THE LOVE OF RUSTY(1947); I LOVE TROUBLE(1947); ANGEL IN EXILE(1948); MEXICAN HAYRIDE(1948); STATION WEST(1948); UP IN CENTRAL PARK(1948); CHINATOWN AT MIDNIGHT(1949); EAST SIDE, WEST SIDE(1949); SCENE OF THE CRIME(1949); SPECIAL AGENT(1949); DESTINATION MOON(1950); NEVADAN, THE(1950); RIGHT CROSS(1950); FIGHTING COAST GUARD(1951); STRIP, THE(1951); TALL TARGET, THE(1951); WELL, THE(1951); BAL TABA-RIN(1952); DEADLINE–U.S.A.(1952); DENVER AND RIO GRANDE(1952); DI-PLOMATIC COURIER(1952); FABULOUS SENORITA, THE(1952); HORIZONS WEST(1952); JET JOB(1952); PHONE CALL FROM A STRANGER(1952); STEEL TRAP, THE(1952); WAC FROM WALLA WALLA, THE(1952); WE'RE NOT MAR-RIED(1952); DONOVAN'S BRAIN(1953); HANNAH LEE(1953); JULIUS CA-ESAR(1953); LAST POSSE, THE(1953); MARKSMAN, THE(1953); SCARED STIFF(1953); SEA OF LOST SHIPS(1953); LUCKY ME(1954); AMERICANO, THE(1955); NEW YORK CONFIDENTIAL(1955); TEN WANTED MEN(1955)
Misc. Talkies
SON OF RUSTY, THE(1947)
Silents
AUCTION BLOCK, THE(1917)
Misc. Silents
IN THE SHADOW OF BIG BEN(1914, Brit.); BARNABY RUDGE(1915); LANCA-SHIRE LASS, A(1915, Brit.); REDEEMED(1915, Brit.)
Vici Powers
MEAL, THE(1975)
Vicki Powers
Misc. Talkies
DEADLY ENCOUNTER(1979)
William Powers
Silents
TRAFFIC IN SOULS(1913)
Misc. Silents
ROSALEEN DHU(1920, Brit.), a, d
Brian Powley
UNDER SECRET ORDERS(1943, Brit.)
Bryan Powley
POISONED DIAMOND, THE(1934, Brit.); CROSS CURRENTS(1935, Brit.); ALL IN(1936, Brit.); TO CATCH A THIEF(1936, Brit.); YOU MUST GET MARRIED(1936, Brit.); LOVE FROM A STRANGER(1937, Brit.); WHEN THE DEVIL WAS WELL(1937, Brit.); DARTS ARE TRUMPS(1938, Brit.); MOONLIGHT SONATA(1938, Brit.); MR. SATAN(1938, Brit.); STRANGE BOARDERS(1938, Brit.); YOU'RE THE DOCTOR(1938, Brit.); OLD MOTHER RILEY JOINS UP(1939, Brit.); WE DIVE AT DAWN(1943, Brit.)
Silents
FANCY DRESS(1919, Brit.); JOYOUS ADVENTURES OF ARISTIDE PUJOL, THE(1920, Brit.); OLD CURIOSITY SHOP, THE(1921, Brit.); NONENTITY, THE(1922, Brit.); OPEN COUNTRY(1922, Brit.)
Byran Powley
CONQUEST OF THE AIR(1940)
Leon Pownall
GREAT BIG THING, A(1968, U.S./Can.)
Stephen Powys
THREE BLIND MICE(1938), w; MOON OVER MIAMI(1941), w; THREE LITTLE GIRLS IN BLUE(1946), w
Donna Poyet
GIRL MOST LIKELY, THE(1957)
Jim Poyner
BUG(1975)
John Poyner
SATURDAY NIGHT OUT(1964, Brit.), ed
Robert L. Poyner
LAWYER, THE(1969)
Stephanie-Stacie Poyner
1984
COUNTRY(1984)
Beulah Poynter
HER SPLENDID FOLLY(1933), w; LOVE IS LIKE THAT(1933), w; DANCING MAN(1934), w
Misc. Silents
HEARTS AND FLOWERS(1914); LITTLE GIRL THAT HE FORGOT, THE(1914); HEARTS OF MEN(1915)
Guy Kingsley Poynter
FLOODS OF FEAR(1958, Brit.); INVITATION TO MURDER(1962, Brit.); GIRL HUNTERS, THE(1963, Brit.)
Roy Poynter
SUBURBAN WIVES(1973, Brit.), ph
Sema Poyraz
1984
FLIGHT TO BERLIN(1984, Ger./Brit.)
Lasse Poysti
SWEDISH WEDDING NIGHT(1965, Swed.)
Mike Pozen
CRIME AGAINST JOE(1956), ed; GHOST TOWN(1956), ed; MUSTANG(1959), ed; HEAD(1968), ed; BLACK VEIL FOR LISA, A(1969 Ital./Ger.), ed; VENUS IN FURS(1970, Ital./Brit./Ger.), ed; LATE LIZ, THE(1971), ed; TOP OF THE HEAP(1972), ed

John G. Pozhke
SPASMS(1983, Can.), p
Vladimir Pozner
CONSPIRATORS, THE(1944), w; DARK MIRROR, THE(1946), w; ANOTHER PART OF THE FOREST(1948), w; DAUGHTERS OF DESTINY(1954, Fr./Ital.), w
W.A. Pozner
NO GREATER LOVE(1944, USSR), w
Ela Poznerova
SWEET LIGHT IN A DARK ROOM(1966, Czech.); DEATH OF TARZAN, THE(1968, Czech)
Angel Del Pozo
EL CONDOR(1970)
Lajos Pozsar
FATHER(1967, Hung.)
Paolo Pozzesi
WIND FROM THE EAST(1970, Fr./Ital./Ger.)
Renato Pozzeto
LA BABY SITTER(1975, Fr./Ital./Ger.)
Diego Pozzetto
BEN HUR(1959)
Renato Pozzetto
MIDNIGHT PLEASURES(1975, Ital.); IMMORTAL BACHELOR, THE(1980, Ital.)
G. Pozzi
GREAT WHITE, THE(1982, Ital.), spec eff
Mario Pozzi
MIRAGE(1972, Peru), set d
Mrs. Pozzi
Silents
SIDESHOW OF LIFE, THE(1924)
Ilja Prachar
TRANSPORT FROM PARADISE(1967, Czech.); FIFTH HORSEMAN IS FEAR, THE(1968, Czech.); SIGN OF THE VIRGIN(1969 Czech.)
Jana Pracharova
FIFTH HORSEMAN IS FEAR, THE(1968, Czech.); REPORT ON THE PARTY AND THE GUESTS, A(1968, Czech.)
Rudolf Prack
CONGRESS DANCES(1957, Ger.); HEIDI(1968, Aust.)
Jose Maria Prada
DIABOLICAL DR. Z, THE(1966 Span./Fr.); HUNT, THE(1967, Span.); VILLA RI-DES(1968); NARCO MEN, THE(1969, Span./Ital.); BRIEF VACATION, A(1975, Ital.); PANCHO VILLA(1975, Span.)
Jose Prada
CARMEN(1949, Span.)
Vittoria Prada
SWEET ECSTASY(1962, Fr.)
Vittorio Prada
FRUIT IS RIPE, THE(1961, Fr./Ital.)
Marie Prade
Silents
GOLD DIGGERS, THE(1923)
Vittoria Prade
DULCINEA(1962, Span.)
Yair Pradelsky
RABBI AND THE SHIKSE, THE(1976, Israel), p
Isabelle Prades
1984
A NOS AMOURS(1984, Fr.)
Jaime Prades
SAVAGE PAMPAS(1967, Span./Arg.), p; ASSIGNMENT TERROR(1970, Ger./Span./Ital.), p
James Prades
NATIVE SON(1951, U.S., Arg.), p
Sunila Pradhan
GANDHI(1982)
Perette Pradier
BEHOLD A PALE HORSE(1964); THAT MAN IN ISTANBUL(1966, Fr./Ital./Span.)
Perrette Pradier
CRIME DOES NOT PAY(1962, Fr.); SEVEN CAPITAL SINS(1962, Fr./Ital.); OSS 117–MISSION FOR A KILLER(1966, Fr./Ital.); TIGHT SKIRTS, LOOSE PLEASU-RES(1966, Fr.); HOUSE OF CARDS(1969)
Perrette Pradier
GAME OF TRUTH, THE(1961, Fr.)
Dominique Prado
MAN WHO LIES, THE(1970, Czech./Fr.)
Francisco Prado
FORMULA, THE(1980); SURVIVORS, THE(1983)
Jose Bolanos Prado
LA CUCARACHA(1961, Mex.), w
Juliet Prado
FLIGHT TO FURY(1966, U.S./Phil.)
Lilia Prado
ILLUSION TRAVELS BY STREETCAR, THE(1977, Mex.)
Lucia Prado
DIABOLICAL DR. Z, THE(1966 Span./Fr.); SAVAGE PAMPAS(1967, Span./Arg.)
Perez Prado
CHA-CHA-CHA BOOM(1956); $100 A NIGHT(1968, Ger.), m
Irene Prador
LET'S MAKE A NIGHT OF IT(1937, Brit.); NO ORCHIDS FOR MISS BLAND-ISH(1948, Brit.); LILLI MARLENE(1951, Brit.); SOMETHING MONEY CAN'T BUY(1952, Brit.); TEARS FOR SIMON(1958, Brit.); SNORKEL, THE(1958, Brit.); DEVIL'S DAFFODIL, THE(1961, Brit./Ger.); JET STORM(1961, Brit.); NICE GIRL LIKE ME, A(1969, Brit.); LAST VALLEY, THE(1971, Brit.); HIDING PLACE, THE(1975); TO THE DEVIL A DAUGHTER(1976, Brit./Ger.); NIGHT CROSSING(1982)
Marcelle Pradot
Misc. Silents
L'HOMME DU LARGE(1920, Fr.); ELDORADO(1921, Fr.); DON JUAN ET FAUST(1923, Fr.); LA MARCHAND DE PLAISIR(1923, Fr.); LATE MATTHEW PASCAL, THE(1925, Fr.)

Fritz Praetorius
BELLA DONNA(1983, Ger.)
Anne Prager
TOOTSIE(1982)
Colonel Manny Prager
STOLEN HARMONY(1935)
Sally Prager
FROM THE MIXED-UP FILES OF MRS. BASIL E. FRANKWEILER(1973)
Stanley Prager
EVE OF ST. MARK, THE(1944); IN THE MEANTIME, DARLING(1944); TAKE IT OR LEAVE IT(1944); BELL FOR ADANO, A(1945); DOLL FACE(1945); JUNIOR MISS(1945); BEHIND GREEN LIGHTS(1946); DO YOU LOVE ME?(1946); SHOCKING MISS PILGRIM, THE(1947); STORK BITES MAN(1947); FORCE OF EVIL(1948); FOREIGN AFFAIR, A(1948); JOE PALOOKA IN WINNER TAKE ALL(1948); YOU GOTTA STAY HAPPY(1948); GUN CRAZY(1949); JOE PALOOKA IN THE BIG FIGHT(1949), w; LADY TAKES A SAILOR, THE(1949); THEY LIVE BY NIGHT(1949); DARK CITY(1950); HUMPHREY TAKES A CHANCE(1950); I'LL GET BY(1950); JOE PALOOKA IN THE SQUARED CIRCLE(1950); THREE HUSBANDS(1950); BANG BANG KID, THE(1968 U.S./Span./Ital.), d; MADIGAN'S MILLIONS(1970, Span./Ital.), d
Willi Prager
MARRIAGE IN THE SHADOWS(1948, Ger.)
Herbert Prah
FINNEGANS WAKE(1965)
Mark Praid
BLACK WINDMILL, THE(1974, Brit.)
Peggy Praigg
JACK AND THE BEANSTALK(1970), cos
Marcel Praince
CAGE OF NIGHTINGALES, A(1947, Fr.)
Marcelle Praince
ENTENTE CORDIALE(1939, Fr.); SEVEN DEADLY SINS, THE(1953, Fr./Ital.); LOVE IN THE AFTERNOON(1957)
Bailey Prairie Kid
BLACK RODEO(1972)
Jan Praise
FIRST NUDIE MUSICAL, THE(1976)
Nigam Prakash
GANDHI(1982)
Joe Praml
TRAIL OF THE PINK PANTHER, THE(1982); FUNNY MONEY(1983, Brit.)
1984
FLETCH(1984)
Kukrit Pramoj
UGLY AMERICAN, THE(1963), a, tech adv
Janet Mary Prance
THIRTEEN FRIGHTENED GIRLS(1963)
Gordon W. Prange
TORA! TORA! TORA!(1970, U.S./Jap.), w
Laurie Prange
LOOKING FOR MR. GOODBAR(1977); PILGRIM, FAREWELL(1980)
Janelle Pransky
BURY ME AN ANGEL(1972)
Giacinto Prantelli
JOAN AT THE STAKE(1954, Ital./Fr.)
Pisan Prasingh
1 2 3 MONSTER EXPRESS(1977, Thai.), ph
Leonard Praskins
CHARLATAN, THE(1929), w; SHADY LADY, THE(1929), w; CHAMP, THE(1931), w; GENTLEMAN'S FATE(1931), w; BIRD OF PARADISE(1932), w; EMMA(1932), w; FLESH(1932), w; ADVICE TO THE LOVELORN(1933), w; MAN HUNT(1933), w; SECRETS(1933), w; HERE COMES THE GROOM(1934), w; LAST GENTLEMAN, THE(1934), w; LOOKING FOR TROUBLE(1934), w; TREASURE ISLAND(1934), w; WE LIVE AGAIN(1934), w; CALL OF THE WILD(1935), w; O'SHAUGHNESSY'S BOY(1935), w; ONE IN A MILLION(1936), w; STABLEMATES(1938), w; ICE FOLLIES OF 1939(1939), w; SO THIS IS WASHINGTON(1943), w; BIG BONANZA, THE(1944), w; MY PAL, WOLF(1944), w; DOLL FACE(1945), w; MOLLY AND ME(1945), w; WINNER'S CIRCLE, THE(1948), w; IT GROWS ON TREES(1952), w; CLOWN, THE(1953), w; IT HAPPENS EVERY THURSDAY(1953), w; MR. SCOUTMAS-TER(1953), w; GORILLA AT LARGE(1954), w; THREE VIOLENT PEOPLE(1956), w; CHAMP, THE(1979), w
Gloria Prat
CURIOUS DR. HUMPP(1967, Arg.)
Jack Prat
Silents
DARING CHANCES(1924)
Mario Pratesi
LA VIACCIA(1962, Fr./Ital.), w
Joan Prather
BIG BAD MAMA(1974); DEVIL'S RAIN, THE(1975, U.S./Mex.); SMILE(1975); RAB-BIT TEST(1978); TAKE THIS JOB AND SHOVE IT(1981)
Misc. Talkies
SINGLE GIRLS(1973)
Lee Prather
SPANISH CAPE MYSTERY(1935); BORN TO THE WEST(1937); GAME THAT KILLS, THE(1937); GIRLS CAN PLAY(1937); PAID TO DANCE(1937); TWO GUN LAW(1937); JUVENILE COURT(1938); PENITENTIARY(1938); SERGEANT MUR-PHY(1938); WOMEN IN PRISON(1938); HOMICIDE BUREAU(1939); RIO GRAN-DE(1939); ROMANCE OF THE REDWOODS(1939); TEXAS STAMPEDE(1939); BULLETS FOR RUSTLERS(1940); ISLAND OF DOOMED MEN(1940); FACE BEHIND THE MASK, THE(1941); KING OF DODGE CITY(1941); OUTLAWS OF THE PANHAN-DLE(1941); RICHEST MAN IN TOWN(1941); TALK OF THE TOWN(1942); CLOSE TO MY HEART(1951)
Misc. Talkies
JUST MY LUCK(1936); TEXAS RENEGADES(1940)
Pat Prather
SHORT EYES(1977), set d

Ron Prather
RETURN TO MACON COUNTY(1975)
Pamela Prati
MONSIGNOR(1982)
Gil Pratley
COME SPY WITH ME(1967)
Vasco Pratolini
PAISAN(1948, Ital.), w; LA VIACCIA(1962, Fr./Ital.), w; FAMILY DIARY(1963 Ital.), w; FOUR DAYS OF NAPLES, THE(1963, US/Ital.), w; DIARY OF AN ITALIAN(1972, Ital.), d&w
Pratt
DUKE WORE JEANS, THE(1958, Brit.), m
Amanda Pratt
MY BRILLIANT CAREER(1980, Aus.)
Anthony Pratt
LAST GRENADE, THE(1970, Brit.), art d; LOOT(1971, Brit.), art d; NIGHT DIGGER, THE(1971, Brit.), art d; SOMETHING TO HIDE(1972, Brit.), art d; BAXTER(1973, Brit.), art d; ZARDOZ(1974, Brit.), prod d; CAT AND THE CANARY, THE(1979, Brit.), set d; EXCALIBUR(1981), prod d
1984
GIVE MY REGARDS TO BROAD STREET(1984, Brit.), prod d
Aurora Pratt
Silents
KENTUCKY CINDERELLA, A(1917)
Barbara Pratt
ROAD TO RIO(1947)
Beverly Pratt
HENRY ALDRICH GETS GLAMOUR(1942)
Charles A. Pratt
WALKING TALL, PART II(1975), p; FINAL CHAPTER–WALKING TALL zero(1977), p; MEAN DOG BLUES(1978), p; GREAT SANTINI, THE(1979), p
Charles Pratt, Jr.
1984
INITIATION, THE(1984), w
Curgie Pratt
WHITE LINE FEVER(1975, Can.)
Deborah Pratt
SPACEHUNTER: ADVENTURES IN THE FORBIDDEN ZONE(1983)
E.R. Pratt
TRIAL OF JOAN OF ARC(1965, Fr.)
Gil Pratt
LAW OF THE NORTH(1932); SAPS AT SEA(1940), w
Gilbert Pratt
ELMER AND ELSIE(1934), d; TIMOTHY'S QUEST(1936), w; BOYS WILL BE GIRLS(1937, Brit.), d
Silents
CLANCY'S KOSHER WEDDING(1927), w; JUST MARRIED(1928), w; PARTNERS IN CRIME(1928), w
Gilbert W. Pratt
Silents
KEEP SMILING(1925), d
Graham Pratt
BOXCAR BERTHA(1972)
Grahame Pratt
SKYJACKED(1972)
Hawley Pratt
INCREDIBLE MR. LIMPET, THE(1964), spec eff
Jack Pratt
DESERT SONG, THE(1929); MAMBO(1955, Ital.), cos
Silents
RIP-TIDE, THE(1923), d; WESTERN WHIRLWIND, THE(1927)
Misc. Silents
MAN'S MAKING, THE(1915), d; GODS OF FATE, THE(1916), d; HER BLEEDING HEART(1916), d; LOYALTY(1918), d; BRIGHT SKIES(1920); HEART OF A WOMAN, THE(1920), d; THIRD GENERATION, THE(1920); WOMAN UNTAMED, THE(1920), d; HUSH(1921); BACK TO YELLOW JACKET(1922); YANKEE DOODLE, JR.(1922), d; RED RIDER, THE(1925); RIDIN' THUNDER(1925); ROUGH AND READY(1927); MADE-TO-ORDER HERO, A(1928)
James Pratt
TONKA(1958), p
Jessie Pratt
Silents
SPINDLE OF LIFE, THE(1917)
Jill Pratt
ASH WEDNESDAY(1973)
John H. Pratt
Silents
DAN(1914); LOVE'S TOLL(1916), d
Misc. Silents
SHORE ACRES(1914), d; RIGHTS OF MAN, THE(1915), d
John Pratt
BETWEEN FIGHTING MEN(1932); MEET THE NAVY(1946, Brit.); WHISPERING CITY(1947, Can.); SINS OF THE FATHERS(1948, Can.); MAN CALLED FLINTSTONE, THE(1966), ph
Misc. Silents
SOLDIERS OF FORTUNE(1914)
Judson Pratt
I CONFESS(1953); FOUR GIRLS IN TOWN(1956); GREAT AMERICAN PASTIME, THE(1956); OUTSIDE THE LAW(1956); SOMEBODY UP THERE LIKES ME(1956); TOY TIGER(1956); MAN AFRAID(1957); FLOOD TIDE(1958); MONSTER ON THE CAMPUS(1958); HORSE SOLDIERS, THE(1959); RISE AND FALL OF LEGS DIA-MOND, THE(1960); SERGEANT RUTLEDGE(1960); KID GALAHAD(1962); PUBLIC AFFAIR, A(1962); UGLY AMERICAN, THE(1963); CHEYENNE AUTUMN(1964); DISTANT TRUMPET, A(1964); HANG YOUR HAT ON THE WIND(1969); BAREFOOT EXECUTIVE, THE(1971); VIGILANTE FORCE(1976)
Laura Pratt
RED RUNS THE RIVER(1963)

Michael Pratt
DUKE WORE JEANS, THE(1958, Brit.), w; DANDY IN ASPIC, A(1968, Brit.)
Mike Pratt
FACE OF A STRANGER(1964, Brit.); THIS IS MY STREET(1964, Brit.); REPULSION(1965, Brit.); PARTY'S OVER, THE(1966, Brit.); FIXER, THE(1968); GOODBYE GEMINI(1970, Brit.); SITTING TARGET(1972, Brit.); VAULT OF HORROR, THE(1973, Brit.)
Morris Pratt
ON THE YARD(1978)
Norma Pratt
STUCK ON YOU(1983); SURVIVORS, THE(1983)
1984
STUCK ON YOU(1984)
Parnell Pratt
RED-HAIRED ALIBI, THE(1932)
Purnell B. Pratt
ALIBI(1929); IS EVERYBODY HAPPY?(1929); ON WITH THE SHOW(1929); COMMON CLAY(1930); LAWFUL LARCENY(1930); PAID(1930); SINNER'S HOLIDAY(1930); DANCE, FOOLS, DANCE(1931); PRODIGAL, THE(1931); UP FOR MURDER(1931); EMMA(1932); GRAND HOTEL(1932); CHIEF, THE(1933); LAZY RIVER(1934); IT'S IN THE AIR(1935)
Purnell Pratt
FAST LIFE(1929); LOCKED DOOR, THE(1929); PAINTED FACES(1929); THRU DIFFERENT EYES(1929); TRESPASSER, THE(1929); FURIES, THE(1930); PUTTIN' ON THE RITZ(1930); ROAD TO PARADISE(1930); SILVER HORDE, THE(1930); BACHELOR APARTMENT(1931); FIVE STAR FINAL(1931); GAY DIPLOMAT, THE(1931); GORILLA, THE(1931); PUBLIC DEFENDER, THE(1931); PUBLIC ENEMY, THE(1931); SECRET WITNESS, THE(1931); SPIDER, THE(1931); TRAVELING HUSBANDS(1931); FALSE FACES(1932); FAMOUS FERGUSON CASE, THE(1932); HAT CHECK GIRL(1932); LADIES OF THE BIG HOUSE(1932); ROADHOUSE MURDER, THE(1932); SCARFACE(1932); UNWRITTEN LAW, THE(1932); HEADLINE SHOOTER(1933); I COVER THE WATERFRONT(1933); LOVE, HONOR, AND OH BABY!(1933); MIDSHIPMAN JACK(1933); PICK-UP(1933); SHRIEK IN THE NIGHT, A(1933); SON OF A SAILOR(1933); SWEETHEART OF SIGMA CHI(1933); CRIMSON ROMANCE(1934); HELL CAT, THE(1934); MIDNIGHT ALIBI(1934); NAME THE WOMAN(1934); WITCHING HOUR, THE(1934); BEHIND GREEN LIGHTS(1935); BLACK FURY(1935); CASINO MURDER CASE, THE(1935); DEATH FLIES EAST(1935); DIAMOND JIM(1935); FRISCO WATERFRONT(1935); LADIES CRAVE EXCITEMENT(1935); MAGNIFICENT OBSESSION(1935); MAN WHO RECLAIMED HIS HEAD, THE(1935); NIGHT AT THE OPERA, A(1935); RED SALUTE(1935); RENDEZVOUS AT MIDNIGHT(1935); SCHOOL FOR GIRLS(1935); SECRET BRIDE, THE(1935); WATERFRONT LADY(1935); WINNING TICKET, THE(1935); $1,000 A MINUTE(1935); DANCING FEET(1936); HOLLYWOOD BOULEVARD(1936); MURDER WITH PICTURES(1936); RETURN OF SOPHIE LANG, THE(1936); STRAIGHT FROM THE SHOULDER(1936); WEDDING PRESENT(1936); WIVES NEVER KNOW(1936); FORLORN RIVER(1937); HIGH, WIDE AND HANDSOME(1937); JOIN THE MARINES(1937); KING OF GAMBLERS(1937); LET'S MAKE A MILLION(1937); MURDER GOES TO COLLEGE(1937); NIGHT OF MYSTERY(1937); PLAINSMAN, THE(1937); ROSALIE(1937); UNDER SUSPICION(1937); COLORADO SUNSET(1939); COME ON RANGERS(1939); MY WIFE'S RELATIVES(1939); SECOND FIDDLE(1939); GRAND OLE OPRY(1940); LIFE BEGINS FOR ANDY HARDY(1941); POT O' GOLD(1941); RINGSIDE MAISIE(1941)
Robert Pratt
RED RUNS THE RIVER(1963); HIRED HAND, THE(1971)
Roger Pratt
SENDER, THE(1982, Brit.), ph
Roosevelt Pratt
FAREWELL, MY LOVELY(1975)
Sondra Pratt
WHEN THE LEGENDS DIE(1972)
Theodore Pratt
MERCY ISLAND(1941), w; JUKE GIRL(1942), w; MR. WINKLE GOES TO WAR(1944), w; BAREFOOT MAILMAN, THE(1951), w; INCREDIBLE MR. LIMPET, THE(1964), w
Thomas Pratt
TERROR, THE(1928), ed; ARGYLE CASE, THE(1929), ed; GAMBLERS, THE(1929), ed; HEARTS IN EXILE(1929), ed; TIGER ROSE(1930), ed; HOT HEIRESS(1931), ed; CROWD ROARS, THE(1932), ed; TIGER SHARK(1932), ed; WINNER TAKE ALL(1932), ed; COLLEGE COACH(1933), ed; ELMER THE GREAT(1933), ed; GOODBYE AGAIN(1933), ed; LAWYER MAN(1933), ed; WILD BOYS OF THE ROAD(1933), ed; 42ND STREET(1933), ed; DESIRABLE(1934), ed; FRIENDS OF MR. SWEENEY(1934), ed; MANDALAY(1934), ed; MERRY WIVES OF RENO, THE(1934), ed; MURDER IN THE CLOUDS(1934), ed; ALIBI IKE(1935), ed; FLORENTINE DAGGER, THE(1935), ed; GOLDEN ARROW, THE(1936), ed; MOONLIGHT ON THE PRAIRIE(1936), ed; PUBLIC ENEMY'S WIFE(1936), ed; WALKING DEAD, THE(1936), ed; WIDOW FROM MONTE CARLO, THE(1936), ed; PENROD AND SAM(1937), ed; SHE LOVED A FIREMAN(1937), ed; SINGING MARINE, THE(1937), ed; ACCIDENTS WILL HAPPEN(1938), ed; BROADWAY MUSKETEERS(1938), ed; TORCHY BLANE IN PANAMA(1938), ed; RETURN OF DR. X, THE(1939), ed; WOMEN IN THE WIND(1939), ed; BRITISH INTELLIGENCE(1940), ed; EAST OF THE RIVER(1940), ed; FUGITIVE FROM JUSTICE, A(1940), ed; MAN WHO TALKED TOO MUCH, THE(1940), ed; CASE OF THE BLACK PARROT, THE(1941), ed; SHADOWS ON THE STAIRS(1941), ed; UNDERGROUND(1941), ed; ALWAYS IN MY HEART(1942), ed; HARD WAY, THE(1942), ed; ACTION IN THE NORTH ATLANTIC(1943), ed; MISS ROBIN CRUSOE(1954), ed; WINDWALKER(1980), prod d
Tom Pratt
NO DEFENSE(1929), ed; FORT DEFIANCE(1951), ed
Tommy Pratt
ON TRIAL(1928), ed; WOMEN THEY TALK ABOUT(1928), ed; REDEEMING SIN, THE(1929), ed
Tony Pratt
HELL IN THE PACIFIC(1968), art d; DEEP END(1970 Ger./U.S.), art d; HELL BOATS(1970, Brit.), art d; BILLY TWO HATS(1973, Brit.), art d; CROSSED SWORDS(1978), prod d; DEATHWATCH(1980, Fr./Ger.), art d
Willie Pratt
SENSATIONS OF 1945(1944)
Anna-Maria Pravda
BEFORE WINTER COMES(1969, Brit.)

George Pravda
TANK FORCE(1958, Brit.); FOLLOW THAT HORSE!(1960, Brit.); MISSILE FROM HELL(1960, Brit.); PASSWORD IS COURAGE, THE(1962, Brit.); PLAYBACK(1962, Brit.); AGENT 8 3/4(1963, Brit.); REACH FOR GLORY(1963, Brit.); HIDE AND SEEK(1964, Brit.); THUNDERBALL(1965, Brit.); WHERE THE SPIES ARE(1965, Brit.); INSPECTOR CLOUSEAU(1968, Brit.); SHOES OF THE FISHERMAN, THE(1968); DECLINE AND FALL... OF A BIRD WATCHER(1969, Brit.); FRANKENSTEIN MUST BE DESTROYED!(1969, Brit.); SUMARINE X-1(1969, Brit.); TASTE OF EXCITEMENT(1969, Brit.); KREMLIN LETTER, THE(1970); UNDERGROUND(1970, Brit.); S(1974); NEXT MAN, THE(1976); HANOVER STREET(1979, Brit.); HOPSCOTCH(1980); FIREFOX(1982)
Hanna-Maria Pravda
AND SOON THE DARKNESS(1970, Brit.); KREMLIN LETTER, THE(1970)
Elsa Prawitz
DOLL, THE(1964, Swed.); WOMAN OF DARKNESS(1968, Swed.); MY FATHER'S MISTRESS(1970, Swed.), w
Mira Prawluk
CANNIBAL GIRLS(1973)
Praxis
JAWS 3-D(1983), spec eff
Chris Pray
AMERICAN GRAFFITI(1973)
Christopher E. Pray
DIE LAUGHING(1980)
Christopher Pray
FOOLS(1970); STRAWBERRY STATEMENT, THE(1970); DIRTY HARRY(1971); SUDDEN IMPACT(1983)
Cris Pray
CRACKING UP(1977)
John R. Pray
STRAWBERRY STATEMENT, THE(1970)
Leonie Pray
ONE HOUR WITH YOU(1932)
Preacher Smith's Deacons
ROCK BABY, ROCK IT(1957)
Chris F. Prebazac
CINDERELLA LIBERTY(1973)
Fred Prebble
HOUSE OF ERRORS(1942), art d
John Prebble
WHITE FEATHER(1955), w; MYSTERIOUS ISLAND(1961, U.S./Brit.), w; ZULU(1964, Brit.), w; GYPSY GIRL(1966, Brit.), w
Simon Prebble
ATTACK ON THE IRON COAST(1968, U.S./Brit.); HIGH ROAD TO CHINA(1983)
Nicholas Prebezac
SLENDER THREAD, THE(1965)
Ed Preble
ODDS AGAINST TOMORROW(1959)
Fred Preble
FACE IN THE FOG, A(1936), set d; KELLY OF THE SECRET SERVICE(1936), set d; ROGUES' TAVERN, THE(1936), set d; TERROR OF TINY TOWN, THE(1938), art d; TORTURE SHIP(1939), art d; DEATH RIDES THE RANGE(1940), art d; ISLE OF DESTINY(1940), art d; THAT GANG OF MINE(1940), set d; FLYING WILD(1941), set d; MAD MONSTER, THE(1942), art d; TOO MANY WOMEN(1942), art d; HITLER'S MADMAN(1943), art d; ISLE OF FORGOTTEN SINS(1943), art d; TRAIL OF TERROR(1944), art d; OUTLAW COUNTRY(1949), art d; SHEP COMES HOME(1949), art d; SON OF A BADMAN(1949), art d; SON OF BILLY THE KID(1949), art d; SQUARE DANCE JUBILEE(1949), art d; ZAMBA(1949), art d; FAST ON THE DRAW(1950), art d; GIRL FROM SAN LORENZO, THE(1950), art d; GUNFIRE(1950), art d; HOSTILE COUNTRY(1950), art d; MARSHAL OF HELDORADO(1950), art d; WEST OF THE BRAZOS(1950), art d; HOODLUM, THE(1951), art d; KOREA PATROL(1951), art d; VANISHING OUTPOST, THE(1951), art d
Jacques Preboist
LOVE IN THE AFTERNOON(1957); RISE OF LOUIS XIV, THE(1970, Fr.)
Paul Preboist
CARTOUCHE(1962, Fr./Ital.); SEVEN CAPITAL SINS(1962, Fr./Ital.); HOW NOT TO ROB A DEPARTMENT STORE(1965, Fr./Ital.); UP TO HIS EARS(1966, Fr./Ital.); WEEKEND AT DUNKIRK(1966, Fr./Ital.); TWO OF US, THE(1968, Fr.); DON'T LOOK NOW(1969, Brit./Fr.); LES MISERABLES(1982, Fr.)
Pierre Preboist
DAYDREAMER, THE(1975, Fr.)
Rose-Marie Precht
PRELUDE TO ECSTASY(1963, Fin.)
Rosemary Precht
MAKE LIKE A THIEF(1966, Fin.)
Herbert Prechtel
SAVAGE(1962), ed
Volker Prechtel
CRIME AND PASSION(1976, U.S., Ger.)
Djama Precigout
OLIVE TREES OF JUSTICE, THE(1967, Fr.)
Vladimir Preclik
MARTYRS OF LOVE(1968, Czech.)
George Preddy
GENERAL CRACK(1929), w
James Preddy
MOONSHINE MOUNTAIN(1964)
Masha Predit
DEATH IN VENICE(1971, Ital./Fr.)
Donna Preece
I, MAUREEN(1978, Can.)
Heather Preece
MEATBALLS(1979, Can.)
Michael Preece
SKULLDUGGERY(1970); PRIZE FIGHTER, THE(1979), d
Tim Preece
CROSSPLOT(1969, Brit.); BRIMSTONE AND TREACLE(1982, Brit.)

Evelyn Preer
BLONDE VENUS(1932); LADIES OF THE BIG HOUSE(1932)
Misc. Talkies
GEORGIA ROSE(1930)
Misc. Silents
GUNSAULUS MYSTERY, THE(1921); HOMESTEADER, THE(1922); DECEIT(1923); BIRTHRIGHT(1924); BRUTE, THE(1925); DEVIL'S DISCIPLE, THE(1926); SPIDER'S WEB, THE(1927)

Robert Pregadio
KISS THE GIRLS AND MAKE THEM DIE(1967, U.S./Ital.), md

Roberto Pregadio
GLASS SPHINX, THE(1968, Egypt/Ital./Span.), m

Eric Anthony Pregent
NIGHT OF EVIL(1962)

Janey Preger
THAT SUMMER(1979, Brit.), w

Roger Pregor
LA MARSEILLAISE(1938, Fr.)

Ana Prehan
LAZARILLO(1963, Span.)

Frank Prehoda
TOYS IN THE ATTIC(1963), makeup; YOU'RE MY EVERYTHING(1949), makeup; SEPARATE TABLES(1958), makeup; ON THE BEACH(1959), makeup; MISFITS, THE(1961), makeup; CAPE FEAR(1962), makeup; STALKING MOON, THE(1969), makeup; I WALK THE LINE(1970), makeup; SHOOT OUT(1971), makeup

Jim Preiean
RIO LOBO(1970)

Hubert Preiler
GOLGOTHA(1937, Fr.)

Milos Preininger
DO YOU KEEP A LION AT HOME?(1966, Czech.)

Jacques Preisach
MATTER OF DAYS, A(1969, Fr./Czech.), set d

Ruzena Preislerova
FIFTH HORSEMAN IS FEAR, THE(1968, Czech.)

Frederick Preisley
HIDE AND SEEK(1964, Brit.)

Jack Preisner
MACHISMO—40 GRAVES FOR 40 GUNS(1970), m&md; INSIDE AMY(1975), m

Wolfgang Preiss
CANARIS(1955, Ger.); DAS LETZTE GEHEIMNIS(1959, Ger.); MISTRESS OF THE WORLD(1959, Ital./Fr./Ger.); PRISONER OF THE VOLGA(1960, Fr./Ital.); DEAD RUN(1961, Fr./Ital./Ger.); RETURN OF DR. MABUSE, THE(1961, Ger./Fr./Ital.); ROSES FOR THE PROSECUTOR(1961, Ger.); VOR SONNENUNTERGANG(1961, Ger); COUNTERFEIT TRAITOR, THE(1962); CARDINAL, THE(1963); LAFAYETTE(1963, Fr.); MILL OF THE STONE WOMEN(1963, Fr./Ital.); DR. MABUSE'S RAYS OF DEATH(1964, Ger./Fr./Ital.); BACKFIRE(1965, Fr.); INVISIBLE DR. MABUSE, THE(1965, Ger.); MAD EXECUTIONERS, THE(1965, Ger.); TERROR OF DR. MABUSE, THE(1965, Ger.); TRAIN, THE(1965, Fr./Ital./U.S.); VON RYAN'S EXPRESS(1965); CAVE OF THE LIVING DEAD(1966, Yugo./Ger.); IS PARIS BURNING?(1966, U.S./Fr.); JACK OF DIAMONDS(1967, U.S./Ger.); ANZIO(1968, Ital.); HANNIBAL BROOKS(1969, Brit.); RAID ON ROMMEL(1971); SALZBURG CONNECTION, THE(1972); MASTER TOUCH, THE(1974, Ital./Ger.); BRIDGE TOO FAR, A(1977, Brit.); BLOODLINE(1979); FORMULA, THE(1980)

Wolfgang Preiss [Lupo Prezzo]
THOUSAND EYES OF DR. MABUSE, THE(1960, Fr./Ital./Ger.)

June Preisser
BABES IN ARMS(1939); DANCING CO-ED(1939); JUDGE HARDY AND SON(1939); GALLANT SONS(1940); STRIKE UP THE BAND(1940); HENRY ALDRICH FOR PRESIDENT(1941); SWEATER GIRL(1944); BABES ON SWING STREET(1944); MURDER IN THE BLUE ROOM(1944); I'LL TELL THE WORLD(1945); LET'S GO STEADY(1945); FREDDIE STEPS OUT(1946); HIGH SCHOOL HERO(1946); JUNIOR PROM(1946); SARGE GOES TO COLLEGE(1947); TWO BLONDES AND A REDHEAD(1947); VACATION DAYS(1947); CAMPUS SLEUTH(1948); MUSIC MAN(1948); SMART POLITICS(1948)

Patrick Prejan
LEGEND OF FRENCHIE KING, THE(1971, Fr./Ital./Span./Brit.)

Albert Prejean
UNDER THE ROOFS OF PARIS(1930, Fr.); DRAGNET NIGHT(1931, Fr.); THREEPENNY OPERA, THE(1931, Ger./U.S.); ALIBI, THE(1939, Fr.); HATRED(1941, Fr.)
Silents
ITALIAN STRAW HAT, AN(1927, Fr.)
Misc. Silents
PARIS QUI DORT(1924, Fr.); LE VOYAGE IMAGINAIRE(1926, Fr.); LES NOUVEAUX MESSIEURS(1929, Fr.); VERDUN, VISIONS D'HISTOIRE(1929, Fr.)

Patrick Prejean
SHADOWMAN(1974, Fr./Ital.)

Jerry M. Prell
CONCORDE, THE–AIRPORT '79(

Karen Prell
1984
MUPPETS TAKE MANHATTAN, THE(1984)

Micheline Prelle [Presle]
UNDER MY SKIN(1950)

Bakshi Prem
LONG DUEL, THE(1967, Brit.)

Eric Lee Preminger
ROSEBUD(1975), w

Erik Lee Preminger
HEARTBREAK KID, THE(1972)

Hope Bryce Preminger
SUCH GOOD FRIENDS(1971), cos

Ingo Preminger
M(1970), p; SALZBURG CONNECTION, THE(1972), p

Otto Preminger
UNDER YOUR SPELL(1936), d; DANGER–LOVE AT WORK(1937), d; PIED PIPER, THE(1942); MARGIN FOR ERROR(1943), a, d; THEY GOT ME COVERED(1943); IN THE MEANTIME, DARLING(1944), p&d; LAURA(1944), p&d; FALLEN ANGEL(1945), p&d; ROYAL SCANDAL, A(1945), d; WHERE DO WE GO FROM HERE?(1945); CENTENNIAL SUMMER(1946), p&d; DAISY KENYON(1947), p&d;

FOREVER AMBER(1947), d; THAT LADY IN ERMINE(1948), d; FAN, THE(1949), p&d; WHIRLPOOL(1949), p&d; WHERE THE SIDEWALK ENDS(1950), p&d; THIRTEENTH LETTER, THE(1951), p&d; ANGEL FACE(1953), p&d; MOON IS BLUE, THE(1953), p, d; STALAG 17(1953); CARMEN JONES(1954), p&d; RIVER OF NO RETURN(1954), d; COURT-MARTIAL OF BILLY MITCHELL, THE(1955), d; MAN WITH THE GOLDEN ARM, THE(1955), p&d; SAINT JOAN(1957), p&d; BONJOUR TRISTESSE(1958), p, d; ANATOMY OF A MURDER(1959), p&d; PORGY AND BESS(1959), d; EXODUS(1960), p&d; ADVISE AND CONSENT(1962), p & d; CARDINAL, THE(1963), p&d; BUNNY LAKE IS MISSING(1965), p&d; IN HARM'S WAY(1965), p&d; HURRY SUNDOWN(1967), p&d; SKIDOO(1968), p&d; TELL ME THAT YOU LOVE ME, JUNIE MOON(1970), p&d; SUCH GOOD FRIENDS(1971), p&d; ROSEBUD(1975), p&d; HUMAN FACTOR, THE(1979, Brit.), p&d

Betty Prendergast
Silents
MODERN CINDERELLA, A(1917)

Derek Prendergast
FRONT LINE KIDS(1942, Brit.)

Gerard Prendergast
TIME WALKER(1982)

James Prendergast
1984
MOSCOW ON THE HUDSON(1984)

Lester Prendergast
DR. NO(1962, Brit.)

Teresa Prendergast
HIS MAJESTY O'KEEFE(1953)

Tessa Prendergast
MANFISH(1956)

Luis Prendes
KING OF KINGS(1961); MIGHTY URSUS(1962, Ital./Span.); PYRO(1964, U.S./Span.); FICKLE FINGER OF FATE, THE(1967, Span./U.S.); MAN WHO KILLED BILLY THE KID, THE(1967, Span./Ital.); TALL WOMEN, THE(1967, Aust./Ital./Span.); CHRISTMAS KID, THE(1968, U.S., Span.); DR. COPPELIUS(1968, U.S./Span.); FEW BULLETS MORE, A(1968, Ital./Span.); JAGUAR LIVES(1979)

Paulette Preney
STOLEN LIFE(1939, Brit.)

Joe Preninger
ROSE BOWL(1936)

Armand Prenny
LAST MAN, THE(1968, Fr.), ed

Derek Prentice
FOUR AGAINST FATE(1952, Brit.); NORMAN CONQUEST(1953, Brit.); PENNY PRINCESS(1953, Brit.); SAILOR OF THE KING(1953, Brit.); DELAYED ACTION(1954, Brit.); MEET MR. MALCOLM(1954, Brit.); PROFILE(1954, Brit.); YOU LUCKY PEOPLE(1955, Brit.); RICHARD III(1956, Brit.); BREAK IN THE CIRCLE, THE(1957, Brit.); DOCTOR'S DILEMMA, THE(1958, Brit.); GIDEON OF SCOTLAND YARD(1959, Brit.); LADY IS A SQUARE, THE(1959, Brit.); TOP FLOOR GIRL(1959, Brit.); SECRET OF MONTE CRISTO, THE(1961, Brit.)

Keith Prentice
BOYS IN THE BAND, THE(1970); LEGEND OF NIGGER CHARLEY, THE(1972); CRUISING(1980)

Marvleen Prentice
SON OF SINBAD(1955)

Ann Prentiss
ANY WEDNESDAY(1966); IF HE HOLLERS, LET HIM GO(1968); OUT OF TOWNERS, THE(1970); CALIFORNIA SPLIT(1974)

Chris Prentiss
GOIN' HOME(1976), p,d&w, ph, ed

David Prentiss
DR. TERROR'S GALLERY OF HORRORS(1967), w; JOURNEY TO THE CENTER OF TIME(1967), w; HELL'S CHOSEN FEW(1968), w; MIGHTY GORGA, THE(1969), w

Ed Prentiss
VIOLENT ROAD(1958); FBI STORY, THE(1959); WESTBOUND(1959); MAN ON A STRING(1960); SUNRISE AT CAMPOBELLO(1960); GATHERING OF EAGLES, A(1963); PROJECT X(1968); BAREFOOT EXECUTIVE, THE(1971); MARRIAGE OF A YOUNG STOCKBROKER, THE(1971)

Edward Prentiss
ONE MAN'S WAY(1964)

Eleanor Prentiss
SOMETHING TO SING ABOUT(1937); LET'S FACE IT(1943)

Gregory Prentiss
CULPEPPER CATTLE COMPANY, THE(1972), w

Lew Prentiss
MICKEY ONE(1965)

Paul E. Prentiss
WAKAMBA!(1955)

Paul Prentiss
WHAT'S NEW, PUSSYCAT?(1965, U.S./Fr.)

Paula Prentiss
WHERE THE BOYS ARE(1960); BACHELOR IN PARADISE(1961); HONEYMOON MACHINE, THE(1961); HORIZONTAL LIEUTENANT, THE(1962); FOLLOW THE BOYS(1963); LOOKING FOR LOVE(1964); MAN'S FAVORITE SPORT [?](1964); WORLD OF HENRY ORIENT, THE(1964); IN HARM'S WAY(1965); CATCH-22(1970); MOVE(1970); BORN TO WIN(1971); LAST OF THE RED HOT LOVERS(1972); CRAZY JOE(1974); PARALLAX VIEW, THE(1974); STEPFORD WIVES, THE(1975); BLACK MARBLE, THE(1980); BUDDY BUDDY(1981); SATURDAY THE 14TH(1981)

Richard Prentout
WOMEN AND WAR(1965, Fr.), w

Olga Preobrajenskaya
COSSACKS OF THE DON(1932, USSR), d

Olga Preobrazhenskaya
Misc. Silents
NEST OF NOBLEMEN, A(1915, USSR); PLEBIAN(1915, USSR); MISS PEASANT(1916, USSR), d; WOMEN OF RYAZAN(1927, USSR), d

Sofya Preobrazhenskaya
QUEEN OF SPADES(1961, USSR)

Preobrazhensky
Misc. Silents
TALE OF PRIEST PANKRATI(1918, USSR), a, d

Evgeni Preov
LAST HILL, THE(1945, USSR)

Rajendra Presade
TARZAN GOES TO INDIA(1962, U.S./Brit./Switz.)

Melvin Presar
GONG SHOW MOVIE, THE(1980)

Eugene Wiley Presbrey
RAFFLES(1930), w

Pearl Prescod
PASSIONATE SUMMER(1959, Brit.); EXORCISM AT MIDNIGHT(1966, Brit. revised 1973, U.S.)

Ellen Prescott
WAKE UP AND LIVE(1937); RAMPARTS WE WATCH, THE(1940)

Elsa Prescott
PETER IBBETSON(1935)

Elsie Prescott
THIRTEEN WOMEN(1932); LIMEHOUSE BLUES(1934); THOU SHALT NOT KILL(1939); WATERLOO BRIDGE(1940); NONE BUT THE LONELY HEART(1944)

George Prescott
HUCKLEBERRY FINN(1974)

Guy Prescott
ROGUE COP(1954); RAGE AT DAWN(1955); SHOTGUN(1955); FLIGHT TO HONG KONG(1956); SCANDAL INCORPORATED(1956); OUTLAW'S SON(1957); PHARAOH'S CURSE(1957); TALL STRANGER, THE(1957); UNEARTHLY, THE(1957); FORT MASSACRE(1958); JET ATTACK(1958); QUANTRILL'S RAIDERS(1958); THE HYPNOTIC EYE(1960)

Jack Prescott
Silents
OVERALLS(1916)
Misc. Silents
POWDER(1916)

Jean Prescott
CONFIRM OR DENY(1941); THIS ABOVE ALL(1942); FOREVER AND A DAY(1943); GUY NAMED JOE, A(1943); WHITE CLIFFS OF DOVER, THE(1944); MOLLY AND ME(1945); CLUNY BROWN(1946); COME TO THE STABLE(1949)

John Prescott
Misc. Silents
TORCH BEARER, THE(1916), d

Kerrigan Prescott
FIEND WITHOUT A FACE(1958); SUBWAY IN THE SKY(1959, Brit.)

Kirchy Prescott
PROMISE, THE(1979)

Nina Prescott
LADY TAKES A SAILOR, THE(1949)

Norm Prescott
PINOCCHIO IN OUTER SPACE(1965, U.S./Bel.), p; JOURNEY BACK TO OZ(1974), p, w; MIGHTY MOUSE IN THE GREAT SPACE CHASE(1983), p

Norman Prescott
DISC JOCKEY(1951)

Paul Prescott
I WANT WHAT I WANT(1972, Brit.)

Robert Prescott
1984
JOY OF SEX(1984)

Russ Prescott
TANK COMMANDOS(1959); WAR IS HELL(1964)

Sy Prescott
HUD(1963); HANGUP(1974)

Thad Prescott
SEXTETTE(1978), prod d

Captain C. P. Prescott-Richardson
UNASHAMED(1938), w

Antonia Preser
PARSIFAL(1983, Fr.)

Catharina Preser
PARSIFAL(1983, Fr.)

The Preseration Hall Jazz Band of New Orleans
WUSA(1970)

Peter Preses
MAGIC FACE, THE(1951, Aust.); NO TIME FOR FLOWERS(1952); 5 SINNERS(1961, Ger.)

The Presidential Philharmonic Orchestra of Turkey
DRY SUMMER(1967, Turkey), m

Robin Presky
SUNDAY BLOODY SUNDAY(1971, Brit.)

Michelin Presle
DONKEY SKIN(1975, Fr.)

Micheline Presle
ANGEL AND SINNER(1947, Fr.); LES JEUX SONT FAITS(1947, Fr.); FOOLISH HUSBANDS(1948, Fr.); DEVIL IN THE FLESH, THE(1949, Fr.); AMERICAN GUERRILLA IN THE PHILIPPINES, AN(1950); ADVENTURES OF CAPTAIN FABIAN(1951); FRENCH WAY, THE(1952, Fr.); NAPOLEON(1955, Fr.); ROYAL AFFAIRS IN VERSAILLES(1957, Fr.); BRIDE IS MUCH TOO BEAUTIFUL, THE(1958, Fr.); DEMONIAQUE(1958, Fr.); CHRISTINE(1959, Fr.); MISTRESS OF THE WORLD(1959, Ital./Fr./Ger.); CHANCE MEETING(1960, Brit.); ASSASSIN, THE(1961, Ital./Fr.); DEVIL AND THE TEN COMMANDMENTS, THE(1962, Fr.); IF A MAN ANSWERS(1962); SEVEN CAPITAL SINS(1962, Fr./Ital.); IMPERIAL VENUS(1963, Ital./Fr.); PRIZE, THE(1963); TIME OUT FOR LOVE(1963, Ital./Fr.); DARK PURPOSE(1964); MISTRESS FOR THE SUMMER, A(1964, Fr./Ital.); HAIL MAFIA(1965, Fr./Ital.); MALE HUNT(1965, Fr./Ital.); KING OF HEARTS(1967, Fr./Ital.); LEGEND OF FRENCHIE KING, THE(1971, Fr./Ital./Span./Brit.); NUN, THE(1971, Fr.)

Henri Presles
THEY MET ON SKIS(1940, Fr.)

Elvis Presley
TROUBLE WITH GIRLS(AND HOW TO GET INTO IT), THE*1/2 (1969); LOVE ME TENDER(1956); JAILHOUSE ROCK(1957); LOVING YOU(1957); KING CREOLE(1958); FLAMING STAR(1960); G.I. BLUES(1960); BLUE HAWAII(1961); WILD IN THE COUNTRY(1961); FOLLOW THAT DREAM(1962); GIRLS! GIRLS! GIRLS!(1962); KID GALAHAD(1963); FUN IN ACAPULCO(1963); IT HAPPENED AT THE WORLD'S FAIR(1963); KISSIN' COUSINS(1964); ROUSTABOUT(1964); VIVA LAS VEGAS(1964); GIRL HAPPY(1965); HARUM SCARUM(1965); TICKLE ME(1965); FRANKIE AND JOHNNY(1966); PARADISE, HAWAIIAN STYLE(1966); SPINOUT(1966); CLAMBAKE(1967); DOUBLE TROUBLE(1967); EASY COME, EASY GO(1967); LIVE A LITTLE, LOVE A LITTLE(1968); SPEEDWAY(1968); STAY AWAY, JOE(1968); CHANGE OF HABIT(1969); CHARRO(1969)

Gladys Presley
LOVING YOU(1957)

Jacquie Presly
PAPERBACK HERO(1973, Can.)

Phil Presly
JUD(1971)

Elie Presman
VERY PRIVATE AFFAIR, A(1962, Fr./Ital.)

E.G. Presnell
SLIGHTLY HONORABLE(1940), w

Harve Presnell
UNSINKABLE MOLLY BROWN, THE(1964); GLORY GUYS, THE(1965); WHEN THE BOYS MEET THE GIRLS(1965); PAINT YOUR WAGON(1969); BLOOD BATH(1976)

Robert Presnell
BIG POND, THE(1930), w; YOUNG MAN OF MANHATTAN(1930), w; BARGAIN, THE(1931), w; LEFTOVER LADIES(1931), w; LOST SQUADRON, THE(1932), w; MAN CALLED BACK, THE(1932), w; BUREAU OF MISSING PERSONS(1933), w; EMPLOYEE'S ENTRANCE(1933), w; EVER IN MY HEART(1933), w; KENNEL MURDER CASE, THE(1933), p, w; KEYHOLE, THE(1933), w; NARROW CORNER, THE(1933), w; TERROR ABOARD(1933), w; WILD BOYS OF THE ROAD(1933), p; HI, NELLIE!(1934), p; KEY, THE(1934), p; MANDALAY(1934), p; MASSACRE(1934), p; SMARTY(1934), p; MANHATTAN MOON(1935), w; MARY JANE'S PA(1935), p; PAROLE(1936), p; POSTAL INSPECTOR(1936), p, w; CARNIVAL QUEEN(1937), p; GIRL OVERBOARD(1937), p; NIGHT KEY(1937), p; THAT'S MY STORY(1937), p; DISBARRED(1939), w; REAL GLORY, THE(1939), w; THEY SHALL HAVE MUSIC(1939), w; THOU SHALT NOT KILL(1939), w; MONEY AND THE WOMAN(1940), w; MEET JOHN DOE(1941), w; HURRICANE SMITH(1942), w; BIG BONANZA, THE(1944), w; HIGH TIDE(1947), w; MICHIGAN KID, THE(1947), w

Robert Presnell, Sr.
CUBAN PETE(1946), w; FOR YOU I DIE(1947), p, w; GUILTY, THE(1947), w; SOFIA(1948), p; GIRL ON THE RUN(1961), p

Sherry Presnell
WILLARD(1971)

Barbara Press
MARCH OF THE SPRING HARE(1969); ROOMMATES(1971)

Gordon Press
ARTHUR(1981)
1984
NEW YORK NIGHTS(1984)

Joel Press
ME AND MY BROTHER(1969)

Marvin Press
NORTHWEST OUTPOST(1947); SONG OF SCHEHERAZADE(1947); SEA TIGER(1952); TREASURE OF LOST CANYON, THE(1952); MEXICAN MANHUNT(1953); DRAGON'S GOLD(1954); MORITURI(1965)

Vlodek Press
1984
AMERICAN DREAMER(1984)

Arnold Pressburger
DIVINE SPARK, THE(1935, Brit./Ital.), p; MY HEART IS CALLING(1935, Brit.), p; RETURN OF THE SCARLET PIMPERNEL(1938, Brit.), p; PRISON WITHOUT BARS(1939, Brit.), p; SHANGHAI GESTURE, THE(1941), p; IT HAPPENED TOMORROW(1944), p; THREE HOURS(1944, Fr.), p; SCANDAL IN PARIS, A(1946), p; LOST ONE, THE(1951, Ger.), p

Emeric Pressburger
BEAUTIFUL ADVENTURE(1932, Ger.), w; ONE RAINY AFTERNOON(1936), w; CHALLENGE, THE(1939, Brit.), w; SPY FOR A DAY(1939, Brit.), w; U-BOAT 29(1939, Brit.), w; BLACKOUT(1940, Brit.), w; ATLANTIC FERRY(1941, Brit.), w; INVADERS, THE,(1941), w; ONE OF OUR AIRCRAFT IS MISSING(1942, Brit.), p,d&w; ADVENTURE IN BLACKMAIL(1943, Brit.), w; SQUADRON LEADER X(1943, Brit.), w; CANTERBURY TALE, A(1944, Brit.), p,d&w; COLONEL BLIMP(1945, Brit.), p, w; SILVER FLEET, THE(1945, Brit.), p; STAIRWAY TO HEAVEN(1946, Brit.), p,d&w; WANTED FOR MURDER(1946, Brit.), w; BLACK NARCISSUS(1947, Brit.), p,d&w; END OF THE RIVER, THE(1947, Brit.), p; I KNOW WHERE I'M GOING(1947, Brit.), p,d&w; RED SHOES, THE(1948, Brit.), p&d, w; HOUR OF GLORY(1949, Brit.), p,d&w; FIGHTING PIMPERNEL, THE(1950, Brit.), d&w; TALES OF HOFFMANN, THE(1951, Brit.), p,d&w; WILD HEART, THE(1952, Brit.), w; TWICE UPON A TIME(1953, Brit.), p,d&w; OH ROSALINDA(1956, Brit.), p,d&w; MIRACLE IN SOHO(1957, Brit.), p, w; PURSUIT OF THE GRAF SPEE(1957, Brit.), p,d&w; NIGHT AMBUSH(1958, Brit.), p,d&w; BEHOLD A PALE HORSE(1964), w; THEY'RE A WEIRD MOB(1966, Aus.), w; BOY WHO TURNED YELLOW, THE(1972, Brit.), w

Fred Pressburger
IT HAPPENED TOMORROW(1944), ed; FABIOLA(1951, Ital.), w; CROWDED PARADISE(1956), d

Fred Pressel
BLOCK BUSTERS(1944)

Louis "Babe" Pressley
HARLEM GLOBETROTTERS, THE(1951)

Edward Pressman
OUT OF IT(1969), p; REVOLUTIONARY, THE(1970, Brit.), p

Edward R. Pressman
DEALING: OR THE BERKELEY-TO-BOSTON FORTY-BRICK LOST-BAG BLUES(1971), p; SISTERS(1973), p; PHANTOM OF THE PARADISE(1974), p; OLD BOYFRIENDS(1979), p; HAND, THE(1981), p

Eugene Pressman
DOCTOR DETROIT(1983)

Gary Pressman
1984
DUBEAT-E-O(1984), ph

Lawrence Pressman
MAKING IT(1971); SHAFT(1971); CRAZY WORLD OF JULIUS VROODER, THE(1974); MAN IN THE GLASS BOOTH, THE(1975); WALK PROUD(1979); NINE TO FIVE(1980)

Michael Pressman
GREAT TEXAS DYNAMITE CHASE, THE(1976), d; BAD NEWS BEARS IN BREAKING TRAINING, THE(1977), d; BOULEVARD NIGHTS(1979), d; THOSE LIPS, THOSE EYES(1980), p, d; SOME KIND OF HERO(1982), d; DOCTOR DETROIT(1983), d

Jason Presson
1984
STONE BOY, THE(1984)

Jay Presson
ANGEL COMES TO BROOKLYN, AN(1945)

Ron Presson
1984
STONE BOY, THE(1984)

Pat Prest
HEAVENLY DAYS(1944); CHILD OF DIVORCE(1946); LADY LUCK(1946); ON DANGEROUS GROUND(1951)

Patricia Prest
BOSS OF BIG TOWN(1943); CHETNIKS(1943); INCENDIARY BLONDE(1945); SON OF LASSIE(1945)

Ben Prestbury
SEDUCTION OF JOE TYNAN, THE(1979)

Antonio Prester
NIGHT OF THE SHOOTING STARS, THE(1982, Ital.)

Joe Lo Presti
DREAMS OF GLASS(1969)

Sam Presti
ALICE IN THE CITIES(1974, W. Ger.)

Mel Prestige
GHOST OF THE CHINA SEA(1958); HONG KONG CONFIDENTIAL(1958)

Shirley Prestio
CHEECH AND CHONG'S NICE DREAMS(1981)

Alan Preston
LIQUID SKY(1982)

"Amarillo Slim" Preston
CALIFORNIA SPLIT(1974)

Ann Preston
MAGNIFICENT BRUTE, THE(1936); PAROLE(1936)

Anne Preston
COQUETTE(1929), w

Billy Preston
ST. LOUIS BLUES(1958); SGT. PEPPER'S LONELY HEARTS CLUB BAND(1978); J-MEN FOREVER(1980), m
1984
BLAME IT ON THE NIGHT(1984)

Clinton Preston
Silents
SEATS OF THE MIGHTY, THE(1914); FAMILY CUPBOARD, THE(1915)

David Preston
SPACEHUNTER: ADVENTURES IN THE FORBIDDEN ZONE(1983), w

Dibbs Preston
1984
WHERE THE BOYS ARE '84(1984)

Don Preston
TWO HUNDRED MOTELS(1971, Brit.); ANDROID(1982), m; BEING, THE(1983), m

Duncan Preston
1984
SCANDALOUS(1984)

Earl G. Preston
FORTUNE AND MEN'S EYES(1971, U.S./Can.), prod d

Earl Preston
WAITING FOR CAROLINE(1969, Can.), art d; PYX, THE(1973, Can.), prod d; WHY ROCK THE BOAT?(1974, Can.), set d; SHOOT(1976, Can.), art d; ANGRY MAN, THE(1979 Fr./Can.), art d; HAPPY BIRTHDAY TO ME(1981), prod d

Harry Preston
Silents
REST CURE, THE(1923, Brit.)

Hugh Preston
HEAD OFFICE(1936, Brit.), w

J. A. Preston
MISSISSIPPI SUMMER(1971); SPOOK WHO SAT BY THE DOOR, THE(1973); TWO-MINUTE WARNING(1976); REAL LIFE(1979); BODY HEAT(1981)
Misc. Talkies
WHITE LIONS(1981)

Jan Preston
PICTURES(1982, New Zealand), m

Jim Preston
MR. SMITH GOES TO WASHINGTON(1939), tech adv

Joey Preston
NO LEAVE, NO LOVE(1946); FIESTA(1947); CAMPUS SLEUTH(1948)

John Preston
TIMBER TERRORS(1935)
Misc. Talkies
BEAST OF BORNEO(1935); COURAGE OF THE NORTH(1935)

June Preston
ANNE OF GREEN GABLES(1934)

Kelly Preston
CHRISTINE(1983); METALSTORM: THE DESTRUCTION OF JARED-SYN(1983)

Leonard Preston
PRIVATES ON PARADE(1982)

Leslie Preston
MANHATTAN MELODRAMA(1934)

Linda Preston
TWO GALS AND A GUY(1951)

Michael Preston
LAST OF THE KNUCKLEMEN, THE(1981, Aus.)

Mike Preston
DUET FOR FOUR(1982, Aus.); ROAD WARRIOR, THE(1982, Aus.); METALSTORM: THE DESTRUCTION OF JARED-SYN(1983)

Misc. Talkies
SURABAYA CONSPIRACY(1975)

Paul Preston
MAKO: THE JAWS OF DEATH(1976)

Paula Preston
RIVERRUN(1968)

Ray Preston
HOOKED GENERATION, THE(1969), w; NAKED ZOO, THE(1970), w

Robert Preston
ILLEGAL TRAFFIC(1938); KING OF ALCATRAZ(1938); BEAU GESTE(1939); DISBARRED(1939); UNION PACIFIC(1939); MOON OVER BURMA(1940); NORTHWEST MOUNTED POLICE(1940); TYPHOON(1940); LADY FROM CHEYENNE(1941); MIDNIGHT ANGEL(1941); NIGHT OF JANUARY 16TH(1941); PARACHUTE BATTALION(1941); NIGHT PLANE FROM CHUNGKING(1942); PACIFIC BLACKOUT(1942); REAP THE WILD WIND(1942); STAR SPANGLED RHYTHM(1942); THIS GUN FOR HIRE(1942); WAKE ISLAND(1942); MACOMBER AFFAIR, THE(1947); VARIETY GIRL(1947); WILD HARVEST(1947); BIG CITY(1947); BLOOD ON THE MOON(1948); WHISPERING SMITH(1948); LADY GAMBLES, THE(1949); TULSA(1949); SUNDOWNERS, THE(1950); BEST OF THE BADMEN(1951); MY BROTHER, THE OUTLAW(1951); WHEN I GROW UP(1951); CLOUDBURST(1952, Brit.); LAST FRONTIER, THE(1955); DARK AT THE TOP OF THE STAIRS, THE(1960); HOW THE WEST WAS WON(1962); MUSIC MAN, THE(1962); ALL THE WAY HOME(1963); ISLAND OF LOVE(1963); CHILD'S PLAY(1972); JUNIOR BONNER(1972); MAME(1974); SEMITOUGH(1977); S.O.B.(1981); VICTOR/VICTORIA(1982)
1984
LAST STARFIGHTER, THE(1984)

Robert Preston, Jr.
NEW YORK TOWN(1941)

Stanley J. Preston
Misc. Silents
CLEAN GUN, THE(1917)

Stephen Preston
DON'T KNOCK THE TWIST(1962)

Steve Preston
SCREAM AND SCREAM AGAIN(1970, Brit.)

Trevor Preston
NIGHT HAIR CHILD(1971, Brit.), w
1984
SLAYGROUND(1984, Brit.), w

Wade Preston
MAN CALLED SLEDGE, A(1971, Ital.)

Ward Preston
SOME KIND OF A NUT(1969), set d; MONTE WALSH(1970), art d; STONE KILLER, THE(1973), art d; TOWERING INFERNO, THE(1974), art d; CAPONE(1975), art d; WON TON TON, THE DOG WHO SAVED HOLLYWOOD(1976), art d; VIVA KNIEVEL!(1977), prod d; THAT CHAMPIONSHIP SEASON(1982), prod d
1984
PURPLE RAIN(1984), prod d
Misc. Talkies
MAN ON THE SPYING TRAPEZE(1965)

Wayde Preston
ANZIO(1968, Ital.); TODAY IT'S ME...TOMORROW YOU!(1968, Ital.); LONG RIDE FROM HELL, A(1970, Ital.)
Misc. Talkies
TODAY WE KILL...TOMORROW WE DIE(1971)

William Preston
MALATESTA'S CARNIVAL(1973)

Greg Prestopino
YOUNG NURSES, THE(1973), m

Camillus Pretal
ABIE'S IRISH ROSE(1928)

Gian Carlo Prete
MASSACRE IN ROME(1973, Ital.)

Giancarlo Prete
HORNET'S NEST(1970); CONFESSIONS OF A POLICE CAPTAIN(1971, Ital.); BLACK BELLY OF THE TARANTULA, THE(1972, Ital.); LOVES AND TIMES OF SCARAMOUCHE, THE(1976, Ital.)
Misc. Talkies
ANONYMOUS AVENGER, THE(1976, Ital.)

Billy Pretorious
KIMBERLEY JIM(1965, South Africa)

Arline Pretty
Silents
IN AGAIN-OUT AGAIN(1917); CHALLENGE OF CHANCE, THE(1919); WHEN THE DEVIL DRIVES(1922); STORMSWEPT(1923); TIPPED OFF(1923); WHITE FLOWER, THE(1923); GIRL ON THE STAIRS, THE(1924)
Misc. Silents
MAN WHO FOUND HIMSELF, THE(1915); DAWN OF FREEDOM, THE(1916); SUPRISES OF AN EMPTY HOTEL, THE(1916); LIFE(1920); VALLEY OF DOUBT, THE(1920); BETWEEN TWO HUSBANDS(1922); LOVE IN THE DARK(1922); WAGES OF SIN, THE(1922); BUCKING THE BARRIER(1923); PRIMROSE PATH, THE(1925)

Violet Pretty [Anne Heywood]
LADY GODIVA RIDES AGAIN(1955, Brit.)

Bruce Pretty Bird
MAN CALLED HORSE, A(1970)

Pretty Things
MONSTER CLUB, THE(1981, Brit.)

The Pretty Things
WHAT'S GOOD FOR THE GOOSE(1969, Brit.)

Jeff Prettyman
1984
SUBURBIA(1984)

Max Pretzfelder
SUMMER STORM(1944), cos

Dana Preu
GAL YOUNG UN(1979)

Edith Terry Preuss
HOLLYWOOD MYSTERY(1934)

Jose Preval
LIQUID SKY(1982)

Jacques Prevert
CRIME OF MONSIEUR LANGE, THE(1936, Fr.), w; MYSTERIOUS MR. DAVIS, THE(1936, Brit.), w; PORT OF SHADOWS(1938, Fr.), w; BIZARRE BIZARRE(1939, Fr.), w; DAYBREAK(1940, Fr.), w; LUMIERE D'ETE(1943, Fr.), w; CHILDREN OF PARADISE(1945, Fr.), w; STORMY WATERS(1946, Fr.), w; BELLMAN, THE(1947, Fr.), w; DEVIL'S ENVOYS, THE(1947, Fr.), w; L'ATALANTE(1947, Fr.); GATES OF THE NIGHT(1950, Fr.), w; LOVERS OF VERONA, THE(1951, Fr.), w; HUNCHBACK OF NOTRE DAME, THE(1957, Fr.), w

Pierre Prevert
L'ATALANTE(1947, Fr.); L'AGE D'OR(1979, Fr.)

Gisele Preville
AGAINST THE WIND(1948, Brit.)

Giselle Preville
DANCING YEARS, THE(1950, Brit.); FIVE MILES TO MIDNIGHT(1963, U.S./Fr./ Ital.)

Andre Previn
THOROUGHLY MODERN MILLIE(1967), md; KISSING BANDIT, THE(1948), m; BORDER INCIDENT(1949), m; CHALLENGE TO LASSIE(1949), m; GREAT SINNER, THE(1949), md; SCENE OF THE CRIME(1949), m; SECRET GARDEN, THE(1949), md; SUN COMES UP, THE(1949), m; TENSION(1949), m; DIAL 1119(1950), m; KIM(1950), m; MALAYA(1950), md; OUTRIDERS, THE(1950), m; SHADOW ON THE WALL(1950), m; THREE LITTLE WORDS(1950), md; CAUSE FOR ALARM(1951), m; GIRL WHO HAD EVERYTHING, THE(1953), m; GIVE A GIRL A BREAK(1953), md; KISS ME KATE(1953), md; SMALL TOWN GIRL(1953), md; BAD DAY AT BLACK ROCK(1955), m; IT'S ALWAYS FAIR WEATHER(1955), md; KISMET(1955), md; CATERED AFFAIR, THE(1956), m; FASTEST GUN ALIVE(1956), m; INVITATION TO THE DANCE(1956), m, md; DESIGNING WOMAN(1957), m; HOT SUMMER NIGHT(1957), m; HOUSE OF NUMBERS(1957), md; SILK STOCKINGS(1957), md; GIGI(1958), md; PORGY AND BESS(1959), md; ELMER GANTRY(1960), m; PE-PE(1960), md; SUBTERRANEANS, THE(1960), a, m; WHO WAS THAT LADY?(1960), m; ALL IN A NIGHT'S WORK(1961), m; ONE, TWO, THREE(1961), m, md; FOUR HORSEMEN OF THE APOCALYPSE, THE(1962), m; LONG DAY'S JOURNEY INTO NIGHT(1962), m; TWO FOR THE SEESAW(1962), m; IRMA LA DOUCE(1963), m; DEAD RINGER(1964), m; GOODBYE CHARLIE(1964), m; KISS ME, STUPID(1964), m; MY FAIR LADY(1964), md; INSIDE DAISY CLOVER(1965), m; FORTUNE COOK-IE, THE(1966), m; WAY WEST, THE(1967), md; MRS. POLLIFAX-SPY(1971), m; MUSIC LOVERS, THE(1971, Brit.), md; JESUS CHRIST, SUPERSTAR(1973), md; ROLLERBALL(1975), m, md; ONE-TRICK PONY(1980), md

Anre Previn
ONE-TRICK PONY(1980), m

Charles Previn
FLYING HOSTESS(1936), m; MY MAN GODFREY(1936), m, md; POSTAL INSPEC-TOR(1936), md; AS GOOD AS MARRIED(1937), md; GIRL OVERBOARD(1937), md; GIRL WITH IDEAS, A(1937), md; LOVE IN A BUNGALOW(1937), md; MAN IN BLUE, THE(1937), md; MERRY-GO-ROUND OF 1938(1937), md; MYSTERIOUS CROSSING(1937), md; PRESCRIPTION FOR ROMANCE(1937), md; ROAD BACK,-THE(1937), md; THREE SMART GIRLS(1937), md; TOP OF THE TOWN(1937), md; WE HAVE OUR MOMENTS(1937), md; WESTLAND CASE, THE(1937), md; WHEN LOVE IS YOUNG(1937), md; WILDCATTER, THE(1937), md; WINGS OVER HONOLULU(1937), md; YOU'RE A SWEETHEART(1937), md; 100 MEN AND A GIRL(1937), md; CRIME OF DR. HALLET(1938), md; DANGER ON THE AIR(1938), md; DEVIL'S PARTY, THE(1938), md; FRESHMAN YEAR(1938), md; LAST WARN-ING, THE(1938), md; LITTLE TOUGH GUY(1938), md; LITTLE TOUGH GUYS IN SOCIETY(1938), md; MIDNIGHT INTRUDER(1938), md; NURSE FROM BROOK-LYN(1938), md; PERSONAL SECRETARY(1938), md; RAGE OF PARIS, THE(1938), md; ROAD TO RENO, THE(1938), md; SECRETS OF A NURSE(1938), md; SINNERS IN PARADISE(1938), md; SPY RING, THE(1938), md; STATE POLICE(1938), md; STORM, THE(1938), md, art d; SWING, SISTER, SWING(1938), md; THAT CERTAIN AGE(1938), md; WIVES UNDER SUSPICION(1938), md; YOUNG FUGITIVES(1938), md; YOUTH TAKES A FLING(1938), md; DESTRY RIDES AGAIN(1939), md; EAST SIDE OF HEAVEN(1939), md; FAMILY NEXT DOOR, THE(1939), md; FIRST LO-VE(1939), md; FOR LOVE OR MONEY(1939), md; FORGOTTEN WOMAN, THE(1939), md; GAMBLING SHIP(1939), md; HAWAIIAN NIGHTS(1939), md; LAUGH IT OFF(1939), md; LITTLE ACCIDENT(1939), md; NEWSBOY'S HOME(1939), md; OK-LAHOMA FRONTIER(1939), md; RIO(1939), md; SOCIETY SMUGGLERS(1939), md; SPIRIT OF CULVER, THE(1939), md; SUN NEVER SETS, THE(1939), md; THREE SMART GIRLS GROW UP(1939), md; TOWER OF LONDON(1939), md; UNDER-PUP, THE(1939), md; UNEXPECTED FATHER(1939), md; YOU CAN'T CHEAT AN HON-EST MAN(1939), md; BOYS FROM SYRACUSE(1940), md; DARK STREETS OF CAIRO(1940), m; GIVE US WINGS(1940), md; I CAN'T GIVE YOU ANYTHING BUT LOVE, BABY(1940), m&md; IF I HAD MY WAY(1940), md; I'M NOBODY'S SWEET-HEART NOW(1940), md; INVISIBLE MAN RETURNS, THE(1940), md; IT'S A DA-TE(1940), m; LA CONGA NIGHTS(1940), md; LITTLE BIT OF HEAVEN, A(1940), a, md; MA, HE'S MAKING EYES AT ME(1940), md; MY LITTLE CHICK-ADEE(1940), md; OH JOHNNY, HOW YOU CAN LOVE!(1940), md; ONE NIGHT IN THE TROPICS(1940), md; PONY POST(1940), md; SANDY IS A LADY(1940), md; SEVEN SINNERS(1940), md; SON OF ROARING DAN(1940), md; SPRING PARA-DE(1940), md; CRACKED NUTS(1941), md; DANGEROUS GAME, A(1941), md; DON'T GET PERSONAL(1941), m; FLAME OF NEW ORLEANS, THE(1941), md; IT STARTED WITH EVE(1941), md; LADY FROM CHEYENNE(1941), m, md; LUCKY DEVILS(1941), md; MAN MADE MONSTER(1941), m; MAN WHO LOST HIMSELF, THE(1941), md; MOONLIGHT IN HAWAII(1941), md; NEVER GIVE A SUCKER AN EVEN BREAK(1941), md; NICE GIRL?(1941), md; SING ANOTHER CHORUS(1941), m; SIX LESSONS FROM MADAME LA ZONGA(1941), md; SOUTH OF TAHITI(1941), md; UNFINISHED BUSINESS(1941), md; WHERE DID YOU GET THAT GIRL?(1941), md; WOLF MAN, THE(1941), m; ARABIAN NIGHTS(1942), md; BEHIND THE EIGHT BALL(1942), md; BETWEEN US GIRLS(1942), m; BROADWAY(1942), m; EAGLE SQUADRON(1942), md; ESCAPE FROM HONG KONG(1942), md; GET HEP TO LOVE(1942), md; GHOST OF FRANKENSTEIN, THE(1942), md; GIVE OUT, SISTERS(1942), md; JUKE BOX JENNY(1942), md; LADY IN A JAM(1942), md; MISSISSIPPI GAMBLER(1942), md; MOONLIGHT IN HAVANA(1942), md; PARDON MY SARONG(1942), md; PITTSBURGH(1942), md; RIDE 'EM COWBOY(1942), md; SABOTEUR(1942), m; SHERLOCK HOLMES AND THE SECRET WEAPON(1942), md; SHERLOCK HOLMES AND THE VOICE OF TERROR(1942), md; SPOILERS, THE(1942), md; WHAT'S COOKIN'?(1942), md; AMAZING MRS. HOLLIDAY(1943), md; CRAZY HOUSE(1943), md; FIRED WIFE(1943), md; FLESH AND FAN-TASY(1943), md; FOLLOW THE BAND(1943), md; GALS, INCORPORATED(1943), md; GOOD MORNING, JUDGE(1943), md; HERS TO HOLD(1943), md; HE'S MY

GUY(1943), md; HI, BUDDY(1943), md; HIS BUTLER'S SISTER(1943), art d; HIT THE ICE(1943), md; IT AIN'T HAY(1943), md; IT COMES UP LOVE(1943), md; LARCENY WITH MUSIC(1943), md; MR. BIG(1943), m, md; RHYTHM OF THE ISLANDS(1943), md; SHADOW OF A DOUBT(1943), md; SHERLOCK HOLMES IN WASHING-TON(1943), md; SHE'S FOR ME(1943), md; SING A JINGLE(1943), md; SO'S YOUR UNCLE(1943), md; TOP MAN(1943), m, md; WE'VE NEVER BEEN LICKED(1943), md; WHEN JOHNNY COMES MARCHING HOME(1943), md; WHITE SAVAGE(1943), md; YOU'RE A LUCKY FELLOW, MR. SMITH(1943), md; SONG OF THE OPEN ROAD(1944), md; THIS IS THE LIFE(1944), md; 3 IS A FAMILY(1944), md; DELIGHT-FULLY DANGEROUS(1945), m, md; IT'S IN THE BAG(1945), md; TWO SISTERS FROM BOSTON(1946), w; B. F.'S DAUGHTER(1948), md; HOMECOMING(1948), md; BLACK BOOK, THE(1949), md; THAT MIDNIGHT KISS(1949), md

Steven Previn
ALMOST ANGELS(1962), d

Ludvig Previs
DYBBUK THE(1938, Pol.), p

Abbe Antoine-Francois Prevost
MANON(1950, Fr.), w

Abbe Prevost
MANON 70(1968, Fr.), w

Silents
MANON LESCAUT(1914), w

Edwin Prevost
1984
CITY HEAT(1984)

Francoise Prevost
ENEMY GENERAL, THE(1960); GAME OF TRUTH, THE(1961, Fr.); BON VOYA-GE(1962); GIRL WITH THE GOLDEN EYES, THE(1962, Fr.); PARIS BELONGS TO US(1962, Fr.); PAYROLL(1962, Brit.); CONDEMNED OF ALTONA, THE(1963); PLAY-TIME(1963, Fr.); SEASON FOR LOVE, THE(1963, Fr.); TIME OUT FOR LOVE(1963, Ital./Fr.); VERONA TRIAL, THE(1963, Ital.); GALIA(1966, Fr./Ital.); MURDER CLIN-IC, THE(1967, Ital./Fr.); OTHER ONE, THE(1967,Fr.); ITALIAN SECRET SER-VICE(1968, Ital.); SPIRITS OF THE DEAD(1969, Fr./Ital.); WINTER WIND(1970, Fr./Hung.); WOMAN ON FIRE, A(1970, Ital.); JOHNNY HAMLET(1972, Ital.)

Marie Prevost
FLYING FOOL(1929); GODLESS GIRL, THE(1929); LADIES OF LEISURE(1930); PAID(1930); PARTY GIRL(1930); SWEETHEARTS ON PARADE(1930); WAR NUR-SE(1930); GENTLEMAN'S FATE(1931); GOOD BAD GIRL, THE(1931); IT'S A WISE CHILD(1931); RECKLESS LIVING(1931); RUNAROUND, THE(1931); SIN OF MADEL-ON CLAUDET, THE(1931); SPORTING BLOOD(1931); WEST OF THE ROCKIES(1931); CARNIVAL BOAT(1932); HELL DIVERS(1932); THREE WISE GIRLS(1932); ELEV-ENTH COMMANDMENT(1933); ONLY YESTERDAY(1933); PAROLE GIRL(1933); SLIGHTLY MARRIED(1933); HANDS ACROSS THE TABLE(1935); TANGO(1936); THIRTEEN HOURS BY AIR(1936); TEN LAPS TO GO(1938)

Misc. Talkies
DIVORCE MADE EASY(1929); CALL OF THE ROCKIES(1931)

Silents
NOBODY'S FOOL(1921); SMALL TOWN IDOL, A(1921); BEAUTIFUL AND DAMNED, THE(1922); DON'T GET PERSONAL(1922); KISSED(1922); RED LIGHTS(1923); WANTERS, THE(1923); MARRIAGE CIRCLE, THE(1924); KISS ME AGAIN(1925); RECOMPENSE(1925); ALMOST A LADY(1926); CAVEMAN, THE(1926); HIS JAZZ BRIDE(1926); MAN BAIT(1926); NIGHT BRIDE, THE(1927); RUSH HOUR, THE(1927); ON TO RENO(1928); RACKET, THE(1928)

Misc. Silents
DOWN ON THE FARM(1920); LOVE, HONOR AND BEHAVE(1920); MOONLIGHT FOLLIES(1921); PARISIAN SCANDAL, A(1921); DANGEROUS LITTLE DEMON, THE(1922); HER NIGHT OF NIGHTS(1922); HEROES OF THE STREET(1922); MAR-RIED FLAPPER, THE(1922); BRASS(1923); BEING RESPECTABLE(1924); COR-NERED(1924); DARK SWAN, THE(1924); DAUGHTERS OF PLEASURE(1924); HOW TO EDUCATE A WIFE(1924); TARNISH(1924); THREE WOMEN(1924); BOBBED HAIR(1925); SEVEN SINNERS(1925); FOR WIVES ONLY(1926); OTHER WOMEN'S HUSBANDS(1926); UP IN MABEL'S ROOM(1926); GETTING GERTIE'S GAR-TER(1927); GIRL IN THE PULLMAN, THE(1927); BLONDE FOR A NIGHT, A(1928); SIDESHOW, THE(1928); CALL OF THE ROCKIES(1931)

Marjorie Prevost
Silents
OLD SWIMMIN' HOLE, THE(1921); FOG, THE(1923)

Minnie Prevost
Silents
FOOD FOR SCANDAL(1920); IF ONLY JIM(1921); GIRL OF THE GOLDEN WEST, THE(1923)

Robert Prevost
LITTLE GIRL WHO LIVES DOWN THE LANE, THE(1977, Can.), art d

Jacques Prevot
SUNDAYS AND CYBELE(1962, Fr.)

Chris Prey
CANDIDATE, THE(1972)

Gertrude Prey
TOXI(1952, Ger.)

Hermann Prey
BARBER OF SEVILLE, THE(1973, Ger./Fr.)

Jacques Preyer
EXPOSED(1983)

Benito Prezia
VON RYAN'S EXPRESS(1965); WHAT DID YOU DO IN THE WAR, DADDY?(1966)

Benito Prezie
TWO WEEKS IN ANOTHER TOWN(1962)

Horace [Horacio] Priani
HEAT(1970, Arg.)

A. Pribylovsky
BRIDE WITH A DOWRY(1954, USSR)

Adm. John Dale Price
WINGS OF EAGLES, THE(1957), tech adv

Alan Price
O LUCKY MAN!(1973, Brit.), a, m; ALFIE DARLING(1975, Brit.), a, m; BRITTANIA HOSPITAL(1982, Brit.), m
1984
PLAGUE DOGS, THE(1984, U.S./Brit.), m

Alison Price
GREASE 2(1982)
1984
UNFAITHFULLY YOURS(1984)
Allan Price
CANNIBAL GIRLS(1973)
Alonzo Price
FORGOTTEN FACES(1936); HUMAN CARGO(1936); BLACK LEGION, THE(1937); MIDNIGHT MADONNA(1937); NAVY BLUES(1937); SLIM(1937); FORBIDDEN VALLEY(1938); MARIE ANTOINETTE(1938); TEST PILOT(1938); PENALTY, THE(1941); JOHNNY EAGER(1942)
Ann Price
Silents
SMART SET, THE(1928), w; THUNDER(1929), w
Art Price
Silents
GOLD RUSH, THE(1925)
Arthur Price
OEDIPUS REX(1957, Can.), art d
Bamlet L. Price
ONE WAY TICKET TO HELL(1955), p,d&w
Bamlet L. Price, Jr.
ONE WAY TICKET TO HELL(1955)
Bobby Price
MELODY AND ROMANCE(1937, Brit.); DOWN OUR ALLEY(1939, Brit.)
Brendan Price
Misc. Talkies
NAUGHTY WIVES(1974)
Brent Price
1984
BUDDY SYSTEM, THE(1984)
Carol Price
SKY RIDERS(1976, U.S./Gr.)
Catherine Price
DREAM GIRL(1947)
Charles Price
NOWHERE TO GO(1959, Brit.); ROOM 43(1959, Brit.); ROAD TO FORT ALAMO, THE(1966, Fr./Ital.), w
Chris Price
SKY RIDERS(1976, U.S./Gr.)
Curtiss Price
SWEET JESUS, PREACHER MAN(1973)
Daria Price
NESTING, THE(1981), w
David F. Price
MOMMIE DEAREST(1981); FAST TIMES AT RIDGEMONT HIGH(1982)
David Price
NINE TO FIVE(1980)
Debbie Price
PIGEON THAT TOOK ROME, THE(1962); MY SIX LOVES(1963)
Dennis Price
CANTERBURY TALE, A(1944, Brit.); ECHO MURDERS, THE(1945, Brit.); PLACE OF ONE'S OWN, A(1945, Brit.); CARAVAN(1946, Brit.); BAD SISTER(1947, Brit.); DEAR MURDERER(1947, Brit.); HOLIDAY CAMP(1947, Brit.); HUNGRY HILL(1947, Brit.); MAGIC BOW, THE(1947, Brit.); MASTER OF BANKDAM, THE(1947, Brit.); EASY MONEY(1948, Brit.); JASSY(1948, Brit.); BAD LORD BYRON, THE(1949, Brit.); HELTER SKELTER(1949, Brit.); KIND HEARTS AND CORONETS(1949, Brit.); SNOWBOUND(1949, Brit.); DANCING YEARS, THE(1950, Brit.); GOOD TIME GIRL(1950, Brit.); LOST PEOPLE, THE(1950, Brit.); ADVENTURERS, THE(1951, Brit.); I'LL NEVER FORGET YOU(1951); MURDER WITHOUT CRIME(1951, Brit.); FRIGHTENED BRIDE, THE(1952, Brit.); MAGIC BOX, THE(1952, Brit.); BACHELOR IN PARIS(1953, Brit.); MURDER AT 3 A.M.(1953, Brit.); NOOSE FOR A LADY(1953, Brit.); FOR BETTER FOR WORSE(1954, Brit.); INTRUDER, THE(1955, Brit.); LADY GODIVA RIDES AGAIN(1955, Brit.); THAT LADY(1955, Brit.); CHARLEY MOON(1956, Brit.); OH ROSALINDA(1956, Brit.); PORT AFRIQUE(1956, Brit.); PRIVATE'S PROGRESS(1956, Brit.); TOUCH OF THE SUN, A(1956, Brit.); ROCK AROUND THE WORLD(1957, Brit.); SHE PLAYED WITH FIRE(1957, Brit.); TIME IS MY ENEMY(1957, Brit.); HELLO LONDON(1958, Brit.); YOUR PAST IS SHOWING(1958, Brit.); DON'T PANIC CHAPS!(1959, Brit.); I'M ALL RIGHT, JACK(1959, Brit.); BREAKOUT(1960, Brit.); MILLIONAIRESS, THE(1960, Brit.); OSCAR WILDE(1960, Brit.); PICCADILLY THIRD STOP(1960, Brit.); SCHOOL FOR SCOUNDRELS(1960, Brit.); TUNES OF GLORY(1960, Brit.); CALL ME GENIUS(1961, Brit.); DOUBLE BUNK(1961, Brit.); FIVE GOLDEN HOURS(1961, Brit.); NO LOVE FOR JOHNNIE(1961, Brit.); PURE HELL OF ST. TRINIAN'S, THE(1961, Brit.); VICTIM(1961, Brit.); WATCH IT, SAILOR!(1961, Brit.); GO TO BLAZES(1962, Brit.); KILL OR CURE(1962, Brit.); POT CARRIERS, THE(1962, Brit.); WHAT A CARVE UP!(1962, Brit.); COOL MIKADO, THE(1963, Brit.); CRACKSMAN, THE(1963, Brit.); DOCTOR IN DISTRESS(1963, Brit.); PLAY IT COOL(1963, Brit.); V.I.P.s, THE(1963, Brit.); WRONG ARM OF THE LAW, THE(1963, Brit.); COMEDY MAN, THE(1964); EARTH DIES SCREAMING, THE(1964, Brit.); HORROR OF IT ALL, THE(1964, Brit.); JOLLY BAD FELLOW, A(1964, Brit.); MURDER MOST FOUL(1964, Brit.); TAMAHINE(1964, Brit.); AMOROUS MR. PRAWN, THE(1965, Brit.); CURSE OF THE VOODOO(1965, Brit.); TEN LITTLE INDIANS(1965, Brit.); JUST LIKE A WOMAN(1967, Brit.); THOSE FANTASTIC FLYING FOOLS(1967, Brit); HORROR HOUSE(1970, Brit.); HORROR OF FRANKENSTEIN, THE(1970, Brit.); MAGIC CHRISTIAN, THE(1970, Brit.); RISE AND RISE OF MICHAEL RIMMER, THE(1970, Brit.); SOME WILL, SOME WON'T(1970, Brit.); VENUS IN FURS(1970, Ital./Brit./Ger.); TWINS OF EVIL(1971, Brit.); ADVENTURES OF BARRY McKENZIE(1972, Austral.); DRACULA VERSUS FRANKENSTEIN(1972, Span.); PULP(1972, Brit.); HORROR HOSPITAL(1973, Brit.); THEATRE OF BLOOD(1973, Brit.); SON OF DRACULA(1974, Brit.); BEYOND THE FOG(1981, Brit.)
Misc. Talkies
GO FOR A TAKE(1972, Brit.)
Dick Price
BEGGAR STUDENT, THE(1958, Ger.); THREE PENNY OPERA(1963, Fr./Ger.), ch
Dilys Price
UNDER MILK WOOD(1973, Brit.)
Donald Price
HELL, HEAVEN OR HOBOKEN(1958, Brit.)

Dorothy Price
PAPER MOON(1973)
Eastman Price
INSIDE AMY(1975)
Edward Price
SMARTEST GIRL IN TOWN(1936); CONFESSION(1937); EVER SINCE EVE(1937); GO-GETTER, THE(1937); KID GALAHAD(1937); SINGING MARINE, THE(1937); THAT GIRL FROM PARIS(1937)
Eugene Price
GUESS WHAT WE LEARNED IN SCHOOL TODAY?(1970), w; CORKY(1972), w; STOOLIE, THE(1972), w
Evadne Price
PHANTOM LIGHT, THE(1935, Brit.), w; WOLF'S CLOTHING(1936, Brit.), w; MERRY COMES TO STAY(1937, Brit.), w; BLONDES FOR DANGER(1938, Brit.), w; LIGHTNING CONDUCTOR(1938, Brit.), w; SILVER TOP(1938, Brit.), w; ONCE A CROOK(1941, Brit.), w; NOT WANTED ON VOYAGE(1957, Brit.), w
Frank Price
SULLIVAN'S EMPIRE(1967), p; GREAT WALDO PEPPER, THE(1975), stunts
Fred Price
COOL HAND LUKE(1967), set d; PRIVATE NAVY OF SGT. O'FARRELL, THE(1968), set d; SKIDOO(1968), set d; BIG DADDY(1969), set d; MITCHELL(1975), set d; POSSE(1975), set d; PORKY'S II: THE NEXT DAY(1983), art d
1984
KIDCO(1984), prod d
Fred R. Price
TRADER HORN(1973), set d; NORMAN...IS THAT YOU?(1976), set d; BAD NEWS BEARS IN BREAKING TRAINING, THE(1977), set d
Gene Price
BUDDY BUDDY(1981)
George S. Price
GUYANA, CULT OF THE DAMNED(1980, Mex./Span./Panama), m
Ginger Price
PRINCE OF PEACE, THE(1951)
Grant Price
NATE AND HAYES(1983, U.S./New Zealand)
Hal Price
NIGHT RIDE(1930); PARTY GIRL(1930); CITY STREETS(1931); PLATINUM BLONDE(1931); TEN CENTS A DANCE(1931); CARNIVAL BOAT(1932); LADY AND GENT(1932); LAST MAN(1932); SIN'S PAYDAY(1932); STRANGERS OF THE EVENING(1932); THIS SPORTING AGE(1932); UNDER-COVER MAN(1932); WIDOW IN SCARLET(1932); BOWERY, THE(1933); GIRL IN 419(1933); RANGER'S CODE, THE(1933); RIDERS OF DESTINY(1933); TUGBOAT ANNIE(1933); CLEOPATRA(1934); FIFTEEN WIVES(1934); FOG OVER FRISCO(1934); HELL BENT FOR LOVE(1934); IT HAPPENED ONE NIGHT(1934); SAGEBRUSH TRAIL(1934); WEST OF THE DIVIDE(1934); CAVALRY(1936); CROOKED TRAIL, THE(1936); DEATH FROM A DISTANCE(1936); FUGITIVE SHERIFF, THE(1936); HEIR TO TROUBLE(1936); LONE WOLF RETURNS, THE(1936); MYSTERIOUS AVENGER, THE(1936); NAVY BORN(1936); RETURN OF SOPHIE LANG, THE(1936); ROSE BOWL(1936); WILDCAT TROOPER(1936); DESERT PHANTOM(1937); MELODY OF THE PLAINS(1937); PUBLIC COWBOY NO. 1(1937); RECKLESS RANGER(1937); RIDIN' THE LONE TRAIL(1937); STARS OVER ARIZONA(1937); SUNDOWN SAUNDERS(1937); TROUBLE IN TEXAS(1937); TRUSTED OUTLAW, THE(1937); WHERE TRAILS DIVIDE(1937); BORN TO FIGHT(1938); CALL THE MESQUITEERS(1938); DANGER VALLEY(1938); GUNSMOKE TRAIL(1938); MAN FROM MUSIC MOUNTAIN(1938); PIONEER TRAIL(1938); PRAIRIE MOON(1938); ACROSS THE PLAINS(1939); HOME ON THE PRAIRIE(1939); IN OLD MONTEREY(1939); LUCKY NIGHT(1939); MAN FROM TEXAS, THE(1939); NEW FRONTIER(1939); NIGHT RIDERS, THE(1939); OVERLAND MAIL(1939); SOUTH OF THE BORDER(1939); WILD HORSE CANYON(1939); ARIZONA FRONTIER(1940); CARSON CITY KID(1940); FRONTIER CRUSADER(1940); LONE STAR RAIDERS(1940); MAD YOUTH(1940); MY SON IS GUILTY(1940); OUT WEST WITH THE PEPPERS(1940); WE WHO ARE YOUNG(1940); BILLY THE KID IN SANTA FE(1941); BILLY THE KID'S FIGHTING PALS(1941); DEVIL BAT, THE(1941); FORBIDDEN TRAILS(1941); GANGS OF SONORA(1941); JUNGLE MAN(1941); LONE RIDER AMBUSHED, THE(1941); LONE RIDER FIGHTS BACK, THE(1941); MEET JOHN DOE(1941); PARSON OF PANAMINT, THE(1941); RIDERS OF THE BADLANDS(1941); RIDING THE CHEROKEE TRAIL(1941); SECRETS OF THE WASTELANDS(1941); SIERRA SUE(1941); SINGING HILL, THE(1941); SIS HOPKINS(1941); ARIZONA ROUNDUP(1942); COWBOY SERENADE(1942); HOME IN WYOMIN'(1942); ICE-CAPADES REVUE(1942); LAW AND ORDER(1942); LONE RIDER AND THE BANDIT, THE(1942); RAIDERS OF THE RANGE(1942); RAIDERS OF THE WEST(1942); SHERIFF OF SAGE VALLEY(1942); THUNDER RIVER FEUD(1942); VALLEY OF HUNTED MEN(1942); BLACK MARKET RUSTLERS(1943); DEAD MEN WALK(1943); MY SON, THE HERO(1943); ONE DANGEROUS NIGHT(1943); OUTLAWS OF STAMPEDE PASS(1943); ROBIN HOOD OF THE RANGE(1943); TWO FISTED JUSTICE(1943); WAGON TRACKS WEST(1943); WESTERN CYCLONE(1943); FUZZY SETTLES DOWN(1944); LAW OF THE VALLEY(1944); MAN FROM FRISCO(1944); MARSHAL OF RENO(1944); MOJAVE FIREBRAND(1944); OUTLAW TRAIL(1944); RUSTLER'S HIDEOUT(1944); SILVER CITY KID(1944); SONORA STAGECOACH(1944); WESTWARD BOUND(1944); WILD HORSE PHANTOM(1944); CORPUS CHRISTI BANDITS(1945); LONE TEXAS RANGER(1945); SHERIFF OF CIMARRON(1945); WILDFIRE(1945); SUN VALLEY CYCLONE(1946); WHITE STALLION(1947); SUNDOWN RIDERS(1948); FATHER MAKES GOOD(1950); FRISCO TORNADO(1950); TARNISHED(1950); ROUGH RIDERS OF DURANGO(1951); JUNCTION CITY(1952); OKLAHOMA ANNIE(1952)
Misc. Talkies
TEXAS RENEGADES(1940); PRAIRIE GUNSMOKE(1942); FUGITIVE OF THE PLAINS(1943)
Harry F. Price
LAW MEN(1944); PARTNERS OF THE TRAIL(1944); RANGE LAW(1944)
Henri Price
ROPE OF FLESH(1965), md; MOONWOLF(1966, Fin./Ger.), m
Henry Price
INCREDIBLY STRANGE CREATURES WHO STOPPED LIVING AND BECAME CRAZY MIXED-UP ZOMBIES, THE(1965), m; THRILL KILLERS, THE(1965), m; RAT PFINK AND BOO BOO(1966), m
Herbert Price
ESCAPED FROM DARTMOOR(1930, Brit.), w

Howard Price
ELOPEMENT(1951); SHE'S BACK ON BROADWAY(1953); TO HELL AND BACK(1955); D-DAY, THE SIXTH OF JUNE(1956); EDDY DUCHIN STORY, THE(1956); FEAR STRIKES OUT(1957); YOUNG STRANGER, THE(1957)

Hu Price
MONEY MOVERS(1978, Aus.)

Isabel Price
LITTLE SEX, A(1982)
1984
VAMPING(1984)

Janet Lees Price
STRANGE AFFAIR, THE(1968, Brit.)

Jeffrey Price
TRENCHCOAT(1983), w

John Price
MAN WHO THOUGHT LIFE, THE(1969, Den.); REMEMBRANCE(1982, Brit.)

Adm. John Dale Price, USN
MISTER ROBERTS(1955), tech adv

K. Hamilton Price
VICAR OF BRAY, THE(1937, Brit.)

Karen Price
SWAMP THING(1982)

Kate Price
SHOW GIRL(1928); COHENS AND KELLYS IN ATLANTIC CITY, THE(1929); GODLESS GIRL, THE(1929); COHENS AND KELLYS IN AFRICA, THE(1930); COHENS AND KELLYS IN SCOTLAND, THE(1930); DANCING SWEETIES(1930); ROGUE SONG, THE(1930); SHADOW RANCH(1930); LADIES OF THE JURY(1932); HAVE A HEART(1934); REMEMBER LAST NIGHT(1935); GREAT GUY(1936); EASY LIVING(1937); LIVE, LOVE AND LEARN(1937)
Silents
NIGHT OUT, A(1916); AMARILLY OF CLOTHESLINE ALLEY(1918); ARIZONA(1918); DINTY(1920); LITTLE LORD FAUNTLEROY(1921); COME ON OVER(1922); NEW TEACHER, THE(1922); PAID BACK(1922); ENEMIES OF CHILDREN(1923); HER FATAL MILLIONS(1923); NEAR LADY, THE(1923); DESERT FLOWER, THE(1925); ARIZONA SWEEPSTAKES(1926); COHENS AND KELLYS, THE(1926); IRENE(1926); LOVE'S BLINDNESS(1926); MEMORY LANE(1926); PARADISE(1926); THIRD DEGREE, THE(1926); QUALITY STREET(1927); SEA TIGER, THE(1927); COHENS AND THE KELLYS IN PARIS, THE(1928); THANKS FOR THE BUGGY RIDE(1928); LINDA(1929)
Misc. Silents
SEAL OF SILENCE, THE(1918); BRIGHT SKIES(1920); GUTTERSNIPE, THE(1922); GOOD-BY GIRLS!(1923); RIDERS UP(1924); PERFECT CLOWN, THE(1925); CASEY JONES(1927); FRISCO SALLY LEVY(1927); MOUNTAINS OF MANHATTAN(1927); ANYBODY HERE SEEN KELLY?(1928)

Katherine Price
PRINCESS O'ROURKE(1943)

Koland C. Price
PENITENTE MURDER CASE, THE(1936), w

Lauri Price
1984
HOT DOG...THE MOVIE(1984)

Lonny Price
1984
MUPPETS TAKE MANHATTAN, THE(1984)

Lorin E. Price
NIGHT OF THE ZOMBIES(1981), a, p

Lucile Price
ONE WAY TICKET TO HELL(1955)

Mark Price
Silents
SCALES OF JUSTICE, THE(1914)

Martin Price
1984
HADLEY'S REBELLION(1984), art d

Mary Wilson Price
BEYOND THE LAW(1968)

May Price
Silents
HANDY ANDY(1921, Brit.); LOVE AT THE WHEEL(1921, Brit.)

Nanci Price
GIRL IN THE SHOW, THE(1929); CAUGHT SHORT(1930); IN GAY MADRID(1930); PUBLIC ENEMY, THE(1931); HUMAN TARGETS(1932)

Nancy Price
AMERICAN PRISONER, THE(1929 Brit.); DOCTOR'S SECRET(1929); THREE LIVE GHOSTS(1929); LOVES OF ROBERT BURNS, THE(1930, Brit.); SUCH IS THE LAW(1930, Brit.); SPECKLED BAND, THE(1931, Brit.); DOWN OUR STREET(1932, Brit.); CRUCIFIX, THE(1934, Brit.); DEAD MAN'S SHOES(1939, Brit.); STARS LOOK DOWN, THE(1940, Brit.); SECRET MISSION(1944, Brit.); MADONNA OF THE SEVEN MOONS(1945, Brit.); CARNIVAL(1946, Brit.); YANK IN LONDON, A(1946, Brit.); I KNOW WHERE I'M GOING(1947, Brit.); MASTER OF BANKDAM, THE(1947, Brit.); THREE WEIRD SISTERS, THE(1948, Brit.); CRASH OF SILENCE(1952, Brit.); NAKED HEART, THE(1955, Brit.)
Silents
HUNTINGTOWER(1927, Brit.); HIS HOUSE IN ORDER(1928, Brit.)
Misc. Silents
LYONS MAIL, THE(1916, Brit.); BELPHEGOR THE MOUNTEBANK(1921, Brit.)

Paige Price
ALL THE RIGHT MOVES(1983)

Paul B. Price
RITZ, THE(1976)
1984
JOHNNY DANGEROUSLY(1984)

Paul Price
LOVE WITH THE PROPER STRANGER(1963); BUTCH AND SUNDANCE: THE EARLY DAYS(1979); SO FINE(1981)
Silents
ARE CHILDREN TO BLAME?(1922), d&w

Peggy Price
PACK, THE(1977)

Peter Edward Price
GREAT CARUSO, THE(1951)

Peter Price
DAYDREAK(1948, Brit.), ed; CHANCE OF A LIFETIME(1950, Brit.), ed; LOVE THAT BRUTE(1950); NEW MEXICO(1951); SUNNY SIDE OF THE STREET(1951); PHANTOM STALLION, THE(1954)

Ray Price
FORTY ACRE FEUD(1965); HONKYTONK MAN(1982)

Richard Price
BLOODBROTHERS(1978), w; WANDERERS, THE(1979), a, w

Roger Price
MAME(1974); MIXED COMPANY(1974); DAY OF THE LOCUST, THE(1975); PETE'S DRAGON(1977); CAT FROM OUTER SPACE, THE(1978)

Roland C. Price
PENITENTE MURDER CASE, THE(1936), p, ph

Roland Price
HELD FOR RANSOM(1938), ph; BRONZE BUCKAROO, THE(1939), ph; HARLEM RIDES THE RANGE(1939), ph; SON OF INGAGI(1940), ph; BRIDE AND THE BEAST, THE(1958), ph; SPRING AFFAIR(1960), ph
Silents
TORRENT, THE(1921), ph; DOWN BY THE RIO GRANDE(1924), ph; OTHER KIND OF LOVE, THE(1924), ph; SWORD OF VALOR, THE(1924), ph

Rosalinda Price
ROARIN' GUNS(1936)

Scott Price
MARATHON MAN(1976)

Sherman Price
GIRL FEVER(1961), p, d; "IMP"PROBABLE MR. WEE GEE, THE(1966), p,d&w; JUDY'S LITTLE NO-NO(1969), d&w

Sherwood Price
REVOLT OF MAMIE STOVER, THE(1956); CITY OF FEAR(1959); BLUEPRINT FOR ROBBERY(1961); ERRAND BOY, THE(1961); MAN FROM GALVESTON, THE(1964); PATSY, THE(1964); ICE STATION ZEBRA(1968)
Misc. Talkies
SCORCHING FURY(1952)

Stanley Price
THREE ON A MATCH(1932); HOLLYWOOD MYSTERY(1934); LITTLE MISS MARKER(1934); GOIN' TO TOWN(1935); SHE GETS HER MAN(1935); STRAIGHT FROM THE HEART(1935); RIFF-RAFF(1936); CHAMPAGNE WALTZ(1937); FIREFLY, THE(1937); LAST TRAIN FROM MADRID, THE(1937); TOUGH TO HANDLE(1937); HUNTED MEN(1938); TIP-OFF GIRLS(1938); RANGE WAR(1939); RIDE 'EM COW-GIRL(1939); SINGING COWGIRL, THE(1939); STAR MAKER, THE(1939); SUDDEN MONEY(1939); TOM SAWYER, DETECTIVE(1939); UNDERCOVER DOCTOR(1939); WATER RUSTLERS(1939); GOLDEN TRAIL, THE(1940); MOON OVER BURMA(1940); ONE MAN'S LAW(1940); SEVENTEEN(1940); TEXAS RANGERS RIDE AGAIN(1940); WAY OF ALL FLESH, THE(1940); DRIFTIN' KID, THE(1941); DYNAMITE CA-NYON(1941); EMERGENCY LANDING(1941); GREAT COMMANDMENT, THE(1941); MEET JOHN DOE(1941); RAIDERS OF THE DESERT(1941); SUNSET MURDER CASE(1941); WANDERERS OF THE WEST(1941); GLASS KEY, THE(1942); JOHNNY EAGER(1942); LONE STAR LAW MEN(1942); OUTLAWS OF PINE RIDGE(1942); ROAD TO MOROCCO(1942); BLACK MARKET RUSTLERS(1943); FALLEN SPAR-ROW, THE(1943); FIGHTING VALLEY(1943); FRONTIER BADMEN(1943); PASS-PORT TO SUEZ(1943); RIDING HIGH(1943); THEY GOT ME COVERED(1943); WILD HORSE RUSTLERS(1943); RAIDERS OF THE BORDER(1944); RAINBOW IS-LAND(1944); RANGE LAW(1944); STORY OF DR. WASSELL, THE(1944); TEXAS KID, THE(1944); CORNERED(1945); FRONTIER FEUD(1945); PHANTOM OF 42ND STREET, THE(1945); SUNSET IN EL DORADO(1945); ALIAS BILLY THE KID(1946); IN FAST COMPANY(1946); MAGNIFICENT DOLL(1946); ROMANCE OF THE WEST(1946); STAGECOACH TO DENVER(1946); EASY COME, EASY GO(1947); HIGH WALL, THE(1947); SCARED TO DEATH(1947); STATE OF THE UNION(1948); GRAND CANYON(1949); RIMFIRE(1949); TOUGH ASSIGNMENT(1949); CHEROKEE UPPRISING(1950); COLORADO RANGER(1950); CROOKED RIVER(1950); DALTON'S WOMEN, THE(1950); FAST ON THE DRAW(1950); GAMBLING HOUSE(1950); HOS-TILE COUNTRY(1950); KIM(1950); MARSHAL OF HELDORADO(1950); OUTLAWS OF TEXAS(1950); SUNDOWNERS, THE(1950); WEST OF THE BRAZOS(1950); ABI-LENE TRAIL(1951); NEVADA BADMEN(1951); OKLAHOMA JUSTICE(1951); ROAR-ING CITY(1951); STAGE TO BLUE RIVER(1951); TEXAS LAWMEN(1951); DEAD MAN'S TRAIL(1952); FARGO(1952); HELLGATE(1952); LAWLESS COWBOYS(1952); MAN FROM BLACK HILLS, THE(1952); NIGHT RAIDERS(1952); TEXAS CITY(1952); WACO(1952); HOMESTEADERS, THE(1953); MARKSMAN, THE(1953); REBEL CI-TY(1953); STAR OF TEXAS(1953); TEN COMMANDMENTS, THE(1956); ARA-BESQUE(1966), w; GOLD(1974, Brit.), w; DEVIL WITHIN HER, THE(1976, Brit.), w; SHOUT AT THE DEVIL(1976, Brit.), w; GOLDEN RENDEZVOUS(1977), w
Misc. Talkies
BLAZING BULLETS(1951)
Misc. Silents
YOUR BEST FRIEND(1922)

Tony Price
SEVENTH DAWN, THE(1964)

Vincent Price
TROUBLE WITH GIRLS(AND HOW TO GET INTO IT), THE*1/2 (1969); SERVICE DE LUXE(1938); PRIVATE LIVES OF ELIZABETH AND ESSEX, THE(1939); TOWER OF LONDON(1939); BRIGHAM YOUNG-FRONTIERSMAN(1940); GREEN HELL(1940); HOUSE OF THE SEVEN GABLES, THE(1940); HUDSON'S BAY(1940); INVISIBLE MAN RETURNS, THE(1940); SONG OF BERNADETTE, THE(1943); EVE OF ST. MARK, THE(1944); KEYS OF THE KINGDOM, THE(1944); LAURA(1944); WILSON(1944); ROYAL SCANDAL, A(1945); DRAGONWYCH(1946); LEAVE HER TO HEAVEN(1946); SHOCK(1946); LONG NIGHT, THE(1947); MOSS ROSE(1947); WEB, THE(1947); ABBOTT AND COSTELLO MEET FRANKENSTEIN(1948); ROGUES' REGIMENT(1948); THREE MUSKETEERS, THE(1948); UP IN CENTRAL PARK(1948); BAGDAD(1949); BRIBE, THE(1949); BARON OF ARIZONA, THE(1950); CHAMPAGNE FOR CAESAR(1950); CURTAIN CALL AT CACTUS CREEK(1950); ADVENTURES OF CAPTAIN FABIAN(1951); HIS KIND OF WOMAN(1951); LAS VEGAS STORY, THE(1952); HOUSE OF WAX(1953); CASANOVA'S BIG NIGHT(1954); DANGEROUS MISSION(1954); MAD MAGICIAN, THE(1954); SON OF SINBAD(1955); SERENADE(1956); TEN COMMANDMENTS, THE(1956); VAGABOND KING, THE(1956); WHILE THE CITY SLEEPS(1956); STORY OF MANKIND, THE(1957); FLY, THE(1958); HOUSE ON HAUNTED HILL(1958); BAT, THE(1959); BIG CIRCUS,

THE(1959); RETURN OF THE FLY(1959); TINGLER, THE(1959); HOUSE OF USHER(1960); MASTER OF THE WORLD(1961); PIT AND THE PENDULUM, THE(1961); CONFESSIONS OF AN OPIUM EATER(1962); CONVICTS FOUR(1962); TALES OF TERROR(1962); TOWER OF LONDON(1962); DIARY OF A MADMAN(1963); HAUNTED PALACE, THE(1963); RAGE OF THE BUCCANEERS(1963, Ital.); RAVEN, THE(1963); TWICE TOLD TALES(1963); COMEDY OF TERRORS, THE(1964); LAST MAN ON EARTH, THE(1964, U.S./Ital.); MASQUE OF THE RED DEATH, THE(1964, U.S./Brit.); QUEEN OF THE NILE(1964, Ital.); CITY UNDER THE SEA(1965, Brit.); DR. GOLDFOOT AND THE BIKINI MACHINE(1965); TOMB OF LIGEIA, THE(1965, Brit.); DR. GOLDFOOT AND THE GIRL BOMBS(1966, Ital.); HOUSE OF 1,000 DOLLS(1967, Ger./Span./Brit.); JACKALS, THE(1967, South Africa); CONQUEROR WORM, THE(1968, Brit.); MORE DEAD THAN ALIVE(1968); OBLONG BOX, THE(1969, Brit.); SPIRITS OF THE DEAD(1969, Fr./Ital.); CRY OF THE BANSHEE(1970, Brit.); SCREAM AND SCREAM AGAIN(1970, Brit.); ABOMINABLE DR. PHIBES, THE(1971, Brit.); DOCTOR PHIBES RISES AGAIN(1972, Brit.); THEATRE OF BLOOD(1973, Brit.); MADHOUSE(1974, Brit.); JOURNEY INTO FEAR(1976, Can); IT'S NOT THE SIZE THAT COUNTS(1979, Brit.); SCAVENGER HUNT(1979); MONSTER CLUB, THE(1981, Brit.); HOUSE OF LONG SHADOWS, THE(1983, Brit.)
1984
BLOODBATH AT THE HOUSE OF DEATH(1984, Brit.)

Walter Price
SUGAR HILL(1974)
Will Price
STRANGE BARGAIN(1949), d; TRIPOLI(1950), d; ROCK, ROCK, ROCK!(1956), d
William Price
EYES THAT KILL(1947, Brit.); SNOWBOUND(1949, Brit.)
Dick Prichard
PLATINUM BLONDE(1931)
Hesketh Prichard
Silents
DON Q, SON OF ZORRO(1925), w
Kate Prichard
Silents
DON Q, SON OF ZORRO(1925), w
Maudie Pricket
LOST IN ALASKA(1952)
Maude Prickett
GOLD MINE IN THE SKY(1938); LONE HAND TEXAN, THE(1947); ONE SUNDAY AFTERNOON(1948); WHIPLASH(1948); SLATTERY'S HURRICANE(1949); MESSENGER OF PEACE(1950); MONTANA(1950); MODEL AND THE MARRIAGE BROKER, THE(1951); STARS AND STRIPES FOREVER(1952); WAIT 'TIL THE SUN SHINES, NELLIE(1952); WOMAN'S WORLD(1954); GOOD MORNING, MISS DOVE(1955)
Maudie Prickett
TIME OUT OF MIND(1947); SONG OF IDAHO(1948); COWBOY AND THE INDIANS, THE(1949); HARVEY(1950); HER FIRST ROMANCE(1951); PECOS RIVER(1951); WEEKEND WITH FATHER(1951); NO ESCAPE(1953); SCANDAL AT SCOURIE(1953); DEEP IN MY HEART(1954); MAN CALLED PETER, THE(1955); MAN WITH THE GUN(1955); NAVY WIFE(1956); KISS THEM FOR ME(1957); PHANTOM STAGECOACH, THE(1957); THUNDERING JETS(1958); LEGEND OF TOM DOOLEY, THE(1959); NORTH BY NORTHWEST(1959); I'LL TAKE SWEDEN(1965); GNOMEMOBILE, THE(1967); MALTESE BIPPY, THE(1969); RASCAL(1969); SWEET CHARITY(1969)
Oliver B. Prickett [Blake]
CASABLANCA(1942); CASTLE IN THE DESERT(1942); GET HEP TO LOVE(1942); I MARRIED AN ANGEL(1942); SABOTEUR(1942); CORVETTE K-225(1943); GREENWICH VILLAGE(1944); UP IN ARMS(1944); CONFLICT(1945); INSIDE JOB(1946); SENATOR WAS INDISCREET, THE(1947)
Sorin Serene Pricopie
1984
UNFAITHFULLY YOURS(1984), stunts
V. Pridayevich
FAREWELL, DOVES(1962, USSR)
Jerry Priddy
WINNING TEAM, THE(1952)
Jimmy Priddy
SUN VALLEY SERENADE(1941)
Nancy Priddy
JAWS OF SATAN(1980)
Charley Pride
FROM NASHVILLE WITH MUSIC(1969)
Dion Pride
THE DOUBLE McGUFFIN(1979)
Franz Priegel
GERMANY IN AUTUMN(1978, Ger.)
Alfonso Rosas Priego
SANTO CONTRA LA INVASION DE LOS MARCIANOS(1966, Mex.), p
Alfredo Rosas Priego
VAMPIRE'S COFFIN, THE(1958, Mex.), ed; CREATURE OF THE WALKING DEAD(1960, Mex.), ed; WITCH'S MIRROR, THE(1960, Mex.), ed; CURSE OF THE DOLL PEOPLE, THE(1968, Mex.), ed; CURSE OF THE CRYING WOMAN, THE(1969, Mex.), ed; LIVING HEAD, THE(1969, Mex.), ed; POLITICAL ASYLUM(1975, Mex./Guatemalan), ed; RUN FOR THE ROSES(1978), ed
Gunther Prien
U-47 LT. COMMANDER PRIEN(1967, Ger.), w
Wolf Priess
MAN WHO KNEW TOO MUCH, THE(1956)
Wolfgang Priess
LONGEST DAY, THE(1962)
Bobbie Priest
MAN FROM OKLAHOMA, THE(1945); EASTER PARADE(1948)
Dan Priest
BLACK LIKE ME(1964); RATTLERS(1976)
Misc. Talkies
RATTLERS(1976)
Dolores Priest
BORN TO THE SADDLE(1953)

Emmett Priest
LIFE STUDY(1973)
Ernie Priest
WOMAN TO WOMAN(1946, Brit.); GREEN FINGERS(1947); NO ROOM AT THE INN(1950, Brit.)
High Priest
MR. MOTO TAKES A CHANCE(1938)
Kim Priest
ROAD WARRIOR, THE(1982, Aus.), spec eff
Lynda Priest
I AM A GROUPIE(1970, Brit.)
Martin Priest
NOTHING BUT A MAN(1964)
Natalie Priest
WRONG MAN, THE(1956); PATERNITY(1981)
Pat Priest
EASY COME, EASY GO(1967); INCREDIBLE TWO-HEADED TRANSPLANT, THE(1971); SOME CALL IT LOVING(1973)
Robert Priest
QUADROON(1972)
Robin Priest
SUBMARINE SEAHAWK(1959)
Stefanie Priest
RIVERRUN(1968)
J.B. Priestley
OLD DARK HOUSE, THE(1932), w; GOOD COMPANIONS(1933, Brit.), w; SING AS WE GO(1934, Brit.), w; DANGEROUS CORNER(1935), w; LOOK UP AND LAUGH(1935, Brit.), w; LABURNUM GROVE(1936, Brit.), w; JAMAICA INN(1939, Brit.), w; LET THE PEOPLE SING(1942, Brit.), w; BATTLE FOR MUSIC(1943, Brit.); SOMEWHERE IN FRANCE(1943, Brit.), w; WHEN WE ARE MARRIED(1943, Brit.), w; THEY CAME TO A CITY(1944, Brit.), a, w; LAST HOLIDAY(1950, Brit.), p, w; INSPECTOR CALLS, AN(1954, Brit.), w; GOOD COMPANIONS, THE(1957, Brit.), w; OLD DARK HOUSE, THE(1963, Brit.), w; SEVERED HEAD, A(1971, Brit.), w
Jack Priestley
NO WAY TO TREAT A LADY(1968), ph; SUBJECT WAS ROSES, THE(1968), ph; STILETTO(1969), ph; WHERE'S POPPA?(1970), ph; ACROSS 110TH STREET(1972), ph; MIDNIGHT MAN, THE(1974), ph; FIRST DEADLY SIN, THE(1980), ph
Robert Priestley
MAN'S FAVORITE SPORT [(?)$rb (1964), set d; ONCE UPON A TIME(1944), set d; SECRET COMMAND(1944), set d; MYSTERIOUS INTRUDER(1946), set d; THRILL OF BRAZIL, THE(1946), set d; WALLS CAME TUMBLING DOWN, THE(1946), set d; INTRIGUE(1947), set d; TENDER YEARS, THE(1947), set d; PITFALL(1948), set d; MRS. MIKE(1949), set d; WITHOUT HONOR(1949), set d; CRAZY OVER HORSES(1951), set d; SIROCCO(1951), set d; AFRICAN TREASURE(1952), set d; NO HOLDS BARRED(1952), set d; JALOPY(1953), set d; MAN IN THE DARK(1953), set d; PARIS PLAYBOYS(1954), set d; EDDY DUCHIN STORY, THE(1956), set d; CAT ON A HOT TIN ROOF(1958), set d; HIGH COST OF LOVING, THE(1958), set d; SOME CAME RUNNING(1959), set d; COMANCHEROS, THE(1961), set d; ADVENTURES OF A YOUNG MAN(1962), set d; WALK, DON'T RUN(1966), set d; IN THE HEAT OF THE NIGHT(1967), set d
Tom Priestley
UNEARTHLY STRANGER, THE(1964, Brit.), ed; MORGAN!(1966, Brit.), ed; PERSECUTION AND ASSASSINATION OF JEAN-PAUL MARAT AS PERFORMED BY THE INMATES OF THE ASYLUM OF CHARENTON UNDER THE DIRECTION OF THE MARQUIS DE SADE, THE(1967, Brit.), ed; ISADORA(1968, Brit.), ed; O LUCKY MAN!(1973, Brit.), ed; VOYAGE OF THE DAMNED(1976, Brit.), ed; EXORCIST II: THE HERETIC(1977), ed; JUBILEE(1978, Brit.), ed; LOVE AND BULLETS(1979, Brit.), ed; TIMES SQUARE(1980), ed
1984
ANOTHER TIME, ANOTHER PLACE(1984, Brit.), ed; 1984(1984, Brit.), ed
Tom Priestley, Jr.
1984
BEAT STREET(1984), ph
Bertha Priestly
DR. CHRISTIAN MEETS THE WOMEN(1940); EVER SINCE VENUS(1944)
Jack Priestly
MAN CALLED ADAM, A(1966), ph; BORN TO WIN(1971), ph
Joseph Priestly
STILL OF THE NIGHT(1982)
Mandy Priestly
ROOM AT THE TOP(1959, Brit.)
Robert Priestly
MAN'S FAVORITE SPORT(?)**1/2 (1964), set d; YOU CAN'T RUN AWAY FROM IT(1956), set d; GILDA(1946), set d; ON OUR MERRY WAY(1948), set d; RANCHO NOTORIOUS(1952), set d; RIOT IN CELL BLOCK 11(1954), set d; PICNIC(1955), set d; SAYONARA(1957), set d; TUNNEL OF LOVE, THE(1958), set d; GATHERING OF EAGLES, A(1963), set d; WAY WEST, THE(1967), set d; P.J.(1968), set d
Tom Priestly
FATHER CAME TOO(1964, Brit.), ed; OUR MOTHER'S HOUSE(1967, Brit.), ed; LEO THE LAST(1970, Brit.), ed; DELIVERANCE(1972), ed; ALPHA BETA(1973, Brit.), ed; RETURN OF THE PINK PANTHER, THE(1975, Brit.), ed; TESS(1980, Fr./Brit.), ed; ANOTHER TIME, ANOTHER PLACE(1983, Brit.), ed
Jose Priete [Joseph Prieto]
FIREBALL JUNGLE(1968), d
Antonio Prieto
FISTFUL OF DOLLARS, A(1964, Ital./Ger./Span.)
Jenaro Prieto
MYSTERIOUS MR. DAVIS, THE(1936, Brit.), w; ASSOCIATE, THE(1982 Fr./Ger.), w
Jose Prieto
OUR MAN IN HAVANA(1960, Brit.)
Joseph G. Prieto
RUN FOR THE ROSES(1978), w
Misc. Talkies
MISS LESLIE'S DOLLS(1972), d
Joseph Prieto
SHANTY TRAMP(1967), d; SAVAGES FROM HELL(1968), d&w
Raul Prieto
REVENGERS, THE(1972, U.S./Mex.)

Stuart Prieto
EYE FOR AN EYE, AN(1981)
Georges Prieur
SECOND BUREAU(1936, Fr.); RASPUTIN(1939, Fr.)
Andre Priez
LOVE IN THE AFTERNOON(1957)
Norman Priggen
PROFESSIONALS, THE(1960, Brit.), p; PAYROLL(1962, Brit.), p; KING AND COUN-
TRY(1964, Brit.), p; SERVANT, THE(1964, Brit.), p; ACCIDENT(1967, Brit.), p;
BOOM!(1968), p; SECRET CEREMONY(1968, Brit.), p; GO-BETWEEN, THE(1971,
Brit.), p; BLACK GUNN(1972), p; TALES THAT WITNESS MADNESS(1973, Brit.), p
V. Prikhodko
OPTIMISTIC TRAGEDY, THE(1964, USSR); WAR AND PEACE(1968, USSR)
Herbert Prikopa
FOREVER MY LOVE(1962); MIRACLE OF THE WHITE STALLIONS(1963)
Frances Prim
Silents
PRAIRIE WIFE, THE(1925)
Monique Prim
DIVA(1982, Fr.), ed; MOON IN THE GUTTER, THE(1983, Fr./Ital.), ed
Suzy Prim
LOWER DEPTHS, THE(1937, Fr.); MAYERLING(1937, Fr.); CROSSROADS(1938, Fr.);
BETRAYAL(1939, Fr.); HEART OF A NATION, THE(1943, Fr.)
Louis Prima
RHYTHM ON THE RANGE(1936); YOU CAN'T HAVE EVERYTHING(1937); ROSE
OF WASHINGTON SQUARE(1939); SENIOR PROM(1958); HEY BOY! HEY
GIRL!(1959); TWIST ALL NIGHT(1961); JUNGLE BOOK, THE(1967)
Prima Symphony
TRANS-EUROP-EXPRESS(1968, Fr.)
Tom Priman
SOME LIKE IT COOL(1979, Ger./Aust./Ital./Fr.), w
Nanda Primavera
GUILT IS NOT MINE(1968, Ital.)
Roberta Primavera
NAKED MAJA, THE(1959, Ital./U.S.)
Robert Primes
1984
DUBEAT-E-O(1984), ph
Frances Primm
Silents
MERRY WIDOW, THE(1925)
Aileen Primple
WAVE, A WAC AND A MARINE, A(1944)
Alec Primrose
TEENAGE GANG DEBS(1966)
Dorothy Primrose
COME BACK PETER(1952, Brit.)
Anna Primula
WHITE SHEIK, THE(1956, Ital.)
Barry Primus
BROTHERHOOD, THE(1968); PUZZLE OF A DOWNFALL CHILD(1970); VON
RICHTHOFEN AND BROWN(1970); BOXCAR BERTHA(1972); GRAVY TRAIN,
THE(1974); BEEN DOWN SO LONG IT LOOKS LIKE UP TO ME(1977); NEW YORK,
NEW YORK(1977); AVALANCHE(1978); ROSE, THE(1979); HEARTLAND(1980);
NIGHT GAMES(1980); ABSENCE OF MALICE(1981)
1984
RIVER, THE(1984)
Misc. Talkies
AUTOPSY(1980, Ital.)
Ruda Princ
LEMONADE JOE(1966, Czech.); SWEET LIGHT IN A DARK ROOM(1966, Czech.)
Prince
COUNTRY BEYOND, THE(1936); COUNTRY GENTLEMEN(1937); LITTLE ARK,
THE(1972)
1984
PURPLE RAIN(1984)
Andrew Prince
CRYPT OF THE LIVING DEAD zero(1973)
Arthur Prince
REGAL CAVALCADE(1935, Brit.)
Barry Harte Prince
DREAMER, THE(1970, Israel), ed
Charles H. Prince
Misc. Silents
MAN AND HIS SOUL(1916)
Charles Prince
Silents
ROYAL FAMILY, A(1915); STORK'S NEST, THE(1915)
Misc. Silents
QUITTER, THE(1916); TURMOIL, THE(1916)
Dale Prince
STRIPES(1981)
David Prince
MISS JESSICA IS PREGNANT(1970), ph
Doris Prince
Silents
AHEAD OF THE LAW(1926)
Edna Prince
HARMONY HEAVEN(1930, Brit.)
Ellen Prince
PINOCCHIO(1969, E. Ger.), a, w
Misc. Talkies
PINOCCHIO'S STORYBOOK ADVENTURES(1979)
Elsie Prince
LUCKY SWEEP, A(1932, Brit.)
Forrest Prince
YOU'LL NEVER GET RICH(1941)

Frank Prince
SHOOT THE WORKS(1934); STOLEN HARMONY(1935)
George Prince
NIGHT TRAIN TO MUNDO FINE(1966)
Ginger Prince
LAWTON STORY, THE(1949); ONE TOO MANY(1950)
Harold Prince
SOMETHING FOR EVERYONE(1970), d; LITTLE NIGHT MUSIC, A(1977, Aust./
U.S./Ger.), d
Hughie Prince
BUCK PRIVATES(1941)
John Prince
1984
RENO AND THE DOC(1984, Can.)
Silents
LITTLE EVA ASCENDS(1922); EAST SIDE–WEST SIDE(1923); JACK
O'HEARTS(1926)
Misc. Silents
HEARTLESS HUSBANDS(1925)
John T. Prince
Silents
DOCTOR JACK(1922); LAWFUL CHEATERS(1925); DAME CHANCE(1926); PROWL-
ERS OF THE NIGHT(1926); KING OF KINGS, THE(1927); RAMONA(1928)
Misc. Silents
BATTLING ORIOLES, THE(1924)
Jonathan Prince
HALLOWEEN II(1981); PRIVATE SCHOOL(1983)
Lawrence Chevis Prince
SMALL CIRCLE OF FRIENDS, A(1980)
Maurice Prince
WIFE WANTED(1946); IT HAD TO BE YOU(1947)
Michael Prince
ANDERSON TAPES, THE(1971); THREE DAYS OF THE CONDOR(1975); GREEK
TYCOON, THE(1978); HOMETOWN U.S.A.(1979); HERO AT LARGE(1980); FORCE:
FIVE(1981); ROLLOVER(1981); DEATH WISH II(1982); SECOND THOUGHTS(1983);
TWO OF A KIND(1983)
Nicola Prince
1984
KIPPERBANG(1984, Brit.)
Norman Prince
MY AIN FOLK(1944, Brit.)
Patrick Prince
SCARED TO DEATH(1981), ph
1984
KILLERS, THE(1984), ph
Paul Prince
1984
SIGNAL 7(1984)
Philippe Prince
MURDER AT 45 R.P.M.(1965, Fr.); MY BABY IS BLACK!(1965, Fr.)
Richard Prince
TRAP DOOR, THE(1980); VORTEX(1982)
Robert Prince
STRANGERS IN THE CITY(1962), m; YOU'RE A BIG BOY NOW(1966), m; GREAT
BIG THING, A(1968, U.S./Can.), m; NEWMAN'S LAW(1974), m; J.D.'S REVEN-
GE(1976), m; SQUIRM(1976), m
Ron Prince
HOT POTATO(1976); TUNNELVISION(1976); CRACKING UP(1977)
Ronald Prince
NEW YORK, NEW YORK(1977)
Steven Prince
TAXI DRIVER(1976); NEW YORK, NEW YORK(1977)
Ursula Prince
KENNER(1969)
William Prince
DESTINATION TOKYO(1944); HOLLYWOOD CANTEEN(1944); VERY THOUGHT
OF YOU, THE(1944); OBJECTIVE, BURMA!(1945); PILLOW TO POST(1945); CIN-
DERELLA JONES(1946); SHADOW OF A WOMAN(1946); CARNEGIE HALL(1947);
DEAD RECKONING(1947); LUST FOR GOLD(1949); CYRANO DE BERGERAC(1950);
SECRET OF TREASURE MOUNTAIN(1956); VAGABOND KING, THE(1956);
MACABRE(1958); SACCO AND VANZETTI(1971, Ital./Fr.); HEARTBREAK KID,
THE(1972); BLADE(1973); STEPFORD WIVES, THE(1975); FAMILY PLOT(1976);
NETWORK(1976); FIRE SALE(1977); GAUNTLET, THE(1977); ROLLERCOAST-
ER(1977); CAT FROM OUTER SPACE, THE(1978); PROMISE, THE(1979); BRONCO
BILLY(1980); KISS ME GOODBYE(1982); LOVE AND MONEY(1982); SOLDIER,
THE(1982)
Prince a Dog
PRIVATE NUMBER(1936)
Prince Lei Lani
WAIKIKI WEDDING(1937)
Prince of Wales
Silents
POWER OF RIGHT, THE(1919, Brit.)
Prince the Dog
WOLF DOG(1958, Can.)
Silents
CAROLYN OF THE CORNERS(1919)
Prince the Great Dane
NEVER GIVE A SUCKER AN EVEN BREAK(1941)
Prince the Horse
WESTERN MAIL(1942)
"Prince"
LITTLE LORD FAUNTLEROY(1936)
Gertrude Princell
LOVE BEFORE BREAKFAST(1936), w
Pamela Princess
Misc. Talkies
COUNTRY CUZZINS(1972)

Princess Baba [Valerie Brooke/Valerie Gregory]
YOU CAN'T CHEAT AN HONEST MAN(1939)
Princess Bluebird
KING OF THE STALLIONS(1942)
Princess Fatosh
BANANAS(1971)
Princess Luana
TRADE WINDS(1938); HAWAIIAN NIGHTS(1939); KEEP 'EM FLYING(1941)
The Princess of Monaco
Silents
GREAT LOVE, THE(1918)
Princess Pearl
HONEYMOON MERRY-GO-ROUND(1939, Brit.)
Princess Yasmin Khan
HAPPY THIEVES, THE(1962)
Liliane Princet
MOUCHETTE(1970, Fr.)
Carl Princi
CHICAGO CONFIDENTIAL(1957); FLIGHT THAT DISAPPEARED, THE(1961); TENDER IS THE NIGHT(1961); STATE FAIR(1962); HOW TO SUCCEED IN BUSINESS WITHOUT REALLY TRYING(1976)
Marc Princi
SQUEEZE, THE(1980, Ital.), w; GREAT WHITE, THE(1982, Ital.), w
Victoria Principal
LIFE AND TIMES OF JUDGE ROY BEAN, THE(1972); NAKED APE, THE(1973); EARTHQUAKE(1974); I WILL ...I WILL ...FOR NOW(1976); VIGILANTE FORCE(1976)
Albino Principe
RED CLOAK, THE(1961, Ital./Fr.), w
Mimi Princz
BLUE IDOL, THE(1931, Hung.)
Don Prindle
UGLY ONES, THE(1968, Ital./Span.), w
James Prindle
ORCHESTRA WIVES(1942), w
Charles Prindley
Silents
NEW DISCIPLE, THE(1921)
Andrew Prine
MIRACLE WORKER, THE(1962); ADVANCE TO THE REAR(1964); TEXAS ACROSS THE RIVER(1966); BANDOLERO!(1968); DEVIL'S BRIGADE, THE(1968); GENERATION(1969); THIS SAVAGE LAND(1969); CHISUM(1970); SIMON, KING OF THE WITCHES(1971); SQUARES(1972); ONE LITTLE INDIAN(1973); BARN OF THE NAKED DEAD(1976); GRIZZLY(1976); TOWN THAT DREADED SUNDOWN, THE(1977); EVIL, THE(1978); AMITYVILLE II: THE POSSESSION(1982)
1984
THEY'RE PLAYING WITH FIRE(1984)
Misc. Talkies
HANNAH–QUEEN OF THE VAMPIRES(1972); CENTERFOLD GIRLS, THE(1974); RIDING WITH DEATH(1976); WINDS OF AUTUMN, THE(1976)
James Prine
LITTLEST HORSE THIEVES, THE(1977), animal t
Yannis Prineas
ANNA OF RHODES(1950, Gr.)
Gerald Pring
WELL DONE, HENRY(1936, Brit.); HUMAN MONSTER, THE(1940, Brit.); ECHO MURDERS, THE(1945, Brit.); LOYAL HEART(1946, Brit.); MY BROTHER'S KEEPER(1949, Brit.)
Silents
BRONZE BELL, THE(1921); DESERT BLOSSOMS(1921); NUT, THE(1921); ALWAYS THE WOMAN(1922); JUNE MADNESS(1922); BOLIBAR(1928, Brit.)
Misc. Silents
FIGHTING STREAK, THE(1922); BETRAYAL, THE(1929)
Aileen Pringle
NIGHT PARADE(1929, Brit.); WALL STREET(1929); PRINCE OF DIAMONDS(1930); PUTTIN' ON THE RITZ(1930); SOLDIERS AND WOMEN(1930); CONVICTED(1931); MURDER AT MIDNIGHT(1931); SUBWAY EXPRESS(1931); AGE OF CONSENT(1932); FAME STREET(1932); PHANTOM OF CRESTWOOD, THE(1932); BY APPOINTMENT ONLY(1933); LOVE PAST THIRTY(1934); ONCE TO EVERY BACHELOR(1934); JANE EYRE(1935); SONS OF STEEL(1935); PICCADILLY JIM(1936); UNGUARDED HOUR, THE(1936); WIFE VERSUS SECRETARY(1936); JOHN MEADE'S WOMAN(1937); LAST OF MRS. CHEYNEY, THE(1937); SHE'S NO LADY(1937); THANKS FOR LISTENING(1937); MAN-PROOF(1938); TOO HOT TO HANDLE(1938); CALLING DR. KILDARE(1939); HARDYS RIDE HIGH, THE(1939); NIGHT OF NIGHTS, THE(1939); SHOULD A GIRL MARRY?(1939); THEY DIED WITH THEIR BOOTS ON(1942); DR. GILLESPIE'S CRIMINAL CASE(1943); YOUNGEST PROFESSION, THE(1943); LAURA(1944); SINCE YOU WENT AWAY(1944)
Silents
OATH-BOUND(1922); STRANGER'S BANQUET(1922); DON'T MARRY FOR MONEY(1923); MY AMERICAN WIFE(1923); SOULS FOR SALE(1923); TIGER'S CLAW, THE(1923); HIS HOUR(1924); MARRIED FLIRTS(1924); KISS IN THE DARK, A(1925); ONE YEAR TO LIVE(1925); SOUL MATES(1925); TIN GODS(1926); WILDERNESS WOMAN, THE(1926); ADAM AND EVIL(1927); TEA FOR THREE(1927); SHOW PEOPLE(1928); SINGLE MAN, A(1929)
Misc. Silents
THREE WEEKS(1924); TRUE AS STEEL(1924); WIFE OF THE CENTAUR(1924); MYSTIC, THE(1925); THIEF IN PARADISE, A(1925); WILDFIRE(1925); GREAT DECEPTION, THE(1926); BODY AND SOUL(1927); BABY CYCLONE, THE(1928); BEAU BROADWAY(1928); DREAM OF LOVE(1928); WICKEDNESS PREFERRED(1928)
Angela Pringle
COUNTESS FROM HONG KONG, A(1967, Brit.); ON A CLEAR DAY YOU CAN SEE FOREVER(1970)
Brian Pringle
BRAIN, THE(1965, Ger./Brit.)
Bryan Pringle
IT TAKES A THIEF(1960, Brit.); SATURDAY NIGHT AND SUNDAY MORNING(1961, Brit.); DAMN THE DEFIANT(1962, Brit.); FRENCH DRESSING(1964, Brit.); EARLY BIRD, THE(1965, Brit.); HOW I WON THE WAR(1967, Brit.); DIAMONDS FOR BREAKFAST(1968, Brit.); CROMWELL(1970, Brit.); SPRING AND PORT WINE(1970, Brit.); BOY FRIEND, THE(1971, Brit.); MR. QUILP(1975, Brit.); JABBER-

WOCKY(1977, Brit.)
Conrad Pringle
LE MANS(1971)
Douglas Pringle
FAR SHORE, THE(1976, Can.), m
Eileen Pringle
HAPPY LAND(1943)
Sgt. George A. Pringle, NWMP
NORTHWEST MOUNTED POLICE(1940), tech adv
H. L. Pringle
Silents
LURE OF LONDON, THE(1914, Brit.)
Ian Pringle
Misc. Talkies
PLAINS OF HEAVEN, THE(1982), d
Jessie Pringle
DEVIL'S HOLIDAY, THE(1930); FUGITIVE LADY(1934); HANDY ANDY(1934); PADDY O'DAY(1935)
Joan Pringle
J.D.'S REVENGE(1976)
Norman Pringle
FIGHTER SQUADRON(1948), makeup; PRIVATE EYES(1953), makeup; PALM SPRINGS WEEKEND(1963), makeup; CHEYENNE AUTUMN(1964), makeup
Samuel Pringle
LIMPING MAN, THE(1931, Brit.)
Val Pringle
SHOOT IT: BLACK, SHOOT IT: BLUE(1974); LAST REMAKE OF BEAU GESTE, THE(1977); RAGTIME(1981)
Aileen Prinple
WOMEN, THE(1939)
Co Prins
VICTORY(1981)
Kees Prins
LIFT, THE(1983, Neth.); STILL SMOKIN'(1983)
Sandra Prinsloo
1984
GODS MUST BE CRAZY, THE(1984, Botswana)
Yvonne Printemps
VOYAGE TO AMERICA(1952, Fr.)
Yuri Printsev
THEY CALL ME ROBERT(1967, USSR), w
Florence Printy
Misc. Silents
SINGLE CODE, THE(1917)
John Printz
WHITE ZOMBIE(1932)
Olga Printzlau
HEARTS OF HUMANITY(1932), w; BROKEN DREAMS(1933), w; MARRIAGE ON APPROVAL(1934), w
Silents
JOHN NEEDHAM'S DOUBLE(1916), w; NAKED HEARTS(1916), w; ONE MORE AMERICAN(1918), w; JACK STRAW(1920), w; MIDSUMMER MADNESS(1920), w; WHAT EVERY WOMAN KNOWS(1921), w; BEAUTIFUL AND DAMNED, THE(1922), w; BURNING SANDS(1922), w; CRADLE, THE(1922), w; LITTLE CHURCH AROUND THE CORNER(1923), w; MOTHERS-IN-LAW(1923), w; BEAUTIFUL CHEAT, THE(1926), w; CAMILLE(1927), w; TRAGEDY OF YOUTH, THE(1928), w
Eddie Prinz
GONE WITH THE WIND(1939), ch; SHUT MY BIG MOUTH(1942), ch; TOP O' THE MORNING(1949), ch; LULLABY OF BROADWAY, THE(1951), ch
Edward Prinz
MADAME SATAN(1930); DANCING LADY(1933), ch; HELLZAPOPPIN'(1941), ch; MOONLIGHT IN HAVANA(1942), ch
Hansi Prinz
$100 A NIGHT(1968, Ger.)
Larry Prinz
HELEN MORGAN STORY, THE(1959), m
Le Roy Prinz
MY WILD IRISH ROSE(1947), ch; TWO GUYS FROM TEXAS(1948), ch
LeRoy J. Prinz
STOLEN HARMONY(1935), ch
LeRoy Prinz
INNOCENTS OF PARIS(1929), ch; MADAME SATAN(1930), ch; COLLEGE RHYTHM(1934), ch; SEARCH FOR BEAUTY(1934), ch; ALL THE KING'S HORSES(1935), ch; BIG BROADCAST OF 1936, THE(1935), ch; CORONADO(1935), ch; LIVES OF A BENGAL LANCER(1935), ch; RUMBA(1935), ch; COLLEGE HOLIDAY(1936), ch; SHOW BOAT(1936), a, ch; ARTISTS AND MODELS(1937), ch; BIG BROADCAST OF 1938, THE(1937), ch; CHAMPAGNE WALTZ(1937), ch; DOUBLE OR NOTHING(1937), ch; HIGH, WIDE AND HANDSOME(1937), ch; THIS WAY PLEASE(1937), ch; THRILL OF A LIFETIME(1937), ch; TURN OFF THE MOON(1937), ch; WAIKIKI WEDDING(1937), spec eff; COLLEGE SWING(1938), ch; EVERY DAY'S A HOLIDAY(1938), md; GIVE ME A SAILOR(1938), ch; TROPIC HOLIDAY(1938), ch; GREAT VICTOR HERBERT, THE(1939), ch; MAN ABOUT TOWN(1939), ch; ST. LOUIS BLUES(1939), ch; ZAZA(1939), ch; BUCK BENNY RIDES AGAIN(1940), ch; ROAD TO SINGAPORE(1940), ch; TOO MANY GIRLS(1940), ch; ROAD TO ZANZIBAR(1941), ch; TIME OUT FOR RHYTHM(1941), ch; HARD WAY, THE(1942), ch; YANKEE DOODLE DANDY(1942), ch; DESERT SONG, THE(1943), ch; MISSION TO MOSCOW(1943), ch; THANK YOUR LUCKY STARS(1943), ch; THIS IS THE ARMY(1943), ch; HOLLYWOOD CANTEEN(1944), ch; SHINE ON, HARVEST MOON(1944), ch; RHAPSODY IN BLUE(1945), ch; SAN ANTONIO(1945), ch; NIGHT AND DAY(1946), ch; TIME, THE PLACE AND THE GIRL, THE(1946), ch; ESCAPE ME NEVER(1947), ch; ALWAYS LEAVE THEM LAUGHING(1949), ch; IT'S A GREAT FEELING(1949), ch; LOOK FOR THE SILVER LINING(1949), ch; MY DREAM IS YOURS(1949), ch; DAUGHTER OF ROSIE O'GRADY, THE(1950), ch; TEA FOR TWO(1950), ch; WEST POINT STORY, THE(1950), ch; I'LL SEE YOU IN MY DREAMS(1951), ch; ON MOONLIGHT BAY(1951), ch; PAINTING THE CLOUDS WITH SUNSHINE(1951), ch; STARLIFT(1951), ch; SHE'S WORKING HER WAY THROUGH COLLEGE(1952), ch; STOP, YOU'RE KILLING ME(1952), ch; APRIL IN PARIS(1953), ch; DESERT SONG, THE(1953), ch; EDDIE CANTOR STORY, THE(1953), ch; JAZZ SINGER, THE(1953), ch; SHE'S BACK ON BROADWAY(1953), ch; SO THIS IS LOVE(1953), ch; THREE SAILORS AND A

GIRL(1953), ch; TEN COMMANDMENTS, THE(1956), ch; SAYONARA(1957), ch; SOUTH PACIFIC(1958), ch; HELEN MORGAN STORY, THE(1959), ch

Angelo Prioli
MIRACLE IN MILAN(1951, Ital.)

Allan Prior
BRIDE OF THE REGIMENT(1930); KING SOLOMON'S TREASURE(1978, Can.), w

Candida Prior
Misc. Talkies
FERN, THE RED DEER(1977, Brit.)

Diane Prior
DOBERMAN GANG, THE(1972)

F. Prior
MARIGOLD(1938, Brit.), w

Herbert Prior
STAND UP AND CHEER(1934 80m FOX bw); THIS SIDE OF HEAVEN(1934); VIVA VILLA!(1934)
Silents
EUGENE ARAM(1915); GREAT EXPECTATIONS(1917); POOR LITTLE RICH GIRL, A(1917); LITTLE 'FRAID LADY, THE(1920); POLLYANNA(1920); MADE IN HEAVEN(1921); NOT GUILTY(1921); GARRISON'S FINISH(1923); SLAVE OF DESIRE(1923); DOUBLING WITH DANGER(1926); DUKE STEPS OUT, THE(1929)
Misc. Silents
TEST, THE(1915); MESSAGE TO GARCIA, A(1916); GHOST OF OLD MORRO, THE(1917); LAST SENTENCE, THE(1917); ROYAL PAUPER, THE(1917); AFTER THE WAR(1918); MENACE, THE(1918); MODEL'S CONFESSION, THE(1918); SOCIETY FOR SALE(1918); CREAKING STAIRS(1919); LOVE HUNGER, THE(1919); THAT'S GOOD(1919); ROSE OF NOME(1920); SNOWSHOE TRAIL, THE(1922); LITTLE JOHNNY JONES(1923); TEARING THROUGH(1925); WILD BULL'S LAIR, THE(1925); LAST OUTLAW, THE(1927); ALL AT SEA(1929)

J. Redmond Prior
CHAIN LIGHTNING(1950), w

James Prior
REUNION(1932, Brit.)
Silents
LADY NOGGS-PEERESS(1929, Brit.)

Peggy Prior
GERALDINE(1929), w; SQUARE SHOULDERS(1929), w

Christopher Priore
THERE'S ALWAYS VANILLA(1972)

Hal Priore
HUNGRY WIVES(1973)

Albert Prisco
Silents
JOLT, THE(1921); LOVE LIGHT, THE(1921); LEGALLY DEAD(1923); SONG OF LOVE, THE(1923); WHITE BLACK SHEEP, THE(1926); DON MIKE(1927); SOFT CUSHIONS(1927)
Misc. Silents
GOSSIP(1923); PRAIRIE KING, THE(1927)

Marty Prisco
WORLD'S GREATEST SINNER, THE(1962)

Albert Priscoe
Silents
NUT-CRACKER, THE(1926); KING OF KINGS, THE(1927)
Misc. Silents
THAT DEVIL QUEMADO(1925)

Lynda Prish
SATIN MUSHROOM, THE(1969)

Robert Pritch
ROCKABILLY BABY(1957), ed

Ann Pritchard
JOURNEY(1977, Can.), set d

Anne Pritchard
APPRENTICESHIP OF DUDDY KRAVITZ, THE(1974, Can.), prod d; FAR SHORE, THE(1976, Can.), prod d; MAN, A WOMAN, AND A BANK, A(1979, Can.), prod d; WHO HAS SEEN THE WIND(1980, Can.), art d; ATLANTIC CITY(1981, U.S./Can.), prod d; DISAPPEARANCE, THE(1981, Brit./Can.), prod d; OF UNKNOWN ORIGIN(1983, Can.), prod d; THRESHOLD(1983, Can.), prod d

David Pritchard
DEVIL'S BRIGADE, THE(1968)

Dick Pritchard
RACETRACK(1933)

Hilary Pritchard
VANDERGILT DIAMOND MYSTERY, THE(1936); YOU MUST GET MARRIED(1936, Brit.); ELDER BROTHER, THE(1937, Brit.); MILL ON THE FLOSS(1939, Brit.); TORSO MURDER MYSTERY, THE(1940, Brit.); MY BROTHER JONATHAN(1949, Brit.); WINSLOW BOY, THE(1950); WHAT'S GOOD FOR THE GOOSE(1969, Brit.); OPTIMISTS, THE(1973, Brit.)

Hillary Pritchard
Misc. Talkies
SHE'LL FOLLOW YOU ANYWHERE(1971)

Josephine Pritchard
CHANGE PARTNERS(1965, Brit.)

June Pritchard
JOURNEY AMONG WOMEN(1977, Aus.)

Michael Pritchard
1984
MASSIVE RETALIATION(1984)

Miranda Pritchard
1984
CONSTANCE(1984, New Zealand)

Owen Pritchard
EDDIE CANTOR STORY, THE(1953)

Sally Pritchard
DOUBLES(1978)

Terry Pritchard
ALL THE RIGHT NOISES(1973, Brit.), art d; FRENCH LIEUTENANT'S WOMAN, THE(1981), art d; WAGNER(1983, Brit./Hung./Aust.), art d
1984
OXFORD BLUES(1984), prod d; RIDDLE OF THE SANDS, THE(1984, Brit.), art d

Anne Pritcherd
ACT OF THE HEART(1970, Can.), art

Jim Pritchett
LISETTE(1961)

Paula Pritchett
CHAPPAQUA(1967); ADRIFT(1971, Czech.); WRATH OF GOD, THE(1972)

Carol Pritikin
1984
NIGHTMARE ON ELM STREET, A(1984)

Karen Pritikin
1984
WHAT YOU TAKE FOR GRANTED(1984), m

Steve Pritko
HALF ANGEL(1951); WE'RE NOT MARRIED(1952)

Norbert Pritz
NOT RECONCILED, OR "ONLY VIOLENCE HELPS WHERE IT RULES"(1969, Ger.)

Lucien Priual
PARTY GIRL(1930)

Bert Prival
EMPEROR WALTZ, THE(1948)

Lucian Prival
EVERY DAY'S A HOLIDAY(1938); WHITE GODDESS(1953)

Lucien Prival
HELL'S ANGELS(1930); IN THE NEXT ROOM(1930); LAST OF THE LONE WOLF(1930); LOTUS LADY(1930); PRINCESS AND THE PLUMBER, THE(1930); YOUNG SINNERS(1931); HOLLYWOOD SPEAKS(1932); SECRETS OF THE FRENCH POLICE(1932); SHERLOCK HOLMES(1932); WESTERN LIMITED(1932); WORLD AND THE FLESH, THE(1932); GRAND SLAM(1933); SPHINX, THE(1933); CRIME OF HELEN STANLEY(1934); MERRY WIDOW, THE(1934); BORN TO GAMBLE(1935); CHAMPAGNE FOR BREAKFAST(1935); DARKEST AFRICA(1936); HIGH FLYERS(1937); HISTORY IS MADE AT NIGHT(1937); TRAPPED BY G-MEN(1937); MR. WONG, DETECTIVE(1938); BEASTS OF BERLIN(1939); CONFESSIONS OF A NAZI SPY(1939); ESPIONAGE AGENT(1939); NURSE EDITH CAVELL(1939); MORTAL STORM, THE(1940); SKY MURDER(1940); MAN HUNT(1941); SOUTH OF PANAMA(1941); PANAMA HATTIE(1942); SUBMARINE BASE(1943); STORM OVER LISBON(1944); FALCON'S ALIBI, THE(1946); ON OUR MERRY WAY(1948); HIGH NOON(1952)
Silents
PUPPETS(1926); AMERICAN BEAUTY(1927); ADORATION(1928); RACKET, THE(1928); PEACOCK FAN(1929)
Misc. Silents
MAN OF QUALITY, A(1926); HIGH HAT(1927)

Vladimir Privaltsev
FATHER OF A SOLDIER(1966, USSR)

Daliah Priver
TRUNK TO CAIRO(1966, Israel/Ger.), makeup

Eytan Priver
THEY WERE TEN(1961, Israel); TRUNK TO CAIRO(1966, Israel/Ger.)

Eugeniusz Priwiezencew
CONTRACT, THE(1982, Pol.)

Eugeniusz Priwieziencew
SOPHIE'S CHOICE(1982)

Hans Priwin
MAIL TRAIN(1941, Brit.), w

Hans Wolfgang Priwin
INSPECTOR HORNLEIGH ON HOLIDAY(1939, Brit.), w

Eugenivze Priwizencew
1984
AMERICAN DREAMER(1984)

John Prizer
UNHOLY ROLLERS(1972), p; SWITCHBLADE SISTERS(1975), p

Diane Prizio
HORROR OF PARTY BEACH, THE(1964)

Henry Proach
INCIDENT, THE(1967); DIRTY LITTLE BILLY(1972)

Galina Probandt-Frank
QUESTION 7(1961, U.S./Ger.)

George Probert
MR. MAGOO'S HOLIDAY FESTIVAL(1970), ed
Silents
KING'S GAME, THE(1916)
Misc. Silents
NEDRA(1915); SPENDER OR THE FORTUNES OF PETER, THE(1915); MADAME PEACOCK(1920)

Graham Probst
ULYSSES(1967, U.S./Brit.), art d

Brian Probyn
LONG DAY'S DYING, THE(1968, Brit.), ph; POOR COW(1968, Brit.), ph; DOWNHILL RACER(1969), ph; REVOLUTIONARY, THE(1970, Brit.), ph; JERUSALEM FILE, THE(1972, U.S./Israel), ph; INNOCENT BYSTANDERS(1973, Brit.), ph; MAN AT THE TOP(1973, Brit.), ph; BADLANDS(1974), ph; FRANKENSTEIN AND THE MONSTER FROM HELL(1974, Brit.), ph; INN OF THE DAMNED(1974, Aus.), ph; STRAIGHT ON TILL MORNING(1974, Brit.), ph; CALL HIM MR. SHATTER(1976, Hong Kong), ph; COUNT DRACULA AND HIS VAMPIRE BRIDE(1978, Brit.), ph; MANGO TREE, THE(1981, Aus.), ph

Marietta Procaccini
CURSE OF THE BLOOD GHOULS(1969, Ital.)

John Procaccino
THE RUNNER STUMBLES(1979)

Frantisek Prochazka
DIAMONDS OF THE NIGHT(1968, Czech.)

Jan Prochazka
ON THE COMET(1970, Czech.), w

Zdenka Prochazkova
LOST FACE, THE(1965, Czech.); FIFTH HORSEMAN IS FEAR, THE(1968, Czech.)

Lidia Prochnicka
GROUP, THE(1966)

Misc. Talkies
KILLING TOUCH, THE(1983)
Susan Prorett
SIR HENRY AT RAWLINSON END(1980, Brit.)
Irene Prosen
SAMSON(1961, Ital.)
Chip Proser
1984
ICEMAN(1984), w
Robert J. Prosky
MONSIGNOR(1982)
Robert Prosky
THIEF(1981); HANKY-PANKY(1982); CHRISTINE(1983); KEEP, THE(1983); LORDS OF DISCIPLINE, THE(1983)
1984
NATURAL, THE(1984)
Jean-Marie Proslier
MAXIME(1962, Fr.); HERBIE GOES TO MONTE CARLO(1977); CHANEL SOLITAIRE(1981); CHARLES AND LUCIE(1982, Fr.); BANZAI(1983, Fr.)
Frank [Francisco] Prosper
MR. ARKADIN(1962, Brit./Fr./Span.), set d; SUPERSONIC MAN(1979, Span.), set d
Frank Prosper
SUPERSONIC MAN(1979, Span.), spec eff
Paul Prosper
1984
LITTLE DRUMMER GIRL, THE(1984)
Franco Prosperi
WONDERS OF ALADDIN, THE(1961, Fr./Ital.), w; EVIL EYE(1964 Ital.), w; HERCULES IN THE HAUNTED WORLD(1964, Ital.), w; TIKO AND THE SHARK(1966, U.S./Ital./Fr.), w; RIPPED-OFF(1971, Ital.), d
G. Prosperi
VERGINITA(1953, Ital.), w
Giorgio Prosperi
INDISCRETION OF AN AMERICAN WIFE(1954, U.S./Ital.), w; DEFEND MY LOVE(1956, Ital.), w; SEVEN HILLS OF ROME, THE(1958), w; NAKED MAJA, THE(1959, Ital./U.S.), w; VIOLENT SUMMER(1961, Fr./Ital.), w; SODOM AND GOMORRAH(1962, U.S./Fr./Ital.), w; GOLDEN ARROW, THE(1964, Ital.), w; TIKO AND THE SHARK(1966, U.S./Ital./Fr.), w; MAIDEN FOR A PRINCE, A(1967, Fr./Ital.), w; SENSO(1968, Ital.), w
Mario Prosperi
LEAP INTO THE VOID(1982, Ital.)
Sergio Prosperi
DUEL OF THE TITANS(1963, Ital.), w
David Prosser
MATTER OF INNOCENCE, A(1968, Brit.)
Don Prosser
JUST IMAGINE(1930)
Hugh Prosser
NIGHT RIDERS, THE(1939); SIERRA SUE(1941); WEST OF CIMARRON(1941); BOSS OF HANGTOWN MESA(1942); SABOTAGE SQUAD(1942); LOST CANYON(1943); NORTHERN PURSUIT(1943); RIDERS OF THE DEADLINE(1943); SO PROUDLY WE HAIL(1943); THEY CAME TO BLOW UP AMERICA(1943); THEY GOT ME COVERED(1943); ADVENTURES OF KITTY O'DAY(1944); DESTINATION TOKYO(1944); LAND OF THE OUTLAWS(1944); RANGE LAW(1944); CODE OF THE LAWLESS(1945); CORNERED(1945); DILLINGER(1945); PARDON MY PAST(1945); MONSIEUR BEAUCAIRE(1946); MY REPUTATION(1946); SUSPENSE(1946); SINBAD THE SAILOR(1947); UNCONQUERED(1947); VACATION DAYS(1947); DAREDEVILS OF THE CLOUDS(1948); SIX-GUN LAW(1948); SAMSON AND DELILAH(1949); WESTERN RENEGADES(1949); ACROSS THE BADLANDS(1950); OUTLAW GOLD(1950); CANYON AMBUSH(1952); GREATEST SHOW ON EARTH, THE(1952); PRISONER OF ZENDA, THE(1952); TREASURE OF LOST CANYON, THE(1952)
Misc. Talkies
GUNS ALONG THE BORDER(1952)
George Prost
PEOPLE THAT TIME FORGOT, THE(1977, Brit.), makeup
Francois Protat
TOMORROW NEVER COMES(1978, Brit./Can.), ph; JACOB TWO-TWO MEETS THE HOODED FANG(1979, Can.), ph; FANTASTICA(1980, Can./Fr.), ph; TULIPS(1981, Can), ph; RUNNING BRAVE(1983, Can.), ph
1984
SURROGATE, THE(1984, Can.), ph
M. A. Protat
KING SOLOMON'S TREASURE(1978, Can.), makeup
Yakov A. Protazanov
Misc. Silents
AELITA(1929, USSR), d
Yakov Protazanov
Misc. Silents
NIKOLAI STAVROGIN(1915, USSR), d; PLEBIAN(1915, USSR), d; WAR AND PEACE(1915, USSR), d; QUEEN OF SPADES, THE(1916, USSR), d; WOMAN WITH A DAGGER(1916, USSR), d; ANDREI KOZHUKHOV(1917, USSR), d; BLOOD NEED NOT BE SPILLED(1917, USSR), d; CURSED MILLIONS(1917, USSR), d; PUBLIC PROSECUTOR(1917, USSR), d; FATHER SERGIUS(1918, USSR), d; QUEEN'S SECRET, THE(1919, USSR), d; BROKEN CHAINS(1925, USSR), d; FORTY-FIRST, THE(1927, USSR), d; WHITE EAGLE, THE(1928, USSR), d; RANKS AND PEOPLE(1929, USSR), d
Anthony Protenza
LAW AND DISORDER(1974), ed
Brian Protheroe
SUPERMAN(1978)
Pierre Prothon
OLIVE TREES OF JUSTICE, THE(1967, Fr.)
Adolfo Torres Protillo
VAMPIRES, THE(1969, Mex.), w
Protopopov
Silents
BATTLESHIP POTEMKIN, THE(1925, USSR)

Jacob Protozanoff
Misc. Silents
L'ANGOISSANTE AVENTURE(1920, Fr.), d; JUSTICE D'ABORD(1921, Fr.), d; LE SENS DE LA MORT(1921, Fr.), d; POUR UNE NUIT(1921, Fr.), d; L'OMBRE DU PECHE(1922), d
J.A. Protozanov
DIARY OF A REVOLUTIONIST(1932, USSR), w
Serge Protzenko
NORTH STAR, THE(1943)
Peter Proud
SOMETHING ALWAYS HAPPENS(1934, Brit.), art d; STRAUSS' GREAT WALTZ(1934, Brit.), set d; MAN WHO KNEW TOO MUCH, THE(1935, Brit.), art d & set d; GREEN FOR DANGER(1946, Brit.), prod d; ESTHER WATERS(1948, Brit.), d; WOMAN IN THE HALL, THE(1949, Brit.), prod d; OUTPOST IN MALAYA(1952, Brit.), w; LEAGUE OF GENTLEMEN, THE(1961, Brit.), prod d, art d; LIFE IN DANGER(1964, Brit.), art d; SATURDAY NIGHT OUT(1964, Brit.), art d; DIE, DIE, MY DARLING(1965, Brit.), prod d; CANDIDATE FOR MURDER(1966, Brit.), art d; NAKED RUNNER, THE(1967, Brit.), art d
Patty Proudfoot
UP IN SMOKE(1978)
Roger Proudlock
HANGMAN WAITS, THE(1947, Brit.), p; MATTER OF MURDER, A(1949, Brit.), p; YOU CAN'T FOOL AN IRISHMAN(1950, Ireland), p; FOUR DAYS(1951, Brit.), p; SIX MEN, THE(1951, Brit.), p; SMART ALEC(1951, Brit.), p; SCHOOL FOR BRIDES(1952, Brit.), p; SECOND MRS. TANQUERAY, THE(1952, Brit.), p; BACHELOR IN PARIS(1953, Brit.), p; ADVENTURE IN THE HOPFIELDS(1954, Brit.), p; BLACK 13(1954, Brit.), p; THEY CAN'T HANG ME(1955, Brit.), p; BLACK ICE, THE(1957, Brit.), p; LIGHT FINGERS(1957, Brit.), p; TIME IS MY ENEMY(1957, Brit.), p; SPANIARD'S CURSE, THE(1958, Brit.), p; JUST JOE(1960, Brit.), p; NOT A HOPE IN HELL(1960, Brit.), p
Michel Prouix
DEATH SHIP(1980, Can.), art d
Michael Proulux
STRANGE SHADOWS IN AN EMPTY ROOM(1977, Can./Ital.), art d
Denise Proulx
1984
HEY BABE!(1984, Can.)
Michael Proulx
TOMORROW NEVER COMES(1978, Brit./Can.), art d
Michel Proulx
VISITING HOURS(1982, Can.), art d; CROSS COUNTRY(1983, Can.), prod d
1984
COVERGIRL(1984, Can.), art d
Monique Proulx
Misc. Talkies
DARK SUNDAY(1978)
Derek Prouse
CHAMPAGNE MURDERS, THE(1968, Fr.), w
Peter Prouse
FRANCIS(1949); DESTINATION BIG HOUSE(1950); MOB, THE(1951); MAN WHO FELL TO EARTH, THE(1976, Brit.); NIGHTWING(1979)
Athenodoros Proussalis
APOLLO GOES ON HOLIDAY(1968, Ger./Swed.)
Colette Proust
PLAYTIME(1973, Fr.)
Marcel Proust
1984
SWANN IN LOVE(1984, Fr.Ger.), w
Victor Prout
Silents
NATURE OF THE BEAST, THE(1919, Brit.)
Misc. Silents
BOUNDARY HOUSE(1918, Brit.)
Jed Prouty
BROADWAY MELODY, THE(1929); FALL OF EVE, THE(1929); GIRL IN THE SHOW, THE(1929); HIS CAPTIVE WOMAN(1929); SONNY BOY(1929); TWO WEEKS OFF(1929); WHY LEAVE HOME?(1929); DEVIL'S HOLIDAY, THE(1930); FLORODORA GIRL, THE(1930); IT'S A GREAT LIFE(1930); TRUE TO THE NAVY(1930); ANNABELLE'S AFFAIRS(1931); NIGHT NURSE(1931); SECRET CALL, THE(1931); STRANGERS MAY KISS(1931); BUSINESS AND PLEASURE(1932); HOLD'EM JAIL(1932); MANHATTAN TOWER(1932); BIG BLUFF, THE(1933); JIMMY AND SALLY(1933); MORNING GLORY(1933); SKYWAY(1933); HOLLYWOOD PARTY(1934); I BELIEVED IN YOU(1934); MURDER ON THE BLACKBOARD(1934); MUSIC IN THE AIR(1934); PRIVATE SCANDAL(1934); ALIBI IKE(1935); BLACK SHEEP(1935); GEORGE WHITE'S 1935 SCANDALS(1935); LIFE BEGINS AT 40(1935); ONE HOUR LATE(1935); BACK TO NATURE(1936); CAN THIS BE DIXIE?(1936); COLLEGE HOLIDAY(1936); EDUCATING FATHER(1936); EVERY SATURDAY NIGHT(1936); HIS BROTHER'S WIFE(1936); LITTLE MISS NOBODY(1936); PIGSKIN PARADE(1936); SPECIAL INVESTIGATOR(1936); TEXAS RANGERS, THE(1936); UNDER YOUR SPELL(1936); BIG BUSINESS(1937); BORROWING TROUBLE(1937); CRIME NOBOBY SAW, THE(1937); DANGEROUS HOLIDAY(1937); HAPPY-GO-LUCKY(1937); HOT WATER(1937); LIFE BEGINS IN COLLEGE(1937); OFF TO THE RACES(1937); SMALL TOWN BOY(1937); SOPHIE LANG GOES WEST(1937); STAR IS BORN, A(1937); YOU CAN'T HAVE EVERYTHING(1937); 100 MEN AND A GIRL(1937); DANGER ON THE AIR(1938); DOWN ON THE FARM(1938); DUKE OF WEST POINT, THE(1938); GOODBYE BROADWAY(1938); KEEP SMILING(1938); LOVE ON A BUDGET(1938); SAFETY IN NUMBERS(1938); TRIP TO PARIS, A(1938); WALKING DOWN BROADWAY(1938); EVERYBODY'S BABY(1939); EXILE EXPRESS(1939); GRACIE ALLEN MURDER CASE(1939); HOLLYWOOD CAVALCADE(1939); JONES FAMILY IN HOLLYWOOD, THE(1939); QUICK MILLIONS(1939); TOO BUSY TO WORK(1939); BARNYARD FOLLIES(1940); LONE WOLF KEEPS A DATE, THE(1940); YOUNG AS YOU FEEL(1940); BACHELOR DADDY(1941); GO WEST, YOUNG LADY(1941); LOOK WHO'S LAUGHING(1941); OBLIGING YOUNG LADY(1941); POT O' GOLD(1941); REMEDY FOR RICHES(1941); ROAR OF THE PRESS(1941); UNEXPECTED UNCLE(1941); IT HAPPENED IN FLATBUSH(1942); MOONLIGHT MASQUERADE(1942); OLD HOMESTEAD, THE(1942); SCATTERGOOD RIDES HIGH(1942); MUG TOWN(1943); GUILTY BYSTANDER(1950)

Misc. Talkies
CITY LIMITS(1941); FATHER STEPS OUT(1941)
Silents
KICK IN(1922); GIRL OF THE GOLDEN WEST, THE(1923); GOLD DIGGERS, THE(1923); SOULS FOR SALE(1923); KNOCKOUT, THE(1925); UNGUARDED HOUR, THE(1925); ELLA CINDERS(1926); MISS NOBODY(1926); SMILE, BROTHER, SMILE(1927); NAME THE WOMAN(1928)
Misc. Silents
HER GAME(1919); SADIE LOVE(1920); SCARLET SAINT(1925); BRED IN OLD KENTUCKY(1926); SIREN, THE(1927); DOMESTIC MEDDLERS(1928)
Olive Higgins Prouty
STELLA DALLAS(1937), w; NOW, VOYAGER(1942), w
Silents
STELLA DALLAS(1925), w
Elisabeth Prouvost
ONE SINGS, THE OTHER DOESN'T(1977, Fr.), ph
David Proval
CINDERELLA LIBERTY(1973); MEAN STREETS(1973); HARRY AND WALTER GO TO NEW YORK(1976); WIZARDS(1977); NUNZIO(1978); HEY, GOOD LOOKIN'(1982); STAR CHAMBER, THE(1983)
Ludwig Provaznik
MR. BELVEDERE RINGS THE BELL(1951)
William Provaznik
MR. BELVEDERE RINGS THE BELL(1951)
Denise Provence
LANDRU(1963, Fr./Ital); RAVISHING IDIOT, A(1966, Ital./Fr.); LEGEND OF FRENCHIE KING, THE(1971, Fr./Ital./Span./Brit.); ADVENTURES OF RABBI JACOB, THE(1973, Fr.)
Martin Provensen
FANTASIA(1940), art d, anim; DUMBO(1941), art d
Martin Provenson
PINOCCHIO(1940), art d
Enzo Provenzale
SALVATORE GIULIANO(1966, Ital.), w; SUCKER, THE(1966, Fr./Ital.), p
Aldo Provenzano
JACKTOWN(1962), m, md
Dorothy Provine
BONNIE PARKER STORY, THE(1958); LIVE FAST, DIE YOUNG(1958); RIOT IN JUVENILE PRISON(1959); THIRTY FOOT BRIDE OF CANDY ROCK, THE(1959); IT'S A MAD, MAD, MAD, MAD WORLD(1963); WALL OF NOISE(1963); GOOD NEIGHBOR SAM(1964); GREAT RACE, THE(1965); THAT DARN CAT(1965); ONE SPY TOO MANY(1966); KISS THE GIRLS AND MAKE THEM DIE(1967, U.S./Ital.); WHO'S MINDING THE MINT?(1967); NEVER A DULL MOMENT(1968)
David Provis
MRS. BROWN, YOU'VE GOT A LOVELY DAUGHTER(1968, Brit.), art d
George Provis
YOU CAN'T DO WITHOUT LOVE(1946, Brit.), art d; DEAR MURDERER(1947, Brit.), art d; GIRL IN THE PAINTING, THE(1948, Brit.), art d; JASSY(1948, Brit.), art d; MY BROTHER'S KEEPER(1949, Brit.), art d; ONCE UPON A DREAM(1949, Brit.), art d; QUARTET(1949, Brit.), art d; SNOWBOUND(1949, Brit.), art d; OBSESSED(1951, Brit.), art d; SO LONG AT THE FAIR(1951, Brit.), art d; ISLAND RESCUE(1952, Brit.), art d; STORY OF ESTHER COSTELLO, THE(1957, Brit.), art d; TRUTH ABOUT WOMEN, THE(1958, Brit.), art d; SUBWAY IN THE SKY(1959, Brit.), art d; NEVER LET GO(1960, Brit.), art d; S.O.S. PACIFIC(1960, Brit.), art d; OFFBEAT(1961, Brit.), art d; DOG AND THE DIAMONDS, THE(1962, Brit.), art d; HOT MONEY GIRL(1962, Brit./Ger.), art d; TARZAN GOES TO INDIA(1962, U.S./Brit./Switz.), art d; EYES OF ANNIE JONES, THE(1963, Brit.), art d; MURDER CAN BE DEADLY(1963, Brit.), art d; EARTH DIES SCREAMING, THE(1964, Brit.), art d; HIDE AND SEEK(1964, Brit.), art d; JOLLY BAD FELLOW, A(1964, Brit.), art d; NIGHT TRAIN TO PARIS(1964, Brit.), art d; WITCHCRAFT(1964, Brit.), art d; WOMAN WHO WOULDN'T DIE, THE(1965, Brit.), art d; DALEKS–INVASION EARTH 2155 A.D.(1966, Brit.), art d; EXORCISM AT MIDNIGHT(1966, Brit. revised 1973, U.S.), art d; IDOL, THE(1966, Brit.), art d; VIKING QUEEN, THE(1967, Brit.), prod d; HOSTILE WITNESS(1968, Brit.), art d; FILE OF THE GOLDEN GOOSE, THE(1969, Brit.), art d; OBLONG BOX, THE(1969, Brit.), art d; CRY OF THE BANSHEE(1970, Brit.), art d; WHO SLEW AUNTIE ROO?(1971, U.S./Brit.), art d; CRAZE(1974, Brit.), art d
F. Provorov
MAGIC VOYAGE OF SINBAD, THE(1962, USSR), ph
Guy Provost
ORDERS, THE(1977, Can.)
Heinz Provost
INTERMEZZO(1937, Swed.), m
Jeanne Provost
HEART OF PARIS(1939, Fr.)
Jon Provost
BACK FROM ETERNITY(1956); TOWARD THE UNKNOWN(1956); ALL MINE TO GIVE(1957); ESCAPADE IN JAPAN(1957); LASSIE'S GREAT ADVENTURE(1963); THIS PROPERTY IS CONDEMNED(1966); COMPUTER WORE TENNIS SHOES, THE(1970); SECRET OF THE SACRED FOREST, THE(1970)
Jonathan Provost
COUNTRY GIRL, THE(1954)
Beverly Prowse
OPERATION BULLSHINE(1963, Brit.)
Dave Prowse
CARRY ON HENRY VIII(1970, Brit.); VAMPIRE CIRCUS(1972, Brit.); SWEET SUZY(1973); FRANKENSTEIN AND THE MONSTER FROM HELL(1974, Brit.); JABBERWOCKY(1977, Brit.)
David Prowse
HAMMERHEAD(1968); HORROR OF FRANKENSTEIN, THE(1970, Brit.); CLOCKWORK ORANGE, A(1971, Brit.); CONFESSIONS OF A POP PERFORMER(1975, Brit.); PEOPLE THAT TIME FORGOT, THE(1977, Brit.); STAR WARS(1977); EMPIRE STRIKES BACK, THE(1980); RETURN OF THE JEDI(1983)
Juliet Prowse
CAN-CAN(1960); G.I. BLUES(1960); FIERCEST HEART, THE(1961); RIGHT APPROACH, THE(1961); SECOND TIME AROUND, THE(1961); AMERICAN WIFE, AN(1965, Ital.); DINGAKA(1965, South Africa); WHO KILLED TEDDY BEAR?(1965); RUN FOR YOUR WIFE(1966, Fr./Ital.)

Peter Prowse
WALLET, THE(1952, Brit.); I AM A CAMERA(1955, Brit.); NOT WANTED ON VOYAGE(1957, Brit.); COUNT FIVE AND DIE(1958, Brit.); SWORD OF LANCELOT(1963, Brit.); CHRISTINE KEELER AFFAIR, THE(1964, Brit.); UNDERWORLD INFORMERS(1965, Brit.)
Freddie Prozesky
HELLIONS, THE(1962, Brit.); KIMBERLEY JIM(1965, South Africa)
Nikolai Prozorvsky
Misc. Silents
WINGS OF A SERF(1926, USSR)
Jaroslav Prucha
SKELETON ON HORSEBACK(1940, Czech.); KRAKATIT(1948, Czech.)
Tilo Pruckner
1984
NEVERENDING STORY, THE(1984, Ger.)
Anna Prucnal
CITY OF WOMEN(1980, Ital./Fr.); SNOW(1983, Fr.)
Cameron Prud'Homme
BACK FROM ETERNITY(1956); POWER AND THE PRIZE, THE(1956); RAINMAKER, THE(1956); CARDINAL, THE(1963)
June Prud'Homme
KING OF COMEDY, THE(1983)
Emile Prud'Hommee
COUNSEL FOR ROMANCE(1938, Fr.)
A. Sears Pruden
Misc. Silents
GRANDEE'S RING, THE(1915)
Cameron Prudhomme
ABRAHAM LINCOLN(1930)
Elizabeth Prudhomme
RAINS OF RANCHIPUR, THE(1955)
Emile Prudhomme
LOVE AT NIGHT(1961, Fr.)
Tilo Prueckner
DIE HAMBURGER KRANKHEIT(1979, Ger./Fr.)
James Pruett
1984
BIRDY(1984)
Jeanne Pruett
Misc. Talkies
SWEET COUNTRY ROAD(1981)
Winston Pruett
DOUBLE EXPOSURE(1982), art d
H. Prugar
BARRIER(1966, Pol.), ed
Halina Prugar
YOUNG GIRLS OF WILKO, THE(1979, Pol./Fr.), ed; CONDUCTOR, THE(1981, Pol.), ed; MAN OF IRON(1981, Pol.), ed
Halina Prugar-Ketling
DANTON(1983), ed
1984
LOVE IN GERMANY, A(1984, Fr./Ger.), ed
Barry Pruitt
ENDLESS LOVE(1981)
Floyd Pruitt
WHERE THERE'S LIFE(1947)
Kermit Pruitt
CARIBBEAN(1952)
Lucille S. Prumbs
MY GIRL TISA(1948), w
Olivierio Prunas
CRAZY DESIRE(1964, Ital.)
Oliviero Prunas
EIGHTEEN IN THE SUN(1964, Ital.)
Joseph Prus
HARDCORE(1979)
Lola Prussac
THERESE(1963, Fr.), cos
Louise Prussing
BEFORE MORNING(1933)
Silents
OUT YONDER(1920); RECKLESS YOUTH(1922)
Misc. Silents
HIS WIFE'S MONEY(1920); GIRL FROM NOWHERE, THE(1921); JAN OF THE BIG SNOWS(1922); THOROUGHBRED, THE(1928, Brit.); WOMAN IN WHITE, THE(1929, Brit.)
Margaret Prussing
Misc. Silents
RING OF THE BORGIAS, THE(1915)
Iosif Prut
SPRINGTIME ON THE VOLGA(1961, USSR), w
Ivan Prut
THIRTEEN, THE(1937, USSR), w
Stephen C. Prutting
TOOTSIE(1982)
Gosta Pruzelius
SMILES OF A SUMMER NIGHT(1957, Swed.); LESSON IN LOVE, A(1960, Swed.); SHAME(1968, Swed.); FANNY AND ALEXANDER(1983, Swed./Fr./Ger.)
Bradley Pryce
BLUE LAGOON, THE(1980)
Edythe Pryce
WEDNESDAY'S LUCK(1936, Brit.), w
Hu Pryce
RAW DEAL(1977, Aus.)
Jonathan Pryce
BREAKING GLASS(1980, Brit.); LOOPHOLE(1981, Brit.); PRAYING MANTIS(1982, Brit.); SOMETHING WICKED THIS WAY COMES(1983)
1984
PLOUGHMAN'S LUNCH, THE(1984, Brit.)

Richard Pryce
Silents
SUDS(1920), w
Lev Prygunov
ITALIANO BRAVA GENTE(1965, Ital./USSR)
Ken Prymus
MODEL SHOP, THE(1969); M(1970)
Hugh Pryne
PLYMOUTH ADVENTURE(1952)
Anita Prynne
FILE OF THE GOLDEN GOOSE, THE(1969, Brit.)
Ainslie Pryor
GIRL IN THE RED VELVET SWING, THE(1955); FOUR GIRLS IN TOWN(1956); LAST HUNT, THE(1956); RANSOM(1956); WALK THE PROUD LAND(1956); GUNS OF FORT PETTICOAT, THE(1957); SHADOW ON THE WINDOW, THE(1957); COLE YOUNGER, GUNFIGHTER(1958); KATHY O'(1958); LEFT-HANDED GUN, THE(1958); ONIONHEAD(1958)
Barbara Pryor
WISHBONE CUTTER(1978), p
Beatrix Pryor
Silents
STELLA DALLAS(1925)
Buddy Pryor
MY BLUE HEAVEN(1950)
Christine Pryor
DON'T RAISE THE BRIDGE, LOWER THE RIVER(1968, Brit.); ADDING MACHINE, THE(1969)
Edward Pryor
BEGGAR'S OPERA, THE(1953)
H.L. Pryor
Misc. Silents
EASY MONEY(1922)
Herbert Pryor
CAUGHT SHORT(1930); STUDENT TOUR(1934)
Silents
ACROSS THE PACIFIC(1926); KING OF KINGS, THE(1927)
Hugh Pryor
NORTH BY NORTHWEST(1959)
Joseph A. Pryor
YOUNG GIRLS OF ROCHEFORT, THE(1968, Fr.)
Maura Pryor
FINNEGANS WAKE(1965)
Maureen Pryor
LADY WITH A LAMP, THE(1951, Brit.); DOCTOR IN THE HOUSE(1954, Brit.); WEAK AND THE WICKED, THE(1954, Brit.); DOCTOR AT LARGE(1957, Brit.); HEART OF A CHILD(1958, Brit.); SECRET PLACE, THE(1958, Brit.); ORDERS ARE ORDERS(1959, Brit.); WALK IN THE SHADOW(1966, Brit.); THREE BITES OF THE APPLE(1967); MUSIC LOVERS, THE(1971, Brit.); LADY CAROLINE LAMB(1972, Brit./Ital.); NATIONAL HEALTH, OR NURSE NORTON'S AFFAIR, THE(1973, Brit.); BLACK WINDMILL, THE(1974, Brit.)
Nicholas Pryor
WAY WE LIVE NOW, THE(1970); MAN ON A SWING(1974); HAPPY HOOKER, THE(1975); SMILE(1975); GUMBALL RALLY, THE(1976); DAMIEN–OMEN II(1978); FISH THAT SAVED PITTSBURGH, THE(1979); RISKY BUSINESS(1983)
Richard "Cactus" Pryor
GREEN BERETS, THE(1968); HELLFIGHTERS(1968)
Richard Pryor
WIZ, THE(1978); BUSYBODY, THE(1967); WILD IN THE STREETS(1968); PHYNX, THE(1970); YOU'VE GOT TO WALK IT LIKE YOU TALK IT OR YOU'LL LOSE THAT BEAT(1971); LADY SINGS THE BLUES(1972); HIT(1973); MACK, THE(1973); SOME CALL IT LOVING(1973); BLAZING SADDLES(1974), w; UPTOWN SATURDAY NIGHT(1974); ADIOS AMIGO(1975); BINGO LONG TRAVELING ALL-STARS AND MOTOR KINGS, THE(1976); CARWASH(1976); SILVER STREAK(1976); GREASED LIGHTNING(1977); WHICH WAY IS UP?(1977); BLUE COLLAR(1978); CALIFORNIA SUITE(1978); MUPPET MOVIE, THE(1979); IN GOD WE TRUST(1980); STIR CRA-ZY(1980); WHOLLY MOSES(1980); BUSTIN' LOOSE(1981), a, p; SOME KIND OF HERO(1982); TOY, THE(1982); SUPERMAN III(1983)
Roger Pryor
MOONLIGHT AND PRETZELS(1933); BELLE OF THE NINETIES(1934); GIFT OF GAB(1934); I LIKE IT THAT WAY(1934); I'LL TELL THE WORLD(1934); LADY BY CHOICE(1934); ROMANCE IN THE RAIN(1934); WAKE UP AND DREAM(1934); CASE OF THE MISSING MAN, THE(1935); DINKY(1935); GIRL FRIEND, THE(1935); HEADLINE WOMAN, THE(1935); STRAIGHT FROM THE HEART(1935); STRANGE WIVES(1935); TO BEAT THE BAND(1935); $1,000 A MINUTE(1935); MISSING GIRLS(1936); RETURN OF JIMMY VALENTINE, THE(1936); SITTING ON THE MOON(1936); TICKET TO PARADISE(1936); MAN THEY COULD NOT HANG, THE(1939); BOWERY BOY(1940); FUGITIVE FROM JUSTICE, A(1940); GAMBLING ON THE HIGH SEAS(1940); GLAMOUR FOR SALE(1940); LONE WOLF MEETS A LADY, THE(1940); MAN WITH NINE LIVES, THE(1940); MONEY AND THE WOM-AN(1940); SUED FOR LIBEL(1940); BULLETS FOR O'HARA(1941); FLYING BLIND(1941); GAMBLING DAUGHTERS(1941); OFFICER AND THE LADY, THE(1941); POWER DIVE(1941); RICHEST MAN IN TOWN(1941); SHE COULDN'T SAY NO(1941); SOUTH OF PANAMA(1941); I LIVE ON DANGER(1942); LADY BODYGUARD(1942); MAN'S WORLD, A(1942); MEET THE MOB(1942); SUBMARINE ALERT(1943); CISCO KID RETURNS, THE(1945); HIGH POWERED(1945); IDENTITY UNKNOWN(1945); KID SISTER, THE(1945); MAN FROM OKLAHOMA, THE(1945); SCARED STIFF(1945); THOROUGHBREDS(1945)
Misc. Talkies
BROKEN HEARTS(1933)
Roger Pryor, Jr.
SMART ALECKS(1942)
Hugh Pryse
SCHOOL FOR SECRETS(1946, Brit.); CALLING PAUL TEMPLE(1948, Brit.); JAS-SY(1948, Brit.); STORY OF SHIRLEY YORKE, THE(1948, Brit.); THREE WEIRD SISTERS, THE(1948, Brit.); CHRISTOPHER COLUMBUS(1949, Brit.); DARK SE-CRET(1949, Brit.); WOMAN IN THE HALL, THE(1949, Brit.); BOTANY BAY(1953); BROKEN HORSESHOE, THE(1953, Brit.); GOOD BEGINNING, THE(1953, Brit.); MARILYN(1953, Brit.); MEN ARE CHILDREN TWICE(1953, Brit.); HAPPINESS OF THREE WOMEN, THE(1954, Brit.); PORT OF ESCAPE(1955, Brit.); THREE CASES OF MURDER(1955, Brit.)

L. Prysonow
THREE DAYS OF VIKTOR TSCHERNIKOFF(1968, USSR)
Suzanne Prystup
HUCKLEBERRY FINN(1974)
Frank Prythetch
GOODBYE PORK PIE(1981, New Zealand)
Agneta Prytz
DOLL, THE(1964, Swed.); RAVEN'S END(1970, Swed.); EMIGRANTS, THE(1972, Swed.); NEW LAND, THE(1973, Swed.)
Peter Pryzgodda
LEFT-HANDED WOMAN, THE(1980, Ger.), ed
1984
PARIS, TEXAS(1984, Ger./Fr.), ed
S. Przedwojewski
WALKOVER(1969, Pol.)
Jerzy Przybylski
SARAGOSSA MANUSCRIPT, THE(1972, Pol.)
Stanislawa Przybyszewska
DANTON(1983), w
Peter Przygodda
ALICE IN THE CITIES(1974, W. Ger.), ed; LOST HONOR OF KATHARINA BLUM, THE(1975, Ger.), ed; KINGS OF THE ROAD(1976, Ger.), ph; AMERICAN FRIEND, THE(1977, Ger.), ed
1984
FLIGHT TO BERLIN(1984, Ger./Brit.), ed
Armand Psenay
DEATHWATCH(1980, Fr./Ger.), ed
Armand Psenny
WOMAN OF SIN(1961, Fr.), ed; FIRST TASTE OF LOVE(1962, Fr.), ed; OBJECTIVE 500 MILLION(1966, Fr.), ed; LET JOY REIGN SUPREME(1977, Fr.), ed; QUESTION, THE(1977, Fr.), ed; JUDGE AND THE ASSASSIN, THE(1979, Fr.), ed; COUP DE TORCHON(1981, Fr.), ed
1984
SUNDAY IN THE COUNTRY, A(1984, Fr.), ed
Lenita Psillakis
1984
MELVIN, SON OF ALVIN(1984, Aus.)
Wojciech Pszoniak
GOLEM(1980, Pol.); DANTON(1983)
Wolcech Pszoniak
TIN DRUM, THE(1979, Ger./Fr./Yugo./Pol.)
Kim Ptak
BUTTERFLY(1982)
Aleksandr Ptushko
DAY THE EARTH FROZE, THE(1959, Fin./USSR), d; SWORD AND THE DRAGON, THE(1960, USSR), p&d; MAGIC VOYAGE OF SINBAD, THE(1962,USSR), d
Santini Puailoa
RAINBOW ISLAND(1944)
Satini Puailoa
REAL GLORY, THE(1939); LURE OF THE ISLANDS(1942); ROAD TO BALI(1952)
Satini Pualioa
ELEPHANT WALK(1954)
Dick Puanaki
1984
UTU(1984, New Zealand)
Sue Puccinelli
GIRL, THE BODY, AND THE PILL, THE(1967)
Puccini
DREAM OF BUTTERFLY, THE(1941, Ital.), m; UNA SIGNORA DELL'OVEST(1942, Ital), w
Aldo Puccini
HURRICANE(1979), spec eff
Duffy Puccini
ENDLESS LOVE(1981)
Giacomo Puccini
MADAME BUTTERFLY(1932), m; MIMI(1935, Brit.), m; BROKEN LOVE(1946, Ital.), m; BEFORE HIM ALL ROME TREMBLED(1947, Ital.), m; MADAME BUTTER-FLY(1955 Ital./Jap.), w; LA BOHEME(1965, Ital.), m
Gianni Puccini
BITTER RICE(1950, Ital.), w; BEHIND CLOSED SHUTTERS(1952, Ital.), w; OSSESS-IONE(1959, Ital.), w; DOUBLE BED, THE(1965, Fr./Ital.), d; LOVE IN 4 DIMEN-SIONS(1965 Fr./Ital.), d&w; LOVE AND MARRIAGE(1966, Ital.), d, w; MY WIFE'S ENEMY(1967, Ital.), d, w
Luciano Puccini
ROMEO AND JULIET(1968, Brit./Ital.), art d; FINE PAIR, A(1969, Ital.), art d; TEOREMA(1969, Ital.), art d; RETURN OF SABATA(1972, Ital./Fr./Ger.), art d
Norman Puchalski
LIFE AND TIMES OF CHESTER-ANGUS RAMSGOOD, THE(1971, Can.)
Werner Puchath
Misc. Talkies
WOMEN FOR SALE(1975)
Jesus Puche
SUNSCORCHED(1966, Span./Ger.)
Maria Puchol
HAND IN THE TRAP, THE(1963, Arg./Span.)
Vladimir Pucholt
LOVES OF A BLONDE(1966, Czech.); SIGN OF THE VIRGIN(1969, Czech.)
Don Puckett
BENJI(1974)
Jean Rosone- Puckett
1984
OH GOD! YOU DEVIL(1984), cos
Joan Puckett
DRACULA(THE DIRTY OLD MAN) (1969)
Hugh C. Puckler
Silents
GARDEN OF RESURRECTION, THE(1919, Brit.)

Alan Pudney
1984
DON'T OPEN TILL CHRISTMAS(1984, Brit.), ph

John Pudney
PROJECT M7(1953, Brit.), w; FUSS OVER FEATHERS(1954, Brit.), w; NAVY HEROES(1959, Brit.), w; STOLEN AIRLINER, THE(1962, Brit.), d&w

V.I. Pudovkin
GENERAL SUVOROV(1941, USSR), d
Silents
STORM OVER ASIA(1929, USSR), d

Vsevolod Pudovkin
IVAN THE TERRIBLE(Part I, 1947, USSR); DESERTER(1934, USSR), d; ADMIRAL NAKHIMOV(1948, USSR), a, d
Misc. Silents
SICKLE AND HAMMER(1921, USSR); MOTHER(1926, USSR), d; END OF ST. PETERSBURG, THE(1927, USSR), d; HEIR TO JENGHIS-KHAN, THE(1928, USSR), d; LIVING CORPSE, A(1931, USSR)

Rodrigo Puebla
MAGNIFICENT ONE, THE(1974, Fr./Ital.)
1984
EL NORTE(1984); EVIL THAT MEN DO, THE(1984); ROMANCING THE STONE(1984)

Jesus Puente
ADIOS GRINGO(1967, Ital./Fr./Span.); COBRA, THE(1968); SEVEN GUNS FOR THE MACGREGORS(1968, Ital./Span.); HATCHET FOR A HONEYMOON(1969, Span./Ital.); NARCO MEN, THE(1969, Span./Ital.)

Lara Puente
RUMBA(1935)

Luis Lopez Puente
YOUNG AND EVIL(1962, Mex.)

Antonio Pueo
MURDERS IN THE RUE MORGUE(1971), cos

Tony Pueo
CAPTAIN APACHE(1971, Brit.), cos; HUNTING PARTY, THE(1977, Brit.), cos; WIDOWS' NEST(1977, U.S./Span.), cos

Henri Puff
ME(1970, Fr.)

Lon Puff
TOM SAWYER(1930)

Charles Puffy
Silents
OPEN ALL NIGHT(1924); ROSE OF PARIS, THE(1924); MAN WHO LAUGHS, THE(1927); MOCKERY(1927); LOVE ME AND THE WORLD IS MINE(1928)
Misc. Silents
ARCTIC ADVENTURE(1922)

Halina Pugarowa
MAN OF MARBLE(1979, Pol.), ed

Jack Pugeat
LAST OF SHEILA, THE(1973)

Arthur Pugh
1984
PLACES IN THE HEART(1984)

David Pugh
LOVING MEMORY(1970, Brit.)
Misc. Talkies
LOVE PILL, THE(1971)

George Pugh
LIMPING MAN, THE(1936, Brit.)

Marshall Pugh
SILENT ENEMY, THE(1959, Brit.), d&w; GUNS AT BATASI(1964, Brit.), w

Mavis Pugh
CLASS OF MISS MAC MICHAEL, THE(1978, Brit./U.S.); BROTHERS AND SISTERS(1980, Brit.)

Nella Pugh
CINDERELLA LIBERTY(1973)

Robert Pugh
NIGHTHAWKS(1981); GIRO CITY(1982, Brit.)

Sylvia Pugh
PAUL TEMPLE RETURNS(1952, Brit.)

Ted Pugh
SOMETHING SHORT OF PARADISE(1979)

Willard Pugh
1984
TOY SOLDIERS(1984)

George Pughe
SOME DAY(1935, Brit.); HOT NEWS(1936, Brit.); REMBRANDT(1936, Brit.); FALSE EVIDENCE(1937, Brit.); STORM IN A TEACUP(1937, Brit.); THANK EVANS(1938, Brit.); STRANGLER, THE(1941, Brit.); FRONT LINE KIDS(1942, Brit.); GIVE ME THE STARS(1944, Brit.)

Frank Puglia
WITHOUT RESERVATIONS(1946); WHITE SISTER, THE(1933); MEN IN WHITE(1934); STAMBOUL QUEST(1934); VIVA VILLA!(1934); BORDERTOWN(1935); CAPTAIN BLOOD(1935); MELODY LINGERS ON, THE(1935); BULLDOG EDITION(1936); DEVIL IS A SISSY, THE(1936); FATAL LADY(1936); GAY DESPERADO(1936); HIS BROTHER'S WIFE(1936); LOVE ON THE RUN(1936); WIFE VERSUS SECRETARY(1936); BRIDE WORE RED, THE(1937); BULLDOG DRUMMOND'S REVENGE(1937); DOCTOR'S DIARY, A(1937); FIREFLY, THE(1937); KING OF GAMBLERS(1937); LANCER SPY(1937); MAMA STEPS OUT(1937); MAYTIME(1937); SEVENTH HEAVEN(1937); SONG OF THE CITY(1937); THIN ICE(1937); WHEN YOU'RE IN LOVE(1937); YOU CAN'T HAVE EVERYTHING(1937); BAREFOOT BOY(1938); DRAMATIC SCHOOL(1938); RASCALS(1938); SHARPSHOOTERS(1938); SHINING HOUR, THE(1938); SPAWN OF THE NORTH(1938); TROPIC HOLIDAY(1938); CODE OF THE SECRET SERVICE(1939); FORGED PASSPORT(1939); GIRL AND THE GAMBLER, THE(1939); IN NAME ONLY(1939); IN OLD CALIENTE(1939); MAISIE(1939); MYSTERY OF THE WHITE ROOM(1939); PIRATES OF THE SKIES(1939); ZAZA(1939); ARISE, MY LOVE(1940); CHARLIE CHAN IN PANAMA(1940); DOWN ARGENTINE WAY(1940); FATAL HOUR, THE(1940); LOVE, HONOR AND OH, BABY(1940); MARK OF ZORRO, THE(1940); MEET THE WILDCAT(1940); NO, NO NANETTE(1940); RANGERS OF FORTUNE(1940); 'TIL WE MEET AGAIN(1940); TORRID ZONE(1940); BILLY THE KID(1941); LAW OF THE TROPICS(1941); PARSON OF PANAMINT, THE(1941); THAT NIGHT IN RIO(1941); ALWAYS IN MY HEART(1942); BOOGIE MAN WILL GET YOU, THE(1942); CASABLANCA(1942); ESCAPE FROM HONG KONG(1942); FLIGHT LIEUTENANT(1942); JUNGLE BOOK(1942); NOW, VOYAGER(1942); SECRET AGENT OF JAPAN(1942); WHO IS HOPE SCHUYLER?(1942); ACTION IN THE NORTH ATLANTIC(1943); AROUND THE WORLD(1943); BACKGROUND TO DANGER(1943); FOR WHOM THE BELL TOLLS(1943); IRON MAJOR, THE(1943); MISSION TO MOSCOW(1943); PHANTOM OF THE OPERA(1943); PILOT NO. 5(1943); PRINCESS O'ROURKE(1943); TARZAN'S DESERT MYSTERY(1943); ALI BABA AND THE FORTY THIEVES(1944); BRAZIL(1944); DRAGON SEED(1944); PASSAGE TO MARSEILLE(1944); STORY OF DR. WASSELL, THE(1944); TALL IN THE SADDLE(1944); THIS IS THE LIFE(1944); TOGETHER AGAIN(1944); BLOOD ON THE SUN(1945); ROUGHLY SPEAKING(1945); SONG TO REMEMBER, A(1945); WEEKEND AT THE WALDORF(1945); BRUTE FORCE(1947); DREAM GIRL(1947); ESCAPE ME NEVER(1947); FIESTA(1947); LOST MOMENT, THE(1947); MY FAVORITE BRUNETTE(1947); ROAD TO RIO(1947); STALLION ROAD(1947); JOAN OF ARC(1948); BAGDAD(1949); BRIDE OF VENGEANCE(1949); COLORADO TERRITORY(1949); SPECIAL AGENT(1949); BLACK HAND, THE(1950); CAPTAIN CAREY, U.S.A(1950); DESERT HAWK, THE(1950); FEDERAL AGENT AT LARGE(1950); WALK SOFTLY, STRANGER(1950); BANDITS OF CORSICA, THE(1953); CADDY, THE(1953); SON OF BELLE STARR(1953); STEEL LADY, THE(1953); CASANOVA'S BIG NIGHT(1954); JUBILEE TRAIL(1954); SHANGHAI STORY, THE(1954); STAR IS BORN, A(1954); ACCUSED OF MURDER(1956); BURNING HILLS, THE(1956); FIRST TEXAN, THE(1956); SERENADE(1956); DUEL AT APACHE WELLS(1957); 20 MILLION MILES TO EARTH(1957); BLACK ORCHID(1959); CRY TOUGH(1959); GIRLS! GIRLS! GIRLS!(1962); SWORD OF ALI BABA, THE(1965); SPY IN THE GREEN HAT, THE(1966); MR. RICCO(1975)
Silents
ORPHANS OF THE STORM(1922); ISN'T LIFE WONDERFUL(1924); ROMOLA(1925); MAN WHO LAUGHS, THE(1927)
Misc. Silents
BEAUTIFUL CITY, THE(1925)

Alberto Pugliese
NUDE ODYSSEY(1962, Fr./Ital.), p; PISTOL FOR RINGO, A(1966, Ital./Span.), p; RETURN OF RINGO, THE(1966, Ital./Span.), p; RUTHLESS FOUR, THE(1969, Ital./Ger.), p

Sergio Pugliese
LOVE AND LARCENY(1963, Fr./Ital.), w

Aldo Puglisi
MARRIAGE–ITALIAN STYLE(1964, Fr./Ital.); SEDUCED AND ABANDONED(1964, Fr./Ital.); GIRL WITH A PISTOL, THE(1968, Ital.); THREE NIGHTS OF LOVE(1969, Ital.)

M. Pugovkin
SONG OVER MOSCOW(1964, USSR)

Mikhail Pugovkin
THEY CALL ME ROBERT(1967, USSR)

William Pugsley
BLOOD OF FRANKENSTEIN(1970), w

Jerri Puhara
BLACK OAK CONSPIRACY(1977), cos

Hui Pui
1984
AH YING(1984, Hong Kong)

Eva Puig
I WANT A DIVORCE(1940); NORTHWEST MOUNTED POLICE(1940); TEXAS RANGERS RIDE AGAIN(1940); HOLD BACK THE DAWN(1941); MOB TOWN(1941); ROMANCE OF THE RIO GRANDE(1941); SINGAPORE WOMAN(1941); ARABIAN NIGHTS(1942); BELOW THE BORDER(1942); RIO RITA(1942); UNDERCOVER MAN(1942); CISCO KID RETURNS, THE(1945); MEDAL FOR BENNY, A(1945); SNAFU(1945); PLAINSMAN AND THE LADY(1946); WILD BEAUTY(1946)

Robert Puig
DEADLY DECOYS, THE(1962, Fr.)

S. Puik
DEAD MOUNTAINEER HOTEL, THE(1979, USSR)

Rene Pujal
ONE RAINY AFTERNOON(1936), w

Rene Pujol
MAN STOLEN(1934, Fr.), w

Jerzy Pujszo
1984
AMERICAN DREAMER(1984)

E. Pukhalsky
Misc. Silents
RUSLAN I LUDMILA(1915, USSR)

Napoleon Pukui
BIRD OF PARADISE(1932)

Frank Pulaski
DESERT RATS, THE(1953); ROBE, THE(1953); SARACEN BLADE, THE(1954)

Enzo Pulcrano
Misc. Talkies
MISTER SCARFACE(1977)

K.L. Puldi
YOL(1982, Turkey), p

Johnny Puleo
TRAPEZE(1956)

Don Pulford
VIGILANTE FORCE(1976); STAR CHAMBER, THE(1983)

Lee Pulford
THEY ONLY KILL THEIR MASTERS(1972); PARALLAX VIEW, THE(1974); STUNTS(1977)

Jose Pulido
UP IN SMOKE(1978); SONG OF MEXICO(1945); TEN DAYS TO TULARA(1958)

Magdalena Pulido
LAZARILLO(1963, Span.), ed; WEB OF VIOLENCE(1966, Ital./Span.), ed; FEW BULLETS MORE, A(1968, Ital./Span.), ed

Meyito Pulito
TALL MEN, THE(1955)

Anthony Pullen
SPY WHO LOVED ME, THE(1977, Brit.)
Bill Pullen
THOSE REDHEADS FROM SEATTLE(1953)
Fred Pullen
BOOLOO(1938)
Jack Pullen
PARIS AFTER DARK(1943)
Jacqueline Pullen
MELODY(1971, Brit.)
Purv Pullen
STOLEN HARMONY(1935)
William August Pullen
STRATEGIC AIR COMMAND(1955)
William Pullen
EVERYBODY DOES IT(1949); I WAS A MALE WAR BRIDE(1949); ALL ABOUT EVE(1950); NO WAY OUT(1950); MOB, THE(1951); CARIBBEAN(1952); LAWLESS BREED, THE(1952); FARMER TAKES A WIFE, THE(1953); WAR PAINT(1953); RIDE CLEAR OF DIABLO(1954); CANYON CROSSROADS(1955); COURT JESTER, THE(1956); HELL CANYON OUTLAWS(1957); JOKER IS WILD, THE(1957); SHORT CUT TO HELL(1957)
Darcy Pulliam
EATING RAOUL(1982)
Gordon Pulliam
1984
THIEF OF HEARTS(1984)
Pauline Pulliam
Silents
CAROLYN OF THE CORNERS(1919)
Frank Pulliam, Jr.
O.S.S.(1946)
Darcy Pulliam
THERESE AND ISABELLE(1968, U.S./Ger.)
Norah Pulling
ONE WISH TOO MANY(1956, Brit.), w
Kimberly Pullins
1984
TEACHERS(1984)
B.S. Pully
FOUR JILLS IN A JEEP(1944); GREENWICH VILLAGE(1944); IN THE MEANTIME, DARLING(1944); TAKE IT OR LEAVE IT(1944); WING AND A PRAYER(1944); DON JUAN QUILLIGAN(1945); NOB HILL(1945); TREE GROWS IN BROOKLYN, A(1945); WITHIN THESE WALLS(1945); DO YOU LOVE ME?(1946); TAXI(1953); GUYS AND DOLLS(1955); HOLE IN THE HEAD, A(1959); BELLBOY, THE(1960); LOVE GOD?, THE(1969)
Jack Pulman
BEST OF ENEMIES, THE(1962), w; KISS THE GIRLS AND MAKE THEM DIE(1967, U.S./Ital.), w; MATCHLESS(1967, Ital.), w; DAVID COPPERFIELD(1970, Brit.), w; EXECUTIONER, THE(1970, Brit.), w; JANE EYRE(1971, Brit.), w; KIDNAPPED(1971, Brit.), w
Tony Pulo
RED SUN(1972, Fr./Ital./Span.), cos
Gianni Pulone
SERAFINO(1970, Fr./Ital.)
Petronella Pulsford
DOCTOR FAUSTUS(1967, Brit.)
Enid Pulver
SO YOUNG, SO BAD(1950)
Herman Pulver
PARSON AND THE OUTLAW, THE(1957)
Lilo Pulver
AFFAIRS OF JULIE, THE(1958, Ger.); TIME TO LOVE AND A TIME TO DIE, A(1958); ONE, TWO, THREE(1961); GLOBAL AFFAIR, A(1964)
Lisa Pulver
CONFESSIONS OF FELIX KRULL, THE(1957, Ger.)
Liselotte Pulver
GAMBLER, THE(1958, Fr.); SPESSART INN, THE(1961, Ger.); ARMS AND THE MAN(1962, Ger.); GLASS OF WATER, A(1962, Cgr.); WHERE THE TRUTH LIES(1962, Fr.); LAFAYETTE(1963, Fr.); MONSIEUR(1964, Fr.); MAN FROM COCODY(1966, Fr/Ital.); WEEKEND, ITALIAN STYLE(1967, Fr./Ital./Span.); NUN, THE(1971, Fr.)
Lisolotte Pulver
ADVENTURES OF ARSENE LUPIN(1956, Fr./Ital.)
Mary Brecht Pulver
Silents
MAN HATER, THE(1917), w
Pumpkin
TORTILLA FLAT(1942)
Rito Punay
DANGEROUS MONEY(1946); SAIGON(1948)
Angela Punch
NEWSFRONT(1979, Aus.); CHANT OF JIMMIE BLACKSMITH, THE(1980, Aus.)
Mme. Pung-Peng-Cheng
YOUR SHADOW IS MINE(1963, Fr./Ital.)
Bernard Punsley
DEAD END(1937); ANGELS WITH DIRTY FACES(1938); LITTLE TOUGH GUY(1938); ANGELS WASH THEIR FACES(1939); DEAD END KIDS ON DRESS PARADE(1939); HELL'S KITCHEN(1939); THEY MADE ME A CRIMINAL(1939); GIVE US WINGS(1940); YOU'RE NOT SO TOUGH(1940); HIT THE ROAD(1941); MOB TOWN(1941); TOUGH AS THEY COME(1942); MUG TOWN(1943)
Bernard Punsly
CRIME SCHOOL(1938)
Salvatore Puntillo
STRANGER IN TOWN, A(1968, U.S./Ital.)
A. Puntus
DESTINY OF A MAN(1961, USSR)
Javanart Punynchoti
BRIDGE ON THE RIVER KWAI, THE(1957)

Bruno Punzalah
BLACK MAMA, WHITE MAMA(1973)
Bruno Punzalan
NO MAN IS AN ISLAND(1962); MORO WITCH DOCTOR(1964, U.S./Phil.); AMBUSH BAY(1966); MISSION BATANGAS(1968); WARKILL(1968, U.S./Phil.); IMPASSE(1969); MAD DOCTOR OF BLOOD ISLAND, THE(1969, Phil./U.S.); BEAST OF BLOOD(1970, U.S./Phil.); SECRET OF THE SACRED FOREST, THE(1970); SUPERBEAST(1972); WONDER WOMEN(1973, Phil.)
Misc. Talkies
OMEGANS, THE(1968)
Henri Puopon
ANGELE(1934 Fr.)
Piccola Pupa
GHOST IN THE INVISIBLE BIKINI(1966)
D.M. Pupillo
PRIMITIVE LOVE(1966, Ital.), w
John Pupillo
IDEA GIRL(1946)
Massimo Pupillo
BLOODY PIT OF HORROR, THE(1965, Ital.), d
Mary Kay Pupo
WHY WOULD I LIE(1980)
The Puppetoons
WONDERFUL WORLD OF THE BROTHERS ERIMM, THE(1962)
Romano Puppo
TRAMPLERS, THE(1966, Ital.); BIG GUNDOWN, THE(1968, Ital.); DEATH RIDES A HORSE(1969, Ital.); SABATA(1969, Ital.); DEAF SMITH AND JOHNNY EARS(1973, Ital.); LOVES AND TIMES OF SCARAMOUCHE, THE(1976, Ital.); STREET PEOPLE(1976, U.S./Ital.); ORCA(1977), stunts; GIRL FROM TRIESTE, THE(1983, Ital.)
Misc. Talkies
ANONYMOUS AVENGER, THE(1976, Ital.)
Colin Purbrook
ALL NIGHT LONG(1961, Brit.)
Andrew Purcell
GREAT PONY RAID, THE(1968, Brit.)
Bob Purcell
FLAMING FURY(1949)
Charles Purcell
YANKS ARE COMING, THE(1942)
David Purcell
CONDUCT UNBECOMING(1975, Brit.)
1984
LOOSE CONNECTIONS(1984, Brit.)
Dick Purcell [Richard Purcell]
DOORWAY TO HELL(1930); CEILNG ZERO(1935); BENGAL TIGER(1936); BRIDES ARE LIKE THAT(1936); BULLETS OR BALLOTS(1936); CASE OF THE VELVET CLAWS, THE(1936); JAILBREAK(1936); KING OF HOCKEY(1936); LAW IN HER HANDS, THE(1936); MAN HUNT(1936); PUBLIC ENEMY'S WIFE(1936); SNOWED UNDER(1936); TIMES SQUARE PLAYBOY(1936); ALCATRAZ ISLAND(1937); CAPTAIN'S KID, THE(1937); MELODY FOR TWO(1937); MEN IN EXILE(1937); MISSING WITNESSES(1937); NAVY BLUES(1937); PUBLIC WEDDING(1937); REPORTED MISSING(1937); SLIM(1937); WINE, WOMEN AND HORSES(1937); ACCIDENTS WILL HAPPEN(1938); AIR DEVILS(1938); BROADWAY MUSKETEERS(1938); DAREDEVIL DRIVERS(1938); FLIGHT INTO NOWHERE(1938); GARDEN OF THE MOON(1938); MYSTERY HOUSE(1938); NANCY DREW–DETECTIVE(1938); OVER THE WALL(1938); PENROD'S DOUBLE TROUBLE(1938); VALLEY OF THE GIANTS(1938); BLACKWELL'S ISLAND(1939); HEROES IN BLUE(1939); IRISH LUCK(1939); STREETS OF NEW YORK(1939); TOUGH KID(1939); ARISE, MY LOVE(1940); BANK DICK, THE(1940); FLIGHT COMMAND(1940); NEW MOON(1940); OUTSIDE THE 3-MILE LIMIT(1940); PRIVATE AFFAIRS(1940); BULLETS FOR O'HARA(1941); FLYING BLIND(1941); KING OF THE ZOMBIES(1941); NO HANDS ON THE CLOCK(1941); PITTSBURGH KID, THE(1941); TWO IN A TAXI(1941); I LIVE ON DANGER(1942); IN OLD CALIFORNIA(1942); OLD HOMESTEAD, THE(1942); PHANTOM KILLER(1942); TORPEDO BOAT(1942); X MARKS THE SPOT(1942); AERIAL GUNNER(1943); HIGH EXPLOSIVE(1943); IDAHO(1943); MYSTERY OF THE 13TH GUEST, THE(1943); NO PLACE FOR A LADY(1943); REVEILLE WITH BEVERLY(1943); OLD TEXAS TRAIL, THE(1944); TIMBER QUEEN(1944); TROCADERO(1944)
Evelyn Purcell
RENEGADE GIRLS(1974), p; FIGHTING MAD(1976), p
Gertrude Purcell
FOLLOW THE LEADER(1930), w; ROYAL FAMILY OF BROADWAY, THE(1930), w; SAP FROM SYRACUSE, THE(1930), w; GIRL HABIT(1931), w; HONOR AMONG LOVERS(1931), w; NIGHT MAYOR, THE(1932), w; VANITY STREET(1932), w; ANOTHER LANGUAGE(1933), w; CHILD OF MANHATTAN(1933), w; COCKTAIL HOUR(1933), w; NO MORE ORCHIDS(1933), w; PALOOKA(1934), w; SHE WAS A LADY(1934), w; GIRL FRIEND, THE(1935), w; REDHEADS ON PARADE(1935), w; IF YOU COULD ONLY COOK(1936), w; MAKE WAY FOR A LADY(1936), w; WITNESS CHAIR, THE(1936), w; HITTING A NEW HIGH(1937), w; MUSIC FOR MADAME(1937), w; STELLA DALLAS(1937), w; SUPER SLEUTH(1937), w; MOTHER CAREY'S CHICKENS(1938), w; SERVICE DE LUXE(1938), w; DESTRY RIDES AGAIN(1939), w; LADY AND THE MOB, THE(1939), w; LITTLE BIT OF HEAVEN, A(1940), w; ONE NIGHT IN THE TROPICS(1940), w; ARKANSAS JUDGE(1941), w; ELLERY QUEEN AND THE MURDER RING(1941), w; INVISIBLE WOMAN, THE(1941), w; ICE-CAPADES REVUE(1942), w; IN OLD CALIFORNIA(1942), w; FOLLOW THE BOYS(1944), w; RECKLESS AGE(1944), w; PARIS UNDERGROUND(1945), w; WINTER WONDERLAND(1947), w
Harold Purcell
LISBON STORY, THE(1946, Brit.), w; LET'S MAKE UP(1955, Brit.), w; LADY IS A SQUARE, THE(1959, Brit.), w
Henry Purcell
KRAMER VS. KRAMER(1979), m
Irene Purcell
JUST A GIGOLO(1931); MAN IN POSSESSION, THE(1931); BACHELOR'S AFFAIRS(1932); CROOKED CIRCLE(1932); PASSIONATE PLUMBER(1932); WESTWARD PASSAGE(1932)
James Purcell
S.O.B.(1981)

Joe Purcell
VIENNESE NIGHTS(1930); CAPTAIN MILKSHAKE(1970)spec eff

Lee Purcell
ADAM AT 6 A.M.(1970); DIRTY LITTLE BILLY(1972); NECROMANCY(1972); STAND UP AND BE COUNTED(1972); KID BLUE(1973); MR. MAJESTYK(1974); ALMOST SUMMER(1978); BIG WEDNESDAY(1978); STIR CRAZY(1980); HOMEWORK(1982); EDDIE MACON'S RUN(1983); VALLEY GIRL(1983)

Mara Purcell
EYES OF ANNIE JONES, THE(1963, Brit.)

Noel Purcell
JIMMY BOY(1935, Brit.); IRELAND'S BORDER LINE(1939, Ireland); CAPTAIN BOYCOTT(1947, Brit.); BLUE LAGOON, THE(1949, Brit.); SAINTS AND SINNERS(1949, Brit.); ENCORE(1951, Brit.); CRIMSON PIRATE, THE(1952); FATHER'S DOING FINE(1952, Brit.); ISLAND RESCUE(1952, Brit.); NO RESTING PLACE(1952, Brit.); PICKWICK PAPERS, THE(1952, Brit.); YOU CAN'T BEAT THE IRISH(1952, Brit.); DECAMERON NIGHTS(1953, Brit.); MAD ABOUT MEN(1954, Brit.); DOCTOR AT SEA(1955, Brit.); LAND OF FURY(1955 Brit.); SVENGALI(1955, Brit.); WICKED WIFE(1955, Brit.); JACQUELINE(1956, Brit.); LUST FOR LIFE(1956); MOBY DICK(1956, Brit.); DOCTOR AT LARGE(1957, Brit.); RISING OF THE MOON, THE(1957, Ireland); KEY, THE(1958, Brit.); MAD LITTLE ISLAND(1958, Brit.); MERRY ANDREW(1958); ROONEY(1958, Brit.); FERRY TO HONG KONG(1959, Brit.); SHAKE HANDS WITH THE DEVIL(1959, Ireland); MAKE MINE MINK(1960, Brit.); MILLIONAIRESS, THE(1960, Brit.); TOMMY THE TOREADOR(1960, Brit.); BEWARE OF CHILDREN(1961, Brit.); DOUBLE BUNK(1961, Brit.); MAN IN THE MOON(1961, Brit.); WATCH YOUR STERN(1961, Brit.); MUTINY ON THE BOUNTY(1962); CEREMONY, THE(1963, U.S./Span.); LIST OF ADRIAN MESSENGER, THE(1963); RUNNING MAN, THE(1963, Brit.); SWINGIN' MAIDEN, THE(1963, Brit.); NURSE ON WHEELS(1964, Brit.); JOHNNY NOBODY(1965, Brit.); ARRIVEDERCI, BABY!(1966, Brit.); CARNABY, M.D.(1967, Brit.); SINFUL DAVEY(1969, Brit.); VIOLENT ENEMY, THE(1969, Brit.); WHERE'S JACK?(1969, Brit.); MC KENZIE BREAK, THE(1970); FLIGHT OF THE DOVES(1971); MACKINTOSH MAN, THE(1973, Brit.)

Pat Purcell
ODE TO BILLY JOE(1976)

Paul Purcell
SLAVES OF BABYLON(1953); GANGSTER STORY(1959), w

Robert Purcell
RED MENACE, THE(1949); MARK OF THE GORILLA(1950); QUICK GUN, THE(1964), art d

Roy Purcell
ALF'S BABY(1953, Brit.); CAPTAIN'S PARADISE, THE(1953, Brit.); PARIS EXPRESS, THE(1953, Brit.); BEYOND MOMBASA(1957); I'M ALL RIGHT, JACK(1959, Brit.); CLUE OF THE TWISTED CANDLE(1968, Brit.); DEADLY FEMALES, THE(1976, Brit.)

Theodore Purcell
MANFISH(1956)

Gertrude Purcell)
BRINGING UP BABY(1938), w

Bruce Purchase
OTHELLO(1965, Brit.); MACBETH(1971, Brit.); MARY, QUEEN OF SCOTS(1971, Brit.); OPTIMISTS, THE(1973, Brit.); MEETINGS WITH REMARKABLE MEN(1979, Brit.)

Reginald Purdell
MIDDLE WATCH, THE(1930, Brit.); NIGHT IN MONTMARTE, A(1931, Brit.); CONGRESS DANCES(1932, Ger.); LOVE ON THE SPOT(1932, Brit.), w; CRIME ON THE HILL(1933, Brit.); MY LUCKY STAR(1933, Brit.); THREE MEN IN A BOAT(1933, Brit.), w; UP TO THE NECK(1933, Brit.); LUCK OF A SAILOR, THE(1934, Brit.); ON THE AIR(1934, Brit.); GET OFF MY FOOT(1935, Brit.); KEY TO HARMONY(1935, Brit.); OLD CURIOSITY SHOP, THE(1935, Brit.); RADIO FOLLIES(1935, Brit.), w; REGAL CAVALCADE(1935, Brit.); RUNAWAY QUEEN, THE(1935, Brit.); CROWN VS STEVENS(1936); DEBT OF HONOR(1936, Brit.); HAIL AND FAREWELL(1936, Brit.), a, w; WHERE'S SALLY?(1936, Brit.); COMPULSORY WIFE, THE(1937, Brit.), w; DON'T GET ME WRONG(1937, Brit.), d, w; PATRICIA GETS HER MAN(1937, Brit.), d; SIDE STREET ANGEL(1937, Brit.); DARK STAIRWAY, THE(1938, Brit.); IT'S IN THE BLOOD(1938, Brit.), w; MANY TANKS MR. ATKINS(1938, Brit.), a, w; QUIET PLEASE(1938, Brit.), a, w; SIMPLY TERRIFIC(1938, Brit.); VIPER, THE(1938, Brit.), a, w; ANYTHING TO DECLARE?(1939, Brit.), a, w; CLOUDS OVER EUROPE(1939, Brit.); HIS BROTHER'S KEEPER(1939, Brit.); MIDDLE WATCH, THE(1939, Brit.); FINGERS(1940, Brit.); MISSING PEOPLE, THE(1940, Brit.); PACK UP YOUR TROUBLES(1940, Brit.), a, w; BELL-BOTTOM GEORGE(1943, Brit.); DARK TOWER, THE(1943, Brit.); IT'S IN THE BAG(1943, Brit.); WE DIVE AT DAWN(1943, Brit.); CANDLES AT NINE(1944, Brit.); DREAMING(1944, Brit.), w; 2,000 WOMEN(1944, Brit.); HERE COMES THE SUN(1945, Brit.); VARIETY JUBILEE(1945, Brit.); BRIGHTON ROCK(1947, Brit.); CAPTAIN BOYCOTT(1947, Brit.); HOLIDAY CAMP(1947, Brit.); LADY SURRENDERS, A(1947, Brit.); MAN ABOUT THE HOUSE, A(1947, Brit.); ROOT OF ALL EVIL, THE(1947, Brit.); FILES FROM SCOTLAND YARD(1951, Brit.); MY HEART GOES CRAZY(1953, Brit.)

Robert Purdie
Misc. Silents
STRIFE ETERNAL, THE(1915, Brit.)

Edmond Purdom
EGYPTIAN. THE(1954)

Edmund Purdom
TITANIC(1953); ATHENA(1954); STUDENT PRINCE, THE(1954); KING'S THIEF, THE(1955); PRODIGAL, THE(1955); STRANGE INTRUDER(1956); COSSACKS, THE(1960, It.); HEROD THE GREAT(1960, Ital.); TRAPPED IN TANGIERS(1960, Ital./Span.); LAST OF THE VIKINGS, THE(1962, Fr./Ital.); LOVES OF SALAMMBO, THE(1962, Fr./Ital.); MALAGA(1962, Brit.); NIGHT THEY KILLED RASPUTIN, THE(1962, Fr./Ital.); WHITE SLAVE SHIP(1962, Fr./Ital.); FURY OF THE PAGANS(1963, Ital.); LAFAYETTE(1963, Fr.); SULEIMAN THE CONQUEROR(1963, Ital.); COMEDY MAN, THE(1964); QUEEN OF THE NILE(1964, Ital.); YELLOW ROLLS-ROYCE, THE(1965, Brit.); BEAUTY JUNGLE, THE(1966, Brit.); MAN WHO LAUGHS, THE(1966, Ital.); HOUSE OF FREAKS(1973, Ital.); NIGHT CHILD(1975, Brit./Ital.); PIECES(1983, Span./Puerto Rico)
1984
AFTER THE FALL OF NEW YORK(1984, Ital./Fr.); DON'T OPEN TILL CHRISTMAS(1984, Brit.), a, d
Misc. Talkies
EVIL FINGERS(1975); MISTER SCARFACE(1977); ATOR: THE FIGHTING EAGLE(1983)

Herbert Purdom
DALTON GIRLS, THE(1957), w

Edmund Purdon
JULIUS CAESAR(1953)

Herbert Purdum
TARGET HONG KONG(1952), w; EL ALAMEIN(1954), w

Ralph Purdum
SPORTING CLUB, THE(1971)

Constance Purdy
TRUE TO LIFE(l943); LLOYDS OF LONDON(1936); BASHFUL BACHELOR, THE(1942); NOW, VOYAGER(1942); RINGS ON HER FINGERS(1942); DOUGHBOYS IN IRELAND(1943); SHADOW OF A DOUBT(1943); WHITE SAVAGE(1943); LOUISIANA HAYRIDE(1944); MY BUDDY(1944); SENSATIONS OF 1945(1944); TOGETHER AGAIN(1944); BEDSIDE MANNER(1945); LOVE LETTERS(1945); SCARLET STREET(1945); SWING OUT, SISTER(1945); THIS LOVE OF OURS(1945); TREE GROWS IN BROOKLYN, A(1945); SHOCKING MISS PILGRIM, THE(1947); THAT HAGEN GIRL(1947); UNCONQUERED(1947); FAMILY HONEYMOON(1948); HOLLOW TRIUMPH(1948); I REMEMBER MAMA(1948); JIGGS AND MAGGIE IN SOCIETY(1948); MADAME BOVARY(1949)

Dick Purdy
SUNBURN(1979), set d; CATTLE ANNIE AND LITTLE BRITCHES(1981), set d

Philip Purdy
OUT ALL NIGHT(1933)

Sharon Purdy
THRESHOLD(1983, Can.), cos

William Purdy
DATE WITH DEATH, A(1959)

Pure Hell
EDUCATION OF SONNY CARSON, THE(1974)

Praprapon Pureem
NIGHT IN BANGKOK(1966, Jap.)

Nat Purefoy
BLACK RODEO(1972)

Amrish Puri
GANDHI(1982)
1984
INDIANA JONES AND THE TEMPLE OF DOOM(1984)

Carlo Puri
ASH WEDNESDAY(1973); COUNT OF MONTE CRISTO(1976, Brit.)

Om Puri
GANDHI(1982)

Bill Purington
WOMAN'S SECRET, A(1949)

Gerhard Puritz
MAN WHO NEVER WAS, THE(1956, Brit.)

Dana Purkis
1984
CONSTANCE(1984, New Zealand)

Linda Purl
JORY(1972); CRAZY MAMA(1975); W.C. FIELDS AND ME(1976); LEO AND LOREE(1980); HIGH COUNTRY, THE(1981, Can.); VISITING HOURS(1982, Can.)

Frankie Purnell
Silents
WHEN SCOUTING WON(1930, Brit.)

Louise Purnell
THREE SISTERS(1974, Brit.)

Purnima
GUIDE, THE(1965, U.S./India)

Colette Purpera
EASY RIDER(1969)

Kathleen Purrman
LITTLE SEX, A(1982)

David Pursall
COUNT FIVE AND DIE(1958, Brit.), w; MURDER SHE SAID(1961, Brit.), w; SECRET PARTNER, THE(1961, Brit.), w; KILL OR CURE(1962, Brit.), w; VILLAGE OF DAUGHTERS(1962, Brit.), w; MURDER AT THE GALLOP(1963, Brit.), w; MURDER AHOY(1964, Brit.), w; MURDER MOST FOUL(1964, Brit.), w; ALPHABET MURDERS, THE(1966), w; BLUE MAX, THE(1966); SOUTHERN STAR, THE(1969, Fr./Brit.), w; CARRY ON ENGLAND(1976, Brit.), w; WHAT CHANGED CHARLEY FARTHING?(1976, Brit.), w; TOMORROW NEVER COMES(1978, Brit./Can.), w

Karin Purschke
TOXI(1952, Ger.)

David Pursel
LONGEST DAY, THE(1962), w

Ivan Purser
COUNTRY BOY(1966)

Jimmy Pursey
RUDE BOY(1980, Brit.)

Maurice Purtill
SUN VALLEY SERENADE(1941)

Bob Purvey
Misc. Talkies
FOLLOW ME(1969)

Edna Purviance
MONSIEUR VERDOUX(1947)
Silents
KID, THE(1921); PILGRIM, THE(1923); WOMAN OF PARIS, A(1923)
Misc. Silents
CARMEN(1916); ESSANAY-CHAPLIN REVUE OF 1916, THE(1916); SHOULDER ARMS(1917); WOMAN OF THE SEA, A(1926); EDUCATION DE PRINCE(1927, Fr.)

Harry Purvis
KID FOR TWO FARTHINGS, A(1956, Brit.)

Henry Purvis
I AM A CAMERA(1955, Brit.)

Jack Purvis
STAR WARS(1977); EMPIRE STRIKES BACK, THE(1980); TIME BANDITS(1981, Brit.); RETURN OF THE JEDI(1983)

GLORY(1957), art d; HOT SUMMER NIGHT(1957), art d; INVISIBLE BOY, THE(1957), art d; NORTH BY NORTHWEST(1959), art d; YOUR CHEATIN' HEART(1964), art d; ONE SPY TOO MANY(1966), art d; SPY WITH MY FACE, THE(1966), art d; TO TRAP A SPY(1966), art d; DOUBLE TROUBLE(1967), art d; FASTEST GUITAR ALIVE, THE(1967), art d; HOT RODS TO HELL(1967), art d; RIOT ON SUNSET STRIP(1967), art d; POWER, THE(1968), art d; YOUNG RUNAWAYS, THE(1968), art d

Silents

TORRENT, THE(1926), set d; ANNIE LAURIE(1927), art d; SMART SET, THE(1928), set d; TRAIL OF '98, THE(1929), art d

Peter Pye

SUMMER LOVERS(1982)

Mike Pyeatt

COWBOYS, THE(1972)

Albert Pyke

FOREVER DARLING(1956), art d

Charles F. Pyke

DEVIL THUMBS A RIDE, THE(1947), art d; THUNDER MOUNTAIN(1947), art d; UNDER THE TONTO RIM(1947), art d; THREAT, THE(1949), art d

Hy Pyke

FIRST NUDIE MUSICAL, THE(1976); NIGHTMARE IN BLOOD(1978); SLITHIS(1978); BLADE RUNNER(1982)

Misc. Talkies

AMOROUS ADVENTURES OF DON QUIXOTE AND SANCHO PANZA, THE(1976)

Monte Pyke

THE LADY DRACULA(1974)

Rex Pyke

PERFECT FRIDAY(1970, Brit.), ed; TAKE A GIRL LIKE YOU(1970, Brit,), ed; STORIES FROM A FLYING TRUNK(1979, Brit.), ed

Samuel M. Pyke

Silents

PRIDE OF SUNSHINE ALLEY(1924), w

Jean Vander Pyl

HEY THERE, IT'S YOGI BEAR(1964)

Leonid Pylajew

JOURNEY, THE(1959, U.S./Aust.)

Denver Pyle

DEVIL SHIP(1947); GUILT OF JANET AMES, THE(1947); MAN FROM COLORADO, THE(1948); MARSHAL OF AMARILLO(1948); TRAIN TO ALCATRAZ(1948); FLAME OF YOUTH(1949); HELLFIRE(1949); RED CANYON(1949); RIM OF THE CANYON(1949); STREETS OF SAN FRANCISCO(1949); TOO LATE FOR TEARS(1949); CUSTOMS AGENT(1950); DYNAMITE PASS(1950); FEDERAL AGENT AT LARGE(1950); FLYING SAUCER, THE(1950); OLD FRONTIER, THE(1950); HILLS OF UTAH(1951); MILLION DOLLAR PURSUIT(1951); ROUGH RIDERS OF DURANGO(1951); CANYON AMBUSH(1952); DESERT PASSAGE(1952); FARGO(1952); LUSTY MEN, THE(1952); MAN FROM BLACK HILLS, THE(1952); MAVERICK, THE(1952); OKLAHOMA ANNIE(1952); GOLDTOWN GHOST RIDERS(1953); PERILOUS JOURNEY, A(1953); REBEL CITY(1953); TEXAS BAD MAN(1953); TOPEKA(1953); VIGILANTE TERROR(1953); JOHNNY GUITAR(1954); RIDE CLEAR OF DIABLO(1954); RAGE AT DAWN(1955); RUN FOR COVER(1955); TEN WANTED MEN(1955); TO HELL AND BACK(1955); TOP GUN(1955); I KILLED WILD BILL HICKOK(1956); NAKED HILLS, THE(1956); PLEASE MURDER ME(1956); SEVENTH CAVALRY(1956); YAQUI DRUMS(1956); DESTINATION 60,000(1957); DOMINO KID(1957); GUN DUEL IN DURANGO(1957); JET PILOT(1957); LONELY MAN, THE(1957); CHINA DOLL(1958); FORT MASSACRE(1958); GOOD DAY FOR A HANGING(1958); LEFT-HANDED GUN, THE(1958); PARTY CRASHERS, THE(1958); CAST A LONG SHADOW(1959); HORSE SOLDIERS, THE(1959); KING OF THE WILD STALLIONS(1959); ALAMO, THE(1960); GERONIMO(1962); MAN WHO SHOT LIBERTY VALANCE, THE(1962); TERRIFIED!(1963); CHEYENNE AUTUMN(1964); MAIL ORDER BRIDE(1964); GREAT RACE, THE(1965); ROUNDERS, THE(1965); SHENANDOAH(1965); GUNPOINT(1966); INCIDENT AT PHANTOM HILL(1966); MARA OF THE WILDERNESS(1966); BONNIE AND CLYDE(1967); TAMMY AND THE MILLIONAIRE(1967); WELCOME TO HARD TIMES(1967); BANDOLERO!(1968); FIVE CARD STUD(1968); SOMETHING BIG(1971); WHO FEARS THE DEVIL(1972); CAHILL, UNITED STATES MARSHAL(1973); ESCAPE TO WITCH MOUNTAIN(1975); ADVENTURES OF FRONTIER FREMONT, THE(1976); BUFFALO BILL AND THE INDIANS, OR SITTING BULL'S HISTORY LESSON(1976); HAWMPS!(1976); WELCOME TO L.A.(1976); WINTERHAWK(1976); GUARDIAN OF THE WILDERNESS(1977)

Misc. Talkies

LEGEND OF THE WILD(1981)

Ed Pyle

FOUR FOR THE MORGUE(1962)

Ernie Pyle

STORY OF G.I. JOE, THE(1945), w

Frances Pyle

HOMECOMING(1948)

Howard Pyle

BLACK SHIELD OF FALWORTH, THE(1954), w

John Pyle

UNDER THE RAINBOW(1981)

Karen Pyles

CARNIVAL OF SOULS(1962)

Walter Pym

END PLAY(1975, Aus.); MOUTH TO MOUTH(1978, Aus.); PATRICK(1979, Aus.); THIRST(1979, Aus.); EARTHLING, THE(1980)

Francine Pyne

HOUSE IS NOT A HOME, A(1964)

Frederick Pyne

DANCE OF DEATH, THE(1971, Brit.)

Joe Pyne

MOTHER GOOSE A GO-GO(1966); LOVE-INS, THE(1967)

Natasha Pyne

DEVIL-SHIP PIRATES, THE(1964, Brit.); IDOL, THE(1966, Brit.); WHO KILLED THE CAT?(1966, Brit.); TAMING OF THE SHREW, THE(1967, U.S./Ital.); MADHOUSE(1974, Brit.); ONE OF OUR DINOSAURS IS MISSING(1975, Brit.)

Misc. Talkies

FATHER DEAR FATHER(1973, Brit.)

Keith Pyott

CALL OF THE BLOOD(1948, Brit.); DISTANT TRUMPET(1952, Brit.); SPIDER AND THE FLY, THE(1952, Brit.); HOUSE OF THE ARROW, THE(1953, Brit.); SEA DEVILS(1953); JOHN WESLEY(1954, Brit.); COLDITZ STORY, THE(1955, Brit.); BLUEBEARD'S TEN HONEYMOONS(1960, Brit.); OPERATION AMSTERDAM(1960, Brit.); WEEKEND WITH LULU, A(1961, Brit.); INVITATION TO MURDER(1962, Brit.); PIRATES OF BLOOD RIVER, THE(1962, Brit.); MASQUERADE(1965, Brit.); CHIMES AT MIDNIGHT(1967, Span.,Switz.); DEVIL'S BRIDE, THE(1968, Brit.)

George Pyper

Silents

CAPTAIN'S COURAGE, A(1926), w; AVENGING FANGS(1927), w; ISLE OF LOST MEN(1928), w

George W. Pyper

Silents

AIR HAWK, THE(1924), w; RIDERS OF MYSTERY(1925), w; GALLANT FOOL, THE(1926), w; WHEEL OF DESTINY, THE(1927), w; INTO THE NIGHT(1928), w; OUTLAWED(1929), w

Peter Pyper

HIGH(1968, Can.)

Erik Pyriev

IVAN THE TERRIBLE(Part I, 1947, USSR)

Ivan Pyriev

IDIOT, THE(1960, USSR), d&w

Misc. Silents

DELUGE, THE(1925, USSR), d

K. Pyryev

DEVOTION(1955, USSR), d, w

Albert Pyun

SWORD AND THE SORCERER, THE(1982), d, w

 **Q**

Faith Quabius
MAD BOMBER, THE(1973); SOYLENT GREEN(1973)

Hua Quach
1984
PERILS OF GWENDOLINE, THE(1984, Fr.)

Larry Quackenbush
LINCOLN CONSPIRACY, THE(1977)

Stan Quackenbush
SNOW WHITE AND THE SEVEN DWARFS(1937), anim

John Quade
HAMMER(1972); HIGH PLAINS DRIFTER(1973); PAPILLON(1973); STING, THE(1973); RANCHO DELUXE(1975); 92 IN THE SHADE(1975, U.S./Brit.); LAST HARD MEN, THE(1976); OUTLAW JOSEY WALES, THE(1976); SPECIAL DELIVERY(1976); ANY WHICH WAY YOU CAN(1980); CATTLE ANNIE AND LITTLE BRITCHES(1981)

Will Quadflieg
LOLA MONTES(1955, Fr./Ger.); FAUST(1963, Ger.)

Alex Quaglia
QUEST FOR FIRE(1982, Fr./Can.)

Licia Quaglia
PISTOL FOR RINGO, A(1966, Ital./Span.), ed

Paole Quagliero
WAR AND PEACE(1956, Ital./U.S.)

Jose Quaglio
CONFORMIST, THE(1971, Ital., Fr)
1984
BASILEUS QUARTET(1984, Ital.)

Buddy Quaid
LOCAL HERO(1983, Brit.)

David Quaid
SANTA CLAUS CONQUERS THE MARTIANS(1964), ph; PRETTY POISON(1968), ph; SWIMMER, THE(1968), ph; JENNY(1969), ph; COPS AND ROBBERS(1973), ph; I AM THE CHEESE(1983), ph; NIGHT IN HEAVEN, A(1983), ph

Dennis Quaid
9/30/55(1977); OUR WINNING SEASON(1978); SENIORS, THE(1978); BREAKING AWAY(1979); GORP(1980); LONG RIDERS, THE(1980); ALL NIGHT LONG(1981); CAVEMAN(1981); NIGHT THE LIGHTS WENT OUT IN GEORGIA, THE(1981); JAWS 3-D(1983); RIGHT STUFF, THE(1983); TOUGH ENOUGH(1983)
1984
DREAMSCAPE(1984)
Misc. Talkies
SENIORS, THE(1978)

Randall R. "Randy" Quaid
WHAT'S UP, DOC?(1972)

Randy Quaid
LAST PICTURE SHOW, THE(1971); LAST DETAIL, THE(1973); LOLLY-MADONNA XXX(1973); PAPER MOON(1973); APPRENTICESHIP OF DUDDY KRAVITZ, THE(1974, Can.); BREAKOUT(1975); BOUND FOR GLORY(1976); MISSOURI BREAKS, THE(1976); CHOIRBOYS, THE(1977); THREE WARRIORS(1977); MIDNIGHT EXPRESS(1978, Brit.); FOXES(1980); LONG RIDERS, THE(1980); HEARTBEEPS(1981); NATIONAL LAMPOON'S VACATION(1983)
1984
WILD LIFE, THE(1984)

Joanne C. Quakenbush
PATSY, THE(1964)

Ragnar Quale
MAN I MARRIED, THE(1940)

J.M. "John" Qualen
HE WAS HER MAN(1934)

John Qualen
ARROWSMITH(1931); STREET SCENE(1931); COUNSELLOR-AT-LAW(1933); DEVIL'S BROTHER, THE(1933); LET'S FALL IN LOVE(1934); OUR DAILY BREAD(1934); SERVANTS' ENTRANCE(1934); 365 NIGHTS IN HOLLYWOOD(1934); BLACK FURY(1935); CHASING YESTERDAY(1935); DOUBTING THOMAS(1935); FARMER TAKES A WIFE, THE(1935); GREAT HOTEL MURDER(1935); MAN OF IRON(1935); ORCHIDS TO YOU(1935); SILK HAT KID(1935); THREE MUSKETEERS, THE(1935); THUNDER IN THE NIGHT(1935); CHEERS OF THE CROWD(1936); COUNTRY DOCTOR, THE(1936); GIRLS' DORMITORY(1936); MEET NERO WOLFE(1936); REUNION(1936); RING AROUND THE MOON(1936); ROAD TO GLORY, THE(1936); WHIPSAW(1936); WIFE VERSUS SECRETARY(1936); ANGEL'S HOLIDAY(1937); FIFTY ROADS TO TOWN(1937); FIT FOR A KING(1937); NOTHING SACRED(1937); SEVENTH HEAVEN(1937); SHE HAD TO EAT(1937); BAD MAN OF BRIMSTONE(1938); CHASER, THE(1938); FIVE OF A KIND(1938); JOY OF LIVING(1938); MAD MISS MANTON, THE(1938); TEXANS, THE(1938); HONEYMOON IN BALI(1939); LET US LIVE(1939); MICKEY, THE KID(1939); STAND UP AND FIGHT(1939); STRANGE CASE OF DR. MEADE(1939); THUNDER AFLOAT(1939); ANGELS OVER BROADWAY(1940); BABIES FOR SALE(1940); BLONDIE ON A BUDGET(1940); GRAPES OF WRATH(1940); HIS GIRL FRIDAY(1940); KNUTE ROCKNE–ALL AMERICAN(1940); LONG VOYAGE HOME, THE(1940); ON THEIR OWN(1940); SKI PATROL(1940); YOUTH WILL BE SERVED(1940); DEVIL AND DANIEL WEBSTER, THE(1941); MILLION DOLLAR BABY(1941); MODEL WIFE(1941); NEW WINE(1941); OUT OF THE FOG(1941); SHEPHERD OF THE HILLS, THE(1941); ARABIAN NIGHTS(1942); CASABLANCA(1942); JUNGLE BOOK(1942); LARCENY, INC.(1942); TORTILLA FLAT(1942); SWING SHIFT MAISIE(1943); AMERICAN ROMANCE, AN(1944); DARK WATERS(1944); IMPOSTER, THE(1944); ADVENTURE(1945); CAPTAIN KIDD(1945); RIVER GANG(1945); ROUGHLY SPEAKING(1945); FUGITIVE, THE(1947); HIGH CONQUEST(1947); SONG OF SCHEHERAZADE(1947); ALIAS A GENTLEMAN(1948); HOLLOW TRIUMPH(1948); MY GIRL TISA(1948); SIXTEEN FATHOMS DEEP(1948); BIG STEAL, THE(1949); CAPTAIN CHINA(1949); BUCCANEER'S GIRL(1950); FLYING MISSILE(1950); JACKPOT, THE(1950); WOMAN ON THE RUN(1950); BELLE LE GRAND(1951); GOODBYE, MY FANCY(1951); HANS CHRISTIAN ANDERSEN(1952); AMBUSH AT TOMAHAWK GAP(1953); I, THE JURY(1953); HIGH AND THE MIGHTY, THE(1954); OTHER WOMAN, THE(1954); PASSION(1954); STUDENT PRINCE, THE(1954); AT GUN-

POINT(1955); SEA CHASE, THE(1955); UNCHAINED(1955); JOHNNY CONCHO(1956); SEARCHERS, THE(1956); BIG LAND, THE(1957); GUN RUNNERS, THE(1958); MY WORLD DIES SCREAMING(1958); REVOLT IN THE BIG HOUSE(1958); ANATOMY OF A MURDER(1959); HELL BENT FOR LEATHER(1960); NORTH TO ALASKA(1960); TWO RODE TOGETHER(1961); MAN WHO SHOT LIBERTY VALANCE, THE(1962); PRIZE, THE(1963); CHEYENNE AUTUMN(1964); SEVEN FACES OF DR. LAO(1964); THOSE CALLOWAYS(1964); I'LL TAKE SWEDEN(1965); PATCH OF BLUE, A(1965); SONS OF KATIE ELDER, THE(1965); BIG HAND FOR THE LITTLE LADY, A(1966); ADVENTURES OF BULLWHIP GRIFFIN, THE(1967); FIRECREEK(1968); P.J.(1968); HAIL, HERO!(1969); FRASIER, THE SENSUOUS LION(1973)
Misc. Talkies
OUTSIDE THE LAW(1938)

John M. Qualen
SING AND LIKE IT(1934); UPPER WORLD(1934); CHARLIE CHAN IN PARIS(1935); ONE MORE SPRING(1935)

Kathy Qualen
BAD AND THE BEAUTIFUL, THE(1952); YOU FOR ME(1952)

Jose Qualglio
VICE AND VIRTUE(1965, Fr./Ital.)

Gertrude Quality
GODLESS GIRL, THE(1929)
Silents
SCARLET LILY, THE(1923); KING OF KINGS, THE(1927)

John Qualls
WILD AND THE INNOCENT, THE(1959)
1984
LOVE STREAMS(1984)

Helmut Qualtinger
CASTLE, THE(1969, Ger.); END OF THE GAME(1976, Ger./Ital.)

James Quamo
1984
NATURAL, THE(1984)

Helen Quan
ADVENTURES OF MARCO POLO, THE(1938)

Henry Quan
PORTRAIT IN BLACK(1960)

Henry S. Quan
LEFT HAND OF GOD, THE(1955); LOVE IS A MANY-SPLENDORED THING(1955)

Ke Huy Quan
1984
INDIANA JONES AND THE TEMPLE OF DOOM(1984)

Moon Quan
GOLDEN GATE GIRL(1941), a, w, ed

Stella Quan
1984
EL NORTE(1984)

Mohy Quandour
SPECTRE OF EDGAR ALLAN POE, THE(1974), p&d, w

Paul Quandt
MY BODYGUARD(1980)

Mohy Quandur
Misc. Talkies
SPECTRE OF EDGAR ALLAN POE(1973), d

Mary Quant
HAUNTING, THE(1963), cos; SING AND SWING(1964, Brit.), cos; GEORGY GIRL(1966, Brit.), cos; TWO FOR THE ROAD(1967, Brit.), cos

Gianni Quaranta
BROTHER SUN, SISTER MOON(1973, Brit./Ital.), art d; LA TRAVIATA(1982), art d; TEMPEST(1982), art d

Lidia Quaranta
Silents
CABIRIA(1914, Ital.)

Isabella Quarantotti
YESTERDAY, TODAY, AND TOMORROW(1964, Ital./Fr.), w; KISS THE OTHER SHEIK(1968, Fr./Ital.), w

Lincoln Quarberg
I'LL TELL THE WORLD(1934), w

Aaron Quarles
1984
GOODBYE PEOPLE, THE(1984), makeup

Caetano Quarraro
SECRET SEVEN, THE(1966, Ital./Span.)

Iain Quarrier
FLEDGLINGS(1965, Brit.); SEPARATION(1968, Brit.); ONE PLUS ONE(1969, Brit.), a, p; WONDERWALL(1969, Brit.)

Iain Quarrier
CUL-DE-SAC(1966, Brit.); FEARLESS VAMPIRE KILLERS, OR PARDON ME BUT YOUR TEETH ARE IN MY NECK, THE(1967)

Robert Quarry
HOUSE OF BAMBOO(1955); SOLDIER OF FORTUNE(1955); KISS BEFORE DYING, A(1956); CRIME OF PASSION(1957); AGENT FOR H.A.R.M.(1966); WINNING(1969); COUNT YORGA, VAMPIRE(1970); RETURN OF COUNT YORGA, THE(1971); DEATHMASTER, THE(1972); DOCTOR PHIBES RISES AGAIN(1972, Brit.); MADHOUSE(1974, Brit.); MIDNIGHT MAN, THE(1974); SUGAR HILL(1974); ROLLERCOASTER(1977)

Hugh Quarshie
DOGS OF WAR, THE(1980, Brit.)

William Quarshie
1984
ELEMENT OF CRIME, THE(1984, Den.), w

Gaetano Quartaro
OMICRON(1963, Ital.)

Gladys Quartaro
Silents
DRIFTIN' SANDS(1928)

Nena Quartaro
MEN OF THE NORTH(1930); BACHELOR FATHER(1931); GOD'S GIFT TO WOMEN(1931); MEN ARE LIKE THAT(1931); CYCLONE RANGER(1935); THREE MESQUITEERS, THE(1936); TWO IN A CROWD(1936); WIFE VERSUS SECRETARY(1936);

LEFT-HANDED LAW(1937); GREEN HELL(1940)

Nina Quartaro
GOLDEN DAWN(1930); MAN FROM MONTEREY, THE(1933)
Misc. Talkies
UNDERWORLD TERROR(1936)
Silents
RED MARK, THE(1928); ETERNAL WOMAN, THE(1929)

Charles Quartermaine
BISHOP MURDER CASE, THE(1930); REDEMPTION(1930); MAN OF MAY-
FAIR(1931, Brit.); DRAKE THE PIRATE(1935, Brit.); CITADEL, THE(1938)
Silents
AUCTION MART, THE(1920, Brit.); FACE AT THE WINDOW, THE(1920, Brit.);
ELEVENTH COMMANDMENT, THE(1924, Brit.)
Misc. Silents
LADY CLARE, THE(1919, Brit.); WESTWARD HO!(1919, Brit.)

Leon Quartermaine
DARK WORLD(1935, Brit.); ESCAPE ME NEVER(1935, Brit.); AS YOU LIKE IT(1936,
Brit.)
Misc. Silents
SETTLED OUT OF COURT(1925, Brit.)

Nena Quartero
VIRGINIAN, THE(1929); FIGHTING SHERIFF, THE(1931); TRAPPED(1931); DE-
VIL'S BROTHER, THE(1933); MONKEY'S PAW, THE(1933); UNDER SECRET OR-
DERS(1933); PHANTOM OF SANTA FE(1937); OUTLAW, THE(1943)

Nina Quartero
FROZEN RIVER(1929); ONE STOLEN NIGHT(1929); REDEEMING SIN, THE(1929);
ISLE OF ESCAPE(1930); LADY TAKES A CHANCE, A(1943)

Harry Quashie
DIAMOND CITY(1949, Brit.); STRANGER IN BETWEEN, THE(1952, Brit.); SIM-
BA(1955, Brit.); SAFARI(1956); PASSIONATE SUMMER(1959, Brit.)

Maria Quasimodo
PULP(1972, Brit.)

Salvatore Quasimodo
LA NOTTE(1961, Fr./Ital.)

John Quastler
SHOOT IT: BLACK, SHOOT IT: BLUE(1974)

Charles Quatermaine
THIRTEENTH CHAIR, THE(1930)

Marisa Quattrini
PLAYGIRLS AND THE VAMPIRE(1964, Ital.)

Paola Quattrini
STORMBOUND(1951, Ital.)

Frank Quattrocchi
PROJECTED MAN, THE(1967, Brit.), w

Joe Quattromani
TRENCHCOAT(1983)

Asa Quawee
GLORIA(1980)

Anna Quayle
HARD DAY'S NIGHT, A(1964, Brit.); ARRIVEDERCI, BABY!(1966, Brit.); SAND-
WICH MAN, THE(1966, Brit.); CASINO ROYALE(1967, Brit.); SMASHING TIME(1967
Brit.); CHITTY CHITTY BANG BANG(1968, Brit.); UP THE CHASTITY BELT(1971,
Brit.); SEVEN-PER-CENT SOLUTION, THE(1977, Brit.)
Misc. Talkies
MISTRESS PAMELA(1974)

Anthony Quayle
PYGMALION(1938, Brit.); HAMLET(1948, Brit.); SARABAND(1949, Brit.); OH ROSA-
LINDA(1956, Brit.); WRONG MAN, THE(1956); NO TIME FOR TEARS(1957, Brit.);
PURSUIT OF THE GRAF SPEE(1957, Brit.); WOMEN IN A DRESSING GOWN(1957,
Brit.); DESERT ATTACK(1958, Brit.); MAN WHO WOULDN'T TALK, THE(1958, Brit.);
TARZAN'S GREATEST ADVENTURE(1959, Brit.); IT TAKES A THIEF(1960, Brit.);
GUNS OF NAVARONE, THE(1961); DAMN THE DEFIANT!(1962, Brit.); IMMORAL
CHARGE(1962, Brit.); LAWRENCE OF ARABIA(1962, Brit.); EAST OF SUDAN(1964,
Brit.); FALL OF THE ROMAN EMPIRE, THE(1964); OPERATION CROSSBOW(1965,
U.S./Ital.); POPPY IS ALSO A FLOWER, THE(1966); STUDY IN TERROR, A(1966,
Brit./Ger.); ANNE OF THE THOUSAND DAYS(1969, Brit.); BEFORE WINTER
COMES(1969, Brit.); MACKENNA'S GOLD(1969); EVERYTHING YOU ALWAYS
WANTED TO KNOW ABOUT SEX, BUT WE'RE AFRAID TO ASK(1972); NELSON
AFFAIR, THE(1973, Brit.); TAMARIND SEED, THE(1974, Brit.); GREAT EXPECTA-
TIONS(1975, Brit.); EAGLE HAS LANDED, THE(1976, Brit.); MOSES(1976, Brit./Ital.);
CHOSEN, THE(1978, Brit./Ital.); MURDER BY DECREE(1979, Brit.)

Bernard Quayle
TRAVELLER'S JOY(1951, Brit.), w

Deborah Quayle
1984
DELIVERY BOYS(1984)

John Quayle
NIGHT TRAIN TO PARIS(1964, Brit.); PRIVATES ON PARADE(1982)
1984
PRIVATES ON PARADE(1984, Brit.)

Lawrie Quayle
REMEMBRANCE(1982, Brit.)

Harriet Qubeka
PENNYWHISTLE BLUES, THE(1952, South Africa)

William C. Quealy
MY FAVORITE SPY(1951)

Gilles Queant
EAGLE WITH TWO HEADS(1948, Fr.); RUY BLAS(1948, Fr.); ODETTE(1951, Brit.);
NIGHT WITHOUT STARS(1953, Brit.); ROYAL AFFAIRS IN VERSAILLES(1957, Fr.);
LAST YEAR AT MARIENBAD(1962, Fr./Ital.); VERY PRIVATE AFFAIR, A(1962,
Fr./Ital.); MY LIFE TO LIVE(1963, Fr.); SIX IN PARIS(1968, Fr.)

Eunice Quedens [Eve Arden]
SONG OF LOVE, THE(1929)

Ellery Queen
SPANISH CAPE MYSTERY(1935), w; CRIME NOBOBY SAW, THE(1937), w; MAN-
DARIN MYSTERY, THE(1937), w; ELLERY QUEEN. MASTER DETECTIVE(1940), w;
ELLERY QUEEN AND THE MURDER RING(1941), w; ELLERY QUEEN AND THE
PERFECT CRIME(1941), w; ELLERY QUEEN'S PENTHOUSE MYSTERY(1941), w;
CLOSE CALL FOR ELLERY QUEEN, A(1942), w; DESPERATE CHANCE FOR
ELLERY QUEEN, A(1942), w; ENEMY AGENTS MEET ELLERY QUEEN(1942), w

Ellery Queen [Frederic Dannay and Manfred B. Lee]
TEN DAYS' WONDER(1972, Fr.), w

Elizabeth Queen [Flora Caroselli]
TOMB OF TORTURE(1966, Ital.)

Queen Mary Dancers
DARK SIDE OF TOMORROW, THE(1970), m

Edward Queen-Mason
HIGH ROLLING(1977, Aus.), ed; PATRICK(1979, Aus.), ed

Queenie the Dog
Silents
PECK'S BAD BOY(1921); DESERTED AT THE ALTAR(1922); TROUBLE(1922)

Alice Queensberry
Silents
GENTLEMAN OF LEISURE, A(1923)

Ann Queensberry
JULIA(1977)

Edgar M. Queeny
WAKAMBA!(1955), p&d, ph

Alain Queffeleah
FIRE WITHIN, THE(1964, Fr./Ital.), p

Alain Queffelean
1984
ERENDIRA(1984, Mex./Fr./Ger.), p

Antonio Queipo
HYPNOSIS(1966, Ger./Sp./Ital.)

Gabriel Queiroz
TARZAN AND THE JUNGLE BOY(1968, US/Switz.), spec eff

German Quejido
TOWN CALLED HELL, A(1971, Span./Brit.), set d

Daneil Quenaud
BRIEF VACATION, A(1975, Ital.)

Raymond Queneau
LOVERS, HAPPY LOVERS!(1955, Brit.), w; GINA(1961, Fr./Mex.), w; ZAZIE(1961,
Fr.), w; LANDRU(1963, Fr./Ital); DEATH IN THE GARDEN(1977, Fr./Mex.), w

Valerie Quenessen
LIKE A TURTLE ON ITS BACK(1981, Fr.)

Yvonne Quenet
SECRETS OF SEX(1970, Brit.)
Misc. Talkies
BIZARRE(1969)

Peter Quennell
BAD LORD BYRON, THE(1949, Brit.), w

Valerie Quennessen
FRENCH POSTCARDS(1979); SUMMER LOVERS(1982)

Isa Quensel
MAKE WAY FOR LILA(1962, Swed./Ger.); TO LOVE(1964, Swed.); TWO LIVING,
ONE DEAD(1964, Brit./Swed.); SWEDISH WEDDING NIGHT(1965, Swed.); LOVING
COUPLES(1966, Swed.); LOVE MATES(1967, Swed.); WOMAN OF DARKNESS(1968,
Swed.)

Alexis Quentin
1984
A NOS AMOURS(1984, Fr.)

Caroline Quentin
PARTY PARTY(1983, Brit.)

Dolores Quentin
I NEVER PROMISED YOU A ROSE GARDEN(1977)

John Quentin
ISADORA(1968, Brit.); MAN AT THE TOP(1973, Brit.); TERRORISTS, THE(1975,
Brit.); DOGS OF WAR, THE(1980, Brit.)

Patrick Quentin
HOMICIDE FOR THREE(1948), w; BLACK WIDOW(1954), w; FEMALE
FIENDS(1958, Brit.), w; MAN IN THE NET, THE(1959), w

Shirley Quentin
NO WAY BACK(1949, Brit.); TEMPTRESS, THE(1949, Brit.)

Stanley Quentin
LOOK BEFORE YOU LOVE(1948, Brit.)

Therese Quentin
LAST ADVENTURE, THE(1968, Fr./Ital.); WANDERER, THE(1969, Fr.)

Elias Querejeta
HUNT, THE(1967, Span.), p

Ellas Querejeta
SPIRIT OF THE BEEHIVE, THE(1976, Span.), p

Francisco J. Querejeta
SPIRIT OF THE BEEHIVE, THE(1976, Span.), w

Cynette Quero
CHILDREN OF PARADISE(1945, Fr.)

Giovanni Querrel
LA DOLCE VITA(1961, Ital./Fr.)

Aludin Quershi
LIVING FREE(1972, Brit.)

Cesareo Quesada
LITTLE RED RIDING HOOD AND THE MONSTERS(1965, Mex.); TOM
THUMB(1967, Mex.)

Milo Quesada
YOUNG RACERS, THE(1963); EVIL EYE(1964 Ital.); TENTH VICTIM, THE(1965,
Fr./Ital.); DJANGO KILL(1967, Ital./Span.); SAVAGE PAMPAS(1967, Span./Arg.);
MERCENARY, THE(1970, Ital./Span.); CAULDRON OF BLOOD(1971, Span.)

Hans Quest
MAGIC FIRE(1956); ETERNAL LOVE(1960, Ger.); SERPENT'S EGG, THE(1977,
Ger./U.S.)

John Quested
LEOPARD IN THE SNOW(1979, Brit./Can.), p; PASSAGE, THE(1979, Brit.), p;
LOOPHOLE(1981, Brit.), d
Misc. Talkies
PHILADELPHIA HERE I COME(1975), d

Mae Questel
MAJORITY OF ONE, A(1961); IT'S ONLY MONEY(1962); FUNNY GIRL(1968);
MOVE(1970)

Hugues Quester
LA NUIT DE VARENNES(1983, Fr./Ital.)
Giulio Questi
LA DOLCE VITA(1961, Ital./Fr.); DJANGO KILL(1967, Ital./Span.), p&d
Guilio Questi
PLUCKED(1969, Fr./Ital.), d, w
Roberto Quezada
UNSEEN, THE(1981), ph
Bob Do Qui
CLARENCE, THE CROSS-EYED LION(1965)
Robert Do Qui
CINCINNATI KID, THE(1965)
Quianna
ARCTIC MANHUNT(1949)
Kevin Quibel
1984
GRANDVIEW, U.S.A.(1984), spec eff
Al Quick
GLORY STOMPERS, THE(1967); CURIOUS FEMALE, THE(1969)
Diana Quick
NICHOLAS AND ALEXANDRA(1971, Brit.); PRIVATE ENTERPRISE, A(1975, Brit.); DUELLISTS, THE(1977, Brit.); BIG SLEEP, THE½(1978, Brit.); ODD JOB, THE(1978, Brit.)
1984
ORDEAL BY INNOCENCE(1984, Brit.); 1919(1984, Brit.)
Eldon Quick
IN THE HEAT OF THE NIGHT(1967); VIVA MAX!(1969); HOMEBODIES(1974); DOC SAVAGE... THE MAN OF BRONZE(1975); HOW COME NOBODY'S ON OUR SIDE?(1975)
Jean Quick
NEOPOLITAN CAROUSEL(1961, Ital.)
Jim Quick
ROAD HUSTLERS, THE(1968)
Louise Quick
SWEET CHARITY(1969); CABARET(1972)
Celia Quicke
HOUSE OF WHIPCORD(1974, Brit.)
Ian Quicke
HANNIE CALDER(1971, Brit.), w
Gisela Quicker
GREAT BRITISH TRAIN ROBBERY, THE(1967, Ger.), ed
Leslie Quickley
FAME(1980)

Quicksilver Messenger Service
CAPTAIN MILKSHAKE(1970), m
Kruno Quien
KAYA, I'LL KILL YOU(1969, Yugo./Fr.), w; EVENT, AN(1970, Yugo.), w
Dan Quig
HER LUCKY NIGHT(1945)
Dan Quigg
THEY WERE EXPENDABLE(1945); POSTMAN ALWAYS RINGS TWICE, THE(1946); HIGH WALL, THE(1947); HOMECOMING(1948)
Baby Jane "Juanita" Quigley
IMITATION OF LIFE(1934); MAN WHO RECLAIMED HIS HEAD, THE(1935); STRAIGHT FROM THE HEART(1935); BORN TO DANCE(1936); DEVIL DOLL, THE(1936); RIFF-RAFF(1936); DEVIL'S PARTY, THE(1938); HAVING WONDERFUL TIME(1938); HAWAII CALLS(1938); MEN WITH WINGS(1938); THAT CERTAIN AGE(1938); WOMAN AGAINST WOMAN(1938); YOU AND ME(1938); CODE OF THE STREETS(1939); FAMILY NEXT DOOR, THE(1939); OH JOHNNY, HOW YOU CAN LOVE!(1940); BACHELOR DADDY(1941); VANISHING VIRGINIAN, THE(1941); YANK AT ETON, A(1942); HAPPY LAND(1943); WHISPERING FOOTSTEPS(1943); LADY AND THE MONSTER, THE(1944); NATIONAL VELVET(1944); LUXURY LINER(1948); MYSTERY STREET(1950)
Bob Quigley
LAND OF MISSING MEN, THE(1930), w; AT THE RIDGE(1931), w
Charles Quigley
SADDLE BUSTER, THE(1932); AND SUDDEN DEATH(1936); CHARLIE CHAN'S SECRET(1936); KING OF BURLESQUE(1936); LADY FROM NOWHERE(1936); FIND THE WITNESS(1937); GAME THAT KILLS, THE(1937); GIRLS CAN PLAY(1937); SHADOW, THE(1937); SPEED TO SPARE(1937); CONVICTED(1938); HEROES IN BLUE(1939); SPECIAL INSPECTOR(1939); KITTY FOYLE(1940); MEN AGAINST THE SKY(1940); MEXICAN SPITFIRE OUT WEST(1940); PLAY GIRL(1940); FOOTLIGHT FEVER(1941); SAINT IN PALM SPRINGS, THE(1941); SECRET EVIDENCE(1941); YOKEL BOY(1942); I LOVE A SOLDIER(1944); NATIONAL BARN DANCE(1944); DUFFY'S TAVERN(1945); AFFAIRS OF GERALDINE(1946); CYCLOTRODE X(1946); LARCENY IN HER HEART(1946); DANGER STREET(1947); THREE ON A TICKET(1947); COWBOY AND THE INDIANS, THE(1949); DAVID HARDING, COUNTERSPY(1950); UNMASKED(1950)
Misc. Talkies
BROKEN HEARTS(1933)
Clint Quigley
LOST, LONELY AND VICIOUS(1958)
Don Quigley
1984
MUPPETS TAKE MANHATTAN, THE(1984)
George P. Quigley
SARUMBA(1950), p
Misc. Talkies
MURDER WITH MUSIC(1941), d
Godfrey Quigley
SAINTS AND SINNERS(1949, Brit.); RISING OF THE MOON, THE(1957, Ireland); ROONEY(1958, Brit.); BROTH OF A BOY(1959, Brit.); SIEGE OF SIDNEY STREET, THE(1960, Brit.); DEAD MAN'S EVIDENCE(1962, Brit.); NOTHING BUT THE BEST(1964, Brit.); COUNTERFEIT CONSTABLE, THE(1966, Fr.); DALEKS–INVASION EARTH 2155 A.D.(1966, Brit.); GUNS IN THE HEATHER(1968, Brit.); CLOCKWORK ORANGE, A(1971, Brit.); GET CARTER(1971, Brit.); RECKONING, THE(1971, Brit.); BARRY LYNDON(1975, Brit.); EDUCATING RITA(1983)

Lee Quigley
SUPERMAN(1978)
Linnea Quigley
YOUNG WARRIORS(1983)
1984
BLACK ROOM, THE(1984); SAVAGE STREETS(1984); SILENT NIGHT, DEADLY NIGHT(1984)
Misc. Talkies
FAIRY TALES(1979); DON'T GO NEAR THE PARK(1981)
Rita Quigley
HOWARDS OF VIRGINIA, THE(1940); SUSAN AND GOD(1940); THIRD FINGER, LEFT HAND(1940); BLONDE INSPIRATION(1941); JENNIE(1941); RIDE, KELLY, RIDE(1941); RIOT SQUAD(1941); HENRY ALDRICH, EDITOR(1942); KEEPER OF THE FLAME(1942); HUMAN COMEDY, THE(1943); ISLE OF FORGOTTEN SINS(1943); WHISPERING FOOTSTEPS(1943); WOMEN IN BONDAGE(1943); TRAP, THE(1947)
Robert Quigley
NEAR THE TRAIL'S END(1931), w; SHOTGUN PASS(1932), w; RUSTY RIDES ALONE(1933), w; BEFORE MIDNIGHT(1934), w; GUN JUSTICE(1934), w
Jean-Roland Quignon
THUNDER IN THE BLOOD(1962, Fr.), art d
John Quihas
COOL AND THE CRAZY, THE(1958)
John M. Quijada
HUD(1963)
John Michael Quijada
ONE-EYED JACKS(1961)
Folco Quilici
TIKO AND THE SHARK(1966, U.S./Ital./Fr.), d, w
John Quill
ALICE'S RESTAURANT(1969)
John E. Quill
NATURAL ENEMIES(1979), p
Baby Bobby Quillan
SWISS FAMILY ROBINSON(1940)
Eddie Quillan
SHOW FOLKS(1928); GERALDINE(1929); GODLESS GIRL, THE(1929); NOISY NEIGHBORS(1929); SOPHOMORE, THE(1929); BIG MONEY(1930); NIGHT WORK(1930); BIG SHOT, THE(1931); SWEEPSTAKES(1931); TIP-OFF, THE(1931); GIRL CRAZY(1932); BROADWAY TO HOLLYWOOD(1933); STRICTLY PERSONAL(1933); HOLLYWOOD PARTY(1934); GRIDIRON FLASH(1935); MUTINY ON THE BOUNTY(1935); BIG CITY(1937); LONDON BY NIGHT(1937); MANDARIN MYSTERY, THE(1937); SWING, SISTER, SWING(1938); ALLEGHENY UPRISING(1939); FAMILY NEXT DOOR, THE(1939); FLYING IRISHMAN, THE(1939); HAWAIIAN NIGHTS(1939); MADE FOR EACH OTHER(1939); YOUNG MR. LINCOLN(1939); DANCING ON A DIME(1940); DARK STREETS OF CAIRO(1940); GRAPES OF WRATH(1940); LA CONGA NIGHTS(1940); MARGIE(1940); FLAME OF NEW ORLEANS, THE(1941); FLYING BLIND(1941); SIX LESSONS FROM MADAME LA ZONGA(1941); TOO MANY BLONDES(1941); WHERE DID YOU GET THAT GIRL?(1941); KID GLOVE KILLER(1942); PRIORITIES ON PARADE(1942); ALASKA HIGHWAY(1943); FOLLOW THE BAND(1943); HERE COMES KELLY(1943); HI' YA, SAILOR(1943); IT AIN'T HAY(1943); MELODY PARADE(1943); DARK MOUNTAIN(1944); HI, GOOD-LOOKIN'(1944); IMPOSTER, THE(1944); MOONLIGHT AND CACTUS(1944); SLIGHTLY TERRIFIC(1944); THIS IS THE LIFE(1944); TWILIGHT ON THE PRAIRIE(1944); DIXIE JAMBOREE(1945); SENSATION HUNTERS(1945); SONG OF THE SARONG(1945); GUY COULD CHANGE, A(1946); SIDESHOW(1950); BRIGADOON(1954); LADIES MAN, THE(1961); WHO'S GOT THE ACTION?(1962); MOVE OVER, DARLING(1963); PROMISES, PROMISES(1963); SUMMER MAGIC(1963); ADVANCE TO THE REAR(1964); GUNFIGHT AT COMANCHE CREEK(1964); VIVA LAS VEGAS(1964); BOUNTY KILLER, THE(1965); GHOST AND MR. CHICKEN, THE(1966); GUIDE FOR THE MARRIED MAN, A(1967); DID YOU HEAR THE ONE ABOUT THE TRAVELING SALESLADY?(1968); ANGEL IN MY POCKET(1969); HOW TO FRAME A FIGG(1971)
Edward Quillan
GENTLEMAN FROM LOUISIANA(1936)
John Quillan
PAGE MISS GLORY(1935); LIVE, LOVE AND LEARN(1937); THIS IS MY AFFAIR(1937)
Joseph Quillan
SHOW BUSINESS(1944), w; SON OF PALEFACE(1952), w; OUR MISS BROOKS(1956), w
Marie Quillan
HURRICANE HORSEMAN(1931); CHEYENNE CYCLONE, THE(1932); SADDLE BUSTER, THE(1932); SINGING VAGABOND, THE(1935)
Ira M. Quillen II
1984
RIVER, THE(1984)
Marie Quillen
MELODY TRAIL(1935)
Silents
CAMPUS KNIGHTS(1929)
Robert Quillen
LIFE BEGINS AT 40(1935), w
Thomas Quillen
PURSUIT(1975), d
Arthur Quiller-Couch
Silents
TRUE TILDA(1920, Brit.), w
Denis Quilley
LIFE AT THE TOP(1965, Brit.); ANNE OF THE THOUSAND DAYS(1969, Brit.); BLACK WINDMILL, THE(1974, Brit.); MURDER ON THE ORIENT EXPRESS(1974, Brit.); EVIL UNDER THE SUN(1982, Brit.); PRIVATES ON PARADE(1982)
1984
MEMED MY HAWK(1984, Brit.)
Dennis Quilley
1984
PRIVATES ON PARADE(1984, Brit.)

John Quillian
SHE COULDN'T TAKE IT(1935)
Veronica Quilligan
MALACHI'S COVE(1973, Brit.); LISZTOMANIA(1975, Brit.); ROBIN AND MA-RIAN(1976, Brit.); CANDLESHOE(1978); ANGEL(1982, Irish)
Ted Quillin
MY SIX LOVES(1963)
David Quilter
DEADLY AFFAIR, THE(1967, Brit.); GIRO CITY(1982, Brit.)
Robert Quilter
INN OF THE DAMNED(1974, Aus.)
Jennifer Quilty
1984
TEACHERS(1984)
Fred Quimby
DANGEROUS WHEN WET(1953), anim; INVITATION TO THE DANCE(1956), anim.
Margaret Quimby
LUCKY BOY(1929); TWO MEN AND A MAID(1929); LADIES LOVE BRUTES(1930); RAMPANT AGE, THE(1930); TRAILING TROUBLE(1930)
Silents
WHAT HAPPENED TO JONES(1926); NEW YORK(1927); WESTERN WHIRLWIND, THE(1927); SALLY OF THE SCANDALS(1928); TRAGEDY OF YOUTH, THE(1928)
Misc. Silents
TIRED BUSINESS MAN, THE(1927); WORLD AT HER FEET, THE(1927)
Richard Quime
FULL OF LIFE(1956), d
Don Quin
GALLIPOLI(1981, Aus.)
John Quin
TIGER BAY(1933, Brit.), w; CHILDREN OF THE FOG(1935, Brit.), d; IMMORTAL GENTLEMAN(1935, Brit.), w; LIVE AGAIN(1936, Brit.), w; ON VELVET(1938, Brit.), w
Louis Quince
DEADLINE AT DAWN(1946); NIGHT AND DAY(1946); NORA PRENTISS(1947)
Peter Quince
CARRY ON ENGLAND(1976, Brit.)
Blaine Quincy
TORTURE ME KISS ME(1970)
Dorothy Quincy
Silents
MAN FROM HOME, THE(1914)
Misc. Silents
ALL FOR A HUSBAND(1917)
Stockton Quincy
Silents
DRIFTER, THE(1916)
Quine
SOUND OFF(1952), w
Don Quine
SULLIVAN'S EMPIRE(1967)
Norma Quine
PROPER TIME, THE(1959)
Richard Quine
COUNSELLOR-AT-LAW(1933); DINKY(1935); DOG OF FLANDERS, A(1935); JANE EYRE(1935); LITTLE MEN(1935); KING OF THE UNDERWORLD(1939); LIFE RE-TURNS(1939); BABES ON BROADWAY(1941); DR. GILLESPIE'S NEW ASSIS-TANT(1942); FOR ME AND MY GAL(1942); MY SISTER EILEEN(1942); STAND BY FOR ACTION(1942); TISH(1942); WE'VE NEVER BEEN LICKED(1943); COCKEYED MIRACLE, THE(1946); COMMAND DECISION(1948); LEATHER GLOVES(1948), p&d; CLAY PIGEON, THE(1949); FLYING MISSILE(1950); NO SAD SONGS FOR ME(1950); ROOKIE FIREMAN(1950); PURPLE HEART DIARY(1951), d; SUNNY SIDE OF THE STREET(1951), d; RAINBOW 'ROUND MY SHOULDER(1952), d, w; SOUND OFF(1952), d; ALL ASHORE(1953), d, w; CRUISIN' DOWN THE RI-VER(1953), d, w; SIREN OF BAGDAD(1953), d; DRIVE A CROOKED ROAD(1954), d, w; PUSHOVER(1954), d; SO THIS IS PARIS(1954), d; BRING YOUR SMILE ALONG(1955), w; MY SISTER EILEEN(1955), d, w; HE LAUGHED LAST(1956), w; SOLID GOLD CADILLAC, THE(1956), d; OPERATION MAD BALL(1957), d; BELL, BOOK AND CANDLE(1958), d; IT HAPPENED TO JANE(1959), p&d; JUKE BOX RHYTHM(1959), m; STRANGERS WHEN WE MEET(1960), p&d; WORLD OF SUZIE WONG, THE(1960), d; NOTORIOUS LANDLADY, THE(1962), d; PARIS WHEN IT SIZZLES(1964), p, d; SEX AND THE SINGLE GIRL(1964), d; HOW TO MURDER YOUR WIFE(1965), d; SYNANON(1965), p&d; HOTEL(1967), d; OH DAD, POOR DAD, MAMA'S HUNG YOU IN THE CLOSET AND I'M FEELIN' SO SAD(1967), d; MOONSHINE WAR, THE(1970), d; W(1974), d; PRISONER OF ZENDA, THE(1979), d
Tom Quine
SEX AND THE SINGLE GIRL(1964); HOW TO STUFF A WILD BIKINI(1965); PARTY, THE(1968)
Bill Quinlan
VIA PONY EXPRESS(1933)
Gertrude Quinlan
Silents
BACK HOME AND BROKE(1922)
Joe Quinlan
METALSTORM: THE DESTRUCTION OF JARED-SYN(1983), spec eff
John L. Quinlan III
SUGARLAND EXPRESS, THE(1974)
Joyce Quinlan
PROJECT X(1949)
Kathleen Quinlan
LIFEGUARD(1976); AIRPORT '77(1977); I NEVER PROMISED YOU A ROSE GARDEN(1977); PROMISE, THE(1979); THE RUNNER STUMBLES(1979); SUNDAY LOVERS(1980, Ital./Fr.); HANKY-PANKY(1982); INDEPENDENCE DAY(1983)
Misc. Talkies
LAST WINTER, THE(1983)
Kathy Quinlan
AMERICAN GRAFFITI(1973)

Noel Quinlan
MAN FROM HONG KONG(1975), m; S.T.A.B.(1976, Hong Kong/Thailand), m
Siobhan Quinlan
ASSAULT(1971, Brit.)
William Quinlan
RED PONY, THE(1949)
Joe Quinlavin
HOSPITAL MASSACRE(1982), spec eff; WACKO(1983), spec eff
Charles Quinlivan
ZERO HOUR!(1957); SEVEN GUNS TO MESA(1958); ALL THE YOUNG MEN(1960)
Joe Quinlivan
REVENGE OF THE NINJA(1983), spec eff
Aidan Quinn
1984
RECKLESS(1984)
Aileen Quinn
ANNIE(1982)
Almeria Quinn
TOP OF THE HEAP(1972)
Anita Quinn
PROUD AND THE DAMNED, THE(1972)
Anthony Quinn
MILKY WAY, THE(1936); NIGHT WAITRESS(1936); PAROLE(1936); SWORN ENE-MY(1936); DAUGHTER OF SHANGHAI(1937); LAST TRAIN FROM MADRID, THE(1937); PARTNERS IN CRIME(1937); PLAINSMAN, THE(1937); SWING HIGH, SWING LOW(1937); WAIKIKI WEDDING(1937); BUCCANEER, THE(1938); BULL-DOG DRUMMOND IN AFRICA(1938); DANGEROUS TO KNOW(1938); HUNTED MEN(1938); KING OF ALCATRAZ(1938); TIP-OFF GIRLS(1938); ISLAND OF LOST MEN(1939); KING OF CHINATOWN(1939); TELEVISION SPY(1939); UNION PACIF-IC(1939); EMERGENCY SQUAD(1940); GHOST BREAKERS, THE(1940); PAROLE FIXER(1940); ROAD TO SINGAPORE(1940); TEXAS RANGERS RIDE AGAIN(1940); BLOOD AND SAND(1941); BULLETS FOR O'HARA(1941); CITY, FOR CON-QUEST(1941); KNOCKOUT(1941); PERFECT SNOB, THE(1941); THIEVES FALL OUT(1941); BLACK SWAN, THE(1942); LARCENY, INC.(1942); ROAD TO MOROC-CO(1942); THEY DIED WITH THEIR BOOTS ON(1942); GUADALCANAL DIA-RY(1943); OX-BOW INCIDENT, THE(1943); BUFFALO BILL(1944); IRISH EYES ARE SMILING(1944); LADIES OF WASHINGTON(1944); ROGER TOUHY, GANG-STER(1944); BACK TO BATAAN(1945); CHINA SKY(1945); WHERE DO WE GO FROM HERE?(1945); CALIFORNIA(1946); BLACK GOLD(1947); IMPERFECT LADY, THE(1947); SINBAD THE SAILOR(1947); TYCOON(1947); BRAVE BULLS, THE(1951); HIGH TREASON(1951, Brit.); MASK OF THE AVENGER(1951); AGAINST ALL FLAGS(1952); BRIGAND, THE(1952); VIVA ZAPATA!(1952); WORLD IN HIS ARMS, THE(1952); BLOWING WILD(1953); CITY BENEATH THE SEA(1953); EAST OF SUMATRA(1953); FATAL DESIRE(1953); RIDE, VAQUERO!(1953); SEMINOLE(1953); LONG WAIT, THE(1954); MAGNIFICENT MATADOR, THE(1955); NAKED STREET, THE(1955); SEVEN CITIES OF GOLD(1955); ULYSSES(1955, Ital.); ANGELS OF DARKNESS(1956, Ital.); LA STRADA(1956, Ital.); LUST FOR LIFE(1956); MAN FROM DEL RIO(1956); WILD PARTY, THE(1956); HUNCHBACK OF NOTRE DAME, THE(1957, Fr.); RIDE BACK, THE(1957); RIVER'S EDGE, THE(1957); WILD IS THE WIND(1957); ATTILA(1958, Ital.); BUCCANEER, THE(1958), d; HOT SPELL(1958); BLACK ORCHID(1959); LAST TRAIN FROM GUN HILL(1959); WARLOCK(1959); HELLER IN PINK TIGHTS(1960); PORTRAIT IN BLACK(1960); SAVAGE INNO-CENTS, THE(1960, Brit.); GUNS OF NAVARONE, THE(1961); BARABBAS(1962, Ital.); LAWRENCE OF ARABIA(1962, Brit.); REQUIEM FOR A HEAVYWEIGHT(1962); BEHOLD A PALE HORSE(1964); VISIT, THE(1964, Ger./Fr./Ital./U.S.), a, p; ZORBA THE GREEK(1964, U.S./Gr.); HIGH WIND IN JAMAICA, A(1965); LOST COMMAND, THE(1966); MARCO THE MAGNIFICENT(1966, Ital./Fr./Yugo./Egypt/Afghanistan); HAPPENING, THE(1967); ROVER, THE(1967, Ital.); 25TH HOUR, THE(1967, Fr./Ital./Yugo.); GUNS FOR SAN SEBASTIAN(1968, U.S./Fr./Mex./Ital.); MAGUS, THE(1968, Brit.); SHOES OF THE FISHERMAN, THE(1968); DREAM OF KINGS, A(1969); SECRET OF SANTA VITTORIA, THE(1969); FLAP(1970); R.P.M.(1970); WALK IN THE SPRING RAIN, A(1970); ACROSS 110TH STREET(1972); DEAF SMITH AND JOHNNY EARS(1973, Ital.); DON IS DEAD, THE(1973); DESTRUCTORS, THE(1974, Brit.); MOHAMMAD, MESSENGER OF GOD(1976, Lebanon/Brit.); CARAVANS(1978, U.S./Iranian); CHILDREN OF SANCHEZ, THE(1978, U. S./Mex.); GREEK TYCOON, THE(1978); INHERITANCE, THE(1978, Ital.); PASSAGE, THE(1979, Brit.); CON ARTISTS, THE(1981, Ital.); HIGH RISK(1981); LION OF THE DESERT(1981, Libya/Brit.); SALAMANDER, THE(1983, U.S./Ital./Brit.)
Misc. Talkies
TARGET OF AN ASSASSIN(1978, S. Africa)
Arthur Quinn
Silents
KENNEDY SQUARE(1916), ph
Barbara Quinn
WILD PARTY, THE(1975); SQUIRM(1976); HE KNOWS YOU'RE ALONE(1980)
Bill Quinn
MOUNTAIN ROAD, THE(1960); DARK INTRUDER(1965); LOVE IS A FUNNY THING(1970, Fr./Ital.); HOW TO FRAME A FIGG(1971); ACE ELI AND RODGER OF THE SKIES(1973); PSYCHIC KILLER(1975); BUSTIN' LOOSE(1981); DEAD AND BURIED(1981); TWILIGHT ZONE-THE MOVIE(1983)
Misc. Talkies
BIG CALIBRE(1935)
Billy Quinn
SWEET JESUS, PREACHER MAN(1973)
Bob Quinn
CRY FOR HAPPY(1961); POITIN(1979, Irish), p&d, ed
Charles Lee Quinn
Misc. Silents
BRONCHO BUSTER, THE(1927)
Dermot Quinn
WHITE HUNTRESS(1957, Brit.), w; DAYLIGHT ROBBERY(1964, Brit.), w
Derry Quinn
YOUNG, WILLING AND EAGER(1962, Brit.), w; OPERATION CROSSBOW(1965, U.S./Ital.), w; TRYGON FACTOR, THE(1969, Brit.), w
Don Quinn
LOOK WHO'S LAUGHING(1941), w; HEAVENLY DAYS(1944), w; PUBLIC PIGEON NO. 1(1957), w

Duncan Quinn
CARAVANS(1978, U.S./Iranian); ECHOES(1983)
Edward Quinn
Misc. Silents
EMPTY CRADLE, THE(1923)
Frank Quinn
HURRY UP OR I'LL BE 30(1973)
Frank P. Quinn
TEACHER'S PET(1958)
Freddy Quinn
FREDDY UNTER FREMDEN STERNEN(1962, Ger.)
George Quinn
SQUARE ROOT OF ZERO, THE(1964)
Howard Quinn
SECRET FURY, THE(1950)
J. C. Quinn
ON THE YARD(1978); FIREPOWER(1979, Brit.); BRUBAKER(1980); TIMES SQUARE(1980); EDDIE MACON'S RUN(1983); SILKWOOD(1983)
1984
C.H.U.D.(1984); PLACES IN THE HEART(1984)
Jack Quinn
EXPOSED(1932)
James Quinn
ARGYLE CASE, THE(1929); JEALOUSY(1934); FURY(1936); TWO IN A CROWD(1936); TOAST OF NEW YORK, THE(1937); TEXANS, THE(1938); HEROSTRATUS(1968, Brit.), p; OVERLORD(1975, Brit.), p; HAMMETT(1982)
Silents
AFRAID TO FIGHT(1922); SECOND HAND LOVE(1923)
James T. Quinn
DANCE OF LIFE, THE(1929)
Jean Quinn
NEANDERTHAL MAN, THE(1953)
Jill Quinn
RAT FINK(1965)
Jimmie Quinn
Silents
PRETTY LADIES(1925); GINSBERG THE GREAT(1927)
Jimmy Quinn
SPIELER, THE(1929); HOLD EVERYTHING(1930)
Silents
RAGS TO RICHES(1922); BROADWAY AFTER DARK(1924); ON THIN ICE(1925); TWO FLAMING YOUTHS(1927)
Misc. Silents
COME AND GET IT(1929)
Joe Quinn
STRAWBERRY STATEMENT, THE(1970); PRETTY MAIDS ALL IN A ROW(1971)
Silents
ARGYLE CASE, THE(1917)
Misc. Silents
UNKNOWN WIFE, THE(1921)
Don Quinn
HERE WE GO AGAIN(1942), w
John Quinn
WEDDING PARTY, THE(1969)
Johnny Quinn
CLINIC, THE(1983, Aus.)
Lewis Quinn
TERROR IN THE JUNGLE(1968), ph
Li Quinn
FISTS OF FURY(1973, Chi.)
Louis Quinn
KILROY WAS HERE(1947), w; TOO MUCH, TOO SOON(1958); AL CAPONE(1959); CROWDED SKY, THE(1960); OCEAN'S ELEVEN(1960); DONDI(1961); GYPSY(1962); FOR THOSE WHO THINK YOUNG(1964); BIRDS DO IT(1966); LAS VEGAS HILLBILLYS(1966); WELCOME TO THE CLUB(1971); UNHOLY ROLLERS(1972); SUPERCHICK(1973)
Misc. Talkies
KEEP OFF! KEEP OFF!(1975)
Mary Quinn
PLOUGH AND THE STARS, THE(1936)
Maureen Quinn
1984
HAMBONE AND HILLIE(1984)
Michael Quinn
WAKE ME WHEN IT'S OVER(1960); DAY OF THE LOCUST, THE(1975); RETURN OF THE JEDI(1983)
Mike Quinn
GREAT MUPPET CAPER, THE(1981); DARK CRYSTAL, THE(1982, Brit.)
Oonagh Quinn
VIOLENT PLAYGROUND(1958, Brit.)
Pat Quinn
ALICE'S RESTAURANT(1969); SHOOT OUT(1971); ZACHARIAH(1971); UNMARRIED WOMAN, AN(1978)
Patricia Quinn
ROCKY HORROR PICTURE SHOW, THE(1975, Brit.); OUTSIDER, THE(1980); SHOCK TREATMENT(1981); MONTY PYTHON'S THE MEANING OF LIFE(1983, Brit.)
Peter Quinn
RED DRESS, THE(1954, Brit.), w
Phyllis Quinn
REAL LIFE(1979)
Ray Quinn
TARANTULA(1955); I'VE LIVED BEFORE(1956)
Raymond J. Quinn
GHOST STORY(1981)
Regina Quinn
Silents
AMERICAN BUDS(1918); BRAVE AND BOLD(1918); OTHER MEN'S DAUGHTERS(1918); OTHER MAN'S WIFE, THE(1919)

Misc. Silents
PRIDE OF NEW YORK, THE(1917); I'LL SAY SO(1918); FROM NOW ON(1920)
Rick Quinn
Misc. Talkies
BUFFALO RIDER(1978)
Spencer Quinn
UNHOLY ROLLERS(1972), art d; LITTLE DRAGONS, THE(1980), art d; SECONDHAND HEARTS(1981)
Tandra Quinn
PROBLEM GIRLS(1953); MESA OF LOST WOMEN, THE(1956)
Teddy Quinn
MADAME X(1966); TAMMY AND THE MILLIONAIRE(1967); BALLAD OF JOSIE(1968); 80 STEPS TO JONAH(1969)
Misc. Talkies
BLACK HOOKER(1974)
Terry Quinn
NECROMANCY(1972)
Thomas Quinn
WESTLAND CASE, THE(1937); SPIRIT OF STANFORD, THE(1942); PRACTICALLY YOURS(1944); SOUP FOR ONE(1982)
Thomas R. Quinn
COUNTY FAIR, THE(1932)
Tom Quinn
TRADE WINDS(1938); VIVACIOUS LADY(1938); IRENE(1940); KITTY FOYLE(1940); I WANTED WINGS(1941); DOUGHGIRLS, THE(1944); GHOST GUNS(1944); LAND OF THE OUTLAWS(1944); LAW OF THE VALLEY(1944); SHINE ON, HARVEST MOON(1944); FLAME OF THE WEST(1945); NAVAJO TRAIL, THE(1945); BORDER BANDITS(1946); KID FROM BOOKLYN, THE(1946); MAN I LOVE, THE(1946); MY REPUTATION(1946); SONG OF ARIZONA(1946); TWO SMART PEOPLE(1946); UNDER NEVADA SKIES(1946); HIGH WALL, THE(1947); MICHIGAN KID, THE(1947); CRASHING THRU(1949); STRIP, THE(1951); STORY OF THREE LOVES, THE(1953); LOVE IN A GOLDFISH BOWL(1961); KING OF THE GYPSIES(1978); NUNZIO(1978); ...AND JUSTICE FOR ALL(1979); VOICES(1979)
Misc. Talkies
PICK-UP(1975)
Tommy Quinn
KING OF THE TURF(1939); GIRL, A GUY AND A GOB, A(1941); DEADLINE AT DAWN(1946)
Tony Quinn
LEST WE FORGET(1934, Brit.); NON-STOP NEW YORK(1937, Brit.); RIVER OF UNREST(1937, Brit.); DANNY BOY(1941, Brit.); UNPUBLISHED STORY(1942, Brit.); IT'S IN THE BAG(1943, Brit.); SAINT MEETS THE TIGER, THE(1943, Brit.); THUNDER ROCK(1944, Brit.); WELCOME, MR. WASHINGTON(1944, Brit.); HUNGRY HILL(1947, Brit.); UNEASY TERMS(1948, Brit.); DIAMOND CITY(1949, Brit.); SAINTS AND SINNERS(1949, Brit.); DON'T SAY DIE(1950, Brit.); YOU CAN'T FOOL AN IRISHMAN(1950, Ireland); LAVENDER HILL MOB, THE(1951, Brit.); LONG DARK HALL, THE(1951, Brit.); GENTLE GUNMAN, THE(1952, Brit.); GLORY AT SEA(1952, Brit.); TREASURE HUNT(1952, Brit.); YOU CAN'T BEAT THE IRISH(1952, Brit.); SEE HOW THEY RUN(1955, Brit.); SHADOW OF A MAN(1955, Brit.); THE BEACHCOMBER(1955, Brit.); LAST MAN TO HANG, THE(1956, Brit.); TONS OF TROUBLE(1956, Brit.); BOOBY TRAP(1957, Brit.); MAN WITHOUT A BODY, THE(1957, Brit.); OPERATION MURDER(1957, Brit.); RISING OF THE MOON, THE(1957, Ireland); STORY OF ESTHER COSTELLO, THE(1957, Brit.); UNDERCOVER GIRL(1957, Brit.); LIFE IN EMERGENCY WARD 10(1959, Brit.); CIRCLE OF DECEPTON(1961, Brit.); TRUNK, THE(1961, Brit.); UNSTOPPABLE MAN, THE(1961, Brit.); GREAT VAN ROBBERY, THE(1963, Brit.); HIDE AND SEEK(1964, Brit.); IN TROUBLE WITH EVE(1964, Brit.); MURDER AHOY(1964, Brit.); RUNAWAY, THE(1964, Brit.)
William Quinn
LAW AND LAWLESS(1932); FLYING FONTAINES, THE(1959); FROM THE TERRACE(1960); YOUNG SAVAGES, THE(1961); ADVISE AND CONSENT(1962); FIVE FINGER EXERCISE(1962); FBI CODE 98(1964)
Silents
ARIZONA CATCLAW, THE(1919); DEVIL'S TRAIL, THE(1919); OLD MAID'S BABY, THE(1919); CHORUS GIRL'S ROMANCE, A(1920); OCCASIONALLY YOURS(1920); KINGFISHER'S ROOST, THE(1922); LURE OF GOLD(1922); WOLF LAW(1922); NO MOTHER TO GUIDE HER(1923); GYPSY OF THE NORTH(1928); MY HOME TOWN(1928)
Misc. Silents
HERITAGE OF HATE, THE(1916); LOVE'S LARIAT(1916); SIRENS OF THE SEA(1917); MARRIAGE LIE, THE(1918); WINNING GRANDMA(1918); SAWDUST DOLL, THE(1919); HELL'S OASIS(1920); HEART OF A TEXAN, THE(1922); HEART OF LINCOLN, THE(1922); TABLE TOP RANCH(1922); WEST OF THE PECOS(1922); FIGHTING STRAIN, THE(1923)
William J. Quinn
Misc. Silents
CALLED BACK(1914)
William Jack Quinn
Silents
NO-GUN MAN, THE(1924)
William T. Quinn
WHEN THE BOYS MEET THE GIRLS(1965)
Ken Quinnell
CATHY'S CHILD(1979, Aus.), w; HOODWINK(1981, Aus.), w
Richard Quinnell
THX 1138(1971)
Valerie Quinnessen
CONAN THE BARBARIAN(1982)
Quino
NEST, THE(1982, Span.)
Adolfo "Shabba Doo" Quinones
1984
BREAKIN'(1984)
Bill Quinones
1984
BAD MANNERS(1984)
Delia Esther Quinones
Misc. Talkies
TWO WORLDS OF ANGELITA, THE(1982)

Jaime Gonzalez Quinones
SEVEN CITIES OF GOLD(1955); CURSE OF THE AZTEC MUMMY, THE(1965, Mex.); ROBOT VS. THE AZTEC MUMMY, THE(1965, Mex.)

Lou Quinones
AARON LOVES ANGELA(1975)

Harvey Quintal
MILESTONES(1975)

Elvira Quintana
CURSE OF THE DOLL PEOPLE, THE(1968, Mex.)

Ernie Quintana
TIMERIDER(1983)

Gene Quintana
COMIN' AT YA!(1981), a, w

Gustavo Quintana
FACE OF TERROR(1964, Span.), p; CHIMES AT MIDNIGHT(1967, Span.,Switz.), prod d

Manuel Quintana
TEXICAN, THE(1966, U.S./Span.)

Baby Quintanilla
BOOM TOWN(1940); FORTY LITTLE MOTHERS(1940)

Barbara Quintanilla
WAGONS ROLL AT NIGHT, THE(1941)

Beverly Quintanilla
WAGONS ROLL AT NIGHT, THE(1941)

Gene Quintano
TREASURE OF THE FOUR CROWNS(1983, Span./U.S.), a, p, w
1984
MAKING THE GRADE(1984), p, w

Jose Quintero
ROMAN SPRING OF MRS. STONE, THE(1961, U.S./Brit.), d

Justo Robles Quintero
SHIP OF FOOLS(1965)

Aroclaw Radio Quintet
ASHES AND DIAMONDS(1961, Pol.), m

Jones Quintet
RACING BLOOD(1938)

Raymond Scott Quintet
ALI BABA GOES TO TOWN(1937)

Quintet from the Hot Club of France
LACOMBE, LUCIEN(1974)

Raymond Scott Quintette
SALLY, IRENE AND MARY(1938)

Quintino
INDISCREET(1958), cos

Robert Quintley [Roberto Cinquini]
SECRET AGENT FIREBALL(1965, Fr./Ital.), ed

Albert Quinton
W.I.A.(WOUNDED IN ACTION)*1/2 (1966)

Dolores Quinton
FOR PETE'S SAKE!(1966)

Adolfo "Shabba-Doo" Quiones
1984
BREAKIN' 2: ELECTRIC BOOGALOO(1984)

Charles Quipley
WOMAN'S FACE(1941)

Rita Quiqley
FIVE LITTLE PEPPERS IN TROUBLE(1940)

Gaston Quiribet
Silents
ONCE ABOARD THE LUGGER(1920, Brit.), d; MR. JUSTICE RAFFLES(1921, Brit.), d

Billy Quirk
Silents
AT THE STAGE DOOR(1921); MAN WORTH WHILE, THE(1921); BRIDE FOR A NIGHT, A(1923); SUCCESS(1923)
Misc. Silents
WEB OF LIFE, THE(1917)

Bobby Quirk
ROAD TO RUIN(1934)

Charles Quirk
SUDDENLY IT'S SPRING(1947); JOAN OF ARC(1948); SOMEBODY LOVES ME(1952); SON OF PALEFACE(1952); SHANE(1953)

Evans Quirk
Silents
KID, THE(1921)

Josephine Quirk
Silents
HER MAD BARGAIN(1921), w; QUESTION OF HONOR, A(1922), w; BLUFF(1924), w

Robert Quirk
ARE THESE OUR CHILDREN?(1931); WOMAN ACCUSED(1933)

William Quirk
Silents
SALOMY JANE(1923)

Pauline Quirke
ELEPHANT MAN, THE(1980, Brit.); RETURN OF THE SOLDIER, THE(1983, Brit.)

Alicia Quiroga
SELF-PORTRAIT(1973, U.S./Chile)

Hector Quiroga
MURIETA(1965, Span.); LOST COMMAND, THE(1966); RETURN OF THE SEVEN(1966, Span.); SON OF A GUNFIGHTER(1966, U.S./Span.); SAVAGE PAMPAS(1967, Span./Arg.); NARCO MEN, THE(1969, Span./Ital.)

Salvador Quiros
LOS OLVIDADOS(1950, Mex.)

Pierre Quiroule
SEXTON BLAKE AND THE HOODED TERROR(1938, Brit.), w

Charley Quirt
TRAIL TO GUNSIGHT(1944); TRIGGER TRAIL(1944)

Max Quismundo
AMBUSH BAY(1966)

David Quitak
TOWN ON TRIAL(1957, Brit.)

Oscar Quitak
OUTSIDER, THE(1949, Brit.); SOMETHING MONEY CAN'T BUY(1952, Brit.); SO LITTLE TIME(1953, Brit.); TOP OF THE FORM(1953, Brit.); ZARAK(1956, Brit.); TOWN ON TRIAL(1957, Brit.); ACCURSED, THE(1958, Brit.); REVENGE OF FRANKENSTEIN, THE(1958, Brit.); OPERATION AMSTERDAM(1960, Brit.)
1984
BLOODBATH AT THE HOUSE OF DEATH(1984, Brit.)

Antonio Quitana
BLOOD WEDDING(1981, Sp.)

Katherine Quittner
PUNISHMENT PARK(1971)

Chris Quivak
YEAR OF LIVING DANGEROUSLY, THE(1982, Aus.)

Marvel Quivey
Silents
NEW LIVES FOR OLD(1925)

Beulah Quo
TWO WEEKS IN ANOTHER TOWN(1962); GIRLS! GIRLS! GIRLS!(1962); SEVENTH DAWN, THE(1964); SAND PEBBLES, THE(1966); CHINATOWN(1974); MAC ARTHUR(1977); YES, GIORGIO(1982)

Marianne Quon
CHINA(1943); CHARLIE CHAN IN THE SECRET SERVICE(1944)

Rose Quong
ELIZA'S HOROSCOPE(1975, Can.)

Don Qureshi
YOU PAY YOUR MONEY(1957, Brit.)

Le Quynh
QUIET AMERICAN, THE(1958); HOA-BINH(1971, Fr.)

John Quzlen
ON OUR MERRY WAY(1948)

A. Martin Qweiback
1984
ULTIMATE SOLUTION OF GRACE QUIGLEY, THE(1984), w

R

Kurt Raab
AMERICAN SOLDIER, THE(1970 Ger.), a, prod d; BITTER TEARS OF PETRA VON KANT, THE(1972, Ger.), art d; EFFI BRIEST(1974, Ger.), art d; FOX AND HIS FRIENDS(1976, Ger.); MOTHER KUSTERS GOES TO HEAVEN(1976, Ger.), a, w, art d; JAIL BAIT(1977, Ger.), a, art d; WHY DOES HERR R. RUN AMOK?(1977, Ger.), a, prod d; BELLA DONNA(1983, Ger.)

Leonid Raab
CRY WOLF(1947, md; HE WALKED BY NIGHT(1948), m; FOLLOW ME QUIET-LY(1949), m; RETURN TO PEYTON PLACE(1961), md

Max Raab
ALL THE RIGHT NOISES(1973, Brit.), p

Elenore Raabe
SPRING BREAK(1983)

Jennifer Raach
PARALLELS(1980, Can.)

Youssef Raad
CIRCLE OF DECEIT(1982, Fr./Ger.)

Henke Raaf
ZERO IN THE UNIVERSE(1966)

Vici Raaf
CHAMPAGNE FOR CAESAR(1950); HE RAN ALL THE WAY(1951); LET'S MAKE IT LEGAL(1951); SECOND WOMAN, THE(1951); DREAMBOAT(1952); CLOWN, THE(1953); LADY WANTS MINK, THE(1953); RUN FOR THE HILLS(1953); FOX-FIRE(1955); ONE DESIRE(1955); SQUAD CAR(1961); YELLOW CANARY, THE(1963)

Vickie Raaf
MAN BEHIND THE GUN, THE(1952)

Jagdish Raaj
TARZAN GOES TO INDIA(1962, U.S./Brit./Switz.)

Prayag Raaj
HOUSEHOLDER, THE(1963, US/India); SHAKESPEARE WALLAH(1966, India); GURU, THE(1969, U.S./India)

Mario Rabaglia
MAYA(1982)

Alberto Rabagliati
STREET ANGEL(1928); BAREFOOT CONTESSA, THE(1954); CROSSED SWORDS(1954); MONTE CARLO STORY, THE(1957, Ital.); JESSICA(1962, U.S./Ital./Fr.); CHRISMAS THAT ALMOST WASN'T. THE(1966, Ital.)

Francesco Rabal
N. P.(1971, Ital.)

Francisco Rabal
MIGHTY CRUSADERS, THE(1961, Ital.); ECLIPSE(1962, Fr./Ital.); VIRIDIA-NA(1962, Mex./Span.); HAND IN THE TRAP, THE(1963, Arg./Span.); MATHIAS SANDORF(1963, Fr.); BELLE DE JOUR(1968, Fr.); NAZARIN(1968, Mex.); WITCHES, THE(1969, Fr./Ital.); YOUNG REBEL, THE(1969, Fr./Ital./Span.); BIG AND THE BAD, THE(1971, Ital./Fr./Span.); NUN, THE(1971, Fr.); EAGLE OVER LONDON(1973, Ital.); EXORCISM'S DAUGHTER zero(1974, Span.); TEMPTER, THE(1974, Ital./Brit.); DEVIL IS A WOMAN, THE(1975, Brit./Ital.); DESERT OF THE TARTARS, THE(1976 Fr./Ital./Iranian); SORCERER(1977); CITY OF THE WALKING DEAD(1983, Span./Ital.); TREASURE OF THE FOUR CROWNS(1983, Span./U.S.)
1984
HOLY INNOCENTS, THE(1984, Span.)
Misc. Talkies
REBORN(1978)

Teresa Rabal
VIRIDIANA(1962, Mex./Span.); WHITE SISTER(1973, Ital./Span./Fr.)

Paco Rabanne
TWO FOR THE ROAD(1967, Brit.), cos; LAST ADVENTURE, THE(1968, Fr./Ital.), cos

Marie Rabasse
RAZOR'S EDGE, THE(1946); FRENCH LINE, THE(1954)

Toni Rabatoni
LOLLIPOP(1966, Braz.), ph

Rene Rabault
RISE OF LOUIS XIV, THE(1970, Fr.)

Herr Rabb
FREUD(1962)

Martin Rabb
WIRE SERVICE(1942), p

Frank Rabbit, Jr.
MAN CALLED HORSE, A(1970)

Tony Rabbitt
1984
SILENT ONE, THE(1984, New Zealand), prod d

Tseven Rabdan
SON OF MONGOLIA(1936, USSR)

David Rabe
I'M DANCING AS FAST AS I CAN(1982), w; STREAMERS(1983), w

Du Vernet Rabell
Silents
RAGE OF PARIS, THE(1921), w; IF I WERE QUEEN(1922), w

Jose Rabelo
VOICES(1979); DOGS OF WAR, THE(1980, Brit.); FORT APACHE, THE BRONX(1981); I OUGHT TO BE IN PICTURES(1982)
1984
MOSCOW ON THE HUDSON(1984)

Peer Raben
AMERICAN SOLDIER, THE(1970 Ger.), m; FOX AND HIS FRIENDS(1976, Ger.), m; MOTHER KUSTERS GOES TO HEAVEN(1976, Ger.), m; CHINESE ROULETTE(1977, Ger.), m; JAIL BAIT(1977, Ger.), m; WHY DOES HERR R. RUN AMOK?(1977, Ger.); DESPAIR(1978, Ger.), m; MARRIAGE OF MARIA BRAUN, THE(1979, Ger.), m; IN A YEAR OF THIRTEEN MOONS(1980, Ger.), m; LILI MARLEEN(1981, Ger.), m; LO-LA(1982, Ger.), m; VERONIKA VOSS(1982, Ger.), m; MALOU(1983), a, m; QUE-RELLE(1983, Ger./Fr.), m

1984
WOMAN IN FLAMES, A(1984, Ger.), m

Arthur Maria Rabenalt
ALRAUNE(1952, Ger.), d

Arthur-Maria Rabenalt
HIPPODROME(1961, Aust./Ger.), p&d

Catherine Rabett
1984
REAL LIFE(1984, Brit.)

Jean Rabier
CLEO FROM 5 TO 7(1961, Fr.), ph; SEVEN CAPITAL SINS(1962, Fr./Ital.), ph; LANDRU(1963, Fr./Ital), ph; THIRD LOVER, THE(1963, Fr./Ital.), ph; BAY OF ANGELS(1964, Fr.), ph; OPHELIA(1964, Fr.), ph; UMBRELLAS OF CHERBOURG, THE(1964, Fr./Ger.), ph; LE BONHEUR(1966, Fr.), ph; BEAUTIFUL SWINDLERS, THE(1967, Fr./Ital./Jap./Neth.), ph; CHAMPAGNE MURDERS, THE(1968, Fr.), ph; LES BICHES(1968, Fr.), ph; SIX IN PARIS(1968, Fr.), ph; LA FEMME IN-FIDELE(1969, Fr./Ital.), ph; THIS MAN MUST DIE(1970, Fr./Ital.), ph; WHO'S GOT THE BLACK BOX?(1970, Fr./Gr./Ital.), ph; LE BOUCHER(1971, Fr./Ital.), ph; DOC-TEUR POPAUL(1972, Fr.), ph; TEN DAYS' WONDER(1972, Fr.), ph; COLD SWEAT(1974, Ital., Fr.), ph; NADA GANG, THE(1974, Fr./Ital.), ph; JUST BEFORE NIGHTFALL(1975, Fr./Ital.), ph; DIRTY HANDS(1976, Fr/Ital./Ger.), ph; TWIST, THE(1976, Fr.), ph; ALICE, OR THE LAST ESCAPADE(1977, Fr.), ph; BLOOD RELA-TIVES(1978, Fr./Can.), ph; VIOLETTE(1978, Fr.), ph; HORSE OF PRIDE(1980, Fr.), ph; HATTER'S GHOST, THE(1982, Fr.), ph

Richard Rabiere
HAPPY BIRTHDAY TO ME(1981)

Paul Rabiger
KILLERS OF KILIMANJARO(1960, Brit.), makeup; GOLDFINGER(1964, Brit.), makeup; WOMAN OF STRAW(1964, Brit.), makeup; BLOW-UP(1966, Brit.), makeup; YOU ONLY LIVE TWICE(1967, Brit.), makeup; DULCIMA(1971, Brit.), makeup; SITTING TARGET(1972, Brit.), makeup; O LUCKY MAN!(1973, Brit.), makeup

J.R. Rabin
HOME OF THE BRAVE(1949), spec eff

Jack A. Rabin
UNKNOWN WORLD(1951), p, spec eff

Jack Rabin
ROCKETSHIP X-M(1950), spec eff; MAN FROM PLANET X, THE(1951), spec eff; CAT WOMEN OF THE MOON(1953), p, w; INVADERS FROM MARS(1953), spec eff; PARIS MODEL(1953), spec eff; ROBOT MONSTER(1953), spec eff; NIGHT OF THE HUNTER, THE(1955), spec eff; WORLD WITHOUT END(1956), spec eff; HELL BOUND(1957), spec eff; INVISIBLE BOY, THE(1957), spec eff; KRONOS(1957), p, spec eff; VOODOO ISLAND(1957), spec eff; DESERT HELL(1958), spec eff; FORT BOWIE(1958), spec eff; MACABRE(1958), spec eff; MONSTER FROM THE GREEN HELL(1958), spec eff; WAR OF THE SATELLITES(1958), p, w, spec eff; THIRTY FOOT BRIDE OF CANDY ROCK, THE(1959), w, spec eff; ATOMIC SUBMARINE, THE(1960), spec eff; BEES, THE(1978), spec eff; DEATHSPORT(1978), spec eff

Jack R. Rabin
HE WALKED BY NIGHT(1948), spec eff

Lenny Rabin
GOLDFINGER(1964, Brit.); SPY WHO LOVED ME, THE(1977, Brit.)

Michel Rabin
HORSE OF PRIDE(1980, Fr.)

Mark Rabiner
1984
AMERICAN TABOO(1984)

Isaac Rabinovich
SON OF MONGOLIA(1936, USSR), m

N. Rabinovich
HAMLET(1966, USSR), md

Gregor Rabinovitch
PORT OF SHADOWS(1938, Fr.), p; I WAS AN ADVENTURESS(1940), w; THREE RUSSIAN GIRLS(1943), p

Bila Rabinovitz
DREAMER, THE(1970, Israel)

Gregor Rabinowicz
EPISODE(1937, Aust.), p

Joseph Rabinowitch
1984
RENO AND THE DOC(1984, Can.)

Harry Rabinowitz
FUNERAL IN BERLIN(1966, Brit.), md; PUPPET ON A CHAIN(1971, Brit.), md; SIGN OF FOUR, THE(1983, Brit.), m
1984
ELECTRIC DREAMS(1984)

Max Rabinowitz
LOST HORIZON(1937)

Mort Rabinowitz
CASTLE KEEP(1969), art d; BABY MAKER, THE(1970), art d; FLAP(1970), art d; MOLLY AND LAWLESS JOHN(1972), prod d; SANTEE(1973), art d

Morton Rabinowitz
FUNHOUSE, THE(1981), prod. d

Diana Rabito
HYPNOSIS(1966, Ger./Sp./Ital.); FOR A FEW DOLLARS MORE(1967, Ital./Ger./Span.)

Stan Rabjohn
WHERE DOES IT HURT?(1972), ed

Stanley Rabjohn
BULLFIGHTERS, THE(1945), ed; BEHIND GREEN LIGHTS(1946), ed; FIGHTER ATTACK(1953), ed

Stanley E. Rabjohn
DEADLY COMPANIONS, THE(1961), ed; X-15(1961), ed

Jean Rabler
BANANA PEEL(1965, Fr.), ph

Al Raboch
ROCKY RHODES(1934), d; CRIMSON TRAIL, THE(1935), d

Alfred Raboch
Silents
COWARD, THE(1927), d; ALBANY NIGHT BOAT, THE(1928), d

Misc. Silents
OBEY THE LAW(1926), d; GREEN GRASS WIDOWS(1928), d; THEIR HOUR(1928), d

Ernest Raboff
MAN WITH THE GOLDEN ARM, THE(1955)

Jan Rabson
1984
RACING WITH THE MOON(1984)

Ali Raby
Misc. Silents
WHEN THE LAD CAME HOME(1922)

Claudio Racca
WARRIORS FIVE(1962), ph; PRIMITIVE LOVE(1966, Ital.), ph; COBRA, THE(1968), ph

Ilya Racek
DEATH OF TARZAN, THE(1968, Czech)

Francine Racette
FOUR FLIES ON GREY VELVET(1972, Ital.); ALIEN THUNDER(1975, US/Can.); LUMIERE(1976, Fr.); DISAPPEARANCE, THE(1981, Brit./Can.)

Pater Rachback
DUCHESS AND THE DIRTWATER FOX, THE(1976)

Hamed Rachedi
Z(1969, Fr./Algeria), p

Carmen Rachel
HAIRY APE, THE(1944)

Carol Rachell
POPDOWN(1968, Brit.)

Diane Rachell
KING OF COMEDY, THE(1983)

Bernie Rachelle
ROLLOVER(1981)

Francesco Rachini
SUPERFLY T.N.T.(1973)

Pascuale Rachini
LA GRANDE BOUFFE(1973, Fr.), ph

Nicole Rachline
MY NIGHT AT MAUD'S(1970, Fr.), art d; MEN PREFER FAT GIRLS(1981, Fr.), art d

Christian Rachman
DON'T CRY WITH YOUR MOUTH FULL(1974, Fr.), ph

Rachmaninoff
BRIEF ENCOUNTER(1945, Brit.), m

Sergei Rachmaninoff
RHAPSODY(1954), m; ROMEO AND JULIET(1968, Ital./Span.), m

Sergei Vassilievich Rachmaninoff
I'VE ALWAYS LOVED YOU(1946), m

Sergey Rachmaninoff
STORY OF THREE LOVES, THE(1953), m

Lewis A. Rachmil
THREE MEN FROM TEXAS(1940), art d

Lewis J. Rachmil
MINE WITH THE IRON DOOR, THE(1936), art d; GIRL SAID NO, THE(1937), art d; BAR 20 JUSTICE(1938), art d; FRONTIERSMAN, THE(1938), art d; IN OLD MEXICO(1938), art d; HERITAGE OF THE DESERT(1939), art d; SUNSET TRAIL(1938), art d; SILVER ON THE SAGE(1939), art d; WAY DOWN SOUTH(1939), art d; HIDDEN GOLD(1940), art d; LIGHT OF WESTERN STARS, THE(1940), art d; LLANO KID, THE(1940), art d; SHOWDOWN, THE(1940), art d; DOOMED CARAVAN(1941), art d; IN OLD COLORADO(1941), art d; PIRATES ON HORSEBACK(1941), art d; DEVIL'S PLAYGROUND, THE(1946), p; FOOL'S GOLD(1946), p; UNEXPECTED GUEST(1946), p; DANGEROUS VENTURE(1947), p; HOPPY'S HOLIDAY(1947), p; MARAUDERS, THE(1947), p; BORROWED TROUBLE(1948), p; DEAD DON'T DREAM, THE(1948), p; FALSE PARADISE(1948), p; SILENT CONFLICT(1948), p; SINISTER JOURNEY(1948), p; STRANGE GAMBLE(1948), p; BUNCO SQUAD(1950), p; HUNT THE MAN DOWN(1950), p; ROADBLOCK(1951), p; WHIP HAND, THE(1951), p; PACE THAT THRILLS, THE(1952), p; GUN FURY(1953), p; HUMAN DESIRE(1954), p; THEY RODE WEST(1954), p; TIGHT SPOT(1955), p; VIOLENT MEN, THE(1955), p; OVER-EXPOSED(1956), p; REPRISAL(1956), p; BROTHERS RICO, THE(1957), p; GIDGET(1959), p; THIRTY FOOT BRIDE OF CANDY ROCK, THE(1959), p; KINGS OF THE SUN(1963), p; RAGE TO LIVE, A(1965), p; RETURN FROM THE ASHES(1965, U.S./Brit.), p; 1,000 PLANE RAID, THE(1969), p; HELL BOATS(1970, Brit.), p; MOSQUITO SQUADRON(1970, Brit.), p; TRADER HORN(1973), p
1984
FOOTLOOSE(1984), p

Lewis Rachmil
MURDER BY TELEVISION(1935), art d; CALL OF THE PRAIRIE(1936), art d; HILLS OF OLD WYOMING(1937), art d; NORTH OF THE RIO GRANDE(1937), art d; RUSTLER'S VALLEY(1937), art d; TEXAS TRAIL(1937), art d; CASSIDY OF BAR 20(1938), art d; HAWAII CALLS(1938), art d; MYSTERIOUS RIDER, THE(1938), art d; PARTNERS OF THE PLAINS(1938), art d; SANTA FE MARSHAL(1940), art d; VILLAIN STILL PURSUED HER, THE(1940), art d; INSPECTOR CLOUSEAU(1968, Brit.), p

Michael Rachmil
1984
RUNAWAY(1984), p

B. Rachwalska
LAST STOP, THE(1949, Pol.); EVE WANTS TO SLEEP(1961, Pol.)

Vicki Racimo
WHAT'S SO BAD ABOUT FEELING GOOD?(1968)
Misc. Talkies
G.I. EXECUTIONER, THE(1971)

Victoria Racimo
MAGIC GARDEN OF STANLEY SWEETHART, THE(1970); RED SKY AT MORNING(1971); JOURNEY THROUGH ROSEBUD(1972); DAY OF THE DOLPHIN, THE(1973); HIGH VELOCITY(1977); PROPHECY(1979); MOUNTAIN MEN, THE(1980)

Racine
WICKED DIE SLOW, THE(1968)

Roger Racine
FORBIDDEN JOURNEY(1950, Can.), ph; SEIZURE(1974), ph

Antonio Racioppi
WOMAN ON FIRE, A(1970, Ital.), w

Aldo Raciti
STORMBOUND(1951, Ital.), p

Joe Raciti
FIREBRAND, THE(1962)

Lisa Rack
FLESH MERCHANT, THE(1956)

Tom Rack
LUCKY STAR, THE(1980, Can.)
1984
BAY BOY(1984, Can.)

Kurt Rackelmann
FIRST SPACESHIP ON VENUS(1960, Ger./Pol.)

Donald Rackerby
LITTLE MEN(1940)

Ted Rackerby
Silents
FIGHTING CHEAT, THE(1926)

Martin Rackin
BUY ME THAT TOWN(1941), w; AIR RAID WARDENS(1943), w; BOMBARDIER(1943), w; MARINE RAIDERS(1944), w; DESPERATE(1947), w; RIFFRAFF(1947), w; FIGHTER SQUADRON(1948), w; FIGHTING FATHER DUNNE(1948), w; RACE STREET(1948), w; DANGEROUS PROFESSION, A(1949), w; THREE SECRETS(1950), w; DISTANT DRUMS(1951), w; ENFORCER, THE(1951), w; SAILOR BEWARE(1951), w; LOAN SHARK(1952), w; STOOGE, THE(1952), w; CLOWN, THE(1953), w; GREAT DIAMOND ROBBERY(1953), w; LONG JOHN SILVER(1954, Aus.), w; HELL ON FRISCO BAY(1956), w; LISBON(1956), w; SANTIAGO(1956), p, w; BIG LAND, THE(1957), w; TOP SECRET AFFAIR(1957), p; DARBY'S RANGERS(1958), p; DEEP SIX, THE(1958), p, w; FORT DOBBS(1958), p; HELEN MORGAN STORY, THE(1959), p; HORSE SOLDIERS, THE(1959), p, w; NORTH TO ALASKA(1960), w; STAGECOACH(1966), p; ROUGH NIGHT IN JERICHO(1967), p; TWO MULES FOR SISTER SARA(1970), p; REVENGERS, THE(1972, U.S./Mex.), p

Steve Rackman
LAST OF THE KNUCKLEMEN, THE(1981, Aus.)

Steve Rackmann
ESCAPE 2000(1983, Aus.)

David Racksin
ACROSS THE WIDE MISSOURI(1951), m

Oscar Raclin
EVELYN PRENTICE(1934), m

Racquel
FLASH GORDON(1980)

Chip Radaelli
HANGAR 18(1980), art d

Eldrick Radage
YELLOW SUBMARINE(1958, Brit.), animation

Serjei Radamsky
FOLLIES GIRL(1943)

Imre Raday
Misc. Silents
AT THE EDGE OF THE WORLD(1929, Ger.)

Veronica Radbrook
GHASTLY ONES, THE(1968)

Veronica Radburn
ANNIE HALL(1977)

I. Radchenko
LULLABY(1961, USSR)

Irina Radchenko
DARK IS THE NIGHT(1946, USSR)

Eleanor Radcliff
CHICAGO CALLING(1951)

Frank Radcliff
MY SIX LOVES(1963); SWEET CHARITY(1969)

E. J. Radcliffe
Silents
OUT OF A CLEAR SKY(1918); LOVE, HONOR AND OBEY(1920); NEGLECTED WIVES(1920); EVERYMAN'S PRICE(1921); WOMAN WHO WALKED ALONE, THE(1922); FOUR FEATHERS(1929)
Misc. Silents
DIVORCEE, THE(1919); EVEN AS EVE(1920); HELP YOURSELF(1920); IMP, THE(1920); WIT WINS(1920); EXPERIENCE(1921); FRAMED(1927)

Frank Radcliffe
DREAMBOAT(1952); JUPITER'S DARLING(1955)

Fred Radcliffe
Silents
BALLET GIRL, THE(1916)
Misc. Silents
LOVE'S CONQUEST(1918)

Jack Radcliffe
WEE GEORDIE(1956, Brit.)

R. Radcliffe
Misc. Silents
MARKED WOMAN, THE(1914)

Stanley Radcliffe
MELODY OF MY HEART(1936, Brit.); SONG OF THE FORGE(1937, Brit.)

Synn Radcliffe
PURSUIT OF D.B. COOPER, THE(1981)

Violet Radcliffe
Silents
GRETCHEN, THE GREENHORN(1916); LITTLE SCHOOL MA'AM, THE(1916); JACK AND THE BEANSTALK(1917)
Misc. Silents
CHILDREN OF THE FEUD(1916); ALADDIN AND THE WONDERFUL LAMP(1917); BABES IN THE WOODS(1917); TREASURE ISLAND(1917); FAN FAN(1918)

Ronald Radd
SMALL WORLD OF SAMMY LEE, THE(1963, Brit.); UP JUMPED A SWAG-MAN(1965, Brit.); WHERE THE SPIES ARE(1965, Brit.); DOUBLE MAN, THE(1967); MISTER TEN PERCENT(1967, Brit.); SEA GULL, THE(1968); KREMLIN LETTER, THE(1970); OFFENSE, THE(1973, Brit.); SPIRAL STAIRCASE, THE(1975, Brit.); OPERATION DAYBREAK(1976, U.S./Brit./Czech.)

Carl Raddatz
DEAD MELODY(1938, Ger.); ROSEMARY(1960, Ger.); COUNTERFEIT TRAITOR, THE(1962)

Celene Radding
SPECTER OF THE ROSE(1946)

Anthony Radecki
RHUBARB(1951); IT GROWS ON TREES(1952); SOUTH SEA WOMAN(1953); FRANCIS JOINS THE WACS(1954)

R.A. Radecki
POINT OF TERROR(1971), ed

R. Rademachr
LEMONADE JOE(1966, Czech.)

Fons Rademakers
DAUGHTERS OF DARKNESS(1971, Bel./ Fr./ Ger./ Ital.); MYSTERIES(1979, Neth.)
Misc. Talkies
BECAUSE OF THE CATS(1974), d

Mike Raden
STING II, THE(1983)

Allan Rader
VOICE OF THE WHISTLER(1945), w

Gary Rader
PROLOGUE(1970, Can.)

Gene Rader
SUGARLAND EXPRESS, THE(1974); CLOSE ENCOUNTERS OF THE THIRD KIND(1977); OUTLAW BLUES(1977); HONEYSUCKLE ROSE(1980)

Jack Rader
EDGE, THE(1968); GRAY LADY DOWN(1978); ONION FIELD, THE(1979); HARD COUNTRY(1981)
Misc. Talkies
BARBARA(1970)

Vulo Radev
PEACH THIEF, THE(1969, Bulgaria), d&w

Art Radford
SMELL OF HONEY, A SWALLOW OF BRINE! A(1966), ph

Basil Radford
BARNUM WAS RIGHT(1929); SEVEN DAYS LEAVE(1930); SOUTHERN MAID, A(1933, Brit.); THERE GOES THE BRIDE(1933, Brit.); LEAVE IT TO SMITH(1934); BROKEN BLOSSOMS(1936, Brit.); DISHONOR BRIGHT(1936, Brit.); CAPTAIN'S ORDERS(1937, Brit.); WHEN THIEF MEETS THIEF(1937, Brit.); CLIMBING HIGH(1938, Brit.); CONVICT 99(1938, Brit.); LADY VANISHES, THE(1938, Brit.); YOUNG AND INNOCENT(1938, Brit.); GIRL WHO FORGOT, THE(1939, Brit.); JAMAICA INN(1939, Brit.); JUST WILLIAM(1939, Brit.); LET'S BE FAMOUS(1939, Brit.); SHE COULDN'T SAY NO(1939, Brit.); TROUBLE BREWING(1939, Brit.); AMONG HUMAN WOLVES(1940 Brit.); CROOKS TOUR(1940, Brit.); FLYING SQUAD, THE(1940, Brit.); NIGHT TRAIN(1940, Brit.); ROOM FOR TWO(1940, Brit.); SECRET FOUR, THE(1940, Brit.); SPIES OF THE AIR(1940, Brit.); GIRL IN THE NEWS, THE(1941, Brit.); FLYING FORTRESS(1942, Brit.); NEXT OF KIN(1942, Brit.); UNPUBLISHED STORY(1942, Brit.); MILLIONS LIKE US(1943, Brit.); TWILIGHT HOUR(1944, Brit.); JOHNNY IN THE CLOUDS(1945, Brit.); RANDOLPH FAMILY, THE(1945, Brit.); DEAD OF NIGHT(1946, Brit.); CAPTIVE HEART, THE(1948, Brit.); IT'S NOT CRICKET(1949, Brit.); PASSPORT TO PIMLICO(1949, Brit.); QUARTET(1949, Brit.); STOP PRESS GIRL(1949, Brit.); TIGHT LITTLE ISLAND(1949, Brit.); CHANCE OF A LIFETIME(1950, Brit.); WINSLOW BOY, THE(1950); GALLOPING MAJOR, THE(1951, Brit.), a, w; WHITE CORRIDORS(1952, Brit.)

E. Radford
SIX MEN, THE(1951, Brit.), w

George Radford
RELUCTANT HEROES(1951, Brit.)

James Q. Radford
NAKED DAWN, THE(1955), p

Lynne Radford
1984
1984(1984, Brit.)

M.A. Radford
SIX MEN, THE(1951, Brit.), w

Maizie Radford
Misc. Silents
WILD GIRL OF THE SIERRAS, A(1916)

Michael Radford
DAY THE FISH CAME OUT, THE(1967. Brit./Gr.); ANOTHER TIME, ANOTHER PLACE(1983, Brit.), d&w
1984
ANOTHER TIME, ANOTHER PLACE(1984, Brit.), d&w; 1984(1984, Brit.), d, w

Radha
RIVER, THE(1951)

Dusan Radic
GENGHIS KHAN(U.S./Brit./Ger./Yugo), m; SQUARE OF VIOLENCE(1963, U.S./Yugo.), m; LONG SHIPS, THE(1964, Brit./Yugo.), m

Gisa Levi Radicchi
LA TRAVIATA(1968, Ital.), ed; UGLY ONES, THE(1968, Ital./Span.), ed

Renie Radich
THREE THE HARD WAY(1974); SWINGING BARMAIDS, THE(1976)

Raymond Radiguet
DEVIL IN THE FLESH, THE(1949, Fr.), w

Charles H. Radilac
MR. SARDONICUS(1961); SHIP OF FOOLS(1965); TORN CURTAIN(1966)

N.M. Radin
HOUSE OF DEATH(1932, USSR)

Nikolai Radin
Misc. Silents
PLEBIAN(1915, USSR); ALARM, THE(1917, USSR)

Oscar Radin
WET PARADE, THE(1932, md; SOCIETY DOCTOR(1935), m

Paul B. Radin
PHASE IV(1974), p

Paul Radin
BORN FREE(1966), p; LIVING FREE(1972, Brit.), p

Radio Free Europe
TAKING TIGER MOUNTAIN(1983, U.S./Welsh), m

Radio Male Voice Choir
SHIPMATES O' MINE(1936, Brit.)

Radio Rascals
DISCOVERIES(1939, Brit.)

The Radio Revellers
HIGH JINKS IN SOCIETY(1949, Brit.)

Radio Rogues
O, MY DARLING CLEMENTINE(1943)

The Radio Rogues
BLOSSOMS ON BROADWAY(1937); HARVEST MELODY(1943); REVEILLE WITH BEVERLY(1943); SHE HAS WHAT IT TAKES(1943); TROCADERO(1944)

Radio Three
VARIETY PARADE(1936, Brit.); OKAY FOR SOUND(1937, Brit.)

Bob Radley
OPERATION CROSS EAGLES(1969, U.S./Yugo.), art d

Alexis Radlin
STONE COLD DEAD(1980, Can.)

D. Radlov
QUEEN OF SPADES(1961, USSR)

Peter Radmall
NIGHTHAWKS(1978, Brit.)

Gilda Radner
LAST DETAIL, THE(1973); FIRST FAMILY(1980); HANKY-PANKY(1982)
1984
WOMAN IN RED, THE(1984)

Brad Radnitz
WACKIEST WAGON TRAIN IN THE WEST, THE(1976), w

Robert B. Radnitz
MISTY(1961), p; ISLAND OF THE BLUE DOLPHINS(1964), p, w; AND NOW MIGUEL(1966), p; MY SIDE OF THE MOUNTAIN(1969), p; LITTLE ARK, THE(1972), p; SOUNDER(1972), p; WHERE THE LILIES BLOOM(1974), p; BIRCH INTERVAL(1976), p; HERO AIN'T NOTHIN' BUT A SANDWICH, A(1977), p; CROSS CREEK(1983), p

Robert D. Radnitz
DOG OF FLANDERS, A(1959), p

Robert Radnitz
WINK OF AN EYE(1958), w

Barry Rado
YOUNG MAN WITH IDEAS(1952)

James Rado
LIONS LOVE(1969); HAIR(1979), w

Jorge Rado
SANTO CONTRA BLUE DEMON EN LA ATLANTIDA(1968, Mex.); SANTO Y BLUE DEMON CONTRA LOS MONSTRUOS(1968, Mex.); POR MIS PISTOLAS(1969, Mex.)

Norman Rado
YOUNG MAN WITH IDEAS(1952)

Bill Radobich
FATHER WAS A FULLBACK(1949)

Alfred Radok
DISTANT JOURNEY(1950, Czech.), d, w

Bernice Radom
Silents
NO WOMAN KNOWS(1921); PENROD(1922)

Winston Radom
Silents
PENROD(1922)

Hans Radon
CRIME DOCTOR'S MAN HUNT(1946), art d; JUST BEFORE DAWN(1946), art d; MYSTERIOUS INTRUDER(1946), art d; SECRET OF THE WHISTLER(1946), art d; SHADOWED(1946), art d; FOR THE LOVE OF RUSTY(1947), art d; KING OF THE WILD HORSES(1947), art d; 13TH HOUR, THE(1947), art d

Branislav Radovic
GENGHIS KHAN(U.S./Brit./Ger./Yugo)

Bill Radovich
AGAINST ALL FLAGS(1952); WORLD IN HIS ARMS, THE(1952); BACK TO GOD'S COUNTRY(1953); GOLDEN BLADE, THE(1953); GUNSMOKE(1953); TROUBLE ALONG THE WAY(1953)

Dem Radulescu
FANTASTIC COMEDY, A(1975, Rum.)

Viktoria Radunskaya
UNCOMMON THIEF, AN(1967, USSR)

A. Radunskiy
NIGHT BEFORE CHRISTMAS, A(1963, USSR)

Aleksandr Radunskiy
LITTLE HUMPBACKED HORSE, THE(1962, USSR), a, p,d&w

Geva Radvanyi
SPECIAL DELIVERY(1955, Ger.), w

Geza Radvanyi
MAEDCHEN IN UNIFORM(1965, Ger./Fr.), d

Jerzy Radzilwilowicz
PASSION(1983, Fr./Switz.)

Elsa Radzin
HAMLET(1966, USSR)

Medea Radzina
Silents
BEDROOM WINDOW, THE(1924)

A. Radzinowicz
BORDER STREET(1950, Pol.), art d

Jerzy Radziwilowicz
MAN OF MARBLE(1979, Pol.); MAN OF IRON(1981, Pol.)
V. Radziyevskiy
KATERINA IZMAILOVA(1969, USSR)
Alice Rae
Misc. Silents
CHILDREN IN THE HOUSE, THE(1916); LOVE SUBLIME, A(1917)
Barbara Rae
HIDE IN PLAIN SIGHT(1980)
Berth Rae
Misc. Silents
DEADSHOT CASEY(1928)
Bud Rae
NEW MEXICO(1951)
Charlotte Rae
JENNY(1969); BANANAS(1971); HOT ROCK, THE(1972); SIDEWINDER ONE(1977); RABBIT TEST(1978); HAIR(1979)
Charolette Rae
HELLO DOWN THERE(1969)
Claude Rae
DANGEROUS AGE, A(1960, Can.); NOBODY WAVED GOODBYE(1965, Can.); DEAD ZONE, THE(1983)
Icilma Rae
Silents
FATAL FINGERS(1916. Brit.)
James Rae
JOY(1983, Fr./Can.)
Jock Rae
FLAME IN THE HEATHER(1935, Brit.)
John Rae
NEUTRAL PORT(1941, Brit.); HE SNOOPS TO CONQUER(1944, Brit.); SOLDIER, SAILOR(1944, Brit.); GREEN FOR DANGER(1946, Brit.); I KNOW WHERE I'M GOING(1947, Brit.); TAWNY PIPIT(1947, Brit.); BONNIE PRINCE CHARLIE(1948, Brit.); BRAVE DON'T CRY, THE(1952, Brit.); GREAT GILBERT AND SULLIVAN, THE(1953, Brit.); HEART OF THE MATTER, THE(1954, Brit.); HIGH AND DRY(1954, Brit.); LITTLE KIDNAPPERS, THE(1954, Brit.); ESCAPADE(1955, Brit.); BIG CHANCE, THE(1957, Brit.); ENEMY FROM SPACE(1957, Brit.); STOWAWAY GIRL(1957, Brit.); HARRY BLACK AND THE TIGER(1958, Brit.); INNOCENT SINNERS(1958, Brit.); BRIDAL PATH, THE(1959, Brit.); QUESTION OF ADULTERY, A(1959, Brit.); MANIA(1961, Brit.); REACH FOR GLORY(1963, Brit.), a, w; FAHRENHEIT 451(1966, Brit.); MORGAN!(1966, Brit.); OH! WHAT A LOVELY WAR(1969, Brit.); FRAGMENT OF FEAR(1971, Brit.); LOLA(1971, Brit./Ital.); SUNDAY BLOODY SUNDAY(1971, Brit.)
Michael Rae
SCRUFFY(1938, Brit.); SKYDIVERS, THE(1963); LASERBLAST(1978), d
Mistress Zoe Rae
Silents
KAISER, BEAST OF BERLIN, THE(1918)
Rada Rae
Silents
CRAIG'S WIFE(1928)
Misc. Silents
DEATH VALLEY(1927)
Sharron Rae
J.W. COOP(1971)
Taija Rae
1984
DELIVERY BOYS(1984)
Thomas Rae
Silents
WHITE YOUTH(1920), ph
Tony Rae
SWING OUT, SISTER(1945)
Zoe Rae
Misc. Silents
BUGLER OF ALGIERS, THE(1916); GLORIANA(1916); CIRCUS OF LIFE, THE(1917); CRICKET, THE(1917); LITTLE PIRATE, THE(1917); MY LITTLE BOY(1917); SILENT LADY, THE(1917); DANGER WITHIN(1918); MAGIC EYE, THE(1918)
Wendy Raebeck
IF EVER I SEE YOU AGAIN(1978); SHOCK TREATMENT(1981)
Boyd Raeburn
ISLAND WOMEN(1958), md
Frances Raeburn
SEVEN SWEETHEARTS(1942); SWING OUT, SISTER(1945)
Gene Raeburn
IT HAPPENED TO JANE(1959)
Henzie Raeburn
ORDERS TO KILL(1958, Brit.)
Mavis Raeburn
TILLY OF BLOOMSBURY(1940, Brit.)
Michael Raeburn
GRASS IS SINGING, THE(1982, Brit./Swed.), d&w
Miriam Raeburn
DREAMS THAT MONEY CAN BUY(1948)
Robin Rael
1984
HOT DOG...THE MOVIE(1984)
The Raelets
BLUES FOR LOVERS(1966, Brit.)
Robert Raetano
1984
ULTIMATE SOLUTION OF GRACE QUIGLEY, THE(1984), ed
Baby Alice Raetz
STAND UP AND CHEER(1934 80m FOX bw)
T. Raewyn
TRICK BABY(1973), w
Roger Rafal
JOUR DE FETE(1952, Fr.)

Soraya Rafat
DESIGN FOR LOVING(1962, Brit.)
Bob Rafelson
HEAD(1968), p, d, w; FIVE EASY PIECES(1970), p, d, w; KING OF MARVIN GARDENS, THE(1972), p&d, w; STAY HUNGRY(1976), p, d, w; POSTMAN ALWAYS RINGS TWICE, THE(1981), p, d
Roby Carr Rafelson
GOIN' SOUTH(1978), prod d
Tobi Carr Rafelson
RENEGADE GIRLS(1974)
Toby Carr Rafelson
KING OF MARVIN GARDENS, THE(1972), art d; ALICE DOESN'T LIVE HERE ANYMORE(1975), prod d; STAY HUNGRY(1976), prod d
Toby Rafelson
I NEVER PROMISED YOU A ROSE GARDEN(1977), prod d; MELVIN AND HOWARD(1980), prod d; UNDER FIRE(1983), art d
Mike Rafetto
Silents
TILLIE'S PUNCTURED ROMANCE(1928)
Robert H. Raff
BUS IS COMING, THE(1971), w
Nancy Raffa
1984
SPLASH(1984)
Alain Raffael
TIGHT SKIRTS, LOOSE PLEASURES(1966, Fr.)
Builiano Raffael
MAN COULD GET KILLED, A(1966)
Erika Raffael
BIG SWITCH, THE(1970, Brit.); MAN OF VIOLENCE(1970, Brit.)
Giuliano Raffaelli
ROMAN HOLIDAY(1953); WILD, WILD PLANET, THE(1967, Ital.); WATERLOO(1970, Ital./USSR)
Guiliano Raffaelli
BLOOD AND BLACK LACE(1965, Ital.)
Claudine Raffali
JOY(1983, Fr./Can.)
Anthony Raffell
MIKADO, THE(1967, Brit.)
Isabelle Rafferty
FAR FROM DALLAS(1972, Fr.), ed
Chips Rafferty
FORTY THOUSAND HORSEMEN(1941, Aus.); OVERLANDERS, THE(1946, Brit./Aus.); BUSH CHRISTMAS(1947, Brit.); LOVES OF JOANNA GODDEN, THE(1947, Brit.); MASSACRE HILL(1949, Brit.); BITTER SPRINGS(1950, Aus.); RATS OF TOBRUK(1951, Aus.); KANGAROO(1952); DESERT RATS, THE(1953); PHANTOM STOCKMAN, THE(1953, Aus.); KING OF THE CORAL SEA(1956, Aus.), a, p, w; SMILEY(1957, Brit.); WALK INTO HELL(1957, Aus.), a, p; SMILEY GETS A GUN(1959, Brit.); SUNDOWNERS, THE(1960); WACKIEST SHIP IN THE ARMY, THE(1961); MUTINY ON THE BOUNTY(1962); THEY'RE A WEIRD MOB(1966, Aus.); DOUBLE TROUBLE(1967); KONA COAST(1968); SKULLDUGGERY(1970); OUTBACK(1971, Aus.)
Frances Rafferty
EYES IN THE NIGHT(1942); SEVEN SWEETHEARTS(1942); WAR AGAINST MRS. HADLEY, THE(1942); DR. GILLESPIE'S CRIMINAL CASE(1943); GIRL CRAZY(1943); HITLER'S MADMAN(1943); SLIGHTLY DANGEROUS(1943); THOUSANDS CHEER(1943); YOUNG IDEAS(1943); BARBARY COAST GENT(1944); DRAGON SEED(1944); MRS. PARKINGTON(1944); ABBOTT AND COSTELLO IN HOLLYWOOD(1945); HIDDEN EYE, THE(1945); BAD BASCOMB(1946); ADVENTURES OF DON COYOTE(1947); LOST HONEYMOON(1947); LADY AT MIDNIGHT(1948); MONEY MADNESS(1948); OLD-FASHIONED GIRL, AN(1948); RODEO(1952); SHANGHAI STORY, THE(1954); WINGS OF CHANCE(1961, Can.)
Frank Rafferty
LASSIE'S GREAT ADVENTURE(1963), set d
Marcy Rafferty
KINGDOM OF THE SPIDERS(1977)
Tom Rafferty
BIG SLEEP, THE(1946)
Wayne Rafferty
MY THIRD WIFE GEORGE(1968), w
Michael Raffeto
FOREIGN AFFAIR, A(1948)
Michael Raffetto
TODAY I HANG(1942); SEVEN DOORS TO DEATH(1944); PIRATES OF MONTEREY(1947); I WAS A SHOPLIFTER(1950); STORM CENTER(1956); ISTANBUL(1957)
Mike Raffetto
EYES OF THE UNDERWORLD(1943)
Ali Raffi
ONE SINGS, THE OTHER DOESN'T(1977, Fr.)
Anita Raffi
GLASS HOUSES(1972)
Joseph Raffill
HIGH RISK(1981), p
Stewart Raffill
TENDER WARRIOR, THE(1971), d, w; NAPOLEON AND SAMANTHA(1972), w; ADVENTURES OF THE WILDERNESS FAMILY, THE(1975), d&w; HIGH RISK(1981), d&w
1984
ICE PIRATES, THE(1984), d, w; PHILADELPHIA EXPERIMENT, THE(1984), d
Misc. Talkies
WHEN THE NORTH WIND BLOWS(1974), d
Deborah Raffin
FORTY CARATS(1973); DOVE, THE(1974, Brit.); ONCE IS NOT ENOUGH(1975); GOD TOLD ME TO(1976); MANIAC!(1977); SENTINEL, THE(1977); TOUCHED BY LOVE(1980); DANCE OF THE DWARFS(1983, U.S., Phil.)
Raffine
TORTURE DUNGEON(1970), cos

Raffles
BAREFOOT EXECUTIVE, THE(1971)
Gerry Raffles
SPARROWS CAN'T SING(1963, Brit.)
Antoinette Raffone
1984
BROADWAY DANNY ROSE(1984)
Francois Raffoul
PROMISE AT DAWN(1970, U.S./Fr.)
Bozorgmeh Rafia
CARAVANS(1978, U.S./Iranian)
Joseph C. Rafill
SEA GYPSIES, THE(1978), p
Stewart Rafill
ACROSS THE GREAT DIVIDE(1976), d&w; SEA GYPSIES, THE(1978), d&w
Rafine
MAN WITH TWO HEADS, THE(1972), cos; RATS ARE COMING! THE WERE-WOLVES ARE HERE!, THE(1972), cos
Alan Rafkin
SKI PARTY(1965), d; GHOST AND MR. CHICKEN, THE(1966), d; RIDE TO HANG-MAN'S TREE, THE(1967), d; NOBODY'S PERFECT(1968), d; SHAKIEST GUN IN THE WEST, THE(1968), d; ANGEL IN MY POCKET(1969), d; HOW TO FRAME A FIGG(1971), d
George Raft
QUEEN OF THE NIGHTCLUBS(1929); GOLDIE(1931); HUSH MONEY(1931); PALMY DAYS(1931); QUICK MILLIONS(1931); DANCERS IN THE DARK(1932); IF I HAD A MILLION(1932); LOVE IS A RACKET(1932); MADAME RACKETEER(1932); NIGHT AFTER NIGHT(1932); NIGHT WORLD(1932); SCARFACE(1932); TAXI!(1932); UNDER-COVER MAN(1932); BOWERY, THE(1933); MIDNIGHT CLUB(1933); PICK-UP(1933); ALL OF ME(1934); BOLERO(1934); LIMEHOUSE BLUES(1934); TRUMPET BLOWS, THE(1934); EVERY NIGHT AT EIGHT(1935); GLASS KEY, THE(1935); RUMBA(1935); SHE COULDN'T TAKE IT(1935); STOLEN HARMONY(1935); IT HAD TO HAPPEN(1936); YOURS FOR THE ASKING(1936); SOULS AT SEA(1937); SPAWN OF THE NORTH(1938); YOU AND ME(1938); EACH DAWN I DIE(1939); I STOLE A MILLION(1939); LADY'S FROM KENTUCKY, THE(1939); HOUSE ACROSS THE BAY, THE(1940); INVISIBLE STRIPES(1940); THEY DRIVE BY NIGHT(1940); MAN-POWER(1941); BROADWAY(1942); BACKGROUND TO DANGER(1943); STAGE DOOR CANTEEN(1943); FOLLOW THE BOYS(1944); JOHNNY ANGEL(1945); NOB HILL(1945); MR. ACE(1946); NOCTURNE(1946); WHISTLE STOP(1946); CHRISTMAS EVE(1947); INTRIGUE(1947); RACE STREET(1948); DANGEROUS PROFESSION, A(1949); JOHNNY ALLEGRO(1949); NOUS IRONS A PARIS(1949, Fr.); OUTPOST IN MOROCCO(1949); RED LIGHT(1949); LUCKY NICK CAIN(1951); LOAN SHARK(1952); I'LL GET YOU(1953, Brit.); MAN FROM CAIRO, THE(1953); BLACK WIDOW(1954); ROGUE COP(1954); BULLET FOR JOEY, A(1955); AROUND THE WORLD IN 80 DAYS(1956); SOME LIKE IT HOT(1959); JET OVER THE ATLAN-TIC(1960); OCEAN'S ELEVEN(1960); LADIES MAN, THE(1961); FOR THOSE WHO THINK YOUNG(1964); PATSY, THE(1964); CASINO ROYALE(1967, Brit.); FIVE GOLDEN DRAGONS(1967, Brit.); UPPER HAND, THE(1967, Fr./Ital./Ger.); SKI-DOO(1968); MADIGAN'S MILLIONS(1970, Span./Ital); HAMMERSMITH IS OUT(1972); SEXTETTE(1978); MAN WITH BOGART'S FACE, THE(1980); DEADHEAD MILES(1982)
Tommy Moe Raft
Misc. Talkies
BLACK CONNECTION, THE(1974)
Raft-Lombard
RUMBA(1935), ch
Louis Raftis
RAGING BULL(1980)
Anna Raftopoulou
300 SPARTANS, THE(1962)
Eskandar Rafu
CARAVANS(1978, U.S./Iranian)
Mohammed Ragaky
LITTLE MISS DEVIL(1951, Egypt), d
Michael Ragan
DAKOTA KID, THE(1951); TEXANS NEVER CRY(1951); LOAN SHARK(1952)
Mike Ragan
OVER THE BORDER(1950); TARGET(1952); LAW AND ORDER(1953); BITTER CREEK(1954); GANG BUSTERS(1955); RAGE AT DAWN(1955); TALL MAN RI-DING(1955); FRONTIER GUN(1958); STAGECOACH TO DANCER'S PARK(1962); DARK INTRUDER(1965); GUNPOINT(1966)
Mike Ragan [Holly Bane]
SON OF BELLE STARR(1953); VIVA LAS VEGAS(1964)
Martin Ragaway
ABBOTT AND COSTELLO IN THE FOREIGN LEGION(1950), w; MA AND PA KETTLE GO TO TOWN(1950), w; MILKMAN, THE(1950), w; LOST IN ALASKA(1952), w; MA AND PA KETTLE AT THE FAIR(1952), w
Elemer Ragalyi
1984
BRADY'S ESCAPE(1984, U.S./Hung.), ph
Jusupoff Ragazzi
CONJUGAL BED, THE(1963, Ital.)
Hugh Raggett
CHARGE OF THE LIGHT BRIGADE, THE(1968, Brit.), ed
Mark Raggett
1984
1984(1984, Brit.), set d
Michael Raghan
DON'T SAY DIE(1950, Brit.); WHISTLE DOWN THE WIND(1961, Brit.)
G. Raghaven
TARZAN GOES TO INDIA(1962, U.S./Brit./Switz.)
Osman Ragheb
MAGIC FOUNTAIN, THE(1961); I DEAL IN DANGER(1966); METEOR(1979); AMERICAN SUCCESS COMPANY, THE(1980); HOPSCOTCH(1980); NIGHT CROSS-ING(1982)
Dave Ragin
BEHIND THAT CURTAIN(1929), ph; ON THE LEVEL(1930), ph; PRINCESS AND THE PLUMBER, THE(1930), ph

David Ragin
COWBOY FROM LONESOME RIVER(1944), ph
John S. Ragin
EARTHQUAKE(1974); MOVING VIOLATION(1976)
Daphne Raglan
CHANGE FOR A SOVEREIGN(1937, Brit.); FALSE EVIDENCE(1937, Brit.); MEET MR. PENNY(1938, Brit.); DOWN OUR ALLEY(1939, Brit.); NORTH SEA PATROL(1939, Brit.)
James Raglan
LAST HOUR, THE(1930, Brit.); CHINESE PUZZLE, THE(1932, Brit.); WORLD, THE FLESH, AND THE DEVIL, THE(1932, Brit.); ADMIRAL'S SECRET, THE(1934, Brit.); POWER(1934, Brit.); ROLLING HOME(1935, Brit.); FLYING DOCTOR, THE(1936, Aus.); MORALS OF MARCUS, THE(1936, Brit.); LOVERS AND LUGGERS(1938, Aus.); MR. CHEDWORTH STEPS OUT(1939, Aus.); VENGEANCE OF THE DEEP(1940, Aus.); CELIA(1949, Brit.); DICK BARTON STRIKES BACK(1949, Brit.); DR. MORELLE-THE CASE OF THE MISSING HEIRESS(1949, Brit.); WHISPERING SMITH VERSUS SCOTLAND YARD(1952, Brit.); BROKEN HORSESHOE, THE(1953, Brit.); FLOATING DUTCHMAN, THE(1953, Brit.); OPERATION DIPLOMAT(1953, Brit.); FABIAN OF THE YARD(1954, Brit.)
Silents
MAN WHO CHANGED HIS NAME, THE(1928, Brit.)
Misc. Silents
FORGER, THE(1928, Brit.); RED ACES(1929, Brit.)
Robert Raglan
CIRCUS BOY(1947, Brit.); GOOD BEGINNING, THE(1953, Brit.); CHILD'S PLAY(1954, Brit.); YELLOW ROBE, THE(1954, Brit.); HANDCUFFS, LONDON(1955, Brit.); DEADLIEST SIN, THE(1956, Brit.); 23 PACES TO BAKER STREET(1956); BIG CHANCE, THE(1957, Brit.); THERE'S ALWAYS A THURSDAY(1957, Brit.); THUN-DER OVER TANGIER(1957, Brit.); UNDERCOVER GIRL(1957, Brit.); ZOO BABY(1957, Brit.); COUNT FIVE AND DIE(1958, Brit.); STRANGE CASE OF DR. MANNING, THE(1958, Brit.); CHILD AND THE KILLER, THE(1959, Brit.); GIDEON OF SCOT-LAND YARD(1959, Brit.); HIDDEN HOMICIDE(1959, Brit.); HIGH JUMP(1959, Brit.); INNOCENT MEETING(1959, Brit.); NO SAFETY AHEAD(1959, Brit.); WEB OF SUSPICION(1959, Brit.); WOMAN'S TEMPTATION, A(1959, Brit.); TASTE OF MONEY, A(1960, Brit.); CORRIDORS OF BLOOD(1962, Brit.); INFORMATION RE-CEIVED(1962, Brit.); GREAT VAN ROBBERY, THE(1963, Brit.); TRAITORS, THE(1963, Brit.); JIG SAW(1965, Brit.); WHERE THE SPIES ARE(1965, Brit.); PREHIS-TORIC WOMEN(1967, Brit.); SUBTERFUGE(1969, US/Brit.); HORROR HOUSE(1970, Brit.); MAGIC CHRISTIAN, THE(1970, Brit.); CATCH ME A SPY(1971, Brit./Fr.); LOOT(1971, Brit.)
Rags Ragland
RINGSIDE MAISIE(1941); WHISTLING IN THE DARK(1941); BORN TO SING(1942); MAISIE GETS HER MAN(1942); PANAMA HATTIE(1942); SOMEWHERE I'LL FIND YOU(1942); SUNDAY PUNCH(1942); WAR AGAINST MRS. HADLEY, THE(1942); WHISTLING IN DIXIE(1942); DU BARRY WAS A LADY(1943); GIRL CRAZY(1943); WHISTLING IN BROOKLYN(1943); CANTERVILLE GHOST, THE(1944); MEET THE PEOPLE(1944); THREE MEN IN WHITE(1944); ANCHORS AWEIGH(1945); HER HIGHNESS AND THE BELLBOY(1945); HOODLUM SAINT, THE(1946)
Robert O. Ragland
WEEKEND WITH THE BABYSITTER(1970), m; THING WITH TWO HEADS, THE(1972), m; ABBY(1974), m; RETURN TO MACON COUNTY(1975), m; SEVEN ALONE(1975), m; SHARK'S TREASURE(1975), m; GRIZZLY(1976), m; MANSION OF THE DOOMED(1976), m; PONY EXPRESS RIDER(1976), m; PROJECT: KILL(1976), m; JAGUAR LIVES(1979), m; MOUNTAIN FAMILY ROBINSON(1979), m; ONLY ONCE IN A LIFETIME(1979), m; GLOVE, THE(1980), m; Q(1982), m; BRAIN-WAVES(1983), m; HYSTERICAL(1983), m; TIME TO DIE, A(1983), m; 10 TO MID-NIGHT(1983), m
Robert Oliver Ragland
DAY OF THE LOCUST, THE(1975)
Robert Raglen
RECOIL(1953)
Arne Ragneborn
DEVIL'S WANTON, THE(1962, Swed.)
Frank Ragney
ROSE MARIE(1954)
Gerome Ragni
HAMLET(1964); LIONS LOVE(1969); HAIR(1979), w
Carlo Ragno
OPIATE '67(1967, Fr./Ital.)
Joe Ragno
LAW AND DISORDER(1974); WINTER KILLS(1979); DEATH VENGEANCE(1982)
Joseph Ragno
MELVIN AND HOWARD(1980); WHERE THE BUFFALO ROAM(1980)
Laurence Ragon
GREEN ROOM, THE(1979, Fr.)
Claudio Ragona
CONFESSIONS OF A POLICE CAPTAIN(1971, Ital.), ph; GOODNIGHT, LADIES AND GENTLEMEN(1977, Ital.), ph; PASSION OF LOVE(1982, Ital./Fr.), ph
Ubaldo Ragona
LAST MAN ON EARTH, THE(1964, U.S./Ital.), d
Paul Ragonese
1984
CORRUPT(1984, Ital.)
Nadiege Ragoo
YOUNG WORLD, A(1966, Fr./Ital.)
Felicja Ragowska
JOAN OF THE ANGELS(1962, Pol.), ed
Ed Ragozzini
SASQUATCH(1978), d
Rags
Silents
PATRIOT, THE(1916)
Rags the Dog
WELL DONE, HENRY(1936, Brit.); LET'S LIVE AGAIN(1948)
Silents
TIMOTHY'S QUEST(1922)
Howard Ragsdale
BADLANDS(1974)

Lulah Ragsdale
Silents
MISS DULCIE FROM DIXIE(1919), w

Angelo Ragusa
1990: THE BRONX WARRIORS(1983, Ital.)

Concetta Ragusa
LA DOLCE VITA(1961, Ital./Fr.)

Mady Rahl
HIPPODROME(1961, Aust./Ger.); PLAYGIRLS AND THE BELLBOY, THE(1962,Ger.); SITUATION HOPELESS–BUT NOT SERIOUS(1965)

Abdul Rahman
OPERATION CROSS EAGLES(1969, U.S./Yugo.)

Capt. Mohamed Abdel Rahman
CAIRO(1963)

Rahman Rahman
LITTLE JUNGLE BOY(1969, Aus.)

Salah Rahmouni
1984
MISUNDERSTOOD(1984)

Ferydoun Rahnema
SIAVASH IN PERSEPOLIS(1966, Iran), d

Humi Raho
BARON BLOOD(1972, Ital.)

Umberto Raho
GIDGET GOES TO ROME(1963); SEVEN SEAS TO CALAIS(1963, Ital.); DUEL OF CHAMPIONS(1964 Ital./Span.); QUEEN OF THE NILE(1964, Ital.); DARLING(1965, Brit.); THAT MAN IN ISTANBUL(1966, Fr./Ital./Span.); MISSION BLOODY MARY(1967, Fr./Ital./Span.); WILD, WILD PLANET, THE(1967, Ital.); CHASTITY BELT, THE(1968, Ital.); ROMEO AND JULIET(1968, Ital./Span.); SONS OF SATAN(1969, Ital./Fr./Ger.); CONFESSION, THE(1970, Fr.); DIARY OF A SCHIZOPHRENIC GIRL(1970, Ital.); MADIGAN'S MILLIONS(1970, Span./Ital); NIGHT EVELYN CAME OUT OF THE GRAVE, THE(1973, Ital.); BREAD AND CHOCOLATE(1978, Ital.)

Franz Raht
SISTERS, OR THE BALANCE OF HAPPINESS(1982, Ger.), ph

Rahuis
PERFECT FRIDAY(1970, Brit.), cos

Rahvis
WOMAN TO WOMAN(1929), cos; WOMAN TO WOMAN(1946, Brit.), cos; UNEASY TERMS(1948, Brit.), cos; GOOD DIE YOUNG, THE(1954, Brit.), cos

Himansu Rai
KARMA(1933, Brit./India), a, p, w
Misc. Silents
SHIRAZ(1929)

Paul Raibaud
MR. PEEK-A-BOO(1951, Fr.), spec eff

Jerry Raibourn
HEARTACHES(1981, Can.), p

Henri Raichi
ZAZIE(1961, Fr.), ph; IMMORAL MOMENT, THE(1967, Fr.), ph; THAT MAN GEORGE!(1967, Fr./Ital./Span.), ph; VISCOUNT, THE(1967, Fr./Span./Ital./Ger.), ph

Raider the Horse
MEDICO OF PAINTED SPRINGS, THE(1941)

Victor Raider-Wexler
BENJI(1974)

Erika Raifael
HERE WE GO ROUND THE MULBERRY BUSH(1968, Brit.)

Robert Raiff
SWING SHIFT MAISIE(1943), w

Napier Raikes
BOOLOO(1938)

Raymond Raikes
WATER GYPSIES, THE(1932, Brit.); POISONED DIAMOND, THE(1934, Brit.); IT'S A BET(1935, Brit.)

Robert Raikes
ACCOUNT RENDERED(1957, Brit.); ENEMY FROM SPACE(1957, Brit.); LINKS OF JUSTICE(1958); INNOCENT MEETING(1959, Brit.); TOP FLOOR GIRL(1959, Brit.); MISSILE FROM HELL(1960, Brit.)

Jack Railey
PAL JOEY(1957); DAYS OF WINE AND ROSES(1962)

Curtis Railing
HONOLULU LU(1941); WIFE TAKES A FLYER, THE(1942)

Hyacinthe Railla
FOREVER FEMALE(1953)

Michael Railsback
STUNT MAN, THE(1980); TRICK OR TREATS(1982), set d

Steve Railsback
VISITORS, THE(1972); ANGELA(1977, Can.); STUNT MAN, THE(1980); ESCAPE 2000(1983, Aus.); GOLDEN SEAL, THE(1983)
1984
TORCHLIGHT(1984)
Misc. Talkies
DEADLY GAMES(1980); ELIMINATOR, THE(1982); TRICK OR TREATS(1983)

John Railton
HAMLET(1969, Brit.)

3000 Railway Workmen
Silents
IRON HORSE, THE(1924)

Toni Raimando
SLAVE GIRL(1947)

Lucien Raimbourg
CARTOUCHE(1962, Fr./Ital.); MONKEY IN WINTER, A(1962, Fr.); ELUSIVE CORPORAL, THE(1963, Fr.); HIGHWAY PICKUP(1965, Fr./Ital.); CHECKERBOARD(1969, Fr.)

Luciene Raimbourg
DEVIL'S NIGHTMARE, THE(1971 Bel./Ital.)

Sam Raimi
EVIL DEAD, THE(1983), d&w

Larry Raimond
STAKEOUT ON DOPE STREET(1958); GET OUTTA TOWN(1960), ph; AIRBORNE(1962), ph

Lawrence Raimond
LOVE AND THE MIDNIGHT AUTO SUPPLY(1978), ph

Gianni Raimondi
LA BOHEME(1965, Ital.)

Maria Raimondi
8 ½(1963, Ital.)

Ruggero Raimondi
DON GIOVANNI(1979, Fr./Ital./Ger.)
1984
BIZET'S CARMEN(1984, Fr./Ital.); LIFE IS A BED OF ROSES(1984, Fr.)

Arthur Raimondo
HEAT OF THE SUMMER(1961, Fr.), ph; HOT HOURS(1963, Fr.), ph

Raimu
CESAR(1936, Fr.); UN CARNET DE BAL(1938, Fr.); HEART OF PARIS(1939, Fr.); BAKER'S WIFE, THE(1940, Fr.); CONFESSIONS OF A NEWLYWED(1941, Fr.); HEART OF A NATION, THE(1943, Fr.); ETERNAL HUSBAND, THE(1946, Fr.); WELL-DIGGER'S DAUGHTER, THE(1946, Fr.); COLONEL CHABERT(1947, Fr.); FANNY(1948, Fr.); STRANGERS IN THE HOUSE(1949, Fr.)

Jules Raimu
MARIUS(1933, Fr.)

Ruggero Raimundi
TROUT, THE(1982, Fr.)

Douglas Rain
OEDIPUS REX(1957, Can.); ONE PLUS ONE(1961, Can.); 2001: A SPACE ODYSSEY(1968, U.S./Brit.)
1984
2010(1984)
Misc. Talkies
LOVE AND LARCENY(1983)

Jeramie Rain
LAST HOUSE ON THE LEFT(1972)

Leslie Rain
1984
CHEECH AND CHONG'S THE CORSICAN BROTHERS(1984)

Frank Rainboth
BIG TRAIL, THE(1930)

Joaquin Rainbow
WOLFEN(1981)

John Rainbow
Silents
OLD CODE, THE(1928)

The Rainbow Four
NAUGHTY NINETIES, THE(1945)

Allen Raine
Silents
WELSH SINGER, A(1915, Brit.), w

Jack Raine
HARMONY HEAVEN(1930, Brit.); HATE SHIP, THE(1930, Brit.); MIDDLE WATCH, THE(1930, Brit.); RAISE THE ROOF(1930); SUSPENSE(1930, Brit.); LEAP OF FAITH(1931, Brit.); NIGHT BIRDS(1931, Brit.); FIRES OF FATE(1932, Brit.); HER NIGHT OUT(1932, Brit.); FORTUNATE FOOL, THE(1933, Brit.); HOUSE OF TRENT, THE(1933, Brit.); OUT OF THE PAST(1933, Brit.); DANGEROUS GROUND(1934, Brit.); GHOUL, THE(1934, Brit.); LILIES OF THE FIELD(1934, Brit.); LITTLE FRIEND(1934, Brit.); CLAIRVOYANT, THE(1935, Brit.); MIMI(1935, Brit.); DOUBLE OR QUITS(1938, Brit.); MEET MR. PENNY(1938, Brit.); FOR FREEDOM(1940, Brit.); NEUTRAL PORT(1941, Brit.); I DIDN'T DO IT(1945, Brit.); SEND FOR PAUL TEMPLE(1946, Brit.); HOLIDAY CAMP(1947, Brit.); CALLING PAUL TEMPLE(1948, Brit.); EASY MONEY(1948, Brit.); MINE OWN EXECUTIONER(1948, Brit.); STORY OF SHIRLEY YORKE, THE(1948, Brit.); MY BROTHER'S KEEPER(1949, Brit.); NO WAY BACK(1949, Brit.); QUARTET(1949, Brit.); GOOD TIME GIRL(1950, Brit.); HAPPY TIME, THE(1952); HOLIDAY FOR SINNERS(1952); LES MISERABLES(1952); ROGUE'S MARCH(1952); ABOVE AND BEYOND(1953); DANGEROUS WHEN WET(1953); DESTINATION GOBI(1953); JULIUS CAESAR(1953); STORY OF THREE LOVES, THE(1953); ELEPHANT WALK(1954); RHAPSODY(1954); SILVER CHALICE, THE(1954); GIRL IN THE RED VELVET SWING, THE(1955); INTERRUPTED MELODY(1955); NOT AS A STRANGER(1955); PRINCE OF PLAYERS(1955); SOLDIER OF FORTUNE(1955); POWER AND THE PRIZE, THE(1956); WOMAN OBSESSED(1959); TARAS BULBA(1962); MY FAIR LADY(1964); SCANDALOUS JOHN(1971)

Jennifer Raine
SCARLET COAT, THE(1955); LIST OF ADRIAN MESSENGER, THE(1963)

Leo Raine
ILLEGAL(1932, Brit.)

Natalie Raine
HA' PENNY BREEZE(1950, Brit.)

Norman Reilly Raine
TUGBOAT ANNIE(1933), w; WHITE WOMAN(1933), w; GOD'S COUNTRY AND THE WOMAN(1937), w; LIFE OF EMILE ZOLA, THE(1937), w; MOUNTAIN JUSTICE(1937), w; PERFECT SPECIMEN, THE(1937), w; ADVENTURES OF ROBIN HOOD, THE(1938), w; MEN ARE SUCH FOOLS(1938), w; EACH DAWN I DIE(1939), w; ISLAND OF LOST MEN(1939), w; PRIVATE LIVES OF ELIZABETH AND ESSEX, THE(1939), w; FIGHTING 69TH, THE(1940), w; TUGBOAT ANNIE SAILS AGAIN(1940), w; VIRGINIA CITY(1940), w; CAPTAINS OF THE CLOUDS(1942), w; EAGLE SQUADRON(1942), w; WE'VE NEVER BEEN LICKED(1943), w; LADIES COURAGEOUS(1944), w; BELL FOR ADANO, A(1945), w; CAPTAIN KIDD(1945), w; NOB HILL(1945), w; M(1951), w; WOMAN OF THE NORTH COUNTRY(1952), w; SEA OF LOST SHIPS(1953), w

Patricia Raine
IT HAPPENED IN SOHO(1948, Brit.); VICE VERSA(1948, Brit.); FOOLS RUSH IN(1949, Brit.); HELTER SKELTER(1949, Brit.); MADELEINE(1950, Brit.); ENCORE(1951, Brit.); PANDORA AND THE FLYING DUTCHMAN(1951, Brit.); CARETAKERS DAUGHTER, THE(1952, Brit.); DAY TO REMEMBER, A(1953, Brit.)

William MacLeod Raine
THREE YOUNG TEXANS(1954), w; MAN FROM BITTER RIDGE, THE(1955), w
Silents
PURE GRIT(1923), w; MAN FROM WYOMING, THE(1924), w; RIDGEWAY OF MONTANA(1924), w; DESERT'S PRICE, THE(1926), w; FIGHTING EDGE(1926), w; MAN FOUR-SQUARE, A(1926), w

Iris Rainer
MOUSE AND HIS CHILD, THE(1977)
Jeanne Rainer
TOUCH OF FLESH, THE(1960)
Joe Rainer
1984
BEAR, THE(1984)
John Rainer
UNDER MILK WOOD(1973, Brit.)
Klaus Rainer
1984
BURIED ALIVE(1984, Ital.)
Leo Rainer
JOURNEYS FROM BERLIN–1971(1980)
Leon Rainer
GERMANY IN AUTUMN(1978, Ger.)
Lorraine Rainer
THIS MAN MUST DIE(1970, Fr./Ital.)
Luise Rainer
ESCAPADE(1935); GREAT ZIEGFELD, THE(1936); BIG CITY(1937); EMPEROR'S
CANDLESTICKS, THE(1937); GOOD EARTH, THE(1937); DRAMATIC SCHOOL(1938);
GREAT WALTZ, THE(1938); TOY WIFE, THE(1938); HOSTAGES(1943)
Margrit Rainer
HEIDI(1954, Switz.); HEIDI AND PETER(1955, Switz.)
Peter Rainer
JOYRIDE(1977), w
Yvonne Rainer
JOURNEYS FROM BERLIN–1971(1980), a, d, ed
Ruth Rainero
JOURNEYS FROM BERLIN–1971(1980)
Christina Raines
TOUCHED BY LOVE(1980)
1984
REAL LIFE(1984, Brit.)
Cristina Raines
STACEY!(1973); STONE KILLER, THE(1973); NASHVILLE(1975); RUSSIAN ROU-
LETTE(1975); DUELLISTS, THE(1977, Brit.); SENTINEL, THE(1977); SILVER DREAM
RACER(1982, Brit.); NIGHTMARES(1983)
David Raines
GREY FOX, THE(1983, Can.)
Ella Raines
UNCLE HARRY(1945); CORVETTE K-225(1943); CRY HAVOC(1943); ENTER AR-
SENE LUPIN(1944); HAIL THE CONQUERING HERO(1944); PHANTOM LADY(1944);
SUSPECT, THE(1944); TALL IN THE SADDLE(1944); RUNAROUND, THE(1946);
WHITE TIE AND TAILS(1946); BRUTE FORCE(1947); SENATOR WAS INDISCREET,
THE(1947); TIME OUT OF MIND(1947); WEB, THE(1947); DANGEROUS PROFES-
SION, A(1949); IMPACT(1949); WALKING HILLS, THE(1949); SECOND FACE,
THE(1950); SINGING GUNS(1950); FIGHTING COAST GUARD(1951); RIDE THE
MAN DOWN(1952); MAN IN THE ROAD, THE(1957, Brit.)
Fred Raines
Silents
WELSH SINGER, A(1915, Brit.); ROGUE IN LOVE, A(1922, Brit.); AUDACIOUS MR.
SQUIRE, THE(1923, Brit.)
Larry S. Raines
1984
TANK(1984)
Steve Raines
UNDER COLORADO SKIES(1947); FRONTIER REVENGE(1948); SHERIFF OF
WICHITA(1949); SON OF A BADMAN(1949); SHANE(1953); NAKED GUN, THE(1956);
CATTLE EMPIRE(1958); STREET OF DARKNESS(1958)
Misc. Talkies
BORDER FENCE(1951)
Steven Raines
COUNT THREE AND PRAY(1955)
Ford Rainey
3:10 TO YUMA(1957); WHITE HEAT(1949); PERFECT STRANGERS(1950); ROBE,
THE(1953); BADLANDERS, THE(1958); JOHN PAUL JONES(1959); LAST MILE,
THE(1959); FLAMING STAR(1960); ADA(1961); CLAUDELLE INGLISH(1961); DEAD
TO THE WORLD(1961); PARRISH(1961); TWO RODE TOGETHER(1961); FORTY
POUNDS OF TROUBLE(1962); KINGS OF THE SUN(1963); GUNPOINT(1966); JOHN-
NY TIGER(1966); SAND PEBBLES, THE(1966); GYPSY MOTHS, THE(1969); NAKED
ZOO, THE(1970); TRAVELING EXECUTIONER, THE(1970); GLORY BOY(1971); LIKE
A CROW ON A JUNE BUG(1972); PARALLAX VIEW, THE(1974); GUARDIAN OF THE
WILDERNESS(1977); HALLOWEEN 11(1981)
Joe Rainey
1984
GO TELL IT ON THE MOUNTAIN(1984), set d
Kathleen Rainey
TROUBLE WITH GIRLS(AND HOW TO GET INTO IT), THE*1/2 (1969)
Norman Rainey
TROUBLE WITH WOMEN, THE(1947); THAT FORSYTE WOMAN(1949); WAKE OF
THE RED WITCH(1949); LORNA DOONE(1951); BREAKDOWN(1953)
Pat Rainey
Misc. Talkies
DREAMER, THE(1947)
Shugfoot Rainey
COMMON LAW WIFE(1963)
Sue Rainey
WORDS AND MUSIC(1929)
Ralph Rainger
FAREWELL TO ARMS, A(1932), m; THIS IS THE NIGHT(1932), m; BOLERO(1934),
m; COME ON, MARINES(1934), m; KISS AND MAKE UP(1934), m; LITTLE MISS
MARKER(1934), m; SIX OF A KIND(1934), m; DEVIL IS A WOMAN, THE(1935), m;
RUGGLES OF RED GAP(1935), m; BIG BROADCAST OF 1938, THE(1937), m/l Leo
Robin; EBB TIDE(1937), m
Lorraine Rainier
VON RICHTHOFEN AND BROWN(1970)

Hedley Rainnie
JIGSAW(1949)
Daniel Rainor
UNHOLY ROLLERS(1972)
Chick Rains
TILL DEATH(1978), m
Claude Rains
INVISIBLE MAN, THE(1933); CRIME WITHOUT PASSION(1934); CLAIRVOYANT,
THE(1935, Brit.); LAST OUTPOST, THE(1935); MAN WHO RECLAIMED HIS HEAD,
THE(1935); MYSTERY OF EDWIN DROOD, THE(1935); ANTHONY ADVERSE(1936);
HEARTS DIVIDED(1936); PRINCE AND THE PAUPER, THE(1937); STOLEN HOLI-
DAY(1937); THEY WON'T FORGET(1937); ADVENTURES OF ROBIN HOOD,
THE(1938); FOUR DAUGHTERS(1938); GOLD IS WHERE YOU FIND IT(1938);
WHITE BANNERS(1938); DAUGHTERS COURAGEOUS(1939); FOUR WIVES(1939);
JUAREZ(1939); MR. SMITH GOES TO WASHINGTON(1939); THEY MADE ME A
CRIMINAL(1939); LADY WITH RED HAIR(1940); SATURDAY'S CHILDREN(1940);
SEA HAWK, THE(1940); FOUR MOTHERS(1941); HERE COMES MR. JORDAN(1941);
WOLF MAN, THE(1941); CASABLANCA(1942); KING'S ROW(1942); MOON-
TIDE(1942); NOW, VOYAGER(1942); FOREVER AND A DAY(1943); PHANTOM OF
THE OPERA(1943); MR. SKEFFINGTON(1944); PASSAGE TO MARSEILLE(1944);
STRANGE HOLIDAY(1945); THIS LOVE OF OURS(1945); ANGEL ON MY SHOUL-
DER(1946); CAESAR AND CLEOPATRA(1946, Brit.); DECEPTION(1946); NOTORI-
OUS(1946); UNSUSPECTED, THE(1947); ONE WOMAN'S STORY(1949, Brit.); ROPE
OF SAND(1949); SONG OF SURRENDER(1949); WHERE DANGER LIVES(1950);
WHITE TOWER, THE(1950); SEALED CARGO(1951); PARIS EXPRESS, THE(1953,
Brit.); LISBON(1956); THIS EARTH IS MINE(1959); LOST WORLD, THE(1960);
BATTLE OF THE WORLDS(1961, Ital.); LAWRENCE OF ARABIA(1962, Brit.); TWI-
LIGHT OF HONOR(1963); GREATEST STORY EVER TOLD, THE(1965)
Darby Lloyd Rains
Misc. Talkies
CHORUS CALL(1979)
Fred Rains
CLUE OF THE NEW PIN, THE(1929, Brit.); VERDICT OF THE SEA(1932, Brit.);
ROYAL DEMAND, A(1933, Brit.); BROKEN ROSARY, THE(1934, Brit.); IMMORTAL
GENTLEMAN(1935, Brit.); CHICK(1936, Brit.)
Silents
GREAT ADVENTURE, THE(1915, Brit.); DOORSTEPS(1916, Brit.); INDIAN LOVE
LYRICS, THE(1923, Brit.); MONEY HABIT, THE(1924, Brit.); NELL GWYNNE(1926,
Brit.); ONLY WAY, THE(1926, Brit.); INSEPARABLES, THE(1929, Brit.); BARNES
MURDER CASE, THE(1930, Brit.)
Misc. Silents
JADE HEART, THE(1915, Brit.); LAND OF MY FATHERS(1921, Brit.), d; RUNA-
WAY PRINCESS, THE(1929, Brit.)
Jessica Rains
KOTCH(1971); PORTNOY'S COMPLAINT(1972); STAND UP AND BE COUN-
TED(1972); SLEEPER(1973); ISLANDS IN THE STREAM(1977); LITTLE MISS MARK-
ER(1980); HONKY TONK FREEWAY(1981)
Alice Raintree
MAIDSTONE(1970)
Cpl. Dennis D. Rainwater, USMC
BACK TO BATAAN(1945)
Wallace Rairden
MILLION DOLLAR LEGS(1939); MYSTERY SEA RAIDER(1940)
Wally Rairdon
DEVIL BAT, THE(1941)
Raisa
DARK CORNER, THE(1946)
Kenneth Raisbeck
Silents
KNOCKOUT REILLY(1927), w
Bill Raisch
LONELY ARE THE BRAVE(1962)
N. RaiskayaDore
GREAT CITIZEN, THE(1939, USSR)
Yuri Raisman
DREAM OF A COSSACK(1982, USSR), d
Dorothy Raison
EVERYBODY'S DANCIN'(1950), w; GIRLS ON THE LOOSE(1958), w
Milton M. Raison
SULTAN'S DAUGHTER, THE(1943), w; SPOILERS OF THE NORTH(1947), w; WEB
OF DANGER, THE(1947), w; TOPEKA(1953), w
Milton Raison
STRICTLY DYNAMITE(1934), w; COUNTRY GENTLEMEN(1937), w; SHADOW,
THE(1937), w; GIRL FROM RIO, THE(1939), w; UNDERCOVER AGENT(1939), w;
MURDER ON THE YUKON(1940), w; WEST OF CARSON CITY(1940), w; DOUBLE
CROSS(1941), w; TUMBLEDOWN RANCH IN ARIZONA(1941), w; BOMBS OVER
BURMA(1942), w; JUNGLE SIREN(1942), w; ROLLING DOWN THE GREAT DI-
VIDE(1942), w; SHERIFF OF SAGE VALLEY(1942), w; LADY FROM CHUNG-
KING(1943), w; HIGH POWERED(1945), w; PHANTOM OF 42ND STREET,
THE(1945), w; MYSTERIOUS MR. VALENTINE, THE(1946), w; BIG TOWN SCAN-
DAL(1948), w; DYNAMITE(1948), w; MR. RECKLESS(1948), w; SPEED TO SPA-
RE(1948), w; LAWTON STORY, THE(1949), w; SPECIAL AGENT(1949), w; STATE
DEPARTMENT–FILE 649(1949), w; WESTERN PACIFIC AGENT(1950), w; PRINCE
OF PEACE, THE(1951), w; STREET BANDITS(1951), w; OLD OKLAHOMA
PLAINS(1952), w; HOMESTEADERS, THE(1953), w; OLD OVERLAND TRAIL(1953),
w
Robert Raison
THIS LOVE OF OURS(1945)
Ronald Raison
KING OF THE MOUNTAIN(1981)
Emily Rait
Silents
WALL FLOWER, THE(1922)
Takazo Raita
MADAME BUTTERFLY(1955 Ital./Jap.), cos
Frank Raiter
LADY IN CEMENT(1968); MC MASTERS, THE(1970)

Vladimir Raiteric-Kraus
BATTLE OF THE NERETVA(1971, Yugo./Ital./Ger.), m
Istvan Raits
FATHER(1967, Hung.)
Anne Raitt
BLEAK MOMENTS(1972, Brit.)
Bonnie Raitt
SGT. PEPPER'S LONELY HEARTS CLUB BAND(1978); URBAN COWBOY(1980)
Jimmy Raitt
KING OF COMEDY, THE(1983); TRADING PLACES(1983)
John Raitt
LITTLE NELLIE KELLY(1940); H.M. PULHAM, ESQ.(1941); MINSTREL MAN(1944); PAJAMA GAME, THE(1957)
Yuli Raizman
Misc. Silents
KATORGA(1928, USSR), d
Yuri Raizman
TRAIN GOES EAST, THE(1949, USSR), d
Jagdish Raj
NINE HOURS TO RAMA(1963, U.S./Brit.)
Rajah the Bengal Tiger
TIGER WALKS, A(1964)
Saeed Rajai
1984
MISSION, THE(1984)
A. Rajan
RIVER, THE(1961, India), ed
Albert Rajau
UP FROM THE BEACH(1965), prod d; LIFE LOVE DEATH(1969, Fr./Ital.); TENANT, THE(1976, Fr.), art d
W. Rajewski
PORTRAIT OF LENIN(1967, Pol./USSR)
Adam Rajhona
FORTRESS, THE(1979, Hung.)
Iveco Rajkovic
RAT SAVIOUR, THE(1977, Yugo.), ph
Thomas Rajna
JET STORM(1961, Brit.), m, md
Johns Rajohnson
FIENDISH PLOT OF DR. FU MANCHU, THE(1980)
1984
CHEECH AND CHONG'S THE CORSICAN BROTHERS(1984)
Pierre-Loup Rajot
1984
A NOS AMOURS(1984, Fr.)
Peggy Rajski
1984
BROTHER FROM ANOTHER PLANET, THE(1984), p
Dunja Rajter
APACHE GOLD(1965, Ger.); FRONTIER HELLCAT(1966, Fr./Ital./Ger./Yugo.)
Janos Rajz
DIALOGUE(1967, Hung.)
Joachim Rake
GLASS OF WATER, A(1962, Cgr.)
Hugh Raker [Cy Endfield]
MASTER PLAN, THE(1955, Brit.), d, w
Loren Raker
COWBOY SERENADE(1942); CHICKEN EVERY SUNDAY(1948)
Lorin L. Raker
VARIETY GIRL(1947)
Lorin Raker
WITHOUT RESERVATIONS(1946); GANG WAR(1928); MOTHER'S BOY(1929); SIX CYLINDER LOVE(1931); IMPATIENT MAIDEN(1932); LITTLE GIANT, THE(1933); LOVE IS LIKE THAT(1933); MY WOMAN(1933); RACING STRAIN, THE(1933); I'VE BEEN AROUND(1935); LES MISERABLES(1935); MAN ON THE FLYING TRAPEZE, THE(1935); NUT FARM, THE(1935); HONEYMOON LIMITED(1936); CALIFORNIA STRAIGHT AHEAD(1937); PRIMROSE PATH(1940); IN THE NAVY(1941); SIX LESSONS FROM MADAME LA ZONGA(1941); TWO-FACED WOMAN(1941); GIVE OUT, SISTERS(1942); TAKE A LETTER, DARLING(1942); COWBOY IN MANHATTAN(1943); NEVER A DULL MOMENT(1943); NO TIME FOR LOVE(1943); YOU'RE A LUCKY FELLOW, MR. SMITH(1943); STANDING ROOM ONLY(1944); I'LL TELL THE WORLD(1945); MEN IN HER DIARY(1945); LADY LUCK(1946); NOCTURNE(1946); I'LL BE YOURS(1947); FAMILY HONEYMOON(1948); FULLER BRUSH GIRL, THE(1950); CHICAGO CALLING(1951); JOURNEY INTO LIGHT(1951); TALES OF ROBIN HOOD(1951); HERE COME THE NELSONS(1952); STEEL TOWN(1952)
Napier Rakes
RULERS OF THE SEA(1939)
Vasili Rakhals
Silents
BATTLESHIP POTEMKIN, THE(1925, USSR), art d
Arkady Rakhman
STRIPES(1981)
Leonid Rakhmanov
BALTIC DEPUTY(1937, USSR), w
Olga Rakhmanova
Misc. Silents
LIFE FOR A LIFE, A(1916, USSR)
Laya Raki
UP TO HIS NECK(1954, Brit.); LAND OF FURY(1955 Brit.); QUENTIN DURWARD(1955); GREH(1962, Ger./Yugo.); GALLANT ONE, THE(1964, U.S./Peru); POPPY IS ALSO A FLOWER, THE(1966); SAVAGE PAMPAS(1967, Span./Arg.)
R. Rakitin
SUN SHINES FOR ALL, THE(1961, USSR)
Alvin Rakoff
ROOM 43(1959, Brit.), d; HOT MONEY GIRL(1962, Brit./Ger.), d; WORLD IN MY POCKET, THE(1962, Fr./Ital./Ger.), d; COMEDY MAN, THE(1964), d; CROSSPLOT(1969, Brit.), d; HOFFMAN(1970, Brit.), d; SAY HELLO TO YESTERDAY(1971, Brit.), d, w; KING SOLOMON'S TREASURE(1978, Can.), d; CITY ON FIRE(1979 Can.), d; DEATH SHIP(1980, Can.), d; DIRTY TRICKS(1981, Can.), d

Ian Rakoff
FLIGHT OF THE EAGLE(1983, Swed.), w
M. Rakovskiy
SHADOWS OF FORGOTTEN ANCESTORS(1967, USSR), art d
Pola Raksa
SARAGOSSA MANUSCRIPT, THE(1972, Pol.)
David Raksin
UNTIL THEY SAIL(1957), m; TWO WEEKS IN ANOTHER TOWN(1962), m; SAN QUENTIN(1937), m; MEN IN HER LIFE, THE(1941), md; DR. RENAULT'S SECRET(1942), m; UNDYING MONSTER, THE(1942), m; SOMETHING TO SHOUT ABOUT(1943), m; LAURA(1944), m; TAMPICO(1944), m; DON JUAN QUILLIGAN(1945), m; FALLEN ANGEL(1945), m; WHERE DO WE GO FROM HERE?(1945), m; SMOKY(1946), m; DAISY KENYON(1947), m; FOREVER AMBER(1947), m; HOMESTRETCH, THE(1947), m; SECRET LIFE OF WALTER MITTY, THE(1947), m; APARTMENT FOR PEGGY(1948), m; FORCE OF EVIL(1948), m; FURY AT FURNACE CREEK(1948), m; WHIRLPOOL(1949), m; LADY WITHOUT PASSPORT, A(1950), m; MAGNIFICENT YANKEE, THE(1950), m; REFORMER AND THE REDHEAD, THE(1950), m; RIGHT CROSS(1950), m; IT'S A BIG COUNTRY(1951), m; KIND LADY(1951), m; MAN WITH A CLOAK, THE(1951), m; BAD AND THE BEAUTIFUL, THE(1952), m; CARRIE(1952), m; GIRL IN WHITE, THE(1952), m; PAT AND MIKE(1952), m; APACHE(1954), m; PASSION(1954), m; SUDDENLY(1954), m; BIG COMBO, THE(1955), m; BIGGER THAN LIFE(1956), m; HILDA CRANE(1956), m; JUBAL(1956), m; GUNSIGHT RIDGE(1957), m; MAN ON FIRE(1957), m; VINTAGE, THE(1957), m; SEPARATE TABLES(1958), m; TWILIGHT FOR THE GODS(1958), m, md; AL CAPONE(1959), m; PAY OR DIE(1960), m, md; TOO LATE BLUES(1962), m; NIGHT TIDE(1963), m; INVITATION TO A GUNFIGHTER(1964), m; PATSY, THE(1964), m; LOVE HAS MANY FACES(1965), m; REDEEMER, THE(1965, Span.), m; SYLVIA(1965), m; BIG HAND FOR THE LITTLE LADY, A(1966), m; WILL PENNY(1968), m; WHAT'S THE MATTER WITH HELEN?(1971), m; GLASS HOUSES(1972), m
Ruby Raksin
VALLEY OF THE DRAGONS(1961), m; LOLLIPOP COVER, THE(1965), m
Hortense Raky
BURG THEATRE(1936, Ger.)
M.W. Rale [Rayle]
Silents
MADAME BUTTERFLY(1915); AWAY GOES PRUDENCE(1920)
Cecil Raleigh
Silents
SINS OF SOCIETY(1915), w
H.M. Raleigh
EXCESS BAGGAGE(1933, Brit.), w
Joe Raleigh
Silents
JANICE MEREDITH(1924)
Mrs. Cecil Raleigh
Silents
CLEMENCEAU CASE, THE(1915)
Saba Raleigh
Silents
PROFIT AND THE LOSS(1917, Brit.); NOBODY'S CHILD(1919, Brit.); ROAD TO LONDON, THE(1921, Brit.)
Misc. Silents
PRINCESS OF NEW YORK, THE(1921 US/Brit.)
Mohamed Ralem
STRANGER, THE(1967, Algeria/Fr./Ital.)
Lillette Zoe Raley
SILENT RAGE(1982)
Don Ralke
C'MON, LET'S LIVE A LITTLE(1967), m
Donald Ralke
SNOOPY, COME HOME(1972), m
Marilyn Rall
SMITHEREENS(1982)
Tommy Rall
GET HEP TO LOVE(1942); KISS ME KATE(1953); SEVEN BRIDES FOR SEVEN BROTHERS(1954); MY SISTER EILEEN(1955); SECOND GREATEST SEX, THE(1955); INVITATION TO THE DANCE(1956); WALK THE PROUD LAND(1956); WORLD IN MY CORNER(1956); MERRY ANDREW(1958); PENNIES FROM HEAVEN(1981)
Anna Marie Ralli
NINE MILES TO NOON(1963)
Giovanna Ralli
GENERALE DELLA ROVERE(1960, Ital./Fr.); WARRIORS FIVE(1962); LET'S TALK ABOUT WOMEN(1964, Fr./Ital.); VERY HANDY MAN, A(1966, Fr./Ital.); WHAT DID YOU DO IN THE WAR, DADDY?(1966); CAPER OF THE GOLDEN BULLS, THE(1967); MY WIFE'S ENEMY(1967, Ital.); DEADFALL(1968, Brit.); CANNON FOR CORDOBA(1970); MERCENARY, THE(1970, Ital./Span.)
Giovanni Ralli
LA FUGA(1966, Ital.)
Lillia Ralli
PHAEDRA(1962, U.S./Gr./Fr.)
Paul Ralli
MARRIED IN HOLLYWOOD(1929)
Silents
SHOW PEOPLE(1928)
Misc. Silents
MONTMARTE ROSE(1929)
Dean Rallis, Jr.
FRATERNITY ROW(1977)
Orestes Rallis
BOY ON A DOLPHIN(1957)
Debra Ralls
Misc. Talkies
BOD SQUAD, THE(1976)
Le Rallye Boissiere
RISE OF LOUIS XIV, THE(1970, Fr.)
Larry Ralmond
BRAIN EATERS, THE(1958), ph

Anna Ralph
MANGANINNIE(1982, Aus.)
George Ralph
Silents
BALLET GIRL, THE(1916)
Misc. Silents
HER MATERNAL RIGHT(1916)
Hanna Ralph
Silents
KRIEMHILD'S REVENGE(1924, Ger.); SIEGFRIED(1924, Ger.)
Misc. Silents
ALGOL(1920, Ger.)
Hannah Ralph
Silents
DECAMERON NIGHTS(1924, Brit.)
Jessie Ralph
ANN CARVER'S PROFESSION(1933); CHILD OF MANHATTAN(1933); COCKTAIL HOUR(1933); ELMER THE GREAT(1933); AFFAIRS OF CELLINI, THE(1934); COMING OUT PARTY(1934); EVELYN PRENTICE(1934); MURDER AT THE VANITIES(1934); NANA(1934); ONE NIGHT OF LOVE(1934); WE LIVE AGAIN(1934); CAPTAIN BLOOD(1935); DAVID COPPERFIELD(1935); ENCHANTED APRIL(1935); I FOUND STELLA PARISH(1935); I LIVE MY LIFE(1935); JALNA(1935); LES MISERABLES(1935); METROPOLITAN(1935); PARIS IN SPRING(1935); VANESSA, HER LOVE STORY(1935); AFTER THE THIN MAN(1936); BUNKER BEAN(1936); GARDEN MURDER CASE, THE(1936); LITTLE LORD FAUNTLEROY(1936); SAN FRANCISCO(1936); UNGUARDED HOUR, THE(1936); WALKING ON AIR(1936); YELLOW DUST(1936); CAMILLE(1937); DOUBLE WEDDING(1937); GOOD EARTH, THE(1937); LAST OF MRS. CHEYNEY, THE(1937); HOLD THAT KISS(1938); LOVE IS A HEADACHE(1938); PORT OF SEVEN SEAS(1938); CAFE SOCIETY(1939); DRUMS ALONG THE MOHAWK(1939); FOUR GIRLS IN WHITE(1939); KID FROM TEXAS, THE(1939); MICKEY, THE KID(1939); ST. LOUIS BLUES(1939); BANK DICK, THE(1940); GIRL FROM AVENUE A(1940); I CAN'T GIVE YOU ANYTHING BUT LOVE, BABY(1940); I WANT A DIVORCE(1940); STAR DUST(1940); LADY FROM CHEYENNE(1941); THEY MET IN BOMBAY(1941)
Silents
NEW YORK(1916); SUCH A LITTLE QUEEN(1921)
Misc. Silents
MARY'S LAMB(1915)
Joseph Ralph
LOYAL HEART(1946, Brit.)
Julia Ralph
Silents
SO'S YOUR OLD MAN(1926)
Louis Ralph
CRUISER EMDEN(1932, Ger.), a, d, w
Silents
GHOST TRAIN, THE(1927, Brit.); SPIES(1929, Ger.)
Misc. Silents
GHOST TRAIN, THE(1927, Brit.); RUSSIA(1929, Ger.)
Ronnie Ralph
DARK HORSE, THE(1946); IT'S A WONDERFUL LIFE(1946); NIGHT EDITOR(1946); RETURN OF THE BADMEN(1948); RUSTY SAVES A LIFE(1949); RUSTY'S BIRTHDAY(1949); MISTER 880(1950)
Ralph Edwards and Co.
SEVEN DAYS LEAVE(1942); RADIO STARS ON PARADE(1945)
Ralph Goldsmith and His Band
PICCADILLY NIGHTS(1930, Brit.)
Ralph Rogers Trio
LORDS OF FLATBUSH, THE(1974)
Ralston
GOD TOLD ME TO(1976), cos
Alfred Ralston
OH! WHAT A LOVELY WAR(1969, Brit.), m, md; YOUNG WINSTON(1972, Brit.), m, md
Bradford Ralston
Silents
PENROD(1922)
Bud Ralston
KIND OF LOVING, A(1962, Brit.)
David Ralston
FOREVER AMBER(1947); IVY(1947); SINGAPORE(1947)
Denis Ralston
PLAYERS(1979)
Esther Ralston
MIGHTY, THE(1929); WHEEL OF LIFE, THE(1929); LONELY WIVES(1931); PRODIGAL, THE(1931); AFTER THE BALL(1932, Brit.); BLACK BEAUTY(1933); ROME EXPRESS(1933, Brit.); TO THE LAST MAN(1933); BY CANDLELIGHT(1934); ROMANCE IN THE RAIN(1934); SADIE MCKEE(1934); FORCED LANDING(1935); LADIES CRAVE EXCITEMENT(1935); MARINES ARE COMING, THE(1935); MR. DYNAMITE(1935); STRANGE WIVES(1935); STREAMLINE EXPRESS(1935); TOGETHER WE LIVE(1935); GIRL FROM MANDALAY(1936); HOLLYWOOD BOULEVARD(1936); REUNION(1936); AS GOOD AS MARRIED(1937); SHADOWS OF THE ORIENT(1937); WE'RE IN THE LEGION NOW(1937); LETTER OF INTRODUCTION(1938); SLANDER HOUSE(1938); TIN PAN ALLEY(1940); SAN FRANCISCO DOCKS(1941)
Silents
HUCKLEBERRY FINN(1920); CROSSING TRAILS(1921); KID, THE(1921); OLIVER TWIST(1922); PRISONER, THE(1923); PURE GRIT(1923); RAILROADED(1923); JACK O' CLUBS(1924); MARRIAGE CIRCLE, THE(1924); PETER PAN(1924); BEGGAR ON HORSEBACK(1925); WOMANHANDLED(1925); AMERICAN VENUS, THE(1926); BLIND GODDESS, THE(1926); KISS FOR CINDERELLA, A(1926); OLD IRONSIDES(1926); QUARTERBACK, THE(1926); CHILDREN OF DIVORCE(1927); HALF A BRIDE(1928); LOVE AND LEARN(1928)
Misc. Silents
WHISPERING DEVILS(1920); DARING DANGER(1922); PALS OF THE WEST(1922); BLINKY(1923); HEART BUSTER, THE(1924); $50,000 Reward(1924); BEST PEOPLE, THE(1925); GOOSE HANGS HIGH, THE(1925); LITTLE FRENCH GIRL, THE(1925); LUCKY DEVIL(1925); TROUBLE WITH WIVES(1925); FASHIONS FOR WOMEN(1927); FIGURES DON'T LIE(1927); SPOTLIGHT, THE(1927); TEN MODERN COMMANDMENTS(1927); SAWDUST PARADISE, THE(1928); SOMETHING AL-

WAYS HAPPENS(1928); BETRAYAL(1929); CASE OF LENA SMITH, THE(1929)
Gil Ralston
KONA COAST(1968), w; SPECIAL DELIVERY(1976), w
Gilbert A. Ralston
WILLARD(1971), w; BEN(1972), w
Hal Ralston
HELL NIGHT(1981)
Henry Ralston
Silents
STOP THIEF(1920)
Howard Ralston
Silents
POLLYANNA(1920); CRIMSON CHALLENGE, THE(1922)
Misc. Silents
IT'S A GREAT LIFE(1920); DAUGHTER OF LUXURY, A(1922)
James Ralston
NIGHT OF THE STRANGLER(1975)
1984
TERMINATOR, THE(1984)
Jane Ralston
FIRST NUDIE MUSICAL, THE(1976); SUNSET COVE(1978); JONI(1980)
Jobyna Ralston
COLLEGE COQUETTE, THE(1929); ROUGH WATERS(1930)
Silents
WHY WORRY(1923); GIRL SHY(1924); HOT WATER(1924); FRESHMAN, THE(1925); FOR HEAVEN'S SAKE(1926); KID BROTHER, THE(1927); PRETTY CLOTHES(1927); RACING ROMEO(1927); SPECIAL DELIVERY(1927); WINGS(1927); NIGHT FLYER, THE(1928); POWER OF THE PRESS, THE(1928); TOILERS, THE(1928)
Misc. Silents
GIGOLO(1926); SWEET DADDIES(1926); LIGHTING(1927); LITTLE MICKEY GROGAN(1927); BIG HOP, THE(1928); BLACK BUTTERFLIES(1928); COUNT OF TEN, THE(1928); SOME MOTHER'S BOY(1929)
Johnny Ralston
PIRANHA II: THE SPAWNING(1981, Neth.)
Ken Ralston
STAR TREK II: THE WRATH OF KHAN(1982), spec eff; RETURN OF THE JEDI(1983), spec eff
Marcia Ralston
CALL IT A DAY(1937); EVER SINCE EVE(1937); FLY-AWAY BABY(1937); SH! THE OCTOPUS(1937); SINGING MARINE, THE(1937); CRIME TAKES A HOLIDAY(1938); FOOLS FOR SCANDAL(1938); GOLD IS WHERE YOU FIND IT(1938); MEN ARE SUCH FOOLS(1938); KEEP 'EM FLYING(1941); KID FROM KANSAS, THE(1941); NEVER GIVE A SUCKER AN EVEN BREAK(1941); PARIS CALLING(1941); SUNDAY PUNCH(1942); OUT OF THE BLUE(1947)
Rudy Ralston
BUCKAROO SHERIFF OF TEXAS(1951), p; DAKOTA KID, THE(1951), p; DESPERADOES OUTPOST(1952), p; THUNDERING CARAVANS(1952), p; WILD HORSE AMBUSH(1952), p; DOWN LAREDO WAY(1953), p; EL PASO STAMPEDE(1953), p; MARSHAL OF CEDAR ROCK(1953), p; RED RIVER SHORE(1953), p; SAVAGE FRONTIER(1953), p; SHADOWS OF TOMBSTONE(1953), p; PHANTOM STALLION, THE(1954), p; GUNFIRE AT INDIAN GAP(1957), p; HELL'S CROSSROADS(1957), p; LAST STAGECOACH WEST, THE(1957), p; LAWLESS EIGHTIES, THE(1957), p; CROOKED CIRCLE, THE(1958), p; MAN WHO DIED TWICE, THE(1958), p; NOTORIOUS MR. MONKS, THE(1958), p
Vera Hruba Ralston
LADY AND THE MONSTER, THE(1944); STORM OVER LISBON(1944); DAKOTA(1945); MURDER IN THE MUSIC HALL(1946); GUNFIRE AT INDIAN GAP(1957)
Vera Ralston
LAKE PLACID SERENADE(1944); PLAINSMAN AND THE LADY(1946); WYOMING(1947); ANGEL ON THE AMAZON(1948); FLAME, THE(1948); I, JANE DOE(1948); FIGHTING KENTUCKIAN, THE(1949); SURRENDER(1950); BELLE LE GRAND(1951); HOODLUM EMPIRE(1952); WILD BLUE YONDER, THE(1952); FAIR WIND TO JAVA(1953); PERILOUS JOURNEY, A(1953); JUBILEE TRAIL(1954); TIMBERJACK(1955); ACCUSED OF MURDER(1956); SPOILERS OF THE FOREST(1957); MAN WHO DIED TWICE, THE(1958); NOTORIOUS MR. MONKS, THE(1958)
Buck Ram
CARNIVAL ROCK(1957), m
Mildred Ram
STARS OVER BROADWAY(1935), w
Rudy Rama
UNDERCURRENT(1946); FIESTA(1947); PRISONERS IN PETTICOATS(1950); SEPTEMBER AFFAIR(1950); HOODLUM, THE(1951); MY FAVORITE SPY(1951); OPERATION SECRET(1952); DREAM WIFE(1953)
Adria Ramaccia
GIDGET GOES TO ROME(1963)
Loretta Ramaciotti
LA DOLCE VITA(1961, Ital./Fr.)
S. Ramadanov
DEVOTION(1955, USSR)
Makara Kwaiha Ramadhani
LION, THE(1962, Brit.)
Cecil Ramage
BRITANNIA OF BILLINGSGATE(1933, Brit.); SECRET AGENT(1933, Brit.); FREEDOM OF THE SEAS(1934, Brit.); LUCK OF A SAILOR, THE(1934, Brit.); WHAT HAPPENED THEN?(1934, Brit.); HELL'S CARGO(1935, Brit.); SINGING THROUGH(1935, Brit.); KING OF THE DAMNED(1936, Brit.); LOVE IN EXILE(1936, Brit.); SECRET OF STAMBOUL, THE(1936, Brit.); APRIL BLOSSOMS(1937, Brit.); CAFE COLETTE(1937, Brit.); LAST ROSE OF SUMMER, THE(1937, Brit.); SCOTLAND YARD COMMANDS(1937, Brit.); MILL ON THE FLOSS(1939, Brit.); FACE BEHIND THE SCAR(1940, Brit.); YANK IN LONDON, A(1946, Brit.); NICHOLAS NICKLEBY(1947, Brit.); KIND HEARTS AND CORONETS(1949, Brit.)
Misc. Talkies
BE CAREFUL, MR. SMITH(1935)
Jack Ramage
DEATH COLLECTOR(1976); SLOW DANCING IN THE BIG CITY(1978); KRAMER VS. KRAMER(1979)

Lee Ramage
JEALOUSY(1934)
Walter Ramage
MISFITS, THE(1961)
Suzie Ramagos
EASY RIDER(1969)
Ramakrishna
JUNGLE, THE(1952)
G. Ramanathan
JUNGLE, THE(1952), m
Vic Ramano
PANIC IN NEEDLE PARK(1971)
Steve Ramanuskas
QUEST FOR FIRE(1982, Fr./Can.)
Crystal Ramar
Misc. Talkies
BURNOUT(1979)
Josef Ramart
CARAVAN(1946, Brit.)
Yusef Ramart
QUEEN OF SPADES(1948, Brit.)
Alexander Ramati
REBELS AGAINST THE LIGHT(1964), p,d&w; SANDS OF BEERSHEBA(1966, U.S./Israel), p,d&w; TRUNK TO CAIRO(1966, Israel/Ger.), w; DESPERATE ONES, THE(1968 U.S./Span.), a, p,d&w; MARTYR, THE(1976, Ger./Israel), w
Didi Ramati
TO HELL AND BACK(1955); ISTANBUL(1957); REBELS AGAINST THE LIGHT(1964); SANDS OF BEERSHEBA(1966, U.S./Israel)
Enrique Rambal
EMPTY STAR, THE(1962, Mex.); MAN AND THE MONSTER, THE(1965, Mex.); EXTERMINATING ANGEL, THE(1967, Mex.)
J.P. Rambal
HOW NOT TO ROB A DEPARTMENT STORE(1965, Fr./Ital.)
Jean-Pierre Rambal
JOKER, THE(1961, Fr.); MAGNIFICENT ONE, THE(1974, Fr./Ital.); LE GENDARME ET LES EXTRATERRESTRES(1978, Fr.)
Carlo Rambaldi
DEEP RED(1976, Ital.), spec eff; KING KONG(1976), cos; ALIEN(1979), spec eff; NIGHTWING(1979), spec eff; HAND, THE(1981), spec eff; E.T. THE EXTRA-TERRESTRIAL(1982), cos
Else Rambausek
HOUSE OF THE THREE GIRLS, THE(1961, Aust.)
Richard Rambaut
BLEAK MOMENTS(1972, Brit.), art d; GUMSHOE(1972, Brit.), art d
Doris Rambeau
MARRIAGE OF A YOUNG STOCKBROKER, THE(1971), cos
Lillian Rambeau
Silents
JENNY BE GOOD(1920); OCCASIONALLY YOURS(1920)
Marjorie Rambeau
HER MAN(1930); MIN AND BILL(1930); EASIEST WAY, THE(1931); INSPIRATION(1931); LAUGHING SINNERS(1931); LEFTOVER LADIES(1931); SECRET SIX, THE(1931); SILENCE(1931); SON OF INDIA(1931); STRANGERS MAY KISS(1931); TAILOR MADE MAN, A(1931); THIS MODERN AGE(1931); HELL DIVERS(1932); MAN'S CASTLE, A(1933); STRICTLY PERSONAL(1933); WARRIOR'S HUSBAND, THE(1933); GRAND CANARY(1934); MODERN HERO, A(1934); PALOOKA(1934); READY FOR LOVE(1934); UNDER PRESSURE(1935); DIZZY DAMES(1936); FIRST LADY(1937); MERRILY WE LIVE(1938); WOMAN AGAINST WOMAN(1938); HEAVEN WITH A BARBED WIRE FENCE(1939); LAUGH IT OFF(1939); RAINS CAME, THE(1939); SUDDEN MONEY(1939); EAST OF THE RIVER(1940); PRIMROSE PATH(1940); SANTA FE MARSHAL(1940); TUGBOAT ANNIE SAILS AGAIN(1940); TWENTY MULE TEAM(1940); THREE SONS O'GUNS(1941); TOBACCO ROAD(1941); BROADWAY(1942); IN OLD OKLAHOMA(1943); ARMY WIVES(1944); OH, WHAT A NIGHT(1944); SALOME, WHERE SHE DANCED(1945); WALLS OF JERICHO(1948); ABANDONED(1949); ANY NUMBER CAN PLAY(1949); LUCKY STIFF, THE(1949); FOREVER FEMALE(1953); TORCH SONG(1953); BAD FOR EACH OTHER(1954); MAN CALLED PETER, THE(1955); VIEW FROM POMPEY'S HEAD, THE(1955); SLANDER(1956); MAN OF A THOUSAND FACES(1957)
Silents
SYNCOPATING SUE(1926)
Misc. Silents
DAZZLING MISS DAVISON, THE(1917); DEBT, THE(1917); GREATER WOMAN, THE(1917); MARY MORELAND(1917); MIRROR, THE(1917); MOTHERHOOD(1917); FORTUNE TELLER, THE(1920); ON HER HONOR(1922)
Patricia Ann Rambeau
KID MILLIONS(1934)
Regina Rambeau
MAN WHO BROKE THE BANK AT MONTE CARLO, THE(1935)
Richard Rambeau
S(1974), art d
Ballet Rambert
WOMAN TO WOMAN(1946, Brit.)
Mme. Rambert
RED SHOES, THE(1948, Brit.)
Tennessee Ramblers
RIDE, RANGER, RIDE(1936)
Bobby Rambo
1984
SONGWRITER(1984)
Dack Rambo
WHICH WAY TO THE FRONT?(1970); NIGHTMARE HONEYMOON(1973)
Misc. Talkies
DEADLY HONEYMOON(1974)
Dan Rambo
NOBODY'S PERFEKT zero(1981); SMOKEY AND THE BANDIT–PART 3(1983)
Natacha Rambova
Silents
SALOME(1922), art d, set d, cos; MONSIEUR BEAUCAIRE(1924), art d; COBRA(1925)

Misc. Silents
WHEN LOVE GROWS COLD(1925)
Natasha Rambova
Misc. Silents
WOMAN IN CHAINS, THE(1923)
Catalina Rambula
LAUGHING BOY(1934)
Franca Rame
LOVE IN 4 DIMENSIONS(1965 Fr./Ital.)
Rameau
MANULESCU(1933, Ger.), w
Emil Rameau
GASLIGHT(1944); GREENWICH VILLAGE(1944); HER HIGHNESS AND THE BELLBOY(1945); SCOTLAND YARD INVESTIGATOR(1945, Brit.); TWO SMART PEOPLE(1946); GHOST GOES WILD, THE(1947); MAIN STREET KID, THE(1947); TIME OUT OF MIND(1947); WHERE THERE'S LIFE(1947); GREAT SINNER, THE(1949); LADY TAKES A SAILOR, THE(1949); SWORD IN THE DESERT(1949)
Emile Rameau
MISSION TO MOSCOW(1943)
Hans Rameau
WORLD WITHOUT A MASK, THE(1934, Ger.), w; MOONLIGHT SONATA(1938, Brit.), w; RAT, THE(1938, Brit.), w; WATERLOO BRIDGE(1940), w; WE WERE DANCING(1942), w
Jean Philippe Rameau
LA MARSEILLAISE(1938, Fr.), m
Paul H. Rameau
MADAME CURIE(1943), w; GABY(1956), w
Hermann Ramelow
CELESTE(1982, Ger.), ph
Henry Ramer
CHANGE OF MIND(1969); APPRENTICESHIP OF DUDDY KRAVITZ, THE(1974, Can.); WHY ROCK THE BOAT?(1974, Can.); IT SEEMED LIKE A GOOD IDEA AT THE TIME(1975, Can.); WELCOME TO BLOOD CITY(1977, Brit./Can.); STARSHIP INVASIONS(1978, Can.)
1984
COVERGIRL(1984, Can.); RENO AND THE DOC(1984, Can.)
Misc. Talkies
MY PLEASURE IS MY BUSINESS(1974, Can.)
Neva Rames
GUN THE MAN DOWN(1957), cos; ESCORT WEST(1959), cos; GNOME-MOBILE, THE(1967), cos; MONKEYS, GO HOME!(1967), cos
Guido Rametta
LAST WAVE, THE(1978, Aus.)
Ed Ramey
DELIVERANCE(1972)
Gene Ramey
MY GAL SAL(1942); ANNE OF THE INDIES(1951)
Rick Ramey
1984
SOLDIER'S STORY, A(1984)
Joe Ramezani
KING OF THE GYPSIES(1978)
R. Rami-Shor
Misc. Silents
WANDERING STARS(1927, USSR)
Jordan Ramin
SCENT OF MYSTERY(1960), m
Sid Ramin
STILETTO(1969), m
Angel Ramirez
BUSTIN' LOOSE(1981)
Anthony Ramirez
CHRISTMAS KID, THE(1968, U.S., Span.), ed
Antonio Ramirez
DESERT WARRIOR(1961 Ital./Span.), ed; COUNTERFEITERS OF PARIS, THE(1962, Fr., Ital.); DEVIL MADE A WOMAN, THE(1962, Span.), ed; SON OF CAPTAIN BLOOD, THE(1964, U.S./Ital./Span.), ed; DRUMS OF TABU, THE(1967, Ital./Span.), ed; TALL WOMEN, THE(1967, Aust./Ital./Span.), ed; SEVEN GUNS FOR THE MACGREGORS(1968, Ital./Span.), ed; MADIGAN'S MILLIONS(1970, Span./Ital), ed; SAGA OF DRACULA, THE(1975, Span.), ed
Ariel Ramirez
WRATH OF GOD, THE(1972), m
Carlos Ramirez
BATHING BEAUTY(1944); TWO GIRLS AND A SAILOR(1944); ANCHORS AWEIGH(1945); WHERE DO WE GO FROM HERE?(1945); EASY TO WED(1946); NIGHT AND DAY(1946)
Dario Ramirez
BULLFIGHTER AND THE LADY(1951)
David Ramirez
NEW YORK, NEW YORK(1977), ed; AMERICAN POP(1981), ed; BARBAROSA(1982), ed; STILL SMOKIN'(1983), ed
Efrain Ramirez
FLIGHT(1960)
Francisco Ramirez
KILL SQUAD(1982)
Frank Ramirez
SMITH(1969); WRATH OF GOD, THE(1972)
Luis Ramirez
MR. MAJESTYK(1974)
Monica Ramirez
HANG YOUR HAT ON THE WIND(1969)
Monika Ramirez
FANTASTIC PLANET(1973, Fr./Czech.); JOE PANTHER(1976); SEED OF INNOCENCE(1980)
Ramiro Ramirez Ramirez
1984
UNDER THE VOLCANO(1984)

Ramon Ramirez
GIANT(1956)
Raul Ramirez
GINA(1961, Fr./Mex.); DEATH IN THE GARDEN(1977, Fr./Mex.)
Ray Ramirez
FAME(1980); LOVESICK(1983)
1984
BROTHER FROM ANOTHER PLANET, THE(1984)
Ricardo Ramirez
UNDER FIRE(1983)
Roberto Ramirez
LOS AUTOMATAS DE LA MUERTE(1960, Mex.); NEUTRON CONTRA EL DR. CARONTE(1962, Mex.); NEUTRON EL ENMASCARADO NEGRO(1962, Mex.); SANTO CONTRA EL CEREBRO DIABOLICO zero(1962, Mex.)
Rosita Ramirez
Silents
MARE NOSTRUM(1926)
Harold Ramis
NATIONAL LAMPOON'S ANIMAL HOUSE(1978), w; MEATBALLS(1979, Can.), w; CADDY SHACK(1980), d, w; HEAVY METAL(1981, Can.); STRIPES(1981), a, w; NATIONAL LAMPOON'S VACATION(1983), d
1984
GHOSTBUSTERS(1984), a, w
Rammellzee
1984
STRANGER THAN PARADISE(1984, U.S./Ger.)
Gudrun Rammler
PINOCCHIO(1969, E. Ger.), w
Clo Ramoin
TEMPTATION(1962, Fr.), cos
Matome "Tommy" Ramokgopa
PENNYWHISTLE BLUES, THE(1952, South Africa), m
Beatriz Ramon
SHE-DEVIL ISLAND(1936, Mex.)
Gordon Ramon
Misc. Talkies
HEADLESS EYES, THE(1983)
Laon Ramon
WIND, THE(1928)
Mitsusaburo Ramon
UGETSU(1954, Jap.)
Ramon & Rosita
GOLD DIGGERS OF 1935(1935)
Ramona
SOCIAL REGISTER(1934)
Ramona the Chimp
BELA LUGOSI MEETS A BROOKLYN GORILLA(1952)
Harold Ramond
FRENCHMAN'S CREEK(1944)
Phil Ramone
HAPPINESS CAGE, THE(1972), m
Phillip Ramone
SIDELONG GLANCES OF A PIGEON KICKER, THE(1970), md
Cenen Ramones
1984
BONA(1984, Phil.), w
The Ramones
ROCK 'N' ROLL HIGH SCHOOL(1979), a, m
Jose Oritz Ramons
CREATURE OF THE WALKING DEAD(1960, Mex.), ph
Apache Ramos
WARRIORS, THE(1979)
Beatriz Ramos
PORTRAIT OF MARIA(1946, Mex.); SOMBRERO(1953)
Benjamin Ramos
SCALPHUNTERS, THE(1968)
Bob Ramos
Misc. Talkies
WEAPONS OF DEATH(1982)
Bobby Ramos
SUSPENSE(1946)
Carlos Rodriguez Ramos
SUMMER LOVERS(1982)
Charles Ramos
UNDER THE PAMPAS MOON(1935)
Ely Ramos, Jr.
WALLS OF HELL, THE(1964, U.S./Phil.)
Fernando Ramos
PAN-AMERICANA(1945); LOVES OF CARMEN, THE(1948)
1984
GABRIELA(1984, Braz.)
Graciliano Ramos
1984
MEMOIRS OF PRISON(1984, Braz.), w
Jess Ramos
BLACK MAMA, WHITE MAMA(1973)
Jose Ortez Ramos
SANTO EN EL MUSEO DE CERA(1963, Mex.), ph
Jose Ortiz Ramos
MY BROTHER, THE OUTLAW(1951), ph; LAST REBEL, THE(1961, Mex.), ph; LOS INVISIBLES(1961, Mex.), ph; LITTLE RED RIDING HOOD AND HER FRIENDS(1964, Mex.), ph; CHIQUTTO PERO PICOSO(1967, Mex.), ph; TOM THUMB(1967, Mex.), ph; CURSE OF THE CRYING WOMAN, THE(1969, Mex.), ph; LIVING HEAD, THE(1969, Mex.), ph; VENGEANCE OF THE VAMPIRE WOMEN, THE(1969, Mex.), ph; DAUGHTER OF DECEIT(1977, Mex.), ph
Jose Orty Ramos
ONE BIG AFFAIR(1952), ph

Jose Ramos
POR MIS PISTOLAS(1969, Mex.), ph
Joseph Ramos
RENEGADES OF THE WEST(1932)
Juan Angel Martinez Ramos
1984
UNDER THE VOLCANO(1984)
Kim Ramos
TWILIGHT PEOPLE(1972, Phil.)
Luis Ramos
1984
MOSCOW ON THE HUDSON(1984)
Nardo Ramos
NO MAN IS AN ISLAND(1962)
Paula Ramos
MARGIN, THE,(1969, Braz.)
R. Ramos
DIAMOND HEAD(1962)
Richard Ramos
GHASTLY ONES, THE(1968); KLUTE(1971); GOOD DISSONANCE LIKE A MAN, A(1977)
Richard Russell Ramos
HANKY-PANKY(1982); I, THE JURY(1982)
Rudy Ramos
DRIVER, THE(1978); DEFIANCE(1980)
Vic Ramos
SIN OF MONA KENT, THE(1961)
Victor Ramos
TOO SOON TO LOVE(1960), art d
Victor Ramos, Jr.
FABLE, A(1971), p
Josephine Ramous
RENEGADES OF THE WEST(1932)
Charlotte Rampling
ROTTEN TO THE CORE(1956, Brit.); KNACK ... AND HOW TO GET IT, THE(1965, Brit.); LONG DUEL, THE(1967, Brit.); SARDINIA: RANSOM(1968, Ital.); THREE(1969, Brit.); SKI BUM, THE(1971); ASYLUM(1972, Brit.); CORKY(1972); HENRY VIII AND HIS SIX WIVES(1972, Brit.); GIORDANO BRUNO(1973, Ital.); 'TIS A PITY SHE'S A WHORE(1973, Ital.); CARAVAN TO VACCARES(1974, Brit./Fr); NIGHT PORTER, THE(1974, Ital./U.S.); ZARDOZ(1974, Brit.); FAREWELL, MY LOVELY(1975); FOX-TROT(1977, Mex./Swiss); ORCA(1977); PURPLE TAXI, THE(1977, Fr./Ital./Ireland); STARDUST MEMORIES(1980); TARGET: HARRY(1980); VERDICT, THE(1982)
Joe Ramrog
FRONT, THE(1976)
Al Ramrus
HALLS OF ANGER(1970), w; ISLAND OF DR. MOREAU, THE(1977), w; GOIN' SOUTH(1978), w
Alexander Ramsay
SAILING ALONG(1938, Brit.)
Alicia Ramsay
YELLOW STOCKINGS(1930, Brit.), w
Allan Ramsay
THROWBACK, THE(1935)
Harold Ramsay
SUNSHINE AHEAD(1936, Brit.)
J. Nelson Ramsay
Silents
ALL ROADS LEAD TO CALVARY(1921, Brit.); LADY OF THE LAKE, THE(1928, Brit.)
Remak Ramsay
STEPFORD WIVES, THE(1975); SIMON(1980); CLASS(1983)
Robin Ramsay
MAD DOG MORGAN(1976,Aus.); 20TH CENTURY OZ(1977, Aus.)
Todd Ramsay
ESCAPE FROM NEW YORK(1981), ed; THING, THE(1982), ed
John Ramsbottom
KILL AND KILL AGAIN(1981)
Roger Ramsdell
HAMLET(1948, Brit.), set d; THERE WAS A CROOKED MAN(1962, Brit.), set d
Frances Ramsden
KISMET(1944); LOST IN A HAREM(1944); MAD WEDNESDAY(1950)
Jackie Ramsden
DEVIL DOLL(1964, Brit.)
Gena Ramsel
COME BACK TO THE 5 & DIME, JIMMY DEAN, JIMMY DEAN(1982)
Al Ramsen
CITY ACROSS THE RIVER(1949)
Allan Ramsen
ISLAND OF TERROR(1967, Brit.), w
Bobby Ramsen
GOD TOLD ME TO(1976); NOBODY'S PERFEKT zero(1981)
Alicia Ramsey
Silents
EVE'S DAUGHTER(1918), w; ROB ROY(1922, Brit.), w; SILENT EVIDENCE(1922, Brit.), w; FIRES OF FATE(1923, Brit.), w; MONEY HABIT, THE(1924, Brit.), w; KING OF THE CASTLE(1925, Brit.), w; PRESUMPTION OF STANLEY HAY, MP, THE(1925, Brit.), w; ONE COLUMBO NIGHT(1926, Brit.), w
Allan Ramsey
JUVENILE COURT(1938); MY FAVORITE BLONDE(1942)
Anne Ramsey
WHEN YOU COMIN' BACK, RED RYDER?(1979); UP THE SANDBOX(1972); FOR PETE'S SAKE(1977); FUN WITH DICK AND JANE(1977); GOIN' SOUTH(1978); ANY WHICH WAY YOU CAN(1980); BLACK MARBLE, THE(1980); NATIONAL LAMPOON'S CLASS REUNION(1982)
1984
KILLERS, THE(1984)
Bill Ramsey
OLD SHATTERHAND(1968, Ger./Yugo./Fr./Ital.)

Clark Ramsey
HARLEM RIDES THE RANGE(1939), ph; MEN OF SAN QUENTIN(1942), ph; TAKE MY LIFE(1942), ph; FEDERAL MAN(1950), ph; FIGHTING STALLION, THE(1950), ph; FORBIDDEN JUNGLE(1950), ph; HOODLUM, THE(1951), ph; SUPERMAN AND THE MOLE MEN(1951), ph; OUTLAW TREASURE(1955), ph; HIDDEN GUNS(1956), ph; PARSON AND THE OUTLAW, THE(1957), ph; MA BARKER'S KILLER BROOD(1960), ph; CHOPPERS, THE(1961), ph

Maj. Clark Ramsey
GOLD FEVER(1952), ph

David Ramsey
LINE, THE(1982)

Douglas Ramsey
KANGAROO(1952)

Eileen Ramsey
FIRST NUDIE MUSICAL, THE(1976)

Freddy Ramsey
WALK IN THE SHADOW(1966, Brit.)

George Ramsey
THIS MAN'S NAVY(1945); PERILOUS WATERS(1948); LOVABLE CHEAT, THE(1949); BACK AT THE FRONT(1952); SCARLET ANGEL(1952); IT HAPPENS EVERY THURSDAY(1953); CONGO CROSSING(1956); MARACAIBO(1958)

Gordon Ramsey
IF EVER I SEE YOU AGAIN(1978)

Ian Ramsey
OLIVER!(1968, Brit.); CAPTAIN NEMO AND THE UNDERWATER CITY(1969, Brit.); SCRAMBLE(1970, Brit.)

James Ramsey
THAT SINKING FEELING(1979, Brit.)

Jeff Ramsey
ELECTRA GLIDE IN BLUE(1973); HERBIE GOES BANANAS(1980); LEGEND OF THE LONE RANGER, THE(1981)
1984
FIRESTARTER(1984); ROMANCING THE STONE(1984); STARMAN(1984)

John Ramsey
RED, WHITE AND BLACK, THE(1970); TWO-MINUTE WARNING(1976)
1984
C.H.U.D.(1984)

Logan Ramsey
HOODLUM PRIEST, THE(1961); SOMETHING WILD(1961); BANNING(1967); HEAD(1968); CHILDISH THINGS(1969); PENDULUM(1969); REIVERS, THE(1969); TRAVELING EXECUTIONER, THE(1970); JUMP(1971); SPORTING CLUB, THE(1971); WHAT'S THE MATTER WITH HELEN?(1971); GLASS HOUSES(1972); OUTSIDE IN(1972); SOME CALL IT LOVING(1973); WALKING TALL(1973); BUSTING(1974); CORNBREAD, EARL AND ME(1975); FAREWELL, MY LOVELY(1975); WALKING TALL, PART II(1975); FINAL CHAPTER–WALKING TALL zero(1977); ANY WHICH WAY YOU CAN(1980); JOYSTICKS(1983)
Misc. Talkies
CONFESSIONS OF TOM HARRIS(1972)

Margaretta Ramsey
WILD SCENE, THE(1970)

Marion Ramsey
1984
POLICE ACADEMY(1984)

Nelson Ramsey
Silents
GOD AND THE MAN(1918, Brit.); INDIAN LOVE LYRICS, THE(1923, Brit.); PRESUMPTION OF STANLEY HAY, MP, THE(1925, Brit.); QUALIFIED ADVENTURER, THE(1925, Brit.)
Misc. Silents
TWELVE POUND LOOK, THE(1920, Brit.)

Quen Ramsey
PRAIRIE LAW(1940); WHEN THE DALTONS RODE(1940); TUMBLEDOWN RANCH IN ARIZONA(1941); UNFINISHED BUSINESS(1941)

R. Ramsey
Silents
JILT, THE(1922), w

Reagan Ramsey
UNHINGED(1982), w

Remak Ramsey
TIGER MAKES OUT, THE(1967); FRONT, THE(1976)

Rex Ramsey
LOVE BUG, THE(1968)

Robert Ramsey
MADRON(1970, U.S./Israel), art d; MADE FOR EACH OTHER(1971), art d; SITTING TARGET(1972, Brit.)
Misc. Silents
FLASHING FANGS(1926)

Thea Ramsey
MANIAC(1934)

Theodore Ramsey
TOM, DICK AND HARRY(1941)

Todd Ramsey
STAR TREK: THE MOTION PICTURE(1979), ed

Wade K. Ramsey
RED RUNS THE RIVER(1963), ph

Ward Ramsey
DINOSAURUS(1960); GREAT IMPOSTOR, THE(1960); SEVEN WAYS FROM SUNDOWN(1960); FLOWER DRUM SONG(1961); LOVER COME BACK(1961); POSSE FROM HELL(1961); TAMMY, TELL ME TRUE(1961); CAPE FEAR(1962); MARY-JANE(1968); SPEEDWAY(1968)

Willis Alan Ramsey
SECOND-HAND HEARTS(1981), m

C.S. Ramsey-Hill
EXILE, THE(1947)

Maj. Cyril Seys Ramsey-Hill
WHITE CLIFFS OF DOVER, THE(1944), tech adv

Ramsey Wallace
Silents
WHAT WIVES WANT(1923)

Maurice Ramsford
DANGEROUS CROSSING(1953), art d

Bob Ramsing
OPERATION CAMEL(1961, Den.), w; CRAZY PARADISE(1965, Den.), w; ERIC SOYA'S "17"(1967, Den.), w

Ramsingh
TIGER AND THE FLAME, THE(1955, India)

Emil Ramu
SO DARK THE NIGHT(1946)

Nick Ramus
APPLE DUMPLING GANG RIDES AGAIN, THE(1979); WINDWALKER(1980)

Igor Stravinsky C.F. Ramuz
SOLDIER'S TALE, THE(1964, Brit.), w

Ahmed Ramy
LITTLE MISS DEVIL(1951, Egypt), m

Ahmed Ramzy
SLAVE, THE(1963, Ital.)

Ray Ranahan
RUNAROUND, THE(1931), ph

Dr. Josef Ranald
HANDS OF DESTINY(1954, Brit.), a, w

Frederick Ranalow
AUTUMN CROCUS(1934, Brit.); LOST CHORD, THE(1937, Brit.); WHO'S YOUR LADY FRIEND?(1937, Brit.); INHERITANCE, THE(1951, Brit.)

Sid Rancer
WOLFMAN(1979)

Misc. Talkies
TRUCKIN' MAN(1975)

The Ranch Boys
IN OLD MONTEREY(1939)

Federica Ranchi
GOLIATH AND THE DRAGON(1961, Ital./Fr.); VIOLENT SUMMER(1961, Fr./Ital.)

Frederica Ranchi
SON OF SAMSON(1962, Fr./Ital./Yugo.)

Alenka Rancic
ROMANCE OF A HORSE THIEF(1971)

Jules Rancourt
Silents
RANGER OF THE NORTH(1927)

Richard Rancyd [Haydn]
MISS TATLOCK'S MILLIONS(1948)

Ayn Rand
NIGHT OF JANUARY 16TH(1941), w; LOVE LETTERS(1945), w; YOU CAME ALONG(1945), w; FOUNTAINHEAD, THE(1949), w

Corey Rand
STRAIGHT TIME(1978)
1984
CLOAK AND DAGGER(1984)

Ed Rand
UNDERCOVER GIRL(1950); HIS KIND OF WOMAN(1951); COLUMN SOUTH(1953); THOSE REDHEADS FROM SEATTLE(1953)

Edwin Rand
RENDEZVOUS WITH ANNIE(1946); CRIMSON KEY, THE(1947); BROKEN ARROW(1950); CAPTURE, THE(1950); RETURN OF THE FRONTIERSMAN(1950); TARANTULA(1955)

Ellen Rand
WEDDING PARTY, THE(1969), cos

Fat Thomas Rand
GANG THAT COULDN'T SHOOT STRAIGHT, THE(1971); SHAMUS(1973)

Hal Rand
DIXIE(1943); LET'S FACE IT(1943); SAINTED SISTERS, THE(1948); CHICAGO DEADLINE(1949); ERRAND BOY, THE(1961)

John Rand
MODERN TIMES(1936)
Silents
GOLD RUSH, THE(1925); CIRCUS, THE(1928); CITY LIGHTS(1931)
Misc. Silents
CARMEN(1916)

Linda Rand
FUN IN ACAPULCO(1963); ROUSTABOUT(1964)

Michael Rand
MEET BOSTON BLACKIE(1941)

Pere Rand
SECOND CHANCE(1953)

Sally Rand
HOTEL VARIETY(1933); BOLERO(1934); SUNSET MURDER CASE(1941)
Silents
MAN BAIT(1926); KING OF KINGS, THE(1927); NIGHT OF LOVE, THE(1927); GIRL IN EVERY PORT, A(1928); NAMELESS MEN(1928)
Misc. Silents
TEXAS BEARCAT, THE(1925); EL RELICARIO(1926); GALLOPING FURY(1927); GETTING GERTIE'S GARTER(1927); HEROES IN BLUE(1927); BLACK FEATHER(1928); CRASHING THROUGH(1928); GOLF WIDOWS(1928)

Ted Rand
MASQUERADE IN MEXICO(1945); MY FAVORITE BRUNETTE(1947)

Theodore "Pete" Rand
ANGELS WITH DIRTY FACES(1938); CODE OF THE SECRET SERVICE(1939); ONE NIGHT IN THE TROPICS(1940); CROSSROADS(1942); RAINBOW ISLAND(1944); DUFFY'S TAVERN(1945); JOHNNY ANGEL(1945); OUR HEARTS WERE GROWING UP(1946); JET PILOT(1957)

Thomas Rand
SEVEN UPS, THE(1973)

Tom Rand
FRENCH LIEUTENANT'S WOMAN, THE(1981), cos; PIRATES OF PENZANCE, THE(1983), cos

Torchy Rand
OH, YOU BEAUTIFUL DOLL(1949)

Cestmir Randa
DEVIL'S TRAP, THE(1964, Czech.); STOLEN DIRIGIBLE, THE(1966, Czech.); TRANSPORT FROM PARADISE(1967, Czech.); FIFTH HORSEMAN IS FEAR, THE(1968, Czech.); ON THE COMET(1970, Czech.); DIVINE EMMA, THE(1983, Czech,)
Tom Randa
UNCOMMON VALOR(1983)
Antonio Randaccio
GARDEN OF THE FINZI-CONTINIS, THE(1976, Ital./Ger.), cos
Monica Randal
SUPERARGO VERSUS DIABOLICUS(1966, Ital./Span.); DOS COSMONAUTAS A LA FUERZA(1967, Span./*Ital.); SEA PIRATE, THE(1967, Fr./Span./Ital.)
Teri Randal
INCREDIBLY STRANGE CREATURES WHO STOPPED LIVING AND BECAME CRAZY MIXED-UP ZOMBIES, THE(1965)
Terry Randal
NOTHING VENTURE(1948, Brit.); SCHOOL FOR RANDLE(1949, Brit.); WOMAN IN THE HALL, THE(1949, Brit.)
Addison [Jack] Randall
ANOTHER FACE(1935); DON'T TURN'EM LOOSE(1936); FLYING HOSTESS(1936); FOLLOW THE FLEET(1936); HIS FAMILY TREE(1936); LOVE ON A BET(1936); NAVY BORN(1936); TWO IN THE DARK(1936); BLAZING BARRIERS(1937); RED LIGHTS AHEAD(1937); HIGH EXPLOSIVE(1943)
Al Randall
PROPER TIME, THE(1959)
Amy Randall
RENEGADE GIRLS(1974)
Andre Randall
BUTLER'S DILEMMA, THE(1943, Brit.); MAN FROM MOROCCO, THE(1946, Brit.); HER MAN GILBEY(1949, Brit.); AMAZING MONSIEUR FABRE, THE(1952, Fr.); UTOPIA(1952, Fr./Ital.); GOODBYE AGAIN(1961)
Silents
ODDS AGAINST HER, THE(1919, Brit.)
Ann Randall
DOOMSDAY VOYAGE(1972)
Anne Randall
SPLIT, THE(1968); MODEL SHOP, THE(1969); HELL'S BLOODY DEVILS(1970); CHRISTIAN LICORICE STORE, THE(1971); TIME FOR DYING, A(1971); GET TO KNOW YOUR RABBIT(1972); STACEY!(1973); WESTWORLD(1973)
Barney Randall
Misc. Silents
TOGETHER(1918)
Bernard Randall
SHOW GIRL(1928); BIG TOWN(1932); HOTEL VARIETY(1933)
Silents
QUESTION, THE(1916); AUCTION BLOCK, THE(1917); MASTER MIND, THE(1920); WHISPERS(1920); FRENCH DOLL, THE(1923); PRETTY LADIES(1925); SKYROCKET, THE(1926)
Misc. Silents
BLUE-EYED MARY(1918); OH, YOU WOMEN!(1919); WITS VS. WITS(1920); CLOSED DOORS(1921); UNMARRIED WIVES(1924)
Bob Randall
BLACK RAVEN, THE(1943); FAN, THE(1981), w; ZORRO, THE GAY BLADE(1981), w
Bruce Randall
MEN OF THE NIGHT(1934)
Carl Randall
RECKLESS(1935), a, ch; MERRY-GO-ROUND OF 1938(1937), ch; SHOW GOES ON, THE(1937, Brit.); YOU'RE A SWEETHEART(1937), ch; PEACE KILLERS, THE(1971), prod d
Celestine Randall
GIRO CITY(1982, Brit.)
Charles Randall
NEXT MAN, THE(1976); NATURAL ENEMIES(1979)
Chris G. Randall
BATTLE STATIONS(1956)
Chris Randall
KENTUCKY JUBILEE(1951); BLACKBOARD JUNGLE, THE(1955); RACERS, THE(1955); RUNNING WILD(1955); RIGHT HAND OF THE DEVIL, THE(1963)
Corky Randall
HORSEMEN, THE(1971), animal trainer
David Randall
ROAD TO HONG KONG, THE(1962, U.S./Brit.); MODEL MURDER CASE, THE(1964, Brit.)
Dick Randall
SHANGRI-LA(1961), p; PARIS OOH-LA-LA!(1963, U.S./Fr.); PRIMITIVE LOVE(1966, Ital.), p; LADY FRANKENSTEIN(1971, Ital.), w; CROCODILE(1979, Thai./Hong Kong), p; SUPERSONIC MAN(1979, Span.), p; PIECES(1983, Span./Puerto Rico), p, w
1984
DON'T OPEN TILL CHRISTMAS(1984, Brit.), p
Florence Engel Randall
WATCHER IN THE WOODS, THE(1980, Brit.), w
Frank Randall
Silents
SHOPSOILED GIRL, THE(1915, Brit.); PLEYDELL MYSTERY, THE(1916, Brit.)
Misc. Silents
DAUGHTER OF ENGLAND, A(1915, Brit.)
Frankie Randall
WILD ON THE BEACH(1965)
Gene Randall
THREE DESPERATE MEN(1951)
George Randall
HARLEM ON THE PRAIRIE(1938); INTO THE STRAIGHT(1950, Aus.); SCALPS(1983)
Glenn Randall
RAIDERS OF THE LOST ARK(1981), stunts; RETURN OF THE JEDI(1983), stunts
Glenn Randall, Jr.
UGLY DACHSHUND, THE(1966), animal t.

Glenn H. Randall, Jr.
WHAT'S UP, DOC?(1972)
1984
MRS. SOFFEL(1984), stunts
Greta Randall
COME BLOW YOUR HORN(1963); DIARY OF A BACHELOR(1964)
J.R. Randall
DUEL AT DIABLO(1966)
Jack Randall
HOLD YOUR MAN(1933); RIDERS OF THE DAWN(1937); STARS OVER ARIZONA(1937); DANGER VALLEY(1938); GUN PACKER(1938); GUNSMOKE TRAIL(1938); LAND OF FIGHTING MEN(1938); MAN'S COUNTRY(1938); MEXICALI KID, THE(1938); WHERE THE WEST BEGINS(1938); ACROSS THE PLAINS(1939); DRIFTING WESTWARD(1939); OKLAHOMA TERROR(1939); OVERLAND MAIL(1939); TRIGGER SMITH(1939); WILD HORSE CANYON(1939); CHEYENNE KID, THE(1940); COVERED WAGON TRAILS(1940); KID FROM SANTA FE, THE(1940); LAND OF THE SIX GUNS(1940); PIONEER DAYS(1940); RIDERS FROM NOWHERE(1940)
Misc. Talkies
LAND OF SIX GUNS(1940); WILD HORSE RANGE(1940)
Misc. Silents
HIS GREATEST BATTLE(1925)
James Randall
Misc. Talkies
DEAFULA(1975)
Jerry Randall
HELL'S ANGELS '69(1969); HELL'S BELLES(1969); HAROLD AND MAUDE(1971)
Judith Randall
IN MACARTHUR PARK(1977), set d
Karen Randall
THIS LOVE OF OURS(1945)
Kathy Randall
SINISTER URGE, THE(1961)
Larry Randall
LIKELY STORY, A(1947)
Leslie Randall
JUST JOE(1960, Brit.); BILLY LIAR(1963, Brit.); MYSTERY SUBMARINE(1963, Brit.)
Lorraine Randall
NORTH OF THE RIO GRANDE(1937); WHERE TRAILS DIVIDE(1937)
Lynn Randall
TOWN WITHOUT PITY(1961, Ger./Switz./U.S.)
Margaret Randall
ROMANCE IN THE DARK(1938); YOU AND ME(1938)
Marilyn Randall
MIKEY AND NICKY(1976)
1984
DELIVERY BOYS(1984)
Meg Randall
ABANDONED(1949); CRISS CROSS(1949); LIFE OF RILEY, THE(1949); MA AND PA KETTLE(1949); MA AND PA KETTLE GO TO TOWN(1950); MA AND PA KETTLE BACK ON THE FARM(1951); WITHOUT WARNING(1952); CHAIN OF EVIDENCE(1957); LAST OF THE BADMEN(1957)
Monica Randall
FIVE GIANTS FROM TEXAS(1966, Ital./Span.); RED SUN(1972, Fr./Ital./Span.)
Norma Randall
BIG HEAT, THE(1953)
Pamela Randall
HEARTS OF HUMANITY(1936, Brit.); LAST WALTZ, THE(1936, Brit.); LIVE AGAIN(1936, Brit.); RHYTHM RACKETEER(1937, Brit.); LADY IN DISTRESS(1942, Brit.)
Pat Randall
REIVERS, THE(1969); ADAM AT 6 A.M.(1970)
Phillip Randall
ATTIC, THE(1979), p
Phyllis Randall
PLEASURE PLANTATION(1970)
Rae Randall
GODLESS GIRL, THE(1929)
Silents
KING OF KINGS, THE(1927)
Rebel Randall
SIN TOWN(1942); HI, BUDDY(1943); HIT THE ICE(1943); DEAD OR ALIVE(1944); SEVEN DOORS TO DEATH(1944); ADVENTURE(1945); HERE COME THE CO-EDS(1945); NIGHT AND DAY(1946); SHADOW RETURNS, THE(1946); ROARING CITY(1951)
Renee Randall
O.S.S.(1946); VARIETY GIRL(1947); NIGHT HAS A THOUSAND EYES(1948); SAIGON(1948)
Robert D. Randall
CHILD'S PLAY(1972)
Robert Randall
BORROWED WIVES(1930); SUNNY SKIES(1930); HOUSE OF FREAKS(1973, Ital.), p
Robert Shelby Randall
THEY WERE EXPENDABLE(1945)
Ron Randall
Misc. Talkies
TO CHASE A MILLION(1967)
Scott Randall
LONG ROPE, THE(1961); SNIPER'S RIDGE(1961)
Shawn Randall
LONELY LADY, THE(1983), w
Stephanie Randall
PREHISTORIC WOMEN(1967, Brit.)
Steven Randall
YOUNG MR. LINCOLN(1939)

Stuart Randall
BELLS OF CORONADO(1950); RIDER FROM TUCSON(1950); RUSTLERS ON HORSEBACK(1950); STORM WARNING(1950); ARIZONA MANHUNT(1951); HOODLUM, THE(1951); ROUGH RIDERS OF DURANGO(1951); TOMAHAWK(1951); TOMORROW IS ANOTHER DAY(1951); WELLS FARGO GUNMASTER(1951); BUGLES IN THE AFTERNOON(1952); BUSHWHACKERS, THE(1952); CAPTIVE WOMEN(1952); CARBINE WILLIAMS(1952); DIPLOMATIC COURIER(1952); HIAWATHA(1952); HURRICANE SMITH(1952); KID MONK BARONI(1952); O. HENRY'S FULL HOUSE(1952); PARK ROW(1952); PONY SOLDIER(1952); PRIDE OF ST. LOUIS, THE(1952); RANCHO NOTORIOUS(1952); ARENA(1953); CAPTAIN JOHN SMITH AND POCAHONTAS(1953); DESTINATION GOBI(1953); HANNAH LEE(1953); MEXICAN MANHUNT(1953); PICKUP ON SOUTH STREET(1953); PONY EXPRESS(1953); SWORD OF VENUS(1953); VICKI(1953); NAKED ALIBI(1954); SOUTHWEST PASSAGE(1954); THEY RODE WEST(1954); THIS IS MY LOVE(1954); CHIEF CRAZY HORSE(1955); FAR COUNTRY, THE(1955); FEMALE ON THE BEACH(1955); HEADLINE HUNTERS(1955); INDESTRUCTIBLE MAN, THE(1956); PARDNERS(1956); STAR IN THE DUST(1956); RUN OF THE ARROW(1957); BIG FISHERMAN, THE(1959); I'LL GIVE MY LIFE(1959); VERBOTEN!(1959); FROM THE TERRACE(1960); HOME FROM THE HILL(1960); FRONTIER UPRISING(1961); POSSE FROM HELL(1961); TAGGART(1964); FLUFFY(1965)

Sue Randall
DESK SET(1957); DATE BAIT(1960)

Suze Randall
CHLOE IN THE AFTERNOON(1972, Fr.)

Terry Randall
MILLIONS LIKE US(1943, Brit.); THURSDAY'S CHILD(1943, Brit.); WHEN WE ARE MARRIED(1943, Brit.); I'LL TURN TO YOU(1946, Brit.); DARK SECRET(1949, Brit.); WHAT A CARRY ON!(1949, Brit.); MISS PILGRIM'S PROGRESS(1950, Brit.)

Thora Randall
ETERNAL SUMMER(1961)

Tony Randall
TWO WEEKS IN ANOTHER TOWN(1962); NO DOWN PAYMENT(1957); OH, MEN! OH, WOMEN!(1957); WILL SUCCESS SPOIL ROCK HUNTER?(1957); MATING GAME, THE(1959); PILLOW TALK(1959); ADVENTURES OF HUCKLEBERRY FINN, THE(1960); LET'S MAKE LOVE(1960); LOVER COME BACK(1961); BOYS' NIGHT OUT(1962); ISLAND OF LOVE(1963); BRASS BOTTLE, THE(1964); ROBIN AND THE SEVEN HOODS(1964); SEND ME NO FLOWERS(1964); SEVEN FACES OF DR. LAO(1964); FLUFFY(1965); ALPHABET MURDERS, THE(1966); BANG, BANG, YOU'RE DEAD(1966); HELLO DOWN THERE(1969); EVERYTHING YOU ALWAYS WANTED TO KNOW ABOUT SEX, BUT WE'RE AFRAID TO ASK(1972); SCAVENGER HUNT(1979); FOOLIN' AROUND(1980); KING OF COMEDY, THE(1983)

W. L. Randall
Silents
PEG OF THE PIRATES(1918), w

W. R. Randall
Silents
MISS CRUSOE(1919)

Walter Randall
HAND, THE(1960, Brit.); SECRET OF MONTE CRISTO, THE(1961, Brit.); HANDS OF ORLAC, THE(1964, Brit./Fr.)

Warwick Randall
PETERSEN(1974, Aus.)

Randall Sisters
STAND UP AND CHEER(1934 80m FOX bw)

Teddy Randazzo
ROCK, ROCK, ROCK!(1956); MISTER ROCK AND ROLL(1957); HEY, LET'S TWIST!(1961)

Anthony Randel
SPACE RAIDERS(1983), ed

Robert Randel
GLAMOUR GIRL(1938, Brit.)

C. Randell
STRANGERS ON A HONEYMOON(1937, Brit.), ed

Carl Randell
LIVING BETWEEN TWO WORLDS(1963), set d

Cyril Randell
STORM IN A TEACUP(1937, Brit.), ed

Frank Randell
Silents
VEILED WOMAN, THE(1917, Brit.)

Margaret Randell
TIP-OFF GIRLS(1938)

Pamela Randell
WOMEN IN WAR(1940)

Rebel Randell
GOOD MORNING, JUDGE(1943); TANGIER(1946)

Robert Randell
Silents
BABBITT(1924)

Ron Randell
STORY OF DR. WASSELL, THE(1944); SMITHY(1946, Aus.); IT HAD TO BE YOU(1947); PACIFIC ADVENTURE(1947, Aus.); LOVES OF CARMEN(1948); MATING OF MILLIE, THE(1948); SIGN OF THE RAM, THE(1948); LONE WOLF AND HIS LADY, THE(1949); MAKE BELIEVE BALLROOM(1949); OMOO OMOO, THE SHARK GOD(1949); COUNTERSPY MEETS SCOTLAND YARD(1950); TYRANT OF THE SEA(1950); CHINA CORSAIR(1951); LORNA DOONE(1951); BRIGAND, THE(1952); CAPTIVE WOMEN(1952); GIRL ON THE PIER, THE(1953, Brit.); KISS ME KATE(1953); MISSISSIPPI GAMBLER, THE(1953); THREE CORNERED FATE(1954, Brit.); YELLOW ROBE, THE(1954, Brit.); COUNT OF TWELVE(1955, Brit.); DESERT SANDS(1955); FINAL COLUMN, THE(1955, Brit.); I AM A CAMERA(1955, Brit.); ONE JUST MAN(1955, Brit.); BERMUDA AFFAIR(1956, Brit.); HOSTAGE, THE(1956, Brit.); QUINCANNON, FRONTIER SCOUT(1956); SHE-CREATURE, THE(1956); BEYOND MOMBASA(1957); GIRL IN BLACK STOCKINGS(1957); STORY OF ESTHER COSTELLO, THE(1957, Brit.); DAVY(1958, Brit.); STRANGE CASE OF DR. MANNING, THE(1958, Brit.); KING OF KINGS(1961); MOST DANGEROUS MAN ALIVE, THE(1961); LONGEST DAY, THE(1962); FOLLOW THE BOYS(1963); GALLANT ONE, THE(1964, U.S./Peru), p; GOLD FOR THE CAESARS(1964); PHONY AMERICAN, THE(1964, Ger.); SAVAGE PAMPAS(1967, Span./Arg.); SEVEN MINUTES, THE(1971); EXPOSED(1983)

Misc. Talkies
BULLDOG DRUMMOND AT BAY(1947); BULLDOG DRUMMOND STRIKES BACK(1947)

Bella Randels
NAKED PREY, THE(1966, U.S./South Africa)

Don Randi
BLOODY MAMA(1970), m; UP IN THE CELLAR(1970), m; J.W. COOP(1971), m; SANTEE(1973), m; STACEY!(1973), m

Ermanno Randi
BRIEF RAPTURE(1952, Ital.)

Lucia Randi
CAESAR THE CONQUEROR(1963, Ital.)

Randian
FREAKS(1932)

Ric Randig
1984
SPLATTER UNIVERSITY(1984)

Massimo Randisi
HEART AND SOUL(1950, Ital.)

Bill Randle
SING, BOY, SING(1958)

Frank Randle
SOMEWHERE IN ENGLAND(1940, Brit.); SOMEWHERE IN CAMP(1942, Brit.), a, w; SOMEWHERE ON LEAVE(1942, Brit.), a, w; SOMEWHERE IN CIVVIES(1943, Brit.); HOME SWEET HOME(1945, Brit.), a, w; WHEN YOU COME HOME(1947, Brit.), a, w; HOLIDAYS WITH PAY(1948, Brit.), a, w; SCHOOL FOR RANDLE(1949, Brit.), a, w; SOMEWHERE IN POLITICS(1949, Brit.), a, w; IT'S A GRAND LIFE(1953, Brit.), a, w

Karen Randle
STORM OVER LISBON(1944); FRONTIER GAL(1945); LADY ON A TRAIN(1945); SALOME, WHERE SHE DANCED(1945); NIGHT IN PARADISE, A(1946); SONG OF SCHEHERAZADE(1947); MEXICAN HAYRIDE(1948); BLONDE DYNAMITE(1950); COWBOY AND THE PRIZEFIGHTER(1950); HURRICANE ISLAND(1951)

Bob Randles
METAMORPHOSES(1978), md

Larry Randles
COWBOYS, THE(1972); ULZANA'S RAID(1972); LEGEND OF THE LONE RANGER, THE(1981)

George Randol
EXILE, THE(1931); GREEN PASTURES(1936); DARK MANHATTAN(1937), p, w
Misc. Talkies
MIDNIGHT SHADOW(1939), d

Tom Randol
1984
GIMME AN 'F'(1984), art d

Anders Randolf
JAZZ SINGER, THE(1927); NOAH'S ARK(1928); DANGEROUS CURVES(1929); FOUR DEVILS(1929); SHANGHAI LADY(1929); YOUNG NOWHERES(1929); MAYBE IT'S LOVE(1930); SON OF THE GODS(1930); WAY OF ALL MEN, THE(1930); GOING WILD(1931)
Silents
WHEELS OF JUSTICE(1915); ONE LAW FOR BOTH(1917); ERSTWHILE SUSAN(1919); IDOL DANCER, THE(1920); LOVE FLOWER, THE(1920); MADONNAS AND MEN(1920); JIM THE PENMAN(1921); NOTORIETY(1922); REFEREE, THE(1922); SHERLOCK HOLMES(1922); STREETS OF NEW YORK, THE(1922); ETERNAL STRUGGLE, THE(1923); BLACK PIRATE, THE(1926); JOHNSTOWN FLOOD, THE(1926); RANSON'S FOLLY(1926); WOMANPOWER(1926); OLD SAN FRANCISCO(1927); SLIGHTLY USED(1927); CRIMSON CITY, THE(1928); GATEWAY OF THE MOON, THE(1928); POWDER MY BACK(1928); KISS, THE(1929); SIN SISTER, THE(1929)
Misc. Silents
CROWN PRINCE'S DOUBLE, THE(1916); DARING OF DIANA, THE(1916); HERO OF SUBMARINE D-2, THE(1916); ISLAND OF SURPRISE, THE(1916); SUSPECT, THE(1916); VITAL QUESTION, THE(1916); BELGIAN, THE(1917); DAUGHTER OF DESTINY(1917); GIRL PHILIPPA, THE(1917); WHO'S YOUR NEIGHBOR?(1917); WITHIN THE LAW(1917); RECLAIMED(1918); SAFETY CURTAIN, THE(1918); SPLENDID SINNER, THE(1918); FROM HEADQUARTERS(1919); LION AND THE MOUSE, THE(1919); THIRD DEGREE, THE(1919); CINEMA MURDER, THE(1920); COMMON SIN, THE(1920); MIGHTY LAK' A ROSE(1923); NONE SO BLIND(1923); BY DIVINE RIGHT(1924); HAPPY WARRIOR, THE(1925); HER MARKET VALUE(1925); SEVEN KEYS TO BALDPATE(1925); COLLEGE WIDOW, THE(1927); DEARIE(1927); LOVE OF SUNYA, THE(1927); SINEWS OF STEEL(1927); POWER OF SILENCE, THE(1928)

Gary Randolf
GREEN SLIME, THE(1969)

Scott Randolf
1984
EXTERMINATOR 2(1984)

Amanda Randolph
NO WAY OUT(1950); BOMBA AND THE JUNGLE GIRL(1952); IRON MISTRESS, THE(1952); SHE'S WORKING HER WAY THROUGH COLLEGE(1952); MR. SCOUTMASTER(1953); MAN CALLED PETER, THE(1955); HELLER IN PINK TIGHTS(1960); LAST CHALLENGE, THE(1967)
Misc. Talkies
LYING LIPS(1939)

Anders Randolph
WOMEN THEY TALK ABOUT(1928); LAST PERFORMANCE, THE(1929); WEST OF THE ROCKIES(1931)
Misc. Talkies
CALL OF THE ROCKIES(1931)
Silents
BURIED TREASURE(1921); PEACOCK ALLEY(1922); SLIM SHOULDERS(1922); IN HOLLYWOOD WITH POTASH AND PERLMUTTER(1924); BROKEN HEARTS OF HOLLYWOOD(1926); MISS NOBODY(1926); TENDER HOUR, THE(1927); THREE SINNERS(1928)
Misc. Silents
RETURN OF MAURICE DONNELLY, THE(1915); MAN FROM GLENGARRY, THE(1923); DOROTHY VERNON OF HADDON HALL(1924); BIG KILLING, THE(1928); ME, GANGSTER(1928); VIKING, THE(1929); CALL OF THE ROCKIES(1931)

Barbara Randolph
GUESS WHO'S COMING TO DINNER(1967)
Betsey Randolph
Misc. Silents
GOLDEN ROSARY, THE(1917)
Bill Randolph
DRESSED TO KILL(1980); FRIDAY THE 13TH PART II(1981); FIRST TIME, THE(1983)
Boots Randolph
THAT TENNESSEE BEAT(1966)
Bryson Randolph
THERE'S ALWAYS VANILLA(1972)
Charles Randolph
GOLDEN BOY(1939); INVITATION TO HAPPINESS(1939); KID FROM KOKOMO, THE(1939); SINGIN' IN THE CORN(1946)
Clay Randolph
BELLES ON THEIR TOES(1952); REVOLT AT FORT LARAMIE(1957)
Clemence Randolph
RAIN(1932), w
Silents
SADIE THOMPSON(1928), w
David Randolph
THEY CALL ME BRUCE(1982), w
Don Randolph
UNDER THE GUN(1951); SILVER CHALICE, THE(1954); TOPAZ(1969, Brit.)
Donald Randolph
13 RUE MADELEINE(1946); FOR THE LOVE OF MARY(1948); BRIDE OF VENGEANCE(1949); DESERT HAWK, THE(1950); GAMBLING HOUSE(1950); ROGUES OF SHERWOOD FOREST(1950); FOURTEEN HOURS(1951); GOLDEN HORDE, THE(1951); PRINCE WHO WAS A THIEF, THE(1951); TEN TALL MEN(1951); ASSIGNMENT-PARIS(1952); BRIGAND, THE(1952); HAREM GIRL(1952); NIGHT WITHOUT SLEEP(1952); ALL-AMERICAN, THE(1953); CADDY, THE(1953); DREAM WIFE(1953); GUNSMOKE(1953); ADVENTURES OF HAJJI BABA(1954); GAMBLER FROM NATCHEZ, THE(1954); KHYBER PATROL(1954); MAD MAGICIAN, THE(1954); PHFFFT!(1954); CHIEF CRAZY HORSE(1955); PURPLE MASK, THE(1955); SON OF SINBAD(1955); OVER-EXPOSED(1956); RAWHIDE YEARS, THE(1956); DEADLY MANTIS, THE(1957); FLAME OF STAMBOUL(1957); MY GUN IS QUICK(1957); COWBOY(1958)
Ed Randolph
LONE WOLF SPY HUNT, THE(1939); MR. SMITH GOES TO WASHINGTON(1939); ONLY ANGELS HAVE WINGS(1939); ALONG CAME JONES(1945); BLUE DAHLIA, THE(1946); DESERT FURY(1947); HAZARD(1948); ABBOTT AND COSTELLO MEET THE KILLER, BORIS KARLOFF(1949); DRIFTER, THE(1966); SHE BEAST, THE(1966, Brit./Ital./Yugo.); DR. HECKYL AND MR. HYPE(1980)
Eddie Randolph
YOU CAN'T TAKE IT WITH YOU(1938); CASBAH(1948); KNOCK ON ANY DOOR(1949)
Edwin Randolph
THAT WONDERFUL URGE(1948); UNDERCOVER MAN, THE(1949)
Elsie Randolph
BROTHER ALFRED(1932, Brit.); LIFE GOES ON(1932, Brit.); RICH AND STRANGE(1932, Brit.); NIGHT OF THE GARTER(1933, Brit.); THAT'S A GOOD GIRL(1933, Brit.); YES, MR. BROWN(1933, Brit.); THIS'LL MAKE YOU WHISTLE(1938, Brit.); LARCENY STREET(1941, Brit.); CHEER THE BRAVE(1951, Brit.)
Ginny Randolph
1984
STRANGERS KISS(1984), art d
Henry Randolph
LOVE ME OR LEAVE ME(1955); BRAIN EATERS, THE(1958)
Idabel Randolph
HOOSIER HOLIDAY(1943)
Isabel Randolph
BARNYARD FOLLIES(1940); SANDY GETS HER MAN(1940); YESTERDAY'S HEROES(1940); LOOK WHO'S LAUGHING(1941); SMALL TOWN DEB(1941); HENRY ALDRICH GETS GLAMOUR(1942); HERE WE GO AGAIN(1942); MY FAVORITE BLONDE(1942); RIDE 'EM COWBOY(1942); TAKE A LETTER, DARLING(1942); FOLLOW THE BAND(1943); O, MY DARLING CLEMENTINE(1943); SHADOW OF A DOUBT(1943); JAMBOREE(1944); PRACTICALLY YOURS(1944); STANDING ROOM ONLY(1944); WILSON(1944); MAN WHO WALKED ALONE, THE(1945); MISS SUSIE SLAGLE'S(1945); MISSING CORPSE, THE(1945); TELL IT TO A STAR(1945); DARK CORNER, THE(1946); OUR HEARTS WERE GROWING UP(1946); DEAR RUTH(1947); SUDDENLY IT'S SPRING(1947); HAZARD(1948); IF YOU KNEW SUSIE(1948); NOOSE HANGS HIGH, THE(1948); SITTING PRETTY(1948); THAT WONDERFUL URGE(1948); CRISS CROSS(1949); LITTLE WOMEN(1949); MARY RYAN, DETECTIVE(1949); THAT FORSYTE WOMAN(1949); FULLER BRUSH GIRL, THE(1950); SECRETS OF MONTE CARLO(1951); TWO DOLLAR BETTOR(1951); TWO TICKETS TO BROADWAY(1951); THUNDERING CARAVANS(1952); LADY WANTS MINK, THE(1953); SHANGHAI STORY, THE(1954); AIN'T MISBEHAVIN'(1955); YOU'RE NEVER TOO YOUNG(1955); HOT SHOTS(1956)
Misc. Talkies
FEUDIN' RHYTHM(1949); BORDER CITY RUSTLERS(1953)
Isobel Randolph
ON THEIR OWN(1940); RIDE, TENDERFOOT, RIDE(1940)
Jane Randolph
DIVE BOMBER(1941); MANPOWER(1941); CAT PEOPLE(1942); FALCON'S BROTHER, THE(1942); HIGHWAYS BY NIGHT(1942); MALE ANIMAL, THE(1942); FALCON STRIKES BACK, THE(1943); CURSE OF THE CAT PEOPLE, THE(1944); IN THE MEANTIME, DARLING(1944); JEALOUSY(1945); SPORTING CHANCE, A(1945); FOOL'S GOLD(1946); IN FAST COMPANY(1946); RAILROADED!(1947); T-MEN(1947); ABBOTT AND COSTELLO MEET FRANKENSTEIN(1948); OPEN SECRET(1948)
John Randolph
NAKED CITY, THE(1948); SECONDS(1966); PRETTY POISON(1968); GAILY, GAILY(1969); NUMBER ONE(1969); SMITH(1969); THERE WAS A CROOKED MAN(1970); ESCAPE FROM THE PLANET OF THE APES(1971); LITTLE MURDERS(1971); CONQUEST OF THE PLANET OF THE APES(1972); SERPICO(1973); EARTHQUAKE(1974); KING KONG(1976); HEAVEN CAN WAIT(1978); FRANCES(1982)
Misc. Talkies
LOVELY BUT DEADLY(1983)

Lillian Randolph
AM I GUILTY?(1940); LITTLE MEN(1940); ALL-AMERICAN CO-ED(1941); GENTLEMAN FROM DIXIE(1941); WEST POINT WIDOW(1941); GLASS KEY, THE(1942); GREAT GILDERSLEEVE, THE(1942); HI, NEIGHBOR(1942); MEXICAN SPITFIRE SEES A GHOST(1942); GILDERSLEEVE ON BROADWAY(1943); GILDERSLEEVE'S BAD DAY(1943); HAPPY GO LUCKY(1943); HOOSIER HOLIDAY(1943); NO TIME FOR LOVE(1943); GILDERSLEEVE'S GHOST(1944); THREE LITTLE SISTERS(1944); UP IN ARMS(1944); SONG FOR MISS JULIE, A(1945); CHILD OF DIVORCE(1946); IT'S A WONDERFUL LIFE(1946); BACHELOR AND THE BOBBY-SOXER, THE(1947); LET'S LIVE A LITTLE(1948); SLEEP, MY LOVE(1948); ONCE MORE, MY DARLING(1949); DEAR BRAT(1951); THAT'S MY BOY(1951); HUSH... HUSH, SWEET CHARLOTTE(1964); HOW TO SEDUCE A WOMAN(1974); ONCE IS NOT ENOUGH(1975); RAFFERTY AND THE GOLD DUST TWINS(1975); WILD McCULLOCHS, THE(1975); MAGIC(1978); ONION FIELD, THE(1979)
Misc. Talkies
MR. SMITH GOES GHOST(1940)
Linda Randolph
SHOCK CORRIDOR(1963)
Marge Randolph
WILD IS MY LOVE(1963)
Marion Randolph
OH! SUSANNA(1951)
Renita Randolph
Misc. Silents
DEVOTION(1921)
Roy Randolph
NOBODY'S BABY(1937), ch
Virginia Randolph
POSTMAN ALWAYS RINGS TWICE, THE(1946); SECRET HEART, THE(1946); SUNSET BOULEVARD(1950)
Bob Random
RESTLESS ONES, THE(1965); SYLVIA(1965); VILLAGE OF THE GIANTS(1965); THIS PROPERTY IS CONDEMNED(1966); ...TICK...TICK...TICK...(1970); TIME FOR DYING, A(1971)
Ida Random
BIG CHILL, THE(1983), prod d
1984
BODY DOUBLE(1984), prod d; IRRECONCILABLE DIFFERENCES(1984), a, a, prod d
Robert Random
TIME WALKER(1982)
Ida Randon
FRANCES(1982), art d
Salvo Randone
ASSASSIN, THE(1961, Ital./Fr.); FAMILY DIARY(1963 Ital.); VERONA TRIAL, THE(1963, Ital.); CASTLE OF BLOOD(1964, Fr./Ital.); MAGNIFICENT CUCKOLD, THE(1965, Fr./Ital.); TENTH VICTIM, THE(1965, Fr./Ital.); SALVATORE GIULIANO(1966, Ital.); WE STILL KILL THE OLD WAY(1967, Ital.); FELLINI SATYRICON(1969, Fr./Ital.); SPIRITS OF THE DEAD(1969, Fr./Ital.); INVESTIGATION OF A CITIZEN ABOVE SUSPICION(1970, Ital.); LOVE PROBLEMS(1970, Ital.); MACHINE GUN McCAIN(1970, Ital.)
Della Rands
SKY BIKE, THE(1967, Brit.)
Wanda Rands
SHE SHALL HAVE MURDER(1950, Brit.); WALLET, THE(1952, Brit.)
Maurice Randsford
DESK SET(1957), art d
Patricia Rane
MUSCLE BEACH PARTY(1964)
Emil Raneau
CRY OF THE CITY(1948)
Ali Raner
THREE(1967, Yugo.)
Boris Ranevsky
TESHA(1929, Brit.); TWO WORLD(1930, Brit.); NIGHT LIKE THIS, A(1932, Brit.); RIVER HOUSE MYSTERY, THE(1935, Brit.); FORBIDDEN TERRITORY(1938, Brit.); OH BOY!(1938, Brit.); VIPER, THE(1938, Brit.); SLEEPING CAR TO TRIESTE(1949, Brit.); OPERATION CONSPIRACY(1957, Brit.); ORDERS TO KILL(1958, Brit.)
Silents
PARADISE(1928, Brit.)
Sue Raney
ROAD HUSTLERS, THE(1968)
Zetta Raney
URBAN COWBOY(1980)
Sonia Rangan
CHATO'S LAND(1972)
Rangda
WAJAN(1938, South Bali)
The Range Ranglers
CYCLONE OF THE SADDLE(1935)
A. Soto Rangel
TREASURE OF THE SIERRA MADRE, THE(1948)
Arturo Rangel
SOMBRERO(1953)
Arturo Soto Rangel
PORTRAIT OF MARIA(1946, Mex.)
Germinal Rangel
HOT MILLIONS(1968, Brit.), cos; TRAVELS WITH MY AUNT(1972, Brit.), cos; LOVE AND PAIN AND THE WHOLE DAMN THING(1973), cos
Lucy Rangel
MARGIN, THE,(1969, Braz.)
Ranger
Silents
ONE MAN DOG, THE(1929)
Misc. Silents
FLAMING FURY(1926); FLASHING FANGS(1926); SWIFT SHADOW, THE(1927); WHEN A DOG LOVES(1927); DOG JUSTICE(1928); LAW OF FEAR(1928); TRACKED(1928); FURY OF THE WILD(1929)

Ranger,the Dog
Silents
AFLAME IN THE SKY(1927); OUTLAW DOG, THE(1927); RANGER OF THE NORTH(1927); DOG LAW(1928); FANGS OF THE WILD(1928)
Clark Ranger
NEW FACES(1954)
The Ranger Chorus of Forty
RIDE 'EM COWBOY(1942)
Puni Rangiaho
1984
UTU(1984, New Zealand)
Terry Rangno
SOMEBODY UP THERE LIKES ME(1956); LONG, HOT SUMMER, THE(1958); LITTLE SAVAGE, THE(1959); REMARKABLE MR. PENNYPACKER, THE(1959)
Rango
RANGO(1931)
Devika Rani
KARMA(1933, Brit./India)
Estrellita Rania
PRETTY MAIDS ALL IN A ROW(1971)
Jeanne Ranier
WHAT DID YOU DO IN THE WAR, DADDY?(1966); I SAILED TO TAHITI WITH AN ALL GIRL CREW(1969)
Giuseppe Ranieri
ATOM AGE VAMPIRE(1961, Ital.), art d; NUDE ODYSSEY(1962, Fr./Ital.), set d; PASSIONATE THIEF, THE(1963, Ital.), art d; PLAYGIRLS AND THE VAMPIRE(1964, Ital.), art d; 00-2 MOST SECRET AGENTS(1965, Ital.), art d; EMBALMER, THE(1966, Ital.), art d; SIX DAYS A WEEK(1966, Fr./Ital./Span.); CURSE OF THE BLOOD GHOULS(1969, Ital.), art d
Guiseppe Ranieri
HOURS OF LOVE, THE(1965, Ital.), set d
Massimo Ranieri
LIGHT AT THE EDGE OF THE WORLD, THE(1971, U.S./Span./Lichtenstein); DEATH RACE(1978, Ital.); PRIEST OF LOVE(1981, Brit.)
Peppino Ranieri
TRAMPLERS, THE(1966, Ital.), art d
Raoul Ranieri
SANDOKAN THE GREAT(1964, Fr./Ital./Span.), makeup; MERCENARY, THE(1970, Ital./Span.), makeup
Thelma Raniero
JACK AND THE BEANSTALK(1970), set d; THUMBELINA(1970), set d
Branislav Ranisavljev
TWILIGHT TIME(1983, U.S./Yugo.)
T. Ranjana
OUTCAST OF THE ISLANDS(1952, Brit.), ch
Claude Rank
MAN FROM COCODY(1966, Fr/Ital.), w; WHO'S GOT THE BLACK BOX?(1970, Fr./Gr./Ital.), w
J. Arthur Rank
BUSH CHRISTMAS(1947, Brit.), p; CALENDAR, THE(1948, Brit.), p; ALL FOR MARY(1956, Brit.), p
Joseph Arthur Rank
SHIELD OF FAITH, THE(1956, Brit.), w
Lord Rank
CROWNING GIFT, THE(1967, Brit.), p
Ursula Rank
MILLION EYES OF SU-MURU, THE(1967, Brit.)
Andrew Rankin
THIRD WALKER, THE(1978, Can.)
Art Rankin
MY LUCKY STAR(1938)
Arthur Rankin
FALL OF EVE, THE(1929); MEXICALI ROSE(1929); WOLF OF WALL STREET, THE(1929); FIGHTING FOOL, THE(1932); UNWRITTEN LAW, THE(1932); TERROR TRAIL(1933); THRILL HUNTER, THE(1933); CRIME OF HELEN STANLEY(1934); MEN OF THE NIGHT(1934); STRAIGHTAWAY(1934); CASE OF THE MISSING MAN, THE(1935); GRAND EXIT(1935); PUBLIC MENACE(1935); SHE COULDN'T TAKE IT(1935); LONE WOLF RETURNS, THE(1936); MEET NERO WOLFE(1936); ROAMING LADY(1936); LOST HORIZON(1937); LOVE IS NEWS(1937); SECOND HONEYMOON(1937); SING AND BE HAPPY(1937); THIS IS MY AFFAIR(1937); ALEXANDER'S RAGTIME BAND(1938); HOTEL FOR WOMEN(1939); WIFE, HUSBAND AND FRIEND(1939)
Misc. Talkies
TRAILING NORTH(1933)
Silents
AMATEUR WIFE, THE(1920); ENCHANTMENT(1921); JIM THE PENMAN(1921); ENTER MADAME(1922); LITTLE MISS SMILES(1922); TO HAVE AND TO HOLD(1922); FEARLESS LOVER, THE(1925); OLD LOVES AND NEW(1926); VOLGA BOATMAN, THE(1926); ADVENTUROUS SOUL, THE(1927); SLIGHTLY USED(1927); WOMAN WHO DID NOT CARE, THE(1927); MAKING THE VARSITY(1928); RUNAWAY GIRLS(1928); WALKING BACK(1928)
Misc. Silents
LURE OF JADE, THE(1921); DISCONTENTED HUSBANDS(1924); VANITY'S PRICE(1924); PURSUED(1925); SPEED(1925); HIDDEN WAY, THE(1926); MAN IN THE SHADOW, THE(1926); MILLIONAIRE POLICEMAN, THE(1926); SPORTING LOVER, THE(1926); LOVE WAGER, THE(1927); RIDING TO FAME(1927); CODE OF THE AIR(1928); SAY IT WITH SABLES(1928); BELOW THE DEADLINE(1929); BROTHERS(1929)
Arthur Rankin, Jr.
WILLIE MCBEAN AND HIS MAGIC MACHINE(1965, U.S./Jap.), p,d&w; DAYDREAMER, THE(1966), p, w; MAD MONSTER PARTY(1967), p, w; WACKY WORLD OF MOTHER GOOSE, THE(1967), p; KING KONG ESCAPES(1968, Jap.), p, d; MARCO(1973), p; BUSHIDO BLADE, THE(1982 Brit./U.S.), p; LAST UNICORN, THE(1982), p&d, prod d
Arthur T. Rankin
GLAD RAG DOLL, THE(1929)
Caroline Rankin
LONE STAR RANGER, THE(1930); MEDICINE MAN, THE(1930); FINISHING SCHOOL(1934)

Silents
WITHOUT HOPE(1914); NINE O'CLOCK TOWN, A(1918); WHEN DO WE EAT?(1918); MIND OVER MOTOR(1923); MISS NOBODY(1926)
Misc. Silents
BE MY WIFE(1921)
Caroline "Spike" Rankin
MEN WITHOUT NAMES(1935)
Carolyn Rankin
KISS BEFORE THE MIRROR, THE(1933)
Catherine Rankin
Misc. Silents
THREE MUST-GET-THERES, THE(1922)
Doris Rankin
LOVE AT FIRST SIGHT(1930); NIGHT ANGEL, THE(1931); SALESLADY(1938); YOU CAN'T TAKE IT WITH YOU(1938); SOCIETY SMUGGLERS(1939)
Misc. Talkies
HER UNBORN CHILD(1933)
Silents
JIM THE PENMAN(1921)
Misc. Silents
COPPERHEAD, THE(1920); DEVIL'S GARDEN, THE(1920); GREAT ADVENTURE, THE(1921)
Douglas Rankin
SCHOOL FOR SCOUNDRELS(1960, Brit.), p
Dugald Rankin
ALFIE DARLING(1975, Brit.), p
Gil Rankin
ACCUSED OF MURDER(1956); DANCE WITH ME, HENRY(1956); BLACK PATCH(1957); MIDNIGHT COWBOY(1969)
Gilman H. Rankin
GHOST TOWN(1956)
Grace Rankin
Silents
HABIT OF HAPPINESS, THE(1916)
Janette Rankin
THAT SINKING FEELING(1979, Brit.)
Joe Rankin
LILITH(1964)
Molly Rankin
RETURN TO YESTERDAY(1940, Brit.); BONNIE PRINCE CHARLIE(1948, Brit.)
Simon Rankin
THIRD WALKER, THE(1978, Can.)
William M. Rankin
SOUTH SEA WOMAN(1953), w
William Rankin
I'VE GOT YOUR NUMBER(1934), w; COUNTERFEIT(1936), w; GIRL WITH IDEAS, A(1937), w; LOVE IN A BUNGALOW(1937), w; TIME OUT FOR ROMANCE(1937), w; ONLY ANGELS HAVE WINGS(1939), w; ST. LOUIS BLUES(1939), w; STREET OF MISSING MEN(1939), w; DIXIE(1943), w; HI BEAUTIFUL(1944), w; HARVEY GIRLS, THE(1946), w; FIGHTING FATHER DUNNE(1948), w
Caroline Ranklin
Silents
KINDRED OF THE DUST(1922)
Edmond Rannania
EMBASSY(1972, Brit.)
Lafayette Ranney
Silents
JOHN HALIFAX, GENTLEMAN(1915, Brit.)
Greta Rannigen
BROKEN ENGLISH(1981)
Saara Rannon
KREMLIN LETTER, THE(1970)
Jerry Rannow
WIZARD OF MARS(1964)
Umberto Rano
BIRD WITH THE CRYSTAL PLUMAGE, THE(1970, Ital./Ger.)
Maggie Ranone
1984
BROADWAY DANNY ROSE(1984)
W. V. Ranous
Silents
LITTLE ANGEL OF CANYON CREEK, THE(1914)
Misc. Silents
CHALICE OF COURAGE, THE(1915)
Chuck Ransdell
NIGHT THEY ROBBED BIG BERTHA'S, THE zero(1975)
Judith Ransdell
HARDCORE(1979)
Maurice Ransford
BRIGHAM YOUNG–FRONTIERSMAN(1940), art d; LITTLE TOKYO, U.S.A.(1942), art d; PIED PIPER, THE(1942), art d; HE HIRED THE BOSS(1943), art d; IMMORTAL SERGEANT, THE(1943), art d; MOON IS DOWN, THE(1943), art d; WINTERTIME(1943), art d; LIFEBOAT(1944), art d; SWEET AND LOWDOWN(1944), art d; HANGOVER SQUARE(1945), art d; LEAVE HER TO HEAVEN(1946), art d; SOMEWHERE IN THE NIGHT(1946), art d; 13 RUE MADELEINE(1946), art d; FOXES OF HARROW, THE(1947), art d; ROAD HOUSE(1948), art d; WALLS OF JERICHO(1948), art d; MOTHER IS A FRESHMAN(1949), art d; OH, YOU BEAUTIFUL DOLL(1949), art d; TWELVE O'CLOCK HIGH(1949), art d; PANIC IN THE STREETS(1950), art d; UNDER MY SKIN(1950), art d; DESERT FOX, THE(1951), art d; I'D CLIMB THE HIGHEST MOUNTAIN(1951), art d; THIRTEENTH LETTER, THE(1951), art d; DREAMBOAT(1952), art d; WAIT 'TIL THE SUN SHINES, NELLIE(1952), art d; KING OF THE KHYBER RIFLES(1953), art d; NIAGARA(1953), art d; TITANIC(1953), art d; BROKEN LANCE(1954), art d; GIRL IN THE RED VELVET SWING, THE(1955), art d; LEFT HAND OF GOD, THE(1955), art d; MAN CALLED PETER, THE(1955), art d; LOVE ME TENDER(1956), art d; 23 PACES TO BAKER STREET(1956), art d; KISS THEM FOR ME(1957), art d; OH, MEN! OH, WOMEN!(1957), art d; HUNTERS, THE(1958), art d; LONG, HOT SUMMER, THE(1958), art d; MAN WHO UNDERSTOOD WOMEN, THE(1959), art d; SOUND AND THE FURY, THE(1959), art d; FROM THE TERRACE(1960), art d; MARRIAGE-GO-ROUND, THE(1960), art d; MISTY(1961), art d; SNOW WHITE AND THE THREE

STOOGES(1961), art d
Mike Ranshaw
Misc. Talkies
ARNOLD'S WRECKING CO.(1973)
Martin Ransley
RETURN OF THE SOLDIER, THE(1983, Brit.)
Queenie Ransley
DOWN OUR ALLEY(1939, Brit.)
Martin Ransohoff
BOYS' NIGHT OUT(1962), p; WHEELER DEALERS, THE(1963), p; AMERICANIZA-
TION OF EMILY, THE(1964), p; CINCINNATI KID, THE(1965), p; LOVED ONE,
THE(1965); SANDPIPER, THE(1965), p, w; DON'T MAKE WAVES(1967), p; EYE OF
THE DEVIL(1967, Brit.), p; ICE STATION ZEBRA(1968), p; CASTLE KEEP(1969), p;
MIDSUMMER NIGHT'S DREAM, A(1969, Brit.), p; CATCH-22(1970), p; MOONSHINE
WAR, THE(1970), p; SEE NO EVIL(1971, Brit.), p; 10 RILLINGTON PLACE(1971,
Brit.), p; WHITE DAWN, THE(1974), p, w; NIGHTWING(1979), p; WANDERERS,
THE(1979), p; CHANGE OF SEASONS, A(1980), p, w; AMERICAN POP(1981), p;
HANKY-PANKY(1982), p; CLASS(1983), p
Aileen Ransom
MADAME SATAN(1930)
David Ransom
"RENT-A-GIRL"(1965)
Douglas Ransom
SOAPBOX DERBY(1958, Brit.), ph
Frank Ransom
KANGAROO(1952); LONG JOHN SILVER(1954, Aus.); SMILEY GETS A GUN(1959,
Brit.)
Glenn Ransom
MONSTER(1979)
Herbert Ransom
SOPHIE LANG GOES WEST(1937)
Jean Ransom
LOCKET, THE(1946)
JoAnn Ransom
VERY YOUNG LADY, A(1941)
John Ransom
Silents
$5,000,000 COUNTERFEITING PLOT, THE(1914)
Malcolm Ransom
UP THE CREEK(1958, Brit.)
Suzanne Ransom
ONCE A LADY(1931); PRODIGAL, THE(1931)
Arthur Ransome
SWALLOWS AND AMAZONS(1977, Brit.), w
Douglas Ransome
MAN'S AFFAIR, A(1949, Brit.), ph
Ethel Ransome
TREASURE ISLAND(1934)
Frank Ransome
OVERLANDERS, THE(1946, Brit./Aus.); KANGAROO KID, THE(1950, Aus./U.S.);
GLENROWAN AFFAIR, THE(1951, Aus.)
Jean Ransome
KITTY(1945); MISSING CORPSE, THE(1945); O.S.S.(1946); TEMPTATION(1946);
JOAN OF ARC(1948); LETTER FROM AN UNKNOWN WOMAN(1948); THAT FOR-
SYTE WOMAN(1949); TO PLEASE A LADY(1950); TURNING POINT, THE(1952)
Prunella Ransome
FAR FROM THE MADDING CROWD(1967, Brit.); ALFRED THE GREAT(1969, Brit.);
MAN IN THE WILDERNESS(1971, U.S./Span.); ISLAND OF THE DAMNED(1976,
Span.)
Stephen Ransome
WHO IS HOPE SCHUYLER?(1942), w
Sydney L. Ransome
Silents
AVE MARIA(1918, Brit.)
Sydney Lewis Ransome
Silents
QUEEN MOTHER, THE(1916, Brit.); STILL WATERS RUN DEEP(1916, Brit.); IF
THOU WERT BLIND(1917, Brit.); FRAILTY(1921, Brit.)
Misc. Silents
MASTER OF MEN, A(1917, Brit.)
Arthur Ranson
OUTSIDE THE LAW(1956)
Barbara Ranson
INTERVAL(1973, Mex./U.S.)
Guy Ranson
REASON TO LIVE, A REASON TO DIE, A(1974, Ital./Fr./Ger./Span.)
Lois Ranson
EARL OF PUDDLESTONE(1940); FRIENDLY NEIGHBORS(1940); GRAND OLE
OPRY(1940); GRANDPA GOES TO TOWN(1940); MEET THE MISSUS(1940); MONEY
TO BURN(1940); UNDER TEXAS SKIES(1940); ANGELS WITH BROKEN
WINGS(1941); CHEERS FOR MISS BISHOP(1941); PETTICOAT POLITICS(1941);
PIERRE OF THE PLAINS(1942)
Misc. Talkies
RENEGADE, THE(1943); CODE OF THE PLAINS(1947)
Malcolm Ranson
GIDEON OF SCOTLAND YARD(1959, Brit.); WOMAN'S TEMPTATION, A(1959,
Brit.); PIPER'S TUNE, THE(1962, Brit.)
Marcelle Ranson
NAKED AUTUMN(1963, Fr.)
Mavis Ranson
GIDEON OF SCOTLAND YARD(1959, Brit.); PIPER'S TUNE, THE(1962, Brit.)
Mary C. Ransone
NO GREATER SIN(1941), w
Fenya Ranyevskaya
SPRING(1948, USSR)
Jo Ranzato
OSS 117–MISSION FOR A KILLER(1966, Fr./Ital.), cos

Uma Rao
MAYA(1966)
Irma Raouch
ANDREI ROUBLOV(1973, USSR)
Sal Rapaglia
IF EVER I SEE YOU AGAIN(1978)
Azaria Rapaport
HILL 24 DOESN'T ANSWER(1955, Israel)
Erno Rapee
MOTHER KNOWS BEST(1928), m; MAKING THE GRADE(1929), m; WHISPERING
WINDS(1929), m; OLD ENGLISH(1930), md; SUNNY(1930), md; TOP SPEED(1930),
md; LITTLE CAESAR(1931), m; MEN OF THE SKY(1931), md; DEAD MARCH,
THE(1937), m
Silents
IRON HORSE, THE(1924), m; WHAT PRICE GLORY(1926), m
Mary-Linda Rapelye
IN COLD BLOOD(1967); MAROONED(1969)
Robert Rapelye
RAMPARTS WE WATCH, THE(1940)
Harry Rapf
CHAMP, THE(1931), p; CHIEF, THE(1933), p; CHRISTOPHER BEAN(1933), p; TUG-
BOAT ANNIE(1933), p; TURN BACK THE CLOCK(1933), p; HOLLYWOOD PAR-
TY(1934), p; WICKED WOMAN, A(1934), p; MURDER MAN(1935), p; NIGHT IS
YOUNG, THE(1935), p; PERFECT GENTLEMAN, THE(1935), p; MAD HOLI-
DAY(1936), p; OLD HUTCH(1936), p; PICCADILLY JIM(1936), p; THREE WISE
GUYS, THE(1936), p; TOUGH GUY(1936), p; WE WENT TO COLLEGE(1936), P;
WHIPSAW(1936), p; ESPIONAGE(1937), p; GOOD OLD SOAR, THE(1937), p; LIVE,
LOVE AND LEARN(1937), p; THEY GAVE HIM A GUN(1937), p; THOROUGHBREDS
DON'T CRY(1937), p; BAD MAN OF BRIMSTONE(1938), p; EVERYBODY
SING(1938), p; GIRL DOWNSTAIRS, THE(1938), p; STABLEMATES(1938), p; BURN
'EM UP O'CONNER(1939), p; ICE FOLLIES OF 1939(1939), p; LET FREEDOM
RING(1939), p; FORTY LITTLE MOTHERS(1940), p; SCENE OF THE CRIME(1949), p
Silents
SCHOOL DAYS(1921), p; RAGS TO RICHES(1922), p
Mathew Rapf
DESPERATE SEARCH(1952), p
Matthew Rapf
ADVENTURES OF GALLANT BESS(1948), w; SELLOUT, THE(1951), w; BIG LEA-
GUER(1953), p; HALF A HERO(1953), p
Maurice Rapf
DIVORCE IN THE FAMILY(1932), w; WE WENT TO COLLEGE(1936), w; THEY
GAVE HIM A GUN(1937), w; BAD MAN OF BRIMSTONE(1938), w; SHARPSHOOT-
ERS(1938), w; NORTH OF SHANGHAI(1939), w; WINTER CARNIVAL(1939), w;
DANCING ON A DIME(1940), w; JENNIE(1941), w; CALL OF THE CANYON(1942),
w; SONG OF THE SOUTH(1946), w; SO DEAR TO MY HEART(1949), w
George Raph
Silents
JAZZLAND(1928)
Harry Raph
GALLANT BESS(1946), p
Albert Raphael
GOLD(1974, Brit.); SAFARI 3000(1982)
Frederic Raphael
BACHELOR OF HEARTS(1958, Brit.), w; NOTHING BUT THE BEST(1964, Brit.), w;
WHY BOTHER TO KNOCK(1964, Brit.), w; DARLING(1965, Brit.), w; FAR FROM
THE MADDING CROWD(1967, Brit.), w; TWO FOR THE ROAD(1967, Brit.), w;
SEVERED HEAD, A(1971, Brit.), w; DAISY MILLER(1974), w; RICHARD'S
THINGS(1981, Brit.), w
John Nathaniel Raphael
PETER IBBETSON(1935), w
Mickey Raphael
HONEYSUCKLE ROSE(1980)
1984
SONGWRITER(1984)
Pat Raphael
MADAME LOUISE(1951, Brit.)
Victor Raphael
SHEILA LEVINE IS DEAD AND LIVING IN NEW YORK(1975)
Olga Raphael-Linden
Misc. Silents
PRESIDENT, THE(1918, Den.)
Samson Raphaelson
JAZZ SINGER, THE(1927), w; SMILING LIEUTENANT, THE(1931), w; BROKEN
LULLABY(1932), w; ONE HOUR WITH YOU(1932), w; TROUBLE IN PARADIS-
E(1932), w; CARAVAN(1934), w; MERRY WIDOW, THE(1934), w; SERVANTS' EN-
TRANCE(1934), w; ACCENT ON YOUTH(1935), w; DRESSED TO THRILL(1935), w;
LADIES LOVE DANGER(1935), w; RUNAWAY QUEEN, THE(1935, Brit.), w; AN-
GEL(1937), w; LAST OF MRS. CHEYNEY, THE(1937), w; SHOP AROUND THE
CORNER, THE(1940), w; SKYLARK(1941), w; SUSPICION(1941), w; HEAVEN CAN
WAIT(1943), w; ZIEGFELD FOLLIES(1945), w; HARVEY GIRLS, THE(1946), w; PER-
FECT MARRIAGE, THE(1946), w; GREEN DOLPHIN STREET(1947), w; THAT LADY
IN ERMINE(1948), w; IN THE GOOD OLD SUMMERTIME(1949), w; MR. MU-
SIC(1950), w; BANNERLINE(1951), w; JAZZ SINGER, THE(1953), w; MAIN STREET
TO BROADWAY(1953), w; HILDA CRANE(1956), d&w; BUT NOT FOR ME(1959), w;
JAZZ SINGER, THE(1980), w
Samuel Raphaelson
MAGNIFICENT LIE(1931), w
Jerome Raphel
CONNECTION, THE(1962); COOL WORLD, THE(1963); HALLELUJAH THE
HILLS(1963); DOUBLE-BARRELED DETECTIVE STORY, THE(1965); TELL THEM
WILLIE BOY IS HERE(1969)
The Rapiers
HE WHO RIDES A TIGER(1966, Brit.)
Martine Rapin
1984
LE DERNIER COMBAT(1984, Fr.), cos
Sara Rapisarda
ALL SCREWED UP(1976, Ital.)

John Rapley
LADY CAROLINE LAMB(1972, Brit./Ital.); ELEPHANT MAN, THE(1980, Brit.)
Azaria Rapoport
TEL AVIV TAXI(1957, Israel)
I.C. Rapoport
TO KILL A CLOWN(1972), w
Joe Raposo
POSSESSION OF JOEL DELANEY, THE(1972), m, md; SAVAGES(1972), m
Helen Rapoza
PAGAN LOVE SONG(1950)
Brian Rapp
RUN, ANGEL, RUN(1969)
Carl Rapp
WITCH WITHOUT A BROOM, A(1967, U.S./Span.); CHRISTMAS KID, THE(1968, U.S., Span.); LAST DAY OF THE WAR, THE(1969, U.S./Ital./Span.); WIND AND THE LION, THE(1975)
Doug Rapp
MISS JESSICA IS PREGNANT(1970), w
Jeannie Rapp
CARNY(1980)
Jimmy Rapp
CARNY(1980)
Joe Rapp
BREAKHEART PASS(1976)
Joel Rapp
HIGH SCHOOL BIG SHOT(1959), d&w; BATTLE OF BLOOD ISLAND(1960), d&w; WILD RACERS, THE(1968), p
Judy Rapp
UNHOLY ROLLERS(1972)
Larry Rapp
1984
ONCE UPON A TIME IN AMERICA(1984)
Neil Rapp
INDEPENDENCE DAY(1976), p
Paul Rapp
CURIOUS FEMALE, THE(1969), p&d
Phil Rapp
ZIEGFELD FOLLIES(1945), w
Philip Rapp
STRIKE ME PINK(1936), w; START CHEERING(1938), w; THERE'S ALWAYS A WOMAN(1938), w; WONDER MAN(1945), w; INSPECTOR GENERAL, THE(1949), w; AIN'T MISBEHAVIN'(1955), w
Phillip Rapp
WILD AND WONDERFUL(1964), w
Richard Rapp
MIDSUMMER NIGHT'S DREAM, A(1966); UNHOLY ROLLERS(1972)
Ray Rappa
WILD GYPSIES(1969)
Azaria Rappaport
SABRA(1970, Fr./Ital./Israel)
David Rappaport
CUBA(1979); MYSTERIES(1979, Neth.); TIME BANDITS(1981, Brit.)
1984
SWORD OF THE VALIANT(1984, Brit.)
Gerbert Rappaport
SONG OVER MOSCOW(1964, USSR), d
Herbert Rappaport
TAXI TO HEAVEN(1944, USSR), d
Mark Rappaport
VIRGIN PRESIDENT, THE(1968), ed; LOCAL COLOR(1978), p,d&w, ed; SCENIC ROUTE, THE(1978), p,d&w, ed; IMPOSTORS(1979), p,d&w, ed
Michele Rappaport
OLD BOYFRIENDS(1979), p
V. Rappaport
NO GREATER LOVE(1944, USSR), ph
Virginia Rappe
Silents
PARADISE GARDEN(1917)
Carolyn Rappel
DON QUIXOTE(1973, Aus.)
Malvina Rappel
MOTEL, THE OPERATOR(1940)
Elizabeth Rappeneau
SAVAGE, THE(1975, Fr.), w
Jean-Paul Rappeneau
ZAZIE(1961, Fr.), w; VERY PRIVATE AFFAIR, A(1962, Fr./Ital.), w; THAT MAN FROM RIO(1964, Fr./Ital.), w; MARCO THE MAGNIFICENT(1966, Ital./Fr./Yugo./Egypt/Afghanistan), w; LA VIE DE CHATEAU(1967, Fr.), d, w; SAVAGE, THE(1975, Fr.), d, w
Irving Rapper
LIFE OF EMILE ZOLA, THE(1937), d; ONE FOOT IN HEAVEN(1941), d; SHINING VICTORY(1941), d; GAY SISTERS, THE(1942), d; NOW, VOYAGER(1942), d; ADVENTURES OF MARK TWAIN, THE(1944), d; CORN IS GREEN, THE(1945), d; RHAPSODY IN BLUE(1945), d; DECEPTION(1946), d; VOICE OF THE TURTLE, THE(1947), d; ANNA LUCASTA(1949), d; GLASS MENAGERIE, THE(1950), d; ANOTHER MAN'S POISON(1952, Brit.), d; FOREVER FEMALE(1953), d; BAD FOR EACH OTHER(1954), d; BRAVE ONE, THE(1956), d; STRANGE INTRUDER(1956), d; MARJORIE MORNINGSTAR(1958), d; MIRACLE, THE(1959), d; STORY OF JOSEPH AND HIS BRETHREN THE(1962, Ital.), d; PONTIUS PILATE(1967, Fr./Ital.), d; CHRISTINE JORGENSEN STORY, THE(1970), d; BORN AGAIN(1978), d
Mario Rappini
SCHOOLGIRL DIARY(1947, Ital.), set d; MADAME(1963, Fr./Ital./Span.), art d
Lillian Rapple
ULYSSES(1967, U.S./Brit.); PADDY(1970, Irish); QUACKSER FORTUNE HAS A COUSIN IN THE BRONX(1970)
E. Rappoport
GORDEYEV FAMILY, THE(1961, U.S.S.R.), cos

Fred Rapport
LADY IN QUESTION, THE(1940); MR. LUCKY(1943); THREE HEARTS FOR JULIA(1943); MRS. PARKINGTON(1944); STORM OVER LISBON(1944); TWO GIRLS AND A SAILOR(1944); WOMAN IN THE WINDOW, THE(1945); UNKNOWN MAN, THE(1951); MARJORIE MORNINGSTAR(1958)
Michael Rapport
1984
HARDBODIES(1984)
Jean Rapstead
Misc. Talkies
THURSDAY MORNING MURDERS, THE(1976)
Edouard Raquello
Silents
GIRL FROM RIO, THE(1927)
Misc. Silents
SOUTH OF PANAMA(1928)
Edward Raquello
LAST EXPRESS, THE(1938); TORCHY GETS HER MAN(1938); WESTERN JAMBOREE(1938); GIRL AND THE GAMBLER, THE(1939); GIRL FROM MEXICO, THE(1939); IDIOT'S DELIGHT(1939); MISSING DAUGHTERS(1939); CALLING PHILO VANCE(1940)
Edward Raquelo
CHARLIE CHAN AT MONTE CARLO(1937); PATIENT IN ROOM 18, THE(1938)
John Rarig
IRISH EYES ARE SMILING(1944)
Eva Ras
LOVE AFFAIR; OR THE CASE OF THE MISSING SWITCHBOARD OPERATOR(1968, Yugo.)
Salvatore Rasa
UP THE DOWN STAIRCASE(1967)
Janet Rasak
STATE OF THINGS, THE(1983)
Tony Rasato
NOTHING PERSONAL(1980, Can.)
Vladimir Rasbevsky
ARCH OF TRIUMPH(1948)
Mars Rasca
BACK DOOR TO HELL(1964), ph
Mars B. Rasca
IMPASSE(1969), ph
Nonong Rasca
LOSERS, THE(1970), ph; DAUGHTERS OF SATAN(1972), ph; SUPERBEAST(1972), ph
Harmonica Rascals
TRAMP, TRAMP, TRAMP(1942)
Renato Rascel
GRAN VARIETA(1955, Ital.); MONTE CARLO STORY, THE(1957, Ital.); SEVEN HILLS OF ROME, THE(1958); SECRET OF SANTA VITTORIA, THE(1969)
Albertina Rasch
DEVIL MAY CARE(1929), ch; OUR BLUSHING BRIDES(1930), ch; STAGE MOTHER(1933), ch; MERRY WIDOW, THE(1934), ch; AFTER THE DANCE(1935), ch; BROADWAY MELODY OF 1936(1935), ch; KING STEPS OUT, THE(1936), ch; FIREFLY, THE(1937), ch; ROSALIE(1937), ch; GIRL OF THE GOLDEN WEST, THE(1938), ch; GREAT WALTZ, THE(1938), ch; MARIE ANTOINETTE(1938), ch; SWEETHEARTS(1938), ch
Budd Rasch
STARLIGHT OVER TEXAS(1938)
Carlos Rasch
SIGNALS-AN ADVENTURE IN SPACE(1970, E. Ger./Pol.), w
Carola Rasch
SHADOWS GROW LONGER, THE(1962, Switz./Ger.)
Kai Rasch
GOLDEN MOUNTAINS(1958, Den.), set d; CRAZY PARADISE(1965, Den.), art d; GERTRUD(1966, Den.), art d; SUDDENLY, A WOMAN!(1967, Den.), art d
Pete Rasch
SHE LEARNED ABOUT SAILORS(1934)
Wilson D. Rasch
DOWN THE WYOMING TRAIL(1939)
David Rasche
MANHATTAN(1979); SOMETHING SHORT OF PARADISE(1979); JUST TELL ME WHAT YOU WANT(1980); HONKY TONK FREEWAY(1981); DEATH VENGEANCE(1982)
1984
BEST DEFENSE(1984)
Julius Rascheff
LYDIA(1964, Can.), p, w, ph; LIFT, THE(1965, Brit./Can.), p, ph; OLIVE TREES OF JUSTICE, THE(1967, Fr.), ph
Renato Raschel
BEAR, THE(1963, Fr.)
Krafft Raschig
Silents
PANDORA'S BOX(1929, Ger.)
Kraft Raschig
THREEPENNY OPERA, THE(1931, Ger./U.S.)
Irmgard H.H. Raschke
JUNGLE JIM IN THE FORBIDDEN LAND(1952)
Judith Rascoe
ROAD MOVIE(1974), w; WHO'LL STOP THE RAIN?(1978), w; PORTRAIT OF THE ARTIST AS A YOUNG MAN, A(1979, Ireland), w; ENDLESS LOVE(1981), w
Linda Rascoe
Misc. Talkies
DISCIPLES OF DEATH(1975)
Mark Rascovich
BEDFORD INCIDENT, THE(1965, Brit.), w
Kendall S. Rase
IN SEARCH OF HISTORIC JESUS(1980), ed
Val Raset
SAN FRANCISCO(1936), ch; BRIDE WORE RED, THE(1937), ch; GOOD OLD SOAK, THE(1937), ch; MAYTIME(1937), ch; SHOPWORN ANGEL(1938), ch; SWISS MISS(1938), a, ch; NEW MOON(1940), ch; MY GAL SAL(1942), ch; SING YOUR

WORRIES AWAY(1942), ch; YOU WERE NEVER LOVELIER(1942), ch; HELLO, FRISCO, HELLO(1943), ch; COVER GIRL(1944), cos $ch; HEY, ROOKIE(1944), ch; BLACK BART(1948), ch; HIT PARADE OF 1951(1950), ch; HELLER IN PINK TIGHTS(1960), ch

Jean Rasey
HINDENBURG, THE(1975); ROLLERCOASTER(1977)

Steve Rash
BUDDY HOLLY STORY, THE(1978), d; UNDER THE RAINBOW(1981), d

Burt Rashby
VIRGIN PRESIDENT, THE(1968), ed

N. Rashevskaya
GREAT CITIZEN, THE(1939, USSR)

Natalia Rashevskaya
FATHERS AND SONS(1960, USSR), p&d, w

Rashkovsky-Kaleva
LIQUID SKY(1982), makeup

Andy Rashleigh
ACCEPTABLE LEVELS(1983, Brit.)
1984
PLOUGHMAN'S LUNCH, THE(1984, Brit.)

Rex Rashley
KEY MAN, THE(1957, Brit.)

Gordana Rashovich
HEAVEN'S GATE(1980)

Bruno Rasia
PIRATE AND THE SLAVE GIRL, THE(1961, Fr./Ital.), w, art d

Eddy Rasimi
LES MAINS SALES(1954, Fr.); NIGHT WATCH, THE(1964, Fr./Ital.)

A. Raskin
SPRING(1948, USSR), w

Damon Bradley Raskin
NORTH AVENUE IRREGULARS, THE(1979)

Dolores Raskin
CROSS AND THE SWITCHBLADE, THE(1970)

Kenneth Raskin
SQUEEZE PLAY(1981)

Sherman Raskin
TAKE A GIANT STEP(1959); TIGER MAKES OUT, THE(1967)

Karen Raskind
ROMANTIC COMEDY(1983)

Savo Raskovitch
WAR AND PEACE(1956, Ital./U.S.)

Mikhail Rasmuny
BLUE SKIES(1946)

Eric Rasmussen
SCALPS(1983), m

Frank Rasmussen
TOAST OF NEW YORK, THE(1937); MARINES COME THROUGH, THE(1943)

Frode Rasmussen
CHILDREN OF GOD'S EARTH(1983, Norwegian)

Manon Rasmussen
1984
ELEMENT OF CRIME, THE(1984, Den.), cos

Mark Rasmussen
SERIAL(1980)

Maurine Rasmussen
Silents
BREWSTER'S MILLIONS(1914)

Mike Rasmussen
MEAL, THE(1975)

Niels Rasmussen
REVENGE OF THE SHOGUN WOMEN(1982, Taiwan), ed

Tom Rasmussen
RUBY(1977), art d, cos; YOU LIGHT UP MY LIFE(1977), art d, set d; HARPER VALLEY, P.T.A.(1978), art d, cos; ATTIC, THE(1979), art d; GOOD LUCK, MISS WYCKOFF(1979), cos

Richard Rasof
MAN IN THE GLASS BOOTH, THE(1975); SHEILA LEVINE IS DEAD AND LIVING IN NEW YORK(1975)

Fritz Rasp
EMIL AND THE DETECTIVE(1931, Ger.); KARAMAZOV(1931, Ger.); THREEPENNY OPERA, THE(1931, Ger./U.S.); MAGIC FIRE(1956)
Silents
METROPOLIS(1927, Ger.); SPIES(1929, Ger.); WOMAN ON THE MOON, THE(1929, Ger.)
Misc. Silents
LOVE OF JEANNE NEY, THE(1927, Ger.); MYSTIC MIRROR, THE(1928, Ger.)

James Raspberry
Misc. Talkies
I WAS A ZOMBIE FOR THE F.B.I.(1982)

Larry Raspberry
THIS IS ELVIS(1982)
Misc. Talkies
I WAS A ZOMBIE FOR THE F.B.I.(1982)

Horst Raspe
CELESTE(1982, Ger.)

Hans Raspotnik
BIMBO THE GREAT(1961, Ger.), w

Ivan Rasputin
MIGHTY JOE YOUNG(1949); FRIENDLY PERSUASION(1956)

Inge Rassaert
$100 A NIGHT(1968, Ger.)

Jean-Pierre Rassam
TOUT VA BIEN(1973, Fr.), p; DON'T TOUCH WHITE WOMEN!(1974, Fr.), p; LANCELOT OF THE LAKE(1975, Fr.), p

S. Rassatov
Misc. Silents
SINGED WINGS(1915, USSR)

Val Rasset
TONIGHT AND EVERY NIGHT(1945), ch

Ivan Rassimov
PLANET OF THE VAMPIRES(1965, U.S./Ital./Span.); NEXT!(1971, Ital./Span.); TORMENTED, THE(1978, Ital.); BEYOND THE DOOR II(1979, Ital.); HUMANOID, THE(1979, Ital.)
Misc. Talkies
SPASMO(1976); MAFIA JUNCTION(1977)

R. Rassimov
STRANGER'S GUNDOWN, THE(1974, Ital.)

Rada Rassimov
GOOD, THE BAD, AND THE UGLY, THE(1967, Ital./Span.); SEED OF MAN, THE(1970, Ital.); CAT O'NINE TAILS(1971, Ital./Ger./Fr.); BARON BLOOD(1972, Ital.)

George Rassman
ARNELO AFFAIR, THE(1947), m

Froda Rassmussen
SUMMER RUN(1974)

Tom Rassmussen
FIRST NUDIE MUSICAL, THE(1976), art d, cos

Bobby Rast
FIREBALL JUNGLE(1968)

Dohle Rast
FIREBALL JUNGLE(1968)

Pat Rast
FIREBALL JUNGLE(1968)

Wendy Rastatter
OUR WINNING SEASON(1978)

Schell Rasten
TO FIND A MAN(1972)

Thalmus Rasulala
BLACULA(1972); COOL BREEZE(1972); WILLIE DYNAMITE(1973); ADIOS AMIGO(1975); BUCKTOWN(1975); CORNBREAD, EARL AND ME(1975); FRIDAY FOSTER(1975); MR. RICCO(1975); LAST HARD MEN, THE(1976); FUN WITH DICK AND JANE(1977)

Jay Rasumny
1984
BREAKIN' 2: ELECTRIC BOOGALOO(1984); NINJA III–THE DOMINATION(1984); STRANGERS KISS(1984)

Mikhail Rasumny
COMRADE X(1940); FORCED LANDING(1941); HOLD BACK THE DAWN(1941); ONE NIGHT IN LISBON(1941); SHANGHAI GESTURE, THE(1941); ROAD TO MOROCCO(1942); THIS GUN FOR HIRE(1942); WAKE ISLAND(1942); YOKEL BOY(1942); FOR WHOM THE BELL TOLLS(1943); HOSTAGES(1943); AND THE ANGELS SING(1944); HENRY ALDRICH PLAYS CUPID(1944); PRACTICALLY YOURS(1944); MASQUERADE IN MEXICO(1945); MEDAL FOR BENNY, A(1945); ROYAL SCANDAL, A(1945); STORK CLUB, THE(1945); UNSEEN, THE(1945); ANNA AND THE KING OF SIAM(1946); HEARTBEAT(1946); HOLIDAY IN MEXICO(1946); OUR HEARTS WERE GROWING UP(1946); HER HUSBAND'S AFFAIRS(1947); PIRATES OF MONTEREY(1947); SONG OF MY HEART(1947); VARIETY GIRL(1947); KISSING BANDIT, THE(1948); SAIGON(1948); FREE FOR ALL(1949); PIRATES OF CAPRI, THE(1949); HIT PARADE OF 1951(1950); ANYTHING CAN HAPPEN(1952); STARS ARE SINGING, THE(1953); TONIGHT WE SING(1953); HOT BLOOD(1956)

Gamil Ratab
TRAPEZE(1956)

Chitra Ratana
RED-DRAGON(1967, Ital./Ger./US)

Wayne Ratay
WIZARD OF GORE, THE(1970)

Carl Ratcliff
ICE PALACE(1960)

Eric Ratcliff
LITTLE SEX, A(1982)

Sandy Ratcliff
FAMILY LIFE(1971, Brit.); LAST DAYS OF MAN ON EARTH, THE(1975, Brit.); RADIO ON(1980, Brit./Ger.)

E. J. Ratcliffe
JAZZ AGE, THE(1929); SALLY(1929); SKINNER STEPS OUT(1929); COHENS AND KELLYS IN SCOTLAND, THE(1930); ONE HYSTERICAL NIGHT(1930); WIDE OPEN(1930); I LOVED A WOMAN(1933)
Silents
AMAZING LOVERS(1921); IDOL OF THE NORTH, THE(1921); INTRODUCE ME(1925); MAN ON THE BOX, THE(1925); BLACK PIRATE, THE(1926); ROLLING HOME(1926); SKINNER'S DRESS SUIT(1926); WINNING OF BARBARA WORTH, THE(1926); CHEATING CHEATERS(1927); HELD BY THE LAW(1927); NO CONTROL(1927); NOTORIOUS LADY, THE(1927); SMILE, BROTHER, SMILE(1927); HEAD MAN, THE(1928)
Misc. Silents
IN THE PALACE OF THE KING(1915); MARRIAGE WHIRL, THE(1925); MORE PAY - LESS WORK(1926); THRILL HUNTER, THE(1926); 30 BELOW ZERO(1926); PRINCE OF HEADWAITERS, THE(1927); PUBLICITY MADNESS(1927)

Jane Ratcliffe
UNCLE, THE(1966, Brit.)

Sandy Ratcliffe
YESTERDAY'S HERO(1979, Brit.)
Misc. Talkies
DOLL'S EYE(1982)

Stanley Ratcliffe
WARNING TO WANTONS, A(1949, Brit.)

Lynn Ratener
ME AND MY BROTHER(1969), ed

E. J. Rath
CLEAR THE DECKS(1929), w; WHAT A MAN(1930), w; WHOOPEE(1930), w; FAST LIFE(1932), w

Earl Rath
UP IN THE CELLAR(1970), ph; RAID ON ROMMEL(1971), ph; SHOOT OUT(1971), ph; BUSTING(1974), ph; PEEPER(1975), ph

Franz Rath
YOUNG TORLESS(1968, Fr./Ger.), ph; DEGREE OF MURDER, A(1969, Ger.), ph; PILGRIM, FAREWELL(1980), ph; GERMAN SISTERS, THE(1982, Ger.), ph; WAR AND PEACE(1983, Ger.), ph

Fred Rath
GIVE OUT, SISTERS(1942), w; SING A JINGLE(1943), w

Virginia Rath
MACABRE(1958), w

Kagen Rathak
TWO DAUGHTERS(1963, India)

Carol Rathaus
DICTATOR, THE(1935, Brit./Ger.), m

Karol Rathaus
KARAMAZOV(1931, Ger.), m; TRUNKS OF MR. O.F., THE(1932, Ger.), m; LET US LIVE(1939), m

Basil Rathbone
LAST OF MRS. CHEYNEY, THE(1929); BISHOP MURDER CASE, THE(1930); FLIRTING WIDOW, THE(1930); LADY OF SCANDAL, THE(1930); LADY SURRENDERS, A(1930); NOTORIOUS AFFAIR, A(1930); SIN TAKES A HOLIDAY(1930); THIS MAD WORLD(1930); AFTER THE BALL(1932, Brit.); WOMAN COMMANDS, A(1932); ONE PRECIOUS YEAR(1933, Brit.); LOYALTIES(1934, Brit.); ANNA KARENINA(1935); CAPTAIN BLOOD(1935); DAVID COPPERFIELD(1935); FEATHER IN HER HAT, A(1935); KIND LADY(1935); LAST DAYS OF POMPEII, THE(1935); TALE OF TWO CITIES, A(1935); GARDEN OF ALLAH, THE(1936); PRIVATE NUMBER(1936); ROMEO AND JULIET(1936); CONFESSION(1937); LOVE FROM A STRANGER(1937, Brit.); MAKE A WISH(1937); TOVARICH(1937); ADVENTURES OF MARCO POLO, THE(1938); ADVENTURES OF ROBIN HOOD, THE(1938); DAWN PATROL, THE(1938); IF I WERE KING(1938); ADVENTURES OF SHERLOCK HOLMES, THE(1939); HOUND OF THE BASKERVILLES, THE(1939); RIO(1939); SON OF FRANKENSTEIN(1939); SUN NEVER SETS, THE(1939); TOWER OF LONDON(1939); MARK OF ZORRO, THE(1940); RHYTHM ON THE RIVER(1940); BLACK CAT, THE(1941); INTERNATIONAL LADY(1941); MAD DOCTOR, THE(1941); PARIS CALLING(1941); CROSSROADS(1942); FINGERS AT THE WINDOW(1942); SHERLOCK HOLMES AND THE SECRET WEAPON(1942); SHERLOCK HOLMES AND THE VOICE OF TERROR(1942); ABOVE SUSPICION(1943); CRAZY HOUSE(1943); SHERLOCK HOLMES FACES DEATH(1943); SHERLOCK HOLMES IN WASHINGTON(1943); BATHING BEAUTY(1944); FRENCHMAN'S CREEK(1944); PEARL OF DEATH, THE(1944); SCARLET CLAW, THE(1944); SHERLOCK HOLMES AND THE SPIDER WOMAN(1944); HOUSE OF FEAR, THE(1945); PURSUIT TO ALGIERS(1945); WOMAN IN GREEN, THE(1945); DRESSED TO KILL(1946); HEARTBEAT(1946); TERROR BY NIGHT(1946); ADVENTURES OF ICHABOD AND MR. TOAD(1949); CASANOVA'S BIG NIGHT(1954); WE'RE NO ANGELS(1955); BLACK SLEEP, THE(1956); COURT JESTER, THE(1956); LAST HURRAH, THE(1958); MAGIC SWORD, THE(1962); TALES OF TERROR(1962); COMEDY OF TERRORS, THE(1964); VOYAGE TO THE PREHISTORIC PLANET(1965); GHOST IN THE INVISIBLE BIKINI(1966); QUEEN OF BLOOD(1966); HILLBILLYS IN A HAUNTED HOUSE(1967); PONTIUS PILATE(1967, Fr./Ital.)
Silents
INNOCENT(1921, Brit.)
Misc. Silents
FRUITFUL VINE, THE(1921, Brit.); SCHOOL FOR SCANDAL, THE(1923, Brit.); TROUPING WITH ELLEN(1924); MASKED BRIDE, THE(1925); GREAT DECEPTION, THE(1926)

Lorna Rathbone
Silents
ALL ROADS LEAD TO CALVARY(1921, Brit.)

Mary Rathbone
OH, HEAVENLY DOG!(1980)

Nigel Rathbone
NO BLADE OF GRASS(1970, Brit.)

Eldon Rathburn
DRYLANDERS(1963, Can.), m; NOBODY WAVED GOODBYE(1965, Can.), m; WAITING FOR CAROLINE(1969, Can.), m; COLD JOURNEY(1975, Can.), m; WHO HAS SEEN THE WIND(1980, Can.), m

Dolly Rathebe
PENNYWHISTLE BLUES, THE(1952, South Africa)

Isabelle Rathery
SPERMULA(1976, Fr.), ed

Gustav Rathje
M(1933, Ger.), ph

Clifford Rathjen
THEY WERE EXPENDABLE(1945)

John Rathmell
LOST JUNGLE, THE(1934), w; CONFIDENTIAL(1935), w; IN OLD SANTA FE(1935), w; LADIES CRAVE EXCITEMENT(1935), w; MARINES ARE COMING, THE(1935), w; DARKEST AFRICA(1936), w; DANGEROUS ADVENTURE, A(1937), w; GHOST TOWN GOLD(1937), w; RIDERS OF THE WHISTLING SKULL(1937), w; TRAPPED(1937), w; PAINTED DESERT, THE(1938), w; STARLIGHT OVER TEXAS(1938), w; FIGHTING MAD(1939), w; RENEGADE TRAIL(1939), w; SONG OF THE BUCKAROO(1939), w; SOUTHWARD HO!(1939), w; BULLETS FOR RUSTLERS(1940), w; RANGE BUSTERS, THE(1940), w; UNDERGROUND RUSTLERS(1941), w

John B. Rathmell
TWO GUN LAW(1937), w

Willy Rathnov
WEEKEND(1964, Den.); SCANDAL IN DENMARK(1970, Den.)

Akos Rathony
DON'T BLAME THE STORK(1954, Brit.), d; DEVIL'S DAFFODIL, THE(1961, Brit./Ger.), d

Robert Rathonyi
WITNESS, THE(1982, Hung.)

Zsuzsa Rathonyi
FATHER(1967, Hung.)

Jean-Paul Raths
1984
CLASS ENEMY(1984, Ger.)

Helen H. Rathvon
SUN SETS AT DAWN, THE(1950), p

N. Peter Rathvon
1984(1956, Brit.), p

Gamil Ratib
LAWRENCE OF ARABIA(1962, Brit.); SHADOW OF EVIL(1967, Fr./Ital.); TO COMMIT A MURDER(1970, Fr./Ital./Ger.); L'ETOILE DU NORD(1983, Fr.)

Donald Ratka
TOO YOUNG, TOO IMMORAL!(1962)

Tracey Ratley
HARDCORE(1979)

Dwayne Ratliff
I DON'T CARE GIRL, THE(1952)

Paul Ratliff
TO BE OR NOT TO BE(1983)

Herb Ratner
JOE LOUIS STORY, THE(1953)

Herbert Ratner
SLEEPING CITY, THE(1950)

Gregory Ratoff
UNDER TWO FLAGS(1936); ONCE IN A LIFETIME(1932); SECRETS OF THE FRENCH POLICE(1932); SKYSCRAPER SOULS(1932); SYMPHONY OF SIX MILLION(1932); UNDER-COVER MAN(1932); WHAT PRICE HOLLYWOOD?(1932); BROADWAY THROUGH A KEYHOLE(1933); GIRL WITHOUT A ROOM(1933); HEADLINE SHOOTER(1933); I'M NO ANGEL(1933); PROFESSIONAL SWEETHEART(1933); SITTING PRETTY(1933); SWEEPINGS(1933); GEORGE WHITE'S SCANDALS(1934); GREAT FLIRTATION, THE(1934), w; LET'S FALL IN LOVE(1934); HELLO SWEETHEART(1935, Brit.); REMEMBER LAST NIGHT(1935); 18 MINUTES(1935, Brit.), a, p, w; HERE COMES TROUBLE(1936); KING OF BURLESQUE(1936); ROAD TO GLORY, THE(1936); SING, BABY, SING(1936); SINS OF MAN(1936), d; TROUBLE AHEAD(1936, Brit.); UNDER YOUR SPELL(1936); CAFE METROPOLE(1937), a, w; LANCER SPY(1937), d; SEVENTH HEAVEN(1937); TOP OF THE TOWN(1937); YOU CAN'T HAVE EVERYTHING(1937), w; FORBIDDEN TERRITORY(1938, Brit.); GATEWAY(1938); SALLY, IRENE AND MARY(1938); BARRICADE(1939), d; DAY-TIME WIFE(1939), d; HOTEL FOR WOMEN(1939), d; INTERMEZZO: A LOVE STORY(1939), d; ROSE OF WASHINGTON SQUARE(1939), d; WIFE, HUSBAND AND FRIEND(1939), d; GREAT PROFILE, THE(1940); I WAS AN ADVENTURESS(1940), d; PUBLIC DEB NO. 1(1940), d; ADAM HAD FOUR SONS(1941), d; CORSICAN BROTHERS, THE(1941), d; MEN IN HER LIFE, THE(1941), p&d; FOOTLIGHT SERENADE(1942), d; TWO YANKS IN TRINIDAD(1942), d; HEAT'S ON, THE(1943), d; SOMETHING TO SHOUT ABOUT(1943), p&d; SONG OF RUSSIA(1943), d; IRISH EYES ARE SMILING(1944), d; PARIS UNDERGROUND(1945), d; WHERE DO WE GO FROM HERE?(1945), d; DO YOU LOVE ME?(1946), d; CARNIVAL IN COSTA RICA(1947), d; MOSS ROSE(1947), d; BLACK MAGIC(1949), p, d; ALL ABOUT EVE(1950); IF THIS BE SIN(1950, Brit.), p&d; OPERATION X(1951, Brit.), a, p&d; O. HENRY'S FULL HOUSE(1952); MOON IS BLUE, THE(1953); TAXI(1953), d; ABDULLAH'S HAREM(1956, Brit./Egypt.), a, p&d; SUN ALSO RISES, THE(1957); EXODUS(1960); ONCE MORE, WITH FEELING(1960); OSCAR WILDE(1960, Brit.), d; BIG GAMBLE, THE(1961)

V. Ratomskiy
LULLABY(1961, USSR)

V. Ratomsky
DREAM OF A COSSACK(1982, USSR)

Suzanna Ratoni
TRUNK TO CAIRO(1966, Israel/Ger.)

Andrew Ratoucheff
PUFNSTUF(1970)

Peter Ratray
TRAIN RIDE TO HOLLYWOOD(1975)

Paul Rattee
STAND UP VIRGIN SOLDIERS(1977, Brit.)

Harry Rattenberry
Silents
OLIVER TWIST(1916); HIGH SPEED(1917); M'LISS(1918); PLAYING THE GAME(1918); HEARTS OF MEN(1919); SOUL OF THE BEAST(1923)
Misc. Silents
MARKED MAN, A(1917); '49 - '17(1917); LAW'S OUTLAW, THE(1918); POOR SIMP, THE(1920); HIS PAJAMA GIRL(1921); MOTION TO ADJOURN, A(1921)

Harry Rattenbury
Silents
ALMOST MARRIED(1919); HUCKLEBERRY FINN(1920); ABRAHAM LINCOLN(1924)
Misc. Silents
DELICIOUS LITTLE DEVIL, THE(1919)

Henry Rattenbury
Silents
WATCH YOUR STEP(1922)

F. M. Ratti
LOST HAPPINESS(1948, Ital.), d

Robert Ratti
NEXT OF KIN(1983, Aus.)

Isabelle Rattier
THAT OBSCURE OBJECT OF DESIRE(1977, Fr./Span.)

Jo Rattigan
DOWN TO EARTH(1947)

Terence Rattigan
BELLES OF ST. CLEMENTS, THE(1936, Brit.), w; GYPSY(1937, Brit.), w; FRENCH WITHOUT TEARS(1939, Brit.), w; QUIET WEDDING(1941, Brit.), w; AVENGERS, THE(1942, Brit.), w; UNCENSORED(1944, Brit.), w; JOHNNY IN THE CLOUDS(1945, Brit.), w; JOURNEY TOGETHER(1946, Brit.), w; BRIGHTON ROCK(1947, Brit.), w; BOND STREET(1948, Brit.), w; HER MAN GILBEY(1949, Brit.), w; WHILE THE SUN SHINES(1950, Brit.), w; WINSLOW BOY, THE(1950), w; BREAKING THE SOUND BARRIER(1952), w; FINAL TEST, THE(1953, Brit.), w; DEEP BLUE SEA, THE(1955, Brit.), w; MAN WHO LOVED REDHEADS, THE(1955, Brit.), w; PRINCE AND THE SHOWGIRL, THE(1957, Brit.), w; SEPARATE TABLES(1958), w; V.I.P.s, THE(1963, Brit.), w; YELLOW ROLLS-ROYCE, THE(1965, Brit.), w; GOODBYE MR. CHIPS(1969, U.S./Brit.), w; NELSON AFFAIR, THE(1973, Brit.), w

Terrence Rattigan
BROWNING VERSION, THE(1951, Brit.), w

Anton Rattinger
GERMAN SISTERS, THE(1982, Ger.)

Heather Rattray
ACROSS THE GREAT DIVIDE(1976); FURTHER ADVENTURES OF THE WILDERNESS FAMILY–PART TWO(1978); SEA GYPSIES, THE(1978); MOUNTAIN FAMILY ROBINSON(1979)

John Ratzenberger
RITZ, THE(1976); TWILIGHT'S LAST GLEAMING(1977, U.S./Ger.); SUPER-MAN(1978); WARLORDS OF ATLANTIS(1978, Brit.); ARABIAN ADVENTURE(1979, Brit.); HANOVER STREET(1979, Brit.); YANKS(1979); EMPIRE STRIKES BACK, THE(1980); MOTEL HELL(1980); SUPERMAN II(1980); OUTLAND(1981); BATTLE-TRUCK(1982); FIREFOX(1982)
Andrea Rau
DAUGHTERS OF DARKNESS(1971, Bel./ Fr./ Ger./ Ital.)
Gretchen Rau
1984
ONCE UPON A TIME IN AMERICA(1984), set d
Jim Rau
WIZARD OF GORE, THE(1970)
Margaret Rau
COLD TURKEY(1971), w
Neil Rau
FOREVER YOURS(1945), w; COLD TURKEY(1971), w
Rama Rau
Misc. Silents
SHIRAZ(1929)
Santha Rama Rau
1984
PASSAGE TO INDIA, A(1984, Brit.), d&w
Umberto Rau
LAST MAN ON EARTH, THE(1964, U.S./Ital.)
Francois Rauber
JACQUES BREL IS ALIVE AND WELL AND LIVING IN PARIS(1975), md
Judy Rauch
Misc. Talkies
NAUGHTY SCHOOL GIRLS(1977)
Samuel Rauch
Misc. Talkies
ALIEN CONTAMINATION(1981)
Siegfried Rauch
PATTON(1970); LE MANS(1971); LITTLE MOTHER(1973, U.S./Yugo./Ger.); EAGLE HAS LANDED, THE(1976, Brit.); BIG RED ONE, THE(1980); ALIEN CONTAMINA-TION(1982, Ital.)
Sigi Rauch
ESCAPE TO ATHENA(1979, Brit.)
Herman Raucher
SWEET NOVEMBER(1968), w; WATERMELON MAN(1970), w; SUMMER OF '42(1971), w; CLASS OF '44(1973), w; ODE TO BILLY JOE(1976), w; OTHER SIDE OF MIDNIGHT, THE(1977), w
Jules Raucourt
CAFE METROPOLE(1937); ARTISTS AND MODELS ABROAD(1938)
Misc. Silents
AT FIRST SIGHT(1917); LA TOSCA(1918); MY WIFE(1918)
Max Rauffer
UNWILLING AGENT(1968, Ger.), makeup
Stanley Rauh
CROSS COUNTRY CRUISE(1934), w; LAUGHING IRISH EYES(1936), w; HOLD THAT KISS(1938), w; CISCO KID AND THE LADY, THE(1939), w; QUICK MIL-LIONS(1939), w; TOO BUSY TO WORK(1939), w; CHARTER PILOT(1940), w; MICHA-EL SHAYNE, PRIVATE DETECTIVE(1940), w; PIER 13(1940), w; YOUNG AS YOU FEEL(1940), w; CADET GIRL(1941), w; DANCE HALL(1941), w; DRESSED TO KILL(1941), w; HARMON OF MICHIGAN(1941), w; SLEEPERS WEST(1941), w; A-HAUNTING WE WILL GO(1942), w; CAREER GIRL(1944), w
Mikhail Rafailovich Raukhverger
MORNING STAR(1962, USSR), w, m
Georges Raulet
UNDER THE ROOFS OF PARIS(1930, Fr.), ph; MILLION, THE(1931, Fr.), ph
Warren Raum
ROBBY(1968)
Bridget Wienst Raume
HAREM BUNCH; OR WAR AND PIECE, THE(1969)
Fritz Raup
SOMEWHERE IN BERLIN(1949, E. Ger.)
Angelo Raupenas
Misc. Silents
STEPAN KHALTURIN(1925, USSR)
Georges Rauquie
LOVE IN A HOT CLIMATE(1958, Fr./Span.), d
Lotte Rausch
LOST ONE, THE(1951, Ger.)
Erdner Rauschalle
UNDERGROUND U.S.A.(1980), p
Marketa Rauschgoldova
WISHING MACHINE(1971, Czech.)
Jaroslav Rauser
TRANSPORT FROM PARADISE(1967, Czech.)
William Rausher
Silents
DIMPLES(1916)
Serge Rausseau
SLEEPING CAR MURDER THE(1966, Fr.)
V. Rautbart
GARNET BRACELET, THE(1966, USSR)
Jans Rautenbach
WILD SEASON(1968, South Africa), p
Bart M. Rauw
REFORM SCHOOL(1939), ed
Rauzena
BATTLE OF THE RAILS(1949, Fr.); GYPSY FURY(1950, Fr.)
Fernand Rauzena
CONFESSIONS OF A ROGUE(1948, Fr.)
Fernard Rauzena
CHEAT, THE(1950, Fr.)

Marie-Claude Rauzier
MY NIGHT AT MAUD'S(1970, Fr.)
Isarco Ravaioli
VAMPIRE AND THE BALLERINA, THE(1962, Ital.); VERY PRIVATE AFFAIR, A(1962, Fr./Ital.); MY SON, THE HERO(1963, Ital./Fr.); WILD, WILD PLANET, THE(1967, Ital.); DANGER: DIABOLIK(1968, Ital./Fr.); HOW TO SEDUCE A PLAY-BOY(1968, Aust./Fr./Ital.); INVINCIBLE SIX, THE(1970, U.S./Iran)
Iscaro Ravaioli
SNOW DEVILS, THE(1965, Ital.)
Francis Raval
VIVA LAS VEGAS(1964)
Blanche Ravalec
MOONRAKER(1979, Brit.)
Mario Ravasco
LA STRADA(1956, Ital.), art d; MAFIOSO(1962, Ital.), set d
Carla Ravasi
RED DESERT(1965, Fr./Ital.)
Mario Ravasio
LEAP INTO THE VOID(1982, Ital.)
Hillel Rave
CAST A GIANT SHADOW(1966)
Ravel
ALLEGRO NON TROPPO(1977, Ital.), m
Alfred Ravel
GREAT CATHERINE(1968, Brit.)
Alicia Ravel
MADAME DEATH(1968, Mex.)
Boyer and Ravel
LUCKY JADE(1937, Brit.)
Francis Ravel
LES GIRLS(1957); THIRD VOICE, THE(1960); NEW KIND OF LOVE, A(1963)
Gaston Ravel
Misc. Silents
DOCUMENT SECRET(1916, Fr.), d; DU RIRE AUX LARMES(1917, Fr.), d; L'HOMME QUI REVIENT DE LION(1917, Fr.), d; LA MAISON D'ARGILE(1918, Fr.), d; UNE FEMME INCONNUE(1918, Fr.), d; LE GEOLE(1921, Fr.), d; L'EN-VOLEE(1921, Fr.), d; A L'OMBRE DE VATICAN(1922, Fr.), d; FERRAGUS(1923, Fr.), d; LE GARDIN DU FEU(1924, Fr.), d; ON NE BADINE PAS AVEC L'AMOUR(1924, Fr.), d; AMOURS, DELICES ET ORGUES(1925, Fr.), d; CHOUCHOU POIDS PLUME(1925, Fr.), d; L'AVOCAT(1925, Fr.), d; LA FAUTEUIL 47(1926, Fr.), d; MADEMOISELLE JOSETTE MA FEMME(1926, Fr.), d; JOCASTE(1927, Fr.), d; LE BONHEUR DU JOUR(1927, Fr.), d; LE ROMAN D'UN JEUNE HOMME PAUV-RE(1927, Fr.), d; MADAME RECAMIER(1928, Fr.), d; FIGARO(1929, Fr.), d
Jean Ravel
TEMPTATION(1962, Fr.), ed; LIARS, THE(1964, Fr.), ed; CLOPORTES(1966, Fr., Ital.), ed; SHAMELESS OLD LADY, THE(1966, Fr.), tech adv; TWO WEEKS IN SEPTEMBER(1967, Fr./Brit.), ed; PARIS IN THE MONTH OF AUGUST(1968, Fr.), ed; BLUEBEARD(1972), ed; LA CAGE(1975, Fr.), ed; WOMAN AT HER WINDOW, A(1978, Fr./Ital./Ger.), ed; L'ETOILE DU NORD(1983, Fr.), ed
Jeanne Ravel
SILK NOOSE, THE(1950, Brit.)
Marcel Ravel
WISE GUYS(1969, Fr./Ital.), spec eff
Maurice Ravel
BOLERO(1934), m
Sandra Ravel
L'ENIGMATIQUE MONSIEUR PARKES(1930); THOSE THREE FRENCH GIRLS(1930); SINGLE SIN(1931); THIS MODERN AGE(1931); BALL AT THE CAST-LE(1939, Ital.)
Stelita Ravel
MOONRISE(1948)
Jacqueline Ravell
SPEED CRAZY(1959)
Rex Ravelle
SONG OF SCHEHERAZADE(1947)
Marissa Ravelli
1984
BLAME IT ON THE NIGHT(1984)
Juan Munoz Ravelo
MACARIO(1961, Mex.), spec eff; EXTERMINATING ANGEL, THE(1967, Mex.), spec eff
Raven
TEXAS TORNADO(1934)
Charles Raven
Silents
WANTED FOR MURDER(1919)
Elsa Raven
HONEYMOON KILLERS, THE(1969); GANG THAT COULDN'T SHOOT STRAIGHT, THE(1971); LADY LIBERTY(1972, Ital./Fr.); AMERICAN POP(1981); PATER-NITY(1981); POSTMAN ALWAYS RINGS TWICE, THE(1981); SECOND THOUGHTS(1983); TWILIGHT ZONE–THE MOVIE(1983)
Harry Raven
JOAN OF ARC(1948); FLESH AND FURY(1952); INCREDIBLE PETRIFIED WORLD, THE(1959)
John Raven
RANCHO NOTORIOUS(1952); SAN FRANCISCO STORY, THE(1952); HOT BLOOD(1956)
Karen Raven
TANGIER(1946)
Mike Raven
CRUCIBLE OF TERROR(1971, Brit.); I, MONSTER(1971, Brit.); LUST FOR A VAMPIRE(1971, Brit.); DISCIPLE OF DEATH(1972, Brit.)
Sheila Raven
TYCOON(1947)
Simon Raven
ON HER MAJESTY'S SECRET SERVICE(1969, Brit.), w; INCENSE FOR THE DAMNED(1970, Brit.), w; UNMAN, WITTERING AND ZIGO(1971, Brit.), w

Terry Raven
LIES MY FATHER TOLD ME(1960, Brit.); MONSTER OF HIGHGATE PONDS, THE(1961, Brit.); CRIMSON CULT, THE(1970, Brit.)
Raven the Horse
HURRICANE HORSEMAN(1931)
Silents
WESTERN ROVER, THE(1927)
Florence Ravenel
TWONKY, THE(1953); VIOLENT SATURDAY(1955); GOING STEADY(1958)
Domenico Ravenna
SWEET BODY OF DEBORAH, THE(1969, Ital./Fr.)
Giuseppe Ravenna
SWEET BODY OF DEBORAH, THE(1969, Ital./Fr.)
Charles de Ravenne
ARTISTS AND MODELS ABROAD(1938)
Thurl Ravenscroft
ROSE MARIE(1954); ONE HUNDRED AND ONE DALMATIANS(1961); MAN FROM BUTTON WILLOW, THE(1965); ARISTOCATS, THE(1970)
B. Ravenskikh
BRIDE WITH A DOWRY(1954, USSR), d
David Ravenswood
PETERSEN(1974, Aus.)
Phillip Raves
1984
DUBEAT-E-O(1984), md
Louis Ravet
Silents
PASSION OF JOAN OF ARC, THE(1928, Fr.)
Irving Ravetch
LIVING IN A BIG WAY(1947), w; OUTRIDERS, THE(1950), w; VENGEANCE VALLEY(1951), w; LONE HAND, THE(1953), w; RUN FOR COVER(1955), w; TEN WANTED MEN(1955), w; LONG, HOT SUMMER, THE(1958), w; SOUND AND THE FURY, THE(1959), w; DARK AT THE TOP OF THE STAIRS, THE(1960), w; HUD(1963), p, w; HOMBRE(1967), p, w; HOUSE OF CARDS(1969), w; REIVERS, THE(1969), p, w; COWBOYS, THE(1972), w; CONRACK(1974), w; SPIKES GANG, THE(1974), w; NORMA RAE(1979), w
Joe Ravetz
ANGELS HARD AS THEY COME(1971), ed
Merolyn Ravetz
SWEET JESUS, PREACHER MAN(1973), set d
Marco Raviart
STORY OF A WOMAN(1970, U.S./Ital.)
H. Ravich
GENERAL SUVOROV(1941, USSR), w
Tom Ravick
BEYOND THE TIME BARRIER(1960)
Ravinder
1984
GREYSTOKE: THE LEGEND OF TARZAN, LORD OF THE APES(1984)
Tony Ravish
BIG LEAGUER(1953)
Anna Raviv
CAN SHE BAKE A CHERRY PIE?(1983)
Janes Ravn
MAN WHO THOUGHT LIFE, THE(1969, Den.), d, w
Lotte Ravnholt
PEOPLE MEET AND SWEET MUSIC FILLS THE HEART(1969, Den./Swed.), cos
Brian Ravok
SOMETHING'S ROTTEN(1979, Can.), ed; PROM NIGHT(1980), ed; SCREW-BALLS(1983), ed
William Benegal Raw
ESCAPE TO BURMA(1955)
Tom Rawe
HAIR(1979)
Ousama Rawi
PULP(1972, Brit.), ph; GOLD(1974, Brit.), ph; ALFIE DARLING(1975, Brit.), ph; SKY RIDERS(1976, U.S./Gr.), ph; POWER PLAY(1978, Brit./Can.), ph; ZULU DAWN(1980, Brit.), ph
Outsama Rawi
BLACK WINDMILL, THE(1974, Brit.), ph
Qusama Rawi
HUMAN FACTOR, THE(1975), ph
Raad Rawi
1984
MISUNDERSTOOD(1984)
Rawicz
STREET SINGER, THE(1937, Brit.), m
Rawicz & Landauer
HOME SWEET HOME(1945, Brit.)
Rawicz and Landauer
SKY'S THE LIMIT, THE(1937, Brit.); STREET SINGER, THE(1937, Brit.)
Rawiri
1984
UTU(1984, New Zealand)
Patrick Rawiri
LAND OF FURY(1955 Brit.)
Ousami Rawl
FOURTEEN, THE(1973, Brit.), ph
Jeff Rawle
HITCH IN TIME, A(1978, Brit.)
Sid Rawle
WINSTANLEY(1979, Brit.)
Carrie E. Rawles
Silents
LITTLE BIG HORN(1927), w
Dennon Rawles
HISTORY OF THE WORLD, PART 1(1981); STAYING ALIVE(1983), ch

Sayhber Rawles
STAYING ALIVE(1983), ch
David Rawley
PIECE OF THE ACTION, A(1977), cos
Donald Rawley
VICE SQUAD(1982)
James Rawley
CREATURE WALKS AMONG US, THE(1956); THERE'S ALWAYS TOMOR-ROW(1956); THOMAS CROWN AFFAIR, THE(1968); CAR, THE(1977)
Peter Rawley
TERRORISTS, THE(1975, Brit.), p; PURPLE TAXI, THE(1977, Fr./Ital./Ireland), p
Alice Rawlings
WHERE ANGELS GO...TROUBLE FOLLOWS(1968)
Frederick Rawlings
MAN WHO COULD CHEAT DEATH, THE(1959, Brit.); MUMMY, THE(1959, Brit.)
Harriet Rawlings
STARTING OVER(1979)
1984
MUPPETS TAKE MANHATTAN, THE(1984)
Jerry Rawlings
ALIEN(1979), ed
John Rawlings
LUCKY LADIES(1932, Brit.), d; GOING STRAIGHT(1933, Brit.), d; SECRETS OF THE WASTELANDS(1941)
Kathy Rawlings
1984
WILD HORSES(1984, New Zealand)
Keith Rawlings
BATTLE HELL(1956, Brit.)
Margaret Rawlings
WAY OF LOST SOULS, THE(1929, Brit.); WOMAN HE SCORNED, THE(1930, Brit.); ROMAN HOLIDAY(1953); BEAUTIFUL STRANGER(1954, Brit.); NO ROAD BACK(1957, Brit.); HANDS OF THE RIPPER(1971, Brit.); PUBLIC EYE, THE(1972, Brit.)
Marjorie Kinnan Rawlings
YEARLING, THE(1946), w; SUN COMES UP, THE(1949), w; CROSS CREEK(1983), w
Richard L. Rawlings
KILLERS, THE(1964), ph; COCKEYED COWBOYS OF CALICO COUNTY, THE(1970), ph
Terence Rawlings
SENTINEL, THE(1977), ed
Terry Rawlings
WATERSHIP DOWN(1978, Brit.), ed; AWAKENING, THE(1980), ed; CHARRIOTS OF FIRE(1981, Brit.), ed; BLADE RUNNER(1982), ed; YENTL(1983), ed
Adrian Rawlins
PALM BEACH(1979, Aus.)
Dave Rawlins
URBAN COWBOY(1980), ed
David Rawlins
LOST LAGOON(1958), ed; PUFNSTUF(1970), ed; BINGO LONG TRAVELING ALL-STARS AND MOTOR KINGS, THE(1976), ed; SATURDAY NIGHT FEVER(1977), ed; CHINA SYNDROME, THE(1979), ed; SOUP FOR ONE(1982), ed; OSTERMAN WEEK-END, THE(1983), ed
1984
FIRESTARTER(1984), ed
Herbert Rawlins
HI BEAUTIFUL(1944)
Jack Rawlins
LINEUP, THE(1934), ed; SPEED WINGS(1934), ed; MILLS OF THE GODS(1935), ed; TROUBLE AT MIDNIGHT(1937), ed
John Rawlins
ISLE OF LOST SHIPS(1929), ed; LOVE RACKET, THE(1929), ed; MURDER AT MIDNIGHT(1931), ed; HIGH SOCIETY(1932, Brit.), d; ABOVE THE CLOUDS(1934), ed; AMONG THE MISSING(1934), ed; DEFENSE HESTS, THE(1934), ed; FUGITIVE LADY(1934), ed; HELL CAT, THE(1934), ed; NAME THE WOMAN(1934), ed; SHAD-OWS OF SING SING(1934), ed; VOICE IN THE NIGHT(1934), ed; DEATH FLIES EAST(1935), ed; GIRL FRIEND, THE(1935), ed; MEN OF THE HOUR(1935), ed; ONE-WAY TICKET(1935), ed; FINAL HOUR, THE(1936), ed; PENNIES FROM HEAV-EN(1936), ed; YOU MAY BE NEXT(1936), ed; LET THEM LIVE(1937), ed; AIR DEVILS(1938), d; MISSING GUEST, THE(1938), d; STATE POLICE(1938), d; YOUNG FUGITIVES(1938), d; WHISPERING ENEMIES(1939), w; ISLE OF DESTINY(1940), ed; LEATHER-PUSHERS, THE(1940), d; DANGEROUS GAME, A(1941), d; MEN OF THE TIMBERLAND(1941), d; MR. DYNAMITE(1941), d; MUTINY IN THE ARC-TIC(1941), d; RAIDERS OF THE DESERT(1941), d; SIX LESSONS FROM MADAME LA ZONGA(1941), d; ARABIAN NIGHTS(1942), d; BOMBAY CLIPPER(1942), d; GREAT IMPERSONATION, THE(1942), d; HALF WAY TO SHANGHAI(1942), d; MISSISSIPPI GAMBLER(1942), d; SHERLOCK HOLMES AND THE VOICE OF TERROR(1942), d; TORPEDO BOAT(1942), d; UNSEEN ENEMY(1942), d; WE'VE NEVER BEEN LICKED(1943), d; LADIES COURAGEOUS(1944), d; SUDAN(1945), d; HER ADVENTUROUS NIGHT(1946), d; STRANGE CONQUEST(1946), d; DICK TRACY MEETS GRUESOME(1947), d; DICK TRACY'S DILEMMA(1947), d; ARIZO-NA RANGER, THE(1948), d; MICHAEL O'HALLORAN(1948), d; MASSACRE RI-VER(1949), d; BOY FROM INDIANA(1950), d; FORT DEFIANCE(1951), d; ROGUE RIVER(1951), d; SHARK RIVER(1953), p&d; LOST LAGOON(1958), p&d, w
Silents
ADORATION(1928), ed
Joy Rawlins
RED SHOES, THE(1948, Brit.)
Judith Rawlins
20,000 EYES(1961)
Lester Rawlins
DIARY OF A MAD HOUSEWIFE(1970); THEY MIGHT BE GIANTS(1971); GOD TOLD ME TO(1976); LOVESICK(1983)
Monte Rawlins
Misc. Talkies
ADVENTURES OF THE MASKED PHANTOM, THE(1939)

Phil Rawlins
FORT DEFIANCE(1951); GUN FURY(1953)

A. B. Rawlinson
SPOT OF BOTHER, A(1938, Brit.), w; CHINESE DEN, THE(1940, Brit.), w

A. R. Rawlinson
LEAP YEAR(1932, Brit.), w; THIRD STRING, THE(1932, Brit.), w; BLARNEY KISS(1933, Brit.), w; CUCKOO IN THE NEST, THE(1933, Brit.), w; ALONG CAME SALLY(1934, Brit.), w; POWER(1934, Brit.), w; WHEN LONDON SLEEPS(1934, Brit.), w; MAN OF THE MOMENT(1935, Brit.), w; MAN WHO KNEW TOO MUCH, THE(1935, Brit.), w; TWO HEARTS IN HARMONY(1935, Brit.), w; KING OF THE DAMNED(1936, Brit.), w; INCIDENT IN SHANGHAI(1937, Brit.), w; KING SOLOMON'S MINES(1937, Brit.), w; LANCASHIRE LUCK(1937, Brit.), w; LAST CURTAIN, THE(1937, Brit.), w; MISSING, BELIEVED MARRIED(1937, Brit.), w; TICKET OF LEAVE MAN, THE(1937, Brit.), w; YOU'RE IN THE ARMY NOW(1937, Brit.), w; JOHN HALIFAX–GENTLEMAN(1938, Brit.), w; MAN WITH 100 FACES, THE(1938, Brit.), w; SEXTON BLAKE AND THE HOODED TERROR(1938, Brit.), w; STRANGE BOARDERS(1938, Brit.), w; FACE AT THE WINDOW, THE(1939, Brit.), w; GASLIGHT(1940, Brit.), w; SPIES OF THE AIR(1940, Brit.), w; THIS ENGLAND(1941, Brit.), w; CALLING PAUL TEMPLE(1948, Brit.), w; MY SISTER AND I(1948, Brit.), w; STORY OF SHIRLEY YORKE, THE(1948, Brit.), w; CELIA(1949, Brit.), w; DARK SECRET(1949, Brit.), w; MEET SIMON CHERRY(1949, Brit.), w; SOMEONE AT THE DOOR(1950, Brit.), w; WHAT THE BUTLER SAW(1950, Brit.), w; PAUL TEMPLE'S TRIUMPH(1951, Brit.), w; SCARLET THREAD(1951, Brit.), w; BROKEN HORSESHOE(1953, Brit.), w; OPERATION DIPLOMAT(1953, Brit.), w; THERE WAS A YOUNG LADY(1953, Brit.), p; BLACK RIDER, THE(1954, Brit.), p&w; FAST AND LOOSE(1954, Brit.), w; STOCK CAR(1955, Brit.), p, w; OPERATION CONSPIRACY(1957, Brit.), p, w; GAOLBREAK(1962, Brit.), w

Brian Rawlinson
DANGEROUS EXILE(1958, Brit.); BEWARE OF CHILDREN(1961, Brit.); SWORD OF SHERWOOD FOREST(1961, Brit.); UNSTOPPABLE MAN, THE(1961, Brit.); SWINGIN' MAIDEN, THE(1963, Brit.); CARRY ON CLEO(1964, Brit.); LADIES WHO DO(1964, Brit.); LIFE IN DANGER(1964, Brit.); NURSE ON WHEELS(1964, Brit.); BIG JOB, THE(1965, Brit.); CARRY ON COWBOY(1966, Brit.); FAR FROM THE MADDING CROWD(1967, Brit.); SEE NO EVIL(1971, Brit.)

Gerald Rawlinson
ALF'S CARPET(1929, Brit.); DEVIL'S MAZE, THE(1929, Brit.); YOUNG WOODLEY(1930, Brit.); BATTLE OF GALLIPOLI(1931, Brit.); BROWN SUGAR(1931, Brit.); DANGEROUS SEAS(1931, Brit.); GABLES MYSTERY, THE(1931, Brit.); LIMPING MAN, THE(1931, Brit.); CALLBOX MYSTERY, THE(1932, Brit.); COLLISION(1932, Brit.); OLD MAN, THE(1932, Brit.); THREADS(1932, Brit.); DAUGHTERS OF TODAY(1933, Brit.); EXCESS BAGGAGE(1933, Brit.); SLEEPLESS NIGHTS(1933, Brit.); EASY MONEY(1934, Brit.); YOU MADE ME LOVE YOU(1934, Brit.); SAY IT WITH DIAMONDS(1935, Brit.); WHEN THE DEVIL WAS WELL(1937, Brit.); HIS LORDSHIP REGRETS(1938, Brit.)
Misc. Silents
LIFE'S A STAGE(1929, Brit.); SILENT HOUSE, THE(1929, Brit.); YOUNG WOODLEY(1929, Brit.)

Herb Rawlinson
COLT COMRADES(1943); WOMAN OF THE TOWN, THE(1943)

Herbert Rawlinson
MOONLIGHT AND PRETZELS(1933); ENLIGHTEN THY DAUGHTER(1934); CONFIDENTIAL(1935); CONVENTION GIRL(1935); MEN WITHOUT NAMES(1935); PEOPLE'S ENEMY, THE(1935); SHOW THEM NO MERCY(1935); BULLETS OR BALLOTS(1936); DANCING FEET(1936); FOLLOW THE FLEET(1936); HITCH HIKE TO HEAVEN(1936); HOLLYWOOD BOULEVARD(1936); MAD HOLIDAY(1936); SON COMES HOME, A(1936); TICKET TO PARADISE(1936); GO-GETTER, THE(1937); GOD'S COUNTRY AND THE WOMAN(1937); KID COMES BACK, THE(1937); LOVE IS ON THE AIR(1937); MAKE A WISH(1937); MYSTERIOUS CROSSING(1937); NOBODY'S BABY(1937); OVER THE GOAL(1937); SOMETHING TO SING ABOUT(1937); THAT CERTAIN WOMAN(1937); EVERY DAY'S A HOLIDAY(1938); HARD TO GET(1938); HAWAII CALLS(1938); MARIE ANTOINETTE(1938); SECRETS OF AN ACTRESS(1938); TORCHY GETS HER MAN(1938); UNDER THE BIG TOP(1938); WOMEN ARE LIKE THAT(1938); DARK VICTORY(1939); NAUGHTY BUT NICE(1939); ORPHANS OF THE STREET(1939); SECRET SERVICE OF THE AIR(1939); YOU CAN'T GET AWAY WITH MURDER(1939); FIVE LITTLE PEPPERS AT HOME(1940); FRAMED(1940); FREE, BLONDE AND 21(1940); I WANT A DIVORCE(1940); MONEY TO BURN(1940); SEVEN SINNERS(1940); SWISS FAMILY ROBINSON(1940); ARIZONA CYCLONE(1941); BAD MAN OF DEADWOOD(1941); FLYING WILD(1941); GENTLEMAN FROM DIXIE(1941); I WANTED WINGS(1941); RIOT SQUAD(1941); SCATTERGOOD MEETS BROADWAY(1941); BROADWAY BIG SHOT(1942); FOREIGN AGENT(1942); HELLO ANNAPOLIS(1942); I KILLED THAT MAN(1942); LADY GANGSTER(1942); PANTHER'S CLAW, THE(1942); PRIDE OF THE ARMY(1942); SILVER QUEEN(1942); SMART ALECKS(1942); STAGECOACH BUCKAROO(1942); TRAMP, TRAMP, TRAMP(1942); WE WERE DANCING(1942); DAYS OF OLD CHEYENNE(1943); DOUGHBOYS IN IRELAND(1943); LOST CANYON(1943); OLD ACQUAINTANCE(1943); REVEILLE WITH BEVERLY(1943); RIDERS OF THE DEADLINE(1943); TWO WEEKS TO LIVE(1943); WHERE ARE YOUR CHILDREN?(1943); FORTY THIEVES(1944); GOIN' TO TOWN(1944); LUMBERJACK(1944); MARSHAL OF GUNSMOKE(1944); MARSHAL OF RENO(1944); NABONGA(1944); OKLAHOMA RAIDERS(1944); SAILOR'S HOLIDAY(1944); SHAKE HANDS WITH MURDER(1944); SHERIFF OF SUNDOWN(1944); ACCOMPLICE(1946); ARGYLE SECRETS, THE(1948); COUNTERFEITERS, THE(1948); GALLANT LEGION, THE(1948); JOAN OF ARC(1948); SILENT CONFLICT(1948); SINISTER JOURNEY(1948); STRANGE GAMBLE(1948); BRIMSTONE(1949); FIGHTING MAN OF THE PLAINS(1949); GENE AUTRY AND THE MOUNTIES(1951); STRANGER WORE A GUN, THE(1953); JAIL BAIT(1954)
Misc. Talkies
BLIND FOOLS(1940, Brit.)
Silents
SEA-WOLF, THE(1913); DAMON AND PYTHIAS(1914); OPENED SHUTTERS, THE(1914); MAN AND HIS WOMAN(1920); CHARGE IT(1921); CHEATED HEARTS(1921); CONFLICT, THE(1921); MILLIONAIRE, THE(1921); PLAYTHINGS OF DESTINY(1921); WEALTH(1921); SCRAPPER, THE(1922); CLEAN UP, THE(1923); NOBODY'S BRIDE(1923); PRISONER, THE(1923); RAILROADED(1923); SCARLET CAR, THE(1923); DARK STAIRWAYS(1924); JACK O' CLUBS(1924); ADVENTUROUS SEX(1925); EVERY MAN'S WIFE(1925); PRAIRIE WIFE, THE(1925); GILDED BUTTERFLY, THE(1926)
Misc. Silents
MONTE CRISTO(1912); CALLED BACK(1914); SPY, THE(1914); EAGLE'S WINGS, THE(1916); LITTLE EVE EDGARTON(1916); COME THROUGH(1917); FLIRTING

WITH DEATH(1917); HIGH SIGN, THE(1917); LIKE WILDFIRE(1917); MAN TRAP, THE(1917); SCARLET CRYSTAL, THE(1917); BACK TO THE WOODS(1918); BRACE UP(1918); COMMON CAUSE, THE(1918); FLASH OF FATE, THE(1918); KISS OR KILL(1918); MATING, THE(1918); OUT OF THE NIGHT(1918); SMASHING THROUGH(1918); TURN OF THE WHEEL, THE(1918); DANGEROUS AFFAIR, A(1919); GOOD GRACIOUS ANNABELLE(1919); HOUSE DIVIDED, A(1919); PASSERS-BY(1920); POPPY TRAIL, THE(1920); WAKEFIELD CASE, THE(1921); YOU FIND IT EVERYWHERE(1921); ANOTHER MAN'S SHOES(1922); BLACK BAG, THE(1922); CONFIDENCE(1922); DON'T SHOOT(1922); MAN UNDER COVER, THE(1922); ONE WONDERFUL NIGHT(1922); FOOLS AND RICHES(1923); HIS MYSTERY'S GIRL(1923); MILLION TO BURN, A(1923); VICTOR, THE(1923); DANCING CHEAT, THE(1924); HIGH SPEED(1924); STOLEN SECRETS(1924); TOMBOY, THE(1924); GREAT JEWEL ROBBERY, THE(1925); MAN IN BLUE, THE(1925); MY NEIGHBOR'S WIFE(1925); UNNAMED WOMAN, THE(1925); BELLE OF BROADWAY, THE(1926); HER BIG ADVENTURE(1926); HER SACRIFICE(1926); MEN OF THE NIGHT(1926); MIDNIGHT THIEVES(1926); MILLIONAIRE POLICEMAN, THE(1926); BUGLE CALL, THE(1927); BURNING GOLD(1927); HOUR OF RECKONING, THE(1927); WAGES OF CONSCIENCE(1927)

Sally Rawlinson
UNCONQUERED(1947); VARIETY GIRL(1947); SORROWFUL JONES(1949); MATING SEASON, THE(1951)

Frank Rawls
MYSTERY SUBMARINE(1950); NIGHT STAGE TO GALVESTON(1952)

Hardy Rawls
1984
LONELY GUY, THE(1984)

Lou Rawls
ANGEL, ANGEL, DOWN WE GO(1969)

Wilson Rawls
WHERE THE RED FERN GROWS(1974), w

David Rawnsley
SOUTHERN MAID, A(1933, Brit.), art d; DANCE BAND(1935, Brit.), art d; APRIL BLOSSOMS(1937, Brit.), set d; ROMANCE AND RICHES(1937, Brit.), art d; INVADERS, THE(1941), art d; ONE OF OUR AIRCRAFT IS MISSING(1942, Brit.), art d; WINGS AND THE WOMAN(1942, Brit.), art d; THEY WERE SISTERS(1945, Brit.), art d; WAY AHEAD, THE(1945, Brit.), art d

Clayton Rawson
MIRACLES FOR SALE(1939), w; MAN WHO WOULDN'T DIE, THE(1942), w

Ethel Rawson
SYLVIA SCARLETT(1936)

Janet Rawson
FRENCH LIEUTENANT'S WOMAN, THE(1981)

Joe Rawson
FIGHTING BACK(1983, Brit.)

Ruth Rawson
SATAN'S BED(1965)

S. Charles Rawson
LET'S ROCK(1958), ed

Stratton Rawson
1984
VAMPING(1984), p, prod d

Tristan Rawson
GREEN SCARF, THE(1954, Brit.)

Tristram Rawson
TIME GENTLEMEN PLEASE!(1953, Brit.); FRONT PAGE STORY(1954, Brit.)
Misc. Silents
FAIR MAID OF PERTH, THE(1923, Brit.)

Alan Rawsthorne
SCHOOL FOR SECRETS(1946, Brit.), m; SARABAND(1949, Brit.), m; INHERITANCE, THE(1951, Brit.), m; PANDORA AND THE FLYING DUTCHMAN(1951, Brit.), m, md; IVORY HUNTER(1952, Brit.), m; CRUEL SEA, THE(1953), m; LEASE OF LIFE(1954, Brit.), m; WEST OF ZANZIBAR(1954, Brit.), m; FLOODS OF FEAR(1958, Brit.), m

Antonio Raxel
LOS ASTRONAUTAS(1960, Mex.)

Antonio Raxell
VAMPIRE'S COFFIN, THE(1958, Mex.); LAST REBEL, THE(1961, Mex.); QUEEN'S SWORDSMEN, THE(1963, Mex.); PUSS 'N' BOOTS(1964, Mex.); LIVING COFFIN, THE(1965, Mex.); LIVING HEAD, THE(1969, Mex.)

Adele Ray
Silents
MOTH AND THE FLAME, THE(1915); SEALED LIPS(1915); SPRINGTIME(1915)

Agnes Ray
42ND STREET(1933)

Al Ray
WEST OF SINGAPORE(1933), d
Misc. Talkies
GUILTY OR NOT GUILTY(1932), d; ST. LOUIS WOMAN(1935), d
Silents
MORE TROUBLE(1918); WHEN DO WE EAT?(1918); COURTSHIP OF MILES STANDISH, THE(1923), w
Misc. Silents
GAME'S UP, THE(1919)

Alan Ray
I'LL TELL THE WORLD(1945); UNSUSPECTED, THE(1947); G.I. JANE(1951); GIRL ON THE BRIDGE, THE(1951); TEN TALL MEN(1951)

Albert Ray
MOLLY AND ME(1929), d; KATHLEEN MAVOURNEEN(1930), d; HOLD'EM JAIL(1932), w; THIRTEENTH GUEST, THE(1932), d; UNHOLY LOVE(1932), d; SHRIEK IN THE NIGHT, A(1933), d; DANCING MAN(1934), d, w; EVERYMAN'S LAW(1936), d; UNDERCOVER MAN(1936), d; LAWLESS LAND(1937), d; 45 FATHERS(1937), w; ARIZONA WILDCAT(1938), w; CHANGE OF HEART(1938), w; ISLAND IN THE SKY(1938), w; KEEP SMILING(1938), w; WHILE NEW YORK SLEEPS(1938), w; CHARLIE CHAN IN RENO(1939), w; DESPERATE TRAILS(1939), p&d; OKLAHOMA FRONTIER(1939), p; WINNER TAKE ALL(1939), w; GOOD MORNING, JUDGE(1943); CHEATERS, THE(1945), w
Misc. Talkies
CALL OF THE WEST(1930), d; MARRIAGE BARGAIN, THE(1935), d

Silents
TAILOR MADE MAN, A(1922), w; LOVE MAKES 'EM WILD(1927), d; NONE BUT THE BRAVE(1928), d; WOMAN WISE(1928), d
Misc. Silents
BE A LITTLE SPORT(1919); LOST PRINCESS, THE(1919); LOVE IS LOVE(1919); MARRIED IN HASTE(1919); VAGABOND LUCK(1919); WORDS AND MUSIC BY...(1919); HONEY BEE, THE(1920); NIGHT RIDERS, THE(1920, Brit.); TIN PAN ALLEY(1920); UGLY DUCKLING, THE(1920, Brit.); MORE PAY - LESS WORK(1926), d; WHISPERING WIRES(1926), d; PUBLICITY MADNESS(1927), d; RICH BUT HONEST(1927), d; THIEF IN THE DARK, A(1928), d

Aldo Ray
MARRYING KIND, THE(1952); PAT AND MIKE(1952); LET'S DO IT AGAIN(1953); MISS SADIE THOMPSON(1953); BATTLE FLAME(1955); THREE STRIPES IN THE SUN(1955); WE'RE NO ANGELS(1955); NIGHTFALL(1956); MEN IN WAR(1957); GOD'S LITTLE ACRE(1958); NAKED AND THE DEAD, THE(1958); DAY THEY ROBBED THE BANK OF ENGLAND, THE(1960, Brit.); FOUR DESPERATE MEN(1960, Brit.); NIGHTMARE IN THE SUN(1964); JOHNNY NOBODY(1965, Brit.); SYLVIA(1965); DEAD HEAT ON A MERRY-GO-ROUND(1966); WHAT DID YOU DO IN THE WAR, DADDY?(1966); KILL A DRAGON(1967); RIOT ON SUNSET STRIP(1967); WELCOME TO HARD TIMES(1967); GREEN BERETS, THE(1968); POWER, THE(1968); ANGEL UNCHAINED(1970); AND HOPE TO DIE(1972 Fr/US) TOM(1973); INSIDE OUT(1975, Brit.); MAN WHO WOULD NOT DIE, THE(1975); PSYCHIC KILLER(1975); SEVEN ALONE(1975); HAUNTED(1976); WON TON TON, THE DOG WHO SAVED HOLLYWOOD(1976); HAUNTS(1977); GLOVE, THE(1980); HUMAN EXPERIMENTS(1980); BOXOFFICE(1982); MONGREL(1982); SECRET OF NIMH, THE(1982)
1984
EXECUTIONER PART II, THE(1984)
Misc. Talkies
CENTERFOLD GIRLS, THE(1974); DYNAMITE BROTHERS, THE(1974); BAD BUNCH, THE(1976); GONE WITH THE WEST(1976); LUCIFER COMPLEX, THE(1978); GLOVE, THE(1980); FREEZE BOMB(1980); STRAIGHT JACKET(1980); DON'T GO NEAR THE PARK(1981); GREAT SKYCOPTER RESCUE, THE(1982); EVILS OF THE NIGHT(1983); VULTURES IN PARADISE(1984)

Alfred Ray
INTRUDER, THE(1932), d

Allan Ray
STORY OF DR. WASSELL, THE(1944); FACE OF MARBLE, THE(1946); SCENE OF THE CRIME(1949); WOMAN ON PIER 13, THE(1950); MR. IMPERIUM(1951); THING, THE(1951); FAR COUNTRY, THE(1955); GANG BUSTERS(1955); WRONG MAN, THE(1956); FRONTIER UPRISING(1961); CAPE FEAR(1962)

Allen Ray
DIXIE(1943); LET'S FACE IT(1943); NOBODY LIVES FOREVER(1946); CROSS-FIRE(1947); VELVET TOUCH, THE(1948); SORROWFUL JONES(1949); DUCHESS OF IDAHO, THE(1950); CARRIE(1952); FRENCH LINE, THE(1954); MIRACLE IN THE RAIN(1956)

Allene Ray
OVERLAND BOUND(1929); WESTWARD BOUND(1931)
Misc. Silents
HONEYMOON RANCH(1920); WEST OF THE RIO GRANDE(1921); PARTNERS OF THE SUNSET(1922); 40TH DOOR, THE(1924); HAWK OF THE HILLS(1929)

Andrew Ray
MUDLARK, THE(1950, Brit.); YELLOW BALLOON, THE(1953, Brit.); ESCAPE BY NIGHT(1954, Brit.); ESCAPADE(1955, Brit.); PRIZE OF GOLD, A(1955); WOMEN IN A DRESSING GOWN(1957, Brit.); YOUNG AND THE GUILTY, THE(1958, Brit.); GIDE-ON OF SCOTLAND YARD(1959, Brit.); IMMORAL CHARGE(1962, Brit.); PRIVATE POOLEY(1962, Brit./E. Ger.); TWICE AROUND THE DAFFODILS(1962, Brit.); GIRL GETTERS, THE(1966, Brit.); UNHOLY FOUR, THE(1969, Ital.); TARZANA, THE WILD GIRL(1973); GREAT EXPECTATIONS(1975, Brit.); ROUGH CUT(1980, Brit.)

Andrew Ray [Andrea Aureli]
SABATA(1969, Ital.); SINGAPORE, SINGAPORE(1969, Fr./Ital.)

Annita Ray
SHAKE, RATTLE, AND ROCK!(1957)

Anthony Ray
MEN IN WAR(1957); TRUE STORY OF JESSE JAMES, THE(1957); SHADOWS(1960); SPOOK WHO SAT BY THE DOOR, THE(1973)

Arthur Ray
DUKE IS THE TOPS, THE(1938); ONE DARK NIGHT(1939); SON OF INGAGI(1940); MR. WASHINGTON GOES TO TOWN(1941); TAKE MY LIFE(1942)
Misc. Talkies
PROFESSOR CREEPS(1942)
Misc. Silents
TIES OF BLOOD(1921)

Arthur T. Ray
AM I GUILTY?(1940)

Barbara Ray
MILLIONS IN THE AIR(1935)

Bernard "B. B." Ray
WOMEN MEN MARRY(1931), ed; MYSTERY RANCH(1932), p; PRIVATE SCAN-DAL, A(1932), ph; ARIZONA NIGHTS(1934), p&d; MYSTIC HOUR, THE(1934), ph; COYOTE TRAILS(1935), p&d; CARYL OF THE MOUNTAINS(1936), p&d; FAST BULLETS(1936), p; MILLIONAIRE KID(1936), p&d; SPEED REPORTER(1936), p&d; PINTO RUSTLERS(1937), p; RIDING ON(1937), p; SANTA FE BOUND(1937), p; SKULL AND CROWN(1938), p; SMOKY TRAILS(1939), d; DANGEROUS LA-DY(1941), p&d; FOOLS OF DESIRE(1941), d&w; LAW OF THE TIMBER(1941), p&d; HOUSE OF ERRORS(1942), p&d; TOO MANY WOMEN(1942), p&d; BUFFALO BILL RIDES AGAIN(1947), d; HOLLYWOOD BARN DANCE(1947), d, w; TIMBER FU-RY(1950), p&d; BUFFALO BILL IN TOMAHAWK TERRITORY(1952), p, d; MOVIE STUNTMEN(1953), d, w; SPRING AFFAIR(1960), p,d&w
Misc. Talkies
GIRL TROUBLE(1933), d; LOSER'S END(1934), d; POTLUCK PARDS(1934), d; RAWHIDE MAIL(1934), d; WEST ON PARADE(1934), d; MIDNIGHT PHANTOM, THE(1935), d; NOW OR NEVER(1935), d; RIO RATTLER(1935), d; SILVER BULLET, THE(1935), d; TEXAS JACK(1935), d; RIDIN' ON(1936), d; ROAMIN' WILD(1936), d; VENGEANCE OF RANNAH(1936), d; SANTA FE RIDES(1937), d; IT'S ALL IN YOUR MIND(1938), d; BROKEN STRINGS(1940), d; HOLLYWOOD THRILL-MAKERS(1954), d

Bill Ray
POOR LITTLE RICH GIRL(1936)

Billy Ray
SECRET BRIDE, THE(1935); ADAM HAD FOUR SONS(1941); LYDIA(1941); MAJOR AND THE MINOR, THE(1942)

Bob Ray
Misc. Talkies
SATAN'S CHILDREN(1975)

Bobby Ray
HIS PRIVATE SECRETARY(1933), ed

Bud Ray
OUR DAILY BREAD(1934)

Buddy Ray
FLOOD, THE(1931)

Cecilia Ray
LILITH(1964)

Ceil Ray
LILITH(1964)

Charles Ray
LADIES SHOULD LISTEN(1934); TICKET TO CRIME(1934); BY YOUR LEA-VE(1935); SCHOOL FOR GIRLS(1935); WELCOME HOME(1935); HOLLYWOOD BOULEVARD(1936); LITTLE BIT OF HEAVEN, A(1940); MARRIED BA-CHELOR(1941); HARVARD, HERE I COME(1942); TENNESSEE JOHNSON(1942)
Misc. Talkies
JUST MY LUCK(1936)
Silents
FORBIDDEN ADVENTURE, THE(1915); PAINTED SOUL, THE(1915); CORNER IN COLLEENS, A(1916); DIVIDEND, THE(1916); HOME(1916); PEGGY(1916); PINCH HITTER, THE(1917); FAMILY SKELETON, THE(1918); NINE O'CLOCK TOWN, A(1918); PLAYING THE GAME(1918); ALARM CLOCK ANDY(1920); NINETEEN AND PHYLLIS(1920); OLD FASHIONED BOY, AN(1920); PARIS GREEN(1920); RED HOT DOLLARS(1920); OLD SWIMMIN' HOLE, THE(1921); TWO MINUTES TO GO(1921), a, d; ALIAS JULIUS CAESAR(1922), a, d; TAILOR MADE MAN, A(1922), a, d; COURTSHIP OF MILES STANDISH, THE(1923); BRIGHT LIGHTS(1925); AUCTION BLOCK, THE(1926); SWEET ADELINE(1926); NOBODY'S WIDOW(1927); VANI-TY(1927)
Misc. Silents
COWARD, THE(1915); DESERTER, THE(1916); HONOR THY NAME(1916); HONOR-ABLE ALGY, THE(1916); PLAIN JANE(1916); WOLF WOMAN, THE(1916); BACK OF THE MAN(1917); CLODHOPPER, THE(1917); HIS MOTHER'S BOY(1917); MIL-LIONAIRE VAGRANT, THE(1917); SON OF HIS FATHER, THE(1917); SUDDEN JIM(1917); WEAKER SEX, THE(1917); CLAWS OF THE HUN, THE(1918); HIRED MAN, THE(1918); HIS OWN HOME TOWN(1918); LAW OF THE NORTH, THE(1918); STRING BEANS(1918); BILL HENRY(1919); BUSHER, THE(1919); EGG CRATE WALLOP, THE(1919); GIRL DODGER, THE(1919); GREASED LIGHTING(1919); HAY FOOT, STRAW FOOT(1919); SHERIFF'S SON, THE(1919); HOMER COMES HO-ME(1920); PEACEFUL VALLEY(1920); VILLAGE SLEUTH, A(1920); 45 MINUTES FROM BROADWAY(1920); MIDNIGHT BELL, A(1921), a, d; R.S.V.P.(1921), a, d; SCRAP IRON(1921), a, d; BARNSTORMER, THE(1922), a, d; DEUCE OF SPADES, THE(1922), a, d; GAS, OIL AND WATER(1922), a, d; SMUDGE(1922), a, d; GIRL I LOVED, THE(1923); DYNAMITE SMITH(1924); PERCY(1925); SOME PUN'KINS(1925); FIRE BRIGADE, THE(1926); PARIS(1926); GETTING GERTIE'S GARTER(1927); COUNT OF TEN, THE(1928)

Cherita Alden Ray
I COVER CHINATOWN(1938)

Cyril Ray
EDGE OF THE WORLD, THE(1937, Brit.), md

David Ray
BLADE(1973), ed; ONE-TRICK PONY(1980), ed; SCARFACE(1983), ed

Dolores Ray
VANITY STREET(1932)

Dorothy Ray
OLD-FASHIONED WAY, THE(1934)

Ellen Ray
ON THE RIVERA(1951); OPPOSITE SEX, THE(1956)

Elynne Ray
SUMMER STOCK(1950); BAND WAGON, THE(1953)

Emma Ray
SO BIG(1932); OLD-FASHIONED WAY, THE(1934)

Frank Ray
SUBMARINE SEAHAWK(1959)

Frankie Ray
NEW ORLEANS UNCENSORED(1955); CARNIVAL ROCK(1957); INVASION OF THE STAR CREATURES(1962)

Fred Olen Ray
IT FELL FROM THE SKY(1980), p&d; SCALPS(1983), d&w
Misc. Talkies
BIO-HAZARD(1984), d

Gdeh Ray
WAJAN(1938, South Bali), d

Gene Anthony Ray
FAME(1980)

Gordon Ray
NIGHT OF MAGIC, A(1944, Brit.)

Harry Ray
WITHOUT HONOR(1949), makeup; WITNESS FOR THE PROSECUTION(1957), makeup; IRMA LA DOUCE(1963), makeup; UNDER THE YUM-YUM TREE(1963), makeup; GOOD NEIGHBOR SAM(1964); ODD COUPLE, THE(1968), makeup; ON A CLEAR DAY YOU CAN SEE FOREVER(1970), makeup; KOTCH(1971), makeup; AVANTI!(1972); WAR BETWEEN MEN AND WOMEN, THE(1972), makeup; SAVE THE TIGER(1973), makeup

Hismansu Ray
Misc. Silents
THROW OF THE DICE(1930, Brit.)

Jack Ray
WE'VE NEVER BEEN LICKED(1943)
1984
MAKING THE GRADE(1984)

Jacki Ray
IN LIKE FLINT(1967)
Jackie Ray
Misc. Talkies
KILLING AT OUTPOST ZETA, THE(1980); BEYOND THE UNIVERSE(1981)
Jacquelyn Mary Ray
GNOME-MOBILE, THE(1967)
James Ray
STRAIGHT TIME(1978); CHARLIE CHAN AND THE CURSE OF THE DRAGON QUEEN(1981); HARRY'S WAR(1981)
1984
MASS APPEAL(1984)
Jane Ray
KEEP YOUR POWDER DRY(1945)
Jean Ray
DOWN OUR ALLEY(1939, Brit.); MALPERTIUS(1972, Bel./Fr.), w
Jimmy Ray
SITTING ON THE MOON(1936); DIXIE(1943); PEOPLE THAT TIME FORGOT, THE(1977, Brit.)
Jody Ray
Misc. Talkies
LITTLE GIRL, BIG TEASE(1977)
Joe Ray
JOHNNY ANGEL(1945); LOCKET, THE(1946); HOLIDAY AFFAIR(1949); KANSAS CITY CONFIDENTIAL(1952)
Silents
KING SPRUCE(1920); REPUTATION(1921); BURNING SANDS(1922); OVER THE BORDER(1922)
Misc. Silents
GENTLEMAN FROM INDIANA, A(1915)
Joey Ray
MONKEY'S PAW, THE(1933); PALS OF THE RANGE(1935); SWING TIME(1936); I STOLE A MILLION(1939); LITTLE ACCIDENT(1939); KITTY FOYLE(1940); MUSIC IN MY HEART(1940); NO, NO NANETTE(1940); SEVENTEEN(1940); BLONDE CO-MET(1941); CAUGHT IN THE ACT(1941); DOUBLE DATE(1941); GAY FALCON, THE(1941); LADY SCARFACE(1941); SAINT IN PALM SPRINGS, THE(1941); SHADOW OF THE THIN MAN(1941); UNEXPECTED UNCLE(1941); MOONLIGHT IN HAVANA(1942); NAVY COMES THROUGH, THE(1942); STRICTLY IN THE GROOVE(1942); GILDERSLEEVE'S BAD DAY(1943); KEEP 'EM SLUGGING(1943); SECRETS OF THE UNDERGROUND(1943); IRISH EYES ARE SMILING(1944); MEET THE PEOPLE(1944); ROGER TOUHY, GANGSTER!(1944); THEY WERE EXPENDA-BLE(1945); DEADLINE FOR MURDER(1946); DOUBLE LIFE, A(1947); FEAR IN THE NIGHT(1947); FORCE OF EVIL(1948); NIGHT HAS A THOUSAND EYES(1948); STATION WEST(1948); RED, HOT AND BLUE(1949); WHERE DANGER LIVES(1950); ACCORDING TO MRS. HOYLE(1951); HIS KIND OF WOMAN(1951); LET'S GO NAVY(1951); RACKET, THE(1951); ROADBLOCK(1951); ARMY BOUND(1952); BLAZING FOREST, THE(1952); HAS ANYBODY SEEN MY GAL?(1952); STEEL TRAP, THE(1952); LET'S DO IT AGAIN(1953); RIDE, VAQUERO!(1953); LUCY GALLANT(1955); SEA CHASE, THE(1955); CRASHING LAS VEGAS(1956); CHICAGO CONFIDENTIAL(1957); JET PILOT(1957); GIRL IN THE WOODS(1958); OLD MAN AND THE SEA, THE(1958); TOUGHEST GUN IN TOMBSTONE(1958)
Joey S. Ray
CALCUTTA(1947)
John Ray
WHOOPEE(1930)
Johnny Ray
THERE'S NO BUSINESS LIKE SHOW BUSINESS(1954); LAST PICTURE SHOW, THE(1971), m
Joseph Ray
COME BACK CIHARLESTON BLUE(1972)
Julia Ray
Misc. Silents
MR. DOLAN OF NEW YORK(1917)
Kali Charan Ray
APARAJITO(1959, India)
Katherine Ray
Silents
BLUEBEARD'S SEVEN WIVES(1926)
Laurence Ray
MAN ON THE RUN(1949, Brit.)
Lawrence Ray
FRANCHISE AFFAIR, THE(1952, Brit.)
Leah Ray
ONE IN A MILLION(1936); HOLY TERROR, THE(1937); SING AND BE HAPPY(1937); THIN ICE(1937); WAKE UP AND LIVE(1937); HAPPY LANDING(1938); WALKING DOWN BROADWAY(1938)
Linda Ray
THEY ALL LAUGHED(1981); SOUP FOR ONE(1982)
Lois Ray
PROUD ONES, THE(1956)
Man Ray
DREAMS THAT MONEY CAN BUY(1948), w
Marc B. Ray
WILD GYPSIES(1969), d&w; STOOLIE, THE(1972), w
Misc. Talkies
SCREAM BLOODY MURDER(1973), d
Marcelle Ray
HAUNTED HOUSE, THE(1940)
Mariane Ray
JETLAG(1981, U.S./Span.)
Mary Ellen Ray
LORDS OF DISCIPLINE, THE(1983)
Mary Ray
$1,000 A TOUCHDOWN(1939)
Mavis Ray
ANNIE(1982)
Michael Ray
TIN STAR, THE(1957)

Michel Ray
DIVIDED HEART, THE(1955, Brit.); BRAVE ONE, THE(1956); FLOOD TIDE(1958); SPACE CHILDREN, THE(1958); LAWRENCE OF ARABIA(1962, Brit.)
Mona Ray
PARDON MY GUN(1930); LI'L ABNER(1940)
Natalia Ray
STRANGERS, THE(1955, Ital.)
Nicholas Ray
KNOCK ON ANY DOOR(1949), d; THEY LIVE BY NIGHT(1949), d; WOMAN'S SECRET, A(1949), d; BORN TO BE BAD(1950), d; IN A LONELY PLACE(1950), d; FLYING LEATHERNECKS(1951), d; ON DANGEROUS GROUND(1951), d, w; RACKET, THE(1951), d; LUSTY MEN, THE(1952), d; MACAO(1952), d; JOHNNY GUITAR(1954), d; REBEL WITHOUT A CAUSE(1955), d; RUN FOR COVER(1955), d; BIGGER THAN LIFE(1956), d; HOT BLOOD(1956), d; TRUE STORY OF JESSE JAMES, THE(1957), d; BITTER VICTORY(1958, Fr.), d, w; PARTY GIRL(1958), d; WIND ACROSS THE EVERGLADES(1958), d; SAVAGE INNOCENTS, THE(1960, Brit.), d, w; KING OF KINGS(1961), d; 55 DAYS AT PEKING(1963), a, d; CIRCUS WORLD(1964), w; AMERICAN FRIEND, THE(1977, Ger.); HAIR(1979)
Nick Ray
TREE GROWS IN BROOKLYN, A(1945)
Nicole Ray
PLAYTIME(1973, Fr.)
Niranjan Ray
RIVER, THE(1961, India)
Nita Ray
OKLAHOMA CYCLONE(1930)
Ola Ray
NIGHT SHIFT(1982); 48 HOURS(1982); 10 TO MIDNIGHT(1983)
1984
FEAR CITY(1984)
Pat Ray
GALLOPING MAJOR, THE(1951, Brit.)
Paula Ray
POSTMAN ALWAYS RINGS TWICE, THE(1946); PERILS OF PAULINE, THE(1947)
Peggy Ray
WRONG BOX, THE(1966, Brit.)
Phil Ray
SEXTON BLAKE AND THE BEARDED DOCTOR(1935, Brit.); NOT SO DUSTY(1936, Brit.); TROOPSHIP(1938, Brit.); NURSEMAID WHO DISAPPEARED, THE(1939, Brit.); WANTED BY SCOTLAND YARD(1939, Brit.); CHAMBER OF HORRORS(1941, Brit.); SEND FOR PAUL TEMPLE(1946, Brit.)
Philip Ray
OLD ROSES(1935, Brit.); FIND THE LADY(1936, Brit.); HEAD OFFICE(1936, Brit.); TWELVE GOOD MEN(1936, Brit.); DARK JOURNEY(1937, Brit.); MAN WHO MADE DIAMONDS, THE(1937, Brit.); PERFECT CRIME, THE(1937, Brit.); DOUBLE OR QUITS(1938, Brit.); JAMAICA INN(1939, Brit.); MYSTERY OF ROOM 13(1941, Brit.); OCTOBER MAN, THE(1948, Brit.); NO PLACE FOR JENNIFER(1950, Brit.); WINSLOW BOY, THE(1950); NO HIGHWAY IN THE SKY(1951, Brit.); FAKE, THE(1953, Brit.); GREAT GILBERT AND SULLIVAN, THE(1953, Brit.); PROJECT M7(1953, Brit.); GOOD DIE YOUNG, THE(1954, Brit.); HELL BELOW ZERO(1954, Brit.); PASSAGE HOME(1955, Brit.); WHERE THERE'S A WILL(1955, Brit.); EXTRA DAY, THE(1956, Brit.); SHADOW OF FEAR(1956, Brit.); NO ROAD BACK(1957, Brit.); NIGHT TO REMEMBER, A(1958, Brit.); SECRET PLACE, THE(1958, Brit.); DATE AT MIDNIGHT(1960, Brit.); SONS AND LOVERS(1960, Brit.); MIND BENDERS, THE(1963, Brit.); DEVIL DOLL(1964, Brit.); IN THE DOGHOUSE(1964, Brit.); FRANKENSTEIN CREATED WOMAN(1965, Brit.); DRACULA–PRINCE OF DARKNESS(1966, Brit.); PANIC(1966, Brit.)
Phillip Ray
ADVENTURERS, THE(1951, Brit.); FOUR AGAINST FATE(1952, Brit.)
Rachel Ray
MIDNIGHT MAN, THE(1974)
Raymond Ray
MAN UPSTAIRS, THE(1959, Brit.); MARY HAD A LITTLE(1961, Brit.); JOLLY BAD FELLOW, A(1964, Brit.)
Rene Ray
HIGH TREASON(1929, Brit.); YOUNG WOODLEY(1930, Brit.); KEEPERS OF YOUTH(1931, Brit.); BORN LUCKY(1932, Brit.); DANCE PRETTY LADY(1932, Brit.); HERE'S GEORGE(1932, Brit.); TONIGHT'S THE NIGHT(1932, Brit.); WHEN LONDON SLEEPS(1932, Brit.); EXCESS BAGGAGE(1933, Brit.); KING'S CUP, THE(1933, Brit.); TIGER BAY(1933, Brit.); WIVES BEWARE(1933, Brit.); EASY MONEY(1934, Brit.); NINE FORTY-FIVE(1934, Brit.); ROLLING IN MONEY(1934, Brit.); FULL CIRCLE(1935, Brit.); ONCE IN A NEW MOON(1935, Brit.); REGAL CAVALCADE(1935, Brit.); STREET SONG(1935, Brit.); BELOVED IMPOSTER(1936, Brit.); CRIME OVER LONDON(1936, Brit.); PASSING OF THE THIRD FLOOR BACK, THE(1936, Brit.); JENIFER HALE(1937, Brit.); MAN OF AFFAIRS(1937, Brit.); PLEASE TEACHER(1937, Brit.); BANK HOLIDAY(1938, Brit.); HOUSEMASTER(1938, Brit.); MOUNTAINS O'MOURNE(1938, Brit.); RAT, THE(1938, Brit.); RETURN OF THE FROG, THE(1938, Brit.); TROOPSHIP(1938, Brit.); WEDDINGS ARE WONDERFUL(1938, Brit.); HOME FROM HOME(1939, Brit.); OLD BILL AND SON(1940, Brit.); GREEN COCKATOO, THE(1947, Brit.); I BECAME A CRIMINAL(1947); IF WINTER COMES(1947); GALLOPING MAJOR, THE(1951, Brit.); TWILIGHT WOMEN(1953, Brit.); GOOD DIE YOUNG, THE(1954, Brit.); COSMIC MONSTERS(1958, Brit.), w; CIRCLE, THE(1959, Brit.)
Misc. Silents
VARSITY(1930, Brit.)
Renee Ray
SUBSTITUTION(1970)
Richard G. Ray
BORN TO FIGHT(1938), ed
Robert Ray
AMBUSH(1939), w
Misc. Silents
DUGAN OF THE DUGOUTS(1928), d; RILEY OF THE RAINBOW DIVISION(1928), d
Robin Ray
WATCH YOUR STERN(1961, Brit.); HARD DAY'S NIGHT, A(1964, Brit.)
Robyn Ray
PIRANHA(1978)

Roger Ray
HOODLUM PRIEST, THE(1961); THERE'S ALWAYS VANILLA(1972)

Roland Ray
OREGON TRAIL, THE(1936); STREETS OF LAREDO(1949), makeup; RING OF TERROR(1962), makeup; THREE WEEKS OF LOVE(1965)

Rolin Ray
STAND UP AND CHEER(1934 80m FOX bw)

Rosalie Ray
GEORGE WHITE'S SCANDALS(1945)

S. Ray
ADVERSARY, THE(1973, Ind.), m

Sandhya Ray
RIVER, THE(1961, India)

Satyajit Ray
PATHER PANCHALI(1958, India), p,d&w; APARAJITO(1959, India), p,d&w; WORLD OF APU, THE(1960, India), p,d&w; GODDESS, THE(1962, India), p&d, w; BIG CITY, THE(1963, India), d&w; MUSIC ROOM, THE(1963, India), p,d&w; TWO DAUGHTERS(1963, India), p,d&w, m; KANCHENJUNGHA(1966, India), p,d&w, m; SHAKESPEARE WALLAH(1966, India), m; ADVERSARY, THE(1973, Ind.), d&w; CHESS PLAYERS, THE(1978, India), d&w, m
1984
HOME AND THE WORLD, THE(1984, India), d&w, m

Sonny Ray
OLIVER TWIST(1933)

Soumendu Ray
ADVERSARY, THE(1973, Ind.), ph

Sudipta Ray
APARAJITO(1959, India)

Sylvia Ray
NOTHING BUT A MAN(1964)

Ted Ray
RADIO FOLLIES(1935, Brit.); TONIGHT AT 8:30(1953, Brit.); ESCAPE BY NIGHT(1954, Brit.); CROWNING TOUCH, THE(1959, Brit.); PLEASE TURN OVER(1960, Brit.); CARRY ON TEACHER(1962, Brit.); MY WIFE'S FAMILY(1962, Brit.)

Terrance Ray
GIRLS DEMAND EXCITEMENT(1931); YOUNG AS YOU FEEL(1931); LIFE BEGINS(1932); HELLO SISTER!(1933); THEY ALL KISSED THE BRIDE(1942); UP IN ARMS(1944)

Terrence Ray
IT'S TOUGH TO BE FAMOUS(1932); LOVE IS A RACKET(1932); TWO KINDS OF WOMEN(1932)

Terry Ray
SEAS BENEATH, THE(1931); MAKE WAY FOR TOMORROW(1937); LADY HAS PLANS, THE(1942); LUCKY JORDAN(1942); WING AND A PRAYER(1944)

Terry Ray [Ellen Drew]
ROSE BOWL(1936); MURDER GOES TO COLLEGE(1937); NIGHT OF MYSTERY(1937); DANGEROUS TO KNOW(1938); CAUGHT IN THE DRAFT(1941)

Thelma Ray
LILITH(1964)

Tim Ray
PRETTY MAIDS ALL IN A ROW(1971)
Misc. Talkies
PREMONITION(1972)

Tom Ray
PHANTOM TOLLBOOTH, THE(1970), anim; BUGS BUNNY'S THIRD MOVIE–1001 RABBIT TALES(1982), anim

Tony Ray
WAR HUNT(1962); WE SHALL RETURN(1963); NEXT STOP, GREENWICH VILLAGE(1976), p; UNMARRIED WOMAN, AN(1978), p; WILLIE AND PHIL(1980), p

Trevor Ray
LOCK UP YOUR DAUGHTERS(1969, Brit.)

Vivian Ray
AVENGERS, THE(1950)
Silents
OKLAHOMA KID, THE(1929)
Misc. Silents
PARTING OF THE TRAILS(1930)

Wallace Ray
Silents
OVER THE HILL TO THE POORHOUSE(1920); SHACKLES OF GOLD(1922); CRITICAL AGE, THE(1923)
Misc. Silents
UNDER THE WESTERN SKIES(1921)

Warwick Ray
HIS MAJESTY O'KEEFE(1953)

Wendell Ray
PERSONAL BEST(1982)

Ray Anthony and his Orchestra
THIS COULD BE THE NIGHT(1957)

Ray Anthony Orchestra
DADDY LONG LEGS(1955)

The Ray Charles Orchestra
BLUES FOR LOVERS(1966, Brit.)

Ray Eberle and His Orchestra
HI' YA, SAILOR(1943); THIS IS THE LIFE(1944)

The Ray Ellington Quartet
WALKING ON AIR(1946, Brit.); PAPER ORCHID(1949, Brit.)

Ray Heatherton and Band
FOLLIES GIRL(1943)

Ray Lewis & The Trekkers
GONKS GO BEAT(1965, Brit.)

Ray McKinley and Orchestra
HIT PARADE OF 1943(1943)

Ray Noble and His Orchestra
PRIDE OF THE YANKEES, THE(1942)

Ray Noble and Orchestra
LAKE PLACID SERENADE(1944)

Ray Noble's band
BIG BROADCAST OF 1936, THE(1935)

Ray Ventura and His Orchestra
MONTE CARLO BABY(1953, Fr.)

Ray Ventura's Orchestra
WHIRLWIND OF PARIS(1946, Fr.)

Ray Venture and Orchestra
NOUS IRONS A PARIS(1949, Fr.)

Ray Whitley and His Bar-6 Cowboys
TRIGGER TRAIL(1944)

Ray Whitley and his Range Ramblers
HITTIN' THE TRAIL(1937); MYSTERY OF THE HOODED HORSEMEN, THE(1937); WHERE THE WEST BEGINS(1938)

Ray Whitley's Bar-6 Cowboys
RIDERS OF THE SANTA FE(1944); RENEGADES OF THE RIO GRANDE(1945)

Bette Raya
BUDDY BUDDY(1981)

Nita Raya
ENTENTE CORDIALE(1939, Fr.)

Andrew Rayan
GOLIATHON(1979, Hong Kong), spec eff

Peg Rayborn
PASSION HOLIDAY(1963)

Harry Raybould
GIRL IN THE WOODS(1958)

Basil Rayburn
DULCIMA(1971, Brit.), p

Jules Raycourt
Silents
PRUNELLA(1918)

Janet Raycraft
TENTACLES(1977, Ital.)

A. Raydanov
SHADOWS OF FORGOTTEN ANCESTORS(1967, USSR)

Carol Raye
WALTZ TIME(1946, Brit.); GREEN FINGERS(1947); WHILE I LIVE(1947, Brit.); SPRINGTIME(1948, Brit.)

Carole Raye
STRAWBERRY ROAN(1945, Brit.)

Don Raye
BUCK PRIVATES(1941)

Helen Raye
FLIGHT OF THE DOVES(1971)

Martha Raye
CONCORDE, THE–AIRPORT '79(; BIG BROADCAST OF 1937, THE(1936); COLLEGE HOLIDAY(1936); RHYTHM ON THE RANGE(1936); ARTISTS AND MODELS(1937); BIG BROADCAST OF 1938, THE(1937); DOUBLE OR NOTHING(1937); HIDEAWAY GIRL(1937); MOUNTAIN MUSIC(1937); WAIKIKI WEDDING(1937); COLLEGE SWING(1938); GIVE ME A SAILOR(1938); TROPIC HOLIDAY(1938); NEVER SAY DIE(1939); $1,000 A TOUCHDOWN(1939); BOYS FROM SYRACUSE(1940); FARMER'S DAUGHTER, THE(1940); HELLZAPOPPIN'(1941); KEEP 'EM FLYING(1941); NAVY BLUES(1941); FOUR JILLS IN A JEEP(1944); PIN UP GIRL(1944); MONSIEUR VERDOUX(1947); JUMBO(1962); PHYNX, THE(1970); PUFNSTUF(1970)

Soretta Raye
GILDA(1946)

Susan Raye
FROM NASHVILLE WITH MUSIC(1969)

Terry Raye
HOTEL HAYWIRE(1937)

Thelma Raye
Silents
ROMOLA(1925)

Billy Rayes
DAD AND DAVE COME TO TOWN(1938, Aus.); MEN IN HER LIFE, THE(1941)

Yevgeniya Rayevskaya
Misc. Silents
POLIKUSHKA(1919, USSR)

David Rayfiel
CASTLE KEEP(1969), w; VALDEZ IS COMING(1971), w; THREE DAYS OF THE CONDOR(1975), w; LIPSTICK(1976), w; DEATHWATCH(1980, Fr./Ger.), w

Alma Rayford
LAW AND LAWLESS(1932)
Silents
ACE OF ACTION(1926); HAUNTED RANGE, THE(1926); VANISHING HOOFS(1926); YOUNG WHIRLWIND(1928)
Misc. Silents
HEARTS O' THE RANGE(1921); LONE RIDER, THE(1922); PASSING OF WOLF MACLEAN, THE(1924); DEMON RIDER, THE(1925); RATTLER, THE(1925); CYCLONE BOB(1926); DEUCE HIGH(1926); SPEEDY SPURS(1926); TRUMPIN' TROUBLE(1926); BETWEEN DANGERS(1927); PHANTOM BUSTER, THE(1927)

Ernest Rayford III
THINGS ARE TOUGH ALL OVER(1982)

Michele Ray-Gavras
HANNAH K.(1983, Fr.), p

Tom Rayhall
SPLIT IMAGE(1982); MR. MOM(1983)

Ye. Raykov
TSAR'S BRIDE, THE(1966, USSR)

Herman C. Raymaker
TRAILING THE KILLER(1932), d
Silents
HIS JAZZ BRIDE(1926), d; NIGHT CRY, THE(1926), d; GAY OLD BIRD, THE(1927), d
Misc. Silents
RACING LUCK(1924), d; TRACKED IN THE SNOW COUNTRY(1925), d; HERO OF THE BIG SNOWS, A(1926), d; MILLIONAIRES(1926), d; FLYING LUCK(1927), d; SIMPLE SIS(1927), d; UNDER THE TONTO RIM(1928), d

Herman Raymaker
Silents
BELOW THE LINE(1925), d; KEEP SMILING(1925), w
Misc. Silents
LOVE HOUR, THE(1925), d
Karyn Raymakers
1984
UNFAITHFULLY YOURS(1984), stunts
Lois Rayman
PILLOW TALK(1959)
Sylvia Rayman
TWILIGHT WOMEN(1953, Brit.), w
Les Raymaster
OH, MEN! OH, WOMEN!(1957)
Billy Rayment
I'M ALL RIGHT, JACK(1959, Brit.)
Raymond
MAN WHO TURNED TO STONE, THE(1957), w
A. Raymond
JUNGLE JIM(1948), w; FURY OF THE CONGO(1951), w; JUNGLE MAN-
HUNT(1951), w; JUNGLE JIM IN THE FORBIDDEN LAND(1952), w
Al Raymond
RETURN TO CAMPUS(1975)
Alex Raymond
FLASH GORDON(1936), w; PYGMY ISLAND(1950), w; KILLER APE(1953), w; SAV-
AGE MUTINY(1953), w; VALLEY OF THE HEADHUNTERS(1953), w; FLASH GOR-
DON(1980), w
Art Raymond
DUKE OF WEST POINT, THE(1938)
Barry Raymond
VIOLENT STRANGER(1957, Brit.); IPCRESS FILE, THE(1965, Brit.)
Betty Raymond
NIGHT MOVES(1975)
1984
WHERE THE BOYS ARE '84(1984)
Bill Raymond
BLUE LAGOON, THE(1949, Brit.); INSPECTOR CALLS, AN(1954, Brit.)
Misc. Talkies
STRONG MEDICINE(1981)
Butch Raymond
PORKY'S(1982)
Candy Raymond
DON'S PARTY(1976, Aus.); GETTING OF WISDOM, THE(1977, Aus.); MONEY
MOVERS(1978, Aus.); PLUMBER, THE(1980, Aus.); MONKEY GRIP(1983, Aus.)
Charles Raymond
Misc. Silents
MYSTERY OF THE DIAMOND BELT(1914, Brit.), d; STOLEN HEIRLOOMS,
THE(1915, Brit.), d; TRAFFIC(1915, Brit.), d; BETTA THE GYPSY(1918, Brit.), d
Clare Raymond
HARRIET CRAIG(1950)
Cyril Raymond
HAPPY ENDING, THE(1931, Brit.); MAN OF MAYFAIR(1931, Brit.); THESE
CHARMING PEOPLE(1931, Brit.); CONDEMNED TO DEATH(1932, Brit.); CRIMINAL
AT LARGE(1932, Brit.); GHOST TRAIN(1933, Brit.); HOME, SWEET HOME(1933,
Brit.); LURE, THE(1933, Brit.); MAN OUTSIDE, THE(1933, Brit.); MIXED DOU-
BLES(1933, Brit.); STRIKE IT RICH(1933, Brit.); KEEP IT QUIET(1934, Brit.); TRAN-
SATLANTIC TUNNEL(1935, Brit.); ACCUSED(1936, Brit.); IT'S LOVE AGAIN(1936,
Brit.); SHADOW, THE(1936, Brit.); TOMORROW WE LIVE(1936, Brit.); DREAMING
LIPS(1937, Brit.); THUNDER IN THE CITY(1937, Brit.); HE LOVED AN AC-
TRESS(1938, Brit.); NIGHT ALONE(1938, Brit.); COME ON GEORGE(1939, Brit.);
GOODBYE MR. CHIPS(1939, Brit.); U-BOAT 29(1939, Brit.); SALOON BAR(1940, Brit.);
BRIEF ENCOUNTER(1945, Brit.); JACK OF DIAMONDS, THE(1949, Brit.), a, w;
QUARTET(1949, Brit.); THIS WAS A WOMAN(1949, Brit.); KISENGA, MAN OF
AFRICA(1952, Brit.); SHOOT FIRST(1953, Brit.); ANGELS ONE FIVE(1954, Brit.);
CROWDED DAY, THE(1954, Brit.); GAY DOG, THE(1954, Brit.); HEART OF THE
MATTER, THE(1954, Brit.); LEASE OF LIFE(1954, Brit.); ONE JUST MAN(1955, Brit.);
CHARLEY MOON(1956, Brit.); BABY AND THE BATTLESHIP, THE(1957, Brit.);
DUNKIRK(1958, Brit.); SAFECRACKER, THE(1958, Brit.); BEWARE OF CHIL-
DREN(1961, Brit.); DON'T TALK TO STRANGE MEN(1962, Brit.); NIGHT TRAIN TO
PARIS(1964, Brit.)
Misc. Silents
DISRAELI(1916, Brit.); MORALS OF WEYBURY, THE(1916, Brit.); HIS LAST
DEFENCE(1919, Brit.); I WILL(1919, Brit.); SCARLET KISS, THE(1920, Brit.); MOTH
AND RUST(1921, Brit.); SONIA(1921, Brit.); WHILE LONDON SLEEPS(1922, Brit.)
Dalton Raymond
SONG OF THE SOUTH(1946), w
Dean Raymond
CRIME OF DR. CRESPI, THE(1936)
Silents
CONQUERED HEARTS(1918)
Misc. Silents
WILD GIRL, THE(1917)
Don Raymond
HIGH HAT(1937)
Ernest Raymond
ATLANTIC(1929 Brit.), w; BATTLE OF GALLIPOLI(1931, Brit.), w; FOR THEM
THAT TRESPASS(1949, Brit.), w
Eve Raymond
STOCK CAR(1955, Brit.)
Felice Raymond
LOADED PISTOLS(1948); COW TOWN(1950)
Ford Raymond
JOAN OF ARC(1948)
Frances Raymond
ILLUSION(1929); GEORGE WHITE'S SCANDALS(1934); LOVE IN BLOOM(1935);
CAFE SOCIETY(1939); STAR MAKER, THE(1939); LADY EVE, THE(1941); WEST
POINT WIDOW(1941)
Silents
SKINNER'S DRESS SUIT(1917); LADY IN LOVE, A(1920); MISS HOBBS(1920); ONE
A MINUTE(1921); ONE WILD WEEK(1921); SHADOWS(1922); MONEY! MONEY!

MONEY!(1923); ABRAHAM LINCOLN(1924); EXCITEMENT(1924); GIRL ON THE
STAIRS, THE(1924); BEHIND THE FRONT(1926); WHAT HAPPENED TO JO-
NES(1926); GAY OLD BIRD, THE(1927); STAGE KISSES(1927); THREE'S A
CROWD(1927); WANDERING GIRLS(1927); WEB OF FATE(1927)
Misc. Silents
BEST MAN, THE(1919); LOVE INSURANCE(1920); MIDLANDERS, THE(1920);
GARMENTS OF YOUTH(1921); SMILING ALL THE WAY(1921); CHAPTER IN HER
LIFE, A(1923); GRAIL, THE(1923); FLIRTING WITH LOVE(1924); RICH MEN'S
SONS(1927)
Frank Raymond
HE SNOOPS TO CONQUER(1944, Brit.); JONI(1980), ph
Frankie Raymond
YOU CAN'T TAKE IT WITH YOU(1938); DIMBOOLA(1979, Aus.)
Misc. Talkies
SWEET DREAMERS(1981)
Silents
SEVEN CHANCES(1925)
Misc. Silents
CHAPERON, THE(1916); BURNING THE CANDLE(1917); FOOLS FOR LUCK(1917);
MAN WHO WAS AFRAID, THE(1917); SADIE GOES TO HEAVEN(1917); SAINT'S
ADVENTURE, THE(1917); LAST OF THE DUANES, THE(1919)
Fred Raymond
THERE GOES THE BRIDE(1933, Brit.), w, m
Gary Raymond
MOONRAKER, THE(1958, Brit.); LOOK BACK IN ANGER(1959); SUDDENLY, LAST
SUMMER(1959, Brit.); MILLIONAIRESS, THE(1960, Brit.); EL CID(1961, U.S./Ital.);
JASON AND THE ARGONAUTS(1963, Brit.); PLAYBOY OF THE WESTERN WORLD,
THE(1963, Ireland); GREATEST STORY EVER TOLD, THE(1965); TRAITOR'S GA-
TE(1966, Brit./Ger.)
Misc. Talkies
TWO FACES OF EVIL, THE(1981, Brit.)
Gene Raymond
PERSONAL MAID(1931); FORGOTTEN COMMANDMENTS(1932); IF I HAD A
MILLION(1932); LADIES OF THE BIG HOUSE(1932); NIGHT OF JUNE 13(1932); RED
DUST(1932); ANN CARVER'S PROFESSION(1933); BRIEF MOMENT(1933); EX-
LADY(1933); FLYING DOWN TO RIO(1933); HOUSE ON 56TH STREET, THE(1933);
ZOO IN BUDAPEST(1933); COMING OUT PARTY(1934); I AM SUZANNE(1934);
SADIE MCKEE(1934); TRANSATLANTIC MERRY-GO-ROUND(1934); WAY OF THE
WEST, THE(1934); BEHOLD MY WIFE(1935); HOORAY FOR LOVE(1935); SEVEN
KEYS TO BALDPATE(1935); TRANSIENT LADY(1935); WOMAN IN RED, THE(1935);
BRIDE WALKS OUT, THE(1936); LOVE ON A BET(1936); SMARTEST GIRL IN
TOWN(1936); WALKING ON AIR(1936); LIFE OF THE PARTY, THE(1937); THAT
GIRL FROM PARIS(1937); THERE GOES MY GIRL(1937); SHE'S GOT EVERY-
THING(1938); STOLEN HEAVEN(1938); CROSS COUNTRY ROMANCE(1940); MR.
AND MRS. SMITH(1941); SMILIN' THROUGH(1941); LOCKET, THE(1946); AS-
SIGNED TO DANGER(1948); MILLION DOLLAR WEEKEND(1948), a, d, w; SO-
FIA(1948); HIT THE DECK(1955); PLUNDER ROAD(1957); BEST MAN, THE(1964); I'D
RATHER BE RICH(1964); GUN RIDERS, THE(1969)
Guy Raymond
MARJORIE MORNINGSTAR(1958); 4D MAN(1959); SAIL A CROOKED SHIP(1961);
GYPSY(1962); IT HAPPENED AT THE WORLD'S FAIR(1963); RUSSIANS ARE
COMING, THE RUSSIANS ARE COMING, THE(1966); RELUCTANT ASTRONAUT,
THE(1967); BALLAD OF JOSIE(1968); BANDOLERO!(1968); UNDEFEATED,
THE(1969)
Helen Raymond
Silents
DANGEROUS TO MEN(1920); TWIN BEDS(1920); HER MAD BARGAIN(1921);
ABLEMINDED LADY, THE(1922); WILD HONEY(1922); HUNTRESS, THE(1923)
Misc. Silents
MY LADY FRIENDS(1921); THROUGH THE BACK DOOR(1921)
Jack Raymond
WILD PARTY, THE(1929); SPLINTERS(1929, Brit.), d; YOUNGER GENERA-
TION(1929); GREAT GAME, THE(1930), d; ALMOST A DIVORCE(1931, Brit.), d;
FRENCH LEAVE(1931, Brit.), d; MISCHIEF(1931, Brit.), d; SPECKLED BAND,
THE(1931, Brit.), d; TILLY OF BLOOMSBURY(1931, Brit.), p&d; UP FOR THE
CUP(1931, Brit.), a, d; LIFE GOES ON(1932, Brit.), d; SAY IT WITH MUSIC(1932,
Brit.), d; IT'S A KING(1933, Brit.), d; JUST MY LUCK(1933, Brit.), d; NIGHT OF THE
GARTER(1933, Brit.), d; SCARLET RIVER(1933); UP TO THE NECK(1933, Brit.), d;
DEATH OF THE DIAMOND(1934); GIRLS PLEASE!(1934, Brit.), d; KING OF PARIS,
THE(1934, Brit.), d; SORRELL AND SON(1934, Brit.), d; COME OUT OF THE
PANTRY(1935, Brit.), d; FOLIES DERGERE(1935); HOPE OF HIS SIDE(1935, Brit.), d;
MILLIONS IN THE AIR(1935); ONE HOUR LATE(1935); PARIS IN SPRING(1935);
RUMBA(1935); CHICK(1936, Brit.), d; PREVIEW MURDER MYSTERY(1936); PRIN-
CESS COMES ACROSS, THE(1936); RETURN OF SOPHIE LANG, THE(1936); EASY
LIVING(1937); FROG, THE(1937, Brit.), d; INTERNES CAN'T TAKE MONEY(1937);
MEET THE BOY FRIEND(1937); NIGHT CLUB SCANDAL(1937); TALK OF THE
DEVIL(1937, Brit.), p; BLONDES FOR DANGER(1938, Brit.), d; NO PARKING(1938,
Brit.), d; RAT, THE(1938, Brit.), d; ROYAL DIVORCE, A(1938, Brit.), d; SHINING
HOUR, THE(1938); HONEYMOON IN BALI(1939); LADY'S FROM KENTUCKY,
THE(1939); HE STAYED FOR BREAKFAST(1940); LADY IN QUESTION, THE(1940);
MISSING PEOPLE, THE(1940, Brit.), d; MYSTERIOUS MR. REEDER, THE(1940,
Brit.), d; HONOLULU LU(1941); YOU WILL REMEMBER(1941, Brit.), d; 'NEATH
BROOKLYN BRIDGE(1942); WHEN KNIGHTS WERE BOLD(1942, Brit.), d; SLEEPY
LAGOON(1943); SHAKE HANDS WITH MURDER(1944); HOLLYWOOD AND VI-
NE(1945); MAN WHO WALKED ALONE, THE(1945); ROGUES GALLERY(1945);
NIGHTMARE ALLEY(1947); OMOO OMOO, THE SHARK GOD(1949); SET-UP,
THE(1949); ABBOTT AND COSTELLO IN THE FOREIGN LEGION(1950); DESERT
HAWK, THE(1950); UP FOR THE CUP(1950, Brit.), d; RELUCTANT HEROES(1951,
Brit.), d; TAKE ME TO PARIS(1951, Brit.), d; WORM'S EYE VIEW(1951, Brit.), d;
LITTLE BIG SHOT(1952, Brit.), d
Silents
ROULETTE(1924); LOVER'S ISLAND(1925); ONLY WAY, THE(1926, Brit.); SOME-
HOW GOOD(1927, Brit.); LAST COMMAND, THE(1928); SALLY OF THE SCAN-
DALS(1928); THANKS FOR THE BUGGY RIDE(1928); ZERO(1928, Brit.), d; PEEP
BEHIND THE SCENES, A(1929, Brit.), d; POINTS WEST(1929)
Misc. Silents
IN THE SHADOW OF BIG BEN(1914, Brit.); HER FATHER'S KEEPER(1917);
LITTLE TERROR, THE(1917); LIGHTS OF HOME, THE(1920, Brit.); HIS OTHER
WIFE(1921); SECOND TO NONE(1926, Brit.), d; LUNATIC AT LARGE,
THE(1927)

Jean Raymond
FRENCH CANCAN(1956, Fr.)
Jill Raymond
WOMAN IN THE HALL, THE(1949, Brit.); STRANGER AT MY DOOR(1950, Brit.)
Jim Raymond
ONCE YOU KISS A STRANGER(1969)
Ken Raymond
ISLAND OF LOVE(1963)
Lee Raymond
SHE FREAK(1967)
Lina Raymond
EMBRYO(1976); TWO-MINUTE WARNING(1976); OTHER SIDE OF MIDNIGHT, THE(1977)
Louis Raymond
RISE OF LOUIS XIV, THE(1970, Fr.)
Marc Raymond
HARRY'S WAR(1981)
Marie Josee Raymond
ALIEN THUNDER(1975, US/Can.), p
Marjorie Raymond
LADY OF BURLESQUE(1943); UP IN ARMS(1944)
Maryse Raymond
FIRST TIME, THE(1978, Fr.)
Michael Raymond
EMERGENCY SQUAD(1940), w
Moore Raymond
GEORGE IN CIVVY STREET(1946, Brit.); SMILEY(1957, Brit.), w; SMILEY GETS A GUN(1959, Brit.), w
Nick Raymond
NIGHT TRAIN TO MUNDO FINE(1966); HELLCATS, THE(1968)
Pamela Raymond
NORTH TO ALASKA(1960); SANCTUARY(1961)
Paul Raymond
SONS OF NEW MEXICO(1949); CLOWN, THE(1953); FOUR FAST GUNS(1959)
Paula Raymond
BLONDIE'S SECRET(1948); RACING LUCK(1948); RUSTY LEADS THE WAY(1948); ADAM'S RIB(1949); CHALLENGE OF THE RANGE(1949); EAST SIDE, WEST SIDE(1949); CRISIS(1950); DEVIL'S DOORWAY(1950); DUCHESS OF IDAHO, THE(1950); GROUNDS FOR MARRIAGE(1950); INSIDE STRAIGHT(1951); SELLOUT, THE(1951); TALL TARGET, THE(1951); TEXAS CARNIVAL(1951); BANDITS OF CORSICA, THE(1953); BEAST FROM 20,000 FATHOMS, THE(1953); CITY THAT NEVER SLEEPS(1953); STORY OF THREE LOVES, THE(1953); HUMAN JUNGLE, THE(1954); KING RICHARD AND THE CRUSADERS(1954); GUN THAT WON THE WEST, THE(1955); FLIGHT THAT DISAPPEARED, THE(1961); HAND OF DEATH(1962); SPY WITH MY FACE, THE(1966); BLOOD OF DRACULA'S CASTLE(1967); GUN RIDERS, THE(1969)
Pete Raymond
Silents
ON WITH THE DANCE(1920)
Ray Raymond
DOSS HOUSE(1933, Brit.); HEARTS OF HUMANITY(1936, Brit.)
Richard Raymond
NEW YORK, NEW YORK(1977)
Robert Raymond
VIXENS, THE(1969)
Robin Raymond
FOR LOVE OR MONEY(1939); ARABIAN NIGHTS(1942); CALLING DR. GILLESPIE(1942); JOHNNY EAGER(1942); MOONTIDE(1942); SUNDAY PUNCH(1942); GIRLS IN CHAINS(1943); HIS BUTLER'S SISTER(1943); LET'S FACE IT(1943); SECRETS OF THE UNDERGROUND(1943); SLIGHTLY DANGEROUS(1943); ARE THESE OUR PARENTS?(1944); LADIES OF WASHINGTON(1944); STANDING ROOM ONLY(1944); LETTER FOR EVIE, A(1945); MEN IN HER DIARY(1945); ROGUES GALLERY(1945); MAN I LOVE, THE(1946); TALK ABOUT A LADY(1946); JOHNNY O'CLOCK(1947); LIKELY STORY, A(1947); WEB, THE(1947); FRENCH LEAVE(1948); PRINCE OF THIEVES, THE(1948); WABASH AVENUE(1950); SNIPER, THE(1952); GLASS WALL, THE(1953); THERE'S NO BUSINESS LIKE SHOW BUSINESS(1954); YOUNG AT HEART(1955); BEYOND A REASONABLE DOUBT(1956); JAILHOUSE ROCK(1957); HIGH SCHOOL CONFIDENTIAL(1958); WILD IN THE COUNTRY(1961); TWILIGHT OF HONOR(1963); CANDIDATE, THE(1964); YOUNG DILLINGER(1965); PENDULUM(1969)
Robyn Raymond
PSYCHIC KILLER(1975)
Ronnie Raymond
MURDER SHE SAID(1961, Brit.)
Roy Raymond
Misc. Silents
LORNA DOONE(1920, Brit.)
Royal Raymond
RED MENACE, THE(1949)
Sid Raymond
SPELL OF THE HYPNOTIST(1956); FOUR BOYS AND A GUN(1957); GODDESS, THE(1958); PRIZE, THE(1963); HOT STUFF(1979); FUNHOUSE, THE(1981); EASY MONEY(1983)
Suzanna Raymond
PETER RABBIT AND TALES OF BEATRIX POTTER(1971, Brit.)
Vicki Raymond
SIDECAR RACERS(1975, Aus.)
William Raymond
1984
FAR FROM POLAND(1984)
Misc. Silents
WOMAN IN 47, THE(1916)
William Joseph Raymond
BABY, IT'S YOU(1983)
1984
C.H.U.D.(1984)
Raymond Maurel and the Cimini Male Chorus
STREET GIRL(1929)

Raymond Paige and His Orchestra
HOLLYWOOD HOTEL(1937)
Raymond Scott and His Quintet
NOTHING SACRED(1937); HAPPY LANDING(1938)
Raymond Scott Quartet
REBECCA OF SUNNYBROOK FARM(1938)
Catherine Raymonde
PEEK-A-BOO(1961, Fr.), cos
Raymone
THIS MAN MUST DIE(1970, Fr./Ital.)
Carol Raymont
PERSECUTION AND ASSASSINATION OF JEAN-PAUL MARAT AS PERFORMED BY THE INMATES OF THE ASYLUM OF CHARENTON UNDER THE DIRECTION OF THE MARQUIS DE SADE, THE(1967, Brit.)
Rayna
DAYTONA BEACH WEEKEND(1965)
Laura Raynair
VAGABOND KING, THE(1956)
Jackie Raynal
SATURDAY NIGHT AT THE BATHS(1975), ed
Jacquie Raynal
LA COLLECTIONNEUSE(1971, Fr.), ed
Nadine Raynaud
BIRD WATCH, THE(1983, Fr.)
Michel Rayne
DANCING HEART, THE(1959, Ger.)
Susan Rayne
HELL BELOW ZERO(1954, Brit.)
Ben Rayner
MAYERLING(1968, Brit./Fr.), ed
Christine Rayner
Silents
QUEEN OF MY HEART(1917, Brit.); IMPOSSIBLE WOMAN, THE(1919, Brit.); NATURE OF THE BEAST, THE(1919, Brit.); ANNA THE ADVENTURESS(1920, Brit.); KIPPS(1921, Brit.)
Misc. Silents
VICAR OF WAKEFIELD, THE(1913, Brit.); KINSMAN, THE(1919, Brit.); LAND OF MYSTERY(1920, Brit.)
Constance Rayner
Silents
FALSE EVIDENCE(1922, Brit.)
D.A. Rayner
ENEMY BELOW, THE(1957), w
Desmond Rayner
STOLEN ASSIGNMENT(1955, Brit.)
John Rayner
COUNTDOWN(1968); TRACKDOWN(1976)
Martin Rayner
VICTOR/VICTORIA(1982)
Minnie Rayner
SYMPHONY IN TWO FLATS(1930, Brit.); GABLES MYSTERY, THE(1931, Brit.); SHERLOCK HOLMES' FATAL HOUR(1931, Brit.); STRANGLEHOLD(1931, Brit.); THESE CHARMING PEOPLE(1931, Brit.); EXCESS BAGGAGE(1933, Brit.); I LIVED WITH YOU(1933, Brit.); THIS WEEK OF GRACE(1933, Brit.); MURDER AT THE INN(1934, Brit.); SOMETIMES GOOD(1934, Brit.); SONG AT EVENTIDE(1934, Brit.); BARNACLE BILL(1935, Brit.); FLOOD TIDE(1935, Brit.); SMALL MAN, THE(1935, Brit.); TRIUMPH OF SHERLOCK HOLMES, THE(1935, Brit.); DREAMS COME TRUE(1936, Brit.); HOUSE OF THE SPANIARD, THE(1936, Brit.); IF I WERE RICH(1936); TWO WHO DARED(1937, Brit.); GASLIGHT(1940); OLD MOTHER RILEY IN SOCIETY(1940, Brit.); MURDER AT THE BASKERVILLES(1941, Brit.)
Silents
MY OLD DUTCH(1915, Brit.); AUCTION MART, THE(1920, Brit.); MARY LATIMER, NUN(1920, Brit.); OLD CURIOSITY SHOP, THE(1921, Brit.); IF YOUTH BUT KNEW(1926, Brit.)
Molly Rayner
WOMAN TO WOMAN(1946, Brit.)
Fred Raynham
Silents
EDGE O'BEYOND(1919, Brit.); PASSIONATE FRIENDS, THE(1922, Brit.); INDIAN LOVE LYRICS, THE(1923, Brit.); DAUGHTER OF LOVE, A(1925, Brit.); PRESUMPTION OF STANLEY HAY, MP, THE(1925, Brit.); QUALIFIED ADVENTURER, THE(1925, Brit.); FLAG LIEUTENANT, THE(1926, Brit.); FURTHER ADVENTURES OF THE FLAG LIEUTENANT(1927, Brit.)
Misc. Silents
ROMANCE OF WASTDALE, A(1921, Brit.); EXPIATION(1922, Brit.); LITTLE BROTHER OF GOD(1922, Brit.); SIGN OF FOUR, THE(1923, Brit.); SEN YAN'S DEVOTION(1924, Brit.); CONFESSIONS(1925, Brit.); ROMANCE OF THE MAYFAIR, A(1925, Brit.); SOMEBODY'S DARLING(1925, Brit.)
Glen Raynham
HOT NEWS(1936, Brit.); MUSIC HALL PARADE(1939, Brit.)
Jack Raynold
LAST GANGSTER, THE(1937)
Christopher Raynolds
THUNDER AND LIGHTNING(1977)
Albert E. Raynor
Silents
KING OF THE CASTLE(1925, Brit.)
Bill Raynor
CASA MANANA(1951), w; RHYTHM INN(1951), w; WITHOUT WARNING(1952), w; FANGS OF THE ARCTIC(1953), w; MURDER WITHOUT TEARS(1953), w; PHANTOM FROM SPACE(1953), w; KILLERS FROM SPACE(1954), w; YUKON VENGEANCE(1954), w
Grace Raynor
TEN DAYS TO TULARA(1958)
Marshall Raynor
FANNY HILL: MEMOIRS OF A WOMAN OF PLEASURE zero(1965); MERRY WIVES OF WINDSOR, THE(1966, Aust.)

Minnie Raynor
MISSING REMBRANDT, THE(1932, Brit.); IT HAPPENED IN PARIS(1935, Brit.)
Molly Raynor
WE'LL MEET AGAIN(1942, Brit.); SCARLET WEB, THE(1954, Brit.)
Sheila Raynor
THEY KNEW MR. KNIGHT(1945, Brit.); MARK OF CAIN, THE(1948, Brit.); MAD-
NESS OF THE HEART(1949, Brit.); DEAD ON COURSE(1952, Brit.); LEASE OF
LIFE(1954, Brit.); VALUE FOR MONEY(1957, Brit.); RELUCTANT DEBUTANTE,
THE(1958); THREE MEN IN A BOAT(1958, Brit.); VIOLENT PLAYGROUND(1958,
Brit.); ROOM AT THE TOP(1959, Brit.); OCTOBER MOTH(1960, Brit.); CLOCKWORK
ORANGE, A(1971, Brit.); DULCIMA(1971, Brit.); MAN IN THE WILDERNESS(1971,
U.S./Span.); FLAME(1975, Brit.); OMEN, THE(1976)
Timothy L. Raynor
FINAL EXAM(1981)
William Raynor
SNOW DOG(1950), w; YUKON MANHUNT(1951), w; NORTHWEST TER-
RITORY(1952), w; YUKON GOLD(1952), w; PRISONERS OF THE CASBAH(1953), w;
SON OF BELLE STARR(1953), w; TARGET EARTH(1954), w; FRANCIS IN THE
HAUNTED HOUSE(1956), w; ROCK, PRETTY BABY(1956), w; KETTLES ON OLD
MACDONALD'S FARM, THE(1957), w; ROCK BABY, ROCK IT(1957), w; SUMMER
LOVE(1958), w; WACKIEST SHIP IN THE ARMY, THE(1961), w
Raynor Lehr Circus
TRIGGER, JR.(1950)
Edythe Raynore
ROAD TO GLORY, THE(1936)
Mirra Rayo
GOIN' TO TOWN(1935)

Benjamin Rayson
LOVESICK(1983)
1984
UNFAITHFULLY YOURS(1984)
David Rayson
MIKADO, THE(1967, Brit.)
Dwayne Rayven
NOTORIOUS CLEOPATRA, THE(1970), ph, ed
Abraham Raz
NEITHER BY DAY NOR BY NIGHT(1972, U.S./Israel), w
Mati Raz
CLOUDS OVER ISRAEL(1966, Israel), p
Vladimar Raz
SWEET LIGHT IN A DARK ROOM(1966, Czech.)
Andy Razaf
1984
PHILADELPHIA EXPERIMENT, THE(1984), m/l
Spiro Razatos
1984
STREETS OF FIRE(1984)
Virendra Razdan
GANDHI(1982)
Stella Razeto
Misc. Silents
SUPREME TEST, THE(1915)
Stella Razetto
Misc. Silents
CIRCULAR STAIRCASE, THE(1915); THREE GODFATHERS, THE(1916)
Amity Razi
JESUS CHRIST, SUPERSTAR(1973)
Alexander Razumni
Misc. Silents
LIFE AND DEATH OF LIEUTENANT SCHMIDT(1917, USSR), d; UPRISING(1918,
USSR), d; MOTHER(1920, USSR), d; BEAUTY AND THE BOLSHEVIK(1923, USSR),
d
Gustavo Re
THAT MAN IN ISTANBUL(1966, Fr./Ital./Span.); THEY CAME TO ROB LAS
VEGAS(1969, Fr./Ital./Span./Ger.)
Charles Rea
IPCRESS FILE, THE(1965, Brit.)
Chris Rea
CROSS COUNTRY(1983, Can.), m
David C. Rea
Misc. Talkies
SHE'LL FOLLOW YOU ANYWHERE(1971), d
Elena Rea
UMBERTO D(1955, Ital.)
Gennard Rea
WEST OF RAINBOW'S END(1938), w
Gennaro Rea
WHERE THE WEST BEGINS(1938), w
Isabel Rea
Silents
FIRE AND SWORD(1914)
Mabel Lillian Rea
DEVIL'S HAIRPIN, THE(1957)
Mabel Rea
JOKER IS WILD, THE(1957); SUBMARINE SEAHAWK(1959)
Peggy Rea
SEVEN FACES OF DR. LAO(1964); STRANGE BEDFELLOWS(1965); WALK, DON'T
RUN(1966); VALLEY OF THE DOLLS(1967); LEARNING TREE, THE(1969); COLD
TURKEY(1971); WHAT'S THE MATTER WITH HELEN?(1971)
Peter W. Rea
1984
GRANDVIEW, U.S.A.(1984), p
Stephen Rea
CRY OF THE BANSHEE(1970, Brit.); ANGEL(1982, Irish)
1984
FOUR DAYS IN JULY(1984); LOOSE CONNECTIONS(1984, Brit.)

Thelma Rea
RANDOLPH FAMILY, THE(1945, Brit.); MIRANDA(1949, Brit.)
John Reach
LIZZIE(1957); BOUNTY KILLER, THE(1965); SILENCERS, THE(1966)
Manuel Reachi
TOAST TO LOVE(1951, Mex.), p
Maria Reachi
EAST SIDE, WEST SIDE(1949)
Renita Reachi
YOURS, MINE AND OURS(1968), cos
Art Read
DEATH IN THE SKY(1937), ph; MISBEHAVING HUSBANDS(1941), ph
Barbara Read
MAKE WAY FOR TOMORROW(1937); MAN WHO CRIED WOLF, THE(1937);
MERRY-GO-ROUND OF 1938(1937); MIGHTY TREVE, THE(1937); ROAD BACK,-
THE(1937); THREE SMART GIRLS(1937); CRIME OF DR. HALLET(1938); MIDNIGHT
INTRUDER(1938); SORORITY HOUSE(1939); SPELLBINDER, THE(1939); CURTAIN
CALL(1940); MARRIED AND IN LOVE(1940); RUBBER RACKETEERS(1942); TOO
MANY WOMEN(1942); BEHIND THE MASK(1946)
Beatrice Read
Misc. Silents
AFTER DARK(1915, Brit.)
Carol Read
RETURN OF THE JEDI(1983)
Darryl Read
DAYLIGHT ROBBERY(1964, Brit.); LOST CONTINENT, THE(1968, Brit.)
David Read
ALICE IN WONDERLAND(1951, Fr.)
Donald Read
MURDER BY ROPE(1936, Brit.)
Douglas Read
GAME IS OVER, THE(1967, Fr.); MILKY WAY, THE(1969, Fr./Ital.)
Dudley Read
Silents
ONCE UPON A TIME(1922), ph
George Read
COLONEL EFFINGHAM'S RAID(1945)
J. Parker Read
Silents
CIVILIZATION(1916), d
Misc. Silents
HIS OWN LAW(1920), d
J. Parker Read, Jr.
TRUMPET BLOWS, THE(1934), w
Jackson Read
Misc. Silents
FIGHTING LOVER, THE(1921)
James Read
1984
INITIATION, THE(1984)
Jan Read
HELTER SKELTER(1949, Brit.), w; WHITE CORRIDORS(1952, Brit.), w; BLOOD
ORANGE(1953, Brit.), w; BOTH SIDES OF THE LAW(1953, Brit.), w; SECRET TENT,
THE(1956, Brit.), w; ZOO BABY(1957, Brit.), w; HAUNTED STRANGLER, THE(1958,
Brit.), w; ROMAN SPRING OF MRS. STONE, THE(1961, U.S./Brit.), w; THAT KIND
OF GIRL(1963, Brit.), w; FIRST MEN IN THE MOON(1964, Brit.), w
John Read
CROSSROADS TO CRIME(1960, Brit.), p; JOURNEY TO THE FAR SIDE OF THE
SUN(1969, Brit.), ph
Josie Read
BLUE MURDER AT ST. TRINIAN'S(1958, Brit.)
Lois Read
WHISTLE DOWN THE WIND(1961, Brit.)
Margaret Read
KISS OF EVIL(1963, Brit.); THAT TENDER TOUCH(1969)
Mary Read
HALF SHOT AT SUNRISE(1930), ch
Nicholas Read
RETURN OF THE JEDI(1983)
Opie Read
Silents
ALMOST A HUSBAND(1919), w
Peter Read
DEMENTIA 13(1963)
Roberta Read
HARD STEEL(1941, Brit.)
Roland Read
MISSING GIRLS(1936), ed
Ava Readdy
LAS VEGAS LADY(1976); ROLLERCOASTER(1977); WHEN TIME RAN OUT(1980)
Carmelo Reade
RETURN OF SABATA(1972, Ital./Fr./Ger.)
Charles Reade
LYONS MAIL, THE(1931, Brit.), w; PEG OF OLD DRURY(1936, Brit.), w; IT'S
NEVER TOO LATE TO MEND(1937, Brit.), w
Janet Reade
SMILING LIEUTENANT, THE(1931)
Lillian Reade
Silents
CIVILIZATION(1916)
Nicki Reade
RETURN OF THE JEDI(1983)
Anna Reader
Silents ›
SENTIMENTAL LADY, THE(1915)
Jim Reader
THAT TENNESSEE BEAT(1966); GLORY STOMPERS, THE(1967)
Misc. Talkies
JENNIE, WIFE/CHILD(1968)

Ralph Reader
SLEEPLESS NIGHTS(1933, Brit.), ch; BLUE SQUADRON, THE(1934, Brit.); BACKS-TAGE(1937, Brit.); SPLINTERS IN THE AIR(1937, Brit.), a, w; GANG, THE(1938, Brit.), a, w; FOUR AGAINST FATE(1952, Brit.); DANGEROUS YOUTH(1958, Brit.)

Bobby Readick
HARRIGAN'S KID(1943); CANTERVILLE GHOST, THE(1944)

Frank Readick
JOURNEY INTO FEAR(1942)

Tony Readin
GREEK TYCOON, THE(1978), art d

Anthony Reading
RAGTIME(1981), art d

Bertice Reading
MOON IN THE GUTTER, THE(1983, Fr./Ital.)

Donna Reading
CONQUEROR WORM, THE(1968, Brit.); SUBTERFUGE(1969, US/Brit.)

Tony Reading
PAPER TIGER(1975, Brit.), art d; KRULL(1983), art d
1984
BOUNTY, THE(1984), art d; SCREAM FOR HELP(1984), art d

Reading and Grant
OLD MOTHER RILEY'S CIRCUS(1941, Brit.)

Lorelei Readoux
MAD YOUTH(1940)

Mike Ready
Silents
WARMING UP(1928)

Roger Ready
MARS NEEDS WOMEN(1966)

Barry Reagan
COLT .45(1950); ENFORCER, THE(1951); I WAS A COMMUNIST FOR THE F.B.I.(1951)

Charles Reagan
TREASURE OF MONTE CRISTO(1949)

Deborah Reagan
STARTING OVER(1979); TRADING PLACES(1983)

George P. Reagan, Jr.
SPEED LIMITED(1940), p

Kevin Reagan
LONG WEEKEND(1978, Aus.), cos

Neil Reagan
TUGBOAT ANNIE SAILS AGAIN(1940); DOUGHBOYS IN IRELAND(1943)

Ray Reagan
LAST CHANCE, THE(1945, Switz.)

Ronald Reagan
HOLLYWOOD HOTEL(1937); LOVE IS ON THE AIR(1937); ACCIDENTS WILL HAPPEN(1938); AMAZING DR. CLITTERHOUSE, THE(1938); BOY MEETS GIRL(1938); BROTHER RAT(1938); COWBOY FROM BROOKLYN(1938); GIRLS ON PROBATION(1938); SERGEANT MURPHY(1938); SWING YOUR LADY(1938); AN-GELS WASH THEIR FACES(1939); CODE OF THE SECRET SERVICE(1939); DARK VICTORY(1939); GOING PLACES(1939); HELL'S KITCHEN(1939); NAUGHTY BUT NICE(1939); SECRET SERVICE OF THE AIR(1939); SMASHING THE MONEY RING(1939); ANGEL FROM TEXAS, AN(1940); KNUTE ROCKNE–ALL AMERI-CAN(1940); MURDER IN THE AIR(1940); SANTA FE TRAIL(1940); TUGBOAT ANNIE SAILS AGAIN(1940); BAD MAN, THE(1941); INTERNATIONAL SQUADRON(1941); MILLION DOLLAR BABY(1941); NINE LIVES ARE NOT ENOUGH(1941); DESPER-ATE JOURNEY(1942); JUKE GIRL(1942); KING'S ROW(1942); THIS IS THE AR-MY(1943); STALLION ROAD(1947); THAT HAGEN GIRL(1947); VOICE OF THE TURTLE, THE(1947); GIRL FROM JONES BEACH, THE(1949); HASTY HEART, THE(1949); IT'S A GREAT FEELING(1949); JOHN LOVES MARY(1949); NIGHT UNTO NIGHT(1949); LOUISA(1950); STORM WARNING(1950); BEDTIME FOR BON-ZO(1951); HONG KONG(1951); LAST OUTPOST, THE(1951); SHE'S WORKING HER WAY THROUGH COLLEGE(1952); WINNING TEAM, THE(1952); LAW AND OR-DER(1953); TROPIC ZONE(1953); CATTLE QUEEN OF MONTANA(1954); PRISONER OF WAR(1954); TENNESSEE'S PARTNER(1955); HELLCATS OF THE NAVY(1957); YOUNG DOCTORS, THE(1961); KILLERS, THE(1964)

Terry Reagan
V.D.(1961)

Real
UMBRELLAS OF CHERBOURG, THE(1964, Fr./Ger.), cos

Alma Real
STORM OVER THE ANDES(1935); DANCING PIRATE(1936)

Louise Real
Silents
SIN(1915)

Rita Real
TENTACLES(1977, Ital.)

Sophie Real
FIVE MILES TO MIDNIGHT(1963, U.S./Fr./Ital.)

Florence Real Bird
DIRTY DINGUS MAGEE(1970)

Genevieve Reale
BILLY IN THE LOWLANDS(1979); DOZENS, THE(1981)

Joe Reale
WHEN A STRANGER CALLS(1979)

Joseph Reale
STRAWBERRY STATEMENT, THE(1970)

Paolo Reale
ISLAND OF PROCIDA, THE(1952, Ital.)

Carlo Reali
BARON BLOOD(1972, Ital.), ed; TWITCH OF THE DEATH NERVE(1973, Ital.), w

Grace Reals
Silents
OH, BOY!(1919); RIGHT TO LIE, THE(1919); KENTUCKIANS, THE(1921)
Misc. Silents
MASTER OF THE HOUSE, THE(1915)

Andrew Ream
1984
TEACHERS(1984)

Ronald Reame
GIVE HER A RING(1936, Brit.), ph

Cynthia Reams
10 TO MIDNIGHT(1983)

Lee Roy Reams
SWEET CHARITY(1969)

Reanda
LEOPARD, THE(1963, Ital.), cos

Andre Reanne
Misc. Silents
CINDERS(1926, Brit.)

Brad Reardon
SILENT SCREAM(1980)
1984
TERMINATOR, THE(1984)

Caspar Reardon
YOU'RE A SWEETHEART(1937)

Craig Reardon
DEAD KIDS(1981 Aus./New Zealand), spec eff & makeup; UNSEEN, THE(1981), makeup; DANCE OF THE DWARFS(1983, U.S., Phil.), makeup; TWILIGHT ZONE–THE MOVIE(1983), makeup
1984
DREAMSCAPE(1984), spec eff

Dennis Reardon
HAPPINESS CAGE, THE(1972), w

Don Reardon
TARAWA BEACHHEAD(1958)

Harry Reardon
STALAG 17(1953); SUMMER CAMP(1979)

Herk Reardon
GOOD TIMES(1967)

James Reardon
FEATHER, THE(1929, Brit.); THIRD STRING, THE(1932, Brit.), w
Misc. Silents
ROGUE IN LOVE, A(1916, Brit.); GLAD EYE, THE(1920, Brit.); SHADOW OF EVIL(1921, Brit.), d; NAUGHTY HUSBANDS(1930, Brit.)

John "Beans" Reardon
KID FROM LEFT FIELD, THE(1953)

Leslie Reardon
Silents
POWER OF RIGHT, THE(1919, Brit.)

Marjorie Reardon
PARACHUTE NURSE(1942); PARDON MY SARONG(1942)

Michael Reardon
SCROOGE(1970, Brit.)

Mildred Reardon
Silents
MALE AND FEMALE(1919); NUMBER 17(1920)
Misc. Silents
SILK HUSBANDS AND CALICO WIVES(1920); HIS RISE TO FAME(1927)

Ned Reardon
Silents
SUBURBAN, THE(1915)
Misc. Silents
MARBLE HEART, THE(1915)

Peter Brady Reardon
1984
PREPPIES(1984)

Stephen Reardon
Misc. Silents
BRIDGE OF SIGHS, THE(1915)

Teri Reardon
Misc. Talkies
LEFT-HANDED(1972)

Thomas Reardon
SUPERCHICK(1973)

Wally Reardon
DAWN PATROL, THE(1938)

Walt Rearick
NIGHT OF EVIL(1962)

Rex Reason
STORM OVER TIBET(1952); CHINA VENTURE(1953); MISSION OVER KO-REA(1953); SALOME(1953); KISS OF FIRE(1955); LADY GODIVA(1955); SMOKE SIGNAL(1955); THIS ISLAND EARTH(1955); CREATURE WALKS AMONG US, THE(1956); RAW EDGE(1956); BADLANDS OF MONTANA(1957); BAND OF AN-GELS(1957); UNDER FIRE(1957); RAWHIDE TRAIL, THE(1958); THUNDERING JETS(1958); MIRACLE OF THE HILLS, THE(1959); SAD HORSE, THE(1959)
Misc. Talkies
RAWHIDE TRAIL, THE(1950)

Rhodes Reason
LADY GODIVA(1955); CRIME AGAINST JOE(1956); DESPERADOES ARE IN TOWN, THE(1956); EMERGENCY HOSPITAL(1956); FLIGHT TO HONG KONG(1956); JUNGLE HEAT(1957); VOODOO ISLAND(1957); BIG FISHERMAN, THE(1959); YEL-LOWSTONE KELLY(1959); FEVER IN THE BLOOD, A(1961); KING KONG ES-CAPES(1968, Jap.); DELTA FACTOR, THE(1970); CAT MURKIL AND THE SILKS(1976)
Misc. Talkies
MAN EATER(1958)

Alma Reat
YANKEE DON(1931)

Woolie Reatherman
PINOCCHIO(1940), anim d

Milly Reauclaire
SINBAD THE SAILOR(1947)

Robert Reault
Misc. Silents
FANGS OF FATE(1928)

Katy Reaves
  HOT STUFF(1979)
Theodore Reaves
  NIGHT PLANE FROM CHUNGKING(1942), w
Arthur Reavis
  CEREMONY, THE(1963, U.S./Span.), spec eff
Rebane
  M(1933, Ger.)
A. Rebane
  WAR AND PEACE(1968, USSR)
Angelica Rebane
  DEVONSVILLE TERROR, THE(1983)
Bill Rebane
  MONSTER A GO-GO(1965), p&d; GIANT SPIDER INVASION, THE(1975), p, d; DEMONS OF LUDLOW, THE(1983), d
Misc. Talkies
  ALPHA INCIDENT, THE(1976), d; INVASION FROM INNER EARTH(1977), d; CAPTURE OF BIGFOOT, THE(1979), d
Alex Rebar
  INCREDIBLE MELTING MAN, THE(1978); DEMENTED(1980), p, w; TO ALL A GOODNIGHT(1980), w
Ann Rebbot
  FRENCH CONNECTION, THE(1971)
Saddy Rebbot
  MY LIFE TO LIVE(1963, Fr.)
Sady Rebbot
  FRIENDS(1971, Brit.); ONCE IN PARIS(1978)
Martial Rebe
  RASPUTIN(1939, Fr.); PARDON MY FRENCH(1951, U.S./Fr.)
"Rebel"
  CHEYENNE TORNADO(1935)
Bernard Rebel
  CROOKS TOUR(1940, Brit.); COLONEL MARCH INVESTIGATES(1952,Brit.); MOULIN ROUGE(1952); CAPTAIN'S PARADISE, THE(1953, Brit.); MR. POTTS GOES TO MOSCOW(1953, Brit.); CASE OF THE RED MONKEY(1955, Brit.); IT'S A WONDERFUL WORLD(1956, Brit.); MARK OF THE PHOENIX(1958, Brit.); ORDERS TO KILL(1958, Brit.); CURSE OF THE MUMMY'S TOMB, THE(1965, Brit.)
Chris Rebello
  JAWS(1975)
Arthur Maria Rebenalt
  BETWEEN TIME AND ETERNITY(1960, Ger.), d
Georg Rebentisch
  EMIL AND THE DETECTIVES(1964)
Dwight Reber
  MORE AMERICAN GRAFFITI(1979)
James Rebhorn
  HE KNOWS YOU'RE ALONE(1980); SOUP FOR ONE(1982); SILKWOOD(1983)
Mrs. Reta Rebia
Silents
  GREED(1925)
A. Rebikova
Misc. Silents
  SHACKLED BY FILM(1918, USSR)
Gisele Rebillon
  LA GUERRE EST FINIE(1967, Fr./Swed.), p
Albert Rebla
  JUST FOR A SONG(1930, Brit.); MIDSHIPMAID GOB(1932, Brit.); WOMAN IN COMMAND, THE(1934 Brit.); WHILE PARENTS SLEEP(1935, Brit.)
Arthur Rebner
  EIGHT GIRLS IN A BOAT(1932, Ger.), m; EIGHT GIRLS IN A BOAT(1934), w, m
Gary Rebstock
  STAR CHAMBER, THE(1983)
Harry Rebuas [Sauber]
  SING FOR YOUR SUPPER(1941), w
Harry Rebuas
  FIVE LITTLE PEPPERS IN TROUBLE(1940), w; OUT WEST WITH THE PEPPERS(1940), w; TRAMP, TRAMP, TRAMP(1942), w; TWO BLONDES AND A REDHEAD(1947), w
Hershel Rebuas
  YOUTH ON PAROLE(1937), w
Stewart Reburn
  SECOND FIDDLE(1939)
Lanny Reca
  CALIFORNIA FIREBRAND(1948)
Danilo Recanatesi
  LA CAGE AUX FOLLES II(1981, Ital./Fr.)
Ron Recasner
1984
  2010(1984)
Bob Rech
  SHADOWS(1960), a, set d
Edmond Rechad
  KILL! KILL! KILL!(1972, Fr./Ger./Ital./Span.), ph
Otto Rechenberg
  AMY(1981)
Roy Rechkemmer
1984
  COUNTRY(1984)
Coby Recht
  APPLE, THE(1980 U.S./Ger.), a, m
Iris Recht
  APPLE, THE(1980 U.S./Ger.), a, m
Joe Recht
  MOB TOWN(1941); SING ANOTHER CHORUS(1941); MY FAVORITE BLONDE(1942); STRANGE CASE OF DR. RX, THE(1942); DESPERATE(1947); EGG AND I, THE(1947); MY FAVORITE BRUNETTE(1947); B. F.'S DAUGHTER(1948); LADY FROM SHANGHAI, THE(1948); PEGGY(1950); UNION STATION(1950); PAINTING THE CLOUDS WITH SUNSHINE(1951); PLACE IN THE SUN, A(1951); STARLIFT(1951); DREAMBOAT(1952)

Ray Recht
  AMITYVILLE II: THE POSSESSION(1982), art d
Joe Rechts
  RECKLESS MOMENTS, THE(1949)
Seymour Rechtzeit
Misc. Talkies
  LIVE AND LAUGH(1933); SONG OF SONGS(1935); JEWISH MELODY, THE(1940)
Stefan Reck
1984
  CLASS ENEMY(1984, Ger.)
Betty Recklaw
  WORDS AND MUSIC(1929)
Fritz Reck-Malleczewen
  BOMBARDMENT OF MONTE CARLO, THE(1931, Ger.), w
Lloyd Reckord
  WHAT A WHOPPER(1961, Brit.)
Baby Reckvell
  GERMANY, YEAR ZERO(1949, Ger.)
Alain Recoing
  RETURN OF MARTIN GUERRE, THE(1983, Fr.)
Don Record
  SUMMERTREE(1971), d
Tony Recorder
  GRAVEYARD OF HORROR(1971, Span.), p
Mireille Recton
  RABID(1976, Can.), makeup
George Rector
  EVERY DAY'S A HOLIDAY(1938)
Charles Red
  EMPIRE OF THE ANTS(1977)
Lois Red Elk
  THREE WARRIORS(1977)
Red Donahue and His Mule Uno
  LAS VEGAS NIGHTS(1941)
Red Donahue and Mule
  MOUNTAIN MUSIC(1937)
Red Dust the Dog
  STARS ARE SINGING, THE(1953)
Red Foley's Saddle Pals
  PIONEERS, THE(1941)
Sailors of the Red Navy
  SEEDS OF FREEDOM(1943, USSR)
Silents
  BATTLESHIP POTEMKIN, THE(1925, USSR)
Red Norvo Trio
  TEXAS CARNIVAL(1951)
Red River Dave
  SWING IN THE SADDLE(1944)
Red Wing
Silents
  WHEN KNIGHTHOOD WAS IN FLOWER(1922)
McKee "Kiko" Red Wing
  THREE WARRIORS(1977)
Habib Reda
  Z(1969, Fr./Algeria)
Joe Di Reda
  GABY(1956)
Jay Redack
  RABBIT TEST(1978), w
Michael Redbourn
  CREEPING FLESH,THE(1973, Brit.), p
Eugene Redd
  CHRISTMAS EVE(1947), set d; ON OUR MERRY WAY(1948), set d
Frances Redd
Misc. Talkies
  MIDNIGHT SHADOW(1939)
Freddie Redd
  CONNECTION, THE(1962), a, m
Gene Redd
  WESTBOUND(1959), set d
James Redd
  DAKOTA(1945), set d; NORTHWEST OUTPOST(1947), set d; MACBETH(1948), set d; OKLAHOMA BADLANDS(1948), set d; SONS OF ADVENTURE(1948), set d; I SHOT JESSE JAMES(1949), set d; NAVAJO TRAIL RAIDERS(1949), set d; OUTCASTS OF THE TRAIL(1949), set d; POST OFFICE INVESTIGATOR(1949), set d; RED MENACE, THE(1949), set d; SAN ANTONE AMBUSH(1949), set d; SOUTH OF RIO(1949), set d; TRAIL OF ROBIN HOOD(1950), set d; DESPERADOES OUTPOST(1952), set d; OLD OKLAHOMA PLAINS(1952), set d; SOUTH PACIFIC TRAIL(1952), set d; TROPICAL HEAT WAVE(1952), set d; WAC FROM WALLA WALLA, THE(1952), set d; GHOST OF ZORRO(1959), set d
James S. Redd
  KILLERS, THE(1964), set d; MC HALE'S NAVY(1964), set d; MC HALE'S NAVY JOINS THE AIR FORCE(1965), set d; WILD SEED(1965), set d; TEXAS ACROSS THE RIVER(1966), set d; CLAMBAKE(1967), set d; ROUGH NIGHT IN JERICHO(1967), set d; HELLFIGHTERS(1968), set d; PINK JUNGLE, THE(1968), set d
John Redd
  THUNDERING CARAVANS(1952), set d
Mary Robin Redd
  J.W. COOP(1971); GREAT NORTHFIELD, MINNESOTA RAID, THE(1972); CANNONBALL(1976, U.S./Hong Kong)
Mary-Robin Redd
  GROUP, THE(1966)
1984
  MIRRORS(1984)
Misc. Talkies
  MIRRORS(1978)
Richard Redd
  MR. SYCAMORE(1975)

Manfred Reddeman
HAGBARD AND SIGNE(1968, Den./Iceland/Swed.)

Manfred Reddemann
BATTLE OF BRITAIN, THE(1969, Brit.)

Arthur Redden
Silents
PURPLE CIPHER, THE(1920)

Billy Redden
DELIVERANCE(1972)

Bill Reddick
SUNSHINE BOYS, THE(1975); SHOOT THE MOON(1982); SUDDEN IMPACT(1983)

Cecil Reddick
UNHOLY ROLLERS(1972); VAN NUYS BLVD.(1979)

Gerri Reddick
TRAIN RIDE TO HOLLYWOOD(1975)

Kenneth Reddin
ANOTHER SHORE(1948, Brit.), w

Eugene Redding
Silents
RED WIDOW, THE(1916)

Jack N. Reddish
LE MANS(1971), p; HARRY'S WAR(1981), p

Jack Reddish
HARRY'S WAR(1981)

Don Reddy
BENJI(1974), ph; HAWMPS!(1976), ph; FOR THE LOVE OF BENJI(1977), ph; THE DOUBLE McGUFFIN(1979), ph; OH, HEAVENLY DOG!(1980), ph

Helen Reddy
AIRPORT 1975(1974); PETE'S DRAGON(1977); SGT. PEPPER'S LONELY HEARTS CLUB BAND(1978)

Quinn Redecker
SLAMS, THE(1973)

Quinn K. Redeker
DEER HUNTER, THE(1978), w

Quinn Redeker
THREE STOOGES MEET HERCULES, THE(1962); SPIDER BABY(1968); CHRISTINE JORGENSEN STORY, THE(1970); CANDIDATE, THE(1972); LIMIT, THE(1972); MIDNIGHT MAN, THE(1974); AT LONG LAST LOVE(1975); ROLLERCOASTER(1977); ELECTRIC HORSEMAN, THE(1979); COAST TO COAST(1980); ORDINARY PEOPLE(1980); WHERE THE BUFFALO ROAM(1980)

Nelly Redel
BLUE IDOL, THE(1931, Hung.)

Gigi Reder
FAST AND SEXY(1960, Fr./Ital.); CAFE EXPRESS(1980, Ital.)

Linda Redfearn
OMEGA MAN, THE(1971)

Linda Moon Redfearn
WHITE BUFFALO, THE(1977)

Adam Redfield
MIDSUMMER NIGHT'S SEX COMEDY, A(1982)

Billy Redfield
BACK DOOR TO HEAVEN(1939)

Dennis Redfield
PRIVATE DUTY NURSES(1972); UNHOLY ROLLERS(1972); SUMMER RUN(1974); WILD McCULLOCHS, THE(1975); MOVING VIOLATION(1976); DEAD AND BURIED(1981); MAN, WOMAN AND CHILD(1983)
1984
BEST DEFENSE(1984)

Marilyn Redfield
TEX(1982)

William Redfield
CONQUEST OF SPACE(1955); PROUD AND THE PROFANE, THE(1956); I MARRIED A WOMAN(1958); CONNECTION, THE(1962); HAMLET(1964); MORITURI(1965); DUEL AT DIABLO(1966); FANTASTIC VOYAGE(1966); ALL WOMAN(1967); SIDELONG GLANCES OF A PIGEON KICKER, THE(1970); NEW LEAF, A(1971); SUCH GOOD FRIENDS(1971); HOT ROCK, THE(1972); DEATH WISH(1974); ONE FLEW OVER THE CUCKOO'S NEST(1975); FOR PETE'S SAKE(1977); MR. BILLION(1977)

Basil Redford
GIRL IN A MILLION, A(1946, Brit.)

H.E.D. Redford
HANGAR 18(1980); EARTHBOUND(1981)
1984
FOOTLOOSE(1984); SILENT NIGHT, DEADLY NIGHT(1984)

Liam Redford
ADVENTURESS, THE(1946, Brit.)

Robert Redford
WAY WE WERE, THE(1973); WAR HUNT(1962); INSIDE DAISY CLOVER(1965); SITUATION HOPELESS–BUT NOT SERIOUS(1965); CHASE, THE(1966); THIS PROPERTY IS CONDEMNED(1966); BAREFOOT IN THE PARK(1967); BUTCH CASSIDY AND THE SUNDANCE KID(1969); DOWNHILL RACER(1969); TELL THEM WILLIE BOY IS HERE(1969); LITTLE FAUSS AND BIG HALSY(1970); CANDIDATE, THE(1972); HOT ROCK, THE(1972); JEREMIAH JOHNSON(1972); STING, THE(1973); GREAT GATSBY, THE(1974); GREAT WALDO PEPPER, THE(1975); THREE DAYS OF THE CONDOR(1975); ALL THE PRESIDENT'S MEN(1976); BRIDGE TOO FAR, A(1977, Brit.); ELECTRIC HORSEMAN, THE(1979); BRUBAKER(1980); ORDINARY PEOPLE(1980), d
1984
NATURAL, THE(1984)

Charles Redgie
HAPPY EVER AFTER(1932, Ger./Brit.); LE DENIER MILLIARDAIRE(1934, Fr.)

Rockets Redglare
1984
STRANGER THAN PARADISE(1984, U.S./Ger.)

Corin Redgrave
CROOKS IN CLOISTERS(1964, Brit.); MAN FOR ALL SEASONS, A(1966, Brit.); DEADLY AFFAIR, THE(1967, Brit.); CHARGE OF THE LIGHT BRIGADE, THE(1968, Brit.); GIRL WITH A PISTOL, THE(1968, Ital.); MAGUS, THE(1968, Brit.); OH! WHAT A LOVELY WAR(1969, Brit.); DAVID COPPERFIELD(1970, Brit.); VON RICHTHOFEN AND BROWN(1970); VACATION, THE(1971, Ital.); WHEN EIGHT BELLS

TOLL(1971, Brit.); EXCALIBUR(1981); EUREKA(1983, Brit.); WAGNER(1983, Brit./Hung./Aust.)

Jeannette Redgrave
YOU CAN'T DO WITHOUT LOVE(1946, Brit.)

Lynn Redgrave
TOM JONES(1963, Brit.); GIRL WITH GREEN EYES(1964, Brit.); GEORGY GIRL(1966, Brit.); DEADLY AFFAIR, THE(1967, Brit.); SMASHING TIME(1967 Brit.); VIRGIN SOLDIERS, THE(1970, Brit.); EVERY LITTLE CROOK AND NANNY(1972); EVERYTHING YOU ALWAYS WANTED TO KNOW ABOUT SEX, BUT WE'RE AFRAID TO ASK(1972); NATIONAL HEALTH, OR NURSE NORTON'S AFFAIR, THE(1973, Brit.); DON'T TURN THE OTHER CHEEK(1974, Ital./Ger./Span.); HAPPY HOOKER, THE(1975); BIG BUS, THE(1976); SUNDAY LOVERS(1980, Ital./Fr.)

Michael Redgrave
SECRET AGENT, THE(1936, Brit.); CLIMBING HIGH(1938, Brit.); LADY VANISHES, THE(1938, Brit.); STOLEN LIFE(1939, Brit.); STARS LOOK DOWN, THE(1940, Brit.); ATLANTIC FERRY(1941, Brit.); GIRL IN DISTRESS(1941, Brit.); BIG BLOCKADE, THE(1942, Brit.); LADY IN DISTRESS(1942, Brit.); REMARKABLE MR. KIPPS(1942, Brit.); THUNDER ROCK(1944, Brit.); JOHNNY IN THE CLOUDS(1945, Brit.); DEAD OF NIGHT(1946, Brit.); FAME IS THE SPUR(1947, Brit.); MOURNING BECOMES ELECTRA(1947); YEARS BETWEEN, THE(1947, Brit.); CAPTIVE HEART, THE(1948, Brit.); SECRET BEYOND THE DOOR(1948); SMUGGLERS, THE(1948, Brit.); BROWNING VERSION, THE(1951, Brit.); IMPORTANCE OF BEING EARNEST, THE(1952, Brit.); MAGIC BOX, THE(1952, Brit.); GREEN SCARF, THE(1954, Brit.); DAM BUSTERS, THE(1955, Brit.); NIGHT MY NUMBER CAME UP, THE(1955, Brit.); SEA SHALL NOT HAVE THEM, THE(1955, Brit.); OH ROSALINDA(1956, Brit.); 1984(1956, Brit.); HAPPY ROAD, THE(1957); TIME WITHOUT PITY(1957, Brit.); BEHIND THE MASK(1958, Brit.); LAW AND DISORDER(1958, Brit.); QUIET AMERICAN, THE(1958); SHAKE HANDS WITH THE DEVIL(1959, Ireland); WRECK OF THE MARY DEAR, THE(1959); INNOCENTS, THE(1961, U.S.); LONELINESS OF THE LONG DISTANCE RUNNER, THE(1962, Brit.); MR. ARKADIN(1962, Brit./Fr./Span.); NO, MY DARLING DAUGHTER(1964, Brit.); HEROES OF TELEMARK, THE(1965, Brit.); HILL, THE(1965, Brit.); YOUNG CASSIDY(1965, U.S./Brit.); 25TH HOUR, THE(1967, Fr./Ital./Yugo.); ASSIGNMENT K(1968, Brit.); BATTLE OF BRITAIN, THE(1969, Brit.); GOODBYE MR. CHIPS(1969, U.S./Brit.); OH! WHAT A LOVELY WAR(1969, Brit.); DAVID COPPERFIELD(1970, Brit.); GOODBYE GEMINI(1970, Brit.); CONNECTING ROOMS(1971, Brit.); GO-BETWEEN, THE(1971, Brit.); NICHOLAS AND ALEXANDRA(1971, Brit.); UNCLE VANYA(1977, Brit.)

Vanessa Redgrave
BEHIND THE MASK(1958, Brit.); BLOW-UP(1966, Brit.); MAN FOR ALL SEASONS, A(1966, Brit.); MORGAN!(1966, Brit.); CAMELOT(1967); SAILOR FROM GIBRALTAR, THE(1967, Brit.); CHARGE OF THE LIGHT BRIGADE, THE(1968, Brit.); ISADORA(1968, Brit.); SEA GULL, THE(1968); OH! WHAT A LOVELY WAR(1969, Brit.); QUIET PLACE IN THE COUNTRY, A(1970, Ital./Fr.); MARY, QUEEN OF SCOTS(1971, Brit.); TROJAN WOMEN, THE(1971); VACATION, THE(1971, Ital.); MURDER ON THE ORIENT EXPRESS(1974, Brit.); OUT OF SEASON(1975, Brit.); JULIA(1977); SEVEN-PER-CENT SOLUTION, THE(1977, Brit.); AGATHA(1979, Brit.); YANKS(1979); BEAR ISLAND(1980, Brit.-Can.); WAGNER(1983, Brit./Hung./Aust.)
1984
BOSTONIANS, THE(1984)
Misc. Talkies
DEVILS, THE(1971)

Riccardo Redi
HAWKS AND THE SPARROWS, THE(1967, Ital.)

John Redick
CAREER GIRL(1960)

Juli Reding
TORMENTED(1960)

Julie Reding
WHY MUST I DIE?(1960)
Misc. Talkies
MISSION IN MOROCCO(1959)

Donald Redinger
MIDNIGHT(1983), p

Julie Redings
VICE RAID(1959)

Dagmar Redinova
INTIMATE LIGHTING(1969, Czech.)

Forest Redlich
HIGH ROLLING(1977, Aus.), w

Ricky Redlich
FAST TIMES AT RIDGEMONT HIGH(1982)

Dwayne Redlin
CAT, THE(1966)

William Redlin
THIRD OF A MAN(1962), p; TIME TRAVELERS, THE(1964), p; CAT, THE(1966), w

Amanda Redman
RICHARD'S THINGS(1981, Brit.)
1984
GIVE MY REGARDS TO BROAD STREET(1984, Brit.)

Anthony Redman
THUNDER AND LIGHTNING(1977), ed; EYE FOR AN EYE, AN(1981), ed; INCREDIBLE SHRINKING WOMAN, THE(1981), ed; LONE WOLF McQUADE(1983), ed
1984
FEAR CITY(1984), ed

Crispin Redman
1984
ANOTHER COUNTRY(1984, Brit.)

Dick Redman
SECOND FIDDLE(1939)

Frank L. Redman
TWO THOROUGHBREDS(1939), ph

Frank Redman
CRASHING HOLLYWOOD(1937), ph; I'M FROM THE CITY(1938), ph; LITTLE ORPHAN ANNIE(1938), ph; MAID'S NIGHT OUT(1938), ph; SAINT IN NEW YORK, THE(1938), ph; BAD LANDS(1939), ph; BEAUTY FOR THE ASKING(1939), ph; CAREER(1939), ph; CONSPIRACY(1939), ph; SAINT STRIKES BACK, THE(1939), ph; ANNE OF WINDY POPLARS(1940), ph; MARINES FLY HIGH, THE(1940), ph; MEN AGAINST THE SKY(1940), ph; TOO MANY GIRLS(1940), ph; ALONG THE RIO GRANDE(1941), ph; LOOK WHO'S LAUGHING(1941), ph; PLAYMATES(1941), ph; GREAT GILDERSLEEVE, THE(1942), ph; HERE WE GO AGAIN(1942), ph; SING

YOUR WORRIES AWAY(1942), ph; FALCON IN DANGER, THE(1943), ph; GOVERN-MENT GIRL(1943), ph; LADY TAKES A CHANCE, A(1943), ph; PETTICOAT LARCE-NY(1943), ph; THIS LAND IS MINE(1943), ph; FALCON IN MEXICO, THE(1944), ph; FALCON OUT WEST, THE(1944), ph; NIGHT OF ADVENTURE, A(1944), ph; DICK TRACY(1945), ph; HAVING WONDERFUL CRIME(1945), ph; MAN ALIVE(1945), ph; PAN-AMERICANA(1945), ph; PATRICK THE GREAT(1945), ph; SING YOUR WAY HOME(1945), ph; BAMBOO BLONDE, THE(1946), ph; CRIMINAL COURT(1946), ph; DING DONG WILLIAMS(1946), ph; FALCON'S ADVENTURE, THE(1946), ph; FAL-CON'S ALIBI, THE(1946), ph; SAN QUENTIN(1946), ph; STEP BY STEP(1946), ph; SUNSET PASS(1946), ph; TRUTH ABOUT MURDER, THE(1946), ph; BEAT THE BAND(1947), ph; DICK TRACY MEETS GRUESOME(1947), ph; DICK TRACY'S DILEMMA(1947), ph; WILD HORSE MESA(1947), ph; IF YOU KNEW SUSIE(1948), ph; LADIES OF THE CHORUS(1948), ph; SHED NO TEARS(1948), ph; DOUBLE DEAL(1950), ph; PACE THAT THRILLS, THE(1952), ph
Silents
EYES OF THE UNDERWORLD(1929), ph
Fred Redman
SAINT TAKES OVER, THE(1940), ph; POWDER TOWN(1942), ph
George Redman
Silents
MONTY WORKS THE WIRES(1921, Brit.), p; HEAD OF THE FAMILY, THE(1922, Brit.), p; SKIPPER'S WOOING, THE(1922, Brit.), p; MONKEY'S PAW, THE(1923, Brit.), p
Joyce Redman
ONE OF OUR AIRCRAFT IS MISSING(1942, Brit.); SPELL OF AMY NUGENT, THE(1945, Brit.); TOM JONES(1963, Brit.); OTHELLO(1965, Brit.); PRUDENCE AND THE PILL(1968, Brit.)
Lee Redman
PLUNDERERS OF PAINTED FLATS(1959); TANK COMMANDOS(1959)
Malcolm Redman
LEO THE LAST(1970, Brit.)
Marcia Redman
LEO THE LAST(1970, Brit.)
Minna Redman
Silents
CHARM SCHOOL, THE(1921); RAGS TO RICHES(1922); STEPPING FAST(1923); SUPREME TEST, THE(1923)
Misc. Silents
DANGER AHEAD(1921); BORDER VENGENCE(1925); ACE OF CLUBS, THE(1926)
Renee Redman
PANIC IN THE CITY(1968)
Robert Redman
LEO THE LAST(1970, Brit.)
Tony Redman
DATE WITH DEATH, A(1959); FAST CHARLIE... THE MOONBEAM RIDER(1979), ed
Willie Redman
MACK, THE(1973)
Danny Redmon
ROLLOVER(1981)
Douglas Redmond
Silents
DOLL'S HOUSE, A(1918); GUILTY OF LOVE(1920); LOVE'S PENALTY(1921)
Douglas Redmond, Jr.
Silents
APPEARANCE OF EVIL(1918)
Frank Redmond
DOUBLE DANGER(1938), ph; FUGITIVES FOR A NIGHT(1938), ph; YOU'LL FIND OUT(1940), ph; EIGER SANCTION, THE(1975)
Granville Redmond
Silents
KID, THE(1921)
Harry Redmond
LITTLE WOMEN(1933), spec eff; LAST DAYS OF POMPEII, THE(1935), spec eff; JACK LONDON(1943), spec eff; DARK WATERS(1944), spec eff; HAIRY APE, THE(1944), spec eff
Harry Redmond, Jr.
ANGEL ON MY SHOULDER(1946), spec eff; RAMROD(1947), ph; DONOVAN'S BRAIN(1953), spec eff; GOG(1954), spec eff; RIDERS TO THE STARS(1954), spec eff
John Redmond
WE DIVE AT DAWN(1943, Brit.)
Liam Redmond
CAPTAIN BOYCOTT(1947, Brit.); DAUGHTER OF DARKNESS(1948, Brit.); SAINTS AND SINNERS(1949, Brit.); SWORD IN THE DESERT(1949); TWENTY QUESTIONS MURDER MYSTERY, THE(1950, Brit.); HIGH TREASON(1951, Brit.); GENTLE GUNMAN, THE(1952, Brit.); CRUEL SEA, THE(1953); DEVIL ON HORSEBACK(1954, Brit.); FINAL APPOINTMENT(1954, Brit.); PASSING STRANGER, THE(1954, Brit.); TONIGHT'S THE NIGHT(1954, Brit.); DIVIDED HEART, THE(1955, Brit.); GLASS TOMB, THE(1955, Brit.); BLONDE SINNER(1956, Brit.); JACQUELINE(1956, Brit.); SAFARI(1956); 23 PACES TO BAKER STREET(1956); LONG HAUL, THE(1957, Brit.); CURSE OF THE DEMON(1958); DESERT ATTACK(1958, Brit.); DIPLOMATIC CORPSE, THE(1958, Brit.); ROONEY(1958, Brit.); BOY AND THE BRIDGE, THE(1959, Brit.); SCENT OF MYSTERY(1960); UNDER TEN FLAGS(1960, U.S./Ital.); ALIVE AND KICKING(1962, Brit.); KID GALAHAD(1962); PHANTOM OF THE OPERA, THE(1962, Brit.); SHE DIDN'T SAY NO!(1962, Brit.); VALIANT, THE(1962, Brit./Ital.); PLAYBOY OF THE WESTERN WORLD, THE(1963, Ireland); LUCK OF GINGER COFFEY, THE(1964, U.S./Can.); NO TREE IN THE STREET(1964, Brit.); AMOROUS ADVENTURES OF MOLL FLANDERS, THE(1965); GHOST AND MR. CHICKEN, THE(1966); TOBRUK(1966); ADVENTURES OF BULLWHIP GRIFFIN, THE(1967); LAST SAFARI, THE(1967, Brit.); SKY BIKE, THE(1967, Brit.); 25TH HOUR, THE(1967, Fr./Ital./Yugo.); ALF 'N' FAMILY(1968, Brit.); DAVID COPPERFIELD(1970, Brit.)
Misc. Talkies
PHILADELPHIA HERE I COME(1975)
Marge Redmond
SANCTUARY(1961); FORTUNE COOKIE, THE(1966); TROUBLE WITH ANGELS, THE(1966); ADAM AT 6 A.M.(1970); JOHNNY GOT HIS GUN(1971); FAMILY PLOT(1976)

Mary Redmond
Silents
MY DAD(1922)
Moira Redmond
DOCTOR IN LOVE(1960, Brit.); PIT OF DARKNESS(1961, Brit.); FREUD(1962); KILL OR CURE(1962, Brit.); NIGHTMARE(1963, Brit.); SHOT IN THE DARK, A(1964); JIG SAW(1965, Brit.); SHARE OUT, THE(1966, Brit.); VIOLENT MOMENT(1966, Brit.); WINTER'S TALE, THE(1968, Brit.); LIMBO LINE, THE(1969, Brit.); MARRIAGE OF CONVENIENCE(1970, Brit.)
Misc. Talkies
PARTNERS IN CRIME(1961, Brit.)
Maurice Redmund
Silents
SQUIBS' HONEYMOON(1926, Brit.)
Redon
BATTLE OF THE RAILS(1949, Fr.)
Jean Redon
BACK TO THE WALL(1959, Fr.), w; HORROR CHAMBER OF DR. FAUSTUS, THE(1962, Fr./Ital.), w
Anthony Redondo
HOW TO BE VERY, VERY, POPULAR(1955)
Emiliano Redondo
ANTONY AND CLEOPATRA(1973, Brit.); LOVE AND PAIN AND THE WHOLE DAMN THING(1973); TREASURE OF THE FOUR CROWNS(1983, Span./U.S.)
Emilio Redondo
NARCO MEN, THE(1969, Span./Ital.)
Modesto Perez Redondo
HOUSE OF PSYCHOTIC WOMEN, THE zero(1973, Span.), p
Patricia Redpath
RODEO RHYTHM(1941)
Phil Redrow
1984
BODY DOUBLE(1984)
Willy Redstone
FLYING DOCTOR, THE(1936, Aus.), m
Redwing
JAGUAR(1956)
Silents
SQUAW MAN, THE(1914)
Rod Redwing
RAINBOW ISLAND(1944); WE WERE STRANGERS(1949); KIM(1950); LITTLE BIG HORN(1951); BUFFALO BILL IN TOMAHAWK TERRITORY(1952); HELL-GATE(1952); LAST OF THE COMANCHES(1952); SAGINAW TRAIL(1953); COPPER SKY(1957)
Rodd Redwing
SONORA STAGECOACH(1944); SINGIN' IN THE CORN(1946); LAST ROUND-UP, THE(1947); PATHFINDER, THE(1952); CONQUEST OF COCHISE(1953); NAKED JUNGLE, THE(1953); WINNING OF THE WEST(1953); CATTLE QUEEN OF MON-TANA(1954); CREATURE FROM THE BLACK LAGOON(1954); ELEPHANT WALK(1954); MOLE PEOPLE, THE(1956); FLAME BARRIER, THE(1958); FLAMING STAR(1960); HELLER IN PINK TIGHTS(1960); ONE-EYED JACKS(1961), tech adv; SERGEANTS 3(1962); JOHNNY RENO(1966); SHALAKO(1968, Brit.); CHARRO(1969)
Roderic Redwing
APACHE CHIEF(1949)
Rodric Redwing
STORY OF DR. WASSELL, THE(1944); OBJECTIVE, BURMA!(1945); OUT OF THE DEPTHS(1946); KEY LARGO(1948); SONG OF INDIA(1949); RANCHO NOTORI-OUS(1952); FLIGHT TO TANGIER(1953)
John Henry Redwood
PORKY'S(1982)
Manning Redwood
SHINING, THE(1980); OUTLAND(1981); SHOCK TREATMENT(1981); NEVER SAY NEVER AGAIN(1983)
Vicky Redwood
BIG CITY, THE(1963, India)
Captain Harry Ree
SCHOOL FOR DANGER(1947, Brit.)
Ma Ree
NIGHT IN HONG KONG, A(1961, Jap.)
Max Ree
BARKER, THE(1928), cos; SHOW GIRL(1928), cos; BROADWAY BABIES(1929), cos; MAN AND THE MOMENT, THE(1929); NIGHT PARADE(1929, Brit.), art d; RIO RITA(1929), art d&cos; SIDE STREET(1929), cos; STREET GIRL(1929), cos; TANNED LEGS(1929), art d; VAGABOND LOVER(1929), art d; VERY IDEA, THE(1929), art d; WEARY RIVER(1929), cos; BEAU BANDIT(1930), art d; INSIDE THE LINES(1930), art d; LEATHERNECKING(1930), art d; LOVIN' THE LADIES(1930), art d; PAY OFF, THE(1930), art d; SHE'S MY WEAKNESS(1930), art d; SHOOTING STRAIGHT(1930), art d; SILVER HORDE, THE(1930), art d; CIMARRON(1931), art d & cos; SECRET SERVICE(1931), art d; GIRL CRAZY(1932), art d; LOST SQUADRON, THE(1932), cos; WAY BACK HOME(1932), art d; MIDSUMMER'S NIGHT'S DREAM, A(1935), cos
Silents
SCARLET LETTER, THE(1926), cos; STOLEN BRIDE, THE(1927), cos; WEDDING MARCH, THE(1927), cos; QUEEN KELLY(1929), cos
Bob Reece
CAPTAIN MILKSHAKE(1970)
Brian Reece
CASE FOR PC 49, A(1951, Brit.); FAST AND LOOSE(1954, Brit.); WEE GEOR-DIE(1956, Brit.); CARRY ON ADMIRAL(1957, Brit.); ORDERS ARE ORDERS(1959, Brit.); WATCH IT, SAILOR!(1961, Brit.)
Cornelius Reece
COWBOY STAR, THE(1936), w
Dizzy Reece
NOWHERE TO GO(1959, Brit.), m
Edward Reece, Jr.
SHEBA BABY(1975)
Kathryn Reece
ANIMAL CRACKERS(1930)

Robert G. Reece
EAGLE HAS LANDED, THE(1976, Brit.)

Robert Reece
CRAZY MAMA(1975)
Misc. Talkies
PRISONERS(1975)

Ruth Reece
GENTLEMAN FROM ARIZONA, THE(1940)

Simon Reece
1984
VIGIL(1984, New Zealand), ed; WILD HORSES(1984, New Zealand), ed

Adam Reed
SIDELONG GLANCES OF A PIGEON KICKER, THE(1970); LADY LIBERTY(1972, Ital./Fr.); SMILE(1975)

Alan Reed
DAYS OF GLORY(1944); POSTMAN ALWAYS RINGS TWICE, THE(1946); EMER-GENCY WEDDING(1950); PERFECT STRANGERS(1950); REDHEAD AND THE COWBOY, THE(1950); HERE COMES THE GROOM(1951); ACTORS AND SIN(1952); VIVA ZAPATA!(1952); GERALDINE(1953); I, THE JURY(1953); WOMAN'S WORLD(1954); DESPERATE HOURS, THE(1955); FAR HORIZONS, THE(1955); KISS OF FIRE(1955); LADY AND THE TRAMP(1955); HE LAUGHED LAST(1956); REVOLT OF MAMIE STOVER, THE(1956); TIMETABLE(1956); TARNISHED ANGELS, THE(1957); MARJORIE MORNINGSTAR(1958); 1001 ARABIAN NIGHTS(1959); SEN-IORS, THE(1978)

Alan "Falstaff Openshaw" Reed
NOB HILL(1945)

Alan Reed, Jr.
ROCK, PRETTY BABY(1956); PEYTON PLACE(1957); GOING STEADY(1958); NEW INTERNS, THE(1964)

Alan Reed, Sr.
BREAKFAST AT TIFFANY'S(1961); MAN CALLED FLINTSTONE, THE(1966); DREAM OF KINGS, A(1969)

Alana Reed
FIRST NUDIE MUSICAL, THE(1976)

Albert Reed
AIRPORT(1970); WHERE DOES IT HURT?(1972)

Alexander B. Reed
1984
UNFAITHFULLY YOURS(1984)

Allen Reed
SHINBONE ALLEY(1971)

April Reed
SHARKY'S MACHINE(1982)

Art Reed
GOLD(1932), ph; FRONTIER JUSTICE(1936), ph; LUCKY TERROR(1936), ph; SWIFTY(1936), ph; TENDERFOOT GOES WEST, A(1937), ph; FIGHTING RENE-GADE(1937), ph; FLAMING LEAD(1939), ph; SIX-GUN RHYTHM(1939), ph; DEATH RIDES THE RANGE(1940), ph; EAST SIDE KIDS(1940), ph; STRAIGHT SHOO-TER(1940), ph; BABY FACE MORGAN(1942), ph; BLACK DRAGONS(1942), ph; CORPSE VANISHES, THE(1942), ph; LET'S GET TOUGH(1942), ph; MR. WISE GUY(1942), ph; GHOST OF HIDDEN VALLEY(1946), ph

Arthur Reed
GIRL IN THE SHOW, THE(1929), ph; MADAME X(1929), ph; UTAH KID, THE(1930), ph; ALIAS THE BAD MAN(1931), ph; DRUMS OF JEOPARDY(1931), ph; FIGHTING THRU(1931), ph; RANGE LAW(1931), ph; POCATELLO KID(1932), ph; SUNSET TRAIL(1932), ph; HONG KONG NIGHTS(1935), ph; MURDER BY TELEVI-SION(1935), ph; RED BLOOD OF COURAGE(1935), ph; WILDERNESS MAIL(1935), ph; PHANTOM PATROL(1936), ph; SONG OF THE TRAIL(1936), ph; WILDCAT TROOPER(1936), ph; DARK MANHATTAN(1937), ph; RANGER COURAGE(1937), ph; WILD HORSE ROUND-UP(1937), ph; WITH LOVE AND KISSES(1937), ph; BORN TO FIGHT(1938), ph; HELD FOR RANSOM(1938), ph; I COVER CHINATOWN(1938), ph; GIRLS' TOWN(1942), ph
Silents
MORGAN'S LAST RAID(1929), ph; OVERLAND TELEGRAPH, THE(1929), ph; SI-OUX BLOOD(1929), ph

Barbara Reed
DEATH VALLEY(1946); MISSING LADY, THE(1946); SHADOW RETURNS, THE(1946); GINGER(1947); KEY WITNESS(1947); CORONER CREEK(1948)

Barry Reed
VERDICT, THE(1982), w

Bernard Reed
TROUBLEMAKER, THE(1964)

Beverlee Reed
1984
IRRECONCILABLE DIFFERENCES(1984)

Bika Reed
MAYA(1982), m

Billy Edward Reed
MEXICAN SPITFIRE'S BLESSED EVENT(1943)

Billy Reed
CARDINAL, THE(1963)

Bob Reed
SUPER SPOOK(1975)
Silents
KILTIES THREE(1918, Brit.); REST CURE, THE(1923, Brit.)
Misc. Silents
HOW COULD YOU UNCLE?(1918, Brit.); RUSSIA - LAND OF TOMORROW(1919, Brit.)

Booty Reed
NEW YORK, NEW YORK(1977)

Bruce Reed
LORDS OF FLATBUSH, THE(1974); FADE TO BLACK(1980)

Bunny Reed
THEATRE OF BLOOD(1973, Brit.)

Carol Reed
IT HAPPENED IN PARIS(1935, Brit.), d; LABURNUM GROVE(1936, Brit.), d; TALK OF THE DEVIL(1937, Brit.), d, w; WHO'S YOUR LADY FRIEND?(1937, Brit.), d; BANK HOLIDAY(1938, Brit.), d; CLIMBING HIGH(1938, Brit.), d; NO PAR-KING(1938, Brit.), w; PENNY PARADISE(1938, Brit.), d; NIGHT TRAIN(1940, Brit.), d; STARS LOOK DOWN, THE(1940, Brit.), d; GIRL IN THE NEWS(1941, Brit.), d;

GIRL MUST LIVE, A(1941, Brit.), d; REMARKABLE MR. KIPPS(1942, Brit.), d; YOUNG MR. PITT, THE(1942, Brit.), d; WAY AHEAD, THE(1945, Brit.), d; ODD MAN OUT(1947, Brit.), p&d; FALLEN IDOL, THE(1949, Brit.), p, d; THIRD MAN, THE(1950, Brit.), p, d; MEN OF THE SEA(1951, Brit.), d; OUTCAST OF THE IS-LANDS(1952, Brit.), d; MAN BETWEEN, THE(1953, Brit.), p&d; KID FOR TWO FARTHINGS, A(1956, Brit.), p&d; TRAPEZE(1956), d; KEY, THE(1958, Brit.), d; OUR MAN IN HAVANA(1960, Brit.), p&d; RUNNING MAN, THE(1963, Brit.), p&d; AGO-NY AND THE ECSTASY, THE(1965), p&d; OLIVER!(1968, Brit.), d; FLAP(1970), d; PUBLIC EYE, THE(1972, Brit.), d

Caroline Reed
1984
CANNONBALL RUN II(1984)

Charles Reed
HOW TO STUFF A WILD BIKINI(1965)

Clarence Reed
Misc. Talkies
DAUGHTER OF THE CONGO, A(1930)

Dan Reed
H.O.T.S.(1979)

Daniel Reed
YOUNG MAN OF MANHATTAN(1930), w; FOG OVER FRISCO(1934), d; MAYBE IT'S LOVE(1935), w

David Reed
YOUTH ON TRIAL(1945); GAS HOUSE KIDS(1946); MURDER IS MY BUSI-NESS(1946); WHAT'S UP FRONT(1964); DEADWOOD'76(1965); RAT FINK(1965); TALES OF A SALESMAN(1965)

Dean Reed
BOUNTY HUNTERS, THE(1970, Ital.); ADIOS SABATA(1971, Ital./Span.)

Deborah Reed
MONDAY'S CHILD(1967, U.S., Arg.)

Diana J. Reed
OEDIPUS THE KING(1968, Brit.)

Diana Reed
Silents
JESSE JAMES AS THE OUTLAW(1921); JESSE JAMES UNDER THE BLACK FLAG(1921)

Dolores Reed
HIT AND RUN(1957); PARTY GIRL(1958); INVASION OF THE STAR CREATU-RES(1962)

Don Reed
JUVENILE COURT(1938); FORTUNE COOKIE, THE(1966); TRACKDOWN(1976)

Donald Reed
SHOW GIRL(1928); EVANGELINE(1929); MOST IMMORAL LADY, A(1929); LITTLE JOHNNY JONES(1930); TEXAN, THE(1930); MAN FROM MON-TEREY, THE(1933); RACING STRAIN, THE(1933); HAPPY LANDING(1934); UNCER-TAIN LADY(1934); CYCLONE RANGER(1935); DEVIL IS A WOMAN, THE(1935); ONE RAINY AFTERNOON(1936); CRUSADE AGAINST RACKETS(1937); FIREFLY, THE(1937); LAW AND LEAD(1937); RENFREW OF THE ROYAL MOUNTED(1937); SPECIAL AGENT K-7(1937); UNDER STRANGE FLAGS(1937)
Misc. Talkies
PLAYTHINGS OF HOLLYWOOD(1931); SIX GUN JUSTICE(1935)
Silents
CONVOY(1927); NIGHT WATCH, THE(1928); EVANGELINE(1929); HARD-BOILED(1929)
Misc. Silents
NAUGHTY BUT NICE(1927); MAD HOUR(1928)

Donna Reed
BABES ON BROADWAY(1941); BUGLE SOUNDS, THE(1941); GET-AWAY, THE(1941); SHADOW OF THE THIN MAN(1941); APACHE TRAIL(1942); CALLING DR. GILLESPIE(1942); COURTSHIP OF ANDY HARDY, THE(1942); EYES IN THE NIGHT(1942); MOKEY(1942); DR. GILLESPIE'S CRIMINAL CASE(1943); HUMAN COMEDY, THE(1943); MAN FROM DOWN UNDER, THE(1943); THOUSANDS CHEER(1943); GENTLE ANNIE(1944); SEE HERE, PRIVATE HARGROVE(1944); PICTURE OF DORIAN GRAY, THE(1945); THEY WERE EXPENDABLE(1945); FAITHFUL IN MY FASHION(1946); IT'S A WONDERFUL LIFE(1946); GREEN DOLPHIN STREET(1947); BEYOND GLORY(1948); CHICAGO DEADLINE(1949); SATURDAY'S HERO(1951); HANGMAN'S KNOT(1952); SCANDAL SHEET(1952); CADDY, THE(1953); FROM HERE TO ETERNITY(1953); GUN FURY(1953); RAIDERS OF THE SEVEN SEAS(1953); TROUBLE ALONG THE WAY(1953); LAST TIME I SAW PARIS, THE(1954); THEY RODE WEST(1954); THREE HOURS TO KILL(1954); FAR HORIZONS, THE(1955); BACKLASH(1956); BENNY GOODMAN STORY, THE(1956); RANSOM(1956); BEYOND MOMBASA(1957); WHOLE TRUTH, THE(1958, Brit.); RIDE LONESOME(1959); PEPE(1960)

Dorothy E. Reed
PIE IN THE SKY(1964), p

Ed Reed
PAPER MOON(1973)

Edmund Reed
MAN IN THE WATER, THE(1963)

Edwin E. Reed
Misc. Silents
BLUEBIRD, THE(1918)

Emma Reed
SECRET SERVICE(1931)

Eunice Reed
ENLIGHTEN THY DAUGHTER(1934)

Floyd Reed, Sr.
Misc. Talkies
DEATH RIDERS(1976)

Florence Reed
GREAT EXPECTATIONS(1934); FRANKIE AND JOHNNY(1936)
Silents
NEW YORK(1916); ETERNAL SIN, THE(1917); TODAY(1917)
Misc. Silents
AT BAY(1915); DANCING GIRL, THE(1915); HER OWN WAY(1915); WOMAN'S LAW, THE(1916); STRUGGLE EVERLASTING, THE(1918); WIVES OF MEN(1918); HER CODE OF HONOR(1919); HER GAME(1919); WOMAN UNDER OATH, THE(1919); BLACK PANTHER'S CUB, THE(1921); ETERNAL MOTHER, THE(1921); INDISCRETION(1921)

Gavin Reed
CARRY ON LOVING(1970, Brit.); TATTOO(1981); TOOTSIE(1982)
Misc. Talkies
BODY BENEATH, THE(1970)
Gayle Reed
JOHNNY ONE-EYE(1950); BECAUSE OF YOU(1952)
Gene Reed
CAPTAIN SINDBAD(1963), ch
Geoffrey Reed
FILE OF THE GOLDEN GOOSE, THE(1969, Brit.); MACBETH(1971, Brit.)
George H. Reed
JUDGE PRIEST(1934); GLASS KEY, THE(1935); SHOW BOAT(1936); WINGS OVER
HONOLULU(1937); JOSETTE(1938); TOY WIFE, THE(1938); DR. KILDARE GOES
HOME(1940); DR. KILDARE'S STRANGE CASE(1940); SPORTING BLOOD(1940); DR.
KILDARE'S VICTORY(1941); DR. KILDARE'S WEDDING DAY(1941); PEOPLE VS.
DR. KILDARE, THE(1941); DR. GILLESPIE'S NEW ASSISTANT(1942); TAKE A
LETTER, DARLING(1942); WE WERE DANCING(1942); HOME IN INDIANA(1944);
THREE MEN IN WHITE(1944); DANGEROUS PARTNERS(1945); STRANGE ILLU-
SION(1945)
Silents
HUCKLEBERRY FINN(1920)
George Reed
RIVER OF ROMANCE(1929); FATHER'S SON(1931); OVER THE HILL(1931); HOLD
YOUR MAN(1933); LAST TRAIL, THE(1934); MRS. WIGGS OF THE CABBAGE
PATCH(1934); TWENTIETH CENTURY(1934); RED SALUTE(1935); WINGS IN THE
DARK(1935); GORGEOUS HUSSY, THE(1936); GREEN PASTURES(1936); SARATO-
GA(1937); CITY GIRL(1938); KENTUCKY(1938); GOING PLACES(1939); SECRET OF
DR. KILDARE, THE(1939); SWANEE RIVER(1939); DR. KILDARE'S CRISIS(1940);
MANHATTAN HEARTBEAT(1940); MARYLAND(1940); GREAT LIE, THE(1941);
KISS THE BOYS GOODBYE(1941); IN THIS OUR LIFE(1942); REAP THE WILD
WIND(1942); TALES OF MANHATTAN(1942); THEY DIED WITH THEIR BOOTS
ON(1942); IS EVERYBODY HAPPY?(1943); MORE THE MERRIER, THE(1943);
SOMEONE TO REMEMBER(1943); HEAVENLY DAYS(1944); NOB HILL(1945);
SARATOGA TRUNK(1945); DARK DELUSION(1947); HOMESTRETCH, THE(1947);
SEA OF GRASS, THE(1947)
Misc. Talkies
TRAILS OF THE GOLDEN WEST(1931)
Silents
RED LIGHTS(1923); SCARS OF JEALOUSY(1923); HELEN'S BABIES(1924); ISLE OF
HOPE, THE(1925); ABSENT(1928)
Misc. Silents
CLEAN-UP MAN, THE(1928)
Gus Reed
MARY BURNS, FUGITIVE(1935); AND SO THEY WERE MARRIED(1936); NEW
YORK TOWN(1941); SULLIVAN'S TRAVELS(1941)
Hal Reed
DOBERMAN GANG, THE(1972)
Henry Reed
JOHN WESLEY(1954, Brit.), m
Hetty Langford Reed
Silents
QUEEN OF MY HEART(1917, Brit.), w
Ione Reed
WEST OF THE ROCKIES(1929); MELODY TRAIL(1935)
Silents
BUCKING THE TRUTH(1926)
Misc. Silents
CHASING TROUBLE(1926); DESPERATE CHANCE(1926); FIGHTING LUCK(1926);
ACROSS THE PLAINS(1928); TEXAS FLASH(1928); CAPTAIN COWBOY(1929); OK-
LAHOMA COWBOY, AN(1929); RIDERS OF THE STORM(1929); MAN FROM NO-
WHERE, THE(1930)
Ira Reed
HELL'S ANGELS(1930); HANDS ACROSS THE TABLE(1935)
J. Theodore Reed
THOSE WERE THE DAYS(1940), p&d; SONG OF MY HEART(1947), p
J.D. Reed
PURSUIT OF D.B. COOPER, THE(1981), w
J.T. Reed
LADY BE CAREFUL(1936), p&d
Jack Reed
HAPPY BIRTHDAY, DAVY(1970)
James Reed
TARZANA, THE WILD GIRL(1973), d
Jan Reed
JASON AND THE ARGONAUTS(1963, Brit.), w
Jared Reed
Misc. Talkies
BIG FUN CARNIVAL, THE(1957)
Jay Theodore Reed
WHAT A LIFE(1939), p&d; LIFE WITH HENRY(1941), p&d
Jerry Reed
W. W. AND THE DIXIE DANCEKINGS(1975); GATOR(1976); SMOKEY AND THE
BANDIT(1977), a, m; HIGH-BALLIN'(1978); HOT STUFF(1979); SMOKEY AND THE
BANDIT II(1980); SMOKEY AND THE BANDIT–PART 3(1983); SURVIVORS,
THE(1983)
Joel Reed
BLOOD BATH(1976), d&w
Joel M. Reed
NIGHT OF THE ZOMBIES(1981), a, d&w; BLOODSUCKING FREAKS(1982), d&w
Misc. Talkies
G.I. EXECUTIONER, THE(1971), d; CAREER BED(1972), d
John Reed
PLACE IN THE SUN, A(1951); MIKADO, THE(1967, Brit.)
Misc. Talkies
RUDDIGORE(1967, Brit.)
Misc. Silents
GAMBLE IN LIVES, A(1920, Brit.)

John F. Reed
FANTASIA(1940), spec eff
Joyce Reed
BALLAD OF A GUNFIGHTER(1964)
Katharine Reed
Silents
GREATER THAN FAME(1920), w
Katherine Reed
Silents
LORNA DOONE(1927), w
Kathy Reed
ASK ANY GIRL(1959)
Lady Reed
DOLEMITE(1975); HUMAN TORNADO, THE(1976); PETEY WHEATSTRAW(1978)
Langford Reed
DREYFUS CASE, THE(1931, Brit.), ed; HE SNOOPS TO CONQUER(1944, Brit.), w
Silents
LASS O' THE LOOMS, A(1919, Brit.), w; POTTER'S CLAY(1922, Brit.), w
Misc. Silents
CHASE ME CHARLIE(1918, Brit.), d
Larry Reed
HOLLYWOOD BARN DANCE(1947); SOME OF MY BEST FRIENDS ARE...(1971)
Les Reed
GIRL ON A MOTORCYCLE, THE(1968, Fr./Brit.), m; BUSHBABY, THE(1970), m;
ONE MORE TIME(1970, Brit.), m
Lewis Reed
TARZAN AND THE GREAT RIVER(1967, U.S./Switz.), w
Linda Reed
PARDON MY RHYTHM(1944); RECKLESS AGE(1944)
Lone Reed
FIRST YANK INTO TOKYO(1945)
Lou Reed
ONE-TRICK PONY(1980); GET CRAZY(1983)
Luther A. Reed
Silents
PAIR OF CUPIDS, A(1918), w; ALMOST MARRIED(1919), w; AMATEUR ADVEN-
TURESS, THE(1919), w
Luther Reed
RIO RITA(1929), d, w; DIXIANA(1930), d&w; HELL'S ANGELS(1930), d; HIT THE
DECK(1930), d&w; BACHELOR MOTHER(1933), w; SWEETHEART OF SIGMA
CHI(1933), w; CONVENTION GIRL(1935), d
Silents
IN FOR THIRTY DAYS(1919), w; BEAU REVEL(1921), w; ENCHANTMENT(1921),
w; LURE OF YOUTH, THE(1921), w; WHEN KNIGHTHOOD WAS IN FLOWER(1922),
w; ADAM AND EVA(1923), w; WOMANHANDLED(1925), w; ACE OF CADS,
THE(1926), d; KID BOOTS(1926), w; LET'S GET MARRIED(1926), w; EVENING
CLOTHES(1927), d; NEW YORK(1927), d
Misc. Silents
HONEYMOON HATE(1927), d; SHANGHAI BOUND(1927), d; WORLD AT HER
FEET, THE(1927), d; SAWDUST PARADISE, THE(1928), d
Lydia Reed
GOOD MORNING, MISS DOVE(1955); SEVEN LITTLE FOYS, THE(1955); HIGH
SOCIETY(1956); VAMPIRE, THE(1957)
Mark Reed
PETTICOAT FEVER(1936), w; YES, MY DARLING DAUGHTER(1939), w
Marshal Reed
LARAMIE TRAIL, THE(1944); SUNDOWN RIDERS(1948)
Marshall J. Reed
TEXAS CITY(1952)
Marshall Reed
DEATH VALLEY MANHUNT(1943); GUY NAMED JOE, A(1943); WAGON TRACKS
WEST(1943); GANGSTERS OF THE FRONTIER(1944); GHOST GUNS(1944); LAW
MEN(1944); LAW OF THE VALLEY(1944); MARSHAL OF RENO(1944); MOJAVE
FIREBRAND(1944); MY BUDDY(1944); PARTNERS OF THE TRAIL(1944); RANGE
LAW(1944); TEXAS KID, THE(1944); TUCSON RAIDERS(1944); DRIFTING
ALONG(1946); GENTLEMAN FROM TEXAS(1946); IN OLD SACRAMENTO(1946);
ANGEL AND THE BADMAN(1947); CHEYENNE TAKES OVER(1947); FIGHTING
VIGILANTES, THE(1947); LAND OF THE LAWLESS(1947); ON THE OLD SPANISH
TRAIL(1947); PRAIRIE EXPRESS(1947); RAIDERS OF THE SOUTH(1947); SONG OF
THE WASTELAND(1947); STAGE TO MESA CITY(1947); WYOMING(1947); BACK
TRAIL(1948); BOLD FRONTIERSMAN, THE(1948); COURTIN' TROUBLE(1948);
DEAD MAN'S GOLD(1948); FIGHTING RANGER, THE(1948); GALLANT LEGION,
THE(1948); HAWK OF POWDER RIVER, THE(1948); MARK OF THE LASH(1948);
PARTNERS OF THE SUNSET(1948); RANGERS RIDE, THE(1948); RENEGADES OF
SONORA(1948); SONG OF THE DRIFTER(1948); TORNADO RANGE(1948); BRAND
OF FEAR(1949); DALTON GANG, THE(1949); FRONTIER INVESTIGATOR(1949);
GUN RUNNER(1949); HIDDEN DANGER(1949); LAW OF THE WEST(1949); NAVAJO
TRAIL RAIDERS(1949); RIDERS OF THE DUSK(1949); ROARING WEST-
WARD(1949); SQUARE DANCE JUBILEE(1949); STAMPEDE(1949); WEST OF EL
DORADO(1949); WESTERN RENEGADES(1949); CHEROKEE UPRISING(1950);
COWBOY AND THE PRIZEFIGHTER(1950); HOT ROD(1950); I WAS A SHOPLIF-
TER(1950); LAW OF THE PANHANDLE(1950); OUTLAW GOLD(1950); OVER THE
BORDER(1950); RADAR SECRET SERVICE(1950); RIDER FROM TUCSON(1950);
SAVAGE HORDE, THE(1950); SILVER RAIDERS(1950); TEXAS DYNAMO(1950);
ABILENE TRAIL(1951); CANYON RAIDERS(1951); GUNPLAY(1951); HURRICANE
ISLAND(1951); LONGHORN, THE(1951); MONTANA DESPERADO(1951); NEVADA
BADMEN(1951); OH! SUSANNA(1951); OKLAHOMA JUSTICE(1951); PURPLE
HEART DIARY(1951); SAILOR BEWARE(1951); TEXAS LAWMEN(1951); WHIS-
TLING HILLS(1951); CANYON AMBUSH(1952); KANSAS TERRITORY(1952); LARA-
MIE MOUNTAINS(1952); LAWLESS COWBOYS(1952); LUSTY MEN, THE(1952);
NIGHT RAIDERS(1952); ROUGH, TOUGH WEST, THE(1952); SOUND OFF(1952);
COW COUNTRY(1953); ROSE MARIE(1954); NIGHT THE WORLD EXPLODED,
THE(1957); LINEUP, THE(1958); GHOST OF ZORRO(1959); THIRD OF A MAN(1962);
WILD WESTERNERS, THE(1962); FATE IS THE HUNTER(1964); THEY SAVED
HITLER'S BRAIN(1964); HALLELUJAH TRAIL, THE(1965); TIME FOR KILLING,
A(1967); HARD RIDE, THE(1971); TILL DEATH(1978)
Misc. Talkies
SHADOWS ON THE RANGE(1946); TRAILING DANGER(1947); TRIGGER-
MAN(1948)

Mary Reed
END OF THE AFFAIR, THE(1955, Brit.)
Max Reed
REVOLT OF MAMIE STOVER, THE(1956); MR. MAJESTYK(1974)
Maxwell Reed
DEAR MURDERER(1947, Brit.); YEARS BETWEEN, THE(1947, Brit.); BROTHERS, THE(1948, Brit.); DAUGHTER OF DARKNESS(1948, Brit.); DAYDREAK(1948, Brit.); NIGHT BEAT(1948, Brit.); SHOWTIME(1948, Brit.); MADNESS OF THE HEART(1949, Brit.); BLACKOUT(1950, Brit.); CLOUDED YELLOW, THE(1950, Brit.); LOST PEOPLE, THE(1950, Brit.); DARK MAN, THE(1951, Brit.); FLAME OF ARABY(1951); MARILYN(1953, Brit.); SEA DEVILS(1953); BRAIN MACHINE, THE(1955, Brit.); SQUARE RING, THE(1955, Brit.); HELEN OF TROY(1956, Ital); SHADOW OF FEAR(1956, Brit.); PIRATES OF TORTUGA(1961); NOTORIOUS LANDLADY, THE(1962); PICTURE MOMMY DEAD(1966)
Michael Reed
DEVIL'S BAIT(1959, Brit.), ph; UGLY DUCKLING, THE(1959, Brit.), ph; OCTOBER MOTH(1960, Brit.), ph; TRAITORS, THE(1963, Brit.), ph; DEVIL-SHIP PIRATES, THE(1964, Brit.), ph; GORGON, THE(1964, Brit.), ph; MOON-SPINNERS, THE(1964), ph; DRACULA–PRINCE OF DARKNESS(1966, Brit.), ph; PLEASURE GIRLS, THE(1966, Brit.), ph; RASPUTIN–THE MAD MONK(1966, Brit.), ph; MALPAS MYSTERY, THE(1967, Brit.), ph; PREHISTORIC WOMEN(1967, Brit.), ph; GUNS IN THE HEATHER(1968, Brit.), ph; TWO A PENNY(1968, Brit.), ph; ON HER MAJESTY'S SECRET SERVICE(1969, Brit.), ph; MC KENZIE BREAK, THE(1970), ph; VON RICHTHOFEN AND BROWN(1970), ph; GROUNDSTAR CONSPIRACY, THE(1972, Can.), ph; Z.P.G.(1972), ph; HIRELING, THE(1973, Brit.), ph; GALILEO(1975, Brit.), ph; HIDING PLACE, THE(1975), ph; NO LONGER ALONE(1978), ph; STICK UP, THE(1978, Brit.), ph; LOOPHOLE(1981, Brit.), ph
Mike Reed
ADDING MACHINE, THE(1969); SHOUT AT THE DEVIL(1976, Brit.), ph; PASSAGE, THE(1979, Brit.), ph
Moira Reed
HAIL AND FAREWELL(1936, Brit.); FATAL HOUR, THE(1937, Brit.); UNDER A CLOUD(1937, Brit.)
Myrtle Reed
MR. POTTS GOES TO MOSCOW(1953, Brit.); DELAYED ACTION(1954, Brit.); WEAPON, THE(1957, Brit.); CAST A DARK SHADOW(1958, Brit.); PLEASE TURN OVER(1960, Brit.); SNOWBALL(1960, Brit.); EYES OF ANNIE JONES, THE(1963, Brit.); PAIR OF BRIEFS, A(1963, Brit.); SLIPPER AND THE ROSE, THE(1976, Brit.)
Silents
LAVENDER AND OLD LACE(1921), w
Nora Reed
Silents
BEYOND PRICE(1921)
Misc. Silents
MIRACLE OF MANHATTAN, THE(1921)
Oliver Reed
HELLO LONDON(1958, Brit.); SQUARE PEG, THE(1958, Brit.); ANGRY SILENCE, THE(1960, Brit.); CALL ME GENIUS(1961, Brit.); CURSE OF THE WEREWOLF, THE(1961); HIS AND HERS(1961, Brit.); SWORD OF SHERWOOD FOREST(1961, Brit.); NIGHT CREATURES(1962, Brit.); PIRATES OF BLOOD RIVER, THE(1962, Brit.); PARANOIAC(1963, Brit.); CRIMSON BLADE, THE(1964, Brit.); BRIGAND OF KANDAHAR, THE(1965, Brit.); THESE ARE THE DAMNED(1965, Brit.); GIRL GETTERS, THE(1966, Brit.); PARTY'S OVER, THE(1966, Brit.); I'LL NEVER FORGET WHAT'S 'IS NAME(1967, Brit.); JOKERS, THE(1967, Brit.); TRAP, THE(1967, Can./Brit.); OLIVER!(1968, Brit.); SHUTTERED ROOM, THE(1968, Brit.); ASSASSINATION BUREAU, THE(1969, Brit.); HANNIBAL BROOKS(1969, Brit.); WOMEN IN LOVE(1969, Brit.); LADY IN THE CAR WITH GLASSES AND A GUN, THE(1970, U.S./Fr.); TAKE A GIRL LIKE YOU(1970, Brit,); SITTING TARGET(1972, Brit.); Z.P.G.(1972); BLUE BLOOD(1973, Brit.); TRIPLE ECHO, THE(1973, Brit.); MAHLER(1974, Brit.); THREE MUSKETEERS, THE(1974, Panama); BLOOD IN THE STREETS(1975, Ital./Fr.); FOUR MUSKETEERS, THE(1975); ROYAL FLASH(1975, Brit.); TEN LITTLE INDIANS(1975, Ital./Fr./Span./Ger.); TOMMY(1975, Brit.); BURNT OFFERINGS(1976); GREAT SCOUT AND CATHOUSE THURSDAY, THE(1976); SELL OUT, THE(1976); HUNTING PARTY, THE(1977, Brit.); MANIAC!(1977); BIG SLEEP, THE½(1978, Brit.); CLASS OF MISS MAC MICHAEL, THE(1978, Brit./U.S.); CROSSED SWORDS(1978); TOMORROW NEVER COMES(1978, Brit./Can.); BROOD, THE(1979, Can.); DR. HECKYL AND MR. HYPE(1980); CONDORMAN(1981); LION OF THE DESERT(1981, Libya/Brit.); VENOM(1982, Brit.); SPASMS(1983, Can.); STING II, THE(1983); TWO OF A KIND(1983)
Misc. Talkies
DEVILS, THE(1971); AGE OF PISCES(1972); ONE RUSSIAN SUMMER(1973)
Pamela Reed
LONG RIDERS, THE(1980); MELVIN AND HOWARD(1980); EYEWITNESS(1981); YOUNG DOCTORS IN LOVE(1982); RIGHT STUFF, THE(1983)
1984
GOODBYE PEOPLE, THE(1984)
Paul Reed
FITZWILLY(1967); RIDE TO HANGMAN'S TREE, THE(1967); DID YOU HEAR THE ONE ABOUT THE TRAVELING SALESLADY?(1968)
Philip Reed
IT'S A DEAL(1930); FEMALE(1933); FASHIONS OF 1934(1934); JIMMY THE GENT(1934); JOURNAL OF A CRIME(1934); MAYBE IT'S LOVE(1935); MADAME X(1937); MERRILY WE LIVE(1938); LITTLE MISS MOLLY(1940); ALOMA OF THE SOUTH SEAS(1941); WEEKEND FOR THREE(1941); GENTLEMAN AFTER DARK, A(1942); OLD ACQUAINTANCE(1943); PEOPLE ARE FUNNY(1945); HOT CARGO(1946); RENDEZVOUS WITH ANNIE(1946); I COVER BIG TOWN(1947); PIRATES OF MONTEREY(1947); SONG OF SCHEHERAZADE(1947); BODYGUARD(1948); UNKNOWN ISLAND(1948); DAUGHTER OF THE WEST(1949); MANHANDLED(1949); DAVY CROCKETT, INDIAN SCOUT(1950); TRIPOLI(1950); TAKE ME TO TOWN(1953); GIRL IN THE RED VELVET SWING, THE(1955); TATTERED DRESS, THE(1957); HARUM SCARUM(1965)
Phillip Reed
HOUSE ON 56TH STREET, THE(1933); AFFAIRS OF A GENTLEMAN(1934); BIG HEARTED HERBERT(1934); BRITISH AGENT(1934); DOCTOR MONICA(1934); GAMBLING LADY(1934); GLAMOUR(1934); LOST LADY, A(1934); REGISTERED NURSE(1934); ACCENT ON YOUTH(1935); CASE OF THE CURIOUS BRIDE, THE(1935); GIRL FROM TENTH AVENUE, THE(1935); SWEET MUSIC(1935); WOMAN IN RED, THE(1935); KLONDIKE ANNIE(1936); LAST OF THE MOHICANS, THE(1936); LUCKIEST GIRL IN THE WORLD, THE(1936); MURDER OF DR. HARRIGAN, THE(1936); HER SISTER'S SECRET(1946); BIG TOWN(1947); BIG TOWN AFTER DARK(1947);

SONG OF THE THIN MAN(1947); BIG TOWN SCANDAL(1948); BANDIT QUEEN(1950)
Ralph Reed
SINCE YOU WENT AWAY(1944); TWO DOLLAR BETTOR(1951); BECAUSE YOU'RE MINE(1952); HIGH NOON(1952); LONE STAR(1952); RED SKIES OF MONTANA(1952); SCANDAL SHEET(1952); SAGINAW TRAIL(1953); TORPEDO ALLEY(1953); ENEMY BELOW, THE(1957); NOT OF THIS EARTH(1957); REFORM SCHOOL GIRL(1957); TALL STRANGER, THE(1957); CRY BABY KILLER, THE(1958); LONG, HOT SUMMER, THE(1958); NORTH BY NORTHWEST(1959)
Rex Reed
SUPERMAN(1978); INCHON(1981)
1984
IRRECONCILABLE DIFFERENCES(1984)
Richard Reed
SEDUCTION, THE(1982)
Robbie Reed
TROUBLEMAKER, THE(1964); CHILD'S PLAY(1972)
Robert Reed
HUNTERS, THE(1958); BLOODLUST(1959); HURRY SUNDOWN(1967); JOURNEY INTO DARKNESS(1968, Brit.); STAR!(1968); MALTESE BIPPY, THE(1969); CONQUEST OF THE EARTH(1980)
Robert S. Reed
STREAMERS(1983)
Roland Reed
FIFTEEN WIVES(1934), ed; IN LOVE WITH LIFE(1934), ed; IN THE MONEY(1934), ed; STOLEN SWEETS(1934), ed; TWIN HUSBANDS(1934), ed; CIRCUMSTANTIAL EVIDENCE(1935), ed; GHOST WALKS, THE(1935), ed; GIRL WHO CAME BACK, THE(1935), ed; HAPPINESS C.O.D.(1935), ed; LADY IN SCARLET, THE(1935), ed; ONE IN A MILLION(1935), ed; PORT OF LOST DREAMS(1935), ed; PUBLIC OPINION(1935), ed; SHOT IN THE DARK, A(1935), ed; SOCIETY FEVER(1935), a, ed; WORLD ACCUSES, THE(1935), ed; DEATH FROM A DISTANCE(1936), ed; LITTLE RED SCHOOLHOUSE(1936), ed; MURDER AT GLEN ATHOL(1936), ed; RING AROUND THE MOON(1936), ed; TANGO(1936), ed; MESSENGER OF PEACE(1950), p
Misc. Talkies
IN PARIS, A.W.O.L.(1936), d
Roland C. Reed
SECRETS OF WU SIN(1932), ed
Roland D. Reed
CONDEMNED TO LIVE(1935), ed; FALSE PRETENSES(1935), ed; DARK HOUR, THE(1936), ed; EASY MONEY(1936), ed; HITCH HIKE TO HEAVEN(1936), ed; IT COULDN'T HAVE HAPPENED–BUT IT DID(1936), ed; LADY LUCK(1936), ed; THREE OF A KIND(1936), ed; HOUSE OF SECRETS, THE(1937), d; RED LIGHTS AHEAD(1937), d
Ronald Reed
SONS OF STEEL(1935), ed
Roxanne Reed
WOMEN OF PITCAIRN ISLAND, THE(1957)
Sandra Reed
BUS IS COMING, THE(1971)
Sandy Reed
FIREBALL 590(1966); THUNDER ALLEY(1967); SPEEDWAY(1968)
Misc. Talkies
TOUGH(1974)
Stanley Reed
WINSTANLEY(1979, Brit.)
Steven Reed
BABY, IT'S YOU(1983)
Susan Reed
GLAMOUR GIRL(1947)
Susanne Reed
UP FROM THE DEPTHS(1979, Phil.)
1984
KILLERS, THE(1984)
Taylor Reed
EASY MONEY(1983)
Ted Reed
Silents
KNICKERBOCKER BUCKAROO, THE(1919)
Theodora Reed
TROPIC HOLIDAY(1938), d
Theodore Reed
DOUBLE OR NOTHING(1937), d; I'M FROM MISSOURI(1939), d; HER FIRST BEAU(1941), d
Silents
NUT, THE(1921), d
Thomas Reed
NIGHT PEOPLE(1954), w
Toby Reed
ROUSTABOUT(1964)
Tom Reed
WATERLOO BRIDGE(1931), w; LONESOME(1928), w; CHARLATAN, THE(1929), w; LAST PERFORMANCE, THE(1929), w; LAST WARNING, THE(1929), w; PHANTOM OF THE OPERA, THE(1929), w; SCANDAL(1929), w; SHOW BOAT(1929), w; BOUDOIR DIPLOMAT(1930), w; EAST IS WEST(1930), w; HELL'S HEROES(1930), w; BAD SISTER(1931), w; HOMICIDE SQUAD(1931), w; LASCA OF THE RIO GRANDE(1931), w; RECKLESS LIVING(1931), w; AFRAID TO TALK(1932), w; LAW AND ORDER(1932), w; MURDERS IN THE RUE MORGUE(1932), w; RADIO PATROL(1932), w; LAUGHTER IN HELL(1933), w; S.O.S. ICEBERG(1933), w; BOMBAY MAIL(1934), w; MAN WITH TWO FACES, THE(1934), w; CASE OF THE CURIOUS BRIDE, THE(1935), w; FLORENTINE DAGGER, THE(1935), w; MARY JANE'S PA(1935), w; CASE OF THE VELVET CLAWS, THE(1936), w; LOVE BEGINS AT TWENTY(1936), w; CAPTAIN'S KID, THE(1937), w; GREAT O'MALLEY, THE(1937), w; MARRY THE GIRL(1937), w; DEAD END KIDS ON DRESS PARADE(1939), w; CALLING PHILO VANCE(1940), w; MAN WHO TALKED TOO MUCH, THE(1940), w; HELLO ANNAPOLIS(1942), w; LOVES OF EDGAR ALLAN POE, THE(1942), w; PITTSBURGH(1942), w; SPOILERS, THE(1942), w; TWO TICKETS TO LONDON(1943), w; UP IN MABEL'S ROOM(1944), w; MOSS ROSE(1947), w; SPIRIT OF WEST POINT, THE(1947), w; UNTAMED BREED, THE(1948), w; RED STALLION IN THE ROCKIES(1949), w; DAVID HARDING, COUNTERSPY(1950), w; LIGHT

TOUCH, THE(1951), w; SOLDIERS THREE(1951), w; BACK TO GOD'S COUN-
TRY(1953), w
Silents
ACQUITTAL, THE(1923), w; PHANTOM OF THE OPERA, THE(1925), t; LONE
EAGLE, THE(1927), t; PAINTED PONIES(1927), t; RAWHIDE KID, THE(1928), t;
RED LIPS(1928), t; STOP THAT MAN(1928), t; THANKS FOR THE BUGGY RI-
DE(1928), t

Toni Reed
CONVENTION GIRL(1935)

David Reed III
WHAT'S UP FRONT(1964), art d; DEADWOOD'76(1965), art d

Tracy Reed
DR. STRANGELOVE: OR HOW I LEARNED TO STOP WORRYING AND LOVE THE
BOMB(1964); SHOT IN THE DARK, A(1964); DEVILS OF DARKNESS, THE(1965,
Brit.); YOU MUST BE JOKING!(1965, Brit.); MAIN CHANCE, THE(1966, Brit.);
CASINO ROYALE(1967, Brit.); MAROC 7(1967, Brit.); HAMMERHEAD(1968); MELO-
DY(1971, Brit.); PERCY(1971, Brit.); 1,000 CONVICTS AND A WOMAN zero(1971,
Brit.); ADAM'S WOMAN(1972, Austral.); TROUBLE MAN(1972); TAKE, THE(1974);
TRAIN RIDE TO HOLLYWOOD(1975); CARWASH(1976); DEADLY FEMALES,
THE(1976, Brit.); NO WAY BACK(1976); PIECE OF THE ACTION, A(1977); ...ALL THE
MARBLES(1981)
Misc. Talkies
OUR MAN IN THE CARIBBEAN(1962)

Violet Reed
Silents
RIGHT TO LIE, THE(1919)
Misc. Silents
MORE TRUTH THAN POETRY(1917); SILENCE SELLERS, THE(1917); UNDYING
FLAME, THE(1917); MAN WHO LOST HIMSELF, THE(1920)

Virginia Reed
KID MILLIONS(1934)

Vivian Reed
HEADIN' FOR BROADWAY(1980); AFRICAN, THE(1983, Fr.)
Silents
LAST EGYPTIAN, THE(1914); IT'S A BEAR(1919)
Misc. Silents
HIS MAJESTY, THE SCARECROW OF OZ(1914); LAD AND THE LION, THE(1917);
LITTLE LOST SISTER(1917); PRINCESS OF PATCHES, THE(1917); GUILTY MAN,
THE(1918)

Walter Reed
ARMY SURGEON(1942); MAYOR OF 44TH STREET, THE(1942); MEXICAN SPIT-
FIRE'S ELEPHANT(1942); MY FAVORITE SPY(1942); SEVEN DAYS LEAVE(1942);
BOMBARDIER(1943); MEXICAN SPITFIRE'S BLESSED EVENT(1943); PETTICOAT
LARCENY(1943); CHILD OF DIVORCE(1946); BANJO(1947); NIGHT SONG(1947);
ANGEL ON THE AMAZON(1948); FIGHTER SQUADRON(1948); MYSTERY IN
MEXICO(1948); RETURN OF THE BADMEN(1948); WESTERN HERITAGE(1948);
EAGLE AND THE HAWK, THE(1950); LAWLESS, THE(1950); SUN SETS AT DAWN,
THE(1950); TORCH, THE(1950); TRIPOLI(1950); YOUNG MAN WITH A HORN(1950);
SUBMARINE COMMAND(1951); SUPERMAN AND THE MOLE MEN(1951); WELLS
FARGO GUNMASTER(1951); BLAZING FOREST, THE(1952); CARIBBEAN(1952);
DESERT PASSAGE(1952); HORIZONS WEST(1952); TARGET(1952); THUNDER-
BIRDS(1952); CLOWN, THE(1953); FOREVER FEMALE(1953); SEMINOLE(1953);
THOSE REDHEADS FROM SEATTLE(1953); WAR PAINT(1953); DANGEROUS MIS-
SION(1954); RETURN FROM THE SEA(1954); YELLOW TOMAHAWK, THE(1954);
BOBBY WARE IS MISSING(1955); FAR HORIZONS, THE(1955); HELL'S IS-
LAND(1955); DANCE WITH ME, HENRY(1956); EMERGENCY HOSPITAL(1956);
ROCK, PRETTY BABY(1956); SEVEN MEN FROM NOW(1956); LAWLESS EIGHTIES,
THE(1957); SLIM CARTER(1957); DEEP SIX, THE(1958); HOW TO MAKE A MON-
STER(1958); SUMMER LOVE(1958); ARSON FOR HIRE(1959); HORSE SOLDIERS,
THE(1959); WESTBOUND(1959); MACUMBA LOVE(1960); SERGEANT RUTLED-
GE(1960); THIRTEEN FIGHTING MEN(1960); HOW THE WEST WAS WON(1962);
CHEYENNE AUTUMN(1964); WHERE LOVE HAS GONE(1964); CONVICT STA-
GE(1965); FORT COURAGEOUS(1965); MOMENT TO MOMENT(1966); MONEY TRAP,
THE(1966); OSCAR, THE(1966); SAND PEBBLES, THE(1966); DESTRUCTORS,
THE(1968); PANIC IN THE CITY(1968)

Mark Reedall
GATHERING OF EAGLES, A(1963), makeup; YOUNG LOVERS, THE(1964), make-
up; SECONDS(1966), makeup; FINE PAIR, A(1969, Ital.), makeup; THEY CALL ME
MISTER TIBBS(1970), makeup; FLIGHT OF THE DOVES(1971), makeup; SLAUGH-
TERHOUSE-FIVE(1972), makeup

Rosemarie Reede
ASSIGNMENT K(1968, Brit.); CRIMSON CULT, THE(1970, Brit.)

Arlene Reeder
MIDNIGHT COWBOY(1969)

Nancy Reeder
WEDDING PARTY, THE(1969)

John Reeding
Silents
HOW MOLLY MADE GOOD(1915)

Beverly Reedy
MAN FROM OKLAHOMA, THE(1945)

Fred Reefe
KING KONG(1933), spec eff; SON OF KONG(1933), spec eff

George Reehm
Silents
TRAIL'S END(1922); ABRAHAM LINCOLN(1924)

Douglas Reekie
TWIN FACES(1937, Brit.), w

Frederick Reel, Jr.
Silents
TIPPED OFF(1923), w
Misc. Silents
BORDER RIDER, THE(1924), d; DESERT SECRET, THE(1924), d; LAST MAN,
THE(1924), d; EYES OF THE DESERT(1926), d; GASOLINE COWBOY(1926), d

Frances Irene Reels
Silents
DANGEROUS AGE, THE(1922), w; SONG OF LIFE, THE(1922), w; HUSBANDS
AND LOVERS(1924), w

Harry Reems
Misc. Talkies
R.S.V.P.(1984)

Angharad Rees
ATCH ME A SPY(1971, Brit./Fr.); HANDS OF THE RIPPER(1971, Brit.); UNDER
MILK WOOD(1973, Brit.); MOMENTS(1974, Brit.)

Anna Rees
REMEMBRANCE(1982, Brit.)

Arthur Rees
FAREWELL TO CINDERELLA(1937, Brit.)

Betty Anne Rees
DEATHMASTER, THE(1972); UNHOLY ROLLERS(1972); SUGAR HILL(1974)

Bill Rees
HEARTS IN EXILE(1929), ph; UNDER A TEXAS MOON(1930), ph

Billy Rees
ESTHER WATERS(1948, Brit.)

Carol Rees
DIPLOMATIC LOVER, THE(1934, Brit.); TOO MANY HUSBANDS(1938, Brit.)

Carol L. Rees
1984
FOOTLOOSE(1984)

Charles Rees
HAMLET(1969, Brit.), ed; NED KELLY(1970, Brit.), ed; GUMSHOE(1972, Brit.), ed;
PRIVATE ENTERPRISE, A(1975, Brit.), ed; ASCENDANCY(1983, Brit.), ed

Christine Rees
VAMPIRE, THE(1957)

Clive Rees
BLOCKHOUSE, THE(1974, Brit.), d, w

Danny Rees
KING'S PIRATE(1967); HARRY AND WALTER GO TO NEW YORK(1976)

Donogh Rees
1984
CONSTANCE(1984, New Zealand)

Ed Rees
I, JANE DOE(1948); MOONRISE(1948)

Edward Rees
LAST DAYS OF DOLWYN, THE(1949, Brit.); THEY CAME FROM BEYOND
SPACE(1967, Brit.)

Gwen Rees
RED RUNS THE RIVER(1963)

Hubert Rees
UNMAN, WITTERING AND ZIGO(1971, Brit.); UNDER MILK WOOD(1973, Brit.);
GREAT TRAIN ROBBERY, THE(1979, Brit.)
1984
CHAMPIONS(1984)

Joan Rees
BAD SISTER(1947, Brit.); LADY SURRENDERS, A(1947, Brit.); LOOK BEFORE YOU
LOVE(1948, Brit.); MAN OF EVIL(1948, Brit.); MY SISTER AND I(1948, Brit.), a, w

John Rees
LONG AND THE SHORT AND THE TALL, THE(1961, Brit.); PRIVATE POO-
LEY(1962, Brit./E. Ger.); PRIZE OF ARMS, A(1962, Brit.); IMPACT(1963, Brit.);
QUILLER MEMORANDUM, THE(1966, Brit.); ALFRED THE GREAT(1969, Brit.);
PASSENGER, THE(1970, Pol.); UNDER MILK WOOD(1973, Brit.); SHOUT, THE(1978,
Brit.); HANOVER STREET(1979, Brit.); EYE OF THE NEEDLE(1981); RAIDERS OF
THE LOST ARK(1981)

Lannie Rees
Misc. Talkies
MY DOG SHEP(1948)

Lanny Rees
TIME OF YOUR LIFE, THE(1948); HOME IN OKLAHOMA(1946); LITTLE
IODINE(1946); LIKELY STORY, A(1947); LIFE OF RILEY, THE(1949)
Misc. Talkies
LAW COMES TO GUNSIGHT, THE(1947)

Llewellyn Rees
YOU CAN'T ESCAPE(1955, Brit.); STRICTLY CONFIDENTIAL(1959, Brit.); HOUSE
IN MARSH ROAD, THE(1960, Brit.); PRICE OF SILENCE, THE(1960, Brit.); DOUBLE,
THE(1963, Brit); SALT & PEPPER(1968, Brit.); RULING CLASS, THE(1972, Brit.);
DRESSER, THE(1983); RETURN OF THE SOLDIER, THE(1983, Brit.)

Llewelwn Rees
NAVY LARK, THE(1959, Brit.)

Llewelyn Rees
CROMWELL(1970, Brit.)
1984
ANOTHER COUNTRY(1984, Brit.)

Olwen Rees
UNDER MILK WOOD(1973, Brit.)

Patricia Rees
Misc. Talkies
SINS OF RACHEL, THE(1975)

Paul Rees
GIRL MOST LIKELY, THE(1957); MY SIX LOVES(1963)

R.F.W. Rees
FEAR SHIP, THE(1933, Brit.), w

Roger Rees
STAR 80(1983)

Sonia Rees
YOUNG AND THE GUILTY, THE(1958, Brit.)

Trevor Crole Rees
UNEARTHLY STRANGER, THE(1964, Brit.), makeup

William Rees
FROM HEADQUARTERS(1929), ph; HARDBOILED ROSE(1929), ph; IT'S A
DEAL(1930), ph; OFFICE WIFE, THE(1930), ph; ROUGH WATERS(1930), ph; SCAR-
LET PAGES(1930), ph; EXPENSIVE WOMEN(1931), ph; MALTESE FALCON,
THE(1931), ph; MURDER AT MIDNIGHT(1931), ph; SIT TIGHT(1931), ph; CASE OF
THE HOWLING DOG, THE(1934), ph; FASHIONS OF 1934(1934), ph;
HOUSEWIFE(1934), ph; MIDNIGHT ALIBI(1934), ph; MODERN HERO, A(1934), ph;
PERSONALITY KID, THE(1934), ph; DON'T BET ON BLONDES(1935), ph; GOING
HIGHBROW(1935), ph; MEET THE MAYOR(1938), ph; SMILEY(1957, Brit.); SMILEY
GETS A GUN(1959, Brit.)

Yvette Rees
WITCHCRAFT(1964, Brit.); CURSE OF THE FLY(1965, Brit.); SEVERED HEAD, A(1971, Brit.)

Michael Reesburg
1984
SONGWRITER(1984)

Bill Reese
HELLCATS, THE(1968); PSYCHOTRONIC MAN, THE(1980), ed

Bob Reese
RENEGADE GIRLS(1974)

Catherine Reese
Misc. Silents
OUR MUTUAL FRIEND(1921, Swed.)

Della Reese
LET'S ROCK(1958); PSYCHIC KILLER(1975)

Gregory Reese
SHAFT'S BIG SCORE(1972)

James Reese
YOUNG DON'T CRY, THE(1957)

Jeffrey Reese
DARK, THE(1979)

John Reese
SEA TIGER(1952); GOOD DAY FOR A HANGING(1958), w; YOUNG LAND, THE(1959), w; CHARLEY VARRICK(1973), w

John H. Reese
1984
FALLING IN LOVE(1984)

Johnny Reese
Silents
HONOR SYSTEM, THE(1917); INNOCENT SINNER, THE(1917)

Joy Reese
DOCKS OF NEW YORK(1945); YOUTH AFLAME(1945)

Kathryn Reese
SAP FROM SYRACUSE, THE(1930)

Lawrence Reese
HOUNDS... OF NOTRE DAME, THE(1980, Can.)

Max Reese
PIRATES OF TORTUGA(1961), md

Ray Reese
FIRST TO FIGHT(1967)

Rhoda Reese
SKY'S THE LIMIT, THE(1943)

Rob Reese
LAST AMERICAN VIRGIN, THE(1982)

Robert Reese
GAY DECEIVERS, THE(1969)

Sammy Reese
CAPTAIN NEWMAN, M.D.(1963); PT 109(1963); KING RAT(1965); TRAVELING EXECUTIONER, THE(1970)

Tom Reese
FLAMING STAR(1960); MARINES, LET'S GO(1961); FORTY POUNDS OF TROUBLE(1962); BLOOD ON THE ARROW(1964); TAGGART(1964); GREATEST STORY EVER TOLD, THE(1965); MONEY TRAP, THE(1966); MURDERERS' ROW(1966); ST. VALENTINE'S DAY MASSACRE, THE(1967); VANISHING POINT(1971); OUTFIT, THE(1973); WILD PARTY, THE(1975)

Tony Reese
GEORGE RAFT STORY, THE(1961); WHEN THE BOYS MEET THE GIRLS(1965); LONGEST YARD, THE(1974)

William Reese
GAMBLERS, THE(1929), ph; CONVENTION CITY(1933), ph; FROM HEADQUARTERS(1933), ph; KENNEL MURDER CASE, THE(1933), ph
Silents
ATTA BOY!(1926), ph

Ethel Reese-Burns
WOMAN AGAINST THE WORLD(1938)

Ada Reeve
THEY CAME TO A CITY(1944, Brit.); MEET ME AT DAWN(1947, Brit.); WHEN THE BOUGH BREAKS(1947, Brit.); DEAR MR. PROHACK(1949, Brit.); NIGHT AND THE CITY(1950, Brit.); I BELIEVE IN YOU(1953, Brit.); TERROR ON A TRAIN(1953); EYEWITNESS(1956, Brit.); NOVEL AFFAIR, A(1957, Brit.)

Alice Means Reeve
JOHNNY DOESN'T LIVE HERE ANY MORE(1944), w

Arthur B. Reeve
UNMASKED(1929), w
Silents
GRIM GAME, THE(1919), w

Christopher Reeve
GRAY LADY DOWN(1978); SUPERMAN(1978); SOMEWHERE IN TIME(1980); SUPERMAN II(1980); DEATHTRAP(1982); MONSIGNOR(1982); SUPERMAN III(1983)
1984
BOSTONIANS, THE(1984)

Connie Reeve
SUPERMAN(1978), makeup

Geoffrey Reeve
PUPPET ON A CHAIN(1971, Brit.), d; CARAVAN TO VACCARES(1974, Brit./Fr.), p, d

John Reeve
Misc. Talkies
YOUNG JACOBITES(1959), d

Judi Reeve
FEELIN' GOOD(1966)

Leonard Reeve
NO HAUNT FOR A GENTLEMAN(1952, Brit.), d, w; SOULS IN CONFLICT(1955, Brit.), d&w

Paul Reeve
1984
SCANDALOUS(1984)

Ronald T. Reeve
YOUNG GIRLS OF ROCHEFORT, THE(1968, Fr.)

Spencer Reeve
DAY OF THE TRIFFIDS, THE(1963), ed; FRANKENSTEIN CREATED WOMAN(1965, Brit.), ed; DEVIL'S BRIDE, THE(1968, Brit.), ed; DRACULA HAS RISEN FROM HIS GRAVE(1968, Brit.), ed; FIVE MILLION YEARS TO EARTH(1968, Brit.), ed; MOON ZERO TWO(1970, Brit.), ed; LUST FOR A VAMPIRE(1971, Brit.), ed; TWINS OF EVIL(1971, Brit.), ed

Winifred Eaton Reeve
EAST IS WEST(1930), w

Winifred Reeve
MISSISSIPPI GAMBLER(1929), w; SHANGHAI LADY(1929), w; UNDERTOW(1930), w; YOUNG DESIRE(1930), w

Art Reeves
MEDICINE MAN, THE(1930), ph; SWELLHEAD, THE(1930), ph
Silents
OUT OF THE SILENT NORTH(1922), ph; BOWERY CINDERELLA(1927), ph

Arthur Reeves
SUNNY SKIES(1930), ph; WINGS OF ADVENTURE(1930), ph
Silents
AFRAID TO FIGHT(1922), ph; GALLOPING KID, THE(1922), ph; PRIDE OF SUNSHINE ALLEY(1924), ph; FIGHTING BOOB, THE(1926), ph; POWER OF THE WEAK, THE(1926), ph; PHANTOM OF THE NORTH(1929), ph

Bernard Reeves
ABOMINABLE DR. PHIBES, THE(1971, Brit.), art d

Bob Reeves
CANYON HAWKS(1930); LONESOME TRAIL, THE(1930); RANGE FEUD, THE(1931); POCATELLO KID(1932); KID MILLIONS(1934); SMOKING GUNS(1934); TRAIL DRIVE, THE(1934); MARY BURNS, FUGITIVE(1935); WESTERN COURAGE(1935); HEROES OF THE RANGE(1936); AMAZING DR. CLITTERHOUSE, THE(1938); NEW FRONTIER(1939); MY LITTLE CHICKADEE(1940); SON OF ROARING DAN(1940); WHEN THE DALTONS RODE(1940); DAYS OF OLD CHEYENNE(1943); LONE STAR TRAIL, THE(1943); DESTINY(1944); SHINE ON, HARVEST MOON(1944); DICK TRACY(1945); SARATOGA TRUNK(1945); CANON CITY(1948); FORCE OF EVIL(1948); GHOST OF ZORRO(1959)
Silents
NO-GUN MAN, THE(1924)
Misc. Silents
AMBUSHED(1926); CYCLONE BOB(1926); DESPERATE CHANCE(1926); FIGHTING LUCK(1926); IRON FIST(1926); RIDIN' STRAIGHT(1926); RIDING FOR LIFE(1926)

Crystal Reeves
SING WHILE YOU DANCE(1946); DREAMBOAT(1952)

Dale Reeves
CAYMAN TRIANGLE, THE(1977)

Del Reeves
FORTY ACRE FEUD(1965); SECOND FIDDLE TO A STEEL GUITAR(1965); GOLD GUITAR, THE(1966); LAS VEGAS HILLBILLYS(1966); COTTONPICKIN' CHICKEN-PICKERS(1967); SAM WHISKEY(1969)

Dick Reeves
LONG NIGHT, THE(1947); SHE'S WORKING HER WAY THROUGH COLLEGE(1952); I DIED A THOUSAND TIMES(1955); MA AND PA KETTLE AT WAIKIKI(1955); TOP GUN(1955); HOUSE IS NOT A HOME, A(1964); PRINCESS AND THE MAGIC FROG, THE(1965)

E. R. Reeves
MANY WATERS(1931, Brit.)

Edith Reeves
Misc. Silents
MORAL FABRIC, THE(1916)

Eve Reeves
BEHIND LOCKED DOORS(1976, S. Africa)
Misc. Talkies
ANY BODY...ANY WAY(1968)

George Reeves
GONE WITH THE WIND(1939); RETURN OF DR. X, THE(1939); ALWAYS A BRIDE(1940); ARGENTINE NIGHTS(1940); CALLING ALL HUSBANDS(1940); CALLING PHILO VANCE(1940); FATHER IS A PRINCE(1940); FIGHTING 69TH, THE(1940); GAMBLING ON THE HIGH SEAS(1940); KNUTE ROCKNE–ALL AMERICAN(1940); LADIES MUST LIVE(1940); MAN WHO TALKED TOO MUCH, THE(1940); TEAR GAS SQUAD(1940); 'TIL WE MEET AGAIN(1940); TORRID ZONE(1940); VIRGINIA CITY(1940); BLOOD AND SAND(1941); BLUE, WHITE, AND PERFECT(1941); DEAD MEN TELL(1941); LYDIA(1941); MAN AT LARGE(1941); STRAWBERRY BLONDE, THE(1941); MAD MARTINDALES, THE(1942); BAR 20(1943); BORDER PATROL(1943); BUCKSKIN FRONTIER(1943); COLT COMRADES(1943); HOPPY SERVES A WRIT(1943); LEATHER BURNERS, THE(1943); SO PROUDLY WE HAIL(1943); VARIETY GIRL(1947); JUNGLE GODDESS(1948); JUNGLE JIM(1948); SAINTED SISTERS, THE(1948); GREAT LOVER, THE(1949); MUTINEERS, THE(1949); SAMSON AND DELILAH(1949); SPECIAL AGENT(1949); THUNDER IN THE PINES(1949); GOOD HUMOR MAN, THE(1950); DAY THE EARTH STOOD STILL, THE(1951); SUPERMAN AND THE MOLE MEN(1951); BUGLES IN THE AFTERNOON(1952); RANCHO NOTORIOUS(1952); BLUE GARDENIA, THE(1953); FOREVER FEMALE(1953); FROM HERE TO ETERNITY(1953); WESTWARD HO THE WAGONS!(1956)

Charles Regan
HIS NIGHT OUT(1935); FOR LOVE OR MONEY(1939); MILLION DOLLAR LEGS(1939); RAIDERS OF THE DESERT(1941); INVISIBLE AGENT(1942); GHOST SHIP, THE(1943); OUT OF THE PAST(1947); JOLSON SINGS AGAIN(1949); SCENE OF THE CRIME(1949); TAKE ME OUT TO THE BALL GAME(1949); DOUBLE DYNAMITE(1951); CAPTIVE CITY(1952); LUCY GALLANT(1955)

Harry Reeves
FUN AND FANCY FREE(1947), w; MELODY TIME(1948), w; ADVENTURES OF ICHABOD AND MR. TOAD(1949), w; CINDERELLA(1950), w

Isabel Reeves
DOCTORS DON'T TELL(1941), w

J. Harold Reeves
HAPPY DAYS(1930); JUST IMAGINE(1930)

Jack Reeves
DARKER THAN AMBER(1970), p; FIRST NUDIE MUSICAL, THE(1976), p

Jan Reeves
KISS THEM FOR ME(1957)
Jim Reeves
KIMBERLEY JIM(1965, South Africa)
Kynaston Reeves
SIGN OF FOUR, THE(1932, Brit.); CRIMSON CANDLE, THE(1934, Brit.); DARK WORLD(1935, Brit.); WOLVES OF THE UNDERWORLD(1935, Brit.); TAKE A CHANCE(1937, Brit.); CITADEL, THE(1938); HOUSEMASTER(1938, Brit.); INSPECTOR HORNLEIGH ON HOLIDAY(1939, Brit.); SONS OF THE SEA(1939, Brit.); FLYING SQUAD, THE(1940, Brit.); PRIME MINISTER, THE(1941, Brit.); THIS ENGLAND(1941, Brit.); YOUNG MR. PITT, THE(1942, Brit.); NIGHT INVADER, THE(1943, Brit); ECHO MURDERS, THE(1945, Brit.); NOTORIOUS GENTLEMAN(1945, Brit.); QUERY(1945, Brit.); STRAWBERRY ROAN(1945, Brit.); BEDELIA(1946, Brit.); MURDER IN REVERSE(1946, Brit.); DEVIL'S PLOT, THE(1948, Brit.); VICE VERSA(1948, Brit.); BADGER'S GREEN(1949, Brit.); FOR THEM THAT TRESPASS(1949, Brit.); MADNESS OF THE HEART(1949, Brit.); OUTSIDER, THE(1949, Brit.); THIS WAS A WOMAN(1949, Brit.); WEAKER SEX, THE(1949, Brit.); BLACKOUT(1950, Brit.); MADELEINE(1950, Brit.); MUDLARK, THE(1950, Brit.); TWENTY QUESTIONS MURDER MYSTERY, THE(1950, Brit.); WINSLOW BOY, THE(1950); CAPTAIN HORATIO HORNBLOWER(1951, Brit.); SMART ALEC(1951, Brit.); TONY DRAWS A HORSE(1951, Brit.); FOUR SIDED TRIANGLE(1953, Brit.); MR. POTTS GOES TO MOSCOW(1953, Brit.); PENNY PRINCESS(1953, Brit.); TOP OF THE FORM(1953, Brit.); BURNT EVIDENCE(1954, Brit.); CROWDED DAY, THE(1954, Brit.); SCOTCH ON THE ROCKS(1954, Brit.); FUN AT ST. FANNY'S(1956, Brit.); GUILTY?(1956, Brit.); BROTHERS IN LAW(1957, Brit.); HIGH FLIGHT(1957, Brit.); LIGHT FINGERS(1957, Brit.); FIEND WITHOUT A FACE(1958); RX MURDER(1958, Brit.); QUESTION OF ADULTERY, A(1959, Brit.); IN THE NICK(1960, Brit.); MAN IN A COCKED HAT(1960, Bri.); SCHOOL FOR SCOUNDRELS(1960, Brit.); CARRY ON REGARDLESS(1961, Brit.); NIGHT WE GOT THE BIRD, THE(1961, Brit.); SHADOW OF THE CAT, THE(1961, Brit.); GO TO BLAZES(1962, Brit.); HIDE AND SEEK(1964, Brit.); IN THE DOGHOUSE(1964, Brit.); WHY BOTHER TO KNOCK(1964, Brit.); HOT MILLIONS(1968, Brit.); ANNE OF THE THOUSAND DAYS(1969, Brit.); PRIVATE LIFE OF SHERLOCK HOLMES, THE(1970, Brit.)
Misc. Talkies
UNDEFEATED, THE(1951, Brit.)
Lisa Reeves
POM POM GIRLS, THE(1976); CHICKEN CHRONICLES, THE(1977); YOU LIGHT UP MY LIFE(1977)
Martha Reeves
Misc. Talkies
FAIRY TALES(1979)
Michael Reeves
CASTLE OF THE LIVING DEAD(1964, Ital./Fr.), d; SHE BEAST, THE(1966, Brit./Ital./Yugo.), d; SORCERERS, THE(1967, Brit.), d, w; CONQUEROR WORM, THE(1968, Brit.), d, w; TELL ME LIES(1968, Brit.), md
Myrtle Reeves
Silents
ETERNAL LOVE(1917); KENTUCKY CINDERELLA, A(1917)
Misc. Silents
PLAYTHINGS(1918); BACHELOR'S WIFE, A(1919)
Nina Reeves
ROLLOVER(1981)
P. Kynaston Reeves
POWER(1934, Brit.); PHANTOM FIEND, THE(1935, Brit.); VINTAGE WINE(1935, Brit.); DEAD MEN ARE DANGEROUS(1939, Brit.); LOST ON THE WESTERN FRONT(1940, Brit.); OUTSIDER, THE(1940, Brit.); TWO FOR DANGER(1940, Brit.)
Pat Reeves
GIANT GILA MONSTER, THE(1959)
Peter Reeves
BROTHERLY LOVE(1970, Brit.); ONE MORE TIME(1970, Brit.); DULCIMA(1971, Brit.)
Richard Reeves
DOUBLE DEAL(1950); FINDERS KEEPERS(1951); RACKET, THE(1951); CARBINE WILLIAMS(1952); FARGO(1952); HOODLUM EMPIRE(1952); MAVERICK, THE(1952); PRIDE OF ST. LOUIS, THE(1952); WE'RE NOT MARRIED(1952); FAIR WIND TO JAVA(1953); GLASS WALL, THE(1953); JACK SLADE(1953); PERILOUS JOURNEY, A(1953); DESTRY(1954); LOOPHOLE(1954); TARGET EARTH(1954); CITY OF SHADOWS(1955); TARZAN'S HIDDEN JUNGLE(1955); DANCE WITH ME, HENRY(1956); MAN IS ARMED, THE(1956); RUNNING TARGET(1956); BUCKSKIN LADY, THE(1957); GUNSMOKE IN TUCSON(1958); RIOT IN JUVENILE PRISON(1959); ROOKIE, THE(1959); TWELVE HOURS TO KILL(1960); HARUM SCARUM(1965); BILLY THE KID VS. DRACULA(1966)
Richard J. Reeves
MONEY FROM HOME(1953); GUNFIGHT AT THE O.K. CORRAL(1957)
Rob Reeves
MAD WEDNESDAY(1950)
Robert Reeves
SON OF DR. JEKYLL, THE(1951)
Robyn Reeves
LIANNA(1983)
Roy Reeves
STACY'S KNIGHTS(1983)
Sgt. George Reeves
WINGED VICTORY(1944)
Spencer Reeves
KING IN NEW YORK, A(1957, Brit.), ed
Steve Reeves
ATHENA(1954); JAIL BAIT(1954); HERCULES(1959, Ital.); GIANT OF MARATHON, THE(1960, Ital.); GOLIATH AND THE BARBARIANS(1960, Ital.); HERCULES UNCHAINED(1960, Ital./Fr.); LAST DAYS OF POMPEII, THE(1960, Ital.); MORGAN THE PIRATE(1961, Fr./Ital.); THIEF OF BAGHDAD, THE(1961, Ital./Fr.); WHITE WARRIOR, THE(1961, Ital./Yugo.); AVENGER, THE(1962, Fr./Ital.); TROJAN HORSE, THE(1962, Fr./Ital.); DUEL OF THE TITANS(1963, Ital.); SLAVE, THE(1963, Ital.); SANDOKAN THE GREAT(1964, Fr./Ital./Span.); LONG RIDE FROM HELL, A(1970, Ital.), a, w
Theodore Reeves
SOCIETY DOCTOR(1935), w; AND SUDDEN DEATH(1936), w; DANGEROUS WATERS(1936), w; BLOSSOMS ON BROADWAY(1937), w; INTERNES CAN'T TAKE MONEY(1937), w; SHE ASKED FOR IT(1937), w; STORM, THE(1938), w; DOCTORS DON'T TELL(1941), w; ALMOST MARRIED(1942), w; NATIONAL VELVET(1944), w;

DEVOTION(1946), w; I WALK ALONE(1948), w; DOCTOR AND THE GIRL, THE(1949), w; BERNARDINE(1957), w
Tommy Reeves
LONG DUEL, THE(1967, Brit.)
Vaughn Reeves
1984
SOLDIER'S STORY, A(1984)
Walter Reeves
SAMSON(1961, Ital.)
H. Reeves-Smith
RETURN OF SHERLOCK HOLMES(1936)
Silents
NO MORE WOMEN(1924)
Olive Reeves-Smith
MY FAIR LADY(1964)
Joe Refalo
2001: A SPACE ODYSSEY(1968, U.S./Brit.)
The Reflections
WINTER A GO-GO(1965)
The Reg Wale Four
MURDER REPORTED(1958, Brit.)
Rega
MUSIC IS MAGIC(1935), cos
Bill Rega
LATE LIZ, THE(1971), w
Della Rega
MY LUCKY STAR(1933, Brit.)
Jules Regal
1984
CONSTANCE(1984, New Zealand)
Joe Regalbuto
CHEAPER TO KEEP HER(1980); SCHIZOID(1980); HONKYTONK MAN(1982); MISSING(1982); SIX WEEKS(1982); SWORD AND THE SORCERER, THE(1982); STAR CHAMBER, THE(1983)
1984
LASSITER(1984)
Joseph Regalbuto
GOODBYE GIRL, THE(1977)
Maurice Regamey
VILLAGE, THE(1953, Brit./Switz.)
Barry Regan
NONE BUT THE LONELY HEART(1944); CLOWN, THE(1953); LOVE ME OR LEAVE ME(1955); SCARLET COAT, THE(1955); SQUARE JUNGLE, THE(1955)
Douglas Regan
VARIETY GIRL(1947)
Elizabeth Regan
CREEPSHOW(1982)
Gretchen Regan
MINI-AFFAIR, THE(1968, Brit.)
James Regan
UNDER THE RED ROBE(1937, Brit.)
Jane Regan
CLEOPATRA(1934)
Jayne Regan
DANTE'S INFERNO(1935); LADIES IN LOVE(1936); STOWAWAY(1936); SECOND HONEYMOON(1937); THANK YOU, MR. MOTO(1937); YOU CAN'T HAVE EVERYTHING(1937); BOOLOO(1938); JOSETTE(1938); MR. MOTO'S GAMBLE(1938); WALKING DOWN BROADWAY(1938)
Misc. Talkies
CACTUS KID, THE(1934); WEST ON PARADE(1934); SILVER BULLET, THE(1935); TEXAS JACK(1935)
Jim Regan
GAOL BREAK(1936, Brit.); MAN WHO MADE DIAMONDS, THE(1937, Brit.)
Joan Regan
HELLO LONDON(1958, Brit.); 6.5 SPECIAL(1958, Brit.)
Ken Regan
YESTERDAY'S HERO(1979, Brit.), p
Linda Regan
CONFESSIONS OF A POP PERFORMER(1975, Brit.); CARRY ON ENGLAND(1976, Brit.)
Martin Regan
Misc. Silents
POLITICIANS, THE(1915)
Mary Regan
1984
HEART OF THE STAG(1984, New Zealand)
Mike Regan
RIDE CLEAR OF DIABLO(1954)
Patrick Regan
FARMER, THE(1977), w
Patty Regan
HOW SWEET IT IS(1968); THOMAS CROWN AFFAIR, THE(1968)
Paul Regan
MEET THE PEOPLE(1944); DEVIL'S CARGO, THE(1948)
Phil Regan
DAMES(1934); HOUSEWIFE(1934); PERSONALITY KID, THE(1934); STUDENT TOUR(1934); BROADWAY HOSTESS(1935); GO INTO YOUR DANCE(1935); IN CALIENTE(1935); STARS OVER BROADWAY(1935); SWEET ADELINE(1935); WE'RE IN THE MONEY(1935); LAUGHING IRISH EYES(1936); HAPPY-GO-LUCKY(1937); HIT PARADE, THE(1937); MANHATTAN MERRY-GO-ROUND(1937); OUTSIDE OF PARADISE(1938); FLIGHT AT MIDNIGHT(1939); SHE MARRIED A COP(1939); LAS VEGAS NIGHTS(1941); SWEET ROSIE O'GRADY(1943); SUNBONNET SUE(1945); SWEETHEART OF SIGMA CHI(1946); SWING PARADE OF 1946(1946); THREE LITTLE WORDS(1950)
Russ Regan
1984
BREAKIN' 2: ELECTRIC BOOGALOO(1984), m

Tony Regan
ERRAND BOY, THE(1961); FOLLOW ME, BOYS!(1966)
Suzanna M. Regard
48 HOURS(1982)
George Regas
UNDER TWO FLAGS(1936); CAUGHT CHEATING(1931); CITY STREETS(1931); MOUNTED FURY(1931); BULLDOG DRUMMOND STRIKES BACK(1934); KID MILLIONS(1934); SIXTEEN FATHOMS DEEP(1934); VIVA VILLA!(1934); FIGHTING TROOPER, THE(1935); LIVES OF A BENGAL LANCER(1935); MARINES ARE COMING, THE(1935); RED BLOOD OF COURAGE(1935); CHARGE OF THE LIGHT BRIGADE, THE(1936); DANIEL BOONE(1936); GIRL FROM MANDALAY(1936); HELL-SHIP MORGAN(1936); ISLE OF FURY(1936); NIGHT CARGO(1936); ROBIN HOOD OF EL DORADO(1936); ROSE MARIE(1936); SWORN ENEMY(1936); CALIFORNIAN, THE(1937); LEFT-HANDED LAW(1937); LEGION OF MISSING MEN(1937); LOVE UNDER FIRE(1937); WAIKIKI WEDDING(1937); CLIPPED WINGS(1938); FOUR MEN AND A PRAYER(1938); HAWAIIAN BUCKAROO(1938); TORCHY BLANE IN PANAMA(1938); TOY WIFE, THE(1938); ADVENTURES OF SHERLOCK HOLMES, THE(1939); BEAU GESTE(1939); CAT AND THE CANARY, THE(1939); CODE OF THE SECRET SERVICE(1939); GUNGA DIN(1939); LIGHT THAT FAILED, THE(1939); RAINS CAME, THE(1939); MAD EMPRESS, THE(1940); MARK OF ZORRO, THE(1940); NORTHWEST MOUNTED POLICE(1940); 'TIL WE MEET AGAIN(1940); TORRID ZONE(1940); VIRGINIA CITY(1940)
Jack Regas
ZIEGFELD FOLLIES(1945); STRIP, THE(1951); MY SIX LOVES(1963), ch; PARADISE, HAWAIIAN STYLE(1966), ch; LIVE A LITTLE, LOVE A LITTLE(1968), ch
P. Regas
POCKET MONEY(1972)
Paul Regas
GILDA(1946); HELL'S ISLAND(1955)
Pedro Regas
TWO-FISTED JUSTICE(1931); FLYING DOWN TO RIO(1933); VIVA VILLA!(1934); UNDER THE PAMPAS MOON(1935); WEST OF THE PECOS(1935); SUTTER'S GOLD(1936); TRAITOR, THE(1936); WAIKIKI WEDDING(1937); GIRL OF THE GOLDEN WEST, THE(1938); TROPIC HOLIDAY(1938); CODE OF THE SECRET SERVICE(1939); ONLY ANGELS HAVE WINGS(1939); RAINS CAME, THE(1939); ROAD TO SINGAPORE(1940); THEY DRIVE BY NIGHT(1940); FOR WHOM THE BELL TOLLS(1943); TIGER FANGS(1943); MASK OF DIMITRIOS, THE(1944); TO HAVE AND HAVE NOT(1944); SOUTH OF THE RIO GRANDE(1945); PERILOUS HOLIDAY(1946); FRENCH LEAVE(1948); KISSING BANDIT, THE(1948); MEXICAN HAYRIDE(1948); SECRET BEYOND THE DOOR, THE(1948); VIVA ZAPATA!(1952); THEY SAVED HITLER'S BRAIN(1964); HELL WITH HEROES, THE(1968); ANGEL UNCHAINED(1970); FLAP(1970)
Ismet Regeila
ABDULLAH'S HAREM(1956, Brit./Egypt.), w
Joachim Regelien
1984
LOOSE CONNECTIONS(1984, Brit.)
Walter Regelsberger
ALMOST ANGELS(1962); FOREVER MY LOVE(1962)
Regensburg Domspatzen Choir
WONDERFUL WORLD OF THE BROTHERS ERIMM, THE(1962)
Robert Regent
I'LL SELL MY LIFE(1941); CORN IS GREEN, THE(1945); TALK ABOUT A LADY(1946)
John Patrick Reger
1984
HOT DOG...THE MOVIE(1984)
Aldo Reggiani
CAT O'NINE TAILS(1971, Ital./Ger./Fr.)
Serge Reggiani
CHILDREN OF CHAOS(1950, Fr.); GATES OF THE NIGHT(1950, Fr.); MANON(1950, Fr.); LOVERS OF VERONA, THE(1951, Fr.); SECRET PEOPLE(1952, Brit.); ACT OF LOVE(1953); ANITA GARIBALDI(1954, Ital.); LA RONDE(1954, Fr.); CASQUE D'OR(1956, Fr.); PARIS BLUES(1961); WICKED GO TO HELL, THE(1961, Fr.); EVERYBODY GO HOME!(1962, Fr./Ital.); WARRIORS FIVE(1962); FINGERMAN, THE(1963, Fr.); LEOPARD, THE(1963, Ital.); DOULOS THE FINGER MAN(1964, Fr./Ital.); DOLL THAT TOOK THE TOWN, THE(1965, Ital.); LORD JIM(1965, Brit.); 25TH HOUR, THE(1967, Fr./Ital./Yugo.); DAY OF THE OWL, THE(1968, Ital./Fr.); LAST ADVENTURE, THE(1968, Fr./Ital.); L'ARMEE DES OMBRES(1969, Fr./Ital.); MAFIA(1969, Fr./Ital.); DON'T TOUCH WHITE WOMEN!(1974, Fr.); CAT AND MOUSE(1978, Fr.); FANTASTICA(1980, Can./Fr.)
Reggie the Horse
IT'S A GREAT LIFE(1943)
Cathy Reghin
PLAYMATES(1969, Fr./Ital.)
Serge Regianni
NAPOLEON(1955, Fr.)
Nadja Regin
MAN WITHOUT A BODY, THE(1957, Brit.); DON'T PANIC CHAPS!(1959, Brit.); FUR COLLAR, THE(1962, Brit.); NUMBER SIX(1962, Brit.); STRANGLEHOLD(1962, Brit.); FROM RUSSIA WITH LOVE(1963, Brit.); DOWNFALL(1964, Brit.); GOLDFINGER(1964, Brit.); SOLO FOR SPARROW(1966, Brit.)
Paul Regina
CHANGE OF SEASONS, A(1980)
Reginald Forsyth and His Band
JIMMY BOY(1935, Brit.); BIG NOISE, THE(1936, Brit.)
Regine
FIVE MILES TO MIDNIGHT(1963, U.S./Fr./Ital.); KILLING GAME, THE(1968, Fr.); MARRY ME! MARRY ME!(1969, Fr.); SEVEN-PER-CENT SOLUTION, THE(1977, Brit.)
1984
MY NEW PARTNER(1984, Fr.)
Alix Regis
1984
SUGAR CANE ALLEY(1984, Fr.), p
Angelina Regis
VILLA!(1958)
Charlita Regis
SIX BLACK HORSES(1962)

Clair Regis
MURDER WITHOUT TEARS(1953)
Colette Regis
LA BETE HUMAINE(1938, Fr.); ATTILA(1958, Ital.); TOMORROW IS MY TURN(1962, Fr./Ital./Ger.); LES ABYSSES(1964, Fr.); FIVE WILD GIRLS(1966, Fr.)
Collette Regis
MODERATO CANTABILE(1964, Fr./Ital.)
Diane Regis
LIMIT, THE(1972)
John Regis
MORITURI(1965)
Francois Regis-Bastide
JE T'AIME, JE T'AIME(1972, Fr./Swed.)
Claude Register
Misc. Talkies
VERNON, FLORIDA(1982)
Florence Regnart
Silents
EAST OF SUEZ(1925)
Nicole Regnault
MY UNCLE(1958, Fr.); LADIES OF THE PARK(1964, Fr.)
Andre Regnier
TRIAL OF JOAN OF ARC(1965, Fr.)
Carola Regnier
SITUATION HOPELESS–BUT NOT SERIOUS(1965)
1984
WOMAN IN FLAMES, A(1984, Ger.)
Misc. Talkies
HINDERED(1974)
Charles Regnier
CANARIS(1955, Ger.); MAGIC FIRE(1956); TIME TO LOVE AND A TIME TO DIE, A(1958); JOURNEY, THE(1959, U.S./Aust.); REST IS SILENCE, THE(1960, Ger.); SECRET WAYS, THE(1961); COUNTERFEIT TRAITOR, THE(1962); COURT MARTIAL(1962, Ger.); FREUD(1962); INVISIBLE MAN, THE(1963, Ger.); MIRACLE OF THE WHITE STALLIONS(1963); TERROR OF DR. MABUSE, THE(1965, Ger.); STUDY IN TERROR, A(1966, Brit./Ger.); RUN LIKE A THIEF(1968, Span.); DUCK RINGS AT HALF PAST SEVEN, THE(1969, Ger./Ital.); STEPPENWOLF(1974); SERPENT'S EGG, THE(1977, Ger./U.S.)
Georges Regnier
LULU(1962, Aus.)
Marthe Regnier
MAYERLING(1937, Fr.)
Roy Regnier
MA AND PA KETTLE AT THE FAIR(1952); PROBLEM GIRLS(1953)
Yves Regnier
PEPPERMINT SODA(1979, Fr.)
Piero Regnoli
DEVIL'S COMMANDMENT, THE(1956, Ital.), w; PLAYGIRLS AND THE VAMPIRE(1964, Ital.), d&w
Dinorah Rego
TOO MANY BLONDES(1941)
Luis Rego
MEN PREFER FAT GIRLS(1981, Fr.)
Roland Rego
LAST TRAIN FROM MADRID, THE(1937)
Costas Regopoulos
MATCHMAKING OF ANNA, THE(1972, Gr.)
Francisco Reguerra
PEPE(1960)
Homer Regus
STOLEN LIFE(1939, Brit.)
Philo Reh
LARCENY, INC.(1942)
Frantisek Rehak
CAPRICIOUS SUMMER(1968, Czech.); DIVINE EMMA, THE(1983, Czech,)
Christopher B. Rehbaum
1984
NATURAL, THE(1984)
Hans Michael Rehberg
WAR AND PEACE(1983, Ger.)
Curt Rehfeld
GENERAL CRACK(1929)
Silents
FOUR HORSEMEN OF THE APOCALYPSE, THE(1921); ALL THE BROTHERS WERE VALIANT(1923)
Rehfisch
DREYFUS CASE, THE(1931, Brit.), w
Hans Rehfisch
GUILTY MELODY(1936, Brit.), w
Wal Wally Rehg
FAST COMPANY(1929)
Al Rehin
SET-UP, THE(1949)
Rehkopf
M(1933, Ger.)
Paul Rehkopf
TESTAMENT OF DR. MABUSE, THE(1943, Ger.)
Silents
ISN'T LIFE WONDERFUL(1924); SPIES(1929, Ger.)
Werner Rehm
TIN DRUM, THE(1979, Ger./Fr./Yugo./Pol.)
Waheeda Rehman
GUIDE, THE(1965, U.S./India)
Hans Rehmann
WAY OF LOST SOULS, THE(1929, Brit.); WOMAN HE SCORNED, THE(1930, Brit.)
Sandra Rehn
STREET OF SINNERS(1957)

Zdenek Rehor
MAN FROM THE FIRST CENTURY, THE(1961, Czech.)

Josef Rehorek
FIREMAN'S BALL, THE(1968, Czech.)

Miri Rei
WAIKIKI WEDDING(1937); TAHITIAN, THE(1956)

To Man Rei
LET'S GO, YOUNG GUY!(1967, Jap.)

Rafi Reibenbach
WORLDS APART(1980, U.S., Israel), p

Ludwig Reiber
DECISION BEFORE DAWN(1951), art d; PATHS OF GLORY(1957), art d; BIG SHOW, THE(1961), art d

Albert Reich
GIRLS IN CHAINS(1943), w; GAY BLADES(1946), w

Christopher Reich
TRAIL OF THE PINK PANTHER, THE(1982); NEVER SAY NEVER AGAIN(1983)

George Reich
BLACK TIGHTS(1962, Fr.)

Georges Reich
JULIE THE REDHEAD(1963, Fr.), ch

Gunter Reich
MOSES AND AARON(1975, Ger./Fr./Ital.)

Hans Leo Reich
Silents
METROPOLIS(1927, Ger.)

Richard Reich
PETS(1974), w

William C. Reich
NIGHT CHILD(1975, Brit./Ital.), p

Paul Reichardt
COUNTERFEIT TRAITOR, THE(1962)

Poul Reichardt
WHILE THE ATTORNEY IS ASLEEP(1945, Den.)

Stephane Reichel
FIRST BLOOD(1982), art d

Susi Reichel
MARRIAGE OF MARIA BRAUN, THE(1979, Ger.), cos

Hardy Reichelt
RUTHLESS FOUR, THE(1969, Ital./Ger.)

Francois Reichenbach
FORTY DEUCE(1982), ph

Harry Reichenbach
HALF-NAKED TRUTH, THE(1932), w

Ernst Reicher
RASPUTIN(1932, Ger.)

Frank Reicher
UNDER TWO FLAGS(1936); SINS OF THE FATHERS(1928); BLACK WATERS(1929); HIS CAPTIVE WOMAN(1929); MISTER ANTONIO(1929), a, d; PARIS BOUND(1929), w; STRANGE CARGO(1929); GIRL OF THE PORT(1930), w; GRAND PARADE, THE(1930), d; HER PRIVATE AFFAIR(1930); GENTLEMAN'S FATE(1931); MATA HARI(1931); SUICIDE FLEET(1931); CROOKED CIRCLE(1932); RASPUTIN AND THE EMPRESS(1932); SCARLET DAWN(1932); WOMAN COMMANDS, A(1932); BEFORE DAWN(1933); CAPTURED(1933); EMPLOYEE'S ENTRANCE(1933); EVER IN MY HEART(1933); JENNIE GERHARDT(1933); KING KONG(1933); SON OF KONG(1933); TOPAZE(1933); BRITISH AGENT(1934); CASE OF THE HOWLING DOG, THE(1934); COUNTESS OF MONTE CRISTO, THE(1934); FOUNTAIN, THE(1934); HI, NELLIE!(1934); JOURNAL OF A CRIME(1934); LET'S TALK IT OVER(1934); LITTLE MAN, WHAT NOW?(1934); NO GREATER GLORY(1934); RETURN OF THE TERROR(1934); CHARLIE CHAN IN EGYPT(1935); DOG OF FLANDERS, A(1935); FLORENTINE DAGGER, THE(1935); GREAT IMPERSONATION, THE(1935); I AM A THIEF(1935); KIND LADY(1935); MAGNIFICENT OBSESSION(1935); MAN WHO BROKE THE BANK AT MONTE CARLO, THE(1935); MILLS OF THE GODS(1935); REMEMBER LAST NIGHT(1935); RENDEZVOUS(1935); SECRET OF THE CHATEAU(1935); STAR OF MIDNIGHT(1935); STRAIGHT FROM THE HEART(1935); ANTHONY ADVERSE(1936); COUNTRY DOCTOR, THE(1936); DEVIL DOLL, THE(1936); EX-MRS. BRADFORD, THE(1936); GIRLS' DORMITORY(1936); LONE WOLF RETURNS, THE(1936); MURDER OF DR. HARRIGAN, THE(1936); MURDER ON A BRIDLE PATH(1936); OLD HUTCH(1936); SECOND WIFE(1936); STAR FOR A NIGHT(1936); STORY OF LOUIS PASTEUR, THE(1936); SUTTER'S GOLD(1936); THE INVISIBLE RAY(1936); TILL WE MEET AGAIN(1936); EMPEROR'S CANDLESTICKS, THE(1937); ESPIONAGE(1937); FIT FOR A KING(1937); GREAT O'MALLEY, THE(1937); LANCER SPY(1937); LAUGHING AT TROUBLE(1937); LIFE OF EMILE ZOLA, THE(1937); MIDNIGHT MADONNA(1937); NIGHT KEY(1937); ON SUCH A NIGHT(1937); PRESCRIPTION FOR ROMANCE(1937); ROAD BACK,THE(1937); STAGE DOOR(1937); STOLEN HOLIDAY(1937); UNDER COVER OF NIGHT(1937); WESTBOUND LIMITED(1937); CITY STREETS(1938); I'LL GIVE A MILLION(1938); LETTER OF INTRODUCTION(1938); PRISON NURSE(1938); RASCALS(1938); SUEZ(1938); TORCHY GETS HER MAN(1938); ESCAPE, THE(1939); EVERYTHING HAPPENS AT NIGHT(1939); JUAREZ(1939); LIFE RETURNS(1939); MAGNIFICENT FRAUD, THE(1939); MYSTERY OF THE WHITE ROOM(1939); NEVER SAY DIE(1939); NINOTCHKA(1939); NURSE EDITH CAVELL(1939); OUR NEIGHBORS–THE CARTERS(1939); SOCIETY SMUGGLERS(1939); SOUTH OF THE BORDER(1939); UNEXPECTED FATHER(1939); WOMAN DOCTOR(1939); ALL THIS AND HEAVEN TOO(1940); DEVIL'S ISLAND(1940); DR. CYCLOPS(1940); DR. EHRLICH'S MAGIC BULLET(1940); LADY IN QUESTION, THE(1940); MAN I MARRIED, THE(1940); SKY MURDER(1940); SOUTH TO KARANGA(1940); TYPHOON(1940); FACE BEHIND THE MASK, THE(1941); FATHER TAKES A WIFE(1941); FLIGHT FROM DESTINY(1941); NURSE'S SECRET, THE(1941); SHINING VICTORY(1941); THEY DARE NOT LOVE(1941); UNDERGROUND(1941); BEYOND THE BLUE HORIZON(1942); DANGEROUSLY THEY LIVE(1942); GAY SISTERS, THE(1942); I MARRIED AN ANGEL(1942); MUMMY'S TOMB, THE(1942); MYSTERY OF MARIE ROGET, THE(1942); NAZI AGENT(1942); NIGHT MONSTER(1942); SCATTERGOOD SURVIVES A MURDER(1942); SECRET ENEMIES(1942); TO BE OR NOT TO BE(1942); ABOVE SUSPICION(1943); BACKGROUND TO DANGER(1943); BOMBER'S MOON(1943); MISSION TO MOSCOW(1943); SONG OF BERNADETTE, THE(1943); TORNADO(1943); WATCH ON THE RHINE(1943); YANKS AHOY(1943); ADDRESS UNKNOWN(1944); BIG BONANZA, THE(1944); CONSPIRATORS, THE(1944); GILDERSLEEVE'S GHOST(1944); HOUSE OF FRANKENSTEIN(1944); IN OUR TIME(1944); MRS. PARKINGTON(1944); MUMMY'S GHOST, THE(1944); BLONDE RANSOM(1945); HOTEL

BERLIN(1945); JADE MASK, THE(1945); MEDAL FOR BENNY, A(1945); STRANGE MR. GREGORY, THE(1945); TIGER WOMAN, THE(1945); HOME IN OKLAHOMA(1946); MR. DISTRICT ATTORNEY(1946); MY PAL TRIGGER(1946); SHADOW RETURNS, THE(1946); SISTER KENNY(1946); ESCAPE ME NEVER(1947); MONSIEUR VERDOUX(1947); SECRET LIFE OF WALTER MITTY, THE(1947); VIOLENCE(1947); YANKEE FAKIR(1947); CARSON CITY RAIDERS(1948); FIGHTING MAD(1948); I, JANE DOE(1948); BARBARY PIRATE(1949); SAMSON AND DELILAH(1949); ARIZONA COWBOY, THE(1950); CARGO TO CAPETOWN(1950); KISS TOMORROW GOODBYE(1950); LADY AND THE BANDIT, THE(1951); SUPERMAN AND THE MOLE MEN(1951)
Silents
WISE HUSBANDS(, d; SECRET ORCHARD(1915), d; ALIEN SOULS(1916), d; DUPE, THE(1916), d; AMERICAN WIDOW, AN(1917), d; PRODIGAL WIFE, THE(1918), d; AMERICAN WAY, THE(1919), d; IDLE HANDS(1921), d; BEAU SABREUR(1928); FOUR SONS(1928)
Misc. Silents
MR. GREX OF MONTE CARLO(1915), d; FOR THE DEFENCE(1916), d; LOVE MASK, THE(1916), d; PUBLIC OPINION(1916), d; PUDD'NHEAD WILSON(1916), d; STORM, THE(1916), d; VICTORY OF CONSCIENCE, THE(1916), d; WITCHCRAFT(1916), d; BETTY TO THE RESCUE(1917), d; BLACK WOLF, THE(1917), d; CASTLES FOR TWO(1917), d; ETERNAL MOTHER, THE(1917), d; INNER SHRINE, THE(1917), d; SACRIFICE(1917), d; TROUBLE BUSTER, THE(1917), d; UNCONQUERED(1917), d; CLAIM, THE(1918), d; ONLY ROAD, THE(1918), d; SEA WAIF, THE(1918), d; TREASURE(1918), d; TREASURE OF THE SEA(1918), d; BATTLER, THE(1919), d; BLACK CIRCLE, THE(1919), d; SUSPENCE(1919), d; TRAP, THE(1919), d; EMPTY ARMS(1920), d; IDLE HANDS(1920), d; BEHIND MASKS(1921), d; MASKS OF THE DEVIL, THE(1928)

Hedwig Reicher
GODLESS GIRL, THE(1929); DRACULA'S DAUGHTER(1936)
Silents
LOVER'S OATH, A(1925); KING OF KINGS, THE(1927); LEOPARD LADY, THE(1928)

Hedwiga Reicher
LUCKY STAR(1929); SPORTING CHANCE(1931); HOUSE OF A THOUSAND CANDLES, THE(1936); I MARRIED A DOCTOR(1936)

Otto Reicher
PARIS AFTER DARK(1943)

Heinz Reichert
STRAUSS' GREAT WALTZ(1934, Brit.), w

Julia Reichert
1984
BREAKIN' 2: ELECTRIC BOOGALOO(1984), w

Kittens Reichert
Silents
AMBITION(1916); ETERNAL SAPHO, THE(1916); TIGER WOMAN, THE(1917); LES MISERABLES(1918); SO'S YOUR OLD MAN(1926)
Misc. Silents
BROKEN FETTERS(1916); FORBIDDEN FRUIT(1916); GREAT PROBLEM, THE(1916); EVERY GIRL'S DREAM(1917); PEDDLER, THE(1917); SCARLET LETTER, THE(1917); UNKNOWN 274(1917)

Kitty Reichert
Silents
SONG OF THE WAGE SLAVE, THE(1915)

Mark Reichert
UNION CITY(1980), d&w

Whit Reichert
STUCKEY'S LAST STAND(1980)

Peter Reichhardt
1984
ZAPPA(1984, Den.)

Poul Reichhardt
SUDDENLY, A WOMAN!(1967, Den.); HAGBARD AND SIGNE(1968, Den./Iceland/Swed.); VENOM(1968, Den.)

Ruth Reichl
CRY DR. CHICAGO(1971)

Art Reichle
YOUNG LIONS, THE(1958)

Helen Reichman
TEN TALL MEN(1951); HAREM GIRL(1952)

Joe Reichman
OUT OF THIS WORLD(1945)

Max Reichmann
ALLURING GOAL, THE(1930, Germ.), d

Wolfgang Reichmann
TRIAL, THE(1963, Fr./Ital./Ger.); NUN, THE(1971, Fr.); SIGNS OF LIFE(1981, Ger.)

Otto Reichow
ARIZONA GANGBUSTERS(1940); INTERNATIONAL LADY(1941); MAN HUNT(1941); PARIS CALLING(1941); UNDERGROUND(1941); YANK IN THE R.A.F., A(1941); DESPERATE JOURNEY(1942); INVISIBLE AGENT(1942); JOAN OF OZARK(1942); LUCKY JORDAN(1942); MY FAVORITE BLONDE(1942); ONCE UPON A HONEYMOON(1942); PIED PIPER, THE(1942); SEVEN MILES FROM ALCATRAZ(1942); SHIP AHOY(1942); TO BE OR NOT TO BE(1942); ABOVE SUSPICION(1943); BACKGROUND TO DANGER(1943); BOMBER'S MOON(1943); FIRST COMES COURAGE(1943); FIVE GRAVES TO CAIRO(1943); HANGMEN ALSO DIE(1943); MOON IS DOWN, THE(1943); TARZAN TRIUMPHS(1943); THEY CAME TO BLOW UP AMERICA(1943); AND THE ANGELS SING(1944); CONSPIRATORS, THE(1944); HOUR BEFORE THE DAWN, THE(1944); TAMPICO(1944); UNWRITTEN CODE, THE(1944); VOICE IN THE WIND(1944); NOB HILL(1945); PARIS UNDERGROUND(1945); SON OF LASSIE(1945); WITHIN THESE WALLS(1945); CLOAK AND DAGGER(1946); DANGEROUS MILLIONS(1946); RENDEZVOUS 24(1946); SEARCHING WIND, THE(1946); 13 RUE MADELEINE(1946); GOLDEN EARRINGS(1947); JEWELS OF BRANDENBURG(1947); WHERE THERE'S LIFE(1947); ROGUES' REGIMENT(1948); SEALED VERDICT(1948); SILVER RIVER(1948); ALASKA PATROL(1949); I WAS A MALE WAR BRIDE(1949); KING RICHARD AND THE CRUSADERS(1954); NIGHT PEOPLE(1954); LOVE ME OR LEAVE ME(1955); MAN IN THE GREY FLANNEL SUIT, THE(1956); NEVER SAY GOODBYE(1956); BACK FROM THE DEAD(1957); ISTANBUL(1957); LOOKING FOR DANGER(1957); OPERATION MAD BALL(1957); YOUNG LIONS, THE(1958); OPERATION EICHMANN(1961); HITLER(1962); JUMBO(1962); PRIZE, THE(1963); 36 HOURS(1965); ULZANA'S RAID(1972)

Werner Reichow
ENEMY BELOW, THE(1957); 36 HOURS(1965)
Esther Reichstadt
EXODUS(1960)
Kittens Reickert
Silents
ETERNAL CITY, THE(1915)
Ace Reid
PONY EXPRESS RIDER(1976)
Alan Reid
MAYTIME IN MAYFAIR(1952, Brit.)
Alastair Reid
BABY LOVE(1969, Brit.), d, w; SHOUT AT THE DEVIL(1976, Brit.), w
Alistair Reid
NIGHT DIGGER, THE(1971, Brit.), d; SOMETHING TO HIDE(1972, Brit.), d&w
Arthur Reid
FLY AWAY PETER(1948, Brit.), w; LOVE IN WAITING(1948, Brit.), w
Barbara Reid
PAD, THE(AND HOW TO USE IT)* (1966, Brit.)
Beryl Reid
BELLES OF ST. TRINIAN'S, THE(1954, Brit.); EXTRA DAY, THE(1956, Brit.); TWO-WAY STRETCH(1961, Brit.); TRIAL AND ERROR(1962, Brit.); INSPECTOR CLOUSEAU(1968, Brit.); STAR!(1968); ASSASSINATION BUREAU, THE(1969, Brit.); ENTERTAINING MR. SLOANE(1970, Brit.); BEAST IN THE CELLAR, THE(1971, Brit.); DOCTOR PHIBES RISES AGAIN(1972, Brit.); PSYCHOMANIA(1974, Brit.); JOSEPH ANDREWS(1977, Brit.); CARRY ON EMANUELLE(1978, Brit.); NO SEX PLEASE–WE'RE BRITISH(1979, Brit.); YELLOWBEARD(1983)
Billy Reid
Silents
MASKED AVENGER, THE(1922)
Cal Benton Reid
WICHITA(1955)
Carl Benton Reid
LITTLE FOXES, THE(1941); NORTH STAR, THE(1943); CONVICTED(1950); FLYING MISSILE(1950); FULLER BRUSH GIRL, THE(1950); IN A LONELY PLACE(1950); KILLER THAT STALKED NEW YORK, THE(1950); STAGE TO TUCSON(1950); CRIMINAL LAWYER(1951); FAMILY SECRET, THE(1951); GREAT CARUSO, THE(1951); INDIAN UPRISING(1951); LORNA DOONE(1951); SMUGGLER'S GOLD(1951); BOOTS MALONE(1952); BRIGAND, THE(1952); CARBINE WILLIAMS(1952); FIRST TIME, THE(1952); SNIPER, THE(1952); STORY OF WILL ROGERS, THE(1952); ESCAPE FROM FORT BRAVO(1953); MAIN STREET TO BROADWAY(1953); ATHENA(1954); BROKEN LANCE(1954); COMMAND, THE(1954); EGYPTIAN, THE(1954); LEFT HAND OF GOD, THE(1955); ONE DESIRE(1955); SPOILERS, THE(1955); DAY OF FURY, A(1956); FIRST TEXAN, THE(1956); LAST WAGON, THE(1956); STRANGE INTRUDER(1956); BATTLE HYMN(1957); SPOILERS OF THE FOREST(1957); TIME LIMIT(1957); LAST OF THE FAST GUNS, THE(1958); TARZAN'S FIGHT FOR LIFE(1958); TRAP, THE(1959); BRAMBLE BUSH, THE(1960); GALLANT HOURS, THE(1960); PRESSURE POINT(1962); UNDERWATER CITY, THE(1962); UGLY AMERICAN, THE(1963); MADAME X(1966)
Charles H. Reid
REAL LIFE(1979)
Clara Reid
PRIDE AND PREJUDICE(1940); WATERLOO BRIDGE(1940); SUSPICION(1941); MRS. MINIVER(1942); PRACTICALLY YOURS(1944); TO EACH HIS OWN(1946); LIFE WITH FATHER(1947)
Cliff Reid
LOST PATROL, THE,(1934), p; ANNIE OAKLEY(1935), p; ANOTHER FACE(1935), p; ARIZONIAN, THE(1935), p; CHASING YESTERDAY(1935), p; GRAND OLD GIRL(1935), p; INFORMER, THE(1935), p; POWDERSMOKE RANGE(1935), p; RED MORNING(1935), p; STRANGERS ALL(1935), p; THREE MUSKETEERS, THE(1935), p; WEST OF THE PECOS(1935), p; HIS FAMILY TREE(1936), p; PLOUGH AND THE STARS, THE(1936), p; SPECIAL INVESTIGATOR(1936), p; WANTED: JANE TURNER(1936), p; WITHOUT ORDERS(1936), p; WITNESS CHAIR, THE(1936), p; YELLOW DUST(1936), p; BEHIND THE HEADLINES(1937), p; CHINA PASSAGE(1937), p; CRASHING HOLLYWOOD(1937), p; CRIMINAL LAWYER(1937), p; HIDEAWAY(1937), p; MAN WHO FOUND HIMSELF, THE(1937), p; BLIND ALIBI(1938), p; CRIME RING(1938), p; LAW WEST OF TOMBSTONE, THE(1938), p; NEXT TIME I MARRY(1938), p; THIS MARRIAGE BUSINESS(1938), p; ALMOST A GENTLEMAN(1939), p; CONSPIRACY(1939), p; FIXER DUGAN(1939), p; GIRL AND THE GAMBLER, THE(1939), p; GREAT MAN VOTES, THE(1939), p; MEXICAN SPITFIRE(1939), p; PANAMA LADY(1939), p; SPELLBINDER, THE(1939), p; TWO THOROUGHBREDS(1939), p; ANNE OF WINDY POPLARS(1940), p; CROSS COUNTRY ROMANCE(1940), p; LADDIE(1940), p; MEXICAN SPITFIRE OUT WEST(1940), p; ONE CROWDED NIGHT(1940), p; PLAY GIRL(1940), p; SAINT'S DOUBLE TROUBLE, THE(1940), p; SUED FOR LIBEL(1940), p; WILDCAT BUS(1940), p; YOU CAN'T FOOL YOUR WIFE(1940), p; LADY SCARFACE(1941), p; PLAYMATES(1941), p; REPENT AT LEISURE(1941), p; MAYOR OF 44TH STREET, THE(1942), p; MEXICAN SPITFIRE AT SEA(1942), p; MEXICAN SPITFIRE SEES A GHOST(1942), p; POWDER TOWN(1942), p; SING YOUR WORRIES AWAY(1942), p; HOODLUM SAINT, THE(1946), p
Don Reid
SMOKEY AND THE BANDIT II(1980); FIGHTING BACK(1983, Brit.)
Donald Gordon Reid
Silents
CHALLENGE ACCEPTED, THE(1918), w
Donald Reid
BOOTS! BOOTS!(1934, Brit.)
Dorothy Reid
SUCKER MONEY(1933), d; RED HEAD(1934), p; WOMEN MUST DRESS(1935), w; HONEYMOON LIMITED(1936), w; BRIDE FOR HENRY, A(1937), p; PARADISE ISLE(1937), p; PRISON BREAK(1938), w; DRUMS OF THE DESERT(1940), w; HAUNTED HOUSE, THE(1940), w; ON THE SPOT(1940), w; TOMBOY(1940), w; OLD SWIMMIN' HOLE, THE(1941), w; REDHEAD(1941), w; WHO KILLED "DOC" ROBBIN?(1948), w; IMPACT(1949), w; RHUBARB(1951), w; FOOTSTEPS IN THE FOG(1955, Brit.), w
Ella Reid
RENEGADE GIRLS(1974)

Elliot Reid
DOUBLE LIFE, A(1947); VICKI(1953); WOMAN'S WORLD(1954)
Elliott Reid
RAMPARTS WE WATCH, THE(1940); YOUNG IDEAS(1943); STORY OF DR. WASSELL, THE(1944); SIERRA(1950); WHIP HAND, THE(1951); GENTLEMEN PREFER BLONDES(1953); INHERIT THE WIND(1960); ABSENT-MINDED PROFESSOR, THE(1961); MOVE OVER, DARLING(1963); SON OF FLUBBER(1963); THRILL OF IT ALL, THE(1963); WHEELER DEALERS, THE(1963); WHO'S BEEN SLEEPING IN MY BED?(1963); FOLLOW ME, BOYS!(1966); BLACKBEARD'S GHOST(1968); SOME KIND OF A NUT(1969); HEAVEN CAN WAIT(1978)
Elma Reid
SECRET OF THE LOCH, THE(1934, Brit.)
Fiona Cunningham Reid
PRIVILEGED(1982, Brit.), ph
Fiona Reid
Misc. Talkies
ACCIDENT(1983)
Frances Reid
MAN-PROOF(1938); WRONG MAN, THE(1956); SECONDS(1966)
1984
WHAT YOU TAKE FOR GRANTED(1984), ph
Frances Whiting Reid
BIG TOWN GIRL(1937), w
George Reid
PUBLIC COWBOY NO. 1(1937), ed; SILVER STAR, THE(1955), ed
Gregory Reid
THIS, THAT AND THE OTHER(1970, Brit.)
Gus Reid
WHEN YOU'RE IN LOVE(1937)
Hal Reid
Silents
DAN(1914), a, w; PROHIBITION(1915), w; LITTLE MISS HOOVER(1918); EVERY WOMAN'S PROBLEM(1921), w
Misc. Silents
TIME LOCK NO. 776(1915), d; TWO BRIDES, THE(1919)
Harold Reid
SMOKEY AND THE BANDIT II(1980)
Lt. Cmdr. J. Reid, R.N.
SHIPS WITH WINGS(1942, Brit.), tech adv
Jane Reid
SINS OF THE CHILDREN(1930); MAID TO ORDER(1932)
Misc. Silents
LAW OF FEAR(1928); TERROR(1928); TERROR MOUNTAIN(1928); WHEN THE LAW RIDES(1928)
John Reid
MIDDLE AGE SPREAD(1979, New Zealand), d
Johnny Reid
Silents
PUPPET MAN, THE(1921, Brit.)
Justin Reid
TORMENTED, THE(1978, Ital.), p
Kate Reid
DANGEROUS AGE, A(1960, Can.); ONE PLUS ONE(1961, Can.); THIS PROPERTY IS CONDEMNED(1966); SIDELONG GLANCES OF A PIGEON KICKER, THE(1970); ANDROMEDA STRAIN, THE(1971); DELICATE BALANCE, A(1973); RAINBOW BOYS, THE(1973, Can.); SHOOT(1976, Can.); "EQUUS"(1977); PLAGUE(1978, Can.); CIRCLE OF TWO(1980, Can.); DEATH SHIP(1980, Can.); DOUBLE NEGATIVE(1980, Can.); ATLANTIC CITY(1981, U.S./Can.); MONKEY GRIP(1983, Aus.)
1984
HIGHPOINT(1984, Can.)
Misc. Talkies
PAPER PEOPLE, THE(1969); M3: THE GEMINI STRAIN(1980)
Kathy Reid
HAPPY BIRTHDAY TO ME(1981)
Kenneth A. Reid
FACTS OF LIFE, THE(1960), art d; MODEL SHOP, THE(1969), prod d; LIBERATION OF L.B. JONES, THE(1970), prod d; OUTSIDE MAN, THE(1973, U.S./FR.), art d
Margaret Reid
SLEEPY LAGOON(1943)
Margot Reid
COLOR ME DEAD(1969, Aus.)
Maria Reid
WRONG MAN, THE(1956)
Marita Reid
CROWDED PARADISE(1956)
Maxwell Reid
LUPE(1967)
Medea Reid
LUPE(1967)
Mickser Reid
SINFUL DAVEY(1969, Brit.)
Milton Reid
UNDERCOVER GIRL(1957, Brit.); FERRY TO HONG KONG(1959, Brit.); SWISS FAMILY ROBINSON(1960); PASSPORT TO CHINA(1961, Brit.); TERROR OF THE TONGS, THE(1961, Brit.); WONDERS OF ALADDIN, THE(1961, Fr./Ital.); NIGHT CREATURES(1962, Brit.); THREE FACES OF SIN(1963, Fr./Ital.); PANIC(1966, Brit.); BERSERK(1967); DEADLIER THAN THE MALE(1967, Brit.); GREAT CATHERINE(1968, Brit.); ASSASSINATION BUREAU, THE(1969, Brit.); HORSEMEN, THE(1971); DOCTOR PHIBES RISES AGAIN(1972, Brit.); RETURN OF THE PINK PANTHER, THE(1975, Brit.); PEOPLE THAT TIME FORGOT, THE(1977, Brit.); SPY WHO LOVED ME, THE(1977, Brit.); ARABIAN ADVENTURE(1979, Brit.); TERROR(1979, Brit.); TARGET: HARRY(1980)
P. R. Reid
COLDITZ STORY, THE(1955, Brit.), w
Pat Ann Reid
GNOME-MOBILE, THE(1967)
Pat Reid
THREADS(1932, Brit.)

Paula Reid
SOMEWHERE IN THE NIGHT(1946)
Phil Reid
THIRST(1979, Aus.), ed
Philip Reid
DAY AFTER HALLOWEEN, THE(1981, Aus.), ed; FIRE IN THE STONE, THE(1983, Aus.), ed
Ralph Reid
HOW TO MARRY A MILLIONAIRE(1953)
Sam Reid
Misc. Silents
MONEY MASTER, THE(1915)
Sheila Reid
OTHELLO(1965, Brit.); TOUCH, THE(1971, U.S./Swed.); I WANT WHAT I WANT(1972, Brit.); Z.P.G.(1972); THREE SISTERS(1974, Brit.); SIR HENRY AT RAWLINSON END(1980, Brit.); FIVE DAYS ONE SUMMER(1982); DRESSER, THE(1983)
Sue Reid
HELP!(1965, Brit.)
Susan Reid
HAND IN HAND(1960, Brit.); HAND, THE(1960, Brit.)
Taylor Reid
ROADBLOCK(1951)
Toni Reid
HAIL(1973); STEPFORD WIVES, THE(1975)
Trevor Reid
DANGEROUS CARGO(1954, Brit.); DELAYED ACTION(1954, Brit.); GILDED CAGE, THE(1954, Brit.); MEET MR. CALLAGHAN(1954, Brit.); HORNET'S NEST, THE(1955, Brit.); BEHIND THE HEADLINES(1956, Brit.); HIDEOUT, THE(1956, Brit.); NARROWING CIRCLE, THE(1956, Brit.); PASSPORT TO TREASON(1956, Brit.); SATELLITE IN THE SKY(1956); HOW TO MURDER A RICH UNCLE(1957, Brit.); MURDER REPORTED(1958, Brit.); BOBBIKINS(1959, Brit.); QUESTION OF ADULTERY, A(1959, Brit.); PICCADILLY THIRD STOP(1960, Brit.); MARY HAD A LITTLE(1961, Brit.); LONGEST DAY, THE(1962); FAST LADY, THE(1963, Brit.); NIGHT TRAIN TO PARIS(1964, Brit.); WALK A TIGHTROPE(1964, U.S./Brit.); MARRIAGE OF CONVENIENCE(1970, Brit.)
Violet Reid
Misc. Silents
GAMBLER OF THE WEST, THÉ(1915)
Virginia Reid
ROBERTA(1935)
Vivian Reid
MAN WHO DARED, THE(1933); SWEETHEARTS(1938); VIVACIOUS LADY(1938)
Vivien Reid
STUDENT TOUR(1934)
Wallace Reid
Silents
BIRTH OF A NATION, THE(1915); CARMEN(1915); GOLDEN CHANCE, THE(1915); INTOLERANCE(1916); JOAN THE WOMAN(1916); NAN OF MUSIC MOUNTAIN(1917); ALIAS MIKE MORAN(1919); HAWTHORNE OF THE U.S.A.(1919); ROARING ROAD, THE(1919); ALWAYS AUDACIOUS(1920); EXCUSE MY DUST(1920); WHAT'S YOUR HURRY?(1920); AFFAIRS OF ANATOL(1921); CHARM SCHOOL, THE(1921); DON'T TELL EVERYTHING(1921); TOO MUCH SPEED(1921); ACROSS THE CONTINENT(1922); DICTATOR, THE(1922); NICE PEOPLE(1922); THIRTY DAYS(1922); WORLD'S CHAMPION, THE(1922)
Misc. Silents
ENOCH ARDEN(1915); LOST HOUSE, THE(1915); OLD HEIDELBERG(1915); YANKEE FROM THE WEST, A(1915); HOUSE OF THE GOLDEN WINDOWS, THE(1916); LOVE MASK, THE(1916); MARIA ROSA(1916); SELFISH WOMAN, THE(1916); TO HAVE AND TO HOLD(1916); YELLOW PAWN, THE(1916); BIG TIMBER(1917); DEVIL STONE, THE(1917); GOLDEN FETTER, THE(1917); HOSTAGE, THE(1917); PRISON WITHOUT WALLS, THE(1917); SQUAW MAN'S SON, THE(1917); WOMAN GOD FORGOT, THE(1917); WORLD APART, THE(1917); BELIEVE ME, XANTIPPE(1918); FIREFLY OF FRANCE, THE(1918); HOUSE OF SILENCE, THE(1918); LESS THAN KIN(1918); MAN FROM FUNERAL RANGE, THE(1918); RIMROCK JONES(1918); SOURCE, THE(1918); THINGS WE LOVE, THE(1918); TOO MANY MILLIONS(1918); DUB, THE(1919); LOTTERY MAN, THE(1919); LOVE BURGLAR, THE(1919); VALLEY OF THE GIANTS, THE(1919); YOU'RE FIRED(1919); DANCIN' FOOL, THE(1920); DOUBLE SPEED(1920); SICK ABED(1920); FOREVER(1921); HELL DIGGERS, THE(1921); LOVE SPECIAL, THE(1921); CLARENCE(1922); GHOST BREAKER, THE(1922); RENT FREE(1922)
Wallace Reid, Jr.
HOOSIER SCHOOLMASTER(1935); GOLD RUSH MAISIE(1940); NORTHWEST MOUNTED POLICE(1940)
Mrs. Wallace Reid [Dorothy Davenport]
DUDE WRANGLER, THE(1930), p; MAN HUNT(1933); RACING STRAIN, THE(1933), w; ROAD TO RUIN(1934), d; WOMEN MUST DRESS(1935), p; HONEYMOON LIMITED(1936), p; HOUSE OF A THOUSAND CANDLES, THE(1936), p
Misc. Talkies
WOMAN CONDEMNED(1934), d
Silents
MASKED AVENGER, THE(1922); RED KIMONO(1925); LINDA(1929), d
Misc. Silents
HUMAN WRECKAGE(1923); BROKEN LAWS(1924); SATIN WOMAN, THE(1927); HELLSHIP BRONSON(1928)
Wally Reid, Jr.
RACING STRAIN, THE(1933); OUTLAW, THE(1943)
Richard Reide
FINDERS KEEPERS(1951), art d
Richard H. Reidel
THAT'S THE SPIRIT(1945), art d; SHE WROTE THE BOOK(1946), art d; TIME OF THEIR LIVES, THE(1946), art d; PIRATES OF MONTEREY(1947), art d; FRANCIS(1949), art d; SADDLE TRAMP(1950), art d; SASKATCHEWAN(1954), art d; MAN WITHOUT A STAR(1955), art d
Richard Reidel
LARCENY(1948), art d; CALAMITY JANE AND SAM BASS(1949), art d
Ed Reider
HOT ROD GIRL(1956)

Marcia Reider
BOOGENS, THE(1982)
Marcia Yvette Reider
1984
FOOTLOOSE(1984)
Francesca Reidy
EDGE OF THE WORLD, THE(1937, Brit.)
Gabrielle Reidy
EDUCATING RITA(1983)
Jamie Reidy
BANK SHOT(1974)
Jean Reiet
GERVAISE(1956, Fr.)
E. H. Reif
SWING IT, PROFESSOR(1937), art d; BIG SHOW-OFF, THE(1945), set d; THUNDER TOWN(1946), set d
Elias H. Reif
STRANGE ILLUSION(1945), set d; MURDER IS MY BUSINESS(1946), set d; FEAR IN THE NIGHT(1947), set d; THREE ON A TICKET(1947), set d; MONEY MADNESS(1948), art d
Elias Reif
MIRACULOUS JOURNEY(1948), set d
Harry Reif
WATERFRONT(1944), set d; PHANTOM OF 42ND STREET, THE(1945), set d; THREE IN THE SADDLE(1945), set d; DEATH VALLEY(1946), art d; SCARED TO DEATH(1947), art d; PREJUDICE(1949), set d; MACHINE GUN KELLY(1958), set d; MISSILE TO THE MOON(1959), set d; ATOMIC SUBMARINE, THE(1960), set d; MA BARKER'S KILLER BROOD(1960), set d; FIVE MINUTES TO LIVE(1961), set d; MASTER OF THE WORLD(1961), set d; PIT AND THE PENDULUM, THE(1961), set d; SILENT CALL, THE(1961), set d; SNIPER'S RIDGE(1961), set d; YOU HAVE TO RUN FAST(1961), set d; 20,000 EYES(1961), set d; AIR PATROL(1962), set d; DEADLY DUO(1962), set d; FIREBRAND, THE(1962), set d; GUN STREET(1962), set d; HAND OF DEATH(1962), set d; INCIDENT IN AN ALLEY(1962), set d; PREMATURE BURIAL, THE(1962), set d; PUBLIC AFFAIR, A(1962), set d; SAINTLY SINNERS(1962), set d; WOMAN HUNT(1962), set d; "X"–THE MAN WITH THE X-RAY EYES(1963), set d; DAY MARS INVADED EARTH, THE(1963), set d; HAUNTED PALACE, THE(1963), set d; POLICE NURSE(1963), set d; RAVEN, THE(1963), set d; TERROR, THE(1963), set d; YOUNG GUNS OF TEXAS(1963), set d; YOUNG SWINGERS, THE(1963), set d; COMEDY OF TERRORS, THE(1964), set d; MUSCLE BEACH PARTY(1964), set d; PAJAMA PARTY(1964), set d; RAIDERS FROM BENEATH THE SEA(1964), set d; SURF PARTY(1964), set d; BILLY THE KID VS. DRACULA(1966), set d; DESTINATION INNER SPACE(1966), set d; FIREBALL 590(1966), set d; JESSE JAMES MEETS FRANKENSTEIN'S DAUGHTER(1966), set d; WOMEN OF THE PREHISTORIC PLANET(1966), set d; IT'S A BIKINI WORLD(1967), set d; THUNDER ALLEY(1967), set d; WHAT AM I BID?(1967), set d; 40 GUNS TO APACHE PASS(1967), set d; MARYJANE(1968), set d; WILD IN THE STREETS(1968), set d; DEVIL'S 8, THE(1969), set d; HELL'S BELLES(1969), set d; 2000 YEARS LATER(1969), set d; NEW CENTURIONS, THE(1972), set d
Harry H. Reif
MURDER IS MY BEAT(1955), set d
Helena Reif
1984
HAMBONE AND HILLIE(1984), prod d
Rudolf Reif
SHOEMAKER AND THE ELVES, THE(1967, Ger.)
Lyle B. Reifsnider
THAT HAGEN GIRL(1947), set d; FIGHTER SQUADRON(1948), set d; IT'S A GREAT FEELING(1949), set d; STORY OF SEABISCUIT, THE(1949), set d; TEA FOR TWO(1950), set d; I WAS A COMMUNIST FOR THE F.B.I.(1951), set d; LULLABY OF BROADWAY, THE(1951), set d; MARA MARU(1952), set d
Claire Reigbert
AFFAIRS OF DR. HOLL(1954, Ger.)
Helene Reigh
HER SISTER'S SECRET(1946)
James Reigle
ANDROID(1982), w
Vickie Reigle
CANNONBALL RUN, THE(1981)
Will Reigle
ANDROID(1982), w
Ado Reigler
SHOEMAKER AND THE ELVES, THE(1967, Ger.)
Francisco Reiguera
BRAVE BULLS, THE(1951); ENCHANTED ISLAND(1958); GINA(1961, Fr./Mex.); VIVA MARIA(1965, Fr./Ital.); GUNS FOR SAN SEBASTIAN(1968, U.S./Fr./Mex./Ital.)
Kay Reihl
RED MENACE, THE(1949)
Hill Reihs-Oromes
DON JUAN(1956, Aust.), cos
Reihsig
M(1933, Ger.)
Andrew Reilly
LISZTOMANIA(1975, Brit.)
Betty Reilly
ON AN ISLAND WITH YOU(1948)
Charles Nelson Reilly
TWO TICKETS TO PARIS(1962); TIGER MAKES OUT, THE(1967)
1984
CANNONBALL RUN II(1984)
Claire Reilly
NATURAL ENEMIES(1979)
Diane Reilly
ICE CASTLES(1978)
Frank Reilly
Silents
BAR SINISTER, THE(1917)

Gina Reilly
Misc. Silents
FACE AT YOUR WINDOW(1920)
Hugh Reilly
JOHNNY STOOL PIGEON(1949); SLEEPING CITY, THE(1950); BRIGHT VIC-
TORY(1951); LASSIE'S GREAT ADVENTURE(1963); CHUKA(1967)
Jack Reilly
STORY OF G.I. JOE, THE(1945); WELL-GROOMED BRIDE, THE(1946); ROYAL
WEDDING(1951)
Jane Reilly
FINNEGANS WAKE(1965)
Jean Burt Reilly
MAJORITY OF ONE, A(1961), makeup
Joan T. Reilly
ROSEMARY'S BABY(1968)
John Reilly
GREAT WALDO PEPPER, THE(1975); MAIN EVENT, THE(1979)
John R. Reilly
THIRTY SECONDS OVER TOKYO(1944)
Luke Reilly
NIGHTHAWKS(1981)
Maureen O Reilly
WITNESS IN THE DARK(1959, Brit.)
Pat Reilly
TOUGH ENOUGH(1983)
Misc. Talkies
HIDEOUT IN THE SUN(1960)
Patricia Reilly
BIG BUSINESS GIRL(1931), w
Robert Reilly
LILITH(1964); FRANKENSTEIN MEETS THE SPACE MONSTER(1965)
Robert T. Reilly
FIGHTING PRINCE OF DONEGAL, THE(1966, Brit.), w
Teddy Reilly
HEARTS OF HUMANITY(1936, Brit.)
Thomas Reilly
VERDICT, THE(1946), ed; APRIL SHOWERS(1948), ed; EMBRACEABLE
YOU(1948), ed; HOMICIDE(1949), ed; NIGHT UNTO NIGHT(1949), ed; BACK-
FIRE(1950), ed; CHAIN LIGHTNING(1950), ed; THREE SECRETS(1950), ed; ALONG
THE GREAT DIVIDE(1951), ed; LIGHTNING STRIKES TWICE(1951), ed; ON MOON-
LIGHT BAY(1951), ed; RATON PASS(1951), ed; ABOUT FACE(1952), ed; BUGLES IN
THE AFTERNOON(1952), ed; CATTLE TOWN(1952), ed; MIRACLE OF OUR LADY
OF FATIMA, THE(1952), ed; SO BIG(1953), ed; CRIME WAVE(1954), ed;
THEM!(1954), ed; ILLEGAL(1955), ed; HELEN OF TROY(1956, Ital), ed; MIRACLE IN
THE RAIN(1956), ed; BOMBERS B-52(1957), ed; GREEN-EYED BLONDE, THE(1957),
ed
Tom Reilly
MY BODYGUARD(1980); YOUNG WARRIORS(1983)
Tommy Reilly
YOUNG MAN OF MANHATTAN(1930); IT ALL CAME TRUE(1940); GANGSTER,
THE(1947); NAVY LARK, THE(1959, Brit.), m
Walter Reilly
VELVET TOUCH, THE(1948), w
William C. Reilly
Misc. Talkies
BROAD COALITION, THE(1972); WHAT DO I TELL THE BOYS AT THE STA-
TION(1972)
Brigitta Reim
ODDO(1967)
Inga Reim
WEEKEND(1964, Den.)
Vicki Reim
TALES OF A SALESMAN(1965)
Eric Reiman
FORTY THOUSAND HORSEMEN(1941, Aus.); LONG JOHN SILVER(1954, Aus.)
Ethel K. Reiman
ROAD TO BALI(1952)
Johannes Reimann
Misc. Silents
SCANDAL IN PARIS(1929, Ger.)
Walter Reimann
Silents
CABINET OF DR. CALIGARI, THE(1921, Ger.), art d, cos; ETERNAL LOVE(1929),
set d&cos
Birgitte Reimar
LESSON IN LOVE, A(1960, Swed.)
Bill Reimbold
NASTY HABITS(1976, Brit.); RAGTIME(1981); RAIDERS OF THE LOST ARK(1981);
SUPERMAN III(1983)
Anton Reimer
UNWILLING AGENT(1968, Ger.)
Bob Reimer
1984
ICEMAN(1984)
Elin Reimer
PEOPLE MEET AND SWEET MUSIC FILLS THE HEART(1969, Den./Swed.)
James Reimer
QUEEN OF THE AMAZONS(1947), art d
Maureen Lynn Reimer
DARLING, HOW COULD YOU!(1951)
Ed Reimers
LOVED ONE, THE(1965); $1,000,000 DUCK(1971)
Edwin Reimers
HARD, FAST, AND BEAUTIFUL(1951); ON THE LOOSE(1951)
George Reimers
Misc. Silents
QUEEN OF SIN AND THE SPECTACLE OF SODOM AND GOMORRAH, THE(1923,
Aust.)

Silke Rein
COUSINS IN LOVE(1982)
Silvano Reina
WONDERS OF ALADDIN, THE(1961, Fr./Ital.), w
Ed Reinach
FOLIES DERGERE(1935)
Edward Reinach
Silents
FOOLISH WIVES(1920)
Ed Reinarch
Silents
DEVIL'S PASSKEY, THE(1920)
Michael Reinbold
BRONCO BILLY(1980)
Jeremy Scott Reinbolt
MOMMIE DEAREST(1981)
Therese Reinch
PRIME CUT(1972)
Heinz Reincke
ALWAYS VICTORIOUS(1960, Ital.); LONGEST DAY, THE(1962); FAUST(1963, Ger.);
DOCTOR OF ST. PAUL, THE(1969, Ger.); PRIEST OF ST. PAULI(1970, Ger.)
Carl Reindel
HE RIDES TALL(1964); FOLLOW ME, BOYS!(1966); BULLITT(1968); SPEED-
WAY(1968); GYPSY MOTHS, THE(1969); 1,000 PLANE RAID, THE(1969); CHEYENNE
SOCIAL CLUB, THE(1970); TORA! TORA! TORA!(1970, U.S./Jap.)
Josef Reindl
GIVEN WORD, THE(1964, Braz.), spec eff
Herbert Reinecker
CANARIS(1955, Ger.), w; BOOMERANG(1960, Ger.), w; BRAINWASHED(1961,
Ger.), w; UNWILLING AGENT(1968, Ger.), w
Gary Reineke
SUNDAY IN THE COUNTRY(1975, Can.); CLOWN MURDERS, THE(1976, Can.);
WHY SHOOT THE TEACHER(1977, Can.); POWER PLAY(1978, Brit./Can.); CREEPER,
THE(1980, Can.); KIDNAPPING OF THE PRESIDENT, THE(1980, Can.); BELLS(1981,
Can.); GREY FOX, THE(1983, Can.)
1984
SURROGATE, THE(1984, Can.)
Ann Reiner
PASTOR HALL(1940, Brit.), w
Carl Reiner
GAZEBO, THE(1959); HAPPY ANNIVERSARY(1959); GIDGET GOES HA-
WAIIAN(1961); IT'S A MAD, MAD, MAD, MAD WORLD(1963); THRILL OF IT ALL,
THE(1963), a, w; ART OF LOVE, THE(1965), a, w; DON'T WORRY, WE'LL THINK
OF A TITLE(1966); RUSSIANS ARE COMING, THE RUSSIANS ARE COMING,
THE(1966); ENTER LAUGHING(1967), p, d, w; GUIDE FOR THE MARRIED MAN,
A(1967); COMIC, THE(1969), a, p, d, w; GENERATION(1969); WHERE'S POP-
PA?(1970), d; OH, GOD!(1977), a, d; END, THE(1978); ONE AND ONLY, THE(1978), d;
JERK, THE(1979), a, d; DEAD MEN DON'T WEAR PLAID(1982), a, d, w; MAN
WITH TWO BRAINS, THE(1983), D, w
1984
ALL OF ME(1984), d
Misc. Talkies
ALICE OF WONDERLAND IN PARIS(1966)
Erwin Reiner
WORLD OWES ME A LIVING, THE(1944, Brit.), w
Estelle Reiner
MAN WITH TWO BRAINS, THE(1983); TO BE OR NOT TO BE(1983)
Ethel Linder Reiner
BOMB IN THE HIGH STREET(1961, Brit.), p
Fritz Reiner
CARNEGIE HALL(1947); CATCH-22(1970), md
Gigette Reiner
RUN FOR YOUR WIFE(1966, Fr./Ital.)
Hannah Reiner
WHERE ANGELS GO...TROUBLE FOLLOWS(1968), ch
Irwin Reiner
TROJAN BROTHERS, THE(1946), w
Ivan Reiner
SNOW DEVILS, THE(1965, Ital.), w; WILD, WILD PLANET, THE(1967, Ital.), w;
GREEN SLIME, THE(1969), p; WAR BETWEEN THE PLANETS(1971, Ital.), w
Maxine Reiner
CHARLIE CHAN AT THE CIRCUS(1936); FLYING HOSTESS(1936); GIRL ON THE
FRONT PAGE, THE(1936); IT HAD TO HAPPEN(1936); SINS OF MAN(1936)
Rob Reiner
ENTER LAUGHING(1967); HALLS OF ANGER(1970); WHERE'S POPPA?(1970);
SUMMERTREE(1971); HOW COME NOBODY'S ON OUR SIDE?(1975); FIRE SA-
LE(1977)
1984
THIS IS SPINAL TAP(1984), a, d, w, m, m/l
Susan Reiner
EDGE, THE(1968)
Thomas Reiner
BLOOD AND BLACK LACE(1965, Ital.)
Tracy Reiner
1984
FLAMINGO KID, THE(1984)
Arlette Reinerg
TENANT, THE(1976, Fr.)
Dennis Reiners
J.W. COOP(1971)
Kai Reiners
LOVING COUPLES(1966, Swed.)
E. E. Reinert
TALE OF FIVE WOMEN, A(1951, Brit.), d; DANGER IS A WOMAN(1952, Fr.), d&w
Emil E. Reinert
GYPSY MELODY(1936, Brit.), p; TREACHERY ON THE HIGH SEAS(1939, Brit.), d
Emile Edwin Reinert
VIENNA WALTZES(1961, Aust.), d

Sisse Reingaard
HAGBARD AND SIGNE(1968, Den./Iceland/Swed.); VENOM(1968, Den.)
Beth Reinglass
10 TO MIDNIGHT(1983)
Jacob Reinglass
DANGEROUS AGE, A(1960, Can.)
Arthur Reinhard
Silents
METROPOLIS(1927, Ger.)
Frank Reinhard
HONKYTONK MAN(1982)
Betty Reinhardt
EVERYBODY'S BABY(1939), w; PARDON OUR NERVE(1939), w; GOLD RUSH
MAISIE(1940), w; MAISIE WAS A LADY(1941), w; MAISIE GETS HER MAN(1942),
w; HIS BUTLER'S SISTER(1943), w; LAURA(1944), w
Django Reinhardt
LACOMBE, LUCIEN(1974), m
Elizabeth Reinhardt
CLUNY BROWN(1946), w; SENTIMENTAL JOURNEY(1946), w; CARNIVAL IN
COSTA RICA(1947), w; GIVE MY REGARDS TO BROADWAY(1948), w; WHEN MY
BABY SMILES AT ME(1948), w; HIT PARADE OF 1951(1950), w
Gottfried Reinhardt
COMRADE X(1940), p
Gottfried Reinhardt
I LIVE MY LIFE(1935), w; GREAT WALTZ, THE(1938), w; BRIDAL SUITE(1939), w;
RAGE IN HEAVEN(1941), p; TWO-FACED WOMAN(1941), p; BIG JACK(1949), p;
GREAT SINNER, THE(1949), p; RED BADGE OF COURAGE, THE(1951), p; INVITA-
TION(1952), d; YOUNG MAN WITH IDEAS(1952), p; STORY OF THREE LOVES,
THE(1953), d; BETRAYED(1954), p&d; TOWN WITHOUT PITY(1961, Ger./Switz./
U.S.), p&d; VOR SONNENUNTERGANG(1961, Ger), d; SITUATION HOPELESS–BUT
NOT SERIOUS(1965), p&d
Janis Reinhardt
WILD SEASON(1968, South Africa)
John Reinhardt
CLIMAX, THE(1930); MAMBA(1930), w; IO ... TU ... Y ... ELLA(1933), d; NADA MAS
QUE UNA MUJER(1934), w; TWO AND ONE TWO(1934), d; TANGO BAR(1935), d;
CAPTAIN CALAMITY(1936), d; PRESCRIPTION FOR ROMANCE(1937), w; MR.
MOTO IN DANGER ISLAND(1939), w; FOR YOU I DIE(1947), p, d; GUILTY,
THE(1947), d; HIGH TIDE(1947), d; OPEN SECRET(1948), d; SOFIA(1948), p, d;
CHICAGO CALLING(1951), d, w
Silents
ACCORDING TO LAW(1916); MISCHIEF MAKER, THE(1916); EYE FOR EYE(1918)
Misc. Silents
PRINCE OF HEARTS, THE(1929)
Max Reinhardt
MIDSUMMER'S NIGHT'S DREAM, A(1935), p, d
Ray Reinhardt
DOUBLE-BARRELLED DETECTIVE STORY, THE(1965); TIME AFTER TIME(1979,
Brit.); CARDIAC ARREST(1980); CHU CHU AND THE PHILLY FLASH(1981)
Richard Reinhardt
OKLAHOMA BLUES(1948)
Silvia Reinhardt
TOWN WITHOUT PITY(1961, Ger./Switz./U.S.), w; SITUATION HOPELESS–BUT
NOT SERIOUS(1965), w
Stephen Reinhardt
SONG OF NORWAY(1970)
Wolfgang Reinhardt
JUAREZ(1939), w; MY LOVE CAME BACK(1940), p; THREE STRANGERS(1946), p;
CAUGHT(1949), p; TRAPP FAMILY, THE(1961, Ger.), p; FREUD(1962), p, w; HI-
TLER: THE LAST TEN DAYS(1973, Brit./Ital.), p, w
Dick Reinhart
RIDIN' DOWN THE TRAIL(1947); OUTLAW BRAND(1948); SONG OF THE DRIFT-
ER(1948)
J. Reinhart
Silents
MAN WHO FORGOT, THE(1917)
John Reinhart
LOVE, LIVE AND LAUGH(1929); TOWER OF TERROR, THE(1942, Brit.), w
Silents
SCALES OF JUSTICE, THE(1914), w
Misc. Silents
TWO MEN AND A WOMAN(1917)
Richard Reinhart
SIX LESSONS FROM MADAME LA ZONGA(1941)
Alice Reinheart
LIEUTENANT WORE SKIRTS, THE(1956); BACHELOR FLAT(1962); HOUSE IS
NOT A HOME, A(1964); RAT FINK(1965)
Henry Reinheimer
1984
LOOSE CONNECTIONS(1984, Brit.)
Ernst Reinhold
U-47 LT. COMMANDER PRIEN(1967, Ger.)
Heinze Reinhold
ALWAYS IN MY HEART(1942), m
Judge Reinhold
STRIPES(1981); FAST TIMES AT RIDGEMONT HIGH(1982); PANDEMONI-
UM(1982); LORDS OF DISCIPLINE, THE(1983)
1984
BEVERLY HILLS COP(1984); GREMLINS(1984); ROADHOUSE 66(1984)
Misc. Talkies
RUNNING SCARED(1980)
Gert Reinholm
SLEEPING BEAUTY(1965, Ger.)
George Reinholt
LOOKING UP(1977)
Lotte Reiniger
UNA SIGNORA DELL'OVEST(1942, Ital), w
Misc. Silents
ADVENTURES OF PRINCE ACHMED, THE(1926, Ger.), d

Scott Reiniger
DAWN OF THE DEAD(1979); KNIGHTRIDERS(1981)
Rex Reinit
THREE IN ONE(1956, Aus.), w
Rex Reinits
OUT OF THE CLOUDS(1957, Brit.), w
Gary Reinke
AGENCY(1981, Can.)
Heinz Reinke
BRIDGE AT REMAGEN, THE(1969)
Ann Reinking
MOVIE MOVIE(1978); ALL THAT JAZZ(1979); ANNIE(1982)
1984
MICKI AND MAUDE(1984)
Wilhelm Reinking
FIDELIO(1970, Ger.), art d
Henrik Reinkwell
SWEET SMELL OF LOVE(1966, Ital./Ger.)
Harald Reinl
RETURN OF DR. MABUSE, THE(1961, Ger./Fr./Ital.), d; APACHE GOLD(1965,
Ger.), d; DESPERADO TRAIL, THE(1965, Ger./Yugo.), d; LAST TOMAHAWK,
THE(1965, Ger./Ital./Span.), d; TREASURE OF SILVER LAKE(1965, Fr./Ger./Yugo.),
d; U-47 LT. COMMANDER PRIEN(1967, Ger.), d
Harold Reinl
INVISIBLE DR. MABUSE, THE(1965, Ger.), d; LAST OF THE RENEGADES(1966,
Fr./Ital./Ger./Yugo.), d; BLOOD DEMON(1967, Ger.), d
Ed Reinoch
PAROLE(1936)
Frantisek Reinstein
FIREMAN'S BALL, THE(1968, Czech.)
Constant Reiny
CLANDESTINE(1948, Fr.)
Denis Reis
SECRETS D'ALCOVE(1954, Fr./Ital.), ed
Echio Reis
EARTH ENTRANCED(1970, Braz.)
Irving Reis
KING OF ALCATRAZ(1938), w; TIME OUT FOR MURDER(1938), w; GRAND JURY
SECRETS(1939), w; KING OF CHINATOWN(1939), w; I'M STILL ALIVE(1940), d;
ONE CROWDED NIGHT(1940), d; DATE WITH THE FALCON, A(1941), d; FOOT-
LIGHT FEVER(1941), d; GAY FALCON, THE(1941), d; WEEKEND FOR
THREE(1941), d; BIG STREET, THE(1942), d; FALCON TAKES OVER, THE(1942), d;
GAMBLER'S CHOICE(1944), w; CRACK-UP(1946), d; BACHELOR AND THE BOBBY-
SOXER, THE(1947), d; ALL MY SONS(1948), d; ENCHANTMENT(1948), d; DANC-
ING IN THE DARK(1949), d; ROSEANNA McCOY(1949), d; THREE HUS-
BANDS(1950), d; NEW MEXICO(1951), d; FOUR POSTER, THE(1952), d;
INVITATION TO THE DANCE(1956), anim.
Silents
TOO MUCH BUSINESS(1922), ph
Misc. Silents
BUSINESS OF LOVE, THE(1925), d
Irving G. Reis
BARKLEYS OF BROADWAY, THE(1949), anim; IT'S ALWAYS FAIR WEA-
THER(1955), spec eff; FORBIDDEN PLANET(1956), spec eff
Oscar Reis
BYE-BYE BRASIL(1980, Braz.)
Ray Reis
DARKENED SKIES(1930), ph
Silents
GALLOPING GOBS, THE(1927), ph
Vivian Reis
MIDDLE AGE CRAZY(1980, Can.); CURTAINS(1983, Can.)
William Reis
FANCY BAGGAGE(1929), ph
G. Reisch
FIRST SPACESHIP ON VENUS(1960, Ger./Pol.), w
Steve Reisch
PARTNERS(1982)
Walter Reisch
THAT UNCERTAIN FEELING(1941), w; BECAUSE I LOVED YOU(1930, Ger.), w;
TEMPORARY WIDOW, THE(1930, Ger./Brit.), w; HAPPY EVER AFTER(1932, Ger./
Brit.), w; EMPRESS AND I, THE(1933, Ger.), w; F.P. 1(1933, Brit.), w; F.P. 1 DOESN'T
ANSWER(1933, Ger.), w; HEART SONG(1933, Brit.), w; PRINCE OF ARCADIA(1933,
Brit.), w; SONG YOU GAVE ME, THE(1934, Brit.), w; DIVINE SPARK, THE(1935,
Brit./Ital.), w; ESCAPADE(1935), w; EPISODE(1937, Aust.), d&w; MEN ARE NOT
GODS(1937, Brit.), d, w; GATEWAY(1938), w; GREAT WALTZ, THE(1938), w; NI-
NOTCHKA(1939), w; COMRADE X(1940), w; MY LOVE CAME BACK(1940), w; THAT
HAMILTON WOMAN(1941), w; SEVEN SWEETHEARTS(1942), w; SOMEWHERE
I'LL FIND YOU(1942), w; HEAVENLY BODY, THE(1943), w; GASLIGHT(1944), w;
SONG OF SCHEHERAZADE(1947), d&w; COUNTESS OF MONTE CRISTO,
THE(1948), w; FAN, THE(1949), w; MATING SEASON, THE(1951), w; MODEL AND
THE MARRIAGE BROKER, THE(1951), w; NIAGARA(1953), w; TITANIC(1953), w;
UNFINISHED SYMPHONY, THE(1953, Aust./Brit.), w; GIRL IN THE RED VELVET
SWING, THE(1955), w; TEENAGE REBEL(1956), w; SILK STOCKINGS(1957), w;
STOPOVER TOKYO(1957), p, w; FRAULEIN(1958), p; JOURNEY TO THE CENTER
OF THE EARTH(1959), w; REMARKABLE MR. PENNYPACKER, THE(1959), w
Geri Reischi
BROTHERHOOD OF SATAN, THE(1971)
Geri Reischl
I DISMEMBER MAMA(1974)
Brian Reise
1984
NIGHTMARE ON ELM STREET, A(1984)
Lee Reisen
SUMMER SOLDIERS(1972, Jap.)
R. Reisen
Misc. Silents
CHRYSANTHEMUMS(1914, USSR)

Felix Reisenberg
SKYLINE(1931), w
Sandor Reisenbuchler
LES MAITRES DU TEMPS(1982, Fr./Switz./Ger.), spec eff
Dr. Hugo Reisenfeld
WANDERING JEW, THE(1935, Brit.), m
Hugo Reisenfeld
ABRAHAM LINCOLN(1930), m; LET'S SING AGAIN(1936), md; ROSE OF THE RIO GRANDE(1938), md
Elmer L. Reisenstein [Elmer Rice]
Silents
ON TRIAL(1917), w
Ann Reiser
WHY ROCK THE BOAT?(1974, Can.)
Edgar Reiser
GEORGE(1973, U.S./Switz.)
Hans Reiser
GREAT ESCAPE, THE(1963); THREE PENNY OPERA(1963, Fr./Ger.); I DEAL IN DANGER(1966); GREAT BRITISH TRAIN ROBBERY, THE(1967, Ger.)
Paul Reiser
DINER(1982)
1984
BEVERLY HILLS COP(1984)
Robert Reiser
HARRAD SUMMER, THE(1974)
Bert Reisfeld
TALES OF THE UNCANNY(1932, Ger.); AS LONG AS YOU'RE NEAR ME(1956, Ger.), w
G. Reisgoff
ANNA CROSS, THE(1954, USSR), ph
Del Reisman
TAKE, THE(1974), w
Leo Reisman
ONLY SAPS WORK(1930), md
Philip Reisman, Jr.
TATTOOED STRANGER, THE(1950), w; SPECIAL DELIVERY(1955, Ger.), w; ALL THE WAY HOME(1963), w; P.J.(1968), w
Rose Judell Reisman
DANCING MAN(1934), p
Allen Reisner
ALL MINE TO GIVE(1957), d; ST. LOUIS BLUES(1958), d
Charles Reisner
NOISY NEIGHBORS(1929), d; EVERYBODY DANCE(1936, Brit.), d; MEET THE PEOPLE(1944), d
Silents
MAN ON THE BOX, THE(1925), d; OH, WHAT A NURSE!(1926), d
Misc. Silents
FOOLS FOR LUCK(1928), d
Charles Reisner, Jr.
EVERYBODY DANCE(1936, Brit.)
Charles "Chuck" Reisner
Silents
BETTER 'OLE, THE(1926), d, w
Charles F. Reisner
CHASING RAINBOWS(1930), d; LOVE IN THE ROUGH(1930), d; FLYING HIGH(1931), d, w; REDUCING(1931), d; DIVORCE IN THE FAMILY(1932), d; CHIEF, THE(1933), d; STUDENT TOUR(1934), d; WINTER CARNIVAL(1939), d; HARRIGAN'S KID(1943), d; BURY ME DEAD(1947), p; COBRA STRIKES, THE(1948), d
Misc. Talkies
BROTHERLY LOVE(1928), d; STEPPING OUT(1931), d
Silents
MAN ON THE BOX, THE(1925); FORTUNE HUNTER, THE(1927), d; WHAT EVERY GIRL SHOULD KNOW(1927), d; STEAMBOAT BILL, JR.(1928), d
Misc. Silents
MISSING LINK, THE(1927), d; CHINA BOUND(1929), d
Chuck Reisner
Silents
PILGRIM, THE(1923); JUSTICE OF THE FAR NORTH(1925)
Chuck Reisner, Jr.
SQUARE SHOULDERS(1929)
Dean Reisner
BILL AND COO(1947), d, w; GUNFIRE(1950); OPERATION HAYLIFT(1950), w; YOUNG MAN WITH A HORN(1950); SKIPALONG ROSENBLOOM(1951), w; HELEN MORGAN STORY, THE(1959), w; COOGAN'S BLUFF(1968), w; PLAY MISTY FOR ME(1971), w; ENFORCER, THE(1976), w
Dorothy Jean Reisner
OUR HEARTS WERE GROWING UP(1946)
Dorothy Reisner
DOUGHGIRLS, THE(1944); NIGHT AND DAY(1946)
Amanda Reiss
TWICE AROUND THE DAFFODILS(1962, Brit.); NURSE ON WHEELS(1964, Brit.)
Hein Reiss
BATTLE OF BRITAIN, THE(1969, Brit.)
Henry Reiss
1984
OH GOD! YOU DEVIL(1984)
Janine Reiss
DON GIOVANNI(1979, Fr./Ital./Ger.)
Marilyn Reiss
SUMMER STOCK(1950)
Stuart A. Reiss
WHAT PRICE GLORY?(1952), set d; HOUSE OF BAMBOO(1955), set d; SEVEN YEAR ITCH, THE(1955), set d; SOLDIER OF FORTUNE(1955), set d; MAN IN THE GREY FLANNEL SUIT, THE(1956), set d; TEENAGE REBEL(1956), set d; KISS THEM FOR ME(1957), set d; OH, MEN! OH, WOMEN!(1957), set d; TRUE STORY OF JESSE JAMES, THE(1957), set d; RALLY 'ROUND THE FLAG, BOYS!(1958), set d; YOUNG LIONS, THE(1958), set d; WARLOCK(1959), set d; WOMAN OBSESSED(1959), set d; NORTH TO ALASKA(1960), set d; SEVEN THIEVES(1960), set d; FIERCEST HEART, THE(1961), set d; MISTY(1961), set d; SECOND TIME AROUND,

THE(1961), set d; WILD IN THE COUNTRY(1961), set d; FIVE WEEKS IN A BALLOON(1962), set d; MR. HOBBS TAKES A VACATION(1962), set d; STRIPPER, THE(1963), set d; TAKE HER, SHE'S MINE(1963), set d; FATE IS THE HUNTER(1964), set d; JOHN GOLDFARB, PLEASE COME HOME(1964), set d; PLEASURE SEEKERS, THE(1964), set d; WHAT A WAY TO GO(1964), set d; STAGECOACH(1966), set d; WAY...WAY OUT(1966), set d; DOCTOR DOLITTLE(1967), set d; SWEET RIDE, THE(1968), set d; THE BOSTON STRANGLER, THE(1968), set d; CHE!(1969), set d; M(1970), set d; ESCAPE FROM THE PLANET OF THE APES(1971), set d
1984
MICKI AND MAUDE(1984), set d
Stuart Reiss
GHOST AND MRS. MUIR, THE(1942), set d; NIGHTMARE ALLEY(1947), set d; FATHER WAS A FULLBACK(1949), set d; IT HAPPENS EVERY SPRING(1949), set d; AMERICAN GUERRILLA IN THE PHILIPPINES, AN(1950), set d; DESERT FOX, THE(1951), set d; RAWHIDE(1951), set d; DIPLOMATIC COURIER(1952), set d; MY WIFE'S BEST FRIEND(1952), set d; NIAGARA(1953), set d; TITANIC(1953), set d; WHITE WITCH DOCTOR(1953), set d; BROKEN LANCE(1954), set dr; HELL AND HIGH WATER(1954), set d; OH, GOD!(1977), set d; VIVA KNIEVEL!(1977), set d; SWARM, THE(1978), set d; WHEN TIME RAN OUT(1980), set d
Stuart M. Reiss
PRIVATE'S AFFAIR, A(1959), set d
Torleif Reiss
Misc. Silents
LOVE ONE ANOTHER(1922, Den.)
Dora Reisser
WHO WAS MADDOX?(1964, Brit.); GIRL GETTERS, THE(1966, Brit.); DIRTY DOZEN, THE(1967, Brit.)
Karel Reisz
SATURDAY NIGHT AND SUNDAY MORNING(1961, Brit.), d; THIS SPORTING LIFE(1963, Brit.), p; NIGHT MUST FALL(1964, Brit.), p, d; MORGAN!(1966, Brit.), d; ISADORA(1968, Brit.), d; GAMBLER, THE(1974), d; WHO'LL STOP THE RAIN?(1978), d; FRENCH LIEUTENANT'S WOMAN, THE(1981), d
Ursula Reit
WILLY WONKA AND THE CHOCOLATE FACTORY(1971)
Robert Reitano
NIGHT SCHOOL(1981), ed; TERROR EYES(1981), ed
Bill Reiter
BY DESIGN(1982)
Frank Reiter
DETECTIVE, THE(1968)
Kath Reiter
WORLD ACCORDING TO GARP, The(1982)
Robrrt Reiter
BLADE RUNNER(1982)
Antonia Reith
Silents
EUGENE ARAM(1914, Brit.)
Douglas Reith
INTERNATIONAL VELVET(1978, Brit.)
Tonie Reith
Silents
MESSAGE FROM MARS, A(1913, Brit.)
Bruno Reithaar
BLACK SPIDER, THE(1983, Swit.), spec eff
Bruce Reitherman
JUNGLE BOOK, THE(1967)
Richard Reitherman
SWORD IN THE STONE, THE(1963)
Robert Reitherman
SWORD IN THE STONE, THE(1963)
Wolfgang Reitherman
SNOW WHITE AND THE SEVEN DWARFS(1937), anim; FANTASIA(1940), anim; DUMBO(1941), anim d; RELUCTANT DRAGON, THE(1941), anim; FUN AND FANCY FREE(1947), anim d; ALICE IN WONDERLAND(1951), anim; PETER PAN(1953), anim; LADY AND THE TRAMP(1955), anim; SLEEPING BEAUTY(1959), d; ONE HUNDRED AND ONE DALMATIANS(1961), d; SWORD IN THE STONE, THE(1963), d; JUNGLE BOOK, THE(1967), d; ARISTOCATS, THE(1970), p, d; ROBIN HOOD(1973), p&d; RESCUERS, THE(1977), p, d; FOX AND THE HOUND, THE(1981), p
Ben L. Reitman
BOXCAR BERTHA(1972), w
Ivan Reitman
FOXY LADY(1971, Can.), p&d, m, ed; CANNIBAL GIRLS(1973), d; THEY CAME FROM WITHIN(1976, Can.), p; HOUSE BY THE LAKE, THE(1977, Can.), p; NATIONAL LAMPOON'S ANIMAL HOUSE(1978), p; MEATBALLS(1979, Can.), d; HEAVY METAL(1981, Can.), p; STRIPES(1981), p, d
1984
GHOSTBUSTERS(1984), p&d
Edgar Reitz
GERMANY IN AUTUMN(1978, Ger.), d
Jack Reitzen
SLAVE GIRL(1947); APPOINTMENT WITH MURDER(1948); ARGYLE SECRETS, THE(1948); HOLIDAY RHYTHM(1950); ONE TOO MANY(1950); SHAKEDOWN(1950); DANGER ZONE(1951); G.I. JANE(1951); KENTUCKY JUBILEE(1951); MASK OF THE DRAGON(1951); NAKED JUNGLE, THE(1953); CAPTAIN KIDD AND THE SLAVE GIRL(1954); FEMALE ON THE BEACH(1955)
Sylvia Reize
STEPPENWOLF(1974)
Franz Reizenstein
MUMMY, THE(1959, Brit.), m; CIRCUS OF HORRORS(1960, Brit.), m; MUMMY'S SHROUD, THE(1967, Brit.), m
Lou Reizner
BLACK JOY(1977, Brit.), md
Rejane
Misc. Silents
ALSACE(1916, FR.); GYPSY PASSION(1922, Fr.)
Lubomir Rejthar
FANTASTIC PLANET(1973, Fr./Czech.), ph

V. Reka
KATERINA IZMAILOVA(1969, USSR)
Winston Rekert
SUZANNE(1980, Can.); HEARTACHES(1981, Can.); LOVE(1982, Can.)
Rod Rekofski
RECOMMENDATION FOR MERCY(1975, Can.)
Frances Rel
SINGIN' IN THE CORN(1946)
Jean Relet
DEVIL IN THE FLESH, THE(1949, Fr.)
Hugh Relicker
GO-GETTER, THE(1937), art d
Marie-Theres Relin
1984
SECRET PLACES(1984, Brit.)
Harry Relis
CAPTAIN SINDBAD(1963), w
Sheila Reljac
SWEET SUBSTITUTE(1964, Can.), ed
Santa Relli
JOUR DE FETE(1952, Fr.)
Chris P. Rellias
POSTMAN ALWAYS RINGS TWICE, THE(1981)
Rellys
LETTERS FROM MY WINDMILL(1955, Fr.)
Emma Relph
EUREKA(1983, Brit.)
George Relph
TOO DANGEROUS TO LIVE(1939, Brit.); GIVE US THE MOON(1944, Brit.); NICHOLAS NICKLEBY(1947, Brit.); FINAL TEST, THE(1953, Brit.); I BELIEVE IN YOU(1953, Brit.); TITFIELD THUNDERBOLT, THE(1953, Brit.); DOCTOR AT LARGE(1957, Brit.); DAVY(1958, Brit.); BEN HUR(1959)
Misc. Silents
PAYING THE PRICE(1916); CANDYTUFT, I MEAN VERONICA(1921, Brit.); DOOR THAT HAS NO KEY, THE(1921, Brit.)
Michael Relph
BELLS GO DOWN, THE(1943, Brit.), art d; MY LEARNED FRIEND(1943, Brit.), art d; THEY CAME TO A CITY(1944, Brit.), art d; DEAD OF NIGHT(1946, Brit.), art d; FRIEDA(1947, Brit.), p; NICHOLAS NICKLEBY(1947, Brit.), art d; SARABAND(1949, Brit.), p, d, art d; POOL OF LONDON(1951, Brit.), p; GENTLE GUNMAN, THE(1952, Brit.), p&d; I BELIEVE IN YOU(1953, Brit.), p&d, w; RAINBOW JACKET, THE(1954, Brit.), p; SQUARE RING, THE(1955, Brit.), p&d; SHIP THAT DIED OF SHAME, THE(1956, Brit.), p&d, w; WHO DONE IT?(1956, Brit.), p; OUT OF THE CLOUDS(1957, Brit.), p, d, w; SMALLEST SHOW ON EARTH, THE(1957, Brit.), p; DAVY(1958, Brit.), d; MAD LITTLE ISLAND(1958, Brit.), d; VIOLENT PLAYGROUND(1958, Brit.), p; SAPPHIRE(1959, Brit.), p; DESERT MICE(1960, Brit.), d; ALL NIGHT LONG(1961, Brit.), d; LEAGUE OF GENTLEMEN, THE(1961, Brit.), p; MAN IN THE MOON(1961, Brit.), p, w; SECRET PARTNER, THE(1961, Brit.), p; VICTIM(1961, Brit.), p; MIND BENDERS, THE(1963, Brit.), p; PLACE TO GO, A(1964, Brit.), p, w; WOMAN OF STRAW(1964, Brit.), p, w; MASQUERADE(1965, Brit.), p, w; WALK IN THE SHADOW(1966, Brit.), p; ASSASSINATION BUREAU, THE(1969, Brit.), p, w, art d; MAN WHO HAUNTED HIMSELF, THE(1970, Brit.), p, w; UNSUITABLE JOB FOR A WOMAN, AN(1982, Brit.), p
Phyllis Relph
Misc. Silents
LIGHTS O' LONDON, THE(1914, Brit.)
Simon Relph
PRIVATES ON PARADE(1982), p; RETURN OF THE SOLDIER, THE(1983, Brit.), p
1984
PLOUGHMAN'S LUNCH, THE(1984, Brit.), p; PRIVATES ON PARADE(1984, Brit.), p; SECRET PLACES(1984, Brit.), p
Robert E. Relyea
REIVERS, THE(1969), exec p
Robert Relyea
DAY OF THE DOLPHIN, THE(1973), p; SEVEN(1979)
Kandy Remacle
MY FAVORITE YEAR(1982), set d
Gary Remal
1984
BREAKIN'(1984), m
James Remar
ON THE YARD(1978); WARRIORS, THE(1979); CRUISING(1980); LONG RIDERS, THE(1980); WINDWALKER(1980); PARTNERS(1982); 48 HOURS(1982)
1984
COTTON CLUB, THE(1984)
Erich Maria Remarque
ALL QUIET ON THE WESTERN FRONT(1930), w; ROAD BACK,THE(1937), w; THREE COMRADES(1938), w; SO ENDS OUR NIGHT(1941), w; OTHER LOVE, THE(1947), w; ARCH OF TRIUMPH(1948), w; LAST TEN DAYS, THE(1956, Ger.), w; TIME TO LOVE AND A TIME TO DIE, A(1958), a, w; BOBBY DEERFIELD(1977), w
Erika Remberg
CIRCUS OF HORRORS(1960, Brit.); MAKE WAY FOR LILA(1962, Swed./Ger.); SATURDAY NIGHT OUT(1964, Brit.); CANDIDATE FOR MURDER(1966, Brit.); CAVE OF THE LIVING DEAD(1966, Yugo./Ger.)
George Rembert, Jr.
THUNDER IN CAROLINA(1960)
Maximilian Remen
DESERTER AND THE NOMADS, THE(1969, Czech./Ital.), ed; ASSISTANT, THE(1982, Czech.), ed
Joja Remenar
KAYA, I'LL KILL YOU(1969, Yugo./Fr.), ed
Dot Remey
SQUARE DANCE JUBILEE(1949)
Jean-Francois Remi
LA GUERRE EST FINIE(1967, Fr./Swed.); VERDICT(1975, Fr./Ital.)
Ricardo Remias
STRYKER(1983, Phil.), ph

Lee Remick
TRIBUTE(1980, Can.); FACE IN THE CROWD, A(1957); LONG, HOT SUMMER, THE(1958); ANATOMY OF A MURDER(1959); THESE THOUSAND HILLS(1959); WILD RIVER(1960); SANCTUARY(1961); DAYS OF WINE AND ROSES(1962); EXPERIMENT IN TERROR(1962); RUNNING MAN, THE(1963, Brit.); WHEELER DEALERS, THE(1963); BABY, THE RAIN MUST FALL(1965); HALLELUJAH TRAIL, THE(1965); DETECTIVE, THE(1968); NO WAY TO TREAT A LADY(1968); HARD CONTRACT(1969); LOOT(1971, Brit.); SEVERED HEAD, A(1971, Brit.); SOMETIMES A GREAT NOTION(1971); DELICATE BALANCE, A(1973); TOUCH ME NOT(1974, Brit.); HENNESSY(1975, Brit.); OMEN, THE(1976); TELEFON(1977); MEDUSA TOUCH, THE(1978, Brit.); EUROPEANS, THE(1979, Brit.); COMPETITION, THE(1980)
William Remick
VERTIGO(1958); NOOSE FOR A GUNMAN(1960); EXPERIMENT IN TERROR(1962)
Patrizia Remiddi
MONSTER OF THE ISLAND(1953, Ital.)
Jean Remignard
AU HASARD, BALTHAZAR(1970, Fr.)
Greta Remin
FIRE DOWN BELOW(1957, U.S./Brit.)
Al Remington
BEAST OF YUCCA FLATS, THE(1961), m
Colt Remington
CROSSED TRAILS(1948), w
Peggy Remington
THOUSANDS CHEER(1943); SECRET BEYOND THE DOOR, THE(1948); EASY TO LOVE(1953)
Rick Remington
UP FROM THE DEPTHS(1979, Phil.), ph
Manuel M. Remis
TREASURE OF MAKUBA, THE(1967, U.S./Span.), w
Nicholai Remisoff
TURNABOUT(1940), art d; PARIS UNDERGROUND(1945), prod d
Nicholas Remisoff
NO MINOR VICES(1948), art d
Nick Remisoff
PLEASE MURDER ME(1956), art d; TROOPER HOOK(1957), art d
Nicolai Remisoff
OF MICE AND MEN(1939), art d; MY LIFE WITH CAROLINE(1941), prod d; HEAT'S ON, THE(1943), prod d; SOMETHING TO SHOUT ABOUT(1943), prod d; GUEST IN THE HOUSE(1944), prod d; STRANGE WOMAN, THE(1946), art d; DISHONORED LADY(1947), prod d & art d; LURED(1947), art d; OCEAN BREAKERS(1949, Swed.), art d; MOON IS BLUE, THE(1953), prod d; APACHE(1954), art d; JOHNNY CONCHO(1956), art d; BLACK PATCH(1957), art d; DESTINATION 60,000(1957), art d; PAWNEE(1957), art d; UNDERSEA GIRL(1957), art d; PORK CHOP HILL(1959), prod d; OCEAN'S ELEVEN(1960), art d
Nikolai Remisoff
YOUNG WIDOW(1946), prod d, art d
Frank Remley
MY BLUE HEAVEN(1950); LET'S DO IT AGAIN(1953)
Ralph M. Remley
AWAKENING OF JIM BURKE(1935); WHOLE TOWN'S TALKING, THE(1935); BULLETS OR BALLOTS(1936); POPPY(1936)
Ralph Remley
DOUBLE DOOR(1934); KEEP 'EM ROLLING(1934); KEY, THE(1934); READY FOR LOVE(1934); BEHOLD MY WIFE(1935); DR. SOCRATES(1935); HOME ON THE RANGE(1935); PRINCESS O'HARA(1935); I MARRIED A DOCTOR(1936); ROBIN HOOD OF EL DORADO(1936); TIMOTHY'S QUEST(1936); YOURS FOR THE ASKING(1936); LET THEM LIVE(1937); MAKE WAY FOR TOMORROW(1937); SWING HIGH, SWING LOW(1937); WAIKIKI WEDDING(1937); OUTSIDE OF PARADISE(1938); TEXANS, THE(1938); KING OF THE UNDERWORLD(1939); STORY OF ALEXANDER GRAHAM BELL, THE(1939)
Andrew Remo
Silents
KING TUT-ANKH-AMEN'S EIGHTH WIFE(1923), d, w
Jean Remoleux
MY UNCLE(1958, Fr.)
Jean-Claude Remoleux
TRIAL, THE(1963, Fr./Ital./Ger.)
Fritz Remond
RATS, THE(1955, Ger.)
Remo Remotti
MASOCH(1980, Ital.); LEAP INTO THE VOID(1982, Ital.)
Jim Rempe
BALTIMORE BULLET, THE(1980)
Frank Remsden
NEW MOON(1940)
Bert Remsen
TESS OF THE STORM COUNTRY(1961); MOON PILOT(1962); DEAD RINGER(1964); LOLLIPOP COVER, THE(1965); BREWSTER McCLOUD(1970); STRAWBERRY STATEMENT, THE(1970); MC CABE AND MRS. MILLER(1971); FUZZ(1972); CALIFORNIA SPLIT(1974); THIEVES LIKE US(1974); NASHVILLE(1975); BABY BLUE MARINE(1976); BUFFALO BILL AND THE INDIANS, OR SITTING BULL'S HISTORY LESSON(1976); HARRY AND WALTER GO TO NEW YORK(1976); UNCLE JOE SHANNON(1978); WEDDING, A(1978); FAST BREAK(1979); BORDERLINE(1980); CARNY(1980); INSIDE MOVES(1980); JONI(1980); SECOND-HAND HEARTS(1981); LOOKIN' TO GET OUT(1982); INDEPENDENCE DAY(1983); STING II, THE(1983)
1984
LIES(1984, Brit.); PLACES IN THE HEART(1984)
Guy Remsen
PRETTY MAIDS ALL IN A ROW(1971)
1984
LIES(1984, Brit.)
Marie Remsen
DRUMS O' VOODOO(1934)
Bert Remson
PORK CHOP HILL(1959)
Dudley Remus
ANGEL BABY(1961); GATOR(1976); SMOKEY AND THE BANDIT II(1980); CANNONBALL RUN, THE(1981)

Albert Remy
CHILDREN OF PARADISE(1945, Fr.); IT HAPPENED AT THE INN(1945, Fr.); DEVIL'S DAUGHTER(1949, Fr.); FRENCH CANCAN(1956, Fr.); HUNCHBACK OF NOTRE DAME, THE(1957, Fr.); LE CIEL EST A VOUS(1957, Fr.); PARIS DOES STRANGE THINGS(1957, Fr./Ital.); FOUR HUNDRED BLOWS, THE(1959); COW AND I, THE(1961, Fr., Ital., Ger.); FOUR HORSEMEN OF THE APOCALYPSE, THE(1962); GIGOT(1962); SHOOT THE PIANO PLAYER(1962, Fr.); TOMORROW IS MY TURN(1962, Fr./Ital./Ger.); LAFAYETTE(1963, Fr.); SEVENTH JUROR, THE(1964, Fr.); HOW NOT TO ROB A DEPARTMENT STORE(1965, Fr./Ital.); MATA HARI(1965, Fr./Ital.); TRAIN, THE(1965, Fr./Ital./U.S.); GRAND PRIX(1966); IS PARIS BURNING?(1966, U.S./Fr.); WEEKEND AT DUNKIRK(1966, Fr./Ital.); 25TH HOUR, THE(1967, Fr./Ital./Yugo.)

Christian Remy
TRAIN, THE(1965, Fr./Ital./U.S.)

Constant Remy
DRAGNET NIGHT(1931, Fr.); RECORD 413(1936, Fr.); ROYAL AFFAIRS IN VERSAILLES(1957, Fr.)

Diemut Remy
1984
NEVERENDING STORY, THE(1984, Ger.), cos

Geza Remy
FIGHTER SQUADRON(1948)

Helene Remy
ALWAYS VICTORIOUS(1960, Ital.); LAST OF THE VIKINGS, THE(1962, Fr./Ital.); VAMPIRE AND THE BALLERINA, THE(1962, Ital.); BORSALINO(1970, Fr.)

J. R. Remy
CHECKERED FLAG, THE(1963), ph; SHANTY TRAMP(1967), ph; SAVAGES FROM HELL(1968), ph

Jacques Remy
DAMNED, THE(1948, Fr.), w; NIGHT HEAVEN FELL, THE(1958, Fr.), w; CAT, THE(1959, Fr.), w; LOVE AND THE FRENCHWOMAN(1961, Fr.), p; MARCO THE MAGNIFICENT(1966, Ital./Fr./Yugo./Egypt/Afghanistan), w; THE DIRTY GAME(1966, Fr./Ital./Ger.), w

Jean-Jacques Remy
THERESE(1963, Fr.)

Louise Remy
TROUBLE-FETE(1964, Can.)

Maurice Remy
TOPAZE(1935, Fr.)

Ronald Remy
NO MAN IS AN ISLAND(1962); BLOOD DRINKERS, THE(1966, U.S./Phil.); MAD DOCTOR OF BLOOD ISLAND, THE(1969, Phil./U.S.)

Pete Renaday
CAT FROM OUTER SPACE, THE(1978); APPLE DUMPLING GANG RIDES AGAIN, THE(1979); LAST FLIGHT OF NOAH'S ARK, THE(1980)
1984
RIVER RAT, THE(1984)

Ray Renahan
VOGUES OF 1938(1937), ph; DUEL IN THE SUN(1946), ph

Rene Renal
SEVENTH JUROR, THE(1964, Fr.)

Tina Renaldi
Misc. Silents
TOILER, THE(1932, Ital.)

Avando Renaldo
TEXAS WILDCATS(1939)

Duncan Renaldo
BRIDGE OF SAN LUIS REY, THE(1929); TRADER HORN(1931); MOTH, THE(1934); PUBLIC STENOGRAPHER(1935); LADY LUCK(1936); MOONLIGHT MURDER(1936); CRIME AFLOAT(1937), a, w; MILE A MINUTE LOVE(1937), a, w; SPECIAL AGENT K-7(1937); TWO MINUTES TO PLAY(1937); REBELLION(1938); ROSE OF THE RIO GRANDE(1938); SPAWN OF THE NORTH(1938); TEN LAPS TO GO(1938); TROPIC HOLIDAY(1938); COWBOYS FROM TEXAS(1939); KANSAS TERRORS, THE(1939); ROUGH RIDERS' ROUNDUP(1939); SOUTH OF THE BORDER(1939); ZAZA(1939); COVERED WAGON DAYS(1940); GAUCHO SERENADE(1940); HEROES OF THE SADDLE(1940); MAD EMPRESS, THE(1940); OKLAHOMA RENEGADES(1940); PIONEERS OF THE WEST(1940); ROCKY MOUNTAIN RANGERS(1940); DOWN MEXICO WAY(1941); GAUCHOS OF EL DORADO(1941); OUTLAWS OF THE DESERT(1941); SOUTH OF PANAMA(1941); WE WERE DANCING(1942); YANK IN LIBYA, A(1942); AROUND THE WORLD(1943); BORDER PATROL(1943); DESERT SONG, THE(1943); FOR WHOM THE BELL TOLLS(1943); HANDS ACROSS THE BORDER(1943); MISSION TO MOSCOW(1943); TIGER FANGS(1943); CALL OF THE SOUTH SEAS(1944); FIGHTING SEABEES, THE(1944); SAN ANTONIO KID, THE(1944); SHERIFF OF SUNDOWN(1944); CISCO KID RETURNS, THE(1945); IN OLD NEW MEXICO(1945); SOUTH OF THE RIO GRANDE(1945); TWO YEARS BEFORE THE MAST(1946); JUNGLE FLIGHT(1947); SWORD OF THE AVENGER(1948); VALIANT HOMBRE, THE(1948); DARING CABALLERO, THE(1949); GAY AMIGO, THE(1949); SATAN'S CRADLE(1949); CAPTURE, THE(1950); GIRL FROM SAN LORENZO, THE(1950); LADY AND THE BANDIT, THE(1951), w
Misc. Talkies
REBELLION(1936)
Silents
PALS OF THE PRAIRIE(1929)
Misc. Silents
NAUGHTY DUCHESS, THE(1928)

Tito Renaldo
APACHE TRAIL(1942); SUNDAY PUNCH(1942); TORTILLA FLAT(1942); FOR WHOM THE BELL TOLLS(1943); ADVENTURE(1945); SOUTH OF THE RIO GRANDE(1945); STORY OF G.I. JOE, THE(1945); ANNA AND THE KING OF SIAM(1946); RIDE THE PINK HORSE(1947); OLD LOS ANGELES(1948); BRIBE, THE(1949); HOLIDAY IN HAVANA(1949); TENSION(1949); WE WERE STRANGERS(1949); ONE WAY STREET(1950); TARZAN AND THE SLAVE GIRL(1950); CALIFORNIA CONQUEST(1952); FABULOUS SENORITA, THE(1952)

Carla Renalli
DAVID AND GOLIATH(1961, Ital.), ch

Simone Renant
PEARLS OF THE CROWN(1938, Fr.); APRES L'AMOUR(1948, Fr.); JENNY LAMOUR(1948, Fr.); BEDEVILLED(1955); IF PARIS WERE TOLD TO US(1956, Fr.); LES LIAISONS DANGEREUSES(1961, Fr./Ital.); LOVE AND THE FRENCHWOMAN(1961, Fr.); THAT MAN FROM RIO(1964, Fr./Ital.); LOVE IS A FUNNY THING(1970,

Fr./Ital.); DEAR DETECTIVE(1978, Fr.); THREE MEN TO DESTROY(1980, Fr.)

Colette Renard
BACK TO THE WALL(1959, Fr.)

David A. Renard
HANGUP(1974)

David Renard
FRONTIER UPRISING(1961); LONG ROPE, THE(1961); DEADLY DUO(1962); SHIP OF FOOLS(1965); COUNTERFEIT KILLER, THE(1968); CHANGE OF HABIT(1969)

Dorothy Renard
PROJECT X(1949)

Emily Renard
WORDS AND MUSIC(1929)

Ervin Renard
CAPTAIN OF THE GUARD(1930)
Silents
LIGHTNING LARIATS(1927); OLD CODE, THE(1928)
Misc. Silents
ROAD TO BROADWAY, THE(1926)

H. Renard
Silents
UNDER FIRE(1926)

Irvin Renard
Misc. Silents
COWBOY COP, THE(1926); MAN FROM THE WEST, THE(1926)

Jacques Renard
MOTHER AND THE WHORE, THE(1973, Fr.), a, ph; CELINE AND JULIE GO BOATING(1974, Fr.), ph

Jason Renard
TRICK OR TREATS(1982)

Jules Renard
POIL DE CAROTTE(1932, Fr.), w

Kaye Renard
GLORIFYING THE AMERICAN GIRL(1930)

Ken Renard
LYDIA BAILEY(1952); SOMETHING OF VALUE(1957); THESE THOUSAND HILLS(1959); HOME FROM THE HILL(1960); PAPA'S DELICATE CONDITION(1963); CHASE, THE(1966); SULLIVAN'S EMPIRE(1967); TRUE GRIT(1969); SPARKLE(1976); EXORCIST II: THE HERETIC(1977); FARMER, THE(1977)

Louis Miehe Renard
JOURNEY TO THE SEVENTH PLANET(1962, U.S./Swed.)

Maurice Renard
MAD LOVE(1935), w

Ray Renard
HELL'S ANGELS '69(1969)

Renee Renard
1984
FIRST NAME: CARMEN(1984, Fr.), cos; LOVE ON THE GROUND(1984,Fr.), cos

Roy Renard
PORTRAIT OF A MOBSTER(1961)

Simone Renard
FLY NOW, PAY LATER(1969)

Yvette Renard
ONE TOUCH OF VENUS(1948)

Renata
LAST METRO, THE(1981, Fr.)

Anne Renate
EROTIQUE(1969, Fr.)

Renaud
Silents
STRANGERS OF THE NIGHT(1923), t

Eadie Renaud
LILITH(1964)

Gilles Renaud
ONE MAN(1979, Can.)

Henri Renaud
NAKED HEARTS(1970, Fr.), m; MURMUR OF THE HEART(1971, Fr./Ital./Ger.), m

Madeleine Renaud
LA MATERNELLE(1933, Fr.); LUMIERE D'ETE(1943, Fr.); STORMY WATERS(1946, Fr.); WOMAN WHO DARED(1949, Fr.); LE PLAISIR(1954, Fr.); LE CIEL EST A VOUS(1957, Fr.); DEVIL BY THE TAIL, THE(1969, Fr./Ital.)

Madeline Renaud
LONGEST DAY, THE(1962)

Jack Renault
Silents
KNOCKOUT REILLY(1927)

Michel Renault
PLEASE, NOT NOW!(1963, Fr./Ital.), ch

Patrice Renault
1984
HERE COMES SANTA CLAUS(1984), set d

Patricia Renaut
COP, A(1973, Fr.), ed; DIRTY MONEY(1977, Fr.), ed

Georges Renavent
RIO RITA(1929); SCOTLAND YARD(1930); EAST OF BORNEO(1931); RICH ARE ALWAYS WITH US, THE(1932); WHISTLIN' DAN(1932); EVER IN MY HEART(1933); PRIVATE DETECTIVE 62(1933); QUEEN CHRISTINA(1933); FASHIONS OF 1934(1934); HOUSE OF ROTHSCHILD, THE(1934); MOULIN ROUGE(1934); STAMBOUL QUEST(1934); CAPTAIN BLOOD(1935); FOLIES DERGERE(1935); FRONT PAGE WOMAN(1935); LAST OUTPOST, THE(1935); WHITE COCKATOO(1935); CHARGE OF THE LIGHT BRIGADE, THE(1936); LLOYDS OF LONDON(1936); SKY PARADE(1936); THE INVISIBLE RAY(1936); WHIPSAW(1936); CAFE METROPOLE(1937); CHARLIE CHAN AT MONTE CARLO(1937); FIGHT FOR YOUR LADY(1937); HISTORY IS MADE AT NIGHT(1937); KING AND THE CHORUS GIRL, THE(1937); LOVE AND HISSES(1937); LOVE UNDER FIRE(1937); SEVENTH HEAVEN(1937); SHEIK STEPS OUT, THE(1937); SHE'S DANGEROUS(1937); THAT CERTAIN WOMAN(1937); THIN ICE(1937); WIFE, DOCTOR AND NURSE(1937); ARTISTS AND MODELS ABROAD(1938); GOLD DIGGERS IN PARIS(1938); I'LL GIVE A MILLION(1938); JEZEBEL(1938); YOUNG IN HEART, THE(1938); ADVENTURES OF JANE ARDEN(1939); EVERYTHING HAPPENS AT NIGHT(1939); INDIANAPOLIS SPEEDWAY(1939); MR. MOTO'S LAST WARNING(1939); PACK UP YOUR TROU-

BLES(1939); THREE MUSKETEERS, THE(1939); TOPPER TAKES A TRIP(1939); CHRISTMAS IN JULY(1940); HOUSE ACROSS THE BAY, THE(1940); SON OF MONTE CRISTO(1940); TURNABOUT(1940); GREAT LIE, THE(1941); NIGHT OF JANUARY 16TH(1941); PARIS CALLING(1941); ROAD TO ZANZIBAR(1941); SULLIVAN'S TRAVELS(1941); THAT HAMILTON WOMAN(1941); THAT NIGHT IN RIO(1941); NOW, VOYAGER(1942); SILVER QUEEN(1942); BACKGROUND TO DANGER(1943); DESERT SONG, THE(1943); MISSION TO MOSCOW(1943); WINTERTIME(1943); EXPERIMENT PERILOUS(1944); MASK OF DIMITRIOS, THE(1944); OUR HEARTS WERE YOUNG AND GAY(1944); STORM OVER LISBON(1944); 'TILL WE MEET AGAIN(1944); CORNERED(1945); SARATOGA TRUNK(1945); THIS LOVE OF OURS(1945); THOSE ENDEARING YOUNG CHARMS(1945); HOODLUM SAINT, THE(1946); PERFECT MARRIAGE, THE(1946); TARZAN AND THE LEOPARD WOMAN(1946); THE CATMAN OF PARIS(1946); FOXES OF HARROW, THE(1947); LADIES' MAN(1947); ROPE OF SAND(1949); FORTUNES OF CAPTAIN BLOOD(1950); SECRETS OF MONTE CARLO(1951); STRANGERS ON A TRAIN(1951); MARA MARU(1952)
Silents
SEVEN SISTERS, THE(1915); ERSTWHILE SUSAN(1919)
Misc. Silents
LIGHT, THE(1919)
Liz Renay
DATE WITH DEATH, A(1959); DAY OF THE NIGHTMARE(1965); THRILL KILLERS, THE(1965); HARD ROAD, THE(1970); BLACKENSTEIN(1973); PEEPER(1975)
Paul Renay
TORRID ZONE(1940); TALES OF MANHATTAN(1942)
Derek Rencher
ROMEO AND JULIET(1966, Brit.)
Nicholas Rend
SECRET INVASION, THE(1964)
John Rendall
CHRISTIAN THE LION(1976, Brit.)
Peter Rendall
INNOCENTS IN PARIS(1955, Brit.)
Robert Rendel
HOUND OF THE BASKERVILLES(1932, Brit.); BORROW A MILLION(1934, Brit.); DEATH AT A BROADCAST(1934, Brit.); WAY OF YOUTH, THE(1934, Brit.); HONOURS EASY(1935, Brit.); PRICE OF WISDOM, THE(1935, Brit.); BLACK ROSES(1936, Ger.); TWICE BRANDED(1936, Brit.); DARK STAIRWAY, THE(1938, Brit.); MR. SATAN(1938, Brit.); SINGING COP, THE(1938, Brit.); THANK EVANS(1938, Brit.); ALL AT SEA(1939, Brit.); FOUR FEATHERS, THE(1939, Brit.); U-BOAT 29(1939, Brit.); LION HAS WINGS, THE(1940, Brit.); SALOON BAR(1940, Brit.); SECOND MR. BUSH, THE(1940, Brit.); THREE COCKEYED SAILORS(1940, Brit.); MISSING TEN DAYS(1941, Brit.)
F. Rendell
GUILTY MELODY(1936, Brit.)
Robert Rendell
CRIMSON CIRCLE, THE(1936, Brit.); FIRE OVER ENGLAND(1937, Brit.)
Adelaide Rendelle
Misc. Silents
MY HOME TOWN(1925)
Les Rendelstein
PRIVATE PARTS(1972), w
Rudy Render
TORCH SONG(1953)
Vince Render
SATIN MUSHROOM, THE(1969)
R. Rendi
STALKER(1982, USSR)
Victor Rendina
JENNIFER ON MY MIND(1971); GODFATHER, THE(1972)
1984
RACING WITH THE MOON(1984)
Aldo Rendine
INVESTIGATION OF A CITIZEN ABOVE SUSPICION(1970, Ital.); AVANTI!(1972); MR. BILLION(1977)
Jana Rendlova
WISHING MACHINE(1971, Czech.)
Gilbert Rendon
EDDIE MACON'S RUN(1983)
Rene
LEFT-HANDED WOMAN, THE(1980, Ger.)
Alexis Rene
Misc. Silents
LOVE'S FLAME(1920)
Fernand Rene
ROYAL AFFAIRS IN VERSAILLES(1957, Fr.)
Hugh Rene
EYES OF FATE(1933, Brit.)
Joel Rene
WE WERE STRANGERS(1949)
Yves Rene
1984
BROTHER FROM ANOTHER PLANET, THE(1984)
Joseph Rene-Corail
1984
SUGAR CANE ALLEY(1984, Fr.)
Renee
BODY SNATCHER, THE(1945), cos; DIARY OF A SCHIZOPHRENIC GIRL(1970, Ital.), w
Silents
PASSION OF JOAN OF ARC, THE(1928, Fr.)
Bobby Renee
WORDS AND MUSIC(1929)
Joan Renee
Misc. Silents
OUTLAW EXPRESS, THE(1926); SILVER TREASURE, THE(1926)
Renati Renee
Misc. Silents
RASPUTIN(1929, Ger.)

Ricky Renee
GOODBYE GEMINI(1970, Brit.); CABARET(1972)
Pat Renella
X-15(1961); SILENCERS, THE(1966); RIOT ON SUNSET STRIP(1967); BULLITT(1968); DAYTON'S DEVILS(1968); MOONCHILD(1972)
Misc. Talkies
THOROUGHBREDS, THE(1977)
Tom Renesto
VEILS OF BAGDAD, THE(1953)
Nesa Renet
FEMALE BUNCH, THE(1969)
Sinitta Renet
SHOCK TREATMENT(1981)
Robert Renfield [Roger Wilson]
SATAN'S BED(1965)
John Renforth
NIGHT OF EVIL(1962); WHEN THE LEGENDS DIE(1972)
Denise Renfro
HICKEY AND BOGGS(1972)
Kristin Renfro
1984
SONGWRITER(1984)
Marli Renfro
PSYCHO(1960); TONIGHT FOR SURE(1962)
Ruth Renick
WEST OF BROADWAY(1931); CANNONBALL EXPRESS(1932)
Silents
HAWTHORNE OF THE U.S.A.(1919); MOLLYCODDLE, THE(1920); BAR NOTHIN'(1921); CHILDREN OF THE NIGHT(1921); WHAT'S A WIFE WORTH?(1921); WITCHING HOUR, THE(1921); RAGS TO RICHES(1922); LONG LIVE THE KING(1923); ROUGH SHOD(1925)
Misc. Silents
JUCKLINS, THE(1920); GOLDEN SNARE, THE(1921); FIRE BRIDE, THE(1922); MEN OF ZANSIBAR, THE(1922); CONDUCTOR 1492(1924)
Sammy Renick
WIND ACROSS THE EVERGLADES(1958)
Renie
DON'T TELL THE WIFE(1937), cos; SATURDAY'S HEROES(1937), cos; GO CHASE YOURSELF(1938), cos; HAVING WONDERFUL TIME(1938), cos; QUICK MONEY(1938), cos; ROOM SERVICE(1938), cos; TARNISHED ANGEL(1938), cos; ROOKIE COP, THE(1939), cos; TWELVE CROWDED HOURS(1939), cos; KITTY FOYLE(1940), cos; MARRIED AND IN LOVE(1940), cos; PRIMROSE PATH(1940), cos; SUED FOR LIBEL(1940), cos; SAINT IN PALM SPRINGS, THE(1941), cos; TOM, DICK AND HARRY(1941), cos; MAYOR OF 44TH STREET, THE(1942), cos; NAVY COMES THROUGH, THE(1942), cos; SEVEN DAYS LEAVE(1942), cos; MR. LUCKY(1943), cos; SEVENTH VICTIM, THE(1943), cos; TENDER COMRADE(1943), cos; THIS LAND IS MINE(1943), cos; MASTER RACE, THE(1944), cos; MUSIC IN MANHATTAN(1944), cos; MY PAL, WOLF(1944), cos; NEVADA(1944), cos; NIGHT OF ADVENTURE, A(1944), cos; NONE BUT THE LONELY HEART(1944), cos; CORNERED(1945), cos; PAN-AMERICANA(1945), cos; CRACK-UP(1946), cos; DEADLINE AT DAWN(1946), cos; NOCTURNE(1946), cos; STEP BY STEP(1946), cos; RIFFRAFF(1947), cos; SO WELL REMEMBERED(1947, Brit.), cos; MIRACLE OF THE BELLS, THE(1948), cos; MYSTERY IN MEXICO(1948), cos; RETURN OF THE BADMEN(1948), cos; STATION WEST(1948), cos; ROUGHSHOD(1949), cos; MR. BELVEDERE RINGS THE BELL(1951), cos; NIGHT WITHOUT SLEEP(1952), cos; RETURN OF THE TEXAN(1952), cos; WAIT 'TIL THE SUN SHINES, NELLIE(1952), cos; MR. SCOUTMASTER(1953), cos; PRESIDENT'S LADY, THE(1953), cos; TONIGHT WE SING(1953), cos; VICKI(1953), cos; SIEGE AT RED RIVER, THE(1954), cos; MAN CALLED PETER, THE(1955), cos; UNTAMED(1955), cos; KING AND FOUR QUEENS, THE(1956), cos; GIRL MOST LIKELY, THE(1957), cos; THREE FACES OF EVE, THE(1957), cos; BIG FISHERMAN, THE(1959), cos; SNOW WHITE AND THE THREE STOOGES(1961), cos; CIRCUS WORLD(1964), cos; PLEASURE SEEKERS, THE(1964), cos; SAND PEBBLES, THE(1966), cos; LEGEND OF LYLAH CLARE, THE(1968), cos; WHAT EVER HAPPENED TO AUNT ALICE?(1969), cos
Yves Renier
STORY OF THE COUNT OF MONTE CRISTO, THE(1962, Fr./Ital.)
Renies
BACK TO BATAAN(1945), cos
V. Renin
WAR AND PEACE(1968, USSR)
Jean Renior
Misc. Silents
LE BLED(1929, Fr.), d
Cyril Renison
THEY CAN'T HANG ME(1955, Brit.); SECOND FIDDLE(1957, Brit.); SONG OF NORWAY(1970); O LUCKY MAN!(1973, Brit.)
Claudia Renito
LOVE IS A CAROUSEL(1970)
A. Renkov
DAY THE EARTH FROZE, THE(1959, Fin./USSR), spec eff
Adrianne Renn
WIFE OF GENERAL LING, THE(1938, Brit.)
Charles G. Renn
SANTA CLAUS CONQUERS THE MARTIANS(1964)
Katherina Renn
RISE OF LOUIS XIV, THE(1970, Fr.)
Peter Renn
OLIVER!(1968, Brit.)
Cosimo Renna
WHAT DID YOU DO IN THE WAR, DADDY?(1966)
Ray Rennahan
VAGABOND KING, THE(1930), ph; WHOOPEE(1930), ph; FANNY FOLEY HERSELF(1931), ph; DOCTOR X(1932), ph; MYSTERY OF THE WAX MUSEUM, THE(1933), ph; EBB TIDE(1937), ph; WINGS OF THE MORNING(1937, Brit.), ph; HER JUNGLE LOVE(1938), ph; KENTUCKY(1938), ph; DRUMS ALONG THE MOHAWK(1939), ph; BLUE BIRD, THE(1940), ph; DOWN ARGENTINE WAY(1940), ph; MARYLAND(1940), ph; BELLE STARR(1941), ph; BLOOD AND SAND(1941), ph; LOUISIANA PURCHASE(1941), ph; THAT NIGHT IN RIO(1941), ph; FOR WHOM THE BELL TOLLS(1943), ph; BELLE OF THE YUKON(1944), ph; LADY IN THE DARK(1944), ph; THREE CABALLEROS, THE(1944), ph; UP IN ARMS(1944), ph;

INCENDIARY BLONDE(1945), ph; IT'S A PLEASURE(1945), ph; THOUSAND AND ONE NIGHTS, A(1945), ph; CALIFORNIA(1946), ph; PERILS OF PAULINE, THE(1947), ph; UNCONQUERED(1947), ph; PALEFACE, THE(1948), ph; CONNECTICUT YANKEE IN KING ARTHUR'S COURT, A(1949), ph; STREETS OF LAREDO(1949), ph; GREAT MISSOURI RAID, THE(1950), ph; WHITE TOWER, THE(1950), ph; AT SWORD'S POINT(1951), ph; FLAMING FEATHER(1951), ph; SILVER CITY(1951), ph; WARPATH(1951), ph; DENVER AND RIO GRANDE(1952), ph; HURRICANE SMITH(1952), ph; ARROWHEAD(1953), ph; FLIGHT TO TANGIER(1953), ph; PONY EXPRESS(1953), ph; LAWLESS STREET, A(1955), ph; RAGE AT DAWN(1955), ph; STRANGER ON HORSEBACK(1955); TEXAS LADY(1955), ph; SEVENTH CAVALRY(1956), ph; GUNS OF FORT PETTICOAT, THE(1957), ph; HALLIDAY BRAND, THE(1957), ph; TERROR IN A TEXAS TOWN(1958), ph

Silents
TEN COMMANDMENTS, THE(1923), ph; MERRY WIDOW, THE(1925), ph

George Renne
1984
SAM'S SON(1984), art d

Ray Rennehan
BECKY SHARP(1935), ph; WHISPERING SMITH(1948), ph

Beth Renner
KEEP YOUR POWDER DRY(1945); WHOSE LIFE IS IT ANYWAY?(1981)

Linda Rennhofer
DR. FRANKENSTEIN ON CAMPUS(1970, Can.); LOVE(1982, Can.)

John Rennick
NATIVE LAND(1942)

Nancy Rennick
YOUNG LOVERS, THE(1964)

Rennie
JOHNNY ANGEL(1945), cos; HOUSE ON TELEGRAPH HILL(1951), cos

Alan Rennie
HAPPY DAYS ARE HERE AGAIN(1936, Brit.), w

Barbara Rennie
1984
SACRED HEARTS(1984, Brit.), d&w

Guy Rennie
GROUNDS FOR MARRIAGE(1950); ROOGIE'S BUMP(1954); NIGHT FREIGHT(1955); INVASION OF THE BODY SNATCHERS(1956); LENNY(1974)

Hilary Rennie
DRAGON OF PENDRAGON CASTLE, THE(1950, Brit.)

James Rennie
BAD MAN, THE(1930); GIRL OF THE GOLDEN WEST(1930); LASH, THE(1930); ILLICIT(1931); PARTY HUSBAND(1931); LITTLE DAMOZEL, THE(1933, Brit.); SKYLARK(1941); CROSSROADS(1942); NOW, VOYAGER(1942); TALES OF MANHATTAN(1942); WILSON(1944); BELL FOR ADANO, A(1945)
Silents
FLYING PAT(1920); STARDUST(1921); DUST FLOWER, THE(1922); ARGENTINE LOVE(1924); CLOTHES MAKE THE PIRATE(1925)
Misc. Silents
REMODELING HER HUSBAND(1920); HIS CHILDREN'S CHILDREN(1923); MIGHTY LAK' A ROSE(1923); MORAL SINNER, THE(1924); RESTLESS WIVES(1924); SHARE AND SHARE ALIKE(1925)

Maggie Rennie
WICKED LADY, THE(1983, Brit.)
1984
JIGSAW MAN, THE(1984, Brit.)

Michael Rennie
BANK HOLIDAY(1938, Brit.); THIS MAN IN PARIS(1939, Brit.); CONQUEST OF THE AIR(1940); TURNED OUT NICE AGAIN(1941, Brit.); BIG BLOCKADE, THE(1942, Brit.); SHIPS WITH WINGS(1942, Brit.); SUICIDE SQUADRON(1942, Brit.); TOWER OF TERROR, THE(1942, Brit.); I'LL BE YOUR SWEETHEART(1945, Brit.); CAESAR AND CLEOPATRA(1946, Brit.); WICKED LADY, THE(1946, Brit.); HIGH FURY(1947, Brit.); PATIENT VANISHES, THE(1947, Brit.); ROOT OF ALL EVIL, THE(1947, Brit.); IDOL OF PARIS(1948, Brit.); UNEASY TERMS(1948, Brit.); GOLDEN MADONNA, THE(1949, Brit.); BLACK ROSE, THE(1950); BODY SAID NO!, THE(1950, Brit.); MISS PILGRIM'S PROGRESS(1950, Brit.); DAY THE EARTH STOOD STILL, THE(1951); DESERT FOX, THE(1951); I'LL NEVER FORGET YOU(1951); THIRTEENTH LETTER, THE(1951); FIVE FINGERS(1952); LES MISERABLES(1952); PHONE CALL FROM A STRANGER(1952); DANGEROUS CROSSING(1953); KING OF THE KHYBER RIFLES(1953); ROBE, THE(1953); SAILOR OF THE KING(1953, Brit.); DEMETRIUS AND THE GLADIATORS(1954); DESIREE(1954); PRINCESS OF THE NILE(1954); MAMBO(1955, Ital.); RAINS OF RANCHIPUR, THE(1955); SEVEN CITIES OF GOLD(1955); SOLDIER OF FORTUNE(1955); TEENAGE REBEL(1956); ISLAND IN THE SUN(1957); OMAR KHAYYAM(1957); THIRD MAN ON THE MOUNTAIN(1959); LOST WORLD, THE(1960); MISSILE FROM HELL(1960, Brit.); MARY, MARY(1963); CYBORG 2087(1966); RIDE BEYOND VENGEANCE(1966); HOTEL(1967); DEVIL'S BRIGADE, THE(1968); POWER, THE(1968); YOUNG, THE EVIL AND THE SAVAGE, THE(1968, Ital.); SUBTERFUGE(1969, US/Brit.); ASSIGNMENT TERROR(1970, Ger./Span./Ital.)
Misc. Talkies
BATTLE OF EL ALAMEIN(1971); DEADLY GAME, THE(1974); SURABAYA CONSPIRACY(1975)

Ruth Rennie
MEATBALLS(1979, Can.)

Vincent Renno
ABBOTT AND COSTELLO MEET THE KILLER, BORIS KARLOFF(1949); CRISS CROSS(1949); GREAT SINNER, THE(1949); CONVICTED(1950); FRENCHIE(1950); I'LL GET BY(1950); GREAT CARUSO, THE(1951); SIROCCO(1951); MY SIX CONVICTS(1952)

Janice Renny
1984
CRIMES OF PASSION(1984)

Reno the Horse
UNDER ARIZONA SKIES(1946)

Darlene Dana Reno
STARK FEAR(1963)

Jean Reno
1984
LE DERNIER COMBAT(1984, Fr.)

Silents
HUNTED MEN(1930); OKLAHOMA SHERIFF, THE(1930)

Kelly Reno
BLACK STALLION, THE(1979); BLACK STALLION RETURNS, THE(1983)
1984
BRADY'S ESCAPE(1984, U.S./Hung.)

Teddy Reno
LADY DOCTOR, THE(1963, Fr./Ital./Span.)

Teddy Reno [Ricordi Ferruccio]
MY WIFE'S ENEMY(1967, Ital.)

Walt Reno, Jr.
FEVER HEAT(1968)

Claude Renoir
DOCTEUR LAENNEC(1949, Fr.), ph; MONSIEUR VINCENT(1949, Fr.), ph; WAYS OF LOVE(1950, Ital./Fr.), ph; RIVER, THE(1951), ph; GREEN GLOVE, THE(1952), ph; GOLDEN COACH, THE(1953, Fr./Ital.), ph; KNOCK(1955, Fr.), ph; MADAME BUTTERFLY(1955 Ital./Jap.), ph; PARIS DOES STRANGE THINGS(1957, Fr./Ital.), ph; BLOOD AND ROSES(1961, Fr./Ital.), ph; CHEATERS, THE(1961, Fr.), ph; END OF DESIRE(1962 Fr./Ital.), ph; LOVERS OF TERUEL, THE(1962, Fr.), ph; LAFAYETTE(1963, Fr.), ph; CIRCUS WORLD(1964), ph; SYMPHONY FOR A MASSACRE(1965, Fr./Ital.), ph; GAME IS OVER, THE(1967, Fr.), ph; BARBARELLA(1968, Fr./Ital.), ph; PARIS IN THE MONTH OF AUGUST(1968, Fr.), ph; TONI(1968, Fr.), ph; DON'T LOOK NOW(1969, Brit./Fr.), ph; MADWOMAN OF CHAILLOT, THE(1969), ph; SPIRITS OF THE DEAD(1969, Fr./Ital.), ph; ADVENTURERS, THE(1970), ph; LADY IN THE CAR WITH GLASSES AND A GUN, THE(1970, U.S./Fr.), ph; HORSEMEN, THE(1971), ph; BURGLARS, THE(1972, Fr./Ital.), ph; IMPOSSIBLE OBJECT(1973, Fr.), ph; SERPENT, THE(1973, Fr./Ital./Ger.), ph; PAUL AND MICHELLE(1974, Fr./Brit.), ph; FRENCH CONNECTION 11(1975), ph; SPY WHO LOVED ME, THE(1977, Brit.), ph; ATTENTION, THE KIDS ARE WATCHING(1978, Fr.), ph; NO TIME FOR BREAKFAST(1978, Fr.), ph

Dido Renoir
CHRISTIAN LICORICE STORE, THE(1971)

Jean Renoir
CRIME OF MONSIEUR LANGE, THE(1936, Fr.), d, w; LOWER DEPTHS, THE(1937, Fr.), d, w; GRAND ILLUSION(1938, Fr.), d, w; LA BETE HUMAINE(1938, Fr.), a, d&w; LA MARSEILLAISE(1938, Fr.), d, w; RULES OF THE GAME, THE(1939, Fr.), a, d, w; SWAMP WATER(1941), d; THIS LAND IS MINE(1943), p, d; SOUTHERNER, THE(1945), d, w; DIARY OF A CHAMBERMAID(1946), d; WOMAN ON THE BEACH, THE(1947), d, w; WAYS OF LOVE(1950, Ital./Fr.), a, d, w; RIVER, THE(1951), d, w; GOLDEN COACH, THE(1953, Fr./Ital.), d, w; FRENCH CANCAN(1956, Fr.), d, w; PARIS DOES STRANGE THINGS(1957, Fr./Ital.), d, w; PICNIC ON THE GRASS(1960, Fr.), d&w; ELUSIVE CORPORAL, THE(1963), d, w; BOUDU SAVED FROM DROWNING(1967, Fr.), d, w; TONI(1968, Fr.), d, w; CHRISTIAN LICORICE STORE, THE(1971); LE PETIT THEATRE DE JEAN RENOIR(1974, Fr.), d&w; LA CHIENNE(1975, Fr.), d, w, and
Misc. Silents
LA FILLE DE L'EAU(1924, Fr.), d; NANA(1926, Fr.), d; MARQUITTA(1927, Fr.), d; LE TORNOI(1928, Fr.), d; TIRE AU FLANC(1929, Fr.), d

Leon Renoir
THIEF OF VENICE, THE(1952)

Louis Renoir
TERROR ON TIPTOE(1936, Brit.), d

Marguerite Renoir
CRIME OF MONSIEUR LANGE, THE(1936, Fr.), ed; GRAND ILLUSION(1938, Fr.), ed; LA BETE HUMAINE(1938, Fr.), ed; LA MARSEILLAISE(1938, Fr.), ed; RULES OF THE GAME, THE(1939, Fr.), ed; ANTOINE ET ANTOINETTE(1947 Fr.), ed; WAYS OF LOVE(1950, Ital./Fr.), a, ed; EDWARD AND CAROLINE(1952, Fr.), ed; ALI BABA(1954, Fr.), ed; CASQUE D'OR(1956, Fr.), ed; GINA(1961, Fr./Mex.), ed; MODIGLIANI OF MONTPARNASSE(1961, Fr./Ital.), ed; NIGHT WATCH, THE(1964, Fr./Ital.), ed; THANK HEAVEN FOR SMALL FAVORS(1964, Fr.), ed; MASCULINE FEMININE(1966, Fr./Swed.), ed; BOUDU SAVED FROM DROWNING(1967, Fr.), ed; TONI(1968, Fr.), ed; SOLO(1970, Fr.), ed; LA CHIENNE(1975, Fr.), ed; DEATH IN THE GARDEN(1977, Fr./Mex.), ed

Pierre Renoir
LA MARSEILLAISE(1938, Fr.); SACRIFICE OF HONOR(1938, Fr.); ESCAPE FROM YESTERDAY(1939, Fr.); PERSONAL COLUMN(1939, Fr.); HATRED(1941, Fr.); CHILDREN OF PARADISE(1945, Fr.); FOOLISH HUSBANDS(1948, Fr.); KNOCK(1955, Fr.)

Rita Renoir
SWEET AND SOUR(1964, Fr./Ital.); RED DESERT(1965, Fr./Ital.); CHAPPAQUA(1967)

Sophie Renoir
ATTENTION, THE KIDS ARE WATCHING(1978, Fr.); LE BEAU MARIAGE(1982, Fr.)

Gaby Renom
ZOMBIE CREEPING FLESH(1981, Ital./Span.); NIGHT OF THE ZOMBIES(1983, Span./Ital.)

Renee Renor
GUYS AND DOLLS(1955)

Theresa Renouard
SOFT SKIN, THE(1964, Fr.)

Pete L. Renoudet
LT. ROBIN CRUSOE, U.S.N.(1966)

Pete Renoudet
LOVE BUG, THE(1968); COMPUTER WORE TENNIS SHOES, THE(1970); BAREFOOT EXECUTIVE, THE(1971); $1,000,000 DUCK(1971); PSYCHOPATH, THE(1973)

Rene Renous
IF PARIS WERE TOLD TO US(1956, Fr.), set d

Rene Renoux
LILIOM(1935, Fr.), art d; FRIC FRAC(1939, FR.), prod d; SYMPHONIE PASTORALE(1948, Fr.), set d; MAN ON THE EIFFEL TOWER, THE(1949), art d; MONSIEUR VINCENT(1949, Fr.), set d; ANGELS OF THE STREETS(1950, Fr.), art d; WAGES OF FEAR, THE(1955, Fr./Ital.), prod d; HUNCHBACK OF NOTRE DAME, THE(1957, Fr.), art d; ROYAL AFFAIRS IN VERSAILLES(1957, Fr.), set d; BEAR, THE(1963, Fr.), art d; THIS SPECIAL FRIENDSHIP(1967, Fr.), art d; TRIPLE CROSS(1967, Fr./Brit.), prod d

Dan Rense
ONE TOO MANY(1950)

Danny Rense
GOLD FEVER(1952)
Elaine Renshaw
DR. EHRLICH'S MAGIC BULLET(1940)
Violent Rensing
SINGING NUN, THE(1966)
Violet Rensing
DESIREE(1954); BEAST OF BUDAPEST, THE(1958); WHEN HELL BROKE LOO-SE(1958)
Barbara Renson
TRIP, THE(1967)
Paul Rensy
DANCE, GIRL, DANCE(1940)
Joe Renteria
HANGUP(1974)
David Renton
NEPTUNE FACTOR, THE(1973, Can.)
Shirley Renton
TROJAN BROTHERS, THE(1946)
Patience Rentoul
LOVE IN WAITING(1948, Brit.); HANGMAN'S WHARF(1950, Brit.); HAPPIEST DAYS OF YOUR LIFE(1950, Brit.); NO HAUNT FOR A GENTLEMAN(1952, Brit.)
Mickey Rentschiler
WEST OF CIMARRON(1941)
Michael Rentschler
MADE FOR EACH OTHER(1939)
Mickey Rentschler
HIS PRIVATE SECRETARY(1933); KID MILLIONS(1934); MODERN HERO, A(1934); SCARLET LETTER, THE(1934); FOLLOW YOUR HEART(1936); SINS OF MAN(1936); ADVENTURES OF TOM SAWYER, THE(1938); BOYS TOWN(1938); DEVIL'S PARTY, THE(1938); PECK'S BAD BOY WITH THE CIRCUS(1938); I MARRIED A WITCH(1942); SEE HERE, PRIVATE HARGROVE(1944); TWO GIRLS AND A SAIL-OR(1944); REDHEAD FROM MANHATTAN(1954)
Robin Renucci
ENTRE NOUS(1983, Fr.)
David W. Renwick
FIEND(, spec eff
Anthony Renya
MAIN EVENT, THE(1979)
Blanche Renze
SON OF PALEFACE(1952)
Gastone Renzelli
BELLISSIMA(1952, Ital.)
Joe Renzetti
BUDDY HOLLY STORY, THE(1978), md; EXTERMINATOR, THE(1980), m; FAT-SO(1980), m; DEAD AND BURIED(1981), m; UNDER THE RAINBOW(1981), m
Eva Renzi
FUNERAL IN BERLIN(1966, Brit.); PINK JUNGLE, THE(1968); THAT WO-MAN(1968, Ger.); BIRD WITH THE CRYSTAL PLUMAGE, THE(1970, Ital./Ger.); DEATH TOOK PLACE LAST NIGHT(1970, Ital./Ger.)
Misc. Talkies
LOVE, VAMPIRE STYLE(1971)
Eve Renzi
Misc. Talkies
NIGHT OF THE ASSASSIN, THE(1972)
Maggie Renzi
RETURN OF THE SECAUCUS SEVEN(1980); LIANNA(1983), a, p
1984
BROTHER FROM ANOTHER PLANET, THE(1984), a, p; SWING SHIFT(1984)
Marta Renzi
HAIR(1979); LIANNA(1983), a, ch
R. Renzi
ANITA GARIBALDI(1954, Ital.), w
Robert Renzo
TALE OF FIVE WOMEN, A(1951, Brit.), art d
Frank Renzulli
1984
BROADWAY DANNY ROSE(1984)
Mario Renzullo
JUNKET 89(1970, Brit.)
Leonida Repaci
LA DOLCE VITA(1961, Ital./Fr.); EMPTY CANVAS, THE(1964, Fr./Ital.)
Maison Repetto
IMPOSSIBLE ON SATURDAY(1966, Fr./Israel), cos
A. Repina
SOUND OF LIFE, THE(1962, USSR), w
Alexander Repinov
THIRTEEN, THE(1937, USSR)
Repnikova
Silents
BATTLESHIP POTEMKIN, THE(1925, USSR)
Art Repola
1984
INDIANA JONES AND THE TEMPLE OF DOOM(1984)
Arthur Repola
RETURN OF THE JEDI(1983), ed
Weather Report
WATCHED(1974), m
Earl Repp
CHEROKEE STRIP(1937), w
Ed Earl Repp
MAN FROM HELL, THE(1934), w; DEVIL'S SADDLE LEGION, THE(1937), w; EMPTY HOLSTERS(1937), w; OLD WYOMING TRAIL, THE(1937), w; PRAIRIE THUNDER(1937), w; CALL OF THE ROCKIES(1938), w; CATTLE RAIDERS(1938), w; OUTLAWS OF THE PRAIRIE(1938), w; WEST OF CHEYENNE(1938), w; RAWHIDE RANGERS(1941), w; LONE PRAIRIE, THE(1942), w; SILVER CITY RAIDERS(1943), w; SIX GUN GOSPEL(1943), w; LAST HORSEMAN, THE(1944), w; TRIGGER TRAIL(1944), w; LONE HAND TEXAN, THE(1947), w; GUNS OF HATE(1948), w; TIOGA KID, THE(1948), w; CHALLENGE OF THE RANGE(1949), w; LAW OF THE BADLANDS(1950), w; RIDER FROM TUCSON(1950), w; STORM OVER WYO-MING(1950), w; GUNPLAY(1951), w; SADDLE LEGION(1951), w; KID FROM BROK-EN GUN, THE(1952), w

Edward Earl Repp
CYCLONE FURY(1951), ph
Guy Repp
ARISE, MY LOVE(1940); HE STAYED FOR BREAKFAST(1940); YOUNG AS YOU FEEL(1940)
Jack Repp
STATUE, THE(1971, Brit.)
Pierre Repp
CARTOUCHE(1962, Fr./Ital.); CHARLES AND LUCIE(1982, Fr.)
Stafford Repp
MAN WITH THE GUN(1955); HARDER THEY FALL, THE(1956); PRICE OF FEAR, THE(1956); STAR IN THE DUST(1956); STEEL JUNGLE, THE(1956); GREEN-EYED BLONDE, THE(1957); PLUNDER ROAD(1957); HOT SPELL(1958); I WANT TO LIVE!(1958); CRIMSON KIMONO, THE(1959); EXPLOSIVE GENERATION, THE(1961); VERY SPECIAL FAVOR, A(1965); BATMAN(1966)
Jim Reppert
NATCHEZ TRACE(1960)
Republic Rhythm Riders
LAST MUSKETEER, THE(1952); WAC FROM WALLA WALLA, THE(1952)
The Republic Rhythm Riders
BORDER SADDLEMATES(1952); COLORADO SUNDOWN(1952); OLD OKLAHOMA PLAINS(1952); OLD OVERLAND TRAIL(1953)
Charles Requa
SOUTH OF THE RIO GRANDE(1932); ARE WE CIVILIZED?(1934); MERRY WIDOW, THE(1934); RIP TIDE(1934); VIVA VILLA!(1934); ESCAPADE(1935); YOURS FOR THE ASKING(1936); MAYTIME(1937); PERSONAL PROPERTY(1937)
Silents
EAST OF SUEZ(1925); SON OF THE SHEIK(1926); KING OF KINGS, THE(1927)
Misc. Silents
COUNT OF LUXEMBOURG, THE(1926)
Carlos Requelme
WOMAN'S DEVOTION, A(1956)
Georgy Rerberg
UNCLE VANYA(1972, USSR), ph
Reri
HURRICANE, THE(1937)
Gayne Rescher
FACE IN THE CROWD, A(1957), ph; MAN ON A STRING(1960), ph; MURDER, INC.(1960), ph; FIEND OF DOPE ISLAND(1961), ph; OPEN THE DOOR AND SEE ALL THE PEOPLE(1964), ph; TROUBLEMAKER, THE(1964), ph; RACHEL, RACH-EL(1968), ph; NEW LEAF, A(1971), ph; SUCH GOOD FRIENDS(1971), ph; BOXCAR BERTHA(1972); BOOK OF NUMBERS(1973), ph; CLAUDINE(1974), ph; NORMAN.-..IS THAT YOU?(1976), ph; OLLY, OLLY, OXEN FREE(1978), ph; STAR TREK II: THE WRATH OF KHAN(1982), ph
Jay Rescher
POCOMANIA(1939), ph
Silents
WET GOLD(1921), ph
Gayne Rescherm
JOHN AND MARY(1969), ph
Lillian Reschm
Silents
GOLD RUSH, THE(1925)
Gayne Reschner
MAD DOG COLL(1961), ph
Ben Resella
DELTA FACTOR, THE(1970), art d
Benjamin Resella
NO MAN IS AN ISLAND(1962), art d
Bruno Resenter
FIRST TIME, THE(1978, Fr.)
Lukas Resetarits
Misc. Talkies
UPPERCRUST, THE(1982)
Aziz Resh
HORSEMEN, THE(1971)
Gabe Resh
CHINATOWN(1974), set d
Robert Resh
CHINATOWN(1974), set d; SHAMPOO(1975), set d
M. Reshetin
QUEEN OF SPADES(1961, USSR)
Don ReSimpson
REVENGE OF THE NINJA(1983)
Dan Resin
RICHARD(1972); HAIL(1973); CRAZY JOE(1974); HAPPY HOOKER, THE(1975); SUNSHINE BOYS, THE(1975); GOD TOLD ME TO(1976); IF EVER I SEE YOU AGAIN(1978); CADDY SHACK(1980); DEADHEAD MILES(1982)
Antonio Resines
1984
SKYLINE(1984, Spain)
Andres Resino [Andrew Reese]
WEREWOLF VS. THE VAMPIRE WOMAN, THE(1970, Span./Ger.)
John Resko
CONVICTS FOUR(1962), d&w
Arthur Resley
DEVIL'S MISTRESS, THE(1968)
Edward Resmini
APPRENTICESHIP OF DUDDY KRAVITZ, THE(1974, Can.)
A.J. Buster Resmondo
COURT JESTER, THE(1956)
Alain Resnais
HIROSHIMA, MON AMOUR(1959, Fr./Jap.), d; LAST YEAR AT MARIENBAD(1962, Fr./Ital.), d; MURIEL(1963, Fr./Ital.), d; LA GUERRE EST FINIE(1967, Fr./Swed.), d; JE T'AIME, JE T'AIME(1972, Fr./Swed.), d, w; STAVISKY(1974, Fr.), d; PROVI-DENCE(1977, Fr.), d; MON ONCLE D'AMERIQUE(1980, Fr.), d

1984
LIFE IS A BED OF ROSES(1984, Fr.), d
Lawrence Resner
GUN BATTLE AT MONTEREY(1957), w
Eli Resnick
ZELIG(1983)
Gershon Resnick
GAS(1981, Can.)
Judith Resnick
CARNIVAL OF BLOOD(1976)
Leona Resnick
SCREAM, BABY, SCREAM(1969)
Marcia Resnick
OFFENDERS, THE(1980); TRAP DOOR, THE(1980)
Matt Resnick
STAKEOUT ON DOPE STREET(1958)
Patricia Resnick
WEDDING, A(1978), a, w; NINE TO FIVE(1980), w
Robert Resnick
CHICKEN CHRONICLES, THE(1977)
Gershon Resnik
KIDNAPPING OF THE PRESIDENT, THE(1980, Can.)
Muriel Resnik
ANY WEDNESDAY(1966), w; HOW SWEET IT IS(1968), w
Sam Resnik
SWORD IN THE DESERT(1949)
Adalberto Martinez Resortes
LOS PLATILLOS VOLADORES(1955, Mex.)
Franco Ressel
ASSASSIN, THE(1961, Ital./Fr.); WONDERS OF ALADDIN, THE(1961, Fr./Ital.); DAMON AND PYTHIAS(1962); ERIK THE CONQUEROR(1963, Fr./Ital.); SAMSON AND THE SEVEN MIRACLES OF THE WORLD(1963, Fr./Ital.); BLOOD AND BLACK LACE(1965, Ital.); UPPER HAND, THE(1967, Fr./Ital./Ger.); WAR ITALIAN STYLE(1967, Ital.); WILD, WILD PLANET, THE(1967, Ital.); NARCO MEN, THE(1969, Span./Ital.); SABATA(1969, Ital.); MERCENARY, THE(1970, Ital./Span.); TRINITY IS STILL MY NAME(1971, Ital.); TRAFFIC(1972, Fr.)
Frank Ressel
TARZANA, THE WILD GIRL(1973)
Harrison Ressler
NIGHT THEY ROBBED BIG BERTHA'S, THE(1975)
Tony Restaino
BRAIN THAT WOULDN'T DIE, THE(1959), m
Carmela Restivo
SPY HUNT(1950)
Thelma Reston
LOLLIPOP(1966, Braz.); EARTH ENTRANCED(1970, Braz.)
Restopino
GATES OF HELL, THE(1983, U.S./Ital.), makeup
Rosario Restopino
DR. BUTCHER, M.D.(1982, Ital.), spec eff
Hughie Restorick
MY CHILDHOOD(1972, Brit.); MY AIN FOLK(1974, Brit.)
Eddie Retacy
NO MAN'S LAND(1964)
Norman Retchin
LEATHER SAINT, THE(1956), p, w; URANIUM BOOM(1956), w; RIDE OUT FOR REVENGE(1957), p, w
Jan Retel
GIRL WITH THE RED HAIR, THE(1983, Neth.)
Joe Reteria
CAT MURKIL AND THE SILKS(1976)
Ella Retford
DARBY AND JOAN(1937, Brit.); POISON PEN(1941, Brit.); I'LL BE YOUR SWEETHEART(1945, Brit.); VARIETY JUBILEE(1945, Brit.); PAPER ORCHID(1949, Brit.); SHADOW OF THE PAST(1950, Brit.); SILK NOOSE, THE(1950, Brit.)
Catherine Rethi
LE BEAU MARIAGE(1982, Fr.)
Gary Rethmeier
OH! CALCUTTA!(1972)
Hugh Reticher
DANGEROUSLY THEY LIVE(1942), art d
Hugh Reticke, Jr.
ROAD GANG(1936), art d
Hugh Reticker
CASE OF THE LUCKY LEGS, THE(1935), art d; MAN OF IRON(1935), art d; RED HOT TIRES(1935), art d; STRANDED(1935), art d; DANGEROUS(1936), art d; PUBLIC ENEMY'S WIFE(1936), art d; WALKING DEAD, THE(1936), art d; WIDOW FROM MONTE CARLO, THE(1936), art d; BACK IN CIRCULATION(1937), art d; EXPENSIVE HUSBANDS(1937), art d; GREAT O'MALLEY, THE(1937), art d; GIRLS ON PROBATION(1938), art d; GOING PLACES(1939), art d; WAGONS ROLL AT NIGHT, THE(1941), art d; ACROSS THE PACIFIC(1942), art d; MURDER IN THE BIG HOUSE(1942), art d; SECRET ENEMIES(1942), art d; BACKGROUND TO DANGER(1943), art d; TRUCK BUSTERS(1943), art d; DOUGHGIRLS, THE(1944), art d; IN OUR TIME(1944), art d; HORN BLOWS AT MIDNIGHT, THE(1945), art d; HUMORESQUE(1946), art d; NOBODY LIVES FOREVER(1946), art d; OF HUMAN BONDAGE(1946), art d; SHADOW OF A WOMAN(1946), art d; WALLFLOWER(1948), art d; HOMICIDE(1949), art d; NIGHT UNTO NIGHT(1949), art d
Misc. Silents
RIGHT OFF THE BAT(1915), d
Hugo Reticker
HELL'S KITCHEN(1939), art d; YOU CAN'T GET AWAY WITH MURDER(1939), art d
Jill Reties
Silents
HIS HOUR(1924)
Gerhard Retschy
EMIL AND THE DETECTIVES(1964)

John Retsek
PRIVATE PARTS(1972), set d; HOMEBODIES(1974), art d
Hugh Retticher
LITTLE BIG SHOT(1935), art d
Earl Rettig
RELUCTANT DRAGON, THE(1941), ed
Tommy Rettig
FOR HEAVEN'S SAKE(1950); JACKPOT, THE(1950); PANIC IN THE STREETS(1950); TWO WEEKS WITH LOVE(1950); ELOPEMENT(1951); STRIP, THE(1951); WEEKEND WITH FATHER(1951); GOBS AND GALS(1952); PAULA(1952); LADY WANTS MINK, THE(1953); SO BIG(1953); 5,000 FINGERS OF DR. T. THE(1953); EGYPTIAN. THE(1954); RAID, THE(1954); RIVER OF NO RETURN(1954); AT GUNPOINT(1955); COBWEB, THE(1955); LAST WAGON, THE(1956)
Albach Retty
Misc. Silents
MYSTIC MIRROR, THE(1928, Ger.)
Raoul Retzer
SECRET WAYS, THE(1961); $100 A NIGHT(1968, Ger.); SALZBURG CONNECTION, THE(1972)
Alma Reuben
Misc. Silents
MASTER OF HIS HOME(1917)
Dr. David Reuben
EVERYTHING YOU ALWAYS WANTED TO KNOW ABOUT SEX, BUT WE'RE AFRAID TO ASK(1972), d&w
Faenza Reuben
1984
UTU(1984, New Zealand)
J. Walter Reuben
BAD MAN OF BRIMSTONE(1938), d
Robert Reuben
STORY OF G.I. JOE, THE(1945)
Reuben Castang and His Apes
NO MONKEY BUSINESS(1935, Brit.)
Alma Reubens
Silents
JUDITH OF THE CUMBERLANDS(1916)
Paul Reubens
CHEECH AND CHONG'S NEXT MOVIE(1980); CHEECH AND CHONG'S NICE DREAMS(1981); DREAM ON(1981); PANDEMONIUM(1982)
1984
MEATBALLS PART II(1984)
Eva Reuber-Staier
SLIPPER AND THE ROSE, THE(1976, Brit.); SPY WHO LOVED ME, THE(1977, Brit.); FOR YOUR EYES ONLY(1981); OCTOPUSSY(1983, Brit.)
Emely Reuer
FOUNTAIN OF LOVE, THE(1968, Aust.); OFFICE GIRLS(1974)
Kevin Reul
BUGSY MALONE(1976, Brit.)
Peter Reusch
I'M GOING TO GET YOU ... ELLIOT BOY(1971, Can.), ph
Antoinette Reuss
WALK WITH LOVE AND DEATH, A(1969)
Francis Reusser
JONAH–WHO WILL BE 25 IN THE YEAR 2000(1976, Switz.)
Bjarne Reuter
1984
ZAPPA(1984, Den.), w
Walter Reuter
VIRGIN SACRIFICE(1959), ph; TIME AND THE TOUCH, THE(1962), ph
Georg M. Reuther
MAKE WAY FOR LILA(1962, Swed./Ger.), p; COUSINS IN LOVE(1982), p
Germaine Reuver
PRIZE, THE(1952, Fr.)
Ichiro Reuzaki
TORA! TORA! TORA!(1970, U.S./Jap.)
Marcel Reuze
LE PLAISIR(1954, Fr.)
Zeev Revan
JERUSALEM FILE, THE(1972, U.S./Israel)
Jacques Revaux
YOUNG GIRLS OF ROCHEFORT, THE(1968, Fr.)
Gerard Reve
1984
FOURTH MAN, THE(1984, Neth.), w
Rick Reveke
WONDER WOMEN(1973, Phil.)
Francis Revel
PAN-AMERICANA(1945)
Harry Revel
BROADWAY THROUGH A KEYHOLE(1933), m; SITTING PRETTY(1933); OLD-FASHIONED WAY, THE(1934), m; PARIS IN SPRING(1935), m
Mara Revel
SOUND OF TRUMPETS, THE(1963, Ital.)
Maurice Revel
LES ENFANTS TERRIBLES(1952, Fr.)
Reni Revel
PARIS UNDERGROUND(1945)
Fred N. Revelala
HURRICANE SMITH(1952)
Fred Revelala
KISS TOMORROW GOODBYE(1950)
Freddie Revelala
I WAS AN AMERICAN SPY(1951)
Nellie Revell
MIGHTY, THE(1929), w
Terry Revell
SINCE YOU WENT AWAY(1944)

Hamilton Revelle
Silents
KISMET(1920); TELEPHONE GIRL, THE(1927)
Misc. Silents
LA DUBARRY(1914, Ital.); DUBARRY(1915); ENEMY TO SOCIETY, AN(1915); HALF MILLION BRIBE, THE(1916); PRICE OF MALICE, THE(1916); BLACK STORK, THE(1917); THAIS(1917); LEST WE FORGET(1918); SPLENDID SINNER, THE(1918); GOOD WOMEN(1921)

The Revels
EXILES, THE(1966), m

Larry Revene
1984
DELIVERY BOYS(1984), ph; HOLLYWOOD HOT TUBS(1984), ph; PREPPIES(1984), ph

Gianfranco Reverberi
THE DIRTY GAME(1966, Fr./Ital./Ger.), m

Anne Revere
DOUBLE DOOR(1934); HOWARDS OF VIRGINIA, THE(1940); ONE CROWDED NIGHT(1940); DESIGN FOR SCANDAL(1941); DEVIL COMMANDS, THE(1941); FLAME OF NEW ORLEANS, THE(1941); H.M. PULHAM, ESQ.(1941); MEN OF BOYS TOWN(1941); REMEMBER THE DAY(1941); ARE HUSBANDS NECESSARY?(1942); FALCON TAKES OVER, THE(1942); GAY SISTERS, THE(1942); MEET THE STEWARTS(1942); STAR SPANGLED RHYTHM(1942); MEANEST MAN IN THE WORLD, THE(1943); OLD ACQUAINTANCE(1943); SHANTYTOWN(1943); SONG OF BERNADETTE, THE(1943); KEYS OF THE KINGDOM, THE(1944); NATIONAL VELVET(1944); RAINBOW ISLAND(1944); STANDING ROOM ONLY(1944); SUNDAY DINNER FOR A SOLDIER(1944); THIN MAN GOES HOME, THE(1944); DON JUAN QUILLIGAN(1945); FALLEN ANGEL(1945); DRAGONWYCH(1946); BODY AND SOUL(1947); CARNIVAL IN COSTA RICA(1947); FOREVER AMBER(1947); GENTLEMAN'S AGREEMENT(1947); SHOCKING MISS PILGRIM, THE(1947); DEEP WATERS(1948); SCUDDA-HOO! SCUDDA-HAY!(1948); SECRET BEYOND THE DOOR, THE(1948); YOU'RE MY EVERYTHING(1949); GREAT MISSOURI RAID, THE(1950); PLACE IN THE SUN, A(1951); MACHO CALLAHAN(1970); TELL ME THAT YOU LOVE ME, JUNIE MOON(1970); BIRCH INTERVAL(1976)

Carla Revere
OPEN CITY(1946, Ital.)

Jed Prouty Reverend
LIFE OF VERGIE WINTERS, THE(1934)

Marta Reves
RIO 70(1970, U.S./Ger./Span.)

Ravinder Singh Revett
OCTOPUSSY(1983, Brit.)

Alex Revides
FAREWELL TO ARMS, A(1957); EVA(1962, Fr./Ital.)

Dorothy Revier
DANCE OF LIFE, THE(1929); DONOVAN AFFAIR, THE(1929); FATHER AND SON(1929); IRON MASK, THE(1929); LIGHT FINGERS(1929); MIGHTY, THE(1929); TANNED LEGS(1929); BAD MAN, THE(1930); HOLD EVERYTHING(1930); MURDER ON THE ROOF(1930); SQUEALER, THE(1930); VENGEANCE(1930); WAY OF ALL MEN, THE(1930); ANYBODY'S BLONDE(1931); AVENGER, THE(1931); BLACK CAMEL, THE(1931); GRAFT(1931); LEFTOVER LADIES(1931); ARM OF THE LAW(1932); BEAUTY PARLOR(1932); KING MURDER, THE(1932); LAST RIDE, THE(1932); NIGHT WORLD(1932); NO LIVING WITNESS(1932); SALLY OF THE SUBWAY(1932); SCARLET WEEKEND, A(1932); SECRETS OF WU SIN(1932); SIN'S PAYDAY(1932); WIDOW IN SCARLET(1932); LOVE IS LIKE THAT(1933); THRILL HUNTER, THE(1933); ABOVE THE CLOUDS(1934); BY CANDLELIGHT(1934); FIGHTING RANGER, THE(1934); GREEN EYES(1934); UNKNOWN BLONDE(1934); WHEN A MAN SEES RED(1934); CIRCUMSTANTIAL EVIDENCE(1935); CURTAIN FALLS, THE(1935); LADY IN SCARLET, THE(1935); COWBOY AND THE KID,-THE(1936); EAGLE'S BROOD, THE(1936)
Misc. Talkies
CIRCUS SHADOWS(1935); $20 A WEEK(1935)
Silents
SUPREME TEST, THE(1923); DOWN BY THE RIO GRANDE(1924); MARRY IN HASTE(1924); OTHER KIND OF LOVE, THE(1924); ROSE OF PARIS, THE(1924); SWORD OF VALOR, THE(1924); ENEMY OF MEN, AN(1925); JUST A WOMAN(1925); FAR CRY, THE(1926); WHEN THE WIFE'S AWAY(1926); CLOWN, THE(1927); DROPKICK, THE(1927); STOLEN PLEASURES(1927); WANDERING GIRLS(1927); WARNING, THE(1927); SINNER'S PARADE(1928)
Misc. Silents
BROADWAY MADONNA, THE(1922); WILD PARTY, THE(1923); CALL OF THE MATE(1924); COWBOY AND THE FLAPPER, THE(1924); MAN FROM GOD'S COUNTRY(1924); THAT WILD WEST(1924); VIRGIN, THE(1924); DANGER SIGNAL, THE(1925); DANGEROUS PLEASURE(1925); FATE OF A FLIRT, THE(1925); SEALED LIPS(1925); STEPPIN' OUT(1925); WHEN HUSBANDS FLIRT(1925); BETTER WAY, THE(1926); FALSE ALARM, THE(1926); POOR GIRLS(1927); PRICE OF HONOR, THE(1927); SIREN, THE(1927); TIGRESS, THE(1927); BEWARE OF BLONDES(1928); SUBMARINE(1928); QUITTER, THE(1929)

Harry J. Revier
BILL'S LEGACY(1931, Brit.), d; PENITENTE MURDER CASE, THE(1936), p, d
Misc. Silents
LUST OF THE AGES, THE(1917), d

Harry Revier
LONE WOLF'S DAUGHTER, THE(1929), w; CONVICT'S CODE(1930), d
Misc. Talkies
CHILD BRIDE(1937), d
Silents
CHALLENGE OF CHANCE, THE(1919), d; ROMANCE OF THE AIR, A(1919), d
Misc. Silents
WEAKNESS OF STRENGTH, THE(1916), d; WHAT SHALL WE DO WITH HIM?(1919), d; RETURN OF TARZAN, THE(1920), d; HEART OF THE NORTH, THE(1921), d; LIFE'S GREATEST QUESTION(1921), d; BROADWAY MADONNA, THE(1922), d; JUNGLE TRAIL OF THE SON OF TARZAN(1923), d; DANGEROUS PLEASURE(1925), d; SLAVER, THE(1927), d; THRILL SEEKERS, THE(1927), d; WHAT PRICE LOVE(1927), d

Dorothy Reviere
Misc. Talkies
CALL OF THE WEST(1930); WIDOW IN SCARLET(1932)

Silents
BORDER WOMEN(1924)

Ramon Revilia
Misc. Talkies
HUSTLER SQUAD(1976)

Clive Revill
REACH FOR THE SKY(1957, Brit.); HEADLESS GHOST, THE(1959, Brit.); BUNNY LAKE IS MISSING(1965); FINE MADNESS, A(1966); KALEIDOSCOPE(1966, Brit.); MODESTY BLAISE(1966, Brit.); DOUBLE MAN, THE(1967); FATHOM(1967); HIGH COMMISSIONER, THE(1968, U.S./Brit.); ITALIAN SECRET SERVICE(1968, Ital.); SHOES OF THE FISHERMAN, THE(1968); ASSASSINATION BUREAU, THE(1969, Brit.); PRIVATE LIFE OF SHERLOCK HOLMES, THE(1970, Brit.); BUTTERCUP CHAIN, THE(1971, Brit.); SEVERED HEAD, A(1971, Brit.); AVANTI!(1972); ESCAPE TO THE SUN(1972, Fr./Ger./Israel); LEGEND OF HELL HOUSE, THE(1973, Brit.); BLACK WINDMILL, THE(1974, Brit.); LITTLE PRINCE, THE(1974, Brit.); GALILEO(1975, Brit.); ONE OF OUR DINOSAURS IS MISSING(1975, Brit.); MATILDA(1978); EMPIRE STRIKES BACK, THE(1980); ZORRO, THE GAY BLADE(1981)

Alma Reville
ROMANCE OF SEVILLE, A(1929, Brit.), w; JUNO AND THE PAYCOCK(1930, Brit.), w; MURDER(1930, Brit.), w; SALLY IN OUR ALLEY(1931, Brit.), w; SKIN GAME, THE(1931, Brit.), w; NINE TILL SIX(1932, Brit.), w; NUMBER SEVENTEEN(1932, Brit.), w; RICH AND STRANGE(1932, Brit.), w; WATER GYPSIES, THE(1932, Brit.), w; OUTSIDER, THE(1933, Brit.), w; STRAUSS' GREAT WALTZ(1934, Brit.), w; 39 STEPS, THE(1935, Brit.), w; PASSING OF THE THIRD FLOOR BACK, THE(1936, Brit.), w; SABOTAGE(1937, Brit.), w; FORBIDDEN TERRITORY(1938, Brit.), w; LADY VANISHES, THE(1938, Brit.), w; YOUNG AND INNOCENT(1938, Brit.), w; JAMAICA INN(1939, Brit.), w; SUSPICION(1941), w; SHADOW OF A DOUBT(1943), w; IT'S IN THE BAG(1945), w; PARADINE CASE, THE(1947), w; STAGE FRIGHT(1950, Brit.), w
Silents
RING, THE(1927, Brit.), w; AFTER THE VERDICT(1929, Brit.), w
Misc. Silents
LIFE STORY OF DAVID LLOYD GEORGE, THE(1918, Brit.)

Vanna Revilli
LAND OF THE MINOTAUR(1976, Gr.)

Frank Revis
CONFESSIONS OF A WINDOW CLEANER(1974, Brit.), prod d

Ethel Revnell
FATHER O'FLYNN(1938, Irish); SO THIS IS LONDON(1940, Brit.); BALLOON GOES UP, THE(1942, Brit.); UP WITH THE LARK(1943, Brit.)

Maurice Revnes
AWFUL TRUTH, THE(1929), p; SUZY(1936), p

Max Revol
SIMPLE CASE OF MONEY, A(1952, Fr.)

The Revolving Band
1984
MAKING THE GRADE(1984)

Bernard Revon
MIDNIGHT FOLLY(1962, Fr.), w; DOUBLE DECEPTION(1963, Fr.), w; TIGHT SKIRTS, LOOSE PLEASURES(1966, Fr.), w; STOLEN KISSES(1969, Fr.), w; BED AND BOARD(1971, Fr.), w

Peter Revson
GRAND PRIX(1966)

Leon Revuelta
NUN AT THE CROSSROADS, A(1970, Ital./Span.), cos; MYSTERIOUS ISLAND OF CAPTAIN NEMO, THE(1973, Fr./Ital. 87m Span./Cameroon), cos

Rosaura Revueltas
SOMBRERO(1953); SALT OF THE EARTH(1954)

The Revuers
GREENWICH VILLAGE(1944)

L. Revutsky
Silents
EARTH(1930, USSR), m

Richard Revy
INHERITANCE IN PRETORIA(1936, Ger.)

Rex
PARADE OF THE WEST(1930); KING OF THE SIERRAS(1938); TWO THOROUGHBREDS(1939); WOMAN DOCTOR(1939); SCATTERGOOD PULLS THE STRINGS(1941); SOUTHERNER, THE(1945)
Silents
KING OF THE WILD HORSES, THE(1924); LIGHTNING ROMANCE(1924); BLACK CYCLONE(1925)
Misc. Silents
THREE IN EXILE(1925); DEVIL HORSE, THE(1926); SILENT GUARDIAN, THE(1926); GUARDIANS OF THE WILD(1928); TWO OUTLAWS, THE(1928)

Rex the Dog
KING OF THE WILD HORSES, THE(1934); POLICE DOG(1955, Brit.)
Silents
FACTORY MAGDALEN, A(1914); WILD GIRL, THE(1925); WEST OF THE RAINBOW'S END(1926); CODE OF THE RANGE(1927); WESTERN ROVER, THE(1927); ARIZONA KID, THE(1929)

Rex the Horse
Silents
WILD BLOOD(1929)

Rex the Wonder Horse
STORMY(1935)
Silents
NO MAN'S LAW(1927); HARVEST OF HATE, THE(1929); HOOFBEATS OF VENGEANCE(1929)

Bert Rex
Misc. Silents
STOLEN HEIRLOOMS, THE(1915, Brit.); WIRELESS(1915, Brit.)

Billy Rex
Silents
OLD CURIOSITY SHOP, THE(1913, Brit.)

Eugen Rex
CONGRESS DANCES(1932, Ger.)

Eugene Rex
ECHO OF A DREAM(1930, Ger.)
Gerald Rex
FACING THE MUSIC(1941, Brit.); GERT AND DAISY'S WEEKEND(1941, Brit.); FRONT LINE KIDS(1942, Brit.); DUAL ALIBI(1947, Brit.); SOMETHING IN THE CITY(1950, Brit.); MADAME LOUISE(1951, Brit.); OLD MOTHER RILEY'S JUNGLE TREASURE(1951, Brit.); PAUL TEMPLE'S TRIUMPH(1951, Brit.); SCARLET THREAD(1951, Brit.); TAKE ME TO PARIS(1951, Brit.); PAUL TEMPLE RETURNS(1952, Brit.); THERE WAS A YOUNG LADY(1953, Brit.)
Jack Rex
MYSTERY OF THE BLACK JUNGLE(1955)
Knud Rex
HIDDEN FEAR(1957); HUNGER(1968, Den./Norway/Swed.); OPERATION LOVEBIRDS(1968, Den.); PEOPLE MEET AND SWEET MUSIC FILLS THE HEART(1969, Den./Swed.)
Roberta Rex
CHILDREN OF THE DAMNED(1963, Brit.)
Rex and Starlight
Silents
PLUNGING HOOFS(1929)
Rex Burrows and His Orchestra
ON VELVET(1938, Brit.)
Fred Rexer
1984
RED DAWN(1984)
Joane Rexer
CHICAGO DEADLINE(1949)
Robert Rexer
CHICAGO DEADLINE(1949)
Rexiane
CARNIVAL OF SINNERS(1947, Fr.)
Jim Rexrode
WHOLE SHOOTIN' MATCH, THE(1979), art d
Alejandro Rey
END OF INNOCENCE(1960, Arg.); BATTLE AT BLOODY BEACH(1961); FUN IN ACAPULCO(1963); SYNANON(1965); BLINDFOLD(1966); WILD PACK, THE(1972); MR. MAJESTYK(1974); BREAKOUT(1975); HIGH VELOCITY(1977); SWARM, THE(1978); CUBA(1979); SUNBURN(1979); NINTH CONFIGURATION, THE(1980)
1984
MOSCOW ON THE HUDSON(1984)
Misc. Talkies
STEPMOTHER, THE(1973)
Alvino Rey
SYNCOPATION(1942); FOLLOW THE BAND(1943)
Antonia Rey
COOGAN'S BLUFF(1968); POPI(1969); DOC(1971); KLUTE(1971); WHO SAYS I CAN'T RIDE A RAINBOW!(1971); TO FIND A MAN(1972); LORDS OF FLATBUSH, THE(1974); MONEY, THE(1975); KING OF THE GYPSIES(1978); HAIR(1979)
1984
BEAT STREET(1984); GARBO TALKS(1984); MOSCOW ON THE HUDSON(1984)
Barbara Rey
HORROR OF THE ZOMBIES(1974, Span.)
Brandon Rey
1984
MOSCOW ON THE HUDSON(1984)
Bruno Rey
SORCERESS(1983)
Misc. Talkies
SORCERESS(1983)
Dolores Rey
BY WHOSE HAND?(1932)
Edith Rey
SPACEHUNTER: ADVENTURES IN THE FORBIDDEN ZONE(1983), w
1984
HEY BABE!(1984, Can.), w
Elisabeth Rey
TWO OF US, THE(1968, Fr.)
Etienne Rey
BEAUTIFUL ADVENTURE(1932, Ger.), w
Fernando Rey
MAD QUEEN, THE(1950, Span.); TANGIER ASSIGNMENT(1954, Brit.); LAST DAYS OF POMPEII, THE(1960, Ital.); REVOLT OF THE SLAVES, THE(1961, Ital./Span./Ger.); SAVAGE GUNS, THE(1962, U.S./Span.); VIRIDIANA(1962, Mex./Span.); CASTILIAN, THE(1963, Span./U.S.); CEREMONY, THE(1963, U.S./Span.); GOLIATH AGAINST THE GIANTS(1963, Ital./Span.); RUNNING MAN, THE(1963, Brit.); FACE OF TERROR(1964, Span.); BACKFIRE(1965, Fr.); SCHEHERAZADE(1965, Fr./Ital./Span.); EL GRECO(1966, Ital./Fr.); RETURN OF THE SEVEN(1966, Span.); SON OF A GUNFIGHTER(1966, U.S./Span.); ATTACK OF THE ROBOTS(1967, Fr./Span.); CHIMES AT MIDNIGHT(1967, Span.,Switz.); NAVAJO JOE(1967, Ital./Span.); VISCOUNT, THE(1967, Fr./Span./Ital./Ger.); DESPERATE ONES, THE(1968 U.S./Span.); RUN LIKE A THIEF(1968, Span.); VILLA RIDES(1968); GUNS OF THE MAGNIFICENT SEVEN(1969); IMMORTAL STORY, THE(1969, Fr.); LAND RAIDERS(1969); PRICE OF POWER, THE(1969, Ital./Span.); YOUNG REBEL, THE(1969, Fr./Ital./Span.); ADVENTURERS, THE(1970); TRISTANA(1970, Span./Ital./Fr.); FRENCH CONNECTION, THE(1971); LIGHT AT THE EDGE OF THE WORLD, THE(1971, U.S./Span./Lichtenstein); TOWN CALLED HELL, A(1971, Span./Brit.); DISCREET CHARM OF THE BOURGEOISIE, THE(1972, Fr.); ANTONY AND CLEOPATRA(1973, Brit.); WHITE SISTER(1973, Ital./Span./Fr.); DRAMA OF THE RICH(1975, Ital./Fr.); FRENCH CONNECTION 11(1975); DESERT OF THE TARTARS, THE(1976 Fr./Ital./Iranian); MATTER OF TIME, A(1976, Ital./U.S.); SEVEN BEAUTIES(1976, Ital.); VOYAGE OF THE DAMNED(1976, Brit.); LA GRANDE BOURGEOISE(1977, Ital.); THAT OBSCURE OBJECT OF DESIRE(1977, Fr./Span.); WOMAN WITH RED BOOTS, THE(1977, Fr./Span.); QUINTET(1979); CABOBLANCO(1981); MONSIGNOR(1982)
Misc. Talkies
ASSIGNMENT, THE(1978)
Florian Rey
CARMEN(1949, Span.), d&w; MANOLETE(1950, Span.), d

Frances Rey
MY DARLING CLEMENTINE(1946); RAZOR'S EDGE, THE(1946); LAST ROUND-UP, THE(1947); LOVES OF CARMEN, THE(1948)
Gaston Rey
ROYAL AFFAIRS IN VERSAILLES(1957, Fr.); LOVE AT NIGHT(1961, Fr.); MY WIFE'S HUSBAND(1965, Fr./Ital.)
Gustavo Rey
DAY THE HOTLINE GOT HOT, THE(1968, Fr./Span.)
Henri-Francois Rey
TIME BOMB(1961, Fr./Ital.), w; NO TIME FOR ECSTASY(1963, Fr.), w; UNINHIBITED, THE(1968, Fr./Ital./Span.), w
Lee Rey
Misc. Talkies
FORBIDDEN UNDER THE CENSORSHIP OF THE KING(1973)
Marcela Lopez Rey
TERRACE, THE(1964, Arg.)
Mariano Garcia Rey
VALDEZ IS COMING(1971), makeup; LOVE AND PAIN AND THE WHOLE DAMN THING(1973), makeup
Mony Rey
MADEMOISELLE(1966, Fr./Brit.)
Nita Rey
Misc. Silents
BRASA DORMIDA(1928, Braz.)
Pauline Rey
NUDE ODYSSEY(1962, Fr./Ital.)
Roberto Rey
CASTILIAN, THE(1963, Span./U.S.); GUNFIGHTERS OF CASA GRANDE(1965, U.S./Span.)
Rosa Rey
FACE OF MARBLE, THE(1946); GILDA(1946); TWO YEARS BEFORE THE MAST(1946); FIESTA(1947); SECRET BEYOND THE DOOR, THE(1948); SECRET OF THE INCAS(1954); ROSE TATTOO, THE(1955)
Rosalie Rey
STOLEN LIFE, A(1946)
Rubina Rey
GRIM REAPER, THE(1981, Ital.)
Sylvia Rey
THIRD VOICE, THE(1960)
Tatiana Rey
Misc. Silents
LIMITE(1930, Braz.)
Tiel Rey
1984
FLASH OF GREEN, A(1984)
Genevieve Rey-Penchenat
1984
LE BAL(1984, Fr./Ital./Algeria)
Andre Reybas
CLANDESTINE(1948, Fr.); STRANGERS IN THE HOUSE(1949, Fr.); WE ARE ALL MURDERERS(1957, Fr.)
Noel Reyburn
LAWLESS, THE(1950); MY BLUE HEAVEN(1950); SATURDAY'S HERO(1951); FLAMING TEEN-AGE, THE(1956)
Nicolas Reye
CREATURE OF THE WALKING DEAD(1960, Mex.), spec eff
Walter Reyer
JOURNEY TO THE LOST CITY(1960, Ger./Fr./Ital.)
Walther Reyer
FOREVER MY LOVE(1962); THIRD LOVER, THE(1963, Fr./Ital.)
Chito Reyes
DAUGHTERS OF SATAN(1972)
Chuy Reyes
THAT'S MY BABY(1944); FREDDIE STEPS OUT(1946)
Eddy Reyes
MR. MAJESTYK(1974)
Efren Reyes
SCAVENGERS, THE(1959, U.S./Phil.); RAIDERS OF LEYTE GULF(1963 U.S./Phil.)
Franc Reyes
1984
BEAT STREET(1984)
Gene Reyes
DOC(1971)
James Reyes
FAMILY HONOR(1973)
Johnny Reyes
CRY FREEDOM(1961, Phil.)
Luis Reyes
WALK PROUD(1979)
Paco Reyes
PRIDE AND THE PASSION, THE(1957), ch
Patricia Reyes
RETURN OF A MAN CALLED HORSE, THE(1976)
Patricio Reyes
Silents
DAWN OF THE EAST(1921)
Stanley J. Reyes
PANIC IN THE STREETS(1950); OBSESSION(1976)
Stanley Reyes
MANDINGO(1975); FRENCH QUARTER(1978)
Georges Reygnier
PORTRAIT OF INNOCENCE(1948, Fr.)
Francisco Reyguera
LAST OF THE FAST GUNS, THE(1958); MAJOR DUNDEE(1965)
Ferdinand Reyher
FUGITIVE LOVERS(1934), w; RENDEZVOUS AT MIDNIGHT(1935), w; STRANDED(1935), w; DON'T TURN'EM LOOSE(1936), w; SPECIAL INVESTIGATOR(1936), w; TWO IN REVOLT(1936), w; YOU MAY BE NEXT(1936), w; RIDE A CROOKED MILE(1938), w; OUTSIDE THESE WALLS(1939), w; WAIT 'TIL THE SUN SHINES, NELLIE(1952), w; WORLD, THE FLESH, AND THE DEVIL, THE(1959), w

Martin Reymert
LEGACY OF BLOOD(1978)
Maurice Reyna
BOY WHO STOLE A MILLION, THE(1960, Brit.)
Tim Reyna
MY BODYGUARD(1980)
Maurice Reynac
ROYAL AFFAIRS IN VERSAILLES(1957, Fr.)
Jackie Reynal
MY LIFE TO LIVE(1963, Fr.), makeup; SIX IN PARIS(1968, Fr.), ed; NIGHT OF THE FOLLOWING DAY, THE(1969, Brit.), makeup; GIVE HER THE MOON(1970, Fr./Ital.), makeup; TWO OR THREE THINGS I KNOW ABOUT HER(1970, Fr.), makeup
Christopher Reynalds
NIGHT DIGGER, THE(1971, Brit.)
Paul Reynall
JEDDA, THE UNCIVILIZED(1956, Aus.)
Yvette Reynard
DOUBLE LIFE, A(1947); COME TO THE STABLE(1949)
Janine Reynaud
SIX DAYS A WEEK(1966, Fr./Ital./Span.)
Alain Reynaud-Fourton
SYMPHONY FOR A MASSACRE(1965, Fr./Ital.), w
John Reynders
BLACKMAIL(1929, Brit.), m; MURDER(1930, Brit.), m; RICH AND STRANGE(1932, Brit.), md
Mary Jane Reyner
1984
COMFORT AND JOY(1984, Brit.), cos
Ferdinand Reyney
ALL-AMERICAN, THE(1932), w
Reyno
FORT APACHE, THE BRONX(1981)
Craig Reynold
LOST WEEKEND, THE(1945)
Abe Reynolds
LOVE AT FIRST SIGHT(1930); SWING TIME(1936); RICHEST MAN IN TOWN(1941); IT HAPPENED ON 5TH AVENUE(1947); MY DEAR SECRETARY(1948)
Adelaide De Walt Reynolds
GIRL FROM MANHATTAN(1948)
Adeline de Walt Reynolds
COME LIVE WITH ME(1941); SHADOW OF THE THIN MAN(1941); ICELAND(1942); STREET OF CHANCE(1942); TALES OF MANHATTAN(1942); SON OF DRACULA(1943); KIM(1950); LYDIA BAILEY(1952); PONY SOLDIER(1952); WITNESS TO MURDER(1954)
Adeline Reynolds
BEHIND THE RISING SUN(1943); HAPPY LAND(1943); GOING MY WAY(1944)
Alan Reynolds
TOBOR THE GREAT(1954); CULT OF THE COBRA(1955); TIGHT SPOT(1955); EARTH VS. THE FLYING SAUCERS(1956); CAPE FEAR(1962)
Arthur Reynolds
MADNESS OF THE HEART(1949, Brit.); DARK INTERVAL(1950, Brit.), p; GREAT MANHUNT, THE(1951, Brit.); WILD HEART, THE(1952, Brit.)
Audrey Reynolds
MAID OF SALEM(1937)
Babby Reynolds
Misc. Silents
THEN YOU'LL REMEMBER ME(1918, Brit.)
Babs Reynolds
Misc. Silents
HER BENNY(1920, Brit.)
Mrs. Bailey Reynolds
Silents
DAUGHTER PAYS, THE(1920), w
Mrs. Baillie Reynolds
Silents
NOTORIOUS MISS LISLE, THE(1920), w
Ben Reynolds
LITTLE WILDCAT, THE(1928), ph; CARELESS AGE(1929), ph; IS EVERYBODY HAPPY?(1929), ph; KID GLOVES(1929), ph; SONNY BOY(1929), ph; STOLEN KISSES(1929), ph; VENGEANCE(1930), ph; MAN OF THE FOREST(1933), ph; TO THE LAST MAN(1933), ph; COME ON, MARINES(1934), ph; THUNDERING HERD, THE(1934), ph; WITCHING HOUR, THE(1934), ph; MC FADDEN'S FLATS(1935), ph; MEN WITHOUT NAMES(1935), ph; ONE HOUR LATE(1935), ph; WANDERER OF THE WASTELAND(1935), ph; IT'S A GREAT LIFE(1936), ph
Silents
DEVIL'S PASSKEY, THE(1920), ph; FOOLISH WIVES(1920), ph; WONDERFUL WIFE, A(1922), ph; MERRY-GO-ROUND(1923), m; STORMSWEPT(1923), ph; SIGNAL TOWER, THE(1924), ph; HIS SECRETARY(1925), ph; MERRY WIDOW, THE(1925), ph; WANING SEX, THE(1926), ph; WEDDING MARCH, THE(1927), ph; FREEDOM OF THE PRESS(1928), ph; NAME THE WOMAN(1928), ph; WAY OF THE STRONG, THE(1928), ph; QUEEN KELLY(1929), ph
Ben F. Reynolds
Silents
BLIND HUSBANDS(1919), ph; GREED(1925), ph
Benjamin Reynolds
TILLIE AND GUS(1933), ph; MENACE(1934), ph; OLD-FASHIONED WAY, THE(1934), ph
Silents
LONG CHANCE, THE(1922), ph; PRISONER, THE(1923), ph
Bill Reynolds
FEMALE RESPONSE, THE(1972), m; OLD BOYFRIENDS(1979), ed
"Brown Jug" Reynolds
YELLOW ROSE OF TEXAS, THE(1944); PAINTED HILLS, THE(1951)
Bruce Reynolds
Silents
CLAY DOLLARS(1921)
Burt Reynolds
ANGEL BABY(1961); ARMORED COMMAND(1961); OPERATION CIA(1965); NAVAJO JOE(1967, Ital./Span.); IMPASSE(1969); SAM WHISKEY(1969); 100 RIFLES(1969); SHARK(1970, U.S./Mex.); SKULLDUGGERY(1970); DELIVERANCE(1972); EVERY-

THING YOU ALWAYS WANTED TO KNOW ABOUT SEX, BUT WE'RE AFRAID TO ASK(1972); FUZZ(1972); MAN WHO LOVED CAT DANCING, THE(1973); SHAMUS(1973); WHITE LIGHTNING(1973); LONGEST YARD, THE(1974); AT LONG LAST LOVE(1975); HUSTLE(1975); LUCKY LADY(1975); W. W. AND THE DIXIE DANCEKINGS(1975); GATOR(1976, a, d; NICKELODEON(1976); SILENT MOVIE(1976); SEMI-TOUGH(1977); SMOKEY AND THE BANDIT(1977); END, THE(1978), a, d; HOOPER(1978); STARTING OVER(1979); ROUGH CUT(1980, Brit.); SMOKEY AND THE BANDIT II(1980); CANNONBALL RUN, THE(1981); PATERNITY(1981); BEST FRIENDS(1982); BEST LITTLE WHOREHOUSE IN TEXAS, THE(1982); SHARKY'S MACHINE(1982), a, d; MAN WHO LOVED WOMEN, THE(1983); SMOKEY AND THE BANDIT–PART 3(1983); STROKER ACE(1983)
1984
CANNONBALL RUN II(1984); CITY HEAT(1984)
Misc. Talkies
FADE-IN(1968)
Buster Reynolds
1984
GODS MUST BE CRAZY, THE(1984, Botswana), ph
Carla Reynolds
NIGHT GAMES(1980)
Cecil Reynolds
STUDY IN SCARLET, A(1933)
Charles Reynolds
MR. H. C. ANDERSEN(1950, Brit.); CHELSEA STORY(1951, Brit.); p; BLIND MAN'S BLUFF(1952, Brit.), p; COME BACK PETER(1952, Brit.), p; HOT ICE(1952, Brit.), p; MOULIN ROUGE(1952); NO HAUNT FOR A GENTLEMAN(1952, Brit.), p; SCARLET SPEAR, THE(1954, Brit.), p; GIRL HUNTERS, THE(1963, Brit.), p; BATTLE BENEATH THE EARTH(1968, Brit.), p
Clarence C. "Renn" Reynolds
SLAUGHTER(1972), ed
Clark Reynolds
VISCOUNT, THE(1967, Fr./Span./Ital./Ger.), w; OPERATION THUNDERBOLT(1978, ISRAEL), w
Clark E. Reynolds
DISC JOCKEY(1951), w; SHOTGUN(1955), w; GUNMEN FROM LAREDO(1959), w
Clarke Reynolds
GENGHIS KHAN(U.S./Brit./Ger./Yugo), w; GUNFIGHTERS OF CASA GRANDE(1965, U.S./Span.), w; SON OF A GUNFIGHTER(1966, U.S./Span.), w; VIKING QUEEN, THE(1967, Brit.), w; SHALAKO(1968, Brit.), w; DESPERADOS, THE(1969), w; NIGHT GAMES(1980), a, w
Craig Reynolds [Hugh Enfield]
UNCLE HARRY(1945); DON'T BET ON LOVE(1933); CASE OF THE LUCKY LEGS, THE(1935); CEILNG ZERO(1935); MAN OF IRON(1935); STARS OVER BROADWAY(1935); BRIDES ARE LIKE THAT(1936); CASE OF THE BLACK CAT, THE(1936); DANGEROUS(1936); GOLDEN ARROW, THE(1936); HERE COMES CARTER(1936); JAILBREAK(1936); SONS O' GUNS(1936); STAGE STRUCK(1936); TIMES SQUARE PLAYBOY(1936); TREACHERY RIDES THE RANGE(1936); BACK IN CIRCULATION(1937); CASE OF THE STUTTERING BISHOP, THE(1937); FOOTLOOSE HEIRESS, THE(1937); GO-GETTER, THE(1937); GREAT GARRICK, THE(1937); GREAT O'MALLEY, THE(1937); MELODY FOR TWO(1937); PENROD AND SAM(1937); SLIM(1937); SMART BLONDE(1937); UNDER SUSPICION(1937); FEMALE FUGITIVE(1938); GOLD MINE IN THE SKY(1938); MAKING THE HEADLINES(1938); ROMANCE ON THE RUN(1938); SLANDER HOUSE(1938); I AM A CRIMINAL(1939); MYSTERY OF MR. WONG, THE(1939); NAVY SECRETS(1939); WALL STREET COWBOY(1939); FATAL HOUR, THE(1940); GENTLEMAN FROM ARIZONA, THE(1940); I TAKE THIS OATH(1940); SON OF THE NAVY(1940); NEVADA(1944); DIVORCE(1945); JUST BEFORE DAWN(1946); QUEEN OF BURLESQUE(1946); MAN FROM COLORADO, THE(1948)
Misc. Talkies
HOUSE OF MYSTERY, THE(1938)
Dale Reynolds
1984
REPO MAN(1984)
Debbie Reynolds
JUNE BRIDE(1948); DAUGHTER OF ROSIE O'GRADY, THE(1950); THREE LITTLE WORDS(1950); TWO WEEKS WITH LOVE(1950); MR. IMPERIUM(1951); SINGIN' IN THE RAIN(1952); SKIRTS AHOY!(1952); AFFAIRS OF DOBIE GILLIS, THE(1953); GIVE A GIRL A BREAK(1953); I LOVE MELVIN(1953); ATHENA(1954); SUSAN SLEPT HERE(1954); HIT THE DECK(1955); TENDER TRAP, THE(1955); BUNDLE OF JOY(1956); CATERED AFFAIR, THE(1956); MEET ME IN LAS VEGAS(1956); TAMMY AND THE BACHELOR(1957); THIS HAPPY FEELING(1958); GAZEBO, THE(1959); IT STARTED WITH A KISS(1959); MATING GAME, THE(1959); SAY ONE FOR ME(1959); PEPE(1960); RAT RACE, THE(1960); PLEASURE OF HIS COMPANY, THE(1961); SECOND TIME AROUND, THE(1961); HOW THE WEST WAS WON(1962); MARY, MARY(1963); MY SIX LOVES(1963); GOODBYE CHARLIE(1964); UNSINKABLE MOLLY BROWN, THE(1964); SINGING NUN, THE(1966); DIVORCE AMERICAN STYLE(1967); HOW SWEET IT IS(1968); WHAT'S THE MATTER WITH HELEN?(1971); CHARLOTTE'S WEB(1973)
Diana Reynolds
RETURN OF THE JEDI(1983)
Dick Reynolds
FINNEY(1969), m
Don Kay Reynolds
LAST ROUND-UP, THE(1947); FIGHTING REDHEAD, THE(1950)
Don Reynolds
ROMANCE OF THE WEST(1946); BEYOND THE PURPLE HILLS(1950); STREETS OF GHOST TOWN(1950); SNAKE RIVER DESPERADOES(1951)
1984
HEART OF THE STAG(1984, New Zealand), p
Don Kay "Little Brown Jug" Reynolds
RIDE, RYDER, RIDE!(1949); ROLL, THUNDER, ROLL(1949)
Dorothy Reynolds
LADY L(1965, Fr./Ital.); OH! WHAT A LOVELY WAR(1969, Brit.)
Dr. Cecil Reynolds
MODERN TIMES(1936)
E. Vivian Reynolds
Silents
GOD AND THE MAN(1918, Brit.)

Misc. Silents
BLEAK HOUSE(1920, Brit.)
Evelyn Reynolds
TERROR IN THE WAX MUSEUM(1973)
Francisco Reynolds
DALTON THAT GOT AWAY(1960)
Frank Reynolds
HIT THE DECK(1955)
Freddy Reynolds
CHANT OF JIMMIE BLACKSMITH, THE(1980, Aus.)
Frederick Reynolds
DR. SIN FANG(1937, Brit.), w
Gary Reynolds
1984
BROADWAY DANNY ROSE(1984)
Gene Reynolds
SINS OF MAN(1936); THANK YOU, JEEVES(1936); CAPTAINS COURA-
GEOUS(1937); THUNDER TRAIL(1937); BOYS TOWN(1938); CROWD ROARS,
THE(1938); IN OLD CHICAGO(1938); LOVE FINDS ANDY HARDY(1938); OF HUMAN
HEARTS(1938); BAD LITTLE ANGEL(1939); FLYING IRISHMAN, THE(1939); SPIRIT
OF CULVER, THE(1939); THEY SHALL HAVE MUSIC(1939); EDISON, THE
MAN(1940); GALLANT SONS(1940); MORTAL STORM, THE(1940); SANTA FE
TRAIL(1940); ADVENTURE IN WASHINGTON(1941); ANDY HARDY'S PRIVATE
SECRETARY(1941); PENALTY, THE(1941); EAGLE SQUADRON(1942); TUTTLES OF
TAHITI(1942); JUNGLE PATROL(1948); BIG CAT, THE(1949); SLATTERY'S HURRI-
CANE(1949); 99 RIVER STREET(1953); COUNTRY GIRL, THE(1954); DOWN THREE
DARK STREETS(1954); DIANE(1955)
Genevieve Reynolds
Silents
CAPRICE OF THE MOUNTAINS(1916)
George Reynolds
FUZZ(1972); CLEOPATRA JONES(1973); SMOKEY AND THE BANDIT(1977)
Gerald H. Reynolds
GOIN' SOUTH(1978)
Gilbert Reynolds
CHARTROOSE CABOOSE(1960)
H. Reynolds
ROAD TO SINGAPORE(1931)
Harold Reynolds
STEAGLE, THE(1971)
Harrington Reynolds
OLD ENGLISH(1930); DAUGHTER OF THE DRAGON(1931); MYSTERY OF MR. X,
THE(1934); TWO SINNERS(1935); SYLVIA SCARLETT(1936); RIDE 'EM COW-
GIRL(1939)
Harry Reynolds
GIRL IN THE SHOW, THE(1929), ed; THEIR OWN DESIRE(1929), ed; SEA BAT,
THE(1930), ed; THIRTEENTH CHAIR, THE(1930), ed; BACHELOR FATHER(1931),
ed; MANHATTAN TOWER(1932), ed; DOWN ON THE FARM(1938), ed; ISLAND IN
THE SKY(1938), ed; KEEP SMILING(1938), ed; LOVE ON A BUDGET(1938), ed;
SAFETY IN NUMBERS(1938), ed; CHARLIE CHAN IN THE CITY OF DARK-
NESS(1939), ed; MR. MOTO IN DANGER ISLAND(1939), ed; PARDON OUR NER-
VE(1939), ed; QUICK MILLIONS(1939), ed; CHARLIE CHAN'S MURDER
CRUISE(1940), ed; GAY CABALLERO, THE(1940), ed; HIGH SCHOOL(1940), ed;
YOUNG AS YOU FEEL(1940), ed; COWBOY AND THE BLONDE, THE(1941), ed;
DEAD MEN TELL(1941), ed; MURDER AMONG FRIENDS(1941), ed; LITTLE
TOKYO, U.S.A.(1942), ed; UNDYING MONSTER, THE(1942), ed; ROGER TOUHY,
GANGSTER!(1944), ed; TAKE IT OR LEAVE IT(1944), ed; FALLEN ANGEL(1945), ed;
HANGOVER SQUARE(1945), ed; WITHIN THESE WALLS(1945), ed; CENTENNIAL
SUMMER(1946), ed; BRASHER DOUBLOON, THE(1947), ed; GAS HOUSE KIDS GO
WEST(1947), ed; KILLER AT LARGE(1947), ed; TOO MANY WINNERS(1947), ed;
HOUSE OF DARKNESS(1948, Brit.), ed; NOOSE HANGS HIGH, THE(1948), ed; MAN
FROM YESTERDAY, THE(1949, Brit.), p; OLD MOTHER RILEY, HEADMIS-
TRESS(1950, Brit.), p; DANGER ZONE(1951), ed; FINGERPRINTS DON'T LIE(1951),
ed; PIER 23(1951), ed; ROARING CITY(1951), ed; OLD MOTHER RILEY(1952, Brit.),
p; DOUBLE CONFESSION(1953, Brit.), p
Silents
LONDON AFTER MIDNIGHT(1927), ed; UNKNOWN, THE(1927), ed; BIG CITY,
THE(1928), ed; FOUR WALLS(1928), ed; WEST OF ZANZIBAR(1928), ed; WHERE
EAST IS EAST(1929), ed
Helen Reynolds
HEAVEN CAN WAIT(1943)
Helene Reynolds
CONFIRM OR DENY(1941); GIRL TROUBLE(1942); MAN WHO WOULDN'T DIE,
THE(1942); MOONTIDE(1942); ROXIE HART(1942); TALES OF MANHATTAN(1942);
DIXIE DUGAN(1943); MEANEST MAN IN THE WORLD, THE(1943); WINTER-
TIME(1943); BERMUDA MYSTERY(1944)
Herb Reynolds
1984
BROADWAY DANNY ROSE(1984)
Herbert Reynolds
DEEP IN MY HEART(1954), lyrics
Hilary Reynolds
EDUCATING RITA(1983)
Jack Reynolds
GANGSTER, THE(1947); IN A LONELY PLACE(1950); MILITARY ACADEMY WITH
THAT TENTH AVENUE GANG(1950); NO MAN OF HER OWN(1950); SUN SETS AT
DAWN, THE(1950); I WAS AN AMERICAN SPY(1951); IT GROWS ON TREES(1952);
BULLWHIP(1958); GANG WAR(1958)
Misc. Talkies
TRAIL OF THE ARROW(1952)
James E. Reynolds
ILLUSTRATED MAN, THE(1969), spec eff
James Hooks Reynolds
1984
CITY HEAT(1984)
Jay Reynolds
WINNING(1969); REINCARNATE, THE(1971, Can.)

Jeff Reynolds
ZOOT SUIT(1981)
Jim Reynolds
MR. MAJESTYK(1974)
Joan Reynolds
EDDY DUCHIN STORY, THE(1956); HOT BLOOD(1956); JUST JOE(1960, Brit.)
Joe Reynolds
BOXCAR BERTHA(1972)
John Reynolds
MANOS, THE HANDS OF FATE(1966)
John W. Reynolds
COUNTRY GIRL, THE(1954)
Jonathan Reynolds
LOVESICK(1983)
1984
MICKI AND MAUDE(1984), w
Joy Reynolds
FLESH MERCHANT, THE(1956)
Joyce Reynolds
GEORGE WASHINGTON SLEPT HERE(1942); YANKEE DOODLE DANDY(1942);
CONSTANT NYMPH, THE(1943); THANK YOUR LUCKY STARS(1943); ADVEN-
TURES OF MARK TWAIN, THE(1944); HOLLYWOOD CANTEEN(1944); JANIE(1944);
ALWAYS TOGETHER(1947); WALLFLOWER(1948); GIRLS' SCHOOL(1950)
Kay Reynolds
HOW TO SUCCEED IN BUSINESS WITHOUT REALLY TRYING(1976)
Ken Reynolds
PSYCH-OUT(1968), ed
Kenneth E. Reynolds
INDEPENDENCE DAY(1983)
Kevin Reynolds
1984
RED DAWN(1984), w
Kristina Reynolds
LIVING LEGEND(1980)
Kristine Reynolds
WOLFMAN(1979)
Larry Reynolds
CHANGE OF MIND(1969); MY SIDE OF THE MOUNTAIN(1969); HOMER(1970);
SHOOT(1976, Can.); MY BLOODY VALENTINE(1981, Can.); SILENCE OF THE
NORTH(1981, Can.)
Lee Reynolds
SANTA FE UPRISING(1946)
Lester Cole Quentin Reynolds
SECRETS OF A NURSE(1938), w
Liam Reynolds
NED KELLY(1970, Brit.); OUTBACK(1971, Aus.)
Lynn F. Reynolds
Silents
GREATER LAW, THE(1917), d&w; OVERLAND RED(1920), d&w; NIGHT HORSE-
MAN, THE(1921), d&w; JUST TONY(1922), d&w
Misc. Silents
ROMANCE OF BILLY GOAT HILL, A(1916), d; SECRET OF THE SWAMP,
THE(1916), d; BROADWAY ARIZONA(1917), d; MR. OPP(1917), d; MUTINY(1917), d;
SHOW-DOWN, THE(1917), d; SOUTHERN JUSTICE(1917), d; UP OR DOWN(1917), d;
FAST COMPANY(1918), d; GOWN OF DESTINY, THE(1918), d; BRUTE BREAKER,
THE(1919), d; COMING OF THE LAW, THE(1919), d; FORBIDDEN ROOM,
THE(1919), d; LITTLE BROTHER OF THE RICH, A(1919), d; MISS ADVEN-
TURE(1919), d; REBELLIOUS BRIDE, THE(1919), d; TREAT 'EM ROUGH(1919), d;
BULLET-PROOF(1920), d; TEXAN, THE(1920), d; TRAILIN'(1921), d; BRASS COM-
MANDMENTS(1923), d; GUNFIGHTER, THE(1923), d
Lynn Reynolds
KID GALAHAD(1962), makeup; IT'S A MAD, MAD, MAD, MAD WORLD(1963),
makeup; YELLOW CANARY, THE(1963), makeup; PARTY, THE(1968), makeup;
DARLING LILI(1970), makeup; SEVEN MINUTES, THE(1971), makeup; TIME AFT-
ER TIME(1979, Brit.), makeup
Silents
FAME AND FORTUNE(1918), d; RED LANE, THE(1920), d, w; SKY HIGH(1922),
d&w; HUNTRESS, THE(1923), d; RAINBOW TRAIL, THE(1925), d&w; RIDERS OF
THE PURPLE SAGE(1925), d; HEY! HEY! COWBOY(1927), d&w
Misc. Silents
END OF THE RAINBOW, THE(1916), d; GIRL OF LOST LAKE, THE(1916), d; IT
HAPPENED IN HONOLULU(1916), d; GOD'S CRUCIBLE(1917), d; ACE HIGH(1918),
d; MR. LOGAN, USA(1918), d; WESTERN BLOOD(1918), d; BIG TOWN ROUND-
UP(1921), d; ROAD DEMON, THE(1921), d; ARABIA(1922), d; FOR BIG STA-
KES(1922), d; UP AND GOING(1922), d; DEADWOOD COACH, THE(1924), d; LAST
OF THE DUANES, THE(1924), d; DURAND OF THE BAD LANDS(1925), d; BUCK-
AROO KID, THE(1926), d; CHIP OF THE FLYING U(1926), d; COMBAT, THE(1926),
d; MAN IN THE SADDLE, THE(1926), d; PRISONERS OF THE STORM(1926), d;
TEXAS STREAK, THE(1926), d; SILENT RIDER, THE(1927), d
Malcolm Reynolds
OTHELLO(1965, Brit.); DANCE OF DEATH, THE(1971, Brit.)
Marie Reynolds
CHAPTER TWO(1979)
Marjorie Reynolds [Peg Riley]
COLLEGE HOLIDAY(1936); MURDER IN GREENWICH VILLAGE(1937); TEX
RIDES WITH THE BOY SCOUTS(1937); BLACK BANDIT(1938); DELINQUENT
PARENTS(1938); GUILTY TRAILS(1938); LAST STAND, THE(1938); MAN'S COUN-
TRY(1938); OVERLAND EXPRESS, THE(1938); REBELLIOUS DAUGHTERS(1938);
SIX SHOOTIN' SHERIFF(1938); WESTERN TRAILS(1938); DANGER FLIGHT(1939);
GONE WITH THE WIND(1939); MR. WONG IN CHINATOWN(1939); MYSTERY
PLANE(1939); PHANTOM STAGE, THE(1939); RACKETEERS OF THE RANGE(1939);
SKY PATROL(1939); STREETS OF NEW YORK(1939); STUNT PILOT(1939); TIMBER
STAMPEDE(1939); CHASING TROUBLE(1940); DOOMED TO DIE(1940); ENEMY
AGENT(1940); FATAL HOUR, THE(1940); MIDNIGHT LIMITED(1940); UP IN THE
AIR(1940); CYCLONE ON HORSEBACK(1941); DUDE COWBOY(1941); GREAT SWIN-
DLE, THE(1941); LAW OF THE TIMBER(1941); ROBIN HOOD OF THE PECOS(1941);
SECRET EVIDENCE(1941); TILLIE THE TOILER(1941); TOP SERGEANT MULLI-
GAN(1941); HOLIDAY INN(1942); STAR SPANGLED RHYTHM(1942); DIXIE(1943);
UP IN MABEL'S ROOM(1944); 3 IS A FAMILY(1944); BRING ON THE GIRLS(1945);
DUFFY'S TAVERN(1945); MINISTRY OF FEAR(1945); MEET ME ON BROAD-

WAY(1946); MONSIEUR BEAUCAIRE(1946); TIME OF THEIR LIVES, THE(1946); HEAVEN ONLY KNOWS(1947); BAD MEN OF TOMBSTONE(1949); THAT MIDNIGHT KISS(1949); CUSTOMS AGENT(1950); GREAT JEWEL ROBBER, THE(1950); ROOKIE FIREMAN(1950); HIS KIND OF WOMAN(1951); HOME TOWN STORY(1951); MODELS, INC.(1952); NO HOLDS BARRED(1952); MOBS INC(1956); JUKE BOX RHYTHM(1959); SILENT WITNESS, THE(1962)

Marthe Reynolds
1984
THREE CROWNS OF THE SAILOR(1984, Fr.)

Mary Beth Reynolds
BLUE, WHITE, AND PERFECT(1941)

Michael Reynolds
BEAR ISLAND(1980, Brit.-Can.)

Michael J. Reynolds
NEPTUNE FACTOR, THE(1973, Can.); WHY SHOOT THE TEACHER(1977, Can.); PLAGUE(1978, Can.); KIDNAPPING OF THE PRESIDENT, THE(1980, Can.); VISITING HOURS(1982, Can.); RUNNING BRAVE(1983, Can.)
1984
POLICE ACADEMY(1984)
Misc. Talkies
M3: THE GEMINI STRAIN(1980)

Mij Reynolds
1984
GODS MUST BE CRAZY, THE(1984, Botswana), cos

Mike Reynolds
STACY'S KNIGHTS(1983)

Muriel Reynolds
Silents
NIGHT WATCH, THE(1926)

Naida Reynolds
STRIKE UP THE BAND(1940); MELVIN AND HOWARD(1980)

Nancy Reynolds
CRIME OF PASSION(1957)

Nip Reynolds
FOURTH HORSEMAN, THE(1933)

Norman Reynolds
WARM DECEMBER, A(1973, Brit.), set d; LITTLE PRINCE, THE(1974, Brit.), art d; LUCKY LADY(1975), art d; MR. QUILP(1975, Brit.), art d; INCREDIBLE SARAH, THE(1976, Brit.), art d; STAR WARS(1977), art d; EMPIRE STRIKES BACK, THE(1980), prod d; RAIDERS OF THE LOST ARK(1981), prod d; RETURN OF THE JEDI(1983), prod d

O'Carroll Reynolds
Silents
IN THE DAYS OF SAINT PATRICK(1920, Brit.)

Owen Reynolds
BLACK SHEEP OF WHITEHALL, THE(1941 Brit.); YOUNG MR. PITT, THE(1942, Brit.); OLD MOTHER RILEY, DETECTIVE(1943, Brit.); SOMEWHERE IN FRANCE(1943, Brit.); THEATRE ROYAL(1943, Brit.); DULCIMER STREET(1948, Brit.); HA'PENNY BREEZE(1950, Brit.)

Paddy Reynolds
HEY! HEY! U.S.A.(1938, Brit.)

Patricia Reynolds
WOMAN OF DISTINCTION, A(1950)

Peter Reynolds
DARK ROAD, THE(1948, Brit.); THINGS HAPPEN AT NIGHT(1948, Brit.); OUTSIDER, THE(1949, Brit.); ADAM AND EVELYNE(1950, Brit.); GUILT IS MY SHADOW(1950, Brit.); FOUR DAYS(1951, Brit.); SMART ALEC(1951, Brit.); MAGIC BOX, THE(1952, Brit.); MAN BAIT(1952, Brit.); AFFAIR IN MONTE CARLO(1953, Brit.); GOOD BEGINNING, THE(1953, Brit.); BLACK 13(1954, Brit.); DELAVINE AFFAIR, THE(1954, Brit.); DESTINATION MILAN(1954, Brit.); DEVIL GIRL FROM MARS(1954, Brit.); EGYPTIAN, THE(1954); SILVER CHALICE, THE(1954); WOMAN'S ANGLE, THE(1954, Brit.); ONE JUST MAN(1955, Brit.); YOU CAN'T ESCAPE(1955, Brit.); LONG HAUL, THE(1957, Brit.); BANK RAIDERS, THE(1958, Brit.); SHAKE HANDS WITH THE DEVIL(1959, Ireland); WRONG NUMBER(1959, Brit.); IT TAKES A THIEF(1960, Brit.); BREAKING POINT, THE(1961, Brit.); HIGHWAY TO BATTLE(1961, Brit.); QUESTION OF SUSPENSE, A(1961, Brit.); SPARE THE ROD(1961, Brit.); GAOLBREAK(1962, Brit.); MURDER CAN BE DEADLY(1963, Brit.); WEST 11(1963, Brit.); GREAT ARMORED CAR SWINDLE, THE(1964); HANDS OF ORLAC, THE(1964, Brit./Fr.); MAN WHO COULDN'T WALK, THE(1964, Brit.); YOUR MONEY OR YOUR WIFE(1965, Brit.); PRIVATE COLLECTION(1972, Aus.)
Misc. Talkies
BORN FOR TROUBLE(1955)

Quentin Reynolds
BIG BLOCKADE, THE(1942, Brit.); EAGLE SQUADRON(1942); GOLDEN EARRINGS(1947); CALL NORTHSIDE 777(1948), w; MIRACLE OF THE BELLS, THE(1948), w

Randall Reynolds
HAPPY DAYS(1930)

Rebecca Reynolds
DRACULA(THE DIRTY OLD MAN) (1969)

Reginald Reynolds
RAMPARTS WE WATCH, THE(1940)

Renn Reynolds
KILLERS THREE(1968), ed; SAVAGE SEVEN, THE(1968), ed; GAY DECEIVERS, THE(1969), ed; RUN, ANGEL, RUN(1969), ed; SIMON, KING OF THE WITCHES(1971), ed

Robert Reynolds
COUNTERSPY MEETS SCOTLAND YARD(1950); FAT ANGELS(1980, U.S./Span.)
Misc. Talkies
FAT CHANCE(1982)

Ross Reynolds
STUNT MAN, THE(1980)

Sheldon Reynolds
FOREIGN INTRIGUE(1956), p&d; w; ASSIGNMENT TO KILL(1968), d&w
Misc. Talkies
KILLER'S CARNIVAL(1965), d

Snake Reynolds
Misc. Talkies
VERNON, FLORIDA(1982)

"Spooky" Reynolds
FIGHTING REDHEAD, THE(1950)

Stephen Reynolds
ROUGH CUT(1980, Brit.)

Steve Reynolds
Misc. Silents
CRIMSON SKULL, THE(1921)

Suzanne Reynolds
WRONG IS RIGHT(1982)

Tom Reynolds
PERFECT ALIBI, THE(1931, Brit.); DARK PASSAGE(1947); NIAGARA(1953); SPELL OF THE HYPNOTIST(1956)
Silents
ONWARD CHRISTIAN SOLDIERS(1918, Brit.); MRS. THOMPSON(1919, Brit.); AUNT RACHEL(1920, Brit.); LAST ROSE OF SUMMER, THE(1920, Brit.); PRIDE OF THE FANCY, THE(1920, Brit.); GAME OF LIFE, THE(1922, Brit.); KNOCKOUT, THE(1923, Brit.); WINNING GOAL, THE(1929, Brit.)
Misc. Silents
LYONS MAIL, THE(1916, Brit.); TINKER, TAILOR, SOLDIER, SAILOR(1918, Brit.); MEMBER OF THE TATTERSALL'S, A(1919, Brit.); RIGHT ELEMENT, THE(1919, Brit.); HUSBAND HUNTER, THE(1920, Brit.); TEMPORARY GENTLEMAN, A(1920, Brit.); FOR HER FATHER'S SAKE(1921, Brit.); MR. PIM PASSES BY(1921, Brit.); TILLY OF BLOOMSBURY(1921, Brit.); BACHELOR'S BABY, A(1922, Brit.); COST OF BEAUTY, THE(1924, Brit.)

Tommy Reynolds
TOMBOY AND THE CHAMP(1961), p, w; EXILES, THE(1966)

Valerie Reynolds
UNTAMED YOUTH(1957)

Vera Reynolds
TONIGHT AT TWELVE(1929); BORROWED WIVES(1930); LAST DANCE, THE(1930); LONE RIDER, THE(1930); HELL BENT FOR 'FRISCO(1931); LAWLESS WOMAN, THE(1931); NECK AND NECK(1931); DRAGNET PATROL(1932); GORILLA SHIP, THE(1932); MONSTER WALKS, THE(1932); TANGLED DESTINIES(1932)
Silents
ICEBOUND(1924); NIGHT CLUB, THE(1925); CORPORAL KATE(1926); JAZZLAND(1928)
Misc. Silents
PRODIGAL DAUGHTERS(1923); CHEAP KISSES(1924); FEET OF CLAY(1924); FLAPPER WIVES(1924); GOLDEN BED, THE(1925); LIMITED MAIL, THE(1925); MILLION DOLLAR HANDICAP, THE(1925); ROAD TO YESTERDAY, THE(1925); WITHOUT MERCY(1925); RISKY BUSINESS(1926); SILENCE(1926); STEEL PREFERRED(1926); SUNNYSIDE UP(1926); ALMOST HUMAN(1927); LITTLE ADVENTURESS, THE(1927); MAIN EVENT, THE(1927); DIVINE SINNER(1928); GOLF WIDOWS(1928); BACK FROM SHANGHAI(1929)

Vivian Reynolds
GIRL THIEF, THE(1938)
Silents
AMATEUR GENTLEMAN, THE(1920, Brit.)

Walt Reynolds
TRADE WINDS(1938), ed

Walter Reynolds
STAGECOACH(1939), ed

Wiley Reynolds III
1984
HARD CHOICES(1984)

William Reynolds
52ND STREET(1937), ed; ALGIERS(1938), ed; SO ENDS OUR NIGHT(1941), ed; MOONTIDE(1942), ed; CARNIVAL IN COSTA RICA(1947), ed; GIVE MY REGARDS TO BROADWAY(1948), ed; STREET WITH NO NAME, THE(1948), ed; YOU WERE MEANT FOR ME(1948), ed; COME TO THE STABLE(1949), ed; MOTHER IS A FRESHMAN(1949), ed; CIMARRON KID, THE(1951); DAY THE EARTH STOOD STILL, THE(1951), ed; DEAR BRAT(1951); DESERT FOX, THE(1951); FROGMEN, THE(1951), ed; HALLS OF MONTEZUMA(1951), ed; NO QUESTIONS ASKED(1951); TAKE CARE OF MY LITTLE GIRL(1951), ed; BATTLE AT APACHE PASS, THE(1952); CARRIE(1952); FRANCIS GOES TO WEST POINT(1952); HAS ANYBODY SEEN MY GAL?(1952); OUTCASTS OF POKER FLAT, THE(1952), ed; RAIDERS, THE(1952); RED SKIES OF MONTANA(1952), ed; SON OF ALI BABA(1952); BENEATH THE 12-MILE REEF(1953), ed; GUNSMOKE(1953); KID FROM LEFT FIELD, THE(1953), ed; MISSISSIPPI GAMBLER, THE(1953); DESIREE(1954), ed; THREE COINS IN THE FOUNTAIN(1954), ed; ALL THAT HEAVEN ALLOWS(1955); CULT OF THE COBRA(1955); DADDY LONG LEGS(1955), ed; GOOD MORNING, MISS DOVE(1955), ed; LOVE IS A MANY-SPLENDORED THING(1955), ed; AWAY ALL BOATS(1956); CAROUSEL(1956); THERE'S ALWAYS TOMORROW(1956); LAND UNKNOWN, THE(1957); MISTER CORY(1957); TIME LIMIT(1957), p; BIG BEAT, THE(1958); IN LOVE AND WAR(1958), ed; THING THAT COULDN'T DIE, THE(1958); BELOVED INFIDEL(1959), ed; BLUE DENIM(1959), ed; COMPULSION(1959), ed; WILD RIVER(1960), ed; TENDER IS THE NIGHT(1961), ed; TARAS BULBA(1962), ed; KINGS OF THE SUN(1963), ed; DISTANT TRUMPET, A(1964); ENSIGN PULVER(1964), ed; FBI CODE 98(1964); HARLOW(1965), makeup; SOUND OF MUSIC, THE(1965), ed; FOLLOW ME, BOYS!(1966); SAND PEBBLES, THE(1966), ed; HOW SWEET IT IS(1968), makeup; STAR!(1968), ed; HELLO, DOLLY!(1969), ed; GREAT WHITE HOPE, THE(1970), ed; GODFATHER, THE(1972), ed; STING, THE(1973), ed; TWO PEOPLE(1973), ed; GREAT WALDO PEPPER, THE(1975), ed; MASTER GUNFIGHTER, THE(1975), ed; TURNING POINT, THE(1977), ed; LITTLE ROMANCE, A(1979, U.S./Fr.), ed; HEAVEN'S GATE(1980), ed; NIJINSKY(1980, Brit.), ed; AUTHOR! AUTHOR!(1982), ed; YELLOWBEARD(1983), ed
1984
LITTLE DRUMMER GIRL, THE(1984), ed; LONELY GUY, THE(1984), ed

William H. Reynolds
DANGEROUS CROSSING(1953), ed; FANNY(1961), ed; WHAT'S THE MATTER WITH HELEN?(1971), ed; MAKING LOVE(1982), ed

William "Red" Reynolds
CHARTROOSE CABOOSE(1960), d

Williams Reynolds
OUR MAN FLINT(1966), ed

Wilson Reynolds
Silents
JANICE MEREDITH(1924)

David Reynoso
ORLAK, THE HELL OF FRANKENSTEIN(1960, Mex.); INVASION OF THE VAM-PIRES, THE(1961, Mex.); RAGE(1966, U.S./Mex.); BLUE DEMON VERSUS THE INFERNAL BRAINS(1967, Mex.); NAZARIN(1968, Mex.)

Herman Reynoso
MAN CALLED SLEDGE, A(1971, Ital.)

Marie-Laure Reyre
POSSESSION(1981, Fr./Ger.), p

Otto Reysser
SLEEPING BEAUTY(1965, Ger.), art d

Claude Reytinas
LOVE AND DEATH(1975), set d

Jose Maria Reyzabal
NUN AT THE CROSSROADS, A(1970, Ital./Span.), p

Al Rezek
RAGGEDY ANN AND ANDY(1977), ph

Rui Rezende
DONA FLOR AND HER TWO HUSHANDS(1977, Braz.)

Lily Rezillot
TESTAMENT OF DR. MABUSE, THE(1943, Ger.)

David Rfjwan
JESUS CHRIST, SUPERSTAR(1973)

Rhaden
M(1933, Ger.)

Ving Rhames
1984
GO TELL IT ON THE MOUNTAIN(1984)

Phoebus Rhazis
ELECTRA(1962, Gr.)

Bunny Rhea
CAPE FEAR(1962)

Pamela Rhea
GIRL, THE BODY, AND THE PILL, THE(1967)

Dana Rheaume
RETURN, THE(1980), spec eff; WACKO(1983), spec eff

Dell Rheaume
INVASION OF THE BODY SNATCHERS(1978), spec eff

Delwyn Rheaume
AMITYVILLE HORROR, THE(1979), spec eff

Joyce Rhed
JESSE JAMES' WOMEN(1954)

Al Rheim
PHANTOM SUBMARINE, THE(1941)

Lili Rheims
RED DESERT(1965, Fr./Ital.)

V.J. Rheims
DRAGSTRIP RIOT(1958), w

Al Rhein
ONLY ANGELS HAVE WINGS(1939); ANGELS OVER BROADWAY(1940); FACE BEHIND THE MASK, THE(1941); NORTH FROM LONE STAR(1941); TALK OF THE TOWN(1942); MR. LUCKY(1943); NONE BUT THE LONELY HEART(1944); JOHNNY ANGEL(1945); LADY LUCK(1946); NOCTURNE(1946); INTRIGUE(1947); EVERY GIRL SHOULD BE MARRIED(1948); RACE STREET(1948); LADY GAMBLES, THE(1949); SURRENDER(1950)

Alan Rhein
BALL OF FIRE(1941)

Alexander Rhein
GIRL RUSH, THE(1955)

Mitchell Rhein
HIGH BARBAREE(1947); LAS VEGAS STORY, THE(1952)

John Rheinard
Silents
AS A WOMAN SOWS(1916)

Samuel Rheiner
INNER SANCTUM(1948), p

William Rheinhold
KRONOS(1957), spec eff

J. Rhems
VIRGIN SACRIFICE(1959), w

V. Rhems
VIRGIN SACRIFICE(1959), w

V.J. Rhems
GANGSTER STORY(1959), w

Alicia Rhett
GONE WITH THE WIND(1939)

Bobby Rhia
ONE AND ONLY GENUINE ORIGINAL FAMILY BAND, THE(1968)

Marty Rhiel
TWO TICKETS TO BROADWAY(1951)

Burke Rhind
CHASTITY(1969)

Larry Rhine
CHIP OF THE FLYING U(1940), w; DEVIL'S PIPELINE, THE(1940), w; LEATHER-PUSHERS, THE(1940), w; DANGEROUS GAME, A(1941), w; SIX LESSONS FROM MADAME LA ZONGA(1941), w; TIMBER(1942), w; TOP SERGEANT(1942), w; SIREN OF BAGDAD(1953), w

William Rhine
Silents
TERROR OF BAR X, THE(1927)
Misc. Silents
RIP SNORTER, THE(1925)

O'leta Rhinehart
CRIME OF THE CENTURY(1946), w; PASSKEY TO DANGER(1946), w

William Rhinehart
MR. SOFT TOUCH(1949); UNDERCOVER MAN, THE(1949); JUBAL(1956)

Stella Rho
MURDER IN THE OLD RED BARN(1936, Brit.)

Stello Rho
DEMON BARBER OF FLEET STREET, THE(1939, Brit.)

Arthur S. Rhoades
OLD MAN AND THE SEA, THE(1958), spec eff

Barbara Rhoades
DON'T JUST STAND THERE(1968); SHAKIEST GUN IN THE WEST, THE(1968); THERE WAS A CROOKED MAN(1970); SCREAM BLACULA SCREAM(1973); HARRY AND TONTO(1974); SERIAL(1980)

Elizabeth Rhoades
VAGABOND LADY(1935)

Georgette Rhoades
LONELY WIVES(1931)

Hilda Rhoades
UNDERCURRENT(1946)

Nell Rhoades
FOLIES DERGERE(1935)

Quentin Rhoades
1984
STONE BOY, THE(1984)

Gloria Rhoads
GIRLS' TOWN(1959)

Sybil Rhoda
Silents
WHEN BOYS LEAVE HOME(1928, Brit.)
Misc. Silents
SAHARA LOVE(1926, Brit.)

Wayne John Rhodda
Z.P.G.(1972)

Fred J. Rhode
FIXED BAYONETS(1951), set d

E. C. Rhoden, Jr.
COOL AND THE CRAZY, THE(1958), p

Neil Rhoden
UNDERCOVERS HERO(1975, Brit.), m

Andrew Rhodes
1984
RUNAWAY(1984)

Barbara Rhodes
UP THE SANDBOX(1972); CHOIRBOYS, THE(1977); GOODBYE GIRL, THE(1977)

Betty Jane Rhodes
OH JOHNNY, HOW YOU CAN LOVE!(1940); ALONG THE RIO GRANDE(1941); MOUNTAIN MOONLIGHT(1941); FLEET'S IN, THE(1942)

Betty Rhodes
HAVING WONDERFUL TIME(1938); PRIORITIES ON PARADE(1942); STAR SPAN-GLED RHYTHM(1942); SWEATER GIRL(1942); SALUTE FOR THREE(1943); YOU CAN'T RATION LOVE(1944)

Billie Rhodes
Misc. Silents
LION'S BREATH, THE(1916); GIRL OF MY DREAMS, THE(1918); HOOP-LA(1919); IN SEARCH OF ARCADY(1919); LAMB AND THE LION, THE(1919); LOVE CALL, THE(1919); BLUE BONNET, THE(1920); NOBODY'S GIRL(1920); HIS PAJAMA GIRL(1921); STAR REPORTER, THE(1921); FIRES OF YOUTH(1924); LEAVE IT TO GERRY(1924)

Billy Rhodes
SKIMPY IN THE NAVY(1949, Brit.)

Bob Rhodes
Misc. Silents
WOMEN FIRST(1924)

Bobby Rhodes
HERCULES(1983)
1984
LAST HUNTER, THE(1984, Ital.)
Misc. Talkies
ENDGAME(1984)

Brian Rhodes
CLUE OF THE TWISTED CANDLE(1968, Brit.), ph; MARRIAGE OF CONVENI-ENCE(1970, Brit.), ph

Carl Rhodes
BRUTE FORCE(1947)

Chris Rhodes
HEART OF THE MATTER, THE(1954, Brit.)

Chrisopher Rhodes
MOULIN ROUGE(1952)

Christopher Rhodes
BETRAYED(1954); DEATH OF MICHAEL TURBIN, THE(1954, Brit.); LAUGHING ANNE(1954, Brit./U.S.); COLDITZ STORY, THE(1955, Brit.); GENTLE TOUCH, THE(1956, Brit.); TIGER IN THE SMOKE(1956, Brit.); DUNKIRK(1958, Brit.); NAKED EARTH, THE(1958, Brit.); NIGHT AMBUSH(1958, Brit.); WONDERFUL THINGS!(1958, Brit.); JOHN PAUL JONES(1959); LADY IS A SQUARE, THE(1959, Brit.); SHAKE HANDS WITH THE DEVIL(1959, Ireland); TIGER BAY(1959, Brit.); NIGHT FIGHTERS, THE(1960); OPERATION AMSTERDAM(1960, Brit.); EL CID(1961, U.S./Ital.); GORGO(1961, Brit.); GUNS OF NAVARONE, THE(1961); PIPER'S TUNE, THE(1962, Brit.); CRACKSMAN, THE(1963, Brit.); SWORD OF LANCELOT(1963, Brit.); BECKET(1964, Brit.)

Cynthia Rhodes
FLASHDANCE(1983); STAYING ALIVE(1983)
1984
RUNAWAY(1984)

Dave Rhodes
KEY MAN, THE(1957, Brit.)

Denys Rhodes
SYNDICATE, THE(1968, Brit.), w

Don Rhodes
REPRISAL(1956); 27TH DAY, THE(1957)

Donnelly Rhodes
GUNFIGHT IN ABILENE(1967); BUTCH CASSIDY AND THE SUNDANCE KID(1969); CHANGE OF MIND(1969); HARD PART BEGINS, THE(1973, Can.); NEPTUNE FACTOR, THE(1973, Can.); OH, HEAVENLY DOG!(1980)

Dotty Rhodes
Misc. Talkies
IT HAPPENED IN HARLEM(1945)
Douglas Rhodes
GRAND FINALE(1936, Brit.)
Dusty Rhodes
WRESTLER, THE(1974)
Earl Rhodes
DARK PLACES(1974, Brit.); SAILOR WHO FELL FROM GRACE WITH THE SEA, THE(1976, Brit.); MEDUSA TOUCH, THE(1978, Brit.)
Ebby Rhodes
VOODOO HEARTBEAT(1972)
Elizabeth Rhodes
Silents
NIGHT LIFE IN HOLLYWOOD(1922)
Erik Rhodes
GAY DIVORCEE, THE(1934); ANOTHER FACE(1935); CHARLIE CHAN IN PARIS(1935); NIGHT AT THE RITZ, A(1935); NITWITS, THE(1935); OLD MAN RHYTHM(1935); TOP HAT(1935); CHATTERBOX(1936); GIVE HER A RING(1936, Brit.); ONE RAINY AFTERNOON(1936); SECOND WIFE(1936); SMARTEST GIRL IN TOWN(1936); SPECIAL INVESTIGATOR(1936); TWO IN THE DARK(1936); BEG, BORROW OR STEAL(1937); CRIMINAL LAWYER(1937); FIGHT FOR YOUR LADY(1937); MUSIC FOR MADAME(1937); WOMAN CHASES MAN(1937); DRAMATIC SCHOOL(1938); MEET THE GIRLS(1938); MYSTERIOUS MR. MOTO(1938); SAY IT IN FRENCH(1938); ON YOUR TOES(1939)
Esther Rhodes
Silents
RINGER, THE(1928, Brit.)
Eugene Manlove Rhodes
FOUR FACES WEST(1948), w
Silents
WALLOP, THE(1921), w; MYSTERIOUS WITNESS, THE(1923), w
Frank Rhodes
I MARRIED A DOCTOR(1936)
George Rhodes
MAN CALLED ADAM, A(1966)
Georgette Rhodes
ROAD TO PARADISE(1930); WORLD MOVES ON, THE(1934); MAGNIFICENT OBSESSION(1935); MAN WHO BROKE THE BANK AT MONTE CARLO, THE(1935); SPLENDOR(1935); STRAIGHT FROM THE HEART(1935); GOD'S COUNTRY AND THE WOMAN(1937); KING AND THE CHORUS GIRL, THE(1937); WE'RE ON THE JURY(1937); THERE'S THAT WOMAN AGAIN(1938); PARIS UNDERGROUND(1945)
Gloria Rhodes
TOUGHEST GUN IN TOMBSTONE(1958)
Gordon Rhodes
HIGH WALL, THE(1947)
Grandin Rhodes
HOLLYWOOD AND VINE(1945)
Grandon Rhodes
SHIP AHOY(1942); SHADOW OF A DOUBT(1943); DOUGHGIRLS, THE(1944); FOLLOW THE BOYS(1944); IMPOSTER, THE(1944); LADIES COURAGEOUS(1944); LADY IN THE DARK(1944); SENSATIONS OF 1945(1944); MAGNIFICENT DOLL(1946); BORN TO KILL(1947); RIDE THE PINK HORSE(1947); SONG OF MY HEART(1947); TOO MANY WINNERS(1947); BLONDIE'S SECRET(1948); GENTLEMAN FROM NOWHERE, THE(1948); LARCENY(1948); ROAD HOUSE(1948); WALK A CROOKED MILE(1948); ALL THE KING'S MEN(1949); AND BABY MAKES THREE(1949); CANADIAN PACIFIC(1949); CLAY PIGEON, THE(1949); DANCING IN THE DARK(1949); MISS MINK OF 1949(1949); SLATTERY'S HURRICANE(1949); STREETS OF LAREDO(1949); TELL IT TO THE JUDGE(1949); TUCSON(1949); WHITE HEAT(1949); EAGLE AND THE HAWK, THE(1950); FLYING MISSILE(1950); LOST VOLCANO, THE(1950); STORM WARNING(1950); TRIPOLI(1950); WOMAN FROM HEADQUARTERS(1950); BORN YESTERDAY(1951); CRIMINAL LAWYER(1951); DETECTIVE STORY(1951); GUY WHO CAME BACK, THE(1951); TAKE CARE OF MY LITTLE GIRL(1951); CRIPPLE CREEK(1952); SNIPER, THE(1952); BLUEPRINT FOR MURDER, A(1953); HOUSE OF WAX(1953); ON TOP OF OLD SMOKY(1953); SO BIG(1953); THREE SAILORS AND A GIRL(1953); HUMAN DESIRE(1954); SECRET OF THE INCAS(1954); STAR IS BORN, A(1954); MAN ALONE, A(1955); REVENGE OF THE CREATURE(1955); TEXAS LADY(1955); TRIAL(1955); EARTH VS. THE FLYING SAUCERS(1956); THESE WILDER YEARS(1956); JAILHOUSE ROCK(1957); WAYWARD GIRL, THE(1957); 27TH DAY, THE(1957); NOTORIOUS MR. MONKS, THE(1958); BRAMBLE BUSH, THE(1960); OKLAHOMA TERRITORY(1960); TESS OF THE STORM COUNTRY(1961)
Hari [Harry] Rhodes
RETURN TO PEYTON PLACE(1961); SHOCK CORRIDOR(1963); SATAN BUG, THE(1965); TAFFY AND THE JUNGLE HUNTER(1965); SHARKY'S MACHINE(1982)
Hari Rhodes
THIS REBEL BREED(1960); FIERCEST HEART, THE(1961); NUN AND THE SERGEANT, THE(1962); DRUMS OF AFRICA(1963); MIRAGE(1965); BLINDFOLD(1966); CONQUEST OF THE PLANET OF THE APES(1972); DETROIT 9000(1973)
Harrison Rhodes
Silents
GENTLEMAN FROM MISSISSIPPI, THE(1914), w; ADVENTURE IN HEARTS, AN(1919), w
Harry Rhodes
COMA(1978)
Hilda Rhodes
YOU CANT TAKE IT WITH YOU(1938); POSTMAN ALWAYS RINGS TWICE, THE(1946)
Ila Rhodes
DARK VICTORY(1939); HELL'S KITCHEN(1939); OFF THE RECORD(1939); SECRET SERVICE OF THE AIR(1939); WOMEN IN THE WIND(1939)
James Rhodes
AT THE RIDGE(1931), w
Jane Rhodes
ARIZONA RAIDERS, THE(1936); FORGOTTEN FACES(1936); LIFE OF THE PARTY, THE(1937); STAGE DOOR(1937)
Jennifer Rhodes
NIGHT CREATURE(1979)

Misc. Talkies
SKETCHES OF A STRANGLER(?)
Jimmy Rhodes
OLD MOTHER RILEY, DETECTIVE(1943, Brit.); STOP PRESS GIRL(1949, Brit.); SHE SHALL HAVE MURDER(1950, Brit.)
Joan Rhodes
JOHNNY, YOU'RE WANTED(1956, Brit.); ELEPHANT MAN, THE(1980, Brit.)
John Rhodes
TWELVE GOOD MEN(1936, Brit.), w; HAPPIEST DAYS OF YOUR LIFE(1950, Brit.)
Jordan Rhodes
ANGEL UNCHAINED(1970); 1776(1972); TERMINAL MAN, THE(1974)
Jordon Rhodes
MR. MAJESTYK(1974)
Kathlyn Rhodes
Silents
AFTERWARDS(1928, Brit.), w
Kenneth Rhodes
DEATH RIDES THE RANGE(1940)
Lea Rhodes
THREE SECRETS(1950), cos
Leah Rhodes
MURDER ON THE WATERFRONT(1943), cos; NORTHERN PURSUIT(1943), cos; CONSPIRATORS, THE(1944), cos; EXPERIMENT PERILOUS(1944), cos; PASSAGE TO MARSEILLE(1944), cos; ROUGHLY SPEAKING(1945), cos; SARATOGA TRUNK(1945), cos; BIG SLEEP, THE(1946), cos; CLOAK AND DAGGER(1946), cos; MY REPUTATION(1946), cos; NEVER SAY GOODBYE(1946), cos; PURSUED(1947), cos;THAT WAY WITH WOMEN(1947), cos; VOICE OF THE TURTLE, THE(1947), cos; KEY LARGO(1948), cos; MY GIRL TISA(1948), cos; ONE SUNDAY AFTERNOON(1948), cos; WALLFLOWER(1948), cos; GIRL FROM JONES BEACH, THE(1949), cos; NIGHT UNTO NIGHT(1949), cos; STORY OF SEABISCUIT, THE(1949), cos; WHITE HEAT(1949), cos; BREAKING POINT, THE(1950), cos; CHAIN LIGHTNING(1950), cos; TEA FOR TWO(1950), cos; COME FILL THE CUP(1951), cos; I'LL SEE YOU IN MY DREAMS(1951), cos; STARLIFT(1951), cos; STRANGERS ON A TRAIN(1951), cos; ROOM FOR ONE MORE(1952), cos; WINNING TEAM, THE(1952), cos; SO THIS IS LOVE(1953), cos; FORTY GUNS(1957), cos; KINGS GO FORTH(1958), cos; TICKLE ME(1965), cos; VILLAGE OF THE GIANTS(1965), cos; PICTURE MOMMY DEAD(1966), cos; GOOD TIMES(1967), cos
Lee Rhodes
FROM HELL IT CAME(1957)
Little Billy Rhodes
COURT JESTER, THE(1956)
Liz Rhodes
Misc. Talkies
BLACK BIRD DESCENDING: TENSE ALIGNMENT(1977)
Margery Rhodes
FOOTSTEPS IN THE FOG(1955, Brit.)
Marjorie Rhodes
POISON PEN(1941, Brit.); BUTLER'S DILEMMA, THE(1943, Brit.); ESCAPE TO DANGER(1943, Brit.); OLD MOTHER RILEY, DETECTIVE(1943, Brit.); SQUADRON LEADER X(1943, Brit.); THEATRE ROYAL(1943, Brit.); WHEN WE ARE MARRIED(1943, Brit.); IT HAPPENED ONE SUNDAY(1944, Brit.); ON APPROVAL(1944, Brit.); GREAT DAY(1945, Brit.); LOVE ON THE DOLE(1945, Brit.); SCHOOL FOR SECRETS(1946, Brit.); TAWNY PIPIT(1947, Brit.); ENCHANTMENT(1948); ESCAPE(1948, Brit.); PRIVATE ANGELO(1949, Brit.); THIS WAS A WOMAN(1949, Brit.); CURE FOR LOVE, THE(1950, Brit.); INHERITANCE, THE(1951, Brit.); THOSE PEOPLE NEXT DOOR(1952, Brit.); BOTH SIDES OF THE LAW(1953, Brit.); DECAMERON NIGHTS(1953, Brit.); GIRL ON THE PIER, THE(1953, Brit.); TIME GENTLEMEN PLEASE!(1953, Brit.); YELLOW BALLOON, THE(1953, Brit.); CHILDREN GALORE(1954, Brit.); WEAK AND THE WICKED, THE(1954, Brit.); ROOM IN THE HOUSE(1955, Brit.); BLONDE SINNER(1956, Brit.); CASH ON DELIVERY(1956, Brit.); IT'S A GREAT DAY(1956, Brit.); IT'S GREAT TO BE YOUNG(1956, Brit.); NOW AND FOREVER(1956, Brit.); AFTER THE BALL(1957, Brit.); GOOD COMPANIONS, THE(1957, Brit.); JUST MY LUCK(1957, Brit.); NO TIME FOR TEARS(1957, Brit.); NOVEL AFFAIR, A(1957, Brit.); TEARS FOR SIMON(1957, Brit.); THERE'S ALWAYS A THURSDAY(1957, Brit.); HELL DRIVERS(1958, Brit.); GIDEON OF SCOTLAND YARD(1959, Brit.); OVER THE ODDS(1961, Brit.); WATCH IT, SAILOR!(1961, Brit.); ALIVE AND KICKING(1962, Brit.); I'VE GOTTA HORSE(1965, Brit.); THOSE MAGNIFICENT MEN IN THEIR FLYING MACHINES; OR HOW I FLEW FROM LONDON TO PARIS IN 25 HOURS AND 11 MINUTES(1965, Brit.); FAMILY WAY, THE(1966, Brit.); MRS. BROWN, YOU'VE GOT A LOVELY DAUGHTER(1968, Brit.); SPRING AND PORT WINE(1970, Brit.); HANDS OF THE RIPPER(1971, Brit.)
Maurice Rhodes
HI, GANG!(1941, Brit.); RHYTHM SERENADE(1943, Brit.)
Michael Rhodes
ATTIC, THE(1979)
Mike Rhodes
BUS IS COMING, THE(1971), w, ph
Percy Rhodes
DEATH AT A BROADCAST(1934, Brit.); SILENT PASSENGER, THE(1935, Brit.)
Silents
HAMLET(1913, Brit.)
Misc. Silents
HOUR OF THE TRIAL, THE(1920, Brit.)
Phil Rhodes
ONE-EYED JACKS(1961), makeup; REFLECTIONS IN A GOLDEN EYE(1967), makeup; MARLOWE(1969), makeup
Philip Rhodes
WON TON TON, THE DOG WHO SAVED HOLLYWOOD(1976), makeup; SUPERMAN(1978), makeup
Phillip Rhodes
GODFATHER, THE(1972), makeup; MECHANIC, THE(1972), makeup
Speck Rhodes
1984
RHINESTONE(1984)
Suzanne Rhodes
TWO FOR TONIGHT(1935)
Terence Rhodes
MILLIONS LIKE US(1943, Brit.)

Vivian Rhodes
WATERMELON MAN(1970)
William Rhodes
NOTHING BUT A MAN(1964), prod d
William R. Rhodes
SLENDER THREAD, THE(1965)
Yokki Rhodes
SUBURBAN WIVES(1973, Brit.)
Carolyn Rhodimer
WITCHMAKER, THE(1969)
Gloria Rhods
INTERRUPTED MELODY(1955)
Geoff Rhoe
PUBERTY BLUES(1983, Aus.)
Rudolf Rhomberg
MAN WHO WALKED THROUGH THE WALL, THE(1964, Ger.); GIRL AND THE LEGEND, THE(1966, Ger.)
Patrice Rhomm
DEVIL'S NIGHTMARE, THE(1971 Bel./Ital.), w
Paul Rhone
STATE FAIR(1962); THOMAS CROWN AFFAIR, THE(1968)
Trevor D. Rhone
HARDER THEY COME, THE(1973, Jamaica), w; SMILE ORANGE(1976, Jamaican), d, w
Rhonda Rhoton
COAL MINER'S DAUGHTER(1980)
Gypsy Rhouma
WHITE CARGO(1930, Brit.)
Misc. Silents
WHITE CARGO(1929, Brit.)
Angela Rhu
HERCULES AGAINST THE SONS OF THE SUN(1964, Span./Ital.)
Roger Rhu
1984
OH GOD! YOU DEVIL(1984)
Rhubarb
COMEDY OF TERRORS, THE(1964)
Paul Rhudy
MARVIN AND TIGE(1983), art d
Madlyn Rhue
OPERATION PETTICOAT(1959); LADIES MAN, THE(1961); MAJORITY OF ONE, A(1961); ESCAPE FROM ZAHRAIN(1962); IT'S A MAD, MAD, MAD, MAD WORLD(1963); HE RIDES TALL(1964); KENNER(1969); STAND UP AND BE COUNT-ED(1972)
Jane Rhum
GRAND THEFT AUTO(1977), cos
Slim Rhyder
VARIETY JUBILEE(1945, Brit.)
Henrik Rhyn
BLACK SPIDER, THE(1983, Swit.)
Scott Rhyne
VERDICT, THE(1982)
Jean Rhys
QUARTET(1981, Brit./Fr.), w
Margot Rhys
HERITAGE(1935, Aus.); UNCIVILISED(1937, Aus.)
Noel Rhys
Silents
DECAMERON NIGHTS(1924, Brit.), w
Robert Rhys
PASSAGE, THE(1979, Brit.)
John Rhys-Davies
BLACK WINDMILL, THE(1974, Brit.); RAIDERS OF THE LOST ARK(1981); SPHINX(1981); VICTOR/VICTORIA(1982)
1984
SAHARA(1984); SWORD OF THE VALIANT(1984, Brit.)
The Rhythm Brothers
UNDER YOUR HAT(1940, Brit.)
The Rhythm Rascals
NOBODY'S BABY(1937)
Rhythm Sisters
AROUND THE TOWN(1938, Brit.)
The Rhythmaires
RELUCTANT DRAGON, THE(1941); ADVENTURES OF ICHABOD AND MR. TOAD(1949); SO DEAR TO MY HEART(1949)
Arthur Rhytis
SOMEBODY KILLED HER HUSBAND(1978)
C. Riabinkin
GREAT CITIZEN, THE(1939, USSR)
Tatiana Riabouchinska
MAKE MINE MUSIC(1946)
Alexandre Riachi
CIRCLE OF DECEIT(1982, Fr./Ger.), art d
Candice Rialson
EIGER SANCTION, THE(1975); HOLLYWOOD BOULEVARD(1976); MOONSHINE COUNTY EXPRESS(1977); STUNTS(1977); SUMMER SCHOOL TEACHERS(1977); WINTER KILLS(1979)
Misc. Talkies
CANDY STRIPE NURSES(1974); CHATTERBOX(1977)
Candy Rialson
PETS(1974)
La Riana
WOLF MAN, THE(1941)
Rene Riano
SONG FOR MISS JULIE, A(1945)
Renie Riano
TIME OF YOUR LIFE, THE(1948); MY DEAR MISS ALDRICH(1937); TOVA-RICH(1937); YOU'RE A SWEETHEART(1937); FOUR'S A CROWD(1938); MEN ARE SUCH FOOLS(1938); NANCY DREW–DETECTIVE(1938); OUTSIDE OF PARADIS-E(1938); ROAD TO RENO, THE(1938); SPRING MADNESS(1938); STRANGE FA-

CES(1938); THANKS FOR EVERYTHING(1938); DAY-TIME WIFE(1939); DISPUTED PASSAGE(1939); HONEYMOON IN BALI(1939); HONEYMOON'S OVER, THE(1939); NANCY DREW AND THE HIDDEN STAIRCASE(1939); NANCY DREW, TROUBLE SHOOTER(1939); TELL NO TALES(1939); WIFE, HUSBAND AND FRIEND(1939); WINGS OF THE NAVY(1939); WOMEN, THE(1939); DOCTOR TAKES A WIFE(1940); KIT CARSON(1940); LITTLE BIT OF HEAVEN, A(1940); MAN WHO WOULDN'T TALK, THE(1940); OH JOHNNY, HOW YOU CAN LOVE!(1940); SHOP AROUND THE CORNER, THE(1940); ADAM HAD FOUR SONS(1941); AFFECTIONATELY YOURS(1941); ICE-CAPADES(1941); REMEDY FOR RICHES(1941); UNFINISHED BUSINESS(1941); YOU BELONG TO ME(1941); YOU'RE THE ONE(1941); ZIEGFELD GIRL(1941); THERE'S ONE BORN EVERY MINUTE(1942); THEY DIED WITH THEIR BOOTS ON(1942); WHISPERING GHOSTS(1942); MAN FROM MUSIC MOUN-TAIN(1943); JAM SESSION(1944); NONE BUT THE LONELY HEART(1944); TAKE IT OR LEAVE IT(1944); 3 IS A FAMILY(1944); ANCHORS AWEIGH(1945); PICTURE OF DORIAN GRAY, THE(1945); BRINGING UP FATHER(1946); CLUB HAVANA(1946); SO GOES MY LOVE(1946); WINTER WONDERLAND(1947); JIGGS AND MAGGIE IN SOCIETY(1948); JIGGS AND MAGGIE OUT WEST(1950); AS YOUNG AS YOU FEEL(1951); BAREFOOT MAILMAN, THE(1951); CLIPPED WINGS(1953); PAJAMA PARTY(1964); FAMILY JEWELS, THE(1965); FIREBALL 590(1966); THREE ON A COUCH(1966)
Misc. Talkies
JIGGS AND MAGGIE IN COURT(1948); JIGGS AND MAGGIE IN JACKPOT JITTERS(1949)
Renio Riano
BAD BASCOMB(1946)
The Rias Dance Orchestra
SCHLAGER-PARADE(1953)
Helen Riaume
Misc. Silents
WHERE ARE MY CHILDREN?(1916)
V. Riazanov
SLEEPING BEAUTY, THE(1966, USSR)
John Riazzi
SCAVENGERS, THE(1969)
Shayiaw Riba
CRY, THE BELOVED COUNTRY(1952, Brit.)
Marian Ribas
SAVAGE PAMPAS(1967, Span./Arg.), cos; DR. COPPELIUS(1968, U.S./Span.), cos
V. Ribe
MARIUS(1933, Fr.)
Catherine Ribeiro
BUFFALO BILL, HERO OF THE FAR WEST(1962, Ital.); WE ARE ALL NAKED(1970, Can./Fr.)
Isabel Ribeiro
ALL NUDITY SHALL BE PUNISHED(1974, Brazil)
Milton Ribeiro
THAT MAN FROM RIO(1964, Fr./Ital.)
G. Ribemont-Dessaignes
LA MARIE DU PORT(1951, Fr.), w
Bente Riber
CRAZY PARADISE(1965, Den.), cos
Catherine Ribero
LES CARABINIERS(1968, Fr./Ital.)
Tito Ribero
DARK RIVER(1956, Arg.), m
Jacques Riberolles
GAME FOR SIX LOVERS, A(1962, Fr.); DOUBLE DECEPTION(1963, Fr.); PLEASE, NOT NOW!(1963, Fr./Ital.); SEVENTH JUROR, THE(1964, Fr.); GALIA(1966, Fr./Ital.); OSS 117–MISSION FOR A KILLER(1966, Fr.); YOUNG GIRLS OF ROCHEFORT, THE(1968, Fr.); SECRET WORLD(1969, Fr.)
Christiane Ribes
LE DENIER MILLIARDAIRE(1934, Fr.)
Philippe Ribes
1984
LES COMPERES(1984, Fr.)
Ivan Ribic
SERGEANT JIM(1962, Yugo.), w
Lisa Riblet
NIGHT THE LIGHTS WENT OUT IN GEORGIA, THE(1981)
Gladys Ribley
GREAT MR. HANDEL, THE(1942, Brit.)
Ronald Ribman
ANGEL LEVINE, THE(1970), w
Maurice Ribot
QUARTET(1981, Brit./Fr.)
Ettore Ribotta
SON OF CAPTAIN BLOOD, THE(1964, U.S./Ital./Span.); THAT SPLENDID NOVEM-BER(1971, Ital./Fr.)
Hector [Ettore] Ribotta
LAST MAN ON EARTH, THE(1964, U.S./Ital.)
Malka Ribovska
PARIS BELONGS TO US(1962, Fr.); SUNDAYS AND CYBELE(1962, Fr.); SHAME-LESS OLD LADY, THE(1966, Fr.); OTHER ONE, THE(1967,Fr.); HIT(1973); TWO MEN IN TOWN(1973, Fr.)
Katherina Ribraka
ANGELO MY LOVE(1983)
Yvonne Ribuca
LT. ROBIN CRUSOE, U.S.N.(1966)
Enrico Ribulzi
ARTURO'S ISLAND(1963, Ital.), w
Adrian Ricard
DEAD MEN DON'T WEAR PLAID(1982); MAN WITH TWO BRAINS, THE(1983)
Albert Rene Ricard
CHELSEA GIRLS, THE(1967)
Eduardo Ricard
WALK PROUD(1979); DEAL OF THE CENTURY(1983)
1984
BEST DEFENSE(1984)

Rene Ricard
UNDERGROUND U.S.A.(1980)
Molly Ricardel
I LOVED YOU WEDNESDAY(1933), w
Ricky Ricardi
STRANGE LOVE OF MARTHA IVERS, THE(1946)
Bertha Ricardo
SINGING THROUGH(1935, Brit.); DODGING THE DOLE(1936, Brit.)
Misc. Talkies
BE CAREFUL, MR. SMITH(1935)
Diana Ricardo
1984
SCREAM FOR HELP(1984); SUPERGIRL(1984)
Joy Ricardo
ONE NIGHT WITH YOU(1948, Brit), cos; TAKE MY LIFE(1948, Brit.), cos
Rona Ricardo
CLEANING UP(1933, Brit.)
Sergio Ricardo
EARTH ENTRANCED(1970, Braz.), m
Sally Ricca
PIRANHA II: THE SPAWNING(1981, Neth.); NIGHT IN HEAVEN, A(1983)
Thomas Riccabona
LITTLE NIGHT MUSIC, A(1977, Aust./U.S./Ger.), art d
Joseph Riccardi
Silents
MY COUSIN(1918)
Michele Riccardini
GREAT DAWN, THE(1947, Ital.); VOICE IN YOUR HEART, A(1952, Ital.); ULYSSES(1955, Ital.); OSSESSIONE(1959, Ital.)
Rick Riccardo
MAN WHO FELL TO EARTH, THE(1976, Brit.)
Valeria Riccardo
MAYA(1982)
Luciano Ricceri
JULIET OF THE SPIRITS(1965, Fr./Ital./W.Ger.), set d; TIGER AND THE PUSSYCAT, THE(1967, U.S., Ital.), art d; MOTIVE WAS JEALOUSY, THE(1970 Ital./Span.), art d; PIZZA TRIANGLE, THE(1970, Ital./Span.), art d; MOST WONDERFUL EVENING OF MY LIFE, THE(1972, Ital./Fr.), art d; ROCCO PAPALEO(1974, Ital./Fr.), art d; MIDNIGHT PLEASURES(1975, Ital.), art d; SPECIAL DAY, A(1977, Ital./Can.), prod d, art d; VIVA ITALIA(1978, Ital.), prod d&set d; IMMORTAL BACHELOR, THE(1980, Ital.), art d
1984
LE BAL(1984, Fr./Ital./Algeria), prod d
Vinicio Ricchi
FACTS OF MURDER, THE(1965, Ital.)
Luciano Ricchieri
DEVIL IN LOVE, THE(1968, Ital.), art d
Ricci
ETERNAL MELODIES(1948, Ital.), md; THAT WOMAN(1968, Ger.)
Aldo Ricci
FIVE GIANTS FROM TEXAS(1966, Ital./Span.), p
Bill Ricci
DON'T GO IN THE HOUSE(1980)
Lina Ricci
TREE OF WOODEN CLOGS, THE(1979, Ital.)
Luciano Ricci
STORY OF JOSEPH AND HIS BRETHREN THE(1962, Ital.), d
Luigi Ricci
DREAM OF BUTTERFLY, THE(1941, Ital.), md; BEFORE HIM ALL ROME TREMBLED(1947, Ital.), md
Nina Ricci
MAGNIFICENT CUCKOLD, THE(1965, Fr./Ital.), cos
Nora Ricci
BIRDS, THE BEES AND THE ITALIANS, THE(1967); GIRL WHO COULDN'T SAY NO, THE(1969, Ital.); WITCHES, THE(1969, Fr./Ital.); DEATH IN VENICE(1971, Ital./Fr.); LUDWIG(1973, Ital./Ger./Fr.); NIGHT PORTER, THE(1974, Ital./U.S.)
Paolo Ricci
SHOOT LOUD, LOUDER... I DON'T UNDERSTAND(1966, Ital.)
1984
AFTER THE FALL OF NEW YORK(1984, Ital./Fr.), spec eff; BLACK CAT, THE(1984, Ital./Brit.), spec eff; NOSTALGHIA(1984, USSR/Ital.), spec eff
Paul Ricci
SUBWAY RIDERS(1981)
Renzo Ricci
L'AVVENTURA(1960, Ital.); SANDRA(1966, Ital.)
Riccardo Ricci
FALL OF ROME, THE(1963, Ital.)
Richard Ricci
THERE'S ALWAYS VANILLA(1972)
Rudolph J. Ricci
THERE'S ALWAYS VANILLA(1972), w
Luciano Ricci [Herbert Wise]
CASTLE OF THE LIVING DEAD(1964, Ital./Fr.), d
Franco Ricciardi
LA BOHEME(1965, Ital.)
Mirella Ricciardi
ECLIPSE(1962, Fr./Ital.)
William Ricciardi
UNDER TWO FLAGS(1936); STRICTLY DISHONORABLE(1931); AS YOU DESIRE ME(1932); CROONER(1932); SCARLET DAWN(1932); TIGER SHARK(1932); SCOUNDREL, THE(1935); STARS OVER BROADWAY(1935); ANTHONY ADVERSE(1936); SAN FRANCISCO(1936); MAN OF THE PEOPLE(1937)
Silents
SIDESHOW OF LIFE, THE(1924); PUPPETS(1926)
Misc. Silents
HUMMING BIRD, THE(1924)
Frederick Riccio
TEENAGE MOTHER(1967)

Guido Riccioli
GUILT IS NOT MINE(1968, Ital.)
Enzo Riccioni
PROSTITUTION(1965, Fr.), ph
Emy Ricciotti
MAGIC WORLD OF TOPO GIGIO, THE(1961, Ital.), animation
Stefano Ricciotti
SWEPT AWAY...BY AN UNUSUAL DESTINY IN THE BLUE SEA OF AUGUST(1975, Ital.), ph
Frank Ricco
SECRET OF THE PURPLE REEF, THE(1960)
Adam Rice
1984
PURPLE HEARTS(1984)
Adnia Rice
MUSIC MAN, THE(1962)
Albert Rice
MEET THE MISSUS(1937), w; HOW'S ABOUT IT?(1943), w; GAY BLADES(1946), w
Alfred Rice [Alfredo Rizzo]
TERROR-CREATURES FROM THE GRAVE(1967, U.S./Ital.)
Alice Hegan Rice
MRS. WIGGS OF THE CABBAGE PATCH(1934), w
Andy Rice
MC FADDEN'S FLATS(1935), w
Andy Rice, Jr.
FOOTLIGHTS AND FOOLS(1929); SPEED LIMITED(1940)
Autumn Rice
UNTAMED WOMEN(1952)
Bill Rice
OFFENDERS, THE(1980); TRAP DOOR, THE(1980); SUBWAY RIDERS(1981); VORTEX(1982)
Brett Rice
1984
BEAR, THE(1984)
Charles J. Rice
WALK ON THE WILD SIDE(1962), ed
Craig Rice
FALCON'S BROTHER, THE(1942), w; FALCON IN DANGER, THE(1943), w; HAVING WONDERFUL CRIME(1945), w; HOME SWEET HOMICIDE(1946), w; TENTH AVENUE ANGEL(1948), w; LUCKY STIFF, THE(1949), w; MRS. O'MALLEY AND MR. MALONE(1950), w; WHIPPED, THE(1950), w
Cy Rice
W.C. FIELDS AND ME(1976), w
Darlene Rice
BROTHER JOHN(1971)
Darol Rice
SOUTH PACIFIC TRAIL(1952)
Don Rice
LADY LUCK(1946); LET'S DO IT AGAIN(1953)
Durant Rice
13 RUE MADELEINE(1946)
Edward Rice
LITTLE MEN(1940)
Elmer Rice
ON TRIAL(1928), w; OH! SAILOR, BEHAVE!(1930), w; STREET SCENE(1931), w; COUNSELLOR-AT-LAW(1933), w; ON TRIAL(1939), w; HOLIDAY INN(1942), w; DREAM GIRL(1947), w
Silents
DOUBLING FOR ROMEO(1921), w; IT IS THE LAW(1924), w
Florence Rice
FUGITIVE LADY(1934); AWAKENING OF JIM BURKE(1935); BEST MAN WINS, THE(1935); CARNIVAL(1935); DEATH FLIES EAST(1935); ESCAPE FROM DEVIL'S ISLAND(1935); GUARD THAT GIRL(1935); SUPERSPEED(1935); UNDER PRESSURE(1935); BLACKMAILER(1936); LONGEST NIGHT, THE(1936); PRIDE OF THE MARINES(1936); SWORN ENEMY(1936); WOMEN ARE TROUBLE(1936); BEG, BORROW OR STEAL(1937); DOUBLE WEDDING(1937); MAN OF THE PEOPLE(1937); MARRIED BEFORE BREAKFAST(1937); NAVY BLUE AND GOLD(1937); RIDING ON AIR(1937); UNDER COVER OF NIGHT(1937); FAST COMPANY(1938); PARADISE FOR THREE(1938); SWEETHEARTS(1938); VACATION FROM LOVE(1938); AT THE CIRCUS(1939); FOUR GIRLS IN WHITE(1939); KID FROM TEXAS, THE(1939); LITTLE ACCIDENT(1939); MIRACLES FOR SALE(1939); STAND UP AND FIGHT(1939); BROADWAY MELODY OF 1940(1940); CHEROKEE STRIP(1940); GIRL IN 313(1940); PHANTOM RAIDERS(1940); SECRET SEVEN, THE(1940); BLONDE FROM SINGAPORE, THE(1941); BORROWED HERO(1941); DOCTORS DON'T TELL(1941); FATHER TAKES A WIFE(1941); MR. DISTRICT ATTORNEY(1941); LET'S GET TOUGH(1942); TRAMP, TRAMP, TRAMP(1942); BOSS OF BIG TOWN(1943); GHOST AND THE GUEST(1943)
Misc. Talkies
STAND BY ALL NETWORKS(1942)
Frank Rice
WAGON MASTER, THE(1929); FIGHTING LEGION, THE(1930); PARADE OF THE WEST(1930); SHADOW RANCH(1930); SONG OF THE CABELLERO(1930); SONS OF THE SADDLE(1930); BORDER LAW(1931); WHOOPEE(1930); CONQUERING HORDE, THE(1931); CORSAIR(1931); MOUNTED FURY(1931); RIDERS OF THE NORTH(1931); SQUAW MAN, THE(1931); FREIGHTERS OF DESTINY(1932); HELLO TROUBLE(1932); PACK UP YOUR TROUBLES(1932); SHOTGUN PASS(1932); SUNSET TRAIL(1932); KING OF THE ARENA(1933); PHANTOM THUNDERBOLT, THE(1933); ROBBERS' ROOST(1933); SOMEWHERE IN SONORA(1933); BELLE OF THE NINETIES(1934); FIDDLIN' BUCKAROO, THE(1934); FIGHTING RANGER, THE(1934); LAST ROUND-UP, THE(1934); THUNDERING HERD, THE(1934); TRAIL DRIVE, THE(1934); WHARF ANGEL(1934); WHEELS OF DESTINY(1934); BORDER BRIGANDS(1935); HARD ROCK HARRIGAN(1935); IVORY-HANDLED GUN(1935); ONE HOUR LATE(1935); POWDERSMOKE RANGE(1935); PRINCESS O'HARA(1935); RUGGLES OF RED GAP(1935); SHE COULDN'T TAKE IT(1935); STONE OF SILVER CREEK(1935); TRAILS OF THE WILD(1935); FORBIDDEN TRAIL(1936); NEVADA(1936); OREGON TRAIL, THE(1936); TRAIL OF THE LONESOME PINE, THE(1936); MONKEY HUSTLE, THE(1976)
Misc. Talkies
LOSER'S END(1934); TERROR OF THE PLAINS(1934)

Silents
AIR HAWK, THE(1924); DYNAMITE DAN(1924); GALLOPING ACE, THE(1924); GOLD RUSH, THE(1925); RIDERS OF MYSTERY(1925); SPOOK RANCH(1925); BOY RIDER, THE(1927); SKY-HIGH SAUNDERS(1927); BANTAM COWBOY, THE(1928); ORPHAN OF THE SAGE(1928); YOUNG WHIRLWIND(1928); LAWLESS LEGION, THE(1929); OVERLAND TELEGRAPH, THE(1929); PALS OF THE PRAIRIE(1929); ROYAL RIDER, THE(1929); STAIRS OF SAND(1929)
Misc. Silents
DESERT RIDER(1923); FORBIDDEN TRAIL, THE(1923); RED WARNING, THE(1923); CALL OF COURAGE, THE(1925); FLYING HIGH(1926); SLINGSHOT KID, THE(1927); WOLF FANGS(1927); PINTO KID, THE(1928); ROUGH RIDIN' RED(1928); WON IN THE CLOUDS(1928); VAGABOND CUB, THE(1929)

Frank G. Rice
DOCTOR DETROIT(1983)

Grantland Rice
MADISON SQUARE GARDEN(1932); FOLLOW THE SUN(1951)

Greg Rice
HARDLY WORKING(1981)

Henry Milton Rice
EXTRAORDINARY SEAMAN, THE(1969), set d

Herb Rice
RUMBLE FISH(1983)

Herbert Rice
YOUNGBLOOD(1978)
Silents
RAINBOW PRINCESS, THE(1916)

Howard Rice
BROTHER JOHN(1971)

Jack Rice
THEY WON'T BELIEVE ME(1947); FLYING DOWN TO RIO(1933); SWING TIME(1936); WALKING ON AIR(1936); STAGE DOOR(1937); ARSON GANG BUSTERS(1938); MAD MISS MANTON, THE(1938); DANGER ON WHEELS(1940); ELLERY QUEEN. MASTER DETECTIVE(1940); FIVE LITTLE PEPPERS AT HOME(1940); FOREIGN CORRESPONDENT(1940); HE STAYED FOR BREAKFAST(1940); LADY IN QUESTION, THE(1940); MONEY TO BURN(1940); WE WHO ARE YOUNG(1940); MEN OF THE TIMBERLAND(1941); NEW YORK TOWN(1941); YOU'LL NEVER GET RICH(1941); LUCKY LEGS(1942); TAKE A LETTER, DARLING(1942); GILDERSLEEVE'S BAD DAY(1943); GOOD MORNING, JUDGE(1943); HONEYMOON LODGE(1943); PASSPORT TO SUEZ(1943); REVEILLE WITH BEVERLY(1943); SHE HAS WHAT IT TAKES(1943); SO'S YOUR UNCLE(1943); TWO WEEKS TO LIVE(1943); COVER GIRL(1944); EVER SINCE VENUS(1944); GOIN' TO TOWN(1944); HI BEAUTIFUL(1944); HAT CHECK HONEY(1944); LADY, LET'S DANCE(1944); LOUISIANA HAYRIDE(1944); PRACTICALLY YOURS(1944); SAN DIEGO, I LOVE YOU(1944); SWINGTIME JOHNNY(1944); WEEKEND PASS(1944); EVE KNEW HER APPLES(1945); HER LUCKY NIGHT(1945); LEAVE IT TO BLONDIE(1945); NAUGHTY NINETIES, THE(1945); UNDER WESTERN SKIES(1945); BLONDIE KNOWS BEST(1946); BLONDIE'S LUCKY DAY(1946); LIFE WITH BLONDIE(1946); MEET ME ON BROADWAY(1946); RUNAROUND, THE(1946); BLONDIE'S ANNIVERSARY(1947); BLONDIE'S BIG MOMENT(1947); BLONDIE'S HOLIDAY(1947); HER HUSBAND'S AFFAIRS(1947); IT HAD TO BE YOU(1947); LIKELY STORY, A(1947); PILGRIM LADY, THE(1947); BLONDIE'S REWARD(1948); BLONDIE'S SECRET(1948); BLONDIE'S BIG DEAL(1949); TAKE ME OUT TO THE BALL GAME(1949); TAKE ONE FALSE STEP(1949); BEWARE OF BLONDIE(1950); SHAKEDOWN(1950); CORKY OF GASOLINE ALLEY(1951); PRIDE OF ST. LOUIS, THE(1952); STARS AND STRIPES FOREVER(1952); MARKSMAN, THE(1953); SILVER WHIP, THE(1953); CRASHING LAS VEGAS(1956); FIRST TRAVELING SALESLADY, THE(1956); TOO MUCH, TOO SOON(1958); THIRTY FOOT BRIDE OF CANDY ROCK, THE(1959); THAT TOUCH OF MINK(1962); SON OF FLUBBER(1963)

Jeff Rice
PSYCHOPATH, THE(1973)

Joan Rice
BLACKMAILED(1951, Brit.); ONE WILD OAT(1951, Brit.); CURTAIN UP(1952, Brit.); GLORY AT SEA(1952, Brit.); STORY OF ROBIN HOOD, THE(1952, Brit.); DAY TO REMEMBER, A(1953, Brit.); HIS MAJESTY O'KEEFE(1953); STEEL KEY, THE(1953, Brit.); CROWDED DAY, THE(1954, Brit.); ONE GOOD TURN(1955, Brit.); POLICE DOG(1955, Brit.); BLONDE BAIT(1956, U.S./Brit.); LONG KNIFE, THE(1958, Brit.); PAYROLL(1962, Brit.); OPERATION BULLSHINE(1963, Brit.); HORROR OF FRANKENSTEIN, THE(1970, Brit.)

Joel S. Rice
FINAL EXAM(1981)

John Rice
ETERNALLY YOURS(1939); THIS LAND IS MINE(1943); LODGER, THE(1944); KITTY(1945); NOCTURNE(1946); SEA OF GRASS, THE(1947); HARDLY WORKING(1981)

Johnny Rice
EXCUSE MY GLOVE(1936, Brit.)

Josephine Rice
Silents
BIG TREMAINE(1916)

Marie Rice
LEAVENWORTH CASE, THE(1936); HOLD THAT WOMAN(1940)

Mark O. Rice
RUN FOR THE HILLS(1953), p

Mary Alice Rice
FLYING HOSTESS(1936); LOVE LETTERS OF A STAR(1936)

Maurice Rice
1984
SPLASH(1984)

Milt Rice
INVASION OF THE BODY SNATCHERS(1956), spec eff; SOME LIKE IT HOT(1959), spec eff; MAGNIFICENT SEVEN, THE(1960), spec eff; ONE, TWO, THREE(1961), spec eff; KID GALAHAD(1962), spec eff; MAGIC SWORD, THE(1962), spec eff; GRAND PRIX(1966), spec eff; MAYA(1966), spec eff; VILLA RIDES(1968), spec eff; HEX(1973), spec eff; W. W. AND THE DIXIE DANCEKINGS(1975), spec eff; DAMNATION ALLEY(1977), spec eff; ONE-TRICK PONY(1980), spec eff

Milton Rice
WORLD WITHOUT END(1956), spec eff; IRMA LA DOUCE(1963), spec eff; KISS ME, STUPID(1964), spec eff; LAST MOVIE, THE(1971), spec eff; OUTLAW BLUES(1977), spec eff

Miriam Rice
Misc. Talkies
BORDER MENACE, THE(1934)

Nick Rice
MAN, A WOMAN, AND A BANK, A(1979, Can.)

Nicolas Rice
GREY FOX, THE(1983, Can.)

Norman Rice
MIRACLE OF OUR LADY OF FATIMA, THE(1952)

Peter Rice
THREE MEN IN A BOAT(1958, Brit.), cos

Robert Rice
COUNTERSPY MEETS SCOTLAND YARD(1950)

Ron Rice
FLOWER THIEF, THE(1962), p,d,w,&ed
Misc. Talkies
QUEEN OF SHEBA MEETS THE ATOM MAN, THE(1963), d

Roy Rice
ON PROBATION(1935); DESERT GUNS(1936)
Silents
HONOR SYSTEM, THE(1917)

Sam Rice
MISS PACIFIC FLEET(1935); POLO JOE(1936); CONFESSION(1937); EVER SINCE EVE(1937); MAGNIFICENT AMBERSONS, THE(1942)

Stan Rice
BILLY JACK(1971)

Taft Rice
TEMPTATION(1936)

Tim Rice
JESUS CHRIST, SUPERSTAR(1973), w; ENTERTAINER, THE(1975), m

Timothy Rice
D.C. CAB(1983)

Rice & Cady
THIS IS MY AFFAIR(1937)

Mandy Rice-Davies
RABBI AND THE SHIKSE, THE(1976, Israel)

Mandy Rice-Davis
NANA(1983, Ital.)

Ricet-Barrier
ARMY GAME, THE(1963, Fr.), a, m

Adam Rich
DEVIL AND MAX DEVLIN, THE(1981)

Allan Rich
SERPICO(1973); GAMBLER, THE(1974); HAPPY HOOKER, THE(1975); UNCLE JOE SHANNON(1978); FRISCO KID, THE(1979); VOICES(1979); HERO AT LARGE(1980); LEO AND LOREE(1980); EATING RAOUL(1982); ENTITY, THE(1982); FRANCES(1982)

Anthony Rich
TANK COMMANDOS(1959)

Arnold Rich
MAN AND BOY(1972), ph

Bernie Rich
SABU AND THE MAGIC RING(1957)

Bob Rich
MATING SEASON, THE(1951)

Buddy Rich
HOW'S ABOUT IT?(1943)

Charles G. Rich
Silents
LOYAL LIVES(1923), w

Charlie Rich
TAKE THIS JOB AND SHOVE IT(1981)

Claude Rich
LOVE AND THE FRENCHWOMAN(1961, Fr.); SEVEN CAPITAL SINS(1962, Fr./Ital.); ELUSIVE CORPORAL, THE(1963, Fr.); MALE HUNT(1965, Fr./Ital.); MATA HARI(1965, Fr./Ital.); IS PARIS BURNING?(1966, U.S./Fr.); WEB OF FEAR(1966, Fr./Span.); BRIDE WORE BLACK, THE(1968, Fr./Ital.); GIRL GAME(1968, Braz./Fr./Ital.); JE T'AIME, JE T'AIME(1972, Fr./Swed.); STAVISKY(1974, Fr.); 1★2?(1975, Fr.)
1984
LE CRABE TAMBOUR(1984, Fr.)

David Lowell Rich
CONCORDE, THE–AIRPORT '79(, d; NO TIME TO BE YOUNG(1957), d; SENIOR PROM(1958), d; HAVE ROCKET, WILL TRAVEL(1959), d; HEY BOY! HEY GIRL!(1959), d; MADAME X(1966), d; PLAINSMAN, THE(1966), d; ROSIE!(1967), d; LOVELY WAY TO DIE, A(1968), d; THREE GUNS FOR TEXAS(1968), d; EYE OF THE CAT(1969), d; THAT MAN BOLT(1973), d; CHU CHU AND THE PHILLY FLASH(1981), d

Dick Rich
HEADIN' EAST(1937); ADVENTURES OF MARCO POLO, THE(1938); ANGELS WITH DIRTY FACES(1938); HARD TO GET(1938); HUNTED MEN(1938); SWEETHEARTS(1938); ANGELS WASH THEIR FACES(1939); EACH DAWN I DIE(1939); HELL'S KITCHEN(1939); LET FREEDOM RING(1939); SMASHING THE MONEY RING(1939); BRIGHAM YOUNG–FRONTIERSMAN(1940); CHAD HANNA(1940); DANGER AHEAD(1940); DARK COMMAND, THE(1940); DEVIL'S ISLAND(1940); GRAPES OF WRATH(1940); LUCKY CISCO KID(1940); MAN WHO TALKED TOO MUCH, THE(1940); MORTAL STORM, THE(1940); MURDER IN THE AIR(1940); PUBLIC DEB NO. 1(1940); TEAR GAS SQUAD(1940); DRESSED TO KILL(1941); HIGHWAY WEST(1941); MOB TOWN(1941); RIDE ON VAQUERO(1941); RISE AND SHINE(1941); STRANGE ALIBI(1941); WESTERN UNION(1941); I WAKE UP SCREAMING(1942); MURDER IN THE BIG HOUSE(1942); RIO RITA(1942); RUBBER RACKETEERS(1942); IN OLD OKLAHOMA(1943); SECRETS OF THE UNDERGROUND(1943); THANK YOUR LUCKY STARS(1943); THREE HEARTS FOR JULIA(1943); CRIME BY NIGHT(1944); JOHNNY DOESN'T LIVE HERE ANY MORE(1944); PRINCESS AND THE PIRATE, THE(1944); ROGER TOUHY, GANGSTER!(1944); STORY OF G.I. JOE, THE(1945); THIS MAN'S NAVY(1945); WITHIN THESE WALLS(1945); BURNING CROSS, THE(1947); KILLER AT LARGE(1947); VIOLENCE(1947); WALLS OF JERICHO(1948); OH, YOU BEAUTIFUL DOLL(1949); KISS TOMORROW GOODBYE(1950); BUGLES IN THE AFTERNOON(1952); OUTCASTS OF POKER FLAT, THE(1952); DREAM WIFE(1953); FIGHTING LAWMAN, THE(1953); NEANDERTHAL MAN, THE(1953); STEEL LADY, THE(1953); OVER-

LAND PACIFIC(1954); SEVEN BRIDES FOR SEVEN BROTHERS(1954); BLACK TUESDAY(1955); INSIDE DETROIT(1955); MAN ALONE, A(1955); RANSOM(1956); JAILHOUSE ROCK(1957)

Doris Rich
SANTA CLAUS CONQUERS THE MARTIANS(1964)

Dorothy Rich
STUDENT BODIES(1981)

Elisa Rich
SINGLE ROOM FURNISHED(1968)

Frances Rich
THIRTEENTH GUEST, THE(1932); UNHOLY LOVE(1932); DIAMOND TRAIL(1933); OFFICER 13(1933); ZOO IN BUDAPEST(1933)

Francis Rich
PILGRIMAGE(1933)

Frank Rich
SMALL CIRCLE OF FRIENDS, A(1980)

Fred Rich
JACK LONDON(1943), md

Freddie Rich
STAGE DOOR CANTEEN(1943), m

Freddy Rich
WAVE, A WAC AND A MARINE, A(1944), m, md

Frederic Efrem Rich
WALK IN THE SUN, A(1945), m

Gary Rich
MAHLER(1974, Brit.)

Gloria Rich
DESPERATE ADVENTURE, A(1938); KING OF THE NEWSBOYS(1938); OLD BARN DANCE, THE(1938); OUTLAWS OF SONORA(1938)

Irene Rich
PERFECT CRIME, THE(1928); WOMEN THEY TALK ABOUT(1928); THEY HAD TO SEE PARIS(1929); AMOS 'N' ANDY(1930); ON YOUR BACK(1930); SO THIS IS LONDON(1930); BEAU IDEAL(1931); CHAMP, THE(1931); FATHER'S SON(1931); FIVE AND TEN(1931); MAD PARADE, THE(1931); STRANGERS MAY KISS(1931); WICKED(1931); DOWN TO EARTH(1932); HER MAD NIGHT(1932); MANHATTAN TOWER(1932); THAT CERTAIN AGE(1938); EVERYBODY'S HOBBY(1939); LADY IN QUESTION, THE(1940); MORTAL STORM, THE(1940); QUEEN OF THE YUKON(1940); KEEPING COMPANY(1941); THREE SONS O'GUNS(1941); THIS TIME FOR KEEPS(1942); ANGEL AND THE BADMAN(1947); CALENDAR GIRL(1947); NEW ORLEANS(1947); FORT APACHE(1948); JOAN OF ARC(1948)
Silents
OLD WIVES FOR NEW(1918); MAN IN THE OPEN, A(1919); STOP THIEF(1920); INVISIBLE POWER, THE(1921; JUST OUT OF COLLEGE(1921); POVERTY OF RICHES, THE(1921); TALE OF TWO WORLDS, A(1921); VOICE IN THE DARK(1921); ONE CLEAR CALL(1922); TRAP, THE(1922); BOY OF MINE(1923); ROSITA(1923); YESTERDAY'S WIFE(1923); BEAU BRUMMEL(1924); CAPTAIN JANUARY(1924); CYTHEREA(1924); LOST LADY, A(1924); COMPROMISE(1925); EVE'S LOVER(1925); LADY WINDERMERE'S FAN(1925); WOMAN WHO SINNED, A(1925); SILVER SLAVE, THE(1927); CRAIG'S WIFE(1928); POWDER MY BACK(1928); EXALTED FLAPPER, THE(1929); NED MCCOBB'S DAUGHTER(1929)
Misc. Silents
GIRL IN HIS HOUSE, THE(1918); TODD OF THE TIMES(1919); BLUE BONNET, THE(1920); JES' CALL ME JIM(1920); STRANGE BORDER, THE(1920); STREET CALLED STRAIGHT, THE(1920); WATER, WATER, EVERYWHERE(1920); BOYS WILL BE BOYS(1921); DESPERATE TRAILS(1921); ONE MAN IN A MILLION(1921); SUNSET JONES(1921); BRAWN OF THE NORTH(1922); CALL OF HOME, THE(1922); FOOL THERE WAS, A(1922); STRENGTH OF THE PINES(1922); WHILE JUSTICE WAITS(1922); YOSEMITE TRAIL, THE(1922); BRASS(1923); DANGEROUS TRAILS(1923); DEFYING DESTINY(1923); LUCRETIA LOMBARD(1923); MICHAEL O'HALLORAN(1923); BEHOLD THIS WOMAN(1924); BEING RESPECTABLE(1924); CYTHEREA(1924); PAL O'MINE(1924); THIS WOMAN(1924); WHAT THE BUTLER SAW(1924, Brit.); MAN WITHOUT A CONSCIENCE, THE(1925); MY WIFE AND I(1925); PLEASURE BUYERS, THE(1925); WIFE WHO WASN'T WANTED, THE(1925); HONEYMOON EXPRESS, THE(1926); MY OFFICIAL WIFE(1926); SILKEN SHACKLES(1926); CLIMBERS, THE(1927); DEARIE(1927); DESIRED WOMAN, THE(1927); DON'T TELL THE WIFE(1927); BEWARE OF MARRIED MEN(1928); DAUGHTERS OF DESIRE(1929); SHANGHAI ROSE(1929)

Jack Rich
Silents
MILLION FOR LOVE, A(1928)

John Rich
WOMAN IN THE DARK(1952), ed; GOLDEN BLADE, THE(1953), w; SECURITY RISK(1954), w; WIVES AND LOVERS(1963), d; NEW INTERNS, THE(1964), d; ROUSTABOUT(1964), d; BOEING BOEING(1965), d; EASY COME, EASY GO(1967), d

Lee Rich
MAN, THE(1972), p; CHOIRBOYS, THE(1977), p

Lee M. Rich
SPORTING CLUB, THE(1971), p

Lillian Rich
HIGH SEAS(1929, Brit.); GRIEF STREET(1931); ONCE A LADY(1931); DEVIL PAYS, THE(1932); RIP TIDE(1934); SHE MARRIED HER BOSS(1935); ARSENE LUPIN RETURNS(1938); LUCKY NIGHT(1939); DR. KILDARE'S CRISIS(1940)
Misc. Talkies
MARK OF THE SPUR(1932)
Silents
RED LANE, THE(1920); BEYOND(1921); BLAZING TRAIL, THE(1921); MILLIONAIRE, THE(1921); AFRAID TO FIGHT(1922); KENTUCKY DERBY, THE(1922); MAN TO MAN(1922); MAN FROM WYOMING, THE(1924); NEVER SAY DIE(1924); KISS IN THE DARK, A(1925); ISLE OF RETRIBUTION, THE(1926); WHISPERING SMITH(1926); WANTED–A COWARD(1927); WEB OF FATE(1927); OLD CODE, THE(1928); RED PEARLS(1930, Brit.)
Misc. Silents
DAY SHE PAID, THE(1919); DICE OF DESTINY(1920); FELIX O'DAY(1920); HALF A CHANCE(1920); GO STRAIGHT(1921); RUSE OF THE RATTLER, THE(1921); SAGE HEN, THE(1921); BEARCAT, THE(1922); CATCH MY SMOKE(1922); ONE WONDERFUL NIGHT(1922); CHEAP KISSES(1924); LOVE MASTER, THE(1924); PHANTOM HORSEMAN, THE(1924); BRAVEHEART(1925); GOLDEN BED, THE(1925); LOVE GAMBLE, THE(1925); SEVEN DAYS(1925); SHIP OF SOULS(1925); SIMON THE JESTER(1925); SOFT SHOES(1925); DANCING DAYS(1926); EXCLUSIVE RIGHTS(1926); GOLDEN WEB, THE(1926); GOD'S GREAT WILDERNESS(1927);

SNOWBOUND(1927); WOMAN'S LAW(1927); FORGER, THE(1928, Brit.); THAT'S MY DADDY(1928)

Margaret Rich
DREAMS OF GLASS(1969)

Marilyn Rich
TO PLEASE A LADY(1950)

Max Rich
WINK OF AN EYE(1958)

Mert Rich
1984
JOHNNY DANGEROUSLY(1984)

Michael Rich
SINGLE ROOM FURNISHED(1968)

Mila Rich
AMAZING MRS. HOLLIDAY(1943)

Monica Rich
NIGHT OF DARK SHADOWS(1971)

Nils Rich
'TILL WE MEET AGAIN(1944)

Pat Rich
VIOLATED(1953), ph

Phil Rich
ESCAPE FROM FORT BRAVO(1953); LONG, LONG TRAILER, THE(1954); SEVEN BRIDES FOR SEVEN BROTHERS(1954); TALL MAN RIDING(1955)

Richard Rich
FOX AND THE HOUND, THE(1981), d

Robert Rich
DREAM GIRL(1947); COUNTESS OF MONTE CRISTO, THE(1948)

Robert Rich III
1984
NATURAL, THE(1984)

Robert Rich "Dalton Trumbo"
BRAVE ONE, THE(1956), w

Ron Rich
FORTUNE COOKIE, THE(1966); CHUBASCO(1968)

Roy Rich
IT'S NOT CRICKET(1949, Brit.), d; MY BROTHER'S KEEPER(1949, Brit.), d

Royce Rich
1984
MOSCOW ON THE HUDSON(1984)

Shirley Rich
PUZZLE OF A DOWNFALL CHILD(1970)

Sigmund Rich
PUNISHMENT PARK(1971)

Ted Rich
CREATION OF THE HUMANOIDS(1962), art d

Tony Rich
WAR IS HELL(1964)

Vernon Rich
SELLOUT, THE(1951); DREAM WIFE(1953); WAR OF THE WORLDS, THE(1953); JOHNNY DARK(1954); FAR HORIZONS, THE(1955); I'LL CRY TOMORROW(1955); SCARLET COAT, THE(1955); STRATEGIC AIR COMMAND(1955); TALL MAN RIDING(1955); TARANTULA(1955); I'VE LIVED BEFORE(1956); OUTSIDE THE LAW(1956); LOVING YOU(1957); PERFECT FURLOUGH, THE(1958); 10 NORTH FREDERICK(1958); ONE MAN'S WAY(1964)

Vido Rich
AMAZING MRS. HOLLIDAY(1943)

Vivian Rich
Misc. Talkies
HELL'S VALLEY(1931)
Silents
MAN FROM MONTANA, THE(1917); LAST STRAW, THE(1920); LONE WAGON, THE(1924); OLD AGE HANDICAP(1928)
Misc. Silents
BRANDED SOUL, A(1917); PRICE OF SILENCE, THE(1917); CRIME OF THE HOUR(1918); CODE OF THE YUKON(1919); MINTS OF HELL, THE(1919); WORLD OF FOLLY, A(1920); WOULD YOU FORGIVE?(1920); BLIND CIRCUMSTANCES(1922); SHELL SHOCKED SAMMY(1923); UNBLAZED TRAIL(1923); MILE A MINUTE MORGAN(1924); MUST WE MARRY?(1928)

Rich & Galvin
MONEY TALKS(1933, Brit.)

Richard
SMOKEY AND THE BANDIT II(1980), stunts

Albert Richard
13TH HOUR, THE(1947), set d

Alexander Richard
CAGE OF EVIL(1960), w

Claude Maroel Richard
EXTERMINATORS, THE(1965 Fr.), w

Cliff Richard
EXPRESSO BONGO(1959, Brit.); IMMORAL CHARGE(1962, Brit.); WONDERFUL TO BE YOUNG!(1962, Brit.); SUMMER HOLIDAY(1963, Brit.); SWINGER'S PARADISE(1965, Brit.); FINDERS KEEPERS(1966, Brit.); TWO A PENNY(1968, Brit.); TAKE ME HIGH(1973, Brit.)

Cyril Richard
WINSLOW BOY, THE(1950)

Dawn Richard
I WAS A TEENAGE WEREWOLF(1957); LEGION OF THE DOOMED(1958); LIVE FAST, DIE YOUNG(1958)

Dick Richard
SNOW WHITE AND THE SEVEN DWARFS(1937), w

Ed Richard
OX-BOW INCIDENT, THE(1943); SAVAGE(1962), m

Edmond Richard
TRIAL, THE(1963, Fr./Ital./Ger.), ph; NIGHT OF LUST(1965, Fr.), ph; CHIMES AT MIDNIGHT(1967, Span.,Switz.), ph; DE L'AMOUR(1968, Fr./Ital.), ph; MANON 70(1968, Fr.), ph; YOUNG REBEL, THE(1969, Fr./Ital./Span.), ph; DISCREET CHARM OF THE BOURGEOISIE, THE(1972, Fr.), ph; PHANTOM OF LIBERTY, THE(1974, Fr.), ph; THAT OBSCURE OBJECT OF DESIRE(1977, Fr./Span.), ph; LES MISERABLES(1982, Fr.), ph

Eric Richard
FINAL CONFLICT, THE(1981); VENOM(1982, Brit.)
1984
KIPPERBANG(1984, Brit.); NUMBER ONE(1984, Brit.)
Frida Richard
AFFAIRS OF MAUPASSANT(1938, Aust.)
Silents
SIEGFRIED(1924, Ger.)
Misc. Silents
LEAP INTO LIFE(1924, Ger.); PEAKS OF DESTINY(1927, Ger.)
Frieda Richard
UNFINISHED SYMPHONY, THE(1953, Aust./Brit.)
Misc. Silents
NEW YEAR'S EVE(1923, Ger.); CINDERELLA(1926, Ger.)
Fritz Richard
Misc. Silents
GYPSY BLOOD(1921, Ger.)
Jack Richard
Misc. Silents
SUDDEN GENTLEMAN, THE(1917)
Jacques Richard
CROSS OF THE LIVING(1963. Fr)/; POSTMAN GOES TO WAR, THE(1968, Fr.); CHECKERBOARD(1969, Fr.); THINGS OF LIFE, THE(1970, Fr./Ital./Switz.); NO TIME FOR BREAKFAST(1978, Fr.)
1984
AVE MARIA(1984, Fr.), d, w
Jean Louis Richard
FAHRENHEIT 451(1966, Brit.), w
Jean Richard
SEVEN DEADLY SINS, THE(1953, Fr./Ital.); PARIS DOES STRANGE THINGS(1957, Fr./Ital.); ROYAL AFFAIRS IN VERSAILLES(1957, Fr.); LA BELLE AMERICAINE(1961, Fr.); CANDIDE(1962, Fr.); DIE GANS VON SEDAN(1962, Fr/Ger.); WAR OF THE BUTTONS(1963, Fr./Ital.); SWEET AND SOUR(1964, Fr./Ital.); DOUBLE BED, THE(1965, Fr./Ital.); COUNTERFEIT CONSTABLE, THE(1966, Fr.); OLDEST PROFESSION, THE(1968, Fr./Ital./Ger.)
Jean-Louis Richard
BREATHLESS(1959, Fr.); JULES AND JIM(1962, Fr.); SOFT SKIN, THE(1964, Fr.), a, w; MATA HARI(1965, Fr./Ital.), d, w; BRIDE WORE BLACK, THE(1968, Fr./Ital.), w; DIANE'S BODY(1969, Fr./Czech.), d; JE T'AIME, JE T'AIME(1972, Fr./Swed.); DAY FOR NIGHT(1973, Fr.), w; LAST METRO, THE(1981, Fr.); CONFIDENTIALLY YOURS(1983, Fr.)
1984
SWANN IN LOVE(1984, Fr.Ger.)
Jefferson Richard
Misc. Talkies
IN SEARCH OF GOLDEN SKY(1984), d
John Richard
VAMPIRE'S NIGHT ORGY, THE(1973, Span./Ital.)
Keith Richard
SNOW CREATURE, THE,(1954)
Little Richard
DON'T KNOCK THE ROCK(1956); GIRL CAN'T HELP IT, THE(1956); MISTER ROCK AND ROLL(1957); CATALINA CAPER, THE(1967)
Pat Richard
TEN COMMANDMENTS, THE(1956)
Philippe Richard
PEPE LE MOKO(1937, Fr.); CONFLICT(1939, Fr.); ROYAL AFFAIRS IN VERSAILLES(1957, Fr.)
Phillippe Richard
ALIBI, THE(1939, Fr.)
Pierre Richard
JOHNNY FRENCHMAN(1946, Brit.); HOT HOURS(1963, Fr.); VERY HAPPY ALEXANDER(1969, Fr.); TALL BLOND MAN WITH ONE BLACK SHOE, THE(1973, Fr.); DAYDREAMER, THE(1975, Fr.), a, p&d, w
1984
LES COMPERES(1984, Fr.)
Sweet Richard
ISLAND WOMEN(1958)
Thomas Richard
FLIGHT FROM DESTINY(1941), ed
Wally Richard
WAR OF THE WORLDS, THE(1953); BUCCANEER, THE(1958)
Walter Richard
QUERELLE(1983, Ger./Fr.), art d
Wendy Richard
NO BLADE OF GRASS(1970, Brit.); GUMSHOE(1972, Brit.)
Richard & The Taxmen
LOOKS AND SMILES(1982, Brit.), m
Richard Williams Studio
MURDER ON THE ORIENT EXPRESS(1974, Brit.), art d; PINK PANTHER STRIKES AGAIN, THE(1976, Brit.), anim
Pierre Richard-Willm
ANNE-MARIE(1936, Fr.); COURRIER SUD(1937, Fr.)
Tessa Richarde
BRONCO BILLY(1980); BEACH GIRLS(1982); CAT PEOPLE(1982); LAST AMERICAN VIRGIN, THE(1982); MAX DUGAN RETURNS(1983); NATIONAL LAMPOON'S VACATION(1983)
Addison Richards
BEYOND THE LAW(1934); BRITISH AGENT(1934); CASE OF THE HOWLING DOG, THE(1934); GENTLEMEN ARE BORN(1934); LET'S BE RITZY(1934); LONE COWBOY(1934); LOST LADY, A(1934); LOVE CAPTIVE, THE(1934); OUR DAILY BREAD(1934); ST. LOUIS KID, THE(1934); 365 NIGHTS IN HOLLYWOOD(1934); ALIAS MARY DOW(1935); CEILNG ZERO(1935); CRUSADES, THE(1935); DINKY(1935); DOG OF FLANDERS, A(1935); FRECKLES(1935); FRISCO KID(1935); FRONT PAGE WOMAN(1935); G-MEN(1935); HERE COMES THE BAND(1935); HOME ON THE RANGE(1935); LITTLE BIG SHOT(1935); SOCIETY DOCTOR(1935); SWEET MUSIC(1935); WHITE COCKATOO(1935); ANTHONY ADVERSE(1936); BULLETS OR BALLOTS(1936); CHINA CLIPPER(1936); COLLEEN(1936); EAGLE'S BROOD, THE(1936); HOT MONEY(1936); JAILBREAK(1936); LAW IN HER HANDS, THE(1936); MAN HUNT(1936); PETRIFIED FOREST, THE(1936); PUBLIC ENEMY'S

WIFE(1936); ROAD GANG(1936); SONG OF THE SADDLE(1936); SUTTER'S GOLD(1936); TRAILIN' WEST(1936); WALKING DEAD, THE(1936); ALCATRAZ ISLAND(1937); BARRIER, THE(1937); BLACK LEGION, THE(1937); DANCE, CHARLIE, DANCE(1937); DRAEGERMAN COURAGE(1937); EMPTY HOLSTERS(1937); GOD'S COUNTRY AND THE WOMAN(1937); HER HUSBAND'S SECRETARY(1937); LOVE IS ON THE AIR(1937); MR. DODD TAKES THE AIR(1937); READY, WILLING AND ABLE(1937); SINGING MARINE, THE(1937); SMART BLONDE(1937); WHITE BONDAGE(1937); WINE, WOMEN AND HORSES(1937); BLACK DOLL, THE(1938); BOYS TOWN(1938); FLIGHT TO FAME(1938); LAST EXPRESS, THE(1938); PRISON NURSE(1938); VALLEY OF THE GIANTS(1938); BAD LANDS(1939); BURN 'EM UP O'CONNER(1939); ESPIONAGE AGENT(1939); EXILE EXPRESS(1939); FOR LOVE OR MONEY(1939); GERONIMO(1939); INSIDE INFORMATION(1939); MYSTERY OF THE WHITE ROOM(1939); NICK CARTER, MASTER DETECTIVE(1939); OFF THE RECORD(1939); TELL NO TALES(1939); THEY ALL COME OUT(1939); THEY MADE HER A SPY(1939); THUNDER AFLOAT(1939); TWELVE CROWDED HOURS(1939); WHEN TOMORROW COMES(1939); WHISPERING ENEMIES(1939); ANDY HARDY MEETS DEBUTANTE(1940); ARIZONA(1940); CHARLIE CHAN IN PANAMA(1940); CHEROKEE STRIP(1940); EDISON, THE MAN(1940); FLIGHT ANGELS(1940); FLIGHT COMMAND(1940); GANGS OF CHICAGO(1940); GIRL FROM HAVANA(1940); GIVE US WINGS(1940); ISLAND OF DOOMED MEN(1940); LONE WOLF STRIKES, THE(1940); MAN FROM DAKOTA, THE(1940); MAN FROM MONTREAL, THE(1940); MOON OVER BURMA(1940); MY LITTLE CHICKADEE(1940); NORTHWEST PASSAGE(1940); PUBLIC DEB NO. 1(1940); SANTA FE TRAIL(1940); SLIGHTLY HONORABLE(1940); SOUTH TO KARANGA(1940); WYOMING(1940); ANDY HARDY'S PRIVATE SECRETARY(1941); BACK IN THE SADDLE(1941); BADLANDS OF DAKOTA(1941); BALL OF FIRE(1941); DIVE BOMBER(1941); GREAT LIE, THE(1941); HER FIRST BEAU(1941); I WANTED WINGS(1941); INTERNATIONAL SQUADRON(1941); MEN OF BOYS TOWN(1941); MUTINY IN THE ARCTIC(1941); SEALED LIPS(1941); SHERIFF OF TOMBSTONE(1941); STRAWBERRY BLONDE, THE(1941); TALL, DARK AND HANDSOME(1941); TEXAS(1941); TRIAL OF MARY DUGAN, THE(1941); WESTERN UNION(1941); A-HAUNTING WE WILL GO(1942); CLOSE CALL FOR ELLERY QUEEN, A(1942); COWBOY SERENADE(1942); FLYING TIGERS(1942); FRIENDLY ENEMIES(1942); LADY HAS PLANS, THE(1942); MAN WITH TWO LIVES, THE(1942); MEN OF TEXAS(1942); MY FAVORITE BLONDE(1942); PACIFIC RENDEZVOUS(1942); PRIDE OF THE ARMY(1942); PRIDE OF THE YANKEES, THE(1942); RIDIN' DOWN THE CANYON(1942); SECRET AGENT OF JAPAN(1942); SECRET ENEMIES(1942); SECRETS OF A CO-ED(1942); SEVEN DAYS LEAVE(1942); SHIP AHOY(1942); THEY DIED WITH THEIR BOOTS ON(1942); TOP SERGEANT(1942); UNDERGROUND AGENT(1942); WAR DOGS(1942); AIR FORCE(1943); ALWAYS A BRIDESMAID(1943); CORVETTE K-225(1943); DEERSLAYER(1943); DESTROYER(1943); GUY NAMED JOE, A(1943); HEADIN' FOR GOD'S COUNTRY(1943); MAD GHOUL, THE(1943); MYSTERY BROADCAST(1943); MYSTERY OF THE 13TH GUEST, THE(1943); SMART GUY(1943); WHERE ARE YOUR CHILDREN?(1943); ARE THESE OUR PARENTS?(1944); BARBARY COAST GENT(1944); FIGHTING SEABEES, THE(1944); FOLLOW THE BOYS(1944); MARRIAGE IS A PRIVATE AFFAIR(1944); MOON OVER LAS VEGAS(1944); MUMMY'S CURSE, THE(1944); NIGHT OF ADVENTURE, A(1944); ROGER TOUHY, GANGSTER!(1944); SINCE YOU WENT AWAY(1944); SULLIVANS, THE(1944); THREE LITTLE SISTERS(1944); THREE MEN IN WHITE(1944); ADVENTURES OF RUSTY(1945); BELLS OF ROSARITA(1945); BETRAYAL FROM THE EAST(1945); BEWITCHED(1945); CHICAGO KID, THE(1945); COME OUT FIGHTING(1945); DANGER SIGNAL(1945); DIVORCE(1945); DUFFY'S TAVERN(1945); GRISSLY'S MILLIONS(1945); I'LL REMEMBER APRIL(1945); LADY ON A TRAIN(1945); MEN IN HER DIARY(1945); ROUGH, TOUGH AND READY(1945); SHANGHAI COBRA, THE(1945); SPELLBOUND(1945); STRANGE CONFESSION(1945); TIGER WOMAN, THE(1945); ANGEL ON MY SHOULDER(1946); ANNA AND THE KING OF SIAM(1946); BLACK MARKET BABIES(1946); COURAGE OF LASSIE(1946); CRIMINAL COURT(1946); DON'T GAMBLE WITH STRANGERS(1946); DRAGONWYCH(1946); HOODLUM SAINT, THE(1946); LEAVE HER TO HEAVEN(1946); LOVE LAUGHS AT ANDY HARDY(1946); RENEGADES(1946); SECRETS OF A SORORITY GIRL(1946); STEP BY STEP(1946); MILLERSON CASE, THE(1947); MONSIEUR VERDOUX(1947); CALL NORTHSIDE 777(1948); IF YOU KNEW SUSIE(1948); LULU BELLE(1948); SAXON CHARM, THE(1948); SOUTHERN YANKEE, A(1948); HENRY, THE RAINMAKER(1949); MIGHTY JOE YOUNG(1949); RUSTLERS(1949); DAVY CROCKETT, INDIAN SCOUT(1950); FORT YUMA(1955); HIGH SOCIETY(1955); ILLEGAL(1955); BROKEN STAR(1956); EVERYTHING BUT THE TRUTH(1956); FASTEST GUN ALIVE(1956); FURY AT GUNSIGHT PASS(1956); REPRISAL(1956); TEN COMMANDMENTS, THE(1956); WALK THE PROUD LAND(1956); WHEN GANGLAND STRIKES(1956); GUNSIGHT RIDGE(1957); LAST OF THE BADMEN(1957); SAGA OF HEMP BROWN, THE(1958); OREGON TRAIL, THE(1959); ALL THE FINE YOUNG CANNIBALS(1960); DARK AT THE TOP OF THE STAIRS, THE(1960); FLIGHT THAT DISAPPEARED, THE(1961); FRONTIER UPRISING(1961); GAMBLER WORE A GUN, THE(1961); SAINTLY SINNERS(1962); FOR THOSE WHO THINK YOUNG(1964); RAIDERS, THE(1964)
Misc. Talkies
RIOT SQUAD(1933); BORDERTOWN TRAIL(1944)
Alexander Richards
THUNDER IN CAROLINA(1960), w
Allen Richards
RUN HOME SLOW(1965)
Ann Richards
DR. GILLESPIE'S NEW ASSISTANT(1942); RANDOM HARVEST(1942); THREE HEARTS FOR JULIA(1943); AMERICAN ROMANCE, AN(1944); LOVE LETTERS(1945); BADMAN'S TERRITORY(1946); SEARCHING WIND, THE(1946); LOST HONEYMOON(1947); LOVE FROM A STRANGER(1947); SORRY, WRONG NUMBER(1948); BREAKDOWN(1953)
Misc. Talkies
HIDEOUT IN THE SUN(1960)
Anthony Richards
Misc. Talkies
ONE PAGE OF LOVE(1979)
Aubrey Richards
LAST DAYS OF DOLWYN, THE(1949, Brit.); IPCRESS FILE, THE(1965, Brit.); IT!(1967, Brit.); MAN WHO HAUNTED HIMSELF, THE(1970, Brit.); SAVAGE MESSIAH(1972, Brit.); UNDER MILK WOOD(1973, Brit.)
B. Richards
PALM SPRINGS WEEKEND(1963), cos

B.W. Richards
HEADLEYS AT HOME, THE(1939), p
Beah Richards
TAKE A GIANT STEP(1959); MIRACLE WORKER, THE(1962); GONE ARE THE DAYS(1963); GUESS WHO'S COMING TO DINNER(1967); HURRY SUNDOWN(1967); IN THE HEAT OF THE NIGHT(1967); GREAT WHITE HOPE, THE(1970); BISCUIT EATER, THE(1972); MAHOGANY(1975)
Bernie Richards
PARRISH(1961)
Bessie Richards
FINAL RECKONING, THE(1932, Brit.)
Silents
FLAMES OF FEAR(1930, Brit.)
Bill Richards
KISSES FOR MY PRESIDENT(1964); PENNIES FROM HEAVEN(1981)
Bill K. Richards
TO BE OR NOT TO BE(1983)
Billie Richards
WILLIE MCBEAN AND HIS MAGIC MACHINE(1965, U.S./Jap.)
Bob Richards
SNOWFIRE(1958), cos; HANNIE CALDER(1971, Brit.), w
Bobby Richards
SATURDAY NIGHT OUT(1964, Brit.), m, md; SCHOOL FOR UNCLAIMED GIRLS(1973, Brit.), m
C. M. Pennington Richards
HEADLINE HUNTERS(1968, Brit.), w
Misc. Talkies
SKY PIRATES(1977, Brit.), d
C. Pennington Richards
SALT TO THE DEVIL(1949, Brit.), ph; WOMAN IN THE HALL, THE(1949, Brit.), ph; SOMETHING MONEY CAN'T BUY(1952, Brit.), ph; WHITE CORRIDORS(1952, Brit.), ph; DESPERATE MOMENT(1953, Brit.), ph; HORSE'S MOUTH, THE(1953, Brit.), d; FORBIDDEN CARGO(1954, Brit.), ph; HOUR OF DECISION(1957, Brit.), d
Carl Richards
Silents
EXIT SMILING(1926)
Claire Richards
DOLLY SISTERS, THE(1945); SHOCK(1946); I WONDER WHO'S KISSING HER NOW(1947); DANCING IN THE DARK(1949)
Colin Richards
RUDE BOY(1980, Brit.)
Cully Richards
STOLEN HARMONY(1935); IT HAD TO HAPPEN(1936); SING, BABY, SING(1936); HERE'S FLASH CASEY(1937); PICK A STAR(1937); SOMETHING TO SING ABOUT(1937); SWEETHEART OF THE NAVY(1937); SWING IT SAILOR(1937); ALEXANDER'S RAGTIME BAND(1938); MY LUCKY STAR(1938); HERO FOR A DAY(1939); LET'S FACE IT(1943); PIRATE, THE(1948); RACE STREET(1948); YOUNG RUNAWAYS, THE(1968)
Danny Richards, Jr.
CLOWN, THE(1953); HELL SHIP MUTINY(1957)
Darroll Richards
FACING THE MUSIC(1933, Brit.)
David Richards
SANDY THE SEAL(1969, Brit.)
Dennis Richards
YOUNG AND THE BRAVE, THE(1963)
Diane Richards
GIRLS IN PRISON(1956)
Dick Richards
HER KIND OF MAN(1946), ed; GIRL FEVER(1961); "IMP"PROBABLE MR. WEE GEE, THE(1966); GRASSHOPPER, THE(1970); CULPEPPER CATTLE COMPANY, THE(1972), d, w; FAREWELL, MY LOVELY(1975), d; RAFFERTY AND THE GOLD DUST TWINS(1975), d; MARCH OR DIE(1977, Brit.), p, d, w; TOOTSIE(1982), p; MAN, WOMAN AND CHILD(1983), d
Silents
KING OF KINGS, THE(1927)
Don Richards
IT SHOULD HAPPEN TO YOU(1954)
Doreen Richards
THREE WEIRD SISTERS, THE(1948, Brit.); LAST DAYS OF DOLWYN, THE(1949, Brit.); LITTLE BALLERINA, THE(1951, Brit.)
E. G. Richards
HUMAN MONSTER, THE(1940, Brit.), ed
E.G. Richards
WANTED BY SCOTLAND YARD(1939, Brit.), ed
Earl Richards
FIFTH AVENUE GIRL(1939); THAT TENNESSEE BEAT(1966)
Misc. Talkies
GIRL FROM TOBACCO ROW, THE(1966)
Earl "Snake" Richards
WHITE LIGHTNIN' ROAD(1967)
Elizabeth Richards
MONEY, THE(1975)
Emil Richards
1984
EL NORTE(1984), m
Evan Richards
TWILIGHT ZONE–THE MOVIE(1983)
Frances Richards
LIVING GHOST, THE(1942)
Francis Richards
MAN WITH TWO LIVES, THE(1942)
Frank Richards
BEFORE I HANG(1940); HOLD THAT GHOST(1941); PUBLIC ENEMIES(1941); CAIRO(1942); MAN'S WORLD, A(1942); HOUSE ON 92ND STREET, THE(1945); GUNMAN'S CODE(1946), art d; DOUBLE LIFE, A(1947); APPOINTMENT WITH MURDER(1948); COWBOY AND THE INDIANS, THE(1949); PRISON WARDEN(1949); SET-UP, THE(1949); SLATTERY'S HURRICANE(1949); THIEVES' HIGHWAY(1949); THREAT, THE(1949); TOUGH ASSIGNMENT(1949); FATHER OF THE BRIDE(1950); KIM(1950); NO WAY OUT(1950); WESTERN PACIFIC AGENT(1950);

SCARF, THE(1951); SOUTH OF CALIENTE(1951); CARBINE WILLIAMS(1952); PAT AND MIKE(1952); STOP, YOU'RE KILLING ME(1952); CLIPPED WINGS(1953); MONEY FROM HOME(1953); PRISONERS OF THE CASBAH(1953); SAVAGE, THE(1953); SYSTEM, THE(1953); DESTRY(1954); REDHEAD FROM MANHATTAN(1954); TENNESSEE CHAMP(1954); GANG BUSTERS(1955); GUYS AND DOLLS(1955); MAN WITH THE GOLDEN ARM, THE(1955); PIRATES OF TRIPOLI(1955); THUNDER OVER SANGOLAND(1955); DAVY CROCKETT AND THE RIVER PIRATES(1956); MAN FROM DEL RIO(1956); RUNNING TARGET(1956); SPY CHASERS(1956); HARD MAN, THE(1957); PERSUADER, THE(1957); STORM RIDER, THE(1957); CRY BABY KILLER, THE(1958); ESCAPE FROM RED ROCK(1958); LONELYHEARTS(1958); REVOLT IN THE BIG HOUSE(1958); TEACHER'S PET(1958); ARSON FOR HIRE(1959); WOMAN UNDER THE INFLUENCE, A(1974)
Frank A. Richards
RUSTLER'S ROUNDUP(1946), art d; BUCK PRIVATES COME HOME(1947), art d; VIGILANTES RETURN, THE(1947), art d; FEUDIN', FUSSIN' AND A-FIGHTIN'(1948), art d; TAP ROOTS(1948), art d; RED CANYON(1949), art d
Fred Richards
MISSING WITNESSES(1937), ed; BELOVED BRAT(1938), ed; ALIMONY(1949)
Frederick B. Richards
BLAZING SIXES(1937), ed
Frederick Richards
GIRLS ON PROBATION(1938), ed; TORCHY BLANE IN CHINATOWN(1938), ed; CODE OF THE SECRET SERVICE(1939), ed; KID NIGHTINGALE(1939), ed; GAMBLING ON THE HIGH SEAS(1940), ed; BODY DISAPPEARS, THE(1941), ed; LAW OF THE TROPICS(1941), ed; PASSAGE FROM HONG KONG(1941), ed; WAGONS ROLL AT NIGHT, THE(1941), ed; MASK OF DIMITRIOS, THE(1944), ed; CORN IS GREEN, THE(1945), ed; HOTEL BERLIN(1945), ed; TWO MRS. CARROLLS, THE(1947), ed; UNSUSPECTED(1947), ed; DECISION OF CHRISTOPHER BLAKE, THE(1948), ed; ONE LAST FLING(1949), ed; YOUNGER BROTHERS, THE(1949), ed; MONTANA(1950), ed
Gavin Richards
TRIPLE ECHO, THE(1973, Brit.)
Gladys Richards
BIGGER THAN LIFE(1956)
Gordon Richards
WIFE TAKES A FLYER, THE(1942); DREAMING(1944, Brit.); FRENCHMAN'S CREEK(1944); MRS. PARKINGTON(1944); NATIONAL VELVET(1944); KITTY(1945); MOLLY AND ME(1945); WEEKEND AT THE WALDORF(1945); WHITE PONGO(1945); FLIGHT TO NOWHERE(1946); LARCENY IN HER HEART(1946); NIGHT AND DAY(1946); UNDERCURRENT(1946); GOLDEN EARRINGS(1947); IMPERFECT LADY, THE(1947); LINDA BE GOOD(1947); THIRTEEN LEAD SOLDIERS(1948); WOMEN IN THE NIGHT(1948); BIG HANGOVER, THE(1950); KISS TOMORROW GOODBYE(1950); MAN WHO CHEATED HIMSELF, THE(1951); MILLION DOLLAR MERMAID(1952); PRISONER OF ZENDA, THE(1952); DREAM WIFE(1953); TITANIC(1953); RAINBOW JACKET, THE(1954, Brit.); ROSE MARIE(1954); PRODIGAL, THE(1955); SCARLET COAT, THE(1955); TENDER TRAP, THE(1955); HIGH SOCIETY(1956); OPPOSITE SEX, THE(1956)
Grant Richards
HOPALONG CASSIDY RETURNS(1936); LOVE ON TOAST(1937); NIGHT OF MYSTERY(1937); ON SUCH A NIGHT(1937); MY OLD KENTUCKY HOME(1938); UNDER THE BIG TOP(1938); INSIDE INFORMATION(1939); RISKY BUSINESS(1939); ISLE OF DESTINY(1940); JUST OFF BROADWAY(1942); GUNS, GIRLS AND GANGSTERS(1958); FOUR SKULLS OF JONATHAN DRAKE, THE(1959); INSIDE THE MAFIA(1959); MUSIC BOX KID, THE(1960); OKLAHOMA TERRITORY(1960); TWELVE HOURS TO KILL(1960); SECRET OF DEEP HARBOR(1961); YOU HAVE TO RUN FAST(1961)
Gwil Richards
IT'S ALIVE(1974); MOTEL HELL(1980); MAN, WOMAN AND CHILD(1983)
Hal Richards
MAN OF CONFLICT(1953), w; PEACEMAKER, THE(1956), w
Hugh Richards
SOUTHERN STAR, THE(1969, Fr./Brit.), makeup; PUBLIC EYE, THE(1972, Brit.), makeup
Irene Richards
MONEY MEANS NOTHING(1932, Brit.)
Ivor Richards
TELL ME LIES(1968, Brit.)
Jack L. Richards
MONKEY HUSTLE, THE(1976), ph; BEAST WITHIN, THE(1982), ph
Jack Richards
FINNEY(1969), ph; ON THE RIGHT TRACK(1981), ph
Jackie Richards
GIRL GRABBERS, THE(1968)
Jackson Richards
TRAILING THE KILLER(1932), w
Janelle Richards
SOME CAME RUNNING(1959); THIS EARTH IS MINE(1959)
Janet Richards
YOU KNOW WHAT SAILORS ARE(1954, Brit.)
Jay Richards
FORCE OF ARMS(1951)
Jean Richards
CAESAR AND CLEOPATRA(1946, Brit.)
Jeff Richards
FIGHTER SQUADRON(1948); GIRL FROM JONES BEACH, THE(1949); ANGELS IN THE OUTFIELD(1951); PEOPLE AGAINST O'HARA, THE(1951); SELLOUT, THE(1951); STRIP, THE(1951); TALL TARGET, THE(1951); DESPERATE SEARCH(1952); ABOVE AND BEYOND(1953); BATTLE CIRCUS(1953); BIG LEAGUER(1953); CODE TWO(1953); CREST OF THE WAVE(1954, Brit.); SEVEN BRIDES FOR SEVEN BROTHERS(1954); BAR SINISTER, THE(1955); MANY RIVERS TO CROSS(1955); MARAUDERS, THE(1955); OPPOSITE SEX, THE(1956); BORN RECKLESS(1959); ISLAND OF LOST WOMEN(1959); SECRET OF THE PURPLE REEF, THE(1960); WACO(1966); DON'T GO NEAR THE WATER(1975)
Jennifer Richards
Misc. Talkies
C.O.D.(1983)
Jill Richards
STARLIFT(1951)

Jocelyn Richards
LOOK BACK IN ANGER(1959), cos; SAILOR FROM GIBRALTAR, THE(1967, Brit.), cos; BLISS OF MRS. BLOSSOM, THE(1968, Brit.), cos; INTERLUDE(1968, Brit.), cos; SUNDAY BLOODY SUNDAY(1971, Brit.), cos

Johnny Richards
GOLD FEVER(1952), m

Jon Richards
I NEVER SANG FOR MY FATHER(1970); SHAFT(1971); ANNIE(1982)

Joseph Richards
COLORADO RANGER(1950)

Kathie Richards
DARK, THE(1979)

Keith Richards
BUY ME THAT TOWN(1941); NOTHING BUT THE TRUTH(1941); ONE NIGHT IN LISBON(1941); SECRETS OF THE WASTELANDS(1941); SKYLARK(1941); WEST POINT WIDOW(1941); FOREST RANGERS, THE(1942); HENRY ALDRICH GETS GLAMOUR(1942); LADY HAS PLANS, THE(1942); LUCKY JORDAN(1942); PALM BEACH STORY, THE(1942); REAP THE WILD WIND(1942); STAR SPANGLED RHYTHM(1942); STREET OF CHANCE(1942); TAKE A LETTER, DARLING(1942); WAKE ISLAND(1942); AERIAL GUNNER(1943); ALASKA HIGHWAY(1943); LOST CANYON(1943); NO TIME FOR LOVE(1943); MIRACLE OF MORGAN'S CREEK, THE(1944); DANGER WOMAN(1946); QUEEN OF THE AMAZONS(1947); ROAD TO THE BIG HOUSE(1947); SEVEN WERE SAVED(1947); TWILIGHT ON THE RIO GRANDE(1947); GAY RANCHERO, THE(1948); SONS OF ADVENTURE(1948); TAP ROOTS(1948); WALK A CROOKED MILE(1948); CAPTAIN CHINA(1949); DUKE OF CHICAGO(1949); SHADOWS OF THE WEST(1949); TRAIL'S END(1949); BLONDE BANDIT, THE(1950); NORTH OF THE GREAT DIVIDE(1950); SPOILERS OF THE PLAINS(1951); TALES OF ROBIN HOOD(1951); WHEN WORLDS COLLIDE(1951); GREATEST SHOW ON EARTH, THE(1952); BLADES OF THE MUSKETEERS(1953); REBEL CITY(1953); AT GUNPOINT(1955); YAQUI DRUMS(1956); BUSTER KEATON STORY, THE(1957); UNTAMED YOUTH(1957); AMBUSH AT CIMARRON PASS(1958); GAMBLER WORE A GUN, THE(1961); INCIDENT IN AN ALLEY(1962)

Kim Richards
ESCAPE TO WITCH MOUNTAIN(1975); ASSAULT ON PRECINCT 13(1976); NO DEPOSIT, NO RETURN(1976); SPECIAL DELIVERY(1976); CAR, THE(1977); RETURN FROM WITCH MOUNTAIN(1978)
1984
MEATBALLS PART II(1984)

Kyle Richards
CAR, THE(1977); HALLOWEEN(1978); WATCHER IN THE WOODS, THE(1980, Brit.); HALLOWEEN II(1981)

Laura E. Richards
CAPTAIN JANUARY(1935), w

Laura Elizabeth Richards
Silents
CAPTAIN JANUARY(1924), w

Leoda Richards
LET'S DO IT AGAIN(1953); FRENCH LINE, THE(1954)

Lexford Richards
SPECIAL DELIVERY(1955, Ger.)

Lilia Richards
WILD BUNCH, THE(1969)

Lisa Blake Richards
HEAVEN CAN WAIT(1978); MAN WHO LOVED WOMEN, THE(1983)

Lisa Richards
HOUSE OF DARK SHADOWS(1970); ROLLING THUNDER(1977)

Lorrie Richards
MAGIC SWORD, THE(1962); TRAUMA(1962)

Lou Richards
SENIORS, THE(1978)
Misc. Talkies
SENIORS, THE(1978)

Louanne Richards
HALF A SIXPENCE(1967, Brit.)

Lowri Ann Richards
BREAKING GLASS(1980, Brit.)

Gerald Richards
Misc. Talkies
ALL THE YOUNG WIVES(1975); NAKED RIVER(1977)

Joanna Richards
Misc. Talkies
NAUGHTY GIRLS ON THE LOOSE(1976)

Mae Richards
MEET THE NAVY(1946, Brit.)

Malcolm Richards
BUSH CHRISTMAS(1983, Aus.), ph

Marc Richards
FIVE MAN ARMY, THE(1970, Ital.), w

Marcella Richards
SHE'S IN THE ARMY(1942)

Martin Richards
BOYS FROM BRAZIL, THE(1978), p; FORT APACHE, THE BRONX(1981), p

Marty Richards
SOME OF MY BEST FRIENDS ARE...(1971), p

Mary Richards
Misc. Silents
BURDEN OF PROOF, THE(1918)

Michael Richards
YOUNG DOCTORS IN LOVE(1982)

Mike Richards
THAT'S THE WAY OF THE WORLD(1975)

Moe Richards
WIRE SERVICE(1942)

Nellie Richards
Silents
MANXMAN, THE(1929, Brit.)

Otto Richards
STEAMBOAT ROUND THE BEND(1935)

Paul E. Richards
STRANGE ONE, THE(1957); BEACH GIRLS(1982)

Paul Richards
FIXED BAYONETS(1951); WAR PAINT(1953); DEMETRIUS AND THE GLADIATORS(1954); PHANTOM OF THE RUE MORGUE(1954); PLAYGIRL(1954); PUSHOVER(1954); KISS ME DEADLY(1955); TALL MAN RIDING(1955); BLACK WHIP, THE(1956); HOUSTON STORY, THE(1956); SCANDAL INCORPORATED(1956); TENSION AT TABLE ROCK(1956); HOT SUMMER NIGHT(1957); MONKEY ON MY BACK(1957); UNKNOWN TERROR, THE(1957); BLOOD ARROW(1958); FOUR FAST GUNS(1959); ALL THE YOUNG MEN(1960); ST. VALENTINE'S DAY MASSACRE, THE(1967); BENEATH THE PLANET OF THE APES(1970)
Misc. Talkies
TRIANGLE(1971)

Peggy Richards
Silents
TAILOR OF BOND STREET, THE(1916, Brit.)
Misc. Silents
DO UNTO OTHERS(1915, Brit.); STOLEN SACRIFICE, THE(1916, Brit.)

Pennington Richards
FRIGHTENED BRIDE, THE(1952, Brit.), ph

Phillip Herzog Richards
1984
HOT MOVES(1984), cos

Phillip Richards
MOLLY MAGUIRES, THE(1970)

Phylip Richards
ROCKERS(1980)

R. Astley Richards
BAD BOY(1938, Brit.), w

Ramona Richards
WANDA NEVADA(1979)

Rex Richards
WILD WOMEN OF WONGO, THE(1959)

Robert Richards
LOUISIANA HUSSY(1960); INCREDIBLE MR. LIMPET, THE(1964), cos; BLACK TORMENT, THE(1965, Brit.), m; GOOD GUYS AND THE BAD GUYS, THE(1969), cos

Robert L. Richards
RAMPARTS WE WATCH, THE(1940), w; LAST CROOKED MILE, THE(1946), w; ONE SUNDAY AFTERNOON(1948), w; ACT OF VIOLENCE(1949), w; JOHNNY STOOL PIGEON(1949), w; KANSAS RAIDERS(1950), w; WINCHESTER '73(1950), w; AIR CADET(1951), w

Roberta Richards
RHUBARB(1951)

Rolf Richards
HOTEL SAHARA(1951, Brit.)

Rosa Richards
Misc. Silents
FORBIDDEN LOVE(1927, Brit.)

Sal Richards
EYES OF LAURA MARS(1978); DEATH VENGEANCE(1982)
1984
OVER THE BROOKLYN BRIDGE(1984)

Shary Richards
PSYCHO A GO-GO!(1965)

Sheila Richards
MY HANDS ARE CLAY(1948, Irish)

Shirley Ann Richards
IT ISN'T DONE(1937, Aus.); TALL TIMBERS(1937, Aus.); DAD AND DAVE COME TO TOWN(1938, Aus.); LOVERS AND LUGGERS(1938, Aus.); ANTS IN HIS PANTS(1940, Aus.)
Misc. Talkies
TIMBERLAND TERROR(1940, Aus.)

Shirley Ann Richards [Ann Richards]
VENGEANCE OF THE DEEP(1940, Aus.)

Silvia Richards
POSSESSED(1947), w; SECRET BEYOND THE DOOR, THE(1948), w; TOMAHAWK(1951), w; RUBY GENTRY(1952), w

Sindee Anne Richards
FOOL KILLER, THE(1965)

Stan Richards
MOVE OVER, DARLING(1963)

Stephen Richards
DESTINATION TOKYO(1944); GOD IS MY CO-PILOT(1945); PRIDE OF THE MARINES(1945)

Stephen Richards [Mark Stevens]
DOUGHGIRLS, THE(1944)

Steve Richards
HOLLYWOOD CANTEEN(1944)

Stewart Richards
DEVIL AND DANIEL WEBSTER, THE(1941)

Stoney Richards
1984
BEST DEFENSE(1984)

Susan Richards
ROCKING HORSE WINNER, THE(1950, Brit.); VILLAGE OF THE DAMNED(1960, Brit.); PART-TIME WIFE(1961, Brit.); HAUNTING, THE(1963); NEVER PUT IT IN WRITING(1964); DEVIL WITHIN HER, THE(1976, Brit.)
1984
WINTER FLIGHT(1984, Brit.), p

Sylvia Richards
RANCHO NOTORIOUS(1952), w

Ted Richards
HILLS OF DONEGAL, THE(1947, Brit.), ed; WHEN YOU COME HOME(1947, Brit.), ed

Ted Richards III
DIFFERENT STORY, A(1978)

Terry Richards
IDOL, THE(1966, Brit.); KIDNAPPED(1971, Brit.); LAST VALLEY, THE(1971, Brit.); 1,000 CONVICTS AND A WOMAN(1971, Brit.); PINK PANTHER STRIKES AGAIN, THE(1976, Brit.); FLASH GORDON(1980); RAIDERS OF THE LOST ARK(1981); HIGH

ROAD TO CHINA(1983)

Thomas Richards
KEY, THE(1934), ed; BORDERTOWN(1935), ed; DINKY(1935), ed; DON'T BET ON BLONDES(1935), ed; PERSONAL MAID'S SECRET(1935), ed; GOLD DIGGERS OF 1937(1936), ed; KING AND THE CHORUS GIRL, THE(1937), ed; LAND BEYOND THE LAW(1937), ed; MR. DODD TAKES THE AIR(1937), ed; THEY WON'T FORGET(1937), ed; HARD TO GET(1938), ed; WHITE BANNERS(1938), ed; WOMEN ARE LIKE THAT(1938), ed; EACH DAWN I DIE(1939), ed; NAUGHTY BUT NICE(1939), ed; OFF THE RECORD(1939), ed; CASTLE ON THE HUDSON(1940), ed; IT ALL CAME TRUE(1940), ed; THEY DRIVE BY NIGHT(1940), ed; BRIDE CAME C.O.D., THE(1941), ed; MALTESE FALCON, THE(1941), ed; ICE-CAPADES REVUE(1942), ed; MALE ANIMAL, THE(1942), ed; HIT PARADE OF 1943(1943), ed; SHANTY-TOWN(1943), ed; THUMBS UP(1943), ed; SEVENTH CROSS, THE(1944), ed

Toby Richards
SERGEANT RUTLEDGE(1960)

Tom Richards
BRITISH AGENT(1934), ed; SINGING KID, THE(1936), ed; STAGE STRUCK(1936), ed; ARCTIC FLIGHT(1952); DAWN(1979, Aus.)
Misc. Talkies
PLUNGE INTO DARKNESS(1977)

Tommy Richards
JIMMY THE GENT(1934), ed; BOULDER DAM(1936), ed; DANGEROUS(1936), ed

Verne Richards
WITHOUT RESERVATIONS(1946)

Vicky Richards
CRIMSON CULT, THE(1970, Brit.)

Vikki Richards
SWEET SUZY(1973)

W. Richards
NIGHT OF MAGIC, A(1944, Brit.), ph

Ward Richards
HER MAN GILBEY(1949, Brit.), art d

Jack Richardsan
GOODBYE CHARLIE(1964)

Abby Sage Richardson
Silents
PRIDE OF JENNICO, THE(1914), w

Adam Richardson
1984
SECRET PLACES(1984, Brit.)

Al Richardson
HAMMER(1972)
Misc. Talkies
BLACK HEAT(1976)

Albert Richardson
COUNTY FAIR(1933, Brit.)

Amos Richardson
1984
DARK ENEMY(1984, Brit.), ph

Angela Richardson
Misc. Talkies
WEST IS STILL WILD, THE(1977)

Anna S. Richardson
FATHER IS A PRINCE(1940), w

Anna Steese Richardson
BIG HEARTED HERBERT(1934), w
Silents
MAN'S HOME, A(1921), w

Anthony Richardson
LATE EXTRA(1935, Brit.), w; OLD ROSES(1935, Brit.), w; SHADOW OF MIKE EMERALD, THE(1935, Brit.), w; TWICE BRANDED(1936, Brit.), w; OPERATION DIAMOND(1948, Brit.), w

Arthur Richardson
FAREWELL TO CINDERELLA(1937, Brit.), w

Brian Richardson
EMIL AND THE DETECTIVES(1964)

Bruce Richardson
FLESH AND FURY(1952)

Charles Richardson
SATELLITE IN THE SKY(1956); HIGH TIDE AT NOON(1957, Brit.); COOL WORLD, THE(1963)
Silents
SPIDER AND THE ROSE, THE(1923), ph
Misc. Silents
WOMAN OF FLESH, A(1927)

Cliff John Richardson
DAY OF THE JACKAL, THE(1973, Brit./Fr.), spec eff

Cliff Richardson
FRIEDA(1947, Brit.), spec eff; LOVES OF JOANNA GODDEN, THE(1947, Brit.), spec eff; NICHOLAS NICKLEBY(1947, Brit.), spec eff; IT ALWAYS RAINS ON SUNDAY(1949, Brit.), spec eff; SEA SHALL NOT HAVE THEM, THE(1955, Brit.), spec eff; ALEXANDER THE GREAT(1956), spec eff; FIRE DOWN BELOW(1957, U.S./Brit.), spec eff; HIGH FLIGHT(1957, Brit.), spec eff; TANK FORCE(1958, Brit.), spec eff; HORROR HOTEL(1960, Brit.), spec eff; KILLERS OF KILIMANJARO(1960, Brit.), spec eff; SCENT OF MYSTERY(1960), spec eff; SIEGE OF SIDNEY STREET, THE(1960, Brit.), spec eff; DESERT PATROL(1962, Brit.), spec eff; TARZAN'S THREE CHALLENGES(1963), spec eff; VICTORS, THE(1963), spec eff; SEVENTH DAWN, THE(1964), spec eff; HELP!(1965, Brit.), spec eff; JUDITH(1965), spec eff; LORD JIM(1965, Brit.), spec eff; SANDS OF THE KALAHARI(1965, Brit.), spec eff; FUNNY THING HAPPENED ON THE WAY TO THE FORUM, A(1966), spec eff; DIRTY DOZEN, THE(1967, Brit.), spec eff; LOST CONTINENT, THE(1968, Brit.), spec eff; BATTLE OF BRITAIN, THE(1969, Brit.), spec eff; ADVENTURERS, THE(1970), spec eff; PRIVATE LIFE OF SHERLOCK HOLMES, THE(1970, Brit.), spec eff; ZEPPELIN(1971, Brit.), spec eff; YOUNG WINSTON(1972, Brit.), spec eff

David Richardson
SPRING FEVER(1983, Can.)

Denis Richardson
TOGETHER(1956, Brit.)

Duncan Richardson
SEA OF GRASS, THE(1947); THIS TIME FOR KEEPS(1947); MY DREAM IS YOURS(1949); GUNMEN OF ABILENE(1950); THREE CAME HOME(1950); THREE SECRETS(1950); PRIDE OF MARYLAND(1951); GLASS WEB, THE(1953); WHITE LIGHTNING(1953); SOMETHING OF VALUE(1957)

Ed Richardson
THE DOUBLE McGUFFIN(1979), art d; AMERICAN GIGOLO(1980), art d; SCARFACE(1983), art d

Edna Richardson
TRUCK TURNER(1974); DARKTOWN STRUTTERS(1975)
Misc. Talkies
GET DOWN AND BOOGIE(1977)

Edward Richardson
HARD COUNTRY(1981), prod d; MODERN ROMANCE(1981), prod d; CAT PEOPLE(1982), art d
1984
THIEF OF HEARTS(1984), art d

Elizabeth Richardson
1984
SCANDALOUS(1984)

Ellis Richardson
SIDELONG GLANCES OF A PIGEON KICKER, THE(1970)

Emery Richardson
Misc. Talkies
SOULS OF SIN(1949)

Emory Richardson
BEWARE(1946); SEPIA CINDERELLA(1947); LOST BOUNDARIES(1949); FUGITIVE KIND, THE(1960)

Ervin Richardson
NIGHT SONG(1947)

Florence Richardson
Silents
PRICE OF A PARTY, THE(1924)

Frank Richardson
FOX MOVIETONE FOLLIES(1929); SUNNY SIDE UP(1929); FOX MOVIETONE FOLLIES OF 1930(1930); HAPPY DAYS(1930); LET'S GO PLACES(1930); DON'T BE A DUMMY(1932, Brit.), d; HER FIRST AFFAIRE(1932, Brit.), p; RIVER HOUSE GHOST, THE(1932, Brit.), d; MONEY MAD(1934, Brit.), d; OH, WHAT A NIGHT(1935), d; HOWARD CASE, THE(1936, Brit.), d; THAT'S THE TICKET(1940, Brit.), w; BAIT(1950, Brit.), d, w; VILLAGE OF THE GIANTS(1965), cos
Misc. Silents
CANDYTUFT, I MEAN VERONICA(1921, Brit.), d; WHITE HEN, THE(1921, Brit.), d; KING OF THE PACK(1926), d; RACING BLOOD(1926), d

Frank A. Richardson
FOR LOVE OF YOU(1933, Brit.), p; KISS ME GOODBYE(1935, Brit.), p; MAN WHO MADE DIAMONDS, THE(1937, Brit.), w

Frankland A. Richardson
Silents
SHEER BLUFF(1921), d
Misc. Silents
IN THE NIGHT(1920, Brit.), d; BLACK TULIP, THE(1921, Brit.), d

Freshey Richardson
COUNTRYMAN(1982, Jamaica)

Gary Richardson
MISSING(1982)

George Richardson
NIJINSKY(1980, Brit.), art d; OH, HEAVENLY DOG!(1980), art d; HIGH ROAD TO CHINA(1983), art d

Gordon Richardson
HIGH WIND IN JAMAICA, A(1965); I START COUNTING(1970, Brit.)

Harry Richardson
TEN SECONDS TO HELL(1959), ed

Henry Handel Richardson
RHAPSODY(1954), w; GETTING OF WISDOM, THE(1977, Aus.), w

Henry Richardson
PASSPORT TO TREASON(1956, Brit.), ed; HIGH TERRACE(1957, Brit.), ed; SHADOW OF FEAR(1963, Brit.), ed; SMALL WORLD OF SAMMY LEE, THE(1963, Brit.), ed; LITTLE ONES, THE(1965, Brit.), ed; POPPY IS ALSO A FLOWER, THE(1966), ed; STUDY IN TERROR, A(1966, Brit./Ger.), ed; AFRICA–TEXAS STYLE!(1967 U.S./Brit.), ed; VALLEY OF GWANGI, THE(1969), ed; REVOLUTIONARY, THE(1970, Brit.), ed; CRAZE(1974, Brit.), ed; GHOUL, THE(1975, Brit.), ed; BEYOND THE FOG(1981, Brit.), ed; OCTOPUSSY(1983, Brit.), ed

Ian Richardson
PERSECUTION AND ASSASSINATION OF JEAN-PAUL MARAT AS PERFORMED BY THE INMATES OF THE ASYLUM OF CHARENTON UNDER THE DIRECTION OF THE MARQUIS DE SADE, THE(1967, Brit.); MIDSUMMER NIGHT'S DREAM, A(1969, Brit.); DARWIN ADVENTURE, THE(1972, Brit.); MAN OF LA MANCHA(1972); HOUND OF THE BASKERVILLES, THE(1983, Brit.); SIGN OF FOUR, THE(1983, Brit.)

Ilsa Richardson
TWICE UPON A TIME(1953, Brit.)

Irene Richardson
GUTTER GIRLS(1964, Brit.)

Jack Richardson
MELODY OF LOVE, THE(1928); LEATHERNECK, THE(1929); PAINTED FACES(1929); SAILORS' HOLIDAY(1929); DUDE WRANGLER, THE(1930); FOURTH ALARM, THE(1930); ONLY SAPS WORK(1930); TRIGGER TRICKS(1930); MYSTERY TRAIN(1931); UNFAITHFUL(1931); LAND OF WANTED MEN(1932); LAST MAN(1932); MAID TO ORDER(1932); MAN FROM NEW MEXICO, THE(1932); SCANDAL FOR SALE(1932); WITHOUT HONORS(1932); GUN JUSTICE(1934); KANSAS CITY PRINCESS(1934); STAND UP AND CHEER(1934 80m FOX bw); GOOSE AND THE GANDER, THE(1935); LIVING ON VELVET(1935); PERFECT CLUE, THE(1935); STRANDED(1935); ANOTHER DAWN(1937); CALL IT A DAY(1937); CASE OF THE STUTTERING BISHOP, THE(1937); CONFESSION(1937); PATIENT IN ROOM 18, THE(1938); SERGEANT MURPHY(1938); CODE OF THE SECRET SERVICE(1939); TORCHY PLAYS WITH DYNAMITE(1939); UNION PACIFIC(1939); GUN CODE(1940); MAN WHO TALKED TOO MUCH, THE(1940); RANGERS OF FORTUNE(1940); LADY EVE, THE(1941); MEET JOHN DOE(1941); MR. CELEBRITY(1942); FEAR(1946); NIGHT AND DAY(1946); ROMANCE OF THE WEST(1946); SUSPENSE(1946); CRASHING THRU(1949); MATING SEASON, THE(1951); PROUD AND THE PROFANE, THE(1956); VERTIGO(1958); SUMMER

PLACE, A(1959); CAPE FEAR(1962); BEYOND THE LAW(1968); MAIDSTONE(1970); FOREPLAY(1975), w

Misc. Talkies
LIGHTNIN' SMITH RETURNS(1931)

Silents
IMMEDIATE LEE(1916); ASHES OF HOPE(1917); ONE SHOT ROSS(1917); MAN ABOVE THE LAW(1918); RECKONING DAY, THE(1918); END OF THE GAME, THE(1919); GO WEST, YOUNG MAN(1919); OLD MAID'S BABY, THE(1919); TOLL GATE, THE(1920); STING OF THE LASH(1921); TOO MUCH SPEED(1921); GIRL FROM THE WEST(1923); NO MOTHER TO GUIDE HER(1923); SOULS FOR SALE(1923); BORDER WOMEN(1924); DOWN BY THE RIO GRANDE(1924); DYNAMITE DAN(1924); MIDNIGHT EXPRESS, THE(1924); KNOCKOUT KID, THE(1925); HEART OF A COWARD, THE(1926); HURRICANE, THE(1926); NIGHT WATCH, THE(1926); RAINMAKER, THE(1926); AVENGING FANGS(1927); EAGER LIPS(1927); SONORA KID, THE(1927); MARKED MONEY(1928); PARTNERS IN CRIME(1928); ONE SPLENDID HOUR(1929)

Misc. Silents
LAND O' LIZARDS(1916); FIGHTING BACK(1917); GIVING BECKY A CHANCE(1917); GOLDEN RULE KATE(1917); LOVE OR JUSTICE(1917); SAWDUST RING, THE(1917); DESERT LAW(1918); HIS ENEMY THE LAW(1918); PAINTED LILY, THE(1918); SEA PANTHER, THE(1918); YOU CAN'T BELIEVE EVERYTHING(1918); LONG LANE'S TURNING, THE(1919); MAYOR OF FILBERT, THE(1919); WIFE OR COUNTRY(1919); DANGEROUS HOURS(1920); HEART OF A WOMAN, THE(1920); TOLL GATE, THE(1920); NO DEFENSE(1921); CRIMSON CLUE(1922); HAIR TRIGGER CASEY(1922); COUNTERFEIT LOVE(1923); COWBOY AND THE FLAPPER, THE(1924); CRASHIN' THROUGH(1924); FIRE PATROL, THE(1924); LIGHTNIN' JACK(1924); LOOPED FOR LIFE(1924); MIDNIGHT SECRETS(1924); NORTH OF ALASKA(1924); THAT WILD WEST(1924); TIGER THOMPSON(1924); BEYOND THE BORDER(1925); BORDER VENGENCE(1925); COLD FURY(1925); GENTLEMAN ROUGHNECK, A(1925); HIS GREATEST BATTLE(1925); RIDIN' WILD(1925); SAGEBRUSH LADY, THE(1925); TEXAS BEARCAT, THE(1925); WHERE ROMANCE RIDES(1925); BROADWAY GALLANT, THE(1926); MILLIONAIRE ORPHAN, THE(1926); WALLOPING KID(1926); BLACK TEARS(1927); SNARL OF HATE, THE(1927); WILFUL YOUTH(1927); ACROSS THE PLAINS(1928); MIDNIGHT ADVENTURE, THE(1928); TRIAL MARRIAGE(1928); WOMEN WHO DARE(1928); SEX MADNESS(1929)

Jack H. Richardson
GOING HIGHBROW(1935); RIGHT TO LIVE, THE(1935); MAID OF SALEM(1937); SMART BLONDE(1937); OUR LEADING CITIZEN(1939)

James Richardson
HELL SQUAD(1958), m

James G. Richardson
ONE ON ONE(1977); METEOR(1979)

Jim Richardson
SUPERFLY(1972)

Joely Richardson
1984
HOTEL NEW HAMPSHIRE, THE(1984)

John Richardson
BACHELOR OF HEARTS(1958, Brit.); NIGHT TO REMEMBER, A(1958, Brit.); OPERATION AMSTERDAM(1960, Brit.); THIRTY NINE STEPS, THE(1960, Brit.); BLACK SUNDAY(1961, Ital.); PIRATES OF TORTUGA(1961); TENDER IS THE NIGHT(1961); SHE(1965, Brit.); ONE MILLION YEARS B.C.(1967, Brit./U.S.); CHASTITY BELT, THE(1968, Ital.); DUFFY(1968, Brit.), spec eff; VENGEANCE OF SHE, THE(1968, Brit.); LEO THE LAST(1970, Brit.), spec eff; NUN AT THE CROSSROADS, A(1970, Ital./Span.); ON A CLEAR DAY YOU CAN SEE FOREVER(1970); RAILWAY CHILDREN, THE(1971, Brit.), spec eff; JUGGERNAUT(1974), spec eff; PHASE IV(1974), spec eff; TORSO(1974, Ital.); ROLLERBALL(1975), spec eff; DUCH IN ORANGE SAUCE(1976, Ital.); OMEN, THE(1976), spec eff; PEOPLE THAT TIME FORGOT, THE(1977, Brit.), spec eff; EYEBALL(1978, Ital.); WARLORDS OF ATLANTIS(1978, Brit.), spec eff; MOONRAKER(1979, Brit.), spec eff; FFOLKES(1980, Brit.), spec. eff.; RAISE THE TITANIC(1980, Brit.), spec eff; WATCHER IN THE WOODS, THE(1980, Brit.), spec eff; OCTOPUSSY(1983, Brit.), spec eff
1984
SLAYGROUND(1984, Brit.), spec eff

John J. Richardson
Silents
BEAU BRUMMEL(1924)

Joyce Richardson
RADIO FOLLIES(1935, Brit.)

Keith Richardson
GOODBYE PORK PIE(1981, New Zealand)

Ken Richardson
NONE BUT THE BRAVE(1963), d, w

Kimberley Richardson
STAR 80(1983), set d
1984
ICEMAN(1984), set d

Lee Richardson
MIDDLE OF THE NIGHT(1959); NETWORK(1976); BRUBAKER(1980); PRINCE OF THE CITY(1981); DANIEL(1983); I AM THE CHEESE(1983)

Lloyd L. Richardson
SO DEAR TO MY HEART(1949), ed; HANG YOUR HAT ON THE WIND(1969), ed; $1,000,000 DUCK(1971), ed

Marcus Richardson
ROMANTIC ENGLISHWOMAN, THE(1975, Brit./Fr.)

Mark Richardson
DATELINE DIAMONDS(1966, Brit.)

Michael Richardson
EARTHQUAKE(1974); HINDENBURG, THE(1975); MIDWAY(1976); AIRPORT '77(1977)

Natasha Richardson
1984
EVERY PICTURE TELLS A STORY(1984, Brit.)

Patricia Richardson
1984
C.H.U.D.(1984)

Patty Richardson
YOU BETTER WATCH OUT(1980)

Paul Richardson
1984
ON THE LINE(1984, Span.)

Pete Richardson
KING BLANK(1983)

Peter Richardson
1984
BROTHER FROM ANOTHER PLANET, THE(1984)

Ralph Richardson
FRIDAY THE 13TH(1934, Brit.); GHOUL, THE(1934, Brit.); KING OF PARIS, THE(1934, Brit.); RETURN OF BULLDOG DRUMMOND, THE(1934, Brit.); ALIAS BULLDOG DRUMMOND(1935, Brit.); JAVA HEAD(1935, Brit.); THINGS TO COME(1936, Brit.); MAN WHO COULD WORK MIRACLES, THE(1937, Brit.); ROMANCE AND RICHES(1937, Brit.); THUNDER IN THE CITY(1937, Brit.); CITADEL, THE(1938, Brit.); DIVORCE OF LADY X, THE(1938, Brit.); SOUTH RIDING(1938, Brit.); CLOUDS OVER EUROPE(1939, Brit.); FOUR FEATHERS, THE(1939, Brit.); FUGITIVE, THE(1940, Brit.); LION HAS WINGS, THE(1940, Brit.); AVENGERS, THE(1942, Brit.); SILVER FLEET, THE(1945, Brit.), a, p; SCHOOL FOR SECRETS(1946, Brit.); ANNA KARENINA(1948, Brit.); FALLEN IDOL, THE(1949, Brit.); HEIRESS, THE(1949); BREAKING THE SOUND BARRIER(1952); OUTCAST OF THE ISLANDS(1952, Brit.); MURDER ON MONDAY(1953, Brit.), a, d; HOLLY AND THE IVY, THE(1954, Brit.); RICHARD III(1956, Brit.); NOVEL AFFAIR, A(1957, Brit.); SMILEY(1957, Brit.); EXODUS(1960); OSCAR WILDE(1960, Brit.); OUR MAN IN HAVANA(1960, Brit.); LONG DAY'S JOURNEY INTO NIGHT(1962); 300 SPARTANS, THE(1962); WOMAN OF STRAW(1964, Brit.); DOCTOR ZHIVAGO(1965); KHARTOUM(1966, Brit.); WRONG BOX, THE(1966, Brit.); CHIMES AT MIDNIGHT(1967, Span.,Switz.); BATTLE OF BRITAIN, THE(1969, Brit.); BED SITTING ROOM, THE(1969, Brit.); MIDAS RUN(1969); OH! WHAT A LOVELY WAR(1969, Brit.); DAVID COPPERFIELD(1970, Brit.); LOOKING GLASS WAR, THE(1970, Brit.); EAGLE IN A CAGE(1971, U.S./Yugo.); WHO SLEW AUNTIE ROO?(1971, U.S./Brit.); ALICE'S ADVENTURES IN WONDERLAND(1972, Brit.); LADY CAROLINE LAMB(1972, Brit./Ital.); TALES FROM THE CRYPT(1972, Brit.); DOLL'S HOUSE, A(1973); O LUCKY MAN!(1973, Brit.); ROLLERBALL(1975); DRAGONSLAYER(1981); TIME BANDITS(1981, Brit.); WAGNER(1983, Brit./Hung./Aust.)
1984
GIVE MY REGARDS TO BROAD STREET(1984, Brit.); GREYSTOKE: THE LEGEND OF TARZAN, LORD OF THE APES(1984)

Regina Richardson
1984
TIGHTROPE(1984)

Richard A. Richardson
MAN, A WOMAN AND A KILLER, A(1975), a, w

Rickey Richardson
HOT BOX, THE(1972, U.S./Phil.)

Rico L. Richardson
1984
SCARRED(1984)

Robert Richardson
GULLIVER'S TRAVELS(1977, Brit., Bel.), ed

Rod Richardson
CLINIC, THE(1983, Aus.)

Sallye Richardson
TEXAS CHAIN SAW MASSACRE, THE(1974), ed

Samuel Richardson
JANE AUSTEN IN MANHATTAN(1980), w

Sandra Richardson
NONE BUT THE BRAVE(1963), w

Sir Ralph Richardson
WATERSHIP DOWN(1978, Brit.)

Susan Richardson
AMERICAN GRAFFITI(1973)

Sy Richardson
NOCTURNA(1979); MY BROTHER'S WEDDING(1983)
1984
REPO MAN(1984)
Misc. Talkies
FAIRY TALES(1979)

Terry Richardson
WHERE THERE'S A WILL(1937, Brit.)

Tony Richardson
LOOK BACK IN ANGER(1959), d; ENTERTAINER, THE(1960, Brit.), d; SANCTUARY(1961), d; SATURDAY NIGHT AND SUNDAY MORNING(1961, Brit.), p; LONELINESS OF THE LONG DISTANCE RUNNER, THE(1962, Brit.), p&d; TASTE OF HONEY, A(1962, Brit.), p&d, w; TOM JONES(1963, Brit.), p&d; LOVED ONE, THE(1965), d; MADEMOISELLE(1966, Fr./Brit.), d; SAILOR FROM GIBRALTAR, THE(1967, Brit.), d, w; CHARGE OF THE LIGHT BRIGADE, THE(1968, Brit.), d; HAMLET(1969, Brit.), d; NED KELLY(1970, Brit.), d, w; DELICATE BALANCE, A(1973), d; JOSEPH ANDREWS(1977, Brit.), d, w; BORDER, THE(1982), d
1984
HOTEL NEW HAMPSHIRE, THE(1984), d&w
Misc. Talkies
DEAD CERT(1974, Brit.), d

Virgil Richardson
TARZAN'S DEADLY SILENCE(1970)

W. Lyle Richardson
ZERO TO SIXTY(1978), w

Walter Richardson
Misc. Silents
ALIAS MISS DODD(1920)

Warren Richardson
CASEY'S SHADOW(1978)

William Richardson
SONG TO REMEMBER, A(1945)

Henri Richaud
LILIOM(1935, Fr.)

Alan Riche
YOUNGBLOOD(1978), p
Nicole Riche
NANA(1957, Fr./Ital.)
Roger Richebe
KOENIGSMARK(1935, Fr.), p; MARKED GIRLS(1949, Fr.), p; MONSEIG-NEUR(1950, Fr.), p,d&w
Myrtle Richell
Misc. Silents
THEY LIKE 'EM ROUGH(1922)
Myrtle Richelle
Misc. Silents
HAPPINESS A LA MODE(1919)
Adam Richens
Misc. Talkies
SKY PIRATES(1977, Brit.)
Jean Richepin
OPEN ROAD, THE(1940, Fr.), w
Clement Richer
TIKO AND THE SHARK(1966, U.S./Ital./Fr.), w; BEYOND THE REEF(1981), w
Gaston Richer
SLEEPING CAR TO TRIESTE(1949, Brit.); SECRET PEOPLE(1952, Brit.); CRUEL SEA, THE(1953); SWORD AND THE ROSE, THE(1953)
Janette Richer
CONSTANT HUSBAND, THE(1955, Brit.)
Jean-Jose Richer
FRENCH POSTCARDS(1979); LAST METRO, THE(1981, Fr.)
Albert Richerd
RENEGADES(1946), set d
Herbert Richers
TRAIN ROBBERY CONFIDENTIAL(1965, Braz.), p; LOLLIPOP(1966, Braz.), p
Barbara Richert
WINTER KILLS(1979)
Bill Richert
LAW AND DISORDER(1974)
Rosa Richert
BEADS OF ONE ROSARY, THE(1982, Pol.)
Ted Richert
EYES OF A STRANGER(1980); PIRANHA II: THE SPAWNING(1981, Neth.)
William Richert
LAW AND DISORDER(1974), p, w; HAPPY HOOKER, THE(1975), w; WINTER KILLS(1979), d&w; AMERICAN SUCCESS COMPANY, THE(1980), a, d, w
Arnold Riches
FIRST MRS. FRASER, THE(1932, Brit.); HER FIRST AFFAIRE(1932, Brit.); GOOD COMPANIONS(1933, Brit.)
Jack Richesim
Misc. Talkies
MIDNIGHT PLOWBOY(1973)
Alice Richey
MA AND PA KETTLE GO TO TOWN(1950); BRIGHT VICTORY(1951)
Grace Richey
ZAZA(1939)
Jean Richey
ON STAGE EVERYBODY(1945); CASA MANANA(1951)
Edwin Richfield
HA' PENNY BREEZE(1950, Brit.); BLUE PARROT, THE(1953, Brit.); FLANNEL-FOOT(1953, Brit.); NORMAN CONQUEST(1953, Brit.); BLACK RIDER, THE(1954, Brit.); DEVIL'S HARBOR(1954, Brit.); FUSS OVER FEATHERS(1954, Brit.); WHAT EVERY WOMAN WANTS(1954, Brit.); BRAIN MACHINE, THE(1955, Brit.); RACE FOR LIFE, A(1955, Brit.); FIND THE LADY(1956, Brit.); HIDEOUT, THE(1956, Brit.); ENEMY FROM SPACE(1957, Brit.); X THE UNKNOWN(1957, Brit.); ADVENTURES OF HAL 5, THE(1958, Brit.); UP THE CREEK(1958, Brit.); INNOCENT MEETING(1959, Brit.); NAVY HEROES(1959, Brit.); BOY WHO STOLE A MILLION, THE(1960, Brit.); INN FOR TROUBLE(1960, Brit.); MODEL FOR MURDER(1960, Brit.); TOMMY THE TOREADOR(1960, Brit.); SWORD OF SHERWOOD FOREST(1961, Brit.); BREAK, THE(1962, Brit.); LIFE IS A CIRCUS(1962, Brit.); CALCULATED RISK(1963, Brit.), w; JUST FOR FUN(1963, Brit.); NO TREE IN THE STREET(1964, Brit.); SECRET OF BLOOD ISLAND, THE(1965, Brit.); FIVE MILLION YEARS TO EARTH(1968, Brit.)
1984
CHAMPIONS(1984)
Clint Richie
BANDOLERO!(1968)
Donald Richie
THRONE OF BLOOD(1961, Jap.), titles
Estelle Richie
STAGE STRUCK(1958)
Ronald Richie
SELF-MADE LADY(1932, Brit.)
Francois Richier
ARISE, MY LOVE(1940)
Jack Richisen
Misc. Talkies
COUNTRY CUZZINS(1972)
Vera Richkova
MISSION TO MOSCOW(1943)
Marfa Richler
JACOB TWO-TWO MEETS THE HOODED FANG(1979, Can.)
Mordecai Richler
NO LOVE FOR JOHNNIE(1961, Brit.), w; TIARA TAHITI(1962, Brit.), w; YOUNG AND WILLING(1964, Brit.), w; LIFE AT THE TOP(1965, Brit.), w; APPRENTICESHIP OF DUDDY KRAVITZ, THE(1974, Can.), w; FUN WITH DICK AND JANE(1977, w; JACOB TWO-TWO MEETS THE HOODED FANG(1979, Can.), w
Maurice Richlin
OPERATION PETTICOAT(1959), w; PILLOW TALK(1959), w; ALL IN A NIGHT'S WORK(1961), w; COME SEPTEMBER(1961), w; SOLDIER IN THE RAIN(1963), w; PINK PANTHER, THE(1964), w; WHAT DID YOU DO IN THE WAR, DADDY?(1966), w; DON'T MAKE WAVES(1967), w; INSPECTOR CLOUSEAU(1968, Brit.), w; FOR PETE'S SAKE(1977), w

Albert Richman
LADY SURRENDERS, A(1930), w; PENAL CODE, THE(1933); LOVE BEFORE BREAKFAST(1936)
Arthur Richman
AWFUL TRUTH, THE(1929), w; LADY SURRENDERS, A(1930), w; LADY'S MOR-ALS, A(1930), w; LAUGHING LADY, THE(1930), w; RECKLESS HOUR, THE(1931), w; ONLY YESTERDAY(1933), w; GAY DECEPTION, THE(1935), w; HERE'S TO ROMANCE(1935), w; AWFUL TRUTH, THE(1937), w; LET'S DO IT AGAIN(1953), w
Silents
AWFUL TRUTH, THE(1925), w; NOT SO LONG AGO(1925), w; FAR CRY, THE(1926), w
Bert Richman
SLAVE GIRL(1947)
Brett Richman
SECOND THOUGHTS(1983)
Charles Richman
STRUGGLE, THE(1931); HIS DOUBLE LIFE(1933); PRESIDENT VANISHES, THE(1934); AFTER OFFICE HOURS(1935); BECKY SHARP(1935); BIOGRAPHY OF A BACHELOR GIRL(1935); CASE OF THE CURIOUS BRIDE, THE(1935); GEORGE WHITE'S 1935 SCANDALS(1935); GLASS KEY, THE(1935); IN OLD KENTUCK-Y(1935); THANKS A MILLION(1935); DON'T TURN'EM LOOSE(1936); EX-MRS. BRADFORD, THE(1936); I'D GIVE MY LIFE(1936); IN HIS STEPS(1936); MY MAR-RIAGE(1936); PAROLE(1936); SING ME A LOVE SONG(1936); UNDER YOUR SPELL(1936); LADY BEHAVE(1937); LIFE OF EMILE ZOLA, THE(1937); MAKE A WISH(1937); ADVENTURES OF TOM SAWYER, THE(1938); BLONDES AT WORK(1938); COWBOY AND THE LADY, THE(1938); HOLIDAY(1938); DARK VICTO-RY(1939); EXILE EXPRESS(1939); I AM NOT AFRAID(1939); TORCHY RUNS FOR MAYOR(1939); DEVIL'S ISLAND(1940)
Silents
MAN FROM HOME, THE(1914); BATTLE CRY OF PEACE, THE(1915); STRANGER THAN FICTION(1921), w; HAS THE WORLD GONE MAD!(1923)
Misc. Silents
HEIGHTS OF HAZARDS, THE(1915); DAWN OF FREEDOM, THE(1916); HERO OF SUBMARINE D-2, THE(1916); SUPRISES OF AN EMPTY HOTEL, THE(1916); MORE EXCELLENT WAY, THE(1917); OVER THERE(1917); PUBLIC BE DAMNED(1917); ECHO OF YOUTH, THE(1919); HIDDEN TRUTH, THE(1919); CURTAIN(1920); HALF AN HOUR(1920); HARRIET AND THE PIPER(1920); SIGN ON THE DOOR, THE(1921); TRUST YOUR WIFE(1921); MY FRIEND, THE DEVIL(1922)
Harold Richman
OLD SPANISH CUSTOM, AN(1936, Brit.), p
Harry Richman
PUTTIN' ON THE RITZ(1930); MUSIC GOES ROUND, THE(1936)
Howard Richman
FROM THE TERRACE(1960), art d
Jeffrey Richman
SEDUCTION, THE(1982)
Marian Richman
GOG(1954)
Mark Richman
FRIENDLY PERSUASION(1956); GIRLS ON THE LOOSE(1958); BLACK OR-CHID(1959); DARK INTRUDER(1965); AGENT FOR H.A.R.M.(1966); FOR SINGLES ONLY(1968)
Peter Mark Richman
Misc. Talkies
PSI FACTOR(1980, Brit.)
[Peter] Mark Richman
STRANGE ONE, THE(1957)
Roger Richman
PIRANHA(1978)
Sandy Richman
1984
BROADWAY DANNY ROSE(1984)
Stuart Richman
REDS(1981); DRESSER, THE(1983)
Ace Richmond
PRAIRIE ROUNDUP(1951)
Al Richmond
SATURDAY'S MILLIONS(1933); MISSISSIPPI(1935)
Misc. Silents
BORDER RIDER, THE(1924); RIP ROARIN' ROBERTS(1924); EYES OF THE DES-ERT(1926); GASOLINE COWBOY(1926); TWISTED TRIGGERS(1926); DEADSHOT CASEY(1928)
Anthony Richmond
BANG! YOU'RE DEAD(1954, Brit.); DEVIL GIRL FROM MARS(1954, Brit.); GLASS TOMB, THE(1955, Brit.); ONE WISH TOO MANY(1956, Brit.); DON'T LOOK NOW(1973, Brit./Ital.), ph; MAN WHO FELL TO EARTH, THE(1976, Brit.), ph; SILVER BEARS(1978), ph; AMERICAN SUCCESS COMPANY, THE(1980), ph; HEAD ON(1981, Can.), ph; IMPROPER CHANNELS(1981, Can.), ph
1984
SLAPSTICK OF ANOTHER KIND(1984), ph
Anthony Richmond [Tonino Ricci]
1984
RUSH(1984, Ital.), d
Bill Richmond
BELLBOY, THE(1960); ERRAND BOY, THE(1961), w; LADIES MAN, THE(1961), w; NUTTY PROFESSOR, THE(1963), w; PATSY, THE(1964), w; FAMILY JEWELS, THE(1965), w; BIG MOUTH, THE(1967), w; SMORGASBORD(1983), a, w
Bill W. Richmond
1984
TERMINATOR, THE(1984)
Branscombe Richmond
CHICKEN CHRONICLES, THE(1977)
1984
STAR TREK III: THE SEARCH FOR SPOCK(1984)
Carol Richmond
DOCTOR AT LARGE(1957, Brit.)
Charles Richmond
TAKE A CHANCE(1933)

Misc. Silents
NEW ADAM AND EVE, THE(1915)
Doyle Richmond
SPY WHO LOVED ME, THE(1977, Brit.)
Edna Richmond
Silents
PRICE OF A PARTY, THE(1924); SPIDER WEBS(1927)
Eric Richmond
RED, WHITE AND BLACK, THE(1970)
Felice Richmond
ON STAGE EVERYBODY(1945); FIGHTING VIGILANTES, THE(1947); I SHOT BILLY THE KID(1950); PEGGY(1950); ROOM FOR ONE MORE(1952); SON OF PALEFACE(1952); MOTORCYCLE GANG(1957); WESTBOUND(1959)
Fiona Richmond
HISTORY OF THE WORLD, PART 1(1981)
Misc. Talkies
HOUSE ON STRAW HILL, THE(1976)
George Richmond
SHOCK WAVES(1977), art d
Harold Richmond
TONY DRAWS A HORSE(1951, Brit.); DISTANT TRUMPET(1952, Brit.), p; I'M A STRANGER(1952, Brit.), p; NIGHT WON'T TALK, THE(1952, Brit.), p; THREE STEPS IN THE DARK(1953, Brit.), p
Harry Richmond
PLAYBOY, THE(1942, Brit.)
Howard Richmond
HIGH FURY(1947, Brit.), makeup; NOT AS A STRANGER(1955), art d; DOMINO KID(1957), art d; MAN ON THE PROWL(1957), art d; CHINA DOLL(1958), art d; GUN RUNNERS, THE(1958), art d; STORY ON PAGE ONE, THE(1959), art d; CONVICTS FOUR(1962), art d; HELL IS FOR HEROES(1962), art d
Irene Richmond
SATURDAY NIGHT AND SUNDAY MORNING(1961, Brit.); NIGHTMARE(1963, Brit.); BRAIN, THE(1965, Ger./Brit.); DARLING(1965, Brit.); DR. TERROR'S HOUSE OF HORRORS(1965, Brit.); HYSTERIA(1965, Brit.); O LUCKY MAN!(1973, Brit.)
J.A. Richmond
Misc. Silents
BARKER, THE(1917), d
John Richmond
MR. BROWN COMES DOWN THE HILL(1966, Brit.); MURDER GAME, THE(1966, Brit.)
Silents
MANHATTAN MADNESS(1916)
June Richmond
Misc. Talkies
DREAMER, THE(1947); REET, PETITE AND GONE(1947)
Kane Richmond
FOR THE DEFENSE(1930); CAVALIER OF THE WEST(1931); POLITICS(1931); STRANGERS MAY KISS(1931); HUDDLE(1932); CRIME OF HELEN STANLEY(1934); DEVIL TIGER(1934); I CAN'T ESCAPE(1934); LET'S FALL IN LOVE(1934); VOICE IN THE NIGHT(1934); FORCED LANDING(1935); PRIVATE NUMBER(1936); THUNDERBOLT(1936); ANYTHING FOR A THRILL(1937); HEADLINE CRASHER(1937); NANCY STEELE IS MISSING(1937); TOUGH TO HANDLE(1937); WITH LOVE AND KISSES(1937); YOUNG DYNAMITE(1937); BORN TO FIGHT(1938); I AM THE LAW(1938); JUVENILE COURT(1938); LETTER OF INTRODUCTION(1938); RACING BLOOD(1938); THREE LOVES HAS NANCY(1938); CHARLIE CHAN IN RENO(1939); CHICKEN WAGON FAMILY(1939); ESCAPE, THE(1939); RETURN OF THE CISCO KID(1939); TAIL SPIN(1939); WINNER TAKE ALL(1939); 20,000 MEN A YEAR(1939); CHARLIE CHAN IN PANAMA(1940); KNUTE ROCKNE—ALL AMERICAN(1940); MURDER OVER NEW YORK(1940); PLAY GIRL(1940); SAILOR'S LADY(1940); DOUBLE CROSS(1941); GREAT GUNS(1941); HARD GUY(1941); MOUNTAIN MOONLIGHT(1941); RIDERS OF THE PURPLE SAGE(1941); GENTLEMAN AT HEART, A(1942); ACTION IN THE NORTH ATLANTIC(1943); THERE'S SOMETHING ABOUT A SOLDIER(1943); THREE RUSSIAN GIRLS(1943); LADIES COURAGEOUS(1944); ROGER TOUHY, GANGSTER!(1944); TIGER WOMAN, THE(1945); BEHIND THE MASK(1946); BLACK MARKET BABIES(1946); DON'T GAMBLE WITH STRANGERS(1946); MISSING LADY, THE(1946); PASSKEY TO DANGER(1946); SHADOW RETURNS, THE(1946); TRAFFIC IN CRIME(1946); BLACK GOLD(1947); STAGE STRUCK(1948)
Misc. Talkies
CIRCUS SHADOWS(1935); SILENT CODE, THE(1935)
Ken Richmond
NIGHT AND THE CITY(1950, Brit.); MAD ABOUT MEN(1954, Brit.)
Kim Richmond
NEW GIRL IN TOWN(1977), m
Leo C. Richmond
DAUGHTER OF THE JUNGLE(1949); WAKE OF THE RED WITCH(1949)
Leo Richmond
MARA MARU(1952)
Linda Richmond
WALKABOUT(1971, Aus./U.S.), makeup
Peter Richmond [John Carradine]
TOL'ABLE DAVID(1930); HEAVEN ON EARTH(1931); TO THE LAST MAN(1933)
Ralph Richmond
JIM, THE WORLD'S GREATEST(1976); KENNY AND CO.(1976); PHANTASM(1979)
Robin Richmond
MYSTERY AT THE BURLESQUE(1950, Brit.)
Steven Richmond
PHANTOM OF THE PARADISE(1974)
Susan Richmond
LIFE IN HER HANDS(1951, Brit.); CROW HOLLOW(1952, Brit.); GIDEON OF SCOTLAND YARD(1959, Brit.)
T. H. Richmond
CAUGHT IN THE ACT(1941), p; GAMBLING DAUGHTERS(1941), p; JUNGLE MAN(1941), p; SOUTH OF PANAMA(1941), p; SHE'S IN THE ARMY(1942), p
Ted Richmond
SIX-GUN RHYTHM(1939), w; TRIGGER PALS(1939), w; KANSAS CITY KITTY(1944), p; MEET MISS BOBBY SOCKS(1944), p; ONE MYSTERIOUS NIGHT(1944), p; SHE'S A SWEETHEART(1944), p; SOUL OF A MONSTER, THE(1944), p; BLONDE FROM BROOKLYN(1945), p; HIT THE HAY(1945), p; LET'S GO STEADY(1945), p; YOUTH ON TRIAL(1945), p; BOSTON BLACKIE AND THE LAW(1946), p; DANGER-

OUS BUSINESS(1946), p; IT'S GREAT TO BE YOUNG(1946), p; NIGHT EDITOR(1946), p; NOTORIOUS LONE WOLF, THE(1946), p; SINGIN' IN THE CORN(1946), p; SO DARK THE NIGHT(1946), p; KING OF THE WILD HORSES(1947), p; LONE WOLF IN LONDON(1947), p; ADVENTURES IN SILVERADO(1948), p; BEST MAN WINS(1948), p; THUNDERHOOF(1948), p; BLONDIE HITS THE JACKPOT(1949), p; BLONDIE'S BIG DEAL(1949), p; HOLIDAY IN HAVANA(1949), p; MAKE BELIEVE BALLROOM(1949), p; BLONDIE'S HERO(1950), p; KANSAS RAIDERS(1950), p; MILKMAN, THE(1950), p; SHAKEDOWN(1950), p; CIMARRON KID, THE(1951), p; SMUGGLER'S ISLAND(1951), p; STRANGE DOOR, THE(1951), p; WEEKEND WITH FATHER(1951), p; BONZO GOES TO COLLEGE(1952), p; BRONCO BUSTER(1952), p; HAS ANYBODY SEEN MY GAL?(1952), p; NO ROOM FOR THE GROOM(1952), p; COLUMN SOUTH(1953), p; DESERT LEGION(1953), p; FORBIDDEN(1953), p; MISSISSIPPI GAMBLER, THE(1953), p; WALKING MY BABY BACK HOME(1953), p; BENGAL BRIGADE(1954), d; FRANCIS JOINS THE WACS(1954), p; RAILS INTO LARAMIE(1954), p; COUNT THREE AND PRAY(1955), p; NIGHTFALL(1956), p; BACHELOR IN PARADISE(1961), p; IT HAPPENED AT THE WORLD'S FAIR(1963), p; ADVANCE TO THE REAR(1964), p; RETURN OF THE SEVEN(1966, Span.), p; VILLA RIDES(1968), p; RED SUN(1972, Fr./Ital./Span.), p; BEHIND THE IRON MASK(1977), p
Tim Richmond
STROKER ACE(1983)
Tom Richmond
1984
HARDBODIES(1984), ph; HIGHWAY TO HELL(1984), ph; RUNNING HOT(1984), ph
Tony Richmond
ONLY WHEN I LARF(1968, Brit.), ph; ONE PLUS ONE(1969, Brit.), ph; STARDUST(1974, Brit.), ph; OLD DRACULA(1975, Brit.), ph; EAGLE HAS LANDED, THE(1976, Brit.), ph; GREEK TYCOON, THE(1978), ph
W. P. Richmond
Silents
MANHATTAN MADNESS(1916)
Warner Richmond
BIG NEWS(1929); REDEEMING SIN, THE(1929); STARK MAD(1929); STRANGE CARGO(1929); MEN WITHOUT WOMEN(1930); STRICTLY MODERN(1930); HUCKLEBERRY FINN(1931); QUICK MILLIONS(1931); BEAST OF THE CITY, THE(1932); HELL'S HIGHWAY(1932); NIGHT COURT(1932); STRANGERS OF THE EVENING(1932); WOMAN FROM MONTE CARLO, THE(1932); CORRUPTION(1933); FAST WORKERS(1933); KING OF THE JUNGLE(1933); LIFE IN THE RAW(1933); MAMA LOVES PAPA(1933); POLICE CALL(1933); THIS DAY AND AGE(1933); FUGITIVE LADY(1934); GIFT OF GAB(1934); HAPPY LANDING(1934); LOST JUNGLE, THE(1934); COURAGEOUS AVENGER, THE(1935); HEADLINE WOMAN, THE(1935); MISSISSIPPI(1935); NEW FRONTIER, THE(1935); RAINBOW'S END(1935); SINGING VAGABOND, THE(1935); SMOKEY SMITH(1935); SO RED THE ROSE(1935); STRAIGHT FROM THE HEART(1935); UNDER PRESSURE(1935); BELOW THE DEADLINE(1936); HEARTS IN BONDAGE(1936); IN HIS STEPS(1936); SONG OF THE GRINGO(1936); WHITE LEGION, THE(1936); DOOMED AT SUNDOWN(1937); FEDERAL BULLETS(1937); GOLD RACKET, THE(1937); HEADIN' FOR THE RIO GRANDE(1937); HEART OF THE WEST(1937); LAWMAN IS BORN, A(1937); RIDERS OF THE DAWN(1937); STARS OVER ARIZONA(1937); TRAIL OF VENGEANCE(1937); WALLABY JIM OF THE ISLANDS(1937); WHERE TRAILS DIVIDE(1937); PRAIRIE MOON(1938); SIX SHOOTIN' SHERIFF(1938); WOLVES OF THE SEA(1938); FIGHTING MAD(1939); RIDE 'EM COWGIRL(1939); SINGING COWGIRL, THE(1939); TRIGGER SMITH(1939); WATER RUSTLERS(1939); WILD HORSE CANYON(1939); GOLDEN TRAIL, THE(1940); PALS OF THE SILVER SAGE(1940); RAINBOW OVER THE RANGE(1940); RHYTHM OF THE RIO GRANDE(1940); OUTLAW TRAIL(1944); COLORADO SERENADE(1946); WILD WEST(1946); PRAIRIE OUTLAWS(1948)
Silents
ROMANCE OF THE AIR, A(1919); WOMAN'S BUSINESS, A(1920); HEART OF MARYLAND, THE(1921); TOL'ABLE DAVID(1921); LUCK(1921); PACE THAT THRILLS, THE(1925); GOOD AND NAUGHTY(1926); IRISH HEARTS(1927); SLIDE, KELLY, SLIDE(1927); WHITE FLANNELS(1927); APACHE, THE(1928); CHICAGO(1928); SHADOWS OF THE NIGHT(1928); STOP THAT MAN(1928)
Misc. Silents
BROWN IN HARVARD(1917); SPORTING LIFE(1918); GRAY TOWERS MYSTERY, THE(1919); MY LADY'S GARTER(1920); CHALLENGE, THE(1922); JAN OF THE BIG SNOWS(1922); MARK OF THE BEAST(1923); DAUGHTERS OF THE NIGHT(1924); SPEED SPOOK, THE(1924); MAKING OF O'MALLEY, THE(1925); HEART OF MARYLAND, THE(1927); HEARTS OF MEN(1928); YOU CAN'T BEAT THE LAW(1928)
Warner P. Richmond
BILLY THE KID(1930); REMOTE CONTROL(1930)
Silents
SPRINGTIME(1915)
Misc. Silents
MAN FROM GLENGARRY, THE(1923)
Wyn Richmond
LOOKING ON THE BRIGHT SIDE(1932, Brit.)
Richard Richonne
PURPLE MASK, THE(1955); GIRL IN THE KREMLIN, THE(1957)
Gary Richrath
FM(1978)
Elfi Richsteiger
EIGHT GIRLS IN A BOAT(1932, Ger.)
Rose Richtel
Silents
BATTLE OF THE SEXES, THE(1914), ed
Rose Richtell
Silents
AVENGING CONSCIENCE, THE(1914), ed
Arno Richter
LIFE BEGINS ANEW(1938, Ger.), cos; DEVIL IN SILK(1968, Ger.), art d
Belle Richter
REAL LIFE(1979)
Carol Richter
OCTOPUSSY(1983, Brit.)
Caroline Richter
WAKE ME WHEN IT'S OVER(1960); ERRAND BOY, THE(1961); LADIES MAN, THE(1961); HOUSE OF WOMEN(1962)

Conrad Richter
SEA OF GRASS, THE(1947), w; ONE DESIRE(1955), w; LIGHT IN THE FOREST, THE(1958), w
Daniel Richter
2001: A SPACE ODYSSEY(1968, U.S./Brit.)
Debi Richter
HOMETOWN U.S.A.(1979); SWAP MEET(1979); GORP(1980)
1984
HOT MOVES(1984)
Eise Ilse Richter
GROUNDSTAR CONSPIRACY, THE(1972, Can.), cos
Elise Richter
BATTLE IN OUTER SPACE(1960)
Ellen Richter
CASE VAN GELDERN(1932, Ger.), a, p; MANULESCU(1933, Ger.), a, p
Misc. Silents
BRIDE OF VENGEANCE(1923); HEADS UP, CHARLIE(1926, Ger.); CARNIVAL OF CRIME(1929, Ger.)
Frederic Richter
ADVENTURES OF TARTU(1943, Brit.)
Frederick Richter
SQUADRON LEADER X(1943, Brit.); WARN THAT MAN(1943, Brit.); MR. EMMANUEL(1945, Brit.); HER MAN GILBEY(1949, Brit.)
Georg Richter
TROMBA, THE TIGER MAN(1952, Ger.), p; KING IN SHADOW(1961, Ger.), p; GLASS OF WATER, A(1962, Cgr.), p; TWO IN A SLEEPING BAG(1964, Ger.), p; GIRL AND THE LEGEND, THE(1966, Ger.), p
George Richter
Silents
BOY OF MINE(1923), ph
Hans Richter
EMIL AND THE DETECTIVE(1931, Ger.); COURT CONCERT, THE(1936, Ger.); DREAMS THAT MONEY CAN BUY(1948), p&d, w
Harold Richter
PASSION HOLIDAY(1963)
Heinrich Richter
KARAMAZOV(1931, Ger.), set d
Ilse Richter
EXPLOSION(1969, Can.), cos; RAINBOW BOYS, THE(1973, Can.), cos; SHADOW OF THE HAWK(1976, Can.), cos
Josef Richter
OCTOPUSSY(1983, Brit.)
Kurt Richter
Silents
PASSION(1920, Ger.), set d
Mildred Richter
LOVE IN THE DESERT(1929), ed
Paul Richter
CASE VAN GELDERN(1932, Ger.)
Silents
SIEGFRIED(1924, Ger.)
Misc. Silents
FORBIDDEN LOVE(1927, Brit.)
Ralph Richter
DAS BOOT(1982)
Svyatoslav Richter
MAN OF MUSIC(1953, USSR)
W. D. Richter
SLITHER(1973), w; PEEPER(1975), w; NICKELODEON(1976), w; INVASION OF THE BODY SNATCHERS(1978), w; DRACULA(1979), w; BRUBAKER(1980), w; ALL NIGHT LONG(1981), w
1984
ADVENTURES OF BUCKAROO BANZAI: ACROSS THE 8TH DIMENSION, THE(1984), p, d
Anna Richter-Visser
DINGAKA(1965, South Africa), cos; KIMBERLEY JIM(1965, South Africa), cos
Marta Richterova
TRANSPORT FROM PARADISE(1967, Czech.)
Richard Richtsfeld
RED-DRAGON(1967, Ital./Ger./US), spec eff; WHO?(1975, Brit./Ger.), spec eff; CROSS OF IRON(1977, Brit., Ger.), spec eff; SLAVERS(1977, Ger.), spec eff
Maria Richwine
BUDDY HOLLY STORY, THE(1978)
Frank Richwood
1984
NO SMALL AFFAIR(1984), art d; RHINESTONE(1984), art d
Alice Richy
STALLION CANYON(1949)
Mike Ricigliano
ANGEL COMES TO BROOKLYN, AN(1945)
Ruth Rickaby
ISLAND OF LOST MEN(1939); LAUGH IT OFF(1939); SMILIN' THROUGH(1941); DIAMOND HORSESHOE(1945); JUNIOR MISS(1945); CHICKEN EVERY SUNDAY(1948)
Ed Rickard
DOUBLE OR NOTHING(1937); REUNION IN FRANCE(1942); YOUNG LIONS, THE(1958)
Edward Rickard
TREASURE OF LOST CANYON, THE(1952)
Marilyn Rickard
Misc. Talkies
TOUCHABLES, THE(1968, Brit.)
Jocelyn Rickards
FROM RUSSIA WITH LOVE(1963, Brit.), cos; KNACK ... AND HOW TO GET IT, THE(1965, Brit.), cos; BLOW-UP(1966, Brit.), cos; MADEMOISELLE(1966, Fr./Brit.), cos; ALFRED THE GREAT(1969, Brit.), cos; WONDERWALL(1969, Brit.), cos; RYAN'S DAUGHTER(1970, Brit.), cos

Ron Rickards
SUMMER WISHES, WINTER DREAMS(1973)
Tony Rickards
CLINIC, THE(1983, Aus.)
1984
SQUIZZY TAYLOR(1984, Aus.)
Gordon Rickarts
Silents
NONENTITY, THE(1922, Brit.)
Ricky Rickerby
LAST SHOT YOU HEAR, THE(1969, Brit.), makeup
Albert Rickerd
ONE WAY TO LOVE(1946), set d
Frank Rickert
Misc. Silents
SOULS IN PAWN(1917)
John F. Rickert
MISTRESS OF THE APES(1981), p
Shirley Rickert
ROYAL WEDDING(1951)
Shirley Jean Rickert
SCARLET LETTER, THE(1934); STRAIGHT FROM THE HEART(1935); FIVE LITTLE PEPPERS IN TROUBLE(1940)
Shirley Jeanne Rickert
ONE HOUR LATE(1935)
G. M. Ricketts
Silents
GREATER LAW, THE(1917)
Thomas Rickett's
Misc. Silents
BUZZARD'S SHADOW, THE(1915), d
Charles Ricketts
MIKADO, THE(1967, Brit.), cos
Rose Ricketts
ODD ANGRY SHOT, THE(1979, Aus.)
Shirley Ricketts [Shirley Jane Rickey]
'NEATH THE ARIZONA SKIES(1934)
Thomas Ricketts
GLAD RAG DOLL, THE(1929); RED HOT SPEED ½(1929); VAGABOND KING, THE(1930); LITTLE MAN, WHAT NOW?(1934)
Misc. Talkies
NOW OR NEVER(1935)
Silents
DAMAGED GOODS(1915), d; SHAM(1921); FOOLS OF FORTUNE(1922); PUTTING IT OVER(1922); SHATTERED IDOLS(1922); TAILOR MADE MAN, A(1922); ALICE ADAMS(1923); STRANGERS OF THE NIGHT(1923); GIRL WHO WOULDN'T WORK, THE(1925); NEVER THE TWAIN SHALL MEET(1925); WAS IT BIGAMY?(1925); NUT-CRACKER, THE(1926); WHEN THE WIFE'S AWAY(1926); FREEDOM OF THE PRESS(1928)
Misc. Silents
END OF THE ROAD, THE(1915), d; LURE OF THE MASK, THE(1915), d; SECRETARY OF FRIVOLOUS AFFAIRS, THE(1915), d; LIFE'S BLIND ALLEY(1916), d; OTHER SIDE OF THE DOOR, THE(1916), d; SINGLE CODE, THE(1917), d; PARISH PRIEST, THE(1921); BLACK OXEN(1924); FATE OF A FLIRT, THE(1925)
Thomas [Tom] Ricketts
Misc. Silents
BROTH FOR SUPPER(1919), d
Thomas H. Ricketts
Misc. Silents
CRIME OF THE HOUR(1918), d
Tom Ricketts
BULLDOG DRUMMOND(1929); LIGHT FINGERS(1929); PRINCE OF DIAMONDS(1930); SEA LEGS(1930); AMBASSADOR BILL(1931); MAN OF THE WORLD(1931); SIDE SHOW(1931); SURRENDER(1931); FAREWELL TO ARMS, A(1932); FORBIDDEN(1932); IF I HAD A MILLION(1932); LOVE ME TONIGHT(1932); MERRILY WE GO TO HELL(1932); THRILL OF YOUTH(1932); FORGOTTEN(1933); HE LEARNED ABOUT WOMEN(1933); LAUGHTER IN HELL(1933); MAMA LOVES PAPA(1933); SECRET SINNERS(1933); WOMEN WON'T TELL(1933); IN LOVE WITH LIFE(1934); IT HAPPENED ONE NIGHT(1934); NANA(1934); NO GREATER GLORY(1934); STOLEN SWEETS(1934); VIVA VILLA!(1934); WHOM THE GODS DESTROY(1934); CURTAIN FALLS, THE(1935); ESCAPADE(1935); FORSAKING ALL OTHERS(1935); GOIN' TO TOWN(1935); GREAT IMPERSONATION, THE(1935); MAN WHO RECLAIMED HIS HEAD, THE(1935); SONS OF STEEL(1935); TALE OF TWO CITIES, A(1935); TOP HAT(1935); AFTER THE THIN MAN(1936); CASE AGAINST MRS. AMES, THE(1936); GOLD DIGGERS OF 1937(1936); HI GAUCHO!(1936); HUMAN CARGO(1936); MORE THAN A SECRETARY(1936); PENNIES FROM HEAVEN(1936); TROUBLE FOR TWO(1936); WE WENT TO COLLEGE(1936); BREAKFAST FOR TWO(1937); DEAD END(1937); HOUSE OF SECRETS, THE(1937); LADY ESCAPES, THE(1937); MAID OF SALEM(1937); PERSONAL PROPERTY(1937); TOAST OF NEW YORK, THE(1937); YOUNG FUGITIVES(1938); YOUNG IN HEART, THE(1938); SON OF FRANKENSTEIN(1939); ZAZA(1939)
Silents
BEATING THE GAME(1921); KILLER, THE(1921); LAVENDER BATH LADY, THE(1922); OH, DOCTOR(1924); WAGES FOR WIVES(1925); CAT'S PAJAMAS, THE(1926); LADIES AT PLAY(1926); LOVE'S BLINDNESS(1926); OLD SOAK, THE(1926); CHILDREN OF DIVORCE(1927); SAILOR'S SWEETHEART, A(1927); JUST MARRIED(1928)
Misc. Silents
CIRCE THE ENCHANTRESS(1924); BUSINESS OF LOVE, THE(1925); FIGHT TO THE FINISH, A(1925); SECRETS OF THE NIGHT(1925); WHEN HUSBANDS FLIRT(1925); GOING THE LIMIT(1926); POKER FACES(1926); LAW AND THE MAN(1928)
Alice Rickey
NO ROOM FOR THE GROOM(1952)
Don Rickles
RUN SILENT, RUN DEEP(1958); RABBIT TRAP, THE(1959); RAT RACE, THE(1960); "X"–THE MAN WITH THE X-RAY EYES(1963); BIKINI BEACH(1964); MUSCLE BEACH PARTY(1964); PAJAMA PARTY(1964); BEACH BLANKET BINGO(1965); ENTER LAUGHING(1967); MONEY JUNGLE, THE(1968); WHERE IT'S AT(1969); KELLY'S HEROES(1970, U.S./Yugo.)

Howard Rickman
GOLDEN HOOFS(1941)
Joseph Rickman
TEXAS RANGERS, THE(1936)
Kathy Rickman
DELIVERANCE(1972)
Thomas Rickman
KANSAS CITY BOMBER(1972), w; LAUGHING POLICEMAN, THE(1973), w; W. W. AND THE DIXIE DANCEKINGS(1975), w; HOOPER(1978), w
1984
RIVER RAT, THE(1984), d&w
Archie Ricks
LONG, LONG TRAIL, THE(1929); GOLD(1932); SHOTGUN PASS(1932); CRASHING BROADWAY(1933); WEST OF THE DIVIDE(1934); DAWN RIDER(1935); SMOKEY SMITH(1935); HITTIN' THE TRAIL(1937); RIDERS FROM NOWHERE(1940)
Misc. Talkies
BRAND OF HATE(1934)
Misc. Silents
RIP SNORTER, THE(1925); VIC DYSON PAYS(1925); IN BRONCHO LAND(1926), d
Ruth Ricksby
COUNTRY GIRL, THE(1954)
Lucille Ricksen
Silents
STRANGER'S BANQUET(1922); RENDEZVOUS, THE(1923); JUDGMENT OF THE STORM(1924)
Misc. Silents
BEHIND THE CURTAIN(1924); HILL BILLY, THE(1924); IDLE TONGUES(1924); YOUNG IDEAS(1924)
Joe Rickson
LONE STAR RANGER, THE(1930); TRAILS OF DANGER(1930); WILD HORSE(1931); FARGO EXPRESS(1933); BAR 20 RIDES AGAIN(1936); HOPALONG CASSIDY RETURNS(1936); ARIZONA LEGION(1939); OKLAHOMA KID, THE(1939)
Silents
ACTION GALORE(1925); RIDERS OF THE PURPLE SAGE(1925); LARIAT KID, THE(1929)
Misc. Silents
BAREE, SON OF KAZAN(1918); HOME TRAIL, THE(1918); FLOWER OF THE NORTH(1921); RIP ROARIN' ROBERTS(1924); ROUGH RIDIN'(1924); BAREE, SON OF KAZAN(1925); FAST FIGHTIN'(1925); DAVY CROCKETT AT THE FALL OF THE ALAMO(1926); RAWHIDE(1926)
Joseph Rickson
UNDER THE PAMPAS MOON(1935); STAGECOACH(1939)
Misc. Silents
GO GET 'EM GARRINGER(1919); OUTLAWED(1921); BORDER BLACK-BIRDS(1927); LAND OF THE LAWLESS(1927)
Lucille Rickson
Misc. Silents
TRIMMED IN SCARLET(1923); DENIAL, THE(1925)
Michael Rickwood
1984
BREAKOUT(1984, Brit.), art d
Don Rico
MARY, MARY, BLOODY MARY(1975, U.S./Mex.), w
John Rico
GUN RUNNER(1969)
Luis Rico
TRISTANA(1970, Span./Ital./Fr.)
Mona Rico
SHANGHAI LADY(1929); DEVIL WITH WOMEN, A(1930); THUNDER BELOW(1932); GOIN' TO TOWN(1935)
Silents
ETERNAL LOVE(1929)
Paquita Rico
SAVAGE GUNS, THE(1962, U.S./Span.)
Paquito Rico
MANOLETE(1950, Span.)
Rigobert Rico
RETURN OF A MAN CALLED HORSE, THE(1976)
Maria Ricossa
CLASS(1983)
Henriette Ridard
VICE DOLLS(1961, Fr.), cos
Jim Ridarsick
HOT STUFF(1979)
Whitney Ridbeck
1941(1979)
Michael Riddall
FAMILY LIFE(1971, Brit.)
George Riddell
Silents
MY FOUR YEARS IN GERMANY(1918)
Jill Riddick
HOVERBUG(1970, Brit.)
Bill Riddle
ROAD HOUSE(1948), makeup; NICKELODEON(1976)
Lt. Carroll Riddle
WINGED VICTORY(1944)
Charles G. Riddle
1984
RIVER, THE(1984)
George Riddle
ARTHUR(1981)
Hal Riddle
COP HATER(1958); DR. GOLDFOOT AND THE BIKINI MACHINE(1965); GREAT RACE, THE(1965)
1984
JOHNNY DANGEROUSLY(1984)

James Riddle
GENTLE GIANT(1967)
Jimmy Riddle
SMOKY MOUNTAIN MELODY(1949)
K.K. Riddle
PSYCHO A GO-GO!(1965)
Mel Riddle
THIS MARRIAGE BUSINESS(1938), w
Nelson Riddle
OCEAN BREAKERS(1949, Swed.), m, md; FLAME OF THE ISLANDS(1955), md; JOHNNY CONCHO(1956), m, md; LISBON(1956), m; GIRL MOST LIKELY, THE(1957), md; PAL JOEY(1957), m; MERRY ANDREW(1958), md; ST. LOUIS BLUES(1958), md; HOLE IN THE HEAD, A(1959), m; LI'L ABNER(1959), m, md; CAN-CAN(1960), md; OCEAN'S ELEVEN(1960), m&md; LOLITA(1962), m; COME BLOW YOUR HORN(1963), m; FOUR FOR TEXAS(1963), m; PARIS WHEN IT SIZZLES(1964), m; ROBIN AND THE SEVEN HOODS(1964), m, md; WHAT A WAY TO GO(1964), m; HARLOW(1965), m; MARRIAGE ON THE ROCKS(1965), m, md; RAGE TO LIVE, A(1965), m; RED LINE 7000(1965), m; BATMAN(1966), m; SPY IN THE GREEN HAT, THE(1966), m; EL DORADO(1967), m; GREAT BANK ROBBERY, THE(1969), m; MALTESE BIPPY, THE(1969), m, md; PAINT YOUR WAGON(1969), md; HELL'S BLOODY DEVILS(1970), m; ON A CLEAR DAY YOU CAN SEE FOREVER(1970), md; HOW TO SUCCEED IN BUSINESS WITHOUT REALLY TRYING(1976), m; HARPER VALLEY, P.T.A.(1978), m; GUYANA, CULT OF THE DAMNED zero(1980, Mex./Span./Panama), m; ROUGH CUT(1980, Brit.), m
1984
CHATTANOOGA CHOO CHOO(1984), m
Rock Riddle
VAN, THE(1977); BLUE COLLAR(1978)
Ronna Riddle
THIS STUFF'LL KILL YA!(1971); YEAR OF THE YAHOO(1971)
Sam Riddle
CLAMBAKE(1967); TUNNELVISION(1976)
June Riddols
WAY WE LIVE, THE(1946, Brit.)
Armand Ridel
RISE OF LOUIS XIV, THE(1970, Fr.), ed
Ruth Ridenour
BOLERO(1934), w
Bob Rideout
FURY AND THE WOMAN(1937); CONVICTED(1938); MANHATTAN SHAKE-DOWN(1939); SPECIAL INSPECTOR(1939)
Doug Rideout
WALK THE ANGRY BEACH(1961)
Ransom Rideout
HALLELUJAH(1929), w
Robert Rideout
WHAT PRICE VENGEANCE?(1937)
Martin Good Rider
SUSANNAH OF THE MOUNTIES(1939)
Mary Rider
Silents
GLADIOLA(1915), w
Sandra Rider
MORE AMERICAN GRAFFITI(1979)
Sid Rider
CANDIDATE FOR MURDER(1966, Brit.), set d
Warrant Officer Sid Rider
JOURNEY TOGETHER(1946, Brit.)
Fritzi Rideway
Misc. Silents
HATE TRAIL, THE(1922)
John David Ridge
HAPPY HOOKER GOES TO WASHINGTON, THE(1977), cos
Walter Ridge
POSTMAN ALWAYS RINGS TWICE, THE(1946); SET-UP, THE(1949); CLOWN, THE(1953); SLIGHT CASE OF LARCENY, A(1953); JEANNE EAGELS(1957)
Cleo Ridgeley
Silents
BEAUTIFUL AND DAMNED, THE(1922)
Misc. Silents
HOUSE OF THE GOLDEN WINDOWS, THE(1916)
John Ridgeley
INDIANAPOLIS SPEEDWAY(1939); CHILD IS BORN, A(1940); THEY DRIVE BY NIGHT(1940); HIGH WALL, THE(1947); IRON CURTAIN, THE(1948); AS YOU WERE(1951)
Richard Ridgeley
Silents
EUGENE ARAM(1915), d&w
Misc. Silents
MAGIC SKIN, THE(1915), d; HEART OF THE HILLS, THE(1916), d
Bob Ridgely
HIGH ANXIETY(1977); MOUSE AND HIS CHILD, THE(1977)
Misc. Talkies
GREAT LESTER BOGGS, THE(1975)
Cleo Ridgely
JUVENILE COURT(1938)
Silents
MARRIAGE OF KITTY, THE(1915); JOAN THE WOMAN(1916); OCCASIONALLY YOURS(1920); SLEEPWALKER, THE(1922)
Misc. Silents
LOVE MASK, THE(1916); SELFISH WOMAN, THE(1916); VICTORIA CROSS, THE(1916); VICTORY OF CONSCIENCE, THE(1916); DANGEROUS PASTIME(1922); FORGOTTEN LAW, THE(1922); LAW AND THE WOMAN(1922)
John Ridgely
HOLLYWOOD HOTEL(1937); KID GALAHAD(1937); SUBMARINE D-1(1937); THEY WON'T FORGET(1937); BLONDES AT WORK(1938); COWBOY FROM BROOK-LYN(1938); CRIME SCHOOL(1938); HARD TO GET(1938); HE COULDN'T SAY NO(1938); INVISIBLE MENACE, THE(1938); LITTLE MISS THOROUGHBRED(1938); MY BILL(1938); PATIENT IN ROOM 18, THE(1938); TORCHY BLANE IN PANA-MA(1938); TORCHY GETS HER MAN(1938); WESTERN TRAILS(1938); WHITE

BANNERS(1938); ADVENTURES OF JANE ARDEN(1939); ANGELS WASH THEIR FACES(1939); CONFESSIONS OF A NAZI SPY(1939); COWBOY QUARTER-BACK(1939); DARK VICTORY(1939); EACH DAWN I DIE(1939); EVERYBODY'S HOBBY(1939); GOING PLACES(1939); KID FROM KOKOMO, THE(1939); KID NIGHT-INGALE(1939); KING OF THE UNDERWORLD(1939); NANCY DREW AND THE HIDDEN STAIRCASE(1939); NAUGHTY BUT NICE(1939); PRIVATE DETEC-TIVE(1939); RETURN OF DR. X, THE(1939); SECRET SERVICE OF THE AIR(1939); SMASHING THE MONEY RING(1939); THEY MADE ME A CRIMINAL(1939); TORCHY PLAYS WITH DYNAMITE(1939); WINGS OF THE NAVY(1939); WOMEN IN THE WIND(1939); YOU CAN'T GET AWAY WITH MURDER(1939); BROTHER ORCHID(1940); FATHER IS A PRINCE(1940); FLIGHT ANGELS(1940); INVISIBLE STRIPES(1940); KNUTE ROCKNE–ALL AMERICAN(1940); LADY WITH RED HAIR(1940); LETTER, THE(1940); MAN WHO TALKED TOO MUCH, THE(1940); NO TIME FOR COMEDY(1940); RIVER'S END(1940); 'TIL WE MEET AGAIN(1940); TORRID ZONE(1940); GREAT MR. NOBODY, THE(1941); HERE COMES HAPPI-NESS(1941); HIGHWAY WEST(1941); INTERNATIONAL SQUADRON(1941); KNOCKOUT(1941); NAVY BLUES(1941); NINE LIVES ARE NOT ENOUGH(1941); STRANGE ALIBI(1941); WAGONS ROLL AT NIGHT, THE(1941); BIG SHOT, THE(1942); BULLET SCARS(1942); DANGEROUSLY THEY LIVE(1942); MAN WHO CAME TO DINNER, THE(1942); SECRET ENEMIES(1942); WINGS FOR THE EA-GLE(1942); AIR FORCE(1943); NORTHERN PURSUIT(1943); ARSENIC AND OLD LACE(1944); DESTINATION TOKYO(1944); DOUGHGIRLS, THE(1944); HOLLY-WOOD CANTEEN(1944); DANGER SIGNAL(1945); GOD IS MY CO-PILOT(1945); PRIDE OF THE MARINES(1945); BIG SLEEP, THE(1946); MAN I LOVE, THE(1946); MY REPUTATION(1946); CHEYENNE(1947); CRY WOLF(1947); NORA PREN-TISS(1947); POSSESSED(1947); THAT WAY WITH WOMEN(1947); THAT'S MY MAN(1947); COMMAND DECISION(1948); LUXURY LINER(1948); NIGHT WIND(1948); SEALED VERDICT(1948); TROUBLE MAKERS(1948); BORDER INCI-DENT(1949); ONCE MORE, MY DARLING(1949); TASK FORCE(1949); TUCSON(1949); BACKFIRE(1950); BEAUTY ON PARADE(1950); EDGE OF DOOM(1950); LOST VOL-CANO, THE(1950); PETTY GIRL, THE(1950); ROOKIE FIREMAN(1950); SADDLE TRAMP(1950); SOUTH SEA SINNER(1950); AL JENNINGS OF OKLAHOMA(1951); HALF ANGEL(1951); LAST OUTPOST, THE(1951); PLACE IN THE SUN, A(1951); THUNDER IN GOD'S COUNTRY(1951); WHEN THE REDSKINS RODE(1951); WHEN WORLDS COLLIDE(1951); FORT OSAGE(1952); GREATEST SHOW ON EARTH, THE(1952); OUTCASTS OF POKER FLAT, THE(1952); ROOM FOR ONE MORE(1952); OFF LIMITS(1953)

Richard Ridgely
Silents
RANSON'S FOLLY(1915), d&w; ENVY(1917), d
Misc. Silents
GREAT PHYSICIAN, THE(1913), d; GREEN EYE OF THE YELLOW GOD, THE(1913), d; DESTROYING ANGEL, THE(1915), d; SHADOWS FROM THE PAST(1915), d; WRONG WOMAN, THE(1915), d; MARTYRDOM OF PHILLIP STRONG, THE(1916), d; MESSAGE TO GARCIA, A(1916), d; MASTER PASSION, THE(1917), d; MYSTIC HOUR, THE(1917), d; PASSION(1917), d

Robert Ridgely
FBI CODE 98(1964); CHROME AND HOT LEATHER(1971); MELVIN AND HOW-ARD(1980)
1984
WILD LIFE, THE(1984)

Stanely C. Ridges
NICK CARTER, MASTER DETECTIVE(1939); EYES IN THE NIGHT(1942); SUS-PECT, THE(1944)

Stanley Ridges
YELLOW JACK(1938); CRIME WITHOUT PASSION(1934); SCOUNDREL, THE(1935); SINNER TAKE ALL(1936); WINTERSET(1936); INTERNES CAN'T TAKE MONEY(1937); IF I WERE KING(1938); MAD MISS MANTON, THE(1938); THERE'S THAT WOMAN AGAIN(1938); DUST BE MY DESTINY(1939); EACH DAWN I DIE(1939); ESPIONAGE AGENT(1939); I STOLE A MILLION(1939); LET US LI-VE(1939); SILVER ON THE SAGE(1939); UNION PACIFIC(1939); BLACK FRI-DAY(1940); MR. DISTRICT ATTORNEY(1941); SEA WOLF, THE(1941); SERGEANT YORK(1941); BIG SHOT, THE(1942); EAGLE SQUADRON(1942); LADY IS WILLING, THE(1942); THEY DIED WITH THEIR BOOTS ON(1942); TO BE OR NOT TO BE(1942); AIR FORCE(1943); FALSE FACES(1943); TARZAN TRIUMPHS(1943); THIS IS THE ARMY(1943); I'LL BE SEEING YOU(1944); MASTER RACE, THE(1944); STORY OF DR. WASSELL, THE(1944); WILSON(1944); CAPTAIN EDDIE(1945); GOD IS MY CO-PILOT(1945); PHANTOM SPEAKS, THE(1945); BECAUSE OF HIM(1946); CAN-YON PASSAGE(1946); MR. ACE(1946); POSSESSED(1947); ACT OF MURDER, AN(1948); STREETS OF LAREDO(1949); TASK FORCE(1949); YOU'RE MY EVERY-THING(1949); FILE ON THELMA JORDAN, THE(1950); NO WAY OUT(1950); PAID IN FULL(1950); GROOM WORE SPURS, THE(1951)
Silents
SUCCESS(1923)

Darla Ridgeway
WAR ARROW(1953)
Fred Ridgeway
BLUEPRINT FOR MURDER, A(1953)
Freddy Ridgeway
FANGS OF THE WILD(1954)
Fritz Ridgeway
NO RANSOM(1935)
Fritzi Ridgeway
RED HOT SPEED ½(1929); THIS IS HEAVEN(1929); HELL'S HEROES(1930); PRINCE OF DIAMONDS(1930); MAD PARADE, THE(1931); LADIES OF THE BIG HOUSE(1932); HOUSE OF MYSTERY(1934); WE LIVE AGAIN(1934)
Silents
HIGH SPEED(1917); REAL FOLKS(1918); PETAL ON THE CURRENT, THE(1919); JUDY OF ROGUES' HARBOUR(1920); BRING HIM IN(1921); RUGGLES OF RED GAP(1923); MAN BAIT(1926); ENEMY, THE(1927); NOBODY'S WIDOW(1927); FLY-ING ROMEOS(1928)
Misc. Silents
LEARNIN' OF JIM BENTON, THE(1917); UP OR DOWN(1917); DANGER ZONE, THE(1918); FAITH AND ENDURIN'(1918); LAW'S OUTLAW, THE(1918); WHEN DOCTORS DISAGREE(1919); FATAL 30, THE(1921); BOOMERANG JUSTICE(1922); BRANDED MAN(1922); MENACING PAST, THE(1922); OLD HOMESTEAD, THE(1922); CRICKET ON THE HEARTH, THE(1923); TRIFLING WITH HONOR(1923); FACE VALUE(1927)

Linda Ridgeway
MECHANIC, THE(1972)
Michael Ridgeway
PUMPKIN EATER, THE(1964, Brit.); GOODBYE MR. CHIPS(1969, U.S./Brit.)
Philip Ridgeway
SWITCH, THE(1963, Brit.), p, w
Philip Ridgeway, Jr.
YANK AT OXFORD, A(1938)
Susan Ridgeway
TIJUANA STORY, THE(1957)
Suzanne Ridgeway
ROAD TO MOROCCO(1942); DUCHESS OF IDAHO, THE(1950); LIEUTENANT WORE SKIRTS, THE(1956)
Audrey Ridgewell
HIS DOUBLE LIFE(1933)
George Ridgewell
Misc. Silents
ROOT OF EVIL, THE(1919), d
Cleo Ridgley
I REMEMBER MAMA(1948)
Silents
GOLDEN CHANCE, THE(1915); PUPPET CROWN, THE(1915); SECRET OR-CHARD(1915)
Misc. Silents
STOLEN GOODS(1915); YELLOW PAWN, THE(1916)
John Ridgley
FORBIDDEN VALLEY(1938); MILLION DOLLAR BABY(1941); THEY DIED WITH THEIR BOOTS ON(1942)
Richard Ridgley
Misc. Silents
TRAGEDIES OF THE CRYSTAL GLOBE, THE(1915), d; GHOST OF OLD MORRO, THE(1917), d; GOD OF LITTLE CHILDREN(1917), d; GREAT BRADLEY MYSTERY, THE(1917), d; PRIDE(1917), d
Edna Ridgway
KIND OF LOVING, A(1962, Brit.)
Fritzie Ridgway
Misc. Silents
HERO OF THE HOUR, THE(1917)
Jack Ridgway
Silents
BABY MINE(1917)
Misc. Silents
UNKNOWN QUANTITY, THE(1919); LITTLE ITALY(1921)
Margaret Ridgway
NAUGHTY ARLETTE(1951, Brit.)
Suzanne Ridgway
HOLD'EM NAVY!(1937); RAIDERS OF THE DESERT(1941); MEXICAN HAYRI-DE(1948); MY FAVORITE SPY(1951); FROM HELL IT CAME(1957)
George Ridgwell
CRIME AT BLOSSOMS, THE(1933, Brit.)
Silents
AMAZING PARTNERSHIP, THE(1921, Brit.), d; CRIMSON CIRCLE, THE(1922, Brit.), d; ELEVENTH HOUR, THE(1922, Brit.), d; POINTING FINGER, THE(1922, Brit.), d; NOTORIOUS MRS. CARRICK, THE(1924, Brit.), d
Misc. Silents
MYSTERY OF ROOM 13, THE(1915), d; SOMEWHERE IN GEORGIA(1916), d; FRUITS OF PASSION(1919), d; WATER LILY, THE(1919), d; GAMBLE IN LIVES, A(1920, Brit.), d; SWORD OF DAMOCLES, THE(1920, Brit.), d; FOUR JUST MEN, THE(1921, Brit.), d; GREATHEART(1921, Brit.), d; CRIMSON CIRCLE, THE(1922, Brit.), d; DON'T BLAME YOUR CHILDREN(1922, Brit.), p; KNIGHT ERRANT, THE(1922, Brit.), d; LOST LEADER, A(1922, Brit.), d; PETTICOAT LOOSE(1922, Brit.), d; BECKET(1923, Brit.), d; LILY OF KILLARNEY(1929, Brit.), d
Richard Ridings
1984
LASSITER(1984)
Diane Ridler
MY WAY(1974, South Africa)
Anne Ridley
SQUADRON 633(1964, U.S./Brit.); 633 SQUADRON(1964)
Arnold Ridley
FLYING FOOL, THE(1931, Brit.), w; KEEPERS OF YOUTH(1931, Brit.), w; THIRD TIME LUCKY(1931, Brit.), w; GHOST TRAIN, THE(1933, Brit.), w; BLIND JUS-TICE(1934, Brit.), w; WARREN CASE, THE(1934, Brit.), w; DOMMED CARGO(1936, Brit.), w; ROYAL EAGLE(1936, Brit.), d, w; SHADOWED EYES(1939, Brit.), w; GHOST TRAIN, THE(1941, Brit.), w; EASY MONEY(1948, Brit.), w; INTERRUPTED JOURNEY, THE(1949, Brit.), w; GREEN GROW THE RUSHES(1951, Brit.); STOLEN FACE(1952, Brit.); MEET MR. LUCIFER(1953, Brit.), w; WINGS OF MYSTERY(1963, Brit.); CROOKS IN CLOISTERS(1964, Brit.); WHO KILLED THE CAT?(1966, Brit.), w; DAD'S ARMY(1971, Brit.)
Silents
GHOST TRAIN, THE(1927, Brit.), w
Arthur Ridley
MRS. PYM OF SCOTLAND YARD(1939, Brit.); MAN WHO KNEW TOO MUCH, THE(1956)
Christopher Ridley
ESCAPADE(1955, Brit.)
Douglas Ridley
CARRY ON HENRY VIII(1970, Brit.); LOOT(1971, Brit.)
Giles Ridley
KILLER FORCE(1975, Switz./Ireland)
Judith Ridley
NIGHT OF THE LIVING DEAD(1968)
Justin Ridley
MONKEY GRIP(1983, Aus.)
Phil Ridley
HOUNDS... OF NOTRE DAME, THE(1980, Can.)
Giovanni Ridolfi
MARRIAGE–ITALIAN STYLE(1964, Fr./Ital.); YESTERDAY, TODAY, AND TO-MORROW(1964, Ital./Fr.)

Sara Ridolfi
DIARY OF A SCHIZOPHRENIC GIRL(1970, Ital.)
Relly Ridon
Misc. Silents
OTHER, THE(1912, Ger.)
William Ridoutt
TO THE DEVIL A DAUGHTER(1976, Brit./Ger.)
Antonio Sanz Ridruejo
LOST COMMAND, THE(1966), adv
Chris Ridsdale
1984
REFLECTIONS(1984, Brit.), ed
Harry Riebauer
GREAT ESCAPE, THE(1963); MAD EXECUTIONERS, THE(1965, Ger.)
Loren Riebe
SHE COULDN'T TAKE IT(1935); COME ON, COWBOYS(1937); GUNSMOKE RANCH(1937); STRANGER FROM ARIZONA, THE(1938)
Barbara Riebling
COME BACK BABY(1968)
J. T. Riebling
COME BACK BABY(1968), m
John Terry Riebling
COME BACK BABY(1968)
Arthur Rieck
SCHOOL FOR SECRETS(1946, Brit.)
Cordula Riedel
MALOU(1983)
Georg Riedel
SWEDISH WEDDING NIGHT(1965, Swed.), m; WOMAN OF DARKNESS(1968, Swed.), m; PIPPI IN THE SOUTH SEAS(1974, Swed./Ger.), m
George Riedel
NIGHT GAMES(1966, Swed.), m
R.H. Riedel
SUN NEVER SETS, THE(1939), art d
Richard Riedel
BETWEEN US GIRLS(1942), art d; NIGHT MONSTER(1942), art d; FLESH AND FANTASY(1943), art d; DESTINY(1944), art d; WEIRD WOMAN(1944), art d; LAWLESS BREED, THE(1952), art d; RAIDERS, THE(1952), art d; FORBIDDEN(1953), art d; MISSISSIPPI GAMBLER, THE(1953), art d; SHOWDOWN AT ABILENE(1956), art d; THIS HAPPY FEELING(1958), art d; PILLOW TALK(1959), art d; PRIVATE LIVES OF ADAM AND EVE, THE(1961), art d
Richard A. Riedel
ILLEGAL ENTRY(1949), art d
Richard E. Riedel
SOUTH SEA SINNER(1950), art d
Richard H. Riedel
SPRING PARADE(1940), art d; NEVER GIVE A SUCKER AN EVEN BREAK(1941), art d; ALI BABA AND THE FORTY THIEVES(1944), art d; GHOST CATCHERS(1944), art d; HER PRIMITIVE MAN(1944), art d; FRONTIER GAL(1945), art d; HERE COME THE CO-EDS(1945), art d; MEN IN HER DIARY(1945), art d; SHADY LADY(1945), art d; SUDAN(1945), art d; CANYON PASSAGE(1946), art d; IDEA GIRL(1946), art d; IVY(1947), art d; FAMILY HONEYMOON(1948), art d; FAT MAN, THE(1951), art d; HOLLYWOOD STORY(1951), art d; TOMAHAWK(1951), art d; NO ROOM FOR THE GROOM(1952), art d; RED BALL EXPRESS(1952), art d; THUNDER BAY(1953), art d; TUMBLEWEED(1953), art d; SHRIKE, THE(1955), art d; SMOKE SIGNAL(1955), art d; THIS ISLAND EARTH(1955), art d; I'VE LIVED BEFORE(1956), art d; RAWHIDE YEARS, THE(1956), art d; TOY TIGER(1956), art d; GREAT MAN, THE(1957), art d; LAND UNKNOWN, THE(1957), art d; MY MAN GODFREY(1957), art d; TAMMY AND THE BACHELOR(1957), art d; LADY TAKES A FLYER, THE(1958), art d; VOICE IN THE MIRROR(1958), art d; IMITATION OF LIFE(1959), art d; STRANGER IN MY ARMS(1959), art d; PORTRAIT IN BLACK(1960), art d
Joseph Rieder
Silents
PIERRE OF THE PLAINS(1914)
Hertha Riedle
SEVEN DARING GIRLS(1962, Ger.)
Gerhard Riedmann
MAGIC FIRE(1956); BEGGAR STUDENT, THE(1958, Ger.); HIPPODROME(1961, Aust./Ger.)
Francis Riedy
MY HANDS ARE CLAY(1948, Irish)
Leni Riefenstahl
BLUE LIGHT, THE(1932, Ger.), a, p, d; S.O.S. ICEBERG(1933)
Misc. Silents
PEAKS OF DESTINY(1927, Ger.)
Charles Riegal
Silents
HEART RAIDER, THE(1923)
Charles Riegel
Silents
POLLY OF THE CIRCUS(1917)
Cindy Riegel
DR. HECKYL AND MR. HYPE(1980); SCHIZOID(1980)
Kenneth Riegel
DON GIOVANNI(1979, Fr./Ital./Ger.)
Roy Riegels
TOUCHDOWN!(1931)
August Rieger
5 SINNERS(1961, Ger.), p, w; $100 A NIGHT(1968, Ger.), w
Peter Riegert
NATIONAL LAMPOON'S ANIMAL HOUSE(1978); AMERICATHON(1979); CHILLY SCENES OF WINTER(1982); LOCAL HERO(1983, Brit.)
1984
CITY GIRL, THE(1984)
Gloria Riegger
KING, MURRAY(1969)
Olav Riego
TORMENT(1947, Swed.)

Ted Riehert
FINAL COUNTDOWN, THE(1980)
Kay Riehl
SHAKEDOWN(1950); DREAM WIFE(1953); HANNAH LEE(1953); STAR, THE(1953); SABRINA(1954); TEEN-AGE CRIME WAVE(1955)
Richard Riehle
JOYRIDE(1977)
Mario Van Riel
EL CID(1961, U.S./Ital.), makeup; FALL OF THE ROMAN EMPIRE, THE(1964), makeup
Margot Rielscher
DEVIL MAKES THREE, THE(1952)
Jack Riely
1984
NIGHT PATROL(1984)
Johannes Riemann
MAID HAPPY(1933, Brit.); DAY AFTER THE DIVORCE, THE(1940, Ger.)
Anita Rieneck
CHRISTINE KEELER AFFAIR, THE(1964, Brit.)
Estelle Riener
FATSO(1980)
Rex Rienits
WIDE BOY(1952, Brit.), w; NOOSE FOR A LADY(1953, Brit.), w; FABIAN OF THE YARD(1954, Brit.), w; RIVER BEAT(1954), w; COUNT OF TWELVE(1955, Brit.), w; CROSS CHANNEL(1955, Brit.), w; NO SMOKING(1955, Brit.), w; WALK INTO HELL(1957, Aus.), w; SMILEY GETS A GUN(1959, Brit.), w; JAZZ BOAT(1960, Brit.), w
Rex Rientis
ASSASSIN FOR HIRE(1951, Brit.), w
Virgilio Riento
ANYTHING FOR A SONG(1947, Ital.); PEDDLIN' IN SOCIETY(1949, Ital.); MIRACLE IN MILAN(1951, Ital.); BREAD, LOVE AND DREAMS(1953, Ital.); CENTO ANNI D'AMORE(1954, Ital.); FRISKY(1955, Ital.); SIGN OF VENUS, THE(1955, Ital.); MILLER'S WIFE, THE(1957, Ital.); DAY IN COURT, A(1965, Ital.)
Eva Rienzi
TASTE OF EXCITEMENT(1969, Brit.)
Albert Riera
L'ATALANTE(1947, Fr.), w
Carlos Riera
NARCO MEN, THE(1969, Span./Ital.)
Marien Perez Riera
Misc. Talkies
TWO WORLDS OF ANGELITA, THE(1982)
Miteira Riera
JETLAG(1981, U.S./Span.), art d
Carol Ries
NAKED ANGELS(1969)
Irving Ries
MYSTERIOUS ISLAND(1929), spec eff; PLYMOUTH ADVENTURE(1952), spec eff
Irving G. Ries
SCARAMOUCHE(1952), spec eff; SINGIN' IN THE RAIN(1952), spec eff
Ray Ries
Silents
ON THE GO(1925), ph; ACE OF ACTION(1926), ph
Harry E. Riesberg
CITY BENEATH THE SEA(1953), w
Robert Riesel
CRAZY JOE(1974)
Hugo Riesenfeld
CAVALIER, THE(1928), m; SINS OF THE FATHERS(1928), m; ALIBI(1929), m; IRON MASK, THE(1929), m; MIDSTREAM(1929), m; MOLLY AND ME(1929), m; THIS IS HEAVEN(1929), m; TWO MEN AND A MAID(1929), m; BAD ONE, THE(1930), m; HELL'S ANGELS(1930), m; LOTTERY BRIDE, THE(1930), md; PUTTIN' ON THE RITZ(1930), m; WHITE ZOMBIE(1932), m; PRESIDENT VANISHES, THE(1934), md; DANIEL BOONE(1936), md; DEVIL ON HORSEBACK, THE(1936), md; HEARTS IN BONDAGE(1936), m; PRESIDENT'S MYSTERY, THE(1936), md; RIDERS OF THE WHISTLING SKULL(1937), m; HAWAII CALLS(1938), m; TARZAN'S REVENGE(1938), md; SUNSET MURDER CASE(1941), m
Silents
REPUTATION(1921), m; PONY EXPRESS, THE(1925), m; BEAU GESTE(1926), m; OLD SAN FRANCISCO(1927), m; SUNRISE–A SONG OF TWO HUMANS(1927), m; AWAKENING, THE(1928), m; BATTLE OF THE SEXES, THE(1928), m; TEMPEST(1928), m; TWO LOVERS(1928), m; ETERNAL LOVE(1929), m; EVANGELINE(1929), m; RESCUE, THE(1929), m; TABU(1931), m
Dr. Hugo Riesenfeld
LUCKY BOY(1929), m; LITTLE MEN(1935), m; FOLLOW YOUR HEART(1936), md; RAINBOW ON THE RIVER(1936), md; WHITE LEGION, THE(1936), md; MAKE A WISH(1937), md; WIDE OPEN FACES(1938), md
Jose Riesgo
CEREMONY, THE(1963, U.S./Span.); MERCENARY, THE(1970, Ital./Span.); TRISTANA(1970, Span./Ital./Fr.)
Michael Riesman
PLEASANTVILLE(1976), m
Charles F Riesner
CAUGHT SHORT(1930), d; POLITICS(1931), d; SHOW-OFF, THE(1934), d; YOU CAN'T BUY EVERYTHING(1934), d; IT'S IN THE AIR(1935), d; MANHATTAN MERRY-GO-ROUND(1937), d; RAILROADED(1947), p; IN THIS CORNER(1948), d; TRAVELING SALESWOMAN(1950), d
Charles Riesner
WINNING TICKET, THE(1935), p, d; MURDER GOES TO COLLEGE(1937), d; SOPHIE LANG GOES WEST(1937), d; BIG STORE, THE(1941), d; THIS TIME FOR KEEPS(1942), d; LOST IN A HAREM(1944), d
Silents
KID, THE(1921)
Dean Riesner
TRAVELING SALESWOMAN(1950); PARIS HOLIDAY(1958), w; MAN FROM GALVESTON, THE(1964), w; DIRTY HARRY(1971), w; CHARLEY VARRICK(1973), w

Heinrich Riethmueller
ETERNAL LOVE(1960, Ger.), md
Carol Riethof
TEACHER AND THE MIRACLE, THE(1961, Ital./Span.), p&d
Peter Riethof
HEIDI AND PETER(1955, Switz.), p; MYSTERIANS, THE(1959, Jap.), p; TEACHER AND THE MIRACLE, THE(1961, Ital./Span.), p&d
Vittorio Rieti
CUCKOO CLOCK, THE(1938, Ital.), m
Bobby Rietti
EMIL(1938, Brit.)
Ronald Rietti
FROZEN ALIVE(1966, Brit./Ger.), p; SUNSCORCHED(1966, Span./Ger.), p
Victor Rietti
TWO HEARTS IN HARMONY(1935, Brit.); JUGGERNAUT(1937, Brit.); ROOM FOR TWO(1940, Brit.); TWENTY-ONE DAYS TOGETHER(1940, Brit.); MAN ABOUT THE HOUSE, A(1947, Brit.); STORY OF ESTHER COSTELLO, THE(1957, Brit.); YOUR PAST IS SHOWING(1958, Brit.)
Vittorio [Robert] Rietti
POWER(1934, Brit.)
Robert Rietty
CROOKED ROAD, THE(; CALL OF THE BLOOD(1948, Brit.); SALT TO THE DEVIL(1949, Brit.); PRELUDE TO FAME(1950, Brit.); STOCK CAR(1955, Brit.); CHECKPOINT(1957, Brit.); SNORKEL, THE(1958, Brit.); TANK FORCE(1958, Brit.); TRUTH ABOUT WOMEN, THE(1958, Brit.); BLUEBEARD'S TEN HONEY-MOONS(1960, Brit.); BOY WHO STOLE A MILLION, THE(1960, Brit.); MIDDLE COURSE, THE(1961, Brit.); LIGHT IN THE PIAZZA(1962); ON THE BEAT(1962, Brit.); STORY OF JOSEPH AND HIS BRETHREN THE(1962, Ital.); TIME TO REMEM-BER(1962, Brit.); CRIMSON BLADE, THE(1964, Brit.); BIBLE...IN THE BEGINNING, THE(1966); ITALIAN JOB, THE(1969, Brit.); ON HER MAJESTY'S SECRET SER-VICE(1969, Brit.); SONG OF NORWAY(1970); SUNDAY BLOODY SUNDAY(1971, Brit.); HIDING PLACE, THE(1975); OMEN, THE(1976); GULLIVER'S TRAVELS(1977, Brit., Bel.); NO LONGER ALONE(1978); NEVER SAY NEVER AGAIN(1983)
Victor Rietty
MR. H. C. ANDERSEN(1950, Brit.)
Robert Rietz
PAL JOEY(1957)
Jeon Rieuben
GATES OF PARIS(1958, Fr./Ital.)
Jean Rieubon
LOVE IN THE AFTERNOON(1957)
Kenny Rieve
RASPUTIN(1932, Ger.)
Klaus Rifbjerg
WEEKEND(1964, Den.), w
Jon Riffel
GAL WHO TOOK THE WEST, THE(1949; SQUARE DANCE KATY(1950)
W.L. Riffs
MAN CALLED DAGGER, A(1967), w
Iva Rifkin
STING II, THE(1983)
Ron Rifkin
DEVIL'S 8, THE(1969); FLAREUP(1969); SILENT RUNNING(1972); SUNSHINE BOYS, THE(1975); BIG FIX, THE(1978); CHOSEN, THE(1982); STING II, THE(1983)
Stephanie Rifkinson
THUNDER ISLAND(1963)
Al Rigali
DEAD MARCH, THE(1937)
Francesco Rigamonti
8 ½(1963, Ital.)
Evi Rigano
EVA(1962, Fr./Ital.); TENTH VICTIM, THE(1965, Fr./Ital.)
Ileana Rigano
THAT SPLENDID NOVEMBER(1971, Ital./Fr.)
Franco Riganti
DAMON AND PYTHIAS(1962), w
Giorgio Riganti
NEVER TAKE NO FOR AN ANSWER(1952, Brit./Ital.)
George Rigas
ACQUITTED(1929); SEA FURY(1929); WOLF SONG(1929); LONESOME TRAIL, THE(1930); BEAU IDEAL(1931); RIDERS OF THE NORTH(1931); GOLDEN WEST, THE(1932); DESTINATION UNKNOWN(1933); WAY TO LOVE, THE(1933); ARREST BULLDOG DRUMMOND(1939, Brit.); OKLAHOMA KID, THE(1939)
Silents
LOVE LIGHT, THE(1921); RIP-TIDE, THE(1923); "THAT ROYLE GIRL"(1925); RESCUE, THE(1929)
Misc. Silents
DANGEROUS MOMENT, THE(1921)
Kostas Rigas
BAREFOOT BATTALION, THE(1954, Gr.)
Peter Rigas
TRAILING THE KILLER(1932)
George Rigaud
MASQUERADE IN MEXICO(1945); PARIS UNDERGROUND(1945); I WALK ALONE(1948); NATIVE SON(1951, U.S., Arg.); JOHN PAUL JONES(1959); HAPPY THIEVES, THE(1962); CASTILIAN, THE(1963, Span./U.S.); SAVAGE PAMPAS(1967, Span./Arg.); UP THE MACGREGORS(1967, Ital./Span.); SANTO CONTRA EL DOC-TOR MUERTE(1974, Span./Mex.); EYEBALL(1978, Ital.)
George [Jorge] Rigaud
OPERATION DELILAH(1966, U.S./Span.); ONE STEP TO HELL(1969, U.S./Ital./Span.)
Georges Rigaud
LIVING CORPSE, THE(1940, Fr.); RIFF RAFF GIRLS(1962, Fr./Ital.); THAT MAN IN ISTANBUL(1966, Fr./Ital./Span.); WEB OF FEAR(1966, Fr./Span.); GRAND SLAM(1968, Ital., Span., Ger.); SEVEN GUNS FOR THE MACGREGORS(1968, Ital./Span.); LAST MERCENARY, THE(1969, Ital./Span.); TOWN CALLED HELL, A(1971, Span./Brit.)

Jorge Rigaud
COLOSSUS OF RHODES, THE(1961, Ital., Fr., Span.); FINGER ON THE TRIG-GER(1965, US/Span.); LOST COMMAND, THE(1966); PLACE CALLED GLORY, A(1966, Span./Ger.); TEXICAN, THE(1966, U.S./Span.); SEA PIRATE, THE(1967, Fr./Span./Ital.); TALL WOMEN, THE(1967, Aust./Ital./Span.); THAT MAN GEOR-GE!(1967, Fr./Ital./Span.); GUNS OF THE MAGNIFICENT SEVEN(1969); LAST DAY OF THE WAR, THE(1969, U.S./Ital./Span.); YOUNG REBEL, THE(1969, Fr./Ital./Span.); NICHOLAS AND ALEXANDRA(1971, Brit.); HORROR EXPRESS(1972, Span./Brit.)
Arthur Rigby
LOVE LIES(1931, Brit.), w; DEPUTY DRUMMER, THE(1935, Brit.), a, w; TRUST THE NAVY(1935, Brit.), a, w; WHO'S YOUR FATHER?(1935, Brit.), w; WOLVES OF THE UNDERWORLD(1935, Brit.), w; HOT NEWS(1936, Brit.), w; HOLD MY HAND(1938, Brit.), w; LUCKY TO ME(1939, Brit.), w; SMALL TOWN STORY(1953, Brit.); DANGEROUS CARGO(1954, Brit.); CROSSROADS TO CRIME(1960, Brit.)
Arthur Rigby, Jr.
YOU MADE ME LOVE YOU(1934, Brit.); PRISONER OF CORBAL(1939, Brit.)
David Rigby
STRANGE BREW(1983)
Edward Rigby
LORNA DOONE(1935, Brit.); NO LIMIT(1935, Brit.); WINDFALL(1935, Brit.); AC-CUSED(1936, Brit.); FORBIDDEN MUSIC(1936, Brit.); GAY OLD DOG(1936, Brit.); HEIRLOOM MYSTERY, THE(1936, Brit.); IRISH FOR LUCK(1936, Brit.); QUEEN OF HEARTS(1936, Brit.); THIS GREEN HELL(1936, Brit.); FATAL HOUR, THE(1937, Brit.); MR. SMITH CARRIES ON(1937, Brit.); SHOW GOES ON, THE(1937, Brit.); UNDER A CLOUD(1937, Brit.); WHEN THIEF MEETS THIEF(1937, Brit.); SMILING ALONG(1938, Brit.); YANK AT OXFORD, A(1938); YELLOW SANDS(1938, Brit.); YOUNG AND INNOCENT(1938, Brit.); THERE AIN'T NO JUSTICE(1939, Brit.); WARE CASE, THE(1939, Brit.); CONVOY(1940); FINGERS(1940, Brit.); SAILOR'S DON'T CARE(1940, Brit.); SECRET FOUR, THE(1940, Brit.); STARS LOOK DOWN, THE(1940, Brit.); COMMON TOUCH, THE(1941, Brit.); COURAGEOUS MR. PENN, THE(1941, Brit.); FARMER'S WIFE, THE(1941, Brit.); MAJOR BARBARA(1941, Brit.); POISON PEN(1941, Brit.); PROUD VALLEY, THE(1941, Brit.); FLYING FORTRESS(1942, Brit.); LET THE PEOPLE SING(1942, Brit.); PLAYBOY, THE(1942, Brit.); REMARKABLE MR. KIPPS(1942, Brit.); SALUTE JOHN CITIZEN(1942, Brit.); GET CRACKING(1943, Brit.); YOUNG MAN'S FANCY(1943, Brit.); CANTERBURY TALE, A(1944, Brit.); DON'T TAKE IT TO HEART(1944, Brit.); 48 HOURS(1944, Brit.); QUERY(1945, Brit.); THEY MET IN THE DARK(1945, Brit.); VACATION FROM MARRIAGE(1945, Brit.); MURDER IN REVERSE(1946, Brit.); YANK IN LONDON, A(1946, Brit.); GREEN FINGERS(1947); LOVES OF JOANNA GODDEN, THE(1947, Brit.); YEARS BE-TWEEN, THE(1947, Brit.); DAYDREAK(1948, Brit.); EASY MONEY(1948, Brit.); PICCADILLY INCIDENT(1948, Brit.); QUIET WEEKEND(1948, Brit.); THREE WEIRD SISTERS, THE(1948, Brit.); AGITATOR, THE(1949); ALL OVER THE TOWN(1949, Brit.); CHRISTOPHER COLUMBUS(1949, Brit.); DON'T EVER LEAVE ME(1949, Brit.); TEMPTATION HARBOR(1949, Brit.); HAPPIEST DAYS OF YOUR LIFE(1950, Brit.); IT'S HARD TO BE GOOD(1950, Brit.); MUDLARK, THE(1950, Brit.); RUN FOR YOUR MONEY, A(1950, Brit.); SILK NOOSE, THE(1950, Brit.); WHAT THE BUTLER SAW(1950, Brit.); CIRCLE OF DANGER(1951, Brit.); MAN IN THE DINGHY, THE(1951, Brit.); TONY DRAWS A HORSE(1951, Brit.); DOUBLE CONFESSION(1953, Brit.)
George Rigby
UNEASY TERMS(1948, Brit.)
Gordon Rigby
SKIN DEEP(1929), w; DANCING SWEETIES(1930), w; MAMMY(1930), w; SONG OF THE FLAME(1930), w; UNDER A TEXAS MOON(1930), w; CAPTAIN THUN-DER(1931), w; COMMAND PERFORMANCE(1931), w; GOLDEN WEST, THE(1932), w; ORCHIDS TO YOU(1935), w; GENTLEMAN FROM LOUISIANA(1936), w; HITCH HIKE LADY(1936), w; WRONG ROAD, THE(1937), w; FLIGHT INTO NO-WHERE(1938), w; REFORMATORY(1938), w; HIDDEN POWER(1939), w; STRANGE CASE OF DR. MEADE(1939), w; TRAPPED IN THE SKY(1939), w; WHISPERING ENEMIES(1939), w; SING, DANCE, PLENTY HOT(1940), w; NAVAL ACADE-MY(1941), w; MAN WHO RETURNED TO LIFE, THE(1942), w; MILLERSON CASE, THE(1947), w; OUT OF THE STORM(1948), w
Graham Rigby
KIND OF LOVING, A(1962, Brit.)
Harry Rigby
OPEN THE DOOR AND SEE ALL THE PEOPLE(1964)
L. G. Rigby
Silents
DARK STAIRWAYS(1924), w; ADVENTURE(1925), w; WINGS OF THE STORM(1926), w; AUCTIONEER, THE(1927), w; NEVADA(1927), w; GRAIN OF DUST, THE(1928), w; TOILERS, THE(1928), w
Ray Rigby
HILL, THE(1965, Brit.), w; OPERATION CROSSBOW(1965, U.S./Ital.), w
Terence Rigby
ACCIDENT(1967, Brit.); GET CARTER(1971, Brit.); HOMECOMING, THE(1973); WATERSHIP DOWN(1978, Brit.); DOGS OF WAR, THE(1980, Brit.); SIGN OF FOUR, THE(1983, Brit.)
Gertrude Rigdon
HOLD ME TIGHT(1933), w
Thelma Rigdon
MRS. O'MALLEY AND MR. MALONE(1950)
Arthur Rigel
ADVENTURES OF SCARAMOUCHE, THE(1964, Fr.), w
Carl Rigg
OBLONG BOX, THE(1969, Brit.); SUMARINE X-1(1969, Brit.); CRY OF THE BAN-SHEE(1970, Brit.); SONG OF NORWAY(1970); TOOMORROW(1970, Brit.); MADE(1972, Brit.)
Daphne Rigg
DOLL'S HOUSE, A(1973)
Diana Rigg
ASSASSINATION BUREAU, THE(1969, Brit.); MIDSUMMER NIGHT'S DREAM, A(1969, Brit.); ON HER MAJESTY'S SECRET SERVICE(1969, Brit.); JULIUS CA-ESAR(1970, Brit.); HOSPITAL, THE(1971); THEATRE OF BLOOD(1973, Brit.); LITTLE NIGHT MUSIC, A(1977, Aust./U.S./Ger.); GREAT MUPPET CAPER, THE(1981); EVIL UNDER THE SUN(1982, Brit.)
Misc. Talkies
OUR MAN IN THE CARIBBEAN(1962)

Nancy Rigg
Silents
ARCADIANS, THE(1927, Brit.)
Misc. Silents
SKIRTS(1928, Brit.)
Rebecca Rigg
MONKEY GRIP(1983, Aus.)
Misc. Talkies
DOCTORS AND NURSES(1983)
Marshal Riggan
SO SAD ABOUT GLORIA(1973), w
Frank Riggi
THEY MADE ME A CRIMINAL(1939); KNOCKOUT(1941); KID FROM BOOKLYN, THE(1946)
Aileen Riggin
ROMAN SCANDALS(1933)
Jerry Riggin
MAN-EATER OF KUMAON(1948)
Kathy Riggins
HITCH-HIKER, THE(1953)
Jerry Riggio
ROMANCE OF THE WEST(1946); TANGIER(1946); ENCHANTED VALLEY, THE(1948); SON OF BILLY THE KID(1949); CRISIS(1950); WAR AND PEACE(1956, Ital./U.S.); HOW SWEET IT IS(1968)
Jess Riggle
POSSE(1975)
Betty Riggs [Evelyn Brent]
Silents
SHOOTING OF DAN MCGREW, THE(1915)
Bobby Riggs
RACQUET(1979)
Daphne Riggs
TWO A PENNY(1968, Brit.); PRIVATE LIFE OF SHERLOCK HOLMES, THE(1970, Brit.)
Jack Riggs
PURPLE HILLS, THE(1961)
Lynn Riggs
STINGAREE(1934), w; GARDEN OF ALLAH, THE(1936), w; PLAINSMAN, THE(1937), w; DESTINATION UNKNOWN(1942), w; MADAME SPY(1942), w; SHERLOCK HOLMES AND THE VOICE OF TERROR(1942), w; SHERLOCK HOLMES IN WASHINGTON(1943), w; OKLAHOMA(1955), w
M.A. Riggs
BAYOU(1957), p
Ralph Riggs
LOST BOUNDARIES(1949); SIDE STREET(1950)
Rita Riggs
HAPPY ENDING, THE(1969), cos; MODEL SHOP, THE(1969), cos; NUMBER ONE(1969), cos; COLD TURKEY(1971), cos; CINDERELLA LIBERTY(1973), cos; ELECTRA GLIDE IN BLUE(1973), cos; NIGHT MOVES(1975), cos; DOMINO PRINCIPLE, THE(1977), cos; IDOLMAKER, THE(1980), cos; CATTLE ANNIE AND LITTLE BRITCHES(1981), cos; YES, GIORGIO(1982), cos
Sarah Riggs
QUADROON(1972), w
Seth Riggs
WHAT EVER HAPPENED TO AUNT ALICE?(1969)
Sidney Riggs
SAP FROM SYRACUSE, THE(1930)
Tommy Riggs
GOODBYE BROADWAY(1938)
Gennaro Righelli
PEDDLIN' IN SOCIETY(1949, Ital.), d
Massimo Righi
ATLAS AGAINST THE CYCLOPS(1963, Ital.); BLACK SABBATH(1963, Ital.); BLOOD AND BLACK LACE(1965, Ital.); PLANET OF THE VAMPIRES(1965, U.S./Ital./Span.); CONQUERED CITY(1966, Ital.); SPY IN YOUR EYE(1966, Ital.)
The Righteous Brothers
SWINGIN' SUMMER, A(1965)
Alexander Rignault
RASPUTIN(1939, Fr.)
Alexandre Rignault
CRIME AND PUNISHMENT(1935, Fr.); LILIOM(1935, Fr.); DR. KNOCK(1936, Fr.); COURRIER SUD(1937, Fr.); ROBBER SYMPHONY, THE(1937, Brit.); ETERNAL RETURN, THE(1943, Fr.); VOLPONE(1947, Fr.); RUY BLAS(1948, Fr.); HOLIDAY FOR HENRIETTA(1955, Fr.); HAPPY ROAD, THE(1957, Fr.); WE ARE MURDERERS(1957, Fr.); HORROR CHAMBER OF DR. FAUSTUS, THE(1962, Fr./Ital.); LA CHIENNE(1975, Fr.); NUMBER TWO(1975, Fr.); MON ONCLE D'AMERIQUE(1980, Fr.)
Bill Rigney
MAIN STREET TO BROADWAY(1953)
Kevin Rigney
PATERNITY(1981)
John Rigol
WOMEN AND BLOODY TERROR(1970)
George Rigon
ROUGH WATERS(1930)
Gordon Rigsby
Misc. Talkies
TIME TO RUN(1974)
Howard Rigsby
LAST SUNSET, THE(1961), w
Henk Rigters
GIRL WITH THE RED HAIR, THE(1983, Neth.)
Bobby Riha
SANTA AND THE THREE BEARS(1970)
Bobby Riha, Jr.
COUNTDOWN(1968)
Jan Riha
DIAMONDS OF THE NIGHT(1968, Czech.)

Jill Riha
DIRTY HARRY(1971)
Mansoureh Rihai
MARCO THE MAGNIFICENT(1966, Ital./Fr./Yugo./Egypt/Afghanistan)
Brad Rijn
1984
PERFECT STRANGERS(1984); SPECIAL EFFECTS(1984)
Lineke Rijxman
GIRL WITH THE RED HAIR, THE(1983, Neth.)
Dominique Rika
ROMAN HOLIDAY(1953)
Robert Rikas
Misc. Talkies
LEFT-HANDED(1972)
Robin Riker
ALLIGATOR(1980)
Shlomo Riklis
HILL 24 DOESN'T ANSWER(1955, Israel), md
Alrick Riley
SCUM(1979, Brit.)
Art Riley
THREE CABALLEROS, THE(1944), art d; FUN AND FANCY FREE(1947), art d
Bruce Riley
DOUBLE LIFE, A(1947); EXILE, THE(1947); SENATOR WAS INDISCREET, THE(1947); DESERT HAWK, THE(1950)
Coleen Riley
DEADLY BLESSING(1981)
Don Riley
THE RUNNER STUMBLES(1979)
Doug Riley
FOXY LADY(1971, Can.), m; CANNIBAL GIRLS(1973), m; SHOOT(1976, Can.), m
Elaine Riley
FALCON AND THE CO-EDS, THE(1943); HIGHER AND HIGHER(1943); FALCON OUT WEST, THE(1944); GIRL RUSH(1944); HEAVENLY DAYS(1944); SEVEN DAYS ASHORE(1944); SHOW BUSINESS(1944); STEP LIVELY(1944); HAVING WONDERFUL CRIME(1945); PAN-AMERICANA(1945); TWO O'CLOCK COURAGE(1945); WHAT A BLONDE(1945); DEVIL'S PLAYGROUND, THE(1946); DANGER STREET(1947); DANGEROUS VENTURE(1947); VARIETY GIRL(1947); BIG CLOCK, THE(1948); BORROWED TROUBLE(1948); EVERY GIRL SHOULD BE MARRIED(1948); FALSE PARADISE(1948); SINISTER JOURNEY(1948); STRANGE GAMBLE(1948); RIDER FROM TUCSON(1950); WHERE DANGER LIVES(1950); HILLS OF UTAH(1951); LEADVILLE GUNSLINGER(1952); STEEL TOWN(1952); CLIPPED WINGS(1953); TEXAS BAD MAN(1953); DIAL RED O(1955); PARDNERS(1956)
Eleanor Riley
TURNABOUT(1940)
Eve Riley
LOVE AT SEA(1936, Brit.)
Gary Riley
1984
WILD LIFE, THE(1984)
George Riley
ALIBI IKE(1935); STAGE STRUCK(1936); TIME OUT FOR ROMANCE(1937); WAGONS ROLL AT NIGHT, THE(1941); OVER MY DEAD BODY(1942); GOVERNMENT GIRL(1943); FOLLOW THE BOYS(1944); RHAPSODY IN BLUE(1945); NIGHT AND DAY(1946); GUILT OF JANET AMES, THE(1947); MEET ME AT THE FAIR(1952); WOMAN HUNT(1962); DAY MARS INVADED EARTH, THE(1963)
Misc. Silents
BRANDED MAN(1928)
Harrison Riley
BACHELOR GIRL, THE(1929), art d
Harry Riley
HARD STEEL(1941, Brit.)
Hugh Riley
FATAL HOUR, THE(1940), w
Jack Riley
CATCH-22(1970); MC CABE AND MRS. MILLER(1971); TODD KILLINGS, THE(1971); LONG GOODBYE, THE(1973); BANK SHOT(1974); CALIFORNIA SPLIT(1974); SILENT MOVIE(1976); HIGH ANXIETY(1977); WORLD'S GREATEST LOVER, THE(1977); ATTACK OF THE KILLER TOMATOES(1978); HISTORY OF THE WORLD, PART 1(1981); FRANCES(1982); TO BE OR NOT TO BE(1983)
1984
FINDERS KEEPERS(1984)
Silents
BROKEN DOLL, A(1921)
Jackie Riley
TURN ON TO LOVE(1969)
James Whitcomb Riley
Silents
OLD SWIMMIN' HOLE, THE(1921), w
Janet Riley
SEARCH FOR BRIDEY MURPHY, THE(1956)
Jay Riley
SHE BEAST, THE(1966, Brit./Ital./Yugo.)
Jeannine Riley
FIVE FINGER EXERCISE(1962); BIG MOUTH, THE(1967); FEVER HEAT(1968); COMIC, THE(1969); ELECTRA GLIDE IN BLUE(1973); WACKIEST WAGON TRAIN IN THE WEST, THE(1976)
Misc. Talkies
STRIKE ME DEADLY(1963)
Joseph Riley
BURNT OFFERINGS(1976)
Juanita Riley
Misc. Talkies
BLOOD OF JESUS(1941)
Katherine Riley
SMITHEREENS(1982)
Kay Riley
LEAVE HER TO HEAVEN(1946); SHOCKING MISS PILGRIM, THE(1947); WALLS OF JERICHO(1948)

Ken Riley
COAL MINER'S DAUGHTER(1980)
Kirk Riley
GOLDTOWN GHOST RIDERS(1953)
Larry Riley
1984
CRACKERS(1984); SOLDIER'S STORY, A(1984)
Lawrence Riley
GO WEST, YOUNG MAN(1936), w; EVER SINCE EVE(1937), w; PERFECT SPECI-
MEN, THE(1937), w; ON YOUR TOES(1939), w; YOU'RE A LUCKY FELLOW, MR.
SMITH(1943), w
Maggie Riley
DANCE OF DEATH, THE(1971, Brit.)
Mike Riley
MUSIC GOES ROUND, THE(1936); THAT'S MY BABY(1944)
Miranda Riley
FLASH GORDON(1980)
Miss Riley
10 RILLINGTON PLACE(1971, Brit.)
Nicola Riley
SEASIDE SWINGERS(1965, Brit.)
P. Riley
Silents
GANGSTERS OF NEW YORK, THE(1914)
Paul Riley
1984
PHAR LAP(1984, Aus.)
Penny Riley
MAROC 7(1967, Brit.); COME BACK PETER(1971, Brit.)
Robin Riley
PLUNDER ROAD(1957)
Skip Riley
SUPER VAN(1977)
Stella Riley
DECAMERON NIGHTS(1953, Brit.); GREAT GILBERT AND SULLIVAN, THE(1953,
Brit.)
Terry Riley
LIFESPAN(1975, U.S./Brit./Neth.), m
Tim Riley
PARADES(1972); TAPS(1981); LINE, THE(1982)
W. Riley
AGITATOR, THE(1949), w
William J. Riley
GREATEST SHOW ON EARTH, THE(1952)
William McKeever Riley
THEY WERE EXPENDABLE(1945); HIGH BARBAREE(1947); LADY IN THE LA-
KE(1947)
William Riley
TWO SMART PEOPLE(1946)
Wilma Riley
RANCHO DELUXE(1975)
Eli Rill
SLIPSTREAM(1974, Can.); POWER PLAY(1978, Brit./Can.)
Ethel Rill
SIDE STREETS(1934), w
Walter Rilla
VICTORIA THE GREAT(1937, Brit.); DIE MANNER UM LUCIE(1931); RENDEZ-
VOUS(1932, Ger.); ABDUL THE DAMNED(1935, Brit.); SCARLET PIMPERNEL,
THE(1935, Brit.); SIXTY GLORIOUS YEARS(1938, Brit.); BLACK EYES(1939, Brit.);
DANGEROUS CARGO(1939, Brit.); FALSE RAPTURE(1941); HOUSE OF MYS-
TERY(1941, Brit.); AMAZING MR. FORREST, THE(1943, Brit.); CANDLELIGHT IN
ALGERIA(1944, Brit.); MR. EMMANUEL(1945, Brit.); LISBON STORY, THE(1946,
Brit.); GOLDEN SALAMANDER(1950, Brit.); GREAT MANHUNT, THE(1951, Brit.);
LUCKY NICK CAIN(1951); OPERATION X(1951, Brit.); ASSASSIN, THE(1953, Brit.);
DESPERATE MOMENT(1953, Brit.); GREEN BUDDHA, THE(1954, Brit.); SHADOW
OF THE EAGLE(1955, Brit.); GAMMA PEOPLE, THE(1956); STAR OF INDIA(1956,
Brit.); TRACK THE MAN DOWN(1956, Brit.); CONFESSIONS OF FELIX KRULL,
THE(1957, Ger.); SONG WITHOUT END(1960); SECRET WAYS, THE(1961); WONDER-
FUL WORLD OF THE BROTHERS ERIMM, THE(1962); CAIRO(1963); SAN-
DERS(1963, Brit.); SCOTLAND YARD HUNTS DR. MABUSE(1963, Ger.); CODE 7,
VICTIM 5(1964, Brit.); FACE OF FU MANCHU, THE(1965, Brit.); TERROR OF DR.
MABUSE, THE(1965, Ger.); FROZEN ALIVE(1966, Brit./Ger.); DAY OF ANGER(1970,
Ital./Ger.); MALPERTIUS(1972, Bel./Fr.)
Misc. Silents
LEAP INTO LIFE(1924, Ger.); ART OF LOVE, THE(1928, Ger.); SAJENKO THE
SOVIET(1929, Ger.)
Water Rilla
WESTMINSTER PASSION PLAY–BEHOLD THE MAN, THE(1951, Brit), d, w
Wolf Rilla
GLAD TIDINGS(1953, Brit.), d, w; LARGE ROPE, THE(1953, Brit.), d; MARI-
LYN(1953, Brit.), d&w; NOOSE FOR A LADY(1953, Brit.), d; BLACK RIDER,
THE(1954, Brit.), d; END OF THE ROAD, THE(1954, Brit.), d; STOCK CAR(1955,
Brit.), d; PACIFIC DESTINY(1956, Brit.), d; BACHELOR OF HEARTS(1958, Brit.), d;
NAVY HEROES(1959, Brit.), d; STRANGE AFFECTION(1959, Brit.), d&w; WITNESS
IN THE DARK(1959, Brit.), d; PICCADILLY THIRD STOP(1960, Brit.), d; VILLAGE
OF THE DAMNED(1960, Brit.), d, w; WATCH IT, SAILOR!(1961, Brit.), d; CAI-
RO(1963), d; PUSSYCAT ALLEY(1965, Brit.), d&w
Misc. Talkies
NAUGHTY WIVES(1974), d
Walter Rills
ADVENTURES OF TARTU(1943, Brit.)
Carlo Rim
SEVEN DEADLY SINS, THE(1953, Fr./Ital.), d, w; DAUGHTERS OF DES-
TINY(1954, Fr./Ital.), w
Carlo Rima
BREAK THE NEWS(1938, Brit.), w
Ciro Rimac
DOLL FACE(1945)

Robert Rimbaud
PEPPERMINT SODA(1979, Fr.); GIRL FROM LORRAINE, A(1982, Fr./Switz.)
Phyllis Rimedy
NEVER STEAL ANYTHING SMALL(1959)
Walter Rimi
S.O.S. ICEBERG(1933)
Stevan Rimkus
1984
CAL(1984, Ireland)
Walter Riml
LONE CLIMBER, THE(1950, Brit./Aust.), ph
Lucien Rimmels
PALACE OF NUDES(1961, Fr./Ital.), w
Jean Rimmer
DEADLY FEMALES, THE(1976, Brit.)
Robert H. Rimmer
HARRAD EXPERIMENT, THE(1973), w
Shane Rimmer
FLAMING FRONTIER(1958, Can.); DANGEROUS AGE, A(1960, Can.); DR. STRAN-
GELOVE: OR HOW I LEARNED TO STOP WORRYING AND LOVE THE BOMB(1964);
THUNDERBIRD 6(1968, Brit.); THUNDERBIRDS ARE GO(1968, Brit.); DIAMONDS
ARE FOREVER(1971, Brit.); S(1974); HUMAN FACTOR, THE(1975); ROLLER-
BALL(1975); NASTY HABITS(1976, Brit.); JULIA(1977); PEOPLE THAT TIME FOR-
GOT, THE(1977, Brit.); SPY WHO LOVED ME, THE(1977, Brit.); TWILIGHT'S LAST
GLEAMING(1977, U.S./Ger.); SILVER BEARS(1978); WARLORDS OF ATLAN-
TIS(1978, Brit.); ARABIAN ADVENTURE(1979, Brit.); HANOVER STREET(1979,
Brit.); DOGS OF WAR, THE(1980, Brit.); SUPERMAN II(1980); PRIEST OF LOVE(1981,
Brit.); REDS(1981); GANDHI(1982); HUNGER, THE(1983); LONELY LADY,
THE(1983); SUPERMAN III(1983)
Noelle Rimmington
MACBETH(1971, Brit.)
Tony Rimmington
JUDITH(1965), art d
Adriano Rimoldi
CARMEN(1946, Ital.); LITTLE MARTYR, THE(1947, Ital.); UTOPIA(1952, Fr./Ital.);
KING OF KINGS(1961); UNSATISFIED, THE(1964, Span.)
Rimski-Korsakov
DEVIL IS A WOMAN, THE(1935), m
Nikolai Andreevich Rimski-Korsakov
INVITATION TO THE DANCE(1956), m; WOMAN OF STRAW(1964, Brit.), m
Nicholas Rimsky
HEART OF PARIS(1939, Fr.)
Nicolas Rimsky
Misc. Silents
LES CONTES LES MILLES ET UNE NUITS(1922, Fr.); CE COCHON DE MO-
RIN(1924, Fr.); JIM LA HOULETTE, ROI DES VOLEURS(1926, Fr.); MINUIT...PLACE
PIGALLE(1928, Fr.)
Nikolai Rimsky
Misc. Silents
ANDREI KOZHUKHOV(1917, USSR); CURSED MILLIONS(1917, USSR); QUEEN'S
SECRET, THE(1919, USSR)
Rimsky-Korsakov
TSAR'S BRIDE, THE(1966, USSR), m
Nicolai Andreyevich Rimsky-Korsakov
LOST IN A HAREM(1944), m
Nikolai Andreevich Rimsky-Korsakov
TSAR'S BRIDE, THE(1966, USSR), w
Taro Rin
GALAXY EXPRESS(1982, Jap.), d
Rin-Tin-Tin
LAND OF THE SILVER FOX(1928); FROZEN RIVER(1929); MILLION DOLLAR
COLLAR, THE(1929); ROUGH WATERS(1930); TIGER ROSE(1930); HUMAN TAR-
GETS(1932)
Silents
MY DAD(1922); LIGHTHOUSE BY THE SEA, THE(1924); BELOW THE LINE(1925);
NIGHT CRY, THE(1926); DOG OF THE REGIMENT(1927); HILLS OF KENTUCK-
Y(1927); JAWS OF STEEL(1927)
Misc. Silents
FIND YOUR MAN(1924); CLASH OF THE WOLVES(1925); TRACKED IN THE
SNOW COUNTRY(1925); HERO OF THE BIG SNOWS, A(1926); WHILE LONDON
SLEEPS(1926); TRACKED BY THE POLICE(1927); RACE FOR LIFE, A(1928); RINTY
OF THE DESERT(1928)
Rin Tin Tin, Jr.
PRIDE OF THE LEGION, THE(1932); CARYL OF THE MOUNTAINS(1936); TOUGH
GUY(1936); SILVER TRAIL, THE(1937); SKULL AND CROWN(1938); DEATH GOES
NORTH(1939)
Misc. Talkies
VENGEANCE OF RANNAH(1936)
Rin Tin Tin III
RETURN OF RIN TIN TIN, THE(1947)
Ita Rina
RAT(1960, Yugo.)
Misc. Silents
EROTIKON(1929, Czech.)
A. Rinaldi
DR. GOLDFOOT AND THE GIRL BOMBS(1966, Ital.), ph
Antonio Rinaldi
PLANET OF THE VAMPIRES(1965, U.S./Ital./Span.), ph; KILL BABY KILL(1966,
Ital.), ph; KNIVES OF THE AVENGER(1967, Ital.), ph; DANGER: DIABOLIK(1968,
Ital./Fr.), ph
Atilio Rinaldi
NO EXIT(1962, U.S./Arg.), ed
Carlos Rinaldi
MALE AND FEMALE SINCE ADAM AND EVE(1961, Arg.), d
Joe Rinaldi
MELODY TIME(1948), w; ADVENTURES OF ICHABOD AND MR. TOAD(1949), w;
CINDERELLA(1950), w; ALICE IN WONDERLAND(1951), w; PETER PAN(1953), w;
LADY AND THE TRAMP(1955), w; BABES IN TOYLAND(1961), w

Manuela Rinaldi
JESSICA(1962, U.S./Ital./Fr.)
Tina Rinaldi
Silents
ROMOLA(1925)
Alice Rinaldi
Misc. Silents
CONSCIENCE OF JOHN DAVID, THE(1916)
Fred Rinaldo
BACHELOR DADDY(1941), w; BLACK CAT, THE(1941), w; INVISIBLE WOMAN, THE(1941), w; JUKE BOX JENNY(1942), w; NO TIME FOR LOVE(1943), w; JUMPING JACKS(1952), w
Frederic I. Rinaldo
STREET OF MEMORIES(1940), w; HOLD THAT GHOST(1941), w; HIT THE ICE(1943), w; BUCK PRIVATES COME HOME(1947), w; WISTFUL WIDOW OF WAGON GAP, THE(1947), w; ABBOTT AND COSTELLO MEET FRANKENSTEIN(1948), w; HOLIDAY IN HAVANA(1949), w; ABBOTT AND COSTELLO MEET THE INVISIBLE MAN(1951), w; COMIN' ROUND THE MOUNTAIN(1951), w
Frederick L. Rinaldo
CRAZY HOUSE(1943), w
Saverio Rinaldo
ARTISTS AND MODELS ABROAD(1938)
Rinaldo Rincon
Misc. Talkies
ASSAULT WITH A DEADLY WEAPON(1983)
Laurin Rinder
NEW YEAR'S EVIL(1980), m; ENTER THE NINJA(1982), m; REVENGE OF THE NINJA(1983), m
Lydia Rindina
Misc. Silents
NIKOLAI STAVROGIN(1915, USSR)
Jessie Rindom
CASE OF THE 44'S, THE(1964 Brit./Den.)
Jochen Rindt
GRAND PRIX(1966)
Harry Rinehardt
Silents
WEDDING MARCH, THE(1927)
Dick Rinehart
SAGA OF DEATH VALLEY(1939); STICK TO YOUR GUNS(1941); SONG OF THE WASTELAND(1947)
Mary Roberts Rinehart
BAT WHISPERS, THE(1930), w; I TAKE THIS WOMAN(1931), w; MISS PINKERTON(1932), w; ELINOR NORTON(1935), w; MR. COHEN TAKES A WALK(1936, Brit.), w; 23 ½ HOURS LEAVE(1937), w; NURSE'S SECRET, THE(1941), w; BAT, THE(1959), w
Silents
ACQUITTED(1916), w; BAB'S BURGLAR(1917), w; BAB'S DIARY(1917), w; LONG LIVE THE KING(1923), w; MIND OVER MOTOR(1923), w; BREAKING POINT, THE(1924), w; K–THE UNKNOWN(1924), w; BAT, THE(1926), w; AFLAME IN THE SKY(1927), w; WHAT HAPPENED TO FATHER(1927), w
Richard Robert Rinehart
LAUGH YOUR BLUES AWAY(1943)
Roberts Rinehart
TISH(1942), w
Ronald A. Riner
HEART IS A LONELY HUNTER, THE(1968)
Cathy Riney
STORY OF A WOMAN(1970, U.S./Ital.)
Michael Riney
TIMES SQUARE(1980)
Louise Rinfret
PYX, THE(1973, Can.)
Amanda Ring
GETTING OF WISDOM, THE(1977, Aus.)
Blanche Ring
IF I HAD MY WAY(1940); HAVING WONDERFUL CRIME(1945)
Silents
IT'S THE OLD ARMY GAME(1926)
Misc. Silents
YANKEE GIRL, THE(1915)
Cy Ring
WEDDING PRESENT(1936); HOUSE ACROSS THE BAY, THE(1940); GIRL, A GUY AND A GOB, A(1941); PUBLIC ENEMIES(1941); BOSTON BLACKIE GOES HOLLYWOOD(1942); ICE-CAPADES REVUE(1942); SABOTAGE SQUAD(1942); IRON MAJOR, THE(1943); MELODY PARADE(1943); SHE HAS WHAT IT TAKES(1943); MAN IN HALF-MOON STREET, THE(1944); ONCE UPON A TIME(1944); HOLLYWOOD AND VINE(1945); SENORITA FROM THE WEST(1945); GIRL ON THE SPOT(1946); OUR HEARTS WERE GROWING UP(1946); BODY AND SOUL(1947); HOLLYWOOD BARN DANCE(1947); HOLLOW TRIUMPH(1948); RED, HOT AND BLUE(1949); IRON MAN, THE(1951)
Cyril Ring
COCOANUTS, THE(1929); SOCIAL LION, THE(1930); TOP SPEED(1930); DON'T BET ON WOMEN(1931); BUSINESS AND PLEASURE(1932); EMERGENCY CALL(1933); NEIGHBORS' WIVES(1933); TILLIE AND GUS(1933); TOO MUCH HARMONY(1933); HOLLYWOOD MYSTERY(1934); DON'T BET ON BLONDES(1935); GILDED LILY, THE(1935); GOIN' TO TOWN(1935); MURDER MAN(1935); OIL FOR THE LAMPS OF CHINA(1935); RENDEZVOUS(1935); BORDER PATROLMAN, THE(1936); COLLEEN(1936); MORE THAN A SECRETARY(1936); PALM SPRINGS(1936); POLO JOE(1936); POPPY(1936); LAST GANGSTER, THE(1937); NOTHING SACRED(1937); WHEN YOU'RE IN LOVE(1937); CITY GIRL(1938); I AM THE LAW(1938); SHINING HOUR, THE(1938); SWEETHEARTS(1938); TEST PILOT(1938); THREE LOVES HAS NANCY(1938); TOO HOT TO HANDLE(1938); TRADE WINDS(1938); YOUNG DR. KILDARE(1938); LET FREEDOM RING(1939); LIGHT THAT FAILED, THE(1939); MIRACLES FOR SALE(1939); OUR LEADING CITIZEN(1939); ROARING TWENTIES, THE(1939); SECOND FIDDLE(1939); WINTER CARNIVAL(1939); IRENE(1940); LADY WITH RED HAIR(1940); MY FAVORITE WIFE(1940); NO, NO NANETTE(1940); ONE NIGHT IN THE TROPICS(1940); ROAD TO SINGAPORE(1940); SAILOR'S LADY(1940); THIRD FINGER, LEFT HAND(1940); THOSE WERE THE DAYS(1940); TWO GIRLS ON BROADWAY(1940); FOR BEAUTY'S SAKE(1941); GREAT LIE,

THE(1941); MAN WHO LOST HIMSELF, THE(1941); NEW YORK TOWN(1941); SAN ANTONIO ROSE(1941); ARMY SURGEON(1942); HOME IN WYOMIN'(1942); I WAKE UP SCREAMING(1942); JOAN OF OZARK(1942); LIFE BEGINS AT 8:30(1942); LUCKY LEGS(1942); MY GAL SAL(1942); NAVY COMES THROUGH, THE(1942); NIGHT TO REMEMBER, A(1942); OVER MY DEAD BODY(1942); SABOTEUR(1942); SECRET AGENT OF JAPAN(1942); SLEEPYTIME GAL(1942); THIS GUN FOR HIRE(1942); WOMAN OF THE YEAR(1942); YOKEL BOY(1942); DIXIE(1943); GOOD MORNING, JUDGE(1943); LET'S FACE IT(1943); MAD GHOUL, THE(1943); MYSTERY OF THE 13TH GUEST, THE(1943); SWEET ROSIE O'GRADY(1943); FOLLOW THE BOYS(1944); HERE COME THE WAVES(1944); HOT RHYTHM(1944); IN SOCIETY(1944); LAURA(1944); MR. SKEFFINGTON(1944); SECRET COMMAND(1944); DUFFY'S TAVERN(1945); HAVING WONDERFUL CRIME(1945); MISS SUSIE SLAGLE'S(1945); NAUGHTY NINETIES, THE(1945); WHERE DO WE GO FROM HERE?(1945); NIGHT AND DAY(1946); NOBODY LIVES FOREVER(1946); FLAME, THE(1948); RETURN OF THE BADMEN(1948)
Silents
BACK HOME AND BROKE(1922); EXCITERS, THE(1923); BREAKING POINT, THE(1924); NEWS PARADE, THE(1928)
Misc. Silents
HIT AND RUN(1924)
Cyrus Ring
TEXAS KID, THE(1944)
Donna Ring
SHE'S WORKING HER WAY THROUGH COLLEGE(1952)
Jeff Ring
HIDE IN PLAIN SIGHT(1980)
John Ring
FORT APACHE, THE BRONX(1981)
1984
GARBO TALKS(1984)
William E. Ring
ROCKY(1976)
Israel Ringel
RABBI AND THE SHIKSE, THE(1976, Israel), p
Pierre Ringel
STRANGERS IN THE HOUSE(1949, Fr.)
Thomas Ringelmann
1984
LOVE IN GERMANY, A(1984, Fr./Ger.)
Claude Ringer
CARMEN, BABY(1967, Yugo./Ger.)
Nora Ringgenberry
BREAKING AWAY(1979)
Gene Ringgold
NEW KIND OF LOVE, A(1963)
John Ringham
COMING-OUT PARTY, A(
Walter Ringham
HOUSE OF SECRETS(1929)
Silents
HAMLET(1913, Brit.)
Misc. Silents
FLESH AND SPIRIT(1922)
Sanna Ringhaver
BLOOD WATERS OF DOCTOR Z(1982)
Rudy Joe Ringo
FIVE ON THE BLACK HAND SIDE(1973)
Francine Ringold
TEX(1982)
Mary Rings
SKIN GAME(1971); PSYCHOPATH, THE(1973)
Beth Ringwald
1984
SIXTEEN CANDLES(1984)
Molly Ringwald
TEMPEST(1982); SPACEHUNTER: ADVENTURES IN THE FORBIDDEN ZONE(1983)
1984
SIXTEEN CANDLES(1984)
Monika Ringwald
CONFESSIONS OF A WINDOW CLEANER(1974, Brit.); GIRL FROM STARSHIP VENUS, THE(1975, Brit.)
Bob Ringwood
EXCALIBUR(1981), cos; DRAUGHTSMAN'S CONTRACT, THE(1983, Brit.), art d
1984
DUNE(1984), cos
David Rini
CALIFORNIA SUITE(1978)
Robert Rinier
GOING HOME(1971)
Rink
INCREDIBLE JOURNEY, THE(1963)
Brad Rinn
SMITHEREENS(1982)
Nicolas Rinsky
Misc. Silents
PARIS EN CINQ JOURS(1926, Fr.)
David W. Rintels
SCORPIO(1973), w
David Rintoul
Misc. Talkies
LEGEND OF THE WEREWOLF(1974)
Rinty the dog
BIG PAYOFF, THE(1933)
Claude Rio
RISE OF LOUIS XIV, THE(1970, Fr.)
Dolores Del Rio
Misc. Silents
HIGH STEPPERS(1926); RED DANCE, THE(1928)

Eddie Rio
JOLSON STORY, THE(1946); FIGHTING FOOLS(1949); SORROWFUL JONES(1949)
Frank Rio
CASA MANANA(1951)
Jim Rio
CASA MANANA(1951)
Joanne Rio
SEMINOLE UPRISING(1955)
Larry Rio
COVER GIRL(1944); DOUGHGIRLS, THE(1944); LADY IN THE DARK(1944); MILDRED PIERCE(1945); TOO YOUNG TO KNOW(1945); JOHN LOVES MARY(1949); KISS IN THE DARK, A(1949); MISSISSIPPI RHYTHM(1949); NIGHT UNTO NIGHT(1949); YOUNG MAN WITH A HORN(1950); CASA MANANA(1951); BUSTER KEATON STORY, THE(1957)
Rita Rio [Dona Drake]
STRIKE ME PINK(1936)
Bill Riola
NOTHING BUT A MAN(1964)
Ricardo Rioli
CROSSED SWORDS(1954)
Riccardo Rioli
GOLDEN COACH, THE(1953, Fr./Ital.); BAREFOOT CONTESSA, THE(1954)
Caroline Riollot
PARSIFAL(1983, Fr.)
Guillemette Riollot
PARSIFAL(1983, Fr.)
David Riondino
NIGHT OF THE SHOOTING STARS, THE(1982, Ital.)
Christopher Riordan
CURIOUS FEMALE, THE(1969); GAY DECEIVERS, THE(1969)
Daniel Riordan
1984
BREAKIN' 2: ELECTRIC BOOGALOO(1984)
Joan Riordan
NIGHT THE LIGHTS WENT OUT IN GEORGIA, THE(1981)
1984
TANK(1984)
Joel Riordan
PRIZE OF GOLD, A(1955)
Joel McGinnis Riordan
Misc. Talkies
BOARDING HOUSE(1984)
Marjorie Riordan
STAGE DOOR CANTEEN(1943); MR. SKEFFINGTON(1944); PURSUIT TO ALGIERS(1945); THREE STRANGERS(1946); HOODLUM, THE(1951)
Misc. Talkies
SOUTH OF MONTEREY(1946)
Naomi Riordan
JANE AUSTEN IN MANHATTAN(1980)
Robert Riordan
SHOOT TO KILL(1947); SMART WOMAN(1948); WINTER MEETING(1948); ARSON FOR HIRE(1959); MANCHURIAN CANDIDATE, THE(1962); I'D RATHER BE RICH(1964); DESTRUCTORS, THE(1968)
Aldana Rios
THREE DARING DAUGHTERS(1948)
Edward C. Rios
MARK OF THE RENEGADE(1951)
Elvira Rios
TROPIC HOLIDAY(1938); REAL GLORY, THE(1939); STAGECOACH(1939)
Juan Rios
ZOOT SUIT(1981)
Lalo Rios
BANDIT QUEEN(1950); LAWLESS, THE(1950); LAW AND THE LADY, THE(1951); ONE MINUTE TO ZERO(1952); RING, THE(1952); BIG LEAGUER(1953); CITY BENEATH THE SEA(1953); PRISONER OF WAR(1954); TOUCH OF EVIL(1958); LONELY ARE THE BRAVE(1962)
Lolita Rios
DIRTY HARRY(1971)
M. E. Rios
MISSING(1982)
Patricia Rios
SILVER RAIDERS(1950)
Raymond Rios
1984
CRACKERS(1984)
S. Pondal Rios
ROMANCE ON THE HIGH SEAS(1948), w
Sixto Pondal Rios
YOU WERE NEVER LOVELIER(1942), w
Rios and Santos
SUNSHINE AHEAD(1936, Brit.)
Louise Rioton
LA FEMME INFIDELE(1969, Fr./Ital.); LADY IN THE CAR WITH GLASSES AND A GUN, THE(1970, U.S./Fr.)
Kevin Riou
WHO SAYS I CAN'T RIDE A RAINBOW!(1971)
Joseph Riozet
LETTERS FROM MY WINDMILL(1955, Fr.)
Rip
COGNASSE(1932, Fr.), w
Joseph Rip
HAREM BUNCH; OR WAR AND PIECE, THE(1969)
The Rip Chords
SWINGIN' SUMMER, A(1965)
Robert Ripa
MODIGLIANI OF MONTPARNASSE(1961, Fr./Ital.)
Jean-Marc Ripart
MARRIAGE CAME TUMBLING DOWN, THE(1968, Fr.), ph

Therese Ripaud
1984
ONE DEADLY SUMMER(1984, Fr.), cos
Colette Ripert
LES JEUX SONT FAITS(1947, Fr.); MY SEVEN LITTLE SINS(1956, Fr./Ital.)
Jean-Marc Ripert
SOPHIE'S WAYS(1970, Fr.), ph
Minnie Riperton
SGT. PEPPER'S LONELY HEARTS CLUB BAND(1978)
Arthur Ripley
BARNUM WAS RIGHT(1929), w; CAPTAIN OF THE GUARD(1930), w; HIDE-OUT, THE(1930), w; HYPNOTIZED(1933), w; I MET MY LOVE AGAIN(1938), w; WATERFRONT(1939), w; PRISONER OF JAPAN(1942), d, w; BEHIND PRISON WALLS(1943), p; VOICE IN THE WIND(1944), p, d, w; CHASE, THE(1946), d; THUNDER ROAD(1958), d
Silents
FOOLISH WIVES(1920), ed; LIFE'S DARN FUNNY(1921), w; STRONG MAN, THE(1926), w; LONG PANTS(1927), w; THREE'S A CROWD(1927), w; CHASER, THE(1928), w; HEART TROUBLE(1928), w
Clement Ripley
BLACK MOON(1934), w; GOLD IS WHERE YOU FIND IT(1938), w
Clements Ripley
DEVIL WITH WOMEN, A(1930), w; JEZEBEL(1938), w; LOVE, HONOR AND BEHAVE(1938), w; BUFFALO BILL(1944), w; OLD LOS ANGELES(1948), w; JOHN PAUL JONES(1959), w
Heather Ripley
CHITTY CHITTY BANG BANG(1968, Brit.)
Jay Ripley
YOUNG FURY(1965); DUEL AT DIABLO(1966); TIME FOR KILLING, A(1967); TRUE GRIT(1969); NORWOOD(1970); APPLE DUMPLING GANG RIDES AGAIN, THE(1979)
Patricia Ripley
NO WAY TO TREAT A LADY(1968); HAIL(1973)
Ray Ripley
Silents
BLAZING TRAIL, THE(1921); HEADS UP(1925); SMILIN' AT TROUBLE(1925); STOLEN PLEASURES(1927)
Misc. Silents
FELIX O'DAY(1920); MARRIAGE PIT, THE(1920); WHY TRUST YOUR HUSBAND?(1921); WESTERN PLUCK(1926)
Raymond Ripley
Misc. Silents
GREAT AIR ROBBERY, THE(1920)
Antonio Ripoll
MAFIA, THE(1972, Arg.), ed
Pablo Ripoll
TREASURE OF MAKUBA, THE(1967, U.S./Span.), ph
Silvia Ripoll
1984
DEATHSTALKER, THE(1984), ed
Michael Ripper
BUSMAN'S HOLIDAY(1936, Brit.); HEIRLOOM MYSTERY, THE(1936, Brit.); NOTHING LIKE PUBLICITY(1936, Brit.); PRISON BREAKER(1936, Brit.); TO CATCH A THIEF(1936, Brit.); TOUCH OF THE MOON, A(1936, Brit.); TWICE BRANDED(1936, Brit.); FIFTY-SHILLING BOXER(1937, Brit.); PEARLS BRING TEARS(1937, Brit.); RACING ROMANCE(1937, Brit.); STRANGE ADVENTURES OF MR. SMITH, THE(1937, Brit.); WHY PICK ON ME?(1937, Brit.); DARTS ARE TRUMPS(1938, Brit.); EASY RICHES(1938, Brit.); HIS LORDSHIP REGRETS(1938, Brit.); IF I WERE BOSS(1938, Brit.); MERELY MR. HAWKINS(1938, Brit.); MIRACLES DO HAPPEN(1938, Brit.); PAID IN ERROR(1938, Brit.); ROMANCE A LA CARTE(1938, Brit.); WEDDINGS ARE WONDERFUL(1938, Brit.); YOU'RE THE DOCTOR(1938, Brit.); HIS LORDSHIP GOES TO PRESS(1939, Brit.); NORTH SEA PATROL(1939, Brit.); DARK ROAD, THE(1948, Brit.); HISTORY OF MR. POLLY, THE(1949, Brit.); EYE WITNESS(1950, Brit.); SILK NOOSE, THE(1950, Brit.); OLD MOTHER RILEY'S JUNGLE TREASURE(1951, Brit.); FOUR AGAINST FATE(1952, Brit.); SECRET PEOPLE(1952, Brit.); TREASURE HUNT(1952, Brit.); FOLLY TO BE WISE(1953); GREAT GILBERT AND SULLIVAN, THE(1953, Brit.); RAINBOW JACKET, THE(1954, Brit.); TALE OF THREE WOMEN, A(1954, Brit.); CONSTANT HUSBAND, THE(1955, Brit.); INTRUDER, THE(1955, Brit.); LADY GODIVA RIDES AGAIN(1955, Brit.); SEA SHALL NOT HAVE THEM, THE(1955, Brit.); SECRET VENTURE(1955, Brit.); BLONDE SINNER(1956, Brit.); RICHARD III(1956, Brit.); WEE GEORDIE(1956, Brit.); 1984(1956, Brit.); ENEMY FROM SPACE(1957, Brit.); GREEN MAN, THE(1957, Brit.); NOT WANTED ON VOYAGE(1957, Brit.); REACH FOR THE SKY(1957, Brit.); WOMEN IN A DRESSING GOWN(1957, Brit.); X THE UNKNOWN(1957, Brit.); DANGEROUS YOUTH(1958, Brit.); FURTHER UP THE CREEK!(1958, Brit.); GIRLS AT SEA(1958, Brit.); I ONLY ASKED!(1958, Brit.); REVENGE OF FRANKENSTEIN, THE(1958, Brit.); STEEL BAYONET, THE(1958, Brit.); UP THE CREEK(1958, Brit.); BOBBIKINS(1959, Brit.); MAN WHO COULD CHEAT DEATH, THE(1959, Brit.); MUMMY, THE(1959, Brit.); UGLY DUCKLING, THE(1959, Brit.); BRIDES OF DRACULA, THE(1960, Brit.); DEAD LUCKY(1960, Brit.); JACKPOT(1960, Brit.); ANATOMIST, THE(1961, Brit.); CIRCLE OF DECEPTON(1961, Brit.); CURSE OF THE WEREWOLF, THE(1961); PETTICOAT PIRATES(1961, Brit.); PURE HELL OF ST. TRINIAN'S, THE(1961, Brit.); MATTER OF WHO, A(1962, Brit.); NIGHT CREATURES(1962, Brit.); PHANTOM OF THE OPERA, THE(1962, Brit.); PIRATES OF BLOOD RIVER, THE(1962, Brit.); PRIZE OF ARMS, A(1962, Brit.); MACBETH(1963); PUNCH AND JUDY MAN, THE(1963, Brit.); WHAT A CRAZY WORLD(1963, Brit.); CRIMSON BLADE, THE(1964, Brit.); DEVIL-SHIP PIRATES, THE(1964, Brit.); AMOROUS MR. PRAWN, THE(1965, Brit.); CURSE OF THE MUMMY'S TOMB, THE(1965, Brit.); SEASIDE SWINGERS(1965, Brit.); SECRET OF BLOOD ISLAND, THE(1965, Brit.); SPY WHO CAME IN FROM THE COLD, THE(1965, Brit.); TWO LEFT FEET(1965, Brit.); GREAT ST. TRINIAN'S TRAIN ROBBERY, THE(1966, Brit.); PLAGUE OF THE ZOMBIES, THE(1966, Brit.); REPTILE, THE(1966, Brit.); WHERE THE BULLETS FLY(1966, Brit.); DEADLY BEES,THE(1967, Brit.); MUMMY'S SHROUD, THE(1967, Brit.); DRACULA HAS RISEN FROM HIS GRAVE(1968, Brit.); INSPECTOR CLOUSEAU(1968, Brit.); LOST CONTINENT, THE(1968, Brit.); TORTURE GARDEN(1968, Brit.); MOON ZERO TWO(1970, Brit.); MUMSY, NANNY, SONNY, AND GIRLY(1970, Brit.); SCARS OF DRACULA, THE(1970, Brit.); TASTE THE BLOOD OF DRACULA(1970, Brit.)
Walter Ripperger
I'LL SELL MY LIFE(1941), w

Otto Rippert
Misc. Silents
PEST IN FLORENZ(1919, Ger.), d
Carleton Ripple
NICKELODEON(1976)
Frank Ripploh
KAMIKAZE '89(1983, Ger.); QUERELLE(1983, Ger./Fr.)
Don Ripps
SMART POLITICS(1948)
M.A. Ripps
SCUM OF THE EARTH(1976), p
Michael Ripps
1984
STREETS OF FIRE(1984), ed
Mike Ripps
Misc. Talkies
ALL THE YOUNG WIVES(1975), d
Frazier Rippy
8 ½(1963, Ital.)
Leon Rippy
1984
FIRESTARTER(1984)
Alfred Ripstein, Jr.
BLACK PIT OF DOCTOR M(1958, Mex.), p
Arturo Ripstein
CASTLE OF PURITY(1974, Mex.), d, w; FOXTROT(1977, Mex./Swiss), d, w
Newton Rique
DONA FLOR AND HER TWO HUSBANDS(1977, Braz.), p
Carlos Riquelme
CRIMINAL LIFE OF ARCHIBALDO DE LA CRUZ, THE(1962, Mex.)
1984
UNDER THE VOLCANO(1984)
Francisco Riquerio
TARZAN AND THE VALLEY OF GOLD(1966 U.S./Switz.)
Georges Riquier
MATA HARI(1965, Fr./Ital.); DEAR DETECTIVE(1978, Fr.)
Tatjena Rirah
Silents
ARE CHILDREN TO BLAME?(1922)
Remo Risaliti
JULIET OF THE SPIRITS(1965, Fr./Ital./W.Ger.)
Michel Risbourg
LONG ABSENCE, THE(1962, Fr./Ital.)
Maurice Risch
LE GENDARME ET LES EXTRATERRESTRES(1978, Fr.); BEAU PERE(1981, Fr.); LAST METRO, THE(1981, Fr.)
1984
TO CATCH A COP(1984, Fr.)
Peter D. Risch
SOMETHING WICKED THIS WAY COMES(1983)
Pierre Risch
SOFT SKIN, THE(1964, Fr.)
Henry Rische
MESSENGER OF PEACE(1950), w
Roberto Risco
SEVEN DWARFS TO THE RESCUE, THE(1965, Ital.)
Arthur Riscoe
FOR LOVE OF YOU(1933, Brit.); FOR THE LOVE OF MIKE(1933, Brit.); KISS ME GOODBYE(1935, Brit.); PUBLIC NUISANCE NO. 1(1936, Brit.); STREET SINGER, THE(1937, Brit.); GAIETY GIRLS, THE(1938, Brit.); REMARKABLE MR. KIPPS(1942, Brit.)
Barbara Riscoe
CROOKS IN CLOISTERS(1964, Brit.)
Maureen Riscoe
MATTER OF MURDER, A(1949, Brit.); OLD MOTHER RILEY(1952, Brit.); IDOL ON PARADE(1959, Brit.)
Carlton Risdon
GOIN' SOUTH(1978)
Elisabeth Risdon
GUARD THAT GIRL(1935); CRAIG'S WIFE(1936); FINAL HOUR, THE(1936); LADY OF SECRETS(1936); MOUNTAIN JUSTICE(1937); THEY WON'T FORGET(1937); AFFAIRS OF ANNABEL(1938); COWBOY FROM BROOKLYN(1938); GIRLS ON PROBATION(1938); MY BILL(1938); DISPUTED PASSAGE(1939); FIVE CAME BACK(1939); FULL CONFESSION(1939); GREAT MAN VOTES, THE(1939); MAN WHO DARED, THE(1939); ROARING TWENTIES, THE(1939); SORORITY HOUSE(1939); TOM SAWYER, DETECTIVE(1939); ABE LINCOLN IN ILLINOIS(1940); HONEYMOON DEFERRED(1940); HOWARDS OF VIRGINIA, THE(1940); LET'S MAKE MUSIC(1940); SING, DANCE, PLENTY HOT(1940); SLIGHTLY TEMPTED(1940); FOOTLIGHT FEVER(1941); HIGH SIERRA(1941); MR. DYNAMITE(1941); NICE GIRL?(1941); PARIS CALLING(1941); ARE HUSBANDS NECESSARY?(1942); JAIL HOUSE BLUES(1942); JOURNEY FOR MARGARET(1942); LADY IS WILLING, THE(1942); REAP THE WILD WIND(1942); AMAZING MRS. HOLLIDAY(1943); NEVER A DULL MOMENT(1943); BLONDE FEVER(1944); CANTERVILLE GHOST, THE(1944); IN THE MEANTIME, DARLING(1944); TALL IN THE SADDLE(1944); WEIRD WOMAN(1944); FIGHTING GUARDSMAN, THE(1945); GRISSLY'S MILLIONS(1945); MAMA LOVES PAPA(1945); SONG FOR MISS JULIE, A(1945); UNSEEN, THE(1945); LOVER COME BACK(1946); THEY MADE ME A KILLER(1946); WALLS CAME TUMBLING DOWN, THE(1946); EGG AND I, THE(1947); HIGH WALL, THE(1947); LIFE WITH FATHER(1947); EVERY GIRL SHOULD BE MARRIED(1948); DOWN DAKOTA WAY(1949); BUNCO SQUAD(1950); MILKMAN, THE(1950); SECRET FURY, THE(1950); SIERRA(1950); BANNERLINE(1951); IN OLD AMARILLO(1951); IT'S A BIG COUNTRY(1951); MY TRUE STORY(1951)
Elizabeth Risdon
CRIME AND PUNISHMENT(1935); DON'T GAMBLE WITH LOVE(1936); KING STEPS OUT, THE(1936); THEODORA GOES WILD(1936); DEAD END(1937); MAKE WAY FOR TOMORROW(1937); MANNEQUIN(1937); WOMAN I LOVE, THE(1937); MAD ABOUT MUSIC(1938); FORGOTTEN WOMAN, THE(1939); GIRL FROM MEXICO, THE(1939); HUCKLEBERRY FINN(1939); I AM NOT AFRAID(1939); MEXICAN SPITFIRE(1939); MA, HE'S MAKING EYES AT ME(1940); MAN WHO WOULDN'T

TALK, THE(1940); MEXICAN SPITFIRE OUT WEST(1940); SATURDAY'S CHILDREN(1940); MEXICAN SPITFIRE'S BABY(1941); I LIVE ON DANGER(1942); MAN WHO RETURNED TO LIFE, THE(1942); MEXICAN SPITFIRE AT SEA(1942); MEXICAN SPITFIRE SEES A GHOST(1942); MEXICAN SPITFIRE'S ELEPHANT(1942); RANDOM HARVEST(1942); HIGHER AND HIGHER(1943); MEXICAN SPITFIRE'S BLESSED EVENT(1943); LOST ANGEL(1944); ROLL ON TEXAS MOON(1944); MOURNING BECOMES ELECTRA(1947); ROMANCE OF ROSY RIDGE, THE(1947); SHOCKING MISS PILGRIM, THE(1947); BODYGUARD(1948); SEALED VERDICT(1948); GUILTY OF TREASON(1950); HILLS OF OKLAHOMA(1950); SCARAMOUCHE(1952)
Silents
LOVE IN A WOOD(1915, Brit.); PRINCESS OF HAPPY CHANCE, THE(1916, Brit.)
Misc. Silents
IDOL OF PARIS, THE(1914, Brit.); LOSS OF THE BIRKENHEAD, THE(1914, Brit.); PRICE OF JUSTICE, THE(1914, Brit.); SUICIDE CLUB, THE(1914, Brit.); CHARITY ANN(1915, Brit.); CHRISTIAN, THE(1915, Brit.); FINE FEATHERS(1915, Brit.); FLORENCE NIGHTINGALE(1915, Brit.); FROM SHOPGIRL TO DUCHESS(1915, Brit.); GRIP(1915, Brit.); HER NAMLESS CHILD(1915, Brit.); WILL OF HER OWN, A(1915, Brit.); DESPERATION(1916, Brit.); MANXMAN, THE(1916, Brit.); MORALS OF WEYBURY, THE(1916, Brit.); MOTHER OF DARTMOOR, THE(1916, Brit.); MOTHER-LOVE(1916, Brit.); SMITH(1917, Brit.)
Leif Rise
STARFIGHTERS, THE(1964), ph; TO THE SHORES OF HELL(1966), ph; HELL ON WHEELS(1967), ph
Miriam Riselle
SINGING BLACKSMITH(1938); TEVYA(1939)
Naomi Riseman
LOOKING UP(1977)
Paul Riser
WHICH WAY IS UP?(1977), m
Dick Rish
OX-BOW INCIDENT, THE(1943)
Myrtle Rishell
Silents
NANCY COMES HOME(1918)
Misc. Silents
DAUGHTER ANGELE(1918); HIGH STAKES(1918)
Sara Risher
1984
NIGHTMARE ON ELM STREET, A(1984), p
Edward Rishon
WINDFLOWERS(1968)
Dino Risi
ANNA(1951, Ital.), d; SIGN OF VENUS, THE(1955, Ital.), d; MONTE CARLO STORY, THE(1957, Ital.), w; SCANDAL IN SORRENTO(1957, Ital./Fr.), d, w; ANNA OF BROOKLYN(1958, Ital.), w; EASY LIFE, THE(1963, Ital.), d, w; LOVE AND LARCENY(1963, Fr./Ital.), d; BAMBOLE!(1965, Ital.), d; OPIATE '67(1967, Ital./Fr.), d, w; TIGER AND THE PUSSYCAT, THE(1967, U.S., Ital.), d, w; WEEKEND, ITALIAN STYLE(1967, Fr./Ital./Span.), d, w; TREASURE OF SAN GENNARO(1968, Fr./Ital./Ger.), d, w; PRIEST'S WIFE, THE(1971, Ital./Fr.), d, w; SCENT OF A WOMAN(1976, Ital.), d, w; VIVA ITALIA(1978, Ital.), d; SUNDAY LOVERS(1980, Ital./Fr.), d
Misc. Talkies
PROPHET, THE(1976), d
Fernando Risi
LOVES OF THREE QUEENS, THE(1954, Ital./Fr.), ph
Nelo Risi
DEAD OF SUMMER(1970 Ital./Fr.), d, w; DIARY OF A SCHIZOPHRENIC GIRL(1970, Ital.), d, w
Lawrence Rising
Silents
PROUD FLESH(1925), w
Robert Rising
1984
PALLET ON THE FLOOR(1984, New Zealand), w
W. Rising
Silents
AMERICA(1924)
William S. Rising
Silents
IN THE STRETCH(1914)
Jeff Risk
KILL SQUAD(1982)
Linda Sue Risk
TROUBLE WITH GIRLS(AND HOW TO GET INTO IT), THE*1/2 (1969); MARY-JANE(1968)
Victoria Risk
REFLECTION OF FEAR, A(1973)
Everett Riskin
FEATHER IN HER HAT, A(1935), p; SHE MARRIED HER BOSS(1935), p; IF YOU COULD ONLY COOK(1936), p; MORE THAN A SECRETARY(1936), p; THEODORA GOES WILD(1936), p; I'LL TAKE ROMANCE(1937), p; LET'S GET MARRIED(1937), p; WHEN YOU'RE IN LOVE(1937), p; HOLIDAY(1938), p; I AM THE LAW(1938), p; AMAZING MR. WILLIAMS(1939), p; HERE COMES MR. JORDAN(1941), p; GUY NAMED JOE, A(1944), p; KISMET(1944), p; THIN MAN GOES HOME, THE(1944), p; HIGH BARBAREE(1947), p; JULIA MISBEHAVES(1948), p; THUNDER IN THE EAST(1953), p
Everett J. Riskin
I'LL LOVE YOU ALWAYS(1935), p
R. Riskin
WHEN YOU'RE IN LOVE(1937), w
Robert Riskin
YOU CAN'T RUN AWAY FROM IT(1956), w; ILLICIT(1931), w; MANY A SLIP(1931), w; MEN ARE LIKE THAT(1931), w; MEN IN HER LIFE(1931), w; MIRACLE WOMAN, THE(1931), w; PLATINUM BLONDE(1931), w; AMERICAN MADNESS(1932), w; NIGHT CLUB LADY(1932), w; SHOPWORN(1932), w; THREE WISE GIRLS(1932), w; VIRTUE(1932), w; ANN CARVER'S PROFESSION(1933), w; EX-LADY(1933), w; LADY FOR A DAY(1933), w; BROADWAY BILL(1934), w; IT HAPPENED ONE NIGHT(1934), w; CARNIVAL(1935), w; WHOLE TOWN'S TALKING, THE(1935), w; MR. DEEDS GOES TO TOWN(1936), w; LOST HORIZON(1937), w; WHEN YOU'RE IN LOVE(1937), d; YOU CAN'T TAKE IT WITH YOU(1938), w; THEY

SHALL HAVE MUSIC(1939), p; MEET JOHN DOE(1941), w; THIN MAN GOES HOME, THE(1944), w; MAGIC TOWN(1947), p, w; MISTER 880(1950), w; RIDING HIGH(1950), w; HALF ANGEL(1951), w; HERE COMES THE GROOM(1951), w; POCKETFUL OF MIRACLES(1961), w

Ann Risley
OLIVER'S STORY(1978); SIMON(1980); HONKY TONK FREEWAY(1981); RICH AND FAMOUS(1981); COME BACK TO THE 5 & DIME, JIMMY DEAN, JIMMY DEAN(1982)

Rispal
BED AND BOARD(1971, Fr.)

Jacques Rispal
LA GUERRE EST FINIE(1967, Fr./Swed.); ZITA(1968, Fr.); MILKY WAY, THE(1969, Fr./Ital.); STOLEN KISSES(1969, Fr.); CONFESSION, THE(1970, Fr.); DISCREET CHARM OF THE BOURGEOISIE, THE(1972, Fr.); GOING PLACES(1974, Fr.); LACOMBE, LUCIEN(1974); CAT, THE(1975, Fr.); INVITATION, THE(1975, Fr./Switz.); PEPPERMINT SODA(1979, Fr.); POURQUOI PAS!(1979, Fr.)

Dan Riss
PINKY(1949); KILLER THAT STALKED NEW YORK, THE(1950); KISS TOMORROW GOODBYE(1950); LOVE THAT BRUTE(1950); PANIC IN THE STREETS(1950); WHEN WILLIE COMES MARCHING HOME(1950); WYOMING MAIL(1950); APPOINTMENT WITH DANGER(1951); ENFORCER, THE(1951); GO FOR BROKE(1951); LITTLE EGYPT(1951); ONLY THE VALIANT(1951); CARBINE WILLIAMS(1952); CONFIDENCE GIRL(1952); OPERATION SECRET(1952); SCARLET ANGEL(1952); TALK ABOUT A STRANGER(1952); WASHINGTON STORY(1952); GIRL WHO HAD EVERYTHING, THE(1953); MAN IN THE DARK(1953); VICE SQUAD(1953); HUMAN DESIRE(1954); MIAMI STORY, THE(1954); RIDERS TO THE STARS(1954); THREE YOUNG TEXANS(1954); YELLOW TOMAHAWK, THE(1954); PRICE OF FEAR, THE(1956); KELLY AND ME(1957); MAN ON FIRE(1957); BADMAN'S COUNTRY(1958); STORY ON PAGE ONE, THE(1959); MA BARKER'S KILLER BROOD(1960)

Don Riss
ARCTIC FURY(1949)

Germaine Risse
ARMY GAME, THE(1963, Fr.)

Marguerite Risser
Misc. Silents
THREADS OF DESTINY(1914)

Wee Risser
GIANT GILA MONSTER, THE(1959), spec eff

Mark M. Rissi
BLACK SPIDER, THE(1983, Swit.), d

Edward Rissien
CRAZY WORLD OF JULIUS VROODER, THE(1974), p

Edward L. Rissien
SNOW JOB(1972), p

Pierre Rissient
ONE NIGHT STAND(1976, Fr.), d, w

Danton Rissner
UP THE ACADEMY(1980), p

John Risso
STREET OF CHANCE(1930)

Richard Risso
DESPERATE WOMEN, THE(?)

Robert Risso
LUXURY GIRLS(1953, Ital.); BREATH OF SCANDAL, A(1960)

Roberto Risso
BREAD, LOVE AND DREAMS(1953, Ital.); FRISKY(1955, Ital.); ANGELS OF DARKNESS(1956, Ital.); VALIANT, THE(1962, Brit./Ital.); CAPTIVE CITY, THE(1963, Ital.); GLADIATOR OF ROME(1963, Ital.); CONQUERED CITY(1966, Ital.)

Till Risso
SWING OUT THE BLUES(1943)

Checco Rissone
BITTER RICE(1950, Ital.); EVA(1962, Fr./Ital.)

Francesco Rissone
CUCKOO CLOCK, THE(1938, Ital.); MIRACLE IN MILAN(1951, Ital.); MAN WHO CAME FOR COFFEE, THE(1970, Ital.)

Giuditta Rissone
SCHOOLGIRL DIARY(1947, Ital.); 8 ½(1963, Ital.); ENGAGEMENT ITALIANO(1966, Fr./Ital.)

Christian Rist
QUESTION, THE(1977, Fr.)

Gary Rist
YOUNG GRADUATES, THE(1971)

Robbie Rist
MEMORY OF US(1974); CONQUEST OF THE EARTH(1980)
Misc. Talkies
HE IS MY BROTHER(1976)

Sepp Rist
S.O.S. ICEBERG(1933); DEVIL MAKES THREE, THE(1952)

Tom Riste
HORIZONS WEST(1952)

Tommy Riste
SIERRA BARON(1958)

Claude Rister
ONE WAY TRAIL, THE(1931), w; TOMBSTONE CANYON(1932), w; PRESCOTT KID, THE(1936), w; TRAPPED(1937), w

Vincent Risterucci
1984
L'ARGENT(1984, Fr./Switz.)

Debbie Ristick
ANGELO MY LOVE(1983)

Johnny Ristick
ANGELO MY LOVE(1983)

Yelka Ristick
ANGELO MY LOVE(1983)

Emilia Ristori
RICE GIRL(1963, Fr./Ital.)

R. J'Acurio Ristori
THIS WINE OF LOVE(1948, Ital.), w

"Rita"
POINTING FINGER, THE(1934, Brit.), w; DARBY AND JOAN(1937, Brit.), d&w

Rita and Rubins
LUCKY LEGS(1942)

Joseph Ritai
1984
VIGIL(1984, New Zealand)

David Ritch
STRANGER'S MEETING(1957, Brit.); SNORKEL, THE(1958, Brit.); STEEL BAYONET, THE(1958, Brit.)

Ocee Ritch
INTRUDER, THE(1962)

Steve Ritch
BATTLE OF ROGUE RIVER(1954); MASSACRE CANYON(1954); SEMINOLE UPRISING(1955); SAFE AT HOME(1962), w

Steven Ritch
CONQUEST OF COCHISE(1953); VALLEY OF THE HEADHUNTERS(1953); CROOKED WEB, THE(1955); WEREWOLF, THE(1956); BAILOUT AT 43,000(1957); HELL ON DEVIL'S ISLAND(1957), w; PLUNDER ROAD(1957), a, w; MURDER BY CONTRACT(1958); CITY OF FEAR(1959), a, w; STUDS LONIGAN(1960)

Cyril Ritchard
BLACKMAIL(1929, Brit.); JUST FOR A SONG(1930, Brit.); SYMPHONY IN TWO FLATS(1930, Brit.); PICCADILLY(1932, Brit.); RESERVED FOR LADIES(1932, Brit.); DANNY BOY(1934, Brit.); IT'S A GRAND OLD WORLD(1937, Brit.); SHOW GOES ON, THE(1937, Brit.); DANGEROUS MEDICINE(1938, Brit.); I SEE ICE(1938); WOMAN HATER(1949, Brit.); HALF A SIXPENCE(1967, Brit.)
Misc. Talkies
HANS BRINKER AND THE SILVER SKATES(1969)

Michael Ritchie
DOWNHILL RACER(1969), d

Rose Ritchel
Silents
ESCAPE, THE(1914), ed; HOME SWEET HOME(1914), ed

Kurt Ritcher
Silents
ONE ARABIAN NIGHT(1921, Ger.), set d

Bruce Ritchey
CHILD IS WAITING, A(1963); SILENCERS, THE(1966)

Lee Ritchey
SPLIT IMAGE(1982)

Will M. Ritchey
Silents
JOY AND THE DRAGON(1916), w; ALIAS MIKE MORAN(1919), w; EXCUSE MY DUST(1920), w; KEEPING UP WITH LIZZIE(1921), w; MAN WHO SAW TOMORROW, THE(1922), w; WOMAN WHO WALKED ALONE, THE(1922), w; RACING HEARTS(1923), w; WHITE SISTER, THE(1923), t; ROMOLA(1925), w; WHISPERING SMITH(1926), w; JIM THE CONQUEROR(1927), w; AFTER THE STORM(1928), w

William M. Ritchey
Silents
WHITE AND UNMARRIED(1921), w

Al Ritchie
DEAD MARCH, THE(1937)

Barbara Ritchie
SHE'S WORKING HER WAY THROUGH COLLEGE(1952)

Bill Ritchie
HOW TO BEAT THE HIGH COST OF LIVING(1980)

Clint Ritchie
ALVAREZ KELLY(1966); FIRST TO FIGHT(1967); ST. VALENTINE'S DAY MASSACRE, THE(1967); PATTON(1970); PEACE KILLERS, THE(1971); JOE KIDD(1972); POCO...LITTLE DOG LOST(1977); FORCE OF ONE, A(1979)

Donna Ritchie
HAIR(1979); WARRIORS, THE(1979)

Edith Ritchie
Silents
CLIMBERS, THE(1915)
Misc. Silents
COLLEGE WIDOW, THE(1915); EVANGELIST, THE(1915)

Eloise Ritchie
Misc. Talkies
TIGHTROPE TO TERROR(1977, Brit.)

Ethel Ritchie
Silents
ONCE A PLUMBER(1920); WONDERFUL WIFE, A(1922)
Misc. Silents
UNDERSTUDY, THE(1917); MIDNIGHT BURGLAR, THE(1918); NO CHILDREN WANTED(1918); HUNGER OF THE BLOOD, THE(1921); STRANGER OF THE HILLS, THE(1922)

Franklin Ritchie
Silents
NOT MY SISTER(1916)
Misc. Silents
INNER STRUGGLE, THE(1916); LIGHT, THE(1916); LYING LIPS(1916); UNDERTOW, THE(1916)

Franklyn Ritchie
Misc. Silents
DUST(1916); RECLAMATION, THE(1916)

Jack Ritchie
NEW LEAF, A(1971), w

Jean Ritchie
RHYTHM INN(1951)

Joe Ritchie
TRAITOR'S GATE(1966, Brit./Ger.); WHERE THE BULLETS FLY(1966, Brit.); BIG SLEEP, THE½(1978, Brit.)

John B. Ritchie
Silents
PRICE MARK, THE(1917), w

June Ritchie
KIND OF LOVING, A(1962, Brit.); LIVE NOW–PAY LATER(1962, Brit.); MOUSE ON THE MOON, THE(1963, Brit.); THREE PENNY OPERA(1963, Fr./Ger.); THIS IS MY STREET(1964, Brit.); PUSSYCAT ALLEY(1965, Brit.); SYNDICATE, THE(1968, Brit.)

Misc. Talkies
KENYA–COUNTRY OF TREASURE(1964)
Larry Ritchie
CONNECTION, THE(1962)
Lee Ritchie
BEST LITTLE WHOREHOUSE IN TEXAS, THE(1982)
Les Ritchie
BLESS 'EM ALL(1949, Brit.); SKIMPY IN THE NAVY(1949, Brit.)
Margaret Ritchie
PINK STRING AND SEALING WAX(1950, Brit.)
Michael Ritchie
CANDIDATE, THE(1972), d; PRIME CUT(1972), d; SMILE(1975), p&d; BAD NEWS BEARS, THE(1976), d; SEMI-TOUGH(1977), d; BAD NEWS BEARS GO TO JAPAN, THE(1978), p; ALMOST PERFECT AFFAIR, AN(1979), d, w; ISLAND, THE(1980), d; SURVIVORS, THE(1983), d
1984
FLETCH(1984), d
Richard Ritchie
SMITH'S WIVES(1935, Brit.)
Robert Ritchie
WHITE DOG(1982)
Ronald Ritchie
MAN WITHOUT A FACE, THE(1935, Brit.); NIGHT JOURNEY(1938, Brit.)
Roy Ritchie
JOURNEY AMONG WOMEN(1977, Aus.), m; MOUTH TO MOUTH(1978, Aus.), m
Stan Ritchie
MR. BILLION(1977); NIGHTMARE IN BLOOD(1978)
Stanley E. Ritchie
LITTLE MISS MARKER(1980)
Welles W. Ritchie
Silents
DOWN GRADE, THE(1927), w
Wells Ritchie
Silents
CROSS BREED(1927), w
Will M. Ritchie
Silents
HANDLE WITH CARE(1922), w
William M. Ritchie
Silents
NORTH OF THE RIO GRANDE(1922), w
Willie Ritchie
Misc. Silents
MAN WHO BEAT DAN DOLAN, THE(1915)
Viktor Ritelis
CRUCIBLE OF HORROR(1971, Brit.), d
Dorris Riter
UNTIL THEY SAIL(1957)
Kristen Riter
STUDENT BODIES(1981)
Ted Fio Rito
YOUNG AND BEAUTIFUL(1934)
Riton
GET OUT YOUR HANDKERCHIEFS(1978, Fr.)
Jennifer Ritt
YOUNG GRADUATES, THE(1971)
Martin Ritt
EDGE OF THE CITY(1957), d; NO DOWN PAYMENT(1957), d; LONG, HOT SUMMER, THE(1958), d; BLACK ORCHID(1959), d; SOUND AND THE FURY, THE(1959), d; FIVE BRANDED WOMEN(1960), d; PARIS BLUES(1961), d; ADVENTURES OF A YOUNG MAN(1962), d; HUD(1963), p, d; OUTRAGE, THE(1964), d; SPY WHO CAME IN FROM THE COLD, THE(1965, Brit.), p&d; HOMBRE(1967), p, d; BROTHERHOOD, THE(1968), d; GREAT WHITE HOPE, THE(1970), d; MOLLY MAGUIRES, THE(1970), p, d; PETE 'N' TILLIE(1972), d; SOUNDER(1972), d; CONRACK(1974), p, d; END OF THE GAME(1976, Ger./Ital.); FRONT, THE(1976), p&d; CASEY'S SHADOW(1978), d; NORMA RAE(1979), d; BACK ROADS(1981), d; CROSS CREEK(1983), d
Pfc. Martin Ritt
WINGED VICTORY(1944)
Tina Ritt
CHEAP DETECTIVE, THE(1978); FM(1978)
Guenther Rittau
GOLD(1934, Ger.), ph
Gunther Rittau
BLUE ANGEL, THE(1930, Ger.), ph; BOMBARDMENT OF MONTE CARLO, THE(1931, Ger.), ph; HAPPY EVER AFTER(1932, Ger./Brit.), ph; TEMPEST(1932, Ger.), ph; F.P. 1 DOESN'T ANSWER(1933, Ger.), ph
Silents
KRIEMHILD'S REVENGE(1924, Ger.), ph; SIEGFRIED(1924, Ger.), ph; METROPOLIS(1927, Ger.), ph
Ritter
M(1933, Ger.)
Fred Ritter
FORTY-NINERS, THE(1932); CAROLINA MOON(1940); HANDS ACROSS THE BORDER(1944), art d; PISTOL PACKIN' MAMA(1943), art d; HIDDEN VALLEY OUTLAWS(1944), art d; LARAMIE TRAIL, THE(1944), art d; MOJAVE FIREBRAND(1944), art d; OUTLAWS OF SANTA FE(1944), art d; PRIDE OF THE PLAINS(1944), art d; THOROUGHBREDS(1945), art d; NORTHWEST OUTPOST(1947), art d; SADDLE PALS(1947), art d; WILD FRONTIER, THE(1947), art d; MACBETH(1948), art d, cos; OMOO OMOO, THE SHARK GOD(1949), art d; RIMFIRE(1949), art d
Fred A. Ritter
END OF THE ROAD(1944), art d; GOODNIGHT SWEETHEART(1944), art d; SHERIFF OF SUNDOWN(1944), art d; SILVER CITY KID(1944), art d; SONG OF NEVADA(1944), md; VIGILANTES OF DODGE CITY(1944), art d; YELLOW ROSE OF TEXAS, THE(1944), art d; GREAT STAGECOACH ROBBERY(1945), art d; MAN FROM OKLAHOMA, THE(1945), art d; SHERIFF OF CIMARRON(1945), art d; TRAIL OF KIT CARSON(1945), art d; DAYS OF BUFFALO BILL(1946), art d; EL PASO KID, THE(1946), art d; INNER CIRCLE, THE(1946), art d; NIGHT TRAIN TO MEMPHIS(1946), art d; RED RIVER RENEGADES(1946), art d; SANTA FE UPRISING(1946), art d; SHERIFF OF REDWOOD VALLEY(1946), art d; HOME-

STEADERS OF PARADISE VALLEY(1947), art d; LAST FRONTIER UPRISING(1947), art d; VIGILANTES OF BOOMTOWN(1947), art d; TRAIN TO ALCATRAZ(1948), art d; NAVAJO TRAIL RAIDERS(1949), art d; PRINCE OF THE PLAINS(1949), art d; RODEO KING AND THE SENORITA(1951), art d; SECRETS OF MONTE CARLO(1951), art d; LEADVILLE GUNSLINGER(1952), art d; WAC FROM WALLA WALLA, THE(1952), art d; GHOST OF ZORRO(1959), art
Gerhard Ritter
KING IN SHADOW(1961, Ger.)
James A. Ritter
PRINCE OF THE PLAINS(1949), set d
Joe Ritter
PLAINSONG(1982), ph
John Ritter
BAREFOOT EXECUTIVE, THE(1971); SCANDALOUS JOHN(1971); OTHER, THE(1972); STONE KILLER, THE(1973); NICKELODEON(1976); BREAKFAST IN BED(1978); AMERICATHON(1979); HERO AT LARGE(1980); WHOLLY MOSES(1980); THEY ALL LAUGHED(1981)
Mary Ritter
LITTLE SEX, A(1982)
Tex Ritter
SONG OF THE GRINGO(1936); ARIZONA DAYS(1937); HEADIN' FOR THE RIO GRANDE(1937); HITTIN' THE TRAIL(1937); MYSTERY OF THE HOODED HORSEMEN, THE(1937), a, m; RIDERS OF THE ROCKIES(1937); SING, COWBOY, SING(1937); TEX RIDES WITH THE BOY SCOUTS(1937); TROUBLE IN TEXAS(1937); FRONTIER TOWN(1938); ROLLIN' PLAINS(1938); STARLIGHT OVER TEXAS(1938); UTAH TRAIL(1938); WHERE THE BUFFALO ROAM(1938); DOWN THE WYOMING TRAIL(1939); MAN FROM TEXAS, THE(1939); RIDERS OF THE FRONTIER(1939); ROLL, WAGONS, ROLL(1939); ROLLIN' WESTWARD(1939); SONG OF THE BUCKAROO(1939); SUNDOWN ON THE PRAIRIE(1939); ARIZONA FRONTIER(1940); COWBOY FROM SUNDOWN(1940); GOLDEN TRAIL, THE(1940); PALS OF THE SILVER SAGE(1940); RAINBOW OVER THE RANGE(1940); RHYTHM OF THE RIO GRANDE(1940); WESTBOUND STAGE(1940); KING OF DODGE CITY(1941); PIONEERS, THE(1941); RIDING THE CHEROKEE TRAIL(1941); ROLLIN' HOME TO TEXAS(1941); DEEP IN THE HEART OF TEXAS(1942); DEVIL'S TRAIL, THE(1942); LITTLE JOE, THE WRANGLER(1942); LONE STAR VIGILANTES, THE(1942); ARIZONA TRAIL(1943); CHEYENNE ROUNDUP(1943); FRONTIER BADMEN(1943); LONE STAR TRAIL, THE(1943); OLD CHISHOLM TRAIL(1943); RAIDERS OF SAN JOAQUIN(1943); TENTING TONIGHT ON THE OLD CAMP GROUND(1943); COWBOY CANTEEN(1944); DEAD OR ALIVE(1944); GANGSTERS OF THE FRONTIER(1944); MARSHAL OF GUNSMOKE(1944); OKLAHOMA RAIDERS(1944); WHISPERING SKULL, THE(1944); ENEMY OF THE LAW(1945); FLAMING BULLETS(1945); FRONTIER FUGITIVES(1945); MARKED FOR MURDER(1945); THREE IN THE SADDLE(1945); HOLIDAY RHYTHM(1950); APACHE AMBUSH(1955); NASHVILLE REBEL(1966); WHAT AM I BID?(1967)
Misc. Talkies
TAKE ME BACK TO OKLAHOMA(1940); ROARING FRONTIERS(1941); BULLETS FOR BANDITS(1942); NORTH OF THE ROCKIES(1942); VENGEANCE OF THE WEST(1942); GIRL FROM TOBACCO ROW, THE(1966)
Thelma Ritter
MIRACLE ON 34TH STREET, THE(1947); LETTER TO THREE WIVES, A(1948); CITY ACROSS THE RIVER(1949); FATHER WAS A FULLBACK(1949); ALL ABOUT EVE(1950); I'LL GET BY(1950); PERFECT STRANGERS(1950); AS YOUNG AS YOU FEEL(1951); MATING SEASON, THE(1951); MODEL AND THE MARRIAGE BROKER, THE(1951); WITH A SONG IN MY HEART(1952); FARMER TAKES A WIFE, THE(1953); PICKUP ON SOUTH STREET(1953); TITANIC(1953); REAR WINDOW(1954); DADDY LONG LEGS(1955); LUCY GALLANT(1955); PROUD AND THE PROFANE, THE(1956); HOLE IN THE HEAD, A(1959); PILLOW TALK(1959); MISFITS, THE(1961); SECOND TIME AROUND, THE(1961); BIRDMAN OF ALCATRAZ(1962); HOW THE WEST WAS WON(1962); FOR LOVE OR MONEY(1963); MOVE OVER, DARLING(1963); NEW KIND OF LOVE, A(1963); BOEING BOEING(1965); INCIDENT, THE(1967); WHAT'S SO BAD ABOUT FEELING GOOD?(1968)
Michael Ritterman
HIGHLY DANGEROUS(1950, Brit.); ISLAND RESCUE(1952, Brit.); MYSTERY SUBMARINE(1963, Brit.); SPY WHO CAME IN FROM THE COLD, THE(1965, Brit.)
Philip Ritti
REUNION(1932, Brit.)
Rudolf Rittner
Silents
KRIEMHILD'S REVENGE(1924, Ger.)
Rudolph Rittner
Misc. Silents
CHRONICLES OF THE GRAY HOUSE, THE(1923, Ger.)
Mary Ritts
ERRAND BOY, THE(1961)
Paul Ritts
ERRAND BOY, THE(1961)
Wulf Rittscher
SLEEPING BEAUTY(1965, Ger.)
Rosemary Rityo
ALICE, SWEET ALICE(1978), w
Al Ritz
YOU CAN'T HAVE EVERYTHING(1937); GORILLA, THE(1939); BEHIND THE EIGHT BALL(1942); HI'YA, CHUM(1943); NEVER A DULL MOMENT(1943)
Harry Ritz
YOU CAN'T HAVE EVERYTHING(1937); GORILLA, THE(1939); BEHIND THE EIGHT BALL(1942); HI'YA, CHUM(1943); NEVER A DULL MOMENT(1943); SILENT MOVIE(1976)
Misc. Talkies
BLAZING STEWARDESSES(1975)
James Ritz
REAL LIFE(1979); LEO AND LOREE(1980), w
1984
SPLASH(1984)
Jim Ritz
GRAND THEFT AUTO(1977); NIGHT SHIFT(1982)
Jimmy Ritz
YOU CAN'T HAVE EVERYTHING(1937); GORILLA, THE(1939); BEHIND THE EIGHT BALL(1942); HI'YA, CHUM(1943); NEVER A DULL MOMENT(1943)

Joan Ritz-

Misc. Talkies
BLAZING STEWARDESSES(1975)
Joan Ritz
Silents
FLYING FROM JUSTICE(1915, Brit.); OLD ARM CHAIR, THE(1920, Brit.)
Misc. Silents
MASTER AND MAN(1915, Brit.); ROGUE'S WIFE, A(1915, Brit.); ROYAL LOVE(1915, Brit.); TRUMPET CALL, THE(1915, Brit.); HOBSON'S CHOICE(1920, Brit.); CROXLEY MASTER, THE(1921, Brit.)
Lyle Ritz
NO DRUMS, NO BUGLES(1971), m
Ritz Brothers
LIFE BEGINS IN COLLEGE(1937); THREE MUSKETEERS, THE(1939)
The Ritz Brothers
ON THE AVENUE(1937); GOLDWYN FOLLIES, THE(1938); KENTUCKY MOONSHINE(1938); STRAIGHT, PLACE AND SHOW(1938); PACK UP YOUR TROUBLES(1939); ARGENTINE NIGHTS(1940); WON TON TON, THE DOG WHO SAVED HOLLYWOOD(1976)
Anna Riva
TOUCH OF HER FLESH, THE(1967), p, ph
Anna Riva [Roberta Findley]
SATAN'S BED(1965)
Emmanuelle Riva
HIROSHIMA, MON AMOUR(1959, Fr./Jap.); THERESE(1963, Fr.); KAPO(1964, Ital./Fr./Yugo.); HOURS OF LOVE, THE(1965, Ital.); LOVE A LA CARTE(1965, Ital.); EYES, THE MOUTH, THE(1982, Ital./Fr.)
J. Michael Riva
BAD BOYS(1983), prod d
1984
ADVENTURES OF BUCKAROO BANZAI: ACROSS THE 8TH DIMENSION, THE(1984), prod d
John Michael Riva
HAND, THE(1981), prod d
Mario Riva
TIMES GONE BY(1953, Ital.)
Michael Riva
BARE KNUCKLES(1978), prod d; FAST CHARLIE... THE MOONBEAM RIDER(1979), art d; ORDINARY PEOPLE(1980), art d; HALLOWEEN II(1981), prod d
Winni Riva
LEOPARD, THE(1963, Ital.)
Ross Rival
WONDER WOMEN(1973, Phil.)
Giorgio Rivalta
COSSACKS, THE(1960, It.), d; PHAROAH'S WOMAN, THE(1961, Ital.), d; AVENGER, THE(1962, Fr./Ital.), d
L. Rivanera
HONEYMOON DEFERRED(1951, Brit.)
Mary Rivard
WARM IN THE BUD(1970)
Robert Rivard
NIKKI, WILD DOG OF THE NORTH(1961, U.S./Can.); WHY ROCK THE BOAT?(1974, Can.)
Steve Rivard
WICKED DIE SLOW, THE(1968)
Carlos Rivas
FURY IN PARADISE(1955, U.S./Mex.); BEAST OF HOLLOW MOUNTAIN, THE(1956); KING AND I, THE(1956); BIG BOODLE, THE(1957); BLACK SCORPION, THE(1957); DEERSLAYER, THE(1957); PANAMA SAL(1957); MACHETE(1958); MIRACLE, THE(1959); DALTON THAT GOT AWAY(1960); PEPE(1960); UNFORGIVEN, THE(1960); THEY SAVED HITLER'S BRAIN(1964); TARZAN AND THE VALLEY OF GOLD(1966 U.S./Switz.); HANG YOUR HAT ON THE WIND(1969); TOPAZ(1969, Brit.); TRUE GRIT(1969); UNDEFEATED, THE(1969); GATLING GUN, THE(1972); DOC SAVAGE... THE MAN OF BRONZE(1975)
Domingo Rivas
DESERT WARRIOR(1961 Ital./Span.)
Gabry Rivas
THUNDER BELOW(1932)
Jose Maria Linares Rivas
CRIMINAL LIFE OF ARCHIBALDO DE LA CRUZ, THE(1962, Mex.)
Jose Maria Linares Rivas
DOCTOR CRIMEN(1953, Mex.)
Kip Rivas
Misc. Talkies
BED OF VIOLENCE(1967)
Linda Rivas
MAYOR OF 44TH STREET, THE(1942); MEXICAN SPITFIRE SEES A GHOST(1942)
Ramiro Rivas
KISMET(1944); SALOME(1953)
Richard Rivas
SALOME(1953)
Rogelio Barriga Rivas
IMPORTANT MAN, THE(1961, Mex.), w
Ruben T. Rivas
SALOME(1953)
William Rivas
KISMET(1944)
Pascale Rivault
LADY CHATTERLEY'S LOVER(1981, Fr./Brit.)
Kenneth Rive
BOYS, THE(1962, Brit.), p; DURING ONE NIGHT(1962, Brit.), p; DEVIL DOLL(1964, Brit.), p; CURSE OF THE VOODOO(1965, Brit.), p
Silents
EMERALD OF THE EAST(1928, Brit.)
Madeleine Rive
SOMEWHERE IN FRANCE(1943, Brit.)
Michel Rivelin
TWO OF US, THE(1968, Fr.), w

Amparo Rivelles
TRAPPED IN TANGIERS(1960, Ital./Span.)
Rafael Rivelles
CARMEN(1949, Span.); REVOLT OF THE SLAVES, THE(1961, Ital./Span./Ger.); EL GRECO(1966, Ital., Fr.)
Luisa Rivelli
WHERE THE HOT WIND BLOWS(1960, Fr., Ital.); POPPY IS ALSO A FLOWER, THE(1966); BIG GUNDOWN, THE(1968, Ital.)
W.L. River
NAVY BLUES(1930), w; WAY FOR A SAILOR(1930), w; REACHING FOR THE SUN(1941), w; ADVENTURES OF MARTIN EDEN, THE(1942), w; GREAT MAN'S LADY, THE(1942), w; CITY WITHOUT MEN(1943), w
William River
OUTLAW: THE SAGE OF GISLI(1982, Iceland), ed
Amelia Rivera
SCALPHUNTERS, THE(1968)
Amos Rivera
FIEND OF DOPE ISLAND(1961)
Ana Maria Rivera
SWEET SUGAR(1972)
Annette Rivera
ROSELAND(1977)
Anthony Rivera
1984
KILLPOINT(1984)
Carlos Rivera
OLD MAN AND THE SEA, THE(1958)
Cecilia Rivera
AGUIRRE, THE WRATH OF GOD(1977, W. Ger.)
Chita Rivera
SWEET CHARITY(1969); SGT. PEPPER'S LONELY HEARTS CLUB BAND(1978)
Eduardo Rivera
AMERICAN GUERRILLA IN THE PHILIPPINES, AN(1950)
Emilio Rivera
THUNDER AND LIGHTNING(1977)
Fermin Rivera
BRAVE ONE, THE(1956)
Gita Rivera
THEY'RE A WEIRD MOB(1966, Aus.)
Greg Rivera
NORSEMAN, THE(1978)
Linda Rivera
REFORM SCHOOL GIRL(1957); FUN IN ACAPULCO(1963); CURSE OF THE VAMPIRES(1970, Phil., U.S.)
Louis Rivera
HOUSE OF 1,000 DOLLS(1967, Ger./Span./Brit.); VAN NUYS BLVD.(1979)
Silents
OUT OF THE SILENT NORTH(1922)
Luis Rivera
SUNSCORCHED(1966, Span./Ger.); FEW BULLETS MORE, A(1968, Ital./Span.); RUN LIKE A THIEF(1968, Span.); GUNS OF THE MAGNIFICENT SEVEN(1969); MURDERS IN THE RUE MORGUE(1971); TOWN CALLED HELL, A(1971, Span./Brit.); BAD MAN'S RIVER(1972, Span.)
Marcelino Rivera
1984
MIXED BLOOD(1984)
Marika Rivera
GIRL ON A MOTORCYCLE, THE(1968, Fr./Brit.); FIDDLER ON THE ROOF(1971)
Mike Rivera
NORSEMAN, THE(1978)
Primy Rivera
1984
OLD ENOUGH(1984)
Roberto G. Rivera
INVISIBLE MAN, THE(1958, Mex.); FRANKENSTEIN, THE VAMPIRE AND CO.(1961, Mex.); CURSE OF THE DOLL PEOPLE, THE(1968, Mex.)
Rudolfo Toledo Rivera
MASSACRE(1956)
Stella Rivera
EYES OF A STRANGER(1980)
Tony Rivera
MR. MAGOO'S HOLIDAY FESTIVAL(1970), prod d
Georges Rivere
AND SUDDENLY IT'S MURDER!(1964, Ital.)
Anna Rivero
WE STILL KILL THE OLD WAY(1967, Ital.)
Carlos Rivero
KANSAS CITY CONFIDENTIAL(1952); RAIDERS, THE(1952); NAKED JUNGLE, THE(1953); ELEPHANT WALK(1954); SECRET OF THE INCAS(1954); HELL'S ISLAND(1955)
Carmen Rivero
REWARD, THE(1965)
Charles Rivero
DOWN MEXICO WAY(1941); MEXICAN HAYRIDE(1948); CRISIS(1950)
Enrico Rivero
BLOOD OF A POET, THE(1930, Fr.)
Enrique Rivero
Misc. Silents
LE TORNOI(1928, Fr.); LE BLED(1929, Fr.)
George Rivero
Misc. Talkies
TARGET EAGLE(1982)
Jorge Rivero
RIO LOBO(1970); SOLDIER BLUE(1970); LAST HARD MEN, THE(1976); PRIEST OF LOVE(1981, Brit.)
1984
CONQUEST(1984, Ital./Span./Mex.)

Jose Antonio Rivero
AFFAIR IN HAVANA(1957)
Julian Rivero
DUGAN OF THE BAD LANDS(1931); GOD'S COUNTRY AND THE MAN(1931); YANKEE DON(1931); BEYOND THE ROCKIES(1932); BROKEN WING, THE(1932); KID FROM SPAIN, THE(1932); LAW AND LAWLESS(1932); MAN FROM HELL'S EDGES(1932); NIGHT RIDER, THE(1932); SON OF OKLAHOMA(1932); WINNER TAKE ALL(1932); FLYING DOWN TO RIO(1933); HOLD THE PRESS(1933); LUCKY LARRIGAN(1933); VIA PONY EXPRESS(1933); COWBOY HOLIDAY(1934); NADA MAS QUE UNA MUJER(1934); VIVA VILLA!(1934); GOIN' TO TOWN(1935); RED SALUTE(1935); SAGEBRUSH TROUBADOR(1935); WESTERN JUSTICE(1935); DANCING PIRATE(1936); GUN PLAY(1936); HI GAUCHO!(1936); PHANTOM PATROL(1936); SONG OF THE SADDLE(1936); WOMAN TRAP(1936); LAND BEYOND THE LAW(1937); LAWLESS LAND(1937); MIGHTY TREVE, THE(1937); RIDIN' THE LONE TRAIL(1937); HEROES OF THE ALAMO(1938); OUTLAW EXPRESS(1938); CODE OF THE SECRET SERVICE(1939); DRIFTING WESTWARD(1939); GIRL AND THE GAMBLER, THE(1939); SOUTH OF THE BORDER(1939); ARIZONA GANGBUSTERS(1940); DEATH RIDES THE RANGE(1940); GAUCHO SERENADE(1940); GREEN HELL(1940); MAD EMPRESS, THE(1940); WESTERNER, THE(1940); YOUNG BUFFALO BILL(1940); BILLY THE KID'S FIGHTING PALS(1941); BILLY THE KID'S RANGE WAR(1941); DOWN MEXICO WAY(1941); LONE RIDER CROSSES THE RIO, THE(1941); RIDERS OF BLACK MOUNTAIN(1941); OVERLAND STAGECOACH(1942); RIO RITA(1942); UNDERGROUND AGENT(1942); HANDS ACROSS THE BORDER(1943); OUTLAW, THE(1943); SONG OF BERNADETTE, THE(1943); FALCON IN MEXICO, THE(1944); MACHINE GUN MAMA(1944); PAN-AMERICANA(1945); THAT NIGHT WITH YOU(1945); ANNA AND THE KING OF SIAM(1946); CAPTAIN FROM CASTILE(1947); LOST MOMENT, THE(1947); RIDE THE PINK HORSE(1947); RIFFRAFF(1947); CHECKERED COAT, THE(1948); KISSING BANDIT, THE(1948); MEXICAN HAYRIDE(1948); OLD LOS ANGELES(1948); PERILOUS WATERS(1948); SECRET BEYOND THE DOOR, THE(1948); TREASURE OF THE SIERRA MADRE, THE(1948); DEVIL'S HENCHMEN, THE(1949); WE WERE STRANGERS(1949); BORDER TREASURE(1950); KILLER SHARK(1950); WHERE DANGER LIVES(1950); MILLIONAIRE FOR CHRISTY, A(1951); TEXAS RANGERS, THE(1951); SNOWS OF KILIMANJARO, THE(1952); WILD HORSE AMBUSH(1952); SHADOWS OF TOMBSTONE(1953); BROKEN LANCE(1954); THREE HOURS TO KILL(1954); GUYS AND DOLLS(1955); MAN ALONE, A(1955); TEN WANTED MEN(1955); VANISHING AMERICAN, THE(1955); GIANT(1956); THUNDER OVER ARIZONA(1956); HOUSEBOAT(1958); REWARD, THE(1965)
Misc. Talkies
MAN OF ACTION(1933); BORN TO BATTLE(1935); TRAIL TO MEXICO(1946)
Silents
NIGHT SHIP, THE(1925)
Lorraine Rivero
ONE MILLION B.C.(1940)
Silents
CHICAGO AFTER MIDNIGHT(1928); LADIES OF THE MOB(1928)
R. Rivero
CHRISTMAS KID, THE(1968, U.S., Span.), w
Santiago Rivero
DEVIL MADE A WOMAN, THE(1962, Span.); DEADFALL(1968, Brit.)
Anthony Rivers
NAKED CITY, THE(1948)
Clarice Rivers
ROUND TRIP(1967)
David Rivers
SUDDEN IMPACT(1983)
Ferdinand Rivers
PASTEUR(1936, Fr.), p
Fernand Rivers
BONNE CHANCE(1935, Fr.), p; OPEN ROAD, THE(1940, Fr.), p&d; LES MAINS SALES(1954, Fr.), p&d, w; ADORABLE LIAR(1962, Fr.), p
Fletcher Rivers
CABIN IN THE SKY(1943)
Jack Rivers
SONG OF THE SIERRAS(1946); WEST OF THE ALAMO(1946); SONG OF THE WASTELAND(1947); OUTLAW BRAND(1948); PARTNERS OF THE SUNSET(1948)
Joan Rivers
SWIMMER, THE(1968); RABBIT TEST(1978), a, d, w; UNCLE SCAM(1981)
1984
MUPPETS TAKE MANHATTAN, THE(1984)
Joe Rivers
BIG CITY(1937)
1984
GIRLS NIGHT OUT(1984), ph
John Rivers
ONCE UPON A COFFEE HOUSE(1965)
Johnny Rivers
SGT. PEPPER'S LONELY HEARTS CLUB BAND(1978)
Larry Rivers
ROUND TRIP(1967); LOVESICK(1983)
Leo Rivers
BLACK ANGELS, THE(1970), p; GUESS WHAT HAPPENED TO COUNT DRACULA(1970), p
Marcia Rivers
Misc. Talkies
DYNAMITE(1972)
Robert Rivers
SUDDEN IMPACT(1983)
Vic Rivers
GRAND THEFT AUTO(1977)
Victor Rivers
GRAND THEFT AUTO(1977), stunts
1984
FEAR CITY(1984)
Gilberte Rivet
LACOMBE, LUCIEN(1974)
Marcel Rivet
LOVER'S NET(1957, Fr.), w

Jacques Rivette
PARIS BELONGS TO US(1962, Fr.), d, w; NUN, THE(1971, Fr.), d, w; CELINE AND JULIE GO BOATING(1974, Fr.), d, w
1984
LOVE ON THE GROUND(1984,Fr.), d, w
Jean Riveyre
DIARY OF A COUNTRY PRIEST(1954, Fr.)
Anne Riviere
TWO ARE GUILTY(1964, Fr.)
Carine Riviere
FIRST TIME, THE(1978, Fr.)
Daniel Riviere
LA PRISONNIERE(1969, Fr./Ital.)
Gaston Riviere
Silents
HEARTS OF THE WORLD(1918)
George Riviere
ANATOMY OF A MARRIAGE(MY DAYS WITH JEAN-MARC AND MY NIGHTS WITH FRANCOISE)**1/2 (1964 Fr.); GIRL CAN'T STOP, THE(1966, Fr./Gr.)
Georges Riviere
GAME OF TRUTH, THE(1961, Fr.); LONGEST DAY, THE(1962); TOMORROW IS MY TURN(1962, Fr./Ital./Ger.); LAFAYETTE(1963, Fr.); CASTLE OF BLOOD(1964, Fr./Ital.); HORROR CASTLE(1965, Ital.); MINNESOTA CLAY(1966, Ital./Fr./Span.); JOURNEY BENEATH THE DESERT(1967, Fr./Ital.)
Isabelle Riviere
WANDERER, THE(1969, Fr.), w
Jorge Riviere
JOHN PAUL JONES(1959)
Marie Riviere
AVIATOR'S WIFE, THE(1981, Fr.)
Marie-France Riviere
24 HOURS IN A WOMAN'S LIFE(1968, Fr./Ger.), w
Richard Riviere
OLD MOTHER RILEY IN PARIS(1938, Brit.)
Lucille Rivin
1984
HOME FREE ALL(1984)
Alan Rivkin
BAD BOY(1935), w
Allen Rivkin
DEVIL IS DRIVING, THE(1932), w; IS MY FACE RED?(1932), w; MADISON SQUARE GARDEN(1932), w; NIGHT WORLD(1932), w; 70,000 WITNESSES(1932), w; DANCING LADY(1933), w; GIRL IN 419(1933), w; HEADLINE SHOOTER(1933), w; MEET THE BARON(1933), w; MELODY CRUISE(1933), w; PICTURE SNATCHER(1933), w; CHEATING CHEATERS(1934), w; BLACK SHEEP(1935), w; OUR LITTLE GIRL(1935), w; CHAMPAGNE CHARLIE(1936), w; HALF ANGEL(1936), w; LOVE UNDER FIRE(1937), w; THIS IS MY AFFAIR(1937), w; STRAIGHT, PLACE AND SHOW(1938), w; IT COULD HAPPEN TO YOU(1939), w; LET US LIVE(1939), w; DANCING ON A DIME(1940), w; TYPHOON(1940), w; HIGHWAY WEST(1941), w; SINGAPORE WOMAN(1941), w; JOE SMITH, AMERICAN(1942), w; KID GLOVE KILLER(1942), w; SUNDAY PUNCH(1942), w; THIS MAN'S NAVY(1945), w; THRILL OF BRAZIL, THE(1946), w; TILL THE END OF TIME(1946), w; DEAD RECKONING(1947), w; FARMER'S DAUGHTER, THE(1947), w; GUILT OF JANET AMES, THE(1947), w; MY DREAM IS YOURS(1949), w; TENSION(1949), w; GAMBLING HOUSE(1950), w; GROUNDS FOR MARRIAGE(1950), w; IT'S A BIG COUNTRY(1951), w; STRIP, THE(1951), w; BATTLE CIRCUS(1953), w; PRISONER OF WAR(1954), w; ETERNAL SEA, THE(1955), w; ROAD TO DENVER, THE(1955), w; TIMBERJACK(1955), w; GIRLS ON THE LOOSE(1958), w; LIVE FAST, DIE YOUNG(1958), w; BIG OPERATOR, THE(1959), w,Robert Smith
Stephen Rivkin
1984
HOT DOG...THE MOVIE(1984), ed
Stephen E. Rivkin
PERSONALS, THE(1982), ed
Leora Rivlin
DREAMER, THE(1970, Israel)
Y. Rivosh
DEFENSE OF VOLOTCHAYEVSK, THE(1938, USSR), prod d
Alexander Rix
ETERNAL WALTZ, THE(1959, Ger.), w
Brian Rix
RELUCTANT HEROES(1951, Brit.); UP TO HIS NECK(1954, Brit.); WHAT EVERY WOMAN WANTS(1954, Brit.); DRY ROT(1956, Brit.); NOT WANTED ON VOYAGE(1957, Brit.); AND THE SAME TO YOU(1960, Brit.); NIGHT WE GOT THE BIRD, THE(1961, Brit.), a, p; NOTHING BARRED(1961, Brit.), a, p; MAKE MINE A DOUBLE(1962, Brit.); DON'T JUST LIE THERE, SAY SOMETHING!(1973, Brit.)
Colin Rix
END OF THE LINE, THE(1959, Brit.); STRICTLY CONFIDENTIAL(1959, Brit.); OPERATION CUPID(1960, Brit.); STRONGROOM(1962, Brit.); PANIC(1966, Brit.); HENRY VIII AND HIS SIX WIVES(1972, Brit.); MEDUSA TOUCH, THE(1978, Brit.); EYE OF THE NEEDLE(1981)
George Rix
Silents
TORRENT, THE(1921), w
Jack Rix
LEASE OF LIFE(1954, Brit.), p; SHIRALEE, THE(1957, Brit.), p
Jonathan Rix
COVER-UP(1949), w
Jonathan Rix [Dennis O'Keefe]
ANGELA(1955, Ital.), w
Paul Rix
VIRGINIA CITY(1940)
Cheryl Rixon
SWAP MEET(1979); USED CARS(1980)
Benjamin R. Rixson
SHAFT(1971)
Angelo Rizacos
HOG WILD(1980, Can.); TICKET TO HEAVEN(1981)

George Rizard
Silents
TRUTH WAGON, THE(1914), ph; THIS HERO STUFF(1919), ph; OLD SWIMMIN' HOLE, THE(1921), ph; TWO MINUTES TO GO(1921), ph; ALIAS JULIUS CAESAR(1922), ph; TAILOR MADE MAN, A(1922), ph; COURTSHIP OF MILES STANDISH, THE(1923), ph; HELD TO ANSWER(1923), ph

Sam Rizhallah
BRUTE FORCE(1947)

N. Rizhov
VOW, THE(1947, USSR.)

Samir Rizkallah
TEMPTATION(1946); CASBAH(1948)

Kent Rizley
ENDANGERED SPECIES(1982)

Luis Rizo
VIVA MARIA(1965, Fr./Ital.)

Nikos Rizos
SISTERS, THE(1969, Gr.)

Walter Rizzati
1990: THE BRONX WARRIORS(1983, Ital.), m
1984
HOUSE BY THE CEMETERY, THE(1984, Ital.), m

Gene Rizzi
SAINT IN PALM SPRINGS, THE(1941); TEN GENTLEMEN FROM WEST POINT(1942); TO BE OR NOT TO BE(1942); CRASH DIVE(1943); OUTLAW, THE(1943)

Gigi Rizzi
DEATH TOOK PLACE LAST NIGHT(1970, Ital./Ger.)

Nicoletta Rizzi
THANK YOU, AUNT(1969, Ital.)

Elena Rizzieri
GLASS MOUNTAIN, THE(1950, Brit)

Alfredo Rizzo
ROMAN HOLIDAY(1953); WAR AND PEACE(1956, Ital./U.S.); PICKUP ALLEY(1957, Brit.); LA DOLCE VITA(1961, Ital./Fr.); PLAYGIRLS AND THE VAMPIRE(1964, Ital.); SEVEN SLAVES AGAINST THE WORLD(1965, Ital.); CURSE OF THE BLOOD GHOULS(1969, Ital.)

Anthony Rizzo
SLEEPING BEAUTY(1959), art d; ONE HUNDRED AND ONE DALMATIANS(1961), art d; SWORD IN THE STONE, THE(1963), art d

Carl Rizzo
DIRTY HARRY(1971); UNHOLY ROLLERS(1972)

Carlo Rizzo
DEPORTED(1950); WHEN IN ROME(1952); ROMAN HOLIDAY(1953); RAINS OF RANCHIPUR, THE(1955); MONTE CARLO STORY, THE(1957, Ital.); SEVEN HILLS OF ROME, THE(1958); NAKED MAJA, THE(1959, Ital./U.S.); FAST AND SEXY(1960, Fr./Ital.); DAMON AND PYTHIAS(1962); SWORDSMAN OF SIENA, THE(1962, Fr./Ital.); BIGGEST BUNDLE OF THEM ALL, THE(1968)

Carmine Rizzo
IT HAPPENED IN CANADA(1962, Can.), m

Giacomo Rizzo
AVANTI!(1972)

Gianna Rizzo
THREE STEPS NORTH(1951)

Gianni Rizzo
CITY OF PAIN(1951, Ital.); HEAD OF A TYRANT(1960, Fr./Ital.); PIRATE AND THE SLAVE GIRL, THE(1961, Fr./Ital.); REQUIEM FOR A SECRET AGENT(1966, Ital.); FACE TO FACE(1967, Ital.); MISSION STARDUST(1968, Ital./Span./Ger.); SABATA(1969, Ital.); ADIOS SABATA(1971, Ital./Span.); RETURN OF SABATA(1972, Ital./Fr./Ger.)

Giovanni Rizzo
LONELY LADY, THE(1983)

Jilly Rizzo
TONY ROME(1967); DETECTIVE, THE(1968)
1984
CANNONBALL RUN II(1984)

Peter Rizzo
1984
VARIETY(1984)

Angela Rizzoli
8 ½(1963, Ital.), p

Angelo Rizzoli
LA DOLCE VITA(1961, Ital./Fr.), p; JULIET OF THE SPIRITS(1965, Fr./Ital./W.Ger.), p; ITALIAN SECRET SERVICE(1968, Ital.), p

Raissa Rjasanova
MOSCOW DOES NOT BELIEVE IN TEARS(1980, USSR)

Agusto Roa
ALIAS BIG SHOT(1962, Argen.), w

Joaquin Roa
VIRIDIANA(1962, Mex./Span.)

Al Roach
Silents
PATCHWORK GIRL OF OZ, THE(1914)

Bert Roach
ARGYLE CASE, THE(1929); LAST WARNING, THE(1929); SO LONG LETTY(1929); TIME, THE PLACE AND THE GIRL, THE(1929); TWIN BEDS(1929); YOUNG NOWHERES(1929); FREE LOVE(1930); HOLD EVERYTHING(1930); LAWFUL LARCENY(1930); LILIOM(1930); NO, NO NANETTE(1930); PRINCESS AND THE PLUMBER, THE(1930); SONG OF THE FLAME(1930); VIENNESE NIGHTS(1930); ARROWSMITH(1931); BAD SISTER(1931); CAPTAIN THUNDER(1931); COMPROMISED(1931); SIX CYLINDER LOVE(1931); THREE GIRLS LOST(1931); BIRD OF PARADISE(1932); EVENINGS FOR SALE(1932); HAT CHECK GIRL(1932); HOTEL CONTINENTAL(1932); IMPATIENT MAIDEN(1932); LOVE ME TONIGHT(1932); MURDERS IN THE RUE MORGUE(1932); NIGHT WORLD(1932); DARING DAUGHTERS(1933); EASY MILLIONS(1933); HALLELUJAH, I'M A BUM(1933); ONLY YESTERDAY(1933); SECRET SINNERS(1933); GIRL FROM MISSOURI, THE(1934); HALF A SINNER(1934); MARRYING WIDOWS(1934); PARIS INTERLUDE(1934); THIN MAN, THE(1934); GOIN' TO TOWN(1935); GUARD THAT GIRL(1935); PUBLIC HERO NO. 1(1935); TRAVELING SALESLADY, THE(1935); FURY(1936); GORGEOUS HUSSY, THE(1936); HOLLYWOOD BOULEVARD(1936); LOVE BEFORE BREAKFAST(1936); SAN FRANCISCO(1936); SONS O' GUNS(1936); DOUBLE WED-

DING(1937); EMPEROR'S CANDLESTICKS, THE(1937); GIRL SAID NO, THE(1937); GOD'S COUNTRY AND THE WOMAN(1937); MANNEQUIN(1937); PRESCRIPTION FOR ROMANCE(1937); SARATOGA(1937); SING WHILE YOU'RE ABLE(1937); ALGIERS(1938); GREAT WALTZ, THE(1938); INTERNATIONAL SETTLEMENT(1938); JOY OF LIVING(1938); JURY'S SECRET, THE(1938); MAD ABOUT MUSIC(1938); ROMANCE ON THE RUN(1938); SAY IT IN FRENCH(1938); SLIGHT CASE OF MURDER, A(1938); STOLEN HEAVEN(1938); HOTEL IMPERIAL(1939); INSIDE STORY(1939); MAN IN THE IRON MASK, THE(1939); NURSE EDITH CAVELL(1939); ROSE OF WASHINGTON SQUARE(1939); THEY MADE ME A CRIMINAL(1939); MORTAL STORM, THE(1940); SANDY GETS HER MAN(1940); YESTERDAY'S HEROES(1940); BACHELOR DADDY(1941); HELLZAPOPPIN'(1941); THERE'S MAGIC IN MUSIC(1941); DR. RENAULT'S SECRET(1942); FINGERS AT THE WINDOW(1942); I MARRIED AN ANGEL(1942); MY FAVORITE SPY(1942); ONCE UPON A HONEYMOON(1942); QUIET PLEASE, MURDER(1942); WIFE TAKES A FLYER, THE(1942); HI DIDDLE DIDDLE(1943); FALCON OUT WEST, THE(1944); MUSIC IN MANHATTAN(1944); PRINCESS AND THE PIRATE, THE(1944); SENSATIONS OF 1945(1944); SHINE ON, HARVEST MOON(1944); BEDSIDE MANNER(1945); LADY ON A TRAIN(1945); WHERE DO WE GO FROM HERE?(1945); DECOY(1946); DUEL IN THE SUN(1946); GIRL ON THE SPOT(1946); LITTLE GIANT(1946); MAN FROM RAINBOW VALLEY, THE(1946); MISSING LADY, THE(1946); RENDEZVOUS 24(1946); SING WHILE YOU DANCE(1946); STRANGE LOVE OF MARTHA IVERS, THE(1946); WIFE WANTED(1946); PERILS OF PAULINE, THE(1947); GOOD SAM(1948); SHOW BOAT(1951)
Silents
MILLIONAIRE, THE(1921); ROWDY, THE(1921); SMALL TOWN IDOL, A(1921); FLIRT, THE(1922); EXCITEMENT(1924); STORM DAUGHTER, THE(1924); TAXI DANCER, THE(1927); TILLIE THE TOILER(1927); TWELVE MILES OUT(1927); CROWD, THE(1928); LATEST FROM PARIS, THE(1928); TELLING THE WORLD(1928); DESERT RIDER, THE(1929); HONEYMOON(1929)
Misc. Silents
DOWN ON THE FARM(1920); BLACK BAG, THE(1922); HIGH SPEED(1924); DENIAL, THE(1925); DON'T(1925); MONEY TALKS(1926); TIN HATS(1926); UNDER THE BLACK EAGLE(1928); WICKEDNESS PREFERRED(1928)

Daryl Roach
1984
ICE PIRATES, THE(1984)

Earl Roach
SING YOU SINNERS(1938)

Frank Roach
Misc. Talkies
FROZEN SCREAM(1980), d

Gladys Roach
CAGED(1950); NEW KIND OF LOVE, A(1963)

Hal Roach
MEN OF THE NORTH(1930), d; ROGUE SONG, THE(1930), p&d; PARDON US(1931), a, p; PACK UP YOUR TROUBLES(1932), p; DEVIL'S BROTHER, THE(1933), p, d; SONS OF THE DESERT(1933), p; BABES IN TOYLAND(1934), p; BONNIE SCOTLAND(1935), p; BOHEMIAN GIRL, THE(1936), p; KELLY THE SECOND(1936), p; MISTER CINDERELLA(1936), p; GENERAL SPANKY(1937), p; NOBODY'S BABY(1937), p; PICK A STAR(1937), p; TOPPER(1937), p; BLOCKHEADS(1938), p; MERRILY WE LIVE(1938), p; SWISS MISS(1938), p, d, w; THERE GOES MY HEART(1938), p; CAPTAIN FURY(1939), p&d; HOUSEKEEPER'S DAUGHTER(1939), p&d; TOPPER TAKES A TRIP(1939), p; ZENOBIA(1939), p; CHUMP AT OXFORD, A(1940), p; SAPS AT SEA(1940), p; TURNABOUT(1940), p&d; BROADWAY LIMITED(1941), p; ROAD SHOW(1941), p, d; TANKS A MILLION(1941), p; TOPPER RETURNS(1941), p; ABOUT FACE(1942), p; BROOKLYN ORCHID(1942), p; DEVIL WITH HITLER, THE(1942), p; DUDES ARE PRETTY PEOPLE(1942), p; FLYING WITH MUSIC(1942), p; YANKS AHOY(1943), p
Silents
SAMSON(1914); SAILOR-MADE MAN, A(1921), w; DOCTOR JACK(1922), p, w; GRANDMA'S BOY(1922), w; SAFETY LAST(1923), w; KING OF THE WILD HORSES, THE(1924), p, w; BLACK CYCLONE(1925), w
Misc. Silents
WHITE SHEEP, THE(1924), d

Hal Roach, Jr.
ONE MILLION B.C.(1940), d; ROAD SHOW(1941), d; DUDES ARE PRETTY PEOPLE(1942), d; HERE COMES TROUBLE(1948), p; WHO KILLED "DOC" ROBBIN?(1948), p; AS YOU WERE(1951), p; TALES OF ROBIN HOOD(1951), p; MR. WALKIE TALKIE(1952), p; BLADES OF THE MUSKETEERS(1953), p; MOBS INC(1956), p

Hal Roach, Sr.
ONE MILLION B.C.(1940), d, p

Hal Roach [Le Roy Prinz]
ALL-AMERICAN CO-ED(1941), p&d

J. Anthony Roach
Silents
FAIR ENOUGH(1918), w; CYCLONE, THE(1920), w; FAITH(1920), w

Jack Roach
Silents
RAINBOW(1921); DESERT'S TOLL, THE(1926), ph

James Roach
FRONTIER UPRISING(1961), set d; HOUSE IS NOT A HOME, A(1964), set d; STAGE TO THUNDER ROCK(1964), set d

Joe Roach
SOMEWHERE IN SONORA(1933), w; SUMMER STOCK(1950); TEXAS CARNIVAL(1951); FROM HERE TO ETERNITY(1953); DEEP IN MY HEART(1954)

John Roach
MERRY WIDOW, THE(1934)

John F. Roach
PARADISE ALLEY(1978), p

Jonathan Roach [Endfield]
IMPULSE(1955, Brit.), w

Joseph Anthony Roach
JAWS OF JUSTICE(1933), w; FEROCIOUS PAL(1934), w
Silents
BULLET MARK, THE(1928), w

Joseph Roach
TAKE ME OUT TO THE BALL GAME(1949); SHOW BOAT(1951)

Lesley Roach
MOON OVER THE ALLEY(1980, Brit.)
Misc. Talkies
MR. HORATIO KNIBBLES(1971)
Leslie Roach
MELODY(1971, Brit.)
Margaret Roach
CAPTAIN FURY(1939); FAST AND FURIOUS(1939); RIDERS FROM NO-WHERE(1940); TURNABOUT(1940); ROAD SHOW(1941)
Neil Roach
SILENT RAGE(1982), ph
Pat Roach
UNIDENTIFIED FLYING ODDBALL, THE(1979, Brit.); CLASH OF THE TITANS(1981); RAIDERS OF THE LOST ARK(1981); NEVER SAY NEVER AGAIN(1983)
1984
CONAN THE DESTROYER(1984); INDIANA JONES AND THE TEMPLE OF DOOM(1984)
Sarah Roache
CHARIOTS OF FIRE(1981, Brit.)
Viola Roache
GOODBYE, MY FANCY(1951); ROYAL WEDDING(1951)
"Baby" Roacho
UNHOLY ROLLERS(1972)
Michael Road
GILDERSLEEVE ON BROADWAY(1943); IRON MAJOR, THE(1943); MUSIC IN MANHATTAN(1944); HALLS OF MONTEZUMA(1951); TRUE AND THE FALSE, THE(1955, Swed.), a, d
Mike Road
DESTINATION INNER SPACE(1966); PICKUP ON 101(1972)
Betty Roadman
TRADE WINDS(1938); FIVE LITTLE PEPPERS AND HOW THEY GREW(1939); FORGOTTEN WOMAN, THE(1939); HEADLEYS AT HOME, THE(1939); I STOLE A MILLION(1939); LAUGH IT OFF(1939); FOOLS OF DESIRE(1941); LAW OF THE TIMBER(1941); DOWN RIO GRANDE WAY(1942); HITLER'S CHILDREN(1942); MAN WHO CAME TO DINNER, THE(1942); LEOPARD MAN, THE(1943); MISSION TO MOSCOW(1943); SEVENTH VICTIM, THE(1943); WINTERTIME(1943); BURNING CROSS, THE(1947)
Misc. Talkies
IT'S ALL IN YOUR MIND(1938); RETURN OF THE DURANGO KID(1945)
Toni Roam
Misc. Talkies
SEX DU JOUR(1976)
Shula Roan
Misc. Talkies
SINTHIA THE DEVIL'S DOLL(1970)
Vinegar Roan
ROBBERS' ROOST(1933); UNDER THE PAMPAS MOON(1935); GUNSMOKE RANCH(1937)
Margie Roanberg
PICK A STAR(1937)
Andre Roanne
ACCUSED–STAND UP(1930, Fr.); COGNASSE(1932, Fr.); ENTENTE CORDIALE(1939, Fr.); PERSONAL COLUMN(1939, Fr.); IT HAPPENED IN GIBRALTAR(1943, Fr.); VICE DOLLS(1961, Fr.); BACK STREETS OF PARIS(1962, Fr.)
Misc. Silents
VIOLETTES IMPERIALES(1924, Fr.); LA TERRE PROMISE(1925, Fr.); VENUS(1929, Fr.)
Sean Roantree
ALFIE DARLING(1975, Brit.)
Annie Roar
EMBEZZLED HEAVEN(1959,Ger.)
Bob Roark
FAT MAN, THE(1951); SCREAMING EAGLES(1956)
Edith Roark
KID FROM SPAIN, THE(1932)
Garland Roark
WAKE OF THE RED WITCH(1949), w; FAIR WIND TO JAVA(1953), w
Patrick Roark
MEGAFORCE(1982), ed
Robert Roark
FORCE OF ARMS(1951); KILLERS FROM SPACE(1954); PRINCESS OF THE NILE(1954); TARGET EARTH(1954); LONG GRAY LINE, THE(1955); MISTER ROBERTS(1955); BLACKJACK KETCHUM, DESPERADO(1956); GIRL IN LOVER'S LANE, THE(1960), p
Adam Roarke
FLUFFY(1965); CYBORG 2087(1966); WOMEN OF THE PREHISTORIC PLANET(1966); EL DORADO(1967); HELL'S ANGELS ON WHEELS(1967); PSYCH-OUT(1968); SAVAGE SEVEN, THE(1968); HELL'S BELLES(1969); BULLET FOR PRETTY BOY, A(1970); LOSERS, THE(1970); FROGS(1972); PLAY IT AS IT LAYS(1972); THIS IS A HIJACK(1973); DIRTY MARY, CRAZY LARRY(1974); HOW COME NOBODY'S ON OUR SIDE?(1975); FOUR DEUCES, THE(1976); STUNT MAN, THE(1980)
Misc. Talkies
HUGHES AND HARLOW: ANGELS IN HELL(1978)
C. F. Roarke
Silents
GOLD RUSH, THE(1925)
Richard Roat
WESTWORLD(1973)
Roau
TIKO AND THE SHARK(1966, U.S./Ital./Fr.)
Yvonne Rob
KISS OF DEATH(1947); CAGED(1950)
Jean Marie Robain
PARIS BELONGS TO US(1962, Fr.)
Jean-Marie Robain
LES ENFANTS TERRIBLES(1952, Fr.)

Maciej Robakiewica
CONTRACT, THE(1982, Pol.)
Glenn Robards
MARATHON MAN(1976); ST. IVES(1976); LONG RIDERS, THE(1980)
Jason Robards
PARIS(1929); CRAZY THAT WAY(1930); LAST DANCE, THE(1930); EX-BAD BOY(1931); DISCARDED LOVERS(1932); DOCKS OF SAN FRANCISCO(1932); UNHOLY LOVE(1932); CARNIVAL LADY(1933); DEVIL'S MATE(1933); CRIMSON ROMANCE(1934); LADIES CRAVE EXCITEMENT(1935); DAMAGED LIVES(1937); CIPHER BUREAU(1938); CLIPPED WINGS(1938); FLIGHT TO FAME(1938); DANGER FLIGHT(1939); I STOLE A MILLION(1939); LONG SHOT, THE(1939); FATAL HOUR, THE(1940); MUSIC IN MANHATTAN(1944); GAME OF DEATH, A(1945); MAN ALIVE(1945); BEDLAM(1946); DING DONG WILLIAMS(1946); FALCON'S ADVENTURE, THE(1946); FALCON'S ALIBI, THE(1946); FARMER'S DAUGHTER, THE(1947); RIFFRAFF(1947); GUNS OF HATE(1948); ALASKA PATROL(1949); IMPACT(1949); RIDERS OF THE WHISTLING PINES(1949)
Silents
GILDED LILY, THE(1921); STELLA MARIS(1925); THIRD DEGREE, THE(1926); HILLS OF KENTUCKY(1927); JAWS OF STEEL(1927); WHITE FLANNELS(1927)
Misc. Silents
LAND OF HOPE, THE(1921); CASEY JONES(1927); HEART OF MARYLAND, THE(1927); POLLY OF THE MOVIES(1927); TRACKED BY THE POLICE(1927); SOME MOTHER'S BOY(1929); TRAIL MARRIAGE(1929)
Jason Robards, Jr.
JOURNEY, THE(1959, U.S./Aust.); BY LOVE POSSESSED(1961); TENDER IS THE NIGHT(1961); LONG DAY'S JOURNEY INTO NIGHT(1962); ACT ONE(1964); THOUSAND CLOWNS, A(1965); ANY WEDNESDAY(1966); BIG HAND FOR THE LITTLE LADY(1966); DIVORCE AMERICAN STYLE(1967); HOUR OF THE GUN(1967); ST. VALENTINE'S DAY MASSACRE, THE(1967); ISADORA(1968); NIGHT THEY RAIDED MINSKY'S, THE(1968); ONCE UPON A TIME IN THE WEST(1969, U.S./Ital.); BALLAD OF CABLE HOGUE(1970); FOOLS(1970); JULIUS CAESAR(1970); TORA! TORA! TORA!(1970, U.S./Jap.); JOHNNY GOT HIS GUN(1971); MURDERS IN THE RUE MORGUE(1971); WAR BETWEEN MEN AND WOMEN, THE(1972); PAT GARRETT AND BILLY THE KID(1973); BOY AND HIS DOG(1975); MR. SYCAMORE(1975); ALL THE PRESIDENT'S MEN(1976); JULIA(1977); COMES A HORSEMAN(1978); HURRICANE(1979); MELVIN AND HOWARD(1980); RAISE THE TITANTIC(1980); CABOBLANCO(1981); LEGAND OF THE LONE RANGER(1981); MAX DUGAN RETURNS(1983); SOMETHING WICKED THIS WAY COMES(1983)
Misc. Talkies
OPERATION SNAFU(1970, Ital./Yugo.)
DEATH OF A STRANGER(1976)

Jason Robards, Sr.
ON TRIAL(1928); FLYING MARINE, THE(1929); GAMBLERS, THE(1929); ISLE OF LOST SHIPS(1929); ABRAHAM LINCOLN(1930); JAZZ CINDERELLA(1930); LIGHTNIN'(1930); PEACOCK ALLEY(1930); SISTERS(1930); CAUGHT PLASTERED(1931); CHARLIE CHAN CARRIES ON(1931); LAW OF THE TONG(1931); SALVATION NELL(1931); SUBWAY EXPRESS(1931); CONQUERORS, THE(1932); KLONDIKE(1932); PRIDE OF THE LEGION, THE(1932); STRANGE ADVENTURE(1932); WHITE EAGLE(1932); DANCE MALL HOSTESS(1932); SHIP OF WANTED MEN(1933); SLIGHTLY MARRIED(1933); WAY TO LOVE, THE(1933); MERRY WIDOW, THE(1934); PRESIDENT VANISHES, THE(1934); TAKE THE STAND(1934); WOMAN UNAFRAID(1934); CRUSADES, THE(1935); ONE EXCITING ADVENTURE(1935); PUBLIC STENOGRAPHER(1935); SAN FRANCISCO(1936); WHITE LEGION, THE(1936); FIREFLY, THE(1937); MAN WHO CRIED WOLF, THE(1937); SWEETHEART OF THE NAVY(1937); ADVENTURES OF MARCO POLO, THE(1938); LITTLE TOUGH GUY(1938); MYSTERY PLANE(1939); RANGE WAR(1939); SKY PATROL(1939); STUNT PILOT(1939); I LOVE YOU AGAIN(1940); MAD EMPRESS, THE(1940); SAN ANTONIO ROSE(1941); GIVE OUT, SISTERS(1942); JOAN OF OZARK(1942); SILVER QUEEN(1942); SING A JINGLE(1943); MADEMOISELLE FIFI(1944); MASTER RACE, THE(1944); BETRAYAL FROM THE EAST(1945); DICK TRACY(1945); ISLE OF THE DEAD(1945); JOHNNY ANGEL(1945); WANDERER OF THE WASTELAND(1945); WHAT A BLONDE(1945); DEADLINE AT DAWN(1946); STEP BY STEP(1946); VACATION IN RENO(1946); DESPERATE(1947); DICK TRACY'S DILEMMA(1947); LIKELY STORY, A(1947); SEVEN KEYS TO BALDPATE(1947); THUNDER MOUNTAIN(1947); TRAIL STREET(1947); UNDER THE TONTO RIM(1947); WILD HORSE MESA(1947); FIGHTING FATHER DUNNE(1948); IF YOU KNEW SUSIE(1948); MR. BLANDINGS BUILDS HIS DREAM HOUSE(1948); RACE STREET(1948); RETURN OF THE BADMEN(1948); SON OF GOD'S COUNTRY(1948); WESTERN HERITAGE(1948); POST OFFICE INVESTIGATOR(1949); RIMFIRE(1949); SOUTH OF DEATH VALLEY(1949); HORSEMEN OF THE SIERRAS(1950); SECOND WOMAN, THE(1951)
Misc. Talkies
WOMAN CONDEMNED(1934)
Silents
IRISH HEARTS(1927)
Misc. Silents
FOOTLOOSE WIDOWS(1926)
Jason Robards III
STRANGER IS WATCHING, A(1982)
Sam Robards
TEMPEST(1982)
Willis Robards
FIVE GUNS TO TOMBSTONE(1961)
Silents
DESERT BLOSSOMS(1921); EVERY WOMAN'S PROBLEM(1921), a, d; THREE MUSKETEERS, THE(1921); MAN TO MAN(1922)
Misc. Silents
MOTHERS OF MEN(1917), a, d
Bobby Robb
MANPOWER(1941)
David Robb
CONDUCT UNBECOMING(1975, Brit.)
Deon Robb
JEANNE EAGELS(1957)
E.M. Robb
Silents
GOLD RUSH, THE(1925)

Gordon Robb
HUNCH, THE(1967, Brit.)
Jill Robb
1984
CAREFUL, HE MIGHT HEAR YOU(1984, Aus.), p
John Robb
PROLOGUE(1970, Can.)
John David Robb
HENRY ALDRICH'S LITTLE SECRET(1944)
Lotus Robb
STAR IS BORN, A(1954)
Lou Robb
RUN, ANGEL, RUN(1969)
R. D. Robb
CHRISTMAS STORY, A(1983)
Robert Lincoln Robb
WORLD IS JUST A 'B' MOVIE, THE(1971)
Peter Robb-King
TOMMY(1975, Brit.), makeup; OCTOPUSSY(1983, Brit.), makeup
Peggie Robb-Smith
UNDER THE GREENWOOD TREE(1930, Brit.)
Alain Robbe-Grillet
LAST YEAR AT MARIENBAD(1962, Fr./Ital.), w; TRANS-EUROP-EXPRESS(1968, Fr.), a, d&w; L'IMMORTELLE(1969, Fr./Ital./Turkey), d&w; MAN WHO LIES, THE(1970, Czech./Fr.), d&w; JE T'AIME, JE T'AIME(1972, Fr./Swed.); BEAUTIFUL PRISONER, THE(1983, Fr.), d, w
Misc. Talkies
TENDER DRACULA OR CONFESSIONS OF A BLOOD DRINKER(1974, Fr.), d
Catherine Robbe-Grillet
TRANS-EUROP-EXPRESS(1968, Fr.); MAN WHO LIES, THE(1970, Czech./Fr.); JE T'AIME, JE T'AIME(1972, Fr./Swed.)
Robbie the Dog
ROOGIE'S BUMP(1954)
Christopher Robbie
WHERE HAS POOR MICKEY GONE?(1964, Brit.); SUDDEN TERROR(1970, Brit.)
Joseph Robbie
BLACK SUNDAY(1977)
Seymour Robbie
C. C. AND COMPANY(1971), d; MARCO(1973), d
Anatole Robbins
INVADERS FROM MARS(1953), makeup
Arch Robbins
HIS NIGHT OUT(1935)
Archie Robbins
SHE GETS HER MAN(1935); LEAVENWORTH CASE, THE(1936); LONE WOLF RETURNS, THE(1936); ROOGIE'S BUMP(1954)
Cpl. Archie Robbins
WINGED VICTORY(1944)
Art Robbins
Silents
ONE MAN DOG, THE(1929)
Barbara Robbins
HAT, COAT AND GLOVE(1934)
Bill Robbins
BOILING POINT, THE(1932)
Budd Robbins
KID VENGEANCE(1977), w
Christmas Robbins
DEMON LOVER, THE(1977)
Cindy Robbins
DINO(1957); GUNSIGHT RIDGE(1957); I WAS A TEENAGE WEREWOLF(1957); ROCKABILLY BABY(1957); THIS EARTH IS MINE(1959)
Clarence Aaron Robbins
Silents
UNHOLY THREE, THE(1925), w
Deanna Robbins
FINAL EXAM(1981)
Debbie Robbins
TAKING OFF(1971)
Dick Robbins
C.H.O.M.P.S.(1979), w
Ed Robbins
SEVEN FACES(1929), ed
Edward H. Robbins
IT HAPPENED IN PARIS(1935, Brit.); MUSIC FOR MADAME(1937)
Edwin Robbins
Silents
IRENE(1926), ed; ESCAPE, THE(1928), ed; NO OTHER WOMAN(1928), ed
Edwina Robbins
Silents
LIGHTS OF NEW YORK, THE(1916)
Misc. Silents
NAN WHO COULDN'T BEAT GOD, THE(1915)
Eva Robbins
HERCULES(1983)
Fred Robbins
DISC JOCKEY(1951)
Gale Robbins
IN THE MEANTIME, DARLING(1944); MR. HEX(1946); MY DEAR SE-CRETARY(1948); MY GIRL TISA(1948); RACE STREET(1948); BARKLEYS OF BROADWAY, THE(1949); OH, YOU BEAUTIFUL DOLL(1949); BETWEEN MID-NIGHT AND DAWN(1950); FULLER BRUSH GIRL, THE(1950); THREE LITTLE WORDS(1950); STRICTLY DISHONORABLE(1951); BELLE OF NEW YORK, THE(1952); BRIGAND, THE(1952); CALAMITY JANE(1953); DOUBLE JEOPAR-DY(1955); GIRL IN THE RED VELVET SWING, THE(1955); GUNSMOKE IN TUC-SON(1958); QUANTRILL'S RAIDERS(1958)
Garry Robbins
HUMONGOUS(1982, Can.)

Gregory Robbins
1984
TERMINATOR, THE(1984)
Harold Robbins
ER LOVE A STRANGER(1958), p, w; KING CREOLE(1958), w; PUSHER, THE(1960), w; CARPETBAGGERS, THE(1964), w; WHERE LOVE HAS GONE(1964), w; STILET-TO(1969), w; ADVENTURERS, THE(1970), w; BETSY, THE(1978), p, w; LONELY LADY, THE(1983), w
Herb Robbins
DOLL SQUAD, THE(1973)
Misc. Talkies
BODY FEVER(1981)
J. Edwin Robbins
MAKING THE GRADE(1929), ed; PLEASURE CRAZED(1929), ed; SPEAKEA-SY(1929), ed; BIG PARTY, THE(1930), w; MAN TROUBLE(1930), ed; SIX CYLINDER LOVE(1931), ed; SWEETHEART OF SIGMA CHI(1933), ed
Jack Robbins
JANIE(1944)
James Robbins
GO-GETTER, THE(1937); KID COMES BACK, THE(1937); MARKED WOMAN(1937); PUBLIC WEDDING(1937); SAN QUENTIN(1937); SINGING MARINE, THE(1937); SLIM(1937); WINE, WOMEN AND HORSES(1937); LADY IN THE MORGUE(1938); BAD BOY(1939); BARBARIAN AND THE GEISHA, THE(1958)
Jane Marla Robbins
ROCKY(1976)
1984
ADVENTURES OF BUCKAROO BANZAI: ACROSS THE 8TH DIMENSION, THE(1984); THIEF OF HEARTS(1984)
Janine Robbins
LITTLE SEX, A(1982)
Jean Robbins
BATTLE CRY(1959)
Jenny Robbins
CLEGG(1969, Brit.); PRAISE MARX AND PASS THE AMMUNITION(1970, Brit.)
Jerome Robbins
ON THE TOWN(1949), w; KING AND I, THE(1956), ch; WEST SIDE STORY(1961), d, ch
Jess Robbins
Silents
TOO MUCH BUSINESS(1922), d
Misc. Silents
LADDER JINX, THE(1922), d; SKIRTS(1928, Brit.), d
Jesse Robbins
Silents
FRONT PAGE STORY, A(1922), d; LAW FORBIDS, THE(1924), d
Misc. Silents
BUSINESS OF LOVE, THE(1925), d
John Franklin Robbins
PUMPKIN EATER, THE(1964, Brit.)
John Robbins
Misc. Talkies
THAT'S YOUR FUNERAL(1974, Brit.), d
Katherine L. Robbins
Silents
GILDED DREAM, THE(1920), w; IN FOLLY'S TRAIL(1920), w
Katherine Lazer Robbins
Silents
RISKY ROAD, THE(1918), w
Lois Robbins
WHOLLY MOSES(1980)
Mac Robbins
LADY IN CEMENT(1968)
Marc Robbins
Silents
JUDGE NOT OR THE WOMAN OF MONA DIGGINGS(1915); MEASURE OF A MAN, THE(1916); SECRET LOVE(1916); AMERICAN METHODS(1917); TALE OF TWO CITIES, A(1917); LES MISERABLES(1918), w; ALIAS JIMMY VALENTINE(1920); RIDERS OF THE DAWN(1920); SCARLET CAR, THE(1923)
Misc. Silents
BUSINESS IS BUSINESS(1915); CRIPPLED HAND, THE(1916); INTERNATIONAL MARRIAGE, AN(1916); HER SOUL'S INSPIRATION(1917); WHEN A MAN SEES RED(1917); RIDERS OF THE PURPLE SAGE(1918); MAN HUNTER, THE(1919); TONG MAN, THE(1919); GIRL WHO RAN WILD, THE(1922); MARRIAGE MARKET, THE(1923)
Marlene Robbins
STREET FIGHTER(1959)
Marty Robbins
BADGE OF MARSHAL BRENNAN, THE(1957); RAIDERS OF OLD CALIFOR-NIA(1957); BUFFALO GUN(1961); BALLAD OF A GUNFIGHTER(1964); HELL ON WHEELS(1967); FROM NASHVILLE WITH MUSIC(1969); GUNS OF A STRAN-GER(1973); HONKYTONK MAN(1982)
Misc. Talkies
ROAD TO NASHVILLE(1967); COUNTRY MUSIC(1972)
Matthew Robbins
SUGARLAND EXPRESS, THE(1974), w; BINGO LONG TRAVELING ALL-STARS AND MOTOR KINGS, THE(1976), w; MAC ARTHUR(1977), w; CORVETTE SUM-MER(1978), d, w; DRAGONSLAYER(1981), d, w
Michael Robbins
LUNCH HOUR(1962, Brit.); RATTLE OF A SIMPLE MAN(1964, Brit.); WHISPER-ERS, THE(1967, Brit.); ALF 'N' FAMILY(1968, Brit.); UP THE JUNCTION(1968, Brit.); LOOKING GLASS WAR, THE(1970, Brit.); VILLAIN(1971, Brit.); ZEPPELIN(1971, Brit.); ON THE BUSES(1972, Brit.); PINK PANTHER STRIKES AGAIN, THE(1976, Brit.); NO SEX PLEASE—WE'RE BRITISH(1979, Brit.); GREAT MUPPET CAPER, THE(1981); VICTOR/VICTORIA(1982)
Pattie Robbins
TEN CENTS A DANCE(1945)
Peter Robbins
TICKLISH AFFAIR, A(1963); AND NOW MIGUEL(1966); MOMENT TO MO-MENT(1966); GOOD TIMES(1967); BOY NAMED CHARLIE BROWN, A(1969)

Rex Robbins
SHAFT(1971); 1776(1972); SIMON(1980); FIRST TIME, THE(1983); REUBEN, REUBEN(1983)

Richard Robbins
WRONG MAN, THE(1956); EUROPEANS, THE(1979, Brit.), m; JANE AUSTEN IN MANHATTAN(1980), m; QUARTET(1981, Brit./Fr.), m; HEAT AND DUST(1983, Brit.), m
1984
BOSTONIANS, THE(1984), m

Ronny Robbins
GUNS OF A STRANGER(1973)

Ruby Robbins
SUGARLAND EXPRESS, THE(1974)

Sam Robbins
BAD MAN FROM RED BUTTE(1940), w; LADY GREY(1980), art d

Sheila Robbins
SUDDENLY, LAST SUMMER(1959, Brit.)

Skeeter Bill Robbins
HARD HOMBRE(1931); LOCAL BAD MAN(1932); MAN'S LAND, A(1932); COWBOY COUNSELOR(1933); DUDE BANDIT, THE(1933); FIGHTING PARSON, THE(1933)

Tacey Robbins
PSYCHO A GO-GO!(1965)

Ted Robbins
FREAKS(1932), w

Tim Robbins
1984
NO SMALL AFFAIR(1984); TOY SOLDIERS(1984)

"Tod" Clarence Aaron Robbins
UNHOLY THREE, THE(1930), w

Walt Robbins
IRON MAJOR, THE(1943)
Silents
JUST TONY(1922)

Walter Robbins
SARATOGA(1937); OX-BOW INCIDENT, THE(1943)

Robby the Robot
FORBIDDEN PLANET(1956)

Chief Red Robe
GOOD MORNING, JUDGE(1943)

Cliff Robeitson
GIRL MOST LIKELY, THE(1957)

Bernard Robel
LAUGHING ANNE(1954, Brit./U.S.)

David Robel
ROSE MARIE(1936); DADDY LONG LEGS(1955), ch; GIRL IN THE RED VELVET SWING, THE(1955), ch; VERY SPECIAL FAVOR, A(1965), ch

Davie Robel
MY FAIR LADY(1964)

Albin Robeling
WHITE TIE AND TAILS(1946); HOLLYWOOD BARN DANCE(1947); NIGHTMARE ALLEY(1947); SITTING PRETTY(1948); EASY LIVING(1949); TURNING POINT, THE(1952)

Miguel Robelo
ONLY ONCE IN A LIFETIME(1979)

Mike Robelo
MACHISMO–40 GRAVES FOR 40 GUNS(1970); ON THE NICKEL(1980)

The Robenis
OKAY FOR SOUND(1937, Brit.)

Emmerich Robenz
TRIAL, THE(1948, Aust.), w

Richard Rober
APRIL SHOWERS(1948); CALL NORTHSIDE 777(1948); EMBRACEABLE YOU(1948); LARCENY(1948); SMART GIRLS DON'T TALK(1948); ILLEGAL ENTRY(1949); PORT OF NEW YORK(1949); TASK FORCE(1949); BACKFIRE(1950); DEPORTED(1950); DIAL 1119(1950); FILE ON THELMA JORDAN, THE(1950); SIERRA(1950); WATCH THE BIRDIE(1950); WOMAN ON PIER 13, THE(1950); FATHER'S LITTLE DIVIDEND(1951); MAN IN THE SADDLE(1951); PASSAGE WEST(1951); TALL TARGET, THE(1951); WELL, THE(1951); DEVIL MAKES THREE, THE(1952); KID MONK BARONI(1952); O. HENRY'S FULL HOUSE(1952); OUTLAW WOMEN(1952); ROSE BOWL STORY, THE(1952); SAVAGE, THE(1953); JET PILOT(1957)

John Roberdeau
LULU(1978)

Thomas Roberdeau
LULU(1978)

Smoky Roberds
PROUD AND THE DAMNED, THE(1972)

Alben Roberling
THEY WON'T BELIEVE ME(1947)

Charles Roberson
COW TOWN(1950)

Charles "Chuck" Roberson
SONG OF SCHEHERAZADE(1947); FRONTIER OUTPOST(1950); OUTCAST OF BLACK MESA(1950)

Chuck Roberson
PLAINSMAN AND THE LADY(1946); FIGHTING KENTUCKIAN, THE(1949); I SHOT JESSE JAMES(1949); STAMPEDE(1949); WESTERN RENEGADES(1949); BANDIT QUEEN(1950); LIGHTNING GUNS(1950); RIO GRANDE(1950); FORT DODGE STAMPEDE(1951); RIDIN' THE OUTLAW TRAIL(1951); LUSTY MEN, THE(1952); GUN BELT(1953); SIGN OF THE PAGAN(1954); FAR COUNTRY, THE(1955); PRODIGAL, THE(1955); RAWHIDE YEARS, THE(1956); SEARCHERS, THE(1956); SEVEN MEN FROM NOW(1956); FORTY GUNS(1957); NIGHT PASSAGE(1957); RUN OF THE ARROW(1957); WINGS OF EAGLES, THE(1957); BIG COUNTRY, THE(1958); MAN OF THE WEST(1958); WONDERFUL COUNTRY, THE(1959); ALAMO, THE(1960); SERGEANT RUTLEDGE(1960); SPARTACUS(1960); MISFITS, THE(1961), stunts; TWO RODE TOGETHER(1961); HOW THE WEST WAS WON(1962); MAN WHO SHOT LIBERTY VALANCE, THE(1962); MERRILL'S MARAUDERS(1962); DONOVAN'S REEF(1963); MC LINTOCK!(1963); SHOCK CORRIDOR(1963); ADVANCE TO THE REAR(1964); CHEYENNE AUTUMN(1964); BLACK SPURS(1965); CAT BALLOU(1965); SMOKY(1966); EL DORADO(1967); WAR WAGON, THE(1967); GREEN BERETS, THE(1968); HELLFIGHTERS(1968); SCALPHUNTERS, THE(1968); UN-

DEFEATED, THE(1969); HAWAIIANS, THE(1970), stunts; RIO LOBO(1970); MC Q(1974); 99 AND 44/100% DEAD(1974)

Donald W. Roberson
GLORY GUYS, THE(1965), makeup; WAR WAGON, THE(1967), makeup

James Roberson
TERROR ON TOUR(1980), ph

James W. Roberson
MOUNTAIN FAMILY ROBINSON(1979), ph

Jim Roberson
SO SAD ABOUT GLORIA(1973), ph; GRAYEAGLE(1977), ph&ed; TOWN THAT DREADED SUNDOWN, THE(1977), ph; WISHBONE CUTTER(1978), ph
Misc. Talkies
LEGEND OF ALFRED PACKER, THE(1979), d

Ken Roberson
1984
YELLOW HAIR AND THE FORTRESS OF GOLD(1984)

Liz Roberson
TIME AFTER TIME(1979, Brit.); HAMMETT(1982)

Lou Roberson
LAWLESS RIDER, THE(1954)

Steve Roberson
Misc. Talkies
BLUE MONEY(1975)

Virgil Roberson
1984
PREPPIES(1984)

Robert
LONG NIGHT, THE(1947), p

A. Robert
WAYS OF LOVE(1950, Ital./Fr.)

Alfredo Robert
Misc. Silents
PASSION OF ST. FRANCIS(1932, Ital.)

Dan Robert
RICH AND FAMOUS(1981), set d

Daniel Robert
KING OF COMEDY, THE(1983), set d

Elaine Robert
FLYING LEATHERNECKS(1951)

Harold G. Robert
RAMSBOTTOM RIDES AGAIN(1956, Brit.), w

Helene Robert
FRIC FRAC(1939, FR.)

Jacqueline Robert
MARK OF CAIN, THE(1948, Brit.); DAY TO REMEMBER, A(1953, Brit.)

Jacques Robert
DEFEND MY LOVE(1956, Ital.), w; GORILLA GREETS YOU, THE(1958, Fr.), w; GUTS IN THE SUN(1959, Fr.); NATHALIE, AGENT SECRET(1960, Fr.), w; LOVE AND THE FRENCHWOMAN(1961, Fr.), w; NIGHT AFFAIR(1961, Fr.), w; SEVENTH JUROR, THE(1964, Fr.), w; TO COMMIT A MURDER(1970, Fr./Ital./Ger.), w, ed; SOMEONE BEHIND THE DOOR(1971, Fr./Brit.), w
Misc. Silents
LA VIVANTE EPINGLE(1921, Fr.), d; LA BOUQUETIERE DES INNOCENTS(1922, Fr.), d; COUSIN PONS(1924, Fr.), d; LE COMTE KOSTIA(1925, Fr.), d; LA CHEVRE AUX PIEDS D'OR(1926, Fr.), d; EN PLONGEE(1927, Fr.), d

Marcel Robert
CHARLES, DEAD OR ALIVE(1972, Switz.)

Marie-Christine Robert
1984
CHEECH AND CHONG'S THE CORSICAN BROTHERS(1984)

Melville Robert
FLYING LEATHERNECKS(1951)

Muriel Robert
PEPPER(1936)

Paulette Robert
DIARY OF A COUNTRY PRIEST(1954, Fr.), ed; IF PARIS WERE TOLD TO US(1956, Fr.), ed; CANDIDE(1962, Fr.), ed

Pierre Robert
RUBBER GUN, THE(1977, Can.)

Richard Robert
ANY NUMBER CAN PLAY(1949)

Sam Robert
MAN CALLED ADAM, A(1966), set d; DIARY OF A MAD HOUSEWIFE(1970), set d

Stephen Robert
FILE ON THELMA JORDAN, THE(1950)

T. H. Robert
LIVING CORPSE, THE(1940, Fr.), w

Yves Robert
GRAND MANEUVER, THE(1956, Fr.); FOLIES BERGERE(1958, Fr.); CLEO FROM 5 TO 7(1961, Fr.); GREEN MARE, THE(1961, Fr./Ital.); LOVE AND THE FRENCHWOMAN(1961, Fr.); PASSION OF SLOW FIRE, THE(1962, Fr.); WAR OF THE BUTTONS(1963 Fr.), p, d, w; VERY HAPPY ALEXANDER(1969, Fr.), p, d, w; MAN WITH CONNECTIONS, THE(1970, Fr.); CROOK, THE(1971, Fr.); TALL BLOND MAN WITH ONE BLACK SHOE, THE(1973, Fr.), a, p, d, w; JUDGE AND THE ASSASSIN, THE(1979, Fr.)
1984
WOMAN IN RED, THE(1984), w

Robert B. Mitchell and his St. Brendan's Boys
CAREFREE(1938)

Robert Mitchell Boy Choir
JOAN OF PARIS(1942); GOING MY WAY(1944); SONG OF ARIZONA(1946)

The Robert Mitchell Boy Choir
JOLSON STORY, THE(1946)

The Robert Mitchell Boys Choir
IDAHO(1943)

Robert Mitchell's Boys Choir
BLONDIE IN SOCIETY(1941)

Robert Mitchell's St. Brendan Boys Choir
FRONTIERSMAN, THE(1938)

Charles Robert-Dumas
SECOND BUREAU(1936, Fr.), w; SECOND BUREAU(1937, Brit.), w

Lyda Roberti
DANCERS IN THE DARK(1932); KID FROM SPAIN, THE(1932); MILLION DOLLAR LEGS(1932); THREE-CORNERED MOON(1933); TORCH SINGER(1933); COLLEGE RHYTHM(1934); BIG BROADCAST OF 1936, THE(1935); GEORGE WHITE'S 1935 SCANDALS(1935); NOBODY'S BABY(1937); PICK A STAR(1937); WIDE OPEN FACES(1938)

Manya Roberti
DELICIOUS(1931); SPIDER, THE(1931); HAT CHECK GIRL(1932)

Roberto
LOVERS OF TERUEL, THE(1962, Fr.)

Federico Roberto
WORLD'S GREATEST LOVER, THE(1977)

Fred Roberto
PEPE(1960)

Freddie Roberto
GUN RUNNERS, THE(1958)

Freddy Roberto
TANK COMMANDOS(1959)

Frederico Roberto
CHINATOWN(1974); DOC SAVAGE... THE MAN OF BRONZE(1975)

Willard Roberton
VIRGINIA JUDGE, THE(1935)

The Robertos
SONG FOR MISS JULIE, A(1945)

Adele Roberts
JOLSON STORY, THE(1946)

Adelle Roberts
TOGETHER AGAIN(1944); BOSTON BLACKIE'S RENDEZVOUS(1945); DANCING IN MANHATTAN(1945); OVER 21(1945); DESERT HORSEMAN, THE(1946); JUST BEFORE DAWN(1946); NOTORIOUS LONE WOLF, THE(1946)
Misc. Talkies
GALLOPING THUNDER(1946); ROARING RANGERS(1946); THROW A SADDLE ON A STAR(1946)

Al Roberts
STRANGE INVADERS(1983)

Alan Roberts
DINOSAURUS(1960); ICE PALACE(1960); TWO LOVES(1961); RACQUET(1979), p; HAPPY HOOKER GOES TO HOLLYWOOD, THE(1980), d

Alice Roberts
Silents
PANDORA'S BOX(1929, Ger.)

Allene Roberts
RED HOUSE, THE(1947); MICHAEL O'HALLORAN(1948); SIGN OF THE RAM, THE(1948); BOMBA ON PANTHER ISLAND(1949); KNOCK ON ANY DOOR(1949); UNION STATION(1950); HOODLUM, THE(1951); SANTA FE(1951); KID MONK BARONI(1952); THUNDERBIRDS(1952)

Amy Roberts
STRONGER THAN THE SUN(1980, Brit.), cos; WEATHER IN THE STREETS, THE(1983, Brit.), cos

Ann Roberts
IN SOCIETY(1944); SUDAN(1945); JOAN OF ARC(1948)

Arlyn Roberts
LULLABY OF BROADWAY, THE(1951)

Arlyne Roberts
NIGHT AND DAY(1946)

Arthur Roberts
UP IN SMOKE(1978); DONOVAN AFFAIR, THE(1929), ed; MISTER ANTONIO(1929), ed; YOUNGER GENERATION(1929), ed; HALF SHOT AT SUNRISE(1930), ed; ROYAL BED, THE(1931), ed; BILL OF DIVORCEMENT, A(1932), ed; CHRISTOPHER STRONG(1933), ed; FLYING DEVILS(1933), ed; IF I WERE FREE(1933), ed; ONE MAN'S JOURNEY(1933), ed; DOWN TO THEIR LAST YACHT(1934), ed; TWO ALONE(1934), ed; LIGHTNING STRIKES TWICE(1935), ed; STAR OF MIDNIGHT(1935), ed; BRIDE WALKS OUT, THE(1936), ed; EX-MRS. BRADFORD, THE(1936), ed; SEA DEVILS(1937), ed; WE WHO ARE ABOUT TO DIE(1937), ed; RADIO CITY REVELS(1938), ed; DANGER ON WHEELS(1940); GENTLEMAN AFTER DARK, A(1942), ed; OLD HOMESTEAD, THE(1942), ed; SUNSET SERENADE(1942), ed; X MARKS THE SPOT(1942), ed; DEAD MAN'S GULCH(1943), ed; FALSE FACES(1943), ed; HEADIN' FOR GOD'S COUNTRY(1943), ed; IDAHO(1943), ed; MANTRAP, THE(1943), ed; MYSTERY BROADCAST(1943), ed; O, MY DARLING CLEMENTINE(1943), ed; SCREAM IN THE DARK, A(1943), ed; SECRETS OF THE UNDERGROUND(1943), ed; END OF THE ROAD(1944), ed; GIRL WHO DARED, THE(1944), ed; LADY AND THE MONSTER, THE(1944), ed; LAKE PLACID SERENADE(1944), ed; STORM OVER LISBON(1944), ed; STRANGERS IN THE NIGHT(1944), ed; BANDITS OF THE BADLANDS(1945), ed; BELLS OF ROSARITA(1945), ed; GIRLS OF THE BIG HOUSE(1945), ed; MEXICANA(1945), ed; PHANTOM SPEAKS, THE(1945), ed; TELL IT TO A STAR(1945), ed; MURDER IN THE MUSIC HALL(1946), ed; RENDEZVOUS WITH ANNIE(1946), ed; SONG OF ARIZONA(1946), ed; THAT BRENNAN GIRL(1946), ed; ALONG THE OREGON TRAIL(1947), ed; DRIFTWOOD(1947), ed; PILGRIM LADY, THE(1947), ed; THAT'S MY GAL(1947), ed; TRESPASSER, THE(1947), ed; UNDER COLORADO SKIES(1947), ed; WYOMING(1947), ed; ANGEL IN EXILE(1948), ed; BOLD FRONTIERSMAN, THE(1948), ed; CAMPUS HONEYMOON(1948), ed; INSIDE STORY, THE(1948), ed; OKLAHOMA BADLANDS(1948), ed; PLUNDERERS, THE(1948), ed; SECRET SERVICE INVESTIGATOR(1948), ed; BRIMSTONE(1949), ed; DEATH VALLEY GUNFIGHTER(1949), ed; FRONTIER INVESTIGATOR(1949), ed; LAST BANDIT, THE(1949), ed; NAVAJO TRAIL RAIDERS(1949), ed; CALIFORNIA PASSAGE(1950), ed; FEDERAL AGENT AT LARGE(1950), ed; HARBOR OF MISSING MEN(1950), ed; HILLS OF OKLAHOMA(1950), ed; ROCK ISLAND TRAIL(1950), ed; SAVAGE HORDE, THE(1950), ed; BUCKAROO SHERIFF OF TEXAS(1951), ed; FIGHTING COAST GUARD(1951), ed; OH! SUSANNA(1951), ed; STREET BANDITS(1951), ed; GOBS AND GALS(1952), ed; LADY POSSESSED(1952), ed; MONTANA BELLE(1952), ed; ROSE OF CIMARRON(1952), ed; INVADERS FROM MARS(1953), ed; UNTAMED HEIRESS(1954), ed; BRIDE, THE(1973); BORN AGAIN(1978); GREAT BRAIN, THE(1978); REVENGE OF THE NINJA(1983)

Silents
AFTER THE STORM(1928), ed; MATINEE IDOL, THE(1928), ed; SO THIS IS LOVE(1928), ed

Arthur E. Roberts
CAREER(1939), ed; FLYING IRISHMAN, THE(1939), ed; SON OF MONTE CRISTO(1940), ed; HEADLINE HUNTERS(1955), ed; LAY THAT RIFLE DOWN(1955), ed

Artie Roberts
GIRL CRAZY(1932), ed; GIRL OF THE RIO(1932), ed; HOLD'EM JAIL(1932), ed

Austin Roberts
RUN, ANGEL, RUN(1969)

Ava Roberts
SEMI-TOUGH(1977)

Barbara Roberts
FOLIES DERGERE(1935)
Misc. Talkies
TONTO KID, THE(1935)

Bart Roberts
TAZA, SON OF COCHISE(1954); THIS ISLAND EARTH(1955)

Beatrice Roberts
SAN FRANCISCO(1936); BILL CRACKS DOWN(1937); LOVE TAKES FLIGHT(1937); PARK AVENUE LOGGER(1937); DEVIL'S PARTY, THE(1938); PIONEERS OF THE WEST(1940); MYSTERY OF MARIE ROGET, THE(1942); FRANKENSTEIN MEETS THE WOLF MAN(1943); HE'S MY GUY(1943); IT COMES UP LOVE(1943); PHANTOM OF THE OPERA(1943); DEAD MAN'S EYES(1944); HI BEAUTIFUL(1944); HER PRIMITIVE MAN(1944); RECKLESS AGE(1944); SCARLET STREET(1945); THIS LOVE OF OURS(1945); KILLERS, THE(1946); WHITE TIE AND TAILS(1946); EGG AND I, THE(1947); RIDE THE PINK HORSE(1947); SENATOR WAS INDISCREET, THE(1947); FAMILY HONEYMOON(1948); FOR THE LOVE OF MARY(1948); MR. PEABODY AND THE MERMAID(1948); YOU GOTTA STAY HAPPY(1948); CRISS CROSS(1949)

Ben Roberts
BORROWED HERO(1941), w; GAMBLING DAUGHTERS(1941), w; SOUTH OF PANAMA(1941), w; FLY BY NIGHT(1942), w; CARTER CASE, THE(1947), w; PREJUDICE(1949), w; WHITE HEAT(1949), w; BACKFIRE(1950), w; CAPTAIN HORATIO HORNBLOWER(1951, Brit.), w; COME FILL THE CUP(1951), w; GOODBYE, MY FANCY(1951), w; GLORY AT SEA(1952, Brit.), w; O. HENRY'S FULL HOUSE(1952), w; KING OF THE KHYBER RIFLES(1953), w; WHITE WITCH DOCTOR(1953), w; GREEN FIRE(1955), w; SERENADE(1956), w; BAND OF ANGELS(1957), w; SHAKE HANDS WITH THE DEVIL(1959, Ireland), w; MIDNIGHT LACE(1960), w; PORTRAIT IN BLACK(1960), w; LEGEND OF THE LONE RANGER, THE(1981), w

Bernice Roberts
OUTLAWS OF THE ORIENT(1937)

Bert Roberts
NIGHT OF BLOODY HORROR zero(1969)

Beryl Roberts
Silents
STRIVING FOR FORTUNE(1926); JUST OFF BROADWAY(1929)
Misc. Silents
SODA WATER COWBOY(1927)

Beth Roberts
MANGANINNIE(1982, Aus.), w

Beverly Roberts
CHINA CLIPPER(1936); HOT MONEY(1936); SINGING KID, THE(1936); SONS O' GUNS(1936); TWO AGAINST THE WORLD(1936); EXPENSIVE HUSBANDS(1937); GOD'S COUNTRY AND THE WOMAN(1937); HER HUSBAND'S SECRETARY(1937); PERFECT SPECIMEN, THE(1937); WEST OF SHANGHAI(1937); CALL OF THE YUKON(1938); DAREDEVIL DRIVERS(1938); FLIRTING WITH FATE(1938); MAKING THE HEADLINES(1938); TENTH AVENUE KID(1938); BURIED ALIVE(1939); FIRST OFFENDERS(1939); I WAS A CONVICT(1939); MAIN STREET LAWYER(1939); STRANGE CASE OF DR. MEADE(1939); TROPIC FURY(1939); MOB TOWN(1941)
Misc. Talkies
HOUSE OF MYSTERY, THE(1938); OUTSIDE THE LAW(1938)

Bill Roberts
SNOW WHITE AND THE SEVEN DWARFS(1937), anim; THRILL OF A LIFETIME(1937); TEXANS, THE(1938); FANTASIA(1940), d; PINOCCHIO(1940), d; DUMBO(1941), d; BAMBI(1942), d; JOURNEY INTO FEAR(1942); THREE CABALLEROS, THE(1944), d

Bob Roberts
WHITE SHADOWS IN THE SOUTH SEAS(1928), ph; STAIRWAY TO HEAVEN(1946, Brit.); BODY AND SOUL(1947), p; FORCE OF EVIL(1948), p; CALL ME MISTER(1951); HE RAN ALL THE WAY(1951), p; TUNNEL OF LOVE, THE(1958), m/l; ALL NIGHT LONG(1961, Brit.), p; THIRD OF A MAN(1962); LIFE STUDY(1973)
Misc. Talkies
SWEET SAVIOR(1971), d

Bobby Roberts
GYPSY MOTHS, THE(1969), p; MONTE WALSH(1970), p; HOT ROCK, THE(1972), p; BANK SHOT(1974), p; DEATH WISH(1974), p

Brian Roberts
Misc. Talkies
ADVERSARY, THE(1970)

Bruce Roberts
FIREBALL JUNGLE(1968); THE CRAZIES(1973), m; JINXED!(1982), m

Byron Roberts
VALLEY OF THE DRAGONS(1961), p

C. E. Roberts
MIDNIGHT PATROL, THE(1932), w; WESTERN LIMITED(1932), w; FLAMING SIGNAL(1933), d, w; FIGHTING HERO(1934), w

C. Edward Roberts
Misc. Talkies
ADVENTUROUS KNIGHTS(1935), d

Casey Roberts
PRISONER OF ZENDA, THE(1937), set d; BACKGROUND TO DANGER(1943), set d; MYSTERIOUS DOCTOR, THE(1943), set d; NORTHERN PURSUIT(1943), set d; HOLLYWOOD CANTEEN(1944), set d; IN OUR TIME(1944), set d; TO HAVE AND HAVE NOT(1944), set d; CHRISTMAS IN CONNECTICUT(1945), set d; DEVOTION(1946), set d; NOBODY LIVES FOREVER(1946), set d; SECRET LIFE OF WALTER MITTY, THE(1947), set d

Charles Roberts
FIGHTING TEXANS(1933), w; MUMMY'S BOYS(1936), w; MAMA LOVES PAPA(1945), w; ENTER INSPECTOR DUVAL(1961, Brit.)
Silents
QUICKER'N LIGHTNIN'(1925)

Charles E. Roberts
MEXICAN SPITFIRE(1939), w; MEXICAN SPITFIRE OUT WEST(1940), w; MILLIONAIRE PLAYBOY(1940), w; POP ALWAYS PAYS(1940), w; HURRY, CHARLIE, HURRY(1941), d; MEXICAN SPITFIRE'S BABY(1941), w; MEXICAN SPITFIRE AT SEA(1942), w; MEXICAN SPITFIRE SEES A GHOST(1942), w; MEXICAN SPITFIRE'S ELEPHANT(1942), w; SING YOUR WORRIES AWAY(1942), w; LADIES' DAY(1943), w; MEXICAN SPITFIRE'S BLESSED EVENT(1943), w; GOIN' TO TOWN(1944), w; WHAT A BLONDE(1945), w; PARTNERS IN TIME(1946), w; RIVERBOAT RHYTHM(1946), w; VACATION IN RENO(1946), w; CUBAN FIREBALL(1951), w; HAVANA ROSE(1951), w; HONEYCHILE(1951), w; FABULOUS SENORITA, THE(1952), w; OKLAHOMA ANNIE(1952), w

Charlie Roberts
ULYSSES(1967, U.S./Brit.)

Chris Roberts
MOONLIGHTING WIVES(1966)

Christian Roberts
TO SIR, WITH LOVE(1967, Brit.); ANNIVERSARY, THE(1968, Brit.); DESPERADOS, THE(1969); TWISTED NERVE(1969, Brit.); ADVENTURERS, THE(1970); MIND OF MR. SOAMES, THE(1970, Brit.); LAST VALLEY, THE(1971, Brit.)

Chuck Roberts
FIGHTING PIONEERS(1935), w

Clete Roberts
STORY OF G.I. JOE, THE(1945); PHENIX CITY STORY, THE(1955); LAST HURRAH, THE(1958); MAN ON A STRING(1960); SWINGER, THE(1966); TODD KILLINGS, THE(1971); JERK, THE(1979); METEOR(1979); TIME AFTER TIME(1979, Brit.); TESTAMENT(1983)

Conrad Roberts
UP THE SANDBOX(1972); FIREPOWER(1979, Brit.)

Cyril Roberts
CHRISTOPHER COLUMBUS(1949, Brit.), w; COME DANCE WITH ME(1950, Brit.), w

Dave Roberts
PRINCESS AND THE MAGIC FROG, THE(1965), m

David Roberts
NAKED WORLD OF HARRISON MARKS, THE(1967, Brit.); DRIVE-IN(1976); DEMON SEED(1977)

Davie Roberts
BLOW OUT(1981)

Davis Roberts
MURDER BY CONTRACT(1958); SWEET BIRD OF YOUTH(1962); KILLERS, THE(1964); QUICK, BEFORE IT MELTS(1964); CHASE, THE(1966); HOTEL(1967); GLASS HOUSES(1972); TRIAL OF THE CATONSVILLE NINE, THE(1972); DETROIT 9000(1973); WESTWORLD(1973); WILLIE DYNAMITE(1973); FROM NOON TO THREE(1976); HONKY TONK FREEWAY(1981)
1984
CHATTANOOGA CHOO CHOO(1984)

Denys Roberts
LAW AND DISORDER(1958, Brit.), w

Des Roberts
GUESS WHAT HAPPENED TO COUNT DRACULA(1970), a, m&md

Desmond Roberts
HELL, HEAVEN OR HOBOKEN(1958, Brit.); WAY FOR A SAILOR(1930); ROYAL BED, THE(1931); SQUAW MAN, THE(1931); BUT THE FLESH IS WEAK(1932); BLIND ADVENTURE(1933); CAVALCADE(1933); CHRISTOPHER STRONG(1933); KING'S VACATION, THE(1933); FOUNTAIN, THE(1934); GIRL FROM MISSOURI, THE(1934); GRAND CANARY(1934); HOUSE OF DANGER(1934); KEY, THE(1934); LIMEHOUSE BLUES(1934); MANDALAY(1934); MENACE(1934); OF HUMAN BONDAGE(1934); RIP TIDE(1934); TARZAN AND HIS MATE(1934); CLIVE OF INDIA(1935); JANE EYRE(1935); GAOL BREAK(1936, Brit.); UNDER THE RED ROBE(1937, Brit.); LILY OF LAGUNA(1938, Brit.); GIVE ME THE STARS(1944, Brit.); MY AIN FOLK(1944, Brit.); ECHO MURDERS, THE(1945, Brit.); SCHOOL FOR SECRETS(1946, Brit.); CALENDAR, THE(1948, Brit.); SCOTT OF THE ANTARCTIC(1949, Brit.); MAN IN THE WHITE SUIT, THE(1952); BEAU BRUMMELL(1954); SIMBA(1955, Brit.); HAUNTED STRANGLER, THE(1958, Brit.); TWO-HEADED SPY, THE(1959, Brit.); DOUBLE BUNK(1961, Brit.)
Misc. Silents
CITY OF YOUTH, THE(1928, Brit.); RECKLESS GAMBLE, A(1928, Brit.)

Di Di Roberts
SIX BRIDGES TO CROSS(1955)

Doak Roberts
RAYMIE(1960)

Doc Roberts
Silents
RAINBOW TRAIL, THE(1925)

Don Roberts
NEXT TIME WE LOVE(1936); RETURN OF SOPHIE LANG, THE(1936); GHOST TOWN GOLD(1937); TRUE CONFESSION(1937); MEET JOHN DOE(1941); PROUD AND THE PROFANE, THE(1956)

Donna Mae Roberts
FOOTLIGHT PARADE(1933); 42ND STREET(1933); DON'T GET PERSONAL(1936); NEXT TIME WE LOVE(1936)

Donna Roberts
RECKLESS(1935); ROBERTA(1935)

Doris Roberts
TAKING OF PELHAM ONE, TWO, THREE, THE(1974); SOMETHING WILD(1961); LOVELY WAY TO DIE, A(1968); NO WAY TO TREAT A LADY(1968); HONEYMOON KILLERS, THE(1969); LITTLE MURDERS(1971); NEW LEAF, A(1971); SUCH GOOD FRIENDS(1971); HEARTBREAK KID, THE(1972); HESTER STREET(1975); ONCE IN PARIS(1978); RABBIT TEST(1978); GOOD LUCK, MISS WYCKOFF(1979); ROSE, THE(1979)

Dorothy Roberts
NEW FACES OF 1937(1937)

Eddie Roberts
SOME BLONDES ARE DANGEROUS(1937)

Edith Roberts
WAGON MASTER, THE(1929); THAT HAGEN GIRL(1947), w
Silents
LOVE SWINDLE(1918); HER FIVE-FOOT HIGHNESS(1920); WHITE YOUTH(1920); DANGEROUS AGE, THE(1922); FRONT PAGE STORY, A(1922); SATURDAY NIGHT(1922); SON OF THE WOLF, THE(1922); THORNS AND ORANGE BLOSSOMS(1922); SUNSHINE TRAIL, THE(1923); ROARING RAILS(1924); ROULETTE(1924); NEW CHAMPION(1925); ON THIN ICE(1925); SPEED MAD(1925); WASTED LIVES(1925); JAZZ GIRL, THE(1926); TAXI MYSTERY, THE(1926); MAN FROM HEADQUARTERS(1928); PHANTOM OF THE NORTH(1929)
Misc. Silents
BEANS(1918); DECIDING KISS, THE(1918); SET FREE(1918); BILL HENRY(1919); LASCA(1919); SUE OF THE SOUTH(1919); TASTE OF LIFE, A(1919); ADORABLE SAVAGE, THE(1920); ALIAS MISS DODD(1920); TRIFLERS, THE(1920); FIRE CAT, THE(1921); IN SOCIETY(1921); OPENED SHUTTERS(1921); THUNDER ISLAND(1921); UNKNOWN WIFE, THE(1921); FLESH AND BLOOD(1922); PAWNED(1922); BACKBONE(1923); BIG BROTHER(1923); AGE OF INNOCENCE, THE(1924); $20 A WEEK(1924); HEIR-LOONS(1925); SEVEN KEYS TO BALDPATE(1925); SHATTERED LIVES(1925); THREE KEYS(1925); MYSTERY CLUB, THE(1926); ROAD TO BROADWAY, THE(1926); SHAMEFUL BEHAVIOR?(1926); THERE YOU ARE!(1926)

Edward Barry Roberts
FORSAKING ALL OTHERS(1935), w

Edward Dryhurst Roberts
Misc. Silents
BOYS OF THE OTTER PATROL(1918, Brit.)

Edward Roberts
VANITY STREET(1932), w; CORRUPTION(1933), d, w

Edwin Roberts
JOAN OF ARC(1948), set d

Eric Roberts
NORTH STAR, THE(1943); WATCH ON THE RHINE(1943); SHADOWED(1946); FIGHTING FATHER DUNNE(1948); KING OF THE GYPSIES(1978); RAGGEDY MAN(1981); STAR 80(1983)
1984
POPE OF GREENWICH VILLAGE, THE(1984)

Eric G. Roberts
BREAKING GLASS(1980, Brit.), ch

Evelyn Roberts
SAY IT WITH MUSIC(1932, Brit.); ANNE ONE HUNDRED(1933, Brit.); MELODY MAKER, THE(1933, Brit.); ONE PRECIOUS YEAR(1933, Brit.); PURSE STRINGS(1933, Brit.); BROKEN ROSARY, THE(1934, Brit.); FEATHERED SERPENT, THE(1934, Brit.); SING AS WE GO(1934, Brit.); SORRELL AND SON(1934, Brit.); NO LIMIT(1935, Brit.); KEEP FIT(1937, Brit.); I'VE GOT A HORSE(1938, Brit.); RETURN OF THE SCARLET PIMPERNEL(1938, Brit.); LOST ON THE WESTERN FRONT(1940, Brit.); MIDAS TOUCH, THE(1940, Brit.); SECOND MR. BUSH, THE(1940, Brit.); WINSLOW BOY, THE(1950); CLUE OF THE MISSING APE, THE(1953, Brit.); GREEN SCARF, THE(1954, Brit.); HEART OF THE MATTER, THE(1954, Brit.); MAN OF THE MOMENT(1955, Brit.); TOUCH OF THE SUN, A(1956, Brit.)
Silents
BOLIBAR(1928, Brit.)

Ewan Roberts
DULCIMER STREET(1948, Brit.); CASTLE IN THE AIR(1952, Brit.); COLONEL MARCH INVESTIGATES(1952,Brit.); FOUR AGAINST FATE(1952, Brit.); MAN IN THE WHITE SUIT, THE(1952); TITFIELD THUNDERBOLT, THE(1953, Brit.); HEART OF THE MATTER, THE(1954, Brit.); RIVER BEAT(1954); PORT OF ESCAPE(1955, Brit.); LADYKILLERS, THE(1956, Brit.); HIGH TIDE AT NOON(1957, Brit.); LET'S BE HAPPY(1957, Brit.); CURSE OF THE DEMON(1958); WHAT A WHOPPER(1961, Brit.); DAY OF THE TRIFFIDS, THE(1963); FIVE TO ONE(1963, Brit.); THREE LIVES OF THOMASINA, THE(1963, U.S./Brit.); TRAITORS, THE(1963, Brit.); PARTNER, THE(1966, Brit.); HOSTILE WITNESS(1968, Brit.); BROTHERLY LOVE(1970, Brit.); INTERNECINE PROJECT, THE(1974, Brit.)

Fanya Roberts
HI' YA, SAILOR(1943), w

Florence Roberts
EYES OF THE WORLD, THE(1930); BACHELOR APARTMENT(1931); EVERYTHING'S ROSIE(1931); FANNY FOLEY HERSELF(1931); KEPT HUSBANDS(1931); TOO MANY COOKS(1931); ALL-AMERICAN, THE(1932); MAKE ME A STAR(1932); WESTWARD PASSAGE(1932); WHAT PRICE HOLLYWOOD?(1932); DANGEROUSLY YOURS(1933); DARING DAUGHTERS(1933); EVER IN MY HEART(1933); HOOPLA(1933); MELODY CRUISE(1933); OFFICER 13(1933); TORCH SINGER(1933); BABES IN TOYLAND(1934); CLEOPATRA(1934); FINISHING SCHOOL(1934); MISS FANE'S BABY IS STOLEN(1934); SING AND LIKE IT(1934); STUDENT TOUR(1934); ACCENT ON YOUTH(1935); EVERY NIGHT AT EIGHT(1935); HARMONY LANE(1935); LES MISERABLES(1935); NUT FARM, THE(1935); PUBLIC OPINION(1935); ROCKY MOUNTAIN MYSTERY(1935); SONS OF STEEL(1935); TOP HAT(1935); YOUR UNCLE DUDLEY(1935); BACK TO NATURE(1936); EDUCATING FATHER(1936); EVERY SATURDAY NIGHT(1936); NEXT TIME WE LOVE(1936); NOBODY'S FOOL(1936); BIG BUSINESS(1937); BORROWING TROUBLE(1937); HOT WATER(1937); LIFE OF EMILE ZOLA, THE(1937); NOBODY'S BABY(1937); OFF TO THE RACES(1937); PRISONER OF ZENDA, THE(1937); DOWN ON THE FARM(1938); LOVE ON A BUDGET(1938); PERSONAL SECRETARY(1938); SAFETY IN NUMBERS(1938); STORM, THE(1938); TRIP TO PARIS, A(1938); EVERYBODY'S BABY(1939); JONES FAMILY IN HOLLYWOOD, THE(1939); QUICK MILLIONS(1939); TOO BUSY TO WORK(1939); ABE LINCOLN IN ILLINOIS(1940); ON THEIR OWN(1940); YOUNG AS YOU FEEL(1940)
Silents
SLEEPWALKER, THE(1922)
Misc. Silents
SAPPHO(1913)

Florian Roberts [Robert Florey]
LADY GANGSTER(1942), d

Francis Roberts
FALSE EVIDENCE(1937, Brit.); MURDER TOMORROW(1938, Brit.); SHADOW OF THE PAST(1950, Brit.); FOUR DAYS(1951, Brit.)
Silents
SHIPS THAT PASS IN THE NIGHT(1921, Brit.)

Frank Roberts
WELCOME TO HARD TIMES(1967), cos; EXTRAORDINARY SEAMAN, THE(1969), cos
Freddy Roberts
RUNNING MAN, THE(1963, Brit.)
G. B. Roberts
FIREBALL JUNGLE(1968), p
Gene Roberts
STORK BITES MAN(1947); UNDERCOVER MAISIE(1947)
Geoffrey Roberts
OLD MOTHER RILEY, DETECTIVE(1943, Brit.)
George Roberts
TELL ME IN THE SUNLIGHT(1967); FORTUNE, THE(1975)
George B. Roberts
SIGN OF AQUARIUS(1970), p
Gerald Roberts
NEW FRONTIER, THE(1935), ed; PARADISE CANYON(1935), ed; DUEL AT APACHE WELLS(1957), m, md; GUNFIRE AT INDIAN GAP(1957), md; HELL'S CROSS-ROADS(1957), m; LAST STAGECOACH WEST, THE(1957), md; LAWLESS EIGHTIES, THE(1957), md; PANAMA SAL(1957), md; SPOILERS OF THE FOREST(1957), md; TAMING SUTTON'S GAL(1957), md; CROOKED CIRCLE, THE(1958), md; JUVENILE JUNGLE(1958), m; MAN WHO DIED TWICE, THE(1958), md; NOTORIOUS MR. MONKS, THE(1958), md; WESTBOUND(1959)
Ginny Roberts
STAKEOUT ON DOPE STREET(1958)
Glen Roberts
GIRLS IN THE NIGHT(1953); EVICTORS, THE(1979)
Glenn Roberts
CRATER LAKE MONSTER, THE(1977)
Gordon Roberts
MESQUITE BUCKAROO(1939)
Hank Roberts
TOP BANANA(1954)
Hans Roberts
Misc. Silents
GREAT WHITE TRAIL, THE(1917)
Harold Roberts
CRY BLOOD, APACHE(1970), p, w
Harry Roberts
Silents
SHEFFIELD BLADE, A(1918, Brit.), d
Misc. Silents
BARTON MYSTERY, THE(1920, Brit.), d
Henry Roberts
GANG WAR(1940)
Herb Roberts
NIGHT TRAIN TO MUNDO FINE(1966), ph
Hi Roberts
NEWSBOY'S HOME(1939); ADVENTURE IN DIAMONDS(1940); CHEYENNE SOCIAL CLUB, THE(1970)
Holly Roberts
1984
PROTOCOL(1984)
Howard Roberts
WINK OF AN EYE(1958); LORD SHANGO(1975), m
Iris Roberts
Silents
SIEGFRIED(1924, Ger.)
Irma Roberts
SECRET OF THE INCAS(1954), ph
Irmin Roberts
WAR OF THE WORLDS, THE(1953), spec eff; CONQUEST OF SPACE(1955), spec eff
Ivor Roberts
SAILOR'S RETURN, THE(1978, Brit.); HOPSCOTCH(1980); SWEET WILLIAM(1980, Brit.)
1984
ANOTHER COUNTRY(1984, Brit.)
J.C. Roberts
1984
FINDERS KEEPERS(1984)
J.H. Roberts
CHARLEY'S(BIG-HEARTED) AUNT*1/2 (1940); ALIBI(1931, Brit.); SAFE AFFAIR, A(1931, Brit.), a, p; GREEN PACK, THE(1934, Brit.); IT'S A BOY(1934, Brit.); LUCK OF A SAILOR, THE(1934, Brit.); REGAL CAVALCADE(1935, Brit.); MORALS OF MARCUS, THE(1936, Brit.); POT LUCK(1936, Brit.); JUGGERNAUT(1937, Brit.); DIVORCE OF LADY X. THE(1938, Brit.); RAT, THE(1938, Brit.); TROOPSHIP(1938, Brit.); YOUNG AND INNOCENT(1938, Brit.); NIGHT TRAIN(1940, Brit.); CHAMBER OF HORRORS(1941, Brit.); COURAGEOUS MR. PENN, THE(1941, Brit.); HE FOUND A STAR(1941, Brit.); SUICIDE SQUADRON(1942, Brit.); YOUNG MR. PITT, THE(1942, Brit.); DARK TOWER, THE(1943, Brit.); UNCENSORED(1944, Brit.); GHOSTS OF BERKELEY SQUARE(1947, Brit.); DULCIMER STREET(1948, Brit.); UNEASY TERMS(1948, Brit.); AGITATOR, THE(1949); MARRY ME!(1949, Brit.); QUARTET(1949, Brit.)
J.K. Roberts
Misc. Silents
DEVIL AT HIS ELBOW, THE(1916)
J.N. Roberts
ELECTRA GLIDE IN BLUE(1973)
J. Mark Roberts
DEPTH CHARGE(1960, Brit.)
J. N. Roberts
SOMETIMES A GREAT NOTION(1971); MECHANIC, THE(1972)
Jack Roberts
TRIPLE JUSTICE(1940), w; LUCKY JORDAN(1942); MAN'S WORLD, A(1942), w; STAR SPANGLED RHYTHM(1942); NO TIME FOR LOVE(1943); CHICAGO DEADLINE(1949); SORROWFUL JONES(1949); FILE ON THELMA JORDAN, THE(1950); UNION STATION(1950); BIG CARNIVAL, THE(1951); CARRIE(1952); MONEY FROM HOME(1953); COUNTRY GIRL, THE(1954)

James Roberts
MILL ON THE FLOSS(1939, Brit.)
Jason Roberts
CORRUPTION(1933)
Jeanie Roberts
GIRL O' MY DREAMS(1935); SPLENDOR(1935); RETURN OF JIMMY VALENTINE, THE(1936)
Jennie Roberts
MURDER MAN(1935)
Jessie Roberts
WE OF THE NEVER NEVER(1983, Aus.)
Jim Roberts
PALM BEACH(1979, Aus.)
Joe Roberts
MY TUTOR(1983), w
Silents
OUR HOSPITALITY(1923); THREE AGES, THE(1923)
Misc. Silents
PRIMITIVE LOVER, THE(1922)
John Roberts
IT HAPPENED OUT WEST(1937), w; MIRROR CRACK'D, THE(1980, Brit.), art d
1984
JIGSAW MAN, THE(1984, Brit.), art d
John H. Roberts
HIGH FINANCE(1933, Brit.); WHITE FACE(1933, Brit.); SPITFIRE(1943, Brit.)
Misc. Silents
PAUPER MILLIONAIRE, THE(1922, Brit.)
John K. Roberts
Misc. Silents
LAW THAT FAILED, THE(1917)
John R. Roberts
WHEN YOU'RE SMILING(1950), W
John S. Roberts
TILL THE END OF TIME(1946); DREAM GIRL(1947); SADDLE PALS(1947)
John Storm Roberts
COUNTDOWN AT KUSINI(1976, Nigerian), w
John Todd Roberts
BOY, DID I GET A WRONG NUMBER!(1966); CAT, THE(1966); FORTUNE COOKIE, THE(1966)
Judith Roberts
MINNIE AND MOSKOWITZ(1971); STUDENT BODY, THE(1976); SWINGING BARMAIDS, THE(1976); NEW GIRL IN TOWN(1977)
Judith Anna Roberts
ERASERHEAD(1978)
June Roberts
"RENT-A-GIRL"(1965); EXPERIENCE PREFERRED... BUT NOT ESSENTIAL(1983, Brit.), w
Kathy Roberts
FIREBALL JUNGLE(1968)
Katy Roberts
OFF THE WALL(1977)
Keith Roberts
OLIVER!(1968, Brit.)
Kenneth Roberts
CAPTAIN CAUTION(1940), w; NORTHWEST PASSAGE(1940), w; LYDIA BAILEY(1952), w
Kenny Roberts
SIX BRIDGES TO CROSS(1955)
Kim Roberts
SING AND SWING(1964, Brit.); DON'T GO IN THE HOUSE(1980)
Kurtis Roberts
MONTE WALSH(1970)
Larry Roberts
LADY AND THE TRAMP(1955); PASSION HOLIDAY(1963)
1984
CRACKERS(1984), spec eff
Lee Roberts
DEATH VALLEY RANGERS(1944); CARAVAN TRAIL, THE(1946); DRIFTIN' RIVER(1946); ROMANCE OF THE WEST(1946); STARS OVER TEXAS(1946); TUMBLEWEED TRAIL(1946); WILD WEST(1946); GHOST TOWN RENEGADES(1947); LAW OF THE LASH(1947); WILD COUNTRY(1947); DEADLINE(1948); HARPOON(1948); MARK OF THE LASH(1948); PRAIRIE OUTLAWS(1948); COWBOY AND THE INDIANS, THE(1949); DALTON GANG, THE(1949); MUTINEERS, THE(1949); OUTLAW COUNTRY(1949); RIDERS OF THE DUSK(1949); RIMFIRE(1949); SOUTH OF DEATH VALLEY(1949); SQUARE DANCE JUBILEE(1949); BATTLING MARSHAL(1950); CHEROKEE UPRISING(1950); COVERED WAGON RAID(1950); FIGHTING REDHEAD, THE(1950); LAW OF THE PANHANDLE(1950); ABILENE TRAIL(1951); COLORADO AMBUSH(1951); DISTANT DRUMS(1951); LONGHORN, THE(1951); MONTANA DESPERADO(1951); NEVADA BADMEN(1951); STAGE TO BLUE RIVER(1951); TEXAS LAWMEN(1951); WELLS FARGO GUNMASTER(1951); WHISTLING HILLS(1951); CANYON AMBUSH(1952); DESPERADOES OUTPOST(1952); KANSAS TERRITORY(1952); LAWLESS COWBOYS(1952); LION AND THE HORSE, THE(1952); BATTLE OF ROGUE RIVER(1954); MAGNIFICENT OBSESSION(1954); RETURN FROM THE SEA(1954); FORT YUMA(1955); MAN ALONE, A(1955); MAN WITHOUT A STAR(1955); GUNFIGHT AT THE O.K. CORRAL(1957); SPIRIT OF ST. LOUIS, THE(1957); THREE BRAVE MEN(1957); MISSILE TO THE MOON(1959)
Misc. Talkies
FIGHTING MUSTANG(1948); MAN FROM SONORA(1951); GUNS ALONG THE BORDER(1952)
Leona Roberts
BORDER CAFE(1937); THERE GOES THE GROOM(1937); AFFAIRS OF ANNABEL(1938); BRINGING UP BABY(1938); CONDEMNED WOMEN(1938); CRIME RING(1938); HAVING WONDERFUL TIME(1938); I STAND ACCUSED(1938); KENTUCKY(1938); OF HUMAN HEARTS(1938); THIS MARRIAGE BUSINESS(1938); ESCAPE, THE(1939); GONE WITH THE WIND(1939); OF MICE AND MEN(1939); SWANEE RIVER(1939); THEY MADE HER A SPY(1939); THOU SHALT NOT KILL(1939); ABE LINCOLN IN ILLINOIS(1940); BLONDIE PLAYS CUPID(1940); COMIN' ROUND THE MOUNTAIN(1940); FLIGHT ANGELS(1940); GANGS OF CHICAGO(1940); GOLDEN GLOVES(1940); QUEEN OF THE MOB(1940); SUED FOR

LIBEL(1940); WILDCAT BUS(1940); WEEKEND IN HAVANA(1941); MADONNA'S SECRET, THE(1946); LOVES OF CARMEN, THE(1948); CHICAGO DEADLINE(1949)

Leslie Roberts
YOU'RE IN THE ARMY NOW(1937, Brit.)

Linda Roberts
FIREBALL JUNGLE(1968)

Lionel Roberts
HINDLE WAKES(1931, Brit.)
Misc. Silents
HUMAN CARGO(1929, Brit.)

Lois Roberts
GYPSY(1962); ISLAND OF LOVE(1963)

Luanne Roberts
DARK SIDE OF TOMORROW, THE(1970); WEEKEND WITH THE BABYSIT-TER(1970); SIMON, KING OF THE WITCHES(1971); WELCOME HOME, SOLDIER BOYS(1972); THUNDERBOLT AND LIGHTFOOT(1974)

Lynn Roberts
CALL THE MESQUITEERS(1938); HIGGINS FAMILY, THE(1938); HOLLYWOOD STADIUM MYSTERY(1938); MAMA RUNS WILD(1938); HI-YO SILVER(1940); MOON OVER MIAMI(1941); PORT OF 40 THIEVES, THE(1944)

Lynne Roberts
DANGEROUS HOLIDAY(1937); HEART OF THE ROCKIES(1937); BILLY THE KID RETURNS(1938); EVERYTHING'S ON ICE(1939); BRIDE WORE CRUTCHES, THE(1940); HIGH SCHOOL(1940); STAR DUST(1940); STREET OF MEMORIES(1940); LAST OF THE DUANES(1941); RIDE ON VAQUERO(1941); RIDERS OF THE PURPLE SAGE(1941); ROMANCE OF THE RIO GRANDE(1941); SUN VALLEY SERENA-DE(1941); YANK IN THE R.A.F., A(1941); DR. RENAULT'S SECRET(1942); MAN IN THE TRUNK, THE(1942); QUIET PLEASE, MURDER(1942); YOUNG AMERI-CA(1942); BIG BONANZA, THE(1944); GHOST THAT WALKS ALONE, THE(1944); MY BUDDY(1944); BEHIND CITY LIGHTS(1945); CHICAGO KID, THE(1945); GIRLS OF THE BIG HOUSE(1945); PHANTOM SPEAKS, THE(1945); MAGNIFICENT ROGUE, THE(1946); SIOUX CITY SUE(1946); PILGRIM LADY, THE(1947); ROBIN OF TEX-AS(1947); SADDLE PALS(1947); THAT'S MY GAL(1947); WINTER WONDER-LAND(1947); EYES OF TEXAS(1948); LIGHTNIN' IN THE FOREST(1948); MADONNA OF THE DESERT(1948); SECRET SERVICE INVESTIGATOR(1948); SONS OF AD-VENTURE(1948); TIMBER TRAIL, THE(1948); DANGEROUS PROFESSION, A(1949); TROUBLE PREFERRED(1949); BLAZING SUN, THE(1950); CALL OF THE KLON-DIKE(1950); DYNAMITE PASS(1950); GREAT PLANE ROBBERY(1950); HUNT THE MAN DOWN(1950); BECAUSE OF YOU(1952); BLAZING FOREST, THE(1952); PORT SINISTER(1953)

Lynwood Roberts
LIVE AGAIN(1936, Brit.)

Maclean Roberts
I'LL WALK BESIDE YOU(1943, Brit.), d

Marc L. Roberts
UNDERGROUND(1970, Brit.), w

Marcel Roberts
BRIDE WORE BLACK, THE(1968, Fr./Ital.), p

Marguerite Roberts
JIMMY AND SALLY(1933), w; SAILOR'S LUCK(1933), w; PECK'S BAD BOY(1934), w; COLLEGE SCANDAL(1935), w; MEN WITHOUT NAMES(1935), w; FLORIDA SPECIAL(1936), w; FORGOTTEN FACES(1936), w; HOLLYWOOD BOULE-VARD(1936), w; ROSE BOWL(1936), w; TURN OFF THE MOON(1937), w; WILD MONEY(1937), w; MEET THE GIRLS(1938), w; ESCAPE(1940), w; HONKY TONK(1941), w; ZIEGFELD GIRL(1941), w; SOMEWHERE I'LL FIND YOU(1942), w; DRAGON SEED(1944), w; UNDERCURRENT(1946), w; DESIRE ME(1947), w; IF WINTER COMES(1947), w; SEA OF GRASS, THE(1947), w; BRIBE, THE(1949), w; AMBUSH(1950), w; SOLDIERS THREE(1951), w; DIAMOND HEAD(1962), w; MAIN ATTRACTION, THE(1962, Brit.), w; RAMPAGE(1963), w; LOVE HAS MANY FA-CES(1965), w; FIVE CARD STUD(1968), w; TRUE GRIT(1969), w; NORWOOD(1970), w; RED SKY AT MORNING(1971), w; SHOOT OUT(1971), w

Marilyn Roberts
SKATEBOARD(1978)

Mario Roberts
1984
CANNONBALL RUN II(1984)

Mariwin Roberts
Misc. Talkies
BEACH BUNNIES(1977); ENFORCER FROM DEATH ROW, THE(1978)

Mark Roberts
TAXI(1953); ONIONHEAD(1958); MONEY JUNGLE, THE(1968); GIRL WHO KNEW TOO MUCH, THE(1969); ONCE IS NOT ENOUGH(1975); POSSE(1975)

Meade Roberts
FUGITIVE KIND, THE(1960), w; SUMMER AND SMOKE(1961), w; IN THE COOL OF THE DAY(1963), w; STRIPPER, THE(1963), w; BLUE(1968), w; DANGER ROU-TE(1968, Brit.), w; KILLING OF A CHINESE BOOKIE, THE(1976); OPENING NIGHT(1977)

Mel Roberts
DRIVE A CROOKED ROAD(1954)

Michael Roberts
FINDERS KEEPERS, LOVERS WEEPERS(1968)

Michael D. Roberts
HUNTER, THE(1980); HEARTBREAKER(1983)
1984
ICE PIRATES, THE(1984)

Morgan Roberts
SOMETHING OF VALUE(1957); LET'S DO IT AGAIN(1975); WHICH WAY IS UP?(1977); HUNTER, THE(1980); BUSTIN' LOOSE(1981)

Myrtle Roberts
LONELY HEARTS(1983, Aus.)

Nancy Roberts
PRISON WITHOUT BARS(1939, Brit.); BLACK NARCISSUS(1947, Brit.); WARNING TO WANTONS, A(1949, Brit.); SLASHER, THE(1953, Brit.); IT'S A GREAT DAY(1956, Brit.); SUPERMAN III(1983)
1984
WHERE IS PARSIFAL?(1984, Brit.)

Ned Roberts
RINGSIDE(1949); MARSHAL OF HELDORADO(1950); SEALED CARGO(1951)

Paddy Roberts
GOOD COMPANIONS, THE(1957, Brit.), m

Pamela Roberts
GHOSTS OF BERKELEY SQUARE(1947, Brit.)

Pascale Roberts
FIVE MILES TO MIDNIGHT(1963, U.S./Fr./Ital.); SWEET AND SOUR(1964, Fr./Ital.); SLEEPING CAR MURDER THE(1966, Fr.); SELLERS OF GIRLS(1967, Fr.); BLONDE FROM PEKING, THE(1968, Fr.); THREE(1969, Brit.); FRIENDS(1971, Brit.)

Pat Roberts
HELP!(1965, Brit.)

Patrick Roberts
MAIN ATTRACTION, THE(1962, Brit.), w

Pernell Roberts
DESIRE UNDER THE ELMS(1958); SHEEPMAN, THE(1958); RIDE LONESO-ME(1959); ERRAND BOY, THE(1961); FOUR RODE OUT(1969, US/Span.); MAGIC OF LASSIE, THE(1978)
Misc. Talkies
PACO(1976)

R.A. Roberts
Silents
AULD ROBIN GRAY(1917, Brit.)
Misc. Silents
AULD ROBIN GRAY(1917, Brit.)

Rachel Roberts
LIMPING MAN, THE(1953, Brit.); MEN ARE CHILDREN TWICE(1953, Brit.); CROWDED DAY, THE(1954, Brit.); WEAK AND THE WICKED, THE(1954, Brit.); GOOD COMPANIONS, THE(1957, Brit.); DAVY(1958, Brit.); OUR MAN IN HAVA-NA(1960, Brit.); SATURDAY NIGHT AND SUNDAY MORNING(1961, Brit.); GIRL ON APPROVAL(1962, Brit.); THIS SPORTING LIFE(1963, Brit.); FLEA IN HER EAR, A(1968, Fr.); DOCTORS' WIVES(1971); RECKONING, THE(1971, Brit.); WILD ROV-ERS(1971); ALPHA BETA(1973, Brit.); O LUCKY MAN!(1973, Brit.); MURDER ON THE ORIENT EXPRESS(1974, Brit.); GREAT EXPECTATIONS(1975, Brit.); PICNIC AT HANGING ROCK(1975, Aus.); BELSTONE FOX, THE(1976, Brit.); FOUL PLAY(1978); WHEN A STRANGER CALLS(1979); YANKS(1979); CHARLIE CHAN AND THE CURSE OF THE DRAGON QUEEN(1981)

Ralph Roberts
MAD HATTERS, THE(1935, Brit.); WHERE'S SALLY?(1936, Brit.); INCIDENT IN SHANGHAI(1937, Brit.); PERFECT CRIME, THE(1937, Brit.); MAXWELL ARCHER, DETECTIVE(1942, Brit.); YOUNG MR. PITT, THE(1942, Brit.); DIAL 1119(1950); KILLER'S KISS(1955); BELLS ARE RINGING(1960); MISFITS, THE(1961); GONE ARE THE DAYS(1963); RESURRECTION(1980)

Ralph Arthur Roberts
RENDEZ-VOUS(1932, Ger.)

Randolph Roberts
WICKED, WICKED(1973); LOGAN'S RUN(1976)

Randy Roberts
GREASED LIGHTNING(1977), ed; STRAIGHT TIME(1978), ed; PLAYERS(1979), ed; SMALL CIRCLE OF FRIENDS, A(1980), ed; HAMMETT(1982), ed; ONE FROM THE HEART(1982), ed; JAWS 3-D(1983), ed

Raymond Roberts
IT FELL FROM THE SKY(1980)

Reeka Roberts
Silents
KING OF KINGS, THE(1927)

Renee Roberts
WHAT BECAME OF JACK AND JILL?(1972, Brit.)

Richard Roberts
FIREPOWER(1979, Brit.)

Richard Emery Roberts
LAST FRONTIER, THE(1955), w; SECOND TIME AROUND, THE(1961), w

Ricky Roberts
STRAWBERRY STATEMENT, THE(1970), cos

Robbe Roberts
LAST AMERICAN HERO, THE(1973), ed; BRING ME THE HEAD OF ALFREDO GARCIA(1974), ed; W. W. AND THE DIXIE DANCEKINGS(1975), ed; BIRCH INTER-VAL(1976), ed; ONE ON ONE(1977), ed; CATTLE ANNIE AND LITTLE BRITCH-ES(1981), ed; PURSUIT OF D.B. COOPER, THE(1981), ed

Robert E. Roberts
1984
ADERYN PAPUR(1984, Brit.)

Robin Roberts
HAPPY BIRTHDAY, DAVY(1970)

Roland Roberts
SHELL SHOCK(1964)

Rosalind Roberts
THAT TOUCH OF MINK(1962)

Rosalind C. Roberts
DESERT RAVEN, THE(1965)

Roy Roberts
GUADALCANAL DIARY(1943); ROGER TOUHY, GANGSTER!(1944); SULLIVANS, THE(1944); TAMPICO(1944); WILSON(1944); BELL FOR ADANO, A(1945); CARIB-BEAN MYSTERY, THE(1945); CIRCUMSTANTIAL EVIDENCE(1945); COLONEL EFFINGHAM'S RAID(1945); WITHIN THESE WALLS(1945); BEHIND GREEN LIGHTS(1946); IT SHOULDN'T HAPPEN TO A DOG(1946); JOHNNY COMES FLYING HOME(1946); MY DARLING CLEMENTINE(1946); SMOKY(1946); STRANGE TRIAN-GLE(1946); BRASHER DOUBLOON, THE(1947); CAPTAIN FROM CASTILE(1947); DAISY KENYON(1947); FOXES OF HARROW, THE(1947); GENTLEMAN'S AGREE-MENT(1947); NIGHTMARE ALLEY(1947); SHOCKING MISS PILGRIM, THE(1947); CHICKEN EVERY SUNDAY(1948); FORCE OF EVIL(1948); FURY AT FURNACE CREEK(1948); GAY INTRUDERS, THE(1948); HE WALKED BY NIGHT(1948); JOAN OF ARC(1948); NO MINOR VICES(1948); CALAMITY JANE AND SAM BASS(1949); CHICAGO DEADLINE(1949); FLAMING FURY(1949); KISS FOR CORLISS, A(1949); MISS GRANT TAKES RICHMOND(1949); RECKLESS MOMENTS, THE(1949); BODY-HOLD(1950); BORDERLINE(1950); CHAIN LIGHTNING(1950); KILLER THAT STALKED NEW YORK, THE(1950); PALOMINO, THE(1950); SECOND FACE, THE(1950); SIERRA(1950); STAGE TO TUCSON(1950); WYOMING MAIL(1950); CI-MARRON KID, THE(1951); ENFORCER, THE(1951); FIGHTING COAST GUARD(1951); I WAS A COMMUNIST FOR THE F.B.I.(1951); MAN WITH A CLOAK, THE(1951); MY FAVORITE SPY(1951); SANTA FE(1951); BATTLES OF CHIEF PONTIAC(1952); BIG TREES, THE(1952); CRIPPLE CREEK(1952); HOODLUM EM-

PIRE(1952); MAN BEHIND THE GUN, THE(1952); ONE MINUTE TO ZERO(1952); SKIRTS AHOY!(1952); STARS AND STRIPES FOREVER(1952); GLORY BRIGADE, THE(1953); HOUSE OF WAX(1953); LONE HAND, THE(1953); SAN ANTONE(1953); SEA OF LOST SHIPS(1953); SECOND CHANCE(1953); TUMBLEWEED(1953); DAWN AT SOCORRO(1954); OUTLAW STALLION, THE(1954); THEY RODE WEST(1954); BIG HOUSE, U.S.A.(1955); I COVER THE UNDERWORLD(1955); LAST COMMAND, THE(1955); WYOMING RENEGADES(1955); BOSS, THE(1956); FIRST TEXAN, THE(1956); KING AND FOUR QUEENS, THE(1956); WHITE SQUAW, THE(1956); YAQUI DRUMS(1956); CHAPMAN REPORT, THE(1962); UNDERWATER CITY, THE(1962); IT'S A MAD, MAD, MAD, MAD WORLD(1963); THOSE CALLOWAYS(1964); I'LL TAKE SWEDEN(1965); HOTEL(1967); TAMMY AND THE MILLIONAIRE(1967); SOME KIND OF A NUT(1969); THIS SAVAGE LAND(1969); OUTFIT, THE(1973); CHINATOWN(1974)

Ruth Roberts
NATIVE SON(1951, U.S., Arg.); WINDSPLITTER, THE(1971)

Sandra Ann Roberts
MEDIUM COOL(1969)

Sandy Roberts
LOSERS, THE(1968)

Sarah Roberts
Silents
GIRLS WHO DARE(1929)

Selwyn Roberts
FUNNY MONEY(1983, Brit.), p

Sheila Roberts
DELINQUENT DAUGHTERS(1944); GIRL IN GOLD BOOTS(1968)

Sheilah Roberts
TONIGHT AND EVERY NIGHT(1945)

Shelila Roberts
YOUTH AFLAME(1945)

Shepard Roberts
HI-DE-HO(1947)

Sherry Roberts
MARS NEEDS WOMEN(1966)

Sidney Roberts
STRANGER IN TOWN(1957, Brit.), p

Stahley Roberts
PRAIRIE MOON(1938), w

Stanley Roberts
YOUNG DYNAMITE(1937), w; CODE OF THE RANGERS(1938), w; HEROES OF THE HILLS(1938), w; LAND OF FIGHTING MEN(1938), w; PALS OF THE SADDLE(1938), w; PHANTOM RANGER(1938), w; RED RIVER RANGE(1938), w; WEST OF RAINBOW'S END(1938), w; WHERE THE WEST BEGINS(1938), w; COLORADO SUNSET(1939), w; NIGHT RIDERS, THE(1939), w; THREE TEXAS STEERS(1939), w; FUGITIVE FROM A PRISON CAMP(1940), w; UNDER AGE(1941), w; BEHIND THE EIGHT BALL(1942), w; WHAT'S COOKIN'?(1942), w; WHO DONE IT?(1942), w; HI' YA, SAILOR(1943), w; NEVER A DULL MOMENT(1943), w; PENTHOUSE RHYTHM(1945), w; UNDER WESTERN SKIES(1945), w; SONG OF THE THIN MAN(1947), w; CURTAIN CALL AT CACTUS CREEK(1950), w; LOUISA(1950), w; UP FRONT(1951), w; DEATH OF A SALESMAN(1952), w; STORY OF WILL ROGERS, THE(1952), w; CAINE MUTINY, THE(1954), w; MADE IN PARIS(1966), w
Silents
OLD COUNTRY, THE(1921, Brit.)

Stephen Roberts
LADY AND GENT(1932), d; NIGHT OF JUNE 13(1932), d; SKY BRIDE(1932), d; ONE SUNDAY AFTERNOON(1933), d; STORY OF TEMPLE DRAKE, THE(1933), d; TRUMPET BLOWS, THE(1934), d; MAN WHO BROKE THE BANK AT MONTE CARLO, THE(1935), d; ROMANCE IN MANHATTAN(1935), d; STAR OF MIDNIGHT(1935), d; EX-MRS. BRADFORD, THE(1936), d; LADY CONSENTS, THE(1936), d; SONG OF BERNADETTE, THE(1943); MIRACLE ON 34TH STREET, THE(1947); JOAN OF ARC(1948); CRISS CROSS(1949); TENSION(1949); ROGUE RIVER(1951); PRISONER OF ZENDA, THE(1952); JULIUS CAESAR(1953); WILD AND THE INNOCENT, THE(1959); PORTRAIT OF A MOBSTER(1961); DIARY OF A MADMAN(1963); TERRIFIED!(1963); BRAINSTORM(1965); FIRST TO FIGHT(1967); ROMANTIC COMEDY(1983)

Stephen S. Roberts
IF I HAD A MILLION(1932), d

Stephens Roberts
QUICK GUN, THE(1964)

Steve Roberts
SPY TRAIN(1943); KISS OF DEATH(1947); AT WAR WITH THE ARMY(1950); SHAKEDOWN(1950); WHERE THE SIDEWALK ENDS(1950); HARLEM GLOBETROTTERS, THE(1951); IRON MAN, THE(1951); ON DANGEROUS GROUND(1951); RACKET, THE(1951); ROADBLOCK(1951); JET JOB(1952); JUST ACROSS THE STREET(1952); TWONKY, THE(1953); GOG(1954); COURT-MARTIAL OF BILLY MITCHELL, THE(1955); INSIDE THE MAFIA(1959); ESCAPE FROM THE PLANET OF THE APES(1971); SIR HENRY AT RAWLINSON END(1980, Brit.), d, w

Susan Roberts
SUMMER AND SMOKE(1961)

Tanya Roberts
FORCED ENTRY(1975); FINGERS(1978); CALIFORNIA DREAMING(1979); RACQUET(1979); TOURIST TRAP, THE(1979); BEASTMASTER, THE(1982)
1984
SHEENA(1984)
Misc. Talkies
YUM-YUM GIRLS(1976)

Teal Roberts
1984
HARDBODIES(1984)

Ted Roberts
CAT ATE THE PARAKEET, THE(1972), m; BUSH CHRISTMAS(1983, Aus.), w

Thayer Roberts
CHINESE RING, THE(1947); DOUBLE LIFE, A(1947); JIGGS AND MAGGIE IN SOCIETY(1948); MIRACLE OF THE BELLS, THE(1948); THAT LADY IN ERMINE(1948); SKY HIGH(1952); DIAL M FOR MURDER(1954); LADY GODIVA(1955); THIS IS NOT A TEST(1962)

Thelma Roberts
WORDS AND MUSIC(1929)

Theodore Roberts
NOISY NEIGHBORS(1929)
Silents
CALL OF THE NORTH, THE(1914); CIRCUS MAN, THE(1914); MAN FROM HOME, THE(1914); READY MONEY(1914); WHERE THE TRAIL DIVIDES(1914); AFTER FIVE(1915); ARAB, THE(1915); CAPTIVE, THE(1915); GIRL OF THE GOLDEN WEST, THE(1915); IMMIGRANT, THE(1915); MARRIAGE OF KITTY, THE(1915); SECRET ORCHARD(1915); TEMPTATION(1915); WILD GOOSE CHASE, THE(1915); WOMAN, THE(1915); ANTON THE TERRIBLE(1916); JOAN THE WOMAN(1916); PLOW GIRL, THE(1916); AMERICAN CONSUL, THE(1917); NAN OF MUSIC MOUNTAIN(1917); ARIZONA(1918); M'LISS(1918); OLD WIVES FOR NEW(1918); HAWTHORNE OF THE U.S.A.(1919); MALE AND FEMALE(1919); ROARING ROAD, THE(1919); EXCUSE MY DUST(1920); JUDY OF ROGUES' HARBOUR(1920); SOMETHING TO THINK ABOUT(1920); SUDS(1920); AFFAIRS OF ANATOL(1921); EXIT THE VAMP(1921); SHAM(1921); TOO MUCH SPEED(1921); ACROSS THE CONTINENT(1922); IF YOU BELIEVE IT, IT'S SO(1922); MAN WHO SAW TOMORROW, THE(1922); NIGHT LIFE IN HOLLYWOOD(1922); OUR LEADING CITIZEN(1922); SATURDAY NIGHT(1922); RACING HEARTS(1923); STEPHEN STEPS OUT(1923); TEN COMMANDMENTS, THE(1923); FORTY WINKS(1925); CAT'S PAJAMAS, THE(1926); NED MCCOBB'S DAUGHTER(1929)
Misc. Silents
GHOST BREAKER(1914), d; MAKING OF BOBBY BURNIT, THE(1914); MR. GREX OF MONTE CARLO(1915); UNKNOWN, THE(1915); COMMON GROUND(1916); DREAM GIRL, THE(1916); PUDD'NHEAD WILSON(1916); STORM, THE(1916); TEMPTATION(1916); THOUSAND DOLLAR HUSBAND, THE(1916); TRAIL OF THE LONESOME PINE, THE(1916); UNPROTECTED(1916); COST OF HATRED, THE(1917); LITTLE PRINCESS, THE(1917); VARMINT, THE(1917); WHAT MONEY CAN'T BUY(1917); GIRL WHO CAME BACK, THE(1918); HIDDEN PEARLS(1918); PETTICOAT PILOT, A(1918); SOURCE, THE(1918); SQUAW MAN, THE(1918); SUCH A LITTLE PIRATE(1918); WE CAN'T HAVE EVERYTHING(1918); WILD YOUTH(1918); PEG O' MY HEART(1919); POOR BOOB(1919); SECRET SERVICE(1919); WINNING GIRL, THE(1919); WOMAN THOU GAVEST ME, THE(1919); YOU'RE FIRED(1919); DOUBLE SPEED(1920); LOVE INSURANCE(1920); SWEET LAVANDER(1920); FORBIDDEN FRUIT(1921); HAIL THE WOMAN(1921); LOVE SPECIAL, THE(1921); MISS LULU BETT(1921); OLD HOMESTEAD, THE(1922); GRUMPY(1923); PRODIGAL DAUGHTERS(1923); TO THE LADIES(1923); LOCKED DOORS(1925); MASKS OF THE DEVIL, THE(1928)

Tony Pierce Roberts
MOONLIGHTING(1982, Brit.), ph

Tony Roberts
TAKING OF PELHAM ONE, TWO, THREE, THE(1974); BEACH GIRLS AND THE MONSTER, THE(1965); NAKED WORLD OF HARRISON MARKS, THE(1967, Brit.), art d; STAR SPANGLED GIRL(1971); $1,000,000 DUCK(1971); PLAY IT AGAIN, SAM(1972); SERPICO(1973); SAVAGE, THE(1975, Fr.); ANNIE HALL(1977); JUST TELL ME WHAT YOU WANT(1980); STARDUST MEMORIES(1980); MIDSUMMER NIGHT'S SEX COMEDY, A(1982); AMITYVILLE 3-D(1983)

Tracey Roberts
SIDESHOW(1950); FORT DEFIANCE(1951); QUEEN FOR A DAY(1951); ACTORS AND SIN(1952); MURDER IS MY BEAT(1955); PRODIGAL, THE(1955); FRONTIER GAMBLER(1956); HOLLYWOOD OR BUST(1956); WAYWARD GIRL, THE(1957); GO NAKED IN THE WORLD(1961); SAM WHISKEY(1969); NAKED FLAME, THE(1970, Can.)

Tracy Roberts
ON DANGEROUS GROUND(1951); TENDER HEARTS(1955); EDGE OF HELL(1956)

Valentine Roberts
Silents
KNOCKNAGOW(1918, Ireland)

Vickie Roberts
FINDERS KEEPERS, LOVERS WEEPERS(1968)

Victor Roberts
GRANDAD RUDD(1935, Aus.), w

Vincent Roberts
TAKE DOWN(1979)

W. Roberts
RED SUN(1972, Fr./Ital./Span.), w

W.O. Roberts
FUN AND FANCY FREE(1947), d

Wanda Roberts
RED, WHITE AND BLACK, THE(1970)

Wendy Roberts
SHE MAN, THE(1967)

Whitey Roberts
MASTER MINDS(1949)

Wilfred Roberts
LIGHT THAT FAILED, THE(1939); ADVENTURE IN DIAMONDS(1940); EMERGENCY SQUAD(1940); PAROLE FIXER(1940); UNTAMED(1940)

Will Roberts
Misc. Talkies
FIGHTER PILOTS(1977)

William Roberts
MY LOVE CAME BACK(1940); PACIFIC RENDEZVOUS(1942); SEVEN SWEETHEARTS(1942); TENNESSEE JOHNSON(1942); YANKS ARE COMING, THE(1942); HUMAN COMEDY, THE(1943); LADY IN THE LAKE(1947); SONG OF THE THIN MAN(1947); YOU FOR ME(1952), w; EASY TO LOVE(1953), w; FAST COMPANY(1953), w; HER TWELVE MEN(1954), w; PRIVATE WAR OF MAJOR BENSON, THE(1955), w; SHEEPMAN, THE(1958), w; MATING GAME, THE(1959), w; MAGNIFICENT SEVEN, THE(1960), w; COME FLY WITH ME(1963), w; DEVIL'S BRIGADE, THE(1968), w; BRIDGE AT REMAGEN, THE(1969), w; ONE MORE TRAIN TO ROB(1971), w; LAST AMERICAN HERO, THE(1973), p, w; POSSE(1975); w; LEGEND OF THE LONE RANGER, THE(1981), w; 10 TO MIDNIGHT(1983), w
1984
SCREAM FOR HELP(1984)

Williams Roberts
WONDERFUL WORLD OF THE BROTHERS ERIMM, THE(1962), w

Wink Roberts
FIRST TIME, THE(1969)
Misc. Talkies
DAY IT CAME TO EARTH, THE(1979)

Wyn Roberts
PICNIC AT HANGING ROCK(1975, Aus.); WEEKEND OF SHADOWS(1978, Aus.); FIGHTING BACK(1983, Brit.)
Zelma Roberts
ALWAYS ANOTHER DAWN(1948, Aus.), w; INTO THE STRAIGHT(1950, Aus.), w
Gerald Robertshaw
Silents
ARAB, THE(1924)
Jerold Robertshaw
Misc. Silents
BETRAYAL, THE(1929)
Jerrold Robertshaw
KITTY(1929, Brit.); SHADOW BETWEEN, THE(1932, Brit.)
Silents
MASTER OF CRAFT, A(1922, Brit.); DON QUIXOTE(1923, Brit.); APACHE, THE(1925, Brit.); HUNTINGTOWER(1927, Brit.); MY LORD THE CHAUFFEUR(1927, Brit.); BOLIBAR(1928, Brit.); PALAIS DE DANSE(1928, Brit.); WHEN BOYS LEAVE HOME(1928, Brit.); INSEPARABLES, THE(1929, Brit.); POWER OVER MEN(1929, Brit.)
Misc. Silents
THROUGH FIRE AND WATER(1923, Brit.)
Al Robertson
COAST TO COAST(1980); STING II, THE(1983)
Alan Robertson
VISITOR, THE(1973, Can.)
Andrew Robertson
FAR FROM THE MADDING CROWD(1967, Brit.); OH! WHAT A LOVELY WAR(1969, Brit.)
Annette Robertson
SPARE THE ROD(1961, Brit.); KIND OF LOVING, A(1962, Brit.); WONDERFUL TO BE YOUNG!(1962, Brit.); PARTY'S OVER, THE(1966, Brit.); JOANNA(1968, Brit.)
Arthur Robertson
Misc. Talkies
BLACK HOOKER(1974), d
Ben Robertson
1984
LITTLE DRUMMER GIRL, THE(1984)
Blair Robertson
AGENT FOR H.A.R.M.(1966), w
Chester Robertson
SILENCE OF THE NORTH(1981, Can.)
Chet Robertson
PAPERBACK HERO(1973, Can.)
Chuck Robertson
WINCHESTER '73(1950); SONS OF KATIE ELDER, THE(1965)
Cliff Robertson
WE'VE NEVER BEEN LICKED(1943); PICNIC(1955); AUTUMN LEAVES(1956); NAKED AND THE DEAD, THE(1958); BATTLE OF THE CORAL SEA(1959); GIDGET(1959); AS THE SEA RAGES(1960 Ger.); ALL IN A NIGHT'S WORK(1961); BIG SHOW, THE(1961); UNDERWORLD U.S.A.(1961); INTERNS, THE(1962); MY SIX LOVES(1963); PT 109(1963); SUNDAY IN NEW YORK(1963); BEST MAN, THE(1964); SQUADRON 633(1964, U.S./Brit.); 633 SQUADRON(1964); LOVE HAS MANY FACES(1965); MASQUERADE(1965, Brit.); UP FROM THE BEACH(1965); HONEY POT, THE(1967, Brit.); CHARLY(1968); DEVIL'S BRIGADE, THE(1968); TOO LATE THE HERO(1970); J.W. COOP(1971), a, p&d, w; GREAT NORTHFIELD, MINNESOTA RAID, THE(1972); ACE ELI AND RODGER OF THE SKIES(1973); MAN ON A SWING(1974); OUT OF SEASON(1975, Brit.); THREE DAYS OF THE CONDOR(1975); MIDWAY(1976); OBSESSION(1976); SHOOT(1976, Can.); FRATERNITY ROW(1977); DOMINIQUE(1978, Brit.); PILOT, THE(1979), a, d, w; BRAINSTORM(1983); CLASS(1983); STAR 80(1983)
Dale Robertson
FIGHTING MAN OF THE PLAINS(1949); FLAMINGO ROAD(1949); GIRL FROM JONES BEACH, THE(1949); CARIBOO TRAIL, THE(1950); TWO FLAGS WEST(1950); CALL ME MISTER(1951); GOLDEN GIRL(1951); TAKE CARE OF MY LITTLE GIRL(1951); LYDIA BAILEY(1952); O. HENRY'S FULL HOUSE(1952); OUTCASTS OF POKER FLAT, THE(1952); RETURN OF THE TEXAN(1952); CITY OF BAD MEN(1953); DEVIL'S CANYON(1953); FARMER TAKES A WIFE, THE(1953); SILVER WHIP(1953); GAMBLER FROM NATCHEZ, THE(1954); SITTING BULL(1954); SON OF SINBAD(1955); TOP OF THE WORLD(1955); DAY OF FURY, A(1956); HELL CANYON OUTLAWS(1957); HIGH TERRACE(1957, Brit.); ANNA OF BROOKLYN(1958, Ital.); FAST AND SEXY(1960, Fr./Ital.); BLOOD ON THE ARROW(1964); LAW OF THE LAWLESS(1964); COAST OF SKELETONS(1965, Brit.); MAN FROM BUTTON WILLOW, THE(1965); ONE-EYED SOLDIERS(1967, U.S./Brit./Yugo.)
David Robertson
FIREBIRD 2015 AD(1981), d
Dennis Robertson
WAR PARTY(1965); MAROONED(1969); NORTH AVENUE IRREGULARS, THE(1979)
Misc. Talkies
MADHOUSE(1982)
Don Robertson
VAMPIRE, THE(1957), makeup
Donald Robertson
FLAME IN THE HEATHER(1935, Brit.)
Douglas Robertson
WHILE I LIVE(1947, Brit.), ed; HATTER'S CASTLE(1948, Brit.), ed; CURTAIN UP(1952, Brit.), ed; FLAMING FRONTIER(1958, Can.), ed; WOLF DOG(1958, Can.), ed; CANADIANS, THE(1961, Brit.), ed; FORTUNE AND MEN'S EYES(1971, U.S./Can.), ed; AT LONG LAST LOVE(1975), ed; MUSTANG COUNTRY(1976), ed
E. Arnot Robertson
FOUR FRIGHTENED PEOPLE(1934), w; KISENGA, MAN OF AFRICA(1952, Brit.), w
Eddie Robertson
SPRING AND PORT WINE(1970, Brit.)
Eric Robertson
QUIET DAY IN BELFAST, A(1974, Can.), m; PLAGUE(1978, Can.), m; IF YOU COULD SEE WHAT I HEAR(1982), md

F.G. Robertson
RIVER HOUSE MYSTERY, THE(1935, Brit.), w
Forest Robertson
Misc. Silents
MATING, THE(1918)
Freddie Robertson
LITTLE ONES, THE(1965, Brit.), p, m
Fyffe Robertson
WHAT A WHOPPER(1961, Brit.)
George Robertson
NORMA RAE(1979)
George C. Robertson
WAITING FOR CAROLINE(1969, Can.), w
George R. Robertson
PAPERBACK HERO(1973, Can.)
1984
POLICE ACADEMY(1984)
George Ross Robertson
ROSEMARY'S BABY(1968)
Gordon Robertson
MADELEINE IS(1971, Can.); MC CABE AND MRS. MILLER(1971); INBREAKER, THE(1974, Can.); SUPREME KID, THE(1976, Can.)
Guy Robertson
KING KELLY OF THE U.S.A(1934)
Harry Robertson
HAWK THE SLAYER(1980, Brit.), p, w, m
1984
BREAKOUT(1984, Brit.), m
Hugh A. Robertson
HARVEY MIDDLEMAN, FIREMAN(1965), ed; MIDNIGHT COWBOY(1969), ed; SHAFT(1971), ed; MELINDA(1972), d
Misc. Talkies
BIM(1976), d
James G. Robertson
UP THE ACADEMY(1980)
James L. Robertson, Jr.
SPIRIT OF ST. LOUIS, THE(1957)
Jim Robertson
HOW WILLINGLY YOU SING(1975, Aus.)
John Robertson
BEYOND VICTORY(1931), d; LITTLE ORPHAN ANNIE(1932), d; ONE MAN'S JOURNEY(1933), d; CRIME DOCTOR, THE(1934), d; HIS GREATEST GAMBLE(1934), d; CAPTAIN HURRICANE(1935), d; OUR LITTLE GIRL(1935), d
Misc. Silents
COMBAT, THE(1916); DESTROYERS, THE(1916); ENEMY TO THE KING, AN(1916); BOTTOM OF THE WELL(1917), d; INTRIGUE(1917), d; MAELSTROM, THE(1917); MONEY MILL, THE(1917), d; MENACE, THE(1918), d
John Forbes Robertson
VAMPIRE LOVERS, THE(1970, Brit.); NICHOLAS AND ALEXANDRA(1971, Brit.)
John S. Robertson
SHANGHAI LADY(1929), d; CAPTAIN OF THE GUARD(1930), d; MADONNA OF THE STREETS(1930), d; NIGHT RIDE(1930), d; PHANTOM OF PARIS, THE(1931), d; WEDNESDAY'S CHILD(1934), d; GRAND OLD GIRL(1935), d
Silents
BABY MINE(1917), d; ERSTWHILE SUSAN(1919), d; AWAY GOES PRUDENCE(1920), d; DR. JEKYLL AND MR. HYDE(1920), d; TESS OF THE STORM COUNTRY(1922), d; CLASSMATES(1924), d; ENCHANTED COTTAGE, THE(1924), d; SHORE LEAVE(1925), d; ANNIE LAURIE(1927), d; CAPTAIN SALVATION(1927), d; SINGLE STANDARD, THE(1929), d
Misc. Silents
(, d; BETTER HALF, THE(1918), d; GIRL OF TODAY, THE(1918), d; HERE COMES THE BRIDE(1919), d; LET'S ELOPE(1919), d; MISLEADING WIDOW, THE(1919), d; TEST OF HONOR, THE(1919), d; DARK LANTERN, A(1920), d; SADIE LOVE(1920), d; 39 EAST(1920), d; FOOTLIGHTS(1921), d; MAGIC CUP, THE(1921), d; SENTIMENTAL TOMMY(1921), d; LOVE'S BOOMERANG(1922), d; SPANISH JADE(1922, Brit.), d; BRIGHT SHAWL, THE(1923), d; FIGHTING BLADE, THE(1923), d; TWENTY-ONE(1923), d; NEW TOYS(1925), d; SOUL-FIRE(1925), d; ROAD TO ROMANCE, THE(1927), d
John Stuart Robertson
Silents
LITTLE MISS HOOVER(1918), d
Misc. Silents
MAKE-BELIEVE WIFE, THE(1918), d
Joseph F. Robertson
CRAWLING HAND, THE(1963), p; SLIME PEOPLE, THE(1963), p; AGENT FOR H.A.R.M.(1966), p
Ken Robertson
NIGHTHAWKS(1978, Brit.); FLASH GORDON(1980)
Kimmy Robertson
LAST AMERICAN VIRGIN, THE(1982)
1984
BAD MANNERS(1984)
Les Robertson
THEY SHOOT HORSES, DON'T THEY?(1969)
Lolita Robertson
Silents
HOOSIER SCHOOLMASTER(1914); TRUTH WAGON, THE(1914); NO MOTHER TO GUIDE HER(1923)
Misc. Silents
MAN ON THE BOX, THE(1914); WHAT'S HIS NAME?(1914); JACK CHANTY(1915)
Malcolm Robertson
LAST WAVE, THE(1978, Aus.)
Margaret Robertson
STREET SCENE(1931); LONG SHADOW, THE(1961, Brit.)
Max Robertson
FOUR DESPERATE MEN(1960, Brit.); FRIENDS AND NEIGHBORS(1963, Brit.)
Mike Robertson
HEARTLAND(1980)

Mrs. Robertson
Silents
COUNTERFEIT(1919)
O. Robertson
Silents
BUCKING THE TRUTH(1926)
Peter Forbes Robertson
11 HARROWHOUSE(1974, Brit.)
R.J. Robertson
FORBIDDEN WORLD(1982), w
Ralph Robertson
BIG BROADCAST, THE(1932); GILDERSLEEVE'S BAD DAY(1943)
Robbie Robertson
CARNY(1980), a, p, w; KING OF COMEDY, THE(1983), m, md
Rochelle Robertson
ROMANTIC COMEDY(1983)
1984
UNTIL SEPTEMBER(1984)
Stuart Robertson
AS YOU LIKE IT(1936, Brit.); MILLIONS(1936, Brit.); PEG OF OLD DRURY(1936, Brit.); SPLINTERS IN THE AIR(1937, Brit.); GANG, THE(1938, Brit.); SIXTY GLORIOUS YEARS(1938, Brit.); IRENE(1940); NO, NO NANETTE(1940); CONFIRM OR DENY(1941); YANK IN THE R.A.F., A(1941); BLACK SWAN, THE(1942); ON THE SUNNY SIDE(1942); FOREVER AND A DAY(1943)
T.W. Robertson
CASTE(1930, Brit.), w
Tim Robertson
CARS THAT ATE PARIS, THE(1974, Aus.); PETERSEN(1974, Aus.); DIMBOOLA(1979, Aus.); CHANT OF JIMMIE BLACKSMITH, THE(1980, Aus.)
Warren Robertson
TWO OF A KIND(1983)
Wilbur Robertson
SATURDAY'S HERO(1951)
Willard Robertson
LAST OF THE DUANES(1930); CITY STREETS(1931); FAIR WARNING(1931); GRAFT(1931); MURDER BY THE CLOCK(1931); RULING VOICE, THE(1931); SHANGHAIED LOVE(1931); SILENCE(1931); SKIPPY(1931); SOOKY(1931); BEHIND THE MASK(1932); BROKEN WING, THE(1932); CALL HER SAVAGE(1932); CENTRAL PARK(1932); DOCTOR X(1932); FAMOUS FERGUSON CASE, THE(1932); GAY CABALLERO, THE(1932); GUILTY AS HELL(1932); I AM A FUGITIVE FROM A CHAIN GANG(1932); IF I HAD A MILLION(1932); OKAY AMERICA(1932); RIDER OF DEATH VALLEY(1932); SILVER DOLLAR(1932); SO BIG(1932); STEADY COMPANY(1932); STRANGE LOVE OF MOLLY LOUVAIN, THE(1932); TEXAS BAD MAN(1932); TOM BROWN OF CULVER(1932); VIRTUE(1932); WILD GIRL(1932); ANOTHER LANGUAGE(1933); CENTRAL AIRPORT(1933); DESTINATION UNKNOWN(1933); EAST OF FIFTH AVE.(1933); EVER IN MY HEART(1933); HEROES FOR SALE(1933); LADY KILLER(1933); MAD GAME, THE(1933); ROMAN SCANDALS(1933); SUPERNATURAL(1933); TRICK FOR TRICK(1933); TUGBOAT ANNIE(1933); WILD BOYS OF THE ROAD(1933); WORLD CHANGES, THE(1933); DARK HAZARD(1934); DEATH OF THE DIAMOND(1934); GAMBLING LADY(1934); HAVE A HEART(1934); HE WAS HER MAN(1934); HEAT LIGHTNING(1934); HERE COMES THE NAVY(1934); HOUSEWIFE(1934); I'LL TELL THE WORLD(1934); LET'S TALK IT OVER(1934); MURDER IN THE PRIVATE CAR(1934); ONE IS GUILTY(1934); OPERATOR 13(1934); TWO ALONE(1934); UPPER WORLD(1934); WHIRLPOOL(1934); BIOGRAPHY OF A BACHELOR GIRL(1935); BLACK FURY(1935); DANTE'S INFERNO(1935); FORCED LANDING(1935); HIS NIGHT OUT(1935); LADDIE(1935); MILLION DOLLAR BABY(1935); MILLS OF THE GODS(1935); OIL FOR THE LAMPS OF CHINA(1935); OLD HOMESTEAD, THE(1935); O'SHAUGHNESSY'S BOY(1935); SECRET BRIDE, THE(1935); STRAIGHT FROM THE HEART(1935); DANGEROUS WATERS(1936); FIRST BABY(1936); GORGEOUS HUSSY, THE(1936); I MARRIED A DOCTOR(1936); LAST OF THE MOHICANS, THE(1936); MAN WHO LIVED TWICE(1936); THREE GODFATHERS(1936); WANTED: JANE TURNER(1936); WINTERSET(1936); EXCLUSIVE(1937); GO-GETTER, THE(1937); HOT WATER(1937); JOHN MEADE'S WOMAN(1937); LARCENY ON THE AIR(1937); LAST GANGSTER, THE(1937); PARK AVENUE LOGGER(1937); ROARING TIMBER(1937); THAT GIRL FROM PARIS(1937); THIS IS MY AFFAIR(1937); GANGS OF NEW YORK(1938); ISLAND IN THE SKY(1938); KENTUCKY(1938); MEN WITH WINGS(1938); TORCHY GETS HER MAN(1938); YOU AND ME(1938); EACH DAWN I DIE(1939); HERITAGE OF THE DESERT(1939); JESSE JAMES(1939); MAIN STREET LAWYER(1939); MY SON IS A CRIMINAL(1939); RANGE WAR(1939); TWO BRIGHT BOYS(1939); UNION PACIFIC(1939); BRIGHAM YOUNG–FRONTIERSMAN(1940); CASTLE ON THE HUDSON(1940); LUCKY CISCO KID(1940); MY LITTLE CHICKADEE(1940); NORTHWEST MOUNTED POLICE(1940); REMEMBER THE NIGHT(1940); I WANTED WINGS(1941); MEN OF THE TIMBERLAND(1941); MONSTER AND THE GIRL, THE(1941); NIGHT OF JANUARY 16th(1941); TEXAS(1941); JUKE GIRL(1942); WAKE ISLAND(1942); AIR FORCE(1943); BACKGROUND TO DANGER(1943); NO TIME FOR LOVE(1943); OX-BOW INCIDENT, THE(1943); NINE GIRLS(1944); ALONG CAME JONES(1945); GALLANT JOURNEY(1946); PERILOUS HOLIDAY(1946); RENEGADES(1946); TO EACH HIS OWN(1946); DEEP VALLEY(1947); MY FAVORITE BRUNETTE(1947); FURY AT FURNACE CREEK(1948); SITTING PRETTY(1948)
Willard Robertson
BIG GAME(1921); MOONTIDE(1942), w
William Robertson
HERO AT LARGE(1980); THOSE LIPS, THOSE EYES(1980)
Misc. Talkies
DARK AUGUST(1975)
Rev. William Preston Robertson
1984
BLOOD SIMPLE(1984)
James Robertson–Justice
FOXHOLE IN CAIRO(1960, Brit.); MYSTERY SUBMARINE(1963, Brit.); MAYERLING(1968, Brit./Fr.); SPIRITS OF THE DEAD(1969, Fr./Ital.); TRYGON FACTOR, THE(1969, Brit.)
Kenneth Robeson
DOC SAVAGE... THE MAN OF BRONZE(1975), w
Paul Robeson
EMPEROR JONES, THE(1933); SANDERS OF THE RIVER(1935, Brit.); SHOW BOAT(1936); BIG FELLA(1937, Brit.); KING SOLOMON'S MINES(1937, Brit.); DARK SANDS(1938, Brit.); SONG OF FREEDOM(1938, Brit.); PROUD VALLEY, THE(1941, Brit.); NATIVE LAND(1942); TALES OF MANHATTAN(1942)

Misc. Silents
BODY AND SOUL(1925)
Stephen Robets
SAMSON AND DELILAH(1949)
Ann Robey
SOMETHING SHORT OF PARADISE(1979)
George Robey
MARRY ME(1932, Brit.); CHU CHIN CHOW(1934, Brit.); BIRDS OF A FEATHER(1935, Brit.); DON QUIXOTE(1935, Fr.); REGAL CAVALCADE(1935, Brit.); CALLING THE TUNE(1936, Brit.); MEN OF YESTERDAY(1936, Brit.); SOUTHERN ROSES(1936, Brit.); GIRL MUST LIVE, A(1941, Brit.); SALUTE JOHN CITIZEN(1942, Brit.); THEY MET IN THE DARK(1945, Brit.); VARIETY JUBILEE(1945, Brit.); HENRY V(1946, Brit.); TROJAN BROTHERS, THE(1946); WALTZ TIME(1946, Brit.); PICKWICK PAPERS, THE(1952, Brit.)
Misc. Talkies
ALI BABA NIGHTS(1953)
Silents
DON QUIXOTE(1923, Brit.); REST CURE, THE(1923, Brit.), a, w; PREHISTORIC MAN, THE(1924, Brit.), a, w
Misc. Silents
ONE ARABIAN NIGHT(1923, Brit.)
Lavelle Robey
LAUGHING POLICEMAN, THE(1973)
Michael Robidoux
1984
KINGS AND DESPERATE MEN(1984, Brit.), m
Earl Robie
MY COUSIN RACHEL(1952); LADY WANTS MINK, THE(1953)
Diane Robillard
PRIME OF MISS JEAN BRODIE, THE(1969, Brit.)
Elizabeth Robillard
DAY IN THE DEATH OF JOE EGG, A(1972, Brit.)
Hayward Robillard
EASY RIDER(1969)
Ann Robin
CALLAWAY WENT THATAWAY(1951); GOODBYE, MY FANCY(1951); I WANT YOU(1951)
Barry Robin
SATURDAY NIGHT FEVER(1977), m
Bernard Robin
DIVA(1982, Fr.)
Bill Robin
SHELL SHOCK(1964)
Dany Robin
MAN ABOUT TOWN(1947, Fr.); GATES OF THE NIGHT(1950, Fr.); JUPITER(1952, Fr.); ACT OF LOVE(1953); HENRIETTE'S HOLIDAY(1953, Fr.); CADET-ROUSSELLE(1954, Fr.); FROU-FROU(1955, Fr.); HOLIDAY FOR HENRIETTA(1955, Fr.); NAPOLEON(1955, Fr.); JULIETTA(1957, Fr.); LOVE AND THE FRENCHWOMAN(1961, Fr.); TALES OF PARIS(1962, Fr./Ital.); WALTZ OF THE TOREADORS(1962, Brit.); FOLLOW THE BOYS(1963); DON'T LOSE YOUR HEAD(1967, Brit.); BEST HOUSE IN LONDON, THE(1969, Brit.); TOPAZ(1969, Brit.)
Diane Robin
DOCTOR DETROIT(1983)
Douglas Robin
HIGH AND DRY(1954, Brit.)
Georges Robin
TOMCAT, THE(1968, Brit.), d, w
Gilbert Robin
FOREIGN INTRIGUE(1956)
Jackie Robin
JACKSON COUNTY JAIL(1976)
Jacques Robin
NIGHT ENCOUNTER(1963, Fr./Ital.), ph; THREE FACES OF SIN(1963, Fr./Ital.), ph; LIFE UPSIDE DOWN(1965, Fr.), ph; KILLING GAME, THE(1968, Fr.), ph; PLAYMATES(1969, Fr./Ital.), ph; PARADISE POUR TOUS(1982, Fr.), ph
Jean-Francois Robin
POURQUOI PAS!(1979, Fr.), ph; LIGHT YEARS AWAY(1982, Fr./Switz.), ph
Jill Robin
LOVE HUNGER(1965, Arg.)
Justin Robin
NEW YEAR'S EVIL(1980)
Leo Robin
EBB TIDE(1937), m; OSCAR, THE(1966), m/l Ralph Rainger
Liliane Robin
BREATHLESS(1959, Fr.)
Mark Robin
WHICH WAY IS UP?(1977)
Michel Robin
CONFESSION, THE(1970, Fr.); INVITATION, THE(1975, Fr./Switz.); MAIN THING IS TO LOVE, THE(1975, Ital./Fr.); VERDICT(1975, Fr./Ital.); DEATH OF MARIO RICCI, THE(1983, Ital.)
Sid Robin
CAMPUS SLEUTH(1948), m; SMART POLITICS(1948), m/l
Sidney Robin
THIS IS THE ARMY(1943)
Sue Robin
YOUTH ON PARADE(1943)
Dale Robinette
GORP(1980); JAZZ SINGER, THE(1980)
Misc. Talkies
BILLION DOLLAR THREAT, THE(1979, Brit.)
Byron Robingson
WOMAN IS THE JUDGE, A(1939), ed
Gabrielle Robinne
RASPUTIN(1939, Fr.); PROSTITUTION(1965, Fr.)
Anthony Robinow
RAINBOW BOYS, THE(1973, Can.), p

John Anthony Robinow
LOST AND FOUND(1979)
Andy Robins
CRY OF THE PENGUINS(1972, Brit.)
Barry Robins
BLESS THE BEASTS AND CHILDREN(1971)
Denise Robins
ROAD TO SINGAPORE(1931), w
Dyane Robins
GNOME-MOBILE, THE(1967)
Edward Robins
LOVE ON TOAST(1937)
Edward H. Robins
EXCLUSIVE(1937); MEET THE MISSUS(1937)
Elliot Robins
WHO SAYS I CAN'T RIDE A RAINBOW!(1971); TRAIN RIDE TO HOL-LYWOOD(1975)
Herb Robins
THRILL KILLERS, THE(1965); THOMASINE AND BUSHROD(1974); FUNHOUSE, THE(1981); WORM EATERS, THE(1981), a, d, w
Jennie Robins
ONE PRECIOUS YEAR(1933, Brit.)
Jessie Robins
KITCHEN, THE(1961, Brit.); FEARLESS VAMPIRE KILLERS, OR PARDON ME BUT YOUR TEETH ARE IN MY NECK, THE(1967); UP THE JUNCTION(1968, Brit.)
John Robins
DEATH SHIP(1980, Can.), w
Misc. Talkies
LOVE THY NEIGHBOUR(1973), d; MAN ABOUT HOUSE(1974, Brit.), d
Oliver Robins
AIRPLANE II: THE SEQUEL(1982); POLTERGEIST(1982)
Phyllis Robins
VARIETY(1935, Brit.); MURDER AT THE CABARET(1936, Brit.); I BECAME A CRIMINAL(1947); SHOWTIME(1948, Brit.)
Rochelle Robins
LUGGAGE OF THE GODS(1983)
Rudy Robins
GREEN BERETS, THE(1968)
Sam Robins
RANGE WAR(1939), w; BLACK DIAMONDS(1940), w; ENEMY AGENT(1940), w; BOWERY BLITZKRIEG(1941), w; LUCKY DEVILS(1941), w; MASKED RIDER, THE(1941), w; SING ANOTHER CHORUS(1941), w; CORPSE VANISHES, THE(1942), w; JUNGLE SIREN(1942), w; LAW AND ORDER(1942), w; MR. WISE GUY(1942), w; LADY FROM CHUNGKING(1943), w
Sheila Robins
BAIT(1950, Brit.); NEVER TAKE CANDY FROM A STRANGER(1961, Brit.)
Skeeter Bill Robins
WILD HORSE(1931)
Toby Robins
GAME FOR THREE LOSERS(1965, Brit.); NAKED RUNNER, THE(1967, Brit.); FRIENDS(1971, Brit.); PAUL AND MICHELLE(1974, Fr./Brit.); FOR YOUR EYES ONLY(1981)
1984
SCANDALOUS(1984)
Ina Robinski
GERMAN SISTERS, THE(1982, Ger.)
Alan Robinson
LOVE IN PAWN(1953, Brit.); THREE STEPS IN THE DARK(1953, Brit.); DOUBLE EXPOSURE(1954, Brit.); DEADLIEST SIN, THE(1956, Brit.); NARROWING CIRCLE, THE(1956, Brit.); HIGH TERRACE(1957, Brit.)
Silents
ACCORDING TO LAW(1916)
Allan Robinson
Silents
IDOL OF THE STAGE, THE(1916)
Amy Robinson
MEAN STREETS(1973); CHILLY SCENES OF WINTER(1982), p; BABY, IT'S YOU(1983), p, w; TASTE OF SIN, A(1983)
Andre Robinson, Jr.
1984
BROTHER FROM ANOTHER PLANET, THE(1984)
Andrew Robinson
THIS COULD BE THE NIGHT(1957); MACKINTOSH & T.J.(1975)
Andy Robinson
DIRTY HARRY(1971); CHARLEY VARRICK(1973); DROWNING POOL, THE(1975)
Misc. Talkies
WOMAN FOR ALL MEN, A(1975)
Angela Robinson
48 HOURS(1982); STING II, THE(1983)
1984
JUNGLE WARRIORS(1984, U.S./Ger./Mex.)
Ann Robinson
GLASS WALL, THE(1953); WAR OF THE WORLDS, THE(1953); BAD FOR EACH OTHER(1954); DRAGNET(1954); GUN BROTHERS(1956); JULIE(1956); GUN DUEL IN DURANGO(1957); DAMN CITIZEN(1958)
Armin Robinson
FORBIDDEN MUSIC(1936, Brit.), w
Arthur Robinson
Misc. Silents
LAST WALTZ, THE(1927, Ger.), d
Bartless Robinson
MARLOWE(1969)
Bartlett Robinson
TOWARD THE UNKNOWN(1956); BATTLE HYMN(1957); SPIRIT OF ST. LOUIS, THE(1957); GIRL IN THE WOODS(1958); I WANT TO LIVE!(1958); NO TIME FOR SERGEANTS(1958); STRANGER IN MY ARMS(1959); WARLOCK(1959); ALL HANDS ON DECK(1961); DISTANT TRUMPET, A(1964); READY FOR THE PEOPLE(1964); WHERE LOVE HAS GONE(1964); BIRDS AND THE BEES, THE(1965); JOY IN THE MORNING(1965); FORTUNE COOKIE, THE(1966); BAMBOO SAUCER, THE(1968); SLEEPER(1973)

Bernard Robinson
YESTERDAY'S ENEMY(1959, Brit.), art d; WHILE I LIVE(1947, Brit.), art d; MYSTERY AT THE BURLESQUE(1950, Brit.), art d; SILK NOOSE, THE(1950, Brit.), art d; TONY DRAWS A HORSE(1951, Brit.), art d; DOUBLE CONFESSION(1953, Brit.), art d; HUNDRED HOUR HUNT(1953, Brit.), art d; SLASHER, THE(1953, Brit.), art d; GOOD DIE YOUNG, THE(1954, Brit.), art d; SEA SHALL NOT HAVE THEM, THE(1955, Brit.), art d; SHIP THAT DIED OF SHAME, THE(1956, Brit.), art d; ENEMY FROM SPACE(1957, Brit.), art d; REACH FOR THE SKY(1957, Brit.), art d; HORROR OF DRACULA, THE(1958, Brit.), art d; REVENGE OF FRANKENSTEIN, THE(1958, Brit.), prod d; SHERIFF OF FRACTURED JAW, THE(1958, Brit.), art d; HOUND OF THE BASKERVILLES, THE(1959, Brit.), art d; MUMMY, THE(1959, Brit.), prod d, art d; UGLY DUCKLING, THE(1959, Brit.), art d; CURSE OF THE WEREWOLF, THE(1961), prod d; NEVER TAKE CANDY FROM A STRANGER(1961, Brit.), art d; PASSPORT TO CHINA(1961, Brit.), art d; SCREAM OF FEAR(1961, Brit.), prod d; SHADOW OF THE CAT, THE(1961, Brit.), prod d; TERROR OF THE TONGS, THE(1961, Brit.), prod d; WATCH IT, SAILOR!(1961, Brit.), art d; NIGHT CREATURES(1962, Brit.), prod d; PHANTOM OF THE OPERA, THE(1962, Brit.), prod d; PIRATES OF BLOOD RIVER, THE(1962, Brit.), prod d; KISS OF EVIL(1963, Brit.), prod d; NIGHTMARE(1963, Brit.), prod d; OLD DARK HOUSE, THE(1963, Brit.), art d; PARANOIAC(1963, Brit.), prod d; CRIMSON BLADE, THE(1964, Brit.), prod d; DEVIL-SHIP PIRATES, THE(1964, Brit.), prod d; GORGON, THE(1964, Brit.), prod d; CURSE OF THE MUMMY'S TOMB, THE(1965, Brit.), prod d; FRANKEN-STEIN CREATED WOMAN(1965, Brit.), prod d; SECRET OF BLOOD ISLAND, THE(1965, Brit.), prod d; THESE ARE THE DAMNED(1965, Brit.), prod d; DRACULA-PRINCE OF DARKNESS(1966, Brit.), prod d; PLAGUE OF THE ZOMBIES, THE(1966, Brit.), prod d; RASPUTIN-THE MAD MONK(1966, Brit.), prod d; REPTILE, THE(1966, Brit.), prod d; DEVIL'S OWN, THE(1967, Brit.), prod d; MUMMY'S SHROUD, THE(1967, Brit.), prod d; DEVIL'S BRIDE, THE(1968, Brit.), art d; DRACULA HAS RISEN FROM HIS GRAVE(1968, Brit.), art d; FIVE MILLION YEARS TO EARTH(1968, Brit.), art d; FRANKENSTEIN MUST BE DESTROYED!(1969, Brit.), art d
Bertram Robinson
SHE'S MY WEAKNESS(1930), w
Bertrand Robinson
LOVE, HONOR, AND OH BABY!(1933), w; YOUR UNCLE DUDLEY(1935), w; LADIES' DAY(1943), w
Betsy Julia Robinson
RETURN OF THE SECAUCUS SEVEN(1980); LIANNA(1983)
Betty Robinson
NAKED KISS, THE(1964)
Bill Robinson
DIXIANA(1930); HARLEM IS HEAVEN(1932); BIG BROADCAST OF 1936, THE(1935); HOORAY FOR LOVE(1935); IN OLD KENTUCKY(1935); LITTLEST REBEL, THE(1935); DIMPLES(1936), ch; ONE MILE FROM HEAVEN(1937); JUST AROUND THE CORNER(1938); REBECCA OF SUNNYBROOK FARM(1938); ROAD DEMON(1938); UP THE RIVER(1938); STORMY WEATHER(1943)
Bill "Bojangles" Robinson
LITTLE COLONEL, THE(1935)
Billy Robinson
WRESTLER, THE(1974)
Bob Robinson
EL DIABLO RIDES(1939); TWO O'CLOCK COURAGE(1945); RUSTLERS(1949)
Bruce Robinson
ROMEO AND JULIET(1968, Brit./Ital.); MUSIC LOVERS, THE(1971, Brit.); PRIVATE ROAD(1971, Brit.); DEVIL'S WIDOW, THE(1972, Brit.); STORY OF ADELE H., THE(1975, Fr.); HARRY'S WAR(1981)
1984
KILLING FIELDS, THE(1984, Brit.), w
Bryon Robinson
BORROWED WIVES(1930), ed; DRAGNET PATROL(1932), ed
Budd Robinson
WHERE DOES IT HURT?(1972), w
Byrd Robinson
MOTOR MADNESS(1937), ed
Byron Robinson
SHANNONS OF BROADWAY, THE(1929), ed; PARADISE ISLAND(1930), ed; SOUL OF THE SLUMS(1931), ed; ALIAS MARY SMITH(1932), ed; BEHIND STONE WALLS(1932), ed; DOCKS OF SAN FRANCISCO(1932), ed; DYNAMITE DEN-NY(1932), ed; GORILLA SHIP, THE(1932), ed; HER MAD NIGHT(1932), ed; MIDNIGHT MORALS(1932), ed; MIDNIGHT WARNING, THE(1932), ed; MONSTER WALKS, THE(1932), ed; NIGHT BEAT(1932), ed; NO LIVING WITNESS(1932), ed; SALLY OF THE SUBWAY(1932), ed; SIN'S PAYDAY(1932), ed; TANGLED DESTINIES(1932), ed; WIDOW IN SCARLET(1932), ed; BIG BLUFF, THE(1933), m; DANCE MALL HOSTESS(1933), ed; EASY MILLIONS(1933), ed; JUSTICE TAKES A HOLIDAY(1933), ed; MALAY NIGHTS(1933), ed; THREE KIDS AND A QUEEN(1935), ed; COME CLOSER, FOLKS(1936), ed; MAN WHO LIVED TWICE(1936), ed; GIRLS CAN PLAY(1937), ed; PAID TO DANCE(1937), ed; SHADOW, THE(1937), ed; WOMAN IN DISTRESS(1937), ed; JUVENILE COURT(1938), ed; WHO KILLED GAIL PRESTON?(1938), ed; ROMANCE OF THE REDWOODS(1939), ed
Silents
ALBANY NIGHT BOAT, THE(1928), ed; ALIAS THE DEACON(1928), ed; LINGER-IE(1928), ed
Cardew Robinson
FUN AT ST. FANNY'S(1956, Brit.); HAPPY IS THE BRIDE(1958, Brit.); I'M ALL RIGHT, JACK(1959, Brit.); NAVY LARK, THE(1959, Brit.); FRENCH MISTRESS(1960, Brit.); LET'S GET MARRIED(1960, Brit.); LIGHT UP THE SKY(1960, Brit.); THREE ON A SPREE(1961, Brit.); WALTZ OF THE TOREADORS(1962, Brit.); HEAVENS ABOVE!(1963, Brit.); FATHER CAME TOO(1964, Brit.); GO KART GO(1964, Brit.); HIDE AND SEEK(1964, Brit.); LADIES WHO DO(1964, Brit.); TIME LOST AND TIME REMEMBERED(1966, Brit.); SMASHING TIME(1967 Brit.); THREE BITES OF THE APPLE(1967); CARRY ON, UP THE KHYBER(1968, Brit.); WHERE'S JACK?(1969, Brit.); HOVERBUG(1970, Brit.)
Casey Robinson
LAST PARADE, THE(1931), w; IS MY FACE RED?(1932), w; RENEGADES OF THE WEST(1932), d; GOLDEN HARVEST(1933), w; I LOVE THAT MAN(1933), w; LUCKY DEVILS(1933), w; SONG OF THE EAGLE(1933), w; STRICTLY PERSONAL(1933), w; EIGHT GIRLS IN A BOAT(1934), w; HERE COMES THE GROOM(1934), w; SHE MADE HER BED(1934), w; CAPTAIN BLOOD(1935), w; I FOUND STELLA PARISH(1935), w; GIVE ME YOUR HEART(1936), w; HEARTS DIVIDED(1936), w; I MARRIED A DOCTOR(1936), w; CALL IT A DAY(1937), w; IT'S LOVE I'M AFT-

ER(1937), w; STOLEN HOLIDAY(1937), w; TOVARICH(1937), w; FOUR'S A CROWD(1938), w; DARK VICTORY(1939), w; OLD MAID, THE(1939), w; YES, MY DARLING DAUGHTER(1939), w; ALL THIS AND HEAVEN TOO(1940), w; MILLION DOLLAR BABY(1941), w; ONE FOOT IN HEAVEN(1941), w; KING'S ROW(1942), w; NOW, VOYAGER(1942), w; THIS IS THE ARMY(1943), w; DAYS OF GLORY(1944), p, w; PASSAGE TO MARSEILLE(1944), w; RACKET MAN, THE(1944), w; CORN IS GREEN, THE(1945), w; SARATOGA TRUNK(1945), w; DESIRE ME(1947), w; MACOMBER AFFAIR, THE(1947), p, w; MATING OF MILLIE, THE(1948), p; FATHER WAS A FULLBACK(1949), w; TWO FLAGS WEST(1950), p, w; UNDER MY SKIN(1950), p, w; DIPLOMATIC COURIER(1952), p, w; BULLET IS WAITING, A(1954), w; EGYPTIAN. THE(1954), w; WHILE THE CITY SLEEPS(1956), w; THIS EARTH IS MINE(1959), p, w; SON OF CAPTAIN BLOOD, THE(1964, U.S./Ital./Span.), w; SCOBIE MALONE(1975, Aus.), p, w

Silents
DO YOUR DUTY(1928), t; HEAD OF THE FAMILY, THE(1928), t

Celeste Robinson
LOST LAGOON(1958)

Charles Knox Robinson
DARING DOBERMANS, THE(1973)

Misc. Talkies
PSYCHO SISTERS(1972)

Charles P. Robinson
BLACK GESTAPO, THE(1975)

Charles Robinson
LADY BE CAREFUL(1936), w; SWING YOUR LADY(1938), w; FLEET'S IN, THE(1942), w; FOLLIES GIRL(1943), w; SPLENDOR IN THE GRASS(1961); INTERNS, THE(1962); TAKE HER, SHE'S MINE(1963); DEAR BRIGETTE(1965); SHENANDOAH(1965); SAND PEBBLES, THE(1966); SINGING NUN, THE(1966); FOR SINGLES ONLY(1968); TIME TO SING, A(1968); BROTHERHOOD OF SATAN, THE(1971); DRIVE, HE SAID(1971); SUGAR HILL(1974)

Misc. Talkies
BRIDGE IN THE JUNGLE, THE(1971); TRIANGLE(1971)

Charlie Robinson
50,000 B.C.(BEFORE CLOTHING)* (1963); GRAY LADY DOWN(1978)
1984
RIVER, THE(1984)

Cheryl Robinson
RICH AND FAMOUS(1981)

Chris Robinson
DIARY OF A HIGH SCHOOL BRIDE(1959); BECAUSE THEY'RE YOUNG(1960); LIKE FATHER LIKE SON(1961); LONG ROPE, THE(1961); YOUNG SAVAGES, THE(1961); BIRDMAN OF ALCATRAZ(1962); SHOOT OUT AT BIG SAG(1962); THIRTEEN WEST STREET(1962); YOUNG SINNER, THE(1965); SEVEN AGAINST THE SUN(1968, South Africa); CYCLE SAVAGES(1969); DARKER THAN AMBER(1970); HAWAIIANS, THE(1970); STANLEY(1973); AMY(1981); YOUNG DOCTORS IN LOVE(1982); SAVANNAH SMILES(1983)

Misc. Talkies
REVENGE IS MY DESTINY(1971); SUNSHINE RUN(1979), d

Clarence Robinson
STORMY WEATHER(1943), ch

Clark Robinson
LUCKY IN LOVE(1929), set d; MOTHER'S BOY(1929), set d
Silents
MAN WHO PLAYED GOD, THE(1922), art d; RULING PASSION, THE(1922), art d; REJECTED WOMAN, THE(1924), art d; SECOND YOUTH(1924), art d

Claudia Robinson
COUNTRYMAN(1982, Jamaica)
1984
HARRY AND SON(1984)

Clifford Robinson
1984
PASSAGE TO INDIA, A(1984, Brit.), art d

Clinton Robinson
HOW DO I LOVE THEE?(1970)

Connie Robinson
RACHEL, RACHEL(1968)

Cyril "Chips" Robinson
COOL HAND LUKE(1967)

Daisy Robinson
BITTER TEA OF GENERAL YEN, THE(1933)
Silents
COUNTY CHAIRMAN, THE(1914); CLEVER MRS. CARFAX, THE(1917); WHEN THE CLOUDS ROLL BY(1920); PARTNERS OF THE TIDE(1921); RIP VAN WINKLE(1921); DON'T GET PERSONAL(1922)
Misc. Silents
HAPPINESS OF THREE WOMEN, THE(1917); WORLD OF FOLLY, A(1920)

Dale Robinson
Z.P.G.(1972)

Dar Robinson
PAPILLON(1973); DOC SAVAGE... THE MAN OF BRONZE(1975); ROLLERBALL(1975); ST. IVES(1976); STUNTS(1977); NIGHTHAWKS(1981)

David Robinson
MONSOON(1953), w; DAMN THE DEFIANT!(1962, Brit.); REVENGE OF THE CHEERLEADERS(1976); MEPHISTO(1981, Ger.)

Dennis Robinson
SILENCE OF THE NORTH(1981, Can.)

Dewey Robinson
ENEMIES OF THE LAW(1931); BIG BROADCAST, THE(1932); BLONDE VENUS(1932); CHEATERS AT PLAY(1932); HAT CHECK GIRL(1932); IF I HAD A MILLION(1932); LAW AND ORDER(1932); ONE WAY PASSAGE(1932); PAINTED WOMAN(1932); SCARLET DAWN(1932); SIX HOURS TO LIVE(1932); WOMAN FROM MONTE CARLO, THE(1932); DEVIL'S IN LOVE, THE(1933); DIPLOMANIACS(1933); HER FORGOTTEN PAST(1933); HEROES FOR SALE(1933); LADY KILLER(1933); LADY'S PROFESSION, A(1933); LAUGHING AT LIFE(1933); LAWYER MAN(1933); LITTLE GIANT, THE(1933); SHE DONE HIM WRONG(1933); SOLDIERS OF THE STORM(1933); WOMEN WON'T TELL(1933); BIG SHAKEDOWN, THE(1934); CAT'S PAW, THE(1934); GEORGE WHITE'S SCANDALS(1934); MERRY WIDOW, THE(1934); MURDER ON THE CAMPUS(1934); NOTORIOUS BUT NICE(1934); SHADOWS OF SING SING(1934); STUDENT TOUR(1934); BEHOLD MY WIFE(1935); GOIN' TO TOWN(1935); HIS NIGHT OUT(1935); MIDSUMMER'S NIGHT'S DREAM, A(1935);

PURSUIT(1935); TOO TOUGH TO KILL(1935); ALL-AMERICAN CHUMP(1936); DANGEROUS WATERS(1936); FLORIDA SPECIAL(1936); LOVE ON THE RUN(1936); MISSING GIRLS(1936); POPPY(1936); RETURN OF JIMMY VALENTINE, THE(1936); MARRY THE GIRL(1937); NEW FACES OF 1937(1937); SLAVE SHIP(1937); SUPER SLEUTH(1937); TOAST OF NEW YORK, THE(1937); WHEN YOU'RE IN LOVE(1937); ARMY GIRL(1938); BROADWAY MUSKETEERS(1938); MAMA RUNS WILD(1938); PROFESSOR BEWARE(1938); RIDE A CROOKED MILE(1938); FORGED PASSPORT(1939); NAVY SECRETS(1939); $1,000 A TOUCHDOWN(1939); CHRISTMAS IN JULY(1940); DANCE, GIRL, DANCE(1940); DIAMOND FRONTIER(1940); GREAT McGINTY, THE(1940); I CAN'T GIVE YOU ANYTHING BUT LOVE, BABY(1940); RANGERS OF FORTUNE(1940); SKY BANDITS, THE(1940); STRANGE CARGO(1940); THREE FACES WEST(1940); TIN PAN ALLEY(1940); COME LIVE WITH ME(1941); GIRL, A GUY AND A GOB, A(1941); LADY FOR A NIGHT(1941); SING FOR YOUR SUPPER(1941); SULLIVAN'S TRAVELS(1941); ISLE OF MISSING MEN(1942); JAIL HOUSE BLUES(1942); JUKE GIRL(1942); 'NEATH BROOKLYN BRIDGE(1942); PALM BEACH STORY, THE(1942); RUBBER RACKETEERS(1942); TALES OF MANHATTAN(1942); TALK OF THE TOWN(1942); TREAT 'EM' ROUGH(1942); TWO YANKS IN TRINIDAD(1942); GHOST SHIP, THE(1943); SEVENTH VICTIM, THE(1943); ALASKA(1944); CHINESE CAT, THE(1944); HAIL THE CONQUERING HERO(1944); TIMBER QUEEN(1944); TROCADERO(1944); WHEN STRANGERS MARRY(1944); WILSON(1944); DILLINGER(1945); FASHION MODEL(1945); GREAT JOHN L. THE(1945); HOLLYWOOD AND VINE(1945); INCENDIARY BLONDE(1945); LADY CONFESSES, THE(1945); MURDER, MY SWEET(1945); PARDON MY PAST(1945); SCARLET STREET(1945); THERE GOES KELLY(1945); THOSE ENDEARING YOUNG CHARMS(1945); BEHIND THE MASK(1946); BLACK MARKET BABIES(1946); FEAR(1946); IDEA GIRL(1946); MIGHTY MCGURK, THE(1946); MISSING LADY, THE(1946); MR. HEX(1946); SLIGHTLY SCANDALOUS(1946); SUSPENSE(1946); TWO SISTERS FROM BOSTON(1946); DISHONORED LADY(1947); FIESTA(1947); GANGSTER, THE(1947); I WONDER WHO'S KISSING HER NOW(1947); STALLION ROAD(1947); WISTFUL WIDOW OF WAGON GAP, THE(1947); CHECKERED COAT, THE(1948); FIGHTING MAD(1948); I WALK ALONE(1948); LET'S LIVE AGAIN(1948); RIVER LADY(1948); TEXAS, BROOKLYN AND HEAVEN(1948); BEAUTIFUL BLONDE FROM BASHFUL BEND, THE(1949); HELLFIRE(1949); MA AND PA KETTLE(1949); NEPTUNE'S DAUGHTER(1949); TENSION(1949); TOUGH ASSIGNMENT(1949); AT WAR WITH THE ARMY(1950); BUCCANEER'S GIRL(1950); DALLAS(1950); DARK CITY(1950); FATHER OF THE BRIDE(1950); MAD WEDNESDAY(1950); PAID IN FULL(1950); RIGHT CROSS(1950); STORM WARNING(1950); ROADBLOCK(1951); SKIPALONG ROSENBLOOM(1951); REDHEAD FROM MANHATTAN(1954)

Dick Robinson
Misc. Talkies
BROTHER OF THE WIND(1972), d; MOUNTAIN CHARLIE(1982); ROGUE AND GRIZZLY, THE(1982)

Dorothy Robinson
MONEY MEANS NOTHING(1932, Brit.); TROUBLE(1933, Brit.); NELL GWYN(1935, Brit.); PEG OF OLD DRURY(1936, Brit.)

Doug Robinson
OUTLAND(1981)

Douglas Robinson
PORT OF ESCAPE(1955, Brit.); PICCADILLY THIRD STOP(1960, Brit.); FRIGHTENED CITY, THE(1961, Brit.); GIRL HUNTERS, THE(1963, Brit.), ch; JASON AND THE ARGONAUTS(1963, Brit.); DAYLIGHT ROBBERY(1964, Brit.); MODEL MURDER CASE, THE(1964, Brit.); MACKINTOSH MAN, THE(1973, Brit.)

Durwyn Robinson
MANDINGO(1975)

E.H. Robinson
WINGS IN THE DARK(1935), w

E.R. Robinson
FLESH AND FANTASY(1943), set d; SHADOW OF A DOUBT(1943), set d; BLACK ANGEL(1946), set d; KILLERS, THE(1946), set d; NIGHT IN PARADISE, A(1946), set d

Earl Robinson
AIR CIRCUS, THE(1928)

Ed Robinson
SWEET CHARITY(1969)

Edward G. Robinson
TWO WEEKS IN ANOTHER TOWN(1962); HOLE IN THE WALL(1929); EAST IS WEST(1930); LADY TO LOVE, A(1930); NIGHT RIDE(1930); OUTSIDE THE LAW(1930); WIDOW FROM CHICAGO, THE(1930); FIVE STAR FINAL(1931); LITTLE CAESAR(1931); SMART MONEY(1931); HATCHET MAN, THE(1932); SILVER DOLLAR(1932); TIGER SHARK(1932); TWO SECONDS(1932); I LOVED A WOMAN(1933); LITTLE GIANT, THE(1933); DARK HAZARD(1934); MAN WITH TWO FACES, THE(1934); BARBARY COAST(1935); WHOLE TOWN'S TALKING, THE(1935); BULLETS OR BALLOTS(1936); KID GALAHAD(1937); LAST GANGSTER, THE(1937); THUNDER IN THE CITY(1937, Brit.); AMAZING DR. CLITTERHOUSE, THE(1938); I AM THE LAW(1938); SLIGHT CASE OF MURDER, A(1938); BLACKMAIL(1939); CONFESSIONS OF A NAZI SPY(1939); BROTHER ORCHID(1940); DISPATCH FROM REUTERS, A(1940); DR. EHRLICH'S MAGIC BULLET(1940); MANPOWER(1941); SEA WOLF, THE(1941); UNHOLY PARTNERS(1941); LARCENY, INC.(1942); TALES OF MANHATTAN(1942); DESTROYER(1943); FLESH AND FANTASY(1943); DOUBLE INDEMNITY(1944); MR. WINKLE GOES TO WAR(1944); TAMPICO(1944); OUR VINES HAVE TENDER GRAPES(1945); SCARLET STREET(1945); WOMAN IN THE WINDOW, THE(1945); JOURNEY TOGETHER(1946, Brit.); STRANGER THE(1946); RED HOUSE, THE(1947); ALL MY SONS(1948); KEY LARGO(1948); NIGHT HAS A THOUSAND EYES(1948); HOUSE OF STRANGERS(1949); IT'S A GREAT FEELING(1949); OPERATION X(1951, Brit.); ACTORS AND SIN(1952); BIG LEAGUER(1953); GLASS WEB, THE(1953); VICE SQUAD(1953); BLACK TUESDAY(1955); BULLET FOR JOEY, A(1955); ILLEGAL(1955); TIGHT SPOT(1955); VIOLENT MEN, THE(1955); HELL ON FRISCO BAY(1956); NIGHTMARE(1956); TEN COMMANDMENTS, THE(1956); HOLE IN THE HEAD, A(1959); PEPE(1960); SEVEN THIEVES(1960); MY GEISHA(1962); PRIZE, THE(1963); CHEYENNE AUTUMN(1964); GOOD NEIGHBOR SAM(1964); OUTRAGE, THE(1964); ROBIN AND THE SEVEN HOODS(1964); BOY TEN FEET TALL, A(1965, Brit.); CINCINNATI KID, THE(1965); BIGGEST BUNDLE OF THEM ALL, THE(1968); BLONDE FROM PEKING, THE(1968, Fr.); GRAND SLAM(1968, Ital., Span., Ger.); NEVER A DULL MOMENT(1968); OPERATION ST. PETER'S(1968, Ital.); MACKENNA'S GOLD(1969); SONG OF NORWAY(1970); NEITHER BY DAY NOR BY NIGHT(1972, U.S./Israel); SOYLENT GREEN(1973)

Silents
ARMS AND THE WOMAN(1916)
Misc. Silents
BRIGHT SHAWL, THE(1923)
Edward G. Robinson, Jr.
INVASION U.S.A.(1952); SCREAMING EAGLES(1956); TANK BATTALION(1958); SOME LIKE IT HOT(1959)
Edward R. Robinson
SPOILERS, THE(1942), set d; SLAVE GIRL(1947), set d
Edward Ray Robinson
SPIRIT OF WEST POINT, THE(1947), set d
Edward Stoney Robinson
STONY ISLAND(1978)
Edwin G. Robinson
KIBITZER, THE(1929), w
Eric Robinson
THINGS HAPPEN AT NIGHT(1948, Brit.); COLONEL MARCH INVESTIGATES(1952,Brit.), md; LIMPING MAN, THE(1953, Brit.), m
Ermer Robinson
HARLEM GLOBETROTTERS, THE(1951)
Ernest Robinson
SUDDEN TERROR(1970, Brit.), ph; DIRTY HARRY(1971); WHAT'S UP, DOC?(1972)
1984
LOVELINES(1984)
Ernie Robinson
LADY SINGS THE BLUES(1972); SPOOK WHO SAT BY THE DOOR, THE(1973)
Forrest Robinson
Silents
DAWN OF A TOMORROW, THE(1915); LITTLE MISS HOOVER(1918); TOL'ABLE DAVID(1921); TESS OF THE STORM COUNTRY(1922); ADAM'S RIB(1923); ASHES OF VENGEANCE(1923); SOULS FOR SALE(1923)
Misc. Silents
FIFTH COMMANDMENT, THE(1915); FROM TWO TO SIX(1918); HIDDEN TRUTH, THE(1919); GOOD BAD BOY(1924)
Fran Robinson
1984
MASS APPEAL(1984)
Frances Robinson
MILLIONS IN THE AIR(1935); GIRL WITH IDEAS, A(1937); EXPOSED(1938); FORBIDDEN VALLEY(1938); HIS EXCITING NIGHT(1938); LAST WARNING, THE(1938); LETTER OF INTRODUCTION(1938); PERSONAL SECRETARY(1938); SECRETS OF A NURSE(1938); SERVICE DE LUXE(1938); STRANGE FACES(1938); FAMILY NEXT DOOR, THE(1939); HERO FOR A DAY(1939); I STOLE A MILLION(1939); LITTLE ACCIDENT(1939); RISKY BUSINESS(1939); SOCIETY SMUGGLERS(1939); TOWER OF LONDON(1939); WHEN TOMORROW COMES(1939); GLAMOUR FOR SALE(1940); INVISIBLE MAN RETURNS, THE(1940); LONE WOLF KEEPS A DATE, THE(1940); RIDERS OF PASCO BASIN(1940); SO YOU WON'T TALK(1940); DR. JEKYLL AND MR. HYDE(1941); OUTLAWS OF THE PANHANDLE(1941); SMILIN' THROUGH(1941); LADY IN THE DARK(1944); KEEPER OF THE BEES(1947); SUDDENLY IT'S SPRING(1947); I, JANE DOE(1948); BACKFIRE(1950); BEDTIME STORY(1964); KITTEN WITH A WHIP(1964); LIVELY SET, THE(1964); HAPPIEST MILLIONAIRE, THE(1967)
Francis Robinson
DESPERATE TRAILS(1939)
Frank M. Robinson
POWER, THE(1968), w; TOWERING INFERNO, THE(1974), w
Frank Robinson
PROMISES IN THE DARK(1979)
Frank "Sugarchile" Robinson
NO LEAVE, NO LOVE(1946)
Fred Robinson
INN FOR TROUBLE(1960, Brit.), a, w
Gail Robinson
THUNDER OVER THE PLAINS(1953); SEA CHASE, THE(1955)
Gareth Robinson
SEVENTY DEADLY PILLS(1964, Brit.); I'VE GOTTA HORSE(1965, Brit.); TO SIR, WITH LOVE(1967, Brit.); HERE WE GO ROUND THE MULBERRY BUSH(1968, Brit.)
George Robinson
CHARLATAN, THE(1929), ph; COLLEGE LOVE(1929), ph; HELL'S HEROES(1930), ph; EAST OF BORNEO(1931), ph; HOMICIDE SQUAD(1931), ph; SPIRIT OF NOTRE DAME, THE(1931), ph; ALL-AMERICAN, THE(1932), ph; ONCE IN A LIFETIME(1932), ph; RACING YOUTH(1932), ph; HER FIRST MATE(1933), ph; HORSEPLAY(1933), ph; LOVE, HONOR, AND OH BABY!(1933), ph; NAGANA(1933), ph; CHEATING CHEATERS(1934), ph; CROSS COUNTRY CRUISE(1934), ph; DESIGNING WOMEN(1934, Brit.), w; GIFT OF GAB(1934), ph; GLAMOUR(1934), ph; GREAT EXPECTATIONS(1934), ph; HALF A SINNER(1934), ph; I GIVE MY LOVE(1934), ph; MILLION DOLLAR RANSOM(1934), ph; CHINATOWN SQUAD(1935), ph; DIAMOND JIM(1935), ph; IT HAPPENED IN NEW YORK(1935), ph; MR. DYNAMITE(1935), ph; MYSTERY OF EDWIN DROOD, THE(1935), ph; STRANGE WIVES(1935), ph; THREE KIDS AND A QUEEN(1935), ph; DRACULA'S DAUGHTER(1936), ph; EASY TO TAKE(1936), ph; PAROLE(1936), ph; POSTAL INSPECTOR(1936), ph; SUTTER'S GOLD(1936), ph; THE INVISIBLE RAY(1936), ph; CARNIVAL QUEEN(1937), ph; MAN IN BLUE, THE(1937), ph; MAN WHO CRIED WOLF, THE(1937), ph; NIGHT KEY(1937), ph; PLAINSMAN, THE(1937), ph; REPORTED MISSING(1937), ph; ROAD BACK,THE(1937), ph; SOME BLONDES ARE DANGEROUS(1937), ph; WHEN'S YOUR BIRTHDAY?(1937), ph; GOODBYE BROADWAY(1938), ph; LITTLE TOUGH GUYS IN SOCIETY(1938), ph; ROAD TO RENO, THE(1938), ph; SERVICE DE LUXE(1938), ph; SINNERS IN PARADISE(1938), ph; WIVES UNDER SUSPICION(1938), ph; YOUNG FUGITIVES(1938), ph; CHARLIE MC CARTHY, DETECTIVE(1939), ph; EAST SIDE OF HEAVEN(1939), ph; SON OF FRANKENSTEIN(1939), ph; SUN NEVER SETS, THE(1939), ph; TOWER OF LONDON(1939), ph; UNEXPECTED FATHER(1939), ph; IF I HAD MY WAY(1940), ph; SON OF MONTE CRISTO(1940), ph; BEHIND THE EIGHT BALL(1942), ph; DRUMS OF THE CONGO(1942), ph; FALCON TAKES OVER, THE(1942), ph; GIVE OUT, SISTERS(1942), ph; GREAT IMPERSONATION, THE(1942), ph; MADAME SPY(1942), ph; MUMMY'S TOMB, THE(1942), ph; SIN TOWN(1942), ph; TOP SERGEANT(1942), ph; TREAT EM' ROUGH(1942), ph; ALLERGIC TO LOVE(1943), ph; CAPTIVE WILD WOMAN(1943), ph; EYES OF THE UNDERWORLD(1943), ph; FRANKENSTEIN MEETS THE WOLF MAN(1943), ph; GET GOING(1943), ph; IT COMES UP LOVE(1943), ph; MR. BIG(1943), ph; RHYTHM OF THE ISLANDS(1943), ph; SON OF DRACULA(1943), ph; WHEN JOHNNY COMES MARCHING HOME(1943), ph; ALI BABA AND THE FORTY THIEVES(1944), ph; COBRA WOMAN(1944), ph; DESTINY(1944), ph; GYPSY WILDCAT(1944), ph; HOUSE OF FRANKENSTEIN(1944), ph; MURDER IN THE BLUE ROOM(1944), ph; SCARLET CLAW, THE(1944), ph; FRONTIER GAL(1945), ph; HERE COME THE CO-EDS(1945), ph; HOUSE OF DRACULA(1945), ph; NAUGHTY NINETIES, THE(1945), ph; SUDAN(1945), ph; CAT CREEPS, THE(1946), ph; IDEA GIRL(1946), ph; RUNAROUND, THE(1946), ph; SHE WROTE THE BOOK(1946), ph; SLIGHTLY SCANDALOUS(1946), ph; HEADING FOR HEAVEN(1947), ph; LINDA BE GOOD(1947), ph; SLAVE GIRL(1947), ph; CHALLENGE, THE(1948), ph; CREEPER, THE(1948), ph; OPEN SECRET(1948), ph; THIRTEEN LEAD SOLDIERS(1948), ph; VICIOUS CIRCLE, THE(1948), ph; WALK A CROOKED MILE(1948), ph; FREE FOR ALL(1949), ph; ABBOTT AND COSTELLO IN THE FOREIGN LEGION(1950), ph; ABBOTT AND COSTELLO MEET THE INVISIBLE MAN(1951), ph; COMIN' ROUND THE MOUNTAIN(1951), ph; TALES OF ROBIN HOOD(1951), ph; JACK AND THE BEANSTALK(1952), ph; LOST IN ALASKA(1952), ph; MA AND PA KETTLE ON VACATION(1953), ph; ABBOTT AND COSTELLO MEET DR. JEKYLL AND MR. HYDE(1954), ph; BLACK HORSE CANYON(1954), ph; DESTRY(1954), ph; RICOCHET ROMANCE(1954), ph; YELLOW MOUNTAIN, THE(1954), ph; ABBOTT AND COSTELLO MEET THE MUMMY(1955), ph; SQUARE JUNGLE, THE(1955), ph; TARANTULA(1955), ph; DANCE WITH ME, HENRY(1956), ph; FRANCIS IN THE HAUNTED HOUSE(1956), ph; KETTLES IN THE OZARKS, THE(1956), ph; ROCK, PRETTY BABY(1956), ph; TOY TIGER(1956), ph; GUN FOR A COWARD(1957), ph; JOE DAKOTA(1957), ph; NIGHT RUNNER, THE(1957), ph
Silents
STEELHEART(1921), ph; WHERE MEN ARE MEN(1921), ph; SILENT VOW, THE(1922), ph; PLAYING IT WILD(1923), ph; TIE THAT BINDS, THE(1923), ph; PHYLLIS OF THE FOLLIES(1928), ph; STOP THAT MAN(1928), ph; HARVEST OF HATE, THE(1929), ph; HOOFBEATS OF VENGEANCE(1929), ph; PLUNGING HOOFS(1929), ph; WILD BLOOD(1929), ph
George H. Robinson
YOU'RE A SWEETHEART(1937), ph
George S. Robinson
KING SOLOMON OF BROADWAY(1935), ph
Gertrude Robinson
Silents
CLASSMATES(1914); JUDITH OF BETHULIA(1914); ARAB, THE(1915); MAY BLOSSOM(1915); AS A WOMAN SOWS(1916); ON THIN ICE(1925)
Misc. Silents
CONCEALED TRUTH, THE(1915); HAUNTED MANOR, THE(1916); QUALITY OF FAITH, THE(1916); WOMAN OF IMPULSE, A(1918); MILESTONES(1920)
Gisela Leif Robinson
ROYAL DEMAND, A(1933, Brit.)
Glen Robinson
BAMBOO SAUCER, THE(1968), spec eff; BATTLE OF BRITAIN, THE(1969, Brit.), spec eff; EARTHQUAKE(1974), spec eff; HURRICANE(1979), spec eff; METEOR(1979), spec eff; AMITYVILLE II: THE POSSESSION(1982), spec eff; DEAD MEN DON'T WEAR PLAID(1982), spec eff
Glenn Robinson
ISLAND CLAWS(1981), spec eff
Gordon Robinson
FIRST MEN IN THE MOON(1964, Brit.)
Gus Robinson
TOMORROW AT SEVEN(1933)
Hank Robinson
LAS VEGAS LADY(1976); NEW YORK, NEW YORK(1977); WHICH WAY IS UP?(1977)
Harry Robinson
FILE OF THE GOLDEN GOOSE, THE(1969, Brit.), m; OBLONG BOX, THE(1969, Brit.), m; VAMPIRE LOVERS, THE(1970, Brit.), m; FRIGHT(1971, Brit.), m; LUST FOR A VAMPIRE(1971, Brit.), m; TWINS OF EVIL(1971, Brit.), m; DEMONS OF THE MIND(1972, Brit.), m; GHOUL, THE(1975, Brit.), m; THERE GOES THE BRIDE(1980, Brit.), m
Misc. Silents
HUNS WIHIN OUR GATES(1918)
Helen Robinson
OF HUMAN BONDAGE(1964, Brit.)
Silents
AMAZONS, THE(1917)
Henry Ford Robinson
ZAPPED!(1982)
Henry Morton Robinson
CARDINAL, THE(1963), w
Henry Robinson
LOOKIN' TO GET OUT(1982)
Hugh Robinson
SEVENTH DAWN, THE(1964)
J. Casey Robinson
SQUEALER, THE(1930), w
Jack A. Robinson
TARZAN'S DEADLY SILENCE(1970), w
Jackie Robinson
JACKIE ROBINSON STORY, THE(1950)
Jacques Robinson
SHOCK TREATMENT(1973, Fr.), ph
James Robinson
PENROD AND SAM(1931); MRS. WIGGS OF THE CABBAGE PATCH(1934); LONG SHOT, THE(1939); SOUTH OF SUEZ(1940); DEMONS OF LUDLOW, THE(1983)
Misc. Silents
TENDERFEET(1928)
James "Hambone" Robinson
BECKY SHARP(1935); ON PROBATION(1935)
Jane Robinson
PEPE(1960); TELEFON(1977), cos; MOONLIGHTING(1982, Brit.), cos; BETRAYAL(1983, Brit.), cos
1984
SECRET PLACES(1984, Brit.), cos; 1919(1984, Brit.), cos

Jay Robinson
ROBE, THE(1953); DEMETRIUS AND THE GLADIATORS(1954); VIRGIN QUEEN, THE(1955); WILD PARTY, THE(1956); MY MAN GODFREY(1957); TELL ME IN THE SUNLIGHT(1967); BUNNY O'HARE(1971); EVERYTHING YOU ALWAYS WANTED TO KNOW ABOUT SEX, BUT WE'RE AFRAID TO ASK(1972); THIS IS A HI-JACK(1973); THREE THE HARD WAY(1974); SHAMPOO(1975); TRAIN RIDE TO HOLLYWOOD(1975); BORN AGAIN(1978); MAN WITH BOGART'S FACE, THE(1980); PARTNERS(1982); SWORD AND THE SORCERER, THE(1982)

Jerome C. Robinson
IRON SHERIFF, THE(1957), p

Jimmy Robinson
PHANTOM GOLD(1938)

Jo Ann Robinson
SCALPS(1983)

Jo-Ann Robinson
CROSS AND THE SWITCHBLADE, THE(1970)

Joe Robinson
KID FOR TWO FARTHINGS, A(1956, Brit.); FIGHTING MAD(1957, Brit.); FLESH IS WEAK, THE(1957, Brit.); FEMALE FIENDS(1958, Brit.); MURDER REPORTED(1958, Brit.); ACTION STATIONS(1959, Brit.); SEA FURY(1959, Brit.); BULLDOG BREED, THE(1960, Brit.); HOUSE OF FRIGHT(1961); BARABBAS(1962, Ital.); LONELINESS OF THE LONG DISTANCE RUNNER, THE(1962, Brit.); DOCTOR IN DISTRESS(1963, Brit.); ERIK THE CONQUEROR(1963, Fr./Ital.); DIAMONDS ARE FOREVER(1971, Brit.)
Misc. Talkies
TAUR THE MIGHTY(1960); THOR AND THE AMAZON WOMEN(1960)

Joel Robinson
FULLER BRUSH GIRL, THE(1950); TWO TICKETS TO BROADWAY(1951)

Joet Robinson
UP IN ARMS(1944)

Joette Robinson
LADY OF BURLESQUE(1943)

John Robinson
ALL THAT GLITTERS(1936, Brit.); HEIRLOOM MYSTERY, THE(1936, Brit.); SCARAB MURDER CASE, THE(1936, Brit.); FAREWELL TO CINDERELLA(1937, Brit.); LION HAS WINGS, THE(1940, Brit.); STORY OF SHIRLEY YORKE, THE(1948, Brit.); UNEASY TERMS(1948, Brit.); HAMMER THE TOFF(1952, Brit.); GHOST SHIP(1953, Brit.); HUNDRED HOUR HUNT(1953, Brit.); CONSTANT HUSBAND, THE(1955, Brit.); SHARKFIGHTERS, THE(1956), w; MIDNIGHT STORY, THE(1957), w; SHE PLAYED WITH FIRE(1957, Brit.); DOCTOR'S DILEMMA, THE(1958, Brit.); SAFE-CRACKER, THE(1958, Brit.); AND THE SAME TO YOU(1960, Brit.); LONGEST DAY, THE(1962); CORPSE GRINDERS, THE(1972), prod d; NOTHING BUT THE NIGHT(1975, Brit.)

John M. Robinson
BRIGHT VICTORY(1951)

John Mark Robinson
1984
ROADHOUSE 66(1984), d

Johnjohn Robinson
PUTNEY SWOPE(1969)

Jonathan Robinson
APPRENTICESHIP OF DUDDY KRAVITZ, THE(1974, Can.)

Judy Robinson
HOUSE OF WHIPCORD(1974, Brit.); INTERNECINE PROJECT, THE(1974, Brit.)

Julia Robinson
FAN'S NOTES, A(1972, Can.)

Julia Anne Robinson
KING OF MARVIN GARDENS, THE(1972)

Julie Robinson
KISMET(1955); MAMBO(1955, Ital.); LUST FOR LIFE(1956); SAFE PLACE, A(1971); BUCK AND THE PREACHER(1972)

Kai Robinson
LOVE CRAZY(1941)

Keith Robinson
MAGNET, THE(1950, Brit.)

Ken Robinson
1984
PURPLE RAIN(1984), ed

Kerwin Robinson
MANDINGO(1975)

Ky Robinson
IT HAPPENED ONE NIGHT(1934); JEALOUSY(1934); CASE OF THE CURIOUS BRIDE, THE(1935); SHE COULDN'T TAKE IT(1935); HOMICIDE BUREAU(1939); ONLY ANGELS HAVE WINGS(1939)

Larry Robinson
GOLDBERGS, THE(1950); NIGHT THEY ROBBED BIG BERTHA'S, THE(1975)

Lee Robinson
PHANTOM STOCKMAN, THE(1953, Aus.), d&w; KING OF THE CORAL SEA(1956, Aus.), d, w; WALK INTO HELL(1957, Aus.), d; FOUR DESPERATE MEN(1960, Brit.), w

Lennox Robinson
BLARNEY KISS(1933, Brit.), w

Lenox Robinson
GENERAL JOHN REGAN(1933, Brit.), w

Leon Robinson
ALL THE RIGHT MOVES(1983)
1984
FLAMINGO KID, THE(1984)

Lewis Robinson
HIGH COMMAND(1938, Brit.), w

Liz Robinson
THIS IS ELVIS(1982)

Louis Robinson
FIREMAN, SAVE MY CHILD(1932)

Louise Robinson
TOY WIFE, THE(1938)

Mabel Robinson
WIZ, THE(1978); COTTON COMES TO HARLEM(1970)

Mace Robinson
Silents
YELLOW STAIN, THE(1922)

Madelaine Robinson
TRIAL, THE(1963, Fr./Ital./Ger.)

Madeleine Robinson
LIVING CORPSE, THE(1940, Fr.); LUMIERE D'ETE(1943, Fr.); BELLMAN, THE(1947, Fr.); LOVE STORY(1949, Fr.); DEMONIAQUE(1958, Fr.); LEVIATHAN(1961, Fr.); WEB OF PASSION(1961, Fr.); DEVIL AND THE TEN COMMANDMENTS, THE(1962, Fr.); CROSS OF THE LIVING(1963,Fr.); YOUNG WORLD, A(1966, Fr./Ital.)

Margaret Robinson
VULTURE, THE(1967, U.S./Brit./Can.)

Martha Robinson
SHOW FLAT(1936, Brit.), w

Mary June Robinson
CAPTAIN EDDIE(1945)

Mary Robinson
RUBY(1977)

Matt Robinson
POSSESSION OF JOEL DELANEY, THE(1972), w; AMAZING GRACE(1974), p, w

Max Robinson
HANGAR 18(1980)
1984
SILENT NIGHT, DEADLY NIGHT(1984)

Michael Robinson
STONE(1974, Aus.), a, w

Milton Robinson
1984
POWER, THE(1984)

Molly Robinson
FAST AND SEXY(1960, Fr./Ital.)

Nancy June Robinson
JANE EYRE(1944); SULLIVANS, THE(1944); MAN WHO WALKED ALONE, THE(1945)

Neil Robinson
WITCH'S CURSE, THE(1963, Ital.); 8 ½(1963, Ital.); HORRIBLE DR. HICHCOCK, THE(1964, Ital.)

Norman Robinson
JUST WILLIAM(1939, Brit.); KILL OR BE KILLED(1980), ch; KILL AND KILL AGAIN(1981), a, ch

Ocie Robinson
HANGAR 18(1980)

Ollie Ann Robinson
Misc. Talkies
MIDNIGHT SHADOW(1939)

Paddy Robinson
MC KENZIE BREAK, THE(1970)

Pamela Robinson
ROBE, THE(1953)

Patty Robinson
NAKED KISS, THE(1964)

Percy Robinson
TO WHAT RED HELL(1929, Brit.), w; MURDER AT THE CABARET(1936, Brit.), w; WANTED FOR MURDER(1946, Brit.), w

Pete Robinson
FREAKS(1932)

Peter Robinson
DAY THE FISH CAME OUT, THE(1967. Brit./Gr.); WHAT'S NEXT?(1975, Brit.)

Phil Alden Robinson
1984
ALL OF ME(1984), w; RHINESTONE(1984), w, m/1

Phyllis Robinson
Misc. Talkies
SUNSHINE RUN(1979)

R. D. Robinson
WORLD IS JUST A 'B' MOVIE, THE(1971), w, ed&set d, p&d, ph

Rad Robinson
KNIGHTS OF THE RANGE(1940); LIGHT OF WESTERN STARS, THE(1940); STAGECOACH WAR(1940)

Ralph Robinson
WILD HORSE RODEO(1938)

Ray Robinson
FOUR FACES WEST(1948), set d; M(1951), set d; PARK ROW(1952), set d

Raymone Robinson
NATIONAL LAMPOON'S ANIMAL HOUSE(1978)

Richard Robinson
KINGDOM OF THE SPIDERS(1977), w; HIGH-BALLIN'(1978), w; PIRANHA(1978), w; RETURN OF THE JEDI(1983)
Misc. Talkies
TO HELL YOU PREACH(1972), d; POOR PRETTY EDDIE(1975), d

Robert Robinson
DATE WITH DISASTER(1957, Brit.); FRENCH DRESSING(1964, Brit.); SILVER BEARS(1978)

Robert H. Robinson
CATTLE QUEEN(1951)

Roberta Robinson
DANGEROUS NAN McGREW(1930); HALF SHOT AT SUNRISE(1930); SOCIAL REGISTER(1934)

Robie Robinson
MAROONED(1969), spec eff

Roger Robinson
BELIEVE IN ME(1971); WILLIE DYNAMITE(1973); NEWMAN'S LAW(1974); METEOR(1979); IT'S MY TURN(1980)
1984
LONELY GUY, THE(1984)

Ruth Robinson
CASE OF THE VELVET CLAWS, THE(1936); CHINA CLIPPER(1936); RAMONA(1936); SINS OF MAN(1936); WALKING DEAD, THE(1936); LOST HORIZON(1937); MIDNIGHT MADONNA(1937); ON SUCH A NIGHT(1937); OUTCAST(1937); WINGS

OVER HONOLULU(1937); LONE WOLF IN PARIS, THE(1938); MIDNIGHT INTRUDER(1938); ROLL ALONG, COWBOY(1938); HELL'S KITCHEN(1939); KANSAS TERRORS, THE(1939); OUR LEADING CITIZEN(1939); TORCHY PLAYS WITH DYNAMITE(1939); COVERED WAGON DAYS(1940); FIVE LITTLE PEPPERS IN TROUBLE(1940); TEXAS TERRORS(1940); ACROSS THE SIERRAS(1941); CORSICAN BROTHERS, THE(1941); DOWN MEXICO WAY(1941); ONE FOOT IN HEAVEN(1941); REMEMBER THE DAY(1941); THERE'S MAGIC IN MUSIC(1941); WHISTLING IN THE DARK(1941); IN OLD CALIFORNIA(1942); YANKEE DOODLE DANDY(1942); CHATTERBOX(1943); SONG OF BERNADETTE, THE(1943); DELIGHTFULLY DANGEROUS(1945); KID SISTER, THE(1945); HOODLUM SAINT, THE(1946); SPIDER WOMAN STRIKES BACK, THE(1946); GUILTY, THE(1947); STEPCHILD(1947); HE WALKED BY NIGHT(1948); THREE MUSKETEERS, THE(1948); IMPACT(1949); TRAPPED(1949); SECRET FURY, THE(1950); PHONE CALL FROM A STRANGER(1952); SEARCH FOR BRIDEY MURPHY, THE(1956); FORTY POUNDS OF TROUBLE(1962)
Misc. Silents
TRIAL MARRIAGE(1928)
Ruthie Robinson
TALL STORY(1960)
Ruthy Robinson
MIRACLE OF SANTA'S WHITE REINDEER, THE(1963)
Sam Robinson
Misc. Silents
LITTLE SAMARITAN, THE(1917)
Seymour B. Robinson
STORMY WEATHER(1943), w
Shari Robinson
YOU'RE MY EVERYTHING(1949); GOLDBERGS, THE(1950)
Sidney Robinson
Silents
SPINDLE OF LIFE, THE(1917), w
Spike Robinson
MADISON SQUARE GARDEN(1932)
Silents
IN AGAIN-OUT AGAIN(1917)
Stanford Robinson
HANDS OF ORLAC, THE(1964, Brit./Fr.), md
Steve Robinson
TERROR-CREATURES FROM THE GRAVE(1967, U.S./Ital.)
Stuart K. Robinson
PARADISE ALLEY(1978); DEATH WISH II(1982)
Stuart Robinson
RIVER'S END(1940); ROCKY II(1979); ZELIG(1983), spec eff
Sue Robinson
OH! WHAT A LOVELY WAR(1969, Brit.)
Sugar Ray Robinson
CANDY(1968, Ital./Fr.); DETECTIVE, THE(1968); PAPER LION(1968); TODD KILLINGS, THE(1971)
Susan Robinson
GREAT WALTZ, THE(1972)
T Robinson
CRY BLOOD, APACHE(1970), ed
Terry Robinson
OFFENDERS, THE(1980)
Thelma Robinson
UP GOES MAISIE(1946), w; UNDERCOVER MAISIE(1947), w; BECAUSE OF YOU(1952), w
Tim Robinson
RAW WEEKEND(1964)
Tina Robinson
MY BRILLIANT CAREER(1980, Aus.); OCTOPUSSY(1983, Brit.); PUBERTY BLUES(1983, Aus.)
Tony Robinson
DARWIN ADVENTURE, THE(1972, Brit.)
Vicki Sue Robinson
GOING HOME(1971)
Victor Robinson
SLEEPING CAR TO TRIESTE(1949, Brit.)
Virginia Robinson
STRANGE FACES(1938)
Walter Robinson
Silents
BETTER 'OLE, THE(1926), ph; NIGHT CRY, THE(1926), ph
Whitey Robinson
INCREDIBLY STRANGE CREATURES WHO STOPPED LIVING AND BECAME CRAZY MIXED-UP ZOMBIES, THE(1965)
William A. Robinson
TAHITIAN, THE(1956)
Jose Robio
SUTTER'S GOLD(1936)
Jacques Robiolles
BRIDE WORE BLACK, THE(1968, Fr./Ital.); STOLEN KISSES(1969, Fr.)
Aafa Robis
BECAUSE I LOVED YOU(1930, Ger.), p
Arthur Robison
INFORMER, THE(1929, Brit.), d
Misc. Silents
WARNING SHADOWS(1924, Ger.), d; MANON LESCAUT(1926, Ger.), d
Naomi Robison
CAGED(1950)
Rob Robison
LOST SQUADRON, THE(1932), ph
Roblan
MAN WHO WOULD NOT DIE, THE(1975), spec eff
Lorenzo Robledo
FOR A FEW DOLLARS MORE(1967, Ital./Ger./Span.); NAVAJO JOE(1967, Ital./Span.)

Emmanuel Robles
STRANGER, THE(1967, Algeria/Fr./Ital.), w
Felix Robles
TERRACE, THE(1964, Arg.)
German Robles
CASTLE OF THE MONSTERS(1958, Mex.); VAMPIRE'S COFFIN, THE(1958, Mex.); VAMPIRE, THE(1968, Mex.); LIVING HEAD, THE(1969, Mex.)
Herman Robles
LOSERS, THE(1970)
Jorge Humberto Robles
1984
EVIL THAT MEN DO, THE(1984)
Leticia Robles
GREAT SCOUT AND CATHOUSE THURSDAY, THE(1976)
Maria Robles
LOVE IS A CAROUSEL(1970)
Nester Robles
TASTE OF HELL, A(1973), m
Nestor Robles
PASSIONATE STRANGERS, THE(1968, Phil.), m
Ray Robles
CYCLE SAVAGES(1969), art d
Renato Robles
LOST BATTALION(1961, U.S./Phil.); BLOOD DRINKERS, THE(1966, U.S./Phil.); ONCE BEFORE I DIE(1967, U.S./Phil.)
Richard Robles
UNION PACIFIC(1939); HUNGER, THE(1983)
Roberto Robles
LOST COMMAND, THE(1966)
Rudy Robles
REAL GLORY, THE(1939); SOUTH OF PAGO PAGO(1940); HONOLULU LU(1941); ACROSS THE PACIFIC(1942); MANILA CALLING(1942); SONG OF THE ISLANDS(1942); SUBMARINE RAIDER(1942); WAKE ISLAND(1942); NOCTURNE(1946); SINGAPORE(1947); JUNGLE GODDESS(1948); OMOO OMOO, THE SHARK GOD(1949); RUSTY SAVES A LIFE(1949); OKINAWA(1952)
Walt Robles
SAVAGE SEVEN, THE(1968); CYCLE SAVAGES(1969)
Walter Robles
STUNT MAN, THE(1980); TWO OF A KIND(1983)
1984
CITY HEAT(1984)
Roblin
Silents
NAPOLEON(1927, Fr.)
Louise Roblin
CAT, THE(1959, Fr.); PARIS BELONGS TO US(1962, Fr.)
Antoine Roblot
ZAZIE(1961, Fr.); VERY PRIVATE AFFAIR, A(1962, Fr./Ital.); NAKED AUTUMN(1963, Fr.)
Jacques Robnard
LA GUERRE EST FINIE(1967, Fr./Swed.)
George Robotham
JOAN OF ARC(1948); CHAIN GANG(1950); ROBE, THE(1953); SAVAGE MUTINY(1953); SEVEN BRIDES FOR SEVEN BROTHERS(1954); PRODIGAL, THE(1955); GREAT LOCOMOTIVE CHASE, THE(1956); DEERSLAYER, THE(1957); GARMENT JUNGLE, THE(1957); SPARTACUS(1960); STRANGE BEDFELLOWS(1965); SPLIT, THE(1968); METEOR(1979); PRISONER OF ZENDA, THE(1979)
George N. Robotham
WHAT'S UP, DOC?(1972)
George W. Robotham
DESTINATION TOKYO(1944)
Mike Robotham
EAST OF KILIMANJARO(1962, Brit./Ital.)
Robotic Systems Intl.
1984
RUNAWAY(1984), spec eff,
Dominador Robridillo
YEAR OF LIVING DANGEROUSLY, THE(1982, Aus.)
Margaret Robsahm
PASSIONATE DEMONS, THE(1962, Norway); YOUNG RACERS, THE(1963); CASTLE OF BLOOD(1964, Fr./Ital.)
Ted Robshaw
STIR(1980, Aus.)
Robson
BEDLAM(1946), w
Andrew Robson
Silents
BRANDING BROADWAY(1918)
Andrew Robson
Silents
SALOMY JANE(1914); BROADWAY SCANDAL(1918); LIGHT OF VICTORY(1919); ALARM CLOCK ANDY(1920); STOP THIEF(1920); ALL'S FAIR IN LOVE(1921); ONE A MINUTE(1921)
Misc. Silents
MRS. WIGGS OF THE CABBAGE PATCH(1914); UNWRITTEN LAW, THE(1916); WOMAN WHO DARED, THE(1916); HEART OF JUANITA(1919); JUST SQAW(1919); LAW OF MEN, THE(1919); CUPID, THE COWPUNCHER(1920); GREAT ACCIDENT, THE(1920); WHO'S YOUR SERVANT?(1920); BLACK ROSES(1921)
Campbell Robson
EDGE OF THE WORLD, THE(1937, Brit.)
Edward Robson
Misc. Silents
HOOSIER ROMANCE, A(1918)
Edward V. Robson
SEND FOR PAUL TEMPLE(1946, Brit.)
Flora Robson
GENTLEMAN OF PARIS, A(1931); DANCE PRETTY LADY(1932, Brit.); ONE PRECIOUS YEAR(1933, Brit.); CATHERINE THE GREAT(1934, Brit.); FIRE OVER ENGLAND(1937, Brit.); TROOPSHIP(1938, Brit.); WE ARE NOT ALONE(1939); WUTHERING HEIGHTS(1939); INVISIBLE STRIPES(1940); SEA HAWK, THE(1940); BAHA-

Greer Robson- (continued)

MA PASSAGE(1941); POISON PEN(1941, Brit.); 2,000 WOMEN(1944, Brit.); GREAT DAY(1945, Brit.); SARATOGA TRUNK(1945); CAESAR AND CLEOPATRA(1946, Brit.); BLACK NARCISSUS(1947, Brit.); FRIEDA(1947, Brit.); HOLIDAY CAMP(1947, Brit.); YEARS BETWEEN, THE(1947, Brit.); SARABAND(1949, Brit.); GOOD TIME GIRL(1950, Brit.); FRIGHTENED BRIDE, THE(1952, Brit.); MALTA STORY(1954, Brit.); ROMEO AND JULIET(1954, Brit.); HIGH TIDE AT NOON(1957, Brit.); NO TIME FOR TEARS(1957, Brit.); GYPSY AND THE GENTLEMAN, THE(1958, Brit.); INNOCENT SINNERS(1958, Brit.); MURDER AT THE GALLOP(1963, Brit.); 55 DAYS AT PEKING(1963); GUNS AT BATASI(1964, Brit.); THOSE MAGNIFICENT MEN IN THEIR FLYING MACHINES; OR HOW I FLEWFROM LONDON TO PARIS IN 25 HOURS AND 11 MINUTES(1965, Brit.); YOUNG CASSIDY(1965, U.S./Brit.); SEVEN WOMEN(1966); EYE OF THE DEVIL(1967, Brit.); SHUTTERED ROOM, THE(1968, Brit.); BEAST IN THE CELLAR, THE(1971, Brit.); FRAGMENT OF FEAR(1971, Brit.); ALICE'S ADVENTURES IN WONDERLAND(1972, Brit.); DOMINIQUE(1978, Brit.); CLASH OF THE TITANS(1981)
Misc. Talkies
BELOVED, THE(1972)

Greer Robson
SCARECROW, THE(1982, New Zealand); SMASH PALACE(1982, New Zealand)

James Robson
WAY WE LIVE, THE(1946, Brit.)

Karen Robson
PICNIC AT HANGING ROCK(1975, Aus.)

Ken Robson
FIDDLER ON THE ROOF(1971)

Kenny Robson
MELODY(1971, Brit.)

Linda Robson
JUNKET 89(1970, Brit.)
Misc. Talkies
BATTLE OF BILLY'S POND(1976)

Lynne Robson
SMASH PALACE(1982, New Zealand)

Mark Robson
CITIZEN KANE(1941), ed; CAT PEOPLE(1942), ed; FALCON'S BROTHER, THE(1942), ed; JOURNEY INTO FEAR(1942), ed; MAGNIFICENT AMBERSONS, THE(1942), ed; GHOST SHIP, THE(1943), d; I WALKED WITH A ZOMBIE(1943), ed; LEOPARD MAN, THE(1943), ed; SEVENTH VICTIM, THE(1943), d; YOUTH RUNS WILD(1944), d; ISLE OF THE DEAD(1945), d; BEDLAM(1946), d; CHAMPION(1949), d; HOME OF THE BRAVE(1949), d; MY FOOLISH HEART(1949), d; ROUGHSHOD(1949), d; EDGE OF DOOM(1950), d; BRIGHT VICTORY(1951), d; I WANT YOU(1951), d; RETURN TO PARADISE(1953), p, d; BRIDGES AT TOKO-RI, THE(1954), d; HELL BELOW ZERO(1954, Brit.), d; PHFFFT!(1954), d; PRIZE OF GOLD, A(1955), d; TRIAL(1955), d; HARDER THEY FALL, THE(1956), d; LITTLE HUT, THE(1957), p, d; PEYTON PLACE(1957), d; INN OF THE SIXTH HAPPINESS, THE(1958), d; FROM THE TERRACE(1960), p&d; LISA(1962, Brit.), p; NINE HOURS TO RAMA(1963, U.S./Brit.), p&d; PRIZE, THE(1963), d; VON RYAN'S EXPRESS(1965), d; LOST COMMAND, THE(1966), p&d; VALLEY OF THE DOLLS(1967), d; DADDY'S GONE A-HUNTING(1969), p&d; HAPPY BIRTHDAY, WANDA JUNE(1971), d; LIMBO(1972), d; EARTHQUAKE(1974), p&d; AVALANCHE EXPRESS(1979), p&d

May Robson
SHE-WOLF, THE(1931); IF I HAD A MILLION(1932); LETTY LYNTON(1932); LITTLE ORPHAN ANNIE(1932); RED HEADED WOMAN(1932); STRANGE INTERLUDE(1932); ALICE IN WONDERLAND(1933); BEAUTY FOR SALE(1933); BROADWAY TO HOLLYWOOD(1933); DANCING LADY(1933); DINNER AT EIGHT(1933); LADY FOR A DAY(1933); MEN MUST FIGHT(1933); ONE MAN'S JOURNEY(1933); REUNION IN VIENNA(1933); SOLITAIRE MAN, THE(1933); WHITE SISTER, THE(1933); LADY BY CHOICE(1934); STRAIGHT IS THE WAY(1934); YOU CAN'T BUY EVERYTHING(1934); AGE OF INDISCRETION(1935); ANNA KARENINA(1935); GRAND OLD GIRL(1935); MILLS OF THE GODS(1935); RECKLESS(1935); STRANGERS ALL(1935); THREE KIDS AND A QUEEN(1935); VANESSA, HER LOVE STORY(1935); RAINBOW ON THE RIVER(1936); WIFE VERSUS SECRETARY(1936); CAPTAIN'S KID, THE(1937); PERFECT SPECIMEN, THE(1937); STAR IS BORN, A(1937); WOMAN IN DISTRESS(1937); ADVENTURES OF TOM SAWYER(1938); BRINGING UP BABY(1938); FOUR DAUGHTERS(1938); TEXANS, THE(1938); DAUGHTERS COURAGEOUS(1939); FOUR WIVES(1939); KID FROM KOKOMO, THE(1939); NURSE EDITH CAVELL(1939); THAT'S RIGHT–YOU'RE WRONG(1939); THEY MADE ME A CRIMINAL(1939); YES, MY DARLING DAUGHTER(1939); GRANNY GET YOUR GUN(1940); IRENE(1940); TEXAS RANGERS RIDE AGAIN(1940); FOUR MOTHERS(1941); MILLION DOLLAR BABY(1941); PLAYMATES(1941); JOAN OF PARIS(1942)
Silents
HOW MOLLY MADE GOOD(1915); NIGHT OUT, A(1916), a, w; ANGEL OF BROADWAY, THE(1927); KING OF KINGS, THE(1927); RUBBER TIRES(1927); CHICAGO(1928)
Misc. Silents
LOST BATALLION, THE(1919); PALS IN PARADISE(1926); HARP IN HOCK, A(1927); REJUVINATION OF AUNT MARY, THE(1927)

Michael Robson
GOT IT MADE(1974, Brit.), w; CHOSEN, THE(1978, Brit./Ital.), w; THIRTY NINE STEPS, THE(1978, Brit.), w; WATER BABIES, THE(1979, Brit.), w

Phil Robson
Silents
LIFE'S WHIRLPOOL(1916)

Philip Robson
Silents
LIFE'S WHIRLPOOL(1917)

Phillip Robson
Silents
CAPTAIN SWIFT(1914)

Roberta Robson
POINT OF TERROR(1971)

Rose May Robson
COVER GIRL(1944)

Stuart Robson
Silents
SHOULD A WIFE WORK?(1922)

Victor Robson
Silents
PATRICIA BRENT, SPINSTER(1919, Brit.)
Misc. Silents
GREATER LOVE, THE(1919, Brit.); GOLDEN WEB, THE(1920, Brit.)

Mrs. Stuart Robson
Silents
PRODIGAL WIFE, THE(1918)
Misc. Silents
AT THE OLD CROSSED ROADS(1914)

Wayne Robson
MC CABE AND MRS. MILLER(1971); POPEYE(1980); IMPROPER CHANNELS(1981, Can.); GREY FOX, THE(1983, Can.)
1984
FINDERS KEEPERS(1984); JUST THE WAY YOU ARE(1984); MRS. SOFFEL(1984)

William N. Robson
PRIVATE JONES(1933), w; LAND UNKNOWN, THE(1957), w

Zuleika Robson
ISADORA(1968, Brit.); TERROR FROM UNDER THE HOUSE(1971, Brit.)

Guido Robuschi
CAESAR THE CONQUEROR(1963, Ital.), m; FURY OF THE PAGANS(1963, Ital.), m

Sam Robustelli
SILENCE(1974)

Fred Roby
JOURNEY, THE(1959, U.S./Aust.)

Lavelle Roby
FINDERS KEEPERS, LOVERS WEEPERS(1968); PEACE KILLERS, THE(1971); BLACK GUNN(1972)

Karen Robyn
1984
POLICE ACADEMY(1984)

Laurie Robyn
WORLD ACCORDING TO GARP, The(1982)

William Robyns
EXPERT, THE(1932); HELL FIRE AUSTIN(1932); PHANTOM THUNDERBOLT, THE(1933); ELMER AND ELSIE(1934); LONE COWBOY(1934); YOU'RE TELLING ME(1934)

Felicia Roc
SAVAGE PAMPAS(1967, Span./Arg.)

Patricia Roc
PHANTOM STRIKES, THE(1939, Brit.); REBEL SON, THE ½(1939, Brit.); DR. O'DOWD(1940, Brit.); MISSING PEOPLE, THE(1940, Brit.); MYSTERIOUS MR. REEDER, THE(1940, Brit.); PACK UP YOUR TROUBLES(1940, Brit.); THREE SILENT MEN(1940, Brit.); FARMER'S WIFE, THE(1941, Brit.); IT HAPPENED TO ONE MAN(1941, Brit.); MY WIFE'S FAMILY(1941, Brit.); LADY IN DISTRESS(1942, Brit.); LET THE PEOPLE SING(1942, Brit.); WE'LL MEET AGAIN(1942, Brit.); MILLIONS LIKE US(1943, Brit.); SUSPECTED PERSON(1943, Brit.); 2,000 WOMEN(1944, Brit.); MADONNA OF THE SEVEN MOONS(1945, Brit.); CANYON PASSAGE(1946); JOHNNY FRENCHMAN(1946, Brit.); WICKED LADY, THE(1946, Brit.); HOLIDAY CAMP(1947, Brit.); LADY SURRENDERS, A(1947, Brit.); SO WELL REMEMBERED(1947, Brit.); WHEN THE BOUGH BREAKS(1947, Brit.); BROTHERS, THE(1948, Brit.); JASSY(1948, Brit.); ONE NIGHT WITH YOU(1948, Brit); MAN ON THE EIFFEL TOWER, THE(1949); PERFECT WOMAN, THE(1950, Brit.); CIRCLE OF DANGER(1951, Brit.); CAPTAIN BLACK JACK(1952, U.S./Fr.); SOMETHING MONEY CAN'T BUY(1952, Brit.); CARTOUCHE(1957, Ital./US); HOUSE IN THE WOODS, THE(1957, Brit.); SCOTLAND YARD DRAGNET(1957, Brit.); BLUEBEARD'S TEN HONEYMOONS(1960, Brit.)

Vicente Roca
RUN LIKE A THIEF(1968, Span.); LAST MERCENARY, THE(1969, Ital./Span./Ger.); MERCENARY, THE(1970, Ital./Span.); TRISTANA(1970, Span./Ital./Fr.)

Annalisa Nasalli Rocca
TROJAN WOMEN, THE(1971), cos; JULIA(1977), cos

Claire Rocca
MY UNCLE(1958, Fr.)

Daniela Rocca
CALTIKI, THE IMMORTAL MONSTER(1959, Ital.); GIANT OF MARATHON, THE(1960, Ital.); HEAD OF A TYRANT(1960, Fr./Ital.); LEGIONS OF THE NILE(1960, Ital.); CAPTIVE CITY, THE(1963, Ital.); BEHOLD A PALE HORSE(1964); EMPTY CANVAS, THE(1964, Fr./Ital.); SYMPHONY FOR A MASSACRE(1965, Fr./Ital.); CONQUERED CITY(1966, Ital.); SUCKER, THE(1966, Fr./Ital.); SELLERS OF GIRLS(1967, Fr.)

Daniella Rocca
ESTHER AND THE KING(1960, U.S./Ital.); DIVORCE, ITALIAN STYLE(1962, Ital.)
Misc. Talkies
COLOSSUS AND THE AMAZONS(1960)

Guilio Rocca
CENTO ANNI D'AMORE(1954, Ital.), w

Laura Rocca
FALL OF ROME, THE(1963, Ital.)

Michael Rocca
GIRL IN THE BIKINI, THE(1958, Fr.), ph

Michel Rocca
CHRISTINE KEELER AFFAIR, THE(1964, Brit.), ph; GIRL CAN'T STOP, THE(1966, Fr./Gr.), ph

Orietta Nasalli Rocca
THOSE DARING YOUNG MEN IN THEIR JAUNTY JALOPIES(1969, Fr./Brit./Ital.), cos; STATUE, THE(1971, Brit.), cos

Samuel F. Rocca
JOHNNY ROCCO(1958), w

Albert Roccardi
LOVE PARADE, THE(1929); ROMANCE OF THE RIO GRANDE(1929); JUST LIKE HEAVEN(1930)
Silents
MR. BARNES OF NEW YORK(1914); ARTIE, THE MILLIONAIRE KID(1916); GREATER THAN FAME(1920); DESTINY'S ISLE(1922); PARTNERS IN CRIME(1928)
Misc. Silents
MODERN THELMA, A(1916); MY LADY'S SLIPPER(1916); TANGLED LIVES(1918)

Goffredo Rocchetti
STEPPE, THE(1963, Fr./Ital.), makeup; LOVE ON THE RIVIERA(1964, Fr./Ital.), spec eff; TEOREMA(1969, Ital.), spec eff; WITCHES, THE(1969, Fr./Ital.), makeup; DEATH IN VENICE(1971, Ital./Fr.), makeup

Luigina Rocchi
ARABIAN NIGHTS(1980, Ital./Fr.)

Marina Rocchi
YOR, THE HUNTER FROM THE FUTURE(1983, Ital.)

Rocco
POLICE DOG STORY, THE(1961)

Alex Rocco
MOTOR PSYCHO(1965); ST. VALENTINE'S DAY MASSACRE, THE(1967); BLOOD MANIA(1971); WILD RIDERS(1971); GODFATHER, THE(1972); DETROIT 9000(1973); FRIENDS OF EDDIE COYLE, THE(1973); OUTSIDE MAN, THE(1973, U.S./FR.); SLITHER(1973); STANLEY(1973); FREEBIE AND THE BEAN(1974); THREE THE HARD WAY(1974); HEARTS OF THE WEST(1975); RAFFERTY AND THE GOLD DUST TWINS(1975); FIRE SALE(1977); RABBIT TEST(1978); VOICES(1979); HERBIE GOES BANANAS(1980); STUNT MAN, THE(1980); NOBODY'S PERFEKT zero(1981); ENTITY, THE(1982)
1984
CANNONBALL RUN II(1984)
Misc. Talkies
BRUTE CORPS(1972); WOMAN FOR ALL MEN, A(1975)

Antonino Rocco
ALICE, SWEET ALICE(1978)

Eddie Rocco
GREAT MIKE, THE(1944); DANGEROUS INTRUDER(1945)

Johnny Rocco
NOTORIOUS CLEOPATRA, THE(1970)

Jose Rocco
FEMALE, THE(1960, Fr.), m; UGLY ONES, THE(1968, Ital./Span.), ed

Lilla Rocco
ANNA(1951, Ital.)

Lyla Rocco
RED CLOAK, THE(1961, Ital./Fr.); PLAYGIRLS AND THE VAMPIRE(1964, Ital.)

Mary Rocco
FRIDAY THE 13TH(1980)

Maurice Rocco
52ND STREET(1937); DUFFY'S TAVERN(1945); INCENDIARY BLONDE(1945)

Pat Rocco
SOMEONE(1968), p&d, ph&ed; DRIFTER(1975), p,d,ph&ed

Tony Rocco
METEOR(1979)

Rocco & His Saints
JAMBOREE(1957)

Rocco and Saulters
VOGUES OF 1938(1937)

Mario Roccuzzo
YOUNG SAVAGES, THE(1961); LOVE-INS, THE(1967); THREE THE HARD WAY(1974)

Rocha
THAT MAN IN ISTANBUL(1966, Fr./Ital./Span.)

Annecy Rocha
BRASIL ANNO 2,000(1968, Braz.)

David Rocha
THAT OBSCURE OBJECT OF DESIRE(1977, Fr./Span.)

Glauber Rocha
EARTH ENTRANCED(1970, Braz.), d&w; WIND FROM THE EAST(1970, Fr./Ital./Ger.)

Glauce Rocha
EARTH ENTRANCED(1970, Braz.)

Eric Rochacit
TUSK(1980, Fr.), p

Danielle Rochard
1984
LE BAL(1984, Fr./Ital./Algeria)

Henri Rochard
I WAS A MALE WAR BRIDE(1949), w

Jean Rochard
CARMEN(1946, Ital.)

Francois Rochas
LANCELOT OF THE LAKE(1975, Fr.), p

Joe Rochay
COCK-EYED WORLD, THE(1929); FROZEN JUSTICE(1929)

Arthur Somers Roche
PENTHOUSE(1933), w; SHADOW OF A DOUBT(1935), w; STAR OF MIDNIGHT(1935), w; CASE AGAINST MRS. AMES, THE(1936), w
Silents
KISSED(1922), w; TRAIL'S END(1922), w; ANY WOMAN(1925), w; GIRL FROM CHICAGO, THE(1927), w; WOLF'S CLOTHING(1927), w

Aurora Roche
IN OLD NEW MEXICO(1945)

Barbara Roche
PEOPLE ARE FUNNY(1945)

Betty Roche
ONCE MORE, MY DARLING(1949)

Dominic Roche
MY WIFE'S LODGER(1952, Brit.), a, w; WHAT EVERY WOMAN WANTS(1954, Brit.); QUARE FELLOW, THE(1962, Brit.); PADDY(1970, Irish)

Eugene Roche
HAPPENING, THE(1967); COTTON COMES TO HARLEM(1970); THEY MIGHT BE GIANTS(1971); SLAUGHTERHOUSE-FIVE(1972); NEWMAN'S LAW(1974); W(1974); MR. RICCO(1975); LATE SHOW, THE(1977); CORVETTE SUMMER(1978); FOUL PLAY(1978)
1984
OH GOD! YOU DEVIL(1984)

France Roche
FRENCH CANCAN(1956, Fr.); LOVE AND THE FRENCHWOMAN(1961, Fr.), w; RED CLOAK, THE(1961, Ital./Fr.), w; NUDE IN HIS POCKET(1962, Fr.), w; PLEASURES AND VICES(1962, Fr.); MALE HUNT(1965, Fr./Ital.), w

Frank Roche
PRIME TIME, THE(1960)

Henri-Pierre Roche
JULES AND JIM(1962, Fr.), w; TWO ENGLISH GIRLS(1972, Fr.), w

Joh Roche
COHENS, AND KELLYS IN HOLLYWOOD, THE(1932)

John Roche
AWFUL TRUTH, THE(1929); DONOVAN AFFAIR, THE(1929); THIS THING CALLED LOVE(1929); UNHOLY NIGHT, THE(1929); MONTE CARLO(1930); LADY WITH A PAST(1932); PROSPERITY(1932); WINNER TAKE ALL(1932); BEAUTY FOR SALE(1933); KLONDIKE FURY(1942); WE WERE DANCING(1942); SHERLOCK HOLMES AND THE SPIDER WOMAN(1944); DARK HORSE, THE(1946); IDEA GIRL(1946)
Silents
FLOWING GOLD(1924); K-THE UNKNOWN(1924); LOST LADY, A(1924); KISS ME AGAIN(1925); RECOMPENSE(1925); DON JUAN(1926); RETURN OF PETER GRIMM, THE(1926); DREAM MELODY, THE(1929)
Misc. Silents
BAG AND BAGGAGE(1923); CORNERED(1924); TENTH WOMAN, THE(1924); BOBBED HAIR(1925); BROADWAY BUTTERFLY, A(1925); MARRY ME(1925); MY WIFE AND I(1925); SCANDAL PROOF(1925); MAN UPSTAIRS, THE(1926); MIDNIGHT LOVERS(1926); THEIR HOUR(1928)

Jonathan Roche
ONE WAY OUT(1955, Brit.), w

Marcel Roche
LES ABYSSES(1964, Fr.)

Marga Roche
SOME GIRLS DO(1969, Brit.)

Mary Roche
HEAT'S ON, THE(1943)

Maureen Roche
VON RICHTHOFEN AND BROWN(1970), set d

Paddy Roche
ULYSSES(1967, U.S./Brit.)

Paul Roche
OEDIPUS THE KING(1968, Brit.)

Sean T. Roche
MY BOYS ARE GOOD BOYS(1978)

Simone Roche
1984
UNTIL SEPTEMBER(1984)

Suzzy Roche
SOUP FOR ONE(1982)
1984
ALMOST YOU(1984)

Christiane Rochefort
TOO MANY CROOKS(1959, Brit.), w; TRUTH, THE(1961, Fr./Ital.), w; LOVE ON A PILLOW(1963, Fr./Ital.), w; SOPHIE'S WAYS(1970, Fr.), w

Jean Rochefort
CARTOUCHE(1962, Fr./Ital.); SYMPHONY FOR A MASSACRE(1965, Fr./Ital.); UP TO HIS EARS(1966, Fr./Ital.); DON'T PLAY WITH MARTIANS(1967, Fr.); TWO WEEKS IN SEPTEMBER(1967, Fr./Brit.); DEVIL BY THE TAIL, THE(1969, Fr./Ital.); TALL BLOND MAN WITH ONE BLACK SHOE, THE(1973, Fr.); PHANTOM OF LIBERTY, THE(1974, Fr.); CLOCKMAKER, THE(1976, Fr.); DIRTY HANDS(1976, Fr./Ital./Ger.); MEAN FRANK AND CRAZY TONY(1976, Ital.); LET JOY REIGN SUPREME(1977, Fr.); WHO IS KILLING THE GREAT CHEFS OF EUROPE?(1978, US/Ger.); FRENCH POSTCARDS(1979); TILL MARRIAGE DO US PART(1979, Ital.); I HATE BLONDES(1981, Ital.); I SENT A LETTER TO MY LOVE(1981, Fr.)
1984
LE CRABE TAMBOUR(1984, Fr.)

Ben Rochelle
COWBOY AND THE SENORITA(1944)

Carrie Rochelle
KAREN, THE LOVEMAKER(1970)

Claire Rochelle
BOOTHILL BRIGADE(1937); EMPTY SADDLES(1937); GUNS IN THE DARK(1937); RIDIN' THE LONE TRAIL(1937); SHE'S DANGEROUS(1937); THANKS FOR LISTENING(1937); CODE OF THE FEARLESS(1939); EL DIABLO RIDES(1939); LONG SHOT, THE(1939); MISSING DAUGHTERS(1939); PAL FROM TEXAS, THE(1939); SERGEANT MADDEN(1939); SHOULD A GIRL MARRY?(1939); TELL NO TALES(1939); TWO-GUN TROUBADOR(1939); I LOVE YOU AGAIN(1939); KID FROM SANTA FE, THE(1940); LIGHTNING STRIKES WEST(1940); NEW MOON(1940); FACE BEHIND THE MASK, THE(1941); NORTH FROM LONE STAR(1941); GALLANT LADY(1942); PRISON GIRL(1942); SECRETS OF A CO-ED(1942); HARVEST MELODY(1943); DOUBLE EXPOSURE(1944); MEN ON HER MIND(1944); SHAKE HANDS WITH MURDER(1944); SWING HOSTESS(1944); WATERFRONT(1944); KEEP YOUR POWDER DRY(1945); BLONDE FOR A DAY(1946)
Misc. Talkies
RIDERS OF THE SAGE(1939); BUZZY RIDES THE RANGE(1940); TEXAS JUSTICE(1942)

Edwin Rochelle
WE WERE STRANGERS(1949); NAMU, THE KILLER WHALE(1966)

Jackie Rochelle
HALF A SIXPENCE(1967, Brit.)

Rochelle and Beebe
TAKE IT BIG(1944)

Lionel Rocheman
CHANEL SOLITAIRE(1981)

Rosina Rochette
GIRL FROM LORRAINE, A(1982, Fr./Switz.), w

Rosine Rochette
INVITATION, THE(1975, Fr./Switz.)

Luigi Rochetti
1984
DUNE(1984), makeup

Capt. E. Rochfort-John
CHARGE OF THE LIGHT BRIGADE, THE(1936), tech adv

Paul Rochin
SAXON CHARM, THE(1948)
Diane Rochlin
MAIDSTONE(1970), ph
Jeff Rochlin
TAPS(1981)
Sheldon Rochlin
SMALL HOURS, THE(1962), ph; SQUARE ROOT OF ZERO, THE(1964), ph, ed; MAIDSTONE(1970), ph
Africanis Rocius
Misc. Talkies
JOE'S BED-STUY BARBERSHOP: WE CUT HEADS(1983)
Blossom Rock
HILDA CRANE(1956); SHE DEVIL(1957); FROM THE TERRACE(1960); SECOND TIME AROUND, THE(1961); SNOW WHITE AND THE THREE STOOGES(1961); BEST MAN, THE(1964)
Blossom Rock [Marie Blake]
SWINGIN' ALONG(1962)
Charles Rock
Silents
HOUSE OF TEMPERLEY, THE(1913, Brit.); FIRM OF GIRDLESTONE, THE(1915, Brit.); PRISONER OF ZENDA, THE(1915, Brit.); RUPERT OF HENTZAU(1915, Brit.); TATTERLY(1919, Brit.)
Misc. Silents
CALLED BACK(1914, Brit.); SHE STOOPS TO CONQUER(1914, Brit.); TRILBY(1914, Brit.); HIS VINDICATION(1915, Brit.); MAN IN THE ATTIC, THE(1915, Brit.); MAN OF HIS WORD, A(1915, Brit.); SONS OF SATAN, THE(1915, Brit.); THIRD GENERATION, THE(1915, Brit.); WHOSO DIGGETH A PIT(1915, Brit.); BEAU BROCADE(1916, Brit.); FAIR IMPOSTER, A(1916, Brit.); MORALS OF WEYBURY, THE(1916, Brit.); PARTNERS AT LAST(1916, Brit.); BIG MONEY(1918, Brit.); DECEPTION(1918, Brit.); RILKA(1918, Brit.); GREATER LOVE, THE(1919, Brit.)
Felippa Rock
MOSS ROSE(1947); FAN, THE(1949); PEGGY(1950); BRIDE OF THE GORILLA(1951); FROM THE TERRACE(1960)
Filippa Rock
KISS THE BLOOD OFF MY HANDS(1948)
Harmut Rock
LONGEST DAY, THE(1962)
Helen Eby Rock
MY REPUTATION(1946)
Helyn Eby Rock
THIN MAN GOES HOME, THE(1944); BORN YESTERDAY(1951); OVER-EXPOSED(1956); FOR PETE'S SAKE!(1966)
James Rock
Silents
MARSHAL OF MONEYMINT, THE(1922)
Joe Rock
GREAT POWER, THE(1929), d; CAPTAIN BILL(1935, Brit.), p; STOKER, THE(1935, Brit.), p; STRICTLY ILLEGAL(1935, Brit.), p; EXCUSE MY GLOVE(1936, Brit.), p; MAN BEHIND THE MASK, THE(1936, Brit.), p; ONE GOOD TURN(1936, Brit.), p; BOYS WILL BE GIRLS(1937, Brit.), p; COTTON QUEEN(1937, Brit.), p; EDGE OF THE WORLD, THE(1937, Brit.), p; RHYTHM RACKETEER(1937, Brit.), p; SING AS YOU SWING(1937, Brit.), p; EVERYTHING IS RHYTHM(1940, Brit.), p
Silents
PRETTY CLOTHES(1927), sup; STRANDED(1927), sup
Monte Rock III
SGT. PEPPER'S LONELY HEARTS CLUB BAND(1978)
Monti Rock III
2000 YEARS LATER(1969); SATURDAY NIGHT FEVER(1977); COMEBACK TRAIL, THE(1982)
Monty Rock III
CUBA CROSSING(1980)
Otto Rock
ARIZONA COLT(1965, It./Fr./Span.)
Oz Rock
1984
BODY ROCK(1984)
Philip Rock
MASK OF DIMITRIOS, THE(1944); EXTRAORDINARY SEAMAN, THE(1969), w
Phillip Rock
ESCAPE FROM FORT BRAVO(1953), w; MOST DANGEROUS MAN ALIVE, THE(1961), w
Sheila Rock
VERY NATURAL THING, A(1974)
Tony Rock
BIG TIP OFF, THE(1955)
Warren Rock
I LOVE YOU AGAIN(1940); NEW MOON(1940)
Rock Steady Crew
1984
BEAT STREET(1984)
Angelique Rockas
OUTLAND(1981)
A.L. Rockett
THREE GIRLS LOST(1931), p
Al Rockett
BARKER, THE(1928), p; HIGH SOCIETY BLUES(1930), p; PRINCESS AND THE PLUMBER, THE(1930), p; BUSINESS AND PLEASURE(1932), p; SHE WAS A LADY(1934), p; SUCH WOMEN ARE DANGEROUS(1934), p; LOTTERY LOVER(1935), p
Silents
HANDLE WITH CARE(1922), p; ABRAHAM LINCOLN(1924), p
Norman Rockett
FIVE WEEKS IN A BALLOON(1962), set d; STRIPPER, THE(1963), set d; PLANET OF THE APES(1968), set d; TORA! TORA! TORA!(1970, U.S./Jap.), set d; CONQUEST OF THE PLANET OF THE APES(1972), set d; STONE KILLER, THE(1973), set d; APPLE DUMPLING GANG RIDES AGAIN, THE(1979), art d; NORTH AVENUE IRREGULARS, THE(1979), set d; HERBIE GOES BANANAS(1980), set d
1984
SPLASH(1984), set d

Ray Rockett
GIRL FROM WOOLWORTH'S, THE(1929), p
Silents
HANDLE WITH CARE(1922), p; ABRAHAM LINCOLN(1924), p
Sam Rockett
STORMY CROSSING(1958, Brit.)
Misc. Talkies
BLACK TIDE(1958)
Jeffrey Rockland
DOCTOR ZHIVAGO(1965)
Sheldon Rocklin
GUNS OF THE TREES(1964), ph
Kathy Rockmeier
Misc. Talkies
GETTING IT ON(1983)
Mrs. Knute Rockne
KNUTE ROCKNE–ALL AMERICAN(1940), w
Rose Rockne
WELCOME TO HARD TIMES(1967), cos
Rose Rockney
BORN TO BE LOVED(1959), cos
Jill Rockow
GRADUATION DAY(1981), spec eff
E.A. Rockwell
SALT OF THE EARTH(1954)
Ed Rockwell
HAPPY DAYS(1930); JUST IMAGINE(1930)
Florence Rockwell
Misc. Silents
HE FELL IN LOVE WITH HIS WIFE(1916)
George "Doc" Rockwell
SINGING MARINE, THE(1937)
Jack Rockwell
ALIAS THE BAD MAN(1931); RANGE LAW(1931); HELL FIRE AUSTIN(1932); POCATELLO KID(1932); SUNSET TRAIL(1932); TEXAS GUN FIGHTER(1932); WHISTLIN' DAN(1932); COME ON TARZAN(1933); FARGO EXPRESS(1933); KING OF THE ARENA(1933); LONE AVENGER, THE(1933); OUTLAW JUSTICE(1933); STRAWBERRY ROAN(1933); WHEN A MAN RIDES ALONE(1933); FIDDLIN' BUCKAROO, THE(1934); GUN JUSTICE(1934); HONOR OF THE RANGE(1934); MAN FROM HELL, THE(1934); 'NEATH THE ARIZONA SKIES(1934); ROCKY RHODES(1934); SMOKING GUNS(1934); TRAIL DRIVE, THE(1934); WHEELS OF DESTINY(1934); WHEN A MAN SEES RED(1934); ALIAS JOHN LAW(1935); GALLANT DEFENDER(1935); IN OLD SANTA FE(1935); JUSTICE OF THE RANGE(1935); LAW BEYOND THE RANGE(1935); LAWLESS FRONTIER, THE(1935); NO MAN'S RANGE(1935); OUTLAWED GUNS(1935); TUMBLING TUMBLEWEEDS(1935); GUNS AND GUITARS(1936); HEIR TO TROUBLE(1936); HEROES OF THE RANGE(1936); LAW RIDES, THE(1936); LAWLESS NINETIES, THE(1936); LAWLESS RIDERS(1936); LIGHTNING BILL CARSON(1936); LION'S DEN, THE(1936); LUCKY TERROR(1936); MAN FROM GUN TOWN, THE(1936); MYSTERIOUS AVENGER, THE(1936); PRESCOTT KID, THE(1936); ROARIN' GUNS(1936); SINGING COWBOY, THE(1936); TRAITOR, THE(1936); VALLEY OF THE LAWLESS(1936); WINDS OF THE WASTELAND(1936); BAR Z BAD MEN(1937); DODGE CITY TRAIL(1937); RANGE DEFENDERS(1937); RANGERS STEP IN, THE(1937); RECKLESS RANGER(1937); RED ROPE, THE(1937); RIDERS OF THE ROCKIES(1937); RIO GRANDE RANGER(1937); ROGUE OF THE RANGE(1937); SINGING OUTLAW(1937); SPRINGTIME IN THE ROCKIES(1937); STARS OVER ARIZONA(1937); SUNDOWN SAUNDERS(1937); TEXAS TRAIL(1937); TRAPPED(1937); BLACK BANDIT(1938); GUILTY TRAILS(1938); LAW OF THE PLAINS(1938); MYSTERIOUS RIDER, THE(1938); OUTLAWS OF THE PRAIRIE(1938); PRAIRIE JUSTICE(1938); PRAIRIE MOON(1938); ROLLING CARAVANS(1938); SHINE ON, HARVEST MOON(1938); SUNSET TRAIL(1938); UNDER WESTERN STARS(1938); WEST OF CHEYENNE(1938); WESTERN TRAILS(1938); DAYS OF JESSE JAMES(1939); LONE STAR PIONEERS(1939); MAN FROM SUNDOWN, THE(1939); RENEGADE TRAIL(1939); ROUGH RIDERS' ROUNDUP(1939); SILVER ON THE SAGE(1939); BULLETS FOR RUSTLERS(1940); CARSON CITY KID(1940); CHEROKEE STRIP(1940); DARK COMMAND, THE(1940); DURANGO KID, THE(1940); HIDDEN GOLD(1940); PONY POST(1940); RETURN OF WILD BILL, THE(1940); SANTA FE MARSHAL(1940); STAGECOACH WAR(1940); STRANGER FROM TEXAS, THE(1940); YOUNG BILL HICKOK(1940); BORDER VIGILANTES(1941); BURY ME NOT ON THE LONE PRAIRIE(1941); JESSE JAMES AT BAY(1941); KING OF DODGE CITY(1941); LAW OF THE RANGE(1941); PINTO KID, THE(1941); RAWHIDE RANGERS(1941); RED RIVER VALLEY(1941); SECRETS OF THE WASTELANDS(1941); SHERIFF OF TOMBSTONE(1941); STICK TO YOUR GUNS(1941); THUNDER OVER THE PRAIRIE(1941); TWILIGHT ON THE TRAIL(1941); WIDE OPEN TOWN(1941); BANDIT RANGER(1942); MAN FROM CHEYENNE(1942); SUNDOWN KID, THE(1942); SUNSET SERENADE(1942); UNDERCOVER MAN(1942); BLACK HILLS EXPRESS(1943); DEAD MAN'S GULCH(1943); FIGHTING FRONTIER(1943); FRONTIER BADMEN(1943); MAN FROM THUNDER RIVER, THE(1943); OVERLAND MAIL ROBBERY(1943); RAIDERS OF SUNSET PASS(1943); RED RIVER ROBIN HOOD(1943); SILVER CITY RAIDERS(1943); SON OF DRACULA(1943); WAGON TRACKS WEST(1943); WEST OF TEXAS(1943); COWBOY FROM LONESOME RIVER(1944); FORTY THIEVES(1944); GUNSMOKE MESA(1944); LAW MEN(1944); LUMBERJACK(1944); MY BUDDY(1944); MYSTERY MAN(1944); TRIGGER TRAIL(1944); BEYOND THE PECOS(1945); COLORADO PIONEERS(1945); FLAME OF THE WEST(1945); FRONTIER FEUD(1945); OUTLAWS OF THE ROCKIES(1945); PHANTOM OF THE PLAINS(1945); ROUGH RIDERS OF CHEYENNE(1945); CANYON PASSAGE(1946); CONQUEST OF CHEYENNE(1946); COWBOY BLUES(1946); DRIFTING ALONG(1946); GENTLEMAN FROM TEXAS(1946); LAWLESS EMPIRE(1946); RED RIVER RENEGADES(1946); UNDER ARIZONA SKIES(1946); FLASHING GUNS(1947); LONGEST YARD, THE(1974)
Misc. Talkies
LIGHTNING TRIGGERS(1935); OUTLAW RULE(1935); TONTO KID, THE(1935); BRAND OF THE OUTLAWS(1936); TUMBLEWEED TRAIL(1942); VIGILANTES RIDE, THE(1944); ROARING RANGERS(1946)
Norman Rockwell
STAGECOACH(1966)
Ricky Rockwell
PICKUP ON 101(1972)

Robert Rockwell
YOU GOTTA STAY HAPPY(1948); ALIAS THE CHAMP(1949); RED MENACE, THE(1949); TASK FORCE(1949); BELLE OF OLD MEXICO(1950); BLONDE BANDIT, THE(1950); DESTINATION BIG HOUSE(1950); FEDERAL AGENT AT LARGE(1950); LONELY HEARTS BANDITS(1950); PRISONERS IN PETTICOATS(1950); TRIAL WITHOUT JURY(1950); UNMASKED(1950); WOMAN FROM HEADQUAR-TERS(1950); CALL ME MISTER(1951); FROGMEN, THE(1951); PRINCE WHO WAS A THIEF, THE(1951); WEEKEND WITH FATHER(1951); TURNING POINT, THE(1952); WAR OF THE WORLDS, THE(1953); OUR MISS BROOKS(1956); SOL MADRID(1968)

Sandra Rockwell
PICKUP ON 101(1972)

Serina Rockwell
PICKUP ON 101(1972)

Shayna Rockwell
PICKUP ON 101(1972)

William Rockwell
SALT OF THE EARTH(1954)

Roy Rockwood
HAPPY DAYS(1930); BOMBA ON PANTHER ISLAND(1949), d&w; BOMBA THE JUNGLE BOY(1949), w; BOMBA AND THE HIDDEN CITY(1950), w; LION HUNT-ERS, THE(1951), w; BOMBA AND THE JUNGLE GIRL(1952), d&w; SAFARI DRUMS(1953), w; GOLDEN IDOL, THE(1954), w

"Rocky"
CODE OF THE MOUNTED(1935); HIS FIGHTING BLOOD(1935); RED BLOOD OF COURAGE(1935)

Rocky the Horse
NORTHERN FRONTIER(1935); TRAILS OF THE WILD(1935); WILDERNESS MAIL(1935); PHANTOM PATROL(1936); SONG OF THE TRAIL(1936); TIMBER WAR(1936); WILDCAT TROOPER(1936)

Bembol Roco
YEAR OF LIVING DANGEROUSLY, THE(1982, Aus.)

Cleo Rocos
HISTORY OF THE WORLD, PART 1(1981)
1984
BLOODBATH AT THE HOUSE OF DEATH(1984, Brit.)

Rod La Rocque
HUNCHBACK OF NOTRE DAME, THE(1939)
Misc. Silents
LIFE(1920); SUSPICIOUS WIVES(1921)

Henry Rocquemore
CIMARRON(1931); KID FROM ARIZONA, THE(1931); NEAR THE TRAIL'S END(1931); WILD WEST WHOOPEE(1931); CHEYENNE CYCLONE, THE(1932); SON OF OKLAHOMA(1932); CRASHING BROADWAY(1933); FIGHTING CHAMP(1933); BATTLE OF GREED(1934); ON PROBATION(1935); RAINBOW VALLEY(1935); RAIN-BOW'S END(1935); TEXAS TERROR(1935); GUNSMOKE TRAIL(1938); GIRL AND THE GAMBLER, THE(1939); TRIPLE JUSTICE(1940); COME ON DANGER(1942); LONE STAR TRAIL, THE(1943)
Misc. Talkies
SONGS AND SADDLES(1938)

Einar Rod
Misc. Silents
PARSON'S WIDOW, THE(1920, Den.)

Robert Rodan
MINX, THE(1969)

Ziva Rodann
COURAGE OF BLACK BEAUTY(1957); FORTY GUNS(1957); PHARAOH'S CUR-SE(1957); STORY OF MANKIND, THE(1957); TEENAGE DOLL(1957); KING CREO-LE(1958); BIG OPERATOR, THE(1959); BLOOD AND STEEL(1959); LAST TRAIN FROM GUN HILL(1959); COLLEGE CONFIDENTIAL(1960); MACUMBA LOVE(1960); STORY OF RUTH, THE(1960); PRIVATE LIVES OF ADAM AND EVE, THE(1961); SAMAR(1962); THREE NUTS IN SEARCH OF A BOLT(1964)

Cecilia Rodarte
10 TO MIDNIGHT(1983), set d
1984
SCARRED(1984), art d

Marcia Rodd
LITTLE MURDERS(1971); T.R. BASKIN(1971); CITIZENS BAND(1977); LAST EM-BRACE(1979)
Misc. Talkies
KEEPING ON(1981)

Rosemary Rennel Rodd
LA DOLCE VITA(1961, Ital./Fr.)

Wayne Rodda
BLUE FIN(1978, Aus.)

Franc Roddam
QUADROPHENIA(1979, Brit.), d, w; LORDS OF DISCIPLINE, THE(1983), d

Allison Roddan
MONSIEUR VERDOUX(1947)

Dawn Roddenberry
PRETTY MAIDS ALL IN A ROW(1971)

Gene Roddenberry
PRETTY MAIDS ALL IN A ROW(1971), p, w; STAR TREK: THE MOTION PIC-TURE(1979), p, w; STAR TREK II: THE WRATH OF KHAN(1982), w
1984
STAR TREK III: THE SEARCH FOR SPOCK(1984), w

John Roddick
DOUBLE EXPOSURE(1954, Brit.), d&w; HORNET'S NEST, THE(1955, Brit.), w; DEATH TRAP(1962, Brit.), w; DOUBLE, THE(1963, Brit.), w; RETURN TO SEN-DER(1963, Brit.), w; RIVALS, THE(1963, Brit.), w; PARTNER, THE(1966, Brit.), w

Sheilah Roddick
DELINQUENT DAUGHTERS(1944)

Virginia Roddick
WALKING HILLS, THE(1949), w

Drew Roddy
SERGEANT MADDEN(1939); GREAT McGINTY, THE(1940); MANPOWER(1941); SHE COULDN'T SAY NO(1941); MAGNIFICENT AMBERSONS, THE(1942); NORTH-WEST RANGERS(1942); HI, BUDDY(1943)

James Roddy
TOY, THE(1982)

Jim Roddy
HISTORY OF THE WORLD, PART 1(1981)

Joe Roddy
MAIDSTONE(1970)

Lee Roddy
IN SEARCH OF HISTORIC JESUS(1980), w

Rod Roddy
Misc. Talkies
POSSE FROM HEAVEN(1975)

Alfred Rode
GYPSY MELODY(1936, Brit.), a, w; MAIDEN, THE(1961, Fr.), p&d; FIRE IN THE FLESH(1964, Fr.), p&d

Christian Rode
IS PARIS BURNING?(1966, U.S./Fr.)

David Rode
NORTH AVENUE IRREGULARS, THE(1979); LAST MARRIED COUPLE IN AMERI-CA, THE(1980)

Diane Rode
PROWLER, THE(1981)

Donald R. Rode
BUS IS COMING, THE(1971), ed
1984
TANK(1984), ed

Ebbe Rode
GERTRUD(1966, Den.)

Fred J. Rode
IN THE MEANTIME, DARLING(1944), set d; THUNDERHEAD-SON OF FLICK-A(1945), art d; IT SHOULDN'T HAPPEN TO A DOG(1946), ed; MY DARLING CLEMENTINE(1946), set d; STRANGE TRIANGLE(1946), set d; THIEVES' HIGH-WAY(1949), set d; PANIC IN THE STREETS(1950), set d; THREE CAME HOME(1950), set d; YOU'RE IN THE NAVY NOW(1951), set d; DREAMBOAT(1952), set d; LURE OF THE WILDERNESS(1952), set d; PONY SOLDIER(1952), set d; KING OF THE KHYBER RIFLES(1953), set d

FredJ. Rode
O. HENRY'S FULL HOUSE(1952), set d

Lone Rode
PEOPLE MEET AND SWEET MUSIC FILLS THE HEART(1969, Den./Swed.)

Nina Pens Rode
GERTRUD(1966, Den.)

Soren Rode
OPERATION LOVEBIRDS(1968, Den.)

Walter Rode
O.S.S.(1946); GOLDEN EARRINGS(1947); GREAT SINNER, THE(1949); JOHNNY ALLEGRO(1949); THIRTEEN FRIGHTENED GIRLS(1963)

John Roden
PIRATES OF BLOOD RIVER, THE(1962, Brit.)

Merrill Roden
MASTER RACE, THE(1944)

Molly Roden
WITNESS FOR THE PROSECUTION(1957); CHARLIE CHAN AND THE CURSE OF THE DRAGON QUEEN(1981)

Maureen Roden-Ryan
LONG VOYAGE HOME, THE(1940); SUSPICION(1941); YANK IN THE R.A.F., A(1941)

John Rodenbeck
FRANKENSTEIN MEETS THE SPACE MONSTER(1965), w

Shmuel Rodenski
OPERATION THUNDERBOLT(1978, ISRAEL)

Shmuel Rodensky
TWO KOUNEY LEMELS(1966, Israel); FLYING MATCHMAKER, THE(1970, Israel); SCORPIO(1973); ODESSA FILE, THE(1974, Brit./Ger.); SELL OUT, THE(1976)

Smuel Rodensky
TEL AVIV TAXI(1957, Israel)

Chuck Rodent
CADDY SHACK(1980)

Milan Roder
LIVES OF A BENGAL LANCER(1935), m; ANOTHER DAWN(1937), md; SOULS AT SEA(1937), m; PRIVATE LIVES OF ELIZABETH AND ESSEX, THE(1939), md

Milton Roder
FOUR FRIGHTENED PEOPLE(1934), m

Walter Roderer
MADDEST CAR IN THE WORLD, THE(1974, Ger.)

George Roderick
MISS TULIP STAYS THE NIGHT(1955, Brit.); SEE HOW THEY RUN(1955, Brit.); LADYKILLERS, THE(1956, Brit.); UNDERCOVER GIRL(1957, Brit.); YOU PAY YOUR MONEY(1957, Brit.); CRASH DRIVE(1959, Brit.); IMMORAL CHARGE(1962, Brit.); RATTLE OF A SIMPLE MAN(1964, Brit.); FINDERS KEEPERS(1966, Brit.); OPERA-TION THIRD FORM(1966, Brit.); PRESS FOR TIME(1966, Brit.); 25TH HOUR, THE(1967, Fr./Ital./Yugo.); ADDING MACHINE, THE(1969)

Olga Roderick
FREAKS(1932)

Ray Roderick
1984
FLAMINGO KID, THE(1984)

Alan Roderick-Jones
SAVAGE HARVEST(1981), art d; TARZAN, THE APE MAN(1981), art d; DEADLY FORCE(1983), prod d; TRIUMPHS OF A MAN CALLED HORSE(1983, US/Mex.), prod d
1984
BOLERO(1984), prod d

Milan Rodern
SONG OF SONGS(1933), m

Mildred Rodesky
DEVIL'S SISTERS, THE(1966)

Sarah Elizabeth Rodger
GIRL OVERBOARD(1937), w

Strewan Rodger
WHO IS KILLING THE GREAT CHEFS OF EUROPE?(1978, US/Ger.)
Struan Rodger
CHARRIOTS OF FIRE(1981, Brit.)
Aggie Guerard Rodgers
AMERICAN GRAFFITI(1973), cos; CORVETTE SUMMER(1978), cos; RETURN OF THE JEDI(1983), cos
Aggie Guerrard Rodgers
1984
ADVENTURES OF BUCKAROO BANZAI: ACROSS THE 8TH DIMENSION, THE(1984), cos
Agnes Rodgers
ONE FLEW OVER THE CUCKOO'S NEST(1975), cos; MORE AMERICAN GRAFFITI(1979), cos
Anton Rodgers
ROTTEN TO THE CORE(1956, Brit.); CRASH DRIVE(1959, Brit.); NIGHT TRAIN FOR INVERNESS(1960, Brit.); PART-TIME WIFE(1961, Brit.); PETTICOAT PIRATES(1961, Brit.); TARNISHED HEROES(1961, Brit.); CARRY ON JACK(1963, Brit.); SWINGIN' MAIDEN, THE(1963, Brit.); TRAITORS, THE(1963, Brit.); MAN WHO HAUNTED HIMSELF, THE(1970, Brit.); SCROOGE(1970, Brit.); DAY OF THE JACKAL, THE(1973, Brit./Fr.); EAST OF ELEPHANT ROCK(1976, Brit.)
Misc. Talkies
TO CHASE A MILLION(1967)
Cloda Rodgers
JUST FOR FUN(1963, Brit.)
Daniel Rodgers
RETURN OF THE JEDI(1983)
1984
THIS IS SPINAL TAP(1984)
Dora Rodgers
Misc. Silents
WHO KILLED WALTON?(1918)
Dorothy Rodgers
HAIL, HERO!(1969), cos
Douglas F. Rodgers
PUSHER, THE(1960)
Douglas Rodgers
ER LOVE A STRANGER(1958)
Eric Rodgers
DR. NO(1962, Brit.), md; CARRY ON CABBIE(1963, Brit.), m
Gaby Rodgers
KISS ME DEADLY(1955)
Gene Rodgers
SENSATIONS OF 1945(1944); THAT'S MY BABY(1944); I'LL TELL THE WORLD(1945); SHOOT TO KILL(1947)
Gil Rodgers
LINE, THE(1982)
Herb Rodgers
THUNDER IN DIXIE(1965)
Howard Emmett Rodgers
EASY TO WED(1946), w
Ilona Rodgers
SALT & PEPPER(1968, Brit.); SNOW TREASURE(1968)
1984
UTU(1984, New Zealand)
James Rodgers
PLAYTHING, THE(1929, Brit.), ph
Jeffrey Rodgers
1984
SURF II(1984)
Jimmie Rodgers
LITTLE SHEPHERD OF KINGDOM COME(1961)
John Rodgers
RANCHO DELUXE(1975)
John Wesley Rodgers
UPTIGHT(1968)
Johnny Rodgers
GETTING OVER(1981), m
Joy Rodgers
DEVIL'S PASS, THE(1957, Brit.)
Julie Rodgers
SET, THE(1970, Aus.)
Lise Rodgers
WE OF THE NEVER NEVER(1983, Aus.)
Mark Rodgers
LET'S KILL UNCLE(1966), w; FLAREUP(1969), w
Mary Rodgers
FREAKY FRIDAY(1976), w; DEVIL AND MAX DEVLIN, THE(1981), w
Mic Rodgers
1984
BIRDY(1984); CITY HEAT(1984)
Michael Rodgers
MOVIE MOVIE(1978)
Nile Rodgers
SOUP FOR ONE(1982), m
1984
ALPHABET CITY(1984), m
Pam Rodgers
DR. GOLDFOOT AND THE BIKINI MACHINE(1965)
Pamela Rodgers
OUT OF SIGHT(1966); MALTESE BIPPY, THE(1969)
Richard Rodgers
HEADS UP(1930), w; LEATHERNECKING(1930), w; MELODY MAN(1930), w; SPRING IS HERE(1930), w; HOT HEIRESS(1931), w; TEN CENTS A DANCE(1931), w; HALLELUJAH, I'M A BUM(1933), w; BABES IN ARMS(1939), w; ON YOUR TOES(1939), w; BOYS FROM SYRACUSE(1940), w; TOO MANY GIRLS(1940), w, m; THEY MET IN ARGENTINA(1941), m; I MARRIED AN ANGEL(1942), w, m; MAIN STREET TO BROADWAY(1953); OKLAHOMA(1955), m; KING AND I, THE(1956), w, m; PAL JOEY(1957), w; SLAUGHTER ON TENTH AVENUE(1957), m; SOUTH PACIFIC(1958), w; FLOWER DRUM SONG(1961), m; SOUND OF MUSIC, THE(1965), w, m

Rod Rodgers
YOUTH RUNS WILD(1944)
Sondra Rodgers
ANCHORS AWEIGH(1945); HIDDEN EYE, THE(1945); KEEP YOUR POWDER DRY(1945); EASY TO WED(1946); TAP ROOTS(1948); TAMMY AND THE DOCTOR(1963); COUNTRY BOY(1966)
Steven Rodgers
1984
PURPLE HEARTS(1984)
Stuart Edmond Rodgers
INCREDIBLE MELTING MAN, THE(1978)
Walter Rodgers
Silents
SECRET OF THE HILLS, THE(1921); SILVER CAR, THE(1921); STEELHEART(1921); RUGGED WATER(1925); IRISH HEARTS(1927); WOLF'S CLOTHING(1927)
Ward Rodgers
REAL LIFE(1979)
Warren Rodgers
Silents
LOVER'S OATH, A(1925); RUGGED WATER(1925); KING OF KINGS, THE(1927)
Lazar Rodic
1984
STRIKEBOUND(1984, Aus.)
Paul Rodier
I SPIT ON YOUR GRAVE(1962, Fr.), ph
Roland Rodier
LAFAYETTE(1963, Fr.)
Matilda Rodik
RETURN OF DANIEL BOONE, THE(1941)
Melinda Rodik
RETURN OF DANIEL BOONE, THE(1941)
Merrill Guy Rodin
AMERICAN EMPIRE(1942)
Merrill Rodin
PIED PIPER, THE(1942); CHETNIKS(1943); SAGEBRUSH LAW(1943); SONG OF BERNADETTE, THE(1943); STRANGE DEATH OF ADOLF HITLER, THE(1943); BUFFALO BILL(1944); HAIL THE CONQUERING HERO(1944); IN THE MEANTIME, DARLING(1944); I WONDER WHO'S KISSING HER NOW(1947)
Maureen Rodin-Ryan
LITTLE MISS THOROUGHBRED(1938); HEAVEN CAN WAIT(1943)
Alex Rodine
DEAD HEAT ON A MERRY-GO-ROUND(1966); WALK, DON'T RUN(1966); COLOSSUS: THE FORBIN PROJECT(1969); FUTUREWORLD(1976); HARRY AND WALTER GO TO NEW YORK(1976); MAC ARTHUR(1977); NUDE BOMB, THE(1980); FIREFOX(1982)
Ralph Rodine
SEVEN FACES OF DR. LAO(1964), spec eff
John Rodion
DAWN PATROL, THE(1938); TOWER OF LONDON(1939)
Leva Rodionov
GROWN-UP CHILDREN(1963, USSR)
L. Rodionova
DAY THE WAR ENDED, THE(1961, USSR), ed; FAREWELL, DOVES(1962, USSR), ed
Nilo Rodis-Jamero
RETURN OF THE JEDI(1983), cos
Violet Roditi
TWICE A MAN(1964)
Malcolm Rodker
LORD OF THE FLIES(1963, Brit.)
Howard Rodman
ONE OF OUR SPIES IS MISSING(1966), w; COOGAN'S BLUFF(1968), w; WINNING(1969), w; CHARLEY VARRICK(1973), w
Mary Rodman
FRENCH LINE, THE(1954)
Nancy Rodman
DANIEL BOONE, TRAIL BLAZER(1957); GERONIMO(1962); CHOSEN SURVIVORS(1974 U.S.-Mex.)
Nick Rodman
INDIAN TERRITORY(1950)
Robert Rodman
Silents
OLD AGE HANDICAP(1928)
Victor Rodman
LONG, HOT SUMMER, THE(1958)
Shumel Rodnesky
MOSES(1976, Brit./Ital.)
Rodney
YOUNG AND EVIL(1962, Mex.), ch
Dayle Rodney
CRASH LANDING(1958)
Earl Rodney
Silents
NAUGHTY, NAUGHTY!(1918)
Misc. Silents
BIGGEST SHOW ON EARTH, THE(1918); CITY OF TEARS, THE(1918); KEYS OF THE RIGHTEOUS, THE(1918)
Earle Rodney
MIDNIGHT DADDIES(1929), w; HYPNOTIZED(1933), w
Silents
HEART TROUBLE(1928), w
Eugene B. Rodney
RELENTLESS(1948), p
Col. George B. Rodney
FRONTIER JUSTICE(1936), w
Jack Rodney
CURE FOR LOVE, THE(1950, Brit.); CONCRETE JUNGLE, THE(1962, Brit.); DEVIL-SHIP PIRATES, THE(1964, Brit.); SHARE OUT, THE(1966, Brit.); VIKING QUEEN, THE(1967, Brit.)

John Rodney
PURSUED(1947); FIGHTER SQUADRON(1948); KEY LARGO(1948); CALAMITY JANE AND SAM BASS(1949)
June Rodney
GREAT VAN ROBBERY, THE(1963, Brit.)
V. Rodney
ODDO(1967), ph
Winston Rodney
ROCKERS(1980)
The Rodney Hudson Dancing Girls
SONG OF THE FORGE(1937, Brit.)
Yu. Rodnoy
MARRIAGE OF BALZAMINOV, THE(1966, USSR)
Master Rodon
PASTEUR(1936, Fr.)
Cedomir Rodovic
EARLY WORKS(1970, Yugo.)
Fred Rodrian
TINDER BOX, THE(1968, E. Ger.), w
Luisa Rodrigo
NEST, THE(1982, Span.)
Ric Rodrigo
IGOROTA, THE LEGEND OF THE TREE OF LIFE(1970, Phil.)
Roberto Rodrigo
DIABOLIQUE(1955, Fr.)
Xavier Rodrigo
HERE COME THE TIGERS(1978)
Cheryl Rodrigue
WOMEN AND BLOODY TERROR(1970)
Madeleine Rodrigue
Misc. Silents
PARIS QUI DORT(1924, Fr.)
Alfred Rodrigues
ALLIGATOR NAMED DAISY, AN(1957, Brit.), ch; LET'S BE HAPPY(1957, Brit.), ch
Amalia Rodrigues
LOVER'S NET(1957, Fr.)
Carmen Rodrigues
NADA MAS QUE UNA MUJER(1934)
Dawn Rodrigues
SPY WHO LOVED ME, THE(1977, Brit.)
Diane Rodrigues
WHICH WAY IS UP?(1977)
Fay Rodrigues
1984
MAJDHAR(1984, Brit.), art d
Joffre Rodrigues
PRETTY BUT WICKED(1965, Braz.), p
Maria Rosa Rodrigues
TASTE FOR WOMEN, A(1966, Fr./Ital.); TIGHT SKIRTS, LOOSE PLEASURES(1966, Fr.)
Mario Rodrigues
WE SHALL RETURN(1963)
Nelson Rodrigues
LOLLIPOP(1966, Braz.), w; ALL NUDITY SHALL BE PUNISHED(1974, Brazil), w
Oscar Rodrigues
PICKUP ON 101(1972), cos; ARNOLD(1973), cos
Pedro Rodrigues
HAPPY THIEVES, THE(1962), cos
Percy Rodrigues
COME BACK CIHARLESTON BLUE(1972); WHO FEARS THE DEVIL(1972); RHINOCEROS(1974); DEADLY BLESSING(1981); BRAINWAVES(1983)
Ramon Rodrigues
WE SHALL RETURN(1963); KING OF COMEDY, THE(1983)
Alfred Rodriguez
MADELEINE(1950, Brit.)
Alicia Rodriguez
VAMPIRE'S COFFIN, THE(1958, Mex.)
Angela Rodriguez
SCALPHUNTERS, THE(1968)
Aurelio Rodriguez
SECRET DOOR, THE(1964), ph
Carlos Rodriguez
SECRET DOOR, THE(1964)
Carmen Rodriguez
QUANDO EL AMOR RIE(1933); TWO AND ONE TWO(1934); TANGO BAR(1935)
Celia Rodriguez
PASSIONATE STRANGERS, THE(1968, Phil.)
Charles Rodriguez
WIZ, THE(1978)
Dagoberto Rodriguez
BLUE DEMON VERSUS THE INFERNAL BRAINS(1967, Mex.); VAMPIRES, THE(1969, Mex.)
Diane Rodriguez
ZOOT SUIT(1981)
Dom Rodriguez
ANGEL LEVINE, THE(1970), cos
Domingo Rodriguez
MICKEY ONE(1965), cos; RACHEL, RACHEL(1968), cos; SIDELONG GLANCES OF A PIGEON KICKER, THE(1970), cos
Domingo A. Rodriguez
LANDLORD, THE(1970), cos
Eduardo Rodriguez
TOM THUMB(1967, Mex.)
Emilio Rodriguez
FACE OF TERROR(1964, Span.); GUNFIGHTERS OF CASA GRANDE(1965, U.S./Span.); KID RODELO(1966, U.S./Span.); DOS COSMONAUTAS A LA FUERZA(1967, Span./*Ital.); VISCOUNT, THE(1967, Fr./Span./Ital./Ger.); DEADFALL(1968, Brit.); CORRUPTION OF CHRIS MILLER, THE(1979, Span.), ed

Emma Rodriguez
LITTLE ANGEL(1961, Mex.)
Estelita Rodriguez
ON THE OLD SPANISH TRAIL(1947); GAY RANCHERO, THE(1948); OLD LOS ANGELES(1948); GOLDEN STALLION, THE(1949); SUSANNA PASS(1949); BELLE OF OLD MEXICO(1950); CALIFORNIA PASSAGE(1950); FEDERAL AGENT AT LARGE(1950); HIT PARADE OF 1951(1950); SUNSET IN THE WEST(1950); TWILIGHT IN THE SIERRAS(1950); CUBAN FIREBALL(1951); HAVANA ROSE(1951); PALS OF THE GOLDEN WEST(1952); SOUTH PACIFIC TRAIL(1952); RIO BRAVO(1959)
Misc. Talkies
IN OLD LOS ANGELES(1948)
Frank Rodriguez
WAY OUT(1966)
George Rodriguez
CHIVATO(1961); REBELLION IN CUBA(1961)
Henrich Rodriguez
VAMPIRE, THE(1968, Mex.), w
Irma Rodriguez
DOCTOR OF DOOM(1962, Mex.)
Ismael Rodriguez
DANIEL BOONE, TRAIL BLAZER(1957), d; IMPORTANT MAN, THE(1961, Mex.), p&d, w; LA CUCARACHA(1961, Mex.), p&d, w
J. Rodriguez
SANTO CONTRA EL CEREBRO DIABOLICO zero(1962, Mex.), p
Jesus Rodriguez
LA NAVE DE LOS MONSTRUOS(1959, Mex.)
Joaquin "Cagancho" Rodriguez
MAGNIFICENT MATADOR, THE(1955)
Johnny Rodriguez
NEW GIRL IN TOWN(1977)
Jose Carlos Rodriguez
UNDER FIRE(1983)
Jose Maria Rodriguez
UP THE MACGREGORS(1967, Ital./Span.), w
Jose Rodriguez
DOCTOR OF DOOM(1962, Mex.), art d; UP THE DOWN STAIRCASE(1967); DETECTIVE, THE(1968); CHOSEN SURVIVORS(1974 U.S.-Mex.), art d
Juanita Rodriguez
SATAN'S BED(1965)
Lisa Rodriguez
TERROR ON TOUR(1980)
Lorenzo Rodriguez
TRISTANA(1970, Span./Ital./Fr.)
Luis F. Rodriguez
FOR A FEW DOLLARS MORE(1967, Ital./Ger./Span.)
Marco Rodriguez
ZOOT SUIT(1981)
Maria Rodriguez
CONFESSIONS OF AMANS, THE(1977)
Maria Rosa Rodriguez
EXTERMINATORS, THE(1965 Fr.)
Mario Alberto Rodriguez
MACARIO(1961, Mex.)
Maurice Rodriguez
BURN(1970)
Michel Andel Rodriguez
TOMMY THE TOREADOR(1960, Brit.)
Mike J. Rodriguez
RHYTHM OF THE RIO GRANDE(1940)
Milton Rodriguez
ROSE FOR EVERYONE, A(1967, Ital.)
Nicolas Rodriguez
MAN'S HOPE(1947, Span.)
Norma Rodriguez
1984
VARIETY(1984)
Orlando Rodriguez
BORN RECKLESS(1959)
Oscar Rodriguez
KING AND FOUR QUEENS, THE(1956), cos; RIDE BACK, THE(1957), cos; MAGIC SWORD, THE(1962), cos; WILD HARVEST(1962), cos; WAR WAGON, THE(1967), cos; PRIVATE NAVY OF SGT. O'FARRELL, THE(1968), cos; TERROR IN THE WAX MUSEUM(1973), cos; WALKING TALL(1973), cos; HUSTLE(1975), cos; MAN WITH BOGART'S FACE, THE(1980), cos
Percy Rodriguez
TROUBLE-FETE(1964, Can.); PLAINSMAN, THE(1966); HEART IS A LONELY HUNTER, THE(1968); SWEET RIDE, THE(1968); HUGO THE HIPPO(1976, Hung./U.S.)
1984
INVISIBLE STRANGLER(1984)
Rafael Rodriguez
MAGNIFICENT MATADOR, THE(1955)
Ralph Rodriguez
FIEND OF DOPE ISLAND(1961); HARBOR LIGHTS(1963)
Ramon Rodriguez
WOMAN'S DEVOTION, A(1956), art d; LITTLE SAVAGE, THE(1959), art d
Raymond Rodriguez
TOUCH OF EVIL(1958)
Roberto Rodriguez
LITTLE ANGEL(1961, Mex.), d, w; LITTLE RED RIDING HOOD(1963, Mex.), d; QUEEN'S SWORDSMEN, THE(1963, Mex.), d, w; LITTLE RED RIDING HOOD AND HER FRIENDS(1964, Mex.), d, w; PUSS 'N' BOOTS(1964, Mex.), p, w; LITTLE RED RIDING HOOD AND THE MONSTERS(1965, Mex.), d, w; TRACKDOWN(1976); LAST AMERICAN VIRGIN, THE(1982)
Roman Rodriguez
GLORIA(1980)

Sixto Rodriguez
FAT CITY(1972)
Tino Rodriguez
MAN FRIDAY(1975, Brit.), ch
Yolanda Rodriguez
COOL WORLD, THE(1963)
Jose Rodriguez-Soltero
LUPE(1967), p&d
Chris Rodriquez
WILD PACK, THE(1972)
Estelita Rodriquez
MEXICANA(1945); IN OLD AMARILLO(1951)
Orlando Rodriquez
PILLARS OF THE SKY(1956)
Oscar Rodriquez
HOW TO MAKE A MONSTER(1958), cos
Paul Rodriquez
D.C. CAB(1983)
Pedro Rodriquez
SPANISH AFFAIR(1958, Span.), cos
Ricardo Rodriquez
CEREMONY, THE(1963, U.S./Span.)
Ruben Rodriquez
1984
ERENDIRA(1984, Mex./Fr./Ger.), spec eff
Tony Rodriquez
SECRET BEYOND THE DOOR, THE(1948)
Vidal "Coco" Rodriquez
1984
BREAKIN' 2: ELECTRIC BOOGALOO(1984)
Christian Rodska
RECKONING, THE(1971, Brit.)
Melvin Rodvold
NORTHERN LIGHTS(1978)
G. Rodway
MARK OF CAIN, THE(1948, Brit.), makeup
Geoff Rodway
SWORD AND THE ROSE, THE(1953), makeup
Geoffrey Rodway
VICE VERSA(1948, Brit.), makeup; STORY OF ROBIN HOOD, THE(1952, Brit.), makeup; PURPLE PLAIN, THE(1954, Brit.), makeup; SAVAGE INNOCENTS, THE(1960, Brit.), makeup; WHISTLE DOWN THE WIND(1961, Brit.), makeup; CARRY ON CABBIE(1963, Brit.), makeup; TRAITORS, THE(1963, Brit.), makeup; VULTURE, THE(1967, U.S./Brit./Can.), makeup
Norman Rodway
THIS OTHER EDEN(1959, Brit.); QUESTION OF SUSPENSE, A(1961, Brit.); AMBUSH IN LEOPARD STREET(1962, Brit.); MURDER IN EDEN(1962, Brit.); QUARE FELLOW, THE(1962, Brit.); WEBSTER BOY, THE(1962, Brit.); FOUR IN THE MORNING(1965, Brit.); JOHNNY NOBODY(1965, Brit.); CHIMES AT MIDNIGHT(1967, Span.,Switz.); I'LL NEVER FORGET WHAT'S 'IS NAME(1967, Brit.); PENTHOUSE, THE(1967, Brit.); FINAL OPTION, THE(1983, Brit.)
James Rodwell
BATTLE OF GALLIPOLI(1931, Brit.), ph
S. Rodwell
ESCAPED FROM DARTMOOR(1930, Brit.), ph
Sally Rodwell
1984
VARIETY(1984)
Stanley Rodwell
FLYING FOOL, THE(1931, Brit.), ph; FLAG LIEUTENANT, THE(1932, Brit.), ph
William Rodwell
FOR THOSE IN PERIL(1944, Brit.); HE SNOOPS TO CONQUER(1944, Brit.)
Anna Rodzianko
SGT. PEPPER'S LONELY HEARTS CLUB BAND(1978)
Artur Rodzinski
CARNEGIE HALL(1947)
Danielle Roe
Misc. Talkies
KAHUNA!(1981)
Guy Roe
SCANDAL IN PARIS, A(1946), ph; RAILROADED(1947), ph; WHISPERING CITY(1947, Can.), ph; BEHIND LOCKED DOORS(1948), ph; COBRA STRIKES, THE(1948), ph; IN THIS CORNER(1948), ph; TRAPPED(1949), ph; ARMORED CAR ROBBERY(1950), ph; SOUND OF FURY, THE(1950), ph; QUEEN FOR A DAY(1951), ph; MY SIX CONVICTS(1952), ph; TARGET EARTH(1954), ph; SILVER STAR, THE(1955), ph; TWO-GUN LADY(1956), ph
Patricia Roe
YOUNGEST PROFESSION, THE(1943); TATTOO(1981)
Raymond Roe
TRUE TO LIFE(1943); BACK DOOR TO HEAVEN(1939); MAJOR AND THE MINOR, THE(1942); IT COMES UP LOVE(1943); PARIS AFTER DARK(1943); YOUNGEST PROFESSION, THE(1943); WING AND A PRAYER(1944); JUNE BRIDE(1948); DEAR WIFE(1949); STRANGE BARGAIN(1949); ASPHALT JUNGLE, THE(1950); PRETTY BABY(1950); WEST POINT STORY, THE(1950)
Raymond Russell Roe
CARRIE(1952)
Stephen Roe
BY WHOSE HAND?(1932), w
Vingie Roe
PERILOUS JOURNEY, A(1953), w
Vingie E. Roe
Silents
PRIMAL LURE, THE(1916), w; CRIMSON CHALLENGE, THE(1922), w; NORTH OF THE RIO GRANDE(1922), w; SPLENDID ROAD, THE(1925), w
Carroll Roebke
SWEET CHARITY(1969)
Paul Roebling
TOMORROW(1972), p; PRINCE OF THE CITY(1981); END OF AUGUST, THE(1982); BLUE THUNDER(1983)

C. Disney Roebuck
OTHER PEOPLE'S SINS(1931, Brit.); WOMAN DECIDES, THE(1932, Brit.)
Charles F. Roebuck
Silents
PRICE OF A PARTY, THE(1924), w
Earle Roebuck
Silents
WHIP WOMAN, THE(1928), w
Jimmy Roebuck
MONKEY BUSINESS(1952)
Tiny Roebuck
STRAIGHT, PLACE AND SHOW(1938); TORCHY PLAYS WITH DYNAMITE(1939)
John Roeburt
JIGSAW(1949), w; ST. BENNY THE DIP(1951), w; DEAD TO THE WORLD(1961), w; STRANGERS IN THE CITY(1962)
Sam Roeca
SIDESHOW(1950), w; I WAS AN AMERICAN SPY(1951), w; NAVY BOUND(1951), w; SIERRA PASSAGE(1951), w; SEA TIGER(1952), w; TORPEDO ALLEY(1953), w; OUTLAW'S DAUGHTER, THE(1954), w; RACING BLOOD(1954), w; HIDDEN GUNS(1956), w; RAIDERS OF OLD CALIFORNIA(1957), w; SABU AND THE MAGIC RING(1957), w; MODERN MARRIAGE, A(1962), w
Samuel Roeca
INCIDENT(1948), w; ANGEL BABY(1961), w; WHEN THE GIRLS TAKE OVER(1962), w; FLUFFY(1965), w
Samuel Roecca
TALL TEXAN, THE(1953), w; NIGHT VISITOR, THE(1970, Swed./U.S.), w
Ralph Roeder
OPEN ROAD, THE(1940, Fr.), titles
Rolf Roediger
PUFNSTUF(1970), puppeteer
Nicholas Roeg
DR. CRIPPEN(1963, Brit.), ph; GUEST, THE(1963, Brit.), ph; JUST FOR FUN(1963, Brit.), ph; CODE 7, VICTIM 5(1964, Brit.), ph; CASINO ROYALE(1967, Brit.), ph
Nicolas Roeg
JAZZ BOAT(1960, Brit.), ph; INFORMATION RECEIVED(1962, Brit.), ph; PRIZE OF ARMS, A(1962, Brit.), w; GREAT VAN ROBBERY, THE(1963, Brit.), ph; SANDERS(1963, Brit.), w; MASQUE OF THE RED DEATH, THE(1964, U.S./Brit.), ph; NOTHING BUT THE BEST(1964, Brit.), ph; SEASIDE SWINGERS(1965, Brit.), ph; FAHRENHEIT 451(1966, Brit.), ph; FUNNY THING HAPPENED ON THE WAY TO THE FORUM, A(1966), ph; GIRL GETTERS, THE(1966, Brit.), ph; FAR FROM THE MADDING CROWD(1967, Brit.), ph; PETULIA(1968, U.S./Brit.), ph; WALKABOUT(1971, Aus./U.S.), d, ph; DON'T LOOK NOW(1973, Brit./Ital.), d; MAN WHO FELL TO EARTH, THE(1976, Brit.), d; EUREKA(1983, Brit.), d
Misc. Talkies
PERFORMANCE(1970, Brit.), d
Nicolette Roeg
MY AIN FOLK(1944, Brit.); HOME SWEET HOME(1945, Brit.); HONEYMOON HOTEL(1946, Brit.); I'LL TURN TO YOU(1946, Brit.); ALL THE RIGHT NOISES(1973, Brit.)
Albin Roeheling
LOVABLE CHEAT, THE(1949)
Viola Roehl
NECK AND NECK(1931), ed
Edward Roehm
LOVE BUTCHER, THE(1982)
Misc. Talkies
C.B. HUSTLERS(1978)
Heinz Roehmheld
MARKED WOMAN(1937), m
Franz Roehn
MIRACLE OF THE BELLS, THE(1948); UNFAITHFULLY YOURS(1948); KNOCK ON ANY DOOR(1949); AFFAIR IN TRINIDAD(1952); SALOME(1953); DEEP IN MY HEART(1954); TOBOR THE GREAT(1954); GIRL IN THE KREMLIN, THE(1957); DEEP SIX, THE(1958); FLY, THE(1958); ME AND THE COLONEL(1958); MR. SARDONICUS(1961)
Franz F. Roehn
TURNING POINT, THE(1952)
Franz J. Roehn
DARK CITY(1950)
Peter Roehrig
SLAVERS(1977, Ger.), art d
Wolfram Roehrig
FOXHOLE IN CAIRO(1960, Brit.), m; LOVE FEAST, THE(1966, Ger.), m
Adriana Roel
GIGANTES PLANETARIOS(1965, Mex.); VIVA MARIA(1965, Fr./Ital.)
Augusta Roeland
DOUBLE LIFE, A(1947)
Jorge Roelas
1984
DEMONS IN THE GARDEN(1984, Span.)
Eva Roelens
1984
LOVE ON THE GROUND(1984,Fr.)
Erik Hazelhoff Roelfzema
SOLDIER OF ORANGE(1979, Dutch), w
Charlie Roellinghoff
DAUGHTER OF EVIL(1930, Ger.), w
Charlotte Roellinghoff
SCANDALS OF PARIS(1935, Brit.), w
Al Roelofe
ARIZONA BUSHWHACKERS(1968), art d
Al Roelofs
MAN-TRAP(1961), art d; WHO'S MINDING THE STORE?(1963), art d; LAW OF THE LAWLESS(1964), art d; BLACK SPURS(1965), art d; IN HARM'S WAY(1965), art d; TOWN TAMER(1965), art d; EYE FOR AN EYE, AN(1966), art d; NEVADA SMITH(1966), art d; WACO(1966), art d; FORT UTAH(1967), art d; HOSTILE GUNS(1967), art d; PRESIDENT'S ANALYST, THE(1967), art d; RED TOMAHAWK(1967), art d; $1,000,000 DUCK(1971), art d; BISCUIT EATER, THE(1972), art d; CHARLEY AND THE ANGEL(1973), art d; ISLAND AT THE TOP OF THE WORLD, THE(1974), art d; ESCAPE TO WITCH MOUNTAIN(1975), art d; GUS(1976), art d;

BLACK HOLE, THE(1979), art d; TRON(1982), art d

Al Y. Roelofs
HELL'S ISLAND(1955), art d; YOUNG CAPTIVES, THE(1959), art d

Alexander Roelofs
HOUSE IS NOT A HOME, A(1964), art d

Kate Roemer
UNMASKED(1929)
Misc. Talkies
UNMASKED(1929)

Michael Roemer
NOTHING BUT A MAN(1964), p, d, w; PILGRIM, FAREWELL(1980), d&w

Sylvia Roemer
ARISTOCATS, THE(1970), anim

H. Roemheld
MAKE YOUR OWN BED(1944), m

Heinz Roemheld
BLACK CAT, THE(1934), md; FRONT PAGE WOMAN(1935), m; BULLETS OR BALLOTS(1936), m; DRACULA'S DAUGHTER(1936), m; GOLDEN ARROW, THE(1936), m; TWO AGAINST THE WORLD(1936), m; GREAT O'MALLEY, THE(1937), m; IT'S LOVE I'M AFTER(1937), m; KID GALAHAD(1937), m; PERFECT SPECIMEN, THE(1937), m; SAN QUENTIN(1937), m; STAND-IN(1937), m; COMET OVER BROADWAY(1938), m; FOUR'S A CROWD(1938), m; I MET MY LOVE AGAIN(1938), m; MEN ARE SUCH FOOLS(1938), m; KING OF THE UNDERWORLD(1939), m; NANCY DREW-REPORTER(1939), m; ROARING TWENTIES, THE(1939), m; YOU CAN'T GET AWAY WITH MURDER(1939), m; BRITISH INTELLIGENCE(1940), m; BROTHER ORCHID(1940), m; BROTHER RAT AND A BABY(1940), m; INVISIBLE STRIPES(1940), m; IT ALL CAME TRUE(1940), m; LADY WITH RED HAIR(1940), m; MY LOVE CAME BACK(1940), m; AFFECTIONATELY YOURS(1941), m; KNOCKOUT(1941), m; STRAWBERRY BLONDE, THE(1941), m; THIEVES FALL OUT(1941), m; WAGONS ROLL AT NIGHT, THE(1941), m; GENTLEMAN JIM(1942), m; HARD WAY, THE(1942), m; MALE ANIMAL, THE(1942), m; DESERT SONG, THE(1943), m; JANIE(1944), m; TOO YOUNG TO KNOW(1945), m; BACHELOR'S DAUGHTERS, THE(1946), md; CHASE, THE(1946), md; MR. ACE(1946), m; O.S.S.(1946), m; SCANDAL IN PARIS, A(1946), m; CHRISTMAS EVE(1947), m; DOWN TO EARTH(1947), m; HEAVEN ONLY KNOWS(1947), m; FLAME, THE(1948), m; FULLER BRUSH MAN(1948), m; GIRL FROM MANHATTAN(1948), m; HERE COMES TROUBLE(1948), md; I, JANE DOE(1948), m; LADY FROM SHANGHAI, THE(1948), m; MY DEAR SECRETARY(1948), m; ON OUR MERRY WAY(1948), m; SIREN OF ATLANTIS(1948), md; STATION WEST(1948), m; WHO KILLED "DOC" ROBBIN?(1948), md; MISS GRANT TAKES RICHMOND(1949), m; FULLER BRUSH GIRL(1950), m; GOOD HUMOR MAN, THE(1950), m; ROGUES OF SHERWOOD FOREST(1950), m; CHICAGO CALLING(1951), m; BIG TREES, THE(1952), m; JACK AND THE BEANSTALK(1952), m; RUBY GENTRY(1952), m; THREE FOR BEDROOM C(1952), m; MOONLIGHTER, THE(1953), m, md; HELL'S HORIZON(1955), m, md; SQUARE JUNGLE, THE(1955), m; THERE'S ALWAYS TOMORROW(1956), m; DECISION AT SUNDOWN(1957), m; MONSTER THAT CHALLENGED THE WORLD, THE(1957), m, md; TALL T, THE(1957), m; RIDE LONESOME(1959), m, md; LAD: A DOG(1962), m

William Roerich
THIS IS THE ARMY(1943)

William Roerick
HARDER THEY FALL, THE(1956); NOT OF THIS EARTH(1957); WASP WOMAN, THE(1959); LOVELY WAY TO DIE, A(1968); LOVE MACHINE, THE(1971); SPORTING CLUB, THE(1971); SEPARATE PEACE, A(1972); DAY OF THE DOLPHIN, THE(1973); OTHER SIDE OF THE MOUNTAIN, THE(1975); 92 IN THE SHADE(1975, U.S./Brit.); GOD TOLD ME TO(1976)

Manuel Roero
LOST HAPPINESS(1948, Ital.)

Skip Roessel
1984
VAMPING(1984), ph

Laura Roessing
Silents
CALL OF THE WILD, THE(1923)

Paul Rene Roestad
1984
KAMILLA(1984, Norway), ph

Maurice Roeves
FIGHTING PRINCE OF DONEGAL, THE(1966, Brit.); ULYSSES(1967, U.S./Brit.); OH! WHAT A LOVELY WAR(1969, Brit.); WHEN EIGHT BELLS TOLL(1971, Brit.); YOUNG WINSTON(1972, Brit.); EAGLE HAS LANDED, THE(1976, Brit.); VICTORY(1981); FINAL OPTION, THE(1983, Brit.)

Ernst R. Roff
GLORY GUYS, THE(1965), ed

Susan Roffer
1984
BEAT STREET(1984)

Jack Roffey
EIGHT O'CLOCK WALK(1954, Brit.), w; HOSTILE WITNESS(1968, Brit.), w

Julian Roffman
SARUMBA(1950), p; MASK, THE(1961, Can.), p&d; EXPLOSION(1969, Can.), p; PYX, THE(1973, Can.), p; GLOVE, THE(1980), p, w, stunts

Gina Rogak
GIRLFRIENDS(1978)

Jonathan Rogal
MAN WHO LOVED WOMEN, THE(1983)

Enrique Rogales
W.I.A.(WOUNDED IN ACTION)*1/2 (1966), ph

Nicholas J. Rogalli
ENLIGHTEN THY DAUGHTER(1934), ph

Marty Rogalny
MALIBU BEACH(1978)

Barney Rogan
TARNISHED LADY(1931), ed; FOLLOW THE LEADER(1930), ed; QUEEN HIGH(1930), ed; GIRL HABIT(1931), ed; STRUGGLE, THE(1931), ed; MIRACLE ON MAIN STREET, A(1940), ed

Bernard Rogan
BIG TOWN(1932), ph; HOTEL VARIETY(1933), ed

Beth Rogan
DOCTOR AT LARGE(1957, Brit.); JUST MY LUCK(1957, Brit.); TRUE AS A TURTLE(1957, Brit.); INNOCENT MEETING(1959, Brit.); COMPELLED(1960, Brit.); OPERATION CUPID(1960, Brit.); MYSTERIOUS ISLAND(1961, U.S./Brit.); SALT & PEPPER(1968, Brit.)

Florence Rogan
Silents
SPARROWS(1926)
Misc. Silents
MAN WHO PAID, THE(1922)

George E. Rogan
WHAT'S YOUR RACKET?(1934), w

Josh Rogan
TWILIGHT ZONE-THE MOVIE(1983), w

Peter Rogan
MOLLY MAGUIRES, THE(1970)

Ralph Rogan
LOVE ON SKIS(1933, Brit.)

Rita Rogan
Silents
WILD GOOSE, THE(1921)

Virginia Rogan
WINGS OVER HONOLULU(1937)

Joseph Rogato
GAMBLING HOUSE(1950)

Brita Rogde
TERRORISTS, THE(1975, Brit.)

Leonard Rogel
WEREWOLVES ON WHEELS(1971)

Al Rogell
FLYING MARINE, THE(1929), d; MAMBA(1930), d; ALOHA(1931), d; AIR HOSTESS(1933), d; EAST OF FIFTH AVE.(1933), d; AMONG THE MISSING(1934), d; FUGITIVE LADY(1934), d; NO MORE WOMEN(1934), d; LAST WARNING, THE(1938), d

Albert Rogell
PAINTED FACES(1929), d; SUICIDE FLEET(1931), d; SWEEPSTAKES(1931), d; TIP-OFF, THE(1931), d; CARNIVAL BOAT(1932), d; RIDER OF DEATH VALLEY(1932), d; BELOW THE SEA(1933), d; WRECKER, THE(1933), d; FOG(1934), d; HELL CAT, THE(1934), d; NAME THE WOMAN(1934), d; AIR HAWKS(1935), d; ATLANTIC ADVENTURE(1935), d; ESCAPE FROM DEVIL'S ISLAND(1935), d; UNKNOWN WOMAN(1935), d
Silents
GALLOPING GALLAGHER(1924), d; GEARED TO GO(1924), d; LIGHTNING ROMANCE(1924), d; NORTH OF NEVADA(1924), d; EASY MONEY(1925), d; GOAT GETTER(1925), d; KNOCKOUT KID, THE(1925), d; UNKNOWN CAVALIER, THE(1926), d; SOMEWHERE IN SONORA(1927), d; SUNSET DERBY, THE(1927), d; WESTERN ROVER, THE(1927), d; WESTERN WHIRLWIND, THE(1927), d, w
Misc. Silents
GREATEST MENACE, THE(1923), d; DANGEROUS COWARD, THE(1924), d; FIGHTING SAP, THE(1924), d; MASK OF LOPEZ, THE(1924), d; SILENT STRANGER, THE(1924), d; THUNDERING HOOFS(1924), d; CIRCUS CYCLONE, THE(1925), d; CRACK O'DAWN(1925), d; CYCLONE CAVALIER(1925), d; FEAR FIGHTER, THE(1925), d; FIGHTING FATE(1925), d; SNOB BUSTER, THE(1925), d; SUPER SPEED(1925), d; YOUTH'S GAMBLE(1925), d; MAN FROM THE WEST, THE(1926), d; MEN OF THE NIGHT(1926), d; PATENT LEATHER PUG, THE(1926), d; RED HOT LEATHER(1926), d; SENOR DAREDEVIL(1926), d; WILD HORSE STAMPEDE, THE(1926), d; DEVIL'S SADDLE, THE(1927), d; FIGHTING THREE, THE(1927), d; GRINNING GUNS(1927), d; MEN OF DARING(1927), d; OVERLAND STAGE, THE(1927), d; RED RAIDERS, THE(1927), d; ROUGH AND READY(1927), d; CANYON OF ADVENTURE, THE(1928), d; GLORIOUS TRAIL, THE(1928), d; PHANTOM CITY, THE(1928), d; SHEPHERD OF THE HILL, THE(1928), d; UPLAND RIDER, THE(1928), d; CALIFORNIA MAIL, THE(1929), d; CHEYENNE(1929), d

Albert S. Rogell
LONE WOLF'S DAUGHTER, THE(1929), d; GRAND JURY(1936), d; ROAMING LADY(1936), d; YOU MAY BE NEXT(1936), d; MURDER IN GREENWICH VILLAGE(1937), d; CITY STREETS(1938), d; LONE WOLF IN PARIS, THE(1938), d; START CHEERING(1938), d; FOR LOVE OR MONEY(1939), d; HAWAIIAN NIGHTS(1939), d; LAUGH IT OFF(1939), p&d; ARGENTINE NIGHTS(1940), d; I CAN'T GIVE YOU ANYTHING BUT LOVE, BABY(1940), d; LI'L ABNER(1940), d; PRIVATE AFFAIRS(1940), d; BLACK CAT, THE(1941), d; PUBLIC ENEMIES(1941), d; SAILORS ON LEAVE(1941), d; TIGHT SHOES(1941), d; BUTCH MINDS THE BABY(1942), d; JAIL HOUSE BLUES(1942), d; PRIORITIES ON PARADE(1942), d; SLEEPYTIME GAL(1942), d; TRUE TO THE ARMY(1942), d; HIT PARADE OF 1943(1943), d; IN OLD OKLAHOMA(1943), d; YOUTH ON PARADE(1943), d; LOVE, HONOR AND GOODBYE(1945), d, w; EARL CARROLL SKETCHBOOK(1946), d; MAGNIFICENT ROGUE, THE(1947), d; HEAVEN ONLY KNOWS(1947), d; NORTHWEST STAMPEDE(1948), p&d; SONG OF INDIA(1949), p&d; ADMIRAL WAS A LADY, THE(1950), p, d; SHADOW OF FEAR(1956, Brit.), d

Nicole Rogell
POINT BLANK(1967)

Sid Rogell
DEATH FLIES EAST(1935), p; MAMA LOVES PAPA(1945), p; STEP BY STEP(1946), p; BODYGUARD(1948), p; GUNS OF HATE(1948), p; MYSTERY IN MEXICO(1948), p; STRANGE BARGAIN(1949), p; WHITE TOWER, THE(1950), p; AT SWORD'S POINT(1951), p

Sig Rogell
ROAMING LADY(1936), p; NEVADA(1944), p

Nicholas Rogelli
CONVENTION GIRL(1935), ph

Maggie Rogen
TORTURE DUNGEON(1970)

Roger
ESCAPE TO BURMA(1955); EDUCATION OF SONNY CARSON, THE(1974)

Fanchon Roger
THRILL OF A LIFETIME(1937), p

Jean-Henri Roger
SNOW(1983, Fr.), d

Odette Roger
HARVEST(1939, Fr.); WAYS OF LOVE(1950, Ital./Fr.)

Sandra Roger
LOST HONEYMOON(1947)

Dr. Wallace Roger
I'D CLIMB THE HIGHEST MOUNTAIN(1951)

Wilfred Roger
Misc. Silents
BLACK FRIDAY(1916)

Roger-Pierre
MON ONCLE D'AMERIQUE(1980, Fr.)

Roger-Roger
MAIDEN, THE(1961, Fr.), m; PROSTITUTION(1965, Fr.), m

Rogers
FORCES' SWEETHEART(1953, Brit.), w

Allan Rogers
GIRL SAID NO, THE(1937); EVERY DAY'S A HOLIDAY(1938)

Allen Rogers
Misc. Talkies
FRIDAY ON MY MIND(1970)

Andrew A. Rogers
Misc. Silents
HIS TURNING POINT(1915)

Anthony Rogers
MEN OF THE SEA(1951, Brit.); RED LINE 7000(1965); CAMELOT(1967); EL DORADO(1967)

Anton Rogers
Misc. Talkies
OPERATION STOGIE(1960, Brit.)

Barbara Rogers
FOOTLIGHT PARADE(1933); LITTLE GIANT, THE(1933); PICTURE SNATCHER(1933); 42ND STREET(1933); DARK HAZARD(1934); ONE IN A MILLION(1935); TWO IN A CROWD(1936)
Misc. Talkies
I HATE WOMEN(1934)

Ben Rogers
CANNONBALL RUN, THE(1981)

Betty Blake Rogers
STORY OF WILL ROGERS, THE(1952), w

Bill Rogers
GIRL, THE BODY, AND THE PILL, THE(1967); SHANTY TRAMP(1967); TASTE OF BLOOD, A(1967)

Bogart Rogers
EAGLE AND THE HAWK, THE(1933), w; EVERYBODY'S OLD MAN(1936), p; PIGSKIN PARADE(1936), p; REUNION(1936), p; THIRTEEN HOURS BY AIR(1936), w; WHITE FANG(1936), p; MAN FROM DOWN UNDER, THE(1943), w

Bradford Rogers
ICE-CAPADES REVUE(1942), w

Brooks Rogers
TRUMAN CAPOTE'S TRILOGY(1969)

Buddy Rogers
BEST OF ENEMIES(1933); WEEKEND MILLIONAIRE(1937, Brit.); LITTLE IODINE(1946), p; SUSIE STEPS OUT(1946), p; ADVENTURES OF DON COYOTE(1947), p; STORK BITES MAN(1947), p

Cameron Rogers
CARDINAL RICHELIEU(1935), w; WHITE BANNERS(1938), w; BELLE STARR(1941), w

Carl Rogers
CAPTURE THAT CAPSULE(1961); STARFIGHTERS, THE(1964)

Cecile Rogers
ATHENA(1954); FUNNY FACE(1957); OUTLAW'S SON(1957); SPRING AFFAIR(1960); GEORGE RAFT STORY, THE(1961)

Charles Rogers
ABIE'S IRISH ROSE(1928); FOLLOW THRU(1930); ALONG CAME YOUTH(1931); BIG SHOT, THE(1931), p; REBOUND(1931), p; WORKING GIRLS(1931); BILLION DOLLAR SCANDAL(1932), p; LADY WITH A PAST(1932), p; DEVIL'S BROTHER, THE(1933), d; BABES IN TOYLAND(1934), d; BOHEMIAN GIRL, THE(1936), d; OUR RELATIONS(1936), w; WAY OUT WEST(1937), w; BLOCKHEADS(1938), w; SWISS MISS(1938), w, w; FLYING DEUCES, THE(1939), w; CHUMP AT OXFORD, A(1940), w; SAPS AT SEA(1940), w; DOUBLE TROUBLE(1941); HOUSE OF ERRORS(1942); THEY RAID BY NIGHT(1942); AIR RAID WARDENS(1943), w; DANCING MASTERS, THE(1943); THAT NAZTY NUISANCE(1943); ABROAD WITH TWO YANKS(1944), w; BREWSTER'S MILLIONS(1945); PARSON AND THE OUTLAW, THE(1957), p; THREE ON A SPREE(1961, Brit.), w; SORCERESS(1983)
Silents
SO'S YOUR OLD MAN(1926); MY BEST GIRL(1927)
Misc. Silents
OLIVER TWIST(1912); FASCINATING YOUTH(1926); MORE PAY - LESS WORK(1926)

Charles A. Rogers
MISBEHAVING HUSBANDS(1941), w

Charles Buddy Rogers
VARSITY(1928); CLOSE HARMONY(1929); HALF WAY TO HEAVEN(1929); ILLUSION(1929); RIVER OF ROMANCE(1929); HEADS UP(1930); SAFETY IN NUMBERS(1930); YOUNG EAGLES(1930); LAWYER'S SECRET, THE(1931); ROAD TO RENO(1931); THIS RECKLESS AGE(1932); TAKE A CHANCE(1933); DANCE BAND(1935, Brit.); OLD MAN RHYTHM(1935); LET'S MAKE A NIGHT OF IT(1937, Brit.); THIS WAY PLEASE(1937); GOLDEN HOOFS(1941); MEXICAN SPITFIRE'S BABY(1941); SING FOR YOUR SUPPER(1941); MEXICAN SPITFIRE AT SEA(1942); MEXICAN SPITFIRE SEES A GHOST(1942); DON'T TRUST YOUR HUSBAND(1948); SLEEP, MY LOVE(1948), p; PARSON AND THE OUTLAW, THE(1957); HIGH SCHOOL HELLCATS(1958), p
Silents
WINGS(1927); RED LIPS(1928)
Misc. Silents
GET YOUR MAN(1927); SOMEONE TO LOVE(1928)

Charles E. Rogers
SWEEPSTAKES(1931), p

Charles P. Rogers
DEVIL IS DRIVING, THE(1932), p

Charles R. Rogers
BAD COMPANY(1931), p; COMMON LAW, THE(1931), p; DEVOTION(1931), p; MILLIE(1931), p; SUICIDE FLEET(1931), p; TIP-OFF, THE(1931), p; WOMAN OF EXPERIENCE, A(1931), p; MADISON SQUARE GARDEN(1932), p; PRESTIGE(1932), p; WOMAN COMMANDS, A(1932), p; 70,000 WITNESSES(1932), p; GIRL WITHOUT A ROOM(1933), p; GOLDEN HARVEST(1933), p; I LOVE THAT MAN(1933), p; SITTING PRETTY(1933), p; SONG OF THE EAGLE(1933), p; EIGHT GIRLS IN A BOAT(1934), p; GREAT FLIRTATION, THE(1934), p; HERE COMES THE GROOM(1934), p; PRIVATE SCANDAL(1934), p; HOLD'EM YALE(1935), p; MC FADDEN'S FLATS(1935), p; VIRGINIA JUDGE, THE(1935), p; FLYING HOSTESS(1936), p; FOUR DAYS WONDER(1936), p; GIRL ON THE FRONT PAGE, THE(1936), p; LUCKIEST GIRL IN THE WORLD, THE(1936), p; MAGNIFICENT BRUTE, THE(1936), p; MY MAN GODFREY(1936), p; TWO IN A CROWD(1936), p; ROAD BACK,THE(1937), p; WHEN LOVE IS YOUNG(1937), p; WINGS OVER HONOLULU(1937), p; 100 MEN AND A GIRL(1937), p; OUR NEIGHBORS–THE CARTERS(1939), p; STAR MAKER, THE(1939), p; ADVENTURE IN WASHINGTON(1941), p; SHE KNEW ALL THE ANSWERS(1941), p; POWERS GIRL, THE(1942), p; SONG OF THE OPEN ROAD(1944), p; DELIGHTFULLY DANGEROUS(1945), p; ANGEL ON MY SHOULDER(1946), p
Silents
MAN CRAZY(1927), p; SMILE, BROTHER, SMILE(1927), p; SUNSET DERBY, THE(1927), p; LADY BE GOOD(1928), p

Charles R. Rogers [John W. Rogers]
FABULOUS DORSEYS, THE(1947), p

Charley Rogers
PARDON US(1931); PACK UP YOUR TROUBLES(1932)

Cloda Rogers
IT'S ALL OVER TOWN(1963, Brit.)

Corin Rogers
COOLEY HIGH(1975); ON THE RIGHT TRACK(1981)

Dan Rogers
REVENGE OF THE NINJA(1983)

Danny Rogers
1984
STAR TREK III: THE SEARCH FOR SPOCK(1984)

Debbie Rogers
BIONIC BOY, THE(1977, Hong Kong/Phil.)

Dinah Ann Rogers
SECRET TENT, THE(1956, Brit.)

Dinah Anne Rogers
MY FAIR LADY(1964); STRANGE BEDFELLOWS(1965)

Dora Rogers
Misc. Silents
AFTER THE WAR(1918)

Doris Rogers
LOVE RACE, THE(1931, Brit.); HONEYMOON FOR THREE(1935, Brit.); TRUST THE NAVY(1935, Brit.); GANGWAY(1937, Brit.); MADAME LOUISE(1951, Brit.); MAYTIME IN MAYFAIR(1952, Brit.); FAMILY AFFAIR(1954, Brit.); LYONS IN PARIS, THE(1955, Brit.)

Dorothy Rogers
MEXICAN SPITFIRE'S BLESSED EVENT(1943)
Misc. Silents
SALESLADY, THE(1916)

Ed Rogers
TRADER HORNEE(1970)

Elizabeth Rogers
TOWERING INFERNO, THE(1974); GRAND THEFT AUTO(1977); VAN, THE(1977); OFFICER AND A GENTLEMAN, AN(1982)

Eric Rogers
GENEVIEVE(1953, Brit.), ch; MEET MR. LUCIFER(1953, Brit.), m; CARRY ON JACK(1963, Brit.), m; SWINGIN' MAIDEN, THE(1963, Brit.), m, md; THREE LIVES OF THOMASINA, THE(1963, U.S./Brit.), md; CARRY ON CLEO(1964, Brit.), m; CARRY ON SPYING(1964, Brit.), m; NURSE ON WHEELS(1964, Brit.), m, md; THIS IS MY STREET(1964, Brit.), m; BIG JOB, THE(1965, Brit.), m; THREE HATS FOR LISA(1965, Brit.), m; CARRY ON COWBOY(1966, Brit.), m; CARRY ON SCREAMING(1966, Brit.), m; DON'T LOSE YOUR HEAD(1967, Brit.), m; FOLLOW THAT CAMEL(1967, Brit.), m; CARRY ON DOCTOR(1968, Brit.), m; CARRY ON, UP THE KHYBER(1968, Brit.), m; CARRY ON AGAIN, DOCTOR(1969, Brit.), m; CARRY ON CAMPING(1969, Brit.), m; CARRY ON HENRY VIII(1970, Brit.), m; CARRY ON UP THE JUNGLE(1970, Brit.), m; DOCTOR IN TROUBLE(1970, Brit.), m; ASSAULT(1971, Brit.), m; QUEST FOR LOVE(1971, Brit.), m; CARRY ON EMANUELLE(1978, Brit.), m; NO SEX PLEASE–WE'RE BRITISH(1979, Brit.), m

Erica Rogers
RIVALS, THE(1963, Brit.); HORROR OF IT ALL, THE(1964, Brit.); SPOTS ON MY LEOPARD, THE(1974, S. Africa); KILLER FORCE(1975, Switz./Ireland)

Frederick Rogers
Silents
PURSUING VENGEANCE, THE(1916)

Gayle Rogers
SUPPORT YOUR LOCAL SHERIFF(1969); DIRTY DINGUS MAGEE(1970)

George Rogers
SWINGING THE LEAD(1934, Brit.), a, w; MEXICAN SPITFIRE'S BLESSED EVENT(1943); SHINE ON, HARVEST MOON(1944); DEVONSVILLE TERROR, THE(1983), spec eff

Gerald Rogers
GRAND CANARY(1934); BULLDOG DRUMMOND IN AFRICA(1938); LIGHT THAT FAILED, THE(1939); CHUMP AT OXFORD, A(1940); LOVE FROM A STRANGER(1947)

Gil Rogers
BLAST OF SILENCE(1961); NOTHING BUT A MAN(1964); YOURS, MINE AND OURS(1968); PANIC IN NEEDLE PARK(1971); BELL JAR, THE(1979); CHILDREN, THE(1980); EDDIE MACON'S RUN(1983)

Ginger Rogers
FOLLOW THE LEADER(1930); QUEEN HIGH(1930); SAP FROM SYRACUSE, THE(1930); YOUNG MAN OF MANHATTAN(1930); HONOR AMONG LOVERS(1931); SUICIDE FLEET(1931); TIP-OFF, THE(1931); CARNIVAL BOAT(1932); HAT CHECK GIRL(1932); TENDERFOOT, THE(1932); THIRTEENTH GUEST, THE(1932); YOU SAID A MOUTHFUL(1932); BROADWAY BAD(1933); CHANCE AT HEAVEN(1933);

DON'T BET ON LOVE(1933); FLYING DOWN TO RIO(1933); GOLD DIGGERS OF 1933(1933); PROFESSIONAL SWEETHEART(1933); SHRIEK IN THE NIGHT, A(1933); SITTING PRETTY(1933); 42ND STREET(1933); CHANGE OF HEART(1934); FINISHING SCHOOL(1934); GAY DIVORCEE, THE(1934); RAFTER ROMANCE(1934); TWENTY MILLION SWEETHEARTS(1934); UPPER WORLD(1934); IN PERSON(1935); ROBERTA(1935); ROMANCE IN MANHATTAN(1935); STAR OF MIDNIGHT(1935); TOP HAT(1935); FOLLOW THE FLEET(1936); SWING TIME(1936); SHALL WE DANCE(1937); STAGE DOOR(1937); CAREFREE(1938); HAVING WONDERFUL TIME(1938); VIVACIOUS LADY(1938); BACHELOR MOTHER(1939); FIFTH AVENUE GIRL(1939); STORY OF VERNON AND IRENE CASTLE, THE(1939); KITTY FOYLE(1940); LUCKY PARTNERS(1940); PRIMROSE PATH(1940); TOM, DICK AND HARRY(1941); MAJOR AND THE MINOR, THE(1942); ONCE UPON A HONEYMOON(1942); ROXIE HART(1942); TALES OF MANHATTAN(1942); TENDER COMRADE(1943); I'LL BE SEEING YOU(1944); LADY IN THE DARK(1944); WEEKEND AT THE WALDORF(1945); HEARTBEAT(1946); MAGNIFICENT DOLL(1946); IT HAD TO BE YOU(1947); BARKLEYS OF BROADWAY, THE(1949); PERFECT STRANGERS(1950); STORM WARNING(1950); GROOM WORE SPURS, THE(1951); DREAMBOAT(1952); MONKEY BUSINESS(1952); WE'RE NOT MARRIED(1952); FOREVER FEMALE(1953); BEAUTIFUL STRANGER(1954, Brit.); BLACK WIDOW(1954); TIGHT SPOT(1955); FIRST TRAVELING SALESLADY, THE(1956); TEENAGE REBEL(1956); OH, MEN! OH, WOMEN!(1957); HARLOW(1965); QUICK, LET'S GET MARRIED(1965)
Misc. Talkies
CONFESSION, THE(1964)

Glen Rogers
TWO-LANE BLACKTOP(1971)

Gregory Rogers
G-MEN(1935), w
Silents
JAWS OF STEEL(1927), w

Gregory Rogers [Darryl F. Zanuck]
MIDNIGHT TAXI, THE(1928), w

Harriet Rogers
ONE SUMMER LOVE(1976)

Hazel Rogers
8 ½(1963, Ital.)
Silents
HEADS UP(1925)

Henry Rogers
WE'VE NEVER BEEN LICKED(1943)

Hilda Rogers
TEMPTATION(1936)

Howard Rogers
CALLING ALL CROOKS(1938, Brit.)

Howard Emmet Rogers
BAD ONE, THE(1930), w; ADVENTURES OF TARTU(1943, Brit.), w

Howard Emmett Rogers
FORWARD PASS, THE(1929), w; LOTTERY BRIDE, THE(1930), w; NO, NO NANETTE(1930), w; DANCERS IN THE DARK(1932), w; DON'T BET ON LOVE(1933), w; HOLD YOUR MAN(1933), w; NUISANCE, THE(1933), w; MYSTERY OF MR. X, THE(1934), w; TARZAN AND HIS MATE(1934), w; WHIRLPOOL(1934), w; BRIDE WALKS OUT, THE(1936), w; LIBELED LADY(1936), w; UNGUARDED HOUR, THE(1936), w; WHIPSAW(1936), w; ARSENE LUPIN RETURNS(1938), w; CHASER, THE(1938), w; BILLY THE KID(1941), w; CROSSROADS(1942), w; EYES IN THE NIGHT(1942), w; FOR ME AND MY GAL(1942), w; ASSIGNMENT IN BRITTANY(1943), w; GAMBLER'S CHOICE(1944), w; CALLING BULLDOG DRUMMOND(1951, Brit.), w; TWO DOLLAR BETTOR(1951), w; HOUR OF THIRTEEN, THE(1952), w
Silents
SO'S YOUR OLD MAN(1926), w; GYPSY OF THE NORTH(1928), w; SPEEDY(1928), w

Ira Rogers
THREE TOUGH GUYS(1974, U.S./Ital.); MAHOGANY(1975)

J. Maclean Rogers
ONE EMBARRASSING NIGHT(1930, Brit.), ed

Jack Rogers
TO EACH HIS OWN(1946)

Jaime Rogers
WEST SIDE STORY(1961)
1984
BREAKIN'(1984), ch

James Rogers
LADY FROM THE SEA, THE(1929, Brit.), ph; COMPULSORY HUSBAND, THE(1930, Brit.), ph; NOT SO QUIET ON THE WESTERN FRONT(1930, Brit.), ph; WHY SAILORS LEAVE HOME(1930, Brit.), ph; CAPTIVATION(1931, Brit), ph; FOR LOVE AND MONEY(1967), w

Jamie Rogers
AMERICATHON(1979), ch

Jane Rogers
PURPLE HAZE(1982)

Jane Jordan Rogers
FLIGHT FROM SINGAPORE(1962, Brit.); LISA(1962, Brit.)

Jean Rogers
MANHATTAN MOON(1935); STORMY(1935); DON'T GET PERSONAL(1936); FLASH GORDON(1936); MY MAN GODFREY(1936); TWO IN A CROWD(1936); CONFLICT(1937); MYSTERIOUS CROSSING(1937); NIGHT KEY(1937); REPORTED MISSING(1937); WHEN LOVE IS YOUNG(1937); WILDCATTER, THE(1937); ALWAYS IN TROUBLE(1938); TIME OUT FOR MURDER(1938); WHILE NEW YORK SLEEPS(1938); HEAVEN WITH A BARBED WIRE FENCE(1939); HOTEL FOR WOMEN(1939); INSIDE STORY(1939); STOP, LOOK, AND LOVE(1939); BRIGHAM YOUNG–FRONTIERSMAN(1940); CHARLIE CHAN IN PANAMA(1940); LET'S MAKE MUSIC(1940); MAN WHO WOULDN'T TALK, THE(1940); VIVA CISCO KID(1940); YESTERDAY'S HEROES(1940); DESIGN FOR SCANDAL(1941); DR. KILDARE'S VICTORY(1941); PACIFIC RENDEZVOUS(1942); SUNDAY PUNCH(1942); WAR AGAINST MRS. HADLEY, THE(1942); STRANGER IN TOWN, A(1943); SWING SHIFT MAISIE(1943); WHISTLING IN BROOKLYN(1943); ROUGH, TOUGH AND READY(1945); STRANGE MR. GREGORY, THE(1945); GAY BLADES(1946); HOT CARGO(1946); BACKLASH(1947); FIGHTING BACK(1948); SPEED TO SPARE(1948); SECOND WOMAN, THE(1951)

Jean Scott Rogers
CORRIDORS OF BLOOD(1962, Brit.), w; FLOOD, THE(1963, Brit.), w

Jeffrey Rogers
FRIDAY THE 13TH PART III(1982)
1984
FRIDAY THE 13TH–THE FINAL CHAPTER(1984)

Jimmie Rogers
BACK DOOR TO HELL(1964)

Jimmy Rogers
DUDES ARE PRETTY PEOPLE(1942); FALSE COLORS(1943); RIDERS OF THE DEADLINE(1943); FORTY THIEVES(1944); LUMBERJACK(1944); MYSTERY MAN(1944); TEXAS MASQUERADE(1944)
Silents
DOUBLING FOR ROMEO(1921)
Misc. Silents
STRANGE BORDER, THE(1920)

John Rogers
BEHIND THAT CURTAIN(1929); RAFFLES(1930); SEA WOLF, THE(1930); CHARLIE CHAN CARRIES ON(1931); MURDER BY THE CLOCK(1931); DR. JEKYLL AND MR. HYDE(1932); CHARLIE CHAN IN LONDON(1934); GRAND CANARY(1934); LIMEHOUSE BLUES(1934); LONG LOST FATHER(1934); WHARF ANGEL(1934); FEATHER IN HER HAT, A(1935); JANE EYRE(1935); PEOPLE WILL TALK(1935); CHARLIE CHAN AT THE RACE TRACK(1936); KLONDIKE ANNIE(1936); LOVE BEFORE BREAKFAST(1936); SUZY(1936); BULLDOG DRUMMOND COMES BACK(1937); THINK FAST, MR. MOTO(1937); MYSTERIOUS MR. MOTO(1938); ARREST BULLDOG DRUMMOND(1939, Brit.); HUDSON'S BAY(1940); OUT WEST WITH THE PEPPERS(1940); TYPHOON(1940); HERE COMES MR. JORDAN(1941); MAN HUNT(1941); SCOTLAND YARD(1941); YANK IN THE R.A.F., A(1941); UNDYING MONSTER, THE(1942); LASSIE, COME HOME(1943); LODGER, THE(1944); SHERLOCK HOLMES AND THE SPIDER WOMAN(1944); DANGEROUS INTRUDER(1945); MOSS ROSE(1947); LES MISERABLES(1952); ABBOTT AND COSTELLO MEET DR. JEKYLL AND MR. HYDE(1954); VICTORS, THE(1963); LOVELY WAY TO DIE, A(1968); CHINATOWN(1974)

John B. Rogers
SONG OF THE CITY(1937), ed

John W. Rogers
SPIRIT OF WEST POINT, THE(1947), p; LAW AND ORDER(1953), p; WAR ARROW(1953), p; BLACK HORSE CANYON(1954), p; RIDE CLEAR OF DIABLO(1954), p

Joy Rogers
NO MINOR VICES(1948)

Joyce Rogers
FLAMING LEAD(1939); FOUR FOR TEXAS(1963), cos; PALM SPRINGS WEEKEND(1963), cos

Julia Rogers
SHAKEDOWN, THE(1960, Brit.)

Kasey Rogers
ASK ANY GIRL(1959); NAKED FLAME, THE(1970, Can.)

Kathleen Butler Rogers
STORY OF SHIRLEY YORKE, THE(1948, Brit.), w

Ken Leigh Rogers
PIRATES OF PENZANCE, THE(1983)

Kenny Rogers
SIX PACK(1982)

Kent Rogers
NORTHWEST PASSAGE(1940); ALL-AMERICAN CO-ED(1941); LIFE BEGINS FOR ANDY HARDY(1941); ROAD TO MOROCCO(1942)

Kevin Rogers
1984
DELIVERY BOYS(1984)

L. Rogers
INFORMER, THE(1929, Brit.), ph; CHILDREN OF CHANCE(1930, Brit.), ph

Lambert Rogers
STREET SCENE(1931); HOLD'EM NAVY!(1937)

Larry Rogers
DOCTOR DEATH: SEEKER OF SOULS(1973)

Leda Rogers
SHEILA LEVINE IS DEAD AND LIVING IN NEW YORK(1975)

Lela E. Rogers
WOMEN WON'T TELL(1933), w

Lela Rogers
MAJOR AND THE MINOR, THE(1942); TANGA-TIKA(1953), w

Leo Rogers
6.5 SPECIAL(1958, Brit.), ph

Leonard Rogers
HI-DE-HO(1947)

Lesley Rogers
WEDDING, A(1978); FAN, THE(1981)

Lina Rogers
FIVE BRANDED WOMEN(1960)

Linda Rogers
COMEDY OF TERRORS, THE(1964); PAJAMA PARTY(1964); TICKLE ME(1965); WINTER A GO-GO(1965); WILD, WILD WINTER(1966)

Liz Rogers
RETURN OF COUNT YORGA, THE(1971)

Liza Rogers
TOMCAT, THE(1968, Brit.)

Lorraine Rogers
PSYCHOMANIA(1964)

Lynn Rogers
EFFECT OF GAMMA RAYS ON MAN-IN-THE-MOON MARIGOLDS, THE(1972)

Maclean Rogers
MISCHIEF(1931, Brit.), w; CRIME AT BLOSSOMS, THE(1933, Brit.), p&d; SUMMER LIGHTNING(1933, Brit.), d; TROUBLE(1933, Brit.), d; UP FOR THE DERBY(1933, Brit.), d; FEATHERED SERPENT, THE(1934, Brit.), d; IT'S A COP(1934, Brit.), d; SCOOP, THE(1934, Brit.), p&d; VIRGINIA'S HUSBAND(1934, Brit.), d; LITTLE BIT OF BLUFF, A(1935, Brit.), d; OLD FAITHFUL(1935, Brit.), d; RIGHT AGE TO MARRY, THE(1935, Brit.), d; ALL THAT GLITTERS(1936, Brit.), d; BUSMAN'S HOLIDAY(1936, Brit.), d; HAPPY FAMILY, THE(1936, Brit.), d, w; HEIRLOOM MYSTERY, THE(1936, Brit.), d; NOT SO DUSTY(1936, Brit.), d; NOTHING LIKE PUBLICITY(1936, Brit.), d; TO CATCH A THIEF(1936, Brit.), d; TOUCH OF THE MOON,

A(1936, Brit.), d; TWICE BRANDED(1936, Brit.), d; FAREWELL TO CINDEREL-LA(1937, Brit.), d, w; FATHER STEPS OUT(1937, Brit.), d; FIFTY-SHILLING BOX-ER(1937, Brit.), d; RACING ROMANCE(1937, Brit.), d; STRANGE ADVENTURES OF MR. SMITH, THE(1937, Brit.), d; WHEN THE DEVIL WAS WELL(1937, Brit.), d; WHY PICK ON ME?(1937, Brit.), d; DARTS ARE TRUMPS(1938, Brit.), d; EASY RI-CHES(1938, Brit.), d; HIS LORDSHIP REGRETS(1938, Brit.), d; IF I WERE BOSS(1938, Brit.), d; MERELY MR. HAWKINS(1938, Brit.), d; MIRACLES DO HAPPEN(1938, Brit.), d; PAID IN ERROR(1938, Brit.), d; ROMANCE A LA CARTE(1938, Brit.), d; WEDDINGS ARE WONDERFUL(1938, Brit.), d; HIS LORDSHIP GOES TO PRESS(1939, Brit.), d; OLD MOTHER RILEY JOINS UP(1939, Brit.), d; SHADOWED EYES(1939, Brit.), d; GARRISON FOLLIES(1940, Brit.), d, w; FACING THE MU-SIC(1941, Brit.), p&d, w; GERT AND DAISY'S WEEKEND(1941, Brit.), d, w; FRONT LINE KIDS(1942, Brit.), d; GERT AND DAISY CLEAN UP(1942, Brit.), d; SOME-WHERE IN CIVVIES(1943, Brit.), d; GIVE ME THE STARS(1944, Brit.), d, w; HEAV-EN IS ROUND THE CORNER(1944, Brit.), d; DON CHICAGO(1945, Brit.), d; VARIETY JUBILEE(1945, Brit.), d; TROJAN BROTHERS, THE(1946), d, w; WOMAN TO WOMAN(1946, Brit.), d; CALLING PAUL TEMPLE(1948, Brit.), d; STORY OF SHIRLEY YORKE, THE(1948, Brit.), d; DARK SECRET(1949, Brit.), d; SOMETHING IN THE CITY(1950, Brit.), d; MADAME LOUISE(1951, Brit.), d; OLD MOTHER RILEY'S JUNGLE TREASURE(1951, Brit.), d; PAUL TEMPLE'S TRIUMPH(1951, Brit.), d; DOWN AMONG THE Z MEN(1952, Brit.), d; HAMMER THE TOFF(1952, Brit.), d; PAUL TEMPLE RETURNS(1952, Brit.), d; SALUTE THE TOFF(1952, Brit.), d; ALF'S BABY(1953, Brit.), d; FLANNELFOOT(1953, Brit.), d; FORCES' SWEET-HEART(1953, Brit.), d; JOHNNY ON THE SPOT(1954, Brit.), d&w; LOVE MATCH, THE(1955, Brit.), d; NOT SO DUSTY(1956, Brit.), d&w; CROOKED SKY, THE(1957, Brit.), w; NOT WANTED ON VOYAGE(1957, Brit.), d; YOU PAY YOUR MONEY(1957, Brit.), d&w; MARK OF THE PHOENIX(1958, Brit.), d; NOBODY IN TOYLAND(1958, Brit.), d; JUST JOE(1960, Brit.), d; NOT A HOPE IN HELL(1960, Brit.), d; MILLION DOLLAR MANHUNT(1962, Brit.), d&w
Misc. Talkies
BEHIND THE HEADLINES(1953), d

Maggie Rogers
NAKED WITCH, THE(1964); GHASTLY ONES, THE(1968)

Malcolm Rogers
PRIVILEGE(1967, Brit.)

Marianne Gordon Rogers
BEING, THE(1983)

Marie Rogers
BEST HOUSE IN LONDON, THE(1969, Brit.)

Marilyn Rogers
LADYBUG, LADYBUG(1963)

Marjean Rogers
FOOTLIGHT PARADE(1933)

Marval Rogers
BLACK RODEO(1972)

Melody Rogers
Misc. Talkies
HOOCH(1977)

Merrill Rogers
HER FIRST AFFAIRE(1932, Brit.), w

Michael Rogers
KILLER FISH(1979, Ital./Braz.), w

Mildred Rogers
FIGHTING GENTLEMAN, THE(1932); FORTY-NINERS, THE(1932); GIRL SAID NO, THE(1937)
Misc. Talkies
TEXAS RAMBLER, THE(1935)

Milton "Shorty" Rogers
TIGER MAKES OUT, THE(1967), m

Mimi Rogers
BLUE SKIES AGAIN(1983)

Mitzi Rogers
NIGHT OF THE PROWLER(1962, Brit.)

Molly Rogers
Silents
LIVINGSTONE(1925, Brit.)

Nanci Rogers
MAN WHO LOVED WOMEN, THE(1983)
1984
BODY DOUBLE(1984)

Nate Rogers
Misc. Talkies
TANYA(1976), d

Noelle Rogers
BUFFALO BILL AND THE INDIANS, OR SITTING BULL'S HISTORY LES-SON(1976)

Nora Rogers
CROSS CREEK(1983)

P.M. Rogers
SPECKLED BAND, THE(1931, Brit.), ed

P. Maclean Rogers
LOVES OF ROBERT BURNS, THE(1930, Brit.), w; "W" PLAN, THE(1931, Brit.), ed; MARRY THE GIRL(1935, Brit.), d, w; SHADOW OF MIKE EMERALD, THE(1935, Brit.), d; WIFE OR TWO, A(1935, Brit.), d, w
Misc. Silents
THIRD EYE, THE(1929, Brit.), d

Pamela Rogers
BIG CUBE, THE(1969)

Paul Rogers
MURDER IN THE CATHEDRAL(1952, Brit.); BEAU BRUMMELL(1954); SVEN-GALI(1955, Brit.); THE BEACHCOMBER(1955, Brit.); GIRL IN THE PICTURE, THE(1956, Brit.), w; MAN WITH THE GREEN CARNATION, THE(1960, Brit.); OUR MAN IN HAVANA(1960, Brit.); CIRCLE OF DECEPTON(1961, Brit.); MARK, THE(1961, Brit.); NO LOVE FOR JOHNNIE(1961, Brit.); BILLY BUDD(1962); POT CARRIERS, THE(1962, Brit.); STOLEN HOURS(1963); THIRD SECRET, THE(1964, Brit.); YOUNG AND WILLING(1964, Brit.); HE WHO RIDES A TIGER(1966, Brit.); WALK IN THE SHADOW(1966, Brit.); SHOES OF THE FISHERMAN, THE(1968); DECLINE AND FALL... OF A BIRD WATCHER(1969, Brit.); MIDSUMMER NIGHT'S DREAM, A(1969, Brit.); THREE INTO TWO WON'T GO(1969, Brit.); LOOKING GLASS WAR, THE(1970, Brit.); RECKONING, THE(1971, Brit.); I WANT WHAT I WANT(1972,

Brit.); HOMECOMING, THE(1973); ABDICATION, THE(1974, Brit.); LOST IN THE STARS(1974); MR. QUILP(1975, Brit.)
1984
NOTHING LASTS FOREVER(1984)

Pepper Rogers
TRIAL OF BILLY JACK, THE(1974)

Peter Rogers
DEAR MURDERER(1947, Brit.), w; HOLIDAY CAMP(1947, Brit.), w; WHEN THE BOUGH BREAKS(1947, Brit.), w; HERE COME THE HUGGETTS(1948, Brit.), w; GAY DOG, THE(1954, Brit.), w; YOU KNOW WHAT SAILORS ARE(1954, Brit.), p, w; CASH ON DELIVERY(1956, Brit.), p, w; AFTER THE BALL(1957, Brit.), p; NOVEL AFFAIR, A(1957, Brit.), p; CHAIN OF EVENTS(1958, Brit.), p; SOLITARY CHILD, THE(1958, Brit.), p; CARRY ON NURSE(1959, Brit.), p; CIRCLE, THE(1959, Brit.), p; TIME LOCK(1959, Brit.), p, w; CARRY ON CONSTABLE(1960, Brit.), p; PLEASE TURN OVER(1960, Brit.), p; BEWARE OF CHILDREN(1961, Brit.), p; CARRY ON REGARDLESS(1961, Brit.), p; WATCH YOUR STERN(1961, Brit.), p; CARRY ON CRUISING(1962, Brit.), p; CARRY ON TEACHER(1962, Brit.), p; CIRCUS FRIENDS(1962, Brit.), p, w; DOG AND THE DIAMONDS, THE(1962, Brit.), p; ROOM-MATES(1962, Brit.), p; TWICE AROUND THE DAFFODILS(1962, Brit.), p; CARRY ON CABBIE(1963, Brit.), p; CARRY ON JACK(1963, Brit.), p; SWINGIN' MAIDEN, THE(1963, Brit.), p; CARRY ON CLEO(1964, Brit.), p; CARRY ON SPYING(1964, Brit.), p; NURSE ON WHEELS(1964, Brit.), p; THIS IS MY STREET(1964, Brit.), p; BIG JOB, THE(1965, Brit.), p; CARRY ON COWBOY(1966, Brit.), p; CARRY ON SCREAMING(1966, Brit.), p; DON'T LOSE YOUR HEAD(1967, Brit.), p; FOLLOW THAT CAMEL(1967, Brit.), p; CARRY ON DOCTOR(1968, Brit.), p; CARRY ON, UP THE KHYBER(1968, Brit.), p; CARRY ON AGAIN, DOCTOR(1969, Brit.), p; CARRY ON CAMPING(1969, Brit.), p; CARRY ON HENRY VIII(1970, Brit.), p; CARRY ON LOVING(1970, Brit.), p; CARRY ON UP THE JUNGLE(1970, Brit.), p; ASSAULT(1971, Brit.), p; CARRY ON ENGLAND(1976, Brit.), p; CARRY ON EMANUELLE(1978, Brit.), p

Rena Rogers
Misc. Silents
CRICKET, THE(1917)

Richard Rogers
CAROUSEL(1956), w

Rita Rogers
MACHISMO--40 GRAVES FOR 40 GUNS(1970); HIRED HAND, THE(1971); MAG-NIFICENT SEVEN RIDE, THE(1972); SHOWDOWN(1973); LOSIN' IT(1983)

Robena Rogers
TAPS(1981)

Robert E. Rogers
SCREAMS OF A WINTER NIGHT(1979), ph

Rock Rogers
TWO GALS AND A GUY(1951)

Rod Rogers
IT AIN'T HAY(1943); CRIME, INC.(1945); YOUTH AFLAME(1945); EMBRACEABLE YOU(1948); MILLION DOLLAR MERMAID(1952); WHO SAYS I CAN'T RIDE A RAINBOW!(1971)
Silents
WINGS(1927)

Ron Rogers
BIONIC BOY, THE(1977, Hong Kong/Phil.)

Rosemary Rogers
LIMBO LINE, THE(1969, Brit.)

Roswell Rogers
SO THIS IS WASHINGTON(1943), w; TWO WEEKS TO LIVE(1943), w; JUST ACROSS THE STREET(1952), w; $1,000,000 DUCK(1971), w; CHARLEY AND THE ANGEL(1973), w

Roxanne Rogers
1984
SLOW MOVES(1984)

Roy Rogers
GALLANT DEFENDER(1935); MYSTERIOUS AVENGER, THE(1936); SONG OF THE SADDLE(1936); OLD WYOMING TRAIL, THE(1937); BILLY THE KID RE-TURNS(1938); SHINE ON, HARVEST MOON(1938); UNDER WESTERN STARS(1938); ARIZONA KID, THE(1939); COME ON RANGERS(1939); DAYS OF JESSE JA-MES(1939); FRONTIER PONY EXPRESS(1939); IN OLD CALIENTE(1939); JEEPERS CREEPERS(1939); ROUGH RIDERS' ROUNDUP(1939); SAGA OF DEATH VAL-LEY(1939); SOUTHWARD HO!(1939); WALL STREET COWBOY(1939); BORDER LEGION, THE(1940); CARSON CITY KID(1940); COLORADO(1940); DARK COM-MAND, THE(1940); RANGER AND THE LADY(1940); YOUNG BILL HICK-OK(1940); YOUNG BUFFALO BILL(1940); ARKANSAS JUDGE(1941); BAD MAN OF DEADWOOD(1941); IN OLD CHEYENNE(1941); JESSE JAMES AT BAY(1941); NEVADA CITY(1941); RED RIVER VALLEY(1941); ROBIN HOOD OF THE PE-COS(1941); SHERIFF OF TOMBSTONE(1941); HEART OF THE GOLDEN WEST(1942); MAN FROM CHEYENNE(1942); RIDIN' DOWN THE CANYON(1942); ROMANCE ON THE RANGE(1942); SONS OF THE PIONEERS(1942); SOUTH OF SANTA FE(1942); SUNSET ON THE DESERT(1942); SUNSET SERENADE(1942); HANDS ACROSS THE BORDER(1943); IDAHO(1943); KING OF THE COWBOYS(1943); MAN FROM MUSIC MOUNTAIN(1943); SILVER SPURS(1943); SONG OF TEXAS(1943); BRAZIL(1944); COWBOY AND THE SENORITA(1944); HOLLYWOOD CANTEEN(1944); LAKE PLA-CID SERENADE(1944); LIGHTS OF OLD SANTA FE(1944); SAN FERNANDO VAL-LEY(1944); SONG OF NEVADA(1944); YELLOW ROSE OF TEXAS, THE(1944); ALONG THE NAVAJO TRAIL(1945); BELLS OF ROSARITA(1945); DON'T FENCE ME IN(1945); MAN FROM OKLAHOMA, THE(1945); SUNSET IN EL DORADO(1945); UTAH(1945); HELLDORADO(1946); HOME IN OKLAHOMA(1946); MY PAL TRIG-GER(1946); OUT CALIFORNIA WAY(1946); RAINBOW OVER TEXAS(1946); ROLL ON TEXAS MOON(1946); SONG OF ARIZONA(1946); UNDER NEVADA SKIES(1946); APACHE ROSE(1947); BELLS OF SAN ANGELO(1947); ON THE OLD SPANISH TRAIL(1947); SPRINGTIME IN THE SIERRAS(1947); EYES OF TEXAS(1948); GAY RANCHERO, THE(1948); GRAND CANYON TRAIL(1948); MELODY TIME(1948); NIGHT TIME IN NEVADA(1948); UNDER CALIFORNIA STARS(1948); DOWN DAKOTA WAY(1949); FAR FRONTIER, THE(1949); GOLDEN STALLION, THE(1949); SUSANNA PASS(1949); BELLS OF CORONADO(1950); NORTH OF THE GREAT DIVIDE(1950); SUNSET IN THE WEST(1950); TRAIL OF ROBIN HOOD(1950); TRIGGER, JR.(1950); TWILIGHT IN THE SIERRAS(1950); HEART OF THE ROCK-IES(1951); IN OLD AMARILLO(1951); SOUTH OF CALIENTE(1951); SPOILERS OF THE PLAINS(1951); PALS OF THE GOLDEN WEST(1952); SON OF PALEFACE(1952); ALIAS JESSE JAMES(1959); MACKINTOSH & T.J.(1975)

Roy Rogers, Jr.
ARIZONA BUSHWHACKERS(1968)
Russ Rogers
KING KONG(1933)
Ruth Rogers
COCOANUT GROVE(1938); HUNTED MEN(1938); KING OF ALCATRAZ(1938); MEN WITH WINGS(1938); SAY IT IN FRENCH(1938); TIP-OFF GIRLS(1938); TROPIC HOLIDAY(1938); YOU AND ME(1938); CAFE SOCIETY(1939); MAN FROM TEXAS, THE(1939); NIGHT RIDERS, THE(1939); SILVER ON THE SAGE(1939); HIDDEN GOLD(1940); LIGHT OF WESTERN STARS, THE(1940); NIGHT AT EARL CARROLL'S, A(1940); TEXAS RANGERS RIDE AGAIN(1940); THOSE WERE THE DAYS(1940); THERE'S MAGIC IN MUSIC(1941)
Sally Rogers
WHILE I LIVE(1947, Brit.)
Sam Rogers
BADGER'S GREEN(1949, Brit.)
Sean Rogers
SWEET INNISCARRA(1934, Brit.)
Sharon Rogers
CANDIDATE, THE(1964)
Sheila Rogers
ERRAND BOY, THE(1961); LADIES MAN, THE(1961); MOVE OVER, DARLING(1963); WHO'S MINDING THE STORE?(1963); PATSY, THE(1964); SHOCK TREATMENT(1964); VERY SPECIAL FAVOR, A(1965); HOW TO SUCCEED IN BUSINESS WITHOUT REALLY TRYING(1976); JEKYLL AND HYDE...TOGETHER AGAIN(1982)
Shelley Rogers
BELL JAR, THE(1979)
Sherman Rogers
IT'S A GREAT LIFE(1936), w
Shirley Rogers
LIFT, THE(1965, Brit./Can.)
Shorty Rogers
MAN WITH THE GOLDEN ARM, THE(1955); TARZAN, THE APE MAN(1959), m; TAFFY AND THE JUNGLE HUNTER(1965), m; YOUNG DILLINGER(1965), m; FOOLS(1970), m; TEACHER, THE(1974), m; DR. MINX(1975), m; SPECIALIST, THE(1975), m; ZOOT SUIT(1981), m
Simone Rogers
COCK O' THE NORTH(1935, Brit.)
Sondra Rogers
LOST IN A HAREM(1944); DANGEROUS PARTNERS(1945); AS YOU WERE(1951)
Stan Rogers
STAMBOUL QUEST(1934), art d; O'SHAUGHNESSY'S BOY(1935), art d; OLD HUTCH(1936), art d; LOVE FINDS ANDY HARDY(1938), art d; PARADISE FOR THREE(1938), art d; GO WEST(1940), art d; SPORTING BLOOD(1940), art d; TWO GIRLS ON BROADWAY(1940), art d; JOHNNY EAGER(1942), art d; DARK DELUSION(1947), art d
Stanley Rogers
BATTLE OF GALLIPOLI(1931, Brit.), ph; SALUTE TO THE MARINES(1943), art d
Stanwood Rogers
BROADWAY TO HOLLYWOOD(1933), art d; RIFF-RAFF(1936), art d
Steve Rogers
SKI PARTY(1965); MOVIE STAR, AMERICAN STYLE, OR, LSD I HATE YOU!(1966); ANGELS FROM HELL(1968)
Steven Rogers
GIRLS ON THE BEACH(1965); WILD, WILD WINTER(1966)
Tania Rogers
STUD, THE(1979, Brit.)
Thomas Rogers
PURSUIT OF HAPPINESS, THE(1971), w
Tim Rogers
RED RUNS THE RIVER(1963)
Timmie Rogers
SPARKLE(1976)
Tony Rogers
KILL OR BE KILLED(1967, Ital.)
Tracey Rogers
LEATHER BOYS, THE(1965, Brit.)
Tristan Rogers
Misc. Talkies
THREE DIMENSIONS OF GRETA(1973)
Valerie Rogers
Misc. Talkies
ZEBRA KILLER, THE(1974)
Victor Rogers
THOROUGHLY MODERN MILLIE(1967); MY FAIR LADY(1964); SLUMBER PARTY '57(1977)
Sgt. Victor Rogers, USAF
OPERATION HAYLIFT(1950)
Walter Browne Rogers
ALL QUIET ON THE WESTERN FRONT(1930)
Walter Rogers
SEVEN FACES(1929); SILVER DOLLAR(1932); GOLD IS WHERE YOU FIND IT(1938)
Silents
ABRAHAM LINCOLN(1924); IRON HORSE, THE(1924)
Misc. Silents
SMASHING BARRIERS(1923)
Warren Rogers
MISSISSIPPI(1935)
Silents
RACING HEARTS(1923); FLAMING BARRIERS(1924); WHISPERING SMITH(1926); RACING ROMEO(1927)
Wayne Rogers
ODDS AGAINST TOMORROW(1959); GLORY GUYS, THE(1965); CHAMBER OF HORRORS(1966); COOL HAND LUKE(1967); ASTRO-ZOMBIES, THE(1969), w; POCKET MONEY(1972); ONCE IN PARIS(1978)

Will Rogers
THEY HAD TO SEE PARIS(1929); HAPPY DAYS(1930); LIGHTNIN'(1930); SO THIS IS LONDON(1930); AMBASSADOR BILL(1931); CONNECTICUT YANKEE, A(1931); YOUNG AS YOU FEEL(1931); BUSINESS AND PLEASURE(1932); DOWN TO EARTH(1932); TOO BUSY TO WORK(1932); DR. BULL(1933); MR. SKITCH(1933); STATE FAIR(1933); DAVID HARUM(1934); HANDY ANDY(1934); JUDGE PRIEST(1934); STAND UP AND CHEER(1934 80m FOX bw), w; COUNTY CHAIRMAN, THE(1935); DOUBTING THOMAS(1935); IN OLD KENTUCKY(1935); LIFE BEGINS AT 40(1935); STEAMBOAT ROUND THE BEND(1935)
Silents
ALMOST A HUSBAND(1919); JUBILO(1919); DOUBLING FOR ROMEO(1921), a, t; GUILE OF WOMEN(1921); TEXAS STEER, A(1927), a, t
Misc. Silents
LAUGHING BILL HYDE(1918); CUPID, THE COWPUNCHER(1920); HONEST HUTCH(1920); JES' CALL ME JIM(1920); STRANGE BORDER, THE(1920); WATER, WATER, EVERYWHERE(1920); BOYS WILL BE BOYS(1921); POOR RELATION, A(1921); UNWILLING HERO, AN(1921); HEADLESS HORSEMAN, THE(1922); ONE GLORIOUS DAY(1922); TIPTOES(1927, Brit.)
Will Rogers, Jr.
LOOK FOR THE SILVER LINING(1949); STORY OF WILL ROGERS, THE(1952); EDDIE CANTOR STORY, THE(1953); BOY FROM OKLAHOMA, THE(1954); WILD HERITAGE(1958)
Silents
JACK RIDER, THE(1921)
William Rogers
SEARCH, THE(1948)
The Rogers Adagio Trio
SEE MY LAWYER(1945)
Rogers and Starr
STAIRCASE(1969 U.S./Brit./Fr.)
Rogers Dancers
NEVER A DULL MOMENT(1943)
The Rogers Dancers
BRIDE CAME C.O.D., THE(1941)
The Roy Rogers Riders
IN OLD AMARILLO(1951)
Rogers Trio
SHE'S FOR ME(1943)
Wanda Rogerson
ONE WOMAN'S STORY(1949, Brit.)
Marcell Rogez
LITTLE FRIEND(1934, Brit.)
Marcelle Rogez
I SPY(1933, Brit.); POWER(1934, Brit.); KOENIGSMARK(1935, Fr.); BIG FELLA(1937, Brit.); COTTON QUEEN(1937, Brit.); FINE FEATHERS(1937, Brit.); MR. STRINGFELLOW SAYS NO(1937, Brit.); WHO'S YOUR LADY FRIEND?(1937, Brit.); ALMOST A GENTLEMAN(1938, Brit.)
Bernhard Rogge
UNDER TEN FLAGS(1960, U.S./Ital.), w
Louis Lucien Rogger
PRINCESS COMES ACROSS, THE(1936), w
Charles Roggero
FEMALE TROUBLE(1975), ed; POLYESTER(1981), ed
Fred Roggin
ROCKY III(1982)
Youigi Rogi
SUNBURN(1979)
Frank Rogier
HANSEL AND GRETEL(1954)
[Jeanne] Lorraine Rognan
SALUTE FOR THREE(1943)
[Roy] Rognan
SALUTE FOR THREE(1943)
Gabriel Rognier
GUTS IN THE SUN(1959, Fr.), ed
Rognoni
GENERALS WITHOUT BUTTONS(1938, Fr.); PERSONAL COLUMN(1939, Fr.); CHILDREN OF PARADISE(1945, Fr.); SYLVIA AND THE PHANTOM(1950, Fr.)
Selma Rogoff
HURRY UP OR I'LL BE 30(1973)
Lionel Rogosin
Misc. Talkies
BLACK FANTASY(1974), d
V. Rogov
FORTY-NINE DAYS(1964, USSR)
A. Rogovtseva
SONG OF THE FOREST(1963, USSR)
Leonard Rogowski
NIGHTBEAST(1982), m
Jaromir Rogoz
ECSTASY(1940, Czech.)
Zvonimir Rogoz
MERRY WIVES, THE(1940, Czech.); SON OF SAMSON(1962, Fr./Ital./Yugo.)
N.A. Rogozbin
ALEXANDER NEVSKY(1939)
Z. Rogozikova
SONG OVER MOSCOW(1964, USSR)
Jerzy Rogulski
1984
AMERICAN DREAMER(1984)
Frank Roh
LIMIT, THE(1972)
John Roh
LIMIT, THE(1972)
Reine Rohan
FRUSTRATIONS(1967, Fr./Ital.)
Eva Rohanova
FIFTH HORSEMAN IS FEAR, THE(1968, Czech.)

Julie Rohde
Misc. Talkies
  KAHUNA!(1981)
Peter Rohe
  GEORGE(1973, U.S./Switz.), ph
H. Rohenheld
  FOUR FRIGHTENED PEOPLE(1934), m
Marc Rohm
  ON THE LOOSE(1951)
Maria Rohm
  CITY OF FEAR(1965, Brit.); 24 HOURS TO KILL(1966, Brit.); FIVE GOLDEN DRAGONS(1967, Brit.); HOUSE OF 1,000 DOLLS(1967, Ger./Span./Brit.); BLOOD OF FU MANCHU, THE(1968, Brit.); EVE(1968, Brit./Span.); VENGEANCE OF FU MANCHU, THE(1968, Brit./Ger./Hong Kong/Ireland); JUSTINE(1969, Ital./Span.); DORIAN GRAY(1970, Ital./Brit./Ger./Liechtenstein); RIO 70(1970, U.S./Ger./Span.); VENUS IN FURS(1970, Ital./Brit./Ger.); BLACK BEAUTY(1971, Brit./Ger./Span.); COUNT DRACULA(1971, Sp., Ital., Ger., Brit.); CALL OF THE WILD(1972, Ger./ Span./Ital./ Fr.); TREASURE ISLAND(1972, Brit./Span./Fr./Ger.); TEN LITTLE INDIANS(1975, Ital./Fr./Span./Ger.)
Marie Rohm
  MILLION EYES OF SU-MURU, THE(1967, Brit.)
Renate Rohm
  5 SINNERS(1961, Ger.); $100 A NIGHT(1968, Ger.)
Eric Rohmer
  SIX IN PARIS(1968, Fr.), w&d; MY NIGHT AT MAUD'S(1970, Fr.), d&w; CLAIRE'S KNEE(1971, Fr.), d&w; LA COLLECTIONNEUSE(1971, Fr.), d, w; CHLOE IN THE AFTERNOON(1972, Fr.), d&w; AVIATOR'S WIFE, THE(1981, Fr.), d&w; LE BEAU MARIAGE(1982, Fr.), d&w; PAULINE AT THE BEACH(1983, Fr.), d&w
1984
  FULL MOON IN PARIS(1984, Fr.), d&w
Patrice Rohmer
  HARRAD SUMMER, THE(1974); HUSTLE(1975); JACKSON COUNTY JAIL(1976); REVENGE OF THE CHEERLEADERS(1976); SMALL TOWN IN TEXAS, A(1976)
Sam Rohmer
  RIO 70(1970, U.S./Ger./Span.), w
Sax Rohmer
  MYSTERIOUS DR. FU MANCHU, THE(1929), w; RETURN OF DR. FU MANCHU, THE(1930), w; DAUGHTER OF THE DRAGON(1931), w; MASK OF FU MANCHU, THE(1932), w; DRUMS OF FU MANCHU(1943), w; FACE OF FU MANCHU, THE(1965, Brit.), w; MILLION EYES OF SU-MURU, THE(1967, Brit.), w; VENGEANCE OF FU MANCHU, THE(1968, Brit./Ger./Hong Kong/Ireland), w; FIENDISH PLOT OF DR. FU MANCHU, THE(1980), w
Jackie Rohr
  C. C. AND COMPANY(1971)
Peter Rohr
  DOWNHILL RACER(1969)
Tony Rohr
  MC VICAR(1982, Brit.)
Gunter Rohrbach
  DAS BOOT(1982), p
Andrew Rohrer
  ABDUCTION(1975)
Everett L. Rohrer
  CAT BALLOU(1965)
Manfred Rohri
  YOUNG LORD, THE(1970, Ger.)
Rohrig
  TEMPORARY WIDOW, THE(1930, Ger./Brit.), prod d
Peter Rohrig
  FREDDY UNTER FREMDEN STERNEN(1962, Ger.), art d; DEVIL IN SILK(1968, Ger.), art d
Walter Rohrig
  EMPRESS AND I, THE(1933, Ger.), set d
Silents
  CABINET OF DR. CALIGARI, THE(1921, Ger.), art d; LAST LAUGH, THE(1924, Ger.), art d; FAUST(1926, Ger.), art d; TARTUFFE(1927, Ger.), set d
George R. Rohrs
  LEARNING TREE, THE(1969), ed
George Rohrs
  AMERICAN DREAM, AN(1966), ed; BIG HAND FOR THE LITTLE LADY, A(1966), ed; FIRST TO FIGHT(1967), ed; ASSIGNMENT TO KILL(1968), ed; SKIDOO(1968), ed
Jacques Roibiolles
  SUNDAYS AND CYBELE(1962, Fr.)
Michael Roider
  PARSIFAL(1983, Fr.)
Maruja Roig
  HEAT(1970, Arg.)
Eero Roine
  PRELUDE TO ECSTASY(1963, Fin.)
Anne Richardson Roiphe
  UP THE SANDBOX(1972), w
Odile Roire
1984
  FIRST NAME: CARMEN(1984, Fr.)
Owen Roisman
  TRUE CONFESSIONS(1981), ph
Jacques Roitfeld
  ADORABLE CREATURES(1956, Fr.), p; FOLIES BERGERE(1958, Fr.), p; GIVE ME MY CHANCE(1958, Fr.), p; EMPIRE OF NIGHT, THE(1963, Fr.), p; PLEASE, NOT NOW!(1963, Fr./Ital.), p
Jacques Roitfield
  COUNT OF MONTE-CRISTO(1955, Fr., Ital.), p
Owen Roizman
  TAKING OF PELHAM ONE, TWO, THREE, THE(1974), ph; FRENCH CONNECTION, THE(1971), ph; GANG THAT COULDN'T SHOOT STRAIGHT, THE(1971), ph; HEARTBREAK KID, THE(1972), ph; PLAY IT AGAIN, SAM(1972), ph; STEPFORD WIVES, THE(1975), ph; THREE DAYS OF THE CONDOR(1975), ph; NETWORK(1976), ph; RETURN OF A MAN CALLED HORSE, THE(1976), ph; SGT. PEPPER'S LONELY HEARTS CLUB BAND(1978), ph; STRAIGHT TIME(1978), ph; ELECTRIC HORSEMAN, THE(1979), ph; BLACK MARBLE, THE(1980), ph; AB-

SENCE OF MALICE(1981), ph; TAPS(1981), ph; TOOTSIE(1982), ph
Own Roizman
  EXORCIST, THE(1973), ph
Luis Roja
  FOR WHOM THE BELL TOLLS(1943)
Victoria Merida Roja
  ROBIN AND MARIAN(1976, Brit.)
Alfonso Rojas
  FEW BULLETS MORE, A(1968, Ital./Span.); KILL THEM ALL AND COME BACK ALONE(1970, Ital./Span.)
Alvaro Rojas, Jr.
1984
  CLOAK AND DAGGER(1984)
Carmen Rojas
  DR. COPPELIUS(1968, U.S./Span.)
Diane Rojas
  SWEET SUGAR(1972)
Eduardo Lopez Rojas
  JORY(1972)
1984
  EVIL THAT MEN DO, THE(1984)
Emmanuel Rojas
  SAMAR(1962), ph; YANK IN VIET-NAM, A(1964), ph; AMBUSH BAY(1966), ph; KILL A DRAGON(1967), ph
Emmanuel I. Rojas
  TERROR IS A MAN(1959, U.S./Phil.), ph; OUT OF THE TIGER'S MOUTH(1962), ph
Jose Luis Rojas
  MASSACRE(1956)
Julio Rojas
  LOVES OF CARMEN, THE(1948)
Lucina Rojas
  UNDER FIRE(1983)
Manola Rojas
  MADIGAN'S MILLIONS(1970, Span./Ital), ph
Manolo Rojas
  CON MEN, THE(1973, Ital.,Span.), ph
Manuel Rojas
  MAGNIFICENT MATADOR, THE(1955); BUCHANAN RIDES ALONE(1958); STEEL CLAW, THE(1961), ph; THAT HOUSE IN THE OUTSKIRTS(1980, Span.), ph; TO BEGIN AGAIN(1982, Span.), ph
Mauel Rojas
  FAT ANGELS(1980, U.S./Span.), ph
Minervino Rojas
  JOURNEY THROUGH ROSEBUD(1972), ph
Mini Rojas
  EYES OF A STRANGER(1980), ph
Raquel Rojas
  DAUGHTER OF DECEIT(1977, Mex.), w
Rojo
  KILL THEM ALL AND COME BACK ALONE(1970, Ital./Span.)
Antonio Molino Rojo
  SANDOKAN THE GREAT(1964, Fr./Ital./Span.); FINGER ON THE TRIGGER(1965, US/Span.); PLACE CALLED GLORY, A(1966, Span./Ger.); MINUTE TO PRAY, A SECOND TO DIE, A(1968, Ital.); SEVEN GUNS FOR THE MACGREGORS(1968, Ital./Span.)
Ethel Rojo
  MINNESOTA CLAY(1966, Ital./Fr./Span.)
Gustavo Rojo
  GENGHIS KHAN(U.S./Brit./Ger./Yugo); TARZAN AND THE MERMAIDS(1948); STRONGHOLD(1952, Mex.); ALEXANDER THE GREAT(1956); ACTION OF THE TIGER(1957); IT STARTED WITH A KISS(1959); MIRACLE, THE(1959); NO SURVIVORS, PLEASE(1963, Ger.); DR. MABUSE'S RAYS OF DEATH(1964, Ger./Fr./Ital.); FICKLE FINGER OF FATE, THE(1967, Span./U.S.); TALL WOMEN, THE(1967, Aust./Ital./Span.); WITCH WITHOUT A BROOM, A(1967, U.S./Span.); CHRISTMAS KID, THE(1968, U.S., Span.); OLD SHATTERHAND(1968, Ger./Yugo./Fr./Ital.); LAND RAIDERS(1969); LAST DAY OF THE WAR, THE(1969, U.S./Ital./Span.); VALLEY OF GWANGI, THE(1969); BULLET FOR SANDOVAL, A(1970, Ital./Span.); EL CONDOR(1970); MADIGAN'S MILLIONS(1970, Span./Ital)
Helena Rojo
  MIRAGE(1972, Peru); MARY, MARY, BLOODY MARY(1975, U.S./Mex.); AGUIRRE, THE WRATH OF GOD(1977, W. Ger.); FOXTROT(1977, Mex./Swiss)
J. Antonio Rojo
  CAULDRON OF BLOOD(1971, Span.), ed
Jose Antonio Rojo
  FACE OF TERROR(1964, Span.), ed
Maria Rojo
Misc. Talkies
  CANDY STRIPE NURSES(1974)
Max Rojo
  TWILIGHT PEOPLE(1972, Phil.)
Mercedes Rojo
  CAULDRON OF BLOOD(1971, Span.)
Molina Rojo
  FIVE GIANTS FROM TEXAS(1966, Ital./Span.)
Ruben Rojo
  ALEXANDER THE GREAT(1956); KING OF KINGS(1961); LAST DAY OF THE WAR, THE(1969, U.S./Ital./Span.); THEY CAME TO ROB LAS VEGAS(1969, Fr./Ital./Span./Ger.); DAUGHTER OF DECEIT(1977, Mex.)
Rueben Rojo
  SANTO EN EL MUSEO DE CERA(1963, Mex.)
Ruven Rojo
  CAULDRON OF BLOOD(1971, Span.)
Rennie Roker
  BROTHERS(1977)
Renny Roker
  SKIDOO(1968); ...TICK...TICK...TICK...(1970); MELINDA(1972); HONKY TONK FREEWAY(1981)
Misc. Talkies
  TOUGH(1974); JOEY(1977)

Roxie Roker
CLAUDINE(1974)
Marika Rokk
KISS ME, SERGEANT(1930, Brit.); WHY SAILORS LEAVE HOME(1930, Brit.); DIE FLEDERMAUS(1964, Aust.)
Prince Rokneddine
Silents
JUST SUPPOSE(1926)
Gadi Rol
JESUS(1979)
Joven E. Rola
EVE OF ST. MARK, THE(1944)
Armand Roland
FOR WHOM THE BELL TOLLS(1943)
Arthur Roland
WHAT PRICE CRIME?(1935)
Aurora Roland
YOU LIGHT UP MY LIFE(1977)
Bobs Roland
Misc. Silents
WAY OF THE WORLD, THE(1920, Brit.)
Cherry Roland
JUST FOR FUN(1963, Brit.)
Denyse Roland
FIVE WILD GIRLS(1966, Fr.); LIFE LOVE DEATH(1969, Fr./Ital.)
Eddie Roland
GUILTY GENERATION, THE(1931)
Eric Roland
CRIMINAL AT LARGE(1932, Brit.)
Frederic Roland
MAGNIFICENT OBSESSION(1935); RAINMAKERS, THE(1935)
Frederick Roland
FATAL LADY(1936)
Fritz Roland
IF IT'S TUESDAY, THIS MUST BE BELGIUM(1969), ph
George Roland
WANDERING JEW, THE(1933), d; DYBBUK THE(1938, Pol.), ed; WITHOUT A HOME(1939, Pol.), titles
Misc. Talkies
JOSEPH IN THE LAND OF EGYPT(1932), d; JEWISH DAUGHTER(1933), d; LOVE AND SACRIFICE(1936), d; I WANT TO BE A MOTHER(1937), d
Gilbert Roland
NEW YORK NIGHTS(1929); MEN OF THE NORTH(1930); CALL HER SAVAGE(1932); LIFE BEGINS(1932); NO LIVING WITNESS(1932); PARISIAN ROMANCE, A(1932); PASSIONATE PLUMBER(1932); WOMAN IN ROOM 13, THE(1932); AFTER TONIGHT(1933); GIGOLETTES OF PARIS(1933); IO ... TU ... Y ... ELLA(1933); OUR BETTERS(1933); SHE DONE HIM WRONG(1933); ELINOR NORTON(1935); LADIES LOVE DANGER(1935); MYSTERY WOMAN(1935); LAST TRAIN FROM MADRID, THE(1937); MIDNIGHT TAXI(1937); THUNDER TRAIL(1937); GATEWAY(1938); JUAREZ(1939); GAMBLING ON THE HIGH SEAS(1940); ISLE OF DESTINY(1940); RANGERS OF FORTUNE(1940); SEA HAWK, THE(1940); ANGELS WITH BROKEN WINGS(1941); MY LIFE WITH CAROLINE(1941); ENEMY AGENTS MEET ELLERY QUEEN(1942); ISLE OF MISSING MEN(1942); CAPTAIN KIDD(1945); BEAUTY AND THE BANDIT(1946); HIGH CONQUEST(1947); OTHER LOVE, THE(1947); PIRATES OF MONTEREY(1947); DUDE GOES WEST, THE(1948); KING OF THE BANDITS(1948), a, w; WE WERE STRANGERS(1949); CRISIS(1950); FURIES, THE(1950); MALAYA(1950); TORCH, THE(1950); BULLFIGHTER AND THE LADY(1951); MARK OF THE RENEGADE(1951); TEN TALL MEN(1951); APACHE WAR SMOKE(1952); BAD AND THE BEAUTIFUL, THE(1952); GLORY ALLEY(1952); MIRACLE OF OUR LADY OF FATIMA, THE(1952); MY SIX CONVICTS(1952); BENEATH THE 12-MILE REEF(1953); DIAMOND QUEEN, THE(1953); THUNDER BAY(1953); FRENCH LINE, THE(1954); GLORY ALLEY(1952); RACERS, THE(1955); THAT LADY(1955, Brit.); TREASURE OF PANCHO VILLA, THE(1955); UNDERWATER!(1955); AROUND THE WORLD IN 80 DAYS(1956); BANDIDO(1956); THREE VIOLENT PEOPLE(1956); MIDNIGHT STORY, THE(1957); LAST OF THE FAST GUNS, THE(1958); BIG CIRCUS, THE(1959); WILD AND THE INNOCENT, THE(1959); GUNS OF THE TIMBERLAND(1960); SAMAR(1962); CHEYENNE AUTUMN(1964); REWARD, THE(1965); POPPY IS ALSO A FLOWER, THE(1966); ANY GUN CAN PLAY(1968, Ital./Span.); RUTHLESS FOUR, THE(1969, Ital./Ger.); CHRISTIAN LICORICE STORE, THE(1971); JOHNNY HAMLET(1972, Ital.); RUNNING WILD(1973); ISLANDS IN THE STREAM(1977); CABOBLANCO(1981); BARBAROSA(1982)
Misc. Talkies
GAY CAVALIER, THE(1946); SOUTH OF MONTEREY(1946); RIDING THE CALIFORNIA TRAIL(1947); ROBIN HOOD OF MONTEREY(1947); CATCH ME IF YOU CAN(1959); TREASURE OF TAYOPA(1974); DELIVER US FROM EVIL(1975); BLACK PEARL, THE(1977)
Silents
PLASTIC AGE, THE(1925); CAMPUS FLIRT, THE(1926); CAMILLE(1927)
Misc. Silents
BLONDE SAINT, THE(1926); DOVE, THE(1927); ROSE OF THE GOLDEN WEST(1927); WOMAN DISPUTED, THE(1928)
Glenn Roland, Jr.
1984
DADDY'S DEADLY DARLING(1984), ph
Gyl Roland
BLACK GUNN(1972); DAY OF THE LOCUST, THE(1975); BARN OF THE NAKED DEAD(1976)
Jeanne Roland
CURSE OF THE MUMMY'S TOMB, THE(1965, Brit.); SALT & PEPPER(1968, Brit.); SEBASTIAN(1968, Brit.)
John Roland
HERO AT LARGE(1980); EYEWITNESS(1981)
Joseph Roland
GREEN TREE, THE(1965, Ital.), p&d, w
Marc Roland
BARBERINA(1932, Ger.), m
Oscar Roland
TAKE DOWN(1979)

Pamela Roland
TWILIGHT'S LAST GLEAMING(1977, U.S./Ger.)
Peter Roland
Misc. Talkies
BATTLE OF THE EAGLES(1981)
Reg Roland
CHECKMATE(1973)
Renate Roland
24-HOUR LOVER(1970, Ger.)
Rita Roland
BOEFJE(1939, Ger.), ed; CROWDED PARADISE(1956), ed; HONEYMOON HOTEL(1964), ed; GIRL HAPPY(1965), ed; PATCH OF BLUE, A(1965), ed; PENELOPE(1966), ed; SINGING NUN, THE(1966), ed; SPINOUT(1966), ed; DON'T MAKE WAVES(1967), ed; SPLIT, THE(1968), ed; WHERE WERE YOU WHEN THE LIGHTS WENT OUT?(1968), ed; JUSTINE(1969), ed; MOVE(1970), ed; TO FIND A MAN(1972), ed; ONCE IS NOT ENOUGH(1975), ed; BETSY, THE(1978), ed; GOOD LUCK, MISS WYCKOFF(1979), ed; RESURRECTION(1980), ed; FORT APACHE, THE BRONX(1981), ed; SIX PACK(1982), ed
Ruth Roland
RENO(1930)
Misc. Silents
COMRADE JOHN(1915); MATRIMONIAL MARTYR, A(1916); SULTANA, THE(1916); DEVIL'S BAIT, THE(1917); STOLEN PLAY, THE(1917); FRINGE OF SOCIETY, THE(1918); LOVE AND THE LAW(1919); DOLLAR DOWN(1925); WHERE THE WORST BEGINS(1925)
Sandra Weintraub Roland
HIGH ROAD TO CHINA(1983), w
Steve Roland
SOME KIND OF A NUT(1969)
J. P. Roland-Levy
UNDERGROUND U.S.A.(1980), ed
Roland-Manuel
STORMY WATERS(1946, Fr.), m; LE CIEL EST A VOUS(1957, Fr.), m
Roland-Maunuel
STRANGERS IN THE HOUSE(1949, Fr.), m
Maria Luisa Rolando
NIGHTS OF CABIRIA(1957, Ital.)
Maria Lusia Rolando
VAMPIRE AND THE BALLERINA, THE(1962, Ital.)
Andree Rolane
Misc. Silents
LES MISERABLES(1927, Fr.)
Agapito Roldan
SCALPHUNTERS, THE(1968)
Emma Roldan
RANCHO GRANDE(1938, Mex.); GUADALAJARA(1943, Mex.); ONE WAY STREET(1950); ROBOT VS. THE AZTEC MUMMY, THE(1965, Mex.)
Julio Roldan
STING OF DEATH(1966), ph
Wilfredo Roldan
DEVIL'S EXPRESS(1975)
Lupi Roldano
STORY OF THE COUNT OF MONTE CRISTO, THE(1962, Fr./Ital.)
Arthur Rolen
WHALERS, THE(1942, Swed.)
Andre Rolet
WOMAN IN COMMAND, THE(1934 Brit.)
Ruby Rolevitt
LADY GAMBLES, THE(1949), set d
Sutton Roley
LONERS, THE(1972), d; CHOSEN SURVIVORS(1974 U.S.-Mex.), d
Rolf the Dog
STALKING MOON, THE(1969)
Erik Rolf
ATLANTIC CONVOY(1942); EYES IN THE NIGHT(1942); WIFE TAKES A FLYER, THE(1942); CHANCE OF A LIFETIME, THE(1943); FIRST COMES COURAGE(1943); KANSAS CITY KITTY(1944); NONE SHALL ESCAPE(1944); SECRET COMMAND(1944); SHE'S A SOLDIER TOO(1944); SOUL OF A MONSTER, THE(1944); STRANGE AFFAIR(1944); U-BOAT PRISONER(1944); COUNTER-ATTACK(1945); PRISON SHIP(1945); CLOSE CALL FOR BOSTON BLACKIE, A(1946); SONG OF THE SOUTH(1946); EVERYBODY DOES IT(1949); DAVY CROCKETT, INDIAN SCOUT(1950)
Frederick Rolf
SEDUCTION OF JOE TYNAN, THE(1979)
Fredrick Rolf
BLADE(1973)
Guy Rolf
HUNGRY HILL(1947, Brit.)
Tom Rolf
CLAMBAKE(1967), ed; MC KENZIE BREAK, THE(1970), ed; UNDERGROUND(1970, Brit.), ed; RESURRECTION OF ZACHARY WHEELER, THE(1971), w; HONKERS, THE(1972), ed; LAST AMERICAN HERO, THE(1973), ed; LOLLYMADONNA XXX(1973), ed; MAN WHO LOVED CAT DANCING, THE(1973), ed; TRIAL OF BILLY JACK, THE(1974), ed; VISIT TO A CHIEF'S SON(1974), ed; FRENCH CONNECTION 11(1975), ed; LUCKY LADY(1975), ed; TAXI DRIVER(1976), ed; BLACK SUNDAY(1977), ed; HUNTING PARTY, THE(1977, Brit.), ed; NEW YORK, NEW YORK(1977), ed; BLUE COLLAR(1978), ed; HARDCORE(1979), ed; PROPHECY(1979), ed; HEAVEN'S GATE(1980), ed; GHOST STORY(1981), ed; RIGHT STUFF, THE(1983), ed; WARGAMES(1983), ed
1984
THIEF OF HEARTS(1984), ed
Tutia Rolf
WHALERS, THE(1942, Swed.)
Tutta Rolf
DRESSED TO THRILL(1935); SWEDENHIELMS(1935, Swed.); RHYTHM IN THE AIR(1936, Brit.); DOLLAR(1938, Swed.)
Alan Rolfe
GLORY AT SEA(1952, Brit.); NORMAN CONQUEST(1953, Brit.); HARASSED HERO, THE(1954, Brit.); GIDEON OF SCOTLAND YARD(1959, Brit.); INN FOR TROUBLE(1960, Brit.); PEEPING TOM(1960, Brit.)

B. A. Rolfe
Silents
MADONNAS AND MEN(1920), d; WOMAN'S BUSINESS, A(1920), d; AMAZING LOVERS(1921), d
B.A. Rolfe
Misc. Silents
EVEN AS EVE(1920), d; LOVE WITHOUT QUESTION(1920), d
Charles Rolfe
HARD STEEL(1941, Brit.); INVADERS, THE(1941); NEUTRAL PORT(1941, Brit.); TOWER OF TERROR, THE(1942, Brit.); MEET SEXTON BLAKE(1944, Brit.); MY AIN FOLK(1944, Brit.); CAESAR AND CLEOPATRA(1946, Brit.); GIRL IN A MILLION, A(1946, Brit.); GRAND ESCAPADE, THE(1946, Brit.); DEAR MURDERER(1947, Brit.); SMUGGLERS, THE(1948, Brit.); THEY ARE NOT ANGELS(1948, Fr.); MIRANDA(1949, Brit.); YOU LUCKY PEOPLE(1955, Brit.)
Chick Rolfe
UNEASY TERMS(1948, Brit.)
E.A. Rolfe
SCARF, THE(1951), d&w
Guy Rolfe
YESTERDAY'S ENEMY(1959, Brit.); MEET ME AT DAWN(1947, Brit.); NICHOLAS NICKLEBY(1947, Brit.); ODD MAN OUT(1947, Brit.); BROKEN JOURNEY(1948, Brit.); EASY MONEY(1948, Brit.); GIRL IN THE PAINTING, THE(1948, Brit.); FOOLS RUSH IN(1949, Brit.); SARABAND(1949, Brit.); PRELUDE TO FAME(1950, Brit.); HOME TO DANGER(1951, Brit.); INHERITANCE, THE(1951, Brit.); RELUCTANT WIDOW, THE(1951, Brit.); IVANHOE(1952, Brit.); SPIDER AND THE FLY, THE(1952, Brit.); KING OF THE KHYBER RIFLES(1953); OPERATION DIPLOMAT(1953, Brit.); VEILS OF BAGDAD, THE(1953); YOUNG BESS(1953); DANCE LITTLE LADY(1954, Brit.); YOU CAN'T ESCAPE(1955, Brit.); LIGHT FINGERS(1957, Brit.); GIRLS AT SEA(1958, Brit.); IT'S NEVER TOO LATE(1958, Brit.); STRANGLERS OF BOMBAY, THE(1960, Brit.); KING OF KINGS(1961); MR. SARDONICUS(1961); SNOW WHITE AND THE THREE STOOGES(1961); TARAS BULBA(1962); FALL OF THE ROMAN EMPIRE, THE(1964); ALPHABET MURDERS, THE(1966); LAND RAIDERS(1969); NICHOLAS AND ALEXANDRA(1971, Brit.); AND NOW THE SCREAMING STARTS(1973, Brit.)
John Rolfe
MC VICAR(1982, Brit.)
Sam Rolfe
NAKED SPUR, THE(1953), w; MC CONNELL STORY, THE(1955), w; TARGET ZERO(1955), w; PILLARS OF THE SKY(1956), w; BOMBERS B-52(1957), w; SPY WITH MY FACE, THE(1966), p; TO TRAP A SPY(1966), p, w
Kirsten Rolfes
EPILOGUE(1967, Den.)
Tom Rolfing
HE KNOWS YOU'RE ALONE(1980)
Arthur Rolhsfel
MAN WHO CRIED WOLF, THE(1937), w
Mino Roli
BEYOND THE LAW(1967, Ital.), w; TALL WOMEN, THE(1967, Aust./Ital./Span.), w; GRAND SLAM(1968, Ital., Span., Ger.), w; MACHINE GUN McCAIN(1970, Ital.), w; MASTER TOUCH, THE(1974, Ital./Ger.), w
Hank Rolike
ROCKY(1976); SMALL TOWN IN TEXAS, A(1976); W.C. FIELDS AND ME(1976)
Misc. Talkies
FOX STYLE(1973)
Judie Rolin
IRISH WHISKEY REBELLION(1973)
Gernot Roll
LAST ESCAPE, THE(1970, Brit.), ph
Philip Roll
ADVENTURES OF ROBINSON CRUSOE, THE(1954), w
Steve Roll
1984
BLOOD SIMPLE(1984), set d
Michelle Rolla
MR. HULOT'S HOLIDAY(1954, Fr.)
Philippe Rolla
Silents
NAPOLEON(1927, Fr.)
Rollan
HARVEST(1939, Fr.)
Henri Rollan
FANFAN THE TULIP(1952, Fr.)
Misc. Silents
PARIS QUI DORT(1924, Fr.)
George Rolland
VILNA LEGEND, A(1949, U.S./Pol.), d
Gerard Rolland
PLEASURES AND VICES(1962, Fr.)
Henri Rolland
ADVENTURES OF ARSENE LUPIN(1956, Fr./Ital.)
Jean-Claude Rolland
OBJECTIVE 500 MILLION(1966, Fr.); WISE GUYS(1969, Fr./Ital.)
Monique Rolland
TESTAMENT OF DR. MABUSE, THE(1943, Ger.)
Esther Rolle
NOTHING BUT A MAN(1964); WHO SAYS I CAN'T RIDE A RAINBOW!(1971); CLEOPATRA JONES(1973)
Marian Rolle
1984
DESIREE(1984, Neth.)
Jack Rollens
Silents
WHEN A WOMAN SINS(1918); THELMA(1922)
Misc. Silents
VAGABOND LUCK(1919)
Jacques Rollens
CHARLATAN, THE(1929), w
Cleve Roller
RECESS(1967)

Raymond Rollet
DON'T SAY DIE(1950, Brit.)
Raymond Rollett
PASTOR HALL(1940, Brit.); MASTER OF BANKDAM, THE(1947, Brit.); FIGHTING PIMPERNEL, THE(1950, Brit.); GALLOPING MAJOR, THE(1951, Brit.); MOULIN ROUGE(1952); WILD HEART, THE(1952, Brit.); LIMPING MAN, THE(1953, Brit.); STOLEN ASSIGNMENT(1955, Brit.); THEY CAN'T HANG ME(1955, Brit.); KID FOR TWO FARTHINGS, A(1956, Brit.); CURSE OF FRANKENSTEIN, THE(1957, Brit.); MEN OF SHERWOOD FOREST(1957, Brit.); BLUE MURDER AT ST. TRINIAN'S(1958, Brit.); GIDEON OF SCOTLAND YARD(1959, Brit.); PART-TIME WIFE(1961, Brit.); TICKET TO PARADISE(1961, Brit.); GOLDEN RABBIT, THE(1962, Brit.); RETURN OF A STRANGER(1962, Brit.)
Misc. Talkies
SUPERSONIC SAUCER(1956, Brit.)
Roger Rollie
PROPER TIME, THE(1959)
Rollin
J'ACCUSE(1939, Fr.)
Georges Rollin
ULTIMATUM(1940, Fr.); IT HAPPENED AT THE INN(1945, Fr.); CLANDESTINE(1948, Fr.)
Jean Rollin
Misc. Talkies
CAGED VIRGINS(1972), d
Patrick Rollin
WAGNER(1983, Brit./Hung./Aust.)
The Rolling Robinsons
GLENN MILLER STORY, THE(1953)
The Rolling Stones
ONE PLUS ONE(1969, Brit.), a, m
Gordon Rollings
WEEKEND WITH LULU, A(1961, Brit.); NIGHT CREATURES(1962, Brit.); VALIANT, THE(1962, Brit./Ital.); JUST FOR FUN(1963, Brit.); GREAT CATHERINE(1968, Brit.); BED SITTING ROOM, THE(1969, Brit.); DAVID COPPERFIELD(1970, Brit.); JABBERWOCKY(1977, Brit.); SUPERMAN II(1980); SUPERMAN III(1983)
1984
BLOODBATH AT THE HOUSE OF DEATH(1984, Brit.); GIVE MY REGARDS TO BROAD STREET(1984, Brit.)
Jack Rollings
Silents
ABRAHAM LINCOLN(1924)
Red Rollings
FAST COMPANY(1929)
Bernie Rollins
GETTING OVER(1981), d&w
Bob Rollins
1984
BROADWAY DANNY ROSE(1984)
David Rollins
AIR CIRCUS, THE(1928); BLACK WATCH, THE(1929); FOX MOVIETONE FOLLIES(1929); LOVE, LIVE AND LAUGH(1929); WHY LEAVE HOME?(1929); BIG TRAIL, THE(1930); HAPPY DAYS(1930); MORALS FOR WOMEN(1931); PHANTOM EXPRESS, THE(1932); PROBATION(1932)
Silents
PREP AND PEP(1928); RILEY THE COP(1928); THANKS FOR THE BUGGY RIDE(1928)
Misc. Silents
WIN THAT GIRL(1928)
Etta Rollins
1984
BROADWAY DANNY ROSE(1984)
Howard Rollins, Jr.
1984
HOUSE OF GOD, THE(1984)
Howard E. Rollins, Jr.
RAGTIME(1981)
1984
SOLDIER'S STORY, A(1984)
Jack Rollins
SWEETHEARTS AND WIVES(1930), ed
1984
BROADWAY DANNY ROSE(1984)
Silents
MORE TROUBLE(1918); MAKING THE GRADE(1921); DO AND DARE(1922); GENTLE JULIA(1923); ROUGH SHOD(1925)
Misc. Silents
UNSEEN HANDS(1924); SILVER TREASURE, THE(1926)
Jean Rollins
THE BEACHCOMBER(1955, Brit.)
Jeanette Rollins
TERROR IN THE JUNGLE(1968)
John Rollins
TOO YOUNG TO MARRY(1931), ed
Jorja Rollins
HITLER'S MADMAN(1943)
Lizabeth Rollins
THE BEACHCOMBER(1955, Brit.)
Oneida Rollins
JAWS II(1978)
Sonny Rollins
ALFIE(1966, Brit.), m
Tony Rollins
ISLAND OF LOVE(1963)
Robert Rollis
LA BELLE AMERICAINE(1961, Fr.); DIE GANS VON SEDAN(1962, Fr/Ger.); WAR OF THE BUTTONS(1963 Fr.); TWO ARE GUILTY(1964, Fr.); WHAT'S NEW, PUSSYCAT?(1965, U.S./Fr.); COUNTERFEIT CONSTABLE, THE(1966, Fr.); WEEKEND AT DUNKIRK(1966, Fr./Ital.)

Dick Rollo
SMASH PALACE(1982, New Zealand)
Primula Rollo
HER MAN GILBEY(1949, Brit.)
E. J. Rollow
Silents
FALSE FRIEND, THE(1917)
P.J. Rollow
Misc. Silents
MARRIAGE BOND, THE(1916)
Pip Rolls
EAGLE ROCK(1964, Brit.)
Bobby Rolofson
APPLE DUMPLING GANG RIDES AGAIN, THE(1979); NORTH AVENUE IRREGU-LARS, THE(1979)
Rosalba Rolon
Misc. Talkies
TWO WORLDS OF ANGELITA, THE(1982)
Robert Rolontz
MISTER ROCK AND ROLL(1957), md
Don Rolos
LOVE NOW...PAY LATER(1966), d
Alice Rolph
KENTUCKY RIFLE(1956)
Misc. Talkies
YELLOW HAIRED KID, THE(1952)
Dudley Rolph
IT'S A BET(1935, Brit.); LILY OF LAGUNA(1938, Brit.)
Rolf Rolphs
EMIL AND THE DETECTIVES(1964)
Louis Rolston
1984
CAL(1984, Ireland)
Jacques Roltfield
KNOCK(1955, Fr.), p
Fono Roma
PAYMENT IN BLOOD(1968, Ital.), m
Jess Roma
BLOOD DRINKERS, THE(1966, U.S./Phil.)
Mikhail Romadin
SOLARIS(1972, USSR), art d
Mario Romagnoli
FELLINI SATYRICON(1969, Fr./Ital.)
Claude Romain
LA MARIE DU PORT(1951, Fr.); TO PARIS WITH LOVE(1955, Brit.); LIGHT ACROSSS THE STREET, THE(1957, Fr.)
George Romain
Misc. Silents
RETURN OF TARZAN, THE(1920)
George E. Romain
Silents
DIANE OF STAR HOLLOW(1921)
Misc. Silents
CALL OF THE DANCE, THE(1915)
Jacques Romain
LOVE IN 4 DIMENSIONS(1965 Fr./Ital.), d
Yvonne Romain
PICKUP ALLEY(1957, Brit.); SILENT ENEMY, THE(1959, Brit.); CIRCUS OF HORRORS(1960, Brit.); CURSE OF THE WEREWOLF, THE(1961); FRIGHTENED CITY, THE(1961, Brit.); NIGHT CREATURES(1962, Brit.); RETURN TO SENDER(1963, Brit.); DEVIL DOLL(1964, Brit.); SMOKESCREEN(1964, Brit.); BRIGAND OF KANDA-HAR, THE(1965, Brit.); SWINGER, THE(1966); DOUBLE TROUBLE(1967); LAST OF SHEILA, THE(1973)
Jean Romaine
TAKE CARE OF MY LITTLE GIRL(1951)
John Romaine
KIDNAPPING OF THE PRESIDENT, THE(1980, Can.)
Louis Romaine
Silents
INTOLERANCE(1916)
Ruth Romaine
HAPPY LANDING(1934); LOUDSPEAKER, THE(1934)
Vincent Romaine
MAN CALLED GANNON, A(1969), makeup
Yvonne Romaine
VILLAGE OF DAUGHTERS(1962, Brit.)
Jules Romains
DR. KNOCK(1936, Fr.), w; VOLPONE(1947, Fr.), w; KNOCK(1955, Fr.), w
A. Roman
LULLABY(1961, USSR), art d; SANDU FOLLOWS THE SUN(1965, USSR), art d
Antoine Roman
JUDGE AND THE ASSASSIN, THE(1979, Fr.), art d
Antonio Roman
PLANET OF THE VAMPIRES(1965, U.S./Ital./Span.), w
Candice Roman
BIG BIRD CAGE, THE(1972); UNHOLY ROLLERS(1972)
Misc. Talkies
MANSON MASSACRE, THE(1976)
Candy Roman
BLOOD WEDDING(1981, Sp.)
Eddie Roman
1984
DELIVERY BOYS(1984)
Elsie Roman
DEVIL'S EXPRESS(1975)
Eugene Roman
CHRISTMAS TREE, THE(1969, Fr.), art d; PLAYTIME(1973, Fr.), prod d

Gina Roman
CANDY MAN, THE(1969)
Greg Roman
NAKED AND THE DEAD, THE(1958)
Hugh Roman
SHOW GIRL(1928)
Joe Roman
BON VOYAGE, CHARLIE BROWN(AND DON'T COME BACK)*** (1980), anim; ST. IVES(1976); RACE FOR YOUR LIFE, CHARLIE BROWN(1977), anim; WHITE BUF-FALO, THE(1977)
Jose Roman
1984
DELIVERY BOYS(1984)
Joseph Roman
LOVE AND BULLETS(1979, Brit.)
L. Roman
RED SUN(1972, Fr./Ital./Span.), w
Lawrence Roman
VICE SQUAD(1953), w; DRUMS ACROSS THE RIVER(1954), w; NAKED ALI-BI(1954), w; MAN FROM BITTER RIDGE, THE(1955), w; ONE DESIRE(1955), w; KISS BEFORE DYING, A(1956), w; SHARKFIGHTERS, THE(1956), w; SLAUGHTER ON TENTH AVENUE(1957), w; DAY OF THE BAD MAN(1958), w; UNDER THE YUM-YUM TREE(1963), w; SWINGER, THE(1966), w; PAPER LION(1968), w; WARM DECEMBER, A(1973, Brit.), w; MC Q(1974), p, w
Leticia Roman
G.I. BLUES(1960); GOLD OF THE SEVEN SAINTS(1961); PIRATES OF TOR-TUGA(1961); EVIL EYE(1964 Ital.); SPY IN THE GREEN HAT, THE(1966); PONTIUS PILATE(1967, Fr./Ital.)
Letitia Roman
FANNY HILL: MEMOIRS OF A WOMAN OF PLEASURE zero(1965); FLAMING FRONTIER(1968, Ger./Yugo.)
Manuel San Roman
THUNDERSTORM(1956)
Martin Roman
50,000 B.C.(BEFORE CLOTHING)* (1963), m
Murray Roman
2000 YEARS LATER(1969)
N. Roman
POCKET MONEY(1972)
Nina Roman
CRIMSON KIMONO, THE(1959); MELINDA(1972)
Paul Roman
HEY, GOOD LOOKIN'(1982)
Pedro Roman
ONCE UPON A COFFEE HOUSE(1965)
Penny Roman
FAT SPY(1966)
Peter Roman
YOU GOTTA STAY HAPPY(1948); SUN COMES UP, THE(1949); MISTER 880(1950); SCANDAL AT SCOURIE(1953)
Phil Roman
RACE FOR YOUR LIFE, CHARLIE BROWN(1977), d
Philip Roman
BOY NAMED CHARLIE BROWN, A(1969), anim; PHANTOM TOLLBOOTH, THE(1970), anim
Ric Roman
KISS TOMORROW GOODBYE(1950); LADY PAYS OFF, THE(1951); MASK OF THE AVENGER(1951); MOB, THE(1951); NAVY BOUND(1951); HAREM GIRL(1952); HOODLUM EMPIRE(1952); KANSAS CITY CONFIDENTIAL(1952); LAST OF THE COMANCHES(1952); LONE STAR(1952); SCANDAL SHEET(1952); SPRINGFIELD RIFLE(1952); VIVA ZAPATA!(1952); APPOINTMENT IN HONDURAS(1953); BIG HEAT, THE(1953); SHADOWS OF TOMBSTONE(1953); SLAVES OF BABYLON(1953); ABOUT MRS. LESLIE(1954); DESPERATE HOURS, THE(1955); MA AND PA KETTLE AT WAIKIKI(1955); UNDERWATER!(1955); TERROR AT MIDNIGHT(1956); WIRE-TAPPERS(1956); DUEL AT APACHE WELLS(1957); LIZZIE(1957); UP IN SMO-KE(1957); WAYWARD GIRL, THE(1957); IN THE MONEY(1958); SOME CAME RUNNING(1959)
Ric [Ricardo] Roman
NEVADA SMITH(1966)
Ricardo Roman
YOUNG AND EVIL(1962, Mex.)
Rick Roman
SLAUGHTER TRAIL(1951); SOUTH OF CALIENTE(1951); ACTORS AND SIN(1952)
Ruth Roman
WITHOUT RESERVATIONS(1946); STAGE DOOR CANTEEN(1943); LADIES COURAGEOUS(1944); SINCE YOU WENT AWAY(1944); STORM OVER LIS-BON(1944); INCENDIARY BLONDE(1945); SHE GETS HER MAN(1945); YOU CAME ALONG(1945); GILDA(1946); BELLE STARR'S DAUGHTER(1947); WHITE STAL-LION(1947); GOOD SAM(1948); ALWAYS LEAVE THEM LAUGHING(1949); BEYOND THE FOREST(1949); CHAMPION(1949); WINDOW, THE(1949); BARRICADE(1950); COLT .45(1950); DALLAS(1950); THREE SECRETS(1950); LIGHTNING STRIKES TWICE(1951); STARLIFT(1951); STRANGERS ON A TRAIN(1951); TOMORROW IS ANOTHER DAY(1951); INVITATION(1952); MARA MARU(1952); YOUNG MAN WITH IDEAS(1952); BLOWING WILD(1953); DOWN THREE DARK STREETS(1954); SHANGHAI STORY, THE(1954); TANGANYIKA(1954); FAR COUNTRY, THE(1955); JOE MACBETH(1955); BOTTOM OF THE BOTTLE, THE(1956); GREAT DAY IN THE MORNING(1956); REBEL IN TOWN(1956); FIVE STEPS TO DANGER(1957); BITTER VICTORY(1958, Fr.); DESERT DESPERADOES(1959); LOOK IN ANY WINDOW(1961); LOVE HAS MANY FACES(1965); BABY, THE(1973); KILLING KIND, THE(1973); IMPULSE(1975); DAY OF THE ANIMALS(1977); ECHOES(1983)
Misc. Talkies
KNIFE FOR THE LADIES, A(1973)
Sig Roman
FORTUNE COOKIE, THE(1966)
Star Roman
HARRY'S WAR(1981)
Susan Roman
RABID(1976, Can.); HEAVY METAL(1981, Can.)

Tony Roman- I-2470

Misc. Talkies
ROCK 'N' RULE(1983)
Tony Roman
POPPY IS ALSO A FLOWER, THE(1966), art d; TRIPLE CROSS(1967, Fr./Brit.), art d; MAYERLING(1968, Brit./Fr.), art d; CHRISTMAS TREE, THE(1969, Fr.), art d; LAST OF SHEILA, THE(1973), art d; COLD SWEAT(1974, Ital., Fr.), art d; NIJINSKY(1980, Brit.), art d
Nicholas Romanac
LADY ICE(1973), set d; LENNY(1974), set d; NIGHT IN HEAVEN, A(1983), set d; SPRING BREAK(1983), art d
Nick Romanac
NAKED APE, THE(1973), set d
Viviane Romance
LILIOM(1935, Fr.); DARK EYES(1938, Fr.); THEY WERE FIVE(1938, Fr.); KISS OF FIRE, THE(1940, Fr.); CARMEN(1946, Ital.); PANIQUE(1947, Fr.); MARKED GIRLS(1949, Fr.); CROSSROADS OF PASSION(1951, Fr.); PLEASURES AND VICES(1962, Fr.); ANY NUMBER CAN WIN(1963 Fr.); NADA GANG, THE(1974, Fr./Ital.)
Vivianne Romance
IT HAPPENED IN GIBRALTAR(1943, Fr.)
Elo Romancik
ASSISTANT, THE(1982, Czech.)
Richard Romancito
ROOSTER COGBURN(1975); NIGHTWING(1979)
Beatrice Romand
CLAIRE'S KNEE(1971, Fr.); CHLOE IN THE AFTERNOON(1972, Fr.); ROMANTIC ENGLISHWOMAN, THE(1975, Brit./Fr.); UNDERCOVERS HERO(1975, Brit.); LE BEAU MARIAGE(1982, Fr.)
Gina Romand
LOS ASTRONAUTAS(1960, Mex.); VENGEANCE OF THE VAMPIRE WOMEN, THE(1969, Mex.); SANTO CONTRA LA HIJA DE FRANKENSTEIN(1971, Mex.)
Catherine Romane
SELLERS OF GIRLS(1967, Fr.)
Carla Romanelli
TO KILL OR TO DIE(1973, Ital.); STEPPENWOLF(1974); LONELY LADY, THE(1983)
1984
CORRUPT(1984, Ital.)
Olga Romanelli
SWORD OF THE CONQUEROR(1962, Ital.); LET'S TALK ABOUT WOMEN(1964, Fr./Ital.); VOYAGE, THE(1974, Ital.)
Roland Romanelli
1984
HERE COMES SANTA CLAUS(1984), md
Augusto Romani
JOAN AT THE STAKE(1954, Ital./Fr.)
Carlo Romani
ANYTHING FOR A SONG(1947, Ital.)
Sofia Romani
PARSIFAL(1983, Fr.)
Bruno Romani-Versteeg
PARSIFAL(1983, Fr.)
Sgt. Romaniello
THREE STRIPES IN THE SUN(1955)
Gaia Romanini
WARRIOR EMPRESS, THE(1961, Ital./Fr.), cos; FAMILY DIARY(1963 Ital.), cos; WASTREL, THE(1963, Ital.), cos; HERCULES, SAMSON & ULYSSES(1964, Ital.), cos; OPERATION KID BROTHER(1967, Ital.), cos; ROSE FOR EVERYONE, A(1967, Ital.), cos; SEVEN GOLDEN MEN(1969, Fr./Ital./Span.), cos; LAST REBEL, THE(1971), cos
George Romanis
EIGHT ON THE LAM(1967), m; CHANDLER(1971), m
L. Romanis
BOXER(1971, Pol.), ed
Alessandra Romano
1984
BASILEUS QUARTET(1984, Ital.)
Amelia Romano
NATIVE LAND(1942); NONE BUT THE LONELY HEART(1944); NAKED CITY, THE(1948); TAPS(1981)
Andy Romano
PAJAMA PARTY(1964); HOW TO STUFF A WILD BIKINI(1965); SERGEANT DEADHEAD(1965); GHOST IN THE INVISIBLE BIKINI(1966); BAMBOO SAUCER, THE(1968); ONE MAN JURY(1978); LOVE AND BULLETS(1979, Brit.); OVER THE EDGE(1979)
Anthony Romano
STARTING OVER(1979)
Carlo Romano
LAUGH PAGLIACCI(1948, Ital.); CHILDREN OF CHANCE(1950, Ital.); MELODY OF LOVE(1954, Ital.); VITELLONI(1956, Ital./Fr.); UNFAITHFULS, THE(1960, Ital.); VARIETY LIGHTS(1965, Ital.); VERY HANDY MAN, A(1966, Fr./Ital.), w; ALL THE OTHER GIRLS DO!(1967, Ital.), w
Carlos Romano
HIGH RISK(1981); UNDER FIRE(1983); YELLOWBEARD(1983)
1984
EVIL THAT MEN DO, THE(1984)
Chris Romano
RETURN OF THE JEDI(1983)
1984
THIS IS SPINAL TAP(1984)
Dean Romano
WILD YOUTH(1961), w
Dina Romano
ANNA(1951, Ital.)
John Romano
HOMEWORK(1982); STREET MUSIC(1982)
Marie Romano
1984
CAGED WOMEN(1984, Ital./Fr.)

Michael Romano
IT HAD TO HAPPEN(1936)
Michael R. Romano
BAYOU(1957)
Nina Romano
Silents
WHAT HAPPENED TO JONES(1926)
Misc. Silents
STORM BREAKER, THE(1925); MONEY TO BURN(1926)
Pasquale Romano
RELUCTANT SAINT, THE(1962, U.S./Ital.), art d
Phil Romano
TWO OF A KIND(1983)
Phillip Romano
1984
RACING WITH THE MOON(1984)
Renato Romano
MINUTE TO PRAY, A SECOND TO DIE, A(1968, Ital.); ITALIAN JOB, THE(1969, Brit.); PLUCKED(1969, Fr./Ital.); DORIAN GRAY(1970, Ital./Brit./Ger./Liechtenstein); LAST REBEL, THE(1971); DEAF SMITH AND JOHNNY EARS(1973, Ital.)
Renator Romano
BIRD WITH THE CRYSTAL PLUMAGE, THE(1970, Ital./Ger.)
Tony Romano
RADIO STARS ON PARADE(1945); MAN I LOVE, THE(1946); PURPLE HEART DIARY(1951); ROBBER'S ROOST(1955)
Vic Romano
COOL WORLD, THE(1963)
Vince Romano
DARK SIDE OF TOMORROW, THE(1970)
Andy Romanoff
SOMETHING WEIRD(1967), ph; TASTE OF BLOOD, A(1967), ph; FLESH FEAST(1970), ph
Constantin Romanoff
GANG BUSTER, THE(1931); LONG VOYAGE HOME, THE(1940); PRINCESS AND THE PIRATE, THE(1944); TAMPICO(1944)
Constantine Romanoff
CONDEMNED(1929); WOLF SONG(1929); SHIPS OF HATE(1931); MOVIE CRAZY(1932); TOO BUSY TO WORK(1932); ISLAND OF LOST SOULS(1933); MARY STEVENS, M.D.(1933); SON OF KONG(1933); JUDGE PRIEST(1934); KID MILLIONS(1934); SIXTEEN FATHOMS DEEP(1934); BARBARY COAST(1935); DANTE'S INFERNO(1935); DON'T BET ON BLONDES(1935); NAUGHTY MARIETTA(1935); PEOPLE WILL TALK(1935); STOLEN HARMONY(1935); AFTER THE THIN MAN(1936); OUR RELATIONS(1936); ROAD GANG(1936); SOULS AT SEA(1937); MEET THE GIRLS(1938); PROFESSOR BEWARE(1938); SISTERS, THE(1938); I STOLE A MILLION(1939); KID NIGHTINGALE(1939); LET FREEDOM RING(1939); $1,000 A TOUCHDOWN(1939); FLORIAN(1940); SAPS AT SEA(1940); FOUR JACKS AND A JILL(1941); REAP THE WILD WIND(1942); NORTHWEST OUTPOST(1947); WILD HARVEST(1947)
Silents
KID BROTHER, THE(1927); TENDER HOUR, THE(1927)
Katia Romanoff
NADA GANG, THE(1974, Fr./Ital.)
Lee Romanoff
1984
PURPLE RAIN(1984), makeup
Liz Romanoff
DR. JEKYLL AND SISTER HYDE(1971, Brit.)
Michael Romanoff
FOOLS FOR SCANDAL(1938); OTHER LOVE, THE(1947); ARCH OF TRIUMPH(1948); MOVE OVER, DARLING(1963); GOODBYE CHARLIE(1964); DO NOT DISTURB(1965); VON RYAN'S EXPRESS(1965); CAPRICE(1967); GUIDE FOR THE MARRIED MAN, A(1967); TONY ROME(1967)
Mike Romanoff
IN A LONELY PLACE(1950)
Prince Michael Romanoff
SING WHILE YOU'RE ABLE(1937); DON'T TRUST YOUR HUSBAND(1948); PARIS MODEL(1953)
Sonia Romanoff
MAN WITH THE BALLOONS, THE(1968, Ital./Fr.)
Richard Romanos
HEAVY METAL(1981, Can.)
The Romanos
I WANNA HOLD YOUR HAND(1978)
M. Romanov
SECRET MISSION(1949, USSR)
Richard Romanowsky
HOUSE OF THE THREE GIRLS, THE(1961, Aust.); YOU ARE THE WORLD FOR ME(1964, Aust.)
Alain Romans
MR. HULOT'S HOLIDAY(1954, Fr.), m
Alains Romans
MY UNCLE(1958, Fr.), m
Joe Romantini
CIPHER BUREAU(1938)
Joseph Romantini
ANGEL(1937); EVER SINCE EVE(1937); FIRST LADY(1937); HOLLYWOOD HOTEL(1937); ARTISTS AND MODELS ABROAD(1938); MIDNIGHT(1939)
Richard Romanus
MEAN STREETS(1973); GRAVY TRAIN, THE(1974); RUSSIAN ROULETTE(1975); WIZARDS(1977); SITTING DUCKS(1979), a, m; HEY, GOOD LOOKIN'(1982); PANDEMONIUM(1982)
1984
PROTOCOL(1984); STRANGERS KISS(1984)
Robert Romanus
FOXES(1980); FAST TIMES AT RIDGEMONT HIGH(1982)
M. Romarov
CAPTAIN GRANT'S CHILDREN(1939, USSR)

Charles Romas
STARS OVER ARIZONA(1937)
A. Romashin
HOUSE ON THE FRONT LINE, THE(1963, USSR)
Carlo Romatko
LAST CHANCE, THE(1945, Switz.)
Lina Romay
YOU WERE NEVER LOVELIER(1942); HEAT'S ON, THE(1943); BATHING BEAU-
TY(1944); TWO GIRLS AND A SAILOR(1944); ADVENTURE(1945); WEEKEND AT
THE WALDORF(1945); LOVE LAUGHS AT ANDY HARDY(1946); HONEY-
MOON(1947); EMBRACEABLE YOU(1948); BIG WHEEL, THE(1949); JOE PALOOKA
IN THE BIG FIGHT(1949); LADY TAKES A SAILOR, THE(1949); MAN BEHIND THE
GUN, THE(1952)
Luis Romay
DEATH OF A BUREAUCRAT(1979, Cuba)
Pepito Romay
IMPORTANT MAN, THE(1961, Mex.)
Titina Romay
IMPORTANT MAN, THE(1961, Mex.)
Romana Rombach
DANIELLA BY NIGHT(1962, Fr/Ger.)
Sigmund Romberg
DESERT SONG, THE(1929), m; NEW MOON(1930), w; VIENNESE NIGHTS(1930),
w, m; CHILDREN OF DREAMS(1931), w; MAYTIME(1937), w; NEW MOON(1940), w,
w, m; DESERT SONG, THE(1943), w, m; UP IN CENTRAL PARK(1948), w, m;
DESERT SONG, THE(1953), w, m; DEEP IN MY HEART(1954), m; STUDENT
PRINCE, THE(1954), w, m
Silents
FOOLISH WIVES(1920), m
Hillevi Rombin
ISTANBUL(1957)
Samuel Obiero Romboh
LION, THE(1962, Brit.)
B. Rombouts
LEGACY OF BLOOD(1973), ph
Bert Rome
FAST COMPANY(1929); FORWARD PASS, THE(1929)
Harold Rome
WONDERFUL THINGS!(1958, Brit.), m; FANNY(1961), m
Harold J. Rome
CALL ME MISTER(1951), w
Peter Rome
NEON PALACE, THE(1970, Can.), ed
Stewart Rome
CRIMSON CIRCLE, THE(1930, Brit.); DARK RED ROSES(1930, Brit.); KISSING
CUP'S RACE(1930, Brit.); LAST HOUR, THE(1930, Brit.); PRICE OF THINGS,
THE(1930, Brit.); DEADLOCK(1931, Brit.); GREAT GAY ROAD, THE(1931, Brit.);
OTHER PEOPLE'S SINS(1931, Brit.); BETRAYAL(1932, Brit.); MARRIAGE BOND,
THE(1932, Brit.); REUNION(1932, Brit.); COUNTY FAIR(1933, Brit.); DESIGNING
WOMEN(1934, Brit.); GIRL IN THE FLAT, THE(1934, Brit.); LEST WE FORGET(1934,
Brit.); TEMPTATION(1935, Brit.); DEBT OF HONOR(1936, Brit.); MEN OF YESTER-
DAY(1936, Brit.); DINNER AT THE RITZ(1937, Brit.); MURDER ON DIAMOND
ROW(1937, Brit.); WINGS OF THE MORNING(1937, Brit.); DANCE OF DEATH,
THE(1938, Brit.); CONFIDENTIAL LADY(1939, Brit.); SHADOWED EYES(1939, Brit.);
BANANA RIDGE(1941, Brit.); ONE OF OUR AIRCRAFT IS MISSING(1942, Brit.);
SALUTE JOHN CITIZEN(1942, Brit.); WORLD OWES ME A LIVING, THE(1944, Brit.);
BAD SISTER(1947, Brit.); MAGIC BOW, THE(1947, Brit.); JASSY(1948, Brit.); MY
SISTER AND I(1948, Brit.); WOMAN HATER(1949, Brit.); STICK 'EM UP(1950, Brit.)
Silents
JUSTICE(1914, Brit.); HER BOY(1915, Brit.); IRIS(1915, Brit.); MOLLY BAWN(1916,
Brit.); PENNILESS MILLIONAIRE, THE(1921, Brit.); WHEN GREEK MEETS
GREEK(1922, Brit.); FIRES OF FATE(1923, Brit.); PRODIGAL SON, THE(1923, Brit.);
UNINVITED GUEST, THE(1923, Brit.); ELEVENTH COMMANDMENT, THE(1924,
Brit.); NETS OF DESTINY(1924, Brit.); THOU FOOL(1926, Brit.); SOMEHOW
GOOD(1927, Brit.); MAN WHO CHANGED HIS NAME, THE(1928, Brit.); PASSING OF
MR. QUIN, THE(1928, Brit.); ZERO(1928, Brit.)
Misc. Silents
GREAT POISON MYSTERY, THE(1914, Brit.); HEART OF MIDLOTHIAN, THE(1914,
Brit.); JUSTICE(1914, Brit.); AS THE SUN WENT DOWN(1915, Brit.); BARNABY
RUDGE(1915, Brit.); BOTTLE, THE(1915, Brit.); LANCASHIRE LASS, A(1915, Brit.); NIGH-
TBIRDS OF LONDON, THE(1915, Brit.); SWEET LAVENDER(1915, Brit.); WHITE
HOPE, THE(1915, Brit.); ANNIE LAURIE(1916, Brit.); COMIN' THRO' THE RYE(1916,
Brit.); GRAND BABYLON HOTEL, THE(1916, Brit.); MARRIAGE OF WILLIAM
ASHE, THE(1916, Brit.); SOWING THE WIND(1916, Brit.); TRELAWNEY OF THE
WELLS(1916, Brit.); COBWEB, THE(1917, Brit.); ETERNAL TRIANGLE, THE(1917,
Brit.); HER MARRIAGE LINES(1917, Brit.); MAN BEHIND "THE TIMES", THE(1917,
Brit.); TOUCH OF A CHILD, THE(1918, Brit.); DAUGHTER OF EVE, A(1919, Brit.);
GREAT COUP, A(1919, Brit.); HEARTS AND SADDLES(1919, Brit.); SNOW IN THE
DESERT(1919, Brit.); CASE OF LADY CAMBER, THE(1920, Brit.); GREAT GAY
ROAD, THE(1920, Brit.); HER SON(1920, Brit.); CHRISTIE JOHNSTONE(1921, Brit.);
HER PENALTY(1921, Brit.); IMPERFECT LOVER, THE(1921, Brit.); DICKY MON-
TEITH(1922, Brit.); SON OF KISSING CUP(1922, Brit.); WHITE HOPE, THE(1922,
Brit.); WOMAN WHO OBEYED, THE(1923, Brit.); LOVES OF COLLEEN BAWN,
THE(1924, Brit.); REVEILLE(1924, Brit.); STIRRUP CUP SENSATION, THE(1924,
Brit.); WARE CASE, THE(1928, Brit.)
Sydne Rome
SOME GIRLS DO(1969, Brit.); TIN GIRL, THE(1970, Ital.); CHE?(1973, Ital./Fr./Ger.);
LA BABY SITTER(1975, Fr./Ital./Ger.); THAT LUCKY TOUCH(1975, Brit.); TWIST,
THE(1976, Fr.); JUST A GIGOLO(1979, Ger.)
Misc. Talkies
THEY CALLED HIM AMEN(1972); ORDER TO KILL(1974); PUMA MAN, THE(1980)
Tina Rome
BARON OF ARIZONA, THE(1950); PARK ROW(1952); UNDERWORLD U.S.A.(1961);
LILITH(1964); MAN CALLED ADAM, A(1966), w
Rome Opera Theater Corps de Ballet
NEOPOLITAN CAROUSEL(1961, Ital.)
Alberto Romea
CARMEN(1949, Span.)

Rachel Romen
MOVE OVER, DARLING(1963); SHOCK CORRIDOR(1963); CANDIDATE,
THE(1964); DESERT RAVEN, THE(1965), a, w; GAY DECEIVERS, THE(1969); RUN,
ANGEL, RUN(1969)
Misc. Talkies
GIRL FROM TOBACCO ROW, THE(1966)
Susan Romen
WEEKEND WITH THE BABYSITTER(1970)
Ina Romeo
1984
SAVAGE STREETS(1984)
Marcello Romeo
1984
RUSH(1984, Ital.), p
Fred Romer [Fernando Romero]
GREAT ADVENTURE, THE(1976, Span./Ital.)
Gene Romer
WINDOW, THE(1949), makeup
Jean Romer
EASTER PARADE(1948)
Jean-Claude Romer
JE T'AIME, JE T'AIME(1972, Fr./Swed.)
Jeanne Romer
SABOTEUR(1942); HITCHHIKE TO HAPPINESS(1945); GREAT GATSBY,
THE(1949)
Leila Romer
Silents
ANNE OF GREEN GABLES(1919)
Misc. Silents
PERFECT 36, A(1918)
Lynn Romer
SABOTEUR(1942); HITCHHIKE TO HAPPINESS(1945); EASTER PARADE(1948)
Lynne Romer
GREAT GATSBY, THE(1949)
Marshall Romer
GLASS MENAGERIE, THE(1950)
Piet Romer
LIFT, THE(1983, Neth.)
Rex Romer
WIRE SERVICE(1942)
John Romeril
GREAT MACARTHY, THE(1975, Aus.), w
Alex Romero
AFFAIRS OF DOBIE GILLIS, THE(1953), ch; LOVE ME OR LEAVE ME(1955), ch;
FASTEST GUN ALIVE(1956), ch; TOM THUMB(1958, Brit./U.S.), ch; SAY ONE FOR
ME(1959), ch; PEPE(1960), ch; GEORGE RAFT STORY, THE(1961), ch; FOUR
HORSEMEN OF THE APOCALYPSE, THE(1962), ch; WHATEVER HAPPENED TO
BABY JANE?(1962), ch; WONDERFUL WORLD OF THE BROTHERS ERIMM,
THE(1962), ch; STRIPPER, THE(1963), ch; CLAMBAKE(1967), ch; FOR SINGLES
ONLY(1968), ch; GRISSOM GANG, THE(1971), ch; HUSTLE(1975), ch; LOVE AT
FIRST BITE(1979), ch; ZORRO, THE GAY BLADE(1981), ch
Blanquita Romero
FLIGHT OF THE LOST BALLOON(1961)
Bob Romero
HARD TRAIL(1969)
Carlos Romero
THRILL OF A LIFETIME(1937), ch; WINTERTIME(1943), ch; BOWERY TO BROAD-
WAY(1944), ch; MERRY MONAHANS, THE(1944), ch; MURDER IN THE BLUE
ROOM(1944), ch; MEN IN HER DIARY(1945), ch; SONG OF THE SARONG(1945), ch;
THAT'S THE SPIRIT(1945), ch; GUN RUNNERS, THE(1958); WORLD WAS HIS
JURY, THE(1958); THEY CAME TO CORDURA(1959); YOUNG LAND, THE(1959);
DEADLY DUO(1962); ISLAND OF THE BLUE DOLPHINS(1964); PROFESSIONALS,
THE(1966); DON IS DEAD, THE(1973); SOYLENT GREEN(1973)
Cesar Romero
BRITISH AGENT(1934); CHEATING CHEATERS(1934); THIN MAN, THE(1934);
CARDINAL RICHELIEU(1935); CLIVE OF INDIA(1935); DEVIL IS A WOMAN,
THE(1935); DIAMOND JIM(1935); GOOD FAIRY, THE(1935); HOLD'EM YALE(1935);
METROPOLITAN(1935); RENDEZVOUS(1935); SHOW THEM NO MERCY(1935);
STRANGE WIVES(1935); FIFTEEN MAIDEN LANE(1936); LOVE BEFORE BREAK-
FAST(1936); NOBODY'S FOOL(1936); PUBLIC ENEMY'S WIFE(1936); ARMORED
CAR(1937); DANGEROUSLY YOURS(1937); SHE'S DANGEROUS(1937); WEE WIL-
LIE WINKIE(1937); ALWAYS GOODBYE(1938); FIVE OF A KIND(1938); HAPPY
LANDING(1938); MY LUCKY STAR(1938); CHARLIE CHAN AT TREASURE IS-
LAND(1939); CISCO KID AND THE LADY, THE(1939); FRONTIER MARSHAL(1939);
LITTLE PRINCESS, THE(1939); RETURN OF THE CISCO KID(1939); WIFE, HUS-
BAND AND FRIEND(1939); GAY CABALLERO, THE(1940); HE MARRIED HIS
WIFE(1940); LUCKY CISCO KID(1940); VIVA CISCO KID(1940); DANCE HALL(1941);
GREAT AMERICAN BROADCAST, THE(1941); RIDE ON VAQUERO(1941); RO-
MANCE OF THE RIO GRANDE(1941); TALL, DARK AND HANDSOME(1941);
WEEKEND IN HAVANA(1941); GENTLEMAN AT HEART, A(1942); ORCHESTRA
WIVES(1942); SPRINGTIME IN THE ROCKIES(1942); TALES OF MANHAT-
TAN(1942); CONEY ISLAND(1943); WINTERTIME(1943); CAPTAIN FROM CAS-
TILE(1947); CARNIVAL IN COSTA RICA(1947); DEEP WATERS(1948); JULIA
MISBEHAVES(1948); THAT LADY IN ERMINE(1948); BEAUTIFUL BLONDE FROM
BASHFUL BEND, THE(1949); LOVE THAT BRUTE(1950); ONCE A THIEF(1950); FBI
GIRL(1951); HAPPY GO LOVELY(1951, Brit.); LOST CONTINENT(1951); JUNGLE,
THE(1952); SCOTLAND YARD INSPECTOR(1952, Brit.); PRISONERS OF THE CAS-
BAH(1953); SHADOW MAN(1953, Brit.); VERA CRUZ(1954); AMERICANO,
THE(1955); RACERS, THE(1955); AROUND THE WORLD IN 80 DAYS(1956); LEATH-
ER SAINT, THE(1956); STORY OF MANKIND, THE(1957); VILLA!(1958); OCEAN'S
ELEVEN(1960); PEPE(1960); SEVEN WOMEN FROM HELL(1961); IF A MAN AN-
SWERS(1962); CASTILIAN, THE(1963, Span./U.S.); DONOVAN'S REEF(1963); WE
SHALL RETURN(1963); HOUSE IS NOT A HOME, A(1964); MARRIAGE ON THE
ROCKS(1965); SERGEANT DEADHEAD(1965); TWO ON A GUILLOTINE(1965); BAT-
MAN(1966); HOT MILLIONS(1968, Brit.); SKIDOO(1968); LATITUDE ZERO(1969,
U.S./Jap.); MIDAS RUN(1969); COMPUTER WORE TENNIS SHOES, THE(1970);
MADIGAN'S MILLIONS(1970, Span./Ital); RED, WHITE AND BLACK, THE(1970);
SOPHIE'S PLACE(1970); NOW YOU SEE HIM, NOW YOU DON'T(1972); PROUD AND
THE DAMNED, THE(1972); SPECTRE OF EDGAR ALLAN POE, THE(1974); STRONG-
EST MAN IN THE WORLD, THE(1975); MONSTER(1979); TARGET: HARRY(1980)

Misc. Talkies
SPECTRE OF EDGAR ALLAN POE(1973); TIMBER TRAMPS(1975); KINO, THE PADRE ON HORSEBACK(1977)
Chanda Romero
FIRECRACKER(1981)
Dorian Romero
Misc. Silents
LOVE'S REDEMPTION(1921)
Eddie Romero
TERROR IS A MAN(1959, U.S./Phil.), p; LOST BATTALION(1961, U.S./Phil.), p&d, w; CAVALRY COMMAND(1963, U.S./Phil.), d&w; RAIDERS OF LEYTE GULF(1963 U.S./Phil.), p&d, w, ed; KIDNAPPERS, THE(1964, U.S./Phil.), d; MORO WITCH DOCTOR(1964, U.S./Phil.), p, d, w; WALLS OF HELL, THE(1964, U.S./Phil.), p, d, w; RAVAGERS, THE(1965, U.S./Phil.), d, w; BRIDES OF BLOOD(1968, US/Phil.), p, d; PASSIONATE STRANGERS, THE(1968, Phil.), d&w; MAD DOCTOR OF BLOOD ISLAND, THE(1969, Phil./U.S.), p, d; BEAST OF BLOOD(1970, U.S./Phil.), p,d&w; TWILIGHT PEOPLE(1972, Phil.), p, d, w; BEYOND ATLANTIS(1973, Phil.), p, d; BLACK MAMA, WHITE MAMA(1973), p, d; SAVAGE SISTERS(1974), p, d; WOMAN HUNT, THE(1975, U.S./Phil.), p, d
Misc. Talkies
BEAST OF THE YELLOW NIGHT(1971, U.S./Phil.), d; SUDDEN DEATH(1977), d
Edgar Romero
SCAVENGERS, THE(1959, U.S./Phil.), p, w
Ernesto A. Romero
TREASURE OF THE SIERRA MADRE, THE(1948), tech adv
George Romero
NIGHT OF THE LIVING DEAD(1968), d, w, ph&ed; HUNGRY WIVES(1973), ph, ed; DAWN OF THE DEAD(1979), d&w, ed
George A. Romero
THERE'S ALWAYS VANILLA(1972), d, ph; HUNGRY WIVES(1973), d&w; THE CRAZIES(1973), d,w,ed, ed; DAWN OF THE DEAD(1979); MARTIN(1979), d&w, ed; KNIGHTRIDERS(1981), d&w, ed; CREEPSHOW(1982), d, ed
George J. Romero
THERE'S ALWAYS VANILLA(1972), ed
Graciela Romero
MAD EMPRESS, THE(1940)
Hernan Romero
MIRAGE(1972, Peru)
Ida Romero
PLEASURE SEEKERS, THE(1964)
Joanelle Romero
BARBAROSA(1982); PARASITE(1982)
John Romero
Misc. Talkies
FRIDAY ON MY MIND(1970)
Juan Ruiz Romero
SAUL AND DAVID(1968, Ital./Span.), ph
Martha Romero
VAMPIRES, THE(1969, Mex.)
Nancy M. Romero
HUNGRY WIVES(1973), p
Ned Romero
TALISMAN, THE(1966); HANG'EM HIGH(1968); BIG DADDY(1969); TELL THEM WILLIE BOY IS HERE(1969)
Paul Romero
I AM THE CHEESE(1983)
Peter Romero
LONG RIDERS, THE(1980), art d; RIGHT STUFF, THE(1983), art d
R. Romero
POCKET MONEY(1972)
Ramon Romero
CITY BENEATH THE SEA(1953), w
Silents
APACHE, THE(1928), w
Robby Romero
VALLEY GIRL(1983)
Salvadore Romero
BLIND DEAD, THE(1972, Span.), p; PEOPLE WHO OWN THE DARK(1975, Span.), p
Tina Romero
MISSING(1982)
Tony Romero
WOMAN REBELS, A(1936)
Victor Romero
BURNING AN ILLUSION(1982, Brit.)
Carlos Romeros
HE'S MY GUY(1943), ch
Friedbert Rometsch
MALOU(1983)
France Romilly
PLAYTIME(1973, Fr.)
Romilly Choir
HEARTS OF HUMANITY(1936, Brit.)
Charles Romine
BEHIND LOCKED DOORS(1976, S. Africa), p&d, w
Misc. Talkies
ANY BODY...ANY WAY(1968), d
Rosanne Romine
FLASH GORDON(1980)
Roseanne Romine
PHANTOM OF THE PARADISE(1974)
Woodward Romine
1984
OASIS, THE(1984), prod d
Glen Rominger
AS THE DEVIL COMMANDS(1933), ph
Santa Maria Romitelli
YETI(1977, Ital.), m

Sante Romitelli
HATCHET FOR A HONEYMOON(1969, Span./Ital.), m
Vic Romito
NIGHT SONG(1947); OUT OF THE PAST(1947); DESERT HAWK, THE(1950); CAPTIVE CITY(1952); GOLDEN BLADE, THE(1953); PERFECT FURLOUGH, THE(1958)
Victor Romito
TROPIC HOLIDAY(1938); FRENCHMAN'S CREEK(1944); PIRATES OF MONTEREY(1947); JOAN OF ARC(1948); LES MISERABLES(1952); PRISONER OF ZENDA, THE(1952); FOREVER FEMALE(1953); LAW AND ORDER(1953); WE'RE NO ANGELS(1955); SERENADE(1956); HOW THE WEST WAS WON(1962); HARRY AND WALTER GO TO NEW YORK(1976)
Harry Romm
SENIOR PROM(1958), p; HAVE ROCRET, WILL TRAVEL(1959), p; HEY BOY! HEY GIRL!(1959), p; HEY, LET'S TWIST!(1961), p; TWO TICKETS TO PARIS(1962), p
Harry A. Romm
SWING PARADE OF 1946(1946), p; LADIES OF THE CHORUS(1948), p
Mikahil Romm
DIARY OF A NAZI(1943, USSR), p
Mikhail Romm
THIRTEEN, THE(1937, USSR), d, w; NINE DAYS OF ONE YEAR(1964, USSR), d, w
Karol Rommel
LOTNA(1966, Pol.)
Manfred Rommel
GERMANY IN AUTUMN(1978, Ger.)
Rox Rommel
STAND-IN(1937), md
Heinz Rommheld
FLIGHT FROM DESTINY(1941), m
Rommie
PRACTICALLY YOURS(1944)
Edana Romney
STRANGLER, THE(1941, Brit.); ALIBI, THE(1943, Brit.); CORRIDOR OF MIRRORS(1948, Brit.), a, w
Hugh Romney
CISCO PIKE(1971)
Geets Romo
1984
LISTEN TO THE CITY(1984, Can.)
Paula Romo
EL TOPO(1971, Mex.)
Nicco Romoff
MISSION TO MOSCOW(1943); NORTHWEST OUTPOST(1947)
Wood Romoff
VAMPIRE, THE(1957)
Frank Romolo
BLOOD FEAST(1963), ed
T. Rompainen
DAY THE EARTH FROZE, THE(1959, Fin./USSR)
Romuald
YOUNG GIRLS OF ROCHEFORT, THE(1968, Fr.)
Jose Romulo
SUPERBEAST(1972)
Tommy Romulo
WALLS OF HELL, THE(1964, U.S./Phil.)
"Romulus"
LAND OF NO RETURN, THE(1981)
Jozsef Romvari
DIALOGUE(1967, Hung.), art d; MEPHISTO(1981, Ger.), art d
1984
BRADY'S ESCAPE(1984, U.S./Hung.), art d
Jozsef Romvary
LOVE(1972, Hung.), art d; CONFIDENCE(1980, Hung.), art d
Tal Ron
HANNAH K.(1983, Fr.)
Abraham Ronai
KAZABLAN(1974, Israel)
Avrahan Ronai
BIG RED ONE, THE(1980)
Babs Ronald
Silents
MAN'S SHADOW, A(1920, Brit.)
James Ronald
DEATH CROONS THE BLUES(1937, Brit.), w; MURDER IN THE FAMILY(1938, Brit.), w; WITNESS VANISHES, THE(1939), w; SUSPECT, THE(1944), w; GAY INTRUDERS, THE(1946, Brit.), w
Pat Ronald
TO BE A LADY(1934, Brit.)
Phillip Ronalde
SHE COULDN'T TAKE IT(1935)
Ronaldino
LOVE SPECIALIST, THE(1959, Ital.)
Danny Ronan
NIGHTMARE(1981)
Robert Ronan
KLUTE(1971)
John Ronane
DR. BLOOD'S COFFIN(1961); MARY HAD A LITTLE(1961, Brit.); KIND OF LOVING, A(1962, Brit.); RATTLE OF A SIMPLE MAN(1964, Brit.); SILENT PLAYGROUND, THE(1964, Brit.); KING RAT(1965); HOW I WON THE WAR(1967, Brit.); SOME MAY LIVE(1967, Brit.); CHARLIE BUBBLES(1968, Brit.); SEBASTIAN(1968, Brit.); SPIRAL STAIRCASE, THE(1975, Brit.)
Jason Ronard
CORVETTE SUMMER(1978); ESCAPE FROM ALCATRAZ(1979)
Avraham Ronay
MY MARGO(1969, Israel)
Edina Ronay
NIGHT TRAIN TO PARIS(1964, Brit.); BLACK TORMENT, THE(1965, Brit.); CARRY ON COWBOY(1966, Brit.); HE WHO RIDES A TIGER(1966, Brit.); STUDY IN TERROR, A(1966, Brit./Ger.); OUR MOTHER'S HOUSE(1967, Brit.); PREHISTORIC WO-

MEN(1967, Brit.); THREE(1969, Brit.); PRAISE MARX AND PASS THE AMMUNI-
TION(1970, Brit.)

Gabriel Ronay
COUNTESS DRACULA(1972, Brit.), w

Mac Ronay
ASSASSIN, THE(1961, Ital./Fr.); EVERYBODY GO HOME!(1962, Fr./Ital.); PAS-
SIONATE THIEF, THE(1963, Ital.); AFTER THE FOX(1966, U.S./Brit./Ital.); NIGHT
OF THE GENERALS, THE(1967, Brit./Fr.)

Oscar Roncal
CRY OF BATTLE(1963); WALLS OF HELL, THE(1964, U.S./Phil.)

Neil Ronco
FINAL COUNTDOWN, THE(1980)

L. Ronconi
MAN WHO LAUGHS, THE(1966, Ital.), w

Patrice Rondard
SHADOW OF EVIL(1967, Fr./Ital.), w

Charles R. Rondeau
DEVIL'S PARTNER, THE(1958), d; LITTLEST HOBO, THE(1958), d; GIRL IN
LOVER'S LANE, THE(1960), d; THREAT, THE(1960), p&d

Charles Rondeau
TRAIN RIDE TO HOLLYWOOD(1975), d

Georgette Rondeau
QUEST FOR FIRE(1982, Fr./Can.)

Jeffrey P. Rondeau
OFFICER AND A GENTLEMAN, AN(1982)

R. A. Rondell
9/30/55(1977), stunts; NATIONAL LAMPOON'S ANIMAL HOUSE(1978)
1984
STAR TREK III: THE SEARCH FOR SPOCK(1984), stunts

Reid Rondell
SKATEBOARD(1978)
1984
BIRDY(1984)

Ron Rondell
TO HAVE AND HAVE NOT(1944); ELECTRA GLIDE IN BLUE(1973); OUTFIT,
THE(1973), stunts; NIGHT MOVES(1975)

Ronald Rondell
DANTE'S INFERNO(1935); GILDED LILY, THE(1935)

Ronald R. Rondell
MA AND PA KETTLE AT THE FAIR(1952)

Ronnie Rondell
COCOANUT GROVE(1938); FAST COMPANY(1938); HAVING WONDERFUL TI-
ME(1938); MEN WITH WINGS(1938); BEAU GESTE(1939); LITTLE ACCIDENT(1939);
NIGHT OF NIGHTS, THE(1939); NO, NO NANETTE(1940); MR. AND MRS.
SMITH(1941); OBLIGING YOUNG LADY(1941); WHISTLING IN THE DARK(1941);
FOREST RANGERS, THE(1942); LUCKY JORDAN(1942); MEXICAN SPITFIRE'S
ELEPHANT(1942); SEVEN DAYS LEAVE(1942); GOVERNMENT GIRL(1943); HI,
BUDDY(1943); NO TIME FOR LOVE(1943); FRENCHMAN'S CREEK(1944); HENRY
ALDRICH PLAYS CUPID(1944); ONCE UPON A TIME(1944); OUR HEARTS WERE
YOUNG AND GAY(1944); PRACTICALLY YOURS(1944); ROAD TO UTOPIA(1945);
MA AND PA KETTLE ON VACATION(1953); MA AND PA KETTLE AT WAIKI-
KI(1955); ENEMY BELOW, THE(1957); PAJAMA PARTY(1964); KING'S PIRA-
TE(1967), stunts; LOVE BUG, THE(1968); MINI-SKIRT MOB, THE(1968)
1984
AGAINST ALL ODDS(1984)

Ronnie Rondell, Jr.
ICE STATION ZEBRA(1968)

Ronnie R. Rondell
TOBRUK(1966)

David Ronder
Misc. Talkies
AVALANCHE(1975, Brit.)

Paul Ronder
FINNEGANS WAKE(1965), ed

Brunello Rondi
GREATEST LOVE, THE(1954, Ital.), w; LA DOLCE VITA(1961, Ital./Fr.), w; 8
½(1963, Ital.), w; HOURS OF LOVE, THE(1965, Ital.); JULIET OF THE SPIRITS(1965,
Fr./Ital./W.Ger.), w; FELLINI SATYRICON(1969, Fr./Ital.), w; PLACE FOR LOVERS,
A(1969, Ital./Fr.), w; CITY OF WOMEN(1980, Ital./Fr.), w

Gian Luigi Rondi
MAN WHO WAGGED HIS TAIL, THE(1961, Ital./Span.), w

Giacomo Rondinella
MELODY OF LOVE(1954, Ital.); NEOPOLITAN CAROUSEL(1961, Ital.)

George Rondo
CHEAP DETECTIVE, THE(1978); CHAPTER TWO(1979)

Robert Rondo
THIS MAN MUST DIE(1970, Fr./Ital.); GODSON, THE(1972, Ital./Fr.); DESTRUC-
TORS, THE(1974, Brit.)

Betty Rone
DAMSEL IN DISTRESS, A(1937)

Helen Ronee
ADVENTURERS, THE(1970)

Helena Ronee
ON HER MAJESTY'S SECRET SERVICE(1969, Brit.)

Ann Ronell
STORY OF G.I. JOE, THE(1945), m; MAIN STREET TO BROADWAY(1953), md

Maurice Ronet
PERFECTIONIST, THE(1952, Fr.); LUCRECE BORGIA(1953, Ital./Fr.); DESPERATE
DECISION(1954, Fr.); CARVE HER NAME WITH PRIDE(1958, Brit.); FRANTIC(1961,
Fr.); PURPLE NOON(1961, Fr./Ital.); DEVIL MADE A WOMAN, THE(1962, Span.);
MIDNIGHT MEETING(1962, Fr.); PLEASURES AND VICES(1962, Fr.); TIME OUT
FOR LOVE(1963, Ital./Fr.); VICTORS, THE(1963); FIRE WITHIN, THE(1964, Fr./Ital.);
CIRCLE OF LOVE(1965, Fr.); ENOUGH ROPE(1966, Fr./Ital./Ger.); LOST COMMAND,
THE(1966); IMMORAL MOMENT, THE(1967, Fr.); BIRDS COME TO DIE IN PE-
RU(1968, Fr.); CHAMPAGNE MURDERS, THE(1968, Fr.); HOW SWEET IT IS(1968);
LA FEMME INFIDELE(1969, Fr./Ital.); WHO'S GOT THE BLACK BOX?(1970, Fr./Gr./
Ital.); DEADLY TRAP, THE(1972, Fr./Ital.); DESTRUCTORS, THE(1974, Brit.); BLOOD-
LINE(1979); BEAU PERE(1981, Fr.); SPHINX(1981); LA BALANCE(1983, Fr.)

Maurice Ronetas
SEVEN DEADLY SINS, THE(1953, Fr./Ital.)

Olwen Roney
THUNDER IN CAROLINA(1960)

Gabriel Rongier
COW AND I, THE(1961, Fr., Ital., Ger.), ed; NIGHTS OF SHAME(1961, Fr.), ed; VICE
DOLLS(1961, Fr.), ed; MAXIME(1962, Fr.), ed; TRAIN, THE(1965, Fr./Ital./U.S.), ed;
POSTMAN GOES TO WAR, THE(1968, Fr.), ed; CHECKERBOARD(1969, Fr.), ed;
SINGAPORE, SINGAPORE(1969, Fr./Ital.), ed; TIME OF THE WOLVES(1970, Fr.), ed

Luigi Roni
BARBER OF SEVILLE, THE(1973, Ger./Fr.)

Peter Ronild
Z.P.G.(1972)

G. Roninson
UNCOMMON THIEF, AN(1967, USSR)

Carl Johann Ronn
HUGS AND KISSES(1968, Swed.)

Gale Ronn
GILDED LILY, THE(1935); YOU CAN'T TAKE IT WITH YOU(1938)

Ronna
CHELSEA GIRLS, THE(1967)

Greta Ronnegun
YOU LIGHT UP MY LIFE(1977)

Michael Ronni
MURDER AT THE CABARET(1936, Brit.)

Fred S. Ronnow
FUNNY MONEY(1983, Brit.)
1984
CANNONBALL RUN II(1984)

Edward Ronns
DEAD TO THE WORLD(1961), w

John Rons
BLOOD AND LACE(1971), m

Adele Ronson
Misc. Talkies
HER UNBORN CHILD(1933)

Cleo Ronson
WHAT A WAY TO GO(1964)

Mel Ronson
BEHIND THE EIGHT BALL(1942), w; ALWAYS A BRIDESMAID(1943), w; HOW'S
ABOUT IT?(1943), w; NEVER A DULL MOMENT(1943), w

Peter Ronson
JOURNEY TO THE CENTER OF THE EARTH(1959)

Linda Ronstadt
FM(1978); PIRATES OF PENZANCE, THE(1983)

George Rony
MELODY LANE(1941), w

Frank Ronzio
ESCAPE FROM ALCATRAZ(1979)
1984
HARD TO HOLD(1984)

Roo
HURRICANE(1979)

Leticia Roo
LITTLE RED RIDING HOOD AND HER FRIENDS(1964, Mex.)

Max Rood
TRIAL, THE(1948, Aust.)

Paul Rooff
Silents
AUTUMN OF PRIDE, THE(1921, Brit.), w; IN HIS GRIP(1921, Brit.), w; POINTING
FINGER, THE(1922, Brit.), w

Bernard Rook
MARCH HARE, THE(1956, Brit.)

David Rook
RUN WILD, RUN FREE(1969, Brit.), w

Heidi Rook
ONE AND ONLY GENUINE ORIGINAL FAMILY BAND, THE(1968)

Roger Rook
LOOKIN' TO GET OUT(1982)
1984
SWING SHIFT(1984)

A.J. Rooke
Misc. Silents
ONE MOMENT'S TEMPTATION(1922), d

Arthur Rooke
Silents
KENT, THE FIGHTING MAN(1916, Brit.); HOLY ORDERS(1917, Brit.), a, d; DOU-
BLE LIFE OF MR. ALFRED BURTON, THE(1919, Brit.), d; GARDEN OF RESURREC-
TION, THE(1919, Brit.), d; BRENDA OF THE BARGE(1920, Brit.), d&w; MIRAGE,
THE(1920, Brit.), d; EDUCATION OF NICKY, THE(1921, Brit.), d&w; SPORT OF
KINGS, THE(1921, Brit.), d&w; WEAVERS OF FORTUNE(1922, Brit.), d; SCANDAL,
THE(1923, Brit.), d; GAY CORINTHIAN, THE(1924), d; NETS OF DESTINY(1924,
Brit.), d
Misc. Silents
BLACKMAILERS, THE(1915, Brit.); FIGHTING COBBLER, THE(1915, Brit.);
CHAINS OF BONDAGE(1916, Brit.); KENT THE FIGHTING MAN(1916, Brit.);
TREASURE OF HEAVEN, THE(1916, Brit.); WHEEL OF DEATH, THE(1916, Brit.);
FOR ALL ETERNITY(1917, Brit.), a, d; PIT-BOY'S ROMANCE, A(1917, Brit.), a, d;
STRONG MAN'S WEAKNESS, A(1917, Brit.); THELMA(1918, Brit.), a, d; GOD'S
CLAY(1919, Brit.), a, d; LURE OF CROONING WATER, THE(1920, Brit.), d; BACHE-
LOR'S BABY, A(1922, Brit.), d; SPORTING DOUBLE, A(1922, Brit.), d; SPORTING
INSTINCT, THE(1922, Brit.), d; M'LORD OF THE WHITE ROAD(1923, Brit.), d;
DIAMOND MAN, THE(1924, Brit.), d; EUGENE ARAM(1924, Brit.), d; WINE OF LIFE,
THE(1924, Brit.), d; BLUE PETER, THE(1928, Brit.), d

Bert Rooke
HOUSE OF DARKNESS(1948, Brit.), cos

Irene Rooke
HIGH TREASON(1929, Brit.); ROSARY, THE(1931, Brit.); COLLISION(1932, Brit.);
THREADS(1932, Brit.)

Silents
HALF A TRUTH(1922, Brit.); POINTING FINGER, THE(1922, Brit.); RUNNING WATER(1922, Brit.)
Misc. Silents
LADY WINDERMERE'S FAN(1916, Brit.); BACHELOR HUSBAND, THE(1920 Brit.); ROMANCE OF WASTDALE, A(1921, Brit.); STREET OF ADVENTURE, THE(1921, Brit.)
Valentine Rooke
SCRUFFY(1938, Brit.)
Irene Rookee
Silents
SHIPS THAT PASS IN THE NIGHT(1921, Brit.)
Conrad Rooks
CHAPPAQUA(1967), a, p,d&w; SIDDHARTHA(1972), w, p&d
Joel Rooks
SMITHEREENS(1982)
Virginia Rooks
MR. BIG(1943), w
Abram Room
SILVER DUST(1953, USSR), d; GARNET BRACELET, THE(1966, USSR), d, w
Misc. Silents
BED AND SOFA(1926, USSR), d; DEATH BAY(1926, USSR), d; TRAITOR(1926, USSR), d; GHOST THAT NEVER RETURNS, THE(1930, USSR), d

Alfred Roome
MAN WHO LIVED AGAIN, THE(1936, Brit.), ed; LADY VANISHES, THE(1938, Brit.), ed; HOLIDAY CAMP(1947, Brit.), ed; MAGIC BOW, THE(1947, Brit.), ed; SMUGGLERS, THE(1948, Brit.), ed; IT'S NOT CRICKET(1949, Brit.), d; MY BROTHER'S KEEPER(1949, Brit.), d; WATERLOO ROAD(1949, Brit.), ed; HIGHLY DANGEROUS(1950, Brit.), ed; TRIO(1950, Brit.), ed; ENCORE(1951, Brit.), ed; HOTEL SAHARA(1951, Brit.), ed; OUTPOST IN MALAYA(1952, Brit.), ed; PENNY PRINCESS(1953, Brit.), ed; ALWAYS A BRIDE(1954, Brit.), ed; YOU KNOW WHAT SAILORS ARE(1954, Brit.), ed; BLACK TENT, THE(1956, Brit.), ed; CASH ON DELIVERY(1956, Brit.), ed; ACROSS THE BRIDGE(1957, Brit.), ed; TALE OF TWO CITIES, A(1958, Brit.), ed; ELEPHANT GUN(1959, Brit.), ed; CONSPIRACY OF HEARTS(1960, Brit.), ed; DOCTOR IN LOVE(1960, Brit.), ed; THIRTY NINE STEPS, THE(1960, Brit.), ed; NO LOVE FOR JOHNNIE(1961, Brit.), ed; UPSTAIRS AND DOWNSTAIRS(1961, Brit.), ed; BIG MONEY, THE(1962, Brit.), ed; DOCTOR IN DISTRESS(1963, Brit.), ed; PAIR OF BRIEFS, A(1963, Brit.), ed; NO, MY DARLING DAUGHTER(1964, Brit.), ed; YOUNG AND WILLING(1964, Brit.), ed; UNDERWORLD INFORMERS(1965, Brit.), ed; MC GUIRE, GO HOME!(1966, Brit.), ed; CARNABY, M.D.(1967, Brit.), ed; DEADLIER THAN THE MALE(1967, Brit.), ed; FOLLOW THAT CAMEL(1967, Brit.), ed; CARRY ON DOCTOR(1968, Brit.), ed; CARRY ON, UP THE KHYBER(1968, Brit.), ed; CARRY ON AGAIN, DOCTOR(1969, Brit.), ed; CARRY ON CAMPING(1969, Brit.), ed; CARRY ON HENRY VIII(1970, Brit.), ed; CARRY ON LOVING(1970, Brit.), ed; CARRY ON UP THE JUNGLE(1970, Brit.), ed
Charles Rooner
PEARL, THE(1948, U.S./Mex.); SOFIA(1948); PLUNDER OF THE SUN(1953)
Ann Rooney
FREDDIE STEPS OUT(1946); HIGH SCHOOL HERO(1946)
Anne Rooney
BABES ON BROADWAY(1941); FOR ME AND MY GAL(1942); HENRY ALDRICH GETS GLAMOUR(1942); FOLLOW THE BAND(1943); SLIGHTLY TERRIFIC(1944)
Annie Rooney
ALWAYS A BRIDESMAID(1943)
Frank Rooney
WILD ONE, THE(1953), w
Gilbert Rooney
Misc. Silents
BURNING QUESTION, THE(1919); VOICES(1920); EAST LYNNE(1921)
John Francis Rooney
SHAMUS(1959, Brit.)
Mary Rooney
"IMP"PROBABLE MR. WEE GEE, THE(1966)
Michael Rooney
WHERE EAGLES DARE(1968, Brit.)
Mickey Rooney
BEAST OF THE CITY, THE(1932); FAST COMPANIONS(1932); MY PAL, THE KING(1932); BIG CAGE, THE(1933); BIG CHANCE, THE(1933); BROADWAY TO HOLLYWOOD(1933); CHIEF, THE(1933); LIFE OF JIMMY DOLAN, THE(1933); WORLD CHANGES, THE(1933); BELOVED(1934); BLIND DATE(1934); CHAINED(1934); DEATH OF THE DIAMOND(1934); HALF A SINNER(1934); HIDEOUT(1934); I LIKE IT THAT WAY(1934); LOST JUNGLE, THE(1934); LOVE BIRDS(1934); MANHATTAN MELODRAMA(1934); UPPER WORLD(1934); AH, WILDERNESS!(1935); COUNTY CHAIRMAN, THE(1935); HEALER, THE(1935); MIDSUMMER'S NIGHT'S DREAM, A(1935); RECKLESS(1935); DEVIL IS A SISSY, THE(1936); DOWN THE STRETCH(1936); LITTLE LORD FAUNTLEROY(1936); RIFF-RAFF(1936); CAPTAINS COURAGEOUS(1937); FAMILY AFFAIR, A(1937); HOOSIER SCHOOLBOY(1937); LIVE, LOVE AND LEARN(1937); SLAVE SHIP(1937); THOROUGHBREDS DON'T CRY(1937); BOYS TOWN(1938); HOLD THAT KISS(1938); JUDGE HARDY'S CHILDREN(1938); LORD JEFF(1938); LOVE FINDS ANDY HARDY(1938); LOVE IS A HEADACHE(1938); OUT WEST WITH THE HARDYS(1938); STABLEMATES(1938); YOU'RE ONLY YOUNG ONCE(1938); ANDY HARDY GETS SPRING FEVER(1939); BABES IN ARMS(1939); HARDYS RIDE HIGH, THE(1939); HUCKLEBERRY FINN(1939); JUDGE HARDY AND SON(1939); ANDY HARDY MEETS DEBUTANTE(1940); STRIKE UP THE BAND(1940); YOUNG TOM EDISON(1940); ANDY HARDY'S PRIVATE SECRETARY(1941); BABES ON BROADWAY(1941); LIFE BEGINS FOR ANDY HARDY(1941); MEN OF BOYS TOWN(1941); ANDY HARDY'S DOUBLE LIFE(1942); COURTSHIP OF ANDY HARDY, THE(1942); YANK AT ETON, A(1942); GIRL CRAZY(1943); HUMAN COMEDY, THE(1943); THOUSANDS CHEER(1943); ANDY HARDY'S BLONDE TROUBLE(1944); NATIONAL VELVET(1944); LOVE LAUGHS AT ANDY HARDY(1946); KILLER McCOY(1947); SUMMER HOLIDAY(1948); BIG WHEEL, THE(1949); FIREBALL, THE(1950); HE'S A COCKEYED WONDER(1950); QUICKSAND(1950); MY BROTHER, THE OUTLAW(1951); MY TRUE STORY(1951), d; STRIP, THE(1951); SOUND OFF(1952); ALL ASHORE(1953); OFF LIMITS(1953); SLIGHT CASE OF LARCENY, A(1953); ATOMIC KID, THE(1954); BRIDGES AT TOKO-RI, THE(1954); DRIVE A CROOKED ROAD(1954); TWINKLE IN GOD'S EYE, THE(1955); BOLD AND THE BRAVE, THE(1956); FRANCIS IN THE HAUNTED HOUSE(1956); JAGUAR(1956), p; MAG-

NIFICENT ROUGHNECKS(1956); BABY FACE NELSON(1957); OPERATION MAD BALL(1957); ANDY HARDY COMES HOME(1958); NICE LITTLE BANK THAT SHOULD BE ROBBED, A(1958); BIG OPERATOR, THE(1959); LAST MILE, THE(1959); PLATINUM HIGH SCHOOL(1960); BREAKFAST AT TIFFANY'S(1961); EVERYTHING'S DUCKY(1961); KING OF THE ROARING TWENTIES-THE STORY OF ARNOLD ROTHSTEIN(1961); PRIVATE LIVES OF ADAM AND EVE, THE(1961), a, d; REQUIEM FOR A HEAVYWEIGHT(1962); IT'S A MAD, MAD, MAD, MAD WORLD(1963); SECRET INVASION, THE(1964); HOW TO STUFF A WILD BIKINI(1965); AMBUSH BAY(1966); 24 HOURS TO KILL(1966, Brit.); DEVIL IN LOVE, THE(1968, Ital.); SKIDOO(1968); COMIC, THE(1969); EXTRAORDINARY SEAMAN, THE(1969); 80 STEPS TO JONAH(1969); COCKEYED COWBOYS OF CALICO COUNTY, THE(1970); PULP(1972, Brit.); RICHARD(1972); JOURNEY BACK TO OZ(1974); DOMINO PRINCIPLE, THE(1977); PETE'S DRAGON(1977); MAGIC OF LASSIE, THE(1978); ARABIAN ADVENTURE(1979, Brit.); BLACK STALLION, THE(1979); FOX AND THE HOUND, THE(1981); ODYSSEY OF THE PACIFIC(1983, Can./Fr.)
Misc. Talkies
B.J. LANG PRESENTS(1971); RACHEL'S MAN(1974)
Mickey Rooney, Jr.
HOT RODS TO HELL(1967); HONEYSUCKLE ROSE(1980)
Pat Rooney
CITY GIRL(1930); PARTNERS OF THE TRAIL(1931); SHOW BUSINESS(1944); STRAWBERRY STATEMENT, THE(1970); BLACK EYE(1974), p; CADDIE(1976, Aus.)
Misc. Talkies
RECKLESS RIDER, THE(1932)
Silents
KINDRED OF THE DUST(1922); ACROSS THE DEADLINE(1925); WHAT PRICE GLORY(1926)
Patricia Rooney
ENLIGHTEN THY DAUGHTER(1934), ed
Silents
MONSIEUR BEAUCAIRE(1924), ed; CHARMER, THE(1925), ed; CLOTHES MAKE THE PIRATE(1925), ed; OLD LOVES AND NEW(1926), ed
Philip Rooney
CAPTAIN BOYCOTT(1947, Brit.), w
Teddy Rooney
ANDY HARDY COMES HOME(1958); IT HAPPENED TO JANE(1959); SEVEN WAYS FROM SUNDOWN(1960)
Tim Rooney
KING OF THE ROARING TWENTIES-THE STORY OF ARNOLD ROTHSTEIN(1961); VILLAGE OF THE GIANTS(1965); RIOT ON SUNSET STRIP(1967); LONERS, THE(1972)
Tim Rooney
Misc. Talkies
STORYVILLE(1974)
Virginia Rooney
ZAZA(1939)
Wallace Rooney
DESPERATE CHARACTERS(1971); EXORCIST, THE(1973)
Terry Roop
1984
NIGHT PATROL(1984), cos
Fay Roope
CALLAWAY WENT THATAWAY(1951); DAY THE EARTH STOOD STILL, THE(1951); FROGMEN, THE(1951); INDIAN UPRISING(1951); YOU'RE IN THE NAVY NOW(1951); BRIGAND, THE(1952); CARBINE WILLIAMS(1952); DEADLINE-U.S.A.(1952); MY SIX CONVICTS(1952); VIVA ZAPATA!(1952); WASHINGTON STORY(1952); YOUNG MAN WITH IDEAS(1952); ALL ASHORE(1953); CHARGE AT FEATHER RIVER, THE(1953); CLIPPED WINGS(1953); CLOWN, THE(1953); DOWN AMONG THE SHELTERING PALMS(1953); FROM HERE TO ETERNITY(1953); LION IS IN THE STREETS, A(1953); MAN OF CONFLICT(1953); SEMINOLE(1953); SYSTEM, THE(1953); ALASKA SEAS(1954); ATOMIC KID, THE(1954); BLACK DAKOTAS, THE(1954); LONE GUN, THE(1954); LONG, LONG TRAILER, THE(1954); NAKED ALIBI(1954); MA AND PA KETTLE AT WAIKIKI(1955); PROUD ONES, THE(1956); RACK, THE(1956); FBI STORY, THE(1959)
Eddy Roos
DEVIL BY THE TAIL, THE(1969, Fr./Ital.)
Fred Roos
BACK DOOR TO HELL(1964), p; FLIGHT TO FURY(1966, U.S./Phil.), p, w; GODFATHER, THE, PART II(1974), p; BLACK STALLION, THE(1979), p; HAMMETT(1982), p; ONE FROM THE HEART(1982), p; BLACK STALLION RETURNS, THE(1983), p; OUTSIDERS, THE(1983), p; RUMBLE FISH(1983), p
George Roos
NATIVE SON(1951, U.S., Arg.)
Joanna Roos
TWO WEEKS IN ANOTHER TOWN(1962); PATTERNS(1956); SPLENDOR IN THE GRASS(1961)
Julio Roos
CARMEN(1949, Span.)
Kelley Roos
NIGHT TO REMEMBER, A(1942), w; DANGEROUS BLONDES(1943), w; COME DANCE WITH ME(1960, Fr.), w; SCENT OF MYSTERY(1960), w
Lisele Roos
LAST METRO, THE(1981, Fr.), cos
William Roos
SCENT OF MYSTERY(1960), w
Jeanine Anne Roose
IT'S A WONDERFUL LIFE(1946)
Lesley Roose
MUTATIONS, THE(1974, Brit.)
Olwen Roose
TILLY OF BLOOMSBURY(1931, Brit.)
Misc. Silents
WHEELS OF CHANCE, THE(1922, Brit.)
Ronald Roose
WANDERERS, THE(1979), ed; WORLD ACCORDING TO GARP, The(1982), ed; EASY MONEY(1983), ed
Thirkild Roose
DAY OF WRATH(1948, Den.)

Tom Roosester
CAYMAN TRIANGLE, THE(1977), ph
Andre Roosevelt
MAN HUNTERS OF THE CARIBBEAN(1938), a, d
Misc. Talkies
GOONA-GOONA(1932), d
Buddy Roosevelt
WAY OUT WEST(1930); DISHONORED(1931); WESTWARD BOUND(1931); WILD HORSE MESA(1932); FOURTH HORSEMAN, THE(1932); CIRCLE CANYON(1933); FUGITIVE LADY(1934); LIGHTNING RANGE(1934); OPERATOR 13(1934); TEXAS TORNADO(1934); MEN WITHOUT NAMES(1935); POWDERSMOKE RANGE(1935); RAINBOW'S END(1935); SHE MARRIED HER BOSS(1935); DEVIL'S PLAY-GROUND(1937); OLD CORRAL, THE(1937); KING OF ALCATRAZ(1938); MARIE ANTOINETTE(1938); STAGECOACH(1939); UNION PACIFIC(1939); MAN FROM DAKOTA, THE(1940); BILLY THE KID'S RANGE WAR(1941); KANSAS CY-CLONE(1941); SHADOW OF THE THIN MAN(1941); MONSIEUR BEAUCAIRE(1946); BUCK PRIVATES COME HOME(1947); DOUBLE LIFE, A(1947); HOMESTRETCH, THE(1947); SEA OF GRASS, THE(1947); UNCONQUERED(1947); BERLIN EX-PRESS(1948); FIGHTING FATHER DUNNE(1948); FLAXY MARTIN(1949); GIRL FROM JONES BEACH, THE(1949); ABBOTT AND COSTELLO IN THE FOREIGN LEGION(1950); COLT .45(1950); COPPER CANYON(1950); DALLAS(1950); DESERT HAWK, THE(1950); KANSAS RAIDERS(1950); PRINCE WHO WAS A THIEF, THE(1951); RED BADGE OF COURAGE, THE(1951); BELLE OF NEW YORK, THE(1952); HORIZONS WEST(1952); LAWLESS BREED, THE(1952); OLD WEST, THE(1952); LAW AND ORDER(1953); MISSISSIPPI GAMBLER, THE(1953); RED-HEAD FROM WYOMING, THE(1953); RIDING SHOTGUN(1954); THREE HOURS TO KILL(1954); TALL MAN RIDING(1955); TRIBUTE TO A BADMAN(1956); FLESH AND THE SPUR(1957); SHOOT-OUT AT MEDICINE BEND(1957); WESTBOUND(1959); MAN WHO SHOT LIBERTY VALANCE, THE(1962)
Misc. Talkies
LIGHTNIN' SMITH RETURNS(1931); BOSS COWBOY(1934); LONE RIDER RIDES ON, THE(1941)
Silents
WALLOPING WALLACE(1924); ACTION GALORE(1925); DEVIL'S TOWER(1929)
Misc. Silents
BATTLING BUDDY(; (1924); BIFF BANG BUDDY(1924); CYCLONE BUDDY(1924); RIP ROARIN' ROBERTS(1924); ROUGH RIDIN'(1924); FAST FIGHTIN'(1925); GAL-LOPING JINX(1925); GOLD AND GRIT(1925); RECKLESS COURAGE(1925); THUN-DERING THROUGH(1925); BANDIT BUSTER, THE(1926); DANGEROUS DUB, THE(1926); EASY GOING(1926); HOODOO RANCH(1926); RAMBLIN' GALOOT, THE(1926); TANGLED HERDS(1926); TWIN TRIGGERS(1926); BETWEEN DAN-GERS(1927); CODE OF THE COW COUNTRY(1927); FIGHTIN' COMEBACK, THE(1927); PHANTOM BUSTER, THE(1927); RIDE 'EM HIGH(1927); SMOKING GUNS(1927); COWBOY CAVALIER, THE(1928); LIGHTNIN' SHOT(1928); MYSTERY VALLEY(1928); PAINTED TRAIL(1928); TRAIL RIDERS(1928); TRAILIN' BACK(1928)
James Roosevelt
POT O' GOLD(1941), p
Congressman James Roosevelt
PURPLE GANG, THE(1960)
The Roosters
FRENCH LEAVE(1937, Brit.)
Chet Root
WILD HARVEST(1947)
Elizabeth Root
WOLF HUNTERS, THE(1949); ACTORS AND SIN(1952); SCARLET ANGEL(1952); MAGNETIC MONSTER, THE(1953)
Georges Root
FROM TOP TO BOTTOM(1933, Fr.), p
George Root, Jr.
GANG'S ALL HERE, THE(1943), w
Jerome Root
LADY CONFESSES, THE(1945); DARK HORSE, THE(1946); LOVER COME BACK(1946)
Jerry Root
CARIBOO TRAIL, THE(1950)
Juan Root
WOLF DOG(1958, Can.)
Lynn Root
MILKY WAY, THE(1936), w; ANGEL'S HOLIDAY(1937), w; STEP LIVELY, JEEVES(1937), w; WILD AND WOOLLY(1937), w; WOMAN CHASES MAN(1937), w; DOWN ON THE FARM(1938), w; INTERNATIONAL SETTLEMENT(1938), w; KEEP SMILING(1938), w; WHILE NEW YORK SLEEPS(1938), w; SAINT IN LONDON, THE(1939, Brit.), w; GOLDEN FLEECING(1940), w; LITTLE ORVIE(1940), w; MILLIONAIRES IN PRISON(1940), w; SAINT TAKES OVER, THE(1940), w; DATE WITH THE FALCON, A(1941), w; GAY FALCON, THE(1941), w; FALCON TAKES OVER, THE(1942), w; HIGHWAYS BY NIGHT(1942), w; CABIN IN THE SKY(1943), w; SKY'S THE LIMIT, THE(1943), w; KID FROM BROOKLYN, THE(1946), w; LADY LUCK(1946), w
Lynne Root
CHECKERS(1937), w
Nancy Root
GIRLS' TOWN(1959); COLLEGE CONFIDENTIAL(1960); LADIES MAN, THE(1961); PRIVATE LIVES OF ADAM AND EVE, THE(1961)
Robert Root
PRISM(1971)
Misc. Talkies
PRISM(1971)
Sandy Root
DIAMOND STUD(1970), cos
Wells Root
VARSITY(1928), w; CHASING RAINBOWS(1930), w; PEACOCK ALLEY(1930), w; STORM, THE(1930), w; POLITICS(1931), w; PRODIGAL, THE(1931), w; BIRD OF PARADISE(1932), w; TIGER SHARK(1932), w; I COVER THE WATERFRONT(1933), w; RACETRACK(1933), w; BLACK MOON(1934), w; PARIS INTERLUDE(1934), w; PUBLIC HERO NO. 1(1935), w; PURSUIT(1935), w; SHADOW OF A DOUBT(1935), w; BOLD CABALLERO(1936), d, w; SWORN ENEMY(1936), w; PRISONER OF ZENDA, THE(1937), w; MAN OF CONQUEST(1939), w; SERGEANT MADDEN(1939), w; THUNDER AFLOAT(1939), w; FLIGHT COMMAND(1940), w; BAD MAN, THE(1941), w; GET-AWAY, THE(1941), w; TURNED OUT NICE AGAIN(1941, Brit.), w; MO-

KEY(1942), d, w; TENNESSEE JOHNSON(1942), w; MAN FROM DOWN UNDER, THE(1943), w; SALUTE TO THE MARINES(1943), w; STRONGHOLD(1952, Mex.), w; MAGNIFICENT OBSESSION(1954), w; HELL SHIP MUTINY(1957), w; SECRET OF DEEP HARBOR(1961), w; TEXAS ACROSS THE RIVER(1966), w
Maurice Rootes
LAST DAYS OF DOLWYN, THE(1949, Brit.), ed; TALE OF FIVE WOMEN, A(1951, Brit.), ed; MAN BAIT(1952, Brit.), ed; STOLEN FACE(1952, Brit.), ed; BLOOD ORANGE(1953, Brit.), ed; SPACEWAYS(1953, Brit.), ed; NAKED HEART, THE(1955, Brit.), ed; ABDULLAH'S HAREM(1956, Brit./Egypt.), ed; TWO GROOMS FOR A BRIDE(1957), ed; GREAT VAN ROBBERY, THE(1963, Brit.), ed; JASON AND THE ARGONAUTS(1963, Brit.), ed; SIEGE OF THE SAXONS(1963, Brit.), ed; FIRST MEN IN THE MOON(1964, Brit.), ed; ESCAPE BY NIGHT(1965, Brit.), ed; CUSTER OF THE WEST(1968, U.S., Span.), ed; KRAKATOA, EAST OF JAVA(1969), ed
Maurice Roots
BLACKOUT(1954, Brit.), ed
Huib Rooymans
SOLDIER OF ORANGE(1979, Dutch)
M. Rooz
CLEAR SKIES(1963, USSR), w; GROWN-UP CHILDREN(1963, USSR), w
Harvey Rope
DOOMSDAY MACHINE(1967), p
Ropence
MANOLETE(1950, Span.), ed
Bob Roper
UNDER TEXAS SKIES(1931)
Brian Roper
JUST WILLIAM'S LUCK(1948, Brit.); WILLIAM COMES TO TOWN(1948, Brit.); SECRET GARDEN, THE(1949); MINIVER STORY, THE(1950, Brit./U.S.); GIRL ON THE PIER, THE(1953, Brit.); TIME GENTLEMEN PLEASE!(1953, Brit.); RAINBOW JACKET, THE(1954, Brit.); NAKED HEART, THE(1955, Brit.); NAVY HEROES(1959, Brit.)
Bryan Roper
HONG KONG CONFIDENTIAL(1958)
Charles Hawtrey Roper
GET ON WITH IT(1963, Brit.)
Dan Roper
MY THIRD WIFE GEORGE(1968)
Dix Roper
SKY RIDERS(1976, U.S./Gr.)
Jack Roper
INVITATION TO HAPPINESS(1939); ONE HOUR TO LIVE(1939); WALL STREET COWBOY(1939); ANGELS OVER BROADWAY(1940); HEROES OF THE SAD-DLE(1940); HOLD THAT WOMAN(1940); MY LITTLE CHICKADEE(1940); TIN PAN ALLEY(1940); WEST OF CARSON CITY(1940); NEVER GIVE A SUCKER AN EVEN BREAK(1941); NORTH FROM LONE STAR(1941); PITTSBURGH KID, THE(1941); RIDING THE CHEROKEE TRAIL(1941); SHADOW OF THE THIN MAN(1941); BROADWAY BIG SHOT(1942); ROLLING DOWN THE GREAT DIVIDE(1942); JACK LONDON(1943); NO TIME FOR LOVE(1943); DAKOTA(1945); JOE PALOOKA, CHAMP(1946); KID FROM BROOKLYN, THE(1946); FABULOUS DORSEYS, THE(1947); FIGHTING MAD(1948); JOE PALOOKA IN WINNER TAKE ALL(1948); JOE PALOOKA IN THE BIG FIGHT(1949); JACKPOT, THE(1950); JOE PALOOKA IN THE SQUARED CIRCLE(1950); STOP THAT CAB(1951); QUIET MAN, THE(1952)
Silents
RED MARK, THE(1928); DUKE STEPS OUT, THE(1929)
John Roper
TOPAZ(1969, Brit.); THIEVES LIKE US(1974); ONCE IS NOT ENOUGH(1975); ODE TO BILLY JOE(1976)
Rex Roper
MELODY AND ROMANCE(1937, Brit.)
Robert Roper
Misc. Silents
PRINCE OF BROADWAY, THE(1926)
Tony Roper
WICKER MAN, THE(1974, Brit.)
Bradford Ropes
STAGE MOTHER(1933), w; 42ND STREET(1933), w; GO INTO YOUR DANCE(1935), w; CIRCUS GIRL(1937), w; HIT PARADE, THE(1937), w; MEET THE BOY FRIEND(1937), w; LORD JEFF(1938), w; GAUCHO SERENADE(1940), w; HIT PARADE OF 1941(1940), w; HULLABALOO(1940), w; MELODY AND MOON-LIGHT(1940), w; RANCHO GRANDE(1940), w; SING, DANCE, PLENTY HOT(1940), w; ANGELS WITH BROKEN WINGS(1941), w; GLAMOUR BOY(1941), w; RIDIN' ON A RAINBOW(1941), w; JOAN OF OZARK(1942), w; SHIP AHOY(1942), w; TRUE TO THE ARMY(1942), w; HANDS ACROSS THE BORDER(1943), w; MAN FROM MUSIC MOUNTAIN(1943), w; COWBOY AND THE SENORITA(1944), w; HI, GOOD-LOO-KIN'(1944), w; NOTHING BUT TROUBLE(1944), w; SWING IN THE SADDLE(1944), w; STEPPIN' IN SOCIETY(1945), w; SUNBONNET SUE(1945), w; WHY GIRLS LEAVE HOME(1945), w; SONG OF ARIZONA(1946), w; TIME OF THEIR LIVES, THE(1946), w; BUCK PRIVATES COME HOME(1947), w; PIRATES OF MON-TEREY(1947), w; FLAME OF YOUTH(1949), w; ARIZONA COWBOY, THE(1950), w; BELLE OF OLD MEXICO(1950), w; REDWOOD FOREST TRAIL(1950), w
Jozef Ropog
ASSISTANT, THE(1982, Czech.)
Jacqueline Roque [Jacqueline Picasso]
TESTAMENT OF ORPHEUS, THE(1962, Fr.)
Cliff Roquemore
HUMAN TORNADO, THE(1976), d; PETEY WHEATSTRAW(1978), d&w
Henry Roquemore
WEST OF THE ROCKIES(1929); LAST DANCE, THE(1930); MIN AND BILL(1930); SOCIAL LION, THE(1930); SPORTING CHAN-CE(1931); YOUNG BLOOD(1932); BREED OF THE BORDER(1933); EASY MIL-LIONS(1933); MAN'S CASTLE, A(1933); FEROCIOUS PAL(1934); INSIDE INFORMATION(1934); MANHATTAN MELODRAMA(1934); DEVIL IS A WOMAN, THE(1935); GLASS KEY, THE(1935); GOIN' TO TOWN(1935); MEN WITHOUT NAMES(1935); NAUGHTY MARIETTA(1935); POWDERSMOKE RANGE(1935); RAC-ING LUCK(1935); RUGGLES OF RED GAP(1935); SHE COULDN'T TAKE IT(1935); SINGING VAGABOND, THE(1935); WHAT PRICE CRIME?(1935); WINGS IN THE DARK(1935); WITHOUT REGRET(1935); CRIME PATROL, THE(1936); GREAT GUY(1936); HEARTS IN BONDAGE(1936); LONE WOLF RETURNS, THE(1936); MEET NERO WOLFE(1936); MILKY WAY, THE(1936); NEVADA(1936); ROSE BOWL(1936); SAN FRANCISCO(1936); TOO MANY PARENTS(1936); YOURS FOR

THE ASKING(1936); BANK ALARM(1937); CHAMPAGNE WALTZ(1937); LOVE IN A BUNGALOW(1937); LOVE TAKES FLIGHT(1937); MAYTIME(1937); OH DOCTOR(1937); PRISONER OF ZENDA, THE(1937); SECOND HONEYMOON(1937); SWEETHEART OF THE NAVY(1937); THANKS FOR LISTENING(1937); WHEN YOU'RE IN LOVE(1937); WOMEN OF GLAMOUR(1937); BAREFOOT BOY(1938); GOODBYE BROADWAY(1938); TEST PILOT(1938); TOY WIFE, THE(1938); YOUNG FUGITIVES(1938); BABES IN ARMS(1939); DISBARRED(1939); EXILE EXPRESS(1939); I STOLE A MILLION(1939); LUCKY NIGHT(1939); LURE OF THE WASTELAND(1939); DISPATCH FROM REUTERS, A(1940); HAUNTED HOUSE, THE(1940); MA, HE'S MAKING EYES AT ME(1940); MOON OVER BURMA(1940); STRANGER ON THE THIRD FLOOR(1940); STRIKE UP THE BAND(1940); TEXAS RANGERS RIDE AGAIN(1940); WESTERNER, THE(1940); WOMEN WITHOUT NAMES(1940); HONKY TONK(1941); LITTLE FOXES, THE(1941); MAN WHO LOST HIMSELF, THE(1941); MEET JOHN DOE(1941); MODEL WIFE(1941); NO GREATER SIN(1941); POT O' GOLD(1941); ROAD TO ZANZIBAR(1941); SAINT IN PALM SPRINGS, THE(1941); SKYLARK(1941); SMALL TOWN DEB(1941); WILD MAN OF BORNEO, THE(1941); BROADWAY(1942); GIRL TROUBLE(1942); MAGNIFICENT AMBERSONS, THE(1942); MY FAVORITE SPY(1942); POSTMAN DIDN'T RING, THE(1942); THAT OTHER WOMAN(1942); WE WERE DANCING(1942); WOMAN OF THE YEAR(1942); DIXIE(1943); GIRL CRAZY(1943); HERS TO HOLD(1943); IRON MAJOR, THE(1943); MORE THE MERRIER, THE(1943); RAIDERS OF SAN JOAQUIN(1943); THIS LAND IS MINE(1943)
Silents
IS YOUR DAUGHTER SAFE?(1927); LADIES AT EASE(1927); GYPSY OF THE NORTH(1928); ANNE AGAINST THE WORLD(1929); OKLAHOMA KID, THE(1929)

Larry Roquemore
WEST SIDE STORY(1961)

Susanne Roquette
DOCTOR OF ST. PAUL, THE(1969, Ger.)

Suzanne Roquette
RED-DRAGON(1967, Ital./Ger./US); VENGEANCE OF FU MANCHU, THE(1968, Brit./Ger./Hong Kong/Ireland)

Noel Roquevert
ANTOINE ET ANTOINETTE(1947 Fr.); CARNIVAL OF SINNERS(1947, Fr.); MURDERER LIVES AT NUMBER 21, THE(1947, Fr.); RAVEN, THE(1948, Fr.); STRANGERS IN THE HOUSE(1949, Fr.); FANFAN THE TULIP(1952, Fr.); MADAME DU BARRY(1954 Fr./Ital.); DIABOLIQUE(1955, Fr.); NAPOLEON(1955, Fr.); NANA(1957, Fr./Ital.); LA PARISIENNE(1958, Fr./Ital.); LAW IS THE LAW, THE(1959, Fr.); COME DANCE WITH ME(1960, Fr.); CRAZY FOR LOVE(1960, Fr.); MARIE OF THE ISLES(1960, Fr.); NATHALIE, AGENT SECRET(1960, Fr.); SPUTNIK(1960, Fr.); LOVE AND THE FRENCHWOMAN(1961, Fr.); WOMAN OF SIN(1961, Fr.); CARTOUCHE(1962, Fr./Ital.); DEVIL AND THE TEN COMMANDMENTS, THE(1962, Fr.); MAGNIFICENT TRAMP, THE(1962, Fr./Ital.); MONKEY IN WINTER, A(1962, Fr.); YOUR TURN, DARLING(1963, Fr.); FRIEND OF THE FAMILY(1965, Fr./Ital.); GREAT SPY CHASE, THE(1966, Fr.)

Isabel Scott Rorick
ARE HUSBANDS NECESSARY?(1942), w

Ann Rork
Silents
OLD LOVES AND NEW(1926); NOTORIOUS LADY, THE(1927); TEXAS STEER, A(1927)
Misc. Silents
BLONDE SAINT, THE(1926)

Sam E. Rork
Silents
HEART OF A FOLLIES GIRL, THE(1928), p

Hayden Rorke
LUST FOR GOLD(1949); ROPE OF SAND(1949); SWORD IN THE DESERT(1949); DOUBLE CROSSBONES(1950); KIM(1950); MAGNIFICENT YANKEE, THE(1950); AMERICAN IN PARIS, AN(1951); FATHER'S LITTLE DIVIDEND(1951); FRANCIS GOES TO THE RACES(1951); INSIDE STRAIGHT(1951); LAW AND THE LADY, THE(1951); PRINCE WHO WAS A THIEF, THE(1951); STARLIFT(1951); WHEN WORLDS COLLIDE(1951); ROGUE'S MARCH(1952); ROOM FOR ONE MORE(1952); SKIRTS AHOY!(1952); WILD STALLION(1952); ABOVE AND BEYOND(1953); CONFIDENTIAL CONNIE(1953); GIRL NEXT DOOR, THE(1953); PROJECT MOONBASE(1953); ROBE, THE(1953); SOUTH SEA WOMAN(1953); STORY OF THREE LOVES, THE(1953); DRUM BEAT(1954); LUCKY ME(1954); ETERNAL SEA, THE(1955); RESTLESS YEARS, THE(1958); THIS HAPPY FEELING(1958); PILLOW TALK(1959); STRANGER IN MY ARMS(1959); MIDNIGHT LACE(1960); PARRISH(1961); POCKETFUL OF MIRACLES(1961); TAMMY, TELL ME TRUE(1961); SPENCER'S MOUNTAIN(1963); THRILL OF IT ALL, THE(1963); HOUSE IS NOT A HOME, A(1964); I'D RATHER BE RICH(1964); NIGHT WALKER, THE(1964); UNSINKABLE MOLLY BROWN, THE(1964); YOUNGBLOOD HAWKE(1964)

Ina Rorke
Silents
WOMAN'S PLACE(1921); WHEN THE WIFE'S AWAY(1926)

Irene Rorke
Misc. Silents
PILLARS OF SOCIETY(1920, Brit.)

John Rorke
LIEUTENANT DARING, RN(1935, Brit.); VARIETY(1935, Brit.); VARIETY JUBILEE(1945, Brit.); HONEYMOON HOTEL(1946, Brit.)

Mary Rorke
Silents
BRIDAL CHAIR, THE(1919, Brit.); EDUCATION OF NICKY, THE(1921, Brit.); IF YOUTH BUT KNEW(1926, Brit.); THOU FOOL(1926, Brit.)
Misc. Silents
DR. WAKE'S PATIENT(1916, Brit.); MERELY MRS. STUBBS(1917, Brit.); RIGHT ELEMENT, THE(1919, Brit.); PILLARS OF SOCIETY(1920, Brit.); TESTIMONY(1920, Brit.); BOY WOODBURN(1922, Brit.); CASTLES IN THE AIR(1923, Brit.); FOR VALOUR(1928, Brit.)

Rosanna Rory
COME SEPTEMBER(1961)

Rossana Rory
RIVER CHANGES, THE(1956); BIG BOODLE, THE(1957); HELL CANYON OUTLAWS(1957); BIG DEAL ON MADONNA STREET, THE(1960); ECLIPSE(1962, Fr./Ital.); JESSICA(1962, U.S./Ital./Fr.)

Rossano Rory
ANGEL WORE RED, THE(1960)

Rory Blackwell and The Blackjacks
ROCK YOU SINNERS(1957, Brit.)

Gesomina Ros
OLIVE TREES OF JUSTICE, THE(1967, Fr.)

Ramon Ros
IRON MAJOR, THE(1943); MELODY PARADE(1943); DECEPTION(1946); DARK PASSAGE(1947); NORA PRENTISS(1947); NIGHT UNTO NIGHT(1949); RHYTHM INN(1951)

Alex Rosa
EYEWITNESS(1981)

Ed Rosa
PATSY, THE(1964)

Milia Rosa
BIRD OF PARADISE(1932), song

Orlando Rosa
PIE IN THE SKY(1964)

Tony Rosa
OLD MAN AND THE SEA, THE(1958)

Rudy Rosado
WAY OUT(1966)

Dennis Rosaire
WOMAN FOR JOE, THE(1955, Brit.)

Rosa Rosal
CRY FREEDOM(1961, Phil.)
Misc. Talkies
ETHAN(1971)

Rosalean and Seville
MANHATTAN MERRY-GO-ROUND(1937)

Fernando Rosales
SANTO Y BLUE DEMON CONTRA LOS MONSTRUOS(1968, Mex.)

Lina Rosales
GIRL FROM VALLADOLIO(1958, Span.); GOLIATH AGAINST THE GIANTS(1963, Ital./Span.)

Rocio Rosales
PUSS 'N' BOOTS(1964, Mex.)

Thomas Rosales
NIGHTHAWKS(1981); SWORD AND THE SORCERER, THE(1982)

Thomas Rosales, Jr.
WALK PROUD(1979)

Tom Rosales
HUNTER, THE(1980)

Tom Rosales, Jr.
MAX DUGAN RETURNS(1983)
1984
OH GOD! YOU DEVIL(1984)

Clinton Rosamond
GREEN PASTURES(1936)

Marion Rosamond
THAT NIGHT IN RIO(1941); I MARRIED AN ANGEL(1942); JANE EYRE(1944)

Oscar Rosander
NIGHT IN JUNE, A(1940, Swed.), ed; TORMENT(1947, Swed.), ed; ILLICIT INTERLUDE(1954, Swed.), ed; SMILES OF A SUMMER NIGHT(1957, Swed.), ed; MAGICIAN, THE(1959, Swed.), ed; WILD STRAWBERRIES(1959, Swed.), ed; DEVIL'S EYE, THE(1960, Swed.), ed; LESSON IN LOVE, A(1960, Swed.), ed; VIRGIN SPRING, THE(1960, Swed.), ed; SECRETS OF WOMEN(1961, Swed.), ed; PORT OF CALL(1963, Swed.), ed; TWO LIVING, ONE DEAD(1964, Brit./Swed.), ed

Rosa Rosanova
ABIE'S IRISH ROSE(1928); LUCKY BOY(1929); YOUNGER GENERATION(1929); SO IT'S SUNDAY(1932); FIGHTING HERO(1934)
Silents
BLOOD AND SAND(1922); HUNGRY HEARTS(1922); COBRA(1925); JAKE THE PLUMBER(1927)
Misc. Silents
HIS PEOPLE(1925); PLEASURE BEFORE BUSINESS(1927); SONIA(1928)

Mme. Rosa Rosanova
Silents
JUST AROUND THE CORNER(1921)

Countess Rosanska
NORTHWEST OUTPOST(1947)

Anita Rosar
MOZART STORY, THE(1948, Aust.)

Annie Rosar
LITTLE MELODY FROM VIENNA(1948, Aust.); THIRD MAN, THE(1950, Brit.); DEVIL MAKES THREE, THE(1952); LIFE AND LOVES OF MOZART, THE(1959, Ger.)

Bert Rosario
S.O.B.(1981); BEACH GIRLS(1982)

Jose Ramon Rosario
HOME FREE ALL(1983)
1984
HOME FREE ALL(1984)

Rosario and Antonio
HOLLYWOOD CANTEEN(1944)

Rosarita
MURDER AT THE CABARET(1936, Brit.); TORSO MURDER MYSTERY, THE(1940, Brit.)

Rosarito
LAST BARRICADE, THE(1938, Brit.)

Rosarito and Paula
OLD MOTHER RILEY OVERSEAS(1943, Brit.)

Raymond Rosas
JAGUAR(1956)

Al Rosati
VIXENS, THE(1969), w

Ana Maria Rosati
TWITCH OF THE DEATH NERVE(1973, Ital.)

Gino Rosati
OSSESSIONE(1959, Ital.), art d
Giuseppe Rosati
OUTCRY(1949, Ital.), m; RAPTURE(1950, Ital.), m; OSSESSIONE(1959, Ital.), m
Guiseppe Rosati
THOSE DIRTY DOGS(1974, U.S./Ital./Span.), d, w
Genesia Rosato
NIJINSKY(1980, Brit.)
Lucio Rosato
NAVAJO JOE(1967, Ital./Span.); DESERTER, THE(1971 Ital./Yugo.)
Tony Rosato
HOG WILD(1980, Can.); IMPROPER CHANNELS(1981, Can.)
Greg Rosatti
ZOOT SUIT(1981)
Francoise Rosay
MAGNIFICENT LIE(1931); CARNIVAL IN FLANDERS(1936, Fr.); UN CARNET DE BAL(1938, Fr.); BIZARRE BIZARRE(1939, Fr.); DEVIL IS AN EMPRESS, THE(1939, Fr.); HALF-WAY HOUSE, THE(1945, Brit.); JOHNNY FRENCHMAN(1946, Brit.); PORTRAIT OF A WOMAN(1946, Fr.); QUARTET(1949, Brit.); SARABAND(1949, Brit.); SEPTEMBER AFFAIR(1950); THIRTEENTH LETTER, THE(1951); SEVEN DEADLY SINS, THE(1953, Fr./Ital.); RED, INN, THE(1954, Fr.); NAKED HEART, THE(1955, Brit.); THAT LADY(1955, Brit.); INTERLUDE(1957); SEVENTH SIN, THE(1957); GAMBLER, THE(1958, Fr.); ME AND THE COLONEL(1958); SOUND AND THE FURY, THE(1959); STOP ME BEFORE I KILL!(1961, Brit.); BACK STREETS OF PARIS(1962, Fr.); COUNTERFEITERS OF PARIS, THE(1962, Fr., Ital.); DIE GANS VON SE-DAN(1962, Fr/Ger.); LONGEST DAY, THE(1962); RIFF RAFF GIRLS(1962, Fr./Ital.); END OF MRS. CHENEY(1963, Ger.); UP FROM THE BEACH(1965); CLOPORTES(1966, Fr., Ital.); 25TH HOUR, THE(1967, Fr./Ital./Yugo.); PEDESTRIAN, THE(1974, Ger.)
Misc. Silents
GRIBICHE(1926, Fr.); MADAME RECAMIER(1928, Fr.)
Ettore Rosbach
WIND FROM THE EAST(1970, Fr./Ital./Ger.), p
Charles Rosbher
ZIEGFELD FOLLIES(1945), ph
Al Roscoe
DIRIGIBLE(1931)
Silents
NO TRESPASSING(1922); PAINTED FLAPPER, THE(1924); KING OF THE TURF, THE(1926)
Misc. Silents
HER BODY IN BOND(1918); OVER THE WIRE(1921); ONE GLORIOUS NIGHT(1924); TENTACLES OF THE NORTH(1926); HIS LAST HAUL(1928)
Alan Roscoe
FLIGHT(1929); LOVE IN THE DESERT(1929); VAGABOND LOVER(1929); DANGER LIGHTS(1930); FALL GUY, THE(1930); HALF SHOT AT SUNRISE(1930); PAY OFF, THE(1930); RAIN OR SHINE(1930); SEVEN KEYS TO BALDPATE(1930); HIGH STAKES(1931); PUBLIC DEFENDER, THE(1931); ROYAL BED, THE(1931); SIN SHIP(1931); SUBWAY EXPRESS(1931); HELL DIVERS(1932); HELL FIRE AUS-TIN(1932); LADIES OF THE JURY(1932); LAST MAN(1932); LAST MILE, THE(1932); STRANGE ADVENTURE(1932); STRANGERS OF THE EVENING(1932); DEATH KISS, THE(1933); LUCKY DEVILS(1933)
Misc. Talkies
CALL OF THE WEST(1930)
Silents
LURE OF THE WILD, THE(1925); LONG PANTS(1927)
Misc. Silents
CHORUS LADY, THE(1924); MIRAGE, THE(1924); BEFORE MIDNIGHT(1925); GIRL OF GOLD, THE(1925); TEXAS STREAK, THE(1926); WOLF HUNTERS, THE(1926); DRIFTWOOD(1928); MATING CALL, THE(1928); SIDESHOW, THE(1928)
Albert Roscoe
Silents
WHEN A WOMAN SINS(1918); BRANDING IRON, THE(1920); HER ELEPHANT MAN(1920); LAST OF THE MOHICANS, THE(1920); BURNING SANDS(1922); MAN WHO SAW TOMORROW, THE(1922); JAVA HEAD(1923); NET, THE(1923)
Misc. Silents
CAMILLE(1917); HEART'S DESIRE(1917); DOCTOR AND THE WOMAN, THE(1918); MORTGAGED WIFE, THE(1918); SHE DEVIL, THE(1918); SHUTTLE, THE(1918); SOUL FOR SALE, A(1918); UNDER THE YOKE(1918); CITY OF COMRADES, THE(1919); EVANGELINE(1919); HER PURCHASE PRICE(1919); MAN'S COUNTRY, A(1919); SALOME(1919); SIREN'S SONG, THE(1919); BLACK SHADOWS(1920); HELL SHIP, THE(1920); HER UNWILLING HUSBAND(1920); MADAME X(1920); MOLLY AND I(1920); PALISER CASE, THE(1920); TARNISHED REPUTATIONS(1920); LAST CARD, THE(1921); LOVEBOUND(1923); WIFE'S ROMANCE, A(1923); PAL O'MI-NE(1924)
Allan Roscoe
HURRICANE(1929); DYNAMITE RANCH(1932); HELLO TROUBLE(1932); CHEYENNE KID, THE(1933)
Silents
MARRY THE GIRL(1928)
Misc. Silents
DUTY'S REWARD(1927)
Barbara Roscoe
DOCTOR AT LARGE(1957, Brit.); SCHOOL FOR SCOUNDRELS(1960, Brit.); TWICE AROUND THE DAFFODILS(1962, Brit.); FATHER CAME TOO(1964, Brit.); HIDE AND SEEK(1964, Brit.); SATURDAY NIGHT OUT(1964, Brit.); RICOCHET(1966, Brit.)
Frederick Roscoe
JULIUS CAESAR(1952)
Gene Roscoe
LOVE BUG, THE(1968)
Gerald Roscoe
OH, SUSANNA(1937)
Lee Roscoe
EVENTS(1970); MAIDSTONE(1970)
Judith Roscow
LIFESPAN(1975, U.S./Brit./Neth.), w
Alex Rose
BLACK BELT JONES(1974), w; DRIVE-IN(1976), p; HOT POTATO(1976), w; I WAN-NA HOLD YOUR HAND(1978), p; NORMA RAE(1979), p

Alexander Rose
HUSTLER, THE(1961); WHO'S GOT THE ACTION?(1962), a, w
Allison Rose
MECHANIC, THE(1972)
Amelia Rose
Silents
MISTRESS NELL(1915)
Anna Perrott Rose
ROOM FOR ONE MORE(1952), w
Anna Rose
Misc. Silents
COMING POWER, THE(1914)
Anthony Edward Rose
Silents
PRISONER OF ZENDA, THE(1915, Brit.), w
Arthur Rose
TRUST THE NAVY(1935, Brit.), w
Bernie Rose
Misc. Talkies
ROAD REBELS(1963)
Bert Rose
SALOME(1953)
Bill Rose
FITZCARRALDO(1982)
Blanche Rose
SCARLET EMPRESS, THE(1934); PRISON FARM(1938); WOMEN WITHOUT NAMES(1940); QUEEN OF BROADWAY(1942); GIRL CRAZY(1943); SUMMER HOLI-DAY(1948)
Silents
OLD SWIMMIN' HOLE, THE(1921)
Misc. Silents
UNDER SUSPICION(1919)
Bob Rose
LUCKY DEVILS(1933), a, w; STORY OF WILL ROGERS, THE(1952)
Bobby Rose
IN OLD KENTUCKY(1935); UNDER THE PAMPAS MOON(1935)
Chris Rose
SIR HENRY AT RAWLINSON END(1980, Brit.), ed
Clarkson Rose
DAVY(1958, Brit.)
Cleo Rose
TERROR STREET(1953); HEATWAVE(1954, Brit.)
Clifford Rose
PERSECUTION AND ASSASSINATION OF JEAN-PAUL MARAT AS PERFORMED BY THE INMATES OF THE ASYLUM OF CHARENTON UNDER THE DIRECTION OF THE MARQUIS DE SADE, THE(1967, Brit.); TELL ME LIES(1968, Brit.); WORK IS A FOUR LETTER WORD(1968, Brit.)
David E. Rose
EYE WITNESS(1950, Brit.), p; CIRCLE OF DANGER(1951, Brit.), p; ISLAND OF DESIRE(1952, Brit.), p; SEA DEVILS(1953), p; PORT AFRIQUE(1956, Brit.), p; MARY HAD A LITTLE(1961, Brit.), p; HOSTILE WITNESS(1968, Brit.), p; FILE OF THE GOLDEN GOOSE, THE(1969, Brit.), p
David Rose
PRINCESS AND THE PIRATE, THE(1944), m; WINGED VICTORY(1944), m; WHIPPED, THE(1950), m; IT'S A BIG COUNTRY(1951), m; RICH, YOUNG AND PRETTY(1951), md; TEXAS CARNIVAL(1951), md; EVERYTHING I HAVE IS YOURS(1952), md; JUST THIS ONCE(1952), m; YOUNG MAN WITH IDEAS(1952), m; BRIGHT ROAD(1953), m; CLOWN, THE(1953), m; CONFIDENTIAL CON-NIE(1953), m; JUPITER'S DARLING(1955), m; PUBLIC PIGEON NO. 1(1957), m, md; HEADLESS GHOST, THE(1959, Brit.); HOUSE OF THE SEVEN HAWKS, THE(1959), p; OPERATION PETTICOAT(1959), m; AND WOMEN SHALL WEEP(1960, Brit.); PLEASE DON'T EAT THE DAISIES(1960), m; THIS REBEL BREED(1960), m; QUICK, BEFORE IT MELTS(1964), m, md; NEVER TOO LATE(1965), m; HOMBRE(1967), m, md; CONFESSIONS OF A WINDOW CLEANER(1974, Brit.)
1984
SAM'S SON(1984), m
David W. Rose
STAR 80(1983)
Diana Rose
SEDUCTION, THE(1982)
Donald Rose
BROADWAY HOSTESS(1935)
E. Rose
RULES OF THE GAME, THE(1939, Fr.), m
Edward Rose
PRISONER OF ZENDA, THE(1937), w; UNDER THE RED ROBE(1937, Brit.), w; DARK CITY(1950)
Silents
FIGHTING BOB(1915), w
Edward E. Rose
MURDER IN THE PRIVATE CAR(1934), w
Silents
CAPPY RICKS(1921), w; PRISONER OF ZENDA, THE(1922), w; RED LIGHTS(1923), w
Ethel Rose
Misc. Silents
MIDNIGHT AT MAXIM'S(1915)
Felicitas Rose
ETERNAL LOVE(1960, Ger.), w
Felipe Rose
CAN'T STOP THE MUSIC(1980)
Felissa Rose
SLEEPAWAY CAMP(1983)
Fred Rose
MYSTERY OF THE HOODED HORSEMEN, THE(1937), m; CYCLONE ON HORSEBACK(1941), m; ROBBERS OF THE RANGE(1941), m
Gary Rose
CHRISTIAN LICORICE STORE, THE(1971)

Gene Rose
CRIME OF DR. FORBES(1936), m; GIRL RUSH(1944), m; DOLLY SISTERS, THE(1945), m

George Rose
BEGGAR'S OPERA, THE(1953); DEVIL ON HORSEBACK(1954, Brit.); GOOD DIE YOUNG, THE(1954, Brit.); NIGHT MY NUMBER CAME UP, THE(1955, Brit.); PORT OF ESCAPE(1955, Brit.); SEA SHALL NOT HAVE THEM, THE(1955, Brit.); SQUARE RING, THE(1955, Brit.); WICKED WIFE(1955, Brit.); TRACK THE MAN DOWN(1956, Brit.); BROTHERS IN LAW(1957, Brit.); GOOD COMPANIONS, THE(1957, Brit.); NO TIME FOR TEARS(1957, Brit.); SHIRALEE, THE(1957, Brit.); THIRD KEY, THE(1957, Brit.); ALL AT SEA(1958, Brit.); CAT AND MOUSE(1958, Brit); NIGHT TO REMEMBER, A(1958, Brit.); DEVIL'S DISCIPLE, THE(1959); HEART OF A MAN, THE(1959, Brit.); JACK THE RIPPER(1959, Brit.); DESERT MICE(1960, Brit.); JET STORM(1961, Brit.); MANIA(1961, Brit.); MACBETH(1963); HAMLET(1964); HAWAII(1966); PINK JUNGLE, THE(1968); TREE, THE(1969); NEW LEAF, A(1971); FROM THE MIXED-UP FILES OF MRS. BASIL E. FRANKWEILER(1973); PIRATES OF PENZANCE, THE(1983)

Gordon Rose
SOME OF MY BEST FRIENDS ARE...(1971), m

H. Rose
SLIPPER EPISODE, THE(1938, Fr), w

Harry Rose
CHARING CROSS ROAD(1935, Brit.), ph; GAY LOVE(1936, Brit.), ph; IT'S YOU I WANT(1936, Brit.), ph; JURY'S EVIDENCE(1936, Brit.), ph; SONG OF FREEDOM(1938, Brit.), ph; ANGEL COMES TO BROOKLYN, AN(1945); SIMON, KING OF THE WITCHES(1971)

Helen Rose
PARTY GIRL(1930), cos; HELLO, FRISCO, HELLO(1943), cos; STORMY WEATHER(1943), cos; HARVEY GIRLS, THE(1946), cos; TILL THE CLOUDS ROLL BY(1946), cos; GOOD NEWS(1947), cos; DATE WITH JUDY, A(1948), cos; HOMECOMING(1948), cos; ACT OF VIOLENCE(1949), cos; EAST SIDE, WEST SIDE(1949), cos; ON THE TOWN(1949), cos; RED DANUBE, THE(1949), cos; STRATTON STORY, THE(1949), cos; TAKE ME OUT TO THE BALL GAME(1949), cos; THAT MIDNIGHT KISS(1949), cos; FATHER OF THE BRIDE(1950), cos; LIFE OF HER OWN, A(1950), cos; NANCY GOES TO RIO(1950), cos; PAGAN LOVE SONG(1950), cos; SUMMER STOCK(1950), cos; TO PLEASE A LADY(1950), cos; TOAST OF NEW ORLEANS, THE(1950), cos; TWO WEEKS WITH LOVE(1950), cos; FATHER'S LITTLE DIVIDEND(1951), cos; GREAT CARUSO, THE(1951), cos; PEOPLE AGAINST O'HARA, THE(1951), cos; STRICTLY DISHONORABLE(1951), cos; STRIP, THE(1951), cos; TEXAS CARNIVAL(1951), cos; TOO YOUNG TO KISS(1951), cos; UNKNOWN MAN, THE(1951), cos; BAD AND THE BEAUTIFUL, THE(1952), cos; BELLE OF NEW YORK, THE(1952), cos; MERRY WIDOW, THE(1952), cos; WASHINGTON STORY(1952), cos; DREAM WIFE(1953), cos; ESCAPE FROM FORT BRAVO(1953), cos; GIRL WHO HAD EVERYTHING, THE(1953), cos; JEOPARDY(1953), cos; LATIN LOVERS(1953), cos; MOGAMBO(1953), cos; SOMBRERO(1953), cos; STORY OF THREE LOVES, THE(1953), cos; TORCH SONG(1953), cos; EXECUTIVE SUITE(1954), cos; LAST TIME I SAW PARIS, THE(1954), cos; RHAPSODY(1954), cos; ROGUE COP(1954), cos; ROSE MARIE(1954), cos; GLASS SLIPPER, THE(1955), cos; GREEN FIRE(1955), cos; HIT THE DECK(1955), cos; I'LL CRY TOMORROW(1955), cos; INTERRUPTED MELODY(1955), cos; IT'S ALWAYS FAIR WEATHER(1955), cos; JUPITER'S DARLING(1955), cos; LOVE ME OR LEAVE ME(1955), cos; RAINS OF RANCHIPUR, THE(1955), cos; TENDER TRAP, THE(1955), cos; FORBIDDEN PLANET(1956), cos; HIGH SOCIETY(1956), cos; MEET ME IN LAS VEGAS(1956), cos; OPPOSITE SEX, THE(1956), cos; POWER AND THE PRIZE, THE(1956), cos; RANSOM(1956), cos; SWAN, THE(1956), cos; TEA AND SYMPATHY(1956), cos; THESE WILDER YEARS(1956), cos; DESIGNING WOMAN(1957), w, cos; SILK STOCKINGS(1957), cos; SOMETHING OF VALUE(1957), cos; TEN THOUSAND BEDROOMS(1957), cos; TIP ON A DEAD JOCKEY(1957), cos; CAT ON A HOT TIN ROOF(1958), cos; PARTY GIRL(1958), cos; RELUCTANT DEBUTANTE, THE(1958), cos; SADDLE THE WIND(1958), cos; TUNNEL OF LOVE, THE(1958), cos; ASK ANY GIRL(1959), cos; COUNT YOUR BLESSINGS(1959), cos; GAZEBO, THE(1959), cos; IT STARTED WITH A KISS(1959), cos; MATING GAME, THE(1959), cos; NEVER SO FEW(1959), cos; BUTTERFIELD 8(1960), cos; ADA(1961), cos; GO NAKED IN THE WORLD(1961), cos; HONEYMOON MACHINE, THE(1961), cos; COURTSHIP OF EDDY'S FATHER, THE(1963), cos; GOODBYE CHARLIE(1964), cos; MADE IN PARIS(1966), cos; MISTER BUDDWING(1966), cos; HOW SWEET IT IS(1968), cos; DON'T GO NEAR THE WATER(1975), cos

Herman Rose
LOVE NOW...PAY LATER(1966)

Hermie Rose
PAL JOEY(1957)

Hilary Rose
TELL ME LIES(1968, Brit.)

Hugh Rose
KING SOLOMON'S TREASURE(1978, Can.)

Jack Rose
LADIES' MAN(1947), w; MY FAVORITE BRUNETTE(1947), w; ROAD TO RIO(1947), w; PALEFACE, THE(1948), w; ADVENTURES OF JANE, THE(1949, Brit.), ph; ALWAYS LEAVE THEM LAUGHING(1949), w; GREAT LOVER, THE(1949), w; IT'S A GREAT FEELING(1949), w; SORROWFUL JONES(1949), w; DAUGHTER OF ROSIE O'GRADY, THE(1950), w; RIDING HIGH(1950), w; I'LL SEE YOU IN MY DREAMS(1951), w; ON MOONLIGHT BAY(1951), w; ROOM FOR ONE MORE(1952), w; APRIL IN PARIS(1953), w; TROUBLE ALONG THE WAY(1953), w; LIVING IT UP(1954), w; SEVEN LITTLE FOYS, THE(1955), p, w; BEAU JAMES(1957), p, w; HOUSEBOAT(1958), p, w; FIVE PENNIES, THE(1959), p, w; IT STARTED IN NAPLES(1960), p, w; ON THE DOUBLE(1961), p, w; WHO'S GOT THE ACTION?(1962), p, w; PAPA'S DELICATE CONDITION(1963), p, w; WHO'S BEEN SLEEPING IN MY BED?(1963), p, w; TOUCH OF CLASS, A(1973, Brit.), w; DUCHESS AND THE DIRTWATER FOX, THE(1976), w; LOST AND FOUND(1979), w; GREAT MUPPET CAPER, THE(1981), w; MARRIAGE, A(1983)
Silents
EXCITEMENT(1924), ph

Jackson Rose
GIRL FROM WOOLWORTH'S, THE(1929), ph; GIRL ON THE BARGE, THE(1929), ph; MIDSTREAM(1929), ph; PAINTED FACES(1929), ph; LADY SURRENDERS, A(1930), ph; LOST ZEPPELIN(1930), ph; ONCE A GENTLEMAN(1930), ph; SWELLHEAD, THE(1930), ph; TROOPERS THREE(1930), ph; RECKLESS LIVING(1931), ph; SEED(1931), ph; STRICTLY DISHONORABLE(1931), ph; LAW AND ORDER(1932), ph; RADIO PATROL(1932), ph; TEXAS GUN FIGHTER(1932), ph; DON'T BET ON LOVE(1933), ph; PHANTOM THUNDERBOLT, THE(1933), ph; THREE WISE GUYS,

THE(1936), ph; MAMA STEPS OUT(1937), ph; NORTHWEST RANGERS(1942), ph; UNKNOWN GUEST, THE(1943), ph; MAIN STREET AFTER DARK(1944), ph; TROCADERO(1944), ph; DILLINGER(1945), ph; FEAR(1946), ph; BORN TO SPEED(1947), ph; OUT OF THE BLUE(1947), ph; PHILO VANCE RETURNS(1947), ph; PHILO VANCE'S GAMBLE(1947), ph; PHILO VANCE'S SECRET MISSION(1947), ph; STEPCHILD(1947), ph; CHECKERED COAT, THE(1948), ph; MUSIC MAN(1948), ph; PREJUDICE(1949), ph
Silents
SLIM PRINCESS, THE(1915), ph; SKINNER'S DRESS SUIT(1917), ph; BIG GAME(1921), ph; MARRIAGE OF WILLIAM ASHE, THE(1921), ph; PAID BACK(1922), ph; MEASURE OF A MAN, THE(1924), ph; OLD SOAK, THE(1926), ph; CHEATING CHEATERS(1927), ph; HELD BY THE LAW(1927), ph; ALIAS THE DEACON(1928), ph; LINGERIE(1928), ph

Jackson A. Rose
I CHEATED THE LAW(1949), ph

Jackson C. Rose
BUNGALOW 13(1948), ph

Jackson J. Rose
MAN FROM TEXAS, THE(1948), ph; DESTINATION MURDER(1950), ph; EXPERIMENT ALCATRAZ(1950), ph; GREAT PLANE ROBBERY(1950), ph
Silents
DANGEROUS AGE, THE(1922), ph; BEAUTIFUL CHEAT, THE(1926), ph; LOVE ME AND THE WORLD IS MINE(1928), ph

Jamie Rose
JUST BEFORE DAWN(1980)
1984
HEARTBREAKERS(1984); TIGHTROPE(1984)

Jane Rose
GARDEN OF EDEN(1954); SUMMERTIME(1955); MONTE CARLO STORY, THE(1957, Ital.); ONE PLUS ONE(1961, Can.); FLIPPER(1963); I WALK THE LINE(1970)

Jennifer Rose
THREE DAYS OF THE CONDOR(1975)

Jeremy Rose
DEATHLINE(1973, Brit.), m

Jewel Rose
EAST SIDE, WEST SIDE(1949); JACKPOT, THE(1950); MILKMAN, THE(1950); FOLLOW THE SUN(1951); MEET ME AFTER THE SHOW(1951)

John Rose
COWARDS(1970)
1984
CRIMES OF PASSION(1984)

John Rose [Jaroslav Rozsival]
VOYAGE TO THE END OF THE UNIVERSE(1963, Czech.)

John C. Rose
INCREDIBLE MR. LIMPET, THE(1964), p, w

Julian Rose
LOOKING ON THE BRIGHT SIDE(1932, Brit.); MONEY TALKS(1933, Brit.)

Kingsley Rose
COUNTRYMAN(1982, Jamaica)

Laurie Rose
HOT BOX, THE(1972, U.S./Phil.); ROOMMATES, THE(1973); WORKING GIRLS, THE(1973); POLICEWOMAN(1974); WOMAN HUNT, THE(1975, U.S./Phil.)

Les Rose
PAPERBACK HERO(1973, Can.), w; THREE CARD MONTE(1978, Can.), d; HOG WILD(1980, Can.), d; GAS(1981, Can.), d; TITLE SHOT(1982, Can.), d
1984
ISAAC LITTLEFEATHERS(1984, Can.), d, w

Louis Rose
LAMBETH WALK, THE(1940, Brit.), w

Louisa Rose
SISTERS(1973), w

Margot Rose
48 HOURS(1982)

Max Rose
SLIGHTLY HONORABLE(1940)

Mickey Rose
WHAT'S UP, TIGER LILY?(1966), a, w; TAKE THE MONEY AND RUN(1969), w; BANANAS(1971), w; CONDORMAN(1981), w; STUDENT BODIES(1981), d&w

Murray Rose
RIDE THE WILD SURF(1964); ICE STATION ZEBRA(1968)

Norman Rose
JOE LOUIS STORY, THE(1953); VIOLATORS, THE(1957); PINOCCHIO IN OUTER SPACE(1965, U.S./Bel.); WAR AND PEACE(1968, USSR); FLYING MATCHMAKER, THE(1970, Israel); ANDERSON TAPES, THE(1971); JUMP(1971); WHO KILLED MARY WHAT'SER NAME?(1971); FRONT, THE(1976)
Misc. Talkies
TELEPHONE BOOK, THE(1971)

Patrick Rose
IMPROPER CHANNELS(1981, Can.)

Pauline Rose
Misc. Talkies
HOT T-SHIRTS(1980)

Penny Rose
QUEST FOR FIRE(1982, Fr./Can.), cos
1984
ANOTHER COUNTRY(1984, Brit.), cos; CAL(1984, Ireland), cos

Phil Rose
1984
MEMED MY HAWK(1984, Brit.)

Philip Rose
ACROSS THE BRIDGE(1957, Brit.); RAISIN IN THE SUN, A(1961), p

Phillip Rose
POOR COW(1968, Brit.)

Phyllis Rose
GENTLE SEX, THE(1943, Brit.), w

Polly Rose
SPECTER OF THE ROSE(1946)

Ralph Rose
LET'S SCARE JESSICA TO DEATH(1971), w
Reginald Rose
CRIME IN THE STREETS(1956), w; DINO(1957), w; 12 ANGRY MEN(1957), p, w; MAN OF THE WEST(1958), w; MAN IN THE NET, THE(1959), w; BAXTER(1973, Brit.), w; SOMEBODY KILLED HER HUSBAND(1978), w; WILD GEESE, THE(1978, Brit.), w; SEA WOLVES, THE(1981, Brit.), w; WHOSE LIFE IS IT ANYWAY?(1981), w; FINAL OPTION, THE(1983, Brit.), w
Reva Rose
THREE IN THE ATTIC(1968); IF IT'S TUESDAY, THIS MUST BE BELGIUM(1969); BUNNY O'HARE(1971); HOUSE CALLS(1978)
Misc. Talkies
NINE LIVES OF FRITZ THE CAT, THE(1974)
Robert Rose
WOMAN FROM MONTE CARLO, THE(1932); GUADALCANAL DIARY(1943); GAY RANCHERO, THE(1948); HIS KIND OF WOMAN(1951); ROGUE RIVER(1951); JALOPY(1953); TORPEDO ALLEY(1953)
1984
BAY BOY(1984, Can.)
Misc. Silents
WESTERN PLUCK(1926)
Robin Pearson Rose
ENEMY OF THE PEOPLE, AN(1978)
Robina Rose
HAMLET(1976, Brit.), ph
Roger Rose
MAN WHO LOVED WOMEN, THE(1983)
1984
MICKI AND MAUDE(1984)
Rosalind Rose
EVERYTHING IN LIFE(1936, Brit.)
Ruth Rose
BLIND ADVENTURE(1933), w; KING KONG(1933), w; SON OF KONG(1933), w; LAST DAYS OF POMPEII, THE(1935), w; SHE(1935), w; MIGHTY JOE YOUNG(1949), w; KING KONG(1976), w
Seymour Rose
Misc. Silents
FROZEN WARNING, THE(1918)
Sharon Rose
JANE EYRE(1971, Brit.)
Sherman Rose
CASSIDY OF BAR 20(1938), ed; FRONTIERSMAN, THE(1938), ed; HEART OF ARIZONA(1938), ed; MYSTERIOUS RIDER, THE(1938), ed; HERITAGE OF THE DESERT(1939), ed; PARSON OF PANAMINT, THE(1941), ed; TWO DOLLAR BETTOR(1951), ed; FOR MEN ONLY(1952), ed; RETURN OF DRACULA, THE(1958), ed; SON OF A GUNFIGHTER(1966, U.S./Span.), ed
Sherman A. Rose
RANGE WAR(1939), ed; CHEROKEE STRIP(1940), ed; LIGHT OF WESTERN STARS, THE(1940), ed; LLANO KID, THE(1940), ed; SANTA FE MARSHAL(1940), ed; STAGECOACH WAR(1940), ed; THREE MEN FROM TEXAS(1940), ed; WIDE OPEN TOWN(1941), ph; SILVER QUEEN(1942), ed; BORDER PATROL(1943), ed; COLT COMRADES(1943), ed; HOPPY SERVES A WRIT(1943), ed; LOST CANYON(1943), ed; RAMROD(1947), ed; SENATOR WAS INDISCREET, THE(1947), ed; TARGET EARTH(1954), d, ed; MAGNIFICENT ROUGHNECKS(1956), d, ed; TANK BATTALION(1958), d, ed
Si Rose
IT HAPPENED AT THE WORLD'S FAIR(1963), w; MC HALE'S NAVY(1964), w; DID YOU HEAR THE ONE ABOUT THE TRAVELING SALESLADY?(1968), p; PUFNSTUF(1970), p, w
Simonemarie Rose
MONTE CARLO STORY, THE(1957, Ital.)
Stan Rose
CAMPUS SLEUTH(1948)
Standley Rose
DULCIMER STREET(1948, Brit.)
Stanley Rose
STOP PRESS GIRL(1949, Brit.); DON'T SAY DIE(1950, Brit.); MYSTERY JUNCTION(1951, Brit.); ISLAND RESCUE(1952, Brit.); DEATM GOES TO SCHOOL(1953, Brit.);LANDFALL(1953, Brit.); END OF THE AFFAIR, THE(1955, Brit.); IT'S A GREAT DAY(1956, Brit.); TIGER IN THE SMOKE(1956, Brit.); LONG HAUL, THE(1957, Brit.)
Stephen Bruce Rose
COACH(1978), w
Steven Rose
TELL ME LIES(1968, Brit.)
Misc. Talkies
MAG WHEELS(1978)
Stuart Rose
1984
RAZOR'S EDGE, THE(1984), set d
Tania Rose
LIGHT TOUCH, THE(1955, Brit.), w; IT'S A MAD, MAD, MAD, MAD WORLD(1963), w
Tim Rose
DARK CRYSTAL, THE(1982, Brit.); RETURN OF THE JEDI(1983)
Veronica Rose
CUCKOO IN THE NEST, THE(1933, Brit.); TURKEY TIME(1933, Brit.); CUP OF KINDNESS, A(1934, Brit.); LEAVE IT TO SMITH(1934); FIGHTING STOCK(1935, Brit.); FOR VALOR(1937, Brit.); SECOND BEST BED(1937, Brit.); WEEKEND MILLIONAIRE(1937, Brit.); OLD IRON(1938, Brit.); WARN THAT MAN(1943, Brit.); DARK ROAD, THE(1948, Brit.)
Virginia Rose
SILENT SCREAM(1980)
Wally Rose
TOGETHER AGAIN(1944); KILLERS, THE(1946); NIGHT EDITOR(1946); BRUTE FORCE(1947); STREET WITH NO NAME, THE(1948); WHIPLASH(1948); UNDERCOVER MAN, THE(1949); MILKMAN, THE(1950); MA BARKER'S KILLER BROOD(1960); SPARTACUS(1960); YOUNG DILLINGER(1965); WHAT'S UP, DOC?(1972); DAY OF THE LOCUST, THE(1975); MOVIE MOVIE(1978); CHAMP, THE(1979); MAN WITH BOGART'S FACE, THE(1980)

Warner Rose
50,000 B.C.(BEFORE CLOTHING)* (1963), d; MURDER IN MISSISSIPPI(1965), ph
Werner Rose
OLGA'S GIRLS(1964), ph
Will Rose
STILL OF THE NIGHT(1982)
Willi Rose
FOUR COMPANIONS, THE(1938, Ger.); CAPTAIN FROM KOEPENICK, THE(1956, Ger.); CIRCUS OF LOVE(1958, Ger.); WOZZECK(1962, E. Ger.); JUDGE AND THE SINNER, THE(1964, Ger.)
William L. Rose
"RENT-A-GIRL"(1965), p,d&w
William Rose
ESTHER WATERS(1948, Brit.), w; LUCKY NICK CAIN(1951), w; MANIACS ON WHEELS(1951, Brit.), w; OPERATION X(1951, Brit.), w; GLORY AT SEA(1952, Brit.), w; BACHELOR IN PARIS(1953, Brit.), w; GENEVIEVE(1953, Brit.), w; HIGH AND DRY(1954, Brit.), w; LIGHT TOUCH, THE(1955, Brit.), w; LADYKILLERS, THE(1956, Brit.), w; DECISION AGAINST TIME(1957, Brit.), w; SMALLEST SHOW ON EARTH, THE(1957, Brit.), w; DAVY(1958, Brit.), w; IT'S A MAD, MAD, MAD, MAD WORLD(1963), w; RUSSIANS ARE COMING, THE RUSSIANS ARE COMING, THE(1966), w; FLIM-FLAM MAN, THE(1967), w; GUESS WHO'S COMING TO DINNER(1967), w; SECRET OF SANTA VITTORIA, THE(1969), w
Winston Rose
PINK FLOYD–THE WALL(1982, Brit.)
Rose-Marie
DEAD HEAT ON A MERRY-GO-ROUND(1966)
John Rosearne
SLAVERS(1977, Ger.), art d
Jeb Rosebrook
JUNIOR BONNER(1972), w; BLACK HOLE, THE(1979), w
Jed Rosebrook
BLACK HOLE, THE(1979), Gerry Day
Leon Rosebrook
RIDERS OF THE WHISTLING SKULL(1937), m
Pauline Rosebrook
FOLIES DERGERE(1935)
The People of the Rosebud Sioux Indian Reservation
JOURNEY THROUGH ROSEBUD(1972)
Irene Roseen
I NEVER PROMISED YOU A ROSE GARDEN(1977)
Beryl Rosekelly
WAY WE LIVE, THE(1946, Brit.)
Jack Roseleigh
Silents
SINGING RIVER(1921)
John Roselius
COAST TO COAST(1980)
1984
FEAR CITY(1984); LOVE STREAMS(1984)
Earl Rosell
LITTLE BIG MAN(1970)
Erika Rosell
STORY OF A WOMAN(1970, U.S./Ital.)
Gail Rosella
JOYRIDE(1977)
Rita Roselle
BLACK CAMEL, THE(1931)
William Roselle
Silents
ONE OF OUR GIRLS(1914); AVALANCHE, THE(1919); MAN WHO, THE(1921)
Misc. Silents
QUEST OF THE SACRED GEM, THE(1914)
Rex Roselli
Silents
ROWDY, THE(1921)
Adrian Rosely
MY WEAKNESS(1933); RIP TIDE(1934); GARDEN OF ALLAH, THE(1936)
Ben Roseman
DEMENTIA(1955); NIGHT TIDE(1963)
E. F. Roseman
Silents
TIGER WOMAN, THE(1917)
E. T. Roseman
Silents
ALL FOR A GIRL(1915)
Ed Roseman
Silents
AMERICAN WAY, THE(1919); IMPOSSIBLE CATHERINE(1919); ON THE BANKS OF THE WABASH(1923); AMERICA(1924)
Misc. Silents
LOVE AND THE WOMAN(1919)
Ed F. Roseman
Misc. Silents
WHERE IS MY FATHER?(1916); RED WOMAN, THE(1917)
Edward Roseman
HOUSE OF SECRETS(1929)
Silents
WHEN BROADWAY WAS A TRAIL(1914); PRIDE OF THE CLAN, THE(1917); EMBARRASSMENT OF RICHES, THE(1918); JUNGLE TRAIL, THE(1919); OH, JOHNNY(1919); ANNE OF LITTLE SMOKY(1921); DEVIL'S PARTNER, THE(1923); POLICE PATROL, THE(1925)
Misc. Silents
LABYRINTH, THE(1915); SECRET OF EVE, THE(1917); CALIBRE 38(1919); HIGH POCKETS(1919); FACE AT YOUR WINDOW(1920); VALLEY OF LOST SOULS, THE(1923)
Edward F. Roseman
Silents
GOVERNOR'S BOSS, THE(1915); SPRINGTIME(1915)

Misc. Silents
LIAR, THE(1918)
Leonard Roseman
SAVAGE EYE, THE(1960), m; HELLFIGHTERS(1968), m; LORD OF THE RINGS, THE(1978), m
Ralph Roseman
BLOB, THE(1958)
Hilton Rosemarin
1984
MRS. SOFFEL(1984), set d
Hilton Rosemartin
INCUBUS, THE(1982, Can.), art d
Miguel Rosemberg
TRAIN ROBBERY CONFIDENTIAL(1965, Braz.)
E.T. Rosemon
Misc. Silents
CALL OF THE DANCE, THE(1915)
Clinton Rosemond
ONLY THE BRAVE(1930); SMART MONEY(1931); NO MAN OF HER OWN(1933); HEARTS IN BONDAGE(1936); THEY WON'T FORGET(1937); ACCIDENTS WILL HAPPEN(1938); TOY WIFE, THE(1938); YOUNG DR. KILDARE(1938); GOLDEN BOY(1939); STAND UP AND FIGHT(1939); MARYLAND(1940); SAFARI(1940); SANTA FE TRAIL(1940); ARE HUSBANDS NECESSARY?(1942); YANKEE DOODLE DANDY(1942); FLESH AND FANTASY(1943); I WALKED WITH A ZOMBIE(1943); IS EVERYBODY HAPPY?(1943); HEAVENLY DAYS(1944); COLONEL EFFINGHAM'S RAID(1945); THREE LITTLE GIRLS IN BLUE(1946); HOMESTRETCH, THE(1947); SPORT OF KINGS(1947)
Misc. Talkies
MIDNIGHT SHADOW(1939)
Norman Rosemont
STILETTO(1969), p; COUNT OF MONTE CRISTO(1976, Brit.), p
Clinton Rosemund
CAROLINA(1934); DARK COMMAND, THE(1940); BLOSSOMS IN THE DUST(1941)
Marion Rosemund
MOONTIDE(1942)
Al Rosen
WITHOUT RESERVATIONS(1946); MARY HAD A LITTLE(1961, Brit.), w
Barry Rosen
DEVIL'S EXPRESS(1975), d
Misc. Talkies
YUM-YUM GIRLS(1976), d
Bob Rosen
VON RYAN'S EXPRESS(1965)
Brian Rosen
FATTY FINN(1980, Aus.), p
Charles Rosen
MAN CALLED ADAM, A(1966), art d; PRODUCERS, THE(1967), art d; CHARLY(1968), art d; SEPARATE PEACE, A(1972), art d; TAXI DRIVER(1976), art d; EMPIRE OF THE ANTS(1977), prod d; HEROES(1977), prod d; INVASION OF THE BODY SNATCHERS(1978), prod d; MAIN EVENT, THE(1979), prod d; INSIDE MOVES(1980), prod d; ENTITY, THE(1982), prod d; MY FAVORITE YEAR(1982), prod d; TOY, THE(1982), prod d; FLASHDANCE(1983), prod d
1984
RIVER, THE(1984), prod d
Chips Rosen [Claudia Salte]
ACE ELI AND RODGER OF THE SKIES(1973), w
Danny Rosen
LOVELESS, THE(1982)
1984
STRANGER THAN PARADISE(1984, U.S./Ger.)
E. Rosen
OCEAN BREAKERS(1949, Swed.)
Edward Rosen
Misc. Silents
HER PRICE(1918)
Eric Rosen
DOLLAR(1938, Swed.)
Frank Rosen
TIME TO DIE, A(1983), art d
Hal Rosen
HELLO SISTER(1930), ph
Heinz Rosen
DANCING HEART, THE(1959, Ger.)
Herb Rosen
SYNANON(1965)
Herman Rosen
ELI ELI(1940)
Herschel Rosen
1984
BROADWAY DANNY ROSE(1984)
Hobert Rosen
HANSEL AND GRETEL(1954), anim
I. Rosen
Silents
DEVIL DOGS(1928), ed
Lance Rosen
FIREFOX(1982)
Lisa Rosen
PERMANENT VACATION(1982)
Marc Rosen
FINAL ASSIGNMENT(1980, Can.), w
Mark L. Rosen
NUTCRACKER FANTASY(1979), p; NEW YEAR'S EVIL(1980)
Martin Rosen
GREAT BIG THING, A(1968, U.S./Can.), p; WATERSHIP DOWN(1978, Brit.), p,d&w
1984
PLAGUE DOGS, THE(1984, U.S./Brit.), pd&w

Marton Rosen
Misc. Talkies
PLAGUE DOGS, THE(1982), d
Marvin J. Rosen
COOL AND THE CRAZY, THE(1958)
Michele Rosen
SILENT PARTNER, THE(1979, Can.)
Milt Rosen
DO NOT DISTURB(1965), w
Milton Rosen
LAW OF THE RANGE(1941), m; MASKED RIDER, THE(1941), ph; FIGHTING BILL FARGO(1942), m; ENTER ARSENE LUPIN(1944), m, md; MEN IN HER DIARY(1945), m; ON STAGE EVERYBODY(1945), m, md; SHADY LADY(1945), m, md; SUDAN(1945), m, md; CUBAN PETE(1946), md; DRESSED TO KILL(1946), md; LAWLESS BREED, THE(1946), md; SLIGHTLY SCANDALOUS(1946), md; SPIDER WOMAN STRIKES BACK, THE(1946), md; TANGIER(1946), m, md; TIME OF THEIR LIVES, THE(1946), m, md; WHITE TIE AND TAILS(1946), m&md; PIRATES OF MONTEREY(1947), m; SLAVE GIRL(1947), m; CREEPER, THE(1948), m; THIRTEEN LEAD SOLDIERS(1948), md; MILKMAN, THE(1950), m; EVERYTHING BUT THE TRUTH(1956), md; OUTSIDE THE LAW(1956), md
Perry Rosen
DEATHTRAP(1982)
1984
PREPPIES(1984)
Peter Rosen
Misc. Talkies
BRIGHT COLLEGE YEARS(1971), d
Phil Rosen
PHANTOM IN THE HOUSE, THE(1929), d; EXTRAVAGANCE(1930), d, w; LOTUS LADY(1930), d; RAMPANT AGE, THE(1930), d; WORLDLY GOODS(1930), d; ALIAS THE BAD MAN(1931), d; ARIZONA TERROR(1931), d; BRANDED MEN(1931), d; RANGE LAW(1931), d; SECOND HONEYMOON(1931), d; TWO GUN MAN, THE(1931), d; GAY BUCKAROO, THE(1932), d; KLONDIKE(1932), d; LENA RIVERS(1932), d; MAN'S LAND, A(1932), d; POCATELLO KID(1932), d; TEXAS GUN FIGHTER(1932), d; VANISHING FRONTIER, THE(1932), d; WHISTLIN' DAN(1932), d; YOUNG BLOOD(1932), d; BLACK BEAUTY(1933), d; DEVIL'S MATE(1933), d; HOLD THE PRESS(1933), d; MY MOTHER(1933), d; PHANTOM BROADCAST, THE(1933), d; SPHINX, THE(1933), d; BEGGARS IN ERMINE(1934), d; CHEATERS(1934), d; PICTURE BRIDES(1934), d; SHADOWS OF SING SING(1934), d; TAKE THE STAND(1934), d; WOMAN IN THE DARK(1934), d; BORN TO GAMBLE(1935), d; DANGEROUS CORNER(1935), d; DEATH FLIES EAST(1935), d; LITTLE MEN(1935), d; UNWELCOME STRANGER(1935), d; WEST OF THE PECOS(1935), d; BRIDGE OF SIGHS(1936), d; BRILLIANT MARRIAGE(1936), d; DAN MATTHEWS(1936), d; EASY MONEY(1936), d; IT COULDN'T HAVE HAPPENED–BUT IT DID(1936), d; MISSING GIRLS(1936), d; PRESIDENT'S MYSTERY, THE(1936), d; TANGO(1936), d; THREE OF A KIND(1936), d; IT COULD HAPPEN TO YOU(1937), d; JIM HANVEY, DETECTIVE(1937), d; ROARING TIMBER(1937), d; TWO WISE MAIDS(1937), d; YOUTH ON PAROLE(1937), p&d; FORBIDDEN TERRITORY(1938, Brit.), d; MARINES ARE HERE, THE(1938), d; EX-CHAMP(1939), d; MISSING EVIDENCE(1939), p&d; CROOKED ROAD, THE(1940), d; FORGOTTEN GIRLS(1940), d; PHANTOM OF CHINATOWN(1940), d; QUEEN OF THE YUKON(1940), d; DEADLY GAME, THE(1941), d; MURDER BY INVITATION(1941), d; PAPER BULLETS(1941), d; ROAR OF THE PRESS(1941), d; SPOOKS RUN WILD(1941), d; I KILLED THAT MAN(1942), d; MAN WITH TWO LIVES, THE(1942), d; MYSTERY OF MARIE ROGET, THE(1942), d; ROAD TO HAPPINESS(1942), d; GENTLE GANGSTER, A(1943), d; WINGS OVER THE PACIFIC(1943), d; ARMY WIVES(1944), d; CALL OF THE JUNGLE(1944), d; CHARLIE CHAN IN BLACK MAGIC(1944), d; CHARLIE CHAN IN THE SECRET SERVICE(1944), d; CHINESE CAT, THE(1944), d; RETURN OF THE APE MAN(1944), d; CAPTAIN TUGBOAT ANNIE(1945), d; IN OLD NEW MEXICO(1945), d; JADE MASK, THE(1945), d; SCARLET CLUE, THE(1945), d; STRANGE MR. GREGORY, THE(1945), d; RED DRAGON, THE(1946), d; SHADOW RETURNS, THE(1946), d; STEP BY STEP(1946), d; SINS OF THE FATHERS(1948, Can.), d; SECRET OF THE PURPLE REEF, THE(1960)
Misc. Talkies
SELF DEFENSE(1933), d; CALLING OF DAN MATTHEWS, THE(1936), d; ELLIS ISLAND(1936), d
Silents
ROMEO AND JULIET(1916), ph; DARLING OF PARIS, THE(1917), ph; ETERNAL MAGDALENE, THE(1919), ph; ABRAHAM LINCOLN(1924), d; LOVER'S LANE(1924), d; EXQUISITE SINNER, THE(1926), d; CALIFORNIA OR BUST(1927), d; PRETTY CLOTHES(1927), d; SALVATION JANE(1927), d; STRANDED(1927), d; THUMBS DOWN(1927), d; WOMAN WHO DID NOT CARE, THE(1927), d; APACHE, THE(1928), d; PEACOCK FAN(1929), d
Misc. Silents
THIS WOMAN(1924), d; BRIDGE OF SIGHS, THE(1925), d; HEART OF A SIREN(1925), d; WANDERING FOOTSTEPS(1925), d; WHITE MONKEY, THE(1925), d; ROSE OF THE TENEMENTS(1926), d; WOMAN'S HEART, A(1926), d; CANCELLED DEBT, THE(1927), d; CLOSED GATES(1927), d; HEAVEN ON EARTH(1927), d; IN THE FIRST DEGREE(1927), d; BURNING UP BROADWAY(1928), d; FAKER, THE(1929), d; SECOND HONEYMOON(1930), d
Philip Rosen
DOUBLE ALIBI(1940), d; SECRET OF ST. IVES, THE(1949), d
Silents
SOUL OF BROADWAY, THE(1915), ph; SPREADING DAWN, THE(1917), ph; MIRACLE MAN, THE(1919), ph; ADORABLE DECEIVER, THE(1926), d; MARRY THE GIRL(1928), d
Misc. Silents
PATH SHE CHOSE, THE(1920), d; ROAD TO DIVORCE, THE(1920), d; YOUNG RAHAH, THE(1922), d; BEING RESPECTABLE(1924), d; MODERN MOTHERS(1928), d; UNDRESSED(1928), d
Philip E. Rosen
Silents
ARE ALL MEN ALIKE?(1920), d; HANDLE WITH CARE(1922), d; WORLD'S CHAMPION, THE(1922), d; STOLEN PLEASURES(1927), d
Misc. Silents
EXTRAVAGANCE(1921), d; LITTLE FOOL, THE(1921), d; BONDED WOMAN, THE(1922), d

Phillip E. Rosen
Silents
TIGER WOMAN, THE(1917), ph; LURE OF YOUTH, THE(1921), d; ACROSS THE CONTINENT(1922), d
Robert Rosen
INDEPENDENCE DAY(1976)
1984
RAW COURAGE(1984), p
Robert L. Rosen
TOGETHER BROTHERS(1974), p; FRENCH CONNECTION 11(1975), p; PROPHECY(1979), p; GOING APE!(1981), p
1984
RAW COURAGE(1984), d
Sam Rosen
ACTORS AND SIN(1952); PHANTOM TOLLBOOTH, THE(1970), w
Gina Rosenbach
SALLAH(1965, Israel), cos; IMPOSSIBLE ON SATURDAY(1966, Fr./Israel), cos
Henry Rosenbaum
BULLET FOR PRETTY BOY, A(1970), w; DUNWICH HORROR, THE(1970), w; HANKY-PANKY(1982), w
Ralph Rosenbaum
BORN TO WIN(1971), ed; GREAT BANK HOAX, THE(1977), ed
Simon Rosenbaum
OPERATION CAMEL(1961, Den.), m
Steve Rosenbaum
1984
PURPLE HEARTS(1984)
Aaron Rosenberg
CRACK-UP, THE(1937), spec eff; LARCENY(1948), p; JOHNNY STOOL PIGEON(1949), p; STORY OF MOLLY X, THE(1949), p; OUTSIDE THE WALL(1950), p; WINCHESTER '73(1950), p; AIR CADET(1951), p; CATTLE DRIVE(1951), p; IRON MAN, THE(1951), p; RAGING TIDE, THE(1951), p; BEND OF THE RIVER(1952), p; HERE COME THE NELSONS(1952), p; RED BALL EXPRESS(1952), p; ALL-AMERICAN, THE(1953), p; GLENN MILLER STORY, THE(1953), p; GUNSMOKE(1953), p; MAN FROM THE ALAMO, THE(1953), p; THUNDER BAY(1953), p; WINGS OF THE HAWK(1953), p; SASKATCHEWAN(1954), p; FAR COUNTRY, THE(1955), p; FOXFIRE(1955), p; MAN WITHOUT A STAR(1955), p; SHRIKE, THE(1955), p; SIX BRIDGES TO CROSS(1955), p; TO HELL AND BACK(1955), p; BACKLASH(1956), p; BENNY GOODMAN STORY, THE(1956), p; FOUR GIRLS IN TOWN(1956), p; WALK THE PROUD LAND(1956), p; WORLD IN MY CORNER(1956), p; GREAT MAN, THE(1957), p; JOE BUTTERFLY(1957), p; NIGHT PASSAGE(1957), p; BADLANDERS, THE(1958), p; IT STARTED WITH A KISS(1959), p; NEVER STEAL ANYTHING SMALL(1959), p; GO NAKED IN THE WORLD(1961), p; MOVE OVER, DARLING(1963), p; FATE IS THE HUNTER(1964), p; SHOCK TREATMENT(1964), p; DO NOT DISTURB(1965), p; MORITURI(1965), p; REWARD, THE(1965), p; SMOKY(1966), p; CAPRICE(1967), p; TONY ROME(1967), p; DETECTIVE, THE(1968), p; LADY IN CEMENT(1968), p; BOY WHO CRIED WEREWOLF, THE(1973), p
Alan Rosenberg
WANDERERS, THE(1979); HAPPY BIRTHDAY, GEMINI(1980)
Albert Rosenberg
MAHOGANY(1975)
Arthur Rosenberg
PROMISES IN THE DARK(1979); 10(1979); CUTTER AND BONE(1981); NOBODY'S PERFEKT(1981); CUJO(1983); SECOND THOUGHTS(1983)
1984
FOOTLOOSE(1984)
Boris Rosenberg
SINAI COMMANDOS: THE STORY OF THE SIX DAY WAR(1968, Israel/Ger.)
C. A. Rosenberg
MANIAC(1980), w
Edgar Rosenberg
RABBIT TEST(1978), p
Frank Rosenberg
WHERE THE SIDEWALK ENDS(1950), w
Frank P Rosenberg
MAN-EATER OF KUMAON(1948), p; SECRET OF CONVICT LAKE, THE(1951), p; RETURN OF THE TEXAN(1952), p; FARMER TAKES A WIFE, THE(1953), p; KING OF THE KHYBER RIFLES(1953), p; ILLEGAL(1955), p; GIRL HE LEFT BEHIND, THE(1956), p; MIRACLE IN THE RAIN(1956), p; ONE-EYED JACKS(1961), p; CRITIC'S CHOICE(1963), p; MADIGAN(1968), p; REINCARNATION OF PETER PROUD, THE(1975), p; GRAY LADY DOWN(1978), w
Hilding Rosenberg
TORMENT(1947, Swed.), m; SHORT IS THE SUMMER(1968, Swed.), m
Irving Rosenberg
Silents
GIRLS GONE WILD(1929), ph
Janie Rosenberg
TAKING OFF(1971)
Jeanne Rosenberg
BLACK STALLION, THE(1979), w
Jerry Rosenberg
Misc. Talkies
LIVING ORPHAN, THE(1939)
Larry Rosenberg
TO BE OR NOT TO BE(1983)
Marc Rosenberg
HEATWAVE(1983, Aus.), w
Max Rosenberg
BIRTHDAY PARTY, THE(1968, Brit.), p; MIND OF MR. SOAMES, THE(1970, Brit.), p; HOUSE THAT DRIPPED BLOOD, THE(1971, Brit.), p
Max J. Rosenberg
ROCK, ROCK, ROCK!(1956), p; JAMBOREE(1957), p; LAST MILE, THE(1959), p; GIRL OF THE NIGHT(1960), p; LAD: A DOG(1962), p; DR. TERROR'S HOUSE OF HORRORS(1965, Brit.), p; DR. WHO AND THE DALEKS(1965, Brit.), p; SKULL, THE(1965, Brit.), p; DALEKS–INVASION EARTH 2155 A.D.(1966, Brit.), p; PSYCHOPATH, THE(1966, Brit.), p; DEADLY BEES, THE(1967, Brit.), p; TERRORNAUTS, THE(1967, Brit.), p; THEY CAME FROM BEYOND SPACE(1967, Brit.), p; DANGER ROUTE(1968, Brit.), p; TORTURE GARDEN(1968, Brit.), p; THANK YOU ALL VERY MUCH(1969, Brit.), p; SCREAM AND SCREAM AGAIN(1970, Brit.), p; I, MONSTER(1971, Brit.), p; ASYLUM(1972, Brit.), p; TALES FROM THE CRYPT(1972,

Brit.), p; WHAT BECAME OF JACK AND JILL?(1972, Brit.), p; AND NOW THE SCREAMING STARTS(1973, Brit.), p; VAULT OF HORROR, THE(1973, Brit.), p; BEAST MUST DIE, THE(1974, Brit.), p; FROM BEYOND THE GRAVE(1974, Brit.), p; MADHOUSE(1974, Brit.), p
Michael Rosenberg
CANTOR'S SON, THE(1937); TWO SISTERS(1938)
Misc. Talkies
HIS WIFE'S LOVER(1931); JEWISH DAUGHTER(1933); MIRELE EFROS(1939); MAZEL TOV, JEWS!(1941); THREE DAUGHTERS(1949)
Phil Rosenberg
FOREVER YOUNG, FOREVER FREE(1976, South Afr.), art d; NEXT STOP, GREENWICH VILLAGE(1976), prod d
Philip Rosenberg
WIZ, THE(1978), art d; CHILDRENS GAMES(1969), art d; OWL AND THE PUSSYCAT, THE(1970), art d; ANDERSON TAPES, THE(1971), art d; POSSESSION OF JOEL DELANEY, THE(1972), art d; BADGE 373(1973), art d; FROM THE MIXED-UP FILES OF MRS. BASIL E. FRANKWEILER(1973), art d; SHAMUS(1973), art d; GAMBLER, THE(1974), prod d; NETWORK(1976), prod d; SENTINEL, THE(1977), prod d; ALL THAT JAZZ(1979), set d; EYEWITNESS(1981), prod d; SOUP FOR ONE(1982), prod d; DANIEL(1983), prod d; LOVESICK(1983), prod d
1984
GARBO TALKS(1984), prod d
Phillip D. Rosenberg
1984
NATURAL, THE(1984)
Richard K. Rosenberg
ALICE, SWEET ALICE(1978), p
Rick Rosenberg
ADAM AT 6 A.M.(1970), p; HIDE IN PLAIN SIGHT(1980), p
Stephen Rosenberg
JACOB TWO-TWO MEETS THE HOODED FANG(1979, Can.)
Stuart Rosenberg
MURDER, INC.(1960), d; QUESTION 7(1961, U.S./Ger.), d; COOL HAND LUKE(1967), d; APRIL FOOLS, THE(1969), d; MOVE(1970), d; POCKET MONEY(1972), d; LAUGHING POLICEMAN, THE(1973), p&d; DROWNING POOL, THE(1975), d; VOYAGE OF THE DAMNED(1976, Brit.), d; AMITYVILLE HORROR, THE(1979), d; LOVE AND BULLETS(1979, Brit.), d; BRUBAKER(1980), d
1984
POPE OF GREENWICH VILLAGE, THE(1984), d
Misc. Talkies
ASYLUM FOR A SPY(1967), d
William Rosenberg
CASE OF THE 44'S, THE(1964 Brit./Den.)
Raimund Rosenberger
ROSES FOR THE PROSECUTOR(1961, Ger.), m; JUDGE AND THE SINNER, THE(1964, Ger.), m; MAD EXECUTIONERS, THE(1965, Ger.), m; TERROR OF DR. MABUSE, THE(1965, Ger.), m
Aaron Rosenberry
WORLD IN HIS ARMS, THE(1952), p
Barbara Rosenblat
CARRY ON ENGLAND(1976, Brit.)
Cantor Josef Rosenblatt
JAZZ SINGER, THE(1927)
Marcell Rosenblatt
SOPHIE'S CHOICE(1982)
Martin Rosenblatt
ANNIE HALL(1977)
1984
SPLITZ(1984)
Max Rosenblatt
MOTHERS OF TODAY(1939)
Janet Rosenbloom
ZELIG(1983), set d
Max Rosenbloom
MY SIDE OF THE MOUNTAIN(1969)
Maxie Rosenbloom
KELLY THE SECOND(1936); MUSS 'EM UP(1936); BIG CITY(1937); KID COMES BACK, THE(1937); NOTHING SACRED(1937); TWO WISE MAIDS(1937); AMAZING DR. CLITTERHOUSE, THE(1938); GANGS OF NEW YORK(1938); HIS EXCITING NIGHT(1938); MR. MOTO'S GAMBLE(1938); SUBMARINE PATROL(1938); EACH DAWN I DIE(1939); KID FROM KOKOMO, THE(1939); NAUGHTY BUT NICE(1939); PRIVATE DETECTIVE(1939); WOMEN IN THE WIND(1939); 20,000 MEN A YEAR(1939); GRANDPA GOES TO TOWN(1940); PASSPORT TO ALCATRAZ(1940); PUBLIC DEB NO. 1(1940); LOUISIANA PURCHASE(1941); RINGSIDE MAISIE(1941); STORK PAYS OFF, THE(1941); BOOGIE MAN WILL GET YOU, THE(1942); HARVARD, HERE I COME(1942); SMART ALECKS(1942); TO THE SHORES OF TRIPOLI(1942); YANKS ARE COMING, THE(1942); ALLERGIC TO LOVE(1943); HERE COMES KELLY(1943); MY SON, THE HERO(1943); SWING FEVER(1943); CRAZY KNIGHTS(1944); FOLLOW THE BOYS(1944); IRISH EYES ARE SMILING(1944); NIGHT CLUB GIRL(1944); MEN IN HER DIARY(1945); PENTHOUSE RHYTHM(1945); HAZARD(1948); MR. UNIVERSE(1951); SKIPALONG ROSENBLOOM(1951); ABBOTT AND COSTELLO MEET THE KEYSTONE KOPS(1955); HOLLYWOOD OR BUST(1956); I MARRIED A MONSTER FROM OUTER SPACE(1958); BEAT GENERATION, THE(1959); DON'T WORRY, WE'LL THINK OF A TITLE(1966); SPY IN THE GREEN HAT, THE(1966); COTTONPICKIN' CHICKENPICKERS(1967)
Misc. Talkies
THREE OF A KIND(1944); TROUBLE CHASERS(1945)
Ralph Rosenbloom
COUNTRY MUSIC HOLIDAY(1958), ed; GROUP, THE(1966), ed
Richard Rosenbloom
CATCH MY SOUL(1974), p
Selma Rosenbloom
HOUSE OF SECRETS(1929), ed
Charles Rosenblum
LAST BLITZKRIEG, THE(1958)
Henry Rosenblum
GET CRAZY(1983), w

Irv Rosenblum
BOOK OF NUMBERS(1973), ed
Irving C. Rosenblum
...ALL THE MARBLES(1981), ed; FORCED VENGEANCE(1982), ed
Irving Rosenblum
CHOIRBOYS, THE(1977), ed; LOVE AND THE MIDNIGHT AUTO SUPPLY(1978), ed; FRISCO KID, THE(1979), ed
Leib Rosenblum
MORGAN'S MARAUDERS(1929), art d
Maxie Rosenblum
KING FOR A NIGHT(1933); BELLBOY, THE(1960)
Ralph Rosenblum
MURDER, INC.(1960), ed; PRETTY BOY FLOYD(1960), ed; MAD DOG COLL(1961), ed; JACKTOWN(1962), ed; LONG DAY'S JOURNEY INTO NIGHT(1962), ed; TWO TICKETS TO PARIS(1962), ed; WITHOUT EACH OTHER(1962), ed; GONE ARE THE DAYS(1963), ed; FAIL SAFE(1964), ed; PIE IN THE SKY(1964), ed; FOOL KILLER, THE(1965), ed; PAWNBROKER, THE(1965), ed; THOUSAND CLOWNS, A(1965), ed; PRODUCERS, THE(1967), ed; GREAT BIG THING, A(1968, U.S./Can.), ed; NIGHT THEY RAIDED MINSKY'S, THE(1968), ed; DON'T DRINK THE WATER(1969), ed; GOODBYE COLUMBUS(1969), ed; TAKE THE MONEY AND RUN(1969), ed; TRUMAN CAPOTE'S TRILOGY(1969), ed; SOMETHING FOR EVERYONE(1970), ed; BAD COMPANY(1972), ed; SLEEPER(1973), ed; LOVE AND DEATH(1975), ed; ANNIE HALL(1977), ed; INTERIORS(1978), ed
Aaron Rosenburg
MUTINY ON THE BOUNTY(1962), p
George Rosenburg
1984
BLIND DATE(1984), ed
Karen Rosenburg
LOOKING UP(1977), p
Lise Rosendahl
ERIC SOYA'S "17"(1967, Den.)
Joey Rosendo
PEACE KILLERS, THE(1971)
Rusty Rosene
KINGDOM OF THE SPIDERS(1977), set d; DARK, THE(1979), art d; DAY TIME ENDED, THE(1980, Span.), art d
Natalya Rosenel
Misc. Silents
BEAR'S WEDDING, THE(1926, USSR); MARRIAGE OF THE BEAR, THE(1928, USSR)
George Rosener
SPEAKEASY(1929), w; DOORWAY TO HELL(1930), w; GOT WHAT SHE WANTED(1930), w; SHE GOT WHAT SHE WANTED(1930), w; SINNER'S HOLIDAY(1930), w; ALIAS THE DOCTOR(1932); DEVIL IS DRIVING, THE(1932); DOCTOR X(1932); UNION DEPOT(1932); 70,000 WITNESSES(1932); CIRCUS QUEEN MURDER, THE(1933); GOODBYE LOVE(1934), w; CASE OF THE BLACK CAT, THE(1936); HOUSE OF SECRETS, THE(1937); NEW FACES OF 1937(1937); PARK AVENUE LOGGER(1937); SH! THE OCTOPUS(1937); SUPER SLEUTH(1937); BEASTS OF BERLIN(1939); CONFESSIONS OF A NAZI SPY(1939); FIFTH AVENUE GIRL(1939); FIGHTING MAD(1939), w; IN NAME ONLY(1939); ABE LINCOLN IN ILLINOIS(1940); CARSON CITY KID(1940); FLORIAN(1940); ARKANSAS JUDGE(1941); CITY OF MISSING GIRLS(1941), a, w; GREAT COMMANDMENT, THE(1941); I'LL SELL MY LIFE(1941), w; IN OLD CHEYENNE(1941)
Bob Rosenfarb
BOOGEYMAN II(1983)
Anne Rosenfeld
MONTY PYTHON'S THE MEANING OF LIFE(1983, Brit.)
H. Rosenfeld
GIVE HER A RING(1936, Brit.), w; HAPPY GO LOVELY(1951, Brit.), w
Hilary Rosenfeld
HEARTLAND(1980), cos; ONE-TRICK PONY(1980), cos
Hilary M. Rosenfeld
RICH KIDS(1979), cos
Hillary Rosenfeld
EYEWITNESS(1981), cos
Jane Rosenfeld
STUDENT TEACHERS, THE(1973)
Jerome Rosenfeld
SOME KIND OF A NUT(1969), spec eff
Moishe Rosenfeld
MIDSUMMER NIGHT'S SEX COMEDY, A(1982); SOPHIE'S CHOICE(1982)
Sydney Rosenfeld
Silents
SENATOR, THE(1915), w
Scott Rosenfelt
WALTZ ACROSS TEXAS(1982), p
Scott M. Rosenfelt
1984
ROADHOUSE 66(1984), p
James Rosenfield
WAVELENGTH(1983), p
Jason Rosenfield
COME BACK TO THE 5 & DIME, JIMMY DEAN, JIMMY DEAN(1982), ed
Lois Rosenfield
BANG THE DRUM SLOWLY(1973), p
Marla Rosenfield
ROCK 'N' ROLL HIGH SCHOOL(1979)
Maurice Rosenfield
BANG THE DRUM SLOWLY(1973), a, p
Max Rosenhauer
FOUR COMPANIONS, THE(1938, Ger.)
Paul Rosenhayn
CAREERS(1929), w
David Rosenkranz
RAMRODDER, THE(1969)
Gerrhard Rosenlocher
PINOCCHIO(1969, E. Ger.)

Howard Rosenman
SPARKLE(1976), p, w; RESURRECTION(1980), p
Leonard Rosenman
COBWEB, THE(1955), m; EAST OF EDEN(1955), m; REBEL WITHOUT A CAUSE(1955), m; BOMBERS B-52(1957), m; EDGE OF THE CITY(1957), m; YOUNG STRANGER, THE(1957), m; LAFAYETTE ESCADRILLE(1958), m; PORK CHOP HILL(1959), m; BRAMBLE BUSH, THE(1960), m; CROWDED SKY, THE(1960), m; PLUNDERERS, THE(1960), m, md; RISE AND FALL OF LEGS DIAMOND, THE(1960), m; CHAPMAN REPORT, THE(1962), m; CONVICTS FOUR(1962), m; HELL IS FOR HEROES(1962), m; OUTSIDER, THE(1962), m, md; COVENANT WITH DEATH, A(1966), m; FANTASTIC VOYAGE(1966), m; COUNTDOWN(1968), m; THIS SAVAGE LAND(1969), m; BENEATH THE PLANET OF THE APES(1970), m; MAN CALLED HORSE, A(1970), m; TODD KILLINGS, THE(1971), m; BATTLE FOR THE PLANET OF THE APES(1973), m; BARRY LYNDON(1975, Brit.), m; RACE WITH THE DEVIL(1975), m; BIRCH INTERVAL(1976), m; BOUND FOR GLORY(1976), md; CAR, THE(1977), m; 9/30/55(1977), m; ENEMY OF THE PEOPLE, AN(1978), m; PROMISES IN THE DARK(1979), m; PROPHECY(1979), m; HIDE IN PLAIN SIGHT(1980), m; MAKING LOVE(1982), m; CROSS CREEK(1983), m
1984
HEART OF THE STAG(1984, New Zealand), m
George Rosenor
SHERIFF OF TOMBSTONE(1941)
Barbara Rosenquest
MACHO CALLAHAN(1970), cos
Holger Rosenqvist
LOVING COUPLES(1966, Swed.), a, ch
Ira Rosenstein
WINTER KILLS(1979)
Jaik Rosenstein
SKIDOO(1968)
Allan Rosenthal
APPRENTICESHIP OF DUDDY KRAVITZ, THE(1974, Can.)
Boris Rosenthal
EAST SIDE SADIE(1929)
Carol Rosenthal
1984
STARMAN(1984)
Clara Rosenthal
PROJECTIONIST, THE(1970)
Dan Rosenthal
T.A.G.: THE ASSASSINATION GAME(1982), p
Everett Rosenthal
WHO KILLED TEDDY BEAR?(1965), p; FAT SPY(1966), p; MISSION MARS(1968), p
Harry Rosenthal
MERELY MARY ANN(1931); TAIL SPIN(1939); WIFE, HUSBAND AND FRIEND(1939); CHRISTMAS IN JULY(1940); GREAT McGINTY, THE(1940); JOHNNY APOLLO(1940); LADY EVE, THE(1941); SULLIVAN'S TRAVELS(1941); UNFINISHED BUSINESS(1941); PALM BEACH STORY, THE(1942); GREAT MOMENT, THE(1944); MIRACLE OF MORGAN'S CREEK, THE(1944); HORN BLOWS AT MIDNIGHT, THE(1945); MAD WEDNESDAY(1950), a, m
J. Rosenthal
FLYING FOOL, THE(1931, Brit.), ph
Jack Rosenthal
LOVERS, THE(1972, Brit.), w; LUCKY STAR, THE(1980, Can.), w; YENTL(1983), w
1984
KIPPERBANG(1984, Brit.), w
Joe Rosenthal
DERELICT, THE(1937, Brit.), p
Larry Rosenthal
WILD PARTY, THE(1975), m, md
Laurence Rosenthal
YELLOWNECK(1955), m; NAKED IN THE SUN(1957), md; DARK ODYSSEY(1961), m; RAISIN IN THE SUN, A(1961), m; MIRACLE WORKER, THE(1962), m; REQUIEM FOR A HEAVYWEIGHT(1962), m; BECKET(1964, Brit.), m; HOTEL PARADISO(1966, U.S./Brit.), m, md; COMEDIANS, THE(1967), m, md; THREE(1969, Brit.), m; GUNFIGHT, A(1971), m; MAN OF LA MANCHA(1972), md; ROOSTER COGBURN(1975), m; RETURN OF A MAN CALLED HORSE, THE(1976), m; ISLAND OF DR. MOREAU, THE(1977), m; BRASS TARGET(1978), m; WHO'LL STOP THE RAIN?(1978), m; MEETINGS WITH REMARKABLE MEN(1979, Brit.), m; METEOR(1979), m; CLASH OF THE TITANS(1981), m; EASY MONEY(1983), m; HEART LIKE A WHEEL(1983), m
Rachel Rosenthal
GAMES(1967)
Richard Rosenthal
BAD BOYS(1983), d
Richard L. Rosenthal
1984
JOHNNY DANGEROUSLY(1984)
Rick Rosenthal
HALLOWEEN II(1981), d
1984
AMERICAN DREAMER(1984), d
Robert Rosenthal
POM POM GIRLS, THE(1976), w; BEEN DOWN SO LONG IT LOOKS LIKE UP TO ME(1977), p; VAN, THE(1977), w
Robert J. Rosenthal
MALIBU BEACH(1978), d, w; ZAPPED!(1982), d, w
Francis Rosenwald
DEAD DON'T DREAM, THE(1948), w; PERILOUS WATERS(1948), w; STRIKE IT RICH(1948), w; FOLLOW ME QUIETLY(1949), w; RED STALLION IN THE ROCKIES(1949), w; UNDERCOVER GIRL(1950), w; LEECH WOMAN, THE(1960), w
Franz Rosenwald
WIFE OF MONTE CRISTO, THE(1946), w
Katherine Rosenwink
MAUSOLEUM(1983), w
Barney Rosenzweig
WHO FEARS THE DEVIL(1972), p

Herny Roser
Silents
KID, THE(1921)
J.R. Roser
Misc. Silents
CHILDREN OF THE WHIRLWIND(1925)
Rose Rosett
HIT PARADE OF 1951(1950)
Rosette
AVIATOR'S WIFE, THE(1981, Fr.); PAULINE AT THE BEACH(1983, Fr.)
Benjamin Rosette
TWO OR THREE THINGS I KNOW ABOUT HER(1970, Fr.)
Joseph D. Rosevich
MAYA(1982), a, w
John Rosewarne
ZULU DAWN(1980, Brit.), prod d
Grigori Roshal
Misc. Silents
SEEDS OF FREEDOM(1929, USSR), d; JEW AT WAR, A(1931, USSR); d
Princess Roshanara
CAESAR AND CLEOPATRA(1946, Brit.)
Charles Rosher
ATLANTIC(1929 Brit.), ph; KNOWING MEN(1930, Brit.), ph; PAID(1930), ph; PRICE OF THINGS, THE(1930, Brit.), ph; ROAD IS FINE, THE(1930, Fr.), ph; TWO WORLD(1930, Brit.), ph; WAR NURSE(1930), ph; BELOVED BACHELOR, THE(1931), ph; DANCE, FOOLS, DANCE(1931), ph; HUSBAND'S HOLIDAY(1931), ph; LAUGHING SINNERS(1931), ph; SILENCE(1931), ph; THIS MODERN AGE(1931), ph; VAGABOND QUEEN, THE(1931, Brit.), ph; ROCKABYE(1932), ph; TWO AGAINST THE WORLD(1932), ph; WHAT PRICE HOLLYWOOD?(1932), ph; AFTER TONIGHT(1933), ph; BED OF ROSES(1933), ph; OUR BETTERS(1933), ph; PAST OF MARY HOLMES, THE(1933), ph; SILVER CORD(1933), ph; AFFAIRS OF CELLINI, THE(1934), ph; FLAMING GOLD(1934), ph; MOULIN ROUGE(1934), ph; OUTCAST LADY(1934), ph; WHAT EVERY WOMAN KNOWS(1934), ph; AFTER OFFICE HOURS(1935), ph; BROADWAY MELODY OF 1936(1935), ph; CALL OF THE WILD(1935), ph; LITTLE LORD FAUNTLEROY(1936), ph; SMALL TOWN GIRL(1936), ph; HOLLYWOOD HOTEL(1937), ph; MEN ARE NOT GODS(1937, Brit.), ph; PERFECT SPECIMEN, THE(1937), ph; WOMAN I LOVE, THE(1937), ph; HARD TO GET(1938), ph; WHITE BANNERS(1938), ph; ESPIONAGE AGENT(1939), ph; HELL'S KITCHEN(1939), ph; OFF THE RECORD(1939), ph; YES, MY DARLING DAUGHTER(1939), ph; BROTHER RAT AND A BABY(1940), ph; CHILD IS BORN, A(1940), ph; MY LOVE CAME BACK(1940), ph; THREE CHEERS FOR THE IRISH(1940), ph; FOUR MOTHERS(1941), ph; MILLION DOLLAR BABY(1941), ph; ONE FOOT IN HEAVEN(1941), ph; MOKEY(1942), ph; PIERRE OF THE PLAINS(1942), ph; STAND BY FOR ACTION(1942), ph; ASSIGNMENT IN BRITTANY(1943), ph; SWING FEVER(1943), ph; KISMET(1944), ph; YOLANDA AND THE THIEF(1945), ph; YEARLING, THE(1946), ph; DARK DELUSION(1947), ph; FIESTA(1947), ph; SONG OF THE THIN MAN(1947), ph; ON AN ISLAND WITH YOU(1948), ph; EAST SIDE, WEST SIDE(1949), ph; NEPTUNE'S DAUGHTER(1949), ph; RED DANUBE, THE(1949), ph; ANNIE GET YOUR GUN(1950), ph; PAGAN LOVE SONG(1950), ph; SHOW BOAT(1951), ph; SCARAMOUCHE(1952), ph; KISS ME KATE(1953), ph; STORY OF THREE LOVES, THE(1953), ph; YOUNG BESS(1953), ph; ADAM AT 6 A.M.(1970), ph; PRETTY MAIDS ALL IN A ROW(1971), ph; TOGETHER BROTHERS(1974), ph; WEDDING, A(1978), ph; NIGHTWING(1979), ph; ONION FIELD, THE(1979), ph; HEARTBEEPS(1981), ph; INDEPENDENCE DAY(1983), ph
Silents
MYSTERY OF THE POISON POOL, THE(1914), ph; ANTON THE TERRIBLE(1916), ph; PLOW GIRL, THE(1916), ph; ON RECORD(1917), ph; SECRET GAME, THE(1917), ph; ONE MORE AMERICAN(1918), ph; DADDY LONG LEGS(1919), ph; HOODLUM THE(1919), ph; POLLYANNA(1920), ph; SUDS(1920), ph; LITTLE LORD FAUNTLEROY(1921), ph; LOVE LIGHT, THE(1921), ph; TESS OF THE STORM COUNTRY(1922), ph; ROSITA(1923), ph; LITTLE ANNIE ROONEY(1925), ph; SPARROWS(1926), ph; MY BEST GIRL(1927), ph; SUNRISE–A SONG OF TWO HUMANS(1927), ph; TEMPEST(1928), ph
Charles Rosher, Jr.
BABY MAKER, THE(1970), ph; HEX(1973), ph; SEMI-TOUGH(1977), ph; MOVIE MOVIE(1978), ph
Chuck Rosher
LATE SHOW, THE(1977), ph; THREE WOMEN(1977), ph
Dorothy Rosher
Silents
DADDY LONG LEGS(1919); POLLYANNA(1920); THOU ART THE MAN(1920)
Ariel Roshko
1984
BEST DEFENSE(1984), art d; LITTLE DRUMMER GIRL, THE(1984), art d
Francesco Rosi
ANITA GARIBALDI(1954, Ital.), d; MOMENT OF TRUTH, THE(1965, Ital./Span.), p, d, w; SALVATORE GIULIANO(1966, Ital.), d, w; MORE THAN A MIRACLE(1967, Ital./Fr.), d, w; RE: LUCKY LUCIANO(1974, Fr./Ital.), d, w; EBOLI(1980, Ital.), d, w
1984
BIZET'S CARMEN(1984, Fr./Ital.), d, w
Francisco Rosi
BELLISSIMA(1952, Ital.), w
Stelvio Rosi
LEOPARD, THE(1963, Ital.); CRAZY DESIRE(1964, Ital.); EIGHTEEN IN THE SUN(1964, Ital.); MYTH, THE(1965, Ital.); QUEENS, THE(1968, Ital./Fr.)
Sheyla Rosia
VENGEANCE(1968, Ital./Ger.)
Anna Rosiak
FIRST START(1953, Pol.)
Dzsoko Rosic
1984
BRADY'S ESCAPE(1984, U.S./Hung.)
Jim Rosica
HAIR(1979)
Agnes Rosier
LOULOU(1980, Fr.)
Cathy Rosier
GODSON, THE(1972, Ital./Fr.)

Mel Rosier
INDEPENDENCE DAY(1976)
James Rosin
1984
ADVENTURES OF BUCKAROO BANZAI: ACROSS THE 8TH DIMENSION, THE(1984)
Mark Rosin
GREAT TEXAS DYNAMITE CHASE, THE(1976), w
Lilyan Rosine
Misc. Silents
HELL MORGAN'S GIRL(1917)
Bodil Rosing
BROADWAY BABIES(1929); ALL QUIET ON THE WESTERN FRONT(1930); BISHOP MURDER CASE, THE(1930); HELLO SISTER(1930); LADY'S MORALS, A(1930); OH, FOR A MAN!(1930); PART TIME WIFE(1930); SURRENDER(1931); THREE WHO LOVED(1931); DOWNSTAIRS(1932); GRAND HOTEL(1932); MATCH KING, THE(1932); CRIME OF THE CENTURY, THE(1933); EX-LADY(1933); REUNION IN VIENNA(1933); CRIMSON ROMANCE(1934); LITTLE MAN, WHAT NOW?(1934); MANDALAY(1934); SUCH WOMEN ARE DANGEROUS(1934); FOUR HOURS TO KILL(1935); LET 'EM HAVE IT(1935); NIGHT AT THE RITZ, A(1935); ROBERTA(1935); THUNDER IN THE NIGHT(1935); HEARTS IN BONDAGE(1936); CONQUEST(1937); MICHAEL O'HALLORAN(1937); FIRST 100 YEARS, THE(1938); YOU CAN'T TAKE IT WITH YOU(1938); BEASTS OF BERLIN(1939); CONFESSIONS OF A NAZI SPY(1939); HOTEL IMPERIAL(1939); STAR MAKER, THE(1939); MORTAL STORM, THE(1940); MARRY THE BOSS' DAUGHTER(1941)
Silents
IT MUST BE LOVE(1926); RETURN OF PETER GRIMM, THE(1926); STAGE MADNESS(1927); SUNRISE–A SONG OF TWO HUMANS(1927); LADIES OF THE MOB(1928); LAW OF THE RANGE, THE(1928); ETERNAL LOVE(1929); KING OF THE RODEO(1929); WHY BE GOOD?(1929)
Misc. Silents
BLONDES BY CHOICE(1927); BIG NOISE, THE(1928); FLEET'S IN, THE(1928); WHEEL OF CHANCE(1928)
Bodil Ann Rosing
LIBELED LADY(1936); ROSE BOWL(1936); MAN AT LARGE(1941); NO GREATER SIN(1941); REACHING FOR THE SUN(1941)
Val Rosing
FEATHER YOUR NEST(1937, Brit.)
Vladimir Rosing
INTERRUPTED MELODY(1955), md
Claudio Rosini
ANOTHER TIME, ANOTHER PLACE(1983, Brit.)
1984
ANOTHER TIME, ANOTHER PLACE(1984, Brit.)
Edith Rosita
HER MAN(1930)
Eva Rosita
RIO RITA(1929)
Angelo Rosito
BARON OF ARIZONA, THE(1950)
Angelo S. Rosito
POCKETFUL OF MIRACLES(1961)
"Little Angelo" Rositto
MR. WONG IN CHINATOWN(1939)
Edward M. Roskam
Silents
ORDEAL, THE(1914), w
Misc. Silents
BANKER'S DAUGHTER, THE(1914), d
Edwin Roskam
Silents
SPRINGTIME(1915), d
Ilse Ruth Roskam
RIVER CHANGES, THE(1956)
Vicky Roskilly
OPERATION GANYMED(1977, Ger.)
Rosko
FLAME(1975, Brit.)
Harry Roskolenko
Misc. Talkies
STRONG MEDICINE(1981)
Adrian Rosley
FLYING DOWN TO RIO(1933); GREAT FLIRTATION, THE(1934); HANDY ANDY(1934); MISS FANE'S BABY IS STOLEN(1934); NOTORIOUS SOPHIE LANG, THE(1934); STAMBOUL QUEST(1934); VIVA VILLA!(1934); CHAMPAGNE FOR BREAKFAST(1935); DEATH FLIES EAST(1935); ENTER MADAME(1935); FRONT PAGE WOMAN(1935); GIRL FROM TENTH AVENUE, THE(1935); I LIVE MY LIFE(1935); METROPOLITAN(1935); ROBERTA(1935); STRANDED(1935); GAY DESPERADO, THE(1936); MAGNIFICENT BRUTE, THE(1936); ROSE MARIE(1936); SING ME A LOVE SONG(1936); SINS OF MAN(1936); SMALL TOWN GIRL(1936); WALKING DEAD, THE(1936); KING AND THE CHORUS GIRL, THE(1937); READY, WILLING AND ABLE(1937); STAR IS BORN, A(1937)
Adrien Rosley
GIRL WITHOUT A ROOM(1933)
Wendy-Sue Rosloff
NEW YEAR'S EVIL(1980)
Mark Rosman
HOUSE ON SORORITY ROW, THE(1983), p, w
Milton Rosmer
HIGH TREASON(1929, Brit.); "W" PLAN, THE(1931, Brit.); DREYFUS CASE, THE(1931, Brit.), d; MANY WATERS(1931, Brit.), d; P.C. JOSSER(1931, Brit.), d; PERFECT LADY, THE(1931, Brit.), p&d; AFTER THE BALL(1932, Brit.), d; CHANNEL CROSSING(1934, Brit.), d; GRAND PRIX(1934, Brit.); SECRET OF THE LOCH, THE(1934, Brit.), d; WHAT HAPPENED TO HARKNESS(1934, Brit.), d; PHANTOM LIGHT, THE(1935, Brit.); EVERYTHING IS THUNDER(1936, Brit.), d; MISTER HOBO(1936, Brit.); MURDER IN THE OLD RED BARN(1936, Brit.), d; SILENT BARRIERS(1937, Brit.), d, w; EMIL(1938, Brit.); SOUTH RIDING(1938, Brit.); CHALLENGE, THE(1939, Brit.), d, w; GOODBYE MR. CHIPS(1939, Brit.); LET'S BE FAMOUS(1939, Brit.); LION HAS WINGS, THE(1940, Brit.); RETURN TO YESTERDAY(1940, Brit.); STARS LOOK DOWN, THE(1940, Brit.); ATLANTIC FERRY(1941,

Brit.); END OF THE RIVER, THE(1947, Brit.); FAME IS THE SPUR(1947, Brit.); FRIEDA(1947, Brit.); MONKEY'S PAW, THE(1948, Brit.); HOUR OF GLORY(1949, Brit.); JOHN WESLEY(1954, Brit.); WHO KILLED VAN LOON?(1984, Brit.)
Silents
GREATER NEED, THE(1916, Brit.); STILL WATERS RUN DEEP(1916, Brit.); ODDS AGAINST HER, THE(1919, Brit.); AMAZING PARTNERSHIP, THE(1921, Brit.); DIAMOND NECKLACE, THE(1921, Brit.); GENERAL JOHN REGAN(1921, Brit.); PASSIONATE FRIENDS, THE(1922, Brit.); POINTING FINGER, THE(1922, Brit.); GAMBLE WITH HEARTS, A(1923, Brit.); SHADOW OF EGYPT, THE(1924, Brit.)
Misc. Silents
MYSTERY OF A HANSOM CAB, THE(1915, Brit.); CYNTHIA IN THE WILDERNESS(1916, Brit.); I BELIEVE(1916, Brit.); LADY WINDERMERE'S FAN(1916, Brit.); WHOSO IS WITHOUT SIN(1916, Brit.); CHINESE PUZZLE, THE(1919, Brit.); COLONEL NEWCOME THE PERFECT GENTLEMAN(1920, Brit.); GOLDEN WEB, THE(1920, Brit.); TORN SAILS(1920, Brit.); TWELVE POUND LOOK, THE(1920, Brit.); WITH ALL HER HEART(1920, Brit.); WUTHERING HEIGHTS(1920, Brit.); BELPHEGOR THE MOUNTEBANK(1921, Brit.); ROMANCE OF WASTDALE, A(1921, Brit.); WHY MEN FORGET(1921, Brit.); WILL, THE(1921, Brit.); WOMAN OF NO IMPORTANCE, A(1921, Brit.); JAWS OF HELL(1928, Brit.), d

Antonio Rosmino
THIEF OF BAGHDAD, THE(1961, Ital./Fr.)
Ernesta Rosmino
STRANGE DECEPTION(1953, Ital.)
G.P. Rosmino
HERCULES(1959, Ital.)
Giampaolo Rosmino
GOLDEN ARROW, THE(1964, Ital.)
Judith Rosner
LOOKING FOR MR. GOODBAR(1977), w
Rudolf Rosner
SECRET WAYS, THE(1961)
Sheldon Rosner
VILLAIN, THE(1979)
Willy Rosner
LOLA MONTES(1955, Fr./Ger.); DIE GANS VON SEDAN(1962, Fr./Ger.)
Jacques Rosny
CATHERINE & CO.(1976, Fr.); TENANT, THE(1976, Fr.)
J.H. Rosny, Sr.
QUEST FOR FIRE(1982, Fr./Can.), w
Bianca Rosoff
MAIDSTONE(1970)
Charlie Rosoff
ROSE OF THE RIO GRANDE(1938), m
Peter Rosoff
BEYOND THE LAW(1968); MAIDSTONE(1970)
Frank Rosolino
I WANT TO LIVE!(1958)
Manuel Roson
NO EXIT(1962, U.S./Arg.)
Betty Rosotti
1984
BROADWAY DANNY ROSE(1984)
William Rospigliosi
RING AROUND THE CLOCK(1953, Ital.), w
Rom Rosqui
HEROES(1977)
Tom Rosqui
DAYS OF WINE AND ROSES(1962); CRAZY QUILT, THE(1966); MADIGAN(1968); THOMAS CROWN AFFAIR, THE(1968); PURSUIT OF HAPPINESS, THE(1971); GODFATHER, THE, PART II(1974); GREAT TEXAS DYNAMITE CHASE, THE(1976); MAC ARTHUR(1977)
A. Ross
NIGHT RIDE(1930), ed
Adam Ross
SEDUCTION OF JOE TYNAN, THE(1979)
Adina Ross
VAN, THE(1977)
Adrian Ross
SOUTHERN MAID, A(1933, Brit.), cos
Alec Ross
DICK BARTON–SPECIAL AGENT(1948, Brit.); TRAITOR'S GATE(1966, Brit./Ger.)
Alma Ross
DAUGHTER OF SHANGHAI(1937); HOLD'EM NAVY!(1937); TUTTLES OF TAHITI(1942)
Angelo Ross
WHISTLE AT EATON FALLS(1951), ed; WALK EAST ON BEACON(1952), ed; DIARY OF A BACHELOR(1964), ed; WHO KILLED TEDDY BEAR?(1965), ed; CROSS AND THE SWITCHBLADE, THE(1970), ed; I NEVER SANG FOR MY FATHER(1970), ed; SOME OF MY BEST FRIENDS ARE...(1971), ed; WHO KILLED MARY WHAT'S-ER NAME?(1971), ed; SMOKEY AND THE BANDIT(1977), ed; JAGUAR LIVES(1979), ed
Angie Ross
MISTER ROCK AND ROLL(1957), ed; SPRING BREAK(1983), ed
Ann Ross
OKLAHOMA JIM(1931); TEXAS PIONEERS(1932)
Annabel Ross
VELVET TOUCH, THE(1948), w; TAHITIAN, THE(1956), w
Annabella Ross
DRUMS O' VOODOO(1934)
Anne Ross
NEW KIND OF LOVE, A(1963)
Annie Ross
STRAIGHT ON TILL MORNING(1974, Brit.); ALFIE DARLING(1975, Brit.); YANKS(1979); FUNNY MONEY(1983, Brit.); SUPERMAN III(1983)
Anthony Ross
BOOMERANG(1947); KISS OF DEATH(1947); WINDOW, THE(1949); BETWEEN MIDNIGHT AND DAWN(1950); FLYING MISSILE(1950); GUNFIGHTER, THE(1950); PERFECT STRANGERS(1950); SKIPPER SURPRISED HIS WIFE, THE(1950); VICIOUS YEARS, THE(1950); ON DANGEROUS GROUND(1951); GIRLS IN THE NIGHT(1953); TAXI(1953); COUNTRY GIRL, THE(1954); ROGUE COP(1954); MIN-

NESOTA CLAY(1966, Ital./Fr./Span.)
Archie Ross
SPLINTERS(1929, Brit.), w
Arnie Ross
ABSENCE OF MALICE(1981); PIRANHA II: THE SPAWNING(1981, Neth.)
Arnold Ross
1984
SCREAM FOR HELP(1984), ed
Arthur Ross
STAR SPANGLED RHYTHM(1942), w; VACATION IN RENO(1946), w; RUSTY LEADS THE WAY(1948), w; OKINAWA(1952), w; STAND AT APACHE RIVER, THE(1953), w; CREATURE FROM THE BLACK LAGOON(1954), w; CREATURE WALKS AMONG US, THE(1956), w; THIRTY FOOT BRIDE OF CANDY ROCK, THE(1959), w; THREE WORLDS OF GULLIVER, THE(1960, Brit.), w; GREAT RACE, THE(1965), w; BRUBAKER(1980), w
Arthur A. Ross
SAN QUENTIN(1946), w; KAZAN(1949), w; PORT OF NEW YORK(1949), w; REVENUE AGENT(1950), w
Barney Ross
REQUIEM FOR A HEAVYWEIGHT(1962)
Benny Ross
BELLBOY, THE(1960)
Beth Ross
OPERATION DIAMOND(1948, Brit.); OLD MOTHER RILEY, HEADMISTRESS(1950, Brit.); WHO KILLED VAN LOON?(1984, Brit.)
Betsy King Ross
Misc. Talkies
SMOKE LIGHTNING(1933)
Betty Ross
MASSACRE HILL(1949, Brit.)
Beverly Ross
THREE WOMEN(1977); WEDDING, A(1978); BROKEN ENGLISH(1981)
Bill Ross
ROLLER BOOGIE(1979); JONI(1980), art d
Bob Ross
THREE ON A COUCH(1966), w
Bucky Ross
DEMON SEED(1977), cos
Buddy Ross
Silents
ACCORDING TO HOYLE(1922)
Burt Ross
Silents
SUNSET DERBY, THE(1927)
Catherine Ross
HARLOW(1965)
Charles Ross
Misc. Talkies
MAD BUTCHER, THE(1972)
Charles J. Ross
Silents
HOW MOLLY MADE GOOD(1915); SENATOR, THE(1915); BY WHOSE HAND?(1916)
Chelcie Ross
ON THE RIGHT TRACK(1981)
Chelsea Ross
KEEP MY GRAVE OPEN(1980)
Chris Ross
VIVA MAX!(1969)
Christopher Ross
HOW SWEET IT IS(1968)
Churchill Ross
COLLEGE LOVE(1929); UNDERTOW(1930)
Silents
BLAZING DAYS(1927)
Misc. Silents
FOURFLUSHER, THE(1928)
Clark Ross
SPACE MASTER X-7(1958), cos
Claudette Ross
CRY OF THE CITY(1948)
Corinne Ross
MY FAIR LADY(1964)
Country Al Ross
PSYCHOPATH, THE(1973), m
Danny Ross
LOVE MATCH, THE(1955, Brit.); RAMSBOTTOM RIDES AGAIN(1956, Brit.); FRIENDS AND NEIGHBORS(1963, Brit.)
David Ross
VICE SQUAD(1982)
Dennis Ross
MODEL AND THE MARRIAGE BROKER, THE(1951); SHADOW IN THE SKY(1951); RETURN OF THE TEXAN(1952); SINGIN' IN THE RAIN(1952); LADY WANTS MINK, THE(1953); LONG, LONG TRAILER, THE(1954)
Denny Ross
REBEL ANGEL(1962), a, w
Diana Ross
WIZ, THE(1978); LADY SINGS THE BLUES(1972); MAHOGANY(1975), a, cos
Dick Ross
GOOD SAM(1948); SOULS IN CONFLICT(1955, Brit.), p, d&w; WIRETAPPERS(1956), d; PERSUADER, THE(1957), p&d, w; RESTLESS ONES, THE(1965), p&d; CROSS AND THE SWITCHBLADE, THE(1970), p; LATE LIZ, THE(1971), p&d
Don Ross
WALK THE DARK STREET(1956); ABSENT-MINDED PROFESSOR, THE(1961); WHATEVER HAPPENED TO BABY JANE?(1962)
Dudley Ross
BOUNTY KILLER, THE(1965)
Earl Ross
CAVALRY(1936); STORMY TRAILS(1936)

Earle Ross
RIDERS OF THE WHISTLING SKULL(1937); COURAGEOUS DR. CHRISTIAN, THE(1940)

Ed Ross
PASSION HOLIDAY(1963); MAFIA GIRLS, THE(1969), d; HOW DO I LOVE THEE?(1970)

Eddy Ross
JUDGE AND THE ASSASSIN, THE(1979, Fr.)

Edna Ross
Silents
STARDUST(1921)

Edward Ross [Rossano Brazzi]
PSYCHOUT FOR MURDER(1971, Arg./Ital.), d, w

Eleanor Ross
MIDNIGHT MAN, THE(1974)

Elizabeth Ross
GLASS HOUSES(1972); MAN, THE(1972)

Ellen Ross
UNDERCURRENT(1946); LADY IN THE LAKE(1947); PIRATE, THE(1948)

Ethel Douglas Ross
Silents
AUTOCRAT, THE(1919, Brit.); YE BANKS AND BRAES(1919, Brit.)
Misc. Silents
MASTER OF GRAY, THE(1918, Brit.)

Frances Ross
Silents
GOLD DIGGERS, THE(1923)
Misc. Silents
LIGHTING RIDER, THE(1924)

Frank Ross
SATURDAY NIGHT KID, THE(1929); YOUNG EAGLES(1930); DEVIL AND MISS JONES, THE(1941), p; LADY TAKES A CHANCE, A(1943), p; MORE THE MERRIER, THE(1943), w; FLAME AND THE ARROW, THE(1950), p; LADY SAYS NO, THE(1951), p, d; ROBE, THE(1953), p; DEMETRIUS AND THE GLADIATORS(1954), p; RAINS OF RANCHIPUR, THE(1955), p; KINGS GO FORTH(1958), p; ONE MAN'S WAY(1964), p; MISTER MOSES(1965), p; WALK, DON'T RUN(1966), w; WHERE IT'S AT(1969), p; MAURIE(1973), p

Fred Ross
AMERICAN GRAFFITI(1973)

Frederick Ross
HELP YOURSELF(1932, Brit.); LORD OF THE MANOR(1933, Brit.); MAROONED(1933, Brit.)

Frederic D. Ross
DIRTY HARRY(1971)

Gary Ross
1984
CRACKERS(1984)

Gaylen Ross
DAWN OF THE DEAD(1979); CREEPSHOW(1982); MADMAN(1982)

Gene Ross
CORN IS GREEN, THE(1945); ALASKA PATROL(1949); BULLET FOR PRETTY BOY, A(1970); DON'T LOOK IN THE BASEMENT(1973); ENCOUNTER WITH THE UNKNOWN(1973); SCUM OF THE EARTH(1976), a, w; KEEP MY GRAVE OPEN(1980); PENNIES FROM HEAVEN(1981); PARTNERS(1982); SECOND THOUGHTS(1983)
1984
ANGEL(1984); CLOAK AND DAGGER(1984); FRIDAY THE 13TH-THE FINAL CHAPTER(1984)
Misc. Talkies
DON'T OPEN THE DOOR(1974)

George Ross
BIG FIX, THE(1947), w; RUSTLERS(1949); SPRINGFIELD RIFLE(1952); DRUM BEAT(1954), tech adv; ILLEGAL(1955); LAST WAGON, THE(1956); HELL CANYON OUTLAWS(1957); DAY OF THE OUTLAW(1959); GLORY GUYS, THE(1965); CHANGES(1969), spec eff; EL CONDOR(1970)
Silents
BULLIN' THE BULLSHEVIKI(1919)

George "Smokey" Ross
EDGE OF ETERNITY(1959)

Gordon Ross
STUNT MAN, THE(1980)

Govind Raja Ross
FLAME OVER INDIA(1960, Brit.)

Guy Ross
IF ...(1968, Brit.)

H. Milton Ross
Silents
ALIAS THE NIGHT WIND(1923)

Hal Ross
JAZZ SINGER, THE(1953)

Harold Ross
NEW YORK, NEW YORK(1977)

Harriet Ross
Silents
EMBARRASSMENT OF RICHES, THE(1918); DAWN OF THE EAST(1921)

Harry Ross
VACATION FROM MARRIAGE(1945, Brit.); SPOOK BUSTERS(1946), makeup; ESTHER WATERS(1948, Brit.); GOOD TIME GIRL(1950, Brit.); STRICTLY CONFIDENTIAL(1959, Brit.); WOMAN EATER, THE(1959, Brit.); FIREBRAND, THE(1962), makeup; PLAYGIRLS AND THE BELLBOY, THE(1962,Ger.), p

Hector Ross
BONNIE PRINCE CHARLIE(1948, Brit.); NIGHT BEAT(1948, Brit.); HAPPY GO LOVELY(1951, Brit.); I'M A STRANGER(1952, Brit.); DEADLY NIGHTSHADE(1953, Brit.); STEEL KEY, THE(1953, Brit.); BEN HUR(1959); FUR COLLAR, THE(1962, Brit.); RING OF SPIES(1964, Brit.)

Helen Ross
JULIUS CAESAR(1952)

Herbert Ross
GABLES MYSTERY, THE(1931, Brit.); KEEPERS OF YOUTH(1931, Brit.); SKIN GAME, THE(1931, Brit.); WONDERFUL TO BE YOUNG!(1962, Brit.), ch; SUMMER HOLIDAY(1963, Brit.), ch; INSIDE DAISY CLOVER(1965), ch; DOCTOR DOLITTLE(1967), ch; FUNNY GIRL(1968), ch; GOODBYE MR. CHIPS(1969, U.S./Brit.), d; OWL AND THE PUSSYCAT, THE(1970), d; T.R. BASKIN(1971), d; PLAY IT AGAIN, SAM(1972), d; LAST OF SHEILA, THE(1973), p&d; FUNNY LADY(1975), d; SUNSHINE BOYS, THE(1975), d; GOODBYE GIRL, THE(1977), d; SEVEN-PER-CENT SOLUTION, THE(1977, Brit.), p&d; TURNING POINT, THE(1977), p; CALIFORNIA SUITE(1978), d; NIJINSKY(1980, Brit.), d; PENNIES FROM HEAVEN(1981), p, d; I OUGHT TO BE IN PICTURES(1982), p, d; MAX DUGAN RETURNS(1983), p, d
1984
FOOTLOOSE(1984), d; PROTOCOL(1984), d

Howard Ross
LADY HAMILTON(1969, Ger./Ital./Fr.); MAN CALLED NOON, THE(1973, Brit.); THOSE DIRTY DOGS(1974, U.S./Ital./Span.); STATELINE MOTEL(1976, Ital.); LEGEND OF THE WOLF WOMAN, THE(1977, Span.)

Howard Ross [Renato Rossini]
MAGNIFICENT BANDITS, THE(1969, Ital./Span.); DIRTY HEROES(1971, Ital./Fr./Ger.)

Irene Ross
MARRIED TOO YOUNG(1962)

Irv Ross
FIVE THE HARD WAY(1969)

Irva Ross
Misc. Silents
HUMAN ORCHID, THE(1916)

Ishbel Ross
THREE ON A HONEYMOON(1934), w

J. MacLaren Ross
ELECTRONIC MONSTER. THE(1960, Brit.), w

J. McLaren Ross
FOUR DAYS(1951, Brit.), w; KEY MAN, THE(1957, Brit.), w; FEMALE FIENDS(1958, Brit.), w

J. Milton Ross
Misc. Silents
EXQUISIT THIEF, THE(1919)

Jack Ross
THEY WERE EXPENDABLE(1945)

James B. Ross
Silents
CELEBRATED CASE, A(1914)
Misc. Silents
SCHOOL FOR SCANDAL, THE(1914); WOLFE OR THE CONQUEST OF QUEBEC(1914)

Jamie Ross
HOW THE WEST WAS WON(1962)

Jane Ross
WILD IS MY LOVE(1963); LIGHT FANTASTIC(1964)

Janet Ross
Silents
KING'S DAUGHTER, THE(1916, Brit.); PRINCESS OF HAPPY CHANCE, THE(1916, Brit.)
Misc. Silents
WHEN KNIGHTS WERE BOLD(1916, Brit.)

Jason Ross
MAN WHO LOVED WOMEN, THE(1983)

Jerry Ross
APOCALYPSE NOW(1979)

Jillian Ross
WORLD ACCORDING TO GARP, The(1982)

Jim Ross
FIVE BOLD WOMEN(1960), a, p

Joe Ross
KINGDOM OF THE SPIDERS(1977); PETE'S DRAGON(1977); CHEAP DETECTIVE, THE(1978); PENNIES FROM HEAVEN(1981)

Joe E. Ross
HEAR ME GOOD(1957); MARACAIBO(1958); BELLBOY, THE(1960); ALL HANDS ON DECK(1961); TONY ROME(1967); LOVE BUG, THE(1968); MARYJANE(1968); JUDY'S LITTLE NO-NO(1969); BOATNIKS, THE(1970); NAKED ZOO, THE(1970); FRASIER, THE SENSUOUS LION(1973); HOW TO SEDUCE A WOMAN(1974); SLUMBER PARTY '57(1977); SKATETOWN, U.S.A.(1979)
Misc. Talkies
REVENGE IS MY DESTINY(1971)

Joey Ross
Misc. Talkies
LEGEND OF THE JUGGLER(1978)

John Ross
SEVENTY DEADLY PILLS(1964, Brit.)

Johnny Ross
JOE MACBETH(1955)

Judith Ross
RICH KIDS(1979), w

Judy Ross
THIS ENGLAND(1941, Brit.)

Julie Ross
YOUNG CASSIDY(1965, U.S./Brit.)

Justin Ross
FAN, THE(1981)

Katharine Ross
SHENANDOAH(1965); MISTER BUDDWING(1966); SINGING NUN, THE(1966); GAMES(1967); GRADUATE, THE(1967); BUTCH CASSIDY AND THE SUNDANCE KID(1969); TELL THEM WILLIE BOY IS HERE(1969); FOOLS(1970); GET TO KNOW YOUR RABBIT(1972); THEY ONLY KILL THEIR MASTERS(1972); STEPFORD WIVES, THE(1975); VOYAGE OF THE DAMNED(1976, Brit.); SWARM, THE(1978); LEGACY, THE(1979, Brit.); FINAL COUNTDOWN, THE(1980); WRONG IS RIGHT(1982)

Katherine Ross
HELLFIGHTERS(1968); BETSY, THE(1978)
1984
DADDY'S DEADLY DARLING(1984)
Kay Ross
GIRL, THE BODY, AND THE PILL, THE(1967)
Kelly Ross
HURRY SUNDOWN(1967); HELL'S CHOSEN FEW(1968); ICE HOUSE, THE(1969)
Kenneth Ross
BROTHER SUN, SISTER MOON(1973, Brit./Ital.), w; DAY OF THE JACKAL, THE(1973, Brit./Fr.), w; ODESSA FILE, THE(1974, Brit./Ger.), w; BLACK SUNDAY(1977), w; BREAKER MORANT(1980, Aus.), w
Kimberly Ross
1984
LAST STARFIGHTER, THE(1984)
Lanny Ross
COLLEGE RHYTHM(1934); MELODY IN SPRING(1934); LADY OBJECTS, THE(1938); GULLIVER'S TRAVELS(1939); STAGE DOOR CANTEEN(1943); BANJO(1947)
Larry Ross
FUNHOUSE, THE(1981)
Len Ross
NORTH AVENUE IRREGULARS, THE(1979)
Leonard Q. Ross
THEY GOT ME COVERED(1943), w
Leonard Ross
ALL THROUGH THE NIGHT(1942), w
1984
CHATTANOOGA CHOO CHOO(1984)
Lillian Ross
MR. DEEDS GOES TO TOWN(1936); ZAZA(1939)
Lillian Bos Ross
ZANDY'S BRIDE(1974), w
Lisa Beth Ross
1984
FLAMINGO KID, THE(1984)
Liz Ross
PAPER MOON(1973)
Lynda Ross
HONEYMOON HOTEL(1946, Brit.)
Lynn Ross
LADIES MAN, THE(1961)
Misc. Talkies
INTIMATE PLAYMATES, THE(1976)
Lynne Ross
SPACED OUT(1981, Brit.)
Manning Ross
COURT-MARTIAL OF BILLY MITCHELL, THE(1955); TIME LIMIT(1957)
Marion Ross
FOREVER FEMALE(1953); GLENN MILLER STORY, THE(1953); PUSHOVER(1954); SABRINA(1954); SECRET OF THE INCAS(1954); LUST FOR LIFE(1956); PROUD AND THE PROFANE, THE(1956); GOD IS MY PARTNER(1957); LIZZIE(1957); TEACHER'S PET(1958); OPERATION PETTICOAT(1959); SOME CAME RUNNING(1959); BLUEPRINT FOR ROBBERY(1961); COLOSSUS: THE FORBIN PROJECT(1969); HONKY(1971); GRAND THEFT AUTO(1977)
Marion Ross [Marion Roland]
Silents
OVER THE HILL TO THE POORHOUSE(1920)
Mark Ross
UP THE JUNCTION(1968, Brit.)
Martin Ross
DANCING YEARS, THE(1950, Brit.)
Mary Ross
Misc. Silents
SCHOOL FOR SCANDAL, THE(1914)
Mearl Ross
PURSUIT OF D.B. COOPER, THE(1981)
Merrie Lynn Ross
BOBBIE JO AND THE OUTLAW(1976); CLASS OF 1984(1982, Can.)
Misc. Talkies
LUCIFER COMPLEX, THE(1978)
Michael Ross
MISS GRANT TAKES RICHMOND(1949); STRATTON STORY, THE(1949); BLONDE DYNAMITE(1950); DESERT HAWK, THE(1950); D.O.A.(1950); WABASH AVENUE(1950); ELOPEMENT(1951); GHOST CHASERS(1951); GOLDEN GIRL(1951); LET'S MAKE IT LEGAL(1951); LOVE NEST(1951); MY FAVORITE SPY(1951); WELL, THE(1951); AGAINST ALL FLAGS(1952); DON'T BOTHER TO KNOCK(1952); LOST IN ALASKA(1952); MARA MARU(1952); MY WIFE'S BEST FRIEND(1952); CLIPPED WINGS(1953); FRANCIS COVERS THE BIG TOWN(1953); GIRL NEXT DOOR, THE(1953); GIRLS OF PLEASURE ISLAND, THE(1953); THOSE REDHEADS FROM SEATTLE(1953); BOWERY TO BAGDAD(1955); JAIL BUSTERS(1955); NIGHT FREIGHT(1955); SON OF SINBAD(1955); UNTAMED(1955); FIGHTING TROUBLE(1956); LIEUTENANT WORE SKIRTS, THE(1956); WILD PARTY, THE(1956); KISS THEM FOR ME(1957); PATSY, THE(1964); FAMILY JEWELS, THE(1965); ONLY WHEN I LAUGH(1981)
Michael Ronald Ross
DEATH GAME(1977), w
Michel Ross
PEGGY(1950)
Mike Ross
CRAZY OVER HORSES(1951); I WAS A COMMUNIST FOR THE F.B.I.(1951); BIG HEAT, THE(1953); TANGIER INCIDENT(1953); TARZAN AND THE SHE-DEVIL(1953); CAPTAIN KIDD AND THE SLAVE GIRL(1954); RETURN OF JACK SLADE, THE(1955); HOLLYWOOD OR BUST(1956); BUSTER KEATON STORY, THE(1957); DELICATE DELINQUENT, THE(1957); SHORT CUT TO HELL(1957); ATTACK OF THE 50 FOOT WOMAN(1958); ERRAND BOY, THE(1961); IT'S ONLY MONEY(1962); WHO'S MINDING THE STORE?(1963); DISORDERLY ORDERLY, THE(1964); HOUSE IS NOT A HOME, A(1964); FLEDGLINGS(1965, Brit)

Milton Ross
FEATHERED SERPENT, THE(1948); STREET CORNER(1948)
Silents
PAINTED SOUL, THE(1915); PATRIOT, THE(1916); TRUTHFUL TULLIVER(1917); FALSE FACES(1919); PENALTY, THE(1920); KILLER, THE(1921); ALIAS JULIUS CAESAR(1922); GAY AND DEVILISH(1922); SALOMY JANE(1923); VIRGINIAN, THE(1923); DOWN BY THE RIO GRANDE(1924); HEADS UP(1925)
Misc. Silents
GREEN SWAMP, THE(1916); NARROW TRAIL, THE(1917); TIGER MAN, THE(1918); FORTUNE'S MASK(1922); GIRL FROM ROCKY POINT, THE(1922); BREED OF THE BORDER, THE(1924); CALL OF THE MATE(1924); COWBOY AND THE FLAPPER, THE(1924); MAN FROM GOD'S COUNTRY(1924); THAT WILD WEST(1924); O.U. WEST(1925)
Mina Ross
Silents
LES MISERABLES(1918)
Monty Ross
Misc. Talkies
JOE'S BED-STUY BARBERSHOP: WE CUT HEADS(1983)
Myrna Ross
OCEAN'S ELEVEN(1960); HOW TO STUFF A WILD BIKINI(1965); GHOST IN THE INVISIBLE BIKINI(1966); SWINGER, THE(1966); HOW SWEET IT IS(1968); 2000 YEARS LATER(1969)
Nat Ross
COLLEGE LOVE(1929), d; OUTLAW DEPUTY, THE(1935), p; MAN FROM GUN TOWN, THE(1936), p; DARBY AND JOAN(1937, Brit.), p; REVERSE BE MY LOT, THE(1938, Brit.), p
Silents
GALLOPING KID, THE(1922), d; RIDIN' WILD(1922), d; PURE GRIT(1923), d; APRIL FOOL(1926), d; STRIVING FOR FORTUNE(1926), d; STOP THAT MAN(1928), d
Misc. Silents
GHOST PATROL, THE(1923), d; SIX-FIFTY, THE(1923), d; SLANDERERS, THE(1924), d; TRANSCONTINENTAL LIMITED(1926), d; TWO CAN PLAY(1926), d
Nina Ross
UNDERCURRENT(1946); LADY IN THE LAKE(1947); ON AN ISLAND WITH YOU(1948); THAT FORSYTE WOMAN(1949)
Oriel Ross
FIRST MRS. FRASER, THE(1932, Brit.); PRICE OF A SONG, THE(1935, Brit.); PIMPERNEL SMITH(1942, Brit.)
Oriol Ross
SELF-MADE LADY(1932, Brit.)
Patti Ross
THIEF(1981)
Paul Ross
BEYOND EVIL(1980), w
Peggy Ross
BUSINESS AND PLEASURE(1932)
Philip Ross
PRIVATE LIFE OF SHERLOCK HOLMES, THE(1970, Brit.); POPE JOAN(1972, Brit.)
Phillip Ross
S(1974); LET THE BALLOON GO(1977, Aus.)
R. Ross
MYSTERIOUS ISLAND(1941, USSR)
Richard Ross
AULD LANG SYNE(1937, Brit.); KINGS GO FORTH(1958), p
Misc. Silents
WONDERS OF THE SEA(1922)
Master Richard Ross
Silents
ONE DAY(1916)
Rita Ross
IT HAPPENED ONE NIGHT(1934); SCOTT JOPLIN(1977)
Robert Ross
DANTE'S INFERNO(1935); WOMAN TO WOMAN(1946, Brit.); SCANDAL AT SCOURIE(1953); CAST A GIANT SHADOW(1966)
Robert C. Ross
RUMBLE ON THE DOCKS(1956); WHITE SQUAW, THE(1956); HARRAD EXPERIMENT, THE(1973)
Robert Lee Ross
BLUES FOR LOVERS(1966, Brit.)
Ron Ross
STONE(1974, Aus.); BATTLE BEYOND THE STARS(1980)
Misc. Talkies
JOY RIDE TO NOWHERE(1978); BABY DOLLS(1982)
Ronald C. Ross
SLAUGHTER(1972)
Ronnie Ross
LOSERS, THE(1970)
Rosalind Ross
SAVAGE SEVEN, THE(1968), w
Rose Ross
MOTHER'S DAY(1980)
Ruby Ross
MAFIA GIRLS, THE(1969)
Russell E. Ross
ADVENTURES OF JANE ARDEN(1939), w
Sam Ross
HE RAN ALL THE WAY(1951), w
Sammy Ross
WAR LORD, THE(1965)
Samuel Ross
Misc. Silents
MISFIT EARL, A(1919)
Sandi Ross
1984
COVERGIRL(1984, Can.)

Sarah Ross
RUTHLESS FOUR, THE(1969, Ital./Ger.)
Misc. Talkies
FULLER REPORT, THE(1966)
Sharyn L. Ross
SLEEPAWAY CAMP(1983), ed
Sharyn Leslie Ross
LIQUID SKY(1982), ed
Sherman Ross
MAKING THE GRADE(1929)
Shirley Ross
MANHATTAN MELODRAMA(1934); CALM YOURSELF(1935); BIG BROADCAST OF 1937, THE(1936); DEVIL'S SQUADRON(1936); BIG BROADCAST OF 1938, THE(1937); BLOSSOMS ON BROADWAY(1937); HIDEAWAY GIRL(1937); WAIKIKI WEDDING(1937); PRISON FARM(1938); THANKS FOR THE MEMORY(1938); CAFE SOCIETY(1939); PARIS HONEYMOON(1939); SOME LIKE IT HOT(1939); UNEXPECTED FATHER(1939); KISSES FOR BREAKFAST(1941); SAILORS ON LEAVE(1941); SONG FOR MISS JULIE, A(1945)
Stan Ross
INTRIGUE(1947); LITTLE MISS BROADWAY(1947); MA AND PA KETTLE AT HOME(1954); REQUIEM FOR A HEAVYWEIGHT(1962); GOIN' DOWN THE ROAD(1970, Can.); HAMMERSMITH IS OUT(1972); WHAT'S UP, DOC?(1972); DR. HECKYL AND MR. HYPE(1980); PRIVATE EYES, THE(1980); WHOLLY MOSES(1980); VICE SQUAD(1982)
Stanley Ross
KILLER DILL(1947); PRETENDER, THE(1947)
Stanley Ralph Ross
JOHN GOLDFARB, PLEASE COME HOME(1964); FLIGHT OF THE PHOENIX, THE(1965); TONY ROME(1967); SKIDOO(1968), w; SLEEPER(1973); ROMANTIC COMEDY(1983)
Stephanie Ross
IN GOD WE TRUST(1980)
Steven Ross
LUGGAGE OF THE GODS(1983), ph
Sutherland Ross
CAUGHT IN THE NET(1960, Brit.), w
Ted Ross
WIZ, THE(1978); BINGO LONG TRAVELING ALL-STARS AND MOTOR KINGS, THE(1976); ARTHUR(1981); RAGTIME(1981)
1984
POLICE ACADEMY(1984)
Terence Ross
STRANGE SHADOWS IN AN EMPTY ROOM(1977, Can./Ital.)
Terrence Ross
PROLOGUE(1970, Can.); ONE MAN(1979, Can.)
Terrence G. Ross
RABID(1976, Can.)
Terry Ann Ross
THREE FACES OF EVE, THE(1957); CRY TERROR(1958); DOG'S BEST FRIEND, A(1960)
Thomas Ross
MORTAL STORM, THE(1940); PHANTOM RAIDERS(1940); SEVENTEEN(1940); POWER DIVE(1941)
Thomas W. Ross
BLONDIE TAKES A VACATION(1939); REMEMBER THE NIGHT(1940); SAINT'S DOUBLE TROUBLE, THE(1940); MEET JOHN DOE(1941); RICHEST MAN IN TOWN(1941); UNFINISHED BUSINESS(1941); KING'S ROW(1942); LADY HAS PLANS, THE(1942); REMARKABLE ANDREW, THE(1942)
Silents
CHECKERS(1913), a, p&d; ONLY SON, THE(1914); FINE FEATHERS(1921); WITHOUT LIMIT(1921)
Misc. Silents
FATAL HOUR, THE(1920)
Tiny Ross
FLASH GORDON(1980); TIME BANDITS(1981, Brit.)
Toby Ross
Misc. Talkies
CRUISIN' 57(1975), d
Tom Ross
Misc. Silents
SMOKING TRAIL, THE(1924)
Tony Ross
SANTA CLAUS CONQUERS THE MARTIANS(1964); TRUMAN CAPOTE'S TRILOGY(1969)
Tracey Ross
1984
BEST DEFENSE(1984)
Troyanne Ross
THUNDER IN CAROLINA(1960)
Vera Ross
GIRL SAID NO, THE(1937)
Virgil Ross
BUGS BUNNY'S THIRD MOVIE–1001 RABBIT TALES(1982), anim; HEY, GOOD LOOKIN'(1982), anim
Virginia Ross
Silents
FALSE EVIDENCE(1919)
Vivian Ross
Misc. Silents
BATTLE OF WATERLOO, THE(1913, Brit.)
Wallace Ross
JEANNE EAGELS(1957)
Wally Ross
ESCAPE TO BURMA(1955), animalt
William Ross
TEXAS LADY(1955), art d; GUN DUEL IN DURANGO(1957), art d; IRON SHERIFF, THE(1957), art d; WOLF LARSEN(1958), art d; GREEN SLIME, THE(1969); YAKUZA, THE(1975, U.S./Jap.); WAR OF THE PLANETS(1977, Jap.)

Ross Kills Enemy
MAN CALLED HORSE, A(1970)
Frances Ross-Campbell
WOMAN IN CHAINS(1932, Brit.)
Ross-Gaffney
GAMERA THE INVINCIBLE(1966, Jap.), ed
Kenneth Ross-MacKenzie
RIVER LADY(1948)
Adrian Ross-Magenty
1984
ANOTHER COUNTRY(1984, Brit.)
Marsha Rossa
EVENTS(1970)
Rossario and Antonio
SING ANOTHER CHORUS(1941); PAN-AMERICANA(1945)
Jean Pierre Rossau
LA GRANDE BOUFFE(1973, Fr.), p
Herman Rosse
FRANKENSTEIN(1931), set d; EMPEROR JONES, THE(1933), art d & set d
Victor Rosseau
Silents
DEVIL'S TOWER(1929), w
Renzo Rosselini
GREATEST LOVE, THE(1954, Ital.), m
Roberto Rosselini
GREATEST LOVE, THE(1954, Ital.), p&d, w; AGE OF THE MEDICI, THE(1979, Ital.), d, w
Ingella Rossell
STORY OF A WOMAN(1970, U.S./Ital.)
William Rosselle
Silents
IN SEARCH OF A SINNER(1920)
Renzo Rossellin
AIDA(1954, Ital.), md
Franco Rossellini
LA DOLCE VITA(1961, Ital./Fr.); TEOREMA(1969, Ital.), p; MEDEA(1971, Ital./Fr./Ger.), p; DRIVER'S SEAT, THE(1975, Ital.), p
Isabella Rossellini
MATTER OF TIME, A(1976, Ital./U.S.)
Renzo Rossellini
OPEN CITY(1946, Ital.), m; PAISAN(1948, Ital.), m; GERMANY, YEAR ZERO(1949, Ger.), m; STROMBOLI(1950, Ital.), m; DOCTOR BEWARE(1951, Ital.), m; MAN FROM CAIRO, THE(1953), m; AFFAIRS OF MESSALINA, THE(1954, Ital.), m; SIGN OF VENUS, THE(1955, Ital.), m; STRANGERS, THE(1955, Ital.), m; ANGELS OF DARKNESS(1956, Ital.), m; FEAR(1956, Ger.), m; QUEEN OF BABYLON, THE(1956, Ital.), m; LEGIONS OF THE NILE(1960, Ital.), m; TARTARS, THE(1962, Ital./Yugo.), m; LOVE AT TWENTY(1963, Fr./Ital./Jap./Pol./Ger.), d&w; CITY OF WOMEN(1980, Ital./Fr.), p; LA NUIT DE VARENNES(1983, Fr./Ital.), p
Renzo Rossellini, Jr.
GENERALE DELLA ROVERE(1960, Ital./Fr.), m
Roberto Rossellini
OPEN CITY(1946, Ital.), p&d, w; PAISAN(1948, Ital.), p, d, w; GERMANY, YEAR ZERO(1949, Ger.), p,d&w; STROMBOLI(1950, Ital.), p&d, w; WAYS OF LOVE(1950, Ital./Fr.), d, w; SEVEN DEADLY SINS, THE(1953, Fr./Ital.), d, w; JOAN AT THE STAKE(1954, Ital./Fr.), d&w; STRANGERS, THE(1955, Ital.), p&d, w; FEAR(1956, Ger.), d, w; GENERALE DELLA ROVERE(1960, Ital./Fr.), d; LES CARABINIERS(1968, Fr./Ital.), w; RISE OF LOUIS XIV, THE(1970, Fr.), d; AUGUSTINE OF HIPPO(1973, Ital.), d, w; YEAR ONE(1974, Ital.), d, w
Arthur Rossen
Silents
PRISONERS OF LOVE(1921), d
Carol Rossen
ARRANGEMENT, THE(1969); FURY, THE(1978)
Ellen Rossen
ALEXANDER THE GREAT(1956)
Harold Rossen
CUBAN LOVE SONG,THE(1931), ph; SPORTING BLOOD(1931), ph; PENTHOUSE(1933), ph; DEVIL IS A SISSY, THE(1936), ph; ON THE TOWN(1949), ph
Robert Rossen
MARKED WOMAN(1937), w; THEY WON'T FORGET(1937), w; RACKET BUSTERS(1938), w; DUST BE MY DESTINY(1939), w; ROARING TWENTIES, THE(1939), w; CHILD IS BORN, A(1940), w; BLUES IN THE NIGHT(1941), w; OUT OF THE FOG(1941), w; SEA WOLF, THE(1941), w; EDGE OF DARKNESS(1943), w; WALK IN THE SUN, A(1945), w; STRANGE LOVE OF MARTHA IVERS, THE(1946), w; BODY AND SOUL(1947), d; DESERT FURY(1947), w; JOHNNY O'CLOCK(1947), d, w; ALL THE KING'S MEN(1949), p,d&w; UNDERCOVER MAN, THE(1949), p; BRAVE BULLS, THE(1951), p&d; MAMBO(1955, Ital.), d, w; ALEXANDER THE GREAT(1956), p,d&w; ISLAND IN THE SUN(1957), d; THEY CAME TO CORDURA(1959), d, w; HUSTLER, THE(1961), p&d, w; BILLY BUDD(1962), w; COOL WORLD, THE(1963), w; LILITH(1964), p,d&w
Steven Rossen
DIRTY KNIGHT'S WORK(1976, Brit.), w
Dilys Rosser
SPYLARKS(1965, Brit.)
Ed Rosser
GRENDEL GRENDEL GRENDEL(1981, Aus.)
Felice Rosser
PERMANENT VACATION(1982)
John Rosser
UNTIL THEY SAIL(1957); YOU FOR ME(1952); TORCH SONG(1953); MEN OF THE FIGHTING LADY(1954); PRODIGAL, THE(1955); TRIAL(1955); SOMEBODY UP THERE LIKES ME(1956)
Laura Rosser
TIGER BY THE TAIL(1970), cos
Peter Rosser
STORK TALK(1964, Brit.), w
Susanne Rosser
GEORGE WHITE'S SCANDALS(1945); SUSPENSE(1946)

Suzanne Rosser
NIGHT AND DAY(1946)
Alan Rosset
DESTRUCTORS, THE(1974, Brit.)
Barney Rosset
MAIDSTONE(1970)
Gerard Rosset
PARDON MY FRENCH(1951, U.S./Fr.)
Alan Rossett
LOVE AND DEATH(1975)
Franco Rossette
AVENGER, THE(1966, Ital.), w
Rossetti
DIRTY OUTLAWS, THE(1971, Ital.), w
Franco Rossetti
CONSTANTINE AND THE CROSS(1962, Ital.), w; DUEL OF THE TITANS(1963, Ital.), w; DJANGO(1966 Ital./Span.), w; RINGO AND HIS GOLDEN PISTOL(1966, Ital.), w; UNHOLY FOUR, THE(1969, Ital.), w; DIRTY OUTLAWS, THE(1971, Ital.), p, d
Guiseppe Rossetti
GENERALE DELLA ROVERE(1960, Ital./Fr.)
Horst Rossgerber
SNOW WHITE(1965, Ger.), ed
Alfred Rossi
ESCAPE TO WITCH MOUNTAIN(1975)
Andreina Rossi
PHAROAH'S WOMAN, THE(1961, Ital.); CLEOPATRA'S DAUGHTER(1963, Fr., Ital.)
Antonio Rossi
FEDORA(1946, Ital.), w
C. Alberto Rossi
GOOD COMPANIONS, THE(1957, Brit.), m
Eleonora Rossi
BEHIND CLOSED SHUTTERS(1952, Ital.)
Ernest Lawrence Rossi
NIGHT OF THE WITCHES(1970)
F. Rossi
SLASHER, THE(1975), ph
Fausto Rossi
THREE STOOGES VS. THE WONDER WOMEN(1975, Ital./Chi.), ph; BLOW TO THE HEART(1983, Ital.)
Franco Rossi
COUNTERFEITERS, THE(1953, Ital.), d; CALYPSO(1959, Fr./It.), d; UNFAITH-FULS, THE(1960, Ital.); NUDE ODYSSEY(1962, Fr./Ital.), d, w; FRIENDS FOR LI-FE(1964, Ital.), d, w; BAMBOLE!(1965, Ital.), d; ROSE FOR EVERYONE, A(1967, Ital.), d, w; WITCHES, THE(1969, Fr./Ital.), d, w
G. Rossi
MONKEY'S PAW, THE(1933), set d
George Rossi
1984
COMFORT AND JOY(1984, Brit.)
Giancarlo Rossi
ALLEGRO NON TROPPO(1977, Ital.), ed
Gino Rossi
THIS MAN CAN'T DIE(1970, Ital.), p
Giorgio Rossi
BEYOND THE DOOR(1975, Ital./U.S.), p
Gloria Rossi
TROIKA(1969)
Ingrid Rossi
JOY(1983, Fr./Can.)
John Rossi
MASK OF KOREA(1950, Fr.), d
Leo Rossi
GRAND THEFT AUTO(1977); MR. BILLION(1977); HALLOWEEN II(1981); HEART LIKE A WHEEL(1983)
Silents
HER GREAT CHANCE(1918), ph; CHALLENGE OF CHANCE, THE(1919), ph
Lia Rossi
PRETTY BUT WICKED(1965, Braz.)
Luciano Rossi
ROVER, THE(1967, Ital.); THEY CALL ME TRINITY(1971, Ital.); DEAF SMITH AND JOHNNY EARS(1973, Ital.)
Luigi Rossi
AMARCORD(1974, Ital.)
Luisa Rossi
LAST CHANCE, THE(1945, Switz.); ANYTHING FOR A SONG(1947, Ital.); STRAN-GER ON THE PROWL(1953, Ital.); AWAKENING, THE(1958, Ital.)
Michelle Rossi
YOUNG WARRIORS(1983)
Nino Rossi
TORSO MURDER MYSTERY, THE(1940, Brit.)
Paoli Rossi
REQUIEM FOR A HEAVYWEIGHT(1962)
Peter Rossi
1984
COMFORT AND JOY(1984, Brit.)
Rex Rossi
NAVAJO KID, THE(1946)
Robert Rossi
LAST OF SHEILA, THE(1973)
Stepfano Rossi
LOVE PROBLEMS(1970, Ital.), m
Steve Rossi
LAST OF THE SECRET AGENTS?, THE(1966); MAN FROM O.R.G.Y., THE(1970)
Sylva Rossi
MAKE LIKE A THIEF(1966, Fin.)
Tino Rossi
KISS OF FIRE, THE(1940, Fr.); ROYAL AFFAIRS IN VERSAILLES(1957, Fr.)

Ugo Rossi
APE WOMAN, THE(1964, Ital.)
Vera Rossi
BLOW TO THE HEART(1983, Ital.)
Vittorio Rossi
LAST DAYS OF POMPEII, THE(1960, Ital.), cos; LEGIONS OF THE NILE(1960, Ital.), cos; COLOSSUS OF RHODES, THE(1961, Ital., Fr., Span.), cos; REVOLT OF THE SLAVES, THE(1961, Ital./Span./Ger.), cos; HERCULES AND THE CAPTIVE WOM-EN(1963, Fr./Ital.), cos; MY SON, THE HERO(1963, Ital./Fr.), cos; JOURNEY BENEATH THE DESERT(1967, Fr./Ital.), cos
Zenaide Rossi
DAY FOR NIGHT(1973, Fr.)
Eleanora Rossi-Drago
DAUGHTERS OF DESTINY(1954, Fr./Ital.); CAMILLE 2000(1969); UNCLE TOM'S CABIN(1969, Fr./Ital./Ger./Yugo.)
Elenora Rossi-Drago
HYPNOSIS(1966, Ger./Sp./Ital.)
Eleonora Rossi-Drago
VERGINITA(1953, Ital.); SENSUALITA(1954, Ital.); NAPOLEON(1955, Fr.); UNDER TEN FLAGS(1960, U.S./Ital.); LE AMICHE(1962, Ital.); SWORD OF THE CONQUER-OR(1962, Ital.); LET'S TALK ABOUT WOMEN(1964, Fr./Ital.); LOVE AND MAR-RIAGE(1966, Ital.); LOVE PROBLEMS(1970, Ital.)
Giovanni Rossi-Loti
WAR AND PEACE(1956, Ital./U.S.)
Giacomo Rossi-Stuart
WAR AND PEACE(1956, Ital./U.S.); CALTIKI, THE IMMORTAL MONSTER(1959, Ital.); SILENT ENEMY, THE(1959, Brit.); LAST MAN ON EARTH, THE(1964, U.S./Ital.); SNOW DEVILS, THE(1965, Ital.); NIGHT EVELYN CAME OUT OF THE GRAVE, THE(1973, Ital.)
Claude Rossignol
1984
LES COMPERES(1984, Fr.)
Michelle Rossignol
ANGELA(1977, Can.); SUZANNE(1980, Can.)
Monique Rossignol
TWIST, THE(1976, Fr.), ed
Gastone Rossilli
MIDNIGHT COWBOY(1969)
Paul Rossilli
SERIAL(1980)
Rado Rossimov
1984
BASILEUS QUARTET(1984, Ital.)
Norman Rossington
KEEP IT CLEAN(1956, Brit.); LONG HAUL, THE(1957, Brit.); STRANGER'S MEET-ING(1957, Brit.); I ONLY ASKED!(1958, Brit.); THREE MEN IN A BOAT(1958, Brit.); CARRY ON SERGEANT(1959, Brit.); SATURDAY NIGHT AND SUNDAY MOR-NING(1961, Brit.); GO TO BLAZES(1962, Brit.); LAWRENCE OF ARABIA(1962, Brit.); LONGEST DAY, THE(1962); COMEDY MAN, THE(1964); DAYLIGHT ROBBERY(1964, Brit.); HARD DAY'S NIGHT, A(1964, Brit.); NURSE ON WHEELS(1964, Brit.); CUP FEVER(1965, Brit.); JOEY BOY(1965, Brit.); THOSE MAGNIFICENT MEN IN THEIR FLYING MACHINES; OR HOW I FLEW FROM LONDON TO PARIS IN 25 HOURS AND 11 MINUTES(1965, Brit.); TOBRUK(1966); WRONG BOX, THE(1966, Brit.); DOUBLE TROUBLE(1967); CHARGE OF THE LIGHT BRIGADE, THE(1968, Brit.); NEGATIVES(1968, Brit.); TWO GENTLEMEN SHARING(1969, Brit.); ADVENTURES OF GERARD, THE(1970, Brit.); RISE AND RISE OF MICHAEL RIMMER, THE(1970, Brit.); MAN IN THE WILDERNESS(1971, U.S./Span.); YOUNG WINSTON(1972, Brit.); DEATHLINE(1973, Brit.); DIGBY, THE BIGGEST DOG IN THE WORLD(1974, Brit.); PRISONER OF ZENDA, THE(1979); HOUSE OF LONG SHADOWS, THE(1983, Brit.)
Misc. Talkies
TO CHASE A MILLION(1967); DOUBLE TAKE(1972, Brit.); GO FOR A TAKE(1972, Brit.)
Gabriel Rossini
1984
AFTER THE FALL OF NEW YORK(1984, Ital./Fr.), w
Giacchino Rossini
GREAT DAWN, THE(1947, Ital.), m
Giacomo Rossini
BARBER OF SEVILLE, THE(1947, Ital.), w; BARBER OF SEVILLE, THE(1973, Ger./Fr.), m
Gioacchino Rossini
UNFAITHFULLY YOURS(1948), m; STORIES FROM A FLYING TRUNK(1979, Brit.), m
Jan Rossini
CRY OF THE BANSHEE(1970, Brit.); WHEN DINOSAURS RULED THE EARTH(1971, Brit.)
Janet Rossini
FILE OF THE GOLDEN GOOSE, THE(1969, Brit.); OBLONG BOX, THE(1969, Brit.)
Nino Rossini
SMILING ALONG(1938, Brit.); OLD MOTHER RILEY, DETECTIVE(1943, Brit.); END OF THE RIVER, THE(1947, Brit.)
Renato Rossini
HERCULES VS THE GIANT WARRIORS(1965 Fr./Ital.)
Lillian Rossino
Silents
GOLD RUSH, THE(1925)
Yu. Rossinol
WAR AND PEACE(1968, USSR)
Leonard Rossiter
KIND OF LOVING, A(1962, Brit.); BILLY LIAR(1963, Brit.); THIS SPORTING LIFE(1963, Brit.); JOLLY BAD FELLOW, A(1964, Brit.); KING RAT(1965); HOTEL PARADISO(1966, U.S./Brit.); WRONG BOX, THE(1966, Brit.); DEADLIER THAN THE MALE(1967, Brit.); DEVIL'S OWN, THE(1967, Brit.); WHISPERERS, THE(1967, Brit.); DEADFALL(1968, Brit.); DIAMONDS FOR BREAKFAST(1968, Brit.); OLIVER!(1968, Brit.); 2001: A SPACE ODYSSEY(1968, U.S./Brit.); OTLEY(1969, Brit.); LUTHER(1974); BARRY LYNDON(1975, Brit.); PINK PANTHER STRIKES AGAIN, THE(1976, Brit.); RISING DAMP(1980, Brit.); BRITTANIA HOSPITAL(1982, Brit.); TRAIL OF THE PINK PANTHER, THE(1982)

S. Rossiter-Shepherd
SNOWBOUND(1949, Brit.)
Angelo Rossito
FREAKS(1932); INVASION OF THE SAUCER MEN(1957); CLONES, THE(1973)
Angelo Rossitto
ONE STOLEN NIGHT(1929); SEVEN FOOTPRINTS TO SATAN(1929); SIGN OF THE CROSS, THE(1932); SPOOKS RUN WILD(1941); CORPSE VANISHES, THE(1942); SHERLOCK HOLMES AND THE SPIDER WOMAN(1944); SCARED TO DEATH(1947); MAD WEDNESDAY(1950); CAROUSEL(1956); MESA OF LOST WOMEN, THE(1956); STORY OF MANKIND, THE(1957); MAGIC SWORD, THE(1962); TERRIFIED!(1963); TRIP, THE(1967); PUFNSTUF(1970); BRAIN OF BLOOD(1971, Phil.); SOMETHING WICKED THIS WAY COMES(1983)
Silents
BELOVED ROGUE, THE(1927); OLD SAN FRANCISCO(1927)
Earl Rossman
Misc. Silents
KIVALINA OF THE ICE LANDS(1925), d
Herman Rossman
HELL IN THE HEAVENS(1934), w
Franco Rosso
BABYLON(1980, Brit.), d, w
Neil Rosso
WHAT DID YOU DO IN THE WAR, DADDY?(1966)
Nini Rosso
MYTH, THE(1965, Ital.)
Pierro Rosso
LAST OF SHEILA, THE(1973)
Harold Rossom
BETWEEN TWO WOMEN(1944), ph
Arthur Rosson
LONG, LONG TRAIL, THE(1929), d; CONCENTRATIN' KID, THE(1930), d; MOUNTED STRANGER, THE(1930), d&w; TRAILING TROUBLE(1930), d, w; EBB TIDE(1932, Brit.), d; WOMEN WHO PLAY(1932, Brit.), d; FLAMING GUNS(1933), d; HIDDEN GOLD(1933), d; BOOTS OF DESTINY(1937), d, w; TRAILING TROUBLE(1937), d
Silents
CASSIDY(1917), d; MAN WHO MADE GOOD, THE(1917), d; HEADIN' SOUTH(1918), d; SAHARA(1919), d; DESERT BLOSSOMS(1921), d; ALWAYS THE WOMAN(1922), d&w; GARRISON'S FINISH(1923), d; MEASURE OF A MAN, THE(1924), d; MEDDLER, THE(1925), d; WET PAINT(1926), d; SILK LEGS(1927), d; PLAY GIRL, THE(1928), d; POINTS WEST(1929), d
Misc. Silents
AMERICA - THAT'S ALL(1917), d; CASE AT LAW, A(1917), d; GRAFTERS(1917), d; SUCCESSFUL FAILURE, A(1917), d; FORBIDDEN FIRE(1919), d; MARRIED IN HASTE(1919), d; ROUGH RIDING ROMANCE(1919), d; SPLENDID HAZARD, A(1920), d; FOR THOSE WE LOVE(1921), d; FIGHTING STREAK, THE(1922), d; FIRE BRIDE, THE(1922), d; CONDEMNED(1923), d; LITTLE JOHNNY JONES(1923), d; SATIN GIRL, THE(1923), d; BLASTED HOPES(1924), d; BURNING TRAIL, THE(1925), d; FIGHTING DEMON, THE(1925), d; RIDIN' PRETTY(1925), d; STRAIGHT THROUGH(1925), d; TAMING OF THE WEST, THE(1925), d; TEARING THROUGH(1925), d; STRANDED IN PARIS(1926), d; YOU'D BE SURPRISED(1926), d; LAST OUTLAW, THE(1927), d; SET FREE(1927), d; FARMER'S DAUGHTER, THE(1928), d; WINGED HORSEMAN, THE(1929), d
Arthur H. Rosson
Silents
POLLY OF THE STORM COUNTRY(1920), d
Carol Rosson
STEPFORD WIVES, THE(1975)
Dick Rosson
Silents
PATCHWORK GIRL OF OZ, THE(1914); PRETTY SISTER OF JOSE(1915); CASSIDY(1917); ALIAS MARY BROWN(1918); POLLY OF THE STORM COUNTRY(1920); BEATING THE GAME(1921)
Misc. Silents
MY BEST GIRL(1915); CASE AT LAW, A(1917); HAUNTED HOUSE, THE(1917); GHOST FLOWER, THE(1918); GOOD LOSER, THE(1918); SHOES THAT DANCED, THE(1918); POOR BOOB(1919); SECRET GARDEN, THE(1919); HER FACE VALUE(1921)
Eddie Rosson
COOL HAND LUKE(1967)
Edward C. Rosson
MAN, THE(1972), ph
Edward Rosson
WHITE LIGHTNING(1973), ph; LOVE AT FIRST BITE(1979), ph
Hal Rosson
PASSION FLOWER(1930), ph; THIS MAD WORLD(1930), ph; THIS SIDE OF HEAVEN(1934), ph; AS YOU LIKE IT(1936, Brit.), ph; GHOST GOES WEST, THE(1936), ph; DUEL IN THE SUN(1946), ph; PETE KELLY'S BLUES(1955), ph; BAD SEED, THE(1956), ph; TOWARD THE UNKNOWN(1956), ph
Silents
DAVID HARUM(1915), ph; BURIED TREASURE(1921), ph; CRADLE, THE(1922), ph; HOMESPUN VAMP, A(1922), ph; LAWFUL LARCENY(1923), ph; MANHATTAN(1924), ph; ALMOST A LADY(1926), ph; MAN BAIT(1926), ph; JIM THE CONQUEROR(1927), ph; ROUGH HOUSE ROSIE(1927), ph; GENTLEMEN PREFER BLONDES(1928), ph; FAR CALL, THE(1929), ph
Hall Rosson
Silents
SOCIETY SCANDAL, A(1924), ph
Harold Rosson
ABIE'S IRISH ROSE(1928), ph; FROZEN JUSTICE(1929), ph; SOUTH SEA ROSE(1929), ph; MADAME SATAN(1930), ph; MEN CALL IT LOVE(1931), ph; PRODIGAL, THE(1931), ph; SON OF INDIA(1931), ph; SQUAW MAN, THE(1931), ph; ARE YOU LISTENING?(1932), ph; DOWNSTAIRS(1932), ph; FELLER NEEDS A FRIEND(1932), ph; TARZAN, THE APE MAN(1932), ph; BARBARIAN, THE(1933), ph; BOMBSHELL(1933), ph; HELL BELOW(1933), ph; TURN BACK THE CLOCK(1933), ed,ph; CAT AND THE FIDDLE(1934), ph; TREASURE ISLAND(1934), ph; CAPTAINS COURAGEOUS(1937), ph; EMPEROR'S CANDLESTICKS, THE(1937), ph; MAN WHO COULD WORK MIRACLES, THE(1937, Brit.), ph; THEY GAVE HIM A GUN(1937), ph; TOO HOT TO HANDLE(1938), ph; YANK AT OXFORD, A(1938), ph; WIZARD OF OZ, THE(1939), ph; BOOM TOWN(1940), ph; DR. KILDARE GOES HOME(1940), ph; FLIGHT COMMAND(1940), ph; I TAKE THIS WOMAN(1940), ph; HONKY TONK(1941), ph; MEN OF BOYS TOWN(1941), ph; PENALTY, THE(1941), ph; WASHINGTON MELODRAMA(1941), ph; JOHNNY EAGER(1942), ph; SOMEWHERE I'LL FIND YOU(1942), ph; TENNESSEE JOHNSON(1942), ph; SLIGHTLY DANGEROUS(1943), ph; AMERICAN ROMANCE, AN(1944), ph; THIRTY SECONDS OVER TOKYO(1944), ph; MY BROTHER TALKS TO HORSES(1946), ph; NO LEAVE, NO LOVE(1946), ph; THREE WISE FOOLS(1946), ph; HUCKSTERS, THE(1947), ph; LIVING IN A BIG WAY(1947), ph; COMMAND DECISION(1948), ph; HOMECOMING(1948), ph; ANY NUMBER CAN PLAY(1949), ph; STRATTON STORY, THE(1949), ph; ASPHALT JUNGLE, THE(1950), ph; KEY TO THE CITY(1950), ph; TO PLEASE A LADY(1950), ph; RED BADGE OF COURAGE, THE(1951), ph; LONE STAR(1952), ph; LOVE IS BETTER THAN EVER(1952), ph; SINGIN' IN THE RAIN(1952), ph; ACTRESS, THE(1953), ph; DANGEROUS WHEN WET(1953), ph; I LOVE MELVIN(1953), ph; STORY OF THREE LOVES, THE(1953), ph; MAMBO(1955, Ital.), ph; STRANGE LADY IN TOWN(1955), ph; ULYSSES(1955, Ital.), ph; ENEMY BELOW, THE(1957), ph; NO TIME FOR SERGEANTS(1958), ph; ONIONHEAD(1958), ph; EL DORADO(1967), ph
Silents
POLLY OF THE STORM COUNTRY(1920), ph; GARRISON'S FINISH(1923), ph; DRAGNET, THE(1928), ph
Harold [Hal] Rosson
SCARLET PIMPERNEL, THE(1935, Brit.), ph
Harold G. Rosson
RED DUST(1932), ph; RED HEADED WOMAN(1932), ph; HOLD YOUR MAN(1933), ph
Harry Rosson
KONGO(1932), ph
Helen Rosson
Silents
GET YOUR MAN(1921); RIDIN' MAD(1924)
Misc. Silents
LIGHT, THE(1916); BORROWED CLOTHES(1918); PRICE OF A GOOD TIME, THE(1918); DEVIL DOG DAWSON(1921); DANGER AHEAD(1923)
Helene Rosson
Silents
AT DEVIL'S GORGE(1923); STING OF THE SCORPION, THE(1923)
Misc. Silents
END OF THE ROAD, THE(1915); ABANDONMENT, THE(1916); APRIL(1916); CRAVING, THE(1916); SIGN OF THE SPADE, THE(1916); TRUE NOBILITY(1916); UNDERTOW, THE(1916); WHITE ROSETTE, THE(1916); ONE-MAN TRAIL, THE(1921)
Keith Rosson
ROMEO AND JULIET(1966, Brit.)
Lili Rosson
DIARY OF A HIGH SCHOOL BRIDE(1959)
Richard Rosson
VERY IDEA, THE(1929), d; WEST POINT OF THE AIR(1935), d; COME AND GET IT(1936), d; BEHIND THE HEADLINES(1937), d; HIDEAWAY(1937), d; CORVETTE K-225(1943), d
Silents
ALWAYS THE WOMAN(1922); FINE MANNERS(1926), d; ROLLED STOCKINGS(1927), d; SHOOTIN' IRONS(1927), d; DEAD MAN'S CURVE(1928), d; ESCAPE, THE(1928), d; ROAD HOUSE(1928), d
Misc. Silents
CHASING RAINBOWS(1919); FOR THOSE WE LOVE(1921); BLONDE OR BRUNETTE(1927), d; RITZY(1927), d; WIZARD, THE(1927), d
Roy Rossotti
TWO-WAY STRETCH(1961, Brit.), set d
Rick Rossovich
LORDS OF DISCIPLINE, THE(1983)
1984
STREETS OF FIRE(1984); TERMINATOR, THE(1984)
Tim Rossovich
MAIN EVENT, THE(1979); LONG RIDERS, THE(1980); CHEECH AND CHONG'S NICE DREAMS(1981); LOOKER(1981); NIGHT SHIFT(1982); TRICK OR TREATS(1982); STING II, THE(1983)
1984
CLOAK AND DAGGER(1984)
Rick Rossovitch
LOSIN' IT(1983)
Terry Ann Rossworn
NEVER SAY GOODBYE(1956)
Barbara Rost
RATS, THE(1955, Ger.)
Susanne Rostack
KING BLANK(1983), ed
Kiell Rostad
CIAO MANHATTAN(1973), ph
Hubert Rostaing
LA PARISIENNE(1958, Fr./Ital.), m; CANDIDE(1962, Fr.), m; HAIL MAFIA(1965, Fr./Ital.), m; TENANT, THE(1976, Fr.), md
1984
WHERE IS PARSIFAL?(1984, Brit.), m
Edmond Rostand
CYRANO DE BERGERAC(1950), w
Jean Rostand
LIFE BEGINS TOMORROW(1952, Fr.)
Maurice Rostand
BROKEN LULLABY(1932), w
Silents
GOOD LITTLE DEVIL, A(1914), w
Robert Rostand
KILLER ELITE, THE(1975), w
Leo Rosten
CONSPIRATORS, THE(1944), w; DARK CORNER, THE(1946), w; LURED(1947), w; SLEEP, MY LOVE(1948), w; VELVET TOUCH, THE(1948), w; WHERE DANGER LIVES(1950), w; DOUBLE DYNAMITE(1951), Harry Crane; WALK EAST ON BEACON(1952), w; MISTER CORY(1957), w; CAPTAIN NEWMAN, M.D.(1963), w

Norman Rosten
VIEW FROM THE BRIDGE, A(1962, Fr./Ital.), w
Peter Rosten
T.A.G.: THE ASSASSINATION GAME(1982), p
Nen Rosterdinck
LITTLE ARK, THE(1972), cos
Milton Rosther
DAYDREAK(1948, Brit.)
John Rostill
SWINGER'S PARADISE(1965, Brit.); FINDERS KEEPERS(1966, Brit.)
A. Rostkowska
YOUNG GIRLS OF WILKO, THE(1979, Pol./Fr.)
Lillian Rostkowska
1984
SCRUBBERS(1984, Brit.)
Leonid Rostoff
COLOSSUS: THE FORBIN PROJECT(1969)
Karen Roston
1984
MUPPETS TAKE MANHATTAN, THE(1984), cos
Stanislav Rostostskiy
HOUSE ON THE FRONT LINE, THE(1963, USSR), d
Stanislav Rostotskiy
HOUSE ON THE FRONT LINE, THE(1963, USSR), p
N. Rostovikov
FORTY-NINE DAYS(1964, USSR)
M. Rostovtsev
CZAR WANTS TO SLEEP(1934, U.S., USSR)
Estephen Rosty
LITTLE MISS DEVIL(1951, Egypt)
Marie Rosulkova
DO YOU KEEP A LION AT HOME?(1966, Czech.)
Maggie Roswell
MIDNIGHT MADNESS(1980); FIRE AND ICE(1983)
Rosy-Rosy
MARK OF THE DEVIL II(1975, Ger./Brit.)
Miklos Rosza
KNIGHT WITHOUT ARMOR(1937, Brit.), m; DIVORCE OF LADY X. THE(1938, Brit.), m; BLOOD ON THE SUN(1945), m; KILLERS, THE(1946), m; MINIVER STORY, THE(1950, Brit./U.S.), m; IVANHOE(1952, Brit.), m; JULIUS CAESAR(1953), m; TRIBUTE TO A BADMAN(1956), m; SOMETHING OF VALUE(1957), m; LAST EMBRACE(1979), m
Janusz Roszkowski
NAKED AMONG THE WOLVES(1967, Ger.)
Camillo A. Rota
WATERLOO(1970, Ital./USSR)
Carlo Rota
TREE OF WOODEN CLOGS, THE(1979, Ital.)
Cleopatra Rota
YOUNG APHRODITES(1966, Gr.)
Giovanni Rota
ROMEO AND JULIET(1954, Brit.)
Mino Rota
HIDDEN ROOM, THE(1949, Brit.), m
Nino Rota
TO LIVE IN PEACE(1947, Ital.), m; PIRATES OF CAPRI, THE(1949), m; UNDER THE SUN OF ROME(1949, Ital.), m; WITHOUT PITY(1949, Ital.), m; CHILDREN OF CHANCE(1950, Ital.), m; GLASS MOUNTAIN, THE(1950, Brit), m; MY WIDOW AND I(1950, Ital.), m; TAMING OF DOROTHY, THE(1950, Brit.), m; ANNA(1951, Ital.), m; NEVER TAKE NO FOR AN ANSWER(1952, Brit./Ital.), m; SOMETHING MONEY CAN'T BUY(1952, Brit.), m; VALLEY OF EAGLES(1952, Brit.), m; ASSASSIN, THE(1953, Brit.), m; HIS LAST TWELVE HOURS(1953, Ital.), m; LUXURY GIRLS(1953, Ital.), m; QUEEN OF SHEBA(1953, Ital.), m; CENTO ANNI D'AMORE(1954, Ital.), m; GREAT HOPE, THE(1954, Ital.), m; HELL RAIDERS OF THE DEEP(1954, Ital.), m; LOVES OF THREE QUEENS, THE(1954, Ital./Fr.), m; MAMBO(1955, Ital.), m; STRANGER'S HAND, THE(1955, Brit.), md; LA STRADA(1956, Ital.), m; STAR OF INDIA(1956, Brit.), m; VITELLONI(1956, Ital./Fr.), m; WAR AND PEACE(1956, Ital./U.S.), m; WHITE SHEIK, THE(1956, Ital.), m; NIGHTS OF CABIRIA(1957, Ital.), m; THIS ANGRY AGE(1958, Ital./Fr.), m; HOUSE OF INTRIGUE, THE(1959, Ital.), m; LAW IS THE LAW, THE(1959, Fr.), m; UNDER TEN FLAGS(1960, U.S./Ital.), m; GREAT WAR, THE(1961, Fr., Ital.), m; LA DOLCE VITA(1961, Ital.), m; PURPLE NOON(1961, Fr./Ital.), m; ROCCO AND HIS BROTHERS(1961, Fr./Ital.), m; WHITE NIGHTS(1961, Ital./Fr.), m; BEST OF ENEMIES, THE(1962), m; BOCCACCIO '70(1962/Ital./Fr.), m; MAFIOSO(1962, Ital.), m; MOST WANTED MAN, THE(1962, Fr./Ital.), m; RELUCTANT SAINT, THE(1962, U.S./Ital.), m; SWINDLE, THE(1962, Fr./Ital.), m; LEOPARD, THE(1963, Ital.), m; 8 ½(1963, Ital.), m; FRIENDS FOR LIFE(1964, Ital.), m; JULIET OF THE SPIRITS(1965, Fr./Ital./W.Ger.), m; SHOOT LOUD, LOUDER... I DON'T UNDERSTAND(1966, Ital.), m; TAMING OF THE SHREW, THE(1967, U.S./Ital.), m; KISS THE OTHER SHEIK(1968, Fr./Ital.), m; ROMEO AND JULIET(1968, Brit./Ital.), m; FELLINI SATYRICON(1969, Fr./Ital.), m; SPIRITS OF THE DEAD(1969, Fr./Ital.), m; WATERLOO(1970, Ital./USSR), m, md; GODFATHER, THE(1972), m; ROMA(1972, Ital./Fr.), m; ABDICATION, THE(1974, Brit.), m; AMARCORD(1974, Ital.), m; GODFATHER, THE, PART II(1974), m; LOVE AND ANARCHY(1974, Ital.), m; CASANOVA(1976, Ital.), m; DEATH ON THE NILE(1978, Brit.), m; HURRICANE(1979), m
Janet Rotblatt
1984
EXTERMINATOR 2(1984)
Ed W. Rote
SPOOKS RUN WILD(1941), prod d
Edward W. Rote
ROGUES' TAVERN, THE(1936), p
Ted Roter
GRASS EATER, THE(1961)
Misc. Talkies
CLOSET CASANOVA, THE(1979), d; ONE PAGE OF LOVE(1979), d
Ernest Roters
MURDERERS AMONG US(1948, Ger.), m

A.J. Roth
ROARING CITY(1951)
Abe Roth
JEALOUSY(1934); HERE COMES MR. JORDAN(1941)
Andy Roth
Misc. Talkies
DOUBLE INITIATION(1970)
Ann Roth
WOMEN OF GLAMOUR(1937); WORLD OF HENRY ORIENT, THE(1964), cos; FINE MADNESS, A(1966), cos; UP THE DOWN STAIRCASE(1967), cos; PRETTY POISON(1968), cos; SWEET NOVEMBER(1968), cos; JENNY(1969), cos; MIDNIGHT COWBOY(1969), cos; OWL AND THE PUSSYCAT, THE(1970), cos; PEOPLE NEXT DOOR, THE(1970), cos; KLUTE(1971), cos; PURSUIT OF HAPPINESS, THE(1971), cos; THEY MIGHT BE GIANTS(1971), cos; VALACHI PAPERS, THE(1972, Ital./Fr.), cos; LAW AND DISORDER(1974), cos; DAY OF THE LOCUST, THE(1975), cos; HAPPY HOOKER, THE(1975), cos; MANDINGO(1975), cos; MURDER BY DEATH(1976), cos; GOODBYE GIRL, THE(1977), cos; CALIFORNIA SUITE(1978), cos; COMING HOME(1978), cos; NUNZIO(1978), cos; HAIR(1979), cos; PROMISES IN THE DARK(1979), cos; DRESSED TO KILL(1980), cos; ISLAND, THE(1980), cos; NINE TO FIVE(1980), cos; HONKY TONK FREEWAY(1981), cos; ONLY WHEN I LAUGH(1981), cos; ROLLOVER(1981), cos; WORLD ACCORDING TO GARP, The(1982), cos; MAN WHO LOVED WOMEN, THE(1983), cos; SILKWOOD(1983), cos; SURVIVORS, THE(1983), cos
1984
PLACES IN THE HEART(1984), cos
Arthur Roth
NIGHT FIGHTERS, THE(1960), w
Bernard R. Roth
TOWN WENT WILD, THE(1945), p, w
Bobby Roth
INDEPENDENCE DAY(1976), p, d&w; BOSS'S SON, THE(1978), d&w
1984
HEARTBREAKERS(1984), p, d&w
Misc. Talkies
BRAINWASH(1982, Brit.), d; CIRCLE OF POWER(1984), d
Bosy Roth
PRISON FARM(1938)
Brendon Roth
WORLD ACCORDING TO GARP, The(1982)
Cy Roth
AIR STRIKE(1955), p,d&w; COMBAT SQUAD(1953), d; FIRE MAIDENS FROM OUTER SPACE(1956, Brit.), d&w
Dan Roth
TOP OF THE HEAP(1972); SCREAM BLACULA SCREAM(1973)
Danni Roth
1984
LITTLE DRUMMER GIRL, THE(1984)
Dena Roth
UNSEEN, THE(1981), art d
E. Roth
FREUD(1962)
Edith Roth
BLACK SPIDER, THE(1983, Swit.), cos
Elizabeth Roth
SHADOWS GROW LONGER, THE(1962, Switz./Ger.)
Elliott Roth
GUILTY GENERATION, THE(1931)
Silents
MERTON OF THE MOVIES(1924)
Eric Roth
NICKEL RIDE, THE(1974), w
Erich Roth
CONCORDE, THE–AIRPORT '79(, w
Eugene Roth
LAST BANDIT, THE(1949); FARGO(1952); MAVERICK, THE(1952); ALASKA SEAS(1954); PRINCE VALIANT(1954); GHOST OF ZORRO(1959); ROSIE!(1967)
Eugene [Gene] Roth
MONTANA BELLE(1952)
Eve Roth
Silents
SCARAMOUCHE(1923), cos
Gene Roth
BARON OF ARIZONA, THE(1950); COLORADO RANGER(1950); WEST OF THE BRAZOS(1950); CHICAGO CALLING(1951); BLUE CANADIAN ROCKIES(1952); GOLD FEVER(1952); MUTINY(1952); RED PLANET MARS(1952); RED SNOW(1952); FARMER TAKES A WIFE, THE(1953); JACK McCALL, DESPERADO(1953); PRINCE OF PIRATES(1953); DESIREE(1954); SILVER LODE(1954); STEEL CAGE, THE(1954); JUPITER'S DARLING(1955); LUCY GALLANT(1955); PORT OF HELL(1955); NIGHTFALL(1956); RUNNING TARGET(1956); JET PILOT(1957); ROCKABILLY BABY(1957); UTAH BLAINE(1957); ZOMBIES OF MORA TAU(1957); EARTH VS. THE SPIDER(1958); SHE DEMONS(1958); SPIDER, THE(1958); YOUNG LIONS, THE(1958); ATTACK OF THE GIANT LEECHES(1959); MIRACLE OF THE HILLS, THE(1959); TORMENTED(1960); CAT BURGLAR, THE(1961); HOW THE WEST WAS WON(1962); STAGECOACH TO DANCER'S PARK(1962); THREE STOOGES MEET HERCULES, THE(1962); PRIZE, THE(1963); TWICE TOLD TALES(1963); YOUNG DILLINGER(1965)
Hans Roth
BLUE ANGEL, THE(1930, Ger.)
Howard Roth
OCEAN'S ELEVEN(1960)
Ivan Roth
1984
NIGHT OF THE COMET(1984)
J.D. Roth
1984
FIRSTBORN(1984)
Jack Roth
TWO SISTERS FROM BOSTON(1946)

James Roth
TONY ROME(1967), art d
Jan Roth
MERRY WIVES, THE(1940, Czech.), ph
Jeff Roth
KENNY AND CO.(1976)
Joe Roth
TUNNELVISION(1976), a, p; OUR WINNING SEASON(1978), p; AMERICATH-ON(1979), p; LADIES AND GENTLEMEN, THE FABULOUS STAINS(1982), p; FINAL TERROR, THE(1983), p
1984
STONE BOY, THE(1984), p
Johannes Roth
TEMPORARY WIDOW, THE(1930, Ger./Brit.); DIE FLEDERMAUS(1964, Aust.)
John Roth
WINGS OVER THE PACIFIC(1943)
Johnny Roth
BRIDE AND THE BEAST, THE(1958)
Joseph Roth
SINS OF MAN(1936), w
Joyce Roth
ROSE, THE(1979)
Leon Roth
LUCK OF GINGER COFFEY, THE(1964, U.S./Can.), p; I DISMEMBER MAMA(1974), p
Lillian Roth
ILLUSION(1929); LOVE PARADE, THE(1929); ANIMAL CRACKERS(1930); HO-NEY(1930); MADAME SATAN(1930); SEA LEGS(1930); VAGABOND KING, THE(1930); LADIES THEY TALK ABOUT(1933); TAKE A CHANCE(1933); I'LL CRY TOMORROW(1955), w; ALICE, SWEET ALICE(1978)
Lois Roth
MAYA(1966), w
Marta Roth
MASSACRE(1956)
Martha Roth
BLACK PIRATES, THE(1954, Mex.); MAN AND THE MONSTER, THE(1965, Mex.)
Marty Roth
BOATNIKS, THE(1970), w
Maya Roth
CRY OF THE BANSHEE(1970, Brit.)
Mia Roth
TWILIGHT TIME(1983, U.S./Yugo.)
Michael Henry Roth
HURRY SUNDOWN(1967)
Mickey Roth
RHAPSODY IN BLUE(1945); ANNA AND THE KING OF SIAM(1946); DRAGON-WYCH(1946); MAGIC TOWN(1947); LONG GRAY LINE, THE(1955)
Murray Roth
HOME TOWNERS, THE(1928), w; LIGHTS OF NEW YORK(1928), w; QUEEN OF THE NIGHTCLUBS(1929), w; ROYAL BOX, THE(1930), w; DON'T BET ON LO-VE(1933), d, w; HAROLD TEEN(1934), d; MILLION DOLLAR RANSOM(1934), d; PALOOKA(1934), w; CHINATOWN SQUAD(1935), d; FLYING HOSTESS(1936), d; PEPPER(1936), w; SHE'S DANGEROUS(1937), w
Silents
TRAMP, TRAMP, TRAMP(1926), w; GAY RETREAT, THE(1927), w
Nancy Roth
YOURS, MINE AND OURS(1968)
Nathan Roth
MALIBU BEACH(1978)
Noreen Roth
ZIEGFELD FOLLIES(1945)
Noreen Roth [Nash]
SOUTHERNER, THE(1945)
Patrick Roth
1984
KILLERS, THE(1984), p,d&w
Paul Roth
LONGEST DAY, THE(1962)
Paul Edwin Roth
CITY OF TORMENT(1950, Ger.); OUR DAILY BREAD(1950, Ger.); CONFESS DR. CORDA(1960, Ger.); GREAT BRITISH TRAIN ROBBERY, THE(1967, Ger.)
Phil Roth
CATCH-22(1970); WHAT'S UP, DOC?(1972); ONE FLEW OVER THE CUCKOO'S NEST(1975); TIDAL WAVE(1975, U.S./Jap.)
Philip Roth
GOODBYE COLUMBUS(1969), w; PORTNOY'S COMPLAINT(1972), d&w
Richard Roth
PEER GYNT(1965), ph; YOUNG FRANKENSTEIN(1974); JULIA(1977), p
Richard A. Roth
SUMMER OF '42(1971), p; OUR TIME(1974), p; ADVENTURES OF SHERLOCK HOLMES' SMARTER BROTHER, THE(1975, Brit.), p; WORLD'S GREATEST LOVER, THE(1977); IN GOD WE TRUST(1980); OUTLAND(1981), p
1984
JOHNNY DANGEROUSLY(1984)
Robert Roth
THEY CALL ME BRUCE(1982), ph
Roger J. Roth
STRAWBERRY STATEMENT, THE(1970), ed
Ron Roth
HONKY(1971), p
Rose Renee Roth
ONE, TWO, THREE(1961); TOWN WITHOUT PITY(1961, Ger./Switz./U.S.)
Roxy Roth
SONG TO REMEMBER, A(1945)
Sandy Roth
BEAST OF THE CITY, THE(1932); HELL'S HIGHWAY(1932); MIDNIGHT MA-RY(1933)

Sid Roth
DAY THE EARTH FROZE, THE(1959, Fin./USSR), ph
Stephen Roth
1984
BEDROOM EYES(1984, Can.), p
Stephen J. Roth
AGENCY(1981, Can.), p; PARADISE(1982), p
Toni Roth
END OF THE GAME(1976, Ger./Ital.)
Wanda Roth
HAMLET(1962, Ger.)
Werner Roth
VICTORY(1981)
Paul Rotha
PHANTOM FIEND, THE(1935, Brit.), w; NO RESTING PLACE(1952, Brit.), d, w; CAT AND MOUSE(1958, Brit), p,d&w
Wanda Rotha
MRS. FITZHERBERT(1950, Brit.); SAADIA(1953); CIRCUS WORLD(1964)
S. L. Rothafel
FOUR DEVILS(1929), m; NOT QUITE DECENT(1929), m
Silents
NEW YEAR'S EVE(1929), m
S. L. "Roxy" Rothafel
MOTHER KNOWS BEST(1928), m
Rothauser
TREMENDOUSLY RICH MAN, A(1932, Ger.)
Eduard Rothauser
TRUNKS OF MR. O.F., THE(1932, Ger.)
Julius Rothchild
Silents
AMERICAN MAID(1917), w
Paul A. Rothchild
ROSE, THE(1979), m
Suki Rothchild
WARRIORS, THE(1979)
Anita Rothe
Silents
IMPOSTER, THE(1918)
Misc. Silents
HER SISTER(1917)
Bendt Rothe
GERTRUD(1966, Den.)
Frank Rothe
WIND ACROSS THE EVERGLADES(1958)
Peter Rothe
JUST A GIGOLO(1979, Ger.), art d
1984
MOSCOW ON THE HUDSON(1984), art d
Shari Rothe
MAIDSTONE(1970)
Cal Rothenberg
MOONLIGHT IN VERMONT(1943); PATRICK THE GREAT(1945)
Murray Rothenberg
MR. UNIVERSE(1951)
Anneliese Rothenberger
OH ROSALINDA(1956, Brit.)
Rosemary Rotheray
TELL-TALE HEART, THE(1962, Brit.)
Paul Rothery
MAN, A WOMAN, AND A BANK, A(1979, Can.)
Eduard Rothhauser
Misc. Silents
MANON LESCAUT(1926, Ger.)
Ed Rothkowitz
92 IN THE SHADE(1975, U.S./Brit.), ed
Max Rothlisberger
SHADOWS GROW LONGER, THE(1962, Switz./Ger.), art d
Conrad Rothman
WINTERHAWK(1976), spec eff; PATRICK(1979, Aus.), spec eff; THIRST(1979, Aus.), spec eff
John Rothman
STARDUST MEMORIES(1980); SOPHIE'S CHOICE(1982); ZELIG(1983)
1984
GHOSTBUSTERS(1984)
Joseph Rothman
DYNAMITE DELANEY(1938), d, w
Keith Rothman
BROKEN ENGLISH(1981), p
Marion Rothman
WILD RIDE, THE(1960), w; THE BOSTON STRANGLER, THE(1968), ed; CHE!(1969), ed; BENEATH THE PLANET OF THE APES(1970), ed; BILLY JACK(1971), ed; ESCAPE FROM THE PLANET OF THE APES(1971), ed; PLAY IT AGAIN, SAM(1972), ed; ASH WEDNESDAY(1973), ed; TOM SAWYER(1973), ed; FUNNY LADY(1975), ed; BABY BLUE MARINE(1976), ed; LIPSTICK(1976), ed; IS-LAND OF DR. MOREAU, THE(1977), ed; ORCA(1977), ed; COMES A HORSEMAN(1978), ed; STARTING OVER(1979), ed; ALL NIGHT LONG(1981), ed; CHRISTINE(1983), ed
1984
STARMAN(1984), ed
Michael Rothman
CITIZENS BAND(1977)
Nancy Rothman
TERROR EYES(1981)
Randy Rothman
SORCERESS(1983)
Rose Rothman
LORDS OF FLATBUSH, THE(1974)

Seymour D. Rothman
SECOND FIDDLE TO A STEEL GUITAR(1965), w
Shirley Rothman
WIND AND THE LION, THE(1975)
Stephanie Rothman
BLOOD BATH(1966), d&w; IT'S A BIKINI WORLD(1967), d, w; STUDENT NURSES, THE(1970), p, d, w; VELVET VAMPIRE, THE(1971), w; TERMINAL IS-LAND(1973), d, w; WORKING GIRLS, THE(1973), d&w; RUBY(1977), d; STAR-HOPS(1978), w
Misc. Talkies
GROUP MARRIAGE(1972), d
Michael Rothner
NORMAN LOVES ROSE(1982, Aus.)
Ronald Rotholz
SANTA CLAUS CONQUERS THE MARTIANS(1964)
Baroness Rothschild
MY FAIR LADY(1964)
Elizabeth Rothschild
ZELIG(1983)
The Baroness Rothschild
Silents
GREAT LOVE, THE(1918)
Mrs. Arnold Rothstein
NOW I'LL TELL(1934), w
Richard Rothstein
HUMAN EXPERIMENTS(1980), w; DEATH VALLEY(1982), p, w
1984
HARD TO HOLD(1984), w
Roger M. Rothstein
ONLY WHEN I LAUGH(1981), p; TWO OF A KIND(1983), p
Alan Rothwell
LINDA(1960, Brit.); TWO LIVING, ONE DEAD(1964, Brit./Swed.); ZEPPELIN(1971, Brit.)
Michael Rothwell
START THE REVOLUTION WITHOUT ME(1970); FRAGMENT OF FEAR(1971, Brit.)
Robert Rothwell
THUNDERING JETS(1958); EL DORADO(1967); FOOLS(1970); RIO LOBO(1970); LAST MOVIE, THE(1971); NOW YOU SEE HIM, NOW YOU DON'T(1972); HOW COME NOBODY'S ON OUR SIDE?(1975); BREAKHEART PASS(1976); END, THE(1978); HOT LEAD AND COLD FEET(1978)
Talbor Rothwell
FRIENDS AND NEIGHBORS(1963, Brit.), w
Talbot Rothwell
IS YOUR HONEYMOON REALLY NECESSARY?(1953, Brit.), w; CROWDED DAY, THE(1954, Brit.), w; DON'T BLAME THE STORK(1954, Brit.), w; WHAT EVERY WOMAN WANTS(1954, Brit.), w; ONE GOOD TURN(1955, Brit.), w; STARS IN YOUR EYES(1956, Brit.), w; TOMMY THE TOREADOR(1960, Brit.), w; MY WIFE'S FAMI-LY(1962, Brit.), w; THREE SPARE WIVES(1962, Brit.), w; CARRY ON CABBIE(1963, Brit.), w; CARRY ON JACK(1963, Brit.), w; CARRY ON CLEO(1964, Brit.), w; CARRY ON SPYING(1964, Brit.), w; BIG JOB, THE(1965, Brit.), w; MAKE MINE A MIL-LION(1965, Brit.), w; THREE HATS FOR LISA(1965, Brit.), w; CARRY ON COW-BOY(1966, Brit.), w; CARRY ON SCREAMING(1966, Brit.), w; DON'T LOSE YOUR HEAD(1967, Brit.), w; FOLLOW THAT CAMEL(1967, Brit.), w; CARRY ON DOC-TOR(1968, Brit.), w; CARRY ON, UP THE KHYBER(1968, Brit.), w; CARRY ON AGAIN, DOCTOR(1969, Brit.), w; CARRY ON CAMPING(1969, Brit.), w; CARRY ON HENRY VIII(1970, Brit.), w; CARRY ON LOVING(1970, Brit.), w; CARRY ON UP THE JUNGLE(1970, Brit.), w; UP POMPEII(1971, Brit.), w
Galit Rotman
BIG RED ONE, THE(1980)
Jack Rotmil
DOLLY GETS AHEAD(1931, Ger.), set d
Mario Rotolo
YOU CAN'T TAKE IT WITH YOU(1938)
Cesare Rotondi
DAISY MILLER(1974)
Peter Rotondo
COTTONPICKIN' CHICKENPICKERS(1967), art d
Rotoscope
STAR WARS(1977), anim
V. Rotov
Misc. Silents
SPARTAKIADA(1929, USSR), d
William Rotsler
MANTIS IN LACE(1968), d
Herman Rotsten
UNWRITTEN CODE, THE(1944), d
Fritz Rotter
STRANGE ILLUSION(1945), w; SOMETHING IN THE WIND(1947), w; SEPTEM-BER AFFAIR(1950), w; ALRAUNE(1952, Ger.), w
Stephen Rotter
MISSOURI BREAKS, THE(1976), ed
Stephen A. Rotter
SEVEN UPS, THE(1973), ed; WORLD ACCORDING TO GARP, The(1982), ed; RIGHT STUFF, THE(1983), ed
Sylvia Rotter
DRAUGHTSMAN'S CONTRACT, THE(1983, Brit.)
Yella Rottlander
ALICE IN THE CITIES(1974, W. Ger.)
Victor Rottman
Misc. Silents
SPOTTED LILY, THE(1917)
Giuseppe Rotummo
ROMA(1972, Ital./Fr.), ph
Nick Rotundo
HUMONGOUS(1982, Can.), ed; CROSS COUNTRY(1983, Can.), ed
Oreste Rotundo
LEAP INTO THE VOID(1982, Ital.)

Giuseppe Rotunna
FAST AND SEXY(1960, Fr./Ital.), ph
Giuseppe Rotunno
END OF WORLD(in Our Usual Bed In a Night Full of Rain), THE*1/2 (1978, Ital.), ph; MONTE CARLO STORY, THE(1957, Ital.), ph; SCANDAL IN SORREN-TO(1957, Ital./Fr.), ph; ANNA OF BROOKLYN(1958, Ital.), ph; LOVE SPECIALIST, THE(1959, Ital.), ph; NAKED MAJA, THE(1959, Ital./U.S.), ph; ON THE BEACH(1959), ph; ANGEL WORE RED, THE(1960), ph; FIVE BRANDED WOMEN(1960), ph; GREAT WAR, THE(1961, Fr., Ital.), ph; ROCCO AND HIS BROTHERS(1961, Fr./Ital.), ph; WHITE NIGHTS(1961, Ital./Fr.), ph; FAMILY DIARY(1963 Ital.), ph; LEOPARD, THE(1963, Ital.), ph; ORGANIZER, THE(1964, Fr./Ital./Yugo.), ph; YESTERDAY, TODAY, AND TOMORROW(1964, Ital./Fr.), ph; BIBLE...IN THE BEGINNING, THE(1966), ph; STRANGER, THE(1967, Algeria/Fr./Ital.), ph; ANZIO(1968, Ital.), ph; SENSO(1968, Ital.), ph; FELLINI SATYRICON(1969, Fr./Ital.), ph; SECRET OF SAN-TA VITTORIA, THE(1969), ph; SPIRITS OF THE DEAD(1969, Fr./Ital.), ph; SUN-FLOWER(1970, Fr./Ital.), ph; CARNAL KNOWLEDGE(1971), ph; MAN OF LA MANCHA(1972), ph; AMARCORD(1974, Ital.), ph; LOVE AND ANARCHY(1974, Ital.), ph; CASANOVA(1976, Ital.), ph; ALL THAT JAZZ(1979), ph; DIVINE NYMPH, THE(1979, Ital.), ph; CITY OF WOMEN(1980, Ital./Fr.), ph; POPEYE(1980), ph; ROL-LOVER(1981), ph; FIVE DAYS ONE SUMMER(1982), ph; AND THE SHIP SAILS ON(1983, Ital./Fr.), ph
1984
AMERICAN DREAMER(1984), ph
Giussepe Rotunno
BEST OF ENEMIES, THE(1962), ph
Giusseppe Rotunno
WITCHES, THE(1969, Fr./Ital.), ph
Guiseppe Rotunno
BOCCACCIO '70(1962/Ital./Fr.), ph; CANDY(1968, Ital./Fr.), ph; ALL SCREWED UP(1976, Ital.), ph
Rotwang
1984
MEMOIRS(1984, Can.)
Geoffrey Rotwein
1984
SLOW MOVES(1984)
Aleksandr Rou
NIGHT BEFORE CHRISTMAS, A(1963, USSR), d&w; MAGIC WEAVER, THE(1965, USSR), d; JACK FROST(1966, USSR), d
Theo Roubanis
SAILOR FROM GIBRALTAR, THE(1967, Brit.); LOVE CYCLES(1969, Gr.)
Marty Roubert
TOM BROWN OF CULVER(1932)
Matty Roubert
CLOSE HARMONY(1929); UP POPS THE DEVIL(1931); TOM BROWN OF CUL-VER(1932); EVELYN PRENTICE(1934); JEALOUSY(1934); MEN OF THE NIGHT(1934); MERRY WIDOW, THE(1934); MURDER MAN(1935); ROSE MA-RIE(1936); COUNTY FAIR(1937); CRUSADE AGAINST RACKETS(1937); GIRL WITH IDEAS, A(1937); SHALL WE DANCE(1937); GOLD MINE IN THE SKY(1938); SHINE ON, HARVEST MOON(1938); FRONTIER VENGEANCE(1939); SAGA OF DEATH VALLEY(1939); ONE MAN'S LAW(1940); ROMANCE OF THE WEST(1946); STARS OVER TEXAS(1946); TUMBLEWEED TRAIL(1946); WILD WEST(1946); LAW OF THE LASH(1947)
Silents
JOHN BARLEYCORN(1914)
Misc. Silents
WAIF, THE(1915); BIG SISTER, THE(1916); HERITAGE(1920); FOR YOU MY BOY(1923); STOLEN CHILD, THE(1923)
Ray Roubert
JUNGLE PRINCESS, THE(1936)
William L. Roubert
Misc. Silents
WAIF, THE(1915), d; HERITAGE(1920), d; FOR YOU MY BOY(1923), d
George Roubicek
ONE THAT GOT AWAY, THE(1958, Brit.); CHANCE MEETING(1960, Brit.); VIC-TORS, THE(1963); BEDFORD INCIDENT, THE(1965, Brit.); DIRTY DOZEN, THE(1967, Brit.); SUMARINE X-1(1969, Brit.); SPY WHO LOVED ME, THE(1977, Brit.)
Matty Roubpert
IT HAPPENED ONE NIGHT(1934)
Arthur Rouce
TOPPER(1937), art d
Jean Rouch
ADOLESCENTS, THE(1967, Can.), d&w; SIX IN PARIS(1968, Fr.), d, w
Barren Rouche
SO LONG, BLUE BOY(1973), art d
Lindsay Rouchsey
ELIZA FRASER(1976, Aus.)
Andrew Roud
LOVES OF CARMEN, THE(1948)
Neil Rouda
HARVEY MIDDLEMAN, FIREMAN(1965)
Nicholas Roudakoff
Silents
ITALIAN STRAW HAT, AN(1927, Fr.), ph
Wladimir Roudenko
Silents
NAPOLEON(1927, Fr.)
Gaston Roudes
Misc. Silents
MARTHE(1919, Fr.), d; AU DELA DES LOIS HUMAINES(1920, Fr.), d; LA DET-TE(1920, Fr.), d; LES DEUX BAISERS(1920, Fr.), d; LA VOIX DE LA MER(1921, Fr.), d; MAITRE EVORA(1921, Fr.), d; PRISCA(1921, Fr.), d; LA GUITARE ET LA JAZZ BAND(1922, Fr.), d; LE LAC D'ARGENT(1922, Fr.), d; LE CRIME DES HOMMES(1923, Fr.), d; LE PETIT MOINEAU DE PARIS(1923, Fr.), d; FELIANA L'ESPIONNE(1924, Fr.), d; LES RANTZAU(1924, Fr.), d; L'EVEIL(1924, Fr.), d; L'OM-BRE DU BONHEUR(1924, Fr.), d; LA DOULEUR(1925, Fr.), d; LA MATERNEL-LE(1925, Fr.), d; LES ELUS DE LA MER(1925, Fr.), d; LES PETITS(1925, Fr.), d; OISEAUX DE PASSAGE(1925, Fr.), d; PULCINELLA(1925, Fr.), d; PRINCE ZI-LAH(1926, Fr.), d; COUSINE DE FRANCE(1927, Fr.), d; LE DEDALE(1927, Fr.), d; L'AME DE PIERRE(1928, Fr.), d; LA MAISON DU SOLEIL(1929, Fr.), d

Annie Roudier
LOVE IN THE AFTERNOON(1957)
Francine Roudine
1984
ELLIE(1984), p
Berton Roueche
BIGGER THAN LIFE(1956), w
Reed de Rouen
JOHN PAUL JONES(1959)
Germaine Rouer
ROYAL AFFAIRS IN VERSAILLES(1957, Fr.)
Misc. Silents
LA TERRE(1921, Fr.); AU BONHEUR DES DAMES(1929, Fr.)
Senne Rouffaer
ONE NIGHT... A TRAIN(1968, Fr./Bel.)
Alida Rouffe
MARIUS(1933, Fr.); CESAR(1936, Fr.); FANNY(1948, Fr.)
Jacques Rouffio
WINTER WIND(1970, Fr./Hung.), w
Michael Rougas
I WAS A TEENAGE WEREWOLF(1957); ICE STATION ZEBRA(1968); FLA-REUP(1969); DAY OF THE ANIMALS(1977); STAR TREK: THE MOTION PIC-TURE(1979); SCARFACE(1983)
Jean Rougerie
LACOMBE, LUCIEN(1974); MARCH OR DIE(1977, Brit.); GET OUT YOUR HAND-KERCHIEFS(1978, Fr.); COUSINS IN LOVE(1982); NORTH STAR, THE(1982, Fr.); L'ETOILE DU NORD(1983, Fr.)
1984
AMERICAN DREAMER(1984); EDITH AND MARCEL(1984, Fr.); PERILS OF GWEN-DOLINE, THE(1984, Fr.)
Sylvain Rougerie
CLOCKMAKER, THE(1976, Fr.)
Jean Rougeul
8 ½(1963, Ital.); SHOES OF THE FISHERMAN, THE(1968); DUCK, YOU SUCK-ER!(1972, Ital.)
Jermey Roughton
WRONG BOX, THE(1966, Brit.)
Roger Roughton
SYLVIA SCARLETT(1936)
Owen Roughwood
Silents
QUEEN MOTHER, THE(1916, Brit.)
Misc. Silents
UNDER THE RED ROBE(1915, Brit.)
Rouiched
HASSAN, TERRORIST(1968, Algerian), a, w
Jacqueline Rouillard
BRIDE WORE BLACK, THE(1968, Fr./Ital.); TWO OF US, THE(1968, Fr.); MILKY WAY, THE(1969, Fr./Ital.)
Jean-Paul Rouland
DEAR DETECTIVE(1978, Fr.), w
Raymond Roulean
JUST A BIG, SIMPLE GIRL(1949, Fr.)
Philippe Rouleau
FAR FROM DALLAS(1972, Fr.)
Raymond Rouleau
AFFAIR LAFONT, THE(1939, Fr.); CONFLICT(1939, Fr.); SHANGHAI DRAMA, THE(1945, Fr.); LOVERS OF TERUEL, THE(1962, Fr.), d, w
Dominique Roulet
1984
DOG DAY(1984, Fr.), w
Raoul Roulien
STATE'S ATTORNEY(1932); FLYING DOWN TO RIO(1933)
Raul Roulien
DELICIOUS(1931); CARELESS LADY(1932); PAINTED WOMAN(1932); IT'S GREAT TO BE ALIVE(1933); WORLD MOVES ON, THE(1934); TE QUIERO CON LOCU-RA(1935); ROAD TO RIO(1947)
Alain Roulleau
CHECKERBOARD(1969, Fr.)
Edgar Roulleau
PRICE OF FLESH, THE(1962, Fr.), p
Theodore Roumbanis
ISLAND OF LOVE(1963)
Thomas Round
GREAT GILBERT AND SULLIVAN, THE(1953, Brit.)
The Rounders
BLAZE O' GLORY(1930)
Rounders Quintet
RAINBOW MAN(1929)
David Rounds
CHILD'S PLAY(1972); KING OF THE GYPSIES(1978); SO FINE(1981)
Steve Rounds
Silents
BY PROXY(1918), ph
Richard Roundtree
SHAFT(1971); EMBASSY(1972, Brit.); SHAFT'S BIG SCORE(1972); CHARLEY-ONE-EYE(1973, Brit.); SHAFT IN AFRICA(1973); EARTHQUAKE(1974); DIAMONDS(1975, U.S./Israel); MAN FRIDAY(1975, Brit.); ESCAPE TO ATHENA(1979, Brit.); GAME FOR VULTURES, A(1980, Brit.); EYE FOR AN EYE, AN(1981); INCHON(1981); ONE DOWN TWO TO GO(1982); Q(1982); BIG SCORE, THE(1983); YOUNG WARRIORS(1983)
1984
CITY HEAT(1984); KILLPOINT(1984)
Misc. Talkies
PORTRAIT OF A HITMAN(1984)
Robert Rounseville
TALES OF HOFFMANN, THE(1951, Brit.); CAROUSEL(1956)
Camilla Rountree
WE OF THE NEVER NEVER(1983, Aus.), cos

Larry Roupe
HARRY'S WAR(1981)
Noel Rouquevert
CADET-ROUSSELLE(1954, Fr.)
George Rouquier
BIQUEFARRE(1983, Fr.), d
Georges Rouquier
Z(1969, Fr./Algeria)
Georgette Rouquier
BIQUEFARRE(1983, Fr.)
Henri Rouquier
BIQUEFARRE(1983, Fr.)
Maria Rouquier
BIQUEFARRE(1983, Fr.)
Raymon Rouquier
BIQUEFARRE(1983, Fr.)
Roch Rouquier
BIQUEFARRE(1983, Fr.)
M. Rourie
KID MILLIONS(1934)
Adam Rourke
BEACH GIRLS(1982)
Hayden Rourke
BACK STREET(1961); BAREFOOT EXECUTIVE, THE(1971)
Jack Rourke
WOMAN'S SECRET, A(1949)
Mickey Rourke
1941(1979); FADE TO BLACK(1980); HEAVEN'S GATE(1980); BODY HEAT(1981); DINER(1982); EUREKA(1983, Brit.); RUMBLE FISH(1983)
1984
POPE OF GREENWICH VILLAGE, THE(1984)
Terry Rourke
LADY, STAY DEAD(1982, Aus.), p,d&w
Thomas Rourke
THUNDER BELOW(1932), w
Bucky Rous
FIVE EASY PIECES(1970), cos; OMEGA MAN, THE(1971), cos; DELIVERAN-CE(1972), cos
Charlotte Rouse
FLY NOW, PAY LATER(1969)
Christopher Rouse
1984
WINDY CITY(1984), ed
Graham Rouse
RIDE A WILD PONY(1976, U.S./Aus.); F.J. HOLDEN, THE(1977, Aus.); BLUE FIN(1978, Aus.); WEEKEND OF SHADOWS(1978, Aus.); ODD ANGRY SHOT, THE(1979, Aus.)
Hugh Rouse
HELLIONS, THE(1962, Brit.); DINGAKA(1965, South Africa); SAFARI 3000(1982)
L. Foster Rouse
GIRL IN TROUBLE(1963)
Russell Rouse
NOTHING BUT TROUBLE(1944), w; TOWN WENT WILD, THE(1945), p, w; D.O.-A.(1950), w; GREAT PLANE ROBBERY(1950), w; WELL, THE(1951), d, W; THIEF, THE(1952), d, w; WICKED WOMAN(1953), d, w; NEW YORK CONFIDEN-TIAL(1955), d, w; FASTEST GUN ALIVE(1956), d, w; HOUSE OF NUMBERS(1957), d&w; PILLOW TALK(1959), w; THUNDER IN THE SUN(1959), d, w; HOUSE IS NOT A HOME, A(1964), d, w; OSCAR, THE(1966), d, w; CAPER OF THE GOLDEN BULLS, THE(1967), d; COLOR ME DEAD(1969, Aus.), w
Simon Rouse
BUTLEY(1974, Brit.); RAGMAN'S DAUGHTER, THE(1974, Brit.)
William Merriam Rouse
Silents
JULES OF THE STRONG HEART(1918), ph
Ron Rousel
LITTLE AUSTRALIANS(1940, Aus.)
Raymond Rousenville
Silents
NIGHT WATCH, THE(1926)
Andre Rouseyrol
THAT CERTAIN WOMAN(1937)
Roge Roush
STACY'S KNIGHTS(1983)
Andre Rousimmoff
1984
MICKI AND MAUDE(1984)
Dolores Rousse
Silents
NO MOTHER TO GUIDE HER(1923); AGAINST ALL ODDS(1924); DARK STAIR-WAYS(1924); LADIES TO BOARD(1924); OH, YOU TONY!(1924); MEDDLER, THE(1925)
Beaudion Roussea
RED(1970, Can.)
Annabelle Rousseau
WESTERNER, THE(1940)
Carolle Rousseau
UNDERCOVERS HERO(1975, Brit.); GREEK TYCOON, THE(1978)
Diane Rousseau
SPORTING CLUB, THE(1971)
Don Jack Rousseau
SLAVERS(1977, Ger.)
Jean Jacques Rousseau
LE GAI SAVOIR(1968, Fr.), w
Louis Rousseau
FIGHTING BILL CARSON(1945), w
Louise Rousseau
FUZZY SETTLES DOWN(1944), w; SWING HOSTESS(1944), w; RIDERS OF THE DAWN(1945), w; ROCKIN' IN THE ROCKIES(1945), w; WEST OF THE ALAMO(1946), w; UNDER COLORADO SKIES(1947), w; AIR HOSTESS(1949), w; .MISSISSIPPI RHYTHM(1949), w; PRINCE OF THE PLAINS(1949), w

Louisette Rousseau
PARIS DOES STRANGE THINGS(1957, Fr./Ital.); WAR OF THE BUTTONS(1963 Fr.); AMERICAN WIFE, AN(1965, Ital.); RUN FOR YOUR WIFE(1966, Fr./Ital.)

Marcel Rousseau
13 RUE MADELEINE(1946); PERFECT FURLOUGH, THE(1958)

Mary Rousseau
JUDGE PRIEST(1934)

Pierre Rousseau
LA VIE DE CHATEAU(1967, Fr.)
1984
LE CRABE TAMBOUR(1984, Fr.)

Renee Rousseau
VISITING HOURS(1982, Can.), spec eff

Serge Rousseau
NAKED AUTUMN(1963, Fr.); IS PARIS BURNING?(1966, U.S./Fr.); BRIDE WORE BLACK, THE(1968, Fr./Ital.); STOLEN KISSES(1969, Fr.); BED AND BOARD(1971, Fr.)

Victor Rousseau
Silents
WEST OF THE RAINBOW'S END(1926), w

Henri Roussel
Misc. Silents
LES NOUVEAUX MESSIEURS(1929, Fr.)

Henry Roussel
Misc. Silents
UN HOMME PASSA(1917, Fr.), d; L'AME DU BRONZE(1918, Fr.), d; LE TORRENT(1918, Fr.); LA FAUTE D'ODETTE MARECHAL(1920, Fr.), d; VISAGES VIOLES...AMES CLOSES(1921, Fr.), d; LA VERITE(1922, Fr.), d; LES OPPRIMES(1923, Fr.), d; VIOLETTES IMPERIALES(1924, Fr.), d; LA TERRE PROMISE(1925, Fr.), d; DESTINEE(1926, Fr.), d; L'ILE ENCHANTEE(1927, Fr.), d; LE VALSE DE L'ADIEU(1928, Fr.), d; PARIS GIRLS(1929, Fr.), d

Louis Roussel
STATE FAIR(1962)

Myriem Roussel
PASSION(1983, Fr./Switz.)
1984
FIRST NAME: CARMEN(1984, Fr.)

Pierre Roussel
SUCKER, THE(1966, Fr./Ital.)

Rene Roussel
WE ARE ALL NAKED(1970, Can./Fr.)

Yann Roussel
DIVA(1982, Fr.)

Jean-Jacques Rousselet
ONCE IN PARIS(1978); JOY(1983, Fr./Can.)

Philippe Rousselet
COCKTAIL MOLOTOV(1980, Fr.), ph

Roussell
NIGHT IS OURS(1930, Fr.)

Henry Roussell
NIGHT IS OURS(1930, Fr.), d

Gabrielle Roussellon
SOMBRERO(1953)

Jean Rousselot
MY BABY IS BLACK!(1965, Fr.), w

Philippe Rousselot
PEPPERMINT SODA(1979, Fr.), ph; DIVA(1982, Fr.), ph; GIRL FROM LORRAINE, A(1982, Fr./Switz.), ph; MOON IN THE GUTTER, THE(1983, Fr./Ital.), ph
1984
DREAM ONE(1984, Brit./Fr.), ph

Yves Rousset-Rouard
LITTLE ROMANCE, A(1979, U.S./Fr.), p; GOODBYE EMMANUELLE(1980, Fr.), p; TROUT, THE(1982, Fr.), p

Jean-Paul Roussillon
DEADLIER THAN THE MALE(1957, Fr.); MARRIAGE OF FIGARO, THE(1963, Fr.); WEEKEND AT DUNKIRK(1966, Fr./Ital.); TROUT, THE(1982, Fr.)

Andre Roussin
JUST A BIG, SIMPLE GIRL(1949, Fr.), w; LITTLE HUT, THE(1957), w

Georges Roussos
MADALENA(1965, Gr.), w

Pierre Roustang
LOVE AT TWENTY(1963, Fr./Ital./Jap./Pol./Ger.), p; BEAUTIFUL SWINDLERS, THE(1967, Fr./Ital./Jap./Neth.), p

Paule Rout
ROMA(1972, Ital./Fr.)

The Routers
SURF PARTY(1964)

George Routh
Misc. Silents
CONVICT KING, THE(1915); DEAD SOUL, THE(1915); SAVED FROM THE HAREM(1915); TERRIBLE ONE, THE(1915); BOND WITHIN, THE(1916); FIGHTING ROMEO, THE(1925)

Jonathan Routh
30 IS A DANGEROUS AGE, CYNTHIA(1968, Brit.)

May Routh
LAST REMAKE OF BEAU GESTE, THE(1977), cos; SGT. PEPPER'S LONELY HEARTS CLUB BAND(1978), cos; MY FAVORITE YEAR(1982), cos
1984
SPLASH(1984), cos

Patricia Routledge
TO SIR, WITH LOVE(1967, Brit.); BLISS OF MRS. BLOSSOM, THE(1968, Brit.); DON'T RAISE THE BRIDGE, LOWER THE RIVER(1968, Brit.); MATTER OF INNOCENCE, A(1968, Brit.); 30 IS A DANGEROUS AGE, CYNTHIA(1968, Brit.); IF IT'S TUESDAY, THIS MUST BE BELGIUM(1969); LOCK UP YOUR DAUGHTERS(1969, Brit.); EGGHEAD'S ROBOT(1970, Brit.); GIRL STROKE BOY(1971, Brit.)

Leroy Routly
THING, THE(1982), spec eff

Pierre Rouve
MILLIONAIRESS, THE(1960, Brit.), p; I LIKE MONEY(1962, Brit.), p, w; TRIAL AND ERROR(1962, Brit.), w; BLOW-UP(1966, Brit.), p; COP-OUT(1967, Brit.), d, w; DIAMONDS FOR BREAKFAST(1968, Brit.), p, w

Catherine Rouvel
PICNIC ON THE GRASS(1960, Fr.); LANDRU(1963, Fr./Ital); HIGHWAY PICKUP(1965, Fr./Ital.); BENJAMIN(1968, Fr.); BORSALINO(1970, Fr.); MISTER FREEDOM(1970, Fr.); BORSALINO AND CO.(1974, Fr.); DESTRUCTORS, THE(1974, Brit.); BLACK AND WHITE IN COLOR(1976, Fr.); COUSINS IN LOVE(1982)

Camille Rouvelle
MADAME DU BARRY(1934)

Aurania Rouveral
ANDY HARDY COMES HOME(1958), w

Jean Rouverel
ROAD BACK,THE(1937)

Aurania Rouverol
DANCE, FOOLS, DANCE(1931), w; FAMILY AFFAIR, A(1937), w; YOU'RE ONLY YOUNG ONCE(1938), w; HARDYS RIDE HIGH, THE(1939), w; LIFE BEGINS FOR ANDY HARDY(1941), w; COURTSHIP OF ANDY HARDY, THE(1942), w

Jean Rouverol
IT'S A GIFT(1934); MISSISSIPPI(1935); PRIVATE WORLDS(1935); BAR 20 RIDES AGAIN(1936); FATAL LADY(1936); LEAVENWORTH CASE, THE(1936); STAGE DOOR(1937); ANNABEL TAKES A TOUR(1938); LAW WEST OF TOMBSTONE, THE(1938); WESTERN JAMBOREE(1938); SO YOUNG, SO BAD(1950), w; FIRST TIME, THE(1952), w; FACE IN THE RAIN, A(1963), w; LEGEND OF LYLAH CLARE, THE(1968), w

Simone Rouviere
AZAIS(1931, Fr.)

Antonio Roux
THRILL OF BRAZIL, THE(1946)

J.L. Roux
THIRTEENTH LETTER, THE(1951)

Jacques Roux
LIST OF ADRIAN MESSENGER, THE(1963); SECRET WAR OF HARRY FRIGG, THE(1968); HOUSE OF CARDS(1969); NIGHTHAWKS(1981)

Jean-Louis Roux
PYX, THE(1973, Can.); TWO SOLITUDES(1978, Can.); CORDELIA(1980, Fr., Can.); ODYSSEY OF THE PACIFIC(1983, Can./Fr.)
1984
HOTEL NEW HAMPSHIRE, THE(1984)

Louis Roux
THIRTEENTH LETTER, THE(1951)

Michel Roux
HENRIETTE'S HOLIDAY(1953, Fr.); HOLIDAY FOR HENRIETTA(1955, Fr.); FEMALE, THE(1960, Fr.); PRICE OF FLESH, THE(1962, Fr.)

Tony Roux
IN OLD MEXICO(1938); LAW OF THE PAMPAS(1939); LLANO KID, THE(1940); GAUCHOS OF EL DORADO(1941); HOLD BACK THE DAWN(1941); UNDERCOVER MAN(1942); ALONG CAME JONES(1945); OUT OF THE PAST(1947); MEXICAN HAYRIDE(1948); SURRENDER(1950); CASA MANANA(1951); LONE STAR(1952); CHARGE OF THE LANCERS(1953); HITCH-HIKER, THE(1953); SECOND CHANCE(1953); FIRST TRAVELING SALESLADY, THE(1956)

Andre Rouyer
NIGHT OF LUST(1965, Fr.)

Marcel Rouze
DIARY OF A CHAMBERMAID(1964, Fr./Ital.); LADIES OF THE PARK(1964, Fr.)

Jean-Michel Rouziere
VICE AND VIRTUE(1965, Fr./Ital.); MAYERLING(1968, Brit./Fr.); SIX IN PARIS(1968, Fr.)

Renee Rouzot
VICE DOLLS(1961, Fr.), cos; SOFT SKIN, THE(1964, Fr.), cos

Brian Rovak
MELANIE(1982, Can.), ed

Cesare Rovatti
MATCHLESS(1967, Ital.), cos; THAT SPLENDID NOVEMBER(1971, Ital./Fr.), cos

Camille Rovelle
NIX ON DAMES(1929); WALL STREET(1929); JIMMY THE GENT(1934); SMARTY(1934)

Brandy Roven
THEY ALL LAUGHED(1981)

Charles Roven
HEART LIKE A WHEEL(1983), p

Marcella Rovena
WHITE NIGHTS(1961, Ital./Fr.); LEOPARD, THE(1963, Ital.); PASSIONATE THIEF, THE(1963, Ital.); SHIP OF CONDEMNED WOMEN, THE(1963, ITAL.); EMPTY CANVAS, THE(1964, Fr./Ital.); FRIENDS FOR LIFE(1964, Ital.)

J. Rovensky
ECSTACY OF YOUNG LOVE(1936, Czech.), d; INSPECTOR GENERAL, THE(1937, Czech.)

Josef Rovensky
Misc. Silents
DIARY OF A LOST GIRL(1929, Ger.)

Gina Rovere
HERCULES(1959, Ital.); PASSIONATE THIEF, THE(1963, Ital.); LOVE A LA CARTE(1965, Ital.); ALL THE OTHER GIRLS DO!(1967, Ital.); GOD FORGIVES–I DON'T!(1969, Ital./Span.); CATCH-22(1970)

Liliane Rovere
MARCH OR DIE(1977, Brit.)

Luigi Rovere
BEHIND CLOSED SHUTTERS(1952, Ital.), p; WHITE SHEIK, THE(1956, Ital.), p; ROMMEL'S TREASURE(1962, Ital.), p; KILL OR BE KILLED(1967, Ital.), p

Marcella Rovere
LA STRADA(1956, Ital.)

Patrizia Della Rovere
HERCULES UNCHAINED(1960, Ital./Fr.)

Ermanno Roveri
MAGIC WORLD OF TOPO GIGIO, THE(1961, Ital.)

Sandy Roveta
SWEET CHARITY(1969)

Joseph Roveto
ALL THE RIGHT MOVES(1983), cos

Sandy Rovetta
WORLD'S GREATEST LOVER, THE(1977)
Giovanni Rovini
SANDRA(1966, Ital.)
Randy Rovins
1984
PREY, THE(1984), p
William Rovis
HEROES OF THE SADDLE(1940)
Mabel Row
WHITE CLIFFS OF DOVER, THE(1944)
Mathew Row
FRATERNITY ROW(1977), m
John Rowal
NO EXIT(1930, Brit.); SCHOONER GANG, THE(1937, Brit.); DANCE OF DEATH, THE(1938, Brit.)
Lt. Andrew S. Rowan
MESSAGE TO GARCIA, A(1936), w
Ann Rowan
ULYSSES(1967, U.S./Brit.)
Brian Rowan
LOCAL HERO(1983, Brit.)
Dan Rowan
ONCE UPON A HORSE(1958); MALTESE BIPPY, THE(1969)
Denine Rowan
YOUNG GIANTS(1983), ed
Diana Rowan
BEYOND REASONABLE DOUBT(1980, New Zeal.); BATTLETRUCK(1982)
Don Rowan
AND SUDDEN DEATH(1936); ARIZONA RAIDERS, THE(1936); MURDER WITH PICTURES(1936); RETURN OF SOPHIE LANG, THE(1936); SAN FRANCISCO(1936); WHIPSAW(1936); AFFAIRS OF CAPPY RICKS(1937); DEVIL'S PLAYGROUND(1937); SEA RACKETEERS(1937); WHEN YOU'RE IN LOVE(1937); WHEN'S YOUR BIRTH-DAY?(1937); RACKET BUSTERS(1938); WANTED BY THE POLICE(1938); BURIED ALIVE(1939); EVERYBODY'S HOBBY(1939); NANCY DREW AND THE HIDDEN STAIRCASE(1939); OKLAHOMA TERROR(1939); TOUGH KID(1939); BROTHER OR-CHID(1940); JOHNNY APOLLO(1940); YOU'RE NOT SO TOUGH(1940); NAVY BLUES(1941)
Dorothy Rowan
LORD OF THE MANOR(1933, Brit.), w; DANGEROUS GROUND(1934, Brit.), w
Silents
FAR FROM THE MADDING CROWD(1915, Brit.); GREAT ADVENTURE, THE(1915, Brit.)
Ed Rowan
NOTHING BUT A MAN(1964)
1984
COTTON CLUB, THE(1984)
Frank Rowan
SIDEWALKS OF NEW YORK(1931); HOTEL HAYWIRE(1937); MAMA RUNS WILD(1938), w
Gay Rowan
U-TURN(1973, Can.); SUDDEN FURY(1975, Can.); S.O.B.(1981); SECOND THOUGHTS(1983)
Misc. Talkies
GIRL IN BLUE, THE(1974)
Gerald Rowan
SINS OF THE FATHERS(1948, Can.)
Jerry Rowan
THIRTEENTH LETTER, THE(1951)
Tom Rowan
WIFE VERSUS SECRETARY(1936)
Bill Rowbotham
VACATION FROM MARRIAGE(1945, Brit.); SCHOOL FOR SECRETS(1946, Brit.); DANCING WITH CRIME(1947, Brit.)
George Rowbotham
FIVE CARD STUD(1968)
Jo Rowbottom
BARGEE, THE(1964, Brit.); LIQUIDATOR, THE(1966, Brit.); TWO A PENNY(1968, Brit.); THAT SUMMER(1979, Brit.)
W.C. Rowden
Misc. Silents
DANIEL DERONDA(1921, Brit.), d
Walter Courtenay Rowden
Misc. Silents
CORINTHIAN JACK(1921, Brit.), d
William Courtenay Rowden
Silents
PRISONER OF ZENDA, THE(1915, Brit.), w; RUPERT OF HENTZAU(1915, Brit.), w
Alan Rowe
HENRY VIII AND HIS SIX WIVES(1972, Brit.); DIMBOOLA(1979, Aus.); NEXT OF KIN(1983, Aus.)
Arthur Rowe
ZEPPELIN(1971, Brit.), w; MAGNIFICENT SEVEN RIDE, THE(1972), w; LAND OF THE MINOTAUR(1976, Gr.), w
Bob Rowe
HIGH BARBAREE(1947)
Charles Rowe
S.O.B.(1981)
Clint Rowe
THING, THE(1982)
Doug Rowe
FLAREUP(1969); LEGEND OF NIGGER CHARLEY, THE(1972)
Earl Rowe
BLOB, THE(1958)
Edna Rowe
Silents
GOLD RUSH, THE(1925)

Fanny Rowe
LADY CAROLINE LAMB(1972, Brit./Ital.)
Frances Rowe
THEY CAME TO A CITY(1944, Brit.); MISS ROBIN HOOD(1952, Brit.); NEVER LOOK BACK(1952, Brit.); TECKMAN MYSTERY, THE(1955, Brit); WARRIORS, THE(1955); MOONRAKER, THE(1958, Brit.)
George Rowe
MERMAIDS OF TIBURON, THE(1962)
Misc. Talkies
FORTRESS IN THE SUN(1978), d
Gerald Rowe
ROLLERCOASTER(1977)
Greg Rowe
STORM BOY(1976, Aus.); BLUE FIN(1978, Aus.); LAST WAVE, THE(1978, Aus.); DEAD MAN'S FLOAT(1980, Aus.)
Guy Rowe
AMAZON QUEST(1949), ph
Hansford Rowe
GORDON'S WAR(1973); SIMON(1980); MISSING(1982); OSTERMAN WEEKEND, THE(1983)
Hansford Rowe, Jr.
THREE DAYS OF THE CONDOR(1975)
Iris Rowe
Misc. Silents
ROSE IN THE DUST(1921, Brit.)
Jeremy Rowe
CHIMES AT MIDNIGHT(1967, Span.,Switz.)
Margaret Rowe
MURDER ON APPROVAL(1956, Brit.); THERE'S ALWAYS A THURSDAY(1957, Brit.)
Marilyn Rowe
DON QUIXOTE(1973, Aus.)
Misty Rowe
HITCHHIKERS, THE(1972); GOODBYE, NORMA JEAN(1976); LOOSE SHO-ES(1980); MAN WITH BOGART'S FACE, THE(1980); DOUBLE EXPOSURE(1982); NATIONAL LAMPOON'S CLASS REUNION(1982)
1984
MEATBALLS PART II(1984)
Myrtle Rowe
NO SMOKING(1955, Brit.)
Nevan Rowe
SLEEPING DOGS(1977, New Zealand)
Nick Rowe
1984
ANOTHER COUNTRY(1984, Brit.)
Patrick Rowe
SPACEHUNTER: ADVENTURES IN THE FORBIDDEN ZONE(1983)
Peter Rowe
NEON PALACE, THE(1970, Can.), p,d&w
Phoebe Rowe
INTRUDER, THE(1962)
Prentis Rowe
DUCHESS AND THE DIRTWATER FOX, THE(1976)
Prentiss Rowe
GUARDIAN OF THE WILDERNESS(1977); TAKE DOWN(1979); HARRY'S WAR(1981)
Prentiss E. Rowe
LONG RIDERS, THE(1980)
Tom Rowe
MY SON, THE HERO(1963, Ital./Fr.), w; VIOLATED PARADISE(1963, Ital./Jap.), w; SUDDENLY, A WOMAN!(1967, Den.), w; GREEN SLIME, THE(1969), w; ARIS-TOCATS, THE(1970), w; LIGHT AT THE EDGE OF THE WORLD, THE(1971, U.S./Span./Lichtenstein), w; SERPENT, THE(1973, Fr./Ital./Ger.), w; TARZAN, THE APE MAN(1981), w
Tracy Lee Rowe
USED CARS(1980)
Vern Rowe
BIG MOUTH, THE(1967); SHAGGY D.A., THE(1976)
Janet Rowell
DATE AT MIDNIGHT(1960, Brit.)
Kathleen Rowell
1984
JOY OF SEX(1984), w
Kathleen Knutsen Rowell
OUTSIDERS, THE(1983), w
W. Rowicki
LOTNA(1966, Pol.), md
Adele Rowland
BLONDE FROM SINGAPORE, THE(1941); LUCKY LEGS(1942); FOR THE LOVE OF MARY(1948); SECRET FURY, THE(1950)
Art Rowland
MURDER WITH PICTURES(1936)
Arthur Rowland
RETURN OF SOPHIE LANG, THE(1936)
Baby Helen Rowland
Silents
TIMOTHY'S QUEST(1922)
Betty Rowland
WORLD'S GREATEST SINNER, THE(1962); LOVE AND KISSES(1965)
Beverly Rowland
BEYOND AND BACK(1978)
Beverly Booth Rowland
CHILLY SCENES OF WINTER(1982)
Bill Rowland
SWEET SURRENDER(1935), p
Bruce Rowland
MAN FROM SNOWY RIVER, THE(1983, Aus.), m
1984
PHAR LAP(1984, Aus.), m

Janette Rowsell
WEEKEND WITH LULU, A(1961, Brit.)
Geoffrey Rowson
CAN YOU HEAR ME MOTHER?(1935, Brit.), p; HER LAST AFFAIRE(1935, Brit.), p
Harry Rowson
OFFICER'S MESS, THE(1931, Brit.), p; LUCKY SWEEP, A(1932, Brit.), p; MRS. DANE'S DEFENCE(1933, Brit.), p
Lesie Rowson
GHOST TRAIN, THE(1933, Brit.), ph
Leslie Rowson
CHARLEY'S AUNT(1930), ph; LORD BABS(1932, Brit.), ph; MICHAEL AND MARY(1932, Brit.), ph; WEDDING REHEARSAL(1932, Brit.), ph; MAN FROM TORONTO, THE(1933, Brit.), ph; MAN THEY COULDN'T ARREST, THE(1933, Brit.), ph; NIGHT AND DAY(1933, Brit.), ph; MY OLD DUTCH(1934, Brit.), ph; STRIKE!(1934, Brit.), ph; WOMAN IN COMMAND, THE(1934 Brit.), ph; HER LAST AFFAIRE(1935, Brit.), ph; MAN OF THE MOMENT(1935, Brit.), ph; REGAL CAVALCADE(1935, Brit.), ph; JUST WILLIAM'S LUCK(1948, Brit.), ph; THINGS HAPPEN AT NIGHT(1948, Brit.), ph
Simon Rowson
CAN YOU HEAR ME MOTHER?(1935, Brit.), p; HER LAST AFFAIRE(1935, Brit.), p
Allex Rox
STAR MAKER, THE(1939)
Roxanne
SEVEN YEAR ITCH, THE(1955); YOUNG DON'T CRY, THE(1957)
Willy Roxier
GIRL IN THE BIKINI, THE(1958, Fr.), w
Roxy D.J.
1984
BEAT STREET(1984)
Alain Roy
LES CREATURES(1969, Fr./Swed.)
Alberta Roy
Misc. Silents
JANE EYRE(1914)
Barbara Roy
Misc. Talkies
FORBIDDEN LESSONS(1982)
Billie Roy
UNDER AGE(1941)
Billy Roy
ALOMA OF THE SOUTH SEAS(1941); CROSSROADS(1942); PRIDE OF THE YANKEES, THE(1942); CROSS OF LORRAINE, THE(1943); GOOD LUCK, MR. YATES(1943); HANGMEN ALSO DIE(1943); IRON MAJOR, THE(1943); CONSPIRATORS, THE(1944); PASSAGE TO MARSEILLE(1944); CORN IS GREEN, THE(1945); IT HAPPENED IN BROOKLYN(1947); THAT HAGEN GIRL(1947)
Brian Roy
MOONRUNNERS(1975), ph
Charu Roy
Misc. Silents
SHIRAZ(1929); THROW OF THE DICE(1930, Brit.)
Chuck Roy
HAPPY BIRTHDAY, DAVY(1970), a, p, w
Deep Roy
RETURN OF THE JEDI(1983)
1984
NEVERENDING STORY, THE(1984, Ger.)
Derek Roy
COME DANCE WITH ME(1950, Brit.)
Devraj Roy
ADVERSARY, THE(1973, Ind.)
Don Roy
NIGHT AND DAY(1946)
Ernest G. Roy
CALLING PAUL TEMPLE(1948, Brit.), p; MONKEY'S PAW, THE(1948, Brit.), p; STORY OF SHIRLEY YORKE, THE(1948, Brit.), p; DARK SECRET(1949, Brit.), p; SOMETHING IN THE CITY(1950, Brit.), p; MADAME LOUISE(1951, Brit.), p; PAUL TEMPLE'S TRIUMPH(1951, Brit.), p; SCARLET THREAD(1951, Brit.), p; HAMMER THE TOFF(1952, Brit.), p; PAUL TEMPLE RETURNS(1952, Brit.), p; SALUTE THE TOFF(1952, Brit.), p; BROKEN HORSESHOE, THE(1953, Brit.), p; MARILYN(1953, Brit.), p; OPERATION DIPLOMAT(1953, Brit.), p; THERE WAS A YOUNG LADY(1953, Brit.), p
Esperanza Roy
WITCH WITHOUT A BROOM, A(1967, U.S./Span.)
Gary Roy
NORSEMAN, THE(1978)
Gloria Roy
CHARLIE CHAN'S GREATEST CASE(1933); HOT PEPPER(1933); JIMMY AND SALLY(1933); WILD GOLD(1934); CHARLIE CHAN IN EGYPT(1935); LIFE BEGINS AT 40(1935); THIS IS THE LIFE(1935); THUNDER IN THE NIGHT(1935); CHARLIE CHAN AT THE RACE TRACK(1936); CHARLIE CHAN'S SECRET(1936); SONG AND DANCE MAN, THE(1936); CRACK-UP, THE(1937); FAIR WARNING(1937); HOLY TERROR, THE(1937); CITY GIRL(1938); MR. MOTO TAKES A CHANCE(1938); FRONTIER MARSHAL(1939); GRAPES OF WRATH(1940); LUCKY CISCO KID(1940)
Gopal Roy
TWO DAUGHTERS(1963, India)
Gregor Roy
VERDICT, THE(1982); EASY MONEY(1983)
Harry Roy
RHYTHM RACKETEER(1937, Brit.); EVERYTHING IS RHYTHM(1940, Brit.)
Indrapramit Roy
1984
HOME AND THE WORLD, THE(1984, India)
Jaysree Roy
ADVERSARY, THE(1973, Ind.)
Jean Roy
TROUBLE-FETE(1964, Can.), ph
Jean-Louis Roy
UNKNOWN MAN OF SHANDIGOR, THE(1967, Switz.), d, w

John Roy
FRENCHMAN'S CREEK(1944); THEY WERE EXPENDABLE(1945); TWO YEARS BEFORE THE MAST(1946); JOAN OF ARC(1948); LUCK OF THE IRISH(1948); CRISS CROSS(1949); RECKLESS MOMENTS, THE(1949); JACKPOT, THE(1950); SCARLET ANGEL(1952); SHOOT-OUT AT MEDICINE BEND(1957); EDGE OF ETERNITY(1959)
Mickey Roy
FOND MEMORIES(1982, Can.)
Nell Roy
YOU CAN'T TAKE IT WITH YOU(1938)
Raymond Roy
TARGETS(1968)
Rob Roy
1984
DELIVERY BOYS(1984)
Rosalie Roy
TRANSATLANTIC(1931); YOUNG AS YOU FEEL(1931); ST. LOUIS KID, THE(1934); TWENTY MILLION SWEETHEARTS(1934); WONDER BAR(1934); MY REPUTATION(1946)
Sam Roy
SOPHIE'S WAYS(1970, Fr.), p
Soumandu Roy
1984
HOME AND THE WORLD, THE(1984, India), ph
Soumendu Roy
TWO DAUGHTERS(1963, India), ph; CHESS PLAYERS, THE(1978, India), ph
Walter Roy
ONCE IN A NEW MOON(1935, Brit.); WISE GUYS(1937, Brit.); SHIPBUILDERS, THE(1943, Brit.); HERE COMES THE SUN(1945, Brit.)
Wilfred Roy
TALKING FEET(1937, Brit.)
William Roy
YOUNG DANIEL BOONE(1950)
Roy Acuff and his Smoky Mountain Boys and Girls
COWBOY CANTEEN(1944)
Roy Acuff and his Smoky Mountain Boys with Rachel
GRAND OLE OPRY(1940); SING, NEIGHBOR, SING(1944)
Roy Fox and His Band
BRITANNIA OF BILLINGSGATE(1933, Brit.); ON THE AIR(1934, Brit.); RADIO PIRATES(1935, Brit.)
Roy Knapp's Rough Riders
RODEO RHYTHM(1941)
Roy Rogers Riders
SOUTH OF CALIENTE(1951)
The Roy Rogers Riders
PALS OF THE GOLDEN WEST(1952)
David Roya
BILLY JACK(1971)
Jacqueline Royaards
ONE NIGHT... A TRAIN(1968, Fr./Bel.)
Alan Royal
ONLY THING YOU KNOW, THE(1971, Can.)
Allan Royal
TITLE SHOT(1982, Can.)
Ann Royal
JESSE JAMES' WOMEN(1954), ch
Charles F. Royal
NEW ADVENTURES OF TARZAN(1935), w; TUNDRA(1936), w; TARZAN AND THE GREEN GODDESS(1938), w; GIRL IN THE CASE(1944), w; ARCTIC FURY(1949), w
Charles F. Royal [George F. Royal]
TROUBLE IN SUNDOWN(1939), w
Charles Royal
PHANTOM OF SANTA FE(1937), w; DARK MOUNTAIN(1944), w
Charles Francis Royal
COURAGEOUS AVENGER, THE(1935), w; FIRETRAP, THE(1935), w; WESTERN COURAGE(1935), w; GUNS IN THE DARK(1937), w; LIGHTNIN' CRANDALL(1937), w; OUTLAWS OF THE ORIENT(1937), w; RIDIN' THE LONE TRAIL(1937), w; SHADOWS OF THE ORIENT(1937), w; COLORADO KID(1938), w; COLORADO TRAIL(1938), w; GANGS OF NEW YORK(1938), w; OLD BARN DANCE, THE(1938), w; OUTPOST OF THE MOUNTIES(1939), w; RIO GRANDE(1939), w; TAMING OF THE WEST, THE(1939), w; TEXAS STAMPEDE(1939), w; LONE STAR RAIDERS(1940), w; MAN FROM TUMBLEWEEDS, THE(1940), w; NORTH FROM LONE STAR(1941), w; GOD IS MY PARTNER(1957), w
Diane Royal
PARACHUTE NURSE(1942)
John Royal
GARDEN OF EDEN(1954)
Lloyd Royal
JESSE JAMES' WOMEN(1954), p; NATCHEZ TRACE(1960), p
Michael Royal
LAWLESS CODE(1949)
Patricia Royal
TIMBER WAR(1936)
Royal Ballet
ROMEO AND JULIET(1966, Brit.)
The Royal Ballet Corps
PETER RABBIT AND TALES OF BEATRIX POTTER(1971, Brit.)
Royal Canadian Air Force
JOURNEY TOGETHER(1946, Brit.)
The Royal Cansinos
DANCING PIRATE(1936)
Royal Hawaiian Serenaders
MILLION DOLLAR WEEKEND(1948)
Personnel of the Royal Netherlands Navy
SILVER FLEET, THE(1945, Brit.)
Principals and Chorus of The Royal Opera House
DAVY(1958, Brit.)

Chorus of The Royal Opera House Covent Garden
SINGING COP, THE(1938, Brit.)
The Royal Philharmonic Orchestra
TWO HUNDRED MOTELS(1971, Brit.)
The Royal Teens
LET'S ROCK(1958)
Allan Royale
WELCOME TO BLOOD CITY(1977, Brit./Can.)
Betty Jane Royale
CYBORG 2087(1966); TROUBLE WITH ANGELS, THE(1966)
Ethel Royale
TWICE BRANDED(1936, Brit.); VANDERGILT DIAMOND MYSTERY, THE(1936);
WE'LL SMILE AGAIN(1942, Brit.); TWILIGHT HOUR(1944, Brit.); OLD MOTHER
RILEY, HEADMISTRESS(1950, Brit.)
Pat Royale
REEFER MADNESS(1936)
Silents
OLD ARM CHAIR, THE(1920, Brit.)
Patricia Royale
JEALOUSY(1934); MARY BURNS, FUGITIVE(1935)
William Royale
CRUSADE AGAINST RACKETS(1937)
Royar
CAFE METROPOLE(1937), cos
Arthur I. Royce
OUR RELATIONS(1936), art d; PICK A STAR(1937), art d; WAY OUT WEST(1937),
art d
Brigham Royce
Misc. Silents
HELENE OF THE NORTH(1915)
Christiane Royce
HOUSE OF FREAKS(1973, Ital.)
Dixie Lynn Royce
NIGHTMARES(1983)
Edward Royce
WORDS AND MUSIC(1929), ch, ch; ALONG CAME SALLY(1934, Brit.), ch
Frosty Royce
OKLAHOMA RENEGADES(1940); KING OF DODGE CITY(1941); BLACK MARKET
RUSTLERS(1943); UP IN ARMS(1944); JOE PALOOKA MEETS HUMPHREY(1950);
OUTCASTS OF POKER FLAT, THE(1952); ESCAPE FROM RED ROCK(1958)
John Royce
CLAUDIA(1943); FIRST COMES COURAGE(1943); FIVE GRAVES TO CAIRO(1943);
NORTHERN PURSUIT(1943); FIGHTER SQUADRON(1948); ROGUES' REGI-
MENT(1948); RED DANUBE, THE(1949); SEALED CARGO(1951)
Julian Royce
CRIMINAL AT LARGE(1932, Brit.); CALL ME MAME(1933, Brit.); SHE WAS ONLY
A VILLAGE MAIDEN(1933, Brit.); THIS IS THE LIFE(1933, Brit.); LEAVE IT TO
BLANCHE(1934, Brit.); MISTER CINDERS(1934, Brit.); BIRDS OF A FEATHER(1935,
Brit.); SO YOU WON'T TALK?(1935, Brit.); TWO HEARTS IN HARMONY(1935, Brit.)
Silents
IRON JUSTICE(1915, Brit.); BIGAMIST, THE(1921, Brit.); RUNNING WATER(1922,
Brit.); KNOCKOUT, THE(1923, Brit.)
Misc. Silents
ESTHER REDEEMED(1915, Brit.); LIGHT(1915, Brit.); HONOUR IN PAWN(1916,
Brit.); TEMPTATION'S HOUR(1916, Brit.); DERELICTS(1917, Brit.); NOT NEGOTIA-
BLE(1918, Brit.); PERSISTENT LOVERS, THE(1922, Brit.)
Lionel Royce
MARIE ANTOINETTE(1938); CONFESSIONS OF A NAZI SPY(1939); CON-
SPIRACY(1939); ESPIONAGE AGENT(1939); LET FREEDOM RING(1939); NURSE
EDITH CAVELL(1939); PACK UP YOUR TROUBLES(1939); 6000 ENEMIES(1939);
CHARLIE CHAN IN PANAMA(1940); FOUR SONS(1940); MAN I MARRIED,
THE(1940); SON OF MONTE CRISTO(1940); VICTORY(1940); ROAD TO ZAN-
ZIBAR(1941); SO ENDS OUR NIGHT(1941); SOUTH OF PANAMA(1941); UNDER-
GROUND(1941); HALF WAY TO SHANGHAI(1942); LADY HAS PLANS, THE(1942);
MY FAVORITE BLONDE(1942); MY FAVORITE SPY(1942); ONCE UPON A HONEY-
MOON(1942); UNSEEN ENEMY(1942); CRASH DIVE(1943); HITLER'S MAD-
MAN(1943); LET'S FACE IT(1943); MISSION TO MOSCOW(1943); HITLER GANG,
THE(1944); PASSPORT TO DESTINY(1944); WHITE PONGO(1945); GILDA(1946)
Madge Royce
Silents
LONG ODDS(1922, Brit.)
Margaret Royce
BIG DADDY(1969), ed
Milton Royce
MYSTERY OF MR. X, THE(1934); MAN WHO BROKE THE BANK AT MONTE
CARLO, THE(1935)
Morgan Royce
SONG OF THE LOON(1970)
Ray L. Royce
Misc. Silents
YORK STATE FOLKS(1915)
Riza Royce
HIT PARADE OF 1947(1947); HOUSE OF WAX(1953); CATTLE QUEEN OF MON-
TANA(1954); GIRLS IN PRISON(1956); BAND OF ANGELS(1957); BAT, THE(1959);
GOOD NEIGHBOR SAM(1964)
Silents
SACRED SILENCE(1919)
Robin Royce
HAPPY HOOKER GOES TO WASHINGTON, THE(1977), art d
Robinson Royce
SO LONG, BLUE BOY(1973), art d; DEATH RACE 2000(1975), art d
Roselyn Royce
OFF THE WALL(1983)
Ruth Royce
Silents
SPLENDID SIN, THE(1919); ALL DOLLED UP(1921); IF ONLY JIM(1921); ACTION
GALORE(1925)
Misc. Silents
CALIFORNIA IN '49(1924); FORT FRAYNE(1926)

Virginia Royce
DESPERATE WOMEN, THE(?)
Bryan Royceston
SING ALONG WITH ME(1952, Brit.)
Leslie Roycroft
Misc. Silents
WHAT'S YOUR REPUTATION WORTH?(1921)
Frank Royde
AFTER OFFICE HOURS(1932, Brit.); TIN GODS(1932, Brit.); AREN'T MEN
BEASTS?(1937, Brit.); MY WIFE'S FAMILY(1962, Brit.)
Misc. Silents
VERDICT OF THE HEART, THE(1915, Brit.)
Philip Roye
SERGEANT, THE(1968); LEARNING TREE, THE(1969)
Phillip Roye
BLACK CAESAR(1973)
Beverly Royed
HAPPY DAYS(1930)
Royer
SMOKY(1933), cos; LAST TRAIL, THE(1934), cos; SHE LEARNED ABOUT SAIL-
ORS(1934), cos; SLEEPERS EAST(1934), cos; THREE ON A HONEYMOON(1934), cos;
WILD GOLD(1934), cos; 365 NIGHTS IN HOLLYWOOD(1934), cos; MYSTERY WOM-
AN(1935), cos; LLOYDS OF LONDON(1936), cos; REUNION(1936), cos; SING, BABY,
SING(1936), cos; SINS OF MAN(1936), cos; STOWAWAY(1936), cos; TO MARY–WITH
LOVE(1936), cos; LOVE IS NEWS(1937), cos; SLAVE SHIP(1937), cos; THIN
ICE(1937), cos; THIS IS MY AFFAIR(1937), cos; YOU CAN'T HAVE EVERY-
THING(1937), cos; ALWAYS GOODBYE(1938), cos; IN OLD CHICAGO(1938), cos; MY
LUCKY STAR(1938), cos; SUEZ(1938), cos; BARRICADE(1939), cos; DAY-TIME
WIFE(1939), cos; ROSE OF WASHINGTON SQUARE(1939), cos; SECOND FID-
DLE(1939), cos; STANLEY AND LIVINGSTONE(1939), cos; STORY OF ALEXANDER
GRAHAM BELL, THE(1939), cos; SWANEE RIVER(1939), cos; THREE MUS-
KETEERS, THE(1939), cos; WIFE, HUSBAND AND FRIEND(1939), cos; YOUNG MR.
LINCOLN(1939), cos; LITTLE OLD NEW YORK(1940), cos; SHANGHAI GESTURE,
THE(1941), cos; MISS ANNIE ROONEY(1942), cos
Fanchon Royer
CANNONBALL EXPRESS(1932), p; HONOR OF THE PRESS(1932), p; ALIMONY
MADNESS(1933), p; REVENGE AT MONTE CARLO(1933), p; DEATH IN THE
SKY(1937), p; MILE A MINUTE LOVE(1937), p; TURN OFF THE MOON(1937), p;
MILLION TO ONE, A(1938), p; TEN LAPS TO GO(1938), p; MYSTIC CIRCLE MUR-
DER(1939), p
Franchon Royer
BEHIND JURY DOORS(1933, Brit.), p
James L. Royer
PEACE FOR A GUNFIGHTER(1967), ed
Myra Royl
GOIN' TO TOWN(1935)
Bron Roylance
10(1979), makeup
Nora Roylance
Silents
PRIDE OF THE NORTH, THE(1920, Brit.)
Pamela Roylance
SLUMBER PARTY MASSACRE, THE(1982)
Suzanne Roylance
MY BRILLIANT CAREER(1980, Aus.); CLINIC, THE(1983, Aus.)
Carol Royle
GREEK TYCOON, THE(1978)
Misc. Talkies
TUXEDO WARRIOR(1982)
Derek Royle
WORK IS A FOUR LETTER WORD(1968, Brit.); DON'T JUST LIE THERE, SAY
SOMETHING!(1973, Brit.)
Edwin Milton Royle
SQUAW MAN, THE(1931), w
Silents
SQUAW MAN, THE(1914), w
John Royle
ON THE BEACH(1959)
Selena Royle
MISLEADING LADY, THE(1932); STAGE DOOR CANTEEN(1943); MAIN STREET
AFTER DARK(1944); MRS. PARKINGTON(1944); SULLIVANS, THE(1944); THIRTY
SECONDS OVER TOKYO(1944); THIS MAN'S NAVY(1945); BLUE SIERRA(1946);
COURAGE OF LASSIE(1946); GALLANT JOURNEY(1946); GREEN YEARS,
THE(1946); HARVEY GIRLS, THE(1946); NIGHT AND DAY(1946); NO LEAVE, NO
LOVE(1946); TILL THE END OF TIME(1946); CASS TIMBERLANE(1947); ROMANCE
OF ROSY RIDGE, THE(1947); DATE WITH JUDY, A(1948); JOAN OF ARC(1948);
MOONRISE(1948); SMART WOMAN(1948); SUMMER HOLIDAY(1948); YOU WERE
MEANT FOR ME(1948); BAD BOY(1949); HEIRESS, THE(1949); MY DREAM IS
YOURS(1949); YOU'RE MY EVERYTHING(1949); BIG HANGOVER, THE(1950);
DAMNED DON'T CRY, THE(1950); BRANDED(1951); COME FILL THE CUP(1951); HE
RAN ALL THE WAY(1951); ROBOT MONSTER(1953); MURDER IS MY BEAT(1955)
William Royle
HIS BROTHER'S WIFE(1936); GLORY TRAIL, THE(1937); HOLLYWOOD COW-
BOY(1937); RENFREW OF THE ROYAL MOUNTED(1937); SPECIAL AGENT K-
7(1937); WESTBOUND LIMITED(1937); REBELLION(1938); RED RIVER RAN-
GE(1938); RENEGADE RANGER(1938); ARIZONA LEGION(1939); FIGHTING GRIN-
GO, THE(1939); FRONTIER PONY EXPRESS(1939); I AM NOT AFRAID(1939); LET US
LIVE(1939); MAN IN THE IRON MASK, THE(1939); MEXICALI ROSE(1939); MR.
WONG IN CHINATOWN(1939); MUTINY IN THE BIG HOUSE(1939); PIRATES OF
THE SKIES(1939); RAINS CAME, THE(1939); LUCKY CISCO KID(1940); MAN FROM
DAKOTA, THE(1940); MAN FROM MONTREAL, THE(1940); MURDER ON THE
YUKON(1940); SON OF THE NAVY(1940); MANPOWER(1941); DRUMS OF FU
MANCHU(1943)
Misc. Talkies
REBELLION(1936)
William H. Royle
ARSENE LUPIN RETURNS(1938)

Thomas L. Roysden
1984
ICEMAN(1984), set d; SOLDIER'S STORY, A(1984), set d

Tom Roysden
BUDDY HOLLY STORY, THE(1978), set d

Frosty Royse
RIDING SHOTGUN(1954); MAN FROM LARAMIE, THE(1955)

Vermetta Royster
BLUE COLLAR(1978)

Benny Royston
PRIVATE ANGELO(1949, Brit.), makeup; MOSQUITO SQUADRON(1970, Brit.), makeup

Dennis Royston
SUDDEN IMPACT(1983)

Gerald Royston
Silents
LITTLE LORD FAUNTLEROY(1914, Brit.)

Harry Royston
Silents
JUSTICE(1914, Brit.); JACK TAR(1915, Brit.); DEAD CERTAINTY, A(1920, Brit.)
Misc. Silents
VICAR OF WAKEFIELD, THE(1913, Brit.); JUSTICE(1914, Brit.); AFTER DARK(1915, Brit.); LADY JENNIFER(1915, Brit.)

Jonah Royston
OUTRAGEOUS!(1977, Can.)

Roy Royston
JUST FOR A SONG(1930, Brit.); BIG SPLASH, THE(1935, Brit.); PLAGUE OF THE ZOMBIES, THE(1966, Brit.)
Silents
ONE SUMMER'S DAY(1917, Brit.); MR. WU(1919, Brit.)

Roland Royter
UNDER AGE(1964)

A. Roytman
SUMMER TO REMEMBER, A(1961, USSR), md; LETTER THAT WAS NEVER SENT, THE(1962, USSR), md; RESURRECTION(1963, USSR), md; FORTY-NINE DAYS(1964, USSR), md

Lita Roza
CAST A DARK SHADOW(1958, Brit.)

Gregory Rozakis
AMERICA, AMERICA(1963); DEATH WISH(1974); GAMBLER, THE(1974); ABDUCTION(1975); BELOW THE BELT(1980)
1984
COTTON CLUB, THE(1984)

Dominique Rozan
LA GUERRE EST FINIE(1967, Fr./Swed.); JE T'AIME, JE T'AIME(1972, Fr./Swed.)

Gerta Rozan
PANTHER'S CLAW, THE(1942)

Greta Rozan
SO ENDS OUR NIGHT(1941)

Katrina Rozan
SECRET INVASION, THE(1964)

Micheline Rozan
IMMORTAL STORY, THE(1969, Fr.), p

Rene Rozan
FIRST TASTE OF LOVE(1962, Fr.); LAFAYETTE(1963, Fr.)

A. Rozanov
DON QUIXOTE(1961, USSR)

T. Rozanov
LADY WITH THE DOG, THE(1962, USSR)

Countess Elektra Rozanska
DOUBLE LIFE, A(1947)

Elektra Rozanska
FROM THE TERRACE(1960); SUMMER AND SMOKE(1961)

Nicole Rozay
ACCUSED–STAND UP(1930, Fr.)

Miklos Rozea
GREEN COCKATOO, THE(1947, Brit.), m

Eloise Rozelle
TWO IN A CROWD(1936)

Rita Rozelle
LADIES LOVE DANGER(1935); STRANDED(1935); TOP HAT(1935)

William Rozelle
Misc. Silents
MOONSTONE, THE(1915)

Florene Rozen
SONG OF SCHEHERAZADE(1947)

Lucien Rozenberg
LIFE AND LOVES OF BEETHOVEN, THE(1937, Fr.)

Francois Rozet
Misc. Silents
MADAME RECAMIER(1928, Fr.)

Stanislaw Rozewicz
ECHO, THE(1964, Pol.), d, w

Tadeusz Rozewicz
ECHO, THE(1964, Pol.), w

G. Rozhalin
HUNTING IN SIBERIA(1962, USSR), art d

Nicolai Rozhekov
SYMPHONY OF LIFE(1949, USSR), w

Jacques Rozier
ADIEU PHILLIPINE(1962, Fr./Ital.), d&w

Shiva Rozier
HOW SWEET IT IS(1968)

Willy Rozier
GIRL IN THE BIKINI, THE(1958, Fr.), p&d; GIRL CAN'T STOP, THE(1966, Fr./Gr.), p&d, w

Vincent Roziere
CROOK, THE(1971, Fr.)

Zdenek Rozkopal
JOURNEY TO THE BEGINNING OF TIME(1966, Czech), art d; WISHING MACHINE(1971, Czech.), set d

Georgine Rozman
DUCHESS AND THE DIRTWATER FOX, THE(1976)

John Rozman
BLACK EYE(1974), art d

Shlomo Rozmarin
RABBI AND THE SHIKSE, THE(1976, Israel)

Frank Roznio
1984
FEAR CITY(1984)

Dr. Nathan Rozofsky
HONOR AMONG LOVERS(1931)

V Rozov
CRANES ARE FLYING, THE(1960, USSR), w

Viktor Rozov
LETTER THAT WAS NEVER SENT, THE(1962, USSR), w

Rozsa
DARK WATERS(1944), md

Janos Rozsa
FATHER(1967, Hung.), ed

Miklos Rozsa
MURDER ON DIAMOND ROW(1937, Brit.), m; DRUMS(1938, Brit.), m; FOUR FEATHERS, THE(1939, Brit.), m; U-BOAT 29(1939, Brit.), m; THIEF OF BAGHDAD, THE(1940, Brit.), m; LYDIA(1941), m; SUNDOWN(1941), m; THAT HAMILTON WOMAN(1941), m, md; JUNGLE BOOK(1942), m; TO BE OR NOT TO BE(1942), m; FIVE GRAVES TO CAIRO(1943), m; SAHARA(1943), m; SO PROUDLY WE HAIL(1943), m; DARK WATERS(1944), m; DOUBLE INDEMNITY(1944), m; HOUR BEFORE THE DAWN, THE(1944), m; MAN IN HALF-MOON STREET, THE(1944), m; LADY ON A TRAIN(1945), m; LOST WEEKEND, THE(1945), m; SONG TO REMEMBER, A(1945), m; SPELLBOUND(1945), m; BECAUSE OF HIM(1946), m; STRANGE LOVE OF MARTHA IVERS, THE(1946), m; BRUTE FORCE(1947), m; DESERT FURY(1947), m; DOUBLE LIFE, A(1947), m; MACOMBER AFFAIR, THE(1947), m&md; OTHER LOVE, THE(1947), m; RED HOUSE, THE(1947), m; SONG OF SCHEHERAZADE(1947), md; TIME OUT OF MIND(1947), m; WOMAN'S VENGEANCE, A(1947), m; COMMAND DECISION(1948), m; KISS THE BLOOD OFF MY HANDS(1948), m; NAKED CITY, THE(1948), m; SECRET BEYOND THE DOOR, THE(1948), m; BRIBE, THE(1949), m; CRISS CROSS(1949), m; EAST SIDE, WEST SIDE(1949), m; MADAME BOVARY(1949), m; RED DANUBE, THE(1949), m; ASPHALT JUNGLE, THE(1950), m; CRISIS(1950), m; LIGHT TOUCH, THE(1951), m, md; PLYMOUTH ADVENTURE(1952), m; ALL THE BROTHERS WERE VALIANT(1953), m; KNIGHTS OF THE ROUND TABLE(1953), m; STORY OF THREE LOVES, THE(1953), a, m; YOUNG BESS(1953), m; CREST OF THE WAVE(1954, Brit.), m; MEN OF THE FIGHTING LADY(1954), m; VALLEY OF THE KINGS(1954), m; DIANE(1955), m; KING'S THIEF, THE(1955), m, md; MOONFLEET(1955), m; BHOWANI JUNCTION(1956), m; LUST FOR LIFE(1956), m; SEVENTH SIN, THE(1957), m; TIP ON A DEAD JOCKEY(1957), m; TIME TO LOVE AND A TIME TO DIE, A(1958), m; BEN HUR(1959), m; WORLD, THE FLESH, AND THE DEVIL, THE(1959), m; EL CID(1961, U.S./Ital.), m; KING OF KINGS(1961), m; SODOM AND GOMORRAH(1962, U.S./Fr./Ital.), m; V.I.P.s, THE(1963, Brit.), m; GREEN BERETS, THE(1968), m; POWER, THE(1968), m, md; PRIVATE LIFE OF SHERLOCK HOLMES, THE(1970, Brit.), m; GOLDEN VOYAGE OF SINBAD, THE(1974, Brit.), m; PROVIDENCE(1977, Fr.), m; FEDORA(1978, Ger./Fr.), m; PRIVATE FILES OF J. EDGAR HOOVER, THE(1978), m; TIME AFTER TIME(1979, Brit.), m; EYE OF THE NEEDLE(1981), m; DEAD MEN DON'T WEAR PLAID(1982), m

Mikols Rozsa
GREEN FIRE(1955), m

Kalman Rozsahegyi
SUN SHINES, THE(1939, Hung.)

Jaroslav Rozsival
TRANSPORT FROM PARADISE(1967, Czech.)

Christopher Rozycki
LOCAL HERO(1983, Brit.)

Miklos Rozza
ADAM'S RIB(1949), m

RPM Motorcycle Club of Brooklyn
TEENAGE GANG DEBS(1966)

Robin Ruakere
1984
UTU(1984, New Zealand)

Patricia Ruanne
NIJINSKY(1980, Brit.)

Alfredo Ruanova
LOS AUTOMATAS DE LA MUERTE(1960, Mex.), w; ORLAK, THE HELL OF FRANKENSTEIN(1960, Mex.), w; WITCH'S MIRROR, THE(1960, Mex.), w; NEUTRON CONTRA EL DR. CARONTE(1962, Mex.), w; NEUTRON EL ENMASCARADO NEGRO(1962, Mex.), w; GIGANTES PLANETARIOS(1965, Mex.), w

Robert C. Ruark
SOMETHING OF VALUE(1957), d&w

Christian A. Rub
NO RANSOM(1935)

Christian Rub
CROOKED CIRCLE(1932); MAN FROM YESTERDAY, THE(1932); SECRETS OF THE FRENCH POLICE(1932); SILVER DOLLAR(1932); TRIAL OF VIVIENNE WARE, THE(1932); HUMANITY(1933); KISS BEFORE THE MIRROR, THE(1933); MAN OF SENTIMENT, A(1933); MARY STEVENS, M.D.(1933); NO OTHER WOMAN(1933); TUGBOAT ANNIE(1933); FOUNTAIN, THE(1934); LITTLE MAN, WHAT NOW?(1934); MAN OF TWO WORLDS(1934); MIGHTY BARNUM, THE(1934); MUSIC IN THE AIR(1934); NO GREATER GLORY(1934); NO MORE WOMEN(1934); ROMANCE IN THE RAIN(1934); STAMBOUL QUEST(1934); DOG OF FLANDERS, A(1935); FOUR HOURS TO KILL(1935); LADIES CRAVE EXCITEMENT(1935); LET 'EM HAVE IT(1935); MAN WHO BROKE THE BANK AT MONTE CARLO, THE(1935); MARK OF THE VAMPIRE(1935); METROPOLITAN(1935); NIGHT IS YOUNG, THE(1935); OIL FOR THE LAMPS OF CHINA(1935); PETER IBBETSON(1935); ROMANCE IN MANHATTAN(1935); STOLEN HARMONY(1935); DRACULA'S DAUGHTER(1936); FURY(1936); GIRLS' DORMITORY(1936); HITCH HIKE LADY(1936); LEATHERNECKS HAVE LANDED, THE(1936); MR. DEEDS GOES TO TOWN(1936); MURDER ON A BRIDLE PATH(1936); MURDER WITH PICTURES(1936); NEXT TIME WE LOVE(1936); PAROLE(1936); SINS OF MAN(1936); SUZY(1936); WE'RE ONLY HU-

MAN(1936); CAFE METROPOLE(1937); CAPTAINS COURAGEOUS(1937); HEIDI(1937); IT COULD HAPPEN TO YOU(1937); MAYTIME(1937); OUTCAST(1937); PRESCRIPTION FOR ROMANCE(1937); THIN ICE(1937); TOVARICH(1937); WHEN LOVE IS YOUNG(1937); 100 MEN AND A GIRL(1937); GREAT WALTZ, THE(1938); I'LL GIVE A MILLION(1938); MAD ABOUT MUSIC(1938); PROFESSOR BEWARE(1938); YOU CAN'T TAKE IT WITH YOU(1938); EVERYTHING HAPPENS AT NIGHT(1939); FORGED PASSPORT(1939); HIDDEN POWER(1939); NEVER SAY DIE(1939); NO PLACE TO GO(1939); ALL THIS AND HEAVEN TOO(1940); EARTHBOUND(1940); FOUR SONS(1940); PINOCCHIO(1940); SWISS FAMILY ROBINSON(1940); FATHER'S SON(1941); BERLIN CORRESPONDENT(1942); DANGEROUSLY THEY LIVE(1942); NAZI AGENT(1942); TALES OF MANHATTAN(1942); BOMBER'S MOON(1943); PRINCESS O'ROURKE(1943); JUNGLE WOMAN(1944); ONCE UPON A TIME(1944); 3 IS A FAMILY(1944); RHAPSODY IN BLUE(1945); STRANGE CONFESSION(1945); FALL GUY(1947); SOMETHING FOR THE BIRDS(1952)
Misc. Silents
BELLE OF NEW YORK, THE(1919)
Al Ruban
1,000 SHAPES OF A FEMALE(1963); FACES(1968), ph, ed; MADIGAN(1968); HUSBANDS(1970), p; MINNIE AND MOSKOWITZ(1971), p; KILLING OF A CHINESE BOOKIE, THE(1976), a, p; OPENING NIGHT(1977), p, ph; DAVID(1979, Ger.), ph; JETLAG(1981, U.S./Span.), ph; SWAMP THING(1982)
1984
LOVE STREAMS(1984), a, ph
Joe Rubbo
LAST AMERICAN VIRGIN, THE(1982)
Janine Rubeiz
DEATHWATCH(1980, Fr./Ger.), p
Barbara Rubel
COME BACK BABY(1968)
James L. Rubel
MEDICO OF PAINTED SPRINGS, THE(1941), w; PRAIRIE STRANGER(1941), w; THUNDER OVER THE PRAIRIE(1941), w
Marc Reid Rubel
ALMOST SUMMER(1978), w; XANADU(1980), w
Paul Rubell
FINAL TERROR, THE(1983), ed
1984
STONE BOY, THE(1984), ed
Ruben
ROADHOUSE MURDER, THE(1932), w; JOYRIDE(1977), w
Aaron Ruben
COMIC, THE(1969), p, w
Albert Ruben
JOURNEY THROUGH ROSEBUD(1972), w; SEVEN UPS, THE(1973), w; VISIT TO A CHIEF'S SON(1974), w
Alex Ruben
THIS MARRIAGE BUSINESS(1938), w; TIME OUT FOR RHYTHM(1941), w
Alva Ruben
LIFESPAN(1975, U.S./Brit./Neth.), w
Glynn Ruben
SHARKY'S MACHINE(1982)
J. Walter Ruben
DANCE HALL(1929), w; JAZZ HEAVEN(1929), w; LOVE DOCTOR, THE(1929), w; MARRIAGE PLAYGROUND, THE(1929), w; AMOS 'N' ANDY(1930), w; LOVIN' THE LADIES(1930), w; SHE'S MY WEAKNESS(1930), w; SHOOTING STRAIGHT(1930), w; HIGH STAKES(1931), w; PUBLIC DEFENDER, THE(1931), d; ROYAL BED, THE(1931), w; SECRET SERVICE(1931), d; WHITE SHOULDERS(1931), w; YOUNG DONOVAN'S KID(1931), w; PHANTOM OF CRESTWOOD, THE(1932), d, w; ROADHOUSE MURDER, THE(1932), d; SYMPHONY OF SIX MILLION(1932), w; ACE OF ACES(1933), d; NO MARRIAGE TIES(1933), d; NO OTHER WOMAN(1933), d; RACETRACK(1933), w; MAN OF TWO WORLDS(1934), d; SUCCESS AT ANY PRICE(1934), d; WHERE SINNERS MEET(1934), d; JAVA HEAD(1935, Brit.), d; PUBLIC HERO NO. 1(1935), d, w; OLD HUTCH(1936), d; RIFF-RAFF(1936), d; TROUBLE FOR TWO(1936), d; GOOD OLD SOAK, THE(1937), d; THOROUGHBREDS DON'T CRY(1937), w; MAISIE(1939), p; SERGEANT MADDEN(1939), p; THUNDER AFLOAT(1939), p; CONGO MAISIE(1940), p; FLIGHT COMMAND(1940), p; GOLD RUSH MAISIE(1940), p; TWENTY MULE TEAM(1940), p; BAD MAN, THE(1941), p; BUGLE SOUNDS, THE(1941), p; GET-AWAY, THE(1941), p; MAISIE WAS A LADY(1941), p; RINGSIDE MAISIE(1941), p; FLEET'S IN, THE(1942), p; MAISIE GETS HER MAN(1942), p; MOKEY(1942), p; TENNESSEE JOHNSON(1942), p; ASSIGNMENT IN BRITTANY(1943), p
Silents
GAY RETREAT, THE(1927), w; SHOOTIN' IRONS(1927), w; AVALANCHE(1928), w; STAIRS OF SAND(1929), w; SUNSET PASS(1929), w
Jose Ruben
Misc. Silents
DARK SECRETS(1923); SALOME OF THE TENEMENTS(1925)
Joseph Ruben
SISTER-IN-LAW, THE(1975), p, d&w; POM POM GIRLS, THE(1976), p&d, w; JOYRIDE(1977), d; OUR WINNING SEASON(1978), d; GORP(1980), d
1984
DREAMSCAPE(1984), d, w
Serge Ruben
ENTRE NOUS(1983, Fr.)
Tom Ruben
MORE AMERICAN GRAFFITI(1979)
Walter Ruben
GET-AWAY, THE(1941), w
Asoka Rubener
JULIET OF THE SPIRITS(1965, Fr./Ital./W.Ger.)
Sujata Rubener
JULIET OF THE SPIRITS(1965, Fr./Ital./W.Ger.)
The Rubenettes
BABES ON SWING STREET(1944)
The Rubenettes
SENSATION HUNTERS(1945)

Alam Rubens
Silents
REGGIE MIXES IN(1916)
Alma Rubens
SHE GOES TO WAR(1929); SHOW BOAT(1929)
Silents
INTOLERANCE(1916); AMERICANO, THE(1917); TRUTHFUL TULLIVER(1917); ANSWER, THE(1918); I LOVE YOU(1918); VALLEY OF SILENT MEN, THE(1922); ENEMIES OF WOMEN, THE(1923); UNDER THE RED ROBE(1923); CYTHEREA(1924); IS LOVE EVERYTHING?(1924); REJECTED WOMAN, THE(1924); WINDING STAIR, THE(1925); GILDED BUTTERFLY, THE(1926); 'MARRIAGE LICENSE?'(1926); SIBERIA(1926)
Misc. Silents
HALF BREED, THE(1916); COLD DECK, THE(1917); REGENERATES, THE(1917); TRUTHFUL TULLIVER(1917); FALSE AMBITION(1918); GHOST FLOWER, THE(1918); GOWN OF DESTINY, THE(1918); MADAME SPHINX(1918); PAINTED LILY, THE(1918); DIANE OF THE GREEN VAN(1919); MAN'S COUNTRY, A(1919); RESTLESS SOULS(1919); HUMORESQUE(1920); THOUGHTLESS WOMEN(1920); WORLD AND HIS WIFE, THE(1920); FIND THE WOMAN(1922); CYTHEREA(1924); GERALD CRANSTON'S LADY(1924); PRICE SHE PAID, THE(1924); WEEK END HUSBANDS(1924); DANCERS, THE(1925); EAST LYNNE(1925); FINE CLOTHES(1925); SHE WOLVES(1925); WOMAN'S FAITH, A(1925); HEART OF SALOME, THE(1927); MASKS OF THE DEVIL, THE(1928)
Bernice Rubens
I SENT A LETTER TO MY LOVE(1981, Fr.), w
George Rubens
OLD SPANISH CUSTOM, AN(1936, Brit.), m
Herbert Rubens
VERDICT, THE(1982)
Mary Beth Rubens
FIREBIRD 2015 AD(1981)
Percival Rubens
DEMON, THE(1981, S. Africa), p,d&w
Misc. Talkies
STRANGERS AT SUNRISE(1969), d; MR. KINGSTREET'S WAR(1973), d
Roseline Rubens
BON VOYAGE, CHARLIE BROWN(AND DON'T COME BACK)***(1980)
Arthur B. Rubenstein
GREAT BANK HOAX, THE(1977), m; ON THE RIGHT TRACK(1981), m; BLUE THUNDER(1983), m
Irving B. Rubenstein
Silents
HALDANE OF THE SECRET SERVICE(1923), ph
John Rubenstein
PADDY(1970, Irish), m; JEREMIAH JOHNSON(1972), m; CAR, THE(1977)
Martin Rubenstein
PRIME TIME, THE(1960), m
Paul Rubenstein
SIGN OF AQUARIUS(1970), p, ph
Phil Rubenstein
LAST AMERICAN VIRGIN, THE(1982)
1984
RHINESTONE(1984)
Richard P. Rubenstein
KNIGHTRIDERS(1981), p
Roberto Rubenstein
KID RODELO(1966, U.S./Span.)
Susan Rubenstein
IF EVER I SEE YOU AGAIN(1978)
Zelda Rubenstein
1984
SIXTEEN CANDLES(1984)
Bruno Rubeo
SPRING FEVER(1983, Can.), art d
Anthony Rubes
YENTL(1983)
Jan Rubes
FORBIDDEN JOURNEY(1950, Can.); INCREDIBLE JOURNEY, THE(1963); MR. PATMAN(1980, Can.); AMATEUR, THE(1982)
Misc. Talkies
LIONS FOR BREAKFAST(1977)
Liz Rubey
NIGHT OF THE IGUANA, THE(1964)
Josle Rubic
GOLDEN ARROW, THE(1936)
Jessica Rubicon
PARIS OOH-LA-LA!(1963, U.S./Fr.)
Alfonso Rubie
CHOSEN SURVIVORS(1974 U.S.-Mex.), cos
Howard Rubie
Misc. Talkies
SCALP MERCHANT, THE(1977), d
Les Rubie
WOLF DOG(1958, Can.); TICKET TO HEAVEN(1981); FUNERAL HOME(1982, Can.)
1984
COVERGIRL(1984, Can.); MRS. SOFFEL(1984)
A.S. Rubien
G.I. HONEYMOON(1945), w
Howard Nelson Rubien
WITCH'S CURSE, THE(1963, Ital.); HORRIBLE DR. HICHCOCK, THE(1964, Ital.)
Otta Rubik
SKELETON ON HORSEBACK(1940, Czech.)
Alec Rubin
KILLER'S KISS(1955)
Andrew Rubin
SUNNYSIDE(1979); LITTLE MISS MARKER(1980)
1984
POLICE ACADEMY(1984)

Andrew A. Rubin
CASEY'S SHADOW(1978)
Arthur Rubin
PRODUCERS, THE(1967)
Benny Rubin
THOROUGHLY MODERN MILLIE(1967); MARIANNE(1929); CHILDREN OF PLEASURE(1930); HOT CURVES(1930), a, w; IT'S A GREAT LIFE(1930); LEATHER-NECKING(1930); LORD BYRON OF BROADWAY(1930); LOVE IN THE ROUGH(1930); MONTANA MOON(1930); SUNNY SKIES(1930); THEY LEARNED ABOUT WOMEN(1930); BRIGHT LIGHTS(1935), w; GEORGE WHITE'S 1935 SCANDALS(1935); GIRL FRIEND, THE(1935), w; GO INTO YOUR DANCE(1935); TRAVELING SALESLADY, THE(1935), w; HIGH FLYERS(1937), w; ON AGAIN-OFF AGAIN(1937), w; ADVENTURES OF JANE ARDEN(1939); FIGHTING MAD(1939); HEADLEYS AT HOME, THE(1939); FIGHTING 69TH, THE(1940); LET'S MAKE MUSIC(1940); LUCKY PARTNERS(1940); NO, NO NANETTE(1940); DOUBLE TROUBLE(1941); HERE COMES MR. JORDAN(1941); OBLIGING YOUNG LADY(1941); SUNNY(1941); ZIS BOOM BAH(1941); BASHFUL BACHELOR, THE(1942); BROADWAY(1942); COLLEGE SWEETHEARTS(1942); MR. WISE GUY(1942); HOLLOW TRIUMPH(1948); NOOSE HANGS HIGH, THE(1948); SELLOUT, THE(1951); JUST THIS ONCE(1952); EASY TO LOVE(1953); GLASS WEB, THE(1953); TANGIER INCIDENT(1953); TORCH SONG(1953); ABOUT MRS. LESLIE(1954); EL ALAMEIN(1954); LAW VS. BILLY THE KID, THE(1954); MASTERSON OF KANSAS(1954); SUSAN SLEPT HERE(1954); YANKEE PASHA(1954); TENDER TRAP, THE(1955); MEET ME IN LAS VEGAS(1956); EIGHTEEN AND ANXIOUS(1957); UP IN SMOKE(1957); WILL SUCCESS SPOIL ROCK HUNTER?(1957); IN THE MONEY(1958); PARTY GIRL(1958); HOLE IN THE HEAD, A(1959); PLEASE DON'T EAT THE DAISIES(1960); ERRAND BOY, THE(1961); POCKETFUL OF MIRACLES(1961); DISORDERLY ORDERLY, THE(1964); HOUSE IS NOT A HOME, A(1964); THAT FUNNY FEELING(1965); GHOST IN THE INVISIBLE BIKINI(1966); SHAKIEST GUN IN THE WEST, THE(1968); ANGEL IN MY POCKET(1969); WHICH WAY TO THE FRONT?(1970); HOW TO FRAME A FIGG(1971); SHAGGY D.A., THE(1976)
Silents
NAUGHTY BABY(1929)
Blanche Rubin
LAST AMERICAN VIRGIN, THE(1982)
Bruce Joel Rubin
BRAINSTORM(1983), w
Bruce Rubin
ZAPPED!(1982), w
Cyma Rubin
GREASER'S PALACE(1972), p
Daniel N. Rubin
TEXAN, THE(1930), w; DISHONORED(1931), w; WOMEN GO ON FOREVER(1931), w; NIGHT CLUB SCANDAL(1937), w
Daniel Nathan Rubin
Silents
MIDNIGHT MADNESS(1928), w
Daniel Rubin
GUILTY AS HELL(1932), w
Eddie Rubin
48 HOURS TO LIVE(1960, Brit./Swed.), p
Glynn Rubin
CANNONBALL(1976, U.S./Hong Kong); FOUL PLAY(1978); NIGHTWING(1979); WHEN TIME RAN OUT(1980)
Harry Rubin
SONG AND THE SILENCE, THE(1969)
J. Walter Rubin
BACHELOR APARTMENT(1931), w; HER CARDBOARD LOVER(1942), p
Jack Rubin
BABY FACE MORGAN(1942), w, w; FRENCH LEAVE(1948), w; MURDER BY CONTRACT(1958), spec eff
Jerry Rubin
UNDERCOVER MAN, THE(1949), w
Jessica Rubin
1984
MICKI AND MAUDE(1984)
Jinx Rubin
TAKING OFF(1971)
Koya Yair Rubin
JERUSALEM FILE, THE(1972, U.S./Israel)
Lance Rubin
LEO AND LOREE(1980), m; MOTEL HELL(1980), m; HAPPY BIRTHDAY TO ME(1981), m; MODERN ROMANCE(1981), m
Laura Rubin
MURDER A LA MOD(1968)
Mann Rubin
BEST OF EVERYTHING, THE(1959), w; PSYCHOMANIA(1964), w; WALK A TIGHTROPE(1964, U.S./Brit.), w; BRAINSTORM(1965), w; AMERICAN DREAM, AN(1966), w; WARNING SHOT(1967), w; TODD KILLINGS, THE(1971), w; FIRST DEADLY SIN, THE(1980), w
Marilyn Rubin
H.O.T.S.(1979)
Murray Rubin
HUNTER, THE(1980)
1984
GHOSTBUSTERS(1984)
Pearl Rubin
PASSION HOLIDAY(1963)
Richard A. Rubin
FIGHT FOR YOUR LIFE(1977)
Rita and Rubin
NIGHT AT THE OPERA, A(1935)
Robert Rubin
NOTHING BUT A MAN(1964), p
Ronald Rubin
COUNTESS FROM HONG KONG, A(1967, Brit.); SERGEANT, THE(1968)
Stan Rubin
ROSELAND(1977)

Stanley C. Rubin
SIX LESSONS FROM MADAME LA ZONGA(1941), w
Stanley Crea Rubin
MR. DYNAMITE(1941), w; SAN FRANCISCO DOCKS(1941), w; WHERE DID YOU GET THAT GIRL?(1941), w
Stanley Rubin
DIAMOND FRONTIER(1940), w; SOUTH TO KARANGA(1940), w; BURMA CONVOY(1941), w; FLYING CADETS(1941), w; BOMBAY CLIPPER(1942), w; LUCKY LEGS(1942), w; UNSEEN ENEMY(1942), w; TWO SENORITAS FROM CHICAGO(1943), w; DECOY(1946), w; SLIGHTLY SCANDALOUS(1946), p; VIOLENCE(1947), w; JOE PALOOKA IN WINNER TAKE ALL(1948), w; BEHAVE YOURSELF(1951), p; MACAO(1952), w; MY PAL GUS(1952), p; NARROW MARGIN, THE(1952), p; DESTINATION GOBI(1953), p; DESTRY(1954), p; RIVER OF NO RETURN(1954), p; FRANCIS IN THE NAVY(1955), p; BEHIND THE HIGH WALL(1956), p; RAWHIDE YEARS, THE(1956), p; GIRL MOST LIKELY, THE(1957), p; PROMISE HER ANYTHING(1966, Brit.), p; OH DAD, POOR DAD, MAMA'S HUNG YOU IN THE CLOSET AND I'M FEELIN' SO SAD(1967), p; PRESIDENT'S ANALYST, THE(1967), p
Sydney Rubin
Misc. Talkies
REDNECK MILLER(1977)
Dr. Theodore Isaac Rubin
DAVID AND LISA(1962), w
Fania Rubina
Misc. Talkies
LIVING ORPHAN, THE(1939)
Irving Rubine
TORCHY RUNS FOR MAYOR(1939), w
Saul Rubinek
SLOW RUN(1968), a, m; DEATH SHIP(1980, Can.); NOTHING PERSONAL(1980, Can.); AGENCY(1981, Can.); TICKET TO HEAVEN(1981); BY DESIGN(1982); SOUP FOR ONE(1982); YOUNG DOCTORS IN LOVE(1982)
1984
AGAINST ALL ODDS(1984); HIGHPOINT(1984, Can.)
Rubini
Misc. Silents
KIRA KIRALINA(1927, USSR)
Giulia Rubini
GOLIATH AND THE BARBARIANS(1960, Ital.); DAVID AND GOLIATH(1961, Ital.); NIGHT THEY KILLED RASPUTIN, THE(1962, Fr./Ital.); MYSTERY OF THUG ISLAND, THE(1966, Ital./Ger.); RINGO AND HIS GOLDEN PISTOL(1966, Ital.); JOURNEY BENEATH THE DESERT(1967, Fr./Ital.)
Guilia Rubini
RAGE OF THE BUCCANEERS(1963, Ital.)
Jan Rubini
MERRY WIDOW, THE(1934); CLANCY STREET BOYS(1943); BAL TABARIN(1952)
Michel Rubini
HUNGER, THE(1983), m
Joseph Rubino
FRENCH LINE, THE(1954)
David Rubinoff
THANKS A MILLION(1935); YOU CAN'T HAVE EVERYTHING(1937)
Ramona Rubinoff
THANKS A MILLION(1935)
Marybeth Rubins
PROM NIGHT(1980)
Israel Rubinshik
THEY WERE TEN(1961, Israel)
Rubinskis
SHAME OF THE SABINE WOMEN, THE(1962, Mex.)
Sam Rubinsky
1984
GOODBYE PEOPLE, THE(1984); HOME FREE ALL(1984)
Wolf Rubinsky
EMPTY STAR, THE(1962, Mex.)
Arthur B. Rubinstein
WHOSE LIFE IS IT ANYWAY?(1981), m; DEAL OF THE CENTURY(1983), m; WARGAMES(1983), m
Arthur Rubinstein
FOLLOW THE BOYS(1944)
Artur Rubinstein
CARNEGIE HALL(1947); NIGHT SONG(1947)
Beatrice Rubinstein
JULIE THE REDHEAD(1963, Fr.), w
Donald Rubinstein
MARTIN(1979), m; KNIGHTRIDERS(1981), m
Gabriela Rubinstein
1984
DEATHSTALKER, THE(1984)
Helena Rubinstein
1984
HAMBONE AND HILLIE(1984), art d
John Rubinstein
TROUBLE WITH GIRLS(AND HOW TO GET INTO IT), THE*1/2 (1969); GETTING STRAIGHT(1970); ZACHARIAH(1971); CANDIDATE, THE(1972), m; WILD PACK, THE(1972); KID BLUE(1973), m; KILLER INSIDE ME, THE(1976), m; BOYS FROM BRAZIL, THE(1978); IN SEARCH OF HISTORIC JESUS(1980); DANIEL(1983)
Keith Rubinstein
VICE SQUAD(1982), m
Martin Rubinstein
TOWING(1978), m
Ora Rubinstein
TABLE FOR FIVE(1983)
Paulette Rubinstein
FLYING MATCHMAKER, THE(1970, Israel)
Phil Rubinstein
LOVE IN A TAXI(1980)
Richard P Rubinstein
CREEPSHOW(1982), p

Richard Rubinstein
DAWN OF THE DEAD(1979), p; MARTIN(1979), p
Zelda Rubinstein
UNDER THE RAINBOW(1981); POLTERGEIST(1982)
Alfonso Rubio
TARZAN AND THE VALLEY OF GOLD(1966 U.S./Switz.), cos
Antonio Rubio
GLADIATORS 7(1964, Span./Ital.)
Ben Rubio
DAUGHTERS OF SATAN(1972)
Edie Marie Rubio
1984
BREAKIN' 2: ELECTRIC BOOGALOO(1984)
Jose Rubio
PENITENTE MURDER CASE, THE(1936); ROMEO AND JULIET(1936); MAYTI-
ME(1937); GOLIATH AGAINST THE GIANTS(1963, Ital./Span.)
Olallo Rubio, Jr.
STRONGHOLD(1952, Mex.), p; MASSACRE(1956), p
Tony Rubio
HIGH RISK(1981)
Rita Rubirosa
NIGHT THEY KILLED RASPUTIN, THE(1962, Fr./Ital.)
Janos Rubleszky
FATHER(1967, Hung.)
Al Rubottom
SALLY'S HOUNDS(1968)
Wade Rubottom
STAND-IN(1937), art d; MORTAL STORM, THE(1940), art d; SHOP AROUND THE
CORNER, THE(1940), art d; TWO SMART PEOPLE(1946), art d; TENTH AVENUE
ANGEL(1948), art d
Wade B. Rubottom
IDIOT'S DELIGHT(1939), art d; WOMEN, THE(1939), art d; PHILADELPHIA STO-
RY, THE(1940), art d; WE WHO ARE YOUNG(1940), art d; WOMAN'S FACE(1941),
art d; JOURNEY FOR MARGARET(1942), art d; CLOWN, THE(1953), art d; SCAN-
DAL AT SCOURIE(1953), art d
Ellalee Ruby
LOVE CAPTIVE, THE(1934)
Misc. Talkies
HOWDY BROADWAY(1929)
Harry Ruby
CUCKOOS, THE(1930), w; TOP SPEED(1930), w; BROADMINDED(1931), w; HORSE
FEATHERS(1932), w; KID FROM SPAIN, THE(1932), w; DUCK SOUP(1933), w;
CIRCUS CLOWN(1934), w; HIPS, HIPS, HOORAY(1934), w; BRIGHT LIGHTS(1935),
w; KENTUCKY KERNELS(1935), w; MAN WHO BROKE THE BANK AT MONTE
CARLO, THE(1935), m/l Bert Kalmar; NIGHT AT THE OPERA, A(1935), w; WALK-
ING ON AIR(1936), w, m; LIFE OF THE PARTY, THE(1937), w; MAISIE GOES TO
RENO(1944), w; LOOK FOR THE SILVER LINING(1949), w; THREE LITTLE
WORDS(1950), w; LOVELY TO LOOK AT(1952), w; STORY OF MANKIND, THE(1957)
Herman Ruby
GORILLA, THE(1931), w; MAN OF COURAGE(1943), w
Irving B. Ruby
Silents
MAN FROM BEYOND, THE(1922), ph; ONE EXCITING NIGHT(1922), ph
Kathy Ruby
AMERICAN GUERRILLA IN THE PHILIPPINES, AN(1950)
Les Ruby
PAPERBACK HERO(1973, Can.)
Mike Ruby
ALIAS THE CHAMP(1949); NO HOLDS BARRED(1952)
Thelma Ruby
WHERE THERE'S A WILL(1955, Brit.); JOHNNY, YOU'RE WANTED(1956, Brit.);
MAN WHO LIKED FUNERALS, THE(1959, Brit.); ROOM AT THE TOP(1959, Brit.);
INVASION QUARTET(1961, Brit.); LIVE NOW–PAY LATER(1962, Brit.)
Wade Ruby
COME NEXT SPRING(1956)
Alan Ruck
CLASS(1983)
Barbara Rucker
STEPFORD WIVES, THE(1975)
1984
OVER THE BROOKLYN BRIDGE(1984)
Bo Rucker
SUPERMAN(1978); SOUP FOR ONE(1982); CROSS CREEK(1983); VIGILANTE(1983)
Charles Rucker
SCREAMS OF A WINTER NIGHT(1979)
Christiane Rucker
BLOOD DEMON(1967, Ger.); FOUNTAIN OF LOVE, THE(1968, Aust.); HOW TO
SEDUCE A PLAYBOY(1968, Aust./Fr./Ital.)
Dennis Rucker
YOU'LL LIKE MY MOTHER(1972); MIDWAY(1976); OFFICER AND A GENTLE-
MAN, AN(1982)
Douglas Rucker
LITTLE MEN(1940)
G. Rucker
FIRST SPACESHIP ON VENUS(1960, Ger./Pol.), w
Laddie Rucker
NIGHT AND DAY(1946)
Luther Rucker
1984
ALPHABET CITY(1984)
Washington Rucker
NEW YORK, NEW YORK(1977)
Ernst Ruckert
Misc. Silents
RASPUTIN(1929, USSR)
Nan Ruckman
NO MAN'S LAND(1964), makeup

Ann Elisabeth Rud
ORDET(1957, Den.)
Ove Rud
ORDET(1957, Den.); PEOPLE MEET AND SWEET MUSIC FILLS THE HEART(1969,
Den./Swed.)
Susanne Rud
ORDET(1957, Den.)
A. Rudachenko
VIOLIN AND ROLLER(1962, USSR), spec eff; ITALIANO BRAVA GENTE(1965,
Ital./USSR), spec eff; MEET ME IN MOSCOW(1966, USSR), spec eff; PORTRAIT OF
LENIN(1967, Pol./USSR), spec eff
Nicolas Rudakov
END OF THE WORLD, THE(1930, Fr.), ph
Rosa Rudami
Silents
WEDDING SONG, THE(1925)
Misc. Silents
POOR GIRL'S ROMANCE, A(1926)
Anthony H. Rudd
Silents
SCARS OF JEALOUSY(1923), w
Bailey Rudd
GRANDAD RUDD(1935, Aus.), w
Bobbie Rudd
Silents
SKIPPER'S WOOING, THE(1922, Brit.)
Misc. Silents
SAM'S BOY(1922, Brit.)
Enid Rudd
CROWDED PARADISE(1956)
Hughes Rudd
DESPERATE WOMEN, THE(?)
Michael Rudd
1984
PHILADELPHIA EXPERIMENT, THE(1984)
Norman Rudd
BLONDE BANDIT, THE(1950)
Paul Rudd
BETSY, THE(1978)
Phoebe Rudd
WIFE TAKES A FLYER, THE(1942)
Richard Rudd
TUNES OF GLORY(1960, Brit.)
Ricky Rudd
STROKER ACE(1983)
Sam Rudd
GOOD LUCK, MR. YATES(1943), w
Steele Rudd
ON OUR SELECTION(1930, Aus.), d; GRANDAD RUDD(1935, Aus.), w
Cook Ruddick
HILDUR AND THE MAGICIAN(1969)
Edith Ruddick
LOCAL HERO(1983, Brit.)
John Ruddock
ESCAPE TO DANGER(1943, Brit.); STRAWBERRY ROAN(1945, Brit.); WAY AHEAD,
THE(1945, Brit.); LISBON STORY, THE(1946, Brit.); NIGHT BOAT TO DUBLIN(1946,
Brit.); WALTZ TIME(1946, Brit.); WANTED FOR MURDER(1946, Brit.); FRIEDA(1947,
Brit.); MEET ME AT DAWN(1947, Brit.); FALLEN IDOL, THE(1949, Brit.); UNDER
CAPRICORN(1949); LAUGHING LADY, THE(1950, Brit.); PINK STRING AND SEAL-
ING WAX(1950, Brit.); QUO VADIS(1951); IVANHOE(1952, Brit.); SECRET PEO-
PLE(1952, Brit.); MARTIN LUTHER(1953); LUST FOR LIFE(1956); TREASURE AT
THE MILL(1957, Brit.); QUESTION 7(1961, U.S./Ger.); LAWRENCE OF ARABIA(1962,
Brit.); HORSEMEN, THE(1971)
Albert S. Ruddy
WILD SEED(1965), p; LITTLE FAUSS AND BIG HALSY(1970), p; MAKING
IT(1971), p; GODFATHER, THE(1972), p; LONGEST YARD(1974), p, w; COON-
SKIN(1975), p; MATILDA(1978), p, w; CANNONBALL RUN, THE(1981), p; MEGA-
FORCE(1982), p, w
1984
CANNONBALL RUN II(1984), p, w; LASSITER(1984), p
Dick Rude
1984
NIGHT OF THE COMET(1984); REPO MAN(1984); WILD LIFE, THE(1984)
Dolf Rudeen
I DEAL IN DANGER(1966), ed
Roger Rudel
LE BOUCHER(1971, Fr./Ital.)
Bob Rudelson
CASE OF PATTY SMITH, THE(1962)
Robert Rudelson
FINDERS KEEPERS, LOVERS WEEPERS(1968); FOOLS(1970), w
Ken Ruder
Misc. Talkies
LIPS OF BLOOD(1972), d
Mikhail Ruderman
COUNTER-ATTACK(1945), w
Barnaby Rudge
VERY NATURAL THING, A(1974)
Myles Rudge
DELAYED ACTION(1954, Brit.); YOU PAY YOUR MONEY(1957, Brit.)
Arik Rudich
1984
DRIFTING(1984, Israel), m
Evelyn Rudie
VIEW FROM POMPEY'S HEAD, THE(1955); RESTLESS BREED, THE(1957); WINGS
OF EAGLES, THE(1957); GIFT OF LOVE, THE(1958)
Richard Rudiger
LE MANS(1971)

Andrew Rudin
FELLINI SATYRICON(1969, Fr./Ital.), m
Herman Rudin
STAKEOUT ON DOPE STREET(1958); FLOWER DRUM SONG(1961); FRONTIER UPRISING(1961); SCARFACE MOB, THE(1962); BEAUTY AND THE BEAST(1963); HARD RIDE, THE(1971)
Milton Rudin
ROBIN AND THE SEVEN HOODS(1964)
Scott Rudin
I'M DANCING AS FAST AS I CAN(1982), p
1984
MRS. SOFFEL(1984), p; RECKLESS(1984), p
V. Rudin
SONG OF THE FOREST(1963, USSR)
Barney Ruditsky
MARGIN FOR ERROR(1943)
David Rudkin
FAHRENHEIT 451(1966, Brit.), w
Herb Rudley
FALLING IN LOVE AGAIN(1980)
Herbert Rudley
ABE LINCOLN IN ILLINOIS(1940); MARRIAGE IS A PRIVATE AFFAIR(1944); MASTER RACE, THE(1944); SEVENTH CROSS, THE(1944); BREWSTER'S MILLIONS(1945); RHAPSODY IN BLUE(1945); WALK IN THE SUN, A(1945); DECOY(1946); CASBAH(1948); HOLLOW TRIUMPH(1948); JOAN OF ARC(1948); SILVER CHALICE, THE(1954); ARTISTS AND MODELS(1955); BLACK SLEEP, THE(1956); COURT JESTER, THE(1956); RAW EDGE(1956); THAT CERTAIN FEELING(1956); BRAVADOS, THE(1958); TONKA(1958); YOUNG LIONS, THE(1958); BELOVED INFIDEL(1959); BIG FISHERMAN, THE(1959); JAYHAWKERS, THE(1959); GREAT IMPOSTOR, THE(1960); HELL BENT FOR LEATHER(1960); FOLLOW THAT DREAM(1962)
John Rudling
MAN IN THE WHITE SUIT, THE(1952); TITFIELD THUNDERBOLT, THE(1953, Brit.); LADYKILLERS, THE(1956, Brit.)
Natalya Rudnaya
YOLANTA(1964, USSR); TSAR'S BRIDE, THE(1966, USSR)
Sara Rudner
HAIR(1979)
Nina Rudneva
DAY THE WAR ENDED, THE(1961, USSR), w
Charles Rudnick
NIGHTMARE IN BLOOD(1978), ph
Dr. Abraham Rudnick
BUTTERFLY(1982)
Franz Rudnick
GERMAN SISTERS, THE(1982, Ger.)
Robert Rudnick
1984
NATURAL, THE(1984)
Ruzena Rudnicka
NINTH HEART, THE(1980, Czech.)
Anthony Rudnicky
COSSACKS IN EXILE(1939, Ukrainian), m
Lev Rudnik
DUEL, THE(1964, USSR), d
Oleg Rudnik
1984
MOSCOW ON THE HUDSON(1984); 2010(1984)
A. Rudnitsky
Misc. Silents
HIS EYES(1916, USSR)
Gene Rudolf
TAKING OF PELHAM ONE, TWO, THREE, THE(1974), art d; HOSPITAL, THE(1971), prod d; LAW AND DISORDER(1974), art d; THREE DAYS OF THE CONDOR(1975), art d; FINGERS(1978), prod d; RAGING BULL(1980), prod d; NIGHT THE LIGHTS WENT OUT IN GEORGIA, THE(1981), prod d; AUTHOR! AUTHOR!(1982), prod d; TRADING PLACES(1983), prod d
Helmut Rudolf
LOST ONE, THE(1951, Ger.)
Leopole Rudolf
TRIAL, THE(1948, Aust.)
Oscar Rudolf
HOLY TERROR, THE(1937)
Peter Rudolf
1984
REVOLT OF JOB, THE(1984, Hung./Ger.)
Rudolf Rokl Quartet
MOST BEAUTIFUL AGE, THE(1970, Czech.)
Alan Rudolph
BUFFALO BILL AND THE INDIANS, OR SITTING BULL'S HISTORY LESSON(1976), w; WELCOME TO L.A.(1976), d&w; REMEMBER MY NAME(1978), d&w; ROADIE(1980), d, w; ENDANGERED SPECIES(1982), d, w
1984
CHOOSE ME(1984), d&w; SONGWRITER(1984), d
Misc. Talkies
PREMONITION(1972), d
Amanda Rudolph
Misc. Talkies
COMES MIDNIGHT(1940)
Claude-Oliver Rudolph
DAS BOOT(1982)
Gene Rudolph
LITTLE MURDERS(1971), prod d; COPS AND ROBBERS(1973), art d; SOUL OF NIGGER CHARLEY, THE(1973), art d
Gretchen Rudolph
MY BODY HUNGERS(1967)
Helmut Rudolph
AFFAIR BLUM, THE(1949, Ger.); DEVIL IN SILK(1968, Ger.)

Jerome Rudolph
STOOLIE, THE(1972)
Jim Rudolph
DAN'S MOTEL(1982)
John Rudolph
BORN IN FLAMES(1983)
Niels-Peter Rudolph
STEPPENWOLF(1974)
Oscar Rudolph
SO THIS IS COLLEGE(1929); DIVORCE IN THE FAMILY(1932); THIS DAY AND AGE(1933); CRUSADES, THE(1935); MAGNIFICENT OBSESSION(1935); SHE COULDN'T TAKE IT(1935); TWO FOR TONIGHT(1935); IT'S A GREAT LIFE(1936); RETURN OF SOPHIE LANG, THE(1936); HOTEL HAYWIRE(1937); MAYTIME(1937); SWING HIGH, SWING LOW(1937); EASY COME, EASY GO(1947); ROCKET MAN, THE(1954), d; TWIST AROUND THE CLOCK(1961), d; DON'T KNOCK THE TWIST(1962), d; WILD WESTERNERS, THE(1962), d
Silents
LITTLE ANNIE ROONEY(1925)
Thomas Rudolph
1984
ROSEBUD BEACH HOTEL(1984), w
Tresi Rudolph
INTERMEZZO(1937, Ger.)
Verenice Rudolph
GERMAN SISTERS, THE(1982, Ger.)
Gunter Rudorf
WILLY(1963, U.S./Ger.), w
Viktor Rudoy
TRAIN GOES TO KIEV, THE(1961, USSR)
Martin Rudy
TESTAMENT(1983)
1984
SAM'S SON(1984)
Tomas Rudy
LAST REBEL, THE(1971)
Rudy Sooter and His Californians
RIDERS OF PASCO BASIN(1940)
Rudy Starita's Marimba Band
LET'S MAKE A NIGHT OF IT(1937, Brit.)
Rudy Vallee and His Orchestra
GLORIFYING THE AMERICAN GIRL(1930)
Rudy Vallee's Connecticut Yankees
SWEET MUSIC(1935)
Kazimierz Rudzki
EROICA(1966, Pol.); PORTRAIT OF LENIN(1967, Pol./USSR); PASSENGER, THE(1970, Pol.)
Ed Rue
SOME CALL IT LOVING(1973)
Fontaine La Rue
Silents
HUMAN STUFF(1920)
Joe Rue
STRATTON STORY, THE(1949)
Mabel Rue
NORTHERN LIGHTS(1978)
Romena Rue
Silents
OLDEST LAW, THE(1918), w
Thorbjorn Rue
NORTHERN LIGHTS(1978)
J. Walter Rueben
BAD MAN OF BRIMSTONE(1938), w
Alma Ruebens
Misc. Silents
FIREFLY OF TOUGH LUCK, THE(1917)
Christiane Ruecker
CARMEN, BABY(1967, Yugo./Ger.); DOCTOR OF ST. PAUL, THE(1969, Ger.)
Manuela Ruecker
FUNNYMAN(1967)
Josephine Rueg
I'LL NEVER FORGET WHAT'S 'IS NAME(1967, Brit.)
Heinz Ruehmann
CAPTAIN FROM KOEPENICK, THE(1956, Ger.); JUDGE AND THE SINNER, THE(1964, Ger.); SHIP OF FOOLS(1965); DUCK RINGS AT HALF PAST SEVEN, THE(1969, Ger./Ital.)
William Ruel
RENDEZVOUS AT MIDNIGHT(1935)
Andre Ruelan
DAYDREAMER, THE(1975, Fr.), w
Andre Ruellan
HU-MAN(1975, Fr.), w; PARADISE POUR TOUS(1982, Fr.), w
Emile de Ruello
SUSPENSE(1930, Brit.), ed
Albert Rueprecht
SONG WITHOUT END(1960); HOUSE OF THE THREE GIRLS, THE(1961, Aust.); COUNTERFEIT TRAITOR, THE(1962); FOREVER MY LOVE(1962)
Hans Ruesch
RACERS, THE(1955), w; SAVAGE INNOCENTS, THE(1960, Brit.), w
Jacques Ruet
YESTERDAY, TODAY, AND TOMORROW(1964, Ital./Fr.), ch
Maximilian Ruethlein
POSSESSION(1981, Fr./Ger.)
Barbara Rueting
OPERATION CROSSBOW(1965, U.S./Ital.)
Barbara Ruetting
CANARIS(1955, Ger.); DAS LETZTE GEHEIMNIS(1959, Ger.); ETERNAL LOVE(1960, Ger.)

Liang Ruey
GRAND SUBSTITUTION, THE(1965, Hong Kong)

Alton Ruff
PENNIES FROM HEAVEN(1981); STING II, THE(1983), ch

Kerry Ruff
BASKET CASE(1982)

Leonora Ruff
STAR PILOT(1977, Ital.)

Eddie Ruffal
1984
FEAR CITY(1984)

Joseph Ruffalo
1984
PURPLE RAIN(1984), p

Laurence Ruffel
ROMEO AND JULIET(1966, Brit.)

Frances Ruffelle
1984
KIPPERBANG(1984, Brit.)

Melvin Ruffin
GOIN' HOME(1976)

Roger Ruffin
1984
SLOW MOVES(1984)

Nancy Ruffing
NOTHING BUT A MAN(1964), cos

Claudio Ruffini
SUPER FUZZ(1981)

Marcella Ruffini
WHITE, RED, YELLOW, PINK(1966, Ital.); LOVE FACTORY(1969, Ital.)

Sandro Ruffini
FEDORA(1946, Ital.); SCHOOLGIRL DIARY(1947, Ital.)

Mercedes Ruffino
TORTILLA FLAT(1942)

Jacques Ruffio
LA PASSANTE(1983, Fr./Ger.), d, w

Eleonora Ruffo
GOLIATH AND THE DRAGON(1961, Ital./Fr.)

Ferdinando Ruffo
GIDGET GOES TO ROME(1963), set d; WASTREL, THE(1963, Ital.), set d; HOUSE OF CARDS(1969), set d; SECRET OF SANTA VITTORIA, THE(1969), set d; VALACHI PAPERS, THE(1972, Ital./Fr.), set d

Fernandino Ruffo
FRANCIS OF ASSISI(1961), set d

Leonora Ruffo
QUEEN OF SHEBA(1953, Ital.); VITELLONI(1956, Ital./Fr.); GOLIATH AND THE VAMPIRES(1964, Ital.); HERCULES IN THE HAUNTED WORLD(1964, Ital.)

Rufini
GATES OF HELL, THE(1983, U.S./Ital.), makeup

Franco Rufini
1984
CONQUEST(1984, Ital./Span./Mex.), makeup

Grillo Rufino
JULIET OF THE SPIRITS(1965, Fr./Ital./W.Ger.)

Francine Rufo
OLD ACQUAINTANCE(1943)

Rufus
MISTER FREEDOM(1970, Fr.); EASY LIFE, THE(1971, Fr.); JONAH–WHO WILL BE 25 IN THE YEAR 2000(1976, Switz.); TENANT, THE(1976, Fr.); MARCH OR DIE(1977, Brit.)
1984
ERENDIRA(1984, Mex./Fr./Ger.)

George Marshall Ruge
MY FAVORITE YEAR(1982)

Jack Ruge
JOE BUTTERFLY(1957), w

William Ruge
Misc. Silents
FANTASMA(1914)

Gunter Ruger
NAKED AMONG THE WOLVES(1967, Ger.)

Gil Rugg
SHINBONE ALLEY(1971), anim

James Rugg
SILENT RUNNING(1972), spec eff

Janet Rugg
TASTE OF HONEY, A(1962, Brit.)

Ada Ruggeri
SON OF SAMSON(1962, Fr./Ital./Yugo.)

Giuseppina Ruggeri
TWO WOMEN(1961, Ital./Fr.)

Nino Ruggeri
COPS AND ROBBERS(1973)

Osvaldo Ruggeri
DAMON AND PYTHIAS(1962); DUEL OF CHAMPIONS(1964 Ital./Span.)

Ruggero Ruggeri
SPIRIT AND THE FLESH, THE(1948, Ital.); DISILLUSION(1949, Ital.)

Valerio Ruggeri
LEOPARD, THE(1963, Ital.); QUIET PLACE IN THE COUNTRY, A(1970, Ital./Fr.)

Gene Ruggerio
SHOP AROUND THE CORNER, THE(1940), ed; WINGS OF EAGLES, THE(1957), ed

Fedozzi Ruggero
SONNY AND JED(1974, Ital.)

Happy Ruggero
GREEN TREE, THE(1965, Ital.), m

Francoise Ruggieri
GLOBAL AFFAIR, A(1964); SECONDS(1966)

Alfonse Ruggiero
1984
HEARTBREAKERS(1984)

Eva Ruggiero
ADIOS AMIGO(1975), ed; MOUNTAIN MEN, THE(1980), ed; STRIPES(1981), ed; SAVANNAH SMILES(1983), ed

Gene Ruggiero
GOD IS MY WITNESS(1931), ed; JOE AND ETHEL TURP CALL ON THE PRESIDENT(1939), ed; NINOTCHKA(1939), ed; TARZAN FINDS A SON!(1939), ed; DR. KILDARE'S CRISIS(1940), ed; DR. KILDARE'S STRANGE CASE(1940), ed; I LOVE YOU AGAIN(1940), ed; SKY MURDER(1940), ed; BLONDE INSPIRATION(1941), ed; TARZAN'S SECRET TREASURE(1941), ed; WASHINGTON MELODRAMA(1941), ed; ANDY HARDY'S DOUBLE LIFE(1942), ed; JACKASS MAIL(1942), ed; TARZAN'S NEW YORK ADVENTURE(1942), ed; YANK ON THE BURMA ROAD, A(1942), ed; THREE WISE FOOLS(1946), ed; DARK DELUSION(1947), ed; LADY IN THE LAKE(1947), ed; SONG OF THE THIN MAN(1947), ed; BIG CITY(1948), ed; BIG CLOCK, THE(1948), ed; BRIBE, THE(1949), ed; THAT MIDNIGHT KISS(1949), ed; MRS. O'MALLEY AND MR. MALONE(1950), ed, art d; TOAST OF NEW ORLEANS, THE(1950), ed; GREAT CARUSO, THE(1951), ed; PEOPLE AGAINST O'HARA, THE(1951), ed; RICH, YOUNG AND PRETTY(1951), ed; GLORY ALLEY(1952), ed; ROGUE'S MARCH(1952), ed; CLOWN, THE(1953), ed; EASY TO LOVE(1953), ed; ATHENA(1954), ed; MEN OF THE FIGHTING LADY(1954), ed; STUDENT PRINCE, THE(1954), ed; AROUND THE WORLD IN 80 DAYS(1956), ed; CATERED AFFAIR, THE(1956), ed; GREAT AMERICAN PASTIME, THE(1956), ed; SEVENTH SIN, THE(1957), ed; SEVEN HILLS OF ROME, THE(1958), ed; TORPEDO RUN(1958), ed; FOR THE FIRST TIME(1959, U.S./Ger./Ital.), ed; TARZAN, THE APE MAN(1959), ed; PLATINUM HIGH SCHOOL(1960), ed; THIEF OF BAGHDAD, THE(1961, Ital./Fr.), ed; WONDERS OF ALADDIN, THE(1961, Fr./Ital.), ed; DOG EAT DOG(1963, U.S./Ger./Ital.), ed; LAST MAN ON EARTH, THE(1964, U.S./Ital.), ed; CAST A GIANT SHADOW(1966), ed; HELL'S ANGELS '69(1969), ed; MARLOWE(1969), ed; MAD BOMBER, THE(1973), ed; BLACK EYE(1974), ed; ADIOS AMIGO(1975), ed; MOONSHINE COUNTY EXPRESS(1977), ed

Jack Ruggiero
WITHOUT RESERVATIONS(1946), ed; AMAZING TRANSPARENT MAN, THE(1960), ed; BEYOND THE TIME BARRIER(1960), ed; TEENAGE MILLIONAIRE(1961), ed; OUT OF THE TIGER'S MOUTH(1962), ed; VARAN THE UNBELIEVABLE(1962, U.S./Jap.), ed

Joe Ruggiero
HOT STUFF(1979)

Byron Ruggles
SUDAN(1945)

Charles Ruggles
BATTLE OF PARIS, THE(1929); GENTLEMEN OF THE PRESS(1929); LADY LIES, THE(1929); QUEEN HIGH(1930); ROADHOUSE NIGHTS(1930); YOUNG MAN OF MANHATTAN(1930); HONOR AMONG LOVERS(1931); HUSBAND'S HOLIDAY(1931); SMILING LIEUTENANT, THE(1931); IF I HAD A MILLION(1932); MADAME BUTTERFLY(1932); ONE HOUR WITH YOU(1932); THIS RECKLESS AGE(1932); GIRL WITHOUT A ROOM(1933); MELODY CRUISE(1933); MURDERS IN THE ZOO(1933); FRIENDS OF MR. SWEENEY(1934); PEOPLE WILL TALK(1935); HEARTS DIVIDED(1936); WIVES NEVER KNOW(1936); YOURS FOR THE ASKING(1936); BREAKING THE ICE(1938); BRINGING UP BABY(1938); HIS EXCITING NIGHT(1938); BALALAIKA(1939); SUDDEN MONEY(1939); MARYLAND(1940); NO TIME FOR COMEDY(1940); HONEYMOON FOR THREE(1941); MODEL WIFE(1941); DOUGHGIRLS, THE(1944); OUR HEARTS WERE YOUNG AND GAY(1944); BEDSIDE MANNER(1945); STOLEN LIFE, A(1946); RAMROD(1947); LOVABLE CHEAT, THE(1949); PLEASURE OF HIS COMPANY, THE(1961)
Silents
HEART RAIDER, THE(1923)
Misc. Silents
MAJESTY OF THE LAW, THE(1915); PEER GYNT(1915)

Charlie Ruggles
CHARLEY'S AUNT(1930); HER WEDDING NIGHT(1930); BELOVED BACHELOR, THE(1931); GIRL HABIT(1931); EVENINGS FOR SALE(1932); LOVE ME TONIGHT(1932); MAKE ME A STAR(1932); NIGHT OF JUNE 13(1932); THIS IS THE NIGHT(1932); TROUBLE IN PARADISE(1932); 70,000 WITNESSES(1932); ALICE IN WONDERLAND(1933); MAMA LOVES PAPA(1933); TERROR ABOARD(1933); GOODBYE LOVE(1934); MELODY IN SPRING(1934); MURDER IN THE PRIVATE CAR(1934); PURSUIT OF HAPPINESS, THE(1934); SIX OF A KIND(1934); BIG BROADCAST OF 1936, THE(1935); NO MORE LADIES(1935); RUGGLES OF RED GAP(1935); ANYTHING GOES(1936); EARLY TO BED(1936); EXCLUSIVE(1937); MIND YOUR OWN BUSINESS(1937); TURN OFF THE MOON(1937); SERVICE DE LUXE(1938); BOY TROUBLE(1939); INVITATION TO HAPPINESS(1939); NIGHT WORK(1939); FARMER'S DAUGHTER, THE(1940); OPENED BY MISTAKE(1940); PUBLIC DEB NO. 1(1940); GO WEST, YOUNG LADY(1941); INVISIBLE WOMAN, THE(1941); PARSON OF PANAMINT, THE(1941); PERFECT SNOB, THE(1941); FRIENDLY ENEMIES(1942); DIXIE DUGAN(1943); 3 IS A FAMILY(1944); INCENDIARY BLONDE(1945); GALLANT JOURNEY(1946); MY BROTHER TALKS TO HORSES(1946); IT HAPPENED ON 5TH AVENUE(1947); GIVE MY REGARDS TO BROADWAY(1948); LOOK FOR THE SILVER LINING(1949); ALL IN A NIGHT'S WORK(1961); PARENT TRAP, THE(1961); PAPA'S DELICATE CONDITION(1963); SON OF FLUBBER(1963); I'D RATHER BE RICH(1964); FOLLOW ME, BOYS!(1966); UGLY DACHSHUND, THE(1966)

Charlie Ruggles, Sr.
PERFECT MARRIAGE, THE(1946)

Eleanor Ruggles
PRINCE OF PLAYERS(1955), w

Virginia Ruggles
Silents
STRANGER'S BANQUET(1922)

Wesley Ruggles
CONDEMNED(1929), d; GIRL OVERBOARD(1929), d; SCANDAL(1929), d; STREET GIRL(1929), d; HONEY(1930), d; SEA BAT, THE(1930), d; ARE THESE OUR CHILDREN?(1931), d&w; CIMARRON(1931), d; ROAR OF THE DRAGON(1932), d; COLLEGE HUMOR(1933), d; I'M NO ANGEL(1933), d; MONKEY'S PAW, THE(1933), d; NO MAN OF HER OWN(1933), d; BOLERO(1934), d; SHOOT THE WORKS(1934), d; ACCENT ON YOUTH(1935), d; GILDED LILY, THE(1935), d; BRIDE COMES HOME(1936), p&d; VALIANT IS THE WORD FOR CARRIE(1936), p&d; I MET HIM IN PARIS(1937), p&d; TRUE CONFESSION(1937), d; SING YOU SINNERS(1938), p&d; INVITATION TO HAPPINESS(1939), p&d; ARIZONA(1940), p&d; TOO MANY HUS-

BANDS(1940), p&d; YOU BELONG TO ME(1941), p&d; SOMEWHERE I'LL FIND YOU(1942), d; SLIGHTLY DANGEROUS(1943), d; SEE HERE, PRIVATE HARGROVE(1944), d; MY HEART GOES CRAZY(1953, Brit.), p&d, w

Silents
SUBMARINE PIRATE, A(1915); IF I WERE QUEEN(1922), d; WILD HONEY(1922), d; HEART RAIDER, THE(1923), d; MR. BILLINGS SPENDS HIS DIME(1923), d; SLIPPY MCGEE(1923), d; PLASTIC AGE, THE(1925), d; KICK-OFF, THE(1926), d

Misc. Silents
FOR FRANCE(1917), d; WINCHESTER WOMAN, THE(1919), d; DESPERATE HERO, THE(1920), d; LEOPARD WOMAN, THE(1920), d; LOVE(1920), d; PICCADILLY JIM(1920), d; SOONER OR LATER(1920), d; GREATER CLAIM, THE(1921), d; OVER THE WIRE(1921), d; UNCHARTED SEAS(1921), d; REMITTANCE WOMAN, THE(1923), d; AGE OF INNOCENCE, THE(1924), d; BROADWAY LADY(1925), d; MAN OF QUALITY, A(1926), d; BEWARE OF WINDOWS(1927), d; SILK STOCKINGS(1927), d; FINDERS KEEPERS(1928), d; FOURFLUSHER, THE(1928), d

Wesley Ruggles, Jr.
OUT OF THE TIGER'S MOUTH(1962), p, w

Wesley H. Ruggles
Misc. Silents
BLIND ADVENTURE, THE(1918), d

Paolo Rugiero
DESERTER AND THE NOMADS, THE(1969, Czech./Ital.), w

Pete Rugolo
WHERE THE BOYS ARE(1960), m; SWEET RIDE, THE(1968), m; FOXTROT(1977, Mex./Swiss), m; CHU CHU AND THE PHILLY FLASH(1981), m

Peter Rugolo
MEET ME IN LAS VEGAS(1956)

Folmer Ruhbaek
HAGBARD AND SIGNE(1968, Den./Iceland/Swed.)

Bill Ruhl
MYSTERY OF MARIE ROGET, THE(1942); ADVENTURES OF KITTY O'DAY(1944); BOWERY CHAMPS(1944); DECOY(1946); IMPACT(1949)

Michel Ruhl
YOUR SHADOW IS MINE(1963, Fr./Ital.)

William Ruhl
MAN WHO RECLAIMED HIS HEAD, THE(1935); SPENDTHRIFT(1936); SUTTER'S GOLD(1936); LITTLE TOUGH GUY(1938); I STOLE A MILLION(1939); TOUGH KID(1939); GAUCHO SERENADE(1940); OKLAHOMA RENEGADES(1940); TEXAS TERRORS(1940); CRIMINALS WITHIN(1941); DOUBLE DATE(1941); GAUCHOS OF EL DORADO(1941); HOLD THAT GHOST(1941); PARIS CALLING(1941); PHANTOM SUBMARINE, THE(1941); SAN FRANCISCO DOCKS(1941); BEHIND THE EIGHT BALL(1942); GENTLEMAN AFTER DARK, A(1942); INVISIBLE AGENT(1942); JUKE BOX JENNY(1942); MY FAVORITE SPY(1942); SABOTEUR(1942); TREAT EM' ROUGH(1942); UNSEEN ENEMY(1942); DAYS OF OLD CHEYENNE(1943); MAD GHOUL, THE(1943); RHYTHM OF THE ISLANDS(1943); SO'S YOUR UNCLE(1943); ROGER TOUHY, GANGSTER!(1944); MILDRED PIERCE(1945); BELOW THE DEADLINE(1946); BOWERY BOMBSHELL(1946); DARK ALIBI(1946); IN FAST COMPANY(1946); KILLERS, THE(1946); LITTLE MISS BIG(1946); LIVE WIRES(1946); MR. HEX(1946); HARD BOILED MAHONEY(1947); RIDE THE PINK HORSE(1947); SONG OF MY HEART(1947); VIOLENCE(1947); ALL MY SONS(1948); COWBOY CAVALIER(1948); FRONTIER AGENT(1948); I WOULDN'T BE IN YOUR SHOES(1948); INCIDENT(1948); JINX MONEY(1948); JOE PALOOKA IN WINNER TAKE ALL(1948); ROCKY(1948); SHANGHAI CHEST, THE(1948); SMUGGLERS' COVE(1948); SONG OF THE DRIFTER(1948); TROUBLE MAKERS(1948); ALIMONY(1949); HOLD THAT BABY!(1949); CODE OF THE SILVER SAGE(1950); SIDE STREET(1950)

William H. Ruhl
PRAIRIE EXPRESS(1947); BRAND OF FEAR(1949); SHADOWS OF THE WEST(1949); WESTERN RENEGADES(1949)
Misc. Talkies
HAUNTED TRAILS(1949)

Jane Ruhm
I NEVER PROMISED YOU A ROSE GARDEN(1977), cos

Heinz Ruhmann
BOMBARDMENT OF MONTE CARLO, THE(1931, Ger.); HIS MAJESTY, KING BALLYHOO(1931, Ger.); EMPRESS AND I, THE(1933, Ger.); MAN WHO WAS SHERLOCK HOLMES, THE(1937, Ger.); IT HAPPENED IN BROAD DAYLIGHT(1960, Ger./Switz.); GOOD SOLDIER SCHWEIK, THE(1963, Ger.); MAN WHO WALKED THROUGH THE WALL, THE(1964, Ger.); OPERATION ST. PETER'S(1968, Ital.)

A. Frank RuHo
HAPPY BIRTHDAY, GEMINI(1980)

Astrid Ruhr
1984
WOMAN IN FLAMES, A(1984, Ger.), cos

Barbara Ruick
APACHE WAR SMOKE(1952); FEARLESS FAGAN(1952); INVITATION(1952); YOU FOR ME(1952); ABOVE AND BEYOND(1953); AFFAIRS OF DOBIE GILLIS, THE(1953); CONFIDENTIAL CONNIE(1953); I LOVE MELVIN(1953); CAROUSEL(1956); CALIFORNIA SPLIT(1974)

Mel Ruick
GILDED LILY, THE(1935); PRESIDENT'S MYSTERY, THE(1936); NAVY BLUES(1937); SARATOGA(1937); KITTY FOYLE(1940); MOON OVER MIAMI(1941); REMEMBER THE DAY(1941); SUN VALLEY SERENADE(1941); TWO LATINS FROM MANHATTAN(1941); WHISTLING IN THE DARK(1941); BOMBAY CLIPPER(1942); LADY HAS PLANS, THE(1942); MAN FROM HEADQUARTERS(1942); RINGS ON HER FINGERS(1942); TREAT EM' ROUGH(1942); KISS OF DEATH(1947)

Melville Ruick
MILKY WAY, THE(1936); THERE'S ONE BORN EVERY MINUTE(1942); TAXI(1953)

Walter Ruick
WEST POINT STORY, THE(1950)

Elisa Ruis
LA MARSEILLAISE(1938, Fr.)

Tom Ruisinger
B.S. I LOVE YOU(1971)

Reo Ruiters
KILLER FORCE(1975, Switz./Ireland), stunts

Al Ruiz
TOKYO ROSE(1945); WONDER MAN(1945); KID FROM BOOKLYN, THE(1946); VARIETY GIRL(1947)

Albert Ruiz
DUFFY'S TAVERN(1945); MISS SUSIE SLAGLE'S(1945); BLUE DAHLIA, THE(1946); O.S.S.(1946); HIT PARADE OF 1947(1947); ROAD TO RIO(1947); TROUBLE WITH WOMEN, THE(1947); SUMMER STOCK(1950)

Alex Ruiz
HUSH... HUSH, SWEET CHARLOTTE(1964), ch; SCALPHUNTERS, THE(1968), ch

Alvaro Ruiz
PROUD AND THE DAMNED, THE(1972)

Antonio Ruiz
SUPERZAN AND THE SPACE BOY(1972, Mex.), ph

Antonio Padilla Ruiz
RUNNING MAN, THE(1963, Brit.); LONG DUEL, THE(1967, Brit.); VILLA RIDES(1968)

Emil Ruiz
SUPERSONIC MAN(1979, Span.), spec eff

Emil [Emilio] Ruiz
SUPERSONIC MAN(1979, Span.), set d

Emilio Ruiz
MONSTER ISLAND(1981, Span./U.S.), spec eff

Federico Ruiz
LAST REBEL, THE(1961, Mex.), m

Francisco Ruiz
SANTIAGO(1956)

Isaac Ruiz
FUN WITH DICK AND JANE(1977); RECORD CITY(1978)

Isaac Ruiz, Jr.
CORVETTE SUMMER(1978)

Jorge Lopez Ruiz
TERRACE, THE(1964, Arg.), m

Jose Carlo Ruiz
BUCK AND THE PREACHER(1972)

Jose Carlos Ruiz
MAJOR DUNDEE(1965); EAGLE'S WING(1979, Brit.)

Julian Ruiz
KRAKATOA, EAST OF JAVA(1969), makeup; ROYAL HUNT OF THE SUN, THE(1969, Brit.), makeup; TRISTANA(1970, Span./Ital./Fr.), makeup

Mercedes Ruiz
DOCTOR ZHIVAGO(1965)

Pastora Ruiz
SAVAGE PAMPAS(1967, Span./Arg.)

Raul Ruiz
1984
THREE CROWNS OF THE SAILOR(1984, Fr.), d, w

Rene Ruiz
1984
UNDER THE VOLCANO(1984)

Starr Ruiz
WAY OUT(1966)

Juan Ruiz-Anchia
1984
STONE BOY, THE(1984), ph

Joe Rujas
SPRING FEVER(1983, Can.)

Edith Rujsz
WAGNER(1983, Brit./Hung./Aust.)

Reg Ruka
NATE AND HAYES(1983, U.S./New Zealand)
1984
SILENT ONE, THE(1984, New Zealand)

A.H. Rule
THREE ON A SPREE(1961, Brit.), ed

Albert Rule
TECKMAN MYSTERY, THE(1955, Brit), ed; RAISING A RIOT(1957, Brit.), ed

B.C. Rule
Silents
APE, THE(1928), d
Misc. Silents
ONE HOUR PAST MIDNIGHT(1924), d

Bert Rule
ZARAK(1956, Brit.), ed; HOW TO MURDER A RICH UNCLE(1957, Brit.), ed; MAN INSIDE, THE(1958, Brit.), ed; TANK FORCE(1958, Brit.), ed; BANDIT OF ZHOBE, THE(1959), ed; IDOL ON PARADE(1959, Brit.), ed; TARZAN'S GREATEST ADVENTURE(1959, Brit.), ed; TARZAN THE MAGNIFICENT(1960, Brit.), ed; TWO-WAY STRETCH(1961, Brit.), ed; HELLIONS, THE(1962, Brit.), ed; KILL OR CURE(1962, Brit.), ed; OPERATION SNATCH(1962, Brit.), ed; MURDER AT THE GALLOP(1963, Brit.), ed; CROSSPLOT(1969, Brit.), ed

Bertie Rule
CHARLEY MOON(1956, Brit.), ed

Beverly C. Rule
Misc. Silents
INVISIBLE WEB, THE(1921), d

Charles Rule
1776(1972)

Eliza Rule
HER FIRST AFFAIR(1947, Fr.)

Frederick Rule
TRACKDOWN(1976)

James Rule
SAVAGES(1972), art d

Janice Rule
GOODBYE, MY FANCY(1951); STARLIFT(1951); HOLIDAY FOR SINNERS(1952); ROGUE'S MARCH(1952); WOMAN'S DEVOTION, A(1956); GUN FOR A COWARD(1957); BELL, BOOK AND CANDLE(1958); SUBTERRANEANS, THE(1960); INVITATION TO A GUNFIGHTER(1964); ALVAREZ KELLY(1966); CHASE, THE(1966); AMBUSHERS, THE(1967); WELCOME TO HARD TIMES(1967); SWIMMER, THE(1968); DOCTORS' WIVES(1971); GUMSHOE(1972, Brit.); KID BLUE(1973); THREE WOMEN(1977); MISSING(1982)

Tyde Rule
WORLD'S GREATEST SINNER, THE(1962)
Horatio Ruller
DIRTYMOUTH(1970)
Ruloff
MELODY PARADE(1943)
Jane Rum
HOLLYWOOD BOULEVARD(1976), cos
Siegfried Rumann
MARIE GALANTE(1934); SERVANTS' ENTRANCE(1934); EAST OF JAVA(1935); FARMER TAKES A WIFE, THE(1935); NIGHT AT THE OPERA, A(1935); UNDER PRESSURE(1935); WEDDING NIGHT, THE(1935); PRINCESS COMES ACROSS, THE(1936); REMEMBER?(1939); SHINING VICTORY(1941); CHINA GIRL(1942); CROSSROADS(1942); ENEMY AGENTS MEET ELLERY QUEEN(1942); GOVERNMENT GIRL(1943); THEY CAME TO BLOW UP AMERICA(1943); HOUSE OF FRANKENSTEIN(1944); DOLLY SISTERS, THE(1945); ROYAL SCANDAL, A(1945); FAITHFUL IN MY FASHION(1946); GIVE MY REGARDS TO BROADWAY(1948); IF YOU KNEW SUSIE(1948); BORDER INCIDENT(1949); FATHER IS A BACHELOR(1950); GLENN MILLER STORY, THE(1953); MA AND PA KETTLE ON VACATION(1953); THREE RING CIRCUS(1954); CAROLINA CANNONBALL(1955); ERRAND BOY, THE(1961); LAST OF THE SECRET AGENTS?, THE(1966)
Siegfried [Sig] Rumann
ROYAL BOX, THE(1930); WORLD MOVES ON, THE(1934); SPRING TONIC(1935)
Sig Rumann
THAT UNCERTAIN FEELING(1941); BOLD CABALLERO(1936); DAY AT THE RACES, A(1937); GREAT HOSPITAL MYSTERY, THE(1937); HEIDI(1937); LANCER SPY(1937); LOVE UNDER FIRE(1937); MAYTIME(1937); MIDNIGHT TAXI(1937); NOTHING SACRED(1937); ON THE AVENUE(1937); SEVENTH HEAVEN(1937); THANK YOU, MR. MOTO(1937); THIN ICE(1937); THINK FAST, MR. MOTO(1937); THIS IS MY AFFAIR(1937); GIRLS ON PROBATION(1938); GREAT WALTZ, THE(1938); I'LL GIVE A MILLION(1938); PARADISE FOR THREE(1938); SAINT IN NEW YORK, THE(1938); SUEZ(1938); CONFESSIONS OF A NAZI SPY(1939); HONOLULU(1939); NEVER SAY DIE(1939); NINOTCHKA(1939); ONLY ANGELS HAVE WINGS(1939); BITTER SWEET(1940); COMRADE X(1940); DR. EHRLICH'S MAGIC BULLET(1940); FOUR SONS(1940); I WAS AN ADVENTURESS(1940); OUTSIDE THE 3-MILE LIMIT(1940); VICTORY(1940); LOVE CRAZY(1941); MAN WHO LOST HIMSELF, THE(1941); SO ENDS OUR NIGHT(1941); THIS WOMAN IS MINE(1941); WAGONS ROLL AT NIGHT, THE(1941); WORLD PREMIERE(1941); BERLIN CORRESPONDENT(1942); DESPERATE JOURNEY(1942); REMEMBER PEARL HARBOR(1942); TO BE OR NOT TO BE(1942); WE WERE DANCING(1942); SONG OF BERNADETTE, THE(1943); SWEET ROSIE O'GRADY(1943); TARZAN TRIUMPHS(1943); HITLER GANG, THE(1944); IT HAPPENED TOMORROW(1944); SUMMER STORM(1944); MEN IN HER DIARY(1945); SHE WENT TO THE RACES(1945); NIGHT AND DAY(1946); NIGHT IN CASABLANCA, A(1946); MOTHER WORE TIGHTS(1947); EMPEROR WALTZ, THE(1948); ON THE RIVERA(1951); O. HENRY'S FULL HOUSE(1952); WORLD IN HIS ARMS, THE(1952); HOUDINI(1953); STALAG 17(1953); LIVING IT UP(1954); WHITE CHRISTMAS(1954); MANY RIVERS TO CROSS(1955); SPY CHASERS(1956); WINGS OF EAGLES, THE(1957); ROBIN AND THE SEVEN HOODS(1964); 36 HOURS(1965)
Rosemary Rumbley
PAPER MOON(1973)
Jonathon Rumbold
CREEPING FLESH,THE(1973, Brit.), w
Regine Rumen
NIGHT OF LUST(1965, Fr.)
Leonard Rumery
TROUBLE WITH GIRLS(AND HOW TO GET INTO IT), THE*1/2 (1969)
France Rumilly
GENDARME OF ST. TROPEZ, THE(1966, Fr./Ital.)
Krystyna Rumistrzewicz
DIVIDED HEART, THE(1955, Brit.)
Jeff Rumney
I AM THE CHEESE(1983)
Cindy Lu Rumple
WHERE ANGELS GO...TROUBLE FOLLOWS(1968)
Virginia Rumrill
Misc. Silents
LIFE IN THE ORANGE GROVES(1920)
Bert Rumsey
SHIP OF FOOLS(1965)
Joseph Rumshinsky
TWO SISTERS(1938), m
A. Rumyanova
MUMU(1961, USSR)
K. Rumyanova
RESURRECTION(1963, USSR)
A. Rumyantseva
MEET ME IN MOSCOW(1966, USSR)
K. Rumyantseva
MUMU(1961, USSR)
Nadezhda Rumyantseva
MARRIAGE OF BALZAMINOV, THE(1966, USSR)
Jennie Runacre
PASSENGER, THE(1975, Ital.)
Jenny Runacre
HUSBANDS(1970); MACKINTOSH MAN, THE(1973, Brit.); LAST DAYS OF MAN ON EARTH, THE(1975, Brit.); DUELLISTS, THE(1977, Brit.); JUBILEE(1978, Brit.); LADY VANISHES, THE(1980, Brit.)
Misc. Talkies
HUSSY(1979)
The Runaway Pancake
WANDERLOVE(1970)
Sylvia Rundell
MARS NEEDS WOMEN(1966)
Tommy Rundell
SILVER BEARS(1978)
Todd Rundgren
1984
COLD FEET(1984), m

Cis Rundle
LOOKIN' TO GET OUT(1982); STAR 80(1983)
Dorothea Rundle
FUSS OVER FEATHERS(1954, Brit.); DOUBLE, THE(1963, Brit)
Kenneth Rundquist
MY GAL SAL(1942)
Mikael Rundqvist
HOUR OF THE WOLF, THE(1968, Swed.)
Dr. Harry Rundt
ROYAL BOX, THE(1930), w
Capt. Nils Runelundquist
VICTORS, THE(1963), tech adv
B. Runge
UNCOMMON THIEF, AN(1967, USSR)
B. Runghe
DIARY OF A NAZI(1943, USSR); HEROES ARE MADE(1944, USSR)
Metta Rungrat
HOT POTATO(1976)
Eric Rungren
HATARI!(1962)
Osip Runich
Misc. Silents
SINGED WINGS(1915, USSR); SONG OF TRIUMPHANT LOVE(1915, USSR); LIVING CORPSE, A(1918, USSR); WOMAN WHO INVENTED LOVE, THE(1918, USSR)
Henri Runique
FOLIES DERGERE(1935)
Theodora Van Runkle
JOHNNY GOT HIS GUN(1971), cos
Marina Runne
SWAN LAKE, THE(1967), ed
Dianne Running
JOURNEY THROUGH ROSEBUD(1972)
Joseph Running Fox
SEEMS LIKE OLD TIMES(1980); PORKY'S II: THE NEXT DAY(1983)
Billy Runsabove
RUNNING BRAVE(1983, Can.)
Run RunShaw
FEMALE PRINCE, THE(1966, Hong Kong), p
Damon Runyan
STRAIGHT, PLACE AND SHOW(1938), w
Michael Runyard
1984
BIRDY(1984)
Damon Runyon
GOD IS MY WITNESS(1931), w; MADISON SQUARE GARDEN(1932); LADY FOR A DAY(1933), w; LEMON DROP KID, THE(1934), w; LITTLE MISS MARKER(1934), w; MIDNIGHT ALIBI(1934), w; MILLION DOLLAR RANSOM(1934), w; VERY HONORABLE GUY, A(1934), w; HOLD'EM YALE(1935), w; NO RANSOM(1935), w; PRINCESS O'HARA(1935), w; PROFESSIONAL SOLDIER(1936), w; THREE WISE GUYS, THE(1936), w; RACING LADY(1937), w; SLIGHT CASE OF MURDER, A(1938), w; JOE AND ETHEL TURP CALL ON THE PRESIDENT(1939), w; TIGHT SHOES(1941), w; BIG STREET, THE(1942), p, w; BUTCH MINDS THE BABY(1942), w; IT AIN'T HAY(1943), w; IRISH EYES ARE SMILING(1944), p; SORROWFUL JONES(1949), w; JOHNNY ONE-EYE(1950), w; LEMON DROP KID, THE(1951), w; BLOODHOUNDS OF BROADWAY(1952), w; STOP, YOU'RE KILLING ME(1952), w; MONEY FROM HOME(1953), w; GUYS AND DOLLS(1955), d&w; POCKETFUL OF MIRACLES(1961), w; FORTY POUNDS OF TROUBLE(1962), w; LITTLE MISS MARKER(1980), w
Jennifer Runyon
TO ALL A GOODNIGHT(1980)
1984
GHOSTBUSTERS(1984); UP THE CREEK(1984)
Thomas M. Runyon
TELEFON(1977)
Tom Runyon
GETAWAY, THE(1972); HEART BEAT(1979)
Waltraut Runze-Waitzmann
ESCAPE FROM EAST BERLIN(1962)
Allen Ruoff
Silents
QUALITY STREET(1927), set d
Lane Ruoff
WARRIORS, THE(1979)
Katja Rupe
GERMANY IN AUTUMN(1978, Ger.), a, d
Jean Rupert
LADY L(1965, Fr./Ital.); TO COMMIT A MURDER(1970, Fr./Ital./Ger.)
Mike Rupert
TODD KILLINGS, THE(1971); SUPERDAD(1974)
Sieghardt Rupp
FISTFUL OF DOLLARS, A(1964, Ital./Ger./Span.); FRONTIER HELLCAT(1966, Fr./Ital./Ger./Yugo.); FIVE GOLDEN DRAGONS(1967, Brit.); RED-DRAGON(1967, Ital./Ger./US); FOUNTAIN OF LOVE, THE(1968, Aust.); DEAD PIGEON ON BEETHOVEN STREET(1972, Ger.)
Sieghart Rupp
DON'T LOOK NOW(1969, Brit./Fr.)
Tommy Rupp
$100 A NIGHT(1968, Ger.)
Walter Rupp
CRAZY FOR LOVE(1960, Fr.), p
Achim E. Ruppel
1984
WOMAN IN FLAMES, A(1984, Ger.)
Karl-Ludwig Ruppel
INVISIBLE DR. MABUSE, THE(1965, Ger.), spec eff
Tait Ruppert
DINER(1982)
David Ruprecht
JEKYLL AND HYDE...TOGETHER AGAIN(1982); STAR TREK II: THE WRATH OF KHAN(1982); YOUNG GIANTS(1983)

Martin Rurek
LOST FACE, THE(1965, Czech.)

Peter Ruric
GAMBLING SHIP(1933), w; AFFAIRS OF A GENTLEMAN(1934), w; BLACK CAT, THE(1934), w; TWELVE CROWDED HOURS(1939), w; MADEMOISELLE FIFI(1944), w

Peter Rurie
DARK SANDS(1938, Brit.), w; GRAND CENTRAL MURDER(1942), w; ALIAS A GENTLEMAN(1948), w

Shirley Rus
FIRE DOWN BELOW(1957, U.S./Brit.)

Edward Ruscha
1984
CHOOSE ME(1984)

Al Ruscio
AL CAPONE(1959); FEVER HEAT(1968); NAKED FLAME, THE(1970, Can.); ANY WHICH WAY YOU CAN(1980); IN SEARCH OF HISTORIC JESUS(1980); DEADLY FORCE(1983)

Jeremiah Rusconi
EUROPEANS, THE(1979, Brit.), art d

Martin Rusek
DEATH IS CALLED ENGELCHEN(1963, Czech.); DEATH OF TARZAN, THE(1968, Czech)

Chrystall Rusel
RAGGEDY ANN AND ANDY(1977), anim

William Rusell
Misc. Silents
CRUSADER, THE(1922)

Alice Rush
BLUE COLLAR(1978), cos

Barbara Rush
GOLDBERGS, THE(1950); FIRST LEGION, THE(1951); FLAMING FEATHER(1951); QUEBEC(1951); WHEN WORLDS COLLIDE(1951); IT CAME FROM OUTER SPACE(1953); PRINCE OF PIRATES(1953); BLACK SHIELD OF FALWORTH, THE(1954); MAGNIFICENT OBSESSION(1954); TAZA, SON OF COCHISE(1954); CAPTAIN LIGHTFOOT(1955); KISS OF FIRE(1955); BIGGER THAN LIFE(1956); FLIGHT TO HONG KONG(1956); WORLD IN MY CORNER(1956); NO DOWN PAYMENT(1957); OH, MEN! OH, WOMEN!(1957); HARRY BLACK AND THE TIGER(1958, Brit.); YOUNG LIONS, THE(1958); YOUNG PHILADELPHIANS, THE(1959); BRAMBLE BUSH, THE(1960); STRANGERS WHEN WE MEET(1960); COME BLOW YOUR HORN(1963); ROBIN AND THE SEVEN HOODS(1964); HOMBRE(1967); STRATEGY OF TERROR(1969); MAN, THE(1972); SUPERDAD(1974); CAN'T STOP THE MUSIC(1980); SUMMER LOVERS(1982)

Billy Rush
SAVAGE SEVEN, THE(1968)

Carol Rush
PETTY GIRL, THE(1950)

Celeste Rush
Silents
INVADERS, THE(1929)

Deborah Rush
OLIVER'S STORY(1978); 10(1979); HONKY TONK FREEWAY(1981); SPLIT IMAGE(1982); NIGHT IN HEAVEN, A(1983); ZELIG(1983)

Dennis Rush
MAN OF A THOUSAND FACES(1957); FOLLOW ME, BOYS!(1966)

Dick Rush
KIBITZER, THE(1929); BENSON MURDER CASE, THE(1930); SKY RAIDERS(1931); YOUNG DONOVAN'S KID(1931); MOVIE CRAZY(1932); BEYOND THE LAW(1934); LAST ROUND-UP, THE(1934); MEN OF THE NIGHT(1934); SIX OF A KIND(1934); THIRTY-DAY PRINCESS(1934); THUNDERING HERD, THE(1934); FRISCO KID(1935); JUSTICE OF THE RANGE(1935); RUMBA(1935); COWBOY AND THE KID,THE(1936); FORBIDDEN TRAIL(1936); POPPY(1936); EXCLUSIVE(1937); PAID TO DANCE(1937); SUPER SLEUTH(1937); HUNTED MEN(1938); JURY'S SECRET, THE(1938); SANTA FE STAMPEDE(1938); TRADE WINDS(1938); YOU CAN'T TAKE IT WITH YOU(1938); HOMICIDE BUREAU(1939); LAUGH IT OFF(1939); OFF THE RECORD(1939); PHANTOM STAGE, THE(1939); ENEMY AGENT(1940); HOUSE ACROSS THE BAY, THE(1940); MY LITTLE CHICKADEE(1940); SLIGHTLY HONORABLE(1940); THIRD FINGER, LEFT HAND(1940); BALL OF FIRE(1941); HONKY TONK(1941); MEXICAN SPITFIRE'S BABY(1941); PUBLIC ENEMIES(1941); BROADWAY BIG SHOT(1942); MY FAVORITE BLONDE(1942); THIS GUN FOR HIRE(1942); HENRY ALDRICH HAUNTS A HOUSE(1943); IS EVERYBODY HAPPY?(1943); ONE DANGEROUS NIGHT(1943); SAGEBRUSH LAW(1943); SKY'S THE LIMIT, THE(1943); HEAVENLY DAYS(1944); OH, WHAT A NIGHT(1944); WHAT A MAN!(1944); EVE KNEW HER APPLES(1945); WITHIN THESE WALLS(1945); CRACK-UP(1946); DEADLINE AT DAWN(1946); NOCTURNE(1946); HIGH BARBAREE(1947); LIKELY STORY, A(1947); SEA OF GRASS, THE(1947); SECRET LIFE OF WALTER MITTY, THE(1947)
Silents
PLAYING DOUBLE(1923), d
Misc. Silents
VILLAGE SLEUTH, A(1920)

Jerry Rush
NEARLY EIGHTEEN(1943); THAT'S THE WAY OF THE WORLD(1975)

John Rush
NATE AND HAYES(1983, U.S./New Zealand)

Loretta Rush
ACCIDENTS WILL HAPPEN(1938)

Louise Rush
OPEN THE DOOR AND SEE ALL THE PEOPLE(1964); LIONHEART(1968, Brit.)

Maggie Rush
BUDDY HOLLY STORY, THE(1978), ch

Philip Rush
OPERATION SECRET(1952); VIRGIN ISLAND(1960, Brit.), w

Richard Rush
TOO SOON TO LOVE(1960), p&d, w; OF LOVE AND DESIRE(1963), d, w; FICKLE FINGER OF FATE, THE(1967, Span./U.S.), d; HELL'S ANGELS ON WHEELS(1967), d; MAN CALLED DAGGER, A(1967), d; THUNDER ALLEY(1967), d; PSYCHOUT(1968), d; SAVAGE SEVEN, THE(1968), d; GETTING STRAIGHT(1970), p&d; FREEBIE AND THE BEAN(1974), p&d; STUNT MAN, THE(1980), p&d, w

Robert Lee Rush
DRESSED TO KILL(1980); BAD BOYS(1983)

Sarah Rush
BATTLESTAR GALACTICA(1979); JONI(1980); NUDE BOMB, THE(1980)
1984
PRODIGAL, THE(1984)

Sid Rushakoff
WHAT AM I BID?(1967)

Emily Rushforth
SOMETIMES GOOD(1934, Brit.), w

James "Jimmy" Rushing
LEARNING TREE, THE(1969)

Jerry Rushing
CARNY(1980); LIVING LEGEND(1980); FINAL EXAM(1981); NIGHT THE LIGHTS WENT OUT IN GEORGIA, THE(1981)
1984
ROTWEILER: DOGS OF HELL(1984)
Misc. Talkies
LAST GAME, THE(1983)

Robert W. Rushing
GREATEST SHOW ON EARTH, THE(1952)

N. Rushkovskiy
MOTHER AND DAUGHTER(1965, USSR)

Karen Rushmore
COAST TO COAST(1980)

John Rushton
PETER RABBIT AND TALES OF BEATRIX POTTER(1971, Brit.), ed; BROTHER SUN, SISTER MOON(1973, Brit./Ital.), ed

Roland Rushton
Silents
DOUBLING FOR ROMEO(1921); BEAU BRUMMEL(1924)

William Rushton
IT'S ALL OVER TOWN(1963, Brit.); NOTHING BUT THE BEST(1964, Brit.); THOSE MAGNIFICENT MEN IN THEIR FLYING MACHINES; OR HOW I FLEWFROM LONDON TO PARIS IN 25 HOURS AND 11 MINUTES(1965, Brit.); BLISS OF MRS. BLOSSOM, THE(1968, Brit.); MINI-AFFAIR, THE(1968, Brit.); BEST HOUSE IN LONDON, THE(1969, Brit.); THOSE DARING YOUNG MEN IN THEIR JAUNTY JALOPIES(1969, Fr./Brit./ Ital.); FLIGHT OF THE DOVES(1971)

Buddy Ruskin
CLAY PIGEON(1971), w

Dan Ruskin
ANNIE HALL(1977)

Don Ruskin
USED CARS(1980)

Harry Ruskin
HELLO SISTER!(1933), w; TOO MUCH HARMONY(1933), w; SIX OF A KIND(1934), w; GLASS KEY, THE(1935), w; RUMBA(1935), w; STOLEN HARMONY(1935), w; TWO FOR TONIGHT(1935), w; BIG NOISE, THE(1936, Brit.), w; LADY BE CAREFUL(1936), w; BEG, BORROW OR STEAL(1937), w; MARRIED BEFORE BREAKFAST(1937), w; WOMEN MEN MARRY, THE(1937), w; 23 ½ HOURS LEAVE(1937), w; CHASER, THE(1938), w; LOVE IS A HEADACHE(1938), w; PARADISE FOR THREE(1938), w; YOUNG DR. KILDARE(1938), w; CALLING DR. KILDARE(1939), w; MIRACLES FOR SALE(1939), w; SECRET OF DR. KILDARE, THE(1939), w; DR. KILDARE GOES HOME(1940), w; DR. KILDARE'S CRISIS(1940), w; DR. KILDARE'S STRANGE CASE(1940), w; GHOST COMES HOME, THE(1940), w; ANDY HARDY'S PRIVATE SECRETARY(1941), w; DR. KILDARE'S VICTORY(1941), w; DR. KILDARE'S WEDDING DAY(1941), w; KEEPING COMPANY(1941), w; PENALTY, THE(1941), w; PEOPLE VS. DR. KILDARE, THE(1941), w; CALLING DR. GILLESPIE(1942), w; DR. GILLESPIE'S NEW ASSISTANT(1942), w; THIS TIME FOR KEEPS(1942), w; TISH(1942), w; DR. GILLESPIE'S CRIMINAL CASE(1943), w; ANDY HARDY'S BLONDE TROUBLE(1944), w; BARBARY COAST GENT(1944), w; BETWEEN TWO WOMEN(1944), w; LOST IN A HAREM(1944), w; RATIONING(1944), w; THREE MEN IN WHITE(1944), w; HIDDEN EYE, THE(1945), w; LOVE LAUGHS AT ANDY HARDY(1946), w; POSTMAN ALWAYS RINGS TWICE, THE(1946), w; DARK DELUSION(1947), w; JULIA MISBEHAVES(1948), w; TENTH AVENUE ANGEL(1948), w; HAPPY YEARS, THE(1950), w; WATCH THE BIRDIE(1950), p, w; LADY GODIVA(1955), w; GIRL IN THE KREMLIN, THE(1957), w

Henry Ruskin
GREAT GUY(1936), w

Jeanne Ruskin
RENT CONTROL(1981)

Joseph Ruskin
HELL BENT FOR LEATHER(1960); RISE AND FALL OF LEGS DIAMOND, THE(1960); DIARY OF A MADMAN(1963); ROBIN AND THE SEVEN HOODS(1964)

Sheila Ruskin
THIS, THAT AND THE OTHER(1970, Brit.); SWISS CONSPIRACY, THE(1976, U.S./Ger.); WHO IS KILLING THE GREAT CHEFS OF EUROPE?(1978, US/Ger.); DOGS OF WAR, THE(1980, Brit.)

Shemen Ruskin
CRACK-UP(1946)

Shimen Ruskin
HAVING WONDERFUL TIME(1938); DANCE HALL(1941); LADY FROM LOUISIANA(1941); THEY GOT ME COVERED(1943); WHAT A WOMAN!(1943); IN OUR TIME(1944); HOLD THAT BLONDE(1945); MURDER, MY SWEET(1945); CROSS MY HEART(1946); DEADLINE AT DAWN(1946); MASK OF DIIJON, THE(1946); DARK PASSAGE(1947); JOHNNY O'CLOCK(1947); SLAVE GIRL(1947); FORCE OF EVIL(1948); LETTER FROM AN UNKNOWN WOMAN(1948); GUN CRAZY(1949); FAT MAN, THE(1951); TEN TALL MEN(1951); DONOVAN'S BRAIN(1953); FIDDLER ON THE ROOF(1971); SHAFT(1971); LOVE AND DEATH(1975)

Paul Rusking
WIND AND THE LION, THE(1975)

Cindy Rusler
Misc. Talkies
1ST NOTCH, THE(1977)

Veronica Rusmin
DR. COPPELIUS(1968, U.S./Span.)

Garry Rusoff
EVICTORS, THE(1979), w

Lou Rusoff
APACHE WOMAN(1955), w; GIRLS IN PRISON(1956), w; IT CONQUERED THE WORLD(1956), w; OKLAHOMA WOMAN, THE(1956), w; PHANTOM FROM 10,000 LEAGUES, THE(1956), w; SHE-CREATURE, THE(1956), w; CAT GIRL(1957), w; DRAGSTRIP GIRL(1957), w; MOTORCYCLE GANG(1957), w; RUNAWAY DAUGHTERS(1957), w; SHAKE, RATTLE, AND ROCK!(1957), w; HOT ROD GANG(1958), p, w; SUICIDE BATTALION(1958), p, w; GHOST OF DRAGSTRIP HOLLOW(1959), p, w; SUBMARINE SEAHAWK(1959), w; ALAKAZAM THE GREAT!(1961, Jap.), p, w; PANIC IN YEAR ZERO!(1962), p; BEACH PARTY(1963), p, w; OPERATION BIKINI(1963), p; IN THE YEAR 2889(1966), w

Alessandro Ruspoli
IDENTIFICATION OF A WOMAN(1983, Ital.)

Esmeralda Ruspoli
L'AVVENTURA(1960, Ital.); SEVEN SEAS TO CALAIS(1963, Ital.); THREE FACES OF A WOMAN(1965, Ital.); ADOLESCENTS, THE(1967, Can.); MAIDEN FOR A PRINCE, A(1967, Fr./Ital.); ROMEO AND JULIET(1968, Brit./Ital.); PLACE FOR LOVERS, A(1969, Ital./Fr.); WITHOUT APPARENT MOTIVE(1972, Fr.)

Luisa Ruspoli
MY SON, THE HERO(1963, Ital./Fr.); OPIATE '67(1967, Fr./Ital.)

Cindy Russ
MY BODYGUARD(1980)

Dan Russ
JOHNNY CONCHO(1956)

Debbie Russ
FLYING SORCERER, THE(1974, Brit.)

Don Russ
ANATOMY OF A MURDER(1959)

George Russ
SHOOT-OUT AT MEDICINE BEND(1957)

Martin Russ
SAND CASTLE, THE(1961)

Robert Russ
EGON SCHIELE–EXCESS AND PUNISHMENT(1981, Ger.), p

Toby Russ
DUNWICH HORROR, THE(1970); LADY SINGS THE BLUES(1972)

William Russ
JUST YOU AND ME, KID(1979); CRUISING(1980); CATTLE ANNIE AND LITTLE BRITCHES(1981); BORDER, THE(1982); RIGHT STUFF, THE(1983)
1984
RAW COURAGE(1984)

Russ Columbo and The Boswell Sisters
MOULIN ROUGE(1934)

Russ Henderson Steel Band
DR. TERROR'S HOUSE OF HORRORS(1965, Brit.)

Russ Morgan and his Orchestra
CIGARETTE GIRL(1947)

Russ Morgan Orchestra
SARGE GOES TO COLLEGE(1947)

Russ Saunders Troupe
VEILS OF BAGDAD, THE(1953)

Russ Sisters
BROADWAY RHYTHM(1944)

Francesco Russe
IT'S A WONDERFUL WORLD(1956, Brit.)

Jorge Russek
VILLA!(1958); RAGE(1966, U.S./Mex.); HOUR OF THE GUN(1967); GUNS FOR SAN SEBASTIAN(1968, U.S./Fr./Mex./Ital.); WILD BUNCH, THE(1969); SOLDIER BLUE(1970); WRATH OF GOD, THE(1972); PAT GARRETT AND BILLY THE KID(1973); BRING ME THE HEAD OF ALFREDO GARCIA(1974); RETURN OF A MAN CALLED HORSE, THE(1976); EAGLE'S WING(1979, Brit.); ZORRO, THE GAY BLADE(1981); MISSING(1982)

Rita Russek
FROM THE LIFE OF THE MARIONETTES(1980, Ger.)

Alice Russel
Misc. Talkies
WAGES OF SIN, THE(1929)

Andaluz Russel
UNDER FIRE(1983)

Autumn Russel
TOWARD THE UNKNOWN(1956)

Buck Russel
HERE COME THE MARINES(1952)

Del Russel
HARD RIDE, THE(1971)

Elizabeth Russel
SCREAM IN THE DARK, A(1943)

Evelyn Russel
EAT MY DUST!(1976)

Gail Russel
EL PASO(1949)

Jack Russel
NUDE ODYSSEY(1962, Fr./Ital.)

Jeff Russel
SWORD OF EL CID, THE(1965, Span./Ital.)

Lewis Russel
CORKY OF GASOLINE ALLEY(1951); AGAINST ALL FLAGS(1952)

Mark Russel
TWILIGHT'S LAST GLEAMING(1977, U.S./Ger.)

Persival Russel
LOVE AND DEATH(1975)

Tony Russel
WAR IS HELL(1964); THREE WEEKS OF LOVE(1965)
Misc. Talkies
DAY THE LORD GOT BUSTED, THE(1976)

Bernard Russelet
ALICE, OR THE LAST ESCAPADE(1977, Fr.)

Mr. Russell
Silents
MR. FIX-IT(1918)

A. J. Russell
LOVELY WAY TO DIE, A(1968), w; STILETTO(1969), w

Albert Russell
DARK ANGEL, THE(1935); I CONQUER THE SEA(1936); COURAGE OF THE WEST(1937)
Misc. Silents
LONE FIGHTER(1923), d

Alexander Russell
MUSIC LOVERS, THE(1971, Brit.)

Alice B. Russell
Misc. Talkies
GOD'S STEPCHILDREN(1937)
Misc. Silents
BROKEN VIOLIN, THE(1927)

Allan Russell
VALDEZ IS COMING(1971)

Allen Russell
CAPTAIN APACHE(1971, Brit.); WIND AND THE LION, THE(1975)

Allen E. Russell
SPIKES GANG, THE(1974)

Andy Russell
STORK CLUB, THE(1945); BREAKFAST IN HOLLYWOOD(1946); MAKE MINE MUSIC(1946); COPACABANA(1947)

Anna Russell
HANSEL AND GRETEL(1954); KILL OR CURE(1962, Brit.)

Archie Russell
PUTNEY SWOPE(1969)

Autumn Russell
SCARLET HOUR, THE(1956); SWEET SMELL OF SUCCESS(1957); ZOMBIES OF MORA TAU(1957); SPARTACUS(1960)

Bernard D. Russell
Misc. Silents
BROKEN LAW, THE(1924), d

Bert Russell
MANHATTAN MELODRAMA(1934)

Bertha Russell
DYNAMITERS, THE(1956, Brit.); IT HAPPENED HERE(1966, Brit.)

Betsy Russell
PRIVATE SCHOOL(1983)

Bill Russell
ON THE RIGHT TRACK(1981)

Billy Russell
TAKE OFF THAT HAT(1938, Brit.); FOR FREEDOM(1940, Brit.); NIGHT TRAIN(1940, Brit.); GALLOPING MAJOR, THE(1951, Brit.); JUDGMENT DEFERRED(1952, Brit.); MAN IN THE WHITE SUIT, THE(1952); NEGATIVES(1968, Brit.); I START COUNTING(1970, Brit.); LEO THE LAST(1970, Brit.)

Bing Russell
TARANTULA(1955); BEHIND THE HIGH WALL(1956); FEAR STRIKES OUT(1957); GUNFIGHT AT THE O.K. CORRAL(1957); RIDE A VIOLENT MILE(1957); TEENAGE THUNDER(1957); CATTLE EMPIRE(1958); GOOD DAY FOR A HANGING(1958); SUICIDE BATTALION(1958); HORSE SOLDIERS, THE(1959); LAST TRAIN FROM GUN HILL(1959); RIO BRAVO(1959); MAGNIFICENT SEVEN, THE(1960); STAKE-OUT!(1962); STRIPPER, THE(1963); CHEYENNE AUTUMN(1964); ONE MAN'S WAY(1964); HALLELUJAH TRAIL, THE(1965); EYE FOR AN EYE, AN(1966), w; MADAME X(1966); RIDE TO HANGMAN'S TREE, THE(1967); JOURNEY TO SHILOH(1968); COMPUTER WORE TENNIS SHOES, THE(1970); APPLE DUMPLING GANG, THE(1975)

Blake Russell
THOSE LIPS, THOSE EYES(1980), set d; SCARFACE(1983), set d

Bob Russell
REACH FOR GLORY(1963, Brit.), m
Misc. Silents
USURPER, THE(1919)

Bobby Russell
NIGHT THE LIGHTS WENT OUT IN GEORGIA, THE(1981), w; COUNTRYMAN(1982, Jamaica)

Brian Russell
CHARLIE, THE LONESOME COUGAR(1967)

Bryan Russell
BABES IN TOYLAND(1961); HOW THE WEST WAS WON(1962); SAFE AT HOME(1962); WONDERFUL WORLD OF THE BROTHERS GRIMM, THE(1962); BYE BYE BIRDIE(1963); TICKLISH AFFAIR, A(1963); EMIL AND THE DETECTIVES(1964); ADVENTURES OF BULLWHIP GRIFFIN, THE(1967)

Bryson Russell
Silents
DAUGHTER PAYS, THE(1920)

Byron Russell
MUTINY ON THE BOUNTY(1935); PARNELL(1937); ONE THIRD OF A NATION(1939)
Silents
IT IS THE LAW(1924); JANICE MEREDITH(1924)
Misc. Silents
FAMILY CLOSET, THE(1921)

Campbell Russell
HIS MAJESTY AND CO(1935, Brit.)

Carl Russell
O.S.S.(1946)

Carol Russell
CONFESSIONS OF AN OPIUM EATER(1962)

Charles Russell
SHIPS WITH WINGS(1942, Brit.); BOMBARDIER(1943); LADIES' DAY(1943); WE DIVE AT DAWN(1943, Brit.); PURPLE HEART, THE(1944); CAPTAIN EDDIE(1945); BEHIND GREEN LIGHTS(1946); JOHNNY COMES FLYING HOME(1946); WAKE UP AND DREAM(1946); LATE GEORGE APLEY, THE(1947); CANON CITY(1948); GIVE MY REGARDS TO BROADWAY(1948); INNER SANCTUM(1948); NIGHT WIND(1948); CHINATOWN AT MIDNIGHT(1949); MARY RYAN, DETECTIVE(1949); TROUBLE PREFERRED(1949); TUCSON(1949); GREAT ARMORED CAR SWINDLE, THE(1964); HEARSE, THE(1980), p

Charlie L. Russell
FIVE ON THE BLACK HAND SIDE(1973), w
Charlotte Russell
KID MILLIONS(1934); STRIKE ME PINK(1936)
Chuck Russell
1984
DREAMSCAPE(1984), w
Claire Russell
CONFESSIONS OF A WINDOW CLEANER(1974, Brit.); STARDUST(1974, Brit.)
Clive Russell
NAKED BRIGADE, THE(1965, U.S./Gr.)
Connie Russell
MELODY AND ROMANCE(1937, Brit.); LADY BE GOOD(1941); CRUISIN' DOWN THE RIVER(1953); THIS IS MY LOVE(1954); NIGHTMARE(1956)
Craig Russell
OUTRAGEOUS!(1977, Can.)
David Russell
SOMEONE(1968); DRIFTER(1975)
Dean Russell
FOREST, THE(1983)
Del Russell
CLEOPATRA(1963)
Diana Russell
LADY GODIVA RIDES AGAIN(1955, Brit.)
Don Russell
TALE OF FIVE WOMEN, A(1951, Brit.), art d; SADIST, THE(1963); NO MAN'S LAND(1964), a, art d; TALES OF A SALESMAN(1965), d
Donald Russell
YOU'D BE SURPRISED!(1930, Brit.); TROUBLE IN THE AIR(1948, Brit.), art d
Donna Russell
SURF PARTY(1964); CATALINA CAPER, THE(1967)
Dora Russell
REDS(1981)
Drew Russell
AMOROUS MR. PRAWN, THE(1965, Brit.)
Duke Russell
FANTASIA(1940), art d, anim
Dusty Russell
STEEL ARENA(1973)
Ed Russell
THAT HAGEN GIRL(1947); GREAT JESSE JAMES RAID, THE(1953)
Ed "Strawberry" Russell
ON STAGE EVERYBODY(1945)
Edd Russell
WEDDING PRESENT(1936)
Edith Russell
WILL SUCCESS SPOIL ROCK HUNTER?(1957)
Edmond Russell
MINISTRY OF FEAR(1945)
Elizabeth Russell
FORGOTTEN FACES(1936); GIRL OF THE OZARKS(1936); HIDEAWAY GIRL(1937); DATE WITH THE FALCON, A(1941); CAT PEOPLE(1942); CORPSE VANISHES, THE(1942); MEET THE MOB(1942); HITLER'S MADMAN(1943); SEVENTH VICTIM, THE(1943); SHE HAS WHAT IT TAKES(1943); CURSE OF THE CAT PEOPLE, THE(1944); SUMMER STORM(1944); UNINVITED, THE(1944); WEIRD WOMAN(1944); YOUTH RUNS WILD(1944); ADVENTURE(1945); KEEP YOUR POWDER DRY(1945); OUR VINES HAVE TENDER GRAPES(1945); BEDLAM(1946); SO BIG(1953)
Ethel Russell
Misc. Silents
BROMLEY CASE, THE(1920)
Evangeline Russell
Misc. Silents
FLOODGATES(1924); RED LOVE(1925); BIG SHOW, THE(1926); MARRIED?(1926)
Evelyn Russell
SHEILA LEVINE IS DEAD AND LIVING IN NEW YORK(1975); 92 IN THE SHADE(1975, U.S./Brit.)
Forbesy Russell
BOARDWALK(1979)
Frances Russell
WORLD OF HANS CHRISTIAN ANDERSEN, THE(1971, Jap.)
Frank Russell
HEROES DIE YOUNG(1960), p
Franz Russell
CHANGE OF MIND(1969); PAPERBACK HERO(1973, Can.); SUNDAY IN THE COUNTRY(1975, Can.); AGENCY(1981, Can.)
Gail Russell
HENRY ALDRICH GETS GLAMOUR(1942); LADY IN THE DARK(1944); OUR HEARTS WERE YOUNG AND GAY(1944); UNINVITED, THE(1944); DUFFY'S TAVERN(1945); SALTY O'ROURKE(1945); UNSEEN, THE(1945); BACHELOR'S DAUGHTERS, THE(1946); OUR HEARTS WERE GROWING UP(1946); ANGEL AND THE BADMAN(1947); CALCUTTA(1947); VARIETY GIRL(1947); MOONRISE(1948); NIGHT HAS A THOUSAND EYES(1948); CAPTAIN CHINA(1949); GREAT DAN PATCH, THE(1949); SONG OF INDIA(1949); WAKE OF THE RED WITCH(1949); LAWLESS, THE(1950); AIR CADET(1951); SEVEN MEN FROM NOW(1956); TATTERED DRESS, THE(1957); NO PLACE TO LAND(1958); SILENT CALL, THE(1961)
Geoffrey Russell
DARWIN ADVENTURE, THE(1972, Brit.); ROUGH CUT(1980, Brit.)
George Russell
LONE HAND TEXAN, THE(1947); MONTANA TERRITORY(1952); SON OF PALEFACE(1952); DALTON THAT GOT AWAY(1960); STATE FAIR(1962); FREE, WHITE AND 21(1963); TRIAL OF LEE HARVEY OSWALD, THE(1964); UNDER AGE(1964); BLACK CAT, THE(1966)
Gilbert Russell
EVERYBODY DOES IT(1949); GREAT CARUSO, THE(1951)
Gloria Russell
STORK TALK(1964, Brit.), w

Gordon Russell
HOUSE OF DARK SHADOWS(1970), w
Silents
TESTING BLOCK, THE(1920); KINGDOM WITHIN, THE(1922); SCARLET LILY, THE(1923); SINGER JIM MCKEE(1924); EASY GOING GORDON(1925)
Misc. Silents
SOME LIAR(1919); THREE WORD BRAND(1921); HIS BACK AGAINST THE WALL(1922); TRAIL OF HATE(1922); HARD HITTIN' HAMILTON(1924); FLYING HOOFS(1925)
Grace D. Russell
IN TROUBLE WITH EVE(1964, Brit.)
Grace Denbeigh Russell
MUDLARK, THE(1950, Brit.)
Grace Denbigh Russell
DARK MAN, THE(1951, Brit.); DOUBLE CONFESSION(1953, Brit.); TEARS FOR SIMON(1957, Brit.)
Graham Russell
NOW AND FOREVER(1983, Aus.), m; WHO KILLED VAN LOON?(1984, Brit.)
Harold Russell
BEST YEARS OF OUR LIVES, THE(1946); INSIDE MOVES(1980)
Harriet Russell
CRIME OF DR. CRESPI, THE(1936)
Harry Russell
Misc. Silents
LITTLE BOSS, THE(1919)
Harvey Russell
SEVEN GUNS TO MESA(1958)
Henry Russell
SHIP AHOY(1942), m; NAUGHTY NINETIES, THE(1945); LIVE WIRES(1946); LULU BELLE(1948), m; FIVE(1951), m; STAR IS BORN, A(1954)
Misc. Silents
BOND WITHIN, THE(1916)
Henry T. Russell
HOTEL RESERVE(1946, Brit.)
Hilda Campbell Russell
NO ESCAPE(1936, Brit.)
Howard Russell
STREET SCENE(1931); PERSONALITY KID, THE(1934)
Silents
HEARTS AND FISTS(1926)
Hugh Russell
STRANGE AFFECTION(1959, Brit.)
Ian Russell
ESCAPE(1948, Brit.)
Irene Russell
HAPPY ENDING, THE(1931, Brit.)
Silents
MUMSIE(1927, Brit.)
Iris Russell
ARMCHAIR DETECTIVE, THE(1952, Brit.); YELLOW ROBE, THE(1954, Brit.); GENTLE TOUCH, THE(1956, Brit.); MOONRAKER, THE(1958, Brit.); STOLEN AIRLINER, THE(1962, Brit.); DREAM MAKER, THE(1963, Brit.); DOWNFALL(1964, Brit.)
J. B. Russell
Silents
KID, THE(1921)
J. Buckley Russell
Silents
JACK RIDER, THE(1921); FRESHIE, THE(1922)
J. Gordon Russell
Silents
MEDIATOR, THE(1916); SEA LION, THE(1921); QUICKER'N LIGHTNIN'(1925); TUMBLEWEEDS(1925); LOOKING FOR TROUBLE(1926)
Misc. Silents
MISS JACKIE OF THE NAVY(1916); COLLEEN OF THE PINES(1922); CHASTITY(1923); MILE-A-MINUTE ROMEO(1923); REFUGE(1923); GALLOPING JINX(1925); ROARING ADVENTURE, A(1925); SIGN OF THE CACTUS, THE(1925); SPURS AND SADDLES(1927); SADDLE MATES(1928)
J. H. Russell
NIGHT TRAIN TO MUNDO FINE(1966), ed
Jack Russell
SO THIS IS NEW YORK(1948), ph; GUILTY OF TREASON(1950), ph; ARCTIC FLIGHT(1952), ph; PARK ROW(1952), ph; BEAST FROM 20,000 FATHOMS, THE(1953), ph; OUT OF SIGHT(1966), ph; FRIENDS(1971, Brit.), w
Jack Golden Russell
OCEAN BREAKERS(1949, Swed.), w; OCEAN'S ELEVEN(1960), w
Jackie Russell
TICKLE ME(1965); GUIDE FOR THE MARRIED MAN, A(1967); NEVER A DULL MOMENT(1968); CHEYENNE SOCIAL CLUB, THE(1970); OTHER SIDE OF THE MOUNTAIN–PART 2, THE(1978)
James Gordon Russell
Silents
KINDLED COURAGE(1923); NO-GUN MAN, THE(1924)
Misc. Silents
WESTERN WALLOP, THE(1924); PARISIAN LOVE(1925)
James Russell
MUSIC LOVERS, THE(1971, Brit.)
Jamie Russell
UNDERWATER!(1955); HOT BLOOD(1956); TERROR IN A TEXAS TOWN(1958)
Jane Russell
OUTLAW, THE(1943); YOUNG WIDOW(1946); PALEFACE, THE(1948); DOUBLE DYNAMITE(1951); HIS KIND OF WOMAN(1951); LAS VEGAS STORY, THE(1952); MACAO(1952); MONTANA BELLE(1952); ROAD TO BALI(1952); SON OF PALEFACE(1952); GENTLEMEN PREFER BLONDES(1953); FRENCH LINE, THE(1954); FOXFIRE(1955); GENTLEMEN MARRY BRUNETTES(1955); TALL MEN, THE(1955); UNDERWATER!(1955); HOT BLOOD(1956); REVOLT OF MAMIE STOVER, THE(1956); FUZZY PINK NIGHTGOWN, THE(1957); FATE IS THE HUNTER(1964); JOHNNY RENO(1966); WACO(1966); BORN LOSERS(1967); DARKER THAN AMBER(1970)

Janet Russell
OPERATION CIA(1965)
Jim Russell
GRAND PRIX(1966)
Jimmy Russell
NEW FACES(1954)
Joan Russell
SMALL TOWN GIRL(1936); PERSONAL BEST(1982)
Joe Ed Russell
HOME FROM THE HILL(1960)
John Russell
PAGAN, THE(1929), w; SIDE STREET(1929), w; GIRL OF THE PORT(1930), w; SEA GOD, THE(1930), w; DUKE COMES BACK, THE(1937); ALWAYS GOODBYE(1938); FIVE OF A KIND(1938); PRISON BREAK(1938); I AM NOT AFRAID(1939); JESSE JAMES(1939); MAN WHO DARED, THE(1939); MR. SMITH GOES TO WASHINGTON(1939); FLORIAN(1940); BELL FOR ADANO, A(1945); DON JUAN QUILLIGAN(1945); ROYAL SCANDAL, A(1945); WITHIN THESE WALLS(1945); DARK CORNER, THE(1946); SOMEWHERE IN THE NIGHT(1946); WAKE UP AND DREAM(1946); FOREVER AMBER(1947); SITTING PRETTY(1948); YELLOW SKY(1948); GAL WHO TOOK THE WEST, THE(1949); SLATTERY'S HURRICANE(1949); STORY OF MOLLY X, THE(1949); UNDERTOW(1949); FRENCHIE(1950); SADDLE TRAMP(1950); BAREFOOT MAILMAN, THE(1951); FAT MAN, THE(1951); FIGHTING COAST GUARD(1951); MAN IN THE SADDLE(1951); HOODLUM EMPIRE(1952); OKLAHOMA ANNIE(1952); FAIR WIND TO JAVA(1953); JUBILEE TRAIL(1954); HELL'S OUTPOST(1955); LAST COMMAND, THE(1955); DALTON GIRLS, THE(1957); HELL BOUND(1957); UNTAMED YOUTH(1957); FORT MASSACRE(1958); RIO BRAVO(1959); YELLOWSTONE KELLY(1959); CABINET OF CALIGARI, THE(1962), ph; BILLIE(1965), ph; APACHE UPRISING(1966); FORT UTAH(1967); HOSTILE GUNS(1967); BUCKSKIN(1968); FIREBALL JUNGLE(1968); IF HE HOLLERS, LET HIM GO(1968); BACKTRACK(1969), ph; CANNON FOR CORDOBA(1970); LEGACY OF BLOOD(1973); LORD SHANGO(1975); SMOKE IN THE WIND(1975); UNCLE SCAM(1981); HONKYTONK MAN(1982)
Misc. Talkies
ATTACK AT NOON SUNDAY(1971); NOON SUNDAY(1971)
Silents
EXILES, THE(1923), w; ARGENTINE LOVE(1924), w; IRON HORSE, THE(1924), w; LORD JIM(1925), w; BEAU GESTE(1926), w; PARADISE(1926), w; SORROWS OF SATAN(1926), w; RED MARK, THE(1928), w
John Russell, Jr.
INDESTRUCTIBLE MAN, THE(1956), ph
John L. Russell
MACBETH(1948), ph; MOONRISE(1948), ph; GREEN PROMISE, THE(1949), ph; MAN FROM PLANET X, THE(1951), ph; INVASION U.S.A.(1952), ph; GIRLS' TOWN(1959), ph; PSYCHO(1960), ph; JIGSAW(1968), ph
John L. Russell, Jr.
GOLDEN GLOVES STORY, THE(1950), ph; CHAMP FOR A DAY(1953), ph; CITY THAT NEVER SLEEPS(1953), ph; GERALDINE(1953), ph; PROBLEM GIRLS(1953), ph; SWORD OF VENUS(1953), ph; ATOMIC KID, THE(1954), ph; HELL'S HALF ACRE(1954), ph; MAKE HASTE TO LIVE(1954), ph; TOBOR THE GREAT(1954), ph; DOUBLE JEOPARDY(1955), ph; ETERNAL SEA, THE(1955), ph; HEADLINE HUNTERS(1955), ph; LAY THAT RIFLE DOWN(1955), ph; VANISHING AMERICAN, THE(1955), ph; STAR IN THE DUST(1956), ph; WHEN GANGLAND STRIKES(1956), ph; HELL'S CROSSROADS(1957), ph
John Lowell Russell
Silents
ARIZONA DAYS(1928); MANHATTAN COWBOY(1928)
Johnny Russell
SABOTAGE(1939); LADY WITH RED HAIR(1940); MAN I MARRIED, THE(1940)
Juan Russell
BUS IS COMING, THE(1971)
Judi Russell
1984
TAIL OF THE TIGER(1984, Aus.), prod d
Ken Russell
FRENCH DRESSING(1964, Brit.), d; BILLION DOLLAR BRAIN(1967, Brit.), d; WOMEN IN LOVE(1969, Brit.), d; BOY FRIEND, THE(1971, Brit.), p, d, w; MUSIC LOVERS, THE(1971, Brit.), p&d; SAVAGE MESSIAH(1972, Brit.), p&d; MAHLER(1974, Brit.), d&w; LISZTOMANIA(1975, Brit.), d&w; TOMMY(1975, Brit.), p, d&w; VALENTINO(1977, Brit.), d, w; ALTERED STATES(1980), d
1984
CRIMES OF PASSION(1984), d
Misc. Talkies
DEVILS, THE(1971), d
Kennedy Russell
OLD MOTHER RILEY'S GHOSTS(1941, Brit.), m; LET THE PEOPLE SING(1942, Brit.), m; GRAND ESCAPADE, THE(1946, Brit.), m; NOTHING VENTURE(1948, Brit.), m, md
Kit Russell
PROJECT X(1949)
Kurt Russell
GUNS OF DIABLO(1964); FOLLOW ME, BOYS!(1966); GUNS IN THE HEATHER(1968, Brit.); HORSE IN THE GRAY FLANNEL SUIT, THE(1968); ONE AND ONLY GENUINE ORIGINAL FAMILY BAND, THE(1968); COMPUTER WORE TENNIS SHOES, THE(1970); BAREFOOT EXECUTIVE, THE(1971); FOOLS' PARADE(1971); NOW YOU SEE HIM, NOW YOU DON'T(1972); CHARLEY AND THE ANGEL(1973); SUPERDAD(1974); STRONGEST MAN IN THE WORLD, THE(1975); USED CARS(1980); ESCAPE FROM NEW YORK(1981); FOX AND THE HOUND, THE(1981); THING, THE(1982); SILKWOOD(1983)
1984
SWING SHIFT(1984)
L. Case Russell
Silents
TWO-EDGED SWORD, THE(1916), w
Leon Russell
WHEN YOU COMIN' BACK, RED RYDER?(1979)
Lewis Russell
AFFAIRS OF SUSAN(1945); SHE WOULDN'T SAY YES(1945); IF I'M LUCKY(1946); NIGHT IN CASABLANCA, A(1946); ONE WAY TO LOVE(1946); JEWELS OF BRANDENBURG(1947); LADIES' MAN(1947); TROUBLE WITH WOMEN, THE(1947); NAKED HILLS, THE(1956)

Lewis L. Russell
HOLD THAT BLONDE(1945); LOST WEEKEND, THE(1945); MOLLY AND ME(1945); YOU CAME ALONG(1945); CROSS MY HEART(1946); SHE WROTE THE BOOK(1946); I WONDER WHO'S KISSING HER NOW(1947); KISS THE BLOOD OFF MY HANDS(1948); MY DOG RUSTY(1948); PRINCE OF THIEVES, THE(1948); WHIPPED, THE(1950); WHEN THE REDSKINS RODE(1951); SANGAREE(1953)
Liam Russell
BUTCH AND SUNDANCE: THE EARLY DAYS(1979); CONTINENTAL DIVIDE(1981)
Lillian Russell
Misc. Silents
WILDFIRE(1915)
Lola Russell
CLAY(1964 Aus.); LONELY HEARTS(1983, Aus.)
Loretta Russell
DESPERATE CARGO(1941)
Lyman H. Russell
ROSE BOWL(1936)
Mabel Russell
TILLY OF BLOOMSBURY(1931, Brit.)
Mairhi Russell
WEDDING OF LILLI MARLENE, THE(1953, Brit.)
Malcolm Russell
TROUBLE IN THE AIR(1948, Brit.); SINISTER MAN, THE(1965, Brit.)
Marigold Russell
STRANGER FROM VENUS, THE(1954, Brit.); KID FOR TWO FARTHINGS, A(1956, Brit.); JUST MY LUCK(1957, Brit.); BLUE MURDER AT ST. TRINIAN'S(1958, Brit.); IDOL ON PARADE(1959, Brit.); IT TAKES A THIEF(1960, Brit.); DREAM MAKER, THE(1963, Brit.); OPERATION BULLSHINE(1963, Brit.); KILLER FORCE(1975, Switz./Ireland)
Marion Russell
TABLE FOR FIVE(1983)
Silents
LITTLE CHURCH AROUND THE CORNER(1923), w
Mary Russell
FLIRTATION WALK(1934); HAPPINESS AHEAD(1934); LOST LADY, A(1934); MAN WITH TWO FACES, THE(1934); PERSONALITY KID, THE(1934); ST. LOUIS KID, THE(1934); NIGHT AT THE RITZ, A(1935); SECRET BRIDE, THE(1935); BIG SHOW, THE(1937); MURDER IN GREENWICH VILLAGE(1937); RIDERS OF THE WHISTLING SKULL(1937); ROARIN' LEAD(1937); SILVER TRAIL, THE(1937); EXTORTION(1938); SQUADRON OF HONOR(1938)
Mavis Russell
LAS VEGAS STORY, THE(1952)
Millicent Russell
FOOL AND THE PRINCESS, THE(1948, Brit.)
Muriel Russell
HISTORY OF MR. POLLY, THE(1949, Brit.); MADNESS OF THE HEART(1949, Brit.)
Nancy Russell
NONE BUT THE LONELY HEART(1944)
Neil Russell
$1,000,000 DUCK(1971)
Nipsey Russell
WIZ, THE(1978)
1984
DREAM ONE(1984, Brit./Fr.)
Nita Russell
Silents
ON LEAVE(1918, Brit.)
Misc. Silents
FORDINGTON TWINS, THE(1920, Brit.)
P. Russell
WINDJAMMER, THE(1931, Brit.)
Pat Russell
REACHING OUT(1983), a, p,d&w, ed
Peggy Russell
ZAZA(1939)
Peter Russell
TELL-TALE HEART, THE(1962, Brit.), set d; CALL ME BWANA(1963, Brit.), set d; PLAY IT COOL(1963, Brit.), set d; JUDITH(1965), set d
Philip Russell
RED RUNS THE RIVER(1963)
R.H. Russell
VAGABOND KING, THE(1930), w; VAGABOND KING, THE(1956), w
Ray Russell
MR. SARDONICUS(1961), w; PREMATURE BURIAL, THE(1962), w; ZOTZ!(1962), w; "X"–THE MAN WITH THE X-RAY EYES(1963), w; HORROR OF IT ALL, THE(1964, Brit.), w; CHAMBER OF HORRORS(1966), w; THAT SUMMER(1979, Brit.), m; INCUBUS, THE(1982, Can.), w
Raymond Russell
Silents
PATCHWORK GIRL OF OZ, THE(1914)
Reb Russell
MAN FROM HELL, THE(1934); ARIZONA BADMAN(1935); CHEYENNE TORNADO(1935)
Misc. Talkies
FIGHTING THROUGH(1934); FIGHTING TO LIVE(1934); BLAZING GUNS(1935); BORDER VENGEANCE(1935); LIGHTNING TRIGGERS(1935); OUTLAW RULE(1935); RANGE WARFARE(1935)
Rip Russell
PRIDE OF THE YANKEES, THE(1942)
Robert Russell
MORE THE MERRIER, THE(1943), w; WELL-GROOMED BRIDE, THE(1946), w; LADY SAYS NO, THE(1951), w; SHADOW OF FEAR(1963, Brit.); OTHELLO(1965, Brit.); WALK, DON'T RUN(1966), w; BEDAZZLED(1967, Brit.); WHISPERERS, THE(1967, Brit.); CONQUEROR WORM, THE(1968, Brit.); INSPECTOR CLOUSEAU(1968, Brit.); CARRY ON LOVING(1970, Brit.); SUDDEN TERROR(1970, Brit.); MAN IN THE WILDERNESS(1971, U.S./Span.); SITTING TARGET(1972, Brit.)
Silents
TESS OF THE STORM COUNTRY(1922); INTO THE NIGHT(1928)

Ron Russell
DUNGEONS OF HARROW(1964), a, art d
Rosalind Russell
UNDER TWO FLAGS(1936); EVELYN PRENTICE(1934); PRESIDENT VANISHES, THE(1934); CASINO MURDER CASE, THE(1935); CHINA SEAS(1935); FORSAKING ALL OTHERS(1935); NIGHT IS YOUNG, THE(1935); RECKLESS(1935); RENDEZVOUS(1935); WEST POINT OF THE AIR(1935); CRAIG'S WIFE(1936); IT HAD TO HAPPEN(1936); TROUBLE FOR TWO(1936); LIVE, LOVE AND LEARN(1937); NIGHT MUST FALL(1937); CITADEL, THE(1938); FOUR'S A CROWD(1938); MAN-PROOF(1938); FAST AND LOOSE(1939); WOMEN, THE(1939); HIRED WIFE(1940); HIS GIRL FRIDAY(1940); NO TIME FOR COMEDY(1940); THIS THING CALLED LOVE(1940); DESIGN FOR SCANDAL(1941); FEMININE TOUCH, THE(1941); THEY MET IN BOMBAY(1941); MY SISTER EILEEN(1942); TAKE A LETTER, DARLING(1942); FLIGHT FOR FREEDOM(1943); WHAT A WOMAN!(1943); ROUGHLY SPEAKING(1945); SHE WOULDN'T SAY YES(1945); SISTER KENNY(1946); GUILT OF JANET AMES, THE(1947); MOURNING BECOMES ELECTRA(1947); VELVET TOUCH, THE(1948); TELL IT TO THE JUDGE(1949); WOMAN OF DISTINCTION, A(1950); NEVER WAVE AT A WAC(1952); GIRL RUSH, THE(1955); PICNIC(1955); UNGUARDED MOMENT, THE(1956), w; AUNTIE MAME(1958); MAJORITY OF ONE, A(1961); FIVE FINGER EXERCISE(1962); GYPSY(1962); TROUBLE WITH ANGELS, THE(1966); OH DAD, POOR DAD, MAMA'S HUNG YOU IN THE CLOSET AND I'M FEELIN' SO SAD(1967); ROSIE!(1967); WHERE ANGELS GO...TROUBLE FOLLOWS(1968); MRS. POLLIFAX-SPY(1971)
Roxie Russell
PAY BOX ADVENTURE(1936, Brit.); THIS GREEN HELL(1936, Brit.); SCHOOL FOR HUSBANDS(1939, Brit.)
Roxy Russell
DREAMS COME TRUE(1936, Brit.)
Roy Russell
YOUNG AND BEAUTIFUL(1934); REGAL CAVALCADE(1935, Brit.); FIRE OVER ENGLAND(1937, Brit.); IT'S NEVER TOO LATE TO MEND(1937, Brit.); MEMBER OF THE JURY(1937, Brit.); 13 MEN AND A GUN(1938, Brit.); STOLEN LIFE(1939, Brit.); DREAMING(1944, Brit.); TWILIGHT HOUR(1944, Brit.); THEY WERE SISTERS(1945, Brit.); CAESAR AND CLEOPATRA(1946, Brit.); WALTZ TIME(1946, Brit.); UNEASY TERMS(1948, Brit.); MAN ON THE RUN(1949, Brit.); TEMPTRESS, THE(1949, Brit.); NO HIGHWAY IN THE SKY(1951, Brit.); KNIGHTS OF THE ROUND TABLE(1953); TWILIGHT WOMEN(1953, Brit.); RICHARD III(1956, Brit.); HAUNTED STRANGLER, THE(1958, Brit.)
Sheila Mackay Russell
GENTLE TOUCH, THE(1956, Brit.), w
Sheridan Earl Russell
LORDS OF DISCIPLINE, THE(1983)
Shirley Russell
WOMEN IN LOVE(1969, Brit.), cos; BOY FRIEND, THE(1971, Brit.), cos; MUSIC LOVERS, THE(1971, Brit.), cos; SAVAGE MESSIAH(1972, Brit.), cos; LITTLE PRINCE, THE(1974, Brit.), cos; MAHLER(1974, Brit.), cos; LISZTOMANIA(1975, Brit.), cos; TOMMY(1975, Brit.), cos; VALENTINO(1977, Brit.), cos; CUBA(1979), cos; YANKS(1979), cos; LADY CHATTERLEY'S LOVER(1981, Fr./Brit.), cos; REDS(1981), cos; RETURN OF THE SOLDIER, THE(1983, Brit.), cos; WAGNER(1983, Brit./Hung./Aust.), cos
1984
GREYSTOKE: THE LEGEND OF TARZAN, LORD OF THE APES(1984), cos; RAZOR'S EDGE, THE(1984), cos
Stan Russell
WEDDINGS AND BABIES(1960), ed; STRANGERS IN THE CITY(1962), ed
Stanley Russell
TOGETHER AGAIN(1944), w
Suzanne Russell
CURTAINS(1983, Can.)
Sylvia Russell
WILL ANY GENTLEMAN?(1955, Brit.)
Tanya Russell
SKATEBOARD(1978); BRONCO BILLY(1980); UNDER FIRE(1983)
Theresa Russell
LAST TYCOON, THE(1976); STRAIGHT TIME(1978); EUREKA(1983, Brit.)
1984
RAZOR'S EDGE, THE(1984)
Tina Russell
Misc. Talkies
DARK DREAMS(1971)
Tommie Russell
UNDER AGE(1964); BLACK CAT, THE(1966)
Tony Russell
SECRET SEVEN, THE(1966, Ital./Span.); WILD, WILD PLANET, THE(1967, Ital.); HARD RIDE, THE(1971)
Misc. Talkies
HONEYMOONS WILL KILL YOU(1966)
Vi Russell
ATOMIC BRAIN, THE(1964), w
Victoria Russell
MUSIC LOVERS, THE(1971, Brit.); TOMMY(1975, Brit.)
Vy Russell
INDESTRUCTIBLE MAN, THE(1956), w
Wallace Russell
ONE MINUTE TO ZERO(1952)
Wally Russell
HOT BLOOD(1956)
Wendy Russell
MY FAIR LADY(1964); WHO'S THAT KNOCKING AT MY DOOR?(1968)
Wensley Russell
MELODY OF MY HEART(1936, Brit.); WELL DONE, HENRY(1936, Brit.); SONG OF THE FORGE(1937, Brit.)
William Russell
MIDNIGHT TAXI, THE(1928); STATE STREET SADIE(1928); MADONNA OF AVENUE A(1929); VIRGINIA(1941); JULIUS CAESAR(1952); ONE GOOD TURN(1955, Brit.); ABOVE US THE WAVES(1956, Brit.); MAN WHO NEVER WAS, THE(1956, Brit.); BIG CHANCE, THE(1957, Brit.); ADVENTURES OF HAL 5, THE(1958, Brit.); GREAT ESCAPE, THE(1963); RETURN TO SENDER(1963, Brit.); SHARE OUT, THE(1966, Brit.); SUPERMAN(1978); TERROR(1979, Brit.); DEATHWATCH(1980, Fr./Ger.); TIME TO DIE, A(1983), w

Silents
STRAIGHT ROAD, THE(1914); FRAME UP, THE(1917); IN BAD(1918); ALL THE WORLD TO NOTHING(1919); SACRED SILENCE(1919); THIS HERO STUFF(1919); CHEATER REFORMED, THE(1921); CHILDREN OF THE NIGHT(1921); DESERT BLOSSOMS(1921); SINGING RIVER(1921); GREAT NIGHT, THE(1922); MIXED FACES(1922); ALIAS THE NIGHT WIND(1923); ANNA CHRISTIE(1923); WHEN ODDS ARE EVEN(1923); BIG PAL(1925); ON THIN ICE(1925); WINGS OF THE STORM(1926); GIRL FROM CHICAGO, THE(1927); ESCAPE, THE(1928); HEAD OF THE FAMILY, THE(1928); WOMAN WISE(1928); GIRLS GONE WILD(1929)
Misc. Silents
MOTHS(1913); ROBIN HOOD(1913); DORA THORNE(1915); GARDEN OF LIES, THE(1915); BRUISER, THE(1916); CRAVING, THE(1916); HIGHEST BID, THE(1916), a, d; LONE STAR(1916); LOVE HERMIT, THE(1916); MAN WHO WOULD NOT DIE, THE(1916), a, d; SEQUEL TO THE DIAMOND FROM THE SKY(1916); SOUL MATES(1916), a, d; STRENGTH OF DONALD MCKENZIE, THE(1916), a, d; THOROUGHBRED, THE(1916); TORCH BEARER, THE(1916), a, d; TWINKLER, THE(1916); FATE AND THE CHILD(1917); GYPSY'S TRUST, THE(1917); HIGH PLAY(1917); MASKED HEART, THE(1917); MY FIGHTING GENTLEMAN(1917); NEW YORK LUCK(1917); PRIDE AND THE MAN(1917); SANDS OF SACRIFICE(1917); SEA MASTER, THE(1917); SHACKLES OF TRUTH(1917); SNAP JUDGEMENT(1917); HEARTS OR DIAMONDS?(1918); HOBBS IN A HURRY(1918); MIDNIGHT TRAIL, THE(1918); UP ROMANCE ROAD(1918); BRASS BUTTONS(1919); EASTWARD HO!(1919); SIX FEET FOUR(1919); SOME LIAR(1919); SPORTING CHANCE, A(1919); WHEN A MAN RIDES ALONE(1919); WHERE THE WEST BEGINS(1919); CHALLENGE OF THE LAW, THE(1920); IRON RIDER, THE(1920); LEAVE IT TO ME(1920); LINCOLN HIGHWAYMAN, THE(1920); LIVE WIRE HICK, A(1920); MAN WHO DARED, THE(1920); SHOD WITH FIRE(1920); TWINS OF SUFFERING CREEK(1920); VALLEY OF TOMORROW, THE(1920); BARE KNUCKLES(1920); COLORADO PLUCK(1921); HIGH GEAR JEFFREY(1921); LADY FROM LONGACRE, THE(1921); QUICK ACTION(1921); ROOF TREE(1921); MEN OF ZANSIBAR, THE(1922); MONEY TO BURN(1922); SELF-MADE MAN, A(1922); STRENGTH OF THE PINES(1922); BOSTON BLACKIE(1923); GOOD-BY GIRLS!(1923); MAN'S SIZE(1923); TIMES HAVE CHANGED(1923); BELOVED BRUTE, THE(1924); BEFORE MIDNIGHT(1925); WAY OF A GIRL, THE(1925); BLUE EAGLE, THE(1926); STILL ALARM, THE(1926); BRASS KNUCKLES(1927); DESIRED WOMAN, THE(1927); ROUGH SHOD FIGHTER, A(1927); DANGER PATROL(1928)
William D. Russell
OUR HEARTS WERE GROWING UP(1946), d; DEAR RUTH(1947), d; LADIES' MAN(1947), d; SAINTED SISTERS, THE(1948), d; BRIDE FOR SALE(1949), d; GREEN PROMISE, THE(1949), d; BEST OF THE BADMEN(1951), d
Willy Russell
EDUCATING RITA(1983), w
Xavier Russell
MUSIC LOVERS, THE(1971, Brit.)
Zella Russell
AVENGING WATERS(1936); TAMING THE WILD(1937)
Russell Patterson's Personettos
ARTISTS AND MODELS(1937)
Mara Russell-Tavernan
TRIAL OF MADAM X, THE(1948, Brit.); DEVIL'S JEST, THE(1954, Brit.)
Luigi Russelli
JOHNNY BANCO(1969, Fr./Ital./Ger.), m
Donia Russey
AFFAIRS OF GERALDINE(1946)
Penelope Russianoff
UNMARRIED WOMAN, AN(1978)
Babe Russin
GLENN MILLER STORY, THE(1953)
N. Russinova
BALLAD OF COSSACK GLOOTA(1938, USSR)
Aaron Russo
ROSE, THE(1979), p; PARTNERS(1982), p; TRADING PLACES(1983), p
1984
TEACHERS(1984), p, w
Alfonso Russo
FURY OF THE PAGANS(1963, Ital.), art d
Barry Russo
SPLIT, THE(1968); MAN, THE(1972)
Carlo Russo
EMBALMER, THE(1966, Ital.)
Carole Russo
LOVE CHILD(1982)
Christopher Russo
1984
FIRSTBORN(1984); WINDY CITY(1984)
Claudia Russo
SOLOMON KING(1974)
Daniel Russo
JUDGE AND THE ASSASSIN, THE(1979, Fr.)
Emanuel Russo
THUNDER BAY(1953)
Gianni Russo
GODFATHER, THE(1972); GODFATHER, THE, PART II(1974); LEPKE(1975, U.S./Israel); FOUR DEUCES, THE(1976); LASERBLAST(1978); WINTER KILLS(1979)
Gus Russo
BASKET CASE(1982), m
Irwin Russo
SATURDAY THE 14TH(1981)
1984
TEACHERS(1984), w
J. Duke Russo
DON IS DEAD, THE(1973)
Jackie Russo
OPERATION EICHMANN(1961)
James Russo
FAST TIMES AT RIDGEMONT HIGH(1982); STRANGER IS WATCHING, A(1982); VORTEX(1982); EXPOSED(1983)
1984
BEVERLY HILLS COP(1984); COTTON CLUB, THE(1984); ONCE UPON A TIME IN AMERICA(1984)

Jodean Russo
AIRPORT(1970); JOHNNY GOT HIS GUN(1971); HARRAD SUMMER, THE(1974)

Joe Russo
BEST FRIENDS(1982), art d

Joey Russo
HARUM SCARUM(1965)

John A. Russo
NIGHT OF THE LIVING DEAD(1968), w; THERE'S ALWAYS VANILLA(1972), p; MIDNIGHT(1983), d&w

John Duke Russo
HUSTLE(1975)

Josan F Russo
CARNY(1980), art d

Josan Russo
CUTTER AND BONE(1981), art d
1984
ICEMAN(1984), art d

Margherita Russo
LA DOLCE VITA(1961, Ital./Fr.)

Mariella Russo
SILHOUETTES(1982)

Mario Russo
NAKED MAJA, THE(1959, Ital./U.S.), d

Matt Russo
MAN CALLED ADAM, A(1966); SEVEN UPS, THE(1973); SUPERMAN(1978); KING OF COMEDY, THE(1983)

N.W. Russo
PIPPI ON THE RUN(1977), p

Neno Russo
FOUL PLAY(1978)

Pepe Russo
Misc. Talkies
YOUNG AND WILD(1975)

Salvatore Russo
KILLER FISH(1979, Ital./Braz.), cos

Tony Russo
LAST TRAIN FROM GUN HILL(1959); SIGN OF ZORRO, THE(1960)

Vincent Russo
NUNZIO(1978)

Russo and The Samba Kings
SONG IS BORN, A(1948)

Carolyn Russoff
MONSIGNOR(1982)

Lou Russoff
DAY THE WORLD ENDED, THE(1956), w

Leon Russom
DIRTY HARRY(1971); TRIAL OF THE CATONSVILLE NINE, THE(1972)

Alice Russon
Silents
DEMOCRACY(1918, Brit.); AFTER MANY DAYS(1919, Brit.); ALL MEN ARE LIARS(1919, Brit.)

Clive Rust
OTHELLO(1965, Brit.)

Henri Rust
THREEPENNY OPERA, THE(1931, Ger./U.S.), ed; MAYERLING(1937, Fr.), ed; TOVARICH(1937), ed; WOMAN I LOVE, THE(1937), ed; CHILDREN OF PARADISE(1945, Fr.), ed; GERVAISE(1956, Fr.), ed; GERMINAL(1963, Fr.), ed; JOHNNY BANCO(1969, Fr./Ital./Ger.), ed

Henry Rust
TEMPEST(1958, Ital./Yugo./Fr.), ed

John Rust
1984
SMURFS AND THE MAGIC FLUTE, THE(1984, Fr./Belg.), d, w

Patricia Rust
TERROR EYES(1981)

Richard Rust
LEGEND OF TOM DOOLEY, THE(1959); COMANCHE STATION(1960); THIS REBEL BREED(1960); HOMICIDAL(1961); UNDERWORLD U.S.A.(1961); TARAS BULBA(1962); WALK ON THE WILD SIDE(1962); ALVAREZ KELLY(1966); NAKED ANGELS(1969); STUDENT NURSES, THE(1970); LAST MOVIE, THE(1971); I ESCAPED FROM DEVIL'S ISLAND(1973); KID BLUE(1973); GREAT GUNDOWN, THE(1977)

Mardi Rustam
TOM(1973), p; PSYCHIC KILLER(1975), p; EATEN ALIVE(1976), p, w
Misc. Talkies
EVILS OF THE NIGHT(1983), d

Torstein Rustdal
ONE DAY IN THE LIFE OF IVAN DENISOVICH(1971, U.S./Brit./Norway)

Ruben Rustia
TASTE OF HELL, A(1973)

Carlo Rusticheli
BEHIND CLOSED SHUTTERS(1952, Ital.), m

Carlo Rustichelli
WHITE LINE, THE(1952, Ital.), m; COUNTERFEITERS, THE(1953, Ital.), m; BLACK 13(1954, Brit.), m; DAY THE SKY EXPLODED, THE(1958, Fr./Ital.), m; HANNIBAL(1960, Ital.), m; ACCATTONE!(1961, Ital.), m; MINOTAUR, THE(1961, Ital.), m; QUEEN OF THE PIRATES(1961, Ital./Ger.), m; THIEF OF BAGHDAD, THE(1961, Ital./Fr.), m; AGOSTINO(1962, Ital.), m; DIVORCE, ITALIAN STYLE(1962, Ital.), m; MAMMA ROMA(1962, Ital.), m; PSYCOSISSIMO(1962, Ital.), m; ROMMEL'S TREASURE(1962, Ital.), m; SWORD OF THE CONQUEROR(1962, Ital.), m; SWORDSMAN OF SIENA, THE(1962, Fr./Ital.), md; FOUR DAYS OF NAPLES, THE(1963, US/Ital.), m; MY SON, THE HERO(1963, Ital./Fr.), m; RAGE OF THE BUCCANEERS(1963, Ital.), m; SECRET MARK OF D'ARTAGNAN, THE(1963, Fr./Ital.), m; BEBO'S GIRL(1964, Ital.), m; KAPO(1964, Ital./Fr./Yugo.), m; ORGANIZER, THE(1964, Fr./Ital./Yugo.), m; QUEEN OF THE NILE(1964, Ital.), m; SEDUCED AND ABANDONED(1964, Fr./Ital.), m; TIGER OF THE SEVEN SEAS(1964, Fr./Ital.), m; BLOOD AND BLACK LACE(1965, Ital.), m; CAVERN, THE(1965, Ital./Ger.), m; CONQUEST OF MYCENE(1965, Ital., Fr.), m; EYE OF THE NEEDLE, THE(1965, Ital./Fr.), m; FACTS OF MURDER, THE(1965, Ital.), m; RAILROAD MAN, THE(1965, Ital.), m; KILL BABY KILL(1966, Ital.), m; MYSTERY OF THUG ISLAND, THE(1966, Ital./Ger.), m; BIRDS,

THE BEES AND THE ITALIANS, THE(1967), m; CLIMAX, THE(1967, Fr., Ital.), m; HEAD OF THE FAMILY(1967, Ital./Fr.), m; JOURNEY BENEATH THE DESERT(1967, Fr./Ital.), m; KILL OR BE KILLED(1967, Ital.), m; LION OF ST. MARK(1967, Ital.), m; MADE IN ITALY(1967, Fr./Ital.), m; MINUTE TO PRAY, A SECOND TO DIE, A(1968, Ital.), m; SECRET WAR OF HARRY FRIGG, THE(1968), m; ACE HIGH(1969, Ital.), m; BETTER A WIDOW(1969, Ital.), m; RUTHLESS FOUR, THE(1969, Ital./Ger.), m; SONS OF SATAN(1969, Ital./Fr./Ger.), m; THREE NIGHTS OF LOVE(1969, Ital.), m; CERTAIN, VERY CERTAIN, AS A MATTER OF FACT... PROBABLE(1970, Ital.), m; SERAFINO(1970, Fr./Ital.), m; AVANTI!(1972), m; CALL OF THE WILD(1972, Ger./ Span./Ital./Fr.), m; ALFREDO, ALFREDO(1973, Ital.), m; CLARETTA AND BEN(1983, Ital., Fr.), ed

M. Rustichelli
GRAN VARIETA(1955, Ital.), m

Julie Ruston
Silents
SHEER BLUFF(1921)

Lilian Ruston
Silents
SHEER BLUFF(1921)

Roland Ruston
Silents
BUNTY PULLS THE STRINGS(1921)

Rusty the Horse
ACROSS THE PLAINS(1939); OKLAHOMA TERROR(1939); OVERLAND MAIL(1939); WILD HORSE CANYON(1939); RIDING THE SUNSET TRAIL(1941); WANDERERS OF THE WEST(1941)

Rusty the Wonder Horse
GUN PACKER(1938); DRIFTING WESTWARD(1939); DYNAMITE CANYON(1941)

Ken Ruta
MOUNTAIN MEN, THE(1980)

I. Rutberg
WELCOME KOSTYA!(1965, USSR)

Elana Beth Rutenberg
1984
UNFAITHFULLY YOURS(1984)

Mark Rutenberg
1984
MOSCOW ON THE HUDSON(1984)

Nancy Hall Rutgers
HURRICANE(1979)

Nicholas Rutgers
RUNNING TARGET(1956)

Nick Rutgers
HURRICANE(1979)

Baby Mary Ruth
THERE'S MAGIC IN MUSIC(1941)

George Herman "Babe" Ruth
PRIDE OF THE YANKEES, THE(1942)
Silents
BABE COMES HOME(1927); SPEEDY(1928)
Misc. Silents
HEADIN' HOME(1920)

Jean Ruth
O.S.S.(1946); SUDDENLY IT'S SPRING(1947); AT WAR WITH THE ARMY(1950); FANCY PANTS(1950); NO MAN OF HER OWN(1950); UNION STATION(1950); MATING SEASON, THE(1951)

Jochen Ruth
DEVIL IN SILK(1968, Ger.), w

Kitty Ruth
RACQUET(1979)

Marshall Ruth
BROADWAY MELODY, THE(1929); NIX ON DAMES(1929); WALL STREET(1929); LEMON DROP KID, THE(1934); FALSE PRETENSES(1935); HOLD'EM YALE(1935); RIFF-RAFF(1936); WEDDING PRESENT(1936); I AM THE LAW(1938); NEW YORK TOWN(1941); PLAYMATES(1941); MORE THE MERRIER, THE(1943); COLONEL EFFINGHAM'S RAID(1945); NOB HILL(1945); NIGHT AND DAY(1946); DESPERATE(1947); STATE OF THE UNION(1948)
Silents
RED WINE(1928); JOY STREET(1929)
Misc. Silents
VIRGIN LIPS(1928)

Mary Ruth
SONG OF THE BUCKAROO(1939); THEY SHALL HAVE MUSIC(1939); NOBODY'S CHILDREN(1940); GENTLEMAN FROM DIXIE(1941); POT O' GOLD(1941); RIOT SQUAD(1941)

Nena Ruth
TOMORROW IS FOREVER(1946)

Phyllis Ruth
ALWAYS A BRIDE(1940); IT'S A DATE(1940); CAUGHT IN THE DRAFT(1941); LOUISIANA PURCHASE(1941); FLEET'S IN, THE(1942); LET'S FACE IT(1943); THEY GOT ME COVERED(1943)
Misc. Talkies
WILD HORSE RANGE(1940)

Richard Ruth
TWO-LANE BLACKTOP(1971)

Robert Ruth
SWASHBUCKLER(1976)

Roy Del Ruth
SIDE SHOW(1931), d; CHOCOLATE SOLDIER, THE(1941), d; DU BARRY WAS A LADY(1943), d; STARLIFT(1951), d; ABOUT FACE(1952), d; STOP, YOU'RE KILLING ME(1952), d

Wally Ruth
MY WILD IRISH ROSE(1947)

Ann Rutherford
MELODY TRAIL(1935); SINGING VAGABOND, THE(1935); WATERFRONT LADY(1935); COMIN' ROUND THE MOUNTAIN(1936); DOUGHNUTS AND SOCIETY(1936); DOWN TO THE SEA(1936); HARVESTER, THE(1936); LAWLESS NINETIES, THE(1936); LONELY TRAIL, THE(1936); OREGON TRAIL, THE(1936); BRIDE WORE RED, THE(1937); DEVIL IS DRIVING, THE(1937); LIVE, LOVE AND LEARN(1937); PUBLIC COWBOY NO. 1(1937); CHRISTMAS CAROL, A(1938); DRA-

MATIC SCHOOL(1938); JUDGE HARDY'S CHILDREN(1938); LOVE FINDS ANDY HARDY(1938); OF HUMAN HEARTS(1938); OUT WEST WITH THE HARDYS(1938); YOU'RE ONLY YOUNG ONCE(1938); ANDY HARDY GETS SPRING FEVER(1939); DANCING CO-ED(1939); FOUR GIRLS IN WHITE(1939); GONE WITH THE WIND(1939); HARDYS RIDE HIGH, THE(1939); JUDGE HARDY AND SON(1939); THESE GLAMOUR GIRLS(1939); ANDY HARDY MEETS DEBUTANTE(1940); GHOST COMES HOME, THE(1940); PRIDE AND PREJUDICE(1940); WYOMING(1940); ANDY HARDY'S PRIVATE SECRETARY(1941); BADLANDS OF DAKOTA(1941); KEEPING COMPANY(1941); LIFE BEGINS FOR ANDY HARDY(1941); WASHINGTON MELODRAMA(1941); WHISTLING IN THE DARK(1941); ANDY HARDY'S DOUBLE LIFE(1942); COURTSHIP OF ANDY HARDY, THE(1942); ORCHESTRA WIVES(1942); THIS TIME FOR KEEPS(1942); WHISTLING IN DIXIE(1942); HAPPY LAND(1943); WHISTLING IN BROOKLYN(1943); BERMUDA MYSTERY(1944); BEDSIDE MANNER(1945); TWO O'CLOCK COURAGE(1945); INSIDE JOB(1946); MADONNA'S SECRET, THE(1946); MURDER IN THE MUSIC HALL(1946); SECRET LIFE OF WALTER MITTY, THE(1947); ADVENTURES OF DON JUAN(1949); OPERATION HAYLIFT(1950); THEY ONLY KILL THEIR MASTERS(1972); SLIPPER AND THE ROSE, THE(1976, Brit.); WON TON TON, THE DOG WHO SAVED HOLLYWOOD(1976)

Billie Rutherford
PICCADILLY NIGHTS(1930, Brit.)

Cedric Rutherford
WILD WOMEN OF WONGO, THE(1959), w

Charles Rutherford
LUXURY GIRLS(1953, Ital.); CHEAPER TO KEEP HER(1980), set d

Chuck Rutherford
O'HARA'S WIFE(1983), set d

Douglas Rutherford
HOUSE ON 92ND STREET, THE(1945); JACKTOWN(1962); GROUP, THE(1966); HAIL(1973)

Gene Rutherford
HURRY SUNDOWN(1967); WILL PENNY(1968); LOVE AND MONEY(1982)

Holly Rutherford
ZAPPED!(1982)

Jack Rutherford
MR. LEMON OF ORANGE(1931); COWBOY COUNSELOR(1933); ROMAN SCANDALS(1933); JUSTICE OF THE RANGE(1935); OREGON TRAIL, THE(1936); ROOTIN' TOOTIN' RHYTHM(1937); GOLD IS WHERE YOU FIND IT(1938); RIDERS OF THE FRONTIER(1939); ARIZONA GANGBUSTERS(1940); RIDERS OF BLACK MOUNTAIN(1941); ROLLIN' HOME TO TEXAS(1941); CORREGIDOR(1943); FRONTIER GAL(1945); ROAD TO UTOPIA(1945); UTAH(1945); KISS OF DEATH(1947); UNTAMED FURY(1947)
Silents
THIS MARRIAGE BUSINESS(1927, Brit.)
Misc. Silents
STREETS OF LONDON, THE(1929, Brit.)

John Rutherford
HALF SHOT AT SUNRISE(1930); WHOOPEE(1930); WOMAN FROM MONTE CARLO, THE(1932); AFFAIRS OF CELLINI, THE(1934); CLEOPATRA(1934); CRUSADES, THE(1935); MAN WHO RECLAIMED HIS HEAD, THE(1935); THREE ON THE TRAIL(1936); HEART OF THE WEST(1937); HOPALONG RIDES AGAIN(1937); NORTH OF THE RIO GRANDE(1937); RAW TIMBER(1937)
Silents
GREAT SHADOW, THE(1920)

Lori Rutherford
FREAKY FRIDAY(1976)

Margaret Rutherford
BEAUTY AND THE BARGE(1937, Brit.); CATCH AS CATCH CAN(1937, Brit.); MISSING, BELIEVED MARRIED(1937, Brit.); TALK OF THE DEVIL(1937, Brit.); HIDEOUT IN THE ALPS(1938, Brit.); QUIET WEDDING(1941, Brit.); SPRING MEETING(1941, Brit.); YELLOW CANARY, THE(1944, Brit.); ADVENTURE FOR TWO(1945, Brit.); BLITHE SPIRIT(1945, Brit.); MEET ME AT DAWN(1947, Brit.); HER MAN GILBEY(1949, Brit.); MIRANDA(1949, Brit.); PASSPORT TO PIMLICO(1949, Brit.); HAPPIEST DAYS OF YOUR LIFE(1950, Brit.); TAMING OF DOROTHY, THE(1950, Brit.); WHILE THE SUN SHINES(1950, Brit.); CASTLE IN THE AIR(1952, Brit.); CURTAIN UP(1952, Brit.); IMPORTANCE OF BEING EARNEST, THE(1952, Brit.); MAGIC BOX, THE(1952, Brit.); MISS ROBIN HOOD(1952, Brit.); AUNT CLARA(1954, Brit.); MAD ABOUT MEN(1954, Brit.); RUNAWAY BUS(1954, Brit.); INNOCENTS IN PARIS(1955, Brit.); TROUBLE IN STORE(1955, Brit.); ALLIGATOR NAMED DAISY, AN(1957, Brit.); JUST MY LUCK(1957, Brit.); SMALLEST SHOW ON EARTH, THE(1957, Brit.); I'M ALL RIGHT, JACK(1959, Brit.); MURDER SHE SAID(1961, Brit.); ON THE DOUBLE(1961); MOUSE ON THE MOON, THE(1963, Brit.); MURDER AT THE GALLOP(1963, Brit.); V.I.P.s, THE(1963, Brit.); MURDER AHOY(1964, Brit.); MURDER MOST FOUL(1964, Brit.); ALPHABET MURDERS, THE(1966); CHIMES AT MIDNIGHT(1967, Span.,Switz.); COUNTESS FROM HONG KONG, A(1967, Brit.); WACKY WORLD OF MOTHER GOOSE, THE(1967); ARABELLA(1969, U.S./Ital.)

Michael Rutherford
SHOUT, THE(1978, Brit.), m

Montagu Rutherford
Silents
HAMLET(1913, Brit.)

Tom Rutherford
FIREFLY, THE(1937); ROSALIE(1937); DESPERATE ADVENTURE, A(1938); MARIE ANTOINETTE(1938); TEST PILOT(1938); VACATION FROM LOVE(1938); THOSE WERE THE DAYS(1940); VIRGINIA(1941)

Harry Rutherford-Jones
1984
TREASURE OF THE YANKEE ZEPHYR(1984)

Tom Rutherfurd
BEG, BORROW OR STEAL(1937); TOY WIFE, THE(1938)

Madeleine Ruthven
DANGEROUS CORNER(1935), w; ACCUSING FINGER, THE(1936), w; AND SUDDEN DEATH(1936), w; STRAIGHT FROM THE SHOULDER(1936), w
Silents
MORGAN'S LAST RAID(1929), w

Madeline Ruthven
SHOCK(1934), w

Silents
RENDEZVOUS, THE(1923), w

Ormond Ruthven
DR. KILDARE'S WEDDING DAY(1941), w

Dina Rutic
ROMANCE OF A HORSE THIEF(1971)

Jan Rutkiewicz
GUESTS ARE COMING(1965, Pol.), p&d

Jerry Rutkin
WAY OUT(1966)

Barbara Rutland
Silents
QUEEN MOTHER, THE(1916, Brit.)
Misc. Silents
LADY JENNIFER(1915, Brit.)

George Rutland
SECRETS OF A WINDMILL GIRL(1966, Brit.)

John Rutland
CALCULATED RISK(1963, Brit.); TAKE ME OVER(1963, Brit.); LITTLE OF WHAT YOU FANCY, A(1968, Brit.); CHARRIOTS OF FIRE(1981, Brit.); MEMOIRS OF A SURVIVOR(1981, Brit.); REMEMBRANCE(1982, Brit.)

Clark Rutledge
MANY HAPPY RETURNS(1934)

Don Rutledge
SUMMERDOG(1977)

P. Rutledge
UNCIVILISED(1937, Aus.)

Robin Rutledge
LAST AFFAIR, THE(1976), ph

Rusty Rutledge
48 HOURS TO LIVE(1960, Brit./Swed.)

Edwin Rutt
OH JOHNNY, HOW YOU CAN LOVE!(1940), w

Gordan Ruttan
FINDERS KEEPERS(1966, Brit.)

Gordon Ruttan
DIAMONDS ARE FOREVER(1971, Brit.)

Susan Ruttan
INDEPENDENCE DAY(1983)
1984
BAD MANNERS(1984)

Joseph Ruttenberg
UNTIL THEY SAIL(1957), ph; STRUGGLE, THE(1931), ph; WOMAN IN THE DARK(1934), ph; GIGOLETTE(1935), ph; PEOPLE'S ENEMY, THE(1935), ph; FRANKIE AND JOHNNY(1936), ph; FURY(1936), ph; MAD HOLIDAY(1936), ph; MAN HUNT(1936), ph; PICCADILLY JIM(1936), ph; THREE GODFATHERS(1936), ph; BIG CITY(1937), ph; DAY AT THE RACES, A(1937), ph; EVERYBODY SING(1938), ph; FIRST 100 YEARS, THE(1938), ph; GREAT WALTZ, THE(1938), ph; SHOPWORN ANGEL(1938), ph; SPRING MADNESS(1938), ph; THREE COMRADES(1938), ph; BALALAIKA(1939), ph; ICE FOLLIES OF 1939(1939), ph; ON BORROWED TIME(1939), ph; TELL NO TALES(1939), ph; WOMEN, THE(1939), ph; BROADWAY MELODY OF 1940(1940), ph; COMRADE X(1940), ph; PHILADELPHIA STORY, THE(1940), ph; WATERLOO BRIDGE(1940), ph; TWO-FACED WOMAN(1941), ph; CROSSROADS(1942), ph; MRS. MINIVER(1942), ph; RANDOM HARVEST(1942), ph; WOMAN OF THE YEAR(1942), ph; MADAME CURIE(1943), ph; PRESENTING LILY MARS(1943), ph; GASLIGHT(1944), ph; MRS. PARKINGTON(1944), ph; ADVENTURE(1945), ph; VALLEY OF DECISION, THE(1945), ph; DESIRE ME(1947), ph; KILLER McCOY(1947), ph; B. F.'S DAUGHTER(1948), ph; JULIA MISBEHAVES(1948), ph; BRIBE, THE(1949), ph; THAT FORSYTE WOMAN(1949), ph; MAGNIFICENT YANKEE, THE(1950), ph; MINIVER STORY, THE(1950, Brit./U.S.), ph; SIDE STREET(1950), ph; CAUSE FOR ALARM(1951), ph; GREAT CARUSO, THE(1951), ph; IT'S A BIG COUNTRY(1951), ph; KIND LADY(1951), ph; TOO YOUNG TO KISS(1951), ph; BECAUSE YOU'RE MINE(1952), ph; PRISONER OF ZENDA, THE(1952), ph; YOUNG MAN WITH IDEAS(1952), ph; GREAT DIAMOND ROBBERY(1953), ph; JULIUS CAESAR(1953), ph; LATIN LOVERS(1953), ph; SMALL TOWN GIRL(1953), ph; BRIGADOON(1954), ph; HER TWELVE MEN(1954), ph; LAST TIME I SAW PARIS, THE(1954), ph; INTERRUPTED MELODY(1955), ph; KISMET(1955), ph; PRODIGAL, THE(1955), ph; INVITATION TO THE DANCE(1956), ph; SOMEBODY UP THERE LIKES ME(1956), ph; SWAN, THE(1956), ph; MAN ON FIRE(1957), ph; VINTAGE, THE(1957), ph; GIGI(1958), ph; RELUCTANT DEBUTANTE, THE(1958), ph; GREEN MANSIONS(1959), ph; WRECK OF THE MARY DEAR, THE(1959), ph; BUTTERFIELD 8(1960), ph; SUBTERRANEANS, THE(1960), ph; ADA(1961), ph; BACHELOR IN PARADISE(1961), ph; TWO LOVES(1961), ph; HOOK, THE(1963), ph; WHO'S GOT THE ACTION?(1962), ph; IT HAPPENED AT THE WORLD'S FAIR(1963), ph; WHO'S BEEN SLEEPING IN MY BED?(1963), ph; GLOBAL AFFAIR, A(1964), ph; HARLOW(1965), ph; LOVE HAS MANY FACES(1965), ph; SYLVIA(1965), ph; OSCAR, THE(1966), ph; SPEEDWAY(1968), ph
Silents
DOING THEIR BIT(1918), ph; PEG OF THE PIRATES(1918), ph; BEYOND PRICE(1921), ph; KNOW YOUR MEN(1921), ph; SILVER WINGS(1922), ph; SUMMER BACHELORS(1926), ph

Frank Ruttencutter
CYCLE SAVAGES(1969), ph; HELL'S BLOODY DEVILS(1970), ph

Barrie Rutter
DOING TIME(1979, Brit.)

Ben Rutter
ANGEL LEVINE, THE(1970), set d; PURSUIT OF HAPPINESS, THE(1971), set d

John Rutter
SHOOT(1976, Can.); THREE CARD MONTE(1978, Can.)

Louise Rutter
Misc. Silents
MILESTONES OF LIFE(1915)

Maureen Rutter
NO BLADE OF GRASS(1970, Brit.)

Owen Rutter
ONCE IN A NEW MOON(1935, Brit.), w

Barbara Rutting
LAST BRIDGE, THE(1957, Aust.); TIME TO LOVE AND A TIME TO DIE, A(1958); TOWN WITHOUT PITY(1961, Ger./Switz./U.S.); SHADOWS GROW LONGER, THE(1962, Switz./Ger.); PHANTOM OF SOHO, THE(1967, Ger.)

Misc. Talkies
RIVER OF EVIL(1964)
Walther Ruttman
Silents
SIEGFRIED(1924, Ger.), anim
Maria Rutz
Misc. Silents
GREEN SPIDER, THE(1916, USSR)
Michael Ruud
HANGAR 18(1980); EARTHBOUND(1981)
Sif Ruud
MAGICIAN, THE(1959, Swed.); WILD STRAWBERRIES(1959, Swed.); MAKE WAY FOR LILA(1962, Swed./Ger.); PORT OF CALL(1963, Swed.)
Siv Ruud
FACE TO FACE(1976, Swed.)
Yuliis Ruval
HOMETOWN U.S.A.(1979)
Yulis Ruval
1984
BEST DEFENSE(1984)
Wolf Ruvinskis
LOS AUTOMATAS DE LA MUERTE(1960, Mex.); NEUTRON CONTRA EL DR. CARONTE(1962, Mex.); NEUTRON EL ENMASCARADO NEGRO(1962, Mex.); SANTO CONTRA LA INVASION DE LOS MARCIANOS(1966, Mex.); CHIQUTTO PERO PICOSO(1967, Mex.)
Adam Arkin Ruvinsky
IMPROPER CHANNELS(1981, Can.), w
Morrie Ruvinsky
IMPROPER CHANNELS(1981, Can.), p, w
Salvatore Ruvo
MORE THAN A MIRACLE(1967, Ital./Fr.)
Richard Ruxton
NIGHTBEAST(1982)
Jay Dee Ruybal
1984
RED DAWN(1984)
Ayn Ruymen
PRIVATE PARTS(1972)
Basil Ruysdael
COCOANUTS, THE(1929); COLORADO TERRITORY(1949); COME TO THE STABLE(1949); DOCTOR AND THE GIRL, THE(1949); PINKY(1949); TASK FORCE(1949); BROKEN ARROW(1950); FILE ON THELMA JORDAN, THE(1950); GAMBLING HOUSE(1950); HIGH LONESOME(1950); ONE WAY STREET(1950); HALF ANGEL(1951); MY FORBIDDEN PAST(1951); PEOPLE WILL TALK(1951); RATON PASS(1951); SCARF, THE(1951); BOOTS MALONE(1952); CARRIE(1952); PRINCE VALIANT(1954); SHANGHAI STORY, THE(1954); BLACKBOARD JUNGLE, THE(1955); DAVY CROCKETT, KING OF THE WILD FRONTIER(1955); DIANE(1955); PEARL OF THE SOUTH PACIFIC(1955); VIOLENT MEN, THE(1955); JUBAL(1956); THESE WILDER YEARS(1956); LAST HURRAH, THE(1958); HORSE SOLDIERS, THE(1959); STORY OF RUTH, THE(1960)
Martin Ruzck
ADELE HASN'T HAD HER SUPPER YET(1978, Czech.)
Martin Ruzek
END OF A PRIEST(1970, Czech.)
Gernand Ruzena
NATHALIE(1958, Fr.)
N. Ruzhov
1812(1944, USSR)
Helena Ruzickova
FIFTH HORSEMAN IS FEAR, THE(1968, Czech.); HAPPY END(1968, Czech.); END OF A PRIEST(1970, Czech.); MOST BEAUTIFUL AGE, THE(1970, Czech.)
Giuseppe Ruzzolini
VIOLENT FOUR, THE(1968, Ital.), ph; TEOREMA(1969, Ital.), ph; DUCK, YOU SUCKER!(1972, Ital.), ph; SCIENTIFIC CARDPLAYER, THE(1972, Ital.), ph; CHE?(1973, Ital./Fr./Ger.), ph; MY NAME IS NOBODY(1974, Ital./Fr./Ger.), ph; GENIUS, THE(1976, Ital./Fr./Ger.), ph; ARABIAN NIGHTS(1980, Ital./Fr.), ph; TREASURE OF THE FOUR CROWNS(1983, Span./U.S.), ph
Giuseppi Ruzzolini
TWELVE PLUS ONE(1970, Fr./Ital.), ph
Guiseppe Ruzzolini
1984
FIRESTARTER(1984), ph
Giuseppe Ruzzolino
SUBVERSIVES, THE(1967, Ital.), ph
I. Ryabinin
SUN SHINES FOR ALL, THE(1961, USSR)
Danny Ryais
FACE IN THE RAIN, A(1963)
Dick Ryal
BUS IS COMING, THE(1971)
Richard Ryal
PLAY IT AS IT LAYS(1972)
David Ryall
DANCE OF DEATH, THE(1971, Brit.); ELEPHANT MAN, THE(1980, Brit.)
A. James Ryan
SWEET SUZY(1973), w
Abigail Ryan
MIKADO, THE(1967, Brit.)
Ann Ryan
KINFOLK(1970)
Barry Ryan
1984
WHERE THE BOYS ARE '84(1984)
Ben Ryan
MY WEAKNESS(1933), w; SAILOR'S LUCK(1933), w; MILLION DOLLAR RANSOM(1934), w; PALOOKA(1934), w; CHINATOWN SQUAD(1935), w; I'D GIVE MY LIFE(1936), w; LAUGHING IRISH EYES(1936), w; SHE'S DANGEROUS(1937), w

Bob Ryan
MR. MOTO'S GAMBLE(1938); GOLDEN BOY(1939); RINGS ON HER FINGERS(1942); WALLS CAME TUMBLING DOWN, THE(1946); DOWN TO EARTH(1947)
Charleen Ryan
SWEET CHARITY(1969)
Charlene Ryan
LAST MARRIED COUPLE IN AMERICA, THE(1980)
Chet Ryan
Silents
KINGFISHER'S ROOST, THE(1922); KING'S CREEK LAW(1923); BORDER WOMEN(1924)
Misc. Silents
ACROSS THE BORDER(1922); ROUNDING UP THE LAW(1922); PAYABLE ON DEMAND(1924)
Christopher Ryan
1984
POLICE ACADEMY(1984), cos
Cornelius Ryan
LONGEST DAY, THE(1962), w; BRIDGE TOO FAR, A(1977, Brit.), w
Dick Ryan
MR. WISE GUY(1942); SMART ALECKS(1942); BRINGING UP FATHER(1946); CALL NORTHSIDE 777(1948); CHICKEN EVERY SUNDAY(1948); JIGGS AND MAGGIE IN SOCIETY(1948); YOU WERE MEANT FOR ME(1948); EASY LIVING(1949); FLAMINGO ROAD(1949); TOP O' THE MORNING(1949); BORN TO BE BAD(1950); FOR HEAVEN'S SAKE(1950); MISTER 880(1950); SECRET FURY, THE(1950); WOMAN ON PIER 13, THE(1950); GUY WHO CAME BACK, THE(1951); STARLIFT(1951); LAS VEGAS STORY, THE(1952); STRANGERS ON A TRAIN(1951); WITH A SONG IN MY HEART(1952); GLENN MILLER STORY, THE(1953); ROGUE COP(1954); SEARCH FOR BRIDEY MURPHY, THE(1956); BUSTER KEATON STORY, THE(1957); LOVING YOU(1957); WILD IS THE WIND(1957); ONCE UPON A HORSE(1958); SUMMER AND SMOKE(1961); I'D RATHER BE RICH(1964); LAW OF THE LAWLESS(1964)
Dominic Ryan
2,000 WEEKS(1970, Aus.)
Don Ryan
CARNIVAL BOAT(1932), w; NAGANA(1933), w; UNCERTAIN LADY(1934), w; CASE OF THE STUTTERING BISHOP, THE(1937), w; FLY-AWAY BABY(1937), w; MIDNIGHT COURT(1937), w; MISSING WITNESSES(1937), w; SMART BLONDE(1937), w; BROADWAY MUSKETEERS(1938), w; ON TRIAL(1939), w; YOU CAN'T GET AWAY WITH MURDER(1939), w; DEVIL'S ISLAND(1940), w; TEAR GAS SQUAD(1940), w; CITADEL OF CRIME(1941), w; DEATH VALLEY OUTLAWS(1941), w; WEST OF CIMARRON(1941), w
Silents
MERRY WIDOW, THE(1925); UNKNOWN CAVALIER, THE(1926), t; WEDDING MARCH, THE(1927)
Douglas Ryan
DRIVE, HE SAID(1971)
Ed "Chromedome" Ryan
STEEL ARENA(1973)
Eddie Ryan
HEY! HEY! U.S.A.(1938, Brit.); AVALANCHE(1946); BREAKFAST IN HOLLYWOOD(1946)
Edmon Ryan
CRIME OVER LONDON(1936, Brit.); GANGWAY(1937, Brit.); OH BOY!(1938, Brit.); MURDER IN THE NIGHT(1940, Brit.); HIGHWAY 301(1950); MYSTERY STREET(1950); SIDE STREET(1950); THREE SECRETS(1950); UNDERCOVER GIRL(1950); GUY WHO CAME BACK, THE(1951); GO, MAN, GO!(1954); GOOD DAY FOR A HANGING(1958); TWO FOR THE SEESAW(1962); GLOBAL AFFAIR, A(1964); HOUSE IS NOT A HOME, A(1964); PLAYGROUND, THE(1965); BANNING(1967); TOPAZ(1969, Brit.); TORA! TORA! TORA!(1970, U.S./Jap.)
Edmond Ryan
HUMAN MONSTER, THE(1940, Brit.); BREAKING POINT, THE(1950); AMERICANIZATION OF EMILY, THE(1964)
Edna Ryan
RACE STREET(1948)
Edward Ryan
NON-STOP NEW YORK(1937, Brit.); STRANGERS ON A HONEYMOON(1937, Brit.); SULLIVANS, THE(1944); TAKE IT OR LEAVE IT(1944); CARIBBEAN MYSTERY, THE(1945); WITHIN THESE WALLS(1945); BEYOND GLORY(1948); ANGELS IN DISGUISE(1949)
Misc. Silents
TRUANT HUSBAND, THE(1921)
Edward Ryan, Jr.
IT HAPPENED ON 5TH AVENUE(1947)
Elaine Ryan
MR. DODD TAKES THE AIR(1937), w; LISTEN, DARLING(1938), w; BABES ON BROADWAY(1941), w; VERY YOUNG LADY, A(1941), w; MR. BELVEDERE GOES TO COLLEGE(1949)
Fran Ryan
SCANDALOUS JOHN(1971); $1,000,000 DUCK(1971); PICKUP ON 101(1972); HOW TO SEDUCE A WOMAN(1974); APPLE DUMPLING GANG, THE(1975); BIG WEDNESDAY(1978); GREAT BRAIN, THE(1978); STRAIGHT TIME(1978); LONG RIDERS, THE(1980); STRIPES(1981); TAKE THIS JOB AND SHOVE IT(1981); PRIVATE SCHOOL(1983); SAVANNAH SMILES(1983); TOUGH ENOUGH(1983)
Frank Ryan
MADE FOR EACH OTHER(1939), w; GIRL, A GUY AND A GOB, A(1941), w; OBLIGING YOUNG LADY(1941), w; CALL OUT THE MARINES(1942), d&w; MAYOR OF 44TH STREET, THE(1942), w; AMAZING MRS. HOLLIDAY(1943), w; HERS TO HOLD(1943), d; CAN'T HELP SINGING(1944), d, w; PATRICK THE GREAT(1945), d; SO GOES MY LOVE(1946), d
Silents
REFEREE, THE(1922)
Gertrude Ryan
Misc. Silents
ROSE OF NOME(1920); SNOWDRIFT(1923)
Helen Ryan
LIFT, THE(1965, Brit./Can.); ELEPHANT MAN, THE(1980, Brit.)
1984
MISUNDERSTOOD(1984)

Hilary Ryan
GETTING OF WISDOM, THE(1977, Aus.)
1984
SCANDALOUS(1984)
Irene Ryan
MELODY FOR THREE(1941); MELODY PARADE(1943); O, MY DARLING CLEMEN-
TINE(1943); REVEILLE WITH BEVERLY(1943); SARONG GIRL(1943); SULTAN'S
DAUGHTER, THE(1943); HOT RHYTHM(1944); SAN DIEGO, I LOVE YOU(1944);
THAT NIGHT WITH YOU(1945); THAT'S THE SPIRIT(1945); BEAUTIFUL CHEAT,
THE(1946); DIARY OF A CHAMBERMAID(1946); LITTLE IODINE(1946); HEADING
FOR HEAVEN(1947); WOMAN ON THE BEACH, THE(1947); MY DEAR SE-
CRETARY(1948); OLD-FASHIONED GIRL, AN(1948); TEXAS, BROOKLYN AND
HEAVEN(1948); THERE'S A GIRL IN MY HEART(1949); HALF ANGEL(1951); MEET
ME AFTER THE SHOW(1951); BLACKBEARD THE PIRATE(1952); BONZO GOES TO
COLLEGE(1952); WAC FROM WALLA WALLA, THE(1952); RICOCHET ROMAN-
CE(1954); ROCKABILLY BABY(1957); SPRING REUNION(1957); DESIRE IN THE
DUST(1960); DON'T WORRY, WE'LL THINK OF A TITLE(1966)
J. Ryan
Silents
GOLD RUSH, THE(1925)
J. M. Ryan
LOVING(1970), w
J.W. Ryan
Misc. Silents
DEAD-SHOT BAKER(1917)
Jack Ryan
THAT CERTAIN WOMAN(1937); PROPERTY(1979)
Jacqueline Ryan
JACQUELINE(1956, Brit.)
James Ryan
MANHUNT IN THE JUNGLE(1958); KILL OR BE KILLED(1980); KILL AND KILL
AGAIN(1981)
1984
FALLING IN LOVE(1984)
Misc. Silents
MY PARTNER(1916)
James Dale Ryan
1984
MIKE'S MURDER(1984)
Joe Ryan
LET'S SCARE JESSICA TO DEATH(1971), ed; UNCLE SCAM(1981), w
Misc. Talkies
ALIENS FROM ANOTHER PLANET(1967)
Misc. Silents
TENDERFOOT, THE(1917); LONE FIGHTER(1923); SMASHING BARRIERS(1923)
John Ryan
TIGER MAKES OUT, THE(1967); LOVELY WAY TO DIE, A(1968); WHAT'S SO BAD
ABOUT FEELING GOOD?(1968); FIVE EASY PIECES(1970); KING OF MARVIN
GARDENS, THE(1972); LEGEND OF NIGGER CHARLEY, THE(1972); COPS AND
ROBBERS(1973); DILLINGER(1973); SHAMUS(1973); IT'S ALIVE(1974); PERSECU-
TION(1974, Brit.); FUTUREWORLD(1976); MISSOURI BREAKS, THE(1976); KIDNAP-
PING OF THE PRESIDENT, THE(1980, Can.), p; ON THE NICKEL(1980); STONE
COLD DEAD(1980, Can.), p
1984
COTTON CLUB, THE(1984)
John P. Ryan
IT LIVES AGAIN(1978); LAST FLIGHT OF NOAH'S ARK, THE(1980); POSTMAN
ALWAYS RINGS TWICE, THE(1981); ESCAPE ARTIST, THE(1982); BREATH-
LESS(1983); RIGHT STUFF, THE(1983)
Dr. John W. Ryan
BREAKING AWAY(1979)
Joseph Ryan
Misc. Silents
GIRL ANGLE, THE(1917)
Kathleen Ryan
CAPTAIN BOYCOTT(1947, Brit.); ODD MAN OUT(1947, Brit.); ESTHER WA-
TERS(1948, Brit.); CHRISTOPHER COLUMBUS(1949, Brit.); SALT TO THE DE-
VIL(1949, Brit.); PRELUDE TO FAME(1950, Brit.); SOUND OF FURY, THE(1950);
YELLOW BALLOON, THE(1953, Brit.); SCOTCH ON THE ROCKS(1954, Brit.); CAP-
TAIN LIGHTFOOT(1955); JACQUELINE(1956, Brit.); SAIL INTO DANGER(1957, Brit.)
Kathy Ryan
TREE, THE(1969); SPRING BREAK(1983)
Kelly Ryan [Sheila Connelly]
OUTLAW'S DAUGHTER, THE(1954)
Ken Ryan
NIGHTMARE(1963, Brit.), art d; LAST SHOT YOU HEAR, THE(1969, Brit.), art d;
RING OF BRIGHT WATER(1969, Brit.), art d; HUMAN FACTOR, THE(1979, Brit.), art
d
Lee Ryan
WINDSPLITTER, THE(1971)
Madge Ryan
WITNESS IN THE DARK(1959, Brit.); HAND IN HAND(1960, Brit.); UPSTAIRS AND
DOWNSTAIRS(1961, Brit.); TIARA TAHITI(1962, Brit.); DOCTOR IN DISTRESS(1963,
Brit.); SUMMER HOLIDAY(1963, Brit.); THIS IS MY STREET(1964, Brit.); STRANGE
AFFAIR, THE(1968, Brit.); I START COUNTING(1970, Brit.); CLOCKWORK ORANGE,
A(1971, Brit.); WHO IS KILLING THE GREAT CHEFS OF EUROPE?(1978, US/Ger.);
LADY VANISHES, THE(1980, Brit.)
Mae Ryan
SWEET INNISCARRA(1934, Brit.)
Mari Karen Ryan
1984
CAGED FURY(1984, Phil.)
Marion Ryan
DREAM MAKER, THE(1963, Brit.)
Marissa Ryan
WITHOUT A TRACE(1983)
Mark Ryan
FINAL OPTION, THE(1983, Brit.)

Misc. Talkies
RAWHIDE TRAIL, THE(1958); ALL MEN ARE APES(1965)
Marla Ryan
DRAGSTRIP RIOT(1958)
Marlo Ryan
DATE BAIT(1960)
Mary Ryan
Misc. Silents
STOP THIEF(1915); HOME-KEEPING HEARTS(1921)
Maurice Ryan
Silents
K-THE UNKNOWN(1924); DRESS PARADE(1927); ANNAPOLIS(1928)
Meg Ryan
RICH AND FAMOUS(1981); AMITYVILLE 3-D(1983)
Michael Ryan
SMALL HOURS, THE(1962); STRANGLER, THE(1964); SATAN'S BED(1965); BODY
HEAT(1981); TOOTSIE(1982)
1984
SLAYGROUND(1984, Brit.)
Mike Ryan
VALLEY OF DECISION, THE(1945)
Mildred Ryan
Misc. Silents
LIVE WIRE, THE(1925); BROADWAY BOOB, THE(1926); THEN CAME THE WOM-
AN(1926)
Mitch Ryan
THUNDER ROAD(1958); MONTE WALSH(1970); ENTERTAINER, THE(1975)
Mitchell Ryan
CHANDLER(1971); GLORY BOY(1971); HONKERS, THE(1972); ELECTRA GLIDE IN
BLUE(1973); FRIENDS OF EDDIE COYLE, THE(1973); HIGH PLAINS DRIF-
TER(1973); MAGNUM FORCE(1973); REFLECTION OF FEAR, A(1973); TWO-MI-
NUTE WARNING(1976); HUNTING PARTY, THE(1977, Brit.)
Nancy Ryan
NOTHING BUT THE TRUTH(1929); PANDEMONIUM(1982)
Natasha Ryan
KINGDOM OF THE SPIDERS(1977); AMITYVILLE HORROR, THE(1979); LAST
WORD, THE(1979); DAY TIME ENDED, THE(1980, Span.); ENTITY, THE(1982);
GOING BERSERK(1983)
Nick Ryan
1984
MEATBALLS PART II(1984)
Paddy Ryan
DICK BARTON AT BAY(1950, Brit.); SWORD AND THE ROSE, THE(1953); HELL
BELOW ZERO(1954, Brit.); ROB ROY, THE HIGHLAND ROGUE(1954, Brit.); UNDER-
COVER GIRL(1957, Brit.)
Pat Ryan
LITTLE AUSTRALIANS(1940, Aus.), w; NOVEL AFFAIR, A(1957, Brit.)
Patricia Ryan
IT'S A WONDERFUL WORLD(1956, Brit.); SPIN A DARK WEB(1956, Brit.)
Patrick Ryan
HOW I WON THE WAR(1967, Brit.), w; 2,000 WEEKS(1970, Aus.), p, w
Paul Ryan
STORM CENTER(1956); STARHOPS(1978); PROMISE, THE(1979); CHARLIE CHAN
AND THE CURSE OF THE DRAGON QUEEN(1981); STAR 80(1983)
Paul G. Ryan
1984
HOT DOG...THE MOVIE(1984), ph
Peggy Ryan
TOP OF THE TOWN(1937); WOMEN MEN MARRY, THE(1937); FLYING IRISH-
MAN, THE(1939); SHE MARRIED A COP(1939); GRAPES OF WRATH(1940); SAI-
LOR'S LADY(1940); GET HEP TO LOVE(1942); GIRLS' TOWN(1942); GIVE OUT,
SISTERS(1942); MISS ANNIE ROONEY(1942); PRIVATE BUCKAROO(1942); WHAT'S
COOKIN'?(1942); MR. BIG(1943); TOP MAN(1943); WHEN JOHNNY COMES MARCH-
ING HOME(1943); BABES ON SWING STREET(1944); BOWERY TO BROAD-
WAY(1944); CHIP OFF THE OLD BLOCK(1944); FOLLOW THE BOYS(1944); MERRY
MONAHANS, THE(1944); THIS IS THE LIFE(1944); HERE COME THE CO-EDS(1945);
MEN IN HER DIARY(1945); ON STAGE EVERYBODY(1945); PATRICK THE
GREAT(1945); THAT'S THE SPIRIT(1945); SHAMROCK HILL(1949); THERE'S A
GIRL IN MY HEART(1949); ALL ASHORE(1953)
Phil L. Ryan
SECRET COMMAND(1944), p; PERILOUS HOLIDAY(1946), p; FIGHTING FATHER
DUNNE(1948), p
Philip Ryan
HANDS OF ORLAC, THE(1964, Brit./Fr.); STRANGE AFFAIR, THE(1968, Brit.);
HANDS OF THE RIPPER(1971, Brit.)
R. Hasset Ryan
Misc. Silents
HER SOUL'S INSPIRATION(1917)
Richard Ryan
CONSTANT NYMPH, THE(1943); MISSION TO MOSCOW(1943); ROYAL SCANDAL,
A(1945); MR. PEABODY AND THE MERMAID(1948); LADY TAKES A SAILOR,
THE(1949); LONELY MAN, THE(1957)
Silents
DAVID AND JONATHAN(1920, Brit.); BEAU REVEL(1921)
Robert Ryan
CROOKED ROAD, THE(; GHOST BREAKERS, THE(1940); GOLDEN GLOVES(1940);
NORTHWEST MOUNTED POLICE(1940); QUEEN OF THE MOB(1940); TEXAS
RANGERS RIDE AGAIN(1940); BEHIND THE RISING SUN(1943); BOMBAR-
DIER(1943); GANGWAY FOR TOMORROW(1943); IRON MAJOR, THE(1943); SKY'S
THE LIMIT, THE(1943); TENDER COMRADE(1943); MARINE RAIDERS(1944); LIFE
WITH BLONDIE(1946); CROSSFIRE(1947); DEAD RECKONING(1947); JOHNNY
O'CLOCK(1947); TRAIL STREET(1947); WOMAN ON THE BEACH, THE(1947); BER-
LIN EXPRESS(1948); RETURN OF THE BADMEN(1948); ACT OF VIOLENCE(1949);
BOY WITH THE GREEN HAIR, THE(1949); CAUGHT(1949); SET-UP, THE(1949);
BORN TO BE BAD(1950); SECRET FURY, THE(1950); WOMAN ON PIER 13,
THE(1950); BEST OF THE BADMEN(1951); FLYING LEATHERNECKS(1951); ON
DANGEROUS GROUND(1951); RACKET, THE(1951); BEWARE, MY LOVELY(1952);
CLASH BY NIGHT(1952); HORIZONS WEST(1952); CITY BENEATH THE SEA(1953);
INFERNO(1953); NAKED SPUR, THE(1953); ABOUT MRS. LESLIE(1954); ALASKA
SEAS(1954); HER TWELVE MEN(1954); BAD DAY AT BLACK ROCK(1955); ESCAPE

TO BURMA(1955); HOUSE OF BAMBOO(1955); TALL MEN, THE(1955); BACK FROM ETERNITY(1956); PROUD ONES, THE(1956); MEN IN WAR(1957); GOD'S LITTLE ACRE(1958); LONELYHEARTS(1958); DAY OF THE OUTLAW(1959); ODDS AGAINST TOMORROW(1959); ICE PALACE(1960); CANADIANS, THE(1961, Brit.); KING OF KINGS(1961); BILLY BUDD(1962); LONGEST DAY, THE(1962); BATTLE OF THE BULGE(1965); PROFESSIONALS, THE(1966); THE DIRTY GAME(1966, Fr./Ital./Ger.); BUSYBODY, THE(1967); DIRTY DOZEN, THE(1967, Brit.); HOUR OF THE GUN(1967); ANZIO(1968, Ital.); CUSTER OF THE WEST(1968, U.S., Span.); MINUTE TO PRAY, A SECOND TO DIE, A(1968, Ital.); CAPTAIN NEMO AND THE UNDERWATER CITY(1969, Brit.); WILD BUNCH, THE(1969); LAWMAN(1971); LOVE MACHINE, THE,(1971); AND HOPE TO DIE(1972 Fr/US); EXECUTIVE ACTION(1973); ICEMAN COMETH, THE(1973); LOLLY-MADONNA XXX(1973); OUTFIT, THE(1973); HIGH COUNTRY, THE(1981, Can.), ph

Silents
WOMANPOWER(1926); TOILERS, THE(1928); STRONG BOY(1929)

Robert L. Ryan
1984
BIRDY(1984)

Ron Ryan
WINDOWS(1980); TRUE CONFESSIONS(1981)

Rosemary Ryan
2,000 WEEKS(1970, Aus.), art d

Rusty Ryan
OUTRAGEOUS!(1977, Can.)

Sam Ryan
Misc. Silents
SPENDER OR THE FORTUNES OF PETER, THE(1915); PEGGY, THE WILL O' THE WISP(1917)

Sam J. Ryan
Silents
CHARITY?(1916)
Misc. Silents
WILDFIRE(1915); OPEN DOOR, THE(1919)

Samuel Ryan
Silents
STAIN, THE(1914)

Sheila Ryan
GAY CABALLERO, THE(1940); DEAD MEN TELL(1941); DRESSED TO KILL(1941); GOLDEN HOOFS(1941); GREAT GUNS(1941); SUN VALLEY SERENADE(1941); WE GO FAST(1941); A-HAUNTING WE WILL GO(1942); CAREFUL, SOFT SHOULDERS(1942); FOOTLIGHT SERENADE(1942); LONE STAR RANGER(1942); WHO IS HOPE SCHUYLER?(1942); GANG'S ALL HERE, THE(1943); SONG OF TEXAS(1943); LADIES OF WASHINGTON(1944); SOMETHING FOR THE BOYS(1944); CARIBBEAN MYSTERY, THE(1945); GETTING GERTIE'S GARTER(1945); DEADLINE FOR MURDER(1946); SLIGHTLY SCANDALOUS(1946); BIG FIX, THE(1947); HEARTACHES(1947); LONE WOLF IN MEXICO, THE(1947); PHILO VANCE'S SECRET MISSION(1947); RAILROADED(1947); CAGED FURY(1948); COBRA STRIKES, THE(1948); COWBOY AND THE INDIANS, THE(1949); HIDEOUT(1949); JOE PALOOKA IN THE COUNTERPUNCH(1949); RINGSIDE(1949); MULE TRAIN(1950); SQUARE DANCE KATY(1950); WESTERN PACIFIC AGENT(1950); FINGERPRINTS DON'T LIE(1951); JUNGLE MANHUNT(1951); MASK OF THE DRAGON(1951); ON TOP OF OLD SMOKY(1953); PACK TRAIN(1953); STREET OF DARKNESS(1958)
Misc. Talkies
STREET OF DARKNESS(1958)

Sheilah Ryan
GOLD RAIDERS, THE(1952)

Shelia Ryan
PARDON MY STRIPES(1942)

Steve Ryan
RANGER'S ROUNDUP, THE(1938)

Steven Ryan
TAPS(1981)

Ted Ryan
HURRICANE SMITH(1952); KANSAS CITY CONFIDENTIAL(1952); ONE MINUTE TO ZERO(1952); RED SKIES OF MONTANA(1952); WOMAN THEY ALMOST LYNCHED, THE(1953); CRIME WAVE(1954); MAIL ORDER BRIDE(1964)

Terry Ryan
YEAR OF LIVING DANGEROUSLY, THE(1982, Aus.), cos

Thelma "Pat" Ryan [Nixon]
SMALL TOWN GIRL(1936)

Thomas Ryan
NOCTURNA(1979); WOLFEN(1981)

Thomas A. Ryan
ARMORED COMMAND(1961)

Thomas C. Ryan
PAD, THE(AND HOW TO USE IT)* (1966, Brit.), w; HURRY SUNDOWN(1967), w; HEART IS A LONELY HUNTER, THE(1968), p, w

Tim Ryan
TRUE TO LIFE(1943); BROTHER ORCHID(1940); I'M NOBODY'S SWEETHEART NOW(1940); PRIVATE AFFAIRS(1940); THIRD FINGER, LEFT HAND(1940); DON'T GET PERSONAL(1941); HARMON OF MICHIGAN(1941); ICE-CAPADES(1941); LAST OF THE DUANES(1941); LUCKY DEVILS(1941); MAN BETRAYED, A(1941); MELODY LANE(1941); MR. AND MRS. NORTH(1941); PENALTY, THE(1941); PUBLIC ENEMIES(1941); RISE AND SHINE(1941); SAN ANTONIO ROSE(1941); STRAWBERRY BLONDE, THE(1941); TWO LATINS FROM MANHATTAN(1941); WHERE DID YOU GET THAT GIRL?(1941); YOU'LL NEVER GET RICH(1941); BEDTIME STORY(1942); FOREST RANGERS, THE(1942); GET HEP TO LOVE(1942); I WAKE UP SCREAMING(1942); MAN IN THE TRUNK(1942); NAZI AGENT(1942); SECRET AGENT OF JAPAN(1942); STAND BY FOR ACTION(1942); STRICTLY IN THE GROOVE(1942); SWEETHEART OF THE FLEET(1942); THIS GUN FOR HIRE(1942); THIS TIME FOR KEEPS(1942); TORTILLA FLAT(1942); WE WERE DANCING(1942); YOKEL BOY(1942); HIT PARADE OF 1943(1943); MELODY PARADE(1943), a, w; MYSTERY OF THE 13TH GUEST, THE(1943), a, w; REVEILLE WITH BEVERLY(1943); RIDING HIGH(1943); SARONG GIRL(1943), a, w; SULTAN'S DAUGHTER, THE(1943), a, w; SWING OUT THE BLUES(1943); TWO WEEKS TO LIVE(1943); ADVENTURES OF KITTY O'DAY(1944), a, w; AND THE ANGELS SING(1944); CRAZY KNIGHTS(1944), a, w; DETECTIVE KITTY O'DAY(1944), a, w; HI BEAUTIFUL(1944); HOT RHYTHM(1944), a, w; KANSAS CITY KITTY(1944); LEAVE IT TO THE IRISH(1944), w; SHADOW OF SUSPICION(1944); SWINGTIME JOHNNY(1944); DETOUR(1945); FASHION MODEL(1945), a, w; ROCKIN' IN THE ROCKIES(1945);

SWINGIN' ON A RAINBOW(1945); THERE GOES KELLY(1945), w; BOWERY BOMB-SHELL(1946), w; BRINGING UP FATHER(1946); DARK ALIBI(1946); IDEA GIRL(1946); IN FAST COMPANY(1946), w; LIVE WIRES(1946), w; SPOOK BUSTERS(1946), w; SWING PARADE OF 1946(1946), w; TILL THE END OF TIME(1946); TWO SISTERS FROM BOSTON(1946); WIFE WANTED(1946); BLONDIE'S HOLIDAY(1947); BODY AND SOUL(1947); BOWERY BUCKAROOS(1947), w; CASS TIMBERLANE(1947); HIGH BARBAREE(1947); NEWS HOUNDS(1947), a, w; ANGELS ALLEY(1948), w; FORCE OF EVIL(1948); JIGGS AND MAGGIE IN SOCIETY(1948); JINX MONEY(1948), w; LUCK OF THE IRISH(1948); MYSTERY OF THE GOLDEN EYE, THE(1948); SHANGHAI CHEST, THE(1948); SMUGGLERS' COVE(1948), w; TROUBLE MAKERS(1948), w; DEAR WIFE(1949); FORGOTTEN WOMEN(1949); RED, HOT AND BLUE(1949); SHAMROCK HILL(1949); SKY DRAGON(1949); STAMPEDE(1949); HUMPHREY TAKES A CHANCE(1950); JIGGS AND MAGGIE OUT WEST(1950); MILITARY ACADEMY WITH THAT TENTH AVENUE GANG(1950); PETTY GIRL, THE(1950); TO PLEASE A LADY(1950); CRAZY OVER HORSES(1951), a, w; CUBAN FIREBALL(1951); BELA LUGOSI MEETS A BROOKLYN GORILLA(1952), w; FARGO(1952); FEUDIN' FOOLS(1952), w; HERE COME THE MARINES(1952), a, w; HOLD THAT LINE(1952), w; NO HOLDS BARRED(1952), a, w; FROM HERE TO ETERNITY(1953); JALOPY(1953), w; MARKSMAN, THE(1953); PRIVATE EYES(1953); REDHEAD FROM MANHATTAN(1954); FIGHTING TROUBLE(1956); BUSTER KEATON STORY, THE(1957)
Misc. Talkies
JIGGS AND MAGGIE IN COURT(1948); JIGGS AND MAGGIE IN JACKPOT JITTERS(1949)

Tom Ryan
TENSION(1949)

Tommy Ryan
PRAIRIE MOON(1938); TENTH AVENUE KID(1938); COVERED TRAILER, THE(1939); MICKEY, THE KID(1939); MY WIFE'S RELATIVES(1939); ORPHANS OF THE STREET(1939); SHOULD HUSBANDS WORK?(1939); STREET OF MISSING MEN(1939); EARL OF PUDDLESTONE(1940); GRANDPA GOES TO TOWN(1940); MONEY TO BURN(1940); BALL OF FIRE(1941); STRANGE LOVE OF MARTHA IVERS, THE(1946); TOP BANANA(1954)
Misc. Silents
SAFE GUARDED(1924)

Tony Ryan
WIRE SERVICE(1942), w

Vera Ryan
MIKADO, THE(1967, Brit.)

Whitey Ryan
KING OF COMEDY, THE(1983)

Eddie Ryans
TANGIER(1946)

Eldar Ryazanov
BALLAD OF A HUSSAR(1963, USSR), d; UNCOMMON THIEF, AN(1967, USSR), d, w

G. Rybakov
WAR AND PEACE(1968, USSR)

Gheorghy B. Rybakov
WATERLOO(1970, Ital./USSR)

N. Rybikov
LOSS OF FEELING(1935, USSR)

Alexander Rybin
HYPERBOLOID OF ENGINEER GARIN, THE(1965, USSR), ph; CHEREZ TERNII K SVEZDAM(1981 USSR), ph

Jan Rybkowski
TONIGHT A TOWN DIES(1961, Pol.), d, w

Harry Rybnick
GOLDEN MISTRESS, THE(1954), p; CURUCU, BEAST OF THE AMAZON(1956), p; GIRLS ON THE LOOSE(1958), p; LIVE FAST, DIE YOUNG(1958), p

Nikolay Rybnikov
WAR AND PEACE(1968, USSR)

A. Rybnikow
THREE DAYS OF VIKTOR TSCHERNIKOFF(1968, USSR), m

J. Rybowski
LAST STOP, THE(1949, Pol.), art d

Sheldon Rybowski
"EQUUS"(1977); PROM NIGHT(1980); SPRING FEVER(1983, Can.)

Jan Rychlik
LEMONADE JOE(1966, Czech.), m

Ladislav Rychman
LADY ON THE TRACKS, THE(1968, Czech.), d

Carol Rydall
ROUGH CUT(1980, Brit.)

Derek Rydall
TELEFON(1977)

Stephanie Ann Rydall
TELEFON(1977)

Whitney Rydbeck
SLEEPER(1973); BATTLE BEYOND THE STARS(1980)

Viktor Rydberg
GYPSY FURY(1950, Fr.), w

Georg Rydeberg
DOLLAR(1938, Swed.); WOMAN'S FACE, A(1939, Swed.); WALPURGIS NIGHT(1941, Swed.); APPASSIONATA(1946, Swed.); HOUR OF THE WOLF, THE(1968, Swed.); PEOPLE MEET AND SWEET MUSIC FILLS THE HEART(1969, Den./Swed.)

George Rydeberg
BREAD OF LOVE, THE(1954, Swed.)

Amy Rydell
1984
RIVER, THE(1984)

Bobby Rydell
BYE BYE BIRDIE(1963); MARCO POLO JUNIOR(1973, Aus.)

Charles Rydell
SAND CASTLE, THE(1961); OPEN THE DOOR AND SEE ALL THE PEOPLE(1964); UNION CITY(1980)

Chris Rydell
ON GOLDEN POND(1981)

Christopher Rydell
CINDERELLA LIBERTY(1973); HARRY AND WALTER GO TO NEW YORK(1976)

Evelyn Rydell
HARRY AND WALTER GO TO NEW YORK(1976)

Mark Rydell
CRIME IN THE STREETS(1956); FOX, THE(1967), d; REIVERS, THE(1969), d; COWBOYS, THE(1972), p&d; CINDERELLA LIBERTY(1973), p&d; LONG GOODBYE, THE(1973); HARRY AND WALTER GO TO NEW YORK(1976), d; ROSE, THE(1979), d; ON GOLDEN POND(1981), d
1984
RIVER, THE(1984), d

Alfred Ryden
Misc. Silents
WORLD OF TODAY, THE(1915)

Ryck Ryden
THEM NICE AMERICANS(1958, Brit.)

A. Ryder
Misc. Silents
SOUL OF FRANCE(1929, Fr.), d

Alfred Ryder
T-MEN(1947); STORY ON PAGE ONE, THE(1959); INVITATION TO A GUNFIGHTER(1964); RAIDERS, THE(1964); HOTEL(1967); VALLEY OF MYSTERY(1967); TRUE GRIT(1969); WHO FEARS THE DEVIL(1972); STONE KILLER, THE(1973); W(1974); ESCAPE TO WITCH MOUNTAIN(1975); TRACKS(1977)

Pfc. Alfred Ryder
WINGED VICTORY(1944)

Amy Ryder
1984
ONCE UPON A TIME IN AMERICA(1984)

Amy S. Ryder
1984
OVER THE BROOKLYN BRIDGE(1984)

Bob Ryder
WARRIORS, THE(1979)

Dave Ryder
1984
ICEMAN(1984)

Diane Ryder
HELLCATS, THE(1968)

Eddie Ryder
COUNTRY GIRL, THE(1954); GIRL RUSH, THE(1955); YOUNG STRANGER, THE(1957); TARAWA BEACHHEAD(1958); IT'S A MAD, MAD, MAD, MAD WORLD(1963); SON OF FLUBBER(1963); FBI CODE 98(1964); NEW INTERNS, THE(1964); ONE MAN'S WAY(1964); PATSY, THE(1964); NOT WITH MY WIFE, YOU DON'T!(1966); OSCAR, THE(1966); STACEY!(1973); SILENT MOVIE(1976)

Edward Ryder
KINGS GO FORTH(1958)

Gerald Ryder
VENOM(1982, Brit.)

John Ryder
1984
STREETS OF FIRE(1984)

Kit Ryder
DUSTY AND SWEETS McGEE(1971)

Loren L. Ryder
UNION PACIFIC(1939), spec eff

Paul Ryder
COSMIC MONSTERS(1958, Brit.), w; INFORMATION RECEIVED(1962, Brit.), w; PRIZE OF ARMS, A(1962, Brit.), w; MATTER OF CHOICE, A(1963, Brit.), w

Philip Ryder
Silents
REAL ADVENTURE, THE(1922)

Rob Ryder
SOUTHERN COMFORT(1981)

Scott Ryder
MAKING LOVE(1982)

Shanueille Ryder
DESPERATE CHARACTERS(1971)

Walter Ryder
Silents
TIDES OF FATE(1917)

Win Ryder
EXODUS(1960), spec eff

Carl Rydin
PRIZE, THE(1963)

Viran Rydkvist
NIGHT IN JUNE, A(1940, Swed.)

Rick Rydon
DOUBLE EXPOSURE(1954, Brit.); SATELLITE IN THE SKY(1956)

Ryck Rydon
DELAYED ACTION(1954, Brit.); ONE WAY OUT(1955, Brit.); HIGH TIDE AT NOON(1957, Brit.); SECOND FIDDLE(1957, Brit.); WEAPON, THE(1957, Brit.); CHILD AND THE KILLER, THE(1959, Brit.); DEAD MAN'S EVIDENCE(1962, Brit.), a, p; HARUM SCARUM(1965); UNDERTAKER AND HIS PALS, THE(1966)

Oscar Rydquist
WALPURGIS NIGHT(1941, Swed.), w

Pia Rydwall
MY FATHER'S MISTRESS(1970, Swed.)

Ann Rye
DON'T LOOK NOW(1973, Brit./Ital.)

Jack Rye
Silents
NAPOLEON(1927, Fr.)

Michael Rye
HANDS OF A STRANGER(1962)

Stellan Rye
Misc. Silents
STUDENT OF PRAGUE, THE(1913, Ger.), d

Patrick Ryecart
SILVER DREAM RACER(1982, Brit.)

Richard Ryen
CASABLANCA(1942); CROSS OF LORRAINE, THE(1943); FIRST COMES COURAGE(1943); GANGWAY FOR TOMORROW(1943); HOSTAGES(1943); STRANGE DEATH OF ADOLF HITLER, THE(1943); HITLER GANG, THE(1944); SECRETS OF SCOTLAND YARD(1944); PARIS UNDERGROUND(1945); SALOME, WHERE SHE DANCED(1945); THIS LOVE OF OURS(1945); CRACK-UP(1946)

Ann Ryerson
WEDDING, A(1978); PERFECT COUPLE, A(1979); CADDY SHACK(1980)

Florence Ryerson
CANARY MURDER CASE, THE(1929), w; DANGEROUS CURVES(1929), w; FAST COMPANY(1929), w; MYSTERIOUS DR. FU MANCHU, THE(1929), w; POINTED HEELS(1930), w; RETURN OF DR. FU MANCHU, THE(1930), w; COMPROMISED(1931), w; DRUMS OF JEOPARDY(1931), w; RECKLESS HOUR, THE(1931), w; CRIME OF THE CENTURY, THE(1933), w; HAVE A HEART(1934), w; THIS SIDE OF HEAVEN(1934), w; WICKED WOMAN, A(1934), w; CASINO MURDER CASE, THE(1935), w; MAD HOLIDAY(1936), w; MOONLIGHT MURDER(1936), w; TOUGH GUY(1936), w; EVERYBODY SING(1938), w; HENRY GOES ARIZONA(1939), w; ICE FOLLIES OF 1939(1939), w; KID FROM TEXAS, THE(1939), w; WIZARD OF OZ, THE(1939), w; HER FIRST BEAU(1941), w; SMOOTH AS SILK(1946), w
Silents
OH, WHAT A NIGHT!(1926), w; ADAM AND EVIL(1927), w; BLAZING DAYS(1927), w; JOHNNY GET YOUR HAIR CUT(1927), w; LOVE MAKES 'EM WILD(1927), w; ON ZE BOULEVARD(1927), w; EASY COME, EASY GO(1928), w; HOT NEWS(1928), w; LOVE AND LEARN(1928), w

Forence Ryerson
NOTORIOUS GENTLEMAN, A(1935), w

Robert Ryerson
SPANISH FLY(1975, Brit.), w

Sean Ryerson
1984
RENO AND THE DOC(1984, Can.), a, p

Eli Ryg
EDVARD MUNCH(1976, Norway/Swed.)

Jorgen Ryg
CRAZY PARADISE(1965, Den.)

Ulla Ryghe
THROUGH A GLASS DARKLY(1962, Swed.), ed; WINTER LIGHT, THE(1963, Swed.), ed; SILENCE, THE(1964, Swed.), ed; GUILT(1967, Swed.), ed; PERSONA(1967, Swed.), ed; HOUR OF THE WOLF, THE(1968, Swed.), ed; SHAME(1968, Swed.), ed; THIRD WALKER, THE(1978, Can.), ed

Sharon Ryker
NASTY RABBIT, THE(1964)

V. Rylach
CLEAR SKIES(1963, USSR), spec eff

Celia Rylan
CLEOPATRA(1934)

Cecilia Ryland
HONOR OF THE MOUNTED(1932)

George H. Ryland
HIGH TIDE(1947)

Jim Ryland
FEMALE ON THE BEACH(1955)

Fred C. Ryle
IRON MASK, THE(1929), makeup
Silents
GENERAL, THE(1927), makeup; ISLE OF FORGOTTEN WOMEN(1927), makeup

Fred Ryle
JIGSAW(1949), makeup; ON THE WATERFRONT(1954), makeup

Larry Ryle
SHIELD FOR MURDER(1954)

Lawrence Ryle
HOUDINI(1953); EGYPTIAN. THE(1954); ROCKET MAN, THE(1954)

William Ryle
1984
KILLPOINT(1984)

J. H. Ryley
Silents
HAMLET(1913, Brit.)

James Ryley
Silents
BY WHOSE HAND?(1916)

Madeline Lucette Ryley
Silents
MICE AND MEN(1916), w

Phil Ryley
Silents
JUST FOR TONIGHT(1918)

Reggie Rymal
HOUSE OF WAX(1953)

Brian Ryman
OPENING NIGHT(1977), art d

Herb Ryman
DUMBO(1941), art d

Herbert Ryman
FANTASIA(1940), art d

Luba Rymer
SINGING BLACKSMITH(1938)

George Ryne
THE BOSTON STRANGLER, THE(1968)

Serge Rynecki
BROKEN ENGLISH(1981)

Ann Rynne
GREAT MUPPET CAPER, THE(1981)

Bill Ryno
Silents
LOADED DOOR, THE(1922)

Misc. Silents
TWINS OF SUFFERING CREEK(1920); DARING DANGER(1922); FIGHTING LUCK(1926)
W. H. Ryno
Silents
SPOILERS, THE(1914)
William H. Ryno
Misc. Silents
PEGGY OF THE SECRET SERVICE(1925)
William Ryno
SAGEBRUSH POLITICS(1930); FIGHTING COWBOY(1933); JEALOUSY(1934)
Silents
VANISHING HOOFS(1926); BOY RIDER, THE(1927)
Misc. Silents
LOVE IS LOVE(1919); BULLET-PROOF(1920); KAZAN(1921); HARD HITTIN' HAMILTON(1924)
Morrie Ryskind
PALMY DAYS(1931), w; NIGHT AT THE OPERA, A(1935), w; MY MAN GODFREY(1936), w; STAGE DOOR(1937), w; ROOM SERVICE(1938), w; THERE'S ALWAYS A WOMAN(1938), w; MAN ABOUT TOWN(1939), w; LOUISIANA PURCHASE(1941), w; PENNY SERENADE(1941), w; CLAUDIA(1943), w; IT'S IN THE BAG(1945), w; WHERE DO WE GO FROM HERE?(1945), w; HEARTBEAT(1946), w; MY MAN GODFREY(1957), w
Rex Ryon
MY TUTOR(1983)
1984
BAD MANNERS(1984); BEVERLY HILLS COP(1984)
Otto Ryser
END OF THE GAME(1976, Ger./Ital.)
Arden Ryshpan
IN PRAISE OF OLDER WOMEN(1978, Can.)
Howard Ryshpan
RABID(1976, Can.)
Morris Ryskind
COCOANUTS, THE(1929), w; ANIMAL CRACKERS(1930), w
Gabriella Rysted
HU-MAN(1975, Fr.)
Frederick Ryter
MAN FROM NEW MEXICO, THE(1932), a, w; SCARLET BRAND(1932)
Chishu Ryu
RICKSHAW MAN, THE(1960, Jap.); EARLY AUTUMN(1962, Jap.); OHAYO(1962, Jap.); WISER AGE(1962, Jap.); YOUTH AND HIS AMULET, THE(1963, Jap.); TEA AND RICE(1964, Jap.); TWILIGHT PATH(1965, Jap.); RED BEARD(1966, Jap.); EMPEROR AND A GENERAL, THE(1968, Jap.); FIGHT FOR THE GLORY(1970, Jap.); FLOATING WEEDS(1970, Jap.); SOLDIER'S PRAYER, A(1970, Jap.); TOKYO STORY(1972, Jap.); LATE AUTUMN(1973, Jap.)
Misc. Silents
COLLEGE IS A NICE PLACE(1936, Jap.)
Daisuke Ryu
KAGEMUSHA(1980, Jap.)
Bill M. Ryusaki
SOME KIND OF HERO(1982)
Bill Ryusaki
WRECKING CREW, THE(1968)
I. Ryzhov
SPRINGTIME ON THE VOLGA(1961, USSR)
Ivan Ryzhov
MUMU(1961, USSR)
Konstantin Ryzhov
ARMED AND DANGEROUS(1977, USSR), ph
Jerzy Rzepka
BEADS OF ONE ROSARY, THE(1982, Pol.)
Lidia Rzeszewska
MAN OF MARBLE(1979, Pol.), cos

S

Robert Saab
FORTUNE AND MEN'S EYES(1971, U.S./Can.)

Aziz Saad
UNCLE TOM'S CABIN(1969, Fr./Ital./Ger./Yugo.)

Margit Saad
CALL ME GENIUS(1961, Brit.); CONCRETE JUNGLE, THE(1962, Brit.); PLAY-BACK(1962, Brit.); I DEAL IN DANGER(1966); MAGNIFICENT TWO, THE(1967, Brit.); LAST ESCAPE, THE(1970, Brit.)

Robert Saad
CANNIBAL GIRLS(1973), ph; HARD PART BEGINS, THE(1973, Can.), ph; RAINBOW BOYS, THE(1973, Can.), ph; THEY CAME FROM WITHIN(1976, Can.), ph; HOUSE BY THE LAKE, THE(1977, Can.), ph

Sasi Saad
1984
LITTLE DRUMMER GIRL, THE(1984)

Norbert Saada
DEATH OF MARIO RICCI, THE(1983, Ital.), p
1984
DOG DAY(1984, Fr.), p

Yacef Saadi
BATTLE OF ALGIERS, THE(1967, Ital./Alger.), a, p

Bob Saal
Misc. Talkies
INSTRUCTOR, THE(1983)

William Saal
BETWEEN FIGHTING MEN(1932), p; COME ON TARZAN(1933), p; DRUM TAPS(1933), p; FARGO EXPRESS(1933), p; LONE AVENGER, THE(1933), p; PHANTOM THUNDERBOLT, THE(1933), p; FRANKIE AND JOHNNY(1936), p

Liane Saalborn
MALOU(1983)

Allen Saalburg
GREEN PASTURES(1936), art d

Nell Saalman
Misc. Silents
MISS MISCHIEF MAKER(1918)

Miel Saan
CONFESSIONS OF AN OPIUM EATER(1962)

Tyno Saar
TEST OF PILOT PIRX, THE(1978, Pol./USSR)

Arla Saare
MARRIED COUPLE, A(1969, Can.), ed; WHO HAS SEEN THE WIND(1980, Can.), ed; SILENCE OF THE NORTH(1981, Can.), ed

Ted Saari
1984
TIGHTROPE(1984)

Martti Saarikivi
MAKE LIKE A THIEF(1966, Fin.)

Eric Saarinen
TIDAL WAVE(1975, U.S./Jap.), ph; EAT MY DUST!(1976), ph; SUMMER SCHOOL TEACHERS(1977), ph; YOU LIGHT UP MY LIFE(1977), ph; HILLS HAVE EYES, THE(1978), ph; STARHOPS(1978), ph; REAL LIFE(1979), ph; MODERN ROMANCE(1981), ph; BOXOFFICE(1982), ph; GOLDEN SEAL, THE(1983), ph

Frank Saba
CARS THAT ATE PARIS, THE(1974, Aus,)

Umberto Saba
ERNESTO(1979, Ital.), w

Fabio Sabag
KILLER FISH(1979, Ital./Braz.)

Frank Sabani
BLAZE O' GLORY(1930)

Thalia Sabanieeva
GIRL FROM POLTAVA(1937)

Lellah Sabarathy
IT'S A WONDERFUL WORLD(1956, Brit.)

Robert Sabaroff
SPLIT, THE(1968), w

Luca Sabatelli
DEAD ARE ALIVE, THE(1972, Yugo./Ger./Ital.), cos; WIFEMISTRESS(1979, Ital.), cos; IMMORTAL BACHELOR, THE(1980, Ital.), cos

Luigi Sabatelli
QUEENS, THE(1968, Ital./Fr.), art d

Dario Sabatello
LADY DOCTOR, THE(1963, Fr./Ital./Span.), p, w; LOVE, THE ITALIAN WAY(1964, Ital.), p; TWELVE-HANDED MEN OF MARS, THE(1964, Ital./Span.), p; UP THE MACGREGORS(1967, Ital./Span.), p

R. Sabatier
SLEEPING CAR MURDER THE(1966, Fr.)

William Sabatier
CASQUE D'OR(1956, Fr.); ROAD TO SHAME, THE(1962, Fr.); SERPENT, THE(1973, Fr./Ital./Ger.); CLOCKMAKER, THE(1976, Fr.)

Danilo Sabatine
PLACE CALLED GLORY, A(1966, Span./Ger.), p

Carlo Sabatini
SACCO AND VANZETTI(1971, Ital./Fr.)

Enrico Sabatini
SACCO AND VANZETTI(1971, Ital./Fr.), cos

Rafael Sabatini
CAPTAIN BLOOD(1935), w; PRISONER OF CORBAL(1939, Brit.), w; BLACK SWAN, THE(1942), w; FORTUNES OF CAPTAIN BLOOD(1950), w; CAPTAIN PIRATE(1952), w; SCARAMOUCHE(1952), w; ADVENTURES OF SCARAMOUCHE, THE(1964, Fr.), w; SON OF CAPTAIN BLOOD, THE(1964, U.S./Ital./Span.), w
Silents
SCARAMOUCHE(1923), w

Stefania Sabatini
ADIEU PHILLIPINE(1962, Fr./Ital.); VAMPIRE AND THE BALLERINA, THE(1962, Ital.); HERCULES, SAMSON & ULYSSES(1964, Ital.)

Afredo Sabato
RIVER, THE(1928)

Alfredo Sabato
SPANISH MAIN, THE(1945); CARNIVAL IN COSTA RICA(1947); ESCAPE ME NEVER(1947)

Antonio Sabato
GRAND PRIX(1966); BEYOND THE LAW(1967, Ital.); HATE FOR HATE(1967, Ital.); LADY OF MONZA, THE(1970, Ital.); CRIME BOSS(1976, Ital.)

Bo Sabato
1984
FLAMINGO KID, THE(1984)

Betty Sabba
TAKE ME AWAY, MY LOVE(1962, Gr.)

Miriam J. Sabbage
Silents
BRIDAL CHAIR, THE(1919, Brit.)

Isa Sabbagh
ISLAND OF ALLAH(1956)

Enrico Sabbatini
CANDY(1968, Ital./Fr.), cos; CAMILLE 2000(1969), art d; FINE PAIR, A(1969, Ital.), cos; GHOSTS, ITALIAN STYLE(1969, Ital./Fr.), cos; PLACE FOR LOVERS, A(1969, Ital./Fr.), cos; MACHINE GUN McCAIN(1970, Ital.), cos; SUNFLOWER(1970, Fr./Ital.), cos; MASTER TOUCH, THE(1974, Ital./Ger.), cos; MOSES(1976, Brit./Ital.), cos; SPECIAL DAY, A(1977, Ital./Can.), cos; BLOODLINE(1979), cos

J. Sabben-Clare
LURE, THE(1933, Brit.), w

William Sabbot
HEAVENLY BODY, THE(1943); NORTH STAR, THE(1943)

Jimmy Sabe
DINGAKA(1965, South Africa)
Misc. Talkies
TOKOLOSHE(1973)

Oscar Sabe
COURT CONCERT, THE(1936, Ger.)

Valeria Sabel
NAVAJO JOE(1967, Ital./Span.); YEAR ONE(1974, Ital.)

Virgilio Sabel
MONTE CASSINO(1948, Ital.), w; DAY THE SKY EXPLODED, THE(1958, Fr./Ital.), w

Eric Sabela
NAKED PREY, THE(1966, U.S./South Africa)

Simon Sabela
GOLD(1974, Brit.); FOREVER YOUNG, FOREVER FREE(1976, South Afr.); ZULU DAWN(1980, Brit.)
Misc. Talkies
TARGET OF AN ASSASSIN(1978, S. Africa)

Ernie Sabella
1984
CITY HEAT(1984)

Julio Sabello
Silents
DOWN BY THE RIO GRANDE(1924), w; SWORD OF VALOR, THE(1924), w

Simon Sabelo
ZULU(1964, Brit.)

David Saber
CLOWN, THE(1953); DRANGO(1957)

Sabicas
KNICKERBOCKER HOLIDAY(1944)

Agustin Castellon Sabicas
FOLLOW THE BOYS(1944)

Barbara Sabichi
SCARLET EMPRESS, THE(1934)

Katerine Sabichi
SCARLET EMPRESS, THE(1934)

Charles Sabin
GIRL IN DANGER(1934); MEN OF THE NIGHT(1934); THAT'S GRATITUDE(1934); TOGETHER WE LIVE(1935)

Marc Sabin
KILL SQUAD(1982)

Olga Sabin
BEHIND PRISON WALLS(1943)

Sea Sabin
MISBEHAVING HUSBANDS(1941), w

Martin Sabine
WHO'S YOUR LADY FRIEND?(1937, Brit.), p
Silents
PURSUING VENGEANCE, THE(1916), d
Misc. Silents
HOUSE OF FEAR, THE(1915)

Cheslav Sabinsky
Misc. Silents
HER SACRIFICE(1917, USSR), d; LIVING CORPSE, A(1918, USSR), d; POWER OF DARKNESS, THE(1918, USSR), d; SAVVA(1919, USSR), d; VILLAGE IN CRISIS(1920, USSR), d; ELDER VASILI GRYAZNOV(1924, USSR), d

Lee Sabinson
THIRD OF A MAN(1962); WHO'S GOT THE ACTION?(1962); SUCH GOOD FRIENDS(1971)

Andrew Sabiston
Misc. Talkies
UPS AND DOWNS(1981)

Germaine Sablon
GLORY OF FAITH, THE(1938, Fr.)

Loulette Sablon
FOREIGN CORRESPONDENT(1940); ONE NIGHT IN LISBON(1941); MISSION TO MOSCOW(1943); PARIS UNDERGROUND(1945); THIS LOVE OF OURS(1945); COME TO THE STABLE(1949); UNDER MY SKIN(1950); LAST TIME I SAW PARIS, THE(1954); TO CATCH A THIEF(1955)

Sablotski
M(1933, Ger.)

Joseph Sabo
PINOCCHIO(1940), w

Michael Sabo
FOES(1977), ph

Dick Sabol
COTTON COMES TO HARLEM(1970); COME BACK CIHARLESTON BLUE(1972);
LADY LIBERTY(1972, Ital./Fr.)

Steve Sabol
PAPER LION(1968), ph

Betty Sabor
SON OF SINBAD(1955)

Timmy Sabor
OLD ACQUAINTANCE(1943)

V. Sabot
MAN WHO BROKE THE BANK AT MONTE CARLO, THE(1935)

Marie Sabouret
FROU-FROU(1955, Fr.); RIFIFI(1956, Fr.); WOULD-BE GENTLEMAN, THE(1960, Fr.)

Marcel Sabourin
CORDELIA(1980, Fr., Can.), w

Richard Sabre
ATHENA(1954)

Sabrina
STOCK CAR(1955, Brit.); RAMSBOTTOM RIDES AGAIN(1956, Brit.); JUST MY
LUCK(1957, Brit.); BLUE MURDER AT ST. TRINIAN'S(1958, Brit.); SATAN IN HIGH
HEELS(1962); MAKE MINE A MILLION(1965, Brit.); ICE HOUSE, THE(1969)

Bruce Sabsay
PROUD RIDER, THE(1971, Can.), ed

Sabu
ELEPHANT BOY(1937, Brit.); DRUMS(1938, Brit.); THIEF OF BAGHDAD, THE(1940,
Brit.); ARABIAN NIGHTS(1942); JUNGLE BOOK(1942); WHITE SAVAGE(1943);
COBRA WOMAN(1944); TANGIER(1946); BLACK NARCISSUS(1947, Brit.); END OF
THE RIVER, THE(1947, Brit.); MAN-EATER OF KUMAON(1948); SONG OF IN-
DIA(1949); SAVAGE DRUMS(1951); HELLO, ELEPHANT(1954, Ital.); JAGUAR(1956);
SABU AND THE MAGIC RING(1957); MISTRESS OF THE WORLD(1959, Ital./Fr./
Ger.); RAMPAGE(1963); TIGER WALKS, A(1964)
Misc. Talkies
JUNGLE HELL(1956)

Victor Sabuni
TORRID ZONE(1940)

Y. Sabura
HAPPINESS OF US ALONE(1962, Jap.), ed

Shin Saburi
TEA AND RICE(1964, Jap.); GLOWING AUTUMN(1981, Jap.)

Franco Sacavola
CARMELA(1949, Ital.), m

Giampaolo Saccarola
EYES, THE MOUTH, THE(1982, Ital./Fr.); LEAP INTO THE VOID(1982, Ital.);
IDENTIFICATION OF A WOMAN(1983, Ital.)

Maria Saccenti
FACTS OF MURDER, THE(1965, Ital.)

Dardano Saccheti
1984
HOUSE BY THE CEMETERY, THE(1984, Ital.), w

D. Sacchetti
GATES OF HELL, THE(1983, U.S./Ital.), w

Dardano Sacchetti
CAT O'NINE TAILS(1971, Ital./Ger./Fr.), w
1984
LAST HUNTER, THE(1984, Ital.), w

Joseph Sacchi
GREEN TREE, THE(1965, Ital.), ph

Robert Sacchi
PULP(1972, Brit.); MAN WITH BOGART'S FACE, THE(1980)

Chuck Sacci
CHOIRBOYS, THE(1977); THANK GOD IT'S FRIDAY(1978)

Thomas Saccio
FAN, THE(1981)

Eugene Saccomano
BORSALINO(1970, Fr.), w

Felipe Sacdalan
SCAVENGERS, THE(1959, U.S./Phil.), ph; LOST BATTALION(1961, U.S./Phil.), ph;
CAVALRY COMMAND(1963, U.S./Phil.), ph; CRY OF BATTLE(1963), ph; RAIDERS
OF LEYTE GULF(1963 U.S./Phil.), ph; KIDNAPPERS, THE(1964, U.S./Phil.), ph;
MORO WITCH DOCTOR(1964, U.S./Phil.), ph; BLOOD DRINKERS, THE(1966, U.S./
Phil.), ph; HOT BOX, THE(1972, U.S./Phil.), ph

Felipe J. Sacdalan
WALLS OF HELL, THE(1964, U.S./Phil.), ph; TNT JACKSON(1975), ph

Philip Sacdalan
BIG BIRD CAGE, THE(1972), ph

Orlando Sach
MIRAGE(1972, Peru)

Alexander Sacha
LAURA(1944); DRAGONWYCH(1946)

Claude Sacha
ROSE, THE(1979)

Jean Sacha
OTHELLO(1955, U.S./Fr./Ital.), ed

Orlando Sacha
NO EXIT(1962, U.S./Arg.)

Carl Hans Sachafer
ZIG-ZAG(1975, Fr./Ital.), m

Rod Sachanrnoski
SEABO(1978)

Achla Sachdev
HOUSEHOLDER, THE(1963, US/India); NINE HOURS TO RAMA(1963, U.S./Brit.)

Shelby Sache
HILDUR AND THE MAGICIAN(1969)

Jonathan Sacher
1984
TIGHTROPE(1984)

Toby Sacher
BLOOD MANIA(1971), w

Dardana Sachetti
1990: THE BRONX WARRIORS(1983, Ital.), d

A. Sachicki
BORDER STREET(1950, Pol.), art d

Louis H. Sachin
ADVENTURES OF CASANOVA(1948), ed

Alice Sachs
SEEMS LIKE OLD TIMES(1980); FEAR NO EVIL(1981)

Andrew Sachs
HITLER: THE LAST TEN DAYS(1973, Brit./Ital.); FRIGHTMARE(1974, Brit.);
CONFESSIONAL, THE(1977, Brit.); HISTORY OF THE WORLD, PART 1(1981)

Beryl Sachs
MR. MUGGS STEPS OUT(1943), w; FOLLOW THE LEADER(1944), w; WHAT A
MAN!(1944), w; RADAR SECRET SERVICE(1950), w

Biryl Sachs
SPOTLIGHT SCANDALS(1943), w

David Sachs
ROAD TO SALINA(1971, Fr./Ital.)

Jack Sachs
WILD PARTY, THE(1975)

Leonard Sachs
SECRET OF STAMBOUL, THE(1936, Brit.); GREAT MANHUNT, THE(1951, Brit.);
GREAT GILBERT AND SULLIVAN, THE(1953, Brit.); FIRE OVER AFRICA(1954,
Brit.); JOHN WESLEY(1954, Brit.); COUNT OF TWELVE(1955, Brit.); GENTLEMEN
MARRY BRUNETTES(1955); GAMMA PEOPLE, THE(1956, Brit.); ODONGO(1956, Brit.);
AFTER THE BALL(1957, Brit.); MEN OF SHERWOOD FOREST(1957, Brit.); THUN-
DER OVER TANGIER(1957, Brit.); MAN WHO WOULDN'T TALK, THE(1958, Brit.);
MENACE IN THE NIGHT(1958, Brit.); BEHEMOTH, THE SEA MONSTER(1959, Brit.);
BEYOND THE CURTAIN(1960, Brit.); BULLDOG BREED, THE(1960, Brit.); OSCAR
WILDE(1960, Brit.); SIEGE OF SIDNEY STREET, THE(1960, Brit.); FIVE GOLDEN
HOURS(1961, Brit.); KONGA(1961, Brit.); PIT OF DARKNESS(1961, Brit.); SCREAM
OF FEAR(1961, Brit.); FREUD(1962); NUMBER SIX(1962, Brit.); STRAN-
GLEHOLD(1962, Brit.); AMOROUS ADVENTURES OF MOLL FLANDERS,
THE(1965); THUNDERBALL(1965, Brit.); PANIC(1966, Brit.); ONCE IS NOT
ENOUGH(1975)

Leslie S. Sachs
1984
FLAMINGO KID, THE(1984)

Robin Sachs
HENRY VIII AND HIS SIX WIVES(1972, Brit.); VAMPIRE CIRCUS(1972, Brit.)

Sharon Sachs
GREASER'S PALACE(1972), cos

Stephen Sachs
DORM THAT DRIPPED BLOOD, THE(1983)
Misc. Talkies
PRANKS(1982)

Steve Sachs
1984
PHILADELPHIA EXPERIMENT, THE(1984)

Tom Sachs
LADY VANISHES, THE(1980, Brit.), p

William Sachs
THERE IS NO 13(1977), p, d&w; FORCE BEYOND, THE(1978), d; INCREDIBLE
MELTING MAN, THE(1978), d&w; VAN NUYS BLVD.(1979), d&w; GALAXINA(1980),
d&w
1984
EXTERMINATOR 2(1984), p,d&w
Misc. Talkies
SOUTH OF HELL MOUNTAIN(1971), d

Leopold Sachse
INTERRUPTED MELODY(1955)

Margarete Sachse
JOHNNY STEALS EUROPE(1932, Ger.)

Salli Sachse
MUSCLE BEACH PARTY(1964); HOW TO STUFF A WILD BIKINI(1965); SER-
GEANT DEADHEAD(1965); SKI PARTY(1965); GHOST IN THE INVISIBLE BIKI-
NI(1966); DEVIL'S ANGELS(1967); MILLION EYES OF SU-MURU, THE(1967, Brit.);
TRIP, THE(1967); WILD IN THE STREETS(1968)

Sallie Sachse
FIREBALL 590(1966)

Sally Sachse
DR. GOLDFOOT AND THE BIKINI MACHINE(1965)

Monro Sachson
MC MASTERS, THE(1970), p

Monroe Sachson
PRETTY BOY FLOYD(1960), p; INCIDENT, THE(1967), p; SLAUGHTER(1972), p;
SLAUGHTER'S BIG RIP-OFF(1973), p

Kim Sachtler
NOT RECONCILED, OR "ONLY VIOLENCE HELPS WHERE IT RULES"(1969, Ger.)

Wendelin Sachtler
NOT RECONCILED, OR "ONLY VIOLENCE HELPS WHERE IT RULES"(1969,
Ger.), a, ph

Jessica Sack
SHOCK WAVES(1977), prod d; EYES OF A STRANGER(1980), art d

Nathanael Sack
Silents
MISTRESS NELL(1915)

Nathaniel Sack
Silents
SOCIAL SECRETARY, THE(1916); INNOCENT(1918)

Louis H. Sacken
MAN ON THE EIFFEL TOWER, THE(1949), ed
Jack Sacker
Silents
OLIVER TWIST(1916)
Joseph Sacket
WORM EATERS, THE(1981)
Janet Sackett
MRS. MIKE(1949); LONG, LONG TRAILER, THE(1954)
Judith Sackett
MRS. MIKE(1949)
Judy Sackett
LONG, LONG TRAILER, THE(1954)
Emanuel Sackey
HIPPODROME(1961, Aust./Ger.)
Jerry Sackheim
I CAN'T ESCAPE(1934), w; NOTORIOUS GENTLEMAN, A(1935), p; NOBODY'S
FOOL(1936), w; RICHEST MAN IN TOWN(1941), w; NIGHT BEFORE THE DIVORCE,
THE(1942), w; FATAL WITNESS, THE(1945), w; ROAD TO ALCATRAZ(1945), w;
LAST CROOKED MILE, THE(1946), w; UNDERCOVER WOMAN, THE(1946), w;
MAIN STREET KID, THE(1947), w; SADDLE PALS(1947), w; TRESPASSER,
THE(1947), w; HEART OF VIRGINIA(1948), w; ROOKIE FIREMAN(1950), w;
STRANGE DOOR, THE(1951), w; BLACK CASTLE, THE(1952), w; BOY AND THE
PIRATES, THE(1960), w; YOUNG JESSE JAMES(1960), w; CLOWN AND THE KID,
THE(1961), w
William Sackheim
SMART GIRLS DON'T TALK(1948), w; HOMICIDE(1949), w; ONE LAST
FLING(1949), w; BARRICADE(1950), w; REVENUE AGENT(1950), w; PURPLE
HEART DIARY(1951), w; REUNION IN RENO(1951), w; YANK IN KOREA, A(1951),
w; PAULA(1952), w; COLUMN SOUTH(1953), w; FORBIDDEN(1953), w; MAN IN
THE DARK(1953), w; SKY COMMANDO(1953), w; BORDER RIVER(1954), w; HU-
MAN JUNGLE, THE(1954), w; TANGANYIKA(1954), w; CHICAGO SYN-
DICATE(1955), w; ART OF LOVE, THE(1965), w; IN-LAWS, THE(1979), p;
COMPETITION, THE(1980), p, w; FIRST BLOOD(1982), w; SURVIVORS, THE(1983),
p
1984
NO SMALL AFFAIR(1984), p
William B. Sackheim
LET'S GO STEADY(1945), w; PERSONALITY KID(1946), w
William J. Sackheim
Silents
CAPTAIN JANUARY(1924), t
William R. Sackheim
MY DOG RUSTY(1948), w
Lou Sackin
REFORM GIRL(1933), ed; I CAN'T ESCAPE(1934), ed; CHAMPAGNE FOR BREAK-
FAST(1935), ed; BUNGALOW 13(1948), ed
Louis Sackin
DESPERATE TRAILS(1939), ed; OKLAHOMA FRONTIER(1939), ed; RIDERS OF
PASCO BASIN(1940), ed; EVE OF ST. MARK, THE(1944), ed; AVALANCHE(1946),
ed; RAILROADED(1947), ed; COBRA STRIKES, THE(1948), ed; NEW MEXICO(1951),
ed
Louis H. Sackin
SECRET WITNESS, THE(1931), ed; REPEAT PERFORMANCE(1947), ed; CANON
CITY(1948), ed; THREE HUSBANDS(1950), ed
Howard Sackler
MIDSUMMERS NIGHT'S DREAM, A(1961, Czech), d, w; GREAT WHITE HOPE,
THE(1970), w; JAWS(1975), w; GRAY LADY DOWN(1978), w; JAWS II(1978), w;
SAINT JACK(1979), w
Howard O. Sackler
FEAR AND DESIRE(1953), w; KILLER'S KISS(1955), w
Alan Sacks
1984
DUBEAT-E-O(1984), p&d, w
Bonnie Sacks
BATTLE OF LOVE'S RETURN, THE(1971)
Cy Sacks
Misc. Talkies
TOKOLOSHE(1973)
Ezra Sacks
FM(1978), w; SMALL CIRCLE OF FRIENDS, A(1980), w
Lee Sacks
FOG, THE(1980)
Michael Sacks
SLAUGHTERHOUSE-FIVE(1972); SUGARLAND EXPRESS, THE(1974); PRIVATE
FILES OF J. EDGAR HOOVER, THE(1978); AMITYVILLE HORROR, THE(1979);
HANOVER STREET(1979, Brit.); SPLIT IMAGE(1982)
1984
HOUSE OF GOD, THE(1984)
Misc. Talkies
HOUSE OF GOD, THE(1979)
Patti Sacks
MAN ABOUT TOWN(1939); COVER GIRL(1944)
Paulo Sacks
ALL NUDITY SHALL BE PUNISHED(1974, Brazil)
Ruth Buchanan Sacks
Silents
WOMAN'S MAN(1920), w
Gordon Sackville
Silents
ODYSSEY OF THE NORTH, AN(1914); ARIZONA CATCLAW, THE(1919); GIRL
WHO DARED, THE(1920); POLLYANNA(1920); DR. JIM(1921); SNOB, THE(1924)
Misc. Silents
PAY DIRT(1916); BEST MAN, THE(1917); PETTICOATS AND POLITICS(1918); LAW
THAT DIVIDES, THE(1919); ONE-WAY TRAIL, THE(1920); ANY NIGHT(1922); SLOW
AS LIGHTING(1923); COWBOY COURAGE(1925)
Glenn E. Sacos
Misc. Talkies
KNOCKING AT HEAVEN'S DOOR(1980)

Andree Sacre
ON VELVET(1938, Brit.)
Mauro Sacripante
TOO BAD SHE'S BAD(1954, Ital.); LUCKY TO BE A WOMAN(1955, Ital.)
Umberto Sacripante
ADVENTURE OF SALVATOR ROSA, AN(1940, Ital.); WAR AND PEACE(1956,
Ital./U.S.); GUILT IS NOT MINE(1968, Ital.)
Humbert Sacripanti
THIEF OF VENICE, THE(1952)
Umberto Sacripanti
FAREWELL TO ARMS, A(1957)
Gregorio Sacristan
SOUND OF HORROR(1966, Span.), p, w
Jose Sacristan
WOMAN WITH RED BOOTS, THE(1977, Fr./Span.)
Gracita Sacromonte
RETURN OF THE SEVEN(1966, Span.)
Keiji Sada
HUMAN CONDITION, THE(1959, Jap.); OHAYO(1962, Jap.); ROAD TO ETER-
NITY(1962, Jap.); LATE AUTUMN(1973, Jap.)
Yukata Sada
I LIVE IN FEAR(1967, Jap.)
Yutaka Sada
MAN AGAINST MAN(1961, Jap.); HIGH AND LOW(1963, Jap.); GODZILLA VS. THE
THING(1964, Jap.); DESTROY ALL MONSTERS(1969, Jap.); MOMENT OF TER-
ROR(1969, Jap.)
Michel Saddi
MARGIN, THE,(1969, Braz.), p
The Saddle Pals
WEST OF THE ALAMO(1946); SONG OF THE WASTELAND(1947)
Donald Saddler
BY THE LIGHT OF THE SILVERY MOON(1953), ch; HAPPY HOOKER, THE(1975),
ch
Francois [Marquis de] Sade
VICE AND VIRTUE(1965, Fr./Ital.), w
Robert Sadeoff
BAWDY ADVENTURES OF TOM JONES, THE(1976, Brit.), p
Michael Sadleir
MAN OF EVIL(1948, Brit.), w
Avril Sadler
IT'S A WONDERFUL WORLD(1956, Brit.); HAND OF NIGHT, THE(1968, Brit.)
Barry Sadler
DAYTON'S DEVILS(1968)
Bill Sadler
HANKY-PANKY(1982)
Dee Sadler
1984
LITTLE DRUMMER GIRL, THE(1984)
Dudley Sadler
BOOMERANG(1947); LONE STAR(1952)
Ian Sadler
SHIPBUILDERS, THE(1943, Brit.); I KNOW WHERE I'M GOING(1947, Brit.)
Iris Sadler
HALF A SIXPENCE(1967, Brit.)
James Sadler
GENTLE SEX, THE(1943, Brit.); SAN DEMETRIO, LONDON(1947, Brit.)
Josie Sadler
Misc. Silents
WHAT HAPPENED TO JONES(1915)
Kathryn Sadler
INTENT TO KILL(1958, Brit.)
Paul Sadler
SEPARATE PEACE, A(1972)
Winifred Sadler
Silents
ONCE ABOARD THE LUGGER(1920, Brit.); EDUCATION OF NICKY, THE(1921,
Brit.)
Misc. Silents
CHARITY ANN(1915, Brit.); MAN IN MOTLEY, THE(1916, Brit.)
the Sadler's Wells Ballet
MELBA(1953, Brit.)
The Sadlers Wells Chorus
TALES OF HOFFMANN, THE(1951, Brit.)
Kitty Sadock
HONKERS, THE(1972)
Fred Sadoff
QUIET AMERICAN, THE(1958); DEATHMASTER, THE(1972), p; POSEIDON AD-
VENTURE, THE(1972); CINDERELLA LIBERTY(1973); MARCO(1973); PAPIL-
LON(1973); TERMINAL MAN, THE(1974)
Martin Jay Sadoff
GRADUATION DAY(1981), ed
Jackqueline Sadoul
ORPHEUS(1950, Fr.), ed
Jacqueline Sadoul
LES PARENTS TERRIBLES(1950, Fr.), ed; FEMALE, THE(1960, Fr.), ed
G. Sadovnikova
HOUSE WITH AN ATTIC, THE(1964, USSR), ed
Felix Sadovsky
LAKE PLACID SERENADE(1944)
Krzysztof Sadowski
IDENTIFICATION MARKS: NONE(1969, Pol.), m
Isabelle Sadoyan
THAT OBSCURE OBJECT OF DESIRE(1977, Fr./Span.); RETURN OF MARTIN
GUERRE, THE(1983, Fr.)
Djamshid Sadri
CARAVANS(1978, U.S./Iranian)
Daniel Sadur
Misc. Talkies
SUGAR COOKIES(1973)

Maureen Sadusk
KNIGHTRIDERS(1981)
Golam H. Saedi
CYCLE, THE(1979, Iran), w
Yehye Saeed
PRIVATE ENTERPRISE, A(1975, Brit.)
James Saeger
PHONY AMERICAN, THE(1964, Ger.)
Roy Saeger
WOMAN IN THE WINDOW, THE(1945)
Mark Saegers
SEDUCERS, THE(1962)
Isamu Saeki
GAMERA VERSUS ZIGRA(1971, Jap.)
Anthony Saenz
SCARFACE(1983)
Armando Saenz
SIERRA BARON(1958); JET OVER THE ATLANTIC(1960); LOS AS-
TRONAUTAS(1960, Mex.)
Eddie Saenz
HOUSE OF STRANGERS(1949); ENCHANTED ISLAND(1958)
Fernando Saenz
1984
EVIL THAT MEN DO, THE(1984)
Ignacio Saenz
SOUTH OF TAHITI(1941); THIS WOMAN IS MINE(1941); SON OF FURY(1942)
Jose Saenz
ESCAPE TO BURMA(1955)
Eddie Saeta
DOCTOR DEATH: SEEKER OF SOULS(1973), p&d; MAN WITH BOGART'S FACE,
THE(1980), ed
Odd Geir Saether
EDVARD MUNCH(1976, Norway/Swed.), ph
Sylvia Saetre
DOWN OUR ALLEY(1939, Brit.)
Ali Safa
TARGET: HARRY(1980)
Amedeo Safa
CAMILLE 2000(1969), ed
Craig Safan
GREAT TEXAS DYNAMITE CHASE, THE(1976), m; BAD NEWS BEARS IN
BREAKING TRAINING, THE(1977), m; CORVETTE SUMMER(1978), m; GOOD
GUYS WEAR BLACK(1978), m; GREAT SMOKEY ROADBLOCK, THE(1978), m;
T.A.G.: THE ASSASSINATION GAME(1982), m; NIGHTMARES(1983), m
1984
ANGEL(1984), m; LAST STARFIGHTER, THE(1984), m
Vsevolod Safanov
HYPERBOLOID OF ENGINEER GARIN, THE(1965, USSR)
Aniko Safar
FATHER(1967, Hung.)
Willy Safar
LOULOU(1980, Fr.)
Sartoria Safas
LEOPARD, THE(1963, Ital.), cos
Mimi Saffian
HARRAD SUMMER, THE(1974); MURPH THE SURF(1974)
Emil Safier
GETTING EVEN(1981), p
Zepporah Safier
GETTING EVEN(1981), p
A. Safonov
HOUSE ON THE FRONT LINE, THE(1963, USSR)
V. Safonov
SONS AND MOTHERS(1967, USSR)
Vsevolod Safonov
OPTIMISTIC TRAGEDY, THE(1964, USSR)
Marya Safonova
LADY WITH THE DOG, THE(1962, USSR)
Michael Safra
ROYAL AFFAIR, A(1950), p; SCHEHERAZADE(1965, Fr./Ital./Span.), p
Michel Safra
PERSONAL COLUMN(1939, Fr.), p; BLIND DESIRE(1948, Fr.), p; JUST ME(1950,
Fr.), p; DIARY OF A BAD GIRL(1958, Fr.), p, w; MAGNIFICENT SINNER(1963,
Fr.), p; DIARY OF A CHAMBERMAID(1964, Fr./Ital.), p; DRAGON SKY(1964, Fr.), p;
DIABOLICAL DR. Z, THE(1966 Span./Fr.), p; GALIA(1966, Fr./Ital.), p
Yosef Safra
THEY WERE TEN(1961, Israel)
Dennis Safran
Misc. Talkies
SOLDIER NAMED JOE, A(1970)
Don Safran
HOMEWORK(1982), w
Henri Safran
STORM BOY(1976, Aus.), d; NORMAN LOVES ROSE(1982, Aus.), p, d&w; BUSH
CHRISTMAS(1983, Aus.), d; WILD DUCK, THE(1983, Aus.), d, w
Libuse Safrankova
DAY THAT SHOOK THE WORLD, THE(1977, Yugo./Czech.)
V. Safranov
MEN OF THE SEA(1938, USSR)
Al Safrata
1984
RENO AND THE DOC(1984, Can.)
Dennis Safren
Misc. Talkies
MEAN MOTHER(1974)
Michiko Saga
SAMURAI(PART III)**(1967, Jap.); HOTSPRINGS HOLIDAY(1970, Jap.)

Boris Sagal
DIME WITH A HALO(1963), d; TWILIGHT OF HONOR(1963), d; GUNS OF DIA-
BLO(1964), d; GIRL HAPPY(1965), d; MADE IN PARIS(1966), d; 1,000 PLANE RAID,
THE(1969), d; MOSQUITO SQUADRON(1970, Brit.), d; OMEGA MAN, THE(1971), d;
ANGELA(1977, Can.), d
D. Sagal
CHILDHOOD OF MAXIM GORKY(1938, Russ.); HEROES ARE MADE(1944, USSR)
Daniel Sagal
TARAS FAMILY, THE(1946, USSR)
Daniil Sagal
SONS AND MOTHERS(1967, USSR)
Dmitri Sagal
DAYS AND NIGHTS(1946, USSR)
Liz Sagal
GREASE 2(1982); FLASHDANCE(1983)
Jonathan Sagalle
1984
DRIFTING(1984, Israel); LITTLE DRUMMER GIRL, THE(1984)
Francoise Sagan
BONJOUR TRISTESSE(1958), w; CERTAIN SMILE, A(1958), w; GOODBYE
AGAIN(1961), w; TESTAMENT OF ORPHEUS, THE(1962, Fr.); LANDRU(1963, Fr./
Ital), w; PLAYTIME(1963, Fr.), w; NUTTY, NAUGHTY CHATEAU(1964, Fr./Ital.), w
Leontine Sagan
MAEDCHEN IN UNIFORM(1932, Ger.), d; MEN OF TOMORROW(1935, Brit.), d, ed;
SHOWTIME(1948, Brit.), d
Anthony Sagar
HELL, HEAVEN OR HOBOKEN(1958, Brit.); LAW AND DISORDER(1958, Brit.);
CARRY ON NURSE(1959, Brit.); PLEASE TURN OVER(1960, Brit.); CARRY ON
LOVING(1970, Brit.); VILLAIN(1971, Brit.); OFFENSE, THE(1973, Brit.)
Hisashi Sagara
HAHAKIRI(1963, Jap.), ed
Hishashi Sagara
TWIN SISTERS OF KYOTO(1964, Jap.), ed
G. Sagaradze
THEY WANTED PEACE(1940, USSR)
G. Sagardze
VOW, THE(1947, USSR.)
Byron Sage
COURAGE(1930); FURIES, THE(1930); ONE ROMANTIC NIGHT(1930)
Silents
OUT OF THE PAST(1927)
Delores Sage
1984
BIRDY(1984)
Foy Willing and The Riders of the Purple Sage
UNDER COLORADO SKIES(1947)
Frances Sage
WITHOUT ORDERS(1936); WITNESS CHAIR, THE(1936); MR. SKEFFING-
TON(1944)
Helen Sage
TEENAGERS FROM OUTER SPACE(1959)
Lee Sage
WITHOUT HONORS(1932), a, w
Margo Sage
OUR RELATIONS(1936)
Mavis Sage
MYSTERY ON BIRD ISLAND(1954, Brit.); STOLEN PLANS, THE(1962, Brit.)
Michael Sage
MISS SUSIE SLAGLE'S(1945)
Sally Sage
GIRLS ON PROBATION(1938); ESPIONAGE AGENT(1939); NAUGHTY BUT NI-
CE(1939); WOMEN IN THE WIND(1939); BROTHER RAT AND A BABY(1940); MEET
JOHN DOE(1941)
Willard Sage
NIAGARA(1953); DRAGNET(1954); BAR SINISTER, THE(1955); TENDER TRAP,
THE(1955); BRASS LEGEND, THE(1956); RACK, THE(1956); ZERO HOUR!(1957);
TIMBUKTU(1959); THAT TOUCH OF MINK(1962); FOR LOVE OR MONEY(1963);
COLOSSUS: THE FORBIN PROJECT(1969); DIRTY LITTLE BILLY(1972)
The Sagebrush Serenaders
MAN FROM RAINBOW VALLEY, THE(1946)
Anthony Sager
CARRY ON SERGEANT(1959, Brit.); NEXT TO NO TIME(1960, Brit.)
Cliff Sager
MAIDSTONE(1970)
George Sager
Misc. Talkies
LIFE AND LEGEND OF BUFFALO JONES, THE(1976); BUFFALO RIDER(1978)
Louis Sager
WAY OUT(1966)
Ray Sager
GIRL, THE BODY, AND THE PILL, THE(1967); JUST FOR THE HELL OF IT(1968);
WIZARD OF GORE, THE(1970); THIS STUFF'LL KILL YA!(1971); YEAR OF THE
YAHOO(1971)
1984
AMERICAN NIGHTMARE(1984), p
Misc. Talkies
JUST FOR THE HELL OF IT(1968)
Joanne Sages
SHADOWS(1960)
Bob Saget
SPACED OUT(1981, Brit.), w
Huguette Saget
ANTOINE ET ANTOINETTE(1947 Fr.)
Robert Saget
PEEK-A-BOO(1961, Fr.)
Roger Saget
HAPPY ROAD, THE(1957)

Charles Saggau
GANG'S ALL HERE, THE(1943); HOME IN INDIANA(1944); OUR HEARTS WERE GROWING UP(1946)
Saggy
MIND BENDERS, THE(1963, Brit.)
Sagiaktok
WHITE DAWN, THE(1974)
Salapata Sagigi
KING OF THE CORAL SEA(1956, Aus.)
Rick Sagliani
GUESS WHAT HAPPENED TO COUNT DRACULA(1970), makeup
Alexandre Sagols
OLIVE TREES OF JUSTICE, THE(1967, Fr.)
Thomas Sagone
BATTLE OF THE WORLDS(1961, Ital.), p
Enzo Bulgarelli,Luciano Sagoni
FIVE MAN ARMY, THE(1970, Ital.), cos
Frederica Sagor
Silents
PLASTIC AGE, THE(1925), w; ROLLED STOCKINGS(1927), w; SILK LEGS(1927), w
V. Sagovsky
GIRL IN THE PAINTING, THE(1948, Brit.), ed; CHRISTOPHER COLUMBUS(1949, Brit.), ed; ASTONISHED HEART, THE(1950, Brit.), ed; ADVENTURERS, THE(1951, Brit.), ed; APPOINTMENT IN LONDON(1953, Brit.), ed; SO LITTLE TIME(1953, Brit.), ed; GOLDEN MASK, THE(1954, Brit.), ed; THEY WHO DARE(1954, Brit.), ed; LAND OF THE PHARAOHS(1955), ed
Vladimir Sagovsky
EASY MONEY(1948, Brit.), ed; GOOD TIME GIRL(1950, Brit.), ed
Elena Sagrary
Misc. Silents
FIEVRE(1921, Fr.)
Allan Sague
HARBOR LIGHTS(1963)
John Sahag
EYES OF LAURA MARS(1978)
Jack Sahakian
IRMA LA DOUCE(1963); MOVE OVER, DARLING(1963)
Kenji Sahara
H-MAN, THE(1959, Jap.); MYSTERIANS, THE(1959, Jap.); MOTHRA(1962, Jap.); KING KONG VERSUS GODZILLA(1963, Jap.); ATTACK OF THE MUSHROOM PEOPLE(1964, Jap.); GODZILLA VS. THE THING(1964, Jap.); GHIDRAH, THE THREE-HEADED MONSTER(1965, Jap.); NONE BUT THE BRAVE(1965, U.S./Jap.); SON OF GODZILLA(1967, Jap.); DESTROY ALL MONSTERS(1969, Jap.); GODZILLA'S REVENGE(1969); SPACE AMOEBA, THE(1970, Jap.); WAR OF THE GARGANTUAS, THE(1970, Jap.); YOG-MONSTER FROM SPACE(1970, Jap.); GODZILLA VERSUS THE COSMIC MONSTER(1974, Jap.); MONSTERS FROM THE UNKNOWN PLANET(1975, Jap.)
Sahdji
SERPENTS OF THE PIRATE MOON, THE(1973)
Sally Sahee
CONSTANT HUSBAND, THE(1955, Brit.)
Louise Sahene
THERE'S ALWAYS VANILLA(1972)
Ron Sahewk
CRY OF THE BANSHEE(1970, Brit.)
Michael Sahl
BLOODSUCKING FREAKS(1982), m
1984
FAR FROM POLAND(1984), m
Mort Sahl
IN LOVE AND WAR(1958); ALL THE YOUNG MEN(1960); JOHNNY COOL(1963); DOCTOR, YOU'VE GOT TO BE KIDDING(1967); DON'T MAKE WAVES(1967)
1984
NOTHING LASTS FOREVER(1984)
William J. Sahlein
SMALL CIRCLE OF FRIENDS, A(1980); DOZENS, THE(1981)
Helmo Sahliger
CELESTE(1982, Ger.), ph
Bernard Sahlins
MONITORS, THE(1969), p
Doug Sahm
MORE AMERICAN GRAFFITI(1979)
Douglas Sahm
CISCO PIKE(1971)
Bhisham Sahni
1984
MOHAN JOSHI HAAZIR HO(1984, India)
Sonia Sahni
MAYA(1966)
Hans Sahnle
PHONY AMERICAN, THE(1964, Ger.), art d
Kishore Sahu
GUIDE, THE(1965, U.S./India)
Sai-Yu
SHARK WOMAN, THE(1941)
Anna Saia
BLACK BELLY OF THE TARANTULA, THE(1972, Ital.)
G. Saibulin
THREE DAYS OF VIKTOR TSCHERNIKOFF(1968, USSR)
Said
TABLE FOR FIVE(1983)
Fouad Said
RIGHT HAND OF THE DEVIL, THE(1963), ph; STRANGE LOVERS(1963), ph; THREE NUTS IN SEARCH OF A BOLT(1964), ph; ACROSS 110TH STREET(1972), p; HICKEY AND BOGGS(1972), p; DEADLY TRACKERS(1973), p; ALOHA, BOBBY AND ROSE(1975), p
Hassan Said
STANLEY AND LIVINGSTONE(1939); SAFARI(1940); SOUTH OF SUEZ(1940); SUNDOWN(1941); MACOMBER AFFAIR, THE(1947)

Joe Said
UP TO HIS EARS(1966, Fr./Ital.)
Shunji Saida
1984
WARRIORS OF THE WIND(1984, Jap.), anim
Morris Saidi
STIR(1980, Aus.)
Robert Saidreau
Misc. Silents
LE PREMIERE IDYLLE DE BOUCOT(1920, Fr.), d; MEFIEZ-VOUS DE VOTRE BONNE(1920, Fr.), d; LA PAIX CHEZ SOI(1921, Fr.), d; L'ETRANGE AVENTURE DU DOCTEUR WORKS(1921, Fr.), d; LA NUIT DE SAINT JEAN(1922, Fr.), d; LE BONHEUR CONJUGAL(1922, Fr.), d; COEUR LEGER(1923, Fr.), d; L'IDEE DE FRANCOISE(1923, Fr.), d; MA TANTE D'HONFLEUR(1923, Fr.), d; MONSIEUR LE DIRECTEUR(1924, Fr.), d; UN FIL A LA PATTE(1924, Fr.), d; UNE ETRAN-GERE(1924, Fr.), d; A LA GARE(1925, Fr.), d; JACK(1925, Fr.), d; LA CORDE AU COU(1926, Fr.), d
Fred Saidy
I DOOD IT(1943), w; MEET THE PEOPLE(1944), w; FINIAN'S RAINBOW(1968), w
Susan Saiger
EATING RAOUL(1982)
Al Saijo
THREE CAME HOME(1950)
Bobby Sailes
STAR IS BORN, A(1954)
Georges Saillard
J'ACCUSE(1939, Fr.)
Chuck Sailor
SUBSTITUTION(1970)
Toni Sailor
SKI FEVER(1969, U.S./Aust./Czech.)
Bella Starace Sainati
FURIA(1947, Ital.); CARMELA(1949, Ital.); DISILLUSION(1949, Ital.); BULLET FOR STEFANO(1950, Ital.)
Nina Sainclair
LE MONDE TREMBLERA(1939, Fr.)
Virendra Saini
1984
MOHAN JOSHI HAAZIR HO(1984, India), ph
Jon Sainken
MOUTH TO MOUTH(1978, Aus.), p
Claude Sainlouis
GREEN MARE, THE(1961, Fr./Ital.); HEAT OF THE SUMMER(1961, Fr.); HOT HOURS(1963, Fr.)
John Sainpolis
COQUETTE(1929); BAD ONE, THE(1930); THREE SISTERS, THE(1930); CAPTAIN THUNDER(1931)
Silents
ALL WOMAN(1918); CAPPY RICKS(1921); FOUR HORSEMEN OF THE APOCA-LYPSE, THE(1921); SHADOWS(1922); HELD TO ANSWER(1923); HERO, THE(1923); SOCIAL CODE, THE(1923); SOULS FOR SALE(1923); THREE WISE FOOLS(1923); ALASKAN, THE(1924); IN EVERY WOMAN'S LIFE(1924); ROSE OF PARIS, THE(1924); PHANTOM OF THE OPERA, THE(1925); FAR CRY, THE(1926); WHY BE GOOD?(1929)
Misc. Silents
SOLDIERS OF FORTUNE(1914); BONDWOMEN(1915); WORMWOOD(1915); SALA-MANDER, THE(1916); SOCIAL HIGHWAYMAN, THE(1916); WORLD AGAINST HIM, THE(1916); YELLOW PASSPORT, THE(1916); FORTUNES OF FIFI, THE(1917); LOVE THAT LIVES, THE(1917); MYSTIC HOUR, THE(1917); PUBLIC DEFENDER(1917); SAPHO(1917); SLEEPING FIRES(1917); LAUGHING BILL HYDE(1918); MONEY MAD(1918); RESURRECTION(1918); GREAT LOVER, THE(1920); PRINCE OF A KING, A(1923); UNTAMEABLE, THE(1923); WOMAN-PROOF(1923); MADEMOI-SELLE MIDNIGHT(1924); THREE WEEKS(1924); DIXIE HANDICAP, THE(1925); PAINT AND POWDER(1925)
John F. Sainpolis
Silents
SALAMANDER, THE(1915)
Delia Sainsbury
HALF A SIXPENCE(1967, Brit.)
Eddie Saint
WOMEN WITHOUT NAMES(1940)
Eva Marie Saint
ON THE WATERFRONT(1954); THAT CERTAIN FEELING(1956); HATFUL OF RAIN, A(1957); RAINTREE COUNTY(1957); NORTH BY NORTHWEST(1959); EX-ODUS(1960); ALL FALL DOWN(1962); SANDPIPER, THE(1965); 36 HOURS(1965); GRAND PRIX(1966); RUSSIANS ARE COMING, THE RUSSIANS ARE COMING, THE(1966); STALKING MOON, THE(1969); LOVING(1970); CANCEL MY RESERVA-TION(1972)
Jan Saint
TORTURE ME KISS ME(1970); BELIEVE IN ME(1971)
Arthur Saint Claire
DELINQUENT DAUGHTERS(1944), w
Monique Saint Clare
ADIOS GRINGO(1967, Ital./Fr./Span.)
George Saint George
ABDULLAH'S HAREM(1956, Brit./Egypt.), w
Susan Saint James
P.J.(1968); WHAT'S SO BAD ABOUT FEELING GOOD?(1968); WHERE ANGELS GO...TROUBLE FOLLOWS(1968); LOVE AT FIRST BITE(1979); HOW TO BEAT THE HIGH COST OF LIVING(1980); DON'T CRY, IT'S ONLY THUNDER(1982)
Tony Saint John
Misc. Talkies
SEVEN DOORS OF DEATH(1983)
Cecil Saint Laurent
DE L'AMOUR(1968, Fr./Ital.), a, w
Yves Saint Laurent
VERY SPECIAL FAVOR, A(1965), cos

Saint Luke's Choristers
MRS. PARKINGTON(1944)
John Saint Polis
REAP THE WILD WIND(1942)
John M. Saint Polis
MAGNIFICENT OBSESSION(1935)
Marcella Saint-Amant
POWER PLAY(1978, Brit./Can.)
Richard Saint-Bris
HIT(1973)
Richard Saint-Bris
THERESE(1963, Fr.); WHAT'S NEW, PUSSYCAT?(1965, U.S./Fr.)
Laurent Saint-Cyr
1984
SUGAR CANE ALLEY(1984, Fr.)
Renee Saint-Cyr
LE DENIER MILLIARDAIRE(1934, Fr.); STRANGE BOARDERS(1938, Brit.); SYM-
PHONIE FANTASTIQUE(1947, Fr.); MARKED GIRLS(1949, Fr.); SECRET DOCU-
MENT – VIENNA(1954, Fr.); IF PARIS WERE TOLD TO US(1956, Fr.);
LAFAYETTE(1963, Fr.)
Michel Saint-Denis
SECRET AGENT, THE(1936, Brit.)
Juliette Saint-Ginez
BRIDE IS MUCH TOO BEAUTIFUL, THE(1958, Fr.), w
Daniel Saint-Hamon
1984
PAR OU T'ES RENTRE? ON T'A PAS VUE SORTIR(1984, Fr./Tunisia), w
Saint-Iles
LOWER DEPTHS, THE(1937, Fr.)
Henri Saint-Isles
CRIME OF MONSIEUR LANGE, THE(1936, Fr.)
Guy Saint-Jean
LIFE UPSIDE DOWN(1965, Fr.); KILLING GAME, THE(1968, Fr.)
Cecil Saint-Laurent
LUCRECE BORGIA(1953, Ital./Fr.), w; MATA HARI'S DAUGHTER(1954, Fr./Ital),
w; FROU-FROU(1955, Fr.), w; LOLA MONTES(1955, Fr./Ger.), w; CAROLINE CHER-
IE(1968, Fr.), w
Francoise Saint-Laurent
FRUIT IS RIPE, THE(1961, Fr./Ital.)
Yves Saint-Laurent
NEW KIND OF LOVE, A(1963), cos; LIVE FOR LIFE(1967, Fr./Ital.), cos
Xavier Saint-Macary
MEN PREFER FAT GIRLS(1981, Fr.); CONFIDENTIALLY YOURS(1983, Fr.)
Saint-Saens
RULES OF THE GAME, THE(1939, Fr.), m; FRENCH WAY, THE(1975, Fr.), m
Lucile Saint-Simon
HANDS OF ORLAC, THE(1964, Brit./Fr.); HORROR CASTLE(1965, Ital.); WOMEN
AND WAR(1965, Fr.)
Raoul Saint-Yves
NIGHT AFFAIR(1961, Fr.)
Buffy Sainte-Marie
SPIRIT OF THE WIND(1979), m
Carlos Saintes
BREAKING AWAY(1979)
Louis Sainteve
FORBIDDEN GAMES(1953, Fr.)
Monique Saintey
LOVE IN THE AFTERNOON(1957)
Loudon Sainthill
MAN WHO LOVED REDHEADS, THE(1955, Brit.), cos
H.A. Saintsbury
Misc. Silents
VALLEY OF FEAR, THE(1916, Brit.)
Kathleen Saintsbury
SEPARATION(1968, Brit.)
Marcia Saintz
DOUBLE-BARRELLED DETECTIVE STORY, THE(1965)
Claude Sainval
CARNIVAL IN FLANDERS(1936, Fr.); MURIEL(1963, Fr./Ital.)
Tina Sainz
SAGA OF DRACULA, THE(1975, Span.)
Jose Sainz de Vicuna
MURIETA(1965, Span.), p
David Saire
VIOLENT STRANGER(1957, Brit.); OPERATION CUPID(1960, Brit.); LOSS OF
INNOCENCE(1961, Brit.); RATTLE OF A SIMPLE MAN(1964, Brit.); SECRET OF
BLOOD ISLAND, THE(1965, Brit.)
Warren Saire
MONSTER CLUB, THE(1981, Brit.)
Marian Sais
ENEMY OF WOMEN(1944)
Marin Sais
FIGHTING COWBOY(1933); WHEELS OF DESTINY(1934); CIRCLE OF
DEATH(1935); TRAILING TROUBLE(1937); PHANTOM GOLD(1938); PIONEER
TRAIL(1938); RIDERS OF THE FRONTIER(1939); FIVE LITTLE PEPPERS AT
HOME(1940); MAD EMPRESS, THE(1940); BILLY THE KID IN SANTA FE(1941);
CRACKED NUTS(1941); SADDLEMATES(1941); SIERRA SUE(1941); TWO GUN
SHERIFF(1941); FRONTIER OUTLAWS(1944); BORDER BADMEN(1945); LIGHT-
NING RAIDERS(1945); RENDEZVOUS 24(1946); TERRORS ON HORSEBACK(1946);
RIDE, RYDER, RIDE!(1949); ROLL, THUNDER, ROLL!(1949); FIGHTING REDHEAD,
THE(1950); GREAT JESSE JAMES RAID, THE(1953)
Silents
MEASURE OF A MAN, THE(1924)
Misc. Silents
PITFALL, THE(1915); CITY OF DIM FACE, THE(1918); HIS BIRTHRIGHT(1918);
BONDS OF HONOR(1919); GRAY WOLF'S GHOST, THE(1919); DEAD OR ALI-
VE(1921); SHERIFF OF HOPE ETERNAL, THE(1921); RIDERS OF THE LAW(1922);
GOOD MEN AND BAD(1923); BEHIND TWO GUNS(1924); ROARING ADVENTURE,
A(1925); WILD HORSE STAMPEDE, THE(1926); FIGHTING THREE, THE(1927); MEN
OF DARING(1927); SON OF THE DESERT, A(1928)

Tatjana Sais
ARENT WE WONDERFUL?(1959, Ger.)
Bill Saito
HONG KONG CONFIDENTIAL(1958); BLOOD AND STEEL(1959); GREEN MAN-
SIONS(1959); WRECKING CREW, THE(1968); ROLLERCOASTER(1977)
1984
ALL OF ME(1984)
Haruhiko Saito
ALMOST TRANSPARENT BLUE(1980, Jap.)
Ichiro Saito
UGETSU(1954, Jap.), m; GOLDEN DEMON(1956, Jap.), m; WOMEN IN PRI-
SON(1957, Jap.), m; WAYSIDE PEBBLE, THE(1962, Jap.), m; LIFE OF OHARU(1964,
Jap.), m; YEARNING(1964, Jap.), m, art d; GEISHA, A(1978, Jap.), m
James Saito
1984
ADVENTURES OF BUCKAROO BANZAI: ACROSS THE 8TH DIMENSION,
THE(1984); HOT DOG...THE MOVIE(1984)
Koichi Saito
WHISPERING JOE(1969, Jap.), p,d,w,ph&m
Kosei Saito
TIME SLIP(1981, Jap.), d
Kozo Saito
SANJURO(1962, Jap.), ph
Masami Saito
M(1970)
Niwa Saito
CHILDREN OF HIROSHIMA(1952, Jap.)
Noritake Saito
SPACE AMOEBA, THE(1970, Jap.); YOG-MONSTER FROM SPACE(1970, Jap.)
Ryosuke Saito
SNOW COUNTRY(1969, Jap.), w
Shiko Saito
GOLDEN DEMON(1956, Jap.)
T. Saito
IDIOT, THE(1963, Jap.), ed
Taizo Saito
TOKYO STORY(1972, Jap.), cos
Takanobu Saito
FLOATING WEEDS(1970, Jap.), m; LATE AUTUMN(1973, Jap.), m
Takanori Saito
TOKYO STORY(1972, Jap.), m
Takao Saito
HIGH AND LOW(1963, Jap.), ph; LEGACY OF THE 500,000, THE(1964, Jap.), ph;
RED BEARD(1966, Jap.), ph; KOJIRO(1967, Jap.), ph; MAD ATLANTIC, THE(1967,
Jap.), ph; DODESKA-DEN(1970, Jap.), ph; RED LION(1971, Jap.), ph; KAGEMU-
SHA(1980, Jap.), ph
Tatsuo Saito
TOKYO FILE 212(1951); GEISHA GIRL(1952); THREE STRIPES IN THE SUN(1955);
ESCAPADE IN JAPAN(1957); JOE BUTTERFLY(1957); MY GEISHA(1962); LORD
JIM(1965, Brit.); THREE WEEKS OF LOVE(1965)
Misc. Silents
YOUNG MISS(1930, Jap.); CHORUS OF TOKYO(1931, Jap.); I WAS BORN,
BUT...(1932, Jap.)
William Saito
WALK, DON'T RUN(1966)
Yonejiro Saito
GAMERA THE INVINCIBLE(1966, Jap.), p, w; PASSION(1968, Jap.), p
Ted Saizis
LOST, LONELY AND VICIOUS(1958), ph; WE SHALL RETURN(1963), ph; SHE-
PHERD OF THE HILLS, THE(1964), ph; INTIMACY(1966), ph; BRIGHTY OF THE
GRAND CANYON(1967), ph; DELTA FACTOR, THE(1970), ph
Vince Saizis
DELTA FACTOR, THE(1970), ph
Vincent Saizis
LOST, LONELY AND VICIOUS(1958), ph; WE SHALL RETURN(1963), ph; SHE-
PHERD OF THE HILLS, THE(1964), ph; INTIMACY(1966), ph; BRIGHTY OF THE
GRAND CANYON(1967), ph; RAVAGERS, THE(1979), ph
Kan Saji
FORT GRAVEYARD(1966, Jap.), w
1984
ANTARCTICA(1984, Jap.), w
Keiko Sajita
JUDO SHOWDOWN(1966, Jap.)
Sol Sak
WALK, DON'T RUN(1966), w
Tsuyoshi Saka
TORA! TORA! TORA!(1970, U.S./Jap.), tech adv
Hisako Sakabe
YOUTH AND HIS AMULET, THE(1963, Jap.)
Branimir Sakac
NINTH CIRCLE, THE(1961, Yugo.), m
Yasushi Sakagami
GAMERA VERSUS ZIGRA(1971, Jap.)
Minako Sakaguchi
GIRL I ABANDONED, THE(1970, Jap.)
Seiji Sakaguchi
FORCED VENGEANCE(1982)
Frankie Sakai
DIPLOMAT'S MANSION, THE(1961, Jap.); LAST WAR, THE(1962, Jap.); CHUSHIN-
GURA(1963, Jap.); THIS MADDING CROWD(1964, Jap.); TOPSY-TURVY JOUR-
NEY(1970, Jap.); YOSAKOI JOURNEY(1970, Jap.); MASTERMIND(1977)
Franky Sakai
MOTHRA(1962, Jap.); SNOW IN THE SOUTH SEAS(1963, Jap.)
Sachio Sakai
SAMURAI(PART II)** (1967, Jap.); GODZILLA, RING OF THE MONSTERS(1956,
Jap.); DANGEROUS KISS, THE(1961, Jap.); SECRET OF THE TELEGIAN, THE(1961,
Jap.); WESTWARD DESPERADO(1961, Jap.); TATSU(1962, Jap.); YOG-MONSTER
FROM SPACE(1970, Jap.)

Pierre L. Salas
CURSE OF THE VAMPIRES(1970, Phil., U.S.), w

Yolanda Salas
GIANT GILA MONSTER, THE(1959)

Paul Salata
ANGELS IN THE OUTFIELD(1951); KID FROM LEFT FIELD, THE(1953); EGYPTIAN. THE(1954)

Paul T. Salata
STALAG 17(1953); JOKER IS WILD, THE(1957)

Neomie Salatich
GIRL IN TROUBLE(1963)

Abel Salazar
VAMPIRE'S COFFIN, THE(1958, Mex.), a, p; WITCH'S MIRROR, THE(1960, Mex.), p; MAN AND THE MONSTER, THE(1965, Mex.), a, p, w; VAMPIRE, THE(1968, Mex.), a, p; CURSE OF THE CRYING WOMAN, THE(1969, Mex.), a, p; LIVING HEAD, THE(1969, Mex.), a, p

Alfredo Salazar
AZTEC MUMMY, THE(1957, Mex.), s; INVISIBLE MAN, THE(1958, Mex.), w; FRANKENSTEIN, THE VAMPIRE AND CO.(1961, Mex.), w; DOCTOR OF DOOM(1962, Mex.), w; ATTACK OF THE MAYAN MUMMY(1963, U.S./Mex.), w; CURSE OF THE AZTEC MUMMY, THE(1965, Mex.), w; ROBOT VS. THE AZTEC MUMMY, THE(1965, Mex.), w; CURSE OF THE DOLL PEOPLE, THE(1968, Mex.), w; NIGHT OF THE BLOODY APES(1968, Mex.), p

Angel Salazar
WALK PROUD(1979); SCARFACE(1983)
1984
WILD LIFE, THE(1984)

Carlos Salazar
THUNDER BELOW(1932); IN CALIENTE(1935); PROJECT: KILL(1976)

Rafael Salazar
MURIETA(1965, Span.), art d; GUNS OF THE MAGNIFICENT SEVEN(1969), set d; CANNON FOR CORDOBA(1970), set d; VALDEZ IS COMING(1971), set d; RED SUN(1972, Fr./Ital./Span.), set d

Rita Salazar
1984
COUNTRY(1984), cos

Luciano Salce
TOTO IN THE MOON(1957, Ital./Span.); HERCULES' PILLS(1960, Ital.), d, w; CRAZY DESIRE(1964, Ital.), a, d, w; FASCIST, THE(1965, Ital.), a, d, w; HIGH INFIDELITY(1965, Fr./Ital.), d; HOURS OF LOVE, THE(1965, Ital.), a, d, w; LITTLE NUNS, THE(1965, Ital.), d; EL GRECO(1966, Ital., Fr.), d, w; KISS THE OTHER SHEIK(1968, Fr./Ital.), a, d, w; QUEENS, THE(1968, Ital./Fr.), d; THREE TOUGH GUYS(1974, U.S./Ital.); DUCH IN ORANGE SAUCE(1976, Ital.), d

Felisa Salcedo
CRY OF BATTLE(1963), cos; MAD DOCTOR OF BLOOD ISLAND, THE(1969, Phil./U.S.)

Jose Salcedo
SABINA, THE(1979, Span./Swed.), ed
1984
DEMONS IN THE GARDEN(1984, Span.), ed

Leopoldo Salcedo
W.I.A.(WOUNDED IN ACTION) (1966); LOST BATTALION(1961, U.S./Phil.); CRY OF BATTLE(1963); RAIDERS OF LEYTE GULF(1963 U.S./Phil.); MISSION BATANGAS(1968)
Misc. Talkies
BEAST OF THE YELLOW NIGHT(1971, U.S./Phil.)

Paquito Salcedo
MORO WITCH DOCTOR(1964, U.S./Phil.); MAD DOCTOR OF BLOOD ISLAND, THE(1969, Phil./U.S.); CURSE OF THE VAMPIRES(1970, Phil., U.S.); LOSERS, THE(1970); DAUGHTERS OF SATAN(1972)

Ralph S. Salcido
1984
CANNONBALL RUN II(1984)

Theresa Saldana
I WANNA HOLD YOUR HAND(1978); NUNZIO(1978); DEFIANCE(1980); RAGING BULL(1980)
1984
EVIL THAT MEN DO, THE(1984)

Raul Faustino Saldanha
BOYS FROM BRAZIL, THE(1978)

Iris Salder
MRS. BROWN, YOU'VE GOT A LOVELY DAUGHTER(1968, Brit.)

Susan Saldivar
LOSIN' IT(1983)

Peter Saldutti
STRANGE BEDFELLOWS(1965), cos
1984
RIVER RAT, THE(1984), cos

Charles "Chic" Sale
STAR WITNESS(1931); EXPERT, THE(1932); STRANGER IN TOWN(1932); CHIEF, THE(1933); MEN OF AMERICA(1933); TREASURE ISLAND(1934); ROCKY MOUNTAIN MYSTERY(1935); GENTLEMAN FROM LOUISIANA(1936); IT'S A GREAT LIFE(1936); YOU ONLY LIVE ONCE(1937)
Misc. Silents
HIS NIBS(1921); NEW SCHOOL TEACHER, THE(1924)

Chic Sale
FELLER NEEDS A FRIEND(1932); LUCKY DOG(1933); MAN HUNT(1936); MAN I MARRY, THE(1936)

David Sale
NO. 96(1974, Aus.), w

Fred Sale
MIDSUMMER'S NIGHT'S DREAM, A(1935)

Fred Sale, Jr.
WHEELS OF DESTINY(1934)

Irene Sale
SWINGIN' SUMMER, A(1965)

Richard Sale
FIND THE WITNESS(1937), w; STRANGE CARGO(1940), w; RENDEZVOUS WITH ANNIE(1946), a, w; CALENDAR GIRL(1947), w; DRIFTWOOD(1947), w; NORTHWEST OUTPOST(1947), w; SPOILERS OF THE NORTH(1947), d; CAMPUS HONEY-MOON(1948), d, w, m; DUDE GOES WEST, THE(1948), w; INSIDE STORY, THE(1948), w; LADY AT MIDNIGHT(1948), w; FATHER WAS A FULLBACK(1949), w; MOTHER IS A FRESHMAN(1949), w; MR. BELVEDERE GOES TO COLLEGE(1949), w; I'LL GET BY(1950), d, w; THIS SIDE OF THE LAW(1950), w; TICKET TO TOMAHAWK(1950), d, w; WHEN WILLIE COMES MARCHING HOME(1950), w; HALF ANGEL(1951), d; LET'S MAKE IT LEGAL(1951), d; MEET ME AFTER THE SHOW(1951), d, w; MY WIFE'S BEST FRIEND(1952), d; GIRL NEXT DOOR, THE(1953), d; LET'S DO IT AGAIN(1953), w; FIRE OVER AFRICA(1954, Brit.), d; FRENCH LINE, THE(1954), w; SUDDENLY(1954), w; WOMAN'S WORLD(1954), w; GENTLEMEN MARRY BRUNETTES(1955), p, d, w; OVER-EXPOSED(1956), w; ABANDON SHIP(1957, Brit.), d&w; TORPEDO RUN(1958), w; OSCAR, THE(1966), w; WHITE BUFFALO, THE(1977), w

Richard B. Sale
SHADOWS OVER SHANGHAI(1938), w

Virginia Sale
FANCY BAGGAGE(1929); BACK PAY(1930); DUDE WRANGLER, THE(1930); EMBARRASSING MOMENTS(1930); LOVIN' THE LADIES(1930); MOBY DICK(1930); SHOW GIRL IN HOLLYWOOD(1930); BIG BUSINESS GIRL(1931); BRIGHT LIGHTS(1931); GOLD DUST GERTIE(1931); HER MAJESTY LOVE(1931); MANY A SLIP(1931); MY PAST(1931); SECRET SERVICE(1931); TOO YOUNG TO MARRY(1931); FIREMAN, SAVE MY CHILD(1932); MAN WANTED(1932); THOSE WE LOVE(1932); UNION DEPOT(1932); BACHELOR MOTHER(1933); IRON MASTER, THE(1933); OLIVER TWIST(1933); EMBARRASSING MOMENTS(1934); MADAME DU BARRY(1934); MAN WITH TWO FACES, THE(1934); REGISTERED NURSE(1934); SMARTY(1934); AFTER THE DANCE(1935); IT'S A SMALL WORLD(1935); WE'RE IN THE MONEY(1935); THREE MEN ON A HORSE(1936); ANGEL'S HOLIDAY(1937); DANGEROUS HOLIDAY(1937); LIVE, LOVE AND LEARN(1937); MEET THE MISSUS(1937); OUTCAST(1937); TOPPER(1937); TROUBLE AT MIDNIGHT(1937); WE HAVE OUR MOMENTS(1937); HIS EXCITING NIGHT(1938); JURY'S SECRET, THE(1938); LADY FROM KENTUCKY, THE(1939); LITTLE ACCIDENT(1939); WHEN TOMORROW COMES(1939); CALLING ALL HUSBANDS(1940); DOCTOR TAKES A WIFE(1940); FLOWING GOLD(1940); GOLD RUSH MAISIE(1940); HOWARDS OF VIRGINIA, THE(1940); I CAN'T GIVE YOU ANYTHING BUT LOVE, BABY(1940); STRIKE UP THE BAND(1940); FLAME OF NEW ORLEANS, THE(1941); SKYLARK(1941); BIG SHOT, THE(1942); HARVARD, HERE I COME(1942); MISS ANNIE ROONEY(1942); PITTSBURGH(1942); THEY DIED WITH THEIR BOOTS ON(1942); DESTROYER(1943); GANG'S ALL HERE, THE(1943); HERS TO HOLD(1943); HIT THE ICE(1943); REVEILLE WITH BEVERLY(1943); DARK MOUNTAIN(1944); Hl BEAUTIFUL(1944); HEAVENLY DAYS(1944); JANIE(1944); THIN MAN GOES HOME, THE(1944); TOGETHER AGAIN(1944); WHEN STRANGERS MARRY(1944); DANGER SIGNAL(1945); HER HIGHNESS AND THE BELLBOY(1945); HER LUCKY NIGHT(1945); OUT OF THIS WORLD(1945); RHAPSODY IN BLUE(1945); SHE GETS HER MAN(1945); BADMAN'S TERRITORY(1946); NIGHT AND DAY(1946); TRAIL STREET(1947); ONE MAN'S WAY(1964); BIG DADDY(1969); SLITHER(1973); HOW TO SUCCEED IN BUSINESS WITHOUT REALLY TRYING(1976)
Misc. Talkies
SMOKE LIGHTNING(1933)
Silents
FLOATING COLLEGE, THE(1928); HAROLD TEEN(1928); MIDNIGHT MADNESS(1928); KID'S CLEVER, THE(1929)
Misc. Silents
LEGIONNAIRES IN PARIS(1927)

Abdel Khalek Saleh
CAIRO(1963)

Eva Saleh
SAVAGES(1972)

El Hedi Ben Salem
FEAR EATS THE SOUL(1974, Ger.); JAIL BAIT(1977, Ger.)

George Salem
SILENT WITNESS, THE(1962)

Ibrahim Salem
MOHAMMAD, MESSENGER OF GOD(1976, Lebanon/Brit.), ph

Kario Salem
SOME KIND OF HERO(1982)

Lionel Salem
L'AGE D'OR(1979, Fr.)

Murray Salem
SPY WHO LOVED ME, THE(1977, Brit.)

Pamela Salem
GREAT TRAIN ROBBERY, THE(1979, Brit.); NEVER SAY NEVER AGAIN(1983)

Sarah Salem
CIRCLE OF DECEIT(1982, Fr./Ger.)

Gianfranco Salemi
NIGHT OF THE SHOOTING STARS, THE(1982, Ital.)

Harold Salemson
NUN, THE(1971, Fr.), titles

Laura Salenger
MY BODYGUARD(1980)

Marilyn Salenger
HERO AT LARGE(1980)

Laura Salerni
LOVE IN MOROCCO(1933, Fr.)

Anna Maria Salerno
LA DOLCE VITA(1961, Ital./Fr.)

Charlene Salerno
GAY SISTERS, THE(1942); ADVENTURES OF MARK TWAIN, THE(1944)

Charles Salerno
SHE WENT TO THE RACES(1945), ph; ARNELO AFFAIR, THE(1947), ph; UNDERCOVER MAISIE(1947), ph

Charles Salerno, Jr.
BARBARY COAST GENT(1944), ph; GENTLE ANNIE(1944), ph; NOTHING BUT TROUBLE(1944), ph; BEWITCHED(1945), ph; BOYS' RANCH(1946), ph; FAITHFUL IN MY FASHION(1946), ph

Enrico Maria Salerno
ANGEL WORE RED, THE(1960); ASSASSIN, THE(1961, Ital./Fr.); VIOLENT SUMMER(1961, Fr./Ital.); NUDE ODYSSEY(1962, Fr./Ital.); SIEGE OF SYRACUSE(1962, Fr./Ital.); HERCULES AND THE CAPTIVE WOMEN(1963, Fr./Ital.); OF WAYWARD LOVE(1964, Ital./Ger.); BACKFIRE(1965, Fr.); CASANOVA '70(1965, Ital.); GOSPEL ACCORDING TO ST. MATTHEW, THE(1966, Fr., Ital.); LA FUGA(1966, Ital.); SIX

DAYS A WEEK(1966, Fr./Ital./Span.); BANDIDOS(1967, Ital.); DEATH SENTEN-
CE(1967, Ital.); WEEKEND, ITALIAN STYLE(1967, Fr./Ital./Span.); CANDY(1968,
Ital./Fr.); OLDEST PROFESSION, THE(1968, Fr./Ital./Ger.); QUEENS, THE(1968,
Ital./Fr.); THREE NIGHTS OF LOVE(1969, Ital.); BIRD WITH THE CRYSTAL
PLUMAGE, THE(1970, Ital./Ger.); ANONYMOUS VENETIAN, THE(1971), d, w; AS-
SASSINATION OF TROTSKY, THE(1972 Fr./Ital.)

Enriso Maria Salerno
WARRIOR EMPRESS, THE(1961, Ital./Fr.)

Giambattista Salerno
TIGER AND THE PUSSYCAT, THE(1967, U.S., Ital.)

Henry F. Salerno
FOUR FAST GUNS(1959), ed

Jay Salerno
NEW YORK, NEW YORK(1977)

Thea Salerno
EASY RIDER(1969)

Clifford Sales
NAKED CITY, THE(1948)

Francis Sales
PRIDE OF THE YANKEES, THE(1942); TAKE A LETTER, DARLING(1942)

Gary Sales
MADMAN(1982), p, m

Michel Sales
IS PARIS BURNING?(1966, U.S./Fr.)

Nancy Sales
DAY OF THE ANIMALS(1977), cos

Robin Sales
1984
FOUR DAYS IN JULY(1984), ed

Sammy Sales
BLOODY BROOD, THE(1959, Can.); ONE PLUS ONE(1961, Can.)

Soupy Sales
TWO LITTLE BEARS, THE(1961); BIRDS DO IT(1966)

Virginia Sales
LOVE PAST THIRTY(1934); MARRYING WIDOWS(1934)

Pierre Salet
BIRD WATCH, THE(1983, Fr.), art d

Frank R. Saletri
BLACKENSTEIN(1973), p, w

John Salew
CONTINENTAL EXPRESS(1939, Brit.); SAILOR'S DON'T CARE(1940, Brit.); MAIL
TRAIN(1941, Brit.); NEUTRAL PORT(1941, Brit.); ONCE A CROOK(1941, Brit.);
TURNED OUT NICE AGAIN(1941, Brit.); BACK ROOM BOY(1942, Brit.); LADY IN
DISTRESS(1942, Brit.); ONE OF OUR AIRCRAFT IS MISSING(1942, Brit.); YOUNG
MR. PITT, THE(1942, Brit.); MILLIONS LIKE US(1943, Brit.); NIGHT INVADER,
THE(1943, Brit); SAINT MEETS THE TIGER, THE(1943, Brit.); SQUADRON LEADER
X(1943, Brit.); SUSPECTED PERSON(1943, Brit.); WARN THAT MAN(1943, Brit.); WE
DIVE AT DAWN(1943, Brit.); DON'T TAKE IT TO
HEART(1944, Brit.); GIVE US THE MOON(1944, Brit.); SECRET MISSION(1944, Brit.);
TIME FLIES(1944, Brit.); NOTORIOUS GENTLEMAN(1945, Brit.); QUERY(1945, Brit.);
WAY AHEAD, THE(1945, Brit.); ADVENTURESS, THE(1946, Brit.); BEDELIA(1946,
Brit.); CARAVAN(1946, Brit.); GIRL IN A MILLION, A(1946, Brit.); MURDER IN
REVERSE(1946, Brit.); WANTED FOR MURDER(1946, Brit.); DANCING WITH
CRIME(1947, Brit.); MEET ME AT DAWN(1947, Brit.); NICHOLAS NICKLEBY(1947,
Brit.); TAWNY PIPIT(1947, Brit.); ANNA KARENINA(1948, Brit.); COUNTER
BLAST(1948, Brit.); DEVIL'S PLOT, THE(1948, Brit.); DULCIMER STREET(1948, Brit.);
OCTOBER MAN, THE(1948, Brit.); ALL OVER THE TOWN(1949, Brit.); BAD LORD
BYRON, THE(1949, Brit.); CARDBOARD CAVALIER, THE(1949, Brit.); DARK SE-
CRET(1949, Brit.); DIAMOND CITY(1949, Brit.); DON'T EVER LEAVE ME(1949, Brit.);
FOR THEM THAT TRESPASS(1949, Brit.); IT ALWAYS RAINS ON SUNDAY(1949,
Brit.); KIND HEARTS AND CORONETS(1949, Brit.); MY BROTHER JONA-
THAN(1949, Brit.); NO WAY BACK(1949, Brit.); QUARTET(1949, Brit.); TEMPTATION
HARBOR(1949, Brit.); SILK NOOSE, THE(1950, Brit.); TWENTY QUESTIONS MUR-
DER MYSTERY, THE(1950, Brit.); GREEN GROW THE RUSHES(1951, Brit.); HOTEL
SAHARA(1951, Brit.); INHERITANCE, THE(1951, Brit.); LAVENDER HILL MOB,
THE(1951, Brit.); MYSTERY JUNCTION(1951, Brit.); NIGHT WAS OUR FRIEND(1951,
Brit.); NO HIGHWAY IN THE SKY(1951, Brit.); HIS EXCELLENCY(1952, Brit.); MR.
LORD SAYS NO(1952, Brit.); SPIDER AND THE FLY, THE(1952, Brit.); BLACK
GLOVE(1954, Brit.); DETECTIVE, THE(1954, Qit.); DUEL IN THE JUNGLE(1954,
Brit.); LEASE OF LIFE(1954, Brit.); RED DRESS, THE(1954, Brit.); THREE CASES OF
MURDER(1955, Brit.); IT'S GREAT TO BE YOUNG(1956, Brit.); ROGUE'S YARN(1956,
Brit.); ALIVE ON SATURDAY(1957, Brit.); GOOD COMPANIONS, THE(1957, Brit.);
PORTRAIT IN SMOKE(1957, Brit.); CURSE OF THE DEMON(1958); GYPSY AND THE
GENTLEMAN, THE(1958, Brit.); LEFT, RIGHT AND CENTRE(1959); TREAD SOFTLY
STRANGER(1959, Brit.); SHAKEDOWN, THE(1960, Brit.); THREE ON A SPREE(1961,
Brit.); TOO HOT TO HANDLE(1961, Brit.); ALIVE AND KICKING(1962, Brit.);
IMPERSONATOR, THE(1962, Brit.)

Amedeo Salfa
LITTLE MOTHER(1973, U.S./Yugo./Ger.), ed; GOODNIGHT, LADIES AND GEN-
TLEMEN(1977, Ital.), ed; GIRL FROM TRIESTE, THE(1983, Ital.), ed
1984
NOSTALGHIA(1984, USSR/Ital.), ed

Heinz Salfner
SHOT AT DAWN, A(1934, Ger.)

Maria Rosa Salgado
IT HAPPENED IN BROAD DAYLIGHT(1960, Ger./Switz.)

Marian Salgado
DEMON WITCH CHILD(1974, Span.)

Emilio Salgari
SON OF THE RED CORSAIR(1963, Ital.), w; SANDOKAN THE GREAT(1964,
Fr./Ital./Span.), w; MYSTERY OF THUG ISLAND, THE(1966, Ital./Ger.), w

Emillio Salgari
MYSTERY OF THE BLACK JUNGLE(1955), w

Andre Salgues
GODSON, THE(1972, Ital./Fr.)

Charles Saliba
TRENCHCOAT(1983)

Paul Saliba
DON QUIXOTE(1973, Aus.)

Lucette Salibur
1984
SUGAR CANE ALLEY(1984, Fr.)

Edward Salier
ALICE, SWEET ALICE(1978), ed; KIRLIAN WITNESS, THE(1978), ed; ROLLER
BOOGIE(1979), ed; SILENT SCREAM(1980), ed; LUNCH WAGON(1981), ed; BOXOF-
FICE(1982), ed; SLAYER, THE(1982), ed
1984
LAST HORROR FILM, THE(1984), ed

Vito Salier
CAPTAIN APACHE(1971, Brit.)

Antonio Salieri
1984
AMADEUS(1984), m

Frantz Salieri
DON GIOVANNI(1979, Fr./Ital./Ger.), w

Giancarlo Salimbeni
MIGHTY CRUSADERS, THE(1961, Ital.), cos

Giancarlo Bartolini Salimbeni
COSSACKS, THE(1960, It.), cos; PHAROAH'S WOMAN, THE(1961, Ital.), cos;
QUEEN OF THE PIRATES(1961, Ital./Ger.), cos; SODOM AND GOMORRAH(1962,
U.S./Fr./Ital.), cos; CLEOPATRA'S DAUGHTER(1963, Fr., Ital.), cos; QUEEN OF THE
NILE(1964, Ital.), cos; SANDOKAN THE GREAT(1964, Fr./Ital./Span.), cos; TIGER OF
THE SEVEN SEAS(1964, Fr./Ital.), cos; INVASION 1700(1965, Fr./Ital./Yugo.), cos;
LION OF ST. MARK(1967, Ital.), cos; BULLET FOR SANDOVAL, A(1970, Ital./Span.),
art d; RED TENT, THE(1971, Ital./USSR), art d; GARDEN OF THE FINZI-CONTINIS,
THE(1976, Ital./Ger.), art d

Anne-Claude Salimo
LA BALANCE(1983, Fr.)

V. Salin
SONS AND MOTHERS(1967, USSR)

Salina
BATTLE OF THE RAILS(1949, Fr.)

Norma Jean Salina
TORCH SONG(1953)

Norman Salina
BAD AND THE BEAUTIFUL, THE(1952)

Dom Salinaro
SWEET CHARITY(1969); HISTORY OF THE WORLD, PART 1(1981)

Chucho Salinas
LOS INVISIBLES(1961, Mex.); DOCTOR OF DOOM(1962, Mex.)

Horacio Salinas
HOLY MOUNTAIN, THE(1973, U.S./Mex.)

Ione Salinas
RUY BLAS(1948, Fr.)

Jone Salinas
MAN ABOUT THE HOUSE, A(1947, Brit.)

Michel Saline
ANGEL AND SINNER(1947, Fr.)

Norman Saling
GAY DECEIVERS, THE(1969), cos

Conrad Salinger
TILL THE CLOUDS ROLL BY(1946), m; ON THE TOWN(1949), m; SHOW
BOAT(1951), md; UNKNOWN MAN, THE(1951), m; CARBINE WILLIAMS(1952), m;
WASHINGTON STORY(1952), m; DREAM WIFE(1953), m; LAST TIME I SAW PARIS,
THE(1954), m; TENNESSEE CHAMP(1954), m; SCARLET COAT, THE(1955), m, md;
GABY(1956), m; LONELYHEARTS(1958), m

J.D. Salinger
MY FOOLISH HEART(1949), w

Matt Salinger
1984
REVENGE OF THE NERDS(1984)

Pierre Salinger
DO NOT DISTURB(1965); DESTRUCTORS, THE(1974, Brit.)

Nancy Salis
ZOOT SUIT(1981)

Barbara Salisbury
COCOANUT GROVE(1938); THREE LOVES HAS NANCY(1938); YOU AND ME(1938)

Diana Salisbury
IT STARTED IN PARADISE(1952, Brit.)

Edward A. Salisbury
Misc. Silents
ON THE SPANISH MAIN(1917), d

Francis Salisbury
WIZ, THE(1978)

Monroe Salisbury
Silents
BREWSTER'S MILLIONS(1914); MAN FROM HOME, THE(1914); MASTER MIND,
THE(1914); READY MONEY(1914); ROSE OF THE RANCHO(1914); SQUAW MAN,
THE(1914); VIRGINIAN, THE(1914); AFTER FIVE(1915); GOOSE GIRL, THE(1915);
LAMB, THE(1915); RAMONA(1916); EAGLE, THE(1918); RED, RED HEART,
THE(1918); LIGHT OF VICTORY(1919)
Misc. Silents
COOK OF CANYON CAMP, THE(1917); DESIRE OF THE MOTH, THE(1917);
DEVIL'S ASSISTANT, THE(1917); DOOR BETWEEN, THE(1917); EYES OF THE
WORLD, THE(1917); PRICE OF HER SOUL, THE(1917); SAVAGE, THE(1917); SILENT
LIE, THE(1917); GUILT OF SILENCE(1918); HANDS DOWN(1918); HUGON THE
MIGHTY(1918); HUNGRY EYES(1918); THAT DEVIL, BATEESE(1918); WINNER
TAKES ALL(1918); HIS DIVORCED WIFE(1919); MAN IN THE MOONLIGHT,
THE(1919); MILLIONAIRE PIRATE, THE(1919); SLEEPING LION, THE(1919); SUN-
DOWN TRAIL, THE(1919); PHANTOM MELODY, THE(1920); BARBARIAN,
THE(1921); GREAT ALONE, THE(1922)

Preston Salisbury
TOUGH ENOUGH(1983)

Salkin
TRANS-EUROP-EXPRESS(1968, Fr.)

Leo Salkin
1001 ARABIAN NIGHTS(1959), w
Alexander Salkind
AUSTERLITZ(1960, Fr./Ital./Yugo.), p; TRIAL, THE(1963, Fr./Ital./Ger.), p; BLUE-BEARD(1972), p; FOUR MUSKETEERS, THE(1975), p
Alexandre Salkind
KILL! KILL! KILL!(1972, Fr./Ger./Ital./Span.), p
Ilya Salkind
DREAMS COME TRUE(1936, Brit.), p; KILL! KILL! KILL!(1972, Fr./Ger./Ital./Span.), p; THREE MUSKETEERS, THE(1974, Panama), p
Miguel Salkind
TRIAL, THE(1963, Fr./Ital./Ger.), p; YOUNG REBEL, THE(1969, Fr./Ital./Span.), p
Kae Salkow
THEY MADE ME A KILLER(1946), w; DANGER STREET(1947), w
Sidney Salkow
FOUR DAYS WONDER(1936), d; MURDER WITH PICTURES(1936), w; RHYTHM ON THE RANGE(1936), w; BEHIND THE MIKE(1937), d; EXCLUSIVE(1937), w; GIRL OVERBOARD(1937), d; THAT'S MY STORY(1937), d; COME ON, LEATHER-NECKS(1938), w; NIGHT HAWK, THE(1938), d; PRISON NURSE(1938), w; STORM OVER BENGAL(1938), d; FIGHTING THOROUGHBREDS(1939), d; FLIGHT AT MID-NIGHT(1939), d; SHE MARRIED A COP(1939), d; STREET OF MISSING MEN(1939), d; WOMAN DOCTOR(1939), d; ZERO HOUR, THE(1939), d; CAFE HOSTESS(1940), d; GIRL FROM GOD'S COUNTRY(1940), d; LONE WOLF KEEPS A DATE, THE(1940), d, w; LONE WOLF MEETS A LADY, THE(1940), d; LONE WOLF STRIKES, THE(1940), d; LONE WOLF TAKES A CHANCE, THE(1941), d, w; TILLIE THE TOILER(1941), w; TIME OUT FOR RHYTHM(1941), d; ADVENTURES OF MARTIN EDEN, THE(1942), d; FLIGHT LIEUTENANT(1942), d; CITY WITHOUT MEN(1943), d; FAITHFUL IN MY FASHION(1946), d; MILLIE'S DAUGHTER(1947), d; SWORD OF THE AVENG-ER(1948), p&d; ADMIRAL WAS A LADY, THE(1950), w; FUGITIVE LADY(1951), d; GOLDEN HAWK, THE(1952), d; PATHFINDER, THE(1952), d; SCARLET AN-GEL(1952), d; JACK MCCALL, DESPERADO(1953), d; PRINCE OF PIRATES(1953), d; RAIDERS OF THE SEVEN SEAS(1953), p&d, w; SITTING BULL(1954), d, w; LAS VEGAS SHAKEDOWN(1955), d; ROBBER'S ROOST(1955), d, w; SHADOW OF THE EAGLE(1955, Brit.), d; TOUGHEST MAN ALIVE(1955), d; GUN BROTHERS(1956), d; CHICAGO CONFIDENTIAL(1957), d; GUN DUEL IN DURANGO(1957), d; IRON SHERIFF, THE(1957), d; BIG NIGHT, THE(1960), d; TWICE TOLD TALES(1963), d; BLOOD ON THE ARROW(1964), d; LAST MAN ON EARTH, THE(1964, U.S./Ital.), d; QUICK GUN, THE(1964), d; GREAT SIOUX MASSACRE, THE(1965), d, w; MURDER GAME, THE(1966, Brit.), d
Misc. Talkies
BOY FROM STALINGRAD, THE(1943), d; BULLDOG DRUMMOND AT BAY(1947), d
Sy Salkowitz
READY FOR THE PEOPLE(1964), w; THUNDER ALLEY(1967), w; BIGGEST BUN-DLE OF THEM ALL, THE(1968), w
William Sall
DYNAMITE RANCH(1932), p
Franz Salla
Misc. Silents
PASSION OF ST. FRANCIS(1932, Ital.)
Loris Sallahian
FAME(1980)
Dennis Sallas
SHADOWS(1960); MACHINE GUN McCAIN(1970, Ital.)
Michael Salle
Misc. Talkies
RIDERS OF THE PONY EXPRESS(1949), d
Sandy Sallee
FOURTH HORSEMAN, THE(1933)
Maurilo Salles
DONA FLOR AND HER TWO HUSBANDS(1977, Braz.), ph
Henry Salley
SPOOK WHO SAT BY THE DOOR, THE(1973), cos; GREASED LIGHTNING(1977), cos
Ronald Salley
1984
BEST DEFENSE(1984)
Eddie Sallia
FOLLOW ME, BOYS!(1966)
Robert Sallin
STAR TREK II: THE WRATH OF KHAN(1982), p
Jack Salling
IS EVERYBODY HAPPY?(1943)
Jackie Salling
FISHERMAN'S WHARF(1939)
Norman Salling
DEAD END(1937); JANIE(1944); END, THE(1978), cos; HOOPER(1978), cos; SHARKY'S MACHINE(1982), cos; STROKER ACE(1983), cos
1984
CANNONBALL RUN II(1984), cos; CITY HEAT(1984), cos
Helen Sallinger
Silents
POLLY OF THE CIRCUS(1917)
Crispian Sallis
1984
TOP SECRET!(1984), set d
Peter Sallis
ANASTASIA(1956); DOCTOR'S DILEMMA, THE(1958, Brit.); SCAPEGOAT, THE(1959, Brit.); CURSE OF THE WEREWOLF, THE(1961); I THANK A FOOL(1962, Brit.); MOUSE ON THE MOON, THE(1963, Brit.); V.I.P.s, THE(1963, Brit.); THIRD SECRET, THE(1964, Brit.); ESCAPE BY NIGHT(1965, Brit.); RAPTURE(1965); CHARL-IE BUBBLES(1968, Brit.); INADMISSIBLE EVIDENCE(1968, Brit.); MY LOVER, MY SON(1970, Brit.); SCREAM AND SCREAM AGAIN(1970, Brit.); TASTE THE BLOOD OF DRACULA(1970, Brit.); WUTHERING HEIGHTS(1970, Brit.); NIGHT DIGGER, THE(1971, Brit.); RECKONING, THE(1971, Brit.); INCREDIBLE SARAH, THE(1976, Brit.); FULL CIRCLE(1977, Brit./Can.); WHO IS KILLING THE GREAT CHEFS OF EUROPE?(1978, US/Ger.); HAUNTING OF JULIA, THE(1981, Brit./Can.)

Zoe Sallis
BIBLE...IN THE BEGINNING, THE(1966); STATUE, THE(1971, Brit.)
Angela Salloker
PEDESTRIAN, THE(1974, Ger.)
Massimo Sallusto
BRIEF RAPTURE(1952, Ital.)
Filippo Sallustri
MYTH, THE(1965, Ital.)
Phyllis Sally
WILD SCENE, THE(1970)
Andre Sallyman
OPERATION LOVEBIRDS(1968, Den.)
Lyda Salmanova
Misc. Silents
STUDENT OF PRAGUE, THE(1913, Ger.); HUNCHBACK AND THE DANCER, THE(1920, Ger.); LOST SHADOW, THE(1921, Ger.)
Albert Salmi
BRAVADOS, THE(1958); BROTHERS KARAMAZOV, THE(1958); UNFORGIVEN, THE(1960); WILD RIVER(1960); OUTRAGE, THE(1964); AMBUSHERS, THE(1967); FLIM-FLAM MAN, THE(1967); HOUR OF THE GUN(1967); THREE GUNS FOR TEXAS(1968); DESERTER, THE(1971 Ital./Yugo.); ESCAPE FROM THE PLANET OF THE APES(1971); LAWMAN(1971); SOMETHING BIG(1971); CRAZY WORLD OF JULIUS VROODER, THE(1974); TAKE, THE(1974); BLACK OAK CONSPIRACY(1977); EMPIRE OF THE ANTS(1977); MOONSHINE COUNTY EXPRESS(1977); VIVA KNIEVEL!(1977); LOVE AND BULLETS(1979, Brit.); SWEET CREEK COUNTY WAR, THE(1979); BRUBAKER(1980); CADDY SHACK(1980); CLOUD DANCER(1980); CUBA CROSSING(1980); STEEL(1980); DRAGONSLAYER(1981); ST. HELENS(1981); LOVE CHILD(1982); GUNS AND THE FURY, THE(1983)
1984
HARD TO HOLD(1984)
Misc. Talkies
PLACE WITHOUT PARENTS, A(1974); TRUCKIN'(1975); COMING, THE(1983)
Esko Salminen
PRELUDE TO ECSTASY(1963, Fin.)
Unto Salminen
TIME OF ROSES(1970, Fin.)
Ville Veikko Salminen
TELEFON(1977)
Barry Salmon
1984
SILENT MADNESS(1984), m
Charles Salmon
LAST PICTURE SHOW, THE(1971)
Don Salmon
MAYA(1982), m
John Salmon
ONLY WHEN I LARF(1968, Brit.), w
Michael Salmon
Z.P.G.(1972), ph
Misc. Talkies
BLACK ISLAND(1979, Brit.)
Mike Salmon
GREEN HELMET, THE(1961, Brit.)
Nancy Salmon
OKAY BILL(1971); INJUN FENDER(1973)
Peter Salmon
SONG OF NORWAY(1970)
Scott Salmon
LAST MARRIED COUPLE IN AMERICA, THE(1980), ch; STIR CRAZY(1980), ch
Tehapaitua Salmon
TAHITIAN, THE(1956)
Frank Salmonese
EVERY SPARROW MUST FALL(1964)
Lyda Salmonova
Silents
GOLEM: HOW HE CAME INTO THE WORLD, THE(1920, Ger.)
Misc. Silents
PIED PIPER OF HAMELIN, THE(1917, Ger.); BEYOND THE RIVER(1922, Ger.); WIFE OF THE PHARAOH, THE(1922, Ger.)
Lydia Salmonoya
Misc. Silents
GOLEM, THE(1914, Ger.)
G. F. Salmony
GUILTY MELODY(1936, Brit.), w
Nadia Salnick
I, MAUREEN(1978, Can.), art d
Mario Salo
Misc. Silents
MACISTE IN HELL(1926, Ital.)
Salome
1984
WOMAN IN FLAMES, A(1984, Ger.)
A.M. Salomon
BRIGGS FAMILY, THE(1940, Brit.), p; FINGERS(1940, Brit.), p; GEORGE AND MARGARET(1940, Brit.), p; THAT'S THE TICKET(1940, Brit.), p
Alain Salomon
POURQUOI PAS!(1979, Fr.)
Ammon Salomon
NEITHER BY DAY NOR BY NIGHT(1972, U.S./Israel), ph
M. Salomon
TWO FOR DANGER(1940, Brit.), p
Mikael Salomon
WELCOME TO THE CLUB(1971), ph; ELVIS! ELVIS!(1977, Swed.), ph
Joanasie Salomonie
WHITE DAWN, THE(1974)
Vic Salomonsen
VENOM(1968, Den.)

Alexis Salomos
NEVER ON SUNDAY(1960, Gr.)

Patricia Salonika
DEVIL'S HARBOR(1954, Brit.); BLONDE BLACKMAILER(1955, Brit.)

Syd Salor
EVE KNEW HER APPLES(1945)

Louis Salou
CHILDREN OF PARADISE(1945, Fr.); ANGEL AND SINNER(1947, Fr.); FRIEND WILL COME TONIGHT, A(1948, Fr.); SYLVIA AND THE PHANTOM(1950, Fr.); FABIOLA(1951, Ital.); LOVERS OF VERONA, THE(1951, Fr.)

Gerry Salsberg
LAST DETAIL, THE(1973); PHOBIA(1980, Can.)

Monroe Salsbury
Misc. Silents
BLINDING TRAIL, THE(1919)

Bryan Salspaugh
CROWD ROARS, THE(1932)

Barry Salt
GREAT WALL OF CHINA, THE(1970, Brit.), ph

Brian Salt
TOTO AND THE POACHERS(1958, Brit.), d, w

Jennifer Salt
MURDER A LA MOD(1968); MIDNIGHT COWBOY(1969); WEDDING PARTY, THE(1969); BREWSTER McCLOUD(1970); HI, MOM!(1970); REVOLUTIONARY, THE(1970, Brit.); PLAY IT AGAIN, SAM(1972); SISTERS(1973); IT'S MY TURN(1980)

John Salt
WITNESS, THE(1959, Brit.), w

Stephen Salt
GYPSY GIRL(1966, Brit.)

Theodore Salt
INVADERS, THE,(1941)

Waldo Salt
SHOPWORN ANGEL(1938), w; PHILADELPHIA STORY, THE(1940), w; WILD MAN OF BORNEO, THE(1941), w; TONIGHT WE RAID CALAIS(1943), w; MR. WINKLE GOES TO WAR(1944), w; RACHEL AND THE STRANGER(1948), w; FLAME AND THE ARROW, THE(1950), w; M(1951), w; TARAS BULBA(1962), w; FLIGHT FROM ASHIYA(1964, U.S./Jap.), w; WILD AND WONDERFUL(1964), w; MIDNIGHT COWBOY(1969), w; GANG THAT COULDN'T SHOOT STRAIGHT, THE(1971), w; SERPICO(1973), w; DAY OF THE LOCUST, THE(1975), w; COMING HOME(1978), w

Gino Saltamerenda
BICYCLE THIEF, THE(1949, Ital.); AFFAIRS OF MESSALINA, THE(1954, Ital.)

Louis Saltamerenda
THIEF OF VENICE, THE(1952)

Luigi Saltamerenda
SHOE SHINE(1947, Ital.); CHILDREN OF CHANCE(1950, Ital.)

Felix Salten
STORM IN A WATER GLASS(1931, Aust.), w; EMPRESS AND I, THE(1933, Ger.), w; HEART SONG(1933, Brit.), w; FLORIAN(1940), w; BAMBI(1942), w; SHAGGY DOG, THE(1959), w; SHAGGY D.A., THE(1976), w

Art Salter
STORY ON PAGE ONE, THE(1959); TENDER IS THE NIGHT(1961)

Gaby Salter
KING OF COMEDY, THE(1983)

H.J. Salter
DARK STREETS OF CAIRO(1940), md; FRAMED(1940), md; INVISIBLE MAN RETURNS, THE(1940), m; LAW AND ORDER(1940), md; LEATHER-PUSHERS, THE(1940), md; MARGIE(1940), md; MUMMY'S HAND, THE(1940), md; PONY POST(1940), md; RAGTIME COWBOY JOE(1940), md; BACHELOR DADDY(1941), m; BADLANDS OF DAKOTA(1941), m; HELLO SUCKER(1941), md; HIT THE ROAD(1941), md; LUCKY DEVILS(1941), m; MEN OF THE TIMBERLAND(1941), md; MODEL WIFE(1941), md; MUTINY IN THE ARCTIC(1941), m; PARIS CALLING(1941), md; RAIDERS OF THE DESERT(1941), md; ROAD AGENT(1941), md; SAN FRANCISCO DOCKS(1941), md; TIGHT SHOES(1941), md; DANGER IN THE PACIFIC(1942), md; DEEP IN THE HEART OF TEXAS(1942), md; DRUMS OF THE CONGO(1942), md; FIGHTING BILL FARGO(1942), md; GREAT IMPERSONATION, THE(1942), md; HALF WAY TO SHANGHAI(1942), md; INVISIBLE AGENT(1942), m; LITTLE JOE, THE WRANGLER(1942), md; MUMMY'S TOMB, THE(1942), md; MYSTERY OF MARIE ROGET(1942), m, md; SIN TOWN(1942), md; STAGECOACH BUCKAROO(1942), md; THERE'S ONE BORN EVERY MINUTE(1942), md; TOP SERGEANT(1942), md; AMAZING MRS. HOLLIDAY(1943), m; COWBOY IN MANHATTTAN(1943), md; FRONTIER BADMEN(1943), md; GET GOING(1943), md; GUNG HO!(1943), md; HI'YA, SAILOR(1943), md; HIS BUTLER'S SISTER(1943), m; HI'YA, CHUM(1943), md; LONE STAR TRAIL, THE(1943), md; OLD CHISHOLM TRAIL(1943), md; SHERLOCK HOLMES FACES DEATH(1943), md; TENTING TONIGHT ON THE OLD CAMP GROUND(1943), md; INVISIBLE MAN'S REVENGE(1944), m; MARSHAL OF GUNSMOKE(1944), md; PARDON MY RHYTHM(1944), md; EASY TO LOOK AT(1945), md; FROZEN GHOST, THE(1945), md; I'LL TELL THE WORLD(1945), md; RIVER GANG(1945), md; SEE MY LAWYER(1945), md; THAT NIGHT WITH YOU(1945), md; THIS LOVE OF OURS(1945), m; HOUSE OF HORRORS(1946), md; LITTLE MISS BIG(1946), m

Hans Salter
BLONDE NIGHTINGALE(1931, Ger.), md; SPRING PARADE(1940), m; GREAT COMMANDMENT, THE(1941), m; RECKLESS MOMENTS, THE(1949), m; FRENCHIE(1950), m; FINDERS KEEPERS(1951), m; HUMAN JUNGLE, THE(1954), m; FAR HORIZONS, THE(1955), m; WICHITA(1955), m&md; AUTUMN LEAVES(1956), m; NAVY WIFE(1956), m; OKLAHOMAN, THE(1957), m, md; TALL STRANGER, THE(1957), m; THREE BRAVE MEN(1957), m

Hans J. Salter
UNCLE HARRY(1945), md; BLACK FRIDAY(1940), md; YOU'RE NOT SO TOUGH(1940), md; IT STARTED WITH EVE(1941), m; MAN MADE MONSTER(1941), md; MOB TOWN(1941), md; BOMBAY CLIPPER(1942), m; NIGHT MONSTER(1942), md; PITTSBURGH(1942), md; SILVER BULLET, THE(1942), md; SPOILERS, THE(1942), m; TOUGH AS THEY COME(1942), md; EYES OF THE UNDERWORLD(1943), md; KEEP 'EM SLUGGING(1943), md; MUG TOWN(1943), md; CAN'T HELP SINGING(1944), m; CHRISTMAS HOLIDAY(1944), m; HI, GOOD-LOOKIN'(1944), md; HOUSE OF FRANKENSTEIN(1944), md; MERRY MONAHANS, THE(1944), md; MUMMY'S GHOST, THE(1944), md; PHANTOM LADY(1944), md; SAN DIEGO, I LOVE YOU(1944), md; PATRICK THE GREAT(1945), md; SCARLET STREET(1945), m; THAT'S THE SPIRIT(1945), md; DARK HORSE, THE(1946), md;

HER ADVENTUROUS NIGHT(1946), md; LOVER COME BACK(1946), m; MAGNIFICENT DOLL(1946), m; SO GOES MY LOVE(1946), m, md; MICHIGAN KID, THE(1947), m; THAT'S MY MAN(1947), m; WEB, THE(1947), m; DON'T TRUST YOUR HUSBAND(1948), m; MAN-EATER OF KUMAON(1948), m; COVER-UP(1949), m; BORDERLINE(1950), m; KILLER THAT STALKED NEW YORK, THE(1950), m; PLEASE BELIEVE ME(1950), m; APACHE DRUMS(1951), m; GOLDEN HORDE, THE(1951), m; PRINCE WHO WAS A THIEF, THE(1951), md; THUNDER ON THE HILL(1951), m; TOMAHAWK(1951), m; YOU NEVER CAN TELL(1951), m; AGAINST ALL FLAGS(1952), m; BATTLE AT APACHE PASS, THE(1952), m; BEND OF THE RIVER(1952), m; DUEL AT SILVER CREEK, THE(1952), m; FLESH AND FURY(1952), m; UNTAMED FRONTIER(1952), m; SIGN OF THE PAGAN(1954), m; MOLE PEOPLE, THE(1956), m; RAWHIDE YEARS, THE(1956), m; RED SUNDOWN(1956), m; DAY OF THE BAD MAN(1958); FEMALE ANIMAL, THE(1958), m; RAW WIND IN EDEN(1958), m; GUNFIGHT AT DODGE CITY, THE(1959), m; MAN IN THE NET, THE(1959), m; WILD AND THE INNOCENT, THE(1959), m; COME SEPTEMBER(1961), m; FOLLOW THAT DREAM(1962), m; HITLER(1962), m; IF A MAN ANSWERS(1962), m; SHOWDOWN(1963), m; BEDTIME STORY(1964), m; BEAU GESTE(1966), m; GUNPOINT(1966), m; INCIDENT AT PHANTOM HILL(1966), m

Ivor Salter
HEART WITHIN, THE(1957, Brit.); DOG EAT DOG(1963, U.S./Ger./Ital.); BE MY GUEST(1965, Brit.); HOUSE OF WHIPCORD(1974, Brit.); CONFESSIONAL, THE(1977, Brit.)

J. J. Salter
1984
JOY OF SEX(1984), w

James Salter
HUNTERS, THE(1958), w; APPOINTMENT, THE(1969), w; DOWNHILL RACER(1969), w; THREE(1969, Brit.), d&w; THRESHOLD(1983, Can.), w

June Salter
CADDIE(1976, Aus.)

Malachi Salter
SIEGE(1983, Can.), prod d

Nicholas Salter
DON'T LOOK NOW(1973, Brit./Ital.)

Richard Salter
MOSES AND AARON(1975, Ger./Fr./Ital.)

Thelma Salter
Silents
ALIEN, THE(1915); CRAB, THE(1917); LAST OF THE INGRAHAMS, THE(1917); HUCKLEBERRY FINN(1920)
Misc. Silents
MATRIMONY(1915); HAPPINESS(1917); IN SLUMBERLAND(1917)

Irene Saltern
NIGHT HAWK, THE(1938), cos; PRISON NURSE(1938), cos; ROMANCE ON THE RUN(1938), cos; MYSTERIOUS MISS X, THE(1939), cos; PRIDE OF THE NAVY(1939), cos; WOMAN DOCTOR(1939), cos; HOWARDS OF VIRGINIA, THE(1940), cos; WESTERNER, THE(1940), cos; TIME OUT FOR RHYTHM(1941), cos

John Salthouse
SPY WHO LOVED ME, THE(1977, Brit.)
1984
GIVE MY REGARDS TO BROAD STREET(1984, Brit.)

N. Saltikov
Misc. Silents
TSAR IVAN VASILYEVICH GROZNY(1915, USSR)

Nikolai Saltikov
Misc. Silents
DEATH BAY(1926, USSR)

Ellen Saltonstall
HAIR(1979)

Salty the Chimp
HELL SHIP MUTINY(1957)

Albert J. Saltzer
WOMEN AND BLOODY TERROR(1970), p

J. Saltzer
WOMEN AND BLOODY TERROR(1970), w

Walter Saltzer
SKYJACKED(1972), p

Harry Saltzman
IRON PETTICOAT, THE(1956, Brit.), w; LOOK BACK IN ANGER(1959), p; ENTERTAINER, THE(1960, Brit.), p; DR. NO(1962, Brit.), p; CALL ME BWANA(1963, Brit.), p; FROM RUSSIA WITH LOVE(1963, Brit.), p; GOLDFINGER(1964, Brit.), p; IPCRESS FILE, THE(1965, Brit.), p; FUNERAL IN BERLIN(1966, Brit.), p; BILLION DOLLAR BRAIN(1967, Brit.), p; YOU ONLY LIVE TWICE(1967, Brit.), p; AND THERE CAME A MAN(1968, Ital.), p; BATTLE OF BRITAIN(1969, Brit.), p; ON HER MAJESTY'S SECRET SERVICE(1969, Brit.), p; PLAY DIRTY(1969, Brit.), p; TOOMORROW(1970, Brit.), p; DIAMONDS ARE FOREVER(1971, Brit.), p; LIVE AND LET DIE(1973, Brit.), p; MAN WITH THE GOLDEN GUN, THE(1974, Brit.), p

Philip Saltzman
SWISS CONSPIRACY, THE(1976, U.S./Ger.), w

Bill Saluga
TUNNELVISION(1976); GOING BERSERK(1983)

Renu Saluja
1984
MOHAN JOSHI HAAZIR HO(1984, India), ed

Salvador
BLOOD DRINKERS, THE(1966, U.S./Phil.), ed

Henri Salvador
NOUS IRONS A PARIS(1949, Fr.)

Jaime Salvador
LOS INVISIBLES(1961, Mex.), d; MADAME DEATH(1968, Mex.), d

Jimmy Salvador
DALTON THAT GOT AWAY(1960), d

Julio Salvador
LAST MERCENARY, THE(1969, Ital./Span./Ger.), w

Lou Salvador
NO PLACE TO HIDE(1956)

Philip Salvador
1984
BONA(1984, Phil.)
Phillip Salvador
JAGUAR(1980, Phil.)
Albert Salvadori
CENTURION, THE(1962, Fr./Ital.), ed
Roy Salvadori
GREEN HELMET, THE(1961, Brit.)
Ruggero Salvadori
ROVER, THE(1967, Ital.)
Maurice Salvage
WORDS AND MUSIC(1929)
Jerry Salvail
BRUTE FORCE(1947); DOUBLE LIFE, A(1947)
Lillian Salvaneschi
NOB HILL(1945)
Mario Salvaneschi
NOB HILL(1945)
Renato Salvaroti
ORGANIZER, THE(1964, Fr./Ital./Yugo.)
Keith Salvat
PRIVATE COLLECTION(1972, Aus.), p&d, w
John Salvata
WHIPLASH(1948)
S. Salvati
GATES OF HELL, THE(1983, U.S./Ital.), ph
Sergia Salvati
1984
BLACK CAT, THE(1984, Ital./Brit.), ph
Sergio Salvati
PSYCHIC, THE(1979, Ital.), ph; ZOMBIE(1980, Ital.), ph; 1990: THE BRONX WARRI-ORS(1983, Ital.), ph
1984
HOUSE BY THE CEMETERY, THE(1984, Ital.), ph
Anna Salvatore
LA DOLCE VITA(1961, Ital./Fr.)
Enrico Salvatore
DAMON AND PYTHIAS(1962)
Alberto Salvatori
EARTH CRIES OUT, THE(1949, Ital.), p; MURDER CLINIC, THE(1967, Ital./Fr.), art d
Giulia Salvatori
LA VIE CONTINUE(1982, Fr.)
Renato Salvatori
BIG DEAL ON MADONNA STREET, THE(1960); AND THE WILD, WILD WO-MEN(1961, Ital.); ROCCO AND HIS BROTHERS(1961, Fr./Ital.); TWO WOMEN(1961, Ital./Fr.); FIASCO IN MILAN(1963, Fr./Ital.); OMICRON(1963, Ital.); DISORDER(1964, Fr./Ital.); OF FLESH AND BLOOD(1964, Fr./Ital.); TWO ARE GUILTY(1964, Fr.); HOW TO SEDUCE A PLAYBOY(1968, Aust./Fr./Ital.); THREE NIGHTS OF LOVE(1969, Ital.); Z(1969, Fr./Algeria); BURN(1970); LIGHT AT THE EDGE OF THE WORLD, THE(1971, U.S./Span./Lichtenstein); BURGLARS, THE(1972, Fr./Ital.); STATE OF SIEGE(1973, Fr./U.S./Ital./Ger.); BRIEF VACATION, A(1975, Ital.); ERNESTO(1979, Ital.); LUNA(1979, Ital.); TRAGEDY OF A RIDICULOUS MAN, THE(1982, Ital.)
Juleste Salve
SWEET CHARITY(1969)
Delia Salvi
FROM HERE TO ETERNITY(1953); COMPETITION, THE(1980); LAST MARRIED COUPLE IN AMERICA, THE(1980)
Della Salvi
FATSO(1980)
Emimmo Salvi
GOLIATH AND THE BARBARIANS(1960, Ital.), p, w; DAVID AND GOLIATH(1961, Ital.), p; TARTARS, THE(1962, Ital./Yugo.), w; GIANT OF METROPOLIS, THE(1963, Ital.), p, w; SEVEN TASKS OF ALI BABA, THE(1963, Ital.), d, w; SEVEN RE-VENGES, THE(1967, Ital.), w
Emmimo Salvi
DAVID AND GOLIATH(1961, Ital.), w
Frank Salvi
PRINCE OF FOXES(1949)
Lola Salvi
IN OLD ARIZONA(1929); THRU DIFFERENT EYES(1929)
Misc. Silents
PLASTERED IN PARIS(1928)
Rafael J. Salvia
PLANET OF THE VAMPIRES(1965, U.S./Ital./Span.), w
Ralph Salvia [Rafael Salvia]
FLAME OVER VIETNAM(1967, Span./Ger.), w
Catherine Salviat
SUNDAY LOVERS(1980, Ital./Fr.)
1984
JUST THE WAY YOU ARE(1984)
Vanna Salviati
CHAMP, THE(1979)
Agostino Salvietti
CHILDREN OF CHANCE(1950, Ital.); DISHONORED(1950, Ital.); ISLAND OF PROCIDA, THE(1952, Ital.); LADY DOCTOR, THE(1963, Fr./Ital./Span.); YESTER-DAY, TODAY, AND TOMORROW(1964, Ital./Fr.)
Kevin Salvilla
COAL MINER'S DAUGHTER(1980)
Alexander Salvini
Silents
NERO(1922, U.S./Ital.)
Rocardo Salvino
LEGEND OF FRENCHIE KING, THE(1971, Fr./Ital./Span./Brit.)
Robert Salvio
CHILDREN OF RAGE(1975, Brit.-Israeli)

Giorgio Salvioni
TENTH VICTIM, THE(1965, Fr./Ital.), w; QUEENS, THE(1968, Ital./Fr.), w
John Salvo
Misc. Talkies
DAWN OF THE MUMMY(1981)
Lianne Salvor
Misc. Silents
BLUEBEARD'S 8TH WIFE(1923)
P. Salvucci
THIS WINE OF LOVE(1948, Ital.), w
Y. Salvucci
AIDA(1954, Ital.), w
Jean Salvy
JE T'AIME(1974, Can.), w
Medford Salway
PURPLE HILLS, THE(1961)
Rafael Salzano
SUMMERSKIN(1962, Arg.)
Gerry Salzberg
OUTRAGEOUS!(1977, Can.)
Naomi Salzberger
MY FATHER'S HOUSE(1947, Palestine)
Leonard Salzedo
GLASS TOMB, THE(1955, Brit.), m; RACE FOR LIFE, A(1955, Brit.), m; BLONDE BAIT(1956, U.S./Brit.), m; SHADOW OF FEAR(1956, Brit.), m; CURSE OF FRANKEN-STEIN, THE(1957, Brit.), m; SEA WIFE(1957, Brit.), m; REVENGE OF FRANKEN-STEIN, THE(1958, Brit.), m; STEEL BAYONET, THE(1958, Brit.), m
Albert J. Salzer
NIGHT OF THE STRANGLER(1975), p
Ted Salzis
BAYOU(1957), ph
Vincent Salzis
BAYOU(1957), ph
Esta Salzman
Misc. Talkies
HER SECOND MOTHER(1940)
Morris Salzman
BREAKING AWAY(1979)
Detlef Salzseider
PINOCCHIO(1969, E. Ger.)
Slim and Sam
HELLZAPOPPIN'(1941)
Sam and Dave
ONE-TRICK PONY(1980)
Sam and the Ape Man with Diane De Marco
DR. GOLDFOOT AND THE BIKINI MACHINE(1965)
Sam Butera and the Witnesses
SENIOR PROM(1958); HEY BOY! HEY GIRL!(1959); TWIST ALL NIGHT(1961)
The Sam Stewart Trio
BOY! WHAT A GIRL(1947)
Sam the Parakeet
KISS ME, STUPID(1964)
Sam the Sham & the Pharoahs
WHEN THE BOYS MEET THE GIRLS(1965)
George Samaan
HELL WITH HEROES, THE(1968)
David Samain
OH, HEAVENLY DOG!(1980)
Nicola Samale
GOODNIGHT, LADIES AND GENTLEMEN(1977, Ital.), m
Antonio Samaniego
UNDER THE PAMPAS MOON(1935); BACKGROUND TO DANGER(1943)
Carmen Samaniego
WHEN YOU'RE IN LOVE(1937)
Ramon Samaniegos [Novarro]
Silents
JOAN THE WOMAN(1916); PRISONER OF ZENDA, THE(1922)
Samantha
FRIENDLY PERSUASION(1956)
Gloria Samara
Misc. Talkies
BATTLE OF THE EAGLES(1981)
Ljubisa Samardzic
BATTLE OF THE NERETVA(1971, Yugo./Ital./Ger.); VISITORS FROM THE GALAXY(1981, Yugo.)
Yelena Samarina
HOUSE OF 1,000 DOLLS(1967, Ger./Span./Brit.); WIDOWS' NEST(1977, U.S./Span.)
Velena Samarine
WEREWOLF VS. THE VAMPIRE WOMAN, THE(1970, Span./Ger.)
Carolina Samario
WORLD'S GREATEST SINNER, THE(1962)
Brank Samarovski
YOUNG MONK, THE(1978, Ger.)
Bobby Samarzich
UNDER YOUR SPELL(1936)
Misc. Talkies
BOY FROM STALINGRAD, THE(1943)
Chuck Samata
CHANGE OF MIND(1969)
Alyette Samazeuilh
CLEO FROM 5 TO 7(1961, Fr.), cos
The Samba Kings
ROMANCE ON THE HIGH SEAS(1948)
Mike Sambeck
OPEN SEASON(1974, U.S./Span.)
Isaac Samberg
Misc. Silents
HIS WIFE'S HUSBAND(1913, Pol.)

Issac Samberg
Misc. Silents
FATALNA KLATWA(1913, USSR)
R. Samberg
DYBBUK THE(1938, Pol.)
Sambo
Misc. Silents
MILADY O' THE BEAN STALK(1918)
Little Sambo
Silents
DOLLY'S VACATION(1918); OLD MAID'S BABY, THE(1919)
Boguslaw Samborski
Misc. Silents
10 CONDEMNED(1932, Pol.)
Aldo Sambrell
GUNFIGHTERS OF CASA GRANDE(1965, U.S./Span.); PLACE CALLED GLORY, A(1966, Span./Ger.); SON OF A GUNFIGHTER(1966, U.S./Span.); TEXICAN, THE(1966, U.S./Span.); DEVIL'S MAN, THE(1967, Ital.); FOR A FEW DOLLARS MORE(1967, Ital./Ger./Span.); GOOD, THE BAD, AND THE UGLY, THE(1967, Ital./Span.); HELLBENDERS, THE(1967, U.S./Ital./Span.); LONG DUEL, THE(1967, Brit.); NAVAJO JOE(1967, Ital./Span.); SEA PIRATE, THE(1967, Fr./Span./Ital.); MINUTE TO PRAY, A SECOND TO DIE, A(1968, Ital.); SUPERARGO(1968, Ital./Span.); 100 RIFLES(1969); LIGHT AT THE EDGE OF THE WORLD, THE(1971, U.S./Span./Lichtenstein); TOWN CALLED HELL, A(1971, Span./Brit.); TREASURE ISLAND(1972, Brit./Span./Fr./Ger.); ANTONY AND CLEOPATRA(1973, Brit.); CHARLEY-ONE-EYE(1973, Brit.); MAN CALLED NOON, THE(1973, Brit.); SHAFT IN AFRICA(1973); GOLDEN VOYAGE OF SINBAD, THE(1974, Brit.); WIND AND THE LION, THE(1975)
1984
YELLOW HAIR AND THE FORTRESS OF GOLD(1984)
Harvey Sambrook
WALKING STICK, THE(1970, Brit.)
Samburu Tribe of Kenya Colony
MOGAMBO(1953)
Artur Samedo
STATE OF THINGS, THE(1983)
Udo Samel
1984
CLASS ENEMY(1984, Ger.)
Thomas D. Samford III
NORMA RAE(1979)
Alfred Samgster
GREAT MR. HANDEL, THE(1942, Brit.)
Catherine Samie
WOMAN TIMES SEVEN(1967, U.S./Fr./Ital.); LIFE LOVE DEATH(1969, Fr./Ital.); DAYDREAMER, THE(1975, Fr.)
Louis Samier
LIGHT YEARS AWAY(1982, Fr./Switz.)
Fernando Samillan
GALLANT ONE, THE(1964, U.S./Peru)
Maria Samina
MOULIN ROUGE(1952)
John Samiotis
NAKED BRIGADE, THE(1965, U.S./Gr.), spec eff
Somchai Samipak
1 2 3 MONSTER EXPRESS(1977, Thai.)
Peter Samish
...AND JUSTICE FOR ALL(1979), art d; HEART BEAT(1979), set d
Angela Sammaciccia
SEDUCED AND ABANDONED(1964, Fr./Ital.), cos; CLIMAX, THE(1967, Fr., Ital.), cos; INVESTIGATION OF A CITIZEN ABOVE SUSPICION(1970, Ital.), cos; SERAFINO(1970, Fr./Ital.), cos
Giancarlo Sammartano
LEAP INTO THE VOID(1982, Ital.)
Gerry Sammer
IT'S HOT IN PARADISE(1962, Ger./Yugo.)
Barbara Sammeth
MAD ROOM, THE(1969); YOUR THREE MINUTES ARE UP(1973)
Edward Sammis
ALBERT, R.N.(1953, Brit.), w
Sue Sammon
CHARRIOTS OF FIRE(1981, Brit.)
Emma Samms
ARABIAN ADVENTURE(1979, Brit.)
Oliver Sammuels
COUNTRYMAN(1982, Jamaica)
Saviour Sammut
LAST OF THE KNUCKLEMEN, THE(1981, Aus.)
Sunshine Sammy
BOYS OF THE CITY(1940); I CAN'T GIVE YOU ANYTHING BUT LOVE, BABY(1940)
Sammy Kaye and His Orchestra
ICELAND(1942); SONG OF THE OPEN ROAD(1944)
Tatyana Samoilcva
CRANES ARE FLYING, THE(1960, USSR)
E. Samoilov
ADVENTURE IN ODESSA(1954, USSR)
Eugene Samoilov
SIX P.M.(1946, USSR); ADMIRAL NAKHIMOV(1948, USSR)
Eughenj Samoilov
WATERLOO(1970, Ital./USSR)
G. Samokhina
PEACE TO HIM WHO ENTERS(1963, USSR)
Leonid Samoloff
Silents
SHOULD A WOMAN DIVORCE?(1914)
Zygmunt Samosiuk
GOLEM(1980, Pol.), ph; WAR OF THE WORLDS–NEXT CENTURY, THE(1981, Pol.), ph

Jacques Samossoud
KNICKERBOCKER HOLIDAY(1944), md
Maria Samosvat
TARAS FAMILY, THE(1946, USSR)
Tanya Samova
MISSION TO MOSCOW(1943)
Tatyana Samoylova
LETTER THAT WAS NEVER SENT, THE(1962, USSR); ITALIANO BRAVA GENTE(1965, Ital./USSR)
Antonio L. Sampaio
GIVEN WORD, THE(1964, Braz.)
Virgilio Sampaio
MARGIN, THE,(1969, Braz.)
Guadalupe Munoz Sampedro
SIX DAYS A WEEK(1966, Fr./Ital./Span.)
Matilde M. Sampedro
MAIN STREET(1956, Span.)
Matilde Munoz Sampedro
LAST DAY OF THE WAR, THE(1969, U.S./Ital./Span.); NUN AT THE CROSSROADS, A(1970, Ital./Span.)
Matilde Sampedro-Munoz
ISLAND OF THE DOOMED(1968, Span./Ger.)
Antonio Sampere
DEADFALL(1968, Brit.)
Joseph Samperi
1984
OH GOD! YOU DEVIL(1984)
Salvatore Samperi
THANK YOU, AUNT(1969, Ital.), d, w; MALICIOUS(1974, Ital.), d, w; ERNESTO(1979, Ital.), d, w
Lewis Sample
CHARLIE, THE LONESOME COUGAR(1967)
Sara Sample
Silents
DIAMOND NECKLACE, THE(1921, Brit.)
Misc. Silents
FORTUNE OF CHRISTINA MCNAB, THE(1921, Brit.)
William Samples
BY DESIGN(1982)
Bill Sampson
NAKED KISS, THE(1964); GIRLS ON THE BEACH(1965); SKI PARTY(1965)
Bill Sampson [John Erman]
ACE ELI AND RODGER OF THE SKIES(1973), d
Chet Sampson
RAWHIDE TRAIL, THE(1958)
Edward Sampson
HANNAH LEE(1953), ed; HIGH SCHOOL HELLCATS(1958), ed; DIARY OF A HIGH SCHOOL BRIDE(1959), ed
Edward Sampson, Jr.
DUFFY OF SAN QUENTIN(1954), ed
Edwards Sampson
FAST AND THE FURIOUS, THE(1954), d, ed
Ivan Sampson
WHITE ENSIGN(1934, Brit.); GAY ADVENTURE, THE(1953, Brit.)
Silents
FAKE, THE(1927, Brit.)
Linda Sampson
YOU'VE GOT TO WALK IT LIKE YOU TALK IT OR YOU'LL LOSE THAT BEAT(1971), art d
Paddy Sampson
STRANGE BREW(1983)
Robert Sampson
STRANGERS WHEN WE MEET(1960); LOOK IN ANY WINDOW(1961); BROKEN LAND, THE(1962); HERO'S ISLAND(1962); RESTLESS ONES, THE(1965); FOR PETE'S SAKE!(1966); ZIGZAG(1970); MR. RICCO(1975); GATES OF HELL, THE(1983, U.S./Ital.)
Misc. Talkies
ETHAN(1971)
Roy Sampson
HOPSCOTCH(1980)
Ted Sampson
GHOST OF DRAGSTRIP HOLLOW(1959), ed
Teddy Sampson
Silents
HOME SWEET HOME(1914); PRETTY SISTER OF JOSE(1915); AS IN A LOOKING GLASS(1916)
Misc. Silents
FOX WOMAN, THE(1915); CROSS CURRENTS(1916); HER AMERICAN HUSBAND(1918); FIGHTING FOR GOLD(1919); CHICKEN IN THE CASE, THE(1921)
Wilbur Sampson
KING OF THE CORAL SEA(1956, Aus.), m, md; SMILEY GETS A GUN(1959, Brit.), m
Will Sampson
ONE FLEW OVER THE CUCKOO'S NEST(1975); BUFFALO BILL AND THE INDIANS, OR SITTING BULL'S HISTORY LESSON(1976); OUTLAW JOSEY WALES, THE(1976); ORCA(1977); WHITE BUFFALO, THE(1977); FISH HAWK(1981, Can.)
Muhsen Samrani
WHERE THE SPIES ARE(1965, Brit.)
Craig Sams
LOLITA(1962)
Samson Samsanov
THREE SISTERS, THE(1969, USSR), d&w
Joe Samsil
ELECTRA GLIDE IN BLUE(1973)
Charles J. Samsill
MIXED COMPANY(1974)
Diane Samsoi
TIKO AND THE SHARK(1966, U.S./Ital./Fr.)

Cheryl Samson
TRUCK TURNER(1974)
David Samson
POLYESTER(1981)
Ed Samson
MONSTER FROM THE OCEAN FLOOR, THE(1954), ed
Ivan Samson
MANY WATERS(1931, Brit.); HONOURS EASY(1935, Brit.); MUSIC HATH
CHARMS(1935, Brit.); REGAL CAVALCADE(1935, Brit.); HAIL AND FARE-
WELL(1936, Brit.); STUDENT'S ROMANCE, THE(1936, Brit.); APRIL BLOS-
SOMS(1937, Brit.); STEPPING TOES(1938, Brit.); GREAT MR. HANDEL, THE(1942,
Brit.); WALTZ TIME(1946, Brit.); WINSLOW BOY, THE(1950); BROWNING VERSION,
THE(1951, Brit.); PAUL TEMPLE'S TRIUMPH(1951, Brit.); LANDFALL(1953, Brit.);
INNOCENTS IN PARIS(1955, Brit.); MARCH HARE, THE(1956, Brit.); YOU PAY
YOUR MONEY(1957, Brit.); LIBEL(1959, Brit.)
Misc. Silents
NANCE(1920, Brit.); LOVES OF MARY, QUEEN OF SCOTS, THE(1923); SWORDS
AND THE WOMAN(1923, Brit.)
John Samson
TRAITOR'S GATE(1966, Brit./Ger.), w
Ken Samson
STING, THE(1973)
Lester A. Samson
BATTLE CRY(1959), p, w
Margot Samson
Misc. Talkies
LOST CITY, THE(1982)
Yvonne Samson
GREAT DAWN, THE(1947, Ital.)
Samson Samsonov
OPTIMISTIC TRAGEDY, THE(1964, USSR), d, w
Nina Samsonova
RESURRECTION(1963, USSR)
Bert Samuel
WANDERERS, THE(1979)
Joanne Samuel
Misc. Talkies
ALISON'S BIRTHDAY(1979, Aus.)
Julie Samuel
NIGHTMARE(1963, Brit.); FERRY ACROSS THE MERSEY(1964, Brit.)
Lonnie Samuel
MC MASTERS, THE(1970)
Phil C. Samuel
BLACK KNIGHT, THE(1954), p; PRIZE OF GOLD, A(1955), p; WICKED WIFE(1955,
Brit.), p; TOO HOT TO HANDLE(1961, Brit.), p; MACBETH(1963), p
R.Z. Samuel
SWEET SUGAR(1972), w
Yvon Samuel
LOVE AT TWENTY(1963, Fr./Ital./Jap./Pol./Ger.), w
Bob Samuels
NEW ORLEANS AFTER DARK(1958)
Carol Samuels
TARGETS(1968)
Charles Samuels
MR. CELEBRITY(1942), w; MAN ON A STRING(1960), w
David Samuels
CANDLESHOE(1978)
Don Samuels
TWO-LANE BLACKTOP(1971)
George Samuels
PURE HELL OF ST. TRINIAN'S, THE(1961, Brit.), spec eff
Harry Samuels
OUR DAILY BREAD(1934)
Henri Samuels
FAST BULLETS(1936), d; SPEED REPORTER(1936), w; PINTO RUSTLERS(1937),
d; SANTA FE BOUND(1937), d
Jackson Samuels
DR. FRANKENSTEIN ON CAMPUS(1970, Can.), ph
Lesser Samuels
IT'S LOVE AGAIN(1936, Brit.), w; GANGWAY(1937, Brit.), w; YOU'RE IN THE
ARMY NOW(1937, Brit.), w; CLIMBING HIGH(1938, Brit.), w; SAILING ALONG(1938,
Brit.), w; BITTER SWEET(1940), w; EARL OF CHICAGO, THE(1940), w; STRANGE
CARGO(1940), w; UNHOLY PARTNERS(1941), w; HOUR BEFORE THE DAWN,
THE(1944), w; TONIGHT AND EVERY NIGHT(1945), w; ADVENTURE IN BAL-
TIMORE(1949), w; NO WAY OUT(1950), w; BIG CARNIVAL, THE(1951), w; DAR-
LING, HOW COULD YOU!(1951), w; LONG WAIT, THE(1954), p, w; SILVER
CHALICE, THE(1954), w; GREAT DAY IN THE MORNING(1956), w
Maurice Samuels
HOUSE OF STRANGERS(1949); OH, YOU BEAUTIFUL DOLL(1949); THIEVES'
HIGHWAY(1949); BLACK HAND, THE(1950); MYSTERY STREET(1950); GREAT
CARUSO, THE(1951); INSURANCE INVESTIGATOR(1951); PEOPLE AGAINST O'-
HARA, THE(1951); PICKUP ON SOUTH STREET(1953); SALOME(1953)
Maxine Samuels
PYX, THE(1973, Can.), p
Nancy Samuels
PROSTITUTE(1980, Brit.)
Raymond Samuels [B.B. Ray]
AMBUSH VALLEY(1936), d; SILVER TRAIL, THE(1937), p&d
Taylor Samuels
1984
REVENGE OF THE NERDS(1984)
Ted Samuels
ROAD TO HONG KONG, THE(1962, U.S./Brit.), spec eff; WAR LOVER, THE(1962,
U.S./Brit.), spec eff; DR. WHO AND THE DALEKS(1965, Brit.), spec eff; SKULL,
THE(1965, Brit.), spec eff; TOMB OF LIGEIA(1965, Brit.), spec eff; DALEKS-
INVASION EARTH 2155 A.D.(1966, Brit.), spec eff; PSYCHOPATH, THE(1966, Brit.),
spec eff; TRYGON FACTOR, THE(1969, Brit.), spec eff; MACBETH(1971, Brit.), spec eff

Tom Samuels
LAST RHINO, THE(1961, Brit.)
Walter G. Samuels
FLIRTING WITH FATE(1938), m
G.B. Samuelson
SPANISH EYES(1930, Brit.), d; INQUEST(1931, Brit.), d; JEALOUSY(1931, Brit.),
d&w; OTHER WOMAN, THE(1931, Brit.), d&w; SHOULD A DOCTOR TELL?(1931,
Brit.), w; WICKHAM MYSTERY, THE(1931, Brit.), d; CALLBOX MYSTERY,
THE(1932, Brit.), d; COLLISION(1932, Brit.), d; THREADS(1932, Brit.), d; CRUCIFIX,
THE(1934, Brit.), d, w
Silents
ADMIRABLE CRICHTON, THE(1918, Brit.), d; WAY OF AN EAGLE, THE(1918,
Brit.), d; BRIDAL CHAIR, THE(1919, Brit.), d&w; GAME OF LIFE, THE(1922, Brit.), d,
w; IF FOUR WALLS TOLD(1922, Brit.), p; HOTEL MOUSE, THE(1923, Brit.), p;
KNOCKOUT, THE(1923, Brit.), p; UNWANTED, THE(1924, Brit.), p; EVERY MOTH-
ER'S SON(1926, Brit.), w; IF YOUTH BUT KNEW(1926, Brit.), p; OVER THE
STICKS(1929, Brit.), d, w; WINNING GOAL, THE(1929, Brit.), d
Misc. Silents
IN ANOTHER GIRL'S SHOES(1917, Brit.), d; LITTLE WOMEN(1917, Brit.), d;
CONVICT 99(1919, Brit.), d; FAITHFUL HEART, THE(1922, Brit.), d; AFTER-
GLOW(1923, Brit.), d; COUPLE OF DOWN AND OUTS, A(1923, Brit.), d; I'PAGLIAC-
CI(1923, Brit.), d; PAGLIACCI(1923, Brit.), d; FOR VALOUR(1928, Brit.), d; FORGER,
THE(1928, Brit.), d; TWO LITTLE DRUMMER BOYS(1928, Brit.), d; VALLEY OF THE
GHOSTS(1928, Brit.), d
Peter Samuelson
MAN, A WOMAN, AND A BANK, A(1979, Can.), p
1984
REVENGE OF THE NERDS(1984), p
Richard Samuelson
DIRTY HARRY(1971)
Sydney Samuelson
SECRET OF THE FOREST, THE(1955, Brit.), ph
M.B. Samuylow
WANDERING JEW, THE(1933)
Morris B. Samuylow
Misc. Talkies
ABRAHAM OUR PATRIARCH(1933)
A. Samvellian
COLOR OF POMEGRANATES, THE(1980, Armenian), ph
Jay Samwald
1984
BIG MEAT EATER(1984, Can.)
Liu San
Misc. Talkies
KUNG FU HALLOWEEN(1981), d
Louis San Andres
PAPER LION(1968), ed; WHEN THE LEGENDS DIE(1972), ed
Luis San Andres
BLACK RODEO(1972), ph; CLAUDINE(1974), ed
The San Christobal Marimba Band
TROPIC HOLIDAY(1938)
Pilarin San Clemente
TOMMY THE TOREADOR(1960, Brit.)
Jacinto San Emeterio
REDEEMER, THE(1965, Span.)
Alfonso San Felix
KID RODELO(1966, U.S./Span.)
Manuel San Fernando
STORY OF VICKIE, THE(1958, Aust.), ed; PUSS 'N' BOOTS(1964, Mex.), d; LITTLE
RED RIDING HOOD AND THE MONSTERS(1965, Mex.), d
San Francisco Art Center Ensemble
TROIKA(1969)
The San Francisco Strutters
LAUGHING POLICEMAN, THE(1973)
San Juan
PLEASURES AND VICES(1962, Fr.)
Christina San Juan
SOUP FOR ONE(1982)
Julio San Juan
TEACHER AND THE MIRACLE, THE(1961, Ital./Span.)
Manolo Hernandez San Juan
CHRISTMAS KID, THE(1968, U.S., Span.), ph
Olga San Juan
RAINBOW ISLAND(1944); DUFFY'S TAVERN(1945); BLUE SKIES(1946); ARE YOU
WITH IT?(1948); COUNTESS OF MONTE CRISTO, THE(1948); ONE TOUCH OF
VENUS(1948); BEAUTIFUL BLONDE FROM BASHFUL BEND, THE(1949); THIRD
VOICE, THE(1960)
Maria San Marco
INTRIGUE(1947); SONG OF THE THIN MAN(1947); SLEEP, MY LOVE(1948)
Rossana San Marco
ROSE TATTOO, THE(1955); WRONG MAN, THE(1956)
Carlos San Martin
CHARGE OF THE LIGHT BRIGADE, THE(1936); KING AND THE CHORUS GIRL,
THE(1937); MARKED WOMAN(1937)
Conrado San Martin
CONTRABAND SPAIN(1955, Brit.); LEGIONS OF THE NILE(1960, Ital.); KING OF
KINGS(1961)
1984
CONQUEST(1984, Ital./Span./Mex.)
Maria Eugenia San Martin
SPIRITISM(1965, Mex.)
San-Juana
Misc. Silents
VIOLETTES IMPERIALES(1924, Fr.)
Izzy Sanabria
LAST FIGHT, THE(1983)
Vsevolod Sanayev
GROWN-UP CHILDREN(1963, USSR); OPTIMISTIC TRAGEDY, THE(1964, USSR)

Gus Sanberg
FAST COMPANY(1929)
Henrik Sanberg
OPERATION CAMEL(1961, Den.), p
Hope Sanberry
FANCY PANTS(1950)
Fred Sanborn
CRAZY HOUSE(1943); NIGHT CLUB GIRL(1944)
Helen Sanborn
CHARGE OF THE LIGHT BRIGADE, THE(1936)
Aldo Sanbrell
LOST COMMAND, THE(1966); LAST RUN, THE(1971); RAIN FOR A DUSTY SUMMER(1971, U.S./Span.); BAD MAN'S RIVER(1972, Span.); TRAVELS WITH MY AUNT(1972, Brit.)
Louis Sance
Silents
NAPOLEON(1927, Fr.)
Jenny Sanches
WORLD'S GREATEST SINNER, THE(1962)
Rodolfo Sanches
PIXOTE(1981, Braz.), ph
Alberta Sanchez
1984
BREAKIN' 2: ELECTRIC BOOGALOO(1984)
Angel Sanchez
Misc. Talkies
SKEZAG(1971)
Angela Sanchez
SALT OF THE EARTH(1954)
Anna "Lollipop" Sanchez
1984
BREAKIN'(1984)
Antonio Sanchez
WEST OF THE ROCKIES(1929)
Ben Sanchez
WALLS OF HELL, THE(1964, U.S./Phil.)
Blanca Sanchez
CEREBROS DIABOLICOS(1966, Mex.)
Cary Sanchez
HICKEY AND BOGGS(1972)
Cuco Sanchez
LA CUCARACHA(1961, Mex.)
Elvira Sanchez
TORRID ZONE(1940)
Fernando Sanchez
CEREMONY, THE(1963, U.S./Span.)
Fernando Maria Sanchez
SECRET SEVEN, THE(1966, Ital./Span.)
Francisco Sanchez
I HATE MY BODY(1975, Span./Switz.), ph; SAGA OF DRACULA, THE(1975, Span.), ph; SABINA, THE(1979, Span./Swed.)
Gilbert Sanchez
CHARLES AND LUCIE(1982, Fr.), ph
Jaime Sanchez
DAVID AND LISA(1962); HEROINA(1965); PAWNBROKER, THE(1965); BEACH RED(1967); WILD BUNCH, THE(1969); NEXT MAN, THE(1976); BOBBY DEERFIELD(1977); ON THE NICKEL(1980)
Jose Antonio Sanchez
TRAVELS WITH MY AUNT(1972, Brit.), makeup; ROBIN AND MARIAN(1976, Brit.), makeup; MARCH OR DIE(1977, Brit.), makeup
Jose Maria Sanchez
PRIDE AND THE PASSION, THE(1957), makeup; MURIETA(1965, Span.), makeup; RETURN OF THE SEVEN(1966, Span.), makeup
Juan Sanchez
1984
HOLY INNOCENTS, THE(1984, Span.)
Leon Sanchez
BEES, THE(1978), ph
Luis Sanchez
UNHOLY ROLLERS(1972)
Luis Pena Sanchez
MAD QUEEN, THE(1950, Span.)
Lynette Sanchez
UNHOLY ROLLERS(1972)
Marcelino Sanchez
WARRIORS, THE(1979)
Marguerite Sanchez
Silents
HEART OF MARYLAND, THE(1921)
Mario Sanchez
DOGS OF WAR, THE(1980, Brit.)
Mark Sanchez
PEACE FOR A GUNFIGHTER(1967)
Pedro Sanchez [Ignazio Spalla]
SABATA(1969, Ital.); JOHNNY HAMLET(1972, Ital.); RETURN OF SABATA(1972, Ital./Fr./Ger.)
Pedro Sanchez
ANY GUN CAN PLAY(1968, Ital./Span.); BOUNTY HUNTERS, THE(1970, Ital.); ADIOS SABATA(1971, Ital./Span.)
1984
MIXED BLOOD(1984)
Pedro Maria Sanchez
EVERY DAY IS A HOLIDAY(1966, Span.); FICKLE FINGER OF FATE, THE(1967, Span./U.S.)
Ramon Sanchez
CAPTAIN FROM CASTILE(1947)
Raymond Sanchez
DIME WITH A HALO(1963)

Ref Sanchez
LET'S KILL UNCLE(1966); EVERYTHING YOU ALWAYS WANTED TO KNOW ABOUT SEX, BUT WE'RE AFRAID TO ASK(1972)
Regnier Sanchez
CUBAN REBEL GIRLS(1960)
Salvador Sanchez
LAST FIGHT, THE(1983)
1984
UNDER THE VOLCANO(1984)
Silviano Sanchez
BRAVE BULLS, THE(1951)
Susana Sanchez
1984
HOLY INNOCENTS, THE(1984, Span.)
Tony Sanchez
NOCTURNA(1979)
Vicki Sanchez
FARMER, THE(1977), cos; CHAPTER TWO(1979), cos; BLOW OUT(1981), cos; BORDER, THE(1982), cos; TABLE FOR FIVE(1983), cos
Violetta Sanchez
CHANEL SOLITAIRE(1981)
Alvaro Sanchez-Prieto
1984
DEMONS IN THE GARDEN(1984, Span.)
Alfonso Sanchez-Tello
FURY IN PARADISE(1955, U.S./Mex.), p
Porfiria Sanchis
NUN AT THE CROSSROADS, A(1970, Ital./Span.)
Fernando Sancho
KING OF KINGS(1961); LAWRENCE OF ARABIA(1962, Brit.); GOLIATH AGAINST THE GIANTS(1963, Ital./Span.); 55 DAYS AT PEKING(1963); SON OF CAPTAIN BLOOD, THE(1964, U.S./Ital./Span.); ARIZONA COLT(1965, It./Fr./Span.); BACKFIRE(1965, Fr.); GUNMEN OF THE RIO GRANDE(1965, Fr./Ital./Span.); HE WHO SHOOTS FIRST(1966, Ital.); MINNESOTA CLAY(1966, Ital./Fr./Span.); PISTOL FOR RINGO, A(1966, Ital./Span.); RETURN OF RINGO, THE(1966, Ital./Span.); 10,000 DOLLARS BLOOD MONEY(1966, Ital.); HATE FOR HATE(1967, Ital.); SEA PIRATE, THE(1967, Fr./Span./Ital.); BIG GUNDOWN, THE(1968, Ital.); SEVEN GUNS FOR THE MACGREGORS(1968, Ital./Span.); BOLDEST JOB IN THE WEST, THE(1971, Ital.); DEMON WITCH CHILD(1974, Span.); WHAT CHANGED CHARLEY FARTHING?(1976, Brit.)
Tarak Sancho
1984
MISUNDERSTOOD(1984)
Manuel Cano Sanciriaco
HATCHET FOR A HONEYMOON(1969, Span./Ital.), p
Pilar Sanclemente
LAZARILLO(1963, Span.)
Ezio Sancrotti
VIOLENT FOUR, THE(1968, Ital.)
Ralph Sancuyo
MARA MARU(1952)
Barry Sand
EDDIE AND THE CRUISERS(1983)
Carlton Sand
SHE LOVED A FIREMAN(1937), w; STRANGE CASE OF DR. MEADE(1939), w; MILLERSON CASE, THE(1947), w; FATHER TAKES THE AIR(1951), ed
Froma Sand
FOUR JILLS IN A JEEP(1944), w
George Sand
Silents
FANCHON THE CRICKET(1915), w
Herve Sand
THINGS OF LIFE, THE(1970, Fr./Ital./Switz.); CESAR AND ROSALIE(1972, Fr.)
Jillian Sand
ARE YOU THERE?(1930)
Margit Sand
RED-DRAGON(1967, Ital./Ger./US)
Paul Sand
SUBTERRANEANS, THE(1960); GREAT BIG THING, A(1968, U.S./Can.); VIVA MAX!(1969); EVERY LITTLE CROOK AND NANNY(1972); HOT ROCK, THE(1972); SECOND COMING OF SUZANNE, THE(1974); GREAT BANK HOAX, THE(1977); MAIN EVENT, THE(1979); CAN'T STOP THE MUSIC(1980); WHOLLY MOSES(1980)
Rebecca Sand
NEVER STEAL ANYTHING SMALL(1959); BEDTIME STORY(1964); ALL WOMAN(1967)
Rolf Sand
HUNGER(1968, Den./Norway/Swed.)
The Sand Castle
MIDNIGHT(1983), m
Dominique Sanda
FIRST LOVE(1970, Ger./Switz.); CONFORMIST, THE(1971, Ital., Fr); GENTLE CREATURE, A(1971, Fr.); WITHOUT APPARENT MOTIVE(1972, Fr.); IMPOSSIBLE OBJECT(1973, Fr.); MACKINTOSH MAN, THE(1973, Brit.); STEPPENWOLF(1974); CONVERSATION PIECE(1976, Ital., Fr.); GARDEN OF THE FINZI-CONTINIS, THE(1976, Ital./Ger.); 1900(1976, Ital.); DAMNATION ALLEY(1977); INHERITANCE, THE(1978, Ital.); CABOBLANCO(1981)
1984
BEYOND GOOD AND EVIL(1984, Ital./Fr./Ger.)
William Sanda
LADY ICE(1973), ed
Hiroyuki Sandada
MESSAGE FROM SPACE(1978, Jap.)
Clare Sandars
JOURNEY FOR MARGARET(1942); MRS. MINIVER(1942)
John Sandbach
DOCTOR FAUSTUS(1967, Brit.)
A.W. Sandberg
Misc. Silents
GOLDEN CLOWN, THE(1927, Swed.), d

Serge Sandberg
PEARLS OF THE CROWN(1938, Fr.), p
Suzanne Sandberg
NAKED HEARTS(1970, Fr.), ed
Valdis Sandberg
YOLANTA(1964, USSR)
Olof Sandborg
ONLY ONE NIGHT(1942, Swed.)
J.J. Sandbrook
Silents
CHRISTIAN, THE(1914)
Angel Sande
SQUIRM(1976)
Gillian Sande
GRAND PRIX(1934, Brit.)
Jillian Sande
TO WHAT RED HELL(1929, Brit.); EARLY TO BED(1933, Brit./Ger.)
Julian Sande
GOLDEN CAGE, THE(1933, Brit.)
Philippe Sande
PURPLE TAXI, THE(1977, Fr./Ital./Ireland), m
Serena Sande
GHOST TOWN(1956); OKEFENOKEE(1960)
Walter Sande
ARSON GANG BUSTERS(1938); GOLDWYN FOLLIES, THE(1938); LADIES IN DISTRESS(1938); MAD MISS MANTON, THE(1938); TENTH AVENUE KID(1938); ETERNALLY YOURS(1939); GOOD GIRLS GO TO PARIS(1939); ANGELS OVER BROADWAY(1940); KITTY FOYLE(1940); YOU CAN'T FOOL YOUR WIFE(1940); CONFESSIONS OF BOSTON BLACKIE(1941); DIVE BOMBER(1941); DOWN IN SAN DIEGO(1941); NAVY BLUES(1941); PARACHUTE BATTALION(1941); SEALED LIPS(1941); SERGEANT YORK(1941); SING FOR YOUR SUPPER(1941); ALIAS BOSTON BLACKIE(1942); BOSTON BLACKIE GOES HOLLYWOOD(1942); COMMANDOS STRIKE AT DAWN, THE(1942); FRECKLES COMES HOME(1942); MY SISTER EILEEN(1942); SWEETHEART OF THE FLEET(1942); TIMBER(1942); TO THE SHORES OF TRIPOLI(1942); TORTILLA FLAT(1942); TRAMP, TRAMP, TRAMP(1942); AFTER MIDNIGHT WITH BOSTON BLACKIE(1943); AIR FORCE(1943); CHANCE OF A LIFETIME, THE(1943); CORVETTE K-225(1943); GUNG HO!(1943); GUY NAMED JOE, A(1943); PURPLE V, THE(1943); REVEILLE WITH BEVERLY(1943); SALUTE FOR THREE(1943); SON OF DRACULA(1943); THEY CAME TO BLOW UP AMERICA(1943); I LOVE A SOLDIER(1944); SINGING SHERIFF, THE(1944); TO HAVE AND HAVE NOT(1944); ALONG CAME JONES(1945); DALTONS RIDE AGAIN, THE(1945); SPIDER, THE(1945); WHAT NEXT, CORPORAL HARGROVE?(1945); BLUE DAHLIA, THE(1946); NO LEAVE, NO LOVE(1946); NOCTURNE(1946); CHRISTMAS EVE(1947); KILLER McCOY(1947); RED HOUSE, THE(1947); WILD HARVEST(1947); WOMAN ON THE BEACH, THE(1947); HALF PAST MIDNIGHT(1948); PERILOUS WATERS(1948); PRINCE OF THIEVES, THE(1948); WALLFLOWER(1948); BAD BOY(1949); BLONDE ICE(1949); CANADIAN PACIFIC(1949); JOE PALOOKA IN THE COUNTERPUNCH(1949); MISS MINK OF 1949(1949); RIM OF THE CANYON(1949); STRANGE BARGAIN(1949); TUCSON(1949); DAKOTA LIL(1950); DARK CITY(1950); KID FROM TEXAS, THE(1950); WOMAN OF DISTINCTION, A(1950); BASKETBALL FIX, THE(1951); FORT WORTH(1951); I WANT YOU(1951); PAYMENT ON DEMAND(1951); PLACE IN THE SUN, A(1951); RACKET, THE(1951); RAWHIDE(1951); RED MOUNTAIN(1951); TOMORROW IS ANOTHER DAY(1951); WARPATH(1951); BOMBA AND THE JUNGLE GIRL(1952); DUEL AT SILVER CREEK, THE(1952); MUTINY(1952); RED PLANET MARS(1952); STEEL TRAP, THE(1952); BLUEPRINT FOR MURDER, A(1953); GREAT SIOUX UPRISING, THE(1953); INVADERS FROM MARS(1953); KID FROM LEFT FIELD, THE(1953); POWDER RIVER(1953); WAR OF THE WORLDS, THE(1953); APACHE(1954); OVERLAND PACIFIC(1954); BAD DAY AT BLACK ROCK(1955); TEXAS LADY(1955); WICHITA(1955); ANYTHING GOES(1956); CANYON RIVER(1956); GUN BROTHERS(1956); MAVERICK QUEEN, THE(1956); DRANGO(1957); IRON SHERIFF, THE(1957); JOHNNY TREMAIN(1957); LAST TRAIN FROM GUN HILL(1959); GALLANT HOURS, THE(1960); NOOSE FOR A GUNMAN(1960); OKLAHOMA TERRITORY(1960); SUNRISE AT CAMPOBELLO(1960); I'LL TAKE SWEDEN(1965); YOUNG DILLINGER(1965); NAVY VS. THE NIGHT MONSTERS, THE(1966); DEATH OF A GUNFIGHTER(1969); COLD TURKEY(1971)
Jack Sandeen
AMY(1981), cos
Bill Sandel
DEAD AND BURIED(1981), art d
Bill Sandell
FAST CHARLIE... THE MOONBEAM RIDER(1979), art d; SERIAL(1980), art d
William Sandell
PROMISE, THE(1979), art d; BLOOD BEACH(1981), art d
1984
WILD LIFE, THE(1984), prod d
Erna Sander
CAPTAIN FROM KOEPENICK, THE(1956, Ger.), cos
Helke Sander
ALL-AROUND REDUCED PERSONALITY-OUTTAKES, THE(1978, Ger.), a, d&w
Karl Sander
HIS MAJESTY, KING BALLYHOO(1931, Ger.), ph
Kuli Sander
DIAMONDS(1975, U.S./Israel), art d; PASSOVER PLOT, THE(1976, Israel), art d; OPERATION THUNDERBOLT(1978, ISRAEL), art d; ASHANTI(1979), art d
Otto Sander
TIN DRUM, THE(1979, Ger./Fr./Yugo./Pol.); DAS BOOT(1982)
1984
LOVE IN GERMANY, A(1984, Fr./Ger.)
Peter Sander
DATELINE DIAMONDS(1966, Brit.)
John Sanderford
LOOKER(1981)
1984
FIRESTARTER(1984)
Misc. Talkies
ALCHEMIST, THE(1981)

Maurice Sanderground
Misc. Silents
RUSSIA - LAND OF TOMORROW(1919, Brit.), d
Albert Sanders
PIRANHA II: THE SPAWNING(1981, Neth.)
Andrew Sanders
NED KELLY(1970, Brit.), a, art d; SHOCK TREATMENT(1981), art d; PRIVATES ON PARADE(1982), art d; MERRY CHRISTMAS MR. LAWRENCE(1983, Jap./Brit.), art d
1984
PRIVATES ON PARADE(1984, Brit.), art d
Anita Sanders
TENTH VICTIM, THE(1965, Fr./Ital.); LA FUGA(1966, Ital.)
Misc. Talkies
BANDITS IN ROME(1967, Ital.)
Anna Sanders
1984
GERMANY PALE MOTHER(1984, Ger.)
Anthony C. Sanders
1984
SOLDIER'S STORY, A(1984)
Barbara Ann Sanders
BRIGHT ROAD(1953)
Beverly Sanders
MAGIC(1978); ...AND JUSTICE FOR ALL(1979); LOVE AT FIRST BITE(1979)
Byron Sanders
FLESH EATERS, THE(1964); TRICK BABY(1973)
Casey Sanders
1984
BODY DOUBLE(1984)
Charles Sanders
GOLDEN LINK, THE(1954, Brit.), d
Chris Sanders
LOVE AND DEATH(1975)
Cornelia Sanders
DAMIEN--OMEN II(1978)
David Sanders
HURRY SUNDOWN(1967)
Denis Sanders
NAKED AND THE DEAD, THE(1958), w; CRIME AND PUNISHMENT, U.S.A.(1959), d; WAR HUNT(1962), d; ONE MAN'S WAY(1964), d; SHOCK TREATMENT(1964), d; INVASION OF THE BEE GIRLS(1973), d
Dick Sanders
WHITE NIGHTS(1961, Ital./Fr.), a, ch
Dirk Sanders
BLACK TIGHTS(1962, Fr.); VERY PRIVATE AFFAIR, A(1962, Fr./Ital.); PIERROT LE FOU(1968, Fr./Ital.); CASTLE KEEP(1969), ch; YOU ONLY LIVE ONCE(1969, Fr.), d, w
Douglas Sanders
SORCERESS(1983)
Florida Sanders
CENTENNIAL SUMMER(1946)
George Sanders
UNCLE HARRY(1945); DISHONOR BRIGHT(1936, Brit.); FIND THE LADY(1936, Brit.); LLOYDS OF LONDON(1936); STRANGE CARGO(1936, Brit.); THINGS TO COME(1936, Brit.); LADY ESCAPES, THE(1937); LANCER SPY(1937); LOVE IS NEWS(1937); MAN WHO COULD WORK MIRACLES, THE(1937, Brit.); SLAVE SHIP(1937); FOUR MEN AND A PRAYER(1938); INTERNATIONAL SETTLEMENT(1938); ALLEGHENY UPRISING(1939); CONFESSIONS OF A NAZI SPY(1939); MR. MOTO'S LAST WARNING(1939); NURSE EDITH CAVELL(1939); SAINT IN LONDON, THE(1939, Brit.); SAINT STRIKES BACK, THE(1939); BITTER SWEET(1940); FOREIGN CORRESPONDENT(1940); GREEN HELL(1940); HOUSE OF THE SEVEN GABLES, THE(1940); OUTSIDER, THE(1940, Brit.); REBECCA(1940); SAINT TAKES OVER, THE(1940); SAINT'S DOUBLE TROUBLE, THE(1940); SO THIS IS LONDON(1940, Brit.); SON OF MONTE CRISTO(1940); DATE WITH THE FALCON, A(1941); GAY FALCON, THE(1941); MAN HUNT(1941); RAGE IN HEAVEN(1941); SAINT IN PALM SPRINGS, THE(1941); SUNDOWN(1941); BLACK SWAN, THE(1942); FALCON TAKES OVER, THE(1942); FALCON'S BROTHER, THE(1942); GHOST AND MRS. MUIR, THE(1942); HER CARDBOARD LOVER(1942); MOON AND SIXPENCE, THE(1942); QUIET PLEASE, MURDER(1942); SON OF FURY(1942); TALES OF MANHATTAN(1942); APPOINTMENT IN BERLIN(1943); PARIS AFTER DARK(1943); THEY CAME TO BLOW UP AMERICA(1943); THIS LAND IS MINE(1943); ACTION IN ARABIA(1944); LODGER, THE(1944); SUMMER STORM(1944); HANGOVER SQUARE(1945); PICTURE OF DORIAN GRAY, THE(1945); SCANDAL IN PARIS, A(1946); STRANGE WOMAN, THE(1946); FOREVER AMBER(1947); LURED(1947); PRIVATE AFFAIRS OF BEL AMI, THE(1947); FAN, THE(1949); SAMSON AND DELILAH(1949); ALL ABOUT EVE(1950); I CAN GET IT FOR YOU WHOLESALE(1951); KENTUCKY JUBILEE(1951); LIGHT TOUCH, THE(1951); ASSIGNMENT-PARIS(1952); CAPTAIN BLACK JACK(1952, U.S./Fr.); HOLD THAT LINE(1952); IVANHOE(1952, Brit.); CALL ME MADAM(1953); RUN FOR THE HILLS(1953); KING RICHARD AND THE CRUSADERS(1954, Brit.), w; UNHOLY FOUR, THE(1954, Brit.); WITNESS TO MURDER(1954); BIG TIP OFF, THE(1955); JUPITER'S DARLING(1955); KING'S THIEF, THE(1955); MOONFLEET(1955); NIGHT FREIGHT(1955); SCARLET COAT, THE(1955); STRANGERS, THE(1955, Ital.); DEATH OF A SCOUNDREL(1956); NEVER SAY GOODBYE(1956); THAT CERTAIN FEELING(1956); WHILE THE CITY SLEEPS(1956); SEVENTH SIN, THE(1957); FROM THE EARTH TO THE MOON(1958); OUTCASTS OF THE CITY(1958); ROCK-A-BYE BABY(1958); WHOLE TRUTH, THE(1958, Brit.); THAT KIND OF WOMAN(1959); BLUEBEARD'S TEN HONEYMOONS(1960, Brit.); LAST VOYAGE, THE(1960); TOUCH OF LARCENY, A(1960, Brit.); VILLAGE OF THE DAMNED(1960, Brit.); CALL ME GENIUS(1961, Brit.); FIVE GOLDEN HOURS(1961, Brit.); TROUBLE IN THE SKY(1961, Brit.); IN SEARCH OF THE CASTAWAYS(1962, Brit.); OPERATION SNATCH(1962, Brit.); CAIRO(1963); CRACKSMAN, THE(1963, Brit.); DARK PURPOSE(1964); SHOT IN THE DARK, A(1964); AMOROUS ADVENTURES OF MOLL FLANDERS, THE(1965); GOLDEN HEAD, THE(1965, Hung., U.S.); QUILLER MEMORANDUM, THE(1966, Brit.); TRUNK TO CAIRO(1966, Israel/Ger.); GOOD TIMES(1967); JUNGLE BOOK(1967); WARNING SHOT(1967); BEST HOUSE IN LONDON, THE(1969, Brit.); BODY STEALERS, THE(1969); CANDY MAN, THE(1969); ONE STEP TO HELL(1969, U.S./Ital./Span.); KREMLIN LETTER, THE(1970); RIO 70(1970, U.S./Ger./Span.); ENDLESS NIGHT(1971, Brit.); DOOMWATCH(1972, Brit.); PSYCHOMANIA(1974, Brit.)

Misc. Talkies
OUT OF THIN AIR(1969); NIGHT OF THE ASSASSIN, THE(1972)
Geraldine Sanders
LAST HOUSE ON DEAD END STREET(1977)
Gregg Sanders
MURDER WITHOUT TEARS(1953)
H. P. Sanders
APPOINTMENT IN BERLIN(1943)
Henry Sanders
Misc. Talkies
PANAMA RED(1976)
Col. Harlan Sanders
HELL'S BLOODY DEVILS(1970)
Henry G. Sanders
BOSS'S SON, THE(1978); HARD COUNTRY(1981); ENDANGERED SPECIES(1982)
1984
CHOOSE ME(1984); HEARTBREAKERS(1984); WEEKEND PASS(1984)
Henry Gayle Sanders
INDEPENDENCE DAY(1976)
Hilary St. George Sanders
PARATROOPER(1954, Brit.), w
Hugh Sanders
DAMNED DON'T CRY, THE(1950); GREAT RUPERT, THE(1950); MAGNIFICENT YANKEE, THE(1950); MISTER 880(1950); STORM WARNING(1950); ALONG THE GREAT DIVIDE(1951); I WAS A COMMUNIST FOR THE F.B.I.(1951); INDIAN UPRISING(1951); ONLY THE VALIANT(1951); SELLOUT, THE(1951); STRICTLY DISHONORABLE(1951); SUGARFOOT(1951); THAT'S MY BOY(1951); THREE GUYS NAMED MIKE(1951); TOMORROW IS ANOTHER DAY(1951); BOOTS MALONE(1952); FIGHTER, THE(1952); LAST OF THE COMANCHES(1952); MONTANA TERRITORY(1952); PRIDE OF ST. LOUIS, THE(1952); SOMETHING FOR THE BIRDS(1952); WINNING TEAM, THE(1952); CITY OF BAD MEN(1953); GLASS WEB, THE(1953); GUN BELT(1953); HERE COME THE GIRLS(1953); SCARED STIFF(1953); THUNDER OVER THE PLAINS(1953); WILD ONE, THE(1953); SHIELD FOR MURDER(1954); UNTAMED HEIRESS(1954); CHICAGO SYNDICATE(1955); FINGER MAN(1955); FIVE AGAINST THE HOUSE(1955); GLORY(1955); I COVER THE UNDERWORLD(1955); I DIED A THOUSAND TIMES(1955); LAST COMMAND, THE(1955); TOP GUN(1955); MIAMI EXPOSE(1956); PEACEMAKER, THE(1956); CARELESS YEARS, THE(1957); CHAIN OF EVIDENCE(1957); JAILHOUSE ROCK(1957); PHANTOM STAGECOACH, THE(1957); GOING STEADY(1958); LIFE BEGINS AT 17(1958); VOICE IN THE MIRROR(1958); DON'T GIVE UP THE SHIP(1959); WARLOCK(1959); CAGE OF EVIL(1960); MUSIC BOX KID, THE(1960); MAN-TRAP(1961); PANIC IN YEAR ZERO!(1962); TO KILL A MOCKINGBIRD(1962); WILD WESTERNERS, THE(1962)
Irene Sanders
FINAL TERROR, THE(1983)
Jack Sanders
STORMY(1935)
Jack Frost Sanders
KING OF THE MOUNTAIN(1981), p
Jay Sanders
STARTING OVER(1979)
Jay O. Sanders
HANKY-PANKY(1982); CROSS CREEK(1983); EDDIE MACON'S RUN(1983)
Jean Sanders
Misc. Talkies
HOTWIRE(1980)
Joe Sanders
DARK STAR(1975)
Jonathan Sanders
GOSPEL ROAD, THE(1973)
June Sanders
LOVING COUPLES(1980); ROMANTIC COMEDY(1983)
Kevin Sanders
FOREPLAY(1975)
Kurtis Sanders
USED CARS(1980)
Kurtis Epper Sanders
ANNIE(1982)
Lamar Sanders
KIRLIAN WITNESS, THE(1978), w
Lawrence Sanders
ANDERSON TAPES, THE(1971), w; FIRST DEADLY SIN, THE(1980), w
Loni Sanders
Misc. Talkies
BLONDE GODDESS(1982)
Lugene Sanders
TORMENTED(1960)
Madelyn Sanders
QUADROON(1972)
Nadine Sanders
8 ½(1963, Ital.)
Nedra Sanders
ARABIAN NIGHTS(1942); FLESH AND FANTASY(1943)
Norma Jean Sanders
1984
MEMOIRS(1984, Can.)
Ray Sanders
FAMILY, THE(1974, Fr./Ital.); PARTNERS(1982)
Richard Sanders
NUDE BOMB, THE(1980); VALLEY GIRL(1983)
Robert Sanders
FROGS(1972)
Ron Sanders
SCANNERS(1981, Can.), ed
1984
FIRESTARTER(1984), ed
Ronald Sanders
TITLE SHOT(1982, Can.), ed; VIDEODROME(1983, Can.), ed

Ronnie Sanders
CANNIBALS IN THE STREETS(1982, Ital./Span.)
Rowena Sanders
MOZART(1940, Brit.)
Roy Sanders
GOODBYE PORK PIE(1981, New Zealand)
Sandy Sanders
LAST ROUND-UP, THE(1947); FRONTIER REVENGE(1948); LOADED PISTOLS(1948); OUTLAW COUNTRY(1949); RIDERS IN THE SKY(1949); RIM OF THE CANYON(1949); SON OF A BADMAN(1949); SONS OF NEW MEXICO(1949); BEYOND THE PURPLE HILLS(1950); BLAZING SUN, THE(1950); FIGHTING REDHEAD, THE(1950); INDIAN TERRITORY(1950); MULE TRAIN(1950); HILLS OF UTAH(1951); SILVER CANYON(1951); TEXANS NEVER CRY(1951); VALLEY OF FIRE(1951); BARBED WIRE(1952); FRONTIER PHANTOM, THE(1952); NIGHT STAGE TO GALVESTON(1952); SMOKY CANYON(1952); WAGON TEAM(1952); PRINCE OF PIRATES(1953); CRIME WAVE(1954); MASTERSON OF KANSAS(1954); HARDER THEY FALL, THE(1956); LEGEND OF TOM DOOLEY, THE(1959); NORSEMAN, THE(1978)
Scott Sanders
TALKING FEET(1937, Brit.); COMMON TOUCH, THE(1941, Brit.); MURDER IN REVERSE(1946, Brit.); LET'S MAKE UP(1955, Brit.)
Shep Sanders
VICE RAID(1959); THREE CAME TO KILL(1960); TWELVE HOURS TO KILL(1960); BALTIMORE BULLET, THE(1980)
Shepard Sanders
1984
BLAME IT ON THE NIGHT(1984)
Shepherd Sanders
YOU HAVE TO RUN FAST(1961); SAND PEBBLES, THE(1966); SOL MADRID(1968); KELLY'S HEROES(1970, U.S./Yugo.); ESCAPE TO WITCH MOUNTAIN(1975)
Sherman Sanders
DEVIL AND DANIEL WEBSTER, THE(1941); SWAMP WATER(1941); STAR SPANGLED RHYTHM(1942); STOLEN LIFE, A(1946); BOWERY BUCKAROOS(1947); LURE OF THE WILDERNESS(1952); PRESIDENT'S LADY, THE(1953)
Sherman E. Sanders
RIDE 'EM COWBOY(1942)
Steve Sanders
HURRY SUNDOWN(1967)
Stuart Sanders
ROOM TO LET(1949, Brit.); MR. H. C. ANDERSEN(1950, Brit.); SCOTLAND YARD INSPECTOR(1952, Brit.); CRAWLING EYE, THE(1958, Brit.); MOUSE THAT ROARED, THE(1959, Brit.); RUNAWAY, THE(1964, Brit.); OCTOPUSSY(1983, Brit.)
Sun Sanders
Misc. Talkies
SWEET SOUND OF DEATH(1965, U.S./Span.)
Ted Sanders
VARIETY(1935, Brit.); TWO ON A DOORSTEP(1936, Brit.)
Terry Sanders
NAKED AND THE DEAD, THE(1958), w; CRIME AND PUNISHMENT, U.S.A.(1959), p; WAR HUNT(1962), p
Tessa Sanders
YOU ONLY LIVE ONCE(1969, Fr.)
Troy Sanders
HENRY ALDRICH SWINGS IT(1943), md; MR. MUSIC(1950), m
W. Sanders
POCKET MONEY(1972)
Walter Sanders
ON THE YARD(1978)
The Sanders Twins
STEPPING TOES(1938, Brit.)
Helma Sanders-Brahms
1984
GERMANY PALE MOTHER(1984, Ger.), d&w
Challis Sanderson
MURDER ON THE SECOND FLOOR(1932, Brit.), w; DANNY BOY(1934, Brit.), p&d; COCK O' THE NORTH(1935, Brit.), d
Silents
MONTY WORKS THE WIRES(1921, Brit.), d
Misc. Silents
LAW DIVINE, THE(1920, Brit.), d; THREE MEN IN A BOAT(1920, Brit.), d; SCALLYWAG, THE(1921, Brit.), d; SCRAGS(1930, Brit.), d
David Sanderson
SHIRLEY THOMPSON VERSUS THE ALIENS(1968, Aus.), ph; NIGHT OF THE PROWLER, THE(1979, Aus.), ph; PLUMBER, THE(1980, Aus.), ph
Derek Sanderson
Misc. Talkies
WINTER COMES EARLY(1972)
Harold Sanderson
THUNDERBALL(1965, Brit.)
James Sanderson
HEAD ON(1981, Can.), w
Joan Sanderson
YOUNG WIVES' TALE(1954, Brit.); SHE KNOWS Y'KNOW(1962, Brit.); PLEASE SIR!(1971, Brit.); GREAT MUPPET CAPER, THE(1981)
Julia Sanderson
Misc. Silents
RUNAWAY, THE(1917)
Kent Sanderson
Silents
LURE OF THE YUKON(1924); STRONG BOY(1929)
Lynn Sanderson
Silents
LAW OF THE MOUNTED(1928); MANHATTAN COWBOY(1928); ARIZONA KID, THE(1929)
Martyn Sanderson
NED KELLY(1970, Brit.); SOLO(1978, New Zealand/Aus.), a, w; BEYOND REASONABLE DOUBT(1980, New Zeal.)
1984
HEART OF THE STAG(1984, New Zealand), w; PALLET ON THE FLOOR(1984, New Zealand), w; UTU(1984, New Zealand); WILD HORSES(1984, New Zealand)

Mary Jane Sanderson
Silents
ENTER MADAME(1922)
Paul Sanderson
CHARLIE CHAN AND THE CURSE OF THE DRAGON QUEEN(1981); MAKING LOVE(1982)
Ruth Sanderson
BRUTE FORCE(1947); SMASH-UP, THE STORY OF A WOMAN(1947); GOOD SAM(1948); ABANDONED(1949); ROSEANNA McCOY(1949)
William Sanderson
FIGHT FOR YOUR LIFE(1977); COAL MINER'S DAUGHTER(1980); DEATH HUNT(1981); RAGGEDY MAN(1981); BLADE RUNNER(1982); LONE WOLF McQUADE(1983); SAVAGE WEEKEND(1983)
1984
CITY HEAT(1984); FLETCH(1984)
William J. Sanderson
SEED OF INNOCENCE(1980)
Armine Sandford
TOWN LIKE ALICE, A(1958, Brit.)
Chris Sandford
COOL IT, CAROL!(1970, Brit.)
Christopher Sandford
NEXT TO NO TIME(1960, Brit.); RAPTURE(1965); HALF A SIXPENCE(1967, Brit.); BEFORE WINTER COMES(1969, Brit.); DEEP END(1970 Ger./U.S.); DIE SCREAMING, MARIANNE(1970, Brit.); KREMLIN LETTER, THE(1970); KING, QUEEN, KNAVE(1972, Ger./U.S.); OLD DRACULA(1975, Brit.)
Frances Sandford
'TILL WE MEET AGAIN(1944); SAINTED SISTERS, THE(1948)
Joseph G. Sandford
SIX LESSONS FROM MADAME LA ZONGA(1941), p
Kenneth Sandford
MIKADO, THE(1967, Brit.)
Marjorie Sandford
LASSIE FROM LANCASHIRE(1938, Brit.)
Robert Sandford
LEASE OF LIFE(1954, Brit.); DOG AND THE DIAMONDS, THE(1962, Brit.)
Stanley J. [Tiny] Sandford
IRON MASK, THE(1929); RIO RITA(1929); FIGHTING CARAVANS(1931); PARDON US(1931); THIRTEENTH GUEST, THE(1932); WARRIOR'S HUSBAND, THE(1933); REMEMBER LAST NIGHT(1935); OUR RELATIONS(1936); SHOW BOAT(1936); ROAD BACK,THE(1937)
Silents
WORLD'S CHAMPION, THE(1922)
Maurice Sandground
Silents
KILTIES THREE(1918, Brit.), p&d; LIFE OF ROBERT BURNS, THE(1926, Brit.), d
Misc. Silents
HOW COULD YOU UNCLE?(1918, Brit.), d
Sandhya
TWO EYES, TWELVE HANDS(1958, India)
Josef Sandia
MY FATHER'S HOUSE(1947, Palestine)
Marsha Jo Sandidge
WILD WHEELS(1969)
Robert Sandien
FOXY LADY(1971, Can.), w
Arthur Sandifer
OPERATION DISASTER(1951, Brit.)
Arthur Sandiford
WRONG BOX, THE(1966, Brit.)
Ray Sandiford
LIFE STUDY(1973), ed
Virginia Sandifur
DEADLY HERO(1976)
Will Sandin
HALLOWEEN(1978)
Albert Sandler
FOR YOU ALONE(1945, Brit.); WALTZ TIME(1946, Brit.)
Allan Sandler
FRASIER, THE SENSUOUS LION(1973), p
Barry Sandler
KANSAS CITY BOMBER(1972), w; LONERS, THE(1972), w; DUCHESS AND THE DIRTWATER FOX, THE(1976), w; GABLE AND LOMBARD(1976), w; MIRROR CRACK'D, THE(1980, Brit.), w; MAKING LOVE(1982), w
1984
CRIMES OF PASSION(1984), p, w
Bobby Sandler
PEOPLE NEXT DOOR, THE(1970); LUNCH WAGON(1981)
Ric Sandler
HEY, GOOD LOOKIN'(1982), m
Robert Sandler
CANNIBAL GIRLS(1973), w
Sally Sandlin
LOVE TIME(1934), w; CALL A MESSENGER(1939), w; OFF THE RECORD(1939), w
Peter Sandloff
RETURN OF DR. MABUSE, THE(1961, Ger./Fr./Ital.), m; THREE PENNY OPERA(1963, Fr./Ger.), md; INVISIBLE DR. MABUSE, THE(1965, Ger.), m; MAEDCHEN IN UNIFORM(1965, Ger./Fr.), m
Rune Sandlunds
KREMLIN LETTER, THE(1970)
Lee Sandman
LENNY(1974); ABSENCE OF MALICE(1981); SUPER FUZZ(1981); WITHOUT A TRACE(1983)
Hans Sandmeier
MARRIAGE OF MARIA BRAUN, THE(1979, Ger.), set d
Toralf Sando
HUNGER(1968, Den./Norway/Swed.)

James Sandoe
DOWNHILL RACER(1969)
Augusto Sandoni
Misc. Silents
SCRAGS(1930, Brit.)
Flo Sandons
SHIP OF CONDEMNED WOMEN, THE(1963, ITAL.)
Alfred Sandor
NICKEL QUEEN, THE(1971, Aus.)
Greg Sandor
JUMP(1971), ph; WHO KILLED MARY WHAT'SER NAME?(1971), ph
Gregory Sandor
SECRET FILE: HOLLYWOOD(1962), ph; NAVAJO RUN(1966), ph; RIDE IN THE WHIRLWIND(1966), ph; BORN LOSERS(1967), ph; HOOKED GENERATION, THE(1969), ph; SHOOTING, THE(1971), ph; TO BE FREE(1972), ph; SISTERS(1973), ph; TEARS OF HAPPINESS(1974), ph; FORBIDDEN ZONE(1980), ph
Steve Sandor
ROUGH NIGHT IN JERICHO(1967); IF HE HOLLERS, LET HIM GO(1968); BRIDGE AT REMAGEN, THE(1969); HELL'S ANGELS '69(1969); ONE MORE TRAIN TO ROB(1971); ONLY WAY HOME, THE(1972); NO MERCY MAN, THE(1975); NINTH CONFIGURATION, THE(1980); FIRE AND ICE(1983); STRYKER(1983, Phil.)
Misc. Talkies
BONNIE'S KIDS(1973)
A. Sandoval
POCKET MONEY(1972)
Antonio Sandoval
BANDIDO(1956)
Chico Sandoval
MEDAL FOR BENNY, A(1945)
Douglas Sandoval
HIGH RISK(1981)
Esther Sandoval
THUNDER ISLAND(1963)
Michael Sandoval
1984
REPO MAN(1984)
Miguel Sandoval
TIMERIDER(1983)
Nena Sandoval
WHEN YOU'RE IN LOVE(1937)
Teri Lynn Sandoval
MONEY TRAP, THE(1966)
Sandow
Silents
AVENGING FANGS(1927)
Misc. Silents
CALL OF THE WILDERNESS, THE(1926); CODE OF THE NORTHWEST(1926)
Mari Sandoz
CHEYENNE AUTUMN(1964), w
Maurice Sandoz
CURSE OF THE WRAYDONS, THE(1946, Brit.), w; MAZE, THE(1953), w
Jerry Sandquist
1984
BLIND DATE(1984)
Frantisek Sandr
INTIMATE LIGHTING(1969, Czech.), prod d
Maxine Sandra
LOYALTIES(1934, Brit.)
Gisele Sandre
TALES OF PARIS(1962, Fr./Ital.); LANDRU(1963, Fr./Ital)
Stefani Sandrelli
DESIRE, THE INTERIOR LIFE(1980, Ital,/Ger.)
Stefania Sandrelli
DIVORCE, ITALIAN STYLE(1962, Ital.); SEDUCED AND ABANDONED(1964, Fr./Ital.); FASCIST, THE(1965, Ital.); CLIMAX, THE(1967, Fr., Ital.); TENDER SCOUNDREL(1967, Fr./Ital.); CONFORMIST, THE(1971, Ital., Fr); BLACK BELLY OF THE TARANTULA, THE(1972, Ital.); ALFREDO, ALFREDO(1973, Ital.); POLICE PYTHON 357(1976, Fr.); 1900(1976, Ital.); CASE AGAINST FERRO, THE(1980, Fr.)
Anna Maria Sandri
RED AND THE BLACK, THE(1954, Fr./Ital.); BLACK TENT, THE(1956, Brit.)
Gia Sandri
STRANGER IN TOWN, A(1968, U.S./Ital.)
Jay Sandrich
SEEMS LIKE OLD TIMES(1980), d
Mark Sandrich
TALK OF HOLLYWOOD, THE(1929), d, w; HOLD'EM JAIL(1932), w; AGGIE APPLEBY, MAKER OF MEN(1933), d; MELODY CRUISE(1933), d, w; COCKEYED CAVALIERS(1934), d; GAY DIVORCEE, THE(1934), d; HIPS, HIPS, HOORAY(1934), d; TOP HAT(1935), d; FOLLOW THE FLEET(1936), d; WOMAN REBELS, A(1936), d; SHALL WE DANCE(1937), d; CAREFREE(1938), d; MAN ABOUT TOWN(1939), d; BUCK BENNY RIDES AGAIN(1940), p, d; LOVE THY NEIGHBOR(1940), p&d; SKYLARK(1941), p&d; HOLIDAY INN(1942), p&d; SO PROUDLY WE HAIL(1943), p&d; HERE COME THE WAVES(1944), p&d; I LOVE A SOLDIER(1944), p&d
Silents
RUNAWAY GIRLS(1928), d
Sandrine
FRUIT IS RIPE, THE(1961, Fr./Ital.); DANIELLA BY NIGHT(1962, Fr/Ger.); SOFT SKIN ON BLACK SILK(1964, Fr./Span.); MICHELLE(1970, Fr.)
Luis Sandrini
GAMES MEN PLAY, THE(1968, Arg.)
Adele Sandrock
BEAUTIFUL ADVENTURE(1932, Ger.); TREMENDOUSLY RICH MAN, A(1932, Ger.)
Sharon Sandrock
MONDO TRASHO(1970)
Claude Sandron
MICHELLE(1970, Fr.), w

Anita Sands
DIARY OF A HIGH SCHOOL BRIDE(1959)
Billy Sands
MC HALE'S NAVY(1964); MC HALE'S NAVY JOINS THE AIR FORCE(1965); HOW TO FRAME A FIGG(1971); HARRAD EXPERIMENT, THE(1973); ROCKY(1976); WORLD'S GREATEST LOVER, THE(1977); SERIAL(1980)
Carol Sands
MODIGLIANI OF MONTPARNASSE(1961, Fr./Ital.)
Danny Sands
LAW OF THE BADLANDS(1950); TALL STRANGER, THE(1957); EL DORADO(1967); RIO LOBO(1970)
Danny H. Sands
SON OF PALEFACE(1952)
Diana Sands
RAISIN IN THE SUN, A(1961); AFFAIR OF THE SKIN, AN(1964); ENSIGN PULVER(1964); LANDLORD, THE(1970); DOCTORS' WIVES(1971); GEORGIA, GEORGIA(1972); WILLIE DYNAMITE(1973); HONEYBABY, HONEYBABY(1974)
Dick Sands
CONFIDENTIAL CONNIE(1953); PHANTOM FROM SPACE(1953); DEMETRIUS AND THE GLADIATORS(1954); SNOW CREATURE, THE,(1954)
Eileen Sands
UP TO HIS NECK(1954, Brit.); YOU KNOW WHAT SAILORS ARE(1954, Brit.)
Elizabeth Sands
TOWN CALLED HELL, A(1971, Span./Brit.)
Henry Sands
Misc. Silents
SHARE AND SHARE ALIKE(1925)
Jack Sands
FLOATING DUTCHMAN, THE(1953, Brit.)
Jay "Suave" Sands
1984
BREAKIN' 2: ELECTRIC BOOGALOO(1984)
Jodie Sands
JAMBOREE(1957)
John Sands
LAWLESS, THE(1950); TWO FLAGS WEST(1950); BASKETBALL FIX, THE(1951); TARGET UNKNOWN(1951); ALADDIN AND HIS LAMP(1952)
Johnny Sands
AFFAIRS OF GERALDINE(1946); TILL THE END OF TIME(1946); BACHELOR AND THE BOBBY-SOXER, THE(1947); BLAZE OF NOON(1947); BORN TO SPEED(1947); FABULOUS TEXAN, THE(1947); ADVENTURE IN BALTIMORE(1949); MASSACRE RIVER(1949); ADMIRAL WAS A LADY, THE(1950); SABRE JET(1953)
Julian Sands
PRIVATES ON PARADE(1982)
1984
KILLING FIELDS, THE(1984, Brit.); OXFORD BLUES(1984); PRIVATES ON PARADE(1984, Brit.)
Silents
BACHELOR'S BABY, THE(1927), w
Lee Sands
GIVE OUT, SISTERS(1942), w; SING A JINGLE(1943), w
Leslie Sands
ANOTHER MAN'S POISON(1952, Brit.), w; CLUE OF THE NEW PIN, THE(1961, Brit.); DEATH TRAP(1962, Brit.); RAPTURE(1965); WALK IN THE SHADOW(1966, Brit.); DEADLY AFFAIR, THE(1967, Brit.); DANGER ROUTE(1968, Brit.); ONE MORE TIME(1970, Brit.); RAGMAN'S DAUGHTER, THE(1974, Brit.); LITTLEST HORSE THIEVES, THE(1977)
Sompote Sands
CROCODILE(1979, Thai./Hong Kong), d
Sonnie Sands
BELLBOY, THE(1960)
Sonny Sands
STOOLIE, THE(1972)
Stella Sands
SUBTERFUGE(1969, US/Brit.)
Susan Sands
1984
MISSION, THE(1984)
Tibor Sands
LILITH(1964), ph
Tommy Sands
MARDI GRAS(1958); SING, BOY, SING(1958); BABES IN TOYLAND(1961); LOVE IN A GOLDFISH BOWL(1961); LONGEST DAY, THE(1962); ENSIGN PULVER(1964); NONE BUT THE BRAVE(1965, U.S./Jap.); VIOLENT ONES, THE(1967)
Walter Sands
QUICK GUN, THE(1964)
William Sands
FUNNY GIRL(1968), ed; ONLY GAME IN TOWN, THE(1970), ed; CACTUS IN THE SNOW(1972), ed
Odd Jan Sandsdalen
ONE DAY IN THE LIFE OF IVAN DENISOVICH(1971, U.S./Brit./Norway)
Flora Sandstrom
BAD SISTER(1947, Brit.), w; MADNESS OF THE HEART(1949, Brit.), d&w; JESSICA(1962, U.S./Ital./Fr.), w
Jacques Sandulescu
OWL AND THE PUSSYCAT, THE(1970); THEY MIGHT BE GIANTS(1971); RUSSIAN ROULETTE(1975); TRADING PLACES(1983)
1984
MOSCOW ON THE HUDSON(1984); POPE OF GREENWICH VILLAGE, THE(1984)
Ellen Sandweiss
EVIL DEAD, THE(1983)
Jan Sandwich
USED CARS(1980)
Baby Sandy [Sandra LeeHenville]
UNEXPECTED FATHER(1939); SANDY GETS HER MAN(1940); SANDY IS A LADY(1940); MELODY LANE(1941); JOHNNY DOUGHBOY(1943)
Eris Sandy
GRASSHOPPER, THE(1970)

Gary Sandy
SOME OF MY BEST FRIENDS ARE...(1971); HAIL(1973); GREAT SMOKEY ROADBLOCK, THE(1978)
Keith Sandy
JAMBOREE(1957)
Karl Sandys
MOTHER'S DAY(1980)
Oliver Sandys
BORN LUCKY(1932, Brit.), w
Silents
GREEN CARAVAN, THE(1922, Brit.), w; PLEASURE GARDEN, THE(1925, Brit./Ger.), w
Pat Sandys
CASTLE IN THE AIR(1952, Brit.)
S. Sanfilippo
Misc. Silents
FABIOLA(1923, Ital.)
Rene Sanfiorenzo, Jr.
LORD OF THE FLIES(1963, Brit.)
Barbara Sanford
CRY BLOOD, APACHE(1970)
Blaine Sanford
MAGNETIC MONSTER, THE(1953), m
Butch Sanford
PERFECT COUPLE, A(1979)
Donald S. Sanford
SUMARINE X-1(1969, Brit.), w; 1,000 PLANE RAID, THE(1969), w; MOSQUITO SQUADRON(1970, Brit.), w; MIDWAY(1976), w; RAVAGERS, THE(1979), w
Erskin Sanford
GIRLS OF THE BIG HOUSE(1945)
Erskine Sanford
WITHOUT RESERVATIONS(1946); POP ALWAYS PAYS(1940); CITIZEN KANE(1941); MAGNIFICENT AMBERSONS, THE(1942); WIFE TAKES A FLYER, THE(1942); JANE EYRE(1944); MR. SKEFFINGTON(1944); UNCERTAIN GLORY(1944); MINISTRY OF FEAR(1945); SPELLBOUND(1945); TREE GROWS IN BROOKLYN, A(1945); ANGEL ON MY SHOULDER(1946); BEST YEARS OF OUR LIVES, THE(1946); CRACK-UP(1946); FROM THIS DAY FORWARD(1946); MOURNING BECOMES ELECTRA(1947); POSSESSED(1947); VOICE OF THE TURTLE, THE(1947); KIDNAPPED(1948); LADY FROM SHANGHAI, THE(1948); LETTER FROM AN UNKNOWN WOMAN(1948); MACBETH(1948); TEXAS, BROOKLYN AND HEAVEN(1948); YOU WERE MEANT FOR ME(1948); IMPACT(1949); NIGHT UNTO NIGHT(1949); THEY LIVE BY NIGHT(1949); WAKE OF THE RED WITCH(1949); SIERRA(1950); WOMAN ON PIER 13, THE(1950); MY SON, JOHN(1952)
Frances Sanford
JOAN OF ARC(1948); CHICAGO DEADLINE(1949); WHEN WORLDS COLLIDE(1951)
Gerald Sanford
SINGLE ROOM FURNISHED(1968), w; AARON LOVES ANGELA(1975), w; KILLER FORCE(1975, Switz./Ireland), w
Harry Sanford
APACHE UPRISING(1966), w; WACO(1966), w
Helen Sanford
PROTECTORS, BOOK 1, THE(1981), w
Misc. Talkies
ANGEL OF H.E.A.T.(1982), d
Isabel Sanford
GUESS WHO'S COMING TO DINNER(1967); YOUNG RUNAWAYS, THE(1968); COMIC, THE(1969); PENDULUM(1969); RED, WHITE AND BLACK, THE(1970); HICKEY AND BOGGS(1972); LADY SINGS THE BLUES(1972); NEW CENTURIONS, THE(1972); UP THE SANDBOX(1972); LOVE AT FIRST BITE(1979)
John Sanford
HONKY TONK(1941), w; GLORY BOY(1971), w
Joseph Sanford
LAW AND ORDER(1940), p; MA, HE'S MAKING EYES AT ME(1940), p; RAGTIME COWBOY JOE(1940), p
Joseph G. Sanford
DARK STREETS OF CAIRO(1940), p; I'M NOBODY'S SWEETHEART NOW(1940), p; MARGIE(1940), p; MEET THE WILDCAT(1940), p; SON OF ROARING DAN(1940), p; CRACKED NUTS(1941), p; DOUBLE DATE(1941), p; SWING IT SOLDIER(1941), p; TOO MANY BLONDES(1941), p; WHERE DID YOU GET THAT GIRL?(1941), p; JUKE BOX JENNY(1942), p; STRICTLY IN THE GROOVE(1942), p
Kenneth Sanford
Misc. Talkies
RUDDIGORE(1967, Brit.)
Kim Sanford
MC Q(1974)
Lee Sanford
KISS OF DEATH(1947)
Paula Sanford
9/30/55(1977)
Phil Sanford
Silents
HIS FATHER'S SON(1917)
Philip Sanford
Misc. Silents
BROKEN BARRIERS(1919); DETERMINATION(1920)
Ralph Sanford
ESCAPE BY NIGHT(1937); PRESCRIPTION FOR ROMANCE(1937); SEA RACKETEERS(1937); ANGELS WITH DIRTY FACES(1938); BLONDES AT WORK(1938); GIVE ME A SAILOR(1938); PATIENT IN ROOM 18, THE(1938); RECKLESS LIVING(1938); SWEETHEARTS(1938); DODGE CITY(1939); LITTLE ACCIDENT(1939); SMASHING THE MONEY RING(1939); STAR MAKER, THE(1939); TORCHY PLAYS WITH DYNAMITE(1939); UNDERCOVER AGENT(1939); YOU CAN'T CHEAT AN HONEST MAN(1939); CAROLINA MOON(1940); DANCE, GIRL, DANCE(1940); STRANGER ON THE THIRD FLOOR(1940); THEY DRIVE BY NIGHT(1940); DOWN IN SAN DIEGO(1941); HIGH SIERRA(1941); MR. AND MRS. SMITH(1941); NO HANDS ON THE CLOCK(1941); OBLIGING YOUNG LADY(1941); I LIVE ON DANGER(1942); LUCKY LEGS(1942); MEET THE STEWARTS(1942); MY FAVORITE SPY(1942); NIGHT FOR CRIME, A(1942); THEY ALL KISSED THE BRIDE(1942); TORPEDO BOAT(1942); UNDERGROUND AGENT(1942); WILDCAT(1942); WRECK-

ING CREW(1942); AERIAL GUNNER(1943); ALASKA HIGHWAY(1943); HEAVENLY BODY, THE(1943); HIGH EXPLOSIVE(1943); LADIES' DAY(1943); MINESWEEPER(1943); NO PLACE FOR A LADY(1943); SUBMARINE ALERT(1943); ADVENTURES OF KITTY O'DAY(1944); COVER GIRL(1944); DOUGHGIRLS, THE(1944); LOST IN A HAREM(1944); SWEETHEARTS OF THE U.S.A.(1944); BULLFIGHTERS, THE(1945); HIGH POWERED(1945); NOB HILL(1945); STATE FAIR(1945); THERE GOES KELLY(1945); THUNDERHEAD-SON OF FLICKA(1945); WHERE DO WE GO FROM HERE?(1945); GIRL ON THE SPOT(1946); IT SHOULDN'T HAPPEN TO A DOG(1946); MY PAL TRIGGER(1946); SIOUX CITY SUE(1946); THEY MADE ME A KILLER(1946); TWO SISTERS FROM BOSTON(1946); COPACABANA(1947); HIT PARADE OF 1947(1947); IT'S A JOKE, SON!(1947); LINDA BE GOOD(1947); OUT OF THE BLUE(1947); WEB OF DANGER, THE(1947); FRENCH LEAVE(1948); JOE PALOOKA IN WINNER TAKE ALL(1948); LET'S LIVE AGAIN(1948); SHAGGY(1948); SMART WOMAN(1948); COW TOWN(1950); FATHER'S WILD GAME(1950); GLASS MENAGERIE, THE(1950); HI-JACKED(1950); UNION STATION(1950); DANGER ZONE(1951); FORT DEFIANCE(1951); KENTUCKY JUBILEE(1951); LET'S MAKE IT LEGAL(1951); MY FAVORITE SPY(1951); RHYTHM INN(1951); ROGUE RIVER(1951); SANTA FE(1951); CARRIE(1952); RANCHO NOTORIOUS(1952); SEA TIGER(1952); SPRINGFIELD RIFLE(1952); STOP, YOU'RE KILLING ME(1952); TURNING POINT, THE(1952); COUNT THE HOURS(1953); FARMER TAKES A WIFE, THE(1953); TORPEDO ALLEY(1953); CATTLE QUEEN OF MONTANA(1954); FORTYNINERS, THE(1954); RIVER OF NO RETURN(1954); SILVER LODE(1954); NIGHT FREIGHT(1955); SEVEN YEAR ITCH, THE(1955); SHOTGUN(1955); TO HELL AND BACK(1955); BLACKJACK KETCHUM, DESPERADO(1956); FRIENDLY PERSUASION(1956); LIEUTENANT WORE SKIRTS, THE(1956); URANIUM BOOM(1956); BADLANDS OF MONTANA(1957); UP IN SMOKE(1957); IN THE MONEY(1958); ALASKA PASSAGE(1959); OREGON TRAIL, THE(1959); REMARKABLE MR. PENNYPACKER, THE(1959); CAGE OF EVIL(1960); PURPLE GANG, THE(1960)

Sandy Sanford
LETTER OF INTRODUCTION(1938); UNDERGROUND AGENT(1942)

Stanley Sanford
Silents
GOLD RUSH, THE(1925)

Stanley J. Sanford
MODERN TIMES(1936)
Silents
PAYING THE LIMIT(1924); GINSBERG THE GREAT(1927); CIRCUS, THE(1928); FAR CALL, THE(1929)

Terry Sanford
IT HAPPENED IN SOHO(1948, Brit.), w

Tiny Sanford
HARD HOMBRE(1931); SPIRIT OF THE WEST(1932)
Silents
GATE CRASHER, THE(1928)

William Sanford
PRETTY BOY FLOYD(1960), m

Clifford Sanforth
MURDER BY TELEVISION(1935), d; HIGH HAT(1937), p&d; I DEMAND PAYMENT(1938), p&d; BANDIT OF SHERWOOD FOREST, THE(1946), p

Giuseppina Sangaletti
TREE OF WOODEN CLOGS, THE(1979, Ital.)

Hans Sange
GERMANY, YEAR ZERO(1949, Ger.)

John Sanger
TRACK THE MAN DOWN(1956, Brit.)

Jonathan Sanger
ELEPHANT MAN, THE(1980, Brit.), p; FRANCES(1982), p

Margaret Sanger
Misc. Silents
BIRTH CONTROL(1917)

Mike Sanger
MOUSE AND HIS CHILD, THE(1977), anim

Angelo Sangermano
HERCULES AGAINST THE MOON MEN(1965, Fr./Ital.), w

Anita Sangiola
SMALL CIRCLE OF FRIENDS, A(1980)

Vicente Sangiovani
RAIN FOR A DUSTY SUMMER(1971, U.S./Span.)

Vincente Sangiovanni
DESPERATE ONES, THE(1968 U.S./Span.); GUNS OF THE MAGNIFICENT SEVEN(1969)

Gumby Sangler
GEEK MAGGOT BINGO(1983)

Alfred Sangster
THIRD CLUE, THE(1934, Brit.); YOUNG MR. PITT, THE(1942, Brit.); THUNDER ROCK(1944, Brit.)

James "Jimmy" Sangster
WHO SLEW AUNTIE ROO?(1971, U.S./Brit.), w

Jimmy Sangster
CURSE OF FRANKENSTEIN, THE(1957, Brit.), w; X THE UNKNOWN(1957, Brit.), w; BLOOD OF THE VAMPIRE(1958, Brit.), w; CRAWLING EYE, THE(1958, Brit.), w; HORROR OF DRACULA, THE(1958, Brit.), w; INTENT TO KILL(1958, Brit.), w; REVENGE OF FRANKENSTEIN, THE(1958, Brit.), w; SNORKEL, THE(1958, Brit.), w; JACK THE RIPPER(1959, Brit.), w; MAN WHO COULD CHEAT DEATH, THE(1959, Brit.), w; MUMMY, THE(1959, Brit.), w; BRIDES OF DRACULA, THE(1960, Brit.), w; SIEGE OF SIDNEY STREET, THE(1960, Brit.), a, w; SCREAM OF FEAR(1961, Brit.), p, w; TERROR OF THE TONGS, THE(1961, Brit.), w; CONCRETE JUNGLE, THE(1962, Brit.), w; PIRATES OF BLOOD RIVER, THE(1962, Brit.), w; SAVAGE GUNS, THE(1962, U.S./Span.), p; HELLFIRE CLUB, THE(1963, Brit.), w; MANIAC(1963, Brit.), p, w; NIGHTMARE(1963, Brit.), p, w; PARANOIAC(1963, Brit.), w; DEVIL-SHIP PIRATES, THE(1964, Brit.), w; HYSTERIA(1965, Brit.), p, w; NANNY, THE(1965, Brit.), p, w; DEADLIER THAN THE MALE(1967, Brit.), w; ANNIVERSARY, THE(1968, Brit.), p, w; HORROR OF FRANKENSTEIN, THE(1970, Brit.), p&d, w; LUST FOR A VAMPIRE(1971, Brit.), d; CRESCENDO(1972, Brit.), w; FEAR IN THE NIGHT(1972, Brit.), p&d, w; LEGACY, THE(1979, Brit.), w; PHOBIA(1980, Can.), w; DEVIL AND MAX DEVLIN, THE(1981), w

Margaret Elizabeth Sangster
Silents
NEW TEACHER, THE(1922), w

Helen Sanguineti
BANG, BANG, YOU'RE DEAD(1966)

William Sanguineti
BANG, BANG, YOU'RE DEAD(1966)

Victoria Hernandez Sanguino
ROBIN AND MARIAN(1976, Brit.)

Sani
PACIFIC DESTINY(1956, Brit.)

Amru Sani
NAKED MAJA, THE(1959, Ital./U.S.)

Nick Sanicandro
WOMEN OF DESIRE(1968)

Hank Sanicola
JOHNNY CONCHO(1956), p

Henry Sanicola
X-15(1961), p

Ray Saniger
FANDANGO(1970); TERMINAL ISLAND(1973)

Alexander Sanin
Misc. Silents
POLIKUSHKA(1919, USSR), d

Villorio Sanipoli
GREAT WAR, THE(1961, Fr., Ital.)

Vittorio Sanipoli
WHITE DEVIL, THE(1948, Ital.); CONSTANTINE AND THE CROSS(1962, Ital.); SWORD OF THE CONQUEROR(1962, Ital.); ORGANIZER, THE(1964, Fr./Ital./Yugo.); DOLL THAT TOOK THE TOWN, THE(1965, Ital.); TEN DAYS' WONDER(1972, Fr.); THREE TOUGH GUYS(1974, U.S./Ital.)

Gilbert Sanjakian
GERVAISE(1956, Fr.)

E. Sanjust
MAN WHO LAUGHS, THE(1966, Ital.), w

Filippo Sanjust
MORGAN THE PIRATE(1961, Fr./Ital.), w, cos; THIEF OF BAGHDAD, THE(1961, Ital./Fr.), w; WHITE WARRIOR, THE(1961, Ital./Yugo.), cos; SEVEN SEAS TO CALAIS(1963, Ital.), w, cos; GOLDEN ARROW, THE(1964, Ital.), w; YOUNG LORD, THE(1970, Ger.), cos

Konstantin Sankar
OUT OF THE FOG(1941)

Betty Sanko
TORRID ZONE(1940)

Gina Sanmarco
LA VIACCIA(1962, Fr./Ital.)

Anna Sanmartin
IT HAPPENED IN ROME(1959, Ital.)

Conrado Sanmartin
COLOSSUS OF RHODES, THE(1961, Ital., Fr., Span.); AWFUL DR. ORLOFF, THE(1964, Span./Fr.); REVOLT OF THE MERCENARIES(1964, Ital./Span.)

Giorgio Sanmartin
JOHNNY HAMLET(1972, Ital.)

Douglas Sannachan
THAT SINKING FEELING(1979, Brit.); GREGORY'S GIRL(1982, Brit.)
1984
COMFORT AND JOY(1984, Brit.)

Bertha Sannell
WINTER LIGHT, THE(1963, Swed.); MY FATHER'S MISTRESS(1970, Swed.), cos

Emilie Sannon
Misc. Silents
EN RAEDSOM NAT(1914, Den.)

Frank Sannucci
MESQUITE BUCKAROO(1939), md

Asao Sano
NAKED YOUTH(1961, Jap.); FIRES ON THE PLAIN(1962, Jap.); GIRL I ABANDONED, THE(1970, Jap.)

Shuji Sano
TILL TOMORROW COMES(1962, Jap.); TUNNEL TO THE SUN(1968, Jap.); FIGHT FOR THE GLORY(1970, Jap.)

Yoshikazu Sano
HOUSE WHERE EVIL DWELLS, THE(1982), art d

Sans Souci Girls
PASSION IN THE SUN(1964)

Hope Sansberry
COUNTRY MUSIC HOLIDAY(1958); SAIL A CROOKED SHIP(1961); SON OF FLUBBER(1963)

Hope Sansbury
SHE'S WORKING HER WAY THROUGH COLLEGE(1952)

Luciana Sanseverino
8 ½(1963, Ital.)

John Sansom
TO HAVE AND TO HOLD(1963, Brit.), w; FACE OF A STRANGER(1964, Brit.), w; DRACULA-PRINCE OF DARKNESS(1966, Brit.), w

Ken Sansom
SHINBONE ALLEY(1971); LONG GOODBYE, THE(1973); NUTCRACKER FANTASY(1979)

Lester Sansom
HUMAN JUNGLE, THE(1954), ed

Lester A. Sansom
HOT NEWS(1953), ed; PRIVATE EYES(1953), ed; HIGH SOCIETY(1955), ed; JAIL BUSTERS(1955), ed; SEVEN ANGRY MEN(1955), ed; CRACK IN THE WORLD(1965), p

Robert Sansom
HE FOUND A STAR(1941, Brit.); IN WHICH WE SERVE(1942, Brit.); THEY MET IN THE DARK(1945, Brit.); DUEL IN THE JUNGLE(1954, Brit.); FINAL COLUMN, THE(1955, Brit.); SHADOW OF FEAR(1956, Brit.); HOUR OF DECISION(1957, Brit.); SCOTLAND YARD DRAGNET(1957, Brit.); SHAKEDOWN, THE(1960, Brit.); TRUNK, THE(1961, Brit.)

William Sansom
WILD AFFAIR, THE(1966, Brit.), w

Lester A. Sansome
DIG THAT URANIUM(1956), ed
Ken Sanson
AIRPORT 1975(1974)
Lester A. Sanson
CLIPPED WINGS(1953), ed
Yvonne Sanson
CHILDREN OF CHANCE(1950, Ital.); STAR OF INDIA(1956, Brit.); MILLER'S WIFE, THE(1957, Ital.); THIS ANGRY AGE(1958, Ital./Fr.); WE HAVE ONLY ONE LIFE(1963, Gr.); BIGGEST BUNDLE OF THEM ALL, THE(1968); DAY OF ANGER(1970, Ital./Ger.); CONFORMIST, THE(1971, Ital., Fr)
Alfonso Sansone
CONJUGAL BED, THE(1963, Ital.), p; MAGNIFICENT CUCKOLD, THE(1965, Fr./Ital.), a, p; RUN FOR YOUR WIFE(1966, Fr./Ital.), p; BEYOND THE LAW(1967, Ital.), p; DEATH RIDES A HORSE(1969, Ital.), p; DAY OF ANGER(1970, Ital./Ger.), p
Rosa Sansone
CONJUGAL BED, THE(1963, Ital.), set d; DEATH RIDES A HORSE(1969, Ital.), art d
Vito Sansone
1984
GOODBYE PEOPLE, THE(1984)
Mario Sansoni
FURY OF HERCULES, THE(1961, Ital.), ed; SAMSON(1961, Ital.), ed; GOLIATH AGAINST THE GIANTS(1963, Ital./Span.), ed
Dino Sant'Ambrogio
CURSE OF THE BLOOD GHOULS(1969, Ital.), p
Abel Santa Cruz
VIOLATED LOVE(1966, Arg.), w
Alfredo Santa Cruz
TRISTANA(1970, Span./Ital./Fr.)
Santa Fe Country Sheriff's Posse
COVENANT WITH DEATH, A(1966)
Vincent Robert Santa Lucia
SOMEBODY KILLED HER HUSBAND(1978)
The Santa Monica Lodge of Elks
SONS OF THE DESERT(1933)
Alfonso Santacana
MURIETA(1965, Span.), ed; NOT ON YOUR LIFE(1965, Ital./Span.), ed
Mary Nell Santacroce
GOLD GUITAR, THE(1966); WISE BLOOD(1979, U.S./Ger.); PRIVATE EYES, THE(1980)
1984
NIGHT SHADOWS(1984)
Salvatore Santaella
MAN WHO PLAYED GOD, THE(1932), m
Ildebrando Santafe
FACTS OF MURDER, THE(1965, Ital.); CLIMAX, THE(1967, Fr., Ital.)
Ugo Santalucia
LUDWIG(1973, Ital./Ger./Fr.), p; BLOOD IN THE STREETS(1975, Ital./Fr.), p
Enrick Santamaran
DECOY FOR TERROR(1970, Can.), d
Juan Santamaria
THAT OBSCURE OBJECT OF DESIRE(1977, Fr./Span.)
Miguel Angel Santamaria
1984
SKYLINE(1984, Spain), ed
Al Santana
BORN IN FLAMES(1983), ph
Arnaldo Santana
SCARFACE(1983)
Bruno Della Santana
TENDER IS THE NIGHT(1961)
Jose Santana
NIGHTHAWKS(1981); PRINCE OF THE CITY(1981)
1984
GARBO TALKS(1984); POPE OF GREENWICH VILLAGE, THE(1984)
Tura Santana
DOLL SQUAD, THE(1973)
Silvio Santanelli
JOAN AT THE STAKE(1954, Ital./Fr.)
Melody Santangello
DEATH WISH II(1982)
Guglielmo Santangelo
CONSTANTINE AND THE CROSS(1962, Ital.), w; STORY OF JOSEPH AND HIS BRETHREN THE(1962, Ital.), w; OF WAYWARD LOVE(1964, Ital./Ger.), w
Melody Santangelo
SHAMUS(1973); RHINOCEROS(1974)
Oscar Santaniello
GRIM REAPER, THE(1981, Ital.), p
Tony Santaniello
THAT CHAMPIONSHIP SEASON(1982)
Santanon
LITTLE RED RIDING HOOD(1963, Mex.); LITTLE RED RIDING HOOD AND HER FRIENDS(1964, Mex.); PUSS 'N' BOOTS(1964, Mex.); LITTLE RED RIDING HOOD AND THE MONSTERS(1965, Mex.); SNAKE PEOPLE, THE(1968, Mex./U.S.)
Julissa Santanon
FEAR CHAMBER, THE(1968, US/Mex.)
Dominique Santarelli
HEAT OF MIDNIGHT(1966, Fr.)
Anna Santarsiero
SEVEN SEAS TO CALAIS(1963, Ital.)
Frederic Santaya
LE PETIT THEATRE DE JEAN RENOIR(1974, Fr.)
Jose Villa Sante
KID RODELO(1966, U.S./Span.)
Antonio Santean
GLASS CAGE, THE(1964), d, w; DIRTY MARY, CRAZY LARRY(1974), w

Ross Santee
GENTLEMAN FROM ARIZONA, THE(1940)
Al Santell
Silents
INTRODUCE ME(1925), sup
Misc. Silents
BELOVED ROGUES(1917), d; IT MIGHT HAPPEN TO YOU(1920), d; WILDCAT JORDAN(1922), d; LIGHTS OUT(1923), d; EMPTY HEARTS(1924), d; FOOLS IN THE DARK(1924), d; MAN WHO PLAYED SQUARE, THE(1924), d; PARISIAN NIGHTS(1925), d
Alfred Santell
SHOW GIRL(1928), d; ROMANCE OF THE RIO GRANDE(1929), d; THIS IS HEAVEN(1929), d; TWIN BEDS(1929), d; ARIZONA KID, THE(1930), d; SEA WOLF, THE(1930), d; BODY AND SOUL(1931), d; DADDY LONG LEGS(1931), d; SOB SISTER(1931), d; POLLY OF THE CIRCUS(1932), d; REBECCA OF SUNNYBROOK FARM(1932), d; TESS OF THE STORM COUNTRY(1932), d; BONDAGE(1933), d; RIGHT TO ROMANCE(1933), d; LIFE OF VERGIE WINTERS, THE(1934), d; FEATHER IN HER HAT, A(1935), d; PEOPLE WILL TALK(1935), d; WINTERSET(1936), d; BREAKFAST FOR TWO(1937), d; INTERNES CAN'T TAKE MONEY(1937), d; ARKANSAS TRAVELER, THE(1938), d; COCOANUT GROVE(1938), d; HAVING WONDERFUL TIME(1938), d; OUR LEADING CITIZEN(1939), d; ALOMA OF THE SOUTH SEAS(1941), d; BEYOND THE BLUE HORIZON(1942), d; JACK LONDON(1943), d; HAIRY APE, THE(1944), d; MEXICANA(1945), p&d; THAT BRENNAN GIRL(1946), p&d
Misc. Silents
CLASSIFIED(1925), d; MARRIAGE WHIRL, THE(1925), d; DANCER OF PARIS, THE(1926), d; SUBWAY SADIE(1926), d; SWEET DADDIES(1926), d; GORILLA, THE(1927), d; ORCHIDS AND ERMINE(1927), d; LITTLE SHEPHERD OF KINGDOM COME, THE(1928), d; WHEEL OF CHANCE(1928), d
Alfred A. Santell
Silents
BLUEBEARD'S SEVEN WIVES(1926), d
Lavinia Santell
Misc. Silents
GREATER THAN ART(1915)
Marie Santell
MARK OF THE WITCH(1970)
Gino Santercole
SERAFINO(1970, Fr./Ital.)
Walter Santesso
LA DOLCE VITA(1961, Ital./Fr.); DULCINEA(1962, Span.); LOVE AND LARCENY(1963, Fr./Ital.)
Santi
OPERATION CIA(1965)
Angelo Santi
AND SO TO BED(1965, Ger.); WITCHES, THE(1969, Fr./Ital.)
Jacques Santi
IMMORAL MOMENT, THE(1967, Fr.)
1984
MY NEW PARTNER(1984, Fr.)
Lionello Santi
ITALIANO BRAVA GENTE(1965, Ital./USSR), p
Adalberto Santiago
1984
MOSCOW ON THE HUDSON(1984)
Cirio H. Santiago
CAVALRY COMMAND(1963, U.S./Phil.), p; BLOOD DRINKERS, THE(1966, U.S./Phil.), p; TNT JACKSON(1975), p&d; UP FROM THE DEPTHS(1979, Phil.), p; VAMPIRE HOOKERS, THE(1979, Phil.), d; FIRECRACKER(1981), d; STRYKER(1983, Phil.), p&d
1984
CAGED FURY(1984, Phil.), d
Misc. Talkies
FLY ME(1973), d; COVER GIRL MODELS(1975), d; MUTHERS, THE(1976), d; EBONY, IVORY AND JADE(1977), d; DEATH FORCE(1978), d
Emile Santiago
SALOME(1953), cos; STRANGE LADY IN TOWN(1955), cos; BIG COUNTRY, THE(1958), cos
Emilio Santiago
LAZARILLO(1963, Span.)
Hugo Santiago
1984
THREE CROWNS OF THE SAILOR(1984, Fr.)
Janira Santiago
TROPICS(1969, Ital.)
Jun Santiago
DANCE OF THE DWARFS(1983, U.S., Phil.), spec eff
Manuel Santiago
FORT APACHE, THE BRONX(1981)
1984
OVER THE BROOKLYN BRIDGE(1984); ROMANCING THE STONE(1984)
Patricio Santiago
EL CONDOR(1970)
Saundra Santiago
END OF AUGUST, THE(1982)
1984
BEAT STREET(1984)
Enzo Santianello
ONCE UPON A TIME IN THE WEST(1969, U.S./Ital.)
Diego Santiesteban
NARCO MEN, THE(1969, Span./Ital.)
Alfonso Santilla
MANHUNT IN THE JUNGLE(1958)
Antonio Santillan
VIVA KNIEVEL!(1977), w
Lamberto Santilli
SKY IS RED, THE(1952, Ital.), w

Frank Santillo
CATERED AFFAIR, THE(1956), ed; GUN GLORY(1957), ed; HIRED GUN, THE(1957), ed; RIDE THE HIGH COUNTRY(1962), ed; MAIL ORDER BRIDE(1964), ed; OUTRAGE, THE(1964), ed; SWINGER, THE(1966), ed; HALF A SIXPENCE(1967, Brit.), ed; CANDY(1968, Ital./Fr.), ed; BALLAD OF CABLE HOGUE, THE(1970), ed; DESERTER, THE(1971 Ital./Yugo.), ed; TRAIN ROBBERS, THE(1973), ed

Bruno Santina
VERTIGO(1958)

Gino Santini
STRANGER'S GUNDOWN, THE(1974, Ital.), ph

James Santini
1984
BIRDY(1984)

Pierre Santini
DIRTY HANDS(1976, Fr./Ital./Ger.)
1984
AMERICAN DREAMER(1984)

Pasqualino De Santis
RE: LUCKY LUCIANO(1974, Fr./Ital.), ph; CONVERSATION PIECE(1976, Ital., Fr.), ph

Alfonso Santisteben
GRAVEYARD OF HORROR(1971, Span.), m

Clifford Santley
ROBBERS' ROOST(1933)

Fred Santley
TRUE TO LIFE(1943); UNCLE HARRY(1945); LEATHERNECKING(1930); THREE WHO LOVED(1931); MORNING GLORY(1933); THREE-CORNERED MOON(1933); SUCH WOMEN ARE DANGEROUS(1934); GEORGE WHITE'S 1935 SCANDALS(1935); ONE IN A MILLION(1935); STAGE DOOR(1937); SHE'S GOT EVERYTHING(1938); SWEETHEARTS(1938); SWING, SISTER, SWING(1938); DANGER ON WHEELS(1940); KILLERS OF THE WILD(1940); DOUBLE TROUBLE(1941); UNFINISHED BUSINESS(1941); ZIEGFELD GIRL(1941); FLEET'S IN, THE(1942); JOAN OF OZARK(1942); SLEEPYTIME GAL(1942); WE WERE DANCING(1942); DIXIE(1943); NIGHT AND DAY(1946); LADY IN THE LAKE(1947); FATHER OF THE BRIDE(1950); MYSTERY STREET(1950); IT'S A BIG COUNTRY(1951); TEXAS CARNIVAL(1951)

Frederic Santley
LOVER COME BACK(1931); MEET THE MISSUS(1937); LITTLE ACCIDENT(1939); CALIFORNIA(1946)

Frederick Santley
IF I HAD A MILLION(1932); WALLS OF GOLD(1933)

Fredric Santley
DOUBLE HARNESS(1933); READY FOR LOVE(1934); PRINCE OF THIEVES, THE(1948)

Joe Santley
WALKING ON AIR(1936), d

Joseph Santley
COCOANUTS, THE(1929), d, ch; SWING HIGH(1930), d, w; HOUSE ON 56TH STREET, THE(1933), w; I LIKE IT THAT WAY(1934), w; LOUDSPEAKER, THE(1934), d; YOUNG AND BEAUTIFUL(1934), d, w; HARMONY LANE(1935), d, w; MILLION DOLLAR BABY(1935), d, w; WATERFRONT LADY(1935), d; DANCING FEET(1936), d; HARVESTER, THE(1936), d; HER MASTER'S VOICE(1936), d; LAUGHING IRISH EYES(1936), d; MAD HOLIDAY(1936), w; SMARTEST GIRL IN TOWN(1936), d; LIFE OF THE PARTY, THE(1937), w; MEET THE MISSUS(1937), d; THERE GOES THE GROOM(1937), d; ALWAYS IN TROUBLE(1938), d; BLOND CHEAT(1938), d; RADIO CITY REVELS(1938), m; RETURN OF CAROL DEANE, THE(1938, Brit.), w; SHE'S GOT EVERYTHING(1938), d; SWING, SISTER, SWING(1938), d; FAMILY NEXT DOOR, THE(1939), d; SPIRIT OF CULVER, THE(1939), d; TWO BRIGHT BOYS(1939), d; DANCING ON A DIME(1940), d; MELODY AND MOONLIGHT(1940), d; MELODY RANCH(1940), d; MUSIC IN MY HEART(1940), d; BEHIND THE NEWS(1941), d; DOWN MEXICO WAY(1941), d; ICE-CAPADES(1941), d; PUDDIN' HEAD(1941), d; ROOKIES ON PARADE(1941), d; SIS HOPKINS(1941), d; CALL OF THE CANYON(1942), d; JOAN OF OZARK(1942), d; REMEMBER PEARL HARBOR(1942), d; TRAGEDY AT MIDNIGHT, A(1942), d; YOKEL BOY(1942), d; CHATTERBOX(1943), d; SHANTYTOWN(1943), d; SLEEPY LAGOON(1943), d; THUMBS UP(1943), d; BRAZIL(1944), d; GOODNIGHT SWEETHEART(1944), d; JAMBOREE(1944), d; ROSIE THE RIVETER(1944), d; THREE LITTLE SISTERS(1944), d; EARL CARROLL'S VANITIES(1945), d; HITCHHIKE TO HAPPINESS(1945), d; SHADOW OF A WOMAN(1946), d; MAKE BELIEVE BALLROOM(1949), d; ON THE ISLE OF SAMOA(1950), w; WHEN YOU'RE SMILING(1950), d

Laurene Santley
Misc. Silents
BOLD EMMETT, IRELAND'S MARTYR(1915)

Santo
SANTO CONTRA EL CEREBRO DIABOLICO zero(1962, Mex.); SANTO EN EL MUSEO DE CERA(1963, Mex.); SANTO CONTRA LA INVASION DE LOS MARCIANOS(1966, Mex.); SANTO CONTRA BLUE DEMON EN LA ATLANTIDA(1968, Mex.); SANTO Y BLUE DEMON CONTRA LOS MONSTRUOS(1968, Mex.); SANTO CONTRA LA HIJA DE FRANKENSTEIN(1971, Mex.)

Vincent Santo
TWO THOUSAND MANIACS!(1964)

Gustavo Santolalla
SHE DANCES ALONE(1981, Aust./U.S.), m

Alma Santoli
NAKED MAJA, THE(1959, Ital./U.S.), makeup

Euclide Santoli
NAKED MAJA, THE(1959, Ital./U.S.), makeup; SODOM AND GOMORRAH(1962, U.S./Fr./Ital.), makeup; WILD, WILD PLANET, THE(1967, Ital.), makeup; MAN OF LA MANCHA(1972), makeup

Ornella Polito Santoliquido
LISTEN, LET'S MAKE LOVE(1969, Fr./Ital.)

Bobby Santon
CLOAK AND DAGGER(1946)

Penny Santon
INTERRUPTED MELODY(1955); FULL OF LIFE(1956); WRONG MAN, THE(1956); DINO(1957); THIS EARTH IS MINE(1959); WEST SIDE STORY(1961); CALIFORNIA(1963); CAPTAIN NEWMAN, M.D.(1963); LOVE WITH THE PROPER STRANGER(1963); SPY IN THE GREEN HAT, THE(1966); DON'T JUST STAND THERE(1968); FUNNY GIRL(1968); KOTCH(1971)

1984
FLETCH(1984); RHINESTONE(1984)

Espartaco Santoni
EXORCISM'S DAUGHTER zero(1974, Span.); HOUSE OF EXORCISM, THE(1976, Ital.)

Reni Santoni
ENTER LAUGHING(1967); ANZIO(1968, Ital.); GREAT BIG THING, A(1968, U.S./Can.); GUNS OF THE MAGNIFICENT SEVEN(1969); STUDENT NURSES, THE(1970); DIRTY HARRY(1971); I NEVER PROMISED YOU A ROSE GARDEN(1977); THEY WENT THAT-A-WAY AND THAT-A-WAY(1978); DEAD MEN DON'T WEAR PLAID(1982); BAD BOYS(1983)

Spartaco Santoni
CASTILIAN, THE(1963, Span./U.S.)

Tino Santoni
GIRL WITH A SUITCASE(1961, Fr./Ital.), ph; VIOLENT SUMMER(1961, Fr./Ital.), ph; PSYCOSISSIMO(1962, Ital.), ph; TWO COLONELS, THE(1963, Ital.), ph; LOVE, THE ITALIAN WAY(1964, Ital.), ph; RED LIPS(1964, Fr./Ital.), ph; DOS COSMONAUTAS A LA FUERZA(1967, Span./*Ital.), ph

Carlo Santonocito
GOLIATH AGAINST THE GIANTS(1963, Ital./Span.), art d

Jack Santora
SERENADE(1956)

Dean Santoro
DOGS(1976)

Francesca Santoro
LITTLE MEN(1940); SAPS AT SEA(1940)

Jack Santoro
MIDNIGHT TAXI, THE(1928); WOMEN THEY TALK ABOUT(1928); ONE STOLEN NIGHT(1929); STORY OF LOUIS PASTEUR, THE(1936); MAGNIFICENT AMBERSONS, THE(1942); DEAD RECKONING(1947); IN A LONELY PLACE(1950); OCEAN'S ELEVEN(1960)
Silents
GINSBERG THE GREAT(1927); SLIGHTLY USED(1927)

Michael Santoro
1984
ADVENTURES OF BUCKAROO BANZAI: ACROSS THE 8TH DIMENSION, THE(1984)

Alfredo Santos
MY FAVORITE SPY(1951); PEKING EXPRESS(1951); MACAO(1952); MARA MARU(1952)

Angel Fernandez Santos
SPIRIT OF THE BEEHIVE, THE(1976, Span.), w

Bas Santos
STRYKER(1983, Phil.), ed

Bert Santos
WALK, DON'T RUN(1966); HERBIE GOES BANANAS(1980)

Burt Santos
LAST EMBRACE(1979)
Misc. Talkies
DIE SISTER, DIE(1978)

Carlos Santos
JETLAG(1981, U.S./Span.), m

Carmen Santos
Misc. Silents
LIMITE(1930, Braz.)

Cecile Santos
KING OF THE GYPSIES(1978)

Frank Santos
TATTOO(1981)

Gaston Santos
BLACK PIT OF DOCTOR M(1958, Mex.); LIVING COFFIN, THE(1965, Mex.)

Gervasio Santos
SCAVENGERS, THE(1959, U.S./Phil.), ed; CAVALRY COMMAND(1963, U.S./Phil.), ed; TNT JACKSON(1975), ed

Jack Santos
GIRL FROM MANDALAY(1936); TUNDRA(1936)

Pvt. Jesus Santos, USA
BACK TO BATAAN(1945)

Joe Santos
MOONLIGHTING WIVES(1966); MY BODY HUNGERS(1967); GANG THAT COULDN'T SHOOT STRAIGHT, THE(1971); PANIC IN NEEDLE PARK(1971); LEGEND OF NIGGER CHARLEY, THE(1972); SHAFT'S BIG SCORE(1972); BLADE(1973); DON IS DEAD, THE(1973); FRIENDS OF EDDIE COYLE, THE(1973); SHAMUS(1973); ZANDY'S BRIDE(1974); BLUE THUNDER(1983)
1984
FEAR CITY(1984)
Misc. Talkies
KNIFE FOR THE LADIES, A(1973)

Mario Santos
TROPIC HOLIDAY(1938); HONEYMOON(1947)

Moacir Santos
KAREN, THE LOVEMAKER(1970), m

Raphael Santos
HORNET'S NEST(1970)

Ricardo Santos
SUPERBEAST(1972)

Santiago Santos
BULLET FOR THE GENERAL, A(1967, Ital.); VALDEZ IS COMING(1971)

Tiki Santos
ADVISE AND CONSENT(1962)

Tony Santos
CRY FREEDOM(1961, Phil.)

Zenildo Oliveira Santos
PIXOTE(1981, Braz.)

Hortensia Santovena
LIVING COFFIN, THE(1965, Mex.); TWO MULES FOR SISTER SARA(1970)

Jorge Santoyo
MISSING(1982); UNDER FIRE(1983)

Manuel Santoyo
LITTLE ANGEL(1961, Mex.)

Thomas Santschi
TEN NIGHTS IN A BARROOM(1931)
Silents
SPOILERS, THE(1914); CITY OF PURPLE DREAMS, THE(1918)
Misc. Silents
COUNTRY THAT GOD FORGOT, THE(1916); GARDEN OF ALLAH, THE(1916); BEWARE OF STRANGERS(1918); WHO SHALL TAKE MY LIFE?(1918); BROKEN COMMANDMENTS(1919); EVE IN EXILE(1919); LITTLE ORPHANT ANNIE(1919); LOVE THAT DARES, THE(1919); RAILROADER, THE(1919); ROSE OF THE WEST(1919); CRADLE OF COURAGE, THE(1920)

Tom Santschi
LAND OF THE SILVER FOX(1928); IN OLD ARIZONA(1929); SHANNONS OF BROADWAY, THE(1929); WAGON MASTER, THE(1929); FOURTH ALARM, THE(1930); PARADISE ISLAND(1930); SPOILERS, THE(1930), tech adv; UTAH KID, THE(1930); RIVER'S END(1931); TRAPPED(1931); LAST RIDE, THE(1932)
Misc. Talkies
WHITE RENEGADE(1931)
Silents
NORTH WIND'S MALICE, THE(1920); ARE YOU A FAILURE?(1923); IS DIVORCE A FAILURE?(1923); TIPPED OFF(1923); STORM DAUGHTER, THE(1924); NIGHT SHIP, THE(1925); PATHS TO PARADISE(1925); PRIDE OF THE FORCE, THE(1925); DESERT'S TOLL, THE(1926); HANDS ACROSS THE BORDER(1926); NO MAN'S GOLD(1926); SIBERIA(1926); THIRD DEGREE, THE(1926); ADVENTUROUS SOUL, THE(1927); HILLS OF KENTUCKY(1927); JIM THE CONQUEROR(1927); INTO NO MAN'S LAND(1928); ISLE OF LOST MEN(1928)
Misc. Silents
MONTE CRISTO(1912); CRISIS, THE(1915); HELL CAT, THE(1918); CODE OF THE YUKON(1919); IN SEARCH OF ARCADY(1919); SHADOWS(1919); STRONGER VOW, THE(1919); FOUND GUILTY(1922); TWO KINDS OF WOMEN(1922); BRASS COMMANDMENTS(1923); THUNDERING DAWN(1923); LIFE'S GREATEST GAME(1924); LITTLE ROBINSON CRUSOE(1924); PLUNDERER, THE(1924); RIGHT OF THE STRONGEST, THE(1924); STREET OF TEARS, THE(1924); BEYOND THE BORDER(1925); FRIVOLOUS SAL(1925); HER HONOR THE GOVERNOR(1926); HIDDEN WAY, THE(1926); MY OWN PAL(1926); CRUISE OF THE HELLION, THE(1927); EYES OF THE TOTEM(1927); HAUNTED SHIP, THE(1927); LAND BEYOND THE LAW, THE(1927); LAND OF THE LAWLESS(1927); OVERLAND STAGE, THE(1927); TRACKED BY THE POLICE(1927); HONOR BOUND(1928); LAW AND THE MAN(1928); YELLOWBACK, THE(1929)

Angelo Santucci
MOON IN THE GUTTER, THE(1983, Fr./Ital.), prod d

John Santucci
THIEF(1981)

Nancy Santucci
THIEF(1981)

Gianni Santuccio
CENTURION, THE(1962, Fr./Ital.); IMPERIAL VENUS(1963, Ital./Fr.); REBEL GLADIATORS, THE(1963, Ital.); RICE GIRL(1963, Fr./Ital.); INVESTIGATION OF A CITIZEN ABOVE SUSPICION(1970, Ital.)

Jose Santugini
MAN WHO WAGGED HIS TAIL, THE(1961, Ital./Span.), w

Frank Sanucci
MYSTERY OF THE HOODED HORSEMEN, THE(1937), m; TEX RIDES WITH THE BOY SCOUTS(1937), md; TROUBLE IN TEXAS(1937), md; BLACK BANDIT(1938), md; GUILTY TRAILS(1938), m; WHERE THE BUFFALO ROAM(1938), md; DOWN THE WYOMING TRAIL(1939), m, md; MYSTERY PLANE(1939), m, md; PHANTOM STAGE, THE(1939), md; RIDERS OF THE FRONTIER(1939), md; ROLL, WAGONS, ROLL(1939), m, md; SONG OF THE BUCKAROO(1939), md; ARIZONA FRONTIER(1940), md; COWBOY FROM SUNDOWN(1940), md; RAINBOW OVER THE RANGE(1940), md; RHYTHM OF THE RIO GRANDE(1940), m; TRAILING DOUBLE TROUBLE(1940), md; WEST OF PINTO BASIN(1940), md; WESTBOUND STAGE(1940), m, md; DYNAMITE CANYON(1941), md; FUGITIVE VALLEY(1941), m; RIDING THE SUNSET TRAIL(1941), m; RIOT SQUAD(1941), md; ROLLIN' HOME TO TEXAS(1941), md; SADDLE MOUNTAIN ROUNDUP(1941), m; TONTO BASIN OUTLAWS(1941), m; TRAIL OF THE SILVER SPURS(1941), md; TUMBLEDOWN RANCH IN ARIZONA(1941), md; WANDERERS OF THE WEST(1941), m; WRANGLER'S ROOST(1941), md; LIVING GHOST, THE(1942), md; ONE THRILLING NIGHT(1942), md; PHANTOM KILLER(1942), md; ROCK RIVER RENEGADES(1942), md; TEXAS TO BATAAN(1942), md; THUNDER RIVER FEUD(1942), md; TRAIL RIDERS(1942), md; WESTERN MAIL(1942), md; BLACK MARKET RUSTLERS(1943), m; LAW RIDES AGAIN, THE(1943), md; WILD HORSE STAMPEDE(1943), md; OUTLAW TRAIL(1944), md; SONORA STAGECOACH(1944), md; WESTWARD BOUND(1944), md; BORDER BADMEN(1945), m; FIGHTING BILL CARSON(1945), md; FLAME OF THE WEST(1945), md; NORTHWEST TRAIL(1945), m; SONG OF THE SIERRAS(1946), md; WEST OF THE ALAMO(1946), md; RAINBOW OVER THE ROCKIES(1947), md; SIX GUN SERENADE(1947), md; WHITE STALLION(1947), m&md; DEADLINE(1948), m

Guy Sanvido
CHANGE OF MIND(1969); FIRST TIME, THE(1969); SILENT PARTNER, THE(1979, Can.); HEARTACHES(1981, Can.)

Michael Sanville
1984
FIRST TURN-ON!, THE(1984)

Giuseppe Sanvitale
FELLINI SATYRICON(1969, Fr./Ital.)

Michael Sanvoisin
BIDDY(1983, Brit.), m

Rita Sanwood
Misc. Silents
GHOST BREAKER(1914), d

Pahari Sanyal
KANCHENJUNGHA(1966, India)

Alberto Sanz
TROJAN WOMEN, THE(1971)

Javier Sanz
1984
MIDSUMMER NIGHT'S DREAM, A(1984, Brit./Span.)

Jorge Sanz
CONAN THE BARBARIAN(1982)

Mario Sanz
VALDEZ IS COMING(1971)

Nikki Sanz
INDEPENDENCE DAY(1976)

Paco Sanz
PISTOL FOR RINGO, A(1966, Ital./Span.); LIGHTNING BOLT(1967, Ital./Sp.); FEW BULLETS MORE, A(1968, Ital./Span.); MINUTE TO PRAY, A SECOND TO DIE, A(1968, Ital.); GOD FORGIVES-I DON'T!(1969, Ital./Span.)

Joe Sanza
GAS(1981, Can.)

Jack Saper
CASE OF THE VELVET CLAWS, THE(1936), ed; CAPTAIN'S KID, THE(1937), ed; CASE OF THE STUTTERING BISHOP, THE(1937), ed; MELODY FOR TWO(1937), ed; WINE, WOMEN AND HORSES(1937), ed; ACROSS THE PACIFIC(1942), p; LARCENY, INC.(1942), p; MAN WHO CAME TO DINNER, THE(1942), p

Henry G. Saperstein
GAY PURR-EE(1962), p

Peter Saphier
SCARFACE(1983), p

Al Sapienza
NOCTURNA(1979)

Gilarda Sapienza
BEHIND CLOSED SHUTTERS(1952, Ital.)

Goliarda Sapienza
SENSO(1968, Ital.)

Louis Sapin
ANATOMY OF A MARRIAGE(MY DAYS WITH JEAN-MARC AND MY NIGHTS WITH FRANCOISE) (1964 Fr.), w

Alvin Sapinsley
INVITATION TO A GUNFIGHTER(1964), w

Aldo Saporetti
WAR AND PEACE(1956, Ital./U.S.)

Themi Sapountzakis
FAN, THE(1981)

T. Sapozhnikova
FATHER OF A SOLDIER(1966, USSR)

"Sapper" [H. C. McNeile]
LOVE ON THE SPOT(1932, Brit.), w; WOMAN IN CHAINS(1932, Brit.), w; BULLDOG DRUMMOND STRIKES BACK(1934), w; DEBT OF HONOR(1936, Brit.), w; BULLDOG DRUMMOND AT BAY(1937, Brit.), w; BULLDOG DRUMMOND COMES BACK(1937), w; BULLDOG DRUMMOND'S REVENGE(1937), w; BULLDOG DRUMMOND IN AFRICA(1938), w; BULLDOG DRUMMOND'S PERIL(1938), w; BULLDOG DRUMMOND'S BRIDE(1939), w; BULLDOG DRUMMOND'S SECRET POLICE(1939), w; CHALLENGE, THE(1948), w; SOME GIRLS DO(1969, Brit.), w

Fred Sappho
TULIPS(1981, Can), w

Fay Sappington
OWL AND THE PUSSYCAT, THE(1970)

Margo Sappington
OH! CALCUTTA!(1972), a, ch

Ariane Sapriel
TRANS-EUROP-EXPRESS(1968, Fr.)

Alice Sapritch
GIRL WITH THE GOLDEN EYES, THE(1962, Fr.); TESTAMENT OF ORPHEUS, THE(1962, Fr.); CHECKERBOARD(1969, Fr.); DELUSIONS OF GRANDEUR(1971 Fr.)

Sapru
TIGER AND THE FLAME, THE(1955, India)

Chinsaure Sar
1984
KILLING FIELDS, THE(1984, Brit.)

Sandor Sara
FATHER(1967, Hung.), ph

Arturo Sarabia
1984
UNDER THE VOLCANO(1984)

Fausto Saraceni
ANYONE CAN PLAY(1968, Ital.), d

Iva Jean Saraceni
BRIDE, THE(1973); CREEPSHOW(1982)

Barney Saracky
MOM AND DAD(1948), ph

Damon Sarafian
1984
BEAR, THE(1984)

Deran Sarafian
10 TO MIDNIGHT(1983)

Richard C. Sarafian
COOL AND THE CRAZY, THE(1958), w; MAN WHO DIED TWICE, THE(1958), w; NOTORIOUS MR. MONKS, THE(1958); TERROR AT BLACK FALLS(1962), p&d; ANDY(1965), p,d&w; RUN WILD, RUN FREE(1969, Brit.), d; FRAGMENT OF FEAR(1971, Brit.), d; MAN IN THE WILDERNESS(1971, U.S./Span.), d; VANISHING POINT(1971), d; LOLLY-MADONNA XXX(1973), d; NEXT MAN, THE(1976), a, d, w; SUNBURN(1979), d
1984
SONGWRITER(1984)

Richard Sarafian
1984
BEAR, THE(1984), d

Richard G. Sarafian
MAN WHO LOVED CAT DANCING, THE(1973), d

Enzo Sarafin
STRANGERS, THE(1955, Ital.), ph; AMERICAN WIFE, AN(1965, Ital.), ph

Lillian Sarafinchan
CROWD INSIDE, THE(1971, Can.), art d

Lillian Sarafinchen
MERRY WIVES OF TOBIAS ROUKE, THE(1972, Can.), art d

Kichizaemon Saramaru
TEAHOUSE OF THE AUGUST MOON, THE(1956)
Chris Sarandon
DOG DAY AFTERNOON(1975); LIPSTICK(1976); SENTINEL, THE(1977); CU-BA(1979); OSTERMAN WEEKEND, THE(1983)
1984
PROTOCOL(1984)
Susan Sarandon
JOE(1970); LADY LIBERTY(1972, Ital./Fr.); FRONT PAGE, THE(1974); LOVIN' MOLLY(1974); GREAT WALDO PEPPER, THE(1975); ROCKY HORROR PICTURE SHOW, THE(1975, Brit.); ONE SUMMER LOVE(1976); OTHER SIDE OF MIDNIGHT, THE(1977); CHECKERED FLAG OR CRASH(1978); GREAT SMOKEY ROADBLOCK, THE(1978); KING OF THE GYPSIES(1978); PRETTY BABY(1978); SOMETHING SHORT OF PARADISE(1979); LOVING COUPLES(1980); ATLANTIC CITY(1981, U.S./Can.); TEMPEST(1982); HUNGER, THE(1983)
1984
BUDDY SYSTEM, THE(1984)
Misc. Talkies
HAUNTING OF ROSALIND, THE(1973)
Alessandro Sarandrea
GUNMEN OF THE RIO GRANDE(1965, Fr./Ital./Span.), set d
The Sarango Girls
PARDON MY SARONG(1942)
Yuri Sarantsev
STORM PLANET(1962, USSR)
Fabrizio Saranzani
JOURNEY TO LOVE(1953, Ital.), w
Pasquale Sarao
1990: THE BRONX WARRIORS(1983, Ital.), spec eff
Theo Sarapo
JUDEX(1966, Fr./Ital.)
Michael Sarasin
SLEEPING DOGS(1977, New Zealand), ph
Frank Sarasino
YOUNG DYNAMITE(1937)
Lane Sarasohn
GROOVE TUBE, THE(1974), a, w
M.A. Partha Sarathy
RIVER, THE(1951), m
Louise Saraydar
FORCE OF EVIL(1948); LUSTY MEN, THE(1952); FROM HERE TO ETERNITY(1953)
Louise Sarayder
MY DREAM IS YOURS(1949)
O. Sarbagishev
MORNING STAR(1962, USSR), w
Uran Sarbagishev
MORNING STAR(1962, USSR)
Saheb Sarbib
CITY NEWS(1983), m
John Sarbutt
SPY WHO LOVED ME, THE(1977, Brit.)
Tonko Sarcevic
STORY OF JOSEPH AND HIS BRETHREN THE(1962, Ital.)
Martine Sarcey
THIEF OF PARIS, THE(1967, Fr./Ital.); MAN WITH THE TRANSPLANTED BRAIN, THE(1972, Fr./Ital./Ger.)
Walter Sarch
CASTLE OF BLOOD(1964, Fr./Ital.), p
Kate Sarchel
SMILE(1975)
Kate Sarchet
MAN WITH TWO BRAINS, THE(1983)
Misc. Talkies
SWEATER GIRLS(1978)
Dardano Sarchetti
PSYCHIC, THE(1979, Ital.), w
Massimo Sarchielli
JULIET OF THE SPIRITS(1965, Fr./Ital./W.Ger.); SAILOR FROM GIBRALTAR, THE(1967, Brit.); MINUTE TO PRAY, A SECOND TO DIE, A(1968, Ital.); THANK YOU, AUNT(1969, Ital.); FRAGMENT OF FEAR(1971, Brit.); NIGHT OF THE SHOOTING STARS, THE(1982, Ital.); TRENCHCOAT(1983)
Bernadette Sarcione
HURRICANE(1979)
Richard Sarcione
HURRICANE(1979)
Jerry Sarcone
OH! CALCUTTA!(1972), ph
Steve Sardanis
WORLD'S GREATEST LOVER, THE(1977), art d
Alain Sarde
BAROCCO(1976, Fr.), p; EVERY MAN FOR HIMSELF(1980, Fr.), p; BEAU PE-RE(1981, Fr.), p; CHOICE OF ARMS(1983, Fr.), p; L'ETOILE DU NORD(1983, Fr.), p; PASSION(1983, Fr./Switz.), p
1984
FIRST NAME: CARMEN(1984, Fr.), p; MY BEST FRIEND'S GIRL(1984, Fr.), p; SUNDAY IN THE COUNTRY, A(1984, Fr.), p
Philippe Sarde
THINGS OF LIFE, THE(1970, Fr./Ital./Switz.), m; LA GRANDE BOUFFE(1973, Fr.), m; CAT, THE(1975, Fr.), m; LANCELOT OF THE LAKE(1975, Fr.), m; BAROC-CO(1976, Fr.), m; LIZA(1976, Fr./Ital.), m; DEVIL PROBABLY, THE(1977, FR.), m; MADAME ROSA(1977, Fr.), m; ADOLESCENT, THE(1978, Fr./W.Ger.), m; JUDGE AND THE ASSASSIN, THE(1979, Fr.), a, m; TESS(1980, Fr./Brit.), m; BEAU PE-RE(1981, Fr.), m; COUP DE TORCHON(1981, Fr.), m; GHOST STORY(1981), m; I SENT A LETTER TO MY LOVE(1981, Fr.), m; CHOICE OF ARMS(1983, Fr.), m; L'ETOILE DU NORD(1983, Fr.), m; LOVESICK(1983), m; TALES OF ORDINARY MADNESS(1983, Ital.), m
1984
LE CRABE TAMBOUR(1984, Fr.), m

Phillippe Sarde
DON'T TOUCH WHITE WOMEN!(1974, Fr.), m; TENANT, THE(1976, Fr.), m; BRONTE SISTERS, THE(1979, Fr.), m; QUEST FOR FIRE(1982, Fr./Can.), m
Ivan Sardi
YOUNG LORD, THE(1970, Ger.)
Vincent Sardi
NO WAY TO TREAT A LADY(1968)
1984
MUPPETS TAKE MANHATTAN, THE(1984)
Vincent Sardi, Jr.
JULIA(1977)
Adrian Sardo
MYSTERIOUS HOUSE OF DR. C., THE(1976), md
Cosmo Sardo
CORPSE CAME C.O.D., THE(; HIT THE HAY(1945); OVER 21(1945); SONG TO REMEMBER, A(1945); SPANISH MAIN, THE(1945); STORK CLUB, THE(1945); GILDA(1946); LADY LUCK(1946); LOVES OF CARMEN, THE(1948); MEXICAN HAYRIDE(1948); ON AN ISLAND WITH YOU(1948); DANCING IN THE DARK(1949); JOHNNY ALLEGRO(1949); MISS GRANT TAKES RICHMOND(1949); RECKLESS MOMENTS, THE(1949); SUN COMES UP, THE(1949); EMERGENCY WED-DING(1950); IN A LONELY PLACE(1950); TALK ABOUT A STRANGER(1952); CRASHING LAS VEGAS(1956); JEANNE EAGELS(1957); SILENCERS, THE(1966); SAME TIME, NEXT YEAR(1978)
Cosmos Sardo
TO CATCH A THIEF(1955)
Fernand Sardou
LETTERS FROM MY WINDMILL(1955, Fr.); FORBIDDEN FRUIT(1959, Fr.); PICNIC ON THE GRASS(1960, Fr.); WOMAN OF SIN(1961, Fr.); OF FLESH AND BLOOD(1964, Fr./Ital.); GENDARME OF ST. TROPEZ, THE(1966, Fr./Ital.)
Jakie Sardou
1984
PAR OU T'ES RENTRE? ON T'A PAS VUE SORTIR(1984, Fr./Tunisia)
Victoria Sardou
Misc. Silents
THEODORA(1921, Ital.), d
Victorien Sardou
THAT UNCERTAIN FEELING(1941), w; FEDORA(1946, Ital.), w; MADAME(1963, Fr./Ital./Span.), w
Silents
SONG OF HATE, THE(1915), w; KISS ME AGAIN(1925), w; NIGHT OF MYSTERY, A(1928), w
Barney A. Sarecky
TROUBLE AT MIDNIGHT(1937), p; MISSING GUEST, THE(1938), p; PIRATES OF THE SKIES(1939), p; DRUMS OF FU MANCHU(1943), p; WHAT A MAN!(1944), p; FLASHING GUNS(1947), p; PRAIRIE EXPRESS(1947), p; SONG OF THE WASTE-LAND(1947), p; SHADOWS OF THE WEST(1949), p; TRAIL'S END(1949), p; WEST OF EL DORADO(1949), p; SUPERMAN AND THE MOLE MEN(1951), p
Barney Sarecky
SHOOTING STRAIGHT(1930), w; HONEYMOON LANE(1931), w; RUNAROUND, THE(1931), w; LOST JUNGLE, THE(1934), w; DARKEST AFRICA(1936), p, w; YOUNG FUGITIVES(1938), p; APE MAN, THE(1943), w; BUFFALO BILL RIDES AGAIN(1947), w; CODE OF THE SADDLE(1947), p; LAND OF THE LAWLESS(1947), p; SIX GUN SERENADE(1947), p; BACK TRAIL(1948), p; FIGHTING RANGER, THE(1948), p; FRONTIER AGENT(1948), p; GUN TALK(1948), p; GUNNING FOR JUSTICE(1948), p; CRASHING THRU(1949), p; HIDDEN DANGER(1949), p; LAW OF THE WEST(1949), p; RANGE JUSTICE(1949), p; MOTOR PATROL(1950), p; RADAR SECRET SERVICE(1950), p
Lou Sarecky
NORTH TO THE KLONDIKE(1942), w
Louis Sarecky
BLOCKADE(1929), w; LOVE IN THE DESERT(1929), w; TANNED LEGS(1929), p, w; VAGABOND LOVER(1929), p; CUCKOOS, THE(1930), d; SHOOTING STRAIGHT(1930), p; KEPT HUSBANDS(1931), w; PUBLIC DEFENDER, THE(1931), p; RUNAROUND, THE(1931), p; SECRET SERVICE(1931), p; YOUNG DONOVAN'S KID(1931), p; KANSAS CYCLONE(1941), w
Silents
HEY RUBE!(1928), w; STOCKS AND BLONDES(1928), sup
Louis J. Sarecky
SEVEN KEYS TO BALDPATE(1930), p
Maurice Sarfati
JOURNEY, THE(1959, U.S./Aust.); LOST COMMAND, THE(1966)
Bill Sargant
HARLOW(1965), p
Charles Sargeant
DOWN THE WYOMING TRAIL(1939)
James Sargeant
THOMASINE AND BUSHROD(1974)
Ray Sargeant
Misc. Talkies
SUPER-JOCKS, THE(1980), d
Kate Sargeantson
Misc. Silents
WHO'S WHO IN SOCIETY(1915)
Al Sargent
FROM HERE TO ETERNITY(1953)
Alvin Sargent
WAY WE WERE, THE(1973), w; GAMBIT(1966), w; STALKING MOON, THE(1969), w; STERILE CUCKOO, THE(1969), w; I WALK THE LINE(1970), w; EFFECT OF GAMMA RAYS ON MAN-IN-THE-MOON MARIGOLDS, THE(1972), w; LOVE AND PAIN AND THE WHOLE DAMN THING(1973), w; PAPER MOON(1973), w; BOBBY DEERFIELD(1977), w; JULIA(1977), w; STRAIGHT TIME(1978), w; ORDINARY PEOPLE(1980), w
Anne Sargent
NAKED CITY, THE(1948); THREE GUYS NAMED MIKE(1951)
Bill Sargent
STOP THE WORLD-I WANT TO GET OFF(1966, Brit.), p
Bobby Sargent
PIRANHA(1978)

Brent Sargent
YELLOW JACK(1938); MY DEAR MISS ALDRICH(1937); MARIE ANTOINET-TE(1938); SWEETHEARTS(1938); TEST PILOT(1938); TOY WIFE, THE(1938); IN-TERNS, THE(1962)
Charley Sargent
LAWLESS RANGE(1935)
Dick Sargent
BEAST WITH A MILLION EYES, THE(1956); CAPTAIN NEWMAN, M.D.(1963); BILLIE(1965); FLUFFY(1965); GHOST AND MR. CHICKEN, THE(1966); LIVE A LITTLE, LOVE A LITTLE(1968); PRIVATE NAVY OF SGT. O'FARRELL, THE(1968); YOUNG RUNAWAYS, THE(1968); CLONUS HORROR, THE(1979); HARDCORE(1979)
Misc. Talkies
I'M GOING TO BE FAMOUS(1981)
Frank Sargent
Silents
ACE OF HEARTS, THE(1916, Brit.)
Frederick Sargent
Misc. Silents
DAWN OF THE TRUTH, THE(1920, Brit.)
George Sargent
Misc. Silents
PHILIP HOLDEN - WASTER(1916), d
George L. Sargent
Silents
GENTLEMAN FROM MISSISSIPPI, THE(1914), d; HIGH SPEED(1917), d
Misc. Silents
CALL OF THE DANCE, THE(1915), d; MIDNIGHT AT MAXIM'S(1915), d; SABLE BLESSING, THE(1916), d; GILDED YOUTH, A(1917), d; BROADWAY BUBBLE, THE(1920), d; PREY, THE(1920), d; WHISPER MARKET, THE(1920), d; CHARMING DECEIVER, THE(1921), d; IT ISN'T BEING DONE THIS SEASON(1921), d
Gundel Sargent
DEVIL'S DAFFODIL, THE(1961, Brit./Ger.)
Herb Sargent
HELLO LONDON(1958, Brit.), w
Herbert Sargent
P.C. JOSSER(1931, Brit.), w; JOSSER IN THE ARMY(1932, Brit.), w; JOSSER JOINS THE NAVY(1932, Brit.), w; LETTING IN THE SUNSHINE(1933, Brit.), w; MY OLD DUCHESS(1933, Brit.), w; JOSSER ON THE FARM(1934, Brit.), w; SMITH'S WI-VES(1935, Brit.), w; STRICTLY ILLEGAL(1935, Brit.), w; LOVE UP THE POLE(1936, Brit.), w; ONE GOOD TURN(1936, Brit.), w; BYE BYE BRAVERMAN(1968), w
Jean Sargent
TRANSATLANTIC MERRY-GO-ROUND(1934)
Joe Sargent
FROM HERE TO ETERNITY(1953); TOBRUK(1966)
John Sargent
Silents
EUGENE ARAM(1914, Brit.)
Joseph Sargent
TAKING OF PELHAM ONE, TWO, THREE, THE(1974), d; KATHY O'(1958); ONE SPY TOO MANY(1966), d; SPY IN THE GREEN HAT, THE(1966), d; HELL WITH HEROES, THE(1968), d; COLOSSUS: THE FORBIN PROJECT(1969), d; TRIBES(1970), d; MAN, THE(1972), d; WHITE LIGHTNING(1973), d; MAC ARTHUR(1977), d; GOLDENGIRL(1979), d; COAST TO COAST(1980), d; NIGHTMARES(1983), d
Joseph D. Sargent
PAY OR DIE(1960)
Leo Sargent
Silents
HIGH SPEED(1917), w
Lewis Sargent
MAN FROM NEW MEXICO, THE(1932); NEW ADVENTURES OF TARZAN(1935)
Silents
ALI BABA AND THE FORTY THIEVES(1918); HUCKLEBERRY FINN(1920); SOUL OF YOUTH, THE(1920); JUST AROUND THE CORNER(1921); OLIVER TWIST(1922); RIDIN' THE WIND(1925); MILLION FOR LOVE, A(1928); CAMPUS KNIGHTS(1929); ONE SPLENDID HOUR(1929)
Misc. Silents
CALL OF THE WILDERNESS, THE(1926); SOUTH OF PANAMA(1928); CLEAN-UP, THE(1929)
Louis Sargent
CRASHING BROADWAY(1933)
Misc. Silents
ACE HIGH(1918)
Michael Sargent
TOUCH OF EVIL(1958)
P. D. Sargent
Misc. Silents
BATTLING KING(1922), d
Richard Sargent
BERNARDINE(1957); MARDI GRAS(1958); OPERATION PETTICOAT(1959); GREAT IMPOSTOR, THE(1960); THAT TOUCH OF MINK(1962); FOR LOVE OR MO-NEY(1963); TANYA'S ISLAND(1981, Can.)
Roy Sargent
MR. PERRIN AND MR. TRAILL(1948, Brit.); MY WAY(1974, South Africa), d
Sir Malcolm Sargent
EDWARD, MY SON(1949, U.S./Brit.), md; GREAT GILBERT AND SULLIVAN, THE(1953, Brit.), md
William Sargent
YOUNG SAVAGES, THE(1961); HITLER(1962)
William S. Sargent, Jr.
HAMLET(1964), p
Wes Sarginson
SHARKY'S MACHINE(1982)
Sari
WAJAN(1938, South Bali)
Hrvoje Saric
CAVE OF THE LIVING DEAD(1966, Yugo./Ger.), ph
Sarie and Sallie
IN OLD MONTEREY(1939)

Dinah Saril
SIX IN PARIS(1968, Fr.)
Vic Sarin
HEARTACHES(1981, Can.), ph
May Sariola
GIDGET GOES TO ROME(1963)
Aggeo Sarioli
DOLL THAT TOOK THE TOWN, THE(1965, Ital.), w
George Saris
GLORY BRIGADE, THE(1953); PHAEDRA(1962, U.S./Gr./Fr.)
Marilyn Saris
LAWLESS EIGHTIES, THE(1957)
Kate Sarjeanston
Misc. Silents
PASSERS-BY(1916)
Kali Sarkar
GODDESS, THE(1962, India); MUSIC ROOM, THE(1963, India)
Mimi Sarkisian
ONE FLEW OVER THE CUCKOO'S NEST(1975)
Sos Sarkissian
SOLARIS(1972, USSR)
Toivo Sarkka
PRELUDE TO ECSTASY(1963, Fin.), p,d&w
Zoltan Sarkozy
1984
BRADY'S ESCAPE(1984, U.S./Hung.)
Sidney Sarl
Silents
GIRL WHO TOOK THE WRONG TURNING, THE(1915, Brit.)
Regina Sarle
Silents
NUGGET NELL(1919)
Isabel Sarli
PUT OR SHUT UP(1968, Arg.); HEAT(1970, Arg.)
Alfonso Sarlo
PRIMITIVE LOVE(1966, Ital.)
Walter Sarmel
PIMPERNEL SVENSSON(1953, Swed.)
Jean Sarment
UN CARNET DE BAL(1938, Fr.), w
Valeria Sarmiento
GUNS(1980, Fr.), ed
1984
THREE CROWNS OF THE SAILOR(1984, Fr.), ed
the Sarn Valley peasants
BLUE LIGHT, THE(1932, Ger.)
Michael Sarne
BEWARE OF CHILDREN(1961, Brit.); PLACE TO GO, A(1964, Brit.); OPERATION SNAFU(1965, Brit.); SEASIDE SWINGERS(1965, Brit.); TWO WEEKS IN SEPTEM-BER(1967, Fr./Brit.); JOANNA(1968, Brit.), d&w
Mike Sarne
MOONLIGHTING(1982, Brit.)
1984
SUCCESS IS THE BEST REVENGE(1984, Brit.)
Alexander Sarner
DREYFUS CASE, THE(1931, Brit.); CALLED BACK(1933, Brit.); PASSING OF THE THIRD FLOOR BACK, THE(1936, Brit.); NON-STOP NEW YORK(1937, Brit.)
Sylvia Sarner
ROAD MOVIE(1974), ed
Hector Sarno
UNDER TWO FLAGS(1936); THEY WON'T BELIEVE ME(1947); OKLAHOMA CY-CLONE(1930); DEATH TAKES A HOLIDAY(1934); MERRY WIDOW, THE(1934); CAR 99(1935); CASE OF THE CURIOUS BRIDE, THE(1935); LADIES IN LOVE(1936); FLIGHT INTO NOWHERE(1938); MARK OF ZORRO, THE(1940); CROSS-ROADS(1942); DAKOTA(1945); ESCAPE ME NEVER(1947); NIGHT SONG(1947)
Silents
CHEATED HEARTS(1921); CONFLICT, THE(1921); DIAMONDS ADRIFT(1921); DO AND DARE(1922); STEPPING FAST(1923); AS MAN DESIRES(1925); KING OF KINGS, THE(1927)
Misc. Silents
LITTLE SISTER OF EVERYBODY, A(1918); ROUGH DIAMOND, THE(1921); WISE KID, THE(1922)
Hector V. Sarno
LUCKY STAR(1929); RED HOT SPEED ½(1929); TAXI!(1932); MAN'S CASTLE, A(1933); LADY BY CHOICE(1934); VIVA VILLA!(1934); HUMAN CARGO(1936); EASY LIVING(1937); WEE WILLIE WINKIE(1937); WHEN YOU'RE IN LOVE(1937); PROFESSOR BEWARE(1938); EGG AND I, THE(1947)
Silents
GO WEST, YOUNG MAN(1919); ISLAND OF INTRIGUE, THE(1919); ASHES OF VENGEANCE(1923); GIRL OF THE GOLDEN WEST, THE(1923); SONG OF LOVE, THE(1923); COBRA(1925); TEMPTRESS, THE(1926)
Misc. Silents
CRIMSON GARDENIA, THE(1919); FORFEIT, THE(1919); RIO GRANDE(1920); SONIA(1928), a, d
Jan Sarno
PEOPLE NEXT DOOR, THE(1970)
Janet Sarno
HOSPITAL, THE(1971)
Jay Sarno
DIAMONDS ARE FOREVER(1971, Brit.)
Joe Sarno
SIN YOU SINNERS(1963), w; LOVE MERCHANT, THE(1966), d&w; MOONLIGHT-ING WIVES(1966), d&w; MY BODY HUNGERS(1967), d&w
Misc. Talkies
BED OF VIOLENCE(1967), d; RED ROSES OF PASSION(1967), d; OVERSEX-ED(1974), d; BIBI(1977), d
John Sarno
SEVEN MINUTES, THE(1971)

Jonathan Sarno
KIRLIAN WITNESS, THE(1978), p&d, w
Victor Sarno
MEN WITHOUT LAW(1930)
Misc. Silents
YANKEE DOODLE, JR.(1922)
Hedda Sarnow
SOMEWHERE IN BERLIN(1949, E. Ger.)
Anna Saro
ODDO(1967), cos
Muni Saroff
TWO SENORITAS FROM CHICAGO(1943)
Daina Saronni
SIX DAYS A WEEK(1966, Fr./Ital./Span.)
Leslie Sarony
ROLLING IN MONEY(1934, Brit.); WOMAN IN COMMAND, THE(1934 Brit.); HOPE OF HIS SIDE(1935, Brit.); WHEN YOU COME HOME(1947, Brit.); NOBODY IN TOYLAND(1958, Brit.); GAME FOR THREE LOSERS(1965, Brit.); ALL THINGS BRIGHT AND BEAUTIFUL(1979, Brit.)
1984
GIVE MY REGARDS TO BROAD STREET(1984, Brit.)
Sarossy
BLUE IDOL, THE(1931, Hung.)
Herman Sarotsky
Misc. Talkies
JOSEPH IN THE LAND OF EGYPT(1932)
Don Saroyan
BLAST OF SILENCE(1961)
Isabelle Saroyan
THINGS OF LIFE, THE(1970, Fr./Ital./Switz.)
Lucy Saroyan
ISADORA(1968, Brit.); SOME KIND OF A NUT(1969); MAIDSTONE(1970); KOTCH(1971); GREASED LIGHTNING(1977); BLUE COLLAR(1978); HOPSCOTCH(1980)
William Saroyan
TIME OF YOUR LIFE, THE(1948), w; HUMAN COMEDY, THE(1943), w
Peter Sarpong
1984
WHITE ELEPHANT(1984, Brit.)
Ed Sarquist
HELLCATS, THE(1968)
Farba Sarr
MANDABI(1970, Fr./Senegal)
Gerald Sarracini
SHADOW ON THE WINDOW, THE(1957)
Ernest Sarracino
SLEEPING CITY, THE(1950); SANTIAGO(1956); STRANGERS WHEN WE MEET(1960); CASTLE OF EVIL(1967); DREAM OF KINGS, A(1969)
Richard Sarradet
MIDWAY(1976)
Louis Sarrano
36 HOURS(1965)
Marion Sarraut
WOMAN IS A WOMAN, A(1961, Fr./Ital.)
Anne Sarraute
HIROSHIMA, MON AMOUR(1959, Fr./Jap.), ed
Yvon Sarray
ROAD TO SHAME, THE(1962, Fr.); MALE HUNT(1965, Fr./Ital.)
Michael Sarrazin
FLIM-FLAM MAN, THE(1967); GUNFIGHT IN ABILENE(1967); JOURNEY TO SHILOH(1968); SWEET RIDE, THE(1968); EYE OF THE CAT(1969); MAN CALLED GANNON, A(1969); THEY SHOOT HORSES, DON'T THEY?(1969); IN SEARCH OF GREGORY(1970, Brit./Ital.); BELIEVE IN ME(1971); PURSUIT OF HAPPINESS, THE(1971); SOMETIMES A GREAT NOTION(1971); GROUNDSTAR CONSPIRACY, THE(1972, Can.); HARRY IN YOUR POCKET(1973); REINCARNATION OF PETER PROUD, THE(1975); GUMBALL RALLY, THE(1976); LOVES AND TIMES OF SCARAMOUCHE, THE(1976, Ital.); FOR PETE'S SAKE(1977); CARAVANS(1978, U.S./Iranian); DOUBLE NEGATIVE(1980, Can.); DEATH VENGEANCE(1982); SEDUCTION, THE(1982)
Norman Sarrazin
TOMORROW NEVER COMES(1978, Brit./Can.), set d
Normand Sarrazin
FOND MEMORIES(1982, Can.), art d
Anthony Sarrero
WAITRESS(1982)
Marco Sarri
OUTCRY(1949, Ital.)
Bernard Sarron
ONE WISH TOO MANY(1956, Brit.), art d; TIME WITHOUT PITY(1957, Brit.), art d; SPARROWS CAN'T SING(1963, Brit.), art d; GUTTER GIRLS(1964, Brit.), art d; POOR COW(1968, Brit.), art d; THANK YOU ALL VERY MUCH(1969, Brit.), prod d; CONFESSIONS OF A POP PERFORMER(1975, Brit.), art d
Andre Sarrut
PARDON MY FRENCH(1951, U.S./Fr.), p
Gailard Sartain
HOLLYWOOD KNIGHTS, THE(1980); ROADIE(1980); HARD COUNTRY(1981); ENDANGERED SPECIES(1982); OUTSIDERS, THE(1983)
1984
ALL OF ME(1984); CHOOSE ME(1984); SONGWRITER(1984)
Giorgio Sartarelli
THREE FACES OF A WOMAN(1965, Ital.)
Marcello Sartarelli
WAR OF THE ZOMBIES, THE(1965 Ital.), w
Gilbert Sarthre
MIDNIGHT FOLLY(1962, Fr.), ph
Andre Sarti
Silents
WOMAN ON TRIAL, THE(1927)

Rene Sartoris
SPYLARKS(1965, Brit.); FIDDLER ON THE ROOF(1971)
Jeff Sartorius
BANG THE DRUM SLOWLY(1973)
Hendrick Sartov
Silents
SCARLET LETTER, THE(1926), ph
Hendrik Sartov
Silents
BROKEN BLOSSOMS(1919), ph; WAY DOWN EAST(1920), ph; DREAM STREET(1921), ph; ONE EXCITING NIGHT(1922), ph; ORPHANS OF THE STORM(1922), ph; WHITE ROSE, THE(1923), ph; AMERICA(1924), ph; ISN'T LIFE WONDERFUL(1924), ph; QUALITY STREET(1927), ph; RED MILL, THE(1927), ph
Hendrik Sartow
Silents
HEARTS OF THE WORLD(1918), ph
Anna Raquel Sartre
Misc. Talkies
BLUEBEARD'S CASTLE(1969, Brit.)
Jean Paul Sartre
LES JEUX SONT FAITS(1947, Fr.), w
Jean-Paul Sartre
LIFE BEGINS TOMORROW(1952, Fr.); LES MAINS SALES(1954, Fr.), w; FREUD(1962), w; NO EXIT(1962, U.S./Arg.), w
Charles Sarver
Silents
ANTON THE TERRIBLE(1916), w; AFRAID TO FIGHT(1922), w; NERO(1922, U.S./Ital.), w; WOLF LAW(1922), w
J.D. Sarver
JIM, THE WORLD'S GREATEST(1976)
Ole Sarvig
GERTRUD(1966, Den.)
Rene Sarvil
LETTERS FROM MY WINDMILL(1955, Fr.)
David Sarvis
SALT OF THE EARTH(1954)
Antonio Sarzi-Braga
GIDGET GOES TO ROME(1963), art d
Toni Sarzi-Braga
GENGHIS KHAN(U.S./Brit./Ger./Yugo), set d; JASON AND THE ARGONAUTS(1963, Brit.), art d; PUSSYCAT, PUSSYCAT, I LOVE YOU!(1970), art d
James Sarzotti
1984
ALMOST YOU(1984), makeup
George Sasaki
VARAN THE UNBELIEVABLE(1962, U.S./Jap.); GREAT BANK ROBBERY, THE(1969); HOUSE CALLS(1978); MODERN ROMANCE(1981)
Katsuhiko Sasaki
MONSTERS FROM THE UNKNOWN PLANET(1975, Jap.); GODZILLA VS. MEGALON(1976, Jap.)
Kiyono Sasaki
THREE WEEKS OF LOVE(1965)
Mamoru Sasaki
DIARY OF A SHINJUKU BURGLAR(1969, Jap.), w
Miyoko Sasaki
JUNGLE HEAT(1957)
Shiro Sasaki
1984
FAMILY GAME, THE(1984, Jap.), p
Sumie Sasaki
INSECT WOMAN, THE(1964, Jap.); GIRL I ABANDONED, THE(1970, Jap.)
Takamaru Sasaki
THRONE OF BLOOD(1961, Jap.); PERFORMERS, THE(1970, Jap.)
Takamura Sasaki
PORTRAIT OF CHIEKO(1968, Jap.)
Toshiyuki Sasaki
HOUSE WHERE EVIL DWELLS, THE(1982)
Yoshiko Sasaki
LAST UNICORN, THE(1982), anim
Fred Sasbsoni
WATERLOO BRIDGE(1940)
Sascha
M(1933, Ger.)
Philip Sascombe
LAST OF THE SECRET AGENTS?, THE(1966)
Peter Sasdy
JOURNEY INTO DARKNESS(1968, Brit.), d; TASTE THE BLOOD OF DRACULA(1970, Brit.), d; HANDS OF THE RIPPER(1971, Brit.), d; COUNTESS DRACULA(1972, Brit.), d, w; DOOMWATCH(1972, Brit.), d; NOTHING BUT THE NIGHT(1975, Brit.), d; DEVIL WITHIN HER, THE(1976, Brit.), d; WELCOME TO BLOOD CITY(1977, Brit./Can.), d; LONELY LADY, THE(1983), d
Misc. Talkies
TWO FACES OF EVIL, THE(1981, Brit.), d
Jiri Sasek
90 DEGREES IN THE SHADE(1966, Czech./Brit.)
Vaclav Sasek
LOVES OF A BLONDE(1966, Czech.), w; INTIMATE LIGHTING(1969, Czech.), w
A. Sashin-Nikolsky
ANNA CROSS, THE(1954, USSR)
Gwen Saska
Misc. Talkies
INTERPLAY(1970)
A. Saskin
Silents
AMATEUR WIFE, THE(1920)
Luis Saslavsky
DEMONIAQUE(1958, Fr.), d, w

Alfonso Sasone
BIG AND THE BAD, THE(1971, Ital./Fr./Span.), p

Sasonia
Misc. Silents
BRIDGE OF SIGHS, THE(1922, Ital.)

Edward Sass
Silents
NEW CLOWN, THE(1916, Brit.)
Misc. Silents
HEART OF A CHILD, THE(1915, Brit.)

Heinz-Gueter Sass
CITY OF SECRETS(1963, Ger.), prod d

Herbert Ravenal Sass
RAID, THE(1954), w

Herbert Ravenel Sass
ANNE OF THE INDIES(1951), w

Ilse Sass
FAME(1980)

Paul Sass
TIMES SQUARE(1980)

Jacqueline Sassard
VIOLENT SUMMER(1961, Fr./Ital.); MY SON, THE HERO(1963, Ital./Fr.); SANDO-
KAN THE GREAT(1964, Fr./Ital./Span.); WHITE VOICES(1965, Fr./Ital.); AC-
CIDENT(1967, Brit.)

Jaqueline Sassard
LES BICHES(1968, Fr.)

Fred Sassebo
CHILDREN OF GOD'S EARTH(1983, Norwegian), ed

Marina Sassi
LEAP INTO THE VOID(1982, Ital.)

Sara Sassin
SMITHEREENS(1982)

Dick Sasso
T.R. BASKIN(1971)

Pietro Sasso
IDEA GIRL(1946); STRANGER THE(1946)

Ugo Sasso
DAVID AND GOLIATH(1961, Ital.); PHAROAH'S WOMAN, THE(1961, Ital.); NIGHT
THEY KILLED RASPUTIN, THE(1962, Fr./Ital.); HERCULES, SAMSON & ULYS-
SES(1964, Ital.)

Dina Sassoli
SPIRIT AND THE FLESH, THE(1948, Ital.); ASH WEDNESDAY(1973)
Misc. Talkies
FLYING SQUADRON(1952)

Anne Sassoon
CAESAR AND CLEOPATRA(1946, Brit.)

Janet Sassoon
1984
IMPULSE(1984)

William Sassoon
CARNIVAL(1946, Brit.), p; HER MAN GILBEY(1949, Brit.), p; GIRL ON A MOTOR-
CYCLE, THE(1968, Fr./Brit.), p

Nate Sassover
WAY WE LIVE NOW, THE(1970), m

Jean-Paul Sassy
THUNDER IN THE BLOOD(1962, Fr.), d

Keiko Sata
HUMAN VAPOR, THE(1964, Jap.)

Remow Satan
DEVIL TIGER(1934)

members of the Satan's Choice Motorcycle Club
PROUD RIDER, THE(1971, Can.)

Tura Satana
IRMA LA DOUCE(1963); ASTRO-ZOMBIES, THE(1969)

Swami Satchidananda
CHAPPAQUA(1967)

Sandra Satchwith
SWAPPERS, THE(1970, Brit.)

Kei Sate
NAKED YOUTH(1961, Jap.)

Frank Satenstein
CLOSE-UP(1948), p; OPEN SECRET(1948), p

Erik Satie
FIRE WITHIN, THE(1964, Fr./Ital.), m; RACHEL, RACHEL(1968), m; IMMORTAL
STORY, THE(1969, Fr.), m

Julius Satinsky
ASSISTANT, THE(1982, Czech.)

Satisfaction
GONG SHOW MOVIE, THE(1980)

Sato
Misc. Talkies
SILENT STRANGER, THE(1975)

Chieko Sato
JAPANESE WAR BRIDE(1952)

Gajiro Sato
TORA-SAN PART 2(1970, Jap.)

Gen Sato
ANGRY ISLAND(1960, Jap.)

Hajime Sato
TERROR BENEATH THE SEA(1966, Jap.), d; GOKE, BODYSNATCHER FROM
HELL(1968, Jap.), d

Ichiro Sato
TILL TOMORROW COMES(1962, Jap.), p; TWILIGHT STORY, THE(1962, Jap.), p;
MADAME AKI(1963, Jap.), p; PRESSURE OF GUILT(1964, Jap.), p; THIS MADDING
CROWD(1964, Jap.), p; ILLUSION OF BLOOD(1966, Jap.), p; RIVER OF FORE-
VER(1967, Jap.), p

Kei Sato
ROAD TO ETERNITY(1962, Jap.); HAHAKIRI(1963, Jap.); ONIBABA(1965, Jap.);
PLEASURES OF THE FLESH, THE(1965); SWORD OF DOOM, THE(1967, Jap.);
KUROENKO(1968, Jap); DEVIL'S TEMPLE(1969, Jap.); DIARY OF A SHINJUKU

BURGLAR(1969, Jap.); ZATOICHI'S CONSPIRACY(1974, Jap.)

Keiroku Sato
TORA-SAN PART 2(1970, Jap.)

Kiminobu Sato
YOUTH IN FURY(1961, Jap.), art d

Kosei Sato
1984
BALLAD OF NARAYAMA, THE(1984, Jap.)

Makato Sato
BANDITS ON THE WIND(1964, Jap.); FORT GRAVEYARD(1966, Jap.)

Makoto Sato
I BOMBED PEARL HARBOR(1961, Jap.); MAN FROM THE EAST, THE(1961, Jap.);
WESTWARD DESPERADO(1961, Jap.); OPERATION X(1963, Jap.); WARRING
CLANS(1963, Jap.); OPERATION ENEMY FORT(1964, Jap.); TIGER FLIGHT(1965,
Jap.); OUTPOST OF HELL(1966, Jap.); RISE AGAINST THE SWORD(1966, Jap.);
DAPHNE, THE(1967); MAD ATLANTIC, THE(1967, Jap.); EMPEROR AND A GENER-
AL, THE(1968, Jap.); SIEGE OF FORT BISMARK(1968, Jap.); WHIRLWIND(1968,
Jap.); FALCON FIGHTERS, THE(1970, Jap.); MESSAGE FROM SPACE(1978, Jap.)

Masamichi Sato
TORA! TORA! TORA!(1970, U.S./Jap.), ph

Masaru Sato
H-MAN, THE(1959, Jap.), m; HIDDEN FORTRESS, THE(1959, Jap.), m; THRONE OF
BLOOD(1961, Jap.), m; YOJIMBO(1961, Jap.), m; LOWER DEPTHS, THE(1962, Jap.),
m; SANJURO(1962, Jap.), m; HIGH AND LOW(1963, Jap.), m; CHALLENGE TO
LIVE(1964, Jap.), m; OPERATION ENEMY FORT(1964, Jap.), m; SAMURAI FROM
NOWHERE(1964, Jap.), m; SAMURAI ASSASSIN(1965, Jap.), m; FORT GRAVE-
YARD(1966, Jap.), m; RED BEARD(1966, Jap.), m; I LIVE IN FEAR(1967, Jap.), m;
MAD ATLANTIC, THE(1967, Jap.), m; RIVER OF FOREVER(1967, Jap.), m; SWORD
OF DOOM, THE(1967, Jap.), m; EMPEROR AND A GENERAL, THE(1968, Jap.), m;
KILL(1968, Jap.), m; PORTRAIT OF CHIEKO(1968, Jap.), m; GOYOKIN(1969, Jap.),
m; MOMENT OF TERROR(1969, Jap.), m; UNDER THE BANNER OF SAMURAI(1969,
Jap.), m; LIVE YOUR OWN WAY(1970, Jap.), m; MAGOICHI SAGA, THE(1970,
Jap.), m; SCANDALOUS ADVENTURES OF BURAIKAN, THE(1970, Jap.), m; SONG
FROM MY HEART, THE(1970, Jap.), m; TENCHU!(1970, Jap.), m; RED LION(1971,
Jap.), m; TIDAL WAVE(1975, U.S./Jap.), m

Masau Sato
BAND OF ASSASSINS(1971, Jap.), m

Massaru Sato
OPERATION X(1963, Jap.), m

Mitsuhiko Sato
CREATURE CALLED MAN, THE(1970, Jap.), m

Mitsuru Sato
H-MAN, THE(1959, Jap.)

Orie Sato
LIVE YOUR OWN WAY(1970, Jap.); TORA-SAN PART 2(1970, Jap.)

Reiko Sato
MOTHER DIDN'T TELL ME(1950); WOMAN ON THE RUN(1950); HOUSE OF
BAMBOO(1955); KISMET(1955); HELL TO ETERNITY(1960); FLOWER DRUM
SONG(1961); UGLY AMERICAN, THE(1963)

Tomomi Sato
GOKE, BODYSNATCHER FROM HELL(1968, Jap.); TOPSY-TURVY JOUR-
NEY(1970, Jap.)

Paul Satoff
CRUSADES, THE(1935)

Makoto Satoh
LOST WORLD OF SINBAD, THE(1965, Jap.)

Masaru Satoh
LOST WORLD OF SINBAD, THE(1965, Jap.), m

Jaroslav Satoransky
END OF A PRIEST(1970, Czech.)

Alain Satou
SKY ABOVE HEAVEN(1964, Fr./Ital.), w

Diana Satow
VALUE FOR MONEY(1957, Brit.)

Kiyosho Satow
Silents
WHERE LIGHTS ARE LOW(1921)

Bush Satterfield
9/30/55(1977)

Dion Satterfield
Misc. Talkies
APOCALYPSE 3:16(1964)

Jeanne Satterfield
BORN IN FLAMES(1983)

Katherine Satterfield
9/30/55(1977)

Paul Satterfield
FANTASIA(1940), d; BAMBI(1942), d

Bruce Satterlee
STELLA DALLAS(1937)

Peggy Satterlee
ARABIAN NIGHTS(1942)

Lucille Satterthwaite
Silents
AMERICAN BUDS(1918)

Lonnie Sattin
HUMAN DUPLICATORS, THE(1965)

Ernst Sattler
FINAL CHORD, THE(1936, Ger.); CONFESS DR. CORDA(1960, Ger.)

Janette Sattler
PRIME OF MISS JEAN BRODIE, THE(1969, Brit.)

Ota Sattler
FIFTH HORSEMAN IS FEAR, THE(1968, Czech.)

Lon Satton
FOR LOVE OF IVY(1968); HELLO–GOODBYE(1970); WELCOME TO THE
CLUB(1971); LIVE AND LET DIE(1973, Brit.); REVENGE OF THE PINK PAN-
THER(1978)

Saturday Revue
WILD WHEELS(1969)
Ludwig Satz
Misc. Talkies
HIS WIFE'S LOVER(1931)
Wayne Satz
TUNNELVISION(1976)
Danny Saual
DEVIL AND THE TEN COMMANDMENTS, THE(1962, Fr.)
Harry Sauber
BEAUTY PARLOR(1932), w; RIDERS OF THE GOLDEN GULCH(1932), w; FORGOTTEN(1933), w; OBEY THE LAW(1933), w; HAPPINESS AHEAD(1934), w; I LIKE IT THAT WAY(1934), w; LET'S BE RITZY(1934), w; TWENTY MILLION SWEETHEARTS(1934), w; DINKY(1935), w; MAYBE IT'S LOVE(1935), w; TOMORROW'S YOUTH(1935), w; ADVENTURE IN MANHATTAN(1936), w; HER MASTER'S VOICE(1936), w; SING ME A LOVE SONG(1936), w; MANHATTAN MERRY-GO-ROUND(1937), p, w; RACKETEERS IN EXILE(1937), w; OUTSIDE OF PARADISE(1938), p, w; DISBARRED(1939), w; FIVE LITTLE PEPPERS AT HOME(1940), w; HERE COMES HAPPINESS(1941), w; LAUGH YOUR BLUES AWAY(1943), w; WHAT'S BUZZIN COUSIN?(1943), w; HOW DO YOU DO?(1946), p, w; LOVE AND LEARN(1947), w; LADIES OF THE CHORUS(1948), w
Thomas J. Sauber
1984
IMPULSE(1984)
Tom Sauber
LONG RIDERS, THE(1980)
Jean Saudray
VERY HAPPY ALEXANDER(1969, Fr.); TALL BLOND MAN WITH ONE BLACK SHOE, THE(1973, Fr.)
Fred Sauer
Misc. Silents
DANGERS OF THE ENGAGEMENT PERIOD(1929, Ger.), d
Hank Sauer
WINNING TEAM, THE(1952)
Barbara Sauerbaum
SISTERS, OR THE BALANCE OF HAPPINESS(1982, Ger.)
Carl Sauerman
Silents
AMERICAN WAY, THE(1919)
Joe Sauers
HUDDLE(1932); ACE OF ACES(1933); COLLEGE COACH(1933); CAR 99(1935)
Patricia Sauers
SQUARES(1972)
Patty Sauers
MOONSHINE WAR, THE(1970)
Marc Gilbert Saugajon
DUCH IN ORANGE SAUCE(1976, Ital.), w
Henri Sauguet
LOVERS OF TERUEL, THE(1962, Fr.), m
Janis Saul
ASTRO-ZOMBIES, THE(1969)
Loretta Saul
SIDECAR RACERS(1975, Aus.)
Nitza Saul
1984
UNTIL SEPTEMBER(1984)
Oscar Saul
ONCE UPON A TIME(1944), w; STRANGE AFFAIR(1944), w; DARK PAST, THE(1948), w; ROAD HOUSE(1948), w; LADY GAMBLES, THE(1949), w; ONCE MORE, MY DARLING(1949), w; WOMAN IN HIDING(1949), w; SECRET OF CONVICT LAKE, THE(1951), w; STREETCAR NAMED DESIRE, A(1951), w; THUNDER ON THE HILL(1951), w; AFFAIR IN TRINIDAD(1952), w; LET'S DO IT AGAIN(1953), p; JOKER IS WILD, THE(1957), w; HELEN MORGAN STORY, THE(1959), w; NAKED MAJA, THE(1959, Ital./U.S.), w; SECOND TIME AROUND, THE(1961), w; MAJOR DUNDEE(1965), w; SILENCERS, THE(1966), w; MAN AND BOY(1972), w; DEAF SMITH AND JOHNNY EARS(1973, Ital.), w
Oscar Saul [Luis Marquina]
MR. SUPERINVISIBLE(1974, Ital./Span./Ger.), w
William Saul
STUDY IN SCARLET, A(1933), p
Jacques Saulnier
LOVERS, THE(1959, Fr.), prod d; JOKER, THE(1961, Fr.), art d; WEB OF PASSION(1961, Fr.), art d; LAST YEAR AT MARIENBAD(1962, Fr./Ital.), art d; VIEW FROM THE BRIDGE, A(1962, Fr./Ital.), art d; LANDRU(1963, Fr./Ital.), art d; MURIEL(1963, Fr./Ital.), art d; SEASON FOR LOVE, THE(1963, Fr.), art d; LA BONNE SOUPE(1964, Fr./Ital.), art d; WHAT'S NEW, PUSSYCAT?(1965, U.S./Fr.), art d; CLOPORTES(1966, Fr., Ital.), set d; MADEMOISELLE(1966, Fr./Brit.), art d; MARCO THE MAGNIFICENT(1966, Ital./Fr./Yugo./Egypt/Afghanistan), art d; LA GUERRE EST FINIE(1967, Fr./Swed.), set d; LA VIE DE CHATEAU(1967, Fr.), art d; THIEF OF PARIS, THE(1967, Fr./Ital.), art d; ZITA(1968, Fr.), art d; LA PRISONNIERE(1969, Fr./Ital.), art d; SICILIAN CLAN, THE(1970, Fr.), art d; SERPENT, THE(1973, Fr./Ital./Ger.), prod d; FRENCH CONNECTION 11(1975), prod d; PROVIDENCE(1977, Fr.), art d; MON ONCLE D'AMERIQUE(1980, Fr.), set d; CHANEL SOLITAIRE(1981), art d
1984
LIFE IS A BED OF ROSES(1984, Fr.), art d; SWANN IN LOVE(1984, Fr.Ger.), prod d
Nicole Saulnier
BANZAI(1983, Fr.), ed
1984
MY NEW PARTNER(1984, Fr.), ed
William F. Sauls
POCKETFUL OF MIRACLES(1961)
Rodney Saulsberry
1984
PHILADELPHIA EXPERIMENT, THE(1984)
Dorothy Saulter
52ND STREET(1937)

William Saulter
FOLLOW THE LEADER(1930), art d; QUEEN HIGH(1930), art d; SAP FROM SYRACUSE, THE(1930), art d; YOUNG MAN OF MANHATTAN(1930), art d; TATTOOED STRANGER, THE(1950), art d
Cliff Saum
FLIRTATION WALK(1934); I'VE GOT YOUR NUMBER(1934); ST. LOUIS KID, THE(1934); UPPER WORLD(1934); ALIBI IKE(1935); GOOSE AND THE GANDER, THE(1935); SECRET BRIDE, THE(1935); GOLD DIGGERS OF 1937(1936); SATAN MET A LADY(1936); THREE MEN ON A HORSE(1936); TRAILIN' WEST(1936); TREACHERY RIDES THE RANGE(1936); CALIFORNIA MAIL, THE(1937); GUNS OF THE PECOS(1937); LOVE IS ON THE AIR(1937); PERFECT SPECIMEN, THE(1937); READY, WILLING AND ABLE(1937); SLIM(1937); SMART BLONDE(1937); THAT CERTAIN WOMAN(1937); ACCIDENTS WILL HAPPEN(1938); BOY MEETS GIRL(1938); COWBOY FROM BROOKLYN(1938); GOLD IS WHERE YOU FIND IT(1938); HARD TO GET(1938); PATIENT IN ROOM 18, THE(1938); TORCHY GETS HER MAN(1938); CODE OF THE SECRET SERVICE(1939); EACH DAWN I DIE(1939); HELL'S KITCHEN(1939); KID FROM KOKOMO, THE(1939); KING OF THE UNDERWORLD(1939); NANCY DREW, TROUBLE SHOOTER(1939); NAUGHTY BUT NICE(1939); ON TRIAL(1939); SECRET SERVICE OF THE AIR(1939); THEY MADE ME A CRIMINAL(1939); TORCHY PLAYS WITH DYNAMITE(1939); LADIES MUST LIVE(1940); MAN WHO TALKED TOO MUCH, THE(1940); BRIDE CAME C.O.D., THE(1941); HIGH SIERRA(1941); MANPOWER(1941); MEET JOHN DOE(1941); WAGONS ROLL AT NIGHT, THE(1941); GEORGE WASHINGTON SLEPT HERE(1942); LARCENY, INC.(1942); MALE ANIMAL, THE(1942); MAN WHO CAME TO DINNER, THE(1942); ADVENTURES OF MARK TWAIN, THE(1944)
Clifford Saum
THREE SISTERS, THE(1930)
Clifford P. Saum
Silents
$5,000,000 COUNTERFEITING PLOT, THE(1914); KAISER'S FINISH, THE(1918), d
Alice Saunders
Misc. Silents
DOLLY DOES HER BIT(1918)
Allen Saunders
MURDER WITH PICTURES(1936)
Arlene Saunders
DER FREISCHUTZ(1970, Ger.); MARRIAGE OF FIGARO, THE(1970, Ger.)
Audrey Saunders
VARIETY GIRL(1947); NIGHT HAS A THOUSAND EYES(1948); GREAT WALDO PEPPER, THE(1975), stunts
Basil Saunders
Silents
NOTORIOUS MRS. CARRICK, THE(1924, Brit.)
Billy Saunders
PAY BOX ADVENTURE(1936, Brit.)
Blanche Saunders
VAGABOND KING, THE(1930)
C. Saunders
EVERYTHING IS THUNDER(1936, Brit.), ed
Charles Saunders
NO EXIT(1930, Brit.), p,d&w; MISTER HOBO(1936, Brit.), ed; MURDER IN THE OLD RED BARN(1936, Brit.), ed; YOU'RE IN THE ARMY NOW(1937, Brit.), ed; PHANTOM STRIKES, THE(1939, Brit.), ed; WARE CASE, THE(1939, Brit.), ed; RETURN TO YESTERDAY(1940, Brit.), ed; YOUNG MAN'S FANCY(1943, Brit.), ed; TAWNY PIPIT(1947, Brit.), d&w; FLY AWAY PETER(1948, Brit.), d; TROUBLE IN THE AIR(1948, Brit.), d; DARK INTERVAL(1950, Brit.), d; CHELSEA STORY(1951, Brit.), d; ONE WILD OAT(1951, Brit.), d; BLIND MAN'S BLUFF(1952, Brit.), d; COME BACK PETER(1952, Brit.), d&w; DEATH OF AN ANGEL(1952, Brit.), d; LOVE IN PAWN(1953, Brit.), d; THREE'S COMPANY(1953, Brit.), d; MEET MR. CALLAGHAN(1954, Brit.), d; RED DRESS, THE(1954, Brit.), d; SCARLET WEB, THE(1954, Brit.), d; HORNET'S NEST, THE(1955, Brit.), d; ONE JUMP AHEAD(1955, Brit.), d; TIME TO KILL, A(1955, Brit.), d; BEHIND THE HEADLINES(1956, Brit.), d; FIND THE LADY(1956, Brit.), d; NARROWING CIRCLE, THE(1956, Brit.), d; DATE WITH DISASTER(1957, Brit.), d; MAN WITHOUT A BODY, THE(1957, Brit.), d; THERE'S ALWAYS A THURSDAY(1957, Brit.), d; KILL HER GENTLY(1958, Brit.), d; MURDER REPORTED(1958, Brit.), d; END OF THE LINE, THE(1959, Brit.), d; NAKED FURY(1959, Brit.), d; STRICTLY CONFIDENTIAL(1959, Brit.), d; WOMAN EATER, THE(1959, Brit.), d; GENTLE TRAP, THE(1960, Brit.), d; OPERATION CUPID(1960, Brit.), d; DANGEROUS AFTERNOON(1961, Brit.), d; DANGER BY MY SIDE(1962, Brit.), d; JUNGLE STREET GIRLS(1963, Brit.), d; PLEASURE LOVERS, THE(1964, Brit.), d
Misc. Talkies
BLACK ORCHID(1952), d; ACCUSED, THE(1953), d
Desmond Saunders
RX MURDER(1958, Brit.), ed
Don Saunders
NICKEL QUEEN, THE(1971, Aus.), ed; NORMAN LOVES ROSE(1982, Aus.), ed; WILD DUCK, THE(1983, Aus.), ed
Elizabeth Saunders
CHEER THE BRAVE(1951, Brit.); JOHNNY ON THE RUN(1953, Brit.); HONOURABLE MURDER, AN(1959, Brit.)
Enid Saunders
SUPERMAN III(1983)
Gene Saunders
GOODBYE PORK PIE(1981, New Zealand)
George A. Saunders
EXORCISM AT MIDNIGHT(1966, Brit. revised 1973, U.S.)
Gertrude Saunders
TOY WIFE, THE(1938); SEPIA CINDERELLA(1947)
Gloria Saunders
OUT OF THIS WORLD(1945); O.S.S.(1946); CRAZY OVER HORSES(1951); CRY DANGER(1951); CAPTIVE WOMEN(1952); NORTHWEST TERRITORY(1952); RED SNOW(1952); PRISONERS OF THE CASBAH(1953); ROBE, THE(1953)
Misc. Talkies
SIX-GUN DECISION(1953)
Hal Saunders
STAKEOUT ON DOPE STREET(1958)

Harold Saunders
NIGHT TRAIN TO MUNDO FINE(1966)
Misc. Talkies
RED ZONE CUBA(1972)
Harry Saunders
EXPLOSION(1969, Can.)
J.J. Saunders
THIEF(1981)
Jack Saunders
GUY NAMED JOE, A(1943); PAPER MOON(1973)
Jackie Saunders
Silents
INFAMOUS MISS REVELL, THE(1921); SHATTERED REPUTATIONS(1923); ALIMONY(1924)
Misc. Silents
WILL O' THE WISP, THE(1914); ADVENTURES OF A MADCAP(1915); ILL-STARRED BABBLE(1915); PERILS OF TEMPTATION, THE(1915); SHRINE OF HAPPINESS, THE(1916); TWIN TRIANGLE, THE(1916); BAB THE FIXER(1917); BETTY BE GOOD(1917); BIT OF KINDLING, A(1917); CHECKMATE, THE(1917); SUNNY JANE(1917); WILDCAT, THE(1917); DAD'S GIRL(1919); SOMEONE MUST PAY(1919); DRAG HARLAN(1920); MIRACLE OF LOVE, THE(1920); SCUTTLERS, THE(1920); PUPPETS OF FATE(1921); DEFYING DESTINY(1923); COURAGEOUS COWARD, THE(1924); GREAT DIAMOND MYSTERY, THE(1924)
Jacqueline Saunders
GOLD DIGGERS OF 1937(1936); POLO JOE(1936)
Misc. Silents
BROKEN LAWS(1924)
James Saunders
SAILOR'S RETURN, THE(1978, Brit.), w
Jan Saunders
GIRLFRIENDS(1978), p
Jess Saunders
JESSE JAMES' WOMEN(1954), ch
Joe Saunders
WORLD IS JUST A 'B' MOVIE, THE(1971)
John Monk Saunders
SHE GOES TO WAR(1929), w; DAWN PATROL, THE(1930), w; FINGER POINTS, THE(1931), w; LAST FLIGHT, THE(1931), w; ACE OF ACES(1933), w; EAGLE AND THE HAWK, THE(1933), w; DEVIL DOGS OF THE AIR(1935), w; I FOUND STELLA PARISH(1935), w; WEST POINT OF THE AIR(1935), w; DAWN PATROL, THE(1938), w; CONQUEST OF THE AIR(1940), d, w; HIDDEN MENACE, THE(1940, Brit.), w
Silents
WINGS(1927), w
Kenneth J. Saunders
LADY WHO DARED, THE(1931), w
Lanna Saunders
BODY HEAT(1981)
Lawrence Saunders
SNOWED UNDER(1936), w
Leslie Saunders
Misc. Talkies
CHIFFY KIDS GANG, THE(1983)
Lew Saunders
DEMONOID(1981)
Linda Saunders
GIRLS ON THE BEACH(1965); MARA OF THE WILDERNESS(1966)
Lloyd A. Saunders
TEXAS RANGERS, THE(1936)
Lori Saunders
BLOOD BATH(1966); HEAD ON(1971); FRASIER, THE SENSUOUS LION(1973); So SAD ABOUT GLORIA(1973); WACKIEST WAGON TRAIN IN THE WEST, THE(1976)
Misc. Talkies
CAPTIVE(1980)
Madge Saunders
TONS OF MONEY(1931, Brit.)
Margery Saunders
I BECAME A CRIMINAL(1947), ed; AFFAIRS OF A ROGUE, THE(1949, Brit.), ed; FOR THEM THAT TRESPASS(1949, Brit.), ed; ONE WILD OAT(1951, Brit.), ed; WHITE FIRE(1953, Brit.), ed; KILL HER GENTLY(1958, Brit.), ed; REMARKABLE MR. PENNYPACKER, THE(1959)
Marion Saunders
MY HEART GOES CRAZY(1953, Brit.)
Mary Jane Saunders
SORROWFUL JONES(1949); FATHER IS A BACHELOR(1950); WOMAN OF DISTINCTION, A(1950); GIRL NEXT DOOR, THE(1953); KISS ME, STUPID(1964)
Max Saunders
JOHN OF THE FAIR(1962, Brit.), m
Merl Saunders
BLACK GIRL(1972), m
Michael Saunders
WOMAN'S TEMPTATION, A(1959, Brit.)
Nancy Saunders
LADY LUCK(1946); LOCKET, THE(1946); HER HUSBAND'S AFFAIRS(1947); IT HAD TO BE YOU(1947); LIKELY STORY, A(1947); LONE WOLF IN LONDON(1947); MILLERSON CASE, THE(1947); WHEN A GIRL'S BEAUTIFUL(1947); WOMAN ON THE BEACH, THE(1947); 13TH HOUR, THE(1947); SIX-GUN LAW(1948); WHIRLWIND RAIDERS(1948); OUTLAW COUNTRY(1949); ARIZONA TERRITORY(1950); MRS. O'MALLEY AND MR. MALONE(1950); LOVE IS BETTER THAN EVER(1952)
Misc. Talkies
LAW OF THE CANYON(1947); PRAIRIE RAIDERS(1947); SOUTH OF THE CHISHOLM TRAIL(1947); WEST OF DODGE CITY(1947)
Nellie Peck Saunders
Silents
REAL ADVENTURE, THE(1922); TAILOR MADE MAN, A(1922); WATCH HIM STEP(1922)
Neza Saunders
BUSH CHRISTMAS(1947, Brit.)

Nicholas Saunders
BANANAS(1971)
Pam Saunders
SAMAR(1962)
Pamela Saunders
HAPPY BIRTHDAY, WANDA JUNE(1971)
Peter Saunders
HE FOUND A STAR(1941, Brit.)
Phillip Saunders
TURNING POINT, THE(1977)
R. D. Saunders
Silents
PENROD(1922)
Rai Saunders
LOST BOUNDARIES(1949)
Ramon Saunders
FIGHT FOR YOUR LIFE(1977)
Ramona Saunders
HOLY MOUNTAIN, THE(1973, U.S./Mex.)
Ray Saunders
VARIETY GIRL(1947); JULIA MISBEHAVES(1948); PRICE OF POWER, THE(1969, Ital./Span.)
Raymond Saunders
JOAN OF ARC(1948); NIGHT HAS A THOUSAND EYES(1948)
Rena Saunders
HER LUCKY NIGHT(1945)
Ronald Saunders
DEAD ZONE, THE(1983), ed
Russ Saunders
TOUCHDOWN!(1931); VARIETY GIRL(1947); WEST POINT STORY, THE(1950); SINGIN' IN THE RAIN(1952); HERE COME THE GIRLS(1953); SLIGHT CASE OF LARCENY, A(1953); SEVEN BRIDES FOR SEVEN BROTHERS(1954); SPARTACUS(1960)
Russ M. Saunders
SANTIAGO(1956)
Russell Saunders
MAYBE IT'S LOVE(1930); THAT'S MY BOY(1932); JOAN OF ARC(1948); NIGHT HAS A THOUSAND EYES(1948); BIRDS DO IT(1966)
Sandra Saunders
FOREST, THE(1983), art d
Sharon Saunders
BAD AND THE BEAUTIFUL, THE(1952); CLOWN, THE(1953)
Sherman Saunders
ROSEANNA McCOY(1949)
Smokey Saunders
MR. CELEBRITY(1942)
Stuart Saunders
UNDERCOVER AGENT(1935, Brit.); COURT MARTIAL(1954, Brit.); DEVIL'S HARBOR(1954, Brit.); CONSTANT HUSBAND, THE(1955, Brit.); DOCTOR AT SEA(1955, Brit.); SIMON AND LAURA(1956, Brit.); MOMENT OF INDISCRETION(1958, Brit.); THREE MEN IN A BOAT(1958, Brit.); BOY AND THE BRIDGE, THE(1959, Brit.); GIDEON OF SCOTLAND YARD(1959, Brit.); HONOURABLE MURDER, AN(1959, Brit.); HORRORS OF THE BLACK MUSEUM(1959, U.S./Brit.); MAN ACCUSED(1959); WITNESS IN THE DARK(1959, Brit.); DENTIST IN THE CHAIR(1960, Brit.); NOT A HOPE IN HELL(1960, Brit.); LAWRENCE OF ARABIA(1962, Brit.); MOUSE ON THE MOON, THE(1963, Brit.); OPERATION SNAFU(1965, Brit.); SECOND BEST SECRET AGENT IN THE WHOLE WIDE WORLD, THE(1965, Brit.); SMASHING TIME(1967 Brit.); NOTHING BUT THE NIGHT(1975, Brit.)
1984
SCANDALOUS(1984)
Terry Saunders
KING AND I, THE(1956)
Vicki Saunders
MAN WHO WALKED ALONE, THE(1945)
W. G. Saunders
JOY RIDE(1935, Brit.); VARIETY(1935, Brit.)
Silents
EAST IS EAST(1916, Brit.); MATING OF MARCUS, THE(1924, Brit.); NOT FOR SALE(1924, Brit.); PREHISTORIC MAN, THE(1924, Brit.); JUNGLE WOMAN, THE(1926, Brit.); PEARL OF THE SOUTH SEAS(1927, Brit.)
Misc. Silents
CARROTS(1917, Brit.)
Willie Saunders
KENTUCKY(1938)
Claude Saunier
MATTER OF DAYS, A(1969, Fr./Czech.), ph; ONCE IN PARIS(1978), ph
Hayden Saunier
PURPLE HAZE(1982)
Nicole Saunier
WITHOUT APPARENT MOTIVE(1972, Fr.), ed
Carlos Saura
HUNT, THE(1967, Span.), d, w; BLOOD WEDDING(1981, Sp.), d; CARMEN(1983, Span.), d, w, ch
Wolfgang Saure
TRAIN, THE(1965, Fr./Ital./U.S.); IS PARIS BURNING?(1966, U.S./Fr.)
George Saurel
HOW TO MARRY A MILLIONAIRE(1953)
1984
LONELY GUY, THE(1984)
Georges Saurel
SOUTH SEA WOMAN(1953); PARTY GIRL(1958)
Maurice Saurel
DEVIL'S DAUGHTER(1949, Fr.), d
Sylvia Saurel
LIFE LOVE DEATH(1969, Fr./Ital.)
Alejandra Saurez
1984
UNDER THE VOLCANO(1984)

Jose Saurez
CARTHAGE IN FLAMES(1961, Fr./Ital.)
Sergio Sauro
SIGN OF THE GLADIATOR(1959, Fr./Ger./Ital.)
Eva Saurova
PARSIFAL(1983, Fr.)
Alain Saury
CARVE HER NAME WITH PRIDE(1958, Brit.); ROOTS OF HEAVEN, THE(1958); MARIE OF THE ISLES(1960, Fr.); BIG GAMBLE, THE(1961); TIME BOMB(1961, Fr./Ital.); MAGNIFICENT SINNER(1963, Fr.); BEHOLD A PALE HORSE(1964); VISCOUNT, THE(1967, Fr./Span./Ital./Ger.); MAYERLING(1968, Brit./Fr.); WE ARE ALL NAKED(1970, Can./Fr.)
Jean Saussac
WISE GUYS(1969, Fr./Ital.), art d
Marie-Therese Saussure
POURQUOI PAS!(1979, Fr.)
Eddie Sauter
MICKEY ONE(1965), m
William N. Sauter
JEALOUSY(1929), art d
Yvette Sautereau
PRICE OF FLESH, THE(1962, Fr.)
Claude Sautet
HORROR CHAMBER OF DR. FAUSTUS, THE(1962, Fr./Ital.), w; MONSIEUR(1964, Fr.), w; BANANA PEEL(1965, Fr.), w; SYMPHONY FOR A MASSACRE(1965, Fr./Ital.), w; LA VIE DE CHATEAU(1967, Fr.), w; BORSALINO(1970, Fr.), w; THINGS OF LIFE, THE(1970, Fr./Ital./Switz.), d, w; CESAR AND ROSALIE(1972, Fr.), d, w
Lauren Sautner
LITTLE SEX, A(1982); SOUP FOR ONE(1982)
Carmen Sautoy
MAN WITH THE GOLDEN GUN, THE(1974, Brit.)
Arlette Sauvage
VITELLONI(1956, Ital./Fr.)
Christiane Sauvage
YOUNG GIRLS OF ROCHEFORT, THE(1968, Fr.), makeup
Marianne Sauvage
SURVIVAL RUN(1980)
Dominique Sauvage-Dandieux
DIARY OF A CHAMBERMAID(1964, Fr./Ital.)
Sauvageau
Silents
NAPOLEON(1927, Fr.), cos
M.G. Sauvajon
DEVIL'S DAUGHTER(1949, Fr.), w
Marc-Gilbert Sauvajon
JUST ME(1950, Fr.), d&w; ROYAL AFFAIR, A(1950), d&w; MICHAEL STROGOFF(1960, Fr./Ital./Yugo.), w; YOUR TURN, DARLING(1963, Fr.), w; ADORABLE JULIA(1964, Fr./Aust.), w; SCHEHERAZADE(1965, Fr./Ital./Span.), w
Sauveplane
LA MARSEILLAISE(1938, Fr.), m
Serge Sauvion
WOMAN OF SIN(1961, Fr.); NAKED AUTUMN(1963, Fr.)
Mohamed Sauvr
OLIVE TREES OF JUSTICE, THE(1967, Fr.)
Brian Savagar
1984
LAST HORROR FILM, THE(1984), art d
Alex Savage
TRAVELS WITH MY AUNT(1972, Brit.)
Ann Savage
AFTER MIDNIGHT WITH BOSTON BLACKIE(1943); DANGEROUS BLONDES(1943); FOOTLIGHT GLAMOUR(1943); MORE THE MERRIER, THE(1943); ONE DANGEROUS NIGHT(1943); PASSPORT TO SUEZ(1943); TWO SENORITAS FROM CHICAGO(1943); WHAT A WOMAN!(1943); EVER SINCE VENUS(1944); KLONDIKE KATE(1944); LAST HORSEMAN, THE(1944); TWO-MAN SUBMARINE(1944); UNWRITTEN CODE, THE(1944); APOLOGY FOR MURDER(1945); DANCING IN MANHATTAN(1945); DETOUR(1945); ONE EXCITING NIGHT(1945); SCARED STIFF(1945); SPIDER, THE(1945); DARK HORSE, THE(1946); LADY CHASER(1946); LAST CROOKED MILE, THE(1946); RENEGADE GIRL(1946); JUNGLE FLIGHT(1947); SATAN'S CRADLE(1949); PYGMY ISLAND(1950); PIER 23(1951); WOMAN THEY ALMOST LYNCHED, THE(1953)
Misc. Talkies
SADDLES AND SAGEBRUSH(1943)
Archie Savage
TALES OF MANHATTAN(1942); HIS MAJESTY O'KEEFE(1953); VERA CRUZ(1954); GARMENT JUNGLE, THE(1957); THIS COULD BE THE NIGHT(1957); SOUTH PACIFIC(1958); ASSIGNMENT OUTER SPACE(1960, Ital.); LA DOLCE VITA(1961, Ital./Fr.); SODOM AND GOMORRAH(1962, U.S./Fr./Ital.), ch; SNOW DEVILS, THE(1965, Ital.); WILD, WILD PLANET, THE(1967, Ital.), ch; DEATH RIDES A HORSE(1969, Ital.)
Blane Savage
TO BE OR NOT TO BE(1983)
Booth Savage
STONE COLD DEAD(1980, Can.); SILENCE OF THE NORTH(1981, Can.); CURTAINS(1983, Can.)
Brad Savage
APPLE DUMPLING GANG, THE(1975); OTHER SIDE OF THE MOUNTAIN, THE(1975); ECHOES OF A SUMMER(1976); NO DEPOSIT, NO RETURN(1976); TWO-MINUTE WARNING(1976); ISLANDS IN THE STREAM(1977); RETURN FROM WITCH MOUNTAIN(1978)
1984
RED DAWN(1984)
Carlos Savage
LOS OLVIDADOS(1950, Mex.), ed; ADVENTURES OF ROBINSON CRUSOE, THE(1954), ed; EL(1955, Mex.), ed; LITTLEST OUTLAW, THE(1955), ed; TEN DAYS TO TULARA(1958), ed; FACE OF THE SCREAMING WEREWOLF(1959, Mex.), ed; YOUNG ONE, THE(1961, Mex.), ed; PEARL OF TLAYUCAN, THE(1964, Mex.), ed; MAN AND THE MONSTER, THE(1965, Mex.), ed; RAGE(1966, U.S./Mex.), ed; EXTERMINATING ANGEL, THE(1967, Mex.), ed; NAZARIN(1968, Mex.), ed; SHARK(1970, U.S./Mex.), ed; DAUGHTER OF DECEIT(1977, Mex.), ed

Carlos Savage, Jr.
BIG CUBE, THE(1969), ed
Carol Savage
G.I. WAR BRIDES(1946); MOSS ROSE(1947); MR. PEABODY AND THE MERMAID(1948); JACKPOT, THE(1950); PLEASE BELIEVE ME(1950); I WANT YOU(1951); LET'S MAKE IT LEGAL(1951); MEET ME AFTER THE SHOW(1951); SON OF DR. JEKYLL, THE(1951); MY SIX CONVICTS(1952)
Cary Savage
GOOD MORNING, MISS DOVE(1955)
Charles E. Savage
PANIC IN THE CITY(1968), w; IT TAKES ALL KINDS(1969, U.S./Aus.), w
Daniel Boone Savage
SWING YOUR LADY(1938)
David Savage
PRIME CUT(1972)
Dominic Savage
BARRY LYNDON(1975, Brit.)
Edna Savage
IT'S GREAT TO BE YOUNG(1956, Brit.)
Eva Savage
GAY ADVENTURE, THE(1953, Brit.)
Henry W. Savage
Misc. Silents
EXCUSE ME(1916), d
Houston Savage
LOSERS, THE(1970)
Jack Savage
FRANCIS OF ASSISI(1961)
Jason Savage
1984
GIVE MY REGARDS TO BROAD STREET(1984, Brit.)
Jim Savage
Misc. Silents
BOLSHEVISM ON TRIAL(1919)
Joe Savage
SECRET MENACE(1931)
John Savage
STAKEOUT ON DOPE STREET(1958); LOVE IS A CAROUSEL(1970); BAD COMPANY(1972); KILLING KIND, THE(1973); STEELYARD BLUES(1973); SISTER-IN-LAW, THE(1975); DEER HUNTER, THE(1978); HAIR(1979); ONION FIELD, THE(1979); INSIDE MOVES(1980); CATTLE ANNIE AND LITTLE BRITCHES(1981); AMATEUR, THE(1982)
1984
BRADY'S ESCAPE(1984, U.S./Hung.)
Les Savage
BLACK HORSE CANYON(1954), w
Les Savage, Jr.
HILLS OF UTAH(1951), w; WHITE SQUAW, THE(1956), w; RETURN TO WARBOW(1958), w
Maggie Savage
1984
PRODIGAL, THE(1984)
Margaret Savage
LOST IN A HAREM(1944); TO HAVE AND HAVE NOT(1944)
Mary Savage
DRYLANDERS(1963, Can.)
Mike Savage
CONFESSIONS FROM A HOLIDAY CAMP(1977, Brit.)
Mildred Savage
PARRISH(1961), p,d&w
Nellie Savage
Silents
MAD DANCER(1925); SORROWS OF SATAN(1926)
Nelly Savage
HOLE IN THE WALL(1929)
Nick Savage
FRIDAY THE 13TH PART III(1982)
1984
FRIDAY THE 13TH–THE FINAL CHAPTER(1984)
Norman Savage
DOCTOR ZHIVAGO(1965), ed; WILD AFFAIR, THE(1966, Brit.), ed; THREE BITES OF THE APPLE(1967), ed; PRUDENCE AND THE PILL(1968, Brit.), ed; PRIME OF MISS JEAN BRODIE, THE(1969, Brit.), ed; RYAN'S DAUGHTER(1970, Brit.), ed; LADY CAROLINE LAMB(1972, Brit./Ital.), ed
O.S. Savage
GETAWAY, THE(1972)
Pam Savage
1984
ON THE LINE(1984, Span.), m
Paul Savage
UNTAMED FURY(1947); BETRAYED WOMEN(1955); FAR COUNTRY, THE(1955); NIGHT THE WORLD EXPLODED, THE(1957); WILD COUNTRY, THE(1971), w; MACKINTOSH & T.J.(1975), w; INCHON(1981), w
Peter Savage
NEW LIFE STYLE, THE(1970, Ger.), p, d, w; CRAZY JOE(1974); TAXI DRIVER(1976); NEW YORK, NEW YORK(1977); RAGING BULL(1980), w; VIGILANTE(1983)
Pius Savage
SPIRIT OF THE WIND(1979)
Ray Savage
SPENCER'S MOUNTAIN(1963)
Robert Savage
FANTASM(1976, Aus.)
Roy Savage
CLUE OF THE MISSING APE, THE(1953, Brit.)
Steve Savage
UNDER THE TONTO RIM(1947); GUN SMUGGLERS(1948); ROUGHSHOD(1949)

Tracie Savage
FRIDAY THE 13TH PART III(1982)
Turner Savage
Silents
TUMBLEWEEDS(1925); ARIZONA SWEEPSTAKES(1926); CALLAHANS AND THE MURPHYS, THE(1927)
Vic Savage [A.N. White]
STREET FIGHTER(1959)
Vic Savage [Art J. Nelson]
CREEPING TERROR, THE(1964)
Yvonne Savage
THERE'S ALWAYS A THURSDAY(1957, Brit.)
Wayne Savagne
PRIME CUT(1972)
Paul Savain
CALYPSO(1959, Fr./It.)
Dany Saval
NATHALIE, AGENT SECRET(1960, Fr.); CHEATERS, THE(1961, Fr.); MOON PILOT(1962); TALES OF PARIS(1962, Fr./Ital.); BOEING BOEING(1965); SWEET SKIN(1965, Fr./Ital.); WEB OF FEAR(1966, Fr./Span.); BIG AND THE BAD, THE(1971, Ital./Fr./Span.)
Misc. Talkies
ATOMIC AGENT(1959, Fr.)
George Savalas
GENGHIS KHAN(U.S./Brit./Ger./Yugo); SLENDER THREAD, THE(1965); ROSEMARY'S BABY(1968); DREAM OF KINGS, A(1969); KELLY'S HEROES(1970, U.S./Yugo.); FAMILY, THE(1974, Fr./Ital.)
Telly Savalas
GENGHIS KHAN(U.S./Brit./Ger./Yugo); MAD DOG COLL(1961); YOUNG SAVAGES, THE(1961); BIRDMAN OF ALCATRAZ(1962); CAPE FEAR(1962); INTERNS, THE(1962); JOHNNY COOL(1963); LOVE IS A BALL(1963); MAN FROM THE DINERS' CLUB, THE(1963); JOHN GOLDFARB, PLEASE COME HOME(1964); NEW INTERNS, THE(1964); BATTLE OF THE BULGE(1965); GREATEST STORY EVER TOLD, THE(1965); SLENDER THREAD, THE(1965); BEAU GESTE(1966); DIRTY DOZEN, THE(1967, Brit.); KARATE KILLERS, THE(1967); BUONA SERA, MRS. CAMPBELL(1968, Ital.); SCALPHUNTERS, THE(1968); SOL MADRID(1968); ASSASSINATION BUREAU, THE(1969, Brit.); LAND RAIDERS(1969); MACKENNA'S GOLD(1969); ON HER MAJESTY'S SECRET SERVICE(1969, Brit.); KELLY'S HEROES(1970, U.S./Yugo.); SOPHIE'S PLACE(1970); CLAY PIGEON(1971); PRETTY MAIDS ALL IN A ROW(1971); TOWN CALLED HELL, A(1971, Span./Brit.); HORROR EXPRESS(1972, Span./Brit.); FAMILY, THE(1974, Fr./Ital.); REASON TO LIVE, A REASON TO DIE, A(1974, Ital./Fr./Ger./Span.); SONNY AND JED(1974, Ital.); INSIDE OUT(1975, Brit.); KILLER FORCE(1975, Switz./Ireland); PANCHO VILLA(1975, Span.); REDNECK(1975, Ital./Span.); CRIME BOSS(1976, Ital.); HOUSE OF EXORCISM, THE(1976, Ital.); CAPRICORN ONE(1978); BEYOND THE POSEIDON ADVENTURE(1979); ESCAPE TO ATHENA(1979, Brit.); MUPPET MOVIE, THE(1979)
1984
CANNONBALL RUN II(1984)
Misc. Talkies
LOST WORLD OF LIBRA, THE(1968); BEYOND REASON(1977), d; FAKE-OUT(1982)
Elena Savanarola
IT'S A BIG COUNTRY(1951)
Pierre Savard
HIGH(1968, Can.), ed
Annie Savarin
MURMUR OF THE HEART(1971, Fr./Ital./Ger.)
Jean Savarino
PHANTOM OF THE PARADISE(1974)
Janet Savarion
PHANTOM OF THE PARADISE(1974)
Jerome Savary
EASY LIFE, THE(1971, Fr.), w
Phil Savath
1984
BIG MEAT EATER(1984, Can.), w
Paul Savatier
CONFESSION, THE(1970, Fr.)
Igor Savchenko
DIARY OF A NAZI(1943, USSR), d; LUCKY BRIDE, THE(1948, USSR), d&w
L. Savchenko
HOUSE ON THE FRONT LINE, THE(1963, USSR)
V. Savchenko
HOUSE ON THE FRONT LINE, THE(1963, USSR)
Brian Savegar
BABYLON(1980, Brit.), art d
Carmen Saveiros
WILD PARTY, THE(1975)
Todd Savell
STREAMERS(1983)
O. Savelyev
LAST GAME, THE(1964, USSR)
Era Savelyeva
RESURRECTION(1963, USSR), ph
Lyudmila Savelyeva
WAR AND PEACE(1968, USSR); SUNFLOWER(1970, Fr./Ital.)
Jeff Savenick
1984
WILD LIFE, THE(1984)
Phil Savenick
LOOSE SHOES(1980), animation
Joseph D. Savery
1984
MYSTERY MANSION(1984)
T. Savich
SHE-WOLF, THE(1963, USSR)
John Savident
INADMISSIBLE EVIDENCE(1968, Brit.); BEFORE WINTER COMES(1969, Brit.); OTLEY(1969, Brit.); WATERLOO(1970, Ital./USSR); CLOCKWORK ORANGE, A(1971, Brit.); LONG AGO, TOMORROW(1971, Brit.); HITLER: THE LAST TEN DAYS(1973, Brit./Ital.); BUTLEY(1974, Brit.); INTERNECINE PROJECT, THE(1974, Brit.); DIRTY

KNIGHT'S WORK(1976, Brit.); WICKED LADY, THE(1983, Brit.)
Grace Savieri
Silents
JUNGLE WOMAN, THE(1926, Brit.)
David Savile
WALKING STICK, THE(1970, Brit.); BIG SLEEP, THE½(1978, Brit.)
Edith Savile
HELP!(1965, Brit.)
Jimmy Savile
JUST FOR FUN(1963, Brit.); FERRY ACROSS THE MERSEY(1964, Brit.)
Phillip Savile
BEST HOUSE IN LONDON, THE(1969, Brit.), d
Edith Saville
BIRDS OF A FEATHER(1931, Brit.); SEA WIFE(1957, Brit.); WOMAN POSSESSED, A(1958, Brit.)
George M. Saville
Silents
KISS, THE(1929), w
Gus Saville
LIGHT OF WESTERN STARS, THE(1930)
Silents
ALMOST A HUSBAND(1919); KING SPRUCE(1920); WOLVERINE, THE(1921); TESS OF THE STORM COUNTRY(1922)
Misc. Silents
TWO MOONS(1920)
Liz Saville
ANTI-CLOCK(1980)
Malcolm Saville
TREASURE AT THE MILL(1957, Brit.), w
Philip Saville
MURDER AT 3 A.M.(1953, Brit.); STRAW MAN, THE(1953, Brit.); BANG! YOU'RE DEAD(1954, Brit.); NIGHT OF THE FULL MOON, THE(1954, Brit.); CONTRABAND SPAIN(1955, Brit.); BETRAYAL, THE(1958, Brit.); ON THE RUN(1958, Brit.); THREE CROOKED MEN(1958, Brit.); HONOURABLE MURDER, AN(1959, Brit.); GREAT VAN ROBBERY, THE(1963, Brit.); STOP THE WORLD–I WANT TO GET OFF(1966, Brit.), d; OEDIPUS THE KING(1968, Brit.), d, w; SECRETS(1971), d, w
Sebastian Saville
LIBEL(1959, Brit.); ANTI-CLOCK(1980)
Victor Saville
KITTY(1929, Brit.), p&d; TESHA(1929, Brit.), p&d, w; WOMAN TO WOMAN(1929), p, d, w; WARM CORNER, A(1930, Brit.), d, w; "W" PLAN, THE(1931, Brit.), p&d, w; HINDLE WAKES(1931, Brit.), d, w; SPORT OF KINGS, THE(1931, Brit.), d; LOVE ON WHEELS(1932, Brit.), d&w; MICHAEL AND MARY(1932, Brit.), d; OFFICE GIRL, THE(1932, Brit.), d, w; FAITHFUL HEART(1933, Brit.), d, w; GOOD COMPANIONS(1933, Brit.), d; EVENSONG(1934, Brit.), d; EVERGREEN(1934, Brit.), d; FRIDAY THE 13TH(1934, Brit.), d; I WAS A SPY(1934, Brit.), d; DICTATOR, THE(1935, Brit./Ger.), d; FIRST A GIRL(1935, Brit.), d; IRON DUKE, THE(1935, Brit.), d; ME AND MARLBOROUGH(1935, Brit.), d; IT'S LOVE AGAIN(1936, Brit.), d; ACTION FOR SLANDER(1937, Brit.), p; DARK JOURNEY(1937, Brit.), d; STORM IN A TEACUP(1937, Brit.), p, d; SOUTH RIDING(1938, Brit.), p&d; GOODBYE MR. CHIPS(1939, Brit.), p; BITTER SWEET(1940), p; EARL OF CHICAGO, THE(1940), p; MORTAL STORM, THE(1940), p; CHOCOLATE SOLDIER, THE(1941), p; SMILIN' THROUGH(1941), p; WOMAN'S FACE(1941), p; KEEPER OF THE FLAME(1942), p; WHITE CARGO(1942), p; ABOVE SUSPICION(1943), p; FOREVER AND A DAY(1943), p&d; TONIGHT AND EVERY NIGHT(1945), p&d; GREEN YEARS, THE(1946), d; GREEN DOLPHIN STREET(1947), d; IF WINTER COMES(1947), d; CONSPIRATOR(1949, Brit.), d; KIM(1950), d; CALLING BULLDOG DRUMMOND(1951, Brit.), d; AFFAIR IN MONTE CARLO(1953, Brit.), d; I, THE JURY(1953), p; LONG WAIT, THE(1954), d; SILVER CHALICE, THE(1954), p&d; LOSS OF INNOCENCE(1961, Brit.), p
Silents
ARCADIANS, THE(1927, Brit.), p, d; ROSES OF PICARDY(1927, Brit.), p; SISTER TO ASSIST 'ER, A(1927, Brit.), p
Misc. Silents
FANNY HAWTHORNE(1927, Brit.), d; KITTY(1929, Brit.), d; WOMAN IN THE NIGHT, A(1929), d
Lee Savin
HARLOW(1965), p; BLACK GIRL(1972), p
Pyotr Savin
DESTINY OF A MAN(1961, USSR); WAR AND PEACE(1968, USSR); RED AND THE WHITE, THE(1969, Hung./USSR)
Volodya Savin
TEENAGERS IN SPACE(1975, USSR)
Carlo Savina
HEROD THE GREAT(1960, Ital.), m; EVA(1962, Fr./Ital.), md; DOG EAT DOG(1963, U.S./Ger./Ital.), m; REBEL GLADIATORS, THE(1963, Ital.), m; MORALIST, THE(1964, Ital.), m; RED DESERT(1965, Fr./Ital.), md; SECRET AGENT FIREBALL(1965, Fr./Ital.), m; SWORD OF EL CID, THE(1965, Span./Ital.), m; VERY HANDY MAN, A(1966, Fr./Ital.), m; TALL WOMEN, THE(1967, Aust./Ital./Span.), m; TAMING OF THE SHREW, THE(1967, U.S./Ital.), md; YOUNG, THE EVIL AND THE SAVAGE, THE(1968, Ital.), m; LONG RIDE FROM HELL, A(1970, Ital.), m; NUN AT THE CROSSROADS, A(1970, Ital./Span.), md; GODFATHER, THE(1972), md; ROMA(1972, Ital./Fr.), md; GARDEN OF THE FINZI-CONTINIS, THE(1976, Ital./Ger.), md; HOUSE OF EXORCISM, THE(1976, Ital.), m; COMIN' AT YA!(1981), m
1984
HUNTERS OF THE GOLDEN COBRA, THE(1984, Ital.), m
Zena Savina
CHRISTOPHER STRONG(1933); ROBERTA(1935)
Tom Savini
DEATHDREAM(1972, Can.), makeup; DAWN OF THE DEAD(1979), makeup & spec eff; MARTIN(1979), a, spec eff & makeup; EFFECTS(1980), a, spec eff; FRIDAY THE 13TH(1980), spec eff & stunts; MANIAC(1980), a, makeup; KNIGHTRIDERS(1981); PROWLER, THE(1981), spec eff&makeup; CREEPSHOW(1982), a, makeup; MIDNIGHT(1983), makeup
1984
FRIDAY THE 13TH–THE FINAL CHAPTER(1984), makeup
Savini-Berle-Adams
BEWARE(1946), p

Carlo Savino
IT STARTED IN NAPLES(1960), m
Domenico Savino
PATRIOT, THE(1928), m
Frank Savino
THREE DAYS OF THE CONDOR(1975); ON THE NICKEL(1980)
Jay Savino
PEOPLE NEXT DOOR, THE(1970)
Renato Savino
VENGEANCE(1968, Ital./Ger.), p, w
Katya Savinova
LULLABY(1961, USSR)
Ye. Savinova
MARRIAGE OF BALZAMINOV, THE(1966, USSR)
V. Savinykh
FAREWELL, DOVES(1962, USSR)
Andria Savio
STRYKER(1983, Phil.)
Carlo Savio
HEAD OF A TYRANT(1960, Fr./Ital.), m
Camille Saviola
1984
BROADWAY DANNY ROSE(1984)
Giorgio Savioni
WHITE SHEIK, THE(1956, Ital.)
Alfred Savior
DRESSED TO THRILL(1935), w
Jessica Savitch
NASTY HABITS(1976, Brit.)
Elena Savitskaya
SIX P.M.(1946, USSR)
Helena Savitskaya
SYMPHONY OF LIFE(1949, USSR)
Catherine Savitsky
GOLDEN EARRINGS(1947)
General Savitsky
PROFESSIONAL SOLDIER(1936); HOTEL IMPERIAL(1939)
Sam Savitsky
ROBERTA(1935); CHAMPAGNE WALTZ(1937); I MARRIED AN ANGEL(1942); RINGS ON HER FINGERS(1942); MISSION TO MOSCOW(1943); ROYAL SCANDAL, A(1945); NORTHWEST OUTPOST(1947)
Vaicheslav Savitsky
Silents
LAST COMMAND, THE(1928)
General Wietsheslav Savitsky
Silents
AWAKENING, THE(1928)
Lee Savitz
ESCAPE TO BURMA(1955), spec eff
Ivan Savkin
HUNTING IN SIBERIA(1962, USSR); MY NAME IS IVAN(1963, USSR)
Ann Savo
RESTLESS NIGHT, THE(1964, Ger.); TERROR OF DR. MABUSE, THE(1965, Ger.); MOONWOLF(1966, Fin./Ger.)
Jimmy Savo
ONCE IN A BLUE MOON(1936); MERRY-GO-ROUND OF 1938(1937); RECKLESS LIVING(1938)
John Savoca
12 ANGRY MEN(1957)
Celeste Savoi
LOVES OF CARMEN, THE(1948); RECKLESS MOMENTS, THE(1949)
Alfred Savoir
HERE IS MY HEART(1934), w; KING OF PARIS, THE(1934, Brit.), w; LADIES SHOULD LISTEN(1934), w; BLUEBEARD'S EIGHTH WIFE(1938), w
Silents
GRAND DUCHESS AND THE WAITER, THE(1926), w; TIME TO LOVE(1927), w
Beatriz Savon
10:30 P.M. SUMMER(1966, U.S./Span.); OPEN SEASON(1974, U.S./Span.)
Isabella Savona
THAT SPLENDID NOVEMBER(1971, Ital./Fr.)
Leopold Savona
LUXURY GIRLS(1953, Ital.)
Leopoldo Savona
WARRIORS FIVE(1962), d, w; MONGOLS, THE(1966, Fr./Ital.), d
Elena Savonarola
CRY OF THE CITY(1948)
Gerald Savory
YOUNG AND INNOCENT(1938, Brit.), w; GEORGE AND MARGARET(1940, Brit.), w; URGE TO KILL(1960, Brit.), w
Frank Savoy
SOUTHERN COMFORT(1981)
Marc Savoy
SOUTHERN COMFORT(1981)
Viola Savoy
Silents
SPENDTHRIFT, THE(1915)
Misc. Silents
ALICE IN WONDERLAND(1916)
Savoy & Brennan
Silents
TWO FLAMING YOUTHS(1927)
Savoy Havana Band
Silents
AFTER MANY YEARS(1930, Brit.)
Renee Savoye
PARISIAN, THE(1931, Fr.)
Semyon Savshenko
Silents
EARTH(1930, USSR)

Igor Savtchenko
BALLAD OF COSSACK GLOOTA(1938, USSR), d
Iya Savvina
LADY WITH THE DOG, THE(1962, USSR); GIRL AND THE BUGLER, THE(1967, USSR)
Svetlana Savyolova
FAREWELL, DOVES(1962, USSR)
Eric Saw
ROCK AROUND THE WORLD(1957, Brit.), art d; VIOLENT MOMENT(1966, Brit.), art d; MALPAS MYSTERY, THE(1967, Brit.), art d
Kenji Sawada
MAN WHO STOLE THE SUN, THE(1980, Jap.)
Harald Sawade
PHANTOM OF SOHO, THE(1967, Ger.)
Ron Sawade
DOUBLE NICKELS(1977), ph, ed
Keiko Sawai
KOJIRO(1967, Jap.); MONSTER ZERO(1970, Jap.); SONG FROM MY HEART, THE(1970, Jap.)
Nadim Sawaiha
SINBAD AND THE EYE OF THE TIGER(1977, U.S./Brit.)
Nadim Sawalha
SHAFT IN AFRICA(1973); TOUCH OF CLASS, A(1973, Brit.); GOLD(1974, Brit.); WIND AND THE LION, THE(1975); SPY WHO LOVED ME, THE(1977, Brit.); AWAKENING, THE(1980); SPHINX(1981)
1984
MISUNDERSTOOD(1984)
Haruko Sawamura
Misc. Silents
SOULS ON THE ROAD(1921, Jap.)
Ichisaburo Sawamura
UGETSU(1954, Jap.)
Ikio Sawamura
ETERNITY OF LOVE(1961, Jap.); YOJIMBO(1961, Jap.); GODZILLA VS. THE THING(1964, Jap.); DESTROY ALL MONSTERS(1969, Jap.); MARCO(1973)
K. Sawamura
ANATAHAN(1953, Jap.)
Kunio Sawamura
HOTSPRINGS HOLIDAY(1970, Jap.), p
Mitsuko Sawamura
MEET ME IN LAS VEGAS(1956); TEAHOUSE OF THE AUGUST MOON, THE(1956)
Sadako Sawamura
DANGEROUS KISS, THE(1961, Jap.); STAR OF HONG KONG(1962, Jap.); LIFE OF OHARU(1964, Jap.); WHIRLPOOL OF WOMAN(1966, Jap.); SNOW COUNTRY(1969, Jap.); SONG FROM MY HEART, THE(1970, Jap.)
Sonosuke Sawamura
ZATOICHI(1968, Jap.)
Teiko Sawamura
YOUTH IN FURY(1961, Jap.)
Kenji Sawara
RODAN(1958, Jap.); ATRAGON(1965, Jap.)
Tadashi Sawashima
BAND OF ASSASSINS(1971, Jap.), d
George Sawaya
CONCORDE, THE–AIRPORT '79(, a, stunts; NARROW MARGIN, THE(1952); PRODIGAL, THE(1955); BLACK SLEEP, THE(1956); EMERGENCY HOSPITAL(1956); HOT CARS(1956); WALKING TARGET, THE(1960); EVERYTHING'S DUCKY(1961); POLICE DOG STORY, THE(1961); HANDS OF A STRANGER(1962); DIARY OF A MADMAN(1963); DRUMS OF AFRICA(1963); CONVICT STAGE(1965); FORT COURAGEOUS(1965); LOLLIPOP COVER, THE(1965); BATMAN(1966); MONEY TRAP, THE(1966); YOUNG WARRIORS, THE(1967); PANIC IN THE CITY(1968); SOL MADRID(1968); DIRTY HARRY(1971); PRIVATE DUTY NURSES(1972); DON IS DEAD, THE(1973), stunts; DEVIL'S RAIN, THE(1975, U.S./Mex.); ST. IVES(1976); DOMINO PRINCIPLE, THE(1977); I WANNA HOLD YOUR HAND(1978); DEAD MEN DON'T WEAR PLAID(1982)
1984
REPO MAN(1984)
Joe Sawaya
WE WERE STRANGERS(1949); KING OF THE KHYBER RIFLES(1953); SALOME(1953)
Rick Sawaya
I WANNA HOLD YOUR HAND(1978); WALK PROUD(1979)
Rick Saways
BUSTIN' LOOSE(1981)
Keith Sawbridge
IT'S A WONDERFUL WORLD(1956, Brit.)
Alexander Sawczynski
HIPPODROME(1961, Aust./Ger.), art d
Ray Sawhill
EXPOSED(1983)
Teresa Sawicka
1984
SHIVERS(1984, Pol.)
Katina Sawidis
LONG RIDERS, THE(1980), ch
George Sawley
TRUE TO LIFE(1943), set d; LUCKY BOY(1929), set d; THIRD ALARM, THE(1930), art d; I MARRIED A WITCH(1942), set d; CRYSTAL BALL, THE(1943), set d; RAINBOW ISLAND(1944), set d; STORY OF DR. WASSELL, THE(1944), set d; MURDER, HE SAYS(1945), set d; ROAD TO UTOPIA(1945), set d; UNSEEN, THE(1945), set d; HEARTBEAT(1946), set d; MAGIC TOWN(1947), set d; MOONRISE(1948), set d; SILENT CONFLICT(1948), set d; SIREN OF ATLANTIS(1948), set d; TEXAS, BROOKLYN AND HEAVEN(1948), set d; WHATEVER HAPPENED TO BABY JANE?(1962), set d
Silents
GRAIN OF DUST, THE(1928), set d; LINGERIE(1928), set d; MAN IN HOBBLES, THE(1928), set d; STORMY WATERS(1928), set d; TOILERS, THE(1928), set d

George E. Sawley
Silents
BACKSTAGE(1927), art d; ENCHANTED ISLAND, THE(1927), art d
Stanley J. Sawley
O.S.S.(1946), set d
Stanley Jay Sawley
UNCONQUERED(1947), set d
Paul Sawtell
MEXICAN SPITFIRE(1939), md; MILLIONAIRE PLAYBOY(1940), m; POP ALWAYS PAYS(1940), md; WAGON TRAIN(1940), m; DUDE COWBOY(1941), md; FARGO KID, THE(1941), m; GAY FALCON, THE(1941), m; LAND OF THE OPEN RANGE(1941), md; SIX GUN GOLD(1941), md; BANDIT RANGER(1942), md; HILLBILLY BLITZKRIEG(1942), md; PIRATES OF THE PRAIRIE(1942), md; RIDING THE WIND(1942), md; SCATTERGOOD SURVIVES A MURDER(1942), m; VALLEY OF THE SUN(1942), m; FIGHTING FRONTIER(1943), md; SAGEBRUSH LAW(1943), m; TARZAN TRIUMPHS(1943), m; TARZAN'S DESERT MYSTERY(1943), m; DEAD MAN'S EYES(1944), md; MR. WINKLE GOES TO WAR(1944), m; MUMMY'S CURSE, THE(1944), md; NEVADA(1944), m; OKLAHOMA RAIDERS(1944), md; OLD TEXAS TRAIL, THE(1944), md; PEARL OF DEATH, THE(1944), md; RIDERS OF THE SANTA FE(1944), md; SCARLET CLAW, THE(1944), md; SECRET COMMAND(1944), m; TRAIL TO GUNSIGHT(1944), md; WEIRD WOMAN(1944), md; YOUTH RUNS WILD(1944), m; BEYOND THE PECOS(1945), m; CRIME DOCTOR'S WARNING, THE(1945), md; FIGHTING GUARDSMAN, THE(1945), m; GAME OF DEATH, A(1945), m; HOUSE OF FEAR, THE(1945), md; I LOVE A BANDLEADER(1945), md; JUNGLE CAPTIVE(1945), md; RENEGADES OF THE RIO GRANDE(1945), md; SNAFU(1945), m; TARZAN AND THE AMAZONS(1945), md; WANDERER OF THE WASTELAND(1945), m; WEST OF THE PECOS(1945), m; CAT CREEPS, THE(1946), md; CRIMINAL COURT(1946), m; DANGER WOMAN(1946), m; FALCON'S ADVENTURE, THE(1946), m; PERILOUS HOLIDAY(1946), m; RENEGADES(1946), m; SAN QUENTIN(1946), m; STEP BY STEP(1946), m; STRANGE CONQUEST(1946), m; SUNSET PASS(1946), m; TARZAN AND THE LEOPARD WOMAN(1946), md; VACATION IN RENO(1946), m; BORN TO KILL(1947), m; CODE OF THE WEST(1947), m; DESPERATE(1947), m; DEVIL THUMBS A RIDE, THE(1947), m; DICK TRACY MEETS GRUESOME(1947), m; DICK TRACY'S DILEMMA(1947), m; KEEPER OF THE BEES(1947), m; SEVEN KEYS TO BALDPATE(1947), m; T-MEN(1947), m; TARZAN AND THE HUNTRESS(1947), m, md; THUNDER MOUNTAIN(1947), m; TRAIL STREET(1947), m; UNDER THE TONTO RIM(1947), m; VIGILANTES RETURN, THE(1947), md; WILD HORSE MESA(1947), m; ARIZONA RANGER, THE(1948), m; FOUR FACES WEST(1948), m, md; MYSTERY IN MEXICO(1948), m; NORTHWEST STAMPEDE(1948), m; RAW DEAL(1948), m; RETURN OF THE BADMEN(1948), m; RIVER LADY(1948), m; WALK A CROOKED MILE(1948), m; WESTERN HERITAGE(1948), m; BAD BOY(1949), m; BIG CAT, THE(1949), m; BLACK MAGIC(1949), m; FIGHTING MAN OF THE PLAINS(1949), m; RIDERS OF THE RANGE(1949), m; STAGECOACH KID(1949), m; THREAT, THE(1949), m; BORDER TREASURE(1950), m; CARIBOO TRAIL, THE(1950), m; DAVY CROCKETT, INDIAN SCOUT(1950), m; DYNAMITE PASS(1950), m; GREAT MISSOURI RAID, THE(1950), m; HUNT THE MAN DOWN(1950), m; SOUTHSIDE 1-1000(1950), m; STAGE TO TUCSON(1950), m; TARZAN AND THE SLAVE GIRL(1950), m, md; BEST OF THE BADMEN(1951), m; FLAMING FEATHER(1951), m; FORT DEFIANCE(1951), m; OVERLAND TELEGRAPH(1951), m; RACKET, THE(1951), m; ROADBLOCK(1951), m; ROGUE RIVER(1951), m; SILVER CITY(1951), m; SON OF DR. JEKYLL, THE(1951), m; WARPATH(1951), m; WHIP HAND, THE(1951), m; ANOTHER MAN'S POISON(1952, Brit.), m; DENVER AND RIO GRANDE(1952), m; HALF-BREED, THE(1952), m; HURRICANE SMITH(1952), m; KANSAS CITY CONFIDENTIAL(1952), m; SKY FULL OF MOON(1952), m; TARZAN'S SAVAGE FURY(1952), m; ARROWHEAD(1953), m; DIAMOND QUEEN, THE(1953), m; FLIGHT TO TANGIER(1953), m; HALF A HERO(1953), m; INFERNO(1953), m; PONY EXPRESS(1953), m; RAIDERS OF THE SEVEN SEAS(1953), m; SAVAGE, THE(1953), m; TARZAN AND THE SHE-DEVIL(1953), md; DOWN THREE DARK STREETS(1954), m; RETURN TO TREASURE ISLAND(1954), m; THEY RODE WEST(1954), m; THREE HOURS TO KILL(1954), m; LAWLESS STREET, A(1955), m, md; MARAUDERS, THE(1955), m; RAGE AT DAWN(1955), m, md; TALL MAN RIDING(1955), m; TARZAN'S HIDDEN JUNGLE(1955), m; TEN WANTED MEN(1955), m; TEXAS LADY(1955), m; DESPERADOES ARE IN TOWN, THE(1956), m; SCANDAL INCORPORATED(1956), m; BLACK SCORPION, THE(1957), m; DEERSLAYER, THE(1957), m; FIVE STEPS TO DANGER(1957), m; GHOST DIVER(1957), m; GUN DUEL IN DURANGO(1957), m; HELL SHIP MUTINY(1957), m; KRONOS(1957), m; LAST OF THE BADMEN(1957), m; MONKEY ON MY BACK(1957), m; PAWNEE(1957), m; SHE DEVIL(1957), m; STOPOVER TOKYO(1957), m; STORY OF MANKIND, THE(1957), m, md; AMBUSH AT CIMARRON PASS(1958), m; CATTLE EMPIRE(1958), m; FLY, THE(1958), m; HONG KONG CONFIDENTIAL(1958), m; HUNTERS, THE(1958), m; IT! THE TERROR FROM BEYOND SPACE(1958), m; MACHETE(1958), m; SIERRA BARON(1958), m; VILLA!(1958), m; BIG CIRCUS, THE(1959), m; COSMIC MAN, THE(1959), m; DOG OF FLANDERS, A(1959), m; MIRACLE OF THE HILLS, THE(1959), m; RETURN OF THE FLY(1959), m; SAD HORSE, THE(1959), m; VICE RAID(1959), m; CAGE OF EVIL(1960), m; DOG'S BEST FRIEND, A(1960), m; LOST WORLD, THE(1960), m; MUSIC BOX KID, THE(1960), m; THREE CAME TO KILL(1960), m; BIG SHOW, THE(1961), m; FIVE GUNS TO TOMBSTONE(1961), m; FRONTIER UPRISING(1961), m; GUN FIGHT(1961), m; LONG ROPE, THE(1961), m; MISTY(1961), m; PIRATES OF TORTUGA(1961), m; TESS OF THE STORM COUNTRY(1961), m; VOYAGE TO THE BOTTOM OF THE SEA(1961), m; FIVE WEEKS IN A BALLOON(1962), m; JACK THE GIANT KILLER(1962), m; WILD HARVEST(1962), m; CATTLE KING(1963), m; HARBOR LIGHTS(1963), m; THUNDER ISLAND(1963), m; YOUNG GUNS OF TEXAS(1963), m; ISLAND OF THE BLUE DOLPHINS(1964), m; LAST MAN ON EARTH, THE(1964, U.S./Ital.), m; BUBBLE, THE(1967), m; CHRISTINE JORGENSEN STORY, THE(1970), m
Arthur H. Sawyer
Misc. Silents
SANDRA(1924), d
Bill Sawyer
NEVER TAKE CANDY FROM A STRANGER(1961, Brit.)
Bob Sawyer
HARLEM IS HEAVEN(1932)
Buz Sawyer
INDEPENDENCE DAY(1983)
Connie Sawyer
HOLE IN THE HEAD, A(1959); ADA(1961); FOR PETE'S SAKE!(1966); LAST OF THE SECRET AGENTS?, THE(1966); WAY WEST, THE(1967); FOUL PLAY(1978); ...AND JUSTICE FOR ALL(1979); FAST BREAK(1979)

Don Sawyer
VAN NUYS BLVD.(1979)
Doris Sawyer
Misc. Silents
HAND OF PERIL, THE(1916)
Edgar Sawyer
SHE KNEW WHAT SHE WANTED(1936, Brit.)
Forrest Sawyer
SHARKY'S MACHINE(1982)
Geneva Sawyer
LIFE BEGINS IN COLLEGE(1937), ch; LOVE AND HISSES(1937), ch; ON THE AVENUE(1937), ch; HOLD THAT CO-ED(1938), ch; JOSETTE(1938), ch; LITTLE MISS BROADWAY(1938), ch; SALLY, IRENE AND MARY(1938), ch; STRAIGHT, PLACE AND SHOW(1938), ch; UP THE RIVER(1938), ch; WHILE NEW YORK SLEEPS(1938), ch; SWANEE RIVER(1939), ch; BLUE BIRD, THE(1940), ch; DOWN ARGENTINE WAY(1940), ch; JOHNNY APOLLO(1940); YOUNG PEOPLE(1940), ch; JITTERBUGS(1943), ch; HOME IN INDIANA(1944), ch; IN THE MEANTIME, DARLING(1944), ch
Jacquelyn Sawyer
1984
KILLPOINT(1984)
James Sawyer
FALLEN IDOL, THE(1949, Brit.), prod d
Joan Sawyer
Misc. Silents
LOVE'S LAW(1917)
Joe Sawyer
BLOOD MONEY(1933); NOTORIOUS SOPHIE LANG, THE(1934); BROADWAY GONDOLIER(1935); RECKLESS(1935); GREAT GUY(1936); LAST OUTLAW, THE(1936); PETRIFIED FOREST, THE(1936); TWO IN A CROWD(1936); LADY FIGHTS BACK(1937); SLIM(1937); HEART OF THE NORTH(1938); CONFESSIONS OF A NAZI SPY(1939); FRONTIER MARSHAL(1939); UNION PACIFIC(1939); GRAPES OF WRATH(1940); HONEYMOON DEFERRED(1940); KING OF THE LUMBERJACKS(1940); DOWN MEXICO WAY(1941); SWAMP WATER(1941); TANKS A MILLION(1941); YOU'RE IN THE ARMY NOW(1941); ABOUT FACE(1942); BROOKLYN ORCHID(1942); HAY FOOT(1942); ALASKA HIGHWAY(1943); BUCKSKIN FRONTIER(1943); COWBOY IN MANHATTAN(1943); LET'S FACE IT(1943); OUTLAW, THE(1943); TARZAN'S DESERT MYSTERY(1943); TORNADO(1943); YANKS AHOY(1943); HEY, ROOKIE(1944); MOON OVER LAS VEGAS(1944); SINGING SHERIFF, THE(1944); SOUTH OF DIXIE(1944); BREWSTER'S MILLIONS(1945); HIGH POWERED(1945); NAUGHTY NINETIES, THE(1945); DEADLINE AT DAWN(1946); INSIDE JOB(1946); JOE PALOOKA, CHAMP(1946); RUNAROUND, THE(1946); BIG TOWN AFTER DARK(1947); CHRISTMAS EVE(1947); DOUBLE LIFE, A(1947); ROSES ARE RED(1947); CORONER CREEK(1948); FIGHTING BACK(1948); FIGHTING FATHER DUNNE(1948); HALF PAST MIDNIGHT(1948); HERE COMES TROUBLE(1948); IF YOU KNEW SUSIE(1948); UNTAMED BREED, THE(1948); AND BABY MAKES THREE(1949); DEPUTY MARSHAL(1949); GAY AMIGO, THE(1949); KAZAN(1949); LUCKY STIFF, THE(1949); STAGECOACH KID(1949); TUCSON(1949); BLONDIE'S HERO(1950); CURTAIN CALL AT CACTUS CREEK(1950); FLYING MISSILE(1950); OPERATION HAYLIFT(1950), a, p, w; TRAVELING SALESWOMAN(1950); AS YOU WERE(1951); COMIN' ROUND THE MOUNTAIN(1951); INDIAN UPRISING(1951); PRIDE OF MARYLAND(1951); DEADLINE–U.S.A.(1952); MR. WALKIE TALKIE(1952); RED SKIES OF MONTANA(1952); RIDING SHOTGUN(1954); TAZA, SON OF COCHISE(1954); KETTLES IN THE OZARKS, THE(1956); KILLING, THE(1956); NORTH TO ALASKA(1960); HOW THE WEST WAS WON(1962)
Misc. Talkies
CAMPY KIDS FROM BOOT CAMP(1942); TWO MUGS FROM BROOKLYN(1942)
Joseph Sawyer
SURRENDER(1931); FORGOTTEN COMMANDMENTS(1932); SHOPWORN(1932); COLLEGE HUMOR(1933); SATURDAY'S MILLIONS(1933); SON OF A SAILOR(1933); THREE-CORNERED MOON(1933); COLLEGE RHYTHM(1934); DEATH OF THE DIAMOND(1934); JIMMY THE GENT(1934); LOOKING FOR TROUBLE(1934); OLSEN'S BIG MOMENT(1934); SING AND LIKE IT(1934); STAMBOUL QUEST(1934); WHARF ANGEL(1934); ARIZONIAN, THE(1935); FRISCO KID(1935); GRIDIRON FLASH(1935); I FOUND STELLA PARISH(1935); INFORMER, THE(1935); LITTLE BIG SHOT(1935); MAN OF IRON(1935); MAN ON THE FLYING TRAPEZE, THE(1935); REVENGE RIDER, THE(1935); SPECIAL AGENT(1935); WHOLE TOWN'S TALKING, THE(1935); AND SUDDEN DEATH(1936); BIG BROWN EYES(1936); FRESHMAN LOVE(1936); HIGH TENSION(1936); LEATHERNECKS HAVE LANDED, THE(1936); MOONLIGHT ON THE PRAIRIE(1936); MURDER WITH PICTURES(1936); PRESCOTT KID, THE(1936); PRIDE OF THE MARINES(1936); ROSE BOWL(1936); SPECIAL INVESTIGATOR(1936); WALKING DEAD, THE(1936); WESTERNER, THE(1936); BLACK LEGION, THE(1937); DANGEROUS ADVENTURE, A(1937); MOTOR MADNESS(1937); NAVY BLUES(1937); REPORTED MISSING(1937); SAN QUENTIN(1937); THEY GAVE HIM A GUN(1937); ALWAYS IN TROUBLE(1938); PASSPORT HUSBAND(1938); STOLEN HEAVEN(1938); STORM, THE(1938); TARZAN'S REVENGE(1938); GAMBLING SHIP(1939); I STOLE A MILLION(1939); INSIDE INFORMATION(1939); LADY AND THE MOB, THE(1939); ROARING TWENTIES, THE(1939); SABOTAGE(1939); YOU CAN'T GET AWAY WITH MURDER(1939); BORDER LEGION, THE(1940); DARK COMMAND, THE(1940); HOUSE ACROSS THE BAY, THE(1940); LONG VOYAGE HOME, THE(1940); LUCKY CISCO KID(1940); MAN FROM MONTREAL, THE(1940); MELODY RANCH(1940); SANTA FE TRAIL(1940); WILDCAT BUS(1940); WOMEN WITHOUT NAMES(1940); BELLE STARR(1941); DOWN IN SAN DIEGO(1941); LADY FROM CHEYENNE(1941); LAST OF THE DUANES(1941); SERGEANT YORK(1941); SUNDOWN JIM(1942); THEY DIED WITH THEIR BOOTS ON(1942); WRECKING CREW(1942); HIT THE ICE(1943); SLEEPY LAGOON(1943); G.I. WAR BRIDES(1946); GILDA(1946); IT CAME FROM OUTER SPACE(1953); JOHNNY DARK(1954)
Kathleen Sawyer
DR. FRANKENSTEIN ON CAMPUS(1970, Can.)
Laura Sawyer
Misc. Silents
PORT OF DOOM, THE(1913); ONE OF MILLIONS(1914); WOMAN'S TRIUMPH, A(1914); DAUGHTER OF THE PEOPLE, A(1915)
Margaret Sawyer
AFTER THE BALL(1957, Brit.)
Richard Sawyer
MELVIN AND HOWARD(1980), art d; WHERE THE BUFFALO ROAM(1980), prod d; HAND, THE(1981), art d; OFF THE WALL(1983), prod d; TWILIGHT ZONE–THE MOVIE(1983), art d

Richard Tom Sawyer
THINGS ARE TOUGH ALL OVER(1982), prod d

William A. Sawyer
HAROLD AND MAUDE(1971), ed; HOW TO SEDUCE A WOMAN(1974), ed; WELCOME TO L.A.(1976), ed

William Abbott Sawyer
LANDLORD, THE(1970), ed

Cathy Sawyer-Young
PINK MOTEL(1983)

Arline Sax
GLASS CAGE, THE(1964)

Carrol Sax
Silents
WOMAN WHO DID NOT CARE, THE(1927), sup

Jean Sax
ARIANE, RUSSIAN MAID(1932, Fr.)

Michael Sax
TRON(1982)

Sam Sax
CONFIDENTIAL LADY(1939, Brit.), p; HIS BROTHER'S KEEPER(1939, Brit.), p; HOOTS MON!(1939, Brit.), p; MURDER WILL OUT(1939, Brit.), p; DR. O'DOWD(1940, Brit.), p; MIDAS TOUCH, THE(1940, Brit.), p; WHY GIRLS LEAVE HOME(1945), p
Silents
HIS MASTER'S VOICE(1925), p; DOWN GRADE, THE(1927), p

Sergius Sax
ELISABETH OF AUSTRIA(1931, Ger.)

Lily Saxby
Silents
HARD WAY, THE(1916, Brit.)
Misc. Silents
DUNGEON OF DEATH, THE(1915, Brit.); LIFE OF AN ACTRESS, THE(1915, Brit.); PORT OF MISSING WOMEN, THE(1915, Brit.); TRAFFIC(1915, Brit.); UNDERWORLD OF LONDON, THE(1915, Brit.); WOMAN WHO DID, THE(1915, Brit.); BURNT WINGS(1916, Brit.)

Carl Saxe
FOREST RANGERS, THE(1942); PILOT NO. 5(1943); THOUSANDS CHEER(1943); O.S.S.(1946); DESPERATE(1947); HIGH BARBAREE(1947); JOHNNY O'CLOCK(1947); WHERE THERE'S LIFE(1947); FORCE OF EVIL(1948); RACE STREET(1948); SOUTHERN YANKEE, A(1948); EASY LIVING(1949); NEPTUNE'S DAUGHTER(1949); SAMSON AND DELILAH(1949); WINDOW, THE(1949); WHERE DANGER LIVES(1950); STRIP, THE(1951); SCARLET ANGEL(1952); JALOPY(1953); PRIVATE EYES(1953); YOUNG BESS(1953); EXECUTIVE SUITE(1954); KETTLES ON OLD MACDONALD'S FARM, THE(1957); HUD(1963); SPLIT, THE(1968); WHAT'S UP, DOC?(1972)

Carl H. Saxe
LAST TRAIN FROM GUN HILL(1959)

Erica Saxe
Misc. Talkies
BRANCHES(1971)

Templar Saxe
MEET THE DUKE(1949, Brit.), w
Silents
IN THE BALANCE(1917); WHISPERS(1920); WOMAN GOD CHANGED, THE(1921); WHAT FOOLS MEN ARE(1922); IN SEARCH OF A THRILL(1923); BEAU BRUMMEL(1924); WHITE BLACK SHEEP, THE(1926)
Misc. Silents
FOOTLIGHTS OF FATE, THE(1916); MAN BEHIND THE CURTAIN, THE(1916); BABETTE(1917); INTRIGUE(1917); SIXTEENTH WIFE, THE(1917); ONE THOUSAND DOLLARS(1918); MIND THE PAINT GIRL(1919); TEETH OF THE TIGER, THE(1919); DANGEROUS PARADISE, THE(1920); DEVIL'S ANGEL, THE(1920); SLAVES OF PRIDE(1920); MILLIONAIRE FOR A DAY, A(1921); SIDEWALKS OF NEW YORK(1923); DANCERS, THE(1925)

Aaron Saxon
DESERT SANDS(1955); FLIGHT TO HONG KONG(1956); GUNSLINGER(1956); TRUE STORY OF JESSE JAMES, THE(1957); UNDEAD, THE(1957); GUN FEVER(1958); PARTY GIRL(1958); SPARTACUS(1960); RAVEN, THE(1963)

Al Saxon
I'M ALL RIGHT, JACK(1959, Brit.)

Alvin Saxon
Silents
AFTER MANY YEARS(1930, Brit.), p

Anne Saxon
SISTER-IN-LAW, THE(1975)

David Saxon
IF IT'S TUESDAY, THIS MUST BE BELGIUM(1969), ed; I LOVE MY WIFE(1970), ed; WILLY WONKA AND THE CHOCOLATE FACTORY(1971), ed; ONE IS A LONELY NUMBER(1972), ed

Don Saxon
SUBJECT WAS ROSES, THE(1968)

Elizabeth Saxon
SIMON, KING OF THE WITCHES(1971)

Fred Saxon
DEATH WISH II(1982)

Glenn Saxon
HE WHO SHOOTS FIRST(1966, Ital.)
Misc. Talkies
LYNCHING(1968)

Hugh Saxon
Silents
HER FIVE-FOOT HIGHNESS(1920); SAND(1920); HIGH HEELS(1921); WATCH HIM STEP(1922); CYTHEREA(1924); FIGHTING BOOB, THE(1926); HAIR TRIGGER BAXTER(1926); BULLDOG PLUCK(1927); IS YOUR DAUGHTER SAFE?(1927); KING OF THE HERD(1927); GYPSY OF THE NORTH(1928); ONE SPLENDID HOUR(1929)
Misc. Silents
HEART OF TWENTY, THE(1920)

James Saxon
NESTING, THE(1981)

Johan Lindstrom Saxon
ELVIRA MADIGAN(1967, Swed.), w

John Saxon
IT SHOULD HAPPEN TO YOU(1954); RUNNING WILD(1955); ROCK, PRETTY BABY(1956); UNGUARDED MOMENT, THE(1956); RELUCTANT DEBUTANTE, THE(1958); RESTLESS YEARS, THE(1958); SUMMER LOVE(1958); THIS HAPPY FEELING(1958); BIG FISHERMAN, THE(1959); CRY TOUGH(1959); PLUNDERERS, THE(1960); PORTRAIT IN BLACK(1960); UNFORGIVEN, THE(1960); POSSE FROM HELL(1961); AGOSTINO(1962, Ital.); MR. HOBBS TAKES A VACATION(1962); WAR HUNT(1962); CARDINAL, THE(1963); EVIL EYE(1964 Ital.); BLOOD BEAST FROM OUTER SPACE(1965, Brit.); CAVERN, THE(1965, U.S./Ital.); RAVAGERS, THE(1965, U.S./Phil.); APPALOOSA, THE(1966); QUEEN OF BLOOD(1966); FOR SINGLES ONLY(1968); DEATH OF A GUNFIGHTER(1969); COMPANY OF KILLERS(1970); JOE KIDD(1972); ENTER THE DRAGON(1973); BLACK CHRISTMAS(1974, Can.); MITCHELL(1975); SWISS CONSPIRACY, THE(1976, U.S./Ger.); MOONSHINE COUNTY EXPRESS(1977); STRANGE SHADOWS IN AN EMPTY ROOM(1977, Can./Ital.); BEES, THE(1978); BLACKOUT(1978, Fr./Can.), w; ELECTRIC HORSEMAN, THE(1979); BEYOND EVIL(1980); GLOVE, THE(1980); BLOOD BEACH(1981); CANNIBALS IN THE STREETS(1982, Ital./Span.); WRONG IS RIGHT(1982); BIG SCORE, THE(1983)
1984
NIGHTMARE ON ELM STREET, A(1984)
Misc. Talkies
BLAZING MAGNUM(1976); MR. KINGSTREET'S WAR(1973); FAMILY KILLER(1975); SHALIMAR(1978, India); FAST COMPANY(1979); GLOVE, THE(1979); RUNNING SCARED(1980); INVASION OF THE FLESH HUNTERS(1981); SCORPION WITH TWO TAILS(1982)

Kate Saxon
FACES(1934, Brit.); CROSS CURRENTS(1935, Brit.); GENTLEMAN'S AGREEMENT(1935, Brit.)

Kathleen Saxon
CHELSEA LIFE(1933, Brit.)

Leif Saxon
EGGHEAD'S ROBOT(1970, Brit.), w; TROUBLESOME DOUBLE, THE(1971, Brit.), w

Lyle Saxon
BUCCANEER, THE(1938), w; BUCCANEER, THE(1958), w

Marie Saxon
BROADWAY HOOFER, THE(1929); UNDER SUSPICION(1931)

Mary Ann Saxon
SQUARES(1972), w

Peter Saxon
SCREAM AND SCREAM AGAIN(1970, Brit.), w

Rolf Saxon
LORDS OF DISCIPLINE, THE(1983)
1984
1984(1984, Brit.)

Sharon Saxon
DEVIL'S SISTERS, THE(1966)

Vin Saxon
RAT PFINK AND BOO BOO(1966)

H. Saxon-Snell
CLUE OF THE NEW PIN, THE(1929, Brit.); LOVES OF ROBERT BURNS, THE(1930, Brit.); DEADLOCK(1931, Brit.); JOSSER JOINS THE NAVY(1932, Brit.); RETURN OF RAFFLES, THE(1932, Brit.); VERDICT OF THE SEA(1932, Brit.); LOVE WAGER, THE(1933, Brit.); MAID HAPPY(1933, Brit.); MURDER AT THE INN(1934, Brit.); RETURN OF BULLDOG DRUMMOND, THE(1934, Brit.); HIS MAJESTY AND CO(1935, Brit.); MAD HATTERS, THE(1935, Brit.); ONCE IN A NEW MOON(1935, Brit.); RADIO PIRATES(1935, Brit.); REGAL CAVALCADE(1935, Brit.); ROLLING HOME(1935, Brit.)
Silents
SMASHING THROUGH(1928, Brit.); PEEP BEHIND THE SCENES, A(1929, Brit.)

Aaron Saxton
OKLAHOMA WOMAN, THE(1956)

Charles Saxton
CONCENTRATIN' KID, THE(1930), w; HIGH GEAR(1933), w

John Saxton
HAPPY BIRTHDAY TO ME(1981), w; CLASS OF 1984(1982, Can.), w; TITLE SHOT(1982, Can.), w

Werner Saxtorph
SMILING LIEUTENANT, THE(1931)

Ted Say
CALIFORNIA SPLIT(1974)

Shunji Sayama
FRIENDLY KILLER, THE(1970, Jap.)

Hamid Sayani
SHAKESPEARE WALLAH(1966, India)

Manuel Sayans
HALLUCINATION GENERATION(1966), spec eff

Charlotte Sayce
WHO SLEW AUNTIE ROO?(1971, U.S./Brit.)

Ismet Saydan
DRY SUMMER(1967, Turkey), w

Hamdy Sayed
VIRGIN SACRIFICE(1959)

Diane Sayer
KITTEN WITH A WHIP(1964); MAIL ORDER BRIDE(1964); ROBIN AND THE SEVEN HOODS(1964); STRANGLER, THE(1964); SANDPIPER, THE(1965); MADIGAN(1968); DIRTY DINGUS MAGEE(1970)

Donald Sayer
SEPARATION(1968, Brit.)

Hilda Sayer
Misc. Silents
AUNTIE'S ANTICS(1929, Brit.)

Jay Sayer
SAGA OF THE VIKING WOMEN AND THEIR VOYAGE TO THE WATERS OF THE GREAT SEA SERPENT, THE(1957); TEENAGE DOLL(1957); MACHINE GUN KELLY(1958); WAR OF THE SATELLITES(1958)

Laura Sayer
NIGHT THEY ROBBED BIG BERTHA'S, THE zero(1975); RETURN TO MACON COUNTY(1975)

Philip Sayer
HUNGER, THE(1983); XTRO(1983, Brit.)
1984
SLAYGROUND(1984, Brit.)

Dorothy L. Sayers
SILENT PASSENGER, THE(1935, Brit.), w; BUSMAN'S HONEYMOON(1940, Brit.), w

Eric Sayers
INVISIBLE AVENGER, THE(1958), p; NEW ORLEANS AFTER DARK(1958), p; COMMON LAW WIFE(1963), d; GARBAGE MAN, THE(1963), d&w

Jo Ann Sayers
YOUNG DR. KILDARE(1938); FAST AND LOOSE(1939); HONOLULU(1939); HUCKLEBERRY FINN(1939); WITHIN THE LAW(1939); WOMEN, THE(1939); LIGHT OF WESTERN STARS, THE(1940); MAN WITH NINE LIVES, THE(1940)

Loretta Sayers
FIFTY FATHOMS DEEP(1931); FIGHTING SHERIFF, THE(1931); LOVER COME BACK(1931); MEN ARE LIKE THAT(1931); DEADLINE, THE(1932); HIGH SPEED(1932); WINGS OVER HONOLULU(1937)

Marian Sayers
KID FROM SPAIN, THE(1932); GARDEN OF ALLAH, THE(1936)

Michael Sayers
CASINO ROYALE(1967, Brit.), w

G. Sayfulin
MUMU(1961, USSR)

Anthony Sayger
LONELINESS OF THE LONG DISTANCE RUNNER, THE(1962, Brit.)

Alexei Sayle
GORKY PARK(1983)

Frances Sayles
TEXAS BAD MAN(1932); HOME ON THE RANGE(1935)

Francis Sayles
BLONDE VENUS(1932); STRANGERS OF THE EVENING(1932); HANDS ACROSS THE TABLE(1935); ONE HOUR LATE(1935); ONE IN A MILLION(1936); MORE THAN A SECRETARY(1936); SATAN MET A LADY(1936); YOURS FOR THE ASKING(1936); BLACK LEGION, THE(1937); EASY LIVING(1937); PLAINSMAN, THE(1937); SHADOW, THE(1937); SOULS AT SEA(1937); STELLA DALLAS(1937); TRAPPED(1937); PURPLE VIGILANTES, THE(1938); FOR LOVE OR MONEY(1939); LAUGH IT OFF(1939); NEWSBOY'S HOME(1939); RIDERS OF BLACK RIVER(1939); BALL OF FIRE(1941); PUBLIC ENEMIES(1941); RAGS TO RICHES(1941); SON OF DAVY CROCKETT, THE(1941); DR. BROADWAY(1942); GLASS KEY, THE(1942); MYSTERY OF MARIE ROGET, THE(1942); SOMEWHERE I'LL FIND YOU(1942); STRICTLY IN THE GROOVE(1942); HONEYMOON LODGE(1943); MOONLIGHT IN VERMONT(1943); SECRETS OF THE UNDERGROUND(1943); CASANOVA BROWN(1944); MINISTRY OF FEAR(1945)

John Sayles
PIRANHA(1978), w; LADY IN RED, THE(1979), w; ALLIGATOR(1980), w; BATTLE BEYOND THE STARS(1980), w; RETURN OF THE SECAUCUS SEVEN(1980), a, d&w, ed; HOWLING, THE(1981), w; CHALLENGE, THE(1982), w; BABY, IT'S YOU(1983), d&w; LIANNA(1983), a, d&w, ed
1984
BROTHER FROM ANOTHER PLANET, THE(1984), a, d&w, ed; HARD CHOICES(1984)

Katie Saylor
DIRTY O'NEIL(1974); SWINGING BARMAIDS, THE(1976); SUPER VAN(1977)

Latie A. Saylor
INVASION OF THE BEE GIRLS(1973)

Shannon Saylor
SEA GYPSIES, THE(1978)

Syd Saylor
BORDER LEGION, THE(1930); FOR THE DEFENSE(1930); LIGHT OF WESTERN STARS, THE(1930); MEN WITHOUT LAW(1930); CAUGHT(1931); FIGHTING CARAVANS(1931); I TAKE THIS WOMAN(1931); LAWYER'S SECRET, THE(1931); NO LIMIT(1931); SIDEWALKS OF NEW YORK(1931); UNFAITHFUL(1931); CRUSADER, THE(1932); IF I HAD A MILLION(1932); LADY AND GENT(1932); LAW OF THE SEA(1932); MILLION DOLLAR LEGS(1932); TANGLED DESTINIES(1932); GAMBLING SHIP(1933); HELL BELOW(1933); JUSTICE TAKES A HOLIDAY(1933); MAN OF SENTIMENT, A(1933); NUISANCE, THE(1933); DUDE RANGER, THE(1934); LOST JUNGLE, THE(1934); MARRYING WIDOWS(1934); TRANSATLANTIC MERRY-GO-ROUND(1934); WHEN A MAN SEES RED(1934); YOUNG AND BEAUTIFUL(1934); BRANDED A COWARD(1935); CODE OF THE MOUNTED(1935); GOIN' TO TOWN(1935); HEADLINE WOMAN, THE(1935); LADIES CRAVE EXCITEMENT(1935); STAR OF MIDNIGHT(1935); WILDERNESS MAIL(1935); EX-MRS. BRADFORD, THE(1936); GORGEOUS HUSSY, THE(1936); HIS BROTHER'S WIFE(1936); HITCH HIKE TO HEAVEN(1936); KELLY OF THE SECRET SERVICE(1936); KELLY THE SECOND(1936); NEVADA(1936); PRISON SHADOWS(1936); RHYTHM ON THE RANGE(1936); ROSE BOWL(1936); SKY PARADE(1936); THREE MESQUITEERS, THE(1936); ARIZONA DAYS(1937); BORN TO THE WEST(1937); EXILED TO SHANGHAI(1937); FORLORN RIVER(1937); GUNS IN THE DARK(1937); HEADIN' FOR THE RIO GRANDE(1937); HOUSE OF SECRETS, THE(1937); MEET THE BOY FRIEND(1937); PICK A STAR(1937); SEA RACKETEERS(1937); SECRET VALLEY(1937); TIME OUT FOR ROMANCE(1937); WALLABY JIM OF THE ISLANDS(1937); WILD AND WOOLLY(1937); WRONG ROAD, THE(1937); CRASHIN' THRU DANGER(1938); LITTLE MISS BROADWAY(1938); MEN WITH WINGS(1938); STRANGE FACES(1938); TEST PILOT(1938); THERE GOES MY HEART(1938); YANK AT OXFORD, A(1938); GERONIMO(1939); GOLDEN BOY(1939); LET FREEDOM RING(1939); OUR LEADING CITIZEN(1939); PIRATES OF THE SKIES(1939); STAND UP AND FIGHT(1939); UNION PACIFIC(1939); $1,000 A TOUCHDOWN(1939); ABE LINCOLN IN ILLINOIS(1940); ARIZONA(1940); I TAKE THIS WOMAN(1940); IRENE(1940); YOUNG PEOPLE(1940); DESIGN FOR SCANDAL(1941); GREAT AMERICAN BROADCAST, THE(1941); H.M. PULHAM, ESQ.(1941); HONKY TONK(1941); LAST OF THE DUANES(1941); NEVADA CITY(1941); SIERRA SUE(1941); SUNSET IN WYOMING(1941); WYOMING WILDCAT(1941); GENTLEMAN AT HEART, A(1942); HENRY ALDRICH GETS GLAMOUR(1942); LADY IN A JAM(1942); MAN IN THE TRUNK, THE(1942); PACIFIC RENDEZVOUS(1942); THAT OTHER WOMAN(1942); TIME TO KILL(1942); TRUE TO THE ARMY(1942); YANKEE DOODLE DANDY(1942); DOUGHBOYS IN IRELAND(1943); HARVEST MELODY(1943); HE HIRED THE BOSS(1943); MUG TOWN(1943); SO'S YOUR UNCLE(1943); HEY, ROOKIE(1944); LOUISIANA HAYRIDE(1944); ONCE UPON A TIME(1944); SWINGTIME JOHNNY(1944); BEDSIDE MANNER(1945); MURDER, HE SAYS(1945); NOB HILL(1945); ON STAGE EVERYBODY(1945); SCARLET STREET(1945); SHE GETS HER

MAN(1945); AMBUSH TRAIL(1946); AVALANCHE(1946); CROSS MY HEART(1946); DEADLINE FOR MURDER(1946); HOUSE OF HORRORS(1946); KID FROM BROOKLYN, THE(1946); NAVAJO KID, THE(1946); SIX GUN MAN(1946); THUNDER TOWN(1946); DEAD RECKONING(1947); SECRET LIFE OF WALTER MITTY, THE(1947); UNCONQUERED(1947); FAMILY HONEYMOON(1948); IF YOU KNEW SUSIE(1948); ISN'T IT ROMANTIC?(1948); MIRACLE OF THE BELLS, THE(1948); PALEFACE, THE(1948); PRINCE OF THIEVES, THE(1948); RACING LUCK(1948); SITTING PRETTY(1948); SLEEP, MY LOVE(1948); SNAKE PIT, THE(1948); TRIPLE THREAT(1948); BIG JACK(1949); DANCING IN THE DARK(1949); MISS GRANT TAKES RICHMOND(1949); STRATTON STORY, THE(1949); CHEAPER BY THE DOZEN(1950); FULLER BRUSH GIRL, THE(1950); JACKPOT, THE(1950); MULE TRAIN(1950); THREE LITTLE WORDS(1950); ABBOTT AND COSTELLO MEET THE INVISIBLE MAN(1951); VALLEY OF FIRE(1951); ABBOTT AND COSTELLO MEET CAPTAIN KIDD(1952); BELLES ON THEIR TOES(1952); GREATEST SHOW ON EARTH, THE(1952); HAWK OF WILD RIVER, THE(1952); LAS VEGAS STORY, THE(1952); MA AND PA KETTLE AT THE FAIR(1952); OLD WEST, THE(1952); WAGON TEAM(1952); ABBOTT AND COSTELLO GO TO MARS(1953); REDHEAD FROM WYOMING, THE(1953); TALL TEXAN, THE(1953); THREE HOURS TO KILL(1954); TOUGHEST MAN ALIVE(1955); SHOOT-OUT AT MEDICINE BEND(1957); SPIRIT OF ST. LOUIS, THE(1957); ESCORT WEST(1959); CRAWLING HAND, THE(1963)
Misc. Talkies
LAST ASSIGNMENT, THE(1936)
Silents
JUST OFF BROADWAY(1929)

Christopher Saylors
URBAN COWBOY(1980); SILKWOOD(1983)
1984
ON THE LINE(1984, Span.)

Donald Sayne-Smith
DECLINE AND FALL... OF A BIRD WATCHER(1969, Brit.)

Charles Sayner
I AM A CAMERA(1955, Brit.)

Alan Saynes
DULCIMER STREET(1948, Brit.)

Charles Saynor
CLOUDBURST(1952, Brit.); MAN IN THE WHITE SUIT, THE(1952); INSPECTOR CALLS, AN(1954, Brit.); LEASE OF LIFE(1954, Brit.); KID FOR TWO FARTHINGS, A(1956, Brit.); MARY HAD A LITTLE(1961, Brit.)

Fukuko Sayo
ONCE A RAINY DAY(1968, Jap.); AFFAIR AT AKITSU(1980, Jap.)

Andree Sayre
Silents
BROKEN MELODY, THE(1929, Brit.)

Bigelow Sayre
GREAT JEWEL ROBBER, THE(1950); JACKPOT, THE(1950); UNION STATION(1950); STARLIFT(1951)

G.W. Sayre
BIG TIME OR BUST(1934), w

George Sayre
CODE OF THE MOUNTED(1935), w; RACING LUCK(1935), w; FLYING HOSTESS(1936), w; SONG OF THE TRAIL(1936), w; TORTURE SHIP(1939), w; AM I GUILTY?(1940), w; NEARLY EIGHTEEN(1943), w; CONTENDER, THE(1944), w; FOREVER YOURS(1945), w

George W. Sayre
MAN THEY COULD NOT HANG, THE(1939), w; JUNGLE SIREN(1942), w; SECRETS OF A CO-ED(1942), w; SHERIFF OF SAGE VALLEY(1942), w; WHERE ARE YOUR CHILDREN?(1943), w; BLACK MARKET BABIES(1946), w; ROCKY(1948), w; UNTAMED WOMEN(1952), w

George Wallace Sayre
REFORM GIRL(1933), w; UNSEEN ENEMY(1942), w; WINGS OVER THE PACIFIC(1943), w; ALASKA(1944), w; SHANGHAI COBRA, THE(1945), w; SECRETS OF A SORORITY GIRL(1946), w; STAGE STRUCK(1948), w; MODERN MARRIAGE, A(1962), w

George Warren Sayre
QUEEN OF BROADWAY(1942), w

Jeffrey Sayre
GREAT GUY(1936); CONFESSION(1937); HOLLYWOOD HOTEL(1937); MARKED WOMAN(1937); SUBMARINE D-1(1937); ACCIDENTS WILL HAPPEN(1938); ANGELS WITH DIRTY FACES(1938); I AM THE LAW(1938); INTERNATIONAL SETTLEMENT(1938); DARK VICTORY(1939); MUTINY IN THE BIG HOUSE(1939); OKLAHOMA KID, THE(1939); ROARING TWENTIES, THE(1939); SECRET SERVICE OF THE AIR(1939); MURDER IN THE AIR(1940); 'TIL WE MEET AGAIN(1940); MANPOWER(1941); MEN OF SAN QUENTIN(1942); SABOTEUR(1942); POSTMAN ALWAYS RINGS TWICE, THE(1946); HIGH BARBAREE(1947); JOHNNY O'CLOCK(1947); POSSESSED(1947); SONG OF THE THIN MAN(1947); SONG IS BORN, A(1948); SCENE OF THE CRIME(1949); DARK CITY(1950); MRS. O'MALLEY AND MR. MALONE(1950); FOLLOW THE SUN(1951); FRENCH LINE, THE(1954); TATTERED DRESS, THE(1957); YOUNG LIONS, THE(1958); SEVEN MINUTES, THE(1971)

Joel Sayre
RACKETY RAX(1932), w; COME ON, MARINES(1934), w; ANNIE OAKLEY(1935), w; PAYOFF, THE(1935), w; HIS FAMILY TREE(1936), w; PAROLE(1936), w; ROAD TO GLORY, THE(1936), w; MEET THE MISSUS(1937), w; TOAST OF NEW YORK, THE(1937), w; THERE'S ALWAYS A WOMAN(1938), w; GUNGA DIN(1939), w; FOURTEEN HOURS(1951), w

Stephen Sayre
VALLEY GIRL(1983)

Theodore Burt Sayre
Silents
COMMANDING OFFICER, THE(1915), w

Parviz Sayyad
1984
MISSION, THE(1984), a, p, d&w, ed

Kyu Sazanka
HUMAN CONDITION, THE(1959, Jap.); ODD OBSESSION(1961, Jap.); YOJIMBO(1961, Jap.); FIRES ON THE PLAIN(1962, Jap.); WAYSIDE PEBBLE, THE(1962, Jap.)

Dan Sazarino
WHO?(1975, Brit./Ger.)
Jose Sazatornil
NOT ON YOUR LIFE(1965, Ital./Span.)
Carmela Sazio
PAISAN(1948, Ital.)
Gaetano Sazio
RENDEZVOUS AT MIDNIGHT(1935), w
A. Sazonov
SKY CALLS, THE(1959, USSR), w
James Sbardellati
FRATERNITY ROW(1977, art d; DEATHSTALKER(1983, Arg./U.S.), p
1984
DEATHSTALKER, THE(1984), p
Raphael Sbarge
RISKY BUSINESS(1983)
Giulio Sbarigia
1984
BLACK CAT, THE(1984, Ital./Brit.), p
Galliano Sbarra
ROMA(1972, Ital./Fr.)
Gianni Sbarra
NIGHT OF THE SHOOTING STARS, THE(1982, Ital.), art d
Giovanni Sbarra
PADRE PADRONE(1977, Ital.), art d
Ellen Sberman
DR. TARR'S TORTURE DUNGEON(1972, Mex.)
Giancarlo Sbragia
FALL OF ROME, THE(1963, Ital.); NO WAY OUT(1975, Ital./Fr.); DEATH RACE(1978, Ital.); NEST OF VIPERS(1979, Ital.)
Mattia Sbragia
NEST OF VIPERS(1979, Ital.)
Mario Sbrenna
GOLIATH AND THE SINS OF BABYLON(1964, Ital.), ph
Greta Scacchi
HEAT AND DUST(1983, Brit.)
Mario Scaccia
TOO BAD SHE'S BAD(1954, Ital.); MIGHTY URSUS(1962, Ital./Span.); LOVE AND LARCENY(1963, Fr./Ital.); LOVE, THE ITALIAN WAY(1964, Ital.); MAIDEN FOR A PRINCE, A(1967, Fr./Ital.); WE STILL KILL THE OLD WAY(1967, Ital.); TEMPTER, THE(1978, Ital.)
Louis Scacciandoci
THIEF OF VENICE, THE(1952), art d
Luigi Scaccianoce
EVA(1962, Fr./Ital.), art d; STEPPE, THE(1963, Fr./Ital.), art d; LOVE A LA CARTE(1965, Ital.), art d; TIME OF INDIFFERENCE(1965, Fr./Ital.), art d; GOSPEL ACCORDING TO ST. MATTHEW, THE(1966, Fr., Ital.), art d; LA VISITA(1966, Ital./Fr.), art d; SIX DAYS A WEEK(1966, Fr./Ital./Span.), set d; HAWKS AND THE SPARROWS, THE(1967, Ital.), art d; ANZIO(1968, Ital.), art d; KISS THE OTHER SHEIK(1968, Fr./Ital.), art d; TREASURE OF SAN GENNARO(1968, Fr./Ital./Ger.), art d; FELLINI SATYRICON(1969, Fr./Ital.), art d; SONS OF SATAN(1969, Ital./Fr./Ger.), art d; WITCH, THE(1969, Ital.), art d; SCIENTIFIC CARDPLAYER, THE(1972, Ital.), art d; VOYAGE, THE(1974, Ital.), prod d; INHERITANCE, THE(1978, Ital.), art d; LA CAGE AUX FOLLES II(1981, Ital./Fr.), prod d
Norman Scace
ACT OF MURDER(1965, Brit.); PARTNER, THE(1966, Brit.); DECLINE AND FALL... OF A BIRD WATCHER(1969, Brit.); ROMANTIC ENGLISHWOMAN, THE(1975, Brit./Fr.)
Claudio Scachilli
GOLDEN ARROW, THE(1964, Ital.)
Harry W. Scadden
Silents
ROAD TO RUIN, THE(1913, Brit.)
Luciano Scaffa
AUGUSTINE OF HIPPO(1973, Ital.), w; YEAR ONE(1974, Ital.), w; AGE OF THE MEDICI, THE(1979, Ital.), w
Michele Scaglione
COLOSSUS OF RHODES, THE(1961, Ital., Fr., Span.), p
May Scagnelli
SPARROWS CAN'T SING(1963, Brit.)
Bruno Scagnetti
AMARCORD(1974, Ital.)
Cecil Scaife
NATCHEZ TRACE(1960); THAT TENNESSEE BEAT(1966)
Edward Scaife
MURDER ON MONDAY(1953, Brit.), ph; TRIAL AND ERROR(1962, Brit.), ph; SQUADRON 633(1964, U.S./Brit.), ph; 633 SQUADRON(1964), ph; OPERATION SNAFU(1965, Brit.), ph; TRUTH ABOUT SPRING, THE(1965, Brit.), ph; KHARTOUM(1966, Brit.), ph; DIRTY DOZEN, THE(1967, Brit.), ph; DARK OF THE SUN(1968, Brit.), ph; PLAY DIRTY(1969, Brit.), ph; SINFUL DAVEY(1969, Brit.), ph; HANNIE CALDER(1971, Brit.), ph; CRY OF THE PENGUINS(1972, Brit.), ph; SITTING TARGET(1972, Brit.), ph
Gerald Scaife
1984
BREAKIN'(1984), w
Hugh Scaife
PERFECT FRIDAY(1970, Brit.), set d; SEE NO EVIL(1971, Brit.), set d; SEVERED HEAD, A(1971, Brit.), set d; PAPILLON(1973), set d; ONE OF OUR DINOSAURS IS MISSING(1975, Brit.), ed; LITTLEST HORSE THIEVES, THE(1977), set d; SPY WHO LOVED ME, THE(1977, Brit.), set d; ELEPHANT MAN, THE(1980, Brit.), set d; EYE OF THE NEEDLE(1981), set d
1984
PASSAGE TO INDIA, A(1984, Brit.), set d
Isobel Scaife
OLD FAITHFUL(1935, Brit.); RIGHT AGE TO MARRY, THE(1935, Brit.); BELLES OF ST. CLEMENTS, THE(1936, Brit.); BUSMAN'S HOLIDAY(1936, Brit.); NOT SO DUSTY(1936, Brit.); NOTHING LIKE PUBLICITY(1936, Brit.); TWICE BRANDED(1936, Brit.); FATHER STEPS OUT(1937, Brit.); PEARLS BRING TEARS(1937, Brit.); SHOW GOES ON, THE(1937, Brit.); STRANGE ADVENTURES OF MR. SMITH, THE(1937, Brit.); WHY PICK ON ME?(1937, Brit.); SILVER TOP(1938, Brit.); HIS

LORDSHIP GOES TO PRESS(1939, Brit.); LILAC DOMINO, THE(1940, Brit.)
Ted Scaife
OUTCAST OF THE ISLANDS(1952, Brit.), ph; PASSIONATE SENTRY, THE(1952, Brit.), ph; CAPTAIN'S PARADISE, THE(1953, Brit.), ph; MELBA(1953, Brit.), ph; RINGER, THE(1953, Brit.), ph; BEAUTIFUL STRANGER(1954, Brit.), ph; HOLLY AND THE IVY, THE(1954, Brit.), ph; INSPECTOR CALLS, AN(1954, Brit.), ph; INTRUDER, THE(1955, Brit.), ph; STORM OVER THE NILE(1955, Brit.), ph; KID FOR TWO FARTHINGS, A(1956, Brit.), ph; BIRTHDAY PRESENT, THE(1957, Brit.), ph; SEA WIFE(1957, Brit.), ph; SMILEY(1957, Brit.), ph; HAPPY IS THE BRIDE(1958, Brit.), ph; LAST BLITZKRIEG, THE(1958), ph; LAW AND DISORDER(1958, Brit.), ph; BOY AND THE BRIDGE, THE(1959, Brit.), ph; HOUSE OF THE SEVEN HAWKS, THE(1959), ph; SMILEY GETS A GUN(1959, Brit.), ph; TARZAN'S GREATEST ADVENTURE(1959, Brit.), ph; TWO-HEADED SPY, THE(1959, Brit.), ph; CARRY ON CONSTABLE(1960, Brit.), ph; PLEASE TURN OVER(1960, Brit.), ph; TARZAN THE MAGNIFICENT(1960, Brit.), ph; ALL NIGHT LONG(1961, Brit.), ph; HIS AND HERS(1961, Brit.), ph; WATCH YOUR STERN(1961, Brit.), ph; LION, THE(1962, Brit.), ph; FOLLOW THE BOYS(1963), ph; TARZAN'S THREE CHALLENGES(1963), ph; YOUNG CASSIDY(1965, U.S./Brit.), ph; LIQUIDATOR, THE(1966, Brit.), ph; WALK WITH LOVE AND DEATH, A(1969), ph; KREMLIN LETTER, THE(1970), ph; CATLOW(1971, Span.), ph; WATER BABIES, THE(1979, Brit.), ph
Dolly Scal
PICKPOCKET(1963, Fr.)
Delia Scala
MESSALINE(1952, Fr./Ital.); AFFAIRS OF MESSALINA, THE(1954, Ital.); GRAN VARIETA(1955, Ital.); MY SEVEN LITTLE SINS(1956, Fr./Ital.)
Della Scala
APPOINTMENT FOR MURDER(1954, Ital.)
Domenico Scala
UNDER THE SUN OF ROME(1949, Ital.), ph; COUNTERFEITERS, THE(1953, Ital.), ph; OSSESSIONE(1959, Ital.), ph
Franco Scala
STRANGER RETURNS, THE(1968, U.S./Ital./Ger./Span.)
Gaetano Scala
SAMSON AND THE SLAVE QUEEN(1963, Ital.)
Gia Scala
FOUR GIRLS IN TOWN(1956); NEVER SAY GOODBYE(1956); PRICE OF FEAR, THE(1956); BIG BOODLE, THE(1957); GARMENT JUNGLE, THE(1957); TIP ON A DEAD JOCKEY(1957); RIDE A CROOKED TRAIL(1958); TUNNEL OF LOVE, THE(1958); ANGRY HILLS, THE(1959, Brit.); BATTLE OF THE CORAL SEA(1959); TWO-HEADED SPY, THE(1959, Brit.); I AIM AT THE STARS(1960); GUNS OF NAVARONE, THE(1961); OPERATION DELILAH(1966, U.S./Span.); DON'T GO NEAR THE WATER(1975)
Misc. Talkies
TRIUMPH OF ROBIN HOOD, THE(1960)
Kim Scala
YOUNG AND DANGEROUS(1957)
Michael Scala
WHO'S THAT KNOCKING AT MY DOOR?(1968)
Tina Scala
SECONDS(1966); MIDNIGHT COWBOY(1969)
Michael Scalera
1984
BEST DEFENSE(1984)
Michele Scalera
LE MANS(1971)
John Scales
VOYAGE TO THE END OF THE UNIVERSE(1963, Czech.), cos
Prunella Scales
HOBSON'S CHOICE(1954, Brit.); SCOTCH ON THE ROCKS(1954, Brit.); WHAT EVERY WOMAN WANTS(1954, Brit.); ROOM AT THE TOP(1959, Brit.); WALTZ OF THE TOREADORS(1962, Brit.); LITTLEST HORSE THIEVES, THE(1977); BOYS FROM BRAZIL, THE(1978); HOUND OF THE BASKERVILLES, THE(1980, Brit.); WAGNER(1983, Brit./Hung./Aust.); WICKED LADY, THE(1983, Brit.)
Trixie Scales
GIVE ME THE STARS(1944, Brit.)
Lenny Scaletta
MEAN STREETS(1973)
Jack Scalia
1984
FEAR CITY(1984)
Peter Scalia
MIDNIGHT COWBOY(1969)
Jack Scalici
ONE AND ONLY, THE(1978); CAVEMAN(1981)
Luciana Scalise
WE STILL KILL THE OLD WAY(1967, Ital.)
Paolo Scalondro
MONSIGNOR(1982)
Vincent Scalondro
1984
AFTER THE FALL OF NEW YORK(1984, Ital./Fr.)
Jacky Scalso
NEST OF THE CUCKOO BIRDS, THE(1965)
Roy Scammel
PSYCHO-CIRCUS(1967, Brit.); THOSE DARING YOUNG MEN IN THEIR JAUNTY JALOPIES(1969, Fr./Ital./ Brit.); GLADIATORS, THE(1970, Swed.); CLOCKWORK ORANGE, A(1971, Brit.), stunts
Roy Scammell
O LUCKY MAN!(1973, Brit.); ROLLERBALL(1975); MIDNIGHT EXPRESS(1978, Brit.), stunts; FLASH GORDON(1980); VENOM(1982, Brit.), stunts
1984
SHEENA(1984), stunts
Terence Scammell
MEPHISTO WALTZ, THE(1971)
P. R. Scammon
Silents
AMERICA(1924)

Itala Scandariato
MADAME(1963, Fr./Ital./Span.), cos; PLACE CALLED GLORY, A(1966, Span./Ger.), cos

Romano Scandariato
DR. BUTCHER, M.D.(1982, Ital.), w

Franco Scandurra
SPIRIT AND THE FLESH, THE(1948, Ital.); GOLDEN ARROW, THE(1964, Ital.)

Frank Scanell
SHADOW OF SUSPICION(1944); COUNTRY GIRL, THE(1954)

George Scanlan
DISTANT DRUMS(1951)

Jack Scanlan
CALIFORNIA SUITE(1978)

Jerry Scanlan
HEAVEN CAN WAIT(1978)

Joseph L. Scanlan
SPRING FEVER(1983, Can.), d

Susan Scanlan
1984
BODY ROCK(1984), ch

Valarie Scanlan
DAD AND DAVE COME TO TOWN(1938, Aus.)

E. Scanlon
Silents
AMERICA(1924)

George Scanlon
WORLD IN HIS ARMS, THE(1952)

John Scanlon
DOC(1971); BADGE 373(1973); ESCAPE FROM ALCATRAZ(1979)

John G. Scanlon
1984
CRIMES OF PASSION(1984)

Frank Scannell
JOHNNY DOESN'T LIVE HERE ANY MORE(1944); LOST IN A HAREM(1944); ABBOTT AND COSTELLO IN HOLLYWOOD(1945); ANGEL COMES TO BROOKLYN, AN(1945); BEHIND CITY LIGHTS(1945); THOUSAND AND ONE NIGHTS, A(1945); WITHIN THESE WALLS(1945); LOVER COME BACK(1946); SUSPENSE(1946); HIT PARADE OF 1947(1947); I WONDER WHO'S KISSING HER NOW(1947); KILROY WAS HERE(1947); LINDA BE GOOD(1947); APARTMENT FOR PEGGY(1948); FRENCH LEAVE(1948); LADIES OF THE CHORUS(1948); RACE STREET(1948); TEXAS, BROOKLYN AND HEAVEN(1948); WHEN MY BABY SMILES AT ME(1948); ALIAS THE CHAMP(1949); FLAMINGO ROAD(1949); MY DREAM IS YOURS(1949); TAKE ME OUT TO THE BALL GAME(1949); SECRET FURY, THE(1950); UNKNOWN MAN, THE(1951); BAD AND THE BEAUTIFUL, THE(1952); KANSAS CITY CONFIDENTIAL(1952); PRIDE OF ST. LOUIS, THE(1952); SHE'S WORKING HER WAY THROUGH COLLEGE(1952); REMAINS TO BE SEEN(1953); STORY OF THREE LOVES, THE(1953); STRANGER WORE A GUN, THE(1953); THREE SAILORS AND A GIRL(1953); LAWLESS STREET, A(1955); CRASHING LAS VEGAS(1956); FIRST TRAVELING SALESLADY, THE(1956); MIRACLE IN THE RAIN(1956); INCREDIBLE SHRINKING MAN, THE(1957); NIGHT THE WORLD EXPLODED, THE(1957); TATTERED DRESS, THE(1957); SCREAMING MIMI(1958); ARSON FOR HIRE(1959); HIGH TIME(1960); ERRAND BOY, THE(1961); DISORDERLY ORDERLY, THE(1964); ROBIN AND THE SEVEN HOODS(1964); HARLOW(1965)

Tony Scannell
FLASH GORDON(1980)

Frank Scannon
BAND WAGON, THE(1953)

Patsy Scantlebury
WAY WE LIVE, THE(1946, Brit.)

Piero Scanziani
ROMAN HOLIDAY(1953)

John Scapar
BIMBO THE GREAT(1961, Ger.), ch

Tony Scaponi
Misc. Talkies
SCREAM IN THE STREETS, A(1972)

Sam Scar
GREAT SINNER, THE(1949); EXPERIMENT ALCATRAZ(1950); HOODLUM EMPIRE(1952); KANSAS CITY CONFIDENTIAL(1952); SALOME(1953); FIGHTING CHANCE, THE(1955)

Michele Scarabelli
1984
HOTEL NEW HAMPSHIRE, THE(1984); RENO AND THE DOC(1984, Can.)

Michelle Scarabelli
1984
COVERGIRL(1984, Can.)

Vittorio Scarabello
FACTS OF MURDER, THE(1965, Ital.)

Armando Scarano
ORCA(1977), set d

Silvio Scarano
COMING HOME(1978), cos; TABLE FOR FIVE(1983), cos

Tecia Scarano
LITTLE MARTYR, THE(1947, Ital.)

Tecla Scarano
BELLISSIMA(1952, Ital.); LADY DOCTOR, THE(1963, Fr./Ital./Span.); MARRIAGE–ITALIAN STYLE(1964, Fr./Ital.); YESTERDAY, TODAY, AND TOMORROW(1964, Ital./Fr.); SHOOT LOUD, LOUDER... I DON'T UNDERSTAND(1966, Ital.); MADE IN ITALY(1967, Fr./Ital.)

Tony Scarano
EYE FOR AN EYE, AN(1966), cos; KING OF MARVIN GARDENS, THE(1972), cos; FAREWELL, MY LOVELY(1975), cos; ISLANDS IN THE STREAM(1977), cos; MARCH OR DIE(1977, Brit.), cos; F.I.S.T.(1978), cos

Bob Scarantino
CLAUDINE(1974); NUNZIO(1978); WITHOUT A TRACE(1983)

Sam Scarber
1984
AGAINST ALL ODDS(1984); KARATE KID, THE(1984)

Alma Sioux Scarberry
HIRED WIFE(1934), w

Dorothy Scarborough
WIND, THE(1928), w

George Scarborough
LADY OF THE PAVEMENTS(1929), w; LOCKED DOOR, THE(1929), w
Silents
LURE, THE(1914), w; LUCK AND PLUCK(1919), w; WEST OF CHICAGO(1922), w

George M. Scarborough
SON-DAUGHTER, THE(1932), w

Claudio Scarchilli
FALL OF ROME, THE(1963, Ital.); GOOD, THE BAD, AND THE UGLY, THE(1967, Ital./Span.); HELLBENDERS, THE(1967, U.S./Ital./Span.)

Sandro Scarchilli
GOOD, THE BAD, AND THE UGLY, THE(1967, Ital./Span.)

Nino Scarciofolo
UP THE MACGREGORS(1967, Ital./Span.)

Elio Scardamaglia
GOLIATH AND THE SINS OF BABYLON(1964, Ital.), p; ARIZONA COLT(1965, It./Fr./Span.), p; REVENGE OF THE GLADIATORS(1965, Ital.), p; SEVEN SLAVES AGAINST THE WORLD(1965, Ital.), p; VENGEANCE IS MINE(1969, Ital./Span.), p; BULLET FOR SANDOVAL, A(1970, Ital./Span.), p; KILL THEM ALL AND COME BACK ALONE(1970, Ital./Span.), w; JOHNNY HAMLET(1972, Ital.), p; MIDNIGHT PLEASURES(1975, Ital.), p; CHARLESTON(1978, Ital.), p, w; IMMORTAL BACHELOR, THE(1980, Ital.), p

Francesco Scardamaglia
GOLIATH AND THE SINS OF BABYLON(1964, Ital.), w; JOHNNY HAMLET(1972, Ital.), w; MIDNIGHT PLEASURES(1975, Ital.), w; IMMORTAL BACHELOR, THE(1980, Ital.), w

Valerie Scarden
TASTE OF HONEY, A(1962, Brit.)

Chelo Scardino
HOMER(1970)

Don Scardino
HOMER(1970), a, m; PEOPLE NEXT DOOR, THE(1970); RIP-OFF(1971, Can.); SQUIRM(1976); CRUISING(1980); HE KNOWS YOU'RE ALONE(1980)

Jack Scardino
DEER HUNTER, THE(1978)

Jean Paul Scardino
Misc. Talkies
NAUGHTY SCHOOL GIRLS(1977), d

Paul Scardom
Silents
DESIRED WOMAN, THE(1918), d

Paul Scardon
FARGO KID, THE(1941); LADY FROM LOUISIANA(1941); SON OF DAVY CROCKETT, THE(1941); MRS. MINIVER(1942); MY FAVORITE BLONDE(1942); TODAY I HANG(1942); MAN FROM THE RIO GRANDE, THE(1943); ADVENTURES OF MARK TWAIN, THE(1944); DOWN MISSOURI WAY(1946); MAGIC TOWN(1947); CANON CITY(1948); FIGHTING MAD(1948); HE WALKED BY NIGHT(1948); SECRET BEYOND THE DOOR, THE(1948); SHANGHAI CHEST, THE(1948); SIGN OF THE RAM, THE(1948)
Silents
UNCLE TOM'S CABIN(1914); BATTLE CRY OF PEACE, THE(1915); JUGGERNAUT, THE(1915); SINS OF THE MOTHERS(1915); PRINCE IN A PAWNSHOP, A(1916), d; APARTMENT 29(1917), d; ARSENE LUPIN(1917), d; IN THE BALANCE(1917), d; ALL MAN(1918), d; KING OF DIAMONDS, THE(1918), d; OTHER MAN, THE(1918), d; PARTNERS OF THE NIGHT(1920), d; BREAKING POINT, THE(1921), d; WHEN THE DEVIL DRIVES(1922), d; WONDERFUL WIFE, A(1922), d; HER OWN FREE WILL(1924), d
Misc. Silents
ALIBI, THE(1916), a, d; DAWN OF FREEDOM, THE(1916), d; ENEMY, THE(1916), d; HERO OF SUBMARINE D-2, THE(1916), d; ISLAND OF SURPRISE, THE(1916), d; PHANTOM FORTUNES, THE(1916), d; REDEMPTION OF DAVE DARCEY, THE(1916), d; ROSE OF THE SOUTH(1916), d; GRELL MYSTERY, THE(1917), d; HAWK, THE(1917), d; HER RIGHT TO LIVE(1917), d; LOVE DOCTOR, THE(1917), d; MAELSTROM, THE(1917), d; SOLDIERS OF CHANCE(1917), d; STOLEN TREATY, THE(1917), d; TRANSGRESSION(1917), d; BACHELOR'S CHILDREN, A(1918); GAME WITH FATE, A(1918), d; GOLDEN GOAL, THE(1918), d; GREEN GOD, THE(1918), d; HOARDED ASSETS(1918), d; TANGLED LIVES(1918), d; BEATING THE ODDS(1919), d; BEAUTY PROOF(1919), d; FIGHTING DESTINY(1919), d; GAMBLERS, THE(1919), d; IN HONOR'S WEB(1919), d; MAN WHO WON, THE(1919), d; SILENT STRENGTH(1919), d; BROKEN GATE, THE(1920), d; CHILDREN NOT WANTED(1920), d; DARKEST HOUR, THE(1920), d; HER UNWILLING HUSBAND(1920), d; MILESTONES(1920), d; FALSE KISSES(1921), d; GOLDEN GALLOWS, THE(1922), d; SHATTERED DREAMS(1922), d

Anthony Scaretti
PLEASURE PLANTATION(1970), p

Alan Scarfe
CATHY'S CURSE(1977, Can.); DESERTERS(1983, Can.)
1984
BAY BOY(1984, Can.)

Gerald Scarfe
PINK FLOYD–THE WALL(1982, Brit.), anim

Ferdinando Scarfiotti
KISS THE OTHER SHEIK(1968, Fr./Ital.), art d; DEATH IN VENICE(1971, Ital./Fr.), art d; AVANTI!(1972), art d; DAISY MILLER(1974), art d

Ferninando Scarfiotti
LISTEN, LET'S MAKE LOVE(1969, Fr./Ital.), art d, cos

Ludovico Scarfiotti
GRAND PRIX(1966)

Eduardo Scarfoglio
TIMES GONE BY(1953, Ital.), w

Karen Scargill
SCROOGE(1970, Brit.)

Roberto Scaringella
ACCATTONE!(1961, Ital.)

Lily Scaringi
NIGHTS OF LUCRETIA BORGIA, THE(1960, Ital.)
Alessandro Scarlatti
EXTERMINATING ANGEL, THE(1967, Mex.), m
Domenico Scarlatti
DEVIL'S EYE, THE(1960, Swed.), m
Glauco Scarlini
LA TRAVIATA(1968, Ital.)
Rose Ann Scarmardella
BADGE 373(1973)
Joe Scarpa
1984
MICKI AND MAUDE(1984)
Renato Scarpa
DON'T LOOK NOW(1973, Brit./Ital.); GIORDANO BRUNO(1973, Ital.)
Umberto Scarpeli
DAVID AND GOLIATH(1961, Ital.), w
Scarpelli
IT HAPPENED IN ROME(1959, Ital.), w; GREAT WAR, THE(1961, Fr., Ital.), w; ORGANIZER, THE(1964, Fr./Ital./Yugo.), w; PIZZA TRIANGLE, THE(1970, Ital./Span.), w; VIVA ITALIA(1978, Ital.), w
Argo Scarpelli
BIG DEAL ON MADONNA STREET, THE(1960), w
Furio Scarpelli
BEST OF ENEMIES, THE(1962), w; LOVE AND LARCENY(1963, Fr./Ital.), w; PASSIONATE THIEF, THE(1963, Ital.), w; CASANOVA '70(1965, Ital.), w; HIGH INFIDELITY(1965, Fr./Ital.), w; BIRDS, THE BEES AND THE ITALIANS, THE(1967), w; OPIATE '67(1967, Fr./Ital.), w; TIGER AND THE PUSSYCAT, THE(1967, U.S., Ital.), w; WITCHES, THE(1969, Fr./Ital.), w
1984
CRACKERS(1984), w; LE BAL(1984, Fr./Ital./Algeria), w
Glenn Scarpelli
NUNZIO(1978); THEY ALL LAUGHED(1981)
Henry Scarpelli
FORCED ENTRY(1975), p, w
Marco Scarpelli
TOTO IN THE MOON(1957, Ital./Span.), ph; DAY IN COURT, A(1965, Ital.), ph
Umberto Scarpelli
FURY OF THE PAGANS(1963, Ital.), w; GIANT OF METROPOLIS, THE(1963, Ital.), d
Giovanni Scarpellini
SANDOKAN THE GREAT(1964, Fr./Ital./Span.), ph
Mario Scarpetta
END OF THE WORLD(in Our Usual Bed In a Night Full of Rain), THE (1978, Ital.)
Carmen Scarpita
GIDGET GOES TO ROME(1963)
Guy Scarpita
SENIORS, THE(1978), ed
Nadia Scarpitia
ADVENTURERS, THE(1970)
Carmen Scarpitta
LA CAGE AUX FOLLES(1979, Fr./Ital.)
1984
BEYOND GOOD AND EVIL(1984, Ital./Fr./Ger.)
Guy Scarpitta
DRIVE-IN(1976), ed
S. C. Scarpitta
SONG OF SONGS(1933), cos
David Scarroll
SCALPEL(1976)
Richard Scarso
SOLOMON KING(1974)
Diana Scarwid
PRETTY BABY(1978); HONEYSUCKLE ROSE(1980); INSIDE MOVES(1980); MOMMIE DEAREST(1981); RUMBLE FISH(1983); SILKWOOD(1983); STRANGE INVADERS(1983)
David Scase
NEVER LOOK BACK(1952, Brit.)
Rosalie Scase
TASTE OF HONEY, A(1962, Brit.)
Arnold Scassi
ON A CLEAR DAY YOU CAN SEE FOREVER(1970), cos
Luce Scatena
SELLERS OF GIRLS(1967, Fr.), cos
Angelo Scatigna
Silents
ROMOLA(1925)
Luigi Scattini
PRIMITIVE LOVE(1966, Ital.), a, d, w; WAR ITALIAN STYLE(1967, Ital.), d; GLASS SPHINX, THE(1968, Egypt/Ital./Span.), d
Monica Scattini
1984
LE BAL(1984, Fr./Ital./Algeria)
Aldo Scavarda
L'AVVENTURA(1960, Ital.), ph; FROM A ROMAN BALCONY(1961, Fr./Ital.), ph; BEFORE THE REVOLUTION(1964, Ital.), ph; THANK YOU, AUNT(1969, Ital.), ph; BLOOD IN THE STREETS(1975, Ital./Fr.), ph
Bartolomeo Scavia
1984
LAST HUNTER, THE(1984, Ital.), prod d&cos
Mimmo Scavia
CHINA IS NEAR(1968, Ital.), set d; VIOLENT FOUR, THE(1968, Ital.), prod D
Leo Scavini
OPERATION KID BROTHER(1967, Ital.)
Romano Scavolini
NIGHTMARE(1981), d&w
Sauro Scavolini
10,000 DOLLARS BLOOD MONEY(1966, Ital.), w; JOHNNY YUMA(1967, Ital.), w; FAMILY, THE(1974, Fr./Ital.), w

Luigi Scavran
HONEY POT, THE(1967, Brit.); STATUE, THE(1971, Brit.)
James Scay
HUNT THE MAN DOWN(1950)
Joe Scedi
MEAN FRANK AND CRAZY TONY(1976, Ital.)
Angela Scellars
CREATURE FROM THE HAUNTED SEA(1961), ed
Minerva Scelza
CADDY SHACK(1980)
Filippo Scelzo
LOYALTY OF LOVE(1937, Ital.); EARTH CRIES OUT, THE(1949, Ital.)
Giorgio Scerbanenco
DEATH TOOK PLACE LAST NIGHT(1970, Ital./Ger.), w
Anna Sceusa
1984
BROADWAY DANNY ROSE(1984)
Liselotte Schaack
TREMENDOUSLY RICH MAN, A(1932, Ger.)
Rudolf Schaad
INVISIBLE OPPONENT(1933, Ger.), ed
Bill Schaaf
1984
FLASH OF GREEN, A(1984)
Edward Schaaf
YOUNG CAPTIVES, THE(1959); DESERT RAVEN, THE(1965); IF HE HOLLERS, LET HIM GO(1968)
Geoff Schaaf
1984
SIGNAL 7(1984), ph
Johannes Schaaf
FIRST LOVE(1970, Ger./Switz.)
Liselott Schaak
DAUGHTER OF EVIL(1930, Ger.)
Katrin Schaake
WHAT'S NEW, PUSSYCAT?(1965, U.S./Fr.); BITTER TEARS OF PETRA VON KANT, THE(1972, Ger.)
Ferdinand Schaal
DAS BOOT(1982)
Richard Schaal
RUSSIANS ARE COMING, THE RUSSIANS ARE COMING, THE(1966); VIRGIN PRESIDENT, THE(1968); SLAUGHTERHOUSE-FIVE(1972); STEELYARD BLUES(1973); AMERICATHON(1979); HOLLYWOOD KNIGHTS, THE(1980); O'HARA'S WIFE(1983)
Wendy Schaal
1984
WHERE THE BOYS ARE '84(1984)
Katrin Schaale
AMERICAN SOLDIER, THE(1970 Ger.)
T. Schaank
NIGHT PEOPLE(1954)
Dick Schaap
GAMBLER, THE(1974); SEMI-TOUGH(1977)
Oskar Von Schab
JONATHAN(1973, Ger.)
Robert Schable
LOCKED DOOR, THE(1929)
Silents
MARRIAGE PRICE(1919); ON WITH THE DANCE(1920); WITHOUT LIMIT(1921); SHERLOCK HOLMES(1922); SISTERS(1922); WOMAN WHO FOOLED HERSELF, THE(1922); IN SEARCH OF A THRILL(1923); NOBODY'S MONEY(1923); SILENT PARTNER, THE(1923); SLANDER THE WOMAN(1923); STRANGER, THE(1924); PARTNERS AGAIN(1926)
Misc. Silents
REDHEAD(1919); TEST OF HONOR, THE(1919)
Robert. Schable
MAN AND THE MOMENT, THE(1929)
Max Schach
CLOWN MUST LAUGH, A(1936, Brit.), p; DISHONOR BRIGHT(1936, Brit.), p; FORBIDDEN MUSIC(1936, Brit.), p; I STAND CONDEMNED(1936, Brit.), p; LOVE IN EXILE(1936, Brit.), p; PUBLIC NUISANCE NO. 1(1936, Brit.), p; SOUTHERN ROSES(1936, Brit.), p; DREAMING LIPS(1937, Brit.), p; FOR VALOR(1937, Brit.), p; LOVE FROM A STRANGER(1937, Brit.), p; SECOND BEST BED(1937, Brit.), p; PRISONER OF CORBAL(1939, Brit.), p; LILAC DOMINO, THE(1940, Brit.), p; WHEN KNIGHTS WERE BOLD(1942, Brit.), p; UNDER SECRET ORDERS(1943, Brit.), p
Kim Schachel
Misc. Talkies
NAUGHTY SCHOOL GIRLS(1977)
Frank Schacher
GEORGE(1973, U.S./Switz.)
Rodolphe Schacher
1984
LIFE IS A BED OF ROSES(1984, Fr.)
Franne Schacht
LASERBLAST(1978), w
Gus Schacht
GENERAL CRACK(1929)
James Schacht
SOD SISTERS(1969)
Sam Schacht
PUZZLE OF A DOWNFALL CHILD(1970); TATTOO(1981)
Bradley Schachter
HALLOWEEN III: SEASON OF THE WITCH(1982)
Felice Schachter
ZAPPED!(1982)
Simone Schachter
IF EVER I SEE YOU AGAIN(1978); LITTLE DARLINGS(1980)

Floyd Schackleford
HARDBOILED ROSE(1929); SAVAGE GIRL, THE(1932); SWING TIME(1936); DOUBLE INDEMNITY(1944)
Silents
ABSENT(1928)
Robert Schackleton
WONDER BOY(1951, Brit./Aust.)
Sam Schact
BADGE 373(1973)
Leon Schactman
WHERE IS MY CHILD?(1937)
Marion Schad
MY BRILLIANT CAREER(1980, Aus.)
Betty Schade
Silents
OPENED SHUTTERS, THE(1914); LOVE GIRL, THE(1916); GIRL IN THE DARK, THE(1918); NOBODY'S WIFE(1918); RIDERS OF VENGEANCE(1919); DARLING MINE(1920); SOUL OF YOUTH, THE(1920); WING TOY(1921)
Misc. Silents
MAN FROM BITTER ROOTS, THE(1916); FIGHTING MAD(1917); REWARD OF THE FAITHLESS, THE(1917); SCARLET CRYSTAL, THE(1917); GUILT OF SILENCE, THE(1918); SCARLET DROP, THE(1918); SCARLET ROAD, THE(1918); WINNER TAKES ALL(1918); WOLF AND HIS MATE, THE(1918); BARE FISTS(1919); BONDS OF LOVE(1919); GIRL IN BOHEMIA, A(1919); GIRL WITH NO REGRETS, THE(1919); HAPPINESS A LA MODE(1919); SPOTLIGHT SADIE(1919); WHO WILL MARRY ME?(1919); SHOD WITH FIRE(1920); FIRST LOVE(1921)
Doris Schade
GERMAN SISTERS, THE(1982, Ger.); VERONIKA VOSS(1982, Ger.); FRIENDS AND HUSBANDS(1983, Ger.)
Jens August Schade
PEOPLE MEET AND SWEET MUSIC FILLS THE HEART(1969, Den./Swed.), w
Miss Betty Schade
Silents
DUMB GIRL OF PORTICI(1916)
Ann Schaefer
SATURDAY'S CHILDREN(1929)
Anne Schaefer
SMILING IRISH EYES(1929); AND SO THEY WERE MARRIED(1936)
Silents
CHORUS GIRL'S ROMANCE, A(1920); NOBODY'S KID(1921); WOLVERINE, THE(1921); ORDEAL, THE(1922); LOVE'S WILDERNESS(1924)
Misc. Silents
JOHANNA ENLISTS(1918); PRICE OF A GOOD TIME, THE(1918); SOCIAL BRIARS(1918); FIGHTING COLLEEN, A(1919); OVER THE GARDEN WALL(1919); SOLITARY SIN, THE(1919); WEAKER VESSEL, THE(1919)
Armand Schaefer
HURRICANE HORSEMAN(1931), d; BATTLING BUCKAROO(1932), d; LAW AND LAWLESS(1932), d; SINISTER HANDS(1932), d; FIGHTING TEXANS(1933), d; OUTLAW JUSTICE(1933), d; TERROR TRAIL(1933), d; LOST JUNGLE(1934), d, w; SAGEBRUSH TRAIL(1934), d; SIXTEEN FATHOMS DEEP(1934), d; SINGING VAGABOND, THE(1935), p; EXILED TO SHANGHAI(1937), p; GIT ALONG, LITTLE DOGIES(1937), p; OLD CORRAL, THE(1937), p; ROOTIN' TOOTIN' RHYTHM(1937), p; SEA RACKETEERS(1937), p; YODELIN' KID FROM PINE RIDGE(1937), p; CALL OF THE YUKON(1938), p; DOWN IN ARKANSAW(1938), p; GANGS OF NEW YORK(1938), p; HOLLYWOOD STADIUM MYSTERY(1938), p; STORM OVER BENGAL(1938), p; CALLING ALL MARINES(1939), p; FEDERAL MAN-HUNT(1939), p; FIGHTING THOROUGHBREDS(1939), p; FLIGHT AT MIDNIGHT(1939), p; IN OLD MONTEREY(1939), p; JEEPERS CREEPERS(1939), p; S.O.S. TIDAL WAVE(1939), p; STREET OF MISSING MEN(1939), p; BARNYARD FOLLIES(1940), p; BOWERY BOY(1940), p; FRIENDLY NEIGHBORS(1940), p; GIRL FROM GOD'S COUNTRY(1940), p; GRAND OLE OPRY(1940), p; IN OLD MISSOURI(1940), p; VILLAGE BARN DANCE(1940), p; WAGONS WESTWARD(1940), p; ARKANSAS JUDGE(1941), p; COUNTRY FAIR(1941), p; MAN BETRAYED, A(1941), p; MERCY ISLAND(1941), p; MOUNTAIN MOONLIGHT(1941), p; PITTSBURGH KID, THE(1941), p; TUXEDO JUNCTION(1941), p; GIRL FROM ALASKA(1942), p; HI, NEIGHBOR(1942), p; OLD HOMESTEAD, THE(1942), p; TRAITOR WITHIN, THE(1942), p; HEADIN' FOR GOD'S COUNTRY(1943), p; HERE COMES ELMER(1943), p; HOOSIER HOLIDAY(1943), p; O, MY DARLING CLEMENTINE(1943), p; SWING YOUR PARTNER(1943), p; JAMBOREE(1944), p; ROSIE THE RIVETER(1944), p; PHANTOM SPEAKS, THE(1945), p; AFFAIRS OF GERALDINE(1946), p; G.I. WAR BRIDES(1946), p; MY PAL TRIGGER(1946), p; SIOUX CITY SUE(1946), p; GHOST GOES WILD, THE(1947), p; LAST ROUND-UP, THE(1947), p; THAT'S MY GAL(1947), p; TRAIL TO SAN ANTONE(1947), p; TWILIGHT ON THE RIO GRANDE(1947), p; LOADED PISTOLS(1948), p; STRAWBERRY ROAN, THE(1948), p; BIG SOMBRERO, THE(1949), p; COWBOY AND THE INDIANS, THE(1949), p; RIDERS IN THE SKY(1949), p; RIDERS OF THE WHISTLING PINES(1949), p; RIM OF THE CANYON(1949), p; SONS OF NEW MEXICO(1949), p; BEYOND THE PURPLE HILLS(1950), p; BLAZING SUN, THE(1950), p; COW TOWN(1950), p; INDIAN TERRITORY(1950), p; MULE TRAIN(1950), p; GENE AUTRY AND THE MOUNTIES(1951), p; HILLS OF UTAH(1951), p; SILVER CANYON(1951), p; TEXANS NEVER CRY(1951), p; VALLEY OF FIRE(1951), p; WHIRLWIND(1951), p; APACHE COUNTRY(1952), p; BARBED WIRE(1952), p; BLUE CANADIAN ROCKIES(1952), p; NIGHT STAGE TO GALVESTON(1952), p; OLD WEST, THE(1952), p; WAGON TEAM(1952), p; GOLDTOWN GHOST RIDERS(1953), p; LAST OF THE PONY RIDERS(1953), p; ON TOP OF OLD SMOKY(1953), p; PACK TRAIN(1953), p; SAGINAW TRAIL(1953), p; WINNING OF THE WEST(1953), p
Misc. Talkies
RECKLESS RIDER, THE(1932), d; WYOMING WHIRLWIND(1932), d
Bill Schaefer
CAPTURE THAT CAPSULE(1961), ed
Billy Schaefer
AS GOOD AS MARRIED(1937)
Billy Kent Schaefer
WIND, THE(1928)
Silents
ENEMY, THE(1927); WARMING UP(1928)
Craig Schaefer
STRIPES(1981)

Ed Schaefer
THIRTEEN HOURS BY AIR(1936)
George Schaefer
MACBETH(1963), d, w; GENERATION(1969), d; PENDULUM(1969), d; DOCTORS' WIVES(1971), d; ONCE UPON A SCOUNDREL(1973), d; ENEMY OF THE PEOPLE, AN(1978), p&d
Misc. Talkies
DEADLY GAMES(1982), d
Hal Schaefer
MONEY TRAP, THE(1966), m; AMSTERDAM KILL, THE(1978, Hong Kong), m
Jack Schaefer
SHANE(1953), w; SILVER WHIP, THE(1953), w; TRIBUTE TO A BADMAN(1956), w; TROOPER HOOK(1957), w; ADVANCE TO THE REAR(1964), w
Jack Warner Schaefer
MONTE WALSH(1970), w
Marie Schaefer
Silents
IS LOVE EVERYTHING?(1924)
Natalie Schaefer
FORTY CARATS(1973)
Robert Schaefer
RAIDERS OF TOMAHAWK CREEK(1950), w; LONE RANGER AND THE LOST CITY OF GOLD, THE(1958), w
Rube Schaefer
OVER 21(1945)
William Schaefer
TO THE SHORES OF HELL(1966), m
A. L. Schaeffer
Silents
SPARROWS(1926)
Albert Schaeffer
Misc. Silents
SET-UP, THE(1926)
Ann Schaeffer
PRISONERS(1929); LILIES OF THE FIELD(1930)
Silents
NIGHT FLYER, THE(1928)
Misc. Silents
GHOST CITY(1921); MAN UNCONQUERABLE, THE(1922); SITTING BULL AT THE "SPIRIT LAKE MASSACRE"(1927); WHEEL OF CHANCE(1928)
Anne Schaeffer
Silents
JUNGLE TRAIL, THE(1919)
Armand Schaeffer
CHEYENNE CYCLONE, THE(1932), d; HELL'S HEADQUARTERS(1932), p; MOUNTAIN RHYTHM(1942), p
Billy Kent Schaeffer
Silents
ARIZONA SWEEPSTAKES(1926); HILLS OF KENTUCKY(1927)
Misc. Silents
HOME MAKER, THE(1925)
Charles Schaeffer
GUN RUNNERS, THE(1958), ed
Misc. Silents
WILD BORN(1927); WINGED HORSEMAN, THE(1929)
Chester A. Schaeffer
BECAUSE THEY'RE YOUNG(1960), ed
Chester Schaeffer
WELL, THE(1951), ed; THIEF, THE(1952), ed; HANNAH LEE(1953), ed; WICKED WOMAN(1953), ed; DUFFY OF SAN QUENTIN(1954), ed; STEEL CAGE, THE(1954), ed; CANYON CROSSROADS(1955), ed; DAVY CROCKETT, KING OF THE WILD FRONTIER(1955), ed; DEADLY MANTIS, THE(1957), ed; THUNDER IN THE SUN(1959), ed; HOUSE IS NOT A HOME, A(1964), ed; CAPER OF THE GOLDEN BULLS, THE(1967), ed
Chester W. Schaeffer
CANTERVILLE GHOST, THE(1944), ed; GENTLE ANNIE(1944), ed; LETTER FOR EVIE, A(1945), ed; TWO SMART PEOPLE(1946), ed; BATTLE OF THE CORAL SEA(1959), ed; TINGLER, THE(1959), ed; LET NO MAN WRITE MY EPITAPH(1960), ed; CRY FOR HAPPY(1961), ed; ONE PLUS ONE(1961, Can.), ed; BALCONY, THE(1963), ed; OSCAR, THE(1966), ed
Earl Schaeffer
Silents
PUTTING IT OVER(1922)
Edward Schaeffer
Silents
KING OF KINGS, THE(1927)
Jerome Schaeffer
RIVER OF NO RETURN(1954)
Rosaline Schaeffer
JESSE JAMES(1939), w
Rube Schaeffer
LADIES' DAY(1943); TREASURE OF MONTE CRISTO(1949)
Willi Schaeffers
SCHLAGER-PARADE(1953)
Hanna Schaer
PARSIFAL(1983, Fr.)
Wolfram Schaerf
LUDWIG(1973, Ital./Ger./Fr.)
Wolfran Schaerf
GREAT BRITISH TRAIN ROBBERY, THE(1967, Ger.)
Jerry Schafer
Misc. Talkies
NOT MY DAUGHTER(1975), d
Martin Schafer
ALICE IN THE CITIES(1974, W. Ger.), ph; KINGS OF THE ROAD(1976, Ger.), ph; RADIO ON(1980, Brit./Ger.), ph; UNSUITABLE JOB FOR A WOMAN, AN(1982, Brit.), ph
1984
FLIGHT TO BERLIN(1984, Ger./Brit.), ph

Natalie Schafer
TIME OF YOUR LIFE, THE(1948); BODY DISAPPEARS, THE(1941); REUNION IN FRANCE(1942); MARRIAGE IS A PRIVATE AFFAIR(1944); KEEP YOUR POWDER DRY(1945); MASQUERADE IN MEXICO(1945); MOLLY AND ME(1945); WONDER MAN(1945); DISHONORED LADY(1947); OTHER LOVE, THE(1947); REPEAT PERFORMANCE(1947); SECRET BEYOND THE DOOR, THE(1948); SNAKE PIT, THE(1948); CAUGHT(1949); CALLAWAY WENT THATAWAY(1951); LAW AND THE LADY, THE(1951); PAYMENT ON DEMAND(1951); TAKE CARE OF MY LITTLE GIRL(1951); JUST ACROSS THE STREET(1952); GIRL NEXT DOOR, THE(1953); CASANOVA'S BIG NIGHT(1954); FEMALE ON THE BEACH(1955); ANASTASIA(1956); FOREVER DARLING(1956); BERNARDINE(1957); OH, MEN! OH, WOMEN!(1957); BACK STREET(1961); SUSAN SLADE(1961); DAY OF THE LOCUST, THE(1975)

Reuben Schafer
THERE IS NO 13(1977)

Rose Schafer
DEVIL STRIKES AT NIGHT, THE(1959, Ger.)

Rosl Schafer
UNWILLING AGENT(1968, Ger.)

Rubin Schafer
GOODBYE COLUMBUS(1969)

Willi Schafer
NAKED AMONG THE WOLVES(1967, Ger.), w

Ed Schaff
STAKEOUT ON DOPE STREET(1958)

Johannes Schaff
DREAM TOWN(1973, Ger.), d&w

Leo Schaff
FAN, THE(1981)

Beth Schaffel
MORTUARY(1983)

Robert Schaffel
LOOKIN' TO GET OUT(1982), p; TABLE FOR FIVE(1983), a, p

Robert L. Schaffel
GORDON'S WAR(1973), p; SUNNYSIDE(1979), p, w

Beth Schaffell
1984
THEY'RE PLAYING WITH FIRE(1984)

Allyson Schaffer
YOUNG EAGLES(1930), ed

Glenn Schaffer
SANTA CLAUS CONQUERS THE MARTIANS(1964)

Jane Schaffer
BIG DOLL HOUSE, THE(1971), p; BIG BIRD CAGE, THE(1972), p

Judit Schaffer
BOYS OF PAUL STREET, THE(1969, Hung./US), cos

Marie Schaffer
Silents
CHILD FOR SALE, A(1920)

Peggy Schaffer
Silents
NINE AND THREE-FIFTHS SECONDS(1925); KING OF KINGS, THE(1927)

Rube Schaffer
PLAYMATES(1941); FRENCHMAN'S CREEK(1944); LOST TRIBE, THE(1949); SEMINOLE UPRISING(1955); SPARTACUS(1960)

Sharon Schaffer
1984
CITY HEAT(1984); PLACES IN THE HEART(1984), a, stunts

Joseph Schaffler
REAL LIFE(1979)

Franklin Schaffner
BEST MAN, THE(1964), d

Franklin J. Schaffner
STRIPPER, THE(1963), d; WAR LORD, THE(1965), d; DOUBLE MAN, THE(1967), a, d; PLANET OF THE APES(1968), d; PATTON(1970), d; NICHOLAS AND ALEXANDRA(1971, Brit.), d; PAPILLON(1973), p, d; ISLANDS IN THE STREAM(1977), d; BOYS FROM BRAZIL, THE(1978), d; SPHINX(1981), d; YES, GIORGIO(1982), d

Franz Schafheitlin
MONEY ON THE STREET(1930, Aust.); STORM IN A WATER GLASS(1931, Aust.); ETERNAL MASK, THE(1937, Swiss); AFFAIRS OF DR. HOLL(1954, Ger.); ETERNAL LOVE(1960, Ger.); HAMLET(1962, Ger.)

Renee Schafransky
1984
VARIETY(1984), p

Tony Schafrazi
SUBWAY RIDERS(1981)

June Schafter
THRILL OF A LIFETIME(1937)

Franz Schaftheitlein
WOODEN HORSE, THE(1951)

Riek Schagen
LITTLE ARK, THE(1972)

Karl Schaidler
BARBER OF SEVILLE, THE(1973, Ger./Fr.)

Don Schain
H.O.T.S.(1979), p
Misc. Talkies
ABDUCTORS, THE(1972), d; GINGER(1972), d; GIRLS ARE FOR LOVING(1973), d; TOO HOT TO HANDLE(1976), d

Jack Schaindlin
TERESA(1951), md; WHISTLE AT EATON FALLS(1951), md

Ekkehard Schall
CONDEMNED OF ALTONA, THE(1963)

Ekkerhard Schall
WAGNER(1983, Brit./Hung./Aust.)

Harry Sherman Schall
PICNIC(1955)

Theo Schall
RASPUTIN(1932, Ger.)

Wendy Schall
RECORD CITY(1978)

John Schaller
KISMET(1944)

Ramon Schaller
RIDING HIGH(1943)

Bill Schallert
TUNNELVISION(1976)

Edwin Schallert
NIGHT FOR CRIME, A(1942)

William Schallert
RECKLESS MOMENTS, THE(1949); LONELY HEARTS BANDITS(1950); MAN FROM PLANET X, THE(1951); PEOPLE AGAINST O'HARA, THE(1951); CAPTIVE WOMEN(1952); FLAT TOP(1952); HOODLUM EMPIRE(1952); STORM OVER TIBET(1952); PORT SINISTER(1953); SWORD OF VENUS(1953); TORPEDO ALLEY(1953); GOG(1954); HIGH AND THE MIGHTY, THE(1954); RIOT IN CELL BLOCK 11(1954); SHIELD FOR MURDER(1954); THEM!(1954); TOBOR THE GREAT(1954); BLACK TUESDAY(1955); HELL'S HORIZON(1955); SMOKE SIGNAL(1955); BIGGER THAN LIFE(1956); FRIENDLY PERSUASION(1956); GUNSLINGER(1956); RAW EDGE(1956); WRITTEN ON THE WIND(1956); BAND OF ANGELS(1957); GIRL IN THE KREMLIN, THE(1957); INCREDIBLE SHRINKING MAN, THE(1957); MAN IN THE SHADOW(1957); MONOLITH MONSTERS, THE(1957); STORY OF MANKIND, THE(1957); TARNISHED ANGELS, THE(1957); TATTERED DRESS, THE(1957); CRY TERROR(1958); BLUE DENIM(1959); DAY OF THE OUTLAW(1959); PILLOW TALK(1959); SOME CAME RUNNING(1959); GALLANT HOURS, THE(1960); LONELY ARE THE BRAVE(1962); PARADISE ALLEY(1962); HOUR OF THE GUN(1967); IN THE HEAT OF THE NIGHT(1967); SPEEDWAY(1968); WILL PENNY(1968); COLOSSUS: THE FORBIN PROJECT(1969); SAM WHISKEY(1969); COMPUTER WORE TENNIS SHOES, THE(1970); TRIAL OF THE CATONSVILLE NINE, THE(1972); CHARLEY VARRICK(1973); STRONGEST MAN IN THE WORLD, THE(1975); TWILIGHT ZONE–THE MOVIE(1983)
1984
TEACHERS(1984)

Thomas Schalm
GRASS IS SINGING, THE(1982, Brit./Swed.), ed

Tom Schamp
O.S.S.(1946); STRANGE LOVE OF MARTHA IVERS, THE(1946); DESERT FURY(1947)

M. Schanauer
FREUD(1962)

Sidney Schanberg
1984
KILLING FIELDS, THE(1984, Brit.), w

Warren Schannon
EASY LIVING(1949)

Karl Schanzer
TONIGHT FOR SURE(1962); DEMENTIA 13(1963); SPIDER BABY(1968); INCREDIBLE INVASION, THE(1971, Mex./U.S.), w

Orven Schanzer
YANK IN VIET-NAM, A(1964), ed

Rudolph Schanzer
BRIDE OF THE REGIMENT(1930), w; THAT LADY IN ERMINE(1948), w
Silents
MADAME POMPADOUR(1927, Brit.), w

John Schapar
CAPTAIN SINDBAD(1963)

Rainer Schaper
MALOU(1983), art d
1984
FLIGHT TO BERLIN(1984, Ger./Brit.), art d

Alan Scharf
TENTACLES(1977, Ital.)

Erwin Scharf
INVISIBLE OPPONENT(1933, Ger.), art d; KILL OR BE KILLED(1950), art d

Heidi Scharf
CITY OF TORMENT(1950, Ger.)

Jillian Scharf
1984
FLAMINGO KID, THE(1984)

Sabrina Scharf
HELL'S ANGELS ON WHEELS(1967); EASY RIDER(1969)

Sabrini Scharf
VIRGIN PRESIDENT, THE(1968)

Walter Scharf
FLYING TIGERS(1942), md; ICE-CAPADES REVUE(1942), md; CHATTERBOX(1943), md; HIT PARADE OF 1943(1943), md; IN OLD OKLAHOMA(1943), m; JOHNNY DOUGHBOY(1943), md; NOBODY'S DARLING(1943), md; SECRETS OF THE UNDERGROUND(1943), md; SHANTYTOWN(1943), md; SLEEPY LAGOON(1943), md; SOMEONE TO REMEMBER(1943), md; THUMBS UP(1943), md; ATLANTIC CITY(1944), m; CASANOVA IN BURLESQUE(1944), md; COWBOY AND THE SENORITA(1944), md; FIGHTING SEABEES, THE(1944), m; LADY AND THE MONSTER, THE(1944), m; LAKE PLACID SERENADE(1944), md; STORM OVER LISBON(1944), m; CHEATERS, THE(1945), m; DAKOTA(1945), md; EARL CARROLL'S VANITIES(1945), m; LOVE, HONOR AND GOODBYE(1945), md; MEXICANA(1945), md; WOMAN WHO CAME BACK(1945), md; I'VE ALWAYS LOVED YOU(1946), md; MURDER IN THE MUSIC HALL(1946), md; ARE YOU WITH IT?(1948), m; CASBAH(1948), m; COUNTESS OF MONTE CRISTO, THE(1948), m; MEXICAN HAYRIDE(1948), m, md; SAXON CHARM, THE(1948), m; ABANDONED(1949), m; CITY ACROSS THE RIVER(1949), m; RED CANYON(1949), m; TAKE ONE FALSE STEP(1949), m; CURTAIN CALL AT CACTUS CREEK(1950), m; DEPORTED(1950), m; SIERRA(1950), m; SOUTH SEA SINNER(1950), m; TWO TICKETS TO BROADWAY(1951), m; HANS CHRISTIAN ANDERSEN(1952), md; FRENCH LINE, THE(1954), m; THREE RING CIRCUS(1954), m; ARTISTS AND MODELS(1955), m; YOU'RE NEVER TOO YOUNG(1955), m; HOLLYWOOD OR BUST(1956), m, md; THREE FOR JAMIE DAWN(1956), m; THREE VIOLENT PEOPLE(1956), m, md; TIMETABLE(1956), m, md; JOKER IS WILD, THE(1957), m, md; LOVING YOU(1957), m, md; SAD SACK, THE(1957), m, md; GEISHA BOY, THE(1958), m; KING CREOLE(1958), m; ROCK-A-BYE BABY(1958), m; DON'T GIVE

UP THE SHIP(1959), m; BELLBOY, THE(1960), m; CINDERFELLA(1960), m; ERRAND BOY, THE(1961), m; LADIES MAN, THE(1961), m; POCKETFUL OF MIRACLES(1961), m, md; IT'S ONLY MONEY(1962), m; MY SIX LOVES(1963), m; NUTTY PROFESSOR, THE(1963), m; GUNS OF DIABLO(1964), m; HONEYMOON HOTEL(1964), m, md; WHERE LOVE HAS GONE(1964), m; BIRDS AND THE BEES, THE(1965), m; TICKLE ME(1965), md; IF IT'S TUESDAY, THIS MUST BE BELGIUM(1969), m; PENDULUM(1969), m; CHEYENNE SOCIAL CLUB, THE(1970), m, md; MR. MAGOO'S HOLIDAY FESTIVAL(1970), md; WILLY WONKA AND THE CHOCOLATE FACTORY(1971), m, md; BEN(1972), m; WALKING TALL(1973), m; WALKING TALL, PART II(1975), m; FINAL CHAPTER–WALKING TALL zero(1977), m; THIS IS ELVIS(1982), m; TWILIGHT TIME(1983, U.S./Yugo.), m

Werner Scharfenberger
TURKISH CUCUMBER, THE(1963, Ger.), m

Herman Scharff
FAR HORIZONS, THE(1955)

Lester Scharff
EARTHBOUND(1940); MAN WHO WOULDN'T TALK, THE(1940); GREAT COMMANDMENT, THE(1941); REMEDY FOR RICHES(1941); SECRETS OF THE LONE WOLF(1941); UNHOLY PARTNERS(1941)

Peter Scharff
SERENADE FOR TWO SPIES(1966, Ital./Ger.), art d; PAPER TIGER(1975, Brit.), art d; WHO?(1975, Brit./Ger.), art d

Bobo Scharffe
ONE TOO MANY(1950)

Lester Schariff
Silents
NEW YORK(1927)

Lynda Scharnott
Misc. Talkies
INSTRUCTOR, THE(1983)

Walter Schart
FUNNY GIRL(1968), md

Dore Schary
FOG(1934), w; FURY OF THE JUNGLE(1934), w; HE COULDN'T TAKE IT(1934), w; LET'S TALK IT OVER(1934), w; MOST PRECIOUS THING IN LIFE(1934), w; MURDER IN THE CLOUDS(1934), w; YOUNG AND BEAUTIFUL(1934), w; CHINATOWN SQUAD(1935), w; RED HOT TIRES(1935), w; YOUR UNCLE DUDLEY(1935), w; HER MASTER'S VOICE(1936), w; TIMOTHY'S QUEST(1936), w; BIG CITY(1937), w; GIRL FROM SCOTLAND YARD, THE(1937), w; MIND YOUR OWN BUSINESS(1937), w; OUTCAST(1937), w; BOYS TOWN(1938), w; LADIES IN DISTRESS(1938), w; BROADWAY MELODY OF 1940(1940), w; EDISON, THE MAN(1940), w; YOUNG TOM EDISON(1940), w; MARRIED BACHELOR(1941), w; I'LL BE SEEING YOU(1944), p; LIVE WIRES(1946), w; SPIRAL STAIRCASE, THE(1946), p; TILL THE END OF TIME(1946), p; BACHELOR AND THE BOBBY-SOXER, THE(1947), p; FARMER'S DAUGHTER, THE(1947), p; EVERY GIRL SHOULD BE MARRIED(1948), p; BATTLEGROUND(1949), p; BOY WITH THE GREEN HAIR, THE(1949), p; GO FOR BROKE(1951), p; IT'S A BIG COUNTRY(1951), p; WESTWARD THE WOMEN(1951), p; PLYMOUTH ADVENTURE(1952), p; WASHINGTON STORY(1952), p; DREAM WIFE(1953), p; TAKE THE HIGH GROUND(1953), p; BAD DAY AT BLACK ROCK(1955), p; LAST HUNT, THE(1956), p; SWAN, THE(1956), p; DESIGNING WOMAN(1957), p; LONELYHEARTS(1958), p, w; SUNRISE AT CAMPOBELLO(1960), p, w; ACT ONE(1964), p,d&w

Solveigh Schattmann
TAKE HER BY SURPRISE(1967, Can.)

Lloyd Schattyn
DELIRIUM(1979)

Jack Schatz
PAPER LION(1968), ph

Sam Schatz
TRON(1982)

Willi Schatz
UNCLE TOM'S CABIN(1969, Fr./Ital./Ger./Yugo.), art d

Willy Schatz
LOLA MONTES(1955, Fr./Ger.), art d; JOURNEY TO THE LOST CITY(1960, Ger./Fr./Ital.), art d

Jerry Schatzberg
PUZZLE OF A DOWNFALL CHILD(1970), d, w; PANIC IN NEEDLE PARK(1971), d; SCARECROW(1973), d; DANDY, THE ALL AMERICAN GIRL(1976), p&d; SEDUCTION OF JOE TYNAN, THE(1979), d; HONEYSUCKLE ROSE(1980), d
1984
MISUNDERSTOOD(1984), d; NO SMALL AFFAIR(1984), d

Maureen Ann Schatzberg
1984
NO SMALL AFFAIR(1984)

Sally Schaub
1984
CRACKERS(1984); NO SMALL AFFAIR(1984)

Byron Schauer
Misc. Talkies
ARNOLD'S WRECKING CO.(1973)

Elsie T. Schauffler
PARNELL(1937), w

H.H. Schaufuss
BOCCACCIO(1936, Ger.)

Hans Schaufuss
EMIL AND THE DETECTIVE(1931, Ger.)

Hans H. Schaufuss
COURT CONCERT, THE(1936, Ger.)

Hans Hermann Schaufuss
HIS MAJESTY, KING BALLYHOO(1931, Ger.); TRUNKS OF MR. O.F., THE(1932, Ger.)

Hans Joachim Schaufuss
WHITE DEMON, THE(1932, Ger.)

Eva Schauland
IT'S HOT IN PARADISE(1962, Ger./Yugo.)

Gisela Schauroth
SLEEPING BEAUTY(1965, Ger.)

E. Richard Schayer
SPIRIT OF NOTRE DAME, THE(1931), w
Silents
ABABIAN KNIGHT, AN(1920), w; KILLER, THE(1921), w; MY DAD(1922), w; HOOK AND LADDER(1924), w; RIDE FOR YOUR LIFE(1924), w; RIDGEWAY OF MONTANA(1924), w; SAWDUST TRAIL(1924), w; HURRICANE KID, THE(1925), w; RUSTLER'S RANCH(1926), w; TELL IT TO THE MARINES(1926), w

Richard Schayer
CHILDREN OF PLEASURE(1930), w; FREE AND EASY(1930), w; MEN OF THE NORTH(1930), w; DANCE, FOOLS, DANCE(1931), w; JUST A GIGOLO(1931), w; PARLOR, BEDROOM AND BATH(1931), w; PRIVATE LIVES(1931), w; TRADER HORN(1931), w; ALL-AMERICAN, THE(1932), w; DESTRY RIDES AGAIN(1932), w; IMPATIENT MAIDEN(1932), w; MUMMY, THE(1932), w; MY PAL, THE KING(1932), w; NIGHT WORLD(1932), w; COCKTAIL HOUR(1933), w; PRIVATE JONES(1933), w; MEANEST GAL IN TOWN, THE(1934), w; WINNING TICKET, THE(1935), w; DANGEROUS WATERS(1936), w; DEVIL IS A SISSY, THE(1936), w; BLACK ARROW(1948), w; DAVY CROCKETT, INDIAN SCOUT(1950), w; IROQUOIS TRAIL, THE(1950), w; KIM(1950), w; INDIAN UPRISING(1951), w; LORNA DOONE(1951), w; TEXAS RANGERS, THE(1951), w; CRIPPLE CREEK(1952), w; BANDITS OF CORSICA, THE(1953), w; GUN BELT(1953), w; STEEL LADY, THE(1953), w; KHYBER PATROL(1954), w; LONE GUN, THE(1954), w; TOP GUN(1955), w; GUN BROTHERS(1956), w; FIVE GUNS TO TOMBSTONE(1961), w; GUN FIGHT(1961), w; SWORD OF LANCELOT(1963, Brit.), w; ARIZONA RAIDERS(1965), w
Silents
ON ZE BOULEVARD(1927), w; ACROSS THE SINGAPORE(1928), w; ACTRESS, THE(1928), w; CAMERAMAN, THE(1928), w; LAW OF THE RANGE, THE(1928), w; FLYING FEET, THE(1929), w; HONEYMOON(1929), w; SPITE MARRIAGE(1929), w; WHERE EAST IS EAST(1929), w; WILD ORCHIDS(1929), w

Leon Schechter
Misc. Talkies
PEOPLE THAT SHALL NOT DIE, A(1939)

Jeffrey Schechtman
1984
BODY ROCK(1984), p

Max Scheck
FOOTLIGHTS AND FOOLS(1929), ch; FOX MOVIETONE FOLLIES OF 1930(1930), ch; SWEETHEART OF THE NAVY(1937), ch

Muriel Scheck
SMARTEST GIRL IN TOWN(1936), w

Edie Schecter
SMITHEREENS(1982)

Martin Schecter
SPRING FEVER(1983, Can.)

Jeff Schectman
PIRANHA II: THE SPAWNING(1981, Neth.), p

Ann Schedeen
EMBRYO(1976)

Anne Schedeen
SECOND THOUGHTS(1983)

Sara Schedeen
LITTLE SEX, A(1982)

Karl Schedit
IN A YEAR OF THIRTEEN MOONS(1980, Ger.)

Tamara Schee
UNFAITHFULLY YOURS(1948); HOUSE ON TELEGRAPH HILL(1951)

Rich Scheeland
Misc. Talkies
LIFE AND LEGEND OF BUFFALO JONES, THE(1976); BUFFALO RIDER(1978)

Karlheinz Scheer
MISSION STARDUST(1968, Ital./Span./Ger.), w

Phil Scheer
INVISIBLE INVADERS(1959), makeup

Bob Scheerer
ANGEL COMES TO BROOKLYN, AN(1945)

Bobby Scheerer
HOW'S ABOUT IT?(1943); MOONLIGHT IN VERMONT(1943); MR. BIG(1943); PATRICK THE GREAT(1945)

Richard Scheerer
WORLD'S GREATEST ATHLETE, THE(1973), d

Robert Scheerer
MARGIE(1946); ADAM AT 6 A.M.(1970), d; HOW TO BEAT THE HIGH COST OF LIVING(1980), d

William Scheerr
COME FILL THE CUP(1951), ph

Fritzi Scheff
FOLLIES GIRL(1943)
Silents
PRETTY MRS. SMITH(1915)

Michael Scheff
AIRPORT '77(1977), w

Werner Scheff
JOHNNY STEALS EUROPE(1932, Ger.), w

Dick Scheffer
LIFT, THE(1983, Neth.)

Jean-Jacques Scheffer
1984
LES COMPERES(1984, Fr.)

Stacey Schefflin
SPRING FEVER(1983, Can.)

Eugene Schefftan
NORAH O'NEALE(1934, Brit.), ph

Bert Schefter
TALL TEXAN, THE(1953), m

Georges Schehade
GOHA(1958, Tunisia), w

K.C. Scheibel
PRIVATE SCHOOL(1983), set d
1984
CHOOSE ME(1984), set d

Francis J. Scheid
THEM!(1954), spec eff
Karl Scheid
AMERICAN SOLDIER, THE(1970 Ger.)
Michelle Scheideler
TAKING OFF(1971)
Cynthia Scheider
LAST EMBRACE(1979); EYEWITNESS(1981), ed; CHILLY SCENES OF WINTER(1982), ed; WITHOUT A TRACE(1983), ed
Peter Scheider
BLACK SPIDER, THE(1983, Swit.)
Roy Scheider
CURSE OF THE LIVING CORPSE, THE(1964); STILETTO(1969); LOVING(1970); FRENCH CONNECTION, THE(1971); FRENCH CONSPIRACY, THE(1973, Fr.); OUTSIDE MAN, THE(1973, U.S./FR.); SEVEN UPS(1973); JAWS(1975); SHEILA LEVINE IS DEAD AND LIVING IN NEW YORK(1975); MARATHON MAN(1976); SORCERER(1977); JAWS II(1978); ALL THAT JAZZ(1979); LAST EMBRACE(1979); STILL OF THE NIGHT(1982); BLUE THUNDER(1983)
1984
2010(1984)
Hans Scheikart
MARRIAGE IN THE SHADOWS(1948, Ger.), d&w
Lou Scheimer
JOURNEY BACK TO OZ(1974), p; MIGHTY MOUSE IN THE GREAT SPACE CHASE(1983), p
Loren Schein
MICROWAVE MASSACRE(1983)
Raynor Scheine
LOVESICK(1983)
Andrew Scheinman
AWAKENING, THE(1980), p; MOUNTAIN MEN, THE(1980), p; MODERN ROMANCE(1981), p
Olga Scheinpflugova
FIFTH HORSEMAN IS FEAR, THE(1968, Czech.)
Clemens Scheitz
NOSFERATU, THE VAMPIRE(1979, Fr./Ger.)
Fred Scheiwiller
PRIZE, THE(1963); WHAT'S UP, DOC?(1972); DAY OF THE LOCUST, THE(1975); MOVIE MOVIE(1978)
Witold Schejbal
1984
PLOUGHMAN'S LUNCH, THE(1984, Brit.)
K.C. Schelbel
ANDROID(1982), art d
George Schelderup
SILVER FLEET, THE(1945, Brit.)
Gerik Schelderupp
OPERATION DIAMOND(1948, Brit.)
Linda Scheley
MONOLITH MONSTERS, THE(1957)
Carl Schell
WEREWOLF IN A GIRL'S DORMITORY(1961, Ital./Aust.); QUICK, LET'S GET MARRIED(1965); BLUE MAX, THE(1966)
Misc. Talkies
CONFESSION, THE(1964)
Catherine Schell
BLACK WINDMILL, THE(1974, Brit.); CALLAN(1975, Brit.); RETURN OF THE PINK PANTHER, THE(1975, Brit.); GULLIVER'S TRAVELS(1977, Brit., Bel.); PRISONER OF ZENDA, THE(1979)
Howard Schell
COME SPY WITH ME(1967)
Karl Schell
ESCAPE FROM EAST BERLIN(1962)
Leo Schell
PROWL GIRLS(1968)
Maria Schell
ANGEL WITH THE TRUMPET, THE(1950, Brit.); MAGIC BOX, THE(1952, Brit.); SO LITTLE TIME(1953, Brit.); AFFAIRS OF DR. HOLL(1954, Ger.); HEART OF THE MATTER, THE(1954, Brit.); NAPOLEON(1955, Fr.); RATS, THE(1955, Ger.); AS LONG AS YOU'RE NEAR ME(1956, Ger.); GERVAISE(1956, Fr.); LAST BRIDGE, THE(1957, Aust.); BROTHERS KARAMAZOV, THE(1958); DREADING LIPS(1958, Ger.); HANGING TREE, THE(1959); SINS OF ROSE BERND, THE(1959, Ger.); AS THE SEA RAGES(1960 Ger.); CIMARRON(1960); DAY WILL COME, A(1960, Ger.); MARK, THE(1961, Brit.); WHITE NIGHTS(1961, Ital./Fr.); END OF DESIRE(1962 Fr./Ital.); I, TOO, AM ONLY A WOMAN(1963, Ger.); ONLY A WOMAN(1966, Ger.); DEVIL BY THE TAIL, THE(1969, Fr./Ital.); ODESSA FILE, THE(1974, Brit./Ger.); TWIST, THE(1976, Fr.); VOYAGE OF THE DAMNED(1976, Brit.); SUPERMAN(1978); JUST A GIGOLO(1979, Ger.); LA PASSANTE(1983, Fr./Ger.)
1984
1919(1984, Brit.)
Misc. Talkies
99 WOMEN(1969, Brit./Span./Ger./Ital.)
Maximilian Schell
YOUNG LIONS, THE(1958); JUDGMENT AT NUREMBERG(1961); FIVE FINGER EXERCISE(1962); HAMLET(1962, Ger.); RELUCTANT SAINT, THE(1962, U.S./Ital.); CONDEMNED OF ALTONA, THE(1963); TOPKAPI(1964); RETURN FROM THE ASHES(1965, U.S./Brit.); COUNTERPOINT(1967); DEADLY AFFAIR, THE(1967, Brit.); DESPERATE ONES, THE(1968 U.S./Span.); CASTLE, THE(1969, Ger.), a, p; KRAKATOA, EAST OF JAVA(1969); FIRST LOVE(1970, Ger./Switz.), a, p, d, w; POPE JOAN(1972, Brit.); ODESSA FILE, THE(1974, Brit./Ger.); PEDESTRIAN, THE(1974, Ger.), a, p, d&w; MAN IN THE GLASS BOOTH, THE(1975); END OF THE GAME(1976, Ger./Ital.), p, d, w; ST. IVES(1976); BRIDGE TOO FAR, A(1977, Brit.); CROSS OF IRON(1977, Brit., Ger.); DAY THAT SHOOK THE WORLD, THE(1977, Yugo./Czech.); JULIA(1977); AVALANCHE EXPRESS(1979); BLACK HOLE, THE(1979); PLAYERS(1979); CHOSEN, THE(1982)
Ronnie Schell
GUS(1976); SHAGGY D.A., THE(1976); CAT FROM OUTER SPACE, THE(1978); LOVE AT FIRST BITE(1979); HOW TO BEAT THE HIGH COST OF LIVING(1980); DEVIL AND MAX DEVLIN, THE(1981)

Ruth Schell
MAYA(1982), d, ed
Ted Schell
TASTE OF BLOOD, A(1967)
August Schellenberg
POWER PLAY(1978, Brit./Can.); ONE MAN(1979, Can.); BEAR ISLAND(1980, Brit.-Can.); DEATH HUNT(1981); HEAVY METAL(1981, Can.); CROSS COUNTRY(1983, Can.); RUNNING BRAVE(1983, Can.)
1984
COVERGIRL(1984, Can.); KINGS AND DESPERATE MEN(1984, Brit.)
George Scheller
HAPPY DAYS(1930)
Henning Schellerup
FANDANGO(1970), p; ONLY WAY HOME, THE(1972), ph; SWEET JESUS, PREACHER MAN(1973), d; BLACK SAMSON(1974), ph; KISS OF THE TARANTULA(1975), ph; GUARDIAN OF THE WILDERNESS(1977), ph; LINCOLN CONSPIRACY, THE(1977), ph; BEYOND AND BACK(1978), ph; IN SEARCH OF HISTORIC JESUS(1980), d
1984
SILENT NIGHT, DEADLY NIGHT(1984), ph
Edmund Schellhammer
OPERETTA(1949, Ger.)
Bud Schelling
GLEN OR GLENDA(1953), ed
Charles Schelling
MOTOR PSYCHO(1965), ed; ROPE OF FLESH(1965), ed; BLACK CAT, THE(1966), ed
R. B. Schellinger
Silents
KAISER'S FINISH, THE(1918), ph; NEVER SAY QUIT(1919), ph
Rial Schellinger
Silents
MISCHIEF MAKER, THE(1916), ph; MODERN CINDERELLA, A(1917), ph; MASTER MIND, THE(1920), ph
Rial B. Schellinger
Silents
MY FOUR YEARS IN GERMANY(1918), ph
Erich Schellow
CAPTAIN FROM KOEPENICK, THE(1956, Ger.); VOR SONNENUNTERGANG(1961, Ger.); CITY OF SECRETS(1963, Ger.)
Rosaria Schemmari
PASSION OF LOVE(1982, Ital./Fr.)
Aubrey Schenck
JOHNNY COMES FLYING HOME(1946), p; SHOCK(1946), p; STRANGE TRIANGLE(1946), p; IT'S A JOKE, SON!(1947), p; REPEAT PERFORMANCE(1947), p; T-MEN(1947), p; MICKEY(1948), p; DOWN MEMORY LANE(1949), p; PORT OF NEW YORK(1949), p; UNDERCOVER GIRL(1950), p; WYOMING MAIL(1950), p; FAT MAN, THE(1951), p; SHIELD FOR MURDER(1954), p; BOP GIRL GOES CALYPSO(1957), p; JUNGLE HEAT(1957), p; OUTLAW'S SON(1957), p; UNTAMED YOUTH(1957), p; FORT BOWIE(1958), p; VIOLENT ROAD(1958), p; BORN RECKLESS(1959), p, w; UP PERISCOPE(1959), p; WILD HARVEST(1962), p; ROBINSON CRUSOE ON MARS(1964), p; DAUGHTERS OF SATAN(1972), p
Earl Schenck
GUY NAMED JOE, A(1943); HEAVENLY BODY, THE(1943); ABILENE TOWN(1946); LEAVE HER TO HEAVEN(1946)
Silents
FALSE FRIEND, THE(1917); KAISER'S FINISH, THE(1918); MY FOUR YEARS IN GERMANY(1918); BURIED TREASURE(1921); NO WOMAN KNOWS(1921); SALOME(1922); ASHES OF VENGEANCE(1923); SONG OF LOVE, THE(1923); ABRAHAM LINCOLN(1924)
Misc. Silents
MADNESS OF HELEN, THE(1916); LOVE AND AMBITION(1917); WEAVERS OF LIFE(1917); HARVEST MOON, THE(1920); GOOD WOMEN(1921); LUCKY CARSON(1921); AT THE SIGN OF THE JACK O'LANTERN(1922); YANKEE MADNESS(1924); DOLLAR DOWN(1925); HUNTED WOMAN, THE(1925); TIDES OF PASSION(1925)
Earl O. Schenck
Misc. Silents
HAUNTED MANOR, THE(1916); ISLE OF LOVE, THE(1916)
George Schenck
KILL A DRAGON(1967), w; MORE DEAD THAN ALIVE(1968), w; BARQUERO(1970), w; SUPERBEAST(1972), p,d&w; FUTUREWORLD(1976), w; ESCAPE 2000(1983, Aus.), w
George W. Schenck
DON'T WORRY, WE'LL THINK OF A TITLE(1966), w
Joseph Schenck
Silents
ETERNAL LOVE(1929), p
Joseph M. Schenck
LADY OF THE PAVEMENTS(1929), p; BAD ONE, THE(1930), p; DU BARRY, WOMAN OF PASSION(1930), p; INDISCREET(1931), p; KIKI(1931), p; RAIN(1932), p; AS YOU LIKE IT(1936, Brit.), p
Silents
BRANDED WOMAN, THE(1920), p; LESSONS IN LOVE(1921), p; LOVE'S REDEMPTION(1921), p; EAST IS WEST(1922), p; ASHES OF VENGEANCE(1923), p; THREE AGES, THE(1923), p; NAVIGATOR, THE(1924), p; KIKI(1926), p; GENERAL, THE(1927), p
Joseph T. Schenck
THEY LEARNED ABOUT WOMEN(1930)
Stephen Schenck
WELCOME TO BLOOD CITY(1977, Brit./Can.), w
Walter Schenck
HORSE IN THE GRAY FLANNEL SUIT, THE(1968), makeup
Wolfgang Schenck
EFFI BRIEST(1974, Ger.)
Aubrey Schenk
RED STALLION IN THE ROCKIES(1949), p; BIG HOUSE, U.S.A.(1955), p; GIRL IN BLACK STOCKINGS(1957), p

Earl Schenk
Silents
BEYOND(1921)
Joseph M. Schenk
NEW YORK NIGHTS(1929), p; BULLDOG DRUMMOND STRIKES BACK(1934), p
Walter Schenk
ROPE OF FLESH(1965), ph; BLACK CAT, THE(1966), ph
Peter Schenke
ONE OF OUR AIRCRAFT IS MISSING(1942, Brit.)
Calvin Schenkel
TWO HUNDRED MOTELS(1971, Brit.), prod d
Chris Schenkel
GOODBYE COLUMBUS(1969); MAURIE(1973); DREAMER(1979)
Diane Schenker
CINDERELLA LIBERTY(1973)
Ine Schenkkan
SPETTERS(1983, Holland), ed
1984
FOURTH MAN, THE(1984, Neth.), ed
Robert Schenkkan
1984
PLACES IN THE HEART(1984)
Judy Schenz
IN FAST COMPANY(1946)
Fred Schepisi
DEVIL'S PLAYGROUND, THE(1976, Aus.), p,d&w; CHANT OF JIMMIE BLACK-SMITH, THE(1980, Aus.), p,d&w; BARBAROSA(1982), d
1984
ICEMAN(1984), d
Fred A. Schepisi
LIBIDO(1973, Aus.), d
Shawn Schepps
10 TO MIDNIGHT(1983)
1984
RACING WITH THE MOON(1984); TERMINATOR, THE(1984)
Yevgeny Scherbakov
BLUE BIRD, THE(1976)
Eugene Scherer
FIREFOX(1982)
Gene Scherer
STRIPES(1981)
Norbert Scherer
MARRIAGE OF MARIA BRAUN, THE(1979, Ger.), a, art d
Edgar J. Scherick
TAKING OF PELHAM ONE, TWO, THREE, THE(1974), p; FOR LOVE OF IVY(1968), p; JENNY(1969), p; HEARTBREAK KID, THE(1972), p; STEPFORD WIVES, THE(1975), p; AMERICAN SUCCESS COMPANY, THE(1980), p; KING OF COMEDY, THE(1983)
1984
MRS. SOFFEL(1984), p; RECKLESS(1984), p
Kathleen Scherini
BIONIC BOY, THE(1977, Hong Kong/Phil.)
Elsje Scherjon
GIRL WITH THE RED HAIR, THE(1983, Neth.)
Oscar Scherl
PALM BEACH(1979, Aus.), ph
Tom Scherman
INCREDIBLY STRANGE CREATURES WHO STOPPED LIVING AND BECAME CRAZY MIXED-UP ZOMBIES, THE(1965), makeup; THRILL KILLERS, THE(1965), art d
Jules Schermer
SULLIVANS, THE(1944), w; FRAMED(1947), p; MAN FROM COLORADO, THE(1948), p; ILLEGAL ENTRY(1949), p; UNION STATION(1950), p; LYDIA BAI-LEY(1952), p; PRIDE OF ST. LOUIS, THE(1952), p; PICKUP ON SOUTH STREET(1953), p; THESE WILDER YEARS(1956), p; ONIONHEAD(1958), p; DREAM OF KINGS, A(1969), p
Ton Scherpenzeel
SPETTERS(1983, Holland), m
Ivo Scherpiani
RED DESERT(1965, Fr./Ital.)
Margarita Scherr
Misc. Talkies
OUR MAN IN JAMAICA(1965)
Jean Schertler
HOUSE ON SORORITY ROW, THE(1983)
Victor Schertzinger
FASHIONS IN LOVE(1929), d; NOTHING BUT THE TRUTH(1929), d; WHEEL OF LIFE, THE(1929), d; HEADS UP(1930), d; LAUGHING LADY, THE(1930), d; SAFETY IN NUMBERS(1930), d; FRIENDS AND LOVERS(1931), d, m; WOMAN BET-WEEN(1931), d; STRANGE JUSTICE(1932), d, m; UPTOWN NEW YORK(1932), d; COCKTAIL HOUR(1933), d; MY WOMAN(1933), d, m; BELOVED(1934), d, m; ONE NIGHT OF LOVE(1934), d; LET'S LIVE TONIGHT(1935), d; LOVE ME FORE-VER(1935), d, w; MUSIC GOES ROUND, THE(1936), d; SOMETHING TO SING ABOUT(1937), d, w; MIKADO, THE(1939, Brit.), d; RHYTHM ON THE RIVER(1940), d; ROAD TO SINGAPORE(1940), d; BIRTH OF THE BLUES(1941), d; KISS THE BOYS GOODBYE(1941), d; ROAD TO ZANZIBAR(1941), d; FLEET'S IN, THE(1942), d
Misc. Talkies
CONSTANT WOMAN, THE(1933), d
Silents
PINCH HITTER, THE(1917), d; QUICKSANDS(1918), d; BEATING THE GA-ME(1921), d; MADE IN HEAVEN(1921), d; WHAT HAPPENED TO ROSA?(1921), d; KINGDOM WITHIN, THE(1922), d; DOLLAR DEVILS(1923), d; LONELY ROAD, THE(1923), d; LONG LIVE THE KING(1923), d; SCARLET LILY, THE(1923), d; MAN AND MAID(1925), d; RETURN OF PETER GRIMM, THE(1926), d; SIBERIA(1926), d; STAGE MADNESS(1927), d
Misc. Silents
CLODHOPPER, THE(1917), d; SON OF HIS FATHER, THE(1917), d; SUDDEN JIM(1917), d; HOMEBREAKER, THE(1919), d; PEACE OF ROARING RIVER, THE(1919), d; BLOOMING ANGEL, THE(1920), d; BOOTLEGGER'S DAUGHTER, THE(1922), d; HEAD OVER HEELS(1922), d; MR. BARNES OF NEW YORK(1922), d;

SCANDALOUS TONGUES(1922), d; CHASTITY(1923), d; MAN LIFE PASSED BY, THE(1923), d; MAN NEXT DOOR, THE(1923), d; REFUGE(1923), d; BOY OF FLAND-ERS, A(1924), d; BREAD(1924), d; FRIVOLOUS SAL(1925), d; GOLDEN STRAIN, THE(1925), d; THUNDER MOUNTAIN(1925), d; WHEEL, THE(1925), d; LILY, THE(1926), d; HEART OF SALOME, THE(1927), d; SECRET STUDIO, THE(1927), d; FORGOTTEN FACES(1928), d; SHOWDOWN, THE(1928), d; REDSKIN(1929), d
Victor L. Schertzinger
Silents
FAMILY SKELETON, THE(1918), d; NINE O'CLOCK TOWN, A(1918), d, w; PLAY-ING THE GAME(1918), d; EXTRAVAGANCE(1919), d
Misc. Silents
HIS MOTHER'S BOY(1917), d; MILLIONAIRE VAGRANT, THE(1917), d; CLAWS OF THE HUN, THE(1918), d; COALS OF FIRE(1918), d; HIRED MAN, THE(1918), d; HIS OWN HOME TOWN(1918), d; STRING BEANS(1918), d; HARD BOILED(1919), d; JINX(1919), d; LADY OF RED BUTTE, THE(1919), d; OTHER MEN'S WIVES(1919), d; SHERIFF'S SON, THE(1919), d; UPSTAIRS(1919), d; WHEN DOCTORS DISA-GREE(1919), d; PINTO(1920), d; SLIM PRINCESS, THE(1920), d
Charles Schettler
GULLIVER'S TRAVELS(1939), ph
Marie Scheue
LOVES OF CARMEN, THE(1948)
David Scheuer
JOANNA(1968, Brit.); OH! WHAT A LOVELY WAR(1969, Brit.); LOOKING GLASS WAR, THE(1970, Brit.)
Helge Scheuer
CRAZY PARADISE(1965, Den.)
Tom Scheuer
Misc. Talkies
ALICE GOODBODY(1974), d; GOSH(1974), d
Joseph L. Scheuering
NEW ORLEANS UNCENSORED(1955)
Jeff Scheulen
FIRST MONDAY IN OCTOBER(1981)
Reinhold Scheunzel
HANGMEN ALSO DIE(1943)
Hanny Scheuring
BLACK SPIDER, THE(1983, Swit.)
Fred Scheweiller
MONEY TRAP, THE(1966)
Amy Schewel
RETURN OF THE SECAUCUS SEVEN(1980)
Karl Scheydt
EFFI BRIEST(1974, Ger.); FEAR EATS THE SOUL(1974, Ger.); JAIL BAIT(1977, Ger.); QUERELLE(1983, Ger./Fr.)
Gerda Scheyrer
YOU ARE THE WORLD FOR ME(1964, Aust.)
Rosanna Schiaffino
TWO WEEKS IN ANOTHER TOWN(1962); MINOTAUR, THE(1961, Ital.); CRIME DOES NOT PAY(1962, Fr.); LA NOTTE BRAVA(1962, Fr./Ital.); LAFAYETTE(1963, Fr.); VICTORS, THE(1963); LONG SHIPS, THE(1964, Brit./Yugo.); CAVERN, THE(1965, Ital./Ger.); ARRIVEDERCI, BABY!(1966, Brit.); EL GRECO(1966, Ital., Fr.); MANDRAGOLA(1966 Fr./Ital.); RED-DRAGON(1967, Ital./Ger./US); ROVER, THE(1967, Ital.); WITCH, THE(1969, Ital.); NUN AT THE CROSSROADS, A(1970, Ital./Span.); MAN CALLED NOON, THE(1973, Brit.); CAGLIOSTRO(1975, Ital.)
Schiaparelli
EVERY DAY'S A HOLIDAY(1938), cos; PYGMALION(1938, Brit.), cos; MOULIN ROUGE(1952), cos
Vincent Schiavelli
TAKING OFF(1971); GREAT GATSBY, THE(1974); HAPPY HOOKER, THE(1975); ONE FLEW OVER THE CUCKOO'S NEST(1975); FOR PETE'S SAKE(1977); UNMAR-RIED WOMAN, AN(1978); BUTCH AND SUNDANCE: THE EARLY DAYS(1979); SEED OF INNOCENCE(1980); CHU CHU AND THE PHILLY FLASH(1981); FAST TIMES AT RIDGEMONT HIGH(1982); NIGHT SHIFT(1982)
1984
ADVENTURES OF BUCKAROO BANZAI: ACROSS THE 8TH DIMENSION, THE(1984); AMADEUS(1984)
Misc. Talkies
ANGELS(1976)
Vinnie Schiavelli
RETURN, THE(1980)
Gianni Schicchi
FIST IN HIS POCKET(1968, Ital.)
Anton Schich
DIAMONDS OF THE NIGHT(1968, Czech.)
Klaus Schichan
JIMMY ORPHEUS(1966, Ger.)
Ben Schick
1984
RED DAWN(1984)
Dani Schick
SALLAH(1965, Israel), ed; CLOUDS OVER ISRAEL(1966, Israel), ed; TRUNK TO CAIRO(1966, Israel/Ger.), ed
Elliot Schick
RETURN TO MACON COUNTY(1975), p; EARTHLING, THE(1980), p
Elliott Schick
SUGAR HILL(1974), p
David Schickele
FUNNYMAN(1967), ed; OVER-UNDER, SIDEWAYS-DOWN(1977), ed
1984
SIGNAL 7(1984)
Peter Schickele
CRAZY QUILT, THE(1966), m; FUNNYMAN(1967), m; SILENT RUNNING(1972), m
Dieter Schidor
BLACK AND WHITE IN COLOR(1976, Fr.); CROSS OF IRON(1977, Brit., Ger.); FORMULA, THE(1980); VERONIKA VOSS(1982, Ger.); QUERELLE(1983, Ger./Fr.), a, p
David Schied
1984
LAST NIGHT AT THE ALAMO(1984)

Roy Schieder
PUZZLE OF A DOWNFALL CHILD(1970)
Kurt Schiegl
QUEST FOR FIRE(1982, Fr./Can.)
Hannes Schiel
LAST TEN DAYS, THE(1956, Ger.); FIDELIO(1961, Aust.)
Poul Schierbeck
DAY OF WRATH(1948, Den.), m; ORDET(1957, Den.), m
Alfred Schieske
DAY WILL COME, A(1960, Ger.); TOMORROW IS MY TURN(1962, Fr./Ital./Ger.); PIPPI IN THE SOUTH SEAS(1974, Swed./Ger.)
Marty Schiff
CREEPSHOW(1982)
Bob Schiffer
KILLER THAT STALKED NEW YORK, THE(1950), makeup
Robert Schiffer
LADY FROM SHANGHAI, THE(1948), makeup; YOUNG SAVAGES, THE(1961), makeup; FREUD(1962), makeup; PROFESSIONALS, THE(1966), makeup; OH DAD, POOR DAD, MAMA'S HUNG YOU IN THE CLOSET AND I'M FEELIN' SO SAD(1967), makeup; LEGEND OF LYLAH CLARE, THE(1968), makeup; HOW TO SUCCEED IN BUSINESS WITHOUT REALLY TRYING(1976), makeup
Robert J. Schiffer
JUDGMENT AT NUREMBERG(1961), makeup; SCANDALOUS JOHN(1971), makeup; WILD COUNTRY, THE(1971), makeup; $1,000,000 DUCK(1971), makeup; NAPOLEON AND SAMANTHA(1972), makeup; SNOWBALL EXPRESS(1972), makeup; WORLD'S GREATEST ATHLETE, THE(1973), makeup; FREAKY FRIDAY(1976), makeup
Frank Schiffman
EXILE, THE(1931), p
Guillaume Schiffman
WILD CHILD, THE(1970, Fr.); TWO ENGLISH GIRLS(1972, Fr.)
Mathieu Schiffman
WILD CHILD, THE(1970, Fr.); TWO ENGLISH GIRLS(1972, Fr.); INQUISITOR, THE(1982, Fr.)
1984
FULL MOON IN PARIS(1984, Fr.)
Suzanne Schiffman
DAY FOR NIGHT(1973, Fr.), w; DON'T CRY WITH YOUR MOUTH FULL(1974, Fr.), w; STORY OF ADELE H., THE(1975, Fr.), w; MAN WHO LOVED WOMEN, THE(1977, Fr.), w; LOVE ON THE RUN(1980, Fr.), w; LAST METRO, THE(1981, Fr.), w; WOMAN NEXT DOOR, THE(1981, Fr.), w; CONFIDENTIALLY YOURS(1983, Fr.), w
1984
LOVE ON THE GROUND(1984,Fr.), w
Suzanne Schiffmann
SMALL CHANGE(1976, Fr.), w
Ernst G. Schiffner
FOUR COMPANIONS, THE(1938, Ger.)
Simon Schiffrin
BLACK TIGHTS(1962, Fr.), p
Lalo Schifrin
CONCORDE, THE–AIRPORT '79(, m; JOY HOUSE(1964, Fr.), m; RHINO(1964, m, md; CINCINNATI KID, THE(1965), m; DARK INTRUDER(1965), m; ONCE A THIEF(1965), m, md; BLINDFOLD(1966), m; I DEAL IN DANGER(1966), m; LIQUIDATOR, THE(1966, Brit.), m, md; MURDERERS' ROW(1966), m; WAY...WAY OUT(1966), m, md; COOL HAND LUKE(1967), m; FOX, THE(1967), m; PRESIDENT'S ANALYST, THE(1967), m; SULLIVAN'S EMPIRE(1967), m; VENETIAN AFFAIR, THE(1967), m; WHO'S MINDING THE MINT?(1967), m; BROTHERHOOD, THE(1968), m; COOGAN'S BLUFF(1968), m; HELL IN THE PACIFIC(1968), m; SOL MADRID(1968), m; WHERE ANGELS GO...TROUBLE FOLLOWS(1968), m; CHE!(1969), m; EYE OF THE CAT(1969), m; I LOVE MY WIFE(1970), m; KELLY'S HEROES(1970, U.S./Yugo.), m; PUSSYCAT, PUSSYCAT, I LOVE YOU(1970), m, md; BEGUILED, THE(1971), m; CHRISTIAN LICORICE STORE, THE(1971), m; DIRTY HARRY(1971), m; MRS. POLLIFAX-SPY(1971), m, md; PRETTY MAIDS ALL IN A ROW(1971), m; THX 1138(1971), m; JOE KIDD(1972), m; PRIME CUT(1972), m; RAGE(1972), m; TO BE FREE(1972), m; WRATH OF GOD, THE(1972), m; CHARLEY VARRICK(1973), m; ENTER THE DRAGON(1973), m; HARRY IN YOUR POCKET(1973), m; HIT(1973), m; MAGNUM FORCE(1973), m; NEPTUNE FACTOR, THE(1973, Can.), m; GOLDEN NEEDLES(1974), m; MAN ON A SWING(1974), m; FOUR MUSKETEERS, THE(1975), m; MASTER GUNFIGHTER, THE(1975), m; EAGLE HAS LANDED, THE(1976, Brit.), m; SKY RIDERS(1976, U.S./Gr.), m; SPECIAL DELIVERY(1976), m; ST. IVES(1976), m; VOYAGE OF THE DAMNED(1976, Brit.), m; DAY OF THE ANIMALS(1977), m; ROLLERCOASTER(1977), m, md; TELEFON(1977), m; CAT FROM OUTER SPACE, THE(1978), m; MANITOU, THE(1978), m; NUNZIO(1978), m; RETURN FROM WITCH MOUNTAIN(1978), m; AMITYVILLE HORROR, THE(1979), m; BOULEVARD NIGHTS(1979), m; ESCAPE TO ATHENA(1979, Brit.), m; LOVE AND BULLETS(1979, Brit.), m; BIG BRAWL, THE(1980), m; BRUBAKER(1980), m; COMPETITION, THE(1980), m; NUDE BOMB, THE(1980), m; SERIAL(1980), m; WHEN TIME RAN OUT(1980), m; BUDDY BUDDY(1981), m; CAVEMAN(1981), m; LOOPHOLE(1981, Brit.), m; AMITYVILLE II: THE POSSESSION(1982), m; CLASS OF 1984(1982, Can.), m; FAST-WALKING(1982), m; SEDUCTION, THE(1982), m; STRANGER IS WATCHING, A(1982), m; DOCTOR DETROIT(1983), m; OSTERMAN WEEKEND, THE(1983), m; STING II, THE(1983), m; SUDDEN IMPACT(1983), m
1984
TANK(1984), m
Shuya Schigawa
ALMOST TRANSPARENT BLUE(1980, Jap.), ph
Marlyn Schild
YOUTH ON PARADE(1943)
Pierre Schildknecht
Silents
NAPOLEON(1927, Fr.), art d
Joseph Schildkraut
MISSISSIPPI GAMBLER(1929); SHOW BOAT(1929); COCK O' THE WALK(1930); NIGHT RIDE(1930); CARNIVAL(1931, Brit.); BLUE DANUBE(1932, Brit.); CLEOPATRA(1934); SISTERS UNDER THE SKIN(1934); VIVA VILLA!(1934); CRUSADES, THE(1935); GARDEN OF ALLAH, THE(1936); LADY BEHAVE(1937); LANCER SPY(1937); LIFE OF EMILE ZOLA, THE(1937); SLAVE SHIP(1937); SOULS AT SEA(1937); BARONESS AND THE BUTLER, THE(1938); MARIE ANTOINETTE(1938);

MR. MOTO TAKES A VACATION(1938); SUEZ(1938); IDIOT'S DELIGHT(1939); LADY OF THE TROPICS(1939); MAN IN THE IRON MASK, THE(1939); PACK UP YOUR TROUBLES(1939); RAINS CAME, THE(1939); THREE MUSKETEERS, THE(1939); MEET THE WILDCAT(1940); PHANTOM RAIDERS(1940); RANGERS OF FORTUNE(1940); SHOP AROUND THE CORNER, THE(1940); PARSON OF PANAMINT, THE(1941); CHEATERS, THE(1945); FLAME OF THE BARBARY COAST(1945); MONSIEUR BEAUCAIRE(1946); PLAINSMAN AND THE LADY(1946); NORTHWEST OUTPOST(1947); GALLANT LEGION, THE(1948); OLD LOS ANGELES(1948); DIARY OF ANNE FRANK, THE(1959); KING OF THE ROARING TWENTIES–THE STORY OF ARNOLD ROTHSTEIN(1961); GREATEST STORY EVER TOLD, THE(1965)
Misc. Talkies
IN OLD LOS ANGELES(1948)
Silents
ORPHANS OF THE STORM(1922); SONG OF LOVE, THE(1923); KING OF KINGS, THE(1927)
Misc. Silents
ROAD TO YESTERDAY, THE(1925); MEET THE PRINCE(1926); SHIPWRECKED(1926); YOUNG APRIL(1926); HEART THIEF, THE(1927); HIS DOG(1927); BLUE DANUBE, THE(1928); TENTH AVENUE(1928)
Rudolph Schildkraut
CHRISTINA(1929)
Silents
KING OF KINGS, THE(1927)
Misc. Silents
HIS PEOPLE(1925); PALS IN PARADISE(1926); YOUNG APRIL(1926); COUNTRY DOCTOR, THE(1927); HARP IN HOCK, A(1927); MAIN EVENT, THE(1927); TURKISH DELIGHT(1927); SHIP COMES IN, A(1928)
R. Schildkret
Silents
BATTLE OF THE SEXES, THE(1928), m
Henrik Schildt
LOVING COUPLES(1966, Swed.)
Peter Schildt
ADALEN 31(1969, Swed.)
Werner Schilichting
HIPPODROME(1961, Aust./Ger.), art d
John Schilleci
PANIC IN THE STREETS(1950)
Dick Schillemans
SPETTERS(1983, Holland), art d
Alfred Schiller
FLYING DEUCES, THE(1939), w
Danny Schiller
REVENGE OF THE PINK PANTHER(1978); TRAIL OF THE PINK PANTHER, THE(1982); CURSE OF THE PINK PANTHER(1983)
David Schiller
CURSE OF THE PINK PANTHER(1983)
Dorothy Schiller
CAPTURE THAT CAPSULE(1961)
Fannie Schiller
LOVE HAS MANY FACES(1965)
Fanny Schiller
BRAVE BULLS, THE(1951); STRONGHOLD(1952, Mex.); SOMBRERO(1953); LIFE IN THE BALANCE, A(1955); TREASURE OF PANCHO VILLA, THE(1955); WOMAN'S DEVOTION, A(1956); BLACK SCORPION, THE(1957); JET OVER THE ATLANTIC(1960)
Fran Schiller
FURY IN PARADISE(1955, U.S./Mex.)
Fred Schiller
THEY MET ON SKIS(1940, Fr.), w; HEAT'S ON, THE(1943), w; PISTOL PACKIN' MAMA(1943), w; SOMETHING TO SHOUT ABOUT(1943), w; BOSTON BLACKIE'S RENDEZVOUS(1945), w
Frederick Schiller
MR. EMMANUEL(1945, Brit.); DEVIL'S PLOT, THE(1948, Brit.); SECRET PEOPLE(1952, Brit.); ALBERT, R.N.(1953, Brit.); NORMAN CONQUEST(1953, Brit.); WHO DONE IT?(1956, Brit.); LADY OF VENGEANCE(1957, Brit.); SMALL HOTEL(1957, Brit.); ACCURSED, THE(1958, Brit.); CRAWLING EYE, THE(1958, Brit.); LADY IS A SQUARE, THE(1959, Brit.); BOY TEN FEET TALL, A(1965, Brit.); DOUBLE MAN, THE(1967)
Joel Schiller
ROSEMARY'S BABY(1968), art d; ILLUSTRATED MAN, THE(1969), art d; REIVERS, THE(1969), art d; MC MASTERS, THE(1970), prod d, art d; SPORTING CLUB, THE(1971), art d; ACE ELI AND RODGER OF THE SKIES(1973), art d; KID BLUE(1973), prod d; LADY ICE(1973), prod d; REFLECTION OF FEAR, A(1973), art d; LENNY(1974), prod d; MAN ON A SWING(1974), prod d; MAN IN THE GLASS BOOTH, THE(1975), prod d; RAFFERTY AND THE GOLD DUST TWINS(1975), art d; BIG BUS, THE(1976), m; BUDDY HOLLY STORY, THE(1978), prod d; ICE CASTLES(1978), prod d; MUPPET MOVIE, THE(1979), prod d; HONEYSUCKLE ROSE(1980), prod d; SMALL CIRCLE OF FRIENDS, A(1980), prod d; MEGAFORCE(1982), prod d
1984
MISUNDERSTOOD(1984), prod d; SLAPSTICK OF ANOTHER KIND(1984), prod d; SONGWRITER(1984), prod d
Lawrence Schiller
BUTCH CASSIDY AND THE SUNDANCE KID(1969), ph
Miriam Schiller
SPECTER OF THE ROSE(1946); MY FAIR LADY(1964)
Norbert Schiller
UNDERGROUND(1941); EXILE, THE(1947); SINBAD THE SAILOR(1947); SEALED VERDICT(1948); THIEVES' HIGHWAY(1949); MY FAVORITE SPY(1951); THING, THE(1951); DEEP IN MY HEART(1954); RACERS, THE(1955); GIRL IN THE KREMLIN, THE(1957); FRANKENSTEIN 1970(1958); OUTCASTS OF THE CITY(1958); YOUNG LIONS, THE(1958); OPERATION EICHMANN(1961); HITLER(1962); MORITURI(1965); 36 HOURS(1965); TORN CURTAIN(1966); IN ENEMY COUNTRY(1968); PEDESTRIAN, THE(1974, Ger.); YOUNG FRANKENSTEIN(1974); MAN IN THE GLASS BOOTH, THE(1975); END OF THE GAME(1976, Ger./Ital.); WORLD'S GREATEST LOVER, THE(1977)

Norman Schiller
MAGNIFICENT OBSESSION(1954)
Paul Schiller
STREET SINGER, THE(1937, Brit.), w
Tom Schiller
1984
NOTHING LASTS FOREVER(1984), d&w
Wilton Schiller
NEW INTERNS, THE(1964), w
Albert Schilling
HUCKLEBERRY FINN(1974)
Gus Schilling
DR. KILDARE'S CRISIS(1940); MEXICAN SPITFIRE OUT WEST(1940); APPOINT-
MENT FOR LOVE(1941); CITIZEN KANE(1941); DR. KILDARE'S VICTORY(1941);
FLAME OF NEW ORLEANS, THE(1941); HELLZAPOPPIN'(1941); ICE-CAPA-
DES(1941); IT STARTED WITH EVE(1941); LUCKY DEVILS(1941); TOO MANY
BLONDES(1941); BROADWAY(1942); LADY BODYGUARD(1942); MAGNIFICENT
AMBERSONS, THE(1942); THERE'S ONE BORN EVERY MINUTE(1942); YOU WERE
NEVER LOVELIER(1942); AMAZING MRS. HOLLIDAY(1943); CHATTERBOX(1943);
HERS TO HOLD(1943); HI, BUDDY(1943); LARCENY WITH MUSIC(1943); SING A
JINGLE(1943); IT'S A PLEASURE(1945); RIVER GANG(1945); SEE MY LA-
WYER(1945); THOUSAND AND ONE NIGHTS, A(1945); DANGEROUS BUSI-
NESS(1946); CALENDAR GIRL(1947); STORK BITES MAN(1947); ANGEL ON THE
AMAZON(1948); LADY FROM SHANGHAI, THE(1948); MACBETH(1948); RETURN
OF OCTOBER, THE(1948); BRIDE FOR SALE(1949); HIT PARADE OF 1951(1950); OUR
VERY OWN(1950); GASOLINE ALLEY(1951); HONEYCHILE(1951); ON DANGER-
OUS GROUND(1951); ONE BIG AFFAIR(1952); EXECUTIVE SUITE(1954); SHE
COULDN'T SAY NO(1954); GLORY(1955); REBEL WITHOUT A CAUSE(1955); RUN
FOR COVER(1955); SON OF SINBAD(1955); BIGGER THAN LIFE(1956)
Joe Schilling
SALOME(1953)
Margaret Schilling
CHILDREN OF DREAMS(1931)
Marian Schilling
IDAHO KID, THE(1937)
Marion Schilling
HEART PUNCH(1932)
Niklas Schilling
48 HOURS TO ACAPULCO(1968, Ger.), ph; 24-HOUR LOVER(1970, Ger.), ph
Nikolaus Schilling
PIPPI IN THE SOUTH SEAS(1974, Swed./Ger.)
William Schilling
ISLAND, THE(1980); RICH AND FAMOUS(1981); I, THE JURY(1982); TES-
TAMENT(1983)
Max Schillinger
1984
LITTLE DRUMMER GIRL, THE(1984)
Sal Schillizi
THREE DAYS OF THE CONDOR(1975)
Arthur Schilski
TERROR OF DR. MABUSE, THE(1965, Ger.)
Lauretta M. Schimmoler
PARACHUTE NURSE(1942)
Cy Schindell
FUGITIVE LADY(1934); JUVENILE COURT(1938); YOU CAN'T TAKE IT WITH
YOU(1938); SOMEWHERE IN THE NIGHT(1946); JOHNNY O'CLOCK(1947); LIKELY
STORY, A(1947)
Hannes Schindler
DER FREISCHUTZ(1970, Ger.), ph; FIDELIO(1970, Ger.), ph; MARRIAGE OF FIGA-
RO, THE(1970, Ger.), ph
Rudolf Schindler
MOSCOW SHANGHAI(1936, Ger.)
Rudolph Schindler
INTERMEZZO(1937, Ger.)
Sibylle Schindler
IDEAL LODGER, THE(1957, Ger.)
Mia Schioka
ADVENTURES OF MARCO POLO, THE(1938)
Volker Schiondorff
COUP DE GRACE(1978, Ger./Fr.), d
Carlo Schipa
STRICTLY DISHONORABLE(1931)
Silents
LITTLE ANNIE ROONEY(1925); SALLY(1925)
Carlos Schipa
APPOINTMENT WITH MURDER(1948); FEDERAL MAN(1950)
Tito Schipa
SOHO CONSPIRACY(1951, Brit.)
Tino Schipinzi
THREE BROTHERS(1982, Ital.)
Thomas Schippers
MEDIUM, THE(1951), md
Vittorio Schiraldi
SHE AND HE(1969, Ital.), w
Misc. Talkies
FAMILY KILLER(1975), d
Victor Schiro
NEW ORLEANS UNCENSORED(1955)
Alfred Schirokauer
CAREERS(1929), w
Eleanor Schirra
THERE'S ALWAYS VANILLA(1972)
Anton Schirsner
MARRIAGE OF MARIA BRAUN, THE(1979, Ger.)
Murray Schisgal
LUV(1967), w; TIGER MAKES OUT, THE(1967), w; TOOTSIE(1982), a, w
Oscar Schisgall
MAN I MARRIED, THE(1940), w

Florence Schissler
LORDS OF FLATBUSH, THE(1974)
Gerik Schjelderup
NEUTRAL PORT(1941, Brit.); WE DIVE AT DAWN(1943, Brit.); GREAT MANHUNT,
THE(1951, Brit.); CRUEL SEA, THE(1953); OUR MAN IN HAVANA(1960, Brit.);
ASSASSINATION BUREAU, THE(1969, Brit.)
Helga Schlack
DIE FASTNACHTSBEICHTE(1962, Ger.)
Sig Schlager
GIRL FROM CALGARY(1932), w
Morris R. Schlank
DRIFTING(1932), d
Silents
CODE OF THE RANGE(1927), d
Adolf Schlasy
ARIANE(1931, Ger.), ph
George Schlatter
NORMAN...IS THAT YOU?(1976), p&d, w
Maria Rosa Schlauzero
VIOLENT FOUR, THE(1968, Ital.)
Larry Schlechter
NIGHTBEAST(1982), makeup
1984
ALIEN FACTOR, THE(1984), spec eff
W. Schlee
STORM IN A WATER GLASS(1931, Aust.), w
Walter Schlee
BLONDE NIGHTINGALE(1931, Ger.), w; DREAM OF SCHONBRUNN(1933, Aus.),
w
Fritz Schlegel
TINDER BOX, THE(1968, E. Ger.)
Jean Schlegel
JONAH–WHO WILL BE 25 IN THE YEAR 2000(1976, Switz.)
Margarete Schlegel
BERLIN ALEXANDERPLATZ(1933, Ger.)
Misc. Silents
HEAD OF JANUS, THE(1920, Ger.)
Peter Schleger
FRATERNITY ROW(1977)
Karel Schleichert
Misc. Silents
EROTIKON(1929, Czech.)
Wolfgang Schleif
FREDDY UNTER FREMDEN STERNEN(1962, Ger.), d
Lincoln Schleifer
THEY ALL LAUGHED(1981)
Herb Schlein
SO FINE(1981)
Egon G. Schleinitz
PHONY AMERICAN, THE(1964, Ger.), w
Carl Schleipper
CURSE OF THE STONE HAND(1965, Mex/Chile), d
Marianne Schleiss
HIDDEN FEAR(1957)
Martina Schleisser
1984
MY KIND OF TOWN(1984, Can.)
Hans Schlenok
CRUISER EMDEN(1932, Ger.)
Arthur Schlesinger, Jr.
1984
GARBO TALKS(1984)
Emma Schlesinger
SUNDAY BLOODY SUNDAY(1971, Brit.)
I. W. Schlesinger
Silents
AFTER THE VERDICT(1929, Brit.), p
Isidore Schlesinger
BELLS, THE(1931, Brit.), p; FAREWELL TO LOVE(1931, Brit.), p
John Schlesinger
SAILOR OF THE KING(1953, Brit.); DIVIDED HEART, THE(1955, Brit.); LAST MAN
TO HANG, THE(1956, Brit.); KIND OF LOVING, A(1962, Brit.), d; BILLY LIAR(1963,
Brit.), d; DARLING(1965, Brit.), d, w; FAR FROM THE MADDING CROWD(1967,
Brit.), d; MIDNIGHT COWBOY(1969), d; SUNDAY BLOODY SUNDAY(1971, Brit.), d;
DAY OF THE LOCUST, THE(1975), d; MARATHON MAN(1976), d; YANKS(1979), d;
HONKY TONK FREEWAY(1981), d
Kurt Schlesinger
ARTHUR(1981)
Leo Schlesinger
O.S.S.(1946); GOLDEN EARRINGS(1947); ROGUES' REGIMENT(1948)
Leon Schlesinger
BIG STAMPEDE, THE(1932), p; HAUNTED GOLD(1932), p; RIDE HIM, COW-
BOY(1932), p; MAN FROM MONTEREY, THE(1933), p; SOMEWHERE IN SONO-
RA(1933), p; TELEGRAPH TRAIL, THE(1933), p; BIG BROADCAST OF 1938,
THE(1937), anim; WHEN'S YOUR BIRTHDAY?(1937), anim; SHE MARRIED A
COP(1939), anim; HI DIDDLE DIDDLE(1943), anim d
Otto Schlesinger
GIRL, THE BODY, AND THE PILL, THE(1967); TASTE OF BLOOD, A(1967)
Peter Schlesinger
INSIDE OUT(1975, Brit.); JUST A GIGOLO(1979, Ger.)
1984
BIGGER SPLASH, A(1984)
Reva Schlesinger
TOMORROW(1972), ed
Richard Schlesinger
CITY NEWS(1983)
Robert E. Schlesinger
THAT CHAMPIONSHIP SEASON(1982)

Tess Schlesinger
GOOD EARTH, THE(1937), w; ARE HUSBANDS NECESSARY?(1942), w

Jo Schlesser
GRAND PRIX(1966)

Diana Schlessinger
NOT RECONCILED, OR "ONLY VIOLENCE HELPS WHERE IT RULES"(1969, Ger.)

Leo Schlessinger
SPANISH MAIN, THE(1945)

Ranate Schlessinger
NIGHT OF THE ZOMBIES(1981)

Hans Schlettow
ESCAPED FROM DARTMOOR(1930, Brit.)

Hedwig Schlichter
MAEDCHEN IN UNIFORM(1932, Ger.)

Victor Schlichter
MASTER OF HORROR(1965, Arg.), m

Isabella Schlichting
JOURNEY, THE(1959, U.S./Aust.), art d; SECRET WAYS, THE(1961), art d; MIRA-CLE OF THE WHITE STALLIONS(1963), art d

Iscbella Schlichting
GOOD SOLDIER SCHWEIK, THE(1963, Ger.), art d

Werner Schlichting
JOURNEY, THE(1959, U.S./Aust.), art d; SECRET WAYS, THE(1961), art d; GOOD SOLDIER SCHWEIK, THE(1963, Ger.), art d; MIRACLE OF THE WHITE STAL-LIONS(1963), art d

Frederick Schlick
WHARF ANGEL(1934), w

Harold Schlickemeyer
WILSON(1944)

Harold Schlickenmayer
LUCKY NIGHT(1939); LAURA(1944)

Dutch Schlickenmeyer
YELLOW JACK(1938); BULLETS OR BALLOTS(1936); SENATOR WAS INDIS-CREET, THE(1947)

Hedwig Schlicter
EIGHT GIRLS IN A BOAT(1932, Ger.)

Werner Schlieting
FOUR IN A JEEP(1951, Switz.), set d

Werner Schlighting
WONDER BOY(1951, Brit./Aust.), prod d

Dutch Schlikenmeyer
THEY WERE EXPENDABLE(1945)

Jurgen Schling
GLADIATORS, THE(1970, Swed.)

Robert Schlitt
PYX, THE(1973, Can.), w; BEEN DOWN SO LONG IT LOOKS LIKE UP TO ME(1977), w

Schlitzie
FREAKS(1932)

Petrus Schloemp
$(DOLLARS) (1971), ph; WHO?(1975, Brit./Ger.), ph

Volker Schloendorff
LOST HONOR OF KATHARINA BLUM, THE(1975, Ger.), d, w; GERMANY IN AUTUMN(1978, Ger.), d

Herman Schlom
DUKE COMES BACK, THE(1937), p; MICHAEL O'HALLORAN(1937), p; SHEIK STEPS OUT, THE(1937), p; COME ON, LEATHERNECKS(1938), p; PRISON NUR-SE(1938), p; ROMANCE ON THE RUN(1938), p; I WAS A CONVICT(1939), p; MICK-EY, THE KID(1939), p; MYSTERIOUS MISS X, THE(1939), p; ORPHANS OF THE STREET(1939), p; SABOTAGE(1939), p; LI'L ABNER(1940), p; GREAT GILDER-SLEEVE, THE(1942), p; HIGHWAYS BY NIGHT(1942), p; SEVEN MILES FROM ALCATRAZ(1942), p; GILDERSLEEVE ON BROADWAY(1943), p; GILDER-SLEEVE'S BAD DAY(1943), p; GILDERSLEEVE'S GHOST(1944), p; NEVADA(1944), p; NIGHT OF ADVENTURE, A(1944), p; PASSPORT TO DESTINY(1944), p; BRIGH-TON STRANGLER, THE(1945), p; DICK TRACY(1945), p; GAME OF DEATH, A(1945), p; WANDERER OF THE WASTELAND(1945), p; WEST OF THE PECOS(1945), p; BAMBOO BLONDE, THE(1946), p; DICK TRACY VS. CUEBALL(1946), p; DING DONG WILLIAMS(1946), p; FALCON'S ADVENTURE, THE(1946), p; GENIUS AT WORK(1946), p; SUNSET PASS(1946), p; TRUTH ABOUT MURDER, THE(1946), p; BORN TO KILL(1947), p; CODE OF THE WEST(1947), p; DEVIL THUMBS A RIDE, THE(1947), p; DICK TRACY MEETS GRUESOME(1947), p; DICK TRACY'S DILEM-MA(1947), p; SEVEN KEYS TO BALDPATE(1947), p; THUNDER MOUNTAIN(1947), p; UNDER THE TONTO RIM(1947), p; WILD HORSE MESA(1947), p; ARIZONA RANGER, THE(1948), p; GUN SMUGGLERS(1948), p; GUNS OF HATE(1948), p; INDIAN AGENT(1948), p; WESTERN HERITAGE(1948), p; BROTHERS IN THE SADDLE(1949), p; CLAY PIGEON, THE(1949), p; FOLLOW ME QUIETLY(1949), p; MASKED RAIDERS(1949), p; MYSTERIOUS DESPERADO, THE(1949), p; RIDERS OF THE RANGE(1949), p; RUSTLERS(1949), p; STAGECOACH KID(1949), p; AR-MORED CAR ROBBERY(1950), p; BORDER TREASURE(1950), p; DYNAMITE PASS(1950), p; LAW OF THE BADLANDS(1950), p; RIDER FROM TUCSON(1950), p; RIO GRANDE PATROL(1950), p; STORM OVER WYOMING(1950), p; BEST OF THE BADMEN(1951), p; GUNPLAY(1951), p; HOT LEAD(1951), p; OVERLAND TELE-GRAPH(1951), p; PISTOL HARVEST(1951), p; SADDLE LEGION(1951), p; DESERT PASSAGE(1952), p; HALF-BREED, THE(1952), p; ROAD AGENT(1952), p; TAR-GET(1952), p; TRAIL GUIDE(1952), p

Marla Denise Schlom
PSYCHO II(1983), cos
1984
SIXTEEN CANDLES(1984), cos; WHERE THE BOYS ARE '84(1984), cos

Volker Schlondorff
YOUNG TORLESS(1968, Fr./Ger.), d&w; DEGREE OF MURDER, A(1969, Ger.), d, w; TIN DRUM, THE(1979, Ger./Fr./Yugo./Pol.), d, w; CIRCLE OF DECEIT(1982, Fr./Ger.), d, w; WAR AND PEACE(1983, Ger.), d&w
1984
SWANN IN LOVE(1984, Fr.Ger.), d, w

Leopold Schlosberg
LE MONDE TREMBLERA(1939, Fr.), p

Morty Schloss
JOE(1970)

Zander Schloss
1984
REPO MAN(1984)

Lucille Schlossberg
IT'S A BIG COUNTRY(1951), w

Susan Schlossman
SAVAGES(1972), cos

Victor Schlowski
HOUSE OF DEATH(1932, USSR), w

Jam Schlubach
SOLDIER, THE(1982), art d

Jan Schlubach
INSIDE OUT(1975, Brit.), art d

Heening Schlueter
ASH WEDNESDAY(1973)

Eric Schlumberger
MY LIFE TO LIVE(1963, Fr.)

Guylaine Schlumberger
MY LIFE TO LIVE(1963, Fr.)

Jean Schlumberger
SIREN OF ATLANTIS(1948), cos

Valerie Schlumberger
1984
A NOS AMOURS(1984, Fr.), a, cos

Edith Schlussel
WHILE THE ATTORNEY IS ASLEEP(1945, Den.), ed; DAY OF WRATH(1948, Den.), ed; GERTRUD(1966, Den.), ed; ERIC SOYA'S "17"(1967, Den.), ed

Henning Schluten
ONE, TWO, THREE(1961)

Henning Schluter
THREE PENNY OPERA(1963, Fr./Ger.); LUDWIG(1973, Ital./Ger./Fr.)

John Schluter, Jr.
1984
TIGHTROPE(1984)

David Schmalholz
HERE COME THE TIGERS(1978)

Claudia Schmann
PARSIFAL(1983, Fr.)

Dagmar Schmedes
CARDINAL, THE(1963)

Tine Schmedes
VENOM(1968, Den.)

Erich-Lothar Schmekel
RAMPAGE AT APACHE WELLS(1966, Ger./Yugo.), makeup

Max Schmeling
AFFAIRS OF JULIE, THE(1958, Ger.)

John Schmerling
DEADLY SPAWN, THE(1983)

Aglaja Schmid
TRIAL, THE(1948, Aust.)

Alfred Schmid
FABULOUS DORSEYS, THE(1947), spec eff; UNTAMED WOMEN(1952), spec eff
Silents
SEVENTH DAY, THE(1922)

Daniel Schmid
AMERICAN FRIEND, THE(1977, Ger.)

Helmut Schmid
HEAD, THE(1961, Ger.); ONE, TWO, THREE(1961); DANIELLA BY NIGHT(1962, Fr./Ger.); INDECENT(1962, Ger.); PRIZE OF ARMS, A(1962, Brit.); JOURNEY INTO NOWHERE(1963, Brit.); TERROR OF DR. MABUSE, THE(1965, Ger.); MOON-WOLF(1966, Fin./Ger.); SALZBURG CONNECTION, THE(1972)

Robert Schmid
JONAH–WHO WILL BE 25 IN THE YEAR 2000(1976, Switz.)

Tanja Schmidbauer
GERMANY IN AUTUMN(1978, Ger.), ed

Von Schmidel
DECISION BEFORE DAWN(1951)

Alfred Schmidhauser
FIVE DAYS ONE SUMMER(1982)

Hannes Schmidhauser
INVISIBLE MAN, THE(1963, Ger.)

Walter Schmidinger
PEDESTRIAN, THE(1974, Ger.); SERPENT'S EGG, THE(1977, Ger./U.S.); FROM THE LIFE OF THE MARIONETTES(1980, Ger.)

F. L. Schmidlapp
THOSE LIPS, THOSE EYES(1980)

Albert Schmidt
OUTCASTS OF POKER FLAT, THE(1952)

Andre Schmidt
CHARLES, DEAD OR ALIVE(1972, Switz.); DEATH OF MARIO RICCI, THE(1983, Ital.)

Anja Schmidt
JOE HILL(1971, Swed./U.S.)

Arthur Schmidt
ANNE OF GREEN GABLES(1934), ed; FINISHING SCHOOL(1934), ed; CHASING YESTERDAY(1935), ed; IN PERSON(1935), ed; RETURN OF PETER GRIMM, THE(1935), ed; CHATTERBOX(1936), ed; BLONDE TROUBLE(1937), ed; BULLDOG DRUMMOND'S REVENGE(1937), ed; CLARENCE(1937), ed; HIDEAWAY GIRL(1937), ed; HOTEL HAYWIRE(1937), ed; DANGEROUS TO KNOW(1938), ed; TOUCHDOWN, ARMY(1938), ed; ALL WOMEN HAVE SECRETS(1939), ed; BULL-DOG DRUMMOND'S SECRET POLICE(1939), ed; DISBARRED(1939), ed; UNDER-COVER DOCTOR(1939), ed; OPENED BY MISTAKE(1940), ed; QUEEN OF THE MOB(1940), ed; SEVENTEEN(1940), ed; TEXAS RANGERS RIDE AGAIN(1940), ed; ALOMA OF THE SOUTH SEAS(1941), ed; LAS VEGAS NIGHTS(1941), ed; DR. BROADWAY(1942), ed; FLY BY NIGHT(1942), ed; HENRY ALDRICH GETS GLA-MOUR(1942), ed; PRIORITIES ON PARADE(1942), ed; STREET OF CHANCE(1942), ed; GOOD FELLOWS, THE(1943), ed; SALUTE FOR THREE(1943), ed; RAINBOW ISLAND(1944), ed; DUFFY'S TAVERN(1945), ed; MEDAL FOR BENNY, A(1945), ed;

BLUE DAHLIA, THE(1946), ed; MONSIEUR BEAUCAIRE(1946), ed; PERILS OF PAULINE, THE(1947), ed; HAZARD(1948), ed; I WALK ALONE(1948), ed; SORROW-FUL JONES(1949), ed; TOP O' THE MORNING(1949), ed; REDHEAD AND THE COWBOY, THE(1950), ed; SUNSET BOULEVARD(1950), ed; BIG CARNIVAL, THE(1951), ed; WHEN WORLDS COLLIDE(1951), ed; HERE COME THE GIRLS(1953), ed; OFF LIMITS(1953), ed; SAVAGE, THE(1953), ed; STARS ARE SING-ING, THE(1953), ed; RED GARTERS(1954), ed; SABRINA(1954), ed; WE'RE NO AN-GELS(1955), ed; VAGABOND KING, THE(1956), ed; SOME LIKE IT HOT(1959), ed; LAST REMAKE OF BEAU GESTE, THE(1977), ed; JAWS II(1978), ed; FISH THAT SAVED PITTSBURGH, THE(1979), ed; COAL MINER'S DAUGHTER(1980), ed; ES-CAPE ARTIST, THE(1982), ed
1984
  BUDDY SYSTEM, THE(1984), ed; FIRSTBORN(1984), ed
Arthur P. Schmidt
  SAYONARA(1957), ed; SPIRIT OF ST. LOUIS, THE(1957), ed; NAKED AND THE DEAD, THE(1958), ed; OLD MAN AND THE SEA, THE(1958), ed; LI'L ABNER(1959), ed; IT'S ONLY MONEY(1962), ed; FAMILY JEWELS, THE(1965), ed
Artie Schmidt
  CINDERFELLA(1960), ed
Burr Schmidt
  SUNSET COVE(1978)
Caprice Schmidt
  AMERICAN GRAFFITI(1973)
Carl Schmidt
  SCOUNDREL, THE(1935)
Carol Schmidt
  BIG DADDY(1969)
Ellen Schmidt
  YOUNG GO WILD, THE(1962, Ger.), art d; WILLY(1963, U.S./Ger.), art d
Georgia Schmidt
  HOUSE OF THE DAMNED(1963); KANSAS CITY BOMBER(1972); GOIN' SOUTH(1978)
Gerhard Schmidt
  HYPNOSIS(1966, Ger./Sp./Ital.), w
Gitta Schmidt
  CABARET(1972)
Gudrun Schmidt
  MONSTER OF LONDON CITY, THE(1967, Ger.)
Gunther Schmidt
  NAKED AMONG THE WOLVES(1967, Ger.), cos
H. C. Schmidt
Silents
  YOUNG WHIRLWIND(1928), w
Harvey Schmidt
  BAD COMPANY(1972), m
Helmut Schmidt
  BIMBO THE GREAT(1961, Ger.); BASHFUL ELEPHANT, THE(1962, Aust.)
Herb Schmidt
  INDEPENDENCE DAY(1976)
I. Schmidt
Misc. Silents
  HE WHO GETS SLAPPED(1916, USSR), d
Irmin Schmidt
1984
  FLIGHT TO BERLIN(1984, Ger./Brit.), m
Jack Schmidt
  STRAWBERRY STATEMENT, THE(1970)
Jacques Schmidt
  TENANT, THE(1976, Fr.), cos
Jan Priiskorn Schmidt
  OPERATION LOVEBIRDS(1968, Den.)
Jan Schmidt
  END OF AUGUST AT THE HOTEL OZONE, THE(1967, Czech.), d
Joe Schmidt
  PAPER LION(1968)
Joseph Schmidt
  MY SONG GOES ROUND THE WORLD(1934, Brit.); STAR FELL FROM HEAVEN, A(1936, Brit.)
Judith Schmidt
  PARSIFAL(1983, Fr.)
Kai Schmidt
  MURDER WITH PICTURES(1936)
Silents
  MOCKERY(1927)
Misc. Silents
  LAUGHING AT DEATH(1929)
Lena Schmidt
Misc. Silents
  REVOLT, THE(1916)
Leonard Schmidt
  MAN ESCAPED, A(1957, Fr.)
Lillimor Schmidt
  FALLING FOR YOU(1933, Brit.)
Lothar Schmidt [Goldschmidt]
  ONE HOUR WITH YOU(1932), w
Silents
  MARRIAGE CIRCLE, THE(1924), w
Marlene Schmidt
  TEACHER, THE(1974); DR. MINX(1975); SPECIALIST, THE(1975), a, w; SCOR-CHY(1976); FIFTH FLOOR, THE(1980), w; SEPARATE WAYS(1981), w; MOR-TUARY(1983), p, w
1984
  THEY'RE PLAYING WITH FIRE(1984), a, p, w
Michael Schmidt
  SIERRA BARON(1958)
Paul Schmidt
  PLAYGROUND, THE(1965)

Peer Schmidt
  CONFESSIONS OF FELIX KRULL, THE(1957, Ger.); MONSTER OF LONDON CITY, THE(1967, Ger.); THOSE DARING YOUNG MEN IN THEIR JAUNTY JALOPIES(1969, Fr./Brit./ Ital.)
Phoebe Schmidt
Misc. Talkies
  MAG WHEELS(1978)
Ralph Schmidt
  EVEL KNIEVEL(1971)
Richard R. Schmidt
  MAN, A WOMAN AND A KILLER, A(1975), p, d, w, ph&ed
Ron Schmidt
1984
  AMERICAN TABOO(1984), p, ed
Russell Schmidt
  SPECIALIST, THE(1975)
Solomon Schmidt
  STRIPES(1981)
Stan Schmidt
  KILL AND KILL AGAIN(1981), a, ch
Stephen Schmidt
  FUNNYMAN(1967), p; ISLAND OF THE DOOMED(1968, Span./Ger.), w; RIVER-RUN(1968), p
Thomas J. Schmidt
  HOT SUMMER WEEK(1973, Can.), p&d
Walter Robert Schmidt
  HELL TO ETERNITY(1960), w; MONSTER(1979), w
Wayne Schmidt
  DAY TIME ENDED, THE(1980, Span.), p, w
William R. Schmidt
  ALL QUIET ON THE WESTERN FRONT(1930), art d
Silents
  GOOSE WOMAN, THE(1925), art d
Wolf Schmidt
  IDEAL LODGER, THE(1957, Ger.), a, p,d&w; PASSOVER PLOT, THE(1976, Israel), p; RUN FOR THE ROSES(1978), p
Wolfgang Schmidt
  SKI FEVER(1969, U.S./Aust./Czech.), p
Schmidt-Boelcke
  EMIL AND THE DETECTIVE(1931, Ger.), m
Willi Schmidt-Gentner
  BLONDE NIGHTINGALE(1931, Ger.), md; DOLLY GETS AHEAD(1931, Ger.), m, md; EPISODE(1937, Aust.), m; OPERETTA(1949, Ger.), md; ANGEL WITH THE TRUMPET, THE(1950, Brit.), m; WONDER BOY(1951, Brit./Aust.), m; CARNIVAL STORY(1954), m; CIRCUS OF LOVE(1958, Ger.), m
Hans Schmidt-Isserstedt
  MARRIAGE OF FIGARO, THE(1970, Ger.), md
Eva Schmidt-Kaiser
  INVISIBLE OPPONENT(1933, Ger.)
Charlotte Schmidt-Kersten
  RETURN OF DR. MABUSE, THE(1961, Ger./Fr./Ital.), makeup; TRAPP FAMILY, THE(1961, Ger.), makeup; TREASURE OF SILVER LAKE(1965, Fr./Ger./Yugo.), makeup
Jorge Schmidt-Reitwein
  EVERY MAN FOR HIMSELF AND GOD AGAINST ALL(1975, Ger.), ph; GERMANY IN AUTUMN(1978, Ger.), ph; NOSFERATU, THE VAMPIRE(1979, Fr./Ger.), ph
Tanja Schmidtbauer
1984
  WOMAN IN FLAMES, A(1984, Ger.), ed
N. Schmidthof
Misc. Silents
  STEPAN KHALTURIN(1925, USSR)
Christiane Schmidtmer
  STOP TRAIN 349(1964, Fr./Ital./Ger.); FANNY HILL: MEMOIRS OF A WOMAN OF PLEASURE zero(1965); SHIP OF FOOLS(1965); I DEAL IN DANGER(1966); BIG DOLL HOUSE, THE(1971)
Christianne Schmidtmer
  GIANT SPIDER INVASION, THE(1975)
Richard Schmiechen
  ROSELAND(1977), ed
Hans Joachim Schmiedel
  STOP TRAIN 349(1964, Fr./Ital./Ger.); IT HAPPENED HERE(1966, Brit.)
Walter Schmiedinger
  GERMANY IN AUTUMN(1978, Ger.)
Joe Schmieg
1984
  GHOSTBUSTERS(1984)
Eleonore Schminke
  JONATHAN(1973, Ger.)
Sophie Schmit
1984
  LE DERNIER COMBAT(1984, Fr.), ed
Albert B. Schmitt
1984
  COUNTRY(1984)
Don W. Schmitt
  4D MAN(1959), set d
Eloise Schmitt
1984
  SONGWRITER(1984)
Henri Schmitt
  MR. HULOT'S HOLIDAY(1954, Fr.), prod d, art d; MY UNCLE(1958, Fr.), art d
Janis Schmitt
  HISTORY OF THE WORLD, PART 1(1981)
Odile Schmitt
  LIGHT YEARS AWAY(1982, Fr./Switz.)
Liesgret Schmitt-Klink
  DEAD PIGEON ON BEETHOVEN STREET(1972, Ger.), ed

Hubert Schmitz
EMIL AND THE DETECTIVE(1931, Ger.)
John Schmitz
SUNNY SIDE UP(1929), ph; HAPPY DAYS(1930), ph; HANDLE WITH CARE(1932), ph
Larry Schmitz
LOVE BUG, THE(1968)
Sibylle Schmitz
VAMPYR(1932, Fr./Ger.)
Sybille Schmitz
F.P. 1 DOESN'T ANSWER(1933, Ger.); MASTER OF THE WORLD(1935, Ger.)
Paul Schmitzburger
SLIPPER AND THE ROSE, THE(1976, Brit.)
Jonathan Schmock
1984
ROSEBUD BEACH HOTEL(1984)
Otto Schmoele
TRIAL, THE(1948, Aust.); LAST TEN DAYS, THE(1956, Ger.); GOOD SOLDIER SCHWEIK, THE(1963, Ger.)
David Schmoeller
TOURIST TRAP, THE(1979), d, w; DAY TIME ENDED, THE(1980, Span.), w; SEDUCTION, THE(1982), d&w
Shailar Schmoeller
SEDUCTION, THE(1982)
Benjamin Schmoll
JULIE DARLING(1982, Can./Ger.)
Claus-Dieter Schmoller
ETERNAL LOVE(1960, Ger.)
Fritz Schmuck
TEMPORARY WIDOW, THE(1930, Ger./Brit.)
Eli Schmudkler
MY FAVORITE WIFE(1940)
Hans Schnabel
VEILS OF BAGDAD, THE(1953)
Stefan Schnabel
TWO WEEKS IN ANOTHER TOWN(1962); JOURNEY INTO FEAR(1942); IRON CURTAIN, THE(1948); BARBARY PIRATE(1949); LAW OF THE BARBARY COAST(1949); DIPLOMATIC COURIER(1952); HOUDINI(1953); CROWDED PARADISE(1956); 27TH DAY, THE(1957); MUGGER, THE(1958); BIG SHOW, THE(1961); QUESTION 7(1961, U.S./Ger.); SECRET WAYS, THE(1961); TOWN WITHOUT PITY(1961, Ger./Switz./U.S.); COUNTERFEIT TRAITOR, THE(1962); FREUD(1962); NO SURVIVORS, PLEASE(1963, Ger.); RAMPAGE(1963); UGLY AMERICAN, THE(1963); PHONY AMERICAN, THE(1964, Ger.); HAPPY HOOKER, THE(1975); FIREFOX(1982); LOVESICK(1983)
Heinz Schnackertz
NO SURVIVORS, PLEASE(1963, Ger.), ph
Heinz Schnackerz
BEGGAR STUDENT, THE(1958, Ger.), ph
Ida Schnall
Misc. Silents
UNDINE(1916)
Sylvia Schneble
GOLDEN NEEDLES(1974), w
Stephen Schneck
INSIDE OUT(1975, Brit.), w; HIGH-BALLIN'(1978), w
Charles Schnee
UNTIL THEY SAIL(1957), p; TWO WEEKS IN ANOTHER TOWN(1962), w; CROSS MY HEART(1946), w; I WALK ALONE(1948), w; RED RIVER(1948), w; EASY LIVING(1949), w; SCENE OF THE CRIME(1949), w; THEY LIVE BY NIGHT(1949), w; BORN TO BE BAD(1950), w; FURIES, THE(1950), w; PAID IN FULL(1950), w; RIGHT CROSS(1950), w; BANNERLINE(1951), w; WESTWARD THE WOMEN(1951), w; BAD AND THE BEAUTIFUL, THE(1952), w; WHEN IN ROME(1952), w; PRODIGAL, THE(1955), p; TRIAL(1955), p; SOMEBODY UP THERE LIKES ME(1956), p; HOUSE OF NUMBERS(1957), p; WINGS OF EAGLES, THE(1957), p; BUTTERFIELD 8(1960), w; CROWDED SKY, THE(1960), w; BY LOVE POSSESSED(1961), w
Thelma Schnee
DETECTIVE, THE(1954, Qit.), w; COLOSSUS OF NEW YORK, THE(1958), w
Hans Schneeberger
BLUE ANGEL, THE(1930, Ger.), ph; BLUE LIGHT, THE(1932, Ger.), p; FOREVER YOURS(1937, Brit.), ph; TROOPSHIP(1938, Brit.), ph; CONQUEST OF THE AIR(1940), ph; OPERETTA(1949, Ger.), ph; HELP I'M INVISIBLE(1952, Ger.), ph
O. Hans Schneeberger
S.O.S. ICEBERG(1933), ph
Charles H. Schneer
PRINCE OF THIEVES, THE(1948), w; IT CAME FROM BENEATH THE SEA(1955), p; EARTH VS. THE FLYING SAUCERS(1956), p; HELLCATS OF THE NAVY(1957), p; 20 MILLION MILES TO EARTH(1957), p; CASE AGAINST BROOKLYN, THE(1958), p; GOOD DAY FOR A HANGING(1958), p; SEVENTH VOYAGE OF SINBAD, THE(1958), p; TARAWA BEACHHEAD(1958), p; BATTLE OF THE CORAL SEA(1959), p; I AIM AT THE STARS(1960), p; THREE WORLDS OF GULLIVER, THE(1960, Brit.), p; MYSTERIOUS ISLAND(1961, U.S./Brit.), p; JASON AND THE ARGONAUTS(1963, Brit.), p; EAST OF SUDAN(1964, Brit.), p; FIRST MEN IN THE MOON(1964, Brit.), p; YOU MUST BE JOKING!(1965, Brit.), p; HALF A SIXPENCE(1967, Brit.), p; LAND RAIDERS(1969), p; VALLEY OF GWANGI, THE(1969), p; EXECUTIONER, THE(1970, Brit.), p; GOLDEN VOYAGE OF SINBAD, THE(1974, Brit.), p; SINBAD AND THE EYE OF THE TIGER(1977, U.S./Brit.), p; CLASH OF THE TITANS(1981), p
Andrew Schneider
INCREDIBLE TWO-HEADED TRANSPLANT, THE(1971)
Barry Schneider
RUBY(1977), w; ROLLER BOOGIE(1979), w; TAKE THIS JOB AND SHOVE IT(1981), w; DEADLY FORCE(1983), w
Benno Schneider
NOTORIOUS LANDLADY, THE(1962)
Misc. Silents
MABUL(1927, USSR)
Bernadette Schneider
WAGNER(1983, Brit./Hung./Aust.)

Bert Schneider
DAYS OF HEAVEN(1978), p; BROKEN ENGLISH(1981), p
Betty Schneider
LOVE IN THE AFTERNOON(1957); MY UNCLE(1958, Fr.); PARIS BELONGS TO US(1962, Fr.); TOMORROW IS MY TURN(1962, Fr./Ital./Ger.)
Clarence Jay Schneider
FLIGHT INTO NOWHERE(1938), w
Daniel Schneider
1984
MAKING THE GRADE(1984)
Daniele Schneider
FIRST TIME, THE(1978, Fr.)
David Schneider
MACHISMO-40 GRAVES FOR 40 GUNS(1970)
Don Schneider
EEGAH!(1962), ed; NASTY RABBIT, THE(1964), art d; INCREDIBLY STRANGE CREATURES WHO STOPPED LIVING AND BECAME CRAZY MIXED-UP ZOMBIES, THE(1965), ed
Edith Schneider
QUILLER MEMORANDUM, THE(1966, Brit.)
Edwin Schneider
SONG O' MY HEART(1930)
Elfe Schneider
SLEEPING BEAUTY(1965, Ger.)
Eric Schneider
MC CABE AND MRS. MILLER(1971)
Gerda Schneider
LAST STOP, THE(1949, Pol.), w
Gerhard Schneider
GERMANY IN AUTUMN(1978, Ger.)
Hans Schneider
F.P. 1 DOESN'T ANSWER(1933, Ger.)
Harold Schneider
PUNISHMENT PARK(1971); SAFE PLACE, A(1971), p; STAY HUNGRY(1976), p; DAYS OF HEAVEN(1978), p; GOIN' SOUTH(1978), p; ENTITY, THE(1982), p; WARGAMES(1983), p
1984
HOUSE OF GOD, THE(1984), p
Helen Schneider
EDDIE AND THE CRUISERS(1983)
Helmut Schneider
STORY OF JOSEPH AND HIS BRETHREN THE(1962, Ital.); CAPTAIN SINDBAD(1963); SECRET INVASION, THE(1964); IS PARIS BURNING?(1966, U.S./Fr.); ASSIGNMENT K(1968, Brit.); POSTMAN GOES TO WAR, THE(1968, Fr.); UNHOLY FOUR, THE(1969, Ital.); DIRTY HEROES(1971, Ital./Fr./Ger.)
Herman Schneider
NAKED DAWN, THE(1955), w
Joe Schneider
MAN IN THE SHADOW(1957)
John Schneider
EDDIE MACON'S RUN(1983)
Jurgen Schneider
TURNING POINT, THE(1977)
Kurt Schneider
PIRATE MOVIE, THE(1982, Aus.)
Larry Schneider
CROSSROADS(1938, Fr.), titles
Leonard Schneider
JAMBOREE(1957)
Lisa Schneider
LA DOLCE VITA(1961, Ital./Fr.)
Lou Schneider
CROWD ROARS, THE(1932)
Mark Schneider
Misc. Talkies
BURNOUT(1979)
Magda Schneider
BE MINE TONIGHT(1933, Brit.); KISS ME GOODBYE(1935, Brit.); STORY OF VICKIE, THE(1958, Aust.); HOUSE OF THE THREE GIRLS, THE(1961, Aust.); FOREVER MY LOVE(1962); GIRL AND THE LEGEND, THE(1966, Ger.)
Margaret Schneider
1001 ARABIAN NIGHTS(1959), w
Maria Schneider
LA BABY SITTER(1975, Fr./Ital./Ger.); PASSENGER, THE(1975, Ital.); MAMMA DRACULA(1980, Bel./Fr.)
Mark Schneider
PREMONITION, THE(1976); SUPER VAN(1977); YOUNG GIANTS(1983)
Max Schneider
Silents
APPEARANCE OF EVIL(1918), ph; JOURNEY'S END(1918), ph; AMATEUR WIDOW, AN(1919), ph; PRAISE AGENT, THE(1919), ph; RIDDLE: WOMAN, THE(1920), ph; CARDIGAN(1922), ph
Michael Schneider
Misc. Talkies
LAST WINTER, THE(1983)
Milton Schneider
BAYOU(1957)
Moe Schneider
PETE KELLY'S BLUES(1955)
Nina Schneider
NAKED DAWN, THE(1955), w
Paul Schneider
LOOTERS, THE(1955), w; 1001 ARABIAN NIGHTS(1959), w; THAT TENNESSEE BEAT(1966), w
Romy Schneider
STORY OF VICKIE, THE(1958, Aust.); CHRISTINE(1959, Fr.); FOREVER MY LOVE(1962); CARDINAL, THE(1963); MAGNIFICENT SINNER(1963, Fr.); TRIAL, THE(1963, Fr./Ital./Ger.); VICTORS, THE(1963); GOOD NEIGHBOR SAM(1964); MAEDCHEN IN UNIFORM(1965, Ger./Fr.); WHAT'S NEW, PUSSYCAT?(1965, U.S./Fr.); GIRL AND THE LEGEND, THE(1966, Ger.); 10:30 P.M. SUMMER(1966, U.S./Span.);

TRIPLE CROSS(1967, Fr./Brit.); OTLEY(1969, Brit.); MY LOVER, MY SON(1970, Brit.); THINGS OF LIFE, THE(1970, Fr./Ital./Switz.); BLOOMFIELD(1971, Brit./Israel); ASSASSINATION OF TROTSKY, THE(1972 Fr./Ital.); CESAR AND ROSALIE(1972, Fr.); LUDWIG(1973, Ital./Ger./Fr.); FRENCH WAY, THE(1975, Fr.); MAIN THING IS TO LOVE, THE(1975, Ital./Fr.); DIRTY HANDS(1976, Fr/Ital./Ger.); WOMAN AT HER WINDOW, A(1978, Fr./Ital./Ger.); BLOODLINE(1979); WOMANLIGHT(1979, Fr./Ger./Ital.); CLAIR DE FEMME(1980,Fr.); DEATHWATCH(1980, Fr./Ger.); INQUISITOR, THE(1982, Fr.); LA PASSANTE(1983, Fr./Ger.)

Roy Schneider
PAPER LION(1968)
Samuel Schneider
CALTIKI, THE IMMORTAL MONSTER(1959, Ital.), p
Stanley Schneider
HOT ROD HULLABALOO(1966), w; THREE DAYS OF THE CONDOR(1975), p
Virginia Schneider
LILITH(1964)
Walter Schneider
FOUNTAIN OF LOVE, THE(1968, Aust.), w
Wolf Schneider
MAGIC FOUNTAIN, THE(1961), ph
George Schneiderman
BORN RECKLESS(1930), ph; GOOD INTENTIONS(1930), ph; PART TIME WIFE(1930), ph; SCOTLAND YARD(1930), ph; CHARLIE CHAN CARRIES ON(1931), ph; HOLY TERROR, A(1931), ph; RIDERS OF THE PURPLE SAGE(1931), ph; UNDER SUSPICION(1931), ph; GAY CABALLERO, THE(1932), ph; GOLDEN WEST, THE(1932), ph; STEPPING SISTERS(1932), ph; YOUNG AMERICA(1932), ph; DR. BULL(1933), ph; INFERNAL MACHINE(1933), ph; PILGRIMAGE(1933), ph; ROBBERS' ROOST(1933), ph; WALLS OF GOLD(1933), ph; GEORGE WHITE'S SCANDALS(1934), ph; HOLD THAT GIRL(1934), ph; JUDGE PRIEST(1934), ph; ORIENT EXPRESS(1934), ph; WORLD MOVES ON, THE(1934), ph; ELINOR NORTON(1935), ph; GEORGE WHITE'S 1935 SCANDALS(1935), ph; STEAMBOAT ROUND THE BEND(1935), ph; DEVIL IS A SISSY, THE(1936), ph; 52ND STREET(1937), ph; FLIRTING WITH FATE(1938), ph; GLADIATOR, THE(1938), ph; MICHAEL SHAYNE, PRIVATE DETECTIVE(1940), ph
Silents
CHILDREN OF THE NIGHT(1921), ph; QUEENIE(1921), ph; SINGING RIVER(1921), ph; PARDON MY NERVE!(1922), ph; PAWN TICKET 210(1922), ph; HEARTS OF OAK(1924), ph; IRON HORSE, THE(1924), ph; ROUGHNECK, THE(1924), ph; LAZYBONES(1925), ph; JOHNSTOWN FLOOD, THE(1926), ph; AUCTIONEER, THE(1927), ph; IS ZAT SO?(1927), ph; FOUR SONS(1928), ph; ROAD HOUSE(1928), ph
Meryl Schneiderman
TAKING OFF(1971)
Wally Schneiderman
GUNS OF NAVARONE, THE(1961), makup; LISA(1962, Brit.), makeup; NINE HOURS TO RAMA(1963, U.S./Brit.), makeup; MODEL MURDER CASE, THE(1964, Brit.), makeup; SANDS OF THE KALAHARI(1965, Brit.), makeup; WOMAN WHO WOULDN'T DIE, THE(1965, Brit.), makeup; IDOL, THE(1966, Brit.), makeup; ONE MILLION YEARS B.C.(1967, Brit./U.S.), makeup; PREHISTORIC WOMEN(1967, Brit.), makeup; ROBBERY(1967, Brit.), makeup; INSPECTOR CLOUSEAU(1968, Brit.), makeup; WHERE'S JACK?(1969, Brit.), makeup; IN SEARCH OF GREGORY(1970, Brit./Ital.), makeup; LAST GRENADE, THE(1970, Brit.), makeup; SCARS OF DRACULA, THE(1970, Brit.), makeup; LAST VALLEY, THE(1971, Brit.), makeup; ROLLERBALL(1975), makeup
Chaim Schneier
Misc. Talkies
JEWISH DAUGHTER(1933)
Ray Schneir
SINGING BLACKSMITH(1938)
G.H. Schnell
DANTON(1931, Ger.)
Silents
NOSFERATU, THE VAMPIRE(1922, Ger.)
Gary Schnell
OFF THE WALL(1977)
George Schnell
FLAME OF LOVE, THE(1930, Brit.)
Silents
PLEASURE GARDEN, THE(1925, Brit./Ger.)
Ken Schnell
JUD(1971)
Lutz Schnell
DAS BOOT(1982)
Charles Schnettler
MR. BUG GOES TO TOWN(1941), ph
The Schnicketfritz Band
GOLD DIGGERS IN PARIS(1938)
Christiane Schnidtner
BOEING BOEING(1965)
Oscar Schnirch
ETERNAL MASK, THE(1937, Swiss), ph
Avrumie Schnitzer
SUMMER CAMP(1979), w
Borde Schnitzer
SUMMER CAMP(1979), w
Dutch Schnitzer
STEEL ARENA(1973)
Gerald Schnitzer
BOWERY AT MIDNIGHT(1942), w; CORPSE VANISHES, THE(1942), w; SCREAM IN THE DARK, A(1943), w; ANGELS ALLEY(1948), w; JINX MONEY(1948), w; TROUBLE MAKERS(1948), w; ANGELS IN DISGUISE(1949), w; FIGHTING FOOLS(1949), w; HOLD THAT BABY!(1949), w
Gerald J. Schnitzer
KID DYNAMITE(1943), w
Henrietta Schnitzer
Silents
BROKEN HEARTS(1926)

Joseph I. Schnitzer
MEN ARE SUCH FOOLS(1933), p; TOMORROW AT SEVEN(1933), p; GOODBYE LOVE(1934), p
Robert Allen Schnitzer
NO PLACE TO HIDE(1975), p&d, w, ed; PREMONITION, THE(1976), p&d, w
Arthur Schnitzler
DAYBREAK(1931), w; LA RONDE(1954, Fr.), w; CHRISTINE(1959, Fr.), w; CIRCLE OF LOVE(1965, Fr.), w
1984
NEW YORK NIGHTS(1984), w
Silents
AFFAIRS OF ANATOL, THE(1921), w
Peter Schnitzler
CARNIVAL OF SOULS(1962)
Olga Linek Schnoll
Silents
NET, THE(1923), w
Reinhold Schnuzel
VICIOUS CIRCLE, THE(1948)
Franz Schnyder
HEIDI AND PETER(1955, Switz.), d
Andrea Schober
EFFI BRIEST(1974, Ger.); CHINESE ROULETTE(1977, Ger.)
Josef Schober
HIPPODROME(1961, Aust./Ger.), makeup
Olga Schoberova
LEMONADE JOE(1966, Czech.); 25TH HOUR, THE(1967, Fr./Ital./Yugo.)
Olga Schoberove
ADELE HASN'T HAD HER SUPPER YET(1978, Czech.)
Hal Schochet
PUTNEY SWOPE(1969)
Debbie Schock
BILLY JACK(1971)
Rudolf Schock
YOU ARE THE WORLD FOR ME(1964, Aust.)
Rudolph Schock
HOUSE OF THE THREE GIRLS, THE(1961, Aust.)
Larry Schoebel
EMERGENCY CALL(1933)
Herman Schoebrun
DINOSAURUS(1960), set d
Doris Schoeder
JESSE JAMES, JR.(1942), w
Ernest Schoedsack
LIVES OF A BENGAL LANCER(1935), ph
Ernest B. Schoedsack
RANGO(1931), p&d, ed; MOST DANGEROUS GAME, THE(1932), p, d; BLIND ADVENTURE(1933), d; KING KONG(1933), a, p&d; MONKEY'S PAW, THE(1933), d; SON OF KONG(1933), d; LONG LOST FATHER(1934), d; LAST DAYS OF POMPEII, THE(1935), d; OUTLAWS OF THE ORIENT(1937), d; TROUBLE IN MOROCCO(1937), d; DR. CYCLOPS(1940), d; MIGHTY JOE YOUNG(1949), d
Silents
GREED(1925), ph; CHANG(1927), p,d&w, ph; FOUR FEATHERS(1929), d, ph, ed
Fred Schoedsack
Silents
MOON MADNESS(1920), ph
Michael Schoeffling
1984
SIXTEEN CANDLES(1984)
Johnie Schoefield
REAL BLOKE, A(1935, Brit.)
Paul Schoefield
WELLS FARGO(1937), w
Jill Schoelen
D.C. CAB(1983)
1984
HOT MOVES(1984)
Anna Schoeller
1984
SUBURBIA(1984)
Ingrid Schoeller
MY SON, THE HERO(1963, Ital./Fr.); 00-2 MOST SECRET AGENTS(1965, Ital.)
William F. Schoeller
ROYAL BOX, THE(1930)
Gloria Schoeman
CAPTAIN SCARLETT(1953), ed
Gloria Schoemann
PORTRAIT OF MARIA(1946, Mex.), ed; PEARL, THE(1948, U.S./Mex.), ed; INVASION OF THE VAMPIRES, THE(1961, Mex.), ed; MACARIO(1961, Mex.), ed; YOUNG AND EVIL(1962, Mex.), ed
Dorothy Schoemer
OLD ACQUAINTANCE(1943); THANK YOUR LUCKY STARS(1943); DESTINATION TOKYO(1944)
Frank Schoen
SOME OF MY BEST FRIENDS ARE...(1971), set d
Vic Schoen
HOW'S ABOUT IT?(1943), m; SWINGTIME JOHNNY(1944), m
Victor Schoen
COURT JESTER, THE(1956), m
Marianne Schoenauer
TRIAL, THE(1948, Aust.); DON JUAN(1956, Aust.)
Charles Schoenbaum
COMMAND PERFORMANCE(1931), ph; SALVATION NELL(1931), ph; WOMAN HUNGRY(1931), ph; WOMEN GO ON FOREVER(1931), ph; MEN ARE SUCH FOOLS(1933), ph; RACETRACK(1933), ph; TOMORROW AT SEVEN(1933), ph; GOODBYE LOVE(1934), ph; HERE COMES THE BAND(1935), ph; IT'S IN THE AIR(1935), ph; RAINBOW ON THE RIVER(1936), ph; DAUGHTER OF SHANGHAI(1937), ph; LOVE ON TOAST(1937), ph; ON SUCH A NIGHT(1937), ph; SECRET VALLEY(1937), ph; SONS OF THE LEGION(1938), ph; ESCAPE TO PARADISE(1939), ph; FISHERMAN'S WHARF(1939), ph; WAY DOWN SOUTH(1939), ph; ALWAYS A

BRIDE(1940), ph; NEW YORK TOWN(1941), ph; HI DIDDLE DIDDLE(1943), ph; JUNIOR ARMY(1943), ph; SALUTE TO THE MARINES(1943), ph; ABBOTT AND COSTELLO IN HOLLYWOOD(1945), ph; SON OF LASSIE(1945), ph; BAD BASCOMB(1946), ph; MIGHTY MCGURK, THE(1946), ph; CYNTHIA(1947), ph; GOOD NEWS(1947), ph; HILLS OF HOME(1948), ph; SUMMER HOLIDAY(1948), ph; CHALLENGE TO LASSIE(1949), ph; LITTLE WOMEN(1949), ph; DUCHESS OF IDAHO, THE(1950), ph; OUTRIDERS, THE(1950), ph; STARS IN MY CROWN(1950), ph

Silents

ACROSS THE CONTINENT(1922), ph

C. E. Schoenbaum

Silents

BEAU SABREUR(1928), ph

C. Edgar Schoenbaum

SALLY(1929), ph; ROGUE SONG, THE(1930), ph; SHE GOT WHAT SHE WANTED(1930), ph

Silents

ALWAYS AUDACIOUS(1920), ph; MISS HOBBS(1920), ph; CHARM SCHOOL, THE(1921), ph; ADVENTURE(1925), ph; DEVIL'S CARGO, THE(1925), ph; IN THE NAME OF LOVE(1925), ph; NEVADA(1927), ph

C.F. Schoenbaum

GOT WHAT SHE WANTED(1930), ph

Charles E. Schoenbaum

BRIDE OF THE REGIMENT(1930), ph; HELL BOUND(1931), ph

Silents

TOO MUCH SPEED(1921), ph; HEART RAIDER, THE(1923), ph; MR. BILLINGS SPENDS HIS DIME(1923), ph; NOBODY'S MONEY(1923), ph

Charles Edgar Schoenbaum

Silents

EXIT THE VAMP(1921), ph; SHAM(1921), ph; ON THE HIGH SEAS(1922), ph; SIREN CALL, THE(1922), ph; WORLD'S CHAMPION, THE(1922), ph; CODE OF THE SEA(1924), ph; EMPTY HANDS(1924), ph

Charles F. Schoenbaum

SAILOR BE GOOD(1933), ph

Edgar Schoenbaum

Silents

ARIZONA BOUND(1927), ph

Alex Schoenberg

NOTHING SACRED(1937)

Alexander Schoenberg

I MET HIM IN PARIS(1937); CRASHIN' THRU DANGER(1938)

Arnold Schoenberg

MOSES AND AARON(1975, Ger./Fr./Ital.), m

Irving Schoenberg

GEISHA GIRL(1952), ed; FIGHTING CHANCE, THE(1955), ed; TEENAGE THUNDER(1957), ed; TEENAGE MONSTER(1958), ed

Irving M. Schoenberg

EXPOSED(1947), ed; HEART OF VIRGINIA(1948), ed; LIGHTNIN' IN THE FOREST(1948), ed; SUNDOWN IN SANTA FE(1948), ed; BANDIT KING OF TEXAS(1949), ed; RANGER OF CHEROKEE STRIP(1949), ed; CODE OF THE SILVER SAGE(1950), ed; GUNMEN OF ABILENE(1950), ed; ARIZONA MANHUNT(1951), ed; FORT DODGE STAMPEDE(1951), ed; NIGHT RIDERS OF MONTANA(1951), ed; ROUGH RIDERS OF DURANGO(1951), ed; SECRETS OF MONTE CARLO(1951), ed; BRAIN FROM THE PLANET AROUS, THE(1958), ed

Jeremy Schoenberg

SHOOT THE MOON(1982)

Mark Schoenberg

PARALLELS(1980, Can.), d, w

Herman Schoenbrun

LADY FROM SHANGHAI, THE(1948), set d; IT! THE TERROR FROM BEYOND SPACE(1958), set d

Pierre Schoendoerffer

OBJECTIVE 500 MILLION(1966, Fr.), d&w

1984

LE CRABE TAMBOUR(1984, Fr.), d, w

Reiner Schoene

EIGER SANCTION, THE(1975)

Eberhard Schoener

SLAVERS(1977, Ger.), m

Ingeborg Schoener

IT HAPPENED IN ROME(1959, Ital.); LOVE AND MARRIAGE(1966, Ital.); MARK OF THE DEVIL(1970, Ger./Brit.); MR. SUPERINVISIBLE(1974, Ital./Span./Ger.)

Bernard Schoenfeld

DARK CORNER, THE(1946), w; PIER 5, HAVANA(1959), w; MAGIC SWORD, THE(1962), w

Bernard C. Schoenfeld

PHANTOM LADY(1944), w; CAGED(1950), w; MACAO(1952), w; DOWN THREE DARK STREETS(1954), w; THERE'S ALWAYS TOMORROW(1956), w; SPACE CHILDREN, THE(1958), w; THIRTEEN WEST STREET(1962), w

Brent Schoenfeld

BUTTERFLY(1982), ed

Don Schoenfeld

LASSIE'S GREAT ADVENTURE(1963), makeup; SOMETHING BIG(1971), makeup; LADY SINGS THE BLUES(1972), makeup; NECROMANCY(1972), makeup; GAUNTLET, THE(1977), makeup

Gerald Schoenfeld

1984

BROADWAY DANNY ROSE(1984)

Mae Schoenfeld

ELI ELI(1940)

Bruce Schoengarth

HEROES IN BLUE(1939), ed; AFRICAN TREASURE(1952), ed; ARMY BOUND(1952), ed; ROBOT MONSTER(1953), ed; SON OF BELLE STARR(1953), ed; WHITE LIGHTNING(1953), ed

Russell Schoengarth

MEDICINE MAN, THE(1930), ed; PARTY GIRL(1930), ed; WEREWOLF OF LONDON, THE(1935), ed; GREAT GUY(1936), ed; BOY OF THE STREETS(1937), ed; GUNSMOKE RANCH(1937), ed; PARADISE ISLE(1937), ed; THIRTEENTH MAN, THE(1937), ed; GANGSTER'S BOY(1938), ed; MARINES ARE HERE, THE(1938), ed; MR. WONG, DETECTIVE(1938), ed; ROMANCE OF THE LIMBERLOST(1938), ed; SALESLADY(1938), ed; TELEPHONE OPERATOR(1938), ed; UNDER THE BIG

TOP(1938), ed; CONVICT'S CODE(1939), ed; GIRL FROM RIO, THE(1939), ed; I AM A CRIMINAL(1939), ed; IRISH LUCK(1939), ed; MR. WONG IN CHINATOWN(1939), ed; MYSTERY OF MR. WONG, THE(1939), ed; NAVY SECRETS(1939), ed; STAR REPORTER(1939), ed; STREETS OF NEW YORK(1939), ed; TOUGH KID(1939), ed; UNDERCOVER AGENT(1939), ed; APE, THE(1940), ed; FATAL HOUR, THE(1940), ed; HAUNTED HOUSE, THE(1940), ed; ON THE SPOT(1940), ed; QUEEN OF THE YUKON(1940), ed; SON OF THE NAVY(1940), ed; TOMBOY(1940), ed; OLD SWIMMIN' HOLE, THE(1941), ed; UNFINISHED BUSINESS(1941), ed; GREAT IMPERSONATION, THE(1942), ed; LADY IN A JAM(1942), ed; LITTLE JOE, THE WRANGLER(1942), ed; MOONLIGHT IN HAVANA(1942), ed; SHERLOCK HOLMES AND THE VOICE OF TERROR(1942), ed; HONEYMOON LODGE(1943), ed; PHANTOM OF THE OPERA(1943), ed; RAIDERS OF SAN JOAQUIN(1943), ed; WHITE SAVAGE(1943), ed; ALI BABA AND THE FORTY THIEVES(1944), ed; CLIMAX, THE(1944), ed; GYPSY WILDCAT(1944), ed; IMPATIENT YEARS, THE(1944), ed; MY GAL LOVES MUSIC(1944), ed; TRAIL TO GUNSIGHT(1944), ed; HOUSE OF DRACULA(1945), ed; PENTHOUSE RHYTHM(1945), ed; SALOME, WHERE SHE DANCED(1945), ed; STRANGE CONFESSION(1945), ed; TRAIL TO VENGEANCE(1945), ed; CAT CREEPS, THE(1946), ed; DANGER WOMAN(1946), ed; LITTLE MISS BIG(1946), ed; EGG AND I, THE(1947), ed; PIRATES OF MONTEREY(1947), ed; WEB, THE(1947), ed; ARE YOU WITH IT?(1948), ed; BLACK BART(1948), ed; BAGDAD(1949), ed; FIGHTING O'FLYNN, THE(1949), ed; MA AND PA KETTLE(1949), ed; TAKE ONE FALSE STEP(1949), ed; DOUBLE CROSSBONES(1950), ed; MA AND PA KETTLE GO TO TOWN(1950), ed; MILKMAN, THE(1950), ed; UNDERCOVER GIRL(1950), ed; AIR CADET(1951), ed; BRIGHT VICTORY(1951), ed; IRON MAN, THE(1951), ed; LADY PAYS OFF, THE(1951), ed; MA AND PA KETTLE BACK ON THE FARM(1951), ed; WEEKEND WITH FATHER(1951), ed; BEND OF THE RIVER(1952), ed; BLACK CASTLE, THE(1952), ed; DUEL AT SILVER CREEK, THE(1952), ed; HAS ANYBODY SEEN MY GAL?(1952), ed; MEET ME AT THE FAIR(1952), ed; NO ROOM FOR THE GROOM(1952), ed; ABBOTT AND COSTELLO GO TO MARS(1953), ed; GLENN MILLER STORY, THE(1953), ed; THUNDER BAY(1953), ed; WINGS OF THE HAWK(1953), ed; ABBOTT AND COSTELLO MEET DR. JEKYLL AND MR. HYDE(1954), ed; FIREMAN SAVE MY CHILD(1954), ed; FRANCIS JOINS THE WACS(1954), ed; RICOCHET ROMANCE(1954), ed; ABBOTT AND COSTELLO MEET THE MUMMY(1955), ed; FAR COUNTRY, THE(1955), ed; FEMALE ON THE BEACH(1955), ed; LOOTERS, THE(1955), ed; BENNY GOODMAN STORY, THE(1956), ed; RAW EDGE(1956), ed; RAWHIDE YEARS, THE(1956), ed; BATTLE HYMN(1957), ed; BULLET FOR A BADMAN(1964), ed; HE RIDES TALL(1964), ed; WHO FEARS THE DEVIL(1972), ed

Russell F. Schoengarth

MUTINY IN THE BIG HOUSE(1939), ed; WRITTEN ON THE WIND(1956), ed; INTERLUDE(1957), ed; SLAUGHTER ON TENTH AVENUE(1957), ed; TARNISHED ANGELS, THE(1957), ed; RAW WIND IN EDEN(1958), ed; MIDNIGHT LACE(1960), ed; COME SEPTEMBER(1961), ed; SPIRAL ROAD, THE(1962), ed; GATHERING OF EAGLES, A(1963), ed; KITTEN WITH A WHIP(1964), ed; FLUFFY(1965), ed; VERY SPECIAL FAVOR, A(1965), ed; BEAU GESTE(1966), ed; GUNPOINT(1966), ed; KING'S PIRATE(1967), ed; YOUNG WARRIORS, THE(1967), ed; IN ENEMY COUNTRY(1968), ed

Joseph Schoengold

MOTEL, THE OPERATOR(1940)

Albrecht Schoenhals

BOCCACCIO(1936, Ger.); PILLARS OF SOCIETY(1936, Ger.); INTERMEZZO(1937, Ger.)

Dietmar Schoenherr

LONGEST DAY, THE(1962); CODE 7, VICTIM 5(1964, Brit.); COAST OF SKELETONS(1965, Brit.); MONSTER OF LONDON CITY, THE(1967, Ger.)

S.O. Schoening

PILLARS OF SOCIETY(1936, Ger.); INTERMEZZO(1937, Ger.)

Annaliese Schoennenbeck

PHONY AMERICAN, THE(1964, Ger.), ed

Eberhard Schoerer

BENJAMIN(1973, Ger.), m

Johnnie Schofield

TAWNY PIPIT(1947, Brit.); SOMETHING MONEY CAN'T BUY(1952, Brit.)

Don Schoff

DARKER THAN AMBER(1970)

Michael Schoffel

1984

FIRST TURN-ON!, THE(1984)

Leslie Schoffield

STAR WARS(1977)

David Schofield

DOGS OF WAR, THE(1980, Brit.); AMERICAN WEREWOLF IN LONDON, AN(1981)

Frank Schofield

WRONG MAN, THE(1956)

Harry Schofield

BONNIE PRINCE CHARLIE(1948, Brit.)

Joan Schofield

TRIO(1950, Brit.); THREE CORNERED FATE(1954, Brit.); WEAPON, THE(1957, Brit.)

John Schofield

HAWLEY'S OF HIGH STREET(1933, Brit.); PRIDE OF THE FORCE, THE(1933, Brit.); OUTCAST, THE(1934, Brit.); ADVENTURE FOR TWO(1945, Brit.)

Johnnie Schofield

JOSSER ON THE FARM(1934, Brit.); COCK O' THE NORTH(1935, Brit.); JIMMY BOY(1935, Brit.); SEXTON BLAKE AND THE BEARDED DOCTOR(1935, Brit.); VARIETY(1935, Brit.); MELODY OF MY HEART(1936, Brit.); INCIDENT IN SHANGHAI(1937, Brit.); LAST ADVENTURERS, THE(1937, Brit.); MAKE-UP(1937, Brit.); SAM SMALL LEAVES TOWN(1937, Brit.); SONG OF THE ROAD(1937, Brit.); TALKING FEET(1937, Brit.); LASSIE FROM LANCASHIRE(1938, Brit.); MOUNTAINS O'MOURNE(1938, Brit.); NIGHT JOURNEY(1938, Brit.); DOWN OUR ALLEY(1939, Brit.); BOB'S YOUR UNCLE(1941, Brit.); SHEEPDOG OF THE HILLS(1941, Brit.); IN WHICH WE SERVE(1942, Brit.); YOUNG MR. PITT, THE(1942, Brit.); BELLS GO DOWN, THE(1943, Brit.); MILLIONS LIKE US(1943, Brit.); OLD MOTHER RILEY, DETECTIVE(1943, Brit.); UP WITH THE LARK(1943, Brit.); WE DIVE AT DAWN(1943, Brit.); GIVE ME THE STARS(1944, Brit.); UNCENSORED(1944, Brit.); WELCOME, MR. WASHINGTON(1944, Brit.); ECHO MURDERS, THE(1945, Brit.); JOHNNY IN THE CLOUDS(1945, Brit.); VOICE WITHIN, THE(1945, Brit.); WAY AHEAD, THE(1945, Brit.); THIS MAN IS MINE(1946 Brit.); CODE OF SCOTLAND YARD)(1948); LOVE IN WAITING(1948, Brit.); MR. PERRIN AND MR. TRAILL(1948, Brit.); DARK SECRET(1949, Brit.); HER MAN GILBEY(1949, Brit.); WATERLOO ROAD(1949, Brit.); SECOND MATE, THE(1950, Brit.); RELUCTANT WIDOW, THE(1951, Brit.); ISLAND

RESCUE(1952, Brit.); TRAIN OF EVENTS(1952, Brit.); WHITE CORRIDORS(1952, Brit.); MURDER WILL OUT(1953, Brit.); PROJECT M7(1953, Brit.); SMALL TOWN STORY(1953, Brit.); WHEEL OF FATE(1953, Brit.); WHITE FIRE(1953, Brit.); COURT MARTIAL(1954, Brit.); SCARLET WEB, THE(1954, Brit.); SOLUTION BY PHONE(1954, Brit.); SEE HOW THEY RUN(1955, Brit.)

Johnny Schofield
END OF THE ROAD, THE(1936, Brit.); PHANTOM SHIP(1937, Brit.); RHYTHM RACKETEER(1937, Brit.); FATHER O'FLYNN(1938, Irish); SPECIAL EDITION(1938, Brit.); NEXT OF KIN(1942, Brit.); 48 HOURS(1944, Brit.); WHILE I LIVE(1947, Brit.); MARK OF CAIN, THE(1948, Brit.); MY BROTHER JONATHAN(1949, Brit.); FAKE, THE(1953, Brit.)

Katharine Schofield
NICHOLAS AND ALEXANDRA(1971, Brit.); POPE JOAN(1972, Brit.); GREEK TYCOON, THE(1978)

Leslie Schofield
LOLA(1971, Brit./Ital.); VILLAIN(1971, Brit.); RULING CLASS, THE(1972, Brit.)

Madge E. Schofield
CALCUTTA(1947)

Nell Schofield
PUBERTY BLUES(1983, Aus.)

Paul Schofield
SCANDAL(1929), w; FRAMED(1930), w; JIMMY AND SALLY(1933), w; SENSATION HUNTERS(1934), w; SUNSET RANGE(1935), w; MYSTERY PLANE(1939), w
Silents
LAST TRAIL(1921), w; LIGHTS OF THE DESERT(1922), w; MIXED FACES(1922), w; WEST OF CHICAGO(1922), w; EAST OF BROADWAY(1924), w; "THAT ROYLE GIRL"(1925), w; NIGHT LIFE OF NEW YORK(1925), w; BEAU GESTE(1926), w; HEARTS AND FISTS(1926), w; PARADISE(1926), w; TEXAS STEER, A(1927), w; ESCAPE, THE(1928), w

Peter Schofield
ROUGH CUT(1980, Brit.)

Walter Schofield
RAT, THE(1938, Brit.)

Alan Scholefield
VENOM(1982, Brit.), w

Kim Scholes
NESTING, THE(1981), m

Art Scholl
GREAT WALDO PEPPER, THE(1975), stunts

Danny Scholl
NANCY GOES TO RIO(1950); TOP BANANA(1954)

Edward Scholl
Silents
ONE EXCITING NIGHT(1922), spec eff; ORPHANS OF THE STORM(1922), set d; WHITE ROSE, THE(1923), spec eff

Jack Scholl
BLAZING SIXES(1937), m/l M. K. Jerome; CONFESSION(1937), m; MARKED WOMAN(1937), m/l; MUSIC IN MANHATTAN(1944), w; HOLIDAY RHYTHM(1950), d

Mitchell Schollars
WAY WEST, THE(1967)

Christina Schollin
SWEDISH WEDDING NIGHT(1965, Swed.); DEAR JOHN(1966, Swed.); LOVE MATES(1967, Swed.); WOMAN OF DARKNESS(1968, Swed.); SONG OF NORWAY(1970); FANNY AND ALEXANDER(1983, Swed./Fr./Ger.)

Picot Scholling
OUTSIDER, THE(1940, Brit.)

Abe Scholtz
POLICE CALL(1933), ph
Silents
HEARTS AND FISTS(1926), ph

Robert Scholtz
Silents
RAT, THE(1925, Brit.)

Axel Scholz
PHONY AMERICAN, THE(1964, Ger.)

Brigitte Scholz
TRAPP FAMILY, THE(1961, Ger.), cos

Eva Ingeborg Scholz
AMERICAN SOLDIER, THE(1970 Ger.)

Eva-Ingeborg Scholz
LOST ONE, THE(1951, Ger.); DEVIL'S GENERAL, THE(1957, Ger.); GIRL OF THE MOORS, THE(1961, Ger.); CITY OF SECRETS(1963, Ger.); EMIL AND THE DETECTIVES(1964)

Heinz Scholz
NAKED AMONG THE WOLVES(1967, Ger.)

Marcus Scholz
WILLY(1963, U.S./Ger.), w

Robert Scholz
Silents
ISN'T LIFE WONDERFUL(1924)

Gerda Scholz-Grosse
WORLD IN MY POCKET, THE(1962, Fr./Ital./Ger.), makeup

Carl Scholze
DO NOT THROW CUSHIONS INTO THE RING(1970)

Hermann Schomberg
FAUST(1963, Ger.)

Abraham Schomer
TODAY(1930), w
Silents
TODAY(1917), w
Misc. Silents
CHAMBER OF MYSTERY, THE(1920), d

Abraham S. Schomer
Misc. Silents
SACRED FLAME, THE(1919), d; HIDDEN LIGHT(1920), d

E. Schomer
FIGHT FOR ROME(1969, Ger./Rum.), set d

Ernst Schomer
MAD EXECUTIONERS, THE(1965, Ger.), art d; DEFECTOR, THE(1966, Ger./Fr.), art d; CORRUPT ONES, THE(1967, Ger.), art d; MONSTER OF LONDON CITY, THE(1967, Ger.), art d; PHANTOM OF SOHO, THE(1967, Ger.), art d

Kyra Schon
NIGHT OF THE LIVING DEAD(1968)

Margarethe Schon
Silents
KRIEMHILD'S REVENGE(1924, Ger.); SIEGFRIED(1924, Ger.)

Marianne Schonauer
FOUNTAIN OF LOVE, THE(1968, Aust.)

Alex Schonberg
THEY SHALL HAVE MUSIC(1939)

Alexander Schonberg
INTERNES CAN'T TAKE MONEY(1937); MAYTIME(1937); ROMANCE IN THE DARK(1938); NINOTCHKA(1939)
Misc. Talkies
BEAST OF BORNEO(1935)

Hans Schonberger
NOT RECONCILED, OR "ONLY VIOLENCE HELPS WHERE IT RULES"(1969, Ger.)

Paul Schonberger
NORMAN LOVES ROSE(1982, Aus.)

Terry Schonblum
RABID(1976, Can.)

Karl Schonbock
SCHLAGER-PARADE(1953); CONGRESS DANCES(1957, Ger.)

Karl Schonbourg
NUDE ODYSSEY(1962, Fr./Ital.)

Prince Johannes Schonburg-Hartenstein
GREAT WALTZ, THE(1972)

Reiner Schone
RETURN OF SABATA(1972, Ital./Fr./Ger.)

Wolfgang Schone
CHRONICLE OF ANNA MAGDALENA BACH(1968, Ital., Ger.)

Schoneberg
HOW TO SEDUCE A WOMAN(1974)

William Schoneberger
SOME KIND OF HERO(1982)

Rene Schonenberger
1984
WOMAN IN FLAMES, A(1984, Ger.)

Inge Schoner
GEORGE(1973, U.S./Switz.)

Ingeborg Schoner
COW AND I, THE(1961, Fr., Ital., Ger.); KING IN SHADOW(1961, Ger.); MYSTERY OF THUG ISLAND, THE(1966, Ital./Ger.); UNWILLING AGENT(1968, Ger.)

Sonja Schoner
FIDELIO(1961, Aust.)

Friedrich Schonfelder
MAGICIAN OF LUBLIN, THE(1979, Israel/Ger.)

Emmy Schonfield
Misc. Silents
WITCHCRAFT THROUGH THE AGES(1921, Swed.)

Hugh J. Schonfield
PASSOVER PLOT, THE(1976, Israel), w

Hubert Schonger
HANSEL AND GRETEL(1965, Ger.), p; SNOW WHITE(1965, Ger.), p; SHOEMAKER AND THE ELVES, THE(1967, Ger.), p, w

Dietmar Schonherr
THREE MOVES TO FREEDOM(1960, Ger.); BRAINWASHED(1961, Ger.); COMMANDO(1962, Ital., Span., Bel., Ger.); TWO IN A SLEEPING BAG(1964, Ger.); MOZAMBIQUE(1966, Brit.); SKI FEVER(1969, U.S./Aust./Czech.)

Terry Schoolcraft
TENDER MERCIES(1982)

Zvee Schooler
1984
OVER THE BROOKLYN BRIDGE(1984)

Mory Schoolhouse
V.D.(1961)

Picot Schooling
BOAT FROM SHANGHAI(1931, Brit.); LOVE'S OLD SWEET SONG(1933, Brit.)

Skip Schoolnick
BODY AND SOUL(1981), ed

Stuart Schoolnick
AVALANCHE(1978), ed

S. Skip Schoolnik
MEGAFORCE(1982), ed

Skip Schoolnik
DR. HECKYL AND MR. HYPE(1980), ed; HALLOWEEN II(1981), ed; GALAXY EXPRESS(1982, Jap.), ed

Thelma Schoonmaker
FINNEGANS WAKE(1965), ed; VIRGIN PRESIDENT, THE(1968), ed; WHO'S THAT KNOCKING AT MY DOOR?(1968), ed; RAGING BULL(1980), ed; KING OF COMEDY, THE(1983), ed

W.K. Schoonover
MAYBE IT'S LOVE(1930)

Herman Schoop
Silents
WINGS(1927), ph

Lex Schoorel
MODESTY BLAISE(1966, Brit.); LITTLE ARK, THE(1972)

Bernie Schootz
SUBSTITUTION(1970)

Dana Schootz
SUBSTITUTION(1970)

Leslie Schootz
SUBSTITUTION(1970)

Herman Schopp
GIGOLETTES OF PARIS(1933), ph; TOKYO FILE 212(1951), ph
James Schoppe
CORVETTE SUMMER(1978), art d; BEING THERE(1979), art d; OCTAGON, THE(1980), prod d; STUNT MAN, THE(1980), art d; WHY WOULD I LIE(1980), art d; RETURN OF THE JEDI(1983), art d
1984
REVENGE OF THE NERDS(1984), prod d
James L. Schoppe
SOME KIND OF HERO(1982), art d; UNCOMMON VALOR(1983), prod d
Jim Schoppe
ROSE, THE(1979), art d
James Schoppee
LOOKIN' TO GET OUT(1982), art d
Bill Schoppert
PERSONALS, THE(1982)
William Schoppert
IT AIN'T EASY(1972)
Lou Schor
BIGAMIST,THE(1953), w; LADY WANTS MINK, THE(1953), w
Gretl Schorg
HIPPODROME(1961, Aust./Ger.)
Evald Schorm
NIGHTS OF PRAGUE, THE(1968, Czech.), d; REPORT ON THE PARTY AND THE GUESTS, A(1968, Czech.); END OF A PRIEST(1970, Czech.), d, w
Bill Schorr
ZIEGFELD FOLLIES(1945), w
Lester Schorr
QUICK GUN, THE(1964), ph
William Schorr
FORGOTTEN COMMANDMENTS(1932), d; INDIAN FIGHTER, THE(1955), p
William W. Schorr
ULYSSES(1955, Ital.), p
Bob Schott
WORKING GIRLS, THE(1973); FORCE: FIVE(1981)
Werner Schott
F.P. 1 DOESN'T ANSWER(1933, Ger.)
Wayne A. Schotten
Misc. Talkies
FRIDAY ON MY MIND(1970), d
Millie Schottland
Silents
HUNGRY HEARTS(1922)
Pascal Schouteeten
1984
HERE COMES SANTA CLAUS(1984), set d
Lt. Schouwenaar
SILVER FLEET, THE(1945, Brit.)
John Schowest
DAMN CITIZEN(1958)
Barry Schrader
GALAXY OF TERROR(1981), m
Charles Schrader
JANIE(1944)
Genevieve Schrader
MIDSTREAM(1929)
George Schrader
MISSION BATANGAS(1968), ed
Hugo Schrader
ROYAL WALTZ, THE(1936)
Leonard Schrader
YAKUZA, THE(1975, U.S./Jap.), w; BLUE COLLAR(1978), w; OLD BOY-FRIENDS(1979), w; MAN WHO STOLE THE SUN, THE(1980, Jap.), w
Marie Schrader
Silents
SO THIS IS ARIZONA(1922), w
Paul Schrader
YAKUZA, THE(1975, U.S./Jap.), w; OBSESSION(1976), w; TAXI DRIVER(1976), w; ROLLING THUNDER(1977), w; BLUE COLLAR(1978), d, w; HARDCORE(1979), d&w; OLD BOYFRIENDS(1979), w; AMERICAN GIGOLO(1980), d&w; RAGING BULL(1980), w; CAT PEOPLE(1982), d
Rudolph Schrager
MONSIEUR VERDOUX(1947), md; HIGH LONESOME(1950), m
Rudy Schrager
STANLEY AND LIVINGSTONE(1939), m; SNUFFY SMITH, YARD BIRD(1942), md; TAKE IT BIG(1944), m; TOKYO ROSE(1945), m; SWAMP FIRE(1946), m; DANGER-OUS YEARS(1947), m; FEAR IN THE NIGHT(1947), m; GUILTY, THE(1947), m; GUNFIGHTERS, THE(1947), m; HIGH TIDE(1947), m; ROSES ARE RED(1947), m; SLEEP, MY LOVE(1948), m, md; STRIKE IT RICH(1948), m; LAST VOYAGE, THE(1960), m
Charles Schram
TELL ME THAT YOU LOVE ME, JUNIE MOON(1970), makeup; PORTNOY'S COMPLAINT(1972), makeup; THEY ONLY KILL THEIR MASTERS(1972), makeup; THING WITH TWO HEADS, THE(1972), makeup; PAPILLON(1973), makeup; LOOK-ING FOR MR. GOODBAR(1977), makeup; TURNING POINT, THE(1977), makeup; BEING THERE(1979), makeup
Charles H. Schram
MOMMIE DEAREST(1981), makeup
Ethel Schram
Silents
NIGHT WATCH, THE(1926)
Violet Schram
Silents
RIDERS OF THE DAWN(1920); PRIDE OF SUNSHINE ALLEY(1924)
Misc. Silents
BIG HAPPINESS(1920)
Arthur Schramm
MAN ON A TIGHTROPE(1953), makeup; SITUATION HOPELESS–BUT NOT SERI-OUS(1965), makeup; MERRY WIVES OF WINDSOR, THE(1966, Aust.), makeup

Erica Schramm
5 SINNERS(1961, Ger.)
Karla Schramm
Silents
BROKEN BLOSSOMS(1919); HIS MAJESTY THE AMERICAN(1919)
Misc. Silents
JUNGLE TRAIL OF THE SON OF TARZAN(1923)
William Schramm
DRACULA'S DAUGHTER(1936)
Rick Schrand
1984
PHILADELPHIA EXPERIMENT, THE(1984)
Raoul Schranil
DO YOU KEEP A LION AT HOME?(1966, Czech.)
Joseph Schrank
PAGE MISS GLORY(1935), w; HARD TO GET(1938), w; HE COULDN'T SAY NO(1938), w; SLIGHT CASE OF MURDER, A(1938), w; SWING YOUR LADY(1938), w; MAGNIFICENT DOPE, THE(1942), w; RINGS ON HER FINGERS(1942), w; SONG OF THE ISLANDS(1942), w; CABIN IN THE SKY(1943), w; BATHING BEAU-TY(1944), w; CLOCK, THE(1945), w; ZIEGFELD FOLLIES(1945), w
Ernest Schrapps
PICK A STAR(1937), cos
Howard Schraps
TOPPER(1937), cos
Richard Schrayer
DEVIL MAY CARE(1929), w
Max Schreck
Silents
NOSFERATU, THE VAMPIRE(1922, Ger.)
Noldi Schreck
LOVE HAS MANY FACES(1965), set d
Peter Schreck
WE OF THE NEVER NEVER(1983, Aus.), w
Vicki Schreck
WHAT'S THE MATTER WITH HELEN?(1971); FREAKY FRIDAY(1976)
Frederick Schrecker
UNDERCOVER AGENT(1935, Brit.); DIVIDED HEART, THE(1955, Brit.); INNO-CENTS IN PARIS(1955, Brit.); MASTER PLAN, THE(1955, Brit.); FOREIGN IN-TRIGUE(1956); MARK OF THE PHOENIX(1958, Brit.)
Eva Schreckling
FREDDY UNTER FREMDEN STERNEN(1962, Ger.), makeup
Marilyn Schreffler
1984
RUNAWAY(1984)
Alan Schreiber
CRY DR. CHICAGO(1971)
Alfred Schreiber
Misc. Silents
PRINCE AND THE PAUPER, THE(1929, Aust./Czech.)
Avery Schreiber
CONCORDE, THE–AIRPORT '79(; DON'T DRINK THE WATER(1969); MONITORS, THE(1969); SWASHBUCKLER(1976); LAST REMAKE OF BEAU GESTE, THE(1977); SCAVENGER HUNT(1979); GALAXINA(1980); LOOSE SHOES(1980); SILENT SCREAM(1980); CAVEMAN(1981); DEADHEAD MILES(1982); JIMMY THE KID(1982)
1984
CANNONBALL RUN II(1984)
Misc. Talkies
SOUTHERN DOUBLE CROSS(1973)
Bruno Paul Schreiber
Misc. Talkies
MYRTE AND THE DEMONS(1948), d
Catherine Schreiber
1984
WOMAN IN RED, THE(1984)
Edward Schreiber
MAD DOG COLL(1961), p, w
Eva Schreiber
INDECENT(1962, Ger.)
Hans Schreiber
HIDDEN FEAR(1957), m
Harald Schreiber
DOWNHILL RACER(1969)
Helmut Schreiber
SIGNALS-AN ADVENTURE IN SPACE(1970, E. Ger./Pol.)
Norman Schreiber
PUTNEY SWOPE(1969)
Otto Schreiber
IT'S A SMALL WORLD(1950), w
Paul Schreiber
HIGH TIME(1960)
Myrl A. Schreibman
CLONUS HORROR, THE(1979), p, w; PROTECTORS, BOOK 1, THE(1981), p&d
Paul Schreibman
GIGANTIS(1959, Jap./U.S.), p; FIRST SPACESHIP ON VENUS(1960, Ger./Pol.), p
Frederick Schreicher
THIRD MAN, THE(1950, Brit.)
Peter Schreicher
SERENITY(1962)
Alexis Schreiner
SUMMER CAMP(1979)
Elana Schreiner
MA AND PA KETTLE(1949); MA AND PA KETTLE GO TO TOWN(1950); MA AND PA KETTLE AT THE FAIR(1952); MA AND PA KETTLE ON VACATION(1953); MA AND PA KETTLE AT WAIKIKI(1955)
Warner Schreiner
BORN IN FLAMES(1983)

Heinz Schreiter
EMIL AND THE DETECTIVES(1964), m
Emmerich Schrenk
DAS LETZTE GEHEIMNIS(1959, Ger.); ORDERED TO LOVE(1963, Ger.); RESTLESS NIGHT, THE(1964, Ger.); CAVE OF THE LIVING DEAD(1966, Yugo./Ger.)
John Schreyer
DESERT SANDS(1955), ed; WILD YOUTH(1961), d; AMBUSH BAY(1966), ed; APACHE UPRISING(1966), ed; MORE DEAD THAN ALIVE(1968), ed; HELL'S BELLES(1969), ed; I SAILED TO TAHITI WITH AN ALL GIRL CREW(1969), ed
John F. Schreyer
WAR PAINT(1953), ed; BEACHHEAD(1954), ed; SHIELD FOR MURDER(1954), ed; SUDDENLY(1954), ed; YELLOW TOMAHAWK, THE(1954), ed; BIG HOUSE, U.S.A.(1955), ed; FORT YUMA(1955), ed; BLACK SLEEP, THE(1956), ed; BROKEN STAR, THE(1956), ed; EMERGENCY HOSPITAL(1956), ed; QUINCANNON, FRONTIER SCOUT(1956), ed; REBEL IN TOWN(1956), ed; THREE BAD SISTERS(1956), ed; DALTON GIRLS, THE(1957), ed; GIRL IN BLACK STOCKINGS(1957), ed; OUTLAW'S SON(1957), ed; PHARAOH'S CURSE(1957), ed; REVOLT AT FORT LARAMIE(1957), ed; TOMAHAWK TRAIL(1957), ed; UNTAMED YOUTH(1957), ed; VOODOO ISLAND(1957), ed; MACABRE(1958), ed; VIOLENT ROAD(1958), ed; BORN RECKLESS(1959), ed; UP PERISCOPE(1959), ed; CONVICT STAGE(1965), ed; FORT COURAGEOUS(1965), ed; WAR PARTY(1965), ed; FORT UTAH(1967), ed; HOSTILE GUNS(1967), ed; KILL A DRAGON(1967), ed; RED TOMAHAWK(1967), ed; ARIZONA BUSHWHACKERS(1968), ed; IMPASSE(1969), ed; WICKED, WICKED(1973), ed
Linda Schreyer
1984
NEW YORK NIGHTS(1984), m
Friedrich Schreyvogel
ETERNAL WALTZ, THE(1959, Ger.), w
Gov. Henry F. Schricker
JOHNNY HOLIDAY(1949)
Helmut Schrieber
PINOCCHIO(1969, E. Ger.)
Tell Schrieber
KEEPER, THE(1976, Can.)
Capt. Harold G. Schrier, USMC
SANDS OF IWO JIMA(1949)
Leon Schrier
HELL SQUAD(1958); GRASS EATER, THE(1961)
Ben Schrift
CASH ON DELIVERY(1956, Brit.), p
Ray Schrock
IN FAST COMPANY(1946), w; HI-JACKED(1950), w
Raymond Schrock
PHANTOM OF THE OPERA, THE(1929), w; HELL BELOW(1933), w; HAPPY-GO-LUCKY(1937), w; KID NIGHTINGALE(1939), w; PRIVATE DETECTIVE(1939), w; SECRET SERVICE OF THE AIR(1939), w; SMASHING THE MONEY RING(1939), w; DEVIL'S ISLAND(1940), w; MURDER IN THE AIR(1940), w; BULLETS FOR O'-HARA(1941), w; HIDDEN HAND, THE(1942), w; GAS HOUSE KIDS(1946), w; SHADOWS OVER CHINATOWN(1946), w; PRISONERS IN PETTICOATS(1950), w
Silents
LEAP TO FAME(1918), w; WINNING STROKE, THE(1919), w; LONG CHANCE, THE(1922), w; PHANTOM OF THE OPERA, THE(1925), w; DUKE STEPS OUT, THE(1929), w
Raymond L. Schrock
NAVY BLUES(1930), w; PART TIME WIFE(1930), w; BAD SISTER(1931), w; SHIPMATES(1931), w; HARD ROCK HARRIGAN(1935), w; SITTING ON THE MOON(1936), w; ESCAPE FROM CRIME(1942), w; MURDER IN THE BIG HOUSE(1942), w; SECRET ENEMIES(1942), w; WILD BILL HICKOK RIDES(1942), w; ISLE OF FORGOTTEN SINS(1943), w; TRUCK BUSTERS(1943), w; GREAT MIKE, THE(1944), w; LAST RIDE, THE(1944), w; MEN ON HER MIND(1944), w; MINSTREL MAN(1944), w; MISSING CORPSE, THE(1945), w; WHITE PONGO(1945), w; CLUB HAVANA(1946), w; DANNY BOY(1946), w; I RING DOORBELLS(1946), w; LARCENY IN HER HEART(1946), w; SECRET OF THE WHISTLER(1946), w; CRIME DOCTOR'S GAMBLE(1947), w; KEY WITNESS(1947), w; MILLERSON CASE, THE(1947), w; 13TH HOUR, THE(1947), w; DAUGHTER OF THE WEST(1949), w
Silents
JUDY FORGOT(1915), w; ELUSIVE ISABEL(1916), w; IN BAD(1918), w; LUCK AND PLUCK(1919), w; NEVER SAY QUIT(1919), w; BURN 'EM UP BARNES(1921), w; ACQUITTAL, THE(1923), w; KINDLED COURAGE(1923), w; OUT OF LUCK(1923), w; SHOOTIN' FOR LOVE(1923), w; FIGHTING AMERICAN, THE(1924), w; HOOK AND LADDER(1924), w; JACK O' CLUBS(1924), w; K-THE UNKNOWN(1924), w; RIDE FOR YOUR LIFE(1924), w; SAWDUST TRAIL(1924), w; HURRICANE KID, THE(1925), w; LET 'ER BUCK(1925), w; SPOOK RANCH(1925), w; BROKEN HEARTS OF HOLLYWOOD(1926), w; PRIVATE IZZY MURPHY(1926), w; TELLING THE WORLD(1928), w; WEST POINT(1928), w
William L. Schrock
HOLD THAT WOMAN(1940), w
George Schrode
Misc. Silents
FANTASMA(1914)
Adolf Schroder
TEMPORARY WIDOW, THE(1930, Ger./Brit.)
Arnulf Schroder
DECISION BEFORE DAWN(1951)
Carl-Gerrard Schroder
Misc. Silents
HALFBREED(1919, Ger.)
Doris Schroder
PRAIRIE LAW(1940), w
Ernst Schroder
COUNTERFEIT TRAITOR, THE(1962); LONGEST DAY, THE(1962); VISIT, THE(1964, Ger./Fr./Ital./U.S.); ODESSA FILE, THE(1974, Brit./Ger.)
Eva Maria Schroder
FREDDY UNTER FREMDEN STERNEN(1962, Ger.), cos
Friedrich Schroder
SCHLAGER-PARADE(1953)
Fritz Schroder
1984
KILLING HEAT(1984), ph

Grete Schroder
Misc. Silents
LOST SHADOW, THE(1921, Ger.)
Kurt Schroder
TRUNKS OF MR. O.F., THE(1932, Ger.), md; FINAL CHORD, THE(1936, Ger.), m
Ricky Schroder
CHAMP, THE(1979); EARTHLING, THE(1980); LAST FLIGHT OF NOAH'S ARK, THE(1980)
Werner Schroder
RED-DRAGON(1967, Ital./Ger./US), makeup
F.W. Schroder-Schrom
RUMPELSTILTSKIN(1965, Ger.); PUSS 'N' BOOTS(1967, Ger.)
Arthur Schroeck
YOU'RE A BIG BOY NOW(1966), md
Aaron Schroeder
JAMBOREE(1957)
Arnulf Schroeder
ETERNAL WALTZ, THE(1959, Ger.); BASHFUL ELEPHANT, THE(1962, Aust.)
Arthur Schroeder
CANARIS(1955, Ger.)
Barbet Schroeder
LES CARABINIERS(1968, Fr./Ital.); SIX IN PARIS(1968, Fr.), a, p; MORE(1969, Luxembourg), d, w; MY NIGHT AT MAUD'S(1970, Fr.), p; LA COLLECTION-NEUSE(1971, Fr.), p; CELINE AND JULIE GO BOATING(1974, Fr.)
Bill Schroeder
1984
LISTEN TO THE CITY(1984, Can.), w
Catherine Schroeder
STRYKER(1983, Phil.)
David V. Schroeder
FRANCES(1982)
Doris Schroeder
CRIMSON ROMANCE(1934), w; HOPALONG CASSIDY(1935), w; BAR 20 RIDES AGAIN(1936), w; CALL OF THE PRAIRIE(1936), w; THREE ON THE TRAIL(1936), w; HEART OF THE WEST(1937), w; WALL STREET COWBOY(1939), w; BULLET CODE(1940), w; LEGION OF THE LAWLESS(1940), w; OKLAHOMA RENEGADES(1940), w; TEXAS TERRORS(1940), w; GANGS OF SONORA(1941), w; KANSAS CYCLONE(1941), w; PHANTOM COWBOY, THE(1941), w; TWO GUN SHERIFF(1941), w; ARIZONA TERRORS(1942), w; MISSOURI OUTLAW, A(1942), w; PIRATES OF THE PRAIRIE(1942), w; SOMBRERO KID, THE(1942), w; STAGECOACH EXPRESS(1942), w; WESTWARD HO(1942), w; BANDITS OF THE BADLANDS(1945), w; DAYS OF BUFFALO BILL(1946), w; DEATH VALLEY(1946), w; DEVIL'S PLAYGROUND, THE(1946), w; FOOL'S GOLD(1946), w; DANGEROUS VENTURE(1947), w; FALSE PARADISE(1948), w; SINISTER JOURNEY(1948), w; STRANGE GAMBLE(1948), w; GAY AMIGO, THE(1949), w
Silents
GIRL WHO WOULDN'T QUIT, THE(1918), w; GILDED DREAM, THE(1920), w; IN FOLLY'S TRAIL(1920), w; NOBODY'S FOOL(1921), w; REPUTATION(1921), w; ROWDY, THE(1921), w; ALTAR STAIRS, THE(1922), w; DON'T GET PERSONAL(1922), w; KISSED(1922), w; LAVENDER BATH LADY, THE(1922), w; SAWDUST(1923), w; TO THE LAST MAN(1923), w; NAUGHTY NANETTE(1927), w; SALVATION JANE(1927), w
Edward Schroeder
DARK STREETS(1929), ed; DRAG(1929), ed; PARIS(1929), ed; SQUALL, THE(1929), ed; WEARY RIVER(1929), ed; ROAD TO PARADISE(1930), ed; SWEET MAMA(1930), ed; WIDOW FROM CHICAGO, THE(1930), ed; HELL'S HOUSE(1932), ed; MEN OF AMERICA(1933), ed; HOPALONG CASSIDY(1935), ed; NEW ADVENTURES OF TARZAN(1935), ed; BAR 20 RIDES AGAIN(1936), ed; CALL OF THE PRAIRIE(1936), ed; EAGLE'S BROOD, THE(1936), ed; IN HIS STEPS(1936), ed; THREE ON THE TRAIL(1936), ed; GIRL LOVES BOY(1937), ed; HEART OF THE WEST(1937), ed; MILE A MINUTE LOVE(1937), ed; SWEETHEART OF THE NAVY(1937), ed; MILLION TO ONE, A(1938), ed; PRISON TRAIN(1938), ed; TEN LAPS TO GO(1938), ed; DANGER FLIGHT(1939), ed; CYCLONE KID, THE(1942), ed; SONS OF THE PIONEERS(1942), ed; CARSON CITY CYCLONE(1943), ed
Silents
SCARLET SEAS(1929), ed
Edward H. Schroeder
UTAH WAGON TRAIN(1951), ed
Ernst Schroeder
MAN BETWEEN, THE(1953, Brit.); HEIDI(1968, Aust.)
F. W. Schroeder
EIGHT GIRLS IN A BOAT(1932, Ger.)
Franz Schroeder
CAPTAIN FROM KOEPENICK(1933, Ger.), set d
Greta Schroeder
Silents
NOSFERATU, THE VAMPIRE(1922, Ger.)
John-Scott Schroeder
Misc. Talkies
FUGITIVE KILLER(1975)
Karin Schroeder
BEFORE WINTER COMES(1969, Brit.); SIGNALS-AN ADVENTURE IN SPACE(1970, E. Ger./Pol.)
Karl Schroeder
INDECENT(1962, Ger.), ph
Kurt Schroeder
WEDDING REHEARSAL(1932, Brit.), m; PRIVATE LIFE OF HENRY VIII, THE(1933), m
Maria Schroeder
PRIZE, THE(1963); GREAT RACE, THE(1965)
Michael Schroeder
ONE DARK NIGHT(1983), p
1984
TORCHLIGHT(1984), p
Peter Schroeder
SEDUCTION OF JOE TYNAN, THE(1979)
Ulrich Schroeder
PRIEST OF ST. PAULI, THE(1970, Ger.), set d

Franz Schroedter
1914(1932, Ger.), set d; LOST ONE, THE(1951, Ger.), art d

Renata Schroeter
LACEMAKER, THE(1977, Fr.)

Bill Schroff
CRIME WAVE(1954)

Chris Schroll
OPEN THE DOOR AND SEE ALL THE PEOPLE(1964)

Schromm
EIGHT GIRLS IN A BOAT(1932, Ger.)

Ina Schroter
PARSIFAL(1983, Fr.)

Hannelore Schroth
CAPTAIN FROM KOEPENICK, THE(1956, Ger.); VOR SONNENUNTERGANG(1961, Ger); WILLY(1963, U.S./Ger.); GREAT BRITISH TRAIN ROBBERY, THE(1967, Ger.)

Heinrich Schroth
HIS MAJESTY, KING BALLYHOO(1931, Ger.); CAPTAIN FROM KOEPENICK(1933, Ger.)

Henry Schroth
Misc. Silents
CARNIVAL OF CRIME(1929, Ger.)

Karl Heinz Schroth
CITY OF SECRETS(1963, Ger.)

Raymand Schruck
CONTENDER, THE(1944), w

Rudolf Schrympf
LITTLE NIGHT MUSIC, A(1977, Aust./U.S./Ger.)

Schtung
SCARECROW, THE(1982, New Zealand), m

Marianne Schubarth
QUESTION 7(1961, U.S./Ger.)

Mark Schubb
ONLY WHEN I LAUGH(1981); MAKING LOVE(1982)

John Schubeck
BUDDY BUDDY(1981)

Schubert
DREAM OF BUTTERFLY, THE(1941, Ital.), m

Anna Luise Schubert
CAPTAIN SINDBAD(1963)

Arland Schubert
NOTHING BUT A MAN(1964)

Benard Schubert
FANNY FOLEY HERSELF(1931), w

Bernard Schubert
PUBLIC DEFENDER, THE(1931), w; SECRET SERVICE(1931), w; SYMPHONY OF SIX MILLION(1932), w; BAND PLAYS ON, THE(1934), w; PECK'S BAD BOY(1934), w; STRAIGHT IS THE WAY(1934), w; KIND LADY(1935), w; MARK OF THE VAMPIRE(1935), w; HEARTS IN BONDAGE(1936), w; BARRIER, THE(1937), w; MAKE A WISH(1937), w; BREAKING THE ICE(1938), w; FISHERMAN'S WHARF(1939), w; SCATTERGOOD PULLS THE STRINGS(1941), w; SILVER QUEEN(1942), w; BUCKSKIN FRONTIER(1943), w; JUNGLE WOMAN(1944), w; MUMMY'S CURSE, THE(1944), w; FROZEN GHOST, THE(1945), w; SONG OF LOVE(1947), w; SONG OF MY HEART(1947), w

Christine Schubert
KING, QUEEN, KNAVE(1972, Ger./U.S.)

Eddie Schubert
I SELL ANYTHING(1934); ROAD GANG(1936)

Franz Peter Schubert
ISADORA(1968, Brit.), m

Franz Schubert
FANTASIA(1940), w; NEW WINE(1941), m; GREAT DAWN, THE(1947, Ital.), m; UNFINISHED SYMPHONY, THE(1953, Aust./Brit.), m; HOUSE OF THE THREE GIRLS, THE(1961, Aust.), m
1984
BASILEUS QUARTET(1984, Ital.), m

Heidi Schubert
DOUBLE NICKELS(1977)

Heinz Schubert
EMIL AND THE DETECTIVES(1964); FUNERAL IN BERLIN(1966, Brit.); TINDER BOX, THE(1968, E. Ger.); OUR HITLER, A FILM FROM GERMANY(1980, Ger.)

Herbert F. Schubert
JUST A GIGOLO(1979, Ger.), ch

Karin Schubert
COMPANEROS(1970 Ital./Span./Ger.); DELUSIONS OF GRANDEUR(1971 Fr.); BLUEBEARD(1972); TILL MARRIAGE DO US PART(1979, Ital.)

Kathryn Schubert
MEDIUM COOL(1969)

Marina Schubert
LITTLE WOMEN(1933); BRITISH AGENT(1934); ALL THE KING'S HORSES(1935); CAR 99(1935); MILLIONS IN THE AIR(1935); PEOPLE WILL TALK(1935); WANDERER OF THE WASTELAND(1935); WITHOUT REGRET(1935)

Mel Schubert
IRON MAJOR, THE(1943); FOLLOW THE BOYS(1944); FOUR JILLS IN A JEEP(1944); WING AND A PRAYER(1944)

Patrice Schubert
DOUBLE NICKELS(1977), a, w

Peter Schubert
GERMANY IN AUTUMN(1978, Ger.), d

Terry Schubert
SATURN 3(1980), spec eff

John Schuck
BREWSTER McCLOUD(1970); M(1970); MOONSHINE WAR, THE(1970); MC CABE AND MRS. MILLER(1971); HAMMERSMITH IS OUT(1972); BLADE(1973); THIEVES LIKE US(1974); BUTCH AND SUNDANCE: THE EARLY DAYS(1979); JUST YOU AND ME, KID(1979); EARTHBOUND(1981)
1984
FINDERS KEEPERS(1984)

Al Schuckman
BOOK OF NUMBERS(1973), m

Hod David Schudson
ATTIC, THE(1979), m; CLONUS HORROR, THE(1979), m

Eugen Schueftan
FROM TOP TO BOTTOM(1933, Fr.), ph

Rainer Schuelein
PERSECUTION AND ASSASSINATION OF JEAN-PAUL MARAT AS PERFORMED BY THE INMATES OF THE ASYLUM OF CHARENTON UNDER THE DIRECTION OF THE MARQUIS DE SADE, THE(1967, Brit.)

Rudolf Schuendler
KINGS OF THE ROAD(1976, Ger.)

Karl Schueneman
HUNTER, THE(1980)

Emil Schuenemann
CASE VAN GELDERN(1932, Ger.), ph

Reinhold Schuenzel
BEAUTIFUL ADVENTURE(1932, Ger.), w; 1914(1932, Ger.); AMPHYTRYON(1937, Ger.), d, w

Rheinhold Schuenzel
VICTOR/VICTORIA(1982), w

Friedrich Schuetter
DOCTOR OF ST. PAUL, THE(1969, Ger.)

Guenther Schuetz
SISTERS, OR THE BALANCE OF HAPPINESS(1982, Ger.)

Kathy Schuetz
CRY DR. CHICAGO(1971)

Eugene Schuftan
MISTRESS OF ATLANTIS, THE(1932, Ger.), ph; INVISIBLE OPPONENT(1933, Ger.), ph; OLD SPANISH CUSTOM, AN(1936, Brit.), ph; ROBBER SYMPHONY, THE(1937, Brit.), ph; PORT OF SHADOWS(1938, Fr.), ph; SHANGHAI DRAMA, THE(1945, Fr.), ph; SCANDAL IN PARIS, A(1946), ph; ULYSSES(1955, Ital.), makeup
Silents
METROPOLIS(1927, Ger.), spec eff

Schugger-Leo
TIN DRUM, THE(1979, Ger./Fr./Yugo./Pol.)

Thomas Schuhly
VERONIKA VOSS(1982, Ger.), a, p

Oskar Schuirch
TRIAL, THE(1948, Aust.), ph

B. P. Schulberg
GREENE MURDER CASE, THE(1929), p; ILLUSION(1929), p; MADAME BUTTERFLY(1932), p; GIRL IN 419(1933), p; HER BODYGUARD(1933), p; JENNIE GERHARDT(1933), p; LUXURY LINER(1933), p; PICK-UP(1933), p; THREE-CORNERED MOON(1933), p; KISS AND MAKE UP(1934), p; LITTLE MISS MARKER(1934), p; THIRTY-DAY PRINCESS(1934), p; BEHOLD MY WIFE(1935), p; CRIME AND PUNISHMENT(1935), p; ONE-WAY TICKET(1935), p; SHE COULDN'T TAKE IT(1935), p; AND SO THEY WERE MARRIED(1936), p; COUNTERFEIT(1936), p; LADY OF SECRETS(1936), p; MEET NERO WOLFE(1936), p; WEDDING PRESENT(1936), p; BLOSSOMS ON BROADWAY(1937), p; DOCTOR'S DIARY, A(1937), p; GREAT GAMBINI, THE(1937), p; HER HUSBAND LIES(1937), p; JOHN MEADE'S WOMAN(1937), p; SHE ASKED FOR IT(1937), p; SHE'S NO LADY(1937), p; HE STAYED FOR BREAKFAST(1940), p; BEDTIME STORY(1942), p; FLIGHT LIEUTENANT(1942), p; WIFE TAKES A FLYER, THE(1942), p
Silents
RICH MEN'S WIVES(1922), sup; APRIL SHOWERS(1923), p; OLD IRONSIDES(1926), sup; AFRAID TO LOVE(1927), p; ROLLED STOCKINGS(1927), p; ROUGH HOUSE ROSIE(1927), p; ROUGH RIDERS, THE(1927), p; SHOOTIN' IRONS(1927), p; SPECIAL DELIVERY(1927), p; TIME TO LOVE(1927), p; WEDDING BILL$(1927), p; WOMAN ON TRIAL, THE(1927), p; LAST COMMAND, THE(1928), p; RED HAIR(1928), p

Budd Schulberg
NOTHING SACRED(1937), w; STAR IS BORN, A(1937), w; LITTLE ORPHAN ANNIE(1938), w; WINTER CARNIVAL(1939), w; WEEKEND FOR THREE(1941), w; CITY WITHOUT MEN(1943), w; GOVERNMENT GIRL(1943), w; ON THE WATERFRONT(1954), w; HARDER THEY FALL, THE(1956), w; FACE IN THE CROWD, A(1957), w; WIND ACROSS THE EVERGLADES(1958), w

Stuart Schulberg
SPECIAL DELIVERY(1955, Ger.), p; WIND ACROSS THE EVERGLADES(1958), p

Robert Schulenberg
EATING RAOUL(1982), prod d
1984
NOT FOR PUBLICATION(1984), prod d

Christine Schuler
PICNIC AT HANGING ROCK(1975, Aus.)

Fred Schuler
GLORIA(1980), ph, prod d; STIR CRAZY(1980), ph; ARTHUR(1981), ph; LOVE AND MONEY(1982), ph; SOUP FOR ONE(1982), ph; AMITYVILLE 3-D(1983), ph; EASY MONEY(1983), ph; KING OF COMEDY, THE(1983), ph
1984
FLETCH(1984), ph; NOTHING LASTS FOREVER(1984), ph; WOMAN IN RED, THE(1984), ph

Gene Schuler
SOUTH OF SONORA(1930)

Heini Schuler
DOWNHILL RACER(1969)

Richard B. Schull
ANDERSON TAPES, THE(1971)

Frank Schuller
GENTLE GIANT(1967); HELLO DOWN THERE(1969); WHO?(1975, Brit./Ger.); LINCOLN CONSPIRACY, THE(1977); FUNHOUSE, THE(1981)
1984
SWORDKILL(1984)

Hal Schullman
TOWING(1978), ph

Alan Schulman
TATTOOED STRANGER, THE(1950), m

Arnold Schulman
CIMARRON(1960), w; LOVE WITH THE PROPER STRANGER(1963), w; NIGHT THEY RAIDED MINSKY'S, THE(1968), W; GOODBYE COLUMBUS(1969), w; TO FIND A MAN(1972), w; FUNNY LADY(1975), w; WON TON TON, THE DOG WHO SAVED HOLLYWOOD(1976), p, w; PLAYERS(1979), w

Ivy Schulman
ROCK, ROCK, ROCK!(1956)

Josh Schulman
1984
BUDDY SYSTEM, THE(1984)

Dr. Leo Schulman
RETURN OF DR. X, THE(1939), tech adv

Max Schulman
ALWAYS LEAVE THEM LAUGHING(1949), w

Nina Schulman
WEREWOLF OF WASHINGTON(1973), p

Richard Schulman
SECRETS OF SEX(1970, Brit.)
Misc. Talkies
BIZARRE(1969)

Sonny Schulman
UNDERGROUND AGENT(1942)

Rolf Schult
GERMAN SISTERS, THE(1982, Ger.)

Robert Schulte
SPARTACUS(1960), ed; MASK, THE(1961, Can.), ed

Victor R. Schulte
CAT ATE THE PARAKEET, THE(1972)

Edward Schulter
BREACH OF PROMISE(1942, Brit.), art d

Willy Schultes
TURKISH CUCUMBER, THE(1963, Ger.)

Charles Schulthies
WESTWORLD(1973), spec eff

Chuck Schulthies, Jr.
1984
TEACHERS(1984), spec eff

Abe Schultz
HIS PRIVATE SECRETARY(1933), ph

Alan Schultz
BEHIND OFFICE DOORS(1931), w

Astrid Schultz
HOUSE IS NOT A HOME, A(1964)

Berkeley Schultz
CANDLELIGHT IN ALGERIA(1944, Brit.)

Cal Schultz
SEEDS OF EVIL(1981), ed

Carl Schultz
BLUE FIN(1978, Aus.), d
1984
CAREFUL, HE MIGHT HEAR YOU(1984, Aus.), d

Chris Schultz
GANJA AND HESS(1973), p

Chriz Schultz
ANGEL LEVINE, THE(1970), p

Derek Schultz
CARWASH(1976)

Don Schultz
SEPARATE PEACE, A(1972)

Dwight Schultz
FAN, THE(1981); ALONE IN THE DARK(1982)

Frank Schultz
Misc. Talkies
BLOWN SKY HIGH(1984)

Franz Schultz
OFFICE GIRL, THE(1932, Brit.), w; SLEEPING CAR(1933, Brit.), w

Fritz Schultz
CONSTANT NYMPH, THE(1933, Brit.); WALTZ TIME(1933, Brit.)

George Schultz
YOU'VE GOT TO WALK IT LIKE YOU TALK IT OR YOU'LL LOSE THAT BEAT(1971)

Guy Schultz
THUNDER TRAIL(1937)

Harry Schultz
ONE STOLEN NIGHT(1929); MOROCCO(1930); HAT CHECK GIRL(1932); HYPNOTIZED(1933); ONE SUNDAY AFTERNOON(1933); TILLIE AND GUS(1933); CRIMSON ROMANCE(1934); STAMBOUL QUEST(1934); DANTE'S INFERNO(1935); DRILLER KILLER(1979)
Silents
RILEY THE COP(1928)

Jack Schultz
HEARTS OF HUMANITY(1932), art d

Lenny Schultz
COMEBACK TRAIL, THE(1982)

Maurice Schultz
CALL, THE(1938, Fr.)
Silents
PASSION OF JOAN OF ARC, THE(1928, Fr.)

Michael Schultz
HONEYBABY, HONEYBABY(1974), d; COOLEY HIGH(1975), d; CARWASH(1976), d; GREASED LIGHTNING(1977), d; WHICH WAY IS UP?(1977), d; SGT. PEPPER'S LONELY HEARTS CLUB BAND(1978), d; SCAVENGER HUNT(1979), d; CARBON COPY(1981), d
Misc. Talkies
TOGETHER FOR DAYS(1972), d

Philip Schultz
HAROLD AND MAUDE(1971)

Sammy Schultz
EGG AND I, THE(1947)

Samuel Schultz
CUBAN PETE(1946)

Uwe Schultz
CREATURES THE WORLD FORGOT(1971, Brit.), animal t

Edith Schultz-Westrum
SHERLOCK HOLMES AND THE DEADLY NECKLACE(1962, Ger.)

Jack Schultze
SO THIS IS LONDON(1930), art d; YOUNG AS YOU FEEL(1931), art d; SILVER LINING(1932), art d

Klaus Schultze
BARRACUDA(1978), m

Norbert Schultze
KOLBERG(1945, Ger.), m; DANCING HEART, THE(1959, Ger.), m; ROSEMARY(1960, Ger.), m; U-47 LT. COMMANDER PRIEN(1967, Ger.), m

Edith Schultze-Westrum
ESCAPE FROM EAST BERLIN(1962); GREH(1962, Ger./Yugo.); WILLY(1963, U.S./Ger.)

Schulz
DREAM OF SCHONBRUNN(1933, Aus.), p

Bob Schulz
Misc. Talkies
FALCON'S GOLD(1982), d

Charles M. Schulz
BON VOYAGE, CHARLIE BROWN(AND DON'T COME BACK)*** (1980), w; BOY NAMED CHARLIE BROWN, A(1969), w; SNOOPY, COME HOME(1972), w; RACE FOR YOUR LIFE, CHARLIE BROWN(1977), w

Franz Schulz
TWO WORLD(1930, Brit.), w; BOMBARDMENT OF MONTE CARLO, THE(1931, Ger.), w; LOVE ON WHEELS(1932, Brit.), w; MARRY ME(1932, Brit.), w; RENDEZ-VOUS(1932, Ger.); LUCKY NUMBER, THE(1933, Brit.), w; WHAT WOMEN DREAM(1933, Ger.), w; TWO HEARTS IN WALTZ TIME(1934, Brit.), w; LOTTERY LOVER(1935), w; NIGHT IS YOUNG, THE(1935), w; ONE EXCITING ADVENTURE(1935), w; CLOTHES AND THE WOMAN(1937, Brit.), w; ADVENTURE IN DIAMONDS(1940), w

G.H. Clutsam Franz Schulz
APRIL BLOSSOMS(1937, Brit.), w

Jiri Schulz
LEMONADE JOE(1966, Czech.)

Joachim Schulz
LILI MARLEEN(1981, Ger.), spec eff

Lore Schulz
JUDGE AND THE SINNER, THE(1964, Ger.)

Manfred Schulz
MC CABE AND MRS. MILLER(1971)

Nathalie Schulz
HANSEL AND GRETEL(1954), anim

Rolf Schulz
SEDUCTION BY THE SEA(1967, Ger./Yugo.), w

Michael Schulz-Dornburg
LA HABANERA(1937, Ger.)

Christof Schulz-Gellen
RUMPELSTILTSKIN(1965, Ger.), w; PUSS 'N' BOOTS(1967, Ger.), w

Wieland Schulz-Keil
1984
UNDER THE VOLCANO(1984), p

Agnes Schulz-Lichterfeld
M(1933, Ger.)

Fritz Schulz-Reichel
INDECENT(1962, Ger.), m

Jack Schulze
BORN RECKLESS(1930), art d; HAPPY DAYS(1930), art d; ON YOUR BACK(1930), art d
Silents
MY BEST GIRL(1927), art d

John D. Schulze
Silents
MY FOUR YEARS IN GERMANY(1918), art d; INVISIBLE FEAR, THE(1921), art d; JOANNA(1925), art d; LITTLE ANNIE ROONEY(1925), art d; MY SON(1925), art d; IRENE(1926), art d

Klaus Schulze
NEXT OF KIN(1983, Aus.), m

John Ducasse Schulze
TRANSATLANTIC MERRY-GO-ROUND(1934), art d; RED SALUTE(1935), art d; LAST OF THE MOHICANS, THE(1936), art d; RIDING ON AIR(1937), art d; MAN IN THE IRON MASK, THE(1939), art d; KIT CARSON(1940), art d; MY SON, MY SON!(1940), art d; SOUTH OF PAGO PAGO(1940), art d; CHEERS FOR MISS BISHOP(1941), art d; INTERNATIONAL LADY(1941), art d; FRIENDLY ENEMIES(1942), art d; GENTLEMAN AFTER DARK, A(1942), art d; MISS ANNIE ROONEY(1942), art d; TWIN BEDS(1942), art d

Klaus Peter Schulze
LOVE FEAST, THE(1966, Ger.), w

Otto F. Schulze
TO CATCH A THIEF(1955)

Edith Schulze-Westrum
BRIDGE, THE(1961, Ger.)

Jerry Schumacher
PAT AND MIKE(1952); CLOWN, THE(1953); PARTY GIRL(1958)

Joan Schumacher
HOW TO BEAT THE HIGH COST OF LIVING(1980)

Joel Schumacher
WIZ, THE(1978), w; PLAY IT AS IT LAYS(1972), cos; SLEEPER(1973), cos; PRISONER OF SECOND AVENUE, THE(1975), cos; CARWASH(1976), w; SPARKLE(1976), w; INTERIORS(1978), cos; INCREDIBLE SHRINKING WOMAN, THE(1981), d; D.C. CAB(1983), d&w

Lou Schumacher
NIGHT OF THE LEPUS(1972), animal t

Capt. Max Schumacher
LIVELY SET, THE(1964)
Paul Schumacher
HOT TOMORROWS(1978)
Phil Schumacher
BATAAN(1943); THEY WERE EXPENDABLE(1945); SLAVE GIRL(1947); CORONER CREEK(1948); MADAME BOVARY(1949); LOVE ME OR LEAVE ME(1955); DUEL AT DIABLO(1966)
Roger Schumacher
DRACULA'S DOG(1978)
Phil Schumacker
DEERSLAYER, THE(1957)
Ida Schumaker
VELVET TOUCH, THE(1948)
Edith Schuman
LAST MERCENARY, THE(1969, Ital./Span./Ger.), ed
Erik Schuman
RESTLESS NIGHT, THE(1964, Ger.)
Ferdinand Schuman-Heink
BLAZE O' GLORY(1930)
Silents
AWAKENING, THE(1928)
Schumann Choirs
CITY OF TORMENT(1950, Ger.), m
Erik Schumann
MAGIC FIRE(1956); TWO-HEADED SPY, THE(1959, Brit.); QUESTION 7(1961, U.S./Ger.); COUNTERFEIT TRAITOR, THE(1962); MIRACLE OF THE WHITE STALLIONS(1963); FLAMING FRONTIER(1968, Ger./Yugo.); SLAVERS(1977, Ger.); NIGHT OF THE ASKARI(1978, Ger./South African); LILI MARLEEN(1981, Ger.); VERONIKA VOSS(1982, Ger.)
Ferdinand Schumann
STORY OF DR. WASSELL, THE(1944)
Robert Schumann
COURT CONCERT, THE(1936, Ger.), m; SONG OF LOVE(1947), m; INTERLUDE(1957), m; SUMMERSKIN(1962, Arg.), m; MADE IN U.S.A.(1966, Fr.), m; RACHEL, RACHEL(1968), m; LUDWIG(1973, Ital./Ger./Fr.), m
Walter Schumann
BUCK PRIVATES COME HOME(1947), m; I'LL BE YOURS(1947), md; WISTFUL WIDOW OF WAGON GAP, THE(1947), m; NOOSE HANGS HIGH, THE(1948), m; DRAGNET(1954), m; NIGHT OF THE HUNTER, THE(1955), m, md
Willi Schumann
NO TIME FOR FLOWERS(1952)
Mme. Schumann-Heink
HERE'S TO ROMANCE(1935)
Mme. Ernestine Schumann-Heink
Silents
WEDDING MARCH, THE(1927)
Fred Schumann-Heinck
MISSION TO MOSCOW(1943)
Ferdinand Schumann-Heink
MAMBA(1930), w; WORLDLY GOODS(1930); SEAS BENEATH, THE(1931); MY PAL, THE KING(1932); FUGITIVE ROAD(1934); MADAME SPY(1934); WORLD MOVES ON, THE(1934); DON'T BET ON BLONDES(1935); SYMPHONY OF LIVING(1935); TRAVELING SALESLADY, THE(1935); STORY OF LOUIS PASTEUR(1936); TWO AGAINST THE WORLD(1936); WIDOW FROM MONTE CARLO, THE(1936); KING AND THE CHORUS GIRL, THE(1937); SLIM(1937); ARTISTS AND MODELS ABROAD(1938); DESPERATE JOURNEY(1942); INVISIBLE AGENT(1942); NORTH STAR, THE(1943); THIS LAND IS MINE(1943)
Silents
GALLANT FOOL, THE(1926); FOUR SONS(1928); RILEY THE COP(1928)
P. Schumann-Heink
GIGOLETTES OF PARIS(1933)
Harold Schumate
HELL-SHIP MORGAN(1936), w; BUCCANEER'S GIRL(1950), w
Alex Schumberg
OUR DAILY BREAD(1934)
Hans Schumm
SONG OF SONGS(1933); FOLIES DERGERE(1935); REVOLT OF THE ZOMBIES(1936); BEASTS OF BERLIN(1939); FOUR SONS(1940); MAN I MARRIED, THE(1940); MOON OVER BURMA(1940); SO ENDS OUR NIGHT(1941); UNDERGROUND(1941); YANK IN THE R.A.F., A(1941); ALL THROUGH THE NIGHT(1942); ATLANTIC CONVOY(1942); BERLIN CORRESPONDENT(1942); DESPERATE JOURNEY(1942); DESTINATION UNKNOWN(1942); FOREIGN AGENT(1942); INVISIBLE AGENT(1942); ONCE UPON A HONEYMOON(1942); PARDON MY SARONG(1942); UNDERGROUND AGENT(1942); MARGIN FOR ERROR(1943); MISSION TO MOSCOW(1943); MOON IS DOWN, THE(1943); SAHARA(1943); STRANGE DEATH OF ADOLF HITLER, THE(1943); THEY GOT ME COVERED(1943); THIS LAND IS MINE(1943); PASSPORT TO DESTINY(1944); UNCERTAIN GLORY(1944); UP IN ARMS(1944); VOICE IN THE WIND(1944); ESCAPE IN THE DESERT(1945); SON OF LASSIE(1945); CLOAK AND DAGGER(1946); DESIRE ME(1947); GOLDEN EARRINGS(1947); NO ESCAPE(1953); I AIM AT THE STARS(1960); QUESTION 7(1961, U.S./Ger.); BASHFUL ELEPHANT, THE(1962, Aust.); CAPTAIN SINDBAD(1963)
Harry Schumm
Silents
CAMPBELLS ARE COMING, THE(1915)
Ursula Schummat
EIGHT GIRLS IN A BOAT(1932, Ger.)
Robert Schumson
FANNY AND ALEXANDER(1983, Swed./Fr./Ger.), m
Rudolf Schundler
THAT WOMAN(1968, Ger.); AMERICAN FRIEND, THE(1977, Ger.); SUSPIRIA(1977, Ital.); JUST A GIGOLO(1979, Ger.)
Rudolph Schundler
TESTAMENT OF DR. MABUSE, THE(1943, Ger.)
Emil Schunemann
RETURN OF RAFFLES, THE(1932, Brit.), ph
Reinhold Schunzel
THREEPENNY OPERA, THE(1931, Ger./U.S.); BEAUTIFUL ADVENTURE(1932, Ger.), d; FIRST A GIRL(1935, Brit.), w; RICH MAN, POOR GIRL(1938), d; BALALAIKA(1939), d; ICE FOLLIES OF 1939(1939), d; NEW WINE(1941), d; FIRST COMES

COURAGE(1943); HITLER GANG, THE(1944); MAN IN HALF-MOON STREET, THE(1944); DRAGONWYCH(1946); NOTORIOUS(1946); PLAINSMAN AND THE LADY(1946); GOLDEN EARRINGS(1947); BERLIN EXPRESS(1948); WASHINGTON STORY(1952)
Silents
PASSION(1920, Ger.)
Misc. Silents
FIVE SINISTER STORIES(1919, Ger.); CAGLIOSTRO(1920, Ger.), a, d; LAST PAYMENT(1921, Ger.); IMAGINARY BARON, THE(1927, Ger.)
Willi Schur
TREMENDOUSLY RICH MAN, A(1932, Ger.); CAPTAIN FROM KOEPENICK(1933, Ger.); MASTER OF THE WORLD(1935, Ger.); COURT CONCERT, THE(1936, Ger.)
Siegfried Schurenberg
MASTER OF THE WORLD(1935, Ger.); MAN WHO WAS SHERLOCK HOLMES, THE(1937, Ger.); LIFE BEGINS ANEW(1938, Ger.); JOURNEY, THE(1959, U.S./Aust.); BRIDGE, THE(1961, Ger.); TOWN WITHOUT PITY(1961, Ger./Switz./U.S.); OLDEST PROFESSION, THE(1968, Fr./Ital./Ger.)
Rudi Schuricke
SCHLAGER-PARADE(1953)
Michael Schurig
1984
NIGHTMARE ON ELM STREET, A(1984), m/1
David Schurman
MARIE-ANN(1978, Can.)
E. Schurmann
PINOCCHIO IN OUTER SPACE(1965, U.S./Bel.), m
Gerard Schurmann
CAMP ON BLOOD ISLAND, THE(1958, Brit.), m; HORRORS OF THE BLACK MUSEUM(1959, U.S./Brit.), m; TWO-HEADED SPY, THE(1959, Brit.), m; KONGA(1961, Brit.), m; TROUBLE IN THE SKY(1961, Brit.), md; CEREMONY, THE(1963, U.S./Span.), m; BEDFORD INCIDENT, THE(1965, Brit.), m; ATTACK ON THE IRON COAST(1968, U.S./Brit.), m; LOST CONTINENT, THE(1968, Brit.), m; DR. SYN, ALIAS THE SCARECROW(1975), m
Gerbrand Schurmann
DECISION AGAINST TIME(1957, Brit.), m; THIRD KEY, THE(1957, Brit.), m
William Schurr
Silents
ANY WOMAN(1925), ph
Edith Schussel
ORDET(1957, Den.), ed
Franz Schussler
LITTLE NIGHT MUSIC, A(1977, Aust./U.S./Ger.)
Johanna Schussler
LITTLE NIGHT MUSIC, A(1977, Aust./U.S./Ger.)
Helen Schustack
FRANCES(1982)
Bena Schuster
ONE PLUS ONE(1961, Can.)
Betty Schuster
HER STRANGE DESIRE(1931, Brit.)
Friedel Schuster
EMPRESS AND I, THE(1933, Ger.); HEART SONG(1933, Brit.)
Harold Schuster
FOUR DEVILS(1929), ed; FROZEN JUSTICE(1929), ed; RENEGADES(1930), ed; SUCH MEN ARE DANGEROUS(1930), ed; WOMEN EVERYWHERE(1930), ed; AMBASSADOR BILL(1931), ed; DON'T BET ON WOMEN(1931), ed; MAN WHO CAME BACK, THE(1931), ed; CHANDU THE MAGICIAN(1932), ed; DEVIL'S LOTTERY(1932), ed; PASSPORT TO HELL(1932), ed; BERKELEY SQUARE(1933), ed; DANGEROUSLY YOURS(1933), ed; ZOO IN BUDAPEST(1933), ed; ALL MEN ARE ENEMIES(1934), ed; HELLDORADO(1935), ed; WINGS OF THE MORNING(1937, Brit.), d; EXPOSED(1938), d; SWING THAT CHEER(1938), d; DIAMOND FRONTIER(1940), d; FRAMED(1940), d; MA, HE'S MAKING EYES AT ME(1940), d; SOUTH TO KARANGA(1940), d; ZANZIBAR(1940), d; PIRATES OF THE SEVEN SEAS(1941, Brit.), d; SMALL TOWN DEB(1941), d; VERY YOUNG LADY, A(1941), d; GIRL TROUBLE(1942), d; ON THE SUNNY SIDE(1942), d; POSTMAN DIDN'T RING, THE(1942), d; BOMBER'S MOON(1943), d; MY FRIEND FLICKA(1943), d; MARINE RAIDERS(1944), d; BREAKFAST IN HOLLYWOOD(1946), d; TENDER YEARS, THE(1947), d; SO DEAR TO MY HEART(1949), d; KID MONK BARONI(1952), d; JACK SLADE(1953), d; LOOPHOLE(1954), d; SECURITY RISK(1954), d; FINGER MAN(1955), d; PORT OF HELL(1955), d; RETURN OF JACK SLADE, THE(1955), d; TARZAN'S HIDDEN JUNGLE(1955), d; DRAGON WELLS MASSACRE(1957), d; PORTLAND EXPOSE(1957), d
Harold D. Schuster
DINNER AT THE RITZ(1937, Brit.), d
Hugo Schuster
HOTEL RESERVE(1946, Brit.); GIRL IN THE PAINTING, THE(1948, Brit.); PRELUDE TO FAME(1950, Brit.); SECRET PEOPLE(1952, Brit.); HOUSE OF BLACKMAIL(1953, Brit.); PAID TO KILL(1954, Brit.); SECRET VENTURE(1955, Brit.); BLUE MAX, THE(1966)
Allan Schute
JOURNEY FOR MARGARET(1942); MAN OF CONFLICT(1953)
Allen Schute
LOCKET, THE(1946); JOAN OF ARC(1948)
Martin Schute
THERE GOES THE BRIDE(1980, Brit.), p
Martin C. Schute
MACHO CALLAHAN(1970), p
Peter Schutte
CORPSE OF BEVERLY HILLS, THE(1965, Ger.)
Ulrike Schutte
1984
CHINESE BOXES(1984, Ger./Brit.), cos
Schutz
PASTEUR(1936, Fr.)
Adolf Schutz
GIRL OF THE MOORS, THE(1961, Ger.), w; MAKE WAY FOR LILA(1962, Swed./Ger.), w

Maurice Schutz
VAMPYR(1932, Fr./Ger.); IT HAPPENED AT THE INN(1945, Fr.)
Silents
NAPOLEON(1927, Fr.)
Misc. Silents
LE FANTOME DU MOULIN ROUGE(1925, Fr.); MAUPRAT(1926, Fr.)
Ilona Schutze
THIRTEEN FRIGHTENED GIRLS(1963)
Ivan Schuveler
Misc. Silents
CITIES AND YEARS(1931, USSR)
Richard Schuyer
DOUGH BOYS(1930), w
Dorothy Schuyler
BLACK WHIP, THE(1956); RIDE A VIOLENT MILE(1957)
Philip Schuyler
WEST OF THE ROCKIES(1929), w
Silents
LAW OF THE MOUNTED(1928), w; HEADIN' WESTWARD(1929), w
Richard Schuyler
RESURRECTION OF ZACHARY WHEELER, THE(1971)
L. Schvarts
ON HIS OWN(1939, USSR), m
Buddy Schwab
THOROUGHLY MODERN MILLIE(1967); CARDINAL, THE(1963), ch
Jacqueline Schwab
TOO SOON TO LOVE(1960)
Joseph Schwab
MOMENT BY MOMENT(1978)
Laurence Schwab
DESERT SONG, THE(1929), w; FOLLOW THRU(1930), p, d&w; GOOD NEWS(1930), w; NEW MOON(1930), w; QUEEN HIGH(1930), p; TAKE A CHANCE(1933), d, w; NEW MOON(1940), w; DESERT SONG, THE(1943), w; GOOD NEWS(1947), w; DESERT SONG, THE(1953), w
Lonna Schwab
TWILIGHT ZONE–THE MOVIE(1983)
Noeste Schwab
TERRORISTS, THE(1975, Brit.)
Per Schwab
ONE DAY IN THE LIFE OF IVAN DENISOVICH(1971, U.S./Brit./Norway), art d
Sophie Schwab
SO FINE(1981)
Volker Schwab
SISTERS, OR THE BALANCE OF HAPPINESS(1982, Ger.)
Peter Schwabach
PRIVILEGED(1982, Brit.), art d
Leslie Schwabacher
SPY TRAIN(1943), w
Franck Schwacke
HU-MAN(1975, Fr.)
Sol Schwade
PLAYGROUND, THE(1965); OLIVER'S STORY(1978); STARTING OVER(1979)
Slavo Schwaiger
SEVEN DARING GIRLS(1962, Ger.); ISLE OF SIN(1963, Ger.)
Ben Schwalb
BLUE BLOOD(1951), p; ARMY BOUND(1952), p; JET JOB(1952), p; CLIPPED WINGS(1953), p; HOT NEWS(1953), p; JALOPY(1953), p; LOOSE IN LONDON(1953), p; PRIVATE EYES(1953), p; WHITE LIGHTNING(1953), p; BOWERY BOYS MEET THE MONSTERS, THE(1954), p; JUNGLE GENTS(1954), p; PARIS PLAYBOYS(1954), p; BOWERY TO BAGDAD(1955), p; HIGH SOCIETY(1955), p; JAIL BUSTERS(1955), p; SUDDEN DANGER(1955), p; CRASHING LAS VEGAS(1956), p; DIG THAT URANIUM(1956), p; FIGHTING TROUBLE(1956), p; HOT SHOTS(1956), p; SPY CHASERS(1956), p; CHAIN OF EVIDENCE(1957), p; DISEMBODIED, THE(1957), p; FOOTSTEPS IN THE NIGHT(1957), p; HOLD THAT HYPNOTIST(1957), p; LOOKING FOR DANGER(1957), p; SPOOK CHASERS(1957), p; COLE YOUNGER, GUNFIGHTER(1958), p; JOY RIDE(1958), p; QUANTRILL'S RAIDERS(1958), p; QUEEN OF OUTER SPACE(1958), p; KING OF THE WILD STALLIONS(1959), p; THE HYPNOTIC EYE(1960), p; GEORGE RAFT STORY, THE(1961), p; GUNFIGHT AT COMANCHE CREEK(1964), p; TICKLE ME(1965), p
Will Schwalbe
1984
STRANGERS KISS(1984)
Ben Schwalk
CALLING HOMICIDE(1956), p
Thomas Schwalm
BABYLON(1980, Brit.), ed
1984
KILLING HEAT(1984), ed; WHITE ELEPHANT(1984, Brit.), ed
Thomas Schwan
SISTERS, OR THE BALANCE OF HAPPINESS(1982, Ger.), ph
Wolf Schwan
HANSEL AND GRETEL(1965, Ger.), ph; SNOW WHITE(1965, Ger.), ph; SNOW WHITE AND ROSE RED(1966, Ger.), ph; SHOEMAKER AND THE ELVES, THE(1967, Ger.), ph
Vernon Schwanke
PAPER MOON(1973)
Ellen Schwannecke
MAEDCHEN IN UNIFORM(1932, Ger.)
Victor Schwannecke
LOVE WALTZ, THE(1930, Ger.)
Ellen Schwanneke
ROYAL WALTZ, THE(1936)
Fred A. Schwarb
SAFE AT HOME(1962)
Milton Schwartwald
NAKED CITY, THE(1948), md
Abraham Schwartz
Silents
DAUGHTER OF MINE(1919)

Al Schwartz
LOOKIN' TO GET OUT(1982), w
Alan U. Schwartz
HISTORY OF THE WORLD, PART 1(1981)
Albert Schwartz
BIG SCORE, THE(1983), p
Arthur Schwartz
NAVY BLUES(1941), m; THANK YOUR LUCKY STARS(1943), w; COVER GIRL(1944), p; NIGHT AND DAY(1946), p; DANCING IN THE DARK(1949), w; DANGEROUS WHEN WET(1953), m
Bernard Schwartz
EYE OF THE CAT(1969), p; JENNIFER ON MY MIND(1971), p; THAT MAN BOLT(1973), p; BUCKTOWN(1975), p; TRACKDOWN(1976), p; COAL MINER'S DAUGHTER(1980), p
Bernie Schwartz
HICKEY AND BOGGS(1972)
Bonnie Sue Schwartz
ANGEL IN MY POCKET(1969)
Bruce R. Schwartz
IN MACARTHUR PARK(1977), p,d&w; ed
Bruce Schwartz
MUPPET MOVIE, THE(1979)
Dan Schwartz
1984
CHEECH AND CHONG'S THE CORSICAN BROTHERS(1984)
David Schwartz
TRADING PLACES(1983)
David R. Schwartz
ISLAND OF LOVE(1963), w; ROBIN AND THE SEVEN HOODS(1964), w; SEX AND THE SINGLE GIRL(1964), w; THAT FUNNY FEELING(1965), w; BOBO, THE(1967, Brit.), w
Douglas Schwartz
PEACE KILLERS, THE(1971), d,ph&ed
Douglas N. Schwartz
YOUR THREE MINUTES ARE UP(1973), d
Eddie Schwartz
CONTINENTAL DIVIDE(1981)
Elroy Schwartz
WACKIEST WAGON TRAIN IN THE WEST, THE(1976), p, w
Emil Schwartz
CONDEMNED(1929)
Fred Schwartz
FLAME OF LOVE, THE(1930, Brit.); JUNO AND THE PAYCOCK(1930, Brit.); REUNION(1932, Brit.); WISHBONE, THE(1933, Brit.); LOVE UP THE POLE(1936, Brit.); WELL DONE, HENRY(1936, Brit.); SONG OF THE ROAD(1937, Brit.)
Gary Schwartz
QUEST FOR FIRE(1982, Fr./Can.)
George Schwartz
1984
SWING SHIFT(1984)
Hans Schwartz
PRINCE OF ARCADIA(1933, Brit.), d; RETURN OF THE SCARLET PIMPERNEL(1938, Brit.), d
Howard Schwartz
CASE OF PATTY SMITH, THE(1962), ph; PUBLIC AFFAIR, A(1962), ph; BATMAN(1966), ph; FUTUREWORLD(1976), ph; DEVIL AND MAX DEVLIN, THE(1981), ph
Howard R. Schwartz
BIG BOUNCE, THE(1969), ph
Ira B. Schwartz
Silents
PRODIGAL WIFE, THE(1918), ph
Irving Schwartz
1984
ROSEBUD BEACH HOTEL(1984), p, w
Irwin Schwartz
STAKEOUT ON DOPE STREET(1958), w
Jack Schwartz
BABY FACE MORGAN(1942), p; SUBMARINE BASE(1943), p; TIGER FANGS(1943), p; CAREER GIRL(1944), p; ENCHANTED FOREST, THE(1945), p; BUFFALO BILL RIDES AGAIN(1947), p; HEADING FOR HEAVEN(1947), p; ENCHANTED VALLEY, THE(1948), p; FEDERAL MAN(1950), p
Jean-Paul Schwartz
DEAR DETECTIVE(1978, Fr.), ph
John Schwartz
CONDEMNED(1929)
Jonathan Schwartz
HOW TO BEAT THE HIGH COST OF LIVING(1980)
Kenneth Schwartz
X-15(1961), set d
L. Schwartz
HEROES ARE MADE(1944, USSR), m; ANNA CROSS, THE(1954, USSR), m
Leonard A. Schwartz
SILENT CALL, THE(1961), p; BROKEN LAND, THE(1962), p
Lev Schwartz
CHILDHOOD OF MAXIM GORKY(1938, Russ.), m; CONCENTRATION CAMP(1939, USSR), m; UNIVERSITY OF LIFE(1941, USSR), m; RAINBOW, THE(1944, USSR), m; TARAS FAMILY, THE(1946, USSR), m
Lew Schwartz
PETTICOAT PIRATES(1961, Brit.), w; COOL MIKADO, THE(1963, Brit.), w; SOME WILL, SOME WON'T(1970, Brit.), w
Lionel Schwartz
APPRENTICESHIP OF DUDDY KRAVITZ, THE(1974, Can.)
Marvin Schwartz
BLINDFOLD(1966), p; WAR WAGON, THE(1967), p; HARD CONTRACT(1969), p; 100 RIFLES(1969), p; TRIBES(1970), p, w; KID BLUE(1973), p
Maurice Schwartz
MAN BEHIND THE MASK, THE(1936, Brit.); TEVYA(1939), a, d&w; MISSION TO MOSCOW(1943); BIRD OF PARADISE(1951); SALOME(1953); SLAVES OF BABYLON(1953)

Misc. Talkies
UNCLE MOSES(1932)
Silents
BROKEN HEARTS(1926), a, d
Mike Schwartz
JEALOUSY(1934)
Mort Schwartz
1984
IRRECONCILABLE DIFFERENCES(1984), cos
Morty Schwartz
RECESS(1967), ed
Neil J. Schwartz
TO BE OR NOT TO BE(1983)
Norman Schwartz
LIMIT, THE(1972), ed
Peter Schwartz
1984
RAZORBACK(1984, Aus.)
Robert Schwartz
GREAT MAN, THE(1957); WICKED DIE SLOW, THE(1968), m
Russell Schwartz
VAN, THE(1977), art d
Sam Schwartz
VAGABOND KING, THE(1956)
Misc. Talkies
FORCE FOUR(1975)
Samuel Schwartz
BUTTERFIELD 8(1960)
Scott Schwartz
TOY, THE(1982); CHRISTMAS STORY, A(1983)
1984
KIDCO(1984)
Sherwood Schwartz
WACKIEST WAGON TRAIN IN THE WEST, THE(1976), w
Sid Schwartz
MAN MADE MONSTER(1941), w
Stanley Schwartz
LEGACY OF BLOOD(1978)
Stephen Schwartz
GODSPELL(1973), w, m; ECHOES(1983), m
Steve Schwartz
SCARFACE(1983), set d
Terry Schwartz
1984
REPO MAN(1984)
Tom Schwartz
RETURN, THE(1980), makeup; HELL NIGHT(1981), makeup
Victor Schwartz
ONE WAY TICKET TO HELL(1955)
William Schwartz
WHERE DOES IT HURT?(1972), p
Zack Schwartz
FANTASIA(1940), art d
Jack Schwartzman
NEVER SAY NEVER AGAIN(1983), p
John Schwartzman
HUCKLEBERRY FINN(1974)
Mischa Schwartzmann
1984
NO SMALL AFFAIR(1984)
Milton Schwartzwald
JOHNNY STOOL PIGEON(1949), md; STORY OF MOLLY X, THE(1949), m; I WAS A SHOPLIFTER(1950), md; OUTSIDE THE WALL(1950), md
Ron Schwary
ULTIMATE THRILL, THE(1974)
Ronald L. Schwary
CASEY'S SHADOW(1978); CHEAP DETECTIVE, THE(1978); ORDINARY PEOPLE(1980), p; TOOTSIE(1982)
1984
SOLDIER'S STORY, A(1984), p
Frank J. Schwarz
UNIVERSAL SOLDIER(1971, Brit.), p
Hans Schwarz
BOMBARDMENT OF MONTE CARLO, THE(1931, Ger.), d; INVISIBLE DR. MABUSE, THE(1965, Ger.)
Herta Schwarz
JUDGE AND THE SINNER, THE(1964, Ger.), makeup
Jack Schwarz
GIRLS' TOWN(1942), p; BOSS OF BIG TOWN(1943), p; DANGER! WOMEN AT WORK(1943), p; GIRL FROM MONTEREY(1943), p; PAYOFF, THE(1943), p; LADY IN THE DEATH HOUSE(1944), p; MACHINE GUN MAMA(1944), p; DIXIE JAMBOREE(1945), p; HOLLYWOOD BARN DANCE(1947), p; BORDER OUTLAWS(1950), p; FIGHTING STALLION, THE(1950), p; FORBIDDEN JUNGLE(1950), p; I KILLED GERONIMO(1950), p; CATTLE QUEEN(1951), p
Lew Schwarz
CRACKSMAN, THE(1963, Brit.), w; CUCKOO PATROL(1965, Brit.), w
Reiner Schwarz
VIDEODROME(1983, Can.)
Robert Schwarz
LAST CHANCE, THE(1945, Switz.)
Rudolph Schwarz
INVISIBLE OPPONENT(1933, Ger.), m
Willie Schwarz
SUN VALLEY SERENADE(1941)
Wolf Schwarz
GIRL FROM HONG KONG(1966, Ger.), p
Xaver Schwarzenberger
LILI MARLEEN(1981, Ger.), ph; ACE OF ACES(1982, Fr./Ger.), ph; LOLA(1982, Ger.), ph; VERONIKA VOSS(1982, Ger.), ph; KAMIKAZE '89(1983, Ger.), ph; QUERELLE(1983, Ger./Fr.), ph

Arnold Schwarzenegger
STAY HUNGRY(1976); VILLAIN, THE(1979); CONAN THE BARBARIAN(1982)
1984
CONAN THE DESTROYER(1984); TERMINATOR, THE(1984)
Madame Elisabeth Schwarzkopf
SVENGALI(1955, Brit.)
Michael Schwarzmaier
DISORDER AND EARLY TORMENT(1977, Ger.)
Milton Schwarzwald
TOP MAN(1943), p; FAMILY HONEYMOON(1948), md; FOR THE LOVE OF MARY(1948), md; ROGUES' REGIMENT(1948), md; YOU GOTTA STAY HAPPY(1948), md; ABBOTT AND COSTELLO MEET THE KILLER, BORIS KARLOFF(1949), m; ARCTIC MANHUNT(1949), m; CALAMITY JANE AND SAM BASS(1949), md; FIGHTING O'FLYNN, THE(1949), md; ILLEGAL ENTRY(1949), md; JOHNNY STOOL PIGEON(1949), m; MA AND PA KETTLE(1949), m; UNDERTOW(1949), md; WOMAN IN HIDING(1949), md; KID FROM TEXAS, THE(1950), m, md; MA AND PA KETTLE GO TO TOWN(1950), md
Paul Schwed
DECISION BEFORE DAWN(1951)
Herman Schwedt
INTERLUDE(1957)
Paul Schwegeler
DANTE'S INFERNO(1935)
Mark Schweid
EAST SIDE SADIE(1929); CANTOR'S SON, THE(1937), w
Misc. Talkies
WEDDING ON THE VOLGA, THE(1929); UNCLE MOSES(1932)
Bontche Schweig [Ernest Kinoy]
COME BACK CHARLESTON BLUE(1972), w
Heinrich Schweiger
DREAM TOWN(1973, Ger.)
Daniel Schweitzer
Misc. Talkies
GOD'S BLOODY ACRE(1975)
Freddie Schweitzer
SHE SHALL HAVE MUSIC(1935, Brit.)
Freddy Schweitzer
SAY IT WITH MUSIC(1932, Brit.); BAND WAGGON(1940, Brit.)
Richard Schweitzer
LAST CHANCE, THE(1945, Switz.), w; FOUR DAYS LEAVE(1950, Switz.), w
S.S. Schweitzer
CHANGE OF HABIT(1969), w; HELL BOATS(1970, Brit.), w; HORNET'S NEST(1970), w
Richard Schweizer
SEARCH, THE(1948), w; FOUR IN A JEEP(1951, Switz.), w; HEIDI(1954, Switz.), w; HEIDI(1968, Aust.), w
Barbara Schweke
1984
WOMAN IN RED, THE(1984)
Gordon Schwenk
DEADWOOD'76(1965)
Karl-Heinz Schwerdtfeger
HAPPY THIEVES, THE(1962)
Dr. Herman Schwerin
BRIDGE, THE(1961, Ger.), p
Karl Schwetter
NO TIME FOR FLOWERS(1952); DIE FLEDERMAUS(1964, Aust.), p
Werner Schwier
24-HOUR LOVER(1970, Ger.)
Ellen Schwiers
BETWEEN TIME AND ETERNITY(1960, Ger.); COW AND I, THE(1961, Fr., Ital., Ger.); ARMS AND THE MAN(1962, Ger.); INVISIBLE MAN, THE(1963, Ger.); NO TIME TO KILL(1963, Brit./Swed./Ger.); BRAIN, THE(1965, Ger./Brit.)
Richard Schwiezer
HEIDI AND PETER(1955, Switz.), w
Wolfgang V. Schwind
JOHNNY STEALS EUROPE(1932, Ger.)
Michael Schwiner
OPERATION CIA(1965)
Tom Schwoegler
BREAKING AWAY(1979)
Ernest Schworck
PATSY, THE(1964)
Kasper Schyberg
KING LEAR(1971, Brit./Den.), ed
Morton Schyberg
SUDDENLY, A WOMAN!(1967, Den.), p
Hanna Schygulla
BITTER TEARS OF PETRA VON KANT, THE(1972, Ger.); EFFI BRIEST(1974, Ger.); JAIL BAIT(1977, Ger.); WHY DOES HERR R. RUN AMOK?(1977, Ger.); MARRIAGE OF MARIA BRAUN, THE(1979, Ger.); LILI MARLEEN(1981, Ger.); CIRCLE OF DECEIT(1982, Fr./Ger.); FRIENDS AND HUSBANDS(1983, Ger.); LA NUIT DE VARENNES(1983, Fr./Ital.); PASSION(1983, Fr./Switz.)
1984
LOVE IN GERMANY, A(1984, Fr./Ger.)
Adolph Schylssleder
DISORDER AND EARLY TORMENT(1977, Ger.), ed
Rick Sciacca
ROLLER BOOGIE(1979)
Ted Sciafe
CURSE OF THE DEMON(1958), ph
Armando Sciascia
TOMB OF TORTURE(1966, Ital.), m
Leonardo Sciascia
WE STILL KILL THE OLD WAY(1967, Ital.), w; DAY OF THE OWL, THE(1968, Ital./Fr.), w; MAFIA(1969, Fr./Ital.), w
Salvatore Scibetta
MONSTER OF THE ISLAND(1953, Ital.)

Angelo Scibetti
MAN FROM PLANET X, THE(1951), art d
Andrzey Scibor
BATTLE OF BRITAIN, THE(1969, Brit.)
Aleksander Scibor-Rylski
MAN OF MARBLE(1979, Pol.), w; MAN OF IRON(1981, Pol.), w
Glenn Scimonelli
TREE, THE(1969)
Giorgio Sciolette
DANGER: DIABOLIK(1968, Ital./Fr.); WATERLOO(1970, Ital./USSR)
Frank Scioscia
SHAFT'S BIG SCORE(1972); GAMBLER, THE(1974); SISTER-IN-LAW, THE(1975)
Roger Scipion
MADE IN U.S.A.(1966, Fr.)
Bruno Scipioni
ASSASSIN, THE(1961, Ital./Fr.); WARRIORS FIVE(1962); REBEL GLADIATORS, THE(1963, Ital.); BEBO'S GIRL(1964, Ital.); ORGANIZER, THE(1964, Fr./Ital./Yugo.); SEDUCED AND ABANDONED(1964, Fr./Ital.); RED DESERT(1965, Fr./Ital.); EL GRECO(1966, Ital., Fr.); LOVE AND MARRIAGE(1966, Ital.); ROMEO AND JULIET(1968, Ital./Span.); PIZZA TRIANGLE, THE(1970, Ital./Span.); WHITE SISTER(1973, Ital./Span./Fr.)
Andrea Scire
FRIENDS FOR LIFE(1964, Ital.)
Mario Scisci
MAN CALLED SLEDGE, A(1971, Ital.), art d; LUDWIG(1973, Ital./Ger./Fr.), art d
Piergiuseppe Sciume
LAST MERCENARY, THE(1969, Ital./Span./Ger.)
Franca Sciuto
SHE AND HE(1969, Ital.)
Giovanni Sciuto
TEN DAYS' WONDER(1972, Fr.)
Franca Sciutto
WOMAN ON FIRE, A(1970, Ital.); DEAF SMITH AND JOHNNY EARS(1973, Ital.)
Maria Rosa Sclauzero
AVANTI!(1972)
V. Scnitzeff
APOLLO GOES ON HOLIDAY(1968, Ger./Swed.), w
Edith Scob
HORROR CHAMBER OF DR. FAUSTUS, THE(1962, Fr./Ital.); THERESE(1963, Fr.); JUDEX(1966, Fr./Ital.); MILKY WAY, THE(1969, Fr./Ital.)
1984
ONE DEADLY SUMMER(1984, Fr.)
Merle Scobee
DOWN THE WYOMING TRAIL(1939)
Ray Scobee
DOWN THE WYOMING TRAIL(1939)
Scobie
GREAT CATHERINE(1968, Brit.)
Alastair Scobie
MEN AGAINST THE SUN(1953, Brit.), p, w
Brian Scobie
UNSUITABLE JOB FOR A WOMAN, AN(1982, Brit.), w
Lesley Scoble
SHE DIDN'T SAY NO!(1962, Brit.)
Lisa Scoble
ELEPHANT MAN, THE(1980, Brit.)
Teresa Scoble
SHE DIDN'T SAY NO!(1962, Brit.)
Teri Scoble
ELEPHANT MAN, THE(1980, Brit.)
Robin Scoby
EMPIRE STRIKES BACK, THE(1980)
Henry Scofield
Silents
FATE'S PLAYTHING(1920, Brit.)
Paul Scofield
THAT LADY(1955, Brit.); CARVE HER NAME WITH PRIDE(1958, Brit.); TRAIN, THE(1965, Fr./Ital./U.S.); MAN FOR ALL SEASONS, A(1966, Brit.); TELL ME LIES(1968, Brit.); BARTLEBY(1970, Brit.); KING LEAR(1971, Brit./Den.); DELICATE BALANCE, A(1973); SCORPIO(1973)
1984
1919(1984, Brit.)
Silents
BLUEBEARD'S SEVEN WIVES(1926), w
Peter Scofield
O LUCKY MAN!(1973, Brit.)
Rehn Scofield
WHERE'S POPPA?(1970); HOSPITAL, THE(1971)
C. E. Scoggins
TYCOON(1947), w
Charles E. Scoggins
UNTAMED(1929), w
Jarry Scoggins
ON TOP OF OLD SMOKY(1953)
Jerry Scoggins
RIDERS OF THE WHISTLING PINES(1949); WAGON TEAM(1952)
Tracy Scoggins
1984
TOY SOLDIERS(1984)
Gabriel Scognamillo
MERRY WIDOW, THE(1934), set d; SUZY(1936), art d; DRAMATIC SCHOOL(1938), art d; RICH MAN, POOR GIRL(1938), art d; MIRACLES FOR SALE(1939), art d; DOWN IN SAN DIEGO(1941), art; FOR ME AND MY GAL(1942), art d; SINGAPORE(1947), art d; UNDERCOVER MAISIE(1947), art d; WISTFUL WIDOW OF WAGON GAP, THE(1947), art d; LOVE HAPPY(1949), art d; BLACK HAND, THE(1950), art d; MYSTERY STREET(1950), art d; GREAT CARUSO, THE(1951), art d; IT'S A BIG COUNTRY(1951), art d; LIGHT TOUCH, THE(1951), art d; LOVE IS BETTER THAN EVER(1952), art d; LOVELY TO LOOK AT(1952), art d; LATIN LOVERS(1953), art d; STRANGE LADY IN TOWN(1955), art d; THUNDER OF DRUMS, A(1961), art d; TWIST ALL NIGHT(1961), art d; SEVEN FACES OF DR.

LAO(1964), art d; ANGEL, ANGEL, DOWN WE GO(1969), art d; LA CHIENNE(1975, Fr.), art d
James Scognamillo
RIGHT CROSS(1950), art d
Gabriel Scognamilo
HIGH BARBAREE(1947), art d
Sherman Scoit
HOLD THAT WOMAN(1940), d
Scola
HERCULES' PILLS(1960, Ital.), w
Ettore Scola
TWO NIGHTS WITH CLEOPATRA(1953, Ital.), w; EASY LIFE, THE(1963, Ital.), w; LOVE AND LARCENY(1963, Fr./Ital.), w; LET'S TALK ABOUT WOMEN(1964, Fr./Ital.), d, w; OF WAYWARD LOVE(1964, Ital./Ger.), w; HIGH INFIDELITY(1965, Fr./Ital.), w; LOVE A LA CARTE(1965, Ital.), w; MAGNIFICENT CUCKOLD, THE(1965, Fr./Ital.), w; ONE MILLION DOLLARS(1965, Ital.), d, w; LA VISITA(1966, Ital./Fr.), w; MADE IN ITALY(1967, Fr./Ital.), w; OPIATE '67(1967, Fr./Ital.), w; ANYONE CAN PLAY(1968, Ital.), w; DEVIL IN LOVE, THE(1968, Ital.), d, w; MOTIVE WAS JEALOUSY, THE(1970 Ital./Span.), d, w; PIZZA TRIANGLE, THE(1970, Ital./Span.), d, w; MOST WONDERFUL EVENING OF MY LIFE, THE(1972, Ital./Fr.), d, w; ROCCO PAPALEO(1974, Ital./Fr.), d, w; GOODNIGHT, LADIES AND GENTLEMEN(1977, Ital.), d&w; SPECIAL DAY, A(1977, Ital./Can.), d, w; VIVA ITALIA(1978, Ital.), d; PASSION OF LOVE(1982, Ital./Fr.), d, w; LA NUIT DE VARENNES(1983, Fr./Ital.), d, w
1984
LE BAL(1984, Fr./Ital./Algeria), d, w
Kathryn Scola
ONE NIGHT AT SUSIE'S(1930), w; LADY WHO DARED, THE(1931), w; WICKED(1931), w; NIGHT AFTER NIGHT(1932), w; BABY FACE(1933), w; FEMALE(1933), w; LILLY TURNER(1933), w; LUXURY LINER(1933), w; MIDNIGHT MARY(1933), w; FASHIONS OF 1934(1934), w; LOST LADY, A(1934), w; MERRY FRINKS, THE(1934), w; MODERN HERO, A(1934), w; SHADOWS OF SING SING(1934), w; GLASS KEY, THE(1935), w; ONE HOUR LATE(1935), w; IT HAD TO HAPPEN(1936), w; SECOND HONEYMOON(1937), w; WIFE, DOCTOR AND NURSE(1937), w; ALEXANDER'S RAGTIME BAND(1938), w; ALWAYS GOODBYE(1938), w; BARONESS AND THE BUTLER, THE(1938), w; HOTEL FOR WOMEN(1939), w; HOUSE ACROSS THE BAY, THE(1940), w; ONE NIGHT IN THE TROPICS(1940), w; LADY FROM CHEYENNE(1941), w; CONSTANT NYMPH, THE(1943), w; HAPPY LAND(1943), w; COLONEL EFFINGHAM'S RAID(1945), w; NIGHT UNTO NIGHT(1949), w
Maria Scola
1984
CONQUEST(1984, Ital./Span./Mex.)
Peter Scolari
1984
ROSEBUD BEACH HOTEL(1984)
Nino Scolaro
CAESAR THE CONQUEROR(1963, Ital.), w; HERCULES AGAINST THE MOON MEN(1965, Fr./Ital.), w
John Scoletti
EASY MONEY(1983)
Fred Scollay
DEATH WISH(1974); MAN WHO WOULD NOT DIE, THE(1975)
Fred J. Scollay
ODDS AGAINST TOMORROW(1959); TREE, THE(1969); LADY LIBERTY(1972, Ital./Fr.); Q(1982)
Zvee Scooler
ANDY(1965); NO WAY TO TREAT A LADY(1968); DREAM OF KINGS, A(1969); FIDDLER ON THE ROOF(1971); LADY ICE(1973); APPRENTICESHIP OF DUDDY KRAVITZ, THE(1974, Can.); HESTER STREET(1975); LOVE AND DEATH(1975); THIEVES(1977); KING OF THE GYPSIES(1978)
Misc. Talkies
UNCLE MOSES(1932)
Mark Scoones
ALFIE DARLING(1975, Brit.)
Scooter
TORTILLA FLAT(1942)
Robert Scopa
UP THE ACADEMY(1980)
William Scope
PLEASURE PLANTATION(1970)
Alfie Scopp
FIDDLER ON THE ROOF(1971)
Alfred Scopp
ONE PLUS ONE(1961, Can.); WILLIE MCBEAN AND HIS MAGIC MACHINE(1965, U.S./Jap.)
Jean Scoppa
HEARTBREAK KID, THE(1972)
Justin Scoppa
ONE-TRICK PONY(1980), set d; AMITYVILLE 3-D(1983), set d
Justin Scoppa, Jr.
ANNIE HALL(1977), set d; WORLD ACCORDING TO GARP, The(1982), set d
1984
MUPPETS TAKE MANHATTAN, THE(1984), set d
Peter Scoppa
MIKEY AND NICKY(1976)
Sandra Scoppettone
SCARECROW IN A GARDEN OF CUCUMBERS(1972), w
Jack Scordi [Jack Costello]
DO YOU LOVE ME?(1946)
Daphne Scorer
SPORT OF KINGS, THE(1931, Brit.); OFFICE GIRL, THE(1932, Brit.); GOOD COMPANIONS(1933, Brit.); SHE WAS ONLY A VILLAGE MAIDEN(1933, Brit.); MY BROTHER'S KEEPER(1949, Brit.)
Catherine Scorsese
WHO'S THAT KNOCKING AT MY DOOR?(1968); MEAN STREETS(1973); KING OF COMEDY, THE(1983)
Cathy Scorsese
KING OF COMEDY, THE(1983)

Charles Scorsese
  KING OF COMEDY, THE(1983)
Martin Scorsese
  WHO'S THAT KNOCKING AT MY DOOR?(1968), a, d, w; BOXCAR BERTHA(1972),
  a, d; MEAN STREETS(1973), a, d; ALICE DOESN'T LIVE HERE ANYMORE(1975),
  d; CANNONBALL(1976, U.S./Hong Kong); TAXI DRIVER(1976), a, d; NEW YORK,
  NEW YORK(1977), d; RAGING BULL(1980), a, d; KING OF COMEDY, THE(1983), a,
  d
Thomas N. Scortia
  TOWERING INFERNO, THE(1974), w
G.M. Scotese
  GREAT DAWN, THE(1947, Ital.), d
Giuseppe Maria Scotese
  RED CLOAK, THE(1961, Ital./Fr.), d, w
Sybil Scotford
  COUNT YORGA, VAMPIRE(1970); LONG GOODBYE, THE(1973); SCREAM BLACU-
  LA SCREAM(1973)
Col. Alexander Scotland, OBE
  TWO-HEADED SPY, THE(1959, Brit.), tech adv
Scots Kilties Band
  SATURDAY NIGHT REVUE(1937, Brit.); TALKING FEET(1937, Brit.)
Scott
  RALLY 'ROUND THE FLAG, BOYS!(1958), set d; VON RYAN'S EXPRESS(1965), set
  d
Scott & Whaley
  KENTUCKY MINSTRELS(1934, Brit.)
Scott and Whaley
  ON THE AIR(1934, Brit.); TAKE OFF THAT HAT(1938, Brit.)
Adam Scott
  FIDDLER ON THE ROOF(1971)
Adrian Scott
  KEEPING COMPANY(1941), w; PARSON OF PANAMINT, THE(1941), w; WE GO
  FAST(1941), w; MR. LUCKY(1943), w; MY PAL, WOLF(1944), p; CORNERED(1945),
  p; MISS SUSIE SLAGLE'S(1945), w; MURDER, MY SWEET(1945), p; DEADLINE AT
  DAWN(1946), p; CROSSFIRE(1947), p; SO WELL REMEMBERED(1947, Brit.), p
Adrienne Scott
  DOWN AMONG THE Z MEN(1952, Brit.); FLANNELFOOT(1953, Brit.); FORCES'
  SWEETHEART(1953, Brit.); JOHNNY ON THE SPOT(1954, Brit.); FLIGHT FROM
  VIENNA(1956, Brit.); FIGHTING MAD(1957, Brit.); ROCK YOU SINNERS(1957, Brit.)
Misc. Talkies
  BEHIND THE HEADLINES(1953)
Al Scott
  NATCHEZ TRACE(1960); WILD GUITAR(1962); MIDNIGHT COWBOY(1969);
  THIEVES LIKE US(1974); ODE TO BILLY JOE(1976)
Alan Scott
  GOODBYE AGAIN(1933), w; HONEYMOON FOR THREE(1941), w; OPERATION
  PETTICOAT(1959); CLEO FROM 5 TO 7(1961, Fr.); LOLA(1961, Fr./Ital.); FRIENDS
  AND NEIGHBORS(1963, Brit.); PARIS IN THE MONTH OF AUGUST(1968, Fr.)
Misc. Talkies
  TWO VIOLENT MEN(1964)
Alex Scott
  SICILIANS, THE(1964, Brit.); AMOROUS ADVENTURES OF MOLL FLANDERS,
  THE(1965); DARLING(1965, Brit.); FAHRENHEIT 451(1966, Brit.); RICOCHET(1966,
  Brit.); MARRIAGE OF CONVENIENCE(1970, Brit.); ABOMINABLE DR. PHIBES,
  THE(1971, Brit.); TWINS OF EVIL(1971, Brit.); ASPHYX, THE(1972, Brit.); NEXT OF
  KIN(1983, Aus.)
Allan Scott
  LET'S TRY AGAIN(1934), w; BY YOUR LEAVE(1935), w; IN PERSON(1935), w;
  ROBERTA(1935), w; TOP HAT(1935), w; VILLAGE TALE(1935), w; FOLLOW THE
  FLEET(1936), w; SWING TIME(1936), w; QUALITY STREET(1937), w; SHALL WE
  DANCE(1937), w; WISE GIRL(1937), w; CAREFREE(1938), w; JOY OF LIVING(1938),
  w; FIFTH AVENUE GIRL(1939), w; MAN ABOUT TOWN(1939), w; LUCKY PART-
  NERS(1940), w; PRIMROSE PATH(1940), w; REMEMBER THE DAY(1941), w; SKY-
  LARK(1941), w; SO PROUDLY WE HAIL(1943), w; HERE COME THE
  WAVES(1944), w; I LOVE A SOLDIER(1944), w; BLUE SKIES(1946), w; LET'S
  DANCE(1950), w; GUY WHO CAME BACK, THE(1951), w; FOUR POSTER,
  THE(1952), w; WAIT 'TIL THE SUN SHINES, NELLIE(1952), w; 5,000 FINGERS OF
  DR. T. THE(1953), w; TOP SECRET AFFAIR(1957), w; IMITATION OF LIFE(1959), w;
  QUICK, LET'S GET MARRIED(1965), w; MAN WHO HAD POWER OVER WOMEN,
  THE(1970, Brit.), w; DON'T LOOK NOW(1973, Brit./Ital.), w; GIRL FROM PETROV-
  KA, THE(1974), w; SPIRAL STAIRCASE, THE(1975, Brit.), w; JOSEPH AN-
  DREWS(1977, Brit.), w; AWAKENING, THE(1980), w
Andrea Scott
  MINOTAUR, THE(1961, Ital.)
Anita d'Este Scott
Misc. Silents
  WOMAN'S LAW, THE(1916)
Ann Scott
1984
  LAUGHTER HOUSE(1984, Brit.), p; PLOUGHMAN'S LUNCH, THE(1984, Brit.), p
Anne Scott
  JUNGLE STREET GIRLS(1963, Brit.)
Anthony Scott
  LOVING MEMORY(1970, Brit.), d&w; SWEENEY(1977, Brit.)
Antony Scott
  BILLY TWO HATS(1973, Brit.); SUPERMAN(1978)
Art Scott
  MELODY TIME(1948), w
Ashmead Scott
  FOR HEAVEN'S SAKE(1950); HOUSE ON TELEGRAPH HILL(1951)
Audrey Scott
  THIRTEEN WOMEN(1932); DARK ANGEL, THE(1935)
Avis Scott
  MILLIONS LIKE US(1943, Brit.); BRIEF ENCOUNTER(1945, Brit.); MASTER OF
  BANKDAM, THE(1947, Brit.); TO HAVE AND TO HOLD(1951, Brit.); IT STARTED IN
  PARADISE(1952, Brit.); WATERFRONT WOMEN(1952, Brit.); HUNDRED HOUR
  HUNT(1953, Brit.); PAID TO KILL(1954, Brit.); STORM OVER THE NILE(1955, Brit.)

Barbara Scott
  CLOCKWORK ORANGE, A(1971, Brit.); LASERBLAST(1978), cos
1984
  CHILDREN OF THE CORN(1984), cos
Barry Scott
  GOODBYE GEMINI(1970, Brit.)
Beatrice Scott
  ROCK YOU SINNERS(1957, Brit.), w
Betty Scott
  PARDON MY GUN(1930), w
Silents
  ALSTER CASE, THE(1915); RIDIN' THE WIND(1925)
Beverly Scott
  GHOST OF DRAGSTRIP HOLLOW(1959)
Bill Scott
  CAUGHT PLASTERED(1931); SUGARLAND EXPRESS, THE(1974)
Billy J. Scott
  KILLER ELITE, THE(1975)
Billy "Uke" Scott
  NIGHT OF MAGIC, A(1944, Brit.)
Bob Scott
  MICHAEL O'HALLORAN(1948); DETECTIVE STORY(1951); PONY EXPRESS(1953);
  LAST TRAIN FROM GUN HILL(1959)
Bobby Scott
  IT'S A WONDERFUL LIFE(1946); BLONDE BANDIT, THE(1950); SLAVES(1969), m;
  JOE(1970), m, md; WHO SAYS I CAN'T RIDE A RAINBOW!(1971), m
Bonnie Scott
  DONDI(1961)
Brenda Scott
  JOHNNY TIGER(1966); JOURNEY TO SHILOH(1968); THIS SAVAGE LAND(1969);
  SIMON, KING OF THE WITCHES(1971)
Bruce Scott
  HANG'EM HIGH(1968); CRY BLOOD, APACHE(1970), ph; PEOPLE NEXT DOOR,
  THE(1970)
Bryan Scott
  9/30/55(1977)
Bud Scott
  NEW ORLEANS(1947)
C. Robert Scott
  PUTNEY SWOPE(1969)
Candy Scott
  SHAKEDOWN, THE(1960, Brit.); YOUR MONEY OR YOUR WIFE(1965, Brit.)
Carey Scott
1984
  MAKING THE GRADE(1984)
Carl Scott
Misc. Talkies
  HARD WAY TO DIE, A(1980)
Cecil Scott
  SENTIMENTAL BLOKE(1932, Aus.)
Cedric Scott
  LET'S DO IT AGAIN(1975); WELCOME TO L.A.(1976)
Channon Scott
  BLACK ANGELS, THE(1970)
Chuck Scott
  TWO THOUSAND MANIACS!(1964), md
Chuck Scott [Charles Glore]
  MOONSHINE MOUNTAIN(1964)
Churchill Scott
Silents
  LAST CHANCE, THE(1921)
Cliff Scott
Misc. Talkies
  GHOSTS OF HANLEY HOUSE, THE(1974)
Clive Scott
  MY WAY(1974, South Africa); KILLER FORCE(1975, Switz./Ireland)
Clyde Scott
  SLEEPING DOGS(1977, New Zealand); GOODBYE PORK PIE(1981, New Zealand)
Connie Scott
  FLIPPER(1963); BROTHERHOOD, THE(1968)
Cyril Scott
  HIS ROYAL HIGHNESS(1932, Aus.)
Silents
  DAY OF DAYS, THE(1914); HOW MOLLY MADE GOOD(1915)
Misc. Silents
  ARIZONA(1913); NOT GUILTY(1915); LORDS OF HIGH DECISION, THE(1916)
David Scott
  IN GAY MADRID(1930); MELODY LINGERS ON, THE(1935); GARDEN OF ALLAH,
  THE(1936); THAT SINKING FEELING(1979, Brit.); THIS IS ELVIS(1982)
Debbi Scott
  DIRTY HARRY(1971)
Deborah Scott
  E.T. THE EXTRA-TERRESTRIAL(1982), cos
Debralee Scott
  AMERICAN GRAFFITI(1973); CRAZY WORLD OF JULIUS VROODER, THE(1974);
  EARTHQUAKE(1974); OUR TIME(1974); REINCARNATION OF PETER PROUD,
  THE(1975); PANDEMONIUM(1982)
1984
  POLICE ACADEMY(1984)
Misc. Talkies
  INCOMING FRESHMEN(1979); JUST TELL ME YOU LOVE ME(1979)
Dennis Scott
1984
  AGAINST ALL ODDS(1984)
Derek Scott
  LIFE WITH FATHER(1947); PUNCH AND JUDY MAN, THE(1963, Brit.), m; BLACK
  GESTAPO, THE(1975), ph

DeVallon Scott
LETTER FOR EVIE, A(1945), w; SHE WENT TO THE RACES(1945), w; LAWTON STORY, THE(1949), w; HUNT THE MAN DOWN(1950), w; BLACKBEARD THE PIRATE(1952), w; PACE THAT THRILLS, THE(1952), w; CONQUEST OF CO-CHISE(1953), w; PRISONERS OF THE CASBAH(1953), w; SLAVES OF BABY-LON(1953), w; BLACK DAKOTAS, THE(1954), w; IRON GLOVE, THE(1954), w; SARACEN BLADE, THE(1954), w; THEY RODE WEST(1954), w; MAVERICK QUEEN, THE(1956), w; HELL SHIP MUTINY(1957), w

Dick Scott
ALASKA(1944); LAKE PLACID SERENADE(1944); LEAVE IT TO THE IRISH(1944); IDENTITY UNKNOWN(1945); MARSHAL OF LAREDO(1945); GLASS ALIBI, THE(1946)

Donovan Scott
1941(1979); POPEYE(1980); ZORRO, THE GAY BLADE(1981); SAVANNAH SMI-LES(1983)
1984
POLICE ACADEMY(1984); SHEENA(1984)

Dorothy Scott
PRETENDER, THE(1947); MY BODYGUARD(1980)
Silents
BIGAMIST, THE(1921, Brit.)

Douglas Scott
NIGHT WORK(1930); RENO(1930); CIMARRON(1931); DEVOTION(1931); RAN-GO(1931); RULING VOICE, THE(1931); RECKONING, THE(1932); CAVAL-CADE(1933); EAGLE AND THE HAWK, THE(1933); AND SO THEY WERE MARRIED(1936); EASY TO TAKE(1936); LLOYDS OF LONDON(1936); TOO MANY PARENTS(1936); LAST GANGSTER, THE(1937); SLAVE SHIP(1937); WEE WILLIE WINKIE(1937); WILD AND WOOLLY(1937); INTERMEZZO: A LOVE STORY(1939); WE ARE NOT ALONE(1939); WUTHERING HEIGHTS(1939); NAVAL ACADE-MY(1941); GET HEP TO LOVE(1942)
Silents
STRONG BOY(1929)

Douglas Frazer Scott
DYNAMITE(1930)

E. Kerrigan Scott
Misc. Talkies
ALABAMA'S GHOST(1972)

Edith Scott
THUNDER IN CAROLINA(1960)

Edmund Scott
LADY OF CHANCE, A(1928), w

Eileen Scott
TEENAGE GANG DEBS(1966)

Einar Perry Scott
NIGHTHAWKS(1981)

Elizabeth Scott
FINGERS(1940, Brit.); WRONG MAN, THE(1956)

Ella Scott
MORGAN'S MARAUDERS(1929)

Elliot Scott
SAFARI(1956), art d; LITTLE HUT, THE(1957), art d; I ACCUSE(1958, Brit.), art d; SAFECRACKER, THE(1958, Brit.), art d; TOUCH OF LARCENY, A(1960, Brit.), artd; INVASION QUARTET(1961, Brit.), art d; SECRET PARTNER, THE(1961, Brit.), prod d; FOUR HORSEMEN OF THE APOCALYPSE, THE(1962), art d; LISA(1962, Brit.), art d; MATTER OF WHO, A(1962, Brit.), art d; HAUNTING, THE(1963), prod d; NINE HOURS TO RAMA(1963, U.S./Brit.), art d; YELLOW ROLLS-ROYCE, THE(1965, Brit.), art d; EYE OF THE DEVIL(1967, Brit.), art d; THREE BITES OF THE APPLE(1967), art d; NO BLADE OF GRASS(1970, Brit.), art d; POPE JOAN(1972, Brit.), prod d; DOLL'S HOUSE, A(1973), art d; MR. QUILP(1975, Brit.), prod d; PERMISSION TO KILL(1975, U.S./Aust.), prod d; INCREDIBLE SARAH, THE(1976, Brit.), prod d; ARABIAN ADVENTURE(1979, Brit.), prod d; DRAGONSLAYER(1981), prod d; EVIL UNDER THE SUN(1982, Brit.), prod d; PIRATES OF PENZANCE, THE(1983), prod d
1984
INDIANA JONES AND THE TEMPLE OF DOOM(1984), prod d

Elliott Scott
ODONGO(1956, Brit.), art d; SCAPEGOAT, THE(1959, Brit.), art d; GORGO(1961, Brit.), art d; OPERATION CROSSBOW(1965, U.S./Ital.), art d; WARM DECEMBER, A(1973, Brit.), art d; WARLORDS OF ATLANTIS(1978, Brit.), prod d; WATCHER IN THE WOODS, THE(1980, Brit.), prod d

Ernest Scott
FIGHTING COWBOY(1933); CIRCLE CANYON(1934); RIDING SPEED(1934)

Evelyn Scott
WICKED WOMAN(1953); BACK FROM THE DEAD(1957); GREEN-EYED BLONDE, THE(1957); I WANT TO LIVE!(1958); LAS RATAS NO DUERMEN DE NOCHE(1974, Span./Fr.)

Ewing Scott
BORDER FLIGHT(1936), w; HEADIN' EAST(1937), d; HOLLYWOOD COW-BOY(1937), d, w; PARK AVENUE LOGGER(1937), w; WINDJAMMER(1937), d; HOL-LYWOOD ROUNDUP(1938), d; MAN HUNTERS OF THE CARIBBEAN(1938), d; UNTAMED FURY(1947), p&d, w; HARPOON(1948), d, w; ARCTIC MAN-HUNT(1949), d, w; ARCTIC FLIGHT(1952), w; RED SNOW(1952), d

Farnham Scott
FAT ANGELS(1980, U.S./Span.); TOUCHED(1983)
Misc. Talkies
FAT CHANCE(1982)

Francy Scott
ONE-EYED JACKS(1961)

Franklin Scott
PUTNEY SWOPE(1969); SERPICO(1973); EDUCATION OF SONNY CARSON, THE(1974), stunts

Franklyn Scott
KING OF THE GYPSIES(1978); TIMES SQUARE(1980)

Fred Scott
RIO RITA(1929); GRAND PARADE, THE(1930); SWING HIGH(1930); LAST OUT-LAW, THE(1936); ROMANCE RIDES THE RANGE(1936); FIGHTING DEPUTY, THE(1937); MAKE A WISH(1937); MELODY OF THE PLAINS(1937); MOONLIGHT ON THE RANGE(1937); ROAMING COWBOY, THE(1937); SINGING BUCKAROO, THE(1937); RANGER'S ROUNDUP, THE(1938); SONGS AND BULLETS(1938); CODE OF THE FEARLESS(1939); IN OLD MONTANA(1939); KNIGHT OF THE PLAINS(1939); TWO-GUN TROUBADOR(1939); RODEO RHYTHM(1941); THUNDER-ING HOOFS(1941); TOM(1973)
Silents
BRIDE OF THE STORM(1926)

Fred D. Scott
GALAXINA(1980)

Fred Daniel Scott
FIVE ON THE BLACK HAND SIDE(1973)

Freda Scott
ONE-TRICK PONY(1980)

Garland Scott
MONSTER(1979), w

Gary Scott
FINAL EXAM(1981), m; DEADLY FORCE(1983), m
1984
ROADHOUSE 66(1984), m

George C. Scott
ANATOMY OF A MURDER(1959); HANGING TREE, THE(1959); HUSTLER, THE(1961); LIST OF ADRIAN MESSENGER, THE(1963); DR. STRANGELOVE: OR HOW I LEARNED TO STOP WORRYING AND LOVE THE BOMB(1964); YELLOW ROLLS-ROYCE, THE(1965, Brit.); BIBLE...IN THE BEGINNING, THE(1966); NOT WITH MY WIFE, YOU DON'T(1966); FLIM-FLAM MAN, THE(1967); PETULIA(1968, U.S./Brit.); THIS SAVAGE LAND(1969); HOSPITAL, THE(1971); JANE EYRE(1971, Brit.); LAST RUN, THE(1971); THEY MIGHT BE GIANTS(1971); NEW CENTURIONS, THE(1972); RAGE(1972), a, d; DAY OF THE DOLPHIN, THE(1973); OKLAHOMA CRUDE(1973); BANK SHOT(1974); SAVAGE IS LOOSE, THE(1974), a, p&d; HINDEN-BURG, THE(1975); ISLANDS IN THE STREAM(1977); CROSSED SWORDS(1978); MOVIE MOVIE(1978); HARDCORE(1979); CHANGELING, THE(1980, Can.); FOR-MULA, THE(1980); TAPS(1981)
1984
FIRESTARTER(1984)

George C. Scott, Jr.
PATTON(1970)

Ginger Scott
HOT STUFF(1979)

Gordon Scott
TARZAN'S HIDDEN JUNGLE(1955); TARZAN AND THE LOST SAFARI(1957, Brit.); TARZAN'S FIGHT FOR LIFE(1958); TARZAN'S GREATEST ADVENTURE(1959, Brit.); TARZAN THE MAGNIFICENT(1960, Brit.); BUFFALO BILL, HERO OF THE FAR WEST(1962, Ital.); DUEL OF THE TITANS(1963, Ital.); GLADIATOR OF RO-ME(1963, Ital.); HERO OF BABYLON(1963, Ital.); SAMSON AND THE SEVEN MIRACLES OF THE WORLD(1963, Fr./Ital.); GOLIATH AND THE VAMPIRES(1964, Ital.); CONQUEST OF MYCENE(1965, Ital., Fr.); TRAMPLERS, THE(1966, Ital.); LION OF ST. MARK(1967, Ital.); PORTNOY'S COMPLAINT(1972), ed; ZANDY'S BRI-DE(1974), ed; GUMBALL RALLY, THE(1976), ed; SPARKLE(1976), ed

Gordon L.T. Scott
SANDS OF THE DESERT(1960, Brit.), p; PETTICOAT PIRATES(1961, Brit.), p; POT CARRIERS, THE(1962, Brit.), p; PUNCH AND JUDY MAN, THE(1963, Brit.), p; CROOKS IN CLOISTERS(1964, Brit.), p

Gregory Scott
Silents
FLYING FROM JUSTICE(1915, Brit.); ANSWER, THE(1916, Brit.); MUNITION GIRL'S ROMANCE, A(1917, Brit.); WARE CASE, THE(1917, Brit.); DEAD CERTAIN-TY, A(1920, Brit.); KISSING CUP'S RACE(1920, Brit.); PENNILESS MILLIONAIRE, THE(1921, Brit.); GREEN CARAVAN, THE(1922, Brit.); ROGUE IN LOVE, A(1922, Brit.)
Misc. Silents
INCOMPARABLE MISTRESS BELLAIRS, THE(1914, Brit.); SHE STOOPS TO CON-QUER(1914, Brit.); MARRIED FOR MONEY(1915, Brit.); MASTER AND MAN(1915, Brit.); ROGUE'S WIFE, A(1915, Brit.); ROMANY RYE, THE(1915, Brit.); ROYAL LOVE(1915, Brit.); SCORPION'S STING, THE(1915, Brit.); TRUMPET CALL, THE(1915, Brit.); BLACK NIGHT, THE(1916); GREEN ORCHARD, THE(1916, Brit.); HOUSE OPPOSITE, THE(1917, Brit.); NOT NEGOTIABLE(1918, Brit.); GREAT COUP, A(1919, Brit.); HEARTS AND SADDLES(1919, Brit.); CASE OF LADY CAMBER, THE(1920, Brit.); KISSING CUP'S RACE(1920, Brit.); TRENT'S LAST CASE(1920, Brit.); IN FULL CRY(1921, Brit.); LOUDWATER MYSTERY, THE(1921, Brit.); SPORTS-MAN'S WIFE, A(1921, Brit.)

Hampton J. Scott
THAT'S MY MAN(1947)

Harold Scott
WATER GYPSIES, THE(1932, Brit.); DISCORD(1933, Brit.); FACE BEHIND THE SCAR(1940, Brit.); GAY LADY, THE(1949, Brit.); NO PLACE FOR JENNIFER(1950, Brit.); TWENTY QUESTIONS MURDER MYSTERY, THE(1950, Brit.); HER PA-NELLED DOOR(1951, Brit.); WHO DONE IT?(1956, Brit.); SPANISH GARDENER, THE(1957, Span.); BRIDES OF DRACULA, THE(1960, Brit.); HAND, THE(1960, Brit.); WONDERFUL TO BE YOUNG!(1962, Brit.); YELLOW ROLLS-ROYCE, THE(1965, Brit.); MAN WHO FINALLY DIED, THE(1967, Brit.)

Harriet Scott
DRUMS O' VOODOO(1934)

Harrison Scott
HOUSE ON 92ND STREET, THE(1945)

Harry Scott
1984
NUMBER ONE(1984, Brit.)

Harry Scott, Jr.
MAN IN GREY, THE(1943, Brit.)

Hazel Scott
HEAT'S ON, THE(1943); I DOOD IT(1943); SOMETHING TO SHOUT ABOUT(1943); BROADWAY RHYTHM(1944); RHAPSODY IN BLUE(1945); NIGHT AFFAIR(1961, Fr.)

Hedy Scott
FIREBALL 590(1966)

Helen Scott
LITTLE SHEPHERD OF KINGDOM COME(1961); FAHRENHEIT 451(1966, Brit.), w; TWO OR THREE THINGS I KNOW ABOUT HER(1970, Fr.)

Helen G. Scott
STORY OF ADELE H., THE(1975, Fr.)

Hennie Scott
CIRCLE OF DECEPTON(1961, Brit.); MISSING NOTE, THE(1961, Brit.)
Hennis Scott
WINGS OF MYSTERY(1963, Brit.)
Henry Scott
ANNA LUCASTA(1958); HATARI!(1962)
Homer Scott
Silents
HUCK AND TOM(1918), ph; SUZANNA(1922), ph; EXTRA GIRL, THE(1923), ph;
LITTLE CHURCH AROUND THE CORNER(1923), ph
Howard Scott
Silents
INTOLERANCE(1916)
Misc. Silents
TATTLERS, THE(1920)
Ian Scott
Misc. Talkies
BLOODRAGE(1979)
Ivan Scott
BUCK AND THE PREACHER(1972)
Ivy Scott
TOO MANY GIRLS(1940); HIGHER AND HIGHER(1943)
J.B. Scott
WINGS IN THE DARK(1935)
J.M. Scott
SEA WIFE(1957, Brit.), w
Jack Scott
JUMP INTO HELL(1955)
Jacqueline Scott
MACABRE(1958); HOUSE OF WOMEN(1962); FIRECREEK(1968); DEATH OF A
GUNFIGHTER(1969); CHARLEY VARRICK(1973); EMPIRE OF THE ANTS(1977);
TELEFON(1977)
Jacques Scott
YOU CAN'T RUN AWAY FROM IT(1956); JOURNEY TO FREEDOM(1957)
James Scott
SCENE OF THE CRIME(1949)
1984
EVERY PICTURE TELLS A STORY(1984, Brit.), d
James R. Scott
ROPE OF SAND(1949); SEPTEMBER AFFAIR(1950); SILVER CITY(1951); STALAG
17(1953)
Jan Scott
WORLD OF HENRY ORIENT, THE(1964), art d; STILETTO(1969), art d; END,
THE(1978), prod d; LOVING COUPLES(1980), art d; RICH AND FAMOUS(1981), prod
d
1984
GRANDVIEW, U.S.A.(1984), prod d
Jan Andrew Scott
DAY OF THE ANIMALS(1977)
Jana Scott
SUPERCHICK(1973)
Jane Scott
IN SEARCH OF ANNA(1978, Aus.), prod d
Janet Scott
SPELLBOUND(1945); PREHISTORIC WOMEN(1950); ROADBLOCK(1951)
Janette Scott
LAMP STILL BURNS, THE(1943, Brit.); 2,000 WOMEN(1944, Brit.); GAY INTRUD-
ERS, THE(1946, Brit.); NO PLACE FOR JENNIFER(1950, Brit.); GALLOPING MAJOR,
THE(1951, Brit.); NO HIGHWAY IN THE SKY(1951, Brit.); MAGIC BOX, THE(1952,
Brit.); BACKGROUND(1953, Brit.); HELEN OF TROY(1956, Ital); NOW AND FOREV-
ER(1956, Brit.); AS LONG AS THEY'RE HAPPY(1957, Brit.); GOOD COMPANIONS,
THE(1957, Brit.); HAPPY IS THE BRIDE(1958, Brit.); DEVIL'S DISCIPLE, THE(1959);
LADY IS A SQUARE, THE(1959, Brit.); SCHOOL FOR SCOUNDRELS(1960, Brit.);
DOUBLE BUNK(1961, Brit.); HIS AND HERS(1961, Brit.); TWO AND TWO MAKE
SIX(1962, Brit.); DAY OF THE TRIFFIDS, THE(1963); OLD DARK HOUSE, THE(1963,
Brit.); PARANOIAC(1963, Brit.); SIEGE OF THE SAXONS(1963, Brit.); CRACK IN THE
WORLD(1965); BEAUTY JUNGLE, THE(1966, Brit.)
Misc. Talkies
BIKINI PARADISE(1967)
Jay Scott
FANDANGO(1970); KINFOLK(1970); GRAVE OF THE VAMPIRE(1972); KISS OF
THE TARANTULA(1975)
Jay Hutchinson Scott
BERSERK(1967), cos
Jean Scott
LANDSLIDE(1937, Brit.)
Misc. Silents
LOVE NEST, THE(1922); MADNESS OF LOVE, THE(1922)
Jeff Scott
GAMES(1967); YOUNG WARRIORS, THE(1967)
Jeremy Scott
TWISTED NERVE(1969, Brit.), w
Jerome Scott
Misc. Talkies
SINS OF RACHEL, THE(1975)
Jerry Scott
THRILL OF A ROMANCE(1945)
Jesse Scott
CHAMP, THE(1931)
Jessie Scott
MADAME DU BARRY(1934); DIMPLES(1936)
Jill Scott
TICKET TO HEAVEN(1981), art d
Jillian Scott
1984
ALL OF ME(1984-
Jimmy Scott
WRONG BOX, THE(1966, Brit.)

Joan Scott
LOVERS, THE(1972, Brit.); MUTATIONS, THE(1974, Brit.)
Joe Scott
FATE IS THE HUNTER(1964)
John Scott
OPERATION SNATCH(1962, Brit.); TELL-TALE HEART, THE(1962, Brit.); HORROR
OF PARTY BEACH, THE(1964); SKIN GAME, THE(1965, Brit.); STUDY IN TERROR,
A(1966, Brit./Ger.), m; PRIVATE LIFE OF SHERLOCK HOLMES, THE(1970, Brit.);
GIRL STROKE BOY(1971, Brit.), m; LOLA(1971, Brit./Ital.), m, md; OUTBACK(1971,
Aus.), m; ADVENTURES OF BARRY McKENZIE(1972, Austral.), ed; DOOM-
WATCH(1972, Brit.), m; JERUSALEM FILE, THE(1972, U.S./Israel), m; ANTONY
AND CLEOPATRA(1973, Brit.), m; BILLY TWO HATS(1973, Brit.), m; ENGLANO
MADE ME(1973, Brit.), m; CRAZE(1974, Brit.), m; GREAT MACARTHY, THE(1975,
Aus.), ed; HENNESSY(1975, Brit.), m; THAT LUCKY TOUCH(1975, Brit.), m; MAD
DOG MORGAN(1976,Aus.), ed; PURE S(1976, Aus.), ed; SATAN'S SLAVE(1976, Brit.),
m; SYMPTOMS(1976, Brit.), m; JOURNEY AMONG WOMEN(1977, Aus.), ed; PEOPLE
THAT TIME FORGOT, THE(1977, Brit.), m; NEWSFRONT(1979, Aus.), ed; NORTH
DALLAS FORTY(1979), m; FINAL COUNTDOWN, THE(1980), m; MANGO TREE,
THE(1981, Aus.), ed; HORROR PLANET(1982, Brit.), m; EXPERIENCE PRE-
FERRED... BUT NOT ESSENTIAL(1983, Brit.), m; HEATWAVE(1983, Aus.), ed; RE-
TURN OF CAPTAIN INVINCIBLE, THE(1983, Aus./U.S.), ed; YOR, THE HUNTER
FROM THE FUTURE(1983, Ital.), m
1984
GREYSTOKE: THE LEGEND OF TARZAN, LORD OF THE APES(1984), m
John Murray Scott
FIRST MEN IN THE MOON(1964, Brit.)
John-Clay Scott
1984
FOOTLOOSE(1984)
Johnny Scott
ALL NIGHT LONG(1961, Brit.); CARNABY, M.D.(1967, Brit.), md; MILLION EYES
OF SU-MURU, THE(1967, Brit.), m, md; AMSTERDAM AFFAIR, THE(1968 Brit.), m;
TROG(1970, Brit.), m, md
Jonathan Scott
SONG AND THE SILENCE, THE(1969); PINK FLOYD-THE WALL(1982, Brit.)
Joseph Scott
PINOCCHIO(1969, E. Ger.), m
1984
POWER, THE(1984)
Judith Scott
NO TIME FOR TEARS(1957, Brit.)
Judson Scott
I, THE JURY(1982)
Julie Scott
DEVIL'S HAND, THE(1961); NOTORIOUS LANDLADY, THE(1962)
Julienne Scott
Misc. Silents
CONCERT, THE(1921)
Karen Scott
MAVERICK QUEEN, THE(1956); FUNNY FACE(1957); PERFECT FURLOUGH,
THE(1958); QUICK, BEFORE IT MELTS(1964)
Katherine Scott
Silents
PLEASURES OF THE RICH(1926)
Kathryn Leigh Scott
HOUSE OF DARK SHADOWS(1970); GREAT GATSBY, THE(1974); BRAN-
NIGAN(1975, Brit.); GREEK TYCOON, THE(1978)
Misc. Talkies
WITCHES' BREW(1980)
Kay Scott
FEAR IN THE NIGHT(1947); CALLAWAY WENT THATAWAY(1951); PEOPLE
AGAINST O'HARA, THE(1951)
Ken Scott
GUY NAMED JOE, A(1943); SEE HERE, PRIVATE HARGROVE(1944); STOPOVER
TOKYO(1957); THREE FACES OF EVE, THE(1957); WAY TO THE GOLD, THE(1957);
BRAVADOS, THE(1958); FIEND WHO WALKED THE WEST, THE(1958); FROM
HELL TO TEXAS(1958); BELOVED INFIDEL(1959); FIVE GATES TO HELL(1959);
THIS EARTH IS MINE(1959); WOMAN OBSESSED(1959); DESIRE IN THE
DUST(1960); FIERCEST HEART, THE(1961); PIRATES OF TORTUGA(1961); SECOND
TIME AROUND, THE(1961); POLICE NURSE(1963); RAIDERS FROM BENEATH
THE SEA(1964); NAKED BRIGADE, THE(1965, U.S./Gr.); FANTASTIC VOYA-
GE(1966); MURDER GAME, THE(1966, Brit.); ST. VALENTINE'S DAY MASSACRE,
THE(1967); TWO FOR THE ROAD(1967, Brit.), cos; PSYCH-OUT(1968); ROOMMATES,
THE(1973)
Kendall Scott
YOUNG LIONS, THE(1958)
Kenneth Scott
IT'S A PLEASURE(1945)
Kevin Scott
FLOODS OF FEAR(1958, Brit.); PASSPORT TO CHINA(1961, Brit.); CALL ME
BWANA(1963, Brit.); COOL MIKADO, THE(1963, Brit.); MOUSE ON THE MOON,
THE(1963, Brit.); INTERNECINE PROJECT, THE(1974, Brit.)
1984
SUPERGIRL(1984)
Kirk Scott
TARGETS(1968); END OF THE WORLD(1977); ONE MAN JURY(1978)
Kristina Scott
RAVAGERS, THE(1965, U.S./Phil.)
Captain L.G.S. Scott
DAWN PATROL, THE(1938), tech adv
Silents
LILAC TIME(1928), tech adv
Larry Scott
MUSCLE BEACH PARTY(1964); THIEVES(1977)
Larry B. Scott
HERO AIN'T NOTHIN' BUT A SANDWICH, A(1977)
1984
KARATE KID, THE(1984); REVENGE OF THE NERDS(1984)

Lee Scott
EXCUSE MY DUST(1951); RAINBOW 'ROUND MY SHOULDER(1952), ch; CRUISIN' DOWN THE RIVER(1953), ch; LET'S DO IT AGAIN(1953), ch; MISS SADIE THOMPSON(1953), ch; SO THIS IS PARIS(1954), ch; AIN'T MISBEHAVIN'(1955), ch; SECOND GREATEST SEX, THE(1955), ch; SCREAMING MIMI(1958), ch

Leo Scott
STRIP, THE(1951)

Leroy Scott
LADY OF CHANCE, A(1928), w
Silents
PARTNERS OF THE NIGHT(1920), w; POVERTY OF RICHES, THE(1921), w; LIGHTNING LARIATS(1927); 13 WASHINGTON SQUARE(1928), w

Leslie Scott
ISLAND WOMEN(1958); PORGY AND BESS(1959)

Lester Scott, Jr.
GET THAT MAN(1935), p

Lester F. Scott, Jr.
DAUGHTER OF THE TONG(1939), p
Silents
WALLOPING WALLACE(1924), p

Lester F. Scott
BORDER ROMANCE(1930), p

Lewis Scott
Misc. Talkies
THREE WAY LOVE(1977), d

Lincoln Scott
CRY DR. CHICAGO(1971)

Linda Scott
DON'T KNOCK THE TWIST(1962); MAN IN THE WATER, THE(1963); WESTWORLD(1973)

Linda Gaye Scott
RUN HOME SLOW(1965); PSYCH-OUT(1968); LITTLE FAUSS AND BIG HALSY(1970); HAMMERSMITH IS OUT(1972)

Lionel Scott
Misc. Silents
DEFINITE OBJECT, THE(1920, Brit.)

Lita Scott
CRIMSON CULT, THE(1970, Brit.)

Lizabeth Scott
YOU CAME ALONG(1945); STRANGE LOVE OF MARTHA IVERS, THE(1946); DEAD RECKONING(1947); DESERT FURY(1947); VARIETY GIRL(1947); I WALK ALONE(1948); PITFALL(1948); EASY LIVING(1949); TOO LATE FOR TEARS(1949); COMPANY SHE KEEPS, THE(1950); DARK CITY(1950); PAID IN FULL(1950); RACKET, THE(1951); RED MOUNTAIN(1951); TWO OF A KIND(1951); STOLEN FACE(1952, Brit.); SCARED STIFF(1953); BAD FOR EACH OTHER(1954); SILVER LODE(1954); LOVING YOU(1957); WEAPON, THE(1957, Brit.); PULP(1972, Brit.)

Lois Scott
Misc. Silents
WHITE PANTHER, THE(1924)

Luanna Scott
SNIPER, THE(1952)

Mabel Julienne Scott
PAINTED FACES(1929)
Silents
SACRED SILENCE(1919); ROUND UP, THE(1920); NO WOMAN KNOWS(1921); ABYSMAL BRUTE, THE(1923); HIS JAZZ BRIDE(1926); DREAM MELODY, THE(1929)
Misc. Silents
LASH OF DESTINY, THE(1916); RECLAIMED(1918); SIGN INVISIBLE, THE(1918); BEHOLD MY WIFE!(1920); JUCKLINS, THE(1920); SEA WOLF, THE(1920); DON'T NEGLECT YOUR WIFE(1921); POWER OF A LIE, THE(1922); TIMES HAVE CHANGED(1923); SEVEN DAYS(1925); FRONTIER TRAIL, THE(1926); WOMAN'S HEART, A(1926); WALLFLOWERS(1928)

Maggie Scott
DOGS OF WAR, THE(1980, Brit.)

Margareta Scott
RETURN OF THE SCARLET PIMPERNEL(1938, Brit.)

Margaretta Scott
DIRTY WORK(1934, Brit.); PRIVATE LIFE OF DON JUAN, THE(1934, Brit.); PEG OF OLD DRURY(1936, Brit.); THINGS TO COME(1936, Brit.); ACTION FOR SLANDER(1937, Brit.); CONQUEST OF THE AIR(1940); ATLANTIC FERRY(1941, Brit.); GIRL IN THE NEWS, THE(1941, Brit.); QUIET WEDDING(1941); SABOTAGE AT SEA(1942, Brit.); MAN FROM MOROCCO(1946, Brit.); CALLING PAUL TEMPLE(1948, Brit.); COUNTER BLAST(1948, Brit.); DEVIL'S PLOT, THE(1948, Brit.); IDOL OF PARIS(1948, Brit.); MAN OF EVIL(1948, Brit.); STORY OF SHIRLEY YORKE, THE(1948, Brit.); AFFAIRS OF A ROGUE, THE(1949, Brit.); MRS. FITZHERBERT(1950, Brit.); WHERE'S CHARLEY?(1952, Brit.); LANDFALL(1953, Brit.); LAST MAN TO HANG, THE(1956, Brit.); TOWN ON TRIAL(1957, Brit.); WOMAN POSSESSED, A(1958, Brit.); HONOURABLE MURDER, AN(1959, Brit.); STRANGE AFFECTION(1959, Brit.); PERCY(1971, Brit.); CRESCENDO(1972, Brit.)

Mark Scott
KID FROM LEFT FIELD, THE(1953); KILLERS FROM SPACE(1954); HELL'S HORIZON(1955); HARDER THEY FALL, THE(1956); CHICAGO CONFIDENTIAL(1957)

Martha Scott
HOWARDS OF VIRGINIA, THE(1940); OUR TOWN(1940); CHEERS FOR MISS BISHOP(1941); ONE FOOT IN HEAVEN(1941); THEY DARE NOT LOVE(1941); HI DIDDLE DIDDLE(1943); IN OLD OKLAHOMA(1943); STAGE DOOR CANTEEN(1943); SO WELL REMEMBERED(1947, Brit.); STRANGE BARGAIN(1949); WHEN I GROW UP(1951); DESPERATE HOURS, THE(1955); TEN COMMANDMENTS, THE(1956); EIGHTEEN AND ANXIOUS(1957); SAYONARA(1957); BEN HUR(1959); CHARLOTTE'S WEB(1973); AIRPORT 1975(1974); TURNING POINT, THE(1977); FIRST MONDAY IN OCTOBER(1981), p

Marvin Scott
KING OF COMEDY, THE(1983)
1984
ONCE UPON A TIME IN AMERICA(1984)

Mary Scott
KING'S ROW(1942); LAW OF THE LASH(1947); PHILO VANCE RETURNS(1947); APACHE COUNTRY(1952); NO TIME FOR SERGEANTS(1958); NOTORIOUS LANDLADY, THE(1962); JOHNNY COOL(1963)

Mel Scott
SPECIAL DELIVERY(1976)

Michael Scott
POLICE DOG(1955, Brit.); TELL ME LIES(1968, Brit.), w; ONE MAN(1979, Can.), p
Misc. Talkies
FRIDAY ON MY MIND(1970)

Michelle Scott
EVIL OF FRANKENSTEIN, THE(1964, Brit.)

Mickey Scott
1984
FALLING IN LOVE(1984), makeup; FLAMINGO KID, THE(1984), makeup

Millicent Scott
CRIMSON CULT, THE(1970, Brit.)

Morton Scott
BELLS OF CAPISTRANO(1942), md; HEART OF THE GOLDEN WEST(1942), md; LONDON BLACKOUT MURDERS(1942), md; MOUNTAIN RHYTHM(1942), md; RIDIN' DOWN THE CANYON(1942), md; SUNSET SERENADE(1942), md; TRAITOR WITHIN, THE(1942), md; X MARKS THE SPOT(1942), md; FALSE FACES(1943), md; HANDS ACROSS THE BORDER(1943), md; HEADIN' FOR GOD'S COUNTRY(1943), md; HOOSIER HOLIDAY(1943), md; IDAHO(1943), md; KING OF THE COWBOYS(1943), md; MAN FROM MUSIC MOUNTAIN(1943), md; MANTRAP, THE(1943), md; MYSTERY BROADCAST(1943), md; O, MY DARLING CLEMENTINE(1943), md; PISTOL PACKIN' MAMA(1943), md; PURPLE V, THE(1943), md; SILVER SPURS(1943), md; SONG OF TEXAS(1943), md; SWING YOUR PARTNER(1943), m, md; TAHITI HONEY(1943), md; WEST SIDE KID(1943), md; WHISPERING FOOTSTEPS(1943), md; GIRL WHO DARED, THE(1944), md; GOODNIGHT SWEETHEART(1944), m&md; JAMBOREE(1944), md; LIGHTS OF OLD SANTA FE(1944), m, md; MY BEST GAL(1944), md; MY BUDDY(1944), md; PORT OF 40 THIEVES, THE(1944), md; ROSIE THE RIVETER(1944), md; SAN FERNANDO VALLEY(1944), md; SECRETS OF SCOTLAND YARD(1944), md; SILENT PARTNER(1944), md; SING, NEIGHBOR, SING(1944), md; SONG OF NEVADA(1944), m; STORM OVER LISBON(1944), md; STRANGERS IN THE NIGHT(1944), md; THREE LITTLE SISTERS(1944), md; YELLOW ROSE OF TEXAS, THE(1944), md; BELLS OF ROSARITA(1945), md; DON'T FENCE ME IN(1945), m, md; FLAME OF THE BARBARY COAST(1945), m, md; GIRLS OF THE BIG HOUSE(1945), md; GRISSLY'S MILLIONS(1945), md; MAN FROM OKLAHOMA, THE(1945), md; STEPPIN' IN SOCIETY(1945), md; SUNSET IN EL DORADO(1945), md; UTAH(1945), md; AFFAIRS OF GERALDINE(1946), m, md; GAY BLADES(1946), md; G.I. WAR BRIDES(1946), m; HELLDORADO(1946), md; HOME IN OKLAHOMA(1946), md; HOME ON THE RANGE(1946), md; MY PAL TRIGGER(1946), md; NIGHT TRAIN TO MEMPHIS(1946), md; ONE EXCITING WEEK(1946), md; RAINBOW OVER TEXAS(1946), md; ROLL ON TEXAS MOON(1946), md; SIOUX CITY SUE(1946), md; SPECTER OF THE ROSE(1946), md; CRIMSON KEY, THE(1947), md; GHOST GOES WILD, THE(1947), md; INVISIBLE WALL, THE(1947), md; MAIN STREET KID, THE(1947), md; ON THE OLD SPANISH TRAIL(1947), md; ROBIN OF TEXAS(1947), md; SADDLE PALS(1947), md; SPRINGTIME IN THE SIERRAS(1947), md; THAT'S MY GAL(1947), md; TRAIL TO SAN ANTONE(1947), md; TWILIGHT ON THE RIO GRANDE(1947), md; ANGEL ON THE AMAZON(1948), md; DAREDEVILS OF THE CLOUDS(1948), md; DESPERADOES OF DODGE CITY(1948), md; EYES OF TEXAS(1948), md; GALLANT LEGION, THE(1948), md; GAY RANCHERO, THE(1948), md; GRAND CANYON TRAIL(1948), md; HEART OF VIRGINIA(1948), md; HOMICIDE FOR THREE(1948), md; I, JANE DOE(1948), md; INSIDE STORY, THE(1948), md; KING OF THE GAMBLERS(1948), art d; MARSHAL OF AMARILLO(1948), md; NIGHT TIME IN NEVADA(1948), md; OLD LOS ANGELES(1948), md; OUT OF THE STORM(1948), md; PLUNDERERS, THE(1948), md; SONS OF ADVENTURE(1948), md; TRAIN TO ALCATRAZ(1948), md; UNDER CALIFORNIA STARS(1948), m; OUTCASTS OF THE TRAIL(1949), md; SUSANNA PASS(1949), md; TOO LATE FOR TEARS(1949), md; WYOMING BANDIT, THE(1949), md

Nathan Scott
ANGEL ON THE AMAZON(1948), m; BRIMSTONE(1949), m; GOLDEN STALLION, THE(1949), m; KID FROM CLEVELAND, THE(1949), m; RED MENACE, THE(1949), m; WAKE OF THE RED WITCH(1949), m; AVENGERS, THE(1950), m; SINGING GUNS(1950), m; SURRENDER(1950), m; TRAIL OF ROBIN HOOD(1950), m; HOODLUM EMPIRE(1952), m; LADY POSSESSED(1952), m; LAST MUSKETEER, THE(1952), m; MONTANA BELLE(1952), m; OKLAHOMA ANNIE(1952), m, md

Nathan G. Scott
WYOMING(1947), m

Nelson Scott
NAKED HEART, THE(1955, Brit.), p

Noel Scott
RIVER OF UNREST(1937, Brit.), w; LAST AMERICAN VIRGIN, THE(1982)

Norman Scott
FLASHDANCE(1983)

Ottavio Scott
MY SON, THE HERO(1963, Ital./Fr.), set d

Oz Scott
BUSTIN' LOOSE(1981), d

Pat Scott
VAGABOND LADY(1935); PAPERBACK HERO(1973, Can.)

Patricia Scott
KENTUCKY BLUE STREAK(1935); CLOPORTES(1966, Fr., Ital.); TO COMMIT A MURDER(1970, Fr./Ital./Ger.)

Patrick John Scott
BERSERK(1967), m; COP-OUT(1967, Brit.), m; LONG DUEL, THE(1967, Brit.), m, md; THOSE FANTASTIC FLYING FOOLS(1967, Brit), m; SOPHIE'S PLACE(1970), m

Paul Scott
EMERGENCY LANDING(1941); JUNGLE MAN(1941); KEEP 'EM FLYING(1941); PHANTOM SUBMARINE, THE(1941); LADY TAKES A CHANCE, A(1943); SATAN IN HIGH HEELS(1962)

Paula Scott
VIOLENT WOMEN(1960)

Peter Scott
JAMAICA INN(1939, Brit.); CIRCUS BOY(1947, Brit.); GREAT SINNER, THE(1949); IRON MAN, THE(1951); TOM BROWN'S SCHOOLDAYS(1951, Brit.); HELL AND HIGH WATER(1954)

Peter Gordon Scott
GENIE, THE(1953, Brit.), w
Peter Graham Scott
PERFECT WOMAN, THE(1950, Brit.), ed; NEVER TAKE NO FOR AN AN-SWER(1952, Brit./Ital.), ed; SING ALONG WITH ME(1952, Brit.), d; LANDFALL(1953, Brit.), ed; RIVER BEAT(1954), ed; SHADOW OF THE EAGLE(1955, Brit.), ed; HIDE-OUT, THE(1956, Brit.), ed; ACCOUNT RENDERED(1957, Brit.), d; BIG CHANCE, THE(1957, Brit.), d&w; DEVIL'S BAIT(1959, Brit.), d; HEADLESS GHOST, THE(1959, Brit.), d; BIG DAY, THE(1960, Brit.), d; LET'S GET MARRIED(1960, Brit.), d; NIGHT CREATURES(1962, Brit.), d; POT CARRIERS, THE(1962, Brit.), d; CRACKSMAN, THE(1963, Brit.), d; FATHER CAME TOO(1964, Brit.), d; MISTER TEN PER-CENT(1967, Brit.), d; SUBTERFUGE(1969, US/Brit.), d
Misc. Talkies
BREAKOUT(1959), d
Pippa Scott
SEARCHERS, THE(1956); AS YOUNG AS WE ARE(1958); AUNTIE MAME(1958); MY SIX LOVES(1963); QUICK, LET'S GET MARRIED(1965); FOR PETE'S SAKE!(1966); PETULIA(1968, U.S./Brit.); SOME KIND OF A NUT(1969); COLD TURKEY(1971)
Preston Scott
LAUGHING BOY(1934)
R. T. M. Scott
YOU'LL FIND OUT(1940), w
Ramona Scott
1984
NO SMALL AFFAIR(1984)
Randolph Scott
VIRGINIAN, THE(1929); WOMEN MEN MARRY(1931); HOT SATURDAY(1932); SUCCESSFUL CALAMITY, A(1932); WILD HORSE MESA(1932); BROKEN DREAMS(1933); COCKTAIL HOUR(1933); HELLO, EVERYBODY(1933); HERITAGE OF THE DESERT(1933); ISLAND OF LOST SOULS(1933); MAN OF THE FO-REST(1933); MURDERS IN THE ZOO(1933); SUNSET PASS(1933); SUPER-NATURAL(1933); TO THE LAST MAN(1933); LAST ROUND-UP, THE(1934); THUNDERING HERD, THE(1934); WAGON WHEELS(1934); HOME ON THE RANGE(1935); ROBERTA(1935); ROCKY MOUNTAIN MYSTERY(1935); SHE(1935); SO RED THE ROSE(1935); VILLAGE TALE(1935); AND SUDDEN DEATH(1936); FOLLOW THE FLEET(1936); GO WEST, YOUNG MAN(1936); LAST OF THE MOHI-CANS, THE(1936); HIGH, WIDE AND HANDSOME(1937); REBECCA OF SUNNY-BROOK FARM(1938); ROAD TO RENO(1938); TEXANS, THE(1938); COAST GUARD(1939); FRONTIER MARSHAL(1939); JESSE JAMES(1939); SUSANNAH OF THE MOUNTIES(1939); 20,000 MEN A YEAR(1939); MY FAVORITE WIFE(1940); VIRGINIA CITY(1940); WHEN THE DALTONS RODE(1940); BELLE STARR(1941); PARIS CALLING(1941); WESTERN UNION(1941); PITTSBURGH(1942); SPOILERS, THE(1942); TO THE SHORES OF TRIPOLI(1942); BOMBARDIER(1943); CORVETTE K-225(1943); DESPERADOES, THE(1943); GUNG HO!(1943); BELLE OF THE YU-KON(1944); FOLLOW THE BOYS(1944); CHINA SKY(1945); ABILENE TOWN(1946); BADMAN'S TERRITORY(1946); HOME SWEET HOMICIDE(1946); CHRISTMAS EVE(1947); GUNFIGHTERS, THE(1947); TRAIL STREET(1947); ALBUQUER-QUE(1948); CORONER CREEK(1948); RETURN OF THE BADMEN(1948); CANADIAN PACIFIC(1949); DOOLINS OF OKLAHOMA, THE(1949); FIGHTING MAN OF THE PLAINS(1949); WALKING HILLS, THE(1949); CARIBOO TRAIL, THE(1950); COLT .45(1950); NEVADAN, THE(1950); FORT WORTH(1951); MAN IN THE SADDLE(1951); SANTA FE(1951); STARLIFT(1951); SUGARFOOT(1951); CARSON CITY(1952); HANG-MAN'S KNOT(1952); MAN BEHIND THE GUN, THE(1952); STRANGER WORE A GUN, THE(1953); THUNDER OVER THE PLAINS(1953); BOUNTY HUNTER, THE(1954); RIDING SHOTGUN(1954); LAWLESS STREET, A(1955); RAGE AT DAWN(1955); TALL MAN RIDING(1955); TEN WANTED MEN(1955); SEVEN MEN FROM NOW(1956); SEVENTH CAVALRY(1956); DECISION AT SUNDOWN(1957); SHOOT-OUT AT MEDICINE BEND(1957); TALL T, THE(1957); BUCHANAN RIDES ALONE(1958), a, p; RIDE LONESOME(1959); WESTBOUND(1959); COMANCHE STATION(1960), a, p; RIDE THE HIGH COUNTRY(1962)
Silents
FAR CALL, THE(1929)
Ray Scott
BELOW THE BELT(1980); ISLAND CLAWS(1981), spec eff
Raymond Scott
ER LOVE A STRANGER(1958), m; PUSHER, THE(1960), m
Rhea Scott
TWO GALS AND A GUY(1951)
Rhonda Scott
BIG DADDY(1969)
Richard Scott
FOLLOW THE LEADER(1930); MISSISSIPPI(1935); STRANGE IMPERSONA-TION(1946)
Silents
LA POUPEE(1920, Brit.)
Ridley Scott
DUELLISTS, THE(1977, Brit.), d; ALIEN(1979), d; BLADE RUNNER(1982), d
Robert Scott
BROTHER RAT(1938); THOSE WERE THE DAYS(1940); GIRL IN THE CASE(1944); CRIME DOCTOR'S COURAGE, THE(1945); PRISON SHIP(1945); TEN CENTS A DANCE(1945); BANDIT OF SHERWOOD FOREST, THE(1946); CLOSE CALL FOR BOSTON BLACKIE, A(1946); COWBOY BLUES(1946); GILDA(1946); NOTORIOUS LONE WOLF, THE(1946); OUT OF THE DEPTHS(1946); SHADOWED(1946); UN-KNOWN, THE(1946); DEAD RECKONING(1947); EXPOSED(1947); SHED NO TEARS(1948); CALL ME MISTER(1951); UNKNOWN MAN, THE(1951); MA AND PA KETTLE ON VACATION(1953)
1984
JUST THE WAY YOU ARE(1984)
Misc. Talkies
PRAIRIE RAIDERS(1947)
Robert E. Scott
ONE MYSTERIOUS NIGHT(1944); RUSTY SAVES A LIFE(1949)
Col. Robert L. Scott
GOD IS MY CO-PILOT(1945), w
Robert S. Scott
JUST FOR YOU(1952)
Col. Robert Lee Scott, Jr.
GOD IS MY CO-PILOT(1945), tech adv

Rod Scott
MARA OF THE WILDERNESS(1966), w
Roger Scott
WOMEN OF DESIRE(1968), p
Ron Scott
MARS NEEDS WOMEN(1966)
Rosemary Scott
SAVE A LITTLE SUNSHINE(1938, Brit.); MOUSE ON THE MOON, THE(1963, Brit.)
Russell Scott
EAGLE AND THE HAWK, THE(1933)
Samantha Scott
WILD GYPSIES(1969); M(1970)
Sandra Scott
INCREDIBLE JOURNEY, THE(1963); HOUSE IS NOT A HOME, A(1964)
Sandu Scott
RX MURDER(1958, Brit.)
Scott Scott
SING ALONG WITH ME(1952, Brit.), w
Seret Scott
PRETTY BABY(1978)
Misc. Talkies
LOSING GROUND(1982)
Shaun Scott
HANOVER STREET(1979, Brit.)
Shawn Scott
GNOME-MOBILE, THE(1967)
Sherman Scott [Sam Newfield]
BEASTS OF BERLIN(1939), p&d; I TAKE THIS OATH(1940), d; INVISIBLE KILL-ER, THE(1940), d; MARKED MEN(1940), d; BILLY THE KID IN SANTA FE(1941), d; BILLY THE KID WANTED(1941), d; BILLY THE KID'S FIGHTING PALS(1941), d; BILLY THE KID'S ROUNDUP(1941), d; BILLY THE KID TRAPPED(1942), d; LAW AND ORDER(1942), d; MYSTERIOUS RIDER, THE(1942), d; SHERIFF OF SAGE VALLEY(1942), d; KID RIDES AGAIN, THE(1943), d; FLYING SERPENT, THE(1946), d; LADY AT MIDNIGHT(1948), d; STRANGE MRS. CRANE, THE(1948), d; WILD WEED(1949), d
Misc. Talkies
BILLY THE KID'S SMOKING GUNS(1942), d
Sherry Scott
SATAN'S MISTRESS(1982)
Simon Scott
RAID, THE(1954); BLACK TUESDAY(1955); ACCUSED OF MURDER(1956); I'VE LIVED BEFORE(1956); BATTLE HYMN(1957); MAN OF A THOUSAND FACES(1957); COMPULSION(1959); NO NAME ON THE BULLET(1959); HONEYMOON MACHINE, THE(1961); COUCH, THE(1962); MOON PILOT(1962); UGLY AMERICAN, THE(1963); FATHER GOOSE(1964); READY FOR THE PEOPLE(1964); STRANGE BEDFEL-LOWS(1965); DEAD HEAT ON A MERRY-GO-ROUND(1966); IN ENEMY COUN-TRY(1968); COLD TURKEY(1971); MAN, THE(1972); HINDENBURG, THE(1975); TWILIGHT'S LAST GLEAMING(1977, U.S./Ger.)
Skip Scott
GRAND PRIX(1966)
Sondra Scott
CHRISTINE JORGENSEN STORY, THE(1970); RABBIT, RUN(1970)
Steven Scott
MAKE MINE MINK(1960, Brit.); STRANGLERS OF BOMBAY, THE(1960, Brit.); GUNS OF DARKNESS(1962, Brit.); FRIENDS AND NEIGHBORS(1963, Brit.); BOY TEN FEET TALL, A(1965, Brit.); THAT RIVIERA TOUCH(1968, Brit.)
Susan Scott
NOB HILL(1945); WONDER MAN(1945); SLASHER, THE(1975)
Misc. Talkies
THEY'RE COMING TO GET YOU(1976)
Sydna Scott
CRACK IN THE WORLD(1965); 10 TO MIDNIGHT(1983)
Synda Scott
MR. SYCAMORE(1975)
Talmadge Scott
SHOCK WAVES(1977); H.O.T.S.(1979)
Terry Scott
BRIDAL PATH, THE(1959, Brit.); I'M ALL RIGHT, JACK(1959, Brit.); TOO MANY CROOKS(1959, Brit.); AND THE SAME TO YOU(1960, Brit.); DOUBLE BUNK(1961, Brit.); MARY HAD A LITTLE(1961, Brit.); NIGHT WE GOT THE BIRD, THE(1961, Brit.); NOTHING BARRED(1961, Brit.); WHAT A WHOPPER(1961, Brit.); NEARLY A NASTY ACCIDENT(1962, Brit.); PAIR OF BRIEFS, A(1963, Brit.); FATHER CAME TOO(1964, Brit.); MURDER MOST FOUL(1964, Brit.); NO, MY DARLING DAUGHT-ER(1964, Brit.); GONKS GO BEAT(1965, Brit.); GREAT ST. TRINIAN'S TRAIN ROBBERY, THE(1966, Brit.); CARNABY, M.D.(1967, Brit.); CARRY ON, UP THE KHYBER(1968, Brit.); CARRY ON CAMPING(1969, Brit.); CARRY ON HENRY VIII(1970, Brit.); CARRY ON LOVING(1970, Brit.); CARRY ON UP THE JUNGLE(1970, Brit.)
Misc. Talkies
BLESS THIS HOUSE(1972, Brit.); GHOST OF A CHANCE, A(1968, Brit.)
Thelma Scott
RUGGED O'RIORDANS, THE(1949, Aus.)
Thomas Scott
YOUNG AND BEAUTIFUL(1934), ed; IN OLD SANTA FE(1935), ed; MARINES ARE COMING, THE(1935), ed; BEAU GESTE(1939), ed; LIGHT THAT FAILED, THE(1939), ed; MIDNIGHT ANGEL(1941), ed; REACHING FOR THE SUN(1941), ed; GREAT MAN'S LADY, THE(1942), ed; TAKE A LETTER, DARLING(1942), ed; EASY COME, EASY GO(1947), ed; MELODY TIME(1948), ed; SO DEAR TO MY HEART(1949), ed; MOTOR PSYCHO(1965)
Thurman Scott
WEREWOLF OF WASHINGTON(1973); FIREPOWER(1979, Brit.); VOICES(1979)
Thurman E. Scott
THREE TOUGH GUYS(1974, U.S./Ital.)
Tim Scott
DAYS OF HEAVEN(1978); BALLAD OF GREGORIO CORTEZ, THE(1983); EURE-KA(1983, Brit.)
Misc. Talkies
TO HELL YOU PREACH(1972)

Timothy Scott
IN THE HEAT OF THE NIGHT(1967); WAY WEST, THE(1967); BALLAD OF JOSIE(1968); PARTY, THE(1968); BUTCH CASSIDY AND THE SUNDANCE KID(1969); ONE MORE TRAIN TO ROB(1971); VANISHING POINT(1971); WELCOME HOME, SOLDIER BOYS(1972); LOLLY-MADONNA XXX(1973); MACON COUNTY LINE(1974); FARMER, THE(1977); KID VENGEANCE(1977); ELECTRIC HORSE-MAN, THE(1979); NIGHTMARES(1983)
1984
FOOTLOOSE(1984)
Tom Scott
NON-STOP NEW YORK(1937, Brit.); GREEN SLIME, THE(1969); CONQUEST OF THE PLANET OF THE APES(1972), m; CULPEPPER CATTLE COMPANY, THE(1972), m; WEREWOLF OF WASHINGTON(1973); UPTOWN SATURDAY NIGHT(1974), m; SIDECAR RACERS(1975, Aus.), m; HERBIE GOES BANANAS(1980); STIR CRA-ZY(1980), m; HANKY-PANKY(1982), m; GOING BERSERK(1983), m
1984
HARD TO HOLD(1984), m
Tommy Scott
MEN WITH WINGS(1938), ed
Tony Scott
BLUE MURDER AT ST. TRINIAN'S(1958, Brit.); OPERATION BIKINI(1963); HUN-GER, THE(1983), d
1984
NUMBER ONE(1984, Brit.)
Treva Scott
HIGH SCHOOL GIRL(1935)
Vernon Scott
TEACHER'S PET(1958); NEW KIND OF LOVE, A(1963); OPERATION BIKINI(1963); PATSY, THE(1964); LEGEND OF LYLAH CLARE, THE(1968); PRIVATE SCHOOL(1983)
W. Patrick Scott
CASEY'S SHADOW(1978)
Wallace Scott
WITHOUT RESERVATIONS(1946); BIG SHOT, THE(1942); LARCENY, INC.(1942); CANYON PASSAGE(1946); NOBODY LIVES FOREVER(1946); MOSS ROSE(1947); NORA PRENTISS(1947); OUT OF THE PAST(1947); TARZAN AND THE HUN-TRESS(1947); VIGILANTES RETURN, THE(1947); SMART WOMAN(1948); WALLS OF JERICHO(1948); WAKE OF THE RED WITCH(1949)
Silents
SONG OF THE WAGE SLAVE, THE(1915)
Wallace E. Scott
PLACE IN THE SUN, A(1951)
Wally Scott
UNCLE HARRY(1945); INVISIBLE AGENT(1942); SCARLET STREET(1945); KILL-ERS, THE(1946); NIGHT AND DAY(1946); KISS THE BLOOD OFF HIS HANDS(1948); STREET WITH NO NAME, THE(1948); WHIPLASH(1948); MADWOMAN OF CHAIL-LOT, THE(1969), md
Walt Scott
THREE TOUGH GUYS(1974, U.S./Ital.)
Walter Scott
MELODY OF LOVE, THE(1928), ph; HOLD YOUR MAN(1929); WHERE DO WE GO FROM HERE?(1945), set d; DAISY KENYON(1947), set d; BROKEN LANCE(1954), set dr; CAN-CAN(1960), set d; GLORY GUYS, THE(1965); PANIC IN THE CITY(1968); DIRTY HARRY(1971); SUMMER OF '42(1971); BUCK AND THE PREACHER(1972); COWBOYS, THE(1972); CULPEPPER CATTLE COMPANY, THE(1972); ULZANA'S RAID(1972); HARD TIMES(1975); MR. SYCAMORE(1975); NIGHT MOVES(1975); ROLLERBALL(1975); DUCHESS AND THE DIRTWATER FOX, THE(1976); OUTLAW JOSEY WALES, THE(1976), stunts; ANOTHER MAN, ANOTHER CHANCE(1977 Fr/US); COMES A HORSEMAN(1978), stunts; HIDE IN PLAIN SIGHT(1980); THIEF(1981); 48 HOURS(1982); SPACEHUNTER: ADVENTURES IN THE FORBID-DEN ZONE(1983), stunts
Walter Scott, Jr.
BITE THE BULLET(1975)
Sir Walter Scott
IVANHOE(1952, Brit.), w; KING RICHARD AND THE CRUSADERS(1954), w; QUENTIN DURWARD(1955), w
Silents
IVANHOE(1913), w; LADY OF THE LAKE, THE(1928, Brit.), w
Walter F. Scott
GREAT POWER, THE(1929)
Walter M. Scott
HEAVEN CAN WAIT(1943), art d; MOON IS DOWN, THE(1943), set d; LODGER, THE(1944), set d; PURPLE HEART, THE(1944), set d; NOB HILL(1945), set d; FOREV-ER AMBER(1947), set d; HOMESTRETCH, THE(1947), set d; APARTMENT FOR PEGGY(1948), set d; CALL NORTHSIDE 777(1948), set d; LETTER TO THREE WIVES, A(1948), set d; THAT LADY IN ERMINE(1948), set d; THAT WONDERFUL URGE(1948), set d; HOUSE OF STRANGERS(1949), set d; I WAS A MALE WAR BRIDE(1949), set d; WHIRLPOOL(1949), set d; UNDER MY SKIN(1950), set d; WHERE THE SIDEWALK ENDS(1950), set d; PEOPLE WILL TALK(1951), set d; THIRTEENTH LETTER, THE(1951), set d; DEADLINE–U.S.A.(1952), set d; LES MIS-ERABLES(1952), set d; MONKEY BUSINESS(1952), set d; MY COUSIN RA-CHEL(1952), set d; WITH A SONG IN MY HEART(1952), set d; KING OF THE KHYBER RIFLES(1953), set d; EGYPTIAN, THE(1954), set d; HELL AND HIGH WATER(1954), set d; RIVER OF NO RETURN(1954), set d; GOOD MORNING, MISS DOVE(1955), set d; HOUSE OF BAMBOO(1955), set d; LEFT HAND OF GOD, THE(1955), set d; RAINS OF RANCHIPUR, THE(1955), set d; SEVEN YEAR ITCH, THE(1955), set d; SOLDIER OF FORTUNE(1955), set d; TALL MEN, THE(1955), set d; UNTAMED(1955), set d; VIEW FROM POMPEY'S HEAD, THE(1955), set d; KING AND I, THE(1956), set d; MAN IN THE GREY FLANNEL SUIT, THE(1956), set d; TEENAGE REBEL(1956), set d; 23 PACES TO BAKER STREET(1956), set d; AFFAIR TO REMEMBER, AN(1957), set d; DESK SET(1957), set d; FORTY GUNS(1957), set d; KISS THEM FOR ME(1957), set d; KRONOS(1957), set d; OH, MEN! OH, WO-MEN!(1957), set d; PEYTON PLACE(1957), set d; SUN ALSO RISES, THE(1957), set d; THREE FACES OF EVE, THE(1957), set d; TRUE STORY OF JESSE JAMES, THE(1957), set d; GANG WAR(1958), set d; IN LOVE AND WAR(1958), set d; LONG, HOT SUMMER, THE(1958), set d; SHOWDOWN AT BOOT HILL(1958), set d; SOUTH PACIFIC(1958), art d; YOUNG LIONS, THE(1958), set d; 10 NORTH FREDE-RICK(1958), set d; JOURNEY TO THE CENTER OF THE EARTH(1959), set d; MAN WHO UNDERSTOOD WOMEN, THE(1959), set d; PRIVATE'S AFFAIR, A(1959), set d; RETURN OF THE FLY(1959), set d; SAY ONE FOR ME(1959), set d; STORY ON PAGE

ONE, THE(1959), set d; WARLOCK(1959), set d; WOMAN OBSESSED(1959), set d; FLAMING STAR(1960), set d; FROM THE TERRACE(1960), set d; LOST WORLD, THE(1960), set d; NORTH TO ALASKA(1960), set d; SEVEN THIEVES(1960), set d; WILD RIVER(1960), set d; COMANCHEROS, THE(1961), set d; FIERCEST HEART, THE(1961), set d; FRANCIS OF ASSISI(1961), set d; MISTY(1961), set d; PIRATES OF TORTUGA(1961), set d; RETURN TO PEYTON PLACE(1961), set d; RIGHT AP-PROACH, THE(1961), set d; SANCTUARY(1961), set d; SECOND TIME AROUND, THE(1961), set d; SNOW WHITE AND THE THREE STOOGES(1961), set d; TENDER IS THE NIGHT(1961), set d; VOYAGE TO THE BOTTOM OF THE SEA(1961), set d; WILD IN THE COUNTRY(1961), set d; ADVENTURES OF A YOUNG MAN(1962), set d; FIVE WEEKS IN A BALLOON(1962), set d; MADISON AVENUE(1962), set d; MR. HOBBS TAKES A VACATION(1962), set d; STATE FAIR(1962), set d; SWINGIN' ALONG(1962), set d; CLEOPATRA(1963), set d; MOVE OVER, DARLING(1963), set d; STRIPPER, THE(1963), set d; TAKE HER, SHE'S MINE(1963), set d; FATE IS THE HUNTER(1964), set d; GOODBYE CHARLIE(1964), set d; JOHN GOLDFARB, PLEASE COME HOME(1964), set d; PLEASURE SEEKERS, THE(1964), set d; RIO CONCHOS(1964), set d; SHOCK TREATMENT(1964), set d; WHAT A WAY TO GO(1964), set d; DEAR BRIGETTE(1965), set d; DO NOT DISTURB(1965), set d; MORITURI(1965), set d; REWARD, THE(1965), set d; SOUND OF MUSIC, THE(1965), set d; I DEAL IN DANGER(1966), set d; OUR MAN FLINT(1966), set d; SAND PEBBLES, THE(1966), set d; STAGECOACH(1966), set d; WAY...WAY OUT(1966), set d; DOCTOR DOLITTLE(1967), set d; FLIM-FLAM MAN, THE(1967), set d; GUIDE FOR THE MARRIED MAN, A(1967), set d; HOMBRE(1967), set d; IN LIKE FLINT(1967), set d; ST. VALENTINE'S DAY MASSACRE, THE(1967), set d; TONY ROME(1967), set d; VALLEY OF THE DOLLS(1967), set d; DETECTIVE, THE(1968), set d; LADY IN CEMENT(1968), set d; PLANET OF THE APES(1968), set d; SECRET LIFE OF AN AMERICAN WIFE, THE(1968), set d; STAR!(1968), set d; SWEET RIDE, THE(1968), set d; THE BOSTON STRANGLER, THE(1968), set d; BUTCH CASSIDY AND THE SUNDANCE KID(1969), set d; HELLO, DOLLY!(1969), set d; JUSTINE(1969), set d; UNDEFEATED, THE(1969), set d; BENEATH THE PLANET OF THE APES(1970), set d; COVER ME BABE(1970), set d; GREAT WHITE HOPE, THE(1970), set d; M(1970), set d; MOVE(1970), set d; ONLY GAME IN TOWN, THE(1970), set d; TORA! TORA! TORA!(1970, U.S./Jap.), set d; TRIBES(1970), set d; ESCAPE FROM THE PLANET OF THE APES(1971), set d; MARRIAGE OF A YOUNG STOCKBROKER, THE(1971), set d; MEPHISTO WALTZ, THE(1971), set d; SEVEN MINUTES, THE(1971), set d; CULPEPPER CATTLE COMPANY, THE(1972), set d; HEX(1973), set d
Walter S. Scott
CHE!(1969), set d
Warner Scott
CASTLE OF BLOOD(1964, Fr./Ital.), art d
Will Scott
LIMPING MAN, THE(1931, Brit.), w; HIS WIFE'S MOTHER(1932, Brit.), d&w; LIMPING MAN, THE(1936, Brit.), w; LONDON BY NIGHT(1937), w
William Scott
COME ON DANGER!(1932); HOTEL CONTINENTAL(1932); LAST MILE, THE(1932); STRANGERS OF THE EVENING(1932)
Silents
AMARILLY OF CLOTHESLINE ALLEY(1918); FLAMES OF THE FLESH(1920); MAID OF THE WEST(1921); VOICE IN THE DARK(1921); ALIAS JULIUS CA-ESAR(1922); DESERTED AT THE ALTAR(1922); ONLY A SHOP GIRL(1922); INNO-CENCE(1923); YESTERDAY'S WIFE(1923); AGAINST ALL ODDS(1924); DANTE'S INFERNO(1924); AFTER BUSINESS HOURS(1925); AFLAME IN THE SKY(1927); BY WHOSE HAND?(1927); SMOKE BELLEW(1929)
Misc. Silents
DEVIL'S WHEEL, THE(1918); HER ONE MISTAKE(1918); KULTUR(1918); RIDERS OF THE PURPLE SAGE(1918); STRANGE WOMAN, THE(1918); BROKEN COM-MANDMENTS(1919); CALL OF THE SOUL, THE(1919); CHASING RAINBOWS(1919); FORBIDDEN ROOM, THE(1919); PITFALLS OF A BIG CITY(1919); SNEAK, THE(1919); THIEVES(1919); MOTHER OF HIS CHILDREN, THE(1920); ROSE OF NOME(1920); SISTER TO SALOME, A(1920); WHITE LIES(1920); HICKVILLE TO BROADWAY(1921); JACKIE(1921); PARTNERS OF FATE(1921); WHILE THE DEVIL LAUGHS(1921); WINNING WITH WITS(1922); FOURTH MUSKETEER, THE(1923); HIS LAST RACE(1923)
Zachary Scott
HOLLYWOOD CANTEEN(1944); MASK OF DIMITRIOS, THE(1944); DANGER SIGNAL(1945); MILDRED PIERCE(1945); SOUTHERNER, THE(1945); HER KIND OF MAN(1946); CASS TIMBERLANE(1947); STALLION ROAD(1947); UNFAITHFUL, THE(1947); RUTHLESS(1948); WHIPLASH(1948); FLAMINGO ROAD(1949); FLAXY MARTIN(1949); ONE LAST FLING(1949); SOUTH OF ST. LOUIS(1949); BORN TO BE BAD(1950); COLT .45(1950); GUILTY BYSTANDER(1950); PRETTY BABY(1950); SHADOW ON THE WALL(1950); LET'S MAKE IT LEGAL(1951); LIGHTNING STRIKES TWICE(1951); SECRET OF CONVICT LAKE, THE(1951); DEAD ON COURSE(1952); STRONGHOLD(1952, Mex.); APPOINTMENT IN HON-DURAS(1953); FLAME OF THE ISLANDS(1955); SHOTGUN(1955); TREASURE OF RUBY HILLS(1955); BANDIDO(1956); COUNTERFEIT PLAN, THE(1957, Brit.); VIO-LENT STRANGER(1957, Brit.); NATCHEZ TRACE(1960); YOUNG ONE, THE(1961, Mex.); IT'S ONLY MONEY(1962)
Arthur Scott-Cravan
Silents
IVANHOE(1913)
B. Scott-Elder
BLIND MAN'S BLUFF(1936, Brit.), w
A. Scott-Gaddy
THEY DIDN'T KNOW(1936, Brit.)
Alex Scott-Gatty
SYMPHONY IN TWO FLATS(1930, Brit.)
Silents
HAMLET(1913, Brit.)
Noel Scott-Gorman
LADY GODIVA RIDES AGAIN(1955, Brit.)
Jean Scott-Rogers
ONE WAY OUT(1955, Brit.), w
Jonathan Scott-Taylor
DAMIEN–OMEN II(1978)
Misc. Talkies
COPTER KIDS, THE(1976, Brit.)
Mel Scott-Thomas
1984
AGAINST ALL ODDS(1984)

Sheila Scott-Wilkinson
NATIONAL HEALTH, OR NURSE NORTON'S AFFAIR, THE(1973, Brit.); PRESSURE(1976, Brit.)

Marloe Scott-Wilson
KILL AND KILL AGAIN(1981)

Andrea Scotti
HUNS, THE(1962, Fr./Ital.); SAMSON AND THE SLAVE QUEEN(1963, Ital.); HERCULES AGAINST THE SONS OF THE SUN(1964, Span./Ital.); MISSION BLOODY MARY(1967, Fr./Ital./Span.); DIRTY OUTLAWS, THE(1971, Ital.)

Don Scotti
SATURDAY NIGHT AT THE BATHS(1975)

Emy Rossi Scotti
VIOLENT FOUR, THE(1968, Ital.)

Gino Scotti
GOLIATH AND THE BARBARIANS(1960, Ital.)

Ottavio Scotti
DOCTOR BEWARE(1951, Ital.), set d; SIGN OF THE GLADIATOR(1959, Fr./Ger./Ital.), art d; SIEGE OF SYRACUSE(1962, Fr./Ital.), art d; SLAVE, THE(1963, Ital.), art d; GOLD FOR THE CAESARS(1964), art d; MONGOLS, THE(1966, Fr./Ital.), art d; UP THE MACGREGORS(1967, Ital./Span.), art d; SAUL AND DAVID(1968, Ital./Span.), art d; SENSO(1968, Ital.), art d; NUN AT THE CROSSROADS, A(1970, Ital./Span.), art d

Otto Scotti
THIEF OF VENICE, THE(1952), art d

Tino Scotti
ANYTHING FOR A SONG(1947, Ital.); BEFORE HIM ALL ROME TREMBLED(1947, Ital.)

Tony Scotti
VALLEY OF THE DOLLS(1967)

Vito Scotti
TWO WEEKS IN ANOTHER TOWN(1962); CRY OF THE CITY(1948); CRISS CROSS(1949); ILLEGAL ENTRY(1949); STOP THAT CAB(1951); FABULOUS SENORITA, THE(1952); HINDU, THE(1953, Brit.); CONQUEST OF SPACE(1955); PARTY GIRL(1958); PAY OR DIE(1960); WHERE THE BOYS ARE(1960); EXPLOSIVE GENERATION, THE(1961); MASTER OF THE WORLD(1961); CAPTAIN NEWMAN, M.D.(1963); DIME WITH A HALO(1963); PLEASURE SEEKERS, THE(1964); RIO CONCHOS(1964); WILD AND WONDERFUL(1964); VON RYAN'S EXPRESS(1965); BLINDFOLD(1966); WHAT DID YOU DO IN THE WAR, DADDY?(1966); CAPER OF THE GOLDEN BULLS, THE(1967); PERILS OF PAULINE, THE(1967); WARNING SHOT(1967); HEAD(1968); HOW SWEET IT IS(1968); SECRET WAR OF HARRY FRIGG, THE(1968); CACTUS FLOWER(1969); ARISTOCATS, THE(1970); BOATNIKS, THE(1970); GODFATHER, THE(1972); NAPOLEON AND SAMANTHA(1972); WHEN THE LEGENDS DIE(1972); WORLD'S GREATEST ATHLETE, THE(1973); HERBIE RIDES AGAIN(1974); HOW TO SEDUCE A WOMAN(1974); WILD McCULLOCHS, THE(1975); HERBIE GOES BANANAS(1980); NUDE BOMB, THE(1980); CHU CHU AND THE PHILLY FLASH(1981)
Misc. Talkies
I WONDER WHO'S KILLING HER NOW(1975)

Scottish Sextet
DISCOVERIES(1939, Brit.)

The Scottish Sextette
LAUGH IT OFF(1940, Brit.)

Aubrey Scotto
PRIVATE WORLDS(1935), ed; SMART GIRL(1935), d; $1,000 A MINUTE(1935), d; FOLLOW YOUR HEART(1936), d; HITCH HIKE LADY(1936), d; PALM SPRINGS(1936), d; TICKET TO PARADISE(1936), d; BLAZING BARRIERS(1937), d; HAPPY-GO-LUCKY(1937), d; LITTLE MISS ROUGHNECK(1938), d; I WAS A CONVICT(1939), d
Misc. Talkies
UNCLE MOSES(1932), d

Aubrey H. Scotto
GAMBLING SHIP(1939), d
Misc. Talkies
I HATE WOMEN(1934), d

Giovanna Scotto
DISHONORED(1950, Ital.)

Vincent Scotto
CINDERELLA(1937, Fr.), m; PEPE LE MOKO(1937, Fr.), m; ALGIERS(1938), m; RULES OF THE GAME, THE(1939, Fr.), m; BAKER'S WIFE, THE(1940, Fr.), m; KISS OF FIRE, THE(1940, Fr.), m; WELL-DIGGER'S DAUGHTER, THE(1946, Fr.), m; FANNY(1948, Fr.), m

Myrtle Scotton
PHANTASM(1979)

Angela Scoular
CASINO ROYALE(1967, Brit.); COUNTESS FROM HONG KONG, A(1967, Brit.); GREAT CATHERINE(1968, Brit.); HERE WE GO ROUND THE MULBERRY BUSH(1968, Brit.); ADVENTURERS, THE(1970); DOCTOR IN TROUBLE(1970, Brit.)

Angelo Scoular
ON HER MAJESTY'S SECRET SERVICE(1969, Brit.)

Cleo Scouloudi
GUNS OF NAVARONE, THE(1961)

Alexander Scourby
AFFAIR IN TRINIDAD(1952); BECAUSE OF YOU(1952); BIG HEAT, THE(1953); GLORY BRIGADE, THE(1953); REDHEAD FROM WYOMING, THE(1953); SIGN OF THE PAGAN(1954); SILVER CHALICE, THE(1954); GIANT(1956); RANSOM(1956); ME AND THE COLONEL(1958); BIG FISHERMAN, THE(1959); SHAGGY DOG, THE(1959); MAN ON A STRING(1960); SEVEN THIEVES(1960); DEVIL AT FOUR O'CLOCK, THE(1961); EXECUTIONER, THE(1970, Brit.); JESUS(1979)

Scout the Horse
Silents
DARING CHANCES(1924); WHITE OUTLAW, THE(1925); LOOKING FOR TROUBLE(1926); WESTERN WHIRLWIND, THE(1927)

Janet Scoutten
UNHINGED(1982), makeup

Phil Scovelle
Silents
IN THE STRETCH(1914), a, d&w

John Scovern
VELVET TRAP, THE(1966); PEACE FOR A GUNFIGHTER(1967); ELECTRA GLIDE IN BLUE(1973)

Paul Scovil
STARK FEAR(1963)

Sharon Scoville
CARNIVAL OF SOULS(1962)

Enzo Scrafin
ENGAGEMENT ITALIANO(1966, Fr./Ital.), ph

Tecla Scrano
ALONE IN THE STREETS(1956, Ital.)

Susan Scranton
GAS(1981, Can.), w

Derf Scratch
1984
DUBEAT-E-O(1984)

Ivan Scratt [Ivan Scratuglia]
STRANGER IN TOWN, A(1968, U.S./Ital.)

Ivan Scratuglia
TRAMPLERS, THE(1966, Ital.); HELLBENDERS, THE(1967, U.S./Ital./Span.); TIGER AND THE PUSSYCAT, THE(1967, U.S., Ital.); CATCH AS CATCH CAN(1968, Ital.); MINUTE TO PRAY, A SECOND TO DIE, A(1968, Ital.); LISTEN, LET'S MAKE LOVE(1969, Fr./Ital.); RUTHLESS FOUR, THE(1969, Ital./Ger.); TEOREMA(1969, Ital.); LONG RIDE FROM HELL, A(1970, Ital.)

Scriabin
THEY CAME TO A CITY(1944, Brit.), m

Aleksander Nikolaevich Scriabin
RISK, THE(1961, Brit.), m

Aleksandr Nikolaevich Scriabin
ISADORA(1968, Brit.), m

A. E. Scribe
DEVIL MAY CARE(1929), w

Eugene Scribe
GLASS OF WATER, A(1962, Cgr.), w

James Scribner
NIGHTMARES(1983), makeup

Rod Scribner
RACE FOR YOUR LIFE, CHARLIE BROWN(1977), anim

Ronnie Scribner
AMY(1981); SPLIT IMAGE(1982)

Angus Scrimm
PHANTASM(1979)

Frederico Scrobogna
BREAD AND CHOCOLATE(1978, Ital.)

Bobbie Scroggins
FIVE ANGLES ON MURDER(1950, Brit.)

Jerry Scroggins
KID FROM AMARILLO, THE(1951)

Michael Scroggins
BABY MAKER, THE(1970)

Robert Scroggins
DOG AND THE DIAMONDS, THE(1962, Brit.)

V. Scrova
IMMORTAL GARRISON, THE(1957, USSR)

Scruffy
SOMETHING BIG(1971)

Scruffy the Dog
STORM IN A TEACUP(1937, Brit.); SCRUFFY(1938, Brit.); IT'S IN THE AIR(1940, Brit.)

Earl Scruggs
WHERE THE LILIES BLOOM(1974), m

Linda Scruggs
SHOOT IT: BLACK, SHOOT IT: BLUE(1974); SALTY(1975); LAS VEGAS LADY(1976)

Victoria Scruton
SWEET CHARITY(1969)

Leo Scuccuglia
GIANT OF METROPOLIS, THE(1963, Ital.), ed

Margaret Scudamore
ARMS AND THE MAN(1932, Brit.); BEAUTY AND THE BARGE(1937, Brit.); MELODY AND ROMANCE(1937, Brit.); MY WIFE'S FAMILY(1941, Brit.)

Kenyon J. Scudder
UNCHAINED(1955), w

Phillip Scuderi
HERE COME THE TIGERS(1978)

Paul Scull
MAYBE IT'S LOVE(1930)

Stephen Scull
HOWZER(1973), m

George Scullin
GUNFIGHT AT THE O.K. CORRAL(1957), w

Denis Scully
JOURNEY INTO NOWHERE(1963, Brit.), d

Frank Scully
SECRET OF MAGIC ISLAND, THE(1964, Fr./Ital.), w

Joe Scully
MY SON IS GUILTY(1940)

Mary Alice Scully
Silents
STELLA MARIS(1925), w

Norbert Scully
PARIS BOUND(1929), ph

Peter Scully
HENRY, THE RAINMAKER(1949), p, ed; LEAVE IT TO HENRY(1949), p, ed; FATHER MAKES GOOD(1950), p; FATHER'S WILD GAME(1950), p; IT'S A SMALL WORLD(1950), p; FATHER TAKES THE AIR(1951), p; SON OF BELLE STARR(1953), p

Sean Scully
HUNTED IN HOLLAND(1961, Brit.); ALMOST ANGELS(1962); ELIZA FRASER(1976, Aus.)

Terry Scully
NIGHT CREATURES(1962, Brit.); PROJECTED MAN, THE(1967, Brit.); GOODBYE GEMINI(1970, Brit.); NIGHT AFTER NIGHT AFTER NIGHT(1970, Brit.); ASPHYX, THE(1972, Brit.)
Vin Scully
FIREBALL 590(1966)
William J. Scully
Silents
ANNABEL LEE(1921), d
Peter Sculthorpe
AGE OF CONSENT(1969, Austral.), m; MANGANINNIE(1982, Aus.), m
Matthew Scurfield
SWEENEY 2(1978, Brit.); RAIDERS OF THE LOST ARK(1981); MC VICAR(1982, Brit.)
1984
JIGSAW MAN, THE(1984, Brit.); 1984(1984, Brit.)
Jeremy Scuse
LORD OF THE FLIES(1963, Brit.)
M. Scutti
YOR, THE HUNTER FROM THE FUTURE(1983, Ital.), makeup
Mario Scutti
1984
DUNE(1984), makeup
Thomas Scwalm
NELLY'S VERSION(1983, Brit.), ed
Shai Scwartz
1984
AMBASSADOR, THE(1984)
Johnny Sea
WHAT AM I BID?(1967)
Seabiscuit
WINNER'S CIRCLE, THE(1948)
Ellen Seaborn
LIFE AND TIMES OF CHESTER-ANGUS RAMSGOOD, THE(1971, Can.)
Arthur Seabourne
77 PARK LANE(1931, Brit.), ed
John Seabourne
COLONEL BLIMP(1945, Brit.), ed; I KNOW WHERE I'M GOING(1947, Brit.), ed; HISTORY OF MR. POLLY, THE(1949, Brit.), ed; ROCKING HORSE WINNER, THE(1950, Brit.), ed; NIGHT WITHOUT STARS(1953, Brit.), ed; SEA DEVILS(1953), ed; GREEN BUDDHA, THE(1954, Brit.), ed; CROSS CHANNEL(1955, Brit.), ed; SECRET VENTURE(1955, Brit.), ed; TRACK THE MAN DOWN(1956, Brit.), ed; IN THE WAKE OF A STRANGER(1960, Brit.), ed
John Seabourne,Sr.
WOODEN HORSE, THE(1951), ed
Peter Seabourne
WOODEN HORSE, THE(1951), ed; DEVIL'S HARBOR(1954, Brit.), ed; TROUBLE IN STORE(1955, Brit.), ed; DOG AND THE DIAMONDS, THE(1962, Brit.), ed; COUNT-DOWN TO DANGER(1967, Brit.), d&w; ESCAPE FROM THE SEA(1968, Brit.), d&w
Roy Seabright
TOPPER RETURNS(1941), spec eff
Edward Seabrook
MR. WALKIE TALKIE(1952), w
Edward E. Seabrook
TANKS A MILLION(1941), w; ABOUT FACE(1942), w; YANKS AHOY(1943), w; HERE COMES TROUBLE(1948), w
Edward R. Seabrook
AS YOU WERE(1951), w
Gay Seabrook
EASY MILLIONS(1933); EX-LADY(1933); STRICTLY PERSONAL(1933); EMBAR-RASSING MOMENTS(1934); HALF A SINNER(1934); SHE LEARNED ABOUT SAIL-ORS(1934); UNCERTAIN LADY(1934); COUNTY CHAIRMAN, THE(1935); HIGGINS FAMILY, THE(1938); LONG SHOT, THE(1939); RACKETEERS OF THE RANGE(1939); LOVE, HONOR AND OH, BABY(1940)
Sam Seabrook
MAN FRIDAY(1975, Brit.)
William Seabrook
WHITE ZOMBIE(1932), w. Garnett Weston
Forest Seabury
Silents
WILD AND WOOLLY(1917)
Forrest Seabury
Silents
AUCTION BLOCK, THE(1926); RANSON'S FOLLY(1926)
Inez Seabury
THE INVISIBLE RAY(1936)
Warren Seabury
PRETTY MAIDS ALL IN A ROW(1971)
Ymez Seabury
NOW AND FOREVER(1934)
Ynez Seabury
DYNAMITE(1930); MADAME SATAN(1930); DRIFTER, THE(1932); SIGN OF THE CROSS, THE(1932); GIRL OF THE GOLDEN WEST, THE(1938); NORTHWEST MOUNTED POLICE(1940)
Silents
SLANDER THE WOMAN(1923)
Misc. Silents
CALGARY STAMPEDE, THE(1925)
Sandra Seacat
ROSE, THE(1979); FRANCES(1982); GOLDEN SEAL, THE(1983)
1984
COUNTRY(1984)
Sandra Diane Seacat
NIGHT MOVES(1975)
Dorothy Seacombe
LORD RICHARD IN THE PANTRY(1930, Brit.); LOVES OF ROBERT BURNS, THE(1930, Brit.); YELLOW MASK, THE(1930, Brit.); MANY TANKS MR. AT-KINS(1938, Brit.); ANYTHING TO DECLARE?(1939, Brit.); WARE CASE, THE(1939, Brit.)

Silents
FLAG LIEUTENANT, THE(1926, Brit.)
Misc. Silents
THIRD EYE, THE(1929, Brit.)
Dorit Seadia
1984
SAHARA(1984)
Susan Seaforth
TIJUANA STORY, THE(1957); CALIFORNIA(1963); GUNFIGHT AT COMANCHE CREEK(1964); BILLIE(1965); IF HE HOLLERS, LET HIM GO(1968); ANGEL IN MY POCKET(1969)
Elaine Seagal
TORTURE ME KISS ME(1970)
Gwen Seager
KID MILLIONS(1934); LITTLE TOUGH GUY(1938); UNFINISHED BUSINESS(1941); COVER GIRL(1944)
Sandy Seager
CONQUEROR WORM, THE(1968, Brit.)
Sara Seager
LAST CURTAIN, THE(1937, Brit.)
Stella Seager
Silents
AFTER THE SHOW(1921)
Vanya Seager
XTRO(1983, Brit.)
Lisa Seagram
CARPETBAGGERS, THE(1964); HOUSE IS NOT A HOME, A(1964); CAPRICE(1967); 2000 YEARS LATER(1969)
Misc. Talkies
TWO THOUSAND YEARS LATER(1969)
Wilfred Seagram
Misc. Silents
DOOR THAT HAS NO KEY, THE(1921, Brit.)
Clifford Seagrave
MURDER AT THE CABARET(1936, Brit.)
Jay Seagrave
1984
CENSUS TAKER, THE(1984), m
Malcolm Seagrave
PHANTASM(1979), m
Jenny Seagrove
MOONLIGHTING(1982, Brit.); LOCAL HERO(1983, Brit.); NATE AND HAYES(1983, U.S./New Zealand)
Barbara [Hershey] Seagull
CRAZY WORLD OF JULIUS VROODER, THE(1974); DIAMONDS(1975, U.S./Israel)
Misc. Talkies
LOVE COMES QUIETLY(1974); YOU AND ME(1975)
Elinor Seagures
Misc. Talkies
COMES MIDNIGHT(1940)
Roy Seagus
FOLIES DERGERE(1935)
J. Seaholme
HUE AND CRY(1950, Brit.), ph
Jeff Seaholme
GUILTY MELODY(1936, Brit.), ph; OUT OF THE CLOUDS(1957, Brit.), ph
Geoffrey Seahorn
BLOOD OF THE VAMPIRE(1958, Brit.), ph
Ted Seaife
CONSTANT HUSBAND, THE(1955, Brit.), ph
Joe Seakatsie
1984
GODS MUST BE CRAZY, THE(1984, Botswana)
Elizabeth Seal
RADIO CAB MURDER(1954, Brit.); TOWN ON TRIAL(1957, Brit.); TROUBLE IN THE SKY(1961, Brit.); VAMPIRE CIRCUS(1972, Brit.)
Esmond Seal
DIAMOND CITY(1949, Brit.), ed; MY BROTHER'S KEEPER(1949, Brit.), ed
Jean Seal
STUDENT TOUR(1934)
Oliver Seal
TENDER MERCIES(1982)
Peter Seal
ONCE UPON A HONEYMOON(1942); ABOVE SUSPICION(1943); GHOSTS ON THE LOOSE(1943); SALOME, WHERE SHE DANCED(1945); CUBAN PETE(1946); GOLD-EN EARRINGS(1947); NORTHWEST OUTPOST(1947); CALL NORTHSIDE 777(1948); JOAN OF ARC(1948)
Mabel Sealby
CHINESE PUZZLE, THE(1932, Brit.)
Douglas Seale
1984
AMADEUS(1984)
John Seale
ALVIN PURPLE(1974, Aus.), ph; DEATHCHEATERS(1976, Aus.), ph; FATTY FINN(1980, Aus.), ph; BMX BANDITS(1983), ph; FIGHTING BACK(1983, Brit.), ph
1984
CAREFUL, HE MIGHT HEAR YOU(1984, Aus.), ph
Paddy Seale
THUNDERBIRDS ARE GO(1968, Brit.), ph
Franklyn Seales
ONION FIELD, THE(1979); SOUTHERN COMFORT(1981)
Scott Sealey
BOY WHO CRIED WEREWOLF, THE(1973)
Jerry Ian Seals
ON THE BEACH(1959)
Steele L. Seals
STONY ISLAND(1978)

Seals and Croft
SGT. PEPPER'S LONELY HEARTS CLUB BAND(1978)
Allen Seaman
DIRTY HARRY(1971)
Earl Seaman
LAWLESS NINETIES, THE(1936); RANGERS OF FORTUNE(1940)
Helen Seaman
HEARTS IN BONDAGE(1936)
Jack Seaman
PROJECT MOONBASE(1953), p, w
Marjorie Seaman
Misc. Silents
FREE AIR(1922)
Milton Seaman
EASY MONEY(1983)
1984
MUPPETS TAKE MANHATTAN, THE(1984)
Pamela Seaman
I NEVER PROMISED YOU A ROSE GARDEN(1977)
Peter Seaman
TRENCHCOAT(1983), w
Rick Seaman
GRAND THEFT AUTO(1977)
Dorothy Seamans
LOOK OUT SISTER(1948)
"Seamark"
QUERY(1945, Brit.), w; MURDER IN REVERSE(1946, Brit.), w
Darryl Seamen
PORTNOY'S COMPLAINT(1972)
Helen Seamon
STRIKE UP THE BAND(1940); BALL OF FIRE(1941); JOAN OF OZARK(1942)
Maxine Seamon
TWO O'CLOCK COURAGE(1945)
Seamon and Farrell
I THANK YOU(1941, Brit.)
Michael Sean
PARRISH(1961); MR. HOBBS TAKES A VACATION(1962)
Walter Sear
LET'S SCARE JESSICA TO DEATH(1971), m
Walter Sear [Nico Fidenco]
DR. BUTCHER, M.D.(1982, Ital.), m
Joe Searby
LORDS OF DISCIPLINE, THE(1983)
The Searchers
SATURDAY NIGHT OUT(1964, Brit.)
Bernie Searl
OPTIMISTS, THE(1973, Brit.)
Jack Searl
WILD AND WOOLLY(1937); THAT CERTAIN AGE(1938); SMALL TOWN DEB(1941); FABULOUS DORSEYS, THE(1947); HAZARD(1948); PALEFACE, THE(1948)
Jackie Searl
TOM SAWYER(1930); FINN AND HATTIE(1931); HUCKLEBERRY FINN(1931); NEWLY RICH(1931); SCANDAL SHEET(1931); SKIPPY(1931); SOOKY(1931); HEARTS OF HUMANITY(1932); HIGH GEAR(1933); ONE YEAR LATER(1933); RETURN OF CASEY JONES(1933); GREAT EXPECTATIONS(1934); MURDER ON THE BLACKBOARD(1934); NO GREATER GLORY(1934); PECK'S BAD BOY(1934); SHE WAS A LADY(1934); STRICTLY DYNAMITE(1934); GINGER(1935); UNWELCOME STRANGER(1935); GENTLE JULIA(1936); LITTLE LORD FAUNTLEROY(1936); TWO WISE MAIDS(1937); LITTLE TOUGH GUY(1938); LITTLE TOUGH GUYS IN SOCIETY(1938); MILITARY ACADEMY(1940)
Veta Searl
Silents
CHARITY?(1916)
Misc. Silents
SUPERSTITION(1922)
Donald Searle
Silents
FOUR MEN IN A VAN(1921, Brit.); SQUIBS WINS THE CALCUTTA SWEEP(1922, Brit.); MUTINY(1925, Brit.)
Edna Searle
ONE EXCITING ADVENTURE(1935); RUNAWAY LADIES(1935, Brit.); SAILING ALONG(1938, Brit.)
Eric Searle
JUST WILLIAM(1939, Brit.)
Francis Searle
GIRL IN A MILLION, A(1946, Brit.), d; THINGS HAPPEN AT NIGHT(1948, Brit.), d; CELIA(1949, Brit.), d, w; LADY CRAVED EXCITEMENT, THE(1950, Brit.), d, w; MAN IN BLACK, THE(1950, Brit.), d, w; ROSSITER CASE, THE(1950, Brit.), w; SOMEONE AT THE DOOR(1950, Brit.), d; CASE FOR PC 49, A(1951, Brit.), d; CARETAKERS DAUGHTER, THE(1952, Brit.), d; CLOUDBURST(1952, Brit.), d, w; NEVER LOOK BACK(1952, Brit.), d, w; WHISPERING SMITH VERSUS SCOTLAND YARD(1952, Brit.), d; MURDER AT 3 A.M.(1953, Brit.), d; WHEEL OF FATE(1953, Brit.), p&d; FINAL APPOINTMENT(1954, Brit.), p; PROFILE(1954, Brit.), d; ONE WAY OUT(1955, Brit.), d; STOLEN ASSIGNMENT(1955, Brit.), p; DYNAMITERS, THE(1956, Brit.), d; UNDERCOVER GIRL(1957, Brit.), d; DIPLOMATIC CORPSE, THE(1958, Brit.), p; KILL ME TOMORROW(1958, Brit.), p; MURDER AT SITE THREE(1959, Brit.), d; TICKET TO PARADISE(1961, Brit.), p, d; DEAD MAN'S EVIDENCE(1962, Brit.), p, d; EMERGENCY(1962, Brit.), p&d; FREEDOM TO DIE(1962, Brit.), d; GAOLBREAK(1962, Brit.), p, d; NIGHT OF THE PROWLER(1962, Brit.), d; MARKED ONE, THE(1963, Brit.), d; IN TROUBLE WITH EVE(1964, Brit.), d
Humphrey Searle
ABOMINABLE SNOWMAN OF THE HIMALAYAS, THE(1957, Brit.), m; ACTION OF THE TIGER(1957), m; BABY AND THE BATTLESHIP, THE(1957, Brit.), m; BEYOND MOMBASA(1957), m; NOVEL AFFAIR, A(1957, Brit.), m; LAW AND DISORDER(1958, Brit.), m; LEFT, RIGHT AND CENTRE(1959), m; HAUNTING, THE(1963), m, md
Jack Searle
LADY AT MIDNIGHT(1948)

Jackie Searle
DAYBREAK(1931); LOVERS COURAGEOUS(1932); MIRACLE MAN, THE(1932); ALICE IN WONDERLAND(1933); OFFICER 13(1933); TOPAZE(1933); WORLD CHANGES, THE(1933); WICKED WOMAN, A(1934); ANGELS WASH THEIR FACES(1939); MY LITTLE CHICKADEE(1940); GLAMOUR BOY(1941)
Judith Searle
WALK PROUD(1979)
Kamuela Searle
Silents
MALE AND FEMALE(1919)
Kamuela C. Searle
Misc. Silents
JUNGLE TRAIL OF THE SON OF TARZAN(1923)
Nagene Searle
COCK O' THE WALK(1930), w
Pamela Searle
IF A MAN ANSWERS(1962); OPERATION BULLSHINE(1963, Brit.)
Ronald Searle
BLUE MURDER AT ST. TRINIAN'S(1958, Brit.), w; PURE HELL OF ST. TRINIAN'S, THE(1961, Brit.), w; THOSE MAGNIFICENT MEN IN THEIR FLYING MACHINES; OR HOW I FLEWFROM LONDON TO PARIS IN 25 HOURS AND 11 MINUTES(1965, Brit.), titles; GREAT ST. TRINIAN'S TRAIN ROBBERY, THE(1966, Brit.), w
Eddie Searles
NORTHERN PURSUIT(1943); PHFFFT!(1954)
Jefferson Dudley Searles
INVISIBLE BOY, THE(1957)
Jefferson Searles
DELICATE DELINQUENT, THE(1957)
Hank Searls
CROWDED SKY, THE(1960), w; COUNTDOWN(1968), w
Ed Searpa
SWISS MISS(1938)
A.D. Sears
Silents
MARTYRS OF THE ALAMO, THE(1915); PENITENTES, THE(1915); HELL-TO-PAY AUSTIN(1916); INTOLERANCE(1916); REGGIE MIXES IN(1916); CITY OF PURPLE DREAMS, THE(1918)
Misc. Silents
FAILURE, THE(1915); LOST HOUSE, THE(1915); GIRL OF THE TIMBER CLAIMS, THE(1917); WOMAN'S AWAKENING, A(1917)
Allan Sears
SECRETS(1933); LADY BY CHOICE(1934); FIGHTING SHADOWS(1935); JUSTICE OF THE RANGE(1935); LAW BEYOND THE RANGE(1935); LIFE BEGINS AT 40(1935); REVENGE RIDER, THE(1935); SINGING VAGABOND, THE(1935); SUNSET OF POWER(1936); TRAPPED(1937); TWO-FISTED SHERIFF(1937); CATTLE RAIDERS(1938); PRAIRIE ROUNDUP(1951)
Silents
KAISER, BEAST OF BERLIN, THE(1918); RED, RED HEART, THE(1918); AMATEUR ADVENTURESS, THE(1919); JUDY OF ROGUES' HARBOUR(1920); LONG LIVE THE KING(1923); INTO THE NIGHT(1928)
Misc. Silents
SAVAGE, THE(1917); GOWN OF DESTINY, THE(1918); BIG LITTLE PERSON, THE(1919); HEART O' THE HILLS(1919); RIO GRANDE(1920); SCARLET HONEYMOON, THE(1925)
Allen D. Sears
Misc. Silents
LITTLE YANK, THE(1917)
Ann Sears
BRIDGE ON THE RIVER KWAI, THE(1957); LADY OF VENGEANCE(1957, Brit); CAT AND MOUSE(1958, Brit); CRASH DRIVE(1959, Brit.); MAN DETAINED(1961, Brit.); UNSTOPPABLE MAN, THE(1961, Brit.); LAMP IN ASSASSIN MEWS, THE(1962, Brit.); SHE ALWAYS GETS THEIR MAN(1962, Brit.); BRAIN, THE(1965, Ger./Brit.); EXPLOSION(1969, Can.); TALES FROM THE CRYPT(1972, Brit.)
B.J. Sears
1984
MASSIVE RETALIATION(1984), ed
Barbara Sears
SUNDAY DINNER FOR A SOLDIER(1944); BAD MEN OF THE BORDER(1945); CODE OF THE LAWLESS(1945); KEEP YOUR POWDER DRY(1945); THAT NIGHT WITH YOU(1945)
Fred F. Sears
DESERT VIGILANTE(1949), d; ACROSS THE BADLANDS(1950), d; HORSEMEN OF THE SIERRAS(1950), d; LIGHTNING GUNS(1950), d; RAIDERS OF TOMAHAWK CREEK(1950), d; BIG GUSHER, THE(1951); BONANZA TOWN(1951); CYCLONE FURY(1951); KID FROM AMARILLO, THE(1951); PECOS RIVER(1951); PRAIRIE ROUNDUP(1951), d; RIDIN' THE OUTLAW TRAIL(1951), d; SNAKE RIVER DESPERADOES(1951), d; HAWK OF WILD RIVER, THE(1952), d; KID FROM BROKEN GUN, THE(1952), d; LAST TRAIN FROM BOMBAY(1952), d; SMOKY CANYON(1952), d; TARGET HONG KONG(1952), d; AMBUSH AT TOMAHAWK GAP(1953), d; FORTY-NINTH MAN, THE(1953), d; MISSION OVER KOREA(1953), d; NEBRASKAN, THE(1953), d; SKY COMMANDO(1953), d; EL ALAMEIN(1954), d; MASSACRE CANYON(1954), d; MIAMI STORY, THE(1954), d; OUTLAW STALLION, THE(1954), d; OVERLAND PACIFIC(1954), d; APACHE AMBUSH(1955), d; CELL 2455, DEATH ROW(1955), d; CHICAGO SYNDICATE(1955), d; INSIDE DETROIT(1955), d; TEENAGE CRIME WAVE(1955), d; WYOMING RENEGADES(1955), d; CHA-CHA-CHA BOOM(1956), d; DON'T KNOCK THE ROCK(1956), d; EARTH VS. THE FLYING SAUCERS(1956), d; FURY AT GUNSIGHT PASS(1956), d; MIAMI EXPOSE(1956), d; ROCK AROUND THE CLOCK(1956), d; RUMBLE ON THE DOCKS(1956), d; WEREWOLF, THE(1956), d; CALYPSO HEAT WAVE(1957), d; ESCAPE FROM SAN QUENTIN(1957), d; GIANT CLAW, THE(1957), d; NIGHT THE WORLD EXPLODED, THE(1957), d; UTAH BLAINE(1957), d; BADMAN'S COUNTRY(1958), d; CRASH LANDING(1958), d; GHOST OF THE CHINA SEA(1958), d; GOING STEADY(1958), d; WORLD WAS HIS JURY, THE(1958), d
Fred J. Sears
MY TRUE STORY(1951)
Fred Sears
CORPSE CAME C.O.D., THE(; JOLSON STORY, THE(1946); BLONDIE IN THE DOUGH(1947); BLONDIE'S ANNIVERSARY(1947); DOWN TO EARTH(1947); FOR THE LOVE OF RUSTY(1947); HER HUSBAND'S AFFAIRS(1947); IT HAD TO BE YOU(1947); LONE HAND TEXAN, THE(1947); ADVENTURES IN SILVERADO(1948);

GALLANT BLADE, THE(1948); PHANTOM VALLEY(1948); RUSTY LEADS THE WAY(1948); WHIRLWIND RAIDERS(1948); BLAZING TRAIL, THE(1949); BOSTON BLACKIE'S CHINESE VENTURE(1949); JOHNNY ALLEGRO(1949); LARAMIE(1949); LONE WOLF AND HIS LADY, THE(1949); LUST FOR GOLD(1949); RENEGADES OF THE SAGE(1949); SHOCKPROOF(1949); SLIGHTLY FRENCH(1949); SMOKY MOUNTAIN MELODY(1949); SOUTH OF DEATH VALLEY(1949); CONVICTED(1950); COUNTERSPY MEETS SCOTLAND YARD(1950); DAVID HARDING, COUNTERSPY(1950); FRONTIER OUTPOST(1950); HOEDOWN(1950); TEXAS DYNAMO(1950); BANDITS OF EL DORADO(1951); BONANZA TOWN(1951), d; FORT SAVAGE RAIDERS(1951); LARAMIE MOUNTAINS(1952); ROUGH, TOUGH WEST, THE(1952)
Misc. Talkies
LAW OF THE CANYON(1947); WEST OF DODGE CITY(1947)

Heather Sears
DRY ROT(1956, Brit.); STORY OF ESTHER COSTELLO, THE(1957, Brit.); ROOM AT THE TOP(1959, Brit.); FOUR DESPERATE MEN(1960, Brit.); SONS AND LOVERS(1960, Brit.); PHANTOM OF THE OPERA, THE(1962, Brit.); SATURDAY NIGHT OUT(1964, Brit.); BLACK TORMENT, THE(1965, Brit.); GREAT EXPECTATIONS(1975, Brit.)
Misc. Talkies
BLACK TORMENT(1984)

Ian Sears
YENTL(1983)

James Sears
LONG GRAY LINE, THE(1955)

Jim Sears
ALL-AMERICAN, THE(1953)

John "Ziggy" Sears
STRATTON STORY, THE(1949)

Larry Sears
WARRIORS, THE(1979)

Laura Sears
Misc. Silents
FLYING COLORS(1917); IN SLUMBERLAND(1917); FRAMING FRAMERS(1918)

Stephen H. Sears
RUMBLE ON THE DOCKS(1956)

Ted Sears
SNOW WHITE AND THE SEVEN DWARFS(1937), w; PINOCCHIO(1940), w; RELUCTANT DRAGON, THE(1941), w; THREE CABALLEROS, THE(1944), w; FUN AND FANCY FREE(1947), w; MELODY TIME(1948), w; ADVENTURES OF ICHABOD AND MR. TOAD(1949), w; SO DEAR TO MY HEART(1949), w; CINDERELLA(1950), w; ALICE IN WONDERLAND(1951), w; PETER PAN(1953), w

Zelda Sears
DEVIL MAY CARE(1929), w; BISHOP MURDER CASE, THE(1930); DIVORCEE, THE(1930), a, w; ROAD TO PARADISE(1930), w; DAYBREAK(1931), w; INSPIRATION(1931); POLITICS(1931), w; SUSAN LENOX–HER FALL AND RISE(1931), w; EMMA(1932), w; NEW MORALS FOR OLD(1932), w; PROSPERITY(1932), w; BEAUTY FOR SALE(1933), w; DAY OF RECKONING(1933), w; TUGBOAT ANNIE(1933), w; OPERATOR 13(1934), w; SADIE MCKEE(1934), w; THIS SIDE OF HEAVEN(1934), w; WICKED WOMAN, A(1934), a, w; YOU CAN'T BUY EVERYTHING(1934), w
Silents
TRUTH, THE(1920); CORPORAL KATE(1926), w; NIGHT BRIDE, THE(1927), w; NO CONTROL(1927), w; RUBBER TIRES(1927), w; RUSH HOUR, THE(1927), w

Zenas Sears
JAMBOREE(1957); LEGEND OF BLOOD MOUNTAIN, THE(1965)
Misc. Talkies
LEGEND OF BLOOD MOUNTAIN, THE(1965)

Dorothy Seastrom
Silents
PRETTY LADIES(1925); IT MUST BE LOVE(1926)

Victor Seastrom [Sjostrom]
LADY TO LOVE, A(1930), d; UNDER THE RED ROBE(1937, Brit.), d; WALPURGIS NIGHT(1941, Swed.); RAILROAD WORKERS(1948, Swed.)
Silents
HE WHO GETS SLAPPED(1924), d, w; TOWER OF LIES, THE(1925), d; SCARLET LETTER, THE(1926), d; DIVINE WOMAN, THE(1928), d
Misc. Silents
NAME THE MAN(1924), d; CONFESSIONS OF A QUEEN(1925), d; MASKS OF THE DEVIL, THE(1928), d

Charles Seat
WHERE THE RED FERN GROWS(1974)

Dixie Seatle
TICKET TO HEAVEN(1981)

Aileen Seaton
DANGEROUS AGE, A(1960, Can.); WAITING FOR CAROLINE(1969, Can.)

Arthur Seaton
FULL SPEED AHEAD(1936, Brit.); GHOST GOES WEST, THE(1936); HOWARD CASE, THE(1936, Brit.); STORM IN A TEACUP(1937, Brit.); YOU'RE IN THE ARMY NOW(1937, Brit.); BREAKERS AHEAD(1938, Brit.); HARD STEEL(1941, Brit.)

Chuck Seaton
SEPARATE WAYS(1981), art d; FORBIDDEN WORLD(1982), set d

Eula Seaton
END OF AUGUST, THE(1982), w

Frederick Seaton
HIDE IN PLAIN SIGHT(1980)

George Seaton
STUDENT TOUR(1934), w; WINNING TICKET, THE(1935), w; DAY AT THE RACES, A(1937), w; DOCTOR TAKES A WIFE(1940), w; THIS THING CALLED LOVE(1940), w; CHARLEY'S AUNT(1941), w; MOON OVER MIAMI(1941), w; THAT NIGHT IN RIO(1941), w; MAGNIFICENT DOPE, THE(1942), w; TEN GENTLEMEN FROM WEST POINT(1942), w; CONEY ISLAND(1943), w; MEANEST MAN IN THE WORLD, THE(1943), w; SONG OF BERNADETTE, THE(1943), w; EVE OF ST. MARK, THE(1944), w; DIAMOND HORSESHOE(1945), d&w; JUNIOR MISS(1945), d, w; COCKEYED MIRACLE, THE(1946), w; MIRACLE ON 34TH STREET(1947), d, w; SHOCKING MISS PILGRIM, THE(1947), w; APARTMENT FOR PEGGY(1948), d&w; CHICKEN EVERY SUNDAY(1948), d, w; BIG LIFT, THE(1950), d&w; FOR HEAVEN'S SAKE(1950), d&w; RHUBARB(1951), p; AARON SLICK FROM PUNKIN CRICK(1952), p; ANYTHING CAN HAPPEN(1952), d, w; SOMEBODY LOVES ME(1952), p; LITTLE BOY LOST(1953), d&w; COUNTRY GIRL, THE(1954), p, d&w;

PROUD AND THE PROFANE, THE(1956), d&w; TIN STAR, THE(1957), p; TEACHER'S PET(1958), d; BUT NOT FOR ME(1959), p; RAT RACE, THE(1960), p; PLEASURE OF HIS COMPANY, THE(1961), d; COUNTERFEIT TRAITOR, THE(1962), d&w; HOOK, THE(1962), d; TWILIGHT OF HONOR(1963), p; 36 HOURS(1965), d&w; WHAT'S SO BAD ABOUT FEELING GOOD?(1968), p&d, w; AIRPORT(1970), d, w; SHOWDOWN(1973), p&d

John Seaton
THX 1138(1971)

Marc Seaton
WILD ON THE BEACH(1965); CHASE, THE(1966); WHAT'S SO BAD ABOUT FEELING GOOD?(1968); ANGELS HARD AS THEY COME(1971)

Scott Seaton
OTHER TOMORROW, THE(1930); MADAME RACKETEER(1932); WOMAN IN THE WINDOW, THE(1945); JOAN OF ARC(1948); DONOVAN'S REEF(1963)
Silents
THUMBS DOWN(1927)
Misc. Silents
WILD BEAUTY(1927)

Violet Seaton
THIRTEEN WOMEN(1932); GREAT IMPERSONATION, THE(1935); SYLVIA SCARLETT(1936)

Michael Seaver
HARRY BLACK AND THE TIGER(1958, Brit.)

Charles Seaverns
FRANCES(1982)

Michael Seavers
STRANGER AT MY DOOR(1950, Brit.); MOULIN ROUGE(1952)

Carolyn Seaward
OCTOPUSSY(1983, Brit.)

Sidney Seaward
Misc. Silents
OFFICER 666(1914)

Sydney Seaward
CONTRABAND LOVE(1931, Brit.); TRAPPED IN A SUBMARINE(1931, Brit.); FLAW, THE(1933, Brit.)
Silents
AMATEUR GENTLEMAN, THE(1920, Brit.); DEBT OF HONOR(1922, Brit.)
Misc. Silents
HUNDRETH CHANCE, THE(1920, Brit.); TIDAL WAVE, THE(1920, Brit.); YELLOW CLAW, THE(1920, Brit.); GENTLEMAN OF FRANCE, A(1921, Brit.); NIGHT HAWK, THE(1921, Brit.); WOMAN OF HIS DREAM, THE(1921, Brit.)

Sydney Seaword
Misc. Silents
DOC(1914)

Ray Seawright
MERRILY WE LIVE(1938), spec eff

Roy Seawright
OUR RELATIONS(1936), spec eff; NOBODY'S BABY(1937), spec eff; PICK A STAR(1937), spec eff; TOPPER(1937), spec eff; WAY OUT WEST(1937), spec eff; THERE GOES MY HEART(1938), spec eff; CAPTAIN FURY(1939), spec eff; OF MICE AND MEN(1939), spec eff; TOPPER TAKES A TRIP(1939), spec eff; ZENOBIA(1939), spec eff; CAPTAIN CAUTION(1940), spec eff; ONE MILLION B.C.(1940), spec eff; SAPS AT SEA(1940), spec eff; TURNABOUT(1940), spec eff; ROAD SHOW(1941), spec eff; TANKS A MILLION(1941), spec eff; BROOKLYN ORCHID(1942), spec eff; DUDES ARE PRETTY PEOPLE(1942), spec eff; YANKS AHOY(1943), spec eff

Roy E. Seawright
PORT OF NEW YORK(1949), spec eff

Roy W. Seawright
GANGSTER, THE(1947), spec eff; WHO KILLED "DOC" ROBBIN?(1948), spec eff; RED STALLION IN THE ROCKIES(1949), spec eff; TRAPPED(1949), spec eff

Billie Seay
MARRIAGE PLAYGROUND, THE(1929)

Billy Seay
MY MAN(1928); KID MILLIONS(1934)
Silents
UNKNOWN, THE(1927)

Charles M. Seay
Misc. Silents
FANTASMA(1914), d; JAN OF THE BIG SNOWS(1922), d

Charles W. Seay
Silents
DAUGHTER OF THE SEA, A(1915), d

James Seay
EMERGENCY SQUAD(1940); GOLDEN GLOVES(1940); NORTHWEST MOUNTED POLICE(1940); OKLAHOMA RENEGADES(1940); QUEEN OF THE MOB(1940); SON OF MONTE CRISTO(1940); THOSE WERE THE DAYS(1940); WAY OF ALL FLESH, THE(1940); WOMEN WITHOUT NAMES(1940); FACE BEHIND THE MASK, THE(1941); IN OLD COLORADO(1941); KEEP 'EM FLYING(1941); KID FROM KANSAS, THE(1941); TWO IN A TAXI(1941); DANGEROUSLY THEY LIVE(1942); EAGLE SQUADRON(1942); ENEMY AGENTS MEET ELLERY QUEEN(1942); HIGHWAYS BY NIGHT(1942); HOME IN WYOMIN'(1942); MAN FROM CHEYENNE(1942); MR. CELEBRITY(1942); RIDE 'EM COWBOY(1942); RIDIN' DOWN THE CANYON(1942); THEY DIED WITH THEIR BOOTS ON(1942); TIMBER(1942); TIME TO KILL(1942); TRAMP, TRAMP, TRAMP(1942); HEARTACHES(1947); MIRACLE ON 34TH STREET, THE(1947); T-MEN(1947); CHECKERED COAT, THE(1948); COBRA STRIKES, THE(1948); DON'T TRUST YOUR HUSBAND(1948); SECRET BEYOND THE DOOR, THE(1948); SLIPPY MCGEE(1948); STRANGE MRS. CRANE, THE(1948); I CHEATED THE LAW(1949); PREJUDICE(1949); RED CANYON(1949); ASPHALT JUNGLE, THE(1950); FLYING MISSILE(1950); MILITARY ACADEMY WITH THAT TENTH AVENUE GANG(1950); UNION STATION(1950); CLOSE TO MY HEART(1951); DAY THE EARTH STOOD STILL, THE(1951); WHEN THE REDSKINS RODE(1951); BRAVE WARRIOR(1952); MODELS, INC.(1952); VOODOO TIGER(1952); CAPTAIN JOHN SMITH AND POCAHONTAS(1953); FORT TI(1953); HOMESTEADERS, THE(1953); JACK MCCALL, DESPERADO(1953); PHANTOM FROM SPACE(1953); PROBLEM GIRLS(1953); SON OF BELLE STARR(1953); TORPEDO ALLEY(1953); CAPTAIN KIDD AND THE SLAVE GIRL(1954); KILLERS FROM SPACE(1954); RETURN TO TREASURE ISLAND(1954); STEEL CAGE, THE(1954); VERA CRUZ(1954); I DIED A THOUSAND TIMES(1955); KISS ME DEADLY(1955); FRIENDLY PERSUASION(1956); GUN BROTHERS(1956); I'VE LIVED BEFORE(1956); MAN IN THE VAULT(1956); AMAZING COLOSSAL MAN, THE(1957);

BEGINNING OF THE END(1957); PAL JOEY(1957); BUCCANEER, THE(1958); STREET OF DARKNESS(1958); THREAT, THE(1960); SECRET OF DEEP HARBOR(1961); WHATEVER HAPPENED TO BABY JANE?(1962); DESTRUCTORS, THE(1968); PANIC IN THE CITY(1968)
Misc. Talkies
STREET OF DARKNESS(1958)

Jerry Seay
FANDANGO(1970)

Duke Seba
TITANIC(1953)

Maria Sebaldt
CAPTAIN FROM KOEPENICK, THE(1956, Ger.); END OF MRS. CHENEY(1963, Ger.)

Maria Sebalt
AFFAIRS OF JULIE, THE(1958, Ger.)

Josef Sebanek
LOVES OF A BLONDE(1966, Czech.); FIREMAN'S BALL, THE(1968, Czech.); MOST BEAUTIFUL AGE, THE(1970, Czech.)

Manuel Sebares
NUN AT THE CROSSROADS, A(1970, Ital./Span.), w

Ferd Sebashan
FLASH AND THE FIRECAT(1976), p,d&w

Dick Sebast
RESCUERS, THE(1977), w

Edward Sebaster
SEVEN MEN FROM NOW(1956), cos

A.H. Sebastian
Silents
RUBBER TIRES(1927), sup

Beverley Sebastian
FLASH AND THE FIRECAT(1976), p,d&w

Beverly Sebastian
HITCHHIKERS, THE(1972), p,d&w; DELTA FOX(1979), p&d; ON THE AIR LIVE WITH CAPTAIN MIDNIGHT(1979), p,d&w
Misc. Talkies
SINGLE GIRLS(1973), d

Don Sebastian
HOW DO I LOVE THEE?(1970); SUPER FUZZ(1981)

Dorothy Sebastian
HIS FIRST COMMAND(1929); UNHOLY NIGHT, THE(1929); BLUSHING BRIDES(1930); BROTHERS(1930); FREE AND EASY(1930); HELL'S ISLAND(1930); LADIES MUST PLAY(1930); MONTANA MOON(1930); OFFICER O'BRIEN(1930); OUR BLUSHING BRIDES(1930); UTAH KID, THE(1930); BIG GAMBLE, THE(1931); DECEIVER, THE(1931); LIGHTNING FLYER(1931); SHIPS OF HATE(1931); THEY NEVER COME BACK(1932); SHIP OF WANTED MEN(1933); ARIZONA KID, THE(1939); ROUGH RIDERS' ROUNDUP(1939); WOMEN, THE(1939); AMONG THE LIVING(1941); KANSAS CYCLONE(1941); REAP THE WILD WIND(1942); TRUE TO THE ARMY(1942); MIRACLE OF THE BELLS, THE(1948)
Silents
BLUEBEARD'S SEVEN WIVES(1926); ARIZONA WILDCAT(1927); CALIFORNIA(1927); ISLE OF FORGOTTEN WOMEN(1927); ON ZE BOULEVARD(1927); TEA FOR THREE(1927); TWELVE MILES OUT(1927); ADVENTURER, THE(1928); OUR DANCING DAUGHTERS(1928); SHOW PEOPLE(1928); WOMAN OF AFFAIRS, A(1928); DEVIL'S APPLE TREE(1929); MORGAN'S LAST RAID(1929); SINGLE STANDARD, THE(1929); SPITE MARRIAGE(1929)
Misc. Silents
SACKCLOTH AND SCARLET(1925); YOU'D BE SURPRISED(1926); HAUNTED SHIP, THE(1927); HOUSE OF SCANDAL, THE(1928); THEIR HOUR(1928); WYOMING(1928); RAINBOW, THE(1929); SPIRIT OF YOUTH, THE(1929)

Ferd Sebastian
HITCHHIKERS, THE(1972), p,d&w, ph; DELTA FOX(1979), p&d; ON THE AIR LIVE WITH CAPTAIN MIDNIGHT(1979), p,d&w
Misc. Talkies
SINGLE GIRLS(1973), d

John Sebastian
CRY TOUGH(1959); NIGHTMARE IN THE SUN(1964); POM POM GIRLS, THE(1976)
1984
ACT, THE(1984), m

John Sebastian [Curtis Harrington]
VOYAGE TO THE PREHISTORIC PLANET(1965), d&w

Julio Sebastian
KILLER SHARK(1950)

Micky Sebastian
1984
EDITH AND MARCEL(1984, Fr.)

Ray Sebastian
WITNESS FOR THE PROSECUTION(1957), makeup; YOUNG SWINGERS, THE(1963), makeup; NOTORIOUS CLEOPATRA, THE(1970), makeup; SCORCHY(1976)

Ray Sebastian II
SUPERCHICK(1973), makeup

Tracy Sebastian
FLASH AND THE FIRECAT(1976); ON THE AIR LIVE WITH CAPTAIN MIDNIGHT(1979)

Gennaro Sebastiani
LOST SOULS(1961, Ital.)

Celeste Sebastiano
KAREN, THE LOVEMAKER(1970), ph

Ben Sebastion
GATOR BAIT(1974)

Beverly Sebastion
GATOR BAIT(1974), p,d&w

Ferd Sebastion
GATOR BAIT(1974), p,d&w

Tracy Sebastion
GATOR BAIT(1974)

Gregg Sebelious
DAY THE EARTH FROZE, THE(1959, Fin./USSR), d

Jean Seberg
SAINT JOAN(1957); BONJOUR TRISTESSE(1958); BREATHLESS(1959, Fr.); MOUSE THAT ROARED, THE(1959, Brit.); LET NO MAN WRITE MY EPITAPH(1960); IN THE FRENCH STYLE(1963, U.S./Fr.); PLAYTIME(1963, Fr.); TIME OUT FOR LOVE(1963, Ital./Fr.); LILITH(1964); BACKFIRE(1965, Fr.); FINE MADNESS, A(1966); MOMENT TO MOMENT(1966); BIRDS COME TO DIE IN PERU(1968, Fr.); PAINT YOUR WAGON(1969); PENDULUM(1969); AIRPORT(1970); DEAD OF SUMMER(1970 Ital./Fr.); MACHO CALLAHAN(1970); WHO'S GOT THE BLACK BOX?(1970, Fr./Gr./Ital.); KILL! KILL! KILL!(1972, Fr./Ger./Ital./Span.); FRENCH CONSPIRACY, THE(1973, Fr.); WILD DUCK, THE(1977, Ger./Aust.); CORRUPTION OF CHRIS MILLER, THE(1979, Span.)
Misc. Talkies
BEHIND THE SHUTTERS(1976, Span.)

Don Sebesky
PEOPLE NEXT DOOR, THE(1970), m

Annie Sebring
Misc. Talkies
BIBI(1977)

Cami Sebring
GNOME-MOBILE, THE(1967)

K. Sebris
DEAD MOUNTAINEER HOTEL, THE(1979, USSR)

Antonio Secchi
ITALIANO BRAVA GENTE(1965, Ital./USSR), ph; SECRET AGENT SUPER DRAGON(1966, Fr./Ital./Ger./Monaco), ph

Toni Secchi
BULLET FOR THE GENERAL, A(1967, Ital.), ph; DEATH SENTENCE(1967, Ital.), ph; HILLS RUN RED, THE(1967, Ital.), ph

Cesare Seccia
COLOSSUS OF RHODES, THE(1961, Ital., Fr., Span.), w; GOLIATH AGAINST THE GIANTS(1963, Ital./Span.), p, w

Tazio Secciaroli
CASSANDRA CROSSING, THE(1977), spec eff

Edmond Sechan
ADVENTURES OF ARSENE LUPIN(1956, Fr./Ital.), ph; TAMANGO(1959, Fr.), ph; BEAR, THE(1963, Fr.), d, w; LOVE IS A BALL(1963), ph; YOUR SHADOW IS MINE(1963, Fr./Ital.), ph; SKY ABOVE HEAVEN(1964, Fr./Ital.), ph; THAT MAN FROM RIO(1964, Fr./Ital.), ph; BACKFIRE(1965, Fr.), ph; UP TO HIS EARS(1966, Fr./Ital.), ph; TENDER SCOUNDREL(1967, Fr./Ital.), ph; TWO WEEKS IN SEPTEMBER(1967, Fr./Brit.), ph; BLUE COUNTRY, THE(1977, Fr.), ph; PIAF–THE EARLY YEARS(1982, U.S./Fr.), ph; LA BOUM(1983, Fr.), ph

Marguerite Andree Sechehaye
DIARY OF A SCHIZOPHRENIC GIRL(1970, Ital.), w

Allen Secher
SHEILA LEVINE IS DEAD AND LIVING IN NEW YORK(1975)

Abdoulaye Seck
SEVENTH CONTINENT, THE(1968, Czech./Yugo.)

Douta Seck
COMEDIANS, THE(1967); CHECKERBOARD(1969, Fr.)
1984
SUGAR CANE ALLEY(1984, Fr.)

Joe Seckeresh
SUMMER'S CHILDREN(1979, Can.), ph

Bill Seckler
WORDS AND MUSIC(1929)

Andrew Secombe
DEVIL WITHIN HER, THE(1976, Brit.)

Harry Secombe
HELTER SKELTER(1949, Brit.); FAKE'S PROGRESS(1950, Brit.); PENNY POINTS TO PARADISE(1951, Brit.); DOWN AMONG THE Z MEN(1952, Brit.); FORCES' SWEETHEART(1953, Brit.); SVENGALI(1955, Brit.); DAVY(1958, Brit.); JET STORM(1961, Brit.); OLIVER!(1968, Brit.); DOCTOR IN TROUBLE(1970, Brit.); SONG OF NORWAY(1970); MAGNIFICENT SEVEN DEADLY SINS, THE(1971, Brit.); SUNSTRUCK(1973, Aus.)

John H. Secondari
THREE COINS IN THE FOUNTAIN(1954), w; PLEASURE SEEKERS, THE(1964), w

Elena Secota
ESCAPE TO ATHENA(1979, Brit.)

James Secrest
FATE IS THE HUNTER(1964)

Lance Secretan
HIGHLY DANGEROUS(1950, Brit.); STOLEN PLANS, THE(1962, Brit.)

Bishop's Secretary
WOMAN IN HIDING(1953, Brit.)

Kim Secrist
TIMERIDER(1983), ed
1984
THIS IS SPINAL TAP(1984), ed

Larry Secrist
HAUNTS(1977), ph

David Secter
OFFERING, THE(1966, Can.), p&d, w; WINTER KEPT US WARM(1968, Can.), p&d, w
Misc. Talkies
FEELIN' UP(1983), d

David Sector
GETTING TOGETHER(1976), p, d&w

Sholem Secunda
TEVYA(1939), m

Sholom Secunda
ELI ELI(1940), md

Chuck Sedacca
WIRE SERVICE(1942)

Dara Sedaka
1984
WHERE THE BOYS ARE '84(1984)

Neil Sedaka
STING OF DEATH(1966); DECOY FOR TERROR(1970, Can.)

Rolfe Sedan
UNDER TWO FLAGS(1936); IRON MASK, THE(1929); MAKING THE GRADE(1929); MONTE CARLO(1930); ONE HYSTERICAL NIGHT(1930); SWEETHEARTS AND WIVES(1930); JUST A GIGOLO(1931); CENTRAL PARK(1932); GRAND HOTEL(1932); IF I HAD A MILLION(1932); LOVE ME TONIGHT(1932); TROUBLE IN PARADISE(1932); WINNER TAKE ALL(1932); DESIGN FOR LIVING(1933); DEVIL'S BROTHER, THE(1933); LITTLE GIANT, THE(1933); PRIVATE DETECTIVE 62(1933); 42ND STREET(1933); MERRY WIDOW, THE(1934); NOW AND FOREVER(1934); PARIS INTERLUDE(1934); THIN MAN, THE(1934); WONDER BAR(1934); MAN WHO RECLAIMED HIS HEAD, THE(1935); NIGHT AT THE OPERA, A(1935); PARIS IN SPRING(1935); RUGGLES OF RED GAP(1935); TALE OF TWO CITIES, A(1935); $1,000 A MINUTE(1935); ANYTHING GOES(1936); ROSE MARIE(1936); SMARTEST GIRL IN TOWN(1936); CAFE METROPOLE(1937); DOUBLE OR NOTHING(1937); FIREFLY, THE(1937); HIGH, WIDE AND HANDSOME(1937); RHYTHM IN THE CLOUDS(1937); SHALL WE DANCE(1937); SOULS AT SEA(1937); 100 MEN AND A GIRL(1937); DESPERATE ADVENTURE, A(1938); I'LL GIVE A MILLION(1938); LETTER OF INTRODUCTION(1938); STOLEN HEAVEN(1938); STRANGE FACES(1938); UNDER THE BIG TOP(1938); EVERYTHING HAPPENS AT NIGHT(1939); NINOTCHKA(1939); STORY OF VERNON AND IRENE CASTLE, THE(1939); I WAS AN ADVENTURESS(1940); LAUGHING AT DANGER(1940); MAD EMPRESS, THE(1940); LAW OF THE TROPICS(1941); SAN ANTONIO ROSE(1941); THAT FORSYTE WOMAN(1949); LET'S DANCE(1950); MY FAVORITE SPY(1951); SOMETHING TO LIVE FOR(1952); GENTLEMEN PREFER BLONDES(1953); MISSISSIPPI GAMBLER, THE(1953); PHANTOM OF THE RUE MORGUE(1954); SO THIS IS PARIS(1954); 36 HOURS(1965); YOUNG FRANKENSTEIN(1974); WORLD'S GREATEST LOVER, THE(1977); FRISCO KID, THE(1979)
Misc. Talkies
DEVIL ON DECK(1932)
Silents
EXCITEMENT(1924); FLESH AND THE DEVIL(1926); ADORABLE CHEAT, THE(1928)

Maria Sedano
SPRING BREAK(1983)

Sibilla Sedat
FELLINI SATYRICON(1969, Fr./Ital.)

Corinna Seddon
1984
1984(1984, Brit.)

George Seddon
Silents
HIS JAZZ BRIDE(1926)

Jack Seddon
COUNT FIVE AND DIE(1958, Brit.), w; MURDER SHE SAID(1961, Brit.), w; SECRET PARTNER, THE(1961, Brit.), w; KILL OR CURE(1962, Brit.), w; LONGEST DAY, THE(1962), w; VILLAGE OF DAUGHTERS(1962, Brit.), w; MURDER AT THE GALLOP(1963, Brit.), w; MURDER AHOY(1964, Brit.), w; MURDER MOST FOUL(1964, Brit.), w; ALPHABET MURDERS, THE(1966), w; BLUE MAX, THE(1966), w; SOUTHERN STAR, THE(1969, Fr./Brit.), w; CARRY ON ENGLAND(1976, Brit.), w; WHAT CHANGED CHARLEY FARTHING?(1976, Brit.), w; TOMORROW NEVER COMES(1978, Brit./Can.), w

Margaret Seddon
BELLAMY TRIAL, THE(1929); DANCE HALL(1929); SHE GOES TO WAR(1929); AFTER THE FOG(1930); DANCING SWEETIES(1930); DUDE WRANGLER, THE(1930); DIVORCE AMONG FRIENDS(1931); IF I HAD A MILLION(1932); SMILIN' THROUGH(1932); BACHELOR MOTHER(1933); BROADWAY BAD(1933); HEROES FOR SALE(1933); LILLY TURNER(1933); MIDSHIPMAN JACK(1933); RETURN OF CASEY JONES(1933); WALLS OF GOLD(1933); WORST WOMAN IN PARIS(1933); BARRETTS OF WIMPOLE STREET, THE(1934); DAVID COPPERFIELD(1935); FLAME WITHIN, THE(1935); GIRL FRIEND, THE(1935); BIG GAME, THE(1936); MR. DEEDS GOES TO TOWN(1936); WOMAN REBELS, A(1936); DANGER–LOVE AT WORK(1937); LET'S MAKE A MILLION(1937); HAVING WONDERFUL TIME(1938); RAFFLES(1939); BANK DICK, THE(1940); DR. KILDARE'S STRANGE CASE(1940); FRIENDLY NEIGHBORS(1940); STRIKE UP THE BAND(1940); DR. KILDARE'S WEDDING DAY(1941); ROXIE HART(1942); SCATTERGOOD SURVIVES A MURDER(1942); TAKE A LETTER, DARLING(1942); WIFE TAKES A FLYER, THE(1942); HONEYMOON LODGE(1943); MEANEST MAN IN THE WORLD, THE(1943); SHERLOCK HOLMES IN WASHINGTON(1943); HOUSE BY THE RIVER(1950); THREE DESPERATE MEN(1951)
Silents
DAWN OF A TOMORROW, THE(1915); GIRL WITHOUT A SOUL, THE(1917); JUST AROUND THE CORNER(1921); MAN WORTH WHILE, THE(1921); MAN'S HOME, A(1921); SCHOOL DAYS(1921); MAN WHO PLAYED GOD, THE(1922); SONNY(1922); TIMOTHY'S QUEST(1922); GOLD DIGGERS, THE(1923); LITTLE CHURCH AROUND THE CORNER(1923); SNOB, THE(1924); NEW LIVES FOR OLD(1925); PROUD FLESH(1925); WAGES FOR WIVES(1925); REGULAR SCOUT, A(1926); ROLLING HOME(1926); WILD OATS LANE(1926); DRIVEN FROM HOME(1927); MATINEE LADIES(1927); QUALITY STREET(1927); SILK LEGS(1927); WHITE PANTS WILLIE(1927); ACTRESS, THE(1928); GENTLEMEN PREFER BLONDES(1928)
Misc. Silents
MIRACLE OF MONEY, THE(1920); HIGHEST LAW, THE(1921); BOOMERANG BILL(1922); LIGHTS OF NEW YORK, THE(1922); LITTLE JOHNNY JONES(1923); HUMAN TERROR, THE(1924); LADY OF QUALITY, A(1924); NIGHT MESSAGE, THE(1924); THROUGH THE DARK(1924); MIDSHIPMAN, THE(1925); HOME MADE(1927)

David Sederholm
PROWLER, THE(1981)

Alan Sedgwick
JOHNNY IN THE CLOUDS(1945, Brit.); WOMAN TO WOMAN(1946, Brit.); MY WIFE'S LODGER(1952, Brit.)

Angel Sedgwick
DANTON(1983)

Anne Sedgwick
Silents
IMPOSSIBLE WOMAN, THE(1919, Brit.), w

Charles Sedgwick
CHARGE OF THE LIGHT BRIGADE, THE(1936)

Ed Sedgwick
Silents
HAUNTED PAJAMAS(1917)

Edgar Sedgwick
PASSIONATE PLUMBER(1932), d; SPEAK EASILY(1932), d

Edie Sedgwick
CIAO MANHATTAN(1973)
Misc. Talkies
POOR LITTLE RICH GIRL(1965)

Edna Sedgwick
YOU'RE A SWEETHEART(1937); SWING, SISTER, SWING(1938)

Edward Sedgwick
PHANTOM OF THE OPERA, THE(1929), d; DOUGH BOYS(1930), d; FREE AND EASY(1930), d; DANGEROUS AFFAIR, A(1931), d; MAKER OF MEN(1931), d, w; PARLOR, BEDROOM AND BATH(1931), d; HORSEPLAY(1933), d; SATURDAY'S MILLIONS(1933), d; WHAT! NO BEER?(1933), d; DEATH OF THE DIAMOND(1934), d; HERE COMES THE GROOM(1934), d; I'LL TELL THE WORLD(1934), d; POOR RICH, THE(1934), d; FATHER BROWN, DETECTIVE(1935), d; MURDER IN THE FLEET(1935), d, w; VIRGINIA JUDGE, THE(1935), d; MISTER CINDERELLA(1936), d; FIT FOR A KING(1937), d; PICK A STAR(1937), d; RIDING ON AIR(1937), d; GLADIATOR, THE(1938), d; BEWARE SPOOKS(1939), d; BURN 'EM UP O'CONNER(1939), d; SO YOU WON'T TALK(1940), d; AIR RAID WARDENS(1943), d; SOUTHERN YANKEE, A(1948), d; MA AND PA KETTLE BACK ON THE FARM(1951), d
Silents
ROUGH AND READY(1918), w; WINNING STROKE, THE(1919), w; BAR NOTHIN'(1921), d; LIVE WIRES(1921), d, w; CHASING THE MOON(1922), d, w; DO AND DARE(1922), d&w; OUT OF LUCK(1923), d, w; ROMANCE LAND(1923), d; SHOOTIN' FOR LOVE(1923), d, w; HOOK AND LADDER(1924), d, w; RIDE FOR YOUR LIFE(1924), d; SAWDUST TRAIL(1924), d; HURRICANE KID, THE(1925), d; LET 'ER BUCK(1925), d&w; SPOOK RANCH(1925), w; SLIDE, KELLY, SLIDE(1927), d; CAMERAMAN, THE(1928), d; WEST POINT(1928), d; SPITE MARRIAGE(1929), d
Misc. Silents
ROUGH DIAMOND, THE(1921), d; BEARCAT, THE(1922), d; BOOMERANG JUSTICE(1922), d; FLAMING HOUR, THE(1922), d; BLINKY(1923), d; DEAD GAME(1923), d; FIRST DEGREE, THE(1923), d; GENTLEMAN FROM AMERICA, THE(1923), d; RAMBLIN' KID, THE(1923), d; SINGLE HANDED(1923), d; THRILL CHASER, THE(1923), d; BROADWAY OR BUST(1924), d; HIT AND RUN(1924), d; RIDIN' KID FROM POWDER RIVER, THE(1924), d; 40-HORSE HAWKINS(1924), d; LORRAINE OF THE LIONS(1925), d; SADDLE HAWK, THE(1925), d; TWO-FISTED JONES(1925), d; FLAMING FRONTIER, THE(1926), d; RUNAWAY EXPRESS, THE(1926), d; TIN HATS(1926), d; UNDER WESTERN SKIES(1926), d; BUGLE CALL, THE(1927), d; SPRING FEVER(1927), d; CIRCUS ROOKIES(1928), d

Eileen Sedgwick
Silents
FALSE BRANDS(1922); WOLF PACK(1922)
Misc. Silents
HERITAGE OF HATE, THE(1916); MAN AND BEAST(1917); HELL'S CRATER(1918); LOVE'S BATTLE(1920); WHITE RIDER, THE(1920); ARREST NORMA MACGREGOR(1921); JUDGEMENT(1922); MAKING GOOD(1923); SCARRED HANDS(1923); WHEN LAW COMES TO HADES(1923); GIRL OF THE WEST(1925); LURE OF THE WEST(1925); SAGEBRUSH LADY, THE(1925); THUNDERING SPEED(1926); WHEN DANGER CALLS(1927); WHITE FLAME(1928)

Josephine Sedgwick
Silents
SUNSHINE TRAIL, THE(1923)
Misc. Silents
CRIMSON CLUE(1922)

Josie Sedgwick
SON OF OKLAHOMA(1932)
Silents
ASHES OF HOPE(1917); ONE SHOT ROSS(1917); MAN ABOVE THE LAW(1918); JUBILO(1919); LONE HAND, THE(1920); WESTERN HEARTS(1921); DADDY(1923); SAWDUST TRAIL(1924); LET 'ER BUCK(1925); OUTLAW'S DAUGHTER, THE(1925)
Misc. Silents
INDISCREET CORINNE(1917); BOSS OF THE LAZY Y, THE(1918); HELL'S END(1918); KEITH OF THE BORDER(1918); PAYING HIS DEBT(1918); WILD LIFE(1918); WOLVES OF THE BORDER(1918); DUKE OF CHIMNEY BUTTE, THE(1921); DARING DAYS(1925); SADDLE HAWK, THE(1925)

Katrina Sedgwick
LAST WAVE, THE(1978, Aus.)

Paulita Sedgwick
SAVAGES(1972); QUARTET(1981, Brit./Fr.)

Juan Sedillo
GIRL FROM HAVANA, THE(1929)

Walter Sedimyn
FOX AND HIS FRIENDS(1976, Ger.)

Vendelin Sedivy
DO YOU KEEP A LION AT HOME?(1966, Czech.)

Bohumil Sedja
FANTASTIC PLANET(1973, Fr./Czech.), anim

Lola Sedky
LITTLE MISS DEVIL(1951, Egypt)

Marcela Sedlackova
DO YOU KEEP A LION AT HOME?(1966, Czech.)

Mike Sedlak
GROUND ZERO(1973), m

Bruce Sedley
OUTLAWS IS COMING, THE(1965)

Gerri Sedley
Misc. Talkies
TEENAGE HITCHHIKERS(1975), d

Henry Sedley
GHOST TALKS, THE(1929); TRANSATLANTIC(1931); ONE-MAN LAW(1932); INTERNATIONAL HOUSE(1933); COCKEYED CAVALIERS(1934)
Silents
EMBARRASSMENT OF RICHES, THE(1918); JUST FOR TONIGHT(1918); NOBODY(1921); SILVER LINING, THE(1921); STRAIGHT IS THE WAY(1921); WOMAN GOD CHANGED, THE(1921); JOHN SMITH(1922); DEVIL'S PARTNER, THE(1923); EXCITERS, THE(1923); LIGHT IN THE WINDOW, THE(1927); MARRIED ALIVE(1927); ONE HOUR OF LOVE(1927); WEB OF FATE(1927); MY HOME TOWN(1928); OBEY YOUR HUSBAND(1928)

Misc. Silents
LIFE IN THE ORANGE GROVES(1920); VOICES(1920); BROKEN VIOLIN, THE(1923); FOR ANOTHER WOMAN(1924); FOOL, THE(1925); LOST CHORD, THE(1925); WRONG DOERS, THE(1925); BOY OF THE STREETS, A(1927); MILLION DOLLAR MYSTERY(1927); TROPIC MADNESS(1928)

Walter Sedlmayer
FEAR EATS THE SOUL(1974, Ger.)

Betty Sedlmayr
GIRL FROM THE MARSH CROFT, THE(1935, Ger.)

Jim Sedlow
WINDSPLITTER, THE(1971)

Henry Sedly
Silents
RACKET, THE(1928)

Eileen Sedwick
Misc. Silents
BEYOND ALL ODDS(1926)

Josie Sedwick
Misc. Silents
BEYOND THE SHADOWS(1918)

Shannon Sedwick
1984
BLOOD SIMPLE(1984)

I. Sedykh
LULLABY(1961, USSR)

Natasha Sedykh
JACK FROST(1966, USSR)

Chou See-loke
FEMALE PRINCE, THE(1966, Hong Kong), d

Jette Seear
PERFECT COUPLE, A(1979)

Guido Seeber
STORM IN A WATER GLASS(1931, Aust.), ph
Silents
GOLEM: HOW HE CAME INTO THE WORLD, THE(1920, Ger.), ph

Eva Seeberg
DOLL, THE(1964, Swed.), w

Peter Seeberg
HUNGER(1968, Den./Norway/Swed.), w

Alison Seebohm
HARD DAY'S NIGHT, A(1964, Brit.); MURDER MOST FOUL(1964, Brit.); SERVANT, THE(1964, Brit.); PARTY'S OVER, THE(1966, Brit.); RIDE THE HIGH WIND(1967, South Africa)

Alison Seebohn
ALPHABET MURDERS, THE(1966)

Vilaiwan Seeboonreaung
BRIDGE ON THE RIVER KWAI, THE(1957)

Adelheid Seeck
REST IS SILENCE, THE(1960, Ger.); MAEDCHEN IN UNIFORM(1965, Ger./Fr.); DEVIL IN SILK(1968, Ger.)

Paul Seed
HUMAN FACTOR, THE(1979, Brit.)

Albert Seedman
REPORT TO THE COMMISSIONER(1975)

Alice Seedorf
LA BOHEME(1965, Ital.), ed

The Seeds
PSYCH-OUT(1968)

Max Seefelder
COW AND I, THE(1961, Fr., Ital., Ger.), art d; UNWILLING AGENT(1968, Ger.), art d

Kai S. Seefield
NIGHT PORTER, THE(1974, Ital./U.S.)

Barry Seegar
GALAXY EXPRESS(1982, Jap.)

Miriam Seegar
LOVE DOCTOR, THE(1929); BIG MONEY(1930); CLANCY IN WALL STREET(1930); FOX MOVIETONE FOLLIES OF 1930(1930); SEVEN KEYS TO BALDPATE(1930); SUCH IS THE LAW(1930, Brit.); WHAT A MAN(1930); DAWN TRAIL, THE(1931); LION AND THE LAMB(1931); WOMAN BETWEEN(1931); FAMOUS FERGUSON CASE, THE(1932); OUT OF SINGAPORE(1932); STRANGERS OF THE EVENING(1932)
Misc. Silents
PRICE OF DIVORCE, THE(1928, Brit.); VALLEY OF THE GHOSTS(1928, Brit.); WHEN KNIGHTS WERE BOLD(1929, Brit.)

Roy Seegar
MARRIED IN HOLLYWOOD(1929)

Sanford Seegar
NEVER STEAL ANYTHING SMALL(1959)

Sara Seegar
DEAD MEN TELL NO TALES(1939, Brit.); LARCENY STREET(1941, Brit.); MYSTERY OF ROOM 13(1941, Brit.)

Sarah Seegar
MUSIC MAN, THE(1962)

Hal Seeger
HI-DE-HO(1947), w

Miriam Seeger
FASHIONS IN LOVE(1929)

Pete Seeger
GAVILAN(1968), m; ALICE'S RESTAURANT(1969); TELL ME THAT YOU LOVE ME, JUNIE MOON(1970)

Sanford Seeger
FAT ANGELS(1980, U.S./Span.); SURVIVORS, THE(1983)

Michael Seehan
SWARM, THE(1978)

Rosemarie Seehofer
SNOW WHITE AND ROSE RED(1966, Ger.)

Douta Seek
GUTS IN THE SUN(1959, Fr.)

Charles Seel
COMET OVER BROADWAY(1938); OFF THE RECORD(1939); NOT WANTED(1949); MAN WITH THE GOLDEN ARM, THE(1955); I WAS A TEENAGE FRANKENSTEIN(1958); DARK AT THE TOP OF THE STAIRS, THE(1960); NORTH TO ALASKA(1960); PLEASE DON'T EAT THE DAISIES(1960); SERGEANT RUTLEDGE(1960); WALKING TARGET, THE(1960); RETURN TO PEYTON PLACE(1961); MAN WHO SHOT LIBERTY VALANCE, THE(1962); TAMMY AND THE DOCTOR(1963); CHEYENNE AUTUMN(1964); LADY IN A CAGE(1964); CHAMBER OF HORRORS(1966); MISTER BUDDWING(1966); THIS SAVAGE LAND(1969); WINNING(1969); SSSSSSSS(1973); WESTWORLD(1973)

Blossom Seeley
BROADWAY THROUGH A KEYHOLE(1933)

Clinton Seeley
STORM FEAR(1956), w

E.S. Seeley, Jr.
HIDEOUS SUN DEMON, THE(1959), w

James Seeley
Silents
WIDE-OPEN TOWN, A(1922)
Misc. Silents
CHANNING OF THE NORTHWEST(1922)

Jeannie Seeley
HONEYSUCKLE ROSE(1980)

John Seeley
HIDEOUS SUN DEMON, THE(1959), m

Kay Seeley
CONTINENTAL EXPRESS(1939, Brit.)

Kaye Seeley
STOLEN LIFE(1939, Brit.)

Ralph Seeley
SUPER VAN(1977)

Ruth Seeley
DANCE, GIRL, DANCE(1940)

S.K. Seeley
BLONDE SAVAGE(1947), d; AMAZON QUEST(1949), d

Tim Seeley
1984
KIPPERBANG(1984, Brit.)

Eric Seelig
VILLA RIDES(1968), cos; DREAM OF KINGS, A(1969), cos; GUNS OF THE MAGNIFICENT SEVEN(1969), cos; WILLARD(1971), cos; FRIENDS OF EDDIE COYLE, THE(1973), cos; GREATEST, THE(1977, U.S./Brit.), cos; WHITE BUFFALO, THE(1977), cos; DEER HUNTER, THE(1978), cos

Jerry Seelin
CALL ME MISTER(1951), m/l Rome

Charles R. Seeling
Silents
JACK RIDER, THE(1921), d; WESTERN FIREBRANDS(1921), d; $1,000 REWARD(1923), d; AVENGER, THE(1924), d; EAGLE'S CLAW, THE(1924), d
Misc. Silents
VENGEANCE TRAIL, THE(1921), d; ACROSS THE BORDER(1922), d; COWBOY KING, THE(1922), d; ROUNDING UP THE LAW(1922), d; APACHE DANCER, THE(1923), d; CYCLONE JONES(1923), d; END OF THE ROPE(1923), d; MYSTERIOUS GOODS(1923), d; PURPLE DAWN(1923), d; TANGO CAVALIER(1923), d; DEEDS OF DARING(1924), d; STOP AT NOTHING(1924), d; YANKEE MADNESS(1924), d

Blossom Seely
BLOOD MONEY(1933)

Donald Seely
YANK IN VIET-NAM, A(1964)

Kay Seely
JENIFER HALE(1937, Brit.)

Kaye Seely
MOUNTAINS O'MOURNE(1938, Brit.)

Tim Seely
PLEASE TURN OVER(1960, Brit.); POACHER'S DAUGHTER, THE(1960, Brit.); MUTINY ON THE BOUNTY(1962); AGATHA(1979, Brit.)
1984
LAUGHTER HOUSE(1984, Brit.)

George Seemer
WORLD'S GREATEST SINNER, THE(1962)

Johnny Seemonell [Giovanni Simonelli]
TOMB OF TORTURE(1966, Ital.), w

Anna Seerattan
Misc. Talkies
BIM(1976)

Bud Seese
1984
BIRDY(1984)

Dorothy Seese
LONG GRAY LINE, THE(1955)

Dorothy Ann Seese
FIVE LITTLE PEPPERS AND HOW THEY GREW(1939); DOCTOR TAKES A WIFE(1940); FIVE LITTLE PEPPERS AT HOME(1940); FIVE LITTLE PEPPERS IN TROUBLE(1940); MEET THE MISSUS(1940); OUT WEST WITH THE PEPPERS(1940); BLONDIE'S BLESSED EVENT(1942)
Misc. Talkies
LET'S HAVE FUN(1943)

Charles O. Seessel
Silents
WAY DOWN EAST(1920), art d; SILVER LINING, THE(1921), set d; CLOTHES MAKE THE PIRATE(1925), art d

Charles Osborne Seessel
Silents
SONNY(1922), art d

Linda Seff
HAMLET(1964)
Mannie Seff
WOMAN CHASES MAN(1937), w
Manny Seff
FALCON OUT WEST, THE(1944), w; JAM SESSION(1944), w; SAILOR'S HOLI-DAY(1944), w; HITCHHIKE TO HAPPINESS(1945), w; FALCON'S ALIBI, THE(1946), w; WALK SOFTLY, STRANGER(1950), w
Manuel Seff
BLESSED EVENT(1932), w; COLLEGE COACH(1933), w; FOOTLIGHT PARA-DE(1933), w; GIRL IN 419(1933), w; TERROR ABOARD(1933), w; BEDSIDE(1934), w; EASY TO LOVE(1934), w; HOUSEWIFE(1934), w; KANSAS CITY PRINCESS(1934), w; SIDE STREETS(1934), w; GOLD DIGGERS OF 1935(1935), w; NIGHT AT THE RITZ, A(1935), w; RED SALUTE(1935), w; TRAVELING SALESLADY, THE(1935), w; LOVE ON THE RUN(1936), w; THREE GODFATHERS(1936), w; TROUBLE FOR TWO(1936), w; ESPIONAGE(1937), w; LET'S MAKE A MILLION(1937), w; BREAK-ING THE ICE(1938), w; SLIGHTLY TEMPTED(1940), w; MARRIED BA-CHELOR(1941), w; UNMASKED(1950), w
Nanny Seff
LOUISIANA HAYRIDE(1944), w
Richard Seff
DIFFERENT STORY, A(1978); WHERE THE BUFFALO ROAM(1980)
Carol Seflinger
STORY ON PAGE ONE, THE(1959); LOLLIPOP COVER, THE(1965); JOHNNY TIGER(1966)
Misc. Talkies
SWEATER GIRLS(1978)
Ernest Seftig
THEY WERE EXPENDABLE(1945)
Ernest Sefto
SILENT BARRIERS(1937, Brit.)
Ernest Sefton
OLD SPANISH CUSTOMERS(1932, Brit.); WHY SAPS LEAVE HOME(1932, Brit.); BERMONDSEY KID, THE(1933, Brit.); BRITANNIA OF BILLINGSGATE(1933, Brit.); ENEMY OF THE POLICE(1933, Brit.); GREAT STUFF(1933, Brit.); I ADORE YOU(1933, Brit.); I'LL STICK TO YOU(1933, Brit.); LITTLE MISS NOBODY(1933, Brit.); STRIKE IT RICH(1933, Brit.); BIG BUSINESS(1934, Brit.); GIRL IN POSSES-SION(1934, Brit.); THIRD CLUE, THE(1934, Brit.); HELLO SWEETHEART(1935, Brit.); MURDER AT MONTE CARLO(1935, Brit.); NO LIMIT(1935, Brit.); SAY IT WITH DIAMONDS(1935, Brit.); SHE SHALL HAVE MUSIC(1935, Brit.); STRICTLY ILLE-GAL(1935, Brit.); BROKEN BLOSSOMS(1936, Brit.); CHEER UP!(1936, Brit.); IT'S IN THE BAG(1936, Brit.); MILLIONS(1936, Brit.); WOLF'S CLOTHING(1936, Brit.); DR. SIN FANG(1937, Brit.); FATAL HOUR, THE(1937, Brit.); JENIFER HALE(1937, Brit.); LITTLE MISS SOMEBODY(1937, Brit.); WHO KILLED FEN MARKHAM?(1937, Brit.); BAD BOY(1938, Brit.); I SEE ICE(1938); OLD MOTHER RILEY IN BUSINESS(1940, Brit.); THAT'S THE TICKET(1940, Brit.); OLD MOTHER RILEY'S CIRCUS(1941, Brit.); HERE COMES THE SUN(1945, Brit.); GRAND ESCAPADE, THE(1946, Brit.)
Alex Segal
RANSOM(1956), d; ALL THE WAY HOME(1963), d; HARLOW(1965), d; JOY IN THE MORNING(1965), d
Boris Segal
HELICOPTER SPIES, THE(1968), d
D. Segal
UNIVERSITY OF LIFE(1941, USSR)
David Segal
TEL AVIV TAXI(1957, Israel)
Eric Segal
GAMES, THE(1970), w
Erich Segal
YELLOW SUBMARINE(1958, Brit.), w; LOVE STORY(1970), w; R.P.M.(1970), w; JENNIFER ON MY MIND(1971), a, w; WITHOUT APPARENT MOTIVE(1972, Fr.); OLIVER'S STORY(1978), w; CHANGE OF SEASONS, A(1980), w; MAN, WOMAN AND CHILD(1983), w
Francine Segal
CAT PEOPLE(1982)
Fred Segal
SEPARATE PEACE, A(1972), w; CHANGE OF SEASONS, A(1980), w
George Segal
YOUNG DOCTORS, THE(1961); LONGEST DAY, THE(1962); ACT ONE(1964); INVI-TATION TO A GUNFIGHTER(1964); NEW INTERNS, THE(1964); KING RAT(1965); SHIP OF FOOLS(1965); LOST COMMAND, THE(1966); QUILLER MEMORANDUM, THE(1966, Brit.); WHO'S AFRAID OF VIRGINIA WOOLF?(1966); ST. VALENTINE'S DAY MASSACRE, THE(1967); BYE BYE BRAVERMAN(1968); NO WAY TO TREAT A LADY(1968); UNSTRAP ME(1968); BRIDGE AT REMAGEN, THE(1969); GIRL WHO COULDN'T SAY NO, THE(1969, Ital.); SOUTHERN STAR, THE(1969, Fr./Brit.); LOVING(1970); OWL AND THE PUSSYCAT, THE(1970); WHERE'S POPPA?(1970); BORN TO WIN(1971); HOT ROCK, THE(1972); BLUME IN LOVE(1973); TOUCH OF CLASS, A(1973, Brit.); CALIFORNIA SPLIT(1974); TERMINAL MAN, THE(1974); BLACK BIRD, THE(1975); RUSSIAN ROULETTE(1975); DUCHESS AND THE DIRT-WATER FOX, THE(1976); FUN WITH DICK AND JANE(1977); ROLLERCOAST-ER(1977); WHO IS KILLING THE GREAT CHEFS OF EUROPE?(1978, US/Ger.); LOST AND FOUND(1979); LAST MARRIED COUPLE IN AMERICA, THE(1980); CARBON COPY(1981)
Misc. Talkies
DEADLY GAMES(1982)
Gilles Segal
TOPKAPI(1964); MADWOMAN OF CHAILLOT, THE(1969); WALK WITH LOVE AND DEATH, A(1969); CONFESSION, THE(1970, Fr.); WITHOUT APPARENT MO-TIVE(1972, Fr.)
Harry Segal
FOR HEAVEN'S SAKE(1950), w
Howard Segal
Misc. Talkies
LAST GAME, THE(1983)
Helen Segal
UNSTRAP ME(1968)
Israel Segal
DREAMER, THE(1970, Israel)

Jeffrey Segal
TRAITORS, THE(1963, Brit.)
Jerry Segal
ONE ON ONE(1977), w; DIE LAUGHING(1980), w, m
John Segal
1984
SECRET PLACES(1984, Brit.)
Kathrin King Segal
WITHOUT A TRACE(1983)
Marion Segal
CARBON COPY(1981), ed
Marvin Segal
TOKYO AFTER DARK(1959), p, w
Michael Segal
HIDE AND SEEK(1964, Brit.); CONQUEROR WORM, THE(1968, Brit.); BLACK WINDMILL, THE(1974, Brit.); NOTHING BUT THE NIGHT(1975, Brit.); CAND-LESHOE(1978); PRISONER OF ZENDA, THE(1979)
Misha Segal
1984
NINJA III–THE DOMINATION(1984), m
Moshe Segal
DREAMER, THE(1970, Israel)
Nicholas Segal
1984
BREAKIN' 2: ELECTRIC BOOGALOO(1984)
Sam Segal
PASSION HOLIDAY(1963)
Samuel Segal
CANTOR'S SON, THE(1937), p; EXODUS(1960)
Stephanie Segal
MAKING LOVE(1982)
Stuart A. Segal
SPEEDTRAP(1978), w
Vivienne Segal
BRIDE OF THE REGIMENT(1930); GOLDEN DAWN(1930); SONG OF THE WEST(1930); VIENNESE NIGHTS(1930); CAT AND THE FIDDLE(1934)
Y. Segal
CAPTAIN GRANT'S CHILDREN(1939, USSR)
Zohra Segal
LONG DUEL, THE(1967, Brit.); VENGEANCE OF SHE, THE(1968, Brit.); TALES THAT WITNESS MADNESS(1973, Brit.)
Gianna Segale
ROMAN HOLIDAY(1953); LOVE SLAVES OF THE AMAZONS(1957); GUILT IS NOT MINE(1968, Ital.)
Bernardo Segall
GREAT ST. LOUIS BANK ROBBERY, THE(1959), m; LUCK OF GINGER COFFEY, THE(1964, U.S./Can.), m, md; HALLUCINATION GENERATION(1966), m; CUSTER OF THE WEST(1968, U.S., Span.), m; LOVING(1970), m; JESUS TRIP, THE(1971), m; HOMEBODIES(1974), m
Colette Segall
POIL DE CAROTTE(1932, Fr.)
Harry Segall
UNCERTAIN LADY(1934), w; BABY FACE HARRINGTON(1935), w; DON'T TURN-'EM LOOSE(1936), w; FATAL LADY(1936), w; FIGHT FOR YOUR LADY(1937), w; OUTCASTS OF POKER FLAT, THE(1937), w; SUPER SLEUTH(1937), w; THERE GOES MY GIRL(1937), w; BLIND ALIBI(1938), w; BLOND CHEAT(1938), w; EVERY-BODY'S DOING IT(1938), w; SHE'S GOT EVERYTHING(1938), w; COAST GUARD(1939), w; LONE WOLF STRIKES, THE(1940), w; HERE COMES MR. JOR-DAN(1941), w; SHE KNEW ALL THE ANSWERS(1941), w; POWERS GIRL, THE(1942), w; TWO YANKS IN TRINIDAD(1942), w; WIFE TAKES A FLYER, THE(1942), w; ANGEL ON MY SHOULDER(1946), w; BRIDE WORE BOOTS, THE(1946), w; DOWN TO EARTH(1947), w; MONKEY BUSINESS(1952), w; HEAVEN CAN WAIT(1978), w
Pamela Segall
GREASE 2(1982)
1984
BAD MANNERS(1984)
Ricky Segall
LAST MARRIED COUPLE IN AMERICA, THE(1980)
Stuart Segall
DRIVE-IN MASSACRE(1976), p&d
Misc. Talkies
C.B. HUSTLERS(1978), d
Stillman Segar
LAST OF THE FAST GUNS, THE(1958); SIERRA BARON(1958)
Stilman Segar
DALTON THAT GOT AWAY(1960)
Stim Segar
RAGE(1966, U.S./Mex.)
Giancarlo Segarelli
LOVE PROBLEMS(1970, Ital.), p
Hiroshi Segawa
WOMAN IN THE DUNES(1964, Jap.), ph; FACE OF ANOTHER, THE(1967, Jap.), ph
Junichi Segawa
THREE WEEKS OF LOVE(1965), ph
Shoji Segawa
TOPSY-TURVY JOURNEY(1970, Jap.), d; YOSAKOI JOURNEY(1970, Jap.), d
Stephanie Segel
1984
LONELY GUY, THE(1984)
Yakov Segel
DAY THE WAR ENDED, THE(1961, USSR), d; FAREWELL, DOVES(1962, USSR), d&w
Tore Segelcke
FACE TO FACE(1976, Swed.)
Lucia Seger
BOOMERANG(1947)

Lucia Backus Seger
EAST SIDE SADIE(1929)
Silents
WILD GOOSE, THE(1921); KNOCKOUT REILLY(1927)
Misc. Silents
BROTH FOR SUPPER(1919)
Gosta Segercrantz
Silents
WATCH YOUR WIFE(1926), w
Armand Seggian
MICHELLE(1970, Fr.), m
Zohra Seghal
GURU, THE(1969, U.S./India)
Anna Seghers
SEVENTH CROSS, THE(1944), w
Michele Seghers
BAND OF OUTSIDERS(1966, Fr.)
Paul Segnitz
SLIPPER EPISODE, THE(1938, Fr), m
Alfredo Segoviano
GOD FORGIVES–I DON'T!(1969, Ital./Span.), spec eff
Ric Segreto
1984
MISSING IN ACTION(1984)
Aldo Segri
NIGHTS OF LUCRETIA BORGIA, THE(1960, Ital.), w
Sebastian Segriff
LAST REBEL, THE(1971)
Shoshana Seguev
MATTER OF DAYS, A(1969, Fr./Czech.)
Pierre Segui
DEER HUNTER, THE(1978)
Horace Seguira
ROOMMATES(1962, Brit.)
Roland Segur
MARTIAN IN PARIS, A(1961, Fr.)
Francisco Segura
CURSE OF THE AZTEC MUMMY, THE(1965, Mex.); ROBOT VS. THE AZTEC MUMMY, THE(1965, Mex.)
Gregorio Garcia Segura
DEVIL MADE A WOMAN, THE(1962, Span.), m; SON OF CAPTAIN BLOOD, THE(1964, U.S./Ital./Span.), m; DRUMS OF TABU(1967, Ital./Span.), m; FICKLE FINGER OF FATE, THE(1967, Span./U.S.), m; TALL WOMEN, THE(1967, Aust./Ital./Span.), m; MADIGAN'S MILLIONS(1970, Span./Ital), m
D. A. Segurd
MAN COULD GET KILLED, A(1966)
Antonio Segurini
STORY OF JOSEPH AND HIS BRETHREN THE(1962, Ital.); GIDGET GOES TO ROME(1963)
Nino Segurini
TIGER AND THE PUSSYCAT, THE(1967, U.S., Ital.); SHOCK TROOPS(1968, Ital./Fr.)
Andres De Segurola
Misc. Silents
LOVE OF SUNYA, THE(1927)
Ove H. Sehested
WORLD'S GREATEST SINNER, THE(1962), ph
August Sehven
ENCOUNTER WITH THE UNKNOWN(1973)
Lynn Seibel
ZAPPED!(1982)
Mary Seibel
WEDDING, A(1978)
Matayas Seiber
MALAGA(1962, Brit.), m, md
Matyas Seiber
DIAMOND WIZARD, THE(1954, Brit.), m; ANIMAL FARM(1955, Brit.), m; CHASE A CROOKED SHADOW(1958, Brit.), m; MARK OF THE HAWK, THE(1958), m; ROBBERY UNDER ARMS(1958, Brit.), m, md; TOWN LIKE ALICE, A(1958, Brit.), m
Mary Anne Seibert
COME BACK BABY(1968)
Arthur Seid
THUNDERING FRONTIER(1940), ed; OUTLAWS OF THE PANHANDLE(1941), ed; SING FOR YOUR SUPPER(1941), ed; TIME OUT FOR RHYTHM(1941), ed; TWO LATINS FROM MANHATTAN(1941), ed; BOSTON BLACKIE GOES HOLLYWOOD(1942), ed; HELLO ANNAPOLIS(1942), ed; LUCKY LEGS(1942), ed; MAN WHO RETURNED TO LIFE, THE(1942), ed; UNDERGROUND AGENT(1942), ed; UNKNOWN, THE(1946), ed; FORCE OF EVIL(1948), ed; HERE COMES TROUBLE(1948), ed; WHO KILLED "DOC" ROBBIN?(1948), ed; WALKING TALL, PART II(1975), ed; MONKEY HUSTLE, THE(1976), ed
Earl Seid
SUBWAY EXPRESS(1931)
Sylvia Bernstein Seid
Silents
LARIAT KID, THE(1929), w; ROYAL RIDER, THE(1929), w
Tauhma Seid
GONE ARE THE DAYS(1963), cos
Tom Seidal
TAHITI HONEY(1943)
Joseph Seide
MORGAN'S MARAUDERS(1929), ed
Adolph Seidel
BIG HOUSE, THE(1930)
Ileana Seidel
Misc. Talkies
BEACH HOUSE(1982)
Louise Seidel
ST. LOUIS KID, THE(1934); CEILNG ZERO(1935); STRANDED(1935); COCOANUT GROVE(1938); YOU AND ME(1938); ZAZA(1939); FORTY LITTLE MOTHERS(1940)

Tim Seidel
Misc. Talkies
GHOST RIDER, THE(1943)
Tom Seidel
DAWN PATROL, THE(1938); GONE WITH THE WIND(1939); 20,000 MEN A YEAR(1939); DIVE BOMBER(1941); MODEL WIFE(1941); RIDING THE SUNSET TRAIL(1941); UNHOLY PARTNERS(1941); WANDERERS OF THE WEST(1941); FLYING TIGERS(1942); MAN WITH TWO LIVES, THE(1942); SWEETHEART OF THE FLEET(1942); WESTWARD HO(1942); FALSE COLORS(1943); MARGIN FOR ERROR(1943); SALUTE FOR THREE(1943); SOMEONE TO REMEMBER(1943); YANKS AHOY(1943); MOONLIGHT AND CACTUS(1944); LIFE OF HER OWN, A(1950)
Tommy Seidel
GOOD GIRLS GO TO PARIS(1939); TOM, DICK AND HARRY(1941); HARVARD, HERE I COME(1942); MY GAL SAL(1942); PRISONER OF JAPAN(1942)
Toscha Seidel
MELODY FOR THREE(1941)
Arthur A. Seidelman
HERCULES IN NEW YORK(1970), d
Arthur Allan Seidelman
CHILDREN OF RAGE(1975, Brit.-Israeli), d&w; ECHOES(1983), d
Susan Seidelman
SMITHEREENS(1982), p&d, w, ed
Conrad Seideman
SWISS MISS(1938)
Conrad Seidemann
RIP TIDE(1934)
Joseph Seiden
MOTEL, THE OPERATOR(1940), p&d
Misc. Talkies
KOL NIDRE(1939), d; LIVING ORPHAN, THE(1939), d; PARADISE IN HARLEM(1939), d; GREATER ADVISOR, THE(1940), d; HER SECOND MOTHER(1940), d; JEWISH MELODY, THE(1940), d; MAZEL TOV, JEWS(1941), d; GOD, MAN AND DEVIL(1949), d
Joseph Seiden
Misc. Talkies
THREE DAUGHTERS(1949), d
Leon Seidenberg
MOTHERS OF TODAY(1939)
Maurice Seiderman
ZOMBIES ON BROADWAY(1945), makeup; LOOK IN ANY WINDOW(1961), makeup; THEY SAVED HITLER'S BRAIN(1964), makeup
Conrad Seidermann
FOLIES DERGERE(1935)
Leon Seiditz
DRANGO(1957), ed
Ferard Seidl
LITTLE BOY LOST(1953)
Lea Seidl
CANDLELIGHT IN ALGERIA(1944, Brit.); WOMAN'S ANGLE, THE(1954, Brit.); I AM A CAMERA(1955, Brit.); WAR AND PEACE(1956, Ital./U.S.); I AIM AT THE STARS(1960); GREAT CATHERINE(1968, Brit.)
Alma Seidler
GOOD SOLDIER SCHWEIK, THE(1963, Ger.)
Maren Seidler
PERSONAL BEST(1982)
Maria Seidler
GIRL FROM THE MARSH CROFT, THE(1935, Ger.)
Magda Seidlerova
END OF AUGUST AT THE HOTEL OZONE, THE(1967, Czech.)
Arie Seidman
HILL 24 DOESN'T ANSWER(1955, Israel)
Robert Seidman
1984
ALPHABET CITY(1984), w; VAMPING(1984), w
Irene Seidner
WE WHO ARE YOUNG(1940); ALL THROUGH THE NIGHT(1942); BACKGROUND TO DANGER(1943); PURPLE V, THE(1943); THREE MUSKETEERS, THE(1948); GREAT SINNER, THE(1949); DAUGHTER OF ROSIE O'GRADY, THE(1950); PEOPLE WILL TALK(1951); VICKI(1953); MIRACLE IN THE RAIN(1956); GARMENT JUNGLE, THE(1957); 10 NORTH FREDERICK(1958)
Marian Seidowsky
YOUNG TORLESS(1968, Fr./Ger.)
Kurt Seifert
INTERMEZZO(1937, Ger.)
Bernard Seigel
Silents
ROMANCE RANCH(1924); FREEDOM OF THE PRESS(1928)
Misc. Silents
DIVINE SINNER(1928)
David Seigel
JOKER IS WILD, THE(1957)
Matt Seigel
FOXY LADY(1971, Can.), w
Terri Seigel
TUNNELVISION(1976)
Al Seiger
RENEGADES OF THE WEST(1932), ph
Reinhold Seigert
NO TIME FOR FLOWERS(1952)
Al Seigler
AGAINST THE LAW(1934), ph; BLIND DATE(1934), ph; FUGITIVE LADY(1934), ph; BLACK ROOM, THE(1935), ph; PARTY WIRE(1935), ph
Allen Seigler
MILLS OF THE GODS(1935), ph
Allen E. Seigler
BLACKMAILER(1936), ph
Allen G. Seigler
KILLER AT LARGE(1936), ph; ROAMING LADY(1936), ph; TRAPPED BY TELEVISION(1936), ph; TRAPPED(1937), ph; PASSAGE FROM HONG KONG(1941), ph

Seigner
ENTENTE CORDIALE(1939, Fr.)

Francoise Seigner
WILD CHILD, THE(1970, Fr.); LES MISERABLES(1982, Fr.)

Louis Seigner
ETERNAL HUSBAND, THE(1946, Fr.); RAVEN, THE(1948, Fr.); ANGELS OF THE STREETS(1950, Fr.); LUCRECE BORGIA(1953, Ital./Fr.); SEVEN DEADLY SINS, THE(1953, Fr./Ital.); LE PLAISIR(1954, Fr.); HOLIDAY FOR HENRIETTA(1955, Fr.); ROYAL AFFAIRS IN VERSAILLES(1957, Fr.); NATHALIE(1958, Fr.); WOULD-BE GENTLEMAN, THE(1960, Fr.); TRUTH, THE(1961, Fr./Ital.); ECLIPSE(1962, Fr./Ital.); MOST WANTED MAN, THE(1962, Fr./Ital.); PRICE OF FLESH, THE(1962, Fr.); MARRIAGE OF FIGARO, THE(1963, Fr.); THIS SPECIAL FRIENDSHIP(1967, Fr.); LES MISERABLES(1982, Fr.)

Louis Seignier
GYPSY FURY(1950, Fr.); HENRIETTE'S HOLIDAY(1953, Fr.)

K.J. Seijto
STOPOVER TOKYO(1957)

Conrad Seiler
REDHEAD(1941), w

Heinrich Seiler
HIPPODROME(1961, Aust./Ger.), w

Jacques Seiler
SWEET AND SOUR(1964, Fr./Ital.); VICE AND VIRTUE(1965, Fr./Ital.); CHAPPAQUA(1967)

Lew Seiler
AIR CIRCUS, THE(1928), d; GHOST TALKS, THE(1929), d; MEN WITHOUT LAW(1930), w; DECEPTION(1933), d; FRONTIER MARSHAL(1934), d; HE COULDN'T SAY NO(1938), d

Lewis Seiler
SONG OF KENTUCKY(1929), d; NO GREATER LOVE(1932), d; CHARLIE CHAN IN PARIS(1935), d; GINGER(1935), d; PADDY O'DAY(1935), d; CAREER WOMAN(1936), d; FIRST BABY(1936), d; HERE COMES TROUBLE(1936), d; STAR FOR A NIGHT(1936), d; TURN OFF THE MOON(1937), d; CRIME SCHOOL(1938), d; HEART OF THE NORTH(1938), d; PENROD'S DOUBLE TROUBLE(1938), d; DUST BE MY DESTINY(1939), d; HELL'S KITCHEN(1939), d; KID FROM KOKOMO(1939), d; KING OF THE UNDERWORLD(1939), d; YOU CAN'T GET AWAY WITH MURDER(1939), d; FLIGHT ANGELS(1940), d; IT ALL CAME TRUE(1940), d; MURDER IN THE AIR(1940), d; SOUTH OF SUEZ(1940), d; TUGBOAT ANNIE SAILS AGAIN(1940), d; KISSES FOR BREAKFAST(1941), d; SMILING GHOST, THE(1941), d; YOU'RE IN THE ARMY NOW(1941), d; BIG SHOT, THE(1942), d; PITTSBURGH(1942), d; GUADALCANAL DIARY(1943), d; SOMETHING FOR THE BOYS(1944), d; DOLL FACE(1945), d; MOLLY AND ME(1945), d; IF I'M LUCKY(1946), d; WHIPLASH(1948), d; BREAKTHROUGH(1950), d; TANKS ARE COMING, THE(1951), d; OPERATION SECRET(1952), d; WINNING TEAM, THE(1952), d; SYSTEM, THE(1953), d; BAMBOO PRISON, THE(1955), d; WOMEN'S PRISON(1955), d; BATTLE STATIONS(1956), d; OVER-EXPOSED(1956), d; TRUE STORY OF LYNN STUART, THE(1958), d
Silents
GREAT K & A TRAIN ROBBERY, THE(1926), d; NO MAN'S GOLD(1926), d; LAST TRAIL, THE(1927), d; OUTLAWS OF RED RIVER(1927), d; TUMBLING RIVER(1927), d; GIRLS GONE WILD(1929), d
Misc. Silents
DARWIN WAS RIGHT(1924), d; WOLF FANGS(1927), d; SQUARE CROOKS(1928), d

William Seiler
BIG BUSINESS GIRL(1931), d

Kenneth Seiling
SEED(1931); NICE WOMAN(1932)

Mona Seilitz
HOUR OF THE WOLF, THE(1968, Swed.)

Frank Seiman
NORMAN CONQUEST(1953, Brit.)

Erich Seipmann
I STAND CONDEMNED(1936, Brit.), w

Christian Seipolt
DAS BOOT(1982)

Bal Seirgakar
BWANA DEVIL(1953)

Michael Seirton
GANDHI(1982), set d
1984
FINDERS KEEPERS(1984), set d

Carline Seisser
DIE HAMBURGER KRANKHEIT(1979, Ger./Fr.)

Robert Seiter
PUBLIC AFFAIR, A(1962), ed
Silents
OUT ALL NIGHT(1927); CHICAGO AFTER MIDNIGHT(1928); RED LIPS(1928)

Robert S. Seiter
ONLY THE VALIANT(1951), ed

William Seiter
CAUGHT PLASTERED(1931), d; TOO MANY COOKS(1931), d; HOT SATURDAY(1932), d; IS MY FACE RED?(1932), d; CHANCE AT HEAVEN(1933), d; HELLO, EVERYBODY(1933), d; PROFESSIONAL SWEETHEART(1933), d; RAFTER ROMANCE(1934), d; IF YOU COULD ONLY COOK(1936), d; DEAR BRAT(1951), d
Silents
LITTLE CHURCH AROUND THE CORNER(1923), d; FAMILY SECRET, THE(1924), d
Misc. Silents
BELL BOY 13(1923), d; FAST WORKER, THE(1924), d; HIS FORGOTTEN WIFE(1924), d; WHITE SIN, THE(1924), d

William A. Seiter
FOOTLIGHTS AND FOOLS(1929), d; LOVE RACKET, THE(1929), d; PRISONERS(1929), d; SMILING IRISH EYES(1929), d; BACK PAY(1930), d; FLIRTING WIDOW, THE(1930), d; STRICTLY MODERN(1930), d; SUNNY(1930), d; TRUTH ABOUT YOUTH, THE(1930), d; GOING WILD(1931), d; KISS ME AGAIN(1931), d; PEACH O' RENO(1931), d; GIRL CRAZY(1932), d; IF I HAD A MILLION(1932), d; WAY BACK HOME(1932), d; YOUNG BRIDE(1932), d; DIPLOMANIACS(1933), d; SONS OF THE DESERT(1933), d; LOVE BIRDS(1934), d; RICHEST GIRL IN THE WORLD, THE(1934), d; SING AND LIKE IT(1934), d; WE'RE RICH AGAIN(1934), d;

DARING YOUNG MAN, THE(1935), d; IN PERSON(1935), d; ORCHIDS TO YOU(1935), d; ROBERTA(1935), d; CASE AGAINST MRS. AMES, THE(1936), d; DIMPLES(1936), d; MOON'S OUR HOME, THE(1936), d; STOWAWAY(1936), d; LIFE BEGINS IN COLLEGE(1937), d; LIFE OF THE PARTY, THE(1937), d; ROOM SERVICE(1938), d; THANKS FOR EVERYTHING(1938), d; THREE BLIND MICE(1938), d; ALLEGHENY UPRISING(1939), d; SUSANNAH OF THE MOUNTIES(1939), d; HIRED WIFE(1940), d; IT'S A DATE(1940), d; APPOINTMENT FOR LOVE(1941), d; NICE GIRL?(1941), d; BROADWAY(1942), d; YOU WERE NEVER LOVELIER(1942), d; DESTROYER(1943), d; LADY TAKES A CHANCE, A(1943), d; BELLE OF THE YUKON(1944), p&d; FOUR JILLS IN A JEEP(1944), d; AFFAIRS OF SUSAN(1945), d; IT'S A PLEASURE(1945), d; THAT NIGHT WITH YOU(1945), d; LITTLE GIANT(1946), d; LOVER COME BACK(1946), d; I'LL BE YOURS(1947), d; ONE TOUCH OF VENUS(1948), d; UP IN CENTRAL PARK(1948), d; BORDERLINE(1950), p, d; CHAMP FOR A DAY(1953), p; LADY WANTS MINK, THE(1953), p&d; MAKE HASTE TO LIVE(1954), d
Silents
BEAUTIFUL AND DAMNED, THE(1922), d; GAY AND DEVILISH(1922), d; HELEN'S BABIES(1924), d; ROLLING HOME(1926), d; SKINNER'S DRESS SUIT(1926), d; TAKE IT FROM ME(1926), d; WHAT HAPPENED TO JONES(1926), d; OUT ALL NIGHT(1927), d; OUTCAST(1928), d; THANKS FOR THE BUGGY RIDE(1928), d; WHY BE GOOD?(1929), d
Misc. Silents
KENTUCKY COLONEL, THE(1920), d; EDEN AND RETURN(1921), d; FOOLISH AGE, THE(1921), d; HEARTS AND MASKS(1921), d; PASSING THRU(1921), d; BOY CRAZY(1922), d; UNDERSTUDY, THE(1922), d; UP AND AT 'EM(1922), d; WHEN LOVE COMES(1922), d; DADDIES(1924), d; LISTEN LESTER(1924), d; DANGEROUS INNOCENCE(1925), d; MAD WHIRL, THE(1925), d; TEASER, THE(1925), d; WHERE WAS I?(1925), d; CHEERFUL FRAUD, THE(1927), d; SMALL BACHELOR, THE(1927), d; GOOD MORNING JUDGE(1928), d; HAPPINESS AHEAD(1928), d; WATERFRONT(1928), d; SYNTHETIC SIN(1929), d

William S. Seiter
THIS IS MY AFFAIR(1937), d; SALLY, IRENE AND MARY(1938), d

Leon Seith
HAWMPS!(1976), ed; FOR THE LOVE OF BENJI(1977), ed; THE DOUBLE McGUFFIN(1979), ed; OH, HEAVENLY DOG!(1980), ed

Seitz
IMPERFECT LADY, THE(1947), ph

Cathy Seitz
HILDUR AND THE MAGICIAN(1969)

Chris Seitz
COME SEPTEMBER(1961)

Dran Seitz
I, THE JURY(1953)

Franz Seitz
YOUNG TORLESS(1968, Fr./Ger.), p; PEDESTRIAN, THE(1974, Ger.); DISORDER AND EARLY TORMENT(1977, Ger.), p&d, w; TIN DRUM, THE(1979, Ger./Fr./Yugo./Pol.), p, w

George Seitz
ABSOLUTE QUIET(1936), d

George B. Seitz
YELLOW JACK(1938), d; CIRCUS KID, THE(1928), d; BLOCKADE(1929), d; DANGER LIGHTS(1930), d; GUILTY?(1930), d; MIDNIGHT MYSTERY(1930), d; MURDER ON THE ROOF(1930), d; DRUMS OF JEOPARDY(1931), d; LION AND THE LAMB(1931), d; MEN ARE LIKE THAT(1931), d; SHANGHAIED LOVE(1931), d; BEHIND STONE WALLS(1932), w; DOCKS OF SAN FRANCISCO(1932), d; NIGHT BEAT(1932), d; SIN'S PAYDAY(1932), d; WIDOW IN SCARLET(1932), d; THRILL HUNTER, THE(1933), d; ABOVE THE CLOUDS(1934), w; FIGHTING RANGER, THE(1934), d; FUGITIVE LOVERS(1934), w; LAZY RIVER(1934), d; WOMEN IN HIS LIFE, THE(1934), d; CALM YOURSELF(1935), d; KIND LADY(1935), d; SHADOW OF A DOUBT(1935), d; SOCIETY DOCTOR(1935), d; TIMES SQUARE LADY(1935), d; WOMAN WANTED(1935), d; EXCLUSIVE STORY(1936), d; LAST OF THE MOHICANS, THE(1936), d; MAD HOLIDAY(1936), d; THREE WISE GUYS, THE(1936), d; BETWEEN TWO WOMEN(1937), d; FAMILY AFFAIR, A(1937), d; MY DEAR MISS ALDRICH(1937), d; THIRTEENTH CHAIR, THE(1937), d; UNDER COVER OF NIGHT(1937), d; JUDGE HARDY'S CHILDREN(1938), d; LOVE FINDS ANDY HARDY(1938), d; OUT WEST WITH THE HARDYS(1938), d; YOU'RE ONLY YOUNG ONCE(1938), d; HARDYS RIDE HIGH, THE(1939), d; JUDGE HARDY AND SON(1939), d; THUNDER AFLOAT(1939), d; 6000 ENEMIES(1939), d; ANDY HARDY MEETS DEBUTANTE(1940), d; GALLANT SONS(1940), d; KIT CARSON(1940), d; SKY MURDER(1940), d; ANDY HARDY'S PRIVATE SECRETARY(1941), d; LIFE BEGINS FOR ANDY HARDY(1941), d; ANDY HARDY'S DOUBLE LIFE(1942), d; COURTSHIP OF ANDY HARDY, THE(1942), d; PIERRE OF THE PLAINS(1942), d; YANK ON THE BURMA ROAD, A(1942), d; ANDY HARDY'S BLONDE TROUBLE(1944), d
Misc. Talkies
PASSPORT TO PARADISE(1932), d; WIDOW IN SCARLET(1932), d; TREASON(1933), d
Silents
KING'S GAME, THE(1916), w; NAULAHKA, THE(1918), w; ICE FLOOD, THE(1926), d; GREAT MAIL ROBBERY, THE(1927), d; ISLE OF FORGOTTEN WOMEN(1927), d; JIM THE CONQUEROR(1927), d; WARNING, THE(1927), d&w; AFTER THE STORM(1928), d; HEY RUBE!(1928), d; RANSOM(1928), d, w
Misc. Silents
ROGUES AND ROMANCE(1920), a, d; 40TH DOOR, THE(1924), d; VANISHING AMERICAN, THE(1925), d; WILD HORSE MESA(1925), d; DESERT GOLD(1926), d; LAST FRONTIER, THE(1926), d; PALS IN PARADISE(1926), d; BLOOD SHIP, THE(1927), d; TIGRESS, THE(1927), d; BEWARE OF BLONDES(1928), d; COURT-MARTIAL(1928), d; BLACK MAGIC(1929), d

George R. Seitz
MAMA STEPS OUT(1937), d

Helma Seitz
ESCAPE FROM EAST BERLIN(1962)

Jane Seitz
1984
NEVERENDING STORY, THE(1984, Ger.), ed

John Seitz
CAREERS(1929), ph; HER PRIVATE LIFE(1929), ph; MOST IMMORAL LADY, A(1929), ph; PAINTED ANGEL, THE(1929), ph; SATURDAY'S CHILDREN(1929), ph; SQUALL, THE(1929), ph; BACK PAY(1930), ph; BAD MAN, THE(1930), ph; IN THE NEXT ROOM(1930), ph; MURDER WILL OUT(1930), ph; ROAD TO PARADISE(1930),

ph; EAST LYNNE(1931), ph; HUSH MONEY(1931), ph; MEN OF THE SKY(1931), ph; MERELY MARY ANN(1931), ph; MISBEHAVING LADIES(1931), ph; OVER THE HILL(1931), ph; RIGHT OF WAY, THE(1931), ph; YOUNG SINNERS(1931), ph; CARELESS LADY(1932), ph; PASSPORT TO HELL(1932), ph; SHE WANTED A MILLIONAIRE(1932), ph; SIX HOURS TO LIVE(1932), ph; ADORABLE(1933), ph; DANGEROUSLY YOURS(1933), ph; LADIES THEY TALK ABOUT(1933), ph; MR. SKITCH(1933), ph; PADDY, THE NEXT BEST THING(1933), ph; ALL MEN ARE ENEMIES(1934), ph; COMING OUT PARTY(1934), ph; MARIE GALANTE(1934), ph; SPRINGTIME FOR HENRY(1934), ph; CAPTAIN JANUARY(1935), ph; CURLY TOP(1935), ph; HELLDORADO(1935), ph; LITTLEST REBEL, THE(1935), ph; ONE MORE SPRING(1935), ph; OUR LITTLE GIRL(1935), ph; REDHEADS ON PARA-DE(1935), ph; COUNTRY DOCTOR, THE(1936), ph; FIFTEEN MAIDEN LANE(1936), ph; NAVY WIFE(1936), ph; POOR LITTLE RICH GIRL(1936), ph; BETWEEN TWO WOMEN(1937), ph; MADAME X(1937), ph; NAVY BLUE AND GOLD(1937), ph; CROWD ROARS, THE(1938), ph; LORD JEFF(1938), ph; LOVE IS A HEADA-CHE(1938), ph; STABLEMATES(1938), ph; BAD LITTLE ANGEL(1939), ph; HARDYS RIDE HIGH, THE(1939), ph; HUCKLEBERRY FINN(1939), ph; 6000 ENEMIES(1939), ph; DR. KILDARE'S CRISIS(1940), ph; DR. KILDARE'S STRANGE CASE(1940), ph; LITTLE BIT OF HEAVEN, A(1940), ph; SULLIVAN'S TRAVELS(1941), ph; FLY BY NIGHT(1942), ph; LUCKY JORDAN(1942), ph; THIS GUN FOR HIRE(1942), ph; CASANOVA BROWN(1944), ph; HOME SWEET HOMICIDE(1946), ph; CALCUT-TA(1947), ph; WILD HARVEST(1947), ph; BEYOND GLORY(1948), ph; BIG CLOCK, THE(1948), ph; ON OUR MERRY WAY(1948), ph; CAPTAIN CAREY, U.S.A(1950), ph; APPOINTMENT WITH DANGER(1951), ph; IRON MISTRESS, THE(1952), ph; SAN FRANCISCO STORY, THE(1952), ph; DESERT LEGION(1953), ph; ROCKET MAN, THE(1954), ph; ROGUE COP(1954), ph; SASKATCHEWAN(1954), ph; MANY RIVERS TO CROSS(1955), ph; MC CONNELL STORY, THE(1955), ph; CRY IN THE NIGHT, A(1956), ph; HELL ON FRISCO BAY(1956), ph; SANTIAGO(1956), ph; BIG LAND, THE(1957), ph; BADLANDERS, THE(1958), ph; DEEP SIX, THE(1958), ph; ISLAND OF LOST WOMEN(1959), ph; MAN IN THE NET, THE(1959), ph; GUNS OF THE TIMBERLAND(1960), ph; OUTSIDER, THE(1980); PROWLER, THE(1981)
1984
HARD CHOICES(1984)
Silents
PRICE OF A PARTY, THE(1924), ph; FAIR CO-ED, THE(1927), ph; ACROSS THE SINGAPORE(1928), ph; ADORATION(1928), ph; OUTCAST(1928), ph; TRAIL OF '98, THE(1929), ph

John B. Seitz
KISMET(1930), ph
John F. Seitz
SWEETHEARTS AND WIVES(1930), ph; WOMAN IN ROOM 13, THE(1932), ph; FARMER TAKES A WIFE, THE(1935), ph; YOUNG DR. KILDARE(1938), ph; SER-GEANT MADDEN(1939), ph; THUNDER AFLOAT(1939), ph; MOON AND SIX-PENCE, THE(1942), ph; FIVE GRAVES TO CAIRO(1943), ph; DOUBLE INDEMNITY(1944), ph; HAIL THE CONQUERING HERO(1944), ph; HOUR BEFORE THE DAWN, THE(1944), ph; MIRACLE OF MORGAN'S CREEK, THE(1944), ph; LOST WEEKEND, THE(1945), ph; UNSEEN, THE(1945), ph; WELL-GROOMED BRIDE, THE(1946), ph; NIGHT HAS A THOUSAND EYES(1948), ph; SAIGON(1948), ph; CHICAGO DEADLINE(1949), ph; GREAT GATSBY, THE(1949), ph; GOLDBERGS, THE(1950), ph; SUNSET BOULEVARD(1950), ph; DEAR BRAT(1951), ph; WHEN WORLDS COLLIDE(1951), ph; BOTANY BAY(1953), ph; INVADERS FROM MARS(1953), ph; SAVAGE, THE(1953), ph; GREAT GATSBY, THE(1974), ph
Silents
BRIDE'S SILENCE, THE(1917), ph; CONQUERING POWER, THE(1921), ph; FOUR HORSEMEN OF THE APOCALYPSE, THE(1921), ph; PRISONER OF ZENDA, THE(1922), ph; SCARAMOUCHE(1923), ph; ARAB, THE(1924), ph; CLASS-MATES(1924), ph; MARE NOSTRUM(1926), ph
Lou Seitz
RETURN OF DR. MABUSE, THE(1961, Ger./Fr./Ital.)
Ryan Seitz
BRAINWAVES(1983)
Sophie Seitz
DISORDER AND EARLY TORMENT(1977, Ger.)
Tani Seitz
I, THE JURY(1953); GREENWICH VILLAGE STORY(1963)
Jirina Sejbalova
SWEET LIGHT IN A DARK ROOM(1966, Czech.)
Sobeslav Sejk
LEMONADE JOE(1966, Czech.)
Sekaryongo
KING SOLOMON'S MINES(1950)
Jack Sekely
MIDNIGHT MADNESS(1980), ed
Steve Sekely
MIRACLE ON MAIN STREET, A(1940), d; BEHIND PRISON WALLS(1943), d; REVENGE OF THE ZOMBIES(1943), d; WOMEN IN BONDAGE(1943), d; LADY IN THE DEATH HOUSE(1944), d; LAKE PLACID SERENADE(1944), d; MY BUD-DY(1944), d; WATERFRONT(1944), d; FABULOUS SUZANNE, THE(1946), p&d; HOLLOW TRIUMPH(1948), d; STRONGHOLD(1952, Mex.), d; CARTOUCHE(1957, Ital./US), d; DESERT DESPERADOES(1959), d; DAY OF THE TRIFFIDS, THE(1963), d; KENNER(1969), d
William Sekely
NEW WINE(1941), p; SEEDS OF FREEDOM(1943, USSR), p
Miroslav Sekera
1984
AMADEUS(1984)
Frank Seki
Silents
PURPLE CIPHER, THE(1920)
Kyoko Seki
IKIRU(1960, Jap.)
Misao Seki
Silents
OUTSIDE WOMAN, THE(1921); WHERE LIGHTS ARE LOW(1921)
Misc. Silents
FIVE DAYS TO LIVE(1922); VERMILION PENCIL, THE(1922)
Ginzo Sekiguchi
WOMAN IN THE DUNES(1964, Jap.)

Hiroshi Sekita
WAR OF THE GARGANTUAS, THE(1970, Jap.)
Koichi Sekizawa
MAD ATLANTIC, THE(1967, Jap.), p
Shinichi Sekizawa
BATTLE IN OUTER SPACE(1960), w; SECRET OF THE TELEGIAN, THE(1961, Jap.), w; WESTWARD DESPERADO(1961, Jap.), w; MOTHRA(1962, Jap.), w; VARAN THE UNBELIEVABLE(1962, U.S./Jap.), w; KING KONG VERSUS GODZILLA(1963, Jap.), w; DAGORA THE SPACE MONSTER(1964, Jap.), w; GODZILLA VS. THE THING(1964, Jap.), w; OPERATION ENEMY FORT(1964, Jap.), w; ATRAGON(1965, Jap.), w; GHIDRAH, THE THREE-HEADED MONSTER(1965, Jap.), w; LOST WORLD OF SINBAD, THE(1965, Jap.), ph; GODZILLA VERSUS THE SEA MONSTER(1966, Jap.), w; GULLIVER'S TRAVELS BEYOND THE MOON(1966, Jap.), w; MAD ATLAN-TIC, THE(1967, Jap.), w; SON OF GODZILLA(1967, Jap.), w; GODZILLA'S REVEN-GE(1969), w; LATITUDE ZERO(1969, U.S./Jap.), w; MONSTER ZERO(1970, Jap.), w; WAR OF THE MONSTERS(1972, Jap.), w; GODZILLA VS. MEGALON(1976, Jap.), w
Johnny Sekka
FLAME IN THE STREETS(1961, Brit.); EAST OF SUDAN(1964, Brit.); WOMAN OF STRAW(1964, Brit.); YOUNG AND WILLING(1964, Brit.); KHARTOUM(1966, Brit.); LAST SAFARI, THE(1967, Brit.); SOUTHERN STAR, THE(1969, Fr./Brit.); INCENSE FOR THE DAMNED(1970, Brit.); CHARLEY-ONE-EYE(1973, Brit.); WARM DECEM-BER, A(1973, Brit.); UPTOWN SATURDAY NIGHT(1974); VISIT TO A CHIEF'S SON(1974); MOHAMMAD, MESSENGER OF GOD(1976, Lebanon/Brit.); ASHAN-TI(1979); CHARLIE CHAN AND THE CURSE OF THE DRAGON QUEEN(1981); HANKY-PANKY(1982)
Bounedine Sekkal
OLIVE TREES OF JUSTICE, THE(1967, Fr.)
Alexandra Sekulova
DESERTER AND THE NOMADS, THE(1969, Czech./Ital.)
Aleksandar Sekulovic
SQUARE OF VIOLENCE(1963, U.S./Yugo.), p, ph
Alexander Sekulovic
KAPO(1964, Ital./Fr./Yugo.), ph
Hjalmar Selander
Misc. Silents
SIR ARNE'S TREASURE(1920, Swed.)
Les Selander
RIDE 'EM COWBOY(1936), d; HOPALONG RIDES AGAIN(1937), d
Leslay Selander
COW COUNTRY(1953), d
Lesley Selander
BOSS RIDER OF GUN CREEK(1936), d; BARRIER, THE(1937), d; EMPTY SAD-DLES(1937), d; LEFT-HANDED LAW(1937), d; SANDFLOW(1937), d; SMOKE TREE RANGE(1937), d; BAR 20 JUSTICE(1938), d; CASSIDY OF BAR 20(1938), d; FRON-TIERSMAN, THE(1938), d; HEART OF ARIZONA(1938), d; MYSTERIOUS RIDER, THE(1938), d; PARTNERS OF THE PLAINS(1938), d; PRIDE OF THE WEST(1938), d; SUNSET TRAIL(1938), d; HERITAGE OF THE DESERT(1939), d; RANGE WAR(1939), d; RENEGADE TRAIL(1939), d; SILVER ON THE SAGE(1939), d; CHEROKEE STRIP(1940), d; HIDDEN GOLD(1940), d; KNIGHTS OF THE RANGE(1940), d; LIGHT OF WESTERN STARS, THE(1940), d; SANTA FE MARSHAL(1940), d; STAGE-COACH WAR(1940), d; THREE MEN FROM TEXAS(1940), d; DOOMED CARA-VAN(1941), d; PIRATES ON HORSEBACK(1941), d; ROUNDUP, THE(1941), d; STICK TO YOUR GUNS(1941), d; THUNDERING HOOFS(1941), d; WIDE OPEN TOWN(1941), d; BANDIT RANGER(1942), d; UNDERCOVER MAN(1942), d; BAR 20(1943), d; BORDER PATROL(1943), d; BUCKSKIN FRONTIER(1943), d; COLT COMRADES(1943), d; LOST CANYON(1943), d; RED RIVER ROBIN HOOD(1943), d; RIDERS OF THE DEADLINE(1943), d; CHEYENNE WILDCAT(1944), d; FIRE-BRANDS OF ARIZONA(1944), d; FORTY THIEVES(1944), d; LUMBERJACK(1944), d; SHERIFF OF LAS VEGAS(1944), d; SHERIFF OF SUNDOWN(1944), d; STAGE-COACH TO MONTEREY(1944), d; FATAL WITNESS, THE(1945), d; GREAT STAGE-COACH ROBBERY(1945), d; PHANTOM OF THE PLAINS(1945), d; THREE'S A CROWD(1945), d; TRAIL OF KIT CARSON(1945), d; VAMPIRE'S GHOST, THE(1945), d; NIGHT TRAIN TO MEMPHIS(1946), d; OUT CALIFORNIA WAY(1946), d; PASS-KEY TO DANGER(1946), d; THE CATMAN OF PARIS(1946), d; TRAFFIC IN CRI-ME(1946), d; BELLE STARR'S DAUGHTER(1947), d; BLACKMAIL(1947), d; LAST FRONTIER UPRISING(1947), d; PILGRIM LADY, THE(1947), d; RED STALLION, THE(1947), d; ROBIN OF TEXAS(1947), d; SADDLE PALS(1947), d; GUNS OF HA-TE(1948), d; INDIAN AGENT(1948), d; PANHANDLE(1948), d; STRIKE IT RICH(1948), d; BROTHERS IN THE SADDLE(1949), d; MASKED RAIDERS(1949), d; MYSTERIOUS DESPERADO, THE(1949), d; RIDERS OF THE RANGE(1949), d; RUSTLERS(1949), d; SKY DRAGON(1949), d; STAMPEDE(1949), d; DAKOTA LIL(1950), d; KANGAROO KID, THE(1950, Aus./U.S.), d; LAW OF THE BAD-LANDS(1950), d; RIDER FROM TUCSON(1950), d; RIO GRANDE PATROL(1950), d; SHORT GRASS(1950), d; STORM OVER WYOMING(1950), d; CAVALRY SCOUT(1951), d; FLIGHT TO MARS(1951), d; GUNPLAY(1951), d; HIGHWAYMAN, THE(1951), d; I WAS AN AMERICAN SPY(1951), d; OVERLAND TELEGRAPH(1951), d; PISTOL HARVEST(1951), d; SADDLE LEGION(1951), d; BATTLE ZONE(1952), d; DESERT PASSAGE(1952), d; FLAT TOP(1952), d; FORT OSAGE(1952), d; RAIDERS, THE(1952), d; ROAD AGENT(1952), d; TRAIL GUIDE(1952), d; DRAGONFLY SQUA-DRON(1953), d; FIGHTER ATTACK(1953), d; FORT ALGIERS(1953), d; FORT VEN-GEANCE(1953), d; ROYAL AFRICAN RIFLES, THE(1953), d; WAR PAINT(1953), d; ARROW IN THE DUST(1954), d; RETURN FROM THE SEA(1954), d; YELLOW TOMAHAWK, THE(1954), d; DESERT SANDS(1955), d; FORT YUMA(1955), d; SHOT-GUN(1955), d; TALL MAN RIDING(1955), d; BROKEN STAR, THE(1956), d; QUIN-CANNON, FRONTIER SCOUT(1956), d; OUTLAW'S SON(1957), d; REVOLT AT FORT LARAMIE(1957), d; TAMING SUTTON'S GAL(1957), d; LONE RANGER AND THE LOST CITY OF GOLD, THE(1958), d; CONVICT STAGE(1965), d; FORT COURA-GEOUS(1965), d; TOWN TAMER(1965), d; WAR PARTY(1965), d; TEXICAN, THE(1966, U.S./Span.), d; FORT UTAH(1967), d; ARIZONA BUSHWHACKERS(1968), d
Misc. Talkies
BORDERTOWN TRAIL(1944), d; CALL OF THE ROCKIES(1944), d
Akushula Selayah
TARZAN, THE APE MAN(1981)
Gunard Selberg
HONKY(1971), w
Irving Selbert
WINTER KILLS(1979)

Evelyn Selbie
MYSTERIOUS DR. FU MANCHU, THE(1929); DANGEROUS PARADISE(1930); LOVE COMES ALONG(1930); RETURN OF DR. FU MANCHU, THE(1930); HATCHET MAN, THE(1932); MERRY WIDOW, THE(1934); NOTORIOUS GENTLEMAN, A(1935); TWO IN A CROWD(1936); GIRLS CAN PLAY(1937); SEVENTH HEAVEN(1937); TOWER OF LONDON(1939); YOU'RE NOT SO TOUGH(1940); RAIDERS OF THE DESERT(1941)
Silents
FLASHLIGHT, THE(1917); DEVIL TO PAY, THE(1920); THORNS AND ORANGE BLOSSOMS(1922); TIGER'S CLAW, THE(1923); ROMANCE RANCH(1924); CAMIL-LE(1927); EAGER LIPS(1927); KING OF KINGS, THE(1927); FREEDOM OF THE PRESS(1928); ETERNAL LOVE(1929)
Misc. Silents
PEOPLE VS. JOHN DOE, THE(1916); MYSTERIOUS MRS. M, THE(1917); TWO-SOUL WOMAN, THE(1918); UNCHARTED CHANNELS(1920); DEVIL DOG DAW-SON(1921); WITHOUT BENEFIT OF CLERGY(1921); SNOWDRIFT(1923); CAFE IN CAIRO, A(1924); ROSE OF THE TENEMENTS(1926)

Irving Selbst
LOVING(1970); WATERMELON MAN(1970); BORN TO WIN(1971); GANG THAT COULDN'T SHOOT STRAIGHT, THE(1971); SHAMUS(1973)
1984
BIRDY(1984)

David Selburg
ON THE RIGHT TRACK(1981); TAKE THIS JOB AND SHOVE IT(1981)

David Selby
NIGHT OF DARK SHADOWS(1971); UP THE SANDBOX(1972); U-TURN(1973, Can.); SUPER COPS, THE(1974); RICH KIDS(1979); RAISE THE TITANIC(1980, Brit.); RICH AND FAMOUS(1981)
Misc. Talkies
GIRL IN BLUE, THE(1974)

Gertrude Selby
Silents
EASY TO MAKE MONEY(1919)
Misc. Silents
CHILD OF MYSTERY, A(1916); SIGN OF THE POPPY, THE(1916); DOUBLE-ROOM MYSTERY, THE(1917); KIDDER & KO.(1918); TWENTY-ONE(1918); IT'S EASY TO MAKE MONEY(1919)

Ian Selby
MUDLARK, THE(1950, Brit.)

Nicholas Selby
MIDSUMMER NIGHT'S DREAM, A(1969, Brit.); MACBETH(1971, Brit.)

Norman Selby
PAINTED ANGEL, THE(1929)
Silents
OATH-BOUND(1922)
Misc. Silents
BUCKING THE LINE(1921); STRAIGHT FROM THE SHOULDER(1921); TO A FINISH(1921); ARABIA(1922)

Norman Douglas Selby
LOOSE ANKLES(1930)

Norman "Kid McCoy" Selby
Silents
BROKEN BLOSSOMS(1919)

Sarah Selby
UNCLE HARRY(1945); SEVENTH VICTIM, THE(1943); HER PRIMITIVE MAN(1944); SAN DIEGO, I LOVE YOU(1944); NAUGHTY NINETIES, THE(1945); WONDER MAN(1945); BEAUTIFUL CHEAT, THE(1946); IDEA GIRL(1946); LITTLE IODINE(1946); DOUBLE LIFE, A(1947); STORK BITES MAN(1947); TRAPPED BY BOSTON BLACKIE(1948); BEYOND THE FOREST(1949); PERFECT STRAN-GERS(1950); SIDE STREET(1950); IRON MISTRESS, THE(1952); SNIPER, THE(1952); BATTLE CIRCUS(1953); LION IS IN THE STREETS, A(1953); MR. SCOUTMAS-TER(1953); SYSTEM, THE(1953); MEN OF THE FIGHTING LADY(1954); BATTLE FLAME(1955); GOOD MORNING, MISS DOVE(1955); MC CONNELL STORY, THE(1955); AFFAIR TO REMEMBER, AN(1957); GUNFIRE AT INDIAN GAP(1957); NO TIME TO BE YOUNG(1957); SHORT CUT TO HELL(1957); STOPOVER TO-KYO(1957); MOON PILOT(1962); TOWER OF LONDON(1962); TAGGART(1964); DON'T MAKE WAVES(1967); WORLD'S GREATEST ATHLETE, THE(1973)

Tony Selby
PRESS FOR TIME(1966, Brit.); CONQUEROR WORM, THE(1968, Brit.); HIGH COMMISSIONER, THE(1968, U.S./Brit.); POOR COW(1968, Brit.); BEFORE WINTER COMES(1969, Brit.); IN SEARCH OF GREGORY(1970, Brit./Ital.); VILLAIN(1971, Brit.); ADOLF HITLER–MY PART IN HIS DOWNFALL(1973, Brit.)

Emma Selby-Walker
FOLLOW THAT CAMEL(1967, Brit.), cos

Arno Selco
ACT ONE(1964)

Arthur Seld
HARMON OF MICHIGAN(1941), ed

Margaret Seldeen
TIME TRAVELERS, THE(1964)

Murray Seldeen
LADY TUBBS(1935), ed; MAN WHO RECLAIMED HIS HEAD, THE(1935), ed; ONE EXCITING ADVENTURE(1935), ed; DANGEROUS WATERS(1936), ed; DON'T GET PERSONAL(1936), ed; HARVESTER, THE(1936), ed; LAUGHING IRISH EYES(1936), ed; THREE MESQUITEERS, THE(1936), ed; WINDS OF THE WASTELAND(1936), ed; DUKE COMES BACK, THE(1937), ed; ESCAPE BY NIGHT(1937), ed; IT COULD HAPPEN TO YOU(1937), ed; MANHATTAN MERRY-GO-ROUND(1937), ed; NAVY BLUES(1937), ed; RIDERS OF THE WHISTLING SKULL(1937), ed; SHEIK STEPS OUT, THE(1937), ed; WRONG ROAD, THE(1937), ed; DESPERATE ADVENTURE, A(1938), ed; FEDERAL MAN-HUNT(1939), ed; MICKEY, THE KID(1939), ed; OR-PHANS OF THE STREET(1939), ed; WOMAN DOCTOR(1939), ed; DARK COMMAND, THE(1940), ed; GANGS OF CHICAGO(1940), ed; GRANDPA GOES TO TOWN(1940), ed; HIT PARADE OF 1941(1940), ed; MELODY RANCH(1940), ed; VILLAGE BARN DANCE(1940), ed; WAGONS WESTWARD(1940), ed; ANGELS WITH BROKEN WINGS(1941), ed; ICE-CAPADES(1941), ed; LADY FOR A NIGHT(1941), ed; LADY FROM LOUISIANA(1941), ed; IN OLD CALIFORNIA(1942), ed; TRAGEDY AT MID-NIGHT, A(1942), ed

Josef Selden
ELI ELI(1940), d

Murray Selden
MILLION DOLLAR RANSOM(1934), ed; IT HAPPENED IN NEW YORK(1935), ed; PRESIDENT'S MYSTERY, THE(1936), ed; RHYTHM IN THE CLOUDS(1937), ph

Tom Selden
YOUNG CAPTIVES, THE(1959)

Frank Selder
IN THE LINE OF DUTY(1931)

George Seldes
REDS(1981)

Marian Seldes
TRUE STORY OF JESSE JAMES, THE(1957); YOUNG STRANGER, THE(1957); LIGHT IN THE FOREST, THE(1958); BIG FISHERMAN, THE(1959); CRIME AND PUNISHMENT, U.S.A.(1959); GREATEST STORY EVER TOLD, THE(1965); FIN-GERS(1978)

Irv Seldin
MURDER IN MISSISSIPPI(1965)

Leon Selditz
HOT ANGEL, THE(1958), ed; THEY SAVED HITLER'S BRAIN(1964), ed

Irene Seldner
WINK OF AN EYE(1958)

Seldom Seen Sioux
GIT!(1965)

Haydee Seldon
KANGAROO KID, THE(1950, Aus./U.S.)

Michel Seldow
DEADLIER THAN THE MALE(1957, Fr.); LOVERS ON A TIGHTROPE(1962, Fr.)

Evelyne Selena
MY WIFE'S HUSBAND(1965, Fr./Ital.)

Diane Seletos
MORTUARY(1983), makeup

Mario Seletti
KANSAS CITY CONFIDENTIAL(1952)

F. Seleznev
ON HIS OWN(1939, USSR)

Vitla Seleznev
BALLAD OF COSSACK GLOOTA(1938, USSR)

V. Seleznyov
SUN SHINES FOR ALL, THE(1961, USSR); WAR AND PEACE(1968, USSR)

Bill Self
DECOY(1946); HOMECOMING(1948)

Bobby Self
HOT STUFF(1979)

Cass Self
STARTING OVER(1979)

George Self
GUNMAN HAS ESCAPED, A(1948, Brit.)

Kay Self
JOURNEY AMONG WOMEN(1977, Aus.)

Manny Self
KANSAS CITY KITTY(1944), w

William Self
STORY OF G.I. JOE, THE(1945); LIKELY STORY, A(1947); MARSHAL OF CRIPPLE CREEK, THE(1947); RED RIVER(1948); ADAM'S RIB(1949); FATHER WAS A FULL-BACK(1949); I WAS A MALE WAR BRIDE(1949); SANDS OF IWO JIMA(1949); BREAKTHROUGH(1950); MALAYA(1950); TICKET TO TOMAHAWK(1950); PEOPLE AGAINST O'HARA, THE(1951); THING, THE(1951); BIG SKY, THE(1952); PAT AND MIKE(1952); PLYMOUTH ADVENTURE(1952); RIDE THE HIGH IRON(1956), p; FROM NOON TO THREE(1976), p; SHOOTIST, THE(1976), p

Edgar Selge
WAR AND PEACE(1983, Ger.)

Kurt Selge
GENERALE DELLA ROVERE(1960, Ital./Fr.)

Louis Selgner
ADORABLE CREATURES(1956, Fr.)

Ali Selgur
YOR, THE HUNTER FROM THE FUTURE(1983, Ital.)

Zeynip Selgur
YOR, THE HUNTER FROM THE FUTURE(1983, Ital.)

I. Selianin
SKI BATTALION(1938, USSR)

Col. William N. Selig
Silents
LAST CHANCE, THE(1921), p

Maxwell Seligman
RAGGEDY ANN AND ANDY(1977), ed

Cdr. Morton Seligman
FLIGHT COMMAND(1940), tech adv

Selig J. Seligman
DIAMONDS FOR BREAKFAST(1968, Brit.), p

Arnaud Selignac
1984
DREAM ONE(1984, Brit./Fr.), d, w

Michele Selignac
LOVE IN THE AFTERNOON(1957)

Dennis Selinger
LONG SHOT(1981, Brit.)

Annemarie Selinko
DESIREE(1954), w

George Selk
CITY OF BAD MEN(1953); IT CAME FROM OUTER SPACE(1953); ROGUE COP(1954); I'LL CRY TOMORROW(1955); STORM CENTER(1956); SPIRIT OF ST. LOUIS, THE(1957); VAMPIRE, THE(1957); GUN FEVER(1958); GUNS OF THE TIMBERLAND(1960)

S.N. Selk
NINE HOURS TO RAMA(1963, U.S./Brit.)

Jamie Selkirk
1984
 SILENT ONE, THE(1984, New Zealand), ed
Jill Selkowitz
1984
 HARRY AND SON(1984)
Bernard Sell
 SUSPENSE(1946); UNDERCOVER MAN, THE(1949)
Bernard C. Sell
 KISS OF DEATH(1947)
Bernie Sell
 FOREVER AND A DAY(1943); CRAZY KNIGHTS(1944); DESTINATION TO-KYO(1944); FOUR JILLS IN A JEEP(1944); SUNDAY DINNER FOR A SOL-DIER(1944); GOD IS MY CO-PILOT(1945); JOHNNY COMES FLYING HOME(1946); T-MEN(1947)
Henry G. Sell
Misc. Silents
 TWIN PAWNS, THE(1919); EMPIRE OF DIAMONDS, THE(1920); MONEY MANIAC, THE(1921); FREE AIR(1922)
Jack M. Sell
 PSYCHOTRONIC MAN, THE(1980), d, w, ph
Janie Sell
 LOST AND FOUND(1979)
Alexis Sellan
 WITHOUT APPARENT MOTIVE(1972, Fr.)
Marie Selland
 INVASION OF THE BODY SNATCHERS(1956)
Arnold Sellars
 DOWN OUR ALLEY(1939, Brit.)
Elizabeth Sellars
 FLOODTIDE(1949, Brit.); GUILT IS MY SHADOW(1950, Brit.); MADELEINE(1950, Brit.); NIGHT WAS OUR FRIEND(1951, Brit.); CLOUDBURST(1952, Brit.); GENTLE GUNMAN, THE(1952, Brit.); STRANGER IN BETWEEN, THE(1952, Brit.); BROKEN HORSESHOE, THE(1953, Brit.); LONG MEMORY, THE(1953, Brit.); RECOIL(1953); THREE'S COMPANY(1953, Brit.); BAREFOOT CONTESSA, THE(1954); DESI-REE(1954); FORBIDDEN CARGO(1954, Brit.); PRINCE OF PLAYERS(1955); THREE CASES OF MURDER(1955, Brit.); LAST MAN TO HANG, THE(1956, Brit.); DECISION AGAINST TIME(1957, Brit.); SHIRALEE, THE(1957, Brit.); LAW AND DISOR-DER(1958, Brit.); DAY THEY ROBBED THE BANK OF ENGLAND, THE(1960, Brit.); NEVER LET GO(1960, Brit.); JET STORM(1961, Brit.); WEBSTER BOY, THE(1962, Brit.); 55 DAYS AT PEKING(1963); CHALK GARDEN, THE(1964, Brit.); MUMMY'S SHROUD, THE(1967, Brit.); HIRELING, THE(1973, Brit.)
Lawrence Sellars
 ENDLESS LOVE(1981); ROLLOVER(1981); I'M DANCING AS FAST AS I CAN(1982)
Tom Selleck
 SEVEN MINUTES, THE(1971); DAUGHTERS OF SATAN(1972); TERMINAL IS-LAND(1973); COMA(1978); HIGH ROAD TO CHINA(1983)
1984
 LASSITER(1984); RUNAWAY(1984)
Misc. Talkies
 WASHINGTON AFFAIR, THE(1978)
Charles A. Sellen
Silents
 ROUGHNECK, THE(1924)
Huguette Sellen
 NOT RECONCILED, OR "ONLY VIOLENCE HELPS WHERE IT RULES"(1969, Ger.)
Robert Seller
 CONFESSIONS OF A ROGUE(1948, Fr.); DEVIL'S DAUGHTER(1949, Fr.); PLEAS-URES AND VICES(1962, Fr.)
Thomas Seller
 ANDY HARDY MEETS DEBUTANTE(1940), w; TISH(1942), w; MAN FROM DOWN UNDER, THE(1943), w; BLACK ARROW(1948), w
Alan Sellers
 IT!(1967, Brit.)
Arlene Sellers
 END OF THE GAME(1976, Ger./Ital.), p; HOUSE CALLS(1978), p; SILVER BEARS(1978), p; CUBA(1979), p; BLUE SKIES AGAIN(1983), p
1984
 IRRECONCILABLE DIFFERENCES(1984), p; SCANDALOUS(1984), p
Arthur Sellers
 MODERN PROBLEMS(1981), a, w
Bridget Sellers
 MAN BETWEEN, THE(1953, Brit.), cos; STORM OVER THE NILE(1955, Brit.), cos; DR. STRANGELOVE: OR HOW I LEARNED TO STOP WORRYING AND LOVE THE BOMB(1964), cos; FAMILY WAY, THE(1966, Brit.), cos; GIRL GETTERS, THE(1966, Brit.), cos; RECKONING, THE(1971, Brit.), cos; RETURN OF THE PINK PANTHER, THE(1975, Brit.), cos
Catherine Sellers
 DESTROY, SHE SAID(1969, Fr.)
Kevin Sellers
 BLUE SKIES AGAIN(1983), w
Mark Sellers
1984
 BODY ROCK(1984)
Michael Sellers
 I LIKE MONEY(1962, Brit.)
Mildred Sellers
 EASY TO WED(1946); GAL WHO TOOK THE WEST, THE(1949)
Ollie Sellers
Silents
 NEW DISCIPLE, THE(1921), d; ABLEMINDED LADY, THE(1922), d&ph
Oliver L. Sellers
Silents
 DIANE OF STAR HOLLOW(1921), d
Misc. Silents
 WHEN BEARCAT WENT DRY(1919), d; HOOSIER SCHOOLMASTER, THE(1924), d
Ollie L. Sellers
Misc. Silents
 GIFT SUPREME, THE(1920), d

Ollie O. Sellers
Misc. Silents
 SEEDS OF VENGEANCE(1920), d
Peter Sellers
 PENNY POINTS TO PARADISE(1951, Brit.); DOWN AMONG THE Z MEN(1952, Brit.); LADYKILLERS, THE(1956, Brit.); MAN WHO NEVER WAS, THE(1956, Brit.); JOHN AND JULIE(1957, Brit.); SMALLEST SHOW ON EARTH, THE(1957, Brit.); TOM THUMB(1958, Brit./U.S.); UP THE CREEK(1958, Brit.); YOUR PAST IS SHO-WING(1958, Brit.); I'M ALL RIGHT, JACK(1959, Brit.); MOUSE THAT ROARED, THE(1959, Brit.); ORDERS ARE ORDERS(1959, Brit.); BATTLE OF THE SEXES, THE(1960, Brit.); MAN IN A COCKED HAT(1960, Bri.); MILLIONAIRESS, THE(1960, Brit.); NEVER LET GO(1960, Brit.); TWO-WAY STRETCH(1961, Brit.); I LIKE MO-NEY(1962, Brit.), a, d; LOLITA(1962); ONLY TWO CAN PLAY(1962, Brit.); ROAD TO HONG KONG, THE(1962, U.S./Brit.); TRIAL AND ERROR(1962, Brit.); WALTZ OF THE TOREADORS(1962, Brit.); HEAVENS ABOVE!(1963, Brit.); WRONG ARM OF THE LAW, THE(1963, Brit.); DR. STRANGELOVE: OR HOW I LEARNED TO STOP WORRYING AND LOVE THE BOMB(1964); PINK PANTHER, THE(1964); SHOT IN THE DARK, A(1964); WORLD OF HENRY ORIENT, THE(1964); WHAT'S NEW, PUSSYCAT?(1965, U.S./Fr.); AFTER THE FOX(1966, U.S./Brit./Ital.); WRONG BOX, THE(1966, Brit.); BOBO, THE(1967, Brit.); CASINO ROYALE(1967, Brit.); WOMAN TIMES SEVEN(1967, U.S./Fr./Ital.); I LOVE YOU, ALICE B. TOKLAS!(1968); PARTY, THE(1968); DAY AT THE BEACH, A(1970); HOFFMAN(1970, Brit.); MAGIC CHRIS-TIAN, THE(1970, Brit.), a, w; THERE'S A GIRL IN MY SOUP(1970, Brit.); ALICE'S ADVENTURES IN WONDERLAND(1972, Brit.); WHERE DOES IT HURT?(1972); OPTIMISTS, THE(1973, Brit.); BLOCKHOUSE, THE(1974, Brit.); GREAT MCGONA-GALL, THE(1975, Brit.); RETURN OF THE PINK PANTHER, THE(1975, Brit.); UNDERCOVERS HERO(1975, Brit.); MURDER BY DEATH(1976); PINK PANTHER STRIKES AGAIN, THE(1976, Brit.); REVENGE OF THE PINK PANTHER(1978); BEING THERE(1979); PRISONER OF ZENDA, THE(1979); FIENDISH PLOT OF DR. FU MANCHU, THE(1980); TRAIL OF THE PINK PANTHER, THE(1982)
Misc. Talkies
 GHOST IN THE NOONDAY SUN(1974)
Ronnie Sellers
 SHOOT IT: BLACK, SHOOT IT: BLUE(1974)
Steve Sellers
 EDUCATION OF SONNY CARSON, THE(1974)
William Sellers
 GUNFIGHTER, THE(1950), w
William F. Sellers
 GOLDEN GLOVES STORY, THE(1950), w
Lula Selli
 AVENGER, THE(1962, Fr./Ital.)
Sergio Selli
 TRAMPLERS, THE(1966, Ital.), cos
Charles E. Sellier
 BROTHERS O'TOOLE, THE(1973), p; GUARDIAN OF THE WILDERNESS(1977), p
1984
 SILENT NIGHT, DEADLY NIGHT(1984), d
Georges Sellier
 DOULOS–THE FINGER MAN(1964, Fr./Ital.)
Charles Sellier, Jr.
 ADVENTURES OF FRONTIER FREMONT, THE(1976), p; BEYOND AND BACK(1978), p; IN SEARCH OF HISTORIC JESUS(1980), w
Charles E. Sellier, Jr.
 LIFE AND TIMES OF GRIZZLY ADAMS, THE(1974), p; LINCOLN CONSPIRACY, THE(1977), p, w; FALL OF THE HOUSE OF USHER, THE(1980), p; HANGAR 18(1980), p, w; IN SEARCH OF HISTORIC JESUS(1980), p; BOOGENS, THE(1982), p
Caj Selling
 DR. COPPELIUS(1968, U.S./Span.); MYSTERIOUS HOUSE OF DR. C., THE(1976)
Kenneth Selling
 STREET SCENE(1931)
Michael Sellmann
 GERMAN SISTERS, THE(1982, Ger.)
Erna Sellner
 MURDERERS AMONG US(1948, Ger.)
Gustav Rudolf Sellner
 YOUNG LORD, THE(1970, Ger.), d; PEDESTRIAN, THE(1974, Ger.)
Manuel Sellner
 PEDESTRIAN, THE(1974, Ger.)
Rudolph Sellner
 DAVID(1979, Ger.)
Charles Sellon
 BIG NEWS(1929); BULLDOG DRUMMOND(1929); GAMBLERS, THE(1929); GIRL IN THE GLASS CAGE, THE(1929); HOT STUFF(1929); MAN AND THE MOMENT, THE(1929); MIGHTY, THE(1929); SATURDAY NIGHT KID, THE(1929); SWEE-TIE(1929); VAGABOND LOVER(1929); BORROWED WIVES(1930); BURNING UP(1930); FOR THE LOVE O'LIL(1930); HONEY(1930); LET'S GO NATIVE(1930); LOVE AMONG THE MILLIONAIRES(1930); MEN ARE LIKE THAT(1930); SEA LEGS(1930); SOCIAL LION, THE(1930); TOM SAWYER(1930); UNDER A TEXAS MOON(1930); BEHIND OFFICE DOORS(1931); DUDE RANCH(1931); LAUGH AND GET RICH(1931); MAN TO MAN(1931); PAINTED DESERT, THE(1931); PENROD AND SAM(1931); TIP-OFF, THE(1931); CARNIVAL BOAT(1932); CENTRAL PARK(1932); DARK HORSE, THE(1932); DRIFTER, THE(1932); I AM A FUGITIVE FROM A CHAIN GANG(1932); MAKE ME A STAR(1932); RIDE HIM, COWBOY(1932); SPEED MADNESS(1932); AS THE DEVIL COMMANDS(1933); CENTRAL AIR-PORT(1933); EMPLOYEE'S ENTRANCE(1933); GOLDEN HARVEST(1933); STRICTLY PERSONAL(1933); BRIGHT EYES(1934); CAT'S PAW, THE(1934); ELMER AND ELSIE(1934); IT'S A GIFT(1934); PRIVATE SCANDAL(1934); READY FOR LO-VE(1934); CASINO MURDER CASE, THE(1935); DEVIL IS A WOMAN, THE(1935); DIAMOND JIM(1935); IN OLD KENTUCKY(1935); IT'S A SMALL WORLD(1935); LIFE BEGINS AT 40(1935); ONE HOUR LATE(1935); WELCOME HOME(1935)
Silents
 FLOWING GOLD(1924); MERTON OF THE MOVIES(1924); OLD HOME WEEK(1925); EASY PICKINGS(1927); KING OF KINGS, THE(1927); PAINTED PO-NIES(1927); EASY COME, EASY GO(1928); LOVE ME AND THE WORLD IS MINE(1928); WHAT A NIGHT!(1928)
Misc. Silents
 MYSTERIOUS RIDER, THE(1927); PRAIRIE KING, THE(1927); FEEL MY PUL-SE(1928); HAPPINESS AHEAD(1928); SOMETHING ALWAYS HAPPENS(1928)

Charles A. Sellon
Silents
SOUTH SEA LOVE(1923); LOVER'S LANE(1924); MONSTER, THE(1925); NIGHT SHIP, THE(1925)
Herb Sells
ELECTRA GLIDE IN BLUE(1973)
Brent Sellstrom
FUTUREWORLD(1976), spec eff
Achim Sellus
BREAKTHROUGH(1978, Ger.), p
David Selman
FIGHTING SHADOWS(1935), d; GALLANT DEFENDER(1935), d; JUSTICE OF THE RANGE(1935), d; REVENGE RIDER, THE(1935), d; COWBOY STAR, THE(1936), d; DANGEROUS INTRIGUE(1936), d; KILLER AT LARGE(1936), d; MYSTERIOUS AVENGER, THE(1936), d; PRESCOTT KID, THE(1936), pd; SECRET PATROL(1936), d; SHAKEDOWN(1936), d; WESTERNER, THE(1936), d; FIND THE WITNESS(1937), d; TEXAS TRAIL(1937), d; WOMAN AGAINST THE WORLD(1938), d
Misc. Talkies
RIDING WILD(1935), d; SQUARE SHOOTER(1935), d; TUGBOAT PRINCESS(1936), d
Misc. Silents
REMEMBER(1926), d; PAYING THE PRICE(1927), d
Joseph Selman
Misc. Silents
PLACE OF THE HONEYMOONS, THE(1920)
Linda Selman
FROM THE MIXED-UP FILES OF MRS. BASIL E. FRANKWEILER(1973); SLOW DANCING IN THE BIG CITY(1978)
Gyorgy Selmeczi
ANGI VERA(1980, Hung.), m
Dean Selmeir
MURDERS IN THE RUE MORGUE(1971)
Marcello Selmi
INVASION 1700(1965, Fr./Ital./Yugo.)
Dean Selmier
MAN IN THE WILDERNESS(1971, U.S./Span.); BLOOD SPATTERED BRIDE, THE(1974, Span.); HUNTING PARTY, THE(1977, Brit.)
Herbert Selpin
LOVE CONTRACT, THE(1932, Brit.), d; SERGEANT BERRY(1938, Ger.), d; WATER FOR CANITOGA(1939, Ger.), d
Eric Selten
CAPTAIN MILKSHAKE(1970), m
Morton Selten
RESERVED FOR LADIES(1932, Brit.); SHADOW BETWEEN, THE(1932, Brit.); WEDDING REHEARSAL(1932, Brit.); FALLING FOR YOU(1933, Brit.); LOVE WAGER, THE(1933, Brit.); DIPLOMATIC LOVER, THE(1934, Brit.); ANNIE, LEAVE THE ROOM(1935, Brit.); DARK WORLD(1935, Brit.); HIS MAJESTY AND CO(1935, Brit.); ONCE IN A NEW MOON(1935, Brit.); TEN MINUTE ALIBI(1935, Brit.); GHOST GOES WEST, THE(1936, Brit.); I STAND CONDEMNED(1936, Brit.); IN THE SOUP(1936, Brit.); ACTION FOR SLANDER(1937, Brit.); FIRE OVER ENGLAND(1937, Brit.); JUGGERNAUT(1937, Brit.); DIVORCE OF LADY X. THE(1938, Brit.); YANK AT OXFORD, A(1938); TWO'S COMPANY(1939, Brit.); SHIPYARD SALLY(1940, Brit.); THIEF OF BAGHDAD, THE(1940, Brit.); YOUNG MAN'S FANCY(1943, Brit.)
Paul Seltenhammer
DIE FLEDERMAUS(1964, Aust.), cos; CORRUPT ONES, THE(1967, Ger.), cos
David Selter
OTHER SIDE OF THE MOUNTAIN, THE(1975), w
Dov Selttzer
RABBI AND THE SHIKSE, THE(1976, Israel), m
Barry Seltzer
TO KILL A MOCKINGBIRD(1962)
Charles Alden Seltzer
SILVER SPURS(1936), w
Silents
FAME AND FORTUNE(1918), w; ROUGH SHOD(1925), w
Daniel Seltzer
UNMARRIED WOMAN, AN(1978)
Dave Seltzer
FINAL CONFLICT, THE(1981), w
David Seltzer
KING, QUEEN, KNAVE(1972, Ger./U.S.), w; ONE IS A LONELY NUMBER(1972), w; OMEN, THE(1976), w; PROPHECY(1979), w; SIX WEEKS(1982), w; TABLE FOR FIVE(1983), w
Dov Seltzer
TRUNK TO CAIRO(1966, Israel/Ger.), m; MY MARGO(1969, Israel), m; NOT MINE TO LOVE(1969, Israel), m; SIMCHON FAMILY, THE(1969, Israel), m; ESCAPE TO THE SUN(1972, Fr./Ger./Israel), m; KAZABLAN(1974, Israel), m; MOSES(1976, Brit./Ital.), ch; OPERATION THUNDERBOLT(1978, ISRAEL), m; SAVAGE WEEKEND(1983), m
1984
AMBASSADOR, THE(1984), m
Frank Seltzer
LET'S LIVE AGAIN(1948), p
Frank N. Seltzer
GAY INTRUDERS, THE(1948), p; JUNGLE PATROL(1948), p; 711 OCEAN DRIVE(1950), p; BOSS, THE(1956), p; TERROR IN A TEXAS TOWN(1958), p
Misc. Silents
BREAKING HOME TIES(1922), d
Terrel Seltzer
CHAN IS MISSING(1982), w
Walter Seltzer
NAKED EDGE, THE(1961), p; MAN IN THE MIDDLE(1964, U.S./Brit.), p; WAR LORD, THE(1965), p; BEAU GESTE(1966), p; WILL PENNY(1968), p; NUMBER ONE(1969), p; DARKER THAN AMBER(1970), p; OMEGA MAN, THE(1971), p; SOYLENT GREEN(1973), p; LAST HARD MEN, THE(1976), p
Will Seltzer
BABY BLUE MARINE(1976); CHICKEN CHRONICLES, THE(1977); CITIZENS BAND(1977); ONE AND ONLY, THE(1978); MORE AMERICAN GRAFFITI(1979)

1984
JOHNNY DANGEROUSLY(1984)
Carole Selvester
NAKED CITY, THE(1948)
Evelyn Selvie
PADDY O'DAY(1935)
Min Selvin
PENTHOUSE RHYTHM(1945), w
Samuel Selvon
PRESSURE(1976, Brit.), w
Tonio Selwart
CROSS OF LORRAINE, THE(1943); EDGE OF DARKNESS(1943); HANGMEN ALSO DIE(1943); NORTH STAR, THE(1943); HITLER GANG, THE(1944); STRANGE AFFAIR(1944); TAMPICO(1944); WILSON(1944); MY FAVORITE SPY(1951); BAREFOOT CONTESSA, THE(1954); CONGO CROSSING(1956); HELEN OF TROY(1956, Ital); TEMPEST(1958, Ital./Yugo./Fr.); NAKED MAJA, THE(1959, Ital./U.S.); FIVE BRANDED WOMEN(1960); ROMANOFF AND JULIET(1961); ANZIO(1968, Ital.); SENSO(1968, Ital.)
George Selway
SECRET PLACE, THE(1958, Brit.); I'M ALL RIGHT, JACK(1959, Brit.); TIGER BAY(1959, Brit.); BOTTOMS UP(1960, Brit.); WRONG BOX, THE(1966, Brit.); MAROC 7(1967, Brit.); STRANGE AFFAIR, THE(1968, Brit.); THREE SISTERS(1974, Brit.)
Alan Selwyn
INADMISSIBLE EVIDENCE(1968, Brit.); POOR COW(1968, Brit.)
Charlotte Selwyn
COP-OUT(1967, Brit.); PRIVATE RIGHT, THE(1967, Brit.)
Clarissa Selwyn
CYNARA(1932); EVERYTHING IN LIFE(1936, Brit.); ONE GOOD TURN(1936, Brit.); EVERYTHING IS RHYTHM(1940, Brit.)
Misc. Silents
GLORIANA(1916); DOUBLE STANDARD, THE(1917); BRASS BOTTLE, THE(1923); POOR GIRL'S ROMANCE, A(1926)
Don Selwyn
SLEEPING DOGS(1977, New Zealand); GOODBYE PORK PIE(1981, New Zealand)
Edgar Selwyn
GIRL IN THE SHOW, THE(1929), d; WAR NURSE(1930), d; MEN CALL IT LOVE(1931), d; POSSESSED(1931), w; SIN OF MADELON CLAUDET, THE(1931), d; SKYSCRAPER SOULS(1932), d; BARBARIAN, THE(1933), w; MEN MUST FIGHT(1933), p&d; TURN BACK THE CLOCK(1933), d, w; CHAINED(1934), w; MYSTERY OF MR. X, THE(1934), d; BABY FACE HARRINGTON(1935), p, w; BRIDAL SUITE(1939), p; DANCING CO-ED(1939), p; JOE AND ETHEL TURP CALL ON THE PRESIDENT(1939), p; KID FROM TEXAS, THE(1939), p; DULCY(1940), p; GOLDEN FLEECING, THE(1940), p; WASHINGTON MELODRAMA(1941), p; PIERRE OF THE PLAINS(1942), p, w
Silents
PIERRE OF THE PLAINS(1914), a, w; ARAB, THE(1915), a, w; ARAB, THE(1924), w; NIGHT LIFE OF NEW YORK(1925), w; DANCING MOTHERS(1926), w
Erin Selwyn
EASY LIVING(1949); SCENE OF THE CRIME(1949); FATHER OF THE BRIDE(1950)
Erwin Selwyn
BAD AND THE BEAUTIFUL, THE(1952)
Hugh Selwyn
LIEUTENANT DARING, RN(1935, Brit.)
Jack Selwyn
Silents
OLYMPIC HERO, THE(1928)
Lionel Selwyn
HANNIBAL BROOKS(1969, Brit.), ed; FOREVER YOUNG, FOREVER FREE(1976, South Afr.), ed; GUEST AT STEENKAMPSKRAAL, THE(1977, South Africa), ed; MARIGOLDS IN AUGUST(1980, South Africa), ed; CITY LOVERS(1982, S. African), ed
1984
GUEST, THE(1984, Brit.), ed; MARIGOLDS IN AUGUST(1984, S. Africa), ed
Louis Selwyn
CRY OF THE BANSHEE(1970, Brit.)
Russell Selwyn
MARAUDERS, THE(1955), ed
Ruth Selwyn
FIVE AND TEN(1931); NEW MORALS FOR OLD(1932); POLLY OF THE CIRCUS(1932); SPEAK EASILY(1932); TRIAL OF VIVIENNE WARE, THE(1932); MEN MUST FIGHT(1933); FUGITIVE LOVERS(1934); BABY FACE HARRINGTON(1935)
William E. Selwyn
BOB MATHIAS STORY, THE(1954), p
Clarissa Selwyne
SPORTING LOVE(1936, Brit.)
Clarissa Selwynne
MY MAN(1928); HARD TO GET(1929); ISLE OF LOST SHIPS(1929); LOVE TRAP, THE(1929); LILIES OF THE FIELD(1930); MY PAL, THE KING(1932); SLIGHTLY MARRIED(1933); RIP TIDE(1934); JANE EYRE(1935); MELODY OF MY HEART(1936, Brit.); WOMEN OF GLAMOUR(1937)
Silents
BRIDE'S AWAKENING, THE(1918); LOVE SWINDLE(1918); OUT OF THE STORM(1920); MARRIAGE OF WILLIAM ASHE, THE(1921); QUEENIE(1921); BEAU BRUMMEL(1924); LUCKY HORSESHOE, THE(1925); HEART OF A FOLLIES GIRL, THE(1928); JAZZ MAD(1928); SINNER'S PARADE(1928)
Misc. Silents
HER GREAT MATCH(1915); DRIFTWOOD(1916); CALENDER GIRL, THE(1917); PRINCESS VIRTUE(1917); FACE VALUE(1918); MOTHER, I NEED YOU(1918); BIG LITTLE PERSON, THE(1919); CREAKING STAIRS(1919); HOME(1919); DANGEROUS DAYS(1920); SOCIETY SECRETS(1921); DANGEROUS FLIRT, THE(1924)
Armond Selz
RAW WEEKEND(1964), ph
Dick Selzer
JUVENILE COURT(1938)
Milton Selzer
LAST MILE, THE(1959); YOUNG SAVAGES, THE(1961); YELLOW CANARY, THE(1963); MARNIE(1964); CINCINNATI KID, THE(1965); BIG HAND FOR THE LITTLE LADY, A(1966); IN ENEMY COUNTRY(1968); LEGEND OF LYLAH CLARE, THE(1968); BLOOD AND LACE(1971); LADY SINGS THE BLUES(1972); BLUE COLLAR(1978); EVIL, THE(1978)

1984
BUDDY SYSTEM, THE(1984)
Paula Selzer
SILENT RAGE(1982)
Richard Selzer
LITTLE TOUGH GUY(1938)
David Selznick
CHINATOWN NIGHTS(1929), p; HELL'S HIGHWAY(1932), p
Silents
FOUR FEATHERS(1929), p
David C. Selznick
GONE WITH THE WIND(1939), w
David O. Selznick
DANCE OF LIFE, THE(1929), p; MAN I LOVE, THE(1929), p; STREET OF CHAN-CE(1930), p; ANIMAL KINGDOM, THE(1932), p; BILL OF DIVORCEMENT, A(1932), p; BIRD OF PARADISE(1932), p; CONQUERORS, THE(1932), p; PHANTOM OF CRESTWOOD, THE(1932), p; ROCKABYE(1932), p; STATE'S ATTORNEY(1932), p; THIRTEEN WOMEN(1932), p; WHAT PRICE HOLLYWOOD?(1932), p; YOUNG BRIDE(1932), p; CHRISTOPHER STRONG(1933), p; CROSSFIRE(1933), p; DANCING LADY(1933), p; DINNER AT EIGHT(1933), p; LUCKY DEVILS(1933), p; MEET THE BARON(1933), p; NIGHT FLIGHT(1933), p; NO OTHER WOMAN(1933), p; OUR BETTERS(1933), p; SCARLET RIVER(1933), p; TOPAZE(1933), p; MANHATTAN MELODRAMA(1934), p; VIVA VILLA!(1934), p; ANNA KARENINA(1935), p; DAVID COPPERFIELD(1935), p; RECKLESS(1935), p; TALE OF TWO CITIES, A(1935), p; GARDEN OF ALLAH, THE(1936), p; LITTLE LORD FAUNTLEROY(1936), p; PUBLIC ENEMY'S WIFE(1936), w; NOTHING SACRED(1937), p; PRISONER OF ZENDA, THE(1937), p; STAR IS BORN, A(1937), p, w; ADVENTURES OF TOM SAWYER, THE(1938), p; YOUNG IN HEART, THE(1938), p; GONE WITH THE WIND(1939), p; INTERMEZZO: A LOVE STORY(1939), p; MADE FOR EACH OTHER(1939), p; REBECCA(1940), p; BULLETS FOR O'HARA(1941), w; SINCE YOU WENT AWAY(1944), p, w; SPELLBOUND(1945), p; DUEL IN THE SUN(1946), p, w; PARA-DINE CASE, THE(1947), p, w; FALLEN IDOL, THE(1949, Brit.), p; PORTRAIT OF JENNIE(1949), p; THIRD MAN, THE(1950, Brit.), p; WILD HEART, THE(1952, Brit.), p; FAREWELL TO ARMS, A(1957), p
Joyce Selznick
PROJECT X(1949), w; ROOGIE'S BUMP(1954), w
Myron Selznick
Silents
ONE WEEK OF LOVE(1922), p; REPORTED MISSING(1922), sup; COMMON LAW, THE(1923), sup; RUPERT OF HENTZAU(1923), sup
Phyllis Selznick
HARD RIDE, THE(1971)
Stephen Selznick
CONDEMNED(1929)
Britt Semand
HORROR OF THE BLOOD MONSTERS(1970, U.S./Phil.)
Benjamin Semaskay
RAMPARTS WE WATCH, THE(1940)
John Sembello
VIVA MAX!(1969), m
Ousmane Sembene
MANDABI(1970, Fr./Senegal), d&w; CEDDO(1978, Nigeria), a, d&w
Tricia Sembera
FLASH AND THE FIRECAT(1976)
Sembt
CROSSROADS OF PASSION(1951, Fr.)
Domingo Semedo
JONAH-WHO WILL BE 25 IN THE YEAR 2000(1976, Switz.)
Harry Semek
FOLIES DERGERE(1935)
Harry Semels
UNDER TWO FLAGS(1936); YELLOW JACK(1938); DELIGHTFUL HOGUE(1929); BAD MAN, THE(1930); HELL'S ANGELS(1930); THOSE WHO DANCE(1930); DANCE, FOOLS, DANCE(1931); DRUMS OF JEOPARDY(1931); FIGHTING CARAVANS(1931); LION AND THE LAMB(1931); PLATINUM BLONDE(1931); SMART MONEY(1931); SUBWAY EXPRESS(1931); SUICIDE FLEET(1931); BROADWAY TO CHEYEN-NE(1932); GHOST VALLEY(1932); NIGHT BEAT(1932); SALLY OF THE SUB-WAY(1932); SIN'S PAYDAY(1932); SOUTH OF THE RIO GRANDE(1932); TEXAS BUDDIES(1932); YOUNG BLOOD(1932); BOWERY, THE(1933); DELUGE(1933); DRUM TAPS(1933); FLYING DOWN TO RIO(1933); HOLD YOUR MAN(1933); THRILL HUNTER, THE(1933); DEATH OF THE DIAMOND(1934); DOWN TO THEIR LAST YACHT(1934); KING OF THE WILD HORSES, THE(1934); ROCKY RHODES(1934); TWENTIETH CENTURY(1934); VIVA VILLA!(1934); BARBARY COAST(1935); LAST OUTPOST, THE(1935); LES MISERABLES(1935); MILLIONS IN THE AIR(1935); REVENGE RIDER, THE(1935); SONS OF STEEL(1935); STONE OF SILVER CREEK(1935); WEDDING NIGHT, THE(1935); GAY DESPERADO, THE(1936); HU-MAN CARGO(1936); FIREFLY, THE(1937); HIGH, WIDE AND HANDSOME(1937); HOTEL HAYWIRE(1937); LAST TRAIN FROM MADRID, THE(1937); ROSALIE(1937); SWING HIGH, SWING LOW(1937); KING OF THE NEWSBOYS(1938); SWISS MISS(1938); YOU CAN'T TAKE IT WITH YOU(1938); KING OF THE TURF(1939); MIDNIGHT(1939); NINOTCHKA(1939); OVERLAND MAIL(1939); ROVIN' TUM-BLEWEEDS(1939); HE STAYED FOR BREAKFAST(1940); STRANGE CARGO(1940); BARNACLE BILL(1941); HONKY TONK(1941); CHANCE OF A LIFETIME, THE(1943); PILOT NO. 5(1943); GYPSY WILDCAT(1944); EVE KNEW HER AP-PLES(1945); HONEYMOON AHEAD(1945); SAN ANTONIO(1945); SEARCHING WIND, THE(1946)
Silents
AMERICAN WAY, THE(1919); AMERICA(1924); ISLE OF FORGOTTEN WO-MEN(1927); LAST COMMAND, THE(1928); OUT WITH THE TIDE(1928); ROYAL RIDER, THE(1929)
Misc. Silents
ROGUES AND ROMANCE(1920)
Michel Semeniako
LA CHINOISE(1967, Fr.)
M. Semenikhin
RESURRECTION(1963, USSR)
Simon Semenoff
GREAT JOHN L. THE(1945)

G. Semenov
NO GREATER LOVE(1944, USSR)
Ludmilla Semenova
Misc. Silents
BED AND SOFA(1926, USSR)
Nadezhda Sementsova
CHEREZ TERNII K SVEZDAM(1981 USSR)
Ed Semenza
STACY'S KNIGHTS(1983)
Julian Semilian
DEATH WISH II(1982), ed
Domenico Seminara
TOUGH ENOUGH(1983)
George Seminara
1984
SPLATTER UNIVERSITY(1984)
G. Semionov
GREAT CITIZEN, THE(1939, USSR)
Vladimir Semitjof
INVISIBLE MAN, THE(1963, Ger.), w
W. Semitjov
BREAD OF LOVE, THE(1954, Swed.), w
Anita Semjen
DIALOGUE(1967, Hung.)
Ira Semko
SONG OF THE FOREST(1963, USSR)
Ann Semler
DEATHCHEATERS(1976, Aus.)
Dean Semler
LET THE BALLOON GO(1977, Aus.), ph; ROAD WARRIOR, THE(1982, Aus.), ph
1984
RAZORBACK(1984, Aus.), ph
Martin Semmelrogge
DAS BOOT(1982)
Willy Semmelrogge
UNWILLING AGENT(1968, Ger.); EVERY MAN FOR HIMSELF AND GOD AGAINST ALL(1975, Ger.)
Dean Semmler
HOODWINK(1981, Aus.), ph; KITTY AND THE BAGMAN(1983, Aus.), ph
Irina Semochenko
MISSION TO MOSCOW(1943); SONG OF BERNADETTE, THE(1943); DEVO-TION(1946)
Larry Semon
Silents
WIZARD OF OZ, THE(1925), a, d, w; SPUDS(1927), a, d&w; UNDERWORLD(1927)
Misc. Silents
GIRL IN THE LIMOUSINE, THE(1924); PERFECT CLOWN, THE(1925); STOP, LOOK, AND LISTEN(1926), a, d
Maxine Semon
SPORTING CHANCE, A(1945); GANGSTER, THE(1947); CAMPUS HONEY-MOON(1948); FATHER'S WILD GAME(1950); FATHER TAKES THE AIR(1951); DRAGNET(1974)
Nina Semona
SEVEN DARING GIRLS(1962, Ger.)
James Semour
MOTHER'S BOY(1929), d
William Semour
MYSTERY SUBMARINE(1963, Brit.)
Tanya Semova
PASSPORT TO SUEZ(1943)
Francisco Sempere
HALLUCINATION GENERATION(1966), ph; HYPNOSIS(1966, Ger./Sp./Ital.), ph; ADIOS GRINGO(1967, Ital./Fr./Span.), ph; ROYAL HUNT OF THE SUN, THE(1969, Brit.), ph; VENGEANCE IS MINE(1969, Ital./Span.), ph; BULLET FOR SANDOVAL, A(1970, Ital./Span.), ph; CAULDRON OF BLOOD(1971, Span.), ph
Wilma Sempetery
PHAROAH'S WOMAN, THE(1961, Ital.)
Vincente Sempio
SECRET OF THE SACRED FOREST, THE(1970), a, ph
Ashby Semple
LITTLE ROMANCE, A(1979, U.S./Fr.)
Elmer Jack Semple
MARGIN FOR ERROR(1943)
Jack Semple
THEY WERE EXPENDABLE(1945)
Lorenzo Semple, Jr.
HONEYMOON MACHINE, THE(1961), w; BATMAN(1966), w; FATHOM(1967), w; PRETTY POISON(1968), w; DADDY'S GONE A-HUNTING(1969), w; MARRIAGE OF A YOUNG STOCKBROKER, THE(1971), w; SPORTING CLUB, THE(1971), w; PAPIL-LON(1973), w; PARALLAX VIEW, THE(1974), w; SUPER COPS, THE(1974), w; DROWNING POOL, THE(1975), w; THREE DAYS OF THE CONDOR(1975), w; KING KONG(1976), w; HURRICANE(1979), w; FLASH GORDON(1980), w; NEVER SAY NEVER AGAIN(1983), w
1984
SHEENA(1984), w
Diego G. Sempre
1984
YELLOW HAIR AND THE FORTRESS OF GOLD(1984), p
Colette Semprun
1984
BIZET'S CARMEN(1984, Fr./Ital.), ed
Jorge Semprun
LA GUERRE EST FINIE(1967, Fr./Swed.), a, w; Z(1969, Fr./Algeria), w; CONFES-SION, THE(1970, Fr.), w; JE T'AIME, JE T'AIME(1972, Fr./Swed.); FRENCH CON-SPIRACY, THE(1973, Fr.), w; STAVISKY(1974, Fr.), w; WOMAN AT HER WINDOW, A(1978, Fr./Ital./Ger.), w
Betty Sempsey
WOMAN IN COMMAND, THE(1934 Brit.)

Lev Semyonov
UNCOMMON THIEF, AN(1967, USSR), art d
N. Semyonov
Misc. Silents
DEFENCE OF SEVASTOPOL(1911, USSR)
Vova Semyonov
DIMKA(1964, USSR)
L. Semyonova
VIOLIN AND ROLLER(1962, USSR)
Ludmila Semyonova
Misc. Silents
DEVIL'S WHEEL, THE(1926, USSR); FRAGMENT OF AN EMPIRE(1930, USSR)
Olya Semyonova
GIRL AND THE BUGLER, THE(1967, USSR)
Aparna Sen
GURU, THE(1969, U.S./India); BOMBAY TALKIE(1970, India); HULLABALOO OVER GEORGIE AND BONNIE'S PICTURES(1979, Brit.)
Bachoo Sen
LOVE IS A SPLENDID ILLUSION(1970, Brit.), p, w
Chan Sen
CLEOPATRA JONES AND THE CASINO OF GOLD(1975 U. S. Hong Kong)
Pro Sen
HOUSEHOLDER, THE(1963, US/India)
Tevfik Sen
YOR, THE HUNTER FROM THE FUTURE(1983, Ital.)
Victor Sen Yung
LETTER, THE(1940); DANGEROUS MILLIONS(1946); CONFESSIONS OF AN OPIUM EATER(1962)
Licinio Sena
KILL OR BE KILLED(1950)
Janice Sena-Shannon
SECOND THOUGHTS(1983)
Eugen Senaj
SHOP ON MAIN STREET, THE(1966, Czech.)
Georges Senamaud
PLEASURES AND VICES(1962, Fr.), p
Geroges Senamaud
LOVE AT NIGHT(1961, Fr.), p
Daniele Senatore
IN SEARCH OF GREGORY(1970, Brit./Ital.), p; INVESTIGATION OF A CITIZEN ABOVE SUSPICION(1970, Ital.), p
Kent Senatore
Misc. Talkies
SKATEBOARD MADNESS(1980)
Paola Senatore
ZIG-ZAG(1975, Fr/Ital.); WOMEN IN CELL BLOCK 7(1977, Ital./U.S.)
George Senaut
Misc. Silents
SUCCESSFUL FAILURE, A(1917)
Ludmila Senchina
ARMED AND DANGEROUS(1977, USSR)
Ralph Sencuya
MOON OVER BURMA(1940)
Ralph R. Sencuya
SAIGON(1948)
Koreya Senda
GATE OF HELL(1954, Jap.); H-MAN, THE(1959, Jap.); BATTLE IN OUTER SPACE(1960); VARAN THE UNBELIEVABLE(1962, U.S./Jap.); PRESSURE OF GUILT(1964, Jap.); TORA! TORA! TORA!(1970, U.S./Jap.)
Max A. Sendel
DECOY FOR TERROR(1970, Can.), p
Brenda Senders
SIDECAR RACERS(1975, Aus.); TIM(1981, Aus.)
Blanca Sendino
HOUSE THAT SCREAMED, THE(1970, Span.)
Albert Sendrey
HILLS OF HOME(1948), m; KISSING BANDIT, THE(1948), m; FATHER'S LITTLE DIVIDEND(1951), m; KANSAS PACIFIC(1953), m; OPPOSITE SEX, THE(1956), md
Albert Sendry
MOONWOLF(1966, Fin./Ger.), m
Nar Modou Sene
CEDDO(1978, Nigeria)
Joe Seneca
KRAMER VS. KRAMER(1979); VERDICT, THE(1982)
1984
EVIL THAT MEN DO, THE(1984)
Sjelko Senecic
SCALAWAG(1973, Yugo.), art d
Zeljko Senecic
EVENT, AN(1970, Yugo.), w, art d
1984
NADIA(1984, U.S./Yugo.), art d
Fiorenzo Senese
DIVINE NYMPH, THE(1979, Ital.), prod d; PASSION OF LOVE(1982, Ital./Fr.), art d
Louis Senesi
Misc. Talkies
ROBIN(1979)
Don Senette
SWEET JESUS, PREACHER MAN(1973)
Norman Senfield
MAFIA GIRLS, THE(1969), p
Gunther Senfleben
BRAINWASHED(1961, Ger.), ph
Gunter Senftleben
THREE MOVES TO FREEDOM(1960, Ger.), ph; QUESTION 7(1961, U.S./Ger.), ph; CAPTAIN SINDBAD(1963), ph; EMIL AND THE DETECTIVES(1964), ph; GIRL AND THE LEGEND, THE(1966, Ger.), ph; MAYA(1966), ph; UNWILLING AGENT(1968, Ger.), ph

Lilian Seng
SINS OF ROSE BERND, THE(1959, Ger.), ed; GIRL FROM HONG KONG(1966, Ger.), ed
Lillian Seng
BOOMERANG(1960, Ger.), ed
Seizo Sengen
DIARY OF A SHINJUKU BURGLAR(1969, Jap.), ph
L. S. Senghor
MANDABI(1970, Fr./Senegal), d&w
Noriko Sengoku
DRUNKEN ANGEL(1948, Jap.); SEVEN SAMURAI, THE(1956, Jap.); STRAY DOG(1963, Jap.); SCANDAL(1964, Jap.); I LIVE IN FEAR(1967, Jap.)
Notiko Sengoku
IDIOT, THE(1963, Jap.)
Jean Marie Senia
CELINE AND JULIE GO BOATING(1974, Fr.), m
Jean-Marie Senia
JONAH–WHO WILL BE 25 IN THE YEAR 2000(1976, Switz.), m; COUSINS IN LOVE(1982), m
Phil Senini
TWILIGHT'S LAST GLEAMING(1977, U.S./Ger.)
Anna Senior
DON'S PARTY(1976, Aus.), cos; GETTING OF WISDOM, THE(1977, Aus.), cos; MONEY MOVERS(1978, Aus.), cos; BREAKER MORANT(1980, Aus.), cos; MY BRILLIANT CAREER(1980, Aus.), cos
1984
PHAR LAP(1984, Aus.), cos
Gilbert Senior
SKULLDUGGERY(1970)
Laurie Senit
DOCTOR DETROIT(1983)
Anna Senluk
YOUNG GIRLS OF WILKO, THE(1979, Pol./Fr.)
Suzanne Senn
BROKEN ENGLISH(1981), ed
Wolfgang Senn
JOURNEYS FROM BERLIN–1971(1980), ph
Mack Sennett
MIDNIGHT DADDIES(1929), p&d; HYPNOTIZED(1933), d, w; HOLLYWOOD CAVALCADE(1939), a, d; DOWN MEMORY LANE(1949); ABBOTT AND COSTELLO MEET THE KEYSTONE KOPS(1955)
Silents
TILLIE'S PUNCTURED ROMANCE(1914), d; SUBMARINE PIRATE, A(1915), sup&w; MICKEY(1919), sup; MOLLY O'(1921), sup, w; SMALL TOWN IDOL, A(1921), sup&w; SUZANNA(1922), sup&w; EXTRA GIRL, THE(1923), w; GOOD-BYE KISS, THE(1928), d, w
Misc. Silents
HOME TALENT(1921), d; OH, MABEL BEHAVE(1922), a, d
Susan Sennett
BIG BAD MAMA(1974); TIDAL WAVE(1975, U.S./Jap.)
Herbert Sennewald
DARK EYES OF LONDON(1961, Ger.), p; YOUNG GO WILD, THE(1962, Ger.), p
Senor Wences with Johnny
MOTHER WORE TIGHTS(1947)
Octave Senoret
ROMAN HOLIDAY(1953)
Ottavio Senoret
BEHIND CLOSED SHUTTERS(1952, Ital.)
G. Senotov
MORNING STAR(1962, USSR), spec eff; HAMLET(1966, USSR), spec eff
Barry Senry
KID COURAGEOUS(1935)
A. Sens-Cazenave
CATHY'S CURSE(1977, Can.), w
Roy S. Sensabaugh
Silents
JOURNEY'S END(1918), w; MISS CRUSOE(1919), w
Ursula Sensburg
DEEP END(1970 Ger./U.S.), cos
Mario Sensi
GIANT OF METROPOLIS, THE(1963, Ital.), ph
Dorita Sensier
GUNS OF DARKNESS(1962, Brit.)
Betty Senter
PRIME TIME, THE(1960)
Jack Senter
GUNSMOKE IN TUCSON(1958), art d; DINOSAURUS(1960), art d; HOW TO SEDUCE A WOMAN(1974), art d; STRONGEST MAN IN THE WORLD, THE(1975), art d; FREAKY FRIDAY(1976), art d; NO DEPOSIT, NO RETURN(1976), art d; OBSESSION(1976), art d; GREASED LIGHTNING(1977), art d; OH, GOD!(1977), art d; GO TELL THE SPARTANS(1978), art d; RETURN FROM WITCH MOUNTAIN(1978), art d; MODERN PROBLEMS(1981), prod d; MAN WHO LOVED WOMEN, THE(1983), art d
1984
MICKI AND MAUDE(1984), art d
Jill Senter
Misc. Talkies
PICK-UP(1975)
John Sentesi
STOP THAT CAB(1951), m
Al Sentesy
JOE(1970)
Jean-Pierre Sentier
QUESTION, THE(1977, Fr.); JUDGE AND THE ASSASSIN, THE(1979, Fr.)
Igor Sentjuro
BOOMERANG(1960, Ger.), w
David Sentman
GREEN SLIME, THE(1969)

Brenda Senton
KISS ME GOODBYE(1935, Brit.)
Eileen Senton
OLD ROSES(1935, Brit.)
Ira Senz
SLEEPING CITY, THE(1950), makeup
Grupo Senzala
1984
BLAME IT ON RIO(1984)
Akiko Seo
KARATE, THE HAND OF DEATH(1961)
Seow
SEVENTH DAWN, THE(1964)
Nana Seowg
1984
WHITE ELEPHANT(1984, Brit.)
Dani Seper
THREE SPARE WIVES(1962, Brit.)
S. Sepian
TEARS OF HAPPINESS(1974)
Nikko Seppala
REDS(1981)
Christopher Seppe
Misc. Talkies
TEAM-MATES(1978)
Kathy September
FLASH GORDON(1980)
Ramiro Torres Septien
UNTOUCHED(1956), w
Carl Sepulveda
CODE OF THE CACTUS(1939); DAYS OF JESSE JAMES(1939); RIDERS OF BLACK RIVER(1939); LITTLE JOE, THE WRANGLER(1942); LONE RIDER AND THE BANDIT, THE(1942); RAIDERS OF THE WEST(1942); STAGECOACH BUCK-AROO(1942); VALLEY OF THE SUN(1942); BLACK MARKET RUSTLERS(1943); BORDERTOWN GUNFIGHTERS(1943); LAND OF HUNTED MEN(1943); RAIDERS OF SAN JOAQUIN(1943); SANTA FE SCOUTS(1943); MARSHAL OF RENO(1944); SHERIFF OF SUNDOWN(1944); STAGECOACH TO MONTEREY(1944); PLAINSMAN AND THE LADY(1946); SONG OF THE SIERRAS(1946); LAND OF THE LAWL-ESS(1947); RAINBOW OVER THE ROCKIES(1947); SADDLE PALS(1947); PARTNERS OF THE SUNSET(1948); RIVER LADY(1948); UP IN CENTRAL PARK(1948); SAN ANTONE AMBUSH(1949); CALLAWAY WENT THATAWAY(1951)
Jose Sepulveda
EVERY DAY IS A HOLIDAY(1966, Span.)
Mario Sequi
COBRA, THE(1968), d
Horace Sequiera
JOHN WESLEY(1954, Brit.)
George Sequira
WICKED WIFE(1955, Brit.)
Randy Ser
GAL YOUNG UN(1979); MORTUARY(1983), art d
1984
EXTERMINATOR 2(1984), set d
Henri Sera
ROMANCE OF A HORSE THIEF(1971)
Ian Sera
PIECES(1983, Span./Puerto Rico)
Enzio Serafin
MYSTERIOUS ISLAND OF CAPTAIN NEMO, THE(1973, Fr./Ital. 87m Span./Cameroon), ph
Enzo Serafin
MEDIUM, THE(1951), ph; SEVEN DEADLY SINS, THE(1953, Fr./Ital.), ph; STRAN-GER'S HAND, THE(1955, Brit.), ph; MILLER'S WIFE, THE(1957, Ital.), ph; RAW WIND IN EDEN(1958), ph; LAST OF THE VIKINGS, THE(1962, Fr./Ital.), ph; STEPPE, THE(1963, Fr./Ital.), ph; LOVE ON THE RIVIERA(1964, Fr./Ital.), ph; PANIC BUTTON(1964), ph; RUN FOR YOUR WIFE(1966, Fr./Ital.), ph; BEYOND THE LAW(1967, Ital.), ph; JOURNEY BENEATH THE DESERT(1967, Fr./Ital.), ph; VENETIAN AFFAIR, THE(1967), ph; DAY OF ANGER(1970, Ital./Ger.), ph; LADY WITHOUT CAMELLIAS, THE(1981, Ital.), ph
Tullio Serafin
RIGOLETTO(1949), md
Enzo Serafini
WOMAN OF ROME(1956, Ital.), w
Gabriella Serafini
RED LIPS(1964, Fr./Ital.)
Sandro Serafini
DIRTY OUTLAWS, THE(1971, Ital.)
Sergio Serafini
SACCO AND VANZETTI(1971, Ital./Fr.)
Oresta Seragnoli
SECOND CHANCE(1953)
Oreste Seragnoli
MY COUSIN RACHEL(1952)
Dino Seragusa
MEAN STREETS(1973)
George Serallon
BATTLE OF THE WORLDS(1961, Ital.), ed
Marion Serandei
CENTO ANNI D'AMORE(1954, Ital.), ed
Mario Serandel
BELLISSIMA(1952, Ital.), ed
Giorgio Serandrei
GOLDEN ARROW, THE(1964, Ital.), ed
Mario Serandrei
LA TERRA TREMA(1947, Ital.), ed; WALLS OF MALAPAGA, THE(1950, Fr./Ital.), ed; TIMES GONE BY(1953, Ital.), ed; TOO BAD SHE'S BAD(1954, Ital.), ed; LUCKY TO BE A WOMAN(1955, Ital.), ed; SIGN OF VENUS, THE(1955, Ital.), ed; SCANDAL IN SORRENTO(1957, Ital./Fr.), ed; HERCULES(1959, Ital.), ed; OSSESSIONE(1959, Ital.), ed; GIANT OF MARATHON, THE(1960, Ital.), ed; BLACK SUNDAY(1961, Ital.), w, ed; GIRL WITH A SUITCASE(1961, Fr./Ital.), ed; ROCCO AND HIS BROTHERS(1961,

Fr./Ital.), ed; VIOLENT SUMMER(1961, Fr./Ital.), ed; WHITE NIGHTS(1961, Ital./Fr.), ed; COMMANDO(1962, Ital., Span., Bel., Ger.), ed; CONSTANTINE AND THE CROSS(1962, Ital.), ed; STORY OF JOSEPH AND HIS BRETHREN THE(1962, Ital.), ed; SWINDLE, THE(1962, Fr./Ital.), ed; SWORD OF THE CONQUEROR(1962, Ital.), ed; ATLAS AGAINST THE CYCLOPS(1963, Ital.), ed; BLACK SABBATH(1963, Ital.), ed; ERIK THE CONQUEROR(1963, Fr./Ital.), ed; FAMILY DIARY(1963 Ital.), ed; FIASCO IN MILAN(1963, Fr./Ital.), ed; LEOPARD, THE(1963, Ital.), ed; RICE GIRL(1963, Fr./Ital.), ed; APE WOMAN, THE(1964, Ital.), ed; EVIL EYE(1964 Ital.), ed; HERCULES IN THE HAUNTED WORLD(1964, Ital.), ed; DOLL THAT TOOK THE TOWN, THE(1965, Ital.), ed; ITALIANO BRAVA GENTE(1965, Ital./USSR), ed; MO-MENT OF TRUTH, THE(1965, Ital./Span.), ed; MAN WHO LAUGHS, THE(1966, Ital.), ed; SALVATORE GIULIANO(1966, Ital.), ed; SANDRA(1966, Ital.), ed; TIKO AND THE SHARK(1966, U.S./Ital./Fr.), ed; BATTLE OF ALGIERS, THE(1967, Ital./Alger.), ed; SENSO(1968, Ital.), ed; WITCHES, THE(1969, Fr./Ital.), ed
Mario Serandrel
CALYPSO(1959, Fr./It.), ed
Manuel Serano
BEAT THE DEVIL(1953)
Sergio Serardi
HEART AND SOUL(1950, Ital.)
I. Serasinghe
1984
INDIANA JONES AND THE TEMPLE OF DOOM(1984)
Ida Serasini
OMICRON(1963, Ital.)
Massimo Serata
EL CID(1961, U.S./Ital.)
Sora Serati
BLOOD, SWEAT AND FEAR(1975, Ital.)
Massimo Serato
FUGITIVE LADY(1951); THIEF OF VENICE, THE(1952); MAN FROM CAIRO, THE(1953); LOVES OF THREE QUEENS(1954, Ital./Fr.); MADAME DU BAR-RY(1954 Fr./Ital.); CARTOUCHE(1957, Ital./US); NAKED MAJA, THE(1959, Ital./U.S.); SILENT ENEMY, THE(1959, Brit.); DAVID AND GOLIATH(1961, Ital.); PIRATE AND THE SLAVE GIRL, THE(1961, Fr./Ital.); QUEEN OF THE PIRATES(1961, Ital./Ger.); CONSTANTINE AND THE CROSS(1962, Ital.); SAMSON AND THE SLAVE QUEEN(1963, Ital.); SECRET MARK OF D'ARTAGNAN, THE(1963, Fr./Ital.); 55 DAYS AT PEKING(1963); LOVE, THE ITALIAN WAY(1964, Ital.); GUNMEN OF THE RIO GRANDE(1965, Fr./Ital./Span.); TENTH VICTIM, THE(1965, Fr./Ital.); HYP-NOSIS(1966, Ger./Sp./Ital.); SECRET SEVEN, THE(1966, Ital./Span.); PONTIUS PI-LATE(1967, Fr./Ital.); TERROR OF THE BLACK MASK(1967, Fr./Ital.); WILD, WILD PLANET, THE(1967, Ital.); CATCH AS CATCH CAN(1968, Ital.); CAMILLE 2000(1969); GAMBLERS, THE(1969); DON'T LOOK NOW(1973, Brit./Ital.); NANA(1983, Ital.)
Misc. Talkies
FLYING SQUADRON(1952)
Rudolph Serato
PIRATES OF CAPRI, THE(1949)
Vincenzo Seratrice
DOCTOR BEWARE(1951, Ital.), ph; PIRATE OF THE BLACK HAWK, THE(1961, Fr./Ital.), ph; FURY OF THE PAGANS(1963, Ital.), ph
Roger Serbagi
EFFECT OF GAMMA RAYS ON MAN-IN-THE-MOON MARIGOLDS, THE(1972); SEVEN UPS, THE(1973)
Roger Omar Serbagi
NEXT MAN, THE(1976)
Alex Serbaroli
PRINCE OF FOXES(1949)
Alex Serberoli
FUGITIVE LADY(1951)
Giovanni Serboli
ROMA(1972, Ital./Fr.)
Julia Serda
LOVE WALTZ, THE(1930, Ger.); DREAM OF SCHONBRUNN(1933, Aus.); LA HABANERA(1937, Ger.)
Misc. Silents
IMAGINARY BARON, THE(1927, Ger.)
Sergey Serebrenikov
HOME FOR TANYA, A(1961, USSR), art d; SPRINGTIME ON THE VOLGA(1961, USSR), art d; HOUSE ON THE FRONT LINE, THE(1963, USSR), artd; DIMKA(1964, USSR), art d
Muni Serebroff
ELI ELI(1940)
Misc. Talkies
I WANT TO BE A MOTHER(1937); GREATER ADVISOR, THE(1940); HER SECOND MOTHER(1940)
Nadya Serednichenko
SUNFLOWER(1970, Fr./Ital.)
Jerry Serempa
PLASTIC DOME OF NORMA JEAN, THE(1966)
Serena
FANTASM(1976, Aus.)
Misc. Talkies
DRACULA SUCKS(1979)
Brunello Serena
SEVEN SEAS TO CALAIS(1963, Ital.), set d
Gustavo Serena
Silents
QUO VADIS?(1913, Ital.)
Signor Serena
Silents
WHITE SISTER, THE(1923)
Serene
Misc. Talkies
JIVE TURKEY(1976)
Martin Serene
1984
SUPERGIRL(1984)

Gustavo Sereno
Misc. Silents
TOILER, THE(1932, Ital.), d
John Seresheff
Silents
TWO FLAMING YOUTHS(1927)
Michael Seresin
RAGMAN'S DAUGHTER, THE(1974, Brit.), ph; BUGSY MALONE(1976, Brit.), ph; MIDNIGHT EXPRESS(1978, Brit.), ph; FAME(1980), ph; TATTOO(1981), ph; SHOOT THE MOON(1982), ph
1984
BIRDY(1984), ph
Jacques Sereys
FIRE WITHIN, THE(1964, Fr./Ital.)
Katherine Sergava
18 MINUTES(1935, Brit.)
Kathryn Sergava
BEDSIDE(1934); HI, NELLIE!(1934); WONDER BAR(1934)
Jean Serge
PARIS DOES STRANGE THINGS(1957, Fr./Ital.), w; GAME OF TRUTH, THE(1961, Fr.), w
Serge Jaroff's Don Cossacks
MOSCOW SHANGHAI(1936, Ger.)
George Sergeant
UNASHAMED(1938), ph
Lewis Sergeant
TARZAN AND THE GREEN GODDESS(1938)
Richard Sergeant
GROUNDSTAR CONSPIRACY, THE(1972, Can.)
Katya Sergeiva
COCK OF THE AIR(1932)
Chouky Sergent
ONCE IN PARIS(1978)
Glenna Sergent
ALEX IN WONDERLAND(1970)
Sergey Sergeyeff
Silents
GALLOPING GOBS, THE(1927), w
F. Sergeyev
MARRIAGE OF BALZAMINOV, THE(1966, USSR)
G. Sergeyev
GORDEYEV FAMILY, THE(1961, U.S.S.R.)
Konstantin Sergeyev
SLEEPING BEAUTY, THE(1966, USSR), d, w, ch
Nikolai Sergeyev
FATHERS AND SONS(1960, USSR)
Nikolay Sergeyev
SUMMER TO REMEMBER, A(1961, USSR); SUN SHINES FOR ALL, THE(1961, USSR); RESURRECTION(1963, USSR); NINE DAYS OF ONE YEAR(1964, USSR); THERE WAS AN OLD COUPLE(1967, USSR); RED AND THE WHITE, THE(1969, Hung./USSR)
Brad Sergi
PURSUIT OF D.B. COOPER, THE(1981)
Miguel Sergides
MOON OVER THE ALLEY(1980, Brit.)
Michael Sergio
HOUSE ON SORORITY ROW, THE(1983)
Sergio Mendes and Brazil '66
SULLIVAN'S EMPIRE(1967)
Semone Sergis
Silents
KING OF KINGS, THE(1927)
Nikolai Sergueiev
ANDREI ROUBLOV(1973, USSR)
Yvonne Sergyl
Misc. Silents
MIRACLE OF WOLVES, THE(1925, Fr.)
Mohamed Serhani
PIRATES OF PENZANCE, THE(1983)
Istvan Seri
BOYS OF PAUL STREET, THE(1969, Hung./US)
Maurice Serien
THUNDER IN THE BLOOD(1962, Fr.), ed
Franco Serino
MAGIC WORLD OF TOPO GIGIO, THE(1961, Ital.), pro d
Charles Serio
HOUSE ON SORORITY ROW, THE(1983)
Frank Serio
1984
RUNAWAY(1984)
Renato Serio
ALONE IN THE DARK(1982), m
Nancy Serlin
CLASS(1983)
1984
WINDY CITY(1984)
Carol Serling
TWILIGHT ZONE-THE MOVIE(1983)
Rod Serling
PATTERNS(1956), w; RACK, THE(1956), w; SADDLE THE WIND(1958), w; INCIDENT IN AN ALLEY(1962), w; REQUIEM FOR A HEAVYWEIGHT(1962), w; YELLOW CANARY, THE(1963), w; SEVEN DAYS IN MAY(1964), w; ASSAULT ON A QUEEN(1966), w; PLANET OF THE APES(1968), w; MAN, THE(1972), w; ENCOUNTER WITH THE UNKNOWN(1973); TWILIGHT ZONE-THE MOVIE(1983), w
Ozen Sermet
TARZAN AND THE JUNGLE BOY(1968, US/Switz.), ph
Larry Sermon
Misc. Silents
GIRL IN THE LIMOUSINE, THE(1924), d

Maxine Sermon
OPPOSITE SEX, THE(1956)
Gil Serna
BUCK ROGERS IN THE 25TH CENTURY(1979)
Pepe Serna
STUDENT NURSES, THE(1970); RED SKY AT MORNING(1971); SHOOT OUT(1971); NEW CENTURIONS, THE(1972); HANGUP(1974); DAY OF THE LOCUST, THE(1975); CARWASH(1976); KILLER INSIDE ME, THE(1976); FORCE OF ONE, A(1979); JERK, THE(1979); WALK PROUD(1979); HONEYSUCKLE ROSE(1980); INSIDE MOVES(1980); VICE SQUAD(1982); BALLAD OF GREGORIO CORTEZ, THE(1983); DEAL OF THE CENTURY(1983); HEARTBREAKER(1983); SCARFACE(1983)
1984
ADVENTURES OF BUCKAROO BANZAI: ACROSS THE 8TH DIMENSION, THE(1984); RED DAWN(1984)
Jack Sernas
HELEN OF TROY(1956, Ital)
Jack [Jacques] Sernas
JUMP INTO HELL(1955)
Jacques Sernas
GOLDEN SALAMANDER(1950, Brit.); SKY IS RED, THE(1952, Ital.); LUXURY GIRLS(1953, Ital.); ANITA GARIBALDI(1954, Ital.); CENTO ANNI D'AMORE(1954, Ital.); SIGN OF THE GLADIATOR(1959, Fr./Ger./Ital.); GODDESS OF LOVE, THE(1960, Ital./Fr.); NIGHTS OF LUCRETIA BORGIA, THE(1960, Ital.); LA DOLCE VITA(1961, Ital./Fr.); LOST SOULS(1961, Ital.); CENTURION, THE(1962, Fr./Ital.); HUNS, THE(1962, Fr./Ital.); LOVES OF SALAMMBO, THE(1962, Fr./Ital.); DUEL OF THE TITANS(1963, Ital.); SLAVE, THE(1963, Ital.); 55 DAYS AT PEKING(1963); DUEL OF CHAMPIONS(1964 Ital./Span.); GOLIATH AND THE VAMPIRES(1964, Ital.); THE DIRTY GAME(1966, Fr./Ital./Ger.); MIDAS RUN(1969); HORNET'S NEST(1970); SUPERFLY T.N.T.(1973); CHILDREN OF RAGE(1975, Brit.-Israeli)
Hakan Serner
DEAR JOHN(1966, Swed.); HUGS AND KISSES(1968, Swed.); PIPPI IN THE SOUTH SEAS(1974, Swed./Ger.)
Kazimierz Serocki
KNIGHTS OF THE TEUTONIC ORDER, THE(1962, Pol.), m
Georges Seroff
Misc. Silents
HOUND OF THE BASKERVILLES, THE(1929, Ger.)
Muni Seroff
TWO SISTERS(1938); DOUGHBOYS IN IRELAND(1943); IS EVERYBODY HAPPY?(1943); PHANTOM OF THE OPERA(1943); SONG OF BERNADETTE, THE(1943); WINTERTIME(1943); CHARLIE CHAN IN THE SECRET SERVICE(1944); EVER SINCE VENUS(1944); MOON OVER LAS VEGAS(1944); STORM OVER LISBON(1944); TAMPICO(1944); TILL WE MEET AGAIN(1944); YOUTH ON TRIAL(1945); LINDA BE GOOD(1947); NORTHWEST OUTPOST(1947); SONG IS BORN, A(1948)
Louise Serpa
GREAT SIOUX MASSACRE, THE(1965)
Joanna Serpe
GETTING STRAIGHT(1970)
Pamela Serpe
HOT SUMMER WEEK(1973, Can.); THREE THE HARD WAY(1974)
Ralph Serpe
MISTER ROCK AND ROLL(1957), p; COUNTRY MUSIC HOLIDAY(1958), p; THREE FACES OF A WOMAN(1965, Ital.); DESERTER, THE(1971 Ital./Yugo.), p; ACROSS 110TH STREET(1972), p; DRUM(1976), p; BRINK'S JOB, THE(1978), p
Hawk Serpent
UNSTRAP ME(1968), p
Franco Serpilli
TO LIVE IN PEACE(1947, Ital.)
Domenica Serra
Misc. Silents
MACISTE IN HELL(1926, Ital.)
Eric Serra
1984
LE DERNIER COMBAT(1984, Fr.), m
Fiorenzo Serra
AND THE SHIP SAILS ON(1983, Ital./Fr.)
Gianna Serra
OUR MAN FLINT(1966); HILLS RUN RED, THE(1967, Ital.); GLASS SPHINX, THE(1968, Egypt/Ital./Span.)
Ian Serra
MONSTER ISLAND(1981, Span./U.S.)
Juan Serra
SAVAGE PAMPAS(1967, Span./Arg.), ed; DR. COPPELIUS(1968, U.S./Span.), ed; ONE STEP TO HELL(1969, U.S./Ital./Span.), ed; WIDOWS' NEST(1977, U.S./Span.), ed
Liliana Serra
THREE STOOGES VS. THE WONDER WOMEN(1975, Ital./Chi.), ed
Ray Serra
MARATHON MAN(1976); MANHATTAN(1979); VOICES(1979)
1984
ALPHABET CITY(1984)
Misc. Talkies
HOOCH(1977)
Raymond Serra
GAMBLER, THE(1974); ARTHUR(1981); WOLFEN(1981)
1984
SPLITZ(1984)
Narciso Ibanez Serrador
MASTER OF HORROR(1965, Arg.)
Narciso Ibanez Serrador
HOUSE THAT SCREAMED, THE(1970, Span.), d; ISLAND OF THE DAMNED(1976, Span.), d
Pastor Serrador
TREASURE OF MAKUBA, THE(1967, U.S./Span.)
G. Serralonga
CANNIBALS IN THE STREETS(1982, Ital./Span.), ed
Giorgio Serralonga
ROSE FOR EVERYONE, A(1967, Ital.), ed; THREE NIGHTS OF LOVE(1969, Ital.), ed; WITCHES, THE(1969, Fr./Ital.), ed

Leopaldo Serran
1984
GABRIELA(1984, Braz.), w

Angel Serrano
RIO 70(1970, U.S./Ger./Span.), ed

Charles Serrano
WARRIORS, THE(1979)

Elmer Serrano
SEARCHING WIND, THE(1946)

Enrique Serrano
GAMES MEN PLAY, THE(1968, Arg.)

Louis Serrano
LOVE SLAVES OF THE AMAZONS(1957)

Luis Serrano
NOTORIOUS(1946)

Manuel Serrano
THIRD VOICE, THE(1960); JOHNNY HAMLET(1972, Ital.)

Manuelo Serrano
ADVENTURERS, THE(1970)

Maria Serrano
SERENADE(1956)

Mary Serrano
VOICES(1979)

Maximo Serrano
Misc. Silents
BRASA DORMIDA(1928, Braz.)

Pedro B. Serrano
1984
BEAT STREET(1984)

Rafael Garcia Serrano
GLADIATORS 7(1964, Span./Ital.), w

Ramon Serrano
LONG DUEL, THE(1967, Brit.); GUNS OF THE MAGNIFICENT SEVEN(1969)

Raul Serrano
MAN CALLED HORSE, A(1970), set d

Rosario Serrano
NIGHT WATCH(1973, Brit.)

Sandy Serrano
HOMETOWN U.S.A.(1979); ZAPPED!(1982)
Misc. Talkies
JOY RIDE TO NOWHERE(1978)

Vincent Serrano
Silents
MODERN MONTE CRISTO, A(1917); ONE LAW FOR BOTH(1917); BRANDED WOMAN, THE(1920); CONVOY(1927)
Misc. Silents
LYDIA GILMORE(1916); EYES OF YOUTH(1919); VIRTUOUS MODEL, THE(1919); DEEP PURPLE, THE(1920)

Arthur Varney Serrao
ALMOST A DIVORCE(1931, Brit.), d, w

Massimo Serrato
OUTCRY(1949, Ital.); LUCRECE BORGIA(1953, Ital./Fr.)

Josefina Serratosa
PIZZA TRIANGLE, THE(1970, Ital./Span.)

Michel Serrault
DIABOLIQUE(1955, Fr.); LA BELLE AMERICAINE(1961, Fr.); LOVE AND THE FRENCHWOMAN(1961, Fr.); PEEK-A-BOO(1961, Fr.); LOVE ON A PILLOW(1963, Fr./Ital.); THREE FABLES OF LOVE(1963, Fr./Ital./Span.); DOUBLE BED, THE(1965, Fr./Ital.); HOW NOT TO ROB A DEPARTMENT STORE(1965, Fr./Ital.); MALE HUNT(1965, Fr./Ital.); KING OF HEARTS(1967, Fr./Ital.); MADMAN OF LAB 4, THE(1967, Fr.); LA CAGE AUX FOLLES(1979, Fr./Ital.); LA CAGE AUX FOLLES II(1981, Ital./Fr.); MALEVIL(1981, Fr./Ger.); ASSOCIATE, THE(1982 Fr./Ger.); HATTER'S GHOST, THE(1982, Fr.); INQUISITOR, THE(1982, Fr.)
1984
LE BON PLAISIR(1984, Fr.)

Catherine Serre
MOONRAKER(1979, Brit.)

Claude Serre
PROVIDENCE(1977, Fr.), set d

Henri Serre
JULES AND JIM(1962, Fr.); VERONA TRIAL, THE(1963, Ital.); FIRE WITHIN, THE(1964, Fr./Ital.); FANTOMAS(1966, Fr./Ital.); EASY LIFE, THE(1971, Fr.)

Coline Serreau
POURQUOI PAS!(1979, Fr.), d&w

Michel Serreaul
GET OUT YOUR HANDKERCHIEFS(1978, Fr.)

Jacques Serres
BLUE COUNTRY, THE(1977, Fr.)

John Serret
SLEEPING CAR TO TRIESTE(1949, Brit.); TEMPTRESS, THE(1949, Brit.); LAUGHING LADY, THE(1950, Brit.); LAUGHING ANNE(1954, Brit./U.S.); INNOCENTS IN PARIS(1955, Brit.); ROGUE'S YARN(1956, Brit.); SCOTLAND YARD DRAGNET(1957, Brit.); FEMALE FIENDS(1958, Brit.); FACES IN THE DARK(1960, Brit.); FOLLOW THAT HORSE!(1960, Brit.); CIRCLE OF DECEPTON(1961, Brit.); SCREAM OF FEAR(1961, Brit.); TWO WIVES AT ONE WEDDING(1961, Brit.); RETURN FROM THE ASHES(1965, U.S./Brit.); DARK OF THE SUN(1968, Brit.); NICE GIRL LIKE ME, A(1969, Brit.); THERE'S A GIRL IN MY SOUP(1970, Brit.)
1984
SWORD OF THE VALIANT(1984, Brit.)

Jean Serrett
ONE WOMAN'S STORY(1949, Brit.)

John Serrett
I WAS A MALE WAR BRIDE(1949); SWORD AND THE ROSE, THE(1953); GOLD EXPRESS, THE(1955, Brit.); TRIPLE DECEPTION(1957, Brit.)

Fred Sersem
RAZOR'S EDGE, THE(1946), spec eff

Frank Sersen
BUFFALO BILL(1944), spec eff

Fred Sersen
BIG TRAIL, THE(1930), w, art d; IN OLD CHICAGO(1938), spec eff; SUEZ(1938), spec eff; RAINS CAME, THE(1939), spec eff; LITTLE OLD NEW YORK(1940), spec eff; YANK IN THE R.A.F., A(1941), spec eff; GHOST AND MRS. MUIR, THE(1942), spec eff; CRASH DIVE(1943), spec eff; GANG'S ALL HERE, THE(1943), spec eff; GUADAL-CANAL DIARY(1943), spec eff; HAPPY LAND(1943), spec eff; HELLO, FRISCO, HELLO(1943), spec eff; HOLY MATRIMONY(1943), spec eff; JITTERBUGS(1943), spec eff; MOON IS DOWN, THE(1943), spec eff; PARIS AFTER DARK(1943), spec eff; SONG OF BERNADETTE, THE(1943), spec eff; STORMY WEATHER(1943), spec eff; SWEET ROSIE O'GRADY(1943), spec eff; THEY CAME TO BLOW UP AMERI-CA(1943), spec eff; WINTERTIME(1943), spec eff; BIG NOISE, THE(1944), spec eff; EVE OF ST. MARK, THE(1944), spec eff; FOUR JILLS IN A JEEP(1944), spec eff; GREENWICH VILLAGE(1944), spec eff; IN THE MEANTIME, DARLING(1944), spec eff; IRISH EYES ARE SMILING(1944), spec eff; JANE EYRE(1944), spec eff; KEYS OF THE KINGDOM, THE(1944), spec eff; LADIES OF WASHINGTON(1944), spec eff; LAURA(1944), spec eff; LIFEBOAT(1944), spec eff; LODGER, THE(1944), spec eff; PIN UP GIRL(1944), spec eff; PURPLE HEART, THE(1944), spec eff; ROGER TOUHY, GANGSTER!(1944), spec eff; SULLIVANS, THE(1944), spec eff; SUNDAY DINNER FOR A SOLDIER(1944), spec eff; SWEET AND LOWDOWN(1944), spec eff; TAKE IT OR LEAVE IT(1944), spec eff; TAMPICO(1944), spec eff; WILSON(1944), spec eff; WING AND A PRAYER(1944), spec eff; WINGED VICTORY(1944), spec eff; CAPTAIN EDDIE(1945), spec. eff; DIAMOND HORSESHOE(1945), spec eff; DOLL FACE(1945), spec eff; DON JUAN QUILLIGAN(1945), spec eff; FALLEN ANGEL(1945), spec eff; HANGOVER SQUARE(1945), spec eff; HOUSE ON 92ND STREET, THE(1945), spec eff; JUNIOR MISS(1945), spec eff; MOLLY AND ME(1945), spec eff; NOB HILL(1945), spec eff; ROYAL SCANDAL, A(1945), spec eff; SPIDER, THE(1945), spec eff; STATE FAIR(1945), spec eff; TREE GROWS IN BROOKLYN, A(1945), spec eff; WHERE DO WE GO FROM HERE?(1945), spec eff; WITHIN THESE WALLS(1945), spec eff; ANNA AND THE KING OF SIAM(1946), spec eff; CENTENNIAL SUMMER(1946), spec eff; CLAUDIA AND DAVID(1946), spec eff; CLUNY BROWN(1946), spec eff; DARK CORNER, THE(1946), spec eff; DO YOU LOVE ME?(1946), spec eff; DRAGON-WYCH(1946), spec eff; IT SHOULDN'T HAPPEN TO A DOG(1946), spec eff; JOHNNY COMES FLYING HOME(1946), spec eff; LEAVE HER TO HEAVEN(1946), spec eff; MARGIE(1946), spec eff; MY DARLING CLEMENTINE(1946), spec eff; SHOCK(1946), spec eff; SMOKY(1946), spec eff; SOMEWHERE IN THE NIGHT(1946), spec eff; STRANGE TRIANGLE(1946), spec eff; 13 RUE MADELEINE(1946), spec eff; BRASH-ER DOUBLOON, THE(1947), spec eff; CAPTAIN FROM CASTILE(1947), spec eff; DAISY KENYON(1947), spec eff; FOREVER AMBER(1947), spec eff; FOXES OF HARROW, THE(1947), spec eff; FUGITIVE, THE(1947), spec eff; HOMESTRETCH, THE(1947), spec eff; I WONDER WHO'S KISSING HER NOW(1947), spec eff; KISS OF DEATH(1947), spec eff; LATE GEORGE APLEY, THE(1947), spec eff; MIRACLE ON 34TH STREET, THE(1947), spec eff; MOSS ROSE(1947), spec eff; NIGHTMARE ALLEY(1947), spec eff; CALL NORTHSIDE 777(1948), spec eff; CRY OF THE CI-TY(1948), ph, spec eff; FURY AT FURNACE CREEK(1948), spec eff; IRON CURTAIN, THE(1948), spec eff; LETTER TO THREE WIVES, A(1948), spec eff; LUCK OF THE IRISH(1948), spec eff; ROAD HOUSE(1948), spec eff; SITTING PRETTY(1948), spec eff; STREET WITH NO NAME, THE(1948), spec eff; THAT LADY IN ERMINE(1948), spec eff; THAT WONDERFUL URGE(1948), spec eff; UNFAITHFULLY YOURS(1948), spec eff; WALLS OF JERICHO(1948), spec eff; YELLOW SKY(1948), spec eff; COME TO THE STABLE(1949), spec eff; DANCING IN THE DARK(1949), spec eff; FAN, THE(1949), spec eff; FATHER WAS A FULLBACK(1949), spec eff; HOUSE OF STRAN-GERS(1949), spec eff; I WAS A MALE WAR BRIDE(1949), spec eff; MOTHER IS A FRESHMAN(1949), spec eff; OH, YOU BEAUTIFUL DOLL(1949), ph; PRINCE OF FOXES(1949), spec eff; SLATTERY'S HURRICANE(1949), spec eff; THIEVES' HIGH-WAY(1949), spec eff; WHIRLPOOL(1949), spec eff; YOU'RE MY EVERYTHING(1949), spec eff; AMERICAN GUERRILLA IN THE PHILIPPINES, AN(1950), spec eff; BIG LIFT, THE(1950), spec eff; MISTER 880(1950), spec eff; PANIC IN THE STREETS(1950), spec eff; UNDER MY SKIN(1950), spec eff; WHEN WILLIE COMES MARCHING HOME(1950), spec eff; WHERE THE SIDEWALK ENDS(1950), spec eff; DAVID AND BATHSHEBA(1951), spec eff; DAY THE EARTH STOOD STILL, THE(1951), spec eff; DESERT FOX, THE(1951), spec eff; ELOPEMENT(1951), spec eff; FIXED BAYONETS(1951), spec eff; I CAN GET IT FOR YOU WHOLESALE(1951), spec eff; I'D CLIMB THE HIGHEST MOUNTAIN(1951), spec eff; MEET ME AFTER THE SHOW(1951), spec eff; PEOPLE WILL TALK(1951), spec eff; RAWHIDE(1951), spec eff; THIRTEENTH LETTER, THE(1951), spec eff; YOU'RE IN THE NAVY NOW(1951), spec eff; FIVE FINGERS(1952), spec eff; PRIDE OF ST. LOUIS, THE(1952), spec eff; WITH A SONG IN MY HEART(1952), spec eff; DOWN AMONG THE SHELTERING PALMS(1953), spec eff

Kiyokata Seruwaka
CHUSHINGURA(1963, Jap.), ch

Dagny Servaes
LAUGH PAGLIACCI(1948, Ital.); YOU ARE THE WORLD FOR ME(1964, Aust.)
Misc. Silents
PETER THE GREAT(1923, Ger.)

Jean Servais
ANGELE(1934 Fr.); LES MISERABLES(1936, Fr.); LE PLAISIR(1954, Fr.); RIFI-FI(1956, Fr.); TAMANGO(1959, Fr.); GAME OF TRUTH, THE(1961, Fr.); CRIME DOES NOT PAY(1962, Fr.); LONGEST DAY, THE(1962); WORLD IN MY POCKET, THE(1962, Fr./Ital./Ger.); LIARS, THE(1964, Fr.); THAT MAN FROM RIO(1964, Fr./Ital.); MUR-DER AT 45 R.P.M.(1965, Fr.); LOST COMMAND, THE(1966); SEATED AT HIS RIGHT(1968, Ital.); BETTER A WIDOW(1969, Ital.); THEY CAME TO ROB LAS VEGAS(1969, Fr./Ital./Span./Ger.); DEVIL'S NIGHTMARE, THE(1971 Bel./Ital.)
Misc. Talkies
BLACK JESUS(1971, Ital.)

Adrienne Servantie
MY UNCLE(1958, Fr.); FIRST TASTE OF LOVE(1962, Fr.)

Jean Servat
MAN WHO LOVED WOMEN, THE(1977, Fr.)

Eric Server
HARRAD EXPERIMENT, THE(1973); DOGS(1976); HOT LEAD AND COLD FEET(1978)

Maria Cristina Servera
THIRTEEN FRIGHTENED GIRLS(1963)

Irene Servet
THINGS OF LIFE, THE(1970, Fr./Ital./Switz.), makeup

John Servetnik
INCIDENT, THE(1967); FOR LOVE OF IVY(1968)

Helli Servi
YOU ARE THE WORLD FOR ME(1964, Aust.)
Robert W. Service
SPOILERS, THE(1942)
Silents
SHOOTING OF DAN MCGREW, THE(1915), w; SONG OF THE WAGE SLAVE, THE(1915), w; TRAIL OF '98, THE(1929), w
Robert William Service
Silents
ROUGHNECK, THE(1924), w
Gilbert Servien
LES CARABINIERS(1968, Fr./Ital.)
Michel Servin
THANK HEAVEN FOR SMALL FAVORS(1965, Fr.), w
Helen Servis
VIOLENCE(1947); SNAKE PIT, THE(1948); DAUGHTER OF THE WEST(1949); GAY AMIGO, THE(1949); LOVABLE CHEAT, THE(1949); HANNAH LEE(1953)
Leo Servo
CHRISTINA(1974, Can.)
Marieta Servo
BYE-BYE BRASIL(1980, Braz.)
Mary Servoss
LONE WOLF KEEPS A DATE, THE(1940); IN THIS OUR LIFE(1942); POSTMAN DIDN'T RING, THE(1942); HUMAN COMEDY, THE(1943); SO PROUDLY WE HAIL(1943); EXPERIMENT PERILOUS(1944); FOUR JILLS IN A JEEP(1944); MRS. PARKINGTON(1944); SUMMER STORM(1944); UNCERTAIN GLORY(1944); YOUTH RUNS WILD(1944); CONFLICT(1945); DANGER SIGNAL(1945); MILDRED PIERCE(1945); ROUGHLY SPEAKING(1945); MY REPUTATION(1946); HIGH WALL, THE(1947); ACT OF MURDER, AN(1948); BEYOND THE FOREST(1949)
Shane Serwin
TERMS OF ENDEARMENT(1983)
Brunno Serwing
FLIGHT OF THE EAGLE(1983, Swed.)
V. Seryozhinikov
Misc. Silents
1812(1912, USSR)
A. Seryozhkin
PEACE TO HIM WHO ENTERS(1963, USSR)
Ricardo Vasquez Sese
HANNIE CALDER(1971, Brit.), makeup
Members of the Sesi Tribes
SANDERS OF THE RIVER(1935, Brit.)
Robert Sessa
MAN WITH TWO BRAINS, THE(1983), set d
Hilda Sessack
FANNY HILL: MEMOIRS OF A WOMAN OF PLEASURE zero(1965)
Alex Sessai
1984
DEATHSTALKER, THE(1984), p
Hilde Sessak
GIRL FROM THE MARSH CROFT, THE(1935, Ger.); WATER FOR CANITOGA(1939, Ger.); MAN BETWEEN, THE(1953, Brit.)
Sabina Sesselman
INFORMATION RECEIVED(1962, Brit.)
Sabina Sesselmann
COURT MARTIAL(1962, Ger.); U-47 LT. COMMANDER PRIEN(1967, Ger.)
Len Sesser
MOONSHINE COUNTY EXPRESS(1977)
Bonta Sesshi
TOPSY-TURVY JOURNEY(1970, Jap.)
Jam Session
SARGE GOES TO COLLEGE(1947)
Saturday Session
FARMER, THE(1977)
Almira Sessions
CHAD HANNA(1940); BLOSSOMS IN THE DUST(1941); JENNIE(1941); OBLIGING YOUNG LADY(1941); SHE KNEW ALL THE ANSWERS(1941); SULLIVAN'S TRAVELS(1941); SUN VALLEY SERENADE(1941); THREE GIRLS ABOUT TOWN(1941); I MARRIED AN ANGEL(1942); MY SISTER EILEEN(1942); HAPPY GO LUCKY(1943); HEAT'S ON, THE(1943); MADAME CURIE(1943); MY KINGDOM FOR A COOK(1943); OX-BOW INCIDENT, THE(1943); SLIGHTLY DANGEROUS(1943); DOUGHGIRLS, THE(1944); HENRY ALDRICH'S LITTLE SECRET(1944); I LOVE A SOLDIER(1944); MIRACLE OF MORGAN'S CREEK, THE(1944); SAN DIEGO, I LOVE YOU(1944); DIXIE JAMBOREE(1945); NOB HILL(1945); SHE WOULDN'T SAY YES(1945); SOUTHERNER, THE(1945); STATE FAIR(1945); TWO O'CLOCK COURAGE(1945); WOMAN WHO CAME BACK(1945); CROSS MY HEART(1946); DIARY OF A CHAMBERMAID(1946); DO YOU LOVE ME?(1946); FEAR(1946); IT'S A WONDERFUL LIFE(1946); MISSING LADY, THE(1946); NIGHT AND DAY(1946); CASS TIMBERLANE(1947); FOR THE LOVE OF RUSTY(1947); I WONDER WHO'S KISSING HER NOW(1947); MONSIEUR VERDOUX(1947); APARTMENT FOR PEGGY(1948); ARTHUR TAKES OVER(1948); FAMILY HONEYMOON(1948); GOOD SAM(1948); JULIA MISBEHAVES(1948); LADIES OF THE CHORUS(1948); FOUNTAINHEAD, THE(1949); NIGHT UNTO NIGHT(1949); ROSEANNA McCOY(1949); TAKE ME OUT TO THE BALL GAME(1949); FANCY PANTS(1950); HARVEY(1950); HUMPHREY TAKES A CHANCE(1950); MONTANA(1950); OLD FRONTIER, THE(1950); SUMMER STOCK(1950); MILLIONAIRE FOR CHRISTY, A(1951); OKLAHOMA ANNIE(1952); WAGONS WEST(1952); AFFAIRS OF DOBIE GILLIS, THE(1953); FOREVER FEMALE(1953); RIDE, VAQUERO!(1953); HELL'S OUTPOST(1955); IT'S ALWAYS FAIR WEATHER(1955); PRODIGAL, THE(1955); REBEL WITHOUT A CAUSE(1955); CALLING HOMICIDE(1956); SCARLET HOUR, THE(1956); LOVING YOU(1957); FEMALE ANIMAL, THE(1958); SUMMER AND SMOKE(1961); PARADISE ALLEY(1962); UNDER THE YUM-YUM TREE(1963); LAST OF THE SECRET AGENTS?, THE(1966); ROSEMARY'S BABY(1968); WILLARD(1971)
Almirz Sessions
ON OUR MERRY WAY(1948)
Anne Sessions
MIKADO, THE(1967, Brit.)

Bob Sessions
PERMISSION TO KILL(1975, U.S./Aust.)
John Sessions
1984
BOUNTY, THE(1984)
Hilary Sesta
BLACK WINDMILL, THE(1974, Brit.)
Mario Sestan
WHITE LINE, THE(1952, Ital.)
Otello Sestili
GOSPEL ACCORDING TO ST. MATTHEW, THE(1966, Fr., Ital.)
Wong Ti Set
Silents
LOSER'S END, THE(1924)
Rene Setan
MIND BENDERS, THE(1963, Brit.)
Andrea Setaro
MYSTERY SEA RAIDER(1940), md
Carl Johan Seth
SHORT IS THE SUMMER(1968, Swed.)
Kleg Seth
CROSS AND THE SWITCHBLADE, THE(1970)
Roshan Seth
JUGGERNAUT(1974, Brit.); GANDHI(1982)
1984
INDIANA JONES AND THE TEMPLE OF DOOM(1984); PASSAGE TO INDIA, A(1984, Brit.)
Nitin Sethi
KENNER(1969)
Renu Setna
SHOUT AT THE DEVIL(1976, Brit.); MOONLIGHTING(1982, Brit.)
Javier Seto
CASTILIAN, THE(1963, Span./U.S.), d, w; DRUMS OF TABU, THE(1967, Ital./Span.), d, w
Misc. Talkies
SWEET SOUND OF DEATH(1965, U.S./Span.), d
Louis Seto
FERRY TO HONG KONG(1959, Brit.)
Anya Seton
DRAGONWYCH(1946), w; FOXFIRE(1955), w
Bruce Seton
BLUE SMOKE(1935, Brit.); FLAME IN THE HEATHER(1935, Brit.); SHADOW OF MIKE EMERALD, THE(1935, Brit.); END OF THE ROAD, THE(1936, Brit.); ANNIE LAURIE(1936, Brit.); MELODY OF MY HEART(1936, Brit.); VANDERGILT DIAMOND MYSTERY, THE(1936); WRATH OF JEALOUSY(1936, Brit.); CAFE COLETTE(1937, Brit.); FATHER STEPS OUT(1937, Brit.); FIFTY-SHILLING BOXER(1937, Brit.); LOVE FROM A STRANGER(1937, Brit.); RACING ROMANCE(1937, Brit.); IF I WERE BOSS(1938, Brit.); MIRACLES DO HAPPEN(1938, Brit.); TWO OF US, THE(1938, Brit.); WEDDINGS ARE WONDERFUL(1938, Brit.); YOU'RE THE DOCTOR(1938, Brit.); DEMON BARBER OF FLEET STREET, THE(1939, Brit.); LUCKY TO ME(1939, Brit.); MIDDLE WATCH, THE(1939, Brit.); OLD MOTHER RILEY JOINS UP(1939, Brit.); CURSE OF THE WRAYDONS, THE(1946, Brit.); GREEN COCKATOO, THE(1947, Brit.); BONNIE PRINCE CHARLIE(1948, Brit.); LOOK BEFORE YOU LOVE(1948, Brit.); STORY OF SHIRLEY YORKE, THE(1948, Brit.); SCOTT OF THE ANTARCTIC(1949, Brit.); TIGHT LITTLE ISLAND(1949, Brit.); BLUE LAMP, THE(1950, Brit.); BLACKMAILED(1951, Brit.); HIGH TREASON(1951, Brit.); DELAYED ACTION(1954, Brit.); EIGHT O'CLOCK WALK(1954, Brit.); FABIAN OF THE YARD(1954, Brit.); HANDCUFFS, LONDON(1955, Brit.); MAN OF THE MOMENT(1955, Brit.); BREAKAWAY(1956, Brit.); CROOKED SKY, THE(1957, Brit.); FIGHTING WILDCATS, THE(1957, Brit.); THERE'S ALWAYS A THURSDAY(1957, Brit.); UNDERCOVER GIRL(1957, Brit.); ZOO BABY(1957, Brit.); STRANGE CASE OF DR. MANNING, THE(1958, Brit.); HIDDEN HOMICIDE(1959, Brit.); JOHN PAUL JONES(1959); STRICTLY CONFIDENTIAL(1959, Brit.); JUST JOE(1960, Brit.); OPERATION CUPID(1960, Brit.); FRIGHTENED CITY, THE(1961, Brit.); GORGO(1961, Brit.); GREYFRIARS BOBBY(1961, Brit.); AMBUSH IN LEOPARD STREET(1962, Brit.); DEAD MAN'S EVIDENCE(1962, Brit.); FREEDOM TO DIE(1962, Brit.); IN TROUBLE WITH EVE(1964, Brit.); LIFE IN DANGER(1964, Brit.); MAKE MINE A MILLION(1965, Brit.); VIOLENT MOMENT(1966, Brit.)
Ernest Thompson Seton
KING OF THE GRIZZLIES(1970), w
Frank Seton
STRONGROOM(1962, Brit.)
Graham Seton
"W" PLAN, THE(1931, Brit.), w
Joan Seton
FRENZY(1946, Brit.); LISBON STORY, THE(1946, Brit.); MEET ME AT DAWN(1947, Brit.); MONKEY'S PAW, THE(1948, Brit.)
Maxwell Seton
BEAUTIFUL STRANGER(1954, Brit.), p
Mimi Seton
GOING BERSERK(1983)
Violet Seton
GUY NAMED JOE, A(1943); YOUNGEST PROFESSION, THE(1943); DEVOTION(1946); EASY TO LOVE(1953)
Maxwell Setoon
APPOINTMENT IN LONDON(1953, Brit.), p
Ed Setrakian
PURSUIT OF HAPPINESS, THE(1971); THREE DAYS OF THE CONDOR(1975)
1984
POPE OF GREENWICH VILLAGE, THE(1984)
Goran Setterberg
FLIGHT OF THE EAGLE(1983, Swed.), p
Valda Setterfield
WEDDING PARTY, THE(1969)

George Lee Settle
JANIE(1944)
Georgia Lee Settle
HENRY ALDRICH FOR PRESIDENT(1941); THANK YOUR LUCKY STARS(1943); VERY THOUGHT OF YOU, THE(1944)
Phil Settle
SKATEBOARD(1978)
Virginia Settle
UNHINGED(1982)
Jim Settler
GUESS WHAT HAPPENED TO COUNT DRACULA(1970)
Dudley Setton
ROTTEN TO THE CORE(1956, Brit.)
Max Setton
BEYOND THIS PLACE(1959, Brit.), p
Maxwell Setton
HELL, HEAVEN OR HOBOKEN(1958, Brit.), p; CAIRO ROAD(1950, Brit.), p; SPIDER AND THE FLY, THE(1952, Brit.), p; SO LITTLE TIME(1953, Brit.), p; GOLDEN MASK, THE(1954, Brit.), a, p; THEY WHO DARE(1954, Brit.), p; FOOTSTEPS IN THE FOG(1955, Brit.), p; KEEP IT CLEAN(1956, Brit.), p; LONG HAUL, THE(1957, Brit.), p; PORTRAIT IN SMOKE(1957, Brit.), p; TOWN ON TRIAL(1957, Brit.), p
Gerard Sety
MAIGRET LAYS A TRAP(1958, Fr.); LADY CHATTERLEY'S LOVER(1959, Fr.); MODIGLIANI OF MONTPARNASSE(1961, Fr./Ital.); MY SON, THE HERO(1963, Ital./Fr.); TASTE FOR WOMEN, A(1966, Fr./Ital.); LA GUERRE EST FINIE(1967, Fr./Swed.)
Val Setz
PIRATE, THE(1948); POWDER RIVER(1953)
Pat Setzer
EVEL KNIEVEL(1971)
Pilar Seurat
BATTLE AT BLOODY BEACH(1961); SEVEN WOMEN FROM HELL(1961); YOUNG SAVAGES, THE(1961)
Leonard Seus
COLLEGE SWEETHEARTS(1942)
Lynne Seus
Misc. Talkies
MOUNTAIN CHARLIE(1982)
Eric Sevareid
RIGHT STUFF, THE(1983)
Michael Sevareid
RAID ON ROMMEL(1971)
A. Sevastynov
HUNTING IN SIBERIA(1962, USSR), m
Helen Seveck
ICE PALACE(1960)
N. Sevelov
DREAM OF A COSSACK(1982, USSR)
Bob Seven
MUSCLE BEACH PARTY(1964)
John Barry Seven
6.5 SPECIAL(1958, Brit.)
John Seven
COP HATER(1958); LAST MILE, THE(1959)
Johnny Seven
APARTMENT, THE(1960); GUNS OF THE TIMBERLAND(1960); MUSIC BOX KID, THE(1960); BOY WHO CAUGHT A CROOK(1961); GREATEST STORY EVER TOLD, THE(1965); NAVAJO RUN(1966), a, p&d; WHAT DID YOU DO IN THE WAR, DADDY?(1966); GUNFIGHT IN ABILENE(1967); DESTRUCTORS, THE(1968)
Temperance Seven
TAKE ME OVER(1963, Brit.)
The Seven Ashtons
PUBLIC PIGEON NO. 1(1957)
750 Rit Players
METROPOLIS(1927, Ger.)
Seven Loria Brothers
NEW FACES OF 1937(1937)
Seven Royal Hinustanis
CALLING ALL CROOKS(1938$c Brit.)
Dora Sevening
2,000 WOMEN(1944, Brit.); THEY WERE SISTERS(1945, Brit.); MARK OF CAIN, THE(1948, Brit.); INTERRUPTED JOURNEY, THE(1949, Brit.)
Maurice Seveno
LIVE FOR LIFE(1967, Fr./Ital.); DAY FOR NIGHT(1973, Fr.)
Rex Sevenoaks
TRAP, THE(1967, Can./Brit.)
Septimu Sever
JOY(1983, Fr./Can.)
Stane Sever
CAVE OF THE LIVING DEAD(1966, Yugo./Ger.)
Jacques Severac
WOMAN OF SIN(1961, Fr.), w; SEA PIRATE, THE(1967, Fr./Span./Ital.), w
Tristan Severe
DEVIL IN THE FLESH, THE(1949, Fr.)
Susanna Severeid
DON'T ANSWER THE PHONE(1980)
Susanne Severeid
VAN NUYS BLVD.(1979)
Gilberto Severi
MONTE CASSINO(1948, Ital.)
Gaston Severin
LA MATERNELLE(1933, Fr.); DIARY OF A COUNTRY PRIEST(1954, Fr.)
Severin-Mars
Misc. Silents
LA DIXIEME SYMPHONIE(1918, Fr.); L'AGONIE DES AIGLES(1921, Fr.); LA ROUE(1923, Fr.)
Terens Severine
FOREIGNER, THE(1978)

Attilio Severini
PAYMENT IN BLOOD(1968, Ital.); WATERLOO(1970, Ital./USSR)
Leonardo Severini
SAMSON AND THE SEVEN MIRACLES OF THE WORLD(1963, Fr./Ital.)
Luigi Severini
HORROR CASTLE(1965, Ital.)
Bernard Severn
THAT'LL BE THE DAY(1974, Brit.)
Billy Severn
ENCHANTED FOREST, THE(1945)
Christopher Severn
MRS. MINIVER(1942); AMAZING MRS. HOLLIDAY(1943); GUY NAMED JOE, A(1943); MAN FROM DOWN UNDER, THE(1943); CLUNY BROWN(1946); TITANIC(1953)
Clifford Severn
JALNA(1935); PERFECT GENTLEMAN, THE(1935); PRINCE AND THE PAUPER, THE(1937); QUALITY STREET(1937); MAN ABOUT TOWN(1939); HOW GREEN WAS MY VALLEY(1941); MAN HUNT(1941); ATLANTIC CONVOY(1942); SON OF FURY(1942); FOREVER AND A DAY(1943); THEY LIVE IN FEAR(1944)
Clifford Severn, Jr.
CAPTAIN CAUTION(1940); GAUCHO SERENADE(1940)
Ernest Severn
GUY NAMED JOE, A(1943); HOUR BEFORE THE DAWN, THE(1944); PURSUED(1947)
Maida Severn
MARJORIE MORNINGSTAR(1958); IMITATION OF LIFE(1959); PRIVATE'S AFFAIR, A(1959); MR. HOBBS TAKES A VACATION(1962); DEAR BRIGETTE(1965); NOBODY'S PERFECT(1968)
Raymond Severn
WE ARE NOT ALONE(1939); FOREIGN CORRESPONDENT(1940); YANK AT ETON, A(1942); GUY NAMED JOE, A(1943); HOUR BEFORE THE DAWN, THE(1944); LODGER, THE(1944); SUSPECT, THE(1944)
Venecia Severn
TOWER OF LONDON(1939)
William Severn
EAGLE SQUADRON(1942); JOURNEY FOR MARGARET(1942); STORY OF DR. WASSELL, THE(1944)
William "Billy" Severn
SON OF LASSIE(1945)
Winston Severn
HER SISTER'S SECRET(1946); LOST HONEYMOON(1947); MAN CALLED PETER, THE(1955)
Yvonne Severn
LLOYDS OF LONDON(1936); TOWER OF LONDON(1939); EARL OF CHICAGO, THE(1940); AMAZING MRS. HOLLIDAY(1943); GUY NAMED JOE, A(1943)
Mary Anne Severne
THREE TO GO(1971, Aus.); ADVENTURES OF BARRY McKENZIE(1972, Austral.)
Darl Severns
SWEET SUGAR(1972); ROOMMATES, THE(1973)
N. Severov
DIARY OF A NAZI(1943, USSR), w
Marcie Severson
Misc. Talkies
STARK RAVING MAD(1983)
Bruce Sevier
DREAMS COME TRUE(1936, Brit.), w
Jack Sevier
LOVESICK(1983)
Carmen Sevilla
SPANISH AFFAIR(1958, Span.); DESERT WARRIOR(1961 Ital./Span.); KING OF KINGS(1961); BOLDEST JOB IN THE WEST, THE(1971, Ital.); ANTONY AND CLEOPATRA(1973, Brit.)
Mario Sevilla
CURSE OF THE CRYING WOMAN, THE(1969, Mex.)
Ninon Sevilla
YOUNG AND EVIL(1962, Mex.)
Raphael J. Sevilla
SHE-DEVIL ISLAND(1936, Mex.), d
Raphael Sevilla, Jr.
VILLA!(1958)
Raphael Sevilla
SHE-DEVIL ISLAND(1936, Mex.), w
Jose Gomez Sevillano
MOMENT OF TRUTH, THE(1965, Ital./Span.)
Edith Seville
FOUR SIDED TRIANGLE(1953, Brit.)
Emily Seville
Silents
KISMET(1920)
Tony Seville
SHAME, SHAME, EVERYBODY KNOWS HER NAME(1969)
Jules Sevin
WACKY WORLD OF DR. MORGUS, THE(1962), p
V. Sevostyanov
VIOLIN AND ROLLER(1962, USSR), spec eff; MY NAME IS IVAN(1963, USSR), spec eff
Robert Sevra
I, THE JURY(1982)
Allen D. Sewall
MAID OF SALEM(1937); CARRIE(1952)
Blanche Sewall
DANGEROUS NUMBER(1937), ed
Frederick Sewall
DARK ANGEL, THE(1935); FOREIGN CORRESPONDENT(1940)
Lucille Sewall
HE RAN ALL THE WAY(1951)
Billie Seward
AMONG THE MISSING(1934); FUGITIVE LADY(1934); ONCE TO EVERY WOMAN(1934); TWENTIETH CENTURY(1934); VOICE IN THE NIGHT(1934); AIR HAWKS(1935); BRANDED A COWARD(1935); JUSTICE OF THE RANGE(1935); LAW

BEYOND THE RANGE(1935); MEN OF THE HOUR(1935); REVENGE RIDER, THE(1935); TRAILS OF THE WILD(1935); MAN FROM GUN TOWN, THE(1936); CHARLIE CHAN AT TREASURE ISLAND(1939); LI'L ABNER(1940); ONE CROWDED NIGHT(1940); NO HANDS ON THE CLOCK(1941); JANE EYRE(1944)
Misc. Talkies
RIDING WILD(1935)

Edmond Seward
WALLS OF GOLD(1933), w; THOROUGHBRED(1936, Aus.), w; GULLIVER'S TRAV-ELS(1939), w; BOWERY BOMBSHELL(1946), w; IN FAST COMPANY(1946), w; SPOOK BUSTERS(1946), w; BOWERY BUCKAROOS(1947), w; NEWS HOUNDS(1947), w; ANGELS ALLEY(1948), w; JINX MONEY(1948), w; SMUG-GLERS' COVE(1948), w; TROUBLE MAKERS(1948), w; FIGHTING FOOLS(1949), w

Edmond G. Seward
BELA LUGOSI MEETS A BROOKLYN GORILLA(1952), w

Edmond Seward, Jr.
JALOPY(1953), w

Edmund Seward
DUKE COMES BACK, THE(1937), w; ORPHAN OF THE WILDERNESS(1937, Aus.), w

Florence A. Seward
GOLD FOR THE CAESARS(1964), w

Kathleen Seward
GETTING TOGETHER(1976)
Misc. Talkies
FEELIN' UP(1983)

Sydney Seward
Silents
PIERRE OF THE PLAINS(1914)

Terence Seward
I'LL NEVER FORGET WHAT'S 'IS NAME(1967, Brit.); HANNIBAL BROOKS(1969, Brit.)

George Sewards
OVER THE BORDER(1950)

Jack Sewards
HELL SQUAD(1958)

Terence Sewards
WHERE THE BULLETS FLY(1966, Brit.); DEADLY AFFAIR, THE(1967, Brit.); MAN WHO HAUNTED HIMSELF, THE(1970, Brit.)

Allen B. Sewell
MARKED TRAILS(1944)

Allen D. Sewell
SHINE ON, HARVEST MOON(1944)

Anna Sewell
BLACK BEAUTY(1933), w; BLACK BEAUTY(1946), w; BLACK BEAUTY(1971, Brit./Ger./Span.), w
Silents
BLACK BEAUTY(1921), w

Audrey Sewell
Silents
NIGHT LIFE(1927)

Blanche Sewell
YELLOW JACK(1938), ed; TRIAL OF MARY DUGAN, THE(1929), ed; BIG HOUSE, THE(1930), ed; CHILDREN OF PLEASURE(1930), ed; NOT SO DUMB(1930), ed; SECRET SIX, THE(1931), ed; GRAND HOTEL(1932), ed; HELL DIVERS(1932), ed; RED DUST(1932), ed; RED HEADED WOMAN(1932), ed; BEAUTY FOR SALE(1933), ed; QUEEN CHRISTINA(1933), ed; REUNION IN VIENNA(1933), ed; SECRET OF MADAME BLANCHE, THE(1933), ed; TUGBOAT ANNIE(1933), ed; LAUGHING BOY(1934), ed; TREASURE ISLAND(1934), ed; WHAT EVERY WOMAN KNOWS(1934), ed; FLAME WITHIN, THE(1935), ed; NAUGHTY MARIETTA(1935), ed; BORN TO DANCE(1936), ed; GORGEOUS HUSSY, THE(1936), ed; ROSE MA-RIE(1936), ed; SMALL TOWN GIRL(1936), ed; BROADWAY MELODY OF '38(1937), ed; ROSALIE(1937), ed; LISTEN, DARLING(1938), ed; WIZARD OF OZ, THE(1939), ed; BOOM TOWN(1940), ed; BROADWAY MELODY OF 1940(1940), ed; GO WEST(1940), ed; TWO GIRLS ON BROADWAY(1940), ed; HONKY TONK(1941), ed; THEY MET IN BOMBAY(1941), ed; ZIEGFELD GIRL(1941), ed; PANAMA HAT-TIE(1942), ed; SEVEN SWEETHEARTS(1942), ed; SHIP AHOY(1942), ed; BEST FOOT FORWARD(1943), ed; DU BARRY WAS A LADY(1943), ed; HEAVENLY BODY, THE(1943), ed; BATHING BEAUTY(1944), ed; VALLEY OF DECISION, THE(1945), ed; EASY TO WED(1946), ed; FIESTA(1947), ed; IT HAPPENED IN BROOK-LYN(1947), ed; PIRATE, THE(1948), ed; TAKE ME OUT TO THE BALL GAME(1949), ed
Silents
TELL IT TO THE MARINES(1926), ed; AFTER MIDNIGHT(1927), ed; SINGLE STANDARD, THE(1929), ed

Charles Sewell
JOY RIDE(1935, Brit.); PLAY UP THE BAND(1935, Brit.); TRUST THE NAVY(1935, Brit.); EVERYTHING OKAY(1936, Brit.); DARBY AND JOAN(1937, Brit.); LAST CHANCE, THE(1937, Brit.); OLD MOTHER RILEY(1937, Brit.); PENNY POOL, THE(1937, Brit.); RACING ROMANCE(1937, Brit.); ROMANCE A LA CARTE(1938, Brit.); STEPPING TOES(1938, Brit.); MUSIC HALL PARADE(1939, Brit.); SECOND MATE, THE(1950, Brit.)

Danny Sewell
MAN AT THE TOP(1973, Brit.)

David George Sewell
BARRY LYNDON(1975, Brit.)

George Sewell
SPARROWS CAN'T SING(1963, Brit.); THIS SPORTING LIFE(1963, Brit.); UNDER-WORLD INFORMERS(1965, Brit.); KALEIDOSCOPE(1966, Brit.); ROBBERY(1967, Brit.); POOR COW(1968, Brit.); VENGEANCE OF SHE, THE(1968, Brit.); JOURNEY TO THE FAR SIDE OF THE SUN(1969, Brit.); HORROR HOUSE(1970, Brit.); GET CARTER(1971, Brit.); OPERATION DAYBREAK(1976, U.S./Brit./Czech.)

Gladdy Sewell
MONEY TALKS(1933, Brit.); OUTCAST, THE(1934, Brit.)

Hazel Sewell
SNOW WHITE AND THE SEVEN DWARFS(1937), art d

Sam Sewell
OVERLORD(1975, Brit.)

T.W. Sewell
HANGUP(1974), p

Vernon Sewell
UNDERCOVER AGENT(1935, Brit.), d; BREAKERS AHEAD(1938, Brit.), d; WORLD OWES ME A LIVING, THE(1944, Brit.), d, w; FRENZY(1946, Brit.), d, w; GHOSTS OF BERKELEY SQUARE(1947, Brit.), d; UNEASY TERMS(1948, Brit.), d; JACK OF DIAMONDS, THE(1949, Brit.), a, d; BLACK WIDOW(1951, Brit.), d; DARK LIGHT, THE(1951, Brit.), d&w; FLOATING DUTCHMAN, THE(1953, Brit.), d&w; GHOST SHIP(1953, Brit.), p&d; RADIO CAB MURDER(1954, Brit.), d&w; TERROR SHIP(1954, Brit.), d; WHERE THERE'S A WILL(1955, Brit.), d; HOME AND AWAY(1956, Brit.), d, w; JOHNNY, YOU'RE WANTED(1956, Brit.), d; ROGUE'S YARN(1956, Brit.), a, d, w; SPIN A DARK WEB(1956, Brit.), d&w; WRONG NUM-BER(1959, Brit.), d; MISSILE FROM HELL(1960, Brit.), d; URGE TO KILL(1960, Brit.), d; HOUSE OF MYSTERY(1961, Brit.), d&w; MAN IN THE BACK SEAT, THE(1961, Brit.), d; WIND OF CHANGE, THE(1961, Brit.), d; STRONGROOM(1962, Brit.), d; MATTER OF CHOICE, A(1963, Brit.), d; STRICTLY FOR THE BIRDS(1963, Brit.), d; BLOOD BEAST TERROR, THE(1967, Brit.), d; SOME MAY LIVE(1967, Brit.), d; CRIMSON CULT, THE(1970, Brit.), d; BURKE AND HARE(1972, Brit.), d

Vernon Campbell Sewell
SILVER FLEET, THE(1945, Brit.), d&w

Edward Sewer
WARRIORS, THE(1979)

Andrzej Seweryn
GOLEM(1980, Pol.); CONDUCTOR, THE(1981, Pol.); MAN OF IRON(1981, Pol.); DANTON(1983)

Marysia Seweryn
CONDUCTOR, THE(1981, Pol.)

Earle S. Sewey
MOUNTAIN RHYTHM(1942)

Alexander Sewruk
ASHES AND DIAMONDS(1961, Pol.)

Joseph Sexhauer
MY THIRD WIFE GEORGE(1968)

Carter Sexton
HAPPY DAYS(1930)

Garcy Sexton
WARGAMES(1983)

Gary Sexton
BORDER, THE(1982)

Hazel Sexton
Silents
AMERICAN WAY, THE(1919); ANNE OF GREEN GABLES(1919)

John Sexton
1984
PHAR LAP(1984, Aus.), p

Patrick Sexton
PIRATES OF TORTUGA(1961)

Frances Sey
HAMILE(1965, Ghana)

Charlie Seybert
LAST PICTURE SHOW, THE(1971)

Eleanor Seybolt
Silents
IMPOSTER, THE(1918)

Michael Seydoux
DON GIOVANNI(1979, Fr./Ital./Ger.), p

Katharina Seyferth
NIGHT CROSSING(1982)

Wilfred Seyferth
DEVIL MAKES THREE, THE(1952)

Wilfried Seyferth
TOXI(1952, Ger.); GOLDEN PLAGUE, THE(1963, Ger.)

Fritz Seyfried
MAN ON A TIGHTROPE(1953), makeup

Athene Seyler
PERFECT LADY, THE(1931, Brit.); BE MINE TONIGHT(1933, Brit.); EARLY TO BED(1933, Brit./Ger.); PRIVATE LIFE OF DON JUAN, THE(1934, Brit.); DRAKE THE PIRATE(1935, Brit.); REGAL CAVALCADE(1935, Brit.); SCROOGE(1935, Brit.); I STAND CONDEMNED(1936, Brit.); IRISH FOR LUCK(1936, Brit.); IT'S LOVE AGAIN(1936, Brit.); SENSATION(1936, Brit.); SOUTHERN ROSES(1936, Brit.); APRIL BLOSSOMS(1937, Brit.); HIGH TREASON(1937, Brit.); NON-STOP NEW YORK(1937, Brit.); SKY'S THE LIMIT, THE(1937, Brit.); CITADEL, THE(1938); JANE STEPS OUT(1938, Brit.); SAILING ALONG(1938, Brit.); MILL ON THE FLOSS(1939, Brit.); SAINT IN LONDON, THE(1939, Brit.); WARE CASE, THE(1939, Brit.); CASTLE OF CRIMES(1940, Brit.); LILAC DOMINO, THE(1940, Brit.); TILLY OF BLOOMS-BURY(1940, Brit.); QUIET WEDDING(1941, Brit.); YOUNG MAN'S FANCY(1943, Brit.); RANDOLPH FAMILY, THE(1945, Brit.); NICHOLAS NICKLEBY(1947, Brit.); QUEEN OF SPADES(1948, Brit.); AFFAIRS OF A ROGUE(1949, Brit.); FRAN-CHISE AFFAIR, THE(1952, Brit.); MADE IN HEAVEN(1952, Brit.); PICKWICK PAPERS, THE(1952, Brit.); SECRET PEOPLE(1952, Brit.); TREASURE HUNT(1952, Brit.); BEGGAR'S OPERA, THE(1953); FOR BETTER FOR WORSE(1954, Brit.); WEAK AND THE WICKED, THE(1954, Brit.); YOUNG WIVES' TALE(1954, Brit.); BLONDE SINNER(1956, Brit.); AS LONG AS THEY'RE HAPPY(1957, Brit.); CAMPBELL'S KINGDOM(1957, Brit.); DOCTOR AT LARGE(1957, Brit.); HOW TO MURDER A RICH UNCLE(1957, Brit.); CURSE OF THE DEMON(1958); HAPPY IS THE BRIDE(1958, Brit.); INN OF THE SIXTH HAPPINESS, THE(1958); TALE OF TWO CITIES, A(1958, Brit.); FRENCH MISTRESS(1960, Brit.); MAKE MINE MINK(1960, Brit.); FRANCIS OF ASSISI(1961); PASSPORT TO CHINA(1961, Brit.); GIRL ON THE BOAT, THE(1962, Brit.); I THANK A FOOL(1962, Brit.); SATAN NEVER SLEEPS(1962); TWO AND TWO MAKE SIX(1962, Brit.); NURSE ON WHEELS(1964, Brit.)
Silents
ADVENTURES OF MR. PICKWICK, THE(1921, Brit.)
Misc. Silents
THIS FREEDOM(1923, Brit.)

Clifford Seyler
SQUIBS(1935, Brit.), w
Silents
SQUIBS(1921, Brit.), w

Misc. Silents
TONS OF MONEY(1924, Brit.)

Larry Seymore
TEMPTATION(1936); UNDERWORLD(1937)

Al Seymour
ANGELS OVER BROADWAY(1940); FACE BEHIND THE MASK, THE(1941); KNOCKOUT(1941); MONSTER AND THE GIRL, THE(1941); PENNY SERENADE(1941); TALK OF THE TOWN(1942)

Angela Seymour
TOP OF THE HEAP(1972)

Ann Seymour
SEVEN ALONE(1975)

Anne Seymour
RAINBOW, THE(1944, USSR); ALL THE KING'S MEN(1949); WHISTLE AT EATON FALLS(1951); FOUR BOYS AND A GUN(1957); MAN ON FIRE(1957); DESIRE UNDER THE ELMS(1958); GIFT OF LOVE, THE(1958); HANDLE WITH CARE(1958); ALL THE FINE YOUNG CANNIBALS(1960); HOME FROM THE HILL(1960); POLLYANNA(1960); SUBTERRANEANS, THE(1960); MISTY(1961); GOOD NEIGHBOR SAM(1964); STAGE TO THUNDER ROCK(1964); WHERE LOVE HAS GONE(1964); MIRAGE(1965); BLINDFOLD(1966); WACO(1966); FITZWILLY(1967); STAY AWAY, JOE(1968); MAN, THE(1972); SO LONG, BLUE BOY(1973); HOW TO SUCCEED IN BUSINESS WITHOUT REALLY TRYING(1976); NEVER NEVER LAND(1982); TRIUMPHS OF A MAN CALLED HORSE(1983, US/Mex.)

Arthur Seymour
DREAMS THAT MONEY CAN BUY(1948)

Caroline Seymour
THERE'S A GIRL IN MY SOUP(1970, Brit.)

Carolyn Seymour
ONE BRIEF SUMMER(1971, Brit.); UNMAN, WITTERING AND ZIGO(1971, Brit.); GUMSHOE(1972, Brit.); RULING CLASS, THE(1972, Brit.); STEPTOE AND SON(1972, Brit.); YELLOW DOG(1973, Brit.); ODD JOB, THE(1978, Brit.); ZORRO, THE GAY BLADE(1981); MR. MOM(1983)
Misc. Talkies
ASSIGNMENT, THE(1978); BITCH, THE(1979); CONDOR(1984)

Clarine Seymour
Silents
GIRL WHO STAYED AT HOME, THE(1919); SCARLET DAYS(1919); TRUE HEART SUSIE(1919); IDOL DANCER, THE(1920)

Dan Seymour
WAY WE WERE, THE(1973); BOMBS OVER BURMA(1942); CASABLANCA(1942); ROAD TO MOROCCO(1942); TALK OF THE TOWN(1942); RHYTHM OF THE ISLANDS(1943); TAHITI HONEY(1943); TIGER FANGS(1943); KISMET(1944); KLONDIKE KATE(1944); RAINBOW ISLAND(1944); TO HAVE AND HAVE NOT(1944); CONFIDENTIAL AGENT(1945); SAN ANTONIO(1945); SPANISH MAIN, THE(1945); CLOAK AND DAGGER(1946); NIGHT IN CASABLANCA, A(1946); SEARCHING WIND, THE(1946); HARD BOILED MAHONEY(1947); INTRIGUE(1947); PHILO VANCE'S GAMBLE(1947); SLAVE GIRL(1947); HIGHWAY 13(1948); JOHNNY BELINDA(1948); KEY LARGO(1948); TRAIL OF THE YUKON(1949); ABBOTT AND COSTELLO IN THE FOREIGN LEGION(1950); JOE PALOOKA IN THE SQUARED CIRCLE(1950); YOUNG MAN WITH A HORN(1950); BLUE VEIL, THE(1951); FACE TO FACE(1952); GLORY ALLEY(1952); MARA MARU(1952); RANCHO NOTORIOUS(1952); BIG HEAT, THE(1953); SECOND CHANCE(1953); SYSTEM, THE(1953); TANGIER INCIDENT(1953); HUMAN DESIRE(1954); ABBOTT AND COSTELLO MEET THE MUMMY(1955); MOONFLEET(1955); BEYOND A REASONABLE DOUBT(1956); BUSTER KEATON STORY, THE(1957); SAD SACK, THE(1957); UNDERSEA GIRL(1957); RETURN OF THE FLY(1959); WATUSI(1959); UNHOLY ROLLERS(1972); ESCAPE TO WITCH MOUNTAIN(1975)

Danny Seymour
MUG TOWN(1943)

Francis Seymour
Silents
STORMY SEAS(1923)

Harry Seymour
CENTRAL PARK(1932); MAN AGAINST WOMAN(1932); ONE WAY PASSAGE(1932); TENDERFOOT, THE(1932); THREE ON A MATCH(1932); YOU SAID A MOUTHFUL(1932); FOOTLIGHT PARADE(1933); MARY STEVENS, M.D.(1933); PRIVATE DETECTIVE 62(1933); 42ND STREET(1933); CASE OF THE HOWLING DOG, THE(1934); CROSBY CASE, THE(1934); DOCTOR MONICA(1934); FOG OVER FRISCO(1934); KANSAS CITY PRINCESS(1934); LOST LADY, A(1934); MANHATTAN MELODRAMA(1934); PERSONALITY KID, THE(1934); SIX-DAY BIKE RIDER(1934); TWENTY MILLION SWEETHEARTS(1934); UPPER WORLD(1934); BROADWAY HOSTESS(1935); DEVIL DOGS OF THE AIR(1935); FRISCO KID(1935); FRONT PAGE WOMAN(1935); IRISH IN US, THE(1935); MISS PACIFIC FLEET(1935); SHIPMATES FOREVER(1935); STARS OVER BROADWAY(1935); TRAVELING SALESLADY, THE(1935); WOMAN IN RED, THE(1935); HOT MONEY(1936), d; BOY MEETS GIRL(1938); GIRLS ON PROBATION(1938), d; SLIGHT CASE OF MURDER, A(1938); MAN WHO TALKED TOO MUCH, THE(1940); MANPOWER(1941); STRAWBERRY BLONDE, THE(1941); SULLIVAN'S TRAVELS(1941); BROADWAY(1942); I WAKE UP SCREAMING(1942); PITTSBURGH(1942); CONEY ISLAND(1943); IRISH EYES ARE SMILING(1944); SAN ANTONIO(1945); SPIDER, THE(1945); TREE GROWS IN BROOKLYN, A(1945); BEHIND GREEN LIGHTS(1946); DO YOU LOVE ME?(1946); MY REPUTATION(1946); NIGHT AND DAY(1946); NOBODY LIVES FOREVER(1946); I WONDER WHO'S KISSING HER NOW(1947); MOTHER WORE TIGHTS(1947); CRY OF THE CITY(1948); GIVE MY REGARDS TO BROADWAY(1948); ROAD HOUSE(1948); UNFAITHFULLY YOURS(1948); WHEN MY BABY SMILES AT ME(1948); DANCING IN THE DARK(1949); OH, YOU BEAUTIFUL DOLL(1949); I'LL GET BY(1950); TICKET TO TOMAHAWK(1950); GUY WHO CAME BACK, THE(1951); MONKEY BUSINESS(1952); NIGHT WITHOUT SLEEP(1952); DANGEROUS CROSSING(1953); GENTLEMEN PREFER BLONDES(1953); MR. SCOUTMASTER(1953); STRANGER WORE A GUN, THE(1953); VICKI(1953); RIVER OF NO RETURN(1954); DADDY LONG LEGS(1955); GIRL IN THE RED VELVET SWING, THE(1955); HOW TO BE VERY, VERY, POPULAR(1955); VIOLENT SATURDAY(1955); MARJORIE MORNINGSTAR(1958); NORTH BY NORTHWEST(1959)

Heather Seymour
PRIME OF MISS JEAN BRODIE, THE(1969, Brit.)

Henry Seymour
CRAZE(1974, Brit.), w

James Seymour
ACQUITTED(1929), w; SWING HIGH(1930), w; WHAT A WIDOW(1930), w; CARNIVAL BOAT(1932), w; SYMPHONY OF SIX MILLION(1932), w; CENTRAL AIRPORT(1933), w; FOOTLIGHT PARADE(1933), w; GOLD DIGGERS OF 1933(1933), w; HOUSE ON 56TH STREET, THE(1933), p; LAWYER MAN(1933), w; SON OF A SAILOR(1933), P; 42ND STREET(1933), w; MODERN HERO, A(1934), p; GOOSE AND THE GANDER, THE(1935), p; KING OF BURLESQUE(1936), w; RHYTHM RACKETEER(1937, Brit.), d; GOLD DIGGERS IN PARIS(1938), w; MISSING MILLION, THE(1942, Brit.), w; WE'LL MEET AGAIN(1942, Brit.), w; HAPPIDROME(1943, Brit.), w; SAINT MEETS THE TIGER, THE(1943, Brit.), w; UP WITH THE LARK(1943, Brit.), w; THEY MET IN THE DARK(1945, Brit.), w; MEET THE NAVY(1946, Brit.), w; WOMAN TO WOMAN(1946, Brit.), w; GHOSTS OF BERKELEY SQUARE(1947, Brit.), w; MEET ME AT DAWN(1947, Brit.), w; SPRINGTIME(1948, Brit.), w

James Ed Seymour
PHENIX CITY STORY, THE(1955)

Jane Seymour
BACK DOOR TO HEAVEN(1939); REMEMBER THE DAY(1941); TOM, DICK AND HARRY(1941); NEVER WAVE AT A WAC(1952); ONLY WAY, THE(1970, Panama/Den./U.S.); YOUNG WINSTON(1972, Brit.); LIVE AND LET DIE(1973, Brit.); SINBAD AND THE EYE OF THE TIGER(1977, U.S./Brit.); BATTLESTAR GALACTICA(1979); OH, HEAVENLY DOG!(1980); SOMEWHERE IN TIME(1980)
1984
LASSITER(1984)

John Seymour
SPORTING CLUB, THE(1971)

Jonah Seymour
KING AND COUNTRY(1964, Brit.)

Jonathan Seymour
TOUGHEST MAN ALIVE(1955)

Judy Seymour
BURNING AN ILLUSION(1982, Brit.), ed

Kit Seymour
SWALLOWS AND AMAZONS(1977, Brit.)

Lou Seymour
SHE GETS HER MAN(1935)

Madeleine Seymour
FACES(1934, Brit.); NO ESCAPE(1934, Brit.); SOMETIMES GOOD(1934, Brit.); QUEEN OF HEARTS(1936, Brit.); SIDE STREET ANGEL(1937, Brit.)
Silents
DAWN(1917, Brit.)
Misc. Silents
HOUSE OF PERIL, THE(1922, Brit.)

Madeline Seymour
EVIDENCE(1929); HIS GLORIOUS NIGHT(1929); LAST OF MRS. CHEYNEY, THE(1929); TONIGHT AT TWELVE(1929)

Michael Seymour
ROBBERY(1967, Brit.), art d; ISADORA(1968, Brit.), art d; ENTERTAINING MR. SLOANE(1970, Brit.), prod d; GUMSHOE(1972, Brit.), prod d; THEATRE OF BLOOD(1973, Brit.), prod d; S(1974), prod d; ROSEBUD(1975), prod d; ALIEN(1979), prod d; EUREKA(1983, Brit.), prod d

Ralph Seymour
JUST BEFORE DAWN(1980); BACK ROADS(1981)
1984
FLETCH(1984); MEATBALLS PART II(1984)
Misc. Talkies
LONGSHOT(1982)

Robin Seymour
JAMBOREE(1957)

Sheldon Seymour [Herschell Gordon Lewis]
MONSTER A GO-GO(1965), p&d; TASTE OF BLOOD, A(1967); THIS STUFF'LL KILL YA!(1971), m; YEAR OF THE YAHOO(1971), m

Stanley Seymour
LOST LAGOON(1958)

Stephen Seymour
SO PROUDLY WE HAIL(1943), set d; HAIL THE CONQUERING HERO(1944), set d; MIRACLE OF MORGAN'S CREEK, THE(1944), set d; PRACTICALLY YOURS(1944), set d; UNINVITED, THE(1944), set d; DUFFY'S TAVERN(1945), set d

Steve Seymour
STAR SPANGLED RHYTHM(1942), set d

Tot Seymour
CALL OF THE PRAIRIE(1936), m

Seymour and Corncob
WAY DOWN EAST(1935)

Seyna Seyn
CASANOVA '70(1965, Ital.); JULIET OF THE SPIRITS(1965, Fr./Ital./W.Ger.); DRUMS OF TABU, THE(1967, Ital./Span.); KISS THE GIRLS AND MAKE THEM DIE(1967, U.S./Ital.)

Delphine Seyrig
LAST YEAR AT MARIENBAD(1962, Fr./Ital.); MURIEL(1963, Fr./Ital.); ACCIDENT(1967, Brit.); MILKY WAY, THE(1969, Fr./Ital.); STOLEN KISSES(1969, Fr.); MISTER FREEDOM(1970, Fr.); DAUGHTERS OF DARKNESS(1971, Bel./ Fr./ Ger./ Ital.); DISCREET CHARM OF THE BOURGEOISIE, THE(1972, Fr.); DAY OF THE JACKAL, THE(1973, Brit./Fr.); DOLL'S HOUSE, A(1973, Brit.); BLACK WINDMILL, THE(1974, Brit.); DONKEY SKIN(1975, Fr.); I SENT A LETTER TO MY LOVE(1981, Fr.)

Francis Seyrig
LAST YEAR AT MARIENBAD(1962, Fr./Ital.), m; TRIAL OF JOAN OF ARC(1965, Fr.), m

V. Sez
RESURRECTION(1963, USSR)

Hilde Sezak
INTERMEZZO(1937, Ger.)

A. Sezemann
DAY THE WAR ENDED, THE(1961, USSR); WAR AND PEACE(1968, USSR)

Serif Sezer
YOL(1982, Turkey)

Sezer Sezin
L'IMMORTELLE(1969, Fr./Ital./Turkey)

Yanni Sfinias
LOVESICK(1983)
1984
FALLING IN LOVE(1984)
Corrado Sfogli
1984
ANOTHER TIME, ANOTHER PLACE(1984, Brit.)
Fabrizio Sforza
INVINCIBLE SIX, THE(1970, U.S./Iran), makeup
1984
AFTER THE FALL OF NEW YORK(1984, Ital./Fr.), makeup
Mirella Sforza
VALACHI PAPERS, THE(1972, Ital./Fr.), makeup
Tony Sforzini
FAME IS THE SPUR(1947, Brit.), makeup; HAMLET(1948, Brit.), makeup; MY SISTER AND I(1948, Brit.), makeup; ONE NIGHT WITH YOU(1948, Brit), makeup; WOMAN HATER(1949, Brit.), makeup; TREASURE ISLAND(1950, Brit.), makeup; ENTERTAINER, THE(1960, Brit.), makeup; STOP ME BEFORE I KILL!(1961, Brit.), makeup; STOLEN HOURS(1963), makeup; JIG SAW(1965, Brit.), makeup; WHERE THE SPIES ARE(1965, Brit.), makeup; MIKADO, THE(1967, Brit.), makeup; TOUCH OF CLASS, A(1973, Brit.), makeup
Tony Sfronzini
RICHARD III(1956, Brit.), makeup
Nicholas Sgarro
HAPPY HOOKER, THE(1975), d
Sgt. Maj. Somu
WALK INTO HELL(1957, Aus.)
Anthony Sgueglia
1984
OH GOD! YOU DEVIL(1984)
Ouyang Sh-fei
SHEPHERD GIRL, THE(1965, Hong Kong)
Mali Sha
RETURN OF THE DRAGON(1974, Chin.)
Au-yang Sha-fei
LOVE ETERNE, THE(1964, Hong Kong); MERMAID, THE(1966, Hong Kong)
Sha-Na-Na
GREASE(1978); SGT. PEPPER'S LONELY HEARTS CLUB BAND(1978)
Youssef Shaaban
CAIRO(1963)
Morgan Shaan
BAND OF ANGELS(1957); GAMBLER WORE A GUN, THE(1961); GUN FIGHT(1961)
Mike Shabaga
PAPERBACK HERO(1973, Can.)
L. Shabaldina
TAXI TO HEAVEN(1944, USSR)
Lydia Shaballna
IN THE NAME OF LIFE(1947, USSR)
Martin Shaban
HELL, HEAVEN OR HOBOKEN(1958, Brit.); LONG HAUL, THE(1957, Brit.)
Arkady Shabashev
1984
MOSCOW ON THE HUDSON(1984)
Shabatai-Tevet
IMPOSSIBLE ON SATURDAY(1966, Fr./Israel), w
Betty Shabazz
1984
UNFAITHFULLY YOURS(1984)
Menelik Shabbazz
BURNING AN ILLUSION(1982, Brit.), d, w
David Shaber
SUCH GOOD FRIENDS(1971), w; LAST EMBRACE(1979), w; WARRIORS, THE(1979), w; THOSE LIPS, THOSE EYES(1980), w; NIGHTHAWKS(1981), w; ROLLOVER(1981), w
R. Shablovskaya
KIEV COMEDY, A(1963, USSR)
Mike Shack
RENEGADE GIRLS(1974)
Sam Shack
JOHNNY O'CLOCK(1947); WHIPLASH(1948); SET-UP, THE(1949); DANGEROUS MISSION(1954)
Sammy Shack
SUNDAY PUNCH(1942); LADY LUCK(1946); GANGSTER, THE(1947); HIGH WALL, THE(1947); STREET WITH NO NAME, THE(1948); SHE COULDN'T SAY NO(1954); CATERED AFFAIR, THE(1956); WORLD IN MY CORNER(1956)
Dan Shackelford
DEADLY BLESSING(1981)
Floyd Shackelford
STARK MAD(1929); LONELY TRAIL, THE(1936); VIVACIOUS LADY(1938); LILLIAN RUSSELL(1940); MARYLAND(1940); PASSPORT TO SUEZ(1943); WHITE WITCH DOCTOR(1953)
Silents
WHITE OUTLAW, THE(1925)
J. B. Shackelford
Silents
NEVER THE TWAIN SHALL MEET(1925), ph
Robert Shackelford
COLORADO SERENADE(1946), ph
Richard Shackelton
KID FROM LEFT FIELD, THE(1953)
Floyd Shackleford
FORWARD PASS, THE(1929); MAN HUNTER, THE(1930); SUNDAY PUNCH(1942)
John Shackleford
JUST FOR THE HELL OF IT(1968); SHE-DEVILS ON WHEELS(1968)
Floyd Shackleforth
JUNGLE MAN(1941)
Richard Shackleton
PONY SOLDIER(1952); HOW TO MARRY A MILLIONAIRE(1953); DESPERADO, THE(1954)

Robert Shackleton
WHERE'S CHARLEY?(1952, Brit.)
Simon Shackleton
PRIVILEGED(1982, Brit.)
Harry Shacklock
CARRY ON LOVING(1970, Brit.)
Gene Shacove
WILD IN THE STREETS(1968)
Tim Shadbolt
1984
UTU(1984, New Zealand)
Timothy Shadden
1984
RIVER, THE(1984)
Jayne Shadduck
GOLD DIGGERS OF 1933(1933); LITTLE GIANT, THE(1933); 42ND STREET(1933)
Barry Shade
1984
BEVERLY HILLS COP(1984)
Betty Shade
Silents
AFTER FIVE(1915); DIVORCE TRAP, THE(1919)
Jameson Shade
DOUBLE LIFE, A(1947); WAR OF THE WORLDS, THE(1953)
Jamesson Shade
SEVENTH VICTIM, THE(1943); WILSON(1944); COVER-UP(1949); DAKOTA LIL(1950); WHIP HAND, THE(1951); TURNING POINT, THE(1952)
Jamison Shade
TREASURE OF MONTE CRISTO(1949)
Pat Shade
ONE TOUCH OF VENUS(1948); JOHNNY STOOL PIGEON(1949); ONLY GAME IN TOWN, THE(1970), ed
Floyd Shadelford
VAMPIRE'S GHOST, THE(1945)
Glenn Shadix
POSTMAN ALWAYS RINGS TWICE, THE(1981)
George Shadnoff
SPECTER OF THE ROSE(1946)
Shadow
SABOTEUR(1942)
Grey Shadow
WOLF CALL(1939)
John Shadow
PIECES(1983, Span./Puerto Rico), w
The Shadows
CARNIVAL ROCK(1957); BOYS, THE(1962, Brit.), m; WONDERFUL TO BE YOUNG!(1962, Brit.); SUMMER HOLIDAY(1963, Brit.); SWINGER'S PARADISE(1965, Brit.)
Arthur E. Shadur
Silents
FREEDOM OF THE PRESS(1928), sup
Charles Shadwell
VARIETY JUBILEE(1945, Brit.)
Buster Shaefer
CANCEL MY RESERVATION(1972)
Charles "Rube" Shaefer
HURRICANE HORSEMAN(1931)
Chester Shaeffer
WINK OF AN EYE(1958), ed
Eddie Shaeffer
BELLBOY, THE(1960)
Dino Shafeek
LONG DUEL, THE(1967, Brit.); CHARGE OF THE LIGHT BRIGADE, THE(1968, Brit.); YOUNG WINSTON(1972, Brit.); HIGH ROAD TO CHINA(1983)
Artie Shafer
FIRST NUDIE MUSICAL, THE(1976)
Don Shafer
OSTERMAN WEEKEND, THE(1983)
Martin Shafer
AWAKENING, THE(1980), p; MOUNTAIN MEN, THE(1980), p; MODERN ROMANCE(1981), p
Molly Shafer
Misc. Silents
BIG ADVENTURE, THE(1921)
Philip Shafer
DOC(1971); BEEN DOWN SO LONG IT LOOKS LIKE UP TO ME(1977)
Robert Shafer
DAMN YANKEES(1958)
Albert Shaff
DESPERATE WOMEN, THE(?), ed; GIRL ON THE BRIDGE, THE(1951), ed; RED SNOW(1952), ed; THY NEIGHBOR'S WIFE(1953), ed
M. Shaff
MAN HUNTERS OF THE CARIBBEAN(1938), w
Monroe Shaff
HEADIN' EAST(1937), w; CALIFORNIA FRONTIER(1938), w; CIPHER BUREAU(1938), w; HOLLYWOOD ROUNDUP(1938), w; LAW OF THE TEXAN(1938), p, w; OVERLAND EXPRESS, THE(1938), w; SHE'S GOT EVERYTHING(1938), w; STRANGER FROM ARIZONA, THE(1938), p, w; PANAMA PATROL(1939), w
Monty Shaff
MAN-EATER OF KUMAON(1948), p; NEVER TRUST A GAMBLER(1951), p
Ken Shaffel
PRINCE AND THE PAUPER, THE(1969)
Allison Shaffer
WOMAN TRAP(1929), ed
Allyson Shaffer
MAN I LOVE, THE(1929), ed; RIVER OF ROMANCE(1929), ed
Alyson Shaffer
BEGGARS OF LIFE(1928), ed; TOM SAWYER(1930), ed

Silents
LADIES OF THE MOB(1928), ed
Anthony Shaffer
CRY OF THE PENGUINS(1972, Brit.), w; FRENZY(1972, Brit.), w; SLEUTH(1972, Brit.), w; WICKER MAN, THE(1974, Brit.), w; DEATH ON THE NILE(1978, Brit.), w; ABSOLUTION(1981, Brit.), w; EVIL UNDER THE SUN(1982, Brit.), w
Caren Shaffer
OPERATION MANHUNT(1954)
Diane Shaffer
POPEYE(1980)
Marie Shaffer
Silents
JUNGLE TRAIL, THE(1919); JANE EYRE(1921)
Paul Shaffer
1984
THIS IS SPINAL TAP(1984)
Peter Shaffer
PAD, THE(AND HOW TO USE IT)* (1966, Brit.), w; FIVE FINGER EXERCISE(1962), w; ROYAL HUNT OF THE SUN, THE(1969, Brit.), w; PUBLIC EYE, THE(1972, Brit.), w; "EQUUS"(1977), w
1984
AMADEUS(1984), w
Rosalind Keating Shaffer
LADY KILLER(1933), w
Tracy K. Shaffer
TRADING PLACES(1983)
Karen Shaffner
COMMITMENT, THE(1976), art d
Louis A. Shaffner
COMMITMENT, THE(1976), d, w, ph
Al Shafran
PANIC IN THE CITY(1968)
Josef Shaftel
PARIS EXPRESS, THE(1953, Brit.), p; NAKED HILLS, THE(1956), p,d&w; NO PLACE TO HIDE(1956), p&d; BIGGEST BUNDLE OF THEM ALL, THE(1968), p, w; BLISS OF MRS. BLOSSOM, THE(1968, Brit.), p; GOODBYE GEMINI(1970, Brit.), p; LAST GRENADE, THE(1970, Brit.), p; SAY HELLO TO YESTERDAY(1971, Brit.), p; ASSASSINATION OF TROTSKY, THE(1972 Fr./Ital.), p; SELL OUT, THE(1976), p
Bert Shafter
BUBBLE, THE(1967), m
Patti Shafter
TOP BANANA(1954)
Hushang Shafti
INVINCIBLE SIX, THE(1970, U.S./Iran), prod d
Robert Shafto
MEET ME AT THE FAIR(1952); SABU AND THE MAGIC RING(1957)
Iris Shafton
DESIRE ME(1947)
Jack Shafton
DESIRE ME(1947)
Lyudmila Shagalova
DUEL, THE(1964, USSR); MARRIAGE OF BALZAMINOV, THE(1966, USSR)
Steve Shagan
TARZAN'S JUNGLE REBELLION(1970), p; SAVE THE TIGER(1973), p, w; HUSTLE(1975), w; VOYAGE OF THE DAMNED(1976, Brit.), w; NIGHTWING(1979), w; FORMULA, THE(1980), p, w
Shaggy
SHAGGY DOG, THE(1959)
Shaggy the Dog
SHAGGY(1948)
Michael Shagrir
CAST A GIANT SHADOW(1966)
Kiran Shah
PEOPLE THAT TIME FORGOT, THE(1977, Brit.); RAIDERS OF THE LOST ARK(1981); RETURN OF THE JEDI(1983)
Krishna Shah
RIVALS(1972), d&w; RIVER NIGER, THE(1976), d
Naseeruddin Shah
1984
MOHAN JOSHI HAAZIR HO(1984, India)
R.P. Shah
EXIT THE DRAGON, ENTER THE TIGER(1977, Hong Kong), p
Satish Shah
1984
MOHAN JOSHI HAAZIR HO(1984, India)
Yuseef Shah
MISSIONARY, THE(1982)
Dean Shah-Kee
DRIFTER(1975)
Mel Shahan
MOONSHINE COUNTY EXPRESS(1977)
Rocky Shahan
ROLL, THUNDER, ROLL(1949); JUBILEE TRAIL(1954); RUN FOR COVER(1955); COPPER SKY(1957); DEERSLAYER, THE(1957); RIDE A VIOLENT MILE(1957); STORM RIDER, THE(1957); BLOOD ARROW(1958); CATTLE EMPIRE(1958)
Kismet Shahani
LADY GODIVA RIDES AGAIN(1955, Brit.)
Comdr. John H. Shaheen, USNR
O.S.S.(1946), tech adv
Carol Lee Shahid
LITTLE SEX, A(1982)
Parvi Shahinkhoo
CARAVANS(1978, U.S./Iranian)
Mahin S. Shahrivar
MAN WHO KNEW TOO MUCH, THE(1956)
Anso Shaibu
TOTO AND THE POACHERS(1958, Brit.)

Nick Shaid
MONKEY'S PAW, THE(1933); LAST OUTPOST, THE(1935); PRIVATE WORLDS(1935); JUNGLE PRINCESS, THE(1936); REAL GLORY, THE(1939); MOON OVER BURMA(1940); RAIDERS OF THE DESERT(1941)
M.Y. Shaikh
NINE HOURS TO RAMA(1963, U.S./Brit.)
Mahmud Shaikhaly
ABBOTT AND COSTELLO IN THE FOREIGN LEGION(1950); DESERT HAWK, THE(1950)
Garry Shail
MUSIC MACHINE, THE(1979, Brit.)
Gary Shail
QUADROPHENIA(1979, Brit.); SHOCK TREATMENT(1981)
1984
GIVE MY REGARDS TO BROAD STREET(1984, Brit.)
Forman Shain
GOLDEN BOX, THE(1970)
Harvey Shain
PLANET OF DINOSAURS(1978)
Marcel Shain
JOHNNY VIK(1973), ph
Jack Shaindin
WHISPERING CITY(1947, Can.), md
Jack Shaindlin
LOST BOUNDARIES(1949), md; WALK EAST ON BEACON(1952), md; OPERATION MANHUNT(1954), md; ER LOVE A STRANGER(1958), md; MICKEY ONE(1965), m
Rich Shaine
IF EVER I SEE YOU AGAIN(1978), ed
Rick Shaine
EYES OF A STRANGER(1980), ed
1984
NIGHTMARE ON ELM STREET, A(1984), ed
Mordaunt Shairp
CRIME AT BLOSSOMS, THE(1933, Brit.), w; DARK ANGEL, THE(1935), w; WHITE ANGEL, THE(1936), w; DARK SECRET(1949, Brit.), w
Mike Shak
EVEL KNIEVEL(1971)
Shaka
FLASH GORDON(1980)
Martin Shakar
SATURDAY NIGHT FEVER(1977); CHILDREN, THE(1980); WITHOUT A TRACE(1983)
Shushella Shakari
RAZOR'S EDGE, THE(1946)
Dean Shakenford
RETURN OF THE JEDI(1983)
Pat Shakesby
HE WHO RIDES A TIGER(1966, Brit.)
Joan Shakespeare
HAND OF NIGHT, THE(1968, Brit.), m; CONNECTING ROOMS(1971, Brit.), m, md
John Shakespeare
LOVE IS A WOMAN(1967, Brit.), md; HAND OF NIGHT, THE(1968, Brit.), m; GREAT MCGONAGALL, THE(1975, Brit.), m
Robert Shakespeare
ROCKERS(1980)
William Shakespeare
TAMING OF THE SHREW, THE(1929), w; MIDSUMMER'S NIGHT'S DREAM, A(1935), w; AS YOU LIKE IT(1936, Brit.), w; ROMEO AND JULIET(1936), w; HENRY V(1946, Brit.), w; DOUBLE LIFE, A(1947), w; HAMLET(1948, Brit.), w; MACBETH(1948), w; JULIUS CAESAR(1952), w; MERRY WIVES OF WINDSOR, THE(1952, Ger.), w; JULIUS CAESAR(1953), w; KISS ME KATE(1953), w; ROMEO AND JULIET(1954, Brit.), w; JOE MACBETH(1955), w; OTHELLO(1955, U.S./Fr./Ital.), w; ROMEO AND JULIET(1955, USSR), w; TWELFTH NIGHT(1956, USSR), w; HONOURABLE MURDER, AN(1959, Brit.), w; OTHELLO(1960, U.S.S.R.), w; REST IS SILENCE, THE(1960, Ger.), w; MIDSUMMERS NIGHT'S DREAM, A(1961, Czech), w; THRONE OF BLOOD(1961, Jap.), w; WEST SIDE STORY(1961), w; HAMLET(1962, Ger.), w; MACBETH(1963), w; HAMILE(1965, Ghana), w; OTHELLO(1965, Brit.), w; MERRY WIVES OF WINDSOR, THE(1966, Aust.), w; MIDSUMMER NIGHT'S DREAM, A(1966), w; ROMEO AND JULIET(1966, Brit.), w; CHIMES AT MIDNIGHT(1967, Span.,Switz.), w; TAMING OF THE SHREW, THE(1967, U.S./Ital.), w; ROMEO AND JULIET(1968, Brit./Ital.), w, w; WINTER'S TALE, THE(1968, Brit.), w; HAMLET(1969, Brit.), w; MIDSUMMER NIGHT'S DREAM, A(1969, Brit.), w; JULIUS CAESAR(1970, Brit.), w; KING LEAR(1971, Brit./Den.), w; MACBETH(1971, Brit.), w; JOHNNY HAMLET(1972, Ital.), w; ANTONY AND CLEOPATRA(1973, Brit.), w; CATCH MY SOUL(1974), w; HAMLET(1976, Brit.), w; TEMPEST(1982), w
1984
MIDSUMMER NIGHT'S DREAM, A(1984, Brit./Span.), w
Silents
HAMLET(1913, Brit.), w; LOVE IN A WOOD(1915, Brit.), w; KING LEAR(1916, w; MERCHANT OF VENICE, THE(1916, Brit.), w; ROMEO AND JULIET(1916), w
William Shakespeare
BIG GAME, THE(1936)
Bernard Shakey
HUMAN HIGHWAY(1982), d, w
Fyodor Shakhamagonov
DESTINY OF A MAN(1961, USSR), w
Karen Shakhnazarov
1984
JAZZMAN(1984, USSR), d, w
Shakila
TIGER AND THE FLAME, THE(1955, India)
Floyd Shakleford
Silents
ENCHANTED ISLAND, THE(1927)
Ye. Shalamov
WAR AND PEACE(1968, USSR)

Betty Shale
LOOKING ON THE BRIGHT SIDE(1932, Brit.); WATER GYPSIES, THE(1932, Brit.); TROUBLE(1933, Brit.); EVERGREEN(1934, Brit.); DARK WORLD(1935, Brit.); FULL CIRCLE(1935, Brit.); ROYAL EAGLE(1936, Brit.); ROMANCE A LA CARTE(1938, Brit.); FULL SPEED AHEAD(1939, Brit.); LOVES OF JOANNA GODDEN, THE(1947, Brit.); NIGHT AND THE CITY(1950, Brit.); GREEN GROW THE RUSHES(1951, Brit.); MIRACLE IN SOHO(1957, Brit.); SURGEON'S KNIFE, THE(1957, Brit.)

Kerry Shale
LONELY LADY, THE(1983); YENTL(1983)

Tom Shale
NEVER TROUBLE TROUBLE(1931, Brit.); GOOD COMPANIONS(1933, Brit.)

Virginia Shaler
LOST BOUNDARIES(1949), w; WHISTLE AT EATON FALLS(1951), w; WALK EAST ON BEACON(1952), w; MAN ON A STRING(1960), w

Diane Shalet
REIVERS, THE(1969); LAST TYCOON, THE(1976); DEADHEAD MILES(1982)

David Shalit
1984
LITTLE DRUMMER GIRL, THE(1984)

Theo Shall
JAZZBAND FIVE, THE(1932, Ger,); SPRING IN THE AIR(1934, Brit.); TEN MINUTE ALIBI(1935, Brit.)

Alan Shallcross
WEATHER IN THE STREETS, THE(1983, Brit.), p

Frank Shallenbach
FIREMAN, SAVE MY CHILD(1932)

Tony Shaller
KNICKERBOCKER HOLIDAY(1944)

William Shallert
TOP OF THE WORLD(1955); HANGAR 18(1980)

Karen Shallo
1984
GARBO TALKS(1984); ONCE UPON A TIME IN AMERICA(1984); OVER THE BROOKLYN BRIDGE(1984)

P. Shalnov
WHEN THE TREES WERE TALL(1965, USSR)

Fvodor Shalyapin
Misc. Silents
TSAR IVAN VASILYEVICH GROZNY(1915, USSR)

Charles Shamata
RUNNING(1979, Can.); STONE COLD DEAD(1980, Can.); DEVIL AND MAX DEVLIN, THE(1981); SCANNERS(1981, Can.)

Chuck Shamata
GET BACK(1973, Can.); HOUSE BY THE LAKE, THE(1977, Can.); I MISS YOU, HUGS AND KISSES(1978, Can.); POWER PLAY(1978, Brit./Can.)

Bernard D. Shamberg
FIGHTING MAD(1948), w

Michael Shamberg
HEART BEAT(1979), p; MODERN PROBLEMS(1981), p; BIG CHILL, THE(1983), p

Lucille Shamberger
LIFE WITH FATHER(1947)

Lucille Shamburger
EMERGENCY WEDDING(1950); BUGLES IN THE AFTERNOON(1952)

Lisa Shames
PRETTY BABY(1978)

M. Shamkovich
SONG OVER MOSCOW(1964, USSR), spec eff

Alain Shammas
HORNET'S NEST(1970)

I. Shamo
SONG OF THE FOREST(1963, USSR), m

Jack Shampan
PAYROLL(1962, Brit.), art d; SING AND SWING(1964, Brit.), art d; TOMORROW AT TEN(1964, Brit.), art d; MODESTY BLAISE(1966, Brit.), art d; ADDING MACHINE, THE(1969), art d; BUSHBABY, THE(1970), art d; TAKE A GIRL LIKE YOU(1970, Brit.), art d; PERSECUTION(1974, Brit.), art d; BAWDY ADVENTURES OF TOM JONES, THE(1976, Brit.), art d; CARRY ON EMANUELLE(1978, Brit.), art d; YELLOWBEARD(1983), art d

Jack Shampar
GHOUL, THE(1975, Brit.), art d

Peter L. Shamray
Silents
HEARTS AND FISTS(1926), ed

Franklin Shamroy
Misc. Talkies
NEVER TOO LATE(1935), d

Leon Shamroy
WOMEN MEN MARRY(1931), ph; STOWAWAY(1932), ph; STRANGE ADVENTURE(1932), ph; HER BODYGUARD(1933), ph; JENNIE GERHARDT(1933), ph; THREE-CORNERED MOON(1933), ph; GOOD DAME(1934), ph; KISS AND MAKE UP(1934), ph; MYSTIC HOUR, THE(1934), ph; READY FOR LOVE(1934), ph; THIRTY-DAY PRINCESS(1934), ph; ACCENT ON YOUTH(1935), ph; BEHOLD MY WIFE(1935), ph; MARY BURNS, FUGITIVE(1935), ph; PRIVATE WORLDS(1935), ph; SHE COULDN'T TAKE IT(1935), ph; SHE MARRIED HER BOSS(1935), ph; FATAL LADY(1936), ph; SOAK THE RICH(1936), ph; SPENDTHRIFT(1936), ph; WEDDING PRESENT(1936), ph; BLOSSOMS ON BROADWAY(1937), ph; GREAT GAMBINI, THE(1937), ph; HER HUSBAND LIES(1937), ph; SHE ASKED FOR IT(1937), ph; YOU ONLY LIVE ONCE(1937), ph; YOUNG IN HEART, THE(1938), ph; ADVENTURES OF SHERLOCK HOLMES, THE(1939), ph; MADE FOR EACH OTHER(1939), ph; SECOND FIDDLE(1939), ph; STORY OF ALEXANDER GRAHAM BELL, THE(1939), ph; DOWN ARGENTINE WAY(1940), ph; FOUR SONS(1940), ph; I WAS AN ADVENTURESS(1940), ph; LILLIAN RUSSELL(1940), ph; LITTLE OLD NEW YORK(1940), ph; TIN PAN ALLEY(1940), ph; CONFIRM OR DENY(1941), ph; GREAT AMERICAN BROADCAST, THE(1941), ph; MOON OVER MIAMI(1941), ph; THAT NIGHT IN RIO(1941), ph; YANK IN THE R.A.F.(1941), ph; BLACK SWAN, THE(1942), ph; ROXIE HART(1942), ph; TEN GENTLEMEN FROM WEST POINT(1942), ph; CLAUDIA(1943), ph; CRASH DIVE(1943), ph; STORMY WEATHER(1943), ph; BUFFALO BILL(1944), ph; GREENWICH VILLAGE(1944), ph; WILSON(1944), ph; STATE FAIR(1945), ph; TREE GROWS IN BROOKLYN, A(1945), ph; WHERE DO WE GO FROM HERE?(1945), ph; LEAVE HER TO HEAVEN(1946), ph; DAISY KE-

NYON(1947), ph; FOREVER AMBER(1947), ph; SHOCKING MISS PILGRIM, THE(1947), ph; THAT LADY IN ERMINE(1948), ph; PRINCE OF FOXES(1949), ph; TWELVE O'CLOCK HIGH(1949), ph; CHEAPER BY THE DOZEN(1950), ph; TWO FLAGS WEST(1950), ph; DAVID AND BATHSHEBA(1951), ph; ON THE RIVERA(1951), ph; WAIT 'TIL THE SUN SHINES, NELLIE(1952), ph; WITH A SONG IN MY HEART(1952), ph; CALL ME MADAM(1953), ph; DOWN AMONG THE SHELTERING PALMS(1953), ph; GIRL NEXT DOOR, THE(1953), ph; KING OF THE KHYBER RIFLES(1953), ph; ROBE, THE(1953), ph; TONIGHT WE SING(1953), ph; WHITE WITCH DOCTOR(1953), ph; EGYPTIAN, THE(1954), ph; THERE'S NO BUSINESS LIKE SHOW BUSINESS(1954), ph; DADDY LONG LEGS(1955), ph; GOOD MORNING, MISS DOVE(1955), ph; LOVE IS A MANY-SPLENDORED THING(1955), ph; BEST THINGS IN LIFE ARE FREE, THE(1956), ph; GIRL CAN'T HELP IT, THE(1956), ph; KING AND I, THE(1956), ph; DESK SET(1957), ph; BRAVADOS, THE(1958), ph; RALLY 'ROUND THE FLAG, BOYS!(1958), ph; SOUTH PACIFIC(1958), ph; BELOVED INFIDEL(1959), ph; BLUE ANGEL, THE(1959), ph; PORGY AND BESS(1959), ph; NORTH TO ALASKA(1960), ph; WAKE ME WHEN IT'S OVER(1960), ph; SNOW WHITE AND THE THREE STOOGES(1961), ph; TENDER IS THE NIGHT(1961), ph; CARDINAL, THE(1963), ph; CLEOPATRA(1963), ph; JOHN GOLDFARB, PLEASE COME HOME(1964), ph; WHAT A WAY TO GO(1964), ph; AGONY AND THE ECSTASY, THE(1965), ph; DO NOT DISTURB(1965), ph; GLASS BOTTOM BOAT, THE(1966), ph; CAPRICE(1967), ph; PLANET OF THE APES(1968), ph; SECRET LIFE OF AN AMERICAN WIFE, THE(1968), ph; SKIDOO(1968), ph; JUSTINE(1969), ph
Silents
PIRATES OF THE SKY(1927), ph; OUT WITH THE TIDE(1928), ph

Sam Shamshak
TO ALL A GOODNIGHT(1980)

Mohammed Shamsi
HORSEMEN, THE(1971); MAN WHO WOULD BE KING, THE(1975, Brit.)

Shamsuddin
HULLABALOO OVER GEORGIE AND BONNIE'S PICTURES(1979, Brit.)

Chin Shan
FISTS OF FURY(1973, Chi.)

Kwan Shan
SHEPHERD GIRL, THE(1965, Hong Kong); VERMILION DOOR(1969, Hong Kong)

Peter Shanaberg
1984
HOUSE WHERE DEATH LIVES, THE(1984), p

Ellen Rome Shanahan
1984
WEEKEND PASS(1984), cos

Mahmoun Shanawy
LITTLE MISS DEVIL(1951, Egypt), m

Ian Shand
LIFE AT THE TOP(1965, Brit.); MISCHIEF(1969, Brit.), p, d; KADOYNG(1974, Brit.), d; WOMBLING FREE(1977, Brit.), p

Ron Shand
NO. 96(1974, Aus.)

Pia Shandel
VISITOR, THE(1973, Can.); SHADOW OF THE HAWK(1976, Can.)

Shandor
ONE DARK NIGHT(1983)

Stephane Shandor
ZIG-ZAG(1975, Fr/Ital.)

Carol Shandrew
Misc. Talkies
TRACY RIDES(1935)

Bill Shane
WANTED FOR MURDER(1946, Brit.)

Forman Shane
WHIP'S WOMEN(1968)
Misc. Talkies
HENRY'S NIGHT IN(1969); COCKTAIL HOSTESSES, THE(1976)

Gene Shane
RUN, ANGEL, RUN(1969); HELL'S BLOODY DEVILS(1970); VELVET VAMPIRE, THE(1971)

George Shane
ACCEPTABLE LEVELS(1983, Brit.)
1984
CAL(1984, Ireland); PIGS(1984, Ireland)

Jeff Shane
MAN WHO WOULDN'T TALK, THE(1958, Brit.)

Jerry Shane
SAN DIEGO, I LOVE YOU(1944); WING AND A PRAYER(1944); MOLLY AND ME(1945)

Jim Shane
PALM SPRINGS WEEKEND(1963)

Maxwell Shane
HITTING A NEW HIGH(1937), w; THIS WAY PLEASE(1937), w; YOU CAN'T BEAT LOVE(1937), w; YOU'RE A SWEETHEART(1937), w; ADVENTURE IN SAHARA(1938), w; SHE'S GOT EVERYTHING(1938), w; TIP-OFF GIRLS(1938), w; FEDERAL MAN-HUNT(1939), w; GRAND JURY SECRETS(1939), w; S.O.S. TIDAL WAVE(1939), w; COMIN' ROUND THE MOUNTAIN(1940), w; GOLDEN GLOVES(1940), w; LEATHER-PUSHERS, THE(1940), w; MUMMY'S HAND, THE(1940), w; DANGEROUS GAME, A(1941), w; FLYING BLIND(1941), w; FORCED LANDING(1941), w; NO HANDS ON THE CLOCK(1941), w; POWER DIVE(1941), w; TOO MANY BLONDES(1941), w; I LIVE ON DANGER(1942), w; TOP SERGEANT(1942), w; TORPEDO BOAT(1942), w; WILDCAT(1942), w; WRECKING CREW(1942), w; AERIAL GUNNER(1943), w; ALASKA HIGHWAY(1943), w; COWBOY IN MANHATTAN(1943), w; EYES OF THE UNDERWORLD(1943), w; HIGH EXPLOSIVE(1943), w; MINESWEEPER(1943), w; SUBMARINE ALERT(1943), w; TORNADO(1943), m; DARK MOUNTAIN(1944), w; DOUBLE EXPOSURE(1944), w; GAMBLER'S CHOICE(1944), w; NAVY WAY, THE(1944), w; ONE BODY TOO MANY(1944), w; TIMBER QUEEN(1944), w; FOLLOW THAT WOMAN(1945), w; HIGH POWERED(1945), w; ONE EXCITING NIGHT(1945), w; PEOPLE ARE FUNNY(1945), w; SCARED STIFF(1945), w; TOKYO ROSE(1945), w; MAN WHO DARED, THE(1946), w; ADVENTURE ISLAND(1947), w; BIG TOWN(1947), w; DANGER STREET(1947), w; FEAR IN THE NIGHT(1947), d; SEVEN WERE SAVED(1947), w; MR. RECKLESS(1948), w; SHAGGY(1948), w; CITY ACROSS THE RIVER(1949), p&d; WAIT 'TIL THE SUN SHINES, NELLIE(1952), w; GLASS WALL, THE(1953), d, w; THREE

HOURS TO KILL(1954), w; HELL'S ISLAND(1955), w; NAKED STREET, THE(1955), d&w; NIGHTMARE(1956), d&w

Michael Shane
ONE POTATO, TWO POTATO(1964); WHY WOULD I LIE(1980); LOVE CHILD(1982)

Rick Shane
1984
GOODBYE PEOPLE, THE(1984), ed

Sara Shane
MAGNIFICENT OBSESSION(1954); SIGN OF THE PAGAN(1954); DADDY LONG LEGS(1955); KING AND FOUR QUEENS, THE(1956); THREE BAD SISTERS(1956); AFFAIR IN HAVANA(1957); TARZAN'S GREATEST ADVENTURE(1959, Brit.)

Tamara Shane
MR. ARKADIN(1962, Brit./Fr./Span.)

Ted Shane
Silents
ACROSS THE SINGAPORE(1928), w; SHADOWS OF THE NIGHT(1928), w; DESERT RIDER, THE(1929), w

Shane Fenton and the Fentones
DREAM MAKER, THE(1963, Brit.); PLAY IT COOL(1963, Brit.)

John Shaner
BUCKET OF BLOOD, A(1959); LIVING BETWEEN TWO WORLDS(1963); HALLS OF ANGER(1970), w

John Herman Shaner
ISLAND OF DR. MOREAU, THE(1977), w; LAST MARRIED COUPLE IN AMERICA, THE(1980), p, w

Ho Lang Shang
RETURN OF THE DRAGON(1974, Chin.), ph

Joan Shangold
1984
POPE OF GREENWICH VILLAGE, THE(1984)

Shoshik Shani
OPERATION THUNDERBOLT(1978, ISRAEL)

Bud Shank
I WANT TO LIVE!(1958); WAR HUNT(1962), m

Gregg Shank
DAY MARS INVADED EARTH, THE(1963); FOLLOW ME, BOYS!(1966)

Jon Shank
THOMAS CROWN AFFAIR, THE(1968); REIVERS, THE(1969); DIRT GANG, THE(1972); JESSIE'S GIRLS(1976)

Ravi Shankar
PATHER PANCHALI(1958, India), m; APARAJITO(1959, India), m; WORLD OF APU, THE(1960, India), m; TARZAN GOES TO INDIA(1962, U.S./Brit./Switz.), m; CHAPPAQUA(1967), a, m; DRY SUMMER(1967, Turkey), m; CHARLY(1968), m; GANDHI(1982), m

Shankar-Jaikshan
BOMBAY TALKIE(1970, India), m

Mark Shanker
FIRST DEADLY SIN, THE(1980), p

Richard Shankland
LOVE ISLAND(1952)

Richard W. Shankland
NAKED CITY, THE(1948)

Robert Shankland
TOWN WITHOUT PITY(1961, Ger./Switz./U.S.); STOP TRAIN 349(1964, Fr./Ital./Ger.)

Douglas Alan Shanklin
1984
STAR TREK III: THE SEARCH FOR SPOCK(1984)

Lina Shanklin
SUMMERSPELL(1983), p, d&w

Ray Shanklin
BLACK GIRL(1972), m

Wayne Shanklin
ANGEL BABY(1961), m

Arnold Shanks
MANFISH(1956)

Dan Shanks
REVENGE OF THE NINJA(1983)
Misc. Talkies
LEGEND OF THE WILD(1981)

Don Shanks
LIFE AND TIMES OF GRIZZLY ADAMS, THE(1974); GUARDIAN OF THE WILDERNESS(1977); SWEET SIXTEEN(1983)
Misc. Talkies
ROGUE AND GRIZZLY, THE(1982)

Susan Shanks
1984
BAY BOY(1984, Can.), ed

Valerie Shanks
BRONCO BILLY(1980)

Billy Shanley
SILENT WITNESS, THE(1962)

Fred Shanley
Misc. Talkies
BYE-BYE BUDDY(1929)
Silents
KING OF THE HERD(1927)

Robert Shanley
THIS IS THE ARMY(1943)

Phyllis Shannaw
Silents
SPORT OF KINGS, THE(1921, Brit.)
Misc. Silents
(; CALL OF THE ROAD, THE(1920, Brit.); FIFTH FORM AT ST. DOMINIC'S, THE(1921, Brit.); RIGHT TO LIVE, THE(1921, Brit.)

John Herman Shanner
GOIN' SOUTH(1978), w

Alec Shannon
Misc. Silents
WOMAN OF REDEMPTION, A(1918)

Alex Shannon
Silents
BATTLE OF LIFE, THE(1916); MAN WHO FORGOT, THE(1917)
Misc. Silents
GIRL OF THE SEA(1920)

Alex K. Shannon
Silents
ARE CHILDREN TO BLAME?(1922)
Misc. Silents
SIMP, THE(1921)

Alexander Shannon
Silents
ETERNAL SIN, THE(1917)

Bill Shannon
WITHOUT RESERVATIONS(1946); LIKELY STORY, A(1947); SINBAD THE SAILOR(1947); WOMAN ON THE BEACH, THE(1947); YOUNG AND DANGEROUS(1957); BUCK AND THE PREACHER(1972)

Carol Shannon
HOT CARS(1956)

Carole Shannon
CAGED(1950)

Charles Shannon
Silents
DOWN UPON THE SUWANNEE RIVER(1925)

Cora Shannon
BELLS OF ST. MARY'S, THE(1945); MR. BELVEDERE RINGS THE BELL(1951); SOMETHING TO LIVE FOR(1952); WAR OF THE WORLDS, THE(1953)

Del Shannon
RING-A-DING RHYTHM(1962, Brit.); DAYTONA BEACH WEEKEND(1965); SGT. PEPPER'S LONELY HEARTS CLUB BAND(1978)

Dick Shannon
TROOPER HOOK(1957)

Effie Shannon
WISER SEX, THE(1932)
Silents
MAN WHO PLAYED GOD, THE(1922); SECRETS OF PARIS, THE(1922); SURE FIRE FLINT(1922); JACQUELINE, OR BLAZING BARRIERS(1923); TIE THAT BINDS, THE(1923); ROULETTE(1924); SIDESHOW OF LIFE, THE(1924); SINNERS IN HEAVEN(1925); NEW COMMANDMENT, THE(1925); SALLY OF THE SAWDUST(1925)
Misc. Silents
AFTER THE BALL(1914); SPHINX, THE(1916); HER BOY(1918); MAMA'S AFFAIR(1921); WANDERING FIRES(1925)

Ernest Shannon
VARIETY PARADE(1936, Brit.)

Ethel Shannon
Silents
EASY TO MAKE MONEY(1919); MASTER STROKE, A(1920); OLD FASHIONED BOY, AN(1920); MAN'S LAW AND GOD'S(1922); WATCH HIM STEP(1922); HERO, THE(1923); PLAYING DOUBLE(1923); LIGHTNING ROMANCE(1924); HIGH AND HANDSOME(1925); SILENT POWER, THE(1926); BABE COMES HOME(1927)
Misc. Silents
DAUGHTERS OF THE RICH(1923); MAYTIME(1923); CHARLEY'S AUNT(1925); PHANTOM EXPRESS, THE(1925); SPEED WILD(1925); STOP FLIRTING(1925); TEXAS TRAIL, THE(1925); BUCKAROO KID, THE(1926); DANGER QUEST(1926); HIGH FLYER, THE(1926); SIGN OF THE CLAW, THE(1926); SPEED LIMIT, THE(1926); THROUGH THICK AND THIN(1927)

Fay Shannon
GHOST TOWN RIDERS(1938)

Frank Shannon
RASPUTIN AND THE EMPRESS(1932); G-MEN(1935); MEN WITHOUT NAMES(1935); EAGLE'S BROOD, THE(1936); END OF THE TRAIL(1936); FLASH GORDON(1936); PRISONER OF SHARK ISLAND, THE(1936); TEXAS RANGERS, THE(1936); ADVENTUROUS BLONDE(1937); EVER SINCE EVE(1937); ACCIDENTS WILL HAPPEN(1938); BLONDES AT WORK(1938); HOLIDAY(1938); OUTLAWS OF THE PRAIRIE(1938); TORCHY BLANE IN CHINATOWN(1938); TORCHY BLANE IN PANAMA(1938); TORCHY GETS HER MAN(1938); YOU CAN'T TAKE IT WITH YOU(1938); NIGHT OF NIGHTS, THE(1939); TORCHY PLAYS WITH DYNAMITE(1939); TORCHY RUNS FOR MAYOR(1939); UNION PACIFIC(1939); RETURN OF FRANK JAMES, THE(1940); WILDCAT BUS(1940); FEDERAL FUGITIVES(1941); RAGE IN HEAVEN(1941); RAWHIDE RANGERS(1941); UNFINISHED BUSINESS(1941); IRON MAJOR, THE(1943); CRACK-UP(1946); DANGEROUS PROFESSION, A(1949)
Silents
ICEBOUND(1924); MONSIEUR BEAUCAIRE(1924)
Misc. Silents
BOOMERANG BILL(1922)

Frank Shannon [Franco Prosperi]
HIRED KILLER, THE(1967, Fr./Ital.), d&w

George Shannon
Misc. Talkies
SUGAR COOKIES(1973)

Gregory Shannon
THAT FUNNY FEELING(1965)

Harry Shannon
TRUE TO LIFE(1943); HEADS UP(1930); TAKE A CHANCE(1933); MIDDLETON FAMILY AT THE N.Y. WORLD'S FAIR(1939); CITY OF CHANCE(1940); GAMBLING ON THE HIGH SEAS(1940); GIRL FROM AVENUE A(1940); ONE CROWDED NIGHT(1940); PAROLE FIXER(1940); SAILOR'S LADY(1940); TEAR GAS SQUAD(1940); TOO MANY GIRLS(1940); TUGBOAT ANNIE SAILS AGAIN(1940); YOUNG AS YOU FEEL(1940); YOUNG TOM EDISON(1940); CITIZEN KANE(1941); SAINT IN PALM SPRINGS, THE(1941); FALCON TAKES OVER, THE(1942); IN OLD CALIFORNIA(1942); LADY IS WILLING, THE(1942); MAD MARTINDALES, THE(1942); MRS. WIGGS OF THE CABBAGE PATCH(1942); ONCE UPON A HONEYMOON(1942); POWERS GIRL, THE(1942); THIS GUN FOR HIRE(1942); ALASKA HIGHWAY(1943); DOUGHBOYS IN IRELAND(1943); GOVERNMENT GIRL(1943); HEADIN' FOR GOD'S COUNTRY(1943); HEAT'S ON, THE(1943); IN OLD OKLAHOMA(1943); SOMEONE TO REMEMBER(1943); SONG OF TEXAS(1943); EVE OF

ST. MARK, THE(1944); LADIES OF WASHINGTON(1944); MUMMY'S GHOST, THE(1944); WHEN THE LIGHTS GO ON AGAIN(1944); YELLOW ROSE OF TEXAS, THE(1944); CAPTAIN EDDIE(1945); CRIME, INC.(1945); NOB HILL(1945); WITHIN THESE WALLS(1945); CRACK-UP(1946); I RING DOORBELLS(1946); JOLSON STORY, THE(1946); LAST CROOKED MILE, THE(1946); NIGHT EDITOR(1946); SAN QUENTIN(1946); DANGEROUS YEARS(1947); DEVIL THUMBS A RIDE, THE(1947); EXPOSED(1947); FARMER'S DAUGHTER, THE(1947); INVISIBLE WALL, THE(1947); NORA PRENTISS(1947); RED HOUSE, THE(1947); TIME OUT OF MIND(1947); FEUDIN', FUSSIN' AND A-FIGHTIN'(1948); FIGHTING FATHER DUNNE(1948); LADY FROM SHANGHAI, THE(1948); MR. BLANDINGS BUILDS HIS DREAM HOUSE(1948); NORTHWEST STAMPEDE(1948); RETURN OF THE BADMEN(1948); CHAMPION(1949); DEVIL'S HENCHMEN, THE(1949); MARY RYAN, DETECTIVE(1949); MR. SOFT TOUCH(1949); RUSTLERS(1949); TULSA(1949); COW TOWN(1950); CURTAIN CALL AT CACTUS CREEK(1950); FLYING MISSILE(1950); GUNFIGHTER, THE(1950); HUNT THE MAN DOWN(1950); JACKIE ROBINSON STORY, THE(1950); KILLER THAT STALKED NEW YORK, THE(1950); RIGHT CROSS(1950); SINGING GUNS(1950); TARNISHED(1950); THREE LITTLE WORDS(1950); WHERE DANGER LIVES(1950); WHIPPED, THE(1950); AL JENNINGS OF OKLAHOMA(1951); BLUE BLOOD(1951); LEMON DROP KID, THE(1951); PRIDE OF MARYLAND(1951); SCARF, THE(1951); BOOTS MALONE(1952); FLESH AND FURY(1952); HIGH NOON(1952); LURE OF THE WILDERNESS(1952); CRY OF THE HUNTED(1953); JACK SLADE(1953); KANSAS PACIFIC(1953); ROAR OF THE CROWD(1953); EXECUTIVE SUITE(1954); PHANTOM STALLION, THE(1954); RAILS INTO LARAMIE(1954); WITNESS TO MURDER(1954); AT GUNPOINT(1955); MARAUDERS, THE(1955); TALL MEN, THE(1955); VIOLENT MEN, THE(1955); COME NEXT SPRING(1956); PEACEMAKER, THE(1956); WRITTEN ON THE WIND(1956); DUEL AT APACHE WELLS(1957); HELL'S CROSSROADS(1957); LONELY MAN, THE(1957); MAN OR GUN(1958); TOUCH OF EVIL(1958); YELLOWSTONE KELLY(1959); SUMMER AND SMOKE(1961); WILD IN THE COUNTRY(1961); GYPSY(1962)

Harry J. Shannon
IDAHO(1943)
Harry T. Shannon
OUTCASTS OF POKER FLAT, THE(1952)
Inez Shannon
Misc. Silents
BELOVED ADVENTURESS, THE(1917)
Ivy Shannon
ROYAL DIVORCE, A(1938, Brit.)
Jack Shannon
STORMY(1935); SERGEANT MURPHY(1938); DESPERATE TRAILS(1939); LAW AND ORDER(1940); SON OF ROARING DAN(1940); WEST OF CARSON CITY(1940); MAN FROM MONTANA(1941); SUNDOWN RIDERS(1948)
Jackie De Shannon
SURF PARTY(1964)
James Shannon
KING OF THE GYPSIES(1978)
Jay Shannon
LAST GUNFIGHTER, THE(1961, Can.)
Jimmy Shannon
FLAMING GUNS(1933)
Johnny Shannon
THAT'LL BE THE DAY(1974, Brit.); FLAME(1975, Brit.); RUNNERS(1983, Brit.)
Jon Shannon
C. C. AND COMPANY(1971), cos
Jose Shannon
Misc. Silents
TORN SAILS(1920, Brit.)
Larry Shannon
Silents
CATCH AS CATCH CAN(1927)
Marc Shannon
VOYAGE TO THE PREHISTORIC PLANET(1965)
Marda Shannon
REMARKABLE MR. KIPPS(1942, Brit.)
Mary Shannon
IT'S A DATE(1940)
Michael Shannon
SHOOT IT: BLACK, SHOOT IT: BLUE(1974); THAT LUCKY TOUCH(1975, Brit.); MAKING LOVE(1982)
1984
SHEENA(1984)
Michael J. Shannon
SUPERMAN II(1980); NEVER NEVER LAND(1982)
Moriah Shannon
D.C. CAB(1983)
1984
ALLEY CAT(1984)
Noel Shannon
BEYOND THE CITIES(1930, Brit.), w; FACES(1934, Brit.); GIRL IN THE FLAT, THE(1934, Brit.); LUCKY LOSER(1934, Brit.)
Paul Shannon
OUTLAWS IS COMING, THE(1965)
Peggy Shannon
ROAD TO RENO(1931); SECRET CALL, THE(1931); SILENCE(1931); TOUCHDOWN!(1931); FALSE FACES(1932); HOTEL CONTINENTAL(1932); PAINTED WOMAN(1932); SOCIETY GIRL(1932); THIS RECKLESS AGE(1932); DELUGE(1933); DEVIL'S MATE(1933); GIRL MISSING(1933); TURN BACK THE CLOCK(1933); FURY OF THE JUNGLE(1934); CASE OF THE LUCKY LEGS(1935); NIGHT LIFE OF THE GODS(1935); MAN I MARRY, THE(1936); YOUTH ON PAROLE(1937); GIRLS ON PROBATION(1938); ADVENTURES OF JANE ARDEN(1939); BLACKWELL'S ISLAND(1939); FIXER DUGAN(1939); WOMEN, THE(1939); HOUSE ACROSS THE BAY, THE(1940); TRIPLE JUSTICE(1940)
Misc. Talkies
BACK PAGE(1934); FIGHTING LADY(1935); ELLIS ISLAND(1936)
Richard Shannon
ARROWHEAD(1953); FLIGHT TO TANGIER(1953); FOREVER FEMALE(1953); GIRLS OF PLEASURE ISLAND, THE(1953); HOUDINI(1953); PONY EXPRESS(1953); VANQUISHED, THE(1953); ALASKA SEAS(1954); BRIDGES AT TOKO-RI, THE(1954); WHITE CHRISTMAS(1954); ARTISTS AND MODELS(1955); SEVEN LITTLE FOYS,

THE(1955); STRATEGIC AIR COMMAND(1955); LEATHER SAINT, THE(1956); PROUD AND THE PROFANE, THE(1956); THAT CERTAIN FEELING(1956); VAGABOND KING, THE(1956); BEAU JAMES(1957); KISS THEM FOR ME(1957); RIDE A VIOLENT MILE(1957); RIDE OUT FOR REVENGE(1957); SPRING REUNION(1957); TIN STAR, THE(1957); CATTLE EMPIRE(1958); DESERT HELL(1958); SPACE CHILDREN, THE(1958); DON'T GIVE UP THE SHIP(1959); PROPER TIME, THE(1959); TRAP, THE(1959)
Robert Shannon
LOVER COME BACK(1931), w; TIMES SQUARE LADY(1935), w; RACKETEERS IN EXILE(1937), w; ADVENTURES OF CAPTAIN FABIAN(1951), w
Robert T. Shannon
STRICTLY PERSONAL(1933), w; I SELL ANYTHING(1934), w; KING SOLOMON OF BROADWAY(1935), w; NIGHT AT THE RITZ, A(1935), w; MOONLIGHT MURDER(1936), w; GIRL WITH IDEAS, A(1937), w; LADY FIGHTS BACK(1937), w; MURDER IN GREENWICH VILLAGE(1937), w; PRESCRIPTION FOR ROMANCE(1937), w; INVISIBLE ENEMY(1938), w; BARNYARD FOLLIES(1940), w; GREAT TRAIN ROBBERY, THE(1941), w; ICE-CAPADES REVUE(1942), w; PARDON MY STRIPES(1942), w; SLEEPYTIME GAL(1942), w; SONS OF THE PIONEERS(1942), w; WRECKING CREW(1942), w; X MARKS THE SPOT(1942), w; BLONDE RANSOM(1945), w; FLAME, THE(1948), w; UNKNOWN ISLAND(1948), w
Robert Terry Shannon
Silents
TAXI DANCER, THE(1927), w
Russell Shannon
TRACKDOWN(1976)
William Shannon
GREEN BERETS, THE(1968)
Zyllah Shannon
Misc. Silents
WORLD TO LIVE IN, THE(1919)
Gaye Shannon-Burnett
MY BROTHER'S WEDDING(1983), a, p
R. Shanock
SINGING BLACKSMITH(1938)
Shri V. Shantaram
TWO EYES, TWELVE HANDS(1958, India), a, p&d
Usu Shao-shing
GOLIATHON(1979, Hong Kong)
Tung Shao-yung
MERMAID, THE(1966, Hong Kong), ph
L. Shapalina
NEW TEACHER, THE(1941, USSR)
William Shapard
BEYOND THE TIME BARRIER(1960)
Ziva Shapir
TATTERED DRESS, THE(1957)
Talia Shapira
JESUS(1979)
Barry Shapiro
WAITRESS(1982), art d; STUCK ON YOU(1983), art d
Beverly Shapiro
BLOODEATERS(1980)
Bobbie Shapiro
1984
WHERE THE BOYS ARE '84(1984), ed
Brad Shapiro
CLEOPATRA JONES(1973), m
E. Shapiro
TWELFTH NIGHT(1956, USSR), ph
George Shapiro
IN GOD WE TRUST(1980), p
Helen Shapiro
RING-A-DING RHYTHM(1962, Brit.); PLAY IT COOL(1963, Brit.); LITTLE OF WHAT YOU FANCY, A(1968, Brit.)
Henry Shapiro
SUPERFLY(1972)
Hilary Shapiro
SOUP FOR ONE(1982)
1984
WEEKEND PASS(1984)
Iosif Shapiro
SLEEPING BEAUTY, THE(1966, USSR), w
Irwin Shapiro
ECHOES OF SILENCE(1966)
Ken Shapiro
GROOVE TUBE, THE(1974), a, a, a, p&d, w; MODERN PROBLEMS(1981), d, w
Lionel Shapiro
SEALED VERDICT(1948), w; DEPORTED(1950), w; D-DAY, THE SIXTH OF JUNE(1956), w
Mel Shapiro
SAMMY STOPS THE WORLD zero(1978), d
Melvin Shapiro
EXPLOSIVE GENERATION, THE(1961), ed; RIDER ON A DEAD HORSE(1962), ed; GLORY GUYS, THE(1965), ed; GOOD TIMES(1967), ed; TELL THEM WILLIE BOY IS HERE(1969), ed; MC MASTERS(1970), ed; B.S. I LOVE YOU(1971), ed; KING, QUEEN, KNAVE(1972, Ger./U.S.), ed; ARNOLD(1973), ed; TERROR IN THE WAX MUSEUM(1973), ed; TAXI DRIVER(1976), ed; AMERICAN HOT WAX(1978), ed; ICE CASTLES(1978), ed
1984
NO SMALL AFFAIR(1984), ed; WHERE THE BOYS ARE '84(1984), ed
Michael Joel Shapiro
STAR 80(1983)
Mikhail Shapiro
KATERINA IZMAILOVA(1969, USSR), d
Richard Shapiro
GREAT SCOUT AND CATHOUSE THURSDAY, THE(1976), w
Ron Shapiro
ATTACK OF THE KILLER TOMATOES(1978)

Ronald Shapiro
TENTACLES(1977, Ital.)

Stanley Shapiro
SOUTH SEA WOMAN(1953), w; PERFECT FURLOUGH, THE(1958), w; OPERA-TION PETTICOAT(1959), w; PILLOW TALK(1959), w; COME SEPTEMBER(1961), w; LOVER COME BACK(1961), p, w; THAT TOUCH OF MINK(1962), p, w; BEDTIME STORY(1964), p, w; VERY SPECIAL FAVOR, A(1965), p, w; HOW TO SAVE A MARRIAGE--AND RUIN YOUR LIFE(1968), p, w; ME, NATALIE(1969), p, w; FOR PETE'S SAKE(1977), p, w; SENIORS, THE(1978), p, w; CARBON COPY(1981), p, w

Tatyana Shapiro
BLUE BIRD, THE(1976), ed

Ted Shapiro
TRACKS(1977), p

Tom Shapiro
ONLY WAY HOME, THE(1972), m

Wayne Shapiro
NORMAN LOVES ROSE(1982, Aus.)

Harlow Shapley
OF STARS AND MEN(1961), w

Dr. Harlow Shapley
OF STARS AND MEN(1961)

Lidiya Shaporenko
PEACE TO HIM WHO ENTERS(1963, USSR)

Yuri Shaporin
DESERTER(1934, USSR), m; GENERAL SUVOROV(1941, USSR), m; 1812(1944, USSR), m

G. Shapovalov
HOME FOR TANYA, A(1961, USSR); RESURRECTION(1963, USSR); WHEN THE TREES WERE TALL(1965, USSR); WAR AND PEACE(1968, USSR)

G. Shapovaov
DESTINY OF A MAN(1961, USSR)

Seryozha Shappu
WELCOME KOSTYA!(1965, USSR)

Melvin Shaprio
FINIAN'S RAINBOW(1968), ed

Cyril Shaps
MIRACLE IN SOHO(1957, Brit.); PICKUP ALLEY(1957, Brit.); ROOM 43(1959, Brit.); SILENT ENEMY, THE(1959, Brit.); BOY WHO STOLE A MILLION, THE(1960, Brit.); FOLLOW THAT HORSE!(1960, Brit.); NEVER LET GO(1960, Brit.); S.O.S. PACI-FIC(1960, Brit.); PURSUERS, THE(1961, Brit.); RETURN OF A STRANGER(1962, Brit.); SMALL WORLD OF SAMMY LEE, THE(1963, Brit.); LITTLE ONES, THE(1965, Brit.); UP JUMPED A SWAGMAN(1965, Brit.); TO SIR, WITH LOVE(1967, Brit.); KREMLIN LETTER, THE(1970); LOOKING GLASS WAR, THE(1970, Brit.); ODESSA FILE, THE(1974, Brit./Ger.); 11 HARROWHOUSE(1974, Brit.); OPERATION DAY-BREAK(1976, U.S./Brit./Czech.); SPY WHO LOVED ME, THE(1977, Brit.); UNIDENTI-FIED FLYING ODDBALL, THE(1979, Brit.)

Bill Shapter
BLACK JACK(1979, Brit.), ed; PROSTITUTE(1980, Brit.), ed

William Shapter
MEMOIRS OF A SURVIVOR(1981, Brit.), ed; DEEP IN THE HEART(1983), ed

Mural Sharada
JUNGLE PRINCESS, THE(1936)

Princess Mural Sharado
UNDER THE PAMPAS MOON(1935)

John Sharaf
IN MACARTHUR PARK(1977), ph

Sharaff
BEST YEARS OF OUR LIVES, THE(1946), cos

Irene Sharaff
GIRL CRAZY(1943), cos; MEET ME IN ST. LOUIS(1944), cos; YOLANDA AND THE THIEF(1945), cos; DARK MIRROR, THE(1946), cos; BISHOP'S WIFE, THE(1947), cos; SONG IS BORN, A(1948), cos; STAR IS BORN, A(1954), cos; GUYS AND DOLLS(1955), cos; KING AND I, THE(1956), cos; PORGY AND BESS(1959), cos; CAN-CAN(1960), cos; FLOWER DRUM SONG(1961), cos; WEST SIDE STORY(1961), cos; CLEOPA-TRA(1963), cos; SANDPIPER, THE(1965), cos; WHO'S AFRAID OF VIRGINIA WOOLF?(1966), cos; TAMING OF THE SHREW, THE(1967, U.S./Ital.), cos; FUNNY GIRL(1968), cos; HELLO, DOLLY!(1969), cos; JUSTINE(1969), cos; GREAT WHITE HOPE, THE(1970), cos; OTHER SIDE OF MIDNIGHT, THE(1977), cos; MOMMIE DEAREST(1981), cos

Del Sharbutt
CUBAN PETE(1946); HIT PARADE OF 1947(1947)

Palma Shard
TAKE CARE OF MY LITTLE GIRL(1951)

Kathy Share
RAMRODDER, THE(1969)

Stefan Sharff
ACROSS THE RIVER(1965), p,d&w

Jack Shargel
MOTHERS OF TODAY(1939)

Becky Shargo
1984
FOOTLOOSE(1984), m

Shari
TIGER BAY(1959, Brit.)

Bonnie Shari
BRAIN THAT WOULDN'T DIE, THE(1959)

Omar Sharif
GENGHIS KHAN(U.S./Brit./Ger./Yugo); LAWRENCE OF ARABIA(1962, Brit.); BEHOLD A PALE HORSE(1964); FALL OF THE ROMAN EMPIRE, THE(1964); DOCTOR ZHIVAGO(1965); YELLOW ROLLS-ROYCE, THE(1965, Brit.); MARCO THE MAGNIFICENT(1966, Ital./Fr./Yugo./Egypt/Afghanistan); POPPY IS ALSO A FLOW-ER, THE(1966); MORE THAN A MIRACLE(1967, Ital./Fr.); NIGHT OF THE GENER-ALS, THE(1967, Brit./Fr.); FUNNY GIRL(1968); MAYERLING(1968, Brit./Fr.); APPOINTMENT, THE(1969); CHE!(1969); MACKENNA'S GOLD(1969); HORSEMEN, THE(1971); LAST VALLEY, THE(1971, Brit.); BURGLARS, THE(1972, Fr./Ital.); MYSTERIOUS ISLAND OF CAPTAIN NEMO, THE(1973, Fr./Ital. 87m Span./Came-roon); JUGGERNAUT(1974, Brit.); TAMARIND SEED, THE(1974, Brit.); FUNNY LADY(1975); CRIME AND PASSION(1976, U.S., Ger.); ASHANTI(1979); BLOOD-LINE(1979); BALTIMORE BULLET, THE(1980); OH, HEAVENLY DOG!(1980); GREEN ICE(1981, Brit.)

1984
TOP SECRET!(1984)

Tarek Sharif
DOCTOR ZHIVAGO(1965)

Yevgeny Sharikov
SIGNALS-AN ADVENTURE IN SPACE(1970, E. Ger./Pol.)

Mrs. Sharkey
Silents
KID CANFIELD THE REFORM GAMBLER(1922)

Dan Sharits
Silents
LAW OF THE RANGE, THE(1928), ed; SHADOWS OF THE NIGHT(1928), ed

Billy Ray Sharkey
WARGAMES(1983)
1984
BEST DEFENSE(1984)

Jack Sharkey
Silents
$5,000,000 COUNTERFEITING PLOT, THE(1914)

Myrl Sharkey
SOUNDER(1972)

Ray Sharkey
LORDS OF FLATBUSH, THE(1974); TRACKDOWN(1976); STUNTS(1977); HOT TOMORROWS(1978); PARADISE ALLEY(1978); WHO'LL STOP THE RAIN?(1978); HEART BEAT(1979); IDOLMAKER, THE(1980); WILLIE AND PHIL(1980); LOVE AND MONEY(1982); SOME KIND OF HERO(1982)
1984
BODY ROCK(1984); DUBEAT-E-O(1984)

Sailor Sharkey
Silents
BASHFUL BUCCANEER(1925); ISLE OF LOST MEN(1928)

Terence Sharkey
BLACK TENT, THE(1956, Brit.)

Tom Sharkey
MADISON SQUARE GARDEN(1932)

Sharkey the Seal
PARDON MY SARONG(1942)

Ned Sharks
Silents
LAW FORBIDS, THE(1924)

Gus Sharland
CHILDREN OF CHANCE(1930, Brit.); HARMONY HEAVEN(1930, Brit.); TWO WORLD(1930, Brit.)

Reginald Sharland
WOMAN TO WOMAN(1929); GIRL OF THE PORT(1930); INSIDE THE LINES(1930); BORN TO LOVE(1931); LADY REFUSES, THE(1931); LONG LOST FATHER(1934); SHOCK(1934)

Amar N. Sharma
ROAD TO SINGAPORE(1931)

Barbara Sharma
NORMAN...IS THAT YOU?(1976)

Madhav Sharma
AWAKENING, THE(1980); GIRO CITY(1982, Brit.)

Partap Sharma
SHAKESPEARE WALLAH(1966, India)

Romesh Sharma
SIDDHARTHA(1972)

Subrata Sen Sharma
KANCHENJUNGHA(1966, India)

Anthony Sharman
UP THE JUNCTION(1968, Brit.)

Della Sharman
FIVE GUNS TO TOMBSTONE(1961)

Graham Sharman
IF ...(1968, Brit.)

Harve Sharman
SHOOT(1976, Can.), p

Jim Sharman
SHIRLEY THOMPSON VERSUS THE ALIENS(1968, Aus.), p&d, w; ROCKY HOR-ROR PICTURE SHOW, THE(1975, Brit.), d, w; SUMMER OF SECRETS(1976, Aus.), d; NIGHT OF THE PROWLER, THE zero(1979, Aus.), d; SHOCK TREATMENT(1981), d, w

John Sharman
WE'LL MEET AGAIN(1942, Brit.)

Maisie Sharman
NIGHT JOURNEY(1938, Brit.), w; HEADLINE(1943, Brit.), w; DEATM GOES TO SCHOOL(1953, Brit.), w

Martin Sharman
CLINIC, THE(1983, Aus.)

Irene Sharoff
SECRET LIFE OF WALTER MITTY, THE(1947), cos

Jean Sharon
EVERYBODY'S HOBBY(1939); CHILD IS BORN, A(1940)

Joseph Sharon
FARMER'S OTHER DAUGHTER, THE(1965)

Lee Sharon
ABBOTT AND COSTELLO MEET THE MUMMY(1955)

Shirley Sharon
KID FROM BOOKLYN, THE(1946)

William Sharon
CITIZEN SAINT(1947); EXPERIMENT IN TERROR(1962)

Pietro Sharov
WANDERING JEW, THE(1948, Ital.)

Alan Sharp
HIRED HAND, THE(1971), w; LAST RUN, THE(1971), w; ULZANA'S RAID(1972), w; BILLY TWO HATS(1973, Brit.), w; NIGHT MOVES(1975), w; DAMNATION AL-LEY(1977), w; OSTERMAN WEEKEND, THE(1983), w

Alex Sharp
HARPOON(1948); EASY LIVING(1949); ROCKY MOUNTAIN(1950); WINNING TEAM, THE(1952); SEMINOLE(1953); RED SUNDOWN(1956); NIGHT RUNNER, THE(1957); YOUNG GUNS OF TEXAS(1963); LAW OF THE LAWLESS(1964); VENGEANCE(1964), w; DIRTY HARRY(1971); WHAT'S UP, DOC?(1972); TELEFON(1977)

Andrew Sharp
SUMMER OF SECRETS(1976, Aus.); BUDDIES(1983, Aus.)

Anne Sharp
BLIND SPOT(1958, Brit.); CRAWLING EYE, THE(1958, Brit.); NAKED FURY(1959, Brit.)

Anthony Sharp
MAN WHO WOULDN'T TALK, THE(1958, Brit.); LEFT, RIGHT AND CENTRE(1959); CLUE OF THE SILVER KEY, THE(1961, Brit.); INVASION(1965, Brit.); CARNABY, M.D.(1967, Brit.); HOT MILLIONS(1968, Brit.); DIE SCREAMING, MARIANNE(1970, Brit.); DOCTOR IN TROUBLE(1970, Brit.); NO BLADE OF GRASS(1970, Brit.); CLOCKWORK ORANGE, A(1971, Brit.); GAWAIN AND THE GREEN KNIGHT(1973, Brit.); BARRY LYNDON(1975, Brit.); CONFESSIONAL, THE(1977, Brit.); NEVER SAY NEVER AGAIN(1983)

Archie Sharp
DREAMER(1979), art d

Becky Sharp
LIFE AND TIMES OF CHESTER-ANGUS RAMSGOOD, THE(1971, Can.)

Bill Sharp
MEDIUM COOL(1969)

Clint Sharp
RACKETEERS OF THE RANGE(1939); OX-BOW INCIDENT, THE(1943); SKY'S THE LIMIT, THE(1943); TRIBUTE TO A BADMAN(1956)

Clive Sharp
ONE-EYED SOLDIERS(1967, U.S./Brit./Yugo.), p; SOME MAY LIVE(1967, Brit.), p; LOLA(1971, Brit./Ital.), p

David Sharp
SOUTHERN YANKEE, A(1948)

Dick Sharp
JAWS II(1978), makeup

Dolly Sharp
Misc. Talkies
DYNAMITE(1972)

Don Sharp
HA' PENNY BREEZE(1950, Brit.), a, p, w; OUTPOST IN MALAYA(1952, Brit.); BACKGROUND(1953, Brit.), w; CRUEL SEA, THE(1953); CHILD'S PLAY(1954, Brit.), w; FUSS OVER FEATHERS(1954, Brit.), w; INBETWEEN AGE, THE(1958, Brit.), d, w; NAVY HEROES(1959, Brit.), w; LINDA(1960, Brit.), d; PROFESSIONALS, THE(1960, Brit.), d; STOLEN AIRLINER, THE(1962, Brit.), d&w; DREAM MAKER, THE(1963, Brit.), p; KISS OF EVIL(1963, Brit.), d; DEVIL-SHIP PIRATES, THE(1964, Brit.), d; WITCHCRAFT(1964, Brit.), d; CURSE OF THE FLY(1965, Brit.), d; FACE OF FU MANCHU, THE(1965, Brit.), d; BANG, BANG, YOU'RE DEAD(1966), d; BRIDES OF FU MANCHU, THE(1966, Brit.), d; RASPUTIN-THE MAD MONK(1966, Brit.), d; THOSE FANTASTIC FLYING FOOLS(1967, Brit), d; TASTE OF EXCITEMENT(1969, Brit.), d, w; VIOLENT ENEMY, THE(1969, Brit.), d; PUPPET ON A CHAIN(1971, Brit.), w; DARK PLACES(1974, Brit.), d; PSYCHOMANIA(1974, Brit.), d; HENNESSY(1975, Brit.), d; THIRTY NINE STEPS, THE(1978, Brit.), d; BEAR ISLAND(1980, Brit.-Can.), d, w

F.B.J. Sharp
CARDINAL, THE(1936, Brit.); OLD MOTHER RILEY(1937, Brit.); SONG OF THE ROAD(1937, Brit.); THREE SILENT MEN(1940, Brit.); MAN IN THE WHITE SUIT, THE(1952); JOHN WESLEY(1954, Brit.); LAND OF FURY(1955 Brit.)

Ged Sharp
GOODBYE PORK PIE(1981, New Zealand)

Graham Sharp
DOT AND THE BUNNY(1983, Aus.), anim

Harry Sharp
CASE OF CLARA DEANE, THE(1932), ph; LADIES SHOULD LISTEN(1934), ph; BOOLOO(1938), ph

Henry Sharp
LORD BYRON OF BROADWAY(1930), ph; LOVE IN THE ROUGH(1930), ph; SINS OF THE CHILDREN(1930), ph; WAY OUT WEST(1930), ph; BROKEN WING, THE(1932), ph; DEVIL IS DRIVING, THE(1932), ph; FALSE MADONNA(1932), ph; MADAME RACKETEER(1932), ph; MADISON SQUARE GARDEN(1932), ph; STRANGE CASE OF CLARA DEANE, THE(1932), ph; STRANGERS IN LOVE(1932), ph; THIS RECKLESS AGE(1932), ph; 70,000 WITNESSES(1932), ph; ALICE IN WONDERLAND(1933), ph; FROM HELL TO HEAVEN(1933), ph; SONG OF THE EAGLE(1933), ph; HERE COMES THE GROOM(1934), ph; IT'S A GIFT(1934), ph; LEMON DROP KID, THE(1934), ph; MANY HAPPY RETURNS(1934), ph; MELODY IN SPRING(1934), ph; SIX OF A KIND(1934), ph; ALL THE KING'S HORSES(1935), ph; GLASS KEY, THE(1935), ph; ACCUSING FINGER, THE(1936), ph; EARLY TO BED(1936), ph; ROSE BOWL(1936), ph; BLONDE TROUBLE(1937), ph; HOLD'EM NAVY!(1937), ph; HOTEL HAYWIRE(1937), ph; MURDER GOES TO COLLEGE(1937), ph; PARTNERS IN CRIME(1937), ph; WILD MONEY(1937), ph; HIS EXCITING NIGHT(1938), ph; ILLEGAL TRAFFIC(1938), ph; SCANDAL STREET(1938), ph; BOY TROUBLE(1939), ph; GERONIMO(1939), ph; SUDDEN MONEY(1939), ph; DR. CYCLOPS(1940), ph; GOLDEN GLOVES(1940), ph; ADVENTURE IN WASHINGTON(1941), ph; BROADWAY LIMITED(1941), ph; HENRY ALDRICH, EDITOR(1942), ph; HIDDEN HAND, THE(1942), ph; MYSTERIOUS DOCTOR, THE(1943), ph; MAN IN HALF-MOON STREET, THE(1944), ph; NATIONAL BARN DANCE(1944), ph; 'TILL WE MEET AGAIN(1944), ph; TOMORROW THE WORLD(1944), ph; JEALOUSY(1945), ph; MINISTRY OF FEAR(1945), ph; SONG TO REMEMBER, A(1945), ph; WHAT NEXT, CORPORAL HARGROVE?(1945), ph; WOMAN WHO CAME BACK(1945), ph; GLASS ALIBI, THE(1946), ph; GUILTY, THE(1947), ph; HIGH TIDE(1947), ph; IT HAPPENED ON 5TH AVENUE(1947), ph; VIOLENCE(1947), ph; PERILOUS WATERS(1948), ph; STRIKE IT RICH(1948), ph; LAWTON STORY, THE(1949), ph; FACE IN THE CROWD, A(1957), ph; VIOLATORS, THE(1957); YOUNG LAND, THE(1959), ph
Silents
BEAU REVEL(1921), ph; LYING LIPS(1921), ph; THIRD ALARM, THE(1922), ph; ANNA CHRISTIE(1923), ph; SOUL OF THE BEAST(1923), ph; SUNSHINE TRAIL, THE(1923), ph; JUDGMENT OF THE STORM(1924), ph; DON Q, SON OF ZORRO(1925), ph; BLACK PIRATE, THE(1926), ph; LORNA DOONE(1927), ph; LOVELORN, THE(1927), ph; SLIDE, KELLY, SLIDE(1927), ph; BIG CITY, THE(1928), ph; CROWD, THE(1928), ph; WHILE THE CITY SLEEPS(1928), ph; THUNDER(1929), ph; WHERE EAST IS EAST(1929), ph

Howard Sharp
LONG SHOT(1981, Brit.), ed

Ian Sharp
MUSIC MACHINE, THE(1979, Brit.), d; FINAL OPTION, THE(1983, Brit.), d

John Sharp
EYE WITNESS(1950, Brit.); LEFT, RIGHT AND CENTRE(1959); GOLDEN RABBIT, THE(1962, Brit.); STORK TALK(1964, Brit.); BUNNY LAKE IS MISSING(1965); THREE BITES OF THE APPLE(1967); MRS. BROWN, YOU'VE GOT A LOVELY DAUGHTER(1968, Brit.); SPRING AND PORT WINE(1970, Brit.); BROTHER SUN, SISTER MOON(1973, Brit./Ital.); WICKER MAN, THE(1974, Brit.); BARRY LYNDON(1975, Brit.); FIENDISH PLOT OF DR. FU MANCHU, THE(1980); DRESSER, THE(1983); RETURN OF THE SOLDIER, THE(1983, Brit.)
1984
TOP SECRET!(1984)

Jack Ross Sharp
OTHER SIDE OF THE MOUNTAIN, THE(1975)

John Gerrard Sharp
RUNAWAY, THE(1964, Brit.), w

Len Sharp
HARD STEEL(1941, Brit.); SHEEPDOG OF THE HILLS(1941, Brit.); GIRL IS MINE, THE(1950, Brit.); KING OF THE UNDERWORLD(1952, Brit.); THREE CROOKED MEN(1958, Brit.); STOLEN PLANS, THE(1962, Brit.)

Leonard Sharp
DUMMY TALKS, THE(1943, Brit.); IT'S THAT MAN AGAIN(1943, Brit.); WARN THAT MAN(1943, Brit.); RANDOLPH FAMILY, THE(1945, Brit.); HANGMAN WAITS, THE(1947, Brit.); MUDLARK, THE(1950, Brit.); TAKE ME TO PARIS(1951, Brit.); SING ALONG WITH ME(1952, Brit.); MURDER AT 3 A.M.(1953, Brit.); FOR BETTER FOR WORSE(1954, Brit.); LADYKILLERS, THE(1956, Brit.); SILKEN AFFAIR, THE(1957, Brit.)

Lester Sharp
BASKETBALL FIX, THE(1951)

Margery Sharp
CLUNY BROWN(1946), w; JULIA MISBEHAVES(1948), w; AFFAIRS OF ADELAIDE(1949, U. S./Brit), w; NOTORIOUS LANDLADY, THE(1962, Brit.), w; RESCUERS, THE(1977), w

Marie Sharp
Misc. Talkies
CAFE FLESH(1982)

Mordaunt Sharp
BARRIER, THE(1937), w

Pamela Sharp
NAKED MAJA, THE(1959, Ital./U.S.)

Rich Sharp
ISLANDS IN THE STREAM(1977), makeup
1984
MICKI AND MAUDE(1984), makeup

Rick Sharp
SLAP SHOT(1977), makeup

Rose Sharp
Silents
BRENDA OF THE BARGE(1920, Brit.)

Sally Sharp
END OF AUGUST, THE(1982), a, p

Sandy Sharp
PRIVATE COLLECTION(1972, Aus.), w

Saundra Sharp
LEARNING TREE, THE(1969)

Steven Sharp
PERFECT COUPLE, A(1979)

Thom Sharp
1984
PROTOCOL(1984)

Thom J. Sharp
BODY HEAT(1981)

Anita Sharp-Bolster
SABOTEUR(1942); LOVE FROM A STRANGER(1947); WOMAN IN WHITE, THE(1948); PERFECT WOMAN, THE(1950, Brit.); SCHOOL FOR SCOUNDRELS(1960, Brit.); LIST OF ADRIAN MESSENGER, THE(1963)

Albert Sharpe
RETURN OF OCTOBER, THE(1948); UP IN CENTRAL PARK(1948); ADVENTURE IN BALTIMORE(1949); PORTRAIT OF JENNIE(1949); HIGHWAYMAN, THE(1951); ROYAL WEDDING(1951); YOU NEVER CAN TELL(1951); FACE TO FACE(1952); BRIGADOON(1954); DARBY O'GILL AND THE LITTLE PEOPLE(1959); DAY THEY ROBBED THE BANK OF ENGLAND, THE(1960, Brit.)

Alex Sharpe
PLEASE MURDER ME(1956); HARRY AND WALTER GO TO NEW YORK(1976); SUNBURN(1979)

Anne Sharpe
JACK THE RIPPER(1959, Brit.); SIEGE OF SIDNEY STREET, THE(1960, Brit.); PLEASURE LOVERS, THE(1964, Brit.)

Anthony Sharpe
SWORD AND THE ROSE, THE(1953); I WANT WHAT I WANT(1972, Brit.)

Arthur Sharpe
Silents
SECRET OF THE HILLS, THE(1921)

Ben Sharpe
WINGS IN THE DARK(1935)

Bernard Sharpe
OTLEY(1969, Brit.)

Bruce Sharpe
BIG COMBO, THE(1955); CELL 2455, DEATH ROW(1955)

Buck Sharpe
DEADLY COMPANIONS, THE(1961)

Charles Sharpe
ROBERTA(1935)

Cliff Sharpe
HAND OF NIGHT, THE(1968, Brit.), makeup; 30 IS A DANGEROUS AGE, CYNTHIA(1968, Brit.), makeup; JULIUS CAESAR(1970, Brit.), makeup

Cornelia Sharpe
KANSAS CITY BOMBER(1972); SERPICO(1973); BUSTING(1974); OPEN SEASON(1974, U.S./Span.); REINCARNATION OF PETER PROUD, THE(1975); NEXT MAN, THE(1976); VENOM(1982, Brit.)

Dave Sharpe
PIGSKIN PARADE(1936); IDAHO KID, THE(1937); PROFESSOR BEWARE(1938); I STOLE A MILLION(1939); NEVER GIVE A SUCKER AN EVEN BREAK(1941); RAIDERS OF THE DESERT(1941); TEXAS TO BATAAN(1942); FALCON'S ADVENTURE, THE(1946); WISTFUL WIDOW OF WAGON GAP, THE(1947); TOMAHAWK(1951); MONTANA BELLE(1952); SINGIN' IN THE RAIN(1952); DESERT LEGION(1953); VEILS OF BAGDAD, THE(1953); SPIRAL ROAD, THE(1962); POSEIDON ADVENTURE, THE(1972); TOWERING INFERNO, THE(1974)
Misc. Talkies
SANTA FE RIDES(1937)

David Sharpe
ROARING ROADS(1935), a, w; DESERT JUSTICE(1936); OUR RELATIONS(1936); DOOMED AT SUNDOWN(1937); DRUMS OF DESTINY(1937); GALLOPING DYNAMITE(1937); MELODY OF THE PLAINS(1937); MIND YOUR OWN BUSINESS(1937); TWO MINUTES TO PLAY(1937); WHERE TRAILS DIVIDE(1937); YOUNG DYNAMITE(1937); LAW COMMANDS, THE(1938); MAN'S COUNTRY(1938); SHINE ON, HARVEST MOON(1938); COWBOYS FROM TEXAS(1939); LAW COMES TO TEXAS, THE(1939); LONE STAR PIONEERS(1939); NIGHT RIDERS, THE(1939); ROVIN' TUMBLEWEEDS(1939); THREE TEXAS STEERS(1939); WYOMING OUTLAW(1939); COVERED WAGON TRAILS(1940); RIDERS OF PASCO BASIN(1940); THIEF OF BAGHDAD, THE(1940, Brit.); SILVER STALLION(1941); THUNDER OVER THE PRAIRIE(1941); TRAIL RIDERS(1942); HAUNTED RANCH, THE(1943); RED RIVER ROBIN HOOD(1943); TWO FISTED JUSTICE(1943); COLORADO SERENADE(1946); BELLS OF SAN ANGELO(1947); FULLER BRUSH MAN(1948); YOU GOTTA STAY HAPPY(1948); SUSANNA PASS(1949); GIRL FROM SAN LORENZO, THE(1950); GOOD HUMOR MAN, THE(1950); WILD BLUE YONDER, THE(1952); FORBIDDEN(1953); WAR OF THE WORLDS, THE(1953), a, stunts; IN ENEMY COUNTRY(1968), stunts; LIFE AND TIMES OF JUDGE ROY BEAN, THE(1972)
Misc. Talkies
GUN GRIT(1936)
Silents
MASKED EMOTIONS(1929)

David H. Sharpe
GHOST TOWN(1937)

Don Sharpe
CALLAN(1975, Brit.), d

Edith Sharpe
MUSIC HATH CHARMS(1935, Brit.); OLD MOTHER RILEY(1937, Brit.); TENTH MAN, THE(1937, Brit.); WHEN THE BOUGH BREAKS(1947, Brit.); OUTSIDER, THE(1949, Brit.); IF THIS BE SIN(1950, Brit.); NO PLACE FOR JENNIFER(1950, Brit.); CLOUDBURST(1952, Brit.); ONCE A SINNER(1952, Brit.); LANDFALL(1953, Brit.); BROTHERS IN LAW(1957, Brit.); HAPPY IS THE BRIDE(1958, Brit.); INN OF THE SIXTH HAPPINESS, THE(1958); FRENCH MISTRESS(1960, Brit.); FRANCIS OF ASSISI(1961); CASH ON DEMAND(1962, Brit.); SATAN NEVER SLEEPS(1962)
Silents
EDUCATION OF ELIZABETH, THE(1921)

Geoff Sharpe
NUTCRACKER(1982, Brit.), prod d, cos

Gertie Messinger Sharpe
OUR RELATIONS(1936)

Graham Sharpe
1984
CAMEL BOY, THE(1984, Aus.), ph

Henry Sharpe
IRON MASK, THE(1929), ph; LION AND THE LAMB(1931), ph; MAN CALLED BACK, THE(1932), ph; DUCK SOUP(1933), ph; LADY BE CAREFUL(1936), ph; CAMPUS CONFESSIONS(1938), ph; CRIME BY NIGHT(1944), ph; FABULOUS SUZANNE, THE(1946), ph; DAUGHTER OF THE WEST(1949), ph; SINGING IN THE DARK(1956)

Hope Sharpe
MOUNTAIN, THE(1935, Brit.)

Jeff Sharpe
1984
LAST HORROR FILM, THE(1984), prod d

John Sharpe
HEATWAVE(1954, Brit.)

Karen Sharpe
ARMY BOUND(1952); BOMBA AND THE JUNGLE GIRL(1952); STRANGE FASCINATION(1952); MEXICAN MANHUNT(1953); VANQUISHED, THE(1953); HIGH AND THE MIGHTY, THE(1954); MAD AT THE WORLD(1955); MAN WITH THE GUN(1955); MAN IN THE VAULT(1956); TARAWA BEACHHEAD(1958); DISORDERLY ORDERLY, THE(1964); VALLEY OF MYSTERY(1967)

Kay Sharpe
SNIPER, THE(1952)

Len Sharpe
SEXTON BLAKE AND THE HOODED TERROR(1938, Brit.); NEUTRAL PORT(1941, Brit.)

Leonard Sharpe
REMBRANDT(1936, Brit.); FAKE, THE(1953, Brit.); INTRUDER, THE(1955, Brit.)

Lester Sharpe
CROSSROADS(1942); DESPERATE JOURNEY(1942); REUNION IN FRANCE(1942); TIME TO KILL(1942); HANGMEN ALSO DIE(1943); STRANGE DEATH OF ADOLF HITLER, THE(1943); THIS LAND IS MINE(1943); LADY IN THE DARK(1944); MUMMY'S GHOST, THE(1944); STORM OVER LISBON(1944); LOST WEEKEND, THE(1945); THOROUGHBREDS(1945), p; SONG OF MY HEART(1947); CALL NORTHSIDE 777(1948); GALLANT LEGION, THE(1948); LETTER FROM AN UNKNOWN WOMAN(1948); PORT SAID(1948); ROGUES' REGIMENT(1948); SAIGON(1948); SNAKE PIT, THE(1948); I WAS A MALE WAR BRIDE(1949); SAMSON AND DELILAH(1949); DESERT HAWK, THE(1950); FLYING SAUCER, THE(1950); MYSTERY SUBMARINE(1950); ONE TOO MANY(1950); UNMASKED(1950); VICIOUS YEARS, THE(1950); WHERE THE SIDEWALK ENDS(1950); MASK OF THE AVENGER(1951); CARRIE(1952); PRINCESS OF THE NILE(1954); SILVER CHALICE, THE(1954)

Nigel Sharpe
THEY CAN'T HANG ME(1955, Brit.)

Norah Sharpe
GEORGE RAFT STORY, THE(1961), cos

Rebecca Sharpe
Misc. Talkies
LAST TANGO IN ACAPULCO, THE(1975)

Roy Sharpe
VARIETY(1935, Brit.); MEN OF THE SEA(1951, Brit.)

William Sharpe
DESPERATE WOMEN, THE(?)
Silents
FICKLE WOMEN(1920)

Anita Sharpe-Bolster
BOY CRIED MURDER, THE(1966, Ger./Brit./Yugo.)

Bernard Sharper
FERRY ACROSS THE MERSEY(1964, Brit.)

Dick Sharples
GOLDEN RABBIT, THE(1962, Brit.), w; GEORGE AND MILDRED(1980, Brit.), w

Robert Sharples
MISSILE FROM HELL(1960, Brit.), m; PRIZE OF ARMS, A(1962, Brit.), m

Sammy Sharples
GUMSHOE(1972, Brit.)

Wayne Sharpnack
NIGHT THE LIGHTS WENT OUT IN GEORGIA, THE(1981)

Ben Sharpsteen
SNOW WHITE AND THE SEVEN DWARFS(1937), d; PINOCCHIO(1940), d; DUMBO(1941), d

Len Sharr
GREAT MR. HANDEL, THE(1942, Brit.)

Michael Sharrett
HOT LEAD AND COLD FEET(1978); MAGIC OF LASSIE, THE(1978)

Ian Sharrock
CANDLESHOE(1978)

Don Shartel
WEST POINT STORY, THE(1950)

Michael Sharvell-Martin
FRIGHTMARE(1974, Brit.)

John Shary
DECOY(1946)

V. Sharykina
LAST GAME, THE(1964, USSR); YOLANTA(1964, USSR)

Ed Shashe
I PASSED FOR WHITE(1960)

Alyson Shasser
FOLLOW THRU(1930), ed

Peter Shatalow
SHOOT(1976, Can.), ed

Vladimir Shaternikov
Misc. Silents
ANNA KARENINA(1914, USSR)

M. Shaternikova
CZAR WANTS TO SLEEP(1934, U.S., USSR)

Nina Shaternikova
Misc. Silents
LACE(1928, USSR); BLACK SAIL, THE(1929, USSR)

William Shatner
BROTHERS KARAMAZOV, THE(1958); EXPLOSIVE GENERATION, THE(1961); JUDGMENT AT NUREMBERG(1961); INTRUDER, THE(1962); OUTRAGE, THE(1964); INCUBUS(1966); BIG BAD MAMA(1974); DEVIL'S RAIN, THE(1975, U.S./Mex.); IMPULSE(1975); KINGDOM OF THE SPIDERS(1977); WHALE OF A TALE, A(1977); THIRD WALKER, THE(1978, Can.); STAR TREK: THE MOTION PICTURE(1979); KIDNAPPING OF THE PRESIDENT, THE(1980, Can.); LAND OF NO RETURN, THE(1981); AIRPLANE II: THE SEQUEL(1982); STAR TREK II: THE WRATH OF KHAN(1982); VISITING HOURS(1982, Can.)
1984
STAR TREK III: THE SEARCH FOR SPOCK(1984)
Misc. Talkies
WHITE COMANCHE(1967): RIEL(1979)

I. Shatokhin
SANDU FOLLOWS THE SUN(1965, USSR)

N. Shatskaya
WELCOME KOSTYA!(1965, USSR)

Howard Shatsky
1984
HEARTBREAKERS(1984)

Sarit Shatsky
HANNAH K.(1983, Fr.)

Alan Shatsman
VIRGIN SOLDIERS, THE(1970, Brit.)

Edward Shattuck
DIXIE JAMBOREE(1945)

Ethel Shattuck
DIXIE JAMBOREE(1945)

Richard Shattuck
GHOST THAT WALKS ALONE, THE(1944), w; MACABRE(1958), w

Truly Shattuck
Silents
PAINTED SOUL, THE(1915); PEGGY(1916); SPEED GIRL, THE(1921); WISE FOOL, A(1921)
Misc. Silents
GOLDEN CLAW, THE(1915); IRON STRAIN, THE(1915); GREAT IMPERSONATION, THE(1921); BEAUTY'S WORTH(1922)

William Shatunovsky
AND QUIET FLOWS THE DON(1960 USSR)

M. A. Shauer
THREE CHEERS FOR LOVE(1936), p

Mary Jane Shauer
GIRL WITH IDEAS, A(1937)

Mel Shauer
THIS WAY PLEASE(1937), p; THANKS FOR THE MEMORY(1938), p
Alfred Shaughnessy
END OF THE ROAD, THE(1954, Brit.), p; SCOTCH ON THE ROCKS(1954, Brit.), p, w; ROOM IN THE HOUSE(1955, Brit.). p, w; HOSTAGE, THE(1956, Brit.), w; TOUCH OF THE SUN, A(1956, Brit.), w; CAT GIRL(1957), d; HIGH TERRACE(1957, Brit.), w; JUST MY LUCK(1957, Brit.), w; LIGHT FINGERS(1957, Brit.), w; SUSPENDED ALIBI(1957, Brit.), d; HEART OF A CHILD(1958, Brit.), p; 6.5 SPECIAL(1958, Brit.), d; FOLLOW THAT HORSE!(1960, Brit.), w; IMPERSONATOR, THE(1962, Brit.), d, w; LUNCH HOUR(1962, Brit.), p; CRESCENDO(1972, Brit.), w; FLESH AND BLOOD SHOW, THE(1974, Brit.), w; TIFFANY JONES(1976), w
J. Todd Shaughnessy
CLASS(1983)
Mickey Shaughnessy
UNTIL THEY SAIL(1957); LAST OF THE COMANCHES(1952); MARRYING KIND, THE(1952); FROM HERE TO ETERNITY(1953); CONQUEST OF SPACE(1955); BUR-GLAR, THE(1956); DESIGNING WOMAN(1957); JAILHOUSE ROCK(1957); SLAUGH-TER ON TENTH AVENUE(1957); GUNMAN'S WALK(1958); NICE LITTLE BANK THAT SHOULD BE ROBBED, A(1958); SHEEPMAN, THE(1958); DON'T GIVE UP THE SHIP(1959); EDGE OF ETERNITY(1959); HANGMAN, THE(1959); ADVENTURES OF HUCKLEBERRY FINN, THE(1960); COLLEGE CONFIDENTIAL(1960); NORTH TO ALASKA(1960); SEX KITTENS GO TO COLLEGE(1960); DONDI(1961); KING OF THE ROARING TWENTIES–THE STORY OF ARNOLD ROTHSTEIN(1961); POCKETFUL OF MIRACLES(1961); HOW THE WEST WAS WON(1962); GLOBAL AFFAIR, A(1964); HOUSE IS NOT A HOME, A(1964); NEVER A DULL MOMENT(1968); BOATNIKS, THE(1970); DON'T GO NEAR THE WATER(1975)
Jane Shaulis
FOUL PLAY(1978)
Wallace Shaun
CHEAPER TO KEEP HER(1980)
Michael Shaunessy
SMALL CIRCLE OF FRIENDS, A(1980)
Melville Shavelson
ICE-CAPADES(1941), w; PRINCESS AND THE PIRATE, THE(1944), w; WONDER MAN(1945), w; KID FROM BROOKLYN, THE(1946), w; WHERE THERE'S LIFE(1947), w; ALWAYS LEAVE THEM LAUGHING(1949), w; GREAT LOVER, THE(1949), w; IT'S A GREAT FEELING(1949), w; SORROWFUL JONES(1949), w; DAUGHTER OF ROSIE O'GRADY, THE(1950), w; DOUBLE DYNAMITE(1951), w; I'LL SEE YOU IN MY DREAMS(1951), w; ON MOONLIGHT BAY(1951), w; ROOM FOR ONE MO-RE(1952), w; APRIL IN PARIS(1953), w; TROUBLE ALONG THE WAY(1953), p, w; LIVING IT UP(1954), w; SEVEN LITTLE FOYS, THE(1955), d, w; BEAU JA-MES(1957), d, w; HOUSEBOAT(1958), d, w; FIVE PENNIES, THE(1959), d, w; IT STARTED IN NAPLES(1960), d, w; ON THE DOUBLE(1961), d, w; PIGEON THAT TOOK ROME, THE(1962), p,d&w; NEW KIND OF LOVE, A(1963), p,d&w; CAST A GIANT SHADOW(1966), p, d&w; YOURS, MINE AND OURS(1968), d, w; WAR BE-TWEEN MEN AND WOMEN, THE(1972), d, w; MIXED COMPANY(1974), p&d, w
Nelville Shavelson
RIDING HIGH(1950), w
Helen Shaver
SHOOT(1976, Can.); SUPREME KID, THE(1976, Can.); OUTRAGEOUS!(1977, Can.); HIGH-BALLIN'(1978); IN PRAISE OF OLDER WOMEN(1978, Can.); STARSHIP INVASIONS(1978, Can.); AMITYVILLE HORROR, THE(1979); WHO HAS SEEN THE WIND(1980, Can.); GAS(1981, Can.); HARRY TRACY–DESPERADO(1982, Can.); OST-ERMAN WEEKEND, THE(1983)
1984
BEST DEFENSE(1984)
Charlie Shavers
SEPIA CINDERELLA(1947), m
G. Shavgulidze
THEY WANTED PEACE(1940, USSR); DRAGONFLY, THE(1955 USSR)
Ariela Shavid
EVERY BASTARD A KING(1968, Israel)
V. Shavinsky
Misc. Silents
SLAVE OF PASSION, SLAVE OF VICE(1914, USSR)
Adriana Shaw
NEW CENTURIONS, THE(1972)
Al Shaw
MRS. WIGGS OF THE CABBAGE PATCH(1934); GRACIE ALLEN MURDER CA-SE(1939); DANGER AHEAD(1940); SKIPALONG ROSENBLOOM(1951)
Albert Shaw
LAST EXPRESS, THE(1938)
Alexander Shaw
CONQUEST OF THE AIR(1940), d; SOLDIER, SAILOR(1944, Brit.), d; CURE FOR LOVE, THE(1950, Brit.), w
Anabel Shaw
HOME SWEET HOMICIDE(1946); SHOCK(1946); STRANGE TRIANGLE(1946); DANGEROUS YEARS(1947); HIGH TIDE(1947); KILLER AT LARGE(1947); MOTHER WORE TIGHTS(1947); IN THIS CORNER(1948); SECRET BEYOND THE DOOR, THE(1948); CITY ACROSS THE RIVER(1949); GUN CRAZY(1949); HOLD THAT BABY!(1949); AT GUNPOINT(1955); SIX BRIDGES TO CROSS(1955); TO HELL AND BACK(1955)
Misc. Talkies
BULLDOG DRUMMOND STRIKES BACK(1947)
Ann Shaw
CAVALCADE(1933); CLIVE OF INDIA(1935)
Anna Marie Shaw
FIVE WILD GIRLS(1966, Fr.)
Anne Shaw
BOLERO(1934)
Anthony Shaw
EDUCATED EVANS(1936, Brit.); BITER BIT, THE(1937, Brit.); COMPULSORY WIFE, THE(1937, Brit.); WINDMILL, THE(1937, Brit.); GOOD OLD DAYS, THE(1939, Brit.); THIS MAN IN PARIS(1939, Brit.); TORSO MURDER MYSTERY, THE(1940, Brit.); UNPUBLISHED STORY(1942, Brit.); WINGS AND THE WOMAN(1942, Brit.); ESCAPE TO DANGER(1943, Brit.); SUSPECTED PERSON(1943, Brit.); HOTEL RE-SERVE(1946, Brit.); PATIENT VANISHES, THE(1947, Brit.); MELODY CLUB(1949, Brit.); LONG DARK HALL, THE(1951, Brit.); APPOINTMENT IN LONDON(1953, Brit.); MR. POTTS GOES TO MOSCOW(1953, Brit.); HOW TO MURDER A RICH UNCLE(1957, Brit.); SILKEN AFFAIR, THE(1957, Brit.); HE KNOWS YOU'RE

ALONE(1980)
1984
JIGSAW MAN, THE(1984, Brit.)
Anthony Pullen Shaw
CUBA(1979); FFOLKES(1980, Brit.)
Artie Shaw
DANCING CO-ED(1939)
Barbara Shaw
PEARLS OF THE CROWN(1938, Fr.); ESTHER WATERS(1948, Brit.); HIGH JINKS IN SOCIETY(1949, Brit.); WOMAN IN THE HALL, THE(1949, Brit.); BLIND MAN'S BLUFF(1952, Brit.); NEVER LOOK BACK(1952, Brit.); NO HAUNT FOR A GENTLE-MAN(1952, Brit.)
Barnaby Shaw
HOUSE OF CARDS(1969); VAMPIRE CIRCUS(1972, Brit.)
Barnett Shaw
UNDER AGE(1964); MARS NEEDS WOMEN(1966)
Barry Shaw
WINSTANLEY(1979, Brit.)
Betty Shaw
DAKOTA(1945); CRIME OF THE CENTURY(1946); GUY COULD CHANGE, A(1946)
Bill Shaw
STAKEOUT ON DOPE STREET(1958)
Billy Shaw
Misc. Silents
TEN OF DIAMONDS(1917)
Bob Shaw
TIME AFTER TIME(1979, Brit.)
Bobbi Shaw
PASSION HOLIDAY(1963); PAJAMA PARTY(1964); BEACH BLANKET BIN-GO(1965); HOW TO STUFF A WILD BIKINI(1965); SERGEANT DEADHEAD(1965); SKI PARTY(1965); GHOST IN THE INVISIBLE BIKINI(1966); PIPE DREAMS(1976)
Misc. Talkies
YOU AND ME(1975)
Brinsley Shaw
Silents
SUBURBAN, THE(1915); PRINCE IN A PAWNSHOP, A(1916); ARSENE LU-PIN(1917); FOUR HORSEMEN OF THE APOCALYPSE, THE(1921); CURSE OF DRINK, THE(1922); STRANGER'S BANQUET(1922); TRAVELIN' ON(1922); THREE WISE FOOLS(1923); JIMMIE'S MILLIONS(1925); BUCKING THE TRUTH(1926)
Misc. Silents
WOLF OF DEBT, THE(1915); CLOVER'S REBELLION(1917); MAN OF MYSTERY, THE(1917); HORNET'S NEST, THE(1919); ROGUE'S ROMANCE, A(1919); WOLF, THE(1919); TRIP TO PARADISE, A(1921); LAST OF THE DUANES, THE(1924); STEPPING LIVELY(1924); BEFORE MIDNIGHT(1925)
Bud Shaw
RUMBA(1935)
Misc. Talkies
BYE-BYE BUDDY(1929)
Silents
LITTLE WILD GIRL, THE(1928); OLD AGE HANDICAP(1928)
Misc. Silents
MUST WE MARRY?(1928)
Buddy Shaw
RIDERS OF THE NORTH(1931); DALLAS(1950); TEA FOR TWO(1950); I WAS A COMMUNIST FOR THE F.B.I.(1951)
Misc. Talkies
TWISTED RAILS(1935)
C. Montague Shaw
CYNARA(1932); MASK OF FU MANCHU, THE(1932); PACK UP YOUR TROU-BLES(1932); DANCING LADY(1933); MASQUERADER, THE(1933); FRAME-UP THE(1937); PAROLE RACKET(1937); RIDERS OF THE WHISTLING SKULL(1937); SHEIK STEPS OUT, THE(1937); WHEN YOU'RE IN LOVE(1937); FOUR MEN AND A PRAYER(1938); KIDNAPPED(1938); LITTLE MISS BROADWAY(1938); SUEZ(1938); MR. MOTO'S LAST WARNING(1939); TOWER OF LONDON(1939); BURMA CON-VOY(1941); CHARLEY'S AUNT(1941); BOMBAY CLIPPER(1942); LAW OF THE JUNGLE(1942); ANGEL COMES TO BROOKLYN, AN(1945); TONIGHT AND EVERY NIGHT(1945); IVY(1947); ROAD TO THE BIG HOUSE(1947)
Cecil Shaw
Silents
MAN THE ARMY MADE, A(1917, Brit.), w
Charles Shaw
HEAVEN KNOWS, MR. ALLISON(1957), w
Charles K. Shaw
DEATH IS A NUMBER(1951, Brit.), w
Christine Shaw
CLUE OF THE TWISTED CANDLE(1968, Brit.); REVENGE OF THE PINK PAN-THER(1978)
Colin Shaw
DEEP, THE(1977)
Crystal Shaw
1984
HARDBODIES(1984)
Danny Shaw
SILVER SKATES(1943)
David Shaw
FOREIGN AFFAIR, A(1948), w; TAKE ONE FALSE STEP(1949), w; MAN INSIDE, THE(1958, Brit.), w; IF IT'S TUESDAY, THIS MUST BE BELGIUM(1969), w; KING, QUEEN, KNAVE(1972, Ger./U.S.), w
Denis Shaw
HOUSE OF BLACKMAIL(1953, Brit.); LONG MEMORY, THE(1953, Brit.); COLDITZ STORY, THE(1955, Brit.); KEEP IT CLEAN(1956, Brit.); PORT AFRIQUE(1956, Brit.); WHO DONE IT?(1956, Brit.); DEPRAVED, THE(1957, Brit.); FLESH IS WEAK, THE(1957, Brit.); WEAPON, THE(1957, Brit.); LINKS OF JUSTICE(1958); MOMENT OF INDISCRETION(1958, Brit.); SOAPBOX DERBY(1958, Brit.); WOMAN POS-SESSED, A(1958, Brit.); BANDIT OF ZHOBE, THE(1959); INNOCENT MEETING(1959, Brit.); JACK THE RIPPER(1959, Brit.); MAN WHO COULD CHEAT DEATH, THE(1959, Brit.); MUMMY, THE(1959, Brit.); NAKED FURY(1959, Brit.); NO SAFETY AHEAD(1959, Brit.); ROOM 43(1959, Brit.); BEYOND THE CURTAIN(1960, Brit.); MAKE MINE MINK(1960, Brit.); CURSE OF THE WEREWOLF, THE(1961); MISFITS, THE(1961); TICKET TO PARADISE(1961, Brit.); WEEKEND WITH LULU, A(1961,

Brit.); INVITATION TO MURDER(1962, Brit.); MAKE MINE A DOUBLE(1962, Brit.);
PIRATES OF BLOOD RIVER, THE(1962, Brit.); GREAT VAN ROBBERY, THE(1963,
Brit.); HELLFIRE CLUB, THE(1963, Brit.); IN TROUBLE WITH EVE(1964, Brit.);
RUNAWAY, THE(1964, Brit.); DEADLY AFFAIR, THE(1967, Brit.); VIKING QUEEN,
THE(1967, Brit.); FILE OF THE GOLDEN GOOSE, THE(1969, Brit.)

Dick Shaw
MAKE MINE MUSIC(1946), w; 1001 ARABIAN NIGHTS(1959), w

Dorothy Shaw
HELD IN TRUST(1949, Brit.)

Ed Shaw
FRATERNITY ROW(1977)

Eddie Shaw
WOMAN UNDER THE INFLUENCE, A(1974)

Eddie Ike Shaw
KILLING OF A CHINESE BOOKIE, THE(1976)

Eleanor Shaw
UP IN ARMS(1944)

Elizabeth Lloyd Shaw
FIRE AND ICE(1983)
1984
CHOOSE ME(1984)

Ellen Shaw
SPACE MASTER X-7(1958); PROMISES IN THE DARK(1979)

Eric Shaw
MAN IN THE ROAD, THE(1957, Brit.), art d

Fiona Shaw
1984
SACRED HEARTS(1984, Brit.)

Frank Shaw
CALL OF THE SEA, THE(1930, Brit.), w; CAPTAIN'S ORDERS(1937, Brit.), w; BACK
STREET(1941), p; SNIPER, THE(1952); NIGHT THEY RAIDED MINSKY'S,
THE(1968); FRISCO KID, THE(1979), w

Frank H. Shaw
LIEUTENANT DARING, RN(1935, Brit.), w

Fred Shaw
STONE(1974, Aus.)

Freita Shaw
I PASSED FOR WHITE(1960)

G. Tito Shaw
PETEY WHEATSTRAW(1978)

George Bernard Shaw
ARMS AND THE MAN(1932, Brit.), w; PYGMALION(1938, Brit.), w; MAJOR BAR-
BARA(1941, Brit.), w; CAESAR AND CLEOPATRA(1946, Brit.), w; ANDROCLES AND
THE LION(1952), w; SAINT JOAN(1957), w; DOCTOR'S DILEMMA, THE(1958, Brit.),
w; DEVIL'S DISCIPLE, THE(1959), w; MILLIONAIRESS, THE(1960, Brit.); MRS.
WARREN'S PROFESSION(1960, Ger.), w; ARMS AND THE MAN(1962, Ger.), w; MY
FAIR LADY(1964), w; GREAT CATHERINE(1968, Brit.), w

Glen Byam Shaw
VAGABOND QUEEN, THE(1931, Brit.); LOOK BACK IN ANGER(1959)

Gloria Shaw
DRIVE-IN(1976)

Guy L. Shaw
LETTER FROM AN UNKNOWN WOMAN(1948)

Harold Shaw
Silents
FIRM OF GIRDLESTONE, THE(1915, Brit.), d; LONDON PRIDE(1920, Brit.), d;
PURSUIT OF PAMELA, THE(1920, Brit.), d; TRUE TILDA(1920, Brit.), d; GENERAL
JOHN REGAN(1921, Brit.), d; KIPPS(1921, Brit.), d; FALSE EVIDENCE(1922, Brit.),
d; HELD TO ANSWER(1923), d
Misc. Silents
BOOTLE'S BABY(1914, Brit.), d; INCOMPARABLE MISTRESS BELLAIRS,
THE(1914, Brit.), d; LIBERTY HALL(1914, Brit.), d; TRILBY(1914, Brit.), d; ASHES
OF REVENGE, THE(1915, Brit.), d; DERBY WINNER, THE(1915, Brit.), d; HEART OF
A CHILD, THE(1915, Brit.), d; HEART OF SISTER ANN, THE(1915, Brit.), d; MR.
LYNDON AT LIBERTY(1915, Brit.), d; THIRD GENERATION, THE(1915, Brit.), d;
LAST CHALLENGE, THE(1916, Brit.), d; ME AND M'PAL(1916, Brit.), d; LAND OF
MYSTERY, THE(1920, Brit.), d; DEAR FOOL, A(1921, Brit.), d; WOMAN OF HIS
DREAM, THE(1921, Brit.), d; ROUGED LIPS(1923), d; FOOL'S AWAKENING,
A(1924), d; WINNING A CONTINENT(1924), a, d

Harold M. Shaw
Silents
HOUSE OF TEMPERLEY, THE(1913, Brit.), d
Misc. Silents
WHEELS OF CHANCE, THE(1922, Brit.), d

Hazel Shaw
DESERT HAWK, THE(1950); ARIZONA MANHUNT(1951); TWO TICKETS TO
BROADWAY(1951); LAS VEGAS STORY, THE(1952); SHE'S WORKING HER WAY
THROUGH COLLEGE(1952)

Helen Shaw
TWILIGHT ZONE–THE MOVIE(1983)

Ian Shaw
1984
PREPPIES(1984), m

Irwin Shaw
TWO WEEKS IN ANOTHER TOWN(1962), w; BIG GAME, THE(1936), w; OUT OF
THE FOG(1941), w; COMMANDOS STRIKE AT DAWN, THE(1942), w; TALK OF THE
TOWN(1942), w; EASY LIVING(1949), w; TAKE ONE FALSE STEP(1949), w; I WANT
YOU(1951), w; ACT OF LOVE(1953), w; ULYSSES(1955, Ital.), w; WAR AND PEA-
CE(1956, Ital./U.S.), w; FIRE DOWN BELOW(1957, U.S./Brit.), w; TIP ON A DEAD
JOCKEY(1957), w; DESIRE UNDER THE ELMS(1958), w; THIS ANGRY AGE(1958,
Ital./Fr.), w; YOUNG LIONS, THE(1958), w; BIG GAMBLE, THE(1961), w; IN THE
FRENCH STYLE(1963, U.S./Fr.), p, w; THREE(1969, Brit.), w

Jack Shaw
SUSPENSE(1946), spec eff; DICK BARTON–SPECIAL AGENT(1948, Brit.)

Jakob Shaw
1984
LOVE STREAMS(1984)

James Shaw
WIZ, THE(1978); MY GAL LOVES MUSIC(1944)

Janet Shaw
THEY WON'T BELIEVE ME(1947); CONFESSION(1937); HOLLYWOOD HO-
TEL(1937); SHE LOVED A FIREMAN(1937); ACCIDENTS WILL HAPPEN(1938);
ADVENTURES OF ROBIN HOOD, THE(1938); BOY MEETS GIRL(1938); COMET
OVER BROADWAY(1938); GIRLS ON PROBATION(1938); JEZEBEL(1938); SISTERS,
THE(1938); TORCHY BLANE IN CHINATOWN(1938); GOING PLACES(1939); OLD
MAID, THE(1939); ROOKIE COP, THE(1939); ALIAS THE DEACON(1940); BLONDIE
ON A BUDGET(1940); FLIGHT ANGELS(1940); WATERLOO BRIDGE(1940); GAM-
BLING DAUGHTERS(1941); HOLD THAT GHOST(1941); HONOLULU LU(1941);
LUCKY DEVILS(1941); YOU'RE OUT OF LUCK(1941); JOHNNY EAGER(1942);
MUMMY'S TOMB, THE(1942); NIGHT MONSTER(1942); ARIZONA TRAIL(1943);
BAD MEN OF THUNDER GAP(1943); FALSE FACES(1943); HERS TO HOLD(1943);
KEEP 'EM SLUGGING(1943); SHADOW OF A DOUBT(1943); FOLLOW THE
BOYS(1944); HI, GOOD-LOOKIN'(1944); JOHNNY DOESN'T LIVE HERE ANY MO-
RE(1944); LADIES COURAGEOUS(1944); I'LL TELL THE WORLD(1945); SCARLET
CLUE, THE(1945); DARK ALIBI(1946); HOUSE OF HORRORS(1946); NOCTUR-
NE(1946); TIME OUT OF MIND(1947); GETTING OF WISDOM, THE(1977, Aus.)
Misc. Talkies
THUNDERGAP OUTLAWS(1947)

Jenifer Shaw
SKYJACKED(1972); THEY ONLY KILL THEIR MASTERS(1972); SEMI-
TOUGH(1977)

Jenny Shaw
CRIMSON CULT, THE(1970, Brit.)

Jerrold Robert Shaw
REMBRANDT(1936, Brit.)

Jimmy Shaw
EXIT THE DRAGON, ENTER THE TIGER(1977, Hong Kong), p; FORCED VEN-
GEANCE(1982)
Misc. Talkies
RETURN OF THE TIGER(1979), d

John Shaw
MUSIC IN MANHATTAN(1944); DOT AND THE BUNNY(1983, Aus.), ph
1984
SONGWRITER(1984)

Jonathan Shaw
1984
TIGHTROPE(1984)

Joseph Shaw
CHANGE OF MIND(1969)

Julie Shaw
BIG SWITCH, THE(1970, Brit.)

June Shaw
TOWN LIKE ALICE, A(1958, Brit.)

Kerry Shaw
MEN IN HER DIARY(1945), w; SMOOTH AS SILK(1946), w

Larry Shaw
MUSCLE BEACH PARTY(1964)

Lewis Shaw
MARRIAGE BOND, THE(1932, Brit.); EARLY TO BED(1933, Brit./Ger.); KING'S
CUP, THE(1933, Brit.); STRANGE EVIDENCE(1933, Brit.); ARE YOU A MASON?(1934,
Brit.); NIGHT CLUB QUEEN(1934, Brit.); OPEN ALL NIGHT(1934, Brit.); ONCE A
THIEF(1935, Brit.); MURDER ON THE SET(1936, Brit.); HIGH TREASON(1937, Brit.)
Silents
ZERO(1928, Brit.)

Linda Shaw
1984
BODY DOUBLE(1984)

Lloyd Shaw
DUEL IN THE SUN(1946), a, ch

Lou Shaw
CRYPT OF THE LIVING DEAD zero(1973), p, w; BAT PEOPLE, THE(1974), p, w

Louanne Shaw
HEIRLOOM MYSTERY, THE(1936, Brit.)

Luanne Shaw
PENNY POOL, THE(1937, Brit.)

Lyn Shaw
IL GRIDO(1962, U.S./Ital.)

Marcia Shaw
PIRATES OF PENZANCE, THE(1983)

Marie Shaw
SON OF PALEFACE(1952)

Marion Shaw
I'M ALL RIGHT, JACK(1959, Brit.)

Martha Shaw
WARGAMES(1983)

Martin Shaw
MACBETH(1971, Brit.); GOLDEN VOYAGE OF SINBAD, THE(1974, Brit.); OPERA-
TION DAYBREAK(1976, U.S./Brit./Czech.); HOUND OF THE BASKERVILLES,
THE(1983, Brit.)

Mary Ellen Shaw
PHANTASM(1979)

Mary Shaw
HURRICANE, THE(1937)

Maxwell Shaw
MAN INSIDE, THE(1958, Brit.); TANK FORCE(1958, Brit.); BEN HUR(1959); ONCE
MORE, WITH FEELING(1960); CONCRETE JUNGLE, THE(1962, Brit.); IN SEARCH
OF THE CASTAWAYS(1962, Brit.); BARBER OF STAMFORD HILL, THE(1963, Brit.);
OBLONG BOX, THE(1969, Brit.); START THE REVOLUTION WITHOUT ME(1970);
MR. QUILP(1975, Brit.)

Meta Shaw
HUSBANDS(1970)

Michael Shaw
CIRCLE OF DECEPTON(1961, Brit.); NUMBER SIX(1962, Brit.)

Mildred Shaw
LUCKY DEVILS(1941)

Montague Shaw

BEHIND THAT CURTAIN(1929); SQUARE SHOULDERS(1929); SHERLOCK HOLMES(1932); SILENT WITNESS, THE(1932); BELOVED(1934); CHARLIE CHAN IN LONDON(1934); JEALOUSY(1934); MYSTERY OF MR. X, THE(1934); RIP TIDE(1934); SHOCK(1934); SISTERS UNDER THE SKIN(1934); DARK ANGEL, THE(1935); MAN WHO RECLAIMED HIS HEAD, THE(1935); TALE OF TWO CITIES, A(1935); TWO SINNERS(1935); LEATHERNECKS HAVE LANDED, THE(1936); LOVE ON THE RUN(1936); MY AMERICAN WIFE(1936); STORY OF LOUIS PASTEUR, THE(1936); SYLVIA SCARLETT(1936); UNGUARDED HOUR, THE(1936); NATION AFLAME(1937); RAINS CAME, THE(1939); STANLEY AND LIVINGSTONE(1939); THREE MUSKETEERS, THE(1939); CHARLIE CHAN'S MURDER CRUISE(1940); EARL OF CHICAGO, THE(1940); GAY CABALLERO, THE(1940); MY SON, MY SON!(1940); HARD GUY(1941); PRIDE OF THE YANKEES, THE(1942); RANDOM HARVEST(1942); THUNDER BIRDS(1942); LODGER, THE(1944); IMPERFECT LADY, THE(1947)

Silents

MORGAN'S LAST RAID(1929)

Misc. Silents

WATER HOLE, THE(1928)

Oscar Shaw

COCOANUTS, THE(1929); RHYTHM ON THE RIVER(1940)

Misc. Silents

GREAT WHITE WAY, THE(1924); KING ON MAIN STREET, THE(1925); GOING CROOKED(1926); UPSTAGE(1926)

Patty Shaw

MOONRUNNERS(1975), cos

Misc. Talkies

DEATH DRIVER(1977)

Paula Shaw

ROOMMATES, THE(1973); BEST LITTLE WHOREHOUSE IN TEXAS, THE(1982)

1984

SAVAGE STREETS(1984)

Peggy Shaw

Silents

SKID PROOF(1923); IN HOLLYWOOD WITH POTASH AND PERLMUTTER(1924)

Misc. Silents

STAGE ROMANCE, A(1922); WHO ARE MY PARENTS?(1922); GRAIL, THE(1923); GOLD HEELS(1924); WINNER TAKE ALL(1924); FIGHTING DEMON, THE(1925); SUBWAY SADIE(1926); HIS RISE TO FAME(1927); BALLYHOO BUSTER, THE(1928); LITTLE BUCKAROO, THE(1928)

Peter Shaw

CLIVE OF INDIA(1935); SONS OF THE SEA(1939, Brit.); EXILE, THE(1947); FOREVER AMBER(1947); SPIRAL STAIRCASE, THE(1975, Brit.), p; WATER BABIES, THE(1979, Brit.), p; ENIGMA(1983), p

1984

CHAMPIONS(1984), p

Philip Shaw

TARZANA, THE WILD GIRL(1973), w; SUNDAY LOVERS(1980, Ital./Fr.), ed; BETTER LATE THAN NEVER(1983), ed

1984

NAKED FACE, THE(1984), ed

Phoebe Shaw

DAVID COPPERFIELD(1970, Brit.)

Reta Shaw

PICNIC(1955); ALL MINE TO GIVE(1957); MAN AFRAID(1957); PAJAMA GAME, THE(1957); LADY TAKES A FLYER, THE(1958); POLLYANNA(1960); BACHELOR IN PARADISE(1961); SANCTUARY(1961); GLOBAL AFFAIR, A(1964); MARY POPPINS(1964); LOVED ONE, THE(1965); MARRIAGE ON THE ROCKS(1965); THAT FUNNY FEELING(1965); GHOST AND MR. CHICKEN, THE(1966); MADE IN PARIS(1966); ESCAPE TO WITCH MOUNTAIN(1975)

Richard Shaw

CARIBBEAN MYSTERY, THE(1945); LATE GEORGE APLEY, THE(1947); GAMBLER AND THE LADY, THE(1952, Brit.); HOUR OF THIRTEEN, THE(1952); PARATROOPER(1954, Brit.); HIDEOUT, THE(1956, Brit.); BOOBY TRAP(1957, Brit.); CROOKED SKY, THE(1957, Brit.); DATE WITH DISASTER(1957, Brit.); FIGHTING WILDCATS, THE(1957, Brit.); HIGH TIDE AT NOON(1957, Brit.); HOUR OF DECISION(1957, Brit.); THUNDER OVER TANGIER(1957, Brit.); MAN WITH A GUN(1958, Brit.); SAFECRACKER, THE(1958, Brit.); FIRST MAN INTO SPACE(1959, Brit.); HIDDEN HOMICIDE(1959, Brit.); HOUSE OF THE SEVEN HAWKS, THE(1959); BOTTOMS UP(1960, Brit.); COMPELLED(1960, Brit.); IT TAKES A THIEF(1960, Brit.); CIRCLE OF DECEPTON(1961, Brit.); CONCRETE JUNGLE, THE(1962, Brit.); CRACKSMAN, THE(1963, Brit.); MAN WHO COULDN'T WALK, THE(1964, Brit.); NO TREE IN THE STREET(1964, Brit.); SQUADRON 633(1964, U.S./Brit.); 633 SQUADRON(1964); DON'T LOSE YOUR HEAD(1967, Brit.); MALPAS MYSTERY, THE(1967, Brit.); ATTACK ON THE IRON COAST(1968, U.S./Brit.); I AM A GROUPIE(1970, Brit.)

Robert Shaw

TAKING OF PELHAM ONE, TWO, THREE, THE(1974); BOY FRIEND(1939); HERE I AM A STRANGER(1939); QUICK MILLIONS(1939); ROSE OF WASHINGTON SQUARE(1939); 20,000 MEN A YEAR(1939); GRAPES OF WRATH(1940); JOHNNY APOLLO(1940); LILLIAN RUSSELL(1940); STAR DUST(1940); YOUNG PEOPLE(1940); ADAM HAD FOUR SONS(1941); RIDE ON VAQUERO(1941); RISE AND SHINE(1941); LAVENDER HILL MOB, THE(1951, Brit.); OPERATION SECRET(1952); DAM BUSTERS, THE(1955, Brit.); DOUBLE CROSS(1956, Brit.); HELL IN KOREA(1956, Brit.); LIBEL(1959, Brit.); SEA FURY(1959, Brit.); VALIANT, THE(1962, Brit./Ital.); FROM RUSSIA WITH LOVE(1963, Brit.); GUEST, THE(1963, Brit.); LUCK OF GINGER COFFEY, THE(1964, U.S./Can.); TOMORROW AT TEN(1964, Brit.); BATTLE OF THE BULGE(1965); SITUATION HOPELESS—BUT NOT SERIOUS(1965), w; MAN FOR ALL SEASONS, A(1966, Brit.); BIRTHDAY PARTY, THE(1968, Brit.); CUSTER OF THE WEST(1968, U.S., Span.); BATTLE OF BRITAIN, THE(1969, Brit.); ROYAL HUNT OF THE SUN, THE(1969, Brit.); FIGURES IN A LANDSCAPE(1970, Brit.), a, w; TOWN CALLED HELL, A(1971, Span./Brit.); YOUNG WINSTON(1972, Brit.); HIRELING, THE(1973, Brit.); REFLECTION OF FEAR, A(1973); STING, THE(1973); DIAMONDS(1975, U.S./Israel); JAWS(1975); MAN IN THE GLASS BOOTH, THE(1975), w; END OF THE GAME(1976, Ger./Ital.); ROBIN AND MARIAN(1976, Brit.); SWASHBUCKLER(1976); BLACK SUNDAY(1977); DEEP, THE(1977); FORCE 10 FROM NAVARONE(1978, Brit.); AVALANCHE EXPRESS(1979)

Robert "Buddy" Shaw

MONSIEUR BEAUCAIRE(1946); OCEAN'S ELEVEN(1960); DAYS OF WINE AND ROSES(1962)

Robert J. Shaw

BERMUDA AFFAIR(1956, Brit.), w

Roderick Shaw

VAMPIRE CIRCUS(1972, Brit.)

Roland Shaw

SECRET OF MY SUCCESS, THE(1965, Brit.), md; SONG OF NORWAY(1970), md; STRAIGHT ON TILL MORNING(1974, Brit.), m

Run Run Shaw

MADAME WHITE SNAKE(1963, Hong Kong), p; LAST WOMAN OF SHANG, THE(1964, Hong Kong), p; LOVE ETERNE, THE(1964, Hong Kong), p; EMPRESS WU(1965, Hong Kong), p; ENCHANTING SHADOW, THE(1965, Hong Kong), p; GRAND SUBSTITUTION, THE(1965, Hong Kong), p; LADY GENERAL, THE(1965, Hong Kong), p; SHEPHERD GIRL, THE(1965, Hong Kong), p; LOVERS' ROCK(1966, Taiwan), p; SONS OF GOOD EARTH(1967, Hong Kong), p; VERMILION DOOR(1969, Hong Kong), p; FIVE FINGERS OF DEATH(1973, Hong Kong), p; BLOOD MONEY(1974, U.S./Hong Kong/Ital./Span.), p; SACRED KNIVES OF VENGEANCE, THE(1974, Hong Kong), p; BRUCE LEE AND I(1976, Chi.), p

Runme Shaw

MAGNIFICENT CONCUBINE, THE(1964, Hong Kong), p; EMPRESS WU(1965, Hong Kong), p; MERMAID, THE(1966, Hong Kong), p; INFRA-MAN(1975, Hong Kong), p; BRUCE LEE AND I(1976, Chi.), p; GOLIATHON(1979, Hong Kong), p

Sacha Shaw

Misc. Talkies

THREE DAUGHTERS(1949)

Sam Shaw

I LIVE FOR LOVE(1935); PARIS BLUES(1961), p; WOMAN UNDER THE INFLUENCE, A(1974), p; KILLING OF A CHINESE BOOKIE, THE(1976), prod d; BLACK OAK CONSPIRACY(1977), ed

Sandra Shaw

BLOOD MONEY(1933)

Sandy Shaw

JANIE(1944); BRAINSTORM(1983), cons

Schuyler Shaw

SHE MARRIED HER BOSS(1935)

Sebastian Shaw

CASTE(1930, Brit.); LITTLE MISS NOBODY(1933, Brit.); ADVENTURE LIMITED(1934, Brit.); FOUR MASKED MEN(1934, Brit.); GET YOUR MAN(1934, Brit.); WAY OF YOUTH, THE(1934, Brit.); ACE OF SPADES, THE(1935, Brit.); BIRDS OF A FEATHER(1935, Brit.); BREWSTER'S MILLIONS(1935, Brit.); DEPARTMENT STORE(1935, Brit.); JUBILEE WINDOW(1935, Brit.); LAD, THE(1935, Brit.); THREE WITNESSES(1935, Brit.); JURY'S EVIDENCE(1936, Brit.); TOMORROW WE LIVE(1936, Brit.); MEN ARE NOT GODS(1937, Brit.); MURDER ON DIAMOND ROW(1937, Brit.); TROOPSHIP(1938, Brit.); TOO DANGEROUS TO LIVE(1939, Brit.); U-BOAT 29(1939, Brit.); BULLDOG SEES IT THROUGH(1940, Brit.); FLYING SQUAD, THE(1940, Brit.); THREE SILENT MEN(1940, Brit.); STRANGLER, THE(1941, Brit.); GLASS MOUNTAIN, THE(1950, Brit); LANDFALL(1953, Brit.); SCOTCH ON THE ROCKS(1954, Brit.); IT HAPPENED HERE(1966, Brit.); MIDSUMMER NIGHT'S DREAM, A(1969, Brit.); RETURN OF THE JEDI(1983); WEATHER IN THE STREETS, THE(1983, Brit.)

Misc. Talkies

HOUSE OF DREAMS(1933)

Flight Lt. Sebastian Shaw

JOURNEY TOGETHER(1946, Brit.)

Sonia Shaw

HOW TO BE VERY, VERY, POPULAR(1955), ch

Stan Shaw

TRUCK TURNER(1974); DARKTOWN STRUTTERS(1975); TNT JACKSON(1975); BINGO LONG TRAVELING ALL-STARS AND MOTOR KINGS, THE(1976); ROCKY(1976); BOYS IN COMPANY C, THE(1978, U.S./Hong Kong); GREAT SANTINI, THE(1979); TOUGH ENOUGH(1983)

1984

RUNAWAY(1984)

Steve Shaw

SATAN'S BED(1965); HUSTLE(1975)

Susan D. Shaw

FURTHER ADVENTURES OF THE WILDERNESS FAMILY–PART TWO(1978)

Susan Damante Shaw

ADVENTURES OF THE WILDERNESS FAMILY, THE(1975); MOUNTAIN FAMILY ROBINSON(1979)

Susann Shaw

COVER GIRL(1944)

Sydney Shaw

GRAND ESCAPADE, THE(1946, Brit.)

Sylvia Davis Shaw

OPENING NIGHT(1977)

Tammy Shaw

LONG GOODBYE, THE(1973)

Tony Shaw

TWO FOR DANGER(1940, Brit.)

Vanessa Shaw

HORROR HOSPITAL(1973, Brit.)

Vee King Shaw

CALL HIM MR. SHATTER(1976, Hong Kong), p

Victoria Shaw

EDDY DUCHIN STORY, THE(1956); CRIMSON KIMONO, THE(1959); EDGE OF ETERNITY(1959); BECAUSE THEY'RE YOUNG(1960); I AIM AT THE STARS(1960); ALVAREZ KELLY(1966); TO TRAP A SPY(1966)

Misc. Talkies

RIDE THE TIGER(1971)

Walter Shaw

Silents

MEG(1926, Brit.), p&d

Wilbur Shaw

CROWD ROARS, THE(1932); TO PLEASE A LADY(1950), tech adv

Will Shaw

STUCKEY'S LAST STAND(1980)

William Shaw

CHOPPERS, THE(1961)

William C. Shaw-

Silents
TAR HEEL WARRIOR, THE(1917)
William C. Shaw
YOUNG CAPTIVES, THE(1959)
Wini Shaw
GIFT OF GAB(1934); MILLION DOLLAR RANSOM(1934); THREE ON A HONEY-MOON(1934); WAKE UP AND DREAM(1934); WILD GOLD(1934); BROADWAY HOSTESS(1935)
Winifred Shaw
CASE OF THE CURIOUS BRIDE, THE(1935); FRONT PAGE WOMAN(1935); GOLD DIGGERS OF 1935(1935); IN CALIENTE(1935); SWEET ADELINE(1935); CASE OF THE VELVET CLAWS, THE(1936); SATAN MET A LADY(1936); SINGING KID, THE(1936); SONS O' GUNS(1936); FUGITIVE IN THE SKY(1937); MELODY FOR TWO(1937); READY, WILLING AND ABLE(1937); SMART BLONDE(1937)
Zanne Shaw
SON OF SINBAD(1955)
Shaw and Lee
YOUNG AND BEAUTIFUL(1934); KING AND THE CHORUS GIRL, THE(1937); READY, WILLING AND ABLE(1937); UNDER WESTERN SKIES(1945)
Said Shawa
ISLAND OF ALLAH(1956)
Yasein Shawaf
1984
LITTLE DRUMMER GIRL, THE(1984)
Donita Shawe
TO SIR, WITH LOVE(1967, Brit.)
Paul Shawhan
FOURTH HORSEMAN, THE(1933)
William Shawhan
FORGOTTEN COMMANDMENTS(1932)
James Shawkey
FRONTIER DAYS(1934), w
Joan Shawlee
THIS LOVE OF OURS(1945); SMASH-UP, THE STORY OF A WOMAN(1947); PREHISTORIC WOMEN(1950); WOMAN ON THE RUN(1950); TWO TICKETS TO BROADWAY(1951); MARRYING KIND, THE(1952); SOMETHING FOR THE BIRDS(1952); ALL ASHORE(1953); FROM HERE TO ETERNITY(1953); LOOSE IN LONDON(1953); ABOUT MRS. LESLIE(1954); CASANOVA'S BIG NIGHT(1954); FRANCIS JOINS THE WACS(1954); PRIDE OF THE BLUE GRASS(1954); STAR IS BORN, A(1954); BOWERY TO BAGDAD(1955); FAREWELL TO ARMS, A(1957); SOME LIKE IT HOT(1959); APARTMENT, THE(1960); CRITIC'S CHOICE(1963); IRMA LA DOUCE(1963); WILD ANGELS, THE(1966); RELUCTANT ASTRONAUT, THE(1967); ST. VALENTINE'S DAY MASSACRE, THE(1967); TONY ROME(1967); LIVE A LITTLE, LOVE A LITTLE(1968); ONE MORE TRAIN TO ROB(1971); WILLARD(1971); FAREWELL, MY LOVELY(1975); FLASH AND THE FIRECAT(1976); BUDDY BUD-DY(1981)
1984
CITY HEAT(1984)
Misc. Talkies
BORN FOR TROUBLE(1955); GUERILLAS IN PINK LACE(1964)
John Shawlee
CONQUEST OF SPACE(1955)
Joan Shawlee [Fulton]
LOVER COME BACK(1946)
Robert Shawley
STALAG 17(1953)
Allen Shawn
MY DINNER WITH ANDRE(1981), m
Bill Shawn
EVER SINCE VENUS(1944); JAM SESSION(1944)
Dick Shawn
OPPOSITE SEX, THE(1956); WAKE ME WHEN IT'S OVER(1960); WIZARD OF BAGHDAD, THE(1960); IT'S A MAD, MAD, MAD, MAD WORLD(1963); VERY SPECIAL FAVOR, A(1965); PENELOPE(1966); WAY...WAY OUT(1966); WHAT DID YOU DO IN THE WAR, DADDY?(1966); PRODUCERS, THE(1967); HAPPY ENDING, THE(1969); LOOKING UP(1977); LOVE AT FIRST BITE(1979); YOUNG WARRI-ORS(1983)
1984
ANGEL(1984); SECRET DIARY OF SIGMUND FREUD, THE(1984)
Misc. Talkies
GOODBYE CRUEL WORLD(1983)
Jenny Shawn
NUNZIO(1978)
Michael Shawn
GOODBYE GIRL, THE(1977)
Philip Shawn
SUN SETS AT DAWN, THE(1950)
Shirley J. Shawn
BILLIE(1965)
Ted Shawn
GLORIFYING THE AMERICAN GIRL(1930), ch
Wallace Shawn
MANHATTAN(1979); STARTING OVER(1979); SIMON(1980); ATLANTIC CITY(1981, U.S./Can.); MY DINNER WITH ANDRE(1981), a, w; LITTLE SEX, A(1982); DEAL OF THE CENTURY(1983); FIRST TIME, THE(1983); LOVESICK(1983); STRANGE INVADERS(1983)
1984
BOSTONIANS, THE(1984); CRACKERS(1984); HOTEL NEW HAMPSHIRE, THE(1984); MICKI AND MAUDE(1984)
Wendy Shawn
HOW TO BEAT THE HIGH COST OF LIVING(1980)
Cheryl Shawver
SEA GYPSIES, THE(1978), animal t
David Shawyer
VICTORY(1981)
Barry Shawzin
FIRST MAN INTO SPACE(1959, Brit.); MAN WHO COULD CHEAT DEATH, THE(1959, Brit.); GUNS OF DARKNESS(1962, Brit.); SPANISH SWORD, THE(1962, Brit.); DUFFY(1968, Brit.)

Dorothy Shay
COMIN' ROUND THE MOUNTAIN(1951); WORLD'S GREATEST ATHLETE, THE(1973); MIXED COMPANY(1974)
Jack Shay
MEN OF SAN QUENTIN(1942); SUBMARINE RAIDER(1942); TALK OF THE TOWN(1942); UNDERGROUND AGENT(1942); NO TIME FOR LOVE(1943)
John Shay
BAD MEN OF THE HILLS(1942); CANAL ZONE(1942); STAR SPANGLED RHYTHM(1942); MISSING CORPSE, THE(1945); GIRL ON THE SPOT(1946); CANON CITY(1948); I WOULDN'T BE IN YOUR SHOES(1948); INCIDENT(1948); IRON CURTAIN, THE(1948); SHANGHAI CHEST, THE(1948); ALIAS NICK BEAL(1949); SORROWFUL JONES(1949); CRY BABY KILLER, THE(1958); ROADRACERS, THE(1959); LAST SUNSET, THE(1961); WHATEVER HAPPENED TO BABY JA-NE?(1962)
Mildred Shay
BALALAIKA(1939); WOMEN, THE(1939); IN OLD MISSOURI(1940); RIDE, TEN-DERFOOT, RIDE(1940); PHANTOM SUBMARINE, THE(1941); I MARRIED AN ANGEL(1942); FLIGHT FROM FOLLY(1945, Brit.); VALENTINO(1977, Brit.); CAND-LESHOE(1978); FUNNY MONEY(1983, Brit.)
Patricia Shay
TO HAVE AND HAVE NOT(1944); MILLION DOLLAR WEEKEND(1948)
Paula Shay
Misc. Silents
CITY OF ILLUSION, THE(1916); FORBIDDEN FRUIT(1916); IMMORTAL FLAME, THE(1916)
W. E. Shay
Silents
TELEPHONE GIRL, THE(1927)
William Shay
Misc. Silents
KREUTZER SONATA, THE(1915); RULING PASSION, THE(1916)
William E. Shay
Silents
NEPTUNE'S DAUGHTER(1914); CLEMENCEAU CASE, THE(1915); SIN(1915); SOUL OF BROADWAY, THE(1915); ETERNAL SIN, THE(1917)
Misc. Silents
HEART OF MARYLAND, THE(1915); TWO ORPHANS, THE(1915)
Vladek Shaybal
DEADFALL(1968, Brit.)
Lin Shaye
GOIN' SOUTH(1978); LONG RIDERS, THE(1980); JEKYLL AND HYDE...TOGETH-ER AGAIN(1982)
1984
NIGHTMARE ON ELM STREET, A(1984)
Robert Shaye
STUNTS(1977), w; ALONE IN THE DARK(1982), p
1984
NIGHTMARE ON ELM STREET, A(1984), p
Soraya Shayesteh
1984
MISSION, THE(1984)
A. Shaykevich
TRAIN GOES TO KIEV, THE(1961, USSR), w
Shayne
FANTASM(1976, Aus.)
Brook Shayne
MESSENGER OF PEACE(1950)
Edith Shayne
Silents
BURIED TREASURE(1921); ENCHANTMENT(1921)
Konstantin Shayne
KING OF ALCATRAZ(1938); PARIS HONEYMOON(1939); FIVE GRAVES TO CAIRO(1943); FOR WHOM THE BELL TOLLS(1943); MISSION TO MOSCOW(1943); FALCON IN HOLLYWOOD, THE(1944); MAN IN HALF-MOON STREET, THE(1944); NONE BUT THE LONELY HEART(1944); PASSAGE TO MARSEILLE(1944); SEV-ENTH CROSS, THE(1944); 'TILL WE MEET AGAIN(1944); ESCAPE IN THE FOG(1945); HER HIGHNESS AND THE BELLBOY(1945); DANGEROUS MIL-LIONS(1946); STRANGER, THE(1946); SECRET LIFE OF WALTER MITTY, THE(1947); SONG OF LOVE(1947); ANGEL ON THE AMAZON(1948); CRY OF THE CITY(1948); NIGHT WIND(1948); TO THE VICTOR(1948); RED DANUBE, THE(1949); I WAS A COMMUNIST FOR THE F.B.I.(1951); UNKNOWN MAN, THE(1951); FIVE FIN-GERS(1952); TREASURE OF THE GOLDEN CONDOR(1953); PRICE OF FEAR, THE(1956); VERTIGO(1958)
Linda Shayne
HUMANOIDS FROM THE DEEP(1980); SCREWBALLS(1983), a, w
Lynne Shayne
HOLLYWOOD CANTEEN(1944)
Patti Shayne
YOUR THREE MINUTES ARE UP(1973)
Richard Shayne
SEND FOR PAUL TEMPLE(1946, Brit.); CASE OF CHARLES PEACE, THE(1949, Brit.)
Robert Shayne
KEEP 'EM ROLLING(1934); WEDNESDAY'S CHILD(1934); MISSION TO MOS-COW(1943); MAKE YOUR OWN BED(1944); MR. SKEFFINGTON(1944); SHINE ON, HARVEST MOON(1944); CHRISTMAS IN CONNECTICUT(1945); RHAPSODY IN BLUE(1945); SAN ANTONIO(1945); BEHIND THE MASK(1946); FACE OF MARBLE, THE(1946); I RING DOORBELLS(1946); MY REPUTATION(1946); NOBODY LIVES FOREVER(1946); THREE STRANGERS(1946); WIFE WANTED(1946); BACK-LASH(1947); I COVER BIG TOWN(1947); SMASH-UP, THE STORY OF A WO-MAN(1947); SPIRIT OF WEST POINT, THE(1947); SWORDSMAN, THE(1947); WELCOME STRANGER(1947); BEST MAN WINS(1948); INSIDE STORY, THE(1948); LET'S LIVE A LITTLE(1948); LOADED PISTOLS(1948); SHAGGY(1948); STRANGE MRS. CRANE, THE(1948); FORGOTTEN WOMEN(1949); LAW OF THE BARBARY COAST(1949); THREAT, THE(1949); BIG TIMBER(1950); CUSTOMS AGENT(1950); DYNAMITE PASS(1950); EXPERIMENT ALCATRAZ(1950); FEDERAL MAN(1950); RIDER FROM TUCSON(1950); STATE PENITENTIARY(1950); WHEN YOU'RE SMIL-ING(1950); CRIMINAL LAWYER(1951); DAKOTA KID, THE(1951); INDIAN UPRIS-ING(1951); MISSING WOMEN(1951); MR. WALKIE TALKIE(1952); WITHOUT WARNING(1952); INVADERS FROM MARS(1953); LADY WANTS MINK, THE(1953);

MARSHAL OF CEDAR ROCK(1953); NEANDERTHAL MAN, THE(1953); PRINCE OF PIRATES(1953); TOBOR THE GREAT(1954); MURDER IS MY BEAT(1955); ACCUSED OF MURDER(1956); DANCE WITH ME, HENRY(1956); HOT SHOTS(1956); INDESTRUCTIBLE MAN, THE(1956); FOOTSTEPS IN THE NIGHT(1957); GIANT CLAW, THE(1957); KRONOS(1957); SPOOK CHASERS(1957); HOW TO MAKE A MONSTER(1958); TEENAGE CAVEMAN(1958); WAR OF THE SATELLITES(1958); I, MOBSTER(1959); NORTH BY NORTHWEST(1959); REBEL SET, THE(1959); CAGE OF EVIL(1960); VALLEY OF THE REDWOODS(1960); WHY MUST I DIE?(1960); 20,000 EYES(1961); SON OF FLUBBER(1963); TIGER WALKS, A(1964); RUNAWAY GIRL(1966); BAREFOOT EXECUTIVE, THE(1971)
Misc. Talkies
EYES OF THE JUNGLE(1953)

Ruell Shayne
GIANT CLAW, THE(1957)

Tamara Shayne
GEORGE WHITE'S 1935 SCANDALS(1935); NINOTCHKA(1939); SOMEWHERE I'LL FIND YOU(1942); MISSION TO MOSCOW(1943); JOLSON STORY, THE(1946); IT HAPPENED IN BROOKLYN(1947); NORTHWEST OUTPOST(1947); PIRATES OF MONTEREY(1947); SNAKE PIT, THE(1948); WALK A CROOKED MILE(1948); BLACK MAGIC(1949); JOLSON SINGS AGAIN(1949); RED DANUBE, THE(1949); THIEVES' HIGHWAY(1949); I CAN GET IT FOR YOU WHOLESALE(1951); ANASTASIA(1956); ROMANOFF AND JULIET(1961)

Ye. Shayner
MOTHER AND DAUGHTER(1965, USSR), makeup

Rodion Konstantinovich Shchedrin
LITTLE HUMPBACKED HORSE, THE(1962, USSR), w, m

N. Shchedrin [Mikhail Saltykov]
HOUSE OF GREED(1934, USSR), w

V. Shchennikov
HAMLET(1966, USSR)

V. Shcherbachev
MAN OF MUSIC(1953, USSR), m

Vladimir Shcherbachov
THUNDERSTORM(1934, USSR), m

M. Shcherbakov
MAGIC WEAVER, THE(1965, USSR); JACK FROST(1966, USSR)

Pyotr Shcherbakov
DAY THE WAR ENDED, THE(1961, USSR)
1984
JAZZMAN(1984, USSR)

Alla Shcherbinina
LITTLE HUMPBACKED HORSE, THE(1962, USSR)

Stefan Shcherby
HEAVEN'S GATE(1980)

V. Shchyolokov
LULLABY(1961, USSR)

George Shdanoff
ROYAL SCANDAL, A(1945)

Billy Shea
LOVE ME TONIGHT(1932), ed; MURDER AT THE VANITIES(1934), ed; WILD HARVEST(1947), ed

Buddy Shea
MY FAIR LADY(1964)

Christopher Shea
FIRECREEK(1968); SMITH(1969)

Cindy Shea
INCREDIBLY STRANGE CREATURES WHO STOPPED LIVING AND BECAME CRAZY MIXED-UP ZOMBIES, THE(1965)

Eric Shea
YOURS, MINE AND OURS(1968); GAILY, GAILY(1969); POSEIDON ADVENTURE, THE(1972); ACE ELI AND RODGER OF THE SKIES(1973); CASTAWAY COWBOY, THE(1974); SMILE(1975)

Gloria Shea
BIG CITY BLUES(1932); LIFE BEGINS(1932); NIGHT MAYOR, THE(1932); DANCE, GIRL, DANCE(1933); DUDE BANDIT, THE(1933); ELEVENTH COMMANDMENT(1933); STRANGE PEOPLE(1933); WOMEN WON'T TELL(1933); BIG TIME OR BUST(1934); BOLERO(1934); DEMON FOR TROUBLE, A(1934); FIDDLIN' BUCKAROO, THE(1934); I LIKE IT THAT WAY(1934); MONEY MEANS NOTHING(1934); SMOKING GUNS(1934); SUCCESSFUL FAILURE, A(1934); WE'RE RICH AGAIN(1934); GREAT GOD GOLD(1935); LADDIE(1935); LAST DAYS OF POMPEII, THE(1935); ONE-WAY TICKET(1935); TOMORROW'S YOUTH(1935); DANGEROUS INTRIGUE(1936)
Misc. Talkies
OIL RAIDER, THE(1934); MEN OF ACTION(1935)

Jack Shea
$1,000 A TOUCHDOWN(1939); I WANTED WINGS(1941); PRIDE OF THE YANKEES, THE(1942); LADIES' DAY(1943); THIS LAND IS MINE(1943); THRILL OF A ROMANCE(1945); EASY TO WED(1946); PERILS OF PAULINE, THE(1947); FIGHTING MAD(1948); SCENE OF THE CRIME(1949); TOO LATE FOR TEARS(1949); MALAYA(1950); MYSTERY STREET(1950); YOUNG MAN WITH A HORN(1950); DETECTIVE STORY(1951); MILLION DOLLAR PURSUIT(1951); RACKET, THE(1951); THREE GUYS NAMED MIKE(1951); UNKNOWN MAN, THE(1951); KANSAS CITY CONFIDENTIAL(1952); LUCKY ME(1954); JUPITER'S DARLING(1955); LUCY GALLANT(1955); JET PILOT(1957); SATAN'S SATELLITES(1958); DAYTON'S DEVILS(1968), d; MONITORS, THE(1969), d
1984
NIGHTMARE ON ELM STREET, A(1984)

James K. Shea
SCAVENGERS, THE(1969); PLANET OF DINOSAURS(1978), p&d

Janet Shea
WATERLOO BRIDGE(1940)

Joe Shea
1984
FEAR CITY(1984)

John Shea
SUBMARINE D-1(1937); MISSING(1982)
1984
WINDY CITY(1984)

Misc. Talkies
HUSSY(1979)

Karin Mary Shea
TIME AFTER TIME(1979, Brit.)

Kathleen Shea
MY TUTOR(1983)

Kathleen M. Shea
CANNONBALL RUN, THE(1981)
1984
CANNONBALL RUN II(1984)

Katt Shea
1984
HOLLYWOOD HOT TUBS(1984); PREPPIES(1984)

Lori Shea
PLAYGIRLS AND THE BELLBOY, THE(1962,Ger.)

Mervyn Shea
STRATTON STORY, THE(1949)

Susan Shaw
WALKING ON AIR(1946, Brit.); HOLIDAY CAMP(1947, Brit.); UPTURNED GLASS, THE(1947, Brit.); DULCIMER STREET(1948, Brit.); HERE COME THE HUGGETTS(1948, Brit.); JASSY(1948, Brit.); VOTE FOR HUGGETT(1948, Brit.); HUGGETTS ABROAD, THE(1949, Brit.); IT ALWAYS RAINS ON SUNDAY(1949, Brit.); IT'S NOT CRICKET(1949, Brit.); MARRY ME!(1949, Brit.); MY BROTHER'S KEEPER(1949, Brit.); QUARTET(1949, Brit.); FIVE ANGLES ON MURDER(1950, Brit.); POOL OF LONDON(1951, Brit.); KILLER WALKS, A(1952, Brit.); TRAIN OF EVENTS(1952, Brit.); WATERFRONT WOMEN(1952, Brit.); WIDE BOY(1952, Brit.); LARGE ROPE, THE(1953, Brit.); MY HEART GOES CRAZY(1953, Brit.); SMALL TOWN STORY(1953, Brit.); GOOD DIE YOUNG, THE(1954, Brit.); BLONDE BLACKMAILER(1955, Brit.); INTRUDER, THE(1955, Brit.); STOCK CAR(1955, Brit.); FIRE MAIDENS FROM OUTER SPACE(1956, Brit.); TIME IS MY ENEMY(1957, Brit.); CHAIN OF EVENTS(1958, Brit.); DAVY(1958, Brit.); DIPLOMATIC CORPSE, THE(1958, Brit.); BIG DAY, THE(1960, Brit.); STRANGLEHOLD(1962, Brit.); SWITCH, THE(1963, Brit.); SITTING TARGET(1972, Brit.); JUNKMAN, THE(1982)

Michael Shea
TIGER AND THE FLAME, THE(1955, India); NAMU, THE KILLER WHALE(1966); WELCOME TO HARD TIMES(1967); RIDE A NORTHBOUND HORSE(1969)

Mike Shea
UNHOLY ROLLERS(1972), ph

Olive Shea
LOVE KISS, THE(1930)

Patrick Shea
SWEET TRASH(1970)

Robert Shea
EVERY SPARROW MUST FALL(1964)

Stephen Shea
SNOOPY, COME HOME(1972)

Thomas E. Shea
Misc. Silents
MAN O' WARS MAN, THE(1914)

Timothy Shea
SARAH AND SON(1930), w

Tom Shea
FRIDAY THE 13TH PART II(1981)

Victoria Shea
1984
ALLEY CAT(1984)

William Shea
THAT UNCERTAIN FEELING(1941), ed; CANARY MURDER CASE, THE(1929), ed; HALF WAY TO HEAVEN(1929), ed; VIRGINIAN, THE(1929), ed; WHY BRING THAT UP?(1929), ed; SPOILERS, THE(1930), ed; CITY STREETS(1931), ed; FIGHTING CARAVANS(1931), ed; DR. JEKYLL AND MR. HYDE(1932), ed; ONE HOUR WITH YOU(1932), ed; WAY TO LOVE, THE(1933), ed; LITTLE MISS MARKER(1934), ed; HANDS ACROSS THE TABLE(1935), ed; LOVE IN BLOOM(1935), ed; WINGS IN THE DARK(1935), ed; DESIRE(1936), ed; GIRL OF THE OZARKS(1936), d; ROSE BOWL(1936), ed; ANGEL(1937), ed; BLUEBEARD'S EIGHTH WIFE(1938), ed; GIVE ME A SAILOR(1938), ed; OUR NEIGHBORS–THE CARTERS(1939), ed; ST. LOUIS BLUES(1939), ed; WHAT A LIFE(1939), ed; THOSE WERE THE DAYS(1940), ed; VICTORY(1940), ed; BUY ME THAT TOWN(1941), ed; GLAMOUR BOY(1941), ed; LIFE WITH HENRY(1941), ed; LADY BODYGUARD(1942), ed; LADY HAS PLANS, THE(1942), ed; DIXIE(1943), ed; STANDING ROOM ONLY(1944), ed; BRING ON THE GIRLS(1945), ed; SALTY O'ROURKE(1945), ed; O.S.S.(1946), ed; WELL-GROOMED BRIDE, THE(1946), ed; TROUBLE WITH WOMEN, THE(1947), ed; SAIGON(1948), ed; MAN OF CONFLICT(1953), ed; PEACEMAKER, THE(1956), ed; SHE DEMONS(1958), ed
Silents
NIGHT OUT, A(1916); COURAGE(1921), ed; SINGER JIM MCKEE(1924), ed; GENTLEMEN PREFER BLONDES(1928), ed; JUST MARRIED(1928), ed; LAST COMMAND, THE(1928), ed; PARTNERS IN CRIME(1928), ed
Misc. Silents
C.O.D.(1915); FOOTLIGHTS OF FATE, THE(1916); SALLY IN A HURRY(1917)

Alex Sheafe
MAN WHO WOULD NOT DIE, THE(1975)

Pat Sheahan
GIGI(1958)

Ruth Sheal
UP TO HIS NECK(1954, Brit.)

Al Shean
MUSIC IN THE AIR(1934); IT'S IN THE AIR(1935); PAGE MISS GLORY(1935); SWEET MUSIC(1935); SYMPHONY OF LIVING(1935); TRAVELING SALESLADY, THE(1935); HITCH HIKE TO HEAVEN(1936); LAW IN HER HANDS, THE(1936); SAN FRANCISCO(1936); IT COULD HAPPEN TO YOU(1937); LIVE, LOVE AND LEARN(1937); PRISONER OF ZENDA, THE(1937); ROAD BACK,THE(1937); ROSALIE(1937); STELLA DALLAS(1937); 52ND STREET(1937); GREAT WALTZ, THE(1938); TOO HOT TO HANDLE(1938); BROADWAY SERENADE(1939); JOE AND ETHEL TURP CALL ON THE PRESIDENT(1939); FRIENDLY NEIGHBORS(1940); ZIEGFELD GIRL(1941); TISH(1942); HITLER'S MADMAN(1943); ATLANTIC CITY(1944)

Darcy Shean
DON'T GO IN THE HOUSE(1980)

Alan Shear
BOY NAMED CHARLIE BROWN, A(1969), anim

Barry Shear
KARATE KILLERS, THE(1967), d; WILD IN THE STREETS(1968), d; TODD KILL-
INGS, THE(1971), p&d; ACROSS 110TH STREET(1972), d; DEADLY TRACK-
ERS(1973), d
Misc. Talkies
SWINGIN' IN THE GROOVE(1960), d

Joseph M. Shear
Silents
CURSE OF DRINK, THE(1922), p

Pearl Shear
PAD, THE(AND HOW TO USE IT)* (1966, Brit.); WITH SIX YOU GET EG-
GROLL(1968); MARIGOLD MAN(1970); GET TO KNOW YOUR RABBIT(1972); UP
THE SANDBOX(1972); SAVE THE TIGER(1973); HARRAD SUMMER, THE(1974);
SOME KIND OF HERO(1982)

Ava Sheara
SINGLE ROOM FURNISHED(1968)

Michael Sheard
MC KENZIE BREAK, THE(1970); ENGLANO MADE ME(1973, Brit.); FORCE 10
FROM NAVARONE(1978, Brit.); ESCAPE TO ATHENA(1979, Brit.); EMPIRE
STRIKES BACK, THE(1980); GREEN ICE(1981, Brit.); HIGH ROAD TO CHINA(1983)
1984
RIDDLE OF THE SANDS, THE(1984, Brit.)

Dorothy Shearer
SONG OF BERNADETTE, THE(1943); YOU'RE A LUCKY FELLOW, MR.
SMITH(1943)

Harry Shearer
ROBE, THE(1953); CRACKING UP(1977); REAL LIFE(1979), a, w; LOOSE SHO-
ES(1980); ONE-TRICK PONY(1980); RIGHT STUFF, THE(1983)
1984
THIS IS SPINAL TAP(1984), a, w, m

Lucille Shearer
UNASHAMED(1938)

Moira Shearer
RED SHOES, THE(1948, Brit.); TALES OF HOFFMANN, THE(1951, Brit.); STORY OF
THREE LOVES, THE(1953); MAN WHO LOVED REDHEADS, THE(1955, Brit.);
PEEPING TOM(1960, Brit.); BLACK TIGHTS(1962, Fr.)

Norma Shearer
LADY OF CHANCE, A(1928); LAST OF MRS. CHEYNEY, THE(1929); THEIR OWN
DESIRE(1929); TRIAL OF MARY DUGAN, THE(1929); DIVORCEE, THE(1930); LET
US BE GAY(1930); FREE SOUL, A(1931); PRIVATE LIVES(1931); STRANGERS MAY
KISS(1931); SMILIN' THROUGH(1932); STRANGE INTERLUDE(1932); BARRETTS
OF WIMPOLE STREET, THE(1934); RIP TIDE(1934); ROMEO AND JULIET(1936);
MARIE ANTOINETTE(1938); IDIOT'S DELIGHT(1939); WOMEN, THE(1939); ES-
CAPE(1940); HER CARDBOARD LOVER(1942); WE WERE DANCING(1942)
Silents
FLAPPER, THE(1920); WAY DOWN EAST(1920); DEVIL'S PARTNER, THE(1923);
PLEASURE MAD(1923); WANTERS, THE(1923); BROADWAY AFTER DARK(1924);
EMPTY HANDS(1924); HE WHO GETS SLAPPED(1924); MARRIED FLIRTS(1924);
SNOB, THE(1924); HIS SECRETARY(1925); LADY OF THE NIGHT(1925); PRETTY
LADIES(1925); TOWER OF LIES, THE(1925); WANING SEX, THE(1926); AFTER
MIDNIGHT(1927); ACTRESS, THE(1928); LATEST FROM PARIS, THE(1928)
Misc. Silents
STEALERS, THE(1920); CHANNING OF THE NORTHWEST(1922); MAN WHO
PAID, THE(1922); CLOUDED NAME, A(1923); LUCRETIA LOMBARD(1923); MAN
AND WIFE(1923); BROKEN BARRIERS(1924); TRAIL OF THE LAW(1924); WOLF
MAN, THE(1924); EXCUSE ME(1925); SLAVE OF FASHION, A(1925); WAKING UP
THE TOWN(1925); DEVIL'S CIRCUS, THE(1926); UPSTAGE(1926); DEMI-BRIDE,
THE(1927); STUDENT PRINCE IN OLD HEIDELBERG, THE(1927); TOO MANY
WIVES(1927)

Willie Shearer
PRIVATE LIFE OF SHERLOCK HOLMES, THE(1970, Brit.)

Michael Shearg
DARWIN ADVENTURE, THE(1972, Brit.)

John Shearin
EATING RAOUL(1982); I'M DANCING AS FAST AS I CAN(1982)

Dinah Shearing
BUDDIES(1983, Aus.)

George Shearing
THEATRE ROYAL(1943, Brit.); DISC JOCKEY(1951); 80 STEPS TO JONAH(1969), m

Joseph Shearing
MOSS ROSE(1947), w; BLANCHE FURY(1948, Brit.), w; MARK OF CAIN, THE(1948,
Brit.), w; SO EVIL MY LOVE(1948, Brit.), w

Julie Shearing
BULLDOG BREED, THE(1960, Brit.); JUNGLE STREET GIRLS(1963, Brit.); SHARE
OUT, THE(1966, Brit.)

Alan Shearman
BULLSHOT(1983), a, w

Michael Shearman
PUBERTY BLUES(1983, Aus.)

Roger Shearman
FORCE OF ONE, A(1979), ph; STEEL(1980), ph; EYE FOR AN EYE, AN(1981), ph;
LONE WOLF McQUADE(1983), ph
1984
COUNTRY(1984), ph

V. Shebalin
MAN OF MUSIC(1953, USSR), m; MAGIC VOYAGE OF SINBAD, THE(1962, USSR),
m

Norma Shebbeare
INADMISSIBLE EVIDENCE(1968, Brit.); WOMEN IN LOVE(1969, Brit.); 10 RILL-
INGTON PLACE(1971, Brit.)

Donald Shebib
GOIN' DOWN THE ROAD(1970, Can.), p&d, w, ed; RIP-OFF(1971, Can.), d, ed; GET
BACK(1973, Can.), d, ed; SECOND WIND(1976, Can.), d, ed; FISH HAWK(1981, Can.),
d; HEARTACHES(1981, Can.), d

Y. Shebuyeva
Misc. Silents
QUEEN OF SPADES, THE(1916, USSR)

Marvin Shechter
PERSONALITY KID, THE(1934)

Joey Sheck
TO BE OR NOT TO BE(1983)

Max Sheck
I LIKE IT THAT WAY(1934), ch

Robert Sheckley
DEAD RUN(1961, Fr./Ital./Ger.), w; MAN IN THE WATER, THE(1963), w; TENTH
VICTIM, THE(1965, Fr./Ital.), w; CONDORMAN(1981), w

Arthur Sheckman
GLADIATOR, THE(1938), w

Francine Shed
ONLY WAY HOME, THE(1972)

George C. Shedd
Silents
INCORRIGIBLE DUKANE, THE(1915), w

John Shedden
BROTHERLY LOVE(1970, Brit.)

Ronald Shedio
BACK ROADS(1981), p

Ronald Shedlo
WHISPERERS, THE(1967, Brit.), p; RECKONING, THE(1971, Brit.), p

Florence Shee
Silents
LIKENESS OF THE NIGHT, THE(1921, Brit.)

John Sheean
ISLAND CAPTIVES(1937)

Vincent Sheean
AMBASSADOR BILL(1931), w

Ally Sheedy
BAD BOYS(1983); WARGAMES(1983)
1984
OXFORD BLUES(1984)

Robert Sheedy
SPY WHO LOVED ME, THE(1977, Brit.)

Bill Sheehan
DARK CITY(1950); BIG CARNIVAL, THE(1951); PLACE IN THE SUN, A(1951);
CARRIE(1952); STALAG 17(1953)

Cecil Sheehan
ULYSSES(1967, U.S./Brit.); LOCK UP YOUR DAUGHTERS(1969, Brit.); QUACKSER
FORTUNE HAS A COUSIN IN THE BRONX(1970); PORTRAIT OF THE ARTIST AS
A YOUNG MAN, A(1979, Ireland)

David Sheehan
CALIFORNIA SUITE(1978)

Doris Sheehan
SHOW BUSINESS(1944)

Doug Sheehan
10(1979)

Ed Sheehan
TWELVE HOURS TO KILL(1960)

Howard Sheehan
PT 109(1963), w

Jack Sheehan
LITTLE MISS MARKER(1934); DYNAMITE DELANEY(1938)

James J. Sheehan
Silents
MAN WHO COULD NOT LOSE, THE(1914)

John Sheehan
KISMET(1930); SWING HIGH(1930); CRIMINAL CODE(1931); FAIR WAR-
NING(1931); HOLD'EM JAIL(1932); AS THE DEVIL COMMANDS(1933); DANCING
LADY(1933); GRAND SLAM(1933); HARD TO HANDLE(1933); KEYHOLE, THE(1933);
KING FOR A NIGHT(1933); PAST OF MARY HOLMES, THE(1933); STATE
FAIR(1933); WARRIOR'S HUSBAND, THE(1933); CIRCUS CLOWN(1934); COUNTESS
OF MONTE CRISTO, THE(1934); HOUSE OF MYSTERY(1934); HUMAN SIDE,
THE(1934); SUCH WOMEN ARE DANGEROUS(1934); MURDER MAN(1935); CASE
OF THE BLACK CAT, THE(1936); EX-MRS. BRADFORD, THE(1936); HERE COMES
CARTER(1936); IT HAD TO HAPPEN(1936); LAUGHING IRISH EYES(1936); ROSE
BOWL(1936); THREE GODFATHERS(1936); THREE MEN ON A HORSE(1936); TICK-
ET TO PARADISE(1936); WHIPSAW(1936); ALL OVER TOWN(1937); JOIN THE
MARINES(1937); LOVE TAKES FLIGHT(1937); MARKED WOMAN(1937); MID-
NIGHT COURT(1937); NIGHT CLUB SCANDAL(1937); ON THE AVENUE(1937);
SMART BLONDE(1937); WAKE UP AND LIVE(1937); MAMA RUNS WILD(1938);
THEY MADE ME A CRIMINAL(1939); TORCHY PLAYS WITH DYNAMITE(1939);
WOLF CALL(1939); GOLD RUSH MAISIE(1940); KING OF THE LUMBER-
JACKS(1940); MARGIE(1940); MEN AGAINST THE SKY(1940); MEXICAN SPITFIRE
OUT WEST(1940); SANDY GETS HER MAN(1940); SLIGHTLY HONORABLE(1940);
TIN PAN ALLEY(1940); YOUNG AS YOU FEEL(1940); BROADWAY LIMITED(1941);
HONKY TONK(1941); KISSES FOR BREAKFAST(1941); MOB TOWN(1941); STRAW-
BERRY BLONDE, THE(1941); UNFINISHED BUSINESS(1941); BROADWAY(1942);
MRS. WIGGS OF THE CABBAGE PATCH(1942); THIS GUN FOR HIRE(1942); WAKE
ISLAND(1942); GANGWAY FOR TOMORROW(1943); HEAVENLY BODY, THE(1943);
JOHNNY COME LATELY(1943); LADIES' DAY(1943); MUG TOWN(1943); NEVER A
DULL MOMENT(1943); OUTLAW, THE(1943); PAYOFF, THE(1943); IRISH EYES ARE
SMILING(1944); KNICKERBOCKER HOLIDAY(1944); MAN FROM FRISCO(1944);
MAN IN HALF-MOON STREET, THE(1944); SWINGTIME JOHNNY(1944); KILLERS,
THE(1946); MAGNIFICENT DOLL(1946); CARTER CASE, THE(1947); I WONDER
WHO'S KISSING HER NOW(1947); SHOCKING MISS PILGRIM, THE(1947); SONG
OF THE THIN MAN(1947); I WOULDN'T BE IN YOUR SHOES(1948); NIGHT HAS A
THOUSAND EYES(1948); DOOLINS OF OKLAHOMA, THE(1949); STAGE TO TUC-
SON(1950); WHERE DANGER LIVES(1950); HIS KIND OF WOMAN(1951); PEOPLE
AGAINST O'HARA, THE(1951); SOLDIERS THREE(1951); TWO TICKETS TO BROAD-
WAY(1951)
Silents
LAST CHAPTER, THE(1915)

John J. Sheehan
Misc. Silents
KEY TO YESTERDAY, THE(1914)

Johnny Sheehan
THAT'S GRATITUDE(1934)

Konrad Sheehan
WANDERERS, THE(1979); WARRIORS, THE(1979); BRUBAKER(1980)

Martha Sheehan
LOOKIN' TO GET OUT(1982)

Pat Sheehan
FRENCH LINE, THE(1954)

Perley Poore Sheehan
Silents
BRAVE AND BOLD(1918), w; ALWAYS THE WOMAN(1922), w; IF YOU BELIEVE IT, IT'S SO(1922), w; MAN WHO SAW TOMORROW, THE(1922), w; HUNCHBACK OF NOTRE DAME, THE(1923), w; WAY OF ALL FLESH, THE(1927), w
Misc. Silents
NIGHT MESSAGE, THE(1924), d

Perry Sheehan
MAGIC CARPET, THE(1951); BAD AND THE BEAUTIFUL, THE(1952); WASHINGTON STORY(1952); YOU FOR ME(1952); BATTLE CIRCUS(1953); DREAM WIFE(1953); FAST COMPANY(1953); GIRL WHO HAD EVERYTHING, THE(1953); LONG, LONG TRAILER, THE(1954)

William Sheehan
APARTMENT FOR PEGGY(1948); WALLS OF JERICHO(1948); YOU WERE MEANT FOR ME(1948); SUNSET BOULEVARD(1950)

Winfield Sheehan
CHANGE OF HEART(1934), p; MARIE GALANTE(1934), p; NOW I'LL TELL(1934), p; SERVANTS' ENTRANCE(1934), p; STAND UP AND CHEER(1934 80m FOX bw), p; CURLY TOP(1935), p; ONE MORE SPRING(1935), p; FLORIAN(1940), p

Winfield H. Sheehan
CAPTAIN EDDIE(1945), p

Winfield R. Sheehan
STATE FAIR(1933), p; WORLD MOVES ON, THE(1934), p; FARMER TAKES A WIFE, THE(1935), p; WAY DOWN EAST(1935), p

Arthur Sheekman
MONKEY BUSINESS(1931), w; DUCK SOUP(1933), w; ROMAN SCANDALS(1933), w; KID MILLIONS(1934), w; DIMPLES(1936), w; PIGSKIN PARADE(1936), w; ROSE OF THE RANCHO(1936), w; STOWAWAY(1936), w; WONDER MAN(1945), w; BLUE SKIES(1946), w; BLAZE OF NOON(1947), w; DEAR RUTH(1947), w; DREAM GIRL(1947), w; TROUBLE WITH WOMEN, THE(1947), w; WELCOME STRANGER(1947), w; HAZARD(1948), w; SAIGON(1948), w; DEAR WIFE(1949), w; MR. MUSIC(1950), w; YOUNG MAN WITH IDEAS(1952), w; CALL ME MADAM(1953), w; BUNDLE OF JOY(1956), w; SOME CAME RUNNING(1959), w; ADA(1961), w

Hans Sheel
MAGIC FACE, THE(1951, Aust.)

Mark Sheeler
FROM HELL IT CAME(1957); TANK BATTALION(1958); SPEED CRAZY(1959); WHY MUST I DIE?(1960)

E. E. Sheeley
Silents
FOOLISH WIVES(1920), art d; MAN TO MAN(1922), art d; MERRY-GO-ROUND(1923), art d; GOOSE WOMAN, THE(1925), art d

Charlie Sheen
1984
RED DAWN(1984)

Chris Sheen
SKIMPY IN THE NAVY(1949, Brit.)

Martin Sheen
INCIDENT, THE(1967); SUBJECT WAS ROSES, THE(1968); CATCH-22(1970); NO DRUMS, NO BUGLES(1971); PICKUP ON 101(1972); RAGE(1972); BADLANDS(1974); CASSANDRA CROSSING, THE(1977); LITTLE GIRL WHO LIVES DOWN THE LANE, THE(1977, Can.); APOCALYPSE NOW(1979); EAGLE'S WING(1979, Brit.); FINAL COUNTDOWN, THE(1980); LOOPHOLE(1981, Brit.); GANDHI(1982); THAT CHAMPIONSHIP SEASON(1982); DEAD ZONE, THE(1983); ENIGMA(1983); MAN, WOMAN AND CHILD(1983)
1984
FIRESTARTER(1984)
Misc. Talkies
LEGEND OF EARL DURAND, THE(1974)

John Sheenan
GOOSE AND THE GANDER, THE(1935)

Barry Sheene
Misc. Talkies
SPACE RIDERS(1984)

Randy Sheer
SHAMPOO(1975)

Tony Sheer
THREE CARD MONTE(1978, Can.); SEARCH AND DESTROY(1981)

William Sheer
Silents
BATTLE OF LIFE, THE(1916); DIVORCE TRAP, THE(1919)
Misc. Talkies
PITFALLS OF A BIG CITY(1919); SEALED ENVELOPE, THE(1919)

William A. Sheer
Silents
TIDES OF FATE(1917)

Doris Sheerin
Misc. Silents
PORCELAIN LAMP, THE(1921)

Chad Sheets
1984
MEATBALLS PART II(1984)

Edith Sheets
ABBOTT AND COSTELLO MEET THE INVISIBLE MAN(1951); MY FAVORITE SPY(1951); TEN TALL MEN(1951)

John Sheets
MICHAEL O'HALLORAN(1948), ed

Millard Sheets
SALOME(1953), tech adv

Walter Sheets
ARISTOCATS, THE(1970), md

Bert Sheffer
GREAT JASPER, THE(1933), m

Bill Sheffield
KNUTE ROCKNE–ALL AMERICAN(1940); KING OF THE WILD HORSES(1947); BEST MAN WINS(1948)

Billy Sheffield
BOY WITH THE GREEN HAIR, THE(1949)

Dan B. Sheffield
HEAVENLY BODY, THE(1943)

Flora Sheffield
CHARLEY'S AUNT(1930); EAST LYNNE(1931); GOD IS MY WITNESS(1931)

Jay Sheffield
THREE STOOGES GO AROUND THE WORLD IN A DAZE, THE(1963); TAMMY AND THE MILLIONAIRE(1967)

John Sheffield
BABES IN ARMS(1939); TARZAN FINDS A SON!(1939); KNUTE ROCKNE–ALL AMERICAN(1940); LITTLE ORVIE(1940); LUCKY CISCO KID(1940); MILLION DOLLAR BABY(1941); TARZAN'S SECRET TREASURE(1941); TARZAN'S NEW YORK ADVENTURE(1942); ROUGHLY SPEAKING(1945); SUN COMES UP, THE(1949); THAT FORSYTE WOMAN(1949); SCARAMOUCHE(1952); YOUNG BESS(1953); SILVER CHALICE, THE(1954); SEA CHASE, THE(1955); BLACK SLEEP, THE(1956); MIDNIGHT LACE(1960)

Johnny Sheffield
TARZAN TRIUMPHS(1943); TARZAN'S DESERT MYSTERY(1943); TARZAN AND THE AMAZONS(1945); TARZAN AND THE LEOPARD WOMAN(1946); TARZAN AND THE HUNTRESS(1947); BOMBA ON PANTHER ISLAND(1949); BOMBA THE JUNGLE BOY(1949); BOMBA AND THE HIDDEN CITY(1950); LOST VOLCANO, THE(1950); ELEPHANT STAMPEDE(1951); LION HUNTERS, THE(1951); AFRICAN TREASURE(1952); BOMBA AND THE JUNGLE GIRL(1952); SAFARI DRUMS(1953); GOLDEN IDOL, THE(1954); KILLER LEOPARD(1954); LORD OF THE JUNGLE(1955)

Leo Sheffield
LORD RICHARD IN THE PANTRY(1930, Brit.); COMPROMISED!(1931, Brit.); HIGH SOCIETY(1932, Brit.); FALLING FOR YOU(1933, Brit.); KENTUCKY MINSTRELS(1934, Brit.); WIFE OR TWO, A(1935, Brit.)
Misc. Silents
VALLEY OF THE GHOSTS(1928, Brit.)

Maceo B. Sheffield
HARLEM ON THE PRAIRIE(1938); MR. WASHINGTON GOES TO TOWN(1941)

Maceo Sheffield
REFORM SCHOOL(1939); GANG WAR(1940); LOOK OUT SISTER(1948)
Misc. Talkies
UP JUMPED THE DEVIL(1941)

Nellie Sheffield
DULCIMER STREET(1948, Brit.)

Quinnon Sheffield
SMOKEY AND THE BANDIT(1977)

Reginald Sheffield
GREEN GODDESS, THE(1930); OLD ENGLISH(1930); PARTNERS OF THE TRAIL(1931); CHARLIE CHAN IN LONDON(1934); HOUSE OF ROTHSCHILD, THE(1934); OF HUMAN BONDAGE(1934); DANTE'S INFERNO(1935); LIVES OF A BENGAL LANCER(1935); SOCIETY FEVER(1935); SPLENDOR(1935); WITHOUT REGRET(1935); CHARGE OF THE LIGHT BRIGADE, THE(1936); ANOTHER DAWN(1937); FEMALE FUGITIVE(1938); SERGEANT MURPHY(1938); GUNGA DIN(1939); ARISE, MY LOVE(1940); EARTHBOUND(1940); HUDSON'S BAY(1940); LADY EVE, THE(1941); SCOTLAND YARD(1941); SUSPICION(1941); EYES IN THE NIGHT(1942); RANDOM HARVEST(1942); TAKE A LETTER, DARLING(1942); CRYSTAL BALL, THE(1943); TONIGHT WE RAID CALAIS(1943); GREAT MOMENT, THE(1944); MAN IN HALF-MOON STREET, THE(1944); OUR HEARTS WERE YOUNG AND GAY(1944); WILSON(1944); MY NAME IS JULIA ROSS(1945); CENTENNIAL SUMMER(1946); DEVOTION(1946); SEARCHING WIND, THE(1946); TEMPTATION(1946); THREE STRANGERS(1946); TO EACH HIS OWN(1946); EXILE, THE(1947); SINGAPORE(1947); KISS THE BLOOD OFF MY HANDS(1948); THREE MUSKETEERS, THE(1948); MR. BELVEDERE GOES TO COLLEGE(1949); PRISON WARDEN(1949); THAT FORSYTE WOMAN(1949); FORBIDDEN(1953); SECOND CHANCE(1953); STORY OF THREE LOVES, THE(1953); YOUNG BESS(1953); SECRET OF TREASURE MOUNTAIN(1956); 23 PACES TO BAKER STREET(1956); STORY OF MANKIND, THE(1957); BUCCANEER, THE(1958); MARJORIE MORNINGSTAR(1958)
Silents
CLASSMATES(1924); NEST, THE(1927); ADORABLE CHEAT, THE(1928); SWEET SIXTEEN(1928)
Misc. Silents
PINCH HITTER, THE(1925)

Winstead Sheffield
SPIRIT OF STANFORD, THE(1942)

Marc Sheffler
LAST HOUSE ON THE LEFT(1972)

Leo Shefield
HAWLEY'S OF HIGH STREET(1933, Brit.)

Danny J. Sheflin
Misc. Talkies
REUNION, THE(1977)

Bert Shefter
HOLIDAY RHYTHM(1950), m; ONE TOO MANY(1950), m, md; DANGER ZONE(1951), m; M(1951), md; PIER 23(1951), m; ROARING CITY(1951), m; SKY HIGH(1952), m; GREAT JESSE JAMES RAID, THE(1953), m; NO ESCAPE(1953), m; SINS OF JEZEBEL(1953), m; DESPERADOES ARE IN TOWN, THE(1956), m; SCANDAL INCORPORATED(1956), m; DEERSLAYER, THE(1957), m; GHOST DIVER(1957), m; GUN DUEL IN DURANGO(1957), m; HELL SHIP MUTINY(1957), m; KRONOS(1957), m; MONKEY ON MY BACK(1957), m; SHE DEVIL(1957), m; AMBUSH AT CIMARRON PASS(1958), m; CATTLE EMPIRE(1958), m; HONG KONG CONFIDENTIAL(1958), m; IT! THE TERROR FROM BEYOND SPACE(1958), m; MACHETE(1958), m; SIERRA BARON(1958), m; VILLA!(1958), m; BIG CIRCUS, THE(1959), m; COSMIC MAN, THE(1959), m; DOG OF FLANDERS, A(1959), m; MIRACLE OF THE HILLS, THE(1959), m; RETURN OF THE FLY(1959), m; SAD HORSE, THE(1959), m; VICE RAID(1959), m; DOG'S BEST FRIEND, A(1960), m; LOST WORLD, THE(1960), m; MUSIC BOX KID(1960), m; THREE CAME TO KILL(1960), m; BIG SHOW, THE(1961), m; FRONTIER UPRISING(1961), m; GUN

FIGHT(1961), m; LONG ROPE, THE(1961), m; MISTY(1961), m; PIRATES OF TORTUGA(1961), m; TESS OF THE STORM COUNTRY(1961), m; VOYAGE TO THE BOTTOM OF THE SEA(1961), m; WILD HARVEST(1962), m; CATTLE KING(1963), m; THUNDER ISLAND(1963), m; YOUNG GUNS OF TEXAS(1963), m; LAST MAN ON EARTH, THE(1964, U.S./Ital.), m; CURSE OF THE FLY(1965, Brit.), m; LAST SHOT YOU HEAR, THE(1969, Brit.), m; CHRISTINE JORGENSEN STORY, THE(1970), m

Mark Shegoff
TIME TRAVELERS, THE(1964), makeup
Cynthia Sheider
BREAKING AWAY(1979), ed
Sheik
KING OF THE SIERRAS(1938)
Sheik Abdullah
WEST OF ZANZIBAR(1954, Brit.)
Sheik the Horse
ROLL ALONG, COWBOY(1938)
Kate Sheil
SINGER AND THE DANCER, THE(1977, Aus.)
Ruth Sheil
VALUE FOR MONEY(1957, Brit.)
Derek Sheils
WE'LL MEET AGAIN(1942, Brit.), w
David Sheiner
GREATEST STORY EVER TOLD, THE(1965); ONE SPY TOO MANY(1966); ODD COUPLE, THE(1968); MAN CALLED GANNON, A(1969); WINNING(1969); THEY CALL ME MISTER TIBBS(1970); STONE KILLER, THE(1973); BIG BRAWL, THE(1980); GONG SHOW MOVIE, THE(1980); BLUE THUNDER(1983)
Hal Sheiner
TARGET ZERO(1955)
Marsha Sheiness
HAVE A NICE WEEKEND(1975), w
Jirina Shejbalova
MERRY WIVES, THE(1940, Czech.)
Lo Lita Shek
HONG KONG AFFAIR(1958)
Lolita Shek
OUT OF THE TIGER'S MOUTH(1962)
Lenia Shekhman
BALLAD OF COSSACK GLOOTA(1938, USSR)
Edna Sheklow
PROMISES, PROMISES(1963), w
Mark Shekter
B.S. I LOVE YOU(1971), m
Riki Shelach
Misc. Talkies
LAST WINTER, THE(1983), d
Charles Shelander
LET'S ROCK(1958)
Reginald Shelborne
LINE, THE(1982), w, ed
Carroll Shelby
GRAND PRIX(1966), tech adv
Charlotte Shelby
Silents
DIMPLES(1916)
Jean Shelby
Misc. Silents
SHADOW OF DOUBT, THE(1916)
Margaret Shelby
Silents
AMAZING IMPOSTER, THE(1919); JENNY BE GOOD(1920)
Misc. Silents
FAITH(1916); ROSEMARY CLIMBS THE HEIGHTS(1918)
Miriam Shelby
Silents
MAN FROM MONTANA, THE(1917)
Misc. Silents
BEHIND THE LINES(1916)
Nicole Shelby
TORTURE GARDEN(1968, Brit.); TERROR IN THE WAX MUSEUM(1973)
Jana Shelden
SENDER, THE(1982, Brit.)
Joe Shelderfer
Silents
CAPTAIN'S CAPTAIN, THE(1919), ph; SCARAB RING, THE(1921), ph
Joseph Shelderfer
Silents
TWO-EDGED SWORD, THE(1916), ph
Barbara Sheldon
FLYING DOWN TO RIO(1933); LUCKY TEXAN, THE(1934)
Bert Sheldon
SPRING BREAK(1983)
Bob Sheldon
1984
CANNONBALL RUN II(1984)
Caroline Sheldon
THESE ARE THE DAMNED(1965, Brit.)
Catherine Sheldon
DESIRABLE(1934)
Charles M. Sheldon
IN HIS STEPS(1936), w
David Sheldon
SHEBA BABY(1975), w, p; GRIZZLY(1976), p&w; PROJECT: KILL(1976), p, w; JUST BEFORE DAWN(1980), p
Misc. Talkies
LOVELY BUT DEADLY(1983), d

Dean Sheldon
BLAST OF SILENCE(1961)
Douglas Sheldon
GUTTER GIRLS(1964, Brit.); UP THE JUNCTION(1968, Brit.); SOME GIRLS DO(1969, Brit.); RYAN'S DAUGHTER(1970, Brit.)
E. Lloyd Sheldon
WILD PARTY, THE(1929), w; ILLUSION(1929), w; HER WEDDING NIGHT(1930), p; CITY STREETS(1931), p; CRADLE SONG(1933), p; WHITE WOMAN(1933), p; DEATH TAKES A HOLIDAY(1934), p; MURDER AT THE VANITIES(1934), p; GLASS KEY, THE(1935), p; HANDS ACROSS THE TABLE(1935), p; LAST OUTPOST, THE(1935), p; JUNGLE PRINCESS, THE(1936), p; MILKY WAY, THE(1936), p; THIRTEEN HOURS BY AIR(1936), p; INTERNATIONAL LADY(1941), w; BEYOND THE BLUE HORIZON(1942), w
Silents
EACH PEARL A TEAR(1916), w; ALL WOMAN(1918), w; OTHER MEN'S DAUGHTERS(1918), w; WHEN A WOMAN SINS(1918), w; DAWN OF THE EAST(1921), w; SISTERS(1922), w; LAW OF THE LAWLESS, THE(1923), w; FLAMING WATERS(1925), w; IT(1927), ed
Edith Sheldon
QUEEN HIGH(1930)
Edward Sheldon
ROMANCE(1930), w; SONG OF SONGS(1933), w; DISHONORED LADY(1947), w; LULU BELLE(1948), w
Edward B. Sheldon
SALVATION NELL(1931), w
Edward Brewster Sheldon
Silents
SALVATION NELL(1921), w; ON THE HIGH SEAS(1922), w
Ernie Sheldon
YOUNG BILLY YOUNG(1969), m/1
Forest Sheldon
DYNAMITE RANCH(1932), w; SILVER TRAIL, THE(1937), w
Forrest Sheldon
LONE RIDER, THE(1930), w; DAWN TRAIL, THE(1931), w; LAW OF THE RIO GRANDE(1931), d; TEXAS RANGER, THE(1931), w; BETWEEN FIGHTING MEN(1932), d, w; DYNAMITE RANCH(1932), d; HELL FIRE AUSTIN(1932), d, w; LONE TRAIL, THE(1932), d; LONE AVENGER, THE(1933), w; PHANTOM THUNDERBOLT, THE(1933), w; FIGHTING TROOPER, THE(1935), w; WILDERNESS MAIL(1935), d; PAL FROM TEXAS, THE(1939), w; PORT OF HATE(1939), w; TEXAS STAMPEDE(1939), w; PIONEER DAYS(1940), w
Silents
RAINBOW RANGERS(1924), d&w; DON X(1925), d&w; KNOCKOUT KID, THE(1925), w; WAS IT BIGAMY?(1925), w; AHEAD OF THE LAW(1926), d
Misc. Silents
BLACK GOLD(1924), d; ALWAYS RIDIN' TO WIN(1925), d; MAKERS OF MEN(1925), d; NEVER TOO LATE(1925), d; STAMPEDIN' TROUBLE(1925), d; LAWLESS TRAILS(1926), d; MAN FROM OKLAHOMA, THE(1926), d
Forrest K. Sheldon
Misc. Silents
WHO'S YOUR FRIEND(1925), d; GREY VULTURE, THE(1926), d; HAUNTED SHIP, THE(1927), d
Gene Sheldon
ROBERTA(1935); TELEVISION TALENT(1937, Brit.); LUCKY TO ME(1939, Brit.); HIDDEN MENACE, THE(1940, Brit.); SHOW BUSINESS(1944); DOLLY SISTERS, THE(1945); WHERE DO WE GO FROM HERE?(1945); GOLDEN GIRL(1951); THREE RING CIRCUS(1954); SIGN OF ZORRO, THE(1960); TOBY TYLER(1960); BABES IN TOYLAND(1961)
George Sheldon
Silents
KID, THE(1921)
George V. Sheldon
BRIEF ENCOUNTER(1945, Brit.)
James Sheldon
SINGLE ROOM FURNISHED(1968), m
Silents
OVER THE HILL TO THE POORHOUSE(1920)
Jana Sheldon
SHINING, THE(1980)
Jerome Sheldon
LURE OF THE ISLANDS(1942); ONE THRILLING NIGHT(1942); SENORITA FROM THE WEST(1945); VICKI(1953)
Jerry Sheldon
FORBIDDEN TRAILS(1941); GUN MAN FROM BODIE, THE(1941); MONKEY BUSINESS(1952); LOVE ME TENDER(1956); STORY ON PAGE ONE, THE(1959)
Joan Sheldon
MERRY FRINKS, THE(1934); STUDENT TOUR(1934); FOLIES DERGERE(1935)
Julie Sheldon
STRAIGHT SHOOTER(1940)
Katherine Sheldon
SOCIETY FEVER(1935); DARK HOUR, THE(1936); TANGO(1936)
Kathryn Sheldon
BONNIE SCOTLAND(1935); STRAIGHT FROM THE HEART(1935); BELOW THE DEADLINE(1936); BRILLIANT MARRIAGE(1936); MAID OF SALEM(1937); I'M FROM THE CITY(1938); MARIE ANTOINETTE(1938); QUICK MONEY(1938); SUNSET TRAIL(1938); FRONTIER MARSHAL(1939); OUR LEADING CITIZEN(1939); GOLD RUSH MAISIE(1940); OUT WEST WITH THE PEPPERS(1940); ARIZONA BOUND(1941); LUCKY DEVILS(1941); NEVER GIVE A SUCKER AN EVEN BREAK(1941); PARACHUTE BATTALION(1941); RICHEST MAN IN TOWN(1941); I MARRIED A WITCH(1942); ICE-CAPADES REVUE(1942); MAGNIFICENT AMBERSONS, THE(1942); MISS V FROM MOSCOW(1942); RINGS ON HER FINGERS(1942); TISH(1942); WAKE UP AND DREAM(1946); JACKPOT, THE(1950); NO WAY OUT(1950); SUMMER STOCK(1950); MR. BELVEDERE RINGS THE BELL(1951); HAPPY TIME, THE(1952); RETURN OF THE TEXAN(1952); VICKI(1953); KETTLES IN THE OZARKS, THE(1956)
Misc. Talkies
CITY LIMITS(1941); FATHER STEPS OUT(1941)
Kelsey Sheldon
RHYTHM OF THE SADDLE(1938)

Ed Shelnut
ODE TO BILLY JOE(1976)

Abigail Shelton
WHY MUST I DIE?(1960); MAIL ORDER BRIDE(1964); ZIGZAG(1970)
1984
FRIDAY THE 13TH–THE FINAL CHAPTER(1984)

Anne Shelton
GIRL IN DISTRESS(1941, Brit.); KING ARTHUR WAS A GENTLEMAN(1942, Brit.); MISS LONDON LTD.(1943, Brit.); BEES IN PARADISE(1944, Brit.); COME DANCE WITH ME(1950, Brit.)

Bob Shelton
RIDERS OF THE DAWN(1945)

David Shelton
1984
FLASH OF GREEN, A(1984)

Deborah Shelton
BLOOD TIDE(1982)
1984
BODY DOUBLE(1984)

Don Shelton
YOU GOTTA STAY HAPPY(1948); RED, HOT AND BLUE(1949); MYSTERY STREET(1950); QUEEN FOR A DAY(1951); TWO DOLLAR BETTOR(1951); COMMAND, THE(1954); THEM!(1954); HILDA CRANE(1956); DRAGSTRIP GIRL(1957); INVASION OF THE SAUCER MEN(1957); BULLWHIP(1958); HIGH SCHOOL HELL-CATS(1958)

E. Lloyd Shelton
SINS OF THE FATHERS(1928), w; DOUBLE DOOR(1934), p

Elsie Shelton
PRISON WITHOUT BARS(1939, Brit.)

George Shelton
HOUSE ON 92ND STREET, THE(1945); KISS OF DEATH(1947)

Gil Shelton
SCARED TO DEATH(1981), p

Hall Shelton
INCIDENT(1948), p; LOVE ISLAND(1952), p; BORN TO THE SADDLE(1953), p

Jack Shelton
FREAKY FRIDAY(1976)

Joe Shelton
SPEED LOVERS(1968), ph

John Shelton
KID GALAHAD(1937); DRAMATIC SCHOOL(1938); DR. KILDARE GOES HOME(1940); GHOST COMES HOME, THE(1940); I TAKE THIS WOMAN(1940); WE WHO ARE YOUNG(1940); BLONDE INSPIRATION(1941); KEEPING COMPANY(1941); A-HAUNTING WE WILL GO(1942); FOREIGN AGENT(1942); WHISPERING GHOSTS(1942); TIME OF THEIR LIVES, THE(1946); BIG FIX, THE(1947); LITTLE MISS BROADWAY(1947); ROAD TO THE BIG HOUSE(1947); JOE PALOOKA IN WINNER TAKE ALL(1948); SIREN OF ATLANTIS(1948); SINS OF JEZEBEL(1953)

Joy Shelton
MILLIONS LIKE US(1943, Brit.); BEES IN PARADISE(1944, Brit.); SEND FOR PAUL TEMPLE(1946, Brit.); UNEASY TERMS(1948, Brit.); WATERLOO ROAD(1949, Brit.); NO ROOM AT THE INN(1950, Brit.); CASE FOR PC 49, A(1951, Brit.); MIDNIGHT EPISODE(1951, Brit.); ONCE A SINNER(1952, Brit.); HUNDRED HOUR HUNT(1953, Brit.); NORMAN CONQUEST(1953, Brit.); IMPULSE(1955, Brit.); BEWARE OF CHILDREN(1961, Brit.); FIVE GOLDEN HOURS(1961, Brit.); LOSS OF INNOCENCE(1961, Brit.); DAMN THE DEFIANT!(1962, Brit.)

Katherine Shelton
NOTHING SACRED(1937)

Laura Shelton
FBI CODE 98(1964)

Lillie Shelton
GONG SHOW MOVIE, THE(1980)

Louie Shelton
J.W. COOP(1971), m

Maria Shelton
ESCAPE TO PARADISE(1939); BELLS OF CAPISTRANO(1942); DO YOU LOVE ME?(1946)

Marie Shelton
Silents
SOCIETY SCANDAL, A(1924)

Marla Shelton
FLYING HOSTESS(1936); POSTAL INSPECTOR(1936); DANGEROUS NUMBER(1937); PERSONAL PROPERTY(1937); SONG OF THE CITY(1937); STAND-IN(1937); THERE GOES MY GIRL(1937); UNDER COVER OF NIGHT(1937); VOGUES OF 1938(1937); 52ND STREET(1937); LONE WOLF MEETS A LADY, THE(1940); SECRETS OF THE UNDERGROUND(1943); WHEN JOHNNY COMES MARCHING HOME(1943); SARATOGA TRUNK(1945)

Mildred Shelton
NEW KIND OF LOVE, A(1963)

Reid Shelton
SENTINEL, THE(1977)

Robert Shelton
EL DORADO(1967)

Ron Shelton
UNDER FIRE(1983), w

Shane Shelton
UNDER MILK WOOD(1973, Brit.)

Sloane Shelton
I NEVER SANG FOR MY FATHER(1970); ALL THE PRESIDENT'S MEN(1976); SOMEBODY KILLED HER HUSBAND(1978)
Misc. Talkies
BROAD COALITION, THE(1972); WHAT DO I TELL THE BOYS AT THE STATION(1972)

Terry Shelton
FIRE DOWN BELOW(1957, U.S./Brit.)

Tom Shelton
Silents
OVER THE STICKS(1929, Brit.)

Violet Shelton
SUSPICION(1941)

William Shelton
DRY SUMMER(1967, Turkey), p

Carole Shelyne
OUT OF SIGHT(1966)

Samuel Shem
1984
HOUSE OF GOD, THE(1984), d&w

John A. Shemayme
PROPHECY(1979)

Steve Shemayne
PROPHECY(1979)

Steve Shemayne
TELL THEM WILLIE BOY IS HERE(1969); LITTLE BIG MAN(1970); JOURNEY THROUGH ROSEBUD(1972)

Chen Ching Shen
SACRED KNIVES OF VENGEANCE, THE(1974, Hong Kong), art d

Freda Foh Shen
WITHOUT A TRACE(1983)

Olive Shen
GLORIFYING THE AMERICAN GIRL(1930)

Shelley Shen
FERRY TO HONG KONG(1959, Brit.)

Paul Shenar
LULU(1978); END OF AUGUST, THE(1982); SECRET OF NIMH, THE(1982); DEADLY FORCE(1983); SCARFACE(1983)

William Shenberg
NIGHTMARE IN THE SUN(1964), ed

Aubrey Shenck
FRANKENSTEIN 1970(1958), p, w

Rifat Shenel
SALT & PEPPER(1968, Brit.)

C.R. Sheng
FIGHT TO THE LAST(1938, Chi.), m

Ariadna Shengelaya
GARNET BRACELET, THE(1966, USSR)

Nikolai Shengelaya
Misc. Silents
ELISO(1928, USSR), d

S. Shenin
BRIDE WITH A DOWRY(1954, USSR), ph

Robert Shenley
THIS IS THE ARMY(1943)

Leila Shenna
MARCH OR DIE(1977, Brit.); MOONRAKER(1979, Brit.)

Walter Shenson
INNER SANCTUM(1948), p; KOREA PATROL(1951), p, w; MOUSE THAT ROARED, THE(1959, Brit.), p; MATTER OF WHO, A(1962, Brit.), p; MOUSE ON THE MOON, THE(1963, Brit.), p; HARD DAY'S NIGHT, A(1964, Brit.), p; HELP!(1965, Brit.), p; DON'T RAISE THE BRIDGE, LOWER THE RIVER(1968, Brit.), p; 30 IS A DANGEROUS AGE, CYNTHIA(1968, Brit.), p; WELCOME TO THE CLUB(1971), p, d; DIGBY, THE BIGGEST DOG IN THE WORLD(1974, Brit.), p; CHICKEN CHRONICLES, THE(1977), p; REUBEN, REUBEN(1983), p

Claire Shenstone
MOON ZERO TWO(1970, Brit.)

Susan Shentall
ROMEO AND JULIET(1954, Brit.)

Thomas Shenton
BUCKET OF BLOOD(1934, Brit.)

William Shenton
STRONGER SEX, THE(1931, Brit.), ph; THIRD TIME LUCKY(1931, Brit.), ph

Anthony Shepard
SING AND SWING(1964, Brit.)

Bob Shepard
Misc. Talkies
SUPER SEAL(1976)

Cortland Shepard
STORM RIDER, THE(1957)

Court Shepard
SPACE MASTER X-7(1958)

Courtland Shepard
LEATHER SAINT, THE(1956); SOMEBODY UP THERE LIKES ME(1956); FEAR STRIKES OUT(1957); GUNFIGHT AT THE O.K. CORRAL(1957); ESCAPE FROM RED ROCK(1958)

Elaine Shepard
DARKEST AFRICA(1936); FIGHTING TEXAN(1937); LAW OF THE RANGER(1937); TOPPER(1937); I COVER CHINATOWN(1938); PROFESSOR BEWARE(1938); YOU CAN'T FOOL YOUR WIFE(1940); FALCON IN DANGER, THE(1943); SEVEN DAYS ASHORE(1944); THIRTY SECONDS OVER TOKYO(1944); ZIEGFELD FOLLIES(1945)

Ellen Shepard
LONELY LADY, THE(1983), w

Gerald Shepard
FIVE EASY PIECES(1970), ed

Gerald S. Shepard
HEROES DIE YOUNG(1960), p, d&w

Iva Shepard
Silents
CAPTAIN SWIFT(1914); CONSPIRACY, THE(1914); STRAIGHT ROAD, THE(1914); SALAMANDER, THE(1915); SUBURBAN, THE(1915); DRIFTER, THE(1916); SCARLET ROAD, THE(1916)
Misc. Silents
BONDWOMEN(1915); HAUNTED MANOR, THE(1916); ISLE OF LOVE, THE(1916)

Ivan Shepard
Misc. Silents
NORTHERN LIGHTS(1914)

Ivy Shepard
Silents
THIEF, THE(1915)

J. Shepard
TIKI TIKI(1971, Can.)

Jan Shepard
SABRE JET(1953); KING CREOLE(1958); ATTACK OF THE GIANT LEECHES(1959); THIRD OF A MAN(1962); PARADISE, HAWAIIAN STYLE(1966)

Jewal Shepard
MY TUTOR(1983)
1984
HOLLYWOOD HOT TUBS(1984)

John Shepard
CHETNIKS(1943)

Judith Shepard
UP THE MACGREGORS(1967, Ital./Span.)

Kathleen Shepard
HUMAN CARGO(1936), w; BAD GUY(1937), w

Mary Shepard
ARTISTS AND MODELS(1937)

Michael Shepard
1984
RIVER RAT, THE(1984)

Miles Shepard
RACKET, THE(1951); TWO TICKETS TO BROADWAY(1951); JUST ACROSS THE STREET(1952); JOURNEY TO FREEDOM(1957)

O-Lan Shepard
OUT(1982); SHOOT THE MOON(1982)

Patty Shepard
ASSIGNMENT TERROR(1970, Ger./Span./Ital.); LEGEND OF FRENCHIE KING, THE(1971, Fr./Ital./Span./Brit.); MAN CALLED NOON, THE(1973, Brit.)
Misc. Talkies
HANNAH-QUEEN OF THE VAMPIRES(1972)

Pearl Shepard
Misc. Silents
BREAK THE NEWS TO MOTHER(1919); ECHO OF YOUTH, THE(1919); WAGES OF SIN, THE(1922)

Phil Shepard
ABBOTT AND COSTELLO MEET THE KILLER, BORIS KARLOFF(1949)

Richmond Shepard
SIMON, KING OF THE WITCHES(1971); YOU LIGHT UP MY LIFE(1977)

Richard A. Shepard
HUNGER, THE(1983), p

Sam Shepard
ME AND MY BROTHER(1969), w,Robert Frank; ZABRISKIE POINT(1970), w; OH! CALCUTTA!(1972), w; DAYS OF HEAVEN(1978); RENALDO AND CLARA(1978), a, w; RESURRECTION(1980); RAGGEDY MAN(1981); FRANCES(1982); RIGHT STUFF, THE(1983)
1984
COUNTRY(1984); PARIS, TEXAS(1984, Ger./Fr.), w

"Shep" Shepard
VAGABOND LADY(1935)

Ted Shepard
HANSEL AND GRETEL(1954), anim

Thomas Z. Shepard
TELL ME THAT YOU LOVE ME, JUNIE MOON(1970), md; SUCH GOOD FRIENDS(1971), m

Court Shepart
ALASKA PASSAGE(1959)

Jean Shepeard
THUNDER ROCK(1944, Brit.)

Honor Sheperd
LINKS OF JUSTICE(1958)

William Sheperd
IN THE WAKE OF THE BOUNTY(1933, Aus.), ed

Bill Shephard
FORTY THOUSAND HORSEMEN(1941, Aus.), ed

Randy Shephard
CUTTER AND BONE(1981)

William Shephard
PHANTOM OF THE PARADISE(1974), a, ch

Jean Shepheard
FAME IS THE SPUR(1947, Brit.); SILVER DARLINGS, THE(1947, Brit.); HER PANELLED DOOR(1951, Brit.)

Albert Shepherd
CHARLIE BUBBLES(1968, Brit.)

Ann Shepherd
DREAM NO MORE(1950, Palestine)

Antonio Shepherd
Misc. Talkies
CHORUS CALL(1979), d

Baby Shepherd
Misc. Silents
I HEAR YOU CALLING ME(1919, Brit.)

Bill Shepherd
IDOL ON PARADE(1959, Brit.), m; MINI-AFFAIR, THE(1968, Brit.), md

Bob Shepherd
BOOK OF NUMBERS(1973), art d

Chris Shepherd
BRONCO BULLFROG(1972, Brit.)

Cybill Shepherd
LAST PICTURE SHOW, THE(1971); HEARTBREAK KID, THE(1972); DAISY MILLER(1974); AT LONG LAST LOVE(1975); SPECIAL DELIVERY(1976); TAXI DRIVER(1976); SILVER BEARS(1978); LADY VANISHES, THE(1980, Brit.); RETURN, THE(1980)
Misc. Talkies
ALIEN'S RETURN, THE(1980)

Duncan Shepherd
QUEEN'S GUARDS, THE(1963, Brit.)

Elaine Shepherd
SINGING VAGABOND, THE(1935)

Elizabeth Shepherd
WHAT EVERY WOMAN WANTS(1962, Brit.); MAN IN THE DARK(1963, Brit.); TOMB OF LIGEIA, THE(1965, Brit.); HELL BOATS(1970, Brit.); DAMIEN-OMEN II(1978); DOUBLE NEGATIVE(1980, Can.); KIDNAPPING OF THE PRESIDENT, THE(1980, Can.); LOVE(1982, Can.)

Freda Shepherd
BRONCO BULLFROG(1972, Brit.)

Harvey Shepherd
MRS. PARKINGTON(1944)

Honor Shepherd
CALAMITY THE COW(1967, Brit.)

Horace Shepherd
MUSIC MAKER, THE(1936, Brit.), p, w; FLAMINGO AFFAIR, THE(1948, Brit.), p&d; HATTER'S CASTLE(1948, Brit.), m

Jack Shepherd
ALL NEAT IN BLACK STOCKINGS(1969, Brit.); VIRGIN SOLDIERS, THE(1970, Brit.); LAST VALLEY, THE(1971, Brit.); SOMETHING TO HIDE(1972, Brit.)

Jean Shepherd
INQUEST(1939, Brit.); GREAT DAY(1945, Brit.); NO PLACE FOR JENNIFER(1950, Brit.); LIGHT FANTASTIC(1964); CHRISTMAS STORY, A(1983), w

Jeanne Shepherd
ADVENTURES OF DON JUAN(1949)

K.J. Shepherd
TALKING FEET(1937, Brit.)

Keith Shepherd
NEUTRAL PORT(1941, Brit.); GIVE ME THE STARS(1944, Brit.); MY BROTHER'S KEEPER(1949, Brit.)

Leonard Shepherd
DREYFUS CASE, THE(1931, Brit.); LUCKY JADE(1937, Brit.)

Merrill Shepherd
LAST PICTURE SHOW, THE(1971)

Norma Shepherd
MIRACLE IN HARLEM(1948)

Pauline Shepherd
OPERATION CUPID(1960, Brit.); HOUSE OF FRIGHT(1961); I LIKE MONEY(1962, Brit.); MARRIAGE OF CONVENIENCE(1970, Brit.)

Richard Shepherd
HANGING TREE, THE(1959), p; BREAKFAST AT TIFFANY'S(1961), p; LOVE IN A GOLDFISH BOWL(1961), p; ALEX AND THE GYPSY(1976), p

Richard A. Shepherd
FUGITIVE KIND, THE(1960), p

Robert Shepherd
FIREFOX(1982), spec eff

Roger Shepherd
MIDSUMMERS NIGHT'S DREAM, A(1961, Czech); TO SIR, WITH LOVE(1967, Brit.)

Sally Shepherd
HOUSE OF FEAR, THE(1945); WOMAN IN GREEN, THE(1945); SNAKE PIT, THE(1948)

Sam Shepherd
BRONCO BULLFROG(1972, Brit.)

Sherry Lou Shepherd
ONCE UPON A COFFEE HOUSE(1965)

Simon Shepherd
LORDS OF DISCIPLINE, THE(1983)

Tina Shepherd
MILESTONES(1975)

Tony Shepherd
INFORMATION RECEIVED(1962, Brit.)

Una Shepherd
MISS LONDON LTD.(1943, Brit.)

Valerie Shepherd
HAVE A NICE WEEKEND(1975); THAT'S THE WAY OF THE WORLD(1975)

William Shepherd
VENGEANCE OF THE DEEP(1940, Aus.), ed

Carroll L. Shephird
HOT RODS TO HELL(1967), spec eff

Michael Shepley
SHOT IN THE DARK, A(1933, Brit.); ARE YOU A MASON?(1934, Brit.); BELLA DONNA(1934, Brit.); GREEN PACK, THE(1934, Brit.); LORD EDGEWARE DIES(1934, Brit.); OPEN ALL NIGHT(1934, Brit.); TANGLED EVIDENCE(1934, Brit.); ACE OF SPADES, THE(1935, Brit.); JUBILEE WINDOW(1935, Brit.); LAD, THE(1935, Brit.); LAZYBONES(1935, Brit.); PRIVATE SECRETARY, THE(1935, Brit.); SQUIBS(1935, Brit.); THAT'S MY UNCLE(1935, Brit.); TRIUMPH OF SHERLOCK HOLMES, THE(1935, Brit.); IN THE SOUP(1936, Brit.); BEAUTY AND THE BARGE(1937, Brit.); HIGH TREASON(1937, Brit.); HOUSEMASTER(1938, Brit.); MAN WITH 100 FACES, THE(1938, Brit.); IT'S IN THE AIR(1940, Brit.); QUIET WEDDING(1941, Brit.); GREAT MR. HANDEL, THE(1942, Brit.); WOMEN AREN'T ANGELS(1942, Brit.); ADVENTURE FOR TWO(1945, Brit.); PLACE OF ONE'S OWN, A(1945, Brit.); HENRY V(1946, Brit.); YANK IN LONDON, A(1946, Brit.); NICHOLAS NICKLEBY(1947, Brit.); MINE OWN EXECUTIONER(1948, Brit.); ELIZABETH OF LADYMEAD(1949, Brit.); MAYTIME IN MAYFAIR(1952, Brit.); SECRET PEOPLE(1952, Brit.); MR. DENNING DRIVES NORTH(1953, Brit.); MURDER ON MONDAY(1953, Brit.); TONIGHT'S THE NIGHT(1954, Brit.); TROUBLE IN THE GLEN(1954, Brit.); YOU KNOW WHAT SAILORS ARE(1954, Brit.); DOCTOR AT SEA(1955, Brit.); WHERE THERE'S A WILL(1955, Brit.); DRY ROT(1956, Brit.); ALLIGATOR NAMED DAISY, AN(1957, Brit.); NOT WANTED ON VOYAGE(1957, Brit.); NOVEL AFFAIR, A(1957, Brit.); GIDEON OF SCOTLAND YARD(1959, Brit.); TEENAGE BAD GIRL(1959, Brit.); JUST JOE(1960, Brit.); DOUBLE BUNK(1961, Brit.); WHY BOTHER TO KNOCK(1964, Brit.)

Ruth Shepley
Silents
WHEN KNIGHTHOOD WAS IN FLOWER(1922)
Misc. Silents
ALIAS JIMMY VALENTINE(1915)

John Shepodd
RETURN OF JACK SLADE, THE(1955)

Jon Shepodd
ATTACK!(1956); DRAGON WELLS MASSACRE(1957); GARMENT JUNGLE, THE(1957); OREGON PASSAGE(1958); I'LL GIVE MY LIFE(1959); WHATEVER HAPPENED TO BABY JANE?(1962)

Jon Shepord
MISSISSIPPI GAMBLER, THE(1953)
Archie Shepp
1984
BLESS THEIR LITTLE HEARTS(1984), m
Al Sheppard
1984
CORRUPT(1984, Ital.); EXTERMINATOR 2(1984)
Ann Sheppard
SONS AND LOVERS(1960, Brit.)
Anthony Sheppard
TWO LEFT FEET(1965, Brit.)
Misc. Talkies
MR. HORATIO KNIBBLES(1971)
Artie Sheppard
GEORGIA, GEORGIA(1972)
David P. Sheppard
BLACK ARROW(1948), w
Delia Sheppard
SPOTS ON MY LEOPARD, THE(1974, S. Africa)
Dolores Sheppard
LOVE AND KISSES(1965), cos
Ellen Sheppard
SATURDAY NIGHT AT THE BATHS(1975)
Gordon Sheppard
ELIZA'S HOROSCOPE(1975, Can.), p,d,w&ed
Guy Sheppard
$(DOLLARS), art d
Jim Sheppard
WILD AND THE INNOCENT, THE(1959); HOUR OF THE GUN(1967)
John Sheppard
1984
AMERICAN NIGHTMARE(1984), w
Morgan Sheppard
STRONGROOM(1962, Brit.); PERSECUTION AND ASSASSINATION OF JEAN-PAUL MARAT AS PERFORMED BY THE INMATES OF THE ASYLUM OF CHARENTON UNDER THE DIRECTION OF THE MARQUIS DE SADE, THE(1967, Brit.); TELL ME LIES(1968, Brit.); ELEPHANT MAN, THE(1980, Brit.); HAWK THE SLAYER(1980, Brit.); SEA WOLVES, THE(1981, Brit.); NUTCRACKER(1982, Brit.); KEEP, THE(1983)
1984
LASSITER(1984)
Patty Sheppard
FICKLE FINGER OF FATE, THE(1967, Span./U.S.); CRYPT OF THE LIVING DEAD zero(1973)
Paula Sheppard
ALICE, SWEET ALICE(1978)
Paula E. Sheppard
LIQUID SKY(1982)
Robert Sheppard
NO QUESTIONS ASKED(1951)
Sally Sheppard
MOSS ROSE(1947)
Stephen Sheppard
VILLAIN(1971, Brit.); LADY CAROLINE LAMB(1972, Brit./Ital.)
Patty Sheppaard
WEREWOLF VS. THE VAMPIRE WOMAN, THE(1970, Span./Ger.)
John Shepperd [Shepperd Strudwick]
BELLE STARR(1941); CADET GIRL(1941); MEN IN HER LIFE, THE(1941); REMEMBER THE DAY(1942); DR. RENAULT'S SECRET(1942); LOVES OF EDGAR ALLAN POE, THE(1942); RINGS ON HER FINGERS(1942); TEN GENTLEMEN FROM WEST POINT(1942); HOME SWEET HOMICIDE(1946); STRANGE TRIANGLE(1946)
Carroll Shepphird
KING KONG(1933), spec eff; SON OF KONG(1933), spec eff
Carroll L. Shepphird
WHEN THE BOYS MEET THE GIRLS(1965), spec eff; GLASS BOTTOM BOAT, THE(1966), spec eff; DOUBLE TROUBLE(1967), spec eff; VENETIAN AFFAIR, THE(1967), spec eff; SPEEDWAY(1968), spec eff; WHERE WERE YOU WHEN THE LIGHTS WENT OUT?(1968), spec eff
Sheppie the Dog
I MET A MURDERER(1939, Brit.)
John Shepridge
OTHELLO(1955, U.S./Fr./Ital.), ed
John C. Shepridge
RAPTURE(1950, Ital.), w
Anthony Sher
YANKS(1979)
Antony Sher
SUPERMAN II(1980)
Jack Sher
MY FAVORITE SPY(1951), w; KID FROM LEFT FIELD, THE(1953), w; OFF LIMITS(1953), w; SHANE(1953), w; FOUR GIRLS IN TOWN(1956), d&w; WALK THE PROUD LAND(1956), w; WORLD IN MY CORNER(1956), w; JOE BUTTERFLY(1957), w; KATHY O'(1958), d, w; WILD AND THE INNOCENT, THE(1959), d, w; THREE WORLDS OF GULLIVER, THE(1960, Brit.), d, w; LOVE IN A GOLDFISH BOWL(1961), w; PARIS BLUES(1961), w; CRITIC'S CHOICE(1963), w; MOVE OVER, DARLING(1963), w; SLITHER(1973), p
Mickey Sherard
GUNFIGHT, A(1971), cos
Phil Sherard
COUNTESS OF MONTE CRISTO, THE(1948)
Hugh Sheraton
WITNESS TO MURDER(1954)
V. Sherbachev
MEN OF THE SEA(1938, USSR), m
Maurice Sherbanee
JUD(1971); DON IS DEAD, THE(1973); FIRST FAMILY(1980); MAUSOLEUM(1983)
Sherbet
HIGH ROLLING(1977, Aus.), m

Michael Sherbrooke
IRON STAIR, THE(1933, Brit.)
Vera Sherburne
HOTEL SPLENDIDE(1932, Brit.); JIMMY BOY(1935, Brit.)
Ted Sherdeman
LUST FOR GOLD(1949, w; BREAKTHROUGH(1950), w; SCANDAL SHEET(1952), w; WINNING TEAM, THE(1952), w; EDDIE CANTOR STORY, THE(1953), w; RIDING SHOTGUN(1954), p; THEM!(1954), w; MC CONNELL STORY, THE(1955), w; AWAY ALL BOATS(1956), w; TOY TIGER(1956), w; MARACAIBO(1958), w; ST. LOUIS BLUES(1958), w; DOG OF FLANDERS, A(1959), w; HELL TO ETERNITY(1960), w; BIG SHOW, THE(1961), p, w; MISTY(1961), w; ISLAND OF THE BLUE DOLPHINS(1964), w; AND NOW MIGUEL(1966), w; LATITUDE ZERO(1969, U.S./Jap.), w; MY SIDE OF THE MOUNTAIN(1969), w
The Sherell Sisters
MOON OVER LAS VEGAS(1944)
Tony Sherer
TRADING PLACES(1983)
Edgar J. Sherick
I'M DANCING AS FAST AS I CAN(1982), p
Ann Sheridan
BEHOLD MY WIFE(1935); CAR 99(1935); CRUSADES, THE(1935); FIGHTING YOUTH(1935); GLASS KEY, THE(1935); HOME ON THE RANGE(1935); MISSISSIPPI(1935); ONE HOUR LATE(1935); RED BLOOD OF COURAGE(1935); ROCKY MOUNTAIN MYSTERY(1935); RUMBA(1935); SING ME A LOVE SONG(1936); ALCATRAZ ISLAND(1937); BLACK LEGION, THE(1937); FOOTLOOSE HEIRESS, THE(1937); GREAT O'MALLEY, THE(1937); SAN QUENTIN(1937); SHE LOVED A FIREMAN(1937); WINE, WOMEN AND HORSES(1937); ANGELS WITH DIRTY FACES(1938); BROADWAY MUSKETEERS(1938); COWBOY FROM BROOKLYN(1938); LETTER OF INTRODUCTION(1938); LITTLE MISS THOROUGHBRED(1938); MYSTERY HOUSE(1938); PATIENT IN ROOM 18, THE(1938); ANGELS WASH THEIR FACES(1939); DODGE CITY(1939); INDIANAPOLIS SPEEDWAY(1939); NAUGHTY BUT NICE(1939); THEY MADE ME A CRIMINAL(1939); WINTER CARNIVAL(1939); CASTLE ON THE HUDSON(1940); IT ALL CAME TRUE(1940); THEY DRIVE BY NIGHT(1940); TORRID ZONE(1940); CITY, FOR CONQUEST(1941); HONEYMOON FOR THREE(1941); NAVY BLUES(1941); GEORGE WASHINGTON SLEPT HERE(1942); JUKE GIRL(1942); KING'S ROW(1942); MAN WHO CAME TO DINNER, THE(1942); WINGS FOR THE EAGLE(1942); EDGE OF DARKNESS(1943); THANK YOUR LUCKY STARS(1943); DOUGHGIRLS, THE(1944); SHINE ON, HARVEST MOON(1944); ONE MORE TOMORROW(1946); NORA PRENTISS(1947); UNFAITHFUL, THE(1947); GOOD SAM(1948); SILVER RIVER(1948); TREASURE OF THE SIERRA MADRE, THE(1948); I WAS A MALE WAR BRIDE(1949); STELLA(1950); WOMAN ON THE RUN(1950); JUST ACROSS THE STREET(1952); STEEL TOWN(1952); APPOINTMENT IN HONDURAS(1953); TAKE ME TO TOWN(1953); COME NEXT SPRING(1956); OPPOSITE SEX, THE(1956); WOMAN AND THE HUNTER, THE(1957)
Anne Sheridan
Silents
BANDIT'S SON, THE(1927); CASEY AT THE BAT(1927); WAY OF ALL FLESH, THE(1927); WEDDING BILL$(1927)
Misc. Silents
GALLOPING THUNDER(1927)
Ardell Sheridan
GODFATHER, THE(1972)
Betty Sheridan
JORY(1972)
Cecil Sheridan
ULYSSES(1967, U.S./Brit.); VIKING QUEEN, THE(1967, Brit.)
Clara Lou [Ann] Sheridan
KISS AND MAKE UP(1934); LADIES SHOULD LISTEN(1934); LIMEHOUSE BLUES(1934); MRS. WIGGS OF THE CABBAGE PATCH(1934); MURDER AT THE VANITIES(1934); NOTORIOUS SOPHIE LANG, THE(1934); READY FOR LOVE(1934); SEARCH FOR BEAUTY(1934); SHOOT THE WORKS(1934); WAGON WHEELS(1934)
Clara Lou Sheridan
COME ON, MARINES(1934)
Dan Sheridan
BULLWHIP(1958); COLE YOUNGER, GUNFIGHTER(1958); HELL'S FIVE HOURS(1958); I WANT TO LIVE!(1958); SEVEN GUNS TO MESA(1958); DAY OF THE OUTLAW(1959); KING OF THE WILD STALLIONS(1959); YOUNG CAPTIVES, THE(1959); HOME FROM THE HILL(1960); TEN WHO DARED(1960); LONELY ARE THE BRAVE(1962)
Dani Sheridan
SORCERERS, THE(1967, Brit.); ON HER MAJESTY'S SECRET SERVICE(1969, Brit.)
Daniel M. Sheridan
CALIFORNIA FIREBRAND(1948); HORSEMEN OF THE SIERRAS(1950)
Dinah Sheridan
BEHIND YOUR BACK(1937, Brit.); FATHER STEPS OUT(1937, Brit.); LANDSLIDE(1937, Brit.); IRISH AND PROUD OF IT(1938, Ireland); MERELY MR. HAWKINS(1938, Brit.); FULL SPEED AHEAD(1939, Brit.); SALUTE JOHN CITIZEN(1942, Brit.); GET CRACKING(1943, Brit.); FOR YOU ALONE(1945, Brit.); QUERY(1945, Brit.); MURDER IN REVERSE(1946, Brit.); HILLS OF DONEGAL, THE(1947, Brit.); CALLING PAUL TEMPLE(1948, Brit.); STORY OF SHIRLEY YORKE, THE(1948, Brit.); DARK SECRET(1949, Brit.); FACTS OF LOVE(1949, Brit.); HUGGETTS ABROAD, THE(1949, Brit.); BLACKOUT(1950, Brit.); NO TRACE(1950, Brit.); PAUL TEMPLE'S TRIUMPH(1951, Brit.); BREAKING THE SOUND BARRIER(1952, Brit.); IVORY HUNTER(1952, Brit.); APPOINTMENT IN LONDON(1953, Brit.); GENEVIEVE(1953, Brit.); GREAT GILBERT AND SULLIVAN, THE(1953, Brit.); RAILWAY CHILDREN, THE(1971, Brit.); MIRROR CRACK'D, THE(1980, Brit.)
Frank Sheridan
FAST LIFE(1929); SIDE STREET(1929); DANGER LIGHTS(1930); OTHER TOMORROW, THE(1930); FLOOD, THE(1931); FREE SOUL, A(1931); MURDER BY THE CLOCK(1931); PUBLIC DEFENDER, THE(1931); SILENCE(1931); YOUNG DONOVAN'S KID(1931); AFRAID TO TALK(1932); BROKEN LULLABY(1932); LADIES OF THE BIG HOUSE(1932); LAST MILE, THE(1932); OKAY AMERICA(1932); WASHINGTON MERRY-GO-ROUND(1932); DECEPTION(1933); LADY KILLER(1933); MAMA LOVES PAPA(1933); MAN WHO DARED(1933); WOMAN ACCUSED(1933); CAT'S PAW, THE(1934); MERRY WIDOW, THE(1934); STAND UP AND CHEER(1934 80m FOX bw); UPPER WORLD(1934); WHARF ANGEL(1934); WITCHING HOUR, THE(1934); FRISCO KID(1935); MEN WITHOUT NAMES(1935); PAYOFF, THE(1935); REVENGE RIDER(1935); ROMANCE IN MANHATTAN(1935); SPANISH CAPE MYSTERY(1935); STRANDED(1935); WHISPERING SMITH SPEAKS(1935); WHOLE

TOWN'S TALKING, THE(1935); LEAVENWORTH CASE, THE(1936); LITTLE RED SCHOOLHOUSE(1936); MURDER WITH PICTURES(1936); NEVADA(1936); SAN FRANCISCO(1936); UNDER YOUR SPELL(1936); CONFLICT(1937); COUNTRY GENTLEMEN(1937); FIGHT TO THE FINISH, A(1937); GREAT O'MALLEY, THE(1937); LIFE OF EMILE ZOLA, THE(1937); MAYTIME(1937); WOMAN IN DISTRESS(1937); CITY STREETS(1938); HEROES IN BLUE(1939)
Misc. Talkies
BROKEN HEARTS(1933)
Silents
ANNE OF LITTLE SMOKY(1921); ONE EXCITING NIGHT(1922)
Misc. Silents
AT BAY(1915); MONEY MASTER, THE(1915); PERILS OF DIVORCE(1916); STRUGGLE, THE(1916); ENLIGHTEN THY DAUGHTER(1917); RULER OF THE ROAD(1918); VENGEANCE IS MINE(1918); HER LORD AND MASTER(1921); RIDER OF THE KING LOG, THE(1921); MAN NEXT DOOR, THE(1923); TWO SHALL BE BORN(1924)

Gail Sheridan
HOPALONG CASSIDY RETURNS(1936); THREE MARRIED MEN(1936); HILLS OF OLD WYOMING(1937); PLAINSMAN, THE(1937)
Gale Sheridan
SHE ALWAYS GETS THEIR MAN(1962, Brit.); THREE SPARE WIVES(1962, Brit.)
Gay Sheridan
CEILNG ZERO(1935)
Hugh S. Sheridan
PRESCRIPTION FOR ROMANCE(1937)
Jack Sheridan
DOZENS, THE(1981)
James Sheridan
DAWN RIDER(1935); TIMBER TERRORS(1935); RIDERS OF THE DAWN(1937); WHERE TRAILS DIVIDE(1937); DRIFTING WESTWARD(1939); OVERLAND MAIL(1939); RIDING THE SUNSET TRAIL(1941); WANDERERS OF THE WEST(1941); LONE STAR LAW MEN(1942); WESTERN MAIL(1942)
Misc. Talkies
LONE RIDER, THE(1934); SUNDOWN TRAIL, THE(1975)
Jay Sheridan
VICE RACKET(1937); NASHVILLE REBEL(1966), d, w
Jill Sheridan
LASERBLAST(1978), cos
Jimmy Sheridan
CLOSE-UP(1948)
John Sheridan
HOLLYWOOD CANTEEN(1944); MILDRED PIERCE(1945); OBJECTIVE, BURMA!(1945); PRIDE OF THE MARINES(1945); ROUGHLY SPEAKING(1945); TOO YOUNG TO KNOW(1945); JANIE GETS MARRIED(1946)
Laurie Sheridan
HOUSE OF WOMEN(1962)
Liz Sheridan
JEKYLL AND HYDE...TOGETHER AGAIN(1982); STAR 80(1983)
Margaret Sheridan
THING, THE(1951); ONE MINUTE TO ZERO(1952); I, THE JURY(1953); DIAMOND WIZARD, THE(1954, Brit.); PRIDE OF THE BLUE GRASS(1954); MAN'S FAVORITE SPORT [?](1964)
Mary Sheridan
OVER THE GARDEN WALL(1934, Brit.)
Michael J. Sheridan
CHAMP, THE(1979), ed; ENDLESS LOVE(1981), ed
Michael Sheridan
CRY OF THE CITY(1948); STREET WITH NO NAME, THE(1948)
Noel Sheridan
MURDER IN EDEN(1962, Brit.)
Oscar M. Sheridan
BIG BUSINESS(1930, Brit.), p&d, w; SUCH WOMEN ARE DANGEROUS(1934), w
Otis Sheridan
NIGHT ANGEL, THE(1931); SWEET SURRENDER(1935)
Paul Sheridan
IT HAPPENED IN PARIS(1935, Brit.); LAST WALTZ, THE(1936, Brit.); SUCH IS LIFE(1936, Brit.); WELL DONE, HENRY(1936, Brit.); CATCH AS CATCH CAN(1937, Brit.); TAKE MY TIP(1937, Brit.); HIS LORDSHIP REGRETS(1938, Brit.); IF I WERE BOSS(1938, Brit.); KATE PLUS TEN(1938, Brit.); LAST BARRICADE, THE(1938, Brit.); RAT, THE(1938, Brit.); ROMANCE A LA CARTE(1938, Brit.); THIS MAN IN PARIS(1939, Brit.); SECRET FOUR, THE(1940, Brit.); PETERVILLE DIAMOND, THE(1942, Brit.); CANDLELIGHT IN ALGERIA(1944, Brit.); 2,000 WOMEN(1944, Brit.); LATE AT NIGHT(1946, Brit.); MAN FROM MOROCCO, THE(1946, Brit.); MY BROTHER JONATHAN(1949, Brit.); OLD MOTHER RILEY, HEADMISTRESS(1950, Brit.); GAMBLER AND THE LADY, THE(1952, Brit.); OLD MOTHER RILEY(1952, Brit.); PENNY PRINCESS(1953, Brit.); DESTINATION MILAN(1954, Brit.); PORTRAIT IN SMOKE(1957, Brit.); FRENCH MISTRESS(1960, Brit.); WHO KILLED VAN LOON?(1984, Brit.)
Richard Brinsley Sheridan
SCHOOL FOR SCANDAL, THE(1930, Brit.), w
Sybil Sheridan
Misc. Silents
BEHOLD THE MAN(1921, US/Fr.)
Tommy Sheridan
RED PONY, THE(1949)
William Sheridan
WOLFEN(1981)
Fenn Sherie
BLUE SMOKE(1935, Brit.), w; LATE EXTRA(1935, Brit.), w; SPORTING LOVE(1936, Brit.), w; TERROR ON TIPTOE(1936, Brit.), w; BIG FELLA(1937, Brit.), w; LEAVE IT TO ME(1937, Brit.), w; AROUND THE TOWN(1938, Brit.), w; I'VE GOT A HORSE(1938, Brit.), w; SONG OF FREEDOM(1938, Brit.), w; HOME FROM HOME(1939, Brit.), w
Julian Sherier
LAUGHING ANNE(1954, Brit./U.S.)
Naom Sheriff
CLOUDS OVER ISRAEL(1966, Israel), m

Paul Sheriff
FRENCH WITHOUT TEARS(1939, Brit.), art d; QUIET WEDDING(1941, Brit.), art d; SAINT'S VACATION, THE(1941, Brit.), art d; VOICE IN THE NIGHT, A(1941, Brit.), art d; SAINT MEETS THE TIGER, THE(1943, Brit.), art d; SPITFIRE(1943, Brit.), art d; ADVENTURE FOR TWO(1945, Brit.), art d; JOHNNY IN THE CLOUDS(1945, Brit.), art d; HENRY V(1946, Brit.), art d; HAMLET(1948, Brit.), spec eff; BLACK ROSE, THE(1950), art d; MOULIN ROUGE(1952), art d; CAPTAIN'S PARADISE, THE(1953, Brit.), art d; MAN WHO LOVED REDHEADS, THE(1955, Brit.), set d; THREE CASES OF MURDER(1955, Brit.), prod d; PICKUP ALLEY(1957, Brit.), art d; DOCTOR'S DILEMMA, THE(1958, Brit.), art d; LIBEL(1959, Brit.), art d; GRASS IS GREENER, THE(1960), art d; MILLIONAIRESS, THE(1960, Brit.), prod d; LAST REBEL, THE(1971); SACCO AND VANZETTI(1971, Ital./Fr.)
R.C. Sheriff
JOURNEY'S END(1930), w; INVISIBLE MAN, THE(1933), w; STAND BY FOR ACTION(1942), w; ODD MAN OUT(1947, Brit.), w; BADGER'S GREEN(1949, Brit.), w; TRIO(1950, Brit.), w; NIGHT MY NUMBER CAME UP, THE(1955, Brit.), w; STORM OVER THE NILE(1955, Brit.), w
Sidney Sheriff, Jr.
1984
BROTHER FROM ANOTHER PLANET, THE(1984)
W.C. Sheriff
GOODBYE MR. CHIPS(1939, Brit.), w
Wade Boteler Sheriff
THIS DAY AND AGE(1933)
The Sheriff's Boys Band
GOOD LUCK, MR. YATES(1943)
Elizabeth Sherill
HIDING PLACE, THE(1975), w
Jack Sherill
Misc. Silents
CRUCIBLE OF LIFE, THE(1918); PROFITEER, THE(1919)
John Sherill
HIDING PLACE, THE(1975), w
Martha Sherill
SEDUCTION OF JOE TYNAN, THE(1979)
Edwin Sherin
GLORY BOY(1971), d; VALDEZ IS COMING(1971), d
Leo "Ukie" Sherin
CRAZY OVER HORSES(1951); FEUDIN' FOOLS(1952); NO HOLDS BARRED(1952)
"Ukie" Sherin
BELA LUGOSI MEETS A BROOKLYN GORILLA(1952), w
Gretl Sherk
UNDERGROUND(1941)
Leon Sherkot
DANCE BAND(1935, Brit.); MERRY-G0-ROUND(1948, Brit.)
Charles Sherlock
DEVIL DOGS OF THE AIR(1935); G-MEN(1935); SHE COULDN'T TAKE IT(1935); ROSE BOWL(1936); UNDER YOUR SPELL(1936); WEDDING PRESENT(1936); INTERNES CAN'T TAKE MONEY(1937); THAT CERTAIN WOMAN(1937); I AM THE LAW(1938); CONFESSIONS OF A NAZI SPY(1939); FORGOTTEN WOMAN, THE(1939); GOLDEN BOY(1939); KING OF THE TURF(1939); ONE HOUR TO LIVE(1939); PIRATES OF THE SKIES(1939); CASTLE ON THE HUDSON(1940); I TAKE THIS WOMAN(1940); MURDER IN THE AIR(1940); THEY DRIVE BY NIGHT(1940); 'TIL WE MEET AGAIN(1940); MANPOWER(1941); MODEL WIFE(1941); SAN FRANCISCO DOCKS(1941); MADAME SPY(1942); MOONLIGHT IN HAVANA(1942); NAZI AGENT(1942); PITTSBURGH(1942); SABOTEUR(1942); YOU'RE TELLING ME(1942); FOLLOW THE BAND(1943); GOOD MORNING, JUDGE(1943); DESTINATION TOKYO(1944); IN SOCIETY(1944); LOUISIANA HAYRIDE(1944); CHRISTMAS IN CONNECTICUT(1945); LADY ON A TRAIN(1945); SCARLET CLUE, THE(1945); SHE GETS HER MAN(1945); UNDER WESTERN SKIES(1945); SUSPENSE(1946); STATE OF THE UNION(1948); TASK FORCE(1949); UNDERTOW(1949); CONVICTED(1950); SHAKEDOWN(1950); UNION STATION(1950); DARLING, HOW COULD YOU!(1951); I WAS A COMMUNIST FOR THE F.B.I.(1951); KANSAS CITY CONFIDENTIAL(1952); TURNING POINT, THE(1952)
Charles P. Sherlock
MY BUDDY(1944)
Charlie Sherlock
LETTER OF INTRODUCTION(1938)
Jerry Sherlock
CHARLIE CHAN AND THE CURSE OF THE DRAGON QUEEN(1981), p, w
John Sherlock
LAST GRENADE, THE(1970, Brit.), w
Norman Sherlock
DRIVE-IN MASSACRE(1976)
Sharon Sherlock
BRONCO BILLY(1980)
Tom Sherlock
OUTSIDER, THE(1962)
Laurie Shermain
NIGHT AND DAY(1946)
Aaron Sherman
1984
SWORD OF THE VALIANT(1984, Brit.), spec eff
Al Sherman
SCARLET RIVER(1933), art d; SENSATIONS OF 1945(1944), m
Alan Sherman
Misc. Talkies
PEPPER AND HIS WACKY TAXI(1972)
Alida Sherman
SLAVES(1969), w
Anne Sherman
MURDER CLINIC, THE(1967, Ital./Fr.)
Annyse Sherman
STORM OVER LISBON(1944)
Arthur Sherman
SHADOW VALLEY(1947), w; NORMAN LOVES ROSE(1982, Aus.)
Bob Sherman
KISS ME DEADLY(1955); GREAT GATSBY, THE(1974); PINK PANTHER STRIKES AGAIN, THE(1976, Brit.); SPY WHO LOVED ME, THE(1977, Brit.); FIRST MONDAY IN OCTOBER(1981); FINAL OPTION, THE(1983, Brit.)

1984
SHEENA(1984)
Bobby Sherman
GET CRAZY(1983)
Misc. Talkies
HE IS MY BROTHER(1976)
Charles Sherman
DU BARRY WAS A LADY(1943), w
Claudia Sherman
BABY, IT'S YOU(1983)
Courtney Sherman
DIRTYMOUTH(1970)
Didi Sherman
OPEN SEASON(1974, U.S./Span.)
Don Sherman
ROCKY(1976); ROCKY III(1982); GOING BERSERK(1983)
Editta Sherman
MS. 45(1981)
Ellen Sherman
LOOKING UP(1977)
Eric Sherman
SALLY'S HOUNDS(1968)
Eugene Sherman
JEANNE EAGELS(1957)
Evelyn Sherman
SONG OF THE CABELLERO(1930)
Silents
SCHOOL DAYS(1921); SUZANNA(1922); RENO(1923); PROUD FLESH(1925)
Misc. Silents
SPEED MADNESS(1925)
Eward Sherman
WAVE, A WAC AND A MARINE, A(1944), p
Fred Sherman
HI, NEIGHBOR(1942); SHEPHERD OF THE OZARKS(1942); TOO MANY WO-
MEN(1942); WILDCAT(1942); WRECKING CREW(1942); BEHIND GREEN
LIGHTS(1946); CHAIN LIGHTNING(1950); VALLEY OF FIRE(1951); STRANGER AT
MY DOOR(1956); GUN BATTLE AT MONTEREY(1957); NO TIME TO BE
YOUNG(1957); WAR DRUMS(1957); SPACE MASTER X-7(1958); ALASKA PASS-
AGE(1959); WESTBOUND(1959); WHY MUST I DIE?(1960); TWIST ALL NIGHT(1961)
Fred E. Sherman
LADY IN THE LAKE(1947); MYSTERY STREET(1950); TALL T, THE(1957)
Garry Sherman
HEARTBREAK KID, THE(1972), m; PARADES(1972), m, md
Gary Sherman
DEATHLINE(1973, Brit.), d, w; BEEN DOWN SO LONG IT LOOKS LIKE UP TO
ME(1977), m; PHOBIA(1980, Can.), w
Gary A. Sherman
DEAD AND BURIED(1981), d; VICE SQUAD(1982), d
George Sherman
HEROES OF THE HILLS(1938), d; OUTLAWS OF SONORA(1938), d; OVERLAND
STAGE RAIDERS(1938), d; PALS OF THE SADDLE(1938), d; PURPLE VIGILANTES,
THE(1938), d; RED RIVER RANGE(1938), d; RHYTHM OF THE SADDLE(1938), d;
RIDERS OF THE BLACK HILLS(1938), d; SANTA FE STAMPEDE(1938), d; WILD
HORSE RODEO(1938), d; COLORADO SUNSET(1939), d; COWBOYS FROM TEX-
AS(1939), d; FRONTIER VENGEANCE(1939), d; IN OLD MONTEREY(1939), w; KAN-
SAS TERRORS, THE(1939), d; MEXICALI ROSE(1939), d; NEW FRONTIER(1939), d;
NIGHT RIDERS, THE(1939), d; ROVIN' TUMBLEWEEDS(1939), d; SOUTH OF THE
BORDER(1939), d; THREE TEXAS STEERS(1939), d; WYOMING OUTLAW(1939), d;
COVERED WAGON DAYS(1940), d; GHOST VALLEY RAIDERS(1940), p&d; LONE
STAR RAIDERS(1940), d; ONE MAN'S LAW(1940), d; ROCKY MOUNTAIN RANG-
ERS(1940), d; TEXAS TERRORS(1940), p&d; TRAIL BLAZERS, THE(1940), d; TULSA
KID, THE(1940), d; UNDER TEXAS SKIES(1940), d; APACHE KID, THE(1941),
p&d; CITADEL OF CRIME(1941), p&d; DEATH VALLEY OUTLAWS(1941), p&d;
DESERT BANDIT(1941), p&d; KANSAS CYCLONE(1941), p&d; PHANTOM COW-
BOY, THE(1941), p&d; TWO GUN SHERIFF(1941), p&d; WYOMING WILDCAT(1941),
p&d; ARIZONA TERRORS(1942), p&d; CYCLONE KID, THE(1942), p&d; JESSE
JAMES, JR.(1942), p&d; LONDON BLACKOUT MURDERS(1942), p&d; MISSOURI
OUTLAW, A(1942), p&d; SOMBRERO KID, THE(1942), p&d; STAGECOACH EX-
PRESS(1942), p&d; X MARKS THE SPOT(1942), p&d; FALSE FACES(1943), p&d;
MANTRAP, THE(1943), p&d; MYSTERY BROADCAST(1943), p&d; PURPLE V,
THE(1943), p&d; SCREAM IN THE DARK, A(1943), p&d; WEST SIDE KID(1943),
p&d; LADY AND THE MONSTER, THE(1944), p&d; STORM OVER LISBON(1944),
p&d; CRIME DOCTOR'S COURAGE, THE(1945), d; BANDIT OF SHERWOOD FOR-
EST, THE(1946), d; GENTLEMAN MISBEHAVES, THE(1946), d; PERSONALITY
KID(1946), d; RENEGADES(1946), d; SECRET OF THE WHISTLER(1946), d; TALK
ABOUT A LADY(1946), d; LAST OF THE REDMEN(1947), d; BLACK BART(1948), d;
FEUDIN', FUSSIN' AND A-FIGHTIN'(1948), d; LARCENY(1948), d; RELENT-
LESS(1948), d; RIVER LADY(1948), d; CALAMITY JANE AND SAM BASS(1949), d,
w; RED CANYON(1949), d; SWORD IN THE DESERT(1949), d; YES SIR, THAT'S MY
BABY(1949), d; COMMANCHE TERRITORY(1950), d; SLEEPING CITY, THE(1950),
d; SPY HUNT(1950), d; GOLDEN HORDE, THE(1951), d; RAGING TIDE, THE(1951),
d; TARGET UNKNOWN(1951), d; TOMAHAWK(1951), d; AGAINST ALL
FLAGS(1952), d; BACK AT THE FRONT(1952), d; BATTLE AT APACHE PASS,
THE(1952), d; STEEL TOWN(1952), d; LONE HAND, THE(1953), d; VEILS OF BAG-
DAD, THE(1953), d; WAR ARROW(1953), d; BORDER RIVER(1954), d; DAWN AT
SOCORRO(1954), d; JOHNNY DARK(1954), d; CHIEF CRAZY HORSE(1955), d;
COUNT THREE AND PRAY(1955), d; TREASURE OF PANCHO VILLA, THE(1955),
d; COMANCHE(1956), d; REPRISAL(1956), d; HARD MAN, THE(1957), d; LAST OF
THE FAST GUNS, THE(1958), d; TEN DAYS TO TULARA(1958), p, d; FLYING
FONTAINES, THE(1959), d; SON OF ROBIN HOOD(1959, Brit.), p&d; ENEMY GEN-
ERAL, THE(1960), d; FOR THE LOVE OF MIKE(1960), p&d; HELL BENT FOR
LEATHER(1960), d; WIZARD OF BAGHDAD, THE(1960), d; COMANCHEROS,
THE(1961), p; FIERCEST HEART, THE(1961), p&d; PANIC BUTTON(1964), d;
MURIETA(1965, Span.), d; SMOKY(1966), d; HELLO DOWN THERE(1969), p; BIG
JAKE(1971), d
George L. Sherman
PURSUIT OF HAPPINESS, THE(1971), w

Geraldine Sherman
DEADFALL(1968, Brit.); INTERLUDE(1968, Brit.); POOR COW(1968, Brit.); TAKE A
GIRL LIKE YOU(1970, Brit.); THERE'S A GIRL IN MY SOUP(1970, Brit.); GET
CARTER(1971, Brit.); CRY OF THE PENGUINS(1972, Brit.)
Hal Sherman
WHITE RAT(1972)
Misc. Silents
GLAD EYE, THE(1927, Brit.)
Harold Sherman
ARE WE CIVILIZED?(1934), w
Harold M. Sherman
ADVENTURES OF MARK TWAIN, THE(1944), w
Harry Sherman
LIGHT OF WESTERN STARS, THE(1930), p; HOPALONG CASSIDY(1935), p; BAR
20 RIDES AGAIN(1936), p; CALL OF THE PRAIRIE(1936), p; EAGLE'S BROOD,
THE(1936), p; HOPALONG CASSIDY RETURNS(1936), p; THREE ON THE
TRAIL(1936), p; TRAIL DUST(1936), p; BARRIER, THE(1937), p; BORDER-
LAND(1937), p; HEART OF THE WEST(1937), p; HILLS OF OLD WYOMING(1937), p;
HOPALONG RIDES AGAIN(1937), p; NORTH OF THE RIO GRANDE(1937), p;
RUSTLER'S VALLEY(1937), p; TEXAS TRAIL(1937), p; BAR 20 JUSTICE(1938), p;
CASSIDY OF BAR 20(1938), p; FRONTIERSMAN, THE(1938), p; HEART OF ARIZO-
NA(1938), p; IN OLD MEXICO(1938), p; MYSTERIOUS RIDER, THE(1938), p; PART-
NERS OF THE PLAINS(1938), p; PRIDE OF THE WEST(1938), p; SUNSET
TRAIL(1938), p; HERITAGE OF THE DESERT(1939), p; LAW OF THE PAM-
PAS(1939), p; RANGE WAR(1939), p; RENEGADE TRAIL(1939), p; SILVER ON THE
SAGE(1939), p; CHEROKEE STRIP(1940), p; HIDDEN GOLD(1940), p; KNIGHTS OF
THE RANGE(1940), p; LIGHT OF WESTERN STARS, THE(1940), p; LLANO KID,
THE(1940), p; SANTA FE MARSHAL(1940), p; SHOWDOWN, THE(1940), p; STAGE-
COACH WAR(1940), p; THREE MEN FROM TEXAS(1940), p; BORDER VIGI-
LANTES(1941), p; BOSS OF BULLION CITY(1941), p; DOOMED CARAVAN(1941), p;
IN OLD COLORADO(1941), p; OUTLAWS OF THE DESERT(1941), p; PARSON OF
PANAMINT, THE(1941), p; PIRATES ON HORSEBACK(1941), p; ROUNDUP,
THE(1941), p; SECRETS OF THE WASTELANDS(1941), p; STICK TO YOUR
GUNS(1941), p; TWILIGHT ON THE TRAIL(1941), p; WIDE OPEN TOWN(1941), p;
AMERICAN EMPIRE(1942), p; SILVER QUEEN(1942), p; TOMBSTONE, THE TOWN
TOO TOUGH TO DIE(1942), p; UNDERCOVER MAN(1942), p; BAR 20(1943), p;
BORDER PATROL(1943), p; BUCKSKIN FRONTIER(1943), p; COLT COM-
RADES(1943), p; FALSE COLORS(1943), p; HOPPY SERVES A WRIT(1943), p; KAN-
SAN, THE(1943), p; LEATHER BURNERS, THE(1943), p; LOST CANYON(1943), p;
RIDERS OF THE DEADLINE(1943), p; WOMAN OF THE TOWN, THE(1943), p;
RAMROD(1947), p; FOUR FACES WEST(1948), p
Harry A. Sherman
BUFFALO BILL(1944), p; FORTY THIEVES(1944), p; LUMBERJACK(1944), p;
MYSTERY MAN(1944), p; TEXAS MASQUERADE(1944), p
Hiram Sherman
ONE THIRD OF A NATION(1939); FANFAN THE TULIP(1952, Fr.); SOLID GOLD
CADILLAC, THE(1956); MARY, MARY(1963); OH DAD, POOR DAD, MAMA'S HUNG
YOU IN THE CLOSET AND I'M FEELIN' SO SAD(1967)
Howard Sherman
1984
ULTIMATE SOLUTION OF GRACE QUIGLEY, THE(1984)
Jack Sherman
SELLOUT, THE(1951); PRIDE OF ST. LOUIS, THE(1952); WILD BLUE YONDER,
THE(1952)
Jane Sherman
Silents
HUNCHBACK OF NOTRE DAME, THE(1923); MERRY-GO-ROUND(1923); GOLD
RUSH, THE(1925); VANISHING HOOFS(1926)
Janine Sherman
DR. FRANKENSTEIN ON CAMPUS(1970, Can.)
Jeff Sherman
1984
UP THE CREEK(1984), w
Jenny Sherman
MEAN JOHNNY BARROWS(1976)
John Sherman
HASTY HEART, THE(1949); LES MISERABLES(1952); KNIGHTS OF THE ROUND
TABLE(1953); SCANDAL AT SCOURIE(1953); BLACK ICE, THE(1957, Brit.), w;
MENACE IN THE NIGHT(1958, Brit.), w; JACKPOT(1960, Brit.), w
Jonathan Adam Sherman
DEATH VENGEANCE(1982)
Joseph Sherman
DEATH OF THE DIAMOND(1934), w
Kerry Sherman
SATAN'S CHEERLEADERS(1977); 1941(1979); 48 HOURS(1982)
Lenny Sherman
SHE'S BACK ON BROADWAY(1953)
Leo Sherman
MURDER IN THE FLEET(1935), w
Lew Sherman
IT'S A WONDERFUL DAY(1949, Brit.)
Lou Sherman
GANG WAR(1940), w
Lowell Sherman
LADY OF CHANCE, A(1928); EVIDENCE(1929); GENERAL CRACK(1929); HE
KNEW WOMEN(1930); LADIES OF LEISURE(1930); LAWFUL LARCENY(1930), a, d;
MAMMY(1930); MIDNIGHT MYSTERY(1930); OH! SAILOR, BEHAVE!(1930); PAY
OFF, THE(1930), a, d; BACHELOR APARTMENT(1931), a, d; HIGH STAKES(1931),
a, d; ROYAL BED, THE(1931), a, d; FALSE FACES(1931), a, d; GREEKS HAD A
WORD FOR THEM(1932), a, d; LADIES OF THE JURY(1932), d; WHAT PRICE
HOLLYWOOD?(1932); BROADWAY THROUGH A KEYHOLE(1933), d; MORNING
GLORY(1933), d; SHE DONE HIM WRONG(1933), d; BORN TO BE BAD(1934), d;
NIGHT LIFE OF THE GODS(1935), d
Silents
SOLD(1915); NEW YORK IDEA, THE(1920); WAY DOWN EAST(1920); GILDED
LILY, THE(1921); MOLLY O'(1921); WHAT NO MAN KNOWS(1921); MONSIEUR
BEAUCAIRE(1924); SPITFIRE, THE(1924); LOVE TOY, THE(1926); RECKLESS
LADY, THE(1926); WILDERNESS WOMAN, THE(1926); CONVOY(1927); DIVINE
WOMAN, THE(1928); HEART OF A FOLLIES GIRL, THE(1928); SCARLET DOVE,
THE(1928); WHIP WOMAN, THE(1928)

Misc. Silents
BEHIND THE SCENES(1914); ALWAYS IN THE WAY(1915); BETTER WOMAN, THE(1915); VERA, THE MEDIUM(1916); YES OR NO?(1920); FACE IN THE FOG, THE(1922); MASKED DANCER, THE(1924); TRUTH ABOUT WOMEN, THE(1924); SATAN IN SABLES(1925); LOST AT SEA(1926); YOU NEVER KNOW WOMEN(1926); GIRL FROM GAY PAREE, THE(1927); GARDEN OF EDEN, THE(1928); WHIP, THE(1928)

Lynn Sherman
CAGED(1950)

Marion Sherman
GANG WAR(1958)

May Sherman
Misc. Silents
FIGHTING HEART, A(1924)

Michael Sherman
1984
CALIFORNIA GIRLS(1984), d&w

Miss Sherman
Silents
SIN THAT WAS HIS, THE(1920)

Orville Sherman
BRAIN EATERS, THE(1958); HOME FROM THE HILL(1960); MY FAIR LADY(1964); DEAR BRIGETTE(1965); ONCE YOU KISS A STRANGER(1969); PRETTY MAIDS ALL IN A ROW(1971); WESTWORLD(1973); YOUR THREE MINUTES ARE UP(1973)

Paul Sherman
MARCH OR DIE(1977, Brit.)

Ransom Sherman
SWING YOUR PARTNER(1943); ALWAYS TOGETHER(1947); BACHELOR AND THE BOBBY-SOXER, THE(1947); DISHONORED LADY(1947); HIGH BAR-BAREE(1947); HUCKSTERS, THE(1947); YANKEE FAKIR(1947); ARE YOU WITH IT?(1948); COUNTESS OF MONTE CRISTO, THE(1948); WHIPLASH(1948); WINTER MEETING(1948); ALWAYS LEAVE THEM LAUGHING(1949); FLAMING FURY(1949); ONE LAST FLING(1949); NANCY GOES TO RIO(1950); PRETTY BABY(1950); SIDE STREET(1950)

Ransom M. Sherman
GENTLEMAN'S AGREEMENT(1947)

Ray Sherman
PETE KELLY'S BLUES(1955); SUMMER LOVE(1958)

Reed Sherman
SABRE JET(1953); COMANCHE(1956); BIG DADDY(1969); NAME FOR EVIL, A(1970), a, p

Richard Sherman
TO MARY–WITH LOVE(1936), w; FOUR MEN AND A PRAYER(1938), w; GIRLS' SCHOOL(1938), w; IN NAME ONLY(1939), w; STORY OF VERNON AND IRENE CASTLE, THE(1939), w; FOR ME AND MY GAL(1942), w; JOHNNY IN THE CLOUDS(1945, Brit.), w; TOM SAWYER(1973), m

Richard M. Sherman
HAPPIEST MILLIONAIRE, THE(1967), m; ONE AND ONLY GENUINE ORIGINAL FAMILY BAND, THE(1968), m; CHARLOTTE'S WEB(1973), m; TOM SAWYER(1973), w; HUCKLEBERRY FINN(1974), w; SLIPPER AND THE ROSE, THE(1976, Brit.), w, m; MAGIC OF LASSIE, THE(1978), w

Robert Sherman
FOR MEN ONLY(1952); FANGS OF THE ARCTIC(1953); BATTLE TAXI(1955); BIG KNIFE, THE(1955); AUTUMN LEAVES(1956); CALYPSO JOE(1957); KISS THEM FOR ME(1957); NO TIME FOR SERGEANTS(1958); PICTURE MOMMY DEAD(1966), a, w; TOO LATE THE HERO(1970), w; TOM SAWYER(1973), m; TWILIGHT'S LAST GLEAMING(1977, U.S./Ger.)

Robert B. Sherman
HAPPIEST MILLIONAIRE, THE(1967), m; ONE AND ONLY GENUINE ORIGINAL FAMILY BAND, THE(1968), m; CHARLOTTE'S WEB(1973), m; TOM SAWYER(1973), w; HUCKLEBERRY FINN(1974), w; SLIPPER AND THE ROSE, THE(1976, Brit.), w, m; MAGIC OF LASSIE, THE(1978), w

Robert M. Sherman
SCARECROW(1973), p; NIGHT MOVES(1975), p; MISSOURI BREAKS, THE(1976), p; CONVOY(1978), p
1984
OH GOD! YOU DEVIL(1984), p

Sam Sherman
BRAIN OF BLOOD(1971, Phil.), p

Samuel M. Sherman
BLOOD OF FRANKENSTEIN(1970), w

Sol Sherman
PROUD RIDER, THE(1971, Can.), m

Stanford Sherman
ANY WHICH WAY YOU CAN(1980), w; KRULL(1983), w; MAN WHO WASN'T THERE, THE(1983), w
1984
ICE PIRATES, THE(1984), w

Susan Sherman
STRAIGHT TIME(1978)

Susi Sherman
ESCAPE ARTIST, THE(1982)

Teddi Sherman
WOMAN OF THE TOWN, THE(1943); FOUR FACES WEST(1948), w; MAN FROM BITTER RIDGE, THE(1955), w; TEN SECONDS TO HELL(1959), w; FOUR FOR TEXAS(1963), w; RAGE(1966, U.S./Mex.), w

Tex Sherman
TROUBLE IN TEXAS(1937)

Vincent Sherman
COUNSELLOR-AT-LAW(1933); CRIME OF HELEN STANLEY(1934); GIRL IN DANGER(1934); HELL BENT FOR LOVE(1934); MIDNIGHT ALIBI(1934); SPEED WINGS(1934); CRIME SCHOOL(1938), w; HEART OF THE NORTH(1938), w; MY BILL(1938), w; ADVENTURES OF JANE ARDEN(1939), w; KING OF THE UNDERWORLD(1939), w; PRIDE OF THE BLUEGRASS(1939), w; RETURN OF DR. X, THE(1939), d; MAN WHO TALKED TOO MUCH, THE(1940), d; SATURDAY'S CHILDREN(1940), d; FLIGHT FROM DESTINY(1941), d; UNDERGROUND(1941), d; ACROSS THE PACIFIC(1942), d; ALL THROUGH THE NIGHT(1942), d; HARD WAY, THE(1942), d; OLD ACQUAINTANCE(1943), d; IN OUR TIME(1944), d; PILLOW TO POST(1945), d; JANIE GETS MARRIED(1946), d; NORA PRENTISS(1947), d; UNFAITHFUL, THE(1947), d; ADVENTURES OF DON JUAN(1949), d; HASTY HEART, THE(1949), d; BACKFIRE(1950), d; DAMNED DON'T CRY, THE(1950), d; HARRIET CRAIG(1950), d; GOODBYE, MY FANCY(1951), d; AFFAIR IN TRINIDAD(1952), p&d; LONE STAR(1952), d; GARMENT JUNGLE, THE(1957), d; NAKED EARTH, THE(1958, Brit.), d; YOUNG PHILADELPHIANS, THE(1959), d; ICE PALACE(1960), d; FEVER IN THE BLOOD, A(1961), d; SECOND TIME AROUND, THE(1961), d; YOUNG REBEL, THE(1969, Fr./Ital./Span.), d

Wendy Sherman
MAN WITH TWO BRAINS, THE(1983)

Wilbur Sherman
CRIME SCHOOL(1938), w

Sherman Fisher Girls
MUSIC HALL(1934, Brit.); NIGHT CLUB QUEEN(1934, Brit.); JIMMY BOY(1935, Brit.); VARIETY(1935, Brit.); SHIPMATES O' MINE(1936, Brit.); SUNSHINE AHEAD(1936, Brit.); VARIETY PARADE(1936, Brit.); CAPTAIN'S ORDERS(1937, Brit.); OKAY FOR SOUND(1937, Brit.); SING AS YOU SWING(1937, Brit.); FATHER O'FLYNN(1938, Irish); TAKE OFF THAT HAT(1938, Brit.); BAND WAGGON(1940, Brit.)

Shuma Shermatova
STARS OVER ARIZONA(1937)

Jules Shermer
PUSHOVER(1954), p

Hazel Shermet
STAR IS BORN, A(1954); ROCKABILLY BABY(1957)

Gayna Shernen
UP IN SMOKE(1978)

Terry Shero
GONE WITH THE WIND(1939)

Tom Sherohman
MODERN PROBLEMS(1981), a, w

Milio Sheron
SONG OF SCHEHERAZADE(1947)

Molio Sheron
HEAVENLY DAYS(1944); NORTHWEST OUTPOST(1947)

Francis Sherr [Frantisek Slegr]
FABULOUS WORLD OF JULES VERNE, THE(1961, Czech.)

Mickey Sherrard
TERRIFIED!(1963), cos; LIMBO(1972), cos

Wesley Sherrard
YOUNG GUNS OF TEXAS(1963), cos

Rex Sherren
Silents
PRIDE OF DONEGAL, THE(1929, Brit.)

Arthur Sherrick
GIRL IN TROUBLE(1963), cos

Julian Sherrier
DEVIL'S JEST, THE(1954, Brit.); BEYOND MOMBASA(1957); ROAD TO HONG KONG, THE(1962, U.S./Brit.); NINE HOURS TO RAMA(1963, U.S./Brit.); SQUADRON 633(1964, U.S./Brit.); STOPOVER FOREVER(1964, Brit.); 633 SQUADRON(1964); DEADLY AFFAIR, THE(1967, Brit.)

Sydney Sherrif
LAW AND DISORDER(1974)

P. Sherriff
DIVORCE OF LADY X. THE(1938, Brit.), prod d

Paul Sherriff
WAR IS HELL(1964)

R. G. Sherriff
THIS ABOVE ALL(1942), w

R.C. Sherriff
OLD DARK HOUSE, THE(1932), w; BADGER'S GREEN(1934, Brit.), w; ONE MORE RIVER(1934), w; WINDFALL(1935, Brit.), w; ROAD BACK,THE(1937), w; FOUR FEATHERS, THE(1939, Brit.), w; THAT HAMILTON WOMAN(1941), w; FOREVER AND A DAY(1943), w; QUARTET(1949, Brit.), w; NO HIGHWAY IN THE SKY(1951, Brit.), w; MURDER ON MONDAY(1953, Brit.), w; DAM BUSTERS, THE(1955, Brit.), w; ACES HIGH(1977, Brit.), w

Steven Sherriff
NEON PALACE, THE(1970, Can.)

Babette Sherrill
DEVIL'S SISTERS, THE(1966); DEATH CURSE OF TARTU(1967)

Billy Sherrill
TAKE THIS JOB AND SHOVE IT(1981), m

Diane Sherrill
Misc. Talkies
SMOKEY AND THE GOODTIME OUTLAWS(1978)

Elizabeth Sherrill
CROSS AND THE SWITCHBLADE, THE(1970), w

Jack Sherrill
Silents
JOHN GLAYDE'S HONOR(1915)
Misc. Silents
THEN I'LL COME BACK TO YOU(1916); WITCHING HOUR, THE(1916); ACCOMPLICE, THE(1917); RAINBOW, THE(1917); MOTHER ETERNAL(1921)

John Sherrill
CROSS AND THE SWITCHBLADE, THE(1970), w

Louise Sherrill
BLOOD AND LACE(1971)

Martha Sherrill
SOMETHING SHORT OF PARADISE(1979)
Misc. Talkies
CALL OF THE FOREST(1949)

Palmer Wray Sherrill
I'VE LIVED BEFORE(1956)

The Sherrill Sisters
FOLLOW THE LEADER(1944)

Ned Sherrin
THINK DIRTY(1970, Brit.), p; VIRGIN SOLDIERS, THE(1970, Brit.), p; GIRL STROKE BOY(1971, Brit.), p; UP POMPEII(1971, Brit.), p; UP THE CHASTITY BELT(1971, Brit.), p; RENTADICK(1972, Brit.), p; UP THE FRONT(1972, Brit.), p; NATIONAL HEALTH, OR NURSE NORTON'S AFFAIR, THE(1973, Brit.), p

Edgar Sherrod
PRESIDENT VANISHES, THE(1934); JOE SMITH, AMERICAN(1942); GILDER-SLEEVE'S BAD DAY(1943)
Silents
KID, THE(1921)
Edward Sherrod
POSTMAN ALWAYS RINGS TWICE, THE(1946)
Alden Sherry
Misc. Talkies
TEENAGE GRAFFITI(1977)
Ariel Sherry
WEST OF THE PECOS(1945)
Barney Sherry
Silents
SURE FIRE FLINT(1922); DAUGHTERS WHO PAY(1925)
Misc. Silents
BARBARIAN, THE(1921); JUST OUTSIDE THE DOOR(1921)
Bob Sherry
GOODBYE, NORMA JEAN(1976), ph
Clarice Sherry
ONE IN A MILLION(1936); EMPEROR'S CANDLESTICKS, THE(1937); THIN ICE(1937)
Craighall Sherry
NUMBER SEVENTEEN(1928, Brit./Ger.); INFORMER, THE(1929, Brit.); LOVES OF ROBERT BURNS, THE(1930, Brit.); NELL GWYN(1935, Brit.); REGAL CAVALCADE(1935, Brit.)
Silents
BATTLES OF THE CORONEL AND FALKLAND ISLANDS, THE(1928, Brit.); SPIES(1929, Ger.)
Diane Sherry
HAWAII(1966); PRETTY MAIDS ALL IN A ROW(1971); SUPERMAN(1978)
Edna Sherry
THRU DIFFERENT EYES(1929), w; SUDDEN FEAR(1952), w
Gordon Sherry
BLACK LIMELIGHT(1938, Brit.), w; SCHOOL FOR HUSBANDS(1939, Brit.), w
J. Barney Sherry
BROADWAY SCANDALS(1929); JAZZ HEAVEN(1929)
Misc. Talkies
VOICE WITHIN, THE(1929)
Silents
BATTLE OF GETTYSBURG(1914); CIVILIZATION(1916); ICED BULLET, THE(1917); EVIDENCE(1918); REAL FOLKS(1918); RECKONING DAY, THE(1918); EXTRAVAGANCE(1919); THIS HERO STUFF(1919); DARLING MINE(1920); DINTY(1920); OCCASIONALLY YOURS(1920); BURN 'EM UP BARNES(1921); INNER MAN, THE(1922); JOHN SMITH(1922); NOTORIETY(1922); SECRETS OF PARIS, THE(1922); SHADOWS OF THE SEA(1922); WHAT FOOLS MEN ARE(1922); JACQUELINE, OR BLAZING BARRIERS(1923); WHITE SISTER, THE(1923); LEND ME YOUR HUSBAND(1924); WARRENS OF VIRGINIA, THE(1924); ENEMIES OF YOUTH(1925); SPIDER WEBS(1927); ALEX THE GREAT(1928)
Misc. Silents
BARGAIN, THE(1914); RUMPELSTILSKIN(1915); BETWEEN MEN(1916); CONQUEROR, THE(1916); GREEN SWAMP, THE(1916); BACK OF THE MAN(1917); BORROWED PLUMAGE(1917); FANATICS(1917); FUEL OF LIFE(1917); LOVE OR JUSTICE(1917); MILLIONAIRE VAGRANT, THE(1917); STRANGE TRANSGRESSOR, A(1917); TEN OF DIAMONDS(1917); HARD ROCK BREED, THE(1918); HER DECISION(1918); HIGH STAKES(1918); SECRET CODE, THE(1918); SOUL IN TRUST, A(1918); WHO KILLED WALTON?(1918); FORBIDDEN ROOM, THE(1919); GUNFIGHTIN' GENTLEMAN, A(1919); LITTLE BROTHER OF THE RICH, A(1919); MARY REGAN(1919); MAYOR OF FILBERT, THE(1919); YVONNE FROM PARIS(1919); FORGED BRIDE, THE(1920); GO AND GET IT(1920); RIVER'S END, THE(1920); THUNDERCLAP(1921); BACK PAY(1922); BROKEN SILENCE, THE(1922); TILL WE MEET AGAIN(1922); MIAMI(1924); LITTLE GIRL IN A BIG CITY, A(1925); LIVE WIRE, THE(1925); BROKEN HOMES(1926)
John B. Sherry
BEGUILED, THE(1971), w; HANGUP(1974), w
John Sherry
LAST CHALLENGE, THE(1967), w
Norman Sherry
TOMBOY AND THE CHAMP(1961)
Robert Sherry
CAPTAIN MILKSHAKE(1970), ph
Robert A. Sherry
ONE WAY TICKET TO HELL(1955)
Tom Sherry
E.T. THE EXTRA-TERRESTRIAL(1982)
Sherven Brothers
HOME ON THE PRAIRIE(1939)
Yvonne Sherwell
LIFE STUDY(1973)
David Sherwin
IF ...(1968, Brit.), w; O LUCKY MAN!(1973, Brit.), w; BRITTANIA HOSPITAL(1982, Brit.), w
Derrick Sherwin
CLUE OF THE SILVER KEY, THE(1961, Brit.); SPANISH SWORD, THE(1962, Brit.); ACCIDENTAL DEATH(1963, Brit.); VENGEANCE OF SHE, THE(1968, Brit.)
Louis Sherwin
Silents
ELEVENTH HOUR, THE(1923), w
Manning Sherwin
ONCE UPON A DREAM(1949, Brit.), m
Miriam Sherwin
WESTERNER, THE(1940)
Richard Sherwin
END OF THE ROAD(1944), m
A.L. Sherwood
NIGHT OF NIGHTS, THE(1939)
Angela Sherwood
PARIS HONEYMOON(1939), w

Anthony Sherwood
TERROR TRAIN(1980, Can.)
Billy Sherwood
Silents
DANGER SIGNAL, THE(1915)
Bob Sherwood
NAUGHTY BUT NICE(1939)
Bobby Sherwood
CAMPUS SLEUTH(1948), a, m; PAL JOEY(1957)
C. Blythe Sherwood
Silents
DREAM STREET(1921), art d
C.L. Sherwood
LEMON DROP KID, THE(1934); HOME ON THE RANGE(1935); MORE THAN A SECRETARY(1936); BULLDOG DRUMMOND COMES BACK(1937); RANGE DEFENDERS(1937); LUCKY NIGHT(1939); MAISIE(1939); OUR LEADING CITIZEN(1939)
Silents
LOADED DOOR, THE(1922); MEDDLER, THE(1925)
Choti Sherwood
BILLY THE KID WANTED(1941)
Clarence Sherwood
STORY OF TEMPLE DRAKE, THE(1933); HOME ON THE RANGE(1935); TRUE CONFESSION(1937)
Clarence L. Sherwood
MISSISSIPPI(1935); TWO FOR TONIGHT(1935); YOU CAN'T TAKE IT WITH YOU(1938)
Silents
STAIRS OF SAND(1929)
Misc. Silents
PEGGY OF THE SECRET SERVICE(1925)
Dale Sherwood
RAIDERS OF THE WEST(1942)
Gale Sherwood
BLONDE SAVAGE(1947); SONG OF MY HEART(1947); ROCKY(1948)
George Sherwood
THEY WON'T BELIEVE ME(1947); LITTLE TOUGH GUY(1938); OVERLAND STAGE RAIDERS(1938); CODE OF THE FEARLESS(1939); BALL OF FIRE(1941); EMERGENCY LANDING(1941); WYOMING WILDCAT(1941); ICE-CAPADES REVUE(1942); STARDUST ON THE SAGE(1942); FALLEN SPARROW, THE(1943); HENRY ALDRICH HAUNTS A HOUSE(1943); LEOPARD MAN, THE(1943); NORTHERN PURSUIT(1943); SALUTE FOR THREE(1943); SECRETS OF THE UNDERGROUND(1943); THEY GOT ME COVERED(1943); APOLOGY FOR MURDER(1945); MAN FROM OKLAHOMA, THE(1945); SALOME, WHERE SHE DANCED(1945); CONQUEST OF CHEYENNE(1946); HOODLUM SAINT, THE(1946); KID FROM BOOKLYN, THE(1946); BUFFALO BILL RIDES AGAIN(1947); DOUBLE LIFE, A(1947); HOMECOMING(1948); NAKED CITY, THE(1948); FLAXY MARTIN(1949); FOUNTAINHEAD, THE(1949); MYSTERY STREET(1950); THREE LITTLE WORDS(1950); WHERE DANGER LIVES(1950); QUEEN FOR A DAY(1951); RACKET, THE(1951); SANTA FE(1951); LUSTY MEN, THE(1952); GIRL WHO HAD EVERYTHING, THE(1953); DANGEROUS MISSION(1954); LUCKY ME(1954); SON OF SINBAD(1955)
Silents
WELCOME CHILDREN(1921); WEB OF THE LAW, THE(1923)
Misc. Silents
WILD JUSTICE(1925)
Gregg Sherwood
GOLDEN GLOVES STORY, THE(1950); IRON MAN, THE(1951); MERRY WIDOW, THE(1952); GIRL NEXT DOOR, THE(1953)
Hal Sherwood
GHASTLY ONES, THE(1968), a, w
Herbert Sherwood
ALONG CAME YOUTH(1931)
Misc. Silents
MARCH HARE, THE(1921)
Jim Sherwood
HITCHHIKERS, THE(1972)
John Sherwood
CREATURE WALKS AMONG US, THE(1956), d; RAW EDGE(1956), d; MONOLITH MONSTERS, THE(1957), d
Kay Sherwood
Silents
ENCHANTED ISLAND, THE(1927), w
Lydia Sherwood
YELLOW STOCKINGS(1930, Brit.); KING OF PARIS, THE(1934, Brit.); LITTLE FRIEND(1934, Brit.); SPRING IN THE AIR(1934, Brit.); DON QUIXOTE(1935, Fr.); MIDNIGHT AT THE WAX MUSEUM(1936, Brit.); SECRET FOUR, THE(1940, Brit.); THEATRE ROYAL(1943, Brit.); WHEN WE ARE MARRIED(1943, Brit.); ROMEO AND JULIET(1954, Brit.); LEAGUE OF GENTLEMEN, THE(1961, Brit.); DARLING(1965, Brit.)
Madeleine Sherwood
CAT ON A HOT TIN ROOF(1958); PARRISH(1961); SWEET BIRD OF YOUTH(1962); HURRY SUNDOWN(1967); PENDULUM(1969); WICKED, WICKED(1973)
1984
TEACHERS(1984)
Mark Sherwood
ROBIN AND THE SEVEN HOODS(1964); NURSE SHERRI(1978), p
Mimi Sherwood
Silents
JAVA HEAD(1923)
Mindy Sherwood
MIRACLE WORKER, THE(1962)
Robert Sherwood
SCARLET PIMPERNEL, THE(1935, Brit.), w; THUNDER IN THE CITY(1937, Brit.), w; DIVORCE OF LADY X. THE(1938, Brit.), w; IDIOT'S DELIGHT(1939), w; ADAM HAD FOUR SONS(1941), p; MAGNIFICENT YANKEE, THE(1950); LITTLE BIG HORN(1951); THREE GUYS NAMED MIKE(1951); TWO DOLLAR BETTOR(1951); TRAIL GUIDE(1952); MAN ON A TIGHTROPE(1953), w; JUPITER'S DARLING(1955), w

Robert E. Sherwood
WATERLOO BRIDGE(1931), w; AGE FOR LOVE, THE(1931), w; ROYAL BED, THE(1931), w; COCK OF THE AIR(1932), w; TWO KINDS OF WOMEN(1932), w; REUNION IN VIENNA(1933), w; ROMAN SCANDALS(1933), w; GHOST GOES WEST, THE(1936), w; PETRIFIED FOREST, THE(1936), w; TOVARICH(1937), w; ADVENTURES OF MARCO POLO, THE(1938), w; ABE LINCOLN IN ILLINOIS(1940), w; OVER THE MOON(1940, Brit.), w; REBECCA(1940), w; WATERLOO BRID-GE(1940), w; ESCAPE IN THE DESERT(1945), w; BEST YEARS OF OUR LIVES, THE(1946), w; BISHOP'S WIFE, THE(1947), w; MAIN STREET TO BROAD-WAY(1953), w; GABY(1956), w

Robert Emmett Sherwood
Silents
OH, WHAT A NURSE!(1926), w

Roberta Sherwood
COURTSHIP OF EDDY'S FATHER, THE(1963)

Robin Sherwood
TOURIST TRAP, THE(1979); HERO AT LARGE(1980); SERIAL(1980); DEATH WISH II(1982); LOVE BUTCHER, THE(1982)

Sheri Sherwood
NIGHT OF BLOODY HORROR zero(1969)

Sherry Sherwood
FABULOUS DORSEYS, THE(1947)

Skip Sherwood
AMERICANA(1981), p
Misc. Talkies
DIDN'T YOU HEAR(1983), d

William Sherwood
MAN WITHOUT A BODY, THE(1957, Brit.); DUBLIN NIGHTMARE(1958, Brit.); HORROR OF DRACULA, THE(1958, Brit.); INTENT TO KILL(1958, Brit.)
Silents
BROKEN CHAINS(1916); LOST BRIDEGROOM, THE(1916)
Misc. Silents
SPELL OF THE YUKON, THE(1916); JURY OF FATE, THE(1917); TRIUMPH OF VENUS, THE(1918)

Yorke Sherwood
MAN FROM BLANKLEY'S, THE(1930); TEMPLE TOWER(1930); LION AND THE LAMB(1931); MAN IN POSSESSION, THE(1931); EAGLE AND THE HAWK, THE(1933); BULLDOG DRUMMOND STRIKES BACK(1934); TREASURE IS-LAND(1934); FOLIES DERGERE(1935); LLOYDS OF LONDON(1936); LOVE ON THE RUN(1936); ANOTHER DAWN(1937); QUALITY STREET(1937); SCOTLAND YARD(1941); JANE EYRE(1944); LODGER, THE(1944); NONE BUT THE LONELY HEART(1944); DEVOTION(1946); 23 PACES TO BAKER STREET(1956)
Silents
GENTLEMEN PREFER BLONDES(1928)

The Sherwood Singers
YOUNG SWINGERS, THE(1963)

Sergei Shestopalov
SOUND OF LIFE, THE(1962, USSR)

Bert Sheter
HARBOR LIGHTS(1963), m

Bas Sheva
CATSKILL HONEYMOON(1950)

Shevchenko Opera and Ballet Theatre Chorus
KATERINA IZMAILOVA(1969, USSR)

Burt Shevelove
FUNNY THING HAPPENED ON THE WAY TO THE FORUM, A(1966), w; WRONG BOX, THE(1966, Brit.), w

Elena Shevetsova
LUCKY BRIDE, THE(1948, USSR)

Jean Shevlin
SIDELONG GLANCES OF A PIGEON KICKER, THE(1970); MIKEY AND NICK-Y(1976); GOING IN STYLE(1979)

Laurie Shevlin
MURDER AT THE VANITIES(1934)

Vladimir Shevtsik
1984
JAZZMAN(1984, USSR), ph

G. Shevtsov
TSAR'S BRIDE, THE(1966, USSR)

Kayne Shew
FIXED BAYONETS(1951)

Lee Sheward
1984
TOP SECRET!(1984)

Steve Shewchuk
1984
POLICE ACADEMY(1984), set d

Edward Spencer Shewl
HANDS OF THE RIPPER(1971, Brit.), w

Valdek Sheybal
GULLIVER'S TRAVELS(1977, Brit., Bel.)

Vladek Sheybal
FROM RUSSIA WITH LOVE(1963, Brit.); RETURN FROM THE ASHES(1965, U.S./Brit.); BILLION DOLLAR BRAIN(1967, Brit.); JOURNEY TO THE FAR SIDE OF THE SUN(1969, Brit.); LIMBO LINE, THE(1969, Brit.); WOMEN IN LOVE(1969, Brit.); LEO THE LAST(1970, Brit.); MOSQUITO SQUADRON(1970, Brit.); BOY FRIEND, THE(1971, Brit.); LAST VALLEY, THE(1971, Brit.); PUPPET ON A CHAIN(1971, Brit.); INNOCENT BYSTANDERS(1973, Brit.); SCORPIO(1973); S(1974); WIND AND THE LION, THE(1975); HAMLET(1976, Brit.); SELL OUT, THE(1976); APPLE, THE(1980 U.S./Ger.); LADY VANISHES, THE(1980, Brit.)
1984
MEMED MY HAWK(1984, Brit.); RED DAWN(1984)

Wladyslaw Sheybal
KANAL(1961, Pol.)

Leo Sheynin
MILITARY SECRET(1945, USSR), w

Carol Shiada
SUBSTITUTION(1970)

Kazue Shiba
SON OF GODZILLA(1967, Jap.), w

Shigeharu Shiba
1984
WARRIORS OF THE WIND(1984, Jap.), md

Toshio Shibaki
GODZILLA VERSUS THE SMOG MONSTER(1972, Jap.)

Vladimir Shibankov
FORTY-NINE DAYS(1964, USSR)

George Shibata
HELL TO ETERNITY(1960); WACKIEST SHIP IN THE ARMY, THE(1961); UGLY AMERICAN, THE(1963); AROUND THE WORLD UNDER THE SEA(1966)

Hidekatsu Shibata
LOVE ROBOTS, THE(1965, Jap.)

Makiko Shibata
MUDDY RIVER(1982, Jap.)

Renzaburo Shibata
DUEL AT EZO(1970, Jap.), w

Teruo Shibata
ANGRY ISLAND(1960, Jap.)

Tokuji Shibata
FIRES ON THE PLAIN(1962, Jap.), art d

Etta Shiber
PARIS UNDERGROUND(1945), w

George Shibita
PORK CHOP HILL(1959)

Kenji Shibuya
HAMMETT(1982)

Minoru Shibuya
TWILIGHT PATH(1965, Jap.), d, w

Koji Shidara
OHAYO(1962, Jap.)

Francis Shide
PETRIFIED FOREST, THE(1936)

Charol Shideler
1984
BLIND DATE(1984)

Maxwell Shieff
D.I., THE(1957), cos; MOTHER GOOSE A GO-GO(1966), cos

Kate Shiel
PUBERTY BLUES(1983, Aus.)

Matthews Phipps Shiel
WORLD, THE FLESH, AND THE DEVIL, THE(1959), w

Bob Shield
MAJORITY OF ONE, A(1961)

Ernest Shield
STOLEN HARMONY(1935); TOAST OF NEW YORK, THE(1937)

Ernie Shield
NONE BUT THE LONELY HEART(1944)

Le Roy Shield
DEVIL'S BROTHER, THE(1933), md

LeRoy Shield
PACK UP YOUR TROUBLES(1932), m; OUR RELATIONS(1936), m, md; WAY OUT WEST(1937), m

Robert Shield
HELL'S HALF ACRE(1954); TIGHT SPOT(1955)

Art Shields
REDS(1981)

Arthur Shields
PLOUGH AND THE STARS, THE(1936); DRUMS ALONG THE MOHAWK(1939); LITTLE NELLIE KELLY(1940); LONG VOYAGE HOME, THE(1940); CONFIRM OR DENY(1941); GAY FALCON, THE(1941); HOW GREEN WAS MY VALLEY(1941); LADY SCARFACE(1941); BLACK SWAN, THE(1942); BROADWAY(1942); DR. RE-NAULT'S SECRET(1942); GENTLEMAN JIM(1942); LOVES OF EDGAR ALLAN POE, THE(1942); NIGHTMARE(1942); PACIFIC RENDEZVOUS(1942); RANDOM HAR-VEST(1942); THIS ABOVE ALL(1942); ABOVE SUSPICION(1943); LASSIE, COME HOME(1943); MADAME CURIE(1943); MAN FROM DOWN UNDER, THE(1943); KEYS OF THE KINGDOM, THE(1944); NATIONAL VELVET(1944); WHITE CLIFFS OF DOVER, THE(1944); YOUTH RUNS WILD(1944); CORN IS GREEN, THE(1945); ROUGHLY SPEAKING(1945); TOO YOUNG TO KNOW(1945); VALLEY OF DECI-SION, THE(1945); GALLANT JOURNEY(1946); NEVER SAY GOODBYE(1946); THREE STRANGERS(1946); VERDICT, THE(1946); EASY COME, EASY GO(1947); FABULOUS DORSEYS, THE(1947); SEVEN KEYS TO BALDPATE(1947); SHOCKING MISS PILGRIM, THE(1947); FIGHTING FATHER DUNNE(1948); MY OWN TRUE LOVE(1948); TAP ROOTS(1948); CHALLENGE TO LASSIE(1949); FIGHTING O'-FLYNN, THE(1949); RED LIGHT(1949); SHE WORE A YELLOW RIBBON(1949); TARZAN AND THE SLAVE GIRL(1950); APACHE DRUMS(1951); BAREFOOT MAIL-MAN, THE(1951); BLUE BLOOD(1951); PEOPLE AGAINST O'HARA, THE(1951); RIVER, THE(1951); SEALED CARGO(1951); QUIET MAN, THE(1952); MAIN STREET TO BROADWAY(1953); SCANDAL AT SCOURIE(1953); SOUTH SEA WOMAN(1953); PRIDE OF THE BLUE GRASS(1954); RIVER OF NO RETURN(1954); WORLD FOR RANSOM(1954); LADY GODIVA(1955); KING AND FOUR QUEENS, THE(1956); DAUGHTER OF DR. JEKYLL(1957); ENCHANTED ISLAND(1958); NIGHT OF THE QUARTER MOON(1959); FOR THE LOVE OF MIKE(1960); PIGEON THAT TOOK ROME, THE(1962)

Barbara Shields
KIND LADY(1935)

Brooke Shields
ALICE, SWEET ALICE(1978); KING OF THE GYPSIES(1978); PRETTY BABY(1978); JUST YOU AND ME, KID(1979); TILT(1979); WANDA NEVADA(1979); BLUE LA-GOON, THE(1980); ENDLESS LOVE(1981)
1984
MUPPETS TAKE MANHATTAN, THE(1984); SAHARA(1984)

Edwin Shields
FIVE MINUTES TO LIVE(1961), art d

Ella Shields
MEN OF YESTERDAY(1936, Brit.)

Ernest Shields
JUDGE PRIEST(1934); LIFE BEGINS AT 40(1935)
Silents
PURPLE CIPHER, THE(1920); SUPREME TEST, THE(1923)
Ernie Shields
GREYHOUND LIMITED, THE(1929); PLOUGH AND THE STARS, THE(1936); WEDDING PRESENT(1936); YOU CAN'T TAKE IT WITH YOU(1938); I MARRIED A WITCH(1942)
Silents
FREE LIPS(1928); WOMAN WISE(1928)
Misc. Silents
WRONG DOOR, THE(1916); BIRTH OF PATRIOTISM, THE(1917)
Everett Shields
DEVIL'S PLAYGROUND, THE(1946)
Frank Shields
MURDER IN THE FLEET(1935); COME AND GET IT(1936); AFFAIRS OF CAPPY RICKS(1937); DEAD END(1937); HOOSIER SCHOOLBOY(1937); GOLDWYN FOLLIES, THE(1938)
Fred Shields
THREE CABALLEROS, THE(1944)
Gordon Shields
1984
VIGIL(1984, New Zealand)
Helen Shields
WHISTLE AT EATON FALLS(1951); WRONG MAN, THE(1956)
Jerry Shields
WHITE STALLION(1947)
Loraine Shields
1984
FLETCH(1984)
Martyn Shields
BLOW YOUR OWN TRUMPET(1958, Brit.)
Nicholas Shields
TIME AFTER TIME(1979, Brit.); HEARSE, THE(1980)
Nick Shields
1984
ALL OF ME(1984); BEVERLY HILLS COP(1984)
Pat Shields
FRASIER, THE SENSUOUS LION(1973), d
Peter Shields
CLOCKWORK ORANGE, A(1971, Brit.), art d
Robert Shields
CONVERSATION, THE(1974); TAXI DRIVER(1976)
Russell Shields
LUCKY BOY(1929), ed; MOLLY AND ME(1929), ed; LOVE AT FIRST SIGHT(1930), ed; ENEMIES OF THE LAW(1931), ed; DEVIL TIGER(1934), w
Russell G. Shields
TALK OF HOLLYWOOD, THE(1929), ed
Sonny Shields
CHAMP, THE(1979); METEOR(1979); UNSEEN, THE(1981), stunts
Stan Shields
DEVIL DOLL(1964, Brit.), art d; INVASION(1965, Brit.), spec eff
Sydney Shields
Misc. Silents
BULLDOGS OF THE TRAIL, THE(1915)
Teri Shields
WANDA NEVADA(1979); ENDLESS LOVE(1981)
Tim Shields
LAST SHOT YOU HEAR, THE(1969, Brit.), w
O'Donovan Shiell
END OF THE AFFAIR, THE(1955, Brit.); GIDEON OF SCOTLAND YARD(1959, Brit.)
George Shiels
PROFESSOR TIM(1957, Ireland), w
Una Shiels
Silents
IRISH DESTINY(1925, Brit.)
Marisa Shiero
GRAVEYARD OF HORROR(1971, Span.)
Alfred Shieske
ODETTE(1951, Brit.)
Mickey Shiff
SIGN OF AQUARIUS(1970)
Arlo Shiffen
FRANCHETTE; LES INTRIGUES(1969), p,d&w
Bob Shiffer
SECRET OF ST. IVES, THE(1949), makeup
Robert Shiffer
WE WERE STRANGERS(1949), makeup
Hal Shiffman
MAN CALLED FLINTSTONE, THE(1966), ph
A.B. Shiffrin
CRY MURDER(1936), w
N. Shifirn
QUEEN OF SPADES(1961, USSR), ph
Milton Shifman
LOUISIANA TERRITORY(1953), ed; MADIGAN(1968), ed; STORY OF A WOMAN(1970, U.S./Ital.), ed
Su Shifrin
SUPERMAN(1978)
Akira Shiga
KARATE, THE HAND OF DEATH(1961)
Natsuko Shiga
PERFORMERS, THE(1970, Jap.)
Takashi Shiga
HENTAI(1966, Jap.), d
Takako Shigemori
MUDDY RIVER(1982, Jap.), w

James Shigeta
CRIMSON KIMONO, THE(1959); WALK LIKE A DRAGON(1960); BRIDGE TO THE SUN(1961); CRY FOR HAPPY(1961); FLOWER DRUM SONG(1961); PARADISE, HAWAIIAN STYLE(1966); NOBODY'S PERFECT(1968); LOST HORIZON(1973); YAKUZA, THE(1975, U.S./Jap.); MIDWAY(1976)
Noriko Shigeyama
THREE DOLLS FROM HONG KONG(1966, Jap.)
Michael J. Shigezane
TRIAL OF BILLY JACK, THE(1974)
Hideyuki Shiino
PRESSURE OF GUILT(1964, Jap.), p; THIS MADDING CROWD(1964, Jap.), p; RIVER OF FOREVER(1967, Jap.), p
Akira Shiizuka
1984
ANTARCTICA(1984, Jap.), ph
Baby Shika
TIGER AND THE FLAME, THE(1955, India)
Joseph Shilcach
MY MARGO(1969, Israel)
L. Shildknekht
SONG OVER MOSCOW(1964, USSR), cos
V. Shildknekht
YOLANTA(1964, USSR), spec eff
Nathaniel Shilkret
BOHEMIAN GIRL, THE(1936), m; MARY OF SCOTLAND(1936), md; PLOUGH AND THE STARS, THE(1936), md; SWING TIME(1936), md; WINTERSET(1936), md; WOMAN REBELS, A(1936), md; MUSIC FOR MADAME(1937), md; SHALL WE DANCE(1937), md; THAT GIRL FROM PARIS(1937), m, md; TOAST OF NEW YORK, THE(1937), md; ONE THIRD OF A NATION(1939), m; AIR RAID WARDENS(1943), m; STRANGER IN TOWN, A(1943), m; NOTHING BUT TROUBLE(1944), m; THREE MEN IN WHITE(1944), m; SHE WENT TO THE RACES(1945), m; THIS MAN'S NAVY(1945), m; BOYS' RANCH(1946), m; FAITHFUL IN MY FASHION(1946), m; HOODLUM SAINT, THE(1946), m
Silents
LILAC TIME(1928), m
Abbie Shilling
1984
RAZOR'S EDGE, THE(1984)
Cassie Shilling
1984
RAZOR'S EDGE, THE(1984)
Dave Shilling
HOLLOW TRIUMPH(1948)
Marian Shilling
PARISIAN ROMANCE, A(1932)
Marion Shilling
LORD BYRON OF BROADWAY(1930); ON YOUR BACK(1930); SHADOW OF THE LAW(1930); SWELLHEAD, THE(1930); WISE GIRLS(1930); BEYOND VICTORY(1931); COMMON LAW, THE(1931); SUNDOWN TRAIL(1931); YOUNG DONOVAN'S KID(1931); COUNTY FAIR, THE(1932); FORGOTTEN WOMEN(1932); MAN'S LAND, A(1932); SHOP ANGEL(1932); CURTAIN AT EIGHT(1934); INSIDE INFORMATION(1934); THUNDER OVER TEXAS(1934); KEEPER OF THE BEES(1935); SHOT IN THE DARK, A(1935); SOCIETY FEVER(1935); STONE OF SILVER CREEK(1935); CAVALCADE OF THE WEST(1936); GUN PLAY(1936); GUN SMOKE(1936); ROMANCE RIDES THE RANGE(1936); WESTERNER, THE(1936)
Misc. Talkies
FIGHTING TO LIVE(1934); BLAZING GUNS(1935); CAPTURED IN CHINATOWN(1935); GUNSMOKE ON THE GUADALUPE(1935); RIO RATTLER(1935); I'LL NAME THE MURDERER(1936)
S. K. Shilling
Silents
BROADWAY SCANDAL(1918)
Margaret Shillingford
Misc. Silents
SUDDEN GENTLEMAN, THE(1917)
Michael Shillo
HILL 24 DOESN'T ANSWER(1955, Israel); DUNKIRK(1958, Brit.); WHOLE TRUTH, THE(1958, Brit.); PILLAR OF FIRE, THE(1963, Israel); CAST A GIANT SHADOW(1966); HELL WITH HEROES, THE(1968); ROSEMARY'S BABY(1968); THOMAS CROWN AFFAIR, THE(1968)
Yosef Shiloa
ROSEBUD(1975)
Yossi Shiloa
1984
SAHARA(1984)
Joseph Shiloach
SINAI COMMANDOS: THE STORY OF THE SIX DAY WAR(1968, Israel/Ger.); PARADISE(1982)
Joseph Shiloah
DIAMONDS(1975, U.S./Israel)
1984
AMBASSADOR, THE(1984)
Yossef Shiloah
JESUS(1979)
Yousef Shiloah
MOSES(1976, Brit./Ital.)
V. Shilov
MEET ME IN MOSCOW(1966, USSR)
Kaori Shima
LOST SEX(1968, Jap.)
Kieko Shima
JOE BUTTERFLY(1957)
Koji Shima
GOLDEN DEMON(1956, Jap.), d, w; MYSTERIOUS SATELLITE, THE(1956, Jap.), d
Yvonne Shima
GENGHIS KHAN(U.S./Brit./Ger./Yugo); SAVAGE INNOCENTS, THE(1960, Brit.); WORLD OF SUZIE WONG, THE(1960); PASSPORT TO CHINA(1961, Brit.); DR. NO(1962, Brit.); ROAD TO HONG KONG, THE(1962, U.S./Brit.); COOL MIKADO, THE(1963, Brit.); SINISTER MAN, THE(1965, Brit.)

Akihiko Shimada
GIRARA(1967, Jap.), p
Glen Shimada
HOLLYWOOD BOULEVARD(1976)
Hiroshi Shimada
GIRL I ABANDONED, THE(1970, Jap.)
Joseph Shimada
RIO BRAVO(1959)
Ryuzo Shimada
BUDDHA(1965, Jap.); ZATOICHI(1968, Jap.)
Sab Shimada
CHALLENGE, THE(1982)
Shogo Shimada
EMPEROR AND A GENERAL, THE(1968, Jap.); DUEL AT EZO(1970, Jap.); GATE-WAY TO GLORY(1970, Jap.); PERFORMERS, THE(1970, Jap.); TORA! TORA! TO-RA!(1970, U.S./Jap.); TIDAL WAVE(1975, U.S./Jap.)
Teru Shimada
NIGHT CLUB LADY(1932); MIDNIGHT CLUB(1933); MURDER AT THE VANI-TIES(1934); OIL FOR THE LAMPS OF CHINA(1935); NEXT TIME WE LOVE(1936); REVOLT OF THE ZOMBIES(1936); WHITE LEGION, THE(1936); MR. MOTO'S LAST WARNING(1939); TOKYO JOE(1949); EMERGENCY WEDDING(1950); WAR OF THE WORLDS, THE(1953); BRIDGES AT TOKO-RI, THE(1954); SNOW CREATURE, THE,(1954); HOUSE OF BAMBOO(1955); NAVY WIFE(1956); BATTLE HYMN(1957); DELICATE DELINQUENT, THE(1957); BATTLE OF THE CORAL SEA(1959); TOKYO AFTER DARK(1959); WACKIEST SHIP IN THE ARMY, THE(1961); PRIZE, THE(1963); KING RAT(1965); ONE SPY TOO MANY(1966); WALK, DON'T RUN(1966); YOU ONLY LIVE TWICE(1967, Brit.)
Toru Shimada
FOUR FRIGHTENED PEOPLE(1934)
Kaoru Shimamori
1984
BALLAD OF NARAYAMA, THE(1984, Jap.)
Rytaro Shimamori
1984
BALLAD OF NARAYAMA, THE(1984, Jap.)
Seryozha Shiman
SONG OF THE FOREST(1963, USSR)
Anatoli Shimanyuk
ADVENTURE IN ODESSA(1954, USSR)
Derick Shimatsu
VARAN THE UNBELIEVABLE(1962, U.S./Jap.)
Kay Shimatsu
WALK, DON'T RUN(1966)
Lukas Shimatsu
WALK, DON'T RUN(1966)
Robin Shimatsu
DEVIL AT FOUR O'CLOCK, THE(1961)
Chizu Shimazaki
JOE BUTTERFLY(1957)
Shinpei Shimazaki
JOE BUTTERFLY(1957)
Yukiko Shimazaki
SEVEN SAMURAI, THE(1956, Jap.)
Kiyoshi Shimazu
TOPSY-TURVY JOURNEY(1970, Jap.), p; YOSAKOI JOURNEY(1970, Jap.), p
Masahiko Shimazu
OHAYO(1962, Jap.)
Hiroshi Shimazv
1941(1979)
Eiji Shimba
YOUTH IN FURY(1961, Jap.), w
Shigako Shimegi
SECRETS OF A WOMAN'S TEMPLE(1969, Jap.)
Edward Connell Skip Shimer
EQUINOX(1970)
Gen Shimizu
TOKYO FILE 212(1951); GATE OF HELL(1954, Jap.); SEVEN SAMURAI, THE(1956, Jap.)
Hiroko Shimizu
PLEASURES OF THE FLESH, THE(1965)
K. Shimizu
VARAN THE UNBELIEVABLE(1962, U.S./Jap.), art d
Kunio Shimizu
SHE AND HE(1967, Jap.), w; DAY THE SUN ROSE, THE(1969, Jap.), w
Masao Shimizu
IKIRU(1960, Jap.); SANJURO(1962, Jap.); LIFE OF OHARU(1964, Jap.); I LIVE IN FEAR(1967, Jap.); SANSHO THE BAILIFF(1969 Jap.)
Sachiko Shimizu
LAKE, THE(1970, Jap.), ed
Tetsutaro Shimizu
NUTCRACKER FANTASY(1979), ch
Joanna Shimkus
BOOM!(1968); DE L'AMOUR(1968, Fr./Ital.); HO(1968, Fr.); LAST ADVENTURE, THE(1968, Fr./Ital.); SIX IN PARIS(1968, Fr.); ZITA(1968, Fr.); LOST MAN, THE(1969); VIRGIN AND THE GYPSY, THE(1970, Brit.); MARRIAGE OF A YOUNG STOCKBR-OKER, THE(1971); TIME FOR LOVING, A(1971, Brit.)
Masahiro Shimoda
DOUBLE SUICIDE(1970, Jap.), d, w, p
Yuki Shimoda
AUNTIE MAME(1958); MAJORITY OF ONE, A(1961); SEVEN WOMEN FROM HELL(1961); HORIZONTAL LIEUTENANT, THE(1962); ONCE A THIEF(1965); MAC ARTHUR(1977); LAST FLIGHT OF NOAH'S ARK, THE(1980); OCTAGON, THE(1980)
Tomoo Shimogawara
ODD OBSESSION(1961, Jap.), art d; EARLY AUTUMN(1962, Jap.), art d; FLIGHT FROM ASHIYA(1964, U.S./Jap.); THOUSAND CRANES(1969, Jap.), art d
Shigenori Shimoishizaka
HIKEN YABURI(1969, Jap.), art d; ZATOICHI CHALLENGED(1970, Jap.), art d

Tsutomo Shimomoto
TENCHU!(1970, Jap.)
Akemi Shimomura
MY GEISHA(1962)
K. Shimomura
TERROR BENEATH THE SEA(1966, Jap.), ph
Sab Shimono
LOVING(1970); PARADES(1972); MIDWAY(1976); RABBIT TEST(1978); CHEECH AND CHONG'S NICE DREAMS(1981); LINE, THE(1982)
Kan Shimozawa
SHOWDOWN FOR ZATOICHI(1968, Jap.), w; ZATOICHI(1968, Jap.), w; ZATOICHI CHALLENGED(1970, Jap.), w; ZATOICHI MEETS YOJIMBO(1970, Jap.), w; ZATOI-CHI'S CONSPIRACY(1974, Jap.), w
Hayes G. Shimp
SILHOUETTES(1982), p
Kyo Shimura
SAMURAI(1967, Jap.)
Sachie Shimura
1984
BALLAD OF NARAYAMA, THE(1984, Jap.)
Takaashi Shimura
LOST WORLD OF SINBAD, THE(1965, Jap.)
Takashi Shimura
SAMURAI(PART III) (1967, Jap.); DRUNKEN ANGEL(1948, Jap.); RA-SHOMON(1951, Jap.); GODZILLA, RING OF THE MONSTERS(1956, Jap.); SEVEN SAMURAI, THE(1956, Jap.); HIDDEN FORTRESS, THE(1959, Jap.); IKIRU(1960, Jap.); I BOMBED PEARL HARBOR(1961, Jap.); MAN AGAINST MAN(1961, Jap.); THRONE OF BLOOD(1961, Jap.); YOJIMBO(1961, Jap.); DIFFERENT SONS(1962, Jap.); MO-THRA(1962, Jap.); SANJURO(1962, Jap.); CHUSHINGURA(1963, Jap.); HIGH AND LOW(1963, Jap.); IDIOT, THE(1963, Jap.); STRAY DOG(1963, Jap.); FRANKENSTEIN CONQUERS THE WORLD(1964, Jap./US); GORATH(1964, Jap.); SAGA OF THE VAGABONDS(1964, Jap.); SCANDAL(1964, Jap.); GHIDRAH, THE THREE-HEADED MONSTER(1965, Jap.); KWAIDAN(1965, Jap.); SAMURAI ASSASSIN(1965, Jap.); NIGHT IN BANGKOK(1966, Jap.); RED BEARD(1966, Jap.); I LIVE IN FEAR(1967, Jap.); EMPEROR AND A GENERAL, THE(1968, Jap.); DAREDEVIL IN THE CAST-LE(1969, Jap.); DAY THE SUN ROSE, THE(1969, Jap.); PROPHECIES OF NOS-TRADAMUS(1974, Jap.); ZATOICHI'S CONSPIRACY(1974, Jap.)
Yukie Shimura
1984
BALLAD OF NARAYAMA, THE(1984, Jap.)
Isamu Shimuzu
MESSAGE FROM SPACE(1978, Jap.)
Anna Shin
MANCHURIAN CANDIDATE, THE(1962); NUN AND THE SERGEANT, THE(1962); SPIRAL ROAD, THE(1962); WALK, DON'T RUN(1966)
Kinzo Shin
GOLDEN DEMON(1956, Jap.); ENJO(1959, Jap.); TWILIGHT PATH(1965, Jap.); WHISPERING JOE(1969, Jap.)
Dean Shindel
1984
LOVE STREAMS(1984)
Eitaro Shindo
TRAITORS(1957, Jap.); LIFE OF OHARU(1964, Jap.); SANSHO THE BAILIFF(1969, Jap.); GEISHA, A(1978, Jap.)
Emi Shindo
ONIMASA(1983, Jap.)
Kaneto Shindo
CHILDREN OF HIROSHIMA(1952, Jap.), d&w; ISLAND, THE(1962, Jap.), p, d&w; WAYSIDE PEBBLE, THE(1962, Jap.), w; THIS MADDING CROWD(1964, Jap.), w; ONIBABA(1965, Jap.), d&w, art d; GAMBLING SAMURAI, THE(1966, Jap.), w; KUROENKO(1968, Jap), d&w; LOST SEX(1968, Jap.), d&w; PASSION(1968, Jap.), w; DEVIL'S TEMPLE(1969, Jap.), w; THOUSAND CRANES(1969, Jap.), w
Karie Shindo
NAVY WIFE(1956)
Kenato Shindo
CHALLENGE TO LIVE(1964, Jap.), w
Seigo Shindo
TOKYO FILE 212(1951), art d; MAGIC BOY(1960, Jap.), art d
Tak Shindo
STOPOVER TOKYO(1957), md
Andy Shine
THAT LADY(1955, Brit.); RICHARD III(1956, Brit.)
Bill Shine
LET GEORGE DO IT(1940, Brit.); MAIL TRAIN(1941, Brit.); TURNED OUT NICE AGAIN(1941, Brit.); VACATION FROM MARRIAGE(1945, Brit.); HIDEOUT(1948, Brit.); RED SHOES, THE(1948, Brit.); PASSPORT TO PIMLICO(1949, Brit.); PRIVATE ANGELO(1949, Brit.); UNDER CAPRICORN(1949); SOMETHING IN THE CITY(1950, Brit.); HER PANELLED DOOR(1951, Brit.); OLD MOTHER RILEY'S JUNGLE TREAS-URE(1951, Brit.); SCARLET THREAD(1951, Brit.); CARETAKERS DAUGHTER, THE(1952, Brit.); HOT ICE(1952, Brit.); NEVER LOOK BACK(1952, Brit.); YOU CAN'T BEAT THE IRISH(1952, Brit.); CLUE OF THE MISSING APE, THE(1953, Brit.); THERE WAS A YOUNG LADY(1953, Brit.); DUEL IN THE JUNGLE(1954, Brit.); TONIGHT'S THE NIGHT(1954, Brit.); WOMAN'S ANGLE, THE(1954, Brit.); DEEP BLUE SEA, THE(1955, Brit.); INNOCENTS IN PARIS(1955, Brit.); LOVERS, HAPPY LO-VERS!(1955, Brit.); QUENTIN DURWARD(1955); WHERE THERE'S A WILL(1955, Brit.); LAST MAN TO HANG, THE(1956, Brit.); NOT SO DUSTY(1956, Brit.); RICHARD III(1956, Brit.); HIGH FLIGHT(1957, Brit.); HOUSE IN THE WOODS, THE(1957, Brit.); RAISING A RIOT(1957, Brit.); DIPLOMATIC CORPSE, THE(1958, Brit.); MAN INSIDE, THE(1958, Brit.); BOY AND THE BRIDGE, THE(1959, Brit.); JACK THE RIPPER(1959, Brit.); LEFT, RIGHT AND CENTRE(1959); LIBEL(1959, Brit.); IT TAKES A THIEF(1960, Brit.); DOUBLE BUNK(1961, Brit.); MY SON, THE VAMPIRE(1963, Brit.); IN TROUBLE WITH EVE(1964, Brit.); JOEY BOY(1965, Brit.); SKY BIKE, THE(1967, Brit.)
Billy Shine
FLYING SCOTSMAN, THE(1929, Brit.); GREENWOOD TREE, THE zero(1930, Brit.); LAST HOUR, THE(1930, Brit.); UNDER THE GREENWOOD TREE(1930, Brit.); MANY WATERS(1931, Brit.); THESE CHARMING PEOPLE(1931, Brit.); MONEY FOR NOTH-ING(1932, Brit.); VERDICT OF THE SEA(1932, Brit.); MAN FROM TORONTO, THE(1933, Brit.); MY OLD DUTCH(1934, Brit.); IT HAPPENED IN PARIS(1935, Brit.); LATE EXTRA(1935, Brit.); SCARLET PIMPERNEL, THE(1935, Brit.); FIND THE

LADY(1936, Brit.); GAOL BREAK(1936, Brit.); HIGHLAND FLING(1936, Brit.); SENSATION(1936, Brit.); TO CATCH A THIEF(1936, Brit.); LAST ADVENTURERS, THE(1937, Brit); STRANGE ADVENTURES OF MR. SMITH, THE(1937, Brit.); TROOPSHIP(1938, Brit.); VILLIERS DIAMOND, THE(1938, Brit.); YOUNG AND INNOCENT(1938, Brit.); YOU'RE THE DOCTOR(1938, Brit.); FACE AT THE WINDOW, THE(1939, Brit.); CROOKS TOUR(1940, Brit.); OVER THE MOON(1940, Brit.); CHAMPAGNE CHARLIE(1944, Brit.); FOR YOU ALONE(1945, Brit.); WINSLOW BOY, THE(1950)

Billy Shine, Jr.
STRAUSS' GREAT WALTZ(1934, Brit.)

John L. Shine
Silents
AMAZING LOVERS(1921)
Misc. Silents
LITTLE LADY EILEEN(1916); LIE, THE(1918); MAN AND WOMAN(1921)

John Shine
Misc. Silents
GREATER SINNER, THE(1919)

Wilfred Shine
LADY FROM THE SEA, THE(1929, Brit.); CROSS ROADS(1930, Brit.); GREENWOOD TREE, THE(1930, Brit.); LAST HOUR, THE(1930, Brit.); LOVES OF ROBERT BURNS, THE(1930, Brit.); UNDER THE GREENWOOD TREE(1930, Brit.); BELLS, THE(1931, Brit.); OLD SOLDIERS NEVER DIE(1931, Brit.); MAROONED(1933, Brit.); OUT OF THE PAST(1933, Brit.); OVER THE MOON(1940, Brit.)
Silents
MANXMAN, THE(1929, Brit.)

William Shine
YELLOW MASK, THE(1930, Brit.)

[William] Bill Shine
VICE VERSA(1948, Brit.)

Murv Shiner
SECOND FIDDLE TO A STEEL GUITAR(1965)

Ronald Shiner
DOCTOR'S ORDERS(1934, Brit.); MY OLD DUTCH(1934, Brit.); GENTLEMAN'S AGREEMENT(1935, Brit.); IT'S A BET(1935, Brit.); LINE ENGAGED(1935, Brit.); ONCE A THIEF(1935, Brit.); REGAL CAVALCADE(1935, Brit.); SQUIBS(1935, Brit.); EXCUSE MY GLOVE(1936, Brit.); KING OF HEARTS(1936, Brit.); BEAUTY AND THE BARGE(1937, Brit.); BLACK TULIP, THE(1937, Brit.); DINNER AT THE RITZ(1937, Brit.); DREAMING LIPS(1937, Brit.); THEY DRIVE BY NIGHT(1938, Brit.); YANK AT OXFORD, A(1938); COME ON GEORGE(1939, Brit.); DISCOVERIES(1939, Brit.); FLYING FIFTY-FIVE(1939, Brit.); MIDDLE WATCH, THE(1939, Brit.); PRISON WITHOUT BARS(1939, Brit.); TROUBLE BREWING(1939, Brit.); BULLDOG SEES IT THROUGH(1940, Brit.); CASE OF THE FRIGHTENED LADY, THE(1940. Brit.); LET GEORGE DO IT(1940, Brit.); LION HAS WINGS, THE(1940, Brit.); MISSING PEOPLE, THE(1940, Brit.); MYSTERIOUS MR. REEDER, THE(1940, Brit.); OLD BILL AND SON(1940, Brit.); SPIDER, THE(1940, Brit.); WHO IS GUILTY?(1940, Brit.); SEVENTH SURVIVOR, THE(1941, Brit.); SOUTH AMERICAN GEORGE(1941, Brit.); BALLOON GOES UP, THE(1942, Brit.); KING ARTHUR WAS A GENTLEMAN(1942, Brit.); SABOTAGE AT SEA(1942, Brit.); THOSE KIDS FROM TOWN(1942, Brit.); UNPUBLISHED STORY(1942, Brit.); WINGS AND THE WOMAN(1942, Brit.); YOUNG MR. PITT, THE(1942, Brit.); AMAZING MR. FORREST, THE(1943, Brit.); BUTLER'S DILEMMA, THE(1943, Brit.); GENTLE SEX, THE(1943, Brit.); GET CRACKING(1943, Brit.); MISS LONDON LTD.(1943, Brit.); NIGHT INVADER, THE(1943, Brit); THURSDAY'S CHILD(1943, Brit.); BEES IN PARADISE(1944, Brit.); CAESAR AND CLEOPATRA(1946, Brit.); GEORGE IN CIVVY STREET(1946, Brit.); YANK IN LONDON, A(1946, Brit.); SMUGGLERS, THE(1948, Brit.); FORBIDDEN(1949, Brit.); RELUCTANT HEROES(1951, Brit.); WORM'S EYE VIEW(1951, Brit.); LITTLE BIG SHOT(1952, Brit.); MAGIC BOX, THE(1952, Brit.); TOP OF THE FORM(1953, Brit.); AUNT CLARA(1954, Brit.); LAUGHING ANNE(1954, Brit./U.S.); UP TO HIS NECK(1954, Brit.); INNOCENTS IN PARIS(1955, Brit.); SEE HOW THEY RUN(1955, Brit.); DRY ROT(1956, Brit.); KEEP IT CLEAN(1956, Brit.); CARRY ON ADMIRAL(1957, Brit.); NOT WANTED ON VOYAGE(1957, Brit.); GIRLS AT SEA(1958, Brit.); NAVY LARK, THE(1959, Brit.); NIGHT WE GOT THE BIRD, THE(1961, Brit.); MY WIFE'S FAMILY(1962, Brit.); OPERATION BULLSHINE(1963, Brit.)

Helen Shingler
SILVER DARLINGS, THE(1947, Brit.); QUIET WEEKEND(1948, Brit.); ROSSITER CASE, THE(1950, Brit.); LADY WITH A LAMP, THE(1951, Brit.); CARETAKERS DAUGHTER, THE(1952, Brit.); JUDGMENT DEFERRED(1952, Brit.); BACKGROUND(1953, Brit.); LAUGHING ANNE(1954, Brit./U.S.); ROOM IN THE HOUSE(1955, Brit.); RX MURDER(1958, Brit.)

Wilfred Shingleton
THERE AIN'T NO JUSTICE(1939, Brit.), art d; TROUBLE BREWING(1939, Brit.), art d; LET GEORGE DO IT(1940, Brit.), art d; RETURN TO YESTERDAY(1940, Brit.), art d; SALOON BAR(1940, Brit.), art d; SECRET FOUR, THE(1940, Brit.), art d; SPARE A COPPER(1940, Brit.), art d; THREE COCKEYED SAILORS(1940, Brit.), art d; PROUD VALLEY, THE(1941, Brit.), art d; TURNED OUT NICE AGAIN(1941, Brit.), art d; SHIPS WITH WINGS(1942, Brit.), art d; YOUNG MAN'S FANCY(1943, Brit.), art d; BONNIE PRINCE CHARLIE(1948, Brit.), prod d; TAKE MY LIFE(1948, Brit.), art d; LAST DAYS OF DOLWYN, THE(1949, Brit.), prod d; SAINTS AND SINNERS(1949, Brit.), prod d; CURE FOR LOVE, THE(1950, Brit.), set d; GREAT MANHUNT, THE(1951, Brit.), prod d; PASSIONATE SENTRY, THE(1952, Brit.), prod d; MEET MR. LUCIFER(1953, Brit.), art d; SEA DEVILS(1953), art d; FIRE OVER AFRICA(1954, Brit.), art d; GREEN SCARF, THE(1954, Brit.), art d; HOBSON'S CHOICE(1954, Brit.), prod d; FOOTSTEPS IN THE FOG(1955, Brit.), art d; SHADOW OF THE EAGLE(1955, Brit.), art d; STORM OVER THE NILE(1955, Brit.), prod d, art d; KID FOR TWO FARTHINGS, A(1956, Brit.), art d; PORT AFRIQUE(1956, Brit.), art d; ABANDON SHIP!(1957, Brit.), prod d; SHE PLAYED WITH FIRE(1957, Brit.), art d; KEY, THE(1958, Brit.), prod d; INNOCENTS, THE(1961, U.S./Brit.), prod d, art d; PURE HELL OF ST. TRINIAN'S, THE(1961, Brit.), art d; TROUBLE IN THE SKY(1961, Brit.), art d; TERM OF TRIAL(1962, Brit.), prod d; I COULD GO ON SINGING(1963), prod d, art d; QUEEN'S GUARDS, THE(1963, Brit.), art d; STOLEN HOURS(1963), prod d; GOODBYE GEMINI(1970, Brit.), prod d; MACBETH(1971, Brit.), prod d; SAY HELLO TO YESTERDAY(1971, Brit.), prod d; VOYAGE OF THE DAMNED(1976, Brit.), prod d; LADY VANISHES, THE(1980, Brit.), prod d; EYE OF THE NEEDLE(1981), prod d; HEAT AND DUST(1983, Brit.), prod d

Wilfrid Shingleton
GREAT EXPECTATIONS(1946, Brit.), art d; WALTZ OF THE TOREADORS(1962, Brit.), prod d; TARZAN'S THREE CHALLENGES(1963), prod d; JUDITH(1965), prod d; PROMISE HER ANYTHING(1966, Brit.), prod d; PRUDENCE AND THE PILL(1968, Brit.), prod d; SEBASTIAN(1968, Brit.), prod d; BUTTERCUP CHAIN, THE(1971,

Takumi Shinjo
EAST CHINA SEA(1969, Jap.); TENCHU!(1970, Jap.)

S. Shinkevich
CITY OF YOUTH(1938, USSR)

Everett Shinn
Silents
POLLY OF THE CIRCUS(1917), art d

Jackie Shinn
GAMEKEEPER, THE(1980, Brit.); LOOKS AND SMILES(1982, Brit.)

Masahiro Shinoda
YOUTH IN FURY(1961, Jap.), d; SCANDALOUS ADVENTURES OF BURAIKAN, THE(1970, Jap.), d; DEMON POND(1980, Jap.), d

Mashahero Shinoda
BANISHED(1978, Jap.), d, w

Saburo Shinoda
WAY OUT, WAY IN(1970, Jap.)

Takemo K. Shinohara
MAJORITY OF ONE, A(1961), tech adv

Sozaburo Shinomura
YOSAKOI JOURNEY(1970, Jap.), ph

Nichiei Shinsha
KUROENKO(1968, Jap), p

Jack Shintani
NAVY WIFE(1956)

Micko Shintani
NAVY WIFE(1956)

Sue Shiomi
MESSAGE FROM SPACE(1978, Jap.)

Cory B. Shiozaki
FAREWELL, MY LOVELY(1975)

Reuben Ship
GIRL ON THE BOAT, THE(1962, Brit.), w; THERE WAS A CROOKED MAN(1962, Brit.), w

The Ship's Master
SILVER CHALICE, THE(1954)

Henry Shipes
Misc. Talkies
VERNON, FLORIDA(1982)

Graham Shipham
STOLEN HOURS(1963), ed

Julie Shipley
THAT SUMMER(1979, Brit.)

A.R. Shipman
NO ORCHIDS FOR MISS BLANDISH(1948, Brit.), p; THINGS HAPPEN AT NIGHT(1948, Brit.), p

Barry Shipman
DANGEROUS HOLIDAY(1937), d&w; FRONTIER VENGEANCE(1939), w; HI-YO SILVER(1940), w; LONE STAR RAIDERS(1940), w; ROCKY MOUNTAIN RANGERS(1940), w; TRAIL BLAZERS, THE(1940), w; PRAIRIE PIONEERS(1941), w; CODE OF THE OUTLAW(1942), w; PHANTOM PLAINSMEN, THE(1942), w; RAIDERS OF THE RANGE(1942), w; LUMBERJACK(1944), w; OUT CALIFORNIA WAY(1946), w; SIX-GUN LAW(1948), w; SONG OF IDAHO(1948), w; WEST OF SONORA(1948), w; BLAZING TRAIL, THE(1949), w; LARAMIE(1949), w; SMOKY MOUNTAIN MELODY(1949), w; ACROSS THE BADLANDS(1950), w; FRONTIER OUTPOST(1950), w; HOEDOWN(1950), w; HORSEMEN OF THE SIERRAS(1950), w; OUTCAST OF BLACK MESA(1950), w; RAIDERS OF TOMAHAWK CREEK(1950), w; STREETS OF GHOST TOWN(1950), w; TEXAS DYNAMO(1950), w; BANDITS OF EL DORADO(1951), w; BONANZA TOWN(1951), w; CYCLONE FURY(1951), w; FORT SAVAGE RAIDERS(1951), w; KID FROM AMARILLO, THE(1951), w; PECOS RIVER(1951), w; SNAKE RIVER DESPERADOES(1951), w; JUNCTION CITY(1952), w; KID FROM BROKEN GUN, THE(1952), w; LARAMIE MOUNTAINS(1952), w; MONTANA TERRITORY(1952), w; ROUGH, TOUGH WEST, THE(1952), w; SMOKY CANYON(1952), w; UNTAMED HEIRESS(1954), w; CAROLINA CANNONBALL(1955), w; LAY THAT RIFLE DOWN(1955), w; STRANGER AT MY DOOR(1956), w; GUNFIRE AT INDIAN GAP(1957), w; HELL'S CROSSROADS(1957), w; LAST STAGECOACH WEST, THE(1957), w

Bert Shipman
Silents
BELOW THE LINE(1925), ph

Edna Shipman
Misc. Silents
GOD'S CRUCIBLE(1921)

Gertrude Shipman
Misc. Silents
ARIZONA(1913)

Gwyn Shipman
LAWTON STORY, THE(1949); PRINCE OF PEACE, THE(1951)

Gwynne Shipman
BATTLE OF GREED(1934); TRAIL DUST(1936)

Harry Shipman
SHAKEDOWN(1936), w

Helen Shipman
GREAT POWER, THE(1929); CHRISTOPHER BEAN(1933); DOUBLE DOOR(1934); MEN WITHOUT NAMES(1935); NAUGHTY MARIETTA(1935); SAN FRANCISCO(1936); SMALL TOWN GIRL(1936); WIFE VERSUS SECRETARY(1936); HOUSE ACROSS THE BAY, THE(1940)

Jeanne Shipman
GNOME-MOBILE, THE(1967)

Kenneth Shipman
GIRL GETTERS, THE(1966, Brit.), p; BURKE AND HARE(1972, Brit.), p

Neil Shipman
WINGS IN THE DARK(1935), w

Nell Shipman
Silents
FIRES OF CONSCIENCE(1916)
Misc. Silents
GOD'S COUNTRY AND THE WOMAN(1916); THROUGH THE WALL(1916); BLACK WOLF, THE(1917); BAREE, SON OF KAZAN(1918); CAVANAUGH OF THE FOREST RANGERS(1918); GENTLEMAN'S AGREEMENT, A(1918); GIRL FROM BEYOND,

THE(1918); HOME TRAIL, THE(1918); TIGER OF THE SEA, THE(1918); WILD STRAIN, THE(1918); BACK TO GOD'S COUNTRY(1919 US/Can.); GIRL FROM GOD'S COUNTRY, THE(1921), a, d; GRUB STAKE, THE(1923); GOLDEN YUKON, THE(1927), a, d

Nina Shipman
HUNTERS, THE(1958); VERTIGO(1958); BLUE DENIM(1959); OREGON TRAIL, THE(1959); SAY ONE FOR ME(1959); HIGH TIME(1960)

Sam Shipman
PAY OFF, THE(1930), w; WOMAN IN ROOM 13, THE(1932), w

Samuel Shipman
FAST LIFE(1929), w; EAST IS WEST(1930), w; LAWFUL LARCENY(1930), w; SCARLET PAGES(1930), w; MANHATTAN PARADE(1931), w; LAW OF THE UNDERWORLD(1938), w; FRIENDLY ENEMIES(1942), w
Silents
EAST IS WEST(1922), w; LAWFUL LARCENY(1923), w

Sylvia Shipman
RACHEL, RACHEL(1968)

Gwyn Shipmen
EVERY GIRL SHOULD BE MARRIED(1948)

Mary Shipp
JENNIFER(1953)

Camille Ships
STRYKER(1983, Phil.)

Paul Shipton
SWEET CHARITY(1969)

Masao Shirai
AFFAIR AT AKITSU(1980, Jap.), p

Sono Shirai
NAVY WIFE(1956)

Ymui Shirakawa
MAN AGAINST MAN(1961, Jap.)

Yumi Shirakawa
RODAN(1958, Jap.); H-MAN, THE(1959, Jap.); MYSTERIANS, THE(1959, Jap.); SECRET OF THE TELEGIAN, THE(1961, Jap.); DIFFERENT SONS(1962, Jap.); EARLY AUTUMN(1962, Jap.); LAST WAR, THE(1962, Jap.); CHUSHINGURA(1963, Jap.); WALL-EYED NIPPON(1963, Jap.); CHALLENGE TO LIVE(1964, Jap.); GORATH(1964, Jap.)

Mickey Shirard
AVALANCHE EXPRESS(1979), cos

Yoshio Shirasaka
TWILIGHT PATH(1965, Jap.), w; KOJIRO(1967, Jap.), w

David Shire
TAKING OF PELHAM ONE, TWO, THREE, THE(1974), m; DRIVE, HE SAID(1971), m; ONE MORE TRAIN TO ROB(1971), m; SKIN GAME(1971), m; SUMMERTREE(1971), m; TO FIND A MAN(1972), m; CLASS OF '44(1973), m; SHOWDOWN(1973), m; STEELYARD BLUES(1973), m; TWO PEOPLE(1973), m; CONVERSATION, THE(1974), m; FAREWELL, MY LOVELY(1975), m; FORTUNE, THE(1975), m, md; HINDENBURG, THE(1975), m; ALL THE PRESIDENT'S MEN(1976), m; HARRY AND WALTER GO TO NEW YORK(1976), a, m; SATURDAY NIGHT FEVER(1977), m; STRAIGHT TIME(1978), m; FAST BREAK(1979), m; NORMA RAE(1979), m; OLD BOYFRIENDS(1979), m; PROMISE, THE(1979), m; NIGHT THE LIGHTS WENT OUT IN GEORGIA, THE(1981), m; ONLY WHEN I LAUGH(1981), m; PATERNITY(1981), m; MAX DUGAN RETURNS(1983), m
1984
OH GOD! YOU DEVIL(1984), m; 2010(1984), m

Talia Shire
GODFATHER, THE(1972); OUTSIDE MAN, THE(1973, U.S./FR.); GODFATHER, THE, PART II(1974); ROCKY(1976); OLD BOYFRIENDS(1979); PROPHECY(1979); ROCKY II(1979); WINDOWS(1980); ROCKY III(1982)

Dorinea Shirely
Silents
ZERO(1928, Brit.)

William L. Shirer
MAGIC FACE, THE(1951, Aust.)

Alan Shires
HE LOVED AN ACTRESS(1938, Brit.)

Spencer Shires
SKY BIKE, THE(1967, Brit.)

Yumi Shirikawa
YEARNING(1964, Jap.)

Moti Shirin
1984
LITTLE DRUMMER GIRL, THE(1984)

Adam Hull Shirk
INGAGI(1931), w; HOUSE OF MYSTERY(1934), w; APE, THE(1940), w

Bill Shirk
Misc. Talkies
MODERN DAY HOUDINI(1983)

Shirley
DOWN MISSOURI WAY(1946)

Aleisa Shirley
SPACEHUNTER: ADVENTURES IN THE FORBIDDEN ZONE(1983); SWEET SIXTEEN(1983)

Anne Shirley
ANNE OF GREEN GABLES(1934); CHASING YESTERDAY(1935); STEAMBOAT ROUND THE BEND(1935); CHATTERBOX(1936); MAKE WAY FOR A LADY(1936); M'LISS(1936); MEET THE MISSUS(1937); STELLA DALLAS(1937); TOO MANY WIVES(1937); BOY SLAVES(1938); CONDEMNED WOMEN(1938); GIRLS' SCHOOL(1938); LAW OF THE UNDERWORLD(1938); MAN TO REMEMBER, A(1938); MOTHER CAREY'S CHICKENS(1938); CAREER(1939); SORORITY HOUSE(1939); ANNE OF WINDY POPLARS(1940); SATURDAY'S CHILDREN(1940); VIGIL IN THE NIGHT(1940); DEVIL AND DANIEL WEBSTER, THE(1941); FOUR JACKS AND A JILL(1941); UNEXPECTED UNCLE(1941); WEST POINT WIDOW(1941); LADY BODYGUARD(1942); MAYOR OF 44TH STREET, THE(1942); POWERS GIRL, THE(1942); BOMBARDIER(1943); GOVERNMENT GIRL(1943); MAN FROM FRISCO(1944); MUSIC IN MANHATTAN(1944); MURDER, MY SWEET(1945)

Anne Shirley [Dawn O'Day]
RASPUTIN AND THE EMPRESS(1932)

Arthur Shirley
MY OLD DUTCH(1934, Brit.), w; IT'S NEVER TOO LATE TO MEND(1937, Brit.), w
Silents
JACK TAR(1915, Brit.), w; MY OLD DUTCH(1915, Brit.), a, w; WOMAN AND WINE(1915), d; BRANDING BROADWAY(1918)
Misc. Silents
BAWBS O' BLUE RIDGE(1916); FALL OF A NATION, THE(1916); VALIANTS OF VIRGINIA, THE(1916); BETTY BE GOOD(1917); BIT OF KINDLING, A(1917); WILDCAT, THE(1917); MODERN LOVE(1918); ROPED(1919)

Bill Shirley
DOCTORS DON'T TELL(1941); ROOKIES ON PARADE(1941); SAILORS ON LEAVE(1941); FLYING TIGERS(1942); HI, NEIGHBOR(1942); ICE-CAPADES REVUE(1942); ABBOTT AND COSTELLO MEET CAPTAIN KIDD(1952); I DREAM OF JEANIE(1952); SWEETHEARTS ON PARADE(1953); SLEEPING BEAUTY(1959); MY FAIR LADY(1964)

Catherine Shirley
RING OF BRIGHT WATER(1969, Brit.), makeup

Dorinea Shirley
Silents
OPEN COUNTRY(1922, Brit.); AUDACIOUS MR. SQUIRE, THE(1923, Brit.); NELL GWYNNE(1926, Brit.); AFTERWARDS(1928, Brit.)
Misc. Silents
HIS SUPREME SACRIFICE(1922, Brit.); PETTICOAT LOOSE(1922, Brit.)

Florence Shirley
NINOTCHKA(1939); WOMEN, THE(1939); I TAKE THIS WOMAN(1940); LADY WITH RED HAIR(1940); NEW MOON(1940); OPENED BY MISTAKE(1940); PRIVATE AFFAIRS(1940); THIRD FINGER, LEFT HAND(1940); THREE SONS O'GUNS(1941); WHEN LADIES MEET(1941); MAISIE GETS HER MAN(1942); SECRET AGENT OF JAPAN(1942); WE WERE DANCING(1942); DANCING MASTERS, THE(1943); LET'S FACE IT(1943); DEADLINE–U.S.A.(1952); STARS AND STRIPES FOREVER(1952)

Irene Shirley
MELODY FOR THREE(1941); CROSSROADS(1942); ICE-CAPADES REVUE(1942); SOMEONE TO REMEMBER(1943); KISS OF DEATH(1947)

Jane Shirley
MY BROTHER JONATHAN(1949, Brit.)

Jessie Shirley
Silents
MAN HATER, THE(1917)

John Shirley
BLACKMAILED(1951, Brit.), ed; SCARLET SPEAR, THE(1954, Brit.), ed; REACH FOR THE SKY(1957, Brit.), ed; UP IN THE WORLD(1957, Brit.), ed; CARVE HER NAME WITH PRIDE(1958, Brit.), ed; SHERIFF OF FRACTURED JAW, THE(1958, Brit.), ed; CARRY ON NURSE(1959, Brit.), ed; CARRY ON CONSTABLE(1960, Brit.), ed; PLEASE TURN OVER(1960, Brit.), ed; BEWARE OF CHILDREN(1961, Brit.), ed; CARRY ON REGARDLESS(1961, Brit.), ed; WATCH YOUR STERN(1961, Brit.), ed; CARRY ON CRUISING(1962, Brit.), ed; CARRY ON TEACHER(1962, Brit.), ed; ROOMMATES(1962, Brit.), ed; TWICE AROUND THE DAFFODILS(1962, Brit.), ed; I COULD GO ON SINGING(1963), ed; SEVENTH DAWN, THE(1964), ed; JOEY BOY(1965, Brit.), ed; ARRIVEDERCI, BABY!(1966, Brit.), ed; PROMISE HER ANYTHING(1966, Brit.), ed; DOCTOR FAUSTUS(1967, Brit.), ed; CHITTY CHITTY BANG BANG(1968, Brit.), ed; WHEN EIGHT BELLS TOLL(1971, Brit.), ed; ZEPPELIN(1971, Brit.), ed; FOURTEEN, THE(1973, Brit.), ed; LIVE AND LET DIE(1973, Brit.), ed; INTERNECINE PROJECT, THE(1974, Brit.), ed; MAN WITH THE GOLDEN GUN, THE(1974, Brit.), ed; SQUEEZE, THE(1977, Brit.), ed; TOMORROW NEVER COMES(1978, Brit./Can.), ed; LION OF THE DESERT(1981, Libya/Brit.), ed; EXPERIENCE PREFERRED... BUT NOT ESSENTIAL(1983, Brit.), ed; NATE AND HAYES(1983, U.S./New Zealand), ed
1984
KIPPERBANG(1984, Brit.), ed

Judy Shirley
SHE KNEW WHAT SHE WANTED(1936, Brit.)

Pam Shirley
1984
MAKING THE GRADE(1984)

Peg Shirley
IMITATION OF LIFE(1959); SOMETHING WILD(1961); THOMAS CROWN AFFAIR, THE(1968); RETURN OF COUNT YORGA, THE(1971); COMMITMENT, THE(1976); ZERO TO SIXTY(1978), w

Robert Shirley
Silents
MAN WHO MADE GOOD, THE(1917), w

Tom Shirley
Silents
KING OF KINGS, THE(1927)
Misc. Silents
RED HOT LEATHER(1926)

Wayne Shirley
Misc. Talkies
SKEZAG(1971)

William Shirley
THREE LITTLE SISTERS(1944)

The Shirley Ross Quartet
HOLLYWOOD PARTY(1934)

Shirley the python
FOUL PLAY(1978)

Takashi Shirmura
MYSTERIANS, THE(1959, Jap.)

A. Shirokauer
ELISABETH OF AUSTRIA(1931, Ger.), w

Alfred Shirokauer
IDOL OF PARIS(1948, Brit.), w

S. Shirokova
CONCENTRATION CAMP(1939, USSR)

Masao Shirota
GIGANTIS(1959, Jap./U.S.), spec eff

Stella Shirpsor
LILLIAN RUSSELL(1940)

Gordon Shirreffs
LONG RIDE FROM HELL, A(1970, Ital.), w
Gordon D. Shirreffs
LONESOME TRAIL, THE(1955), w; OREGON PASSAGE(1958), w
Cathie Shirriff
1984
COVERGIRL(1984, Can.); STAR TREK III: THE SEARCH FOR SPOCK(1984)
Cathy Shirriff
OLD DRACULA(1975, Brit.)
Yukoo Shirukaya
SILENCE HAS NO WINGS(1971, Jap.)
V. Shiryayev
KIEV COMEDY, A(1963, USSR)
Joe Shishido
GATE OF FLESH(1964, Jap.)
Boris Shishkin
TAXI TO HEAVEN(1944, USSR)
S. Shishko
Misc. Silents
PALACE AND FORTRESS(1924, USSR); DECEMBRISTS(1927, USSR)
Paula Lee Shiu
PASSPORT TO CHINA(1961, Brit.)
Paula Li Shiu
SOME MAY LIVE(1967, Brit.); BATTLE BENEATH THE EARTH(1968, Brit.)
Shiva
OCEAN'S ELEVEN(1960)
Gil Shiva
END OF THE WORLD(in Our Usual Bed In a Night Full of Rain), THE (1978, Ital.), p
Mark Shivas
RICHARD'S THINGS(1981, Brit.), p; MOONLIGHTING(1982, Brit.), p
Governor Allan Shivers of Texas
LUCY GALLANT(1955)
Shizen
HALLELUJAH THE HILLS(1963), set d
Sheldon Shkolnik
TELL ME A RIDDLE(1980), m
S. Shkurat
TRAIN GOES TO KIEV, THE(1961, USSR)
Stepan Shkurat
Silents
EARTH(1930, USSR)
V. Shkurkin
MEET ME IN MOSCOW(1966, USSR)
I. Shkurya
SANDU FOLLOWS THE SUN(1965, USSR)
H.A. Shlettow
IMMORTAL VAGABOND(1931, Ger.)
M. Shlosberg
Misc. Silents
STEPMOTHER, THE(1914, USSR)
Sonia Shlosberg
Misc. Silents
CANTOR'S DAUGHTER, THE(1913, USSR)
P. Shmakov
DREAM COME TRUE, A(1963, USSR)
G. Shmovanov
WHEN THE TREES WERE TALL(1965, USSR)
Sami Shmueli
MADRON(1970, U.S./Israel)
Tatyana Shmyga
BALLAD OF A HUSSAR(1963, USSR)
Natasha Shneider
1984
2010(1984)
A. Shnitke
UNCLE VANYA(1972, USSR), m
Olga Shoberova
WHO KILLED JESSIE?(1965, Czech.); SIR, YOU ARE A WIDOWER(1971, Czech.)
Shochiku Kagekidan Girls Revue
SAYONARA(1957)
The Shochiku Troupe from Kokusai Theater
HOUSE OF BAMBOO(1955)
Marion Shockley
NEAR THE TRAIL'S END(1931); STAGE DOOR CANTEEN(1943)
Milton Shockley
TO HAVE AND HAVE NOT(1944)
Shope Shodeinde
SAILOR'S RETURN, THE(1978, Brit.)
Ann Shoemaker
CHANCE AT HEAVEN(1933); CHEATING CHEATERS(1934); DOCTOR MONI-CA(1934); ALICE ADAMS(1935); DOG OF FLANDERS, A(1935); STRANDED(1935); WOMAN IN RED, THE(1935); SINS OF MAN(1936); LIFE OF THE PARTY, THE(1937); SHALL WE DANCE(1937); STELLA DALLAS(1937); THEY WON'T FORGET(1937); BABES IN ARMS(1939); ROMANCE OF THE REDWOODS(1939); THEY ALL COME OUT(1939); ANGEL FROM TEXAS, AN(1940); CURTAIN CALL(1940); ELLERY QUEEN. MASTER DETECTIVE(1940); FARMER'S DAUGHTER, THE(1940); GIRL FROM AVENUE A(1940); MARINES FLY HIGH, THE(1940); MY FAVORITE WI-FE(1940); SEVENTEEN(1940); STRIKE UP THE BAND(1940); SCATTERGOOD PULLS THE STRINGS(1941); YOU'LL NEVER GET RICH(1941); ABOVE SUSPICION(1943); MR. WINKLE GOES TO WAR(1944); THIRTY SECONDS OVER TOKYO(1944); CONFLICT(1945); WHAT A BLONDE(1945); MAGIC TOWN(1947); RETURN OF THE WHISTLER, THE(1948); SITTING PRETTY(1948); WALLFLOWER(1948); RECKLESS MOMENTS, THE(1949); SHOCKPROOF(1949); WOMAN'S SECRET, A(1949); HOUSE BY THE RIVER(1950); SUNRISE AT CAMPOBELLO(1960); FORTUNE COOKIE, THE(1966)
Ida Shoemaker
GANGWAY FOR TOMORROW(1943); SKY'S THE LIMIT, THE(1943); THIS LAND IS MINE(1943); NONE BUT THE LONELY HEART(1944); YOUTH RUNS WILD(1944)

Lu Shoemaker
CULPEPPER CATTLE COMPANY, THE(1972)
Joseph Shoengold
Misc. Silents
CHILDREN OF FATE(1926)
Fukuoka Shogo
HOTSPRINGS HOLIDAY(1970, Jap.)
Li Shoh-shoh
Misc. Silents
SONG OF CHINA(1936, Chi.)
Kent Shoji
NAVY WIFE(1956)
Willy Sholanke
SIMBA(1955, Brit.)
Mickey Sholdar
ONE MAN'S WAY(1964)
Jack Sholder
ALONE IN THE DARK(1982), d, w
John Sholder
BURNING, THE(1981), ed
Lee Sholem
TARZAN'S MAGIC FOUNTAIN(1949), d; TARZAN AND THE SLAVE GIRL(1950), d; SUPERMAN AND THE MOLE MEN(1951), d; REDHEAD FROM WYOMING, THE(1953), d; STAND AT APACHE RIVER, THE(1953), d; CANNIBAL AT-TACK(1954), d; JUNGLE MAN-EATERS(1954), d; TOBOR THE GREAT(1954), d; MA AND PA KETTLE AT WAIKIKI(1955), d; CRIME AGAINST JOE(1956), d; EMER-GENCY HOSPITAL(1956), d; HELL SHIP MUTINY(1957), d; PHARAOH'S CUR-SE(1957), d; SIERRA STRANGER(1957), d; LOUISIANA HUSSY(1960), d; CATALINA CAPER, THE(1967), d; DOOMSDAY MACHINE(1967), d
John Maxwell Sholes
ADAM'S RIB(1949)
John Sholle
THEY ALL LAUGHED(1981)
Mikhail Sholokhov
AND QUIET FLOWS THE DON(1960 USSR), d&w
Anne Sholter
IT'S A SMALL WORLD(1950)
Kitty Sholto
Silents
SEALED VALLEY, THE(1915)
Pamela Sholto
L-SHAPED ROOM, THE(1962, Brit.); HIDING PLACE, THE(1975)
Michael Shomacker
1984
ZAPPA(1984, Den.)
Hazel Shon
SAIGON(1948); LOVE IS A MANY-SPLENDORED THING(1955)
Saky Shong
DRAGON SKY(1964, Fr.)
Lindsay Shonteff
LAST GUNFIGHTER, THE(1961, Can.), p,d&w, ed; DEVIL DOLL(1964, Brit.), p, d; CURSE OF THE VOODOO(1965, Brit.), d; SECOND BEST SECRET AGENT IN THE WHOLE WIDE WORLD, THE(1965, Brit.), d, w; RUN WITH THE WIND(1966, Brit.), d; MILLION EYES OF SU-MURU, THE(1967, Brit.), d; CLEGG(1969, Brit.), d
Misc. Talkies
FAST KILL(1973), d; BIG ZAPPER(1974), d
Michael Shoob
PARASITE(1982), w
Roger Shook
TRON(1982), set d
Roger M. Shook
HERBIE GOES BANANAS(1980), set d; MIDNIGHT MADNESS(1980), set d
Warner Shook
KNIGHTRIDERS(1981); CREEPSHOW(1982)
Pamela Shoop
EMPIRE OF THE ANTS(1977); ONE MAN JURY(1978)
Pamela Susan Shoop
HALLOWEEN 11(1981)
Shooting Star
BUFFALO BILL RIDES AGAIN(1947); LARAMIE(1949); TICKET TO TOMA-HAWK(1950)
Percy Shooting Star
SEARCHERS, THE(1956)
Hedi Shope
WEDDING NIGHT, THE(1935)
Herman Shopp
SON OF INGAGI(1940), ph
Dan Shor
BACK ROADS(1981); DEAD KIDS(1981 Aus./New Zealand); TRON(1982); STRANGE INVADERS(1983)
1984
STRANGERS KISS(1984)
Daniel Shor
WISE BLOOD(1979, U.S./Ger.)
1984
MIKE'S MURDER(1984)
R. Shor
SPRINGTIME ON THE VOLGA(1961, USSR), ed
Sol Shor
DRUMS OF FU MANCHU(1943), w; CYCLOTRODE X(1946), w; DAUGHTER OF THE JUNGLE(1949), w; FLAME OF CALCUTTA(1953), w; SAVAGE MUTINY(1953), w; GHOST OF ZORRO(1959), w
Barrie Shore
BROTHERS AND SISTERS(1980, Brit.)
Dave Shore
SUSPENSE(1946)
Dinah Shore
THANK YOUR LUCKY STARS(1943); BELLE OF THE YUKON(1944); FOLLOW THE BOYS(1944); UP IN ARMS(1944); MAKE MINE MUSIC(1946); TILL THE CLOUDS ROLL BY(1946); FUN AND FANCY FREE(1947); AARON SLICK FROM

PUNKIN CRICK(1952); OH, GOD!(1977)

Elaine Shore
TELL ME THAT YOU LOVE ME, JUNIE MOON(1970); EIGER SANCTION, THE(1975); SENTINEL, THE(1977)

Fannie Shore
1984
BAY BOY(1984, Can.)

Fran Shore
LADY IN THE DARK(1944)

Fredric Shore
SURVIVAL RUN(1980), w

Howard Shore
I MISS YOU, HUGS AND KISSES(1978, Can.), m; SCANNERS(1981, Can.), m; VIDEODROME(1983, Can.), m
1984
PLACES IN THE HEART(1984), m

Jean Shore
GO, MAN, GO!(1954)

Maydra Shore
TRIAL, THE(1963, Fr./Ital./Ger.)

Richard Shore
NIGHT OF DARK SHADOWS(1971), ph; BANG THE DRUM SLOWLY(1973), ph

Roberta Shore
BLUE DENIM(1959); SHAGGY DOG, THE(1959); SUMMER PLACE, A(1959); BECAUSE THEY'RE YOUNG(1960); STRANGERS WHEN WE MEET(1960); YOUNG SAVAGES, THE(1961); LOLITA(1962)

Sammy Shore
THUNDER ALLEY(1967); HISTORY OF THE WORLD, PART 1(1981)

Sharon Shore
ART OF LOVE, THE(1965)

Sig Shore
SUPERFLY(1972), a, p; SUPERFLY T.N.T.(1973), w; THAT'S THE WAY OF THE WORLD(1975), p&d
1984
ACT, THE(1984), p, d

Steve Shore
THAT'S THE WAY OF THE WORLD(1975)

Viola Brothers Shore
DANGEROUS CURVES(1929), w; KIBITZER, THE(1929), w; LUCKY BOY(1929), w; NO LIMIT(1931), w; MEN ARE SUCH FOOLS(1933), w; SAILOR BE GOOD(1933), w; SMARTEST GIRL IN TOWN(1936), w; WALKING ON AIR(1936), w; BREAKFAST FOR TWO(1937), w; LIFE OF THE PARTY, THE(1937), w; ARKANSAS TRAVELER, THE(1938), w; BLOND CHEAT(1938), w
Silents
NIGHT LIFE(1927), t; SHIELD OF HONOR, THE(1927), t; NAMELESS MEN(1928), t; SCARLET DOVE, THE(1928), t

Byron Shores
TOO MANY GIRLS(1940); LIFE BEGINS FOR ANDY HARDY(1941); LOVE CRAZY(1941); BROADWAY(1942); JOHNNY EAGER(1942); MAD DOCTOR OF MARKET STREET, THE(1942); MAJOR AND THE MINOR, THE(1942); TISH(1942); TO THE SHORES OF TRIPOLI(1942); FLIGHT FOR FREEDOM(1943); MORE THE MERRIER, THE(1943); SHADOW OF A DOUBT(1943); SO PROUDLY WE HAIL(1943); THEY GOT ME COVERED(1943)

Jeanne Shores
SON OF SINBAD(1955)

Lynn Shores
DELIGHTFUL ROGUE(1929), d; JAZZ AGE, THE(1929), d; SIN SHIP(1931), d; GLORY TRAIL, THE(1937), d; HERE'S FLASH CASEY(1937), d; SHADOW STRIKES, THE(1937), d; WOMAN IN DISTRESS(1937), d; MILLION TO ONE, A(1938), d; REBELLION(1938), d; CHARLIE CHAN AT THE WAX MUSEUM(1940), d; GOLDEN HOOFS(1941), d
Misc. Talkies
REBELLION(1936), d
Silents
SALLY OF THE SCANDALS(1928), d; SKINNER'S BIG IDEA(1928), d
Misc. Silents
SALLY'S SHOULDERS(1928), d; STOLEN LOVE(1928), d; VOICE OF THE STORM, THE(1929), d

Richard Shores
LOOK IN ANY WINDOW(1961), m; TOMBOY AND THE CHAMP(1961), m; LAST CHALLENGE, THE(1967), m

Kathy Shorkey
HOSPITAL MASSACRE(1982), makeup
1984
HOSPITAL MASSACRE(1984), makeup

Lester Shorr
PEACEMAKER, THE(1956), ph; RUNNING TARGET(1956), ph; THREE BAD SISTERS(1956), ph; HOT ROD RUMBLE(1957), ph; LAW OF THE LAWLESS(1964), ph; RIDE BEYOND VENGEANCE(1966), ph; ARIZONA BUSHWHACKERS(1968), ph; TAKE THE MONEY AND RUN(1969), ph; MC MASTERS, THE(1970), ph; PHANTOM TOLLBOOTH, THE(1970), ph

Richard Shorr
Misc. Talkies
WITCHES' BREW(1980), d

Valerie Shorr
MAN WHO WOULD NOT DIE, THE(1975)

Toni Shorrock
STERILE CUCKOO, THE(1969)

Al Short
BORDER ROMANCE(1930), md

Antrim Short
SHE COULDN'T TAKE IT(1935); WINGS IN THE DARK(1935); MILKY WAY, THE(1936); MOON'S OUR HOME, THE(1936); ROSE BOWL(1936); EBB TIDE(1937)
Silents
JOHN BARLEYCORN(1914); WHERE THE TRAIL DIVIDES(1914); AMARILLY OF CLOTHESLINE ALLEY(1918); CUPID BY PROXY(1918); HUCK AND TOM(1918); NARROW PATH, THE(1918); ROMANCE AND ARABELLA(1919); O'MALLEY OF THE MOUNTED(1921); CLASSMATES(1924); JACK O'HEARTS(1926)

Misc. Silents
JESS(1914); FLIRT, THE(1916); JEWEL IN PAWN, A(1917); HUGON THE MIGHTY(1918); YELLOW DOG, THE(1918); DESTINY(1919); PLEASE GET MARRIED(1919); RICH GIRL, POOR GIRL(1921); SON OF WALLINGFORD, THE(1921); BROADWAY BOOB, THE(1926)

Bernadette Short
UNSUITABLE JOB FOR A WOMAN, AN(1982, Brit.)

Bobby Short
CALL ME MISTER(1951)

Cal Short
STORMY(1935)

Charles W. Short
ENFORCER, THE(1976), ph

David Short
SILENT SCREAM(1980), ph

Don Short
Silents
PENALTY, THE(1920), ph; ACE OF HEARTS, THE(1921), ph; GLEAM O'DAWN(1922), ph; OATH-BOUND(1922), ph; YELLOW STAIN, THE(1922), ph; ELEVENTH HOUR, THE(1923), ph; SECOND HAND LOVE(1923), ph; SKID PROOF(1923), ph

Doris Short
HUCKLEBERRY FINN(1931)

Dorothy Short
STUDENT TOUR(1934); SHE MARRIED HER BOSS(1935); MORE THAN A SECRETARY(1936); REEFER MADNESS(1936); BROTHERS OF THE WEST(1938); HEART OF ARIZONA(1938); WHERE THE BUFFALO ROAM(1938); CODE OF THE CACTUS(1939); DAUGHTER OF THE TONG(1939); SINGING COWGIRL, THE(1939); WILD HORSE CANYON(1939); FRONTIER CRUSADER(1940); PHANTOM RANCHER(1940); PONY POST(1940); ALOMA OF THE SOUTH SEAS(1941); LONE RIDER FIGHTS BACK, THE(1941); SPOOKS RUN WILD(1941); TRAIL OF THE SILVER SPURS(1941)
Misc. Talkies
BUZZY AND THE PHANTOM PINTO(1941); BULLETS FOR BANDITS(1942)

Edward Short
FAMILY HONEYMOON(1948); FRENCH LINE, THE(1954)

Edward C. Short
TANGANYIKA(1954)
1984
JOHNNY DANGEROUSLY(1984)

Florence Short
Silents
DAMAGED GOODS(1915); GREAT ADVENTURE, THE(1918); KILDARE OF STORM(1918); IDOL DANCER, THE(1920); LOVE FLOWER, THE(1920); WAY DOWN EAST(1920); LESSONS IN LOVE(1921); WOMAN'S PLACE(1921); CARDIGAN(1922); SILVER WINGS(1922); ENCHANTED COTTAGE, THE(1924)
Misc. Silents
GREAT BRADLEY MYSTERY, THE(1917); LAW THAT FAILED, THE(1917); MYSTIC HOUR, THE(1917); OUTSIDER, THE(1917); FIVE THOUSAND AN HOUR(1918); MAN'S WORLD, A(1918); PAY DAY(1918); WHEN YOU AND I WERE YOUNG(1918); LOVE, HONOR AND ?(1919); DOES IT PAY?(1923)

Gertrude Short
BROADWAY HOOFER, THE(1929); BULLDOG DRUMMOND(1929); GOLD DIGGERS OF BROADWAY(1929); IN OLD CALIFORNIA(1929); LAST DANCE, THE(1930); LITTLE ACCIDENT(1930); ONCE A GENTLEMAN(1930); LAUGHING SINNERS(1931); BLONDE VENUS(1932); GIRL IN 419(1933); SECRET SINNERS(1933); SON OF KONG(1933); KEY, THE(1934); LOVE BIRDS(1934); ST. LOUIS KID, THE(1934); THIN MAN, THE(1934); G-MEN(1935); HELLDORADO(1935); WOMAN WANTED(1935); FOLLOW THE FLEET(1936); THIRTEEN HOURS BY AIR(1936); PARK AVENUE LOGGER(1937); STELLA DALLAS(1937); WILD MONEY(1937); TIP-OFF GIRLS(1938); TOM, DICK AND HARRY(1941); MAN ALIVE(1945); WEEK-END AT THE WALDORF(1945)
Silents
LITTLE ANGEL OF CANYON CREEK, THE(1914); AMARILLY OF CLOTHESLINE ALLEY(1918); YOUTH TO YOUTH(1922); CRINOLINE AND ROMANCE(1923); GOLD DIGGERS, THE(1923); PRISONER, THE(1923); NARROW STREET, THE(1924); BEGGAR ON HORSEBACK(1925); SWEET ADELINE(1926); ADAM AND EVIL(1927); TILLIE THE TOILER(1927); NONE BUT THE BRAVE(1928)
Misc. Silents
JESS(1914); HOSTAGE, THE(1917); HEADIN' WEST(1922); RENT FREE(1922); DANGEROUS FRIENDS(1926); LADIES OF LEISURE(1926); POOR GIRL'S ROMANCE, A(1926); POLLY OF THE MOVIES(1927); WOMEN'S WARES(1927); THREE OUTCASTS, THE(1929)

Gertude Short
Silents
LADIES AT EASE(1927)

Hal Short
Misc. Talkies
SHADOW LAUGHS(1933)

Harry Short
Silents
JUST SUPPOSE(1926)
Misc. Silents
MIGHTY LAK' A ROSE(1923)

Hassard Short
Silents
WAY OF A WOMAN(1919); WOMAN'S PLACE(1921)
Misc. Silents
MOTH, THE(1917)

Jack Short
WEE GEORDIE(1956, Brit.); MAD LITTLE ISLAND(1958, Brit.)

Jackie Short
HELL'S CARGO(1935, Brit.)

Jane Short
MUDLARK, THE(1950, Brit.)

Jean Short
FATAL NIGHT, THE(1948, Brit.); RED SHOES, THE(1948, Brit.); THIRD TIME LUCKY(1950, Brit.)

Jo Anna Short
STOP THE WORLD–I WANT TO GET OFF(1966, Brit.)

John Short
FLASH THE SHEEPDOG(1967, Brit.)

Lew Short
LAW OF THE NORTH(1932)
Silents
CAMPBELLS ARE COMING, THE(1915); ONCE A PLUMBER(1920); BIG CITY, THE(1928)
Misc. Silents
THREE OUTCASTS, THE(1929)

Lewis W. Short
Silents
BRANDING BROADWAY(1918)

Luke Short
HURRY, CHARLIE, HURRY(1941), w; RAMROD(1947), w; ALBUQUERQUE(1948), w; BLOOD ON THE MOON(1948), w; STATION WEST(1948), w; AMBUSH(1950), w; SILVER CITY(1951), w; VENGEANCE VALLEY(1951), w; RIDE THE MAN DOWN(1952), w; HELL'S OUTPOST(1955), w; HANGMAN, THE(1959), w

Marion Short
Silents
OUT YONDER(1920), w

Martin Short
LOST AND FOUND(1979)

Paul Short
BAD BOY(1949), p, w; KID FROM TEXAS, THE(1950), p

Robert Short
SCARED TO DEATH(1981), spec eff; SLAYER, THE(1982), makeup

Robin Short
WITHOUT RESERVATIONS(1946); WING AND A PRAYER(1944); I LOVE A BAND-LEADER(1945); DARK HORSE, THE(1946); GAL WHO TOOK THE WEST, THE(1949); I SHOT JESSE JAMES(1949); AMBUSH(1950); BARON OF ARIZONA, THE(1950); RETURN OF JESSE JAMES, THE(1950); BUCKSKIN LADY, THE(1957); HALLIDAY BRAND, THE(1957)

Sein Short
ROAD TO HONG KONG, THE(1962, U.S./Brit.)

Skip Short
1984
FLASHPOINT(1984), p

Sylvia Short
ENDLESS LOVE(1981)

William Short
TWELVE O'CLOCK HIGH(1949)

Anna Shorter
IN MACARTHUR PARK(1977)

Frank Shorter
PERSONAL BEST(1982)

Ken Shorter
YOU CAN'T SEE 'ROUND CORNERS(1969, Aus.); NED KELLY(1970, Brit.); STONE(1974, Aus.); DRAGONSLAYER(1981)
1984
PLOUGHMAN'S LUNCH, THE(1984, Brit.); SCRUBBERS(1984, Brit.)

Paul Shortino
1984
THIS IS SPINAL TAP(1984)

Steve Shortridge
FRATERNITY ROW(1977)

Barbara L. Shorts
SLAP SHOT(1977)

Marie Shortwell
Misc. Silents
PILLORY, THE(1916)

Shorty
IRMA LA DOUCE(1963)

"Shorty"
LADY FOR A DAY(1933)

Shorty Rogers and His Band
GLASS WALL, THE(1953)

Shorty Thompson and His Saddle Rockin' Rhythm
EL DORADO PASS(1949)

Murray Shostak
CHILD UNDER A LEAF(1975, Can.), p; DEATH HUNT(1981), p; SILENCE OF THE NORTH(1981, Can.), p

Dmitri Shostakovich
DEFENSE OF VOLOTCHAYEVSK, THE(1938, USSR), m; NEW HORIZONS(1939, USSR), m; IRON CURTAIN, THE(1948), m; CONDEMNED OF ALTONA, THE(1963), m; ROLLERBALL(1975), md

Dmitriy Dmitriyevich Shostakovich
SONG OVER MOSCOW(1964, USSR), w, m; HAMLET(1966, USSR), m; KATERINA IZMAILOVA(1969, USSR), w, m

G. Shostko
WAR AND PEACE(1968, USSR)

Mark Shostrom
DEADLY FORCE(1983), spec-makeup eff

Mark Shostrum
TO ALL A GOODNIGHT(1980), makeup

Barbara Shotter
TEARS FOR SIMON(1957, Brit.)

Constance Shotter
FOR THE LOVE OF MIKE(1933, Brit.); MEET MY SISTER(1933, Brit.); BORROWED CLOTHES(1934, Brit.); BRIDES TO BE(1934, Brit.); OFF THE DOLE(1935, Brit.); REGAL CAVALCADE(1935, Brit.)

Marjorie Shotter
SCOOP, THE(1934, Brit.); LITTLE BIT OF BLUFF, A(1935, Brit.)

Winifred Shotter
ON APPROVAL(1930, Brit.); ONE EMBARRASSING NIGHT(1930, Brit.); CHANCE OF A NIGHT-TIME, THE(1931, Brit); MISCHIEF(1931, Brit.); PLUNDER(1931, Brit.); LOVE CONTRACT, THE(1932, Brit.); NIGHT LIKE THIS, A(1932, Brit.); JUST MY LUCK(1933, Brit.); NIGHT AND DAY(1933, Brit.); NIGHT OF THE GARTER(1933, Brit.); SUMMER LIGHTNING(1933, Brit.); UP TO THE NECK(1933, Brit.); LILIES OF

THE FIELD(1934, Brit.); SORRELL AND SON(1934, Brit.); MARRY THE GIRL(1935, Brit.); PETTICOAT FEVER(1936); HIGH TREASON(1937, Brit.); HIS LORDSHIP REGRETS(1938, Brit.); CAPTAIN MOONLIGHT(1940, Brit.); CANDLES AT NINE(1944, Brit.); BODY SAID NO!, THE(1950, Brit.); JOHN AND JULIE(1957, Brit.)

Hudson Shotwell
YELLOW JACK(1938); SHOPWORN ANGEL(1938); TEST PILOT(1938)

Marie Shotwell
Silents
MASTER MIND, THE(1920); SHACKLES OF GOLD(1922); SALLY OF THE SAW-DUST(1925); SHORE LEAVE(1925); ONE WOMAN TO ANOTHER(1927)
Misc. Silents
WITCHING HOUR, THE(1916); MARRIED IN NAME ONLY(1917); WARFARE OF THE FLESH, THE(1917); WOMAN AND THE BEAST, THE(1917); MISS INNOCENCE(1918); ECHO OF YOUTH, THE(1919); THIRTEENTH CHAIR, THE(1919); CHAINS OF EVIDENCE(1920); RUNNING WILD(1927)

Phyllis Shotwell
CALIFORNIA SPLIT(1974), m

Richard Shotwell
HOUSE OF THE BLACK DEATH(1965), p

Mac Shoub
FORBIDDEN JOURNEY(1950, Can.)

Georges Shoucair
COME SPY WITH ME(1967)

Stephanie Shouldus
IMPROPER CHANNELS(1981, Can.)

Col. D.M. Shoup, USMC
SANDS OF IWO JIMA(1949)

Howard Shoup
PERFECT SPECIMEN, THE(1937), cos; SAN QUENTIN(1937), cos; WEST OF SHANGHAI(1937), cos; WINE, WOMEN AND HORSES(1937), cos; GIRLS ON PROBATION(1938), cos; MEN ARE SUCH FOOLS(1938), cos; RACKET BUSTERS(1938), cos; SERGEANT MURPHY(1938), cos; SWING YOUR LADY(1938), cos; TORCHY BLANE IN CHINATOWN(1938), cos; TORCHY GETS HER MAN(1938), cos; WHEN WERE YOU BORN?(1938), cos; EACH DAWN I DIE(1939), cos; NAUGHTY BUT NICE(1939), cos; NO PLACE TO GO(1939), cos; BROTHER ORCHID(1940), cos; MURDER IN THE AIR(1940), cos; TORRID ZONE(1940), cos; CITY, FOR CONQUEST(1941), cos; FOOTSTEPS IN THE DARK(1941), cos; NAVY BLUES(1941), cos; STRANGE ALIBI(1941), cos; CAPTAINS OF THE CLOUDS(1942), cos; JACKASS MAIL(1942), cos; NAZI AGENT(1942), cos; SEVEN SWEETHEARTS(1942), cos; DU BARRY WAS A LADY(1943), cos; YOUNGEST PROFESSION, THE(1943), cos; MIGHTY MCGURK, THE(1946), cos; OCEAN BREAKERS(1949, Swed.), cos; JAZZ SINGER, THE(1953), cos; SO BIG(1953), cos; COURT-MARTIAL OF BILLY MITCHELL, THE(1955), cos; MC CONNELL STORY, THE(1955), cos; PETE KELLY'S BLUES(1955), cos; SINCERELY YOURS(1955), cos; YOUNG AT HEART(1955), cos; BUNDLE OF JOY(1956), cos; SERENADE(1956), cos; BOMBERS B-52(1957), cos; UNHOLY WIFE, THE(1957), cos; DEEP SIX, THE(1958), cos; HOME BEFORE DARK(1958), cos; I MARRIED A WOMAN(1958), cos; MARJORIE MORNINGSTAR(1958), cos; ONIONHEAD(1958), cos; HELEN MORGAN STORY, THE(1959), cos; ISLAND OF LOST WOMEN(1959), cos; WESTBOUND(1959), cos; YOUNG PHILADELPHIANS, THE(1959), cos; BRAMBLE BUSH, THE(1960), cos; CASH McCALL(1960), cos; ICE PALACE(1960), cos; OCEAN'S ELEVEN(1960), cos; RISE AND FALL OF LEGS DIAMOND, THE(1960), cos; CLAUDELLE INGLISH(1961), cos; FEVER IN THE BLOOD, A(1961), cos; PARRISH(1961), cos; PORTRAIT OF A MOBSTER(1961), cos; SUSAN SLADE(1961), cos; GYPSY(1962), cos; ROME ADVENTURE(1962), cos; WALL OF NOISE(1963), cos; DISTANT TRUMPET, A(1964), cos; KISSES FOR MY PRESIDENT(1964), cos; YOUNGBLOOD HAWKE(1964), cos; RAGE TO LIVE, A(1965), cos; COOL HAND LUKE(1967), cos; COOL ONES THE(1967), cos; HOTEL(1967), cos; OH DAD, POOR DAD, MAMA'S HUNG YOU IN THE CLOSET AND I'M FEELIN' SO SAD(1967), cos

Sherry Shourds
BIG PUNCH, THE(1948), d

John Shouse
TENDER WARRIOR, THE(1971), ed

Tom Shouse
SATAN'S MISTRESS(1982), spec eff

Yuval Shousterman
10 VIOLENT WOMEN(1982), ph

David Showacre
CAT PEOPLE(1982)

Max Showalter [Casey Adams]
ALWAYS LEAVE THEM LAUGHING(1949); WITH A SONG IN MY HEART(1952); MOVE OVER, DARLING(1963); MY SIX LOVES(1963); FATE IS THE HUNTER(1964); SEX AND THE SINGLE GIRL(1964); HOW TO MURDER YOUR WIFE(1965); LORD LOVE A DUCK(1966); MOONSHINE WAR, THE(1970); ANDERSON TAPES, THE(1971); SGT. PEPPER'S LONELY HEARTS CLUB BAND(1978); 10(1979)
1984
RACING WITH THE MOON(1984); SIXTEEN CANDLES(1984)

Mary Jane Shower
STAGE DOOR(1937)

Gennadiy Shpalikov
MEET ME IN MOSCOW(1966, USSR), w

Stan Shpetner
LEGEND OF TOM DOOLEY, THE(1959), p, w; TWO RODE TOGETHER(1961), p

Stanley Shpetner
BONNIE PARKER STORY, THE(1958), p&w; PARATROOP COMMAND(1959), w

G. Shpigel
MARRIAGE OF BALZAMINOV, THE(1966, USSR)

Isaac Shpinel
IVAN THE TERRIBLE(Part I, 1947, USSR), art d, cos
Silents
ARSENAL(1929, USSR), art d

P. Shpringfeld
NINE DAYS OF ONE YEAR(1964, USSR); GARNET BRACELET, THE(1966, USSR)

George Shrader
MY FORBIDDEN PAST(1951), ed; LAS VEGAS STORY, THE(1952), ed; TARGET(1952), ed

Henry Shrady
SQUIRM(1976), art d; SLOW DANCING IN THE BIG CITY(1978), art d

Lawrence Shragge
FIREBIRD 2015 AD(1981), m
Bud Shrake
J.W. COOP(1971), w; NIGHTWING(1979), w; TOM HORN(1980), w
1984
SONGWRITER(1984), w
Edwin Shrake
KID BLUE(1973), w
John Shrapnel
NICHOLAS AND ALEXANDRA(1971, Brit.); POPE JOAN(1972, Brit.); HENNESSY(1975, Brit.); WAGNER(1983, Brit./Hung./Aust.)
Peter Shrayder
SEVEN MINUTES, THE(1971)
Craig Shreeve
ICE STATION ZEBRA(1968); SKYJACKED(1972); RAISE THE TITANIC(1980, Brit.); PARTNERS(1982)
Haim Shreiber
PILLAR OF FIRE, THE(1963, Israel), ph
I. Shreter
GARNET BRACELET, THE(1966, USSR), art d
Florence Shreve
FORGOTTEN COMMANDMENTS(1932)
Leo Shreve
QUEEN OF BLOOD(1966), ed; IT'S A BIKINI WORLD(1967), ed; GIRL IN GOLD BOOTS(1968), ed
Leo H. Shreve
PORTRAIT OF A MOBSTER(1961), ed; COUCH, THE(1962), ed; HOUSE OF WOMEN(1962), ed; BLACK GOLD(1963), ed; FBI CODE 98(1964), ed
Lillian Shreve
Misc. Talkies
THREE LIVES(1971)
D. Shridhankar
TIGER AND THE FLAME, THE(1955, India), ed
Chrissie Shrimpton
MOON ZERO TWO(1970, Brit.); MY LOVER, MY SON(1970, Brit.)
Jean Shrimpton
PRIVILEGE(1967, Brit.)
Herb Shriner
MAIN STREET TO BROADWAY(1953)
Indy Shriner
HYSTERICAL(1983)
Kin Shriner
YOUNG DOCTORS IN LOVE(1982)
Ian Shrives
1984
STRIKEBOUND(1984, Aus.)
Ray Shrock
CRIME, INC.(1945), w
Raymond L. Shrock
Silents
CLEAN UP, THE(1923), w
Kurt Shroeder
GIRL FROM MAXIM'S, THE(1936, Brit.), m
Maurice Shrog
HARVEY MIDDLEMAN, FIREMAN(1965)
1984
BROADWAY DANNY ROSE(1984)
Anne Shropshire
SIDELONG GLANCES OF A PIGEON KICKER, THE(1970); TOOTSIE(1982)
Sonny Shroyer
LONGEST YARD, THE(1974); FARMER, THE(1977); LINCOLN CONSPIRACY, THE(1977); DEVIL AND MAX DEVLIN, THE(1981)
Cal Shrum
ROLLIN' HOME TO TEXAS(1941)
Misc. Talkies
SWING, COWBOY, SWING(1944); TROUBLE AT MELODY MESA(1949)
Shanna Shrum
1984
PLACES IN THE HEART(1984)
Walt Shrum
ROLLIN' HOME TO TEXAS(1941)
Misc. Talkies
SWING, COWBOY, SWING(1944); TROUBLE AT MELODY MESA(1949)
Dennis Shryack
GOOD GUYS AND THE BAD GUYS, THE(1969), p, w; CAR, THE(1977), w; GAUNTLET, THE(1977), w; BELLS(1981, Can.), w
Edward Shryver
CHROME AND HOT LEATHER(1971), ed
Makolm Shtgaukh
LUCKY BRIDE, THE(1948, USSR)
L. Shtifanov
TRAIN GOES TO KIEV, THE(1961, USSR), spec eff
D. Shtilman
SPRINGTIME ON THE VOLGA(1961, USSR), md
E. Shtirtskober
SON OF MONGOLIA(1936, USSR), ph
O. Shtoda
THERE WAS AN OLD COUPLE(1967, USSR)
M. Shtraugh
VOW, THE(1947, USSR.)
M. Shtraukh
NEW HORIZONS(1939, USSR)
Misc. Silents
GHOST THAT NEVER RETURNS, THE(1930, USSR)
Maksim Shtraukh
PORTRAIT OF LENIN(1967, Pol./USSR)
Leda Shtykan
ONCE THERE WAS A GIRL(1945, USSR)

Edgar Shtyrtskober
THEY CALL ME ROBERT(1967, USSR), ph
Hsu Shuang-kun
FLYING GUILLOTINE, THE(1975, Chi.)
Eddie Shubart
MURDER IN THE CLOUDS(1934)
Shubert
Silents
AS IN A LOOKING GLASS(1916), p
Arland Shubert
HELL'S BLOODY DEVILS(1970)
Eddie Shubert
CASE OF THE HOWLING DOG, THE(1934); GAMBLING LADY(1934); HEAT LIGHTNING(1934); HERE COMES THE NAVY(1934); JIMMY THE GENT(1934); KANSAS CITY PRINCESS(1934); LOST LADY, A(1934); ST. LOUIS KID, THE(1934); TWENTY MILLION SWEETHEARTS(1934); ALIBI IKE(1935); BLACK FURY(1935); BORDERTOWN(1935); DON'T BET ON BLONDES(1935); FRONT PAGE WOMAN(1935); GOOSE AND THE GANDER, THE(1935); PAYOFF, THE(1935); SWEET ADELINE(1935); WHILE THE PATIENT SLEPT(1935); ALL-AMERICAN CHUMP(1936); BIG NOISE, THE(1936); BULLETS OR BALLOTS(1936); GOLDEN ARROW, THE(1936); LAW IN HER HANDS, THE(1936); LIBELED LADY(1936); MAN HUNT(1936); SATAN MET A LADY(1936); SNOWED UNDER(1936); SONG OF THE SADDLE(1936); TRAILIN' WEST(1936)
Mel Shubert
WEEKEND AT THE WALDORF(1945)
Nancy Shubert
SAGEBRUSH TRAIL(1934)
Elisabeth Shue
1984
KARATE KID, THE(1984)
Edward Shuey
ROSE BOWL(1936)
Gene Shuey
MUSCLE BEACH PARTY(1964)
Ted Shuffle
HELLO LONDON(1958, Brit.), ch
Wally Shufflebottom
HELP!(1965, Brit.)
Andy Shufford
BIG TRAIL, THE(1930)
Andy Shuford
DUGAN OF THE BAD LANDS(1931); HEADIN' FOR TROUBLE(1931); MONTANA KID, THE(1931); OKLAHOMA JIM(1931); RIDER OF THE PLAINS(1931); FELLER NEEDS A FRIEND(1932); GHOST CITY(1932); LAND OF WANTED MEN(1932); LAW OF THE NORTH(1932); MASON OF THE MOUNTED(1932); TEXAS PIONEERS(1932)
Brent Shugar
THEY WERE EXPENDABLE(1945)
Eugene Shugleit
1984
HOT MOVES(1984), ph
Robert F. Shugrue
SULLIVAN'S EMPIRE(1967), ed; DEATH OF A GUNFIGHTER(1969), ed; TWO MULES FOR SISTER SARA(1970), ed; THAT MAN BOLT(1973), ed; RAISE THE TITANIC(1980, Brit.), ed
1984
STAR TREK III: THE SEARCH FOR SPOCK(1984), ed
Tommy Shugrue
DANCE, FOOLS, DANCE(1931)
Leo Shuken
FLYING DEUCES, THE(1939), m; STAGECOACH(1939), m; OUR WIFE(1941), m; SULLIVAN'S TRAVELS(1941), m; MEET THE STEWARTS(1942), m; MIRACLE OF MORGAN'S CREEK, THE(1944), m; GUN CRAZY(1949), md; THOSE REDHEADS FROM SEATTLE(1953), m; CRIMSON KIMONO, THE(1959), md
Phil Shuken
PLUNDERERS OF PAINTED FLATS(1959), w
Phillip Shuken
DOCTOR, YOU'VE GOT TO BE KIDDING(1967), w; SPEEDWAY(1968), w
Vasiliy Shukshin
WHEN THE TREES WERE TALL(1965, USSR)
Lauren Shuler
MR. MOM(1983), p
G. Shulgin
QUEEN OF SPADES(1961, USSR)
V. Shulgin
OPTIMISTIC TRAGEDY, THE(1964, USSR)
John Shulick
WHEN WILLIE COMES MARCHING HOME(1950)
Esther Shulkin
Silents
HUSBAND HUNTERS(1927), w
Bill Shull
DUMBO(1941), anim
Charles Shull
FOXES(1980)
Richard Shull
KLUTE(1971)
Richard B. Shull
B.S. I LOVE YOU(1971); SUCH GOOD FRIENDS(1971); HAIL(1973); SLITHER(1973); SSSSSSSS(1973); BORN TO KILL(1975); FORTUNE, THE(1975); HEARTS OF THE WEST(1975); BIG BUS, THE(1976); PACK, THE(1977); DREAMER(1979); WHOLLY MOSES(1980); HEARTBEEPS(1981); LOVESICK(1983); SPRING BREAK(1983)
1984
GARBO TALKS(1984); SPLASH(1984); UNFAITHFULLY YOURS(1984)
William N. Shull
FANTASIA(1940), anim
Jack Shulla
BURNING CROSS, THE(1947)

Arnold Shulman
WILD IS THE WIND(1957), w; HOLE IN THE HEAD, A(1959), w
Irvin Shulman
COLLEGE CONFIDENTIAL(1960), w
Irving Shulman
CITY ACROSS THE RIVER(1949), w; JOURNEY INTO LIGHT(1951), w; RING, THE(1952), w; CHAMP FOR A DAY(1953), w; REBEL WITHOUT A CAUSE(1955), w; TERROR AT MIDNIGHT(1956), w; BABY FACE NELSON(1957), w; CRY TOUGH(1959), w; HARLOW(1965), w
Jean Shulman
LOVE WITH THE PROPER STRANGER(1963)
Max Shulman
AFFAIRS OF DOBIE GILLIS, THE(1953), w; CONFIDENTIAL CONNIE(1953), w; HALF A HERO(1953), w; TENDER TRAP, THE(1955), w; RALLY 'ROUND THE FLAG, BOYS!(1958), w; HOUSE CALLS(1978), w
Milton Shulman
THINK DIRTY(1970, Brit.), w
Beatrice Shulte
NEW FACES OF 1937(1937)
E. J. Shulter
Silents
HUNCH, THE(1921), art d; LITTLE EVA ASCENDS(1922), art d; SALLY(1925), art d; WHAT FOOLS MEN(1925), art d; ELLA CINDERS(1926), art d; FAR CRY, THE(1926), art d; MISS NOBODY(1926), art d
Edward Shulter
Silents
DESERT FLOWER, THE(1925), art d
Jackie Shultis
DAYS OF HEAVEN(1978)
Tracy Shults
HONKYTONK MAN(1982)
Michael Shultz
TOGETHER FOR DAYS(1972), d
Franz Shulz
PARIS IN SPRING(1935), w; MIDNIGHT(1939), w
J. Shumacher
WITHOUT A HOME(1939, Pol.)
Barbara Shuman
FIEND(
Felix Shuman
DAMIEN–OMEN II(1978); FURY, THE(1978); DREAMER(1979); ON THE RIGHT TRACK(1981)
Jimmy Shuman
MAMMA DRACULA(1980, Bel./Fr.); CHANEL SOLITAIRE(1981)
Mort Shuman
ROMANCE OF A HORSE THIEF(1971), a, m; JACQUES BREL IS ALIVE AND WELL AND LIVING IN PARIS(1975), a, w; LITTLE GIRL WHO LIVES DOWN THE LANE, THE(1977, Can.), a, md; ASSOCIATE, THE(1982 Fr./Ger.), m
Mortimer Shuman
DAY AT THE BEACH, A(1970), m
Roy Shuman
GODDESS, THE(1958); GANG THAT COULDN'T SHOOT STRAIGHT, THE(1971)
F. Shumann-Heink
HELL'S ANGELS(1930)
Harold Shumate
RIVER WOMAN, THE(1928), p, w; HOLD YOUR MAN(1929), w; TIMES SQUARE(1929), p, w; LOVE TRADER(1930), p, w; HIGH SPEED(1932), w; RIDIN' FOR JUSTICE(1932), w; SOUTH OF THE RIO GRANDE(1932), w; WILD HORSE MESA(1932), w; CROSSFIRE(1933), w; HERITAGE OF THE DESERT(1933), w; MAN OF THE FOREST(1933), w; SCARLET RIVER(1933), w; SON OF THE BORDER(1933), w; AGAINST THE LAW(1934), w; BEYOND THE LAW(1934), w; CRIME OF HELEN STANLEY(1934), w; GIRL IN DANGER(1934), w; HELL BENT FOR LOVE(1934), w; MAN'S GAME, A(1934), w; ONE IS GUILTY(1934), w; VOICE IN THE NIGHT(1934), w; AFTER THE DANCE(1935), w; BEHIND THE EVIDENCE(1935), w; HOME ON THE RANGE(1935), w; SUPERSPEED(1935), w; WHITE LIES(1935), w; CRASH DONOVAN(1936), w; DANGEROUS INTRIGUE(1936), w; END OF THE TRAIL(1936), w; FINAL HOUR, THE(1936), w; KILLER AT LARGE(1936), w; PRIDE OF THE MARINES(1936), w; WESTERNER, THE(1936), w; COUNSEL FOR CRIME(1937), w; COUNTERFEIT LADY(1937), w; DODGE CITY TRAIL(1937), w; ESCAPE BY NIGHT(1937), p, w; FIGHT TO THE FINISH, A(1937), w; FRAME-UP(1937), w; PAROLE RACKET(1937), w; BORN TO BE WILD(1938), p; MAIN EVENT, THE(1938), w; ALMOST A GENTLEMAN(1939), w; CHARLIE MC CARTHY, DETECTIVE(1939), w; KONGA, THE WILD STALLION(1939), w; MAN OF CONQUEST(1939), w; CAFE HOSTESS(1940), w; MAN WITH NINE LIVES, THE(1940), w; TRAIL OF THE VIGILANTES(1940), w; WHEN THE DALTONS RODE(1940), w; BADLANDS OF DAKOTA(1941), w; PARSON OF PANAMINT, THE(1941), w; ROUNDUP, THE(1941), w; FOREST RANGERS, THE(1942), w; MEN OF TEXAS(1942), w; RIDE 'EM COWBOY(1942), w; KANSAN, THE(1943), w; ABILENE TOWN(1946), w; RENEGADES(1946), w; BLOOD ON THE MOON(1948), w; SADDLE TRAMP(1950), w; LADY FROM TEXAS(1951), w; LITTLE BIG HORN(1951), w; HALF-BREED, THE(1952), w; PRIDE OF THE BLUE GRASS(1954), w
Silents
OUTLAW'S DAUGHTER, THE(1925), w; MISS BREWSTER'S MILLIONS(1926), w; CIRCUS ACE, THE(1927), w; LOVE MAKES 'EM WILD(1927), w; OUTLAWS OF RED RIVER(1927), w; AFTER THE STORM(1928), w; MIDNIGHT LIFE(1928), sup
Harry Shumate
MY SON IS GUILTY(1940), w
Herman Shumlin
WATCH ON THE RHINE(1943), d; CONFIDENTIAL AGENT(1945), d; REUBEN, REUBEN(1983), w
Hans Shumm
LADY HAS PLANS, THE(1942)
Ryucho Shumputei
NONE BUT THE BRAVE(1965, U.S./Jap.)
Yu. Shumski
Misc. Silents
BENNIE THE HOWL(1927, USSR)

Vyacheslav Shumskiy
CHILDREN OF THE FOG(1935, Brit.), w; HATRED(1941, Fr.), ph; HITLER'S MADMAN(1943), ph; SUMMER STORM(1944), ph; WOMEN IN THE NIGHT(1948), ph, art d, set d; BLOODY BROOD, THE(1959, Can.), ph; HUSTLER, THE(1961), ph; SOMETHING WILD(1961), ph; SPRINGTIME ON THE VOLGA(1961, USSR), ph; HORROR CHAMBER OF DR. FAUSTUS, THE(1962, Fr./Ital.), ph; HOUSE ON THE FRONT LINE, THE(1963, USSR), ph; LILITH(1964), ph
Cora Beach Shumway
DANCE OF LIFE, THE(1929)
Cora Shumway
MADAME RACKETEER(1932); PLAINSMAN, THE(1937)
Donald Shumway
TOO YOUNG, TOO IMMORAL!(1962)
L.C. Shumway
BUFFALO BILL RIDES AGAIN(1947)
Silents
KINGDOM OF LOVE, THE(1918); CONFLICT, THE(1921); TORRENT, THE(1921); OVER THE BORDER(1922); STEP ON IT!(1922)
Misc. Silents
CONVICT KING, THE(1915); DEAD SOUL, THE(1915); RED VIRGIN, THE(1915); SOLDIER'S SONS(1916); GATES OF DOOM, THE(1917); MISS JACKIE OF THE ARMY(1917); PLOW WOMAN, THE(1917); BIRD OF PREY, THE(1918); CONFESSION(1918); FALLEN ANGEL, THE(1918); GIRL WITH THE CHAMPAGNE EYES, THE(1918); SCARLET ROAD, THE(1918); TWO-GUN BETTY(1918); GIRL IN BOHEMIA, A(1919); LOVE HUNGER, THE(1919); RUSTLING A BRIDE(1919); DAREDEVIL, THE(1920); GAMESTERS, THE(1920); GUNFIGHTER, THE(1923); LONE STAR RANGER, THE(1923); SOFT BOILED(1923); VAGABOND TRAIL, THE(1924)
Lee Shumway
EVANGELINE(1929); LEATHERNECK, THE(1929); NIGHT PARADE(1929, Brit.); QUEEN OF THE NIGHTCLUBS(1929); SO THIS IS COLLEGE(1929); LONE STAR RANGER, THE(1930); SANTA FE TRAIL, THE(1930); SHOW GIRL IN HOLLYWOOD(1930); SWEET MAMA(1930); WIDOW FROM CHICAGO, THE(1930); CENTRAL PARK(1932); FIGHTING MARSHAL, THE(1932); I AM A FUGITIVE FROM A CHAIN GANG(1932); PARTNERS(1932); HE WAS HER MAN(1934); LADY BY CHOICE(1934); LEMON DROP KID, THE(1934); MANHATTAN MELODRAMA(1934); MEN OF THE NIGHT(1934); ROCKY RHODES(1934); FRISCO WATERFRONT(1935); GIRL O' MY DREAMS(1935); HARD ROCK HARRIGAN(1935); IN PERSON(1935); IVORY-HANDLED GUN(1935); LIVING ON VELVET(1935); MILLION DOLLAR BABY(1935); MYSTERIOUS MR. WONG(1935); ONE HOUR LATE(1935); O'SHAUGHNESSY'S BOY(1935); OUTLAWED GUNS(1935); SHE COULDN'T TAKE IT(1935); SHOW THEM NO MERCY(1935); GREAT GUY(1936); LONE WOLF RETURNS, THE(1936); MURDER WITH PICTURES(1936); PREVIEW MURDER MYSTERY(1936); SONG OF THE TRAIL(1936); WEDDING PRESENT(1936); DAUGHTER OF SHANGHAI(1937); GHOST TOWN(1937); GIRLS CAN PLAY(1937); HOLLYWOOD COWBOY(1937); LEFT-HANDED LAW(1937); LOVE IS ON THE AIR(1937); NATION AFLAME(1937); NIGHT CLUB SCANDAL(1937); SOULS AT SEA(1937); THIS IS MY AFFAIR(1937); THUNDER TRAIL(1937); WINDJAMMER(1937); CITY GIRL(1938); HOLLYWOOD ROUNDUP(1938); I AM THE LAW(1938); JUVENILE COURT(1938); KENTUCKY(1938); OUTLAWS OF THE PRAIRIE(1938); PAINTED DESERT, THE(1938); PENITENTIARY(1938); RAWHIDE(1938); SPAWN OF THE NORTH(1938); THERE'S THAT WOMAN AGAIN(1938); WHO KILLED GAIL PRESTON?(1938); FRONTIERS OF '49(1939); HOMICIDE BUREAU(1939); HOTEL IMPERIAL(1939); LAW COMES TO TEXAS, THE(1939); LET US LIVE(1939); LONE STAR PIONEERS(1939); NIGHT RIDERS, THE(1939); ROVIN' TUMBLEWEEDS(1939); BRIGHAM YOUNG–FRONTIERSMAN(1940); DANCE, GIRL, DANCE(1940); GRAPES OF WRATH(1940); GREAT McGINTY, THE(1940); LONG VOYAGE HOME, THE(1940); YOUNG AS YOU FEEL(1940); BURY ME NOT ON THE LONE PRAIRIE(1941); DEATH VALLEY OUTLAWS(1941); FACE BEHIND THE MASK, THE(1941); I WANTED WINGS(1941); MURDER BY INVITATION(1941); NO GREATER SIN(1941); NOTHING BUT THE TRUTH(1941); OUTLAWS OF THE CHEROKEE TRAIL(1941); PRAIRIE PIONEERS(1941); TWO GUN SHERIFF(1941); WEST POINT WIDOW(1941); ARIZONA TERRORS(1942); HOME IN WYOMIN'(1942); ICE-CAPADES REVUE(1942); INVISIBLE AGENT(1942); JESSE JAMES, JR.(1942); LADY HAS PLANS, THE(1942); MISSOURI OUTLAW, A(1942); PIRATES OF THE PRAIRIE(1942); PRIORITIES ON PARADE(1942); ROXIE HART(1942); STARDUST ON THE SAGE(1942); BOMBARDIER(1943); DEAD MAN'S GULCH(1943); OUTLAW, THE(1943); DOUBLE INDEMNITY(1944); GENTLE ANNIE(1944); LADIES OF WASHINGTON(1944); MAN FROM FRISCO(1944); MY BUDDY(1944); HOLD THAT BLONDE(1945); OREGON TRAIL(1945); ROAD TO UTOPIA(1945); ANGEL ON MY SHOULDER(1946); ROLL ON TEXAS MOON(1946); DANGEROUS YEARS(1947); SMASH-UP, THE STORY OF A WOMAN(1947); WEB, THE(1947); WYOMING(1947); NAKED CITY, THE(1948); HOODLUM EMPIRE(1952); SAVAGE FRONTIER(1953)
Misc. Talkies
HIT OF THE SNOW(1928)
Silents
AIR HAWK, THE(1924); AMERICAN MANNERS(1924); AIR MAIL, THE(1925); HANDSOME BRUTE, THE(1925); INTRODUCE ME(1925); SMILIN' AT TROUBLE(1925); BAT, THE(1926); ONE MINUTE TO PLAY(1926); GREAT MAIL ROBBERY, THE(1927); LAST TRAIL, THE(1927); LET IT RAIN(1927); OUTLAWS OF RED RIVER(1927); MILLION FOR LOVE, A(1928); EVANGELINE(1929)
Misc. Silents
BIG ADVENTURE, THE(1921); BRAWN OF THE NORTH(1922); BOWERY BISHOP, THE(1924); BAD LANDS, THE(1925); PRICE OF SUCCESS, THE(1925); GLENISTER OF THE MOUNTED(1926); WHISPERING CANYON(1926); SOUTH SEA LOVE(1927); BEYOND LONDON LIGHTS(1928)
Lee C. Shumway
Misc. Silents
WHEN DAWN CAME(1920)
Leonard C. Shumway
Silents
BRIDE OF FEAR, THE(1918)
Misc. Silents
BEGGAR IN PURPLE, A(1920); WANTED AT HEADQUARTERS(1920)
Walter Shumway
HEADIN' NORTH(1930); GHOST CITY(1932); NIGHT RIDER, THE(1932); DEVIL'S BROTHER, THE(1933); OUTLAW JUSTICE(1933); GILDED LILY, THE(1935); MARY BURNS, FUGITIVE(1935); WHIRLWIND HORSEMAN(1938); SIX-GUN RHYTHM(1939); SHOWDOWN, THE(1940); BALL OF FIRE(1941); DOUBLE CROSS(1941); WRANGLER'S ROOST(1941); LADY TAKES A SAILOR, THE(1949)

Silents
PRETTY LADIES(1925); CATCH AS CATCH CAN(1927); KING OF KINGS, THE(1927); APACHE RAIDER, THE(1928)
Misc. Silents
WHAT BECOMES OF THE CHILDREN?(1918); FIGHTING SHERIFF, THE(1925); PRINCE OF THE PLAINS(1927); WANDERER OF THE WEST(1927); GREASED LIGHTING(1928)

Chung Shun
BRUCE LEE–TRUE STORY(1976, Chi.)
Wang Shun
MAGNIFICENT CONCUBINE, THE(1964, Hong Kong), m
Iris Shunn
GEORGE WHITE'S 1935 SCANDALS(1935)
Capt. Charles Shunstrom
STORY OF G.I. JOE, THE(1945), tech adv
Sol Shur
SONS OF ADVENTURE(1948), w
Lisa Shure
BREAKING AWAY(1979); GORP(1980)
Wilfred Shure
HOUND OF THE BASKERVILLES(1932, Brit.)
Dinah Shurey
LAST POST, THE(1929, Brit.), p&d, w
Misc. Silents
CARRY ON!(1927, Brit.), d
Alison Cass Shurpin
WILLIE AND PHIL(1980)
Robert Shurr
GEORGE WASHINGTON CARVER(1940), w
Sewall Shurtz
LAKE PLACID SERENADE(1944)
Sewell Shurtz
THIS LOVE OF OURS(1945)
V. Shurupov
MEET ME IN MOSCOW(1966, USSR)
Edward Shurush
EVERY BASTARD A KING(1968, Israel)
Shurze
FRASIER, THE SENSUOUS LION(1973)
Ronald Shusett
W(1974), w; ALIEN(1979), w; PHOBIA(1980, Can.), w; DEAD AND BURIED(1981), p, w; FINAL TERROR, THE(1983), w
Wolfgang Shushitsky
REBELS AGAINST THE LIGHT(1964), ph
Madame Shushkina
SCOUNDREL, THE(1935)
William Shust
RIVALS(1972); SEVEN UPS, THE(1973); SEDUCTION OF JOE TYNAN, THE(1979)
Harold Shuster
SKYLINE(1931), ed; FARMER TAKES A WIFE, THE(1935), ed; COURAGE OF BLACK BEAUTY(1957), d
Harry Shuster
WANDA(1971), p
Hugo Shuster
BURNT EVIDENCE(1954, Brit.); DETECTIVE, THE(1954, Qit.)
Joe Shuster
SUPERMAN II(1980), w; SUPERMAN III(1983), w
Joel Shuster
SUPERMAN(1978), w
Harry Shutan
ARE THESE OUR CHILDREN?(1931); FIRST AID(1931); GAMBLING SHIP(1933); INFERNAL MACHINE(1933)
Jan Shutan
SEVEN MINUTES, THE(1971); DRACULA'S DOG(1978)
Col. William H. Shutan
REAL GLORY, THE(1939), tech adv
Alan Shute
NIGHT AND DAY(1946)
Anja Shute
COUSINS IN LOVE(1982)
Betty Shute
SNIPER, THE(1952)
James Shute
FOOLS FOR SCANDAL(1938), w
Martin C. Shute
NOT NOW DARLING(1975, Brit.), p
Nevil Shute
SCOTLAND YARD COMMANDS(1937, Brit.), w; PIED PIPER, THE(1942), w; NO HIGHWAY IN THE SKY(1951, Brit.), w; LANDFALL(1953, Brit.), w; TOWN LIKE ALICE, A(1958, Brit.), w; ON THE BEACH(1959), w
Susan Shute
LIVE A LITTLE, LOVE A LITTLE(1968)
Valerie Shute
CARRY ON AGAIN, DOCTOR(1969, Brit.); CARRY ON LOVING(1970, Brit.); ASSAULT(1971, Brit.)
Ye. Shutov
LULLABY(1961, USSR)
Ethel Shutta
WHOOPEE(1930); PLAYGROUND, THE(1965)
Jack Shutta
FALSE PRETENSES(1935); GHOST WALKS, THE(1935); HAPPINESS C.O.D.(1935); SONS OF STEEL(1935); LOVER COME BACK(1946); SLAVE GIRL(1947); WISTFUL WIDOW OF WAGON GAP, THE(1947); RIVER LADY(1948); FRANCIS(1949); ABBOTT AND COSTELLO IN THE FOREIGN LEGION(1950); TATTERED DRESS, THE(1957)
Steve Shuttack
RETURN TO CAMPUS(1975), ph
Bertram Shuttlesworth
MASTER OF BANKDAM, THE(1947, Brit.)

Keri Shuttleton
WHAT'S THE MATTER WITH HELEN?(1971); HICKEY AND BOGGS(1972)
Bertram Shuttleworth
SECRET PEOPLE(1952, Brit.)
Larry Shuttleworth
HELL SQUAD(1958); DIARY OF A HIGH SCHOOL BRIDE(1959); TANK COMMANDOS(1959)
Ernst Shutz
MERRY WIVES OF WINDSOR, THE(1966, Aust.)
Menachem Shuval
THEY WERE TEN(1961, Israel), w
Fusako Shuzui
SUMMER SOLDIERS(1972, Jap.), ed
L. Shvachkin
LITTLE HUMPBACKED HORSE, THE(1962, USSR)
Lev Shvarts
GORDEYEV FAMILY, THE(1961, U.S.S.R.), m
Yevgeniy Shvarts
DON QUIXOTE(1961, USSR), w; MAGIC WEAVER, THE(1965, USSR), w
C.N. Shvedoff
GIRL FROM POLTAVA(1937), m
Michael Shvetz
GIRL FROM POLTAVA(1937); COSSACKS IN EXILE(1939, Ukrainian)
Mikhail Shveytser
RESURRECTION(1963, USSR), d, w
A. Shvorin
CRANES ARE FLYING, THE(1960, USSR)
Alexander Shvorin
SKY CALLS, THE(1959, USSR)
Gus Shy
GOOD NEWS(1930); LADY'S MORALS, A(1930); NEW MOON(1930); I SELL ANYTHING(1934); CAPTAIN'S KID, THE(1937)
Charles Shyer
SMOKEY AND THE BANDIT(1977), w; GOIN' SOUTH(1978), w; HOUSE CALLS(1978), w; PRIVATE BENJAMIN(1980), p
1984
IRRECONCILABLE DIFFERENCES(1984), d, w; PROTOCOL(1984), w
Melville Shyer
SUCKER MONEY(1933), d; GREEN EYES(1934), w; MAN FROM HELL, THE(1934), w; MURDER IN THE MUSEUM(1934), d; ROAD TO RUIN(1934), d; DEAD MAN'S TRAIL(1952), w
Dennis Shyrack
1984
FLASHPOINT(1984), w
Siam
YO YO(1967, Fr.)
Ed Siani
CAPTURE THAT CAPSULE(1961)
Ryp Siani
ROBBY(1968)
Sabrina Siani
1984
CONQUEST(1984, Ital./Span./Mex.)
Misc. Talkies
ATOR: THE FIGHTING EAGLE(1983)
Silvio Siano
ALONE IN THE STREETS(1956, Ital.), d&w
A. Siaskas
STRANDED(1965), ed
El Siaskas
NAKED BRIGADE, THE(1965, U.S./Gr.), ed
Reynaldo Sibal
WALLS OF HELL, THE(1964, U.S./Phil.)
Stefano Sibaldi
MISSION STARDUST(1968, Ital./Span./Ger.)
Laurie Sibbald
UNDER THE YUM-YUM TREE(1963)
Tony Sibbald
CRY OF THE BANSHEE(1970, Brit.); HANOVER STREET(1979, Brit.); SUPERMAN II(1980); REDS(1981); AMIN–THE RISE AND FALL(1982, Kenya); LORDS OF DISCIPLINE, THE(1983)
1984
SCREAM FOR HELP(1984)
Arthur Sibcom
DANGEROUS CORNER(1935), p
S. Sibel
TRAIN GOES TO KIEV, THE(1961, USSR)
Simon Sibela
ONE STEP TO HELL(1969, U.S./Ital./Span.)
Sibelius
ALLEGRO NON TROPPO(1977, Ital.), m
Celia Sibelius
CONFESSIONS OF A NAZI SPY(1939)
Johanna Sibelius
DREADING LIPS(1958, Ger.), w; MRS. WARREN'S PROFESSION(1960, Ger.), w; END OF MRS. CHENEY(1963, Ger.), w; I, TOO, AM ONLY A WOMAN(1963, Ger.), w; AMONG VULTURES(1964, Ger./Ital./Fr./Yugo.), w; FRONTIER HELLCAT(1966, Fr./Ital./Ger./Yugo.), w; ONLY A WOMAN(1966, Ger.), w; 24 HOURS IN A WOMAN'S LIFE(1968, Fr./Ger.), w
Johanna Sibellus
ARMS AND THE MAN(1962, Ger.), w
Serge Siberman
AND HOPE TO DIE(1972 Fr/US), p
Nadia Siberskaia
LA MARSEILLAISE(1938, Fr.)
Roderick Spencer Sibert
WIZ, THE(1978)

N. Sibeykin
WAR AND PEACE(1968, USSR)
Nadia Sibirskaia
CRIME OF MONSIEUR LANGE, THE(1936, Fr.)
Misc. Silents
MENILMONTANT(1926, Fr.); BLIGHTY(1927, Brit.); SABLES(1928, Fr.)
Antoinette Sibley
TURNING POINT, THE(1977)
Dorothy Sibley
Silents
FIFTY CANDLES(1921)
Jim Sibley
STOP THE WORLD—I WANT TO GET OFF(1966, Brit.), ed
John Sibley
THREE CABALLEROS, THE(1944), anim; MAKE MINE MUSIC(1946), anim; FUN
AND FANCY FREE(1947), anim; MELODY TIME(1948), animators; SLEEPING
BEAUTY(1959), anim; ONE HUNDRED AND ONE DALMATIANS(1961), anim
W.M. Sibley
SWISS HONEYMOON(1947, Brit.), p, w
Joseph R. Sicari
WHO IS HARRY KELLERMAN AND WHY IS HE SAYING THOSE TERRIBLE
THINGS ABOUT ME?(1971); PARADES(1972); NIGHT SCHOOL(1981); TERROR
EYES(1981); PARTNERS(1982)
Manuel Sicart
P.O.W., THE(1973)
Mary Siceloff
CARNY(1980)
John Sichel
THREE SISTERS(1974, Brit.), d
Baker Sichol
MATING SEASON, THE(1951)
Jules Sicilia
GOING HOME(1971)
Orlando Sicilia
GIRL RUSH, THE(1955)
Antino Siciliano
GIORDANO BRUNO(1973, Ital.), ed
Antonio Siciliano
CONFESSIONS OF A POLICE CAPTAIN(1971, Ital.), ed; TRINITY IS STILL MY
NAME(1971, Ital.), ed; DUCH IN ORANGE SAUCE(1976, Ital.), ed
Enzo Siciliano
GOSPEL ACCORDING TO ST. MATTHEW, THE(1966, Fr., Ital.)
Flaminia Siciliano
HAWKS AND THE SPARROWS, THE(1967, Ital.)
Sickerts
AMERICAN FRIEND, THE(1977, Ger.), art d
Robert Sickinger
MICKEY ONE(1965); LOVE IN A TAXI(1980), p&d
William Sickinger
MEDIUM COOL(1969)
Luke Sickle
HAZEL'S PEOPLE(1978); WITHOUT A TRACE(1983)
Ken Sicklen
FLASH GORDON(1980)
Luke Sickles
HAPPY AS THE GRASS WAS GREEN(1973)
Roy Sickner
MORITURI(1965)
Roy N. Sickner
WILD BUNCH, THE(1969), w
William Sickner
BORDER BRIGANDS(1935), ph; OUTLAWED GUNS(1935), ph; STORMY(1935), ph;
LEFT-HANDED LAW(1937), ph; BAD MAN FROM RED BUTTE(1940), ph; BLACK
DIAMONDS(1940), ph; CHIP OF THE FLYING U(1940), ph; HOT STEEL(1940), ph;
PONY POST(1940), ph; RIDERS OF PASCO BASIN(1940), ph; SON OF ROARING
DAN(1940), ph; DANGER IN THE PACIFIC(1942), ph; LITTLE JOE, THE WRAN-
GLER(1942), ph; ARIZONA TRAIL(1943), ph; CHEYENNE ROUNDUP(1943), ph;
FRONTIER BADMEN(1943), ph; KEEP 'EM SLUGGING(1943), ph; LONE STAR
TRAIL, THE(1943), ph; OLD CHISHOLM TRAIL(1943), ph; RAIDERS OF SAN JOA-
QUIN(1943), ph; TENTING TONIGHT ON THE OLD CAMP GROUND(1943), ph;
MUMMY'S GHOST, THE(1944), ph; OKLAHOMA RAIDERS(1944), ph; OLD TEXAS
TRAIL, THE(1944), ph; TRIGGER TRAIL(1944), ph; WEEKEND PASS(1944), ph; FAL-
CON IN SAN FRANCISCO, THE(1945), ph; PENTHOUSE RHYTHM(1945), ph; RID-
ERS OF THE DAWN(1945), ph; SOUTH OF THE RIO GRANDE(1945), ph; THERE
GOES KELLY(1945), ph; BOWERY BOMBSHELL(1946), ph; DANGEROUS MO-
NEY(1946), ph; DON'T GAMBLE WITH STRANGERS(1946), ph; IN FAST COMPA-
NY(1946), ph; LIVE WIRES(1946), ph; MISSING LADY, THE(1946), ph; SHADOW
RETURNS, THE(1946), ph; SHADOWS OVER CHINATOWN(1946), ph; BELLE
STARR'S DAUGHTER(1947), ph; BLONDE SAVAGE(1947), ph; CHINESE RING,
THE(1947), ph; GAS HOUSE KIDS GO WEST(1947), ph; KILLER DILL(1947), ph;
KILROY WAS HERE(1947), ph; LOUISIANA(1947), ph; PRAIRIE EXPRESS(1947),
ph; DOCKS OF NEW ORLEANS(1948), ph; FEATHERED SERPENT, THE(1948), ph;
FIGHTING MAD(1948), ph; FRENCH LEAVE(1948), ph; JOE PALOOKA IN WINNER
TAKE ALL(1948), ph; KIDNAPPED(1948), ph; KING OF THE BANDITS(1948), ph;
MYSTERY OF THE GOLDEN EYE, THE(1948), ph; ROCKY(1948), ph; SHANGHAI
CHEST, THE(1948), ph; BLACK MIDNIGHT(1949), ph; BOMBA ON PANTHER IS-
LAND(1949), ph; BOMBA THE JUNGLE BOY(1949), ph; FIGHTING FOOLS(1949),
ph; HENRY, THE RAINMAKER(1949), ph; HOLD THAT BABY!(1949), ph; JOE
PALOOKA IN THE COUNTERPUNCH(1949), ph; LEAVE IT TO HENRY(1949), ph;
MISSISSIPPI RHYTHM(1949), ph; SKY DRAGON(1949), ph; TRAIL OF THE YU-
KON(1949), ph; TUNA CLIPPER(1949), ph; WOLF HUNTERS, THE(1949), ph; BIG
TIMBER(1950), ph; BOMBA AND THE HIDDEN CITY(1950), ph; CALL OF THE
KLONDIKE(1950), ph; FATHER MAKES GOOD(1950), ph; HUMPHREY TAKES A
CHANCE(1950), ph; JOE PALOOKA MEETS HUMPHREY(1950), ph; KILLER
SHARK(1950), ph; SIDESHOW(1950), ph; SNOW DOG(1950), ph; SQUARE DANCE
KATY(1950), ph; CASA MANANA(1951), ph; ELEPHANT STAMPEDE(1951), ph; FA-
THER TAKES THE AIR(1951), ph; JOE PALOOKA IN TRIPLE CROSS(1951), ph;
LION HUNTERS, THE(1951), ph; RHYTHM INN(1951), ph; SIERRA PASSAGE(1951),
ph; YELLOW FIN(1951), ph; YUKON MANHUNT(1951), ph; DESERT PUR-
SUIT(1952), ph; NORTHWEST TERRITORY(1952), ph; STEEL FIST, THE(1952), ph;

FANGS OF THE ARCTIC(1953), ph; JACK SLADE(1953), ph; MEXICAN MAN-
HUNT(1953), ph; NORTHERN PATROL(1953), ph; TANGIER INCIDENT(1953), ph;
TORPEDO ALLEY(1953), ph; CRY VENGEANCE(1954), ph; LOOPHOLE(1954), ph;
FINGER MAN(1955), ph; NIGHT FREIGHT(1955), ph; RETURN OF JACK SLADE,
THE(1955), ph; UNDEAD, THE(1957), ph; MODERN MARRIAGE, A(1962), ph
William A. Sickner
SCARLET CLUE, THE(1945), ph; BEHIND THE MASK(1946), ph; BORDER BAN-
DITS(1946), ph; DARK ALIBI(1946), ph; LAND OF THE LAWLESS(1947), ph
Rocco Siclari
1984
C.H.U.D.(1984)
Marcel Sicot
PROSTITUTION(1965, Fr.), w
Gilbert Sicotte
TI-CUL TOUGAS(1977, Can.); CORDELIA(1980, Fr., Can.)
Jan Sid
TREASURE OF SILVER LAKE(1965, Fr./Ger./Yugo.)
Sid Catlett and Band
BOY! WHAT A GIRL(1947)
Bruno [Bronislaw] Sidar
ROSEMARY'S BABY(1968)
Andy Sidaris
STACEY!(1973), d, w; TWO-MINUTE WARNING(1976); SEVEN(1979), p&d, w
Woody Sidarous
1984
RENO AND THE DOC(1984, Can.)
Robert Sidaway
NICE GIRL LIKE ME, A(1969, Brit.)
John Siddal
1984
SCANDALOUS(1984), art d
John Siddall
PINK PANTHER STRIKES AGAIN, THE(1976, Brit.), art d; REVENGE OF THE
PINK PANTHER(1978), art d; DOGS OF WAR, THE(1980, Brit.), art d; THERE GOES
THE BRIDE(1980, Brit.), art d; TRAIL OF THE PINK PANTHER, THE(1982), art d;
CURSE OF THE PINK PANTHER(1983), art d
J. David Siddon
Misc. Talkies
THEIR ONLY CHANCE(1978), d
Alathea Siddons
BLONDE BLACKMAILER(1955, Brit.)
Audra Siddons
WEST POINT WIDOW(1941)
Betty Siddons
Misc. Silents
CUPID IN CLOVER(1929, Brit.); MASTER AND MAN(1929, Brit.)
Harold Siddons
GLORY AT SEA(1952, Brit.); CLUE OF THE MISSING APE, THE(1953, Brit.);
GENEVIEVE(1953, Brit.); FUSS OVER FEATHERS(1954, Brit.); GOOD DIE YOUNG,
THE(1954, Brit.); MALTA STORY(1954, Brit.); PURPLE PLAIN, THE(1954, Brit.); I AM
A CAMERA(1955, Brit.); LAST MAN TO HANG, THE(1956, Brit.); BABY AND THE
BATTLESHIP, THE(1957, Brit.); VIOLENT STRANGER(1957, Brit.); HARRY BLACK
AND THE TIGER(1958, Brit.); MARK OF THE HAWK, THE(1958); NIGHT TO
REMEMBER, A(1958, Brit.); NAVY HEROES(1959, Brit.); SILENT ENEMY, THE(1959,
Brit.); WHITE TRAP, THE(1959, Brit.); MISSILE FROM HELL(1960, Brit.)
Bob Sidel
UPTIGHT(1968), makeup
Robert Sidell
MAN, THE(1972), makeup
N. Sidelnikov
OVERCOAT, THE(1965, USSR), m
Ron Siden
PRIME TIME, THE(1960)
Delores Sidener
PECOS RIVER(1951)
Conrad Siderman
ARE WE CIVILIZED?(1934)
Doug Sides
BLACK BELT JONES(1974)
Mathilda Sides
FIRST TASTE OF LOVE(1962, Fr.)
Patricia Sides
GUIDE FOR THE MARRIED MAN, A(1967)
Sidewalk Productions
GLORY STOMPERS, THE(1967), m; KILLERS THREE(1968), m; FREE
GRASS(1969), m
Sam Sidman
Silents
SHOW GIRL, THE(1927)
Ann Sidney
SEBASTIAN(1968, Brit.)
Misc. Talkies
PERFORMANCE(1970, Brit.)
Bruce Sidney
GIRLS CAN PLAY(1937); HIGH FLYERS(1937); I'LL TAKE ROMANCE(1937);
WHEN YOU'RE IN LOVE(1937); WOMEN OF GLAMOUR(1937); WHO KILLED GAIL
PRESTON?(1938); YOU CAN'T TAKE IT WITH YOU(1938)
D. J. Sidney
SHOCK WAVES(1977)
Derek Sidney
HOT ICE(1952, Brit.); ABANDON SHIP!(1957, Brit.)
George Sidney
COHENS AND KELLYS IN ATLANTIC CITY, THE(1929); GIVE AND TAKE(1929);
COHENS AND KELLYS IN AFRICA, THE(1930); COHENS AND KELLYS IN
SCOTLAND, THE(1930); CAUGHT CHEATING(1931); COHENS, AND KELLYS IN
HOLLYWOOD, THE(1932); HEART OF NEW YORK(1932); HIGH PRESSURE(1932);
COHENS AND KELLYS IN TROUBLE, THE(1933); MANHATTAN MELO-
DRAMA(1934); RAFTER ROMANCE(1934); DIAMOND JIM(1935); GOOD OLD SOAK,
THE(1937); FREE AND EASY(1941), d; PACIFIC RENDEZVOUS(1942), d; PILOT NO.
5(1943), d; THOUSANDS CHEER(1943), d; BATHING BEAUTY(1944), d; ANCHORS

AWEIGH(1945), d; ZIEGFELD FOLLIES(1945), d; HARVEY GIRLS, THE(1946), d; HOLIDAY IN MEXICO(1946), d; CASS TIMBERLANE(1947), d; THREE MUSKETEERS, THE(1948), d; RED DANUBE, THE(1949), d; ANNIE GET YOUR GUN(1950), d; KEY TO THE CITY(1950), d; SHOW BOAT(1951), d; SCARAMOUCHE(1952), d; KISS ME KATE(1953), d; YOUNG BESS(1953), d; JUPITER'S DARLING(1955), d; EDDY DUCHIN STORY, THE(1956), d; JEANNE EAGELS(1957), p&d; PAL JOEY(1957), d; PEPE(1960), p&d; WHO WAS THAT LADY?(1960), d; BYE BYE BIRDIE(1963), d; TICKLISH AFFAIR, A(1963), d; VIVA LAS VEGAS(1964), p, d; SWINGER, THE(1966), p&d; HALF A SIXPENCE(1967, Brit.), p, d

Misc. Talkies
AROUND THE CORNER(1930)

Silents
IN HOLLYWOOD WITH POTASH AND PERLMUTTER(1924); COHENS AND KELLYS, THE(1926); PARTNERS AGAIN(1926); PRINCE OF PILSEN, THE(1926); AUCTIONEER, THE(1927); CLANCY'S KOSHER WEDDING(1927); COHENS AND THE KELLYS IN PARIS, THE(1928); FLYING ROMEOS(1928); LATEST FROM PARIS, THE(1928)

Misc. Silents
MILLIONAIRES(1926); SWEET DADDIES(1926); FOR THE LOVE OF MIKE(1927); LIFE OF RILEY, THE(1927); LOST AT THE FRONT(1927); WE AMERICANS(1928)

Jay Sidney
NO WAY TO TREAT A LADY(1968)

Jon Sidney
DAY AFTER HALLOWEEN, THE(1981, Aus.)

Louis K. Sidney
HULLABALOO(1940), p; BIG STORE, THE(1941), p

Margaret Sidney
FIVE LITTLE PEPPERS AND HOW THEY GREW(1939), w; FIVE LITTLE PEPPERS AT HOME(1940), w; FIVE LITTLE PEPPERS IN TROUBLE(1940), w; OUT WEST WITH THE PEPPERS(1940), w

Neville Sidney
MELODY IN THE DARK(1948, Brit.)

P. Jay Sidney
JOE LOUIS STORY, THE(1953); BROTHER JOHN(1971); TRADING PLACES(1983)

Robert Sidney
YOU CAN'T RUN AWAY FROM IT(1956), ch; THIS IS THE ARMY(1943), ch; LOVES OF CARMEN, THE(1948), a, ch; SLIGHTLY FRENCH(1949), ch; SUSAN SLEPT HERE(1954), ch; CONQUEROR, THE(1956), ch; OPPOSITE SEX, THE(1956), ch; PARTY GIRL(1958), ch; WHERE THE BOYS ARE(1960), ch; PLEASURE SEEKERS, THE(1964), ch; HOW TO MURDER YOUR WIFE(1965), ch; SILENCERS, THE(1966), ch; SINGING NUN, THE(1966), ch; VALLEY OF THE DOLLS(1967), ch

Scott Sidney
Silents
PAINTED SOUL, THE(1915), d; TARZAN OF THE APES(1918), d; RECKLESS ROMANCE(1924), d; NERVOUS WRECK, THE(1926), d; NO CONTROL(1927), d

Misc. Silents
MATING, THE(1915), d; MATRIMONY(1915), d; TOAST OF DEATH, THE(1915), d; BULLETS AND BROWN EYES(1916), d; GREEN SWAMP, THE(1916), d; ROAD TO LOVE, THE(1916), d; WAIFS, THE(1916), d; HER OWN PEOPLE(1917), d; "813"(1920), d; HOLD YOUR BREATH(1924), d; CHARLEY'S AUNT(1925), d; MADAME BEHAVE(1925), d; MILLION DOLLAR HANDICAP, THE(1925), d; SEVEN DAYS(1925), d; STOP FLIRTING(1925), d; WRONG MR. WRIGHT, THE(1927), d

Steffi Sidney
HOLD BACK TOMORROW(1955); REBEL WITHOUT A CAUSE(1955); PEYTON PLACE(1957); HOT ANGEL, THE(1958); TEACHER'S PET(1958)

Susanne Sidney
ANGELS FROM HELL(1968)

Suzanne Sidney
STUDS LONIGAN(1960)

Sylvia Sidney
THRU DIFFERENT EYES(1929); AMERICAN TRAGEDY, AN(1931); CITY STREETS(1931); CONFESSIONS OF A CO-ED(1931); STREET SCENE(1931); LADIES OF THE BIG HOUSE(1932); MADAME BUTTERFLY(1932); MAKE ME A STAR(1932); MERRILY WE GO TO HELL(1932); MIRACLE MAN, THE(1932); JENNIE GERHARDT(1933); PICK-UP(1933); THIRTY-DAY PRINCESS(1934); ACCENT ON YOUTH(1935); BEHOLD MY WIFE(1935); MARY BURNS, FUGITIVE(1935); TRAIL OF THE LONESOME PINE, THE(1936); DEAD END(1937); SABOTAGE(1937, Brit.); YOU ONLY LIVE ONCE(1937); YOU AND ME(1938); ONE THIRD OF A NATION(1939); WAGONS ROLL AT NIGHT, THE(1941); BLOOD ON THE SUN(1945); MR. ACE(1946); SEARCHING WIND, THE(1946); LOVE FROM A STRANGER(1947); LES MISERABLES(1952); VIOLENT SATURDAY(1955); BEHIND THE HIGH WALL(1956); SUMMER WISHES, WINTER DREAMS(1973); GOD TOLD ME TO(1976); I NEVER PROMISED YOU A ROSE GARDEN(1977); DAMIEN–OMEN II(1978); HAMMETT(1982)

1984
CORRUPT(1984, Ital.)

Karol Sidon
DESERTER AND THE NOMADS, THE(1969, Czech./Ital.), w

Harri Sidonie
SIMON, KING OF THE WITCHES(1971)

M. Sidorchuk
NIGHT BEFORE CHRISTMAS, A(1963, USSR)

V. Sidorchuk
SONG OF THE FOREST(1963, USSR)

Joe Sidore
FROGS(1972), spec eff

M. Sidorkin
VOW, THE(1947, USSR.); RESURRECTION(1963, USSR)

Mikhail Sidorkin
SPRING(1948, USSR)

Itzhak Sidranski
JESUS CHRIST, SUPERSTAR(1973)

Fanyana Sidumo
1984
GODS MUST BE CRAZY, THE(1984, Botswana)

Fanyana H. Sidumo
SAFARI 3000(1982)

Tamara Sie
MAN IN THE WILDERNESS(1971, U.S./Span.)

Josef Sieber
WATER FOR CANITOGA(1939, Ger.); ETERNAL LOVE(1960, Ger.)

Maria Sieber
SCARLET EMPRESS, THE(1934)

Barbara Siebert
DILLINGER(1973), cos

Charles Siebert
DEADLY HERO(1976); OTHER SIDE OF MIDNIGHT, THE(1977); BLUE SUNSHINE(1978); COMA(1978); ...AND JUSTICE FOR ALL(1979); LAST WORD, THE(1979); ALL NIGHT LONG(1981)

Chuck Siebert
LIKE FATHER LIKE SON(1961); YOUNG SINNER, THE(1965)

John Siebert
MOZART STORY, THE(1948, Aust.)

Markus Sieburg
DISORDER AND EARLY TORMENT(1977, Ger.)

Constance Siech
Misc. Talkies
SUPERBUG, THE WILD ONE(1977)

Johannes Siedel
FISTFUL OF DOLLARS, A(1964, Ital./Ger./Span.)

Jim Siedow
TEXAS CHAIN SAW MASSACRE, THE(1974)

Percy Sieff
CODE 7, VICTIM 5(1964, Brit.)
Misc. Talkies
BOESMAN AND LENA(1976)

Claudia Siefried
SCAVENGERS, THE(1969)

Edward Sieg
RING, THE(1952)

Bernard Siegal
EBB TIDE(1937)

Robin Siegal
IF EVER I SEE YOU AGAIN(1978)

Sol C. Siegal
LARCENY ON THE AIR(1937), p; HIGGINS FAMILY, THE(1938), p; CALL ME MADAM(1953), p

Allen S. Siegel
HELL'S HOUSE(1932), ph

Barbara Siegel
WEREWOLF OF WASHINGTON(1973)

Bernard Siegel
PHANTOM OF THE OPERA, THE(1929); SEA FURY(1929); CASE OF SERGEANT GRISCHA, THE(1930); BEAU IDEAL(1931); SHADOW OF A DOUBT(1935); WEDDING NIGHT, THE(1935); JUNGLE PRINCESS, THE(1936); WELLS FARGO(1937)

Silents
FORTUNE HUNTER, THE(1914); CLIMBERS, THE(1915); APARTMENT 29(1917); ARSENE LUPIN(1917); ALL MAN(1918); EVERYBODY'S GIRL(1918); HEART OF MARYLAND, THE(1921); AGAINST ALL ODDS(1924); CRIMSON RUNNER, THE(1925); PHANTOM OF THE OPERA, THE(1925); BLAZING DAYS(1927); KING OF KINGS, THE(1927); RAGTIME(1927); RANGER OF THE NORTH(1927); LAUGH, CLOWN, LAUGH(1928); STAND AND DELIVER(1928); FAR CALL, THE(1929); RESCUE, THE(1929)

Misc. Silents
THIRD DEGREE, THE(1914); THREADS OF DESTINY(1914); OGRE AND THE GIRL, THE(1915); SOULS IN BONDAGE(1916); SONG OF THE SOUL, THE(1918); WOMAN BETWEEN FRIENDS, THE(1918); MAN WHO WON, THE(1919); SILENT STRENGTH(1919); LOVE NEST, THE(1922); MADNESS OF LOVE, THE(1922); SIDEWALKS OF NEW YORK(1923); OPEN RANGE(1927)

Cornelius Siegel
NOSFERATU, THE VAMPIRE(1979, Fr./Ger.), spec eff

Don Siegel
CASABLANCA(1942), art d; EDGE OF DARKNESS(1943), set d; MISSION TO MOSCOW(1943), art d; NORTHERN PURSUIT(1943), spec eff; ADVENTURES OF MARK TWAIN, THE(1944), ph; VERDICT, THE(1946), d; BIG STEAL, THE(1949), d; NIGHT UNTO NIGHT(1949), d; DUEL AT SILVER CREEK, THE(1952), d; NO TIME FOR FLOWERS(1952), d; CHINA VENTURE(1953), d; COUNT THE HOURS(1953), d; PRIVATE HELL 36(1954), d; RIOT IN CELL BLOCK 11(1954), d; ANNAPOLIS STORY, AN(1955), d; CRIME IN THE STREETS(1956), d; INVASION OF THE BODY SNATCHERS(1956), d; GUN RUNNERS, THE(1958), d; LINEUP, THE(1958), d; EDGE OF ETERNITY(1959), d; HOUND-DOG MAN(1959), d; FLAMING STAR(1960), d; HELL IS FOR HEROES(1962), d; TWO MULES FOR SISTER SARA(1970), d; BEGUILED, THE(1971), p&d; DIRTY HARRY(1971), p&d; CHARLEY VARRICK(1973), d; BLACK WINDMILL, THE(1974, Brit.), p&d; SHOOTIST, THE(1976), d; TELEFON(1977), d; INVASION OF THE BODY SNATCHERS(1978); ESCAPE FROM ALCATRAZ(1979), p&d; ROUGH CUT(1980, Brit.), d; JINXED!(1982), d

Donald Siegel
BABY FACE NELSON(1957), d; SPANISH AFFAIR(1958, Span.), d; EDGE OF ETERNITY(1959), d; KILLERS, THE(1964), p&d; COOGAN'S BLUFF(1968), p&d; MADIGAN(1968), d; PLAY MISTY FOR ME(1971); CHARLEY VARRICK(1973); ESCAPE FROM ALCATRAZ(1979)

Gordon Barry Siegel
WINDOWS(1980), w

Jan Siegel
1984
HARRY AND SON(1984)

Jerry Siegel
CHILDRENS GAMES(1969), ed; TOYS ARE NOT FOR CHILDREN(1972), ed; SUPERMAN(1978), w; SUPERMAN II(1980), w; SUPERMAN III(1983), w

Joel Siegel
DEATHTRAP(1982)

Mark Siegel
CRATER LAKE MONSTER, THE(1977)

Max Siegel
INDIANAPOLIS SPEEDWAY(1939), p

Otto Siegel
MYSTERY BROADCAST(1943), set d; PURPLE V, THE(1943), set d; SECRETS OF THE UNDERGROUND(1943), set d; SILVER SPURS(1943), set d; LADY AND THE MONSTER, THE(1944), set d; STEPPIN' IN SOCIETY(1945), set d; UNDER NEVADA SKIES(1946), set d; MYSTERY SUBMARINE(1950), set d; LET'S GO NAVY(1951), set d; THUNDERBIRDS(1952), set d; LAW AND JAKE WADE, THE(1958), set d; SADDLE THE WIND(1958), set d; HORIZONTAL LIEUTENANT, THE(1962), set d; RIDE THE HIGH COUNTRY(1962), set d

Phillip Siegel
JULIA(1977)

Robert J. Siegel
PARADES(1972), p&d; LINE, THE(1982), p&d

Rohama Siegel
WE'RE GOING TO BE RICH(1938, Brit.), w

Sol Siegel
CRY OF THE CITY(1948), p

Sol C. Siegel
COME ON, COWBOYS(1937), p; GUNSMOKE RANCH(1937), p; HEART OF THE ROCKIES(1937), p; PUBLIC COWBOY NO. 1(1937), p; RANGE DEFENDERS(1937), p; SPRINGTIME IN THE ROCKIES(1937), p; TRIGGER TRIO, THE(1937), p; ARMY GIRL(1938), p; OLD BARN DANCE, THE(1938), p; PURPLE VIGILANTES, THE(1938), p; UNDER WESTERN STARS(1938), p; WILD HORSE RODEO(1938), p; MAN OF CONQUEST(1939), p; MY WIFE'S RELATIVES(1939), p; SHE MARRIED A COP(1939), p; SHOULD HUSBANDS WORK?(1939), p; WOMAN DOCTOR(1939), p; ZERO HOUR, THE(1939), p; DARK COMMAND, THE(1940), p; HI-YO SILVER(1940), p; HIT PARADE OF 1941(1940), p; MELODY RANCH(1940), p; THREE FACES WEST(1940), p; WOMEN IN WAR(1940), p; AMONG THE LIVING(1941), p; BUY ME THAT TOWN(1941), p; GLAMOUR BOY(1941), p; HENRY ALDRICH FOR PRESIDENT(1941), p; NIGHT OF JANUARY 16TH(1941), p; WEST POINT WIDOW(1941), p; WORLD PREMIERE(1941), p; DR. BROADWAY(1942), p; FLY BY NIGHT(1942), p; HENRY ALDRICH, EDITOR(1942), p; HENRY AND DIZZY(1942), p; LADY BODYGUARD(1942), p; MRS. WIGGS OF THE CABBAGE PATCH(1942), p; MY HEART BELONGS TO DADDY(1942), p; NIGHT IN NEW ORLEANS, A(1942), p; PACIFIC BLACKOUT(1942), p; PRIORITIES ON PARADE(1942), p; STREET OF CHANCE(1942), p; SWEATER GIRL(1942), p; TRUE TO THE ARMY(1942), p; HOSTAGES(1943), p; KISS AND TELL(1945), p; BLUE SKIES(1946), p; PERILS OF PAULINE, THE(1947), p; WELCOME STRANGER(1947), p; IRON CURTAIN, THE(1948), p; LETTER TO THREE WIVES, A(1948), p; HOUSE OF STRANGERS(1949), p; I WAS A MALE WAR BRIDE(1949), p; PRINCE OF FOXES(1949), p; MY BLUE HEAVEN(1950), p; PANIC IN THE STREETS(1950), p; STELLA(1950), p; FOURTEEN HOURS(1951), p; I CAN GET IT FOR YOU WHOLESALE(1951), p; I'LL NEVER FORGET YOU(1951), p; ON THE RIVERA(1951), p; DEADLINE–U.S.A.(1952), p; DREAMBOAT(1952), p; MONKEY BUSINESS(1952), p; WHAT PRICE GLORY?(1952), p; GENTLEMEN PREFER BLONDES(1953), p; PRESIDENT'S LADY, THE(1953), p; BROKEN LANCE(1954), p; THERE'S NO BUSINESS LIKE SHOW BUSINESS(1954), p; THREE COINS IN THE FOUNTAIN(1954), p; HIGH SOCIETY(1956), p; LES GIRLS(1957), p; MAN ON FIRE(1957), p; MERRY ANDREW(1958), p; SOME CAME RUNNING(1959), p; ALVAREZ KELLY(1966), p; WALK, DON'T RUN(1966), p; NO WAY TO TREAT A LADY(1968), p

Stan Siegel
LORDS OF FLATBUSH, THE(1974), ed

Tom Siegel
SCAVENGERS, THE(1969)

Kurt Siegenberg
WINDOM'S WAY(1958, Brit.)

John Siegfried
HITLER(1962); TRADER HORN(1973)

Norbert Siegfried
MORITURI(1965)

Siegfried and Roy
LOOKIN' TO GET OUT(1982)

Gerda Siegl
HOUSE OF THE THREE GIRLS, THE(1961, Aust.)

Al Sieglar
DAMAGED LIVES(1937), ph

A. Siegler
BEYOND THE LAW(1934), ph

Al Siegler
RUSTY RIDES ALONE(1933), ph; UNKNOWN VALLEY(1933), ph; CRIME OF HELEN STANLEY(1934), ph; FIGHTING CODE, THE(1934), ph; SPEED WINGS(1934), ph; CARNIVAL(1935), ph; DEATH FLIES EAST(1935), ph
Silents
DANGEROUS AGE, THE(1922), ph

Alan Siegler
ANYBODY'S WAR(1930), ph
Silents
RED, RED HEART, THE(1918), ph

All Siegler
MAN'S GAME, A(1934), ph

Allen Siegler
WOLF SONG(1929), ph; BURNING UP(1930), ph; L'ENIGMATIQUE MONSIEUR PARKES(1930), ph; LOVE AMONG THE MILLIONAIRES(1930), ph; POINTED HEELS(1930), ph; SEA LEGS(1930), ph; SOCIAL LION, THE(1930), ph; TAKE THE HEIR(1930), ph; MAKE ME A STAR(1932), ph; MEET THE BARON(1933), ph; DEVIL IS DRIVING, THE(1937), ph; WEST OF SANTA FE(1938), ph; SPOILERS OF THE RANGE(1939), ph; SECRET OF THE WHISTLER(1946), ph; SING WHILE YOU DANCE(1946), ph; BLONDIE'S BIG MOMENT(1947), ph; DEVIL SHIP(1947), ph; LONE WOLF IN MEXICO, THE(1947), ph; MILLIE'S DAUGHTER(1947), ph; PORT SAID(1948), ph; AIR HOSTESS(1949), ph; NEVER TRUST A GAMBLER(1951), ph; SMUGGLER'S GOLD(1951), ph
Silents
SAVING THE FAMILY NAME(1916), ph; GIRL WHO WOULDN'T WORK, THE(1925), ph; PLASTIC AGE, THE(1925), ph; LOVES OF RICARDO, THE(1926), ph; AIN'T LOVE FUNNY?(1927), ph; JESSE JAMES(1927), ph; JUDGMENT OF THE HILLS(1927), ph; NAUGHTY NANETTE(1927), ph

Allen G. Siegler
CASE OF THE MISSING MAN, THE(1935), ph; CASE OF THE BLACK CAT, THE(1936), ph; COWBOY STAR, THE(1936), ph; DAN MATTHEWS(1936), ph; COUNTERFEIT LADY(1937), ph; IT CAN'T LAST FOREVER(1937), ph; MOTOR MADNESS(1937), ph; OLD WYOMING TRAIL, THE(1937), ph; TWO-FISTED SHERIFF(1937), ph; WOMAN IN DISTRESS(1937), ph; LADY OBJECTS, THE(1938), ph; MAIN EVENT, THE(1938), ph; NO TIME TO MARRY(1938), ph; BEHIND PRISON GATES(1939), ph; BEWARE SPOOKS(1939), ph; LONE WOLF SPY HUNT, THE(1939), ph; MY SON IS A CRIMINAL(1939), ph; ROMANCE OF THE REDWOODS(1939), ph; SMASHING THE SPY RING(1939), ph; FIVE LITTLE PEPPERS AT HOME(1940), ph; MILITARY ACADEMY(1940), ph; SO YOU WON'T TALK(1940), ph; BODY DISAPPEARS, THE(1941), ph; DEVIL COMMANDS, THE(1941), ph; FATHER'S SON(1941), ph; SHADOWS ON THE STAIRS(1941), ph; STRANGE ALIBI(1941), ph; UNKNOWN WORLD(1951), ph

Allen S. Siegler
CITY STREETS(1938), ph

Marc Siegler
SKI BUM, THE(1971), a, w; GALAXY OF TERROR(1981), p, w

George Siegman
Silents
BIG PUNCH, THE(1921)

George Siegmann
Silents
AVENGING CONSCIENCE, THE(1914); HOME SWEET HOME(1914); BIRTH OF A NATION, THE(1915); ATTA BOY'S LAST RACE(1916); d; INTOLERANCE(1916); GREAT LOVE, THE(1918); HEARTS OF THE WORLD(1918); SPITFIRE OF SEVILLE, THE(1919); d; LITTLE MISS REBELLION(1920); CONNECTICUT YANKEE AT KING ARTHUR'S COURT, A(1921); QUEEN OF SHEBA, THE(1921); SHAME(1921); THREE MUSKETEERS, THE(1921); CALIFORNIA ROMANCE, A(1922); HUNGRY HEARTS(1922); OLIVER TWIST(1922); ANNA CHRISTIE(1923); EAGLE'S FEATHER, THE(1923); ENEMIES OF CHILDREN(1923); JEALOUS HUSBANDS(1923); MERRY-GO-ROUND(1923); SCARAMOUCHE(1923); SLANDER THE WOMAN(1923); JANICE MEREDITH(1924); MANHATTAN(1924); ON TIME(1924); REVELATION(1924); SAINTED DEVIL, A(1924); SINGER JIM McKEE(1924); NEVER THE TWAIN SHALL MEET(1925); RECOMPENSE(1925); ZANDER THE GREAT(1925); CARNIVAL GIRL, THE(1926); OLD SOAK, THE(1926); CAT AND THE CANARY, THE(1927); KING OF KINGS, THE(1927); MAN WHO LAUGHS, THE(1927); RED MILL, THE(1927); LOVE ME AND THE WORLD IS MINE(1928); STOP THAT MAN(1928)
Misc. Silents
YANKEE FROM THE WEST, A(1915), d; LITTLE YANK, THE(1917), d; SHOULD SHE OBEY?(1917), d; MY UNMARRIED WIFE(1918), d; TREMBLING HOUR, THE(1919), d; WOMAN UNDER COVER, THE(1919), d; UNTAMED, THE(1920); SILENT YEARS(1921); HELL'S HOLE(1923); RIGHT OF THE STRONGEST, THE(1924); MANHATTAN MADNESS(1925); PURSUED(1925); MIDNIGHT SUN, THE(1926); POKER FACES(1926); HOTEL IMPERIAL(1927); UNCLE TOM'S CABIN(1927)

George A. Siegmann
Misc. Silents
MOTHER LOVE AND THE LAW(1917), d

Elie Siegmeister
THEY CAME TO CORDURA(1959), m

George A. Siegmund
Misc. Silents
MOTHER LOVE AND THE LAW(1917)

Frank Sieman
MEET MR. CALLAGHAN(1954, Brit.); THREE CROOKED MEN(1958, Brit.); MUMMY, THE(1959, Brit.); MAIN ATTRACTION, THE(1962, Brit.); KNACK ... AND HOW TO GET IT, THE(1965, Brit.); HE WHO RIDES A TIGER(1966, Brit.); TRAITOR'S GATE(1966, Brit./Ger.); IT!(1967, Brit.); SMASHING TIME(1967 Brit.); CONFESSIONS OF A WINDOW CLEANER(1974, Brit.)

Casey Siemaszko
CLASS(1983)

Curtis Siemens
1984
COUNTRY(1984)

Friedrich Siemers
JUDGE AND THE SINNER, THE(1964, Ger.)

Paul Siemion
SPY WITH MY FACE, THE(1966)

Wojciech Siemion
EROICA(1966, Pol.); SALTO(1966, Pol.)

Frank Siemon
DEAD MAN'S EVIDENCE(1962, Brit.)

Gregory Siena
CASTAWAY COWBOY, THE(1974)

Henry Sienkiewickz
INVASION 1700(1965, Fr./Ital./Yugo.), w

Henryk Sienkiewicz
Silents
QUO VADIS?(1913, Ital.), w

Kinja Sienko
GREAT BIG WORLD AND LITTLE CHILDREN, THE(1962, Pol.)

Bridget Sienna
1984
BAD MANNERS(1984)

Cesare Siepi
DON GIOVANNI(1955, Brit.)

Herman Sieracki
Misc. Silents
HARSH FATHER, THE(1911, USSR)

Tom Sierchio
1984
DELIVERY BOYS(1984)

Detlef Sierck [Douglas Sirk]
GIRL FROM THE MARSH CROFT, THE(1935, Ger.), d; COURT CONCERT, THE(1936, Ger.), d&w; FINAL CHORD, THE(1936, Ger.), d, w; PILLARS OF SOCIETY(1936, Ger.), d; LIFE BEGINS ANEW(1938, Ger.), d, w; BOEFJE(1939, Ger.), d, w

Gregg Sierra
POCKET MONEY(1972); LAUGHING POLICEMAN, THE(1973)

Gregory Sierra
BENEATH THE PLANET OF THE APES(1970); GETTING STRAIGHT(1970); RED SKY AT MORNING(1971); CULPEPPER CATTLE COMPANY, THE(1972); WRATH OF GOD, THE(1972); CLONES, THE(1973); PAPILLON(1973); THIEF WHO CAME TO DINNER, THE(1973); TOWERING INFERNO, THE(1974); MEAN DOG BLUES(1978); PRISONER OF ZENDA, THE(1979)

Martinez Sierra
CRADLE SONG(1933), w; IO ... TU ... Y ... ELLA(1933), w
Melissa Sierra
LAW OF THE TEXAN(1938); ONLY ANGELS HAVE WINGS(1939)
Sara Lopez Sierra
CAVEMAN(1981)
Jost Siethoff
BEGGAR STUDENT, THE(1958, Ger.)
George B. Sietz
SALLY OF THE SUBWAY(1932), d&w
Lance Sieveking
THIRD CLUE, THE(1934, Brit.), w
Bernard Sievel
Misc. Silents
DAWN OF REVENGE(1922), d
Alejandro Sieverina
STATE OF SIEGE(1973, Fr./U.S./Ital./Ger.)
Chris Sievernich
STATE OF THINGS, THE(1983), p
1984
CHINESE BOXES(1984, Ger./Brit.), a, p; FLIGHT TO BERLIN(1984, Ger./Brit.), P
Ille Sievers
WILLY WONKA AND THE CHOCOLATE FACTORY(1971), cos
1984
LITTLE DRUMMER GIRL, THE(1984), cos
Alan Sievewright
WONDERFUL TO BE YOUNG!(1962, Brit.), cos
Helen J. Siff
WHITE DOG(1982)
1984
KARATE KID, THE(1984)
Joe Siffert
GRAND PRIX(1966)
Armando Sifo
CONDEMNED OF ALTONA, THE(1963)
Claire Sifton
MIDNIGHT(1934), w
Elizabeth Sifton
FLIGHT ANGELS(1940); SEA HAWK, THE(1940)
Paul Sifton
MIDNIGHT(1934), w
Eugene Sigaloff
CLEAR ALL WIRES(1933); ROYAL SCANDAL, A(1945); NORTHWEST OUT-POST(1947)
Misc. Talkies
BEAST OF BORNEO(1935)
Sigayev
ENEMIES OF PROGRESS(1934, USSR), ph
Alexander Sigayev
DEFENSE OF VOLOTCHAYEVSK, THE(1938, USSR), ph
Barbara Sigel
Misc. Talkies
TIME TO RUN(1974)
Michael Sigel
BALTIMORE BULLET, THE(1980)
Sigfrit
PEDESTRIAN, THE(1974, Ger.)
Jeff Siggens
SUMMERTREE(1971)
Jeff Siggins
DOUBLE-BARRELLED DETECTIVE STORY, THE(1965); BABY MAKER, THE(1970)
Mietta Sighele
FITZCARRALDO(1982)
Marian Sigler
Misc. Silents
WANTED - A HOME(1916)
Ernie Sigley
DEAD MAN'S FLOAT(1980, Aus.)
Marjorie L. Sigley
NEVER NEVER LAND(1982), w
Marjory Sigley
GEORGY GIRL(1966, Brit.), ch
David Sigmund
1984
SECOND TIME LUCKY(1984, Aus./New Zealand), w
Elsbeth Sigmund
HEIDI(1954, Switz.); HEIDI AND PETER(1955, Switz.)
Eugene Signaloff
ROSE OF THE YUKON(1949)
Christine Signe
LADY BY CHOICE(1934)
Gordon Signer
PRIME CUT(1972); SUPERMAN III(1983)
Bob Signorelli
LAST HARD MEN, THE(1976), set d
James Signorelli
SUPERFLY(1972), ph; BLACK CAESAR(1973), ph; EASY MONEY(1983), d
Robert Signorelli
TOP OF THE HEAP(1972), set d; BITE THE BULLET(1975), set d; WHIFFS(1975), set d; I WILL ...I WILL ...FOR NOW(1976), set d
Tom Signorelli
ST. VALENTINE'S DAY MASSACRE, THE(1967); TRIP, THE(1967); KELLY'S HEROES(1970, U.S./Yugo.); ANDERSON TAPES, THE(1971); BANG THE DRUM SLOWLY(1973); SEVEN UPS, THE(1973); BIG BAD MAMA(1974); LAST PORNO FLICK, THE(1974); ALICE, SWEET ALICE(1978); HIDE IN PLAIN SIGHT(1980); THIEF(1981); ESCAPE ARTIST, THE(1982); ONE DOWN TWO TO GO(1982)
1984
COTTON CLUB, THE(1984)

Tommy Signorelli
HICKEY AND BOGGS(1972)
Signoret
SACRIFICE OF HONOR(1938, Fr.)
Gabriel Signoret
Misc. Silents
LE ROI DE LA MER(1917, Fr.); LE TORRENT(1918, Fr.); LA CIGARETTE(1919, Fr.); LA RAFALE(1920, Fr.); LE SECRET DU 'LONE STAR'(1920, Fr.); LA PERE GORI-OT(1921, Fr.)
Simone Signoret
LIVING CORPSE, THE(1940, Fr.); AGAINST THE WIND(1948, Brit.); DEDEE(1949, Fr.); CHEAT, THE(1950, Fr.); FOUR DAYS LEAVE(1950, Switz.); LA RONDE(1954, Fr.); DIABOLIQUE(1955, Fr.); CASQUE D'OR(1956, Fr.); ADULTERESS, THE(1959, Fr.); ROOM AT THE TOP(1959, Brit.); GINA(1961, Fr./Mex.); BACK STREETS OF PA-RIS(1962, Fr.); TERM OF TRIAL(1962, Brit.); DAY AND THE HOUR, THE(1963, Fr./Ital.); NAKED AUTUMN(1963, Fr.); SWEET AND SOUR(1964, Fr./Ital.); LOVE A LA CARTE(1965, Ital.); SHIP OF FOOLS(1965); IS PARIS BURNING?(1966, U.S./Fr.); SLEEPING CAR MURDER(1966, Fr.); DEADLY AFFAIR, THE(1967, Brit.); GAMES(1967); SEA GULL, THE(1968); L'ARMEE DES OMBRES(1969, Fr./Ital.); CONFESSION, THE(1970, Fr.); MISTER FREEDOM(1970, Fr.); CAT, THE(1975, Fr.); POLICE PYTHON 357(1976, Fr.); DEATH IN THE GARDEN(1977, Fr./Mex.); MADAME ROSA(1977, Fr.); ADOLESCENT, THE(1978, Fr./W.Ger.); CASE AGAINST FERRO, THE(1980, Fr.); I SENT A LETTER TO MY LOVE(1981, Fr.); NORTH STAR, THE(1982, Fr.); L'ETOILE DU NORD(1983, Fr.)
Misc. Talkies
TIME RUNNING OUT(1950)
Irene Signoretti
LADY LIBERTY(1972, Ital./Fr.); TOYS ARE NOT FOR CHILDREN(1972)
Tom Signotelli
CALIFORNIA SPLIT(1974)
Gerhard Maser Signpost
COTTONPICKIN' CHICKENPICKERS(1967), ph
Howard Sigrist
PAL JOEY(1957)
Jacques Siguard
WEB OF FEAR(1966, Fr./Span.), w
Placido Sigueiros
HOLD BACK THE DAWN(1941)
Shawn Sigueiros
1984
REVENGE OF THE NERDS(1984)
Jacques Sigurd
DEDEE(1949, Fr.), w; CHEAT, THE(1950, Fr.), w; LUCRECE BORGIA(1953, Ital./Fr.), w; DESPERATE DECISION(1954, Fr.), w; CHEATERS, THE(1961, Fr.), w; CRIME DOES NOT PAY(1962, Fr.), w; LAFAYETTE(1963, Fr.), w; SWEET SKIN(1965, Fr./Ital.), w
William Sigurgeirson
INBREAKER, THE(1974, Can.), w
Caroline Sihol
CONFIDENTIALLY YOURS(1983, Fr.)
Seija Siikamaki
MAKE LIKE A THIEF(1966, Fin.)
Cynthia Sikes
LADIES AND GENTLEMEN, THE FABULOUS STAINS(1982); MAN WHO LOVED WOMEN, THE(1983)
Misc. Talkies
GOODBYE CRUEL WORLD(1983)
Steve Sikes
MASSACRE AT CENTRAL HIGH(1976)
Gen. Vladimir Sikevitch
COSSACKS IN EXILE(1939, Ukrainian)
Sweet Daddy Siki
NEON PALACE, THE(1970, Can.)
James Sikking
STRANGLER, THE(1964); VON RYAN'S EXPRESS(1965); POINT BLANK(1967); CHARRO(1969); DADDY'S GONE A-HUNTING(1969); CHANDLER(1971); NEW CEN-TURIONS, THE(1972); SCORPIO(1973); TERMINAL MAN, THE(1974)
Misc. Talkies
BOOTS TURNER(1973); BROTHER ON THE RUN(1973)
James B. Sikking
MAGNIFICENT SEVEN RIDE, THE(1972); ELECTRIC HORSEMAN, THE(1979); COMPETITION, THE(1980); ORDINARY PEOPLE(1980); OUTLAND(1981); STAR CHAMBER, THE(1983)
1984
STAR TREK III: THE SEARCH FOR SPOCK(1984); UP THE CREEK(1984)
Joe Sikorra
1984
HARRY AND SON(1984)
Jan Sikorski
VOICE WITHIN, THE(1945, Brit.), ph; LATE AT NIGHT(1946, Brit.), ph; SWISS HONEYMOON(1947, Brit.), d, ph
Sil-Vara
STORY OF VICKIE, THE(1958, Aust.), w
Valeria Sila
WARRIORS FIVE(1962)
Giorgio Silagni
BLACK AND WHITE IN COLOR(1976, Fr.), p
George Silano
RECESS(1967), ph; STOOLIE, THE(1972), d; LAST AMERICAN HERO, THE(1973), ph
Yu. Silantyev
GROWN-UP CHILDREN(1963, USSR), md
Ela Silarova
DO YOU KEEP A LION AT HOME?(1966, Czech.)
Carolyn Silas
REAL LIFE(1979)
E. Silas
DON'T BLAME THE STORK(1954, Brit.), w

Everett Silas
MY BROTHER'S WEDDING(1983)
Louis Silas
FINIAN'S RAINBOW(1968)
Vic Silayan
NO MAN IS AN ISLAND(1962); RAVAGERS, THE(1965, U.S./Phil.); SECRET OF THE SACRED FOREST, THE(1970); PROJECT: KILL(1976)
Vick Silayan
DAUGHTERS OF SATAN(1972)
Adam Silbar
1984
HOT MOVES(1984)
Joel Silberg
1984
BREAKIN'(1984), d
Tusse Silberg
GORKY PARK(1983)
1984
FLIGHT TO BERLIN(1984, Ger./Brit.)
Yoel Silberg
KAZABLAN(1974, Israel), w; RABBI AND THE SHIKSE, THE(1976, Israel), d&w
Morris Silberkasten
WHERE IS MY CHILD?(1937)
Buddy Silberman
1984
WOMAN IN RED, THE(1984)
Irene Silberman
DIVA(1982, Fr.), p
1984
AVE MARIA(1984, Fr.), p
Serge Silberman
DIARY OF A CHAMBERMAID(1964, Fr./Ital.), p; DRAGON SKY(1964, Fr.), p; SCHEHERAZADE(1965, Fr./Ital./Span.), p; DIABOLICAL DR. Z, THE(1966 Span./Fr.), p; GALIA(1966, Fr./Ital.), p; FAREWELL, FRIEND(1968, Fr./Ital.), p; MILKY WAY, THE(1969, Fr./Ital.), p; RIDER ON THE RAIN(1970, Fr./Ital.), p; DISCREET CHARM OF THE BOURGEOISIE, THE(1972, Fr.), p; PHANTOM OF LIBERTY, THE(1974, Fr.), p; THAT OBSCURE OBJECT OF DESIRE(1977, Fr./Span.), p
Marvin Silbersher
RAISE THE TITANIC(1980, Brit.)
Mona Silberstein
TRUNK TO CAIRO(1966, Israel/Ger.)
Denise Silbert
STUCK ON YOU(1983)
1984
STUCK ON YOU(1984)
Liza Silbert
Silents
BROKEN HEARTS(1926)
Theodore Silbert
Silents
BROKEN HEARTS(1926)
Marvin Silbisher
GOD TOLD ME TO(1976)
Anna Silena
ANGELO IN THE CROWD(1952, Ital.)
Mikhail Silenko
LITTLE HUMPBACKED HORSE, THE(1962, USSR), ph
Vira Silenti
MONTE CASSINO(1948, Ital.); VITELLONI(1956, Ital./Fr.); SON OF SAMSON(1962, Fr./Ital./Yugo.); STORY OF JOSEPH AND HIS BRETHREN THE(1962, Ital.); ATLAS AGAINST THE CYCLOPS(1963, Ital.); SON OF THE RED CORSAIR(1963, Ital.); WITCH'S CURSE, THE(1963, Ital.)
Cinda Siler
INDIAN PAINT(1965)
Mario Siletti
ESCAPE ME NEVER(1947); HOUSE OF STRANGERS(1949); BLACK HAND, THE(1950); LADY WITHOUT PASSPORT, A(1950); UNDER MY SKIN(1950); ANNE OF THE INDIES(1951); ENFORCER, THE(1951); FORCE OF ARMS(1951); GREAT CARUSO, THE(1951); HOUSE ON TELEGRAPH HILL(1951); MAN WHO CHEATED HIMSELF, THE(1951); STOP THAT CAB(1951); STRICTLY DISHONORABLE(1951); CAPTAIN PIRATE(1952); CLASH BY NIGHT(1952); DIPLOMATIC COURIER(1952); MY COUSIN RACHEL(1952); WHEN IN ROME(1952); BIG LEAGUER(1953); HOT NEWS(1953); SO THIS IS LOVE(1953); TAXI(1953); THUNDER BAY(1953); WINGS OF THE HAWK(1953); THREE COINS IN THE FOUNTAIN(1954); BRING YOUR SMILE ALONG(1955); EAST OF EDEN(1955); HELL'S ISLAND(1955); NAKED STREET, THE(1955); MAN IN THE GREY FLANNEL SUIT, THE(1956); SERENADE(1956); MAN IN THE SHADOW(1957); PAY OR DIE(1960); TO TRAP A SPY(1966)
L. Silich
SPRINGTIME ON THE VOLGA(1961, USSR), cos
Anja Silja
FIDELIO(1970, Ger.)
Erik Silju
ISLAND AT THE TOP OF THE WORLD, THE(1974)
Geoff Silk
PSYCHO-CIRCUS(1967, Brit.); THOSE DARING YOUNG MEN IN THEIR JAUNTY JALOPIES(1969, Fr./Brit./ Ital.)
Jack Silk
SKULL, THE(1965, Brit.); OUR MOTHER'S HOUSE(1967, Brit.)
Lawrence Silk
SPORTING CLUB, THE(1971), ed
James R. Silke
REVENGE OF THE NINJA(1983), w
1984
NINJA III—THE DOMINATION(1984), w; SAHARA(1984), w
Ron Silkosky
MANIAC!(1977), w
Ronald Silkosky
DUNWICH HORROR, THE(1970), w

Joel Sill
FIRST LOVE(1977), m
Kelly Sill
MONSTER(1979)
Felix Silla
POINT BLANK(1967); SHE FREAK(1967); PUFNSTUF(1970); LITTLE CIGARS(1973); SSSSSSSS(1973); BLACK BIRD, THE(1975); DEMON SEED(1977); BUCK ROGERS IN THE 25TH CENTURY(1979); RETURN OF THE JEDI(1983)
1984
MEATBALLS PART II(1984)
Yuri Sillart
DEAD MOUNTAINEER HOTEL, THE(1979, USSR), ph
Guiseppe Sillato
GODFATHER, THE, PART II(1974)
Drake Silliman
SWEET SIXTEEN(1983), ed
Drake P. Silliman
1984
HOT MOVES(1984), ed
Paul Silliman
SWEET JESUS, PREACHER MAN(1973)
Alan Silliphant
CREEPING TERROR, THE(1964), w
Robert Silliphant
CREEPING TERROR, THE(1964), w; INCREDIBLY STRANGE CREATURES WHO STOPPED LIVING AND BECAME CRAZY MIXED-UP ZOMBIES, THE(1965), w
Stirling Silliphant
JOE LOUIS STORY, THE(1953), p; FIVE AGAINST THE HOUSE(1955), p, w; HUK(1956), w; NIGHTFALL(1956), w; DAMN CITIZEN(1958), w; LINEUP, THE(1958), w; MARACAIBO(1958), w; VILLAGE OF THE DAMNED(1960, Brit.), w; SLENDER THREAD, THE(1965), w; IN THE HEAT OF THE NIGHT(1967), w; CHARLY(1968), w; MARLOWE(1969), w; WALK IN THE SPRING RAIN, A(1970), p, w; MURPHY'S WAR(1971, Brit.), w; NEW CENTURIONS, THE(1972), w; POSEIDON ADVENTURE, THE(1972), w; SHAFT IN AFRICA(1973), w; TOWERING INFERNO, THE(1974), w; KILLER ELITE, THE(1975), w; ENFORCER, THE(1976), w; TELE-FON(1977), w; SWARM, THE(1978), w; CIRCLE OF IRON(1979, Brit.), w; WHEN TIME RAN OUT(1980), w
Alan Sillitoe
SATURDAY NIGHT AND SUNDAY MORNING(1961, Brit.), w; LONELINESS OF THE LONG DISTANCE RUNNER, THE(1962, Brit.), w; COUNTERPOINT(1967), w; RAGMAN'S DAUGHTER, THE(1974, Brit.), w
Frank Sillman
Misc. Talkies
KAHUNA!(1981), d
Leonard Sillman
ANGEL COMES TO BROOKLYN, AN(1945), p; NEW FACES(1954), w
Stirling Sillphant
LIBERATION OF L.B. JONES, THE(1970), w
Deek Sills
TRADER HORNEE(1970)
James Sills
HELLO, FRISCO, HELLO(1943)
Milton Sills
BARKER, THE(1928); HIS CAPTIVE WOMAN(1929); MAN TROUBLE(1930); SEA WOLF, THE(1930)
Silents
ARRIVAL OF PERPETUA, THE(1915); HONOR SYSTEM, THE(1917); DANGEROUS TO MEN(1920); INFERIOR SEX, THE(1920); FAITH HEALER, THE(1921); SAL-VAGE(1921); BURNING SANDS(1922); ENVIRONMENT(1922); ONE CLEAR CALL(1922); WOMAN WHO WALKED ALONE, THE(1922); ADAM'S RIB(1923); ISLE OF LOST SHIPS, THE(1923); LEGALLY DEAD(1923); SOULS FOR SALE(1923); FLOWING GOLD(1924); AS MAN DESIRES(1925); KNOCKOUT, THE(1925); LOVER'S OATH, A(1925), ed; UNGUARDED HOUR, THE(1925); PARADISE(1926); PUP-PETS(1926); SILENT LOVER, THE(1926); SEA TIGER, THE(1927)
Misc. Silents
DEEP PURPLE, THE(1915); PIT, THE(1915); MARRIED IN NAME ONLY(1917); SOULS ADRIFT(1917); CLAW, THE(1918); DIAMONDS AND PEARLS(1918); FRINGE OF SOCIETY, THE(1918); HELL CAT, THE(1918); MYSTERIOUS CLIENT, THE(1918); OTHER WOMAN, THE(1918); REASON WHY, THE(1918); SAVAGE WOMAN, THE(1918); STRUGGLE EVERLASTING, THE(1918); YELLOW TICKET, THE(1918); EYES OF YOUTH(1919); FEAR WOMAN, THE(1919); SATAN JUNIOR(1919); SHAD-OWS(1919); STRONGER VOW, THE(1919); WHAT EVERY WOMAN LEARNS(1919); WOMAN THOU GAVEST ME, THE(1919); BEHOLD MY WIFE!(1920); FURNANCE, THE(1920); HUSHED HOUR, THE(1920); STREET CALLED STRAIGHT, THE(1920); SWEET LAVANDER(1920); WEEK-END, THE(1920); AT THE END OF THE WORLD(1921); GREAT MOMENT, THE(1921); LITTLE FOOL, THE(1921); MISS LULU BETT(1921); BORDERLAND(1922); FORGOTTEN LAW, THE(1922); MARRIAGE CHANCE, THE(1922); SKIN DEEP(1922); FLAMING YOUTH(1923); LAST HOUR, THE(1923); SPOILERS, THE(1923); WHAT A WIFE LEARNED(1923); WHY WOMEN REMARRY(1923); HEART BANDIT, THE(1924); MADONNA OF THE STREETS(1924); SEA HAWK, THE(1924); SINGLE WIVES(1924); I WANT MY MAN(1925); MAKING OF O'MALLEY, THE(1925); MEN OF STEEL(1926); FRAMED(1927); HARD BOILED HAGGERTY(1927); VALLEY OF THE GIANTS, THE(1927); BARKER, THE(1928); BURNING DAYLIGHT(1928); CRASH, THE(1928); HAWK'S NEST, THE(1928); LOVE AND THE DEVIL(1929)
Paula Sills
NO WAY BACK(1976); ONE DOWN TWO TO GO(1982)
Pawnee Sills
LILITH(1964)
Ted Sills
ABROAD WITH TWO YANKS(1944), w
Teddy B. Sills
TO KILL A CLOWN(1972), p
Jon Silo
STORY OF RUTH, THE(1960); THAT TOUCH OF MINK(1962); FORTUNE COOKIE, THE(1966); HOW SWEET IT IS(1968)
Susan Silo
LOVE IN A GOLDFISH BOWL(1961); CONVICTS FOUR(1962); MC HALE'S NAVY JOINS THE AIR FORCE(1965)

Leopold Silos
W.I.A.(WOUNDED IN ACTION)*1/2 (1966), m
Manuel Silos
NO PLACE TO HIDE(1956)
Adalberto Silva
XICA(1982, Braz.)
Billy Silva
BORDER, THE(1982)
Candice L. Silva
ZOOT SUIT(1981)
Carmelo Silva
TREE OF WOODEN CLOGS, THE(1979, Ital.)
Carmen Silva
HOUSE OF EXORCISM, THE(1976, Ital.)
David Silva
PASSION ISLAND(1943, Mex.); TOAST TO LOVE(1951, Mex.); FIRST TEXAN, THE(1956); RAGE(1966, U.S./Mex.); EL TOPO(1971, Mex.)
Franco Silva
MAN FROM CAIRO, THE(1953); QUEEN OF SHEBA(1953, Ital.); HANNIBAL(1960, Ital.); STORY OF THE COUNT OF MONTE CRISTO, THE(1962, Fr./Ital.); MONGOLS, THE(1966, Fr./Ital.)
Geno Silva
THOMASINE AND BUSHROD(1974); WANDA NEVADA(1979); 1941(1979); ZOOT SUIT(1981)
Gino Silva
SCARFACE(1983)
Henry Silva
VIVA ZAPATA!(1952); CROWDED PARADISE(1956); HATFUL OF RAIN, A(1957); TALL T, THE(1957); BRAVADOS, THE(1958); LAW AND JAKE WADE, THE(1958); RIDE A CROOKED TRAIL(1958); GREEN MANSIONS(1959); JAYHAWKERS, THE(1959); CINDERFELLA(1960); OCEAN'S ELEVEN(1960); MANCHURIAN CANDIDATE, THE(1962); SERGEANTS 3(1962); GATHERING OF EAGLES, A(1963); JOHNNY COOL(1963); SECRET INVASION, THE(1964); HAIL MAFIA(1965, Fr./Ital.); RETURN OF MR. MOTO, THE(1965, Brit.); REWARD, THE(1965); PLAINSMAN, THE(1966); HILLS RUN RED, THE(1967, Ital.); MATCHLESS(1967, Ital.); NEVER A DULL MOMENT(1968); ANIMALS, THE(1971); MAN AND BOY(1972); ITALIAN CONNECTION, THE(1973, U.S./Ital./Ger.); ALMOST HUMAN(1974,Ital.); SHOOT(1976, Can.); BUCK ROGERS IN THE 25TH CENTURY(1979); LOVE AND BULLETS(1979, Brit.); THIRST(1979, Aus.); ALLIGATOR(1980); VIRUS(1980, Jap.); MEGAFORCE(1982); SHARKY'S MACHINE(1982); WRONG IS RIGHT(1982); CHAINED HEAT(1983 U.S./Ger.)
1984
CANNONBALL RUN II(1984)
Misc. Talkies
TRAPPED(1982)
Irene K. Silva
ROAD TO BALI(1952)
Jerry Silva
SLEEPAWAY CAMP(1983), p
Jose Silva
LIVING IDOL, THE(1957), ch
Kathy Silva
SOYLENT GREEN(1973)
Maria Silva
AWFUL DR. ORLOFF, THE(1964, Span./Fr.); DOS COSMONAUTAS A LA FUERZA(1967, Span./*Ital.); CURSE OF THE DEVIL(1973, Span./Mex.); I HATE MY BODY(1975, Span./Switz.)
1984
IT'S NEVER TOO LATE(1984, Span.)
Mario Silva
TALK ABOUT A LADY(1946), md; SONG OF LOVE(1947), w; STEPCHILD(1947), m
Marion Silva, Jr.
GENTLEMAN MISBEHAVES, THE(1946), md
Marlene Silva
XICA(1982, Braz.), ch
Michael Silva
MAN CALLED ADAM, A(1966)
Patrick Silva
MEMENTO MEI(1963)
Petra Silva
ARIZONA RAIDERS, THE(1936); SURRENDER(1950)
Roberto Silva
LAST OF THE FAST GUNS, THE(1958), art d; FOR THE LOVE OF MIKE(1960), art d; GERONIMO(1962), art d; OF LOVE AND DESIRE(1963), art d; QUEEN'S SWORDSMEN, THE(1963, Mex.), art d; PUSS 'N' BOOTS(1964, Mex.), set d; GLORY GUYS, THE(1965), art d; LITTLE RED RIDING HOOD AND THE MONSTERS(1965, Mex.), set d; TOM THUMB(1967, Mex.), set d; GUNS FOR SAN SEBASTIAN(1968, U.S./Fr./Mex./Ital.), art d; CURSE OF THE CRYING WOMAN, THE(1969, Mex.), art d; LIVING HEAD, THE(1969, Mex.), art d; I ESCAPED FROM DEVIL'S ISLAND(1973), art d
Rudolph Silva
KID FROM BOOKLYN, THE(1946)
Rudy Silva
SPY HUNT(1950)
Sampaio e Silva
DOVE, THE(1974, Brit.)
Simone Silva
SECRET PEOPLE(1952, Brit.); DESPERATE MOMENT(1953, Brit.); SHADOW MAN(1953, Brit.); DUEL IN THE JUNGLE(1954, Brit.); ESCAPE BY NIGHT(1954, Brit.); GOLDEN MASK, THE(1954, Brit.); WEAK AND THE WICKED, THE(1954, Brit.); DEADLY GAME, THE(1955, Brit.); LADY GODIVA RIDES AGAIN(1955, Brit.); DYNAMITERS, THE(1956, Brit.)
Solomon Silva
THIN RED LINE, THE(1964)
Trinidad Silva
ALAMBRISTA!(1977); WALK PROUD(1979); SECOND THOUGHTS(1983)
1984
CRACKERS(1984); EL NORTE(1984)

Uilani Silva
HAWAII CALLS(1938)
Silvagni
RISE OF LOUIS XIV, THE(1970, Fr.)
Cesare Silvagni
VAMPYR(1932, Fr./Ger.), art d
Giorgio Silvagni
I SENT A LETTER TO MY LOVE(1981, Fr.), p; MEN PREFER FAT GIRLS(1981, Fr.), p; LA VIE CONTINUE(1982, Fr.), p
1984
HEAT OF DESIRE(1984, Fr.), p; LE BAL(1984, Fr./Ital./Algeria), p
Eugene Silvain
Silents
PASSION OF JOAN OF ARC, THE(1928, Fr.)
Silvan
MODESTY BLAISE(1966, Brit.)
Al Silvani
OCEAN'S ELEVEN(1960); CAPE FEAR(1962); ROCKY(1976); EVERY WHICH WAY BUT LOOSE(1978), stunt; ROCKY II(1979), a, technical adviser; RAGING BULL(1980), tech adv; ROCKY III(1982)
Aldo Silvani
ANYTHING FOR A SONG(1947, Ital.); TO LIVE IN PEACE(1947, Ital.); CARMELA(1949, Ital.); GOLDEN MADONNA, THE(1949, Brit.); DIFFICULT YEARS(1950, Ital.); STORMBOUND(1951, Ital.); TERESA(1951); THIEF OF VENICE, THE(1952); WHEN IN ROME(1952); STRANGER ON THE PROWL(1953); VALLEY OF THE KINGS(1954); LA STRADA(1956, Ital.); NIGHTS OF CABIRIA(1957, Ital.); TEMPEST(1958, Ital./Yugo./Fr.); BEN HUR(1959); FIVE BRANDED WOMEN(1960); CARTHAGE IN FLAMES(1961, Fr./Ital.); DAMON AND PYTHIAS(1962); SODOM AND GOMORRAH(1962, U.S./Fr./Ital.); ROBIN AND THE SEVEN HOODS(1964)
Iole Silvani
LUNA(1979, Ital.)
Jole Silvani
WHITE SHEIK, THE(1956, Ital.); CITY OF WOMEN(1980, Ital./Fr.)
Lora Silvani
ANGELO IN THE CROWD(1952, Ital.)
Jonathan Silveira
HOLLYWOOD HIGH(1977), ph
Mozael Silveira
TRAIN ROBBERY CONFIDENTIAL(1965, Braz.)
Ruth Silveira
STRAWBERRY STATEMENT, THE(1970); THX 1138(1971); STEELYARD BLUES(1973); MAN, WOMAN AND CHILD(1983)
1984
MICKI AND MAUDE(1984)
Edward Silveni
UNCIVILISED(1937, Aus.)
Silver the horse
LONE RIDER, THE(1930); MEN WITHOUT LAW(1930); AVENGER, THE(1931); DESERT VENGEANCE(1931); FIGHTING SHERIFF, THE(1931); RANGE FEUD, THE(1931); TEXAS RANGER, THE(1931); DEADLINE, THE(1932); HELLO TROUBLE(1932); MC KENNA OF THE MOUNTED(1932); ONE-MAN LAW(1932); RIDIN' FOR JUSTICE(1932); SOUTH OF THE RIO GRANDE(1932); WHITE EAGLE(1932); SUNDOWN RIDER, THE(1933); UNKNOWN VALLEY(1933); FIGHTING RANGER, THE(1934); MAN TRAILER, THE(1934); ROCKY RHODES(1934); CRIMSON TRAIL, THE(1935); IVORY-HANDLED GUN(1935); STONE OF SILVER CREEK(1935); THROWBACK, THE(1935); COWBOY AND THE KID,THE(1936); FOR THE SERVICE(1936); FORBIDDEN TRAIL(1936); RIDE 'EM COWBOY(1936); SUNSET OF POWER(1936); BOSS OF LONELY VALLEY(1937); EMPTY SADDLES(1937); LAW FOR TOMBSTONE(1937); LEFT-HANDED LAW(1937); SANDFLOW(1937); SMOKE TREE RANGE(1937); LAW OF THE TEXAN(1938); OVERLAND EXPRESS, THE(1938); STRANGER FROM ARIZONA, THE(1938); HI-YO SILVER(1940); FORBIDDEN TRAILS(1941); GUN MAN FROM BODIE, THE(1941); BELOW THE BORDER(1942); DAWN ON THE GREAT DIVIDE(1942); DOWN TEXAS WAY(1942); GHOST TOWN LAW(1942); RIDERS OF THE WEST(1942); WEST OF THE LAW(1942); LONE RANGER AND THE LOST CITY OF GOLD, THE(1958)
Silents
ARIZONA ROMEO, THE(1925); REGULAR SCOUT, A(1926)
Silver Wolf the Dog
ROGUES' TAVERN, THE(1936); KILLERS OF THE WILD(1940)
Adam Silver
IN MACARTHUR PARK(1977)
Borah Silver
BLUE COLLAR(1978); S.O.B.(1981)
Christine Silver
DEAD MEN TELL NO TALES(1939, Brit.); SALUTE JOHN CITIZEN(1942, Brit.); HEAVEN IS ROUND THE CORNER(1944, Brit.); ROOM TO LET(1949, Brit.); STOP PRESS GIRL(1949, Brit.); MYSTERY JUNCTION(1951, Brit.); WHISPERING SMITH VERSUS SCOTLAND YARD(1952, Brit.); COMPANIONS IN CRIME(1954, Brit.); HORNET'S NEST, THE(1955, Brit.)
Silents
PLEYDELL MYSTERY, THE(1916, Brit.); CHICKEN CASEY(1917), w; LABOUR LEADER, THE(1917, Brit.); JUDGE NOT(1920, Brit.)
Misc. Silents
LITTLE WELSH GIRL, THE(1920, Brit.)
Cindy Silver
1984
HARDBODIES(1984)
Clarence Silver
SINCE YOU WENT AWAY(1944), ph
Daniel Silver
Misc. Talkies
MISSION HILL(1982)
Darrell Silver
BELLS OF ST. MARY'S, THE(1945), set d
Dina Silver
1984
OLD ENOUGH(1984), p

Fawn Silver
ORGY OF THE DEAD(1965); TERROR IN THE JUNGLE(1968)

George Silver
GUMSHOE(1972, Brit.); MURDER ON THE ORIENT EXPRESS(1974, Brit.); ADVENTURES OF SHERLOCK HOLMES' SMARTER BROTHER, THE(1975, Brit.); MIRROR CRACK'D, THE(1980, Brit.); VICTOR/VICTORIA(1982); MONTY PYTHON'S THE MEANING OF LIFE(1983, Brit.)

Jeff Silver
YOUNG STRANGER, THE(1957); OUTSIDER, THE(1962)

Joan Micklin Silver
HESTER STREET(1975), d&w; BETWEEN THE LINES(1977), d; ON THE YARD(1978), p; CHILLY SCENES OF WINTER(1982), d&w

Joan Silver
LIMBO(1972), w

Joe Silver
DIARY OF A BACHELOR(1964); MOVE(1970); KLUTE(1971); APPRENTICESHIP OF DUDDY KRAVITZ, THE(1974, Can.); RHINOCEROS(1974); RABID(1976, Can.); THEY CAME FROM WITHIN(1976, Can.); RAGGEDY ANN AND ANDY(1977); YOU LIGHT UP MY LIFE(1977); BOARDWALK(1979); DEATHTRAP(1982)
1984
ALMOST YOU(1984)

Joel Silver
48 HOURS(1982), p
1984
STREETS OF FIRE(1984), p

John Silver
TWO HEARTS IN HARMONY(1935, Brit.), ph; DARBY AND JOAN(1937, Brit.), ph; REVERSE BE MY LOT, THE(1938, Brit.), ph; THOMAS CROWN AFFAIR, THE(1968)

Johnny Silver
GUYS AND DOLLS(1955); WHO'S BEEN SLEEPING IN MY BED?(1963); GREAT RACE, THE(1965); HOW SWEET IT IS(1968); NEVER A DULL MOMENT(1968); PUFNSTUF(1970); HAMMER(1972); LEPKE(1975, U.S./Israel); HISTORY OF THE WORLD, PART 1(1981)

Joseph Silver
RIO CONCHOS(1964), ed; MORITURI(1965), ed; SMOKY(1966), ed

Louis Silver
DISRAELI(1929), m; FROZEN RIVER(1929), m; HOUSE OF HORROR(1929), m; COUNTRY DOCTOR, THE(1936), md; SINS OF MAN(1936), md; SEVENTH HEAVEN(1937), m

Marc Silver
MOTEL HELL(1980)

Marcel Silver
FOX MOVIETONE FOLLIES(1929), d; MARRIED IN HOLLYWOOD(1929), d; ONE MAD KISS(1930), d

Marisa Silver
1984
OLD ENOUGH(1984), d&w

Pat Silver
WIZARD OF BAGHDAD, THE(1960), w; PIRATES OF TORTUGA(1961), w; SEVEN WOMEN FROM HELL(1961), w; LAND RAIDERS(1969), w; CRIME AND PASSION(1976, U.S., Ger.), w

Raphael D. Silver
BETWEEN THE LINES(1977), p; ON THE YARD(1978), d

Ron Silver
TUNNELVISION(1976); SEMI-TOUGH(1977); BEST FRIENDS(1982); ENTITY, THE(1982); SILENT RAGE(1982); LOVESICK(1983); SILKWOOD(1983)
1984
GARBO TALKS(1984); GOODBYE PEOPLE, THE(1984); OH GOD! YOU DEVIL(1984); ROMANCING THE STONE(1984)

Sandy Silver
TONIGHT FOR SURE(1962)

Sonia Silver
"IMP"PROBABLE MR. WEE GEE, THE(1966)

Stew Silver
CROSS AND THE SWITCHBLADE, THE(1970)

Veronique Silver
LIKE A TURTLE ON ITS BACK(1981, Fr.); WOMAN NEXT DOOR, THE(1981, Fr.)

Silver King the Dog
RUSTY RIDES ALONE(1933)

Silver King the Horse
Misc. Talkies
SUNDOWN TRAIL, THE(1975)
Silents
GALLOPING GALLAGHER(1924); NORTH OF NEVADA(1924); RIDIN' THE WIND(1925); HANDS ACROSS THE BORDER(1926); DON MIKE(1927); JESSE JAMES(1927); SILVER COMES THROUGH(1927)

Silver King the Wonder Dog
ON THE GREAT WHITE TRAIL(1938)

C. Silvera
ROPE OF SAND(1949), makeup

Carl Silvera
STREETS OF LAREDO(1949), makeup; NIGHT WALKER, THE(1964), makeup; MUNSTER, GO HOME(1966), makeup; SUMMERTREE(1971), makeup
Silents
SHARK MASTER, THE(1921); PELL STREET MYSTERY, THE(1924); LIGHTNING LARIATS(1927)

Carlos Silvera
Misc. Silents
BEYOND ALL ODDS(1926)

Darrel Silvera
BODY SNATCHER, THE(1945), set d; TILL THE END OF TIME(1946), set d

Darrell Silvera
WITHOUT RESERVATIONS(1946), set d; THEY WON'T BELIEVE ME(1947), set d; FOLLOW THE FLEET(1936), set d; MARY OF SCOTLAND(1936), set d; PLOUGH AND THE STARS, THE(1936), set d; SWING TIME(1936), set d; WOMAN REBELS, A(1936), set d; BREAKFAST FOR TWO(1937), set d; LIFE OF THE PARTY, THE(1937), set d; QUALITY STREET(1937), set d; SHALL WE DANCE(1937), set d; STAGE DOOR(1937), set d; THAT GIRL FROM PARIS(1937), set d; BRINGING UP BABY(1938), set d; CAREFREE(1938), set d; HAVING WONDERFUL TIME(1938), set d; MAD MISS MANTON, THE(1938), set d; ROOM SERVICE(1938), set d; VIVACIOUS

LADY(1938), set d; FIFTH AVENUE GIRL(1939), set d; GUNGA DIN(1939), set d; IN NAME ONLY(1939), set d; STORY OF VERNON AND IRENE CASTLE, THE(1939), set d; KITTY FOYLE(1940), set d; LUCKY PARTNERS(1940), set d; MY FAVORITE WIFE(1940), set d; PRIMROSE PATH(1940), set d; THEY KNEW WHAT THEY WANTED(1940), set d; VIGIL IN THE NIGHT(1940), set d; SUSPICION(1941), set d; TOM, DICK AND HARRY(1941), set d; JOURNEY INTO FEAR(1942), set d; ONCE UPON A HONEYMOON(1942), set d; AROUND THE WORLD(1943), set d; FLIGHT FOR FREEDOM(1943), set d; GHOST SHIP, THE(1943), set d; GOVERNMENT GIRL(1943), set d; HIGHER AND HIGHER(1943), set d; I WALKED WITH A ZOMBIE(1943), set d; IRON MAJOR, THE(1943), set d; LEOPARD MAN, THE(1943), set d; MR. LUCKY(1943), set d; SEVENTH VICTIM, THE(1943), set d; SKY'S THE LIMIT, THE(1943), set d; TENDER COMRADE(1943), set d; THIS LAND IS MINE(1943), set d; EXPERIMENT PERILOUS(1944), set d; HEAVENLY DAYS(1944), set d; MADEMOISELLE FIFI(1944), set d; MARINE RAIDERS(1944), set d; NEVADA(1944), set d; NONE BUT THE LONELY HEART(1944), set d; SEVEN DAYS ASHORE(1944), set d; STEP LIVELY(1944), set d; YOUTH RUNS WILD(1944), set d; BACK TO BATAAN(1945), set d; BETRAYAL FROM THE EAST(1945), set d; CORNERED(1945), set d; DICK TRACY(1945), set d; ENCHANTED COTTAGE, THE(1945), set d; FIRST YANK INTO TOKYO(1945), set d; HAVING WONDERFUL CRIME(1945), set d; ISLE OF THE DEAD(1945), set d; JOHNNY ANGEL(1945), set d; MAN ALIVE(1945), set d; MURDER, MY SWEET(1945), set d; SPANISH MAIN, THE(1945), set d; THOSE ENDEARING YOUNG CHARMS(1945), set d; TWO O'CLOCK COURAGE(1945), set d; WANDERER OF THE WASTELAND(1945), set d; WEST OF THE PECOS(1945), set d; BEDLAM(1946), set d; CRACK-UP(1946), set d; DEADLINE AT DAWN(1946), set d; DICK TRACY VS. CUEBALL(1946), set d; FROM THIS DAY FORWARD(1946), set d; LADY LUCK(1946), set d; LOCKET, THE(1946), set d; NOCTURNE(1946), set d; NOTORIOUS(1946), set d; SAN QUENTIN(1946), set d; SISTER KENNY(1946), set d; SPIRAL STAIRCASE, THE(1946), set d; SUNSET PASS(1946), set d BACHELOR AND THE BOBBY-SOXER, THE(1947), set d; CROSSFIRE(1947), set d; DESPERATE(1947), set d; LIKELY STORY, A(1947), set d; LONG NIGHT, THE(1947), set d; MOURNING BECOMES ELECTRA(1947), set d; NIGHT SONG(1947), set d; OUT OF THE PAST(1947), set d; RIFFRAFF(1947), set d; SINBAD THE SAILOR(1947), set d; TRAIL STREET(1947), set d; UNDER THE TONTO RIM(1947), set d; WILD HORSE MESA(1947), set d; WOMAN ON THE BEACH, THE(1947), set d; BERLIN EXPRESS(1948), set d; EVERY GIRL SHOULD BE MARRIED(1948), set d; I REMEMBER MAMA(1948), set d; MR. BLANDINGS BUILDS HIS DREAM HOUSE(1948), set d; RACE STREET(1948), set d; RACHEL AND THE STRANGER(1948), set d; RETURN OF THE BADMEN(1948), set d; STATION WEST(1948), set d; VELVET TOUCH, THE(1948), set d; WESTERN HERITAGE(1948), set d; DANGEROUS PROFESSION, A(1949), set d; EASY LIVING(1949), set d; FOLLOW ME QUIETLY(1949), set d; SET-UP, THE(1949), set d; STAGECOACH KID(1949), set d; THEY LIVE BY NIGHT(1949), set d; THREAT, THE(1949), set d; WINDOW, THE(1949), set d; WOMAN'S SECRET, A(1949), set d; WHERE DANGER LIVES(1950), set d; WOMAN ON PIER 13, THE(1950), set d; DOUBLE DYNAMITE(1951), set d; HIS KIND OF WOMAN(1951), set d; ON DANGEROUS GROUND(1951), set d; RACKET, THE(1951), set d; ROADBLOCK(1951), set d; THING, THE(1951), set d; TWO TICKETS TO BROADWAY(1951), set d; CLASH BY NIGHT(1952), set d; LAS VEGAS STORY, THE(1952), set d; LUSTY MEN, THE(1952), set d; NARROW MARGIN, THE(1952), set d; ANGEL FACE(1953), set d; MAN WITH THE GOLDEN ARM, THE(1955), set d; SON OF SINBAD(1955), set d; FIRST TRAVELING SALESLADY, THE(1956), set d; BROTHERS RICO, THE(1957), set d; JET PILOT(1957), set d; KINGS GO FORTH(1958), set d; LONELYHEARTS(1958), set d; HAVE ROCKET, WILL TRAVEL(1959), set d; TIMBUKTU(1959), set d; PAY OR DIE(1960), set d; GIDGET GOES HAWAIIAN(1961), set d; HOMICIDAL(1961), set d; MAN WHO SHOT LIBERTY VALANCE, THE(1962), set d; THIRTEEN WEST STREET(1962), set d; WHO'S GOT THE ACTION?(1962), set d; MC LINTOCK!(1963), set d; CHEYENNE AUTUMN(1964), set d; LAW OF THE LAWLESS(1964), set d; RUSSIANS ARE COMING, THE RUSSIANS ARE COMING, THE(1966), set d; IN ENEMY COUNTRY(1968), set d; MOLLY MAGUIRES, THE(1970), set d; GUNFIGHT, A(1971), set d; POCKET MONEY(1972), set d; NICKELODEON(1976), set d; DRIVER, THE(1978), set d; FOOLIN' AROUND(1980), set d

Frank Silvera
TOYS IN THE ATTIC(1963); CIMARRON KID, THE(1951); FIGHTER, THE(1952); MIRACLE OF OUR LADY OF FATIMA, THE(1952); VIVA ZAPATA!(1952); FEAR AND DESIRE(1953); KILLER'S KISS(1955); CROWDED PARADISE(1956); CRIME AND PUNISHMENT, U.S.A.(1959); HELLER IN PINK TIGHTS(1960); KEY WITNESS(1960); MOUNTAIN ROAD, THE(1960); MUTINY ON THE BOUNTY(1962); LONNIE(1963); GREATEST STORY EVER TOLD, THE(1965); APPALOOSA, THE(1966); HOMBRE(1967); ST. VALENTINE'S DAY MASSACRE, THE(1967); UPTIGHT(1968); CHE!(1969); GUNS OF THE MAGNIFICENT SEVEN(1969); STALKING MOON, THE(1969); VALDEZ IS COMING(1971)

Karl Silvera
SUNSET BOULEVARD(1950), makeup; PERSONAL BEST(1982), makeup
Silents
BULLDOG COURAGE(1922); MIDNIGHT MESSAGE, THE(1926)

Rene Silvera
PLAYTIME(1973, Fr.), p

Simone Silvera
MOON ZERO TWO(1970, Brit.)

Jay Silverheels
TOO MANY GIRLS(1940); VALLEY OF THE SUN(1942); NORTHERN PURSUIT(1943); SINGIN' IN THE CORN(1946); CAPTAIN FROM CASTILE(1947); NORTHWEST OUTPOST(1947); UNCONQUERED(1947); FAMILY HONEYMOON(1948); FEATHERED SERPENT, THE(1948); FURY AT FURNACE CREEK(1948); KEY LARGO(1948); PRAIRIE(1948); YELLOW SKY(1948); COWBOY AND THE INDIANS, THE(1949); LARAMIE(1949); LUST FOR GOLD(1949); SAND(1949); TRAIL OF THE YUKON(1949); BROKEN ARROW(1950); BATTLE AT APACHE PASS, THE(1952); BRAVE WARRIOR(1952); LAST OF THE COMANCHES(1952); PATHFINDER, THE(1952); STORY OF WILL ROGERS, THE(1952); WILD BLUE YONDER, THE(1952); YANKEE BUCCANEER(1952); JACK MCCALL, DESPERADO(1953); NEBRASKAN, THE(1953); WAR ARROW(1953); BLACK DAKOTAS(1954); DRUMS ACROSS THE RIVER(1954); FOUR GUNS TO THE BORDER(1954); MASTERSON OF KANSAS(1954); SASKATCHEWAN(1954); LONE RANGER, THE(1955); VANISHING AMERICAN, THE(1955); WALK THE PROUD LAND(1956); LONE RANGER AND THE LOST CITY OF GOLD, THE(1958); RETURN TO WARBOW(1958); ALIAS JESSE JAMES(1959); INDIAN PAINT(1965); SMITH(1969); PHYNX, THE(1970); MAN WHO LOVED CAT DANCING, THE(1973); ONE LITTLE INDIAN(1973); SANTEE(1973)
Misc. Talkies
SINGING SPURS(1948)

Daniela Silverio
IDENTIFICATION OF A WOMAN(1983, Ital.)
Sergio Silverio
STATUE, THE(1971, Brit.)
Bob Silverman
SWEET SUBSTITUTE(1964, Can.); 125 ROOMS OF COMFORT(1974, Can.); RA-BID(1976, Can.); BROOD, THE(1979, Can.)
Charles Silverman
PIPE DREAMS(1976)
Jeff Silverman
FOXES(1980); FANTASIES(1981), m; EXPOSED(1983)
Louis Silverman
TASTE OF FLESH, A(1967), p,d&w, ed
Misc. Talkies
AMAZING TRANSPLANT, THE(1970), d
Manny Silverman
NIGHT OF EVIL(1962)
Margaret Silverman
NIGHT OF EVIL(1962)
Mitchell Silverman
WALK IN THE SPRING RAIN, A(1970)
Noel L. Silverman
ONE-TRICK PONY(1980)
Robert Silverman
PARTNERS(1976, Can.); PROM NIGHT(1980); HEAD ON(1981, Can.); SCAN-NERS(1981, Can.)
Ron Silverman
LIFEGUARD(1976), p; BRUBAKER(1980), p; KRULL(1983), p
Stanley Silverman
SIMON(1980), m; EYEWITNESS(1981), m; I'M DANCING AS FAST AS I CAN(1982), m
Stanley H. Silverman
GUN FEVER(1958), w
Bea Silvern
DESERT RAVEN, THE(1965); COMPETITION, THE(1980)
1984
BREAKIN'(1984)
Clark Silvernail
HELL HARBOR(1930), w
Clarke Silvernail
BEHIND THAT CURTAIN(1929), w; EYES OF THE WORLD, THE(1930), w; SHAD-OW RANCH(1930), w
Frank Silvero
SHAMUS(1973)
Carmen Silveroli, Sr.
MAX DUGAN RETURNS(1983)
Darrell Silvers
DING DONG WILLIAMS(1946), set d
Lou Silvers
DANCING LADY(1933), m&md
Louis Silvers
UNDER TWO FLAGS(1936), m, md; JAZZ SINGER, THE(1927), m; BARKER, THE(1928), m; NOAH'S ARK(1928), m; STATE STREET SADIE(1928), m; REDEEM-ING SIN, THE(1929), m; SMILING IRISH EYES(1929), md; SONNY BOY(1929), m; TIME, THE PLACE AND THE GIRL, THE(1929), m; OLD ENGLISH(1930), md; VIENNESE NIGHTS(1930), md; IT HAPPENED ONE NIGHT(1934), md; ONE NIGHT OF LOVE(1934), m; SISTERS UNDER THE SKIN(1934), md; BLACK ROOM, THE(1935), md; CAPTAIN JANUARY(1935), md; CRIME AND PUNISHMENT(1935), m; LOVE ME FOREVER(1935), m, md; DIMPLES(1936), md; HALF ANGEL(1936), md; LADIES IN LOVE(1936), md; LLOYDS OF LONDON(1936), md; MESSAGE TO GARCIA, A(1936), md; ONE IN A MILLION(1936), md; POOR LITTLE RICH GIRL(1936), md; PRISONER OF SHARK ISLAND, THE(1936), md; PRIVATE NUM-BER(1936), md; PROFESSIONAL SOLDIER(1936), m; ROAD TO GLORY, THE(1936), md; SING, BABY, SING(1936), md; STOWAWAY(1936), md; TO MARY-WITH LO-VE(1936), md; CAFE METROPOLE(1937), md; HEIDI(1937), md; LIFE BEGINS IN COLLEGE(1937), md; LOVE AND HISSES(1937), md; THIN ICE(1937), md; WAKE UP AND LIVE(1937), md; WEE WILLIE WINKIE(1937), m; ALWAYS GOOD-BYE(1938), md; BARONESS AND THE BUTLER, THE(1938), md; BATTLE OF BROADWAY(1938), md; FOUR MEN AND A PRAYER(1938), md; HAPPY LAND-ING(1938), md; I'LL GIVE A MILLION(1938), m, md; IN OLD CHICAGO(1938), md; JUST AROUND THE CORNER(1938), md; KENTUCKY(1938), md; KENTUCKY MOONSHINE(1938), md; LITTLE MISS BROADWAY(1938), md; MY LUCKY STAR(1938), md; STRAIGHT, PLACE AND SHOW(1938), md; SUEZ(1938), md; THANKS FOR EVERYTHING(1938), md; HERE I AM A STRANGER(1939), m; HOLLYWOOD CAVALCADE(1939), md; JESSE JAMES(1939), m, md; LITTLE PRIN-CESS, THE(1939), md; ROSE OF WASHINGTON SQUARE(1939), md; SECOND FID-DLE(1939), md; STANLEY AND LIVINGSTONE(1939), m, md; STORY OF ALEXANDER GRAHAM BELL, THE(1939), md; SUSANNAH OF THE MOUN-TIES(1939), md; SWANEE RIVER(1939), md; TAIL SPIN(1939), md; YOUNG MR. LINCOLN(1939), md; POWERS GIRL, THE(1942), md; MEET THE NAVY(1946, Brit.), m; HOT STUFF(1979)
Silents
WAY DOWN EAST(1920), m; ISN'T LIFE WONDERFUL(1924), m
Olympia Silvers
DEATHMASTER, THE(1972)
Phil Silvers
HIT PARADE OF 1941(1940); STRIKE UP THE BAND(1940); ICE-CAPADES(1941); LADY BE GOOD(1941); PENALTY, THE(1941); TOM, DICK AND HARRY(1941); WILD MAN OF BORNEO, THE(1941); YOU'RE IN THE ARMY NOW(1941); ALL THROUGH THE NIGHT(1942); FOOTLIGHT SERENADE(1942); JUST OFF BROADWAY(1942); MY GAL SAL(1942); ROXIE HART(1942); CONEY ISLAND(1943); LADY TAKES A CHANCE, A(1943); COVER GIRL(1944); FOUR JILLS IN A JEEP(1944); SOMETHING FOR THE BOYS(1944); TAKE IT OR LEAVE IT(1944); DIAMOND HORSESHOE(1945); DON JUAN QUILLIGAN(1945); THOUSAND AND ONE NIGHTS, A(1945); IF I'M LUCKY(1946); SUMMER STOCK(1950); LUCKY ME(1954); TOP BANANA(1954); FORTY POUNDS OF TROUBLE(1962); IT'S A MAD, MAD, MAD, MAD WORLD(1963); FUNNY THING HAPPENED ON THE WAY TO THE FORUM, A(1966); FOLLOW THAT CAMEL(1967, Brit.); GUIDE FOR THE MARRIED MAN, A(1967); BUONA SERA, MRS. CAMPBELL(1968, Ital.); BOATNIKS, THE(1970); STRONGEST MAN IN THE WORLD, THE(1975); WON TON TON, THE DOG WHO SAVED HOL-

LYWOOD(1976); CHICKEN CHRONICLES, THE(1977); CHEAP DETECTIVE, THE(1978); RACQUET(1979); HAPPY HOOKER GOES TO HOLLYWOOD, THE(1980); THERE GOES THE BRIDE(1980, Brit.)
Sid Silvers
DANCING SWEETIES(1930); FOLLOW THE LEADER(1930), w; OH! SAILOR, BEHAVE!(1930), w; MY WEAKNESS(1933), w; TAKE A CHANCE(1933), w; BOTTOMS UP(1934), a, w; TRANSATLANTIC MERRY-GO-ROUND(1934), w; BROADWAY MELO-DY OF 1936(1935), a, w; RENDEZVOUS(1935), w; BORN TO DANCE(1936), a, w; BROADWAY MELODY OF '38(1937), w; 52ND STREET(1937), a, w; GORILLA, THE(1939), w; FLEET'S IN, THE(1942), w; FOR ME AND MY GAL(1942), w; GIRL CRAZY(1943), w; MR. ACE(1946); TWO TICKETS TO BROADWAY(1951), w; STOOGE, THE(1952), w
Boyd Silversmith
TAKE DOWN(1979)
The Silversmith Band
HOPSCOTCH(1980)
Bob Silverstein
PRISM(1971), p
Dave Silverstein
STREAMLINE EXPRESS(1935), w; WOMAN WANTED(1935), w
David Silverstein
DEVIL'S MATE(1933), w; KING KELLY OF THE U.S.A(1934), w; MANHATTAN LOVE SONG(1934), w; SCARLET LETTER, THE(1934), w; UNKNOWN BLON-DE(1934), w; DANCING FEET(1936), w; FIFTEEN MAIDEN LANE(1936), w; TICKET TO PARADISE(1936), w; FLIGHT FROM GLORY(1937), w; SATURDAY'S HERO-ES(1937), w; YOU CAN'T BEAT LOVE(1937), w; ALMOST A GENTLEMAN(1939), w; SHOULD A GIRL MARRY?(1939), w; MELODY AND MOONLIGHT(1940), w; MILI-TARY ACADEMY(1940), w; KID FROM KANSAS, THE(1941), w; MYSTERY SHIP(1941), w; NAVAL ACADEMY(1941), w; I KILLED THAT MAN(1942), w; SA-BOTAGE SQUAD(1942), w
Elliot Silverstein
CAT BALLOU(1965), d; HAPPENING, THE(1967), d; MAN CALLED HORSE, A(1970), d; NIGHTMARE HONEYMOON(1973), d; CAR, THE(1977), p, d
Misc. Talkies
BELLE SOMMERS(1962), d; DEADLY HONEYMOON(1974), d
Helen Silverstein
ME AND MY BROTHER(1969), p, ed
Howard Silverstein
LONGEST YARD, THE(1974)
Jason Silverstein
HAPPENING, THE(1967), cos
Joe Silverstein
BEFORE MORNING(1933), ed; DRUMS O' VOODOO(1934), ed
Louis M. Silverstein
STRANGE BREW(1983), p
Maurice "Red" Silverstein
SWISS CONSPIRACY, THE(1976, U.S./Ger.), p
Shel Silverstein
NED KELLY(1970, Brit.), m; WHO IS HARRY KELLERMAN AND WHY IS HE SAYING THOSE TERRIBLE THINGS ABOUT ME?(1971); THIEVES(1977), m
Silverstein the Loft King
ROUND TRIP(1967)
Lillian Silverstone
THEY ALL LAUGHED(1981)
Silverstone Quartet
SHOW BOAT(1929)
Silverstreak the Dog
Silents
FANGS OF JUSTICE(1926); CROSS BREED(1927)
Larry Silverstri
Q(1982)
Richard Jay Silverthorn
FEAR NO EVIL(1981)
Mabel Silvester
SAILING ALONG(1938, Brit.)
Umberta Silvestra
QUEEN OF SHEBA(1953, Ital.)
Armando Silvestre
WYOMING MAIL(1950); APACHE DRUMS(1951); MARK OF THE RENEGA-DE(1951); THUNDERBIRDS(1952); WHITE ORCHID, THE(1954); FOR THE LOVE OF MIKE(1960); LOS AUTOMATAS DE LA MUERTE(1960, Mex.); GERONIMO(1962); NEUTRON CONTRA EL DR. CARONTE(1962, Mex.); NEUTRON EL ENMASCARADO NEGRO(1962, Mex.); KINGS OF THE SUN(1963); RAGE, THE(1963, U.S./Mex.); RAGE(1966, U.S./Mex.); SMOKY(1966); NIGHT OF THE BLOODY APES(1968, Mex.); SCALPHUNTERS, THE(1968); BARQUERO(1970); TWO MULES FOR SISTER SA-RA(1970)
Armondo Silvestre
DOCTOR OF DOOM(1962, Mex.)
Flor Silvestre
IMPORTANT MAN, THE(1961, Mex.)
Alan Silvestri
DOBERMAN GANG, THE(1972), m; AMAZING DOBERMANS, THE(1976), m; LAS VEGAS LADY(1976), m
1984
ROMANCING THE STONE(1984), m
Alberto Silvestri
DETECTIVE BELLI(1970, Ital.), w
Franco Silvestri
DIRTY HEROES(1971, Ital./Fr./Ger.), w
Gianni Silvestri
DAISY MILLER(1974), set d; LUNA(1979, Ital.), art d; TRAGEDY OF A RIDICU-LOUS MAN, THE(1982, Ital.), prod d
Larry Silvestri
NUNZIO(1978); WARRIORS, THE(1979)
Mario Silvestri
AMARCORD(1974, Ital.)
Umberto Silvestri
ULYSSES(1955, Ital.); CONFORMIST, THE(1971, Ital., Fr)

Mike Silveus
BREAKING AWAY(1979)
Ben Silvey
SPIDER, THE(1945), p; WITHIN THESE WALLS(1945), p
Shirley Silvey
MR. MAGOO'S HOLIDAY FESTIVAL(1970), prod d
Franca Silvi
EVA(1962, Fr./Ital.), ed
Robert Silvi
PIRANHA II: THE SPAWNING(1981, Neth.), ed; OF UNKNOWN ORIGIN(1983, Can.), ed
Roberto Silvi
MASSACRE IN ROME(1973, Ital.), ed; CASSANDRA CROSSING, THE(1977), ed; WISE BLOOD(1979, U.S./Ger.), ed; NINTH CONFIGURATION, THE(1980), ed; VICTORY(1981), ed
1984
UNDER THE VOLCANO(1984), ed
Aldo Silviani
BEAT THE DEVIL(1953)
Evelyn Silvie
GAMBLING SHIP(1933)
Adrien Silvio
CONFIDENTIALLY YOURS(1983, Fr.)
Anselmo Silvio
ORGANIZER, THE(1964, Fr./Ital./Yugo.)
Urszula Silwinska
CONSTANT FACTOR, THE(1980, Pol.), ed
Alastair Sim
FIRE HAS BEEN ARRANGED, A(1935, Brit.); LATE EXTRA(1935, Brit.); PRIVATE SECRETARY, THE(1935, Brit.); RIVERSIDE MURDER, THE(1935, Brit.); BIG NOISE, THE(1936, Brit.); KEEP YOUR SEATS PLEASE(1936, Brit.); MAN IN THE MIRROR, THE(1936, Brit.); MYSTERIOUS MR. DAVIS, THE(1936, Brit.); TROUBLED WATERS(1936, Brit.); WRATH OF JEALOUSY(1936, Brit.); CLOTHES AND THE WOMAN(1937, Brit.); GANGWAY(1937, Brit.); MELODY AND ROMANCE(1937, Brit.); MURDER ON DIAMOND ROW(1937, Brit.); STRANGE EXPERIMENT(1937, Brit.); ALF'S BUTTON AFLOAT(1938, Brit.); CLIMBING HIGH(1938, Brit.); SAILING ALONG(1938, Brit.); INSPECTOR HORNLEIGH(1939, Brit.); INSPECTOR HORNLEIGH ON HOLIDAY(1939, Brit.); THIS MAN IN PARIS(1939, Brit.); THIS MAN IS NEWS(1939, Brit.); LAW AND DISORDER(1940, Brit.); BOMBSIGHT STOLEN(1941, Brit.); MAIL TRAIN(1941, Brit.); TERROR, THE(1941, Brit.); LET THE PEOPLE SING(1942, Brit.); CAPTAIN BOYCOTT(1947, Brit.); DULCIMER STREET(1948, Brit.); WATERLOO ROAD(1949, Brit.); HAPPIEST DAYS OF YOUR LIFE(1950, Brit.); HUE AND CRY(1950, Brit.); STAGE FRIGHT(1950, Brit.); CHRISTMAS CAROL, A(1951, Brit.); LAUGHTER IN PARADISE(1951, Brit.); FOLLY TO BE WISE(1953); BELLES OF ST. TRINIAN'S, THE(1954, Brit.); INSPECTOR CALLS, AN(1954, Brit.); ESCAPADE(1955, Brit.); INNOCENTS IN PARIS(1955, Brit.); LADY GODIVA RIDES AGAIN(1955, Brit.); GREEN MAN, THE(1957, Brit.); BLUE MURDER AT ST. TRINIAN'S(1958, Brit.); LEFT, RIGHT AND CENTRE(1959); MILLIONAIRESS, THE(1960, Brit.); SCHOOL FOR SCOUNDRELS(1960, Brit.); RULING CLASS, THE(1972, Brit.); ROYAL FLASH(1975, Brit.); LITTLEST HORSE THIEVES, THE(1977)
Alistair Sim
CASE OF GABRIEL PERRY, THE(1935, Brit.); LOST ON THE WESTERN FRONT(1940, Brit.); GREEN FOR DANGER(1946, Brit.); WEE GEORDIE(1956, Brit.); DOCTOR'S DILEMMA, THE(1958, Brit.); ANATOMIST, THE(1961, Brit.)
Bert Sim
ROOM IN THE HOUSE(1955, Brit.)
Gerald Sim
JOSEPHINE AND MEN(1955, Brit.); WHISTLE DOWN THE WIND(1961, Brit.); L-SHAPED ROOM, THE(1962, Brit.); I COULD GO ON SINGING(1963); MURDER CAN BE DEADLY(1963, Brit.); PUMPKIN EATER, THE(1964, Brit.); SEANCE ON A WET AFTERNOON(1964 Brit.); AMOROUS MR. PRAWN, THE(1965, Brit.); KING RAT(1965); MURDER GAME, THE(1966, Brit.); WRONG BOX, THE(1966, Brit.); OUR MOTHER'S HOUSE(1967, Brit.); WHISPERERS, THE(1967, Brit.); MADWOMAN OF CHAILLOT, THE(1969); MISCHIEF(1969, Brit.); OH! WHAT A LOVELY WAR(1969, Brit.); DOCTOR IN TROUBLE(1970, Brit.); LAST GRENADE, THE(1970, Brit.); MAN WHO HAUNTED HIMSELF, THE(1970, Brit.); RYAN'S DAUGHTER(1970, Brit.); DR. JEKYLL AND SISTER HYDE(1971, Brit.); LONG AGO, TOMORROW(1971, Brit.); DOCTOR PHIBES RISES AGAIN(1972, Brit.); YOUNG WINSTON(1972, Brit.); SLIPPER AND THE ROSE, THE(1976, Brit.); NO SEX PLEASE—WE'RE BRITISH(1979, Brit.)
Heather Sim
SLOW RUN(1968)
Ray Sim
KILLERS OF KILIMANJARO(1960, Brit.), art d
S.M. Sim
SAINT JACK(1979)
Sheila Sim
CANTERBURY TALE, A(1944, Brit.); GREAT DAY(1945, Brit.); DANCING WITH CRIME(1947, Brit.); DEAR MR. PROHACK(1949, Brit.); OUTSIDER, THE(1949, Brit.); PANDORA AND THE FLYING DUTCHMAN(1951, Brit.); MAGIC BOX, THE(1952, Brit.); WEST OF ZANZIBAR(1954, Brit.); NIGHT MY NUMBER CAME UP, THE(1955, Brit.)
Oskar Sima
ALLURING GOAL, THE(1930, Germ.); PILLARS OF SOCIETY(1936, Ger.); OH ROSALINDA(1956, Brit.); CONGRESS DANCES(1957, Ger.); TURKISH CUCUMBER, THE(1963, Ger.); DIE FLEDERMAUS(1964, Aust.)
A. Simachyov
LITTLE HUMPBACKED HORSE, THE(1962, USSR)
Otto Simanek
13 RUE MADELEINE(1946); WRONG MAN, THE(1956)
Lorna Simans
GIRL RUSH, THE(1955)
Elfrida Simbari
NUN'S STORY, THE(1959)
Barry Simco
MAN WHO WOULD NOT DIE, THE(1975)
Ben Simcoe
MURDER BY CONTRACT(1958), w

Benjamin Simcoe
BOMB IN THE HIGH STREET(1961, Brit.), w
Tom Simcox
SHENANDOAH(1965); INCIDENT AT PHANTOM HILL(1966); ONE LITTLE INDIAN(1973)
David Sime
SOLDIER, SAILOR(1944, Brit.)
Denise Simek
TENDER MERCIES(1982)
Ida Simenfalvy
FATHER(1967, Hung.); ROUND UP, THE(1969, Hung.); WINTER WIND(1970, Fr./Hung.)
Sandor Simenfalvy
ROUND UP, THE(1969, Hung.)
Georges Simenon
PANIQUE(1947, Fr.), w; MAN ON THE EIFFEL TOWER, THE(1949), w; STRANGERS IN THE HOUSE(1949, Fr.), w; TEMPTATION HARBOR(1949, Brit.), w; LA MARIE DU PORT(1951, Fr.), w; MIDNIGHT EPISODE(1951, Brit.), w; PARIS EXPRESS, THE(1953, Brit.), d&w; LIFE IN THE BALANCE, A(1955), w; BROTHERS RICO, THE(1957), w; MAIGRET LAYS A TRAP(1958, Fr.), w; FORBIDDEN FRUIT(1959, Fr.), w; LOVE IS MY PROFESSION(1959, Fr.), w; PASSION OF SLOW FIRE, THE(1962, Fr.), w; COP-OUT(1967, Brit.), w; CAT, THE(1975, Fr.), w; CLOCKMAKER, THE(1976, Fr.), w; HATTER'S GHOST, THE(1982, Fr.), w; L'ETOILE DU NORD(1983, Fr.), w
Simeon
HEART OF PARIS(1939, Fr.)
Andre Simeon
STORY OF THREE LOVES, THE(1953)
Georges Simeon
BOTTOM OF THE BOTTLE, THE(1956), w
Lewis Simeon
RING OF TERROR(1962), w
Virginia Simeon
SUMMERTIME(1955)
Simonetta Simeoni
VERY PRIVATE AFFAIR, A(1962, Fr./Ital.); FURY OF THE PAGANS(1963, Ital.); SON OF CAPTAIN BLOOD, THE(1964, U.S./Ital./Span.)
Bogomil Simeonov
CLOWN AND THE KIDS, THE(1968, U.S./Bulgaria)
Konstantin Simeonov
KATERINA IZMAILOVA(1969, USSR), md
Simi
TARZAN GOES TO INDIA(1962, U.S./Brit./Switz.)
Carlo Simi
DUEL OF THE TITANS(1963, Ital.), set d; MINNESOTA CLAY(1966, Ital./Fr./Span.), art d; FOR A FEW DOLLARS MORE(1967, Ital./Ger./Span.), art d&cos; GOOD, THE BAD, AND THE UGLY, THE(1967, Ital./Span.), art d, cos; ONCE UPON A TIME IN THE WEST(1969, U.S./Ital.), art d, cos; SABATA(1969, Ital.), art d&cos; DAY OF ANGER(1970, Ital./Ger.), cos; BLOOD IN THE STREETS(1975, Ital./Fr.), art d,set d; GENIUS, THE(1976, Ital./Fr./Ger.), art d
1984
ONCE UPON A TIME IN AMERICA(1984), art d
Nikola Simic
SQUARE OF VIOLENCE(1963, U.S./Yugo.)
1984
SECRET DIARY OF SIGMUND FREUD, THE(1984)
Peter Similuk
MYSTERY SUBMARINE(1950)
Simino
LOST COMMAND, THE(1966)
Bruno Simionato
EASY LIFE, THE(1963, Ital.); QUIET PLACE IN THE COUNTRY, A(1970, Ital./Fr.)
Graziella Simionato
QUIET PLACE IN THE COUNTRY, A(1970, Ital./Fr.)
Mirta Simionato
QUIET PLACE IN THE COUNTRY, A(1970, Ital./Fr.)
C. Simionescu
FIGHT FOR ROME(1969, Ger./Rum.), set d
Mme. Simkie
TIGER AND THE FLAME, THE(1955, India), ch
Bob Simm
SMILEY(1957, Brit.)
Jacqui Simm
REVENGE OF THE PINK PANTHER(1978)
Ray Simm
FAITHFUL CITY(1952, Israel), art d; POSTMARK FOR DANGER(1956, Brit.), art d; ABANDON SHIP(1957, Brit.), art d; JAZZ BOAT(1960, Brit.), art d; TARZAN THE MAGNIFICENT(1960, Brit.), art d; MARK, THE(1961, Brit.), art d; WHISTLE DOWN THE WIND(1961, Brit.), art d; KIND OF LOVING, A(1962, Brit.), art d; L-SHAPED ROOM, THE(1962, Brit.), art d; TRIAL AND ERROR(1962, Brit.), art d; HELLFIRE CLUB, THE(1963, Brit.), art d; HARD DAY'S NIGHT, A(1964, Brit.), art d; SEANCE ON A WET AFTERNOON(1964 Brit.), art d; DARLING(1965, Brit.), art d; HELP!(1965, Brit.), art d; WRONG BOX, THE(1966, Brit.), art d; DEADFALL(1968, Brit.), art d, set d; MADWOMAN OF CHAILLOT, THE(1969), prod d; DULCIMA(1971, Brit.), art d; FRAGMENT OF FEAR(1971, Brit.), art d; RECKONING, THE(1971, Brit.), art d; STRAW DOGS(1971, Brit.), prod d; NATIONAL HEALTH, OR NURSE NORTON'S AFFAIR, THE(1973, Brit.), prod d; HENNESSY(1975, Brit.), prod d
Raymond Simm
RISING OF THE MOON, THE(1957, Ireland), art d; SAINT JOAN(1957), art d; BONJOUR TRISTESSE(1958), art d; SLIPPER AND THE ROSE, THE(1976, Brit.), pd
Boucci Simma
FANTASIES(1981)
Oscar Simma
Misc. Silents
THREE LOVES(1931, Ger.)
Johannes Mario Simmel
GIRL AND THE LEGEND, THE(1966, Ger.), w

James Simmerhan
BRONCO BILLY(1980)

Roberto Simmi
DESERTER, THE(1971 Ital./Yugo.)

Charles Simminger
SCENT OF MYSTERY(1960), cos; TOWN CALLED HELL, A(1971, Span./Brit.), cos

Paul Simmion
KING OF COMEDY, THE(1983)

Alan Simmonds
HEAD ON(1981, Can.), p

Annette Simmonds
NO ORCHIDS FOR MISS BLANDISH(1948, Brit.); ADVENTURES OF PC 49, THE(1949, Brit.); BLACKOUT(1950, Brit.); FRIGHTENED MAN, THE(1952, Brit.)

Annette D. Simmonds
TROJAN BROTHERS, THE(1946)

Charles Simmonds
NATIVE SON(1951, U.S., Arg.)

Kathy Simmonds
Misc. Talkies
TOUCHABLES, THE(1968, Brit.)

Leslie Simmonds
IMPORTANT WITNESS, THE(1933), w; ACES AND EIGHTS(1936), p; BORDER CABALLERO(1936), p; GHOST PATROL(1936), p; LIGHTNING BILL CARSON(1936), p; LION'S DEN, THE(1936), p; ROARIN' GUNS(1936), p; TRAITOR, THE(1936), p; CRASHIN' THRU DANGER(1938), p

Nancy Simmonds
SILENT PARTNER, THE(1979, Can.)

Nikolas Simmonds
LOVERS, THE(1972, Brit.)

Philip Simmonds
Misc. Silents
TRUANTS, THE(1922, Brit.)

S. Simmonds
MAN WHO WON, THE(1933, Brit.), ed

Sam Simmonds
MR. DRAKE'S DUCK(1951, Brit.), ed; TIME IS MY ENEMY(1957, Brit.), ed

Samuel Simmonds
EVERYTHING IS RHYTHM(1940, Brit.), ed

Stanley Simmonds
LI'L ABNER(1959); ROLLOVER(1981); ZELIG(1983)

Albert Simmons
FOREIGN INTRIGUE(1956)

Allene Simmons
PORKY'S(1982)

Amy Simmons
Silents
COUNTY CHAIRMAN, THE(1914)

Anthony Simmons
PASSING STRANGER, THE(1954, Brit.), p, w; TIME WITHOUT PITY(1957, Brit.), p; FOUR IN THE MORNING(1965, Brit.), d&w; YOUR MONEY OR YOUR WIFE(1965, Brit.), d; OPTIMISTS, THE(1973, Brit.), d, w; BLACK JOY(1977, Brit.), d, w; GREEN ICE(1981, Brit.), w

Barrie Simmons
VOYAGE, THE(1974, Ital.)

Beverly Simmons
CUBAN PETE(1946); LITTLE MISS BIG(1946); BUCK PRIVATES COME HOME(1947)

Beverly Sue Simmons
FRONTIER GAL(1945)

Bob Simmons
REFORM SCHOOL(1939); SWORD AND THE ROSE, THE(1953); SECRET WAYS, THE(1961), stunts; DR. NO(1962, Brit.), stunts; GREAT VAN ROBBERY, THE(1963, Brit.); THUNDERBALL(1965, Brit.), a; DIAMONDS ARE FOREVER(1971, Brit.), stunts; MURPHY'S WAR(1971, Brit.), stunts; WHEN EIGHT BELLS TOLL(1971, Brit.), stunts; LIVE AND LET DIE(1973, Brit.), stunts; MOONRAKER(1979, Brit.), stunts; ZULU DAWN(1980, Brit.), stunts

Bobby Simmons
ONE DARK NIGHT(1939)

Clarence Simmons
JUST IMAGINE(1930)

Claudia Simmons
EVER SINCE EVE(1937); MR. DODD TAKES THE AIR(1937); THAT CERTAIN WOMAN(1937)

Craig Simmons
POLTERGEIST(1982)

Dan Simmons
FRONTIER GUN(1958); GANG WAR(1958); SHOWDOWN AT BOOT HILL(1958); HIGH-POWERED RIFLE, THE(1960); LITTLE SHEPHERD OF KINGDOM COME(1961)

Dick Simmons
MILLION TO ONE, A(1938); STAND BY FOR ACTION(1942); PILOT NO. 5(1943); THOUSANDS CHEER(1943); YOUNGEST PROFESSION, THE(1943); THIS TIME FOR KEEPS(1947); UNDERCOVER MAISIE(1947); EASTER PARADE(1948); ON AN ISLAND WITH YOU(1948); SOUTHERN YANKEE, A(1948); GREAT SINNER, THE(1949); LOOK FOR THE SILVER LINING(1949); NEPTUNE'S DAUGHTER(1949); DIAL 1119(1950); DUCHESS OF IDAHO, THE(1950); TO PLEASE A LADY(1950); I'LL SEE YOU IN MY DREAMS(1951); MR. IMPERIUM(1951); NO QUESTIONS ASKED(1951); WELL, THE(1951); DESPERATE SEARCH(1952); GLORY ALLEY(1952); ABOVE AND BEYOND(1953); BATTLE CIRCUS(1953); REMAINS TO BE SEEN(1953); THREE SAILORS AND A GIRL(1953); MEN OF THE FIGHTING LADY(1954); REAR WINDOW(1954); ROGUE COP(1954)

Dolly Simmons
OLGA'S GIRLS(1964)

Dori Simmons
VERTIGO(1958)

Ed Simmons
SCARED STIFF(1953), w

Elinor Simmons
TONY ROME(1967), cos

Floyd Simmons
AWAY ALL BOATS(1956); OUTSIDE THE LAW(1956); PILLARS OF THE SKY(1956); WRITTEN ON THE WIND(1956); DEADLY MANTIS, THE(1957); TATTERED DRESS, THE(1957); PARTY GIRL(1958); SOUTH PACIFIC(1958); TWICE TOLD TALES(1963)

Gardner Simmons
1984
RARE BREED(1984), w

Gene Simmons
1984
RUNAWAY(1984)

George Simmons
THAT TOUCH OF MINK(1962); SWARM, THE(1978)

George F. Simmons
CHEAP DETECTIVE, THE(1978)

Georgia Simmons
HEART OF THE ROCKIES(1937); MOUNTAIN MUSIC(1937); ROMANCE ON THE RUN(1938); SWING YOUR LADY(1938); GRAPES OF WRATH(1940); ROSE TATTOO, THE(1955); ALL THE WAY HOME(1963); 8 ½(1963, Ital.); BILLIE(1965)

Grant Simmons
FANTASIA(1940), anim; DUMBO(1941), anim; GAY PURR-EE(1962), anim; HEY THERE, IT'S YOGI BEAR(1964), anim

Jack Simmons
REBEL WITHOUT A CAUSE(1955)

James Simmons
STORY OF SEABISCUIT, THE(1949)

Jean Simmons
UNTIL THEY SAIL(1957); GIVE US THE MOON(1944, Brit.); KISS THE BRIDE GOODBYE(1944, Brit.); MEET SEXTON BLAKE(1944, Brit.); JOHNNY IN THE CLOUDS(1945, Brit.); MR. EMMANUEL(1945, Brit.); CAESAR AND CLEOPATRA(1946, Brit.); GREAT EXPECTATIONS(1946, Brit.); BLACK NARCISSUS(1947, Brit.); HUNGRY HILL(1947, Brit.); HAMLET(1948, Brit.); BLUE LAGOON, THE(1949, Brit.); WOMAN IN THE HALL, THE(1949, Brit.); ADAM AND EVELYNE(1950, Brit.); CAGE OF GOLD(1950, Brit.); CLOUDED YELLOW, THE(1950, Brit.); TRIO(1950, Brit.); INHERITANCE, THE(1951, Brit.); SO LONG AT THE FAIR(1951, Brit.); ANDROCLES AND THE LION(1952); ACTRESS, THE(1953); AFFAIR WITH A STRANGER(1953); ANGEL FACE(1953); ROBE, THE(1953); YOUNG BESS(1953); BULLET IS WAITING, A(1954); DEMETRIUS AND THE GLADIATORS(1954); DESIREE(1954); EGYPTIAN. THE(1954); SHE COULDN'T SAY NO(1954); FOOTSTEPS IN THE FOG(1955, Brit.); GUYS AND DOLLS(1955); HILDA CRANE(1956); THIS COULD BE THE NIGHT(1957); BIG COUNTRY, THE(1958); HOME BEFORE DARK(1958); THIS EARTH IS MINE(1959); ELMER GANTRY(1960); GRASS IS GREENER, THE(1960); SPARTACUS(1960); ALL THE WAY HOME(1963); LIFE AT THE TOP(1965, Brit.); MISTER BUDDWING(1966); DIVORCE AMERICAN STYLE(1967); ROUGH NIGHT IN JERICHO(1967); HAPPY ENDING, THE(1969); SAY HELLO TO YESTERDAY(1971, Brit.); MR. SYCAMORE(1975); DOMINIQUE(1978, Brit.)

John Simmons
XTRO(1983, Brit.), ph

M.L. Simmons
HONOR OF THE PRESS(1932), w

Matty Simmons
NATIONAL LAMPOON'S ANIMAL HOUSE(1978), p; NATIONAL LAMPOON'S CLASS REUNION(1982), p; NATIONAL LAMPOON'S VACATION(1983), p

Maude Simmons
PORTRAIT OF JENNIE(1949); NO WAY OUT(1950)

Michael Simmons
AWAKENING OF JIM BURKE(1935), w; GIRL OF THE OZARKS(1936), w; VENUS MAKES TROUBLE(1937), w; FLIGHT TO FAME(1938), w; SQUADRON OF HONOR(1938), w; MISSING DAUGHTERS(1939), w; SCATTERGOOD SURVIVES A MURDER(1942), w; LANDRUSH(1946), w

Michael L. Simmons
FIRST AID(1931), w; BOWERY, THE(1933), w; ALL-AMERICAN SWEETHEART(1937), w; MURDER IN GREENWICH VILLAGE(1937), w; JUVENILE COURT(1938), w; LITTLE ADVENTURESS, THE(1938), w; LITTLE MISS ROUGHNECK(1938), w; MUTINY ON THE BLACKHAWK(1939), w; ROMANCE OF THE REDWOODS(1939), w; TROPIC FURY(1939), w; SCATTERGOOD BAINES(1941), w; SCATTERGOOD MEETS BROADWAY(1941), w; CINDERELLA SWINGS IT(1942), w; SCATTERGOOD RIDES HIGH(1942), w; EYES OF THE UNDERWORLD(1943), w; TWO WEEKS TO LIVE(1943), w; THEY LIVE IN FEAR(1944), w

Pat Simmons
GIANT GILA MONSTER, THE(1959)

Paul A. Simmons
SWAMP THING(1982), cos

Philip Simmons
Silents
ELEVENTH HOUR, THE(1922, Brit.); HALF A TRUTH(1922, Brit.)

Richard Simmons
LOVE LAUGHS AT ANDY HARDY(1946); LADY IN THE LAKE(1947); THREE MUSKETEERS, THE(1948); I DREAM OF JEANIE(1952); THUNDERBIRDS(1952); FLIGHT NURSE(1953); WOMAN THEY ALMOST LYNCHED, THE(1953); IT'S ALWAYS FAIR WEATHER(1955); LOVE ME OR LEAVE ME(1955); SCARLET COAT, THE(1955); YOU'RE NEVER TOO YOUNG(1955); SERGEANTS 3(1962); LASSIE'S GREAT ADVENTURE(1963); ROBIN AND THE SEVEN HOODS(1964); RESURRECTION OF ZACHARY WHEELER, THE(1971)

Richard Alan Simmons
LADY WANTS MINK, THE(1953), w; THREE'S COMPANY(1953, Brit.), w; WAR PAINT(1953), w; BEACHHEAD(1954), w; BENGAL BRIGADE(1954), w; SHIELD FOR MURDER(1954), w; TANGANYIKA(1954), w; THREE HOURS TO KILL(1954), w; YELLOW TOMAHAWK, THE(1954), w; FEMALE ON THE BEACH(1955), w; LOOTERS, THE(1955), w; PRIVATE WAR OF MAJOR BENSON, THE(1955), w; CONGO CROSSING(1956), w; KING AND FOUR QUEENS, THE(1956), w; FUZZY PINK NIGHTGOWN, THE(1957), w; ISTANBUL(1957), w; OUTLAW'S SON(1957), w; TARAWA BEACHHEAD(1958), w; TRAP, THE(1959), w; ART OF LOVE, THE(1965), w; SKIN GAME(1971), w

Robert Simmons
TANGIER ASSIGNMENT(1954, Brit.); WILBY CONSPIRACY, THE(1975, Brit.), stunts

Robert Dale Simmons
BRONCO BILLY(1980)
Robert Wynne Simmons
BLOOD ON SATAN'S CLAW, THE(1970, Brit.), w
Roger Dale Simmons
BRONCO BILLY(1980)
Roz Simmons
NOBODY'S PERFEKT(1981)
S. Simmons
LOOSE ENDS(1930, Brit.), ed; MIDDLE WATCH, THE(1930, Brit.), ed
Sada Simmons
MEET JOHN DOE(1941); IRON MAJOR, THE(1943); CASANOVA BROWN(1944)
Sam Simmons
GREAT, MEADOW, THE(1931), ed; GREAT MR. HANDEL, THE(1942, Brit.), ed; BLACK 13(1954, Brit.), ed
Sara Simmons
SOME KIND OF HERO(1982)
Stan Simmons
SECRET MAN, THE(1958, Brit.); KISS OF EVIL(1963, Brit.); CURSE OF THE FLY(1965, Brit.)
Tim Simmons
JIM, THE WORLD'S GREATEST(1976)
Warwick Simmons
NATE AND HAYES(1983, U.S./New Zealand)
Al Simms
ALAKAZAM THE GREAT!(1961, Jap.), md; "X"-THE MAN WITH THE X-RAY EYES(1963), md; BIKINI BEACH(1964), m; DR. GOLDFOOT AND THE BIKINI MACHINE(1965), md; SERGEANT DEADHEAD(1965), md; FIREBALL 590(1966), md; THREE IN THE ATTIC(1968), md; CRY OF THE BANSHEE(1970, Brit.), md; FROGS(1972), md
Alice Simms
CHECKERED FLAG, THE(1963), m
Eddie Simms
RINGSIDE MAISIE(1941); SONG OF THE THIN MAN(1947); IRON MAN, THE(1951); SAILOR BEWARE(1951)
Eddie Lou Simms
VIGILANTES OF BOOMTOWN(1947)
Gene Simms
PRIVATE PARTS(1972); BUCKTOWN(1975); DARKTOWN STRUTTERS(1975)
Ginny Simms
THAT'S RIGHT-YOU'RE WRONG(1939); YOU'LL FIND OUT(1940); PLAYMATES(1941); HERE WE GO AGAIN(1942); SEVEN DAYS LEAVE(1942); HIT THE ICE(1943); BROADWAY RHYTHM(1944); SHADY LADY(1945); NIGHT AND DAY(1946); DISC JOCKEY(1951)
Hartwell Simms
HERO AIN'T NOTHIN' BUT A SANDWICH, A(1977)
Heather Simms
STOP THE WORLD-I WANT TO GET OFF(1966, Brit.)
Hilda Simms
NINE TILL SIX(1932, Brit.); JOE LOUIS STORY, THE(1953); BLACK WIDOW(1954)
J.M. Simms
Misc. Silents
LURE OF A WOMAN, THE(1921), d
Jan Simms
ACE ELI AND RODGER OF THE SKIES(1973)
Jay Simms
KILLER SHREWS, THE(1959), w; PANIC IN YEAR ZERO!(1962), w; RESURRECTION OF ZACHARY WHEELER, THE(1971), w
Larry Simms
BLONDIE(1938); BLONDIE BRINGS UP BABY(1939); BLONDIE MEETS THE BOSS(1939); BLONDIE TAKES A VACATION(1939); BLONDIE HAS SERVANT TROUBLE(1940); BLONDIE ON A BUDGET(1940); BLONDIE PLAYS CUPID(1940); BLONDIE GOES LATIN(1941); BLONDIE IN SOCIETY(1941); BLONDIE FOR VICTORY(1942); BLONDIE GOES TO COLLEGE(1942); BLONDIE'S BLESSED EVENT(1942); GAY SISTERS, THE(1942); FOOTLIGHT GLAMOUR(1943); IT'S A GREAT LIFE(1943); LEAVE IT TO BLONDIE(1945); BLONDIE KNOWS BEST(1946); BLONDIE'S LUCKY DAY(1946); IT'S A WONDERFUL LIFE(1946); LIFE WITH BLONDIE(1946); BLONDIE IN THE DOUGH(1947); BLONDIE'S ANNIVERSARY(1947); BLONDIE'S BIG MOMENT(1947); BLONDIE'S HOLIDAY(1947); GOLDEN EARRINGS(1947); BLONDIE'S REWARD(1948); BLONDIE'S SECRET(1948); BLONDIE HITS THE JACKPOT(1949); BLONDIE'S BIG DEAL(1949); MADAME BOVARY(1949); BEWARE OF BLONDIE(1950); BLONDIE'S HERO(1950)
Leslie Simms
POINT OF TERROR(1971); TRACKDOWN(1976); LAST AMERICAN VIRGIN, THE(1982)
Marilyn Simms
THREE FOR JAMIE DAWN(1956)
Marley Simms
MR. MOM(1983)
Mike Simms
BUS IS COMING, THE(1971)
Pat Simms
ROYAL WEDDING(1951)
Phil Simms
MR. MOM(1983)
Ray Simms
MAN INSIDE, THE(1958, Brit.), art d
Sylvia Simms
NIGHT WITHOUT SLEEP(1952)
Tammy Simms
DEVIL'S SISTERS, THE(1966)
William Simms
FRENCH QUARTER(1978)
Irenio Simoes
GIVEN WORD, THE(1964, Braz.)
Abe Simon
ON THE WATERFRONT(1954); SINGING IN THE DARK(1956); ER LOVE A STRANGER(1958); REQUIEM FOR A HEAVYWEIGHT(1962)

Alain Simon
TOUCH, THE(1971, U.S./Swed.)
Alphonse Simon
GREEN ROOM, THE(1979, Fr.)
Barney Simon
CITY LOVERS(1982, S. African), d&w
Benjamin Simon
JOY(1983, Fr./Can.), p
Carly Simon
TAKING OFF(1971)
Carmi Simon
STONY ISLAND(1978)
Charles Simon
ZAZA(1939), w; DARWIN ADVENTURE, THE(1972, Brit.)
Charles J. Simon
ANATOMY OF A PSYCHO(1961)
Christian Simon
GATES OF THE NIGHT(1950, Fr.)
Christine Simon
MILKY WAY, THE(1969, Fr./Ital.)
Claude Robert Simon
JOE(1970)
David Simon
WITHOUT A TRACE(1983)
Ed Simon
MURDER, INC.(1960)
Eric Simon
DE L'AMOUR(1968, Fr./Ital.), art d; TWO PEOPLE(1973), set d; TENANT, THE(1976, Fr.), set d; WOMANLIGHT(1979, Fr./Ger./Ital.), art d; CLAIR DE FEMME(1980,Fr.), art d; COUSINS IN LOVE(1982), art d
Ernie Simon
DISC JOCKEY(1951)
Ernst Simon
YOUNG GO WILD, THE(1962, Ger.), m
Francis Simon
CHICKEN CHRONICLES, THE(1977), d
Francois Simon
CHARLES, DEAD OR ALIVE(1972, Switz.); INVITATION, THE(1975, Fr./Switz.); LUMIERE(1976, Fr.)
1984
BASILEUS QUARTET(1984, Ital.)
Gunther Simon
FIRST SPACESHIP ON VENUS(1960, Ger./Pol.)
Henry R. Simon
Silents
BROADWAY BILLY(1926), w
Jean Marie Simon
NIGHT PORTER, THE(1974, Ital./U.S.), art d
Jean-Daniel Simon
VICE AND VIRTUE(1965, Fr./Ital.); FINO A FARTI MALE(1969, Fr./Ital.), d, w
Jean-Marie Simon
EGLANTINE(1972, Fr.), art d
Jerome Simon
DOUBLE NEGATIVE(1980, Can.), p
Joe Simon
SGT. PEPPER'S LONELY HEARTS CLUB BAND(1978)
John Simon
LAST SUMMER(1969), m; SATAN'S MISTRESS(1982)
Juan Piquer Simon
MONSTER ISLAND(1981, Span./U.S.), p&d; PIECES(1983, Span./Puerto Rico), d
Lauren Simon
CHEAP DETECTIVE, THE(1978)
Leah Simon
Misc. Talkies
TENDER LOVING CARE(1974)
Linda Simon
WAY WE LIVE NOW, THE(1970)
Luc Simon
LANCELOT OF THE LAKE(1975, Fr.)
M. Simon
Misc. Silents
REWARD OF FAITH(1929), d
Marcel Simon
WITH A SMILE(1939, Fr.); ANGEL AND SINNER(1947, Fr.)
Margarete Simon
RED-DRAGON(1967, Ital./Ger./US), cos
Maricza Simon
HIPPOLYT, THE LACKEY(1932, Hung.)
Marla Simon
MICROWAVE MASSACRE(1983)
May Simon
Misc. Silents
GIRL WHO DIDN'T THINK, THE(1917)
Maya Simon
CHARLES, DEAD OR ALIVE(1972, Switz.)
Mayo Simon
I COULD GO ON SINGING(1963), w; MAROONED(1969), w; PHASE IV(1974), w; FUTUREWORLD(1976), w
Michel Simon
FROM TOP TO BOTTOM(1933, Fr.); PORT OF SHADOWS(1938, Fr.); BIZARRE BIZARRE(1939, Fr.); END OF A DAY, THE(1939, Fr.); FRIC FRAC(1939, FR.); KISS OF FIRE, THE(1940, Fr.); UNA SIGNORA DELL'OVEST(1942, Ital); KING'S JESTER, THE(1947, Ital.); L'ATALANTE(1947, Fr.); PANIQUE(1947, Fr.); FRIEND WILL COME TONIGHT, A(1948, Fr.); FABIOLA(1951, Ital.); BEAUTY AND THE DEVIL(1952, Fr./Ital.); SAADIA(1953); ANATOMY OF LOVE(1959, Ital.); AUSTERLITZ(1960, Fr./Ital./Yugo.); IT HAPPENED IN BROAD DAYLIGHT(1960, Ger./Switz.); HEAD, THE(1961, Ger.); CANDIDE(1962, Fr.); DEVIL AND THE TEN COMMANDMENTS, THE(1962, Fr.); TRAIN, THE(1965, Fr./Ital./U.S.); BOUDU SAVED FROM DROWNING(1967, Fr.), a, p; MARRIAGE CAME TUMBLING DOWN, THE(1968, Fr.); TWO OF US, THE(1968, Fr.); BLANCHE(1971, Fr.); MOST WONDERFUL EVENING OF MY

LIFE, THE(1972, Ital./Fr.); LA CHIENNE(1975, Fr.)
Silents
PASSION OF JOAN OF ARC, THE(1928, Fr.)
Misc. Silents
LATE MATTHEW PASCAL, THE(1925, Fr.); TIRE AU FLANC(1929, Fr.)
Miklos Simon
FOUR FRIENDS(1981)
Neil Simon
COME BLOW YOUR HORN(1963), w; AFTER THE FOX(1966, U.S./Brit./Ital.), w; BAREFOOT IN THE PARK(1967), w; ODD COUPLE, THE(1968), w; SWEET CHARITY(1969), w; OUT OF TOWNERS, THE(1970), w; PLAZA SUITE(1971), w; STAR SPANGLED GIRL(1971), w; HEARTBREAK KID, THE(1972), w; LAST OF THE RED HOT LOVERS(1972), w; PRISONER OF SECOND AVENUE, THE(1975), w; SUNSHINE BOYS, THE(1975), w; MURDER BY DEATH(1976), w; GOODBYE GIRL, THE(1977), w; CALIFORNIA SUITE(1978), w; CHEAP DETECTIVE, THE(1978), w; CHAPTER TWO(1979), w; SEEMS LIKE OLD TIMES(1980), w; ONLY WHEN I LAUGH(1981), p, w; I OUGHT TO BE IN PICTURES(1982), p, w; MAX DUGAN RETURNS(1983), p, w
1984
LONELY GUY, THE(1984), w
P. Simon
IT HAPPENED IN GIBRALTAR(1943, Fr.), m
Paul Simon
SHAMPOO(1975), m; ANNIE HALL(1977); ONE-TRICK PONY(1980), a, w, m
Pete Simon
MEN, THE(1950)
Piquer Simon
SUPERSONIC MAN(1979, Span.), d, w; MONSTER ISLAND(1981, Span./U.S.), w
Robert A. Simon
STRICTLY DYNAMITE(1934), w
Robert F. Simon
WHERE THE SIDEWALK ENDS(1950); BRIGHT VICTORY(1951); ROGUE COP(1954); CHIEF CRAZY HORSE(1955); BENNY GOODMAN STORY, THE(1956); BUCCANEER, THE(1958); GUNMAN'S WALK(1958); LAST ANGRY MAN, THE(1959); OPERATION PETTICOAT(1959); FACTS OF LIFE, THE(1960); PAY OR DIE(1960); WIZARD OF BAGHDAD, THE(1960); TESS OF THE STORM COUNTRY(1961); MAN WHO SHOT LIBERTY VALANCE, THE(1962); SPIRAL ROAD, THE(1962); CAPTAIN NEWMAN, M.D.(1963); NEW KIND OF LOVE, A(1963); WALL OF NOISE(1963); FATE IS THE HUNTER(1964); ACROSS THE RIVER(1965); RELUCTANT ASTRONAUT, THE(1967)
Robert S. Simon
ADA(1961)
Robert Simon
BLACK DAKOTAS, THE(1954); ROOGIE'S BUMP(1954); COURT-MARTIAL OF BILLY MITCHELL, THE(1955); FOXFIRE(1955); GIRL IN THE RED VELVET SWING, THE(1955); SEVEN ANGRY MEN(1955); BIGGER THAN LIFE(1956); CATERED AFFAIR, THE(1956); FIRST TRAVELING SALESLADY, THE(1956); NEVER SAY GOODBYE(1956); RACK, THE(1956); EDGE OF THE CITY(1957); SPRING REUNION(1957); COMPULSION(1959); FACE OF FIRE(1959, U.S./Brit.); BLINDFOLD(1966)
Roger L. Simon
JENNIFER ON MY MIND(1971), w; BIG FIX, THE(1978), w; BUSTIN' LOOSE(1981), w
Ruti Simon
RUNNERS(1983, Brit.)
S. J. Simon
HEADIN' NORTH(1930); LAND OF MISSING MEN, THE(1930); GIVE US THE MOON(1944, Brit.), w; GHOSTS OF BERKELEY SQUARE(1947, Brit.), w; ONE NIGHT WITH YOU(1948, Brit), w; GAY LADY, THE(1949, Brit.), w
S. S. Simon
BARKER, THE(1928)
Silents
GREED(1925)
S. Sylvan Simon
GIRL WITH IDEAS, A(1937), d; PRESCRIPTION FOR ROMANCE(1937), d; CRIME OF DR. HALLET(1938), d; NURSE FROM BROOKLYN(1938), d; ROAD TO RENO, THE(1938), d; SPRING MADNESS(1938), d; DANCING CO-ED(1939), d; FOUR GIRLS IN WHITE(1939), d; KID FROM TEXAS, THE(1939), d; THESE GLAMOUR GIRLS(1939), d; DULCY(1940), d; SPORTING BLOOD(1940), d; TWO GIRLS ON BROADWAY(1940), d; BUGLE SOUNDS, THE(1941), d; KEEPING COMPANY(1941), d; WASHINGTON MELODRAMA(1941), d; WHISTLING IN THE DARK(1941), d; GRAND CENTRAL MURDER(1942), d; RIO RITA(1942), d; TISH(1942), d; WHISTLING IN DIXIE(1942), d; SALUTE TO THE MARINES(1943), d; WHISTLING IN BROOKLYN(1943), d; SONG OF THE OPEN ROAD(1944), d; ABBOTT AND COSTELLO IN HOLLYWOOD(1945), d; SON OF LASSIE(1945), d; BAD BASCOMB(1946), d; COCKEYED MIRACLE, THE(1946), d; THRILL OF BRAZIL, THE(1946), d; HER HUSBAND'S AFFAIRS(1947), d; I LOVE TROUBLE(1947), p&d; FULLER BRUSH MAN(1948), d; LUST FOR GOLD(1949), p&d; MISS GRANT TAKES RICHMOND(1949), p; SHOCKPROOF(1949), p; FATHER IS A BACHELOR(1950), p; GOOD HUMOR MAN, THE(1950), p; BORN YESTERDAY(1951), p
Simone Simon
GIRLS' DORMITORY(1936); LADIES IN LOVE(1936); LOVE AND HISSES(1937); SEVENTH HEAVEN(1937); DARK EYES(1938, Fr.); JOSETTE(1938); LA BETE HUMAINE(1938, Fr.); DEVIL AND DANIEL WEBSTER, THE(1941); CAT PEOPLE(1942); TAHITI HONEY(1943); CURSE OF THE CAT PEOPLE, THE(1944); JOHNNY DOESN'T LIVE HERE ANY MORE(1944); MADEMOISELLE FIFI(1944); TEMPTATION HARBOR(1949, Brit.); LA RONDE(1954, Fr.); LE PLAISIR(1954, Fr.); EXTRA DAY, THE(1956, Brit.)
Susan Simon
COCKEYED MIRACLE, THE(1946); HER HUSBAND'S AFFAIRS(1947); SOUTHERN YANKEE, A(1948)
Ted Simon
LOVE HUNGER(1965, Arg.), m&md
William Simon
NO PLACE FOR JENNIFER(1950, Brit.)
Yves Simon
PEPPERMINT SODA(1979, Fr.), m; COCKTAIL MOLOTOV(1980, Fr.), m
William H. Simon, Jr.
CAMPUS HONEYMOON(1948)

Aime Simon-Girard
Misc. Silents
MILADY(1923, Fr.)
Jozef Simoncic
ASSISTANT, THE(1982, Czech.), ph
Walter Simonds
MARTY(1955), art d; YELLOW CANARY, THE(1963), art d; LIVELY SET, THE(1964), art d; FLUFFY(1965), art d; VERY SPECIAL FAVOR, A(1965), art d; FRANKIE AND JOHNNY(1966), art d; EIGHT ON THE LAM(1967), art d; COMIC, THE(1969), prod d; CAHILL, UNITED STATES MARSHAL(1973), art d; MC Q(1974), prod d; ULTIMATE WARRIOR, THE(1975), art d; GUMBALL RALLY, THE(1976), art d
Walter M. Simonds
WAYWARD BUS, THE(1957), art d; FIEND WHO WALKED THE WEST, THE(1958), art d; FROM HELL TO TEXAS(1958), art d; NICE LITTLE BANK THAT SHOULD BE ROBBED, A(1958), art d; HOUND-DOG MAN(1959), art d; PRIVATE'S AFFAIR, A(1959), art d; FLAMING STAR(1960), art d; LOST WORLD, THE(1960), art d; ALL HANDS ON DECK(1961), art d; SECOND TIME AROUND, THE(1961), art d; STATE FAIR(1962), art d; STRIPPER, THE(1963), art d; I SAW WHAT YOU DID(1965), art d; DEAD HEAT ON A MERRY-GO-ROUND(1966), art d; GREEN BERETS, THE(1968), prod d; P.J.(1968), art d; PENDULUM(1969), prod d; HOW DO I LOVE THEE?(1970), art d; OMEGA MAN, THE(1971), art d; NAPOLEON AND SAMANTHA(1972), art d; ONE IS A LONELY NUMBER(1972), art d
William A. Simonds
EDISON, THE MAN(1940), tech adv
Charles Simone
Misc. Silents
IL TROVATORE(1914), d
Dario Simone
MADWOMAN OF CHAILLOT, THE(1969), set d; KREMLIN LETTER, THE(1970), set d
Lisa Simone
GIANT GILA MONSTER, THE(1959); MISSILE TO THE MOON(1959)
Michael Simone
TOO BAD SHE'S BAD(1954, Ital.)
Paulette Dubost Simone
DEAR DETECTIVE(1978, Fr.)
Ralph Simone
FLIGHT LIEUTENANT(1942); CITIZEN SAINT(1947); NAKED CITY, THE(1948)
Sam Simone
THEY WERE EXPENDABLE(1945)
Aupalotak Simonee
WHITE DAWN, THE(1974)
Liborio Simonella
FITZCARRALDO(1982)
George Simonelli
THAT MAN IN ISTANBUL(1966, Fr./Ital./Span.), w; JOHNNY YUMA(1967, Ital.), w; KNIVES OF THE AVENGER(1967, Ital.), w
Georgio C. Simonelli
SAMSON(1961, Ital.), w
Gianni Simonelli
CON MEN, THE(1973, Ital.,Span.), w
Giorgio C. Simonelli
FURY OF HERCULES, THE(1961, Ital.), w
Giovanni Simonelli
GOLIATH AGAINST THE GIANTS(1963, Ital./Span.), w; GUNMEN OF THE RIO GRANDE(1965, Fr./Ital./Span.), w; SEA PIRATE, THE(1967, Fr./Span./Ital.), w; THEY CAME TO ROB LAS VEGAS(1969, Fr./Ital./Span./Ger.), w
John [Giovanni] Simonelli
YOUNG, THE EVIL AND THE SAVAGE, THE(1968, Ital.), w
Eva Simonet
Z(1969, Fr./Algeria)
Martine Simonet
LAST METRO, THE(1981, Fr.)
Claudio Simonetti
NEW BARBARIANS, THE(1983, Ital.), m
1984
CONQUEST(1984, Ital./Span./Mex.), m; WARRIORS OF THE WASTELAND(1984, Ital.), m
Enrico Simonetti
MACUMBA LOVE(1960), m; PLACE FOR LOVERS, A(1969, Ital./Fr.); KAREN, THE LOVEMAKER(1970), m
Giuliano Simonetti
UGLY ONES, THE(1968, Ital./Span.), p
Ario Simoni
MAN WITH A MILLION(1954, Brit.), set d
Dario Simoni
IF THIS BE SIN(1950, Brit.), set d; THIRD MAN, THE(1950, Brit.), set d; MAGIC BOX, THE(1952, Brit.), set d; PURPLE PLAIN, THE(1954, Brit.), set d; QUIET AMERICAN, THE(1958), art d; EXODUS(1960), set d; SCENT OF MYSTERY(1960), set d; LAWRENCE OF ARABIA(1962, Brit.), set d; DOCTOR ZHIVAGO(1965), set d; DOCTOR FAUSTUS(1967, Brit.), set d; TAMING OF THE SHREW, THE(1967, U.S./Ital.), set d; THOSE DARING YOUNG MEN IN THEIR JAUNTY JALOPIES(1969, Fr./Brit./ Ital.), set d; TRAVELS WITH MY AUNT(1972, Brit.), set d
Sara Simoni
ORGANIZER, THE(1964, Fr./Ital./Yugo.)
Jacqueline Simoni-Adamus
1984
THREE CROWNS OF THE SAILOR(1984, Fr.), ed
Albert Simonin
ADVENTURES OF ARSENE LUPIN(1956, Fr./Ital.), w; CANDIDE(1962, Fr.), a, w; COUNTERFEITERS OF PARIS, THE(1962, Fr./Ital.), w; ROAD TO SHAME, THE(1962, Fr.), w; ANY NUMBER CAN WIN(1963 Fr.), w; MALE HUNT(1965, Fr./Ital.), w; CLOPORTES(1966, Fr., Ital.), w; GREAT SPY CHASE, THE(1966, Fr.), w; TENDER SCOUNDREL(1967, Fr./Ital.), w; COLD SWEAT(1974, Ital., Fr.), w
Brigitte Simonin
DIVA(1982, Fr.)

Simono
STOLEN KISSES(1969, Fr.)
1984
CHEECH AND CHONG'S THE CORSICAN BROTHERS(1984)
Albert Simono
PAUL AND MICHELLE(1974, Fr./Brit.)
1984
MY NEW PARTNER(1984, Fr.)
Paul Simonon
LADIES AND GENTLEMEN, THE FABULOUS STAINS(1982)
Konstantin Simonov
LAD FROM OUR TOWN(1941, USSR), d; IMMORTAL GARRISON, THE(1957, USSR), w
M. Simonov
JACK FROST(1966, USSR), animal t
Nikolai Simonov
Misc. Silents
NINTH OF JANUARY(1925, USSR)
Yvetta Simonova
LEMONADE JOE(1966, Czech.)
Konstantin Simonovic
LES ABYSSES(1964, Fr.), md
Anita Simons
Silents
PAINTED FLAPPER, THE(1924)
Dick Simons
ONE MILLION B.C.(1940)
Doris Simons
NAKED GUN, THE(1956)
Margaret Simons
GOOD COMPANIONS, THE(1957, Brit.); OPERATION BULLSHINE(1963, Brit.)
Mary Simons
TEX(1982)
Richard Simons
TOO MANY THIEVES(1968), p
Roger Simons
KEEP, THE(1983), spec eff
Virgil Simons
WINGS IN THE DARK(1935)
William Simons
IVORY HUNTER(1952, Brit.); WEST OF ZANZIBAR(1954, Brit.); NOT SO DUS-
TY(1956, Brit.)
William Simonsen
CURSE OF BIGFOOT, THE(1972)
M. H. Simonson
CAN SHE BAKE A CHERRY PIE?(1983), p
Theodore Simonson
BLOB, THE(1958), w; 4D MAN(1959), w
Thol O. Simonson
MAN IN THE WATER, THE(1963), spec eff; VOICE OF THE HURRICANE(1964), spec eff; GRASSHOPPER, THE(1970), spec eff
Antonio Simont
MIGHTY URSUS(1962, Ital./Span.), art d; GLADIATORS 7(1964, Span./Ital.), art d; PYRO(1964, U.S./Span.), set d; OPERATION DELILAH(1966, U.S./Span.), art d
Juan Antonio Simont
MAN WHO WAGGED HIS TAIL, THE(1961, Ital./Span.), art d
Ida Vera Simonton
WHITE CARGO(1942), w
Vera Simonton
WHITE CARGO(1930, Brit.), w
N. Simonyan
LADY WITH THE DOG, THE(1962, USSR), m
Tony Simotes
WHOSE LIFE IS IT ANYWAY?(1981)
Henri Simoun [Howard Rodman]
MADIGAN(1968), w
Ileana Simova
UMBERTO D(1955, Ital.)
Tomislav Simovic
SEVENTH CONTINENT, THE(1968, Czech./Yugo.), m
The Simp Phonies
COUNTRY FAIR(1941)
The Simp-Phonies
MEDICO OF PAINTED SPRINGS, THE(1941)
Andrew Simpkins
MAN WHO LOVED WOMEN, THE(1983)
George Simpsom-Little
JEDDA, THE UNCIVILIZED(1956, Aus.)
Alan Simpson
SIEGE OF SIDNEY STREET, THE(1960, Brit.); CALL ME GENIUS(1961, Brit.), w; WRONG ARM OF THE LAW, THE(1963, Brit.), w; BARGEE, THE(1964, Brit.), w; SPY WITH A COLD NOSE, THE(1966, Brit.), w; LOOT(1971, Brit.), w; MAGNIFICENT SEVEN DEADLY SINS, THE(1971, Brit.), w; UP THE CHASTITY BELT(1971, Brit.), w; STEPTOE AND SON(1972, Brit.), w
Allan Simpson
AFTER THE FOG(1930)
Silents
EXCITERS, THE(1923); ANOTHER SCANDAL(1924); HER OWN FREE WILL(1924); SOCIETY SCANDAL, A(1924); SEA HORSES(1926); BERTHA, THE SEWING MA-
CHINE GIRL(1927); ONE SPLENDID HOUR(1929)
Misc. Silents
FAMILY UPSTAIRS, THE(1926); BLONDES BY CHOICE(1927); GIRL HE DIDN'T BUY, THE(1928)
Bernadine Simpson
NEVER WAVE AT A WAC(1952)
Berris Simpson
ROCKERS(1980)

Bill Simpson
MOONSHINE MOUNTAIN(1964); PREACHERMAN(1971)
Bob Simpson
HER MASTER'S VOICE(1936), ed; ZANDY'S BRIDE(1974)
Brock Simpson
PROM NIGHT(1980)
Colin Simpson
PINK STRING AND SEALING WAX(1950, Brit.)
Danny Simpson
Misc. Talkies
BEGGING THE RING(1979, Brit.)
David Simpson
HUE AND CRY(1950, Brit.)
Dianne Simpson
MAN'S FAVORITE SPORT(?)(1964); ISLAND OF LOVE(1963); ROUSTABOUT(1964)
Dick Simpson
MARS NEEDS WOMEN(1966)
Don Simpson
FLASHDANCE(1983), p
1984
BEVERLY HILLS COP(1984), p; THIEF OF HEARTS(1984), p
Donald Simpson
MR. BROWN COMES DOWN THE HILL(1966, Brit.); CANNONBALL(1976, U.S./ Hong Kong)
Donald C. Simpson
CANNONBALL(1976, U.S./Hong Kong), w
Dorothy Simpson
Misc. Silents
FINDERS KEEPERS(1921)
Earl Simpson
Silents
KINGFISHER'S ROOST, THE(1922)
Edward Simpson
MIND OF MR. SOAMES, THE(1970, Brit.), w
Evan P. Simpson
UNINVITED, THE(1944)
Evar Simpson
HORRIBLE DR. HICHCOCK, THE(1964, Ital.)
Frank Simpson
WHITE STALLION(1947), w; FAIL SAFE(1964); YOU'RE A BIG BOY NOW(1966); ALICE'S RESTAURANT(1969); EASY MONEY(1983)
George Simpson
1984
ROADHOUSE 66(1984), w
Georgina Simpson
CARRY ON AGAIN, DOCTOR(1969, Brit.); OTLEY(1969, Brit.); WALK A CROOKED PATH(1969, Brit.); PERFECT FRIDAY(1970, Brit.)
Gertrude Simpson
JUNGLE BRIDE(1933); HAPPY LANDING(1934); HOLLYWOOD BOULE-
VARD(1936); EXCLUSIVE(1937); INTERNES CAN'T TAKE MONEY(1937); SARATO-
GA(1937); THUNDER TRAIL(1937); TRUE CONFESSION(1937); WOMEN, THE(1939); SHOP AROUND THE CORNER, THE(1940); THIRD FINGER, LEFT HAND(1940)
Gillian Simpson
WITCH WITHOUT A BROOM, A(1967, U.S./Span.)
Gloria Ann Simpson
TIGHT SPOT(1955); EDDY DUCHIN STORY, THE(1956)
Gloria Simpson
HEART WITHIN, THE(1957, Brit.)
Gregory Simpson
Misc. Talkies
ROGUE, THE(1976), d
Harold Simpson
DERELICT, THE(1937, Brit.), d&w; GIRL THIEF, THE(1938), w; SPY OF NAPOLE-
ON(1939, Brit.), w; TREACHERY ON THE HIGH SEAS(1939, Brit.), w; LOST ON THE WESTERN FRONT(1940, Brit.), w
Silents
PHANTOM PICTURE, THE(1916, Brit.), w; VEILED WOMAN, THE(1917, Brit.), w
Helen Simpson
MURDER(1930, Brit.), w; SABOTAGE(1937, Brit.), w; SARABAND(1949, Brit.), w; UNDER CAPRICORN(1949), w
Henrietta Simpson
Silents
JOAN OF THE WOODS(1918)
Hugh Simpson
TOUGH ASSIGNMENT(1949)
Ivan Simpson
DISRAELI(1929); EVIDENCE(1929); GREEN GODDESS, THE(1930); INSIDE THE LINES(1930); ISLE OF ESCAPE(1930); MANSLAUGHTER(1930); OLD EN-
GLISH(1930); SEA GOD, THE(1930); WAY OF ALL MEN, THE(1930); I LIKE YOUR NERVE(1931); LADY WHO DARED, THE(1931); MILLIONAIRE, THE(1931); RECK-
LESS HOUR, THE(1931); SAFE IN HELL(1931); MAN WHO PLAYED GOD, THE(1932); PASSPORT TO HELL(1932); PHANTOM OF CRESTWOOD, THE(1932); THE CRASH(1932); BLIND ADVENTURE(1933); CHARLIE CHAN'S GREATEST CASE(1933); MIDNIGHT MARY(1933); MONKEY'S PAW, THE(1933); PAST OF MARY HOLMES, THE(1933); SILK EXPRESS, THE(1933); VOLTAIRE(1933); AMONG THE MISSING(1934); BRITISH AGENT(1934); HOUSE OF ROTHSCHILD, THE(1934); MAN OF TWO WORLDS(1934); MYSTERY OF MR. X, THE(1934); WORLD MOVES ON, THE(1934); DAVID COPPERFIELD(1935); EAST OF JAVA(1935); MARK OF THE VAMPIRE(1935); MUTINY ON THE BOUNTY(1935); PERFECT GENTLEMAN, THE(1935); SHADOW OF A DOUBT(1935); SPLENDOR(1935); LITTLE LORD FAUNT-
LEROY(1936); MARY OF SCOTLAND(1936); SMALL TOWN GIRL(1936); TROUBLE FOR TWO(1936); LONDON BY NIGHT(1937); ADVENTURES OF ROBIN HOOD, THE(1938); BARONESS AND THE BUTLER, THE(1938); BOOLOO(1938); INVISIBLE ENEMY(1938); HOUND OF THE BASKERVILLES, THE(1939); MADE FOR EACH OTHER(1939); NEVER SAY DIE(1939); RULERS OF THE SEA(1939); TOWER OF LONDON(1939); EARL OF CHICAGO, THE(1940); INVISIBLE MAN RETURNS, THE(1940); NEW MOON(1940); BODY DISAPPEARS, THE(1941); EAGLE SQUA-
DRON(1942); MALE ANIMAL, THE(1942); NAZI AGENT(1942); NIGHTMARE(1942); RANDOM HARVEST(1942); THEY ALL KISSED THE BRIDE(1942); ABOVE SUSPI-
CION(1943); FOREVER AND A DAY(1943); GOVERNMENT GIRL(1943); MY KING-

DOM FOR A COOK(1943); THIS LAND IS MINE(1943); TWO WEEKS TO LIVE(1943); YOUTH ON PARADE(1943); HOUR BEFORE THE DAWN, THE(1944); JANE EYRE(1944)
Misc. Talkies
HER SECRET(1933)
Silents
OUT OF THE DRIFTS(1916); MAN WHO PLAYED GOD, THE(1922); MISS BLUEBEARD(1925); WOMANHANDLED(1925); KISS FOR CINDERELLA, A(1926)

Ivan F. Simpson
CAPTAIN BLOOD(1935); GREAT IMPERSONATION, THE(1935); LLOYDS OF LONDON(1936); MAID OF SALEM(1937); NIGHT OF MYSTERY(1937); PRINCE AND THE PAUPER, THE(1937); MARIE ANTOINETTE(1938)

Janet Simpson
HARDCORE(1979)

John Simpson
DAY OF THE TRIFFIDS, THE(1963)

Kevin Simpson
GOODBYE PORK PIE(1981, New Zealand)

Lane Simpson
INDEPENDENCE DAY(1983)

Lanny Simpson
SHAMROCK HILL(1949); THERE'S A GIRL IN MY HEART(1949)

Liz Simpson
GOODBYE PORK PIE(1981, New Zealand)

Marcus Simpson
CLUE OF THE MISSING APE, THE(1953, Brit.)

Mark Simpson
1984
BIRDY(1984)

Mary Simpson
KID FROM BOOKLYN, THE(1946)

Mickey Simpson
FREE, BLONDE AND 21(1940); HONOLULU LU(1941); IN THE NAVY(1941); KEEP 'EM FLYING(1941); OBLIGING YOUNG LADY(1941); ARABIAN NIGHTS(1942); FALCON TAKES OVER, THE(1942); NO TIME FOR LOVE(1943); MY DARLING CLEMENTINE(1946); ROAD TO THE BIG HOUSE(1947); SLAVE GIRL(1947); SONG OF SCHEHERAZADE(1947); TARZAN AND THE HUNTRESS(1947); WISTFUL WIDOW OF WAGON GAP, THE(1947); ARGYLE SECRETS, THE(1948); FORT APACHE(1948); RIVER LADY(1948); THAT WONDERFUL URGE(1948); THREE MUSKETEERS, THE(1948); FIGHTING KENTUCKIAN(1949); IT HAPPENS EVERY SPRING(1949); SHE WORE A YELLOW RIBBON(1949); THEY LIVE BY NIGHT(1949); WAKE OF THE RED WITCH(1949); WOMAN'S SECRET, A(1949); SURRENDER(1950); WABASH AVENUE(1950); WAGONMASTER(1950); WHEN WILLIE COMES MARCHING HOME(1950); HIS KIND OF WOMAN(1951); KENTUCKY JUBILEE(1951); MASK OF THE AVENGER(1951); TEN TALL MEN(1951); APACHE COUNTRY(1952); BELA LUGOSI MEETS A BROOKLYN GORILLA(1952); LEADVILLE GUNSLINGER(1952); WHAT PRICE GLORY?(1952); LION IS IN THE STREETS, A(1953); SAGINAW TRAIL(1953); SALOME(1953); STAR OF TEXAS(1953); THREE SAILORS AND A GIRL(1953); PRINCE VALIANT(1954); ROSE MARIE(1954); I DIED A THOUSAND TIMES(1955); LONE RANGER, THE(1955); LONG GRAY LINE, THE(1955); NEW YORK CONFIDENTIAL(1955); TALL MAN RIDING(1955); GIANT(1956); WORLD WITHOUT END(1956); GUNFIGHT AT THE O.K. CORRAL(1957); UNDERSEA GIRL(1957); WARLOCK(1959); HE RIDES TALL(1964); GREATEST STORY EVER TOLD, THE(1965); GREAT BANK ROBBERY, THE(1969)

Mimi Simpson
SCANDAL INCORPORATED(1956)

N.F. Simpson
ONE WAY PENDULUM(1965, Brit.), w; DIAMONDS FOR BREAKFAST(1968, Brit.), w

Napoleon Simpson
EACH DAWN I DIE(1939); ONE HOUR TO LIVE(1939); ABE LINCOLN IN ILLINOIS(1940); AM I GUILTY?(1940); SANTA FE TRAIL(1940); GREAT LIE, THE(1941); DRUMS OF THE CONGO(1942); GREAT IMPERSONATION, THE(1942); IN THIS OUR LIFE(1942); HAPPY GO LUCKY(1943); MUG TOWN(1943); MUMMY'S CURSE, THE(1944); DIVORCE(1945); RED MENACE, THE(1949)

Noelle Simpson
1984
BLIND DATE(1984)

O. J. Simpson
KLANSMAN, THE(1974); TOWERING INFERNO, THE(1974); KILLER FORCE(1975, Switz./Ireland); CASSANDRA CROSSING, THE(1977); CAPRICORN ONE(1978); FIREPOWER(1979, Brit.)
1984
HAMBONE AND HILLIE(1984)

Patrick Simpson
DIAMOND SAFARI(1958)

Peggy Simpson
SLEEPING CAR(1933, Brit.); CAMELS ARE COMING, THE(1934, Brit.); MY OLD DUTCH(1934, Brit.); FIGHTING STOCK(1935, Brit.); TEMPTATION(1935, Brit.); 39 STEPS, THE(1935, Brit.); EVERYTHING IS THUNDER(1936, Brit.); WHERE THERE'S A WILL(1936, Brit); DARBY AND JOAN(1937, Brit.); TWO OF US, THE(1938, Brit.); YOUNG AND INNOCENT(1938, Brit.)

Peter Simpson
PROM NIGHT(1980), p; MELANIE(1982, Can.), p

Peter R. Simpson
CURTAINS(1983, Can.), p

Ray Simpson
CAN'T STOP THE MUSIC(1980)

Raymond E. Simpson
SUGAR HILL(1974)

Reggie Simpson
PRACTICALLY YOURS(1944)

Reginald Simpson
HONOR OF THE PRESS(1932); WHY SAPS LEAVE HOME(1932, Brit.), w; STAND UP AND CHEER(1934 80m FOX bw); LIVING DANGEROUSLY(1936, Brit.), w; PEPPER(1936); NIGHT CLUB SCANDAL(1937); I AM THE LAW(1938); JUVENILE COURT(1938); WHO GOES NEXT?(1938, Brit.), w; CAFE SOCIETY(1939); FIVE LITTLE PEPPERS IN TROUBLE(1940); TAKE A LETTER, DARLING(1942); THEY WERE EXPENDABLE(1945); POSTMAN ALWAYS RINGS TWICE, THE(1946); UNDERCURRENT(1946); MY FAVORITE BRUNETTE(1947); SUMMER STOCK(1950);

DANGEROUS WHEN WET(1953); EASY TO LOVE(1953); TORCH SONG(1953); TENDER TRAP, THE(1955); HIGH SOCIETY(1956)

Rich Simpson
1984
UNFAITHFULLY YOURS(1984), set d

Richard Simpson
MC VICAR(1982, Brit.)

Rick Simpson
SILENT MOVIE(1976), set d; CAPRICORN ONE(1978), set d; COMA(1978), set d; JUST YOU AND ME, KID(1979), set d; HUNTER, THE(1980), set d; SMALL CIRCLE OF FRIENDS, A(1980), set d; TOM HORN(1980), set d; MAKING LOVE(1982), set d; PERSONAL BEST(1982), set d; SOMETHING WICKED THIS WAY COMES(1983), set d; STAR CHAMBER, THE(1983), set d
1984
JOHNNY DANGEROUSLY(1984), set d; 2010(1984), set d

Robert Simpson
BIG BROWN EYES(1936), ed; FOLLOW YOUR HEART(1936), ed; ONE IN A MILLION(1936), ed; PRESIDENT'S MYSTERY, THE(1936), ed; SPENDTHRIFT(1936), ed; LOVE AND HISSES(1937), ed; THIN ICE(1937), ed; WAKE UP AND LIVE(1937), ed; ALWAYS GOODBYE(1938), ed; JOSETTE(1938), ed; SUBMARINE PATROL(1938), ed; THANKS FOR EVERYTHING(1938), ed; DRUMS ALONG THE MOHAWK(1939), ed; HOUND OF THE BASKERVILLES, THE(1939), ed; SECOND FIDDLE(1939), ed; GRAPES OF WRATH(1940), ed; HUDSON'S BAY(1940), ed; MAN I MARRIED, THE(1940), ed; PUBLIC DEB NO. 1(1940), ed; STAR DUST(1940), ed; BELLE STARR(1941), ed; GREAT AMERICAN BROADCAST, THE(1941), ed; FOOTLIGHT SERENADE(1942), ed; I WAKE UP SCREAMING(1942), ed; MY GAL SAL(1942), ed; SONG OF THE ISLANDS(1942), ed; SPRINGTIME IN THE ROCKIES(1942), ed; CLAUDIA(1943), ed; CONEY ISLAND(1943), ed; SWEET ROSIE O'GRADY(1943), ed; GREENWICH VILLAGE(1944), ed; PIN UP GIRL(1944), ed; SOMETHING FOR THE BOYS(1944), ed; DIAMOND HORSESHOE(1945), ed; JUNIOR MISS(1945), ed; CLAUDIA AND DAVID(1946), ed; DO YOU LOVE ME?(1946), ed; HOMESTRETCH, THE(1947), ed; MIRACLE ON 34TH STREET, THE(1947), ed; SHOCKING MISS PILGRIM, THE(1947), ed; APARTMENT FOR PEGGY(1948), ed; CHICKEN EVERY SUNDAY(1948), ed; FURY AT FURNACE CREEK(1948), ed; SLATTERY'S HURRICANE(1949), ed; TAKE ME OUT TO THE BALL GAME(1949); AMERICAN GUERRILLA IN THE PHILIPPINES, AN(1950), ed; BIG LIFT, THE(1950), ed; FOR HEAVEN'S SAKE(1950), ed; WABASH AVENUE(1950), ed; AS YOUNG AS YOU FEEL(1951), ed; I CAN GET IT FOR YOU WHOLESALE(1951), ed; MODEL AND THE MARRIAGE BROKER, THE(1951), ed; RAWHIDE(1951), ed; MY WIFE'S BEST FRIEND(1952), ed; PRIDE OF ST. LOUIS, THE(1952), ed; CALL ME MADAM(1953), ed; GIRL NEXT DOOR, THE(1953), ed; INFERNO(1953), ed; TREASURE OF THE GOLDEN CONDOR(1953), ed; PRINCE VALIANT(1954), ed; THERE'S NO BUSINESS LIKE SHOW BUSINESS(1954), ed; MAN CALLED PETER, THE(1955), ed; VIEW FROM POMPEY'S HEAD, THE(1955), ed; VIRGIN QUEEN, THE(1955), ed; KING AND I, THE(1956), ed; DESK SET(1957), ed; KISS THEM FOR ME(1957), ed; TRUE STORY OF JESSE JAMES, THE(1957), ed; MARDI GRAS(1958), ed; SOUTH PACIFIC(1958), ed; BEST OF EVERYTHING, THE(1959), ed; WOMAN OBSESSED(1959), ed; CANCAN(1960), ed; HIGH TIME(1960), ed; MARINES, LET'S GO(1961), ed; SANCTUARY(1961), ed; CHAPMAN REPORT, THE(1962), ed; MOVE OVER, DARLING(1963), ed; STRIPPER, THE(1963), ed; FATE IS THE HUNTER(1964), ed; DO NOT DISTURB(1965), ed; REWARD, THE(1965), ed; CAPRICE(1967), ed; TONY ROME(1967), ed; DETECTIVE, THE(1968), ed; LADY IN CEMENT(1968), ed; UNDEFEATED, THE(1969), ed; 100 RIFLES(1969), ed; CHISUM(1970), ed; FOOLS' PARADE(1971), ed; ONE MORE TRAIN TO ROB(1971), ed; SOMETHING BIG(1971), ed

Robert J. T. Simpson
TOMAHAWK(1951)

Robert L. Simpson
CAHILL, UNITED STATES MARSHAL(1973), ed

Roger Simpson
1984
SQUIZZY TAYLOR(1984, Aus.), w

Ronald Simpson
MEDICINE MAN, THE(1933, Brit.); ONE PRECIOUS YEAR(1933, Brit.); IT'S A COP(1934, Brit.); LUCKY DAYS(1935, Brit.); CALLING THE TUNE(1936, Brit.); HEAD OFFICE(1936, Brit.); NO ESCAPE(1936, Brit.); SONG OF FREEDOM(1938, Brit.); LOVES OF JOANNA GODDEN, THE(1947, Brit.); MINE OWN EXECUTIONER(1948, Brit.); LAST HOLIDAY(1950, Brit.); I'LL NEVER FORGET YOU(1951); LONG DARK HALL, THE(1951, Brit.); CRUEL SEA, THE(1953); LAST MAN TO HANG, THE(1956, Brit.)

Roy Simpson
CUP FEVER(1965, Brit.), p; KADOYNG(1974, Brit.), p

Russell Simpson
INNOCENTS OF PARIS(1929); NOISY NEIGHBORS(1929); SAP, THE(1929); ABRAHAM LINCOLN(1930); AFTER THE FOG(1930); BILLY THE KID(1930); LONE STAR RANGER, THE(1930); ALEXANDER HAMILTON(1931); GREAT, MEADOW, THE(1931); MAN TO MAN(1931); SUSAN LENOX–HER FALL AND RISE(1931); WEST OF THE ROCKIES(1931); FAMOUS FERGUSON CASE, THE(1932); FLAMES(1932); HELLO TROUBLE(1932); LAW AND ORDER(1932); LENA RIVERS(1932); RIDIN' FOR JUSTICE(1932); RIDING TORNADO, THE(1932); SILVER DOLLAR(1932); WHITE EAGLE(1932); FACE IN THE SKY(1933); HELLO, EVERYBODY(1933); CAROLINA(1934); EVER SINCE EVE(1934); FRONTIER MARSHAL(1934); SIXTEEN FATHOMS DEEP(1934); THREE ON A HONEYMOON(1934); WORLD MOVES ON, THE(1934); COUNTY CHAIRMAN, THE(1935); HOOSIER SCHOOLMASTER(1935); MOTIVE FOR REVENGE(1935); PADDY O'DAY(1935); WAY DOWN EAST(1935); WEST OF THE PECOS(1935); CRIME OF DR. FORBES(1936); GIRL OF THE OZARKS(1936); HARVESTER, THE(1936); MAN HUNT(1936); RAMONA(1936); SAN FRANCISCO(1936); GREEN LIGHT(1937); MAID OF SALEM(1937); MOUNTAIN JUSTICE(1937); PARADISE ISLE(1937); THAT I MAY LIVE(1937); YODELIN' KID FROM PINE RIDGE(1937); GIRL OF THE GOLDEN WEST, THE(1938); GOLD IS WHERE YOU FIND IT(1938); HEART OF THE NORTH(1938); VALLEY OF THE GIANTS(1938); DESPERATE TRAILS(1939); DODGE CITY(1939); DRUMS ALONG THE MOHAWK(1939); GERONIMO(1939); MR. SMITH GOES TO WASHINGTON(1939); WESTERN CARAVANS(1939); YOUNG MR. LINCOLN(1939); BRIGHAM YOUNG–FRONTIERSMAN(1940); GRAPES OF WRATH(1940); SANTA FE TRAIL(1940); THREE FACES WEST(1940); VIRGINIA CITY(1940); WYOMING(1940); BAD MEN OF MISSOURI(1941); CITADEL OF CRIME(1941); LAST OF THE DUANES(1941); SWAMP WATER(1941); TOBACCO ROAD(1941); WILD GEESE CALLING(1941); LONE STAR RANGER(1942); NAZI AGENT(1942); SHUT MY BIG MOUTH(1942); SPOILERS, THE(1942); TENNESSEE JOHNSON(1942); WILD BILL

HICKOK RIDES(1942); BORDER PATROL(1943); MOONLIGHT IN VERMONT(1943); RIDING HIGH(1943); WOMAN OF THE TOWN, THE(1943); BIG BONANZA, THE(1944); MAN FROM FRISCO(1944); TALL IN THE SADDLE(1944); TEXAS MASQUERADE(1944); ALONG CAME JONES(1945); INCENDIARY BLONDE(1945); THEY WERE EXPENDABLE(1945); BAD BASCOMB(1946); DEATH VALLEY(1946); LADY LUCK(1946); MY DARLING CLEMENTINE(1946); BOWERY BUCK-AROOS(1947); FABULOUS TEXAN, THE(1947); MILLERSON CASE, THE(1947); ROMANCE OF ROSY RIDGE, THE(1947); ALBUQUERQUE(1948); CORONER CREEK(1948); JOAN OF ARC(1948); SUNDOWN IN SANTA FE(1948); TAP ROOTS(1948); BEAUTIFUL BLONDE FROM BASHFUL BEND, THE(1949); FREE FOR ALL(1949); GAL WHO TOOK THE WEST, THE(1949); TUNA CLIPPER(1949); CALL OF THE KLONDIKE(1950); SADDLE TRAMP(1950); WAGONMASTER(1950); ACROSS THE WIDE MISSOURI(1951); COMIN' ROUND THE MOUNTAIN(1951); FEUDIN' FOOLS(1952); LONE STAR(1952); MA AND PA KETTLE AT THE FAIR(1952); MEET ME AT THE FAIR(1952); SUN SHINES BRIGHT, THE(1953); BROKEN LANCE(1954); SEVEN BRIDES FOR SEVEN BROTHERS(1954); LAST COMMAND, THE(1955); TALL MEN, THE(1955); BRASS LEGEND, THE(1956); FRIENDLY PERSUASION(1956); THESE WILDER YEARS(1956); LONELY MAN, THE(1957); TIN STAR, THE(1957); HORSE SOLDIERS, THE(1959)
Misc. Talkies
CALL OF THE ROCKIES(1931); CALIFORNIA GOLD RUSH(1946); GHOST OF CROSSBONES CANYON, THE(1952)
Silents
GIRL OF THE GOLDEN WEST, THE(1915); CHALLENGE ACCEPTED, THE(1918); BRANDING IRON, THE(1920); OUT OF THE DUST(1920); BUNTY PULLS THE STRINGS(1921); SHADOWS OF CONSCIENCE(1921); SNOWBLIND(1921); ACROSS THE DEAD-LINE(1922); FOOLS OF FORTUNE(1922); KINGDOM WITHIN, THE(1922); RAGS TO RICHES(1922); CIRCUS DAYS(1923); GIRL OF THE GOLDEN WEST, THE(1923); HUNTRESS, THE(1923); RIP-TIDE, THE(1923); VIRGINIAN, THE(1923); NARROW STREET, THE(1924); PAINTED PEOPLE(1924); SPLENDID ROAD, THE(1925); SOCIAL HIGHWAYMAN, THE(1926); ANNIE LAURIE(1927); NOW WE'RE IN THE AIR(1927); OLD SHOES(1927); KID'S CLEVER, THE(1929); TRAIL OF '98, THE(1929)
Misc. Silents
LOVELY MARY(1916); FOOD GAMBLERS, THE(1917); SALT OF THE EARTH(1917); BREAKERS AHEAD(1918); RIDERS OF THE NIGHT(1918); BILL APPERSON'S BOY(1919); BLUE BANDANNA, THE(1919); BRAND, THE(1919); FIGHTING CRESSY(1919); GODLESS MEN(1921); UNDER THE LASH(1921); HUMAN HEARTS(1922); PEG O' MY HEART(1922); WHEN LOVE IS YOUNG(1922); BEAUTY AND THE BAD MAN(1925); EARTH WOMAN, THE(1926); RUSTLING FOR CU-PID(1926); FIRST AUTO, THE(1927); FRONTIERSMAN, THE(1927); GOD'S GREAT WILDERNESS(1927); WILD GEESE(1927); BUSHRANGER, THE(1928); LIFE'S MOCKERY(1928); CALL OF THE ROCKIES(1931)

Scott Simpson
INDEPENDENCE DAY(1983)

Shirlee Simpson
TREASURE ISLAND(1934)

Shirley Simpson
I FOUND STELLA PARISH(1935)

Sloan Simpson
PUSHER, THE(1960)

Tammy Simpson
HOSPITAL MASSACRE(1982)

Tara Simpson
RICH AND FAMOUS(1981)

Toby Simpson
UNMAN, WITTERING AND ZIGO(1971, Brit.)

Tom Simpson
LONG DARK HALL, THE(1951, Brit.), ed; I'LL GET YOU(1953, Brit.), ed; CONTRA-BAND SPAIN(1955, Brit.), ed; STRANGER'S HAND, THE(1955, Brit.), ed; INTENT TO KILL(1958, Brit.), ed; BLUEBEARD'S TEN HONEYMOONS(1960, Brit.), ed; WEEK-END WITH LULU, A(1961, Brit.), ed; MANIAC(1963, Brit.), ed; BRIGAND OF KAN-DAHAR, THE(1965, Brit.), ed; SECRET OF BLOOD ISLAND, THE(1965, Brit.), ed; FROZEN DEAD, THE(1967, Brit.), ed; IT!(1967, Brit.), ed; ONE MILLION YEARS B.C.(1967, Brit./U.S.), ed

Tomy Simpson
NIGHT AND THE CITY(1950, Brit.)

Tony Simpson
WAY OUT, THE(1956, Brit.)

William Simpson
THREE HUSBANDS(1950)

Bennett Sims
HOMEBODIES(1974), w

Bert Sims
END OF THE ROAD, THE(1954, Brit.)

Corie Sims
MARCO POLO JUNIOR(1973, Aus.)

Dorothea Carolyn Sims
I'D CLIMB THE HIGHEST MOUNTAIN(1951)

Dorothy Rice Sims
FOG(1934), w

Eddie Sims
SHADOW OF THE THIN MAN(1941)

Ernest Sims
ROMANCE ON THE RUN(1938), ed

George Sims
MERRY COMES TO STAY(1937, Brit.); ON VELVET(1938, Brit.); DEVIL'S AN-GELS(1967); HIGH COUNTRY, THE(1981, Can.)

Hilda Sims
Silents
DEBT OF HONOR(1922, Brit.); EXPERIMENT, THE(1922, Brit.)
Misc. Silents
FROM SHOPGIRL TO DUCHESS(1915, Brit.); WILL OF HER OWN, A(1915, Brit.)

Jay Sims
GIANT GILA MONSTER, THE(1959), w

Joan Sims
COLONEL MARCH INVESTIGATES(1952,Brit.); MEET MR. LUCIFER(1953, Brit.); DOCTOR IN THE HOUSE(1954, Brit.); WHAT EVERY WOMAN WANTS(1954, Brit.); DOCTOR AT SEA(1955, Brit.); SEA SHALL NOT HAVE THEM, THE(1955, Brit.); SQUARE RING, THE(1955, Brit.); TROUBLE IN STORE(1955, Brit.); WILL ANY

GENTLEMAN?(1955, Brit.); CASH ON DELIVERY(1956, Brit.); DRY ROT(1956, Brit.); KEEP IT CLEAN(1956, Brit.); STARS IN YOUR EYES(1956, Brit.); AS LONG AS THEY'RE HAPPY(1957, Brit.); CARRY ON ADMIRAL(1957, Brit.); JUST MY LUCK(1957, Brit.); NO TIME FOR TEARS(1957, Brit.); SILKEN AFFAIR, THE(1957, Brit.); TEARS FOR SIMON(1957, Brit.); DAVY(1958, Brit.); YOUR PAST IS SHO-WING(1958, Brit.); CARRY ON NURSE(1959, Brit.); LIFE IN EMERGENCY WARD 10(1959, Brit.); ROOM 43(1959, Brit.); CAPTAIN'S TABLE, THE(1960, Brit.); CARRY ON CONSTABLE(1960, Brit.); DOCTOR IN LOVE(1960, Brit.); PLEASE TURN OVER(1960, Brit.); CARRY ON REGARDLESS(1961, Brit.); HIS AND HERS(1961, Brit.); UPSTAIRS AND DOWNSTAIRS(1961, Brit.); WATCH YOUR STERN(1961, Brit.); CARRY ON TEACHER(1962, Brit.); I LIKE MONEY(1962, Brit.); TWICE AROUND THE DAF-FODILS(1962, Brit.); PAIR OF BRIEFS, A(1963, Brit.); STRICTLY FOR THE BIRDS(1963, Brit.); SWINGIN' MAIDEN, THE(1963, Brit.); CARRY ON CLEO(1964, Brit.); NO, MY DARLING DAUGHTER(1964, Brit.); NURSE ON WHEELS(1964, Brit.); BIG JOB, THE(1965, Brit.); SAN FERRY ANN(1965, Brit.); CARRY ON COWBOY(1966, Brit.); CARRY ON SCREAMING(1966, Brit.); CARNABY, M.D.(1967, Brit.); DON'T LOSE YOUR HEAD(1967, Brit.); FOLLOW THAT CAMEL(1967, Brit.); CARRY ON DOCTOR(1968, Brit.); CARRY ON, UP THE KHYBER(1968, Brit.); CARRY ON AGAIN, DOCTOR(1969, Brit.); CARRY ON CAMPING(1969, Brit.); CARRY ON HENRY VIII(1970, Brit.); CARRY ON LOVING(1970, Brit.); CARRY ON UP THE JUNGLE(1970, Brit.); DOCTOR IN TROUBLE(1970, Brit.); MAGNIFICENT SEVEN DEADLY SINS, THE(1971, Brit.); DON'T JUST LIE THERE, SAY SOMETHING!(1973, Brit.); NOT NOW DARLING(1975, Brit.); ONE OF OUR DINOSAURS IS MISSING(1975, Brit.); CARRY ON ENGLAND(1976, Brit.); CARRY ON EMANUELLE(1978, Brit.)
Misc. Talkies
CARRY ON 'ROUND THE BEND(1972, Brit.); CARRY ON ABROAD(1974, Brit.); CARRY ON GIRLS(1974, Brit.); CARRY ON BEHIND(1975, Brit.); CARRY ON DICK(1975, Brit.)

Larry Sims
LAST GANGSTER, THE(1937)

Lee Sims
DINNER AT THE RITZ(1937, Brit.), m

Marilyn Sims
GIGI(1958)

Marley Sims
HERO AT LARGE(1980); TO BE OR NOT TO BE(1983)

Nelson Sims
TOGETHER BROTHERS(1974)

Patrick Sims
BLACK CAT, THE(1966), p

Sami Sims
JACK AND THE BEANSTALK(1970)

Sylvia Sims
IT HAPPENS EVERY THURSDAY(1953); NO TIME FOR TEARS(1957, Brit.); HOSTILE WITNESS(1968, Brit.); SOME OF MY BEST FRIENDS ARE...(1971)

Timothy Sims
RESTLESS ONES, THE(1965)

Tom Sims
FREEWHEELIN'(1976)

Warrick Sims
FIREFOX(1982)

Warwick Sims
TWO A PENNY(1968, Brit.); WILD RACERS, THE(1968); FIGURES IN A LAND-SCAPE(1970, Brit.); 11 HARROWHOUSE(1974, Brit.); MAN WITH TWO BRAINS, THE(1983)

George Simson
GIRL IN TROUBLE(1963), md

Zoran Simujanovic
FRAGRANCE OF WILD FLOWERS, THE(1979, Yugo.), m

Linda Sina
BELLISSIMA(1952, Ital.)

Eli Sinai
SINAI COMMANDOS: THE STORY OF THE SIX DAY WAR(1968, Israel/Ger.)

Jonathan Sinaiko
CITY NEWS(1983), ph

Hans Sinarowsky
LIFE AND LOVES OF MOZART, THE(1959, Ger.)

Dick Sinatra
KNOCK ON ANY DOOR(1949)

Frank Sinatra
LAS VEGAS NIGHTS(1941); SHIP AHOY(1942); HIGHER AND HIGHER(1943); REVEILLE WITH BEVERLY(1943); STEP LIVELY(1944); ANCHORS AWEIGH(1945); TILL THE CLOUDS ROLL BY(1946); IT HAPPENED IN BROOKLYN(1947); KISSING BANDIT, THE(1948); MIRACLE OF THE BELLS, THE(1948); ON THE TOWN(1949); TAKE ME OUT TO THE BALL GAME(1949); DOUBLE DYNAMITE(1951); MEET DANNY WILSON(1952); FROM HERE TO ETERNITY(1953); SUDDENLY(1954); GUYS AND DOLLS(1955); MAN WITH THE GOLDEN ARM, THE(1955); NOT AS A STRANGER(1955); TENDER TRAP, THE(1955); YOUNG AT HEART(1955); AROUND THE WORLD IN 80 DAYS(1956); HIGH SOCIETY(1956); JOHNNY CONCHO(1956), a, p; MEET ME IN LAS VEGAS(1956); JOKER IS WILD, THE(1957); PAL JOEY(1957); PRIDE AND THE PASSION, THE(1957); KINGS GO FORTH(1958); HOLE IN THE HEAD, A(1959); NEVER SO FEW(1959); SOME CAME RUNNING(1959); CAN-CAN(1960); OCEAN'S ELEVEN(1960); PEPE(1960); DEVIL AT FOUR O'CLOCK, THE(1961); MANCHURIAN CANDIDATE, THE(1962); ROAD TO HONG KONG, THE(1962, U.S./Brit.); SERGEANTS 3(1962), a, p; COME BLOW YOUR HORN(1963); FOUR FOR TEXAS(1963); LIST OF ADRIAN MESSENGER, THE(1963); PARIS WHEN IT SIZZLES(1964); ROBIN AND THE SEVEN HOODS(1964), a, p; MARRIAGE ON THE ROCKS(1965); NONE BUT THE BRAVE(1965, U.S./Jap.), a, p&d; VON RYAN'S EXPRESS(1965); ASSAULT ON A QUEEN(1966); CAST A GIANT SHADOW(1966); OSCAR, THE(1966); NAKED RUNNER, THE(1967, Brit.); TONY ROME(1967); DETEC-TIVE, THE(1968); LADY IN CEMENT(1968); DIRTY DINGUS MAGEE(1970); FIRST DEADLY SIN, THE(1980)
1984
CANNONBALL RUN II(1984)

Frank Sinatra, Jr.
BEACH GIRLS AND THE MONSTER, THE(1965), m; MAN CALLED ADAM, A(1966)
Misc. Talkies
PEPPER AND HIS WACKY TAXI(1972)

Nancy Sinatra
FOR THOSE WHO THINK YOUNG(1964); GET YOURSELF A COLLEGE GIRL(1964); MARRIAGE ON THE ROCKS(1965); GHOST IN THE INVISIBLE BIKINI(1966); LAST OF THE SECRET AGENTS?, THE(1966); OSCAR, THE(1966); WILD ANGELS, THE(1966); SPEEDWAY(1968)

Ray Sinatra
HONEYMOON AHEAD(1945), md

Richard Sinatra
BEAST FROM THE HAUNTED CAVE(1960); OCEAN'S ELEVEN(1960); SKI TROOP ATTACK(1960); ROBIN AND THE SEVEN HOODS(1964); NONE BUT THE BRAVE(1965, U.S./Jap.)

Guglielmo Sinaz
CUCKOO CLOCK, THE(1938, Ital.); BEFORE HIM ALL ROME TREMBLED(1947, Ital.); GREAT DAWN, THE(1947, Ital.)

Jean Sincere
LITTLE NIGHT MUSIC, A(1977, Aust./U.S./Ger.)

Andrea Sinclair
1,000 SHAPES OF A FEMALE(1963)

Andrew Sinclair
BEFORE WINTER COMES(1969, Brit.), w; BLUE BLOOD(1973, Brit.), d&w; MALACHI'S COVE(1973, Brit.), p; UNDER MILK WOOD(1973, Brit.), d&w

Annette Sinclair
1984
THIEF OF HEARTS(1984); WEEKEND PASS(1984)

Arthur Sinclair
M'BLIMEY(1931, Brit.); EVENSONG(1934, Brit.); NORAH O'NEALE(1934, Brit.); SING AS WE GO(1934, Brit.); WILD BOY(1934, Brit.); CHARING CROSS ROAD(1935, Brit.); PEG OF OLD DRURY(1936, Brit.); KING SOLOMON'S MINES(1937, Brit.); LAST CURTAIN, THE(1937, Brit.); SHOW GOES ON, THE(1937, Brit.); WELCOME, MR. WASHINGTON(1944, Brit.); HUNGRY HILL(1947, Brit.)

Barry Sinclair
TENTH MAN, THE(1937, Brit.); HALF A SIXPENCE(1967, Brit.)

Bertrand W. Sinclair
Silents
RAIDERS, THE(1921), w

Berty Sinclair
CITY STREETS(1931)

Betty Sinclair
LIGHTNIN'(1930); 'NEATH BROOKLYN BRIDGE(1942); SMART ALECKS(1942); CRAZY KNIGHTS(1944); WHAT A MAN!(1944); CAPTAIN TUGBOAT ANNIE(1945); DOCKS OF NEW YORK(1945); MR. MUGGS RIDES AGAIN(1945); SOMETHING IN THE CITY(1950, Brit.)

Bob Sinclair
Silents
HARDBOILED(1929)

Carol Sinclair
GO, MAN, GO!(1954)

Charles Sinclair
CHASE A CROOKED SHADOW(1958, Brit.), w; SNOW DEVILS, THE(1965, Ital.), w; GREEN SLIME, THE(1969), w

Claire Sinclair
FRISCO KID(1935)

Diane Sinclair
WASHINGTON MASQUERADE(1932); CRADLE SONG(1933); RUSTLERS' ROUNDUP(1933); FIGHTING CODE, THE(1934); DAMAGED LIVES(1937)

Dorothy Sinclair
PENAL CODE, THE(1933); SEVENTH VEIL, THE(1946, Brit.), cos; DAYBREAK(1948, Brit.), cos; THE BEACHCOMBER(1955, Brit.), cos; MAN OF LA MANCHA(1972)

Edward Sinclair
BELLS, THE(1931, Brit.); FIGHTING GENTLEMAN, THE(1932), w; MARRIAGE ON APPROVAL(1934), w; TOWER OF TERROR, THE(1942, Brit.); SARABAND(1949, Brit.); DAD'S ARMY(1971, Brit.)

Elaine Sinclair
REFORM SCHOOL GIRL(1957)

Elizabeth Sinclair
WICKER MAN, THE(1974, Brit.)
1984
COMFORT AND JOY(1984, Brit.)

Eric Sinclair
FACES IN THE FOG(1944); SINCE YOU WENT AWAY(1944); MISSING CORPSE, THE(1945); YOUTH ON TRIAL(1945); CLUB HAVANA(1946); CYRANO DE BERGERAC(1950); LONELY HEARTS BANDITS(1950); UNKNOWN MAN, THE(1951); MY MAN GODFREY(1957); WAR OF THE SATELLITES(1958); MA BARKER'S KILLER BROOD(1960); BUTCH CASSIDY AND THE SUNDANCE KID(1969)

Fred Sinclair
SILVER TOP(1938, Brit.)

Gordon John Sinclair
THAT SINKING FEELING(1979, Brit.); GREGORY'S GIRL(1982, Brit.)

Grant Sinclair
TOWN THAT DREADED SUNDOWN, THE(1977), art d

Harold Sinclair
HORSE SOLDIERS, THE(1959), w

Horace Sinclair
ONE THIRD OF A NATION(1939)

Hugh Sinclair
OUR BETTERS(1933); ESCAPE ME NEVER(1935, Brit.); STRANGERS ON A HONEYMOON(1937, Brit.); PRISONER OF CORBAL(1939, Brit.); SECRET FOUR, THE(1940, Brit.); GIRL MUST LIVE, A(1941, Brit.); SAINT'S VACATION, THE(1941, Brit.); ALIBI, THE(1943, Brit.); AT DAWN WE DIE(1943, Brit.); SAINT MEETS THE TIGER, THE(1943, Brit.); FLIGHT FROM FOLLY(1945, Brit.); THEY WERE SISTERS(1945, Brit.); CORRIDOR OF MIRRORS(1948, Brit.); DON'T EVER LEAVE ME(1949, Brit.); GAY LADY, THE(1949, Brit.); NO TRACE(1950, Brit.); ROCKING HORSE WINNER, THE(1950, Brit.); CIRCLE OF DANGER(1951, Brit.); JUDGMENT DEFERRED(1952, Brit.); NEVER LOOK BACK(1952, Brit.); SECOND MRS. TANQUERAY, THE(1952, Brit.); THREE STEPS IN THE DARK(1953, Brit.); WOMAN IN HIDING(1953, Brit.)

Ian Sinclair
SUBURBAN WIVES(1973, Brit.)

Irene Sinclair [Griffith]
Silents
WHITE ROSE, THE(1923), w

Ivy Sinclair
Misc. Talkies
TEAM-MATES(1978)

Jan Sinclair
FINDERS KEEPERS, LOVERS WEEPERS(1968)

Jerry Sinclair
Silents
SO'S YOUR OLD MAN(1926)

Joan Sinclair
HOT CARS(1956)

John Gordon Sinclair
LOCAL HERO(1983, Brit.)

John Sinclair
IT PAYS TO ADVERTISE(1931); MILLION DOLLAR LEGS(1932); KISS AND MAKE UP(1934); SECRET SERVICE OF THE AIR(1939); GREAT AMERICAN BROADCAST, THE(1941); HELLO, FRISCO, HELLO(1943); THEY GOT ME COVERED(1943); 1990: THE BRONX WARRIORS(1983, Ital.)

Johnny Sinclair
HAIL THE CONQUERING HERO(1944)
Silents
GOAT GETTER(1925); ROYAL RIDER, THE(1929)
Misc. Silents
FIGHTING FATE(1925); RAPID FIRE ROMANCE(1926)

Joshua Sinclair
GOLDEN LADY, THE(1979, Brit.), w; JUST A GIGOLO(1979, Ger.), w; SOME LIKE IT COOL(1979, Ger./Aust./Ital./Fr.), w; LILI MARLEEN(1981, Ger.), w; GREAT WHITE, THE(1982, Ital.)

Ken Sinclair
MEAN STREETS(1973)

Kenny Sinclair
TOOTSIE(1982)

Key Sinclair
JUST FOR FUN(1963, Brit.), spec eff

Madge Sinclair
CONRACK(1974); CORNBREAD, EARL AND ME(1975); I WILL ...I WILL ...FOR NOW(1976); LEADBELLY(1976); CONVOY(1978); UNCLE JOE SHANNON(1978)

Malcolm Sinclair
1984
SUCCESS IS THE BEST REVENGE(1984, Brit.)

Mary Sinclair
ARROWHEAD(1953)

Nancy Sinclair
ANNIE(1982)

Patricia Sinclair
COSMIC MONSTERS(1958, Brit.)

Peggy Sinclair
PERMISSION TO KILL(1975, U.S./Aust.)

Peter Sinclair
MAN FROM MOROCCO, THE(1946, Brit.); ESCAPE BY NIGHT(1954, Brit.); TROUBLE IN THE GLEN(1954, Brit.); CROSS CHANNEL(1955, Brit.); ONE JUMP AHEAD(1955, Brit.); TIME OF HIS LIFE, THE(1955, Brit.); LET'S BE HAPPY(1957, Brit.); ZOO BABY(1957, Brit.); HEART OF A MAN, THE(1959, Brit.); WEB OF SUSPICION(1959, Brit.); IN THE WAKE OF A STRANGER(1960, Brit.); COURT MARTIAL OF MAJOR KELLER, THE(1961, Brit.); INVASION(1965, Brit.); OPERATION SNAFU(1965, Brit.); SPACED OUT(1981, Brit.), ph

Richard Sinclair
Misc. Silents
SHOPGIRLS; OR, THE GREAT QUESTION(1914, Brit.)

Robert B. Sinclair
DRAMATIC SCHOOL(1938), d; WOMAN AGAINST WOMAN(1938), d; JOE AND ETHEL TURP CALL ON THE PRESIDENT(1939), d; DOWN IN SAN DIEGO(1941), p; I'LL WAIT FOR YOU(1941), d; MR. AND MRS. NORTH(1941), d; WILD MAN OF BORNEO, THE(1941), d; MR. DISTRICT ATTORNEY(1946), d; THAT WONDERFUL URGE(1948), d

Robert Sinclair
AND ONE WAS BEAUTIFUL(1940), d

Robert H. Sinclair
CAPTAIN IS A LADY, THE(1940), d

Ron Sinclair
CAYMAN TRIANGLE, THE(1977)

Ronald Sinclair
THOROUGHBREDS DON'T CRY(1937); CHRISTMAS CAROL, A(1938); FIVE LITTLE PEPPERS AND HOW THEY GREW(1939); LIGHT THAT FAILED, THE(1939); THEY MADE ME A CRIMINAL(1939); TOWER OF LONDON(1939); EARL OF CHICAGO, THE(1940); FIVE LITTLE PEPPERS AT HOME(1940); FIVE LITTLE PEPPERS IN TROUBLE(1940); OUT WEST WITH THE PEPPERS(1940); THAT HAMILTON WOMAN(1941); DESPERATE JOURNEY(1942); LONG WAIT, THE(1954), ed; TOP BANANA(1954), ch; APACHE WOMAN(1955), ed; FIVE GUNS WEST(1955), ed; DAY THE WORLD ENDED, THE(1956), ed; GIRLS IN PRISON(1956), ed; OKLAHOMA WOMAN, THE(1956), ed; SHE-CREATURE, THE(1956), ed; AMAZING COLOSSAL MAN, THE(1957), ed; DRAGSTRIP GIRL(1957), ed; FLESH AND THE SPUR(1957), ed; INVASION OF THE SAUCER MEN(1957), ed; RUNAWAY DAUGHTERS(1957), ed; SAGA OF THE VIKING WOMEN AND THEIR VOYAGE TO THE WATERS OF THE GREAT SEA SERPENT, THE(1957), ed; VOODOO WOMAN(1957), ed; ATTACK OF THE PUPPET PEOPLE(1958), ed; MACHINE GUN KELLY(1958), ed; SPIDER, THE(1958), ed; WAR OF THE COLOSSAL BEAST(1958), ed; SUBMARINE SEAHAWK(1959), ed; INTRUDER, THE(1962), ed; PREMATURE BURIAL, THE(1962), ed; TOWER OF LONDON(1962), ed; HAUNTED PALACE, THE(1963), ed; RAVEN, THE(1963), ed; YOUNG RACERS, THE(1963), ed; SECRET INVASION, THE(1964), ed; BOUNTY KILLER, THE(1965), ed; DR. GOLDFOOT AND THE BIKINI MACHINE(1965), ed; SERGEANT DEADHEAD(1965), ed; THUNDER ALLEY(1967), ed; TRIP, THE(1967), ed; BIG CATCH, THE(1968, Brit.); HOW TO COMMIT MARRIAGE(1969), ed; MALTESE BIPPY, THE(1969), ed; HOW DO I LOVE THEE?(1970), ed; SWEET CREEK COUNTY WAR, THE(1979), ed

Roy Sinclair
Silents
  DREAM STREET(1921), w
Ruth Sinclair
Misc. Silents
  MAN'S LAW, A(1917); SOME BRIDE(1919); HEART LINE, THE(1921); MAS-
  QUERADER, THE(1922)
Sandra Sinclair
  BLOOD FEAST(1963); SCUM OF THE EARTH(1963)
Sidney Sinclair
Misc. Silents
  SHOPGIRLS; OR, THE GREAT QUESTION(1914, Brit.)
Terrie Sinclair
  CLINIC, THE(1983, Aus.)
Tim Sinclair
  PRIVATES ON PARADE(1982)
1984
  PRIVATES ON PARADE(1984, Brit.)
Toni Sinclair
Misc. Talkies
  LOVE PILL, THE(1971)
Upton Sinclair
  WET PARADE, THE(1932), w; DAMAGED GOODS(1937), w; GNOME-MOBILE,
  THE(1967), w
Silents
  JUNGLE, THE(1914), a, w
Vincent L. Sinclair
  WOMEN OF DESIRE(1968), d
Walter A. Sinclair
Silents
  IS THAT NICE?(1926), w
Chrystin Sinclaire
  GOIN' COCONUTS(1978)
Crystin Sinclaire
  RUBY(1977)
Lynda Sinclaire
Misc. Talkies
  HUSTLER SQUAD(1976)
David Sindaha
  HELL WITH HEROES, THE(1968)
Jose Maria Sonzalez Sinde
  FEMALE BUTCHER, THE(1972, Ital./Span.), p
Miguel G. Sinde
  TO BEGIN AGAIN(1982, Span.), ed
R. R. Sinde
  MUSIC ROOM, THE(1963, India), set d
Pearl Sindelar
Misc. Silents
  FOUR-FOOTED RANGER, THE(1928); MADE-TO-ORDER HERO, A(1928)
Gerald Seth Sindell
  DOUBLE STOP(1968), d, w
Misc. Talkies
  TEENAGER(1975), d
Gerald Sindell
  H.O.T.S.(1979), p, d
Rodger I. Sindell
  DOUBLE STOP(1968), p, w
Donald Sinden
  GIRL IN THE PAINTING, THE(1948, Brit.); CRUEL SEA, THE(1953); DAY TO
  REMEMBER, A(1953, Brit.); MOGAMBO(1953); DOCTOR IN THE HOUSE(1954, Brit.);
  MAD ABOUT MEN(1954, Brit.); YOU KNOW WHAT SAILORS ARE(1954, Brit.);
  JOSEPHINE AND MEN(1955, Brit.); SIMBA(1955, Brit.); THE BEACHCOMBER(1955,
  Brit.); ABOVE US THE WAVES(1956, Brit.); BLACK TENT, THE(1956, Brit.); EYEWIT-
  NESS(1956, Brit.); TIGER IN THE SMOKE(1956, Brit.); ALLIGATOR NAMED DAISY,
  AN(1957, Brit.); DOCTOR AT LARGE(1957, Brit.); MAD LITTLE ISLAND(1958, Brit.);
  CAPTAIN'S TABLE, THE(1960, Brit.); SIEGE OF SIDNEY STREET, THE(1960, Brit.);
  MIX ME A PERSON(1962, Brit.); TWICE AROUND THE DAFFODILS(1962, Brit.);
  OPERATION BULLSHINE(1963, Brit.); YOUR MONEY OR YOUR WIFE(1965, Brit.);
  DECLINE AND FALL... OF A BIRD WATCHER(1969, Brit.); VILLAIN(1971, Brit.);
  RENTADICK(1972, Brit.); DAY OF THE JACKAL, THE(1973, Brit./Fr.); NATIONAL
  HEALTH, OR NURSE NORTON'S AFFAIR, THE(1973, Brit.); ISLAND AT THE TOP
  OF THE WORLD, THE(1974); THAT LUCKY TOUCH(1975, Brit.)
Jeremy Sinden
  STAR WARS(1977); CHARIOTS OF FIRE(1981, Brit.)
Marc Sinden
  WICKED LADY, THE(1983, Brit.)
Jules Sindic
  THESE THIRTY YEARS(1934), ph
Carlo Sindici
  OPEN CITY(1946, Ital.)
Ellen Sinding
Misc. Silents
  SYV DAGER FOR ELISABETH(1927, Swed.)
Leif Sinding
Misc. Silents
  SYV DAGER FOR ELISABETH(1927, Swed.), d
Merrill Sindler
  LEGEND OF NIGGER CHARLEY, THE(1972), art d
Vittorio Sindoni
  BURNING YEARS, THE(1979, Ital.), d, w
Elsie Sindora
Silents
  KID, THE(1921)
M. Sinelnikova
Misc. Silents
  SEEDS OF FREEDOM(1929, USSR)
Vova Sinev
  SON OF THE REGIMENT(1948, USSR)

Chan Sing
  AMSTERDAM KILL, THE(1978, Hong Kong)
Chow Sing
  SMILEY(1957, Brit.)
Hop Sing
Silents
  HEARTS OF MEN(1919)
Jesse Tai Sing
  GUY NAMED JOE, A(1943)
Jessie Tai Sing
  CHINA(1943); KISMET(1944)
Mae Tai Sing
  FORBIDDEN(1953)
Mui Kwok Sing
  CLEOPATRA JONES AND THE CASINO OF GOLD(1975 U. S. Hong Kong)
Wong Hok Sing
  GOLDEN GATE GIRL(1941)
Wong Sing
  MAN BEAST(1956)
James Singelis
1984
  ONCE UPON A TIME IN AMERICA(1984), art d
Alexander Singelow
Misc. Silents
  NOMANDIE(1931), d
Alexander Singer
  COLD WIND IN AUGUST(1961), d; PSYCHE 59(1964, Brit.), d; LOVE HAS MANY
  FACES(1965), d; CAPTAIN APACHE(1971, Brit.), d; GLASS HOUSES(1972), d, w
Bob Singer
  CHARLOTTE'S WEB(1973), art d
Bruce Singer
1984
  MEATBALLS PART II(1984), w
Campbell Singer
  OPERATION DIAMOND(1948, Brit.); DICK BARTON AT BAY(1950, Brit.); HANG-
  MAN'S WHARF(1950, Brit.); SOMEONE AT THE DOOR(1950, Brit.); CASE FOR PC 49,
  A(1951, Brit.); QUIET WOMAN, THE(1951, Brit.); MR. LORD SAYS NO(1952, Brit.);
  SCOTLAND YARD INSPECTOR(1952, Brit.); GIRL ON THE PIER(1953, Brit.);
  MURDER ON MONDAY(1953, Brit.); RINGER, THE(1953, Brit.); TERROR ON A
  TRAIN(1953); TITFIELD THUNDERBOLT, THE(1953, Brit.); YELLOW BALLOON,
  THE(1953, Brit.); FUSS OVER FEATHERS(1954, Brit.); INTRUDER, THE(1955, Brit.);
  RAMSBOTTOM RIDES AGAIN(1956, Brit.); DAVY(1958, Brit.); SQUARE PEG,
  THE(1958, Brit.); YOUNG AND THE GUILTY, THE(1958, Brit.); DEVIL'S DAFFODIL,
  THE(1961, Brit./Ger.); ON THE BEAT(1962, Brit.); POT CARRIERS, THE(1962, Brit.);
  FAST LADY, THE(1963, Brit.); GO KART GO(1964, Brit.); HANDS OF ORLAC,
  THE(1964, Brit./Fr.); NO TREE IN THE STREET(1964, Brit.)
Fred Singer
  TEEN-AGE STRANGLER(1967), ph
George Singer
  TEL AVIV TAXI(1957, Israel), md; RACE FOR YOUR LIFE, CHARLIE
  BROWN(1977), anim
George M. Singer, Jr.
  JIM, THE WORLD'S GREATEST(1976)
Howard Singer
  WAKE ME WHEN IT'S OVER(1960), w
Isaac Bashevis Singer
  MAGICIAN OF LUBLIN, THE(1979, Israel/Ger.), w; YENTL(1983), w
Izzy Singer
  RACHEL, RACHEL(1968); LOOKING UP(1977)
Jerry Singer
  STALAG 17(1953)
John Singer
  MY OLD DUTCH(1934, Brit.); DANDY DICK(1935, Brit.); REGAL CAVALCADE(1935,
  Brit.); THIS GREEN HELL(1936, Brit.); WHAT A MAN!(1937, Brit.); EMIL(1938, Brit.);
  SOMEWHERE IN ENGLAND(1940, Brit.); FRONT LINE KIDS(1942, Brit.); SOME-
  WHERE IN CAMP(1942, Brit.); FLY AWAY PETER(1948, Brit.); SCHOOL FOR
  RANDLE(1949, Brit.); DARK MAN, THE(1951, Brit.); BRAVE DON'T CRY, THE(1952,
  Brit.); COME BACK PETER(1952, Brit.); WHISPERING SMITH VERSUS SCOTLAND
  YARD(1952, Brit.); CRUEL SEA, THE(1953); FURTHER UP THE CREEK!(1958, Brit.);
  GET CHARLIE TULLY(1976, Brit.), w
Johnny Singer
  LOVE ON THE SPOT(1932, Brit.); KING OF THE RITZ(1933, Brit.); SOMETHING
  ALWAYS HAPPENS(1934, Brit.); MY HEART IS CALLING(1935, Brit.); STREET
  SONG(1935, Brit.); GAY OLD DOG(1936, Brit.); KING OF THE CASTLE(1936, Brit.);
  NOT SO DUSTY(1936, Brit.); IT'S NEVER TOO LATE TO MEND(1937, Brit.); DARTS
  ARE TRUMPS(1938, Brit.); DEMON BARBER OF FLEET STREET, THE(1939, Brit.)
Judith Singer
  GLASS HOUSES(1972), w
Larry Singer
  HOUSE ON SORORITY ROW, THE(1983)
Loren Singer
  PARALLAX VIEW, THE(1974), w
Lori Singer
1984
  FOOTLOOSE(1984)
Marc Singer
  GO TELL THE SPARTANS(1978); BEASTMASTER, THE(1982); IF YOU COULD SEE
  WHAT I HEAR(1982)
Marion Singer
Misc. Silents
  PRICE OF HAPPINESS, THE(1916)
Patricia Singer
  LAST TYCOON, THE(1976); I NEVER PROMISED YOU A ROSE GARDEN(1977)
Ray Singer
  HOUSE ACROSS THE BAY, THE(1940), spec eff; SHE GETS HER MAN(1945), w;
  NEPTUNE'S DAUGHTER(1949), w; MASK OF THE DRAGON(1951); PRISONERS OF
  THE CASBAH(1953); JUKE BOX RACKET(1960); MALTESE BIPPY, THE(1969), w

Raymond Singer
BLOODBROTHERS(1978); IT'S MY TURN(1980); ENTITY, THE(1982)
Reuben Singer
AUTHOR! AUTHOR!(1982)
Richard Singer
AMERICAN POP(1981)
Misc. Talkies
GIRLS NEXT DOOR, THE(1979)
Robert Singer
GAY PURR-EE(1962), prod d; MR. MAGOO'S HOLIDAY FESTIVAL(1970), prod d;
CUJO(1983), p; INDEPENDENCE DAY(1983), p
Sandy Singer
JAMBOREE(1957)
Simon "Stuffy" Singer
EMERGENCY WEDDING(1950)
Steve Singer
MS. 45(1981)
Steven L. Singer
MEAT CLEAVER MASSACRE(1977), p
Stuffy Singer
HER TWELVE MEN(1954)
Thomas Singer
MICROWAVE MASSACRE(1983), p, w
Tom Singer
MALIBU HIGH(1979), w
The Singer Midgets
WIZARD OF OZ, THE(1939)
Berta Singerman
NADA MAS QUE UNA MUJER(1934)
Jackie Ward Singers
SHINBONE ALLEY(1971)
Ah Singh
Silents
INTOLERANCE(1916)
Amrik Singh
SIDDHARTHA(1972)
Bhoghwan Singh
CALCUTTA(1947)
Bhogwan Singh
JUNGLE PRINCESS, THE(1936); ROAD TO BALI(1952); BWANA DEVIL(1953);
BRIDE AND THE BEAST, THE(1958); DESERT HELL(1958)
Boswhan Singh
LIVES OF A BENGAL LANCER(1935)
Doris Singh
NORTH BY NORTHWEST(1959)
Gurmuks Singh
MAN WHO WOULD BE KING, THE(1975, Brit.)
Hari Singh
ROMAN HOLIDAY(1953)
Indrani Singh
KANCHENJUNGHA(1966, India)
K.N. Singh
GUIDE, THE(1965, U.S./India)
Keshov Singh
NINE HOURS TO RAMA(1963, U.S./Brit.)
Kimat Singh
MAN WHO WOULD BE KING, THE(1975, Brit.)
Kmark Singh
ROMAN HOLIDAY(1953)
Kuljit Singh
KENNER(1969)
Mohan Singh
DEVIL'S BRIDE, THE(1968, Brit.)
Naranjan Singh
VIRGIN SOLDIERS, THE(1970, Brit.)
Niranjan Singh
HIS MAJESTY O'KEEFE(1953)
Parkie Singh
BAKER'S HAWK(1976), ed
Paul Singh
TYPHOON(1940); KISMET(1944); CALCUTTA(1947); MALAYA(1950); CHAPTER
TWO(1979)
R. Singh
CHARGE OF THE LIGHT BRIGADE, THE(1936)
Raj Singh
1984
INDIANA JONES AND THE TEMPLE OF DOOM(1984)
Ram Singh
LIVES OF A BENGAL LANCER(1935); MOON OVER BURMA(1940); RIVER,
THE(1951); RAINS OF RANCHIPUR, THE(1955)
Ranji Singh
Silents
INTOLERANCE(1916)
Ranveer Singh
LONG DUEL, THE(1967, Brit.), w
Reginald Lal Singh
ELEPHANT WALK(1954)
Reginald Singh
DRAGON'S GOLD(1954)
Shuran Singh
BOMBAY CLIPPER(1942)
Suran Singh
CALCUTTA(1947)
Vidya Singh
KANCHENJUNGHA(1966, India)
Eva Maria Singhammer
HEIDI(1968, Aust.)

Frank Singineau
HEART WITHIN, THE(1957, Brit.)
The Singing Buckaroos
SINGING BUCKAROO, THE(1937)
The Singing Constables
HIS FIGHTING BLOOD(1935)
The Singing Indian Braves
SINGIN' IN THE CORN(1946)
Singles People
NO MORE EXCUSES(1968)
Dennis Singletary
ONE DOWN TWO TO GO(1982)
Anthony Singleton
MIND BENDERS, THE(1963, Brit.); MASQUERADE(1965, Brit.)
Doris Singleton
AFFAIR IN RENO(1957); VOICE IN THE MIRROR(1958)
Eddie Singleton
BLUE COLLAR(1978)
Jack Singleton
Silents
LOVES OF RICARDO, THE(1926)
Joe Singleton
Silents
JUDGE NOT OR THE WOMAN OF MONA DIGGINGS(1915); BAIT, THE(1921)
Misc. Silents
SHARK MONROE(1918); OPENED SHUTTERS(1921)
Joe E. Singleton
Silents
SQUAW MAN, THE(1914)
Joseph Singleton
Silents
BREWSTER'S MILLIONS(1914); GIRL FROM HIS TOWN, THE(1915); JORDAN IS A
HARD ROAD(1915); GOOD BAD MAN, THE(1916); REGGIE MIXES IN(1916); WILD
AND WOOLLY(1917); INSIDE THE LINES(1918); TOLL GATE, THE(1920); TREAS-
URE ISLAND(1920)
Misc. Silents
GREAT REDEEMER, THE(1920); TOLL GATE, THE(1920)
Joseph E. Singleton
Silents
INFATUATION(1915)
Misc. Silents
LONESOME HEART(1915); MIRACLE OF LIFE, THE(1915); QUEST, THE(1915)
Keith Singleton
STUDENT BODIES(1981)
Mark Singleton
GAMBLER AND THE LADY, THE(1952, Brit.); TAKE A POWDER(1953, Brit.); YOU
LUCKY PEOPLE(1955, Brit.); MOMENT OF INDISCRETION(1958, Brit.); INNOCENT
MEETING(1959, Brit.); NO SAFETY AHEAD(1959, Brit.); TOP FLOOR GIRL(1959,
Brit.); BLUEBEARD'S TEN HONEYMOONS(1960, Brit.); COMPELLED(1960, Brit.);
SENTENCED FOR LIFE(1960, Brit.); ENTER INSPECTOR DUVAL(1961, Brit.); PART-
TIME WIFE(1961, Brit.); GANG WAR(1962, Brit.); MURDER IN EDEN(1962, Brit.);
NIGHT OF THE PROWLER(1962, Brit.); OPERATION SNATCH(1962, Brit.); TRAI-
TORS, THE(1963, Brit.); LOVE IS A WOMAN(1967, Brit.); SALT & PEPPER(1968, Brit.);
GAME FOR VULTURES, A(1980, Brit.)
Penny Singleton
BLONDIE(1938); BOY MEETS GIRL(1938); GARDEN OF THE MOON(1938); MAD
MISS MANTON, THE(1938); MEN ARE SUCH FOOLS(1938); MR. CHUMP(1938);
OUTSIDE OF PARADISE(1938); RACKET BUSTERS(1938); SECRETS OF AN AC-
TRESS(1938); SWING YOUR LADY(1938); BLONDIE BRINGS UP BABY(1939);
BLONDIE MEETS THE BOSS(1939); BLONDIE TAKES A VACATION(1939); BLON-
DIE HAS SERVANT TROUBLE(1940); BLONDIE ON A BUDGET(1940); BLONDIE
PLAYS CUPID(1940); BLONDIE GOES LATIN(1941); BLONDIE IN SOCIETY(1941);
GO WEST, YOUNG LADY(1941); BLONDIE FOR VICTORY(1942); BLONDIE GOES TO
COLLEGE(1942); BLONDIE'S BLESSED EVENT(1942); FOOTLIGHT GLA-
MOUR(1943); IT'S A GREAT LIFE(1943); LEAVE IT TO BLONDIE(1945); BLONDIE
KNOWS BEST(1946); BLONDIE'S LUCKY DAY(1946); LIFE WITH BLONDIE(1946);
YOUNG WIDOW(1946); BLONDIE IN THE DOUGH(1947); BLONDIE'S ANNIVER-
SARY(1947); BLONDIE'S BIG MOMENT(1947); BLONDIE'S HOLIDAY(1947); BLON-
DIE'S REWARD(1948); BLONDIE'S SECRET(1948); BLONDIE HITS THE
JACKPOT(1949); BLONDIE'S BIG DEAL(1949); BEWARE OF BLONDIE(1950); BLON-
DIE'S HERO(1950); BEST MAN, THE(1964)
Ralph Singleton
TAXI DRIVER(1976)
Rya Singleton
BLUE COLLAR(1978)
Steve Singleton
LOOKS AND SMILES(1982, Brit.), ed
Wilfred Singleton
BEAT THE DEVIL(1953), art d
Zuttie Singleton
STORMY WEATHER(1943)
Zutty Singleton
NEW ORLEANS(1947)
Art Singley
MY MAN GODFREY(1936)
Arthur Singley
RIDE, RANGER, RIDE(1936); THIRTEEN HOURS BY AIR(1936); NATION
AFLAME(1937); WINGS OVER HONOLULU(1937)
Frank Singuineau
SIMBA(1955, Brit.); STORM OVER THE NILE(1955, Brit.); SAFARI(1956); THUNDER
OVER TANGIER(1957, Brit.); MUMMY, THE(1959, Brit.); NUN'S STORY, THE(1959);
PUMPKIN EATER, THE(1964, Brit.); SEANCE ON A WET AFTERNOON(1964 Brit.);
WRONG BOX, THE(1966, Brit.); HOT MILLIONS(1968, Brit.); CARRY ON AGAIN,
DOCTOR(1969, Brit.); O LUCKY MAN!(1973, Brit.); PRESSURE(1976, Brit.); FIREPOW-
ER(1979, Brit.)
Ramon Sinha
PRIVATE ENTERPRISE, A(1975, Brit.)

Shivendra Sinha
LONG DUEL, THE(1967, Brit.); LOST CONTINENT, THE(1968, Brit.)
Linda Sini
STRANGER ON THE PROWL(1953, Ital.); THOUSAND EYES OF DR. MABUSE, THE(1960, Fr./Ital./Ger.); SHERLOCK HOLMES AND THE DEADLY NECK-LACE(1962, Ger.); CONJUGAL BED, THE(1963, Ital.); EASY LIFE, THE(1963, Ital.); LOVE AND LARCENY(1963, Fr./Ital.); MAN WHO LAUGHS, THE(1966, Ital.); DOS COSMONAUTAS A LA FUERZA(1967, Span./*Ital.); WILD, WILD PLANET, THE(1967, Ital.)
Petra Siniawski
FIDDLER ON THE ROOF(1971)
Annie Sinigalia
LOVE AND THE FRENCHWOMAN(1961, Fr.)
Gino Sinimberghi
BEFORE HIM ALL ROME TREMBLED(1947, Ital.); THIS WINE OF LOVE(1948, Ital.)
Jeanine Siniscal
PAPER TIGER(1975, Brit.)
Vincenzo M. Siniscalchi
VACATION, THE(1971, Ital.), w
Robert Sinise
BLOOD FEAST(1963), ed; MOONSHINE MOUNTAIN(1964), ed; TWO THOUSAND MANIACS!(1964), ed; COLOR ME BLOOD RED(1965), ed
Sabine Sinjen
GLASS OF WATER, A(1962, Cgr.); MAEDCHEN IN UNIFORM(1965, Ger./Fr.)
Bernhard Sinkel
GERMANY IN AUTUMN(1978, Ger.), d
Abe Sinkoff
EAST SIDE SADIE(1929)
Imre Sinkovits
DIALOGUE(1967, Hung.)
Albert Sinkys
MS. 45(1981)
Nickelas Sinnerella
Silents
JUNGLE, THE(1914)
Sinoel
LE DENIER MILLIARDAIRE(1934, Fr.); ENTENTE CORDIALE(1939, Fr.); BELL-MAN, THE(1947, Fr.)
Pepe Sinoff
DON'T BET ON LOVE(1933)
Pepi Sinoff
HAVE A HEART(1934); MANHATTAN MELODRAMA(1934); PRINCESS O'HA-RA(1935)
Sherree Sinquefield
HUCKLEBERRY FINN(1974)
Arthur H. C. Sintzenich
Silents
OVER THE HILL TO THE POORHOUSE(1920), ph
Hal Sintzenich
Silents
OUT YONDER(1920), ph; HAS THE WORLD GONE MAD!(1923), ph; WHITE ROSE, THE(1923), ph; AMERICA(1924), ph; ISN'T LIFE WONDERFUL(1924), ph; "THAT ROYLE GIRL"(1925), ph; SALLY OF THE SAWDUST(1925), ph
Shane Sinutko
SHAGGY D.A., THE(1976); SCAVENGER HUNT(1979)
Wallace Sinyella
ULZANA'S RAID(1972)
Curt Siodmak
F.P. 1(1933, Brit.), w; F.P. 1 DOESN'T ANSWER(1933, Ger.), w; GIRLS WILL BE BOYS(1934, Brit.), w; IT'S A BET(1935, Brit.), w; TRANSATLANTIC TUNNEL(1935, Brit.), w; NON-STOP NEW YORK(1937, Brit.), w; HER JUNGLE LOVE(1938, w; LOVES OF MADAME DUBARRY, THE(1938, Brit.), w; APE, THE(1940), w; BLACK FRIDAY(1940), w; INVISIBLE MAN RETURNS, THE(1940), w; ALOMA OF THE SOUTH SEAS(1941), w; INVISIBLE WOMAN, THE(1941), w; MIDNIGHT AN-GEL(1941), w; WOLF MAN, THE(1941), w; INVISIBLE AGENT(1942), w; LONDON BLACKOUT MURDERS(1942), w; PACIFIC BLACKOUT(1942), w; FALSE FA-CES(1943), w; FRANKENSTEIN MEETS THE WOLF MAN(1943), w; I WALKED WITH A ZOMBIE(1943), w; MANTRAP(1943), w; PURPLE V, THE(1943), w; SON OF DRACULA(1943), w; CLIMAX, THE(1944), w; HOUSE OF FRANKEN-STEIN(1944), w; LADY AND THE MONSTER, THE(1944), w; FRISCO SAL(1945), w; SHADY LADY(1945), w; BEAST WITH FIVE FINGERS, THE(1946), w; RETURN OF MONTE CRISTO, THE(1946), w; BERLIN EXPRESS(1948), w; TARZAN'S MAGIC FOUNTAIN(1949), w; FOUR DAYS LEAVE(1950, Switz.), w; BRIDE OF THE GORIL-LA(1951), d&w; DONOVAN'S BRAIN(1953), d&w; MAGNETIC MONSTER, THE(1953), d, w; RIDERS TO THE STARS(1954), w; CREATURE WITH THE ATOM BRAIN(1955), w; CURUCU, BEAST OF THE AMAZON(1956), d&w; EARTH VS. THE FLYING SAUCERS(1956), w; LOVE SLAVES OF THE AMAZONS(1957), p,d&w; SHERLOCK HOLMES AND THE DEADLY NECKLACE(1962), w; BRAIN, THE(1965, Ger./Brit.), w; SKI FEVER(1969, U.S./Aust./Czech.), d, w
Robert Siodmak
UNCLE HARRY(1945), d; TEMPEST(1932, Ger.), d; PERSONAL COLUMN(1939, Fr.), d; HATRED(1941, Fr.), d; WEST POINT WIDOW(1941), d; FLY BY NIGHT(1942), d; MY HEART BELONGS TO DADDY(1942), d; NIGHT BEFORE THE DIVORCE, THE(1942), d; SOMEONE TO REMEMBER(1943), d; SON OF DRACULA(1943), d; CHRISTMAS HOLIDAY(1944), d; COBRA WOMAN(1944), d; PHANTOM LADY(1944), d; SUSPECT, THE(1944), d; CONFLICT(1945), w; DARK MIRROR, THE(1946), d; KILLERS, THE(1946), d; SPIRAL STAIRCASE, THE(1946), d; TIME OUT OF MIND(1947), p&d; CRY OF THE CITY(1948), d; CRISS CROSS(1949), d; GREAT SINNER, THE(1949), d; DEPORTED(1950), d; FILE ON THELMA JORDAN, THE(1950), d; WHISTLE AT EATON FALLS(1951), d; CRIMSON PIRATE, THE(1952), d; FLESH AND THE WOMAN(1954, Fr./Ital.), d; RATS, THE(1955, Ger.), d; DEVIL STRIKES AT NIGHT, THE(1959, Ger.), p&d; PORTRAIT OF A SINNER(1961, Brit.), d; ESCAPE FROM EAST BERLIN(1962, Ger.), d; MAGNIFICENT SINNER(1963, Fr.), d; CUSTER OF THE WEST(1968, U.S., Span.), d; FIGHT FOR ROME(1969, Ger./Rum.), d
Misc. Silents
PEOPLE ON SUNDAY(1929, Ger.), d
Sioux Indians of the Rosebud Reservation
MAN CALLED HORSE, A(1970)

Siouxsie and the Banshees
JUBILEE(1978, Brit.), m
Paul B. Sipe
Silents
OUTSIDE WOMAN, THE(1921), w
Tibor Sipeki
WITNESS, THE(1982, Hung.)
Glenn Sipes
PT 109(1963)
J. Law Siple
Misc. Silents
UNBEATABLE GAME, THE(1925), d
Ralph Sipperly
ME AND MY GAL(1932)
Silents
WOMANPOWER(1926); SUNRISE-A SONG OF TWO HUMANS(1927)
Misc. Silents
CANYON OF LIGHT, THE(1926)
Crete Sipple
LIFE BEGINS AT 40(1935); OUR RELATIONS(1936)
Kasimir Sipush
LOVERS OF TERUEL, THE(1962, Fr.), md
Sir Lancelot
GHOST SHIP, THE(1943); ROMANCE ON THE HIGH SEAS(1948)
Gurdial Sira
OCTOPUSSY(1983, Brit.)
Puneet Sira
ARABIAN ADVENTURE(1979, Brit.)
Yacov Ben Sira
1984
SAHARA(1984)
Joe Siracusa
1001 ARABIAN NIGHTS(1959), ed
Vito Siracusa
MIDNIGHT COWBOY(1969)
Marie Sirago
BON VOYAGE(1962)
Charles Siragusa
RE: LUCKY LUCIANO(1974, Fr./Ital.), a, cons
Mark Sirandrews [Mario Serandrei]
HIRED KILLER, THE(1967, Fr./Ital.), ed
Egon Sirany
ASTRO-ZOMBIES, THE(1969)
Antoine Sire
MAN AND A WOMAN, A(1966, Fr.)
Gerard Sire
MAN AND A WOMAN, A(1966, Fr.); TO BE A CROOK(1967, Fr.); AND NOW MY LOVE(1975, Fr.)
Pehr-Olof Siren
KREMLIN LETTER, THE(1970)
Juan Sires
TERRACE, THE(1964, Arg.), ed
Jeffrey Sirett
HUE AND CRY(1950, Brit.)
Dan Siretta
THOSE LIPS, THOSE EYES(1980), a, ch
Louis Sirgo
NEW ORLEANS AFTER DARK(1958); FOUR FOR THE MORGUE(1962)
Otto Sirgo
HEROINA(1965)
E.A. Sirianni
IF HE HOLLERS, LET HIM GO(1968)
Joree Sirianni
CHEAP DETECTIVE, THE(1978)
Siriaque
KING SOLOMON'S MINES(1950)
Anthony Siricco, Jr.
SO FINE(1981); EXPOSED(1983)
Niroot Sirichanya
1 2 3 MONSTER EXPRESS(1977, Thai.)
Setta Sirichaya
1 2 3 MONSTER EXPRESS(1977, Thai.)
Anthony Sirico
ONE MAN JURY(1978); LAST FIGHT, THE(1983)
Tony Sirico
LOVE AND MONEY(1982)
Del Sirino
PRETTY BOY FLOYD(1960), m
Ulai Sirisombat
1 2 3 MONSTER EXPRESS(1977, Thai.), prod d & art d
Urai Sirisombat
HOT POTATO(1976), art d
Douglas Sirk [Detlef Sierck]
LA HABANERA(1937, Ger.), d; HITLER'S MADMAN(1943), d; SUMMER STORM(1944), d, w; SCANDAL IN PARIS, A(1946), d; LURED(1947), d; SLEEP, MY LOVE(1948), d; SHOCKPROOF(1949), d; SLIGHTLY FRENCH(1949), d; MYSTERY SUBMARINE(1950), d; FIRST LEGION, THE(1951), p&d; LADY PAYS OFF, THE(1951), d; THUNDER ON THE HILL(1951), d; WEEKEND WITH FATHER(1951), d; HAS ANYBODY SEEN MY GAL?(1952), d; MEET ME AT THE FAIR(1952), d; NO ROOM FOR THE GROOM(1952), d; ALL I DESIRE(1953), d; TAKE ME TO TOWN(1953), d; MAGNIFICENT OBSESSION(1954), d; SIGN OF THE PAGAN(1954), d; TAZA, SON OF COCHISE(1954), d; ALL THAT HEAVEN ALLOWS(1955), d; CAPTAIN LIGHTFOOT(1955), d; NEVER SAY GOODBYE(1956), d; THERE'S AL-WAYS TOMORROW(1956), d; WRITTEN ON THE WIND(1956), d; BATTLE HYMN(1957), d; INTERLUDE(1957), d; TARNISHED ANGELS, THE(1957), d; TIME TO LOVE AND A TIME TO DIE, A(1958), d; IMITATION OF LIFE(1959), d
Brian Sirner
ALL CREATURES GREAT AND SMALL(1975, Brit.)

Sandor Siro
SET, THE(1970, Aus.), ph
Anthony Siroco
FINGERS(1978)
Joe Sirola
SEIZURE(1974)
Joseph Sirola
GREATEST STORY EVER TOLD, THE(1965); STRANGE BEDFELLOWS(1965); CHUKA(1967); HANG'EM HIGH(1968); DELTA FACTOR, THE(1970); HAIL(1973); SUPER COPS, THE(1974)
Eleanor Siron
WONDER WOMEN(1973, Phil.)
Alexander Sirotin
SOPHIE'S CHOICE(1982)
Peggy Sirr
HIGH ROAD TO CHINA(1983)
Marina Sirtis
WICKED LADY, THE(1983, Brit.)
1984
BLIND DATE(1984)
Bob Sirucek
HEARTLAND(1980)
Gilles Siry
HEAT OF THE SUMMER(1961, Fr.), w; HOT HOURS(1963, Fr.), w
Ruth Sisberg
1984
POLICE ACADEMY(1984)
Sheila Sisco
CHEAP DETECTIVE, THE(1978)
Otello Sisi
MAIDEN FOR A PRINCE, A(1967, Fr./Ital.), makeup
1984
LE BAL(1984, Fr./Ital./Algeria), makeup
Bob Sisk
CAREER(1939), p
Jan Sisk
NORTHVILLE CEMETERY MASSACRE, THE(1976)
Robert F. Sisk
DON'T TURN 'EM LOOSE(1936), p; CONDEMNED WOMEN(1938), p
Robert Sisk
CHATTERBOX(1936), p; FARMER IN THE DELL, THE(1936), p; LAST OUTLAW, THE(1936), p; M'LISS(1936), p; PLOUGH AND THE STARS, THE(1936), p; TWO IN REVOLT(1936), p; BORDER CAFE(1937), p; DON'T TELL THE WIFE(1937), p; FLIGHT FROM GLORY(1937), p; OUTCASTS OF POKER FLAT, THE(1937), p; SATURDAY'S HEROES(1937), p; YOU CAN'T BEAT LOVE(1937), p; GO CHASE YOURSELF(1938), p; LAW OF THE UNDERWORLD(1938), p; MAID'S NIGHT OUT(1938), p; MAN TO REMEMBER, A(1938), p; MR. DOODLE KICKS OFF(1938), p; NIGHT SPOT(1938), p; SKY GIANT(1938), p; BAD LANDS(1939), p; DAY THE BOOKIES WEPT, THE(1939), p; FIVE CAME BACK(1939), p; FULL CONFESSION(1939), p; GIRL FROM MEXICO, THE(1939), p; PACIFIC LINER(1939), p; RENO(1939), p; SAINT STRIKES BACK, THE(1939), p; SORORITY HOUSE(1939), p; THEY MADE HER A SPY(1939), p; THREE SONS(1939), p; TWELVE CROWDED HOURS(1939), p; MARINES FLY HIGH, THE(1940), p; MARRIED AND IN LOVE(1940), p; MILLIONAIRE PLAYBOY(1940), p; TOM, DICK AND HARRY(1941), p; FOREST RANGERS, THE(1942), p; STRANGER IN TOWN, A(1943), p; YOUNG IDEAS(1943), p; GENTLE ANNIE(1944), p; LOST ANGEL(1944), p; HIDDEN EYE, THE(1945), p; OUR VINES HAVE TENDER GRAPES(1945), p; BLUE SIERRA(1946), p; BOYS' RANCH(1946), p; COURAGE OF LASSIE(1946), p; LOVE LAUGHS AT ANDY HARDY(1946), p; HILLS OF HOME(1948), p; CHALLENGE TO LASSIE(1949), p; SUN COMES UP, THE(1949), p; TENSION(1949), p; SHADOW ON THE WALL(1950), p; ACROSS THE WIDE MISSOURI(1951), p; IT'S A BIG COUNTRY(1951), p; MAN BEHIND THE GUN, THE(1952), p; THIS WOMAN IS DANGEROUS(1952), p
Joe Sison
W.I.A.(WOUNDED IN ACTION)*1/2 (1966); LOST BATTALION(1961, U.S./Phil.); STEEL CLAW, THE(1961); DYNAMITE JOHNSON(1978, Phil.)
Jose Sison
BACK DOOR TO HELL(1964)
Monirak Sisowath
1984
KILLING FIELDS, THE(1984, Brit.)
Einar Sissener
Misc. Silents
BRIDE OF GLOMDAL, THE(1925, Nor.)
Noble Sissle
Misc. Talkies
MURDER WITH MUSIC(1941)
Richard [Shaw] Sisson
RAZOR'S EDGE, THE(1946)
Rosemary Anne Sisson
RIDE A WILD PONY(1976, U.S./Aus.), w; LITTLEST HORSE THIEVES, THE(1977), w; CANDLESHOE(1978), w; WATCHER IN THE WOODS, THE(1980, Brit.), w
Vera Sisson
Silents
PARADISE GARDEN(1917)
Misc. Silents
HIDDEN SPRING, THE(1917); MARRIED VIRGIN, THE(1918); EXPERIMENTAL MARRIAGE(1919); HIS OFFICIAL FIANCEE(1919); FRIVOLOUS WIVES(1920)
Frederick Sistaine
HUNTER, THE(1980)
Sisters "G"
RECAPTURED LOVE(1930); KISS ME AGAIN(1931)
Sibby Sisti
1984
NATURAL, THE(1984)
Frank Sisto
1984
ONCE UPON A TIME IN AMERICA(1984)

Rocco Sisto
1984
SCREAM FOR HELP(1984)
Joseph Sistrom
LONE WOLF SPY HUNT, THE(1939), p; NIGHT OF JANUARY 16TH(1941), p; STAR SPANGLED RHYTHM(1942), p; WAKE ISLAND(1942), p; DOUBLE INDEMNITY(1944), p; INCENDIARY BLONDE(1945), p; SOMETHING IN THE WIND(1947), p; SAXON CHARM, THE(1948), p; SUBMARINE COMMAND(1951), p; ATOMIC CITY, THE(1952), p; BOTANY BAY(1953), p
William Sistrom
RUNAWAY BRIDE(1930), p; CROOKED CIRCLE(1932), p; WHILE PARIS SLEEPS(1932), p; KEEP 'EM ROLLING(1934), p; DOG OF FLANDERS, A(1935), p; HOT TIP(1935), p; SEVEN KEYS TO BALDPATE(1935), p; BUNKER BEAN(1936), p; MURDER ON A BRIDLE PATH(1936), p; PLOT THICKENS, THE(1936), p; FORTY NAUGHTY GIRLS(1937), p; RACING LADY(1937), p; THERE GOES MY GIRL(1937), p; TOO MANY WIVES(1937), p; BLOND CHEAT(1938), p; EVERYBODY'S DOING IT(1938), p; I'M FROM THE CITY(1938), p; SAINT IN NEW YORK, THE(1938), p; SAINT IN LONDON, THE(1939, Brit.), p; LITTLE ORVIE(1940), p; SAINT'S VACATION, THE(1941, Brit.), p; MAXWELL ARCHER, DETECTIVE(1942, Brit.), p; SUICIDE SQUADRON(1942, Brit.), p; ESCAPE TO DANGER(1943, Brit.), p; SAINT MEETS THE TIGER, THE(1943, Brit.), p; MR. EMMANUEL(1945, Brit.), p; HUNGRY HILL(1947, Brit.), p; WOMAN HATER(1949, Brit.), p
Silents
ANGEL OF BROADWAY, THE(1927), p
Otis Sistrunk
CARWASH(1976)
Fred Siterman
WHEN GANGLAND STRIKES(1956)
John Sithebe
DINGAKA(1965, South Africa)
Jose Sithole
NAKED PREY, THE(1966, U.S./South Africa)
Lisa Sitjar
TWO LOVES(1961)
Emil Sitka
FIGHTING MAD(1948); TEXAS DYNAMO(1950); LET'S GO NAVY(1951); SEA HORNET, THE(1951); PERILOUS JOURNEY, A(1953); PRIVATE EYES(1953); JUBILEE TRAIL(1954); JUNGLE GENTS(1954); JAIL BUSTERS(1955); CRASHING LAS VEGAS(1956); 27TH DAY, THE(1957); THREE STOOGES IN ORBIT, THE(1962); THREE STOOGES MEET HERCULES, THE(1962); THIRTEEN FRIGHTENED GIRLS(1963); THREE STOOGES GO AROUND THE WORLD IN A DAZE, THE(1963); OUTLAWS IS COMING, THE(1965); WATERMELON MAN(1970)
B. Sitko
GORDEYEV FAMILY, THE(1961, U.S.S.R.); HUNTING IN SIBERIA(1962, USSR)
William Sittel
HOUSE ON 92ND STREET, THE(1945), set d
Fred Sittenham
Silents
FINE FEATHERS(1921), d; SCARLET LILY, THE(1923), w
Misc. Silents
CLOTHES(1920), d
Doree Sitterly
SMALL CIRCLE OF FRIENDS, A(1980)
Sitting Bull
Silents
TOM AND HIS PALS(1926)
Sir Osbert Sitwell
PLACE OF ONE'S OWN, A(1945, Brit.), w
Patty Siu
WALK, DON'T RUN(1966)
Ronald Siu
SAMURAI(1945)
Michael Siv
BALLAD OF A SOLDIER(1960, USSR), m
Marion Siva
IT HAPPENED IN ATHENS(1962)
D. Sivakov
WAR AND PEACE(1968, USSR)
Laurie Sivell
VICTORY(1981)
Frank Sivera
NEW YORK, NEW YORK(1977)
Frank Sivero
GAMBLER, THE(1974); GODFATHER, THE, PART II(1974); BILLION DOLLAR HOBO, THE(1977); GOING APE!(1981); DEATH VENGEANCE(1982)
1984
FEAR CITY(1984)
Monique Sivers
PARIS OOH-LA-LA!(1963, U.S./Fr.)
Shelley Siverstein
TWO-MINUTE WARNING(1976)
Andriana Sivieri
BITTER RICE(1950, Ital.); BEHIND CLOSED SHUTTERS(1952, Ital.)
Gyorgy Sivo
LOVE(1972, Hung.), ed
Sirppa Sivori-Asp
MAKE LIKE A THIEF(1966, Fin.)
Eugenie Sivyer
MAYTIME IN MAYFAIR(1952, Brit.)
Eva Six
BEACH PARTY(1963); OPERATION BIKINI(1963)
Roger Six
IF IT'S TUESDAY, THIS MUST BE BELGIUM(1969)
The Six Hits
HELLZAPOPPIN'(1941); KEEP 'EM FLYING(1941)
Six Hits and a Miss
HIT PARADE OF 1941(1940); IF I HAD MY WAY(1940); TIME OUT FOR RHYTHM(1941); ZIEGFELD GIRL(1941); CALL OUT THE MARINES(1942)

The Six Metzetti Brothers
BORDER OUTLAWS(1950)
Six Sizzlers Orchestra
TEMPTATION(1936)
The Six Willys
SEE MY LAWYER(1945)
60 Sherman Fisher Girls
CALLING ALL CROOKS(1938$c Brit.)
Sonny Sixkiller
LONGEST YARD, THE(1974)
Henry Size
Misc. Silents
ASIAN SUN, THE(1921, Ger.)
Philip H. Sizeler
PRETTY BABY(1978)
Robert Sizelove
RED RUNS THE RIVER(1963)
Alla Sizova
SLEEPING BEAUTY, THE(1966, USSR)
Dee Sjendery
BURKE AND HARE(1972, Brit.)
Alf Sjoberg
TORMENT(1947, Swed.), d
Gunnar Sjoberg
WOMAN'S FACE, A(1939, Swed.); NIGHT IN JUNE, A(1940, Swed.); CHILDREN, THE(1949, Swed.); WILD STRAWBERRIES(1959, Swed.); BRINK OF LIFE(1960, Swed.); DEVIL'S EYE, THE(1960, Swed.); LOVE MATES(1967, Swed.)
Tore Sjoberg
SWEDISH WEDDING NIGHT(1965, Swed.), p
Ulla Sjoblem
FLIGHT OF THE EAGLE(1983, Swed.)
Tekia Sjoblom
CRIME AND PUNISHMENT(1948, Swed.)
Ulla Sjoblom
MAGICIAN, THE(1959, Swed.); HERE'S YOUR LIFE(1968, Swed.)
Margareta Sjodin
VIBRATION(1969, Swed.)
Gunnar Sjoeberg
WHALERS, THE(1942, Swed.)
Peder Sjogren
BREAD OF LOVE, THE(1954, Swed.), w
Tage Sjogren
HERE'S YOUR LIFE(1968, Swed.)
Jerry Sjolander
TELL ME IN THE SUNLIGHT(1967), art d
Licka Sjoman
FANNY AND ALEXANDER(1983, Swed./Fr./Ger.)
Vilgot Sjoman
SWEDISH MISTRESS, THE(1964, Swed.), d&w; SHAME(1968, Swed.)
Anne-Charlotte Sjorberg
DEVIL, THE(1963)
Inger Sjorstrand
DEVIL, THE(1963)
Victor Sjorstrom
Misc. Silents
HELL SHIP, THE(1923, Swed.)
Per Sjostedt
1984
DELIVERY BOYS(1984), p
Per Sjostrand
WILD STRAWBERRIES(1959, Swed.); TOUCH, THE(1971, U.S./Swed.)
Henning Sjostrom
MY FATHER'S MISTRESS(1970, Swed.)
Rik Sjostrom
DEVIL'S COMMANDMENT, THE(1956, Ital.), w
Victor Sjostrom
WILD STRAWBERRIES(1959, Swed.)
Misc. Silents
GIVE US THIS DAY(1913, Swed.), d; INGEBORG HOLM(1913, Swed.), d; KISS OF DEATH(1916, Swed.), a, d; MAN THERE WAS, A(1917, Swed.), a, d; OUTLAW AND HIS WIFE, THE(1918, Swed.), a, d; KARIN, INGMAR'S DAUGHTER(1920, Swed.), a, d; PHANTOM CARRIAGE, THE(1921, Swed.), a, d; LOVE'S CRUCIBLE(1922, Swed.), d; HELL SHIP, THE(1923, Swed.), d
Maj Sjowall
LAUGHING POLICEMAN, THE(1973), w
Peggy Sjulstad
SWEET CREEK COUNTY WAR, THE(1979), cos
Herbert Skable
LONNIE(1963), p
George Skaff
MAN BEAST(1956); INCREDIBLE PETRIFIED WORLD, THE(1959); CHAMPAGNE MURDERS, THE(1968, Fr.); TOPAZ(1969, Brit.); FROGS(1972); DETROIT 9000(1973); DON IS DEAD, THE(1973); SMILE(1975); OTHER SIDE OF MIDNIGHT, THE(1977); DIFFERENT STORY, A(1978); WRONG IS RIGHT(1982); WAVELENGTH(1983)
Calvin Skaggs
1984
GO TELL IT ON THE MOUNTAIN(1984), p
William V. Skal
CRIPPLE CREEK(1952), ph
Klaramaria Skala
TRIAL, THE(1948, Aust.)
Lilia Skala
CALL ME MADAM(1953); LILIES OF THE FIELD(1963); SHIP OF FOOLS(1965); CAPRICE(1967); CHARLY(1968); DEADLY HERO(1976); ROSELAND(1977); HEARTLAND(1980); END OF AUGUST, THE(1982); FLASHDANCE(1983); TESTAMENT(1983)
Mary Skalek
DISPUTED PASSAGE(1939)

Georges Skalenakis
APOLLO GOES ON HOLIDAY(1968, Ger./Swed.), d; LOVE CYCLES(1969, Gr.), d
William Skall
LITTLE COLONEL, THE(1935), ph; DANCING PIRATE(1936), ph; RAMONA(1936), ph; LITTLE PRINCESS, THE(1939), ph; MIKADO, THE(1939, Brit.), ph; TO THE SHORES OF TRIPOLI(1942), ph; ALL MINE TO GIVE(1957), ph
William V. Skall
NORTHWEST PASSAGE(1940), ph; RETURN OF FRANK JAMES, THE(1940), ph; BILLY THE KID(1941), ph; VIRGINIA(1941), ph; REAP THE WILD WIND(1942), ph; NIGHT AND DAY(1946), ph; TIME, THE PLACE AND THE GIRL, THE(1946), ph; LIFE WITH FATHER(1947), ph; MY WILD IRISH ROSE(1947), ph; SONG OF SCHEHERAZADE(1947), ph; ROPE(1948), ph; TWO GUYS FROM TEXAS(1948), ph; KIM(1950), ph; BRAVE WARRIOR(1952), ph; EVERYTHING I HAVE IS YOURS(1952), ph; GOLDEN HAWK, THE(1952), ph; HALF-BREED, THE(1952), ph; SILVER CHALICE, THE(1954), ph
Skarine
DRAGON SKY(1964, Fr.)
Antonio Skarmeta
JOURNEYS FROM BERLIN-1971(1980); MALOU(1983)
Karin Skarreso
HOUSE OF 1,000 DOLLS(1967, Ger./Span./Brit.)
George Skarstadt
SHAME(1968, Swed.)
Vance Skarsted
BATTLE TAXI(1955)
Georg Skarstedt
OCEAN BREAKERS(1949, Swed.); TWO LIVING, ONE DEAD(1964, Brit./Swed.)
Toby Skarstedt
WHAT A WAY TO GO(1964), makeup
Vance Skarstedt
MAN OR GUN(1958), p, w; NO PLACE TO LAND(1958), w; RAYMIE(1960); SLIME PEOPLE, THE(1963), w; WALLS OF HELL, THE(1964, U.S./Phil.); ONCE BEFORE I DIE(1967, U.S./Phil.), a, w
Jackie Skarvellis
Misc. Talkies
BODY BENEATH, THE(1970)
Jacqueline Skarvellis
RATS ARE COMING! THE WEREWOLVES ARE HERE!, THE(1972)
Hanna Skarzanka
PARTINGS(1962, Pol.)
Jerzy Skarzynski
SARAGOSSA MANUSCRIPT, THE(1972, Pol.), art d
Skating Avalons
DUMMY TALKS, THE(1943, Brit.)
The Skating Avalons
WALKING ON AIR(1946, Brit.)
Skating Vanities
PIN UP GIRL(1944)
Olaf Skavlan
Misc. Silents
YELLOW TRAFFIC, THE(1914); CONTINENTAL GIRL, A(1915); WHY AMERICA WILL WIN(1918)
B. Skay
Misc. Talkies
LOVE, VAMPIRE STYLE(1971)
Brigitte Skay
24-HOUR LOVER(1970, Ger.); TWITCH OF THE DEATH NERVE(1973, Ital.)
Colin Skeaping
SUPERMAN(1978); SENDER, THE(1982, Brit.), stunts
Mary Skeaping
ANNE OF THE THOUSAND DAYS(1969, Brit.), ch
Sue Skeen
DAYTONA BEACH WEEKEND(1965)
Bonnie Skeet
Misc. Talkies
COMES MIDNIGHT(1940)
Norman O. Skeete
ORGANIZATION, THE(1971), spec eff
Roland Skeete
MC HALE'S NAVY(1964), spec eff; MC HALE'S NAVY JOINS THE AIR FORCE(1965), spec eff; JOURNEY TO SHILOH(1968), spec eff
Roy Skeggs
FRANKENSTEIN AND THE MONSTER FROM HELL(1974, Brit.), p; TO THE DEVIL A DAUGHTER(1976, Brit./Ger.), p; RISING DAMP(1980, Brit.), p
Farmer Skein
Silents
FATAL FINGERS(1916. Brit.)
Misc. Silents
REDEMPTION OF HIS NAME, THE(1918, Brit.)
Peter Skellern
EAST OF ELEPHANT ROCK(1976, Brit.), m
1984
LASSITER(1984)
Arrin Skelley
BON VOYAGE, CHARLIE BROWN(AND DON'T COME BACK)*** (1980)
Hal Skelly
DANCE OF LIFE, THE(1929); WOMAN TRAP(1929); BEHIND THE MAKEUP(1930); MEN ARE LIKE THAT(1930); STRUGGLE, THE(1931); HOTEL VARIETY(1933)
Misc. Talkies
SHADOW LAUGHS(1933)
Peter Skelly
RED RUNS THE RIVER(1963)
Geoffrey Skelton
PERSECUTION AND ASSASSINATION OF JEAN-PAUL MARAT AS PERFORMED BY THE INMATES OF THE ASYLUM OF CHARENTON UNDER THE DIRECTION OF THE MARQUIS DE SADE, THE(1967, Brit.), w
Maxine Skelton
MACBETH(1971, Brit.)

Red Skelton
HAVING WONDERFUL TIME(1938); FLIGHT COMMAND(1940); DR. KILDARE'S WEDDING DAY(1941); LADY BE GOOD(1941); PEOPLE VS. DR. KILDARE, THE(1941); WHISTLING IN THE DARK(1941); MAISIE GETS HER MAN(1942); PANAMA HATTIE(1942); SHIP AHOY(1942); WHISTLING IN DIXIE(1942); DU BARRY WAS A LADY(1943); I DOOD IT(1943); THOUSANDS CHEER(1943); WHISTLING IN BROOKLYN(1943); BATHING BEAUTY(1944); ZIEGFELD FOLLIES(1945); SHOW-OFF, THE(1946); MERTON OF THE MOVIES(1947); FULLER BRUSH MAN(1948); SOUTHERN YANKEE, A(1948); NEPTUNE'S DAUGHTER(1949); DUCHESS OF IDAHO, THE(1950); FULLER BRUSH GIRL, THE(1950); THREE LITTLE WORDS(1950); WATCH THE BIRDIE(1950); YELLOW CAB MAN, THE(1950); EXCUSE MY DUST(1951); TEXAS CARNIVAL(1951); LOVELY TO LOOK AT(1952); CLOWN, THE(1953); GREAT DIAMOND ROBBERY(1953); HALF A HERO(1953); AROUND THE WORLD IN 80 DAYS(1956); PUBLIC PIGEON NO. 1(1957); OCEAN'S ELEVEN(1960); THOSE MAGNIFICENT MEN IN THEIR FLYING MACHINES; OR HOW I FLEW FROM LONDON TO PARIS IN 25 HOURS AND 11 MINUTES(1965, Brit.)

Robert Skelton
HIGH BARBAREE(1947); HOMECOMING(1948)

Roy Skelton
THERE'S A GIRL IN MY SOUP(1970, Brit.)

Terence Skelton
VICTOR/VICTORIA(1982)

Terry Skelton
MAN IN THE MIDDLE(1964, U.S./Brit.)

Tiny Skelton
THUNDER OVER TEXAS(1934); WAY OF THE WEST, THE(1934); TIMBER TERRORS(1935)

Carl-Olov Skeppstedt
NAKED NIGHT, THE(1956, Swed.), ed; BRINK OF LIFE(1960, Swed.), ed; DREAMS(1960, Swed.), ed; WOMAN OF DARKNESS(1968, Swed.), ed; DUET FOR CANNIBALS(1969, Swed.), ed

Lena Skerla
FIRE WITHIN, THE(1964, Fr./Ital.); 24 HOURS IN A WOMAN'S LIFE(1968, Fr./Ger.)

Tom Skerrit
DEAD ZONE, THE(1983)

Tom Skerritt
UP IN SMOKE(1978); WAR HUNT(1962); ONE MAN'S WAY(1964); THOSE CALLOWAYS(1964); M(1970); WILD ROVERS(1971); FUZZ(1972); BIG BAD MAMA(1974); THIEVES LIKE US(1974); DEVIL'S RAIN, THE(1975, U.S./Mex.); TURNING POINT, THE(1977); ICE CASTLES(1978); ALIEN(1979); SAVAGE HARVEST(1981); SILENCE OF THE NORTH(1981, Can.); DEATH VENGEANCE(1982)
Misc. Talkies
RUN, RUN, JOE!(1974)

Susan Skersick
GREEN SLIME, THE(1969)

Bartholomew Sketch
IVORY HUNTER(1952, Brit.); ODONGO(1956, Brit.); SAFARI(1956); BEYOND MOMBASA(1957)

Bethlehem Sketch
WEST OF ZANZIBAR(1954, Brit.)

Lea Sketchley
HANGOVER SQUARE(1945)

Les Sketchley
GUNGA DIN(1939); LODGER, THE(1944); MR. WINKLE GOES TO WAR(1944); T-MEN(1947); SNIPER, THE(1952); 23 PACES TO BAKER STREET(1956)

Leslie Sketchley
TIGER ROSE(1930); PRISONER OF ZENDA, THE(1937); MRS. MINIVER(1942); THEY WERE EXPENDABLE(1945); UP IN CENTRAL PARK(1948); ELEPHANT WALK(1954)

Skidaddle
TUNNEL OF LOVE, THE(1958), m/l

Andrew Skidd
RECOMMENDATION FOR MERCY(1975, Can.)

Bob Skidmore
MONDO TRASHO(1970)

Graham Skidmore
MAN IN THE MIDDLE(1964, U.S./Brit.)

Jimmy Skidmore
THEATRE ROYAL(1943, Brit.)

Margie Skidmore
MONDO TRASHO(1970)

George Skier
CITY WITHOUT MEN(1943), w

Oswald Skilbeck
TEMPORARY WIDOW, THE(1930, Ger./Brit.); MURDER ON THE SECOND FLOOR(1932, Brit.)

Marlin Skiles
23 ½ HOURS LEAVE(1937), md; HIT PARADE OF 1943(1943), m; IMPATIENT YEARS, THE(1944), m; KANSAS CITY KITTY(1944), md; MAN FROM FRISCO(1944), m; MEET MISS BOBBY SOCKS(1944), md; STRANGE AFFAIR(1944), m; OVER 21(1945), m; SHE WOULDN'T SAY YES(1945), m; THOUSAND AND ONE NIGHTS, A(1945), m; GALLANT JOURNEY(1946), m; GILDA(1946), ph; WALLS CAME TUMBLING DOWN, THE(1946), m; DEAD RECKONING(1947), m; FRAMED(1947), m; MICKEY(1948), m; CALLAWAY WENT THATAWAY(1951), m; CAVALRY SCOUT(1951), m; FLIGHT TO MARS(1951), m; LION HUNTERS, THE(1951), m, md; ALADDIN AND HIS LAMP(1952), m; ARMY BOUND(1952), m; BATTLE ZONE(1952), m; FLAT TOP(1952), m; FORT OSAGE(1952), m; HIAWATHA(1952), m; RODEO(1952), m; ROSE BOWL STORY, THE(1952), m; WAGONS WEST(1952), m; WILD STALLION(1952), m; FIGHTER ATTACK(1953), m; LOOSE IN LONDON(1953), md; MAZE, THE(1953), m; PRIVATE EYES(1953), md; ROAR OF THE CROWD(1953), m; SAFARI DRUMS(1953), m; SON OF BELLE STARR(1953), m; WHITE LIGHTNING(1953), m; ARROW IN THE DUST(1954), m; CHALLENGE THE WILD(1954), m; JUNGLE GENTS(1954), md; PARIS PLAYBOYS(1954), m, md; PRIDE OF THE BLUE GRASS(1954), m; RETURN FROM THE SEA(1954), m; ANNAPOLIS STORY, AN(1955), m; BOWERY TO BAGDAD(1955), md; DIAL RED O(1955), m; HIGH SOCIETY(1955), md; JAIL BUSTERS(1955), md; LORD OF THE JUNGLE(1955), md; SUDDEN DANGER(1955), m; CALLING HOMICIDE(1956), m; CANYON RIVER(1956), m; CRASHING LAS VEGAS(1956), md; DIG THAT URANIUM(1956), md; HOT SHOTS(1956), m, md; SPY CHASERS(1956), md; YOUNG GUNS, THE(1956), m; CHAIN OF EVIDENCE(1957), m; DISEMBODIED, THE(1957), m; FOOTSTEPS IN THE NIGHT(1957), m; HOLD THAT HYPNOTIST(1957), md; LOOKING FOR DANGER(1957), md; MY GUN IS QUICK(1957), m; SPOOK CHASERS(1957), md; UP IN SMOKE(1957), md; BEAST OF BUDAPEST, THE(1958), m; COLE YOUNGER, GUNFIGHTER(1958), m; IN THE MONEY(1958), m; JOY RIDE(1958), m; MAN FROM GOD'S COUNTRY(1958), m; QUANTRILL'S RAIDERS(1958), m; QUEEN OF OUTER SPACE(1958), m; BATTLE CRY(1959), m; KING OF THE WILD STALLIONS(1959), m; THE HYPNOTIC EYE(1960), m; DEADLY COMPANIONS, THE(1961), m; GUNFIGHT AT COMANCHE CREEK(1964), m; SHEPHERD OF THE HILLS, THE(1964), m; STRANGLER, THE(1964), m; INDIAN PAINT(1965), m; VIOLENT ONES, THE(1967), m; DAYTON'S DEVILS(1968), m; RESURRECTION OF ZACHARY WHEELER, THE(1971), m

Martin Skiles
RELENTLESS(1948), m; JALOPY(1953), m

Merlin Skiles
GREAT GUY(1936), md

Marlin Skilks
FORT MASSACRE(1958), m

George Skillan
DREYFUS CASE, THE(1931, Brit.); SPITFIRE(1943, Brit.)
Silents
MERCHANT OF VENICE, THE(1916, Brit.)

Suzanne Skillen
SCARECROW IN A GARDEN OF CUCUMBERS(1972)

Robert Skilling
THEY ALL LAUGHED(1981)

Skinnay Ennis and His Orchestra
SWING IT SOLDIER(1941)

Skinnay Ennis and the Groove Boys
FOLLOW THE BAND(1943)

Skinnay Ennis Band
RADIO STARS ON PARADE(1945)

Skinnay Ennis' Band
LET'S GO STEADY(1945)

Skinnay Ennis' Orchestra
SLEEPYTIME GAL(1942)

Anita Skinner
GIRLFRIENDS(1978)
1984
SOLE SURVIVOR(1984)

Ann Skinner
RETURN OF THE SOLDIER, THE(1983, Brit.), p
1984
SECRET PLACES(1984, Brit.), p

Arthur Skinner
KID FOR TWO FARTHINGS, A(1956, Brit.); ROTTEN TO THE CORE(1956, Brit.); I'M ALL RIGHT, JACK(1959, Brit.)

Carole Skinner
ELIZA FRASER(1976, Aus.); MY BRILLIANT CAREER(1980, Aus.); HEATWAVE(1983, Aus.); MONKEY GRIP(1983, Aus.)

Colin Skinner
Misc. Talkies
UPS AND DOWNS(1981)

Cornelia Otis Skinner
STAGE DOOR CANTEEN(1943); OUR HEARTS WERE YOUNG AND GAY(1944), w; UNINVITED, THE(1944); GIRL IN THE RED VELVET SWING, THE(1955); PLEASURE OF HIS COMPANY, THE(1961), w; SWIMMER, THE(1968)

Cornelia Skinner
Silents
KISMET(1920)

Edna Skinner
KISSING BANDIT, THE(1948); EASY TO LOVE(1953); LONG, LONG TRAILER, THE(1954); SECOND GREATEST SEX, THE(1955); FRIENDLY PERSUASION(1956)

Frank Skinner
OUTLAW EXPRESS(1938), m; DESTRY RIDES AGAIN(1939), m; FIRST LOVE(1939), m; SON OF FRANKENSTEIN(1939), m; SUN NEVER SETS, THE(1939), m; TOWER OF LONDON(1939), m; INVISIBLE MAN RETURNS, THE(1940), m; MY LITTLE CHICKADEE(1940), m; SEVEN SINNERS(1940), m; APPOINTMENT FOR LOVE(1941), m; FLAME OF NEW ORLEANS, THE(1941), m; NEVER GIVE A SUCKER AN EVEN BREAK(1941), m; ARABIAN NIGHTS(1942), m; EAGLE SQUADRON(1942), m; LADY IN A JAM(1942), m; PITTSBURGH(1942), m; SABOTEUR(1942), m; SHERLOCK HOLMES AND THE SECRET WEAPON(1942), m; SHERLOCK HOLMES AND THE VOICE OF TERROR(1942), m; WHO DONE IT?(1942), m; AMAZING MRS. HOLLIDAY(1943), m; FIRED WIFE(1943), m; GUNG HO!(1943), m; SHERLOCK HOLMES IN WASHINGTON(1943), m; WE'VE NEVER BEEN LICKED(1943), m; WHITE SAVAGE(1943), m; DESTINY(1944), m; SUSPECT, THE(1944), m; BLONDE RANSOM(1945), m; DALTONS RIDE AGAIN, THE(1945), md; FRONTIER GAL(1945), m, md; PILLOW OF DEATH(1945), m; SHE GETS HER MAN(1945), md; STRANGE CONFESSION(1945), md; UNDER WESTERN SKIES(1945), md; BLACK ANGEL(1946), m; CANYON PASSAGE(1946), m, md; IDEA GIRL(1946), md; NIGHT IN PARADISE, A(1946), m&md; RUNAROUND, THE(1946), m; SWELL GUY(1946), m; EGG AND I, THE(1947), m; EXILE, THE(1947), m; I'LL BE YOURS(1947), m; RIDE THE PINK HORSE(1947), m; ABBOTT AND COSTELLO MEET FRANKENSTEIN(1948), m; FAMILY HONEYMOON(1948), m; HAZARD(1948), m; NAKED CITY, THE(1948), m; TAP ROOTS(1948), m; FIGHTING O'FLYNN, THE(1949), m; FRANCIS(1949), m; FREE FOR ALL(1949), m; GAL WHO TOOK THE WEST, THE(1949), m; LADY GAMBLES, THE(1949), m; LIFE OF RILEY, THE(1949), m; ONCE MORE, MY DARLING(1949), m; SWORD IN THE DESERT(1949), m; TULSA(1949), m; WOMAN IN HIDING(1949), m; DESERT HAWK, THE(1950), m; DOUBLE CROSSBONES(1950), m; HARVEY(1950), m; LOUISA(1950), m; ONE WAY STREET(1950), m; SLEEPING CITY, THE(1950), m; BEDTIME FOR BONZO(1951), m; BRIGHT VICTORY(1951), m; FRANCIS GOES TO THE RACES(1951), m; KATIE DID IT(1951), m; LADY PAYS OFF, THE(1951), m, md; MARK OF THE RENEGADE(1951), m; RAGING TIDE, THE(1951), m; WEEKEND WITH FATHER(1951), m; BECAUSE OF YOU(1952), m; BONZO GOES TO COLLEGE(1952), m; IT GROWS ON TREES(1952), m; NO ROOM FOR THE GROOM(1952), m; SALLY AND SAINT ANNE(1952), m; WORLD IN HIS ARMS, THE(1952), m; BACK TO GOD'S COUNTRY(1953), m; DESERT LEGION(1953), m; FORBIDDEN(1953), m; MAN FROM THE ALAMO, THE(1953), m; MISSISSIPPI GAMBLER, THE(1953), m; STAND AT APACHE RIVER, THE(1953), m; THUNDER BAY(1953), m; WINGS OF THE HAWK(1953), m; MAGNIFICENT OBSESSION(1954), m; SIGN OF THE PA-

GAN(1954), m; TAZA, SON OF COCHISE(1954), m; ALL THAT HEAVEN ALLOWS(1955), m; CHIEF CRAZY HORSE(1955), m; FOXFIRE(1955), m; ONE DESIRE(1955), m; SHRIKE, THE(1955), m; AWAY ALL BOATS(1956), m; NEVER SAY GOODBYE(1956), m; RAWHIDE YEARS, THE(1956), m; STAR IN THE DUST(1956), m; WRITTEN ON THE WIND(1956), m; BATTLE HYMN(1957), m; INTERLUDE(1957), m; MAN OF A THOUSAND FACES(1957), m; MY MAN GODFREY(1957), m; TAMMY AND THE BACHELOR(1957), m; TARNISHED ANGELS, THE(1957), m; TATTERED DRESS, THE(1957), m; KATHY O'(1958), m; ONCE UPON A HORSE(1958), m; PERFECT FURLOUGH, THE(1958), m; THIS HAPPY FEELING(1958), m; IMITATION OF LIFE(1959), m; SNOW QUEEN, THE(1959, USSR), m; MIDNIGHT LACE(1960), m; PORTRAIT IN BLACK(1960), m; BACK STREET(1961), m; CAPTAIN NEWMAN, M.D.(1963), m; TAMMY AND THE DOCTOR(1963), m; UGLY AMERICAN, THE(1963), m; BULLET FOR A BADMAN(1964), m; SHENANDOAH(1965), m; SWORD OF ALI BABA, THE(1965), m; APPALOOSA, THE(1966), m; MADAME X(1966), m; RIDE TO HANGMAN'S TREE, THE(1967), m

Gene Skinner
HE'S MY GUY(1943)

Harold Skinner
Misc. Silents
BIRDS' CHRISTMAS CAROL, THE(1917)

Herbert Skinner
SPECIAL AGENT(1935); TAKE MY LIFE(1942)

Jennifer Skinner
ON VELVET(1938, Brit.)

Kay Skinner
MELODY(1971, Brit.)

Keith Skinner
MADEMOISELLE(1966, Fr./Brit.); ROMEO AND JULIET(1968, Brit./Ital.); SLIPPER AND THE ROSE, THE(1976, Brit.)

Ki Skinner
1984
AMERICAN TABOO(1984)

Lew Skinner
DRIFTER, THE(1966)

Llewellyn B. Skinner
BLACK LIKE ME(1964)

Margo Skinner
TERROR EYES(1981)

Marian Skinner
Silents
DANGEROUS TO MEN(1920); MORALS(1921); WHITE AND UNMARRIED(1921); BILLY JIM(1922); STRANGER, THE(1924)
Misc. Silents
SHE HIRED A HUSBAND(1919); LIFE IN THE ORANGE GROVES(1920)

Marie Antoinette Skinner
CHILD IS A WILD THING, A(1976)

Marion Skinner
Silents
SKINNER'S DRESS SUIT(1917); REAL FOLKS(1918); AMATEUR ADVENTURESS, THE(1919); GAMBLING IN SOULS(1919); SPITFIRE OF SEVILLE, THE(1919); BREWSTER'S MILLIONS(1921)
Misc. Silents
SKINNER'S BUBBLE(1917); CLAIM, THE(1918); SLEEPING LION, THE(1919)

Mary Skinner
BEHIND THE MASK(1958, Brit.)

Newton John Skinner
1984
FLESHBURN(1984)

Otis Skinner
KISMET(1930)
Silents
KISMET(1920)

Peter Skinner
CHILD IS A WILD THING, A(1976), ed

Robert Skinner
CROSS MY HEART(1937, Brit.), w

T.B. Skinner
WIZ, THE(1978)

Tom Skinner
DIVE BOMBER(1941); INTERNATIONAL SQUADRON(1941); SONG OF SCHEHERAZADE(1947)

Tony Skios
LIGHT AT THE EDGE OF THE WORLD, THE(1971, U.S./Span./Lichtenstein)

Raymond Skipp
MC VICAR(1982, Brit.); TO BE OR NOT TO BE(1983)
1984
ICE PIRATES, THE(1984)

Tommy Skipp
MELODY(1971, Brit.)

Skipper
WILD PARTY, THE(1975)

William Skipper
UP IN CENTRAL PARK(1948)

Skipper the Dog
MONSTER AND THE GIRL, THE(1941)

Skippy
THIRTY-DAY PRINCESS(1934)

Skippy the Dog
SMILING ALONG(1938, Brit.); TOPPER TAKES A TRIP(1939)

Patrick Skipwith
ANNA KARENINA(1948, Brit.)

Alison Skipworth
DU BARRY, WOMAN OF PASSION(1930); OH, FOR A MAN!(1930); OUTWARD BOUND(1930); RAFFLES(1930); STRICTLY UNCONVENTIONAL(1930); DEVOTION(1931); NIGHT ANGEL, THE(1931); ROAD TO SINGAPORE(1931); TONIGHT OR NEVER(1931); VIRTUOUS HUSBAND(1931); HIGH PRESSURE(1932); MADAME RACKETEER(1932); NIGHT AFTER NIGHT(1932); SINNERS IN THE SUN(1932); UNEXPECTED FATHER(1932); ALICE IN WONDERLAND(1933); HE LEARNED ABOUT WOMEN(1933); LADY'S PROFESSION, A(1933); MIDNIGHT CLUB(1933); SONG OF SONGS(1933); TILLIE AND GUS(1933); TONIGHT IS OURS(1933); CAP-

TAIN HATES THE SEA, THE(1934); COMING OUT PARTY(1934); HERE IS MY HEART(1934); NOTORIOUS SOPHIE LANG, THE(1934); SHOOT THE WORKS(1934); SIX OF A KIND(1934); WHARF ANGEL(1934); BECKY SHARP(1935); CASINO MURDER CASE, THE(1935); DEVIL IS A WOMAN, THE(1935); DOUBTING THOMAS(1935); GIRL FROM TENTH AVENUE, THE(1935); SHANGHAI(1935); DANGEROUS(1936); GORGEOUS HUSSY, THE(1936); HITCH HIKE LADY(1936); PRINCESS COMES ACROSS, THE(1936); SATAN MET A LADY(1936); TWO IN A CROWD(1936); WHITE HUNTER(1936); STOLEN HOLIDAY(1937); TWO WISE MAIDS(1937); KING OF THE NEWSBOYS(1938); LADIES IN DISTRESS(1938); WIDE OPEN FACES(1938)
Misc. Silents
39 EAST(1920)

Dewey Skipworth
SHE MARRIED HER BOSS(1935)

Jack Skirball
BIRTH OF A BABY(1938), p; MIRACLE ON MAIN STREET, A(1940), p

Jack H. Skirball
SABOTEUR(1942), p; SHADOW OF A DOUBT(1943), p; GUEST WIFE(1945), p; IT'S IN THE BAG(1945), p; MAGNIFICENT DOLL(1946), p; SO GOES MY LOVE(1946), p; BRIDE FOR SALE(1949), p; SECRET FURY, THE(1950), p; PAYMENT ON DEMAND(1951), p; MATTER OF TIME, A(1976, Ital./U.S.), p

Margaret Skirvin
Misc. Silents
PARISIAN ROMANCE, A(1916)

Marguerite Skirvin
Silents
PORT OF MISSING MEN(1914)
Misc. Silents
ARISTOCRACY(1914); PASSERS-BY(1916); QUITTER, THE(1916); UPHEAVAL, THE(1916)

Henry Skjaer
ORDET(1957, Den.)

Valdemar Skjerning
WHILE THE ATTORNEY IS ASLEEP(1945, Den.)

Gunnar Skjetne
EDVARD MUNCH(1976, Norway/Swed.)

Espen Skjonberg
ONE DAY IN THE LIFE OF IVAN DENISOVICH(1971, U.S./Brit./Norway)

Jo Skjonberg
ONE DAY IN THE LIFE OF IVAN DENISOVICH(1971, U.S./Brit./Norway)

Pal Skjonberg
HUNGER(1968, Den./Norway/Swed.)

Sam Sklair
AFTER YOU, COMRADE(1967, S. Afr.), m; CONFESSIONS OF A WINDOW CLEANER(1974, Brit.), m

Al Sklar
ATTACK OF THE KILLER TOMATOES(1978)

George Sklar
AFRAID TO TALK(1932), w; FIRST COMES COURAGE(1943), w

Michael Sklar
SCARECROW IN A GARDEN OF CUCUMBERS(1972); L'AMOUR(1973)

William D. Sklar
ULTIMATE THRILL, THE(1974), p

Seth Sklarey
CHILDREN SHOULDN'T PLAY WITH DEAD THINGS(1972)

Vincent Sklena
1984
BREAKIN'(1984), ed

Mike Skloot
KILLING OF A CHINESE BOOKIE, THE(1976)

Carl Sklover
ABBOTT AND COSTELLO MEET FRANKENSTEIN(1948); APPOINTMENT WITH MURDER(1948); FORCE OF EVIL(1948); FIGHTING FOOLS(1949); SET-UP, THE(1949); TENSION(1949); NEVER A DULL MOMENT(1950); PEGGY(1950); SHAKEDOWN(1950); WHERE DANGER LIVES(1950); ABBOTT AND COSTELLO MEET THE INVISIBLE MAN(1951); SEALED CARGO(1951); LAS VEGAS STORY, THE(1952); MEET DANNY WILSON(1952); PLAYGIRL(1954); SHE COULDN'T SAY NO(1954); GIRL IN THE KREMLIN, THE(1957); MARJORIE MORNINGSTAR(1958)

G. Sklyanskiy
TRAIN GOES TO KIEV, THE(1961, USSR)

Igor Sklyar
1984
JAZZMAN(1984, USSR)

Irene Skobline
CHLOE IN THE AFTERNOON(1972, Fr.); COUP DE TORCHON(1981, Fr.)

Irina Skobtseva
OTHELLO(1960, U.S.S.R.); SUMMER TO REMEMBER, A(1961, USSR); MEET ME IN MOSCOW(1966, USSR); WAR AND PEACE(1968, USSR); SILENCE OF DR. EVANS, THE(1973, USSR)

Irina Skobzeva
WATERLOO(1970, Ital./USSR)

Wlodzimierz Skoczylas
KNIGHTS OF THE TEUTONIC ORDER, THE(1962, Pol.)

Albin Skoda
LAST TEN DAYS, THE(1956, Ger.)

Stefan Skodler
STORY OF VICKIE, THE(1958, Aust.)

Milko Skofic
FAST AND SEXY(1960, Fr./Ital.), p

Bibi Skoglund
NIGHT IS MY FUTURE(1962, Swed.)

Gunnar Skoglund
JUNGLE OF CHANG(1951), d

Per Skogsberg
WILD STRAWBERRIES(1959, Swed.)

Sven Skold
CHILDREN, THE(1949, Swed.), m; BREAD OF LOVE, THE(1954, Swed.), m

George Skolimowski
1984
SUCCESS IS THE BEST REVENGE(1984, Brit.)

Jerry Skolimowski
IDENTIFICATION MARKS: NONE(1969, Pol.), art d
Jerzy Skolimowski
KNIFE IN THE WATER(1963, Pol.), w; BARRIER(1966, Pol.), d&w; IDENTIFICA-
TION MARKS: NONE(1969, Pol.), a, d,w; WALKOVER(1969, Pol.), a, d&w; ADVEN-
TURES OF GERARD, THE(1970, Brit.), d, w; DEEP END(1970 Ger./U.S.), d, w; KING,
QUEEN, KNAVE(1972, Ger./U.S.), d; SHOUT, THE(1978, Brit.), d, w; CIRCLE OF
DECEIT(1982, Fr./Ger.); MOONLIGHTING(1982, Brit.), p, d, w
1984
SUCCESS IS THE BEST REVENGE(1984, Brit.), p&d, w
Elsa Skolinstad
FICKLE FINGER OF FATE, THE(1967, Span./U.S.)
Ada Skolmen
HUNGER(1968, Den./Norway/Swed.), cos; ONE DAY IN THE LIFE OF IVAN
DENISOVICH(1971, U.S./Brit./Norway), cos; EDVARD MUNCH(1976, Norway/
Swed.), cos
Harvey Skolnik
MODERN ROMANCE(1981)
Sid Skolsky
TOM, DICK AND HARRY(1941)
Sidney Skolsky
GIFT OF GAB(1934); DARING YOUNG MAN, THE(1935), w; GENERAL DIED AT
DAWN, THE(1936); JOLSON STORY, THE(1946), p; SUNSET BOULEVARD(1950);
EDDIE CANTOR STORY, THE(1953), p, w; TEACHER'S PET(1958); LEGEND OF
LYLAH CLARE, THE(1968)
Vladimir Skomarovsky
1984
2010(1984)
Leena Skoog
Misc. Talkies
THREE DIMENSIONS OF GRETA(1973)
Jan Skopecek
SWEET LIGHT IN A DARK ROOM(1966, Czech.); 90 DEGREES IN THE SHA-
DE(1966, Czech./Brit.)
Achilleas Skordilis
OEDIPUS THE KING(1968, Brit.)
Skorepova
DO YOU KEEP A LION AT HOME?(1966, Czech.), cos
R. Skoretskaya
SHE-WOLF, THE(1963, USSR), ed
M. Skorik
SHADOWS OF FORGOTTEN ANCESTORS(1967, USSR), m
Guy Skornik
TUSK(1980, Fr.), m
Michael Skorobohach
GIRL FROM POLTAVA(1937)
Karin Skorreso
CATCH AS CATCH CAN(1968, Ital.)
Mogens Skot-Hansen
DAY OF WRATH(1948, Den.), w
Robert Skotak
FORBIDDEN WORLD(1982), prod d; STRANGE INVADERS(1983), spec eff
Costas Skouras
LAND OF THE MINOTAUR(1976, Gr.)
Daphne Skouras
GROUCH, THE(1961, Gr.)
Edith Skouras
ALWAYS GOODBYE(1938), w; HIGH SCHOOL(1940), w; MANHATTAN HEART-
BEAT(1940), w; ON THEIR OWN(1940), w
Plato Skouras
APACHE WARRIOR(1957), p; UNDER FIRE(1957), p
Plato A. Skouras
SIERRA BARON(1958), p; VILLA!(1958), p; FRANCIS OF ASSISI(1961), p
Joergen Skov
GOLDEN MOUNTAINS(1958, Den.), ph
Jorgen Skov
OPERATION LOVEBIRDS(1968, Den.), ph
Zbigniew Skowronski
KNIGHTS OF THE TEUTONIC ORDER, THE(1962, Pol.)
Zbigniew Skowronski
ASHES AND DIAMONDS(1961, Pol.); PORTRAIT OF LENIN(1967, Pol./USSR)
Zdzislaw Skowronski
YELLOW SLIPPERS, THE(1965, Pol.), w
Karl Skraup
BURG THEATRE(1936, Ger.)
Olga Skrigin
SQUARE OF VIOLENCE(1963, U.S./Yugo.), ed; TWILIGHT TIME(1983, U.S./Yugo.),
ed
Flora Skrine
WINSTANLEY(1979, Brit.)
Ina Skriver
EMILY(1976, Brit.); VICTOR/VICTORIA(1982)
Christian Skrobek
LAST ESCAPE, THE(1970, Brit.)
N. Skryabin
Misc. Silents
MISS PEASANT(1916, USSR)
Helgi Skulason
OUTLAW: THE SAGE OF GISLI(1982, Iceland)
Frank Skully
LUCKY LEGS(1942)
V. Skulme
LAST GAME, THE(1964, USSR)
Valentino Skulme
WATERLOO(1970, Ital./USSR)
Menasha Skulnick
Misc. Talkies
LIVE AND LAUGH(1933)

A. Skupien
PORTRAIT OF LENIN(1967, Pol./USSR)
I. Skuratov
1812(1944, USSR)
V. Skuridin
OPTIMISTIC TRAGEDY, THE(1964, USSR)
Ron Skurow
LOOKIN' TO GET OUT(1982)
Grzegorz Skurski
MAN OF MARBLE(1979, Pol.)
Victor Skutetzky
YOUNG WIVES' TALE(1954, Brit.), p
Victor Skutezky
IT HAPPENED ONE SUNDAY(1944, Brit.), p, w; QUIET WEEKEND(1948, Brit.), w;
FOR THEM THAT TRESPASS(1949, Brit.), p; TEMPTATION HARBOR(1949, Brit.), p,
w; MURDER WITHOUT CRIME(1951, Brit.), p; FATHER'S DOING FINE(1952,
Brit.), p; LANDFALL(1953, Brit.), p; YELLOW BALLOON, THE(1953, Brit.), p; WEAK
AND THE WICKED, THE(1954, Brit.), p; IT'S GREAT TO BE YOUNG(1956, Brit.), p
Victor Skutzeky
ALIVE AND KICKING(1962, Brit.), p
Frantisek Skvor
BOHEMIAN RAPTURE(1948, Czech.), m
Karel Skvor
DEVIL'S TRAP, THE(1964, Czech.), art d; LEMONADE JOE(1966, Czech.), art d;
SHOP ON MAIN STREET, THE(1966, Czech.), art d; SWEET LIGHT IN A DARK
ROOM(1966, Czech.), art d; TRANSPORT FROM PARADISE(1967, Czech.), art d
Zdena Skvorecka
REPORT ON THE PARTY AND THE GUESTS, A(1968, Czech.); END OF A
PRIEST(1970, Czech.)
Josef Skvorecky
END OF A PRIEST(1970, Czech.), w
N. Skvortsova
NIGHT BEFORE CHRISTMAS, A(1963, USSR)
Sky
HOT SPUR(1968); PRIVATE DUTY NURSES(1972), m
Dawn Little Sky
DUEL AT DIABLO(1966)
Eddie Little Sky
DUEL AT DIABLO(1966)
Helen Sky
DIMBOOLA(1979, Aus.)
George Sky Eagle
KING OF THE STALLIONS(1942)
Paul Skyhorse
WOLFEN(1981)
Barbara Skyler
OPERATION DAMES(1959)
Tristine Skyler
1984
KIDCO(1984); OLD ENOUGH(1984)
Georgiy Slabinyak
SPRINGTIME ON THE VOLGA(1961, USSR)
Igor Slabnjewitsch
MOSCOW DOES NOT BELIEVE IN TEARS(1980, USSR), ph
Arthur Slabotsky
MERRY WIVES OF TOBIAS ROUKE, THE(1972, Can.), w
Ben Slack
ON THE YARD(1978); SEDUCTION OF JOE TYNAN, THE(1979)
1984
OASIS, THE(1984)
Benjamin Slack
MAN ON A SWING(1974)
Bill Slack
CLASH BY NIGHT(1952)
Freddie Slack
HIGH SCHOOL HERO(1946)
William Slack
OPERATION SECRET(1952)
Bernard Slade
TRIBUTE(1980, Can.), w; STAND UP AND BE COUNTED(1972), w; SAME TIME,
NEXT YEAR(1978), w; ROMANTIC COMEDY(1983), w
Betsy Slade
OUR TIME(1974)
Cal Slade
MY THIRD WIFE GEORGE(1968)
Christine Jope Slade
Silents
LIFE'S DARN FUNNY(1921), w
Dumas Slade
MC MASTERS, THE(1970)
Gurney Slade
LOVERS AND LUGGERS(1938, Aus.), w
Hynie Slade
WILD SEASON(1968, South Africa)
Jack Slade
GOLDEN LINK, THE(1954, Brit.), ed; GAMMA PEOPLE, THE(1956), ed; MURDER
ON APPROVAL(1956, Brit.), ed; ODONGO(1956, Brit.), ed; FIRE DOWN BELOW(1957,
U.S./Brit.), ed; HIGH FLIGHT(1957, Brit.), ed; BOY AND THE BRIDGE, THE(1959,
Brit.), ed; KONGA(1961, Brit.), ed; MANIA(1961, Brit.), ed; BOYS, THE(1962, Brit.),
ed; WONDERFUL TO BE YOUNG!(1962, Brit.), ed; SUMMER HOLIDAY(1963, Brit.),
ed; FRENCH DRESSING(1964, Brit.), ed; PUSSYCAT ALLEY(1965, Brit.), ed; SWING-
ER'S PARADISE(1965, Brit.), ed; UP JUMPED A SWAGMAN(1965, Brit.), ed; IDOL,
THE(1966, Brit.), ed; SPY WITH A COLD NOSE, THE(1966, Brit.), ed; JUST LIKE A
WOMAN(1967, Brit.), ed; ASSIGNMENT K(1968, Brit.), ed; SALT & PEPPER(1968,
Brit.), ed; PLAY DIRTY(1969, Brit.), ed; CONNECTING ROOMS(1971, Brit.), ed
Mark Slade
VOYAGE TO THE BOTTOM OF THE SEA(1961); THIRTEEN WEST STREET(1962);
BENJI(1974); SALTY(1975)

1984
FLASHPOINT(1984); INVISIBLE STRANGLER(1984)
Olga Slade
ONE PRECIOUS YEAR(1933, Brit.)
Silents
FARMER'S WIFE, THE(1928, Brit.)
Robert Slade
SUMMER AND SMOKE(1961)
William A. Slade
YELLOWNECK(1955), ed; NAKED IN THE SUN(1957), ed
Marta Sladeckova
ASSISTANT, THE(1982, Czech.)
Lisa Slagle
CLAMBAKE(1967)
John Slan
HIGH-BALLIN'(1978), p
Jon Slan
FISH HAWK(1981, Can.), p; THRESHOLD(1983, Can.), p
Ivor Slaney
BAD BLONDE(1953, Brit.), m; BLOOD ORANGE(1953, Brit.), m; SPACEWAYS(1953, Brit.), m; TERROR STREET(1953), m; BLACKOUT(1954, Brit.), m; HEATWAVE(1954, Brit.), m; PAID TO KILL(1954, Brit.), m; SCARLET SPEAR, THE(1954, Brit.), m; UNHOLY FOUR, THE(1954, Brit.), m; TERROR(1979, Brit.), m
Mike Slaney
CARWASH(1976)
Axel Slangus
VIRGIN SPRING, THE(1960, Swed.)
Ivoy Slanley
SAINT'S GIRL FRIDAY, THE(1954, Brit.), m
Ivan Slapeta
I KILLED EINSTEIN, GENTLEMEN(1970, Czech.), ph
A. Slaska
LAST STOP, THE(1949, Pol.)
Aleksandra Slaska
PASSENGER, THE(1970, Pol.)
Vladimir Slastcheff
INNOCENTS IN PARIS(1955, Brit.)
Henry Slate
FOURTEEN HOURS(1951); FROGMEN, THE(1951); RHUBARB(1951); YOU'RE IN THE NAVY NOW(1951); BELLE OF NEW YORK, THE(1952); BLOODHOUNDS OF BROADWAY(1952); JUST THIS ONCE(1952); LOAN SHARK(1952); SOMEBODY LOVES ME(1952); STOP, YOU'RE KILLING ME(1952); DOWN AMONG THE SHELTERING PALMS(1953); MISS SADIE THOMPSON(1953); PICKUP ON SOUTH STREET(1953); SLIGHT CASE OF LARCENY, A(1953); THREE SAILORS AND A GIRL(1953); THERE'S NO BUSINESS LIKE SHOW BUSINESS(1954); HIT THE DECK(1955); MY SISTER EILEEN(1955); BUS STOP(1956); HE LAUGHED LAST(1956); ROCK AROUND THE CLOCK(1956); WINK OF AN EYE(1958); HEY BOY! HEY GIRL!(1959); BEDTIME STORY(1964); PATSY, THE(1964); SHAGGY D.A., THE(1976); PETE'S DRAGON(1977); CAT FROM OUTER SPACE, THE(1978); NORMA RAE(1979); HERBIE GOES BANANAS(1980); LITTLE MISS MARKER(1980); BACK ROADS(1981)
Pfc. Henry Slate
WINGED VICTORY(1944)
Jack Slate
MOVIE MOVIE(1978); STAR CHAMBER, THE(1983)
Cpl. Jack Slate
WINGED VICTORY(1944)
Jeremy Slate
GIRLS! GIRLS! GIRLS!(1962); WIVES AND LOVERS(1963); I'LL TAKE SWEDEN(1965); SONS OF KATIE ELDER, THE(1965); BORN LOSERS(1967); DEVIL'S BRIGADE, THE(1968); MINI-SKIRT MOB, THE(1968); HELL'S ANGELS '69(1969), a, w; HELL'S BELLES(1969); HOOKED GENERATION, THE(1969); TRUE GRIT(1969)
Misc. Talkies
CURSE OF THE MOON CHILD(1972); CENTERFOLD GIRLS, THE(1974)
Lane Slate
CLAY PIGEON(1971), p&d; THEY ONLY KILL THEIR MASTERS(1972), w; CAR, THE(1977), w
Sid Slate
RUN FOR THE HILLS(1953)
The Slate Brothers
HAPPY DAYS(1930); COLLEGE SWING(1938); MEET ME IN LAS VEGAS(1956)
Frank Slaten
1984
JOHNNY DANGEROUSLY(1984)
Max Slaten
WONDERFUL COUNTRY, THE(1959); DESPERATE ONES, THE(1968 U.S./Span.); HUNTING PARTY, THE(1977, Brit.)
Troy W. Slaten
1984
JOHNNY DANGEROUSLY(1984)
Adam Slater
YOUNG WARRIORS(1983), anim
B. John Slater
LOVE ON THE DOLE(1945, Brit.)
Barbara Slater
LOUISIANA PURCHASE(1941); POWERS GIRL, THE(1942); TOMORROW WE LIVE(1942); LADY OF BURLESQUE(1943); YOUNG AND WILLING(1943); YOUTH ON PARADE(1943); LADY CONFESSES, THE(1945); THOSE ENDEARING YOUNG CHARMS(1945); MONSIEUR VERDOUX(1947)
Barney Slater
IT GROWS ON TREES(1952), w; IT HAPPENS EVERY THURSDAY(1953), w; MR. SCOUTMASTER(1953), w; GORILLA AT LARGE(1954), w; THREE VIOLENT PEOPLE(1956), w; TIN STAR, THE(1957), w; CAHILL, UNITED STATES MARSHAL(1973), w
Bob Slater
Misc. Silents
SQUARE JOE(1921)

Bobbie Slater
LOVE UP THE POLE(1936, Brit.); MELODY OF MY HEART(1936, Brit.)
Bobby Slater
VARIETY(1935, Brit.)
Bud Slater
PANIC IN YEAR ZERO!(1962)
Daphne Slater
COURTNEY AFFAIR, THE(1947, Brit.)
Debbie Slater
POPDOWN(1968, Brit.)
Grant Slater
TICKET TO HEAVEN(1981)
Helen Slater
1984
SUPERGIRL(1984)
Humphrey Slater
CONSPIRATOR(1949, Brit.), w
Ivor Slater
LADY CAROLINE LAMB(1972, Brit./Ital.)
J. Wynn Slater
Silents
HARD TIMES(1915, Brit.)
Jack Slater
SAM'S SONG(1971)
John Slater
FACING THE MUSIC(1941, Brit.); GERT AND DAISY'S WEEKEND(1941, Brit.); FLYING FORTRESS(1942, Brit.); WINGS AND THE WOMAN(1942, Brit.); YOUNG MR. PITT, THE(1942, Brit.); DEADLOCK(1943, Brit.); HUNDRED POUND WINDOW, THE(1943, Brit.); MILLIONS LIKE US(1943, Brit.); SAINT MEETS THE TIGER, THE(1943, Brit.); WE DIVE AT DAWN(1943, Brit.); CANDLELIGHT IN ALGERIA(1944, Brit.); FOR THOSE IN PERIL(1944, Brit.); UNCENSORED(1944, Brit.); UNDERGROUND GUERRILLAS(1944, Brit.); 48 HOURS(1944, Brit.); QUERY(1945, Brit.); MURDER IN REVERSE(1946, Brit.); SEVENTH VEIL, THE(1946, Brit.); YANK IN LONDON, A(1946, Brit.); AGAINST THE WIND(1948, Brit.); ESCAPE(1948, Brit.); IT ALWAYS RAINS ON SUNDAY(1949, Brit.); PASSPORT TO PIMLICO(1949, Brit.); PRELUDE TO FAME(1950, Brit.); SILK NOOSE, THE(1950, Brit.); THIRD VISITOR, THE(1951, Brit.); FAITHFUL CITY(1952, Israel); BAD BLONDE(1953, Brit.); LONG MEMORY, THE(1953, Brit.); RINGER, THE(1953, Brit.); JOHN WESLEY(1954, Brit.); MAN WITH A MILLION(1954, Brit.); JOHNNY, YOU'RE WANTED(1956, Brit.); STAR OF INDIA(1956, Brit.); DEVIL'S PASS, THE(1957, Brit.); VIOLENT PLAYGROUND(1958, Brit.); NIGHT WE GOT THE BIRD, THE(1961, Brit.); NOTHING BARRED(1961, Brit.); THREE ON A SPREE(1961, Brit.); PLACE TO GO, A(1964, Brit.); YELLOW HAT, THE(1966, Brit.)
John J. Slater
FRONT, THE(1976)
Lee Slater
TILL THE END OF TIME(1946)
Leslie Slater
YEAR OF THE YAHOO(1971)
Margo Slater
EXODUS(1960), cos
Montagu Slater
MANIACS ON WHEELS(1951, Brit.), w; BRAVE DON'T CRY, THE(1952, Brit.), w; MAN OF AFRICA(1956, Brit.), w
Montague Slater
DEVIL ON HORSEBACK(1954, Brit.), w
Shirley Slater
WHY WOULD I LIE(1980)
William Slater
WATERLOO(1970, Ital./USSR)
Lucille Slatherwaite
Silents
POLLY OF THE CIRCUS(1917)
Don Slaton
SILKWOOD(1983)
Arthur Slatter
Silents
HER FATAL MILLIONS(1923), w
Charles Slattery
UNMASKED(1929)
Silents
FAIR PRETENDER, THE(1918); NUMBER 17(1920); DREAM STREET(1921); RAGGED EDGE, THE(1923)
Misc. Silents
SWAT THE SPY(1918); TELL IT TO THE MARINES(1918)
Des Slattery
BLOOD ARROW(1958)
Desmond Slattery
AMBUSH AT CIMARRON PASS(1958)
Jack Slattery
PARDON MY RHYTHM(1944); SONG OF THE SARONG(1945)
Joe Slattery
DESERT RAVEN, THE(1965)
Nellie Slattery
Silents
MISCHIEF MAKER, THE(1916)
Misc. Silents
NARROW PATH, THE(1916); WRATH OF LOVE(1917)
Page Slattery
CAPE FEAR(1962); JESSE JAMES MEETS FRANKENSTEIN'S DAUGHTER(1966)
Richard Slattery
TILL THE END OF TIME(1946)
Richard X. Slattery
BUTTERFIELD 8(1960); DISTANT TRUMPET, A(1964); TIME FOR KILLING, A(1967); SECRET WAR OF HARRY FRIGG, THE(1968); THE BOSTON STRANGLER, THE(1968); WALKING TALL(1973); BLACK EYE(1974); BUSTING(1974); HERBIE RIDES AGAIN(1974); NO MERCY MAN, THE(1975); APPLE DUMPLING GANG RIDES AGAIN, THE(1979)

Misc. Talkies
ZEBRA FORCE(1977)
Don Slatton
INDEPENDENCE DAY(1983)
Bob Slatzer
HELLCATS, THE(1968)
Robert F. Slatzer
HELLCATS, THE(1968), d, w; BIG FOOT(1973), d, w
Anna May Slaughter
GRAND CANYON(1949); SKY LINER(1949)
Christopher Slaughter
IT HAPPENED HERE(1966, Brit.)
Frank G. Slaughter
SANGAREE(1953), w; NAKED IN THE SUN(1957), w; DOCTORS' WIVES(1971), w
Richard Slaughter
DARK CRYSTAL, THE(1982, Brit.)
Robert Slaughter
EMMA MAE(1976)
Rulon Slaughter
Silents
ACROSS THE DEADLINE(1925)
Tod Slaughter
CRIMES OF STEPHEN HAWKE, THE(1936, Brit.); MURDER IN THE OLD RED BARN(1936, Brit.); DARBY AND JOAN(1937, Brit.); IT'S NEVER TOO LATE TO MEND(1937, Brit.); SONG OF THE ROAD(1937, Brit.); TICKET OF LEAVE MAN, THE(1937, Brit.); SEXTON BLAKE AND THE HOODED TERROR(1938, Brit.); DEMON BARBER OF FLEET STREET, THE(1939, Brit.); FACE AT THE WINDOW, THE(1939, Brit.); CRIMES AT THE DARK HOUSE(1940, Brit.); CURSE OF THE WRAYDONS, THE(1946, Brit.); GREED OF WILLIAM HART, THE(1948, Brit.); KING OF THE UNDERWORLD(1952, Brit.)
Misc. Talkies
MURDER AT SCOTLAND YARD(1952)
Steve Slauson
ANGELS HARD AS THEY COME(1971)
Brad Slaven
GHOST AND MRS. MUIR, THE(1942); CLUNY BROWN(1946); CHEYENNE TAKES OVER(1947); MOTHER WORE TIGHTS(1947); RETURN OF THE LASH(1947); STAGE TO MESA CITY(1947); TORNADO RANGE(1948)
Buster Slaven
BRINGING UP BABY(1938); JUVENILE COURT(1938); PROFESSOR BEWARE(1938); MY LITTLE CHICKADEE(1940); PRIDE AND PREJUDICE(1940); DOWN IN SAN DIEGO(1941)
Matthew B. Slaven [Brad Slaven]
RIDIN' DOWN THE TRAIL(1947)
Rick Slaven
METEOR(1979)
Robert Slaven
DATE BAIT(1960), w; HIGH SCHOOL CAESAR(1960), w
Buster Slavens
MAYTIME(1937)
Mia Slavenska
LIVING CORPSE, THE(1940, Fr.)
John Slavid
ROUGH CUT(1980, Brit.)
Sandy Slavik
MC HALE'S NAVY(1964)
Brad Slavin
SONG OF THE SIERRAS(1946); BORDER FEUD(1947); LAW OF THE LASH(1947); RANGE BEYOND THE BLUE(1947)
Buster Slavin
DEVIL IS A SISSY, THE(1936)
George Slavin
INTRIGUE(1947), w; RED MOUNTAIN(1951), w; SMOKE SIGNAL(1955), w; SON OF ROBIN HOOD(1959, Brit.), w
George F. Slavin
EXPERIMENT ALCATRAZ(1950), w; MYSTERY SUBMARINE(1950), w; NEVADAN, THE(1950), w; PEGGY(1950), w; WOMAN ON PIER 13(1950), w; WEEKEND WITH FATHER(1951), w; CITY OF BAD MEN(1953), w; THUNDER BAY(1953), w; ROCKET MAN, THE(1954), w; DESERT SANDS(1955), w; URANIUM BOOM(1956), w
George P. Slavin
FIGHTING STALLION, THE(1950), w
George S. Slavin
HALLIDAY BRAND, THE(1957), w
J. Edward Slavin
FIRST OFFENDERS(1939), w
Jo Jo Slavin
FINNEGANS WAKE(1965)
Johnny Slavin
Misc. Silents
BUNCH OF KEYS, A(1915)
Jose Slavin
MAFIA, THE(1972, Arg.)
Lev Slavin
SON OF MONGOLIA(1936, USSR), w
Martin Slavin
INFORMATION RECEIVED(1962, Brit.), m, md; YOUNG, WILLING AND EAGER(1962, Brit.), m; MURDER CAN BE DEADLY(1963, Brit.), m; BOY CRIED MURDER, THE(1966, Ger./Brit./Yugo.), m; WILD AFFAIR, THE(1966, Brit.), m, md
Slick Slavin
EIGHTEEN AND ANXIOUS(1957); BRIDE AND THE BEAST, THE(1958); SPEED CRAZY(1959); INVASION OF THE STAR CREATURES(1962)
Susan Slavin
BLACK ZOO(1963)
K. Slavinskiy
DIMKA(1964, USSR)
A. Slavinsky
Misc. Silents
ESSENTIAL SPARK OF JEWISHNESS, THE(1912, USSR), d

Fedor Slavski
Misc. Silents
TRANSPORT OF FIRE(1931, USSR)
Helen Slayton-Hughes
SHOOT THE MOON(1982)
Alan Slecker
WORLD IS JUST A 'B' MOVIE, THE(1971)
John Sledge
INVISIBLE AVENGER, THE(1958), d; NEW ORLEANS AFTER DARK(1958), d; FOUR FOR THE MORGUE(1962), d
Peter Sledmere
GOODBYE PORK PIE(1981, New Zealand)
Elma Slee
OLD MOTHER RILEY(1937, Brit.)
Phil Sleeman
SAILORS' HOLIDAY(1929); BLONDE CRAZY(1931); YOUNG DONOVAN'S KID(1931)
Silents
KING OF KINGS, THE(1927)
Philip G. Sleeman
SCARLET EMPRESS, THE(1934); MARKED WOMAN(1937)
Philip Sleeman
HALF ANGEL(1936); THIRD FINGER, LEFT HAND(1940)
Misc. Silents
COME ON COWBOYS!(1924)
Phillip Sleeman
COCK O' THE WALK(1930); PRISONER OF ZENDA, THE(1937)
Silents
HOME STUFF(1921); AFTER MIDNIGHT(1927)
Wayne Sleep
VIRGIN SOLDIERS, THE(1970, Brit.); PETER RABBIT AND TALES OF BEATRIX POTTER(1971, Brit.); GREAT TRAIN ROBBERY, THE(1979, Brit.)
Sleep 'n' Eat [Willie Best]
FEET FIRST(1930); MONSTER WALKS, THE(1932); KENTUCKY KERNELS(1935); WEST OF THE PECOS(1935)
Martha Sleeper
TAXI 13(1928); MADAME SATAN(1930); OUR BLUSHING BRIDES(1930); WAR NURSE(1930); CONFESSIONS OF A CO-ED(1931); GIRLS DEMAND EXCITEMENT(1931); TAILOR MADE MAN, A(1931); TEN CENTS A DANCE(1931); HUDDLE(1932); BROKEN DREAMS(1933); MIDNIGHT MARY(1933); PENTHOUSE(1933); SPITFIRE(1934); GREAT GOD GOLD(1935); SCOUNDREL, THE(1935); SUNSET RANGE(1935); TOMORROW'S YOUTH(1935); TWO SINNERS(1935); WEST OF THE PECOS(1935); FOUR DAYS WONDER(1936); RHYTHM ON THE RANGE(1936); BELLS OF ST. MARY'S, THE(1945)
Silents
MAILMAN, THE(1923); SKINNER'S BIG IDEA(1928); AIR LEGION, THE(1929)
Misc. Silents
DANGER STREET(1928); LITTLE YELLOW HOUSE, THE(1928); VOICE OF THE STORM, THE(1929)
Frantisek Slegr
MURDER CZECH STYLE(1968, Czech.)
E. N. Sleight
MAYBE IT'S LOVE(1930)
Jean Slemmon
EASY TO LOOK AT(1945)
Henry Slesar
EYES OF ANNIE JONES, THE(1963, Brit.), w; TWO ON A GUILLOTINE(1965), w; ONE OF OUR SPIES IS MISSING(1966), w; MURDERS IN THE RUE MORGUE(1971), w
Tess Slesinger
BRIDE WORE RED, THE(1937), w; GIRLS' SCHOOL(1938), w; DANCE, GIRL, DANCE(1940), w; REMEMBER THE DAY(1941), w; TREE GROWS IN BROOKLYN, A(1945), w
Philip Slessor
GAY ADVENTURE, THE(1953, Brit.)
Mario Sletti
THIEVES' HIGHWAY(1949)
Gerry Slevin
CHARRIOTS OF FIRE(1981, Brit.)
Jeff Slevin
FIGHT FOR YOUR LIFE(1977), m
Leo Slezak
FOUR COMPANIONS, THE(1938, Ger.); OPERETTA(1949, Ger.)
Margaret Slezak
MAN ON A TIGHTROPE(1953)
Walter Slezak
ONCE UPON A HONEYMOON(1942); FALLEN SPARROW, THE(1943); THIS LAND IS MINE(1943); LIFEBOAT(1944); PRINCESS AND THE PIRATE, THE(1944); STEP LIVELY(1944); 'TILL WE MEET AGAIN(1944); CORNERED(1945); SALOME, WHERE SHE DANCED(1945); SPANISH MAIN, THE(1945); BORN TO KILL(1947); RIFFRAFF(1947); SINBAD THE SAILOR(1947); PIRATE, THE(1948); INSPECTOR GENERAL, THE(1949); ABBOTT AND COSTELLO IN THE FOREIGN LEGION(1950); SPY HUNT(1950); YELLOW CAB MAN, THE(1950); BEDTIME FOR BONZO(1951); PEOPLE WILL TALK(1951); CALL ME MADAM(1953); CONFIDENTIAL CONNIE(1953); WHITE WITCH DOCTOR(1953); STEEL CAGE, THE(1954); TEN THOUSAND BEDROOMS(1957); MIRACLE, THE(1959); COME SEPTEMBER(1961); WONDERFUL WORLD OF THE BROTHERS ERIMM, THE(1962); EMIL AND THE DETECTIVES(1964); SWINGER'S PARADISE(1965, Brit.); VERY SPECIAL FAVOR, A(1965); 24 HOURS TO KILL(1966, Brit.); CAPER OF THE GOLDEN BULLS, THE(1967); DR. COPPELIUS(1968, U.S./Span.); BLACK BEAUTY(1971, Brit./Ger./Span.); TREASURE ISLAND(1972, Brit./Span./Fr./Ger.); MYSTERIOUS HOUSE OF DR. C., THE(1976)
Misc. Silents
QUEEN OF SIN AND THE SPECTACLE OF SODOM AND GOMORRAH, THE(1923, Aust.); MICHAEL(1924, Ger.); CHAINED(1927, Ger.)
Slick and Slack
Misc. Talkies
IT HAPPENED IN HARLEM(1945)

"Slickem"
FIFTEEN WIVES(1934)
Dutch Slickenmeyer
STUDENT TOUR(1934)
Slicker the Seal
SPAWN OF THE NORTH(1938); FISHERMAN'S WHARF(1939)
The Slickers
HARDER THEY COME, THE(1973, Jamaica), m
Clarence Slifer
NORTH STAR, THE(1943), spec eff; PRINCESS AND THE PIRATE, THE(1944), spec eff; SINCE YOU WENT AWAY(1944), spec eff; UP IN ARMS(1944), spec eff; DUEL IN THE SUN(1946), spec eff; PARADINE CASE, THE(1947), spec eff; PORTRAIT OF JENNIE(1949), spec eff; GREATEST STORY EVER TOLD, THE(1965), spec eff
Elisabeth Slifer
MILLION DOLLAR MERMAID(1952)
Elizabeth Slifer
PRISONER OF ZENDA, THE(1952); WAC FROM WALLA WALLA, THE(1952); GLASS WALL, THE(1953); MONEY FROM HOME(1953); STORY OF THREE LOVES, THE(1953); PROUD AND THE PROFANE, THE(1956); FUNNY FACE(1957); JAIL-HOUSE ROCK(1957)
Liz Slifer
LOVE NEST(1951)
Lizz Slifer
FRENCH LINE, THE(1954); HELL'S OUTPOST(1955); BUSTER KEATON STORY, THE(1957); CARELESS YEARS, THE(1957)
Elsie Sligh
NIGHT THE LIGHTS WENT OUT IN GEORGIA, THE(1981)
Memphis Slim
SERGEANT, THE(1968)
Iceberg Slim [Robert Beck]
TRICK BABY(1973), w
Slim Gaillard Trio
SWEETHEART OF SIGMA CHI(1946)
Scott Slimon
SUDDENLY, LAST SUMMER(1959, Brit.), set d; DAY THE EARTH CAUGHT FIRE, THE(1961, Brit.), set d; STOP ME BEFORE I KILL!(1961, Brit.), set d; BOY TEN FEET TALL, A(1965, Brit.), set d; DR. WHO AND THE DALEKS(1965, Brit.), set d; SKULL, THE(1965, Brit.), set d; TERRORNAUTS, THE(1967, Brit.), art d; THEY CAME FROM BEYOND SPACE(1967, Brit.), art d; SALT & PEPPER(1968, Brit.), set d; TORTURE GARDEN(1968, Brit.), art d; CRY OF THE BANSHEE(1970, Brit.), set d
Harold Sline
HOUSE OF WOMEN(1962), ph
Penny Slinger
OTHER SIDE OF THE UNDERNEATH, THE(1972, Brit.)
David Slingsby
ROAD WARRIOR, THE(1982, Aus.)
Mark Slipp
PARALLELS(1980, Can.), ed
Anne Slipyj
STRANGER IN HOLLYWOOD(1968), a, p
Rodion Slipyj
STRANGER IN HOLLYWOOD(1968), d&w
Jiri Slitr
DAISIES(1967, Czech.), m
Hana Slivkova
SHOP ON MAIN STREET, THE(1966, Czech.)
Marie Slivova
FIREMAN'S BALL, THE(1968, Czech.)
Urszula Sliwinska
CONTRACT, THE(1982, Pol.), ed
Charles Sloan
YOUNG DILLINGER(1965)
Edward Sloan
Misc. Silents
HIS PEOPLE(1925), d; BUTTERFLIES IN THE RAIN(1926), d
Estelle Sloan
NIGHT AND DAY(1946)
Goldie Sloan
CAPTAINS COURAGEOUS(1937)
James Sloan
Silents
ZERO(1928, Brit.), p
James B. Sloan
GREAT, MEADOW, THE(1931), p; HARD STEEL(1941, Brit.), p; GREAT MR. HANDEL, THE(1942, Brit.), p; THEY KNEW MR. KNIGHT(1945, Brit.), p
Jean-Pierre Sloan
LIFE LOVE DEATH(1969, Fr./Ital.)
John Sloan
REGAL CAVALCADE(1935, Brit.), p; BEYOND THIS PLACE(1959, Brit.), p
John R. Sloan
WILLIAM COMES TO TOWN(1948, Brit.), p; PAPER ORCHID(1949, Brit.), p; SEA DEVILS(1953), p; BEAUTIFUL STRANGER(1954, Brit.), p; KEEP IT CLEAN(1956, Brit.), p; PORT AFRIQUE(1956, Brit.), p; ABANDON SHIP(1957, Brit.), p; SAFE-CRACKER, THE(1958, Brit.), p; KILLERS OF KILIMANJARO(1960, Brit.), p; LET'S GET MARRIED(1960, Brit.), p; JOHNNY NOBODY(1965, Brit.), p; DAD'S ARMY(1971, Brit.), p; FRAGMENT OF FEAR(1971, Brit.), p; FORCE 10 FROM NAVARONE(1978, Brit.), p; NO SEX PLEASE–WE'RE BRITISH(1979, Brit.), p
Jon Sloan
FOXES(1980); KING OF THE MOUNTAIN(1981)
1984
STRANGERS KISS(1984)
Lisa Sloan
STARTING OVER(1979)
1984
RIVER, THE(1984)
Melvin Sloan
STAKEOUT ON DOPE STREET(1958), ed; FACE IN THE RAIN, A(1963), ed; LONNIE(1963), ed

Michael Sloan
ASSASSIN(1973, Brit.), w; MOMENTS(1974, Brit.), p, w
Olive Sloan
HOUSE IN MARSH ROAD, THE(1960, Brit.)
Patricia Sloan
FOUR BOYS AND A GUN(1957)
Paul Sloan
Silents
MANHATTAN(1924), w
Tod Sloan
MADISON SQUARE GARDEN(1932); MIDNIGHT PATROL, THE(1932)
Silents
KILLER, THE(1921)
Todd Sloan
Misc. Silents
DETERMINATION(1920)
Tot Sloan
DODGING THE DOLE(1936, Brit.)
William Sloan
IS EVERYBODY HAPPY?(1943); COVER GIRL(1944)
Allan Sloane
QUESTION 7(1961, U.S./Ger.), w; HIDING PLACE, THE(1975), w
Allen Sloane
MARTIN LUTHER(1953), w
Barbara Sloane
WIZARDS(1977)
Barton Sloane
4D MAN(1959), spec eff
Everett Sloane
CITIZEN KANE(1941); JOURNEY INTO FEAR(1942); LADY FROM SHANGHAI, THE(1948); JIGSAW(1949); PRINCE OF FOXES(1949); MEN, THE(1950); BIRD OF PARADISE(1951); BLUE VEIL, THE(1951); DESERT FOX, THE(1951); ENFORCER, THE(1951); PRINCE WHO WAS A THIEF, THE(1951); SELLOUT, THE(1951); SIROCCO(1951); WAY OF A GAUCHO(1952); BIG KNIFE, THE(1955); LUST FOR LIFE(1956); PATTERNS(1956); SOMEBODY UP THERE LIKES ME(1956); GUN RUNNERS, THE(1958); MARJORIE MORNINGSTAR(1958); HOME FROM THE HILL(1960); BY LOVE POSSESSED(1961); BRUSHFIRE(1962); MAN FROM THE DINERS' CLUB, THE(1963); DISORDERLY ORDERLY, THE(1964); PATSY, THE(1964); READY FOR THE PEOPLE(1964); MR. MAGOO'S HOLIDAY FESTIVAL(1970)
Misc. Talkies
HERCULES AND THE PRINCESS OF TROY(1966)
J. Sloane
STREET OF WOMEN(1932), set d
John Sloane
Silents
SOMEHOW GOOD(1927, Brit.), p
June Sloane
Silents
ROSE OF THE WORLD(1918)
Michael Sloane
ROUGH RIDERS OF CHEYENNE(1945); DAYS OF BUFFALO BILL(1946)
Olive Sloane
GOOD COMPANIONS(1933, Brit.); BRIDES TO BE(1934, Brit.); FACES(1934, Brit.); MUSIC HALL(1934, Brit.); SING AS WE GO(1934, Brit.); WOMAN IN COMMAND, THE(1934 Brit.); ALIBI INN(1935, Brit.); KEY TO HARMONY(1935, Brit.); HOWARD CASE, THE(1936, Brit.); IN THE SOUP(1936, Brit.); HE LOVED AN ACTRESS(1938, Brit.); MAKE IT THREE(1938, Brit.); INQUEST(1939, Brit.); LET THE PEOPLE SING(1942, Brit.); THOSE KIDS FROM TOWN(1942, Brit.); TOWER OF TERROR, THE(1942, Brit.); DUMMY TALKS, THE(1943, Brit.); THUNDER ROCK(1944, Brit.); THEY KNEW MR. KNIGHT(1945, Brit.); VOICE WITHIN, THE(1945, Brit.); SEND FOR PAUL TEMPLE(1946, Brit.); DEVIL'S PLOT, THE(1948, Brit.); OUTSIDER, THE(1949, Brit.); UNDER CAPRICORN(1949); SEVEN DAYS TO NOON(1950, Brit.); CURTAIN UP(1952, Brit.); FRANCHISE AFFAIR, THE(1952, Brit.); FRIGHTENED BRIDE, THE(1952, Brit.); MY WIFE'S LODGER(1952, Brit.); ONCE A SINNER(1952, Brit.); WATERFRONT WOMEN(1952, Brit.); ALF'S BABY(1953, Brit.); MEET MR. LUCIFER(1953, Brit.); GOLDEN LINK, THE(1954, Brit.); WEAK AND THE WICKED, THE(1954, Brit.); PRIZE OF GOLD, A(1955, Brit.); LAST MAN TO HANG, THE(1956, Brit.); BROTHERS IN LAW(1957, Brit.); MAN IN THE ROAD, THE(1957, Brit.); WRONG NUMBER(1959, Brit.); PRICE OF SILENCE, THE(1960, Brit.); IMMORAL CHARGE(1962, Brit.); HEAVENS ABOVE!(1963, Brit.); YOUR MONEY OR YOUR WIFE(1965, Brit.)
Silents
TRAPPED BY THE MORMONS(1922, Brit.); MONEY ISN'T EVERYTHING(1925, Brit.)
Misc. Silents
GREATHEART(1921, Brit.); ROGUES OF THE TURF(1923, Brit.)
Paul Sloane
HEARTS IN DIXIE(1929), p&d; CUCKOOS, THE(1930), d; HALF SHOT AT SUNRISE(1930), d; THREE SISTERS, THE(1930), d; CONSOLATION MARRIAGE(1931), d; TRAVELING HUSBANDS(1931), d; WAR CORRESPONDENT(1932), d; TERROR ABOARD(1933), d; WOMAN ACCUSED(1933), d; DOWN TO THEIR LAST YACHT(1934), d; LONE COWBOY(1934), d, w; STRAIGHT IS THE WAY(1934), d; HERE COMES THE BAND(1935), d, w; TEXANS, THE(1938), w
1984
STRANGER THAN PARADISE(1984, U.S./Ger.)
Silents
COMING OF AMOS, THE(1925), d; CORPORAL KATE(1926), d
Misc. Silents
MAN MUST LIVE, THE(1925), d; SHOCK PUNCH, THE(1925), d; TOO MANY KISSES(1925), d; CLINGING VINE, THE(1926), d; EVE'S LEAVES(1926), d; MADE FOR LOVE(1926), d; TURKISH DELIGHT(1927), d; BLUE DANUBE, THE(1928), d
Paul H. Sloane
GERONIMO(1939), d&w; SUN SETS AT DAWN, THE(1950), p, d&w
Silents
OVER THE HILL TO THE POORHOUSE(1920), w; BEYOND PRICE(1921), w; KNOW YOUR MEN(1921), w; SHACKLES OF GOLD(1922), w; SILVER WINGS(1922), w; WITHOUT FEAR(1922), w

Robert Sloane
COWBOY FROM BROOKLYN(1938), w; TWO GUYS FROM TEXAS(1948), w
Taylor Sloane
WILD RIDE, THE(1960), ph
W. Sloane
STREET OF WOMEN(1932), set d
William Sloane
DEVIL COMMANDS, THE(1941), w
Carl Sloboda
INFERNAL MACHINE(1933), w
Karl Sloboda
Silents
TEA FOR THREE(1927), w
Madame Slobodskaya
MAGIC BOX, THE(1952, Brit.)
Oda Slobodskaya
MOZART(1940, Brit.)
M. Slobodsky
SPRING(1948, USSR), w
Douglas Slocombe
BIG BLOCKADE, THE(1942, Brit.), ph; FOR THOSE IN PERIL(1944, Brit.), ph; GIRL ON THE CANAL, THE(1947, Brit.), ph; LOVES OF JOANNA GODDEN, THE(1947, Brit.), ph; ANOTHER SHORE(1948, Brit.), ph; CAPTIVE HEART, THE(1948, Brit.), ph; IT ALWAYS RAINS ON SUNDAY(1949, Brit.), ph; KIND HEARTS AND CORONETS(1949, Brit.), ph; SARABAND(1949, Brit.), ph; CAGE OF GOLD(1950, Brit.), ph; DANCE HALL(1950, Brit.), ph; HUE AND CRY(1950, Brit.), ph; RUN FOR YOUR MONEY, A(1950, Brit.), ph; LAVENDER HILL MOB, THE(1951, Brit.), ph; CRASH OF SILENCE(1952, Brit.), ph; HIS EXCELLENCY(1952, Brit.), ph; MAN IN THE WHITE SUIT, THE(1952), ph; TITFIELD THUNDERBOLT, THE(1953, Brit.), ph; LEASE OF LIFE(1954, Brit.), ph; LOVE LOTTERY, THE(1954, Brit.), ph; LIGHT TOUCH, THE(1955, Brit.), ph; DECISION AGAINST TIME(1957, Brit.), ph; PANIC IN THE PARLOUR(1957, Brit.), ph; SMALLEST SHOW ON EARTH, THE(1957, Brit.), ph; ALL AT SEA(1958, Brit.), ph; DAVY(1958, Brit.), ph; TREAD SOFTLY STRANGER(1959, Brit.), ph; BOY WHO STOLE A MILLION, THE(1960, Brit.), ph; CIRCUS OF HORRORS(1960, Brit.), ph; MARK, THE(1961, Brit.), ph; SCREAM OF FEAR(1961, Brit.), ph; FREUD(1962), ph; L-SHAPED ROOM, THE(1962, Brit.), ph; WONDERFUL TO BE YOUNG!(1962, Brit.), ph; GUNS AT BATASI(1964, Brit.), ph; SERVANT, THE(1964, Brit.), ph; THIRD SECRET, THE(1964, Brit.), ph; HIGH WIND IN JAMAICA, A(1965), ph; BLUE MAX, THE(1966), ph; PROMISE HER ANYTHING(1966), ph; FATHOM(1967), ph; FEARLESS VAMPIRE KILLERS, OR PARDON ME BUT YOUR TEETH ARE IN MY NECK, THE(1967), ph; ROBBERY(1967, Brit.), ph; BOOM!(1968), ph; LION IN WINTER, THE(1968, Brit.), ph; ITALIAN JOB, THE(1969, Brit.), ph; BUTTERCUP CHAIN, THE(1971, Brit.), ph; MURPHY'S WAR(1971, Brit.), ph; MUSIC LOVERS, THE(1971, Brit.), ph; TRAVELS WITH MY AUNT(1972, Brit.), ph; JESUS CHRIST, SUPERSTAR(1973), ph; DESTRUCTORS, THE(1974, Brit.), ph; HEDDA(1975, Brit.), ph; MAIDS, THE(1975, Brit.), ph; ROLLERBALL(1975), ph; THAT LUCKY TOUCH(1975, Brit.), ph; BAWDY ADVENTURES OF TOM JONES, THE(1976, Brit.), ph; NASTY HABITS(1976, Brit.), ph; SAILOR WHO FELL FROM GRACE WITH THE SEA, THE(1976, Brit.), ph; CLOSE ENCOUNTERS OF THE THIRD KIND(1977), ph; JULIA(1977), ph; CARAVANS(1978, U.S./Iranian), ph; LOST AND FOUND(1979), ph; LADY VANISHES, THE(1980, Brit.), ph; NIJINSKY(1980, Brit.), ph; RAIDERS OF THE LOST ARK(1981), ph; NEVER SAY NEVER AGAIN(1983), ph; PIRATES OF PENZANCE, THE(1983), ph
1984
INDIANA JONES AND THE TEMPLE OF DOOM(1984), ph
George Slocombe
UNDERGROUND GUERRILLAS(1944, Brit.), w; MURDERER LIVES AT NUMBER 21, THE(1947, Fr.), titles
Jeff Slocombe
Z.P.G.(1972)
Cy Slocum
OUR RELATIONS(1936); WAY OUT WEST(1937); SWISS MISS(1938); MR. BLANDINGS BUILDS HIS DREAM HOUSE(1948)
George Slocum
ALL MY SONS(1948); RED DESERT(1949); BORDER OUTLAWS(1950); KILLER SHARK(1950); MULE TRAIN(1950); TIMBER FURY(1950); TALES OF ROBIN HOOD(1951); PRISONER OF ZENDA, THE(1952)
Hylah Slocum
PALMY DAYS(1931)
Tom Slocum
MOMENT BY MOMENT(1978); CATTLE ANNIE AND LITTLE BRITCHES(1981), m
Robert Slodmak
COMPLIMENTS OF MR. FLOW(1941, Fr.), d
Al Sloey
COWBOY FROM LONESOME RIVER(1944)
Cy Slokum
LADY BY CHOICE(1934)
Anthony Sloman
RADIO ON(1980, Brit./Ger.), ed
Edward Sloman
GIRL ON THE BARGE, THE(1929), d; KIBITZER, THE(1929), d; HELL'S ISLAND(1930), d; LOST ZEPPELIN(1930), d; SOLDIERS AND WOMEN(1930), d; CAUGHT(1931), d; CONQUERING HORDE, THE(1931), d; GUN SMOKE(1931), d; HIS WOMAN(1931), d; MURDER BY THE CLOCK(1931), d; WAYWARD(1932), d; DOG OF FLANDERS, A(1935), d
Silents
FRAME UP, THE(1917), d; FAIR ENOUGH(1918), d; IN BAD(1918), d; MOLLY OF THE FOLLIES(1919), d; MARRIAGE OF WILLIAM ASHE, THE(1921), d; TEN DOLLAR RAISE, THE(1921), d; SHATTERED IDOLS(1922), d; EAGLE'S FEATHER, THE(1923), d; BEAUTIFUL CHEAT, THE(1926), d; OLD SOAK, THE(1926), d; ALIAS THE DEACON(1928), d; LOVE ME AND THE WORLD IS MINE(1928), w
Misc. Silents
CONVICT KING, THE(1915), d; BOND WITHIN, THE(1916), d; DUST(1916), d; EMBODIED THOUGHT, THE(1916), a, d; INNER STRUGGLE, THE(1916), d; LONE STAR(1916), d; LYING LIPS(1916), d; RECLAMATION, THE(1916), d; SEQUEL TO THE DIAMOND FROM THE SKY(1916), d; TWINKLER, THE(1916), d; WOMAN'S DARING, A(1916), d; FATE AND THE CHILD(1917), d; HIGH PLAY(1917), d; MASKED HEART, THE(1917), d; MY FIGHTING GENTLEMAN(1917), d; PRIDE AND THE MAN(1917), d; SHACKLES OF TRUTH(1917), d; SNAP JUDGEMENT(1917), d; GHOST OF ROSY TAYLOR, THE(1918), d; MANTLE OF CHARITY, THE(1918), d; MIDNIGHT TRAIL, THE(1918), d; MONEY ISN'T EVERYTHING(1918), d; PUT UP YOUR HANDS!(1919), d; WESTERNERS, THE(1919), d; BLIND YOUTH(1920), d; BURNING DAYLIGHT(1920), d; LUCK OF GERALDINE LAIRD, THE(1920), d; MUTINY OF THE ELSINORE, THE(1920), d; SAGEBRUSHER, THE(1920), d; STAR ROVER, THE(1920), d; HIGH GEAR JEFFREY(1921), d; OTHER WOMAN, THE(1921), d; PILGRIMS OF THE NIGHT(1921), d; QUICK ACTION(1921), d; WOMAN HE LOVED, THE(1922), d; BACKBONE(1923), d; LAST HOUR, THE(1923), d; PRICE OF PLEASURE, THE(1925), d; STORM BREAKER, THE(1925), d; UP THE LADDER(1925), d; SURRENDER(1927), d; FOREIGN LEGION, THE(1928), d; WE AMERICANS(1928), d; LOST ZEPPELIN, THE(1929), d
Edward H. Sloman
PUTTIN' ON THE RITZ(1930), d
Edward S. Sloman
Misc. Silents
GYPSY'S TRUST, THE(1917), d; NEW YORK LUCK(1917), d; SANDS OF SACRIFICE(1917), d; SEA MASTER, THE(1917), d; BIT OF JADE, A(1918), d
Hilda Hollis Sloman
Misc. Silents
JEWEL(1915)
Robert Sloman
YOUNG AND WILLING(1964, Brit.), w
Roger Sloman
MONSTER CLUB, THE(1981, Brit.); PRIEST OF LOVE(1981, Brit.); REDS(1981)
Susan Sloman
FIDDLER ON THE ROOF(1971)
Ted Sloman [Edward Sloman]
JURY'S SECRET, THE(1938), d
Gisa W. Slonim
NEITHER BY DAY NOR BY NIGHT(1972, U.S./Israel), w
Mordecai Slonim
NEITHER BY DAY NOR BY NIGHT(1972, U.S./Israel), p
Merritt Sloper
KLONDIKE FEVER(1980)
John Slosser
OREGON TRAIL, THE(1959)
R. John Slosser
OCEAN'S ELEVEN(1960)
Nate Slot
HIT THE DECK(1930)
Gene Slott
BITTERSWEET LOVE(1976), p; LAS VEGAS LADY(1976), a, p
Harry M. Slott
YOUNG AND THE BRAVE, THE(1963), w
Nate Slott
NIGHT PARADE(1929, Brit.)
Vaclav Sloup
SWEET LIGHT IN A DARK ROOM(1966, Czech.)
Sam Slovick
1984
RED DAWN(1984)
Vera Slovina
TARAS FAMILY, THE(1946, USSR)
Ye. Slovtsova
QUEEN OF SPADES(1961, USSR), cos
Georgia Slowe
1984
SECRET PLACES(1984, Brit.)
James Sloyan
XANADU(1980)
James J. Sloyan
TRAVELING EXECUTIONER, THE(1970); GANG THAT COULDN'T SHOOT STRAIGHT, THE(1971); STING, THE(1973)
J.M. Slutker
I'M GOING TO GET YOU ... ELLIOT BOY(1971, Can.), p
Oksana Sluzhenko
MOTHER AND DAUGHTER(1965, USSR)
Sly and the Family Stone
MID-DAY MISTRESS(1968), m
Leonard Slye [Roy Rogers]
OLD HOMESTEAD, THE(1935)
Fred Slyter
1776(1972); ULTIMATE WARRIOR, THE(1975); WHOSE LIFE IS IT ANYWAY?(1981)
Gordon Smaaladen
NORTHERN LIGHTS(1978)
Sergio Smacchi
SUPER FUZZ(1981)
David Smader
JERUSALEM FILE, THE(1972, U.S./Israel)
Andre Smagghe
ONE, TWO, THREE(1961), d; SKY ABOVE HEAVEN(1964, Fr./Ital.); ONE-TRICK PONY(1980), d
Mustapha Smaili
OLIVE TREES OF JUSTICE, THE(1967, Fr.)
Ewa Smal
CONTRACT, THE(1982, Pol.), ed
Joellina Smalda
MADWOMAN OF CHAILLOT, THE(1969)
Valerie Smaldone
BORN IN FLAMES(1983)
Amber Smale
ANGEL IN MY POCKET(1969)
Ade Small
DOCTOR DETROIT(1983); GOING BERSERK(1983)
Austin Small
DOWN RIVER(1931, Brit.), w
Bennie Small
DRUMS O' VOODOO(1934)

Bernard Small
CHALLENGE, THE(1948), p; CREEPER, THE(1948), p; THIRTEEN LEAD SOLDIERS(1948), p; IROQUOIS TRAIL, THE(1950), p; INDIAN UPRISING(1951), p; LONE GUN, THE(1954), ed; OVERLAND PACIFIC(1954), ed; FIVE GUNS TO TOMBSTONE(1961), ed

Bob Small
EYES OF A STRANGER(1980)

Brian T. Small
HOUSE ON SORORITY ROW, THE(1983)

Bud Small
PLAINSMAN, THE(1966), ed; MANCHU EAGLE MURDER CAPER MYSTERY, THE(1975), ed

Buddy Small
KANSAS CITY CONFIDENTIAL(1952), ed; RAIDERS OF THE SEVEN SEAS(1953), ed; 99 RIVER STREET(1953), ed

Eddie Small
I'LL TELL THE WORLD(1945)

Edward Small
CLANCY IN WALL STREET(1930), d; COUNT OF MONTE CRISTO, THE(1934), p; TRANSATLANTIC MERRY-GO-ROUND(1934), p; LET 'EM HAVE IT(1935), p; MELODY LINGERS ON, THE(1935), p; RED SALUTE(1935), p; BRIDE WALKS OUT, THE(1936), p; LAST OF THE MOHICANS, THE(1936), p; NEW FACES OF 1937(1937), p; SEA DEVILS(1937), p; SUPER SLEUTH(1937), p; TOAST OF NEW YORK, THE(1937), p; WE WHO ARE ABOUT TO DIE(1937), p; DUKE OF WEST POINT, THE(1938), p; KING OF THE TURF(1939), p; MAN IN THE IRON MASK, THE(1939), p; KIT CARSON(1940), p; MY SON, MY SON!(1940), p; SON OF MONTE CRISTO(1940), p; SOUTH OF PAGO PAGO(1940), p; CORSICAN BROTHERS, THE(1941), p; INTERNATIONAL LADY(1941), p; FRIENDLY ENEMIES(1942), p; GENTLEMAN AFTER DARK, A(1942), p; MISS ANNIE ROONEY(1942), p; TWIN BEDS(1942), p; ABROAD WITH TWO YANKS(1944), p; UP IN MABEL'S ROOM(1944), p; BREWSTER'S MILLIONS(1945), p; GETTING GERTIE'S GARTER(1945), p; TEMPTATION(1946), p; BLACK ARROW(1948), p; FULLER BRUSH MAN(1948), p; RAW DEAL(1948), p; BLACK MAGIC(1949), p; DAVY CROCKETT, INDIAN SCOUT(1950), p; LORNA DOONE(1951), p; TEXAS RANGERS, THE(1951), p; VALENTINO(1951), p; CRIPPLE CREEK(1952), p; KANSAS CITY CONFIDENTIAL(1952), p; SCANDAL SHEET(1952), p; GUN BELT(1953), p; 99 RIVER STREET(1953), p; KHYBER PATROL(1954), p; LONE GUN, THE(1954), p; OVERLAND PACIFIC(1954), p; SOUTHWEST PASSAGE(1954), p; NAKED STREET, THE(1955), p; TOP GUN(1955), p; MONKEY ON MY BACK(1957), p; TIMBUKTU(1959), p; LOSS OF INNOCENCE(1961, Brit.), p; JACK THE GIANT KILLER(1962), p; I'LL TAKE SWEDEN(1965), p; BOY, DID I GET A WRONG NUMBER!(1966), p; FRANKIE AND JOHNNY(1966), p; WICKED DREAMS OF PAULA SCHULTZ, THE(1968), p; CHRISTINE JORGENSEN STORY, THE(1970), p

George Small
LAST RITES(1980), m
1984
SPLITZ(1984), m

Jerome Small
TWILIGHT PEOPLE(1972, Phil.), w

Joan Small
ROCK YOU SINNERS(1957, Brit.)

Lela Small
FIGHT FOR YOUR LIFE(1977)

Louis Small
RECKLESS RANGER(1937)

Louise Small
CRUSADE AGAINST RACKETS(1937); MELODY OF THE PLAINS(1937)

Marya Small
SLEEPER(1973); ONE FLEW OVER THE CUCKOO'S NEST(1975); WILD PARTY, THE(1975); WORLD'S GREATEST LOVER, THE(1977); GREAT SMOKEY ROADBLOCK, THE(1978); THANK GOD IT'S FRIDAY(1978); DREAMER(1979); FADE TO BLACK(1980); AMERICAN POP(1981); NATIONAL LAMPOON'S CLASS REUNION(1982); ZAPPED!(1982)

Michael Small
JENNY(1969), m; OUT OF IT(1969), m, md; PUZZLE OF A DOWNFALL CHILD(1970), m, md; REVOLUTIONARY, THE(1970, Brit.), m&md; DEALING: OR THE BERKELEY-TO-BOSTON FORTY-BRICK LOST-BAG BLUES(1971), m; KLUTE(1971), m; SPORTING CLUB, THE(1971), m; CHILD'S PLAY(1972), m; LOVE AND PAIN AND THE WHOLE DAMN THING(1973), m, md; PARALLAX VIEW, THE(1974), m; DROWNING POOL, THE(1975), m; NIGHT MOVES(1975), m; STEPFORD WIVES, THE(1975), m; MARATHON MAN(1976), m, md; AUDREY ROSE(1977), m; COMES A HORSEMAN(1978), m; DRIVER, THE(1978), m; GIRLFRIENDS(1978), m; GOING IN STYLE(1979), m; THOSE LIPS, THOSE EYES(1980), m; CONTINENTAL DIVIDE(1981), m, m/l; POSTMAN ALWAYS RINGS TWICE, THE(1981), m; ROLLOVER(1981), m; STAR CHAMBER, THE(1983), m
1984
FIRSTBORN(1984), m; KIDCO(1984), m

Neva Small
FIDDLER ON THE ROOF(1971); LOOKING UP(1977)

Norma Small
LIAR'S DICE(1980)

Robert Small
SPRING BREAK(1983)

Small Faces
DATELINE DIAMONDS(1966, Brit.)

Peter Smalley
WILD DUCK, THE(1983, Aus.), w

Phillips Smalley
AVIATOR, THE(1929); HIGH VOLTAGE(1929); CHARLEY'S AUNT(1930); PEACOCK ALLEY(1930); HIGH STAKES(1931); LADY FROM NOWHERE(1931); LAWLESS WOMAN, THE(1931); MIDNIGHT SPECIAL(1931); ESCAPADE(1932); FACE ON THE BARROOM FLOOR, THE(1932); GREEKS HAD A WORD FOR THEM(1932); HELL'S HEADQUARTERS(1932); MIDNIGHT WARNING, THE(1932); MURDER AT DAWN(1932); SINISTER HANDS(1932); THIRTEENTH GUEST, THE(1932); WIDOW IN SCARLET(1932); SECRET SINNERS(1933); SLIGHTLY MARRIED(1933); BIG RACE, THE(1934); BOLERO(1934); CHAINED(1934); FUGITIVE LADY(1934); STOLEN SWEETS(1934); HOLD'EM YALE(1935); IT'S IN THE AIR(1935); NIGHT AT THE OPERA, A(1935); NIGHT LIFE OF THE GODS(1935); TWO FOR TONIGHT(1935); LOVE ON THE RUN(1936); YOURS FOR THE ASKING(1936); HOTEL HAYWIRE(1937); MAKE WAY FOR TOMORROW(1937); SECOND HONEYMOON(1937);

BOOLOO(1938); I AM THE LAW(1938)
Silents
COUNTRY MOUSE, THE(1914), d; FALSE COLORS(1914), a, w; MADCAP BETTY(1915), d; SCANDAL(1915), a, d; DUMB GIRL OF PORTICI(1916), d; HOP, THE DEVIL'S BREW(1916), a, d; JOHN NEEDHAM'S DOUBLE(1916), d; SAVING THE FAMILY NAME(1916), a, d; BLOT, THE(1921), d&w; NOBODY'S BRIDE(1923); TEMPTATION(1923); DAUGHTERS OF TODAY(1924); AWFUL TRUTH, THE(1925); SOUL MATES(1925); STELLA MARIS(1925); QUEEN O' DIAMONDS(1926); TAXI MYSTERY, THE(1926); IRRESISTIBLE LOVER, THE(1927); MAN CRAZY(1927); SENSATION SEEKERS(1927); STAGE KISSES(1927); TEA FOR THREE(1927); HONEYMOON FLATS(1928); SINNERS IN LOVE(1928)
Misc. Silents
MERCHANT OF VENICE, THE(1914), a, d; JEWEL(1915), d; YANKEE GIRL, THE(1915), d; EYE OF GOD, THE(1916), d; FLIRT, THE(1916), d; IDLE WIVES(1916), a, d; WANTED - A HOME(1916), d; WHERE ARE MY CHILDREN?(1916), d; DOUBLE STANDARD, THE(1917), d; HAND THAT ROCKS THE CRADLE, THE(1917), a, d; BORROWED CLOTHES(1918), d; DOCTOR AND THE WOMAN, THE(1918), d; FOR HUSBANDS ONLY(1918), d; PRICE OF A GOOD TIME, THE(1918), d; SCANDAL MONGERS(1918), a, d; FORBIDDEN(1919), d; WHEN A GIRL LOVES(1919), d; TOO WISE WIVES(1921); SELF-MADE WIFE, THE(1923); CHEAP KISSES(1924); FATE OF A FLIRT, THE(1925); BORDER PATROL, THE(1928); BROADWAY DADDIES(1928); TRUE HEAVEN(1929)

Charlie Smalls
WIZ, THE(1978), w; DRUM(1976), md

Beth Smallwood
1984
TANK(1984)

Joe Smallwood
SOME BLONDES ARE DANGEROUS(1937)

Neville Smallwood
GENGHIS KHAN(U.S./Brit./Ger./Yugo), makeup; VIKINGS, THE(1958), makeup; JOHN PAUL JONES(1959), makeup; MAIN ATTRACTION, THE(1962, Brit.), makeup; TAMAHINE(1964, Brit.), makeup; HEROES OF TELEMARK, THE(1965, Brit.), makeup; MODESTY BLAISE(1966, Brit.), makeup; LAST SAFARI, THE(1967, Brit.), makeup; MIDSUMMER NIGHT'S DREAM, A(1969, Brit.), makeup; SINFUL DAVEY(1969, Brit.), makeup; NICHOLAS AND ALEXANDRA(1971, Brit.), makeup; UNMAN, WITTERING AND ZIGO(1971, Brit.), makeup; ZEPPELIN(1971, Brit.), makeup; FROM BEYOND THE GRAVE(1974, Brit.), makeup; MOHAMMAD, MESSENGER OF GOD(1976, Lebanon/Brit.), makeup; ORCA(1977), makeup

Ray C. Smallwood
Misc. Silents
BEST OF LUCK, THE(1920), d; BILLIONS(1920), d; HEART OF A CHILD, THE(1920), d; MADAME PEACOCK(1920), d; CAMILLE(1921), d; MY OLD KENTUCKY HOME(1922), d; QUEEN OF THE MOULIN ROUGE(1922), d; WHEN THE DESERT CALLS(1922), d

Tucker Smallwood
1984
COTTON CLUB, THE(1984)

Yuri Smaltzoff
HOW TO SEDUCE A WOMAN(1974), ch

June Smaney
SAINTED SISTERS, THE(1948); NEW KIND OF LOVE, A(1963); PATSY, THE(1964)

Mabel Smaney
FRAMED(1947); LADY FROM SHANGHAI, THE(1948); EVERYBODY DOES IT(1949); KNOCK ON ANY DOOR(1949); STRATTON STORY, THE(1949); SELLOUT, THE(1951); NEW KIND OF LOVE, A(1963); PATSY, THE(1964)

Bobby Smart
Misc. Silents
HIS GREAT CHANCE(1923)

G. Smart
TILL DEATH(1978), ph

Jack Smart
GIRL OVERBOARD(1937); LOVE IN A BUNGALOW(1937); TOP OF THE TOWN(1937); WHEN LOVE IS YOUNG(1937); WILDCATTER, THE(1937); 100 MEN AND A GIRL(1937); SOME LIKE IT HOT(1939); SHADOW OF A WOMAN(1946); KISS OF DEATH(1947); THAT HAGEN GIRL(1947); FAT MAN, THE(1951)

Jean Smart
1984
FLASHPOINT(1984); PROTOCOL(1984)

John Smart
CIPHER BUREAU(1938)

John E. Smart
PANAMA PATROL(1939)

Leroy Smart
ROCKERS(1980)

Patricia Smart
NOTORIOUS(1946)

Patsy Smart
MAILBAG ROBBERY(1957, Brit.); TELL-TALE HEART, THE(1962, Brit.); WHAT EVERY WOMAN WANTS(1962, Brit.); LEO THE LAST(1970, Brit.); LONG AGO, TOMORROW(1971, Brit.); O LUCKY MAN!(1973, Brit.); PINK PANTHER STRIKES AGAIN, THE(1976, Brit.); LEGACY, THE(1979, Brit.); ELEPHANT MAN, THE(1980, Brit.); TESS(1980, Fr./Brit.)
1984
ELECTRIC DREAMS(1984)

Peter Smart
WHAT'S NEXT?(1975, Brit.)

Ralph Smart
BORN LUCKY(1932, Brit.), w; C.O.D.(1932, Brit.), w; HIS LORDSHIP(1932, Brit.), w; HOTEL SPLENDIDE(1932, Brit.), w; NIGHT OF THE PARTY, THE(1934, Brit.), w; CRIME UNLIMITED(1935, Brit.), w; PHANTOM LIGHT, THE(1935, Brit.), w; ALF'S BUTTON AFLOAT(1938, Brit.), w; CONVICT 99(1938, Brit.), w; GOOD OLD DAYS, THE(1939, Brit.), w; GASBAGS(1940, Brit.), w; OVERLANDERS, THE(1946, Brit./Aus.), p; BUSH CHRISTMAS(1947, Brit.), d, w; BOY, A GIRL AND A BIKE, A(1949 Brit.), d; BITTER SPRINGS(1950, Aus.), d; CURTAIN UP(1952, Brit.), d; IVORY HUNTER(1952, Brit.), w; NEVER TAKE NO FOR AN ANSWER(1952, Brit./Ital.), d, w; ALWAYS A BRIDE(1954, Brit.), d, w
Misc. Silents
WOODPIGEON PATROL, THE(1930, Brit.), d

Roy Smart
BEDKNOBS AND BROOMSTICKS(1971)
Sam Smart
1984
SUCCESS IS THE BEST REVENGE(1984, Brit.)
Tom Smart
QUADROON(1972), ph
Tony Smart
BREAKER MORANT(1980, Aus.), stunts
1984
NEVERENDING STORY, THE(1984, Ger.), stunts
George A. Smathers
MIAMI STORY, THE(1954)
June Smavey
RING OF TERROR(1962)
Bruce Smeaton
CARS THAT ATE PARIS, THE(1974, Aus.), m; GREAT MACARTHY, THE(1975, Aus.), m; PICNIC AT HANGING ROCK(1975, Aus.), m; DEVIL'S PLAYGROUND, THE(1976, Aus.), m; ELIZA FRASER(1976, Aus.), m; TRESPASSERS, THE(1976, Aus.), m; SUMMERFIELD(1977, Aus.), m; CHANT OF JIMMIE BLACKSMITH, THE(1980, Aus.), m; GRENDEL GRENDEL GRENDEL(1981, Aus.), m; LAST OF THE KNUCKLEMEN, THE(1981, Aus.), m; BARBAROSA(1982), m; MONKEY GRIP(1983, Aus.), m
1984
ICEMAN(1984), m; SQUIZZY TAYLOR(1984, Aus.), m
Ken Smedberg
SUMMER SCHOOL TEACHERS(1977)
Melvina Smedley
LAUGHING POLICEMAN, THE(1973)
Richard Smedley
Misc. Talkies
ABDUCTORS, THE(1972)
Michael Smedley-Astin
THEATRE OF DEATH(1967, Brit.), p
Brian Smedley-Aston
GIRL WITH GREEN EYES(1964, Brit.), ed; TIME LOST AND TIME REMEMBERED(1966, Brit.), ed; UNCLE, THE(1966, Brit.), ed; SEBASTIAN(1968, Brit.), ed; SHUTTERED ROOM, THE(1968, Brit.), ed; STRANGE AFFAIR, THE(1968, Brit.), ed; PEOPLE NEXT DOOR, THE(1970), ed; SQUIRM(1976), ed; VAMPYRES, DAUGHTERS OF DRACULA(1977, Brit.), p; MUSIC MACHINE, THE(1979, Brit.), p, ed
E.M. Smedley-Aston
EXTRA DAY, THE(1956, Brit.), p; TWO-WAY STRETCH(1961, Brit.), p; LIFE IS A CIRCUS(1962, Brit.), p; WILDCATS OF ST. TRINIAN'S, THE(1980, Brit.), p
David Smeed
SUMMERFIELD(1977, Aus.)
Enid Smeedon
LADY GODIVA RIDES AGAIN(1955, Brit.)
Derek Smek
MYSTERY SUBMARINE(1963, Brit.)
Donald Smelick
SOUND OF FURY, THE(1950)
Vladimir Smeral
SKELETON ON HORSEBACK(1940, Czech.); MOST BEAUTIFUL AGE, THE(1970, Czech.); BLACK SUN, THE(1979, Czech.)
Ida Smeraldo
VICIOUS YEARS, THE(1950); BRING YOUR SMILE ALONG(1955); RAYMIE(1960)
Ron Smerczak
HOUSE OF WHIPCORD(1974, Brit.)
Bedrich Smetana
VOICE IN THE WIND(1944), m
1984
BASILEUS QUARTET(1984, Ital.), m
Felix Smetana
5 SINNERS(1961, Ger.), art d; $100 A NIGHT(1968, Ger.), art d
Jack Smethurst
KIND OF LOVING, A(1962, Brit.); OPERATION SNAFU(1965, Brit.); MAIN CHANCE, THE(1966, Brit.); RUN WITH THE WIND(1966, Brit.); NIGHT AFTER NIGHT AFTER NIGHT(1970, Brit.); CHARRIOTS OF FIRE(1981, Brit.)
Misc. Talkies
LOVE THY NEIGHBOUR(1973)
Lida Smeyan
WELCOME KOSTYA!(1965, USSR)
Daniel Smid
KREMLIN LETTER, THE(1970)
Jan Smid
TRANSPORT FROM PARADISE(1967, Czech.)
Karel Smid
FIFTH HORSEMAN IS FEAR, THE(1968, Czech.)
Smidgeon the Dog
GREAT AMERICAN PASTIME, THE(1956)
Ulla Smidje
DEVIL, THE(1963); EMIGRANTS, THE(1972, Swed.)
Burr Smidt
YOUNG SAVAGES, THE(1961), art d; REQUIEM FOR A HEAVYWEIGHT(1962), art d; NO WAY TO TREAT A LADY(1968); SLAVES(1969), art d
Smutty Smiff
1984
WHERE THE BOYS ARE '84(1984)
Jack Smight
I'D RATHER BE RICH(1964), d; THIRD DAY, THE(1965), p&d; HARPER(1966), d; KALEIDOSCOPE(1966, Brit.), d; NO WAY TO TREAT A LADY(1968), d; SECRET WAR OF HARRY FRIGG, THE(1968), d; ILLUSTRATED MAN, THE(1969), d; STRATEGY OF TERROR(1969), d; RABBIT, RUN(1970), d; TRAVELING EXECUTIONER, THE(1970), p&d; AIRPORT 1975(1974), d; MIDWAY(1976), d; DAMNATION ALLEY(1977), d; FAST BREAK(1979), a, d; LOVING COUPLES(1980), d
Gina Smika
SWORD AND THE SORCERER, THE(1982)

Kurt Smildsin
1984
SAM'S SON(1984)
Ted Smile
SON OF THE RENEGADE(1953); JUBILEE TRAIL(1954); CATTLE EMPIRE(1958)
Alan Smiler
ROCKET ATTACK, U.S.A.(1961), ed
Finch Smiles
BEHIND THAT CURTAIN(1929); LAST OF MRS. CHEYNEY, THE(1929)
Silents
LOST WORLD, THE(1925); BANDIT'S SON, THE(1927)
Frank Finch Smiles
Silents
MY BEST GIRL(1927)
Anne Smiley
GUILT(1930, Brit.)
Brenda Smiley
MAIDSTONE(1970)
Charles Smiley
Silents
ABRAHAM LINCOLN(1924)
Misc. Silents
SPIRIT OF GOOD, THE(1920)
Charles A. Smiley
Silents
GUILE OF WOMEN(1921); LOADED DOOR, THE(1922)
Delores Smiley
SECOND FIDDLE TO A STEEL GUITAR(1965)
George Smiley
NEW FACES(1954)
Harry Smiley
OUR LEADING CITIZEN(1939)
John Smiley
Silents
GOD'S HALF ACRE(1916); ADOPTED SON, THE(1917); OUT YONDER(1920)
Misc. Silents
GRAY HORROR, THE(1915); HALF MILLION BRIBE, THE(1916); PATSY(1917); UNBROKEN PROMISE, THE(1919)
Joe Smiley
Silents
ISLE OF CONQUEST(1919); LUCK AND PLUCK(1919); NEVER SAY QUIT(1919)
Misc. Silents
PUBLIC BE DAMNED(1917)
John A. Smiley
Misc. Silents
FORTUNATE YOUTH, THE(1916)
Joseph Smiley
Silents
JOAN OF PLATTSBURG(1918); SCARAB RING, THE(1921); WILD GOOSE, THE(1921); WOMAN GOD CHANGED, THE(1921); OLD HOME WEEK(1925); POLICE PATROL, THE(1925); ALOMA OF THE SOUTH SEAS(1926); UNTAMED LADY, THE(1926); POTTERS, THE(1927)
Misc. Silents
GRAY HORROR, THE(1915); LOVE OF WOMEN, THE(1915), d; PATH TO THE RAINBOW, THE(1915), d; RATED AT $10.000.000(1915); VOICES FROM THE PAST(1915), a, d; HEART OF THE WILDS(1918); HITTING THE TRAIL(1918); QUEEN OF HEARTS, THE(1918); POISON PEN, THE(1919); LAW OF THE YUKON, THE(1920); OLD OAKEN BUCKET, THE(1921); RICH SLAVE, THE(1921); BLONDE VAMPIRE, THE(1922)
Joseph W. Smiley
Silents
LIFE WITHOUT SOUL(1916), d
Misc. Silents
THREADS OF DESTINY(1914), d; WHOM THE GODS WOULD DESTROY(1915), d
Pril Smiley
PREMONITION, THE(1976), m
Ralph Smiley
MY FAVORITE SPY(1951); SNIPER, THE(1952); REAR WINDOW(1954); BULLET FOR JOEY, A(1955); FLIGHT TO HONG KONG(1956); PARTY GIRL(1958); MADIGAN(1968)
Robert Smiley
LET'S LIVE AGAIN(1948), w; YOU FOR ME(1952)
Smiley & Kitty
SQUARE DANCE JUBILEE(1949)
James Smilie
JAGUAR LIVES(1979)
Bozo Smiljanic
1984
NADIA(1984, U.S./Yugo.)
Bill Smillie
PIRANHA(1978); WHEN TIME RAN OUT(1980)
1984
PHILADELPHIA EXPERIMENT, THE(1984)
Syd Smillie
1984
SURF II(1984), art d
D.G. Smilnak
PURSUIT OF D.B. COOPER, THE(1981)
David Smilow
SPRING BREAK(1983), w
A.D. Smiranin
Misc. Silents
BREAK-UP, THE(1930, USSR)
Charlie Smirke
GALLOPING MAJOR, THE(1951, Brit.)
Anatole Smirnoff
FIRE DOWN BELOW(1957, U.S./Brit.); FRIENDS AND NEIGHBORS(1963, Brit.)

Yakov Smirnoff
1984
  ADVENTURES OF BUCKAROO BANZAI: ACROSS THE 8TH DIMENSION, THE(1984); MOSCOW ON THE HUDSON(1984)
A. Smirnov
  GORDEYEV FAMILY, THE(1961, U.S.S.R.), makeup; SOUND OF LIFE, THE(1962, USSR); NIGHT BEFORE CHRISTMAS, A(1963, USSR); RESURRECTION(1963, USSR); NINE DAYS OF ONE YEAR(1964, USSR); WELCOME KOSTYA!(1965, USSR); MEET ME IN MOSCOW(1966, USSR); WAR AND PEACE(1968, USSR)
Boris Smirnov
  MAN OF MUSIC(1953, USSR); RESURRECTION(1963, USSR); WAR AND PEACE(1968, USSR); THREE SISTERS, THE(1969, USSR)
E. Smirnov
  MY NAME IS IVAN(1963, USSR), w
Igor Smirnov
  CHILDHOOD OF MAXIM GORKY(1938, Russ.)
N. Smirnov
  SUN SHINES FOR ALL, THE(1961, USSR)
Nikolai Smirnov
  AND QUIET FLOWS THE DON(1960 USSR)
Sergey Smirnov
  ITALIANO BRAVA GENTE(1965, Ital./USSR), w
V. Smirnov
  WAR AND PEACE(1968, USSR)
Vladislav Smirnov
  STAR INSPECTOR, THE(1980, USSR), w
Mme. Smirnova
  DRESSED TO THRILL(1935)
A. Smirnova
  THEY WANTED PEACE(1940, USSR)
Anna Smirnova
  LAD FROM OUR TOWN(1941, USSR); NO GREATER LOVE(1944, USSR); ROAD HOME, THE(1947, USSR)
Dina Smirnova
  SHE GOES TO WAR(1929); SCARLET EMPRESS, THE(1934); SYLVIA SCARLETT(1936); ONCE UPON A HONEYMOON(1942); MASQUERADE IN MEXICO(1945); ROYAL SCANDAL, A(1945); NORTHWEST OUTPOST(1947)
G. Smirnova
  HOUSE WITH AN ATTIC, THE(1964, USSR)
L. Smirnova
  DIARY OF A NAZI(1943, USSR), w
Lida Smirnova
  WELCOME KOSTYA!(1965, USSR)
Lidiya Smirnova
  MARRIAGE OF BALZAMINOV, THE(1966, USSR)
Tina Smirnova
  FOOLS FOR SCANDAL(1938)
Y. Smirnova
  MASSACRE AT CENTRAL HIGH(1976)
Misc. Silents
  ROMANCE OF A RUSSIAN BALLERINA(1913, USSR); CHILD OF THE BIG CITY(1914, USSR)
Z. Smirnova-Nemirovich
  WAR AND PEACE(1968, USSR)
Anna Smirrell
  DOWN OUR ALLEY(1939, Brit.)
Howard Smit
  RENEGADES OF SONORA(1948), makeup; RED MENACE, THE(1949), makeup
John Smit
1984
  QUESTION OF SILENCE(1984, Neth.)
Leonid Smit
  MEN OF THE SEA(1938, USSR)
Smith
  MONGREL(1982), spec eff& makeup
Mrs. Smith
Silents
  THOSE WITHOUT SIN(1917)
A. Barr Smith
  STUDENT TOUR(1934); TILLY OF BLOOMSBURY(1940, Brit.), p
A. George Smith
  FEATHERED SERPENT, THE(1934, Brit.), p; LITTLE BIT OF BLUFF, A(1935, Brit.), p; OLD FAITHFUL(1935, Brit.), p; RIGHT AGE TO MARRY, THE(1935, Brit.), p; SHADOW OF MIKE EMERALD, THE(1935, Brit.), p; VANITY(1935), p; ALL THAT GLITTERS(1936, Brit.), p; BUSMAN'S HOLIDAY(1936, Brit.), p; HEIRLOOM MYSTERY, THE(1936, Brit.), p; NOT SO DUSTY(1936, Brit.), p; NOTHING LIKE PUBLICITY(1936, Brit.), p; PRISON BREAKER(1936, Brit.), p; TO CATCH A THIEF(1936, Brit.), p; TOUCH OF THE MOON, A(1936, Brit.), p; TWICE BRANDED(1936, Brit.), p; FAREWELL TO CINDERELLA(1937, Brit.), p; PEARLS BRING TEARS(1937, Brit.), p; RACING ROMANCE(1937, Brit.), p; WHEN THE DEVIL WAS WELL(1937, Brit.), p; WHY PICK ON ME?(1937, Brit.), p; EASY RICHES(1938, Brit.), p; HIS LORDSHIP REGRETS(1938, Brit.), p; WEDDINGS ARE WONDERFUL(1938, Brit.), p; YOU'RE THE DOCTOR(1938, Brit.), p; HIS LORDSHIP GOES TO PRESS(1939, Brit.), p; SHADOWED EYES(1939, Brit.), p
A. Madeline Smith
1984
  SILENT NIGHT, DEADLY NIGHT(1984)
A. Wayne Smith
  STORY OF VICKIE, THE(1958, Aust.), ed
Adele Smith
  MIRACLE KID(1942)
Adrian Smith
1984
  GIVE MY REGARDS TO BROAD STREET(1984, Brit.), art d
Agnes Smith
Silents
  SHORE LEAVE(1925), t

Al Smith
  SHADOW RANCH(1930); BRANDED(1931); DESERT VENGEANCE(1931); BORDER DEVILS(1932); DYNAMITE RANCH(1932); HELLO TROUBLE(1932); LAST MAN(1932); THRILL HUNTER, THE(1933); HONOR OF THE RANGE(1934); FORBIDDEN TRAIL(1936); TERROR TRAIN(1980, Can.), ph
Silents
  GATE CRASHER, THE(1928); OUTLAWED(1929)
Misc. Silents
  MAN TRACKERS, THE(1921); LAW OF FEAR(1928); TRACKED(1928); DRIFTER, THE(1929)
Alan Smith
  MURDER AT THE BASKERVILLES(1941, Brit.), ed; INCREDIBLY STRANGE CREATURES WHO STOPPED LIVING AND BECAME CRAZY MIXED-UP ZOMBIES, THE(1965), ch; MACKINTOSH & T.J.(1975), art d
Albert Smith
  LINCOLN CONSPIRACY, THE(1977); CARNY(1980)
Albert I. Smith
Silents
  UNDER FIRE(1926), p
Misc. Silents
  GIRL ALASKA, THE(1919), d
Albert J. Smith
  LIGHTNING FLYER(1931); BETWEEN FIGHTING MEN(1932); LAST MILE, THE(1932); SHOTGUN PASS(1932); TELEGRAPH TRAIL, THE(1933); MADAME SPY(1934); PRESCOTT KID, THE(1936); WESTERNER, THE(1936); CODE OF THE RANGE(1937); GOLD RACKET, THE(1937); PRAIRIE THUNDER(1937)
Silents
  MEASURE OF A MAN, THE(1924); BARRIERS OF THE LAW(1925); MEDDLER, THE(1925); SPEED CRAZED(1926); BULLET MARK, THE(1928)
Misc. Silents
  BURNING TRAIL, THE(1925); STRAIGHT THROUGH(1925); HARD FISTS(1927); HILLS OF PERIL(1927); RED CLAY(1927); WHERE TRAILS BEGIN(1927)
Alexis Smith
  LADY WITH RED HAIR(1940); AFFECTIONATELY YOURS(1941); DIVE BOMBER(1941); SHE COULDN'T SAY NO(1941); SMILING GHOST, THE(1941); STEEL AGAINST THE SKY(1941); THREE SONS O'GUNS(1941); GENTLEMAN JIM(1942); CONSTANT NYMPH, THE(1943); THANK YOUR LUCKY STARS(1943); ADVENTURES OF MARK TWAIN, THE(1944); DOUGHGIRLS, THE(1944); HOLLYWOOD CANTEEN(1944); CONFLICT(1945); HORN BLOWS AT MIDNIGHT, THE(1945); RHAPSODY IN BLUE(1945); SAN ANTONIO(1945); NIGHT AND DAY(1946); OF HUMAN BONDAGE(1946); ONE MORE TOMORROW(1946); STALLION ROAD(1947); TWO MRS. CARROLLS, THE(1947); DECISION OF CHRISTOPHER BLAKE, THE(1948); WHIPLASH(1948); WOMAN IN WHITE, THE(1948); ANY NUMBER CAN PLAY(1949); ONE LAST FLING(1949); SOUTH OF ST. LOUIS(1949); MONTANA(1950); UNDERCOVER GIRL(1950); WYOMING MAIL(1950); CAVE OF OUTLAWS(1951); HERE COMES THE GROOM(1951); TURNING POINT, THE(1952); SPLIT SECOND(1953); SLEEPING TIGER, THE(1954, Brit.); ETERNAL SEA, THE(1955); BEAU JAMES(1957); THIS HAPPY FEELING(1958); YOUNG PHILADELPHIANS, THE(1959); ONCE IS NOT ENOUGH(1975); LITTLE GIRL WHO LIVES DOWN THE LANE, THE(1977, Can.); CASEY'S SHADOW(1978); TROUT, THE(1982, Fr.)
Alfred E. Smith
  WILD RIVER(1960)
Alfred J. Smith
  SUTTER'S GOLD(1936)
Alice Smith
Silents
  HEADIN' SOUTH(1918); MR. FIX-IT(1918)
Alice H. Smith
Silents
  NEW DISCIPLE, THE(1921); REPUTATION(1921); ROSE OF PARIS, THE(1924)
Allan Smith
  DAMNED DON'T CRY, THE(1950)
Allen Smith
  ESCAPE FROM ALCATRAZ(1979), prod d
Allen E. Smith
  SAN ANTONIO(1945); ENFORCER, THE(1976), art d; GAUNTLET, THE(1977), art d
Allison Smith
  SCREWBALLS(1983)
Alma Smith
  HARLEM IS HEAVEN(1932)
Alson Jesse Smith
  LAWLESS EIGHTIES, THE(1957), w
Amber Dean Smith
  MOON ZERO TWO(1970, Brit.); ONE MORE TIME(1970, Brit.)
Anderson Smith
Silents
  JOLT, THE(1921)
Misc. Silents
  DANGEROUS LITTLE DEMON, THE(1922)
Andrea Smith
  PRIVATE LIVES OF ADAM AND EVE, THE(1961)
Andrew Smith
  LOOKING UP(1977); MAIN EVENT, THE(1979), w
Andy Smith
  EDDY DUCHIN STORY, THE(1956)
Ann Smith
  NAUGHTY ARLETTE(1951, Brit.); TONY DRAWS A HORSE(1951, Brit.); WARM DECEMBER, A(1973, Brit.)
Anna Deavere Smith
  SOUP FOR ONE(1982)
Annabelle Smith
  DRUMS O' VOODOO(1934)
Anne Smith
  LUCKY LOSER(1934, Brit.), w; TIME OF HIS LIFE, THE(1955, Brit.)
Archie Smith
  ACROSS THE RIVER(1965); SLENDER THREAD, THE(1965)
Art Smith
  MASON OF THE MOUNTED(1932); FIGHTING RANGER, THE(1934); NATIVE LAND(1942); EDGE OF DARKNESS(1943); GOVERNMENT GIRL(1943); BLACK PARACHUTE, THE(1944); MR. WINKLE GOES TO WAR(1944); NONE BUT THE

LONELY HEART(1944); NONE SHALL ESCAPE(1944); UNCERTAIN GLORY(1944); YOUTH RUNS WILD(1944); TREE GROWS IN BROOKLYN, A(1945); BODY AND SOUL(1947); BRUTE FORCE(1947); DOUBLE LIFE, A(1947); FRAMED(1947); RIDE THE PINK HORSE(1947); T-MEN(1947); ANGEL IN EXILE(1948); ARCH OF TRIUMPH(1948); LETTER FROM AN UNKNOWN WOMAN(1948); MR. PEABODY AND THE MERMAID(1948); CAUGHT(1949); MANHANDLED(1949); RED, HOT AND BLUE(1949); SONG OF SURRENDER(1949); SOUTH OF ST. LOUIS(1949); IN A LONELY PLACE(1950); KILLER THAT STALKED NEW YORK, THE(1950); QUICKSAND(1950); SOUND OF FURY, THE(1950); SOUTH SEA SINNER(1950); HALF ANGEL(1951); PAINTED HILLS, THE(1951); JUST FOR YOU(1952); ROSE OF CIMARRON(1952); MOVING FINGER, THE(1963)

Arthur Smith
GENERAL DIED AT DAWN, THE(1936), spec eff; SEABO(1978), m; WOLFMAN(1979), m; LADY GREY(1980), m; ON THE RIGHT TRACK(1981)

Arthur "Fiddlin" Smith
RIDERS OF THE DAWN(1945); SIX GUN SERENADE(1947); OKLAHOMA BLUES(1948); PARTNERS OF THE SUNSET(1948); RANGE RENEGADES(1948); RANGERS RIDE, THE(1948); SONG OF THE DRIFTER(1948)

Aubrey Smith
Silents
REJECTED WOMAN, THE(1924)

Augustus Smith
HI-DE-HO(1947)

Barbara Smith
TICKET TO TOMAHAWK(1950)

Barbara Jane Smith
NEVER WAVE AT A WAC(1952)

Barry R. Smith
1984
FALLING IN LOVE(1984)

Bart Smith
WEREWOLVES ON WHEELS(1971)

Beaumont Smith
SPLENDID FELLOWS(1934, Aus.), p, d, w

Ben Smith
LE BEAU SERGE(1959, Fr.), titles

Bernard Smith
IMMORTAL GENTLEMAN(1935, Brit.), p; MEN WITHOUT HONOUR(1939, Brit.), p; ELMER GANTRY(1960), p; HOW THE WEST WAS WON(1962), p; CHEYENNE AUTUMN(1964), p; SEVEN WOMEN(1966), p; ALFRED THE GREAT(1969, Brit.), p

Bernie Smith
"RENT-A-GIRL"(1965), ph

Beryl Smith
RED RUNS THE RIVER(1963)

Betty Smith
TREE GROWS IN BROOKLYN, A(1945), w; JOY IN THE MORNING(1965), w
1984
COUNTRY(1984)

Betty Leslie Smith
NAUGHTY ARLETTE(1951, Brit.)

Bill Smith
THIN MAN GOES HOME, THE(1944); MATING GAME, THE(1959); ATLANTIS, THE LOST CONTINENT(1961); GO NAKED IN THE WORLD(1961); MAIL ORDER BRIDE(1964); OLIVER!(1968, Brit.); LAST TYCOON, THE(1976), set d
Misc. Talkies
BLACKJACK(1978)

Billy Smith
LAST GANGSTER, THE(1937)

Bo Smith
1984
POPE OF GREENWICH VILLAGE, THE(1984)

Bob Smith
MONEY, WOMEN AND GUNS(1958), art d; TRACK OF THUNDER(1967); GREATEST, THE(1977, U.S./Brit.), prod d

Bobbie Smith
LADY CAROLINE LAMB(1972, Brit./Ital.), hair styles

Brenda Smith
MR. SYCAMORE(1975); HOMETOWN U.S.A.(1979)

Brendan Smith
PLAYBOY OF THE WESTERN WORLD, THE(1963, Ireland), p

Brett Smith
SMALL CIRCLE OF FRIENDS, A(1980)

Brian Smith
NO PLACE FOR JENNIFER(1950, Brit.); BROWNING VERSION, THE(1951, Brit.); GLAD TIDINGS(1953, Brit.); BETRAYED(1954); BATTLE HELL(1956, Brit.); IT'S GREAT TO BE YOUNG(1956, Brit.); BARRETTS OF WIMPOLE STREET, THE(1957); NO TIME FOR TEARS(1957, Brit.); GIDEON OF SCOTLAND YARD(1959, Brit.); FEET OF CLAY(1960, Brit.); RIVALS, THE(1963, Brit.); NIGHT IN HEAVEN, A(1983); PORKY'S II: THE NEXT DAY(1983)

Brian Trenchard Smith
MAN FROM HONG KONG(1975), d&w; DEATHCHEATERS(1976, Aus.), a, p&d, w

Bruce Smith
BARBAROSA(1982)
Misc. Silents
SPELLBOUND(1916); UNDERSTUDY, THE(1917); YELLOW BULLET, THE(1917); WHATEVER THE COST(1918)

Bruce Meredith Smith
CRY, THE BELOVED COUNTRY(1952, Brit.)

Bubba Smith
STROKER ACE(1983)
1984
POLICE ACADEMY(1984)

Bud Smith
PUT UP OR SHUT UP(1968, Arg.), ed; PUTNEY SWOPE(1969), ed; GREASER'S PALACE(1972), ed; EXORCIST, THE(1973), ed; RHINOCEROS(1974), ed; SORCERER(1977), ed; BRINK'S JOB, THE(1978), ed; CRUISING(1980), ed; FALLING IN LOVE AGAIN(1980), ed; DEADHEAD MILES(1982), ed; PERSONAL BEST(1982), ed; DEAL OF THE CENTURY(1983), ed; FLASHDANCE(1983), ed

1984
KARATE KID, THE(1984), ed

Buddy Smith
Silents
ROUGHNECK, THE(1924)

Burnal "Custus" Smith
SKULLDUGGERY(1970)

Butterball Smith
STANLEY(1973)

C. A. R. Smith
LOVE AND DEATH(1975); KING OF THE GYPSIES(1978)

C. Aubrey Smith
SUCH IS THE LAW(1930, Brit.); BACHELOR FATHER(1931); CONTRABAND LOVE(1931, Brit.); DAYBREAK(1931); GUILTY HANDS(1931); JUST A GIGOLO(1931); MAN IN POSSESSION, THE(1931); NEVER THE TWAIN SHALL MEET(1931); PERFECT ALIBI, THE(1931, Brit.); PHANTOM OF PARIS, THE(1931); SON OF INDIA(1931); SQUAW MAN, THE(1931); SURRENDER(1931); TRADER HORN(1931); BUT THE FLESH IS WEAK(1932); LOVE ME TONIGHT(1932); POLLY OF THE CIRCUS(1932); TARZAN, THE APE MAN(1932); TROUBLE IN PARADISE(1932); ADORABLE(1933); BARBARIAN, THE(1933); BOMBSHELL(1933); LUXURY LINER(1933); MONKEY'S PAW, THE(1933); MORNING GLORY(1933); NO MORE ORCHIDS(1933); QUEEN CHRISTINA(1933); SECRETS(1933); THEY JUST HAD TO GET MARRIED(1933); BULLDOG DRUMMOND STRIKES BACK(1934); CARAVAN(1934); CLEOPATRA(1934); CURTAIN AT EIGHT(1934); FIREBIRD, THE(1934); GAMBLING LADY(1934); HOUSE OF ROTHSCHILD, THE(1934); ONE MORE RIVER(1934); SCARLET EMPRESS, THE(1934); WE LIVE AGAIN(1934); CHINA SEAS(1935); CLIVE OF INDIA(1935); CRUSADES, THE(1935); FLORENTINE DAGGER, THE(1935); GILDED LILY, THE(1935); JALNA(1935); LIVES OF A BENGAL LANCER(1935); RIGHT TO LIVE, THE(1935); TRANSATLANTIC TUNNEL(1935, Brit.); GARDEN OF ALLAH, THE(1936); LITTLE LORD FAUNTLEROY(1936); LLOYDS OF LONDON(1936); ROMEO AND JULIET(1936); HURRICANE, THE(1937); PRISONER OF ZENDA, THE(1937); THOROUGHBREDS DON'T CRY(1937); WEE WILLIE WINKIE(1937); FOUR MEN AND A PRAYER(1938); KIDNAPPED(1938); SIXTY GLORIOUS YEARS(1938, Brit.); ANOTHER THIN MAN(1939); BALALAIKA(1939); EAST SIDE OF HEAVEN(1939); ETERNALLY YOURS(1939); FIVE CAME BACK(1939); FOUR FEATHERS, THE(1939, Brit.); SUN NEVER SETS, THE(1939); UNDER-PUP, THE(1939); BEYOND TOMORROW(1940); BILL OF DIVORCEMENT(1940); CITY OF CHANCE(1940); LITTLE BIT OF HEAVEN, A(1940); REBECCA(1940); WATERLOO BRIDGE(1940); DR. JEKYLL AND MR. HYDE(1941); FREE AND EASY(1941); MAISIE WAS A LADY(1941); FLESH AND FANTASY(1943); FOREVER AND A DAY(1943); MADAME CURIE(1943); TWO TICKETS TO LONDON(1943); ADVENTURES OF MARK TWAIN, THE(1944); SECRETS OF SCOTLAND YARD(1944); SENSATIONS OF 1945(1944); WHITE CLIFFS OF DOVER, THE(1944); AND THEN THERE WERE NONE(1945); FOREVER YOURS(1945); SCOTLAND YARD INVESTIGATOR(1945, Brit.); CLUNY BROWN(1946); RENDEZVOUS WITH ANNIE(1946); HIGH CONQUEST(1947); UNCONQUERED(1947); IDEAL HUSBAND, AN(1948, Brit.); LITTLE WOMEN(1949)
Silents
JOHN GLAYDE'S HONOR(1915); RED POTTAGE(1918, Brit.); FACE AT THE WINDOW, THE(1920, Brit.); FLAMES OF PASSION(1922, Brit.); UNWANTED, THE(1924, Brit.)
Misc. Silents
JAFFERY(1915); WITCHING HOUR, THE(1916); CASTLES IN SPAIN(1920, Brit.); SHUTTLE OF LIFE, THE(1920, Brit.); BOHEMIAN GIRL, THE(1922, Brit.); TEMPTATION OF CARLTON EARLYE, THE(1923, Brit.)

Col. C. C. Smith
Silents
RANSON'S FOLLY(1926)

C. D. Smith
HOLLYWOOD BOULEVARD(1976), stunts; SUMMER SCHOOL TEACHERS(1977)

C. Davis Smith
TASTE OF FLESH, A(1967), ph

C.M. Smith
NEVER CRY WOLF(1983), w

Cameron Smith
TOAST OF NEW YORK, THE(1937)

Candice Smith
WILD McCULLOCHS, THE(1975)

Carl Smith
BADGE OF MARSHAL BRENNAN, THE(1957); BUFFALO GUN(1961); FROM NASHVILLE WITH MUSIC(1969)
1984
KILLPOINT(1984)

Carole Smith
WHAT'S NEXT?(1975, Brit.), p

Carole K. Smith
JUNKET 89(1970, Brit.), p

Caroline Smith
BUCK ROGERS IN THE 25TH CENTURY(1979)

Carter Smith
WINDSPLITTER, THE(1971)

Catherine Lee Smith
SOUP FOR ONE(1982)

Cathy Smith
JOE HILL(1971, Swed./U.S.)

Charles Smith
NANCY DREW-REPORTER(1939); SHOP AROUND THE CORNER, THE(1940); STRIKE UP THE BAND(1940); TOM BROWN'S SCHOOL DAYS(1940); ADVENTURE IN WASHINGTON(1941); CHEERS FOR MISS BISHOP(1941); GIRL, A GUY AND A GOB, A(1941); HENRY ALDRICH FOR PRESIDENT(1941); LUCKY DEVILS(1941); YOU BELONG TO ME(1941); CAPTAINS OF THE CLOUDS(1942); HENRY ALDRICH, EDITOR(1942); HENRY AND DIZZY(1942); MAJOR AND THE MINOR, THE(1942); STAR SPANGLED RHYTHM(1942); YANKEE DOODLE DANDY(1942); YOU'RE TELLING ME(1942); GUY NAMED JOE, A(1943); HENRY ALDRICH HAUNTS A HOUSE(1943); SALUTE FOR THREE(1943); YOUTH ON PARADE(1943); HENRY ALDRICH PLAYS CUPID(1944); HENRY ALDRICH'S LITTLE SECRET(1944); LADY IN THE DARK(1944); SAN FERNANDO VALLEY(1944); GOD IS MY CO-PILOT(1945); OUT OF THIS WORLD(1945); THREE LITTLE GIRLS IN BLUE(1946); WAKE UP AND DREAM(1946); OUT OF THE BLUE(1947); TROUBLE WITH WOMEN, THE(1947); TWO BLONDES AND A REDHEAD(1947); CAMPUS HONEYMOON(1948); ADVEN-

Charles B. Smith- (continued)

TURE IN BALTIMORE(1949); DUCHESS OF IDAHO, THE(1950); KEY TO THE CITY(1950); TWO WEEKS WITH LOVE(1950); RHYTHM INN(1951); YOU'RE IN THE NAVY NOW(1951); FRENCH LINE, THE(1954); SUDDENLY(1954); JOHNNY TREMAIN(1957); MODERN MARRIAGE, A(1962); GNOME-MOBILE, THE(1967); GOOD TIMES(1967)
Silents
GENERAL, THE(1927), a, w
Charles B. Smith
DOWN IN SAN DIEGO(1941); UNHOLY PARTNERS(1941); WING AND A PRAYER(1944); CARRIE(1952); CITY OF BAD MEN(1953); APACHE RIFLES(1964), w
Charles H. Smith
CLEAR THE DECKS(1929), w
Silents
NOBODY(1921), w; SILVER LINING, THE(1921), w; NAUGHTY NANETTE(1927), w
Charles Henry Smith
GIRL ON THE BARGE, THE(1929), w
Charles Martin Smith
CULPEPPER CATTLE COMPANY, THE(1972); FUZZ(1972); AMERICAN GRAFFITI(1973); PAT GARRETT AND BILLY THE KID(1973); SPIKES GANG, THE(1974); RAFFERTY AND THE GOLD DUST TWINS(1975); NO DEPOSIT, NO RETURN(1976); BUDDY HOLLY STORY, THE(1978); HAZING, THE(1978); MORE AMERICAN GRAFFITI(1979); HERBIE GOES BANANAS(1980); NEVER CRY WOLF(1983)
1984
STARMAN(1984)
Charles P. Smith
STRATTON STORY, THE(1949)
Charley Smith
HENRY ALDRICH, BOY SCOUT(1944)
Charlie Smith
DOUBLE DATE(1941); HENRY ALDRICH GETS GLAMOUR(1942); HENRY ALDRICH SWINGS IT(1943)
Cheryl Smith
LASERBLAST(1978); MELVIN AND HOWARD(1980); PARASITE(1982); VICE SQUAD(1982); INDEPENDENCE DAY(1983)
Cheryl "Rainbeaux" Smith
THE LADY DRACULA(1974)
"Chief" Tug Smith
SHALAKO(1968, Brit.)
Christ Smith
STIR(1980, Aus.)
Christian Smith
NEW YORK, NEW YORK(1977), makeup
Christina Smith
PERSONAL BEST(1982), makeup
Christine Smith
TOMBOY AND THE CHAMP(1961); LUST FOR A VAMPIRE(1971, Brit.)
Clarence Smith
JUST IMAGINE(1930)
Claude Smith
HOPALONG CASSIDY RETURNS(1936); DUMBO(1941), anim; RELUCTANT DRAGON, THE(1941), anim; SHE FREAK(1967)
Claudia Smith
SUNSET TRAIL(1938)
Clay Smith
SEABO(1978), m; LADY GREY(1980), m
Cliff Smith
Misc. Talkies
TEXAN, THE(1932), d; DEVIL'S CANYON(1935), d; FIVE BAD MEN(1935), d
Silents
DEVIL DODGER, THE(1917), d; ONE SHOT ROSS(1917), d; BY PROXY(1918), d; FLY GOD, THE(1918), d; CYCLONE, THE(1920), d; GIRL WHO DARED, THE(1920), d; LONE HAND, THE(1920), d; CROSSING TRAILS(1921), d; WESTERN HEARTS(1921), d, w; MY DAD(1922), p&d
Misc. Silents
LEARNIN' JIM BENTON, THE(1917), d; MEDICINE MAN, THE(1917), d; BOSS OF THE LAZY Y, THE(1918), d; CACTUS CRANDALL(1918), d; FAITH AND ENDURIN'(1918), d; KEITH OF THE BORDER(1918), d; LAW'S OUTLAW(1918), d; PAYING HIS DEBT(1918), d; PRETENDER, THE(1918), d; RED-HAIRED CUPID, A(1918), d; SILENT RIDER, THE(1918), d; UNTAMED(1918), d; WOLVES OF THE BORDER(1918), d; THREE GOLD COINS(1920), d; STRANGER IN CANYON VALLEY, THE(1921), d; DARING DANGER(1922), d; SCARRED HANDS(1923), a, d; DEMON, THE(1926), d; LOCO LUCK(1927), d
Clifford Smith
RIDERS OF THE GOLDEN GULCH(1932), d
Silents
APOSTLE OF VENGEANCE, THE(1916), d; ARYAN, THE(1916), d; BACK TRAIL, THE(1924), d; WHITE OUTLAW, THE(1925), d; DESERT'S TOLL, THE(1926), d
Misc. Silents
DARKENING TRAIL, THE(1915), d; DISCIPLE, THE(1915), d; WESTERN WALLOP, THE(1924), d; TERROR, THE(1926), d; THREE OUTCASTS, THE(1929), d
Clifford S. Smith
Silents
DARING CHANCES(1924), d; RIDGEWAY OF MONTANA(1924), d; SINGER JIM MCKEE(1924), d; ARIZONA SWEEPSTAKES(1926), d; RUSTLER'S RANCH(1926), d
Misc. Silents
FIGHTING FURY(1924), d; BUSTIN' THRU(1925), d; CALL OF COURAGE, THE(1925), d; DON DARE DEVIL(1925), d; FLYING HOOFS(1925), d; RED RIDER, THE(1925), d; RIDIN' THUNDER(1925), d; ROARING ADVENTURE, A(1925), d; SIGN OF THE CACTUS(1925), d; FIGHTING PEACEMAKER, THE(1926), d; MAN IN THE SADDLE, THE(1926), d; PHANTOM BULLET, THE(1926), d; RIDIN' RASCAL, THE(1926), d; SCRAPPIN' KID, THE(1926), d; SET-UP, THE(1926), d; SIX SHOOTIN' ROMANCE, A(1926), d; SKY HIGH CORRAL, THE(1926), d; OPEN RANGE(1927), d; SPURS AND SADDLES(1927), d; VALLEY OF HELL, THE(1927), d
Clint Smith
48 HOURS(1982); TRADING PLACES(1983)
Clive Smith
MADHOUSE(1974, Brit.), ed; LIQUID SKY(1982), m

Clive A. Smith
Misc. Talkies
ROCK 'N' RULE(1983), d
Clyde Smith
SECOND FIDDLE TO A STEEL GUITAR(1965)
Colby Smith
FINAL COUNTDOWN, THE(1980); DEAD AND BURIED(1981)
Colin Smith
BAND OF THIEVES(1962, Brit.)
Connie Smith
SECOND FIDDLE TO A STEEL GUITAR(1965); LAS VEGAS HILLBILLYS(1966); HELL ON WHEELS(1967)
Misc. Talkies
ROAD TO NASHVILLE(1967)
Constance Smith
JASSY(1948, Brit.); NOW BARABBAS WAS A ROBBER(1949, Brit.); ROOM TO LET(1949, Brit.); DON'T SAY DIE(1950, Brit.); MUDLARK, THE(1950, Brit.); MYSTERY AT THE BURLESQUE(1950, Brit.); PERFECT WOMAN, THE(1950, Brit.); LUCKY NICK CAIN(1951); THIRTEENTH LETTER, THE(1951); LURE OF THE WILDERNESS(1952); RED SKIES OF MONTANA(1952); MAN IN THE ATTIC(1953); TAXI(1953); TREASURE OF THE GOLDEN CONDOR(1953); BIG TIP OFF, THE(1955); IMPULSE(1955, Brit.); CROSS-UP(1958); SHAMPOO(1975)
Cornelia Smith
SONG OF FREEDOM(1938, Brit.)
Crystal Smith
1984
HOT DOG...THE MOVIE(1984)
Cynthia Smith
BENJI(1974); HAWMPS!(1976); FOR THE LOVE OF BENJI(1977)
Cyril Smith
MAYOR'S NEST, THE(1932, Brit.); WHY SAPS LEAVE HOME(1932, Brit.); GOOD COMPANIONS(1933, Brit.); ROOF, THE(1933, Brit.); BLACK ABBOT, THE(1934, Brit.); CHANNEL CROSSING(1934, Brit.); FRIDAY THE 13TH(1934, Brit.); IT'S A COP(1934, Brit.); STRAUSS' GREAT WALTZ(1934, Brit.); WILD BOY(1934, Brit.); ALIAS BULL-DOG DRUMMOND(1935, Brit.); BORN FOR GLORY(1935, Brit.); HELLO SWEET-HEART(1935, Brit.); KEY TO HARMONY(1935, Brit.); LEND ME YOUR WIFE(1935, Brit.); ME AND MARLBOROUGH(1935, Brit.); POT LUCK(1936, Brit.); FROG, THE(1937, Brit.); STORM IN A TEACUP(1937, Brit.); YOU'RE IN THE ARMY NOW(1937, Brit.); NO PARKING(1938, Brit.); RETURN OF THE FROG, THE(1938, Brit.); SWORD OF HONOUR(1938, Brit.); TWO OF US, THE(1938, Brit.); CHALLENGE, THE(1939, Brit.); FLYING SQUAD, THE(1940, Brit.); LAW AND DISORDER(1940, Brit.); SIDEWALKS OF LONDON(1940, Brit.); TORSO MURDER MYSTERY, THE(1940, Brit.); WINGS AND THE WOMAN(1942, Brit.); WHEN WE ARE MARRIED(1943, Brit.); MEET SEXTON BLAKE(1944, Brit.); APPOINTMENT WITH CRIME(1945, Brit.); DON CHICAGO(1945, Brit.); ECHO MURDERS, THE(1945, Brit.); ON STAGE EVERYBODY(1945); MURDER IN REVERSE(1946, Brit.); SCHOOL FOR SECRETS(1946, Brit.); YOU CAN'T DO WITHOUT LOVE(1946, Brit.); I BECAME A CRIMINAL(1947); IF WINTER COMES(1947); ESCAPE(1948, Brit.); AGITATOR, THE(1949); CONSPIRATOR(1949, Brit.); HISTORY OF MR. POLLY, THE(1949, Brit.); INTERRUPTED JOURNEY, THE(1949, Brit.); BODY SAID NO!, THE(1950, Brit.); IT'S HARD TO BE GOOD(1950, Brit.); NO ROOM AT THE INN(1950, Brit.); OLD MOTHER RILEY, HEADMISTRESS(1950, Brit.); ROCKING HORSE WINNER, THE(1950, Brit.); DARK MAN, THE(1951, Brit.); GREEN GROW THE RUSHES(1951, Brit.); MYSTERY JUNCTION(1951, Brit.); NIGHT WAS OUR FRIEND(1951, Brit.); NO HIGHWAY IN THE SKY(1951, Brit.); THIRD VISITOR, THE(1951, Brit.); HOLIDAY WEEK(1952, Brit.); JUDGMENT DEFERRED(1952, Brit.); STOLEN FACE(1952, Brit.); BIG FRAME, THE(1953, Brit.); TWILIGHT WOMEN(1953, Brit.); WHEEL OF FATE(1953, Brit.); BURNT EVIDENCE(1954, Brit.); SVENGALI(1955, Brit.); PANIC IN THE PARLOUR(1957, Brit.); VALUE FOR MONEY(1957, Brit.); LIGHT UP THE SKY(1960, Brit.); OVER THE ODDS(1961, Brit.); PORTRAIT OF A SINNER(1961, Brit.); WATCH IT, SAILOR!(1961, Brit.); SHE KNOWS Y'KNOW(1962, Brit.); MY SON, THE VAMPIRE(1963, Brit.); OPERATION SNAFU(1965, Brit.)
Silents
WALLS OF PREJUDICE(1920, Brit.); FIRES OF FATE(1923, Brit.)
D. Bradley Smith
SCHOOL FOR SECRETS(1946, Brit.)
D. Herbert Smith
ALL AT SEA(1939, Brit.), p&d
Darr Smith
CRAZY OVER HORSES(1951); GIRL ON THE BRIDGE, THE(1951); SAILOR BEWARE(1951); THY NEIGHBOR'S WIFE(1953)
David Smith
Silents
BY THE WORLD FORGOT(1918), d; BLACK BEAUTY(1921), d; IT CAN BE DONE(1921), d; SILVER CAR, THE(1921), d; ANGEL OF CROOKED STREET, THE(1922), d; NINETY AND NINE, THE(1922), d; AVENGING SHADOW, THE(1928), ph
Misc. Silents
BAREE, SON OF KAZAN(1918), d; CHANGING WOMAN, THE(1918), d; DAWN OF UNDERSTANDING, THE(1918), d; GENTLEMAN'S AGREEMENT, A(1918), d; CUPID FORECLOSES(1919), d; ENCHANTED BARN, THE(1919), d; FIGHTING COLLEEN, A(1919), d; LITTLE BOSS, THE(1919), d; OVER THE GARDEN WALL(1919), d; WISHING RING MAN, THE(1919), d; YANKEE PRINCESS, A(1919), d; COURAGE OF MARGE O'DOONE, THE(1920), d; PEGEEN(1920), d; FLOWER OF THE NORTH(1921), d; GUILTY CONSCIENCE, A(1921), d; LITTLE MINISTER, THE(1922), d; MY WILD IRISH ROSE(1922), d; MAN FROM BRODNEY'S, THE(1923), d; MASTERS OF MEN(1923), d; MIDNIGHT ALARM, THE(1923), d; PIONEER TRAILS(1923), d; BORROWED HUSBANDS(1924), d; CAPTAIN BLOOD(1924), d; CODE OF THE WILDERNESS(1924), d; MY MAN(1924), d; BAREE, SON OF KAZAN(1925), d; PAMPERED YOUTH(1925), d; STELLE OF THE ROYAL MOUNTED(1925), d
David E. Smith
NIGHT OF THE ZOMBIES(1981), makeup
Dawn Eisler Smith
1984
IMPULSE(1984)
Dawnis Kaye Smith
TOY, THE(1982)

Dean Smith
EL DORADO(1967); HURRY SUNDOWN(1967); CHEYENNE SOCIAL CLUB, THE(1970); RIO LOBO(1970); BIG JAKE(1971); SOMETIMES A GREAT NOTION(1971); HICKEY AND BOGGS(1972); LIFE AND TIMES OF JUDGE ROY BEAN, THE(1972); SQUARES(1972); ULZANA'S RAID(1972); SUGARLAND EXPRESS, THE(1974); MACKINTOSH & T.J.(1975); SEVEN ALONE(1975); FRATERNITY ROW(1977)
1984
RHINESTONE(1984)
Debbie Smith
ONE AND ONLY GENUINE ORIGINAL FAMILY BAND, THE(1968)
Delos Smith
GOODBYE COLUMBUS(1969); SILVER STREAK(1976)
Delos V. Smith
SGT. PEPPER'S LONELY HEARTS CLUB BAND(1978)
Delos V. Smith, Jr.
ONE FLEW OVER THE CUCKOO'S NEST(1975); PACK, THE(1977)
Delos W. Smith, Jr.
SCOTT JOPLIN(1977)
Denis Smith
SPOTS ON MY LEOPARD, THE(1974, S. Africa)
Derek Smith
TINKER(1949, Brit.); ALFIE DARLING(1975, Brit.); WHO IS KILLING THE GREAT CHEFS OF EUROPE?(1978, US/Ger.)
Dick Smith
IRON CURTAIN, THE(1948), makeup; WHAT A WAY TO GO(1964), makeup; WORLD OF HENRY ORIENT, THE(1964), makeup; ME, NATALIE(1969), makeup; MIDNIGHT COWBOY(1969), makeup; HOUSE OF DARK SHADOWS(1970), makeup; LITTLE BIG MAN(1970), makeup; WHO IS HARRY KELLERMAN AND WHY IS HE SAYING THOSE TERRIBLE THINGS ABOUT ME?(1971), makeup; GODFATHER, THE(1972), makeup; EXORCIST, THE(1973), makeup; POLITICAL ASYLUM(1975, Mex./Guatemalan); STEPFORD WIVES, THE(1975), makeup; SUNSHINE BOYS, THE(1975), makeup; MARATHON MAN(1976), makeup; TAXI DRIVER(1976), makeup; SENTINEL, THE(1977), makeup; ALTERED STATES(1980), makeup; GHOST STORY(1981), makeup; SCANNERS(1981, Can.), spec eff, makeup; SPASMS(1983, Can.), makeup
1984
AMADEUS(1984), makeup
Misc. Talkies
HOT SUMMER IN BAREFOOT COUNTY(1974)
Silents
STOP THAT MAN(1928), w
Digby Smith
ESCAPE DANGEROUS(1947, Brit.), p, d
Dirk Smith
CALL NORTHSIDE 777(1948), makeup
Dodie Smith
CALL IT A DAY(1937), w; UNINVITED, THE(1944), w; RANDOLPH FAMILY, THE(1945, Brit.), w; DARLING, HOW COULD YOU!(1951), w; ONE HUNDRED AND ONE DALMATIANS(1961), w
Don Smith
SECRET OF THE SACRED FOREST, THE(1970); WHO SAYS I CAN'T RIDE A RAINBOW!(1971)
1984
RAZORBACK(1984, Aus.)
Don "Mini Shred" Smith
Misc. Talkies
SKATEBOARD MADNESS(1980)
Donald Smith
MARRIAGE PLAYGROUND, THE(1929)
Donnella Smith
RED RUNS THE RIVER(1963)
Doug Smith
1984
LONELY GUY, THE(1984)
Douglas Bradley Smith
NO HIGHWAY IN THE SKY(1951, Brit.)
Doyle Smith
LOVELESS, THE(1982), ph
Drake Smith
CATTLE QUEEN(1951); WILD HORSE AMBUSH(1952)
Duchyll Smith
MONKEY HUSTLE, THE(1976)
Dudley Smith
Silents
CIRCUS ACE, THE(1927)
Duncan Smith
UNDERGROUND U.S.A.(1980); SCARECROW, THE(1982, New Zealand)
Dutchell Smith
THREE TOUGH GUYS(1974, U.S./Ital.)
Dwan Smith
SPARKLE(1976)
Earl Smith
MACOMBER AFFAIR, THE(1947); SAVAGE WILD, THE(1970), m/l Title song; RAFFERTY AND THE GOLD DUST TWINS(1975)
1984
NINJA III–THE DOMINATION(1984)
Earl E. Smith
LEGEND OF BOGGY CREEK, THE(1973), w; BOOTLEGGERS(1974), a, w; WINTERHAWK(1976), w; TOWN THAT DREADED SUNDOWN, THE(1977), a, w; WISHBONE CUTTER(1978), p, d&w; SUDDEN IMPACT(1983), w
Earl W. Smith
VILLAIN, THE(1979); DEATH VALLEY(1982)
Ebbe Roe Smith
BRUBAKER(1980); RESURRECTION(1980); I'M DANCING AS FAST AS I CAN(1982); PANDEMONIUM(1982); DEAL OF THE CENTURY(1983)
Ed Smith
FLIGHT(1960)

Ed. W. Smith
MADISON SQUARE GARDEN(1932)
Eddie Smith
DIRTY HARRY(1971); UNHOLY ROLLERS(1972); LIVE AND LET DIE(1973, Brit.), stunts; BLACK BELT JONES(1974); TRUCK TURNER(1974); NEW YORK, NEW YORK(1977); WHICH WAY IS UP?(1977); YOUNGBLOOD(1978), stunts; UNDER FIRE(1983)
1984
SWING SHIFT(1984)
Edgar Smith
Silents
TILLIE'S PUNCTURED ROMANCE(1914), w; TILLIE'S PUNCTURED ROMANCE(1928), w
Edna Smith
HERE COME THE NELSONS(1952); KETTLES ON OLD MACDONALD'S FARM, THE(1957)
Edward Smith
PACIFIC ADVENTURE(1947, Aus.); GLENROWAN AFFAIR, THE(1951, Aus.)
Elizabeth Smith
SON OF SINBAD(1955); HAWAIIANS, THE(1970); CASTAWAY COWBOY, THE(1974)
Ella Smith
YOUNG DOCTORS, THE(1961)
Elwood Smith
BOY! WHAT A GIRL(1947)
Emily Smith
Misc. Talkies
LUCIFER'S WOMEN(1978)
Emmett Smith
STANLEY AND LIVINGSTONE(1939); SUNDOWN(1941); GIVE OUT, SISTERS(1942); SON OF DRACULA(1943); ADVENTURES OF MARK TWAIN, THE(1944); HOME IN INDIANA(1944); TO HAVE AND HAVE NOT(1944); CHRISTMAS IN CONNECTICUT(1945); SHADY LADY(1945); JACKIE ROBINSON STORY, THE(1950); NO MAN OF HER OWN(1950); NO WAY OUT(1950); SUNSET BOULEVARD(1950); SNOWS OF KILIMANJARO, THE(1952); REMAINS TO BE SEEN(1953); UNTAMED(1955)
Emmett E. Smith
VOODOO WOMAN(1957)
Emory Smith
THIS IS ELVIS(1982)
Eric Smith
HANGMAN WAITS, THE(1947, Brit.), set d
Eric l'Epine Smith
NAUGHTY ARLETTE(1951, Brit.), p
Ernest Smith
Silents
HEART OF A COWARD, THE(1926), ph; SPEED COP(1926), ph; WHEN SECONDS COUNT(1927), ph
Ernest F. Smith
NEW ADVENTURES OF TARZAN(1935), ph; TARZAN AND THE GREEN GODDESS(1938), ph
Ernest Lee Smith
TOUGH ENOUGH(1983)
Ernie Smith
COMA(1978), spec eff
Essex Smith
CUTTER AND BONE(1981); HALLOWEEN III: SEASON OF THE WITCH(1982)
Esther Smith
VOYAGE TO THE END OF THE UNIVERSE(1963, Czech.), cos
Ethel Smith
BATHING BEAUTY(1944); GEORGE WHITE'S SCANDALS(1945); TWICE BLESSED(1945); CUBAN PETE(1946); EASY TO WED(1946); MELODY TIME(1948); C'MON, LET'S LIVE A LITTLE(1967); SIDELONG GLANCES OF A PIGEON KICKER, THE(1970)
Misc. Talkies
WAGES OF SIN, THE(1929)
Eugene Smith
CRY MURDER(1936); SKIN GAME(1971)
Eve Smith
CAESAR AND CLEOPATRA(1946, Brit.)
1984
ROMANCING THE STONE(1984)
Evelyn Smith
PERMANENT VACATION(1982)
Evelynne Smith
MISSION TO MOSCOW(1943); FIGHTING MAD(1948); WAC FROM WALLA WALLA, THE(1952)
Everet Smith
MR. SYCAMORE(1975)
Everett Smith
SET-UP, THE(1949); CONTINENTAL DIVIDE(1981)
F. Hopkinson Smith
Silents
KENTUCKY CINDERELLA, A(1917), w
F. R. Smith
BORDER LAW(1931)
Floyd Smith
TOUGH ENOUGH(1983), set d
Frank Smith
PEACEMAKER, THE(1956), art d; VALERIE(1957), art d; CAPE CANAVERAL MONSTERS(1960); BOY NAMED CHARLIE BROWN, A(1969), anim
Silents
SUBURBAN, THE(1915)
Misc. Silents
MARBLE HEART, THE(1915)
Frank Leon Smith
MELODY IN SPRING(1934), w

Frank T. Smith
SCARFACE MOB, THE(1962), art d; JOHNNY COOL(1963), art d; HOT LEAD AND COLD FEET(1978), art d; APPLE DUMPLING GANG RIDES AGAIN, THE(1979), art d

Frankie Smith
TRIP, THE(1967)

Frazer Smith
BELOW THE BELT(1980); T.A.G.: THE ASSASSINATION GAME(1982)
1984
ELECTRIC DREAMS(1984)

Fred Smith
COLLEGE LOVERS(1930), ed; ARCTIC FURY(1949); PROLOGUE(1970, Can.); LOVE AND DEATH(1975); CANNONBALL RUN, THE(1981)
Silents
IN BAD(1918); FORTUNE'S CHILD(1919)

Fredelia Smith
WINDWALKER(1980)

Frederick A. Smith
TOWING(1978), p

Frederick E. Smith
DEVIL DOLL(1964, Brit.), w; SQUADRON 633(1964, U.S./Brit.), w; 633 SQUADRON(1964), w

Frederick Y. Smith
SWEET MAMA(1930), ed; TRUTH ABOUT YOUTH, THE(1930), ed; DEVIL DOLL, THE(1936), ed; LIBELED LADY(1936), ed; PETTICOAT FEVER(1936), ed; BIG CITY(1937), ed; MANNEQUIN(1937), ed; PARNELL(1937), ed; DRAMATIC SCHOOL(1938), ed; FAST COMPANY(1938), ed; PORT OF SEVEN SEAS(1938), ed; THREE LOVES HAS NANCY(1938), ed; ANOTHER THIN MAN(1939), ed; KID FROM TEXAS, THE(1939), ed; LET FREEDOM RING(1939), ed; MAISIE(1939), ed; MIRACLES FOR SALE(1939), ed; CONGO MAISIE(1940), ed; EDISON, THE MAN(1940), ed; GOLD RUSH MAISIE(1940), ed; LITTLE NELLIE KELLY(1940), ed; BABES ON BROADWAY(1941), ed; LADY BE GOOD(1941), ed; MAISIE WAS A LADY(1941), ed; MEN OF BOYS TOWN(1941), ed; RINGSIDE MAISIE(1941), ed; MAISIE GETS HER MAN(1942), ed; THIS TIME FOR KEEPS(1942), ed; WHITE CARGO(1942), ed; SALUTE TO THE MARINES(1943), ed; BIG HANGOVER, THE(1950), ed; GROUNDS FOR MARRIAGE(1950), ed; LADY WITHOUT PASSPORT, A(1950), ed; BANNERLINE(1951), ed; IT'S A BIG COUNTRY(1951), ed; HOLIDAY FOR SINNERS(1952), ed; JUST THIS ONCE(1952), ed; SKY FULL OF MOON(1952), ed; YOUNG MAN WITH IDEAS(1952), ed; CODE TWO(1953), ed; CONFIDENTIAL CONNIE(1953), ed; I, THE JURY(1953), ed; FOUR GIRLS IN TOWN(1956), ed; OUR MISS BROOKS(1956), ed; ROCK, PRETTY BABY(1956), ed; FOR THE LOVE OF MIKE(1960), ed; GALLANT HOURS, THE(1960), ed; ALL HANDS ON DECK(1961), ed; MISTY(1961), ed

Frieda Smith
1984
CANNONBALL RUN II(1984)

G. Albert Smith
STOLEN HEAVEN(1931)

G. Turney Smith
GENTLEMEN MARRY BRUNETTES(1955), ed; MANFISH(1956), ed

G. Warren Smith
MIDNIGHT MAN, THE(1974)

Gar Smith
MY LIFE WITH CAROLINE(1941)

Garland Smith
EACH DAWN I DIE(1939); MURDER IN THE AIR(1940); DIVE BOMBER(1941); NAVY BLUES(1941)

Garnett Smith
LADY LIBERTY(1972, Ital./Fr.); SCARFACE(1983)

Garret Smith
OLD HUTCH(1936), w

Gary Smith
UP IN THE AIR(1969, Brit.); ALL AT SEA(1970, Brit.)
Misc. Talkies
MR. HORATIO KNIBBLES(1971)

Geoffrey Smith
NORMAN LOVES ROSE(1982, Aus.)

Georgann Smith
SWEETHEARTS OF THE U.S.A.(1944); WONDER MAN(1945); SLIGHTLY SCANDALOUS(1946)

George Smith
MALAY NIGHTS(1933); VIRGINIA'S HUSBAND(1934, Brit.), p; FATHER STEPS OUT(1937, Brit.), p; FIFTY-SHILLING BOXER(1937, Brit.), p; STRANGE ADVENTURES OF MR. SMITH, THE(1937, Brit.), p; COMING OF AGE(1938, Brit.), p; DARTS ARE TRUMPS(1938, Brit.), p; IF I WERE BOSS(1938, Brit.), p; MERELY MR. HAWKINS(1938, Brit.), p; MIRACLES DO HAPPEN(1938, Brit.), p; PAID IN ERROR(1938, Brit.), p; ROMANCE A LA CARTE(1938, Brit.), p; BLIND FOLLY(1939, Brit.), p; JAMAICA INN(1939, Brit.); KISS OF DEATH(1947); HAWK OF POWDER RIVER, THE(1948), w; MAROONED(1969); ALAMBRISTA!(1977)

George L. Smith
SOMETHING WILD(1961)

George W. Smith
GOIN' SOUTH(1978)

Gerald O. Smith
SUNBONNET SUE(1945)

Gerald Oliver Smith
MAN I MARRY, THE(1936); BEHIND THE MIKE(1937); GIRL OVERBOARD(1937); LADY FIGHTS BACK(1937); TOP OF THE TOWN(1937); WHEN YOU'RE IN LOVE(1937); 100 MEN AND A GIRL(1937); GATEWAY(1938); INVISIBLE ENEMY(1938); FEDERAL FUGITIVES(1941); PUDDIN' HEAD(1941); SINGING HILL, THE(1941); BEYOND THE BLUE HORIZON(1942); MRS. MINIVER(1942); TISH(1942); FOREVER AND A DAY(1943); JANE EYRE(1944); KNICKERBOCKER HOLIDAY(1944); MAN IN HALF-MOON STREET, THE(1944); MRS. PARKINGTON(1944); NATIONAL VELVET(1944); RAINBOW OVER TEXAS(1946); SAILOR TAKES A WIFE, THE(1946); HER HUSBAND'S AFFAIRS(1947); LINDA BE GOOD(1947); MOSS ROSE(1947); SINGAPORE(1947); ENCHANTMENT(1948); THAT FORSYTE WOMAN(1949)
Misc. Silents
MYSTERIOUS MISS TERRY, THE(1917)

Geraldine Smith
LORDS OF FLATBUSH, THE(1974); ONE MAN JURY(1978)
1984
MIXED BLOOD(1984)

Gilbert Smith
MIRACLE OF THE HILLS, THE(1959)

Girard Smith
HARPOON(1948), w

Glen Smith
NIGHTMARE IN WAX(1969), ph; REBEL ROUSERS(1970), ph

Glen R. Smith
HEROES DIE YOUNG(1960), ph

Glenn Allen Smith
1984
ELLIE(1984), w

Gloria Smith
TOP BANANA(1954)

Gordon Smith
1984
CENSUS TAKER, THE(1984), w

Grace Smith
Misc. Silents
MILLIONARE, THE(1927)

Graham Smith
SPYLARKS(1965, Brit.)

Grant K. Smith
NIKKI, WILD DOG OF THE NORTH(1961, U.S./Can.), ed; BIG RED(1962), ed; SAVAGE SAM(1963), ed; THOSE CALLOWAYS(1964), ed; TIGER WALKS, A(1964), ed

Grayce Hampton Smith
HEAVEN CAN WAIT(1943)

Greg Smith
CONFESSIONS OF A WINDOW CLEANER(1974, Brit.), p; CONFESSIONS OF A POP PERFORMER(1975, Brit.), p; CONFESSIONS FROM A HOLIDAY CAMP(1977, Brit.), p; STAND UP VIRGIN SOLDIERS(1977, Brit.), p; THIRTY NINE STEPS, THE(1978, Brit.), p; LAST WORD, THE(1979), w; SHILLINGBURY BLOWERS, THE(1980, Brit.), p; STIR(1980, Aus.); DANGEROUS DAVIES–THE LAST DETECTIVE(1981, Brit.), p

"Grizzly" Smith
Misc. Talkies
WRESTLING QUEEN, THE(1975)

Gunboat Smith
Silents
MANHATTAN(1924); BASHFUL BUCCANEER(1925); GREAT GATSBY, THE(1926); LET'S GET MARRIED(1926); CITY GONE WILD, THE(1927); WE'RE ALL GAMBLERS(1927); WINGS(1927)
Misc. Silents
FEAR FIGHTER, THE(1925); SAY IT AGAIN(1926)

Gwen Smith
BILLY JACK(1971)

H. Allen Smith
RHUBARB(1951), w

H. Reeves Smith
Misc. Silents
THREE WEEKS(1924)

H.M.K. Smith
JEALOUSY(1929), cos

Hagen Smith
Misc. Talkies
TO HELL YOU PREACH(1972); LEGEND OF FRANK WOODS, THE(1977), d

Hal Smith
GOOD LUCK, MR. YATES(1943), w; MUSIC IN MANHATTAN(1944), w; SHE'S A SOLDIER TOO(1944), w; DANGEROUS BUSINESS(1946), w; NIGHT EDITOR(1946), w; STARS OVER TEXAS(1946), w; BLACK EAGLE(1948), w; THUNDERHOOF(1948), w; CUSTOMS AGENT(1950), w; MILKMAN, THE(1950); YOU FOR ME(1952); IT CAME FROM BENEATH THE SEA(1955), w; THERE'S ALWAYS TOMORROW(1956); HOT CAR GIRL(1958); APARTMENT, THE(1960); THREE STOOGES MEET HERCULES, THE(1962); MIRACLE OF SANTA'S WHITE REINDEER, THE(1963); SON OF FLUBBER(1963); HEY THERE, IT'S YOGI BEAR(1964); GREAT RACE, THE(1965); GHOST AND MR. CHICKEN, THE(1966); UGLY DACHSHUND, THE(1966); SANTA AND THE THREE BEARS(1970); SHINBONE ALLEY(1971); $1,000,000 DUCK(1971); FANTASTIC PLANET(1973, Fr./Czech.); OKLAHOMA CRUDE(1973)

Hal J. Smith
O. HENRY'S FULL HOUSE(1952)

Hamilton Smith
Silents
AMERICAN MAID(1917), w; I WANT TO FORGET(1918), w; JUST SYLVIA(1918), w; NEIGHBORS(1918), w; INNER MAN, THE(1922), d
Misc. Silents
ISLE OF DOUBT(1922), d

Hank Smith
BON VOYAGE, CHARLIE BROWN(AND DON'T COME BACK)***(1980), anim; 1001 ARABIAN NIGHTS(1959), anim; GAY PURR-EE(1962), anim; MR. MAGOO'S HOLIDAY FESTIVAL(1970), anim; RACE FOR YOUR LIFE, CHARLIE BROWN(1977), anim

Harold Jacob Smith
RIVER'S EDGE, THE(1957), w; DEFIANT ONES, THE(1958), w; ENCHANTED ISLAND(1958), w; INHERIT THE WIND(1960), w; MC MASTERS, THE(1970), w

Henry Smith
KID BLUE(1973)

Harry B. Smith
SWEETHEARTS(1938), w

Harry G. Smith
LOVE KISS, THE(1930), w

Harry James Smith
TAILOR MADE MAN, A(1931), w
Silents
TAILOR MADE MAN, A(1922), w

Harry Smith
HELL'S HIGHWAY(1932)
Silents
ANOTHER MAN'S BOOTS(1922)
Harry S. Smith [Jay Silverheels]
GOOD MORNING, JUDGE(1943)
Harry W. Smith
LOUISIANA TERRITORY(1953), d, ph; LOST LAGOON(1958), ph
Helen Vreeland Smith
MOON OVER HER SHOULDER(1941), w
Herb Smith
BLADES OF THE MUSKETEERS(1953), ed
Herbert Smith
CLEANING UP(1933, Brit.), p; GREAT STUFF(1933, Brit.), p; I'LL STICK TO
YOU(1933, Brit.), p; MAROONED(1933, Brit.), p; STRIKE IT RICH(1933, Brit.), p;
THAT'S MY WIFE(1933, Brit.), p; THIS IS THE LIFE(1933, Brit.), p; GREEN PACK,
THE(1934, Brit.), p; KEEP IT QUIET(1934, Brit.), p; MAN I WANT, THE(1934, Brit.), p;
ON THE AIR(1934, Brit.), p&d; PASSING SHADOWS(1934, Brit.), p; WARN LON-
DON!(1934, Brit.), p; WITHOUT YOU(1934, Brit.), p; BIG SPLASH, THE(1935, Brit.), p;
CASE OF GABRIEL PERRY, THE(1935, Brit.), p; CHARING CROSS ROAD(1935,
Brit.), p; LINE ENGAGED(1935, Brit.), p; MARRY THE GIRL(1935, Brit.), p; NIGHT
MAIL(1935, Brit.), p&d; WIFE OR TWO, A(1935, Brit.), p; GAY LOVE(1936, Brit.), p;
HAPPY FAMILY, THE(1936, Brit.), p; INTERRUPTED HONEYMOON, THE(1936,
Brit.), p; IT'S YOU I WANT(1936, Brit.), p; JURY'S EVIDENCE(1936, Brit.), p; THEY
DIDN'T KNOW(1936, Brit.), p&d; FINE FEATHERS(1937, Brit.), p; IT'S A GRAND
OLD WORLD(1937, Brit.), d; LEAVE IT TO ME(1937, Brit.), d; MELODY AND
ROMANCE(1937, Brit.), p; VARIETY HOUR(1937, Brit.), p; AROUND THE
TOWN(1938, Brit.), p&d; I'VE GOT A HORSE(1938, Brit.), p&d; HOME FROM HO-
ME(1939, Brit.), p&d; THEY WERE NOT DIVIDED(1951, Brit.), p; CAT GIRL(1957, Brit.),
art d; ROCK AROUND THE WORLD(1957, Brit.), p; ACCURSED, THE(1958, Brit.), art d; 6.5
SPECIAL(1958, Brit.), p; WOMAN EATER, THE(1959, Brit.), art d; TOO YOUNG TO
LOVE(1960, Brit.), p; ROMAN SPRING OF MRS. STONE, THE(1961, U.S./Brit.), art d;
TASTE OF HONEY, A(1962, Brit.); JASON AND THE ARGONAUTS(1963, Brit.), art d;
SEVENTH DAWN, THE(1964), art d; HILL, THE(1965, Brit.), art d; SWINGER'S
PARADISE(1965, Brit.), art d; DUTCHMAN(1966, Brit.), art d; TARZAN AND THE
GREAT RIVER(1967, U.S./Switz.), art d; SHALAKO(1968, Brit.), art d; TARZAN AND
THE JUNGLE BOY(1968, US/Switz.), art d; QUACKSER FORTUNE HAS A COUSIN
IN THE BRONX(1970), art d; CATLOW(1971, Span.), art d; CONNECTING
ROOMS(1971, Brit.), art d; DANCE OF DEATH, THE(1971, Brit.), art d; MUTATIONS,
THE(1974, Brit.), art d; PAPER TIGER(1975, Brit.), prod d
Hinton Smith
IN HIS STEPS(1936), w; GIRL LOVES BOY(1937), w
Howard Smith
LAND OF THE SILVER FOX(1928), w; CRY MURDER(1936); GAMBLER'S CHOI-
CE(1944), ed; NAVY WAY, THE(1944), ed; ONE BODY TOO MANY(1944), ed; TAKE
IT BIG(1944), ed; TIMBER QUEEN(1944), ed; SCARED STIFF(1945), ed; TOKYO
ROSE(1945), ed; HER KIND OF MAN(1946); SWAMP FIRE(1946), ed; THEY MADE
ME A KILLER(1946), ed; ADVENTURE ISLAND(1947), ed; BIG TOWN(1947), ed; BIG
TOWN AFTER DARK(1947), ed; DANGER STREET(1947), ed; FEAR IN THE
NIGHT(1947), ed; I COVER BIG TOWN(1947), ed; JUNGLE FLIGHT(1947), ed; KISS
OF DEATH(1947), ed; SEVEN WERE SAVED(1947), ed; ALBUQUERQUE(1948), ed; BIG
TOWN SCANDAL(1948), ed; CAGED FURY(1948), ed; CALL NORTHSIDE 777(1948);
DISASTER(1948), ed; DYNAMITE(1948), ed; MR. RECKLESS(1948), ed; SHAG-
GY(1948), ed; STATE OF THE UNION(1948); STREET WITH NO NAME, THE(1948);
WATERFRONT AT MIDNIGHT(1948), ed; CAPTAIN CHINA(1949), ed; EL PA-
SO(1949), ed; LUCKY STIFF, THE(1949), ed; MANHANDLED(1949), ed; SPECIAL
AGENT(1949), ed; LAWLESS, THE(1950), ed; TRIPOLI(1950), ed; CROSS-
WINDS(1951), ed; HONG KONG(1951), ed; LAST OUTPOST, THE(1951), ed; PAS-
SAGE WEST(1951), ed; BLAZING FOREST, THE(1952), ed; CARIBBEAN(1952), ed;
DEATH OF A SALESMAN(1952); NEVER WAVE AT A WAC(1952); CADDY,
THE(1953); JAMAICA RUN(1953), ed; SANGAREE(1953), ed; TROPIC ZONE(1953),
ed; GOLDEN MISTRESS, THE(1954), ed; JIVARO(1954), ed; LUCY GALLANT(1955),
ed; NO MAN'S WOMAN(1955), ed; RUN FOR COVER(1955), ed; DAKOTA IN-
CIDENT(1956), ed; HOLLYWOOD OR BUST(1956), ed; STRANGE ADVENTURE,
A(1956), ed; STRANGER AT MY DOOR(1956), ed; DELICATE DELINQUENT,
THE(1957), ed; FACE IN THE CROWD, A(1957); LOVING YOU(1957), ed; I BURY THE
LIVING(1958), ed; MATCHMAKER, THE(1958), ed; NO TIME FOR SERGEANTS(1958);
FACE OF FIRE(1959, U.S./Brit.); THAT KIND OF WOMAN(1959), ed; BREATH OF
SCANDAL, A(1960), ed; HELLER IN PINK TIGHTS(1960), ed; WALK LIKE A
DRAGON(1960), ed; ALL IN A NIGHT'S WORK(1961), ed; BREAKFAST AT TIFFA-
NY'S(1961), ed; HELL IS FOR HEROES(1962), ed; WHO'S GOT THE ACTION?(1962),
ed; BRASS BOTTLE, THE(1964); MARNIE(1964), makeup; MURPH THE SURF(1974),
ed; DON'T GO NEAR THE WATER(1975); MACKINTOSH & T.J.(1975), ed; NIGHT
THE LIGHTS WENT OUT IN GEORGIA, THE(1981), p; TEX(1982), ed; TWILIGHT
ZONE–THE MOVIE(1983), ed
1984
RHINESTONE(1984), p
Silents
SILVER SLAVE, THE(1927), w
Misc. Silents
YOUNG AMERICA(1918)
Howard A. Smith
RIDE THE WILD SURF(1964), ed
Howard Ellis Smith
MAN WHO BROKE THE BANK AT MONTE CARLO, THE(1935), w; IT HAD TO
HAPPEN(1936), w; PROFESSIONAL SOLDIER(1936), w; TO MARY–WITH LO-
VE(1936), w; THINK FAST, MR. MOTO(1937), w
Howard I. Smith
WIND ACROSS THE EVERGLADES(1958); MURDER, INC.(1960); BON VOYA-
GE(1962)
Howard K. Smith
BEST MAN, THE(1964); CANDIDATE, THE(1972); MAN, THE(1972); NASTY HAB-
ITS(1976, Brit.); PURSUIT OF D.B. COOPER, THE(1981); BEST LITTLE WHORE-
HOUSE IN TEXAS, THE(1982)
Hubert Smith
LOST LAGOON(1958), m; STUDENT BODY, THE(1976), w; MOONSHINE COUNTY
EXPRESS(1977), w; NIGHT CREATURE(1979), w; GLOVE, THE(1980), w

Hugh Smith
BLACK OAK CONSPIRACY(1977), w
Misc. Talkies
ZEBRA KILLER, THE(1974)
Ian Smith
CHILD'S PLAY(1954, Brit.)
Ira N. Smith
AMITYVILLE II: THE POSSESSION(1982), p
Irving Smith
SEA OF GRASS, THE(1947); BOOTS MALONE(1952)
J. Smith
GAL YOUNG UN(1979)
J. Augustus Smith
DRUMS O' VOODOO(1934), a, w
J. Brennan Smith
TESTAMENT(1983)
J. J. Smith
Silents
GOLD RUSH, THE(1925)
J. Lewis Smith
SOMEWHERE I'LL FIND YOU(1942); MRS. O'MALLEY AND MR. MALONE(1950);
HARDER THEY FALL, THE(1956); MISFITS, THE(1961); JUMBO(1962); ADVANCE
TO THE REAR(1964)
J. Louis Smith
SHADOW OF THE THIN MAN(1941)
J.W. Smith
WARRIORS, THE(1979); D.C. CAB(1983); DEAL OF THE CENTURY(1983)
Jack Smith
HITTIN' THE TRAIL(1937); TROUBLE IN TEXAS(1937); PAROLED–TO DIE(1938);
FRONTIER SCOUT(1939); LUCKY DEVILS(1941); STICK TO YOUR GUNS(1941);
JOHNNY O'CLOCK(1947); MAKE BELIEVE BALLROOM(1949); ON MOONLIGHT
BAY(1951); WHITE FEATHER(1955), art d; ALIAS JOHN PRESTON(1956), ph; IL-
LIAC PASSION, THE(1968); PERFECT FRIDAY(1970, Brit.), p; BAREFOOT EXECU-
TIVE, THE(1971); CONNECTING ROOMS(1971, Brit.), p; NEITHER THE SEA NOR
THE SAND(1974, Brit.), p; SILENT NIGHT, BLOODY NIGHT(1974); TRAP DOOR,
THE(1980)
1984
CANNONBALL RUN II(1984)
Misc. Talkies
QUEEN OF SHEBA MEETS THE ATOM MAN, THE(1963)
Jack Smith, Jr.
CHINA SYNDROME, THE(1979)
Jack C. Smith
DOOMED AT SUNDOWN(1937); FIGHTING DEPUTY, THE(1937); GIT ALONG,
LITTLE DOGIES(1937); GUNS IN THE DARK(1937); HEADIN' FOR THE RIO
GRANDE(1937); LAWMAN IS BORN, A(1937); LIGHTNIN' CRANDALL(1937); MYS-
TERY OF THE HOODED HORSEMEN, THE(1937); RIO GRANDE RANGER(1937);
ROUNDUP TIME IN TEXAS(1937); SING, COWBOY, SING(1937); TRAIL OF VEN-
GEANCE(1937); ANGELS WITH DIRTY FACES(1938); FEUD MAKER(1938); FRON-
TIER TOWN(1938); HEROES OF THE ALAMO(1938); ROMANCE OF THE
ROCKIES(1938); EACH DAWN I DIE(1939); OUTLAW'S PARADISE(1939); TOWER OF
LONDON(1939); HONKY TONK(1941); PIONEERS, THE(1941); REG'LAR FEL-
LERS(1941); RIOT SQUAD(1941); SIN TOWN(1942); STAGECOACH BUCK-
AROO(1942); STRANGE CASE OF DR. RX, THE(1942); KEEP 'EM SLUGGING(1943)
Jack Martin Smith
YOLANDA AND THE THIEF(1945), art d; ZIEGFELD FOLLIES(1945), art d; HOLI-
DAY IN MEXICO(1946), art d; EASTER PARADE(1948), art d; PIRATE, THE(1948),
art d; SUMMER HOLIDAY(1948), art d; MADAME BOVARY(1949), art d; ON THE
TOWN(1949), art d; NANCY GOES TO RIO(1950), art d; SUMMER STOCK(1950), art
d; ROYAL WEDDING(1951), art d; SHOW BOAT(1951), art d; BELLE OF NEW YORK,
THE(1952), art d; MILLION DOLLAR MERMAID(1952), art d; EASY TO LOVE(1953),
art d; I LOVE MELVIN(1953), art d; SEVEN CITIES OF GOLD(1955), art d; SOLDIER
OF FORTUNE(1955), art d; BIGGER THAN LIFE(1956), art d; MAN IN THE GREY
FLANNEL SUIT, THE(1956), art d; TEENAGE REBEL(1956), art d; AFFAIR TO
REMEMBER, AN(1957), art d; PEYTON PLACE(1957), art d; BARBARIAN AND THE
GEISHA, THE(1958), art d; WOMAN OBSESSED(1959), art d; CAN-CAN(1960), art d;
NORTH TO ALASKA(1960), art d; ALL HANDS ON DECK(1961), art d; COMAN-
CHEROS, THE(1961), art d; MARINES, LET'S GO(1961), art d; PIRATES OF TOR-
TUGA(1961), art d; RETURN TO PEYTON PLACE(1961), art d;
SANCTUARY(1961), art d; SECOND TIME AROUND, THE(1961), art d; SNOW
WHITE AND THE THREE STOOGES(1961), art d; TENDER IS THE NIGHT(1961), art
d; VOYAGE TO THE BOTTOM OF THE SEA(1961), art d; WILD IN THE COUN-
TRY(1961), art d; FIVE WEEKS IN A BALLOON(1962), art d; MR. HOBBS TAKES A
VACATION(1962), art d; STATE FAIR(1962), art d; CLEOPATRA(1963), art d; MOVE
OVER, DARLING(1963), art d; STRIPPER, THE(1963), art d; TAKE HER, SHE'S
MINE(1963), art d; FATE IS THE HUNTER(1964), art d; GOODBYE CHARLIE(1964),
art d; JOHN GOLDFARB, PLEASE COME HOME(1964), art d; PLEASURE SEEKERS,
THE(1964), art d; RIO CONCHOS(1964), art d; SHOCK TREATMENT(1964), art d;
WHAT A WAY TO GO(1964), art d; AGONY AND THE ECSTASY, THE(1965), art d;
DEAR BRIGITTE(1965), art d; DO NOT DISTURB(1965), art d; MORITURI(1965), art
d; REWARD, THE(1965), art d; VON RYAN'S EXPRESS(1965), art d; I DEAL IN
DANGER(1966), art d; OUR MAN FLINT(1966), art d; SMOKY(1966), art d; STAGE-
COACH(1966), art d; WAY...WAY OUT(1966), art d; DOCTOR DOLITTLE(1967), art d;
FLIM-FLAM MAN, THE(1967), art d; GUIDE FOR THE MARRIED MAN, A(1967), art
d; HOMBRE(1967), art d; IN LIKE FLINT(1967), art d; ST. VALENTINE'S DAY
MASSACRE, THE(1967), art d; TONY ROME(1967), art d; VALLEY OF THE
DOLLS(1967), art d; BANDOLERO!(1968), art d; DETECTIVE, THE(1968), art d;
PLANET OF THE APES(1968), art d; PRETTY POISON(1968), art d; SECRET LIFE OF
AN AMERICAN WIFE, THE(1968), art d; SWEET RIDE, THE(1968), art d; THE
BOSTON STRANGLER, THE(1968), art d; BUTCH CASSIDY AND THE SUNDANCE
KID(1969), art d; CHE!(1969), art d; HELLO, DOLLY!(1969), art d; JUSTINE(1969), art
d; BENEATH THE PLANET OF THE APES(1970), art d; COVER ME BABE(1970), art
d; GREAT WHITE HOPE, THE(1970), art d; M(1970), art d; MOVE(1970), art d; TORA!
TORA! TORA!(1970, U.S./Jap.), art d; TRIBES(1970), art d; ESCAPE FROM THE
PLANET OF THE APES(1971), art d; CULPEPPER CATTLE COMPANY, THE(1972),
art d; ACE ELI AND RODGER OF THE SKIES(1973), art d; EMPEROR OF THE
NORTH POLE(1973), art d; ICEMAN COMETH, THE(1973), prod d; LOST IN THE
STARS(1974), art d; RHINOCEROS(1974), prod d; REINCARNATION OF PETER
PROUD, THE(1975), art d; GREAT SCOUT AND CATHOUSE THURSDAY, THE(1976),
prod d; PETE'S DRAGON(1977), art d

Jack W. Smith
Silents
FLAG LIEUTENANT, THE(1919, Brit.), p; HER LONELY SOLDIER(1919, Brit.), p; HER SECRET(1919, Brit.), p; ODDS AGAINST HER, THE(1919, Brit.), p

Jaclyn Smith
GOODBYE COLUMBUS(1969); ADVENTURERS, THE(1970); BOOTLEGGERS(1974)

Jacqueline Smith
GO NAKED IN THE WORLD(1961)

James Smith
LADY OF THE PAVEMENTS(1929), ed; BAT WHISPERS, THE(1930), ed; ONE ROMANTIC NIGHT(1930), ed; COME ON, MARINES(1934), ed; DOUBLE DOOR(1934), ed; MISS FANE'S BABY IS STOLEN(1934), ed; SEARCH FOR BEAUTY(1934), ed; FATHER BROWN, DETECTIVE(1935), ed; SHIP CAFE(1935), ed; TWO FISTED(1935), ed; ARIZONA MAHONEY(1936), ed; FLORIDA SPECIAL(1936), ed; PREVIEW MURDER MYSTERY(1936), ed; CRIME NOBODY SAW, THE(1937), ed; NIGHT OF MYSTERY(1937), ed; RIDE A CROOKED MILE(1938), ed; SCANDAL STREET(1938), ed; DISPUTED PASSAGE(1939), ed; GREAT VICTOR HERBERT, THE(1939), ed; MAGNIFICENT FRAUD, THE(1939), ed; NEVER SAY DIE(1939), ed; THERE'S MAGIC IN MUSIC(1941), ed; DARK WATERS(1944), ed; BEDSIDE MANNER(1945), ed; SONG FOR MISS JULIE, A(1945), ed; DIARY OF A CHAMBERMAID(1946), ed; MR. ACE(1946), ed; CHRISTMAS EVE(1947), ed; MACOMBER AFFAIR, THE(1947), ed; LULU BELLE(1948), ed; ON OUR MERRY WAY(1948), ed; SANDS OF THE KALAHARI(1965, Brit.), cos; DAY THE FISH CAME OUT, THE(1967. Brit./Gr.)
Silents
AVENGING CONSCIENCE, THE(1914), ed; BATTLE OF THE SEXES, THE(1914), ed; ESCAPE, THE(1914), ed; HOME SWEET HOME(1914), ed; JUDITH OF BETHULIA(1914), ed; BIRTH OF A NATION, THE(1915), ed; INTOLERANCE(1916), ed; GREAT LOVE, THE(1918), ed; GREATEST THING IN LIFE, THE(1918), ed; HEARTS OF THE WORLD(1918), ed; BROKEN BLOSSOMS(1919), ed; GIRL WHO STAYED AT HOME, THE(1919), ed; ROMANCE OF HAPPY VALLEY, A(1919), ed; SCARLET DAYS(1919), ed; TRUE HEART SUSIE(1919), ed; GREATEST QUESTION, THE(1920), ed; IDOL DANCER, THE(1920), ed; LOVE FLOWER, THE(1920), ed; SINS OF ROZANNE(1920), ed; WAY DOWN EAST(1920), ed; DREAM STREET(1921), ed; ORPHANS OF THE STORM(1922), a, ed; AMERICA(1924), ed; "THAT ROYLE GIRL"(1925), ed; SALLY OF THE SAWDUST(1925), ed; BATTLE OF THE SEXES, THE(1928), ed

James Bell Smith
Silents
ISLE OF HOPE, THE(1925), w; BLUE STREAK, THE(1926), w; SILENT POWER, THE(1926), w

James E. Smith
NEW WINE(1941), ed; GIRL FROM MANHATTAN(1948), ed

James J. Smith
HAPPY LAND(1943)

Jamie Smith
FAITHFUL CITY(1952, Israel); KILLER'S KISS(1955)

Jan Smith
YOU'VE GOT TO WALK IT LIKE YOU TALK IT OR YOU'LL LOSE THAT BEAT(1971)

Jan Darnley Smith
UP IN THE AIR(1969, Brit.), d, w

Jane Smith
FOLLOW THE BOYS(1944)

Janet M. Smith
DRAGON OF PENDRAGON CASTLE, THE(1950, Brit.), w

Jay Smith
Silents
KAISER, BEAST OF BERLIN, THE(1918)

Jean Smith
Silents
WOMAN WHO SINNED, A(1925), ph

Jean Taylor Smith
ROB ROY, THE HIGHLAND ROGUE(1954, Brit.); IT'S NEVER TOO LATE(1958, Brit.)

Jeffrey S. Smith
1984
PHILADELPHIA EXPERIMENT, THE(1984)

Jem Smith
Misc. Silents
LAST CHALLENGE, THE(1916, Brit.)

Jerry Smith
WEST OF PINTO BASIN(1940)

Jessica Smith
REDS(1981)

Jim Smith
GRASSHOPPER, THE(1970)
1984
PRODIGAL, THE(1984)

Jim B. Smith
VIVA MAX!(1969); MITCHELL(1975)

Jimmie Smith
TROUBLE WITH WOMEN, THE(1947); THUNDERING JETS(1958)

Jimmy Smith
ROMANCE IN THE DARK(1938), ed; SENSATIONS OF 1945(1944), ed; CLOPORTES(1966, Fr., Ital.), m
Misc. Talkies
STREET GIRLS(1975)

Jo Ann Smith
PAL JOEY(1957)

Jo-Jo Smith
SATURDAY NIGHT FEVER(1977), cons

Joanne Smith
SUTTER'S GOLD(1936)

Joe Smith
MANHATTAN PARADE(1931); HEART OF NEW YORK(1932); NOB HILL(1945); TWO TICKETS TO BROADWAY(1951); JAMBOREE(1957); FM(1978); ONE-TRICK PONY(1980)

Silents
GOLD RUSH, THE(1925)

Joe P. Smith
KEY LARGO(1948); OUTCASTS OF POKER FLAT, THE(1952)

Joel Smith
THEM!(1954); COURT-MARTIAL OF BILLY MITCHELL, THE(1955); COURT JESTER, THE(1956); STEEL JUNGLE, THE(1956)

John Smith
WOMAN OF DISTINCTION, A(1950); GUY WHO CAME BACK, THE(1951); HIGH AND THE MIGHTY, THE(1954); DESERT SANDS(1955); SEVEN ANGRY MEN(1955); WE'RE NO ANGELS(1955); WICHITA(1955); BOLD AND THE BRAVE, THE(1956); FRIENDLY PERSUASION(1956); GHOST TOWN(1956); HOT ROD GIRL(1956); QUINCANNON, FRONTIER SCOUT(1956); REBEL IN TOWN(1956); FURY AT SHOWDOWN(1957); KETTLES ON OLD MACDONALD'S FARM, THE(1957); LAWLESS EIGHTIES, THE(1957); TOMAHAWK TRAIL(1957); WOMEN OF PITCAIRN ISLAND, THE(1957); CROOKED CIRCLE, THE(1958); HANDLE WITH CARE(1958); ISLAND OF LOST WOMEN(1959); ROAD TO HONG KONG, THE(1962, U.S./Brit.), ed; CIRCUS WORLD(1964); WACO(1966); LEGACY OF BLOOD(1973); PERSONAL BEST(1982)
1984
PURPLE HEARTS(1984)
Silents
WHAT PRICE GLORY(1926), ph

John C. Smith
BARTLEBY(1970, Brit.), ed

John M. Smith
LEGEND OF THE LONE RANGER, THE(1981)

John Martin Smith
BANDIDO(1956), art d; ADVENTURES OF A YOUNG MAN(1962), art d

Count John Maximillian Smith
NO HOLDS BARRED(1952)

John S. Smith
HE WHO RIDES A TIGER(1966, Brit.), ed; VULTURE, THE(1967, U.S./Brit./Can.), ed; SUMARINE X-1(1969, Brit.), ed; HELL BOATS(1970, Brit.), ed; MOSQUITO SQUADRON(1970, Brit.), ed

John Victor Smith
IT TAKES A THIEF(1960, Brit.), ed; FOLLOW THE BOYS(1963), ed; FURY AT SMUGGLERS BAY(1963, Brit.), ed; FERRY ACROSS THE MERSEY(1964, Brit.), ed; HELP!(1965, Brit.), ed; ALPHABET MURDERS, THE(1966), ed; FUNNY THING HAPPENED ON THE WAY TO THE FORUM, A(1966), ed; HOW I WON THE WAR(1967, Brit.), ed; INSPECTOR CLOUSEAU(1968, Brit.), ed; BED SITTING ROOM, THE(1969, Brit.), ed; MELODY(1971, Brit.), ed; DEVIL'S WIDOW, THE(1972, Brit.), ed; POSSESSION OF JOEL DELANEY, THE(1972), ed; DELICATE BALANCE, A(1973), ed; HARDER THEY COME, THE(1973, Jamaica), ed; OFFENSE, THE(1973, Brit.), ed; THREE MUSKETEERS, THE(1974, Panama), ed; FOUR MUSKETEERS, THE(1975), ed; ROYAL FLASH(1975, Brit.), ed; ROBIN AND MARIAN(1976, Brit.), ed; CUBA(1979), ed; ABSOLUTION(1981, Brit.), ed; COUNTRYMAN(1982, Jamaica), ed; SUPERMAN III(1983), ed
1984
FINDERS KEEPERS(1984), ed

Jonathan Smith
SCARECROW, THE(1982, New Zealand)

Joseph Smith
CAPTAIN KIDD(1945), ed; I WAS A COMMUNIST FOR THE F.B.I.(1951)

Josephine Smith
KING AND I, THE(1956); YOUNG DON'T CRY, THE(1957); CAPE FEAR(1962)

Judith Smith
GAMES THAT LOVERS PLAY(1971, Brit.), p

Justin Smith
JAZZ SINGER, THE(1953); POLICE NURSE(1963); YOUNG SWINGERS, THE(1963); WHAT A WAY TO GO(1964); WILD ON THE BEACH(1965); HOW TO SUCCEED IN BUSINESS WITHOUT REALLY TRYING(1976)

K.L. Smith
UNDER FIRE(1957); BATTLE OF THE CORAL SEA(1959); ROUSTABOUT(1964)

Karen Smith
YOU'VE GOT TO WALK IT LIKE YOU TALK IT OR YOU'LL LOSE THAT BEAT(1971); FREAKY FRIDAY(1976); HOSPITAL MASSACRE(1982)

Karyn Smith
1984
HOSPITAL MASSACRE(1984)

Kate Smith
HELLO, EVERYBODY(1933); THIS IS THE ARMY(1943)

Katherine Smith
INTRUDER, THE(1962)

Kathleen Smith
INCIDENT, THE(1967)

Kay Smith
ESCAPE TO GLORY(1940); THIS LOVE OF OURS(1945)

Keats Smith
POLYESTER(1981)

Keely Smith
SENIOR PROM(1958); THUNDER ROAD(1958); HEY BOY! HEY GIRL!(1959)

Keith Smith
I'M ALL RIGHT, JACK(1959, Brit.); UGLY DUCKLING, THE(1959, Brit.); CONCRETE JUNGLE, THE(1962, Brit.); HAIR OF THE DOG(1962, Brit.); FACE OF A STRANGER(1964, Brit.); FERRY ACROSS THE MERSEY(1964, Brit.); RICOCHET(1966, Brit.); HEADLINE HUNTERS(1968, Brit.); ANIMALS, THE(1971), ph; ONE BRIEF SUMMER(1971, Brit.); WALKING TALL, PART II(1975), ph

Ken Smith
JIGSAW(1949); SANTA CLAUS(1960, Mex.); LITTLE ANGEL(1961, Mex.), d; SUNBURN(1979)

Kendall Smith
RUNNING BRAVE(1983, Can.)

Kenneth L. Smith
PUSHOVER(1954); JUNGLE MOON MEN(1955)

Kenneth Leslie Smith
MAYFAIR MELODY(1937, Brit.), m

Kent Smith
GARDEN MURDER CASE, THE(1936); BACK DOOR TO HEAVEN(1939); CAT PEOPLE(1942); HITLER'S CHILDREN(1942); FOREVER AND A DAY(1943); THIS LAND IS MINE(1943); THREE RUSSIAN GIRLS(1943); CURSE OF THE CAT PEOPLE,

THE(1944); YOUTH RUNS WILD(1944); SPIRAL STAIRCASE, THE(1946); MAGIC TOWN(1947); NORA PRENTISS(1947); VOICE OF THE TURTLE, THE(1947); FOUNTAINHEAD, THE(1949); MY FOOLISH HEART(1949); DAMNED DON'T CRY, THE(1950); THIS SIDE OF THE LAW(1950); PAULA(1952); COMANCHE(1956); SAYONARA(1957); BADLANDERS, THE(1958); IMITATION GENERAL(1958); MUGGER, THE(1958); PARTY GIRL(1958); THIS EARTH IS MINE(1959); STRANGERS WHEN WE MEET(1960); SUSAN SLADE(1961); MOON PILOT(1962); BALCONY, THE(1963); DISTANT TRUMPET, A(1964); YOUNG LOVERS, THE(1964); YOUNGBLOOD HAWKE(1964); COVENANT WITH DEATH, A(1966); TROUBLE WITH ANGELS, THE(1966); GAMES(1967); ASSIGNMENT TO KILL(1968); KONA COAST(1968); MONEY JUNGLE, THE(1968); DEATH OF A GUNFIGHTER(1969); GAMES, THE(1970); PETE 'N' TILLIE(1972); LOST HORIZON(1973); TAKING TIGER MOUNTAIN(1983, U.S./Welsh), d, w, ph

Misc. Talkies
COMPANION, THE(1976); DIE SISTER, DIE(1978)

Kerry Smith
Misc. Talkies
MY NAME IS LEGEND(1975)

Kevin Smith
CRIMSON CULT, THE(1970, Brit.)

Kim Smith
LITTLE ONES, THE(1965, Brit.); SOME MAY LIVE(1967, Brit.); OLIVER!(1968, Brit.); OH! WHAT A LOVELY WAR(1969, Brit.)

Kimry Smith
1984
BEAT STREET(1984)

Kirby Smith
GHOST OF DRAGSTRIP HOLLOW(1959)

Kurtwood Smith
ZOOT SUIT(1981); GOING BERSERK(1983); STAYING ALIVE(1983)
1984
FLASHPOINT(1984)

L.R. Smith
PHANTOM LADY(1944), set d

La Ron A. Smith
1984
BODY ROCK(1984)

La Vergne Smith
NEW ORLEANS AFTER DARK(1958)

Lane Smith
MAIDSTONE(1970); LAST AMERICAN HERO, THE(1973); MAN ON A SWING(1974); ROOSTER COGBURN(1975); NETWORK(1976); BAD NEWS BEARS IN BREAKING TRAINING, THE(1977); BETWEEN THE LINES(1977); BLUE COLLAR(1978); ON THE YARD(1978); HONEYSUCKLE ROSE(1980); ON THE NICKEL(1980); RESURRECTION(1980); PRINCE OF THE CITY(1981); FRANCES(1982); SOGGY BOTTOM U.S.A.(1982)
1984
PLACES IN THE HEART(1984); PURPLE HEARTS(1984); RED DAWN(1984)

Larry K. Smith
PINK MOTEL(1983), m

Lawrence Smith
SATURDAY NIGHT AT THE BATHS(1975)

Lee Smith
TILL THE CLOUDS ROLL BY(1946)

Leigh Smith
BIG BLUFF, THE(1933); REVOLT OF THE ZOMBIES(1936), art d; FRONTIER BADMEN(1943), set d; NAUGHTY NINETIES, THE(1945), set d; PILLOW OF DEATH(1945), set d; SUDAN(1945), set d; CANYON PASSAGE(1946), set d; SHE-WOLF OF LONDON(1946), set d; PIRATES OF MONTEREY(1947), set d

Leigh R. Smith
Silents
DOWN TO THE SEA IN SHIPS(1923)

Lelan Smith
ALL THE PRESIDENT'S MEN(1976)

Len Smith
HOLD'EM JAIL(1932), ph; YOU CAN'T BUY EVERYTHING(1934), ph

Lennie Smith
FOLLOW THE BOYS(1944); SON OF THE RENEGADE(1953); ESCAPE FROM SAN QUENTIN(1957)

Leon Smith
QUEEN OF BLOOD(1966), set d; BENJI(1974), ed

Leonard Smith
IDLE RICH, THE(1929), ph; SO THIS IS COLLEGE(1929), ph; CAUGHT SHORT(1930), ph; DOUGH BOYS(1930), ph; FREE AND EASY(1930), ph; THEY LEARNED ABOUT WOMEN(1930), ph; PARLOR, BEDROOM AND BATH(1931), ph; REDUCING(1931), ph; SIDEWALKS OF NEW YORK(1931), ph; PROSPERITY(1932), ph; SO THIS IS AFRICA(1933), ph; BAND PLAYS ON, THE(1934), ph; MURDER IN THE PRIVATE CAR(1934), ph; DEVIL DOLL, THE(1936), ph; SINNER TAKE ALL(1936), ph; TARZAN ESCAPES(1936), ph; TOUGH GUY(1936), ph; DANGEROUS NUMBER(1937), ph; MARRIED BEFORE BREAKFAST(1937), ph; SONG OF THE CITY(1937), ph; THOROUGHBREDS DON'T CRY(1937), ph; PARADISE FOR THREE(1938), ph; FOUR GIRLS IN WHITE(1939), ph; JOE AND ETHEL TURP CALL ON THE PRESIDENT(1939), ph; MAISIE(1939), ph; STAND UP AND FIGHT(1939), ph; TARZAN FINDS A SON!(1939), ph; CAPTAIN IS A LADY, THE(1940), ph; GHOST COMES HOME, THE(1940), ph; GO WEST(1940), ph; GOLDEN FLEECING, THE(1940), ph; BILLY THE KID(1941), ph; DESIGN FOR SCANDAL(1941), ph; SMILIN' THROUGH(1941), ph; SHIP AHOY(1942), ph; BEST FOOT FORWARD(1943), ph; LASSIE, COME HOME(1943), ph; BROADWAY RHYTHM(1944), ph; NATIONAL VELVET(1944), ph; BLUE SIERRA(1946), ph; COURAGE OF LASSIE(1946), ph; YEARLING, THE(1946), ph; OUR MISS BROOKS(1956); TAKE A HARD RIDE(1975, U.S./Ital.); THAT'S THE WAY OF THE WORLD(1975); HIGH RISK(1981)

Silents
BATTLE CRY OF PEACE, THE(1915), ph; WIZARD OF OZ, THE(1925), ph

Leonard M. Smith
LONDON BY NIGHT(1937), ph; AT THE CIRCUS(1939), ph

Leonard O. Smith
EXTRAORDINARY SEAMAN, THE(1969); ...TICK...TICK...TICK...(1970)

Leslie Smith
BOOGEYMAN II(1983); DEVONSVILLE TERROR, THE(1983)

Lew Smith
MIGHTY MCGURK, THE(1946); HIGH BARBAREE(1947); HOMECOMING(1948); STATE OF THE UNION(1948); TO PLEASE A LADY(1950); THIS COULD BE THE NIGHT(1957)

Lewis Smith
SOUTHERN COMFORT(1981); I OUGHT TO BE IN PICTURES(1982); LOVE CHILD(1982); FINAL TERROR, THE(1983)
1984
ADVENTURES OF BUCKAROO BANZAI: ACROSS THE 8TH DIMENSION, THE(1984)

Lez Smith
FAST COMPANY(1929)

Linda Smith
ANGEL UNCHAINED(1970); HALLS OF ANGER(1970); HARDCORE(1979)

Lindsay Smith
NED KELLY(1970, Brit.); TOGETHER FOR DAYS(1972), w; PETERSEN(1974, Aus.)

Lindzee Smith
SUBWAY RIDERS(1981)

Lionel Smith
YOUNGBLOOD(1978); GALAXINA(1980); POSTMAN ALWAYS RINGS TWICE, THE(1981)

Liz Smith
BLEAK MOMENTS(1972, Brit.); ALL THINGS BRIGHT AND BEAUTIFUL(1979, Brit.); SIR HENRY AT RAWLINSON END(1980, Brit.); FAN, THE(1981); FRENCH LIEUTENANT'S WOMAN, THE(1981); TRAIL OF THE PINK PANTHER, THE(1982); CURSE OF THE PINK PANTHER(1983)

Lois Smith
EAST OF EDEN(1955); STRANGE LADY IN TOWN(1955); FIVE EASY PIECES(1970); WAY WE LIVE NOW, THE(1970); BROTHER JOHN(1971); UP THE SANDBOX(1972); NEXT STOP, GREENWICH VILLAGE(1976); FOXES(1980); RESURRECTION(1980); FOUR FRIENDS(1981); REUBEN, REUBEN(1983)
1984
RECKLESS(1984)

Lonnie Smith
NIGHT THE LIGHTS WENT OUT IN GEORGIA, THE(1981)

Lady Eleanor Smith
RED WAGON(1936), w; GYPSY(1937, Brit.), w; MEN IN HER LIFE, THE(1941), w; MAN IN GREY, THE(1943, Brit.), w; CARAVAN(1946, Brit.), w

Loring Smith
KEEP 'EM FLYING(1941); SHADOW OF THE THIN MAN(1941); CLOSE-UP(1948); PAT AND MIKE(1952); CLOWN, THE(1953); MA AND PA KETTLE AT WAIKIKI(1955); HAPPY ANNIVERSARY(1959); CARDINAL, THE(1963); HURRY SUNDOWN(1967)

Lou Smith
FAST COMPANY(1953)

J. Walter Smith
Misc. Talkies
ABAR–THE FIRST BLACK SUPERMAN(1977)

Lucy Smith
LILITH(1964)

M.U. Smith
SON OF SINBAD(1955)

Maddy Smith
COME BACK PETER(1971, Brit.)

Maddy "Madeleine" Smith
TASTE THE BLOOD OF DRACULA(1970, Brit.)

Madeleine Smith
VAMPIRE LOVERS, THE(1970, Brit.)

Madeline Smith
DRUMS O' VOODOO(1934); MINI-AFFAIR, THE(1968, Brit.); PUSSYCAT, PUSSYCAT, I LOVE YOU(1970); UP POMPEII(1971, Brit.); DEVIL'S WIDOW, THE(1972, Brit.); LIVE AND LET DIE(1973, Brit.); THEATRE OF BLOOD(1973, Brit.); FRANKENSTEIN AND THE MONSTER FROM HELL(1974, Brit.); BAWDY ADVENTURES OF TOM JONES, THE(1976, Brit.)

Madolyn Smith
URBAN COWBOY(1980)
1984
ALL OF ME(1984); 2010(1984)

Maggie Smith
NOWHERE TO GO(1959, Brit.); GO TO BLAZES(1962, Brit.); V.I.P.s, THE(1963, Brit.); PUMPKIN EATER, THE(1964, Brit.); OTHELLO(1965, Brit.); YOUNG CASSIDY(1965, U.S./Brit.); HONEY POT, THE(1967, Brit.); HOT MILLIONS(1968, Brit.); OH! WHAT A LOVELY WAR(1969, Brit.); PRIME OF MISS JEAN BRODIE, THE(1969, Brit.); TRAVELS WITH MY AUNT(1972, Brit.); LOVE AND PAIN AND THE WHOLE DAMN THING(1973); MURDER BY DEATH(1976); CALIFORNIA SUITE(1978); DEATH ON THE NILE(1978, Brit.); CLASH OF THE TITANS(1981); QUARTET(1981, Brit./Fr.); EVIL UNDER THE SUN(1982, Brit.); MISSIONARY, THE(1982); BETTER LATE THAN NEVER(1983)

Malcolm Smith
HEROES DIE YOUNG(1960); CREATION OF THE HUMANOIDS(1962)

Mamie Smith
Misc. Talkies
PARADISE IN HARLEM(1939); MURDER ON LENOX AVENUE(1941); SUNDAY SINNERS(1941)

Manny Smith
TIMERIDER(1983)

Marc Smith
GOLD(1974, Brit.); SPIKES GANG, THE(1974); FINAL CONFLICT, THE(1981); TRAIL OF THE PINK PANTHER, THE(1982)

Margaret Smith
STAGECOACH(1939); UNHOLY ROLLERS(1972)

Maria Smith
LORDS OF FLATBUSH, THE(1974); INCREDIBLE SHRINKING WOMAN, THE(1981)

Marion Owen Smith
MEMOIRS OF A SURVIVOR(1981, Brit.)

Marisa Smith
RETURN OF THE SECAUCUS SEVEN(1980); SOUP FOR ONE(1982); LIANNA(1983)
1984
BROTHER FROM ANOTHER PLANET, THE(1984)
Marjorie Smith
WHO IS KILLING THE GREAT CHEFS OF EUROPE?(1978, US/Ger.)
Mark Smith
Silents
ANNEXING BILL(1918); DAMSEL IN DISTRESS, A(1919)
Misc. Silents
NEARLY MARRIED(1917)
Marshall Smith
SATAN'S BED(1965), d
Martha Smith
NATIONAL LAMPOON'S ANIMAL HOUSE(1978)
Martin Smith
BAND OF ANGELS(1957); SHOWDOWN AT BOOT HILL(1958); GIRL IN TROUBLE(1963); YANKS(1979); UNDER THE RAINBOW(1981), w
Martin Cruz Smith
NIGHTWING(1979), w; GORKY PARK(1983), w
Marty Smith
Misc. Talkies
ONE CHANCE TO WIN(1976)
Mary Smith
MEDIUM COOL(1969)
Mary Ann Smith
INDEPENDENCE DAY(1983)
Mary Jane Smith
SCENE OF THE CRIME(1949); FATHER OF THE BRIDE(1950); MYSTERY STREET(1950)
Mary Louise Smith
NEW FACES OF 1937(1937)
Matthew Smith
BARRETTS OF WIMPOLE STREET, THE(1934); ONLY WAY HOME, THE(1972)
Maura Smith
TOWING(1978), d&w
Maurice Smith
CYCLE SAVAGES(1969), p; DIAMOND STUD(1970), w; HOW COME NOBODY'S ON OUR SIDE?(1975), p; JULIE DARLING(1982, Can./Ger.), p, w; SCREWBALLS(1983), p; SPASMS(1983, Can.), p
Max Smith
IRISH EYES ARE SMILING(1944); ONE HUNDRED AND ONE DALMATIANS(1961)
Maybe Smith
Misc. Talkies
YOUNG AND WILD(1975)
Mel Smith
BABYLON(1980, Brit.); BLOODY KIDS(1983, Brit.); BULLSHOT(1983)
1984
NUMBER ONE(1984, Brit.); SLAYGROUND(1984, Brit.)
Melinda Smith
SHAMPOO(1975)
Merritt Smith
TEACHER'S PET(1958)
Michael Smith
YOUNG LIONS, THE(1958); MA BARKER'S KILLER BROOD(1960); FIGHTING BACK(1983, Brit.)
Mike Smith
HAVING A WILD WEEKEND(1965, Brit.)
1984
KILLPOINT(1984)
Milan Smith
STAGECOACH TO DANCER'S PARK(1962)
Mildred Smith
LILITH(1964); STOOLIE, THE(1972)
Mildred Joanne Smith
NO WAY OUT(1950)
Milton Smith
WILD REBELS, THE(1967); HOOKED GENERATION, THE(1969); MAKO: THE JAWS OF DEATH(1976)
Mitchell Smith
DIRTY KNIGHT'S WORK(1976, Brit.), w
Mittie Smith
RIGHT STUFF, THE(1983)
Morley Smith
CONNECTING ROOMS(1971, Brit.), art d
Muriel Smith
MOULIN ROUGE(1952); CROWNING EXPERIENCE, THE(1960); VOICE OF THE HURRICANE(1964)
Murray Smith
JAZZ CINDERELLA(1930); SOUL OF THE SLUMS(1931); COOL IT, CAROL!(1970, Brit.), w; DIE SCREAMING, MARIANNE(1970, Brit.), w; RABID(1976, Can.); SELL OUT, THE(1976), w; BEAR ISLAND(1980, Brit.-Can.), w; COMEBACK, THE(1982, Brit.), w
Neville Smith
GUMSHOE(1972, Brit.), a, w; LONG SHOT(1981, Brit.)
Nicholas Smith
SALT & PEPPER(1968, Brit.); WALK WITH LOVE AND DEATH, A(1969); TWELVE CHAIRS, THE(1970); I AM THE CHEESE(1983), ed
Nick Smith
DESPERATE CHARACTERS(1971)
Noel Smith
KING OF HOCKEY(1936), d; TRAILIN' WEST(1936), d; BLAZING SIXES(1937), d; CALIFORNIA MAIL, THE(1937), d; CHEROKEE STRIP(1937), d; GUNS OF THE PECOS(1937), d; OVER THE GOAL(1937), d; MYSTERY HOUSE(1938), d; CODE OF THE SECRET SERVICE(1939), d; COWBOY QUARTERBACK(1939), d; DEAD END KIDS ON DRESS PARADE(1939), d; PRIVATE DETECTIVE(1939), d; SECRET SERVICE OF THE AIR(1939), d; TORCHY PLAYS WITH DYNAMITE(1939), d; CALLING ALL HUSBANDS(1940), d; FATHER IS A PRINCE(1940), d; LADIES MUST LIVE(1940), d; CATTLE TOWN(1952), d

Noel M. Smith
ALWAYS A BRIDE(1940), d; BURMA CONVOY(1941), d; CASE OF THE BLACK PARROT, THE(1941), d; HERE COMES HAPPINESS(1941), d; NURSE'S SECRET, THE(1941), d
Noel Mason Smith
Silents
FANGS OF JUSTICE(1926), d; NIGHT PATROL, THE(1926), d; CROSS BREED(1927), d; ONE CHANCE IN A MILLION(1927), d
Misc. Silents
CLASH OF THE WOLVES(1925), d; WHERE TRAILS BEGIN(1927), d; FANGS OF FATE(1928), d; LAW'S LASH, THE(1928), d
Noella Smith
1984
SECRETS(1984, Brit.), w
Nolan Smith
M(1970)
Norman Smith
AMAZING TRANSPARENT MAN, THE(1960); STREAMERS(1983), ed
Norris Smith
DIAMOND CITY(1949, Brit.)
Oliver Smith
HIS DOUBLE LIFE(1933); BAND WAGON, THE(1953), ch; GUYS AND DOLLS(1955), prod d; OKLAHOMA(1955), prod d; PORGY AND BESS(1959), prod d; TURNING POINT, THE(1977), tech adv; GREAT TRAIN ROBBERY, THE(1979, Brit.)
Orriel Smith
SPLIT, THE(1968)
Oscar Smith
CANARY MURDER CASE, THE(1929); CLOSE HARMONY(1929); DANGEROUS CURVES(1929); LET'S GO NATIVE(1930); SHADOW OF THE LAW(1930); GUILTY AS HELL(1932); THIRTEEN WOMEN(1932); NIGHT OF TERROR(1933); NO MAN OF HER OWN(1933); OLD-FASHIONED WAY, THE(1934); READY FOR LOVE(1934); HOLD'EM YALE(1935); MISSISSIPPI(1935); STOLEN HARMONY(1935); MILKY WAY, THE(1936); RHYTHM ON THE RANGE(1936); TEXANS, THE(1938); TOM SAWYER, DETECTIVE(1939); MONSTER AND THE GIRL, THE(1941); NOTHING BUT THE TRUTH(1941); FLEET'S IN, THE(1942); HENRY ALDRICH GETS GLAMOUR(1942); GOOD FELLOWS, THE(1943); DOUBLE INDEMNITY(1944); HENRY ALDRICH PLAYS CUPID(1944)
Silents
FRESHMAN, THE(1925); MARRIAGE CLAUSE, THE(1926); BEAU SABREUR(1928); MIDNIGHT MADNESS(1928)
Paddy Smith
I AM A CAMERA(1955, Brit.)
Pam Smith
MISTY(1961)
Patricia Smith
BACHELOR PARTY, THE(1957); SPIRIT OF ST. LOUIS, THE(1957); GIRL WHO KNEW TOO MUCH, THE(1969); ACE ELI AND RODGER OF THE SKIES(1973); SAVE THE TIGER(1973)
Patty Smith
MIRACLE ON 34TH STREET, THE(1947); SEA OF GRASS, THE(1947)
Paul Smith
SNOW WHITE AND THE SEVEN DWARFS(1937), m; SHE COULDN'T SAY NO(1939, Brit.), w; SHADOW VALLEY(1947); STRANGE MRS. CRANE, THE(1948), md; LOVE HAPPY(1949), md; CINDERELLA(1950), m; THIRD MAN, THE(1950, Brit.); I WANT YOU(1951); BATTLE AT APACHE PASS, THE(1952); YOU FOR ME(1952); MEN OF THE FIGHTING LADY(1954); PILLARS OF THE SKY(1956); SCREAMING EAGLES(1956); STRANGE ADVENTURE, A(1956); THERE'S ALWAYS TOMORROW(1956); DEADLY MANTIS, THE(1957); FUNNY FACE(1957); LOVING YOU(1957); LEFT-HANDED GUN, THE(1958); WINK OF AN EYE(1958); POLLYANNA(1960), m; BON VOYAGE(1962), m; MOON PILOT(1962), m; MIRACLE OF THE WHITE STALLIONS(1963), m; ADVANCE TO THE REAR(1964); BIKINI BEACH(1964); GREAT RACE, THE(1965); MADRON(1970, U.S./Israel); NOW YOU SEE HIM, NOW YOU DON'T(1972); GOSPEL ROAD, THE(1973); STORM BOY(1976, Aus.); MIDNIGHT EXPRESS(1978, Brit.); MONTENEGRO(1981, Brit./Swed.); FIGHTING BACK(1983, Brit.); FIRE IN THE STONE, THE(1983, Aus.); PIECES(1983, Span./Puerto Rico); SALAMANDER, THE(1983, U.S./Ital./Brit.)
1984
DUNE(1984)
Paul F. Smith
DREAM WIFE(1953)
Paul G. Smith
HAROLD TEEN(1934), w
Paul Gerald Smith
WILD BILL HICKOK RIDES(1942), w
Paul Gerard Smith
WELCOME DANGER(1929), w; DANGEROUS NAN McGREW(1930), w; FEET FIRST(1930), w; HEADS UP(1930), w; SIDEWALKS OF NEW YORK(1931), w; SON OF A SAILOR(1933), w; CIRCUS CLOWN(1934), w; HOLD'EM YALE(1935), w; ONE HOUR LATE(1935), w; WELCOME HOME(1935), w; F MAN(1936), w; IT'S A GREAT LIFE(1936), w; SHE KNEW WHAT SHE WANTED(1936, Brit.), w; THRILL OF A LIFETIME(1937), w; TURN OFF THE MOON(1937), w; HIGGINS FAMILY, THE(1938), w; JUST AROUND THE CORNER(1938), w; MAMA RUNS WILD(1938), w; I CAN'T GIVE YOU ANYTHING BUT LOVE, BABY(1940), w; LA CONGA NIGHTS(1940), w; MARGIE(1940), d, w; SANDY GETS HER MAN(1940), d, w; HELLO SUCKER(1941), w; HURRY, CHARLIE, HURRY(1941), w; SAN ANTONIO ROSE(1941), w; SING ANOTHER CHORUS(1941), w; STEEL AGAINST THE SKY(1941), w; TANKS A MILLION(1941), w; TOPPER RETURNS(1941), w; YOU'RE IN THE ARMY NOW(1941), w; GIVE OUT, SISTERS(1942), w; HERE WE GO AGAIN(1942), w; JAIL HOUSE BLUES(1942), w; PRIVATE BUCKAROO(1942), w; HI, GOOD-LOOKIN'(1944), w; LADY, LET'S DANCE(1944), w; MOONLIGHT AND CACTUS(1944), w; OH, WHAT A NIGHT(1944), w; SUNBONNET SUE(1945), w; IT'S A JOKE, SON!(1947), w; UNTAMED FURY(1947), w
Silents
BATTLING BUTLER(1926), w
Paul J. Smith
PINOCCHIO(1940), m; THREE CABALLEROS, THE(1944), md; SONG OF THE SOUTH(1946), m; FUN AND FANCY FREE(1947), m; SO DEAR TO MY HEART(1949), m; CINDERELLA(1950), md; 20,000 LEAGUES UNDER THE SEA(1954), m; GREAT LOCOMOTIVE CHASE, THE(1956), m; LIGHT IN THE FOREST, THE(1958), m; SHAGGY DOG, THE(1959), m; PARENT TRAP, THE(1961), m; THREE LIVES OF

THOMASINA, THE(1963, U.S./Brit.), m

Paul L. Smith
POPEYE(1980)
1984
JUNGLE WARRIORS(1984, U.S./Ger./Mex.)

Paul Lawrence Smith
IN-LAWS, THE(1979)

Paul R. Smith
1984
BLOOD SIMPLE(1984), makeup

Perry Smith
U-BOAT PRISONER(1944), art d; UNWRITTEN CODE, THE(1944), art d; BOSTON
BLACKIE BOOKED ON SUSPICION(1945), art d; BOSTON BLACKIE'S RENDEZ-
VOUS(1945), art d; HIT THE HAY(1945), art d; LEAVE IT TO BLONDIE(1945), art d;
NOTORIOUS LONE WOLF, THE(1946), art d; RENEGADES(1946), art d; BIG FIX,
THE(1947), art d; LOVE FROM A STRANGER(1947), art d; PHILO VANCE RE-
TURNS(1947), art d; PHILO VANCE'S GAMBLE(1947), art d; PHILO VANCE'S
SECRET MISSION(1947), art d; RAILROADED(1947), art d; RED STALLION,
THE(1947), art d; STEPCHILD(1947), art d; JOHNNY ALLEGRO(1949), art d; BLON-
DIE'S HERO(1950), art d; KILL THE UMPIRE(1950), art d; PALOMINO, THE(1950),
art d

Pete Smith
CHAPTER TWO(1979), art d; SEEMS LIKE OLD TIMES(1980), art d; NIGHT
SHIFT(1982), art d
Silents
LYING TRUTH, THE(1922)

Peter Smith
EMBASSY(1972, Brit.); WHAT'S NEXT?(1975, Brit.), d; LAST MARRIED COUPLE IN
AMERICA, THE(1980), art d; PATERNITY(1981), art d
1984
MY KIND OF TOWN(1984, Can.)

Peter K. Smith
PRIVATE ENTERPRISE, A(1975, Brit.), d, w, ed

Peter Lansdown Smith
GOING BERSERK(1983), prod d

Phil Smith
FLYING DOCTOR, THE(1936, Aus.); RANGLE RIVER(1939, Aus.); LOVE STO-
RY(1970), set d; OLIVER'S STORY(1978), set d; STARTING OVER(1979), set d

Philip Smith
JOHN AND MARY(1969), set d; MIDNIGHT COWBOY(1969), set d; LITTLE MUR-
DERS(1971), set d; PANIC IN NEEDLE PARK(1971), set d; GODFATHER, THE(1972),
set d
1984
GARBO TALKS(1984), set d

Polly Smith
1984
MUPPETS TAKE MANHATTAN, THE(1984), cos

Putter Smith
DIAMONDS ARE FOREVER(1971, Brit.)

Queenie Smith
YOU CAN'T RUN AWAY FROM IT(1956); MISSISSIPPI(1935); SHOW BOAT(1936);
SPECIAL AGENT K-7(1937); ON YOUR TOES(1939); FROM THIS DAY FOR-
WARD(1946); KILLERS, THE(1946); NOCTURNE(1946); LONG NIGHT, THE(1947);
SLEEP, MY LOVE(1948); SNAKE PIT, THE(1948); MASSACRE RIVER(1949); CA-
GED(1950); EMERGENCY WEDDING(1950); GREAT RUPERT, THE(1950); PRISON-
ERS IN PETTICOATS(1950); UNION STATION(1950); FIRST LEGION, THE(1951);
WHEN WORLDS COLLIDE(1951); MY SISTER EILEEN(1955); FIGHTING TROU-
BLE(1956); HOT SHOTS(1956); HOLD THAT HYPNOTIST(1957); SWEET SMELL OF
SUCCESS(1957); LEGEND OF LYLAH CLARE, THE(1968); HUSTLE(1975); END,
THE(1978); FOUL PLAY(1978)

Queeny Smith
DAY OF THE LOCUST, THE(1975)

Quentin R. Smith
Misc. Talkies
JUST MY LUCK(1936)

Quinn Smith
BAD NEWS BEARS, THE(1976); BAD NEWS BEARS IN BREAKING TRAINING,
THE(1977)

R. Andrew Smith
FIRST YANK INTO TOKYO(1945), tech adv

R. Cecil Smith
Silents
PLAYING THE GAME(1918), w; QUICKSANDS(1918), w; EXTRAVAGANCE(1919),
w; FIGHTER, THE(1921), w

R. David Smith
METALSTORM: THE DESTRUCTION OF JARED-SYN(1983)

R. Norwood Smith
HUCKLEBERRY FINN(1974)

R.J. Smith
OVERLAND BOUND(1929)

Rainbeaux Smith
UP IN SMOKE(1978); RENEGADE GIRLS(1974); FAREWELL, MY LOVELY(1975);
DRUM(1976); POM POM GIRLS, THE(1976); REVENGE OF THE CHEER-
LEADERS(1976); SLUMBER PARTY '57(1977); INCREDIBLE MELTING MAN,
THE(1978)
Misc. Talkies
SWINGING CHEERLEADERS, THE(1974)

Ray Smith
MURDER CAN BE DEADLY(1963, Brit.); MYSTERY SUBMARINE(1963, Brit.);
TOMORROW AT TEN(1964, Brit.); CANDIDATE FOR MURDER(1966, Brit.); MA-
DE(1972, Brit.); UNDER MILK WOOD(1973, Brit.); OPERATION DAYBREAK(1976,
U.S./Brit./Czech.); SAILOR'S RETURN, THE(1978, Brit.)

Raymond Smith
CALLING ALL CROOKS(1938, Brit.)

Rebecca Dianna Smith
NIGHTMARE HONEYMOON(1973); SHEILA LEVINE IS DEAD AND LIVING IN
NEW YORK(1975)
Misc. Talkies
DEADLY HONEYMOON(1974)

Reginald Smith
HEART SONG(1933, Brit.); MY SONG FOR YOU(1935, Brit.); WEEKEND MIL-
LIONAIRE(1937, Brit.)

Reid Smith
LATE LIZ, THE(1971)
Misc. Talkies
TEENAGER(1975)

Rex Smith
HEADIN' FOR BROADWAY(1980); PIRATES OF PENZANCE, THE(1983)

Richard Lewis Smith
1984
TANK(1984)

Rob "Smitty" Smith
1984
HOT AND DEADLY(1984), ed

Robert Smith
HURRICANE HORSEMAN(1931); HIT THE SADDLE(1937); FOUR JACKS AND A
JILL(1941); GAY FALCON, THE(1941); OBLIGING YOUNG LADY(1941); PARA-
CHUTE BATTALION(1941); CALL OUT THE MARINES(1942); MAYOR OF 44TH
STREET, THE(1942); YOU CAME ALONG(1945), w; I WALK ALONE(1948), w; BIG
WHEEL, THE(1949), w; QUICKSAND(1950), w; MAGIC FACE, THE(1951, Aust.), p,
w; SECOND WOMAN, THE(1951), p, w; INVASION U.S.A.(1952), p, w; SUDDEN
FEAR(1952), w; PARIS MODEL(1953), w; 99 RIVER STREET(1953), w; COURT JEST-
ER, THE(1956); BUSTER KEATON STORY, THE(1957), p, w; LONELY MAN,
THE(1957), w; ST. LOUIS BLUES(1958), p, w; FIVE PENNIES, THE(1959), w; GIRLS'
TOWN(1959), w; PLATINUM HIGH SCHOOL(1960), w; STAGE TO THUNDER
ROCK(1964), art d; FOOL KILLER, THE(1965), prod d; KING RAT(1965), art d; RIO
LOBO(1970), prod d; OFFENDERS, THE(1980); ACCEPTABLE LEVELS(1983, Brit.),
w, ph, art d; XTRO(1983, Brit.), w

Robert B. Smith
SWEETHEARTS(1938), w

Robert C. Smith
Silents
APACHE RAIDER, THE(1928)

Robert E. Smith
COURT JESTER, THE(1956); MOLE PEOPLE, THE(1956), art d; INTERLUDE(1957),
art d; MONOLITH MONSTERS, THE(1957), art d; SLAUGHTER ON TENTH AVE-
NUE(1957), art d; LIVE FAST, DIE YOUNG(1958), art d; SAGA OF HEMP BROWN,
THE(1958), art d; TONKA(1958), art d; NO NAME ON THE BULLET(1959), art d;
LONELY ARE THE BRAVE(1962), art d; FLIM-FLAM MAN, THE(1967), art d;
SKIDOO(1968), art d; GENERATION(1969), prod d; SMITH(1969), art d

Robert Emmet Smith
DUCHESS AND THE DIRTWATER FOX, THE(1976), art d

Robert I. Smith
HOMBRE(1967), art d

Robert Leroy Smith
CLARENCE AND ANGEL(1981)

Robert Paul Smith
TENDER TRAP, THE(1955), w

Roberta Smith
DOWN ON THE FARM(1938); WHAT A LIFE(1939); GIRLS UNDER TWENTY-
ONE(1940); GAMBLING DAUGHTERS(1941); MAYOR OF 44TH STREET, THE(1942);
TALK OF THE TOWN(1942); NOBODY'S DARLING(1943); BLOCK BUSTERS(1944);
DANGEROUS INTRUDER(1945); TOWN WENT WILD(1945)

Roberta J. Smith
1984
WOMAN IN RED, THE(1984)

Roderick Smith
IN SEARCH OF GREGORY(1970, Brit./Ital.)

Rodney Smith
DON QUIXOTE(1973, Aus.)

Roger Smith
MAN OF A THOUSAND FACES(1957); NO TIME TO BE YOUNG(1957); OPERATION
MAD BALL(1957); AUNTIE MAME(1958); CRASH LANDING(1958); NEVER STEAL
ANYTHING SMALL(1959); FOR THOSE WHO THINK YOUNG(1964); UP THE
JUNCTION(1968, Brit.), w; FIRST TIME, THE(1969), p, w; C. C. AND COM-
PANY(1971), p, w
Misc. Talkies
ROGUE'S GALLERY(1968)

Roland "Ozzie" Smith
CHEAPER TO KEEP HER(1980), ph

Rolland Smith
HERO AT LARGE(1980)

Ron Smith
NOTORIOUS CLEOPATRA, THE(1970)

Ronnie Smith
1984
UTU(1984, New Zealand)

Roosevelt Smith
NEW YORK, NEW YORK(1977); PROPHECY(1979); CHEECH AND CHONG'S NICE
DREAMS(1981)

Rose Smith
PAY OFF, THE(1930), ed; POLICE CALL(1933), ed; SHIP OF WANTED MEN(1933),
ed; FOUND ALIVE(1934), ed
Silents
INTOLERANCE(1916), ed; HEARTS OF THE WORLD(1918), ed; WAY DOWN
EAST(1920), ed; DREAM STREET(1921), ed; ORPHANS OF THE STORM(1922), a, ed;
AMERICA(1924), ed

Roy Smith
NON-STOP NEW YORK(1937, Brit.); FAR FROM THE MADDING CROWD(1967,
Brit.), art d; MONTY PYTHON AND THE HOLY GRAIL(1975, Brit.), prod d; JABBER-
WOCKY(1977, Brit.), prod d; HOUND OF THE BASKERVILLES, THE(1980, Brit.),
prod d

Roy Forge Smith
HOUSE BY THE LAKE, THE(1977, Can.), art d; RUNNING(1979, Can.), prod d;
YESTERDAY(1980, Can.), art d; LAST CHASE, THE(1981), art d; FUNERAL HO-
ME(1982, Can.), prod d; MELANIE(1982, Can.), prod d; CURTAINS(1983, Can.), prod d
1984
MRS. SOFFEL(1984), art d

Roylene Smith
RODEO RHYTHM(1941)
Russ Smith
Misc. Talkies
DEATH RIDERS(1976)
Russell Smith
GREAT TEXAS DYNAMITE CHASE, THE(1976), prod d
Russell Smith, Jr.
MAN IN THE WATER, THE(1963)
Russell E. Smith
Silents
DAUGHTER OF THE SEA, A(1915), w; FEMALE OF THE SPECIES(1917), w
S.W. Smith
CLUE OF THE NEW PIN, THE(1929, Brit.), p; SQUEAKER, THE(1930, Brit.), p;
SHOULD A DOCTOR TELL?(1931, Brit.), p; TO OBLIGE A LADY(1931, Brit.), p;
FLYING SQUAD, THE(1932, Brit.), p; OLD MAN, THE(1932, Brit.), p; SALLY BISH-
OP(1932, Brit.), p; AT DAWN WE DIE(1943, Brit.), p; REAL LIFE(1979)
Misc. Silents
PAGLIACCI(1923, Brit.), d
Sally Smith
STORY OF ESTHER COSTELLO, THE(1957, Brit.); SHE ALWAYS GETS THEIR
MAN(1962, Brit.); MY SIX LOVES(1963); FATHER CAME TOO(1964, Brit.); IN
TROUBLE WITH EVE(1964, Brit.); YOUNG, THE EVIL AND THE SAVAGE,
THE(1968, Ital.)
Sammy Smith
ACT ONE(1964); MADE FOR EACH OTHER(1971); GREAT GATSBY, THE(1974);
SUNSHINE BOYS, THE(1975); HOW TO SUCCEED IN BUSINESS WITHOUT REAL-
LY TRYING(1976); IN-LAWS, THE(1979)
1984
GOODBYE PEOPLE, THE(1984)
Samuel W. Smith
ON THE AIR(1934, Brit.), w
Silents
LAND OF HOPE AND GLORY(1927, Brit.), p
Sandy Smith
TEENAGE DOLL(1957)
Sara B. Smith
MY GIRL TISA(1948), w
Savannah Smith
FIVE DAYS FROM HOME(1978); NORTH DALLAS FORTY(1979); LONG RIDERS,
THE(1980)
Scott Smith
TEX(1982)
Sebastian Smith
WHITE CARGO(1930, Brit.); LOVE LIES(1931, Brit.); MAN OF MAYFAIR(1931, Brit.);
TILLY OF BLOOMSBURY(1931, Brit.); BADGER'S GREEN(1934, Brit.); DOUBLE
EVENT, THE(1934, Brit.); VIRGINIA'S HUSBAND(1934, Brit.); PUBLIC NUISANCE
NO. 1(1936, Brit.); BEAUTY AND THE BARGE(1937, Brit.); FAREWELL TO CIN-
DERELLA(1937, Brit.); MUSEUM MYSTERY(1937, Brit.); OH, MR. PORTER!(1937,
Brit.)
Sharon Smith
CISCO KID RETURNS, THE(1945); NIGHTMARE(1981)
Shawn Smith
LONG WAIT, THE(1954); BOTTOM OF THE BOTTLE, THE(1956); WORLD WITH-
OUT END(1956); LAND UNKNOWN, THE(1957); IT! THE TERROR FROM BEYOND
SPACE(1958)
1984
RIVER RAT, THE(1984)
Sheldon Smith
Misc. Silents
FALSE WOMEN(1921)
Shelley Smith
TIGER BAY(1959, Brit.), w; RUNNING MAN, THE(1963, Brit.), w; NATIONAL
LAMPOON'S CLASS REUNION(1982)
Shermann Smith
COOLEY HIGH(1975)
Shirley Smith
PRETTY BOY FLOYD(1960)
Shirley W. Smith
IT HAPPENS EVERY SPRING(1949), w
Sidney Smith
VALERIE(1957); HELLO LONDON(1958, Brit.), d
Silents
NE'ER-DO-WELL, THE(1916); KISMET(1920)
Silverheels Smith [Jay Silverheels]
SONG OF THE SARONG(1945); LAST ROUND-UP, THE(1947)
Solon Smith
LOVE IN THE AFTERNOON(1957)
Stan Smith
36 HOURS(1965), makeup; SUPPORT YOUR LOCAL SHERIFF(1969), makeup
Stanley Smith
SOPHOMORE, THE(1929); SWEETIE(1929); FOLLOW THE LEADER(1930); GOOD
NEWS(1930); HONEY(1930); LOVE AMONG THE MILLIONAIRES(1930); QUEEN
HIGH(1930); SOUP TO NUTS(1930); HOT SATURDAY(1932); STEPPING SIS-
TERS(1932); HARD TO HANDLE(1933); REFORM GIRL(1933); FLIGHT COM-
MAND(1940); DIVE BOMBER(1941); KEEP 'EM FLYING(1941); EAGLE
SQUADRON(1942); SUBMARINE ALERT(1943)
Stephanie Smith
WARM DECEMBER, A(1973, Brit.)
Stephen Smith
1984
SLAYGROUND(1984, Brit.), ph
Stephen Smith, Jr.
Silents
ANGEL OF CROOKED STREET, THE(1922), ph; LITTLE WILDCAT(1922), ph
Stephen Phillip Smith
1984
CHATTANOOGA CHOO CHOO(1984), w

Steve Smith
DINER(1982)
Steve Smith, Jr.
Silents
NINETY AND NINE, THE(1922), ph; ONE STOLEN NIGHT(1923), ph
Steven Phillip Smith
LONG RIDERS, THE(1980), w
Stevie Smith
STEVIE(1978, Brit.), w
Stirling W. Smith
1984
MIRRORS(1984), p
Stuart Smith
Misc. Talkies
JOE'S BED-STUY BARBERSHOP: WE CUT HEADS(1983)
Susanne Smith
TOWING(1978)
Suzanna Smith
STRANGE BREW(1983), art d
Sydney Smith
FROGMEN, THE(1951); FURY AT SHOWDOWN(1957); NO TIME FOR SER-
GEANTS(1958); PARTY GIRL(1958); TONKA(1958); GALLANT HOURS, THE(1960);
WONDERFUL WORLD OF THE BROTHERS ERIMM, THE(1962)
William Smith II
LAST AMERICAN HERO, THE(1973)
"T" Oney Smith
TAKE DOWN(1979)
Ted Smith
HAPPY DAYS(1930); TREACHERY RIDES THE RANGE(1936), art d; SLIM(1937),
art d; VALLEY OF THE GIANTS(1938), art d; WE'RE GOING TO BE RICH(1938, Brit.);
DODGE CITY(1939), art d; FIGHTING 69TH, THE(1940), art d; TORRID ZONE(1940),
art d; VIRGINIA CITY(1940), art d; BRIDE CAME C.O.D., THE(1941), art d; HIGH
SIERRA(1941), art d; GENTLEMAN JIM(1942), art d; LADY GANGSTER(1942), art d;
SPY SHIP(1942), art d; ACTION IN THE NORTH ATLANTIC(1943), art d; MASK OF
DIMITRIOS, THE(1944), art d; CONFLICT(1945), art d; OBJECTIVE, BURMA!(1945),
art d; SAN ANTONIO(1945), art d; HER KIND OF MAN(1946), art d; THREE
STRANGERS(1946), art d; VERDICT, THE(1946), art d; PURSUED(1947), art d;
FIGHTER SQUADRON(1948), art d; SILVER RIVER(1948), art d; FLAXY MAR-
TIN(1949), art d; COUNTERPLOT(1959); CAVALRY COMMAND(1963, U.S./Phil.), ed
Tedd Smith
NO LONGER ALONE(1978), m
Teddy Smith
FUGITIVE, THE(1940, Brit.)
Terence Lore Smith
THIEF WHO CAME TO DINNER, THE(1973), w
Terri Susan Smith
BASKET CASE(1982)
Terry Smith
HOOKED GENERATION, THE(1969)
Thaddeus Smith
FINAL CUT, THE(1980, Aus.); ROAD GAMES(1981, Aus.); PSYCHO II(1983)
Thomas Smith
Silents
IF ONLY JIM(1921)
Thora Smith
LONG JOHN SILVER(1954, Aus.)
Thorne Smith
NIGHT LIFE OF THE GODS(1935), w; TOPPER(1937), w; TOPPER TAKES A
TRIP(1939), w; TURNABOUT(1940), w; TOPPER RETURNS(1941), w; I MARRIED A
WITCH(1942), w
Tody Smith
TOUGH ENOUGH(1983)
Tom Smith
OKLAHOMA FRONTIER(1939); CARSON CITY KID(1940); MELODY RANCH(1940);
YOUNG BILL HICKOK(1940); DEEP IN THE HEART OF TEXAS(1942); DOWN RIO
GRANDE WAY(1942); MAN FROM MUSIC MOUNTAIN(1943); CHEYENNE WILD-
CAT(1944); TRAIL OF TERROR(1944); ROARING WESTWARD(1949)
Tom Smith
TANK FORCE(1958, Brit.), makeup; LIGHT IN THE PIAZZA(1962), makeup; TRIAL
AND ERROR(1962, Brit.), makeup; V.I.P.s, THE(1963, Brit.), makeup; NANNY,
THE(1965, Brit.), makeup; ONE WAY PENDULUM(1965, Brit.), makeup; RETURN
FROM THE ASHES(1965, U.S./Brit.), makeup; SECRET OF MY SUCCESS, THE(1965,
Brit.), makeup; YELLOW ROLLS-ROYCE, THE(1965, Brit.), makeup; STUDY IN
TERROR, A(1966, Brit./Ger.), makeup; CRY OF THE BANSHEE(1970, Brit.), makeup;
HORROR OF FRANKENSTEIN, THE(1970, Brit.), make up; VAMPIRE LOVERS,
THE(1970, Brit.), makeup; SLEUTH(1972, Brit.), makeup; SHINING, THE(1980),
makeup; HOUND OF THE BASKERVILLES, THE(1983, Brit.), makeup; RETURN OF
THE JEDI(1983), makeup; SIGN OF FOUR, THE(1983, Brit.), makeup
Tomaso Smith
LOYALTY OF LOVE(1937, Ital.), w
Tony Smith
AMBUSH BAY(1966)
Tony Stratton Smith
SIR HENRY AT RAWLINSON END(1980, Brit.), p
Tracy Smith
MISS JESSICA IS PREGNANT(1970)
Tracy N. Smith
1984
HOT DOG...THE MOVIE(1984)
Trevor T. Smith
11 HARROWHOUSE(1974, Brit.)
Trixie Smith
BLACK KING(1932); DRUMS O' VOODOO(1934)
Truman Smith
PHENIX CITY STORY, THE(1955); MONTE CARLO STORY, THE(1957, Ital.);
PRETTY BOY FLOYD(1960); ONE PLUS ONE(1961, Can.); GROUP, THE(1966)
Tucker Smith
WEST SIDE STORY(1961); PRODUCERS, THE(1967); HOW TO SUCCEED IN
BUSINESS WITHOUT REALLY TRYING(1976); TO BE OR NOT TO BE(1983)

Tyler Smith
GEEK MAGGOT BINGO(1983), a, spec eff
Valerian Smith
HARD TIMES(1975); TOY, THE(1982)
Valerie Smith
OH! WHAT A LOVELY WAR(1969, Brit.)
Van Smith
POLYESTER(1981), cos
Varley Smith
LOOSE SHOES(1980), w
Verne Smith
NO TIME FOR SERGEANTS(1958)
Vernon Smith
COHENS AND KELLYS IN TROUBLE, THE(1933), w; CALL OF THE PRAI-RIE(1936), w; THREE ON THE TRAIL(1936), w; MISBEHAVING HUSBANDS(1941), w
Silents
DO YOUR DUTY(1928), w
Vic Smith
GUN FEVER(1958)
Victor Smith
SMASHING TIME(1967 Brit.), m; STRANGER IN HOLLYWOOD(1968); WOLF-MAN(1979)
Vincent Smith
PADDY(1970, Irish); UNDERGROUND(1970, Brit.); LIGHT YEARS AWAY(1982, Fr./Switz.)
Virginia Smith
MIKEY AND NICKY(1976)
1984
TEACHERS(1984)
Vivian Smith
HEARTS IN DIXIE(1929)
Vola Smith [Vola Vale]
Misc. Silents
EAGLE'S WINGS, THE(1916)
W. Henry Smith
PREACHERMAN(1971), a, m
W.A. Smith
TIME OF HIS LIFE, THE(1955, Brit.), p
W.C. Smith
PORT OF MISSING GIRLS(1938), ph
Wallace Smith
BIG TIME(1929), w; BULLDOG DRUMMOND(1929), w; DELIGHTFUL HO-GUE(1929), w; NOT QUITE DECENT(1929), w; BEAU BANDIT(1930), w; FRA-MED(1930), w; LOVE COMES ALONG(1930), w; SHOOTING STRAIGHT(1930), w; SILVER HORDE, THE(1930), w; LADY REFUSES, THE(1931), w; ALMOST MAR-RIED(1932), w; LOST SQUADRON, THE(1932), w; MEN OF CHANCE(1932), w; CAP-TAIN HATES THE SEA, THE(1934), w; TRUMPET BLOWS, THE(1934), w; BORDERTOWN(1935), w; SEVEN KEYS TO BALDPATE(1935), w; GAY DE-SPERADO, THE(1936), w; HER HUSBAND LIES(1937), w
Wallis Smith
WILD AFFAIR, THE(1966, Brit.), art d
Walter Smith
NIGHTFALL(1956); BAND OF ANGELS(1957); PATSY, THE(1964); LAS VEGAS LADY(1976)
Walton Hall Smith
HUDDLE(1932), w
Wanda Smith
MOONLIGHT IN VERMONT(1943); WHERE THE SIDEWALK ENDS(1950)
Warren Smith
WITHOUT RESERVATIONS(1946)
Wayne Smith
HEART IS A LONELY HUNTER, THE(1968); MR. SYCAMORE(1975); MISSION GALACTICA: THE CYLON ATTACK(1979), spec eff; CONQUEST OF THE EARTH(1980), spec eff
Web Smith
CAPTURE THAT CAPSULE(1961)
Webb Smith
SNOW WHITE AND THE SEVEN DWARFS(1937), w; PINOCCHIO(1940), w
Whispering Jack Smith
BIG PARTY, THE(1930); CHEER UP AND SMILE(1930); HAPPY DAYS(1930)
Wilber Smith
GOLD(1974, Brit.), w; SHOUT AT THE DEVIL(1976, Brit.), w, w
Wilbur Smith
KINGFISH CAPER, THE(1976, South Africa), w
Wilbur A. Smith
DARK OF THE SUN(1968, Brit.), w
Wiletta Smith
RAIDERS OF THE SEVEN SEAS(1953), ch
Willetta Smith
PRISONERS OF THE CASBAH(1953); DEMETRIUS AND THE GLADIATORS(1954)
William Smith
HARPER(1966), cos; THREE GUNS FOR TEXAS(1968); BACKTRACK(1969); RUN, ANGEL, RUN(1969); ANGELS DIE HARD(1970); DARKER THAN AMBER(1970); LOSERS, THE(1970); C. C. AND COMPANY(1971); CHROME AND HOT LEA-THER(1971); SUMMERTREE(1971); GRAVE OF THE VAMPIRE(1972); HAM-MER(1972); THING WITH TWO HEADS, THE(1972); DEADLY TRACKERS(1973); INVASION OF THE BEE GIRLS(1973); SWEET JESUS, PREACHER MAN(1973); TASTE OF HELL, A(1973); BLACK SAMSON(1974); BOSS NIGGER(1974); POLICE-WOMAN(1974); DR. MINX(1975); ULTIMATE WARRIOR, THE(1975); SCOR-CHY(1976); SWINGING BARMAIDS, THE(1976); TWILIGHT'S LAST GLEAMING(1977, U.S./Ger.); BLOOD AND GUTS(1978, Can.); FRISCO KID, THE(1979); SEVEN(1979); ANY WHICH WAY YOU CAN(1980); CONAN THE BAR-BARIAN(1982); DEATHSTALKER(1983, Arg./U.S.), makeup; OUTSIDERS, THE(1983); RUMBLE FISH(1983)
1984
RED DAWN(1984)
Misc. Talkies
RUNAWAY(1971); PIRANHA, PIRANHA(1972); CAMPER JOHN(1973); CRACKLE OF DEATH(1974); HOLLYWOOD MAN, THE(1976); FAST COMPANY(1979)

William Cooper Smith
LUCKY STAR(1929), ph
William Craig Smith
PROPHECY(1979), prod d; S.O.B.(1981), art d; VICTOR/VICTORIA(1982), art d
William Whistance Smith
WRONG ARM OF THE LAW, THE(1963, Brit.), w
Willie E. Smith
LEGEND OF BOGGY CREEK, THE(1973)
Winchell Smith
LOVE DOCTOR, THE(1929), w; LIGHTNIN'(1930), w; BREWSTER'S MIL-LIONS(1935, Brit.), w; BREWSTER'S MILLIONS(1945), w; THREE ON A SPREE(1961, Brit.), w
Silents
BREWSTER'S MILLIONS(1914), w; FORTUNE HUNTER, THE(1914), w; ONLY SON, THE(1914), w; BREWSTER'S MILLIONS(1921), w; SAPHEAD, THE(1921), p, sup, w; THREE WISE FOOLS(1923), w; WAGES FOR WIVES(1925), w; MISS BREWSTER'S MILLIONS(1926), w; FORTUNE HUNTER, THE(1927), w
Winfield Smith
SNAFU(1945)
Wingate Smith
STEAMBOAT ROUND THE BEND(1935)
Winona Smith
MAGIC CARPET, THE(1951); LOVE ME OR LEAVE ME(1955)
Wonderful Smith
TOP SERGEANT MULLIGAN(1941); OVER MY DEAD BODY(1942); HOWZER(1973)
1984
THIS IS SPINAL TAP(1984)
Wynonna Smith
1984
COTTON CLUB, THE(1984)
Smith Ballew and the Sons of the Sage
UNDER ARIZONA SKIES(1946)
Jennifer Smith-Ashley
1984
LOVE STREAMS(1984), cos
Frederic Smith-Bolton
1984
KINGS AND DESPERATE MEN(1984, Brit.)
Maria Smith-Caffey
NUNZIO(1978)
Davis Smith-Dorrien
IMPROPER DUCHESS, THE(1936, Brit.)
Heather Smith-Harper
1984
BIG MEAT EATER(1984, Can.)
Hallie Smith-Simmons
MAGIC(1978), makeup
Allen Smithee
DEATH OF A GUNFIGHTER(1969), d
Allen Smithee [Jud Taylor]
Misc. Talkies
FADE-IN(1968), d
Allen Smithee [Michael Ritchie]
STUDENT BODIES(1981), p
Jan Smithers
WHERE THE LILIES BLOOM(1974); OUR WINNING SEASON(1978)
Mary Smithers
Silents
ROAD TO RUIN, THE(1913, Brit.)
Sue Smithers
Misc. Talkies
SWEET DREAMERS(1981)
William Smithers
ATTACK!(1956); TROUBLE MAN(1972); PAPILLON(1973); SCORPIO(1973); DEATH-SPORT(1978)
Brian Smithies
DARK CRYSTAL, THE(1982, Brit.), spec eff
1984
DUNE(1984), models
Fred Smithson
BOYS IN COMPANY C, THE(1978, U.S./Hong Kong)
Laura Smithson
OTHER PEOPLE'S SINS(1931, Brit.); CAVALIER OF THE STREETS, THE(1937, Brit.); MEN ARE NOT GODS(1937, Brit.); I SEE ICE(1938); SOUTH RIDING(1938, Brit.)
Silents
BROKEN ROMANCE, A(1929, Brit.)
Mary Smithuysen
BRIDGE TOO FAR, A(1977, Brit.)
Harry W. Smithy
BERMUDA AFFAIR(1956, Brit.), ph
Bill Smitrovich
LITTLE SEX, A(1982); WITHOUT A TRACE(1983)
1984
SPLASH(1984)
Aivars Smits
HEAVEN'S GATE(1980)
Sonja Smits
VIDEODROME(1983, Can.)
Misc. Talkies
PIT, THE(1984)
Theodore R. Smits
ZELIG(1983)
Wessel Smitter
REACHING FOR THE SUN(1941), w
Bob Smitts
SEALED CARGO(1951)
Smitty
CHICAGO CALLING(1951)

Maurice Smity
HARD TRAIL(1969), p
"Smoke"
GUNS OF THE PECOS(1937)
Frank Smokecocks [Franco Fumagalli]
HORRIBLE DR. HICHCOCK, THE(1964, Ital.), art d
The Smokestack Lightnin'
DREAMS OF GLASS(1969)
Smokey
SABOTEUR(1942)
Peter Smokler
PUNISHMENT PARK(1971), ph
1984
THIS IS SPINAL TAP(1984), ph
Innokentiy Smoktunovskiy
LETTER THAT WAS NEVER SENT, THE(1962, USSR); NINE DAYS OF ONE
YEAR(1964, USSR)
Innokenti Smoktunovsky
HAMLET(1966, USSR); CRIME AND PUNISHMENT(1975, USSR); MOSCOW DOES
NOT BELIEVE IN TEARS(1980, USSR)
Innokenty Smoktunovsky
UNCOMMON THIEF, AN(1967, USSR); UNCLE VANYA(1972, USSR); MOSCOW-
CASSIOPEIA(1974, USSR); TEENAGERS IN SPACE(1975, USSR)
Smoky Mountain Boys
NIGHT TRAIN TO MEMPHIS(1946); SMOKY MOUNTAIN MELODY(1949)
Smoky the Dogs
SIGN OF THE WOLF(1941)
Smoky the Horse
SMOKY(1933)
Bruce Smolanoff
1984
EXTERMINATOR 2(1984); PREPPIES(1984)
Jeff Smolek
1984
STREETS OF FIRE(1984)
Don Smolen
GREASER'S PALACE(1972)
Francis Smolen [Erantisek Smdik]
VOYAGE TO THE END OF THE UNIVERSE(1963, Czech.)
Vivian Smolen
MY BODYGUARD(1980)
Frantisek Smolik
MERRY WIVES, THE(1940, Czech.); SKELETON ON HORSEBACK(1940, Czech.);
KRAKATIT(1948, Czech.); SWEET LIGHT IN A DARK ROOM(1966, Czech.)
Janina Smolinska
SONG OF THE FLAME(1930)
Aaron Smolinski
SUPERMAN(1978)
Ken Smolka
HALLOWEEN II(1981); S.O.B.(1981)
Bradley J. Smollen
Silents
STEELHEART(1921), w; LITTLE WILDCAT(1922), w; SILENT VOW, THE(1922), w;
ONE STOLEN NIGHT(1923), w
J. Bradley Smollen
Silents
NIGHT WORKERS, THE(1917), w
Fred Smoot
Misc. Talkies
NINE LIVES OF FRITZ THE CAT, THE(1974)
Reed Smoot
TAKE DOWN(1979), ph; HARRY'S WAR(1981), ph
Ken Smoothy
SHE SHALL HAVE MUSIC(1935, Brit.)
Boris Smorchkov
MOSCOW DOES NOT BELIEVE IN TEARS(1980, USSR)
N. Smorchkov
WAR AND PEACE(1968, USSR)
Irene Smordoni
SHOE SHINE(1947, Ital.)
Rinaldo Smordoni
SHOE SHINE(1947, Ital.)
Tom Smothers
GET TO KNOW YOUR RABBIT(1972); SILVER BEARS(1978); SERIAL(1980); THERE
GOES THE BRIDE(1980, Brit.); PANDEMONIUM(1982)
Misc. Talkies
HURRAY FOR BETTY BOOP(1980)
Reed Smott
WINDWALKER(1980), ph
Montana Smoyer
1984
SAM'S SON(1984)
Jana Smrchova
DIVINE EMMA, THE(1983, Czech,)
Brett Smrz
THEY ALL LAUGHED(1981)
1984
BEAT STREET(1984)
Brian Smrz
THEY ALL LAUGHED(1981)
Karel Smrz
ROCKET TO NOWHERE(1962, Czech.)
Michael Smuin
RUMBLE FISH(1983), ch
1984
COTTON CLUB, THE(1984), ch
Elbert Smuiyh
4D MAN(1959)

Dana Smutna
SWEET LIGHT IN A DARK ROOM(1966, Czech.)
Sarah Smuts-Kennedy
SCARECROW, THE(1982, New Zealand)
Sonia Smyles
1984
OXFORD BLUES(1984)
Jacqueline Smylle
NEXT TIME WE LOVE(1936)
Ann Smyrner
JOURNEY TO THE SEVENTH PLANET(1962, U.S./Swed.); REPTILICUS(1962,
U.S./Den.); SEVEN DARING GIRLS(1962, Ger.); CODE 7, VICTIM 5(1964, Brit.);
BEYOND THE LAW(1967, Ital.); FOUNTAIN OF LOVE, THE(1968, Aust.); MISSION
STARDUST(1968, Ital./Span./Ger.)
Anne Smyrner
HOUSE OF 1,000 DOLLS(1967, Ger./Span./Brit.)
Poul Smyrner
LURE OF THE JUNGLE, THE(1970, Den.)
Dina Smyrnova
PARIS UNDERGROUND(1945)
Joseph Hilton Smyth
I, MOBSTER(1959), w
Patrick Smyth
QUACKSER FORTUNE HAS A COUSIN IN THE BRONX(1970)
Tim Smyth
EVEL KNIEVEL(1971), spec eff; J.W. COOP(1971), spec eff; TOP OF THE
HEAP(1972), spec eff
Zelda Smyth
MY BRILLIANT CAREER(1980, Aus.)
Amanda Jane Smythe
ANNE OF THE THOUSAND DAYS(1969, Brit.)
Florence Smythe
Silents
WILD GOOSE CHASE, THE(1915)
Grace Smythe
Misc. Silents
SPIDER'S WEB, THE(1927)
Norman Smythe
OF HUMAN BONDAGE(1964, Brit.); WHERE'S JACK?(1969, Brit.)
Tim Smythe
MAN CALLED HORSE, A(1970), spec eff
Tony Smythe
HAPPY DAYS ARE HERE AGAIN(1936, Brit.)
Vernon Smythe
LINKS OF JUSTICE(1958); HONOURABLE MURDER, AN(1959, Brit.); INNOCENT
MEETING(1959, Brit.); DATE AT MIDNIGHT(1960, Brit.); SENTENCED FOR LI-
FE(1960, Brit.); CURSE OF THE MUMMY'S TOMB, THE(1965, Brit.)
Seymore Snaer
NORA PRENTISS(1947)
John Snagge
2,000 WOMEN(1944, Brit.); IT HAPPENED HERE(1966, Brit.); MAGIC CHRISTIAN,
THE(1970, Brit.)
T. Snake
HONEYSUCKLE ROSE(1980)
Cecil R. Snape
Silents
CRADLE BUSTER, THE(1922), ed
Martin Snaric
LAST REMAKE OF BEAU GESTE, THE(1977)
Pahari Snayal
HOUSEHOLDER, THE(1963, US/India)
George Snazelle
Silents
DAWN(1917, Brit.)
Gary Snead
BROKEN LAND, THE(1962)
Sam Snead
FOLLOW THE SUN(1951); CADDY, THE(1953)
Brian Sneagle
DERANGED(1974, Can.)
Maurice Sneed
COOL WORLD, THE(1963); YOUNGBLOOD(1978); IN-LAWS, THE(1979); MAIN
EVENT, THE(1979); LUNCH WAGON(1981); HYSTERICAL(1983); MR. MOM(1983)
Lam y Sneegas
CARNIVAL OF SOULS(1962)
Susan Sneers
TIFFANY JONES(1976)
Gregory Snegoff
MONSIGNOR(1982)
Leonid Snegoff
AFTER TONIGHT(1933); GIRL WITHOUT A ROOM(1933); MAN WHO DARED,
THE(1933); SMOKY(1933); DRESSED TO THRILL(1935); GREAT IMPERSONATION,
THE(1935); MAN WHO BROKE THE BANK AT MONTE CARLO, THE(1935); PADDY
O'DAY(1935); RENDEZVOUS(1935); STRANGE WIVES(1935); WEDDING NIGHT,
THE(1935); STORY OF LOUIS PASTEUR, THE(1936); CAFE METROPOLE(1937);
DANGEROUSLY YOURS(1937); EASY LIVING(1937); SEVENTH HEAVEN(1937);
THREE LEGIONNAIRES, THE(1937); SPAWN OF THE NORTH(1938); BAR-
RICADE(1939); FOR WHOM THE BELL TOLLS(1943); MISSION TO MOSCOW(1943);
IN OUR TIME(1944); MASK OF DIMITRIOS, THE(1944); ROYAL SCANDAL, A(1945);
SONG OF MY HEART(1947); SMUGGLERS' COVE(1948); ONE GIRL'S CONFES-
SION(1953)
Misc. Silents
FORBIDDEN WOMAN, THE(1927)
Marc Snegoff
AGENT FOR H.A.R.M.(1966)
Sneh
FLASH GORDON(1980)

Vern J. Sneider
TEAHOUSE OF THE AUGUST MOON, THE(1956), w
Tom Snelgrove
WOLFPEN PRINCIPLE, THE(1974, Can.)
Anthony Snell
BREAKING THE SOUND BARRIER(1952); CRUEL SEA, THE(1953); HEART OF THE MATTER, THE(1954, Brit.); THREE CORNERED FATE(1954, Brit.); HOUR OF DECISION(1957, Brit.)
Bernice Snell
WORDS AND MUSIC(1929)
David Snell
FAMILY AFFAIR, A(1937), m; MADAME X(1937), m; MY DEAR MISS ALDRICH(1937), m; THIRTEENTH CHAIR, THE(1937), m; JUDGE HARDY'S CHILDREN(1938), m; LOVE FINDS ANDY HARDY(1938), m; YOUNG DR. KILDARE(1938), m; YOU'RE ONLY YOUNG ONCE(1938), m; DANCING CO-ED(1939), m; HARDYS RIDE HIGH, THE(1939), m; HENRY GOES ARIZONA(1939), m; JUDGE HARDY AND SON(1939), m; SECRET OF DR. KILDARE, THE(1939), m, md; THESE GLAMOUR GIRLS(1939), m; THUNDER AFLOAT(1939), m; WOMEN, THE(1939), m; DR. KILDARE GOES HOME(1940), md; DR. KILDARE'S CRISIS(1940), m, md; DR. KILDARE'S STRANGE CASE(1940), m, md; GHOST COMES HOME, THE(1940), m; PHANTOM RAIDERS(1940), m; SKY MURDER(1940), m; THIRD FINGER, LEFT HAND(1940), m; TWENTY MULE TEAM(1940), m; BILLY THE KID(1941), m; DOWN IN SAN DIEGO(1941), m; LOVE CRAZY(1941), m; RINGSIDE MAISIE(1941), m; SHADOW OF THE THIN MAN(1941), m; UNHOLY PARTNERS(1941), m; VANISHING VIRGINIAN, THE(1941), m; WILD MAN OF BORNEO, THE(1941), m; BORN TO SING(1942), md; GRAND CENTRAL MURDER(1942), m; JACKASS MAIL(1942), m; KID GLOVE KILLER(1942), m; PACIFIC RENDEZVOUS(1942), m; TARZAN'S NEW YORK ADVENTURE(1942), m, md; WAR AGAINST MRS. HADLEY, THE(1942), m; MAN FROM DOWN UNDER, THE(1943), m; SWING FEVER(1943), md; YOUNG IDEAS(1943), md; YOUNGEST PROFESSION, THE(1943), m; ANDY HARDY'S BLONDE TROUBLE(1944), m; BETWEEN TWO WOMEN(1944), m; GENTLE ANNIE(1944), m; LOST IN A HAREM(1944), md; MAISIE GOES TO RENO(1944), m; RATIONING(1944), m; SEE HERE, PRIVATE HARGROVE(1944), m; THIN MAN GOES HOME, THE(1944), m; DANGEROUS PARTNERS(1945), m; HIDDEN EYE, THE(1945), m; KEEP YOUR POWDER DRY(1945), m; TWICE BLESSED(1945), md; WHAT NEXT, CORPORAL HARGROVE?(1945), m; COCKEYED MIRACLE, THE(1946), m; MIGHTY MCGURK, THE(1946), m; SHOW-OFF, THE(1946), m; UP GOES MAISIE(1946), m; DARK DELUSION(1947), md; KILLER McCOY(1947), m; LADY IN THE LAKE(1947), m; MERTON OF THE MOVIES(1947), m; SONG OF THE THIN MAN(1947), m; UNDERCOVER MAISIE(1947), m; SOUTHERN YANKEE, A(1948), m; HANKY-PANKY(1982)
Davis Snell
WASHINGTON MELODRAMA(1941), m
Earle Snell
CLEAR THE DECKS(1929), w; IT CAN BE DONE(1929), w; EMBARRASSING MOMENTS(1930), w; HOT CURVES(1930), w; ALIAS THE BAD MAN(1931), w; BRANDED MEN(1931), w; RANGE LAW(1931), w; SUBWAY EXPRESS(1931), w; TWO GUN MAN, THE(1931), w; FAST COMPANIONS(1932), w; RACING YOUTH(1932), w; STEADY COMPANY(1932), w; TOMBSTONE CANYON(1932), w; FARGO EXPRESS(1933), w; HER FIRST MATE(1933), w; HALF A SINNER(1934), w; LET'S BE RITZY(1934), w; LOVE PAST THIRTY(1934), w; BRANDED A COWARD(1935), w; ESCAPE FROM DEVIL'S ISLAND(1935), w; GRIDIRON FLASH(1935), w; NIGHT ALARM(1935), w; STONE OF SILVER CREEK(1935), w; BURNING GOLD(1936), w; EVERYMAN'S LAW(1936), w; KING OF THE ROYAL MOUNTED(1936), w; RAINBOW ON THE RIVER(1936), w; ROAMING LADY(1936), w; SUNSET OF POWER(1936), w; TWO IN A CROWD(1936), w; WILD BRIAN KENT(1936), w; DESERT PHANTOM(1937), w; IT HAPPENED OUT WEST(1937), w; MAKE A WISH(1937), w; ROGUE OF THE RANGE(1937), w; SECRET VALLEY(1937), w; WESTERN GOLD(1937), w; GLADIATOR, THE(1938), w; WIDE OPEN FACES(1938), w; DAYS OF JESSE JAMES(1939), w; HOMICIDE BUREAU(1939), w; PRIVATE DETECTIVE(1939), w; TORCHY PLAYS WITH DYNAMITE(1939), w; TORCHY RUNS FOR MAYOR(1939), w; AM I GUILTY?(1940), w; COVERED WAGON DAYS(1940), w; OKLAHOMA RENEGADES(1940), w; ROCKY MOUNTAIN RANGERS(1940), w; TRAIL BLAZERS, THE(1940), w; WEST OF PINTO BASIN(1940), w; BORROWED HERO(1941), w; GAUCHOS OF EL DORADO(1941), w; KID'S LAST RIDE, THE(1941), w; TONTO BASIN OUTLAWS(1941), w; TRAIL OF THE SILVER SPURS(1941), w; WRANGLER'S ROOST(1941), w; BROOKLYN ORCHID(1942), d; RIDING THE WIND(1942), w; ROCK RIVER RENEGADES(1942), w; THUNDER RIVER FEUD(1942), w; THAT NAZTY NUISANCE(1943), w; BOWERY CHAMPS(1944), w; SHADOW OF SUSPICION(1944), w; COLORADO PIONEERS(1945), w; COME OUT FIGHTING(1945), w; PHANTOM OF THE PLAINS(1945), w; ALIAS BILLY THE KID(1946), w; CONQUEST OF CHEYENNE(1946), w; SANTA FE UPRISING(1946), w; SHERIFF OF REDWOOD VALLEY(1946), w; STAGECOACH TO DENVER(1946), w; SUN VALLEY CYCLONE(1946), w; ALONG THE OREGON TRAIL(1947), w; HOMESTEADERS OF PARADISE VALLEY(1947), w; LAST ROUND-UP, THE(1947), w; MARSHAL OF CRIPPLE CREEK, THE(1947), w; OREGON TRAIL SCOUTS(1947), w; ROBIN OF TEXAS(1947), w; RUSTLERS OF DEVIL'S CANYON(1947), w; VIGILANTES OF BOOMTOWN(1947), w; CARSON CITY RAIDERS(1948), w; DESERT VIGILANTE(1949), w; EL DORADO PASS(1949), w; RANGER OF CHEROKEE STRIP(1949), w; RENEGADES OF THE SAGE(1949), w; SOUTH OF DEATH VALLEY(1949), w; VALLEY OF FIRE(1951), w; DESPERADOES ARE IN TOWN, THE(1956), w; WAGON WHEELS WESTWARD(1956), w
Silents
KNOCKOUT, THE(1925), w; LET IT RAIN(1927), w
Erle Snell
SUNNY SKIES(1930), w
Frank Snell
RIVER HOUSE MYSTERY, THE(1935, Brit.)
H. Saxon Snell
MY FRIEND THE KING(1931, Brit.)
Harold Snell
Silents
EUGENE ARAM(1914, Brit.)
James Snell
1984
SUPERGIRL(1984)

Ken Snell
MARRIAGE OF A YOUNG STOCKBROKER, THE(1971)
Kenneth Snell
CHARLIE CHAN AND THE CURSE OF THE DRAGON QUEEN(1981)
Madge Snell
ETERNAL FEMININE, THE(1931, Brit.); LAST WALTZ, THE(1936, Brit.)
Patsy Snell
WRONG BOX, THE(1966, Brit.); CAPTAIN NEMO AND THE UNDERWATER CITY(1969, Brit.)
Peter Snell
WINTER'S TALE, THE(1968, Brit.), p; SUBTERFUGE(1969, US/Brit.), p; GOODBYE GEMINI(1970, Brit.), p; JULIUS CAESAR(1970, Brit.), p; ANTONY AND CLEOPATRA(1973, Brit.), p; WICKER MAN, THE(1974, Brit.), p; HENNESSY(1975, Brit.), p; BEAR ISLAND(1980, Brit.-Can.), p
Ted Snell
Silents
HEROIC LOVER, THE(1929)
Jeffrey Sneller
KINGDOM OF THE SPIDERS(1977), p
Leonard Snelling
GIRLS IN THE STREET(1937, Brit.); GANG, THE(1938, Brit.); GIRL IN THE STREET(1938, Brit.); SHOW GOES ON, THE(1938, Brit.)
Gertrude Snelson
Misc. Talkies
WAGES OF SIN, THE(1929); THIRTY YEARS LATER(1938)
Mortimer Snerd
LETTER OF INTRODUCTION(1938); YOU CAN'T CHEAT AN HONEST MAN(1939)
Leonid Snergoff
Silents
BROKEN HEARTS(1926)
Nakai Snez
ROCKY MOUNTAIN(1950)
William Snickowski
TAKING OF PELHAM ONE, TWO, THREE, THE(1974)
Barry Snider
KLUTE(1971); I, THE JURY(1982)
Bill Snider
SWARM, THE(1978)
Duke Snider
TROUBLE WITH GIRLS(AND HOW TO GET INTO IT), THE*1/2 (1969)
Norman Snider
PARTNERS(1976, Can.), w
Ray Snider
PRAIRIE PIONEERS(1941), ed
Robin Snider
EQUINOX(1970)
Scotty Snider
1984
VARIETY(1984)
Ronald Snijders
1984
DESIREE(1984, Neth.), m
Oskar Snirch
LIFE AND LOVES OF MOZART, THE(1959, Ger.), ph
Robert Sniveley
DEATH WISH II(1982)
Vernon Snively
Silents
NOBODY'S FOOL(1921)
Jan Snizek
ECSTACY OF YOUNG LOVE(1936, Czech.), w
Mike Snodgrass
Misc. Talkies
LEGACY(1963)
Richard Snodgrass
Misc. Talkies
LEGACY(1963), d
Carrie Snodgress
DIARY OF A MAD HOUSEWIFE(1970); RABBIT, RUN(1970); FURY, THE(1978); ATTIC, THE(1979); HOMEWORK(1982); TRICK OR TREATS(1982); NIGHT IN HEAVEN, A(1983)
1984
NADIA(1984, U.S./Yugo.)
Misc. Talkies
TRICK OR TREATS(1983)
Robert Snody
SOCIAL REGISTER(1934), ed
Robert R. Snody
LOVE KISS, THE(1930), d, w; MIDDLETON FAMILY AT THE N.Y. WORLD'S FAIR(1939), d, w
Liz Snoijink
LIFT, THE(1983, Neth.)
Dan Snook
1984
CHILDREN OF THE CORN(1984)
Connie Snow
MADE FOR EACH OTHER(1971)
David Snow
QUADROON(1972); DORM THAT DRIPPED BLOOD, THE(1983)
Misc. Talkies
PRANKS(1982)
G. A. Snow
PHANTOM THIEF, THE(1946), w
Hank Snow
LAST PICTURE SHOW, THE(1971), m
Heber Snow
HITTIN' THE TRAIL(1937)

L. Steven Snyder
SADIST, THE(1963), p
Lillian Snyder
Misc. Silents
HEARTS OF LOVE(1918)
Matt Snyder
Misc. Silents
HEART OF MARYLAND, THE(1915); UNWRITTEN LAW, THE(1916)
Nancy Snyder
KIRLIAN WITNESS, THE(1978)
Ray Snyder
WALL STREET(1929), ed; AVENGER, THE(1931), ed; DESERT VENGEANCE(1931), ed; PRIDE OF THE LEGION, THE(1932), ed; LAUGHING AT LIFE(1933), ed; LAW BEYOND THE RANGE(1935), ed; WESTERNER, THE(1936), ed; DUKE COMES BACK, THE(1937), ed; GENERAL SPANKY(1937), ed; NOBODY'S BABY(1937), ed; COVERED TRAILER, THE(1939), ed; GRAND OLE OPRY(1940), ed; ONE MILLION B.C.(1940), ed; DESERT BANDIT(1941), ed; GANGS OF SONORA(1941), ed; OUT-LAWS OF THE CHEROKEE TRAIL(1941), ed; PALS OF THE PECOS(1941), ed; BROOKLYN ORCHID(1942), ed; GET GOING(1943), ed; KEEP 'EM SLUGGING(1943), ed; LONE STAR TRAIL, THE(1943), ed; OLD CHISHOLM TRAIL(1943), ed; YOU'RE A LUCKY FELLOW, MR. SMITH(1943), ed; HER PRIMITIVE MAN(1944), ed; JUN-GLE WOMAN(1944), ed; MOONLIGHT AND CACTUS(1944), ed; PEARL OF DEATH, THE(1944), ed; RIDERS OF THE SANTA FE(1944), ed; THIS IS THE LIFE(1944), ed; BEYOND THE PECOS(1945), ed; FRONTIER GAL(1945), ed; I'LL TELL THE WORLD(1945), ed; BEAUTIFUL CHEAT, THE(1946), ed; GUN TOWN(1946), ed; LOV-ER COME BACK(1946), ed; SMOOTH AS SILK(1946), ed; SPIDER WOMAN STRIKES BACK, THE(1946), ed; WHITE TIE AND TAILS(1946), ed; FRANCIS IN THE NA-VY(1955), ed; RUNNING WILD(1955), ed; PRICE OF FEAR, THE(1956), ed; SHOW-DOWN AT ABILENE(1956), ed; STAR IN THE DUST(1956), ed
Silents
MIDNIGHT LIFE(1928), ed
Ron Snyder
JAWS II(1978), makeup
Roy Snyder
MEN WITHOUT LAW(1930), ed; JEALOUSY(1934), ed
Sammy Snyder
TOMORROW NEVER COMES(1978, Brit./Can.)
Scotty Snyder
Misc. Talkies
STRONG MEDICINE(1981)
Suzanne Snyder
1984
OASIS, THE(1984)
William Snyder
WHITE SAVAGE(1943), ph; PRINCESS AND THE PIRATE, THE(1944), ph; WON-DER MAN(1945), ph; BANDIT OF SHERWOOD FOREST, THE(1946), ph; BLUE SKIES(1946), ph; RENEGADES(1946), ph; SWORDSMAN, THE(1947), ph; VARIETY GIRL(1947); JULIA MISBEHAVES(1948); LOVES OF CARMEN, THE(1948), ph; MAN FROM COLORADO, THE(1948), ph; RETURN OF OCTOBER, THE(1948), ph; HOUSE ACROSS THE STREET, THE(1949), ph; JOLSON SINGS AGAIN(1949), ph; YOUNG-ER BROTHERS, THE(1949), ph; FLYING MISSILE(1950), ph; PETTY GIRL, THE(1950), ph; TOAST OF NEW ORLEANS, THE(1950), ph; NEW MEXICO(1951), ph; TEN TALL MEN(1951), ph; DANGEROUS MISSION(1954), ph; AMERICANO, THE(1955), ph; SON OF SINBAD(1955), ph; TREASURE OF PANCHO VILLA, THE(1955), ph; BEYOND A REASONABLE DOUBT(1956), ph; BUNDLE OF JOY(1956), ph; CONQUEROR, THE(1956), ph; FIRST TRAVELING SALESLADY, THE(1956), ph; GREAT DAY IN THE MORNING(1956), ph; HUK(1956), ph; RED SUNDOWN(1956), ph; ESCAPADE IN JAPAN(1957), ph; TARZAN'S FIGHT FOR LIFE(1958), ph; TOBY TYLER(1960), ph; BON VOYAGE(1962), ph; MOON PI-LOT(1962), ph; SUMMER MAGIC(1963), ph; TIGER WALKS, A(1964), ph; LT. ROBIN CRUSOE, U.S.N.(1966), ph; KING'S PIRATE(1967); MONKEYS, GO HOME!(1967), ph; HORSE IN THE GRAY FLANNEL SUIT, THE(1968), ph; NEVER A DULL MO-MENT(1968), ph; RASCAL(1969), ph; BOATNIKS, THE(1970), ph; $1,000,000 DUCK(1971), ph
William E. Snyder
FLYING LEATHERNECKS(1951), ph; BLACKBEARD THE PIRATE(1952), ph; ONE MINUTE TO ZERO(1952), ph; SECOND CHANCE(1953), ph; CREATURE FROM THE BLACK LAGOON(1954), ph; APPOINTMENT WITH A SHADOW(1958), ph
William L. Snyder
TINDER BOX, THE(1968, E. Ger.), p
Sammy Snyders
Misc. Talkies
PIT, THE(1984)
Hui So-Kam
1984
AH YING(1984, Hong Kong)
Hui So-Kei
1984
AH YING(1984, Hong Kong)
Hui So-lam
1984
AH YING(1984, Hong Kong)
Hui So-lin
1984
AH YING(1984, Hong Kong)
Hui So-ying
1984
AH YING(1984, Hong Kong)
Terence Soall
GEORGY GIRL(1966, Brit.)
Arthur Soames
Silents
TALE OF TWO WORLDS, A(1921)
Robin Soans
ABSOLUTION(1981, Brit.)
Antonio L. Soares
1984
MEMOIRS OF PRISON(1984, Braz.), ph

Jofre Soares
ANTONIO DAS MORTES(1970, Braz.); EARTH ENTRANCED(1970, Braz.); BYE-BYE BRASIL(1980, Braz.)
1984
GABRIELA(1984, Braz.); MEMOIRS OF PRISON(1984, Braz.)
Laura Soares
ROSE FOR EVERYONE, A(1967, Ital.)
Paulo Gil Soares
EARTH ENTRANCED(1970, Braz.), art d
Zdenek Sob
FANTASTIC PLANET(1973, Fr./Czech.), anim
Boguslaw Sobczuk
MAN OF MARBLE(1979, Pol.); GOLEM(1980, Pol.); MAN OF IRON(1981, Pol.); CAMERA BUFF(1983, Pol.)
Richard Sobek
SUPER VAN(1977)
Harold Sobel
MASSACRE AT CENTRAL HIGH(1976), p
Jack Sobel
THIEVES FALL OUT(1941), w
Ron Sobel
WHEN YOU COMIN' BACK, RED RYDER?(1979)
Jack Sobell
NORA PRENTISS(1947), w
David Sober
PLYMOUTH ADVENTURE(1952)
Gary Sobers
TWO GENTLEMEN SHARING(1969, Brit.); JUNKET 89(1970, Brit.)
Carol Sobieski
CASEY'S SHADOW(1978), w; HONEYSUCKLE ROSE(1980), w; ANNIE(1982), w; TOY, THE(1982), w
James Bem Sobieski
1984
BLAME IT ON THE NIGHT(1984)
Jean Sobieski
SWEET SKIN(1965, Fr./Ital.); GIRL CAN'T STOP, THE(1966, Fr./Gr.); PLUCK-ED(1969, Fr./Ital.); PUSSYCAT, PUSSYCAT, I LOVE YOU(1970)
Jean Sobiewski
ITALIAN SECRET SERVICE(1968, Ital.)
Ron Soble
AL CAPONE(1959); WALK TALL(1960); GUN FIGHT(1961); CINCINNATI KID, THE(1965); NAVAJO RUN(1966); TRUE GRIT(1969); MACHO CALLAHAN(1970); JOE KIDD(1972); PAPILLON(1973); BEAST WITHIN, THE(1982)
Witold Sobocinski
ADVENTURES OF GERARD, THE(1970, Brit.), ph; CATAMOUNT KILLING, THE(1975, Ger.), ph
Louis Sobol
COLLEGE CONFIDENTIAL(1960)
P. Sobolevskiy
DUEL, THE(1964, USSR); OPTIMISTIC TRAGEDY, THE(1964, USSR)
Pvotr Sobolevsky
Misc. Silents
CLUB OF THE BIG DEED, THE(1927, USSR)
Pytor Sobolevsky
Misc. Silents
DEVIL'S WHEEL, THE(1926, USSR); NEW BABYLON, THE(1929, USSR)
Tadeusz Sobolewski
GOLEM(1980, Pol.), w
Arnold Soboloff
DETECTIVE, THE(1968); POPI(1969); NICKELODEON(1976); SILENT MOVIE(1976); CAT FROM OUTER SPACE, THE(1978)
Bohumil Sobotka
DO YOU KEEP A LION AT HOME?(1966, Czech.), w
Ruth Sobotka
KILLER'S KISS(1955)
Jaromir Sobotoa
EMPEROR AND THE NIGHTINGALE, THE(1949, Czech.)
Griyo Sobrinho
STRANGE WORLD(1952)
Gino Soccio
1984
HEY BABE!(1984, Can.), m
Giovanni Soccol
DON'T LOOK NOW(1973, Brit./Ital.), art d
Cheryl Socher
TWILIGHT ZONE-THE MOVIE(1983)
Hylton Socher
MISTER CORY(1957); SUMMER LOVE(1958)
Boguslaw Sochnacki
PASSENGER, THE(1970, Pol.)
Francesco Socinus
Silents
WHITE SISTER, THE(1923)
Sally Sockwell
ROLLOVER(1981)
Frank Socolow
VISIT TO A SMALL PLANET(1960)
Mario Socrate
HUNCHBACK OF ROME, THE(1963, Ital.), w; GOSPEL ACCORDING TO ST. MATTHEW, THE(1966, Fr., Ital.)
Darius Socratos
MALE COMPANION(1965, Fr./Ital.)
Terry Soda
ROCK 'N' ROLL HIGH SCHOOL(1979)
Soda the Bulldog
SINCE YOU WENT AWAY(1944)
Rolf Soder
ISLAND AT THE TOP OF THE WORLD, THE(1974)

Kristina Soderbaum
KOLBERG(1945, Ger.)
Hjalmar Soderberg
GERTRUD(1966, Den.), w
Robert Soderberg
BORN TO BE BAD(1950), w; AIR CADET(1951), w
Robert W. Soderberg
RECKLESS MOMENTS, THE(1949), w
Adele Soderblom
SWEDENHIELMS(1935, Swed.)
Lena Soderblom
SMILES OF A SUMMER NIGHT(1957, Swed.)
Janine Soderhjelm
UNSTRAP ME(1968)
Walter Soderling
TRUE TO LIFE(1943); UNCLE HARRY(1945); CHEROKEE STRIP(1937); CRIMINALS OF THE AIR(1937); MAID OF SALEM(1937); MOUNTAIN JUSTICE(1937); NAVY BLUE AND GOLD(1937); TRUE CONFESSION(1937); WOMAN CHASES MAN(1937); I AM THE LAW(1938); SAY IT IN FRENCH(1938); DEATH OF A CHAMPION(1939); MR. SMITH GOES TO WASHINGTON(1939); ST. LOUIS BLUES(1939); STAND UP AND FIGHT(1939); BLONDIE HAS SERVANT TROUBLE(1940); MEN WITHOUT SOULS(1940); ON THEIR OWN(1940); OUT WEST WITH THE PEPPERS(1940); RAGTIME COWBOY JOE(1940); REMEMBER THE NIGHT(1940); SANTA FE TRAIL(1940); SLIGHTLY TEMPTED(1940); THIRD FINGER, LEFT HAND(1940); TOO MANY HUSBANDS(1940); WHEN THE DALTONS RODE(1940); CONFESSIONS OF BOSTON BLACKIE(1941); FACE BEHIND THE MASK, THE(1941); GAY FALCON, THE(1941); LUCKY DEVILS(1941); MEET JOHN DOE(1941); NINE LIVES ARE NOT ENOUGH(1941); PENNY SERENADE(1941); RETURN OF DANIEL BOONE, THE(1941); THIEVES FALL OUT(1941); THREE GIRLS ABOUT TOWN(1941); I MARRIED AN ANGEL(1942); NO TIME FOR LOVE(1943); THEY GOT ME COVERED(1943); WHAT'S BUZZIN COUSIN?(1943); YOUTH ON PARADE(1943); FALCON IN HOLLYWOOD, THE(1944); NONE BUT THE LONELY HEART(1944); OUTLAWS OF SANTA FE(1944); BLONDE FROM BROOKLYN(1945); DOLLY SISTERS, THE(1945); RHAPSODY IN BLUE(1945); DANNY BOY(1946); DEADLINE AT DAWN(1946); EASY TO WED(1946); FRENCH KEY(1946); GLASS ALIBI, THE(1946); IN FAST COMPANY(1946); SENATOR WAS INDISCREET, THE(1947); YANKEE FAKIR(1947); ALL MY SONS(1948); LEATHER GLOVES(1948); SO DEAR TO MY HEART(1949)
Ulla-Britt Soderlund
HAGBARD AND SIGNE(1968, Den./Iceland/Swed.), cos; PEOPLE MEET AND SWEET MUSIC FILLS THE HEART(1969, Den./Swed.), cos; EMIGRANTS, THE(1972, Swed.), cos; NEW LAND, THE(1973, Swed.), cos
Elmer Soderstrom
1984
CHILDREN OF THE CORN(1984)
Lorna S. Soderstrom
FANTASIA(1940), art d
Joe Sodja
PARSON AND THE OUTLAW, THE(1957), a, m
Harry Sodoni
CURIOUS FEMALE, THE(1969); GAY DECEIVERS, THE(1969)
Giovanna Sodre
1984
BLAME IT ON RIO(1984)
John Soer
DOG OF FLANDERS, A(1959); LITTLE ARK, THE(1972)
Gerard Soeteman
SOLDIER OF ORANGE(1979, Dutch), w; SPETTERS(1983, Holland), w
1984
FOURTH MAN, THE(1984, Neth.), w
Abraham Sofaer
DREYFUS CASE, THE(1931, Brit.); HOUSE OPPOSITE, THE(1931, Brit.); STAMBOUL(1931, Brit.); FLAG LIEUTENANT, THE(1932, Brit.); FLYING SQUAD, THE(1932, Brit.); INSULT(1932, Brit.); ASK BECCLES(1933, Brit.); HIGH FINANCE(1933, Brit.); KARMA(1933, Brit./India); LITTLE MISS NOBODY(1933, Brit.); TROUBLE(1933, Brit.); ADMIRAL'S SECRET, THE(1934, Brit.); OH NO DOCTOR!(1934, Brit.); PRIVATE LIFE OF DON JUAN(1934, Brit.); NELL GWYN(1935, Brit.); WANDERING JEW, THE(1935, Brit.); REMBRANDT(1936, Brit.); THINGS TO COME(1936, Brit.); CROOKS TOUR(1940, Brit.); VOICE IN THE NIGHT, A(1941, Brit.); STAIRWAY TO HEAVEN(1946, Brit.); DUAL ALIBI(1947, Brit.); GHOSTS OF BERKELEY SQUARE(1947, Brit.); CALLING PAUL TEMPLE(1948, Brit.); CHRISTOPHER COLUMBUS(1949, Brit.); CAIRO ROAD(1950, Brit.); PANDORA AND THE FLYING DUTCHMAN(1951, Brit.); QUO VADIS(1951); JUDGMENT DEFERRED(1952, Brit.); HIS MAJESTY O'KEEFE(1953); NAKED JUNGLE, THE(1953); ELEPHANT WALK(1954); BHOWANI JUNCTION(1956); FIRST TEXAN, THE(1956); OMAR KHAYYAM(1957); OUT OF THE CLOUDS(1957, Brit.); SAD SACK, THE(1957); STORY OF MANKIND, THE(1957); TARAS BULBA(1962); CAPTAIN SINDBAD(1963); TWICE TOLD TALES(1963); GREATEST STORY EVER TOLD, THE(1965); JOURNEY TO THE CENTER OF TIME(1967); HEAD(1968); CHE!(1969); JUSTINE(1969); CHISUM(1970)
Don Soffer
HOT STUFF(1979)
Oma Soffian
SINISTER URGE, THE(1961)
Mario Soffici
MAN AND THE BEAST, THE(1951, Arg.), a, p&d, w
Alberto Soffientini
SOUND OF TRUMPETS, THE(1963, Ital.), p
Alan Soffin
CONFESSOR(1973), p,d,ph&ed
Vinicio Sofia
DEAD WOMAN'S KISS, A(1951, Ital.); THIEF OF VENICE, THE(1952)
Jayne Sofiano
JOANNA(1968, Brit.)
Gisella Sofio
RAGE OF THE BUCCANEERS(1963, Ital.); LOVE, THE ITALIAN WAY(1964, Ital.); MY WIFE'S ENEMY(1967, Ital.); STORY OF A WOMAN(1970, U.S./Ital.)

Jaromir Sofr
CLOSELY WATCHED TRAINS(1967, Czech.), ph; REPORT ON THE PARTY AND THE GUESTS, A(1968, Czech.), ph; END OF A PRIEST(1970, Czech.), ph
V. Sofronov
WAR AND PEACE(1968, USSR)
Hisao Soga
YEARNING(1964, Jap.)
Masafumi Soga
ANGRY ISLAND(1960, Jap.), p
Rev. Ryosho S. Sogabe
CRIMSON KIMONO, THE(1959)
Rosita Sogoviz
NEOPOLITAN CAROUSEL(1961, Ital.)
Chanan Singh Sohi
ROAD TO BALI(1952)
Jerry Sohl
TWELVE HOURS TO KILL(1960), w; FRANKENSTEIN CONQUERS THE WORLD(1964, Jap./US), w; DIE, MONSTER, DIE(1965, Brit.), w
Lisa Sohm
HISTORY OF THE WORLD, PART 1(1981)
I. Sohma
Misc. Silents
SLUMS OF TOKYO(1930, Jap.)
Barbara Sohmers
LOVES OF SALAMMBO, THE(1962, Fr./Ital.), w
Hans Sohnie
DAUGHTER OF EVIL(1930, Ger.), art d
Hans Sohnker
FOUR COMPANIONS, THE(1938, Ger.); DAY AFTER THE DIVORCE, THE(1940, Ger.); FILM WITHOUT A NAME(1950, Ger.); FOR THE FIRST TIME(1959, U.S./Ger./Ital.); BRAINWASHED(1961, Ger.); DIE FASTNACHTSBEICHTE(1962, Ger.); SHERLOCK HOLMES AND THE DEADLY NECKLACE(1962, Ger.); PHANTOM OF SOHO, THE(1967, Ger.)
Hans Sohnle
THEY WERE SO YOUNG(1955), art d
Rolf Sohre
PRIVATE POOLEY(1962, Brit./E. Ger.), ph
J. Soifer
Misc. Silents
LEAH'S SUFFERING(1917, USSR)
Josef Soifer
Misc. Silents
BEILIS CASE, THE(1917, USSR), d; DON'T BUILD YOUR HAPPINESS ON YOUR WIFE AND CHILD(1917, USSR), d; BRUISED BY THE STORMS OF LIFE(1918, USSR), d
Joseph Soifer
Misc. Silents
LEAH'S SUFFERING(1917, USSR), d
Joel Soisson
1984
HAMBONE AND HILLIE(1984), w
Sojin
CAREERS(1929); PAINTED FACES(1929); SEVEN FOOTPRINTS TO SATAN(1929); UNHOLY NIGHT, THE(1929); GOLDEN DAWN(1930); WAY FOR A SAILOR(1930)
Silents
THIEF OF BAGDAD, THE(1924); PROUD FLESH(1925); ACROSS THE PACIFIC(1926); SEA BEAST, THE(1926); ALL ABOARD(1927); DRIVEN FROM HOME(1927); FOREIGN DEVILS(1927); KING OF KINGS, THE(1927); OLD SAN FRANCISCO(1927); CRIMSON CITY, THE(1928); OUT WITH THE TIDE(1928); RESCUE, THE(1929)
Misc. Silents
SHIPS OF THE NIGHT(1928); SOMETHING ALWAYS HAPPENS(1928); BACK FROM SHANGHAI(1929); CHINA SLAVER(1929)
Sojin, Jr.
WAIKIKI WEDDING(1937)
Mrs. Sojin
TRADE WINDS(1938)
Ed Sojin, Jr.
I WAS AN AMERICAN SPY(1951)
K. Sojin
DUDE WRANGLER, THE(1930)
Kamiyama Sojin
Silents
EAST OF SUEZ(1925); ROAD TO MANDALAY, THE(1926)
H.R. Sokal
ARMS AND THE MAN(1962, Ger.), p; HELDINNEN(1962, Ger.), p
Henri Sokal
THEY MET ON SKIS(1940, Fr.), p&d
Henry Sokal
WINTER WONDERLAND(1947), p
Narziss Sokatscheff
ESCAPE TO BERLIN(1962, U.S./Switz./Ger.); STOP TRAIN 349(1964, Fr./Ital./Ger.); MAD EXECUTIONERS, THE(1965, Ger.); THAT WOMAN(1968, Ger.)
Ruzica Sokic
LOVE AFFAIR; OR THE CASE OF THE MISSING SWITCHBOARD OPERATOR(1968, Yugo.)
Maria Sokil
COSSACKS IN EXILE(1939, Ukrainian)
Marilyn Sokol
FRONT, THE(1976); GOODBYE GIRL, THE(1977); FOUL PLAY(1978); SOMETHING SHORT OF PARADISE(1979); CAN'T STOP THE MUSIC(1980); LAST MARRIED COUPLE IN AMERICA, THE(1980)
R.L. Sokol
FORBIDDEN FRUIT(1959, Fr.), titles
Rose Sokol
CLEO FROM 5 TO 7(1961, Fr.), titles; COW AND I, THE(1961, Fr., Ital., Ger.), titles; GREEN MARE, THE(1961, Fr./Ital.), titles; LOLA(1961, Fr./Ital.), titles

Yuri Sokol
SILENCE OF DR. EVANS, THE(1973, USSR), ph; LONELY HEARTS(1983, Aus.), ph
1984
MAN OF FLOWERS(1984, Aus.), ph

L. Sokolava
UNCOMMON THIEF, AN(1967, USSR)

Vladimir Sokoloff
CASE VAN GELDERN(1932, Ger.); MISTRESS OF ATLANTIS, THE(1932, Ger.); FROM TOP TO BOTTOM(1933, Fr.); HELL ON EARTH(1934, Ger.); BEG, BORROW OR STEAL(1937); CONQUEST(1937); EXPENSIVE HUSBANDS(1937); LIFE OF EMILE ZOLA, THE(1937); LOWER DEPTHS, THE(1937, Fr.); MAYERLING(1937, Fr.); WEST OF SHANGHAI(1937); AMAZING DR. CLITTERHOUSE, THE(1938); ARSENE LUPIN RETURNS(1938); BLOCKADE(1938); RIDE A CROOKED MILE(1938); SPAWN OF THE NORTH(1938); JUAREZ(1939); REAL GLORY, THE(1939); COMRADE X(1940); COMPLIMENTS OF MR. FLOW(1941, Fr.); LOVE CRAZY(1941); CROSSROADS(1942); ROAD TO MOROCCO(1942); FOR WHOM THE BELL TOLLS(1943); MISSION TO MOSCOW(1943); MR. LUCKY(1943); SONG OF RUSSIA(1943); CONSPIRATORS, THE(1944); PASSAGE TO MARSEILLE(1944); 'TILL WE MEET AGAIN(1944); BACK TO BATAAN(1945); PARIS UNDERGROUND(1945); ROYAL SCANDAL, A(1945); SCARLET STREET(1945); CLOAK AND DAGGER(1946); SCANDAL IN PARIS, A(1946); TWO SMART PEOPLE(1946); TO THE ENDS OF THE EARTH(1948); BARON OF ARIZONA, THE(1950); MACAO(1952); WHILE THE CITY SLEEPS(1956); I WAS A TEENAGE WEREWOLF(1957); ISTANBUL(1957); SABU AND THE MAGIC RING(1957); MONSTER FROM THE GREEN HELL(1958); TWILIGHT FOR THE GODS(1958); BEYOND THE TIME BARRIER(1960); CIMARRON(1960); MAGNIFICENT SEVEN, THE(1960); MAN ON A STRING(1960); MR. SARDONICUS(1961); ESCAPE FROM ZAHRAIN(1962); TARAS BULBA(1962)

Aleksandr Sokolov
OVERCOAT, THE(1965, USSR); KATERINA IZMAILOVA(1969, USSR)

B. Sokolov
LULLABY(1961, USSR)

Maria Sokolov
GIRL FROM PETROVKA, THE(1974)

N. Sokolov
BALLAD OF COSSACK GLOOTA(1938, USSR)

Vladimir Sokolov
THREEPENNY OPERA, THE(1931, Ger./U.S.)
Misc. Silents
LOVE OF JEANNE NEY, THE(1927, Ger.)

L. Sokolova
GORDEYEV FAMILY, THE(1961, U.S.S.R.); SUMMER TO REMEMBER, A(1961, USSR); MEET ME IN MOSCOW(1966, USSR)

Lyubov Sokolova
THREE SISTERS, THE(1969, USSR)

Natasha Sokolova
ONE WOMAN'S STORY(1949, Brit.); SO LONG AT THE FAIR(1951, Brit.); DEAD ON COURSE(1952, Brit.); SPIDER AND THE FLY, THE(1952, Brit.)

Ye. Sokolova
RESURRECTION(1963, USSR)

Richard Sokolove
MAGNIFICENT ROGUE, THE(1946), w; ANNE OF THE THOUSAND DAYS(1969, Brit.), w

Ethel Sokolow
FUNNYMAN(1967); TAKE THE MONEY AND RUN(1969)

Anna Sokolowska
GREAT BIG WORLD AND LITTLE CHILDREN, THE(1962, Pol.), d, w

Helena Sokolowska
PARTINGS(1962, Pol.)

Myra Sokolskaya
NORTHWEST OUTPOST(1947)

Ekali Sokou
DOCTOR AT SEA(1955, Brit.)

Milosh Sokulich
UNDERGROUND GUERRILLAS(1944, Brit.), w

Sol Hoopii and his Native Orchestra
FLIRTATION WALK(1934)

Carlos Miguel Sola
TEXICAN, THE(1966, U.S./Span.)

Catherine Sola
LA BELLE AMERICAINE(1961, Fr.); COUNTERFEIT CONSTABLE, THE(1966, Fr.); CHAMPAGNE MURDERS, THE(1968, Fr.); FAREWELL, FRIEND(1968, Fr./Ital.)

Jose Sola
PYRO(1964, U.S./Span.), m&md; FINGER ON THE TRIGGER(1965, US/Span.), m

Robert Sola
PURSUIT OF D.B. COOPER, THE(1981)

Martial Solal
BREATHLESS(1959, Fr.), m; TESTAMENT OF ORPHEUS, THE(1962, Fr.), m; BACKFIRE(1965, Fr.), m

Ewen Solan
HOUND OF THE BASKERVILLES, THE(1959, Brit.)

Agel Solano
GUNFIGHTERS OF CASA GRANDE(1965, U.S./Span.)

Felipe Solano
TOWN CALLED HELL, A(1971, Span./Brit.); ANTONY AND CLEOPATRA(1973, Brit.); WIND AND THE LION, THE(1975)

Rosalio Solano
PEARL OF TLAYUCAN, THE(1964, Mex.), ph; PUSS 'N' BOOTS(1964, Mex.), ph; LITTLE RED RIDING HOOD AND THE MONSTERS(1965, Mex.), ph; RAGE(1966, U.S./Mex.), ph; VAMPIRE, THE(1968, Mex.), ph; SLAUGHTER(1972), ph; I ESCAPED FROM DEVIL'S ISLAND(1973), ph

Jane Solar
TIMES SQUARE(1980)

Silvia Solar
FINGER ON THE TRIGGER(1965, US/Span.); LAS RATAS NO DUERMEN DE NOCHE(1974, Span./Fr.); EYEBALL(1978, Ital.)
Misc. Talkies
SIGMA III(1966)

Willie Solar
DIAMOND HORSESHOE(1945)

Augustin Martinez Solares
LOS PLATILLOS VOLADORES(1955, Mex.), ph; MIGHTY JUNGLE, THE(1965, U.S./Mex.), ph; NIGHT OF THE BLOODY APES(1968, Mex.)

Gilberto Solares
ATTACK OF THE MAYAN MUMMY(1963, U.S./Mex.), w

Gilberto Martinez Solares
FACE OF THE SCREAMING WEREWOLF(1959, Mex.), d, w; SANTO Y BLUE DEMON CONTRA LOS MONSTRUOS(1968, Mex.), d

Raul Martinez Solares
TARZAN AND THE MERMAIDS(1948), ph; INVISIBLE MAN, THE(1958, Mex.), ph; FACE OF THE SCREAMING WEREWOLF(1959, Mex.), ph; LA NAVE DE LOS MONSTRUOS(1959, Mex.), ph; INVASION OF THE VAMPIRES, THE(1961, Mex.), ph; YOUNG AND EVIL(1962, Mex.), ph; MAN AND THE MONSTER, THE(1965, Mex.), ph; NIGHT OF THE BLOODY APES(1968, Mex.), ph; SANTO CONTRA BLUE DEMON EN LA ATLANTIDA(1968, Mex.), ph; SANTO Y BLUE DEMON CONTRA LOS MONSTRUOS(1968, Mex.), ph; SHARK(1970, U.S./Mex.), ph; SANTO CONTRA LA HIJA DE FRANKENSTEIN(1971, Mex.), ph; ILLUSION TRAVELS BY STREETCAR, THE(1977, Mex.), ph

Corrado Solari
DUCK, YOU SUCKER!(1972, Ital.)

Laura Solari
CUCKOO CLOCK, THE(1938, Ital.); ROMAN HOLIDAY(1953); RETURN OF DR. MABUSE, THE(1961, Ger./Fr./Ital.); DUEL OF THE TITANS(1963, Ital.); VIOLENT FOUR, THE(1968, Ital.)

Rudy Solari
KINGS OF THE SUN(1963); BOSS'S SON, THE(1978)

Gianni Solaro
QUEEN OF THE PIRATES(1961, Ital./Ger.); CENTURION, THE(1962, Fr./Ital.); GLADIATOR OF ROME(1963, Ital.); SEVEN SEAS TO CALAIS(1963, Ital.); ARIZONA COLT(1965, It./Fr./Span.); REVENGE OF THE GLADIATORS(1965, Ital.); SECRET SEVEN, THE(1966, Ital./Span.); JOHNNY YUMA(1967, Ital.)

Lena Lin Solaro
HAWKS AND THE SPARROWS, THE(1967, Ital.)

Libero Solaroli
OSSESSIONE(1959, Ital.), p

Olga Solbelli
SCHOOLGIRL DIARY(1947, Ital.); MILL OF THE STONE WOMEN(1963, Fr./Ital.); SHIP OF CONDEMNED WOMEN, THE(1963, ITAL.)

Sandra Solberg
1984
ONCE UPON A TIME IN AMERICA(1984)

Steve Solberg
1984
MIKE'S MURDER(1984)

Steven Solberg
UNCOMMON VALOR(1983)

Charles Soldani
RIDING HIGH(1943); THANK YOUR LUCKY STARS(1943); BELLE OF THE YUKON(1944); MAN FROM OKLAHOMA, THE(1945); SINBAD THE SAILOR(1947); APACHE CHIEF(1949); DAUGHTER OF THE JUNGLE(1949); BROKEN ARROW(1950); MONTANA BELLE(1952); SALOME(1953); WINNING OF THE WEST(1953); FOXFIRE(1955); ESCORT WEST(1959)

Mario Soldati
CUCKOO CLOCK, THE(1938, Ital.), w; TAMING OF DOROTHY, THE(1950, Brit.), d; WOMAN OF THE RIVER(1954, Fr./Ital.), d, w; STRANGER'S HAND, THE(1955, Brit.), d; OF WAYWARD LOVE(1964, Ital./Ger.), w

Sebastiano Soldati
VIOLENT FOUR, THE(1968, Ital.), cos

Lally Soldavilla
SPIRIT OF THE BEEHIVE, THE(1976, Span.)

Stella Soldi
EAST SIDE, WEST SIDE(1949)

Steve Soldi
TWILIGHT ON THE RIO GRANDE(1947)

Chris Soldo
WINTER KILLS(1979)

Alfred Sole
ALICE, SWEET ALICE(1978), d, w; TANYA'S ISLAND(1981, Can.), d; PANDEMONIUM(1982), d

Judith Soleh
NOT MINE TO LOVE(1969, Israel)

Luc Solente
1984
L'ARGENT(1984, Fr./Switz.)

Andres Soler
BRUTE, THE(1952, Mex.); SOMBRERO(1953); LOS PLATILLOS VOLADORES(1955, Mex.); ORLAK, THE HELL OF FRANKENSTEIN(1960, Mex.); PEARL OF TLAYUCAN, THE(1964, Mex.); MIGHTY JUNGLE, THE(1965, U.S./Mex.)

Domingo Soler
CURSE OF THE CRYING WOMAN, THE(1969, Mex.); ILLUSION TRAVELS BY STREETCAR, THE(1977, Mex.)

Fernando Soler
DAUGHTER OF DECEIT(1977, Mex.)

Fernando Soler, Jr.
INTERVAL(1973, Mex./U.S.)

John Soler
TEXICAN, THE(1966, U.S./Span.), art d

Juan Alberto Soler
SANDOKAN THE GREAT(1964, Fr./Ital./Span.), set d; SWORD OF EL CID, THE(1965, Span./Ital.), art d; PISTOL FOR RINGO, A(1966, Ital./Span.), art d; SUN-SCORCHED(1966, Span./Ger.), art d; SUPERARGO VERSUS DIABOLICUS(1966, Ital./Span.), art d; LIGHTNING BOLT(1967, Ital./Sp.), art d; SEA PIRATE, THE(1967, Fr./Span./Ital.), art d; DAY THE HOTLINE GOT HOT, THE(1968, Fr./Span.), art d; GRAND SLAM(1968, Ital., Span., Ger.), art d; THEY CAME TO ROB LAS VEGAS(1969, Fr./Ital./Span./Ger.), art d; RAIN FOR A DUSTY SUMMER(1971, U.S./Span.), art d&set d

Julian Soler
LOS PLATILLOS VOLADORES(1955, Mex.), d; CASTLE OF THE MONSTERS(1958, Mex.), d; SANTO CONTRA BLUE DEMON EN LA ATLANTIDA(1968, Mex.), d, w

Kathy Sunshine Soler
1984
UP THE CREEK(1984)

Mercedes Soler
VAMPIRE, THE(1968, Mex.)

Toni Soler
ROMEO AND JULIET(1968, Ital./Span.)

Vincente Soler
TEXICAN, THE(1966, U.S./Span.); TRISTANA(1970, Span./Ital./Fr.)

P.J. Soles
BLOOD BATH(1976); CARRIE(1976); HALLOWEEN(1978); OUR WINNING SEASON(1978); BREAKING AWAY(1979); OLD BOYFRIENDS(1979); ROCK 'N' ROLL HIGH SCHOOL(1979); PRIVATE BENJAMIN(1980); STRIPES(1981); SOGGY BOTTOM U.S.A.(1982)
1984
LISTEN TO THE CITY(1984, Can.)

Paul Soles
WILLIE MCBEAN AND HIS MAGIC MACHINE(1965, U.S./Jap.); TICKET TO HEAVEN(1981)
1984
JUST THE WAY YOU ARE(1984)

Ruth Solff
ABDICATION, THE(1974, Brit.), w

Loredana Solfizi
CITY OF WOMEN(1980, Ital./Fr.)

The Solid Gold Dancers
NIGHT SHIFT(1982)

Edda Soligo
WHERE THE HOT WIND BLOWS(1960, Fr., Ital.)

Sergio Solima
BEHIND CLOSED SHUTTERS(1952, Ital.), w

Harvey Solin
IN SEARCH OF HISTORIC JESUS(1980)

V. Solin
INSPECTOR GENERAL, THE(1937, Czech.), w

Franco Solinas
BEHIND CLOSED SHUTTERS(1952, Ital.), w; SAVAGE INNOCENTS, THE(1960, Brit.), w; MADAME(1963, Fr./Ital./Span.), w; KAPO(1964, Ital./Fr./Yugo.), w; SALVATORE GIULIANO(1966, Ital.), w; BATTLE OF ALGIERS, THE(1967, Ital./Alger.), w; BULLET FOR THE GENERAL, A(1967, Ital.), w; BIG GUNDOWN, THE(1968, Ital.), w; BURN(1970), w; MERCENARY, THE(1970, Ital./Span.), w; STATE OF SIEGE(1973, Fr./U.S./Ital./Ger.), w; MR. KLEIN(1976, Fr.), w; HANNAH K.(1983, Fr.), w

Giovanni Solinas
SEVEN DWARFS TO THE RESCUE, THE(1965, Ital.)

Kay Solinas
TARZAN AND THE LEOPARD WOMAN(1946)

Marisa Solinas
SWEET SMELL OF LOVE(1966, Ital./Ger.)

Charito Solis
BUDDHA(1965, Jap.); IGOROTA, THE LEGEND OF THE TREE OF LIFE(1970, Phil.)

Joaquin Solis
MAN IN THE WILDERNESS(1971, U.S./Span.)

Leonardo Rodriguez Solis
DEATHSTALKER(1983, Arg./U.S.), ph
1984
DEATHSTALKER, THE(1984), ph

Martha "Guera" Solis
DOCTOR OF DOOM(1962, Mex.)

Lilibeth Solison
HUNTING PARTY, THE(1977, Brit.)

Bernadino Solitari
BLACK VEIL FOR LISA, A(1969 Ital./Ger.)

Josiane Soll
OLIVE TREES OF JUSTICE, THE(1967, Fr.)

Don Sollars
IN COLD BLOOD(1967)

Amadeo Sollazzo
PRIMITIVE LOVE(1966, Ital.), w

Amedeo Sollazzo
00-2 MOST SECRET AGENTS(1965, Ital.), w; DOS COSMONAUTAS A LA FUERZA(1967, Span./*Ital.), w

Francesca Solleville
SWEET AND SOUR(1964, Fr./Ital.)

Edda Sollgo
GIRL WITH A SUITCASE(1961, Fr./Ital.)

Sergio Sollima
MIGHTY URSUS(1962, Ital./Span.), w; GOLIATH AGAINST THE GIANTS(1963, Ital./Span.), w; REBEL GLADIATORS, THE(1963, Ital.), w; OF WAYWARD LOVE(1964, Ital./Ger.), d; REQUIEM FOR A SECRET AGENT(1966, Ital.), d, w; FACE TO FACE(1967, Ital.), d&w; BIG GUNDOWN, THE(1968, Ital.), d, w; FAMILY, THE(1974, Fr./Ital.), d, w; BLOOD IN THE STREETS(1975, Ital./Fr.), d, w

Bill Sollner
CARNIVAL OF SOULS(1962)

Frederick Solm
NUMBER SEVENTEEN(1928, Brit./Ger.)

Alfred Solman
Silents
MISCHIEF MAKER, THE(1916), w

Kenny Solms
DAY OF THE LOCUST, THE(1975); SHEILA LEVINE IS DEAD AND LIVING IN NEW YORK(1975), w

Rodolphe Solmsen
MINOTAUR, THE(1961, Ital.), p; WHITE SLAVE SHIP(1962, Fr./Ital.), p

Jaroslav Solnicka
MURDER CZECH STYLE(1968, Czech.); MOST BEAUTIFUL AGE, THE(1970, Czech.), p

Victor Solnicki
HOG WILD(1980, Can.), w

Yulia Solntseva
Silents
EARTH(1930, USSR)
Misc. Silents
CIGARETTE GIRL FROM MOSSELPROM(1924, USSR)

J. Solnzeva
Misc. Silents
AELITA(1929, USSR)

Robert H. Solo
SCROOGE(1970, Brit.), p; INVASION OF THE BODY SNATCHERS(1978), p

Robert Solo
AWAKENING, THE(1980), p; I, THE JURY(1982), p; BAD BOYS(1983), p

Peter Solobevski
ISLAND OF DOOM(1933, USSR)

Madeleine Sologne
LE MONDE TREMBLERA(1939, Fr.); CROISIERES SIDERALES(1941, Fr.); ETERNAL RETURN, THE(1943, Fr.); FRIEND WILL COME TONIGHT, A(1948, Fr.); JUST A BIG, SIMPLE GIRL(1949, Fr.); BERNADETTE OF LOURDES(1962, Fr.)

Bruce Soloman
CHILDREN SHOULDN'T PLAY WITH DEAD THINGS(1972)

David Soloman
Silents
KENTUCKY DAYS(1923), d; SOUTH SEA LOVE(1923), d
Misc. Silents
LOVE LETTERS(1924), d

Murray Soloman
LET'S SCARE JESSICA TO DEATH(1971), ed

Nick Solomatin
RIVER CHANGES, THE(1956)

Juri Solomin
RED TENT, THE(1971, Ital./USSR)

Yuri Solomine
SONS AND MOTHERS(1967, USSR); DERSU UZALA(1976, Jap./USSR)

Alan Solomon
MIDNIGHT MADNESS(1980)

Barbara Probst Solomon
1984
ON THE LINE(1984, Span.), w

Bessie Roth Solomon
BOWERY, THE(1933), w

Bruce Solomon
FOUL PLAY(1978)

Cassie Solomon
EVEL KNIEVEL(1971)

Ed Solomon
MR. MAGOO'S HOLIDAY FESTIVAL(1970), anim

George Solomon
HONKY TONK FREEWAY(1981)

J. Solomon
THE BEACHCOMBER(1938, Brit.)

Jesse Solomon
LIANNA(1983)

Joe Solomon
HELL'S ANGELS ON WHEELS(1967), p; GAY DECEIVERS, THE(1969), p; RUN, ANGEL, RUN(1969), p; LOSERS, THE(1970), p; SMALL TOWN IN TEXAS, A(1976), p

Leo Solomon
DARK HORSE, THE(1946), w

Linda Lee Solomon
IT HAPPENED ON 5TH AVENUE(1947)

Louis Solomon
MR. WINKLE GOES TO WAR(1944), w; SNAFU(1945), w; MARK OF THE RENEGADE(1951), w

M. Solomon
Silents
SIGN OF THE ROSE, THE(1922)

Maribeth Solomon
IMPROPER CHANNELS(1981, Can.), m; TICKET TO HEAVEN(1981), m; HARRY TRACY–DESPERADO(1982, Can.), m; THRESHOLD(1983, Can.), m

Mickey Solomon
UTILITIES(1983, Can.), m

Murray Solomon
GODFATHER, THE(1972), ed; STIGMA(1972), ed

Sam Solomon
LEPKE(1975, U.S./Israel)

Shirley Solomon
MIDDLE AGE CRAZY(1980, Can.)

Timothy "Poppin' Pete" Solomon
1984
BREAKIN'(1984)

Tina Solomon
LEO THE LAST(1970, Brit.)

James Solomons
SANDERS OF THE RIVER(1935, Brit.)

Ralph Solomons
VIRGIN WITCH, THE(1973, Brit.), p

Alexis Solomos
DREAM OF PASSION, A(1978, Gr.)

Ewen Solon
DULCIMER STREET(1948, Brit.); ROSSITER CASE, THE(1950, Brit.); ASSASSIN FOR HIRE(1951, Brit.); MYSTERY JUNCTION(1951, Brit.); STORY OF ROBIN HOOD, THE(1952, Brit.); VALLEY OF EAGLES(1952, Brit.); GHOST SHIP(1953, Brit.); SWORD AND THE ROSE, THE(1953); END OF THE ROAD, THE(1954, Brit.); ROB ROY, THE HIGHLAND ROGUE(1954, Brit.); DAM BUSTERS, THE(1955, Brit.); NAKED HEART, THE(1955, Brit.); WARRIORS, THE(1955); BATTLE HELL(1956, Brit.); BEHIND THE HEADLINES(1956, Brit.); JUMPING FOR JOY(1956, Brit.); 1984(1956, Brit.); AC-

COUNT RENDERED(1957, Brit.); BLACK ICE, THE(1957, Brit.); DEVIL'S PASS, THE(1957, Brit.); LONG HAUL, THE(1957, Brit.); TEARS FOR SIMON(1957, Brit.); THERE'S ALWAYS A THURSDAY(1957, Brit.); MARK OF THE HAWK, THE(1958); JACK THE RIPPER(1959, Brit.); SILENT ENEMY, THE(1959, Brit.); STRANGLERS OF BOMBAY, THE(1960, Brit.); SUNDOWNERS, THE(1960); TARZAN THE MAGNIFI-CENT(1960, Brit.); CURSE OF THE WEREWOLF, THE(1961); TERROR OF THE TONGS, THE(1961, Brit.); MYSTERY SUBMARINE(1963, Brit.); MOHAMMAD, MESS-ENGER OF GOD(1976, Lebanon/Brit.); UNIDENTIFIED FLYING ODDBALL, THE(1979, Brit.); LION OF THE DESERT(1981, Libya/Brit.); NUTCRACKER(1982, Brit.); WICKED LADY, THE(1983, Brit.)

Gwen Solon
MURDER REPORTED(1958, Brit.)

Anatoli Solonitsin
STALKER(1982, USSR)

Anatoll Solonitzine
ANDREI ROUBLOV(1973, USSR)

Jesus "Chucho" Solorzano
MAGNIFICENT MATADOR, THE(1955)

Christos Solouroglou
BAREFOOT BATTALION, THE(1954, Gr.)

Solovets
Misc. Silents
LEAH'S SUFFERING(1917, USSR)

V. Soloviev
VOW, THE(1947, USSR.)

Vladimir Soloviev
DAYS AND NIGHTS(1946, USSR)

Yuri Soloviev
SLEEPING BEAUTY, THE(1966, USSR)

Vera Soloviova
Misc. Silents
HIS EYES(1916, USSR)

Valeri Solovtsov
Misc. Silents
CHILDREN OF STORM(1926, USSR); KATKA'S REINETTE APPLES(1926, USSR); HOUSE IN THE SNOW-DRIFTS, THE(1928, USSR); PARISIAN COBBLER(1928, USSR); FRAGMENT OF AN EMPIRE(1930, USSR)

A. Solovyov
GORDEYEV FAMILY, THE(1961, U.S.S.R.)

I. Solovyov
WAR AND PEACE(1968, USSR)

L. Solovyov
OVERCOAT, THE(1965, USSR), w

V. Solovyov
SECRET BRIGADE, THE(1951 USSR)

Vasiliy Solovyov
WAR AND PEACE(1968, USSR), w

Vsevolod Solovyov
1812(1944, USSR), w

Yuriy Solovyov
LULLABY(1961, USSR); QUEEN OF SPADES(1961, USSR)

Eugene Solow
MASTER OF MEN(1933), w; FOG OVER FRISCO(1934), w; GENTLEMEN ARE BORN(1934), w; RETURN OF THE TERROR(1934), w; THUNDER IN THE NIGHT(1935), w; WHILE THE PATIENT SLEPT(1935), w; CRASH DONOVAN(1936), w; LEAGUE OF FRIGHTENED MEN(1937), w; PATIENT IN ROOM 18, THE(1938), w; START CHEERING(1938), w; OF MICE AND MEN(1939), w; BOWERY BOY(1940), w

Murray Solow
NIGHT OF BLOODY HORROR zero(1969)

Victor Solow
SWEET LOVE, BITTER(1967), ph

W. Solski
CASE VAN GELDERN(1932, Ger.), w

Andrew P. Solt
THEY ALL KISSED THE BRIDE(1942), w

Andrew Solt
WITHOUT RESERVATIONS(1946), w; MY KINGDOM FOR A COOK(1943), w; JOL-SON STORY, THE(1946), w; JOAN OF ARC(1948), w; LITTLE WOMEN(1949), w; WHIRLPOOL(1949), w; IN A LONELY PLACE(1950), w; FAMILY SECRET, THE(1951), w; THUNDER ON THE HILL(1951), w; LOVELY TO LOOK AT(1952), w; FOR THE FIRST TIME(1959, U.S./Ger./Ital.), w; THIS IS ELVIS(1982), p,d&w

Harry Solter
Misc. Silents
LASH OF POWER, THE(1917), d; SPOTTED LILY, THE(1917), d; WIFE HE BOUGHT, THE(1918), d

Bertalan Solti
DIALOGUE(1967, Hung.)

Mary Rose Solti
BILLY JACK(1971), p

Ole Soltoft
ERIC SOYA'S "17"(1967, Den.)

Ollie Soltoft
Misc. Talkies
GROOVE ROOM, THE(1974, Brit.)

P. Solvay
MAN COULD GET KILLED, A(1966)

Paolo Solvay
CURSE OF THE BLOOD GHOULS(1969, Ital.)

Paul Solvay
DEVIL'S WEDDING NIGHT, THE(1973, Ital.), d

Maria Solveg
ELISABETH OF AUSTRIA(1931, Ger.)

Larry Solway
FLAMING FRONTIER(1958, Can.)

Vic Solyin
CRY OF BATTLE(1963)

Katalin Solyom
MEPHISTO(1981, Ger.)

Kati Solyom
AGE OF ILLUSIONS(1967, Hung.); FATHER(1967, Hung.)

Alexander Solzhenitsyn
ONE DAY IN THE LIFE OF IVAN DENISOVICH(1971, U.S./Brit./Norway), w

J. Soma
Misc. Silents
CROSSWAYS(1928, Jap.)

Linda Soma
GODDESS, THE(1958)

Jack Somack
GENERATION(1969); DESPERATE CHARACTERS(1971); PURSUIT OF HAPPI-NESS, THE(1971); PORTNOY'S COMPLAINT(1972); FRISCO KID, THE(1979); MAIN EVENT, THE(1979); HERO AT LARGE(1980)

Claire Sombert
INVITATION TO THE DANCE(1956)

Somburu Tribe of Kenya
UP THE SANDBOX(1972)

Josef Somer
STEPFORD WIVES, THE(1975)

Yanti Somer
TRINITY IS STILL MY NAME(1971, Ital.); MAN FROM THE EAST, A(1974, Ital./Fr.); MONSIGNOR(1982)

Christine Somerfield
WHITE RAT(1972)

Beverly Somerman
THIEF(1981)

Ann Somers
PARTY PARTY(1983, Brit.)

Barbara Somers
TRUTH, THE(1961, Fr./Ital.); IN THE FRENCH STYLE(1963, U.S./Fr.); WHAT'S NEW, PUSSYCAT?(1965, U.S./Fr.)

Brett Somers
BUS RILEY'S BACK IN TOWN(1965); RAGE TO LIVE, A(1965)

Bud Somers
CONDEMNED(1929)

Cap Somers
CRACK-UP(1946)

Dalton Somers
Silents
AMATEUR GENTLEMAN, THE(1920, Brit.); AUNT RACHEL(1920, Brit.)

Esther Somers
FORCE OF EVIL(1948); RIVER LADY(1948); SNAKE PIT, THE(1948); MADAME BOVARY(1949); PORTRAIT OF JENNIE(1949); SUN COMES UP, THE(1949); FOR HEAVEN'S SAKE(1950); IROQUOIS TRAIL, THE(1950); SIDE STREET(1950); TAR-NISHED(1950); FOLLOW THE SUN(1951); PEOPLE WILL TALK(1951); VIOLENT SATURDAY(1955)

Capt. F. G. Somers
STRATTON STORY, THE(1949)

Fred Somers
MATCHMAKER, THE(1958)

Fred G. Somers
I WALK ALONE(1948)

Gerald Somers
Misc. Silents
ROMANCE OF ANNIE LAURIE, THE(1920, Brit.), d

Hilda Somers [Helga Sommerfield]
RED-DRAGON(1967, Ital./Ger./US

James Somers
MUTINEERS, THE(1949); MALAYA(1950)

Jerry Somers
MAN WITH BOGART'S FACE, THE(1980)

Julian Somers
ROYAL DIVORCE, A(1938, Brit.); PETERVILLE DIAMOND, THE(1942, Brit.); CARAVAN(1946, Brit.); DIAMOND CITY(1949, Brit.); GAMBLER AND THE LADY, THE(1952, Brit.); STORY OF ROBIN HOOD, THE(1952, Brit.); STRANGER IN BETWEEN, THE(1952, Brit.); CLUE OF THE MISSING APE, THE(1953, Brit.); LONG MEMORY, THE(1953, Brit.); WHITE FIRE(1953, Brit.); MIRACLE IN SOHO(1957, Brit.); TIME WITHOUT PITY(1957, Brit.); ANOTHER TIME, ANOTHER PLACE(1958); MOONRAKER, THE(1958, Brit.); NIGHT TO REMEMBER, A(1958, Brit.); ONE THAT GOT AWAY, THE(1958, Brit.); ROOM AT THE TOP(1959, Brit.); MISSILE FROM HELL(1960, Brit.); FAR FROM THE MADDING CROWD(1967, Brit.)

Julie Somers
DEATH OF AN ANGEL(1952, Brit.)

Kristi Somers
RUMBLE FISH(1983)
1984
HARDBODIES(1984)

Madge Somers
CONCERNING MR. MARTIN(1937, Brit.)

Norman Somers
NEVER LOOK BACK(1952, Brit.)

Paul Somers
DESPERATE MAN, THE(1959, Brit.), w

Robert Somers
1984
COUNTRY(1984)

Sonia Somers
VINTAGE WINE(1935, Brit.); BELLES OF ST. CLEMENTS, THE(1936, Brit.); KING ARTHUR WAS A GENTLEMAN(1942, Brit.)

Steve Somers
VISITOR, THE(1980, Ital./U.S.)

Suzanne Somers
AMERICAN GRAFFITI(1973); YESTERDAY'S HERO(1979, Brit.); NOTHING PER-SONAL(1980, Can.)

W. Dalton Somers
Misc. Silents
RIVER OF STARS, THE(1921, Brit.)

W. Debroy Somers
ROSE OF TRALEE(1938, Ireland), m
C.W. Somerset
Misc. Silents
BY BERWIN BANKS(1920, Brit.)
G. Somerset
Silents
ROAD TO RUIN, THE(1913, Brit.)
John Somerset [John S. Gaisford]
TAKE HER BY SURPRISE(1967, Can.), p
Pat Somerset
BLACK WATCH, THE(1929); FROM HEADQUARTERS(1929); BORN RECK-LESS(1930); GOOD INTENTIONS(1930); HELL'S ANGELS(1930); MEN WITHOUT WOMEN(1930); UP THE RIVER(1930); BODY AND SOUL(1931); DEVOTION(1931); SQUAW MAN, THE(1931); BLONDE VENUS(1932); MERRILY WE GO TO HELL(1932); NIGHT WORLD(1932); TRIAL OF VIVIENNE WARE, THE(1932); DANC-ING LADY(1933); MIDNIGHT CLUB(1933); BULLDOG DRUMMOND STRIKES BACK(1934); KEY, THE(1934); MURDER IN TRINIDAD(1934); MYSTERY OF MR. X, THE(1934); CLIVE OF INDIA(1935); DON'T BET ON BLONDES(1935); GILDED LILY, THE(1935); HERE'S TO ROMANCE(1935); TWO FOR TONIGHT(1935); LIBELED LADY(1936); LONE WOLF RETURNS, THE(1936); SYLVIA SCARLETT(1936); TO MARY–WITH LOVE(1936); DEATH IN THE SKY(1937); FIREFLY, THE(1937); I COVER THE WAR(1937); MAYTIME(1937); PRISONER OF ZENDA, THE(1937); THIN ICE(1937); WEE WILLIE WINKIE(1937); HOWARDS OF VIRGINIA, THE(1940); SWIMMER, THE(1968), ed; FIVE THE HARD WAY(1969), ed; MAD ROOM, THE(1969), ed; DRIVE, HE SAID(1971), ed; BLACK GUNN(1972), ed
Silents
WALLS OF PREJUDICE(1920, Brit.); ONE OF THE BRAVEST(1925)
Misc. Silents
KEY OF THE WORLD, THE(1918, Brit.); SERVING TWO MASTERS(1921); WHITE HEN, THE(1921, Brit.); MOTHER MACHREE(1928)
Patricia Somerset
WEDDING OF LILLI MARLENE, THE(1953, Brit.)
Robert Somerset
ULYSSES(1967, U.S./Brit.); MC KENZIE BREAK, THE(1970); QUACKSER FOR-TUNE HAS A COUSIN IN THE BRONX(1970)
A.W. Somerville
OH, YEAH!(1929), w
H.B. Somerville
Silents
ASHES OF VENGEANCE(1923), w
Karen Somerville
RICH AND FAMOUS(1981)
Mary Somerville
MR. PEABODY AND THE MERMAID(1948)
Phyllis Somerville
ARTHUR(1981)
Roy Somerville
Silents
ACQUITTED(1916), w; INNOCENT MAGDALENE, AN(1916), w; REGGIE MIXES IN(1916), w; EMBARRASSMENT OF RICHES, THE(1918), w; OUR LITTLE WI-FE(1918), w; CHALLENGE OF CHANCE, THE(1919), w; SACRED SILENCE(1919), w
Michael Somes
LITTLE BALLERINA, THE(1951, Brit.); ROMEO AND JULIET(1966, Brit.)
James Somich
LOSERS, THE(1968), p&d
Josef Somio
BE MINE TONIGHT(1933, Brit.), p; ARSENAL STADIUM MYSTERY, THE(1939, Brit.), p
Arnold Somkin
BEST FRIENDS(1975), w
1984
OVER THE BROOKLYN BRIDGE(1984), w
Josef Somlo
NUMBER SEVENTEEN(1928, Brit./Ger.), p; MIKADO, THE(1939, Brit.), p; FUGI-TIVE, THE(1940, Brit.), p; OLD BILL AND SON(1940, Brit.), p; LADY IN DIS-TRESS(1942, Brit.), p; ALIBI, THE(1943, Brit.), p; ONE NIGHT WITH YOU(1948, Brit.), p; INHERITANCE, THE(1951, Brit.), p; MAN WHO LOVED REDHEADS, THE(1955, Brit.), p; TECKMAN MYSTERY, THE(1955, Brit.), p; BEHIND THE MASK(1958, Brit.), p
Tamas Somlo
RED AND THE WHITE, THE(1969, Hung./USSR), ph; ROUND UP, THE(1969, Hung.), ph
Chris Somma
ROCK 'N' ROLL HIGH SCHOOL(1979)
Laurence Somma
MR. BILLION(1977)
Lorenz Somma
REVENGE OF THE SHOGUN WOMEN(1982, Taiwan), ph
Julie Sommars
PAD, THE(AND HOW TO USE IT)* (1966, Brit.); GREAT SIOUX MASSACRE, THE(1965); HERBIE GOES TO MONTE CARLO(1977)
Edith R. Sommer
FROM THIS DAY FORWARD(1946), w
Edith Sommer
BORN TO BE BAD(1950), w; PERFECT STRANGERS(1950), w; TEENAGE RE-BEL(1956), w; BEST OF EVERYTHING, THE(1959), w; BLUE DENIM(1959), w; PLEASURE SEEKERS, THE(1964), w; THIS PROPERTY IS CONDEMNED(1966), w
Elke Sommer
DANIELLA BY NIGHT(1962, Fr./Ger.); SWEET ECSTASY(1962, Fr.); PRIZE, THE(1963); VICTORS, THE(1963); AMONG VULTURES(1964, Ger./Ital./Fr./Yugo.); LOVE, THE ITALIAN WAY(1964, Ital.); SHOT IN THE DARK, A(1964); WHY BOTHER TO KNOCK(1964, Brit.); ART OF LOVE, THE(1965); BAMBOLE!(1965, Ital.); BOY, DID I GET A WRONG NUMBER!(1966); FRONTIER HELLCAT(1966, Fr./Ital./Ger./Yugo.); MONEY TRAP, THE(1966); OSCAR, THE(1966); CORRUPT ONES, THE(1967, Ger.); DEADLIER THAN THE MALE(1967, Brit.); SEDUCTION BY THE SEA(1967, Ger./Yugo.); VENETIAN AFFAIR, THE(1967); WICKED DREAMS OF PAULA SCHULTZ, THE(1968); WRECKING CREW, THE(1968); THEY CAME TO ROB LAS VEGAS(1969, Fr./Ital./Span./Ger.); INVINCIBLE SIX, THE(1970, U.S./Iran); PERCY(1971, Brit.); ZEPPELIN(1971, Brit.); BARON BLOOD(1972, Ital.); TEN LITTLE INDIANS(1975,

Ital./Fr./Span./Ger.); HOUSE OF EXORCISM, THE(1976, Ital.); SWISS CONSPIRACY, THE(1976, U.S./Ger.); I MISS YOU, HUGS AND KISSES(1978, Can.); IT'S NOT THE SIZE THAT COUNTS(1979, Brit.); PRISONER OF ZENDA, THE(1979); THE DOUBLE McGUFFIN(1979)
1984
INVISIBLE STRANGLER(1984)
Misc. Talkies
JAMAICAN GOLD(1971); NIGHTINGALE SANG IN BERKELEY SQUARE, A(1979); ONE AWAY(1980)
Hans Sommer
HER SISTER'S SECRET(1946), m; GAS HOUSE KIDS GO WEST(1947), m; FIRST LEGION, THE(1951), m
Josef Sommer
DIRTY HARRY(1971); MAN ON A SWING(1974); CLOSE ENCOUNTERS OF THE THIRD KIND(1977); OLIVER'S STORY(1978); ABSENCE OF MALICE(1981); REDS(1981); ROLLOVER(1981); HANKY-PANKY(1982); SOPHIE'S CHOICE(1982); STILL OF THE NIGHT(1982); INDEPENDENCE DAY(1983); SILKWOOD(1983)
1984
ICEMAN(1984)
Judi Sommer
LIFE AND TIMES OF CHESTER-ANGUS RAMSGOOD, THE(1971, Can.)
M. Josef Sommer
FRONT, THE(1976)
Robert Sommer
LA TRAVIATA(1982); HANNAH K.(1983, Fr.)
Yanti Sommer
AVANTI!(1972)
Helga Sommerfeld
FREDDY UNTER FREMDEN STERNEN(1962, Ger.); 24 HOURS TO KILL(1966, Brit.); PHANTOM OF SOHO, THE(1967, Ger.)
Diane Sommerfield
LOVE IN A TAXI(1980); BACK ROADS(1981)
Misc. Talkies
BLACKJACK(1978)
Helga Sommerfield
SHADOWS GROW LONGER, THE(1962, Switz./Ger.)
John Sommerfield
BOY, A GIRL AND A BIKE, A(1949 Brit.), w
Barbara Sommers
DESTRUCTORS, THE(1974, Brit.)
Edith Sommers
JESSICA(1962, U.S./Ital./Fr.), w
Capt. Fred Sommers
FORCE OF EVIL(1948)
Harry Sommers
TRIAL OF JOAN OF ARC(1965, Fr.)
Jason Sommers
Misc. Talkies
SWINGING CHEERLEADERS, THE(1974); KINGS OF THE HILL(1976)
Jay Sommers
ALL HANDS ON DECK(1961), w
Joanie Sommers
EVERYTHING'S DUCKY(1961); LIVELY SET, THE(1964)
Kristi Sommers
1984
SAVAGE STREETS(1984)
Laura Lizer Sommers
VILLAIN, THE(1979); CANNONBALL RUN, THE(1981)
Nancy Sommers
CREATURE CALLED MAN, THE(1970, Jap.)
Rick Sommers [Riccardo Domenici]
SECRET AGENT FIREBALL(1965, Fr./Ital.), art d
Russell Sommers
1984
RAZOR'S EDGE, THE(1984); SUPERGIRL(1984); TOP SECRET!(1984)
Evan Sommerville
SMASH PALACE(1982, New Zealand)
Don Sommese
STRAIGHT TIME(1978)
Pearl Somner
CROSS AND THE SWITCHBLADE, THE(1970), cos; LOVE STORY(1970), cos
George Somnes
GIRL IN 419(1933), d; MIDNIGHT CLUB(1933), d; TORCH SINGER(1933), d; WHARF ANGEL(1934), d
T. Somogi
LOTNA(1966, Pol.)
Rudolf Somogyvari
ROUND UP, THE(1969, Hung.)
Georgette Somohano
SIERRA BARON(1958), cos; EXTERMINATING ANGEL, THE(1967, Mex.), cos
Valeriy Somov
ITALIANO BRAVA GENTE(1965, Ital./USSR)
Josef Somr
CLOSELY WATCHED TRAINS(1967, Czech.); NIGHTS OF PRAGUE, THE(1968, Czech.); WHAT WOULD YOU SAY TO SOME SPINACH(1976, Czech.); NINTH HEART, THE(1980, Czech.); DIVINE EMMA, THE(1983, Czech,)
A. K. Sona
MYSTERIOUS ISLAND(1941, USSR)
Lacia Sonami
SLAVE GIRL(1947)
Elvero Sonchez
LAW AND LAWLESS(1932)
Ralph Soncuya
THEY WERE EXPENDABLE(1945)
Mara Sondakoff
STALAG 17(1953)
Roland Sonder-Mahnken
GLASS OF WATER, A(1962, Cgr.), m

Gale Sondergaard
ANTHONY ADVERSE(1936); LIFE OF EMILE ZOLA, THE(1937); MAID OF SALEM(1937); SEVENTH HEAVEN(1937); DRAMATIC SCHOOL(1938); LORD JEFF(1938); CAT AND THE CANARY, THE(1939); JUAREZ(1939); NEVER SAY DIE(1939); BLUE BIRD, THE(1940); LETTER, THE(1940); LLANO KID, THE(1940); MARK OF ZORRO, THE(1940); BLACK CAT, THE(1941); PARIS CALLING(1941); ENEMY AGENTS MEET ELLERY QUEEN(1942); MY FAVORITE BLONDE(1942); NIGHT TO REMEMBER, A(1942); APPOINTMENT IN BERLIN(1943); ISLE OF FORGOTTEN SINS(1943); STRANGE DEATH OF ADOLF HITLER, THE(1943); CHRISTMAS HOLIDAY(1944); CLIMAX, THE(1944); ENTER ARSENE LUPIN(1944); FOLLOW THE BOYS(1944); GYPSY WILDCAT(1944); INVISIBLE MAN'S REVENGE(1944); SHERLOCK HOLMES AND THE SPIDER WOMAN(1944); ANNA AND THE KING OF SIAM(1946); NIGHT IN PARADISE, A(1946); SPIDER WOMAN STRIKES BACK, THE(1946); TIME OF THEIR LIVES, THE(1946); PIRATES OF MONTEREY(1947); ROAD TO RIO(1947); EAST SIDE, WEST SIDE(1949); SLAVES(1969); PLEASANTVILLE(1976); RETURN OF A MAN CALLED HORSE, THE(1976); ECHOES(1983)

Hester Sondergaard
SEEDS OF FREEDOM(1943, USSR); NAKED CITY, THE(1948); JIGSAW(1949)

Quent Sondergaard
FIVE GUNS TO TOMBSTONE(1961)

Quentin Sondergaard
THIS PROPERTY IS CONDEMNED(1966)

Thok Sondergaard
JOURNEY TO THE SEVENTH PLANET(1962, U.S./Swed.), ed

Walter Sondes
HOURS OF LONELINESS(1930, Brit.); BRITANNIA OF BILLINGSGATE(1933, Brit.); FACES(1934, Brit.), a, w; IRON DUKE, THE(1935, Brit.); TOILERS OF THE SEA(1936, Brit.); KATE PLUS TEN; PRISONER OF CORBAL(1939, Brit.)
Silents
UNWANTED, THE(1924, Brit.)

Eugene Sondfield
BAYOU(1957)

Stephen Sondheim
LAST OF SHEILA, THE(1973), w; STAVISKY(1974, Fr.), m; LITTLE NIGHT MUSIC, A(1977, Aust./U.S./Ger.), w; REDS(1981), m

Bill Sondholm
GUN TOWN(1946)

Mal Sondock
TOWN WITHOUT PITY(1961, Ger./Switz./U.S.); PHONY AMERICAN, THE(1964, Ger.)

Harumi Sone
MESSAGE FROM SPACE(1978, Jap.)

John Sone
LOVE IN A FOUR LETTER WORLD(1970, Can.), d, w

Roy Sone
FIXER, THE(1968)

Rodolfo Sonego
ANNA(1951, Ital.), w; NERO'S MISTRESS(1962, Ital.), w; DEVIL, THE(1963), w; AND SUDDENLY IT'S MURDER!(1964, Ital.), w; FLYING SAUCER, THE(1964, Ital.), w; LOVE ON THE RIVIERA(1964, Fr./Ital.), w; MORALIST, THE(1964, Ital.), w; AMERICAN WIFE, AN(1965, Ital.), w; THREE FACES OF A WOMAN(1965, Ital.), w; RUN FOR YOUR WIFE(1966, Fr./Ital.), w; GIRL WITH A PISTOL, THE(1968, Ital.), w; QUEENS, THE(1968, Ital./Fr.), w; SCIENTIFIC CARDPLAYER, THE(1972, Ital.), w; WIFEMISTRESS(1979, Ital.), w

Sonya Sones
1984
FLESHBURN(1984), ed

Joe Sonessa
PARTY CRASHERS, THE(1958)

Joseph Sonessa
TAKE A GIANT STEP(1959)

Jino Soneya
WIFE OF GENERAL LING, THE(1938, Brit.)

Jiro Soneya
MUTINY OF THE ELSINORE, THE(1939, Brit.)

Eugene Sonfield
FOUR FOR THE MORGUE(1962)

Arthur Song
FLOWER DRUM SONG(1961)

Cheryl Song
1984
WEEKEND PASS(1984)

Lim Bun Song
FIENDISH PLOT OF DR. FU MANCHU, THE(1980)

Lovey Song
ON HER BED OF ROSES(1966)

Mary Song
HUNTERS, THE(1958)

Owen Song
HER HUSBAND'S AFFAIRS(1947); ONE MINUTE TO ZERO(1952)

Soo Ah Song
PURPLE PLAIN, THE(1954, Brit.)

Song Spinners
FOLLIES GIRL(1943)

Supakorn Songermvorakul
HOT POTATO(1976)

Cynthia Songey
RENEGADE GIRLS(1974); CRAZY MAMA(1975)

Seksan Sonimsat
1 2 3 MONSTER EXPRESS(1977, Thai.), m

Magda Sonja
ROBBER SYMPHONY, THE(1937, Brit.)
Misc. Silents
OTHER SELF, THE(1918, Aust.)

Anne Sonka
GIANT GILA MONSTER, THE(1959)

Margitta Sonke
PUSS 'N' BOOTS(1967, Ger.)

Hans Sonker
FAITHFUL(1936, Brit.); PATRICIA GETS HER MAN(1937, Brit.)

Paul Sonkilla
HOODWINK(1981, Aus.)

Paul Sonkkila
STIR(1980, Aus.); GALLIPOLI(1981, Aus.); YEAR OF LIVING DANGEROUSLY, THE(1982, Aus.)

Kalu Sonkur, Sr.
REAL GLORY, THE(1939)

Kalu K. Sonkur
BWANA DEVIL(1953); WRECK OF THE MARY DEAR, THE(1959)

Anatoli Sonlinitsin
SOLARIS(1972, USSR)

Gus Sonnenberg
BIG CITY(1937)

Barry Sonnenfeld
1984
BLOOD SIMPLE(1984), ph

Sherry Sonnett
BELOW THE BELT(1980), w

Wim Sonneveld
SILK STOCKINGS(1957)

Johanna Sonnex
STORIES FROM A FLYING TRUNK(1979, Brit.)

Jo-El Sonnier
THEY ALL LAUGHED(1981)

Joseph Sonnleithner
FIDELIO(1970, Ger.), w

Philip Sonntag
BENJAMIN(1973, Ger.)

Ursula Sonntag
KAMIKAZE '89(1983, Ger.), cos & makeup

Sonny
ACES WILD(1937)

Sonny and Cher
WILD ON THE BEACH(1965); GOOD TIMES(1967)

Sonny Farrer and His Band
TALKING FEET(1937, Brit.)

Sonny Stewart's Skiffle Kings
INBETWEEN AGE, THE(1958, Brit.)

Sonny the Marvel Horse
WILD MUSTANG(1935); GHOST TOWN(1937)

Eriko Sono
HARBOR LIGHT YOKOHAMA(1970, Jap.)

Makoto Sono
SAMURAI(1955, Jap.), art d

Mari Sono
LAS VEGAS FREE-FOR-ALL(1968, Jap.)

Ayumi Sonoda
VARAN THE UNBELIEVABLE(1962, U.S./Jap.)

Keisuke Sonoi
GIRARA(1967, Jap.)

Kameo Sonokawa
TORA! TORA! TORA!(1970, U.S./Jap.), tech adv

Sonora
NOTORIOUS CLEOPATRA, THE(1970)

Sons of the Pioneers
OLD HOMESTEAD, THE(1935); RHYTHM ON THE RANGE(1936); OLD CORRAL, THE(1937); CALL OF THE ROCKIES(1938); CATTLE RAIDERS(1938); COLORADO TRAIL(1938); LAW OF THE PLAINS(1938); SOUTH OF ARIZONA(1938); WEST OF CHEYENNE(1938); WEST OF SANTA FE(1938); MAN FROM SUNDOWN, THE(1939); NORTH OF THE YUKON(1939); OUTPOST OF THE MOUNTIES(1939); RIDERS OF BLACK RIVER(1939); RIO GRANDE(1939); SPOILERS OF THE RANGE(1939); TEXAS STAMPEDE(1939); THUNDERING WEST, THE(1939); WESTERN CARAVANS(1939); BLAZING SIX SHOOTERS(1940); DURANGO KID, THE(1940); STRANGER FROM TEXAS, THE(1940); TEXAS STAGECOACH(1940); THUNDERING FRONTIER(1940); TWO-FISTED RANGERS(1940); WEST OF ABILENE(1940); OUTLAWS OF THE PANHANDLE(1941); PINTO KID, THE(1941); CALL OF THE CANYON(1942); MAN FROM CHEYENNE(1942); SONS OF THE PIONEERS(1942); SOUTH OF SANTA FE(1942); SUNSET ON THE DESERT(1942); KING OF THE COWBOYS(1943); HOLLYWOOD CANTEEN(1944); BELLS OF ROSARITA(1945); HELLDORADO(1946); BELLS OF SAN ANGELO(1947); HIT PARADE OF 1947(1947); MELODY TIME(1948); EVERYBODY'S DANCIN'(1950); FIGHTING COAST GUARD(1951)

Lester A. Sonsom
BOWERY BOYS MEET THE MONSTERS, THE(1954), ed

Gerry Sont
1984
MELVIN, SON OF ALVIN(1984, Aus.)

Hedy Sontag
DOC(1971)

Jenny Sontag
SPARROWS CAN'T SING(1963, Brit.)

Susan Sontag
DUET FOR CANNIBALS(1969, Swed.), d&w; ZELIG(1983)
Misc. Talkies
BROTHER CARL(1972), d

Ben Sonten
DEMON BARBER OF FLEET STREET, THE(1939, Brit.)

Victor Sontolda
SNOW DEVILS, THE(1965, Ital.), spec eff

Magda Sonya
Misc. Silents
THAT MURDER IN BERLIN(1929, Ger.)

G. C. Sonzogno
STRANGER ON THE PROWL(1953, Ital.), m

Hayward Soo Soo
CHINA'S LITTLE DEVILS(1945)
Jack Soo
THOROUGHLY MODERN MILLIE(1967); FLOWER DRUM SONG(1961); WHO'S
BEEN SLEEPING IN MY BED?(1963); OSCAR, THE(1966); GREEN BERETS,
THE(1968); RETURN FROM WITCH MOUNTAIN(1978)
Park Jong Soo
SEARCH AND DESTROY(1981)
Misc. Talkies
STRIKING BACK(1981)
Eunice Soo Hoo
KEYS OF THE KINGDOM, THE(1944)
Hayward Soo Hoo
KEYS OF THE KINGDOM, THE(1944)
Willie Soo Hoo
FOLLOW ME, BOYS!(1966)
Surgit Sood
NO BLADE OF GRASS(1970, Brit.)
Edward Soohoo
LITTLE TOKYO, U.S.A.(1942)
Eleanor Soohoo
SUSAN AND GOD(1940); SOMEWHERE I'LL FIND YOU(1942)
Frances Chin Soon
KING OF THE CORAL SEA(1956, Aus.)
Lucille Soong
GENGHIS KHAN(U.S./Brit./Ger./Yugo); DARLING(1965, Brit.); THREE WEEKS
OF LOVE(1965); MINI-AFFAIR, THE(1968, Brit.); ONE MORE TIME(1970, Brit.)
Rudy Sooter
MOONLIGHT ON THE RANGE(1937); ROAMING COWBOY, THE(1937); TROUBLE
IN TEXAS(1937); MAN FROM MUSIC MOUNTAIN(1938); RHYTHM OF THE SAD-
DLE(1938); UTAH TRAIL(1938)
Jeri Sopanen
BLAST OF SILENCE(1961); MAKE A FACE(1971), ph; I COULD NEVER HAVE SEX
WITH ANY MAN WHO HAS SO LITTLE REGARD FOR MY HUSBAND(1973), ph;
MY DINNER WITH ANDRE(1981), ph
Alexander Sopenar
WEDDING, A(1978)
Harn Soper
1984
MASSIVE RETALIATION(1984), m
Margarete Soper
CRIME AND PASSION(1976, U.S., Ger.)
Mark Soper
TEMPEST(1982); WORLD ACCORDING TO GARP, The(1982)
Sophie
SLEEP, MY LOVE(1948), cos; FLASH GORDON(1980)
Sophocles
OEDIPUS REX(1957, Can.), w; OEDIPUS THE KING(1968, Brit.), w
Dolna Sopir
S.T.A.B.(1976, Hong Kong/Thailand)
Michael Sopkiw
1984
AFTER THE FALL OF NEW YORK(1984, Ital./Fr.)
Claudio Sora
SACCO AND VANZETTI(1971, Ital./Fr.)
Luiz Sorace
Misc. Silents
BRASA DORMIDA(1928, Braz.)
Daniel Sorano
PORT OF DESIRE(1960, Fr.); TIME BOMB(1961, Fr./Ital.); DOUBLE DECEP-
TION(1963, Fr.); WOMEN AND WAR(1965, Fr.)
Piella Sorano
LOVERS ON A TIGHTROPE(1962, Fr.)
Camille Soray
NEW FACES OF 1937(1937)
Soraya
THREE FACES OF A WOMAN(1965, Ital.)
Elga Sorbas
AMERICAN SOLDIER, THE(1970 Ger.); LITTLE MOTHER(1973, U.S./Yugo./Ger.)
Joe Sorbello
ROCKY(1976)
Marie-Louise Sorbon
WALPURGIS NIGHT(1941, Swed.)
Cecile Sorci
PEARLS OF THE CROWN(1938, Fr.)
Alberto Sordi
UNDER THE SUN OF ROME(1949, Ital.); TWO NIGHTS WITH CLEOPATRA(1953,
Ital.); GRAN VARIETA(1955, Ital.); SIGN OF VENUS, THE(1955, Ital.); VITEL-
LONI(1956, Ital./Fr.); WHITE SHEIK, THE(1956, Ital.); FAREWELL TO ARMS,
A(1957); IT HAPPENED IN ROME(1959, Ital.); GREAT WAR, THE(1961, Fr., Ital.);
BEST OF ENEMIES, THE(1962); EVERYBODY GO HOME!(1962, Fr./Ital.); MAFI-
OSO(1962, Ital.); NERO'S MISTRESS(1962, Ital.); DEVIL, THE(1963); AND SUDDEN-
LY IT'S MURDER!(1964, Ital.); FLYING SAUCER, THE(1964, Ital.); LOVE ON THE
RIVIERA(1964, Fr./Ital.), a, w; MORALIST, THE(1964, Ital.); DAY IN COURT, A(1965,
Ital.), a, w; THOSE MAGNIFICENT MEN IN THEIR FLYING MACHINES; OR HOW
I FLEWFROM LONDON TO PARIS IN 25 HOURS AND 11 MINUTES(1965, Brit.);
THREE FACES OF A WOMAN(1965, Ital.), a, w; MADE IN ITALY(1967, Fr./Ital.);
QUEENS, THE(1968, Ital./Fr.); WITCHES, THE(1969, Fr./Ital.); MOST WONDERFUL
EVENING OF MY LIFE, THE(1972, Ital./Fr.); ROMA(1972, Ital./Fr.); SCIENTIFIC
CARDPLAYER, THE(1972, Ital.); VIVA ITALIA(1978, Ital.)
Ann Soreen
BLACK TULIP, THE(1937, Brit.)
George Sorel
MAN WHO BROKE THE BANK AT MONTE CARLO, THE(1935); CHARGE OF THE
LIGHT BRIGADE, THE(1936); DRACULA'S DAUGHTER(1936); PRINCESS COMES
ACROSS, THE(1936); SING ME A LOVE SONG(1936); SNOWED UNDER(1936);
ESPIONAGE(1937); I MET HIM IN PARIS(1937); KING AND THE CHORUS GIRL,
THE(1937); SHEIK STEPS OUT, THE(1937); SWING HIGH, SWING LOW(1937);
ANGELS WITH DIRTY FACES(1938); SUEZ(1938); SWISS MISS(1938); IDIOT'S
DELIGHT(1939); SECRET SERVICE OF THE AIR(1939); HITLER–DEAD OR ALI-

VE(1942); ONCE UPON A HONEYMOON(1942); FOR WHOM THE BELL TOLLS(1943);
MISSION TO MOSCOW(1943); PARIS AFTER DARK(1943); SONG OF BERNADETTE,
THE(1943); STRANGE DEATH OF ADOLF HITLER, THE(1943); THIS LAND IS
MINE(1943); TAMPICO(1944); 'TILL WE MEET AGAIN(1944); TO HAVE AND HAVE
NOT(1944); VOICE IN THE WIND(1944); DANGEROUS INTRUDER(1945); BLUE
DAHLIA, THE(1946); DO YOU LOVE ME?(1946); GILDA(1946); MONSIEUR BEAU-
CAIRE(1946); O.S.S.(1946); RAZOR'S EDGE, THE(1946); CALCUTTA(1947); GOLDEN
EARRINGS(1947); NORTHWEST OUTPOST(1947); ROAD TO RIO(1947); SIN-
GAPORE(1947); SONG OF THE THIN MAN(1947); TROUBLE WITH WOMEN,
THE(1947); ALL MY SONS(1948); COBRA STRIKES, THE(1948); SAIGON(1948)
Guy Sorel
THIRTEENTH LETTER, THE(1951); HONEYMOON KILLERS, THE(1969); TELL
ME THAT YOU LOVE ME, JUNIE MOON(1970)
Jacques Sorel
FINO A FARTI MALE(1969, Fr./Ital.)
Jean Sorel
SKY LINER(1949); AMELIE OR THE TIME TO LOVE(1961, Fr.); FROM A ROMAN
BALCONY(1961, Fr./Ital.); I SPIT ON YOUR GRAVE(1962, Fr.); VIEW FROM THE
BRIDGE, A(1962, Fr./Ital.); FOUR DAYS OF NAPLES, THE(1963, US/Ital.); GERMI-
NAL(1963, Fr.); ADORABLE JULIA(1964, Fr./Aust.); DISORDER(1964, Fr./Ital.);
BAMBOLE!(1965, Ital.); CIRCLE OF LOVE(1965, Fr.); HIGHWAY PICKUP(1965,
Fr./Ital.); HYPNOSIS(1966, Ger./Sp./Ital.); MAN WHO LAUGHS, THE(1966, Ital.);
SANDRA(1966, Ital.); MADE IN ITALY(1967, Fr./Ital.); WEEKEND, ITALIAN STY-
LE(1967, Fr./Ital./Span.); BELLE DE JOUR(1968, Fr.); DE L'AMOUR(1968, Fr./Ital.);
QUEENS, THE(1968, Ital./Fr.); SWEET BODY OF DEBORAH, THE(1969, Ital./Fr.);
LOVE PROBLEMS(1970, Ital.); DAY OF THE JACKAL, THE(1973, Brit./Fr.); TRADER
HORN(1973)
Misc. Talkies
TO LOVE, PERHAPS TO DIE(1975)
Jeanne Sorel
AMERICAN MADNESS(1932); PREHISTORIC WOMEN(1950); MODEL SHOP,
THE(1969); B.S. I LOVE YOU(1971)
Louise Sorel
PARTY'S OVER, THE(1966, Brit.); B.S. I LOVE YOU(1971); PLAZA SUITE(1971);
EVERY LITTLE CROOK AND NANNY(1972); AIRPLANE II: THE SEQUEL(1982)
1984
CRIMES OF PASSION(1984); WHERE THE BOYS ARE '84(1984)
Michel Sorel
PIRATES OF CAPRI, THE(1949)
Roger Sorel
Misc. Talkies
BELOW THE HILL(1974)
Sonia Sorel
BLUEBEARD(1944); BLONDE FOR A DAY(1946); CLUB HAVANA(1946); WOMEN
OF PITCAIRN ISLAND, THE(1957)
Ted Sorel
JEREMY(1973)
Theodore Sorel
NETWORK(1976); WITHOUT A TRACE(1983)
Maya Sorell
MAN WHO FINALLY DIED, THE(1967, Brit.)
Sonja Sorell
FOREVER MY LOVE(1962)
William Sorell
Misc. Silents
CONTINENTAL GIRL, A(1915)
Diane Sorelle
1984
LA PETIT SIRENE(1984, Fr.)
William Sorelle
Silents
PRINCE AND THE PAUPER, THE(1915)
Misc. Silents
MUMMY AND THE HUMMINGBIRD, THE(1915); FORTUNES OF FIFI, THE(1917);
HAND INVISIBLE, THE(1919)
William J. Sorelle
Misc. Silents
COMMON SENSE BRACKETT(1916)
William T. Sorelle
Silents
PRIVATE PEAT(1918)
Babita Soren
CHALLENGE, THE(1939, Brit.)
Edith Sorensen
CRAZY PARADISE(1965, Den.), cos
Eva Sorensen
INCREDIBLE TWO-HEADED TRANSPLANT, THE(1971)
Linda Sorensen
MC CABE AND MRS. MILLER(1971)
Monique Sorensen
1984
REVENGE OF THE NERDS(1984)
Paul Sorensen
FLOWER DRUM SONG(1961); STEEL CLAW, THE(1961); MADIGAN(1968); SUP-
POSE THEY GAVE A WAR AND NOBODY CAME?(1970)
1984
STAR TREK III: THE SEARCH FOR SPOCK(1984)
Ragnar Sorensen
PASSIONATE DEMONS, THE(1962, Norway), ph
Rickie Sorensen
MAN OF A THOUSAND FACES(1957); TARZAN'S FIGHT FOR LIFE(1958)
Bill Sorenson
HOUNDS... OF NOTRE DAME, THE(1980, Can.)
Erik Sorenson
CAT BALLOU(1965)
Fred Sorenson
RAIDERS OF THE LOST ARK(1981)

Heidi Sorenson
HISTORY OF THE WORLD, PART 1(1981)
Ingeborg Sorenson
TOP OF THE HEAP(1972); KRAMER VS. KRAMER(1979)
Laura Sorenson
1984
REPO MAN(1984)
Leilani Sorenson
PERSUADER, THE(1957)
Linda Sorenson
MERRY WIVES OF TOBIAS ROUKE, THE(1972, Can.); HARD PART BEGINS, THE(1973, Can.); PAPERBACK HERO(1973, Can.); STONE COLD DEAD(1980, Can.)
Paul Sorenson
DANCE WITH ME, HENRY(1956); BATTLE HYMN(1957); WOMEN OF PITCAIRN ISLAND, THE(1957); HANG'EM HIGH(1968); EXECUTIVE ACTION(1973); ONE LITTLE INDIAN(1973); ESCAPE TO WITCH MOUNTAIN(1975)
Peter Sorenson
DAY THE EARTH FROZE, THE(1959, Fin./USSR)
Rich Sorenson
CAT FROM OUTER SPACE, THE(1978)
Rickie Sorenson
HARD MAN, THE(1957); UNDERWORLD U.S.A.(1961); SWORD IN THE STONE, THE(1963)
Sylvia Sorente
CASTLE OF BLOOD(1964, Fr./Ital.)
Misc. Talkies
BIKINI PARADISE(1967)
Eva Soreny
ASSIGNMENT TO KILL(1968)
Paul Soreze
VERY PRIVATE AFFAIR, A(1962, Fr./Ital.); YOU ONLY LIVE ONCE(1969, Fr.), w
Adam Sorg
MOONSHINE MOUNTAIN(1964)
Dr. Ernst Sorge
S.O.S. ICEBERG(1933), tech adv
Michael Sorgeoff
LIFE AND TIMES OF CHESTER-ANGUS RAMSGOOD, THE(1971, Can.)
Sorges
DR. KNOCK(1936, Fr.)
Alberto Soria
TERROR IN THE JUNGLE(1968), ed
Florentino Soria
CALABUCH(1956, Span./Ital.), w
Mario Soria
OPERATION KID BROTHER(1967, Ital.)
Charo Soriano
VAMPIRE'S NIGHT ORGY, THE(1973, Span./Ital.)
Judy Soriano
Misc. Talkies
FORCE FOUR(1975)
Maria Luisa Soriano
KILL THEM ALL AND COME BACK ALONE(1970, Ital./Span.), ed; GRAVEYARD OF HORROR(1971, Span.), ed
Jim Soriero
1984
DELIVERY BOYS(1984)
Louis Sorin
LUCKY IN LOVE(1929); MOTHER'S BOY(1929); ANIMAL CRACKERS(1930); SEEDS OF FREEDOM(1943, USSR)
Alexandra Sorina
RASPUTIN(1932, Ger.)
Nina Sorina
RED AND THE WHITE, THE(1969, Hung./USSR)
Gaudeline Soriol
GAS(1981, Can.), cos
Marc Sorkin
SEEDS OF FREEDOM(1943, USSR), ed; SHANGHAI DRAMA, THE(1945, Fr.), p
Mare Sorkin
SINGING IN THE DARK(1956), ed
Edward Sorley
Silents
QUEEN'S EVIDENCE(1919, Brit.); NELL GWYNNE(1926, Brit.)
Janet Sorley
LAST HOUSE ON DEAD END STREET(1977)
Misc. Talkies
FUN HOUSE, THE(1977)
Frank Sorman [Francesco Sormano]
SECRET SEVEN, THE(1966, Ital./Span.)
Judy Soroka
NEON PALACE, THE(1970, Can.)
K. Sorokin
MEN OF THE SEA(1938, USSR); TAXI TO HEAVEN(1944, USSR); TRAIN GOES EAST, THE(1949, USSR); BOUNTIFUL SUMMER(1951, USSR); TIGER GIRL(1955, USSR)
Konstantin Sorokin
SONG OVER MOSCOW(1964, USSR); THREE SISTERS, THE(1969, USSR)
N. Sorokin
WAR AND PEACE(1968, USSR)
V. Sorokovov
MEET ME IN MOSCOW(1966, USSR)
Sam Sorono
POWERFORCE(1983)
Sonia Sorrel
STRANGE ILLUSION(1945)
George Sorrell
GOLDEN ARROW, THE(1936); CHARLIE CHAN AT MONTE CARLO(1937); YOUNG IN HEART, THE(1938); NAVY SECRETS(1939); HAIRY APE, THE(1944)

Karen Sorrell
FLIGHT INTO NOWHERE(1938); MYSTERIOUS MR. MOTO(1938); REAL GLORY, THE(1939)
Sally Sorrell
MAIDSTONE(1970)
Sonia Sorrell
CAPTAIN KIDD AND THE SLAVE GIRL(1954); HAROLD AND MAUDE(1971)
Ted Sorrell
LENNY(1974)
William Sorrelle
Misc. Silents
WHERE IS MY FATHER?(1916)
William J. Sorrelle
Misc. Silents
LITTLEST REBEL, THE(1914)
Bill Sorrells
BABY BLUE MARINE(1976); ROLLERCOASTER(1977); HEAVEN CAN WAIT(1978)
1984
FLETCH(1984)
Robert Sorrells
MORITURI(1965); GUNFIGHT IN ABILENE(1967); LAST CHALLENGE, THE(1967); RIDE TO HANGMAN'S TREE, THE(1967); DEATH OF A GUNFIGHTER(1969); MAN CALLED GANNON, A(1969)
William Sorrells
PRETTY POISON(1968)
Robert Sorrels
1984
FLETCH(1984)
Laura Sorrenson
1984
ANGEL(1984)
Paul Sorrenson
EVEL KNIEVEL(1971)
Sylvia Sorrente
SIN ON THE BEACH(1964, Fr.); POPPY IS ALSO A FLOWER, THE(1966)
Alberto Sorrentino
BOCCACCIO '70(1962/Ital./Fr.)
Bob Sorrentino
DAY OF THE ANIMALS(1977), ph
Claudio Sorrentino
MASOCH(1980, Ital.)
Martin Sorrentino
TRENCHCOAT(1983)
Rosanne Sorrentino
ANNIE(1982)
Walter Sors
SCHWEIK'S NEW ADVENTURES(1943, Brit.), p
Joe Della Sorte
GODFATHER, THE, PART II(1974)
Irma Sorter
Misc. Silents
SOUL ENSLAVED, A(1916)
Warren Sortomme
STALAG 17(1953)
Robert Sortsch-Pla
Silents
PASSION(1920, Ger.)
Lilian Sorval
HOT HOURS(1963, Fr.)
Liliane Sorval
MURMUR OF THE HEART(1971, Fr./Ital./Ger.)
George Sorvic
DEATHSTALKER(1983, Arg./U.S.)
1984
DEATHSTALKER, THE(1984)
Paul Sorvino
WHERE'S POPPA?(1970); MADE FOR EACH OTHER(1971); PANIC IN NEEDLE PARK(1971); DAY OF THE DOLPHIN, THE(1973); TOUCH OF CLASS, A(1973, Brit.); GAMBLER, THE(1974); SHOOT IT: BLACK, SHOOT IT: BLUE(1974); I WILL ...I WILL ...FOR NOW(1976); OH, GOD!(1977); BLOODBROTHERS(1978); BRINK'S JOB, THE(1978); SLOW DANCING IN THE BIG CITY(1978); LOST AND FOUND(1979); CRUISING(1980); REDS(1981); I, THE JURY(1982); MELANIE(1982, Can.); THAT CHAMPIONSHIP SEASON(1982); OFF THE WALL(1983)
Geo Anne Sosa
TRIAL OF BILLY JACK, THE(1974); MASTER GUNFIGHTER, THE(1975)
Guillermo Bravo Sosa
RUN FOR THE SUN(1956); ILLUSION TRAVELS BY STREETCAR, THE(1977, Mex.)
Mile Sosa
ROMANCE OF A HORSE THIEF(1971)
Robert Sosa
HIGH RISK(1981)
Roberto Martinez Sosa
1984
UNDER THE VOLCANO(1984)
Susan Sosa
BILLY JACK(1971); TRIAL OF BILLY JACK, THE(1974)
Vladimir Soshalsky
OTHELLO(1960, U.S.S.R.)
Sosimo
ON THE NICKEL(1980)
Henry Soskin
DON'T RAISE THE BRIDGE, LOWER THE RIVER(1968, Brit.)
Paul Soskin
TEN MINUTE ALIBI(1935, Brit.), p; WHILE PARENTS SLEEP(1935, Brit.), p; TWO'S COMPANY(1939, Brit.), p; QUIET WEDDING(1941, Brit.), p; AVENGERS, THE(1942, Brit.), p; WEAKER SEX, THE(1949, Brit.), p, w; HIGH TREASON(1951, Brit.), p; WATERFRONT WOMEN(1952, Brit.), p, w; TOP OF THE FORM(1953, Brit.), p; ALL FOR MARY(1956, Brit.), w; HAPPY IS THE BRIDE(1958, Brit.), p; LAW AND DISORDER(1958, Brit.), p

Pedro Soso
Silents
KAISER, BEAST OF BERLIN, THE(1918)
William Soso
1984
PREPPIES(1984)
Sosor-Rarma
SON OF MONGOLIA(1936, USSR)
P.H. Sosso
Misc. Silents
GIVING BECKY A CHANCE(1917)
Peitro Sosso
FIRST COMES COURAGE(1943)
Pete Sosso
PARIS CALLING(1941); SONG OF THE SARONG(1945); DOUBLE LIFE, A(1947); JOAN OF ARC(1948)
Pietro Sosso
LIGHT FINGERS(1929); LAST OF THE LONE WOLF(1930); MURDER ON THE ROOF(1930); BROKEN WING, THE(1932); JEALOUSY(1934); ADAM HAD FOUR SONS(1941); CODE OF THE LAWLESS(1945); DARK CORNER, THE(1946); MAGNIFICENT DOLL(1946); NIGHT IN PARADISE, A(1946); HIGH BARBAREE(1947)
Silents
RIP VAN WINKLE(1921); MIND OVER MOTOR(1923); ON THE GO(1925)
Misc. Silents
MARCELLINI MILLIONS, THE(1917)
Dina Sossoli
LOST HAPPINESS(1948, Ital.)
Hrovoje Sostaric
SOPHIE'S CHOICE(1982)
Jiri Sotala
BLACK SUN, THE(1979, Czech.), w
Dimas Sotello
BEAUTY AND THE BANDIT(1946); LOVES OF CARMEN, THE(1948); SALOME(1953); SECRET OF THE INCAS(1954)
Calvo Sotelo
GIRL FROM VALLADOLIO(1958, Span.), w
Mia Soteriou
FRENCH LIEUTENANT'S WOMAN, THE(1981)
Ann Sothern
BLIND DATE(1934); HELL CAT, THE(1934); KID MILLIONS(1934); LET'S FALL IN LOVE(1934); MELODY IN SPRING(1934); PARTY'S OVER, THE(1934); EIGHT BELLS(1935); FOLIES DERGERE(1935); GIRL FRIEND, THE(1935); GRAND EXIT(1935); HOORAY FOR LOVE(1935); DON'T GAMBLE WITH LOVE(1936); HELLSHIP MORGAN(1936); MY AMERICAN WIFE(1936); SMARTEST GIRL IN TOWN(1936); WALKING ON AIR(1936); YOU MAY BE NEXT(1936); DANGER–LOVE AT WORK(1937); DANGEROUS NUMBER(1937); FIFTY ROADS TO TOWN(1937); SUPER SLEUTH(1937); THERE GOES MY GIRL(1937); THERE GOES THE GROOM(1937); SHE'S GOT EVERYTHING(1938); TRADE WINDS(1938); FAST AND FURIOUS(1939); HOTEL FOR WOMEN(1939); JOE AND ETHEL TURP CALL ON THE PRESIDENT(1939); MAISIE(1939); BROTHER ORCHID(1940); CONGO MAISIE(1940); DULCY(1940); GOLD RUSH MAISIE(1940); LADY BE GOOD(1941); MAISIE WAS A LADY(1941); RINGSIDE MAISIE(1941); MAISIE GETS HER MAN(1942); PANAMA HATTIE(1942); CRY HAVOC(1943); SWING SHIFT MAISIE(1943); THOUSANDS CHEER(1943); THREE HEARTS FOR JULIA(1943); MAISIE GOES TO RENO(1944); UP GOES MAISIE(1946); UNDERCOVER MAISIE(1947); APRIL SHOWERS(1948); LETTER TO THREE WIVES, A(1948); JUDGE STEPS OUT, THE(1949); NANCY GOES TO RIO(1950); SHADOW ON THE WALL(1950); BLUE GARDENIA, THE(1953); BEST MAN, THE(1964); LADY IN A CAGE(1964); SYLVIA(1965); CHUBASCO(1968); KILLING KIND, THE(1973); GOLDEN NEEDLES(1974); CRAZY MAMA(1975); MANITOU, THE(1978); LITTLE DRAGONS, THE(1980)
E.H. Sothern
Misc. Silents
PRIMROSE PATH, THE(1915); CHATTEL, THE(1916); ENEMY TO THE KING, AN(1916); MAN OF MYSTERY, THE(1917)
Elsie Sothern
Silents
ALL WOMAN(1918)
Harry Sothern
Silents
NEW MOON, THE(1919); SECRETS OF PARIS, THE(1922)
Misc. Silents
BLIND WIVES(1920)
Hugh Sothern
BORDER G-MAN(1938); BUCCANEER, THE(1938); DANGEROUS TO KNOW(1938); FLIGHT TO FAME(1938); JUAREZ(1939); OKLAHOMA KID, THE(1939); $1,000 A TOUCHDOWN(1939); DIAMOND FRONTIER(1940); DISPATCH FROM REUTERS, A(1940); HOUSE OF THE SEVEN GABLES, THE(1940); LEGION OF THE LAWLESS(1940); MAN FROM DAKOTA, THE(1940); NORTHWEST PASSAGE(1940); YOUNG BUFFALO BILL(1940); BAD MEN OF MISSOURI(1941); MAD DOCTOR, THE(1941); MAN WITH TWO LIVES, THE(1942); TENNESSEE JOHNSON(1942); THEY DIED WITH THEIR BOOTS ON(1942)
Jean Sothern
DOWN THE WYOMING TRAIL(1939)
Misc. Silents
TWO ORPHANS, THE(1915); WHOSO TAKETH A WIFE(1916); HER GOOD NAME(1917); MISS DECEPTION(1917); MOTHER'S ORDEAL, A(1917); MUTE APPEAL, A(1917); PEG O' THE SEA(1917)
Lucille Sothern
FRESH FROM PARIS(1955), cos
Sam Sothern
Misc. Silents
DREAM CHEATER, THE(1920)
Hans Sotin
DER FREISCHUTZ(1970, Ger.); FIDELIO(1970, Ger.)
Carmen Sotir
MOONSHINE MOUNTAIN(1964)
Kopi Sotiropulos
PRIVATE BENJAMIN(1980); POSTMAN ALWAYS RINGS TWICE, THE(1981)

Bert Sotlar
SQUARE OF VIOLENCE(1963, U.S./Yugo.)
Angel Domenech Soto
Misc. Talkies
TWO WORLDS OF ANGELITA, THE(1982)
F. Soto
POCKET MONEY(1972)
Fernando Soto
INVASION OF THE VAMPIRES, THE(1961, Mex.); DAUGHTER OF DECEIT(1977, Mex.); ILLUSION TRAVELS BY STREETCAR, THE(1977, Mex.)
Frank Soto
LIFE AND TIMES OF JUDGE ROY BEAN, THE(1972)
Harve Soto
1984
HOME FREE ALL(1984)
Lorenzo Soto
1984
BEAT STREET(1984)
Richard Soto
BALLAD OF GREGORIO CORTEZ, THE(1983), ed
Roberto Soto
TROPIC HOLIDAY(1938)
Rosana Soto
SERIAL(1980)
Paul Sotoff
ANTHONY ADVERSE(1936)
Jesus Sotomayer
SANTO CONTRA BLUE DEMON EN LA ATLANTIDA(1968, Mex.), p
Jesus Sotomayor
CASTLE OF THE MONSTERS(1958, Mex.), p; LA NAVE DE LOS MONSTRUOS(1959, Mex.), p; SANTO Y BLUE DEMON CONTRA LOS MONSTRUOS(1968, Mex.), p
Jim Sotos
FORCED ENTRY(1975), p, d; TEXAS LIGHTNING(1981), p; SWEET SIXTEEN(1983), p&d
1984
HOT MOVES(1984), p&d
Liliane Sottane
UP THE CREEK(1958, Brit.); HEADLESS GHOST, THE(1959, Brit.)
Marilyn Sotto
JOE DAKOTA(1957), cos; KETTLES ON OLD MACDONALD'S FARM, THE(1957), cos; MONOLITH MONSTERS, THE(1957), cos
Rosana Sotto
IN-LAWS, THE(1979)
Tito Sotto
TNT JACKSON(1975), m
Vincent Sotto
CESAR(1936, Fr.), m
Zinedine Soualem
HANNAH K.(1983, Fr.)
Jean-Francois Soubielle
1984
RAZOR'S EDGE, THE(1984)
Cliff Soubier
PENROD AND HIS TWIN BROTHER(1938)
Clifford Soubier
BLACK LEGION, THE(1937); MR. DODD TAKES THE AIR(1937); THEY WON'T FORGET(1937); TOVARICH(1937)
Andre Soubiran
DOCTORS, THE(1956, Fr.), w
Andres Jose Cruz Soublette
TEOREMA(1969, Ital.)
Waslm Soubra
CIRCLE OF DECEIT(1982, Fr./Ger.)
Alain Souchon
1984
ONE DEADLY SUMMER(1984, Fr.)
Gerald Soucie
NATIONAL LAMPOON'S ANIMAL HOUSE(1978), makeup
Jerry Soucie
TILL DEATH(1978), makeup
Erika Soucy
LOVE IS A BALL(1963)
Hector Soucy
CONQUEST OF THE PLANET OF THE APES(1972)
Christine Souder
Misc. Talkies
STREET GIRLS(1975)
Bernard Soufflet
DEATH OF MARIO RICCI, THE(1983, Ital.)
Roger Soui
TANGA-TIKA(1953)
Robert Soukis
CHAFED ELBOWS(1967), ed; NO MORE EXCUSES(1968), ed
Antonin Soukup
MOST BEAUTIFUL AGE, THE(1970, Czech.)
David Soul
JOHNNY GOT HIS GUN(1971); MAGNUM FORCE(1973); DOGPOUND SHUFFLE(1975, Can.); STICK UP, THE(1978, Brit.)
Louis Soulanes
FRUIT IS RIPE, THE(1961, Fr./Ital.), d&w; FIVE WILD GIRLS(1966, Fr.), w; PLAYMATES(1969, Fr./Ital.), d&w
Olan Soule
LADY TAKES A SAILOR, THE(1949); DESTINATION BIG HOUSE(1950); PEGGY(1950); CUBAN FIREBALL(1951); DAY THE EARTH STOOD STILL, THE(1951); YOU NEVER CAN TELL(1951); ATOMIC CITY, THE(1952); DON'T BOTHER TO KNOCK(1952); MONKEY BUSINESS(1952); NEVER WAVE AT A WAC(1952); STARS AND STRIPES FOREVER(1952); STORY OF WILL ROGERS, THE(1952); CALL ME MADAM(1953); DRAGNET(1954); FRANCIS JOINS THE WACS(1954); HUMAN DESIRE(1954); PHFFFT!(1954); CULT OF THE COBRA(1955); DADDY LONG LEGS(1955); PRINCE OF PLAYERS(1955); QUEEN BEE(1955); THIS ISLAND

EARTH(1955); CASH McCALL(1960); THIRTEEN WEST STREET(1962); SHOCK TREATMENT(1964); CINCINNATI KID, THE(1965); BUBBLE, THE(1967); DESTRUCTORS, THE(1968); SEVEN MINUTES, THE(1971); FANTASTIC PLANET(1973, Fr./Czech.); TOWERING INFERNO, THE(1974); APPLE DUMPLING GANG, THE(1975); SHAGGY D.A., THE(1976); ST. IVES(1976)

Peter Soule
STRANGE AFFECTION(1959, Brit.)

Dale Soules
PRISM(1971)
Misc. Talkies
PRISM(1971)

Paul Soulignac
MANDABI(1970, Fr./Senegal), ph

Frederick Soult
Silents
RAIDERS, THE(1921)

Sounds Incorporated
RING-A-DING RHYTHM(1962, Brit.); JUST FOR FUN(1963, Brit.); SING AND SWING(1964, Brit.)

Souplex
CAROLINE CHERIE(1951, Fr.)

Raymond Souplex
MANON(1950, Fr.); MR. PEEK-A-BOO(1951, Fr.); ROYAL AFFAIRS IN VERSAILLES(1957, Fr.); FIRE IN THE FLESH(1964, Fr.)

Francois Sourissier
DIANE'S BODY(1969, Fr./Czech.), w

Tania Sourseva
CHARLES AND LUCIE(1982, Fr.)

Jane Sourza
FRENCH TOUCH, THE(1954, Fr.)

John Philip Sousa
STARS AND STRIPES FOREVER(1952), w; ONCE MORE, WITH FEELING(1960), m; ISADORA(1968, Brit.), m; STING, THE(1973), m; DOC SAVAGE... THE MAN OF BRONZE(1975), m; FIRST FAMILY(1980), m

Lynn Sousa
LATIN LOVERS(1953)

W. Sousania
Silents
YANKEE CLIPPER, THE(1927)

Nicholas Soussainin
Misc. Silents
SPOTLIGHT, THE(1927)

Nicholas Soussanin
UNDER TWO FLAGS(1936); SQUALL, THE(1929); ARE YOU THERE?(1930); CRIMINAL CODE(1931); DAUGHTER OF THE DRAGON(1931); WHITE SHOULDERS(1931); PARISIAN ROMANCE, A(1932); MAN WHO BROKE THE BANK AT MONTE CARLO, THE(1935); ARTISTS AND MODELS ABROAD(1938); THOSE HIGH GREY WALLS(1939); MY LIFE WITH CAROLINE(1941)
Silents
ADORATION(1928); LAST COMMAND, THE(1928); NIGHT WATCH, THE(1928)

Brigitte Sousselier
JONAH–WHO WILL BE 25 IN THE YEAR 2000(1976, Switz.), ed; LIGHT YEARS AWAY(1982, Fr./Switz.), ed

Ali Soussi
ALL AT SEA(1970, Brit.)

Jean Soustre
RISE OF LOUIS XIV, THE(1970, Fr.)

Andrew Soutar
WORLDLY GOODS(1930), w; ALMOST MARRIED(1932), w; MAN CALLED BACK, THE(1932), w
Silents
GREAT GAME, THE(1918, Brit.), w; COURAGE(1921), w; LOVE'S REDEMPTION(1921), w; IN THE BLOOD(1923, Brit.), w

Farren Soutar
BLACK ABBOT, THE(1934, Brit.); CRUCIFIX, THE(1934, Brit.)

John Soutar
LAST JOURNEY, THE(1936, Brit.), w

Renee Soutendijk
GIRL WITH THE RED HAIR, THE(1983, Neth.); SPETTERS(1983, Holland)
1984
FOURTH MAN, THE(1984, Neth.)

Farren Souter
IRON DUKE, THE(1935, Brit.)

Ann South
ANNA KARENINA(1948, Brit.)

Harry South
BIG SWITCH, THE(1970, Brit.), m

Leonard South
HANG'EM HIGH(1968), ph; I SAILED TO TAHITI WITH AN ALL GIRL CREW(1969), ph; FAMILY PLOT(1976), ph

Leonard J. South
HERBIE GOES TO MONTE CARLO(1977), ph; NORTH AVENUE IRREGULARS, THE(1979), ph; AMY(1981), ph

Ivan Southall
LET THE BALLOON GO(1977, Aus.), w

Suzy Southam
1984
CHILDREN OF THE CORN(1984)

T. W. Southam
SUICIDE MISSION(1956, Brit.)

Bennett Southard
Silents
SECOND HAND ROSE(1922); INTO NO MAN'S LAND(1928), w; MAKING THE VARSITY(1928), w

H. D. Southard
Silents
AMERICAN BUDS(1918)

Harry Southard
Silents
SECRET LOVE(1916)
Misc. Silents
BROADWAY PEACOCK, THE(1922)

Ruth Southard
NO SAD SONGS FOR ME(1950), w

Bryan Southcombe
MAN WITH TWO HEADS, THE(1972)

Colin Southcott
MASQUE OF THE RED DEATH, THE(1964, U.S./Brit.), set d; DIE, MONSTER, DIE(1965, Brit.), art d; TOMB OF LIGEIA, THE(1965, Brit.), art d

Fleet Southcott
BLOOD ARROW(1958), ph; VIOLENT ONES, THE(1967), ph

John Souther
SNAFU(1945)

Roy Southerland
Misc. Silents
PRINCESS OF PATCHES, THE(1917)

Eve Southern
HAUNTED HOUSE, THE(1928); WHISPERING WINDS(1929); LILIES OF THE FIELD(1930); MOROCCO(1930); FIGHTING CARAVANS(1931); LAW OF THE SEA(1932); GHOST WALKS, THE(1935)
Misc. Talkies
VOICE WITHIN, THE(1929)
Silents
AFTER THE SHOW(1921); RAGE OF PARIS, THE(1921); NICE PEOPLE(1922); SOULS FOR SALE(1923); GAUCHO, THE(1928); STORMY WATERS(1928)
Misc. Silents
CONSCIENCE(1917); GOLDEN GALLOWS, THE(1922); WOMAN OF THE SEA, A(1926); WILD GEESE(1927); CLOTHES MAKE THE WOMAN(1928); NAUGHTY DUCHESS, THE(1928)

Fred Southern
Silents
EUGENE ARAM(1914, Brit.)

Harry Southern
Silents
WHILE NEW YORK SLEEPS(1920)

Jean Southern
Misc. Silents
DR. RAMEAU(1915)

Jeri Southern
I, MOBSTER(1959)

Kathleen Southern
TOMCAT, THE(1968, Brit.)

Linda Southern
Misc. Talkies
AMAZING TRANSPLANT, THE(1970)

Lucille Southern
ESCAPE TO BURMA(1955), cos

Richard Southern
HANKY-PANKY(1982)

Roland Southern
RENEGADES OF THE WEST(1932)

Sam Southern
Silents
HIS MAJESTY THE AMERICAN(1919)
Misc. Silents
WHISPERING DEVILS(1920)

Terry Southern
DR. STRANGELOVE: OR HOW I LEARNED TO STOP WORRYING AND LOVE THE BOMB(1964), w; CINCINNATI KID, THE(1965), w; LOVED ONE, THE(1965), w; BARBARELLA(1968, Fr./Ital.), w; CANDY(1968, Ital./Fr.), w; EASY RIDER(1969), w; MAGIC CHRISTIAN, THE(1970, Brit.), w

Tom Southern
HARLEM RIDES THE RANGE(1939)

Tommy Southern
LOOK OUT SISTER(1948)

Virginia Southern
Silents
BIG TREMAINE(1916)
Misc. Silents
WYOMING WILDCAT, THE(1925)

Robert Southey
Silents
NELSON(1918, Brit.), w; NELSON(1926, Brit.), w

Michael Southgate
MAHLER(1974, Brit.)

Bennett Southhard
Misc. Silents
DRAGON, THE(1916)

Ben Southland
STEEL HELMET, THE(1951), spec eff

Rev. G.E. Southon
TEN COMMANDMENTS, THE(1956), w

Larry Southwick
JIM, THE WORLD'S GREATEST(1976)

Charlie Southwood
Misc. Talkies
THEY CALL ME HALLELUJAH(1973)

John Southworth
SECRET OF BLOOD ISLAND, THE(1965, Brit.)

Ken Southworth
SHINBONE ALLEY(1971), anim

Tommy Southworth
RAINBOW OVER THE RANGE(1940)

Ignacio Souto
TERRACE, THE(1964, Arg.), ph

Ben Soutten
 TIGER BAY(1933, Brit.); CHILDREN OF THE FOG(1935, Brit.); CRIMES OF STEPHEN HAWKE, THE(1936, Brit.); PHANTOM SHIP(1937, Brit.); UNDER THE RED ROBE(1937, Brit.); MUTINY OF THE ELSINORE, THE(1939, Brit.)
Ben Graham Soutten
 VANDERGILT DIAMOND MYSTERY, THE(1936)
Graham Soutten
 OVERNIGHT(1933, Brit.)
Graham [Ben] Soutten
 SIGN OF FOUR, THE(1932, Brit.)
Marcelle Souty
 Misc. Silents
 NARAYANA(1920, Fr.)
Mathe Souverbie
 POURQUOI PAS!(1979, Fr.)
Art Souvern
 RUSTLERS(1949)
Pierre Souvestre
 FANTOMAS(1966, Fr./Ital.), w
Cecilia Souza
 MEMENTO MEI(1963)
Emory Souza
 DIRTY HARRY(1971); LITTLE CIGARS(1973); EVIL, THE(1978)
A. Sova
 TRAIN GOES TO KIEV, THE(1961, USSR)
Peter Sova
 SHORT EYES(1977), ph; ROCKERS(1980), ph; DINER(1982), ph
Fabijan Sovagovic
 EVENT, AN(1970, Yugo.); SCALAWAG(1973, Yugo.); RAT SAVIOUR, THE(1977, Yugo.); MEETINGS WITH REMARKABLE MEN(1979, Brit.)
Jiri Sovak
 WHO KILLED JESSIE?(1965, Czech.); 90 DEGREES IN THE SHADE(1966, Czech./ Brit.); I KILLED EINSTEIN, GENTLEMEN(1970, Czech.); SIR, YOU ARE A WIDOW-ER(1971, Czech.); WHAT WOULD YOU SAY TO SOME SPINACH(1976, Czech.)
G. Sovchis
 SANDU FOLLOWS THE SUN(1965, USSR)
Victor Soverall
 6.5 SPECIAL(1958, Brit.)
Whitey Sovern
 TEXANS, THE(1938)
Walter Sovkis
 SUSPENSE(1930, Brit.), ed
A. Sovolev
 VOW, THE(1947, USSR.)
Serigne Sow
 MANDABI(1970, Fr./Senegal)
Maj Sowall
 KAMIKAZE '89(1983, Ger.), w
George Sowards
 WILD GIRL(1932); CRIMSON TRAIL, THE(1935); CROOKED RIVER(1950); HOS-TILE COUNTRY(1950)
Jack Sowards
 TANK COMMANDOS(1959)
Jack B. Sowards
 STAR TREK II: THE WRATH OF KHAN(1982), w
Edward Sowders
 Silents
 GREED(1925), art d
Barbara Hudson Sowers
 Misc. Talkies
 MACBETH(1950)
Paula Sowl
 I WAS A COMMUNIST FOR THE F.B.I.(1951); OPERATION SECRET(1952); SPRING-FIELD RIFLE(1952)
Diana Sowle
 WILLY WONKA AND THE CHOCOLATE FACTORY(1971)
Carl Eric Soya
 ERIC SOYA'S "17"(1967, Den.), w
Maj Soya
 WEEKEND(1964, Den.), ed; EPILOGUE(1967, Den.), ed
Wole Soyinka
 KONGI'S HARVEST(1971, U.S./Nigeria), a, w
Marti Soyoa
 D.C. CAB(1983)
Joyce Sozen
 1984
 HOME FREE ALL(1984)
Agnes Spaak
 SWEET ECSTASY(1962, Fr.); WHITE, RED, YELLOW, PINK(1966, Ital.); BETTER A WIDOW(1969, Ital.); LOVE FACTORY(1969, Ital.)
Catherine Spaak
 EASY LIFE, THE(1963, Ital.); THREE FACES OF SIN(1963, Fr./Ital.); CRAZY DESIRE(1964, Ital.); EIGHTEEN IN THE SUN(1964, Ital.); EMPTY CANVAS, THE(1964, Fr./Ital.); NIGHT WATCH, THE(1964, Fr./Ital.); OF WAYWARD LO-VE(1964, Ital./Ger.); CIRCLE OF LOVE(1965, Fr.); LITTLE NUNS, THE(1965, Ital.); SIX DAYS A WEEK(1966, Fr./Ital./Span.); WEEKEND AT DUNKIRK(1966, Fr./Ital.); HOTEL(1967); MADE IN ITALY(1967, Fr./Ital.); DROP DEAD, MY LOVE(1968, Italy); MAN WITH THE BALLOONS, THE(1968, Ital./Fr.); IF IT'S TUESDAY, THIS MUST BE BELGIUM(1969); THREE NIGHTS OF LOVE(1969, Ital.); CERTAIN, VERY CERTAIN, AS A MATTER OF FACT... PROBABLE(1970, Ital.); CAT O'NINE TAILS(1971, Ital./Ger./Fr.); RIPPED-OFF(1971, Ital.); DIARY OF A CLOISTERED NUN(1973, Ital./Fr./Ger.); TAKE A HARD RIDE(1975, U.S./Ital.); SUNDAY LO-VERS(1980, Ital./Fr.)
Charles Spaak
 CARNIVAL IN FLANDERS(1936, Fr.), w; LOWER DEPTHS, THE(1937, Fr.), w; GRAND ILLUSION(1938, Fr.), w; SACRIFICE OF HONOR(1938, Fr.), w; THEY WERE FIVE(1938, Fr.), w; END OF A DAY, THE(1939, Fr.), w; ESCAPE FROM YESTER-DAY(1939, Fr.), w; MAN OF THE HOUR, THE(1940, Fr.), w; TWO WOMEN(1940, Fr.), w; HATRED(1941, Fr.), w; HEART OF A NATION, THE(1943, Fr.), w; ETERNAL HUSBAND, THE(1946, Fr.), w; PANIQUE(1947, Fr.), w; BLIND DESIRE(1948, Fr.), w;

IDIOT, THE(1948, Fr.), w; WOMAN WHO DARED(1949, Fr.), w; CAPTAIN BLACK JACK(1952, U.S./Fr.), w; SEVEN DEADLY SINS, THE(1953, Fr./Ital.), w; FLESH AND THE WOMAN(1954, Fr./Ital.), w; ADORABLE CREATURES(1956, Fr.), w; LE CIEL EST A VOUS(1957, Fr.), w; ADULTERESS, THE(1959, Fr.), w; CHEATERS, THE(1961, Fr.), w; CARTOUCHE(1962, Fr./Ital.), w; GERMINAL(1963, Fr.), w; MAG-NIFICENT SINNER(1963, Fr.), w; MATHIAS SANDORF(1963, Fr.), w; TWO ARE GUILTY(1964, Fr.), w
Dan Spaccarelli
 SYNANON(1965)
Giorgio Spaccarelli
 HELL RAIDERS OF THE DEEP(1954, Ital.)
Arthur Space
 BUGLE SOUNDS, THE(1941); RIOT SQUAD(1941); ANDY HARDY'S DOUBLE LIFE(1942); QUIET PLEASE, MURDER(1942); RANDOM HARVEST(1942); REUNION IN FRANCE(1942); RIO RITA(1942); TISH(1942); TORTILLA FLAT(1942); DANCING MASTERS, THE(1943); GUY NAMED JOE, A(1943); HEAVENLY BODY, THE(1943); THEY CAME TO BLOW UP AMERICA(1943); THIS IS THE ARMY(1943); WHISTLING IN BROOKLYN(1943); BIG NOISE, THE(1944); GENTLE ANNIE(1944); GHOST THAT WALKS ALONE, THE(1944); MARRIAGE IS A PRIVATE AFFAIR(1944); RATION-ING(1944); WILSON(1944); ABBOTT AND COSTELLO IN HOLLYWOOD(1945); CRIM-SON CANARY(1945); LEAVE IT TO BLONDIE(1945); OUR VINES HAVE TENDER GRAPES(1945); WOMAN IN THE WINDOW, THE(1945); BAD BASCOMB(1946); BLACK BEAUTY(1946); BOYS' RANCH(1946); COCKEYED MIRACLE, THE(1946); COURAGE OF LASSIE(1946); HOME IN OKLAHOMA(1946); MAGNIFICENT DOLL(1946); MYSTERIOUS MR. VALENTINE, THE(1946); SECRET OF THE WHIS-TLER(1946); BIG TOWN AFTER DARK(1947); CRIMSON KEY, THE(1947); GUILT OF JANET AMES, THE(1947); HER HUSBAND'S AFFAIRS(1947); I LOVE TROU-BLE(1947); INVISIBLE WALL, THE(1947); MILLIE'S DAUGHTER(1947); RED HOUSE, THE(1947); RUSTLERS OF DEVIL'S CANYON(1947); FIGHTER SQUA-DRON(1948); FULLER BRUSH MAN(1948); HOMECOMING(1948); JOAN OF ARC(1948); PALEFACE, THE(1948); SILVER RIVER(1948); SOUTHERN YANKEE, A(1948); TAP ROOTS(1948); WALK A CROOKED MILE(1948); CHICAGO DEAD-LINE(1949); EL PASO(1949); LONE WOLF AND HIS LADY, THE(1949); LUST FOR GOLD(1949); MARY RYAN, DETECTIVE(1949); MISS GRANT TAKES RICH-MOND(1949); MR. BELVEDERE GOES TO COLLEGE(1949); SHOCKPROOF(1949); SORROWFUL JONES(1949); FATHER IS A BACHELOR(1950); FULLER BRUSH GIRL, THE(1950); GOOD HUMOR MAN, THE(1950); KILLER THAT STALKED NEW YORK, THE(1950); VANISHING WESTERNER, THE(1950); BAREFOOT MAILMAN, THE(1951); HER FIRST ROMANCE(1951); NIGHT RIDERS OF MONTANA(1951); THREE GUYS NAMED MIKE(1951); TOMAHAWK(1951); UTAH WAGON TRAIN(1951); AFRICAN TREASURE(1952); FARGO(1952); FEUDIN' FOOLS(1952); HERE COME THE MARINES(1952); JET JOB(1952); RAINBOW 'ROUND MY SHOUL-DER(1952); SOUND OFF(1952); BACK TO GOD'S COUNTRY(1953); CLIPPED WINGS(1953); CONFIDENTIAL CONNIE(1953); LAST OF THE PONY RIDERS(1953); TARGET EARTH(1954); YANKEE PASHA(1954); FOXFIRE(1955); MAN ALONE, A(1955); SPOILERS, THE(1955); SPIRIT OF ST. LOUIS, THE(1957); 20 MILLION MILES TO EARTH(1957); TWILIGHT FOR THE GODS(1958); DAY OF THE OUT-LAW(1959); SUMMER PLACE, A(1959); GUNFIGHTERS OF ABILENE(1960); TAG-GART(1964); SHAKIEST GUN IN THE WEST, THE(1968); TERROR HOUSE(1972); FRASIER, THE SENSUOUS LION(1973); BAT PEOPLE, THE(1974); MANSION OF THE DOOMED(1976); SWARM, THE(1978); ON THE NICKEL(1980)
Sissy Spacek
 PRIME CUT(1972); GINGER IN THE MORNING(1973); BADLANDS(1974); PHAN-TOM OF THE PARADISE(1974), set d; CARRIE(1976); WELCOME TO L.A.(1976); THREE WOMEN(1977); HEART BEAT(1979); COAL MINER'S DAUGHTER(1980); RAGGEDY MAN(1981); MISSING(1982)
 1984
 RIVER, THE(1984)
John Spacey
 MAN WHO BROKE THE BANK AT MONTE CARLO, THE(1935); CHINA CLIP-PER(1936); MR. DODD TAKES THE AIR(1937); PAROLE RACKET(1937); WOMEN OF GLAMOUR(1937); FOUR MEN AND A PRAYER(1938); WHO KILLED GAIL PRES-TON?(1938); SPECIAL INSPECTOR(1939); STORY OF ALEXANDER GRAHAM BELL, THE(1939)
John G. Spacey
 WIDOW FROM MONTE CARLO, THE(1936); MURDER IS NEWS(1939)
John Graham Spacey
 MOON'S OUR HOME, THE(1936); THANK YOU, JEEVES(1936); SERGEANT MUR-PHY(1938); RAFFLES(1939); BRITISH INTELLIGENCE(1940)
Charles Spadard
 PORKY'S(1982)
Adriana Spadaro
 HERCULES(1983), cos
Giuseppe Spadaro
 SHOE SHINE(1947, Ital.)
Grazia Spadaro
 FATAL DESIRE(1953)
Italia Spadaro
 SEDUCED AND ABANDONED(1964, Fr./Ital.)
Michele Spadaro
 THEY CALL ME TRINITY(1971, Ital.)
Odoardo Spadaro
 GOLDEN COACH, THE(1953, Fr./Ital.); DIVORCE, ITALIAN STYLE(1962, Ital.); CAPTIVE CITY, THE(1963, Ital.); NAKED HOURS, THE(1964, Ital.); CONQUERED CITY(1966, Ital.)
Pepino Spadaro
 RING AROUND THE CLOCK(1953, Ital.)
Umberto Spadaro
 FURIA(1947, Ital.); DIFFICULT YEARS(1950, Ital.); ANGELO(1951, Ital.); ANGELO IN THE CROWD(1952, Ital.); BRIEF RAPTURE(1952, Ital.); FATAL DESIRE(1953); JOURNEY TO LOVE(1953, Ital.); APPOINTMENT FOR MURDER(1954, Ital.); FARE-WELL TO ARMS, A(1957); SEDUCED AND ABANDONED(1964, Fr./Ital.); EYE OF THE NEEDLE, THE(1965, Ital./Fr.); VERY HANDY MAN, A(1966, Fr./Ital.)
Spade Cooley and his Orchestra
 SINGING SHERIFF, THE(1944); SENORITA FROM THE WEST(1945)
Guido Spadea
 WHITE SISTER(1973, Ital./Span./Fr.)

Charlie Spademan
PERMANENT VACATION(1982)
Jimmy Spader
ENDLESS LOVE(1981)
Letizia Spadini
LA DOLCE VITA(1961, Ital./Fr.)
Annabella Spadon
MAGIC WORLD OF TOPO GIGIO, THE(1961, Ital.), animation
Giacomo Spadoni
MR. IMPERIUM(1951)
Luciano Spadoni
WITCH'S CURSE, THE(1963, Ital.), set d; MADE IN ITALY(1967, Fr./Ital.), art d;
ROVER, THE(1967, Ital.), set d; GOODNIGHT, LADIES AND GENTLEMEN(1977,
Ital.), art d; COMIN' AT YA!(1981), art d, cos; LONELY LADY, THE(1983), art d;
TREASURE OF THE FOUR CROWNS(1983, Span./U.S.), art d
1984
SAHARA(1984), prod d
Pierre Spadoni
RISE OF LOUIS XIV, THE(1970, Fr.)
Merrie Spaeth
WORLD OF HENRY ORIENT, THE(1964)
William Spaeth
SALOME(1953)
Dave Spafford
SECRET OF NIMH, THE(1982), anim
Robert Spafford
HEAVEN ON EARTH(1960, Ital./U.S.), d&w; CHRISTINE KEELER AFFAIR,
THE(1964, Brit.), d, w
Anna Spaghetti
MALOU(1983), cos
Genaro Spagneli
I'LL TAKE ROMANCE(1937)
Giuseppe Spagnitti
LEOPARD, THE(1963, Ital.)
A. Spagnoli
GREAT WHITE, THE(1982, Ital.), ph
Albert Spagnoli
DAISY MILLER(1974), ph
Alberto Spagnoli
LA BABY SITTER(1975, Fr./Ital./Ger.), ph; KILLER FISH(1979, Ital./Braz.), ph;
HERCULES(1983), ph
Genaro Spagnoli
RUGGLES OF RED GAP(1935); TOP HAT(1935); LOVE ON THE RUN(1936);
MAYTIME(1937)
Philomena Spagnolo
GLORIA(1980)
Billy Spagnuolo
MANIAC(1980)
Denise Spagnuolo
MANIAC(1980)
Diane Spagnuolo
MANIAC(1980)
Filomena Spagnuolo
NUNZIO(1978); EASY MONEY(1983)
Paul Spahn
PARSON AND THE OUTLAW, THE(1957); MUSTANG(1959)
Fay Spain
ABDUCTORS, THE(1957); DRAGSTRIP GIRL(1957); TEENAGE DOLL(1957);
CROOKED CIRCLE, THE(1958); GOD'S LITTLE ACRE(1958); AL CAPONE(1959);
BEAT GENERATION, THE(1959); PRIVATE LIVES OF ADAM AND EVE, THE(1961);
BLACK GOLD(1963); HERCULES AND THE CAPTIVE WOMEN(1963, Fr./Ital.);
THUNDER ISLAND(1963); FLIGHT TO FURY(1966, U.S./Phil.); GENTLE RAIN,
THE(1966, Braz.); WELCOME TO HARD TIMES(1967); NAKED ZOO, THE zero(1970);
TODD KILLINGS, THE(1971); GODFATHER, THE, PART II(1974)
Mark Spain
BUSH CHRISTMAS(1983, Aus.)
Nancy Spain
SING AND SWING(1964, Brit.)
Roda Spain
SCAVENGERS, THE(1969)
Earl Spainard
HE WALKED BY NIGHT(1948); MEXICAN HAYRIDE(1948); HAS ANYBODY SEEN
MY GAL?(1952); SEMINOLE(1953); SIMON, KING OF THE WITCHES(1971)
George Spalding
WOMAN'S WORLD(1954)
Harry Spalding
FRECKLES(1960), p, w; SEVEN WOMEN FROM HELL(1961), p; FIREBRAND,
THE(1962), w; WOMAN HUNT(1962), w; DAY MARS INVADED EARTH, THE(1963),
w; POLICE NURSE(1963), w; YOUNG SWINGERS, THE(1963), w; EARTH DIES
SCREAMING, THE(1964, Brit.), w; WITCHCRAFT(1964, Brit.), w; CURSE OF THE
FLY(1965, Brit.), w; SPACEFLIGHT IC-1(1965, Brit.), w; MURDER GAME, THE(1966,
Brit.), w; ONE LITTLE INDIAN(1973), w; WATCHER IN THE WOODS, THE(1980,
Brit.), w
Ken Spalding
DIMENSION 5(1966)
Kim Spalding
EXPERIMENT ALCATRAZ(1950); GUNFIGHTER, THE(1950); JACKPOT,
THE(1950); HURRICANE SMITH(1952); OFF LIMITS(1953); MAN ALONE, A(1955); IT!
THE TERROR FROM BEYOND SPACE(1958); TRUE STORY OF LYNN STUART,
THE(1958)
Nellie Parker Spalding
Silents
INNER MAN, THE(1922)
Sherry Spalding
OREGON TRAIL, THE(1959)
Thomas Spalding
BLOB, THE(1958), ph

Thomas E. Spalding
THUNDER IN DIXIE(1965), ph; HOT ROD HULLABALOO(1966), ph; WAY
OUT(1966), ph
Erminio Spalia
DEPORTED(1950)
Timothy Spall
MISSIONARY, THE(1982); REMEMBRANCE(1982, Brit.)
Erminio Spalla
NAKED MAJA, THE(1959, Ital./U.S.); PRISONER OF THE IRON MASK(1962,
Fr./Ital.); SAILOR FROM GIBRALTAR, THE(1967, Brit.)
Ermino Spalla
MIRACLE IN MILAN(1951, Ital.)
Ignazio Spalla
SHOOT LOUD, LOUDER... I DON'T UNDERSTAND(1966, Ital.)
Michael Spalletta
WILD SEASON(1968, South Africa)
Mario Spallino
NIGHT OF THE SHOOTING STARS, THE(1982, Ital.)
Daniele Spallone
STEPPE, THE(1963, Fr./Ital.)
Carlo Spandoni
BLACK VEIL FOR LISA, A(1969 Ital./Ger.)
Luciano Spandoni
GIRL AND THE GENERAL, THE(1967, Fr./Ital.), art d
Georges Spanelly
LA BETE HUMAINE(1938, Fr.); LA MARSEILLAISE(1938, Fr.); DOUBLE CRIME IN
THE MAGINOT LINE(1939, Fr.)
Laurette Spang
BATTLESTAR GALACTICA(1979)
Ron Spang
ANY WHICH WAY YOU CAN(1980), ed; FIREFOX(1982), ed
Joan Spangehl
UNHOLY ROLLERS(1972)
Dick Spangler
CONQUEST OF THE PLANET OF THE APES(1972)
Larry Spangler
SOUL OF NIGGER CHARLEY, THE(1973), p&d, w; JOSHUA(1976), p&d; CHANEL
SOLITAIRE(1981), p
Larry G. Spangler
LAST REBEL, THE(1971), p; LEGEND OF NIGGER CHARLEY, THE(1972), p, w
1984
BEAR, THE(1984), p
Misc. Talkies
KNIFE FOR THE LADIES, A(1973), d
Tod Spangler
1984
BEAR, THE(1984)
Filomena Spanguolo
1984
MOSCOW ON THE HUDSON(1984)
Spanish Peasants
MAN'S HOPE(1947, Span.)
Maarten Spanjer
SPETTERS(1983, Holland)
Patricia Spann
PARADISE ALLEY(1978)
Georges Spannelly
RISE OF LOUIS XIV, THE(1970, Fr.)
Joe Spano
AMERICAN GRAFFITI(1973); NORTHERN LIGHTS(1978); ROADIE(1980)
Misc. Talkies
WARLOCK MOON(1973)
Joseph Spano
ONE IS A LONELY NUMBER(1972)
Vincent Spano
OVER THE EDGE(1979); BABY, IT'S YOU(1983); BLACK STALLION RETURNS,
THE(1983); RUMBLE FISH(1983)
1984
ALPHABET CITY(1984)
Vinnie Spano
THE DOUBLE McGUFFIN(1979)
Isidore Sparber
MR. BUG GOES TO TOWN(1941), w
Izzy Sparber
GULLIVER'S TRAVELS(1939), w
Milko Sparemblek
LOVERS OF TERUEL, THE(1962, Fr.), a, ch
Paul Sparer
LOVING(1970); KING OF THE GYPSIES(1978)
John Sparey
MAN CALLED FLINTSTONE, THE(1966), anim; SHINBONE ALLEY(1971), anim;
HEY, GOOD LOOKIN'(1982), anim
Mary Spargarino
1984
DEATHSTALKER, THE(1984), set d
Donovan R. Sparhawk
INDEPENDENCE DAY(1983)
Lynden Sparhawk
SALUTE TO THE MARINES(1943), art d; LOST ANGEL(1944), art d
Don Spark
27TH DAY, THE(1957)
Muriel Spark
PRIME OF MISS JEAN BRODIE, THE(1969, Brit.), w; NASTY HABITS(1976,
Brit.), w
Muriel Sparke
DRIVER'S SEAT, THE(1975, Ital.), w
Pip Sparke
FATHER GOOSE(1964)

Jim Sparkman
THAT CHAMPIONSHIP SEASON(1982)
Billy Sparks
1984
PURPLE RAIN(1984)
Bob Sparks
WILD REBELS, THE(1967)
Bruce Sparks
LOVE MERCHANT, THE(1966), ph; WINDFLOWERS(1968), ph; CHILDRENS GAMES(1969), ph; MARCH OF THE SPRING HARE(1969), ph; FABLE, A(1971), ph; ROOMMATES(1971), ph
Bruce G. Sparks
SISTER-IN-LAW, THE(1975), ph
Cheryl Sparks
SILENT RUNNING(1972)
Dan Sparks
1984
RED DAWN(1984)
Don Sparks
Misc. Talkies
FAIRY TALES(1979)
Dee Gee Sparks
SON OF SINBAD(1955)
Fay Sparks
REFLECTIONS IN A GOLDEN EYE(1967)
Floyd Sparks
TOMAHAWK(1951)
Frances Sparks
Silents
ROMANCE OF HAPPY VALLEY, A(1919)
Frank Sparks
BLONDIE(1938), p; JAWS II(1978)
Frank James Sparks
1984
STAR TREK III: THE SEARCH FOR SPOCK(1984)
Jack Sparks
SUN VALLEY CYCLONE(1946); RANGERS RIDE, THE(1948); GOLDEN STALLION, THE(1949); SHOWDOWN, THE(1950)
Joselyn Sparks
WISHBONE, THE(1933, Brit.)
Kliss Sparks
SEVEN ALONE(1975)
Martha Lee Sparks
HAPPY DAYS(1930); SO THIS IS LONDON(1930); DADDY LONG LEGS(1931)
Ned Sparks
CANARY MURDER CASE, THE(1929); NOTHING BUT THE TRUTH(1929); STRANGE CARGO(1929); STREET GIRL(1929); CONSPIRACY(1930); DEVIL'S HOLIDAY, THE(1930); DOUBLE CROSS ROADS(1930); FALL GUY, THE(1930); LEATHERNECKING(1930); LOVE COMES ALONG(1930); CORSAIR(1931); IRON MAN, THE(1931); KEPT HUSBANDS(1931); SECRET CALL, THE(1931); BIG CITY BLUES(1932); BLESSED EVENT(1932); CRUSADER, THE(1932); ALICE IN WONDERLAND(1933); GOING HOLLYWOOD(1933); GOLD DIGGERS OF 1933(1933); LADY FOR A DAY(1933); SECRETS(1933); TOO MUCH HARMONY(1933); 42ND STREET(1933); DOWN TO THEIR LAST YACHT(1934); HI, NELLIE!(1934); IMITATION OF LIFE(1934); MARIE GALANTE(1934); PRIVATE SCANDAL(1934); SERVANTS' ENTRANCE(1934); SING AND LIKE IT(1934); GEORGE WHITE'S 1935 SCANDALS(1935); SWEET ADELINE(1935); SWEET MUSIC(1935); BRIDE WALKS OUT, THE(1936); COLLEGIATE(1936); ONE IN A MILLION(1936); THIS WAY PLEASE(1937); WAKE UP AND LIVE(1937); HAWAII CALLS(1938); STAR MAKER, THE(1939); TWO'S COMPANY(1939, Brit.); FOR BEAUTY'S SAKE(1941); STAGE DOOR CANTEEN(1943); MAGIC TOWN(1947)
Silents
IN SEARCH OF A SINNER(1920); WIDE-OPEN TOWN, A(1922); BRIGHT LIGHTS(1925); SOUL MATES(1925); AUCTION BLOCK, THE(1926); LOVE'S BLINDNESS(1926); MIKE(1926); OH, WHAT A NIGHT!(1926); WHEN THE WIFE'S AWAY(1926); ALIAS THE LONE WOLF(1927); ALIAS THE DEACON(1928); MAGNIFICENT FLIRT, THE(1928); ON TO RENO(1928)
Misc. Silents
GOOD REFERENCES(1920); BOND BOY, THE(1922); MONEY TALKS(1926)
Ned A. Sparks
MIRACLE MAN, THE(1932)
Silents
LITTLE MISS BROWN(1915); NOTHING BUT THE TRUTH(1920)
Preston Sparks
KING OF THE MOUNTAIN(1981)
1984
CITY HEAT(1984)
Randy Sparks
THUNDER ROAD(1958); BIG NIGHT, THE(1960); COLLEGE CONFIDENTIAL(1960); ADVANCE TO THE REAR(1964), m; ANGEL UNCHAINED(1970), m; HOW DO I LOVE THEE?(1970), m
Robert Sparks
IF I HAD A MILLION(1932), w; BEWARE SPOOKS(1939), p; BLONDIE BRINGS UP BABY(1939), p; BLONDIE MEETS THE BOSS(1939), p; BLONDIE TAKES A VACATION(1939), p; BLONDIE HAS SERVANT TROUBLE(1940), p; BLONDIE ON A BUDGET(1940), p; BLONDIE PLAYS CUPID(1940), p; BLONDIE GOES LATIN(1941), p; BLONDIE IN SOCIETY(1941), p; GO WEST, YOUNG LADY(1941), p; TILLIE THE TOILER(1941), p; BLONDIE FOR VICTORY(1942), p; BLONDIE GOES TO COLLEGE(1942), p; BLONDIE'S BLESSED EVENT(1942), p; DARING YOUNG MAN, THE(1942), p; MEET THE STEWARTS(1942), p; SHUT MY BIG MOUTH(1942), p; STATION WEST(1948), p; DANGEROUS PROFESSION, A(1949), p; EASY LIVING(1949), p; BORN TO BE BAD(1950), p; WALK SOFTLY, STRANGER(1950), p; HIS KIND OF WOMAN(1951), p; MY FORBIDDEN PAST(1951), p; LAS VEGAS STORY, THE(1952), p; AFFAIR WITH A STRANGER(1953), p; SHE COULDN'T SAY NO(1954), p; SON OF SINBAD(1955), p; HARD RIDE, THE(1971), ph
Tony Sparks
1984
TREASURE OF THE YANKEE ZEPHYR(1984)

Theodor Sparkuhl
ALF'S CARPET(1929, Brit.), ph; FLYING SCOTSMAN, THE(1929, Brit.), ph; INFORMER, THE(1929, Brit.), ph; LADY FROM THE SEA, THE(1929, Brit.), ph; COMPULSORY HUSBAND, THE(1930, Brit.), ph; HARMONY HEAVEN(1930, Brit.), ph; SUSPENSE(1930, Brit.), ph; MIDNIGHT CLUB(1933), ph; CARAVAN(1934), ph; LONE COWBOY(1934), ph; NO MORE WOMEN(1934), ph; COLLEGE SCANDAL(1935), ph; ENTER MADAME(1935), ph; FATHER BROWN, DETECTIVE(1935), ph; FOUR HOURS TO KILL(1935), ph; LAST OUTPOST, THE(1935), ph; SHIP CAFE(1935), ph; BIG BROADCAST OF 1937, THE(1936), ph; COLLEGE HOLIDAY(1936), ph; FORGOTTEN FACES(1936), ph; THIRTEEN HOURS BY AIR(1936), ph; YOURS FOR THE ASKING(1936), ph; HIGH, WIDE AND HANDSOME(1937), ph; INTERNES CAN'T TAKE MONEY(1937), ph; WELLS FARGO(1937), ph; DANGEROUS TO KNOW(1938), ph; IF I WERE KING(1938), ph; TEXANS, THE(1938), ph; TIP-OFF GIRLS(1938), ph; ALL WOMEN HAVE SECRETS(1939), ph; BEAU GESTE(1939), ph; LADY'S FROM KENTUCKY, THE(1939), ph; LIGHT THAT FAILED, THE(1939), ph; RULERS OF THE SEA(1939), ph; ST. LOUIS BLUES(1939), ph; OPENED BY MISTAKE(1940), ph; QUEEN OF THE MOB(1940), ph; RANGERS OF FORTUNE(1940), ph; SECOND CHORUS(1940), ph; WAY OF ALL FLESH, THE(1940), ph; AMONG THE LIVING(1941), ph; BUY ME THAT TOWN(1941), ph; MIDNIGHT ANGEL(1941), ph; THERE'S MAGIC IN MUSIC(1941), ph; WEST POINT WIDOW(1941), ph; DR. BROADWAY(1942), ph; GLASS KEY, THE(1942), ph; NIGHT PLANE FROM CHUNG-KING(1942), ph; REMARKABLE ANDREW, THE(1942), ph; STAR SPANGLED RHYTHM(1942), ph; STREET OF CHANCE(1942), ph; WAKE ISLAND(1942), ph; GOOD FELLOWS, THE(1943), ph; JOHNNY COME LATELY(1943), ph; SALUTE FOR THREE(1943), ph; OUR HEARTS WERE YOUNG AND GAY(1944), ph; 'TILL WE MEET AGAIN(1944), ph; BLOOD ON THE SUN(1945), ph; MURDER, HE SAYS(1945), ph; SALTY O'ROURKE(1945), ph; BACHELOR'S DAUGHTERS, THE(1946), ph; LA CHIENNE(1975, Fr.), ph
Silents
PASSION(1920, Ger.), ph; ONE ARABIAN NIGHT(1921, Ger.), ph
Sparky
RIOT SQUAD(1941)
Elliott Sparling
Misc. Silents
POWER OF LOVE, THE(1922); FORBIDDEN LOVER(1923)
Susan Sparling
COWARDS(1970)
Al Sparlis
SOMEWHERE IN THE NIGHT(1946)
Robert Sparr
SWINGIN' SUMMER, A(1965), d; MORE DEAD THAN ALIVE(1968), d; ONCE YOU KISS A STRANGER(1969), d
Anne Sparrow
Misc. Talkies
SINFUL DWARF, THE(1973)
Anita Sparrow
RECKLESS AGE(1944); SHAKE HANDS WITH MURDER(1944)
Anitra Sparrow
CARRIE(1952)
Bernice Sparrow
WILD, WILD PLANET, THE(1967, Ital.), cos
Bobby Sparrow
STARDUST(1974, Brit.); CONFESSIONS OF A POP PERFORMER(1975, Brit.); TO THE DEVIL A DAUGHTER(1976, Brit./Ger.)
Walter Sparrow
DR. TERROR'S HOUSE OF HORRORS(1965, Brit.)
Wendy Sparrow
INBREAKER, THE(1974, Can.)
Len Sparrowhawk
WILD GEESE, THE(1978, Brit.)
George Spartels
BLUE FIN(1978, Aus.)
Camilla Sparv
DEAD HEAT ON A MERRY-GO-ROUND(1966); MURDERERS' ROW(1966); TROUBLE WITH ANGELS, THE(1966); ASSIGNMENT K(1968, Brit.); HIGH COMMISSIONER, THE(1968, U.S./Brit.); DOWNHILL RACER(1969); MACKENNA'S GOLD(1969); GREEK TYCOON, THE(1978); WINTER KILLS(1979); CABOBLANCO(1981)
Neda Spasojevic
EVENT, AN(1970, Yugo.)
Emanuele Spatafora
THREE TOUGH GUYS(1974, U.S./Ital.)
Rolf Spath
WEEKEND AT DUNKIRK(1966, Fr./Ital.)
Tina Spathi
ASSAULT ON AGATHON(1976, Brit./Gr.)
Linda Spatz
PAYDAY(1972); KISS OF THE TARANTULA(1975)
Nell Spaugh
SUMMER HOLIDAY(1948)
Misc. Silents
FOUR HEARTS(1922)
Bill Spaulding
KNUTE ROCKNE–ALL AMERICAN(1940); JACKIE ROBINSON STORY, THE(1950)
Ernest Spaulding
Misc. Silents
GREAT GAY ROAD, THE(1920, Brit.)
G. S. Spaulding
Silents
MOLLY ENTANGLED(1917)
George Spaulding
CALL NORTHSIDE 777(1948); UP IN CENTRAL PARK(1948); ACCUSED, THE(1949); HOUSE OF STRANGERS(1949); LADY GAMBLES, THE(1949); LADY TAKES A SAILOR, THE(1949); WHITE HEAT(1949); KISS TOMORROW GOODBYE(1950); MAGNIFICENT YANKEE, THE(1950); WHEN WILLIE COMES MARCHING HOME(1950); LURE OF THE WILDERNESS(1952); SCARLET ANGEL(1952); PRESIDENT'S LADY, THE(1953)
George L. Spaulding
CHINESE RING, THE(1947); MYSTERY OF THE GOLDEN EYE, THE(1948); COUNTY FAIR(1950); MEET ME AT THE FAIR(1952)

Harry Spaulding
HOUSE OF THE DAMNED(1963), w; RAIDERS FROM BENEATH THE SEA(1964), w; SURF PARTY(1964), w; WILD ON THE BEACH(1965), w

Kathy Spaulding
BUGSY MALONE(1976, Brit.)

Nellie Spaulding
Misc. Silents
MIDNIGHT BRIDE, THE(1920)

Nellie P. Spaulding
Silents
SCHOOL DAYS(1921)
Misc. Silents
GOOD REFERENCES(1920); POWER WITHIN, THE(1921)

Nellie Parker Spaulding
Silents
HER GREAT CHANCE(1918); BRIDE FOR A NIGHT, A(1923); ONE MILLION IN JEWELS(1923)

Thomas E. Spaulding
BLACK JACK(1973), ph

Colin Spaull
NOBODY IN TOYLAND(1958, Brit.)

Elio Spaziani
GOSPEL ACCORDING TO ST. MATTHEW, THE(1966, Fr., Ital.)

Monique Spaziani
FOND MEMORIES(1982, Can.)

Robert Speaight
MAGIC BOW, THE(1947, Brit.)

Jean L. Speak
DICK TRACY(1945), set d

Tris Speaker
KID FROM CLEVELAND, THE(1949)

John Speaks
DANCING PIRATE(1936), p; LITTLE ORPHAN ANNIE(1938), p

Bernard Spear
ARRIVEDERCI, BABY!(1966, Brit.); BEDAZZLED(1967, Brit.); CHITTY CHITTY BANG BANG(1968, Brit.); GULLIVER'S TRAVELS(1977, Brit., Bel.); WOMBLING FREE(1977, Brit.); YENTL(1983)

Charles Spear
Misc. Silents
MAN WHO WOULDN'T TELL, THE(1918)

David Spear
CREATURE WASN'T NICE,THE(1981), m; FEAR NO EVIL(1981), m
1984
EXTERMINATOR 2(1984), m

Eric Spear
UNDERCOVER AGENT(1935, Brit.), m; GHOST SHIP(1953, Brit.), m; SHADOW MAN(1953, Brit.), m; BANG! YOU'RE DEAD(1954, Brit.), m; GOLDEN LINK, THE(1954; Brit.), m; STRANGER FROM VENUS, THE(1954, Brit.), m; TOO HOT TO HANDLE(1961, Brit.), m; VULTURE, THE(1967, U.S./Brit./Can.), m

Harry Spear
PATSY, THE(1964)

Tony Spear
I'M ALL RIGHT, JACK(1959, Brit.)

Walter Spear
PLAY MISTY FOR ME(1971)

Walter M. Spear
SPEEDTRAP(1978), w

Dorothy Speare
ONE NIGHT OF LOVE(1934), w

James O. Spearing
DEVIL TIGER(1934), w
Silents
SIGNAL TOWER, THE(1924), w; ICE FLOOD, THE(1926), w

Frank H. Spearman
WHISPERING SMITH SPEAKS(1935), w; WHISPERING SMITH(1948), w; WHISPERING SMITH VERSUS SCOTLAND YARD(1952, Brit.), w
Silents
NAN OF MUSIC MOUNTAIN(1917), w

Frank Hamilton Spearman
Silents
WHISPERING SMITH(1926), w; NIGHT FLYER, THE(1928), w

Janet Spearman
SECRETS OF SEX(1970, Brit.)

Bee Spears
HONEYSUCKLE ROSE(1980)
1984
SONGWRITER(1984)

Diana Spears
DEVIL'S HAND, THE(1961)

Hazel Spears
PENITENTIARY(1979)

Jan Spears
GAME OF DEATH, THE(1979), w

Ken Spears
HEY THERE, IT'S YOGI BEAR(1964), ed

Les Spears
THIS ISLAND EARTH(1955)

Paul Allen Spears
KNICKERBOCKER HOLIDAY(1944)

Steve J. Spears
ROAD WARRIOR, THE(1982, Aus.)

Phil Speary
ATTIC, THE(1979)

Jack Specht
STAKEOUT!(1962), ph

Kenneth Specht
MADELEINE IS(1971, Can.), p, w

Wayne Specht
MADELEINE IS(1971, Can.)

Lynda Speciale
SCREWBALLS(1983)

Jan Speck
MODERN PROBLEMS(1981)

John Speckhardt
PURPLE HAZE(1982)

Katherine Specktor
LOVE CHILD(1982), w

Dan Spector
SWAP MEET(1979)

David Spector
AIRPORT '77(1977), w

Don Spector
MR. SYCAMORE(1975)

Jack Spector
MAFIA GIRLS, THE(1969)

Jeannie Spector
SOUTHERN COMFORT(1981)

Phil Spector
EASY RIDER(1969)

Sumner Spector
BLACK ANGELS, THE(1970)

Yiftah Spector
CLOUDS OVER ISRAEL(1966, Israel)

The Spectrum
RECKONING, THE(1971, Brit.)

David Speechley
SPACED OUT(1981, Brit.), p; HORROR PLANET(1982, Brit.), p

Carol Speed
BIG BIRD CAGE, THE(1972); NEW CENTURIONS, THE(1972); MACK, THE(1973); ABBY(1974); BLACK SAMSON(1974)
Misc. Talkies
BUMMER(1973); SAVAGE!(1973)

Carolyn Ann Speed
Misc. Talkies
DYNAMITE BROTHERS, THE(1974)

George Speed
KES(1970, Brit.)

Jacqui Speed
CAULDRON OF BLOOD(1971, Span.)

Pamela Speed
SMITHEREENS(1982)

"Speed" Webb and His Orchestra
SINS OF THE FATHERS(1928)

Speedy
OLD MOTHER RILEY'S CIRCUS(1941, Brit.)

Hermann Speelmans
DANTON(1931, Ger.); CAPTAIN FROM KOEPENICK(1933, Ger.); F.P. 1 DOESN'T ANSWER(1933, Ger.); SHOT AT DAWN, A(1934, Ger.)

Alan Speer
THIS GUN FOR HIRE(1942)

Charlotte Speer
PLANET OF DINOSAURS(1978)

Darryl Speer
CROSS AND THE SWITCHBLADE, THE(1970)

Jane Speer
SOLDIER OF ORANGE(1979, Dutch), ed

Katherine Speer
Silents
NOTHING BUT THE TRUTH(1920), w

Martin Speer
HILLS HAVE EYES, THE(1978)
Misc. Talkies
KILLER'S DELIGHT(1978)

Paul Speer
THOUSANDS CHEER(1943)

Linda Speeris
1984
LAST STARFIGHTER, THE(1984), set d

Robert D. Speers
TOO TOUGH TO KILL(1935), w

Christopher Speeth
MALATESTA'S CARNIVAL(1973), d&w

Albert Spehr
GREAT COMMANDMENT, THE(1941)

Henriett Speidel
DECISION BEFORE DAWN(1951)

Norman R. Speiden
EDISON, THE MAN(1940), tech adv

Dennis Speigel
ROLLERCOASTER(1977)

Larry Speigel
SURVIVAL RUN(1980), d, w

Johnny Speight
FRENCH DRESSING(1964, Brit.), w; PLANK, THE(1967, Brit.); PRIVILEGE(1967, Brit.), w; ALF 'N' FAMILY(1968, Brit.), w

Rosalind Speight
SONG OF NORWAY(1970)

Leslie Speights
ONE DARK NIGHT(1983)

Steven Spielberg
1941(1979), d

Jack Speirs
CHARLIE, THE LONESOME COUGAR(1967), w; KING OF THE GRIZZLIES(1970), w

Bert Speiser
CORN IS GREEN, THE(1945)
Frank Speiser
ELECTRIC HORSEMAN, THE(1979); ROSE, THE(1979)
Jacques Speisser
TROUT, THE(1982, Fr.)
Irmgard Speitel
FLOWERS FOR THE MAN IN THE MOON(1975, Ger.), w
Ulrich Speitel
FLOWERS FOR THE MAN IN THE MOON(1975, Ger.), w
Beate Speith
NOT RECONCILED, OR "ONLY VIOLENCE HELPS WHERE IT RULES"(1969, Ger.)
George Spell
NAKED KISS, THE(1964); THEY CALL ME MISTER TIBBS(1970); ORGANIZATION, THE(1971); BISCUIT EATER, THE(1972); MAN AND BOY(1972)
Wanda Spell
THEY CALL ME MISTER TIBBS(1970); ORGANIZATION, THE(1971); HICKEY AND BOGGS(1972)
Winston Spell
HICKEY AND BOGGS(1972)
Aaron Spelling
VICKI(1953); ALASKA SEAS(1954); BLACK WIDOW(1954); THREE YOUNG TEXANS(1954); TARGET ZERO(1955); WYOMING RENEGADES(1955); SPIRIT OF ST. LOUIS, THE(1957); GUNS OF THE TIMBERLAND(1960), p, w; ONE FOOT IN HELL(1960), w; BABY BLUE MARINE(1976), p
Daniel Spelling
NIGHT GOD SCREAMED, THE(1975)
Leora Spellman
WISE GIRLS(1930)
Martin Spellman
BOYS TOWN(1938); SANTA FE STAMPEDE(1938); TEST PILOT(1938); BEAU GESTE(1939); I AM A CRIMINAL(1939); LET US LIVE(1939); STREETS OF NEW YORK(1939); HOLD THAT WOMAN(1940); SON OF THE NAVY(1940); CONFESSIONS OF BOSTON BLACKIE(1941); MEET THE CHUMP(1941)
Martin Joseph Spellman, Jr.
SHARPSHOOTERS(1938)
Peter Spelson
PSYCHOTRONIC MAN, THE(1980), a, p, w
George Spelvin
REDEMPTION(1930); SUZY(1936); NIGHT OF BLOODY HORROR zero(1969)
Silents
JUST SUPPOSE(1926)
Georgina Spelvin
1984
POLICE ACADEMY(1984)
Misc. Talkies
GIRLS FOR RENT(1974)
Bruce Spence
STORK(1971, Aus.); CARS THAT ATE PARIS, THE(1974, Aus.); FIRM MAN, THE(1975, Aus.); GREAT MACARTHY, THE(1975, Aus.); ELIZA FRASER(1976, Aus.); LET THE BALLOON GO(1977, Aus.); 20TH CENTURY OZ(1977, Aus.); DIMBOOLA(1979, Aus.); ROAD WARRIOR, THE(1982, Aus.); BUDDIES(1983, Aus.)
1984
PALLET ON THE FLOOR(1984, New Zealand)
Claude Spence
FIRST NUDIE MUSICAL, THE(1976)
Dennis Spence
GUNMAN HAS ESCAPED, A(1948, Brit.)
Edwana Spence
PHFFFT!(1954)
George Spence
GIVE ME THE STARS(1944, Brit.); HAUNTED STRANGLER, THE(1958, Brit.); HIDE AND SEEK(1964, Brit.); WHISPERERS, THE(1967, Brit.)
Grace Spence
COAST TO COAST(1980)
Grayce Spence
CANNONBALL RUN, THE(1981)
Hartzell Spence
ONE FOOT IN HEAVEN(1941), w
Ian Spence
STARSTRUCK(1982, Aus.)
Irv Spence
GAY PURR-EE(1962), anim; HEY THERE, IT'S YOGI BEAR(1964), anim; MAN CALLED FLINTSTONE, THE(1966), anim; PHANTOM TOLLBOOTH, THE(1970), anim
Irven Spence
WIZARDS(1977), anim; HEY, GOOD LOOKIN'(1982), anim
James Spence
DERELICT, THE(1937, Brit.), w
Jock Spence
SOLO(1978, New Zealand/Aus.)
John Spence
GIRL GRABBERS, THE(1968)
Johnnie Spence
LIMBO LINE, THE(1969, Brit.), m
Michael Spence
HANGAR 18(1980), ed; BOOGENS, THE(1982), ed; ONE DARK NIGHT(1983), ed
1984
SILENT NIGHT, DEADLY NIGHT(1984), ed
Mike Spence
GRAND PRIX(1966)
Peter Spence
1984
BAY BOY(1984, Can.)
Ralph Spence
LADY OF CHANCE, A(1928), w; FLORODORA GIRL, THE(1930), w; HALF SHOT AT SUNRISE(1930), w; HOOK, LINE AND SINKER(1930), w; WAY OUT WEST(1930), w; CAUGHT PLASTERED(1931), w; EVERYTHING'S ROSIE(1931), w; GORILLA, THE(1931), w; LAUGH AND GET RICH(1931), w; PEACH O' RENO(1931), w; CROOKED CIRCLE(1932), w; FAST LIFE(1932), w; PASSIONATE PLUMBER(1932),

w; SPEAK EASILY(1932), w; HER BODYGUARD(1933), w; MR. SKITCH(1933), w; SAILOR BE GOOD(1933), w; TOMORROW AT SEVEN(1933), w; WARRIOR'S HUSBAND, THE(1933), w; BAND PLAYS ON, THE(1934), w; DEATH OF THE DIAMOND(1934), w; I'LL TELL THE WORLD(1934), w; LOUDSPEAKER, THE(1934), w; MURDER IN THE PRIVATE CAR(1934), w; STAND UP AND CHEER(1934 80m FOX bw), w; STUDENT TOUR(1934), w; BIG BROADCAST OF 1936, THE(1935), w; GOING HIGHBROW(1935), w; HERE COMES THE BAND(1935), w; MILLIONS IN THE AIR(1935); WINNING TICKET, THE(1935), w; EVERYBODY DANCE(1936, Brit.), w; POOR LITTLE RICH GIRL(1936), w; WHERE THERE'S A WILL(1936, Brit), w; KING SOLOMON'S MINES(1937, Brit.), w; SH! THE OCTOPUS(1937), w; SILENT BARRIERS(1937, Brit.), w; SKY'S THE LIMIT, THE(1937, Brit.), w; STRANGERS ON A HONEYMOON(1937, Brit.), w; SWEET DEVIL(1937, Brit.), w; FLYING DEUCES, THE(1939), w; GORILLA, THE(1939), w; DOWN ARGENTINE WAY(1940), w; LADY BE GOOD(1941), w; LARCENY STREET(1941, Brit.), w; FLEET'S IN, THE(1942), w; SEVEN DAYS LEAVE(1942), w; AMAZING MR. FORREST, THE(1943, Brit.), w; AROUND THE WORLD(1943), w; HIGHER AND HIGHER(1943), w; PLAINSMAN AND THE LADY(1946), w
Silents
POOR LITTLE RICH GIRL, A(1917), w; STRANGER THAN FICTION(1921), t, ed; CHASING THE MOON(1922), t, ed; DO AND DARE(1922), t, ed; SURE FIRE FLINT(1922), t; FRIENDLY HUSBAND, A(1923), t, ed; LUCK(1923), t; HIS DARKER SELF(1924), t; ON TIME(1924), t, ed; EARLY BIRD, THE(1925), t; CAMPUS FLIRT, THE(1926), t; FOR HEAVEN'S SAKE(1926), t; IT'S THE OLD ARMY GAME(1926), t; ADAM AND EVIL(1927), t; CALLAHANS AND THE MURPHYS, THE(1927), t; JOHNNY GET YOUR HAIR CUT(1927), t; TAXI DANCER, THE(1927), t; TILLIE THE TOILER(1927), t; BABY MINE(1928), t; EXCESS BAGGAGE(1928), w, t; SHOW PEOPLE(1928), t; VAMPING VENUS(1928), t
Ralph H. Spence
Silents
JACK SPURLOCK, PRODIGAL(1918), w
Sallianne Spence
1984
HIGHPOINT(1984, Can.)
Sandra Spence
NOOSE HANGS HIGH, THE(1948); EAST SIDE, WEST SIDE(1949); FIGHTING COAST GUARD(1951); MA AND PA KETTLE AT WAIKIKI(1955)
Steve Spence
SENDER, THE(1982, Brit.), art d
1984
KILLING FIELDS, THE(1984, Brit.), art d
Tod Spence
IS THIS TRIP REALLY NECESSARY?(1970)
Verne Spence
OLD HOMESTEAD, THE(1935)
Peter Spenceley
CREEPING FLESH,THE(1973, Brit.), w
Spencer
MADHOUSE(1974, Brit.), spec eff
Al Spencer
NIGHT OF THE HUNTER, THE(1955), set d
Alexander Spencer
SOLDIER, THE(1982)
Alfred Spencer
AIR RAID WARDENS(1943), set d; MIGHTY MCGURK, THE(1946), set d; SHOW BOAT(1951), set d; TENNESSEE'S PARTNER(1955), set d; SLIGHTLY SCARLET(1956), set d
Alfred A. Spencer
YOU FOR ME(1952), set d
Alfred D. Spencer
MY BROTHER TALKS TO HORSES(1946), set d
Alfred E. Spencer
IT HAPPENED IN BROOKLYN(1947), set d; SONG OF THE THIN MAN(1947), set d; SCENE OF THE CRIME(1949), set d; CAUSE FOR ALARM(1951), set d; ROYAL WEDDING(1951), set d; STRIP, THE(1951), set d; DREAM WIFE(1953), set d; PARIS MODEL(1953), set d; WITNESS TO MURDER(1954), set d; MACKENNA'S GOLD(1969), set d
Ann Spencer
BIGGER THAN LIFE(1956)
Bert Spencer
JEANNE EAGELS(1957)
Bob Spencer
DEVIL DOGS OF THE AIR(1935); KEEP 'EM SLUGGING(1943); DON'T WORRY, WE'LL THINK OF A TITLE(1966), cos
Misc. Talkies
CONVOY BUDDIES(1977)
Bud Spencer
ACE HIGH(1969, Ital.); BOOT HILL(1969, Ital.); GOD FORGIVES–I DON'T!(1969, Ital./Span.); FIVE MAN ARMY, THE(1970, Ital.); BIG AND THE BAD, THE(1971, Ital./Fr./Span.); FOUR FLIES ON GREY VELVET(1972, Ital.); ALL THE WAY, BOYS(1973, Ital.); REASON TO LIVE, A REASON TO DIE, A(1974, Ital./Fr./Ger./Span.); CHARLESTON(1978, Ital.)
Misc. Talkies
TODAY WE KILL...TOMORROW WE DIE(1971)
Bud Spencer [Carlo Pedersoli]
REVENGE AT EL PASO(1968, Ital.); TODAY IT'S ME...TOMORROW YOU!(1968, Ital.); THEY CALL ME TRINITY(1971, Ital.); TRINITY IS STILL MY NAME(1971, Ital.); TWO SUPER COPS(1978, Ital.)
Cleon Spencer
SUPERMAN II(1980)
David Spencer
CAPTAIN EDDIE(1945); MR. PERRIN AND MR. TRAILL(1948, Brit.)
Dean Spencer
BRIDE FOR HENRY, A(1937), w; ACROSS THE PLAINS(1939); DRIFTING WESTWARD(1939)
Diana Spencer
DON'T GIVE UP THE SHIP(1959)
Don Spencer
STUDENT NURSES, THE(1970), w; BIG DOLL HOUSE, THE(1971), w; SWEET SUGAR(1972), w

Dorothy Spencer

CONCORDE, THE–AIRPORT '79(, ed; MARRIED IN HOLLYWOOD(1929), ed; NIXON DAMES(1929), ed; SHE WAS A LADY(1934), ed; CASE AGAINST MRS. AMES, THE(1936), ed; LUCKIEST GIRL IN THE WORLD, THE(1936), ed; STAND-IN(1937), ed; VOGUES OF 1938(1937), ed; BLOCKADE(1938), ed; TRADE WINDS(1938), ed; ETERNALLY YOURS(1939), ed; STAGECOACH(1939), ed; WINTER CARNIVAL(1939), ed; FOREIGN CORRESPONDENT(1940), ed; HOUSE ACROSS THE BAY, THE(1940), ed; SUNDOWN(1941), ed; GHOST AND MRS. MUIR, THE(1942), ed; TO BE OR NOT TO BE(1942), ed; HAPPY LAND(1943), ed; HEAVEN CAN WAIT(1943), ed; LIFEBOAT(1944), ed; SWEET AND LOWDOWN(1944), ed; ROYAL SCANDAL, A(1945), ed; TREE GROWS IN BROOKLYN, A(1945), ed; CLUNY BROWN(1946), ed; DRAGONWYCH(1946), ed; MY DARLING CLEMENTINE(1946), ed; SNAKE PIT, THE(1948), ed; THAT LADY IN ERMINE(1948), ed; DOWN TO THE SEA IN SHIPS(1949), ed; THREE CAME HOME(1950), ed; UNDER MY SKIN(1950), ed; DECISION BEFORE DAWN(1951), ed; FOURTEEN HOURS(1951), ed; LYDIA BAILEY(1952), ed; MAN ON A TIGHTROPE(1953), ed; TONIGHT WE SING(1953), ed; VICKI(1953), ed; BLACK WIDOW(1954), ed; BROKEN LANCE(1954), ed; DEMETRIUS AND THE GLADIATORS(1954), ed; NIGHT PEOPLE(1954), ed; LEFT HAND OF GOD, THE(1955), ed; PRINCE OF PLAYERS(1955), ed; RAINS OF RANCHIPUR, THE(1955), ed; SOLDIER OF FORTUNE(1955), ed; MAN IN THE GREY FLANNEL SUIT, THE(1956), ed; HATFUL OF RAIN, A(1957), ed; YOUNG LIONS, THE(1958), ed; JOURNEY, THE(1959, U.S./Aust.), ed; PRIVATE'S AFFAIR, A(1959), ed; FROM THE TERRACE(1960), ed; NORTH TO ALASKA(1960), ed; SEVEN THIEVES(1960), ed; WILD IN THE COUNTRY(1961), ed; CLEOPATRA(1963), ed; CIRCUS WORLD(1964), ed; VON RYAN'S EXPRESS(1965), ed; LOST COMMAND, THE(1966), ed; GUIDE FOR THE MARRIED MAN, A(1967), ed; VALLEY OF THE DOLLS(1967), ed; DADDY'S GONE A-HUNTING(1969), ed; HAPPY BIRTHDAY, WANDA JUNE(1971), ed; LIMBO(1972), ed; EARTHQUAKE(1974), ed

Doug Spencer

SMOKY(1946)

Douglas Spencer

MEN AGAINST THE SKY(1940); BIG CLOCK, THE(1948); NIGHT HAS A THOUSAND EYES(1948); SAINTED SISTERS, THE(1948); ALIAS NICK BEAL(1949); BRIDE OF VENGEANCE(1949); CHICAGO DEADLINE(1949); FOLLOW ME QUIETLY(1949); IT HAPPENS EVERY SPRING(1949); MY FRIEND IRMA(1949); RED, HOT AND BLUE(1949); FATHER OF THE BRIDE(1950); PAID IN FULL(1950); REDHEAD AND THE COWBOY, THE(1950); UNION STATION(1950); COME FILL THE CUP(1951); PLACE IN THE SUN, A(1951); THING, THE(1951); WARPATH(1951); MONKEY BUSINESS(1952); SOMETHING TO LIVE FOR(1952); UNTAMED FRONTIER(1952); GLASS WALL, THE(1953); HOUDINI(1953); SHANE(1953); SHE'S BACK ON BROADWAY(1953); TROUBLE ALONG THE WAY(1953); RAID(1954); RIVER OF NO RETURN(1954); KENTUCKIAN, THE(1955); MAN ALONE, A(1955); SMOKE SIGNAL(1955); THIS ISLAND EARTH(1955); MAN FROM DEL RIO(1956); PARDNERS(1956); SHORT CUT TO HELL(1957); THREE FACES OF EVE, THE(1957); UNHOLY WIFE, THE(1957); COLE YOUNGER, GUNFIGHTER(1958); SADDLE THE WIND(1958); DIARY OF ANNE FRANK, THE(1959); SINS OF RACHEL CADE, THE(1960)

Elizabeth Spencer

LIGHT IN THE PIAZZA(1962), w; I, MAUREEN(1978, Can.), w

Silents

INFIDELITY(1917)

Emily Spencer

Misc. Talkies

MEATEATER(1979)

Frank Spencer

PACIFIC BLACKOUT(1942), w; SOMEONE AT THE DOOR(1950, Brit.), m; TO HAVE AND TO HOLD(1951, Brit.), m; CLOUDBURST(1952, Brit.), m; WHISPERING SMITH VERSUS SCOTLAND YARD(1952, Brit.), md; SCOTCH ON THE ROCKS(1954, Brit.), m; "RENT-A-GIRL"(1965)

Franz Spencer

MIDNIGHT ANGEL(1941), w; FIGHTING GUARDSMAN, THE(1945), w; MASQUERADE IN MEXICO(1945), w; INVASION U.S.A.(1952), w

Franz G. Spencer

DOWN IN SAN DIEGO(1941), w; BORN TO SING(1942), w

Fred Spencer

SNOW WHITE AND THE SEVEN DWARFS(1937), anim

George Spencer

Misc. Talkies

IF YOU DON'T STOP IT, YOU'LL GO BLIND(1977)

George S. Spencer

Misc. Silents

THIRD DEGREE, THE(1914)

George Soule Spencer

Silents

DAUGHTERS OF MEN(1914); FORTUNE HUNTER, THE(1914); HOUSE NEXT DOOR, THE(1914); CLIMBERS, THE(1915); CLARION, THE(1916)

Misc. Silents

GAMBLERS, THE(1914); WOLF, THE(1914); COLLEGE WIDOW, THE(1915); DISTRICT ATTORNEY, THE(1915); EVANGELIST, THE(1915); GREAT RUBY, THE(1915); LOVE OF WOMEN, THE(1915); SPORTING DUCHESS, THE(1915); TROOPER 44(1917); WEB OF LIFE, THE(1917)

Gil Spencer, Jr.

1984

GIRLS NIGHT OUT(1984), w

Gillian Spencer

WHAT'S SO BAD ABOUT FEELING GOOD?(1968)

Gladys Spencer

PSYCHE 59(1964, Brit.); ONE MORE TIME(1970, Brit.)

Glenn Spencer

APACHE ROSE(1947), m

Gordon Spencer

Misc. Talkies

MAN OUTSIDE(1965)

Harvey Spencer

UP JUMPED A SWAGMAN(1965, Brit.)

Herbert Spencer

SPRING REUNION(1957), m; M(1970), md; SCROOGE(1970, Brit.), md

J. Russell Spencer

GREAT DICTATOR, THE(1940), art d; CLUNY BROWN(1946), art d; DRAGONWYCH(1946), art d; MARGIE(1946), art d; WAKE UP AND DREAM(1946), art d; LATE GEORGE APLEY, THE(1947), art d; NIGHTMARE ALLEY(1947), art d; GIVE MY REGARDS TO BROADWAY(1948), art d; LETTER TO THREE WIVES, A(1948), art d; LUCK OF THE IRISH(1948), art d; THAT LADY IN ERMINE(1948), art d; IT HAPPENS EVERY SPRING(1949), art d; PINKY(1949), art d; AMERICAN GUERRILLA IN THE PHILIPPINES, AN(1950), art d; WHERE THE SIDEWALK ENDS(1950), art d; YOU'RE IN THE NAVY NOW(1951), art d; LES MISERABLES(1952), art d; LYDIA BAILEY(1952), art d; PHONE CALL FROM A STRANGER(1952), art d

James Spencer

SEA GOD, THE(1930); TWO-FACED WOMAN(1941); PAPER MOON(1973), set d

Silents

ADVENTURE(1925)

James H. Spencer

ROCKY(1976), art d; FIRE SALE(1977), prod d; DIE LAUGHING(1980), prod d; KING OF THE MOUNTAIN(1981), prod d; STRIPES(1981), prod d; POLTERGEIST(1982), prod d; TWILIGHT ZONE–THE MOVIE(1983), art d

1984

GREMLINS(1984), prod d

James P. Spencer

JUNGLE PRINCESS, THE(1936)

Jeanne Spencer

HEART PUNCH(1932), ed; ALIMONY MADNESS(1933), ed; BEHIND JURY DOORS(1933, Brit.), ed; HER RESALE VALUE(1933), ed; HOLLYWOOD MYSTERY(1934), ed

Silents

RAMONA(1928), ed; EVANGELINE(1929), ed

Jeremy Spencer

MAN WHO LOVED REDHEADS, THE(1955, Brit.)

Jessica Spencer

MY BROTHER JONATHAN(1949, Brit.); MAN OF VIOLENCE(1970, Brit.)

Jim Spencer

FROZEN JUSTICE(1929); EBB TIDE(1937); MOONLIGHT IN HAWAII(1941); TUTTLES OF TAHITI(1942)

John Spencer

ECHOES(1983); WARGAMES(1983)

Katherine Spencer

Silents

AT THE STAGE DOOR(1921)

Misc. Silents

BARRICADE, THE(1921)

Kenneth Spencer

BATAAN(1943); CABIN IN THE SKY(1943)

Linbert Spencer

ONE PLUS ONE(1969, Brit.); TWO GENTLEMEN SHARING(1969, Brit.); JULIUS CAESAR(1970, Brit.)

Lou Spencer

CALL ME MISTER(1951)

Marian Spencer

CAPTAIN'S TABLE, THE(1936, Brit.); DAVID LIVINGSTONE(1936, Brit.); AULD LANG SYNE(1937, Brit.); LAST ROSE OF SUMMER, THE(1937, Brit.); LET THE PEOPLE SING(1942, Brit.); THIS WAS PARIS(1942, Brit.); WE'LL MEET AGAIN(1942, Brit.); WHEN WE ARE MARRIED(1943, Brit.); ADVENTURE FOR TWO(1945, Brit.); FLIGHT FROM FOLLY(1945, Brit.); BOND STREET(1948, Brit.); WEAKER SEX, THE(1949, Brit.); DISOBEDIENT(1953, Brit.); SECRET, THE(1955, Brit.); THREE WORLDS OF GULLIVER, THE(1960, Brit.); CORRIDORS OF BLOOD(1962, Brit.); BLAZE OF GLORY(1963, Brit.); SEANCE ON A WET AFTERNOON(1964 Brit.)

Marion Spencer

WIFE OF GENERAL LING, THE(1938, Brit.); SUICIDE SQUADRON(1942, Brit.); SPELL OF AMY NUGENT, THE(1945, Brit.)

Marjorie Spencer

TAKE HER BY SURPRISE(1967, Can.), a, makeup

Mike Spencer

OUT OF THE BLUE(1982)

Mya Mya Spencer

PURPLE PLAIN, THE(1954, Brit.)

Nell Spencer

Misc. Silents

SKYLIGHT ROOM, THE(1917)

Norman Spencer

RAINBOW'S END(1935), d; HOBSON'S CHOICE(1954, Brit.), w; VANISHING POINT(1971), p

Norris Spencer

GOLDEN LADY, THE(1979, Brit.), art d

Oliver Spencer

1984

UNTIL SEPTEMBER(1984)

Omkar Spencer

NOBODY'S PERFEKT(1981)

Pam Spencer

PERSONAL BEST(1982)

Paul Spencer

NO RETURN ADDRESS(1961)

Penny Spencer

COUNTDOWN TO DANGER(1967, Brit.); WHISPERERS, THE(1967, Brit.)

Peter Spencer

LOVE IN MOROCCO(1933, Fr.), w

Prince C. Spencer

HERE COME THE GIRLS(1953)

Raphaelle Spencer

1984

UNTIL SEPTEMBER(1984)

Ray Spencer

CRACK-UP(1946), w

Richard V. Spencer

Silents

PARADISE GARDEN(1917), w

Robert Spencer
GIRL WITH IDEAS, A(1937); LOVE IN A BUNGALOW(1937); MAN WHO CRIED WOLF, THE(1937); REPORTED MISSING(1937); WINGS OVER HONOLULU(1937); JURY'S SECRET, THE(1938); I MARRIED AN ANGEL(1942); LADY IN THE LAKE(1947); VOICE OF THE TURTLE, THE(1947); SAXON CHARM, THE(1948)

Ronald Spencer
Misc. Talkies
COPTER KIDS, THE(1976, Brit.), d

Roy Spencer
BARRY LYNDON(1975, Brit.); SATURN 3(1980), spec eff

Russell Spencer
MODERN TIMES(1936), art d; HAPPY LAND(1943), art d; HOLY MATRIMONY(1943), art d; TONIGHT WE RAID CALAIS(1943), art d; EVE OF ST. MARK, THE(1944), art d; SUNDAY DINNER FOR A SOLDIER(1944), art d; NOB HILL(1945), art d

Sara Spencer
BAD AND THE BEAUTIFUL, THE(1952)

Sarah Spencer
STARLIFT(1951); HOODLUM EMPIRE(1952); WAC FROM WALLA WALLA, THE(1952); LONG, LONG TRAILER, THE(1954)

Scott Spencer
ENDLESS LOVE(1981), w; SPLIT IMAGE(1982), w

Shelley Spencer
LEATHER BURNERS, THE(1943)

Sundown Spencer
JUNIOR BONNER(1972)

Terry Spencer
MYSTERY OF MR. X, THE(1934)

Tim Spencer
GALLANT DEFENDER(1935); MYSTERIOUS AVENGER, THE(1936); SONG OF THE SADDLE(1936); OLD WYOMING TRAIL, THE(1937); TEXAS STAGECOACH(1940); TWO-FISTED RANGERS(1940), m/l; APACHE ROSE(1947), m

Tiphanie Spencer
1984
UNTIL SEPTEMBER(1984)

Tom Spencer
Silents
GRETCHEN, THE GREENHORN(1916)

Vicki Spencer
TEENAGE MILLIONAIRE(1961); TWIST AROUND THE CLOCK(1961)

W.E. Spencer
Silents
MAID OF THE WEST(1921), w

William Spencer, Jr.
HARLEM ON THE PRAIRIE(1938)

William W. Spencer
THUNDER OF DRUMS, A(1961), ph; COUNTDOWN(1968), ph; IF HE HOLLERS, LET HIM GO(1968), ph; 1,000 PLANE RAID, THE(1969), ph; MEPHISTO WALTZ, THE(1971), ph

Zoltan G. Spencer
Misc. Talkies
SATANIST, THE(1968), d

Spencer Davis Group
HERE WE GO ROUND THE MULBERRY BUSH(1968, Brit.)

Noel Spencer-Barnes
CAYMAN TRIANGLE, THE(1977)

M.S.I. Spencer-Hagen
GIRL RUSH, THE(1955), m

Stephen Spender
FOOL AND THE PRINCESS, THE(1948, Brit.), w

J.B. Spendlove
GOOD COMPANIONS(1933, Brit.)

George Spenee
WRONG BOX, THE(1966, Brit.)

Craig Spengel
I WANNA HOLD YOUR HAND(1978)

Kimberly Spengel
I WANNA HOLD YOUR HAND(1978)

Pierre Spengler
CROSSED SWORDS(1978), p, w; SUPERMAN(1978), p; SUPERMAN II(1980), p; SUPERMAN III(1983), p

V. Spengler
CHINESE ROULETTE(1977, Ger.)

Volker Spengler
DESPAIR(1978, Ger.); MARRIAGE OF MARIA BRAUN, THE(1979, Ger.); IN A YEAR OF THIRTEEN MOONS(1980, Ger.); VERONIKA VOSS(1982, Ger.)

Guy Spennato
NUNZIO(1978)

Nora Helen Spens
YOUNG DOCTORS, THE(1961)

David Spenser
FUSS OVER FEATHERS(1954, Brit.); STRANGLERS OF BOMBAY, THE(1960, Brit.); IN SEARCH OF THE CASTAWAYS(1962, Brit.); EARTH DIES SCREAMING, THE(1964, Brit.); SOME MAY LIVE(1967, Brit.); BATTLE BENEATH THE EARTH(1968, Brit.)

Jack Spenser
GURU, THE MAD MONK(1971)

Jeremy Spenser
ANNA KARENINA(1948, Brit.); DANCING YEARS, THE(1950, Brit.); PRELUDE TO FAME(1950, Brit.); PORTRAIT OF CLARE(1951, Brit.); ISLAND RESCUE(1952, Brit.); OUTPOST IN MALAYA(1952, Brit.); SPIDER AND THE FLY, THE(1952, Brit.); BACKGROUND(1953, Brit.); DEVIL ON HORSEBACK(1954, Brit.); ESCAPADE(1955, Brit.); SUMMERTIME(1955); IT'S GREAT TO BE YOUNG(1956, Brit.); PRINCE AND THE SHOWGIRL, THE(1957, Brit.); WONDERFUL THINGS!(1958, Brit.); FERRY TO HONG KONG(1959, Brit.); ROMAN SPRING OF MRS. STONE, THE(1961, U.S./Brit.); KING AND COUNTRY(1964, Brit.); BRAIN, THE(1965, Ger./Brit.); FAHRENHEIT 451(1966, Brit.); HE WHO RIDES A TIGER(1966, Brit.)

Sophia Spentzos
CODE 7, VICTIM 5(1964, Brit.)

Norman Sper
SONG OF THE CABELLERO(1930), w

Mitchell Spera
MADE FOR EACH OTHER(1971)

R.W. Spera
LADY LIBERTY(1972, Ital./Fr.), w

Cinzia Sperapani
CLIMAX, THE(1967, Fr., Ital.)

Milo Sperber
MR. EMMANUEL(1945, Brit.); END OF THE RIVER, THE(1947, Brit.); GAY ADVENTURE, THE(1953, Brit.); BLUEBEARD'S TEN HONEYMOONS(1960, Brit.); IN SEARCH OF THE CASTAWAYS(1962, Brit.); OPERATION CROSSBOW(1965, U.S./Ital.); BILLION DOLLAR BRAIN(1967, Brit.); PROVIDENCE(1977, Fr.); SPY WHO LOVED ME, THE(1977, Brit.)

Nil Sperber
FOREIGN INTRIGUE(1956)

Wendie Jo Sperber
I WANNA HOLD YOUR HAND(1978); 1941(1979); FIRST TIME, THE(1983)

Luther Sperberg
REFUGE(1981), w

George Sperdakos
BLOODY BROOD, THE(1959, Can.); TWO AND TWO MAKE SIX(1962, Brit.); WAR LOVER, THE(1962, U.S./Brit.); WHAT'S SO BAD ABOUT FEELING GOOD?(1968); NUMBER ONE(1969); JOURNEY(1977, Can.); OTHER SIDE OF MIDNIGHT, THE(1977); RESURRECTION(1980)

Denis Sperdouklis
LITTLE GIRL WHO LIVES DOWN THE LANE, THE(1977, Can.), cos

Charles Spere
Silents
DESERT BLOSSOMS(1921)
Misc. Silents
T.N.T(THE NAKED TRUTH) (1924); FIGHTING COLLEEN, A(1919); HELLION, THE(1919); PEGEEN(1920); EVER SINCE EVE(1921); GIRL FROM ROCKY POINT, THE(1922)

George Sperkados
CROSS COUNTRY(1983, Can.)

Edna May Sperl
Silents
HIS DARKER SELF(1924)
Misc. Silents
LONESOME CORNERS(1922)

Hermine Sperler
UNFINISHED SYMPHONY, THE(1953, Aust./Brit.)

Alessandro Sperli
HERCULES AND THE CAPTIVE WOMEN(1963, Fr./Ital.); SPY IN YOUR EYE(1966, Ital.); WAR ITALIAN STYLE(1967, Ital.); VALACHI PAPERS, THE(1972, Ital./Fr.)

Nicola Sperli
HERCULES AND THE CAPTIVE WOMEN(1963, Fr./Ital.)

Dave Sperling
TASTE OF SIN, A(1983), ph

David Sperling
BLOODEATERS(1980), ph, ed; BOOGEY MAN, THE(1980), ph; BOOGEYMAN II(1983), ph; REACHING OUT(1983), ph, ed

Hazel Sperling
HAPPY DAYS(1930)

Karen Sperling
MAKE A FACE(1971), a, p, d, w

Milton Sperling
SING, BABY, SING(1936), w; THIN ICE(1937), w; HAPPY LANDING(1938), w; I'LL GIVE A MILLION(1938), w; HERE I AM A STRANGER(1939), w; RETURN OF THE CISCO KID(1939), w; FOUR SONS(1940), w; GREAT PROFILE, THE(1940), w; SUN VALLEY SERENADE(1941), p; I WAKE UP SCREAMING(1942), p; RINGS ON HER FINGERS(1942), p; CRASH DIVE(1943), p; HELLO, FRISCO, HELLO(1943), p; CLOAK AND DAGGER(1946), p; PURSUED(1947), p; MY GIRL TISA(1948), p; SOUTH OF ST. LOUIS(1949), p; THREE SECRETS(1950), p; DISTANT DRUMS(1951), p; ENFORCER, THE(1951), p; BLOWING WILD(1953), p; COURT-MARTIAL OF BILLY MITCHELL, THE(1955), p, w; MARJORIE MORNINGSTAR(1958), p; BRAMBLE BUSH, THE(1960), p, w; RISE AND FALL OF LEGS DIAMOND, THE(1960), p; MERRILL'S MARAUDERS(1962), p, w; BATTLE OF THE BULGE(1965), p, w; CAPTAIN APACHE(1971, Brit.), p, w

Rae Sperling
HOLLYWOOD HIGH(1977)
Misc. Talkies
HOLLYWOOD HIGH(1976)

Ronnie Sperling
BUDDY BUDDY(1981)

Marvin C. Spero
LOVE IS A CAROUSEL(1970), p

Mike Spero
FIREFOX(1982)

Richard Spero
CORVETTE SUMMER(1978), set d; STUNT MAN, THE(1980), set d

Roberta Speroni
LA NOTTE(1961, Fr./Ital.)

Julie Sperow
1984
BODY ROCK(1984)

Jane Sperr
MYSTERIES(1979, Neth.), ed

Martin Sperr
OUR HITLER, A FILM FROM GERMANY(1980, Ger.); PARSIFAL(1983, Fr.)

Martin Sperzel
IRISH EYES ARE SMILING(1944)

Arlette Spetelbroot
QUARTET(1981, Brit./Fr.)

Myron Speth
STRIKE UP THE BAND(1940)
Bella Spewack
CLEAR ALL WIRES(1933), w; SHOULD LADIES BEHAVE?(1933), w; SOLITAIRE MAN, THE(1933), w; CAT AND THE FIDDLE(1934), w; GAY BRIDE, THE(1934), w; RENDEZVOUS(1935), w; VOGUES OF 1938(1937), w; BOY MEETS GIRL(1938), w; CHASER, THE(1938), w; THREE LOVES HAS NANCY(1938), w; MY FAVORITE WIFE(1940), w; WEEKEND AT THE WALDORF(1945), w; KISS ME KATE(1953), w; MOVE OVER, DARLING(1963), w
Sam Spewack
NUISANCE, THE(1933), w; CAT AND THE FIDDLE(1934), w; GAY BRIDE, THE(1934), w; BOY MEETS GIRL(1938), w; THREE LOVES HAS NANCY(1938), w; MY FAVORITE WIFE(1940), w; WEEKEND AT THE WALDORF(1945), w
Samuel Spewack
SECRET WITNESS, THE(1931), w; CLEAR ALL WIRES(1933), w; SHOULD LADIES BEHAVE?(1933), w; SOLITAIRE MAN, THE(1933), w; RENDEZVOUS(1935), w; VOGUES OF 1938(1937), w; CHASER, THE(1938), w; KISS ME KATE(1953), w; MOVE OVER, DARLING(1963), w
Erica Speyer
SAND CASTLE, THE(1961)
Wilhelm Speyer
HAT, COAT AND GLOVE(1934), w; NIGHT OF ADVENTURE, A(1944), w
Willoughby Speyers
MAID'S NIGHT OUT(1938), w
Renato Spezali
RAILROAD MAN, THE(1965, Ital.)
Renato Speziali
BLOOD AND ROSES(1961, Fr./Ital.); WHITE SLAVE SHIP(1962, Fr./Ital.); HOURS OF LOVE, THE(1965, Ital.)
Linda Spheeris
CRAZY MAMA(1975), set d; REAL LIFE(1979), art d; USED CARS(1980), set d; ALL NIGHT LONG(1981), set d; CONTINENTAL DIVIDE(1981), set d; MISSING(1982), set d
Lynda Spheeris
MISSING(1982)
Penelope Spheeris
REAL LIFE(1979), p
1984
SUBURBIA(1984), d&w
Kostas Sphikas
YOUNG APHRODITES(1966, Gr.), w
Michael Spice
COUNTESS FROM HONG KONG, A(1967, Brit.)
Barry Spicer
IT TAKES ALL KINDS(1969, U.S./Aus.)
Bernard Spicer
AMBUSH IN LEOPARD STREET(1962, Brit.), w
David Spicer
NORMAN LOVES ROSE(1982, Aus.)
Vanetia Spicer
FLASH GORDON(1980)
Astrid Spiegel
ECHOES OF SILENCE(1966)
Barbara Spiegel
TOOTSIE(1982)
Bob Spiegel
BEYOND THE REEF(1981)
Dennis Spiegel
1984
PRODIGAL, THE(1984), m/l
Doris Spiegel
REQUIEM FOR A GUNFIGHTER(1965)
Ed Spiegel
SALT OF THE EARTH(1954), ed
Georgi Spiegel
TAXI TO HEAVEN(1944, USSR); ROAD HOME, THE(1947, USSR)
Larry Spiegel
BOOK OF NUMBERS(1973), w; HAIL(1973), w; DEATH GAME(1977), p
Misc. Talkies
GOD BLESS DR. SHAGETZ(1977), d
Paul Spiegel
SHOPWORN ANGEL(1938)
Sam Spiegel
INVISIBLE OPPONENT(1933, Ger.), p; OLD SPANISH CUSTOM, AN(1936, Brit.), p; ON THE WATERFRONT(1954), p; BRIDGE ON THE RIVER KWAI, THE(1957), p; STRANGE ONE, THE(1957), p; SUDDENLY, LAST SUMMER(1959, Brit.), p; LAWRENCE OF ARABIA(1962, Brit.), p; CHASE, THE(1966), p; NIGHT OF THE GENERALS, THE(1967, Brit./Fr.), p; NICHOLAS AND ALEXANDRA(1971, Brit.), p; LAST TYCOON, THE(1976), p; BETRAYAL(1983, Brit.), p
Leonard Spiegelgass
I'LL FIX IT(1934), w
Karl Spiehs
FOUNTAIN OF LOVE, THE(1968, Aust.), p; HOW TO SEDUCE A PLAYBOY(1968, Aust./Fr./Ital.), p
David Spielberg
EFFECT OF GAMMA RAYS ON MAN-IN-THE-MOON MARIGOLDS, THE(1972); TRIAL OF THE CATONSVILLE NINE, THE(1972); LAW AND DISORDER(1974); NEWMAN'S LAW(1974); HUSTLE(1975); CHOIRBOYS, THE(1977); REAL LIFE(1979); WINTER KILLS(1979); CHRISTINE(1983)
Steven Spielberg
ACE ELI AND RODGER OF THE SKIES(1973), w; SUGARLAND EXPRESS, THE(1974), d, w; JAWS(1975), d; CLOSE ENCOUNTERS OF THE THIRD KIND(1977), d&w; BLUES BROTHERS, THE(1980); RAIDERS OF THE LOST ARK(1981), d; E.T. THE EXTRA-TERRESTRIAL(1982), p, d; POLTERGEIST(1982), p, w; TWILIGHT ZONE–THE MOVIE(1983), p, d
1984
INDIANA JONES AND THE TEMPLE OF DOOM(1984), d

Leonard Spielgass
STINGAREE(1934), w
Ed Spielman
GORDON'S WAR(1973), w; FAST CHARLIE... THE MOONBEAM RIDER(1979), w
Fred Spielman
GREAT RUPERT, THE(1950), m
Bert Spielvogel
DEAD TO THE WORLD(1961), ph; DIRTYMOUTH(1970), ph
Angelica Spier
Misc. Silents
PARISIAN ROMANCE, A(1916)
Carol Spier
HOG WILD(1980, Can.), art d; GAS(1981, Can.), prod d; GREAT MUPPET CAPER, THE(1981), cos; SCANNERS(1981, Can.), art d; FUNNY FARM, THE(1982, Can.), art d; HUMONGOUS(1982, Can.), art d; DEAD ZONE, THE(1983), prod d; RUNNING BRAVE(1983, Can.), prod d; VIDEODROME(1983, Can.), prod d
William Spier
LADY POSSESSED(1952), d; DEVIL'S WIDOW, THE(1972, Brit.), w
Wolfgang Spier
ENDLESS NIGHT, THE(1963, Ger.)
Betty Spiers
DREYFUS CASE, THE(1931, Brit.), ed
Hetty Spiers
Silents
POTTER'S CLAY(1922, Brit.), w
K. C. Spiers
Silents
IF YOUTH BUT KNEW(1926, Brit.), w
Ros Spiers
STONE(1974, Aus.); MAN FROM HONG KONG(1975)
Adrian Spies
DARK OF THE SUN(1968, Brit.), w
Corinna Spies
GERMANY IN AUTUMN(1978, Ger.)
Glen Spies
DESTINATION INNER SPACE(1966)
Manfred Spies
PASSENGER, THE(1975, Ital.)
Walter Spies
WAJAN(1938, South Bali), d
Jacques Spiesser
STAVISKY(1974, Fr.); BLACK AND WHITE IN COLOR(1976, Fr.); LUMIERE(1976, Fr.)
Joan Spiga
FUN WITH DICK AND JANE(1977)
Leonard Spigelgass
HELLO SISTER!(1933), w; PRINCESS O'HARA(1935), p; LETTER OF INTRODUCTION(1938), w; SERVICE DE LUXE(1938), w; UNEXPECTED FATHER(1939), w; BOYS FROM SYRACUSE(1940), w; ONE NIGHT IN THE TROPICS(1940), p; PRIVATE AFFAIRS(1940), w; MILLION DOLLAR BABY(1941), w; TIGHT SHOES(1941), w; ALL THROUGH THE NIGHT(1942), w; BIG STREET, THE(1942), w; BUTCH MINDS THE BABY(1942), w; THEY GOT ME COVERED(1943), w; YOUNGEST PROFESSION, THE(1943), w; PERFECT MARRIAGE, THE(1946), w; SO EVIL MY LOVE(1948, Brit.), w; I WAS A MALE WAR BRIDE(1949), w; MYSTERY STREET(1950), w; LAW AND THE LADY, THE(1951), w; NIGHT INTO MORNING(1951), w; BECAUSE YOU'RE MINE(1952), w; SCANDAL AT SCOURIE(1953), w; ATHENA(1954), w; DEEP IN MY HEART(1954), w; SILK STOCKINGS(1957), w; TEN THOUSAND BEDROOMS(1957), w; PEPE(1960), w; MAJORITY OF ONE, A(1961), w; GYPSY(1962), w
Spike Spigener
THEY ALL LAUGHED(1981)
Hugh Spight
ELEPHANT MAN, THE(1980, Brit.); GREAT MUPPET CAPER, THE(1981); DARK CRYSTAL, THE(1982, Brit.)
Spike Jones
FIREMAN SAVE MY CHILD(1954)
Spike Jones and His City Slickers
THANK YOUR LUCKY STARS(1943); MEET THE PEOPLE(1944); LADIES' MAN(1947); VARIETY GIRL(1947)
Spike Jones Orchestra
BRING ON THE GIRLS(1945)
Spike the Dog
OLD YELLER(1957)
Buddy Spiker
SECOND FIDDLE TO A STEEL GUITAR(1965)
Harriet Spiker
ILLUSION(1929)
Ray Spiker
OUR DAILY BREAD(1934); RIDING HIGH(1943); IRISH EYES ARE SMILING(1944); SAN ANTONIO(1945); SPANISH MAIN, THE(1945); RUSTLER'S ROUNDUP(1946); BRASHER DOUBLOON, THE(1947); BERLIN EXPRESS(1948); RIVER LADY(1948); ON MOONLIGHT BAY(1951); MAN BEHIND THE GUN, THE(1952); SHANE(1953); DEMETRIUS AND THE GLADIATORS(1954); PRINCE VALIANT(1954); MANCHURIAN CANDIDATE, THE(1962)
Barry Spikings
CONDUCT UNBECOMING(1975, Brit.), p; MAN WHO FELL TO EARTH, THE(1976, Brit.), p; DEER HUNTER, THE(1978), p
Otello Spila
VIOLENT FOUR, THE(1968, Ital.), ph; DORIAN GRAY(1970, Ital./Brit./Ger./Liechtenstein), ph
Jim Spillane
FAST BREAK(1979)
Mickey Spillane
I, THE JURY(1953), w; LONG WAIT, THE(1954), w; RING OF FEAR(1954), w; KISS ME DEADLY(1955), w; MY GUN IS QUICK(1957), w; GIRL HUNTERS, THE(1963, Brit.), a, w; DELTA FACTOR, THE(1970), w; I, THE JURY(1982), w
Sherri Spillane
DELTA FACTOR, THE(1970)

Dean Spille
BOY NAMED CHARLIE BROWN, A(1969), anim
Harry Spillman
DIRTYMOUTH(1970); THE CRAZIES(1973); BORN AGAIN(1978)
Evelyn Spillsbury
Silents
PAINTED PICTURES(1930, Brit.)
May Spils
GENGHIS KHAN(U.S./Brit./Ger./Yugo)
Klinton Spilsbury
LEGEND OF THE LONE RANGER, THE(1981)
Grazia Maria Spina
COSSACKS, THE(1960, It.); BIBLE...IN THE BEGINNING, THE(1966)
Harold Spina
52ND STREET(1937), m; JUST AROUND THE CORNER(1938), m; LITTLE MISS
BROADWAY(1938), m
John Spina
PRIVATE NAVY OF SGT. O'FARRELL, THE(1968)
Maria Grazia Spina
SAMSON AND THE SLAVE QUEEN(1963, Ital.); TIGER OF THE SEVEN SEAS(1964,
Fr./Ital.)
Sergio Spina
MERCENARY, THE(1970, Ital./Span.), w
Robert Spindele
TOY WIFE, THE(1938)
Bobby Spindola
LEOPARD MAN, THE(1943)
Robert Spindola
RAMONA(1936); FIREFLY, THE(1937); LIVE, LOVE AND LEARN(1937); PORT OF
SEVEN SEAS(1938)
Joe Spinell
SEVEN UPS, THE(1973); GODFATHER, THE, PART II(1974); FAREWELL, MY
LOVELY(1975); 92 IN THE SHADE(1975, U.S./Brit.); ROCKY(1976); STAY HUN-
GRY(1976); TAXI DRIVER(1976); SORCERER(1977); NUNZIO(1978); ONE MAN
JURY(1978); PARADISE ALLEY(1978); LAST EMBRACE(1979); ROCKY II(1979);
BRUBAKER(1980); CRUISING(1980); FIRST DEADLY SIN, THE(1980); LITTLE
DRAGONS, THE(1980); MANIAC(1980), a, w; NINTH CONFIGURATION, THE(1980);
NIGHTHAWKS(1981); MONSIGNOR(1982); NIGHT SHIFT(1982); ONE DOWN TWO
TO GO(1982); BIG SCORE, THE(1983); EUREKA(1983, Brit.); LAST FIGHT, THE(1983);
LOSIN' IT(1983); VIGILANTE(1983)
1984
LAST HORROR FILM, THE(1984)
Joseph Spinell
COPS AND ROBBERS(1973); RANCHO DELUXE(1975)
Mary Spinell
1984
LAST HORROR FILM, THE(1984)
Frank Spinella
TEENAGE GANG DEBS(1966)
Martin J. Spinelli
SOURDOUGH(1977), d, w
Philip J. Spinelli
1984
EYES OF FIRE(1984), p
Rosella Spinelli
LIGHT IN THE PIAZZA(1962)
Spinelly
AMERICAN LOVE(1932, Fr.)
Brent Spiner
RENT CONTROL(1981)
Victor Spinetti
GENTLE TERROR, THE(1962, Brit.); SPARROWS CAN'T SING(1963, Brit.); BECK-
ET(1964, Brit.); HARD DAY'S NIGHT, A(1964, Brit.); HELP!(1965, Brit.); WILD
AFFAIR, THE(1966, Brit.); TAMING OF THE SHREW, THE(1967, U.S./Ital.); BIGGEST
BUNDLE OF THEM ALL, THE(1968); START THE REVOLUTION WITHOUT
ME(1970); THIS, THAT AND THE OTHER(1970, Brit.); UNDER MILK WOOD(1973,
Brit.); DIGBY, THE BIGGEST DOG IN THE WORLD(1974, Brit.); LITTLE PRINCE,
THE(1974, Brit.); GREAT MCGONAGALL, THE(1975, Brit.); RETURN OF THE PINK
PANTHER, THE(1975, Brit.); EMILY(1976, Brit.); VOYAGE OF THE DAMNED(1976,
Brit.); SOME LIKE IT COOL(1979, Ger./Aust./Ital./Fr.)
Harry Spingler
Silents
CAPTAIN SWIFT(1914); GREYHOUND, THE(1914); ORDEAL, THE(1914); THIEF,
THE(1915); DEVIL'S PLAYGROUND, THE(1918); LES MISERABLES(1918); PERFECT
LADY, A(1918); FLAMES OF THE FLESH(1920)
Misc. Silents
NORTHERN LIGHTS(1914); BONDMAN, THE(1916); DRIFTWOOD(1916); WOMAN
UNDER COVER, THE(1919); MERELY MARY ANN(1920); SHERRY(1920)
Marie Spingold
WIFE TAKES A FLYER, THE(1942)
Brian Spink
1984
PLAGUE DOGS, THE(1984, U.S./Brit.)
George Spink
OUANGA(1936, Brit.)
Misc. Silents
PARDON MY FRENCH(1921)
Margo Spinker
PALM SPRINGS WEEKEND(1963)
James Spinks
CARWASH(1976); DAMIEN—OMEN II(1978); HUNTER, THE(1980); BIG SCORE,
THE(1983); DOCTOR DETROIT(1983)
Joe Spinnell
NEXT STOP, GREENWICH VILLAGE(1976); STARCRASH(1979)
Anthony Spinner
READY FOR THE PEOPLE(1964), p; HELICOPTER SPIES, THE(1968), p; HELL
BOATS(1970, Brit.), w

Marilyn Spinner
WEST POINT OF THE AIR(1935); TEST PILOT(1938)
The Spinners
FISH THAT SAVED PITTSBURGH, THE(1979)
Carroll Spinney
MUPPET MOVIE, THE(1979); GREAT MUPPET CAPER, THE(1981)
Matteo Spinola
HOUSE OF INTRIGUE, THE(1959, Ital.)
Paolo Spinola
TRAPPED IN TANGIERS(1960, Ital./Span.), w; LA FUGA(1966, Ital.), d, w
Dante Spinotti
1984
BASILEUS QUARTET(1984, Ital.), ph
Camilla Spira
TESTAMENT OF DR. MABUSE, THE(1943, Ger.); MERRY WIVES OF WINDSOR,
THE(1952, Ger.); DEVIL'S GENERAL, THE(1957, Ger.); ROSES FOR THE PROSECU-
TOR(1961, Ger.)
Cammila Spira
FREDDY UNTER FREMDEN STERNEN(1962, Ger.)
Daniel Spira
KING OF THE GYPSIES(1978)
Francois Spira
LAST YEAR AT MARIENBAD(1962, Fr./Ital.)
Fritz Spira
JOHNNY STEALS EUROPE(1932, Ger.); RASPUTIN(1932, Ger.)
Heinz Spira
TIME IN THE SUN, A(1970, Swed.)
Lotte Spira
LOVE WALTZ, THE(1930, Ger.)
Serge Spira
WANDERER, THE(1969, Fr.); TENANT, THE(1976, Fr.)
Victoria Spiri-Mercanton
CIRCLE OF LOVE(1965, Fr.), ed
N. Spiridonova
SUMMER TO REMEMBER, A(1961, USSR), spec eff
Olga Spiridonovic
FRAGRANCE OF WILD FLOWERS, THE(1979, Yugo.)
Valentina Spirina
GROWN-UP CHILDREN(1963, USSR), w
Spirit
MODEL SHOP, THE(1969), m
Hugh Spirit
RETURN OF THE JEDI(1983)
Jiri Spirit
DISTANT JOURNEY(1950, Czech.)
Bjorn Spiro
OPERATION LOVEBIRDS(1968, Den.)
Herbert Abbott Spiro
WORLD WAS HIS JURY, THE(1958), w; MUSIC BOX KID, THE(1960), w; CLOWN
AND THE KID, THE(1961), w
Richard Spiro
HIS WOMAN(1931)
Phil Spitalny
WHEN JOHNNY COMES MARCHING HOME(1943)
Richard M. Spitalny
1984
RHINESTONE(1984), p
Eric Spitella
CIRCLE OF DECEIT(1982, Fr./Ger.)
Anthony Spiteri
TRENCHCOAT(1983)
Sharon Spits
THEY ALL LAUGHED(1981)
Emilio Spitz
LOVE HUNGER(1965, Arg.), p
Ernst Spitz
WORLD AND THE FLESH, THE(1932), w
Harry Spitz
OFFENDERS, THE(1980)
Henry Spitz
BIG BOODLE, THE(1957), prod d
Joyce Spitz
EMBRYO(1976)
Oscar Spitz
MAEVA(1961)
Rhonda Spitz
Misc. Talkies
CUTTING LOOSE(1980)
Marian Spitzer
THRU DIFFERENT EYES(1929); DOLLY SISTERS, THE(1945), w; LOOK FOR THE
SILVER LINING(1949), w
Heinz Spitzner
LONGEST DAY, THE(1962)
Murray Spivack
MONKEY'S PAW, THE(1933), m
Alice Spivak
LILITH(1964); TIMES SQUARE(1980)
1984
GARBO TALKS(1984); MUPPETS TAKE MANHATTAN, THE(1984)
Misc. Talkies
FUN AND GAMES(1973)
Bob Spivak
SQUARE ROOT OF ZERO, THE(1964)
Timofei Spivak
STAR INSPECTOR, THE(1980, USSR)
Mme. Spivey
REQUIEM FOR A HEAVYWEIGHT(1962)

Ron Spivey
HARD COUNTRY(1981); SECOND-HAND HEARTS(1981)
Ronald Spivey
DEAD MEN DON'T WEAR PLAID(1982)
Sedena Spivey
LOVE AND THE MIDNIGHT AUTO SUPPLY(1978)
Victoria Spivey
HALLELUJAH(1929)
Spivy
FUGITIVE KIND, THE(1960)
Madame Spivy
ALL FALL DOWN(1962); MANCHURIAN CANDIDATE, THE(1962)
Mme. Spivy
STUDS LONIGAN(1960)
Jack Splangler
MAN WITH BOGART'S FACE, THE(1980), cos
William Splawn
MIDNIGHT MAN, THE(1974)
Tommy Splittberger
RACE WITH THE DEVIL(1975)
Spo-De-Odee
SCOTT JOPLIN(1977); WHICH WAY IS UP?(1977)
Dorothy Spoencer
WHAT PRICE GLORY?(1952), ed
William Spofford
REASON TO LIVE, A REASON TO DIE, A(1974, Ital./Fr./Ger./Span.)
Patrick Spohn
SWEET CHARITY(1969)
Vera Spohr
JAZZBAND FIVE, THE(1932, Ger,)
Walter Spohr
BELLE DE JOUR(1968, Fr.), ed
Jaromir Spol
BOHEMIAN RAPTURE(1948, Czech)
Michael Spolan
CREEPSHOW(1982), ed
Aldo Spoldi
WHIPLASH(1948)
Filippo Spoletini
WHITE VOICES(1965, Fr./Ital.)
Guglielmo Spoletini
WHITE VOICES(1965, Fr./Ital.); HILLS RUN RED, THE(1967, Ital.); SAILOR FROM GIBRALTAR, THE(1967, Brit.); DEATH RIDES A HORSE(1969, Ital.)
Michael [Mischa] Spolianski
PRIVATE LIFE OF DON JUAN, THE(1934, Brit.), m
M. Spoliansky
EVENSONG(1934, Brit.), m; BATTLE OF THE VILLA FIORITA, THE(1965, Brit.), m
Mischa Spoliansky
LUCKY NUMBER, THE(1933, Brit.), m; MY SONG FOR YOU(1935, Brit.), m; SANDERS OF THE RIVER(1935, Brit.), m; FOREVER YOURS(1937, Brit.), m; MAN WHO COULD WORK MIRACLES, THE(1937, Brit.), m; GAIETY GIRLS, THE(1938, Brit.), m; OVER THE MOON(1940, Brit.), m; GIRL IN DISTRESS(1941, Brit.), m; DON'T TAKE IT TO HEART(1944, Brit.), m; SECRET MISSION(1944, Brit.), m; MR. EMMANUEL(1945, Brit.), m; MAN FROM MOROCCO, THE(1946, Brit.), m; WANTED FOR MURDER(1946, Brit.), m; MEET ME AT DAWN(1947, Brit.), m; IDOL OF PARIS(1948, Brit.), m; TEMPTATION HARBOR(1949, Brit.), m; THIS WAS A WOMAN(1949, Brit.), m; ADAM AND EVELYNE(1950, Brit.), m; HAPPIEST DAYS OF YOUR LIFE(1950, Brit.), m; IF THIS BE SIN(1950, Brit.), m; HAPPY GO LOVELY(1951, Brit.), m; MAN IN THE DINGHY, THE(1951, Brit.), m; MIDNIGHT EPISODE(1951, Brit.), m; GAY ADVENTURE, THE(1953, Brit.), m; TURN THE KEY SOFTLY(1954, Brit.), m; TROUBLE IN STORE(1955, Brit.), m; SAINT JOAN(1957), m; WHOLE TRUTH, THE(1958, Brit.), m; FLAME OVER INDIA(1960, Brit.), m; BEST HOUSE IN LONDON, THE(1969, Brit.), m; HITLER: THE LAST TEN DAYS(1973, Brit./Ital.), m
Misha Spoliansky
GHOST GOES WEST, THE(1936), m
Viola Spolin
ALEX IN WONDERLAND(1970)
Branko Spoljar
APACHE GOLD(1965, Ger.); TREASURE OF SILVER LAKE(1965, Fr./Ger./Yugo.); ROMANCE OF A HORSE THIEF(1971)
Mischa Spollansky
DUEL IN THE JUNGLE(1954, Brit.), m
Mel Sponder
BLAST OF SILENCE(1961)
Hilda Spong
Misc. Silents
DIVORCED(1915)
Kuno Sponholtz
NIGHT OF THE ZOMBIES(1981)
Kuno Sponholz
1984
DELIVERY BOYS(1984)
Mario Sponza
STROMBOLI(1950, Ital.)
Spooks
FOLLOW THE BOYS(1944)
Spooks the Dog
FAMILY NEXT DOOR, THE(1939)
Arlene Spooner
ORGY OF THE DEAD(1965)
Cecil Spooner
Silents
NELL OF THE CIRCUS(1914), a, w; ONE LAW FOR THE WOMAN(1924)
David Spooner
Misc. Talkies
BLINKER'S SPY-SPOTTER(1971)

Edna May Spooner
Misc. Silents
MAN AND WIFE(1923)
F.E. Spooner
Silents
AS THE SUN WENT DOWN(1919)
Judy Spooner
PRIVATE LIFE OF SHERLOCK HOLMES, THE(1970, Brit.)
Tina Spooner
PRIVATE LIFE OF SHERLOCK HOLMES, THE(1970, Brit.)
N. Spoor
BETRAYAL, THE(1948), ph
Carl Spore
SAVAGE WILD, THE(1970)
Sport the Dog
Silents
ARE YOU A FAILURE?(1923)
Franco Sportelli
FOUR DAYS OF NAPLES, THE(1963, US/Ital.); AFTER THE FOX(1966, U.S./Brit./Ital.); CHASTITY BELT, THE(1968, Ital.)
Luca Sportelli
00-2 MOST SECRET AGENTS(1965, Ital.)
The Sportsman
WALKING MY BABY BACK HOME(1953)
The Sportsmen
HERE COMES ELMER(1943); MOON OVER LAS VEGAS(1944); WEEKEND PASS(1944); FEUDIN', FUSSIN' AND A-FIGHTIN'(1948); MAKE BELIEVE BALLROOM(1949); FRESH FROM PARIS(1955); PARIS FOLLIES OF 1956(1955)
Murray Douglas Sporup
ROCK BABY, ROCK IT(1957), d
Carletto Sposito
DIFFICULT YEARS(1950, Ital.); MILLER'S WIFE, THE(1957, Ital.)
Luis Spota
EMPTY STAR, THE(1962, Mex.), w
The Spotnicks
JUST FOR FUN(1963, Brit.)
Spotted Elk
SILENT ENEMY, THE(1930)
James Spottiswood
SWEET SURRENDER(1935)
Roger Spottiswoode
STRAW DOGS(1971, Brit.), ed; PAT GARRETT AND BILLY THE KID(1973), ed; GAMBLER, THE(1974), ed; HARD TIMES(1975), ed; TERROR TRAIN(1980, Can.), d; PURSUIT OF D.B. COOPER, THE(1981), d; 48 HOURS(1982), w; UNDER FIRE(1983), d
John Spotton
NOBODY WAVED GOODBYE(1965, Can.), ph, ed
George Louis Spotts
COURT JESTER, THE(1956)
Roger Hamilton Spotts
NATIONAL LAMPOON'S CLASS REUNION(1982)
James Spottswood
THUNDERBOLT(1929); CONVENTION GIRL(1935); ANGELS WITH DIRTY FACES(1938); GIRLS ON PROBATION(1938); HOLLYWOOD STADIUM MYSTERY(1938)
Silents
CLIMBERS, THE(1919)
Michael Spound
WACKO(1983), w
Branko Spoylar
LUM AND ABNER ABROAD(1956)
G.D. Spradlin
WILL PENNY(1968); NUMBER ONE(1969); MONTE WALSH(1970); ZABRISKIE POINT(1970); ONLY WAY HOME, THE(1972), a, p&d; GODFATHER, THE, PART II(1974); HUNTING PARTY, THE(1977, Brit.); MAC ARTHUR(1977); ONE ON ONE(1977); APOCALYPSE NOW(1979); NORTH DALLAS FORTY(1979); FORMULA, THE(1980); WRONG IS RIGHT(1982); LORDS OF DISCIPLINE, THE(1983)
1984
TANK(1984)
J.D. Spradlin
HELL'S ANGELS '69(1969)
Hart Sprager
1984
NOT FOR PUBLICATION(1984)
Chandler Sprague
SONG OF KENTUCKY(1929), p; DANCERS, THE(1930), d; NOT DAMAGED(1930), d; I LIKE IT THAT WAY(1934), w; MENACE(1934), w; EARLY TO BED(1936), w; CHASER, THE(1938), w; BASHFUL BACHELOR, THE(1942), w; GUY NAMED JOE, A(1943), w
Misc. Talkies
THEIR MAD MOMENT(1931), d
Silents
CAMILLE(1927), w; STREET OF SIN, THE(1928), w
Hall T. Sprague
SKY RIDERS(1976, U.S./Gr.), w
Kenneth Sprague
SO LONG, BLUE BOY(1973), p
Milton Sprague
GEORGE WASHINGTON CARVER(1940)
Peter Hans Sprague
SPLIT IMAGE(1982)
Richard Sprague
MOVING VIOLATION(1976), ed; ROLLERCOASTER(1977), ed
Richard M. Sprague
MAN CALLED GANNON, A(1969), ed; RED SKY AT MORNING(1971), ed
Ted Sprague
HISTORY OF THE WORLD, PART 1(1981); TO BE OR NOT TO BE(1983)
William E. Sprague
MOTOR PSYCHO(1965), w; ROPE OF FLESH(1965), w

Thomas Spratley
GOING HOME(1971)
Tom Spratley
HOSPITAL, THE(1971); STING, THE(1973); WHERE THE LILIES BLOOM(1974); SUNSHINE BOYS, THE(1975); MAN WITH TWO BRAINS, THE(1983); MAX DUGAN RETURNS(1983); SUDDEN IMPACT(1983)
1984
CITY HEAT(1984); PROTOCOL(1984)
Tony Spratling
MAN WHO HAUNTED HIMSELF, THE(1970, Brit.), ph; UP THE FRONT(1972, Brit.), ph
Terry Spratt
SHAPE OF THINGS TO COME, THE(1979, Can.)
Nella Spraugh
EGG AND I, THE(1947)
Geraldine Spreckels
SECRETS OF A CO-ED(1942)
Joe Spree
WALTZ TIME(1933, Brit.)
Michael Sprehn
OPERATION LOVEBIRDS(1968, Den.)
Volker Sprengler
QUERELLE(1983, Ger./Fr.)
Penelope Sprerris
NAKED ANGELS(1969)
Elizabeth Spriggs
WORK IS A FOUR LETTER WORD(1968, Brit.); THREE INTO TWO WON'T GO(1969, Brit.); LADY CHATTERLEY'S LOVER(1981, Fr./Brit.); RICHARD'S THINGS(1981, Brit.); UNSUITABLE JOB FOR A WOMAN, AN(1982, Brit.)
Linda Spriggs
RETURN OF THE JEDI(1983)
Deer Spring
LAUGHING BOY(1934)
Frank E. Spring
Silents
DEMOCRACY(1918, Brit.), p; AFTER MANY DAYS(1919, Brit.), p; ALL MEN ARE LIARS(1919, Brit.), p; MAN'S SHADOW, A(1920, Brit.), p; FIRES OF INNOCENCE(1922, Brit.), p
Helen Spring
ABBOTT AND COSTELLO MEET FRANKENSTEIN(1948); COVER-UP(1949); CAGED(1950); EMERGENCY WEDDING(1950); ONE TOO MANY(1950); TO PLEASE A LADY(1950); STRIP, THE(1951); TWO TICKETS TO BROADWAY(1951); SOMETHING TO LIVE FOR(1952); STRANGE LADY IN TOWN(1955); HIGH SOCIETY(1956); HOT ROD GANG(1958); WILLARD(1971)
Howard Spring
MY SON, MY SON!(1940), w; FAME IS THE SPUR(1947, Brit.), w
Kathy Spring
LOVE AND MONEY(1982)
M. Spring
TENTACLES(1977, Ital.), art d
Muriel Spring
Silents
BLUEBEARD'S SEVEN WIVES(1926)
Sylvia Spring
MADELEINE IS(1971, Can.), d, w
Tim Spring
WHITE HUNTER(1965), ph; SPOTS ON MY LEOPARD, THE(1974, S. Africa), d & ed
Arthur Springer
WORDS AND MUSIC(1929)
Edgar Springer
ONLY WAY HOME, THE(1972)
Gary Springer
LAW AND DISORDER(1974); DOG DAY AFTERNOON(1975); BETWEEN THE LINES(1977); JAWS II(1978); HOMETOWN U.S.A.(1979); SMALL CIRCLE OF FRIENDS, A(1980)
Harry Springer
Silents
SPREADING DAWN, THE(1917)
Jim Springer
MOONSHINE COUNTY EXPRESS(1977)
John Springer, Jr.
WHEN TIME RAN OUT(1980)
Louise Springer
STAND UP AND FIGHT(1939)
Norman Springer
HURRICANE(1929), w; SHANGHAIED LOVE(1931), w; STOWAWAY(1932), w; FRONTIER DAYS(1934), w; DEVIL'S PLAYGROUND(1937), w; SCREAM IN THE NIGHT(1943), w
Silents
ISLE OF FORGOTTEN WOMEN(1927), w; SO THIS IS LOVE(1928), w
Patricia Springer
1984
OH GOD! YOU DEVIL(1984)
Philip Springer
KILL A DRAGON(1967), m; MORE DEAD THAN ALIVE(1968), m; I SAILED TO TAHITI WITH AN ALL GIRL CREW(1969), m; IMPASSE(1969), m, md; TELL ME THAT YOU LOVE ME, JUNIE MOON(1970), m; WICKED, WICKED(1973), m
Robert Springer
NO RETURN ADDRESS(1961), w
Winnifred Springetti
SUNDAY IN THE COUNTRY(1975, Can.)
Rick Springfield
BATTLESTAR GALACTICA(1979)
1984
HARD TO HOLD(1984), a, m
Wayne Springfield
ANDROID(1982), art d; FORBIDDEN WORLD(1982), art d; SPACE RAIDERS(1983), art d

The Springfields
IT'S ALL OVER TOWN(1963, Brit.); JUST FOR FUN(1963, Brit.)
Ruth Springford
ONE PLUS ONE(1961, Can.); FIVE CARD STUD(1968); SUNDAY IN THE COUNTRY(1975, Can.); CHANGELING, THE(1980, Can.); IMPROPER CHANNELS(1981, Can.)
Harry Springler
Silents
PLUNDERER, THE(1915); LAST TRAIL(1921)
Elliott White Springs
YOUNG EAGLES(1930), w; BODY AND SOUL(1931), w
Sam Springson
MR. COHEN TAKES A WALK(1936, Brit.); TWELVE GOOD MEN(1936, Brit.); PERFECT CRIME, THE(1937, Brit.)
Pamela Springsteen
FAST TIMES AT RIDGEMONT HIGH(1982)
Pamlea Springsteen
1984
RECKLESS(1984)
R.G. Springsteen
COLORADO PIONEERS(1945), d; MARSHAL OF LAREDO(1945), d; PHANTOM OF THE PLAINS(1945), p; CONQUEST OF CHEYENNE(1946), d; SANTA FE UPRISING(1946), d; SHERIFF OF REDWOOD VALLEY(1946), d; STAGECOACH TO DENVER(1946), d; SUN VALLEY CYCLONE(1946), d; ALONG THE OREGON TRAIL(1947), d; HOMESTEADERS OF PARADISE VALLEY(1947), d; MAIN STREET KID, THE(1947), d; MARSHAL OF CRIPPLE CREEK, THE(1947), d; OREGON TRAIL SCOUTS(1947), d; RUSTLERS OF DEVIL'S CANYON(1947), d; UNDER COLORADO SKIES(1947), d; VIGILANTES OF BOOMTOWN(1947), d; HEART OF VIRGINIA(1948), d; OUT OF THE STORM(1948), d; RENEGADES OF SONORA(1948), d; SECRET SERVICE INVESTIGATOR(1948), d; SON OF GOD'S COUNTRY(1948), d; SUNDOWN IN SANTA FE(1948), d; DEATH VALLEY GUNFIGHTER(1949), d; FLAME OF YOUTH(1949), d; HELLFIRE(1949), d; NAVAJO TRAIL RAIDERS(1949), d; RED MENACE, THE(1949), d; SHERIFF OF WICHITA(1949), d; ARIZONA COWBOY, THE(1950), d; BELLE OF OLD MEXICO(1950), d; COVERED WAGON RAID(1950), d; FRISCO TORNADO(1950), d; HARBOR OF MISSING MEN(1950), d; HILLS OF OKLAHOMA(1950), d; SINGING GUNS(1950), d; HONEYCHILE(1951), d; MILLION DOLLAR PURSUIT(1951), d; STREET BANDITS(1951), d; FABULOUS SENORITA, THE(1952), d; GOBS AND GALS(1952), d; OKLAHOMA ANNIE(1952), d; TOUGHEST MAN IN ARIZONA(1952), d; TROPICAL HEAT WAVE(1952), d; GERALDINE(1953), d; PERILOUS JOURNEY, A(1953), d; CROSS CHANNEL(1955, Brit.), d; DOUBLE JEOPARDY(1955), d; I COVER THE UNDERWORLD(1955), d; SECRET VENTURE(1955, Brit.), d; COME NEXT SPRING(1956), d; TRACK THE MAN DOWN(1956, Brit.), d; WAGON WHEELS WESTWARD(1956), d; WHEN GANGLAND STRIKES(1956), d; AFFAIR IN RENO(1957), d; COLE YOUNGER, GUNFIGHTER(1958), d; REVOLT IN THE BIG HOUSE(1958), d; BATTLE CRY(1959), d; KING OF THE WILD STALLIONS(1959), d; OPERATION EICHMANN(1961), d; SHOWDOWN(1963), d; BULLET FOR A BADMAN(1964), d; HE RIDES TALL(1964), d; TAGGART(1964), d; BLACK SPURS(1965), d; APACHE UPRISING(1966), d; JOHNNY RENO(1966), d; WACO(1966), d; HOSTILE GUNS(1967), d; RED TOMAHAWK(1967), d; TIGER BY THE TAIL(1970), d
Misc. Talkies
CALIFORNIA GOLD RUSH(1946), d
Robert Springsteen
HOME ON THE HANGE(1946), d; MAN FROM RAINBOW VALLEY, THE(1946), d
Larry Sprinkle
1984
FIRESTARTER(1984)
Ove Sprogoe
JOURNEY TO THE SEVENTH PLANET(1962, U.S./Swed.); CRAZY PARADISE(1965, Den.); OPERATION LOVEBIRDS(1968, Den.); ONLY WAY, THE(1970, Panama/Den./U.S.); SCANDAL IN DENMARK(1970, Den.)
Eoin Sprott
JAWS OF SATAN(1980), spec eff
William Sprott
THUNDER IN CAROLINA(1960)
Bert Sprotte
MARRIED IN HOLLYWOOD(1929); PASSPORT TO HELL(1932); CAPTURED(1933); SONG OF THE EAGLE(1933); MANHATTAN MELODRAMA(1934); PURSUIT OF HAPPINESS, THE(1934); BARBARY COAST(1935); DRACULA'S DAUGHTER(1936); LANCER SPY(1937); THIN ICE(1937)
Silents
BREED OF MEN(1919); BLAZING TRAIL, THE(1921); BOB HAMPTON OF PLACER(1921); GUILE OF WOMEN(1921); NIGHT HORSEMAN, THE(1921); O'MALLEY OF THE MOUNTED(1921); WHITE OAK(1921); HUNGRY HEARTS(1922); QUESTION OF HONOR, A(1922); THELMA(1922); PRISONER, THE(1923); ROSITA(1923); SOUL OF THE BEAST(1923); HIS HOUR(1924); SINGER JIM MCKEE(1924); STOLEN BRIDE, THE(1927)
Misc. Silents
SELFISH YATES(1918); BROTH FOR SUPPER(1919); DECEIVER, THE(1920); GOLDEN TRAIL, THE(1920); TWO MOONS(1920); BELOW THE DEAD LINE(1921); BLUE BLAZES(1922); CONQUERING THE WOMAN(1922); FOR BIG STAKES(1922); PURPLE DAWN(1923); SNOWDRIFT(1923); HUMAN TORNADO, THE(1925); WHY WOMEN LOVE(1925); FIGHTING HOMBRE, THE(1927); LIFE OF AN ACTRESS(1927)
Berthold Sprotte
Misc. Silents
SHARK MONROE(1918)
G. Sprotte
Silents
PARADISE GARDEN(1917)
Peter Sproule
IF ...(1968, Brit.); LAND THAT TIME FORGOT, THE(1975, Brit.); TERROR(1979, Brit.); MOUSE AND THE WOMAN, THE(1981, Brit.)
Don Spruance
FATHER GOOSE(1964); PICKUP ON 101(1972)
Donald Spruance
MA BARKER'S KILLER BROOD(1960)
Miklaj Sprudin
BOXER(1971, Pol.), ph

Ray Spruell
MANDINGO(1975); TOY, THE(1982)

Paul Sprunck
UNTAMED WOMEN(1952), art d

Sandy Sprung
LAST AMERICAN VIRGIN, THE(1982)

Paul Sprunk
UNTAMED WOMEN(1952), spec eff

Dick Spry
HOSTAGE, THE(1966)

Nancy Spry
GIRLS ON THE BEACH(1965)

Robin Spry
PROLOGUE(1970, Can.), p, d, w; ONE MAN(1979, Can.), d, w; SUZANNE(1980, Can.), d, w
1984
KINGS AND DESPERATE MEN(1984, Brit.)

Alec Spryce
RINGER, THE(1932, Brit.), ph

Kuno Spunholz
ZELIG(1983)

Charles Spurderson
SKIDOO(1968), spec eff

Charles Spurgeon
KITTEN WITH A WHIP(1964), spec eff; NIGHT WALKER, THE(1964), spec eff; PICTURE MOMMY DEAD(1966), spec eff; OH DAD, POOR DAD, MAMA'S HUNG YOU IN THE CLOSET AND I'M FEELIN' SO SAD(1967), spec eff; PRIVATE NAVY OF SGT. O'FARRELL, THE(1968), spec eff; STERILE CUCKOO, THE(1969), spec eff; UPTOWN SATURDAY NIGHT(1974), spec eff; MARATHON MAN(1976), spec eff; MOONSHINE COUNTY EXPRESS(1977), spec eff

Charlie Spurgeon
DRIVER, THE(1978), spec eff; TERROR ON TOUR(1980), spec eff

Danny Spurlock
SHEPHERD OF THE HILLS, THE(1964)

Shelley Spurlock
ABSENCE OF MALICE(1981)

Sandra Spurr
HUNTED IN HOLLAND(1961, Brit.)

Sharon Spurrell
MAN, A WOMAN, AND A BANK, A(1979, Can.)

Linda Spurrier
JUBILEE(1978, Brit.); PIRATES OF PENZANCE, THE(1983)

Paul Spurrier
WILD GEESE, THE(1978, Brit.)

Johanna Spyri
HEIDI(1937), w; HEIDI(1954, Switz.), w; HEIDI AND PETER(1955, Switz.), w; HEIDI(1968, Aust.), w; HEIDI'S SONG(1982), w

V. Spyropoulos
ANNA OF RHODES(1950, Gr.), w

The Squadronnaires
HIGH JINKS IN SOCIETY(1949, Brit.)

David Square
MOONLIGHTING(1982, Brit.)

Emma-Lindsay Squier
DANCING PIRATE(1936), w

Ken Squier
CANNONBALL RUN, THE(1981); STROKER ACE(1983)

Lucita Squier
Silents
PENROD(1922), w; GAMBLE WITH HEARTS, A(1923, Brit.), w; ROYAL OAK, THE(1923, Brit.), w

Jose Squinquel
PASTEUR(1936, Fr.); DEADLY DECOYS, THE(1962, Fr.)

Anthony Squire
FILES FROM SCOTLAND YARD(1951, Brit.), d; INTRUDER, THE(1955, Brit.), w; DOUBLE CROSS(1956, Brit.), d, w; HELL IN KOREA(1956, Brit.), p, w; MAC-BETH(1963), w; DARLING LILI(1970), ph

David Squire
MEMOIRS OF A SURVIVOR(1981, Brit.)
1984
NUMBER ONE(1984, Brit.)

Jacqueline Squire
NOTORIOUS LANDLADY, THE(1962); MY FAIR LADY(1964)

Jamie Squire
SMALL CIRCLE OF FRIENDS, A(1980)

Janie Squire
PIRANHA(1978)

Jules Squire
MOULIN ROUGE(1952), cos

Julia Squire
PANDORA AND THE FLYING DUTCHMAN(1951, Brit.), cos; MAGIC BOX, THE(1952, Brit.), cos; HEART OF THE MATTER, THE(1954, Brit.), cos; END OF THE AFFAIR, THE(1955, Brit.), cos; PORT AFRIQUE(1956, Brit.), cos

Katherine Squire
STORY ON PAGE ONE, THE(1959); SONG WITHOUT END(1960); STUDS LONI-GAN(1960); DAYS OF WINE AND ROSES(1962); RIDE IN THE WHIRLWIND(1966); THIS SAVAGE LAND(1969); TWO-LANE BLACKTOP(1971); LOLLY-MADONNA XXX(1973)

Luise Squire
SING FOR YOUR SUPPER(1941)

Ronald Squire
WILD BOY(1934, Brit.); COME OUT OF THE PANTRY(1935, Brit.); LOVE IN EXILE(1936, Brit.); ACTION FOR SLANDER(1937, Brit.); FORBIDDEN TER-RITORY(1938, Brit.); HIDEOUT IN THE ALPS(1938, Brit.); VOICE IN THE NIGHT, A(1941, Brit.); FLEMISH FARM, THE(1943, Brit.); DON'T TAKE IT TO HEART(1944, Brit.); JOURNEY TOGETHER(1946, Brit.); AFFAIRS OF A ROGUE, THE(1949, Brit.); WOMAN HATER(1949, Brit.); ROCKING HORSE WINNER, THE(1950, Brit.); WHILE THE SUN SHINES(1950, Brit.); NO HIGHWAY IN THE SKY(1951, Brit.); ENCORE(1951, Brit.); IT STARTED IN PARADISE(1952, Brit.); MY COUSIN RA-CHEL(1952); UNFINISHED SYMPHONY, THE(1953, Aust./Brit.); ALWAYS A BRI-

DE(1954, Brit.); MAN WITH A MILLION(1954, Brit.); SCOTCH ON THE ROCKS(1954, Brit.); FOOTSTEPS IN THE FOG(1955, Brit.); JOSEPHINE AND MEN(1955, Brit.); AROUND THE WORLD IN 80 DAYS(1956); NOW AND FOREVER(1956, Brit.); ISLAND IN THE SUN(1957); RAISING A RIOT(1957, Brit.); SEA WIFE(1957, Brit.); SILKEN AFFAIR, THE(1957, Brit.); INN OF THE SIXTH HAPPINESS, THE(1958); LAW AND DISORDER(1958, Brit.); SHERIFF OF FRACTURED JAW, THE(1958, Brit.); COUNT YOUR BLESSINGS(1959)
Misc. Silents
WHOSO IS WITHOUT SIN(1916, Brit.)

Sydney Squire
1984
PURPLE HEARTS(1984)

William Squire
ALEXANDER THE GREAT(1956); MAN WHO NEVER WAS, THE(1956, Brit.); PURSUIT OF THE GRAF SPEE(1957, Brit.); DUNKIRK(1958, Brit.); CHALLENGE FOR ROBIN HOOD, A(1968, Brit.); WHERE EAGLES DARE(1968, Brit.); ANNE OF THE THOUSAND DAYS(1969, Brit.); THIRTY NINE STEPS, THE(1978, Brit.)

Dorothy Squires
STARS IN YOUR EYES(1956, Brit.)

Douglas Squires
DREAM MAKER, THE(1963, Brit.), ch

Jacey Squires
MUSIC MAN, THE(1962)

Jack Squires
DYNAMITE DELANEY(1938)

Louise Squires
LAUGH YOUR BLUES AWAY(1943)

Lucita Squires
Silents
DAUGHTER OF LOVE, A(1925, Brit.), w

William Squires
LONG DARK HALL, THE(1951, Brit.)

Pasquale Squittierie
GUN, THE(1978, Ital.), p,d,w,&ed

Bohumil Sramek
MIDSUMMERS NIGHT'S DREAM, A(1961, Czech), anim

Milan Srdoc
FRONTIER HELLCAT(1966, Fr./Ital./Ger./Yugo.); TWILIGHT TIME(1983, U.S./Yugo.)

Mirdo Sreckovic
TEMPEST(1958, Ital./Yugo./Fr.)

Felike Srednicki
FIRST START(1953, Pol.), ph

Blagoe Srephanoff
THAT HAMILTON WOMAN(1941), makeup

I. Sretenskiy
GORDEYEV FAMILY, THE(1961, U.S.S.R.)

Patravadi Sritrairatana
1 2 3 MONSTER EXPRESS(1977, Thai.)

Krung Srivilai
S.T.A.B.(1976, Hong Kong/Thailand); 1 2 3 MONSTER EXPRESS(1977, Thai.)

Jiri Srnka
SWEET LIGHT IN A DARK ROOM(1966, Czech.), m

S. Srodka
BORDER STREET(1950, Pol.)

Jerry Sroka
GODSPELL(1973); NOCTURNA(1979)

Alfred Srp
FOREVER MY LOVE(1962), ed; MIRACLE OF THE WHITE STALLIONS(1963), ed; OLD SHATTERHAND(1968, Ger./Yugo./Fr./Ital.), ed; FIGHT FOR ROME(1969, Ger./Rum.), ed

Fred Srp
CORRUPT ONES, THE(1967, Ger.), ed; ESCAPE TO THE SUN(1972, Fr./Ger./Israel), ed; SLAVERS(1977, Ger.), ed; JUST A GIGOLO(1979, Ger.), ed; JULIE DAR-LING(1982, Can./Ger.), ed
1984
CHINESE BOXES(1984, Ger./Brit.), ed

Zdenek Srstka
LEMONADE JOE(1966, Czech.)

Karl Sruss
GIRL IN 419(1933), ph

Raymond St. Albin
PASSAGE TO MARSEILLE(1944)

Joseph St. Amaad
SARATOGA TRUNK(1945), prod d

Joseph St. Amand
THIEF, THE(1952), prod d

Marcella St. Amant
LAND RAIDERS(1969)

Michael St. Angel
GANGWAY FOR TOMORROW(1943); BRIDE BY MISTAKE(1944); FALCON OUT WEST, THE(1944); MARINE RAIDERS(1944); SEVEN DAYS ASHORE(1944); BRIGH-TON STRANGLER, THE(1945); FIRST YANK INTO TOKYO(1945); WHAT A BLONDE(1945); TRUTH ABOUT MURDER, THE(1946); FRENCH LINE, THE(1954); DEAD HEAT ON A MERRY-GO-ROUND(1966)

Bob St. Angelo
LAST MAN(1932); HE STAYED FOR BREAKFAST(1940); ROAD TO SIN-GAPORE(1940); SON OF PALEFACE(1952); VEILS OF BAGDAD, THE(1953); KISS THEM FOR ME(1957)

Robert St. Angelo
SUBWAY EXPRESS(1931); MOUNTAIN MUSIC(1937); NORTHWEST PASS-AGE(1940); RAINBOW ISLAND(1944); ESCAPE ME NEVER(1947); GREATEST SHOW ON EARTH, THE(1952); CHIEF CRAZY HORSE(1955); LAST FRONTIER, THE(1955)
Silents
KING OF KINGS, THE(1927)

Sallee St. Aubin
TOYS ARE NOT FOR CHILDREN(1972)

Robert St. Aubrey
HIDDEN FEAR(1957), p; ALIAS JESSE JAMES(1959), w
Stella St. Audrie
Silents
LITTLE LORD FAUNTLEROY(1914, Brit.); RUPERT OF HENTZAU(1915, Brit.)
Misc. Silents
WORLD, THE FLESH AND THE DEVIL, THE(1914, Brit.); HENRY, KING OF NAVARRE(1924, Brit.)
Jeanne St. Bonnet
AZAIS(1931, Fr.)
St. Brendan's Choir
SWEET ROSIE O'GRADY(1943)
The St. Brendan's Church Choir
ANGELS WITH DIRTY FACES(1938)
H. St. C. Stewart
MAN WHO KNEW TOO MUCH, THE(1935, Brit.), ed
Ada St. Clair
Misc. Silents
RUNAWAY, THE(1917)
Ana St. Clair
ALL THE YOUNG MEN(1960); CARETAKERS, THE(1963)
Arthur St. Clair
MISS V FROM MOSCOW(1942), w; STAGECOACH BUCKAROO(1942), w; SUBMARINE BASE(1943), w; ARSON SQUAD(1945), w; GUNMAN'S CODE(1946), w; PHILO VANCE'S GAMBLE(1947), w; RIMFIRE(1949), w
David St. Clair
LORD OF THE FLIES(1963, Brit.)
Elizabeth St. Clair
STAR!(1968); LOVE MACHINE, THE,(1971); TENDER FLESH(1976)
Eric St. Clair
Misc. Silents
FIND YOUR MAN(1924)
Jean St. Clair
GENTLE GUNMAN, THE(1952, Brit.); EIGHT O'CLOCK WALK(1954, Brit.); MEET MR. MALCOLM(1954, Brit.); IMPULSE(1955, Brit.); DOCTOR AT LARGE(1957, Brit.); HELL DRIVERS(1958, Brit.); YOUNG AND THE GUILTY, THE(1958, Brit.); DENTIST IN THE CHAIR(1960, Brit.); GREAT ST. TRINIAN'S TRAIN ROBBERY, THE(1966, Brit.)
Joan St. Clair
PARIS EXPRESS, THE(1953, Brit.)
Johnny St. Clair
ONE SUNDAY AFTERNOON(1933)
Joyce St. Clair
MELODY OF MY HEART(1936, Brit.)
Kristina St. Clair
COUNTRYMAN(1982, Jamaica)
Leonard St. Clair
INNER CIRCLE, THE(1946), w
Luke St. Clair
Misc. Talkies
BEWARE THE BLACK WIDOW(1968)
Lydia St. Clair
HOUSE ON 92ND STREET, THE(1945)
Mal St. Clair
SIDE STREET(1929), d, w; BORN RECKLESS(1937), d; MEET THE MISSUS(1940), d; SWING OUT THE BLUES(1943), d
Silents
LIGHTHOUSE BY THE SEA, THE(1924), d; AFTER BUSINESS HOURS(1925), d; ON THIN ICE(1925), d
Misc. Silents
GEORGE(, WASHINGTON$c JR. (1924), d; FIND YOUR MAN(1924), d
Malcolm St. Clair
CANARY MURDER CASE, THE(1929), d; NIGHT PARADE(1929, Brit.), d; BOUDOIR DIPLOMAT(1930), d; MONTANA MOON(1930), d; REMOTE CONTROL(1930), d; GOLDIE GETS ALONG(1933), d; OLSEN'S BIG MOMENT(1934), d; CRACK-UP, THE(1937), d; DANGEROUSLY YOURS(1937), d; TIME OUT FOR ROMANCE(1937), d; DOWN ON THE FARM(1938), d; SAFETY IN NUMBERS(1938), d; TRIP TO PARIS, A(1938), d; EVERYBODY'S BABY(1939), d; HOLLYWOOD CAVALCADE(1939), d; JONES FAMILY IN HOLLYWOOD, THE(1939), d; QUICK MILLIONS(1939), d; YOUNG AS YOU FEEL(1940), d; BASHFUL BACHELOR, THE(1942), d; MAN IN THE TRUNK, THE(1942), d; OVER MY DEAD BODY(1942), d; DANCING MASTERS, THE(1943), d; JITTERBUGS(1943), d; TWO WEEKS TO LIVE(1943), d; BIG NOISE, THE(1944), d; BULLFIGHTERS, THE(1945), d; ARTHUR TAKES OVER(1948), d; FIGHTING BACK(1948), d
Silents
ARE PARENTS PEOPLE?(1925), d; GOOD AND NAUGHTY(1926), d; GRAND DUCHESS AND THE WAITER, THE(1926), d; SOCIAL CELEBRITY, A(1926), d; KNOCKOUT REILLY(1927), d; GENTLEMEN PREFER BLONDES(1928), d; SPORTING GOODS(1928), d
Misc. Silents
TROUBLE WITH WIVES, THE(1925), d; WOMAN OF THE WORLD, A(1925), d; POPULAR SIN, THE(1926), d; SHOW OFF, THE(1926), d; BREAKFAST AT SUNRISE(1927), d; BEAU BROADWAY(1928), d
Marie St. Clair
Silents
LOVER'S ISLAND(1925), ed
Maurice St. Clair
LADY, LET'S DANCE(1944); DOCKS OF NEW YORK(1945); TANGIER(1946)
Michael St. Clair
THOROUGHLY MODERN MILLIE(1967); NOTORIOUS LANDLADY, THE(1962); THREE STOOGES GO AROUND THE WORLD IN A DAZE, THE(1963); MY FAIR LADY(1964); VON RYAN'S EXPRESS(1965); OUR MAN FLINT(1966); KING'S PIRATE(1967); MISSION MARS(1968), w; BODY STEALERS, THE(1969), w; SKULLDUGGERY(1970); REFLECTION OF FEAR, A(1973)
Robert St. Clair
SWING IT, PROFESSOR(1937), w; I'M FROM THE CITY(1938), w; WOMEN IN THE NIGHT(1948), w

Sally St. Clair
SHADOW, THE(1937)
Sue St. Clair
SHADOW, THE(1937)
Suzette St. Clair
CONFESSIONS OF A POP PERFORMER(1975, Brit.)
Sylvie St. Clair
CARAVAN(1946, Brit.)
St. Clair & Vilova
THAT'S MY GAL(1947)
Arthur St. Claire
SECRETS OF A MODEL(1940), w; BOSS OF BULLION CITY(1941), w; ROAD AGENT(1941), w; DAWN EXPRESS, THE(1942), w; GALLANT LADY(1942), w; KING OF THE STALLIONS(1942), w; NIGHT FOR CRIME, A(1942), w; PRISON GIRL(1942), w; YANK IN LIBYA, A(1942), w; YANKS ARE COMING, THE(1942), w; MAN OF COURAGE(1943), w; TIGER FANGS(1943), w; SWEETHEARTS OF THE U.S.A.(1944), w; SHADOW OF TERROR(1945), w; MASK OF DIIJON, THE(1946), w; PRAIRIE, THE(1948), w
Dorothy St. Claire
DRUMS O' VOODOO(1934)
Jean St. Claire
HORSE'S MOUTH, THE(1953, Brit.)
Nova St. Claire
CRIMSON CULT, THE(1970, Brit.)
Robert St. Claire
DOUGHNUTS AND SOCIETY(1936), w; DELINQUENT PARENTS(1938), w
Sally St. Claire
SUBWAY EXPRESS(1931)
Silvie St. Claire
AMONG HUMAN WOLVES(1940 Brit.)
Suzette St. Claire
SLIPPER AND THE ROSE, THE(1976, Brit.)
Sylvia St. Claire
THEY CAME BY NIGHT(1940, Brit.)
Pam St. Clement
HEDDA(1975, Brit.)
1984
SCRUBBERS(1984, Brit.)
Lili St. Cyr
SON OF SINBAD(1955); NAKED AND THE DEAD, THE(1958); I, MOBSTER(1959); RUNAWAY GIRL(1966)
Vince St. Cyr
COMANCHE STATION(1960)
Vincent St. Cyr
BILLY TWO HATS(1973, Brit.)
St. David's Singers
I'LL WALK BESIDE YOU(1943, Brit.)
Ruth St. Denis
KITTY(1945)
Silents
INTOLERANCE(1916)
Madelon St. Dennis
DEATH KISS, THE(1933), w
Malila St. Duval
GREAT GUNDOWN, THE(1977)
John St. Elwood
1984
AGAINST ALL ODDS(1984)
Jon St. Elwood
48 HOURS(1982)
1984
REPO MAN(1984)
St. Gall's School Choir
DEVIL'S ROCK(1938, Brit.)
Charles St. George
TALK OF THE TOWN(1942); JOHNNY O'CLOCK(1947)
Clement St. George
FANTASM(1976, Aus.); TIME AFTER TIME(1979, Brit.); SIX WEEKS(1982); MAN WHO WASN'T THERE, THE(1983)
Clive St. George
BLONDE BLACKMAILER(1955, Brit.)
Ernest St. George
GEORGE WASHINGTON CARVER(1940), ph
George St. George
YELLOW ROBE, THE(1954, Brit.), w; THUNDERSTORM(1956), w; ORDERS TO KILL(1958, Brit.), w; 300 SPARTANS, THE(1962), p, w; SEVEN SEAS TO CALAIS(1963, Ital.), w
Jenny St. George
Misc. Silents
SADIE GOES TO HEAVEN(1917)
Malo St. George
LOVE, THE ITALIAN WAY(1964, Ital.)
Philip St. George
ROCKET ATTACK, U.S.A.(1961)
Thomas R. St. George
CAMPUS HONEYMOON(1948), w
Ron St. Germaine
JUMP(1971)
Valerie St. Helene
COME BACK PETER(1971, Brit.)
Ivy St. Helier
BITTER SWEET(1933, Brit.); SINGING COP, THE(1938, Brit.); HENRY V(1946, Brit.); GOLD EXPRESS, THE(1955, Brit.)
Ivy St. Hellier
DULCIMER STREET(1948, Brit.)
Raymond St. Jacques
MISTER MOSES(1965); PAWNBROKER, THE(1965); MISTER BUDDWING(1966); COMEDIANS, THE(1967); GREEN BERETS, THE(1968); IF HE HOLLERS, LET HIM GO(1968); MADIGAN(1968); UPTIGHT(1968); CHANGE OF MIND(1969); COTTON COMES TO HARLEM(1970); COME BACK CIHARLESTON BLUE(1972); COOL

BREEZE(1972); FINAL COMEDOWN, THE(1972); BOOK OF NUMBERS(1973), a, p&d; LOST IN THE STARS(1974); BORN AGAIN(1978); CUBA CROSSING(1980)
1984
EVIL THAT MEN DO, THE(1984)

Sterling St. Jacques
BOOK OF NUMBERS(1973); EYES OF LAURA MARS(1978)

Raymond St. Jacques, Jr.
PRIVATE FILES OF J. EDGAR HOOVER, THE(1978)

Gaylord St. James
LAST HOUSE ON THE LEFT(1972)

Susan St. James
CARBON COPY(1981)

William H. St. James
Silents
OUR MRS. McCHESNEY(1918)

Adela Rogers St. John
SCANDAL(1929), w; FREE SOUL, A(1931), w; WICKED(1931), w; WHAT PRICE HOLLYWOOD?(1932), w; MISS FANE'S BABY IS STOLEN(1934), w; BACK IN CIRCULATION(1937), w; I WANT A DIVORCE(1940), w; GREAT MAN'S LADY, THE(1942), w; GOVERNMENT GIRL(1943), w; SMART WOMAN(1948), w; GIRL WHO HAD EVERYTHING, THE(1953), w
Silents
INEZ FROM HOLLYWOOD(1924), w; LADY OF THE NIGHT(1925), w; PRETTY LADIES(1925), w; BRONCHO TWISTER(1927), w

Adele Rogers St. John
Silents
ARIZONA WILDCAT(1927), w

Al St. John
DANCE OF LIFE, THE(1929); SHE GOES TO WAR(1929); HELL HARBOR(1930); OKLAHOMA CYCLONE(1930); ALOHA(1931); PAINTED DESERT, THE(1931); SON OF THE PLAINS(1931); FAME STREET(1932); RIDERS OF THE DESERT(1932); HIS PRIVATE SECRETARY(1933); PUBLIC STENOGRAPHER(1935); SHE GETS HER MAN(1935); WANDERER OF THE WASTELAND(1935); BAR 20 RIDES AGAIN(1936); FACE IN THE FOG, A(1936); HOPALONG CASSIDY RETURNS(1936); MILLIONAIRE KID(1936); TRAIL DUST(1936); WEST OF NEVADA(1936); FIGHTING DEPUTY, THE(1937); LAWMAN IS BORN, A(1937); MELODY OF THE PLAINS(1937); MOONLIGHT ON THE RANGE(1937); OUTCASTS OF POKER FLAT, THE(1937); PINTO RUSTLERS(1937); SATURDAY'S HEROES(1937); SING, COWBOY, SING(1937); CALL OF THE YUKON(1938); EXPOSED(1938); RANGER'S ROUNDUP, THE(1938); SONGS AND BULLETS(1938); FRONTIER SCOUT(1939); KNIGHT OF THE PLAINS(1939); OKLAHOMA TERROR(1939); TRIGGER PALS(1939); BILLY THE KID IN TEXAS(1940); FRIENDLY NEIGHBORS(1940); MARKED MEN(1940); MURDER ON THE YUKON(1940); TEXAS TERRORS(1940); BILLY THE KID IN SANTA FE(1941); BILLY THE KID WANTED(1941); BILLY THE KID'S FIGHTING PALS(1941); BILLY THE KID'S RANGE WAR(1941); BILLY THE KID'S ROUNDUP(1941); LONE RIDER AMBUSHED, THE(1941); LONE RIDER CROSSES THE RIO, THE(1941); LONE RIDER FIGHTS BACK, THE(1941); LONE RIDER IN GHOST TOWN, THE(1941); ARIZONA TERRORS(1942); BILLY THE KID TRAPPED(1942); JESSE JAMES, JR.(1942); LAW AND ORDER(1942); LONE RIDER AND THE BANDIT, THE(1942); LONE RIDER IN CHEYENNE, THE(1942); MISSOURI OUTLAW, A(1942); PRAIRIE PALS(1942); SHERIFF OF SAGE VALLEY(1942); STAGECOACH EXPRESS(1942); VALLEY OF THE SUN(1942); CATTLE STAMPEDE(1943); KID RIDES AGAIN, THE(1943); MY SON, THE HERO(1943); WESTERN CYCLONE(1943); WILD HORSE RUSTLERS(1943); FUZZY SETTLES DOWN(1944); I'M FROM ARKANSAS(1944); GENTLEMEN WITH GUNS(1946); GHOST OF HIDDEN VALLEY(1946); FRONTIER REVENGE(1948); SON OF BILLY THE KID(1949); DALTON'S WOMEN, THE(1950); KING OF THE BULLWHIP(1950); THUNDERING TRAIL, THE(1951); VANISHING OUTPOST, THE(1951)
Misc. Talkies
LAW OF THE 45'S(1935); FUGITIVE OF THE PLAINS(1943); FRONTIER FIGHTERS(1947)
Silents
TILLIE'S PUNCTURED ROMANCE(1914); AMERICAN BEAUTY(1927)
Misc. Silents
CASEY JONES(1927); PAINTED POST(1928)

Al [Fuzzy] St. John
ROAMING COWBOY, THE(1937); THUNDERING GUN SLINGERS(1944); OUTLAW COUNTRY(1949)

Al "Fuzzy" St. John
LAND OF MISSING MEN, THE(1930); AT THE RIDGE(1931); LAW OF THE NORTH(1932); RIDERS OF DESTINY(1933); GUNSMOKE TRAIL(1938); OVERLAND STAGECOACH(1942); WOLVES OF THE RANGE(1943); BLAZING FRONTIER(1944); DEATH RIDES THE PLAINS(1944); DEVIL RIDERS(1944); DRIFTER, THE(1944); FRONTIER OUTLAWS(1944); LAW OF THE SADDLE(1944); RAIDERS OF RED GAP(1944); RUSTLER'S HIDEOUT(1944); VALLEY OF VENGEANCE(1944); WILD HORSE PHANTOM(1944); BORDER BADMEN(1945); FIGHTING BILL CARSON(1945); HIS BROTHER'S GHOST(1945); LIGHTNING RAIDERS(1945); PRAIRIE RUSTLERS(1945); SHADOWS OF DEATH(1945); STAGECOACH OUTLAWS(1945); OUTLAW OF THE PLAINS(1946); OVERLAND RIDERS(1946); PRAIRIE BADMEN(1946); TERRORS ON HORSEBACK(1946); BORDER FEUD(1947); CHEYENNE TAKES OVER(1947); FIGHTING VIGILANTES, THE(1947); GHOST TOWN RENEGADES(1947); LAW OF THE LASH(1947); PIONEER JUSTICE(1947); RETURN OF THE LASH(1947); STAGE TO MESA CITY(1947); DEAD MAN'S GOLD(1948); MARK OF THE LASH(1948); SON OF A BADMAN(1949); FRONTIER PHANTOM, THE(1952)
Misc. Talkies
TRIGGER TOM(1935); BILLY THE KID OUTLAWED(1940); BILLY THE KID'S GUN JUSTICE(1940); LONE RIDER IN FRONTIER FURY, THE(1941); LONE RIDER RIDES ON, THE(1941); BILLY THE KID'S SMOKING GUNS(1942); BORDER ROUNDUP(1942); LONE RIDER IN BORDER ROUNDUP(1942); OUTLAWS OF BOULDER PASS(1942); TEXAS JUSTICE(1942); RENEGADE, THE(1943); OATH OF VENGEANCE(1944); GANGSTER'S DEN(1945); CODE OF THE PLAINS(1947)

Andrew St. John
BRONCO BULLFROG(1972, Brit.), p

Antoine St. John
WIND AND THE LION, THE(1975)

Barre Lyndon Theodore St. John
GREATEST SHOW ON EARTH, THE(1952), w

Betta St. John
ALL THE BROTHERS WERE VALIANT(1953); DREAM WIFE(1953); ROBE, THE(1953); DANGEROUS MISSION(1954); LAW VS. BILLY THE KID(1954); SARACEN BLADE, THE(1954); STUDENT PRINCE, THE(1954); NAKED DAWN, THE(1955); ALIAS JOHN PRESTON(1956); HIGH TIDE AT NOON(1957, Brit.); TARZAN AND THE LOST SAFARI(1957, Brit.); SNORKEL, THE(1958, Brit.); HORROR HOTEL(1960, Brit.); TARZAN THE MAGNIFICENT(1960, Brit.); CORRIDORS OF BLOOD(1962, Brit.)

Bill St. John
GHOST OF DRAGSTRIP HOLLOW zero(1959)

Cal St. John
WARRIORS, THE(1979)

Christoff St. John
CHAMP, THE(1979)

Christoper St. John
FOR LOVE OF IVY(1968)

Christopher St. John
SHAFT(1971); TOP OF THE HEAP(1972), a, p,d&w

Darby St. John
GIGOLETTES OF PARIS(1933), m

Donte St. John
1984
TEACHERS(1984)

Earl St. John
FORBIDDEN CARGO(1954, Brit.), p; LAND OF FURY(1955 Brit.), p

Edward St. John
CEREMONY, THE(1963, U.S./Span.)

Fuzzy St. John
BLACK LASH, THE(1952)

Greer St. John
EVENTS(1970); MAIDSTONE(1970)

Herbert St. John
FLAW, THE(1955, Brit.)

Howard St. John
SHOCKPROOF(1949); UNDERCOVER MAN, THE(1949); COUNTERSPY MEETS SCOTLAND YARD(1950); CUSTOMS AGENT(1950); DAVID HARDING, COUNTERSPY(1950); MEN, THE(1950); MISTER 880(1950); SUN SETS AT DAWN, THE(1950); 711 OCEAN DRIVE(1950); BIG NIGHT, THE(1951); BORN YESTERDAY(1951); CLOSE TO MY HEART(1951); GOODBYE, MY FANCY(1951); SATURDAY'S HERO(1951); STARLIFT(1951); STRANGERS ON A TRAIN(1951); STOP, YOU'RE KILLING ME(1952); THREE COINS IN THE FOUNTAIN(1954); I DIED A THOUSAND TIMES(1955); ILLEGAL(1955); TENDER TRAP, THE(1955); WORLD IN MY CORNER(1956); LI'L ABNER(1959); CRY FOR HAPPY(1961); LOVER COME BACK(1961); ONE, TWO, THREE(1961); SANCTUARY(1961); MADISON AVENUE(1962); LAFAYETTE(1963, Fr.); FATE IS THE HUNTER(1964); QUICK, BEFORE IT MELTS(1964); SEX AND THE SINGLE GIRL(1964); STRAIT-JACKET(1964); STRANGE BEDFELLOWS(1965); BANNING(1967); MATCHLESS(1967, Ital.); DON'T DRINK THE WATER(1969)

Jessica St. John
1984
LOVE STREAMS(1984)

Jill St. John
SUMMER LOVE(1958); HOLIDAY FOR LOVERS(1959); REMARKABLE MR. PENNYPACKER, THE(1959); LOST WORLD, THE(1960); ROMAN SPRING OF MRS. STONE, THE(1961, U.S./Brit.); TENDER IS THE NIGHT(1961); COME BLOW YOUR HORN(1963); WHO'S BEEN SLEEPING IN MY BED?(1963); WHO'S MINDING THE STORE?(1963); HONEYMOON HOTEL(1964); LIQUIDATOR, THE(1966, Brit.); OSCAR, THE(1966); BANNING(1967); EIGHT ON THE LAM(1967); KING'S PIRATE(1967); TONY ROME(1967); DIAMONDS ARE FOREVER(1971, Brit.); SITTING TARGET(1972, Brit.); CONCRETE JUNGLE, THE(1982)
1984
ACT, THE(1984)

John St. John
PLAYTHING, THE(1929, Brit.); TWO WORLD(1930, Brit.)

Kathleen St. John
MORE THAN A MIRACLE(1967, Ital./Fr.)
1984
ANOTHER COUNTRY(1984, Brit.)

Marco St. John
PLASTIC DOME OF NORMA JEAN, THE(1966); HAPPINESS CAGE, THE(1972); NEXT MAN, THE(1976); NIGHT OF THE JUGGLER(1980)
1984
TIGHTROPE(1984)

Marguerite St. John
LAUGHING LADY, THE(1930)

Martin St. John
MURDER IN MISSISSIPPI(1965)

Mary St. John
TRADING PLACES(1983)
Silents
ANTHING ONCE(1917)

Michael St. John
CONFESSIONS OF AMANS, THE(1977)

Nicholas St. John
DRILLER KILLER(1979), w; MS. 45(1981), w
1984
FEAR CITY(1984), w

Orford St. John
FAME(1936, Brit.), ph

Richard St. John
KISSES FOR MY PRESIDENT(1964); THAT TENDER TOUCH(1969)

Shara St. John
LITTLE FAUSS AND BIG HALSY(1970)

Theodore St. John
FORT ALGIERS(1953), w

Valerie St. John
SWAPPERS, THE(1970, Brit.)

Adela Rogers St. Johns
THAT BRENNAN GIRL(1946), w; REDS(1981)

Silents
RED KIMONO(1925), w; SKYROCKET, THE(1926), w; SINGED(1927), w; HEART OF A FOLLIES GIRL, THE(1928), w; SINGLE STANDARD, THE(1929), w

Ashley St. Jon
1984
WILD LIFE, THE(1984)

Philip St. Jon
NIGHT OF BLOODY HORROR zero(1969), makeup

Ellis St. Joseph
RENO(1939), w; JOAN OF PARIS(1942), w; FLESH AND FANTASY(1943), w; IN OUR TIME(1944), w; SCANDAL IN PARIS, A(1946), w; BARBARIAN AND THE GEISHA, THE(1958), w; CHRISTINE JORGENSEN STORY, THE(1970), w

Martin St. Judge
BROTHERS(1977)

Maurice St. Just
SUPER FUZZ(1981), makeup

Franklyn St. Juste
CHILDREN OF BABYLON(1980, Jamaica), ph

Dea St. Lamont
NEWMAN'S LAW(1974)

Andree St. Laurent
STRANGE SHADOWS IN AN EMPTY ROOM(1977, Can./Ital.)

Cecil St. Laurent
CAROLINE CHERIE(1951, Fr.), w; MANON 70(1968, Fr.), w

Francoise St. Laurent
BERNADETTE OF LOURDES(1962, Fr.)

Michael St. Laurent
ROSE, THE(1979)

Yves St. Laurent
BLACK TIGHTS(1962, Fr.), cos; PINK PANTHER, THE(1964), cos; PROVIDEN-CE(1977, Fr.), cos

Beverly St. Lawrence
CANDIDATE, THE(1964)

Leonard St. Lee
DRIFTING ALONG(1946)

Leonard St. Leo
CHAD HANNA(1940); RIDING HIGH(1943)
Silents
HEROIC LOVER, THE(1929)
Misc. Silents
BACK FROM SHANGHAI(1929)

Florence St. Leonard
Silents
BAR SINISTER, THE(1917); IDOL OF THE NORTH, THE(1921)

Louis St. Louis
WILD PARTY, THE(1975), m; GREASE 2(1982), m

St. Louis Cardinals
DEATH OF THE DIAMOND(1934)

The St. Louis Police Department
GREAT ST. LOUIS BANK ROBBERY, THE(1959)

St. Luke's Choristers
RAINBOW ON THE RIVER(1936); MAKE A WISH(1937); PRINCE AND THE PAUPER, THE(1937); SUNDOWN(1941); MRS. MINIVER(1942); CHEATERS, THE(1945); MEXICANA(1945); OUT CALIFORNIA WAY(1946)

Xavier St. Macary
LOULOU(1980, Fr.)

Lawrence St. Marks
Misc. Talkies
ANDREA(1979)

Adele St. Mauer
HISTORY IS MADE AT NIGHT(1937)

Adele St. Maur
BROKEN DREAMS(1933); WORST WOMAN IN PARIS(1933); GAY DECEPTION, THE(1935); MELODY LINGERS ON, THE(1935); THE INVISIBLE RAY(1936); KING AND THE CHORUS GIRL, THE(1937); NORA PRENTISS(1947); PATHFINDER, THE(1952); LITTLE BOY LOST(1953); CRASHOUT(1955); TO CATCH A THIEF(1955)

Elaine St. Maur
SCARLET EMPRESS, THE(1934)

Ruth St. Moritz
DINGAKA(1965, South Africa), cos

Florence St. Peter
REIVERS, THE(1969); HALLS OF ANGER(1970); TOP OF THE HEAP(1972)

Ross St. Phillip
STAYING ALIVE(1983)

Ross St. Phillips
1984
RHINESTONE(1984)

Monique St. Pierre
MOTEL HELL(1980); STRYKER(1983, Phil.)

Paul St. Pierre
SMITH(1969), w

Phyllis St. Pierre
FRENCH LINE, THE(1954); SON OF SINBAD(1955)

William G. St. Pierre
HEAD ON(1971), m

John St. Polis
MARRIAGE BY CONTRACT(1928); FAST LIFE(1929); DEVIL WITH WOMEN, A(1930); GUILTY?(1930); IN THE NEXT ROOM(1930); KISMET(1930); MELODY MAN(1930); PARTY GIRL(1930); CRIMINAL CODE(1931); DOCTORS' WIVES(1931); HEARTBREAK(1931); MEN OF THE SKY(1931); TRANSGRESSION(1931); ALIAS THE DOCTOR(1932); CRUSADER, THE(1932); FORBIDDEN COMPANY(1932); GAMBLING SEX(1932); IF I HAD A MILLION(1932); LENA RIVERS(1932); SYMPHONY OF SIX MILLION(1932); KING OF THE ARENA(1933); SING SINNER, SING(1933); TERROR TRAIL(1933); WORLD GONE MAD(1933); GUILTY PARENTS(1934); NOTORIOUS BUT NICE(1934); LADY IN SCARLET, THE(1935); BELOW THE DEADLINE(1936); BORDER PATROLMAN, THE(1936); DARK HOUR, THE(1936); DEATH FROM A DISTANCE(1936); THREE ON THE TRAIL(1936); PARADISE ISLE(1937); RUSTLER'S VALLEY(1937); INTERNATIONAL CRIME(1938); MR. WONG, DETECTIVE(1938); PHANTOM RANGER(1938); SALESLADY(1938); THEY SHALL HAVE MUSIC(1939); HAUNTED HOUSE, THE(1940); ON THE SPOT(1940);

ROCKY MOUNTAIN RANGERS(1940); CROSSROADS(1942)
Silents
RETURN OF PETER GRIMM, THE(1926); UNKNOWN, THE(1927); GRAIN OF DUST, THE(1928); GUN RUNNER, THE(1928)

John M. St. Polls
BEAU IDEAL(1931)

Helen St. Rayner
I MARRIED A WITCH(1942); CASANOVA BROWN(1944); MADAME BOVARY(1949)

Vida St. Romaine
HORSEMEN, THE(1971)

Georges St. Saens
WAYS OF LOVE(1950, Ital./Fr.)

Camille St.-Saens
EFFI BRIEST(1974, Ger.), m

Bruno Staab
SMALL CHANGE(1976, Fr.)

James Staahl
MAX DUGAN RETURNS(1983)

Jim Staahl
CRACKING UP(1977); NATIONAL LAMPOON'S CLASS REUNION(1982); NIGHT SHIFT(1982)

Herta Staal
DANCING HEART, THE(1959, Ger.)

Viktor Staal
LIFE BEGINS ANEW(1938, Ger.); GREH(1962, Ger./Yugo.)

Bob Staats
PUTNEY SWOPE(1969)

Robert Staats
PROJECTIONIST, THE(1970); COMEBACK TRAIL, THE(1982)
Misc. Talkies
FAKING OF THE PRESIDENT, THE(1976)

Dinah Stabb
CRY OF THE BANSHEE(1970, Brit.)

Tony Stabeneau
HOLD EVERYTHING(1930)

Joe Stabil
PATSY, THE(1964)

Dick Stabile
STOLEN HARMONY(1935); AT WAR WITH THE ARMY(1950); SAILOR BEWA-RE(1951); HOOK, LINE AND SINKER(1969), m

Ed Stabile
PLAINSONG(1982), d&w

Jim Stabile
NIGHT THE LIGHTS WENT OUT IN GEORGIA, THE(1981)

Mariano Stabile
ROSSINI(1948, Ital.)

John Stableford
LORD OF THE FLIES(1963, Brit.)

Robert Stabler
BLACK WHIP, THE(1956), p; BACK FROM THE DEAD(1957), p; COPPER SKY(1957), p, w; RIDE A VIOLENT MILE(1957), p; UNKNOWN TERROR, THE(1957), p; BLOOD ARROW(1958), p; RESURRECTION OF ZACHARY WHEEL-ER, THE(1971), p

Robert W. Stabler
DESERT HELL(1958), p; ANATOMY OF A PSYCHO(1961); VIOLENT ONES, THE(1967), p; DAYTON'S DEVILS(1968), p

Grigori Stabovoi
Misc. Silents
TWO DAYS(1929, USSR), d

Stacchini
SABATA(1969, Ital.), spec eff

Ivano Staccioli
CENTURION, THE(1962, Fr./Ital.); CLEOPATRA'S DAUGHTER(1963, Fr., Ital.); LIPSTICK(1965, Fr./Ital.); WAR OF THE ZOMBIES, THE(1965 Ital.); ROAD TO SALINA(1971, Fr./Ital.)

Bill Stacey
SCOBIE MALONE(1975, Aus.), ed; ROAD GAMES(1981, Aus.)

Eddie Stacey
PINK PANTHER STRIKES AGAIN, THE(1976, Brit.); FORCE 10 FROM NAVA-RONE(1978, Brit.), stunts; HAWK THE SLAYER(1980, Brit.), stunts; SAFARI 3000(1982), a, stunts
1984
1984(1984, Brit.)

Eric Stacey, Jr.
NATIONAL LAMPOON'S VACATION(1983)

James Stacey
1984
BOLERO(1984)

Jim Stacey
LIKE FATHER LIKE SON(1961)

John Stacey
WAR AND PEACE(1956, Ital./U.S.); JUDITH(1965); YETI(1977, Ital.)

Neil Stacey
MURDER MOST FOUL(1964, Brit.)

Olive Stacey
WRONG MAN, THE(1956)

Patricia Stacey
KING OF THE ZOMBIES(1941)

Susan Stacey
Misc. Talkies
PHANTOM KID, THE(1983)

Virginia Stach
MURDERS IN THE RUE MORGUE(1971)

Elizabeth Stack
RENT CONTROL(1981)

Lenny Stack
C. C. AND COMPANY(1971), m

Liam Stack
EDUCATING RITA(1983)
Patrick Stack
FIRST BLOOD(1982)
Robert Stack
FIRST LOVE(1939); LITTLE BIT OF HEAVEN, A(1940); MORTAL STORM, THE(1940); BADLANDS OF DAKOTA(1941); NICE GIRL?(1941); EAGLE SQUADRON(1942); MEN OF TEXAS(1942); TO BE OR NOT TO BE(1942); DATE WITH JUDY, A(1948); FIGHTER SQUADRON(1948); MISS TATLOCK'S MILLIONS(1948); MR. MUSIC(1950); BULLFIGHTER AND THE LADY(1951); MY BROTHER, THE OUTLAW(1951); BWANA DEVIL(1953); CONQUEST OF COCHISE(1953); SABRE JET(1953); WAR PAINT(1953); HIGH AND THE MIGHTY, THE(1954); IRON GLOVE, THE(1954); GOOD MORNING, MISS DOVE(1955); HOUSE OF BAMBOO(1955); GREAT DAY IN THE MORNING(1956); WRITTEN ON THE WIND(1956); TARNISHED ANGELS, THE(1957); GIFT OF LOVE, THE(1958); JOHN PAUL JONES(1959); LAST VOYAGE, THE(1960); SCARFACE MOB, THE(1962); CARETAKERS, THE(1963); IS PARIS BURNING?(1966, U.S./Fr.); CORRUPT ONES, THE(1967, Ger.); LEATHER AND NYLON(1969, Fr./Ital.); STORY OF A WOMAN(1970, U.S./Ital.); SECOND WIND, A(1978, Fr.); 1941(1979); AIRPLANE!(1980); UNCOMMON VALOR(1983)
Misc. Talkies
ASYLUM FOR A SPY(1967)
Tiare Stack
PLAINSONG(1982), p
Wesley Stack
ROYAL FAMILY OF BROADWAY, THE(1930)
William Stack
DERELICT(1930); SARAH AND SON(1930); PAYMENT DEFERRED(1932); CHARLIE CHAN'S GREATEST CASE(1933); FOUNTAIN, THE(1934); HELL IN THE HEAVENS(1934); MANHATTAN MELODRAMA(1934); MYSTERY OF MR. X, THE(1934); TARZAN AND HIS MATE(1934); WONDER BAR(1934); BECKY SHARP(1935); COLLEGE SCANDAL(1935); I'VE BEEN AROUND(1935); MAGNIFICENT OBSESSION(1935); MAN WHO BROKE THE BANK AT MONTE CARLO, THE(1935); MUTINY ON THE BOUNTY(1935); RENDEZVOUS(1935); HIS BROTHER'S WIFE(1936); LIBELED LADY(1936); MARY OF SCOTLAND(1936); PENNIES FROM HEAVEN(1936); STOWAWAY(1936); CAPTAINS COURAGEOUS(1937); CRIMINAL LAWYER(1937); EMPEROR'S CANDLESTICKS, THE(1937); PERSONAL PROPERTY(1937); SOLDIER AND THE LADY, THE(1937); SOULS AT SEA(1937); BOOLOO(1938); FOUR MEN AND A PRAYER(1938); MAN-PROOF(1938); OF HUMAN HEARTS(1938); SHOPWORN ANGEL(1938); GONE WITH THE WIND(1939); EARL OF CHICAGO, THE(1940); LADY IN QUESTION, THE(1940); AMONG THE LIVING(1941); SO ENDS OUR NIGHT(1941); PICTURE OF DORIAN GRAY, THE(1945)
Silents
GIRL FROM DOWNING STREET, THE(1918, Brit.)
Misc. Silents
FORTUNE'S FOOL(1922, Brit.)
L. Stackell
DARK JOURNEY(1937, Brit.), tech adv
Steven Stacker
BOBBIKINS(1959, Brit.)
Gene Stackleborg
MAN OUTSIDE, THE(1968, Brit.), w
David Stackpole
FOUR SEASONS, THE(1981)
Peter Stackpole
JANIE(1944)
H. DeVere Stacpoole
MAN WHO LOST HIMSELF, THE(1941), w
Silents
SATAN'S SISTER(1925, Brit.), w
Henry Devere Stacpoole
BLUE LAGOON, THE(1949, Brit.), w; TRUTH ABOUT SPRING, THE(1965, Brit.), w; BLUE LAGOON, THE(1980), w
Charles Stacy
TOO BAD SHE'S BAD(1954, Ital.)
Eddie Stacy
FLASH GORDON(1980)
James Stacy
SUMMER MAGIC(1963); SWINGIN' SUMMER, A(1965); WINTER A GO-GO(1965); YOUNG SINNER, THE(1965); FLAREUP(1969); POSSE(1975); DOUBLE EXPOSURE(1982); SOMETHING WICKED THIS WAY COMES(1983)
Jess Stacy
SARGE GOES TO COLLEGE(1947)
John Stacy
THEM NICE AMERICANS(1958, Brit.); CAT GANG, THE(1959, Brit.); HEADLESS GHOST, THE(1959, Brit.); COME SEPTEMBER(1961); ROMMEL'S TREASURE(1962, Ital.); GIDGET GOES TO ROME(1963); 8 ½(1963, Ital.); EVIL EYE(1964 Ital.); AGONY AND THE ECSTASY, THE(1965); MODESTY BLAISE(1966, Brit.); STATUE, THE(1971, Brit.); BIG GAME, THE(1972)
Michelle Stacy
LOGAN'S RUN(1976); DAY OF THE ANIMALS(1977); DEMON SEED(1977); RESCUERS, THE(1977)
Paul Stacy
1984
BOLERO(1984)
William Stacy
FREE SOUL, A(1931)
Gerald Stadden
HISTORY OF THE WORLD, PART 1(1981)
James Stadden
REUNION(1932, Brit.); DOSS HOUSE(1933, Brit.)
Gerald Staddon
RETURN OF THE JEDI(1983)
Josephine Staddon
RETURN OF THE JEDI(1983)
O.B. Stade
VIVA VILLA!(1934), w

Signe Stade
HERE'S YOUR LIFE(1968, Swed.)
John Stadelman
1984
EYES OF FIRE(1984), set d
Paul Stader
HURRICANE, THE(1937); NOCTURNE(1946); ABBOTT AND COSTELLO MEET FRANKENSTEIN(1948); SURRENDER(1950); MONTANA BELLE(1952); DEMETRIUS AND THE GLADIATORS(1954); JUBILEE TRAIL(1954); OUTLAW'S DAUGHTER, THE(1954); HELL'S OUTPOST(1955); PRINCE OF PLAYERS(1955); GHOST DIVER(1957); SPOILERS OF THE FOREST(1957); ENCHANTED ISLAND(1958); SATAN'S SATELLITES(1958); SEVEN MINUTES(1971); WHEN EIGHT BELLS TOLL(1971, Brit.), d; POSEIDON ADVENTURE, THE(1972), stunts; WHAT'S UP, DOC?(1972); TOWERING INFERNO, THE(1974), stunts; SWARM, THE(1978), stunts
Peter T. Stader
MOVIE MOVIE(1978)
Hildegarde Stadie
MANIAC(1934), w
Harry Stading
MY FAIR LADY(1964), ph
Lewis Stadlen
VERDICT, THE(1982)
Lewis J. Stadlen
PARADES(1972); PORTNOY'S COMPLAINT(1972); SAVAGES(1972); SERPICO(1973); BETWEEN THE LINES(1977); LINE, THE(1982); SOUP FOR ONE(1982); TO BE OR NOT TO BE(1983)
1984
WINDY CITY(1984)
Clem Stadler
AMBUSH BAY(1966)
Lt. Col. Clement J. Stadler
OUTSIDER, THE(1962), tech adv
Maria Stadler
HEAD, THE(1961, Ger.)
Rose Marie Stadler
MY BODY HUNGERS(1967)
Suzan Stadner
1984
ALLEY CAT(1984)
Beth Staeheli
1984
ALLEY CAT(1984)
Per Staehr
OPERATION CAMEL(1961, Den.), ph
Zack Staenberg
1984
POLICE ACADEMY(1984), ed
Harry Walker Staff
SCRATCH HARRY(1969)
Ivan Staff
SQUARE RING, THE(1955, Brit.)
Katherine Staff
KIND OF LOVING, A(1962, Brit.)
Kathy Staff
DRESSER, THE(1983)
Murray Staff
HAWAIIANS, THE(1970)
Charles Staffel
SIMBA(1955, Brit.), spec eff; MAN WHO HAUNTED HIMSELF, THE(1970, Brit.), spec eff; YOUNG WINSTON(1972, Brit.), spec eff
Charles Staffell
PURPLE PLAIN, THE(1954, Brit.), spec eff; ZARDOZ(1974, Brit.), makeup
Laurel Staffell
CARRY ON TEACHER(1962, Brit.), cos; LONG AGO, TOMORROW(1971, Brit.), cos
Ann Stafford
SCUM OF THE EARTH(1976); KEEP MY GRAVE OPEN(1980)
Art Stafford
SEA GYPSIES, THE(1978), ed
Baird Stafford
NIGHTMARE(1981)
Bess Stafford
BACHELOR MOTHER(1933); RED HEAD(1934); IT HAPPENED IN NEW YORK(1935); LEAVENWORTH CASE, THE(1936); PRINCESS COMES ACROSS, THE(1936)
Bill Stafford
TOO LATE BLUES(1962)
Bing Stafford
BEAST OF YUCCA FLATS, THE(1961)
Brendan Stafford
FORTUNE LANE(1947, Brit.), ph; THREE'S COMPANY(1953, Brit.), ph; EIGHT O'CLOCK WALK(1954, Brit.), ph; PROFILE(1954, Brit.), ph; HANDCUFFS, LONDON(1955, Brit.), ph; HOSTAGE, THE(1956, Brit.), ph; DATE WITH DISASTER(1957, Brit.), ph; MAN WITHOUT A BODY, THE(1957, Brit.), ph; THERE'S ALWAYS A THURSDAY(1957, Brit.), ph; MURDER REPORTED(1958, Brit.), ph; WITNESS IN THE DARK(1959, Brit.), ph
Brendan J. Stafford
SOMETHING IN THE CITY(1950, Brit.), ph; STRANGER AT MY DOOR(1950, Brit.), d, ph; PAUL TEMPLE'S TRIUMPH(1951, Brit.), ph; ARMCHAIR DETECTIVE, THE(1952, Brit.), d; NIGHT WON'T TALK, THE(1952, Brit.), ph; WALLET, THE(1952, Brit.), ph; GENIE, THE(1953, Brit.), ph; MEN AGAINST THE SUN(1953, Brit.), d, ph; BANG! YOU'RE DEAD(1954, Brit.), ph; CIRCUMSTANIAL EVIDENCE(1954, Brit.), ph; DESTINATION MILAN(1954, Brit.), ph; LAST MOMENT, THE(1954, Brit.), ph; RED DRESS, THE(1954, Brit.), ph; ONE JUMP AHEAD(1955, Brit.), ph; FIND THE LADY(1956, Brit.), ph; HIDEOUT, THE(1956, Brit.), ph; SHAKEDOWN, THE(1960, Brit.), ph; YOUR MONEY OR YOUR WIFE(1965, Brit.), ph; CROSSPLOT(1969, Brit.), ph
Bucko Stafford
STORM CENTER(1956); SPOILERS OF THE FOREST(1957)

Eddie Stafford
DEADLIEST SIN, THE(1956, Brit.)

Fred Stafford
CONAN THE BARBARIAN(1982), ed
1984
NIGHT OF THE COMET(1984), ed

Frederick Stafford
OSS 117–MISSION FOR A KILLER(1966, Fr./Ital.); TOPAZ(1969, Brit.); DIRTY HEROES(1971, Ital./Fr./Ger.); EAGLE OVER LONDON(1973, Ital.); LEGEND OF THE WOLF WOMAN, THE(1977, Span.)
Misc. Talkies
BATTLE OF EL ALAMEIN(1971)

Garry Stafford
SOMETHING OF VALUE(1957)

Gary Stafford
OCEAN'S ELEVEN(1960)

Gilbert Stafford
ENDLESS LOVE(1981)

Gino Stafford
GIANT OF METROPOLIS, THE(1963, Ital.), w

Grace Stafford
DR. SOCRATES(1935); ANTHONY ADVERSE(1936); I MARRIED A DOCTOR(1936); BLONDIE BRINGS UP BABY(1939); CONFESSIONS OF A NAZI SPY(1939); I AM NOT AFRAID(1939); INDIANAPOLIS SPEEDWAY(1939); MAN WHO DARED, THE(1939); DISPATCH FROM REUTERS, A(1940); FLIGHT ANGELS(1940); MARGIE(1940); SANTA FE TRAIL(1940); AFFECTIONATELY YOURS(1941); MODEL WIFE(1941); UNFINISHED BUSINESS(1941); LARCENY, INC.(1942); YOU'RE TELLING ME(1942); DOC SAVAGE... THE MAN OF BRONZE(1975)

Greg Stafford
SABRINA(1954)

Hanley Stafford
LIFE WITH HENRY(1941); SWING IT SOLDIER(1941); LULLABY OF BROADWAY, THE(1951); GIRL IN EVERY PORT, A(1952); HERE COME THE MARINES(1952); JUST THIS ONCE(1952); AFFAIRS OF DOBIE GILLIS, THE(1953); FRANCIS COVERS THE BIG TOWN(1953)

Harry B. Stafford
I STOLE A MILLION(1939); OUR LEADING CITIZEN(1939); NAZI AGENT(1942)

Harry Stafford
UNDER THE GREENWOOD TREE(1930, Brit.); UNDER YOUR SPELL(1936); CHAMPAGNE WALTZ(1937); YOU CAN'T TAKE IT WITH YOU(1938)

Harvey Stafford
Misc. Silents
ACE OF CACTUS RANGE(1924)

Henry Stafford
BLACKMAIL(1929, Brit.), m

Jim Stafford
ANY WHICH WAY YOU CAN(1980)

Jo Stafford
DU BARRY WAS A LADY(1943)

Joe Stafford
LAST PICTURE SHOW, THE(1971), m

John Stafford
BEGGAR STUDENT, THE(1931,Brit.), w; WHERE IS THIS LADY?(1932, Brit.), p, w; DICK TURPIN(1933, Brit.), d; NO FUNNY BUSINESS(1934, Brit.), p, d; SPRING IN THE AIR(1934, Brit.), p; ADMIRALS ALL(1935, Brit.), p; SCANDALS OF PARIS(1935, Brit.), p,d&w; AVENGING HAND, THE(1936, Brit.), p; BALL AT SAVOY(1936, Brit.), p; BELOVED IMPOSTER(1936, Brit.), p; CROUCHING BEAST, THE(1936, U. S./Brit.), p; SECOND BUREAU(1937, Brit.), p; WAKE UP FAMOUS(1937, Brit.), p; WIFE OF GENERAL LING, THE(1938, Brit.), p; WINGS OVER AFRICA(1939), p; FACE BEHIND THE SCAR(1940, Brit.), p; SPITFIRE(1943, Brit.), p; CALL OF THE BLOOD(1948, Brit.), p; GOLDEN MADONNA, THE(1949, Brit.), p; HER PANELLED DOOR(1951, Brit.), p; OUTPOST IN MALAYA(1952, Brit.), p; STRANGER'S HAND, THE(1955, Brit.), p; LOSER TAKES ALL(1956, Brit.), p; ACROSS THE BRIDGE(1957, Brit.), p; ELEPHANT GUN(1959, Brit.), p
Silents
INSEPARABLES, THE(1929, Brit.), d, w

Joseph Stafford
OUTLAW'S SON(1957)

Joseph "Bucko" Stafford
MEN OF THE FIGHTING LADY(1954)

Marian Stafford
Misc. Talkies
BIG FUN CARNIVAL, THE(1957)

Marvel Stafford
Silents
APOSTLE OF VENGEANCE, THE(1916)

Marvin Stafford
UNCLE SCAM(1981)

Nancy Stafford
Q(1982)

Nigel Stafford
WHISTLE DOWN THE WIND(1961, Brit.)

Randy Stafford
NIGHT OF THE WITCHES(1970)

Robert Stafford
BABES IN TOYLAND(1961), ed; SUMMER MAGIC(1963), ed; FOLLOW ME, BOYS!(1966), ed; UGLY DACHSHUND, THE(1966), ed; HORSE IN THE GRAY FLANNEL SUIT, THE(1968), ed; SMITH(1969), ed; BAREFOOT EXECUTIVE, THE(1971), ed; WILD COUNTRY, THE(1971), ed; NAPOLEON AND SAMANTHA(1972), ed; SNOWBALL EXPRESS(1972), ed; ONE LITTLE INDIAN(1973), ed; ISLAND AT THE TOP OF THE WORLD, THE(1974), ed; ESCAPE TO WITCH MOUNTAIN(1975), ed; GUS(1976), ed

Ron Stafford
FEELIN' GOOD(1966)

Ronald Stafford
MEN OF THE FIGHTING LADY(1954)

Tamara Stafford
1984
AGAINST ALL ODDS(1984)

Terry Stafford
WILD WHEELS(1969)

Tim Stafford
DONOVAN'S REEF(1963); HOT RODS TO HELL(1967)

Stafford Sisters
GOLD MINE IN THE SKY(1938); OLD BARN DANCE, THE(1938)

Charles Stafford-Dickens
Misc. Silents
DEFINITE OBJECT, THE(1920, Brit.)

Katarina Stagarovic
WITNESS OUT OF HELL(1967, Ger./Yugo.), ed

Alonzo Stagg
KNUTE ROCKNE–ALL AMERICAN(1940)

Bima Stagg
Misc. Talkies
BLACK TRASH(1978)

Christopher Stagg
STUD, THE(1979, Brit.), w

Clinton H. Stagg
Silents
RACE, THE(1916), w

Robert Stagg
1984
SECRETS(1984, Brit.)

William Stagg
PRECIOUS JEWELS(1969), d&w

Jeff Staggs
1984
DREAMSCAPE(1984), art d; SURF II(1984), prod d

Guido Stagnaro
MAGIC WORLD OF TOPO GIGIO, THE(1961, Ital.), w

Ferruccio Stagni
ULYSSES(1955, Ital.)

Fides Stagni
HAWKS AND THE SPARROWS, THE(1967, Ital.); AMARCORD(1974, Ital.)

Giuseppe Stagnitti
VERY HANDY MAN, A(1966, Fr./Ital.)

Julie Staheli
HANGAR 18(1980), cos; IN SEARCH OF HISTORIC JESUS(1980), cos

Paul Staheli
GUARDIAN OF THE WILDERNESS(1977), art d; HANGAR 18(1980), prod d; IN SEARCH OF HISTORIC JESUS(1980), prod d; REVENGE OF THE NINJA(1983), art d

Randy Staheli
IN SEARCH OF HISTORIC JESUS(1980), set d

Al Stahl
SQUARE ROOT OF ZERO, THE(1964), spec eff

Andy Stahl
1984
RIVER, THE(1984)

Ben Stahl
BLACKBEARD'S GHOST(1968), w

Buck Stahl
KINFOLK(1970)

C. Ray Stahl
GEISHA GIRL(1952), p&d, w

Dick Stahl
FUNNYMAN(1967)

George Stahl
SONG OF MEXICO(1945), ph; ENCHANTED ISLAND(1958), ph; JET OVER THE ATLANTIC(1960), ph; JORY(1972), ph

George Stahl, Jr.
COMANCHE(1956), ph; LITTLE SAVAGE, THE(1959), ph

Irwin Stahl
TOMORROW(1972), m

John Stahl
LADY SURRENDERS, A(1930), d; HOLY MATRIMONY(1943), d; IMMORTAL SERGEANT, THE(1943), d

John M. Stahl
MARRIAGE BY CONTRACT(1928), p; SEED(1931), p&d; STRICTLY DISHONORABLE(1931), d; BACK STREET(1932), d; ONLY YESTERDAY(1933), d; IMITATION OF LIFE(1934), d; MAGNIFICENT OBSESSION(1935), p&d; PARNELL(1937), p&d; LETTER OF INTRODUCTION(1938), p&d; WHEN TOMORROW COMES(1939), p&d; OUR WIFE(1941), p&d; EVE OF ST. MARK, THE(1944), d; KEYS OF THE KINGDOM, THE(1944), d; LEAVE HER TO HEAVEN(1946), d; FOXES OF HARROW, THE(1947), d; WALLS OF JERICHO(1948), d; FATHER WAS A FULLBACK(1949), d; OH, YOU BEAUTIFUL DOLL(1949), d
Silents
DANGEROUS AGE, THE(1922), d; ONE CLEAR CALL(1922), d; SONG OF LIFE, THE(1922), d; WANTERS, THE(1923), d; HUSBANDS AND LOVERS(1924), d, w; MEMORY LANE(1926), d, w; IN OLD KENTUCKY(1927), d
Misc. Silents
SUSPICION(1918), d; WIVES OF MEN(1918), d; HER CODE OF HONOR(1919), d; WOMAN UNDER OATH, THE(1919), d; GREATER THAN LOVE(1920), d; WOMAN IN HIS HOUSE, THE(1920), d; WOMEN MEN FORGET(1920), d; CHILD THOU GAVEST ME, THE(1921), d; SOWING THE WIND(1921), d; SUSPICIOUS WIVES(1921), d; WHY MEN LEAVE HOME(1924), d; FINE CLOTHES(1925), d; GAY DECEIVER, THE(1926), d; LOVERS?(1927), d

Jorge Stahl
ZACHARIAH(1971), ph

Jorge Stahl, Jr.
GARDEN OF EVIL(1954), ph; BEAST OF HOLLOW MOUNTAIN, THE(1956), ph; WOMAN'S DEVOTION, A(1956), ph; SEPTEMBER STORM(1960), ph; WITCH'S MIRROR, THE(1960, Mex.), ph; GINA(1961, Fr./Mex.), ph; SANTO CONTRA LA INVASION DE LOS MARCIANOS(1966, Mex.), ph; LIVING HEAD, THE(1969, Mex.), ph; DEATH IN THE GARDEN(1977, Fr./Mex.), ph

Margaret Stahl
BOY ON A DOLPHIN(1957)

Marvin D. Stahl
BIG FIX, THE(1947), p; BORN TO SPEED(1947), p; HEARTACHES(1947), p
Ray Stahl
SCARLET SPEAR, THE(1954, Brit.), d&w; WHITE HUNTRESS(1957, Brit.), p
Richard Stahl
FIVE EASY PIECES(1970); STUDENT NURSES, THE(1970); SUMMERTREE(1971);
BEWARE! THE BLOB(1972); DIRTY LITTLE BILLY(1972); FUZZ(1972); TERMINAL
ISLAND(1973); HIGH ANXIETY(1977); NINE TO FIVE(1980); UNDER THE RAIN-
BOW(1981); PRIVATE SCHOOL(1983)
1984
FLAMINGO KID, THE(1984)
Walter Stahl
LITTLE MISS ROUGHNECK(1938); BEASTS OF BERLIN(1939); SO ENDS OUR
NIGHT(1941); ONCE UPON A HONEYMOON(1942); PHANTOM OF THE OPE-
RA(1943); WATCH ON THE RHINE(1943)
Rudolf Stahl
GIRL WITH THREE CAMELS, THE(1968, Czech.), ph; ON THE COMET(1970,
Czech.), ph
Walter O. Stahl
I'LL TAKE ROMANCE(1937); LIFE OF EMILE ZOLA, THE(1937); JUAREZ(1939);
DISPATCH FROM REUTERS, A(1940); REUNION IN FRANCE(1942); ABOVE SUSPI-
CION(1943); THEY CAME TO BLOW UP AMERICA(1943)
Walter Richard Stahl
Misc. Silents
WHAT BECOMES OF THE CHILDREN?(1918), d
William Stahl
UNDERGROUND AGENT(1942)
Willy Stahl
NAVY WAY, THE(1944), m; TIMBER QUEEN(1944), m
Ernst Stahl-Nachbaur
DANTON(1931, Ger.); DIE MANNER UM LUCIE(1931); M(1933, Ger.)
Misc. Silents
BERLIN AFTER DARK(1929, Ger.)
Gio Staiano
LA DOLCE VITA(1961, Ital./Fr.)
Libi Staiger
HANKY-PANKY(1982)
Norman Stainback
HEY THERE, IT'S YOGI BEAR(1964), ph; MAN CALLED FLINTSTONE, THE(1966),
ph
Patricia Stainer
STRAWBERRY ROAN(1945, Brit.)
Michael Stainer-Hutchins
DEVIL'S BRIDE, THE(1968, Brit.), spec eff; WORK IS A FOUR LETTER WORD(1968,
Brit.), spec eff
Neale Stainton
FRAULEIN DOKTOR(1969, Ital./Yugo.)
Philip Stainton
NIGHT BEAT(1948, Brit.); BLUE LAGOON, THE(1949, Brit.); DON'T EVER LEAVE
ME(1949, Brit.); PASSPORT TO PIMLICO(1949, Brit.); POET'S PUB(1949, Brit.); SCOTT
OF THE ANTARCTIC(1949, Brit.); FIGHTING PIMPERNEL, THE(1950, Brit.); IS-
LAND RESCUE(1952, Brit.); MADE IN HEAVEN(1952, Brit.); SPIDER AND THE FLY,
THE(1952, Brit.); WHITE CORRIDORS(1952, Brit.); ISN'T LIFE WONDERFUL!(1953,
Brit.); MOGAMBO(1953); MONSOON(1953); ANGELS ONE FIVE(1954, Brit.); HOB-
SON'S CHOICE(1954, Brit.); INNOCENTS IN PARIS(1955, Brit.); WOMAN FOR JOE,
THE(1955, Brit.); LADYKILLERS, THE(1956, Brit.); MOBY DICK(1956, Brit.), a, m;
WHO DONE IT?(1956, Brit.); REACH FOR THE SKY(1957, Brit.); CAST A DARK
SHADOW(1958, Brit.)
Enzo Staiola
BICYCLE THIEF, THE(1949, Ital.); LUCKY NICK CAIN(1951); TIMES GONE
BY(1953, Ital.); VOLCANO(1953, Ital.); BAREFOOT CONTESSA, THE(1954)
William Stair
LEO THE LAST(1970, Brit.), w
Martin Stairn
SHADOW OF FEAR(1963, Brit.), m
Ethel Stairt
Silents
POISON(1924)
Don Staiton
SPY WHO LOVED ME, THE(1977, Brit.)
Enzo Stajola
WHITE LINE, THE(1952, Ital.); JOURNEY TO LOVE(1953, Ital.)
Randall Stake
BIG BRAIN, THE(1933)
Tony Stakenau
EX-BAD BOY(1931)
Ivan Stalenin
Misc. Silents
SCANDAL?(1929, USSR)
Chuck Staley
CRACKING UP(1977), d
Donna Staley
INTERNES CAN'T TAKE MONEY(1937)
James Staley
LAST WORD, THE(1979); HONKY TONK FREEWAY(1981); FIREFOX(1982); NA-
TIONAL LAMPOON'S VACATION(1983)
1984
AMERICAN DREAMER(1984); PROTOCOL(1984)
Joan Staley
MIDNIGHT LACE(1960); OCEAN'S ELEVEN(1960); DONDI(1961); GUN
FIGHT(1961); LADIES MAN, THE(1961); VALLEY OF THE DRAGONS(1961); CAPE
FEAR(1962); JOHNNY COOL(1963); NEW KIND OF LOVE, A(1963); ROUS-
TABOUT(1964); GHOST AND MR. CHICKEN, THE(1966); GUNPOINT(1966)
Lora Staley
THIEF(1981)
1984
AMERICAN NIGHTMARE(1984)
Misc. Talkies
AMERICAN NIGHTMARE(1981, Can.)

Marilyn Staley
SEDUCTION, THE(1982)
Jan Stalich
ECSTASY(1940, Czech.), ph; MOZART(1940, Brit.), ph
Joseph Stalin
EXTRAORDINARY SEAMAN, THE(1969)
Liz Stalker-Mason
PROM NIGHT(1980)
Fred Stall
Misc. Silents
SHAME(1918)
Karl Stall
SMILING LIEUTENANT, THE(1931)
Ernest Stallard
Silents
AMERICAN WIDOW, AN(1917)
Jan Stallich
SILENT PASSENGER, THE(1935, Brit.), ph; GUILTY MELODY(1936, Brit.), ph;
MIDNIGHT AT THE WAX MUSEUM(1936, Brit.), ph; GOLEM, THE(1937, Czech./Fr.),
ph; INSPECTOR GENERAL, THE(1937, Czech.), ph; SCOTLAND YARD COM-
MANDS(1937, Brit.), ph; SHOW GOES ON, THE(1937, Brit.), ph; WHO'S YOUR LADY
FRIEND?(1937, Brit.), ph; MOONLIGHT SONATA(1938, Brit.), ph; SCHOOLGIRL
DIARY(1947, Ital.), ph; EMPEROR AND THE GOLEM, THE(1955, Czech.), ph; SKI
FEVER(1969, U.S./Aust./Czech.), ph
Jan Stallick
TWENTY-ONE DAYS TOGETHER(1940, Brit.), ph
Carl Stalling
GREAT AMERICAN BUGS BUNNY-ROAD RUNNER CHASE(1979), m; BUGS
BUNNY'S THIRD MOVIE–1001 RABBIT TALES(1982), m
George Stallings
SONG OF THE SOUTH(1946), w
Laurence Stallings
COCK-EYED WORLD, THE(1929), w; MARIANNE(1929), w; BILLY THE KID(1930),
w; SONG OF THE WEST(1930), w; WAY FOR A SAILOR(1930), w; BIG EX-
ECUTIVE(1933), w; FAST WORKERS(1933), w; HOT PEPPER(1933), w; AFTER OF-
FICE HOURS(1935), w; SO RED THE ROSE(1935), w; TOO HOT TO
HANDLE(1938), w; MAN FROM DAKOTA, THE(1940), w; NORTHWEST PASS-
AGE(1940), w; JUNGLE BOOK(1942), w; SALOME, WHERE SHE DANCED(1945), w;
CHRISTMAS EVE(1947), w; ON OUR MERRY WAY(1948), w; THREE GODFA-
THERS, THE(1948), w; SHE WORE A YELLOW RIBBON(1949), w; WHAT PRICE
GLORY?(1952); SUN SHINES BRIGHT, THE(1953), w
Silents
OLD IRONSIDES(1926), w; WHAT PRICE GLORY(1926), w; SHOW PEOPLE(1928),
w
Lawrence Stallings
Silents
BIG PARADE, THE(1925), w
Rex Stallings
UNDERCOVERS HERO(1975, Brit.)
Lynn Stallmaster
STEEL HELMET, THE(1951)
Butkus Stallone
ROCKY(1976)
Frank Stallone
ROCKY(1976); ROCKY II(1979); ROCKY III(1982); STAYING ALIVE(1983), a, m
Frank Stallone, Jr.
ROCKY(1976); PARADISE ALLEY(1978)
Sylvester Stallone
LORDS OF FLATBUSH, THE(1974), a, w; CAPONE(1975); DEATH RACE 2000(1975);
FAREWELL, MY LOVELY(1975); NO PLACE TO HIDE(1975); PRISONER OF SE-
COND AVENUE, THE(1975); CANNONBALL(1976, U.S./Hong Kong); ROCKY(1976),
a, w, ch; F.I.S.T.(1978), a, w; PARADISE ALLEY(1978), a, d&w; ROCKY II(1979), a,
d&w, ch; NIGHTHAWKS(1981); VICTORY(1981); FIRST BLOOD(1982); ROCKY
III(1982), a, d&w; STAYING ALIVE(1983), p, d, w
1984
RHINESTONE(1984), a, w
Marjorie Stallor
Misc. Silents
FOR VALOUR(1928, Brit.)
Stu Stallsmith
WALK THE WALK(1970), ph
Larry Stallsworth
TEX(1982)
Frank Stallworth
LOST, LONELY AND VICIOUS(1958)
Roscoe Stallworth
ROOTS OF HEAVEN, THE(1958)
Anne Stallybrass
DAVID COPPERFIELD(1970, Brit.)
Hal Stalmaster
JOHNNY TREMAIN(1957)
Lynn Stalmaster
FLYING LEATHERNECKS(1951)
Charles Stalnaker
THIN RED LINE, THE(1964); CUSTER OF THE WEST(1968, U.S., Span.); SHALA-
KO(1968, Brit.); LAND RAIDERS(1969); CANNON FOR CORDOBA(1970); EL CON-
DOR(1970); CAPTAIN APACHE(1971, Brit.); WIND AND THE LION, THE(1975)
David Stambaugh
BAD NEWS BEARS, THE(1976); BAD NEWS BEARS IN BREAKING TRAINING,
THE(1977); BAD NEWS BEARS GO TO JAPAN, THE(1978)
Jack Stambaugh
MARRIED IN HOLLYWOOD(1929)
Jack Stamberger
ONE POTATO, TWO POTATO(1964); LAW AND DISORDER(1974)
Robert Stambler
STRANGE LOVERS(1963), p, d, w
Antony Stamboulieh
GET CHARLIE TULLY(1976, Brit.)

Tony Stamboulieh
PLAY DIRTY(1969, Brit.)
Anthony Stamboulish
SUDDEN TERROR(1970, Brit.)
Heinz Stamm
THOUSAND EYES OF DR. MABUSE, THE(1960, Fr./Ital./Ger.), makeup; INVISI-
BLE DR. MABUSE, THE(1965, Ger.), makeup; MAEDCHEN IN UNIFORM(1965,
Ger./Fr.), makeup; FROZEN ALIVE(1966, Brit./Ger.), makeup; MONSTER OF LON-
DON CITY, THE(1967, Ger.), makeup
Max Stamm
MOONLIGHT AND PRETZELS(1933)
Raimund Stamm
FIRST BLOOD(1982); EUREKA(1983, Brit.)
Willy Stamm
TERROR OF DR. MABUSE, THE(1965, Ger.), makeup
Dimitri Stamos
SERENITY(1962)
Arnold Stamp
WONDERFUL WORLD OF THE BROTHERS ERIMM, THE(1962)
John Stamp
GREEN GROW THE RUSHES(1951, Brit.); OUTPOST IN MALAYA(1952, Brit.);
STORY OF ROBIN HOOD, THE(1952, Brit.)
Terence Stamp
BILLY BUDD(1962); TERM OF TRIAL(1962, Brit.); COLLECTOR, THE(1965);
MODESTY BLAISE(1966, Brit.); FAR FROM THE MADDING CROWD(1967, Brit.);
BLUE(1968); POOR COW(1968, Brit.); SPIRITS OF THE DEAD(1969, Fr./Ital.); TEORE-
MA(1969, Ital.); MIND OF MR. SOAMES, THE(1970, Brit.); HU-MAN(1975, Fr.);
SUPERMAN(1978); DIVINE NYMPH, THE(1979, Ital.); MEETINGS WITH REMARK-
ABLE MEN(1979, Brit.); SUPERMAN II(1980); MONSTER ISLAND(1981, Span./U.S.)
Will Stamp
LOSS OF INNOCENCE(1961, Brit.)
Enid Stamp-Taylor
YELLOW STOCKINGS(1930, Brit.); MEET MY SISTER(1933, Brit.); POLITICAL
PARTY, A(1933, Brit.); FEATHERED SERPENT, THE(1934, Brit.); VIRGINIA'S HUS-
BAND(1934, Brit.); JIMMY BOY(1935, Brit.); MR. WHAT'S-HIS-NAME(1935, Brit.);
RADIO PIRATES(1935, Brit.); SO YOU WON'T TALK?(1935, Brit.); TWO HEARTS IN
HARMONY(1935, Brit.); WHILE PARENTS SLEEP(1935, Brit.); BLIND MAN'S
BLUFF(1936, Brit.); GAY LOVE(1936, Brit.); HOUSE BROKEN(1936, Brit.); QUEEN OF
HEARTS(1936, Brit.); ACTION FOR SLANDER(1937, Brit.); FEATHER YOUR
NEST(1937, Brit.); OKAY FOR SOUND(1937, Brit.); TAKE A CHANCE(1937, Brit.);
TALKING FEET(1937, Brit.); UNDERNEATH THE ARCHES(1937, Brit.); BLONDES
FOR DANGER(1938, Brit.); CLIMBING HIGH(1938, Brit.); OLD IRON(1938, Brit.);
STEPPING TOES(1938, Brit.); GIRL WHO FORGOT, THE(1939, Brit.); LAMBETH
WALK, THE(1940, Brit.); SOUTH AMERICAN GEORGE(1941, Brit.); SPRING MEET-
ING(1941, Brit.); ALIBI, THE(1943, Brit.); WICKED LADY, THE(1946, Brit.); HAT-
TER'S CASTLE(1948, Brit.)
Silents
EASY VIRTUE(1927, Brit.); BROKEN MELODY, THE(1929, Brit.)
Misc. Silents
COCTAILS(1928, Brit.); YELLOW STOCKINGS(1928, Brit.)
Will Stampe
MAIN CHANCE, THE(1966, Brit.); SMASHING TIME(1967 Brit.); INSPECTOR
CLOUSEAU(1968, Brit.); POOR COW(1968, Brit.); TWELVE CHAIRS, THE(1970); DR.
JEKYLL AND SISTER HYDE(1971, Brit.)
Dave Stamper
MOTHER KNOWS BEST(1928, d; SUCH MEN ARE DANGEROUS(1930), m
George Haymid Stamper
EMPEROR JONES, THE(1933)
Larry Stamper
1984
HOT AND DEADLY(1984), p
Pope Stamper
Silents
PRIDE OF THE FANCY, THE(1920, Brit.); MASTER OF CRAFT, A(1922, Brit.)
Alexander Stampfer
DOWNHILL RACER(1969)
Atilio Stampone
HAND IN THE TRAP, THE(1963, Arg./Span.), m
Larry Stamps
WE'RE NOT MARRIED(1952)
Adam Stan
HARD TRAIL(1969)
Stan Bernard Trio
I AM A CAMERA(1955, Brit.)
Stan Kenton and his Orchestra
TALK ABOUT A LADY(1946); SCHLAGER-PARADE(1953)
Roy Stanard
HANDS OF THE RIPPER(1971, Brit.), art d; DEVIL WITHIN HER, THE(1976,
Brit.), art d
Ivy Stanborough
Misc. Silents
RUGGED PATH, THE(1918, Brit.)
Ray Stancer
THRESHOLD(1983, Can.)
Walt Stanchfield
ARISTOCATS, THE(1970), anim
Nadia Stancioff
ASH WEDNESDAY(1973)
Gianni Standaart
FRIDAY THE 13TH PART III(1982)
Andree Standard
Silents
NAPOLEON(1927, Fr.)
The Standells
GET YOURSELF A COLLEGE GIRL(1964); RIOT ON SUNSET STRIP(1967)
Lionel Stander
GAY DECEPTION, THE(1935); HOORAY FOR LOVE(1935); I LIVE MY LIFE(1935);
PAGE MISS GLORY(1935); SCOUNDREL, THE(1935); WE'RE IN THE MONEY(1935);
IF YOU COULD ONLY COOK(1936); MEET NERO WOLFE(1936); MILKY WAY,
THE(1936); MORE THAN A SECRETARY(1936); MR. DEEDS GOES TO TOWN(1936);

MUSIC GOES ROUND, THE(1936); SOAK THE RICH(1936); THEY MET IN A
TAXI(1936); LAST GANGSTER, THE(1937); LEAGUE OF FRIGHTENED MEN(1937);
STAR IS BORN, A(1937); CROWD ROARS, THE(1938); NO TIME TO MARRY(1938);
PROFESSOR BEWARE(1938); ICE FOLLIES OF 1939(1939); WHAT A LIFE(1939);
BRIDE WORE CRUTCHES, THE(1940); GUADALCANAL DIARY(1943); HANGMEN
ALSO DIE(1943); TAHITI HONEY(1943); BIG SHOW-OFF, THE(1945); BOY, A GIRL,
AND A DOG, A(1946); IN OLD SACRAMENTO(1946); KID FROM BOOKLYN,
THE(1946); SPECTER OF THE ROSE(1946); CALL NORTHSIDE 777(1948); TEXAS,
BROOKLYN AND HEAVEN(1948); TROUBLE MAKERS(1948); UNFAITHFULLY
YOURS(1948); MAD WEDNESDAY(1950); ST. BENNY THE DIP(1951); TWO GALS
AND A GUY(1951); MOVING FINGER, THE(1963); LOVED ONE, THE(1965); CUL-DE-
SAC(1966, Brit.); PROMISE HER ANYTHING(1966, Brit.); BEYOND THE LAW(1967,
Ital.); DANDY IN ASPIC, A(1968, Brit.); GATES TO PARADISE(1968, Brit./Ger.); BOOT
HILL(1969, Ital.); ONCE UPON A TIME IN THE WEST(1969, U.S./Ital.); GANG THAT
COULDN'T SHOOT STRAIGHT, THE(1971); PULP(1972, Brit.); TREASURE IS-
LAND(1972, Brit./Span./Fr./Ger.); CON MEN, THE(1973, Ital.,Span.); BLACK BIRD,
THE(1975); CASSANDRA CROSSING, THE(1977); NEW YORK, NEW YORK(1977);
MATILDA(1978); 1941(1979); SQUEEZE, THE(1980, Ital.)
Misc. Talkies
1931, ONCE UPON A TIME IN NEW YORK(1972); SEVEN TIMES SEVEN(1973, Ital.)
Martin Stander
REPTILICUS(1962, U.S./Den.)
Guy Standeven
ROAD TO HONG KONG, THE(1962, U.S./Brit.); PARTNER, THE(1966, Brit.)
Glenn Standifer
WARGAMES(1983)
Mr. Standing
Misc. Silents
ALONE IN NEW YORK(1914)
Gordon Standing
Silents
ARE CHILDREN TO BLAME?(1922); OUTLAWS OF THE SEA(1923)
Misc. Silents
MAN AND WOMAN(1920)
Sir Guy Standing
CRADLE SONG(1933); EAGLE AND THE HAWK, THE(1933); HELL AND HIGH
WATER(1933); MIDNIGHT CLUB(1933); STORY OF TEMPLE DRAKE, THE(1933);
DEATH TAKES A HOLIDAY(1934); DOUBLE DOOR(1934); NOW AND FORE-
VER(1934); WITCHING HOUR, THE(1934); ANNAPOLIS FAREWELL(1935); CAR
99(1935); LIVES OF A BENGAL LANCER(1935); I'D GIVE MY LIFE(1936); LLOYDS
OF LONDON(1936); PALM SPRINGS(1936); RETURN OF SOPHIE LANG, THE(1936);
BULLDOG DRUMMOND ESCAPES(1937)
Guy Standing, Jr.
TITANIC(1953)
Mrs. Guy Standing
Misc. Silents
HOODMAN BLIND(1913)
Herbert Standing
Silents
CAPRICES OF KITTY, THE(1915); CAPTAIN COURTESY(1915); IT'S NO LAUGH-
ING MATTER(1915); KILMENY(1915); MADCAP BETTY(1915); CODE OF MARCIA
GRAY(1916); TONGUES OF MEN, THE(1916); DOWN TO EARTH(1917); LITTLE
PATRIOT, A(1917); MAN FROM PAINTED POST, THE(1917); AMARILLY OF
CLOTHESLINE ALLEY(1918); STELLA MARIS(1918); ALMOST A HUSBAND(1919);
JANE GOES A' WOOING(1919); ROMANCE OF THE AIR, A(1919); WILD HO-
NEY(1919); JUDY OF ROGUES' HARBOUR(1920); INFAMOUS MISS REVELL,
THE(1921); ONE WILD WEEK(1921); IMPOSSIBLE MRS. BELLEW, THE(1922); TRAP,
THE(1922); WHILE SATAN SLEEPS(1922); JAZZMANIA(1923); SAWDUST(1923)
Misc. Silents
CALL OF THE CUMBERLANDS, THE(1915); GENTLEMAN FROM INDIANA,
A(1915); YANKEE GIRL, THE(1915); BEN BLAIR(1916); DAVID GARRICK(1916);
DAVY CROCKETT(1916); HER FATHER'S SON(1916); INTRIGUE(1916); MADAME
LA PRESIDENTE(1916); RIGHT DIRECTION, THE(1916); REDEEMING LOVE,
THE(1917); SPIRIT OF ROMANCE, THE(1917); HE COMES UP SMILING(1918); HOW
COULD YOU, JEAN?(1918); IN JUDGEMENT OF(1918); WHITE MAN'S LAW,
THE(1918); SPORTING CHANCE, A(1919); THROUGH THE WRONG DOOR(1919);
BLUE MOON, THE(1920); SIMPLE SOULS(1920); MASQUERADER, THE(1922)
Herbert Standing, Jr.
Misc. Silents
HERITAGE(1920)
Jack Standing
Silents
CLIMBERS, THE(1915); HELL'S HINGES(1916); INNOCENT SINNER, THE(1917)
Misc. Silents
EVANGELIST, THE(1915); LOVE OF WOMEN, THE(1915); RATED AT
$10.000.000(1915); CIVILIZATION'S CHILD(1916); ONE TOUCH OF SIN(1917); PRICE
OF HER SOUL, THE(1917)
Joan Standing
FASHIONS IN LOVE(1929); MARRIAGE PLAYGROUND, THE(1929); EXTRAVA-
GANCE(1930); FOR THE LOVE O'LIL(1930); LADY'S MORALS, A(1930); STREET OF
CHANCE(1930); DRACULA(1931); EX-FLAME(1931); NEVER THE TWAIN SHALL
MEET(1931); YOUNG AS YOU FEEL(1931); BROKEN LULLABY(1932); SHOP-
WORN(1932); JANE EYRE(1935); STRAIGHT FROM THE HEART(1935); LITTLE
LORD FAUNTLEROY(1936)
Silents
BRANDING IRON, THE(1920); OLIVER TWIST(1922); NOISE IN NEWBORO,
A(1923); GREED(1925); CAMPUS FLIRT, THE(1926); MEMORY LANE(1926); OUTSID-
ER, THE(1926); SANDY(1926); SKYROCKET, THE(1926); KID'S CLEVER, THE(1929)
Misc. Silents
RITZY(1927); HOME JAMES(1928); RILEY OF THE RAINBOW DIVISION(1928)
John Standing
PAIR OF BRIEFS, A(1963, Brit.); SWINGIN' MAIDEN, THE(1963, Brit.); YOUNG
AND WILLING(1964, Brit.); KING RAT(1965); PSYCHOPATH, THE(1966, Brit.);
WALK, DON'T RUN(1966); TORTURE GARDEN(1968, Brit.); THANK YOU ALL VERY
MUCH(1969, Brit.); X Y & ZEE(1972, Brit.); ALL THE RIGHT NOISES(1973, Brit.);
EAGLE HAS LANDED, THE(1976, Brit.); CLASS OF MISS MAC MICHAEL, THE(1978,
Brit./U.S.); LEGACY, THE(1979, Brit.); ELEPHANT MAN, THE(1980, Brit.); SEA
WOLVES, THE(1981, Brit.); PRIVATES ON PARADE(1982)

1984
PRIVATES ON PARADE(1984, Brit.)
Silents
PLEASURE MAD(1923)
Michael Standing
BAND WAGGON(1940, Brit.); COP-OUT(1967, Brit.); UP THE JUNCTION(1968, Brit.); ITALIAN JOB, THE(1969, Brit.); VIOLENT ENEMY, THE(1969, Brit.); MADE(1972, Brit.)
Percy Standing
FLAME OF LOVE, THE(1930, Brit.); HARMONY HEAVEN(1930, Brit.); COLONEL BLOOD(1934, Brit.)
Silents
EVERYBODY'S GIRL(1918); KAISER'S FINISH, THE(1918); MY FOUR YEARS IN GERMANY(1918); CAPTAIN'S CAPTAIN, THE(1919); MODERN SALOME, A(1920); APPEARANCES(1921); SHEER BLUFF(1921); HALF A TRUTH(1922, Brit.); FIRES OF FATE(1923, Brit.)
Misc. Silents
FALL OF A NATION, THE(1916); BUSINESS OF LIFE, THE(1918); GAME WITH FATE, A(1918); SONG OF THE SOUL, THE(1918); TO THE HIGHEST BIDDER(1918); BONDS OF LOVE(1919); EVERY MOTHER'S SON(1919); ISLAND OF WISDOM, THE(1920, Brit.); MIRACLE OF LOVE, THE(1920)
Percy Darrell Standing
Silents
LIFE WITHOUT SOUL(1916)
Percy G. Standing
Silents
HER FIGHTING CHANCE(1917)
Wyndham Standing
BILLY THE KID(1930); HELL'S ANGELS(1930); SUCH IS THE LAW(1930, Brit.); SILENT WITNESS, THE(1932); DESIGN FOR LIVING(1933); STUDY IN SCARLET, A(1933); IMITATION OF LIFE(1934); KEY, THE(1934); LIMEHOUSE BLUES(1934); SADIE MCKEE(1934); CLIVE OF INDIA(1935); BELOVED ENEMY(1936); MARY OF SCOTLAND(1936); MAN IN THE IRON MASK, THE(1939); NIGHT OF NIGHTS, THE(1939); THEY SHALL HAVE MUSIC(1939); LONG VOYAGE HOME, THE(1940); OUT WEST WITH THE PEPPERS(1940); PRIDE AND PREJUDICE(1940); SON OF MONTE CRISTO(1940); MEET JOHN DOE(1941); RAGE IN HEAVEN(1941); SMILIN' THROUGH(1941); THEY ALL KISSED THE BRIDE(1942); THIS ABOVE ALL(1942); GUY NAMED JOE, A(1943); LAUGH YOUR BLUES AWAY(1943); MADAME CURIE(1943); MRS. PARKINGTON(1944); WEEKEND AT THE WALDORF(1945); WOMAN IN THE WINDOW, THE(1945); LOCKET, THE(1946); SECRET HEART, THE(1946); GREEN DOLPHIN STREET(1947); IVY(1947); LATE GEORGE APLEY, THE(1947); PRIVATE AFFAIRS OF BEL AMI, THE(1947); SEA OF GRASS, THE(1947)
Silents
LAW OF THE LAND, THE(1917); ROSE OF THE WORLD(1918); ISLE OF CONQUEST(1919); MARRIAGE PRICE(1919); OUT OF THE SHADOW(1919); LIFTING SHADOWS(1920); MODERN SALOME, A(1920); JOURNEY'S END, THE(1921); MARRIAGE OF WILLIAM ASHE, THE(1921); INNER MAN, THE(1922); LION'S MOUSE, THE(1922, Brit.); GOLD DIGGERS, THE(1923); REJECTED WOMAN, THE(1924); DARK ANGEL, THE(1925); EARLY BIRD, THE(1925); RECKLESS SEX, THE(1925); UNCHASTENED WOMAN(1925); IF YOUTH BUT KNEW(1926, Brit.); CITY GONE WILD, THE(1927); THUMBS DOWN(1927); POWER OVER MEN(1929, Brit.)
Misc. Silents
SUPREME TEST, THE(1915); BEGGAR OF CAWNPORE, THE(1916); BUGLE CALL, THE(1916); BULLETS AND BROWN EYES(1916); AUCTION OF VIRTUE, THE(1917); EXILE(1917); REDEEMING LOVE, THE(1917); SOUL OF MAGDALEN, THE(1917); TO THE DEATH(1917); WAITING SOUL, THE(1917); GLORIOUS ADVENTURE, THE(1918); HILLCREST MYSTERY, THE(1918); LIFE MASK, THE(1918); EYES OF THE SOUL(1919); PAID IN FULL(1919); TEMPERAMENTAL WIFE, A(1919); WITNESS FOR THE DEFENSE, THE(1919); WOMAN ON THE INDEX, THE(1919); BLACKMAIL(1920); EARTHBOUND(1920); MIRACLE OF LOVE, THE(1920); MY LADY'S GARTER(1920); IRON TRAIL, THE(1921); BRIDE'S PLAY, THE(1922); ISLE OF DOUBT(1922); SMILIN' THROUGH(1922); DAYTIME WIVES(1923); HYPOCRITES, THE(1923, Brit.); LITTLE JOHNNY JONES(1923); FLAMES OF DESIRE(1924); PAGAN PASSIONS(1924); VANITY'S PRICE(1924); DARK ANGEL, THE(1925); CANADIAN, THE(1926); WHITE HEAT(1926, Brit.); PRICE OF DIVORCE, THE(1928, Brit.); WIDECOMBE FAIR(1928, Brit.); FLYING SQUAD, THE(1929)
Dick Standish
HELL BOUND(1957)
Pamela Standish
SIXTY GLORIOUS YEARS(1938, Brit.); PRIME MINISTER, THE(1941, Brit.)
Robert Standish
ELEPHANT WALK(1954), w
Schuyler Standish
BLACK BANDIT(1938); WUTHERING HEIGHTS(1939); LITTLE MEN(1940); BLOOD AND SAND(1941); MELODY FOR THREE(1941)
Shirley Standlee
PATTERNS(1956)
Martha Standner
NOT RECONCILED, OR "ONLY VIOLENCE HELPS WHERE IT RULES"(1969, Ger.)
Wg. Cdr. Robert Standord-Tuck
BATTLE OF BRITAIN, THE(1969, Brit.), tech adv
Barbara Stanek
POSSESSION(1981, Fr./Ger.)
Stanelli
LATIN LOVE(1930, Brit.); HEARTS OF HUMANITY(1936, Brit.); OLD MOTHER RILEY OVERSEAS(1943, Brit.); ADVENTURES OF JANE, THE(1949, Brit.)
Stanelli and His Hornchestra
RADIO FOLLIES(1935, Brit.)
Ken Stanely
MOUSE THAT ROARED, THE(1959, Brit.)
Emilian Stanev
PEACH THIEF, THE(1969, Bulgaria), d&w
Net Stanfield
STORMY WEATHER(1943)
Alan Stanford
EDUCATING RITA(1983)
Arnold Stanford
IRON MAJOR, THE(1943); JANIE(1944)

Chuck Stanford
X-15(1961); LAST ESCAPE, THE(1970, Brit.)
Deborah Stanford
GIRL WITH A PISTOL, THE(1968, Ital.); THANK YOU ALL VERY MUCH(1969, Brit.)
Donald Stanford
TASTE OF BLOOD, A(1967), w
Frank Stanford
IS EVERYBODY HAPPY?(1943)
Henry Stanford
Misc. Silents
WHERE LOVE IS(1917)
Len Stanford
THEY WERE EXPENDABLE(1945)
Leonard Stanford
BATTLE IN OUTER SPACE(1960)
Lillian Stanford
RAZOR'S EDGE, THE(1946)
Robert Stanford
DANGEROUS BLONDES(1943); PASSPORT TO SUEZ(1943); THERE'S SOMETHING ABOUT A SOLDIER(1943)
Thomas Stanford
WEST SIDE STORY(1961), ed; IN THE COOL OF THE DAY(1963), ed; EMIL AND THE DETECTIVES(1964), ed; SLENDER THREAD, THE(1965), ed; TRUTH ABOUT SPRING, THE(1965, Brit.), ed; DON'T MAKE WAVES(1967), ed; FOX, THE(1967), ed; HELL IN THE PACIFIC(1968), ed; REIVERS, THE(1969), ed; STEAGLE, THE(1971), ed; JEREMIAH JOHNSON(1972), ed; YAKUZA, THE(1975, U.S./Jap.), ed; LEGEND OF THE LONE RANGER, THE(1981), ed
Thomas G. Stanford
SUDDENLY, LAST SUMMER(1959, Brit.), ed
Trevor H. Stanford
WEEKEND WITH LULU, A(1961, Brit.), m
Victor Stanford
YANKEE DON(1931); GET THAT GIRL(1932)
Stanford & McNaughton
SATURDAY NIGHT REVUE(1937, Brit.)
Arnold Stang
MY SISTER EILEEN(1942); SEVEN DAYS LEAVE(1942); THEY GOT ME COVERED(1943); LET'S GO STEADY(1945); SO THIS IS NEW YORK(1948); TWO GALS AND A GUY(1951); MAN WITH THE GOLDEN ARM, THE(1955); ALAKAZAM THE GREAT!(1961, Jap.); DONDI(1961); IT'S A MAD, MAD, MAD, MAD WORLD(1963); PINOCCHIO IN OUTER SPACE(1965, U.S./Bel.); SECOND FIDDLE TO A STEEL GUITAR(1965); SKIDOO(1968); HELLO DOWN THERE(1969); HERCULES IN NEW YORK(1970); MARCO POLO JUNIOR(1973, Aus.); RAGGEDY ANN AND ANDY(1977)
Hugh Stange
AFTER TOMORROW(1932), w
Hugh Stanislaus Stange
NEW YORK NIGHTS(1929), w; YOUNG BRIDE(1932), w
Michaelis Stangeland
STAR FOR A NIGHT(1936), w
Barbara Stanger
SAVANNAH SMILES(1983)
Hugo Stanger
VICE SQUAD(1982); JOYSTICKS(1983)
Hugo L. Stanger
1984
BEST DEFENSE(1984); IMPULSE(1984)
Goran Stangertz
FLIGHT OF THE EAGLE(1983, Swed.)
Henrik Stangerup
MAN WHO THOUGHT LIFE, THE(1969, Den.), w
Raimund Stangl
FREUD(1962), makeup; GIRL AND THE LEGEND, THE(1966, Ger.), makeup; SOMETHING FOR EVERYONE(1970), makeup; WILLY WONKA AND THE CHOCOLATE FACTORY(1971), makeup
Ida Stanhope
Misc. Silents
SOULS IN BONDAGE(1916)
Paul Stanhope
MONKEY'S PAW, THE(1933), makeup; WATERFRONT AT MIDNIGHT(1948), makeup; MANHANDLED(1949), makeup; VANISHING OUTPOST, THE(1951), makeup; GREAT WHITE HOPE, THE(1970), makeup
Ted Stanhope
TILLIE AND GUS(1933); ROAD SHOW(1941); TALES OF MANHATTAN(1942); LEAVE IT TO THE IRISH(1944); GLASS ALIBI, THE(1946); BURNING CROSS, THE(1947); WEB, THE(1947); SMART GIRLS DON'T TALK(1948); MA AND PA KETTLE(1949); EMERGENCY WEDDING(1950); ACCORDING TO MRS. HOYLE(1951); MR. BELVEDERE RINGS THE BELL(1951); YOU'RE IN THE NAVY NOW(1951); FLESH AND FURY(1952); HIGH NOON(1952); HOLD THAT LINE(1952); BIG HEAT, THE(1953); SUDDENLY(1954); ILLEGAL(1955); TERROR IN A TEXAS TOWN(1958); GATHERING OF EAGLES, A(1963)
Warren Stanhope
IS YOUR HONEYMOON REALLY NECESSARY?(1953, Brit.); RED DRESS, THE(1954, Brit.); BEDFORD INCIDENT, THE(1965, Brit.); CURSE OF THE FLY(1965, Brit.); GAMES, THE(1970); REVOLUTIONARY, THE(1970, Brit.)
Mila Stanic
EASY LIFE, THE(1963, Ital.)
John Stanier
1984
OXFORD BLUES(1984), ph
Reg Staniford
NO BLADE OF GRASS(1970, Brit.)
Albert Stanislaus
1984
CHOOSE ME(1984)
Jiri Stanislav
MOONLIGHTING(1982, Brit.)
Jacques Stanislavski
VON RYAN'S EXPRESS(1965)

Andrew Stanislavsky
GIRL FROM POLTAVA(1937)
Jacques Stanislawski
CASTLE OF THE LIVING DEAD(1964, Ital./Fr.)
Grazyna Staniszewska
KNIGHTS OF THE TEUTONIC ORDER, THE(1962, Pol.)
Viktor Stanitsyn
WAR AND PEACE(1968, USSR)
Brian John Stankiewicz
YOUNG GIANTS(1983)
Marushka Stankova
1984
HEY BABE!(1984, Can.)
Maruska Stankova
QUINTET(1979)
Marushka Stankove
1984
MRS. SOFFEL(1984)
Bojana Stankovic
TWILIGHT TIME(1983, U.S./Yugo.)
Ernst Stankowski
GOOD SOLDIER SCHWEIK, THE(1963, Ger.)
Penrhyn Stanlaws
Silents
OVER THE BORDER(1922), d; SINGED WINGS(1922), d
Misc. Silents
AT THE END OF THE WORLD(1921), d; HOUSE THAT JAZZ BUILT, THE(1921), d; LITTLE MINISTER, THE(1921), d; LAW AND THE WOMAN, THE(1922), d; PINK GODS(1922), d
Aileen Stanley, Jr.
ABOUT FACE(1952)
Al Stanley
EAST SIDE SADIE(1929)
Alvah Stanley
SWORD AND THE SORCERER, THE(1982)
Art Stanley
CALL ME MISTER(1951)
Arthur Stanley
TRUST THE NAVY(1935, Brit.)
B.F. Stanley
Misc. Silents
OTHER WOMAN'S STORY, THE(1925), d
Barbara Stanley
HARBOR OF MISSING MEN(1950); TRAIN TO TOMBSTONE(1950); VALLEY OF FIRE(1951)
Betty Stanley
LAST DAYS OF DOLWYN, THE(1949, Brit.)
Blanche Stanley
Silents
BRENDA OF THE BARGE(1920, Brit.); MIRAGE, THE(1920, Brit.)
Charles Stanley
23 PACES TO BAKER STREET(1956); SHADOW OF THE CAT, THE(1961, Brit.); ROOMMATES(1962, Brit.); CARRY ON CABBIE(1963, Brit.)
Silents
ADAM BEDE(1918, Brit.)
Clifford "Red" Stanley
MELODY LANE(1941)
Diane Stanley
PLANET OF THE APES(1968)
Dick Stanley
STANLEY AND LIVINGSTONE(1939); SINGIN' IN THE CORN(1946)
Donna Stanley
FANDANGO(1970)
Misc. Talkies
RUNNING WITH THE DEVIL(1973)
Ed Stanley
BULLETS OR BALLOTS(1936); HOT MONEY(1936); LIBELED LADY(1936); ALCATRAZ ISLAND(1937); ONCE A DOCTOR(1937); COMET OVER BROADWAY(1938); STAR MAKER, THE(1939); UNEXPECTED FATHER(1939); I WANT A DIVORCE(1940); MAN WHO TALKED TOO MUCH, THE(1940); MURDER IN THE AIR(1940); FACE BEHIND THE MASK, THE(1941); MAN BETRAYED, A(1941); MEET JOHN DOE(1941); SEALED LIPS(1941); DRUMS OF THE CONGO(1942); GIRL TROUBLE(1942); LOVES OF EDGAR ALLAN POE, THE(1942); THIS GUN FOR HIRE(1942); WHO IS HOPE SCHUYLER?(1942); HEAVENLY DAYS(1944)
Edward Stanley
SECOND WIFE(1936); SOME BLONDES ARE DANGEROUS(1937); WIVES UNDER SUSPICION(1938)
Edwin Stanley
AMATEUR DADDY(1932); IF I HAD A MILLION(1932); ROCKABYE(1932); INTERNATIONAL HOUSE(1933); LUCKY DEVILS(1933); MY WOMAN(1933); NO OTHER WOMAN(1933); JEALOUSY(1934); LIFE OF VERGIE WINTERS, THE(1934); UPPER WORLD(1934); YOU BELONG TO ME(1934); STRANDED(1935); CHINA CLIPPER(1936); TRAILIN' WEST(1936); CHARLIE CHAN ON BROADWAY(1937); EASY LIVING(1937); LOVE IS ON THE AIR(1937); MANDARIN MYSTERY, THE(1937); MARKED WOMAN(1937); ACCIDENTS WILL HAPPEN(1938); ALEXANDER'S RAGTIME BAND(1938); BILLY THE KID RETURNS(1938); BORN TO BE WILD(1938); INTERNATIONAL SETTLEMENT(1938); LITTLE TOUGH GUY(1938); MISSING GUEST, THE(1938); SHINING HOUR, THE(1938); SWEETHEARTS(1938); YOU CAN'T TAKE IT WITH YOU(1938); ESPIONAGE AGENT(1939); ETERNALLY YOURS(1939); KING OF THE UNDERWORLD(1939); NEWSBOY'S HOME(1939); NINOTCHKA(1939); TOO BUSY TO WORK(1939); 20,000 MEN A YEAR(1939); BABIES FOR SALE(1940); CHARLIE CHAN IN PANAMA(1940); YOUTH WILL BE SERVED(1940); ARKANSAS JUDGE(1941); KNOCKOUT(1941); LUCKY DEVILS(1941); MOUNTAIN MOONLIGHT(1941); NIGHT OF JANUARY 16TH(1941); RIDE, KELLY, RIDE(1941); SMALL TOWN DEB(1941); GENTLEMAN JIM(1942); ICE-CAPADES REVUE(1942); MAN WHO CAME TO DINNER, THE(1942); PARDON MY STRIPES(1942); JOHNNY COME LATELY(1943); O, MY DARLING CLEMENTINE(1943); SHADOW OF A DOUBT(1943); SONG OF BERNADETTE(1943); BUFFALO BILL(1944); FOLLOW THE BOYS(1944); JAMBOREE(1944); LOUISIANA HAYRIDE(1944); PRINCESS AND THE PIRATE, THE(1944); STANDING ROOM ONLY(1944); CONFLICT(1945); INCEN-

DIARY BLONDE(1945); YOUTH ON TRIAL(1945); TWO YEARS BEFORE THE MAST(1946)
Silents
KING LEAR(1916); LOVE AUCTION, THE(1919)
Misc. Silents
DIVORCE AND THE DAUGHTER(1916); DUMMY, THE(1917); LAW OF COMPENSATION, THE(1917); MARRIAGES ARE MADE(1918); EVERY MOTHER'S SON(1919)
Eric Stanley
RINGER, THE(1932, Brit.); GOING STRAIGHT(1933, Brit.); OUT OF THE PAST(1933, Brit.); INVITATION TO THE WALTZ(1935, Brit.); LIVING DANGEROUSLY(1936, Brit.); FIRST LADY(1937); OVER THE GOAL(1937); SH! THE OCTOPUS(1937); AMAZING DR. CLITTERHOUSE, THE(1938); BUCCANEER, THE(1938); DAREDEVIL DRIVERS(1938); LITTLE MISS THOROUGHBRED(1938); MEN ARE SUCH FOOLS(1938); MYSTERY HOUSE(1938); PATIENT IN ROOM 18, THE(1938); SLIGHT CASE OF MURDER, A(1938); TORCHY BLANE IN PANAMA(1938); WHEN WERE YOU BORN?(1938)
Erika Stanley
NIGHTMARE IN BLOOD(1978)
Erle Stanley
RIVER HOUSE GHOST, THE(1932, Brit.)
Fergal Stanley
BIG GAMBLE, THE(1961)
Florence Stanley
UP THE DOWN STAIRCASE(1967); DAY OF THE DOLPHIN, THE(1973); FORTUNE, THE(1975); PRISONER OF SECOND AVENUE, THE(1975)
Forrest Stanley
DRAKE CASE, THE(1929); LOVE KISS, THE(1930); MEN ARE LIKE THAT(1931); RACING YOUTH(1932); RIDER OF DEATH VALLEY(1932); SIN'S PAYDAY(1932); SHOW BOAT(1936); OUTLAWS OF THE DESERT(1941); TATTERED DRESS, THE(1957)
Silents
PRETTY MRS. SMITH(1915); CODE OF MARCIA GRAY(1916); TONGUES OF MEN, THE(1916); NOTORIOUS MRS. SANDS, THE(1920); ENCHANTMENT(1921); PRIDE OF PALOMAR, THE(1922); WHEN KNIGHTHOOD WAS IN FLOWER(1922); GIRL WHO WOULDN'T WORK, THE(1925); CAT AND THE CANARY, THE(1927); WHEEL OF DESTINY, THE(1927); INTO THE NIGHT(1928); JAZZLAND(1928)
Misc. Silents
JANE(1915); REFORM CANDIDATE, THE(1915); HE FELL IN LOVE WITH HIS WIFE(1916); HEART OF PAULA, THE(1916); MADAME LA PRESIDENTE(1916); MAKING OF MADDALENA, THE(1916); HIS OFFICIAL FIANCEE(1916); OTHER MEN'S WIVES(1919); RESCUING ANGEL, THE(1919); UNDER SUSPICION(1919); WHAT EVERY WOMAN WANTS(1919); MISFIT WIFE, THE(1920); THIRTIETH PIECE OF SILVER, THE(1920); TRIFLERS, THE(1920); WOMAN WHO UNDERSTOOD, A(1920); HOUSE THAT JAZZ BUILT, THE(1921); BEAUTY'S WORTH(1922); YOUNG DIANA, THE(1922); BAVU(1923); HER ACCIDENTAL HUSBAND(1923); TIGER ROSE(1923); THROUGH THE DARK(1924); WINE(1924); BEAUTY AND THE BAD MAN(1925); FATE OF A FLIRT, THE(1925); UNWRITTEN LAW, THE(1925); UP THE LADDER(1925); WHEN HUSBANDS FLIRT(1925); WITH THIS RING(1925); DANCING DAYS(1926); FOREST HAVOC(1926); SHADOW OF THE LAW, THE(1926); CLIMBERS, THE(1927); PHANTOM OF THE TURF(1928)
Frank Stanley
J.W. COOP(1971), ph; CAREY TREATMENT, THE(1972), ph; SEPARATE PEACE, A(1972), ph; BREEZY(1973), ph; MAGNUM FORCE(1973), ph; TOM SAWYER(1973), ph; WILLIE DYNAMITE(1973), ph; THUNDERBOLT AND LIGHTFOOT(1974), ph; EIGER SANCTION, THE(1975), ph; MR. RICCO(1975), ph; CARWASH(1976), ph; HERO AIN'T NOTHIN' BUT A SANDWICH, A(1977), ph; HEROES(1977), ph; BIG FIX, THE(1978), ph; CORVETTE SUMMER(1978), ph; FISH THAT SAVED PITTSBURGH, THE(1979), ph; 10(1979), ph; WHOLLY MOSES(1980), ph; UNDER THE RAINBOW(1981), ph; GREASE 2(1982), ph
1984
PRODIGAL, THE(1984), ph
Fred Stanley
WALKING ON AIR(1936); LADY IN A JAM(1942)
Silents
NIGHT BRIDE, THE(1927), w; RUSH HOUR, THE(1927), w; NONE BUT THE BRAVE(1928), w; RILEY THE COP(1928), w
Fredric Stanley
DANGEROUS AFFAIR, A(1931)
Gene Stanley
NIGHT AND DAY(1946)
George Stanley
SPIDER, THE(1958)
Silents
LITTLE ANGEL OF CANYON CREEK, THE(1914); WHERE MEN ARE MEN(1921); ANGEL OF CROOKED STREET, THE(1922)
Misc. Silents
SOUL'S CYCLE, THE(1916); COURAGE OF MARGE O'DOONE, THE(1920)
Helene Stanley
THRILL OF A ROMANCE(1945); HOLIDAY IN MEXICO(1946); MY DEAR SECRETARY(1948); ALL THE KING'S MEN(1949); BANDIT KING OF TEXAS(1949); ASPHALT JUNGLE, THE(1950); DIPLOMATIC COURIER(1952); DREAMBOAT(1952); SNOWS OF KILIMANJARO, THE(1952); WAIT 'TIL THE SUN SHINES, NELLIE(1952); ROAR OF THE CROWD(1953); CARNIVAL STORY(1954); DAVY CROCKETT, KING OF THE WILD FRONTIER(1955); DIAL RED O(1955); CIRCUS OF LOVE(1958, Ger.); ONE HUNDRED AND ONE DALMATIANS(1961)
Henry Stanley
Misc. Silents
GIRL WHO DOESN'T KNOW, THE(1917)
Sir Henry Stanley
Silents
GREAT LOVE, THE(1918)
Irwin Stanley
YANKS AHOY(1943)
Jack Stanley
NIGHT ALARM(1935), w; YODELIN' KID FROM PINE RIDGE(1937), m/l; TRIAL OF BILLY JACK, THE(1974)
Misc. Silents
CROXLEY MASTER, THE(1921, Brit.)

Jacqueline Stanley
OLD MOTHER RILEY, HEADMISTRESS(1950, Brit.)
Jann Stanley
BIRCH INTERVAL(1976)
Jean Stanley
GREAT MR. HANDEL, THE(1942, Brit.)
John Stanley
GEORGE WHITE'S SCANDALS(1945); SPECTER OF THE ROSE(1946); VARIETY GIRL(1947); MC LINTOCK!(1963); NIGHTMARE IN BLOOD(1978), p, d, w
Joseph Stanley
WE WENT TO COLLEGE(1936), d; HERE COMES ELMER(1943), d
Judge Stanley
NAKED STREET, THE(1955)
Kim Stanley
GODDESS, THE(1958); TO KILL A MOCKINGBIRD(1962); SEANCE ON A WET AFTERNOON(1964 Brit.); THREE SISTERS, THE(1977); FRANCES(1982); RIGHT STUFF, THE(1983)
Lee Stanley
ICE STATION ZEBRA(1968)
Leo L. Stanley
6000 ENEMIES(1939), w
Lilian Stanley
CURE FOR LOVE, THE(1950, Brit.); HAPPIEST DAYS OF YOUR LIFE(1950, Brit.)
Lillian Stanley
THINGS HAPPEN AT NIGHT(1948, Brit.)
Louise Stanley
CALL IT A DAY(1937); GUN LORDS OF STIRRUP BASIN(1937); LAWLESS LAND(1937); MARRY THE GIRL(1937); ONCE A DOCTOR(1937); PAID TO DANCE(1937); RIDERS OF THE ROCKIES(1937); SING, COWBOY, SING(1937); DANGER ON THE AIR(1938); DURANGO VALLEY RAIDERS(1938); GUN PACKER(1938); GUNSMOKE TRAIL(1938); LAND OF FIGHTING MEN(1938); PENITENTIARY(1938); PERSONAL SECRETARY(1938); START CHEERING(1938); THUNDER IN THE DESERT(1938); CHEYENNE KID, THE(1940); LAND OF THE SIX GUNS(1940); PINTO CANYON(1940); SKY BANDITS, THE(1940); YUKON FLIGHT(1940)
Martha M. Stanley
Silents
MY SON(1925), w
Maxfield Stanley
Silents
BIRTH OF A NATION, THE(1915); INTOLERANCE(1916); GREAT LOVE, THE(1918); JUST OUT OF COLLEGE(1921); WHAT'S A WIFE WORTH?(1921)
Misc. Silents
23 ½ HOURS ON LEAVE(1919)
Michael Stanley
SWISS CONSPIRACY, THE(1976, U.S./Ger.), w
Pamela Stanley
DAVID LIVINGSTONE(1936, Brit.); MARIGOLD(1938, Brit.); LAST GRENADE, THE(1970, Brit.)
Pat Stanley
LADIES MAN, THE(1961)
Paul Stanley
CRY TOUGH(1959), d; THREE GUNS FOR TEXAS(1968), d
1984
ICEMAN(1984)
Misc. Talkies
COTTER(1972), d
Phyllis Stanley
LEAVE IT TO BLANCHE(1934, Brit.); TOO MANY MILLIONS(1934, Brit.); HELLO SWEETHEART(1935, Brit.); COMMAND PERFORMANCE(1937, Brit.); SIDE STREET ANGEL(1937, Brit.); THERE AIN'T NO JUSTICE(1939, Brit.); SIDEWALKS OF LONDON(1940, Brit.); GIRL IN DISTRESS(1941, Brit.); NEXT OF KIN(1942, Brit.); WE'LL SMILE AGAIN(1942, Brit.); THEY MET IN THE DARK(1945, Brit.); YOU CAN'T DO WITHOUT LOVE(1946, Brit.); LOOK BEFORE YOU LOVE(1948, Brit.); IF THIS BE SIN(1950, Brit.); LAW AND THE LADY, THE(1951); THUNDER ON THE HILL(1951); TAKE ME TO TOWN(1953); BLACK SLEEP, THE(1956)
Pippa Stanley
TRUNK, THE(1961, Brit.)
Ralph Stanley
DEAD DON'T DREAM, THE(1948), m; FALSE PARADISE(1948), m; GAY INTRUDERS, THE(1948), m; LET'S LIVE AGAIN(1948), m; NIGHT WIND(1948), m; SHAGGY(1948), m; SHED NO TEARS(1948), md; SILENT CONFLICT(1948), m; ROLL, THUNDER, ROLL(1949), m; TIMBER FURY(1950), md; COP HATER(1958); WILD IS MY LOVE(1963); ANDERSON TAPES, THE(1971)
Rebecca Stanley
ONLY WHEN I LAUGH(1981)
1984
BODY DOUBLE(1984); EYES OF FIRE(1984)
Red Stanley
COCOANUT GROVE(1938); SING FOR YOUR SUPPER(1941)
Richard Stanley
ILLEGAL TRAFFIC(1938); KING OF ALCATRAZ(1938); PERSONS IN HIDING(1939)
Robert Stanley
UNASHAMED(1938)
Ruth Stanley
KINFOLK(1970); GLASS HOUSES(1972)
S. Victor Stanley
WORLD, THE FLESH, AND THE DEVIL, THE(1932, Brit.); GHOST CAMERA, THE(1933, Brit.); HIS GRACE GIVES NOTICE(1933, Brit.); IRON STAIR, THE(1933, Brit.); MEDICINE MAN, THE(1933, Brit.); UMBRELLA, THE(1933, Brit.); LASH, THE(1934, Brit.); WHITE ENSIGN(1934, Brit.); WOLVES OF THE UNDERWORLD(1935, Brit.)
Val Stanley
THERE'S ALWAYS VANILLA(1972)
Victor Stanley
HOUSE OF TRENT, THE(1933, Brit.); THREE MEN IN A BOAT(1933, Brit.); TIMBUCTOO(1933, Brit.); FOUR MASKED MEN(1934, Brit.); WHISPERING TONGUES(1934, Brit.); GENTLEMAN'S AGREEMENT(1935, Brit.); SCHOOL FOR STARS(1935, Brit.); TROPICAL TROUBLE(1936, Brit.); AREN'T MEN BEASTS?(1937, Brit.)

Stanley the Chimp
MONKEY'S UNCLE, THE(1965)
Michael Stanley-Evans
BRIDGE TOO FAR, A(1977, Brit.), p
Frank Stanlow
MISS SADIE THOMPSON(1953); SILENT RAIDERS(1954)
B. Stanmore
Silents
MESSAGE FROM MARS, A(1913, Brit.)
Frank Stanmore
TEMPORARY WIDOW, THE(1930, Ger./Brit.); YOU'D BE SURPRISED!(1930, Brit.); GREAT GAY ROAD, THE(1931, Brit.); HOUSE OPPOSITE, THE(1931, Brit.); WHAT A NIGHT!(1931, Brit.); BRIDEGROOM FOR TWO(1932, Brit.); LUCKY GIRL(1932, Brit.); OLD MAN, THE(1932, Brit.); LOVE WAGER, THE(1933, Brit.); THAT'S A GOOD GIRL(1933, Brit.); DON QUIXOTE(1935, Fr.); IT'S A BET(1935, Brit.); LIVE AGAIN(1936, Brit.); ROMANCE AND RICHES(1937, Brit.); NO PARKING(1938, Brit.)
Silents
LOVE IN A WOOD(1915, Brit.); GRIT OF A JEW, THE(1917, Brit.); HOUSE ON THE MARSH, THE(1920, Brit.); JUDGE NOT(1920, Brit.); LONDON PRIDE(1920, Brit.); ROGUE IN LOVE, A(1922, Brit.); LILY OF THE ALLEY(1923, Brit.); SQUIBS, MP(1923, Brit.); ALLEY OF GOLDEN HEARTS, THE(1924, Brit.); OWD BOB(1924, Brit.); SATAN'S SISTER(1925, Brit.); ONLY WAY, THE(1926, Brit.); SQUIBS' HONEYMOON(1926, Brit.); MR. NOBODY(1927, Brit.); MUMSIE(1927, Brit.); RED PEARLS(1930, Brit.)
Misc. Silents
MOTHERLOVE(1916, Brit.); BLINKEYES(192?); BEYOND THE DREAMS OF AVARICE(1920, Brit.); GOD'S PRODIGAL(1923, Brit.); SCHOOL FOR SCANDAL, THE(1923, Brit.); LITTLE PEOPLE, THE(1926, Brit.); WAIT AND SEE(1928, Brit.); WHAT NEXT?(1928, Brit.); CHAMBER OF HORRORS(1929, Brit.); LIFE'S A STAGE(1929, Brit.); LITTLE MISS LONDON(1929, Brit.); THREE MEN IN A CART(1929, Brit.)
John Stannage
SMITHY(1946, Aus.)
Don Stannard
DON CHICAGO(1945, Brit.); CAESAR AND CLEOPATRA(1946, Brit.); I'LL TURN TO YOU(1946, Brit.); DICK BARTON–SPECIAL AGENT(1948, Brit.); DICK BARTON STRIKES BACK(1949, Brit.); TEMPTRESS, THE(1949, Brit.); DICK BARTON AT BAY(1950, Brit.); PINK STRING AND SEALING WAX(1950, Brit.)
Eliot Stannard
AMERICAN PRISONER, THE(1929 Brit.), w; OFFICER'S MESS, THE(1931, Brit.), w; SAFE AFFAIR, A(1931, Brit.), w
Silents
FATAL FINGERS(1916. Brit.), d&w; SOLDIER AND A MAN, A(1916, Brit.), w; FLAMES(1917, Brit.), w; GAY LORD QUEX, THE(1917, Brit.), w; PROFIT AND THE LOSS(1917, Brit.), d, w; GOD AND THE MAN(1918, Brit.), w; NELSON(1918, Brit.), w; RED POTTAGE(1918, Brit.), w; ARTISTIC TEMPERAMENT, THE(1919, Brit.), w; PATRICIA BRENT, SPINSTER(1919, Brit.), w; ERNEST MALTRAVERS(1920, Brit.), w; GENERAL POST(1920, Brit.), w; MANCHESTER MAN, THE(1920, Brit.), w; ADVENTURES OF MR. PICKWICK, THE(1921, Brit.), w; BACHELORS' CLUB, THE(1921, Brit.), w; HANDY ANDY(1921, Brit.), w; OLD COUNTRY, THE(1921, Brit.), w; PRINCE AND THE BEGGARMAID, THE(1921, Brit.), w; SQUIBS(1921, Brit.), w; MASTER OF CRAFT, A(1922, Brit.), w; AUDACIOUS MR. SQUIRE, THE(1923, Brit.), w; HEARTSTRINGS(1923, Brit.), w; HUTCH STIRS 'EM UP(1923, Brit.), w; PADDY, THE NEXT BEST THING(1923, Brit.), w; GAY CORINTHIAN, THE(1924), w; NETS OF DESTINY(1924, Brit.), w; PLEASURE GARDEN, THE(1925, Brit./Ger.), w; FEAR O' GOD(1926, Brit./Ger.), w; LODGER, THE(1926, Brit.), w; EASY VIRTUE(1927, Brit.), w; MOTORING(1927, Brit.), w; VORTEX, THE(1927, Brit.), w; CHAMPAGNE(1928, Brit.), w; FARMER'S WIFE, THE(1928, Brit.), w; WHEN BOYS LEAVE HOME(1928, Brit.), w; MANXMAN(1929, Brit.), w
Misc. Silents
LAUGHING CAVALIER, THE(1917, Brit.), d
Eliott Stannard
Silents
NOT QUITE A LADY(1928, Brit.), w
Elliot Stannard
Silents
JIMMY(1916, Brit.), d, w; STARTING POINT, THE(1919, Brit.), w
Eloit Stannard
HATE SHIP, THE(1930, Brit.), w
Patricia Stannard
Silents
FANCY DRESS(1919, Brit.)
Roy Stannard
TRYGON FACTOR, THE(1969, Brit.), art d; GAMES, THE(1970), art d; THINK DIRTY(1970, Brit.), art d; MELODY(1971, Brit.), art d; TWINS OF EVIL(1971, Brit.), art d; HENRY VIII AND HIS SIX WIVES(1972, Brit.), prod d; SENDER, THE(1982, Brit.), set d; NEVER SAY NEVER AGAIN(1983), art d
1984
CHAMPIONS(1984), art d
Glen Stannel
SOD SISTERS(1969)
Keith Stanners-Bloxam
AFTER YOU, COMRADE(1967, S. Afr.)
Arthur Stanning
SECRETS OF SCOTLAND YARD(1944)
Valerie Stano
PEPPERMINT SODA(1979, Fr.)
Vera Stanojevic
ROMANCE OF A HORSE THIEF(1971)
Anna Stanovich
VICE GIRLS, LTD.(1964)
Dora Dee Stansauk
STORM CENTER(1956)
Ellen Stansbury
ONE GIRL'S CONFESSION(1953)
Erica Stansbury
SECOND-HAND HEARTS(1981)
Hope Stansbury
FOR LOVE OF IVY(1968); RATS ARE COMING! THE WEREWOLVES ARE HERE!, THE(1972)

Jessica Stansbury
SECOND-HAND HEARTS(1981)
Joyce Stansell
TOP BANANA(1954)
Alice Stansfield
WONDER MAN(1945)
Vivian Stanshall
SIR HENRY AT RAWLINSON END(1980, Brit.), a, w, m
Ralph Stantley
JOE LOUIS STORY, THE(1953)
Ralph Stantly
MISTER ROCK AND ROLL(1957)
Ann Stanton
KILLER AT LARGE(1947)
Barry Stanton
ROBBERY(1967, Brit.); TELL ME LIES(1968, Brit.); KING LEAR(1971, Brit./Den.); HAMLET(1976, Brit.)
Betty Stanton
TROUBLEMAKER, THE(1964)
Bob Stanton
SO DEAR TO MY HEART(1949)
Charlotte Stanton
SEMI-TOUGH(1977)
Dane Stanton
Silents
ANSWER, THE(1916, Brit.), w; STILL WATERS RUN DEEP(1916, Brit.), w
Ernie Stanton
STAGE STRUCK(1936); THANK YOU, JEEVES(1936); DEVIL'S SADDLE LEGION, THE(1937); HATS OFF(1937); PRINCE AND THE PAUPER, THE(1937); SARATOGA(1937); FOREIGN CORRESPONDENT(1940); SOUTH OF SUEZ(1940); CASE OF THE BLACK PARROT, THE(1941); CRACKED NUTS(1941); DESERT BANDIT(1941); HIT THE ROAD(1941); MOONLIGHT IN HAWAII(1941); OBLIGING YOUNG LADY(1941); WOLF MAN, THE(1941); GHOST OF FRANKENSTEIN, THE(1942)
Flo Stanton
SON OF PALEFACE(1952)
Fred Stanton
Silents
SON OF THE WOLF, THE(1922); LITTLE CHURCH AROUND THE CORNER(1923)
Misc. Silents
FIRE BRIDE, THE(1922); CANYON OF THE FOOLS(1923)
Frederick Stanton
Silents
JENNY BE GOOD(1920)
Misc. Silents
SPIRIT OF GOOD, THE(1920)
Hank Stanton
ONE MAN'S WAY(1964)
Harry Stanton
FATHER OF THE BRIDE(1950); ONE TOO MANY(1950); IT'S A BIG COUNTRY(1951); WHEN WORLDS COLLIDE(1951); MY SIX CONVICTS(1952); DREAM WIFE(1953); SECRET OF THE INCAS(1954); WHAT'S THE MATTER WITH HELEN?(1971)
Harry Dean Stanton
WRONG MAN, THE(1956); REVOLT AT FORT LARAMIE(1957); TOMAHAWK TRAIL(1957); PROUD REBEL, THE(1958); PORK CHOP HILL(1959); ADVENTURES OF HUCKLEBERRY FINN, THE(1960); DOG'S BEST FRIEND, A(1960); HERO'S ISLAND(1962); HOW THE WEST WAS WON(1962); MAN FROM THE DINERS' CLUB, THE(1963); HOSTAGE, THE(1966); RIDE IN THE WHIRLWIND(1966); COOL HAND LUKE(1967); TIME FOR KILLING, A(1967); DAY OF THE EVIL GUN(1968); MINISKIRT MOB, THE(1968); KELLY'S HEROES(1970, U.S./Yugo.); REBEL ROUSERS(1970); CISCO PIKE(1971); TWO-LANE BLACKTOP(1971); COUNT YOUR BULLETS(1972); DILLINGER(1973); PAT GARRETT AND BILLY THE KID(1973); GODFATHER, THE, PART II(1974); WHERE THE LILIES BLOOM(1974); ZANDY'S BRIDE(1974); BORN TO KILL(1975); FAREWELL, MY LOVELY(1975); RAFFERTY AND THE GOLD DUST TWINS(1975); RANCHO DELUXE(1975); WIN, PLACE, OR STEAL(1975); 92 IN THE SHADE(1975, U.S./Brit.); MISSOURI BREAKS, THE(1976); RENALDO AND CLARA(1978); STRAIGHT TIME(1978); ALIEN(1979); ROSE, THE(1979); WISE BLOOD(1979, U.S./Ger.); BLACK MARBLE, THE(1980); DEATHWATCH(1980, Fr./Ger.); PRIVATE BENJAMIN(1980); ESCAPE FROM NEW YORK(1981); ONE FROM THE HEART(1982); YOUNG DOCTORS IN LOVE(1982); CHRISTINE(1983)
1984
BEAR, THE(1984); PARIS, TEXAS(1984, Ger./Fr.); RED DAWN(1984); REPO MAN(1984)
Helen Stanton
JUNGLE MOON MEN(1955)
Helene Stanton
BIG COMBO, THE(1955); NEW ORLEANS UNCENSORED(1955); SUDDEN DANGER(1955); FOUR GIRLS IN TOWN(1956); PHANTOM FROM 10,000 LEAGUES, THE(1956)
Jane Stanton
PAT AND MIKE(1952)
Jane C. Stanton
OUR TIME(1974), w
John Stanton
KITTY AND THE BAGMAN(1983, Aus.)
1984
PHAR LAP(1984, Aus.)
Misc. Talkies
BELLAMY: MESSAGE GIRL MURDERS(1980)
Marchita Stanton
RED, WHITE AND BLACK, THE(1970)
Marita Stanton
CARRY ON NURSE(1959, Brit.)
Mary Stanton
PAJAMA GAME, THE(1957)
Myra Stanton
BETRAYAL, THE(1948)

Paul Stanton
MOST PRECIOUS THING IN LIFE(1934); STAND UP AND CHEER(1934 80m FOX bw); THIS SIDE OF HEAVEN(1934); VIVA VILLA!(1934); WEDNESDAY'S CHILD(1934); ANOTHER FACE(1935); LET 'EM HAVE IT(1935); RED SALUTE(1935); STRANGERS ALL(1935); CAREER WOMAN(1936); CHARLIE CHAN AT THE CIRCUS(1936); CRIME OF DR. FORBES(1936); DIMPLES(1936); EVERY SATURDAY NIGHT(1936); HALF ANGEL(1936); IT HAD TO HAPPEN(1936); LONGEST NIGHT, THE(1936); NIGHT WAITRESS(1936); POOR LITTLE RICH GIRL(1936); PRISONER OF SHARK ISLAND, THE(1936); PRIVATE NUMBER(1936); ROAD TO GLORY, THE(1936); SING, BABY, SING(1936); SINS OF MAN(1936); WHIPSAW(1936); AWFUL TRUTH, THE(1937); BLACK LEGION, THE(1937); CRACK-UP, THE(1937); DANGER-LOVE AT WORK(1937); IT COULD HAPPEN TO YOU(1937); MAKE WAY FOR TOMORROW(1937); MAN OF THE PEOPLE(1937); MARRIED BEFORE BREAKFAST(1937); MIDNIGHT TAXI(1937); PAID TO DANCE(1937); PORTIA ON TRIAL(1937); SOULS AT SEA(1937); STAR IS BORN, A(1937); STELLA DALLAS(1937); YOUTH ON PAROLE(1937); ARMY GIRL(1938); CITY GIRL(1938); KENTUCKY MOONSHINE(1938); KING OF THE NEWSBOYS(1938); LAW OF THE UNDERWORLD(1938); MY LUCKY STAR(1938); RASCALS(1938); BACHELOR MOTHER(1939); HOLLYWOOD CAVALCADE(1939); MR. SMITH GOES TO WASHINGTON(1939); ROSE OF WASHINGTON SQUARE(1939); STANLEY AND LIVINGSTONE(1939); STAR MAKER, THE(1939); STORY OF ALEXANDER GRAHAM BELL, THE(1939); STRONGER THAN DESIRE(1939); THEY SHALL HAVE MUSIC(1939); 20,000 MEN A YEAR(1939); AND ONE WAS BEAUTIFUL(1940); I LOVE YOU AGAIN(1940); LADY WITH RED HAIR(1940); MAN WHO WOULDN'T TALK, THE(1940); PUBLIC DEB NO. 1(1940); QUEEN OF THE MOB(1940); BODY DISAPPEARS, THE(1941); MIDNIGHT ANGEL(1941); NIGHT OF JANUARY 16TH(1941); PEOPLE VS. DR. KILDARE, THE(1941); REMEMBER THE DAY(1941); ROAD SHOW(1941); STRANGE ALIBI(1941); WHISTLING IN THE DARK(1941); YOU'RE IN THE ARMY NOW(1941); ACROSS THE PACIFIC(1942); LUCKY JORDAN(1942); MAGNIFICENT DOPE, THE(1942); AIR RAID WARDENS(1943); ALLERGIC TO LOVE(1943); FLIGHT FOR FREEDOM(1943); GOVERNMENT GIRL(1943); SLIGHTLY DANGEROUS(1943); SO'S YOUR UNCLE(1943); MR. WINKLE GOES TO WAR(1944); ONCE UPON A TIME(1944); HIT THE HAY(1945); SHE GETS HER MAN(1945); CRIME OF THE CENTURY(1946); HOLIDAY IN MEXICO(1946); SHADOW OF A WOMAN(1946); SISTER KENNY(1946); CRY WOLF(1947); HER HUSBAND'S AFFAIRS(1947); MY WILD IRISH ROSE(1947); THAT'S MY GAL(1947); WELCOME STRANGER(1947); HERE COMES TROUBLE(1948); FOUNTAINHEAD, THE(1949); SANTA FE(1951); JET JOB(1952)
Misc. Silents
GLORIOUS ADVENTURE, THE(1918)
Penny Stanton
CRY TOUGH(1959)
Peter Stanton
GREAT WALL OF CHINA, THE(1970, Brit.)
Richard Stanton
Silents
ROUGH AND READY(1918), d, w; JUNGLE TRAIL, THE(1919), d
Misc. Silents
BEAST, THE(1916), d; LOVE THIEF, THE(1916), d; DURAND OF THE BAD LANDS(1917), d; HER TEMPTATION(1917), d; NORTH OF FIFTY-THREE(1917), d; ONE TOUCH OF SIN(1917), d; SCARLET PIMPERNEL, THE(1917), d; SPY, THE(1917), d; YANKEE WAY, THE(1917), d; CAILLAUX CASE, THE(1918), d; CHEATING THE PUBLIC(1918), d; WHY AMERICA WILL WIN(1918), d; WHY I WOULD NOT MARRY(1918), d; CHECKERS(1919), d; FACE AT YOUR WINDOW(1920), d; THUNDERCLAP(1921), d; MCGUIRE OF THE MOUNTED(1923), d; AMERICAN PLUCK(1925), d
Richard S. Stanton
Misc. Silents
STOLEN HONOR(1918), d
Robert Stanton
LAWLESS VALLEY(1938); THREE SONS(1939); BULLET CODE(1940); MARINES FLY HIGH, THE(1940); ABBOTT AND COSTELLO IN HOLLYWOOD(1945); BLONDE FROM BROOKLYN(1945); BLONDIE'S LUCKY DAY(1946); GENTLEMAN MISBEHAVES, THE(1946); IT'S GREAT TO BE YOUNG(1946); SING WHILE YOU DANCE(1946); STING OF DEATH(1966); I EAT YOUR SKIN(1971)
Ronald Stanton
GET HEP TO LOVE(1942)
Sylvia Stanton
CAROUSEL(1956)
Val Stanton
STAGE STRUCK(1936); HATS OFF(1937); PRISON TRAIN(1938); DUKE OF THE NAVY(1942); GREAT IMPERSONATION, THE(1942); THIS ABOVE ALL(1942)
Valerie Stanton
TOMCAT, THE(1968, Brit.)
Vera Stanton
Silents
PEEP BEHIND THE SCENES, A(1929, Brit.)
W. Dane Stanton
Misc. Silents
LIFE OF LORD KITCHENER, THE(1917, Brit.), d
Whitney J. Stanton
RED RIVER ROBIN HOOD(1943), w
Will Stanton
PARADISE ISLAND(1930); LION AND THE LAMB(1931); PARDON US(1931); TWO GUN MAN, THE(1931); ME AND MY GAL(1932); ROAR OF THE DRAGON(1932); WILD GIRL(1932); HELLO SISTER!(1933); MONKEY'S PAW, THE(1933); SAILOR'S LUCK(1933); ESCAPADE(1935); IRISH IN US, THE(1935); MAN WHO BROKE THE BANK AT MONTE CARLO, THE(1935); MAN WHO RECLAIMED HIS HEAD, THE(1935); MUTINY ON THE BOUNTY(1935); FURY(1936); LAST OF THE MOHICANS, THE(1936); LLOYDS OF LONDON(1936); WHITE HUNTER(1936); AFFAIRS OF CAPPY RICKS(1937); ANOTHER DAWN(1937); SEVENTH HEAVEN(1937); FOUR MEN AND A PRAYER(1938); STRAIGHT, PLACE AND SHOW(1938); CAPTAIN FURY(1939); LITTLE PRINCESS, THE(1939); DEVIL'S ISLAND(1940); CHARLEY'S AUNT(1941); THIS ABOVE ALL(1942); THANK YOUR LUCKY STARS(1943); LODGER, THE(1944); MR. SKEFFINGTON(1944); OUR HEARTS WERE YOUNG AND GAY(1944); SHINE ON, HARVEST MOON(1944); GUY, A GAL AND A PAL, A(1945); NOB HILL(1945); TO EACH HIS OWN(1946); WIFE WANTED(1946); EXILE, THE(1947); FOREVER AMBER(1947); SLIGHTLY FRENCH(1949); CHARLEY AND THE ANGEL(1973), w

Silents
SADIE THOMPSON(1928)
William Stanton
MAMBA(1930); CAVALCADE(1933)
Charles Stantz
SOUTH OF DIXIE(1944)
Otis Stantz
Silents
NON-STOP FLIGHT, THE(1926)
Claude Stanush
LUSTY MEN, THE(1952), w
Ann Stanville
EGYPT BY THREE(1953)
Peter Stanwick
OLD MOTHER RILEY'S JUNGLE TREASURE(1951, Brit.); MYSTERY SUBMA-
RINE(1963, Brit.)
Dick Stanwood
FINNEY(1969)
Louie R. Stanwood
Silents
KILMENY(1915), w
Michael Stanwood
YOUNG WARRIORS, THE(1967)
Rita Stanwood
Misc. Silents
DESERTER, THE(1916); GRAY WOLF'S GHOST, THE(1919)
Barbara Stanwyck
LOCKED DOOR, THE(1929); MEXICALI ROSE(1929); LADIES OF LEISURE(1930);
ILLICIT(1931); MIRACLE WOMAN, THE(1931); NIGHT NURSE(1931); TEN CENTS A
DANCE(1931); FORBIDDEN(1932); PURCHASE PRICE, THE(1932); SHOP-
WORN(1932); SO BIG(1932); BABY FACE(1933); BITTER TEA OF GENERAL YEN,
THE(1933); EVER IN MY HEART(1933); LADIES THEY TALK ABOUT(1933); GAM-
BLING LADY(1934); LOST LADY, A(1934); ANNIE OAKLEY(1935); RED SALU-
TE(1935); SECRET BRIDE, THE(1935); WOMAN IN RED, THE(1935); BANJO ON MY
KNEE(1936); BRIDE WALKS OUT, THE(1936); HIS BROTHER'S WIFE(1936); MES-
SAGE TO GARCIA, A(1936); PLOUGH AND THE STARS, THE(1936); BREAKFAST
FOR TWO(1937); INTERNES CAN'T TAKE MONEY(1937); STELLA DALLAS(1937);
THIS IS MY AFFAIR(1937); ALWAYS GOODBYE(1938); MAD MISS MANTON,
THE(1938); GOLDEN BOY(1939); UNION PACIFIC(1939); REMEMBER THE
NIGHT(1940); BALL OF FIRE(1941); LADY EVE, THE(1941); MEET JOHN DOE(1941);
YOU BELONG TO ME(1941); GAY SISTERS, THE(1942); GREAT MAN'S LADY,
THE(1942); FLESH AND FANTASY(1943); LADY OF BURLESQUE(1943); DOUBLE
INDEMNITY(1944); HOLLYWOOD CANTEEN(1944); CHRISTMAS IN CONNEC-
TICUT(1945); BRIDE WORE BOOTS, THE(1946); CALIFORNIA(1946); MY REPUTA-
TION(1946); STRANGE LOVE OF MARTHA IVERS, THE(1946); CRY WOLF(1947);
OTHER LOVE, THE(1947); TWO MRS. CARROLLS, THE(1947); VARIETY GIRL(1947);
B. F.'S DAUGHTER(1948); SORRY, WRONG NUMBER(1948); EAST SIDE, WEST
SIDE(1949); LADY GAMBLES, THE(1949); FILE ON THELMA JORDAN, THE(1950);
FURIES, THE(1950); NO MAN OF HER OWN(1950); TO PLEASE A LADY(1950); MAN
WITH A CLOAK, THE(1951); CLASH BY NIGHT(1952); ALL I DESIRE(1953); BLOW-
ING WILD(1953); JEOPARDY(1953); MOONLIGHTER, THE(1953); TITANIC(1953);
CATTLE QUEEN OF MONTANA(1954); EXECUTIVE SUITE(1954); WITNESS TO
MURDER(1954); ESCAPE TO BURMA(1955); VIOLENT MEN, THE(1955); MAVERICK
QUEEN(1956); THERE'S ALWAYS TOMORROW(1956); THESE WILDER
YEARS(1956); CRIME OF PASSION(1957); FORTY GUNS(1957); TROOPER
HOOK(1957); WALK ON THE WILD SIDE(1962); NIGHT WALKER, THE(1964);
ROUSTABOUT(1964)
Jacques Stany
GOLD FOR THE CAESARS(1964); MYTH, THE(1965, Ital.); HOUSE OF CARDS(1969);
HORNET'S NEST(1970); PRIEST'S WIFE, THE(1971, Ital./Fr.); MAHOGANY(1975)
Michel Stany
MAN FROM O.R.G.Y., THE(1970)
Bryan Stanyon
COP-OUT(1967, Brit.)
Karel Stapanek
SALT TO THE DEVIL(1949, Brit.)
Stefan Stapasik
FORTY DEUCE(1982), ph
Huub Stapel
LIFT, THE(1983, Neth.)
Fritz Stapenhorst
GIRL FROM THE MARSH CROFT, THE(1935, Ger.), ed
Gunther Stapenhorst
EMIL AND THE DETECTIVE(1931, Ger.), p; BEAUTIFUL ADVENTURE(1932,
Ger.), p; AMPHYTRYON(1937, Ger.), p; SILENT BARRIERS(1937, Brit.), p; GAIETY
GIRLS, THE(1938, Brit.), p; CHALLENGE, THE(1939, Brit.), p; RESTLESS NIGHT,
THE(1964, Ger.), p
George Stapleford
LIFE AND TIMES OF GRIZZLY ADAMS, THE(1974), ph, ed; ADVENTURES OF
FRONTIER FREMONT, THE(1976), ph
Misc. Talkies
MOUNTAIN CHARLIE(1982), d
Robert Stapler
CATTLE EMPIRE(1958), p
Dan Stapleton
I EAT YOUR SKIN(1971)
James Stapleton
HANDS OF A STRANGER(1962)
Jean Stapleton
DAMN YANKEES(1958); BELLS ARE RINGING(1960); SOMETHING WILD(1961);
UP THE DOWN STAIRCASE(1967); COLD TURKEY(1971); KLUTE(1971)
1984
BUDDY SYSTEM, THE(1984)
Jim Stapleton
EMERGENCY HOSPITAL(1956)
Joan Stapleton
DEVIL'S MISTRESS, THE(1968)

John Stapleton
Silents
GENTLEMAN OF LEISURE, A(1923), w
Marie Stapleton
JAZZ SINGER, THE(1927)
Maureen Stapleton
LONELYHEARTS(1958); FUGITIVE KIND, THE(1960); VIEW FROM THE BRIDGE,
A(1962, Fr./Ital.); BYE BYE BIRDIE(1963); TRUMAN CAPOTE'S TRILOGY(1969);
AIRPORT(1970); PLAZA SUITE(1971); SUMMER OF '42(1971); INTERIORS(1978);
LOST AND FOUND(1979); THE RUNNER STUMBLES(1979); FAN, THE(1981); ON
THE RIGHT TRACK(1981); REDS(1981)
1984
JOHNNY DANGEROUSLY(1984)
Vivian Stapleton
YOUNG, THE EVIL AND THE SAVAGE, THE(1968, Ital.)
Maitland Stapley
Misc. Silents
FORGOTTEN(1914, Brit.)
Richard Stapley
CHALLENGE, THE(1948); THREE MUSKETEERS, THE(1948); LITTLE WO-
MEN(1949); STRANGE DOOR, THE(1951); CHARGE OF THE LANCERS(1953); KING
OF THE KHYBER RIFLES(1953); IRON GLOVE, THE(1954); JUNGLE MAN-EA-
TERS(1954); TARGET ZERO(1955); D-DAY, THE SIXTH OF JUNE(1956)
Babe Stapp
TO PLEASE A LADY(1950), tech adv
Margie Stapp
JOLSON SINGS AGAIN(1949); WITHOUT HONOR(1949)
Marjorie Stapp
BLAZING TRAIL, THE(1949); LARAMIE(1949); MISS GRANT TAKES RICH-
MOND(1949); RIMFIRE(1949); EMERGENCY WEDDING(1950); PORT SINIS-
TER(1953); PROBLEM GIRLS(1953); SWORD OF VENUS(1953); FAR COUNTRY,
THE(1955); ILLEGAL(1955); I'VE LIVED BEFORE(1956); LIEUTENANT WORE
SKIRTS, THE(1956); SCANDAL INCORPORATED(1956); WEREWOLF, THE(1956);
GUN FOR A COWARD(1957); KRONOS(1957); MONSTER THAT CHALLENGED THE
WORLD, THE(1957); SHOOT-OUT AT MEDICINE BEND(1957); SAGA OF HEMP
BROWN, THE(1958); SUICIDE BATTALION(1958); YOUNG CAPTIVES, THE(1959);
BATTLE AT BLOODY BEACH(1961); WILD WESTERNERS, THE(1962); GATHERING
OF EAGLES, A(1963)
Philip Stapp
ANIMAL FARM(1955, Brit.), w
Terrell Stapp
SNOW WHITE AND THE SEVEN DWARFS(1937), art d; FANTASIA(1940), art d;
PINOCCHIO(1940), art d; DUMBO(1941), art d
A. Stapran
JACK FROST(1966, USSR)
Georges Staquet
DAY AND THE HOUR, THE(1963, Fr./ Ital.); BAND OF OUTSIDERS(1966, Fr.); IS
PARIS BURNING?(1966, U.S./Fr.); WEEKEND(1968, Fr./Ital.)
Star
Misc. Silents
MY PAL(1925)
Star the Horse
Silents
ARIZONA KID, THE(1929)
Ben Star
TEXAS ACROSS THE RIVER(1966), w
Black Star
FIREBALL JUNGLE(1968)
Lloyd One Star
MAN CALLED HORSE, A(1970), m
Lynn Star
HOUSE OF ERRORS(1942)
Shooting Star
RIDE, RANGER, RIDE(1936)
White Star
Silents
KING OF THE HERD(1927); OLD AGE HANDICAP(1928)
Gabriela Star-Tyszkiewicz
CAMERA BUFF(1983, Pol.), cos
Shag Starbird
RICH KIDS(1979)
Betty Starbuck
SAP FROM SYRACUSE, THE(1930)
James Starbuck
COURT JESTER, THE(1956), ch
K. Starchuk
SATAN'S MISTRESS(1982)
Viktor Starcic
SQUARE OF VIOLENCE(1963, U.S./Yugo.); 25TH HOUR, THE(1967, Fr./Ital./Yugo.);
SEVENTH CONTINENT, THE(1968, Czech./Yugo.)
John Starck
NO TIME TO KILL(1963, Brit./Swed./Ger.)
Todd Starck
ANGEL IN MY POCKET(1969)
Starcom West
I'M GOING TO GET YOU ... ELLIOT BOY(1971, Can.), art d
Harry Stardling, Jr.
FOOLS' PARADE(1971), ph
The Stardusters
SLIGHTLY TERRIFIC(1944); TROCADERO(1944); MELODY IN THE DARK(1948,
Brit.); REBEL ANGEL(1962), m
Dimos Starenios
300 SPARTANS, THE(1962); ISLAND OF LOVE(1963); OEDIPUS THE KING(1968,
Brit.); LOVE CYCLES(1969, Gr.); THANOS AND DESPINA(1970, Fr./Gr.); GREEK
TYCOON, THE(1978); MIDNIGHT EXPRESS(1978, Brit.)
Dimos Starenlos
ANNA OF RHODES(1950, Gr.)

Jack Starett
BORN LOSERS(1967)

Ladislas Starevitch
Misc. Silents
SNOW MAIDEN, THE(1914, USSR), d

Wladyslaw Starewicz
Misc. Silents
CHRISTMAS EVE(1913, USSR), d; TERRIBLE REVENGE, A(1913, USSR), d; RUSLAN I LUDMILA(1915, USSR), d; ON THE WARSAW HIGHROAD(1916, USSR), d

Stargard
SGT. PEPPER'S LONELY HEARTS CLUB BAND(1978)

Martin Starger
AUTUMN SONATA(1978, Swed.), p; FROM THE LIFE OF THE MARIONETTES(1980, Ger.), p

R. Starik
TRAIN GOES TO KIEV, THE(1961, USSR)

Yevgeny Starikovitch
BLUE BIRD, THE(1976), set d

Mikhaylo Petrovich Staritskiy
KIEV COMEDY, A(1963, USSR), w

Arthur Stark
GREEN SLIME, THE(1969)

Audrine Stark
Silents
SHOOTING OF DAN MCGREW, THE(1915)

Bud Stark
MY FOOLISH HEART(1949); CHICAGO CALLING(1951)

Cecillia Stark
1984
STRANGER THAN PARADISE(1984, U.S./Ger.)

Don Stark
EVILSPEAK(1982)

Douglas Stark
MIDDLETON FAMILY AT THE N.Y. WORLD'S FAIR(1939); REFLECTIONS IN A GOLDEN EYE(1967); REACHING OUT(1983)

Graham Stark
DOWN AMONG THE Z MEN(1952, Brit.); FLANNELFOOT(1953, Brit.); FORCES' SWEETHEART(1953, Brit.); JOHNNY ON THE SPOT(1954, Brit.); MILLIONAIRESS, THE(1960, Brit.); DOUBLE BUNK(1961, Brit.); WATCH IT, SAILOR!(1961, Brit.); WEEKEND WITH LULU, A(1961, Brit.); ONLY TWO CAN PLAY(1962, Brit.); OPERATION SNATCH(1962, Brit.); VILLAGE OF DAUGHTERS(1962, Brit.); GET ON WITH IT(1963, Brit.); MAID FOR MURDER(1963, Brit.); MOUSE ON THE MOON, THE(1963, Brit.); PAIR OF BRIEFS, A(1963, Brit.); STRICTLY FOR THE BIRDS(1963, Brit.); SWORD OF LANCELOT(1963, Brit.); WRONG ARM OF THE LAW, THE(1963, Brit.); BECKET(1964, Brit.); GO KART GO(1964, Brit.); GUNS AT BATASI(1964, Brit.); LADIES WHO DO(1964, Brit.); SHOT IN THE DARK, A(1964); OPERATION SNAFU(1965, Brit.); RUNAWAY RAILWAY(1965, Brit.); SAN FERRY ANN(1965, Brit.); THOSE MAGNIFICENT MEN IN THEIR FLYING MACHINES; OR HOW I FLEW FROM LONDON TO PARIS IN 25 HOURS AND 11 MINUTES(1965, Brit.); YOU MUST BE JOKING!(1965, Brit.); ALFIE(1966, Brit.); FINDERS KEEPERS(1966, Brit.); WRONG BOX, THE(1966, Brit.); PLANK, THE(1967, Brit.); THOSE FANTASTIC FLYING FOOLS(1967, Brit); SALT & PEPPER(1968, Brit.); DOCTOR IN TROUBLE(1970, Brit.); MAGIC CHRISTIAN, THE(1970, Brit.); SCRAMBLE(1970, Brit.); START THE REVOLUTION WITHOUT ME(1970); MAGNIFICENT SEVEN DEADLY SINS, THE(1971, Brit.), p&d, w; RETURN OF THE PINK PANTHER, THE(1975, Brit.); GULLIVER'S TRAVELS(1977, Brit., Bel.); CROSSED SWORDS(1978); REVENGE OF THE PINK PANTHER(1978); PRISONER OF ZENDA, THE(1979); HAWK THE SLAYER(1980, Brit.); THERE GOES THE BRIDE(1980, Brit.); SEA WOLVES, THE(1981, Brit.); TRAIL OF THE PINK PANTHER, THE(1982); VICTOR/VICTORIA(1982); CURSE OF THE PINK PANTHER(1983); SUPERMAN III(1983)
1984
BLOODBATH AT THE HOUSE OF DEATH(1984, Brit.)
Misc. Talkies
GHOST OF A CHANCE, A(1968, Brit.); NAUGHTY WIVES(1974)

James Stark
PEGGY(1950); WHITE RAT(1972), ed

John Stark
MAN I MARRIED, THE(1940); MORTAL STORM, THE(1940); FOREIGN INTRIGUE(1956); FOOD OF THE GODS, THE(1976), set d

Juanita Stark
DIVE BOMBER(1941); MALE ANIMAL, THE(1942); THANK YOUR LUCKY STARS(1943); CRIME BY NIGHT(1944); ONE MORE TOMORROW(1946)

Koo Stark
ROCKY HORROR PICTURE SHOW, THE(1975, Brit.); EMILY(1976, Brit.)
1984
ELECTRIC DREAMS(1984)

Laurie Stark
HOT STUFF(1979); NOBODY'S PERFEKT(1981)

Leighton Stark
Misc. Silents
SOLDIERS OF FORTUNE(1914); DAREDEVIL KATE(1916)

Leonard Stark
SALT OF THE EARTH(1954), ph

Lorie Stark
VELVET TRAP, THE(1966)

Michael Stark
CRY OF THE CITY(1948)

Mike Stark
VICKI(1953)

Pauline Stark
WHAT MEN WANT(1930)

Ray Stark
WAY WE WERE, THE(1973), p; WORLD OF SUZIE WONG, THE(1960), p; NIGHT OF THE IGUANA, THE(1964), p; OH DAD, POOR DAD, MAMA'S HUNG YOU IN THE CLOSET AND I'M FEELIN' SO SAD(1967), p; REFLECTIONS IN A GOLDEN EYE(1967), p; FUNNY GIRL(1968), p; OWL AND THE PUSSYCAT, THE(1970), p; FAT CITY(1972), p; FUNNY LADY(1975), p; SUNSHINE BOYS, THE(1975), p; MURDER BY DEATH(1976), p; GOODBYE GIRL, THE(1977), p; CALIFORNIA SUITE(1978), p; CASEY'S SHADOW(1978), d; CHEAP DETECTIVE, THE(1978), p; CHAPTER TWO(1979), p; ELECTRIC HORSEMAN, THE(1979), p; SEEMS LIKE OLD TIMES(1980), p; ANNIE(1982), p

Richard Stark
1984
SLAYGROUND(1984, Brit.), w

Richard Stark [Donald Westlake]
MADE IN U.S.A.(1966, Fr.), d; POINT BLANK(1967), w; SPLIT, THE(1968), w; OUTFIT, THE(1973), w

Roland Stark
FOURTEEN, THE(1973, Brit.), w

Roxanne Stark
STALLION ROAD(1947)

Wallace Stark
LOST MOMENT, THE(1947)

Wilbur Stark
MY LOVER, MY SON(1970, Brit.), p, w; VAMPIRE CIRCUS(1972, Brit.), p, w

Gusti Stark-Gstettenbauer
VIENNA, CITY OF SONGS(1931, Ger.)

Gustl Stark-Gstettenbauer
Silents
WOMAN ON THE MOON, THE(1929, Ger.)

Gustl Stark-Gstettenbaur
DOLLY GETS AHEAD(1931, Ger.)

Pauline Starke
MYSTERIOUS ISLAND(1929); ROYAL ROMANCE, A(1930); SHE KNEW ALL THE ANSWERS(1941)
Silents
INTOLERANCE(1916); ALIAS MARY BROWN(1918); ATOM, THE(1918); EVIDENCE(1918); CONNECTICUT YANKEE AT KING ARTHUR'S COURT, A(1921); SALVATION NELL(1921); SNOWBLIND(1921); WIFE AGAINST WIFE(1921); IF YOU BELIEVE IT, IT'S SO(1922); KINGDOM WITHIN, THE(1922); LITTLE CHURCH AROUND THE CORNER(1923); ARIZONA EXPRESS, THE(1924); DANTE'S INFERNO(1924); FORBIDDEN PARADISE(1924); HEARTS OF OAK(1924); ADVENTURE(1925); BRIGHT LIGHTS(1925); DEVIL'S CARGO, THE(1925); LOVE'S BLINDNESS(1926); WAR PAINT(1926); CAPTAIN SALVATION(1927)
Misc. Silents
RUMMY, THE(1916); CHEERFUL GIVERS(1917); DAUGHTER ANGELE(1918); INNOCENT'S PROGRESS(1918); MAN WHO WOKE UP, THE(1918); SHOES THAT DANCED, THE(1918); UNTIL THEY GET ME(1918); BROKEN BUTTERFLY, THE(1919); EYES OF YOUTH(1919); LIFE LINE, THE(1919); SOLDIERS OF FORTUNE(1919); WHOM THE GODS WOULD DESTROY(1919); COURAGE OF MARGE O'DOONE, THE(1920); LITTLE SHEPARD OF KINGDOM COME, THE(1920); UNTAMED, THE(1920); FLOWER OF THE NORTH(1921); FORGOTTEN WOMAN(1921); MY WILD IRISH ROSE(1922); EYES OF THE FOREST(1923); IN THE PALACE OF THE KING(1923); LITTLE GIRL NEXT DOOR, THE(1923); LOST AND FOUND ON A SOUTH SEA ISLAND(1923); MISSING DAUGHTERS(1924); MAN WITHOUT A COUNTRY, THE(1925); SUN-UP(1925); HONESTY-THE BEST POLICY(1926); DANCE MAGIC(1927); STREETS OF SHANGHAI(1927); WOMEN LOVE DIAMONDS(1927); MAN, WOMAN AND WIFE(1929); VIKING, THE(1929)

Yvonne Starke
SHE GOES TO WAR(1929)

Jaison Starkes
J.D.'S REVENGE(1976), w; FISH THAT SAVED PITTSBURGH, THE(1979), w

Alan Starkey
DRESSER, THE(1983)

Bert Starkey
SIN SHIP(1931); HELL'S HIGHWAY(1932); SCARFACE(1932); FUGITIVE LADY(1934); IT HAPPENED ONE NIGHT(1934); YOU CAN'T TAKE IT WITH YOU(1938)
Silents
CUB, THE(1915); DARK MIRROR, THE(1920)
Misc. Silents
LEND ME YOUR NAME(1918)

Charles Starkey
BENJI(1974); HAWMPS!(1976)

Max Starkey
LAS VEGAS LADY(1976)

Carol Starkman
BLOODY BROOD, THE(1959, Can.)

Pytor Starkovksy
Misc. Silents
NIKOLAI STAVROGIN(1915, USSR)

Pytor Starkovsky
Misc. Silents
FLOOD(1915, USSR); ELDER VASILI GRYAZNOV(1924, USSR)

Irena Starkowna
PARTINGS(1962, Pol.)

Jack Starkweather
CRY DR. CHICAGO(1971)

Max Starky
SILVER BEARS(1978)

Starlight the Horse
OVERLAND BOUND(1929); PHANTOM OF THE DESERT(1930); RIDIN' LAW(1930); DESERT JUSTICE(1936); SWIFTY(1936)
Silents
KNOCKOUT KID, THE(1925); GREY DEVIL, THE(1926); WEST OF THE RAINBOW'S END(1926); CODE OF THE RANGE(1927); HARVEST OF HATE, THE(1929); HOOFBEATS OF VENGEANCE(1929); WILD BLOOD(1929)
Misc. Silents
WHERE THE NORTH HOLDS SWAY(1927); GUARDIANS OF THE WILD(1928)

The Starlighters
FUN AND FANCY FREE(1947); SONG OF IDAHO(1948)

Clayton Starling
HUCKLEBERRY FINN(1974)

Don Starling
UNDERWATER CITY, THE(1962), ed; MAJOR DUNDEE(1965), ed

Donald Starling
TALK OF THE TOWN(1942), spec eff

Lyn Starling
MORE THAN A SECRETARY(1936), w; CLIMAX, THE(1944), w

Lynn Starling
OH, FOR A MAN!(1930), w; MEET THE WIFE(1931), w; TRANSATLANTIC(1931), w; CYNARA(1932), w; FIRST YEAR, THE(1932), w; TORCH SINGER(1933), w; DOWN TO THEIR LAST YACHT(1934), w; LOVE TIME(1934), w; PRESIDENT VANISHES, THE(1934), w; PRIVATE WORLDS(1935), w; SHANGHAI(1935), w; GIVE US THIS NIGHT(1936), w; AS GOOD AS MARRIED(1937), w; WOMEN OF GLAMOUR(1937), w; THANKS FOR THE MEMORY(1938), w; THREE BLIND MICE(1938), w; CAT AND THE CANARY, THE(1939), w; HE MARRIED HIS WIFE(1940), w; NIGHT AT EARL CARROLL'S, A(1940), w; MOON OVER MIAMI(1941), w; FOOTLIGHT SERENADE(1942), w; WINTERTIME(1943), w; IMPOSTER, THE(1944), w; IT'S A PLEASURE(1945), w; THREE LITTLE GIRLS IN BLUE(1946), w; TIME, THE PLACE AND THE GIRL, THE(1946), w

Pat Starling
ARABIAN NIGHTS(1942); SAN FERNANDO VALLEY(1944); SINGING SHERIFF, THE(1944); SONG OF THE OPEN ROAD(1944); RAINBOW OVER THE ROCKIES(1947); DEADLINE(1948); BATTLING MARSHAL(1950)
Misc. Talkies
SUNSET CARSON RIDES AGAIN(1948)

Patricia Starling
Misc. Talkies
FIGHTING MUSTANG(1948)

Roland Starling
GYPSY GIRL(1966, Brit.)

Lynn Starlings
DUMBBELLS IN ERMINE(1930), w

The Starliters
HEY, LET'S TWIST!(1961); TWO TICKETS TO PARIS(1962)

Inoa Starly
HORRIBLE DR. HICHCOCK, THE(1964, Ital.), cos

Pippo Starnazza
ORGANIZER, THE(1964, Fr./Ital./Yugo.); STORY OF A WOMAN(1970, U.S./Ital.); SUNFLOWER(1970, Fr./Ital.); PRIEST'S WIFE, THE(1971, Ital./Fr.)

Dene Starnes
ORGY OF THE DEAD(1965)

Grady Starnes
I'D CLIMB THE HIGHEST MOUNTAIN(1951)

Leland Starnes
THE CRAZIES(1973); CRUISING(1980)

Alina Starnitzka
DREAMER, THE(1970, Israel)

K. Starostin
MAGIC WEAVER, THE(1965, USSR); JACK FROST(1966, USSR)

N. Starostin
BALLAD OF COSSACK GLOOTA(1938, USSR)

T. Starova
YOLANTA(1964, USSR)

Franciszek Starowieyski
DANTON(1983)

Adam Starr
LOOKER(1981)

Alexandre Starr
GOLD RAIDERS, THE(1952), m

Barbara Starr
Silents
SPLITTING THE BREEZE(1927)
Misc. Silents
LET'S GO GALLAGHER(1925); BLUE BLAZES(1926); ESCAPE, THE(1926)

Beau Starr
HANKY-PANKY(1982)
1984
CITY HEAT(1984); FLETCH(1984); LONELY GUY, THE(1984)

Ben Starr
PAD, THE(AND HOW TO USE IT)*(1966, Brit.), w; OUR MAN FLINT(1966), w; BUSYBODY, THE(1967), w; SPIRIT IS WILLING, THE(1967), w; HOW TO COMMIT MARRIAGE(1969), w

Bernice Starr
NIGHT OF THE IGUANA, THE(1964)

Bill Starr
1984
HIGHPOINT(1984, Can.)

Bruce Starr
BOOGEYMAN II(1983), d

Buck Starr
TASTE OF FLESH, A(1967)

Christopher Starr
OSTERMAN WEEKEND, THE(1983)

D. Starr
POCKET MONEY(1972)

Dave Starr
SINGING IN THE DARK(1956)

David S. Starr
FRATERNITY ROW(1977)

Dixie Starr
LAW AND LAWLESS(1932)

Dolores Starr
ATHENA(1954); VAGABOND KING, THE(1956)

Don Starr
LIFE AND TIMES OF JUDGE ROY BEAN, THE(1972); NIGHT OF THE LEPUS(1972); HAWMPS!(1976)

Ed Starr
FUN AND FANCY FREE(1947), art d

Frances Starr
FIVE STAR FINAL(1931); STAR WITNESS(1931); THIS RECKLESS AGE(1932)

Fred Starr
Silents
ONLY SON, THE(1914); POPPY GIRL'S HUSBAND, THE(1919)

Freddie Starr
SQUEEZE, THE(1977, Brit.)

Frederick Starr
Silents
CROOKED STREETS(1920); MOON MADNESS(1920); RIDERS OF THE DAWN(1920)
Misc. Silents
VIVE LA FRANCE(1918)

Harrison Starr
LADY ICE(1973), p

Helen Starr
Silents
HIGH SPEED(1917), w

Henry Starr
Misc. Silents
DEBTOR TO THE LAW, A(1924)

Irving Starr
TOMBSTONE CANYON(1932), p; BORDER BRIGANDS(1935), p; HIS NIGHT OUT(1935), p; STONE OF SILVER CREEK(1935), p; NOBODY'S FOOL(1936), p; WESTLAND CASE, THE(1937), p; BLACK DOLL, THE(1938), p; DANGER ON THE AIR(1938), p; LADY IN THE MORGUE(1938), p; LAST EXPRESS, THE(1938), p; LAST WARNING, THE(1938), p; GAMBLING SHIP(1939), p; INSIDE INFORMATION(1939), p; MYSTERY OF THE WHITE ROOM(1939), p; WITNESS VANISHES, THE(1939), p; MUSIC IN MY HEART(1940), p; TIME OUT FOR RHYTHM(1941), p; AFFAIRS OF MARTHA, THE(1942), p; FINGERS AT THE WINDOW(1942), p; SUNDAY PUNCH(1942), p; BATAAN(1943), p; HARRIGAN'S KID(1943), p; SWING FEVER(1943), p; FOUR JILLS IN A JEEP(1944), p; SOMETHING FOR THE BOYS(1944), p; COCKEYED MIRACLE, THE(1946), p; GALLANT BLADE, THE(1948), p; JOHNNY ALLEGRO(1949), p; SLIGHTLY FRENCH(1949), p

J.A. Starr
SONNY BOY(1929), titles

Jack Starr
PEACE KILLERS, THE(1971)

James Starr
SKY DEVILS(1932), w

James A. Starr
FANCY BAGGAGE(1929), w; IN THE HEADLINES(1929), w; IS EVERYBODY HAPPY?(1929), w; STOLEN KISSES(1929), w; IN THE NEXT ROOM(1930), w; MAN HUNTER, THE(1930), w; OTHER TOMORROW, THE(1930), w; ROUGH WATERS(1930), w; SHOW GIRL IN HOLLYWOOD(1930), w; SPRING IS HERE(1930), w; SWEETHEARTS ON PARADE(1930), w; WIDE OPEN(1930), w
Silents
HAM AND EGGS AT THE FRONT(1927), w; HUSBANDS FOR RENT(1927), t; CRIMSON CITY, THE(1928), t

Jane Starr
Silents
GUILE OF WOMEN(1921); MAD MARRIAGE, THE(1921); FIGHTING AMERICAN, THE(1924)
Misc. Silents
BANDITS OF THE AIR(1925)

Jeffrey Louis Starr
BAD NEWS BEARS IN BREAKING TRAINING, THE(1977); BAD NEWS BEARS GO TO JAPAN, THE(1978)

Jimmie Starr
LION AND THE MOUSE, THE(1928), w; 365 NIGHTS IN HOLLYWOOD(1934), w

Jimmy Starr
CORPSE CAME C.O.D., THE(, w; THAT'S RIGHT–YOU'RE WRONG(1939); SCATTERBRAIN(1940); NIGHT FOR CRIME, A(1942), a, w; OUT CALIFORNIA WAY(1946); NEW KIND OF LOVE, A(1963)

John Starr
MAKING LOVE(1982)

Jonathan Starr
ODYSSEY OF THE PACIFIC(1983, Can./Fr.)

Judy Starr
1984
NINJA III–THE DOMINATION(1984)

June Starr
RED SNOW(1952), m; OPERATION EICHMANN(1961), m; C'MON, LET'S LIVE A LITTLE(1967), p, w

Kay Starr
MAKE BELIEVE BALLROOM(1949); WHEN YOU'RE SMILING(1950); LAST PICTURE SHOW, THE(1971), m

Lynn Starr
GALLANT LADY(1942); NIGHT FOR CRIME, A(1942); PANTHER'S CLAW, THE(1942); PRISON GIRL(1942); YANKS ARE COMING, THE(1942)

Malcolm Starr
TONY ROME(1967), cos

Mary Starr
HAVING WONDERFUL CRIME(1945)

Michael Starr
BUSHIDO BLADE, THE(1982 Brit./U.S.)
1984
NATURAL, THE(1984)

Mike Starr
CRUISING(1980)

Pat Starr
OUTLAND(1981); REDS(1981); SUPERMAN III(1983)
1984
NADIA(1984, U.S./Yugo.)

Paul Starr
DEADLY AFFAIR, THE(1967, Brit.)

Randy Starr
HARD TRAIL(1969); MACHISMO–40 GRAVES FOR 40 GUNS(1970), a, stunts ch

Rick Starr
NIGHT SHIFT(1982)

Ringo Starr
HARD DAY'S NIGHT, A(1964, Brit.); HELP!(1965, Brit.); CANDY(1968, Ital./Fr.); MAGIC CHRISTIAN, THE(1970, Brit.); TWO HUNDRED MOTELS(1971, Brit.); BLINDMAN(1972, Ital.); SON OF DRACULA(1974, Brit.), a, p; THAT'LL BE THE DAY(1974, Brit.); LISZTOMANIA(1975, Brit.); SEXTETTE(1978); CAVEMAN(1981)
1984
GIVE MY REGARDS TO BROAD STREET(1984, Brit.)

Robert Starr
1984
LAST STARFIGHTER, THE(1984)
Ronald Starr
RIDE THE HIGH COUNTRY(1962)
Sally Starr
SO THIS IS COLLEGE(1929); FOR THE LOVE O'LIL(1930); NIGHT WORK(1930); NOT SO DUMB(1930); PARDON MY GUN(1930); PERSONALITY(1930); SWING HIGH(1930); WOMAN RACKET, THE(1930); SWEETHEART OF SIGMA CHI(1933); IN THE MONEY(1934); OUTLAWS IS COMING, THE(1965)
Silents
RISKY ROAD, THE(1918)
Misc. Silents
MAN TRAP, THE(1917); SMASHING THROUGH(1918)
Samantha Starr
ASH WEDNESDAY(1973)
Sheryle Starr
HAVING WONDERFUL CRIME(1945)
Tex Starr
Misc. Silents
CYCLONE BOB(1926)
Texas Starr
ORGY OF THE DEAD(1965)
Vonnie Starr
SINISTER URGE, THE(1961)
Wally Starr
CAPTAIN MILKSHAKE(1970)
Wanda Starr
Misc. Talkies
GUY FROM HARLEM, THE(1977)
Dimos Starrenios
NEVER ON SUNDAY(1960, Gr.)
Bob Starrett
1984
COMFORT AND JOY(1984, Brit.)
Charles Starrett
FAST AND LOOSE(1930); ROYAL FAMILY OF BROADWAY, THE(1930); AGE FOR LOVE(1931); DAMAGED LOVE(1931); SILENCE(1931); TOUCHDOWN!(1931); VIKING, THE(1931); LADY AND GENT(1932); MASK OF FU MANCHU, THE(1932); SKY BRIDE(1932); JUNGLE BRIDE(1933); MR. SKITCH(1933); OUR BETTERS(1933); RETURN OF CASEY JONES(1933); SWEETHEART OF SIGMA CHI(1933); CALL IT LUCK(1934); DESIRABLE(1934); GENTLEMEN ARE BORN(1934); GREEN EYES(1934); MURDER ON THE CAMPUS(1934); STOLEN SWEETS(1934); THIS MAN IS MINE(1934); THREE ON A HONEYMOON(1934); GALLANT DEFENDER(1935); MAKE A MILLION(1935); ONE IN A MILLION(1935); ONE NEW YORK NIGHT(1935); SHOT IN THE DARK, A(1935); SILVER STREAK, THE(1935); SO RED THE ROSE(1935); SONS OF STEEL(1935); WHAT PRICE CRIME?(1935); COWBOY STAR, THE(1936); MYSTERIOUS AVENGER, THE(1936); SECRET PATROL(1936); STAMPEDE(1936); ALONG CAME LOVE(1937); CODE OF THE RANGE(1937); DODGE CITY TRAIL(1937); OLD WYOMING TRAIL, THE(1937); ONE MAN JUSTICE(1937); TRAPPED(1937); TWO-FISTED SHERIFF(1937); TWO GUN LAW(1937); WESTBOUND MAIL(1937); CALL OF THE ROCKIES(1938); CATTLE RAIDERS(1938); COLORADO TRAIL(1938); LAW OF THE PLAINS(1938); OUTLAWS OF THE PRAIRIE(1938); SOUTH OF ARIZONA(1938); START CHEERING(1938); WEST OF CHEYENNE(1938); WEST OF SANTA FE(1938); MAN FROM SUNDOWN, THE(1939); NORTH OF THE YUKON(1939); OUTPOST OF THE MOUNTIES(1939); RIDERS OF BLACK RIVER(1939); RIO GRANDE(1939); SPOILERS OF THE RANGE(1939); TEXAS STAMPEDE(1939); THUNDERING WEST, THE(1939); WESTERN CARAVANS(1939); BLAZING SIX SHOOTERS(1940); BULLETS FOR RUSTLERS(1940); DURANGO KID, THE(1940); STRANGER FROM TEXAS, THE(1940); TEXAS STAGECOACH(1940); THUNDERING FRONTIER(1940); TWO-FISTED RANGERS(1940); WEST OF ABILENE(1940); MEDICO OF PAINTED SPRINGS, THE(1941); OUTLAWS OF THE PANHANDLE(1941); PINTO KID, THE(1941); PRAIRIE STRANGER(1941); RIDERS OF THE BADLANDS(1941); ROYAL MOUNTED PATROL, THE(1941); THUNDER OVER THE PRAIRIE(1941); BAD MEN OF THE HILLS(1942); DOWN RIO GRANDE WAY(1942); LAWLESS PLAINSMEN(1942); PARDON MY GUN(1942); RIDERS OF THE NORTHLAND(1942); WEST OF TOMBSTONE(1942); COWBOY IN THE CLOUDS(1943); FIGHTING BUCKAROO, THE(1943); HAIL TO THE RANGERS(1943); LAW OF THE NORTHWEST(1943); ROBIN HOOD OF THE RANGE(1943); COWBOY CANTEEN(1944); COWBOY FROM LONESOME RIVER(1944); CYCLONE PRAIRIE RANGERS(1944); RIDING WEST(1944); SUNDOWN VALLEY(1944); OUTLAWS OF THE ROCKIES(1945); DESERT HORSEMAN, THE(1946); LANDRUSH(1946); LAWLESS EMPIRE(1946); LAST DAYS OF BOOT HILL(1947); LONE HAND TEXAN, THE(1947); BUCKAROO FROM POWDER RIVER(1948); PHANTOM VALLEY(1948); SIX-GUN LAW(1948); WEST OF SONORA(1948); WHIRLWIND RAIDERS(1948); BLAZING TRAIL, THE(1949); CHALLENGE OF THE RANGE(1949); DESERT VIGILANTE(1949); EL DORADO PASS(1949); LARAMIE(1949); QUICK ON THE TRIGGER(1949); RENEGADES OF THE SAGE(1949); SOUTH OF DEATH VALLEY(1949); ACROSS THE BADLANDS(1950); FRONTIER OUTPOST(1950); HORSEMEN OF THE SIERRAS(1950); LIGHTNING GUNS(1950); OUTCAST OF BLACK MESA(1950); RAIDERS OF TOMAHAWK CREEK(1950); STREETS OF GHOST TOWN(1950); TEXAS DYNAMO(1950); BANDITS OF EL DORADO(1951); BONANZA TOWN(1951); CYCLONE FURY(1951); FORT SAVAGE RAIDERS(1951); KID FROM AMARILLO, THE(1951); PECOS RIVER(1951); PRAIRIE ROUNDUP(1951); RIDIN' THE OUTLAW TRAIL(1951); SNAKE RIVER DESPERADOES(1951); HAWK OF WILD RIVER, THE(1952); JUNCTION CITY(1952); KID FROM BROKEN GUN, THE(1952); LARAMIE MOUNTAINS(1952); ROUGH, TOUGH WEST, THE(1952); SMOKY CANYON(1952)
Misc. Talkies
DANGEROUS APPOINTMENT(1934); UNDERCOVER MEN(1935); OVERLAND TO DEADWOOD(1942); RIDING THROUGH NEVADA(1942); SADDLE LEATHER LAW(1944); BLAZING THE WESTERN TRAIL(1945); BOTH BARRELS BLAZING(1945); RETURN OF THE DURANGO KID(1945); ROUGH RIDIN' JUSTICE(1945); RUSTLERS OF THE BADLANDS(1945); SAGEBRUSH HEROES(1945); TEXAS PANHANDLE(1945); FIGHTING FRONTIERSMAN, THE(1946); FRONTIER GUNLAW(1946); GALLOPING THUNDER(1946); GUNNING FOR VENGEANCE(1946); HEADING WEST(1946); ROARING WEST(1946); TERROR TRAIL(1946); TWO-FISTED STRANGER(1946); LAW OF THE CANYON(1947); PRAIRIE RAIDERS(1947); RIDERS OF THE LONE STAR(1947); SOUTH OF THE CHISHOLM TRAIL(1947); STRANGER FROM PONCA CITY, THE(1947); WEST OF DODGE CITY(1947); BLAZING ACROSS THE PECOS(1948); TRAIL TO LAREDO(1948); TRAIL OF THE RUSTLERS(1950)

Jack Starrett
LIKE FATHER LIKE SON(1961); YOUNG SINNER, THE(1965); HELL'S ANGELS ON WHEELS(1967); ANGELS FROM HELL(1968); GAY DECEIVERS, THE(1969); GUN RUNNER(1969), ed; RUN, ANGEL, RUN(1969), d; CRY BLOOD, APACHE(1970), a, d; HELL'S BLOODY DEVILS(1970); LOSERS, THE(1970), a, d; SLAUGHTER(1972), d; STRANGE VENEGEANCE OF ROSALIE, THE(1972), d; CLEOPATRA JONES(1973), d; GRAVY TRAIN, THE(1974), a, d; RACE WITH THE DEVIL(1975), a, d; SMALL TOWN IN TEXAS, A(1976), d; FINAL CHAPTER–WALKING TALL zero(1977), d; ROSE, THE(1979); FIRST BLOOD(1982)
1984
RIVER, THE(1984)
Misc. Talkies
HOLLYWOOD MAN, THE(1976), d; KISS MY GRITS(1982), d
Claude Ennis Starrett, Jr.
KID BLUE(1973)
Jennifer Starrett
RUN, ANGEL, RUN(1969); FRIGHTMARE(1983)
Valerie Starrett
RUN, ANGEL, RUN(1969)
Vincent Starrett
GREAT HOTEL MURDER(1935), w
Silents
WANTED–A COWARD(1927), w
Wieslawa Starska
MAN OF IRON(1981, Pol.), cos
Allan Starski
MAN OF MARBLE(1979, Pol.), prod d; YOUNG GIRLS OF WILKO, THE(1979, Pol./Fr.), art d; CONDUCTOR, THE(1981, Pol.), prod d; MAN OF IRON(1981, Pol.), art d; DANTON(1983), art d, set d
1984
LOVE IN GERMANY, A(1984, Fr./Ger.), art d
Ludwik Starski
FIRST START(1953, Pol.), w
Lynn Startling
DON'T BET ON WOMEN(1931), w
A. Startsev
FATHER OF A SOLDIER(1966, USSR)
Jack Stary
ARTISTS AND MODELS(1937)
Edward Stasack
MEMENTO MEI(1963)
Elga Stass
THAT WOMAN(1968, Ger.)
Herbert Stass
INVISIBLE MAN, THE(1963, Ger.)
Robert Stass
QUILLER MEMORANDUM, THE(1966, Brit.)
Paul Stassino
MIRACLE IN SOHO(1957, Brit.); PICKUP ALLEY(1957, Brit.); DESERT ATTACK(1958, Brit.); NIGHT AMBUSH(1958, Brit.); BANDIT OF ZHOBE, THE(1959); MAN WHO LIKED FUNERALS, THE(1959, Brit.); TIGER BAY(1959, Brit.); EXODUS(1960); SANDS OF THE DESERT(1960, Brit.); STRANGLERS OF BOMBAY, THE(1960, Brit.); ECHO OF BARBARA(1961, Brit.); MAN DETAINED(1961, Brit.); ROMAN SPRING OF MRS. STONE, THE(1961, U.S./Brit.); SECRET PARTNER, THE(1961, Brit.); CONCRETE JUNGLE, THE(1962, Brit.); MALAGA(1962, Brit.); GREAT VAN ROBBERY, THE(1963, Brit.); STOLEN HOURS(1963); LONG SHIPS, THE(1964, Brit./Yugo.); MOON-SPINNERS, THE(1964); REBELS AGAINST THE LIGHT(1964); VERDICT, THE(1964, Brit.); BOY TEN FEET TALL, A(1965, Brit.); THUNDERBALL(1965, Brit.); WHERE THE SPIES ARE(1965, Brit.); MC GUIRE, GO HOME!(1966, Brit.); SANDS OF BEERSHEBA(1966, U.S./Israel); MAGUS, THE(1968, Brit.); THAT RIVIERA TOUCH(1968, Brit.); PRIVATE LIFE OF SHERLOCK HOLMES, THE(1970, Brit.); TOUCH OF THE OTHER, A(1970, Brit.); YOU CAN'T WIN 'EM ALL(1970, Brit.)
J. Stastny
LEMONADE JOE(1966, Czech.)
Jack Statham
SCARLET STREET(1945)
Jim Stathis
DOGS(1976); TRACKDOWN(1976)
1984
BLACK ROOM, THE(1984)
Misc. Talkies
BLACK ROOM, THE(1983)
Eleonora Stathopoulou
LION OF THE DESERT(1981, Libya/Brit.)
Inuta Stathopoulou
RECONSTRUCTION OF A CRIME(1970, Ger.)
Jon Statkis
PLEASURE PLANTATION(1970), w
Jennifer Statler
VIOLENT WOMEN(1960)
Marjorie Statler
Misc. Silents
SHE(1925, Brit.)
Mary Statler
CHEYENNE AUTUMN(1964)
The Statler Brothers
THAT TENNESSEE BEAT(1966)
Richard Statman
UGLY DUCKLING, THE(1959, Brit.)
Harry Staton
CLOWN, THE(1953)
Joe Staton
LONG NIGHT, THE(1976), ed
Lyn Statten
7TH COMMANDMENT, THE(1961)

A. F. Statter
Silents
TRUTH, THE(1920), w
A.M. Statter
AFTER THE FOG(1930), w
Arthur Statter
Silents
GALLOPING KID, THE(1922), w; JILT, THE(1922), w; SHOCK, THE(1923), w; CY-CLONE OF THE RANGE(1927), w; PAINTED PONIES(1927), w; MIDNIGHT LI-FE(1928), w; RAWHIDE KID, THE(1928), w
Arthur E. Statter
Silents
VOICE IN THE DARK(1921), w
Arthur F. Statter
Silents
ALL'S FAIR IN LOVE(1921), w; JUST OUT OF COLLEGE(1921), w; MADE IN HEAVEN(1921), w; POVERTY OF RICHES, THE(1921), w; STEP ON IT!(1922), w; WONDERFUL WIFE, A(1922), w
Robert Statts
MR. BILLION(1977)
Arnold "Jigger" Statz
FAST COMPANY(1929)
Franklin Statz
LAST HOUSE ON DEAD END STREET(1977)
Robert Statzel
BRAINSTORM(1983), w
Ralph Staub
SITTING ON THE MOON(1936), d; AFFAIRS OF CAPPY RICKS(1937), d; COUN-TRY GENTLEMEN(1937), d; JOIN THE MARINES(1937), d; MANDARIN MYSTERY, THE(1937), d; MEET THE BOY FRIEND(1937), d; NAVY BLUES(1937), d; MAMA RUNS WILD(1938), d; PRAIRIE MOON(1938), d; WESTERN JAMBOREE(1938), d; CHIP OF THE FLYING U(1940), d; DANGER AHEAD(1940), d; SKY BANDITS, THE(1940), d; YUKON FLIGHT(1940), d
Pete Stauber
1984
SONGWRITER(1984)
Richard Stauch
RUMPELSTILTSKIN(1965, Ger.), m; GOOSE GIRL, THE(1967, Ger.), m; PUSS 'N' BOOTS(1967, Ger.), m
Hannes Staudinger
MERRY WIVES OF WINDSOR, THE(1966, Aust.), ph; AGE OF CONSENT(1969, Austral.), ph
Wolfgang Staudte
SINS OF ROSE BERND, THE(1959, Ger.), d; ALWAYS VICTORIOUS(1960, Ital.), d; ROSES FOR THE PROSECUTOR(1961, Ger.), d, w; THREE PENNY OPERA(1963, Fr./Ger.), d, w
Wolfgang Staudtel
MURDERERS AMONG US(1948, Ger.), d&w
Aubrey Stauffer
Silents
SLEEPWALKER, THE(1922), w
Helen Stauffer
TERMS OF ENDEARMENT(1983)
Jack Stauffer
1984
CHATTANOOGA CHOO CHOO(1984)
Richard Stauffer
HOT ANGEL, THE(1958)
Ted Stauffer
48 HOURS TO ACAPULCO(1968, Ger.)
M. P. Staulcup
Silents
WITHOUT LIMIT(1921), set d
Ann Staunton
PRISONER OF JAPAN(1942); SUMMER STORM(1944); KILLERS, THE(1946); HEARTACHES(1947); PHILO VANCE RETURNS(1947); APARTMENT FOR PEG-GY(1948); CALL NORTHSIDE 777(1948); HOLLOW TRIUMPH(1948); SOUTHERN YANKEE, A(1948); CRISS CROSS(1949); MY WIFE'S BEST FRIEND(1952); DIA-NE(1955); BAND OF ANGELS(1957); VAMPIRE, THE(1957)
Anne Staunton
MIRACLE ON 34TH STREET, THE(1947)
Kim Staunton
1984
BROTHER FROM ANOTHER PLANET, THE(1984)
Jacqueline Staup
THIEF OF PARIS, THE(1967, Fr./Ital.); JULIA(1977)
Mary Stavin
OCTOPUSSY(1983, Brit.)
Charles Stavola
I'M DANCING AS FAST AS I CAN(1982)
Charlie Stavola
GET CRAZY(1983); STAR CHAMBER, THE(1983)
Anna Stavridou
ELECTRA(1962, Gr.)
George Stavrinos
UNION CITY(1980), art d
Anna Stavropoulou
ZORBA THE GREEK(1964, U.S./Gr.), cos
Ari Stavrou
BLOOD TIDE(1982), ph; NEXT ONE, THE(1982, U.S./Gr.), ph
Aris Stavrou
ASSAULT ON AGATHON(1976, Brit./Gr.), ph
Jerzy Stefan Stawinski
KANAL(1961, Pol.), w; KNIGHTS OF THE TEUTONIC ORDER, THE(1962, Pol.), w; LOVE AT TWENTY(1963, Fr./Ital./Jap./Pol./Ger.), w; EROICA(1966, Pol.), w
Josef Stawiski
EVE WANTS TO SLEEP(1961, Pol.), ph

Edith Stayart
Misc. Silents
DANGEROUS PATHS(1921)
Gail Stayden
I COULD NEVER HAVE SEX WITH ANY MAN WHO HAS SO LITTLE REGARD FOR MY HUSBAND(1973), a, p
Martin Stayden
I COULD NEVER HAVE SEX WITH ANY MAN WHO HAS SO LITTLE REGARD FOR MY HUSBAND(1973), a, p
Frank B. Stayer
MONSTER WALKS, THE(1932), d
Linda Stayer
1984
UNFAITHFULLY YOURS(1984)
Stanley Stayle
DEAR WIFE(1949)
Frank Stayton
THREADS(1932, Brit.), w; MIXED DOUBLES(1933, Brit.), w; LAST CHANCE, THE(1937, Brit.), w
Silents
INFERIOR SEX, THE(1920), w; PASSIONATE ADVENTURE, THE(1924, Brit.), w
Angelo Stea
TANYA'S ISLAND(1981, Can.), art d
Colin Stead
BMX BANDITS(1983), m; FIGHTING BACK(1983, Brit.), m
1984
MELVIN, SON OF ALVIN(1984, Aus.), m
Freddie Stead
OLIVER!(1968, Brit.)
Karl Stead
SLEEPING DOGS(1977, New Zealand), w
Douglas Steade
HAPPY DAYS(1930)
Alison Steadman
1984
CHAMPIONS(1984); KIPPERBANG(1984, Brit.); NUMBER ONE(1984, Brit.)
Bob Steadman
HAMMER(1972), ph; DOGS(1976), ph
Don Steadman
RECKONING, THE(1971, Brit.)
John Steadman
THINGS ARE TOUGH ALL OVER(1982); GRISSOM GANG, THE(1971); UNHOLY ROLLERS(1972); EMPEROR OF THE NORTH POLE(1973); OUTFIT, THE(1973); WHITE LIGHTNING(1973); LONGEST YARD, THE(1974); GATOR(1976); ST. IVES(1976); VIGILANTE FORCE(1976); POCO...LITTLE DOG LOST(1977); HILLS HAVE EYES, THE(1978); HOT LEAD AND COLD FEET(1978); FADE TO BLACK(1980); CHU CHU AND THE PHILLY FLASH(1981); DEADHEAD MI-LES(1982)
1984
CHATTANOOGA CHOO CHOO(1984)
Monte Steadman
CARNATION KID(1929), ph
Myrtle Steadman
JAZZ AGE, THE(1929); ONE YEAR LATER(1933)
Silents
CRASHIN' THRU(1923)
Robert Steadman
EXECUTIVE ACTION(1973), ph
Vera Steadman
GREAT GUY(1936); RING AROUND THE MOON(1936); TEXANS, THE(1938)
Silents
NERVOUS WRECK, THE(1926)
Misc. Silents
SCRAP IRON(1921); MEET THE PRINCE(1926)
Sheila Steafel
JUST LIKE A WOMAN(1967, Brit.); FIVE MILLION YEARS TO EARTH(1968, Brit.); BABY LOVE(1969, Brit.); GOODBYE MR. CHIPS(1969, U.S./Brit.); OTLEY(1969, Brit.); SOME WILL, SOME WON'T(1970, Brit.); ATCH ME A SPY(1971, Brit./Fr.); MELO-DY(1971, Brit.); PERCY(1971, Brit.); DIGBY, THE BIGGEST DOG IN THE WORLD(1974, Brit.)
1984
BLOODBATH AT THE HOUSE OF DEATH(1984, Brit.)
Jim Steakley
WILD RIVER(1960)
Robert Steaples
METEOR(1979), spec eff
Vern Stearman
LEGEND OF BOGGY CREEK, THE(1973)
Gordon Stearne
MISSILE FROM HELL(1960, Brit.)
Craig Stearns
HALLOWEEN(1978), set d; FOG, THE(1980), art d; JUST BEFORE DAWN(1980), art d; T.A.G.: THE ASSASSINATION GAME(1982), art d; ONE DARK NIGHT(1983), art d
1984
BODY ROCK(1984), art d; CHILDREN OF THE CORN(1984), art d; TOR-CHLIGHT(1984), art d
Franklin Stearns
IDLE RICH, THE(1929), w
John Stearns
KISS OF DEATH(1947); THEATRE OF BLOOD(1973, Brit.), spec eff
Johnny Stearns
BOOMERANG(1947)
Louis Stearns
Silents
MASTER MIND, THE(1920); ANNABEL LEE(1921)
Michael Stearns
CHROME AND HOT LEATHER(1971)

Misc. Talkies
CHAIN GANG WOMEN(1972)
Minnie Stearns
Silents
KID, THE(1921)
Philip Stearns
WINSTANLEY(1979, Brit.)
Speed Stearns
METALSTORM: THE DESTRUCTION OF JARED-SYN(1983)
Misc. Talkies
BABY DOLLS(1982)
Toby L. Stearns
THX 1138(1971)
Virginia Stearns
Misc. Silents
UP IN MARY'S ATTICK(1920)
John Stears
CALL ME BWANA(1963, Brit.), spec eff; FROM RUSSIA WITH LOVE(1963, Brit.), spec eff; GOLDFINGER(1964, Brit.), spec eff; THUNDERBALL(1965, Brit.), spec eff; YOU ONLY LIVE TWICE(1967, Brit.), spec eff; ON HER MAJESTY'S SECRET SERVICE(1969, Brit.), spec eff; TOOMORROW(1970, Brit.), spec eff; PIED PIPER, THE(1972, Brit.), spec eff; SITTING TARGET(1972, Brit.), spec eff; O LUCKY MAN!(1973, Brit.), spec eff; MAN WITH THE GOLDEN GUN, THE(1974, Brit.), spec eff; SKY RIDERS(1976, U.S./Gr.), spec eff; OUTLAND(1981), spec eff
1984
BOUNTY, THE(1984), spec eff
Anne Stebbins
DESPERADOES ARE IN TOWN, THE(1956); YOUNG LIONS, THE(1958)
Bob Stebbins
FACES IN THE FOG(1944); FORCE OF EVIL(1948)
Bobby Stebbins
MOKEY(1942); BEST FOOT FORWARD(1943); YOUNGEST PROFESSION, THE(1943); STRANGE HOLIDAY(1945)
Candy Stebbins
FIREBALL JUNGLE(1968)
Sidney L. Stebel
1984
MIRRORS(1984), w
Rich Steber
TWILIGHT'S LAST GLEAMING(1977, U.S./Ger.)
Yevgeniy Steblov
MEET ME IN MOSCOW(1966, USSR)
Kim Stebner
1984
BIG MEAT EATER(1984, Can.)
Sophie Steboun
CHAPPAQUA(1967)
H. Tipton Steck
Silents
OUTCASTS OF POKER FLAT, THE(1919), w; FORBIDDEN WOMAN, THE(1920), w; OCCASIONALLY YOURS(1920), w; STING OF THE LASH(1921), w; OUT OF THE PAST(1927), w
Jim Steck
HISTORY OF THE WORLD, PART 1(1981)
1984
ELECTRIC DREAMS(1984)
Joseph T. Steck
WATERHOLE NO. 3(1967), p, w
Leonard Steckel
INVISIBLE OPPONENT(1933, Ger.); M(1933, Ger.); CAPTAIN FROM KOEPENICK, THE(1956, Ger.); ETERNAL WALTZ, THE(1959, Ger.); VISIT, THE(1964, Ger./Fr./Ital./U.S.)
Alan Steckery
WORLD IS JUST A 'B' MOVIE, THE(1971), p&d, ph, ed&set d
Laura Steckler
Misc. Talkies
BLOOD MONSTER(1972)
Linda Steckler
Misc. Talkies
BLOOD MONSTER(1972)
Michael Steckler
FOR THE LOVE OF MIKE(1960)
Doug Steckley
TUNNELVISION(1976)
Walter Stedding
UNDERGROUND U.S.A.(1980), m
Joel Stedman
ROLLOVER(1981); SO FINE(1981)
Lincoln Stedman
TANNED LEGS(1929); WOMAN BETWEEN(1931); SAILOR BE GOOD(1933)
Silents
ATOM, THE(1918); ANNE OF GREEN GABLES(1919); NINETEEN AND PHYLLIS(1920); OUT OF THE STORM(1920); CHARM SCHOOL, THE(1921); OLD SWIMMIN' HOLE, THE(1921); TWO MINUTES TO GO(1921); DANGEROUS AGE, THE(1922); FRESHIE, THE(1922); HOMESPUN VAMP, A(1922); YOUTH TO YOUTH(1922); PRISONER, THE(1923); SCARLET LILY, THE(1923); SOUL OF THE BEAST(1923); WANTERS, THE(1923); CAPTAIN JANUARY(1924); ON PROBATION(1924); DAME CHANCE(1926); ONE MINUTE TO PLAY(1926); LET IT RAIN(1927); HAROLD TEEN(1928); WHY BE GOOD?(1929)
Misc. Silents
PEACEFUL VALLEY(1920); BE MY WIFE(1921); RED HOT TIRES(1925); SEALED LIPS(1925); REMEMBER(1926); WARNING SIGNAL, THE(1926); FARMER'S DAUGHTER, THE(1928)
Marshall Stedman
Silents
COUNTRY MOUSE, THE(1914)
Myrtle Stedman
LOVE RACKET, THE(1929); WHEEL OF LIFE, THE(1929); LITTLE ACCIDENT(1930); LUMMOX(1930); TRUTH ABOUT YOUTH, THE(1930); BEAU IDEAL(1931); ALIAS MARY SMITH(1932); FORBIDDEN COMPANY(1932); KLON-

DIKE(1932); WIDOW IN SCARLET(1932); SCHOOL FOR GIRLS(1935); GOLD DIGGERS OF 1937(1936); POLO JOE(1936); SONG OF THE SADDLE(1936); GO-GETTER, THE(1937); GREEN LIGHT(1937); SHE LOVED A FIREMAN(1937); SLIGHT CASE OF MURDER, A(1938)
Silents
COUNTRY MOUSE, THE(1914); CAPRICES OF KITTY, THE(1915); IT'S NO LAUGHING MATTER(1915); KILMENY(1915); NEARLY A LADY(1915); AS MEN LOVE(1917); SEX(1920); DANGEROUS AGE, THE(1922); NANCY FROM NOWHERE(1922); RECKLESS YOUTH(1922); RICH MEN'S WIVES(1922); SIX DAYS(1923); TEMPORARY MARRIAGE(1923); JUDGMENT OF THE STORM(1924); IF I MARRY AGAIN(1925); SALLY(1925); FAR CRY, THE(1926); PRINCE OF PILSEN, THE(1926); IRRESISTIBLE LOVER, THE(1927); ALIAS THE DEACON(1928); SPORTING GOODS(1928); SIN SISTER, THE(1929)
Misc. Silents
VALLEY OF THE MOON, THE(1914); CALL OF THE CUMBERLANDS, THE(1915); JANE(1915); PEER GYNT(1915); REFORM CANDIDATE, THE(1915); TWAS EVER THUS(1915); AMERICAN BEAUTY, THE(1916); PASQUALE(1916); SOUL OF KURA SAN, THE(1916); HAPPINESS OF THREE WOMEN, THE(1917); PRISON WITHOUT WALLS, THE(1917); WORLD APART, THE(1917); IN THE HOLLOW OF HER HAND(1918); TEETH OF THE TIGER, THE(1919); HARRIET AND THE PIPER(1920); SILVER HORDE, THE(1920); TIGER'S COAT, THE(1920); BLACK ROSES(1921); CONCERT, THE(1921); SOWING THE WIND(1921); WHISTLE, THE(1921); ASHES(1922); FAMOUS MRS. FAIR, THE(1923); BREATH OF A SCANDAL, THE(1924); WINE(1924); GOOSE HANGS HIGH, THE(1925); MAD WHIRL, THE(1925); TESSIE(1925); DON JUAN'S THREE NIGHTS(1926); BLACK DIAMOND EXPRESS, THE(1927); NO PLACE TO GO(1927)
Pat Stedman
DELINQUENTS, THE(1957)
Ursula Stedman
PIRATES OF PENZANCE, THE(1983)
Vera Stedman
ELMER AND ELSIE(1934); FRISCO KID(1935); VICE RACKET(1937)
Jaroslava Stedra
INTIMATE LIGHTING(1969, Czech.)
Max Steeber
GUN HAWK, THE(1963), w; APACHE UPRISING(1966), w
Judy Steed
FAR SHORE, THE(1976, Can.), p
Maggie Steed
BABYLON(1980, Brit.)
Andre Steedman
RIVERSIDE MURDER, THE(1935, Brit.), w
Shirley Steedman
PRIME OF MISS JEAN BRODIE, THE(1969, Brit.)
Tony Steedman
GAWAIN AND THE GREEN KNIGHT(1973, Brit.); ABDICATION, THE(1974, Brit.); THIRTY NINE STEPS, THE(1978, Brit.); MISSIONARY, THE(1982)
Edward Steefe
YOU LIGHT UP MY LIFE(1977)
Ingrid Steeger
Misc. Talkies
YOUNG SEDUCERS, THE(1974)
Aaron Steel
KILLER SHREWS, THE(1959), ed
Agnes Steel
WIFE TAKES A FLYER, THE(1942)
Alan Steel [Sergio Ciani]
SAMSON(1961, Ital.); REBEL GLADIATORS, THE(1963, Ital.); SAMSON AND THE SLAVE QUEEN(1963, Ital.); HERCULES AGAINST THE MOON MEN(1965, Fr./Ital.)
Amy Steel
FAT ANGELS(1980, U.S./Span.); FRIDAY THE 13TH PART II(1981)
1984
FRIDAY THE 13TH–THE FINAL CHAPTER(1984)
Misc. Talkies
FAT CHANCE(1982)
Anthony Steel
GIRL IN THE PAINTING, THE(1948, Brit.); AMAZING MR. BEECHAM, THE(1949, Brit.); DON'T EVER LEAVE ME(1949, Brit.); GAY LADY, THE(1949, Brit.); HELTER SKELTER(1949, Brit.); MARRY ME!(1949, Brit.); ONCE UPON A DREAM(1949, Brit.); POET'S PUB(1949, Brit.); SARABAND(1949, Brit.); MUDLARK, THE(1950, Brit.); LAUGHTER IN PARADISE(1951, Brit.); WOODEN HORSE, THE(1951); ANOTHER MAN'S POISON(1952, Brit.); IVORY HUNTER(1952, Brit.); OUTPOST IN MALAYA(1952, Brit.); ALBERT, R.N.(1953, Brit.); HUNDRED HOUR HUNT(1953, Brit.); MASTER OF BALLANTRAE, THE(1953, U.S./Brit.); MALTA STORY(1954, Brit.); WEST OF ZANZIBAR(1954, Brit.); PASSAGE HOME(1955, Brit.); SEA SHALL NOT HAVE THEM, THE(1955, Brit.); STORM OVER THE NILE(1955, Brit.); BLACK TENT, THE(1956, Brit.); CHECKPOINT(1957, Brit.); OUT OF THE CLOUDS(1957, Brit.); VALERIE(1957); HARRY BLACK AND THE TIGER(1958, Brit.); QUESTION OF ADULTERY, A(1959, Brit.); 48 HOURS TO LIVE(1960, Brit./Swed.); MATTER OF CHOICE, A(1963, Brit.); SWITCH, THE(1963, Brit.); TIGER OF THE SEVEN SEAS(1964, Fr./Ital.); LAST OF THE RENEGADES(1966, Fr./Ital./Ger./Yugo.); HELL IS EMPTY(1967, Brit./Ital); ANZIO(1968, Ital.); QUEENS, THE(1968, Ital./Fr.); MIRROR CRACK'D, THE(1980, Brit.); WORLD IS FULL OF MARRIED MEN, THE(1980, Brit.); MONSTER CLUB, THE(1981, Brit.)
Bret Steel
VELVET TRAP, THE(1966)
Charles Steel
HORSE SOLDIERS, THE(1959); GREAT RACE, THE(1965)
Danielle Steel
NOW AND FOREVER(1983, Aus.), w
Edward Steel
BOY CRIED MURDER, THE(1966, Ger./Brit./Yugo.)
Geoffrey Steel
D-DAY, THE SIXTH OF JUNE(1956)
Gile Steel
DR. JEKYLL AND MR. HYDE(1941), cos
Gordon Steel
WILD GEESE, THE(1978, Brit.)

James Steel
DEAD ON COURSE(1952, Brit.)
John Steel
MURDER IN MISSISSIPPI(1965)
Silents
BROADWAY AFTER DARK(1924)
Kurt Steel
MURDER GOES TO COLLEGE(1937), w; PARTNERS IN CRIME(1937), w
Lee Steel
COPS AND ROBBERS(1973)
Minnie Steel
WIFE TAKES A FLYER, THE(1942)
Pippa Steel
COP-OUT(1967, Brit.); OH! WHAT A LOVELY WAR(1969, Brit.); TAKE A GIRL LIKE YOU(1970, Brit.); LUST FOR A VAMPIRE(1971, Brit.); YOUNG WINSTON(1972, Brit.)
Sylvia Steel
BEAUTY JUNGLE, THE(1966, Brit.)
Tessa Steel
HALF A SIXPENCE(1967, Brit.)
Vernon Steel
LLOYDS OF LONDON(1936)
Silents
BEYOND PRICE(1921); DANGER POINT, THE(1922); THELMA(1922); WHEN THE DEVIL DRIVES(1922)
Misc. Silents
OUT OF THE CHORUS(1921)
Aaron Steele
LONELYHEARTS(1958), ed
Aggie Steele
MONKEY'S PAW, THE(1933)
Agnes Steele
SCARLET EMPRESS, THE(1934); WE LIVE AGAIN(1934)
Silents
THREE'S A CROWD(1927)
Alan Steele
FURY OF HERCULES, THE(1961, Ital.)
Anna Steele
ROMANTIC ENGLISHWOMAN, THE(1975, Brit./Fr.)
Anthony Steele
SOMETHING MONEY CAN'T BUY(1952, Brit.)
Austin Steele
FRIENDS AND NEIGHBORS(1963, Brit.), w
Barbara Steele
BACHELOR OF HEARTS(1958, Brit.); BLACK SUNDAY(1961, Ital.); PIT AND THE PENDULUM, THE(1961); UPSTAIRS AND DOWNSTAIRS(1961, Brit.); 8 ½(1963, Ital.); CASTLE OF BLOOD(1964, Fr./Ital.); HORRIBLE DR. HICHCOCK, THE(1964, Ital.); GHOST, THE(1965, Ital.); HOURS OF LOVE, THE(1965, Ital.); WHITE VOICES(1965, Fr./Ital.); YOUR MONEY OR YOUR WIFE(1965, Brit.); NIGHTMARE CASTLE(1966, Ital.); SHE BEAST, THE(1966, Brit./Ital./Yugo.); TERROR-CREATURES FROM THE GRAVE(1967, U.S./Ital.); YOUNG TORLESS(1968, Fr./Ger.); CRIMSON CULT, THE(1970, Brit.); RENEGADE GIRLS(1974); THEY CAME FROM WITHIN(1976, Can.); I NEVER PROMISED YOU A ROSE GARDEN(1977); PIRANHA(1978); PRETTY BABY(1978); SILENT SCREAM(1980)
Misc. Talkies
ANGEL FOR SATAN, AN(1966, Ital.)
Barry Steele
YESTERDAY'S ENEMY(1959, Brit.); MILLIONS LIKE US(1943, Brit.); CRUEL SEA, THE(1953); ROOM IN THE HOUSE(1955, Brit.); SIMON AND LAURA(1956, Brit.); ORDERS ARE ORDERS(1959, Brit.); TUNES OF GLORY(1960, Brit.)
Bernard Steele
THEY HAD TO SEE PARIS(1929), ch
Bill Steele
WESTERNER, THE(1940); SAN ANTONIO(1945); SEARCHERS, THE(1956)
Bob Steele
HEADIN' NORTH(1930); LAND OF MISSING MEN, THE(1930); NEAR THE RAINBOW'S END(1930); OKLAHOMA CYCLONE(1930); AT THE RIDGE(1931); NEAR THE TRAIL'S END(1931); SUNRISE TRAIL(1931); HIDDEN VALLEY(1932); MAN FROM HELL'S EDGES(1932); RIDERS OF THE DESERT(1932); SON OF OKLAHOMA(1932); SOUTH OF SANTA FE(1932); TEXAS BUDDIES(1932); YOUNG BLOOD(1932); BREED OF THE BORDER(1933); CALIFORNIA TRAIL, THE(1933); FIGHTING CHAMP(1933); GALLANT FOOL, THE(1933); GALLOPING ROMEO(1933); RANGER'S CODE, THE(1933); DEMON FOR TROUBLE, A(1934); ALIAS JOHN LAW(1935); KID COURAGEOUS(1935); NO MAN'S RANGE(1935); POWDERSMOKE RANGE(1935); RIDER OF THE LAW, THE(1935); SMOKEY SMITH(1935); TOMBSTONE TERROR(1935); TRAIL OF TERROR(1935); WESTERN JUSTICE(1935); CAVALRY(1936); KID RANGER, THE(1936); LAST OF THE WARRENS, THE(1936); LAW RIDES, THE(1936); ARIZONA GUNFIGHTER(1937); BORDER PHANTOM(1937); DOOMED AT SUNDOWN(1937); GUN LORDS OF STIRRUP BASIN(1937); GUN RANGER, THE(1937); LIGHTNIN' CRANDALL(1937); RED ROPE, THE(1937); RIDIN' THE LONE TRAIL(1937); SUNDOWN SAUNDERS(1937); TRUSTED OUTLAW, THE(1937); COLORADO KID(1938); DESERT PATROL(1938); DURANGO VALLEY RAIDERS(1938); FEUD MAKER(1938); PAROLED-TO DIE(1938); THUNDER IN THE DESERT(1938); EL DIABLO RIDES(1939); FEUD OF THE RANGE(1939); MESQUITE BUCKAROO(1939); OF MICE AND MEN(1939); PAL FROM TEXAS, THE(1939); SMOKY TRAILS(1939); BILLY THE KID IN TEXAS(1940); CARSON CITY KID(1940); LONE STAR RAIDERS(1940); PINTO CANYON(1940); TRAIL BLAZERS, THE(1940); UNDER TEXAS SKIES(1940); WILD HORSE VALLEY(1940); BILLY THE KID IN SANTA FE(1941); BILLY THE KID'S FIGHTING PALS(1941); BILLY THE KID'S RANGE WAR(1941); CITY, FOR CONQUEST(1941); GANGS OF SONORA(1941); GAUCHOS OF EL DORADO(1941); GREAT TRAIN ROBBERY, THE(1941); OUTLAWS OF THE CHEROKEE TRAIL(1941); PALS OF THE PECOS(1941); PRAIRIE PIONEERS(1941); SADDLEMATES(1941); WEST OF CIMARRON(1941); CODE OF THE OUTLAW(1942); PHANTOM PLAINSMEN, THE(1942); RAIDERS OF THE RANGE(1942); SHADOWS ON THE SAGE(1942); VALLEY OF HUNTED MEN(1942); WESTWARD HO(1942); REVENGE OF THE ZOMBIES(1943); RIDERS OF THE RIO GRANDE(1943); SANTA FE SCOUTS(1943); THUNDERING TRAILS(1943); ARIZONA WHIRLWIND(1944); DEATH VALLEY RANGERS(1944); MARKED TRAILS(1944); OUTLAW TRAIL(1944); SONORA STAGECOACH(1944); WESTWARD BOUND(1944); NORTHWEST TRAIL(1945); WILDFIRE(1945); AMBUSH TRAIL(1946); BIG SLEEP, THE(1946); NAVAJO KID, THE(1946); RIO GRANDE RAIDERS(1946); SHERIFF OF REDWOOD VALLEY(1946);

SIX GUN MAN(1946); THUNDER TOWN(1946); BANDITS OF DARK CANYON(1947); CHEYENNE(1947); EXPOSED(1947); KILLER McCOY(1947); TWILIGHT ON THE RIO GRANDE(1947); SOUTH OF ST. LOUIS(1949); SAVAGE HORDE, THE(1950); CATTLE DRIVE(1951); ENFORCER, THE(1951); FORT WORTH(1951); SILVER CANYON(1951); BUGLES IN THE AFTERNOON(1952); LION AND THE HORSE, THE(1952); ROSE OF CIMARRON(1952); COLUMN SOUTH(1953); ISLAND IN THE SKY(1953); SAN ANTONE(1953); SAVAGE FRONTIER(1953); DRUMS ACROSS THE RIVER(1954); OUTCAST, THE(1954); FIGHTING CHANCE, THE(1955); SPOILERS, THE(1955); LAST OF THE DESPERADOES(1956); PARDNERS(1956); STEEL JUNGLE, THE(1956); BAND OF ANGELS(1957); DUEL AT APACHE WELLS(1957); GUN FOR A COWARD(1957); PARSON AND THE OUTLAW, THE(1957); GIANT FROM THE UNKNOWN(1958); ONCE UPON A HORSE(1958); PORK CHOP HILL(1959); RIO BRAVO(1959); ATOMIC SUBMARINE, THE(1960); HELL BENT FOR LEATHER(1960); COMANCHEROS, THE(1961); SIX BLACK HORSES(1962); WILD WESTERNERS, THE(1962); FOUR FOR TEXAS(1963); MC LINTOCK!(1963); TAGGART(1964); BOUNTY KILLER, THE(1965); REQUIEM FOR A GUNFIGHTER(1965); SHENANDOAH(1965); TOWN TAMER(1965); HANG'EM HIGH(1968); GREAT BANK ROBBERY, THE(1969); RIO LOBO(1970); SOMETHING BIG(1971)
Misc. Talkies
NEVADA BUCKAROO, THE(1931); RIDIN' FOOL, THE(1931); LAW OF THE WEST(1932); TRAILING NORTH(1933); BRAND OF HATE(1934); BIG CALIBRE(1935); BRAND OF THE OUTLAWS(1936); RIDERS OF THE SAGE(1939); BILLY THE KID OUTLAWED(1940); BILLY THE KID'S GUN JUSTICE(1940); BLOCKED TRAIL, THE(1943); TRIGGER LAW(1944); UTAH KID, THE(1944)
Silents
BANDIT'S SON, THE(1927); BREED OF THE SUNSETS(1928); CAPTAIN CARELESS(1928), a, w; DRIFTIN' SANDS(1928); MAN IN THE ROUGH(1928); AMAZING VAGABOND(1929); INVADERS, THE(1929); HUNTED MEN(1930); OKLAHOMA SHERIFF, THE(1930)
Misc. Silents
MOJAVE KID, THE(1927); HEADIN' FOR DANGER(1928); LIGHTING SPEED(1928); RIDING RENEGADE, THE(1928); TRAIL OF COURAGE, THE(1928); COME AND GET IT(1929); COWBOY AND THE OUTLAW, THE(1929); LAUGHING AT DEATH(1929); TEXAS COWBOY, A(1929); BREEZY BILL(1930); MAN FROM NOWHERE, THE(1930)
C. B. Steele
Silents
GOLD RUSH, THE(1925)
Charles Q. Steele
MISSING PEOPLE, THE(1940, Brit.), p; MYSTERIOUS MR. REEDER, THE(1940, Brit.), p; YOU WILL REMEMBER(1941, Brit.), p
Christopher Steele
PEG OF OLD DRURY(1936, Brit.); TWILIGHT HOUR(1944, Brit.); TAWNY PIPIT(1947, Brit.); TURNERS OF PROSPECT ROAD, THE(1947, Brit.); QUIET WEEKEND(1948, Brit.); HORNET'S NEST, THE(1955, Brit.); JACQUELINE(1956, Brit.)
Don Steele
DEATH RACE 2000(1975); GRAND THEFT AUTO(1977); ROCK 'N' ROLL HIGH SCHOOL(1979); EATING RAOUL(1982)
1984
GREMLINS(1984)
Elbert Steele
LONG GRAY LINE, THE(1955)
lp: Evan Steele
Misc. Talkies
TOY BOX, THE(1971)
Frankie Steele
OPERATION LOVEBIRDS(1968, Den.)
Fred Steele
DUFFY'S TAVERN(1945); WHIPLASH(1948)
Misc. Talkies
DEMOLITION(1977)
Freddie Steele
PITTSBURGH KID, THE(1941); HAIL THE CONQUERING HERO(1944); MIRACLE OF MORGAN'S CREEK, THE(1944); STORY OF G.I. JOE, THE(1945); BLACK ANGEL(1946); DESPERATE(1947); CALL NORTHSIDE 777(1948); FOREIGN AFFAIR, A(1948); I WALK ALONE(1948); RACE STREET(1948)
Gay Steele
OFFICE PICNIC, THE(1974, Aus.)
Geoffrey Steele
HOLY MATRIMONY(1943); TERROR BY NIGHT(1946); MY FAIR LADY(1964)
George Steele
TALL TEXAN, THE(1953); RACING BLOOD(1954)
Gile Steele
MARIE ANTOINETTE(1938), cos; BOOM TOWN(1940), cos; EDISON, THE MAN(1940), cos; FLIGHT COMMAND(1940), cos; LITTLE NELLIE KELLY(1940), cos; MAN FROM DAKOTA, THE(1940), cos; MORTAL STORM, THE(1940), cos; NEW MOON(1940), cos; PRIDE AND PREJUDICE(1940), cos; STRIKE UP THE BAND(1940), cos; TWENTY MULE TEAM(1940), cos; WATERLOO BRIDGE(1940), cos; YOUNG TOM EDISON(1940), cos; BLOSSOMS IN THE DUST(1941), cos; H.M. PULHAM, ESQ.(1941), md; HONKY TONK(1941), cos; SMILIN' THROUGH(1941), cos; VANISHING VIRGINIAN, THE(1941), cos; WILD MAN OF BORNEO, THE(1941), cos; FOR ME AND MY GAL(1942), cos; JACKASS MAIL(1942), cos; RIO RITA(1942), cos; TORTILLA FLAT(1942), cos; ABOVE SUSPICION(1943), cos; DU BARRY WAS A LADY(1943), cos; MADAME CURIE(1943), cos; CALIFORNIA(1946), cos; EMPEROR WALTZ, THE(1948), cos; I REMEMBER MAMA(1948), cos; HEIRESS, THE(1949), cos; GREAT CARUSO, THE(1951), cos; MAN WITH A CLOAK, THE(1951), cos; BELLE OF NEW YORK, THE(1952), cos; MERRY WIDOW, THE(1952), cos; SCARAMOUCHE(1952), cos
Hamilton Steele
FIGHTING COWBOY(1933)
Isobel Lillian Steele
I WAS A CAPTIVE IN NAZI GERMANY(1936)
James Steele
1984
PHAR LAP(1984, Aus.)
Jane Steele
DYNAMITE DELANEY(1938)
Jimmy Steele
MADMAN(1982)

Jo Ann Steele
FROM NASHVILLE WITH MUSIC(1969)
Joseph Steele
SOCIETY SMUGGLERS(1939), w
Joseph Henry Steele
NIGHT WAITRESS(1936), p
Karen Steele
CLOWN, THE(1953); MAN CRAZY(1953); MARTY(1955); SHARKFIGHTERS, THE(1956); TOWARD THE UNKNOWN(1956); BAILOUT AT 43,000(1957); DECISION AT SUNDOWN(1957); RIDE LONESOME(1959); WESTBOUND(1959); RISE AND FALL OF LEGS DIAMOND, THE(1960); FORTY POUNDS OF TROUBLE(1962); CYBORG 2087(1966); BOY...A GIRL, A(1969)
Misc. Talkies
TRAP ON COUGAR MOUNTAIN(1972)
Kristopher Steele
MAN FROM SNOWY RIVER, THE(1983, Aus.)
Larry Steele
DARKENED SKIES(1930)
Lee Steele
SHAFT(1971); WHO SAYS I CAN'T RIDE A RAINBOW!(1971); THREE DAYS OF THE CONDOR(1975); MARATHON MAN(1976); NESTING, THE(1981)
1984
FLAMINGO KID, THE(1984)
Lou Steele
FURIES, THE(1950); SEPTEMBER AFFAIR(1950); SOME OF MY BEST FRIENDS ARE...(1971)
Misc. Talkies
PAWN, THE(1968)
Marjorie Steele
TOUGH ASSIGNMENT(1949); FACE TO FACE(1952); NO ESCAPE(1953)
Mary Steele
NO TIME FOR TEARS(1957, Brit.); GIRLS AT SEA(1958, Brit.); INBETWEEN AGE, THE(1958, Brit.)
Michael Steele
COMMAND DECISION(1948); STATION WEST(1948); SADDLE TRAMP(1950); TANKS ARE COMING, THE(1951); WHIP HAND, THE(1951)
Mike Steele
BAT, THE(1959); REVENGE OF THE CHEERLEADERS(1976)
Minnie Steele
SCARLET EMPRESS, THE(1934)
Natasha Steele
SATIN MUSHROOM, THE(1969)
Pauline Steele
HURRICANE, THE(1937)
Pippa Steele
VAMPIRE LOVERS, THE(1970, Brit.)
R.W. Steele
TOMORROW WE LIVE(1936, Brit.)
Radcliffe Steele
Silents
NOTHING BUT THE TRUTH(1920)
Misc. Silents
MAN WHO LOST HIMSELF, THE(1920)
Richard Steele
DEADLY AFFAIR, THE(1967, Brit.); WITH SIX YOU GET EGGROLL(1968); SUMARINE X-1(1969, Brit.)
Misc. Silents
SHOPGIRLS; OR, THE GREAT QUESTION(1914, Brit.)
Richard S. Steele
MAIN EVENT, THE(1979)
Rob Steele
CHANT OF JIMMIE BLACKSMITH, THE(1980, Aus.); FIGHTING BACK(1983, Brit.)
1984
STRIKEBOUND(1984, Aus.)
Rod Steele
THING WITH TWO HEADS, THE(1972)
Rufus Steele
Silents
HOP, THE DEVIL'S BREW(1916), w
Stephanie Steele
POSSE(1975)
Sylvia Steele
EXPRESSO BONGO(1959, Brit.)
Tom Steele
RIDERS OF THE WHISTLING SKULL(1937); WESTBOUND LIMITED(1937); RENEGADE RANGER(1938); I STOLE A MILLION(1939); IN OLD MONTEREY(1939); SOUTH OF TAHITI(1941); OUTLAWS OF PINE RIDGE(1942); RAIDERS OF THE RANGE(1942); TEXAS TO BATAAN(1942); LONE STAR TRAIL, THE(1943); OVERLAND MAIL ROBBERY(1943); WAGON TRACKS WEST(1943); CHEYENNE WILDCAT(1944); CODE OF THE PRAIRIE(1944); HIDDEN VALLEY OUTLAWS(1944); MARSHAL OF RENO(1944); MOJAVE FIREBRAND(1944); SAN ANTONIO KID, THE(1944); SILVER CITY KID(1944); TUCSON RAIDERS(1944); GOD IS MY COPILOT(1945); LONE TEXAS RANGER(1945); TRAIL OF KIT CARSON(1945); BRUTE FORCE(1947); VIGILANTES OF BOOMTOWN(1947); DENVER KID, THE(1948); OUTCASTS OF THE TRAIL(1949); MILKMAN, THE(1950); THING, THE(1951), a, stunts; MONTANA BELLE(1952); CATTLE QUEEN OF MONTANA(1954); PRODIGAL, THE(1955); SATAN'S SATELLITES(1958); GHOST OF ZORRO(1959); SPARTACUS(1960); SPIRAL ROAD, THE(1962); SILENCERS, THE(1966); DIAMONDS ARE FOREVER(1971, Brit.)
Tommy Steele
ROCK AROUND THE WORLD(1957, Brit.); DUKE WORE JEANS, THE(1958, Brit.); KILL ME TOMORROW(1958, Brit.); LIGHT UP THE SKY(1960, Brit.); TOMMY THE TOREADOR(1960, Brit.); DREAM MAKER, THE(1963, Brit.); HALF A SIXPENCE(1967, Brit.); HAPPIEST MILLIONAIRE, THE(1967); FINIAN'S RAINBOW(1968); WHERE'S JACK?(1969, Brit.)
Vernon Steele
BIG NEWS(1929); DESIGN FOR LIVING(1933); KING'S VACATION, THE(1933); SILK EXPRESS, THE(1933); BULLDOG DRUMMOND STRIKES BACK(1934); GREAT FLIRTATION, THE(1934); WHERE SINNERS MEET(1934); CAPTAIN BLOOD(1935); I FOUND STELLA PARISH(1935); TIME OUT FOR ROMANCE(1937); KIDNAP-

PED(1938); NORTH OF THE YUKON(1939); WITNESS VANISHES, THE(1939); MRS. MINIVER(1942); RIDERS OF THE NORTHWEST MOUNTED(1943); THEY WERE EXPENDABLE(1945); LONE WOLF IN LONDON(1947); JOAN OF ARC(1948); TO THE ENDS OF THE EARTH(1948); MADAME BOVARY(1949); THIRTEENTH LETTER, THE(1951)
Silents
POLLY OF THE CIRCUS(1917); ETERNAL MAGDALENE, THE(1919); WONDERFUL WIFE, A(1922); ALICE ADAMS(1923); TEMPTATION(1923); WANTERS, THE(1923); WHAT WIVES WANT(1923); HOUSE OF YOUTH, THE(1924)
Misc. Silents
HER GREAT MATCH(1915); LITTLE LADY EILEEN(1916); SILKS AND SATINS(1916); SUPREME SACRIFICE, THE(1916); PANTHER WOMAN, THE(1919); PHANTOM HONEYMOON, THE(1919); WITNESS FOR THE DEFENSE, THE(1919); HIS HOUSE IN ORDER(1920); HIGHEST BIDDER, THE(1921); FOR THE DEFENSE(1922); GIRL WHO RAN WILD, THE(1922)
Victor Steele
Misc. Silents
MIND THE PAINT GIRL(1919)
Vivie Steele
MRS. MINIVER(1942)
Walter Steele
GOD TOLD ME TO(1976)
Wilbur Daniel Steele
UNDERTOW(1930), w; WAY TO THE GOLD, THE(1957), w
Silents
SHADOWS(1922), w
William Steele
DOUGH BOYS(1930); LONE STAR RANGER, THE(1930); FLAMING GUNS(1933); KING OF THE ARENA(1933); WHEN A MAN SEES RED(1934); ROMANCE RIDES THE RANGE(1936); MARIE ANTOINETTE(1938); OUTLAW, THE(1943); COLT .45(1950); SHOWDOWN, THE(1950)
Silents
RIDING WITH DEATH(1921); PARDON MY NERVE!(1922); SHOOTIN' FOR LOVE(1923)
Misc. Silents
FAST MAIL, THE(1922); SINGLE HANDED(1923); TWO-FISTED JONES(1925); WILD HORSE STAMPEDE, THE(1926); HOOF MARKS(1927); VALLEY OF HELL, THE(1927)
William A. Steele
Silents
HURRICANE KID, THE(1925); LET 'ER BUCK(1925)
Misc. Silents
FIGHTING PEACEMAKER, THE(1926); SIX SHOOTIN' ROMANCE, A(1926); LOCO LUCK(1927); RANGE COURAGE(1927); ROUGH AND READY(1927); CALL OF THE HEART(1928); THUNDER RIDERS(1928)
J. Steeley
TILL DEATH(1978), ph
Jack Steeley
GOLD GUITAR, THE(1966), ph; THAT TENNESSEE BEAT(1966), ph; WEEKEND WITH THE BABYSITTER(1970), ph
Hosea Steelman
Silents
VIRGINIAN, THE(1914)
Phil Steelman
GIRL FROM SCOTLAND YARD, THE(1937)
Peter Steels
GAMEKEEPER, THE(1980, Brit.)
Mary Steelsmith
RABBIT TEST(1978); H.O.T.S.(1979); DEATH VALLEY(1982)
Jack Steely
INCREDIBLE TWO-HEADED TRANSPLANT, THE(1971), ph; THING WITH TWO HEADS, THE(1972), ph
S. A. Steeman
MURDERER LIVES AT NUMBER 21, THE(1947, Fr.), w
Stanislas-Andre Steeman
JENNY LAMOUR(1948, Fr.), w
Bodil Steen
CRAZY PARADISE(1965, Den.); ERIC SOYA'S "17"(1967, Den.)
Derek Steen
MOSQUITO SQUADRON(1970, Brit.); DR. JEKYLL AND SISTER HYDE(1971, Brit.); LOLA(1971, Brit./Ital.)
Irving Steen
FALL OF THE HOUSE OF USHER, THE(1952, Brit.)
Jan Steen
OFFERING, THE(1966, Can.), w
Jessica Steen
THRESHOLD(1983, Can.)
Kristen Steen
EVENTS(1970)
Margaret Steen
MAN FROM MOROCCO, THE(1946, Brit.), w
Michael Steen
THIS PROPERTY IS CONDEMNED(1966)
Mike Steen
TRUE STORY OF JESSE JAMES, THE(1957); SWEET BIRD OF YOUTH(1962); CRACK IN THE WORLD(1965)
Sammy Steen
TOP BANANA(1954)
Mary Steenburgen
GOIN' SOUTH(1978); TIME AFTER TIME(1979, Brit.); MELVIN AND HOWARD(1980); RAGTIME(1981); MIDSUMMER NIGHT'S SEX COMEDY, A(1982); CROSS CREEK(1983); ROMANTIC COMEDY(1983)
E. Burton Steene
HELL'S ANGELS(1930), ph
Silents
BEN-HUR(1925), ph; WINGS(1927), ph
Clarence Steensen
MAKE YOUR OWN BED(1944), set d; HORN BLOWS AT MIDNIGHT, THE(1945), art d; STALLION ROAD(1947), set d; RAW DEAL(1948), set d; SPIRITUALIST, THE(1948), set d; GUN HAWK, THE(1963), set d; GUNFIGHT AT COMANCHE

CREEK(1964), set d; DR. GOLDFOOT AND THE BIKINI MACHINE(1965), set d; GHOST IN THE INVISIBLE BIKINI(1966), set d

Clarence I. Steensen
ACTION IN THE NORTH ATLANTIC(1943), set d; CONFLICT(1945), set d; RISE AND FALL OF LEGS DIAMOND, THE(1960), set d

Charles Steenson
PRIVATE EYES(1953), set d

Clarence Steenson
HUMORESQUE(1946), set d; PHILO VANCE'S SECRET MISSION(1947), set d; CANON CITY(1948), set d; HE WALKED BY NIGHT(1948), set d; HOLLOW TRIUMPH(1948), set d; STEEL HELMET, THE(1951), set d; FACE TO FACE(1952), set d

Amanda Steer
CRY OF THE PENGUINS(1972, Brit.)

Caroline Steer
ROCKING HORSE WINNER, THE(1950, Brit.)

Clifton Steere
SOME OF MY BEST FRIENDS ARE...(1971); EDUCATION OF SONNY CARSON, THE(1974)

A. Harding Steerman
OTHER PEOPLE'S SINS(1931, Brit.)
Silents
IRON JUSTICE(1915, Brit.); BID FOR FORTUNE, A(1917, Brit.); ELUSIVE PIMPERNEL, THE(1919, Brit.); MANCHESTER MAN, THE(1920, Brit.); GOD IN THE GARDEN, THE(1921, Brit.); LOVE AT THE WHEEL(1921, Brit.); OLD CURIOSITY SHOP, THE(1921, Brit.)
Misc. Silents
LIGHT(1915, Brit.); CORNER MAN, THE(1921, Brit.); DIANA OF THE CROSSWAYS(1922, Brit.)

L.W. Steers
Silents
PAIR OF SILK STOCKINGS, A(1918)
Misc. Silents
HAPPINESS OF THREE WOMEN, THE(1917)

Larry Steers
YELLOW JACK(1938); IN OLD CALIFORNIA(1929); WHEEL OF LIFE, THE(1929); LET'S GO PLACES(1930); SEVEN DAYS LEAVE(1930); THOROUGHBRED, THE(1930); FREE SOUL, A(1931); GRIEF STREET(1931); LITTLE CAESAR(1931); SECRET CALL, THE(1931); CENTRAL PARK(1932); IF I HAD A MILLION(1932); STRANGE JUSTICE(1932); TROUBLE IN PARADISE(1932); TWO KINDS OF WOMEN(1932); DANCING LADY(1933); SITTING PRETTY(1933); EVELYN PRENTICE(1934); GIRL FROM MISSOURI, THE(1934); JOURNAL OF A CRIME(1934); GREAT IMPERSONATION, THE(1935); MURDER MAN(1935); PADDY O'DAY(1935); RECKLESS(1935); RENDEZVOUS(1935); MURDER WITH PICTURES(1936); NAVY BORN(1936); PRINCESS COMES ACROSS, THE(1936); TROUBLE FOR TWO(1936); BREAKFAST FOR TWO(1937); LOVE IS NEWS(1937); MUSIC FOR MADAME(1937); SOMETHING TO SING ABOUT(1937); STAGE DOOR(1937); TOAST OF NEW YORK, THE(1937); WRONG ROAD, THE(1937); AMAZING DR. CLITTERHOUSE, THE(1938); FORGOTTEN WOMAN, THE(1939); NIGHT OF NIGHTS, THE(1939); OUR LEADING CITIZEN(1939); IRENE(1940); PLAY GIRL(1940); LOVE CRAZY(1941); WHISTLING IN THE DARK(1941); RIDING THE WIND(1942); GOVERNMENT GIRL(1943); HANDS ACROSS THE BORDER(1943); GYPSY WILDCAT(1944); I LOVE A SOLDIER(1944); MOJAVE FIREBRAND(1944); MY BUDDY(1944); SECRETS OF SCOTLAND YARD(1944); UP IN ARMS(1944); THEY WERE EXPENDABLE(1945); WHITE PONGO(1945); WOMAN IN THE WINDOW, THE(1945); DRAGONWYCH(1946); MAGNIFICENT DOLL(1946); TILL THE CLOUDS ROLL BY(1946); BLONDIE'S ANNIVERSARY(1947); GANGSTER, THE(1947); HIGH BARBAREE(1947); SADDLE PALS(1947); DOCKS OF NEW ORLEANS(1948); FIGHTING MAD(1948); DUCHESS OF IDAHO, THE(1950)
Silents
ELOPE IF YOU MUST(1922); MIND OVER MOTOR(1923); SOUL OF THE BEAST(1923); FLATTERY(1925); NEW BROOMS(1925); BRIDE OF THE STORM(1926); NO CONTROL(1927); JUST OFF BROADWAY(1929)
Misc. Silents
MYSTIC FACES(1918); HEARTSEASE(1919); REDSKIN(1929)

Larry W. Steers
Silents
LITTLE COMRADE(1919)

Lawrence Steers
Silents
WEALTH(1921); SOUTH OF SUVA(1922); HUNTRESS, THE(1923); LODGE IN THE WILDERNESS, THE(1926)

Fred Stefan
SPRING FEVER(1983, Can.), w

George Stefan
IT HAPPENED IN ATHENS(1962)

Ivan Stefan
SEVENTH CONTINENT, THE(1968, Czech./Yugo.), cos

Kismi Stefan
KID FROM BOOKLYN, THE(1946)

Benito Stefanelli
AVENGER, THE(1962, Fr./Ital.); LAST OF THE VIKINGS, THE(1962, Fr./Ital.); SLAVE, THE(1963, Ital.); FISTFUL OF DOLLARS, A(1964, Ital./Ger./Span.); FOR A FEW DOLLARS MORE(1967, Ital./Ger./Span.); GOOD, THE BAD, AND THE UGLY, THE(1967, U.S./Ital./Span.); HELLBENDERS, THE(1967, U.S./Ital./Span.); BIG GUNDOWN, THE(1968, Ital.); DAY OF ANGER(1970, Ital./Ger.); BATTLE OF THE AMAZONS(1973, Ital./Span.)

Benoit Stefanelli
ONCE UPON A TIME IN THE WEST(1969, U.S./Ital.)

Count Stefanelli
MESSAGE TO GARCIA, A(1936); DOWN TO EARTH(1947)

M. Teresa Stefanelli [Gina Lollobrigida]
THAT SPLENDID NOVEMBER(1971, Ital./Fr.), cos

Simonetta Stefanelli
GODFATHER, THE(1972); THREE BROTHERS(1982, Ital.)

Stefano Stefanelli
MASOCH(1980, Ital.)

Andi Stefanescu
CELESTE(1982, Ger.)

Stefani
GINA(1961, Fr./Mex.)

Frederick Stefani
ALL THE KING'S HORSES(1935), w

Joseph Stefani
BABIES FOR SALE(1940); DISPATCH FROM REUTERS, A(1940); SKY BANDITS, THE(1940)

Grigoris Stefanides
DAY THE FISH CAME OUT, THE(1967. Brit./Gr.); OEDIPUS THE KING(1968, Brit.)

Alberto Stefanini
INVASION 1700(1965, Fr./Ital./Yugo.)

Niksa Stefanini
TEMPEST(1958, Ital./Yugo./Fr.); WHITE WARRIOR, THE(1961, Ital./Yugo.); FURY OF THE PAGANS(1963, Ital.); APACHE GOLD(1965, Ger.); LA VIE DE CHATEAU(1967, Fr.)

Peter Stefaniuk
SILENCE OF THE NORTH(1981, Can.)

Joseph Stefano
BLACK ORCHID(1959), w; FAST AND SEXY(1960, Fr./Ital.), w; PSYCHO(1960), w; NAKED EDGE, THE(1961), w; EYE OF THE CAT(1969), w

Rachel Stefanopoli
NUMBER TWO(1975, Fr.)

George Stefans
GANG THAT COULDN'T SHOOT STRAIGHT, THE(1971)

Mark Steffan
SWORD AND THE SORCERER, THE(1982)

Steffani and His Silver Songsters
WHAT DO WE DO NOW?(1945, Brit.)

Steffani's Silver Songsters
DODGING THE DOLE(1936, Brit.)

Peggy Steffans
HALLELUJAH THE HILLS(1963)

Anthony Steffen
LAST TOMAHAWK, THE(1965, Ger./Ital./Span.); NO ROOM TO DIE(1969, Ital.); NIGHT EVELYN CAME OUT OF THE GRAVE, THE(1973, Ital.); STRANGER'S GUNDOWN, THE(1974, Ital.), p; KILLER FISH(1979, Ital./Braz.)
Misc. Talkies
WHY KILL AGAIN?(1965)

Ben Steffen
CASTLE OF BLOOD(1964, Fr./Ital.)

Geary Steffen
WINTERTIME(1943)

Paul Steffen
SEVEN HILLS OF ROME, THE(1958), ch; THIEF OF BAGHDAD, THE(1961, Ital./Fr.), ch

Sirry Steffen
HITLER(1962); CRAWLING HAND, THE(1963)

Roger Steffens
ROLLERCOASTER(1977)

Sandy Steffens
MY FAIR LADY(1964)

Stegani
BEYOND THE LAW(1967, Ital.), w

Giorgio Stegani
TROJAN HORSE, THE(1962, Fr./Ital.), w; MILL OF THE STONE WOMEN(1963, Fr./Ital.), w; BEYOND THE LAW(1967, Ital.), d

Frederic Steger
HIDEOUT(1948, Brit.); ROSSITER CASE, THE(1950, Brit.); SPIDER AND THE FLY, THE(1952, Brit.)

Frederick Steger
CLOUDBURST(1952, Brit.); FINGER OF GUILT(1956, Brit.)

Julius Steger
Misc. Silents
FIFTH COMMANDMENT, THE(1915); MASTER OF THE HOUSE, THE(1915); BLINDNESS OF LOVE, THE(1916); LIBERTINE, THE(1916), d; PRIMA DONNA'S HUSBAND, THE(1916), d; STOLEN TRIUMPH, THE(1916), d; LAW OF COMPENSATION, THE(1917), d; REDEMPTION(1917), d; BURDEN OF PROOF, THE(1918), d; CECILIA OF THE PINK ROSES(1918), d; HER MISTAKE(1918), d; BELLE OF NEW YORK, THE(1919), d; HIDDEN TRUTH, THE(1919), d; LAW OF COMPENSATION(1927), d

Bernice Stegers
CATCH ME A SPY(1971, Brit./Fr.); CITY OF WOMEN(1980, Ital./Fr.); QUARTET(1981, Brit./Fr.); LIGHT YEARS AWAY(1982, Fr./Switz.); XTRO(1983, Brit.)
Misc. Talkies
DOLL'S EYE(1982)

Frank Steggall
SUGARLAND EXPRESS, THE(1974)

Carl Stegger
CASE OF THE 44'S, THE(1964 Brit./Den.)

Karl Stegger
GOLDEN MOUNTAINS(1958, Den.); CRAZY PARADISE(1965, Den.); OPERATION LOVEBIRDS(1968, Den.); VENOM(1968, Den.); LURE OF THE JUNGLE, THE(1970, Den.); SCANDAL IN DENMARK(1970, Den.)

Erika Stegman
SINAI COMMANDOS: THE STORY OF THE SIX DAY WAR(1968, Israel/Ger.), ed

G. F. Stegmann
GENERAL JOHN REGAN(1933, Brit.), ph

Dave Stegstra
COME BACK BABY(1968)

Edgar Stehli
DRUM BEAT(1954); EXECUTIVE SUITE(1954); COBWEB, THE(1955); BROTHERS KARAMAZOV, THE(1958); NO NAME ON THE BULLET(1959); 4D MAN(1959); CASH McCALL(1960); ATLANTIS, THE LOST CONTINENT(1961); PARRISH(1961); POCKETFUL OF MIRACLES(1961); SPIRAL ROAD, THE(1962); TWILIGHT OF HONOR(1963); SECONDS(1966); TIGER MAKES OUT, THE(1967); LOVING(1970)

Penny Stehli
NED KELLY(1970, Brit.)

Miloslav Stehlik
GIRL WITH THREE CAMELS, THE(1968, Czech.), w
Zdenek Stehlik
FABULOUS WORLD OF JULES VERNE, THE(1961, Czech.), ed; JOURNEY TO THE
BEGINNING OF TIME(1966, Czech), ed
Jana Stehnova
DESERTER AND THE NOMADS, THE(1969, Czech./Ital.)
Warren Steibel
HONEYMOON KILLERS, THE(1969), p
Frank Steifel
LORDS OF FLATBUSH, THE(1974)
Milton Steifel
FIEND OF DOPE ISLAND(1961)
Samuel H. Steifel
BIG WHEEL, THE(1949), p
Friedrich Steig
CANARIS(1955, Ger.)
Brad Steiger
VALENTINO(1977, Brit.), w
O.M. Steiger
GOIN' TO TOWN(1935); JOHNNY ANGEL(1945)
Rod Steiger
TERESA(1951); ON THE WATERFRONT(1954); BIG KNIFE, THE(1955); COURT-
MARTIAL OF BILLY MITCHELL, THE(1955); OKLAHOMA(1955); BACK FROM
ETERNITY(1956); HARDER THEY FALL, THE(1956); JUBAL(1956); ACROSS THE
BRIDGE(1957, Brit.); RUN OF THE ARROW(1957); UNHOLY WIFE, THE(1957); CRY
TERROR(1958); AL CAPONE(1959); SEVEN THIEVES(1960); MARK, THE(1961, Brit.);
CONVICTS FOUR(1962); LONGEST DAY, THE(1962); THIRTEEN WEST
STREET(1962); WORLD IN MY POCKET, THE(1962, Fr./Ital./Ger.); DOCTOR ZHIVA-
GO(1965); LOVED ONE, THE(1965); PAWNBROKER, THE(1965); TIME OF INDIF-
FERENCE(1965, Fr./Ital.); GIRL AND THE GENERAL, THE(1967, Fr./Ital.); IN THE
HEAT OF THE NIGHT(1967); AND THERE CAME A MAN(1968, Ital.); NO WAY TO
TREAT A LADY(1968); SERGEANT, THE(1968); ILLUSTRATED MAN, THE(1969);
THREE INTO TWO WON'T GO(1969, Brit.); WATERLOO(1970, Ital./USSR); HAPPY
BIRTHDAY, WANDA JUNE(1971); DUCK, YOU SUCKER!(1972, Ital.); LOLLY-
MADONNA XXX(1973); LAST DAYS OF MUSSOLINI(1974, Ital.); RE: LUCKY
LUCIANO(1974, Fr./Ital.); HENNESSY(1975, Brit.); DIRTY HANDS(1976, Fr./Ital./
Ger.); W.C. FIELDS AND ME(1976); BREAKTHROUGH(1978, Ger.); F.I.S.T.(1978);
AMITYVILLE HORROR, THE(1979); LOVE AND BULLETS(1979, Brit.); KLONDIKE
FEVER(1980); LUCKY STAR, THE(1980, Can.); CATTLE ANNIE AND LITTLE
BRITCHES(1981); LION OF THE DESERT(1981, Libya/Brit.); CHOSEN, THE(1982)
1984
NAKED FACE, THE(1984)
Misc. Talkies
HEROES, THE(1975); WOLF LAKE(1979); PORTRAIT OF A HITMAN(1984)
Vanessa Steiger
GRIM REAPER, THE(1981, Ital.)
Josef Steigl
DO YOU KEEP A LION AT HOME?(1966, Czech.)
Walter Steihl
STUCK ON YOU(1983), cos
Jiri Steimar
LEMONADE JOE(1966, Czech.)
Anna Steimarova
MERRY WIVES, THE(1940, Czech.)
Adolf Steimel
TROMBA, THE TIGER MAN(1952, Ger.), m
Max Steimer
ROUGHLY SPEAKING(1945), m
Andrew Stein
HOLLYWOOD BOULEVARD(1976), m; DEATHSPORT(1978), m
Andy Stein
THUNDER AND LIGHTNING(1977), m
Anna Stein
MISTER CORY(1957)
Ben Stein
1984
WILD LIFE, THE(1984)
Bob Stein
NIGHT MOVES(1975), makeup
Buddy Stein
THREE TOUGH GUYS(1974, U.S./Ital.)
Chris Stein
ROADIE(1980); UNION CITY(1980), m; POLYESTER(1981), m
Daniel Michael Stein
WALL OF NOISE(1963), w
Danny Stein
ENTER LAUGHING(1967)
David Stein
LORDS OF FLATBUSH, THE(1974)
Elliott Stein
NAKED HEARTS(1970, Fr.); SECRETS OF SEX(1970, Brit.), a, w
Misc. Talkies
BIZARRE(1969)
Frankie Stein
BROKEN ENGLISH(1981)
Franz Stein
M(1933, Ger.); GIRL FROM THE MARSH CROFT, THE(1935, Ger.); TESTAMENT OF
DR. MABUSE, THE(1943, Ger.)
George Stein
MAGIC VOYAGE OF SINBAD, THE(1962, USSR), ed
Gisela Stein
1984
GERMANY PALE MOTHER(1984, Ger.)
Gita Stein
CATSKILL HONEYMOON(1950)
Hal Stein
GROUND ZERO(1973)

Herman Stein
IT CAME FROM OUTER SPACE(1953), m; REVENGE OF THE CREATURE(1955),
m; THIS ISLAND EARTH(1955), m; BACKLASH(1956), m; I'VE LIVED BEFO-
RE(1956), m; THERE'S ALWAYS TOMORROW(1956), m; UNGUARDED MOMENT,
THE(1956), m; GREAT MAN, THE(1957), m; QUANTEZ(1957), m; SLIM CAR-
TER(1957), m; LADY TAKES A FLYER, THE(1958), m; NO NAME ON THE BUL-
LET(1959), m; INTRUDER, THE(1962), m; TAGGART(1964), m; LET'S KILL
UNCLE(1966), m
Howard Stein
NIGHTHAWKS(1981)
Ina Stein
THOUSAND EYES OF DR. MABUSE, THE(1960, Fr./Ital./Ger.), cos; DISORDER
AND EARLY TORMENT(1977, Ger.), cos
John Stein
INTERLUDE(1957); PATHS OF GLORY(1957)
Joseph Stein
MRS. GIBBONS' BOYS(1962, Brit.), w; ENTER LAUGHING(1967), p, w; FIDDLER
ON THE ROOF(1971), w
Julian Stein
FLESH EATERS, THE(1964), m
Lee Stein
TOWING(1978)
Leo Stein
MERRY WIDOW, THE(1934), w; MERRY WIDOW, THE(1952), w
Silents
MERRY WIDOW, THE(1925), w
Lotte Stein
ALLERGIC TO LOVE(1943); SWING OUT THE BLUES(1943); CLIMAX, THE(1944);
WEEKEND PASS(1944); CAPTAIN EDDIE(1945); HOTEL BERLIN(1945); EXILE,
THE(1947); MOTHER WORE TIGHTS(1947); CREEPER, THE(1948); LETTER FROM
AN UNKNOWN WOMAN(1948); WALLFLOWER(1948); GREAT SINNER, THE(1949);
MR. BELVEDERE GOES TO COLLEGE(1949); WHITE TOWER, THE(1950); ALL I
DESIRE(1953); BAND WAGON, THE(1953); SO BIG(1953)
Lottie Stein
CLOAK AND DAGGER(1946)
Mary Stein
E.T. THE EXTRA-TERRESTRIAL(1982)
Maurice Stein
LET'S DO IT AGAIN(1953); MAKING IT(1971), makeup; SIMON, KING OF THE
WITCHES(1971), makeup; TOP OF THE HEAP(1972), makeup
Michael Stein
1984
LOVE STREAMS(1984)
Michael H. Stein
1984
WILD LIFE, THE(1984)
Mitch Stein
GAMBLER, THE(1974)
Paul Stein
OFFICE SCANDAL, THE(1929), d; HER PRIVATE AFFAIR(1930), d; LOTTERY
BRIDE, THE(1930), d; LILY CHRISTINE(1932, Brit.), d; SONG YOU GAVE ME,
THE(1934, Brit.), d; HEART'S DESIRE(1937, Brit.), d; BLACK LIMELIGHT(1938,
Brit.), d; JUST LIKE A WOMAN(1939, Brit.), d; IT HAPPENED TO ONE MAN(1941,
Brit.), d; BREACH OF PROMISE(1942, Brit.), d; SAINT MEETS THE TIGER,
THE(1943, Brit.), d; KISS THE BRIDE GOODBYE(1944, Brit.), p&d, w; COUNTER
BLAST(1948, Brit.), d; CAGE OF GOLD(1950, Brit.), w
Misc. Silents
RED PEACOCK, THE(1922, Ger.), d; DON'T TELL THE WIFE(1927), d
Paul L. Stein
SHOW FOLKS(1928), d; THIS THING CALLED LOVE(1929), d; ONE ROMANTIC
NIGHT(1930), d; SIN TAKES A HOLIDAY(1930), d; BORN TO LOVE(1931), d; COM-
MON LAW, THE(1931), d; WOMAN COMMANDS, A(1932), d; MIMI(1935, Brit.), d;
FAITHFUL(1936, Brit.), d; RED WAGON(1936), d; APRIL BLOSSOMS(1937, Brit.), d;
CAFE COLETTE(1937, Brit.), d; JANE STEPS OUT(1938, Brit.), d; OUTSIDER,
THE(1940, Brit.), d; POISON PEN(1941, Brit.), d; TWILIGHT HOUR(1944, Brit.), d;
LISBON STORY, THE(1946, Brit.), d; WALTZ TIME(1946, Brit.), d; DEVIL'S PLOT,
THE(1948, Brit.), d; LAUGHING LADY, THE(1950, Brit.), d; TWENTY QUESTIONS
MURDER MYSTERY, THE(1950, Brit.), d
Silents
MAN-MADE WOMEN(1928), d
Misc. Silents
MY OFFICIAL WIFE(1926), d; CLIMBERS, THE(1927), d
Paul Ludwig Stein
Misc. Silents
DEVIL'S PAWN, THE(1922, Ger.), d
Peter Stein
GOOD DISSONANCE LIKE A MAN, A(1977), ph; FRIDAY THE 13TH PART
II(1981), ph; REUBEN, REUBEN(1983), ph
1984
C.H.U.D.(1984), ph; CLASS ENEMY(1984, Ger.), d, w
Ralph Stein
FIRST YANK INTO TOKYO(1945); MR. BLANDINGS BUILDS HIS DREAM
HOUSE(1948); WOMAN'S SECRET, A(1949)
Rita Stein
SLOW RUN(1968)
Rob Stein
MY BLOODY VALENTINE(1981, Can.)
Robert Stein
1984
STARMAN(1984)
Ron Stein
NICKELODEON(1976); STING II, THE(1983)
1984
STAR TREK III: THE SEARCH FOR SPOCK(1984), stunts
Ronald Stein
APACHE WOMAN(1955), m; DAY THE WORLD ENDED, THE(1956), m; GIRLS IN
PRISON(1956), m; GUNSLINGER(1956), m; IT CONQUERED THE WORLD(1956), m;
OKLAHOMA WOMAN, THE(1956), m; PHANTOM FROM 10,000 LEAGUES,
THE(1956), m; SHE-CREATURE, THE(1956), m; ATTACK OF THE CRAB MON-
STERS(1957), m; DRAGSTRIP GIRL(1957), m; FLESH AND THE SPUR(1957), m;

INVASION OF THE SAUCER MEN(1957), m; NAKED PARADISE(1957), m; NOT OF THIS EARTH(1957), m; REFORM SCHOOL GIRL(1957), m; RUNAWAY DAUGHTERS(1957), m; SORORITY GIRL(1957), m; UNDEAD, THE(1957), m; ATTACK OF THE 50 FOOT WOMAN(1958), m; BONNIE PARKER STORY, THE(1958), m; DEVIL'S PARTNER, THE(1958), m; HOT ROD GANG(1958), m; JET ATTACK(1958), m, md; LITTLEST HOBO, THE(1958), m; SHE-GODS OF SHARK REEF(1958), m; SUICIDE BATTALION(1958), m, md; DIARY OF A HIGH SCHOOL BRIDE(1959), m; GHOST OF DRAGSTRIP HOLLOW(1959), m; LEGEND OF TOM DOOLEY, THE(1959), m; PARATROOP COMMAND(1959), m; TANK COMMANDOS(1959), m; ATLAS(1960), m; DINOSAURUS(1960), m; RAYMIE(1960), m; THREAT, THE(1960), m; TOO SOON TO LOVE(1960), m; PREMATURE BURIAL, THE(1962), m; UNDERWATER CITY, THE(1962), m; DEMENTIA 13(1963), m; DIME WITH A HALO(1963), m; HAUNTED PALACE, THE(1963), m; OF LOVE AND DESIRE(1963), m; TERROR, THE(1963), m; YOUNG AND THE BRAVE, THE(1963), m; WAR IS HELL(1964), m; BOUNTY KILLER, THE(1965), m; RAT FINK(1965), m; REQUIEM FOR A GUNFIGHTER(1965), m; MAN CALLED DAGGER, A(1967), md; PSYCH-OUT(1968), m; SPIDER BABY(1968), m; RAIN PEOPLE, THE(1969), m; GETTING STRAIGHT(1970), m

Ronald S. Stein
LAST WOMAN ON EARTH, THE(1960), m

S. Bernard Stein
WIRE SERVICE(1942), m

Sam Stein
GOIN' TO TOWN(1935); MODERN TIMES(1936)

Sammy Stein
LOST PATROL, THE,(1934); LONG VOYAGE HOME, THE(1940); MEXICAN SPITFIRE OUT WEST(1940); PRAIRIE SCHOONERS(1940); PUBLIC ENEMIES(1941); SIERRA SUE(1941); WILDCAT OF TUCSON(1941); BROADWAY(1942); GENTLEMAN JIM(1942); MY FAVORITE SPY(1942); PITTSBURGH(1942); REMEMBER PEARL HARBOR(1942); ROAD TO MOROCCO(1942); SING YOUR WORRIES AWAY(1942); IT AIN'T HAY(1943); NEVER A DULL MOMENT(1943); NO TIME FOR LOVE(1943); SLEEPY LAGOON(1943); SWING FEVER(1943); FRENCHMAN'S CREEK(1944); KISMET(1944); LOST IN A HAREM(1944); MARINE RAIDERS(1944); PRINCESS AND THE PIRATE, THE(1944); BIG SHOW-OFF, THE(1945); HERE COME THE COEDS(1945); THEY WERE EXPENDABLE(1945); DARK HORSE, THE(1946); FRENCH KEY, THE(1946); SHOOT TO KILL(1947); VARIETY GIRL(1947); MIGHTY JOE YOUNG(1949); VEILS OF BAGDAD, THE(1953)

Selma Stein
SALVATION NELL(1931), w

Sheila Stein
DATE WITH JUDY, A(1948); THAT MIDNIGHT KISS(1949)

William Stein
SATAN'S BED(1965)

Yvonne Stein
PARATROOPER(1954, Brit.)

Alex Steinart
TONIGHT WE SING(1953)

Alexander Steinart
PRAIRIE, THE(1948), m

Peter Steinbach
GERMANY IN AUTUMN(1978, Ger.), w

Fred Steinbacher
BURG THEATRE(1936, Ger.)

Victor Steinback
1984
2010(1984)

Floyd Steinbeck
PICNIC(1955)

John Steinbeck
OF MICE AND MEN(1939), w; GRAPES OF WRATH(1940), w; TORTILLA FLAT(1942), w; MOON IS DOWN, THE(1943), w; LIFEBOAT(1944), w; MEDAL FOR BENNY, A(1945), w; PEARL, THE(1948, U.S./Mex.), w; RED PONY, THE(1949), w; O. HENRY'S FULL HOUSE(1952); VIVA ZAPATA!(1952), w; EAST OF EDEN(1955), w; WAYWARD BUS, THE(1957), w; FLIGHT(1960), w; CANNERY ROW(1982), w

Muriel Steinbeck
SMITHY(1946, Aus.); PACIFIC ADVENTURE(1947, Aus.); INTO THE STRAIGHT(1950, Aus.); WHEREVER SHE GOES(1953, Aus.); LONG JOHN SILVER(1954, Aus.); THEY'RE A WEIRD MOB(1966, Aus.)

Rudolf Steinbeck
SECRET ENEMIES(1942); MISSION TO MOSCOW(1943)

Walter Steinbeck
GREAT YEARNING, THE(1930, Ger.); CASE VAN GELDERN(1932, Ger.); JAZZBAND FIVE, THE(1932, Ger,); JOHNNY STEALS EUROPE(1932, Ger.); DREAMER, THE(1936, Ger.)

Irene Steinbeisser
SERPENT'S EGG, THE(1977, Ger./U.S.)

Betty Steinberg
TWONKY, THE(1953), ed; SIEGE AT RED RIVER, THE(1954), ed; KILLING, THE(1956), ed; MIRACLE OF THE HILLS, THE(1959), ed; OREGON TRAIL, THE(1959), ed; TWELVE HOURS TO KILL(1960), ed; SECOND TIME AROUND, THE(1961), ed; MADISON AVENUE(1962), ed; SWINGIN' ALONG(1962), ed; MAN IN THE WATER, THE(1963), ed

David Steinberg
FEARLESS FRANK(1967); LOST MAN, THE(1969); END, THE(1978); SOMETHING SHORT OF PARADISE(1979); PATERNITY(1981), d; GOING BERSERK(1983), d, w

Dawn Steinberg
FAME(1980)

Dianne Steinberg
SGT. PEPPER'S LONELY HEARTS CLUB BAND(1978)

Ed Steinberg
OFFENDERS, THE(1980), m

Gerhard Steinberg
DECISION BEFORE DAWN(1951)

Irving Steinberg
YOUNG SAVAGES, THE(1961); MANCHURIAN CANDIDATE, THE(1962); SEX AND THE SINGLE GIRL(1964)

Joe Steinberg
TORMENTED(1960), p; CRY OF BATTLE(1963), p

Kalman Steinberg
LUCKY STAR, THE(1980, Can.)

Lawrence Steinberg
GAS(1981, Can.)

Martha Jean Steinberg
DETROIT 9000(1973)

Norman Steinberg
BLAZING SADDLES(1974), w; MY FAVORITE YEAR(1982), w; YES, GIORGIO(1982), a, w
1984
JOHNNY DANGEROUSLY(1984), a, w

Samuel Steinberg
WHERE IS MY CHILD?(1937)

Stewart Steinberg
TWO-MINUTE WARNING(1976); HARDCORE(1979); ISLAND, THE(1980); LOVESICK(1983)

Susan Steinberg
DEADLY HERO(1976), ed; ROCKERS(1980), ed

Charly Steinberger
DEEP END(1970 Ger./U.S.), ph; KING, QUEEN, KNAVE(1972, Ger./U.S.), ph; PAPER TIGER(1975, Brit.), ph; JUST A GIGOLO(1979, Ger.), ph

Helmut Steinberger [Berger]
WITCHES, THE(1969, Fr./Ital.)

Richard Steinbicker
INVISIBLE OPPONENT(1933, Ger.), w

Rudy Steinbock
LOVE CRAZY(1941)

Dick Steinborn
MOONRUNNERS(1975)

David Steinbuck
WALK THE WALK(1970)

Oliver Steindecker
LAST OF THE RED HOT LOVERS(1972)

Howie Steindler
TROUBLE MAN(1972)

Maureen Steindler
WEDDING, A(1978)

Ragheiour Steindorsdottir
OUTLAW: THE SAGE OF GISLI(1982, Iceland)

Arthur Steiner
THIS IS THE ARMY(1943)

Claudio Steiner
NIGHT PORTER, THE(1974, Ital./U.S.)

Dorothy Steiner
JOY OF LIVING(1938)

Eduard Steiner
BLACK SPIDER, THE(1983, Swit.), p

Elio Steiner
CITY OF PAIN(1951, Ital.); LADY WITHOUT CAMELLIAS, THE(1981, Ital.)

Elisabeth Steiner
MARRIAGE OF FIGARO, THE(1970, Ger.)

Eric Steiner
O.S.S.(1946)

Estelle Steiner
JOY OF LIVING(1938)

Fred Steiner
TIME LIMIT(1957), m, md; FIRST TO FIGHT(1967), m; ST. VALENTINE'S DAY MASSACRE, THE(1967), m; SEA GYPSIES, THE(1978), m

Frederick Steiner
MAN FROM DEL RIO(1956), m; RUN FOR THE SUN(1956), m

Ira Steiner
VALDEZ IS COMING(1971), p

J. Steiner
SLEEPING CAR MURDER THE(1966, Fr.)

Jacques Steiner
IMPOSSIBLE ON SATURDAY(1966, Fr./Israel), p, w

Joe Paul Steiner
DESIRE IN THE DUST(1960)

John Steiner
PERSECUTION AND ASSASSINATION OF JEAN-PAUL MARAT AS PERFORMED BY THE INMATES OF THE ASYLUM OF CHARENTON UNDER THE DIRECTION OF THE MARQUIS DE SADE, THE(1967, Brit.); WORK IS A FOUR LETTER WORD(1968, Brit.); MASSACRE IN ROME(1973, Ital.); DEVIL WITHIN HER, THE(1976 Brit.); BEYOND THE DOOR II(1979, Brit.); SALAMANDER, THE(1983, U.S./Ital./Brit.); YOR, THE HUNTER FROM THE FUTURE(1983, Ital.)
1984
HUNTERS OF THE GOLDEN COBRA, THE(1984, Ital.); LAST HUNTER, THE(1984, Ital.)
Misc. Talkies
MAY MORNING(1970)

Leo Steiner
1984
BROADWAY DANNY ROSE(1984)

Mac Steiner
WESTWARD PASSAGE(1932), md

Marcel Steiner
FROM BEYOND THE GRAVE(1974, Brit.)

Max Steiner
DIXIANA(1930), orch; HALF SHOT AT SUNRISE(1930), md; CONSOLATION MARRIAGE(1931), m; FRIENDS AND LOVERS(1931), m; BILL OF DIVORCEMENT, A(1932), m; BIRD OF PARADISE(1932), m; CONQUERORS, THE(1932), m; HOLD'EM JAIL(1932), m; MOST DANGEROUS GAME, THE(1932), md; ROCKABYE(1932), md; SECRETS OF THE FRENCH POLICE(1932), m; SYMPHONY OF SIX MILLION(1932), m; WAY BACK HOME(1932), m; WHAT PRICE HOLLYWOOD?(1932), md; ACE OF ACES(1933), m; AFTER TONIGHT(1933), md; AGGIE APPLEBY, MAKER OF MEN(1933), md; ANN VICKERS(1933), md; BED OF ROSES(1933), md; BEFORE DAWN(1933), md; BLIND ADVENTURE(1933), m; CHANCE AT HEAVEN(1933), md; CHRISTOPHER STRONG(1933), m; DIPLOMANIACS(1933), m; DOUBLE HARNESS(1933), md; FLYING DOWN TO RIO(1933), md; KING KONG(1933), m; LITTLE WOMEN(1933), m; MONKEY'S PAW, THE(1933), md; MORNING GLORY(1933), m;

NO OTHER WOMAN(1933), m; **OUR BETTERS**(1933), md; **PROFESSIONAL SWEETHEART**(1933), md; **SILVER CORD**(1933), m; **SON OF KONG**(1933), m; **SWEEPINGS**(1933), m; **TOPAZE**(1933), m; **ANNE OF GREEN GABLES**(1934), m, md; **BACHELOR BAIT**(1934), md; **DOWN TO THEIR LAST YACHT**(1934), md; **FINISHING SCHOOL**(1934), md; **FOUNTAIN, THE**(1934), m; **GAY DIVORCEE, THE**(1934), md; **HIPS, HIPS, HOORAY!**(1934), m; **LET'S TRY AGAIN**(1934), m; **LIFE OF VERGIE WINTERS, THE**(1934), m; **LITTLE MINISTER, THE**(1934), m; **LOST PATROL, THE,**(1934), m; **MAN OF TWO WORLDS**(1934), md; **MEANEST GAL IN TOWN, THE**(1934), md; **MURDER ON THE BLACKBOARD**(1934), md; **OF HUMAN BONDAGE**(1934), m; **RAFTER ROMANCE**(1934), md; **RICHEST GIRL IN THE WORLD, THE**(1934), md; **SPITFIRE**(1934), m; **STINGAREE**(1934), md; **THIS MAN IS MINE**(1934), m, md; **WORLD MOVES ON, THE**(1934), m; **ALICE ADAMS**(1935), m; **BREAK OF HEARTS**(1935), m; **GRIDIRON FLASH**(1935), m; **I DREAM TOO MUCH**(1935), md; **INFORMER, THE**(1935), m; **ROBERTA**(1935), m; **SHE**(1935), m; **STAR OF MIDNIGHT**(1935), m, md; **THREE MUSKETEERS, THE**(1935), m; **TOP HAT**(1935), m; **CHARGE OF THE LIGHT BRIGADE, THE**(1936), m; **FOLLOW THE FLEET**(1936), md; **GARDEN OF ALLAH, THE**(1936), m; **LITTLE LORD FAUNTLEROY**(1936), m; **MARY OF SCOTLAND**(1936), m; **GREEN LIGHT**(1937), m; **KID GALAHAD**(1937), m; **LIFE OF EMILE ZOLA, THE**(1937), m; **LOST HORIZON**(1937), md; **SLIM**(1937), m; **STAR IS BORN, A**(1937), m; **SUBMARINE D-1**(1937), m; **THAT CERTAIN WOMAN**(1937), m; **TOVARICH**(1937), m; **ADVENTURES OF TOM SAWYER, THE**(1938), m; **AMAZING DR. CLITTERHOUSE, THE**(1938), m; **ANGELS WITH DIRTY FACES**(1938), m; **CRIME SCHOOL**(1938), m; **DAWN PATROL, THE**(1938), m; **FOUR DAUGHTERS**(1938), m; **GOLD IS WHERE YOU FIND IT**(1938), m; **JEZEBEL**(1938), m; **SISTERS, THE**(1938), m; **WHITE BANNERS**(1938), m; **DARK VICTORY**(1939), m; **DAUGHTERS COURAGEOUS**(1939), m; **DODGE CITY**(1939), m; **EACH DAWN I DIE**(1939), m; **FOUR WIVES**(1939), m; **GONE WITH THE WIND**(1939), m; **OKLAHOMA KID, THE**(1939), m; **OLD MAID, THE**(1939), m; **THEY MADE ME A CRIMINAL**(1939), m; **WE ARE NOT ALONE**(1939), m; **ALL THIS AND HEAVEN TOO**(1940), m; **DISPATCH FROM REUTERS, A**(1940), m; **DR. EHRLICH'S MAGIC BULLET**(1940), m; **LETTER, THE**(1940), m; **SANTA FE TRAIL**(1940), m; **TUGBOAT ANNIE SAILS AGAIN**(1940), m; **VIRGINIA CITY**(1940), m; **BRIDE CAME C.O.D., THE**(1941), m; **CITY, FOR CONQUEST**(1941), m; **DIVE BOMBER**(1941), m; **GREAT LIE, THE**(1941), m; **ONE FOOT IN HEAVEN**(1941), m; **SHINING VICTORY**(1941), m; **CAPTAINS OF THE CLOUDS**(1942), m; **CASABLANCA**(1942), m; **DESPERATE JOURNEY**(1942), m; **GAY SISTERS, THE**(1942), m; **IN THIS OUR LIFE**(1942), m; **NOW, VOYAGER**(1942), m; **THEY DIED WITH THEIR BOOTS ON**(1942), m; **ADVENTURES OF MARK TWAIN, THE**(1944), m; **ARSENIC AND OLD LACE**(1944), m; **CONSPIRATORS, THE**(1944), m; **PASSAGE TO MARSEILLE**(1944), m; **SINCE YOU WENT AWAY**(1944), m; **CORN IS GREEN, THE**(1945), m; **MILDRED PIERCE**(1945), m; **SAN ANTONIO**(1945), m; **SARATOGA TRUNK**(1945), m; **BEAST WITH FIVE FINGERS, THE**(1946), m; **BIG SLEEP, THE**(1946), m; **CLOAK AND DAGGER**(1946), m; **MAN I LOVE, THE**(1946), m; **MY REPUTATION**(1946), m; **NIGHT AND DAY**(1946), m; **ONE MORE TOMORROW**(1946), m; **STOLEN LIFE, A**(1946), m; **TOMORROW IS FOREVER**(1946), m; **CHEYENNE**(1947), m; **DEEP VALLEY**(1947), m; **LIFE WITH FATHER**(1947), m; **LOVE AND LEARN**(1947), m; **MY WILD IRISH ROSE**(1947), m; **PURSUED**(1947), m; **UNFAITHFUL, THE**(1947), m; **VOICE OF THE TURTLE, THE**(1947), m; **DECISION OF CHRISTOPHER BLAKE, THE**(1948), m; **FIGHTER SQUADRON**(1948), m; **JOHNNY BELINDA**(1948), m; **KEY LARGO**(1948), m; **MY GIRL TISA**(1948), m; **SILVER RIVER**(1948), m; **TREASURE OF THE SIERRA MADRE, THE**(1948), m; **WINTER MEETING**(1948), m; **WOMAN IN WHITE, THE**(1948), m; **ADVENTURES OF DON JUAN**(1949), m; **BEYOND THE FOREST**(1949), m; **FLAMINGO ROAD**(1949), m; **FOUNTAINHEAD, THE**(1949), m; **KISS IN THE DARK, A**(1949), m; **LADY TAKES A SAILOR, THE**(1949), m; **SOUTH OF ST. LOUIS**(1949), m; **WHITE HEAT**(1949), m; **WITHOUT HONOR**(1949), m&md; **CAGED**(1950), m; **DALLAS**(1950), m; **FLAME AND THE ARROW, THE**(1950), m; **GLASS MENAGERIE, THE**(1950), m; **ROCKY MOUNTAIN**(1950), m; **CLOSE TO MY HEART**(1951), m; **DISTANT DRUMS**(1951), m; **FORCE OF ARMS**(1951), m; **JIM THORPE-ALL AMERICAN**(1951), m; **LIGHTNING STRIKES TWICE**(1951), m; **ON MOONLIGHT BAY**(1951), m; **OPERATION PACIFIC**(1951), m; **RATON PASS**(1951), m; **SUGARFOOT**(1951), m; **IRON MISTRESS, THE**(1952), m; **LION AND THE HORSE, THE**(1952), m; **MARA MARU**(1952), m; **MIRACLE OF OUR LADY OF FATIMA, THE**(1952), m; **ROOM FOR ONE MORE**(1952), m; **SPRINGFIELD RIFLE**(1952), m; **BY THE LIGHT OF THE SILVERY MOON**(1953), m; **CHARGE AT FEATHER RIVER, THE**(1953), m; **DESERT SONG, THE**(1953), m; **SO BIG**(1953), m; **SO THIS IS LOVE**(1953), m; **TROUBLE ALONG THE WAY**(1953), m; **BOY FROM OKLAHOMA, THE**(1954), m; **CAINE MUTINY, THE**(1954), m; **KING RICHARD AND THE CRUSADERS**(1954), m; **BATTLE FLAME**(1955), m; **ILLEGAL**(1955), m; **LAST COMMAND, THE**(1955), m, md; **MC CONNELL STORY, THE**(1955), m; **VIOLENT MEN, THE**(1955), m; **BANDIDO**(1956), m; **COME NEXT SPRING**(1956), m; **DEATH OF A SCOUNDREL**(1956), m; **HELEN OF TROY**(1956, Ital), m; **HELL ON FRISCO BAY**(1956), m; **SEARCHERS, THE**(1956), m; **ALL MINE TO GIVE**(1957), m; **BAND OF ANGELS**(1957), m; **CHINA GATE**(1957), m; **ESCAPADE IN JAPAN**(1957), m; **DARBY'S RANGERS**(1958), m; **FORT DOBBS**(1958), m; **MARJORIE MORNINGSTAR**(1958), m; **FBI STORY, THE**(1959), m; **JOHN PAUL JONES**(1959), m; **SUMMER PLACE, A**(1959), m; **CASH McCALL**(1960), m; **DARK AT THE TOP OF THE STAIRS, THE**(1960), m; **ICE PALACE**(1960), m; **SINS OF RACHEL CADE, THE**(1960), m; **PARRISH**(1961), m; **PORTRAIT OF A MOBSTER**(1961), m; **SUSAN SLADE**(1961), m; **ROME ADVENTURE**(1962), m; **SPENCER'S MOUNTAIN**(1963), m; **DISTANT TRUMPET, A**(1964), m; **FBI CODE 98**(1964), m; **THOSE CALLOWAYS**(1964), m; **YOUNGBLOOD HAWKE**(1964), m; **TWO ON A GUILLOTINE**(1965), m; **PLAY IT AGAIN, SAM**(1972), m

Phil Steiner
GO, MAN, GO!(1954), ph

Rachel Steiner
1984
AMBASSADOR, THE(1984)

Ronald Steiner
DEVIL'S ANGELS(1967), ed

Sherry Steiner
GOD TOLD ME TO(1976)

Sigfrit Steiner
LAST CHANCE, THE(1945, Switz.); VILLAGE, THE(1953, Brit./Switz.); IT HAPPENED IN BROAD DAYLIGHT(1960, Ger./Switz.); BLACK SPIDER, THE(1983, Swit.); WAGNER(1983, Brit./Hung./Aust.)
1984
LOVE IN GERMANY, A(1984, Fr./Ger.)

Walter Steiner
BLONDE NIGHTINGALE(1931, Ger.)

William Steiner
LADY LIES, THE(1929), ph; FAST AND LOOSE(1930), ph; HEADS UP(1930), ph; QUEEN HIGH(1930), ph; ROADHOUSE NIGHTS(1930), ph; HIS WOMAN(1931), ph; NIGHT ANGEL, THE(1931), ph; WAYWARD(1932), ph; HOTEL VARIETY(1933), ph; TAKE A CHANCE(1933), ph; AMBUSH VALLEY(1936), p; RETURN OF SHERLOCK HOLMES(1936), ph; MIDDLETON FAMILY AT THE N.Y. WORLD'S FAIR(1939), ph; WHISPERING CITY(1947, Can.), ph; SINS OF THE FATHERS(1948, Can.), ph; WINDOW, THE(1949), ph; TATTOOED STRANGER, THE(1950), ph
Silents
POISON(1924), p; SURGING SEAS(1924), p

William Steiner, Jr.
RETURN OF SHERLOCK HOLMES(1936), ph
Silents
SOUTH OF NORTHERN LIGHTS(1922), ph

William O. Steiner, Sr.
TWO TICKETS TO PARIS(1962), ph

Alex Steinert
STRANGLER OF THE SWAMP(1945), md

Alexander Steinert
DEVIL BAT'S DAUGHTER, THE(1946), m; DON RICARDO RETURNS(1946), m; LITTLE IODINE(1946), m; TOO YOUNG TO KISS(1951); BECAUSE YOU'RE MINE(1952)

Anni Steinert
WEREWOLF IN A GIRL'S DORMITORY(1961, Ital./Aust.)

Edward Steinfeld
GOING HOME(1971)

Jake Steinfeld
HOME SWEET HOME(1981)

Dave Steingard
PAPERBACK HERO(1973, Can.)

Bjarni Steingrimsson
OUTLAW: THE SAGE OF GISLI(1982, Iceland)

Wolfgang Steinhardt
DANIELLA BY NIGHT(1962, Fr/Ger.), w

Tony Steinhart
WALK PROUD(1979)

Steve Steinhauer
COME BACK BABY(1968)

Bruce Steinhemmer
1984
ALL OF ME(1984), spec eff

Budd Steinhilber
FUNNYMAN(1967)

Hans Steinhoff
Misc. Silents
THREE KINGS, THE(1929, Brit.), d

Ninon Steinhoff
THREEPENNY OPERA, THE(1931, Ger./U.S.), w

Don Steinhouse
GOIN' DOWN THE ROAD(1970, Can.)

Frank Steininger
HIT AND RUN(1957), m, md

Franz Steininger
BORN TO BE LOVED(1959), m; PARADISE ALLEY(1962), m; STAGECOACH TO DANCER'S PARK(1962), m

Fred Steinkamp
MARRIAGE OF A YOUNG STOCKBROKER, THE(1971), ed; HIDE IN PLAIN SIGHT(1980), ed

Fredric Steinkamp
ADVENTURES OF HUCKLEBERRY FINN, THE(1960), ed; WHERE THE BOYS ARE(1960), ed; TWO LOVES(1961), ed; ALL FALL DOWN(1962), ed; PERIOD OF ADJUSTMENT(1962), ed; IT HAPPENED AT THE WORLD'S FAIR(1963), ed; SUNDAY IN NEW YORK(1963), ed; QUICK, BEFORE IT MELTS(1964), ed; UNSINKABLE MOLLY BROWN, THE(1964), ed; ONCE A THIEF(1965), ed; DUEL AT DIABLO(1966), ed; GRAND PRIX(1966), ed; MISTER BUDDWING(1966), ed; DOCTOR, YOU'VE GOT TO BE KIDDING(1967), ed; CHARLY(1968), ed; EXTRAORDINARY SEAMAN, THE(1969), ed; THEY SHOOT HORSES, DON'T THEY?(1969), ed; STRAWBERRY STATEMENT, THE(1970), ed; NEW LEAF, A(1971), ed; FREEBIE AND THE BEAN(1974), ed; THREE DAYS OF THE CONDOR(1975), ed; YAKUZA, THE(1975, U.S./Jap.), ed; BOBBY DEERFIELD(1977), ed; TOOTSIE(1982), ed
1984
AGAINST ALL ODDS(1984), ed

William Steinkamp
HIDE IN PLAIN SIGHT(1980), ed; KING OF THE MOUNTAIN(1981), ed; TOOTSIE(1982), ed
1984
AGAINST ALL ODDS(1984), ed

Hans Steinke
DECEPTION(1933); ISLAND OF LOST SOULS(1933); PEOPLE WILL TALK(1935); RECKLESS(1935); ONCE IN A BLUE MOON(1936); NOTHING SACRED(1937)

Michael Steinke
JOURNEYS FROM BERLIN-1971(1980), ph

Frederic Steinkemp
MIDAS RUN(1969), ed

Jim Steinman
AMERICATHON(1979), m; SMALL CIRCLE OF FRIENDS, A(1980), m

Anna Steinmann
GERMAN SISTERS, THE(1982, Ger.)

Danny Steinmann
1984
SAVAGE STREETS(1984), d, w

Herbert R. Steinmann
LOVE AND ANARCHY(1974, Ital.), p

Shawn Steinmann
WHAT'S THE MATTER WITH HELEN?(1971)

Wilbert Steinmann
GERMAN SISTERS, THE(1982, Ger.)
Bill Steinmetz
CALIFORNIA SUITE(1978)
Dennis Steinmetz
RECORD CITY(1978), d
Herbert Steinmetz
EFFI BRIEST(1974, Ger.); LOLA(1982, Ger.); VERONIKA VOSS(1982, Ger.)
Hans Steinoff
Silents
ALLEY CAT, THE(1929, Brit.), d
Albert Steinruck
Silents
GOLEM: HOW HE CAME INTO THE WORLD, THE(1920, Ger.); DECAMERON NIGHTS(1924, Brit.)
Misc. Silents
GOLEM, THE(1914, Ger.)
Albert Steinrueck
CRIMSON CIRCLE, THE(1930, Brit.)
Misc. Silents
AT THE EDGE OF THE WORLD(1929, Ger.)
Annemarie Steinsieck
ARIANE(1931, Ger.)
Lieselotte Steinweg
DECISION BEFORE DAWN(1951)
Walter Steinweg
FINAL CHORD, THE(1936, Ger.)
Vaclav Stekl
ROCKET TO NOWHERE(1962, Czech.); LEMONADE JOE(1966, Czech.)
Shirley Stelfox
CORRUPTION(1968, Brit.)
1984
1984(1984, Brit.)
Stelita
BORN TO BE WILD(1938); STARLIGHT OVER TEXAS(1938)
Aaron Stell
COWBOY IN THE CLOUDS(1943), ed; COWBOY FROM LONESOME RIVER(1944), ed; CYCLONE PRAIRIE RANGERS(1944), ed; SHE'S A SOLDIER TOO(1944), ed; SUNDOWN VALLEY(1944), ed; SWING IN THE SADDLE(1944), ed; BOSTON BLACKIE'S RENDEZVOUS(1945), ed; I LOVE A MYSTERY(1945), ed; OUTLAWS OF THE ROCKIES(1945), ed; PRISON SHIP(1945), ed; SNAFU(1945), ed; BLONDIE KNOWS BEST(1946), ed; BLONDIE'S LUCKY DAY(1946), ed; IT'S GREAT TO BE YOUNG(1946), ed; SINGIN' IN THE CORN(1946), ed; LAST ROUND-UP, THE(1947), ed; MILLIE'S DAUGHTER(1947), ed; SPORT OF KINGS(1947), ed; JUNGLE JIM(1948), ed; LOADED PISTOLS(1948), ed; SIGN OF THE RAM, THE(1948), ed; SONG OF IDAHO(1948), ed; LOST TRIBE, THE(1949), ed; RIDERS OF THE WHIS-TLING PINES(1949), ed; RIM OF THE CANYON(1949), ed; BEAUTY ON PARA-DE(1950), ed; CHAIN GANG(1950), ed; COUNTERSPY MEETS SCOTLAND YARD(1950), ed; CUSTOMS AGENT(1950), ed; ON THE ISLE OF SAMOA(1950), ed; PALOMINO, THE(1950), ed; ROOKIE FIREMAN(1950), ed; TOUGHER THEY COME, THE(1950), ed; BAREFOOT MAILMAN, THE(1951), ed; BIG GUSHER, THE(1951), ed; CHAIN OF CIRCUMSTANCE(1951), ed; GASOLINE ALLEY(1951), ed; BRAVE WAR-RIOR(1952), ed; EIGHT IRON MEN(1952), ed; SNIPER, THE(1952), ed; YANK IN INDO-CHINA, A(1952), ed; AMBUSH AT TOMAHAWK GAP(1953), ed; JACK MCCALL, DESPERADO(1953), ed; JUGGLER, THE(1953), ed; BLACK DAKOTAS, THE(1954), ed; LAW VS. BILLY THE KID, THE(1954), ed; MASSACRE CA-NYON(1954), ed; OUTLAW STALLION, THE(1954), ed; CREATURE WITH THE ATOM BRAIN(1955), ed; DEVIL GODDESS(1955), ed; HELL'S HORIZON(1955), ed; BOLD AND THE BRAVE, THE(1956), ed; FEAR STRIKES OUT(1957), ed; FIVE STEPS TO DANGER(1957), ed; TIME LIMIT(1957), ed; PROUD REBEL, THE(1958), ed; TARZAN'S FIGHT FOR LIFE(1958), ed; TOUCH OF EVIL(1958), ed; GIANT GILA MONSTER, THE(1959), ed; MY DOG, BUDDY(1960), ed; WAKE ME WHEN IT'S OVER(1960), ed; SECRET WAYS, THE(1961), ed; SIX BLACK HORSES(1962), ed; TO KILL A MOCKINGBIRD(1962), ed; LOVE WITH THE PROPER STRANGER(1963), ed; GALLANT ONE, THE(1964, U.S./Peru), p, d&w; BABY, THE RAIN MUST FALL(1965), ed; INSIDE DAISY CLOVER(1965), ed; NOT WITH MY WIFE, YOU DON'T(1966), ed; WELCOME TO HARD TIMES(1967), ed; FLAREUP(1969), ed; STALKING MOON, THE(1969), ed; GRASSHOPPER, THE(1970), ed; SILENT RUN-NING(1972), ed; TRIAL OF THE CATONSVILLE NINE, THE(1972), ed; WILLIE DYNAMITE(1973), ed; YOUR THREE MINUTES ARE UP(1973), ed; TAKE, THE(1974), ed; CORNBREAD, EARL AND ME(1975), ed; LEPKE(1975, U.S./Israel), ed; KILLER INSIDE ME, THE(1976), ed
G. Calderon Stell
NIGHT OF THE BLOODY APES(1968, Mex.), p
William C. Stell
ROBOT VS. THE AZTEC MUMMY, THE(1965, Mex.), w, p
William Calderon Stell [Guillermo Calderon]
DOCTOR OF DOOM(1962, Mex.), p; CURSE OF THE AZTEC MUMMY, THE(1965, Mex.), p&w; CURSE OF THE DOLL PEOPLE, THE(1968, Mex.), p
Stella
OUTSIDER, THE(1940, Brit.)
Enrico Stella
CRAZY DESIRE(1964, Ital.), w
Ruth Stella
HARLOW(1965), cos; WILL PENNY(1968), cos
Carolyn Stellar
CRY BLOOD, APACHE(1970)
Dawn Stellar
CRY BLOOD, APACHE(1970)
James Stellar
BIG FOOT(1973)
Gian Stellari
CAESAR THE CONQUEROR(1963, Ital.), m; FURY OF THE PAGANS(1963, Ital.), m
Vernon Stelle
Misc. Silents
STUBBORNESS OF GERALDINE, THE(1915)
Katie Stelletello
1984
PREPPIES(1984)

Jean Stelli
IT HAPPENED IN GIBRALTAR(1943, Fr.), w; BLUE VEIL, THE(1947, Fr.), d
Stellina
ALONE IN THE STREETS(1956, Ital.)
William Stelling
HELL IN THE HEAVENS(1934); DEVIL'S SQUADRON(1936); WOMAN I LOVE, THE(1937); BORDER G-MAN(1938); GONE WITH THE WIND(1939); WUTHERING HEIGHTS(1939); FLIGHT COMMAND(1940); FOREIGN CORRESPONDENT(1940); TRIAL OF MARY DUGAN, THE(1941); GHOST AND MRS. MUIR, THE(1942); NIGHT WIND(1948); THIRTEEN LEAD SOLDIERS(1948); GREEK TYCOON, THE(1978)
Martin Stellman
QUADROPHENIA(1979, Brit.), w; BABYLON(1980, Brit.), w
Michael Stellman
WASTREL, THE(1963, Ital.)
Al Stellone
CARWASH(1976)
Carol Stellson
Misc. Silents
UNDINE(1916)
John Stelly
SOUTHERN COMFORT(1981)
Jiri Stelmar
BOHEMIAN RAPTURE(1948, Czech)
Arthur Steloff
CITY OF FEAR(1965, Brit.), p
Skip Steloff
CODE 7, VICTIM 5(1964, Brit.), p; SHARK(1970, U.S./Mex.), p; ISLAND OF DR. MOREAU, THE(1977), p
Donna Stelzer
SHE-DEVILS ON WHEELS(1968)
Hannes Stelzer
DREAMER, THE(1936, Ger.)
John Stember
7254(1971), d
Elisabeth Stemberger
APRIL 1, 2000(1953, Aust.)
R.A. Stemmle
DESIRE(1936), w; MAN WHO WAS SHERLOCK HOLMES, THE(1937, Ger.), w; AFFAIR BLUM, THE(1949, Ger.), w; TOXI(1952, Ger.), d, w; CONFESS DR. COR-DA(1960, Ger.), w; ALMOST ANGELS(1962), w
Robert A. Stemmle
MAD EXECUTIONERS, THE(1965, Ger.), w; TERROR OF DR. MABUSE, THE(1965, Ger.), w; MONSTER OF LONDON CITY, THE(1967, Ger.), w; OLD SHATTER-HAND(1968, Ger./Yugo./Fr./Ital.), w
Robert Adolf Stemmle
DREAMER, THE(1936, Ger.), w
Emil Stemmler
BANG, BANG, YOU'RE DEAD(1966)
Kyra Stempel
1984
WOMAN IN RED, THE(1984)
Sten
JONAH–WHO WILL BE 25 IN THE YEAR 2000(1976, Switz.)
Anna Sten
BOMBARDMENT OF MONTE CARLO, THE(1931, Ger.); KARAMAZOV(1931, Ger.); TEMPEST(1932, Ger.); TRAPEZE(1932, Ger.); NANA(1934); WE LIVE AGAIN(1934); WEDDING NIGHT, THE(1935); TWO WHO DARED(1937, Brit.); EXILE EX-PRESS(1939); MAN I MARRIED, THE(1940); SO ENDS OUR NIGHT(1941); CHET-NIKS(1943); THEY CAME TO BLOW UP AMERICA(1943); THREE RUSSIAN GIRLS(1943); LET'S LIVE A LITTLE(1948); SOLDIER OF FORTUNE(1955); RUNA-WAY DAUGHTERS(1957); NUN AND THE SERGEANT, THE(1962)
Misc. Silents
GIRL WITH THE HAT-BOX(1927, USSR); WHITE EAGLE, THE(1928, USSR)
Birgitta Stenberg
JUST ONCE MORE(1963, Swed.), w
Per Lillo Stenberg
PASSIONATE DEMONS, THE(1962, Norway)
A. Stenbock-Fermor
FIRST SPACESHIP ON VENUS(1960, Ger./Pol.), w
Helen Stenborg
THREE DAYS OF THE CONDOR(1975); EUROPEANS, THE(1979, Brit.); STARTING OVER(1979)
1984
FLASH OF GREEN, A(1984)
Kathleen Stendal
CLOSE TO MY HEART(1951)
Monica Stender
$(DOLLARS) (1971)
Stendhal
LOVERS OF TOLEDO, THE(1954, Fr./Span./Ital.), w; RED AND THE BLACK, THE(1954, Fr./Ital.), w; DE L'AMOUR(1968, Fr./Ital.), w
Walka Stenermann
SEVEN FACES(1929)
Count Stenfenelli
ZIEGFELD FOLLIES(1945)
Christian Stengel
CRIME AND PUNISHMENT(1935, Fr.), w
Leni Stengel
HALF SHOT AT SUNRISE(1930); ROYAL BOX, THE(1930); BEAU IDEAL(1931); BELOVED BACHELOR, THE(1931); CRACKED NUTS(1931); HUSBAND'S HOLI-DAY(1931); JUST A GIGOLO(1931); ROAD TO RENO(1931); ANIMAL KINGDOM, THE(1932); HOLLYWOOD SPEAKS(1932); MAN ABOUT TOWN(1932); BARBARIAN, THE(1933)
Norman Stengel
MAN WHO BROKE THE BANK AT MONTE CARLO, THE(1935)
Mack Stenger
FALL GUY(1947), ph

Mack Stengier
ADVENTURES OF KITTY O'DAY(1944), ph
Jack Stengler
Silents
ONE HOUR OF LOVE(1927), ph
Mack Stengler
BORDER LEGION, THE(1930), ph; HELL HARBOR(1930), ph; ONE-MAN LAW(1932), ph; CAPTAIN CALAMITY(1936), ph; YELLOW CARGO(1936), ph; BANK ALARM(1937), ph; GOLD RACKET, THE(1937), ph; LOVE TAKES FLIGHT(1937), ph; NAVY SPY(1937), ph; WE'RE IN THE LEGION NOW(1937), ph; SONGS AND BULLETS(1938), ph; TERROR OF TINY TOWN, THE(1938), ph; KNIGHT OF THE PLAINS(1939), ph; RIDE 'EM COWGIRL(1939), ph; SINGING COWGIRL, THE(1939), ph; WATER RUSTLERS(1939), ph; DANGER AHEAD(1940), ph; YUKON FLIGHT(1940), ph; CAUGHT IN THE ACT(1941), ph; GAMBLING DAUGHTERS(1941), ph; GANG'S ALL HERE(1941), ph; KING OF THE ZOMBIES(1941), ph; LET'S GO COLLEGIATE(1941), ph; REG'LAR FELLERS(1941), ph; SOUTH OF PANAMA(1941), ph; SUNSET MURDER CASE(1941), ph; TOP SERGEANT MULLIGAN(1941), ph; BOWERY AT MIDNIGHT(1942), ph; DUKE OF THE NAVY(1942), ph; FOREIGN AGENT(1942), ph; LIVING GHOST, THE(1942), ph; LURE OF THE ISLANDS(1942), ph; MEET THE MOB(1942), ph; 'NEATH BROOKLYN BRIDGE(1942), ph; POLICE BULLETS(1942), ph; SMART ALECKS(1942), ph; APE MAN, THE(1943), ph; CAMPUS RYTHM(1943), ph; CLANCY STREET BOYS(1943), ph; KID DYNAMITE(1943), ph; MELODY PARADE(1943), ph; MYSTERY OF THE 13TH GUEST, THE(1943), ph; NEARLY EIGHTEEN(1943), ph; REVENGE OF THE ZOMBIES(1943), ph; RHYTHM PARADE(1943), ph; SARONG GIRL(1943), ph; SILVER SKATES(1943), ph; SMART GUY(1943), ph; SPOTLIGHT SCANDALS(1943), ph; SPY TRAIN(1943), ph; WHERE ARE YOUR CHILDREN?(1943), ph; WINGS OVER THE PACIFIC(1943), ph; WOMEN IN BONDAGE(1943), ph; ALASKA(1944), ph; ARMY WIVES(1944), ph; LADY, LET'S DANCE(1944), ph; OH, WHAT A NIGHT(1944), ph; SONG FOR MISS JULIE, A(1945), ph; WHY GIRLS LEAVE HOME(1945), ph; DEVIL'S PLAYGROUND, THE(1946), ph; FOOL'S GOLD(1946), ph; UNEXPECTED GUEST(1946), ph; DANGEROUS VENTURE(1947), ph; HOPPY'S HOLIDAY(1947), ph; MARAUDERS, THE(1947), ph; SARGE GOES TO COLLEGE(1947), ph; ARGYLE SECRETS, THE(1948), ph; BORROWED TROUBLE(1948), ph; CAMPUS SLEUTH(1948), ph; DEAD DON'T DREAM, THE(1948), ph; GAY INTRUDERS(1948), ph; I WOULDN'T BE IN YOUR SHOES(1948), ph; JUNGLE PATROL(1948), ph; LET'S LIVE AGAIN(1948), ph; SILENT CONFLICT(1948), ph; SINISTER JOURNEY(1948), ph; SMART POLITICS(1948), ph; STRANGE GAMBLE(1948), ph; JOE PALOOKA IN THE BIG FIGHT(1949), ph
Silents
COLLEGE DAYS(1926), ph; JOSSELYN'S WIFE(1926), ph; SILVER COMES THROUGH(1927), ph; KIT CARSON(1928), ph; PIONEER SCOUT, THE(1928), ph; SUNSET LEGION, THE(1928), ph
Mark Stengler
HIRED WIFE(1934), ph; FALSE PARADISE(1948), ph
Max Stengler
FRECKLES COMES HOME(1942), ph; LAW OF THE JUNGLE(1942), ph; GHOSTS ON THE LOOSE(1943), ph
Katherine Stenholm
RED RUNS THE RIVER(1963), d
Misc. Talkies
MACBETH(1950), d
Antonella Steni
TIGER AND THE PUSSYCAT, THE(1967, U.S., Ital.)
Jack Stenlino
B. F.'S DAUGHTER(1948)
Sue Stenmark
NORMAN LOVES ROSE(1982, Aus.)
Ingrid Stenn
THEY WERE SO YOUNG(1955)
Roy Stennard
GOOD LUCK, MISS WYCKOFF(1979), set d
Bob Stenner
CANNONBALL RUN, THE(1981)
Arthur Stenning
TOWER OF LONDON(1939); GUY NAMED JOE, A(1943); PEARL OF DEATH, THE(1944)
Steno
NERO'S MISTRESS(1962, Ital.), d; PSYCOSISSIMO(1962, Ital.), d, w; TWO COLONELS, THE(1963, Ital.), d; DAY IN COURT, A(1965, Ital.), d; GIRL GAME(1968, Braz./Fr./Ital.), d
Stefano Steno
TOTO IN THE MOON(1957, Ital./Span.), d, w; UNFAITHFULS, THE(1960, Ital.), d, w
Glenn Stensel
GUN HAWK, THE(1963); SWINGIN' SUMMER, A(1965)
Yutte Stensgaard
SOME GIRLS DO(1969, Brit.); DOCTOR IN TROUBLE(1970, Brit.); SCREAM AND SCREAM AGAIN(1970, Brit.); THIS, THAT AND THE OTHER(1970, Brit.); BUTTERCUP CHAIN, THE(1971, Brit.); LUST FOR A VAMPIRE(1971, Brit.)
Misc. Talkies
ZETA ONE(1969)
Melanie Stensland
WRONG IS RIGHT(1982)
Peter Stenson
HAUNTING OF M, THE(1979)
Anders Stenstedt
1984
HOT DOG...THE MOVIE(1984)
Akan Stensvold
COUNTRY BOY(1966), ph
Alan Stensvold
AIR STRIKE(1955), ph; SUNDOWN RIDERS(1948), ph; AFFAIR IN HAVANA(1957), ph; THUNDER ROAD(1958), ph; SATURDAY NIGHT IN APPLE VALLEY(1965), ph; DIMENSION 5(1966), ph; IT'S A BIKINI WORLD(1967), ph; TRACK OF THUNDER(1967), ph; DESTRUCTORS, THE(1968), ph; MONEY JUNGLE, THE(1968), ph; PANIC IN THE CITY(1968), ph; PRIVATE NAVY OF SGT. O'FARRELL, THE(1968), ph; GIRL WHO KNEW TOO MUCH, THE(1969), ph; TIGER BY THE TAIL(1970), ph; CHANDLER(1971), ph; CLAY PIGEON(1971), ph

1984
INVISIBLE STRANGLER(1984), ph
Allen Stensvold
PLEASE MURDER ME(1956), ph
Alan Stenvold
EIGHT ON THE LAM(1967), ph
The Step Brothers
HI, BUDDY(1943); IT AIN'T HAY(1943); RHYTHM OF THE ISLANDS(1943); PATSY, THE(1964)
Elisabeth Stepanek
1984
GERMANY PALE MOTHER(1984, Ger.)
Karel Stepanek
AT DAWN WE DIE(1943, Brit.); ESCAPE TO DANGER(1943, Brit.); SECRET MISSION(1944, Brit.); THEY MET IN THE DARK(1945, Brit.); COUNTER BLAST(1948, Brit.); DEVIL'S PLOT, THE(1948, Brit.); CONSPIRATOR(1949, Brit.); FALLEN IDOL, THE(1949, Brit.); CAIRO ROAD(1950, Brit.); GREAT MANHUNT, THE(1951, Brit.); NO HIGHWAY IN THE SKY(1951, Brit.); THIRD VISITOR, THE(1951, Brit.); AFFAIR IN TRINIDAD(1952); WALK EAST ON BEACON(1952); CITY BENEATH THE SEA(1953); GAY ADVENTURE, THE(1953, Brit.); NEVER LET ME GO(1953, U.S./Brit.); SHOOT FIRST(1953, Brit.); DANGEROUS CARGO(1954, Brit.); TALE OF THREE WOMEN, A(1954, Brit.); COCKLESHELL HEROES, THE(1955); MAN OF THE MOMENT(1955, Brit.); PRIZE OF GOLD, A(1955); SECRET VENTURE(1955, Brit.); ANASTASIA(1956); FIGHTING WILDCATS, THE(1957, Brit.); MAN IN THE ROAD, THE(1957, Brit.); ACCURSED, THE(1958, Brit.); I AIM AT THE STARS(1960); OUR MAN IN HAVANA(1960, Brit.); SINK THE BISMARCK!(1960, Brit.); THREE MOVES TO FREEDOM(1960, Ger.); BRAINWASHED(1961, Ger.); DEVIL DOLL(1964, Brit.); HEROES OF TELEMARK, THE(1965, Brit.); OPERATION CROSSBOW(1965, U.S./Ital.); SECOND BEST SECRET AGENT IN THE WHOLE WIDE WORLD, THE(1965, Brit.); TERROR AFTER MIDNIGHT(1965, Ger.); FROZEN DEAD, THE(1967, Brit.); BEFORE WINTER COMES(1969, Brit.); FILE OF THE GOLDEN GOOSE, THE(1969, Brit.); GAMES, THE(1970)
Karl Stepanek
JAZZBAND FIVE, THE(1932, Ger,); CAPTIVE HEART, THE(1948, Brit.)
Lilly Stepanek
VIENNA WALTZES(1961, Aust.)
Zdenek Stepanek
MERRY WIVES, THE(1940, Czech.), a, w; SKELETON ON HORSEBACK(1940, Czech.); EMPEROR AND THE GOLEM, THE(1955, Czech.); TRANSPORT FROM PARADISE(1967, Czech.)
Count Stepanelli
HOUSE OF A THOUSAND CANDLES, THE(1936)
Jana Stepankova
DEATH OF TARZAN, THE(1968, Czech)
I. Stepanov
ROAD TO LIFE(1932, USSR), art d
L. Stepanov
LADY WITH THE DOG, THE(1962, USSR)
M. Stepanov
COSSACKS OF THE DON(1932, USSR)
V. Stepanov
LAD FROM OUR TOWN(1941, USSR); THREE SISTERS, THE(1969, USSR)
A. Stepanova
WAR AND PEACE(1968, USSR)
Aram Stephan
GERVAISE(1956, Fr.); LOVE IS A BALL(1963); 55 DAYS AT PEKING(1963); BEDTIME STORY(1964); MY BABY IS BLACK!(1965, Fr.)
Bruno Stephan
GREH(1962, Ger./Yugo.), ph
Ruth Stephan
TURKISH CUCUMBER, THE(1963, Ger.)
Nicole Stephane
LES ENFANTS TERRIBLES(1952, Fr.); CARVE HER NAME WITH PRIDE(1958, Brit.); LA VIE DE CHATEAU(1967, Fr.), p; OTHER ONE, THE(1967,Fr.), p; DESTROY, SHE SAID(1969, Fr.), p
Stephane Grappelly and his Quintet
FLAMINGO AFFAIR, THE(1948, Brit.)
Frederick Stephani
FIFTEEN WIVES(1934), w; FLASH GORDON(1936), d, w; BEG, BORROW OR STEAL(1937), p; BETWEEN TWO WOMEN(1937), w; LOVE IS NEWS(1937), w; WE HAVE OUR MOMENTS(1937), w; FAST COMPANY(1938), p; LOVE IS A HEADACHE(1938), p; FAST AND FURIOUS(1939), p; FAST AND LOOSE(1939), p; AND ONE WAS BEAUTIFUL, THE(1940), p; CAPTAIN IS A LADY, THE(1940), p; GALLANT SONS(1940), p; PHANTOM RAIDERS(1940), p; SKY MURDER(1940), p; BORN TO SING(1942), p; TARZAN'S NEW YORK ADVENTURE(1942), p; SWEET ROSIE O'-GRADY(1943), w; SHE WENT TO THE RACES(1945), p; IT HAPPENED ON 5TH AVENUE(1947), w; SOFIA(1948), w; THAT WONDERFUL URGE(1948), w; JOHNNY HOLIDAY(1949), w; FORT ALGIERS(1953), w; TWO GROOMS FOR A BRIDE(1957), w
Nick Stephanini
WISE GUYS(1969, Fr./Ital.)
Tony Stephano
REINCARNATION OF PETER PROUD, THE(1975); TRON(1982)
Blagoe Stephanoff
WUTHERING HEIGHTS(1939), makeup; MY FOOLISH HEART(1949), makeup
Blague Stephanoff
EDGE OF DOOM(1950), makeup
Bob Stephanoff
LADY OF BURLESQUE(1943), makeup
Robert Stephanoff
SONG IS BORN, A(1948), makeup
Robert Stephanott
SINCE YOU WENT AWAY(1944), makeup
A. Stephanov
1812(1944, USSR)
Harvey Stephans
STAGECOACH WAR(1940)

Roy Stephens
DURING ONE NIGHT(1962, Brit.); DR. STRANGELOVE: OR HOW I LEARNED TO STOP WORRYING AND LOVE THE BOMB(1964); UP FROM THE BEACH(1965); WHERE THE BULLETS FLY(1966, Brit.); ISADORA(1968, Brit.); TORTURE GARDEN(1968, Brit.)

Sally Stephens
EIGHT O'CLOCK WALK(1954, Brit.); BABY LOVE(1969, Brit.)

Sheila Stephens
BACKFIRE(1950); PRETTY BABY(1950)

Socorro Stephens
CLAUDINE(1974)

Sonia Stephens
TASTE OF HONEY, A(1962, Brit.)

Stephanie Stephens
Silents
FLYING FIFTY-FIVE, THE(1924, Brit.)
Misc. Silents
TRAINER AND THE TEMPTRESS(1925, Brit.)

Tennyson Stephens
STONY ISLAND(1978)

Valdo Stephens
LUM AND ABNER ABROAD(1956)

Vi Stephens
LISA(1962, Brit.); LUNCH HOUR(1962, Brit.)

Vicki Stephens
CALIFORNIA SUITE(1978)

William Stephens
MEET DR. CHRISTIAN(1939), p; COURAGEOUS DR. CHRISTIAN, THE(1940), p; DR. CHRISTIAN MEETS THE WOMEN(1940), p; MELODY FOR THREE(1941), p; REMEDY FOR RICHES(1941), p; THEY MEET AGAIN(1941), p; RETURN OF RIN TIN TIN, THE(1947), p, w; HIGHWAY 13(1948), p; JUNGLE GODDESS(1948), p; ARSON, INC.(1949), p; DEPUTY MARSHAL(1949), p; SKY LINER(1949), p; THUNDER IN THE PINES(1949), p

Carl Stephenson
NAKED JUNGLE, THE(1953), w

Charles Stephenson
INQUEST(1939, Brit.)

Dale Stephenson
D.C. CAB(1983)

David I. Stephenson
COBRA STRIKES, THE(1948), p

David L. Stephenson
IN THIS CORNER(1948), p

Edward Stephenson
DIVORCE AMERICAN STYLE(1967), prod d

Florence Stephenson
CIRCUS BOY(1947, Brit.)

Geoffrey Stephenson
BRIDE, THE(1973), ph
1984
BREED APART, A(1984), ph

George Stephenson
CIRCUS BOY(1947, Brit.)

Hayden Stephenson
WOMAN TRAP(1936)

Henry Stephenson
ANIMAL KINGDOM, THE(1932); BILL OF DIVORCEMENT, A(1932); CYNARA(1932); GUILTY AS HELL(1932); RED HEADED WOMAN(1932); BLIND ADVENTURE(1933); DOUBLE HARNESS(1933); IF I WERE FREE(1933); LITTLE WOMEN(1933); MY LIPS BETRAY(1933); TOMORROW AT SEVEN(1933); ALL MEN ARE ENEMIES(1934); MAN OF TWO WORLDS(1934); MYSTERY OF MR. X, THE(1934); ONE MORE RIVER(1934); OUTCAST LADY(1934); RICHEST GIRL IN THE WORLD, THE(1934); SHE LOVES ME NOT(1934); STINGAREE(1934); THIRTY-DAY PRINCESS(1934); WHAT EVERY WOMAN KNOWS(1934); CAPTAIN BLOOD(1935); FLAME WITHIN, THE(1935); MUTINY ON THE BOUNTY(1935); NIGHT IS YOUNG, THE(1935); O'SHAUGHNESSY'S BOY(1935); PERFECT GENTLEMAN, THE(1935); RECKLESS(1935); RENDEZVOUS(1935); VANESSA, HER LOVE STORY(1935); BELOVED ENEMY(1936); CHARGE OF THE LIGHT BRIGADE, THE(1936); GIVE ME YOUR HEART(1936); HALF ANGEL(1936); HEARTS DIVIDED(1936); LITTLE LORD FAUNTLEROY(1936); WALKING ON AIR(1936); CONQUEST(1937); EMPEROR'S CANDLESTICKS, THE(1937); PRINCE AND THE PAUPER, THE(1937); WHEN YOU'RE IN LOVE(1937); WISE GIRL(1937); BARONESS AND THE BUTLER, THE(1938); DRAMATIC SCHOOL(1938); MARIE ANTOINETTE(1938); SUEZ(1938); YOUNG IN HEART, THE(1938); ADVENTURES OF SHERLOCK HOLMES, THE(1939); PRIVATE LIVES OF ELIZABETH AND ESSEX, THE(1939); TARZAN FINDS A SON!(1939); DOWN ARGENTINE WAY(1940); IT'S A DATE(1940); LITTLE OLD NEW YORK(1940); SPRING PARADE(1940); LADY FROM LOUISIANA(1941); MAN WHO LOST HIMSELF, THE(1941); HALF WAY TO SHANGHAI(1942); RINGS ON HER FINGERS(1942); THIS ABOVE ALL(1942); MANTRAP, THE(1943); MR. LUCKY(1943); HOUR BEFORE THE DAWN, THE(1944); RECKLESS AGE(1944); SECRETS OF SCOTLAND YARD(1944); TWO GIRLS AND A SAILOR(1944); TARZAN AND THE AMAZONS(1945); GREEN YEARS, THE(1946); HEARTBEAT(1946); HER SISTER'S SECRET(1946); LOCKET, THE(1946); NIGHT AND DAY(1946); OF HUMAN BONDAGE(1946); RETURN OF MONTE CRISTO, THE(1946); DARK DELUSION(1947); HOMESTRETCH, THE(1947); IVY(1947); SONG OF LOVE(1947); TIME OUT OF MIND(1947); ENCHANTMENT(1948); JULIA MISBEHAVES(1948); CHALLENGE TO LASSIE(1949); OLIVER TWIST(1951, Brit.)
Silents
SPREADING DAWN, THE(1917)
Misc. Silents
TOWER OF JEWELS, THE(1920); BLACK PANTHER'S CUB, THE(1921); MEN AND WOMEN(1925); WILD, WILD SUSAN(1925)

James Stephenson
MAN WHO MADE DIAMONDS, THE(1937, Brit.); PERFECT CRIME, THE(1937, Brit.); TAKE IT FROM ME(1937, Brit.); YOU LIVE AND LEARN(1937, Brit.); BOY MEETS GIRL(1938); COWBOY FROM BROOKLYN(1938); DARK STAIRWAY, THE(1938, Brit.); HEART OF THE NORTH(1938); IT'S IN THE BLOOD(1938, Brit.); MR. SATAN(1938, Brit.); NANCY DREW–DETECTIVE(1938); TORCHY BLANE IN CHINATOWN(1938); WHEN WERE YOU BORN?(1938); WHITE BANNERS(1938); ADVENTURES OF JANE ARDEN(1939); BEAU GESTE(1939); CONFESSIONS OF A NAZI SPY(1939); ESPIONAGE AGENT(1939); KING OF THE UNDERWORLD(1939); OLD MAID, THE(1939); ON TRIAL(1939); PRIVATE LIVES OF ELIZABETH AND ESSEX, THE(1939); SECRET SERVICE OF THE AIR(1939); WANTED BY SCOTLAND YARD(1939, Brit.); WE ARE NOT ALONE(1939); CALLING PHILO VANCE(1940); DEVIL'S ISLAND(1940); DISPATCH FROM REUTERS, A(1940); LETTER, THE(1940); MURDER IN THE AIR(1940); RIVER'S END(1940); SEA HAWK, THE(1940); SOUTH OF SUEZ(1940); WOLF OF NEW YORK(1940); FLIGHT FROM DESTINY(1941); INTERNATIONAL SQUADRON(1941); SHINING VICTORY(1941)

John Stephenson
I DIED A THOUSAND TIMES(1955); LOOTERS, THE(1955); TEENAGE REBEL(1956); CARELESS YEARS, THE(1957); NIGHT RUNNER, THE(1957); MAN CALLED FLINTSTONE, THE(1966); CHARLOTTE'S WEB(1973); AT LONG LAST LOVE(1975)

Leon Stephenson
1984
BEAT STREET(1984)

Maureen Stephenson
DANGEROUS MISSION(1954); FRENCH LINE, THE(1954); SON OF SINBAD(1955); WILD PARTY, THE(1956)

Pamela Stephenson
PRIVATE COLLECTION(1972, Aus.); STAND UP VIRGIN SOLDIERS(1977, Brit.); HISTORY OF THE WORLD, PART 1(1981); COMEBACK, THE(1982, Brit.); SUPERMAN III(1983)
1984
BLOODBATH AT THE HOUSE OF DEATH(1984, Brit.); FINDERS KEEPERS(1984); SCANDALOUS(1984)

Robert Stephenson
DESPERATE JOURNEY(1942); STATE DEPARTMENT–FILE 649(1949); TAKE ME OUT TO THE BALL GAME(1949); COPPER CANYON(1950); DAVID AND BATHSHEBA(1951); WILD NORTH, THE(1952); LOVE ME OR LEAVE ME(1955)

Robert R. Stephenson
CALCUTTA(1947); SHOCKPROOF(1949); CLOWN, THE(1953); I'LL CRY TOMORROW(1955); TARANTULA(1955)

Ross Stephenson
I'M GOING TO GET YOU ... ELLIOT BOY(1971, Can.)

Sandra Stephenson
MONEY AND THE WOMAN(1940)

Sarah Stephenson
BLEAK MOMENTS(1972, Brit.)

Sheila Stephenson
SEX AND THE SINGLE GIRL(1964); HOW TO STUFF A WILD BIKINI(1965)

Shelagh Stephenson
1984
WINTER FLIGHT(1984, Brit.)

I. Stepnaov
UNIVERSITY OF LIFE(1941, USSR), art d

Chuck Stepney
THAT'S THE WAY OF THE WORLD(1975)

Barbara Stepniakowna
YOUNG GIRLS OF WILKO, THE(1979, Pol./Fr.)

Jirina Stepnickova
TRANSPORT FROM PARADISE(1967, Czech.)

Jarema Stepowski
EVE WANTS TO SLEEP(1961, Pol.); PORTRAIT OF LENIN(1967, Pol./USSR)

Ilse Steppat
MARRIAGE IN THE SHADOWS(1948, Ger.); RATS, THE(1955, Ger.); CONFESSIONS OF FELIX KRULL, THE(1957, Ger.); EIGHTH DAY OF THE WEEK, THE(1959, Pol./Ger.); INVISIBLE MAN, THE(1963, Ger.); ON HER MAJESTY'S SECRET SERVICE(1969, Brit.)

Leila Steppe
DAD AND DAVE COME TO TOWN(1938, Aus.)

Steppenwolf
CANDY(1968, Ital./Fr.)

John Stepping
Silents
GAY OLD BIRD, THE(1927)

Minnie Steppler
Silents
LITTLE WILD GIRL, THE(1928), ed; OLD AGE HANDICAP(1928), ed; GIRLS WHO DARE(1929), ed

Carl Steppling
GUN RUNNER(1969); ANGELS DIE HARD(1970)

John Steppling
Silents
DAMAGED GOODS(1915); CUPID BY PROXY(1918); GOOD NIGHT, PAUL(1918); DIVORCE TRAP, THE(1919); INFERIOR SEX, THE(1920); BLACK BEAUTY(1921); HUNCH, THE(1921); NOBODY'S KID(1921); SILVER CAR, THE(1921); TOO MUCH BUSINESS(1922); ABRAHAM LINCOLN(1924); RECKLESS AGE, THE(1924); EVE'S LOVER(1925); MEMORY LANE(1926); BY WHOSE HAND?(1927); CALIFORNIA OR BUST(1927); WEDDING BILL$(1927)
Misc. Silents
MISS JACKIE OF THE NAVY(1916); BUTTERFLY GIRL, THE(1917); GIRL WHO COULDN'T GROW UP, THE(1917); RESCUING ANGEL, THE(1919); MADAME PEACOCK(1920); SICK ABED(1920); GARMENTS OF YOUTH(1921); SIN FLOOD, THE(1922); BELL BOY 13(1923); BETTER MAN, THE(1926); COLLEGIATE(1926)

Sammy Stept
DANCING FEET(1936), m

Zoreta Steptoe
MR. WASHINGTON GOES TO TOWN(1941)

F. Stepun
FATHER OF A SOLDIER(1966, USSR)
David Sterago
HARRY'S WAR(1981)
Robert Sterbini
SQUEEZE, THE(1980, Ital.), ed
Roberto Sterbini
KILLER FISH(1979, Ital./Braz.), ed
Pierre Sterckx
MAMMA DRACULA(1980, Bel./Fr.), w
Jaroslav Stercl
LEMONADE JOE(1966, Czech.)
Anthony Stergar
SACCO AND VANZETTI(1971, Ital./Fr.)
Erich Stering
GLADIATORS, THE(1970, Swed.)
Jeanette Sterke
LUST FOR LIFE(1956); LIVE NOW–PAY LATER(1962, Brit.)
Jeannette Sterke
FINAL COLUMN, THE(1955, Brit.); PRISONER, THE(1955, Brit.); SAFECRACKER, THE(1958, Brit.); NUN'S STORY, THE(1959, Brit.); DOUBLE, THE(1963, Brit); STITCH IN TIME, A(1967, Brit.); MOMENTS(1974, Brit.)
John Sterland
MAN OUTSIDE, THE(1968, Brit.); TOUCH OF CLASS, A(1973, Brit.)
Hermine Sterler
RASPUTIN(1932, Ger.); DR. EHRLICH'S MAGIC BULLET(1940); MY SON IS GUILTY(1940); JENNIE(1941); SHINING VICTORY(1941); KING'S ROW(1942); NAZI AGENT(1942); SECRET AGENT OF JAPAN(1942); THIS GUN FOR HIRE(1942); RENEGADES(1946); GOLDEN EARRINGS(1947); RAILROADED(1947); LETTER FROM AN UNKNOWN WOMAN(1948); THERE'S ALWAYS TOMORROW(1956)
Misc. Silents
STRAUSS, THE WALTZ KING(1929, Ger.)
Hermone Sterler
HOW TO MARRY A MILLIONAIRE(1953)
Anne Sterling
BLUEBEARD(1944); BOWERY CHAMPS(1944)
Arleen Sterling
RIVERRUN(1968), cos
Barbara Sterling
OCEAN'S ELEVEN(1960)
Dick Sterling
HOW DO I LOVE THEE?(1970)
Edythe Sterling
Silents
NANCY'S BIRTHRIGHT(1916); ARIZONA CATCLAW, THE(1919); GIRL WHO DARED, THE(1920)
Misc. Silents
IN THE WEB OF THE GRAFTERS(1916); STAIN IN THE BLOOD, THE(1916); SECRET MAN, THE(1917); ONE-WAY TRAIL, THE(1920); STRANGER IN CANYON VALLEY, THE(1921); DANGER(1923)
Elaine Sterling
JULIA MISBEHAVES(1948); NEPTUNE'S DAUGHTER(1949)
Ford Sterling
FALL OF EVE, THE(1929); GIRL IN THE SHOW, THE(1929); SALLY(1929); BRIDE OF THE REGIMENT(1930); KISMET(1930); SHOW GIRL IN HOLLYWOOD(1930); SPRING IS HERE(1930); HER MAJESTY LOVE(1931); BEHIND GREEN LIGHTS(1935); BLACK SHEEP(1935); HEADLINE WOMAN, THE(1935)
Silents
STRANGER'S BANQUET(1922); HE WHO GETS SLAPPED(1924); SO BIG(1924); AMERICAN VENUS, THE(1926); GOOD AND NAUGHTY(1926); MIKE(1926); MISS BREWSTER'S MILLIONS(1926); CASEY AT THE BAT(1927); GENTLEMEN PREFER BLONDES(1928); OH, KAY(1928); SPORTING GOODS(1928); WIFE SAVERS(1928)
Misc. Silents
LOVE, HONOR AND BEHAVE(1920); MARRIED LIFE(1920); OH, MABEL BEHAVE(1922), a, d; DESTROYING ANGEL, THE(1923); GALLOPING FISH(1924); LOVE AND GLORY(1924); WILD ORANGES(1924); STEPPIN' OUT(1925); TROUBLE WITH WIVES, THE(1925); EVERYBODY'S ACTING(1926); ROAD TO GLORY, THE(1926); SHOW OFF, THE(1926); STRANDED IN PARIS(1926); DRUMS OF THE DESERT(1927); FIGURES DON'T LIE(1927); FOR THE LOVE OF MIKE(1927); CHICKEN A LA KING(1928)
Gayle Sterling
Misc. Talkies
SIMPLY IRRESISTIBLE(1983)
Georgie Sterling
RANGLE RIVER(1939, Aus.); THAT CERTAIN SOMETHING(1941, Aus.)
Harriet Sterling
Silents
WILDERNESS WOMAN, THE(1926)
Jack Sterling
CAPTAINS COURAGEOUS(1937); O.S.S.(1946); GIRL WHO HAD EVERYTHING, THE(1953); SHANE(1953)
Jan Sterling
JOHNNY BELINDA(1948); CAGED(1950); MYSTERY STREET(1950); SKIPPER SURPRISED HIS WIFE, THE(1950); UNION STATION(1950); APPOINTMENT WITH DANGER(1951); BIG CARNIVAL, THE(1951); MATING SEASON, THE(1951); RHUBARB(1951); FLESH AND FURY(1952); SKY FULL OF MOON(1952); PONY EXPRESS(1953); SPLIT SECOND(1953); VANQUISHED, THE(1953); ALASKA SEAS(1954); HIGH AND THE MIGHTY, THE(1954); HUMAN JUNGLE, THE(1954); RETURN FROM THE SEA(1954); FEMALE ON THE BEACH(1955); MAN WITH THE GUN(1955); WOMEN'S PRISON(1955); HARDER THEY FALL, THE(1956); 1984(1956, Brit.); SLAUGHTER ON TENTH AVENUE(1957); FEMALE ANIMAL, THE(1958); HIGH SCHOOL CONFIDENTIAL(1958); KATHY O'(1958); LOVE IN A GOLDFISH BOWL(1961); INCIDENT, THE(1967); ANGRY BREED, THE(1969); MINX, THE(1969); FIRST MONDAY IN OCTOBER(1981)
Misc. Talkies
SAMMY SOMEBODY(1976)
Jane Sterling
GARDEN OF EDEN(1954)

Joann Sterling
Misc. Talkies
BLUE SUMMER(1973)
John Sterling
MURDER IN EDEN(1962, Brit.); LAST OF THE SECRET AGENTS?, THE(1966); REVENGE OF THE CHEERLEADERS(1976), m
Joseph Sterling
GHOSTS OF BERKELEY SQUARE(1947, Brit.), ed; GREEN FINGERS(1947), ed; TIGHT LITTLE ISLAND(1949, Brit.), ed; OPERATION CONSPIRACY(1957, Brit.), d
Jude Sterling
CONTRABAND LOVE(1931, Brit.)
Leigh Sterling
PILOT NO. 5(1943)
Lewis Sterling
TOMB OF THE UNDEAD(1972)
Linda Sterling
POWERS GIRL, THE(1942)
Marie Sterling
Misc. Silents
OGRE AND THE GIRL, THE(1915); GREAT DIVIDE, THE(1916); SORROWS OF HAPPINESS(1916)
Myrta Sterling
Misc. Silents
SAGE-BRUSH LEAGUE, THE(1919)
Pamela Sterling
THEY ARE NOT ANGELS(1948, Fr.); LOST PEOPLE, THE(1950, Brit.)
Paul Sterling
Misc. Silents
MYSTERY OF EDWIN DROOD, THE(1914)
Phil Sterling
DETECTIVE, THE(1968); ME, NATALIE(1969)
Philip Sterling
GANG THAT COULDN'T SHOOT STRAIGHT, THE(1971); GAMBLER, THE(1974); AUDREY ROSE(1977); METEOR(1979); PROMISES IN THE DARK(1979); COMPETITION, THE(1980)
Richard Sterling
Silents
RAMONA(1916)
Misc. Silents
MADCAP, THE(1916); STORM, THE(1916)
Robert Sterling
BLONDIE BRINGS UP BABY(1939); BLONDIE MEETS THE BOSS(1939); FIRST OFFENDERS(1939); GOLDEN BOY(1939); GOOD GIRLS GO TO PARIS(1939); GAY CABALLERO, THE(1940); MANHATTAN HEARTBEAT(1940); MY SON IS GUILTY(1940); YESTERDAY'S HEROES(1940); DR. KILDARE'S VICTORY(1941); GETAWAY, THE(1941); I'LL WAIT FOR YOU(1941); PENALTY, THE(1941); RINGSIDE MAISIE(1941); TWO-FACED WOMAN(1941); JOHNNY EAGER(1942); SOMEWHERE I'LL FIND YOU(1942); THIS TIME FOR KEEPS(1942); SECRET HEART, THE(1946); ROUGHSHOD(1949); BUNCO SQUAD(1950); SUNDOWNERS, THE(1950); SHOW BOAT(1951); COLUMN SOUTH(1953); RETURN TO PEYTON PLACE(1961); VOYAGE TO THE BOTTOM OF THE SEA(1961); GLOBAL AFFAIR, A(1964)
Stewart Sterling
HAVING WONDERFUL CRIME(1945), w
Thomas Sterling
HONEY POT, THE(1967, Brit.), w
Tisha Sterling
VILLAGE OF THE GIANTS(1965); COOGAN'S BLUFF(1968); JOURNEY TO SHILOH(1968); NAME OF THE GAME IS KILL, THE(1968); BIG DADDY(1969); NORWOOD(1970); WILD PACK, THE(1972); KILLER INSIDE ME, THE(1976)
Misc. Talkies
COMING, THE(1983)
Todd Sterling
STUNT PILOT(1939)
Trish Sterling
CRAZY MAMA(1975)
William Sterling
DOOMED TO DIE(1940); ALICE'S ADVENTURES IN WONDERLAND(1972, Brit.), d&w
Dominick Sterlini
CONCERNING MR. MARTIN(1937, Brit.); JENIFER HALE(1937, Brit.); I SEE ICE(1938); LAST BARRICADE, THE(1938, Brit.)
John Sterlini
CATTLE ANNIE AND LITTLE BRITCHES(1981)
Jimmy Sterman
LURE OF THE JUNGLE, THE(1970, Den.)
Misc. Talkies
BOY OF TWO WORLDS(1970)
Maurice Sterman
1984
GARBO TALKS(1984)
Adam Stern
COMPETITION, THE(1980)
Albert Stern
SECRETS OF A CO-ED(1942), p
Alex Stern
DEAD AND BURIED(1981), w
Alfred Stern
BOMBS OVER BURMA(1942), p; RANGERS TAKE OVER, THE(1942), p; BAD MEN OF THUNDER GAP(1943), p; BORDER BUCKAROOS(1943), p; FIGHTING VALLEY(1943), p; GHOST AND THE GUEST(1943), p; LADY FROM CHUNGKING(1943), p; WEST OF TEXAS(1943), p; BOSS OF THE RAWHIDE(1944), p; MEN ON HER MIND(1944), p; PINTO BANDIT, THE(1944), p; SEVEN DOORS TO DEATH(1944), p; TRAIL OF TERROR(1944), p; LADY CONFESSES, THE(1945), p; MASK OF DIIJON, THE(1946), p; QUEEN OF BURLESQUE(1946), p; SECRETS OF A SORORITY GIRL(1946), p
Annelise Stern
WILD, WILD PLANET, THE(1967, Ital.)

Bernadette Stern
THERESE AND ISABELLE(1968, U.S./Ger.)
Bibiane Stern
SUNDAYS AND CYBELE(1962, Fr.)
Bill Stern
PRIDE OF THE YANKEES, THE(1942); STAGE DOOR CANTEEN(1943); WE'VE NEVER BEEN LICKED(1943); HERE COME THE CO-EDS(1945); SPIRIT OF WEST POINT, THE(1947); GO, MAN, GO!(1954)
Dan Stern
SMALL CIRCLE OF FRIENDS, A(1980)
Daniel Stern
BREAKING AWAY(1979); STARTING OVER(1979); IT'S MY TURN(1980); ONE-TRICK PONY(1980); STARDUST MEMORIES(1980); HONKY TONK FREE-WAY(1981); DINER(1982); I'M DANCING AS FAST AS I CAN(1982); BLUE THUN-DER(1983); GET CRAZY(1983)
1984
C.H.U.D.(1984)
David Stern
FRANCIS(1949), w; FRANCIS GOES TO THE RACES(1951), w; RHUBARB(1951), w; FRANCIS GOES TO WEST POINT(1952), w; FRANCIS COVERS THE BIG TOWN(1953), w; FRANCIS JOINS THE WACS(1954), w; FRANCIS IN THE NA-VY(1955), w; FRANCIS IN THE HAUNTED HOUSE(1956), w; SWAMP WO-MEN(1956), w; O LUCKY MAN!(1973, Brit.)
Don Stern
WIRE SERVICE(1942), ed; DOUBLE STOP(1968), ed
Eddie Stern
OLD MOTHER RILEY, DETECTIVE(1943, Brit.)
Elizabeth Stern
1984
DELIVERY BOYS(1984)
Ellen Stern
DUCHESS AND THE DIRTWATER FOX, THE(1976); JESSIE'S GIRLS(1976)
Emile Stern
MARRY ME! MARRY ME!(1969, Fr.), m
Eric Stern
GARDEN OF THE DEAD(1972)
Erik Stern
LOVE BUTCHER, THE(1982); WARGAMES(1983)
Prof. Ernest Stern
DOLLY GETS AHEAD(1931, Ger.), cos
Ernst Stern
MOZART(1940, Brit.), cos
Eva Stern
VIOLATORS, THE(1957)
G. B. Stern
LONG LOST FATHER(1934), w; MEN ARE NOT GODS(1937, Brit.), w; WOMAN IN THE HALL, THE(1949, Brit.), w
George Stern
GAL WHO TOOK THE WEST, THE(1949); BARRICADE(1950); ROGUE RIVER(1951)
Gladys Bronwyn Stern
UGLY DACHSHUND, THE(1966), w
Gordon Stern
LIBEL(1959, Brit.)
H. George Stern
MY SIX CONVICTS(1952)
Hans Stern
LONG JOHN SILVER(1954, Aus.)
Helmut Stern
LUDWIG(1973, Ital./Ger./Fr.)
Isaac Stern
TONIGHT WE SING(1953)
Jack Stern
CRIMINAL LAWYER(1937), m
Jake Stern
FEEDBACK(1979), m
Joe Stern
HOME TO DANGER(1951, Brit.); LORDS OF FLATBUSH, THE(1974)
Joseph Stern
HERO AT LARGE(1980)
Jozef Stern
GOLEM, THE(1937, Czech./Fr.), p
Kandy Stern
MAX DUGAN RETURNS(1983), set d; TWO OF A KIND(1983), set d
Kimberly Stern
RENT CONTROL(1981); LITTLE SEX, A(1982)
Leonard Stern
ABBOTT AND COSTELLO IN THE FOREIGN LEGION(1950), w; MA AND PA KETTLE GO TO TOWN(1950), w; MILKMAN, THE(1950), w; LOST IN ALASKA(1952), w; MA AND PA KETTLE AT THE FAIR(1952), w; OKINAWA(1952), w; JAZZ SINGER, THE(1953), w; THREE FOR THE SHOW(1955), w; JUST YOU AND ME, KID(1979), d, w
Leonard B. Stern
NUDE BOMB, THE(1980), w
Louis Stern
IN OLD CALIFORNIA(1929)
Silents
EYE FOR EYE(1918); GREAT SHADOW, THE(1920); RIDDLE: WOMAN, THE(1920); WEDDING BILL$(1927); WHERE EAST IS EAST(1929)
Marcel Stern
THUNDER IN THE BLOOD(1962, Fr.), m
Murray Stern
BORN TO WIN(1971), art d
Murray P. Stern
PANIC IN NEEDLE PARK(1971), art d
Otto Stern
IS PARIS BURNING?(1966, U.S./Fr.)
Paul Stern
HERO(1982, Brit.), m

Silents
MANHATTAN COWBOY(1928), ph
Rene Stern
LILIOM(1935, Fr.); COLONEL CHABERT(1947, Fr.)
Richard Stern
TWELVE HOURS TO KILL(1960), w
Robert Victor Stern
FEAR STRIKES OUT(1957)
Sandor Stern
AMITYVILLE HORROR, THE(1979), w; FAST BREAK(1979), w
Sol Stern
COTTON COMES TO HARLEM(1970), spec eff
Steven H. Stern
Misc. Talkies
I WONDER WHO'S KILLING HER NOW?(1975), d
Steven Hillard Stern
B.S. I LOVE YOU(1971), d&w; NEITHER BY DAY NOR BY NIGHT(1972, U.S./Israel), d, w; HARRAD SUMMER, THE(1974), d; RUNNING(1979, Can.), d&w; DEVIL AND MAX DEVLIN, THE(1981), d
Stewart Stern
TERESA(1951), w; REBEL WITHOUT A CAUSE(1955), w; RACK, THE(1956), w; THUNDER IN THE SUN(1959), w; OUTSIDER, THE(1962), w; UGLY AMERICAN, THE(1963), w; RACHEL, RACHEL(1968), w; LAST MOVIE, THE(1971), w; SUMMER WISHES, WINTER DREAMS(1973), w
Theodore Stern
WORM EATERS, THE(1981), m
Tim Stern
VICTOR/VICTORIA(1982)
Tom Stern
HALLELUJAH TRAIL, THE(1965); SPY WHO CAME IN FROM THE COLD, THE(1965, Brit.); YOU'VE GOT TO BE SMART(1967); ANGELS FROM HELL(1968); DEVIL'S BRIGADE, THE(1968); HELL'S ANGELS '69(1969), a, p, w; CLAY PI-GEON(1971), a, p&d; ENTITY, THE(1982)
Toni Stern
LAST MOVIE, THE(1971)
Tony Stern
YANKS ARE COMING, THE(1942), w
Wes Stern
FIRST TIME, THE(1969); UP IN THE CELLAR(1970)
Willy Stern
HERO AT LARGE(1980)
Joseph Sternad
UP IN MABEL'S ROOM(1944), art d; GETTING GERTIE'S GARTER(1945), art d
Rudolph Sternad
MESSAGE TO GARCIA, A(1936), art d; POOR LITTLE RICH GIRL(1936), art d; FIFTY ROADS TO TOWN(1937), art d; LOVE IS NEWS(1937), art d; LOVE UNDER FIRE(1937), art d; THIS IS MY AFFAIR(1937), art d; FOUR MEN AND A PRAYER(1938), art d; IN OLD CHICAGO(1938), art d; SALLY, IRENE AND MA-RY(1938), art d; SUEZ(1938), art d; ROSE OF WASHINGTON SQUARE(1939), art d; TAIL SPIN(1939), art d; LITTLE OLD NEW YORK(1940), art d; YOUNG PEO-PLE(1940), art d; ADAM HAD FOUR SONS(1941), art; YOU'LL NEVER GET RICH(1941), art d; LADY IS WILLING, THE(1942), art d; TALK OF THE TOWN(1942), art d; YOU WERE NEVER LOVELIER(1942), art d; FIRST COMES COURAGE(1943), art d; MORE THE MERRIER, THE(1943), art d; MR. WINKLE GOES TO WAR(1944), art d; OVER 21(1945), art d; THOUSAND AND ONE NIGHTS, A(1945), art d; TONIGHT AND EVERY NIGHT(1945), art d; BANDIT OF SHERWOOD FOREST, THE(1946), art d; PERILOUS HOLIDAY(1946), art d; DEAD RECKONING(1947), art d; DOWN TO EARTH(1947), art d; IT HAD TO BE YOU(1947), art d; PORT SAID(1948), art d; RETURN OF OCTOBER, THE(1948), art d; WALK A CROOKED MILE(1948), art d; HOME OF THE BRAVE(1949), art d; KISS FOR CORLISS, A(1949), art d; DAVY CROCKETT, INDIAN SCOUT(1950), art d; MEN, THE(1950), prod d; THREE HUS-BANDS(1950), art d; SCARF, THE(1951), art d; DEATH OF A SALESMAN(1952), prod d; FOUR POSTER, THE(1952), prod d; HIGH NOON(1952), prod d; SNIPER, THE(1952), prod d; WILD ONE, THE(1953), prod d; 5,000 FINGERS OF DR. T. THE(1953), prod d; NOT AS A STRANGER(1955), prod d; PRIDE AND THE PASSION, THE(1957), prod d; DEFIANT ONES, THE(1958), prod d; ON THE BEACH(1959), prod d; INHERIT THE WIND(1960), prod d, art d; JUDGMENT AT NUREMBERG(1961), prod d; PRESSURE POINT(1962), prod d; CHILD IS WAITING, A(1963), prod d; IT'S A MAD, MAD, MAD, MAD WORLD(1963), prod d; LADY IN A CAGE(1964), prod d
Rudy Sternad
FOOL KILLER, THE(1965), art d
Bert Sternbach
QUEEN OF BROADWAY(1942), p; KID RIDES AGAIN, THE(1943), p; CONTEND-ER, THE(1944), p
Hans Sternberg
BECAUSE I LOVED YOU(1930, Ger.)
Jacques Sternberg
JE T'AIME, JE T'AIME(1972, Fr./Swed.), w
Kurt Sternberg
SHADOWED EYES(1939, Brit.), p; TILLY OF BLOOMSBURY(1940, Brit.), p
Richard Sternberg
EDDY DUCHIN STORY, THE(1956)
Tom Sternberg
BLACK STALLION, THE(1979), p; BLACK STALLION RETURNS, THE(1983), p
Joan Sterndale
WE DIVE AT DAWN(1943, Brit.)
Martin Sterndale
TWO-HEADED SPY, THE(1959, Brit.); OPERATION CUPID(1960, Brit.); TOO HOT TO HANDLE(1961, Brit.); JUNGLE STREET GIRLS(1963, Brit.)
Joan Sterndale-Bennett
TAWNY PIPIT(1947, Brit.); POET'S PUB(1949, Brit.); NO HAUNT FOR A GENTLE-MAN(1952, Brit.); SPIDER'S WEB, THE(1960, Brit.); WHY BOTHER TO KNOCK(1964, Brit.); THOSE FANTASTIC FLYING FOOLS(1967, Brit); DECLINE AND FALL... OF A BIRD WATCHER(1969, Brit.); ALL AT SEA(1970, Brit.)
David Sterne
SINBAD AND THE EYE OF THE TIGER(1977, U.S./Brit.); VENOM(1982, Brit.)
Elaine Sterne
Silents
WITHOUT HOPE(1914), w; SINS OF THE MOTHERS(1915), w; PRIDE OF THE CLAN, THE(1917), w; ON THE BANKS OF THE WABASH(1923), w

Gordon Sterne
FLOODS OF FEAR(1958, Brit.); CHILD AND THE KILLER, THE(1959, Brit.); MURDER AT SITE THREE(1959, Brit.); MILLIONAIRESS, THE(1960, Brit.); FUR COLLAR, THE(1962, Brit.); GREAT VAN ROBBERY, THE(1963, Brit.); V.I.P.s, THE(1963, Brit.); VULTURE, THE(1967, U.S./Brit./Can.); ADDING MACHINE, THE(1969); ASSASSINATION BUREAU, THE(1969); CHAIRMAN, THE(1969); MOSQUITO SQUADRON(1970, Brit.); THIS, THAT AND THE OTHER(1970, Brit.); AMERICAN WEREWOLF IN LONDON, AN(1981)
1984
RAZOR'S EDGE, THE(1984)

Joe Sterne
PASSING STRANGER, THE(1954, Brit.)

Morgan Sterne
NO EXIT(1962, U.S./Arg.); NINE MILES TO NOON(1963); LEARNING TREE, THE(1969); TODD KILLINGS, THE(1971); CAREY TREATMENT, THE(1972)

Richard Sterne
HAMLET(1964)

John W. Sterner
INCREDIBLE PETRIFIED WORLD, THE(1959), w

Roland Sterner
ADVENTURES OF PICASSO, THE(1980, Swed.), ph

Sterner Sisters
NIGHT AT EARL CARROLL'S, A(1940)

Frances Sternhagen
TIGER MAKES OUT, THE(1967); UP THE DOWN STAIRCASE(1967); HOSPITAL, THE(1971); TWO PEOPLE(1973); FEDORA(1978, Ger./Fr.); STARTING OVER(1979); OUTLAND(1981); INDEPENDENCE DAY(1983); ROMANTIC COMEDY(1983)

Jenny Sternling
BRONCO BILLY(1980)

Vincent Sternroyd
PRICE OF THINGS, THE(1930, Brit.); HOWARD CASE, THE(1936, Brit.); PRISONER OF CORBAL(1939, Brit.)

Joseph Sterns
Silents
NO WOMAN KNOWS(1921)

Michael Sterns
BATTLE FOR THE PLANET OF THE APES(1973); HARRY IN YOUR POCKET(1973)

Speed Sterns
STEEL ARENA(1973); BOBBIE JO AND THE OUTLAW(1976), stunts

Jiri Sternwald
TRANSPORT FROM PARADISE(1967, Czech.), m; SIGN OF THE VIRGIN(1969, Czech.), m

Ugo Sterpini
WEEKEND MURDERS, THE(1972, Ital.), art d

Mr. Sterr
WHY DOES HERR R. RUN AMOK?(1977, Ger.)

Mrs. Sterr
WHY DOES HERR R. RUN AMOK?(1977, Ger.)

Walter Sterret
Silents
INVADERS, THE(1929), w; OKLAHOMA KID, THE(1929), w

Charles Sterrett
UNDERWORLD U.S.A.(1961)

Wiske Sterringa
LIFT, THE(1983, Neth.)

Gertrude Sterroll
HIS GRACE GIVES NOTICE(1933, Brit.); SHE WAS ONLY A VILLAGE MAIDEN(1933, Brit.)
Silents
CALL OF YOUTH, THE(1920, Brit.); GLORIOUS ADVENTURE, THE(1922, U.S./Brit.); DAUGHTER IN REVOLT, A(1927, Brit.)

Benno Sterzenbach
FREDDY UNTER FREMDEN STERNEN(1962, Ger.); DON'T LOOK NOW(1969, Brit./Fr.)

Sophie Stesart
CITY OF BEAUTIFUL NONSENSE, THE(1935, Brit.)

Adrea Stetaro
DEVIL IS A WOMAN, THE(1935), m

Al Stetson
MIDNIGHT COWBOY(1969)

Muriel Stetson
HERE COME THE CO-EDS(1945)

Richard Stetson
HARD ROAD, THE(1970), w

Eldean Steuart
Silents
GLADIOLA(1915); EAST LYNNE(1916); ALIAS MRS. JESSOP(1917)
Misc. Silents
HINTON'S DOUBLE(1917); HUNGRY HEART, THE(1917)

Maurice Steuart
Misc. Silents
CHILD IN JUDGEMENT, A(1915)

Maury Steuart
Silents
FLAPPER, THE(1920)
Misc. Silents
BRIDGES BURNED(1917)

Carl Steuber
SNOW WHITE(1965, Ger.), m

Billy Steuer
TOLL OF THE DESERT(1936)

Max Steuer
COMMITTEE, THE(1968, Brit.), p, w

Robert Steuer
GARBAGE MAN, THE(1963), p

Helen Steusloff
MARYJANE(1968)

Bert Stevans
CLASH BY NIGHT(1952)

Norman Stevans
SWEET CHARITY(1969)

Bob Stevanson
GAL WHO TOOK THE WEST, THE(1949)

Wildman Steve
PETEY WHEATSTRAW(1978)

Steve Gibson's Redcaps
DESTINATION MURDER(1950)

Steve Miller Band
CAPTAIN MILKSHAKE(1970), m

Alex Steven
CLAUDINE(1974)

Carl Steven
1984
STAR TREK III: THE SEARCH FOR SPOCK(1984)

Geoff Steven
SKIN DEEP(1978, New Zealand), d, w

Gosta Steven
HONEYSUCKLE ROSE(1980), w

James Steven
Misc. Silents
CALL OF HIS PEOPLE, THE(1922)

Margaret Steven
LONELY HEARTS(1983, Aus.)

Daryl Stevenett
1984
KILLPOINT(1984), m

Diane Stevenett
1984
KILLPOINT(1984), p

Agnes Stevenin
HU-MAN(1975, Fr.)

Jean Francois Stevenin
VICTORY(1981)

Jean-Francois Stevenin
WILD CHILD, THE(1970, Fr.); DAY FOR NIGHT(1973, Fr.); SMALL CHANGE(1976, Fr.); MAIS OU ET DONC ORNICAR(1979, Fr.); DOGS OF WAR, THE(1980, Brit.); LIKE A TURTLE ON ITS BACK(1981, Fr.); PASSION(1983, Fr./Switz.); SNOW(1983, Fr.)
1984
FLIGHT TO BERLIN(1984, Ger./Brit.)

Dora Stevening
FORBIDDEN(1949, Brit.); LONG DARK HALL, THE(1951, Brit.)

A. Kenneth Stevens
BROADWAY(1942)

Alex Stevens
LADY IN CEMENT(1968); LOVELY WAY TO DIE, A(1968); HOUSE OF DARK SHADOWS(1970), stunts; PROJECTIONIST, THE(1970); NIGHT OF DARK SHADOWS(1971), d; LADY LIBERTY(1972, Ital./Fr.); SHAFT'S BIG SCORE(1972), stunts; SHAMUS(1973); AARON LOVES ANGELA(1975), a, stunts; GOD TOLD ME TO(1976); EYES OF LAURA MARS(1978), stunts; THEY ALL LAUGHED(1981); I, THE JURY(1982); LITTLE SEX, A(1982)
1984
ALPHABET CITY(1984)

Aline Stevens
PANIC IN THE STREETS(1950)

Alison Stevens
STARTING OVER(1979)

Andrew Stevens
LAS VEGAS LADY(1976); MASSACRE AT CENTRAL HIGH(1976); VIGILANTE FORCE(1976); DAY OF THE ANIMALS(1977); BOYS IN COMPANY C, THE(1978, U.S./Hong Kong); FURY, THE(1978); DEATH HUNT(1981); SEDUCTION, THE(1982); 10 TO MIDNIGHT(1983)

Angela Stevens
KID FROM BROKEN GUN, THE(1952); WITHOUT WARNING(1952); FROM HERE TO ETERNITY(1953); JACK MCCALL, DESPERADO(1953); MISSISSIPPI GAMBLER, THE(1953); SAVAGE MUTINY(1953); WILD ONE, THE(1953); CREATURE WITH THE ATOM BRAIN(1955); DEVIL GODDESS(1955); NAKED STREET, THE(1955); BLACK-JACK KETCHUM, DESPERADO(1956); SHADOW ON THE WINDOW, THE(1957); UTAH BLAINE(1957)

Anitra Stevens
JAZZ SINGER, THE(1953); EGYPTIAN. THE(1954)

Ann Stevens
THUNDER IN CAROLINA(1960)

Anthony Stevens
LIFE IN HER HANDS(1951, Brit.), w

Art Stevens
PETER PAN(1953), anim; ONE HUNDRED AND ONE DALMATIANS(1961), anim; ROBIN HOOD(1973), anim; RESCUERS, THE(1977), d; FOX AND THE HOUND, THE(1981), p, d

Arthur Stevens
CLUE OF THE MISSING APE, THE(1953, Brit.), ed; MIRACLE IN SOHO(1957, Brit.), ed; NIGHT AMBUSH(1958, Brit.), ed; VIOLENT PLAYGROUND(1958, Brit.), ed; SEA FURY(1959, Brit.), ed; OPERATION AMSTERDAM(1960, Brit.), ed; S.O.S. PACIFIC(1960, Brit.), ed; STOLEN PLANS, THE(1962, Brit.), ed

Babette Stevens
IRISHMAN, THE(1978, Aus.)

Bard Stevens
VON RYAN'S EXPRESS(1965); BUG(1975); SIXTH AND MAIN(1977)

Bee Stevens
GOLD DIGGERS OF 1933(1933)

Bernard Stevens
UPTURNED GLASS, THE(1947, Brit.), m; MARK OF CAIN, THE(1948, Brit.), m; MANIACS ON WHEELS(1951, Brit.), m

Bert Stevens
FOREST RANGERS, THE(1942); LAS VEGAS STORY, THE(1952); TITANIC(1953); DESIREE(1954); WOMAN'S WORLD(1954)

Bill Stevens
LONE TEXAS RANGER(1945); OLD MOTHER RILEY, HEADMISTRESS(1950, Brit.); COOL AND THE CRAZY, THE(1958); THIRD OF A MAN(1962); MURDER CAN BE DEADLY(1963, Brit.)

Bob Stevens
JOLSON STORY, THE(1946); ONE HUNDRED AND ONE DALMATIANS(1961); THERE'S ALWAYS VANILLA(1972)

Bobby Stevens
MY BLUE HEAVEN(1950)
Misc. Talkies
BLACK CONNECTION, THE(1974)

Boyd Stevens
I KNOW WHERE I'M GOING(1947, Brit.)

Branch Stevens
NANA(1934)

Brinke Stevens
SLUMBER PARTY MASSACRE, THE(1982)
1984
BODY DOUBLE(1984)

Burt Stevens
JOAN OF ARC(1948)

Byron Stevens
STAGE DOOR(1937); UNION PACIFIC(1939)

Carol Stevens
SABOTEUR(1942); GOOD SAM(1948); MAIDSTONE(1970)

Casey Stevens
PROM NIGHT(1980)

Cat Stevens
HAROLD AND MAUDE(1971), m

Cathy Stevens
SATAN'S BED(1965)

Cedric Stevens
UNDER YOUR SPELL(1936); FASHION MODEL(1945); FEAR(1946); DOUBLE LIFE, A(1947); SENATOR WAS INDISCREET, THE(1947)

Charles Stevens
IRON MASK, THE(1929); MYSTERIOUS DR. FU MANCHU, THE(1929); TAMING OF THE SHREW, THE(1929); VIRGINIAN, THE(1929); BIG TRAIL, THE(1930); TOM SAWYER(1930); CISCO KID(1931); CONQUERING HORDE, THE(1931); BROKEN WING, THE(1932); GOLDEN WEST, THE(1932); MYSTERY RANCH(1932); SOUTH OF THE RIO GRANDE(1932); STOKER, THE(1932); CALIFORNIA TRAIL, THE(1933); DRUM TAPS(1933); HERITAGE OF THE DESERT(1933); POLICE CALL(1933); WHEN STRANGERS MARRY(1933); TRUMPET BLOWS, THE(1934); VIVA VILLA!(1934); CALL OF THE WILD(1935); LIVES OF A BENGAL LANCER(1935); UNDER THE PAMPAS MOON(1935); BOLD CABALLERO(1936); HERE COMES TROUBLE(1936); LAST TRAIN FROM MADRID, THE(1937); SWING HIGH, SWING LOW(1937); CRIME OF DR. HALLET(1938); FORBIDDEN VALLEY(1938); RENEGADE RANGER(1938); TROPIC HOLIDAY(1938); DESPERATE TRAILS(1939); FRONTIER MARSHAL(1939); GIRL AND THE GAMBLER, THE(1939); MAN OF CONQUEST(1939); REAL GLORY, THE(1939); KIT CARSON(1940); MARK OF ZORRO, THE(1940); UNTAMED(1940); WAGONS WESTWARD(1940); BAD MAN, THE(1941); BLOOD AND SAND(1941); BEYOND THE BLUE HORIZON(1942); MANILA CALLING(1942); PIERRE OF THE PLAINS(1942); MARKED TRAILS(1944); MUMMY'S CURSE, THE(1944); SAN ANTONIO(1945); SOUTH OF THE RIO GRANDE(1945); BORDER BANDITS(1946); MY DARLING CLEMENTINE(1946); TANGIER(1946); BUFFALO BILL RIDES AGAIN(1947); CALCUTTA(1947); EXILE, THE(1947); HOMESTRETCH, THE(1947); RIDE THE PINK HORSE(1947); SINBAD THE SAILOR(1947); FEATHERED SERPENT, THE(1948); FURY AT FURNACE CREEK(1948); RETURN OF THE BADMEN(1948); SAIGON(1948); ROLL, THUNDER, ROLL(1949); WALKING HILLS, THE(1949); AMBUSH(1950); CALIFORNIA PASSAGE(1950); INDIAN TERRITORY(1950); SAVAGE HORDE, THE(1950); SHOWDOWN, THE(1950); OH! SUSANNA(1951); LION AND THE HORSE, THE(1952); SMOKY CANYON(1952); WAGONS WEST(1952); ESCAPE FROM FORT BRAVO(1953); JEOPARDY(1953); RIDE, VAQUERO!(1953); SAVAGE MUTINY(1953); JUBILEE TRAIL(1954); KILLER LEOPARD(1954); GREEN FIRE(1955); VANISHING AMERICAN, THE(1955); PARDNERS(1956); LAST TRAIN FROM GUN HILL(1959)
Silents
BIRTH OF A NATION, THE(1915); GOOD BAD MAN, THE(1916); AMERICANO, THE(1917); MAN FROM PAINTED POST, THE(1917); REACHING FOR THE MOON(1917); WILD AND WOOLLY(1917); MARK OF ZORRO(1920); MOLLYCODDLE, THE(1920); THREE MUSKETEERS, THE(1921); EMPTY HANDS(1924); THIEF OF BAGDAD, THE(1924); DON Q, SON OF ZORRO(1925); RECOMPENSE(1925); ACROSS THE PACIFIC(1926); BLACK PIRATE, THE(1926); KING OF KINGS, THE(1927); GAUCHO, THE(1928); STAND AND DELIVER(1928)
Misc. Silents
DIAMOND HANDCUFFS(1928)

Charley Stevens
OUTSIDER, THE(1962)

Charlie Stevens
FURY OF THE JUNGLE(1934); PLAINSMAN, THE(1937); TICKET TO TOMAHAWK(1950)

Charlotte Stevens
Silents
ONE LAW FOR THE WOMAN(1924); COWARD, THE(1927); ENCHANTED ISLAND, THE(1927)
Misc. Silents
MINE TO KEEP(1923); KING OF THE PACK(1926); MERRY CAVALIER, THE(1926); CANCELLED DEBT, THE(1927); IN A MOMENT OF TEMPTATION(1927); WHERE TRAILS BEGIN(1927); THUNDER RIDERS(1928)

Chuck Stevens
KING OF COMEDY, THE(1983)

Cindy Stevens
MAFIA GIRLS, THE(1969)

Clark Stevens
BUFFALO BILL RIDES AGAIN(1947); SQUARE DANCE JUBILEE(1949)

Clarke Stevens
GANGSTERS OF THE FRONTIER(1944); SUDAN(1945); SON OF BILLY THE KID(1949); DALTON'S WOMEN, THE(1950); HALLS OF MONTEZUMA(1951); THUNDERING TRAIL, THE(1951); VANISHING OUTPOST, THE(1951); BLACK LASH, THE(1952); FRONTIER PHANTOM, THE(1952)

Connie Stevens
YOUNG AND DANGEROUS(1957); DRAGSTRIP RIOT(1958); PARTY CRASHERS, THE(1958); ROCK-A-BYE BABY(1958); PARRISH(1961); SUSAN SLADE(1961); PALM SPRINGS WEEKEND(1963); NEVER TOO LATE(1965); TWO ON A GUILLOTINE(1965); WAY...WAY OUT(1966); GRISSOM GANG, THE(1971); SCORCHY(1976); SGT. PEPPER'S LONELY HEARTS CLUB BAND(1978); GREASE 2(1982)

Constance Stevens [Sally Gray]
SCHOOL FOR SCANDAL, THE(1930, Brit.)

Craig Stevens
MR. SMITH GOES TO WASHINGTON(1939); AFFECTIONATELY YOURS(1941); BODY DISAPPEARS, THE(1941); DIVE BOMBER(1941); LAW OF THE TROPICS(1941); STEEL AGAINST THE SKY(1941); HIDDEN HAND, THE(1942); SECRET ENEMIES(1942); SPY SHIP(1942); DOUGHGIRLS, THE(1944); HOLLYWOOD CANTEEN(1944); SINCE YOU WENT AWAY(1944); GOD IS MY CO-PILOT(1945); ROUGHLY SPEAKING(1945); TOO YOUNG TO KNOW(1945); HUMORESQUE(1946); MAN I LOVE, THE(1946); LOVE AND LEARN(1947); THAT WAY WITH WOMEN(1947); LADY TAKES A SAILOR, THE(1949); NIGHT UNTO NIGHT(1949); BLUES BUSTERS(1950); WHERE THE SIDEWALK ENDS(1950); DRUMS IN THE DEEP SOUTH(1951); KATIE DID IT(1951); LADY FROM TEXAS, THE(1951); PHONE CALL FROM A STRANGER(1952); MURDER WITHOUT TEARS(1953); ABBOTT AND COSTELLO MEET DR. JEKYLL AND MR. HYDE(1954); FRENCH LINE, THE(1954); DUEL ON THE MISSISSIPPI(1955); DEADLY MANTIS, THE(1957); BUCHANAN RIDES ALONE(1958); GUNN(1967); LIMBO LINE, THE(1969, Brit.); S.O.B.(1981); TROUT, THE(1982, Fr.)
Misc. Talkies
FROM THE DESK OF MARGARET TYDING(1958); CONDOR(1984)

Cy Stevens
LETTER FROM AN UNKNOWN WOMAN(1948); FOLLOW ME QUIETLY(1949); STRATTON STORY, THE(1949); SUN COMES UP, THE(1949); CLOWN, THE(1953)

David Stevens
BREAKER MORANT(1980, Aus.), w
Misc. Talkies
ROSES BLOOM TWICE(1977), d

Dennis F. Stevens
HARRAD EXPERIMENT, THE(1973), p; HARRAD SUMMER, THE(1974), p

Dick Stevens
Silents
PAYING THE LIMIT(1924)

Dodie Stevens
HOUND-DOG MAN(1959); ALAKAZAM THE GREAT!(1961, Jap.); CONVICTS FOUR(1962)

Dorinda Stevens
IT STARTED IN PARADISE(1952, Brit.); SCOTLAND YARD INSPECTOR(1952, Brit.); GOLDEN LINK, THE(1954, Brit.); HANDCUFFS, LONDON(1955, Brit.); DEADLIEST SIN, THE(1956, Brit.); NOT WANTED ON VOYAGE(1957, Brit.); HORRORS OF THE BLACK MUSEUM(1959, U.S./Brit.); JACK THE RIPPER(1959, Brit.); CARRY ON CONSTABLE(1960, Brit.); GENTLE TRAP, THE(1960, Brit.); MAKE MINE MINK(1960, Brit.); SHAKEDOWN, THE(1960, Brit.); HIS AND HERS(1961, Brit.); HAIR OF THE DOG(1962, Brit.); NIGHT WITHOUT PITY(1962, Brit.); ROOMMATES(1962, Brit.); OPERATION BULLSHINE(1963, Brit.); NIGHT TRAIN TO PARIS(1964, Brit.); VERDICT, THE(1964, Brit.)

Dorothy Stevens
MURDER WITH PICTURES(1936)

Edmond Stevens
FISH THAT SAVED PITTSBURGH, THE(1979), w

Edmund Stevens
Silents
SLIPPY MCGEE(1923)

Edwin Stevens
Silents
HAWTHORNE OF THE U.S.A.(1919); SAHARA(1919); CHARM SCHOOL, THE(1921); CRAZY TO MARRY(1921); ONE WILD WEEK(1921); STING OF THE LASH(1921); RAGGED HEIRESS, THE(1922); SPIDER AND THE ROSE, THE(1923); LOVER'S OATH, A(1925)
Misc. Silents
DEVIL'S TOY, THE(1916); HONOR OF MARY BLAKE, THE(1916), d; MAN INSIDE, THE(1916); BOY GIRL, THE(1917), d; SUSAN'S GENTLEMAN(1917), d; FAITH(1919); FORBIDDEN FIRE(1919); HOMEBREAKER, THE(1919); LONE WOLF'S DAUGHTER, THE(1919); PROFITEERS, THE(1919); UNPARDONABLE SIN, THE(1919); UPSTAIRS(1919); DUDS(1920); HER UNWILLING HUSBAND(1920); PASSION'S PLAYGROUND(1920); SEEING IT THROUGH(1920); EVERYTHING FOR SALE(1921); LITTLE MINISTER, THE(1921); SNOB, THE(1921); GOLDEN GALLOWS, THE(1922); HANDS OF NARA, THE(1922); VOICE FROM THE MINARET, THE(1923); WOMAN OF BRONZE, THE(1923)

Eileen Stevens
CAGED(1950); THIS WOMAN IS DANGEROUS(1952); PROBLEM GIRLS(1953); INVASION OF THE BODY SNATCHERS(1956); ATTACK OF THE 50 FOOT WOMAN(1958)

Eileene Stevens
RAINTREE COUNTY(1957); ESCAPE FROM RED ROCK(1958)

Elaine Stevens
BILLY LIAR(1963, Brit.)

Emilie Stevens
FUNNY FACE(1957)

Emily Stevens
Silents
ALIAS MRS. JESSOP(1917); OUTWITTED(1917); KILDARE OF STORM(1918)
Misc. Silents
CORA(1915); HOUSE OF TEARS, THE(1915); SOUL OF A WOMAN, THE(1915); WAGER, THE(1916); WHEEL OF THE LAW, THE(1916); SLACKER, THE(1917); SLEEPING MEMORY, A(1917); DAYBREAK(1918); MAN'S WORLD, A(1918); SACRED FLAME, THE(1919); PLACE OF THE HONEYMOONS, THE(1920)

Evan Stevens
WHEN THE LEGENDS DIE(1972)

Fisher Stevens
BURNING, THE(1981); BABY, IT'S YOU(1983)
1984
BROTHER FROM ANOTHER PLANET, THE(1984); FLAMINGO KID, THE(1984)

Ford Stevens
WEREWOLF, THE(1956)
Fran Stevens
GANG THAT COULDN'T SHOOT STRAIGHT, THE(1971); SILENT NIGHT, BLOODY NIGHT(1974)
Francis Stevens
GOOD SAM(1948); SUMMER HOLIDAY(1948)
Frank Stevens
G.I. HONEYMOON(1945)
Frederick Stevens
FRENCH LINE, THE(1954)
Geoffrey Stevens
PSYCH-OUT(1968)
George Stevens
COHENS AND KELLYS IN TROUBLE, THE(1933), d; ALICE ADAMS(1935), d; ANNIE OAKLEY(1935), d; KENTUCKY KERNELS(1935), d; LADDIE(1935), d; NIT-WITS, THE(1935), d; ACES AND EIGHTS(1936); SWING TIME(1936), d; DAMSEL IN DISTRESS, A(1937), d; QUALITY STREET(1937), d; VIVACIOUS LADY(1938), p&d; GUNGA DIN(1939), d; VIGIL IN THE NIGHT(1940), p&d; PENNY SERENADE(1941), p&d; TALK OF THE TOWN(1942), p&d; WOMAN OF THE YEAR(1942), d; MORE THE MERRIER, THE(1943), p&d; I REMEMBER MAMA(1948), p; PLACE IN THE SUN, A(1951), p&d; SOMETHING TO LIVE FOR(1952), p&d; SHANE(1953), p&d; GIANT(1956), p, d; DIARY OF ANNE FRANK, THE(1959), p&d; GREATEST STORY EVER TOLD, THE(1965), p&d, w; SYNDICATE, THE(1968, Brit.), ph; ONLY GAME IN TOWN, THE(1970), d
Silents
DR. JEKYLL AND MR. HYDE(1920); WHISPERS(1920); JAVA HEAD(1923); BLACK CYCLONE(1925), ph; DESERT'S TOLL, THE(1926), ph; NO MAN'S LAW(1927), ph
Misc. Silents
TRAIL OF THE LAW(1924)
Geroge Stevens
BACHELOR BAIT(1934), d
Gosta Stevens
COUNT OF THE MONK'S BRIDGE, THE(1934, Swed.), w; ON THE SUN-NYSIDE(1936, Swed.), w; INTERMEZZO(1937, Swed.), w; INTERMEZZO: A LOVE STORY(1939), w; ONLY ONE NIGHT(1942, Swed.), w
Grace Stevens
Silents
FLORIDA ENCHANTMENT, A(1914); MODERN CINDERELLA, A(1917); FAIR PRETENDER, THE(1918)
Harmon Stevens
FOLLOW THE SUN(1951); HAS ANYBODY SEEN MY GAL?(1952); MESA OF LOST WOMEN, THE(1956)
Harry Stevens
GUN FEVER(1958), w
Harvey Stevens
OMEN, THE(1976)
Helen Stevens
BUTTERFIELD 8(1960)
Helena Stevens
ADDING MACHINE, THE(1969); LORDS OF DISCIPLINE, THE(1983)
Housely Stevens
NATIVE LAND(1942)
Inger Stevens
MAN ON FIRE(1957); BUCCANEER, THE(1958); CRY TERROR(1958); WORLD, THE FLESH, AND THE DEVIL, THE(1959); NEW INTERNS, THE(1964); GUIDE FOR THE MARRIED MAN, A(1967); TIME FOR KILLING, A(1967); FIRECREEK(1968); FIVE CARD STUD(1968); HANG'EM HIGH(1968); MADIGAN(1968); DREAM OF KINGS, A(1969); HOUSE OF CARDS(1969)
Ira Stevens
LITTLE PRINCESS, THE(1939)
J. Stevens
CUCKOO CLOCK, THE(1938, Ital.), ph
Jack Stevens
PARDON US(1931), ph; GAY PURR-EE(1962), ph; PINK PANTHER, THE(1964), set d; WHAT DID YOU DO IN THE WAR, DADDY?(1966), set d; GUNN(1967), set d; WATERHOLE NO. 3(1967), set d; DARLING LILI(1970), set d; ONE MORE TIME(1970, Brit.), prod d; LAST OF THE RED HOT LOVERS(1972), set d; HOMECOMING, THE(1973), art d; NICKEL RIDE, THE(1974), set d; FUN WITH DICK AND JA-NE(1977), set d; 10(1979), set d; LOVE CHILD(1982)
Silents
AMERICAN MANNERS(1924), ph; LAW FORBIDS, THE(1924), ph; ISLE OF HOPE, THE(1925), ph; BLUE STREAK, THE(1926), ph; NIGHT PATROL, THE(1926), ph
James Stevens
CAPTAINS OF THE CLOUDS(1942); BABY AND THE BATTLESHIP, THE(1957, Brit.), m; WEAPON, THE(1957, Brit.), m; SPARROWS CAN'T SING(1963, Brit.), m; THEY CAME FROM BEYOND SPACE(1967, Brit.), m; TWO OF A KIND(1983)
January Stevens
FAT ANGELS(1980, U.S./Span.)
Misc. Talkies
FAT CHANCE(1982)
Jason Stevens
WINDWALKER(1980)
Jean Stevens
MISSING JUROR, THE(1944); DANCING IN MANHATTAN(1945); MEX-ICANA(1945); OVER 21(1945); THAT BRENNAN GIRL(1946)
Misc. Talkies
RETURN OF THE DURANGO KID(1945); FRONTIER GUNLAW(1946)
Jeffrey Stevens
ON MOONLIGHT BAY(1951); BUGSY MALONE(1976, Brit.)
Jessie Stevens
Silents
GLADIOLA(1915); RANSON'S FOLLY(1915); ENVY(1917); OTHER MAN, THE(1918); PAIR OF CUPIDS, A(1918); FORTUNE'S CHILD(1919); SINGLE TRACK, THE(1921)
Misc. Silents
APPLE-TREE GIRL, THE(1917); BILLY AND THE BIG STICK(1917); PUTTING THE BEE IN HERBERT(1917); FIND THE WOMAN(1918); LITTLE RUNAWAY, THE(1918); DOLLARS AND THE WOMAN(1920)

John Stevens
CAVALIER, THE(1928), ph; JOURNEY AHEAD(1947, Brit.); SLEEPING CAR TO TRIESTE(1949, Brit.); WOMAN HATER(1949, Brit.); MR. DENNING DRIVES NORTH(1953, Brit.); WOMEN OF PITCAIRN ISLAND, THE(1957); JUST FOR FUN(1963, Brit.), cos; FATE IS THE HUNTER(1964); DEAR BRIGETTE(1965); LAST MOVIE, THE(1971); BLACK RODEO(1972), ph; BLACULA(1972), ph
1984
MAKING THE GRADE(1984)
Judy Stevens
CORPSE CAME C.O.D., THE(
Julie Stevens
PRIVATE DETECTIVE(1939); HONEYMOON DEFERRED(1940); MURDER IN THE AIR(1940); TEAR GAS SQUAD(1940); CARRY ON CLEO(1964, Brit.)
K.T. Stevens
NAVY BLUE AND GOLD(1937); ADDRESS UNKNOWN(1944); PORT OF NEW YORK(1949); HARRIET CRAIG(1950); TUMBLEWEED(1953); VICE SQUAD(1953); MISSILE TO THE MOON(1959); BOB AND CAROL AND TED AND ALICE(1969); PETS(1974)
1984
THEY'RE PLAYING WITH FIRE(1984)
Misc. Talkies
JUNGLE HELL(1956)
Katharine Stevens
GREAT MAN'S LADY, THE(1942)
Katharine [K.T.] Stevens
KITTY FOYLE(1940)
Kay Stevens
INTERNS, THE(1962); MAN FROM THE DINERS' CLUB, THE(1963); NEW IN-TERNS, THE(1964)
Kaye Stevens
JAWS 3-D(1983)
Ken Stevens
STRICTLY IN THE GROOVE(1942)
Kenneth Stevens
BROADWAY SERENADE(1939); WINTER CARNIVAL(1939)
Kenny Stevens
SWING IT SOLDIER(1941)
Landers Stevens
FROZEN JUSTICE(1929); NEW YORK NIGHTS(1929); TRIAL OF MARY DUGAN, THE(1929); GORILLA, THE(1931); LITTLE CAESAR(1931); PUBLIC ENEMY, THE(1931); HELL DIVERS(1932); RAINBOW TRAIL(1932); MANHATTAN MELO-DRAMA(1934); PERSONALITY KID, THE(1934); FRISCO KID(1935); LET 'EM HAVE IT(1935); SWEET ADELINE(1935); CHARLIE CHAN'S SECRET(1936); COWBOY STAR, THE(1936); PAROLE(1936); SWING TIME(1936); BREAKFAST FOR TWO(1937); JOIN THE MARINES(1937); SLAVE SHIP(1937); THAT GIRL FROM PARIS(1937); WE WHO ARE ABOUT TO DIE(1937); GOLDEN BOY(1939); I STOLE A MILLION(1939); LONE WOLF SPY HUNT, THE(1939); STORY OF ALEXANDER GRAHAM BELL, THE(1939); WHEN TOMORROW COMES(1939); ZERO HOUR, THE(1939); DANGER ON WHEELS(1940)
Silents
KEEPING UP WITH LIZZIE(1921); SHADOWS OF CONSCIENCE(1921); HANDLE WITH CARE(1922); WILD HONEY(1922); WONDERFUL WIFE, A(1922)
Misc. Silents
PRICE OF REDEMPTION, THE(1920); THOUSAND TO ONE, A(1920); VEILED WOMAN, THE(1922); YOUTH MUST HAVE LOVE(1922)
Larry Stevens
CENTENNIAL SUMMER(1946)
Laura Stevens
RAZOR'S EDGE, THE(1946)
Lee E. Stevens
TO BE OR NOT TO BE(1983)
Leith Stevens
SYNCOPATION(1942), md; NIGHT SONG(1947), m; ALL MY SONS(1948), m; BLACK BART(1948), m; FEUDIN', FUSSIN' AND A-FIGHTIN'(1948), m; LAR-CENY(1948), m; NOT WANTED(1949), m; DESTINATION MOON(1950), m; NEVER FEAR(1950), m; SUN SETS AT DAWN, THE(1950), m; NO QUESTIONS ASKED(1951), m; WHEN WORLDS COLLIDE(1951), m; ATOMIC CITY, THE(1952), m; BEWARE, MY LOVELY(1952), m; EIGHT IRON MEN(1952), m; NAVAJO(1952), m; STORM OVER TIBET(1952), m; BIGAMIST,THE(1953), m; CRAZYLEGS, ALL AMERI-CAN(1953), m; GLASS WALL, THE(1953), m; HITCH-HIKER, THE(1953), m; SCARED STIFF(1953), m; WAR OF THE WORLDS, THE(1953), m; WILD ONE, THE(1953), m; PRIVATE HELL 36(1954), m; CRASHOUT(1955), m; TREASURE OF PANCHO VILLA, THE(1955), m; GREAT DAY IN THE MORNING(1956), m; JU-LIE(1956), m; SCARLET HOUR, THE(1956), m; WORLD WITHOUT END(1956), m, md; CARELESS YEARS, THE(1957), m; EIGHTEEN AND ANXIOUS(1957), m; GAR-MENT JUNGLE, THE(1957), m; GREEN-EYED BLONDE, THE(1957), m; LIZ-ZIE(1957), m, md; RIDE OUT FOR REVENGE(1957), m&md; BULLWHIP(1958), m; GUN RUNNERS, THE(1958), m; SEVEN GUNS TO MESA(1958), m; VIOLENT ROAD(1958), m; BUT NOT FOR ME(1959), m; FIVE PENNIES, THE(1959), m; GENE KRUPA STORY, THE(1959), m; HELL TO ETERNITY(1960), m; MAN-TRAP(1961), m; ON THE DOUBLE(1961), m, md; INTERNS, THE(1962), m; IT HAPPENED AT THE WORLD'S FAIR(1963), m; NEW KIND OF LOVE, A(1963), m; NIGHT OF THE GRIZZLY, THE(1966), m; SMOKY(1966), m; CHUKA(1967), m
Lenore Stevens
GAY DECEIVERS, THE(1969); SCANDALOUS JOHN(1971); BEYOND ATLAN-TIS(1973, Phil.)
Leon B. Stevens
BUTTERFIELD 8(1960); MURDER, INC.(1960); DEAD TO THE WORLD(1961); SPORTING CLUB, THE(1971); SEDUCTION OF JOE TYNAN, THE(1979); ENDLESS LOVE(1981)
Leslie Stevens
LEFT-HANDED GUN, THE(1958), w; MARRIAGE-GO-ROUND, THE(1960), p, w; PRIVATE PROPERTY(1960), d&w; HERO'S ISLAND(1962), p, d&w; WAR LORD, THE(1965), w; INCUBUS(1966), d&w; BATTLESTAR GALACTICA(1979), p; BUCK ROGERS IN THE 25TH CENTURY(1979), w
1984
SHEENA(1984), w

Lewis Stevens
HEADS UP(1930), w
Lionel Stevens
OUTSIDER, THE(1949, Brit.)
Lonny Stevens
PHYNX, THE(1970); ROLLERCOASTER(1977)
Louis Stevens
HOT STUFF(1929), w; MEN OF CHANCE(1932), w; STATE'S ATTORNEY(1932), w; FLYING DEVILS(1933), w; HOT TIP(1935), w; MARY BURNS, FUGITIVE(1935), w; SPECIAL INVESTIGATOR(1936), w; TEXAS RANGERS, THE(1936), w; CRIMINAL LAWYER(1937), w; LAST TRAIN FROM MADRID, THE(1937), w; SINNERS IN PARADISE(1938), w; BORDER LEGION, THE(1940), w; COLORADO(1940), w; MASSACRE RIVER(1949), w; STREETS OF LAREDO(1949), w; CIMARRON KID, THE(1951), w; SANTA FE(1951), w; HORIZONS WEST(1952), w; BORDER RIVER(1954), w; CARTOUCHE(1957, Ital./US), w; GUN DUEL IN DURANGO(1957), w; BEAST OF BUDAPEST, THE(1958), w; FLAMING FRONTIER(1958, Can.), w; WOLF DOG(1958, Can.), w
Silents
BRONZE BELL, THE(1921), w; DOLLAR DEVILS(1923), w; HUMAN DESIRES(1924, Brit.), w; BABE COMES HOME(1927), w; EASY PICKINGS(1927), w; SCARLET SEAS(1929), t
Lyda Stevens
THIRD OF A MAN(1962)
Lydia Stevens
GIGI(1958)
M.A.F. Stevens
YELLOW HAT, THE(1966, Brit.), w
Marc Stevens
SURVIVORS, THE(1983)
Margot Stevens
ADULTEROUS AFFAIR(1966), d&w
Mark Stevens
DESTINATION TOKYO(1944); PASSAGE TO MARSEILLE(1944); OBJECTIVE, BURMA!(1945); RHAPSODY IN BLUE(1945); WITHIN THESE WALLS(1945); DARK CORNER, THE(1946); FROM THIS DAY FORWARD(1946); I WONDER WHO'S KISSING HER NOW(1947); SNAKE PIT, THE(1948); STREET WITH NO NAME, THE(1948); DANCING IN THE DARK(1949); OH, YOU BEAUTIFUL DOLL(1949); SAND(1949); BETWEEN MIDNIGHT AND DAWN(1950); PLEASE BELIEVE ME(1950); KATIE DID IT(1951); LITTLE EGYPT(1951); REUNION IN RENO(1951); TARGET UNKNOWN(1951); MUTINY(1952); BIG FRAME, THE(1953, Brit.); JACK SLADE(1953); TORPEDO ALLEY(1953); CRY VENGEANCE(1954), a, d; TIMETABLE(1956), a, p&d; GUNSIGHT RIDGE(1957); GUN FEVER(1958), a, d; GUNSMOKE IN TUCSON(1958); SEPTEMBER STORM(1960); MAN IN THE WATER, THE(1963), a, d; FATE IS THE HUNTER(1964); FROZEN ALIVE(1966, Brit./Ger.); SUNSCORCHED(1966, Span./Ger.), a, d, w
Marti Stevens
ABDULLAH'S HAREM(1956, Brit./Egypt.); ALL NIGHT LONG(1961, Brit.)
Marya Stevens
QUEEN OF OUTER SPACE(1958); MONEY TRAP, THE(1966)
Mel Stevens
MURPH THE SURF(1974)
Mike Stevens
PLAY DIRTY(1969, Brit.)
Morgan Stevens
Misc. Talkies
UP RIVER(1979)
Morton Stevens
LOST BOUNDARIES(1949); RAIDERS, THE(1964), m; WILD AND WONDERFUL(1964), m; SPY WITH MY FACE, THE(1966), m; ONE MAN JURY(1978), m; HARDLY WORKING(1981), m; GREAT WHITE, THE(1982, Ital.), m; SMORGASBORD(1983), m
Morty Stevens
1984
SLAPSTICK OF ANOTHER KIND(1984), m
Nancy Stevens
PROUD AND THE PROFANE, THE(1956)
Naomi Stevens
BLACK ORCHID(1959); APARTMENT, THE(1960); CONVICTS FOUR(1962); ART OF LOVE, THE(1965); VALLEY OF THE DOLLS(1967); BUONA SERA, MRS. CAMPBELL(1968, Ital.); HAWAIIANS, THE(1970); SUPERDAD(1974); HARD TIMES(1975); HUSTLE(1975)
Misc. Talkies
FLY ME(1973)
Nico Stevens
NEW YORK, NEW YORK(1977)
Norman Stevens
LAS VEGAS STORY, THE(1952); VICKI(1953)
Norman L. Stevens
Silents
JOHNNY RING AND THE CAPTAIN'S SWORD(1921), d
Onslow Stevens
UNDER TWO FLAGS(1936); GOLDEN WEST, THE(1932); OKAY AMERICA(1932); ONCE IN A LIFETIME(1932); RADIO PATROL(1932); COUNSELLOR-AT-LAW(1933); NAGANA(1933); ONLY YESTERDAY(1933); PEG O' MY HEART(1933); SECRET OF THE BLUE ROOM(1933); AFFAIRS OF A GENTLEMAN(1934); BOMBAY MAIL(1934); CROSBY CASE, THE(1934); HOUSE OF DANGER(1934); I CAN'T ESCAPE(1934); I'LL TELL THE WORLD(1934); IN LOVE WITH LIFE(1934); THIS SIDE OF HEAVEN(1934); BORN TO GAMBLE(1935); FORCED LANDING(1935); GRAND EXIT(1935); NOTORIOUS GENTLEMAN, A(1935); THREE MUSKETEERS, THE(1935); BRIDGE OF SIGHS(1936); EASY MONEY(1936); F MAN(1936); MURDER WITH PICTURES(1936); STRAIGHT FROM THE SHOULDER(1936); THREE ON THE TRAIL(1936); YELLOW DUST(1936); FLIGHT FROM GLORY(1937); THERE GOES THE GROOM(1937); YOU CAN'T BUY LUCK(1937); LIFE RETURNS(1939); THOSE HIGH GREY WALLS(1939); WHEN TOMORROW COMES(1939); MAN WHO WOULDN'T TALK, THE(1940); MYSTERY SEA RAIDER(1940); WHO KILLED AUNT MAGGIE?(1940); GO WEST, YOUNG LADY(1941); MONSTER AND THE GIRL, THE(1941); SUNSET SERENADE(1942); APPOINTMENT IN BERLIN(1943); HANDS ACROSS THE BORDER(1943); IDAHO(1943); HOUSE OF DRACULA(1945); ANGEL ON MY SHOULDER(1946); CANYON PASSAGE(1946); O.S.S.(1946); CREEPER, THE(1948); GALLANT BLADE, THE(1948); WALK A CROOKED MILE(1948); BOMBA

THE JUNGLE BOY(1949); RED, HOT AND BLUE(1949); MARK OF THE GORILLA(1950); MOTOR PATROL(1950); ONE TOO MANY(1950); REVENUE AGENT(1950); STATE PENITENTIARY(1950); FAMILY SECRET, THE(1951); HILLS OF UTAH(1951); LORNA DOONE(1951); SEALED CARGO(1951); SIROCCO(1951); SAN FRANCISCO STORY, THE(1952); CHARGE AT FEATHER RIVER, THE(1953); LION IS IN THE STREETS, A(1953); FANGS OF THE WILD(1954); THEM!(1954); THEY RODE WEST(1954); NEW YORK CONFIDENTIAL(1955); OUTSIDE THE LAW(1956); TEN COMMANDMENTS, THE(1956); TRIBUTE TO A BADMAN(1956); KELLY AND ME(1957); BUCCANEER, THE(1958); LONELYHEARTS(1958); PARTY CRASHERS, THE(1958); TARAWA BEACHHEAD(1958); ALL THE FINE YOUNG CANNIBALS(1960); COUCH, THE(1962)
Misc. Talkies
ALL THAT I HAVE(1951); MAGNIFICENT ADVENTURE, THE(1952)
Oren Stevens
TIGER MAKES OUT, THE(1967); DARING GAME(1968); DOWNHILL RACER(1969)
Pat Stevens
THEY KNEW MR. KNIGHT(1945, Brit.)
Patricia Stevens
1984
CRIMES OF PASSION(1984)
Paul Stevens
EXODUS(1960); MASK, THE(1961, Can.); MARLOWE(1969); PATTON(1970); CORKY(1972); MELINDA(1972); RAGE(1972); BATTLE FOR THE PLANET OF THE APES(1973)
Pauline Stevens
CONSOLATION MARRIAGE(1931)
Peggy Stevens
ADULTEROUS AFFAIR(1966), makeup; TAKE HER BY SURPRISE(1967, Can.), makeup
Phillip Stevens
Silents
SATAN'S SISTER(1925, Brit.)
Ray Stevens
PICKUP ON SOUTH STREET(1953)
Reginald Stevens
Misc. Silents
LONDON FLAT MYSTERY, A(1915, Brit.)
Rhoda Stevens
WHEN THE LEGENDS DIE(1972)
Rikki Stevens
MISTER BUDDWING(1966)
Rise Stevens
CHOCOLATE SOLDIER, THE(1941); GOING MY WAY(1944); CARNEGIE HALL(1947); JOURNEY BACK TO OZ(1974)
Rita Stevens
AFTER THE BALL(1957, Brit.)
Robert C. Stevens
HEAVEN CAN WAIT(1978)
Robert Stevens
HELLO ANNAPOLIS(1942); SPIRIT OF STANFORD, THE(1942); SWEETHEART OF THE FLEET(1942); FIGHTING BUCKAROO, THE(1943); GILDA(1946); NIGHT EDITOR(1946); SING WHILE YOU DANCE(1946); BLONDIE'S BIG MOMENT(1947); FRAMED(1947); LONE HAND TEXAN, THE(1947); MILLERSON CASE, THE(1947); BIG CAPER, THE(1957), d; ER LOVE A STRANGER(1958), d; I THANK A FOOL(1962, Brit.), d; IN THE COOL OF THE DAY(1963), d; TELL ME IN THE SUNLIGHT(1967), w; CHANGE OF MIND(1969), d
Misc. Talkies
LONE STAR MOONLIGHT(1946); RETURN OF RUSTY, THE(1946)
Silents
WIZARD OF OZ, THE(1925), art d; DREAM MELODY, THE(1929), spec eff
Robert M. Stevens
TOY, THE(1982)
Robin Stevens
MUDLARK, THE(1950, Brit.)
Rock Stevens
Misc. Talkies
HERCULES AND THE TYRANTS OF BABYLON(1964)
Rock Stevens [Peter Lupus]
MUSCLE BEACH PARTY(1964)
Rodney Stevens
MIDNIGHT MAN, THE(1974)
Ronald Stevens
SCARLET WEB, THE(1954, Brit.); BACHELOR OF HEARTS(1958, Brit.)
Ronald [Ronnie] Stevens
NARROWING CIRCLE, THE(1956, Brit.)
Ronald Smokey Stevens
WIZ, THE(1978)
Ronald "Smokey" Stevens
TIMES SQUARE(1980)
Ronnie Stevens
COMING-OUT PARTY, A(; HELL, HEAVEN OR HOBOKEN(1958, Brit.); MADE IN HEAVEN(1952, Brit.); MR. POTTS GOES TO MOSCOW(1953, Brit.); EMBEZZLER, THE(1954, Brit.); FOR BETTER FOR WORSE(1954, Brit.); HORNET'S NEST, THE(1955, Brit.); DOCTOR AT LARGE(1957, Brit.); VALUE FOR MONEY(1957, Brit.); I'M ALL RIGHT, JACK(1959, Brit.); DENTIST IN THE CHAIR(1960, Brit.); DOCTOR IN LOVE(1960, Brit.); NEARLY A NASTY ACCIDENT(1962, Brit.); ON THE BEAT(1962, Brit.); RING-A-DING RHYTHM(1962, Brit. 73m Amicus/COL bw (G.B: IT'S TRAD, DAD!); DOCTOR IN DISTRESS(1963, Brit.); GET ON WITH IT(1963, Brit.); PAIR OF BRIEFS, A(1963, Brit.); SAN FERRY ANN(1965, Brit.); THOSE MAGNIFICENT MEN IN THEIR FLYING MACHINES; OR HOW I FLEW FROM LONDON TO PARIS IN 25 HOURS AND 11 MINUTES(1965, Brit.); CARNABY, M.D.(1967, Brit.); GIVE A DOG A BONE(1967, Brit.); SMASHING TIME(1967 Brit.); GOODBYE MR. CHIPS(1969, U.S./Brit.); SOME GIRLS DO(1969, Brit.)
Rory Stevens
RUBY(1977); MALIBU BEACH(1978)
Rose Anne Stevens
DOWN RIO GRANDE WAY(1942)

Roseanne Stevens
TOMORROW WE LIVE(1942)
Roy Stevens
SUPERMAN(1978)
Ruth Elma Stevens
HARVEY(1950)
Ruthelma Stevens
LIFE BEGINS(1932); NIGHT CLUB LADY(1932); CIRCUS QUEEN MURDER, THE(1933); GRAND SLAM(1933); MIND READER, THE(1933); NO MORE OR-CHIDS(1933); WORKING MAN, THE(1933); CURTAIN AT EIGHT(1934); SCARLET EMPRESS, THE(1934); DANTE'S INFERNO(1935); ORCHIDS TO YOU(1935); PEOPLE WILL TALK(1935); FOUNTAINHEAD, THE(1949); NOT WANTED(1949); TRIAL WITHOUT JURY(1950); APACHE DRUMS(1951); TOO YOUNG TO KISS(1951); JET PILOT(1957)
Sally Stevens
YOUNG GIRLS OF ROCHEFORT, THE(1968, Fr.)
Sandra Stevens
COP HATER(1958)
Sarah Stevens
IMPROPER CHANNELS(1981, Can.)
Scott Stevens
MARVIN AND TIGE(1983), set d
Shari Stevens
KILL, THE(1968)
Shawn Stevens
SAVAGE HARVEST(1981)
Sheila Stevens
CAGED(1950)
Stella Stevens
LI'L ABNER(1959); SAY ONE FOR ME(1959); MAN-TRAP(1961); GIRLS! GIRLS! GIRLS!(1962); TOO LATE BLUES(1962); COURTSHIP OF EDDY'S FATHER, THE(1963); NUTTY PROFESSOR, THE(1963); ADVANCE TO THE REAR(1964); SECRET OF MY SUCCESS, THE(1965, Brit.); SYNANON(1965); RAGE(1966, U.S./Mex.); SILENCERS, THE(1966); HOW TO SAVE A MARRIAGE–AND RUIN YOUR LIFE(1968); SOL MADRID(1968); WHERE ANGELS GO...TROUBLE FOLLOWS(1968); MAD ROOM, THE(1969); BALLAD OF CABLE HOGUE, THE(1970); TOWN CALLED HELL, A(1971, Span./Brit.); POSEIDON ADVENTURE, THE(1972); SLAUGHT-ER(1972); STAND UP AND BE COUNTED(1972); ARNOLD(1973); CLEOPATRA JONES AND THE CASINO OF GOLD(1975 U. S. Hong Kong); LAS VEGAS LA-DY(1976); NICKELODEON(1976); MANITOU, THE(1978); CHAINED HEAT(1983 U.S./Ger.); WACKO(1983)
Misc. Talkies
UNDER THE SIGN OF CAPRICORN(1971)
Steve Stevens
SUNSET PASS(1946); HIGH SCHOOL CAESAR(1960); AGENT FOR H.A.R.M.(1966)
Susan Stevens
HER FIRST ROMANCE(1951)
Theo Stevens
NORMAN LOVES ROSE(1982, Aus.)
Tom Stevens
BAT PEOPLE, THE(1974), ed
1984
A NOS AMOURS(1984, Fr.)
Tony Stevens
BEST LITTLE WHOREHOUSE IN TEXAS, THE(1982), ch; SORCERESS(1983)
1984
WHERE THE BOYS ARE '84(1984), ch
Vi Stevens
MUDLARK, THE(1950, Brit.); HER PANELLED DOOR(1951, Brit.); HAMMER THE TOFF(1952, Brit.); LOVE MATCH, THE(1955, Brit.); IT'S A GREAT DAY(1956, Brit.); CRY FROM THE STREET, A(1959, Brit.); OLD MAC(1961, Brit.)
Virginia Stevens
NATIVE LAND(1942); BLACK ORCHID(1959)
W.L. Stevens
TOPPER(1937), set d
Wade Stevens
NIGHTWING(1979)
Warren Stevens
FOLLOW THE SUN(1951); FROGMEN, THE(1951); MR. BELVEDERE RINGS THE BELL(1951); DEADLINE–U.S.A.(1952); I DON'T CARE GIRL, THE(1952); O. HENRY'S FULL HOUSE(1952); PHONE CALL FROM A STRANGER(1952); RED SKIES OF MONTANA(1952); WAIT 'TIL THE SUN SHINES, NELLIE(1952); SHARK RI-VER(1953); BAREFOOT CONTESSA, THE(1954); GORILLA AT LARGE(1954); BLACK TUESDAY(1955); DUEL ON THE MISSISSIPPI(1955); MAN FROM BITTER RIDGE, THE(1955); ROBBER'S ROOST(1955); WOMEN'S PRISON(1955); ACCUSED OF MUR-DER(1956); FORBIDDEN PLANET(1956); ON THE THRESHOLD OF SPACE(1956); PRICE OF FEAR, THE(1956); CASE AGAINST BROOKLYN, THE(1958); HOT SPELL(1958); INTENT TO KILL(1958, Brit.); MAN OR GUN(1958); NO NAME ON THE BULLET(1959); FORTY POUNDS OF TROUBLE(1962); STAGECOACH TO DANCER'S PARK(1962); AMERICAN DREAM, AN(1966); CYBORG 2087(1966); MADAME X(1966); MADIGAN(1968); SWEET RIDE, THE(1968); STUDENT BODY, THE(1976); STROKER ACE(1983)
Misc. Talkies
BELLE SOMMERS(1962)
Will S. Stevens
Misc. Silents
LIFE'S SHADOWS(1916)
William Stevens
GILDERSLEEVE ON BROADWAY(1943), art d; HEAVENLY DAYS(1944), set d; NEVADA(1944), set d; SEVEN DAYS ASHORE(1944), set d; BETRAYAL FROM THE EAST(1945), set d; JOHNNY ANGEL(1945), set d; TWO O'CLOCK COURAGE(1945), set d; WEST OF THE PECOS(1945), set d; SUNSET PASS(1946), set d; TILL THE END OF TIME(1946), set d; STORK BITES MAN(1947), set d; BERLIN EXPRESS(1948), set d; EVERY GIRL SHOULD BE MARRIED(1948), set d; RACE STREET(1948), set d; WHO KILLED "DOC" ROBBIN?(1948), set d; THREAT, THE(1949), set d; RACKET, THE(1951), set d; THING, THE(1951), set d; NARROW MARGIN, THE(1952), set d; YOUNG AND DANGEROUS(1957); BONNIE PARKER STORY, THE(1958); SHOW-DOWN AT BOOT HILL(1958); SERGEANT WAS A LADY, THE(1961), set d; DEAD RINGER(1964), set d; FBI CODE 98(1964), set d

William L. Stevens
OUR RELATIONS(1936), art d; PICK A STAR(1937), set d; WAY OUT WEST(1937), set d; SWISS MISS(1938), set d; SAPS AT SEA(1940), set d; WEB, THE(1947), set d; MOON PILOT(1962), set d
Bronwyn Stevens-Jones
PALM BEACH(1979, Aus.)
Adlai Stevenson
GLOBAL AFFAIR, A(1964)
Al Stevenson
MISTER BROWN(1972)
Alexandra Stevenson
PREHISTORIC WOMEN(1967, Brit.)
Anson Stevenson
HALLELUJAH(1929), ed; GARDEN OF ALLAH, THE(1936), ed
Audrey Stevenson
SPOOK WHO SAT BY THE DOOR, THE(1973)
Ben Stevenson
SUMMER HOLIDAY(1963, Brit.)
Bob Stevenson
OPERATOR 13(1934); TREASURE ISLAND(1934); BARBARY COAST(1935); GOD'S COUNTRY AND THE WOMAN(1937); BEASTS OF BERLIN(1939); MORTAL STORM, THE(1940); UNDERGROUND(1941); JOAN OF OZARK(1942); ONCE UPON A HONEY-MOON(1942); REUNION IN FRANCE(1942); GHOST SHIP, THE(1943); THIS LAND IS MINE(1943); FRENCHMAN'S CREEK(1944); MAN IN HALF-MOON STREET, THE(1944); VOICE IN THE WIND(1944); GREAT SINNER, THE(1949); SELLOUT, THE(1951); OPERATION SECRET(1952); WHEN HELL BROKE LOOSE(1958); FID-DLER ON THE ROOF(1971)
Bobby Stevenson
KID FROM CANADA, THE(1957, Brit.)
Burton E. Stevenson
CASE OF THE BLACK PARROT, THE(1941), w
Silents
PURSUING VENGEANCE, THE(1916), w
Burton Egbert Stevenson
IN THE NEXT ROOM(1930), w
Charles Stevenson
MYSTERIOUS DR. FU MANCHU, THE(1929)
Silents
NIGHTINGALE, THE(1914); SAILOR-MADE MAN, A(1921); DOCTOR JACK(1922); GRANDMA'S BOY(1922); KICK IN(1922); SAFETY LAST(1923); WHY WORRY(1923); HOT WATER(1924); FRESHMAN, THE(1925)
Misc. Silents
TRUTHFUL LIAR, THE(1922); SHRIEK OF ARABY, THE(1923); PIED PIPER MALONE(1924); WALLFLOWERS(1928)
Charles A. Stevenson
Silents
HER GILDED CAGE(1922); GARRISON'S FINISH(1923); LEGALLY DEAD(1923); BREAKING POINT, THE(1924); AFLAME IN THE SKY(1927)
Misc. Silents
SHORE ACRES(1914); MORE EXCELLENT WAY, THE(1917); GIRL OF TODAY, THE(1918); NYMPH OF THE FOOTHILLS, A(1918); REDHEAD(1919); WHISPERING SHADOWS(1922); BOLTED DOOR, THE(1923); DOOMSDAY(1928)
Deborah Stevenson
ENTITY, THE(1982)
Dick Stevenson
FLOWER THIEF, THE(1962)
Douglas Stevenson
BREAKER! BREAKER!(1977); PROWLER, THE(1981)
Silents
JANICE MEREDITH(1924)
Edward Stevenson
THEY WON'T BELIEVE ME(1947), cos; SALLY(1929), cos; SMILING IRISH EYES(1929), cos; LADIES OF LEISURE(1930), cos; NOTORIOUS AFFAIR, A(1930), cos; SONG OF THE FLAME(1930), cos; PUBLIC ENEMY, THE(1931), cos; WOMAN HUNGRY(1931), cos; FORBIDDEN(1932), cos; BITTER TEA OF GENERAL YEN, THE(1933), cos; MUMMY'S BOYS(1936), cos; NIGHT WAITRESS(1936), cos; SECOND WIFE(1936), cos; BREAKFAST FOR TWO(1937), cos; LIFE OF THE PARTY, THE(1937), cos; THAT GIRL FROM PARIS(1937), cos; THEY WANTED TO MAR-RY(1937), cos; TOAST OF NEW YORK, THE(1937), cos; TOO MANY WIVES(1937), cos; WE WHO ARE ABOUT TO DIE(1937), cos; WE'RE ON THE JURY(1937), cos; YOU CAN'T BEAT LOVE(1937), cos; YOU CAN'T BUY LUCK(1937), cos; CAREFREE(1938), cos; MAD MISS MANTON, THE(1938), cos; MOTHER CAREY'S CHICKENS(1938), cos; RADIO CITY REVELS(1938), cos; SAINT IN NEW YORK, THE(1938), cos; GUNGA DIN(1939), cos; IN NAME ONLY(1939), cos; MURDER WILL OUT(1939, Brit.), cos; PACIFIC LINER(1939), cos; PANAMA LADY(1939), cos; SORORITY HOUSE(1939), cos; STORY OF VERNON AND IRENE CASTLE, THE(1939), cos; THAT'S RIGHT–YOU'RE WRONG(1939), cos; THEY MADE HER A SPY(1939), cos; THREE SONS(1939), cos; NO, NO NANETTE(1940), cos; PLAY GIRL(1940), cos; SWISS FAMILY ROBINSON(1940), cos; THEY KNEW WHAT THEY WANTED(1940), cos; TOO MANY GIRLS(1940), cos; YOU CAN'T FOOL YOUR WIFE(1940), cos; YOU'LL FIND OUT(1940), cos; CITIZEN KANE(1941), cos; MY LIFE WITH CARO-LINE(1941), cos; SUSPICION(1941), cos; JOURNEY INTO FEAR(1942), cos; MAG-NIFICENT AMBERSONS, THE(1942), cos; GHOST SHIP, THE(1943), cos; HIGHER AND HIGHER(1943), cos; EXPERIMENT PERILOUS(1944), cos; MADEMOISELLE FIFI(1944), cos; PASSPORT TO DESTINY(1944), cos; STEP LIVELY(1944), cos; YOUTH RUNS WILD(1944), cos; ISLE OF THE DEAD(1945), cos; MURDER, MY SWEET(1945), cos; WHAT A BLONDE(1945), cos; IT'S A WONDERFUL LIFE(1946), cos; BACHELOR AND THE BOBBY-SOXER, THE(1947), cos; OUT OF THE PAST(1947), cos; I REMEMBER MAMA(1948), cos; RACE STREET(1948), cos; EASY LIVING(1949), cos; WOMAN'S SECRET, A(1949), cos; MUDLARK, THE(1950, Brit.), cos; STELLA(1950), cos; DAVID AND BATHSHEBA(1951), cos; THIRTEENTH LET-TER, THE(1951), cos; AGAINST ALL FLAGS(1952), cos; PONY SOLDIER(1952), cos; WAR ARROW(1953), cos
Frances Stevenson
BREEZY(1973)
George Stevenson
Silents
FIRES OF INNOCENCE(1922, Brit.), w

Gilbert Stevenson
HIGH AND DRY(1954, Brit.)
Hayden Stevenson
COLLEGE LOVE(1929); VENGEANCE(1930); GILDED LILY, THE(1935); EASY LIVING(1937); HOTEL HAYWIRE(1937); MAID OF SALEM(1937); SAY IT IN FRENCH(1938); LIGHT THAT FAILED, THE(1939); OUR LEADING CITIZEN(1939)
Silents
ABYSMAL BRUTE, THE(1923); ACQUITTAL, THE(1923); DARK STAIRWAYS(1924); LAW FORBIDS, THE(1924); RECKLESS AGE, THE(1924); BIG PAL(1925); BEHIND THE FRONT(1926); FREEDOM OF THE PRESS(1928); RED LIPS(1928); SILKS AND SADDLES(1929)
Misc. Silents
GREAT DIVIDE, THE(1916); LONE HAND, THE(1922); TRIFLING WITH HONOR(1923); ON YOUR TOES(1927)
Houseley Stevenson
WITHOUT RESERVATIONS(1946); GHOST AND MRS. MUIR, THE(1942); HAPPY LAND(1943); DAKOTA(1945); LITTLE MISS BIG(1946); SOMEWHERE IN THE NIGHT(1946); YEARLING, THE(1946); BRASHER DOUBLOON, THE(1947); DARK PASSAGE(1947); FOREVER AMBER(1947); TIME OUT OF MIND(1947); APARTMENT FOR PEGGY(1948); CASBAH(1948); CHALLENGE, THE(1948); FOUR FACES WEST(1948); JOAN OF ARC(1948); KIDNAPPED(1948); MOONRISE(1948); PALEFACE, THE(1948); SECRET BEYOND THE DOOR, THE(1948); SMART WOMAN(1948); YOU GOTTA STAY HAPPY(1948); ALL THE KING'S MEN(1949); CALAMITY JANE AND SAM BASS(1949); COLORADO TERRITORY(1949); GAL WHO TOOK THE WEST, THE(1949); KNOCK ON ANY DOOR(1949); LADY GAMBLES, THE(1949); LEAVE IT TO HENRY(1949); MASKED RAIDERS(1949); SORROWFUL JONES(1949); TAKE ONE FALSE STEP(1949); WALKING HILLS, THE(1949); GUNFIGHTER, THE(1950); SIERRA(1950); SUN SETS AT DAWN, THE(1950); CAVE OF OUTLAWS(1951); DARLING, HOW COULD YOU!(1951); HOLLYWOOD STORY(1951); SECRET OF CONVICT LAKE, THE(1951); OKLAHOMA ANNIE(1952); WILD NORTH, THE(1952); ABBOTT AND COSTELLO MEET THE KEYSTONE KOPS(1955); SPECIAL DELIVERY(1976), ed; FINAL CHAPTER–WALKING TALL zero(1977), ed; MEAN DOG BLUES(1978), ed; GREAT SANTINI, THE(1979), ed
Houseley Stevenson, Jr.
ATOMIC CITY, THE(1952); CADDY, THE(1953); WAR OF THE WORLDS, THE(1953)
Houseley Stevenson, Sr.
ISLE OF FURY(1936); ONCE A DOCTOR(1937); EDGE OF DOOM(1950)
Misc. Talkies
ALL THAT I HAVE(1951)
Howard J. Stevenson
HUMAN COMEDY, THE(1943)
Janet Stevenson
COUNTER-ATTACK(1945), w; MAN FROM CAIRO, THE(1953), w
John Stevenson
DAY OF TRIUMPH(1954)
Judy Stevenson
CATHY'S CHILD(1979, Aus.)
Keith Stevenson
SEA WOLVES, THE(1981, Brit.)
Laura Stevenson
MURDER A LA MOD(1968)
Margot Stevenson
SMASHING THE MONEY RING(1939); CALLING PHILO VANCE(1940); CASTLE ON THE HUDSON(1940); FLIGHT ANGELS(1940); GRANNY GET YOUR GUN(1940); INVISIBLE STRIPES(1940); VALLEY OF THE DOLLS(1967); RABBIT, RUN(1970); GOING IN STYLE(1979)
Marion Stevenson
Silents
NO MOTHER TO GUIDE HER(1923)
McLean Stevenson
CHRISTIAN LICORICE STORE, THE(1971); WIN, PLACE, OR STEAL(1975); CAT FROM OUTER SPACE, THE(1978)
Michael Stevenson
CHAPTER TWO(1979), ed
Michael A. Stevenson
CALIFORNIA SUITE(1978), ed; CHEAP DETECTIVE, THE(1978), ed; SEEMS LIKE OLD TIMES(1980), ed; ANNIE(1982), ed; TOY, THE(1982), ed
1984
BEST DEFENSE(1984), ed
Mollie Stevenson
RED, WHITE AND BLACK, THE(1970)
Monica Stevenson
CONSTANT HUSBAND, THE(1955, Brit.); BACHELOR OF HEARTS(1958, Brit.)
Olga Stevenson
HAPPIDROME(1943, Brit.)
Onslow Stevenson
NIGHT HAS A THOUSAND EYES(1948)
Parker Stevenson
SEPARATE PEACE, A(1972); OUR TIME(1974); LIFEGUARD(1976); STROKER ACE(1983)
Paul Stevenson
FREE GRASS(1969), w
Phil Stevenson
KILLER'S KISS(1955)
Philip Stevenson
COUNTER-ATTACK(1945), w; STORY OF G.I. JOE, THE(1945), w; GIRL IN WHITE, THE(1952), w; MAN FROM CAIRO, THE(1953), w
Richard Stevenson
HOUSE OF SECRETS(1929); PRIVILEGED(1982, Brit.), p
Robert Stevenson
LATIN LOVE(1930, Brit.), w; HAPPY EVER AFTER(1932, Ger./Brit.), d; LOVE ON WHEELS(1932, Brit.), w; MICHAEL AND MARY(1932, Brit.), w; OFFICE GIRL, THE(1932, Brit.), w; RINGER, THE(1932, Brit.), w; EARLY TO BED(1933, Brit./Ger.), w; FAITHFUL HEART(1933, Brit.), w; FALLING FOR YOU(1933, Brit.), d, w; F.P. 1(1933, Brit.), w; HEART SONG(1933, Brit.), w; BATTLE, THE(1934, Fr.), w; LITTLE FRIEND(1934, Brit.), p; STUDENT TOUR(1934); WHITE HEAT(1934); GARDEN OF ALLAH, THE(1936); LADY JANE GREY(1936, Brit.), d, w; MAN WHO LIVED AGAIN, THE(1936, Brit.), d; KING SOLOMON'S MINES(1937, Brit.), d; NON-STOP NEW YORK(1937, Brit.), d; GAIETY GIRLS, THE(1938, Brit.), w; TO THE VICTOR(1938, Brit.), d; TWO OF US, THE(1938, Brit.), d; INVITATION TO HAPPINESS(1939);

LADY'S FROM KENTUCKY, THE(1939); WARE CASE, THE(1939, Brit.), d, w; RETURN TO YESTERDAY(1940, Brit.), d, w; TOM BROWN'S SCHOOL DAYS(1940), d, w; BACK STREET(1941), d; JOAN OF PARIS(1942), d; SECRET ENEMIES(1942); VALLEY OF HUNTED MEN(1942); FOREVER AND A DAY(1943), p&d; YOUNG MAN'S FANCY(1943, Brit.), d, w; JANE EYRE(1944), d, w; 'TILL WE MEET AGAIN(1944); DISHONORED LADY(1947), d; TO THE ENDS OF THE EARTH(1948), d; I WAS A MALE WAR BRIDE(1949), d; WALK SOFTLY, STRANGER(1950), d; WOMAN ON PIER 13, THE(1950), d; MY FORBIDDEN PAST(1951), d; THING, THE(1951); LAS VEGAS STORY, THE(1952), d; FANGS OF THE WILD(1954); JOHNNY TREMAIN(1957), d; OLD YELLER(1957), d; ZERO HOUR!(1957); GUN FEVER(1958); DARBY O'GILL AND THE LITTLE PEOPLE(1959), d; KIDNAPPED(1960), d&w; SPARTACUS(1960); ABSENT-MINDED PROFESSOR, THE(1961), d; BOY WHO CAUGHT A CROOK(1961); IN SEARCH OF THE CASTAWAYS(1962, Brit.), d; SON OF FLUBBER(1963), d; MARY POPPINS(1964), d; MISADVENTURES OF MERLIN JONES, THE(1964), d; MONKEY'S UNCLE, THE(1965), d; THAT DARN CAT(1965), d; GNOME-MOBILE, THE(1967), d; BLACKBEARD'S GHOST(1968), d; LOVE BUG, THE(1968), d; BEDKNOBS AND BROOMSTICKS(1971), d; HERBIE RIDES AGAIN(1974), d; ISLAND AT THE TOP OF THE WORLD, THE(1974), d; ONE OF OUR DINOSAURS IS MISSING(1975, Brit.), d; SHAGGY D.A., THE(1976), d
Robert Lewis Stevenson
DR. JEKYLL AND MR. HYDE(1941), w
Silents
DR. JEKYLL AND MR. HYDE(1920), w
Robert Louis Stevenson
DR. JEKYLL AND MR. HYDE(1932), w; TREASURE ISLAND(1934), w; TROUBLE FOR TWO(1936), w; EBB TIDE(1937), w; KIDNAPPED(1938), w; BODY SNATCHER, THE(1945), w; ADVENTURE ISLAND(1947), w; ADVENTURES IN SILVERADO(1948), w; BLACK ARROW(1948), w; KIDNAPPED(1948), w; SECRET OF ST. IVES, THE(1949), w; TREASURE ISLAND(1950, Brit.), w; STRANGE DOOR, THE(1951), w; TREASURE OF LOST CANYON, THE(1952), w; MASTER OF BALLANTRAE, THE(1953, U.S./Brit.), w; ABBOTT AND COSTELLO MEET DR. JEKYLL AND MR. HYDE(1953), w; UGLY DUCKLING(1959, Brit.), w; KIDNAPPED(1960), w; HOUSE OF FRIGHT(1961), w; WRONG BOX, THE(1966, Brit.), w; DR. JEKYLL AND SISTER HYDE(1971, Brit.), w; KIDNAPPED(1971, Brit.), w; MAN WITH TWO HEADS, THE(1972), d&w; TREASURE ISLAND(1972, Brit./Span./Fr./Ger.), w; SCALAWAG(1973, Yugo.), w; JEKYLL AND HYDE...TOGETHER AGAIN(1982), w
Silents
KIDNAPPED(1917), w; TREASURE ISLAND(1920), w; EBB TIDE(1922), w
Robert Louis Stevenson II
WEDDING NIGHT, THE(1935)
Robert R. Stevenson
WHERE DANGER LIVES(1950)
Rosalind A. Stevenson
TWO VOICES(1966), p&d
Rovert Stevenson
WINDBAG THE SAILOR(1937, Brit.), w
Simone Stevenson
1984
RENO AND THE DOC(1984, Can.)
Tom Stevenson
INTERNATIONAL SQUADRON(1941); NINE LIVES ARE NOT ENOUGH(1941); PASSAGE FROM HONG KONG(1941); WOLF MAN, THE(1941); ACROSS THE PACIFIC(1942); COUNTER-ESPIONAGE(1942); EAGLE SQUADRON(1942); HIDDEN HAND, THE(1942); LONDON BLACKOUT MURDERS(1942); NAZI AGENT(1942); FIRST COMES COURAGE(1943); HAPPY LAND(1943); MANTRAP, THE(1943); SONG OF BERNADETTE, THE(1943); GASLIGHT(1944); MR. SKEFFINGTON(1944); MARGIE(1946); O.S.S.(1946); TEMPTATION(1946); TILL THE CLOUDS ROLL BY(1946); FOREVER AMBER(1947); HUCKSTERS, THE(1947); LONE WOLF IN LONDON(1947); MOTHER WORE TIGHTS(1947); MY WILD IRISH ROSE(1947); SWORDSMAN, THE(1947); HOLLOW TRIUMPH(1948); LUCK OF THE IRISH(1948); MATING OF MILLIE, THE(1948); MIRACLE OF THE BELLS, THE(1948); MR. PEABODY AND THE MERMAID(1948); WHEN MY BABY SMILES AT ME(1948); LADY TAKES A SAILOR, THE(1949); SECRET OF ST. IVES, THE(1949); CARGO TO CAPETOWN(1950)
Venetia Stevenson
DARBY'S RANGERS(1958); VIOLENT ROAD(1958); DAY OF THE OUTLAW(1959); ISLAND OF LOST WOMEN(1959); BIG NIGHT, THE(1960); HORROR HOTEL(1960, Brit.); JET OVER THE ATLANTIC(1960); SEVEN WAYS FROM SUNDOWN(1960); STUDS LONIGAN(1960); SERGEANT WAS A LADY, THE(1961)
William H. Stevenson
BUSHBABY, THE(1970), w
Carl Stever
F.J. HOLDEN, THE(1977, Aus.)
Hans Stever
Misc. Silents
PAWNS OF PASSION(1929, Fr./USSR)
Ed Stevlingson
VERTIGO(1958); LAST SUMMER(1969)
Charles Stevns
WARPATH(1951)
Cabin Steward
NEXT TO NO TIME(1960, Brit.)
Don Steward
RED RIVER(1948), spec eff; LAND OF THE PHARAOHS(1955), spec eff; WHATEVER HAPPENED TO BABY JANE?(1962), spec eff
Doug Steward
JINXED!(1982), ed
Edward Steward
EYES THAT KILL(1947, Brit.), art d
Ernest Steward
COMING-OUT PARTY, A(, ph; WEEKEND MILLIONAIRE(1937, Brit.), ph; ISLAND RESCUE(1952, Brit.), ph; DAY TO REMEMBER, A(1953, Brit.), ph; TOP OF THE FORM(1953, Brit.), ph; DOCTOR IN THE HOUSE(1954, Brit.), ph; MAD ABOUT MEN(1954, Brit.), ph; UP TO HIS NECK(1954, Brit.), ph; DOCTOR AT SEA(1955, Brit.), ph; TROUBLE IN STORE(1955, Brit.), ph; ABOVE US THE WAVES(1956, Brit.), ph; CASH ON DELIVERY(1956, Brit.), ph; IRON PETTICOAT, THE(1956, Brit.), ph; SIMON AND LAURA(1956, Brit.), ph; CAMPBELL'S KINGDOM(1957, Brit.), ph; DOCTOR AT LARGE(1957, Brit.), ph; SECRET PLACE, THE(1958, Brit.), ph; TALE OF TWO CITIES, A(1958, Brit.), ph; WIND CANNOT READ, THE(1958, Brit.), ph; PASSIONATE SUMMER(1959, Brit.), ph; CONSPIRACY OF HEARTS(1960,

Brit.), ph; DOCTOR IN LOVE(1960, Brit.), ph; PICCADILLY THIRD STOP(1960, Brit.), ph; THIRTY NINE STEPS, THE(1960, Brit.), ph; NO LOVE FOR JOHNNIE(1961, Brit.), ph; UPSTAIRS AND DOWNSTAIRS(1961, Brit.), ph; MAKE MINE A DOUBLE(1962, Brit.), ph; PAYROLL(1962, Brit.), ph; BITTER HARVEST(1963, Brit.), ph; CROOKS ANONYMOUS(1963, Brit.), ph; DOCTOR IN DISTRESS(1963, Brit.), ph; PAIR OF BRIEFS, A(1963, Brit.), ph; WRONG ARM OF THE LAW, THE(1963, Brit.), ph; NO, MY DARLING DAUGHTER(1964, Brit.), ph; YOUNG AND WILLING(1964, Brit.), ph; FACE OF FU MANCHU, THE(1965, Brit.), ph; I'VE GOTTA HORSE(1965, Brit.), ph; TEN LITTLE INDIANS(1965, Brit.), ph; MC GUIRE, GO HOME!(1966, Brit.), ph; 24 HOURS TO KILL(1966, Brit.), ph; CARNABY, M.D.(1967, Brit.), ph; DEADLIER THAN THE MALE(1967, Brit.), ph; MAGNIFICENT TWO, THE(1967, Brit.), ph; PSYCHO-CIRCUS(1967, Brit.), ph; CARRY ON, UP THE KHYBER(1968, Brit.), ph; HIGH COMMISSIONER, THE(1968, U.S./Brit.), ph; CARRY ON AGAIN, DOCTOR(1969, Brit.), ph; CARRY ON CAMPING(1969, Brit.), ph; SOME GIRLS DO(1969, Brit.), ph; CARRY ON LOVING(1970, Brit.), ph; CARRY ON UP THE JUNGLE(1970, Brit.), ph; DOCTOR IN TROUBLE(1970, Brit.), ph; PERCY(1971, Brit.), ph; QUEST FOR LOVE(1971, Brit.), ph; DARK PLACES(1974, Brit.), ph; HENNESSY(1975, Brit.), ph; CARRY ON ENGLAND(1976, Brit.), ph; GET CHARLIE TULLY(1976, Brit.), ph; WILDCATS OF ST. TRINIAN'S, THE(1980, Brit.), ph

Ernest W. Steward
ONE MORE TIME(1970, Brit.), ph

Ernie Steward
DULCIMER STREET(1948, Brit.), ph

James Steward
COUNTRY BOY(1966)

Kenny Steward
SHORT EYES(1977)

Leslie Steward
Silents
LOVE AT THE WHEEL(1921, Brit.)

Orville Steward
TIME OF THE HEATHEN(1962)

Peggy Steward
MAN ABOUT TOWN(1939)

Peter Steward [Sam Newfield]
FRONTIER CRUSADER(1940), d

Joe Stewardson
AFTER YOU, COMRADE(1967, S. Afr.); WILD SEASON(1968, South Africa); MY WAY(1974, South Africa); CITY LOVERS(1982, S. African)

Joe Stewardson
Misc. Talkies
SUPER-JOCKS, THE(1980)

Michael Stewarry
BYE BYE BIRDIE(1963), w

Al Stewart
MIRACLE WOMAN, THE(1931); WHEN THE LIGHTS GO ON AGAIN(1944); SGT. PEPPER'S LONELY HEARTS CLUB BAND(1978)

Al H. Stewart
MAID OF SALEM(1937)

Alana Stewart
1984
SWING SHIFT(1984); WHERE THE BOYS ARE '84(1984)

Alexandra Stewart
EXODUS(1960); TARZAN THE MAGNIFICENT(1960, Brit.); GAME FOR SIX LOVERS, A(1962, Fr.); PASSION OF SLOW FIRE, THE(1962, Fr.); NAKED AUTUMN(1963, Fr.); SEASON FOR LOVE, THE(1963, Fr.); FIRE WITHIN, THE(1964, Fr./Ital.); SWEET AND SOUR(1964, Fr./Ital.); AND SO TO BED(1965, Ger.); MICKEY ONE(1965); MAROC 7(1967, Brit.); ONLY WHEN I LARF(1968, Brit.); BYE BYE BARBARA(1969, Fr.); WAITING FOR CAROLINE(1969, Can.); MAN WHO HAD POWER OVER WOMEN, THE(1970, Brit.); ZEPPELIN(1971, Brit.); FAR FROM DALLAS(1972, Fr.); DAY FOR NIGHT(1973, Fr.); DESTRUCTORS, THE(1974, Brit.); BLACK MOON(1975, Fr.); UNCANNY, THE(1977, Brit./Can.); IN PRAISE OF OLDER WOMEN(1978, Can.); FINAL ASSIGNMENT(1980, Can.); GOODBYE EMMANUELLE(1980, Fr.); PHOBIA(1980, Can.); AGENCY(1981, Can.); CHANEL SOLITAIRE(1981); LAST CHASE, THE(1981)
1984
LE BON PLAISIR(1984, Fr.)
Misc. Talkies
BECAUSE OF THE CATS(1974)

Alistair Stewart
RANDOLPH FAMILY, THE(1945, Brit.)

Andy Stewart
BATTLE BEYOND THE SUN(1963)

Anita Stewart
Silents
JUGGERNAUT, THE(1915); SINS OF THE MOTHERS(1915); MIDNIGHT ROMANCE, A(1919); IN OLD KENTUCKY(1920); HER MAD BARGAIN(1921); INVISIBLE FEAR, THE(1921); PLAYTHINGS OF DESTINY(1921); QUESTION OF HONOR, A(1922); SOULS FOR SALE(1923); NEVER THE TWAIN SHALL MEET(1925); LODGE IN THE WILDERNESS, THE(1926); PRINCE OF PILSEN, THE(1926); NAME THE WOMAN(1928)
Misc. Silents
MILLION BID, A(1914); COMBAT, THE(1916); DARING OF DIANA, THE(1916); MY LADY'S SLIPPER(1916); SUSPECT, THE(1916); CLOVER'S REBELLION(1917); GIRL PHILIPPA, THE(1917); GLORY OF YOLANDA, THE(1917); MESSAGE OF THE MOUSE, THE(1917); MORE EXCELLENT WAY, THE(1917); FROM HEADQUARTERS(1919); HER KINGDOM OF DREAMS(1919); HUMAN DESIRE, THE(1919); MARY REGAN(1919); MIND THE PAINT GIRL(1919); PAINTED WORLD, THE(1919); SHADOWS OF THE PAST(1919); TWO WOMEN(1919); VIRTUOUS WIVES(1919); FIGHTING SHEPHERDESS, THE(1920); HARRIET AND THE PIPER(1920); YELLOW TAIFUN(1920); YELLOW TYPHOON, THE(1920); SOWING THE WIND(1921); ROSE O' THE SEA(1922); WOMAN HE MARRIED, THE(1922); LOVE PIKER, THE(1923); GREAT WHITE WAY, THE(1924); BAREE, SON OF KAZAN(1925); BOOMERANG, THE(1925); MORGANSON'S FINISH(1926); RUSTLING FOR CUPID(1926); WHISPERING WIRES(1926); ROMANCE OF A ROGUE(1928); SISTERS OF EVE(1928)

Ann Stewart
NEW WINE(1941)

Anna Stewart
Misc. Talkies
SOUTH OF HELL MOUNTAIN(1971)

Anna Marie Stewart
VALLEY OF HUNTED MEN(1942); THREE RUSSIAN GIRLS(1943); MRS. PARKINGTON(1944)

Art Stewart
OCEAN'S ELEVEN(1960); GOLD OF THE SEVEN SAINTS(1961); GREAT RACE, THE(1965)

Athole Stewart
TO WHAT RED HELL(1929, Brit.); CANARIES SOMETIMES SING(1930, Brit.); TEMPORARY WIDOW, THE(1930, Ger./Brit.); SPECKLED BAND, THE(1931, Brit.); FRAIL WOMEN(1932, Brit.); CONSTANT NYMPH, THE(1933, Brit.); FAITHFUL HEART(1933, Brit.); LITTLE DAMOZEL, THE(1933, Brit.); FOUR MASKED MEN(1934, Brit.); LOYALTIES(1934, Brit.); PATH OF GLORY, THE(1934, Brit.); TOO MANY MILLIONS(1934, Brit.); CLAIRVOYANT, THE(1935, Brit.); WHILE PARENTS SLEEP(1935, Brit.); ACCUSED(1936, Brit.); AMATEUR GENTLEMAN(1936, Brit.); WHERE'S SALLY?(1936, Brit.); ACTION FOR SLANDER(1937, Brit.); DOCTOR SYN(1937, Brit.); TENTH MAN, THE(1937, Brit.); BREAK THE NEWS(1938, Brit.); CLIMBING HIGH(1938, Brit.); HIDEOUT IN THE ALPS(1938, Brit.); HIS LORDSHIP REGRETS(1938, Brit.); SINGING COP, THE(1938, Brit.); THISTLEDOWN(1938, Brit.); TWO OF US, THE(1938, Brit.); CONFIDENTIAL LADY(1939, Brit.); U-BOAT 29(1939, Brit.); FACE BEHIND THE SCAR(1940, Brit.); OLD MOTHER RILEY IN SOCIETY(1940, Brit.); SECRET FOUR, THE(1940, Brit.); THEY CAME BY NIGHT(1940, Brit.); TILLY OF BLOOMSBURY(1940, Brit.); WHO IS GUILTY?(1940, Brit.); IT HAPPENED TO ONE MAN(1941, Brit.); POISON PEN(1941, Brit.); MAXWELL ARCHER, DETECTIVE(1942, Brit.)

Avril Stewart
MONTY PYTHON AND THE HOLY GRAIL(1975, Brit.)

Barbara Stewart
LUCY GALLANT(1955)

Barry Stewart
LUCK OF GINGER COFFEY, THE(1964, U.S./Can.)

Blanche Stewart
NIGHT AT EARL CARROLL'S, A(1940); SWING IT SOLDIER(1941); SWEETHEART OF THE FLEET(1942)

Bob Stewart
COUNTRY BOY(1966); TRACK OF THUNDER(1967)
Misc. Talkies
MAN OUTSIDE(1965)

Bobby Stewart
BAMBI(1942)

Brad Stewart
Misc. Talkies
LEGEND OF FRANK WOODS, THE(1977)

Bruce Stewart
HAND OF NIGHT, THE(1968, Brit.), w; SUNSET COVE(1978), m

Bunty Stewart
Misc. Silents
JADE HEART, THE(1915, Brit.); ON THE STEPS OF THE ALTAR(1916, Brit.)

Byron Stewart
FIRE SALE(1977)

Carol "Lynne" Stewart
HANDLE WITH CARE(1964)

Catherine Mary Stewart
NIGHTHAWKS(1981)
1984
LAST STARFIGHTER, THE(1984); NIGHT OF THE COMET(1984)

Cecil Stewart
WOMAN'S FACE(1941); TONIGHT AND EVERY NIGHT(1945); UNSUSPECTED, THE(1947); SUN COMES UP, THE(1949)

Cecile Stewart
CASANOVA BROWN(1944)

Charles Stewart
LINEUP, THE(1958); WAR OF THE COLOSSAL BEAST(1958); PRAISE MARX AND PASS THE AMMUNITION(1970, Brit.), ph; FAMILY LIFE(1971, Brit.), ph; ALPHA BETA(1973, Brit.), ph; PROSTITUTE(1980, Brit.), ph; DEEP IN THE HEART(1983), ph; SAVANNAH SMILES(1983), prod d

Charles J. Stewart
WAR OF THE WORLDS, THE(1953)

Charlie Stewart
WHEN EIGHT BELLS TOLL(1971, Brit.)

Charlotte Stewart
V.D.(1961); SLENDER THREAD, THE(1965); CHEYENNE SOCIAL CLUB, THE(1970); ERASERHEAD(1978); BUDDY BUDDY(1981); HUMAN HIGHWAY(1982)
1984
IRRECONCILABLE DIFFERENCES(1984)

Chris Menges and Charles Stewart
GAMEKEEPER, THE(1980, Brit.), ph

Chuck Stewart
FRIGHTMARE(1983), spec eff,

Cindy Stewart
WOMEN OF DESIRE(1968)

Craig Stewart
STACEY!(1973), ed

Danny Stewart
WILD HARVEST(1947)

Dave Stewart
CLOSE ENCOUNTERS OF THE THIRD KIND(1977), ph; STAR TREK: THE MOTION PICTURE(1979), spec eff

David Stewart
SILVER CHALICE, THE(1954); YOUNG SAVAGES, THE(1961); WHO'S MINDING THE MINT?(1967)

David J. Stewart
CARNIVAL ROCK(1957); MURDER, INC.(1960)

Deborah Stewart
CLASH BY NIGHT(1952)

Dennis Stewart
ZOOT SUIT(1981); D.C. CAB(1983)

Dennis C. Stewart
GREASE(1978); GREASE 2(1982)

Diane Stewart
EXILE, THE(1947); TYCOON(1947); BIG CLOCK, THE(1948); FORCE OF EVIL(1948); CRISS CROSS(1949); CLASH BY NIGHT(1952)

Diane Lee Stewart
DOUBLE LIFE, A(1947); LETTER FROM AN UNKNOWN WOMAN(1948); THREE DARING DAUGHTERS(1948)

Dick Stewart
SHOTGUN PASS(1932); GLASS WEB, THE(1953); GOOD MORNING, MISS DOVE(1955); THAT'S THE WAY OF THE WORLD(1975)

Don Stewart
TOWER OF LONDON(1939); WILD HORSE STAMPEDE(1943); ARIZONA WHIRL-WIND(1944); VALLEY OF MYSTERY(1967)
Misc. Talkies
LOST(1983)

Donald Stewart
DEVOTION(1931); CYNARA(1932); CHRISTOPHER STRONG(1933); FIRST A GIRL(1935, Brit.); FINE FEATHERS(1937, Brit.); FLYING FORTRESS(1942, Brit.); PETERVILLE DIAMOND, THE(1942, Brit.); WELCOME, MR. WASHINGTON(1944, Brit.); YOU CAN'T DO WITHOUT LOVE(1946, Brit.); LUCKY NICK CAIN(1951); THING, THE(1951), spec eff; RAMSBOTTOM RIDES AGAIN(1956, Brit.); TWO GROOMS FOR A BRIDE(1957); CROSS-UP(1958); SHERIFF OF FRACTURED JAW, THE(1958, Brit.); JACKSON COUNTY JAIL(1976), w; DEATHSPORT(1978), w; MISSING(1982), w
Misc. Talkies
WHERE TRAILS END(1942)
Misc. Silents
GIRL-SHY COWBOY, THE(1928)

Donald Ogden Stewart
TARNISHED LADY(1931), w; THAT UNCERTAIN FEELING(1941), w; LAUGHTER(1930), w; NOT SO DUMB(1930); FINN AND HATTIE(1931), w; REBOUND(1931), w; ANOTHER LANGUAGE(1933), w; DINNER AT EIGHT(1933), w; GOING HOLLYWOOD(1933), w; WHITE SISTER, THE(1933), a, w; BARRETTS OF WIMPOLE STREET, THE(1934), w; NO MORE LADIES(1935), a, w; PRISONER OF ZENDA, THE(1937), w; HOLIDAY(1938), w; MARIE ANTOINETTE(1938), w; LOVE AFFAIR(1939), w; NIGHT OF NIGHTS(1939), w; KITTY FOYLE(1940), w; PHILADELPHIA STORY, THE(1940), w; SMILIN' THROUGH(1941), w; WOMAN'S FACE(1941), w; KEEPER OF THE FLAME(1942), w; TALES OF MANHATTAN(1942), w; FOREVER AND A DAY(1943), w; WITHOUT LOVE(1945), w; CASS TIMBERLANE(1947), w; LIFE WITH FATHER(1947), w; EDWARD, MY SON(1949, U.S./Brit.), w; MALAGA(1962, Brit.), w
Silents
BROWN OF HARVARD(1926), w

Doug Stewart
GIRL IN THE WOODS(1958), ed; ROUGH CUT(1980, Brit.), ed

Douglas Stewart
WARN LONDON!(1934, Brit.); ROLLING HOME(1935, Brit.); SCARLET PIMPERNEL, THE(1935, Brit.); WELL DONE, HENRY(1936, Brit.); LITTLE DOLLY DAYDREAM(1938, Brit.); NIGHT JOURNEY(1938, Brit.); OLD MOTHER RILEY IN PARIS(1938, Brit.); STRANGE BOARDERS(1938, Brit.); FRONT LINE KIDS(1942, Brit.); GERT AND DAISY CLEAN UP(1942, Brit.); MYSTERIOUS MR. NICHOLSON, THE(1947, Brit.); MY BROTHER'S KEEPER(1949, Brit.); HITCH-HIKER, THE(1953), ed; EIGHTEEN AND ANXIOUS(1957), ed; NIGHTMARE IN THE SUN(1964), ed; GAMES(1967), ed; CHANGE OF HABIT(1969), ed; GREAT NORTHFIELD, MINNESOTA RAID, THE(1972), ed; WHERE THE RED FERN GROWS(1974), w; WHITE DAWN, THE(1974), ed; SEVEN ALONE(1975), w; SHOOTIST, THE(1976), ed; TELEFON(1977), ed; INVASION OF THE BODY SNATCHERS(1978), ed; WALK PROUD(1979), ed; FAST-WALKING(1982), ed; RIGHT STUFF, THE(1983), ed

Douglas C. Stewart
AGAINST A CROOKED SKY(1975), w

Douglas Day Stewart
OTHER SIDE OF THE MOUNTAIN–PART 2, THE(1978), w; BLUE LAGOON, THE(1980), w; OFFICER AND A GENTLEMAN, AN(1982), w
1984
THIEF OF HEARTS(1984), d&w

Ed Stewart
FROM THE MIXED-UP FILES OF MRS. BASIL E. FRANKWEILER(1973), set d; NEXT STOP, GREENWICH VILLAGE(1976), set d; SENTINEL, THE(1977), set d; WILLIE AND PHIL(1980), set d; SOUP FOR ONE(1982), set d

Edmund Stewart
IVORY HUNTER(1952, Brit.)

Edward Stewart
POSSESSION OF JOEL DELANEY, THE(1972), set d; SHAMUS(1973), set d; GAMBLER, THE(1974), set d; NETWORK(1976), set d; UNMARRIED WOMAN, AN(1978), set d

Elaine Stewart
SAILOR BEWARE(1951); BAD AND THE BEAUTIFUL, THE(1952); DESPERATE SEARCH(1952); EVERYTHING I HAVE IS YOURS(1952); ROGUE'S MARCH(1952); SINGIN' IN THE RAIN(1952); SKY FULL OF MOON(1952); YOU FOR ME(1952); CODE TWO(1953); SLIGHT CASE OF LARCENY, A(1953); TAKE THE HIGH GROUND(1953); YOUNG BESS(1953); ADVENTURES OF HAJJI BABA(1954); BRIGADOON(1954); MEET ME IN LAS VEGAS(1956); NIGHT PASSAGE(1957); TATTERED DRESS, THE(1957); HIGH HELL(1958); ESCORT WEST(1959); RISE AND FALL OF LEGS DIAMOND, THE(1960); MOST DANGEROUS MAN ALIVE, THE(1961); SEVEN REVENGES, THE(1967, Ital.)

Eldean Stewart
Misc. Silents
BLADE O' GRASS(1915)

Eleanor Stewart
LOVE ON THE RUN(1936); ARIZONA DAYS(1937); GUN RANGER, THE(1937); HEADIN' FOR THE RIO GRANDE(1937); HEADLINE CRASHER(1937); RANGE DEFENDERS(1937); RANGERS STEP IN, THE(1937); TRAPPED BY G-MEN(1937); WHERE TRAILS DIVIDE(1937); MEXICALI KID, THE(1938); PAINTED TRAIL, THE(1938); ROLLING CARAVANS(1938); STAGECOACH DAYS(1938); ETERNALLY YOURS(1939); FLAMING LEAD(1939); CAUGHT IN THE DRAFT(1941); LAS VEGAS NIGHTS(1941); LOUISIANA PURCHASE(1941); PIRATES ON HORSEBACK(1941); RIDERS OF THE TIMBERLINE(1941); WEST POINT WIDOW(1941); GREAT MAN'S LADY, THE(1942); MEN OF SAN QUENTIN(1942); SILVER QUEEN(1942); MYSTERY MAN(1944); FRIDAY THE 13TH... THE ORPHAN(1979)
Misc. Talkies
SANTA FE RIDES(1937); FIGHTING DEVIL DOGS(1938)

Eleanore Stewart
WATERLOO BRIDGE(1940)

Elinore Randall Stewart
HEARTLAND(1980), w

Elizabeth Stewart
SWIMMER, THE(1968), cos

Enid Stewart
DEATM GOES TO SCHOOL(1953, Brit.)

Ernest Stewart
CHECKPOINT(1957, Brit.), ph; BRIDES OF FU MANCHU, THE(1966, Brit.), ph

Ethel Stewart
COME OUT OF THE PANTRY(1935, Brit.)
Misc. Silents
IMP, THE(1920)

Evelyn Stewart
HE WHO SHOOTS FIRST(1966, Ital.); ADIOS GRINGO(1967, Ital./Fr./Span.); SWEET BODY OF DEBORAH, THE(1969, Ital./Fr.); UNHOLY FOUR, THE(1969, Ital.); WEEK-END MURDERS, THE(1972, Ital.); EAGLE OVER LONDON(1973, Ital.); CAGLIOSTRO(1975, Ital.); NIGHT CHILD(1975, Brit./Ital.); PSYCHIC, THE(1979, Ital.)
Misc. Talkies
WHY KILL AGAIN?(1965)

Ewan Stewart
THAT SUMMER(1979, Brit.); REMEMBRANCE(1982, Brit.)
1984
FLIGHT TO BERLIN(1984, Ger./Brit.)

Frank Stewart
HONEYSUCKLE ROSE(1980)

Fred Stewart
MISLEADING LADY, THE(1932); SPLENDOR IN THE GRASS(1961); WORLD OF HENRY ORIENT, THE(1964); IN THE HEAT OF THE NIGHT(1967); NEW LEAF, A(1971)

Fred Mustard Stewart
MEPHISTO WALTZ, THE(1971), w; SIX WEEKS(1982), w

Freddie Stewart
FREDDIE STEPS OUT(1946); HIGH SCHOOL HERO(1946); JUNIOR PROM(1946); LOUISIANA(1947); SARGE GOES TO COLLEGE(1947); VACATION DAYS(1947); CAMPUS SLEUTH(1948), a, m; MUSIC MAN(1948); SMART POLITICS(1948), a, m/l

Gary Stewart
TALK ABOUT A STRANGER(1952)

George Stewart
SILVER SKATES(1943)
Silents
ANNE OF GREEN GABLES(1919); MOLLYCODDLE, THE(1920); FIGHTER, THE(1921); SEVENTH DAY, THE(1922); ABYSMAL BRUTE, THE(1923)
Misc. Silents
GILDED LIES(1921); OVER THE WIRE(1921); CROSSED WIRES(1923)

Graham Stewart
COCKLESHELL HEROES, THE(1955); MAN WHO WOULDN'T TALK, THE(1958, Brit.); MAN UPSTAIRS, THE(1959, Brit.); UNSTOPPABLE MAN, THE(1961, Brit.)

Grant Stewart
Silents
RAINBOW PRINCESS, THE(1916); ARMS AND THE GIRL(1917), w

Hamilton Stewart
Silents
HANGING JUDGE, THE(1918, Brit.); KEEPER OF THE DOOR(1919, Brit.)
Misc. Silents
LADY TETLEY'S DEGREE(1920, Brit.)

Harold Stewart
MAN'S AFFAIR, A(1949, Brit.), w

Helen Stewart
WICKED DIE SLOW, THE(1968)

Hommy Stewart
PUFNSTUF(1970)

Horace Stewart
MIND YOUR OWN BUSINESS(1937)

Hugh Stewart
ACTION FOR SLANDER(1937, Brit.), ed; DARK JOURNEY(1937, Brit.), ed; STORM IN A TEACUP(1937, Brit.), ed; SOUTH RIDING(1938, Brit.), ed; CLOUDS OVER EUROPE(1939, Brit.), ed; U-BOAT 29(1939, Brit.), ed; SIDEWALKS OF LONDON(1940, Brit.), ed; MISSING TEN DAYS(1941, Brit.), ed; IT'S IN THE BAG(1943, Brit.); SHOWTIME(1948, Brit.), ed; GAY LADY, THE(1949, Brit.), p; LONG MEMORY, THE(1953, Brit.), p; NIGHT WITHOUT STARS(1953, Brit.), p; UP TO HIS NECK(1954, Brit.), p; MAN OF THE MOMENT(1955, Brit.), p; JUST MY LUCK(1957, Brit.), p; UP IN THE WORLD(1957, Brit.), p; INNOCENT SINNERS(1958, Brit.), p; SQUARE PEG, THE(1958, Brit.), p; FOLLOW A STAR(1959, Brit.), p; MAKE MINE MINK(1960, Brit.), p; BIG MONEY, THE(1962, Brit.), ed; ON THE BEAT(1962, Brit.), p; IN THE DOGHOUSE(1964, Brit.), p; EARLY BIRD, THE(1965, Brit.), p; SPYLARKS(1965, Brit.), p; MAGNIFICENT TWO, THE(1967, Brit.), p; STITCH IN TIME, A(1967, Brit.), p; THAT RIVIERA TOUCH(1968, Brit.), p; ALL AT SEA(1970, Brit.), p; FLYING SORCERER, THE(1974, Brit.), p

Ian Stewart
LOCAL HERO(1983, Brit.)
1984
UTU(1984, New Zealand)

Iva Stewart
THIN ICE(1937); MR. MOTO TAKES A VACATION(1938); SAFETY IN NUMBERS(1938); THREE BLIND MICE(1938); WIFE, HUSBAND AND FRIEND(1939); LITTLE OLD NEW YORK(1940)

Jack Stewart
PRIDE OF THE YANKEES, THE(1942); LADIES' DAY(1943); GORBALS STORY, THE(1950, Brit.); CASE FOR PC 49, A(1951, Brit.); DARK LIGHT, THE(1951, Brit.); BRAVE DON'T CRY, THE(1952, Brit.); STRANGER IN BETWEEN, THE(1952, Brit.); GHOST SHIP(1953, Brit.); HIGH AND DRY(1954, Brit.); LITTLE KIDNAPPERS, THE(1954, Brit.); RADIO CAB MURDER(1954, Brit.); TROUBLE IN THE GLEN(1954, Brit.); FINGER OF GUILT(1956, Brit.); JOHNNY, YOU'RE WANTED(1956, Brit.); HEART WITHIN, THE(1957, Brit.); SPANISH GARDENER, THE(1957, Span.); STEEL

BAYONET, THE(1958, Brit.); BOY AND THE BRIDGE, THE(1959, Brit.); DEVIL'S BAIT(1959, Brit.); KIDNAPPED(1960); FRIGHTENED CITY, THE(1961, Brit.); PIRATES OF BLOOD RIVER, THE(1962, Brit.); STRONGROOM(1962, Brit.); THREE LIVES OF THOMASINA, THE(1963, U.S./Brit.); TOM JONES(1963, Brit.); AMOROUS MR. PRAWN, THE(1965, Brit.)

Jack Stewart [Giacomo Rossi]
KNIVES OF THE AVENGER(1967, Ital.)

James Stewart
MURDER MAN(1935); AFTER THE THIN MAN(1936); BORN TO DANCE(1936); GORGEOUS HUSSY, THE(1936); NEXT TIME WE LOVE(1936); ROSE MARIE(1936); SMALL TOWN GIRL(1936); SPEED(1936); WIFE VERSUS SECRETARY(1936); LAST GANGSTER, THE(1937); SEVENTH HEAVEN(1937); OF HUMAN HEARTS(1938); SHOPWORN ANGEL(1938); VIVACIOUS LADY(1938); YOU CAN'T TAKE IT WITH YOU(1938); DESTRY RIDES AGAIN(1939); ICE FOLLIES OF 1939(1939); IT'S A WONDERFUL WORLD(1939); MADE FOR EACH OTHER(1939); MR. SMITH GOES TO WASHINGTON(1939); MORTAL STORM, THE(1940); NO TIME FOR COMEDY(1940); PHILADELPHIA STORY, THE(1940); SHOP AROUND THE CORNER, THE(1940); COME LIVE WITH ME(1941); POT O' GOLD(1941); ZIEGFELD GIRL(1941); IT'S A WONDERFUL LIFE(1946); MAGIC TOWN(1947); CALL NORTHSIDE 777(1948); ON OUR MERRY WAY(1948); ROPE(1948); YOU GOTTA STAY HAPPY(1948); STRATTON STORY, THE(1949); BROKEN ARROW(1950); HARVEY(1950); JACKPOT, THE(1950); MALAYA(1950); WINCHESTER '73(1950); NO HIGHWAY IN THE SKY(1951, Brit.); BEND OF THE RIVER(1952); CARBINE WILLIAMS(1952); GREATEST SHOW ON EARTH, THE(1952); GLENN MILLER STORY, THE(1953); NAKED SPUR, THE(1953); THUNDER BAY(1953); REAR WINDOW(1954); FAR COUNTRY, THE(1955); MAN FROM LARAMIE, THE(1955); STRATEGIC AIR COMMAND(1955); MAN WHO KNEW TOO MUCH, THE(1956); NIGHT PASSAGE(1957); SPIRIT OF ST. LOUIS, THE(1957); BELL, BOOK AND CANDLE(1958); VERTIGO(1958); ANATOMY OF A MURDER(1959); FBI STORY, THE(1959); MOUNTAIN ROAD, THE(1960); TWO RODE TOGETHER(1961); X-15(1961); HOW THE WEST WAS WON(1962); MAN WHO SHOT LIBERTY VALANCE, THE(1962); MR. HOBBS TAKES A VACATION(1962); TAKE HER, SHE'S MINE(1963); CHEYENNE AUTUMN(1964); DEAR BRIGITTE(1965); FLIGHT OF THE PHOENIX, THE(1965); SHENANDOAH(1965); RARE BREED, THE(1966); BANDOLERO!(1968); FIRECREEK(1968); CHEYENNE SOCIAL CLUB, THE(1970); FOOLS' PARADE(1971); SHOOTIST, THE(1976); MAGIC OF LASSIE, THE(1978)

James C. Stewart
ISLAND OF ALLAH(1956)

James L. Stewart
SECRET OF NIMH, THE(1982), p

Janet Stewart
STRANGERS ON A TRAIN(1951); TAKE CARE OF MY LITTLE GIRL(1951); SMALL TOWN GIRL(1953); THEM!(1954); WOMAN'S WORLD(1954); MAN CALLED PETER, THE(1955)

James Stewart
MAD HATTERS, THE(1935, Brit.), w

James Stewart [Stewart Granger]
SOUTHERN MAID, A(1933, Brit.)

Jaye Stewart
ALL THE PRESIDENT'S MEN(1976)

Jean Stewart
Silents
SEVEN SISTERS, THE(1915); NANETTE OF THE WILDS(1916)

Jean-Pierre Stewart
SOMEBODY KILLED HER HUSBAND(1978); NIGHTHAWKS(1981)

Jerry Stewart
MYSTERY LINER(1934); YOU'RE TELLING ME(1934)

Jimmy Stewart
BIG SLEEP, THE½(1978, Brit.)

Joanne Stewart
WALK THE ANGRY BEACH(1961)

Job Stewart
LIFT, THE(1965, Brit./Can.); LAST SHOT YOU HEAR, THE(1969, Brit.)

John Stewart
FRONT PAGE STORY(1954, Brit.); CRIMSON BLADE, THE(1964, Brit.); SERPICO(1973); WHO?(1975, Brit./Ger.); SGT. PEPPER'S LONELY HEARTS CLUB BAND(1978)

John Michael Stewart
1984
MIKE'S MURDER(1984)

Johna Stewart
1984
IRRECONCILABLE DIFFERENCES(1984)

Johnny Stewart
BOOTS MALONE(1952); LAST OF THE COMANCHES(1952)

Joy Stewart
DARWIN ADVENTURE, THE(1972, Brit.)

Julie Stewart
DEATM GOES TO SCHOOL(1953, Brit.)

Katherine Stewart
Misc. Silents
HOW WOMEN LOVE(1922)

Kathy Stewart
DEMON LOVER, THE(1977)

Kay Stewart
FRESHMAN YEAR(1938); NINOTCHKA(1939); WHAT A LIFE(1939); CHRISTMAS IN JULY(1940); GHOST BREAKERS, THE(1940); THOSE WERE THE DAYS(1940); LIFE WITH HENRY(1941); MR. SCOUTMASTER(1953); PRIVATE WAR OF MAJOR BENSON, THE(1955); SQUARE JUNGLE, THE(1955); SPARTACUS(1960); 40 GUNS TO APACHE PASS(1967)

Ken Stewart
GIRL CRAZY(1943); HARD TRAIL(1969), ed

Larry Stewart
SLEEPY LAGOON(1943); LITTLE BIG HORN(1951); PURPLE HEART DIARY(1951); YANK IN KOREA, A(1951); ONE MINUTE TO ZERO(1952); THIEF OF DAMASCUS(1952); FRANKENSTEIN CREATED WOMAN(1965, Brit.), cos; DESERTER, THE(1971 Ital./Yugo.)
1984
INITIATION, THE(1984), d

Laurence Stewart
HELL ON DEVIL'S ISLAND(1957), p; PLUNDER ROAD(1957), p

Lawrence Stewart
THE INVISIBLE RAY(1936)

Leon Stewart
MALAYA(1950)

Leonora Stewart
Misc. Silents
PRUSSIAN CUR, THE(1918)

Leslie Stewart
Misc. Silents
SECRET CODE, THE(1918)

Lily Stewart
MORE THAN A SECRETARY(1936)

Lucie Stewart
ANNIE(1982)

Lucille Lee Stewart
Silents
SINS OF THE MOTHERS(1915); OUR MRS. McCHESNEY(1918); PERFECT LOVER, THE(1919); WOMAN'S BUSINESS, A(1920); SHAMS OF SOCIETY(1921)
Misc. Silents
CONFLICT, THE(1916); DESTROYERS, THE(1916); HIS WIFE'S GOOD NAME(1916); NINETY AND NINE, THE(1916); FIVE THOUSAND AN HOUR(1918); EASTWARD HO!(1919); SEALED HEARTS(1919); WOMAN GIVES, THE(1920); BAD COMPANY(1925)

Lynn Stewart
I NEVER PROMISED YOU A ROSE GARDEN(1977)

Lynn Marie Stewart
AMERICAN GRAFFITI(1973); TUNNELVISION(1976)

Lynne Stewart
1984
WEEKEND PASS(1984)

Lynne Marie Stewart
YOUR THREE MINUTES ARE UP(1973); LAST MARRIED COUPLE IN AMERICA, THE(1980); YOUNG DOCTORS IN LOVE(1982)

MacLaren Stewart
FANTASIA(1940), art d

Maitland Stewart
DEVIL'S BEDROOM, THE(1964), ph

Margie Stewart
AROUND THE WORLD(1943); FALCON AND THE CO-EDS, THE(1943); FALLEN SPARROW, THE(1943); GILDERSLEEVE'S BAD DAY(1943); MEXICAN SPITFIRE'S BLESSED EVENT(1943); FALCON IN HOLLYWOOD, THE(1944); GILDERSLEEVE'S GHOST(1944); HEAVENLY DAYS(1944); MADEMOISELLE FIFI(1944); MUSIC IN MANHATTAN(1944); NEVADA(1944); HAVING WONDERFUL CRIME(1945); WONDER MAN(1945)

Marian Stewart
Misc. Silents
LA BELLE RUSSE(1919)

Marianne Stewart
RIGHT CROSS(1950); TIMETABLE(1956); BACK FROM THE DEAD(1957); HOT SUMMER NIGHT(1957); BIG FISHERMAN, THE(1959); FACTS OF LIFE, THE(1960); HUSH... HUSH, SWEET CHARLOTTE(1964)

Marjorie Stewart
LITTLE BIG SHOT(1952, Brit.); WEAK AND THE WICKED, THE(1954, Brit.); MASTER PLAN, THE(1955, Brit.); WOMAN FOR JOE, THE(1955, Brit.)

Mark Stewart
TRON(1982)

Marlene Stewart
1984
BODY ROCK(1984), cos

Martha Stewart
LOCKED DOOR, THE(1929); DOLL FACE(1945); JOHNNY COMES FLYING HOME(1946); DAISY KENYON(1947); I WONDER WHO'S KISSING HER NOW(1947); ARE YOU WITH IT?(1948); CONVICTED(1950); IN A LONELY PLACE(1950); AARON SLICK FROM PUNKIN CRICK(1952); SURF PARTY(1964)

Mary Stewart
HOLIDAY AFFAIR(1949); MOON-SPINNERS, THE(1964), w

Maud Stewart
Misc. Silents
REDEEMED(1915, Brit.)

Maurice Stewart
DEATH CURSE OF TARTU(1967)
Silents
MOTH AND THE FLAME, THE(1915)

Maury Stewart, Jr.
Silents
POLLY OF THE CIRCUS(1917)

Maxine Stewart
EVERYTHING'S ON ICE(1939); VIOLATORS, THE(1957)

McLaren Stewart
SNOW WHITE AND THE SEVEN DWARFS(1937), art d; PINOCCHIO(1940), art d; MARY POPPINS(1964), anim

Mel Stewart
ODDS AGAINST TOMORROW(1959); FUNNYMAN(1967); HAMMER(1972); TRICK BABY(1973); NEWMAN'S LAW(1974); LET'S DO IT AGAIN(1975); WHOSE LIFE IS IT ANYWAY?(1981)

Melville Stewart
Misc. Silents
AFTER DARK(1915); GALLOPER, THE(1915)

Melvin Stewart
NOTHING BUT A MAN(1964); LANDLORD, THE(1970); KID BLUE(1973); SCORPIO(1973); STEELYARD BLUES(1973)

Michael Stewart
ONE PLUS ONE(1961, Can.)

Mike Stewart
YELLOW SUBMARINE(1958, Brit.), animation

Morris Walcot Stewart, Jr.
Silents
EVIDENCE(1915)
Muriel Stewart
MARRIAGE BOND, THE(1932, Brit.), w
Nan Stewart
WHO HAS SEEN THE WIND(1980, Can.)
Nancy E. Stewart
SOMETHING'S ROTTEN(1979, Can.), p
Nicholas Stewart
LOOKING GLASS WAR, THE(1970, Brit.)
Nick Stewart
MY SON, THE HERO(1943); I LOVE A BANDLEADER(1945); SHE WOULDN'T SAY YES(1945); NO HOLDS BARRED(1952); CARMEN JONES(1954); FLAME OF THE ISLANDS(1955); PHANTOM OF THE JUNGLE(1955); THUNDER OVER SANGOLAND(1955); SILVER STREAK(1976)
Nicodemus Stewart
GO WEST, YOUNG MAN(1936); STORMY WEATHER(1943); FOLLOW THE BOYS(1944); GILDERSLEEVE'S GHOST(1944); COLONEL EFFINGHAM'S RAID(1945); DAKOTA(1945); CENTENNIAL SUMMER(1946); NIGHT AND DAY(1946); NIGHT TRAIN TO MEMPHIS(1946); SONG OF THE SOUTH(1946); DOWN TO EARTH(1947); VOICE OF THE TURTLE, THE(1947)
Noel Stewart
Silents
JACK O' CLUBS(1924)
Patricia Stewart
GENTLE GUNMAN, THE(1952, Brit.)
Patrick Stewart
HEDDA(1975, Brit.); HENNESSY(1975, Brit.); EXCALIBUR(1981)
1984
DUNE(1984); PLAGUE DOGS, THE(1984, U.S./Brit.)
Paul Stewart
CITIZEN KANE(1941); JOHNNY EAGER(1942); GOVERNMENT GIRL(1943); MR. LUCKY(1943); CHAMPION(1949); EASY LIVING(1949); ILLEGAL ENTRY(1949); TWELVE O'CLOCK HIGH(1949); WINDOW, THE(1949); EDGE OF DOOM(1950); WALK SOFTLY, STRANGER(1950); APPOINTMENT WITH DANGER(1951); BAD AND THE BEAUTIFUL, THE(1952); CARBINE WILLIAMS(1952); DEADLINE-U.S.-A.(1952); LOAN SHARK(1952); WE'RE NOT MARRIED(1952); JOE LOUIS STORY, THE(1953); JUGGLER, THE(1953); DEEP IN MY HEART(1954); PRISONER OF WAR(1954); CHICAGO SYNDICATE(1955); COBWEB, THE(1955); KISS ME DEADLY(1955); HELL ON FRISCO BAY(1956); WILD PARTY, THE(1956); TOP SECRET AFFAIR(1957); KING CREOLE(1958); CHILD IS WAITING, A(1963); GREATEST STORY EVER TOLD, THE(1965); IN COLD BLOOD(1967); JIGSAW(1968); WRECKING CREW, THE(1968), spec eff; HOW TO COMMIT MARRIAGE(1969); FAT CITY(1972), spec eff; MURPH THE SURF(1974); BITE THE BULLET(1975); DAY OF THE LOCUST, THE(1975); W.C. FIELDS AND ME(1976); MR. BILLION(1977), spec eff; OPENING NIGHT(1977); REVENGE OF THE PINK PANTHER(1978); NOBODY'S PERFEKT(1981); S.O.B.(1981); NATIONAL LAMPOON'S CLASS REUNION(1982), spec eff; TEMPEST(1982); TWILIGHT ZONE-THE MOVIE(1983), spec eff
1984
NIGHT SHADOWS(1984), spec eff
Paula Stewart
DIARY OF A BACHELOR(1964); SUPPOSE THEY GAVE A WAR AND NOBODY CAME?(1970); GOING HOME(1971)
Peg Stewart
BOOGENS, THE(1982)
Peggy Stewart
WELLS FARGO(1937); LITTLE TOUGH GUY(1938); LITTLE TOUGH GUYS IN SOCIETY(1938); THAT CERTAIN AGE(1938); EVERYBODY'S HOBBY(1939); ALL THIS AND HEAVEN TOO(1940); BACK STREET(1941); GIRLS IN CHAINS(1943); CHEYENNE WILDCAT(1944); CODE OF THE PRAIRIE(1944); FIREBRANDS OF ARIZONA(1944); SHERIFF OF LAS VEGAS(1944); SILVER CITY KID(1944); STAGECOACH TO MONTEREY(1944); TUCSON RAIDERS(1944); BANDITS OF THE BADLANDS(1945); MARSHAL OF LAREDO(1945); OREGON TRAIL(1945); ROUGH RIDERS OF CHEYENNE(1945); TIGER WOMAN, THE(1945); UTAH(1945); VAMPIRE'S GHOST, THE(1945); ALIAS BILLY THE KID(1946); CONQUEST OF CHEYENNE(1946); DAYS OF BUFFALO BILL(1946); INVISIBLE INFORMER(1946); RED RIVER RENEGADES(1946); SHERIFF OF REDWOOD VALLEY(1946); STAGECOACH TO DENVER(1946); RUSTLERS OF DEVIL'S CANYON(1947); TRAIL TO SAN ANTONE(1947); VIGILANTES OF BOOMTOWN(1947); DEAD MAN'S GOLD(1948); FRONTIER REVENGE(1948); DESERT VIGILANTE(1949); RIDE, RYDER, RIDE!(1949); FIGHTING REDHEAD, THE(1950); MESSENGER OF PEACE(1950); PRIDE OF MARYLAND(1951); BLACK LASH, THE(1952); KANSAS TERRITORY(1952); CLOWN AND THE KID, THE(1961); WHEN THE CLOCK STRIKES(1961); GUN STREET(1962); WAY WEST, THE(1967); ANIMALS, THE(1971); PICKUP ON 101(1972); TERROR IN THE WAX MUSEUM(1973); BOBBIE JO AND THE OUTLAW(1976); BLACK OAK CONSPIRACY(1977)
Misc. Talkies
CALIFORNIA GOLD RUSH(1946); MONTANA INCIDENT(1952)
Penolope Stewart
1984
VIGIL(1984, New Zealand)
Peter Stewart [Sam Newfield]
ARIZONA GANGBUSTERS(1940), d; BILLY THE KID IN TEXAS(1940), d; GUN CODE(1940), d; SAGEBRUSH FAMILY TRAILS WEST, THE(1940), d; BILLY THE KID'S RANGE WAR(1941), d; OUTLAWS OF THE RIO GRANDE(1941), d; RIDERS OF BLACK MOUNTAIN(1941), d; TEXAS MARSHAL, THE(1941), d; PRAIRIE PALS(1942), d; RAIDERS OF THE WEST(1942), d; ROLLING DOWN THE GREAT DIVIDE(1942), d; TEXAS MAN HUNT(1942), d; ADVENTURE ISLAND(1947), d; JUNGLE FLIGHT(1947), d; COUNTERFEITERS, THE(1948), d; MIRACULOUS JOURNEY(1948), d; MONEY MADNESS(1948), d; STATE DEPARTMENT-FILE 649(1949), d
Phillip Stewart
WRONG BOX, THE(1966, Brit.)
Polly Stewart
DR. EHRLICH'S MAGIC BULLET(1940)
Ramona Stewart
DESERT FURY(1947), w; POSSESSION OF JOEL DELANEY, THE(1972), w

Raphael D. Stewart
HESTER STREET(1975), p
Ray Stewart
SPACE RAIDERS(1983)
Richard Stewart
MR. BIG(1943); TERROR SHIP(1954, Brit.); SCOTLAND YARD DRAGNET(1957, Brit.)
Misc. Silents
CITY, THE(1916); FACE TO FACE(1920)
Ritchie Stewart
ULYSSES(1967, U.S./Brit.)
Rob Stewart
DIGBY, THE BIGGEST DOG IN THE WORLD(1974, Brit.)
Robert Stewart
BACKFIRE!(1961, Brit.), w; PLAYBACK(1962, Brit.), w; DOWNFALL(1964, Brit.), w; BRAIN, THE(1965, Ger./Brit.), w; SINISTER MAN, THE(1965, Brit.), w; MARRIAGE OF CONVENIENCE(1970, Brit.), w
1984
SOLDIER'S STORY, A(1984), cos
Robert Banks Stewart
NEVER MENTION MURDER(1964, Brit.), w
Robin Stewart
DAMN THE DEFIANT!(1962, Brit.); TAMAHINE(1964, Brit.); BE MY GUEST(1965, Brit.); CROMWELL(1970, Brit.); HORROR HOUSE(1970, Brit.); DRACULA AND THE SEVEN GOLDEN VAMPIRES(1978, Brit./Chi.)
Rod Stewart
GUEST AT STEENKAMPSKRAAL, THE(1977, South Africa), ph
1984
GUEST, THE(1984, Brit.), ph
Rola Stewart
MASK OF DIMITRIOS, THE(1944)
Ronnie Stewart
ODDS AGAINST TOMORROW(1959)
Rosina Stewart
1984
GIVE MY REGARDS TO BROAD STREET(1984, Brit.)
Roy Stewart
IN OLD ARIZONA(1929); BORN RECKLESS(1930); GREAT DIVIDE, THE(1930); LONE STAR RANGER, THE(1930); MEN WITHOUT WOMEN(1930); ROUGH ROMANCE(1930); FIGHTING CARAVANS(1931); COME ON DANGER!(1932); EXPOSED(1932); MYSTERY RANCH(1932); COME ON TARZAN(1933); FARGO EXPRESS(1933); RUSTLERS' ROUNDUP(1933); ZOO IN BUDAPEST(1933); ONE PLUS ONE(1969, Brit.); JULIUS CAESAR(1970, Brit.); LEO THE LAST(1970, Brit.); TWINS OF EVIL(1971, Brit.); LADY CAROLINE LAMB(1972, Brit./Ital.); LIVE AND LET DIE(1973, Brit.)
Silents
DEVIL DODGER, THE(1917); ONE SHOT ROSS(1917); BY PROXY(1918); FLY GOD, THE(1918); DEVIL TO PAY, THE(1920); LONE HAND, THE(1920); RIDERS OF THE DAWN(1920); MISTRESS OF SHENSTONE, THE(1921); PRISONERS OF LOVE(1921); PURE GRIT(1923); LADY FROM HELL, THE(1926); SPARROWS(1926); LITTLE BIG HORN(1927); MIDNIGHT WATCH, THE(1927); ONE WOMAN TO ANOTHER(1927); STORMY WATERS(1928); PROTECTION(1929)
Misc. Silents
INNER STRUGGLE, THE(1916); MIXED BLOOD(1916); THOROUGHBRED, THE(1916); BOND OF FEAR, THE(1917); DAUGHTER OF THE POOR, A(1917); DOUBLE STANDARD, THE(1917); FOLLOW THE GIRL(1917); HOUSE BUILT UPON SAND, THE(1917); LEARNIN' OF JIM BENTON, THE(1917); MEDICINE MAN, THE(1917); BOSS OF THE LAZY Y, THE(1918); CACTUS CRANDALL(1918); FAITH AND ENDURIN'(1918); KEITH OF THE BORDER(1918); LAW'S OUTLAW, THE(1918); PAYING HIS DEBT(1918); RED-HAIRED CUPID, A(1918); SILENT RIDER, THE(1918); UNTAMED(1918); WOLVES OF THE BORDER(1918); WESTERNERS, THE(1919); BEAUTY MARKET, THE(1920); JUST A WIFE(1920); MONEY CHANGERS, THE(1920); SAGEBRUSHER, THE(1920); U.P. TRAIL, THE(1920); HEART OF THE NORTH, THE(1921); HER SOCIAL VALUE(1921); INNOCENT CHEAT, THE(1921); LIFE'S GREATEST QUESTION(1921); MOTION TO ADJOURN, A(1921); BACK TO YELLOW JACKET(1922); ONE EIGHTH APACHE(1922); SAGEBRUSH TRAIL, THE(1922); SNOWSHOE TRAIL, THE(1922); BURNING WORDS(1923); LOVE BRAND, THE(1923); TRIMMED IN SCARLET(1923); SUNDOWN(1924); KIT CARSON OVER THE GREAT DIVIDE(1925); BUFFALO BILL ON THE U.P. TRAIL(1926); DANIEL BOONE THRU THE WILDERNESS(1926); GENERAL CUSTER AT LITTLE BIG HORN(1926); ROARING FIRES(1927)
Ruth Stewart
Misc. Silents
GOLDEN SHACKLES(1928)
S.S. Stewart
THUNDERBOLT(1929)
Sally Stewart
DON'T BE A DUMMY(1932, Brit.); TROUBLE AHEAD(1936, Brit.); HOLIDAY'S END(1937, Brit.); HIS LORDSHIP REGRETS(1938, Brit.); LADY VANISHES, THE(1938, Brit.); WANTED BY SCOTLAND YARD(1939, Brit.)
Salvin Stewart
SCOTLAND YARD DRAGNET(1957, Brit.)
Sam Stewart
MURDER IN MISSISSIPPI(1965); MID-DAY MISTRESS(1968); PROJECTIONIST, THE(1970)
Sandra Stewart
PAPER MOON(1973), cos; GREATEST, THE(1977, U.S./Brit.), cos
Sandy Stewart
GO, JOHNNY, GO!(1959)
Sophie Stewart
HER LAST AFFAIRE(1935, Brit.); AS YOU LIKE IT(1936, Brit.); MURDER IN THE OLD RED BARN(1936, Brit.); THINGS TO COME(1936, Brit.); MAN WHO COULD WORK MIRACLES, THE(1937, Brit.); UNDER THE RED ROBE(1937, Brit.); MARIGOLD(1938, Brit.); RETURN OF THE SCARLET PIMPERNEL(1938, Brit.); WHO GOES NEXT?(1938, Brit.); NURSE EDITH CAVELL(1939); MY SON, MY SON!(1940); LAMP STILL BURNS, THE(1943, Brit.); STRAWBERRY ROAN(1945, Brit.); INHERITANCE, THE(1951, Brit.); MADE IN HEAVEN(1952, Brit.); DEVIL GIRL FROM MARS(1954, Brit.); BATTLE HELL(1956, Brit.); NO TIME FOR TEARS(1957, Brit.)

Steven Stewart
YOUNG GRADUATES, THE(1971)
Susan Stewart
MANTIS IN LACE(1968); FIRST NUDIE MUSICAL, THE(1976)
Thomas A. Stewart
JAWS II(1978)
Tom Stewart
MAROONED(1969); AMERICAN GIGOLO(1980)
Trish Stewart
MANSION OF THE DOOMED(1976)
Val Stewart
FOR THEM THAT TRESPASS(1949, Brit.), ph
Vera Stewart
Misc. Silents
THIRTY YEARS BETWEEN(1921)
Victor Stewart
Silents
ADVENTURE SHOP, THE(1918); EVERYBODY'S GIRL(1918)
Violet Stewart
Misc. Silents
HOODMAN BLIND(1913)
Wayne Stewart
FARMER, THE(1977)
Wynn Stewart
FROM NASHVILLE WITH MUSIC(1969)
Yvonne Stewart
SATAN'S SADISTS(1969)
Gerald Steyn
REUNION(1932, Brit.)
Penny Steyne
MIDNIGHT EXPRESS(1978, Brit.), makeup
Alexander Sthein
MEN OF THE SEA(1938, USSR), w
Arthur Stibolt
Silents
WOMAN OF PARIS, A(1923), art d
Pat Stich
LONERS, THE(1972)
Patricia Stich
HALLS OF ANGER(1970)
The Stick
STUDENT BODIES(1981)
Amzie Stickland
DRANGO(1957); SLAUGHTER ON TENTH AVENUE(1957)
Gail Stickland
1984
PROTOCOL(1984)
Dorothy Stickney
WORKING GIRLS(1931); WAYWARD(1932); LITTLE MINISTER, THE(1934); MURDER AT THE VANITIES(1934); AND SO THEY WERE MARRIED(1936); MOON'S OUR HOME, THE(1936); I MET MY LOVE AGAIN(1938); WHAT A LIFE(1939); UNINVITED, THE(1944); MISS TATLOCK'S MILLIONS(1948); GREAT DIAMOND ROBBERY(1953); CATERED AFFAIR, THE(1956); REMARKABLE MR. PENNYPACKER, THE(1959); I NEVER SANG FOR MY FATHER(1970)
Edward F. Stidder
SEVENTH CAVALRY(1956)
Ted Stidder
EXPLOSION(1969, Can.)
George Stidham
CHAMP, THE(1979)
Ernest Stidwell
WATCH BEVERLY(1932, Brit.); OH, WHAT A NIGHT(1935)
Rulf Stiefel
BATTLE OF BRITAIN, THE(1969, Brit.)
Vicki Raw Stiener
CAUGHT(1949)
Elisabeth Stiepl
ELUSIVE CORPORAL, THE(1963, Fr.)
Vern Stierman
TOWN THAT DREADED SUNDOWN, THE(1977)
David Stiers
DRIVE, HE SAID(1971)
David Ogden Stiers
THX 1138(1971); OH, GOD!(1977); CHEAP DETECTIVE, THE(1978); MAGIC(1978); HARRY'S WAR(1981)
Art Stifel
MISS JESSICA IS PREGNANT(1970), ph
Nell Stifel
1984
EXTERMINATOR 2(1984), set d
Magnus Stifter
RASPUTIN(1932, Ger.)
Silents
PASSION(1920, Ger.)
Misc. Silents
HEAD OF JANUS, THE(1920, Ger.); GYPSY BLOOD(1921, Ger.)
Stig
OCEAN BREAKERS(1949, Swed.)
Buster Stiggs
STARSTRUCK(1982, Aus.)
France Stiglic
NINTH CIRCLE, THE(1961, Yugo.), d, w; SERGEANT JIM(1962, Yugo.), d
Tugo Stiglic
SERGEANT JIM(1962, Yugo.)
Hugo Stiglitz
NIGHT OF A THOUSAND CATS(1974, Mex.); SURVIVE!(1977, Mex.); TINTORERA...-BLOODY WATERS(1977, Brit./Mex.); GUYANA, CULT OF THE DAMNED zero(1980, Mex./Span./Panama); CITY OF THE WALKING DEAD(1983, Span./Ital.)

1984
UNDER THE VOLCANO(1984)
Misc. Talkies
ROBINSON CRUSOE AND THE TIGER(1972)
Robert Stigwood
JESUS CHRIST, SUPERSTAR(1973), p; TOMMY(1975, Brit.), p; SATURDAY NIGHT FEVER(1977), p; GREASE(1978), p; MOMENT BY MOMENT(1978), p; SGT. PEPPER'S LONELY HEARTS CLUB BAND(1978), p; TIMES SQUARE(1980), p; FAN, THE(1981), p; GALLIPOLI(1981, Aus.), p; GREASE 2(1982), p; STAYING ALIVE(1983), p
Jimmy Stiles
ZEBRA IN THE KITCHEN(1965)
Leslie Stiles
JOSSER JOINS THE NAVY(1932, Brit.)
Silents
POLAR STAR, THE(1919, Brit.), w
Misc. Silents
LES CLOCHES DE CORNEVILLE(1917, Brit.)
Mark Stiles
HEATWAVE(1983, Aus.), w
Robert Stiles
$(DOLLARS) (1971)
Victor Stiles
SANTA CLAUS CONQUERS THE MARTIANS(1964)
Aaron Still
COWBOY CANTEEN(1944), ed
Andy Still
1984
TANK(1984)
Robby Still
SIX PACK(1982)
Georg Stillanudis
HELL ON EARTH(1934, Ger.), ph
Robin Stille
SLUMBER PARTY MASSACRE, THE(1982)
Amy Stiller
LOVERS AND OTHER STRANGERS(1970)
Bettina Stiller
PARSIFAL(1983, Fr.)
Jerry Stiller
TAKING OF PELHAM ONE, TWO, THREE, THE(1974); AIRPORT 1975(1974); NASTY HABITS(1976, Brit.); RITZ, THE(1976); THOSE LIPS, THOSE EYES(1980)
Mauritz Stiller
Silents
TEMPTRESS, THE(1926), d, w; WOMAN ON TRIAL, THE(1927), d; STREET OF SIN, THE(1928), d
Misc. Silents
LOVE AND JOURNALISM(1916, Swed.), d; EROTIKON(1920, Swed.), d; SIR ARNE'S TREASURE(1920, Swed.), d; GUNNAR HEDE'S SAGA(1922, Swed.), d; BLIZZARD, THE(1924, Swed.), d; SAGA OF GOSTA BERLING, THE(1924, Fr.), d; HOTEL IMPERIAL(1927), d; LEGEND OF GOSTA BERLING(1928, Swed.), d
Fred Stillkraut
CROSS OF IRON(1977, Brit., Ger.)
Frances Stillman
GUNS OF THE TREES(1964)
Irene Stillman
1984
SKYLINE(1984, Spain)
Jack Stillman
BUS IS COMING, THE(1971)
Joe Stillman
HI, MOM!(1970)
John Stillman, Jr.
LADY SAYS NO, THE(1951), p
Neil Stillman
INCREDIBLY STRANGE CREATURES WHO STOPPED LIVING AND BECAME CRAZY MIXED-UP ZOMBIES, THE(1965)
Patricia Stillman
ETERNALLY YOURS(1939)
Robert Stillman
SOUND OF FURY, THE(1950), p; QUEEN FOR A DAY(1951), p; AMERICANO, THE(1955), p
Whit Stillman
1984
SKYLINE(1984, Spain)
Bill Stillwell
WOMEN AND BLOODY TERROR(1970)
Gary C. Stillwell
OFFICER AND A GENTLEMAN, AN(1982)
Diane Stilwell
SENTINEL, THE(1977); RICH KIDS(1979)
Ernest Stilwell
LIMPING MAN, THE(1931, Brit.)
Slavco Stimac
CROSS OF IRON(1977, Brit., Ger.)
Viola Kate Stimpson
1984
WOMAN IN RED, THE(1984)
Misc. Talkies
ALCHEMIST, THE(1981)
C.A. Stimson
TAKE THE HEIR(1930), p
Sara Stimson
LITTLE MISS MARKER(1980)
Bertha Stinchfield
NATIONAL VELVET(1944)
Cliff Stine
AIR CADET(1951), ph; MA AND PA KETTLE AT WAIKIKI(1955), ph

Clifford Stine
WITHOUT RESERVATIONS(1946), spec eff; STEP BY STEP(1946), spec eff; MILK-MAN, THE(1950), ph; MYSTERY SUBMARINE(1950), ph; WEEKEND WITH FA-THER(1951), ph; BACK AT THE FRONT(1952), ph; BRONCO BUSTER(1952), ph; HAS ANYBODY SEEN MY GAL?(1952), ph; NO ROOM FOR THE GROOM(1952), ph; ABBOTT AND COSTELLO GO TO MARS(1953), ph; EAST OF SUMATRA(1953), ph; IT CAME FROM OUTER SPACE(1953), ph; LAW AND ORDER(1953), ph; WINGS OF THE HAWK(1953), ph; FIREMAN SAVE MY CHILD(1954), ph; SMOKE SIG-NAL(1955), ph; TARANTULA(1955), spec eff; THIS ISLAND EARTH(1955), ph, spec eff; CREATURE WALKS AMONG US, THE(1956), ph; FOUR GIRLS IN TOWN(1956), spec eff; MOLE PEOPLE, THE(1956), spec eff; WRITTEN ON THE WIND(1956), spec eff; INCREDIBLE SHRINKING MAN, THE(1957), spec eff; KELLY AND ME(1957), ph; MAN OF A THOUSAND FACES(1957), spec eff; MONOLITH MONSTERS, THE(1957), spec eff; NIGHT PASSAGE(1957), ph; TAMMY AND THE BA-CHELOR(1957), spec eff; TARNISHED ANGELS, THE(1957), spec eff; TATTERED DRESS, THE(1957), spec eff; MONSTER ON THE CAMPUS(1958), spec eff; ONCE UPON A HORSE(1958), spec eff; PERFECT FURLOUGH, THE(1958), spec eff; STEP DOWN TO TERROR(1958), spec eff; SUMMER LOVE(1958), spec eff; THING THAT COULDN'T DIE, THE(1958), ph; THIS HAPPY FEELING(1958), spec eff; TIME TO LOVE AND A TIME TO DIE, A(1958), spec eff; TWILIGHT FOR THE GODS(1958), ph; IMITATION OF LIFE(1959), spec eff; NEVER STEAL ANYTHING SMALL(1959), spec eff; OPERATION PETTICOAT(1959), ph; HELL BENT FOR LEATHER(1960), ph; SPARTACUS(1960), ph; POSSE FROM HELL(1961), ph; TAMMY, TELL ME TRUE(1961), ph; FOR LOVE OR MONEY(1963), ph; UGLY AMERICAN, THE(1963), ph; BEDTIME STORY(1964), ph; BRASS BOTTLE, THE(1964), ph; CREEPING TER-ROR, THE(1964), spec eff; FLUFFY(1965), ph; THAT FUNNY FEELING(1965), ph; AND NOW MIGUEL(1966), ph; FOLLOW ME, BOYS!(1966), ph; GAMBIT(1966), ph; KING'S PIRATE(1967), ph; ROSIE!(1967), ph

Eric Stine
SPY WHO LOVED ME, THE(1977, Brit.); HANOVER STREET(1979, Brit.)

Hal Stine
JOHNNY RENO(1966), ph; BUSYBODY, THE(1967), ph; CAPER OF THE GOLDEN BULLS, THE(1967), ph; SPIRIT IS WILLING, THE(1967), ph

Harold Stine
MIGHTY JOE YOUNG(1949), spec eff; ON DANGEROUS GROUND(1951), spec eff; MAN OF CONFLICT(1953), ph; COUCH, THE(1962), ph; BLACK GOLD(1963), ph; HOUSE IS NOT A HOME, A(1964), ph; INCREDIBLE MR. LIMPET, THE(1964), ph; NIGHT WALKER, THE(1964), ph; LAST OF THE SECRET AGENTS?, THE(1966), ph; CHUKA(1967), ph; PROJECT X(1968), ph

Harold E. Stine
FOR THOSE WHO THINK YOUNG(1964), ph; M(1970), ph; TODD KILLINGS, THE(1971), ph; POSEIDON ADVENTURE, THE(1972), ph

Jan Stine
HORSE SOLDIERS, THE(1959); CLAUDELLE INGLISH(1961); SUMMER MA-GIC(1963)

Steven Stinebaugh
VAN, THE(1977)

David Stinehart
IN THE HEAT OF THE NIGHT(1967)

Louise A. Stinetorf
WHITE WITCH DOCTOR(1953), w

Sting
QUADROPHENIA(1979, Brit.); RADIO ON(1980, Brit./Ger.), a, m; BRIMSTONE AND TREACLE(1982, Brit.), a, m
1984
DUNE(1984)

Dewey Stinger, III
BEACH RED(1967)

Michael Stinger
MIRROR CRACK'D, THE(1980, Brit.), prod d

Joe Stington
UNDERTOW(1949), makeup

George Stinson
CRASH DONOVAN(1936)

Jana Stinson
THRESHOLD(1983, Can.)

John Stinson
HAND, THE(1981); SCARED TO DEATH(1981)

Joseph C. Stinson
SUDDEN IMPACT(1983), w
1984
CITY HEAT(1984), w

Colin Stinton
VERDICT, THE(1982); DANIEL(1983)

George Stinton
STRANGE BREW(1983)

J. Stinton
FILE ON THELMA JORDAN, THE(1950), makeup

Joe Stinton
T-MEN(1947), makeup; HE WALKED BY NIGHT(1948), makeup; LET'S LIVE A LITTLE(1948), makeup

Joseph Stinton
STRANGE WOMAN, THE(1946), makeup

Lucki Stipetic
FITZCARRALDO(1982), p

Carmine Stipo
CRUISING(1980)

Marc Stirdivant
CONDORMAN(1981), w

Walter Stiritz
WIFE TAKES A FLYER, THE(1942)

Lt. Col. Stirling
FOUR FEATHERS, THE(1939, Brit.), tech adv

Brand Stirling
WESTWARD HO THE WAGONS!(1956)

Edward Stirling
TWILIGHT HOUR(1944, Brit.); EAGLE WITH TWO HEADS(1948, Fr.)

Helen Stirling
COME SEPTEMBER(1961); DARLING(1965, Brit.)

Linda Stirling
SAN ANTONIO KID, THE(1944); SHERIFF OF SUNDOWN(1944); VIGILANTES OF DODGE CITY(1944); CHEROKEE FLASH, THE(1945); DAKOTA(1945); SANTA FE SADDLEMATES(1945); SHERIFF OF CIMARRON(1945); TOPEKA TERROR, THE(1945); CYCLOTRODE X(1946); INVISIBLE INFORMER(1946); MADONNA'S SECRET, THE(1946); MYSTERIOUS MR. VALENTINE, THE(1946); RIO GRANDE RAIDERS(1946); PRETENDER, THE(1947); WAGON WHEELS WESTWARD(1956)

Michael Joseph Stirling
WEAKER SEX, THE(1949, Brit.), ed

Pamela Stirling
LA MARSEILLAISE(1938, Fr.); CANDLELIGHT IN ALGERIA(1944, Brit.); ECHO MURDERS, THE(1945, Brit.); MADNESS OF THE HEART(1949, Brit.); DIVIDED HEART, THE(1955, Brit.); TO PARIS WITH LOVE(1955, Brit.); KID FROM CANADA, THE(1957, Brit.); SAFECRACKER, THE(1958, Brit.); ELEPHANT GUN(1959, Brit.); RETURN FROM THE ASHES(1965, U.S./Brit.)

Brian Stirner
OVERLORD(1975, Brit.)
1984
PLAGUE DOGS, THE(1984, U.S./Brit.)

Robert Stirrat
REAL LIFE(1979)

Gwen Stith
DARK HORSE, THE(1946)

Alexander Stitt
GRENDEL GRENDEL GRENDEL(1981, Aus.), p, d&w, prod d, anim

Milan Stitt
THE RUNNER STUMBLES(1979), w

Richard Stitt
JONIKO AND THE KUSH TA KA(1969)

Teresa Stitt
JONIKO AND THE KUSH TA KA(1969)

David Stiven
TIM(1981, Aus.), ed; ROAD WARRIOR, THE(1982, Aus.), ed

James Stiver
BONNIE AND CLYDE(1967)

John Stix
GREAT ST. LOUIS BANK ROBBERY, THE(1959), d

Louise Stjensward
PASSENGER, THE(1975, Ital.), cos

Louise Stjernsward
1984
EVERY PICTURE TELLS A STORY(1984, Brit.), prod d

John Stobart
HE LOVED AN ACTRESS(1938, Brit.)

Tom Stobart
Misc. Talkies
GREAT MONKEY RIP-OFF, THE(1979), d

Paul Stober
MAFIA GIRLS, THE(1969)

Charles Stobert
YOUNG SINNER, THE(1965)

Renee Stobrawa
CRUISER EMDEN(1932, Ger.); HELL ON EARTH(1934, Ger.); AFFAIR BLUM, THE(1949, Ger.); SLEEPING BEAUTY(1965, Ger.), a, w; GOOSE GIRL, THE(1967, Ger.)

Alan Stock
WHOSE LIFE IS IT ANYWAY?(1981); SECOND THOUGHTS(1983)

Cynthia Stock
JOY RIDE(1935, Brit.); PLAY UP THE BAND(1935, Brit.); PRICE OF A SONG, THE(1935, Brit.); IMPROPER DUCHESS, THE(1936, Brit.); KING OF THE CAST-LE(1936, Brit.); RADIO LOVER(1936, Brit.); REASONABLE DOUBT(1936, Brit.); SHIPMATES O' MINE(1936, Brit.); INTIMATE RELATIONS(1937, Brit.); LITTLE MISS SOMEBODY(1937, Brit.); MILL ON THE FLOSS(1939, Brit.); OLD MOTHER RILEY MP(1939, Brit.); THREE SILENT MEN(1940, Brit.)

Dennis Stock
LAST MOVIE, THE(1971)

Elwyn Stock
GIRL IS MINE, THE(1950, Brit.)

Freda Stock
GIRL IS MINE, THE(1950, Brit.), p

Gailene Stock
DON QUIXOTE(1973, Aus.)

Herbert L. Stock
BLOOD OF DRACULA(1957), d

Jennifer Stock
SHRIEK OF THE MUTILATED(1974)

L.S. Stock
GRAND PRIX(1934, Brit.), p

Nigel Stock
LANCASHIRE LUCK(1937, Brit.); GOODBYE MR. CHIPS(1939, Brit.); NORTH SEA PATROL(1939, Brit.); SONS OF THE SEA(1939, Brit.); BRIGHTON ROCK(1947, Brit.); LADY WITH A LAMP, THE(1951, Brit.); FOUR AGAINST FATE(1952, Brit.); AUNT CLARA(1954, Brit.); MALTA STORY(1954, Brit.); DAM BUSTERS, THE(1955, Brit.); NIGHT MY NUMBER CAME UP, THE(1955, Brit.); EYEWITNESS(1956, Brit.); PURSUIT OF THE GRAF SPEE(1957, Brit.); SILENT ENEMY, THE(1959, Brit.); NEVER LET GO(1960, Brit.); VICTIM(1961, Brit.); DAMN THE DEFIANT!(1962, Brit.); PASSWORD IS COURAGE, THE(1962, Brit.); GREAT ESCAPE, THE(1963); TO HAVE AND TO HOLD(1963, Brit.); NOTHING BUT THE BEST(1964, Brit.); MC GUIRE, GO HOME!(1966, Brit.); WEEKEND AT DUNKIRK(1966, Fr./Ital.); NIGHT OF THE GENERALS, THE(1967, Brit./Fr.); LION IN WINTER, THE(1968, Brit.); LOST CONTI-NENT, THE(1968, Brit.); CROMWELL(1970, Brit.); RUSSIAN ROULETTE(1975); OP-ERATION DAYBREAK(1976, U.S./Brit./Czech.); MIRROR CRACK'D, THE(1980, Brit.); RED MONARCH(1983, Brit.); YELLOWBEARD(1983)

Nigel Stock, Sr.
NELSON AFFAIR, THE(1973, Brit.)

Ralph Stock
BRITANNIA OF BILLINGSGATE(1933, Brit.), w; ROME EXPRESS(1933, Brit.), d; HIGHLAND FLING(1936, Brit.), w; JENIFER HALE(1937, Brit.), w; EARL OF CHICAGO, THE(1940); GYPSY WILDCAT(1944), w; GIRL IS MINE, THE(1950, Brit.), w
Silents
LOVE FLOWER, THE(1920), w

Werner Stock
COURT CONCERT, THE(1936, Ger.); GLASS TOWER, THE(1959, Ger.)

Carl Stockade
CONDEMNED TO LIVE(1935)

Fanny Stockbridge
Silents
WALL FLOWER, THE(1922)
Misc. Silents
OLD NEST, THE(1921)

Henry Stockbridge
DYNAMITE(1930); MADAME SATAN(1930); NO, NO NANETTE(1930); SECOND CHOICE(1930); EMPLOYEE'S ENTRANCE(1933)

Ann Stockdale
RENEGADE GIRLS(1974)

Carl Stockdale
TERROR, THE(1928); CARNATION KID(1929); LOVE PARADE, THE(1929); ABRAHAM LINCOLN(1930); FURIES, THE(1930); HELL'S ISLAND(1930); HIDE-OUT, THE(1930); SISTERS(1930); RULING VOICE, THE(1931); GET THAT GIRL(1932); PHANTOM EXPRESS, THE(1932); VAMPIRE BAT, THE(1933); BATTLE OF GREED(1934); MANHATTAN MELODRAMA(1934); MONTE CARLO NIGHTS(1934); ROCKY RHODES(1934); STUDENT TOUR(1934); CRIMSON TRAIL, THE(1935); DR. SOCRATES(1935); IVORY-HANDLED GUN(1935); MAD LOVE(1935); MAN WHO RECLAIMED HIS HEAD, THE(1935); MARY JANE'S PA(1935); OUTLAWED GUNS(1935); PUBLIC HERO NO. 1(1935); FURY(1936); LEAVENWORTH CASE, THE(1936); REVOLT OF THE ZOMBIES(1936); RING AROUND THE MOON(1936); SAN FRANCISCO(1936); WHIPSAW(1936); COURAGE OF THE WEST(1937); LAW FOR TOMBSTONE(1937); LOST HORIZON(1937); MOUNTAIN JUSTICE(1937); MY DEAR MISS ALDRICH(1937); NATION AFLAME(1937); OH, SUSANNA(1937); SARATOGA(1937); SINGING OUTLAW(1937); CIPHER BUREAU(1938); HAWAIIAN BUCKAROO(1938); LAW COMMANDS, THE(1938); LAWLESS VALLEY(1938); MARIE ANTOINETTE(1938); RAWHIDE(1938); KING OF THE UNDERWORLD(1939); KONGA, THE WILD STALLION(1939); LADY'S FROM KENTUCKY, THE(1939); LUCKY NIGHT(1939); MARSHAL OF MESA CITY, THE(1939); MR. SMITH GOES TO WASHINGTON(1939); CAPTAIN IS A LADY, THE(1940); PIONEERS OF THE FRONTIER(1940); STAGE TO CHINO(1940); THUNDERING FRONTIER(1940); WAGON TRAIN(1940); ALONG THE RIO GRANDE(1941); BABES ON BROADWAY(1941); DANGEROUS LADY(1941); DEVIL AND DANIEL WEBSTER, THE(1941); FARGO KID, THE(1941); HONKY TONK(1941); RETURN OF DANIEL BOONE, THE(1941); SCATTERGOOD MEETS BROADWAY(1941); SCATTERGOOD PULLS THE STRINGS(1941); DARING YOUNG MAN, THE(1942); OUTLAW, THE(1943)
Silents
GOOD-FOR-NOTHING, THE(1914); ATTA BOY'S LAST RACE(1916); INTOLERANCE(1916); LITTLE LIAR, THE(1916); OLIVER TWIST(1916); AMERICANO, THE(1917); EYES OF JULIA DEEP, THE(1918); IN BAD(1918); AMAZING IMPOSTER, THE(1919); SPITFIRE OF SEVILLE, THE(1919); GREATEST QUESTION, THE(1920); MOLLY O'(1921); OLIVER TWIST(1922); RED HOT ROMANCE(1922); SUZANNA(1922); THORNS AND ORANGE BLOSSOMS(1922); WILD HONEY(1922); EXTRA GIRL, THE(1923); MONEY! MONEY! MONEY!(1923); TIGER'S CLAW, THE(1923); REGULAR FELLOW, A(1925); DESERT'S PRICE, THE(1926); KING OF KINGS, THE(1927); SOMEWHERE IN SONORA(1927); AIR MAIL PILOT, THE(1928); JAZZLAND(1928); MY HOME TOWN(1928)
Misc. Silents
CASEY AT THE BAT(1916); STRANDED(1916); DAUGHTER OF THE POOR, A(1917); LAND OF LONG SHADOWS(1917); LOST AND WON(1917); OPEN PLACES(1917); PEGGY LEADS THE WAY(1917); RANGE BOSS, THE(1917); HEARTS OR DIAMONDS?(1918); POINTING FINGER, THE(1919); WHEN A MAN RIDES ALONE(1919); $30,000(1920); FATAL 30, THE(1921); WHERE IS MY WANDERING BOY TONIGHT?(1922); GRAIL, THE(1923); CAFE IN CAIRO, A(1924); SPIRIT OF THE U.S.A., THE(1924); TRAIL RIDER, THE(1925)

Carlton Stockdale
STAND UP AND CHEER(1934 80m FOX bw)
Misc. Silents
BLACK PEARL, THE(1928)

Frank E. Stockdale
Silents
GOLD RUSH, THE(1925)

Terry Stockdale
SHOOT IT: BLACK, SHOOT IT: BLUE(1974), m

Vaclav Stockel
FIREMAN'S BALL, THE(1968, Czech.)

Wilma Stockenstrom
GUEST AT STEENKAMPSKRAAL, THE(1977, South Africa)
1984
GUEST, THE(1984, Brit.)

John Stocker
KIDNAPPING OF THE PRESIDENT, THE(1980, Can.); JOY(1983, Fr./Can.)
1984
FINDERS KEEPERS(1984)

Stephen Stocker
THAT KIND OF GIRL(1963, Brit.)

Walter Stocker
LASSIE'S GREAT ADVENTURE(1963); THEY SAVED HITLER'S BRAIN(1964); TILL DEATH(1978), p&d

Hank Stockert
DEATHSPORT(1978), spec eff

Betty Stockfeld
77 PARK LANE(1931, Brit.); MAID OF THE MOUNTAINS, THE(1932, Brit.); MONEY FOR NOTHING(1932, Brit.); WOMAN IN CHAINS(1932, Brit.); KING OF THE RITZ(1933, Brit.); LORD OF THE MANOR(1933, Brit.); MAN WHO CHANGED HIS NAME, THE(1934, Brit.); DISHONOR BRIGHT(1936, Brit.); WHO'S YOUR LADY FRIEND?(1937, Brit.); I SEE ICE(1938); GIRL WHO COULDN'T QUITE, THE(1949, Brit.); GUILTY?(1956, Brit.)

Betty Stockfield
FAREWELL TO LOVE(1931, Brit.); LIFE GOES ON(1932, Brit.); ANNE ONE HUNDRED(1933, Brit.); BATTLE, THE(1934, Fr.); BRIDES TO BE(1934, Brit.); LAD, THE(1935, Brit.); RUNAWAY LADIES(1935, Brit.); BELOVED VAGABOND, THE(1936, Brit.); UNDER PROOF(1936, Brit.); SLIPPER EPISODE, THE(1938, Fr); HARD STEEL(1941, Brit.); FLYING FORTRESS(1942, Brit.); EDWARD AND CAROLINE(1952, Fr.); LOVER'S NET(1957, Fr.); TRUE AS A TURTLE(1957, Brit.)

Karl-Heinz Stockhausen
LA CHINOISE(1967, Fr.), m

Chester Stocki
PROUD RIDER, THE(1971, Can.), d, w

Betty Stockield
CAPTIVATION(1931, Brit)

Melissa Stocking
HOWZER(1973)

Roy Stocking
UP IN SMOKE(1978)

Jan Stockl
MOST BEAUTIFUL AGE, THE(1970, Czech.)

Eric Stocklassa
Misc. Silents
SIR ARNE'S TREASURE(1920, Swed.)

Cynthia Stockley
Silents
SINS OF ROZANNE(1920), w; WILD HONEY(1922), w

Matthew Stockley
1984
PERFECT STRANGERS(1984)

Boyd Stockman
LAWLESS EMPIRE(1946); SUNSET PASS(1946); CODE OF THE SADDLE(1947); PRAIRIE EXPRESS(1947); CROSSED TRAILS(1948); FRONTIER AGENT(1948); GUN TALK(1948); GUNNING FOR JUSTICE(1948); OUTLAW BRAND(1948); PARTNERS OF THE SUNSET(1948); RANGERS RIDE, THE(1948); ACROSS THE RIO GRANDE(1949); BRAND OF FEAR(1949); CRASHING THRU(1949); HIDDEN DANGER(1949); RIDERS IN THE SKY(1949); RIM OF THE CANYON(1949); STAMPEDE(1949); TRAIL'S END(1949); WEST OF EL DORADO(1949); INDIAN TERRITORY(1950); LAW OF THE PANHANDLE(1950); RADAR SECRET SERVICE(1950); STAGE TO TUCSON(1950); GENE AUTRY AND THE MOUNTIES(1951); SILVER CANYON(1951); WHIRLWIND(1951); NIGHT RAIDERS(1952); NIGHT STAGE TO GALVESTON(1952); GUN BELT(1953); MAN FROM LARAMIE, THE(1955); WYOMING RENEGADES(1955); SECRET OF TREASURE MOUNTAIN(1956); NIGHT PASSAGE(1957); FRONTIER GUN(1958); ALLIGATOR PEOPLE, THE(1959); LONE TEXAN(1959); RIDE LONESOME(1959); FIVE GUNS TO TOMBSTONE(1961); GAMBLER WORE A GUN, THE(1961); GUN FIGHT(1961); THEY RAN FOR THEIR LIVES(1968), stunts

Carl Stockman
Misc. Silents
MEN OF THE DESERT(1917)

Jerry Stockman
1984
NATURAL, THE(1984)

Paul Stockman
DR. BLOOD'S COFFIN(1961); SKULL, THE(1965, Brit.)

Hardy Stockmann
HOT POTATO(1976)

Dorothy Stockmar
DANTE'S INFERNO(1935)

Betty Stockton
WHOOPEE(1930); PALMY DAYS(1931)

Charles Stockton
PRINCE AND THE PAUPER, THE(1969), art d

Edith Stockton
Silents
ASHAMED OF PARENTS(1921); SHOULD A WIFE WORK?(1922)
Misc. Silents
PUTTING ONE OVER(1919); KEEP TO THE RIGHT(1920); THROUGH THE STORM(1922)

John Stockton
HITLER'S CHILDREN(1942)

John Arthur Stockton
COMMANDOS STRIKE AT DAWN, THE(1942)

Kevin Stockton
WIZ, THE(1978)

Philip Stockton
1984
SILENT MADNESS(1984), ed

J.W. Stockvis
FLYING FOOL, THE(1931, Brit.), ed

L.J.W. Stockviss
DIVORCE OF LADY X. THE(1938, Brit.), ed

Dean Stockwell
ABBOTT AND COSTELLO IN HOLLYWOOD(1945); ANCHORS AWEIGH(1945); VALLEY OF DECISION, THE(1945); GREEN YEARS, THE(1946); HOME SWEET HOMICIDE(1946); MIGHTY MCGURK, THE(1946); ARNELO AFFAIR, THE(1947); GENTLEMAN'S AGREEMENT(1947); ROMANCE OF ROSY RIDGE, THE(1947); SONG OF THE THIN MAN(1947); DEEP WATERS(1948); BOY WITH THE GREEN HAIR, THE(1949); DOWN TO THE SEA IN SHIPS(1949); SECRET GARDEN, THE(1949); HAPPY YEARS, THE(1950); KIM(1950); STARS IN MY CROWN(1950); CATTLE DRIVE(1951); CARELESS YEARS, THE(1957); GUN FOR A COWARD(1957); COMPULSION(1959); SONS AND LOVERS(1960, Brit.); LONG DAY'S JOURNEY INTO NIGHT(1962); RAPTURE(1965); PSYCH-OUT(1968); DUNWICH HORROR, THE(1970); LAST MOVIE, THE(1971); LONERS, THE(1972); WEREWOLF OF WASHINGTON(1973); WIN, PLACE, OR STEAL(1975); WON TON TON, THE DOG WHO SAVED HOLLYWOOD(1976); TRACKS(1977); HUMAN HIGHWAY(1982), a, d, w; WRONG IS RIGHT(1982); ALSINO AND THE CONDOR(1983, Nicaragua)
1984
DUNE(1984); PARIS, TEXAS(1984, Ger./Fr.)
Misc. Talkies
SHE CAME TO THE VALLEY(1979); ONE AWAY(1980); CITIZEN SOLDIER(1984)

Guy Stockwell
PLEASE DON'T EAT THE DAISIES(1960); WAR LORD, THE(1965); AND NOW MIGUEL(1966); BEAU GESTE(1966); BLINDFOLD(1966); PLAINSMAN, THE(1966); TOBRUK(1966); BANNING(1967); KING'S PIRATE(1967); IN ENEMY COUNTRY(1968); MONITORS, THE(1969); GATLING GUN, THE(1972); AIRPORT 1975(1974); IT'S ALIVE(1974)
Misc. Talkies
THREE SWORDS OF ZORRO, THE(1960); COMING, THE(1983)
Harry Stockwell
BROADWAY MELODY OF 1936(1935); HERE COMES THE BAND(1935); ALL OVER TOWN(1937); SNOW WHITE AND THE SEVEN DWARFS(1937)
Jake Stockwell
TOWING(1978)
John Stockwell
SO FINE(1981); CHRISTINE(1983); EDDIE AND THE CRUISERS(1983); LOSIN' IT(1983)
Belle Stoddard
Silents
ANNE AGAINST THE WORLD(1929)
Ed Stoddard
FLIGHT THAT DISAPPEARED, THE(1961); MAN'S FAVORITE SPORT[?](1964)
Harry Stoddard
JUNGLE BRIDE(1933), m
Jean Stoddard
YOU ONLY LIVE ONCE(1937)
Malcolm Stoddard
LUTHER(1974); GODSEND, THE(1980, Can.)
Marie Stoddard
LAW COMMANDS, THE(1938); TO CATCH A THIEF(1955)
Russ Stoddard
THIN RED LINE, THE(1964); CHRISTMAS KID, THE(1968, U.S., Span.)
Dayton Stoddart
RUTHLESS(1948), w
Hugh Stoddart
REMEMBRANCE(1982, Brit.), w
John Stoddart
BARRY MC KENZIE HOLDS HIS OWN(1975, Aus.), prod d; GETTING OF WISDOM, THE(1977, Aus.), prod d
1984
CAREFUL, HE MIGHT HEAR YOU(1984, Aus.), prod d
Michael F. Stodden
KING OF COMEDY, THE(1983)
Sheila Stodden
THEY ALL LAUGHED(1981)
Warren Chetham Stode
BACKGROUND(1953, Brit.), w
John Stodel
KILLER FORCE(1975, Switz./Ireland), art d
Orville Stoeber
LET'S SCARE JESSICA TO DEATH(1971), m
Frank Stoegerer
SEDUCTION OF JOE TYNAN, THE(1979); DINER(1982)
Suzann Stoehr
FOOLS' PARADE(1971)
William Stoermer
Misc. Silents
TIDAL WAVE, THE(1918), d
Ludwig Stoessel
ELISABETH OF AUSTRIA(1931, Ger.); HIS MAJESTY, KING BALLYHOO(1931, Ger.); TRUNKS OF MR. O.F., THE(1932, Ger.)
George Stoetzel
GUERRILLA GIRL(1953), ph; I NEVER SANG FOR MY FATHER(1970), ph
Ernst Stoetzner
1984
CLASS ENEMY(1984, Ger.)
Hank Stohl
BANK SHOT(1974)
Edmund Stoiber
SEEMS LIKE OLD TIMES(1980); FIRST MONDAY IN OCTOBER(1981)
Katarina Stojanovic
LOVE AFFAIR; OR THE CASE OF THE MISSING SWITCHBOARD OPERATOR(1968, Yugo.), ed
Miliovj Stojanovic
TREASURE OF SILVER LAKE(1965, Fr./Ger./Yugo.)
Aca Stojkovic
FRAULEIN DOKTOR(1969, Ital./Yugo.); TWELVE CHAIRS, THE(1970)
Danuta Witold Stok
MOONLIGHTING(1982, Brit.), w
Austin Stoker
BATTLE FOR THE PLANET OF THE APES(1973); ABBY(1974); HORROR HIGH(1974); SHEBA BABY(1975); ASSAULT ON PRECINCT 13(1976); TIME WALKER(1982)
Misc. Talkies
ZEBRA KILLER, THE(1974)
Bram Stoker
DRACULA(1931), w; DRACULA'S DAUGHTER(1936), w; HORROR OF DRACULA, THE(1958, Brit.), w; DRACULA–PRINCE OF DARKNESS(1966, Brit.), w; DRACULA HAS RISEN FROM HIS GRAVE(1968, Brit.), w; VAMPIRES, THE(1969, Mex.), w; SCARS OF DRACULA, THE(1970, Brit.), w; TASTE THE BLOOD OF DRACULA(1970, Brit.), w; COUNT DRACULA(1971, Sp., Ital., Ger., Brit.), w; BLOOD FROM THE MUMMY'S TOMB(1972, Brit.), w; DRACULA A.D. 1972(1972, Brit.), w; JONATHAN(1973, Ger.), w; DRACULA AND SON(1976, Fr.), w; COUNT DRACULA AND HIS VAMPIRE BRIDE(1978, Brit.), w; DRACULA AND THE SEVEN GOLDEN VAMPIRES(1978, Brit./Chi.), w; DRACULA'S DOG(1978), w; DRACULA(1979), w; NOSFERATU, THE VAMPIRE(1979, Fr./Ger.), w; AWAKENING, THE(1980), w
Silents
NOSFERATU, THE VAMPIRE(1922, Ger.), w

H.G. Stoker
ONE PRECIOUS YEAR(1933, Brit.); CHANNEL CROSSING(1934, Brit.); BORN FOR GLORY(1935, Brit.); FIRST OFFENCE(1936, Brit.); IT'S YOU I WANT(1936, Brit.); POT LUCK(1936, Brit.); NON-STOP NEW YORK(1937, Brit.); MAN WITH 100 FACES, THE(1938, Brit.); MOONLIGHT SONATA(1938, Brit.); FULL SPEED AHEAD(1939, Brit.); CALL OF THE BLOOD(1948, Brit.); MADNESS OF THE HEART(1949, Brit.); WOMAN HATER(1949, Brit.); FOUR DAYS(1951, Brit.); RELUCTANT WIDOW, THE(1951, Brit.); WHERE'S CHARLEY?(1952, Brit.)
Al Stokes
GREEN PASTURES(1936)
Barbara Stokes
SHARKY'S MACHINE(1982)
Barry Stokes
CORRUPTION OF CHRIS MILLER, THE(1979, Span.); LADY OSCAR(1979, Fr./Jap.); SPACED OUT(1981, Brit.); GUNS AND THE FURY, THE(1983)
Misc. Talkies
BEHIND THE SHUTTERS(1976, Span.)
Craig Stokes
GREAT TRAIN ROBBERY, THE(1979, Brit.)
1984
SECRETS!(1984, Brit.)
Dorothy Stokes
JACK AND THE BEANSTALK(1970)
Silents
SOCIETY SCANDAL, A(1924)
Ernest Stokes
LONE HAND TEXAN, THE(1947)
Gary Stokes
MOVIE MOVIE(1978)
Irene Stokes
RENEGADE GIRLS(1974)
J. Stokes
WATER BABIES, THE(1979, Brit.), anim
James Stokes, Jr.
MOONSHINE MOUNTAIN(1964)
Jack Stokes
YELLOW SUBMARINE(1958, Brit.), animation d
Leslie Stokes
OSCAR WILDE(1960, Brit.), w
Phil Stokes
WILBY CONSPIRACY, THE(1975, Brit.), spec eff
Robert Stokes
SNOW WHITE AND THE SEVEN DWARFS(1937), anim; FANTASIA(1940), anim
Ron Stokes
MUTINY IN OUTER SPACE(1965); ROSIE!(1967); SPLIT, THE(1968); HARD RIDE, THE(1971)
Sewell Stokes
BRITANNIA OF BILLINGSGATE(1933, Brit.), w; ROLLING IN MONEY(1934, Brit.), w; YOU WILL REMEMBER(1941, Brit.), w; I BELIEVE IN YOU(1953, Brit.), w; OSCAR WILDE(1960, Brit.), w; ISADORA(1968, Brit.), w
Simon Stokes
1984
PLOUGHMAN'S LUNCH, THE(1984, Brit.)
Thomas Stokes
1984
BAD MANNERS(1984)
Vera Stokes
WHEN A GIRL'S BEAUTIFUL(1947); LETTER FROM AN UNKNOWN WOMAN(1948); GAMBLING HOUSE(1950); ON DANGEROUS GROUND(1951)
Mike Stokey
DOUBLE LIFE, A(1947); SENATOR WAS INDISCREET, THE(1947); ESCAPE FROM TERROR(1960)
Susan Stokey
1984
POWER, THE(1984)
Linn Stokke
TIME TO DIE, A(1983)
Tor Stokke
OPERATION CAMEL(1961, Den.); SNOW TREASURE(1968)
Leopold Stokowski
100 MEN AND A GIRL(1937); FANTASIA(1940); CARNEGIE HALL(1947)
J.W. Stokuis
WOMAN DECIDES, THE(1932, Brit.), ed
E. Stokvis
PRISONER OF CORBAL(1939, Brit.), ed
Walter Stokvis
SLEEPLESS NIGHTS(1933, Brit.), ed; LIVING DEAD, THE(1936, Brit.), ed; NORTH SEA PATROL(1939, Brit.), ed
Ludwig Stolarski
BORDER STREET(1950, Pol.), w
Adam Stolarsky
SO FINE(1981)
Paul Stolarsky
1984
MUPPETS TAKE MANHATTAN, THE(1984)
Eduard Stolba
MAGIC FACE, THE(1951, Aust.), art d
Edward Stolba
NO TIME FOR FLOWERS(1952), art d
Mink Stole
MONDO TRASHO(1970); FEMALE TROUBLE(1975); POLYESTER(1981)
Shirley Stoler
HONEYMOON KILLERS, THE(1969); KLUTE(1971); SEVEN BEAUTIES(1976, Ital.); DEER HUNTER, THE(1978); BELOW THE BELT(1980); SEED OF INNOCENCE(1980); SECOND-HAND HEARTS(1981)
1984
SPLITZ(1984)

Andre Stolka
WOLFEN(1981)
David Stoll
DEATH OF AN ANGEL(1952, Brit.)
Freda Stoll
KNICKERBOCKER HOLIDAY(1944); INTERRUPTED MELODY(1955)
Frederic F. Stoll
Misc. Silents
DETERMINATION(1920), d
Frieda Stoll
DARK CORNER, THE(1946); RENDEZVOUS 24(1946); TWO TICKETS TO BROAD-WAY(1951)
George Stoll [Georgie Stoll]
GO WEST, YOUNG MAN(1936), m; MIND YOUR OWN BUSINESS(1937), md; ON SUCH A NIGHT(1937), md; DR. RHYTHM(1938), md; LISTEN, DARLING(1938), md; LADY BE GOOD(1941), md; ROAD SHOW(1941), m; ZIEGFELD GIRL(1941), md; FOR ME AND MY GAL(1942), md; PANAMA HATTIE(1942), md; SHIP AHOY(1942), m, md; GIRL CRAZY(1943), md; I DOOD IT(1943), md; ANCHORS AWEIGH(1945), m; BIG CITY(1948), m; KISSING BANDIT, THE(1948), m, md; LUXURY LINER(1948), md; THREE DARING DAUGHTERS(1948), md; IN THE GOOD OLD SUMMER-TIME(1949), m, md; TOAST OF NEW ORLEANS, THE(1950), md; EXCUSE MY DUST(1951), md; EASY TO LOVE(1953), md; LATIN LOVERS(1953), md; ATHENA(1954), md; FLAME AND THE FLESH(1954), md; STUDENT PRINCE, THE(1954), md; HIT THE DECK(1955), md; TEN THOUSAND BEDROOMS(1957), md; THIS COULD BE THE NIGHT(1957), md; SEVEN HILLS OF ROME, THE(1958), m; FOR THE FIRST TIME(1959, U.S./Ger./Ital.), md; WHERE THE BOYS ARE(1960), m; HORIZONTAL LIEUTENANT, THE(1962), m; COURTSHIP OF EDDY'S FATHER, THE(1963), m; TICKLISH AFFAIR, A(1963), m; VIVA LAS VEGAS(1964), m; GIRL HAPPY(1965), m; MAN FROM BUTTON WILLOW, THE(1965), m, md; MADE IN PARIS(1966), m, md; SPINOUT(1966), m
Georgie Stoll [George Stoll]
PENNIES FROM HEAVEN(1936), md; BROADWAY MELODY OF '38(1937), md; HONOLULU(1939), md; SOCIETY LAWYER(1939), md; GO WEST(1940), md; LITTLE NELLIE KELLY(1940), md; STRIKE UP THE BAND(1940), md; TWO GIRLS ON BROADWAY(1940), md; BABES ON BROADWAY(1941), md; BIG STORE, THE(1941), m; LIFE BEGINS FOR ANDY HARDY(1941), md; CAIRO(1942), md; CABIN IN THE SKY(1943), md; DU BARRY WAS A LADY(1943), md; PRESENTING LILY MARS(1943), md; SWING FEVER(1943), md; MEET ME IN ST. LOUIS(1944), md; MUSIC FOR MILLIONS(1944), md; TWO GIRLS AND A SAILOR(1944), md; HER HIGHNESS AND THE BELLBOY(1945), m; THRILL OF A ROMANCE(1945), m&md; HOLIDAY IN MEXICO(1946), m; NO LEAVE, NO LOVE(1946), md; THIS TIME FOR KEEPS(1947), m, md; DATE WITH JUDY, A(1948); ON AN ISLAND WITH YOU(1948), md; NEPTUNE'S DAUGHTER(1949), md; DUCHESS OF IDAHO, THE(1950), md; NANCY GOES TO RIO(1950), md; TWO WEEKS WITH LOVE(1950), md; WATCH THE BIRDIE(1950), m; FATHER'S LITTLE DIVIDEND(1951), md; STRIP, THE(1951), m; GLORY ALLEY(1952), md; SKIRTS AHOY!(1952), md; DAN-GEROUS WHEN WET(1953), md; I LOVE MELVIN(1953), md; ROSE MARIE(1954), md; LOVE ME OR LEAVE ME(1955), md; MEET ME IN LAS VEGAS(1956), m; LOOKING FOR LOVE(1964), m
Guenther Stoll
PRIEST OF ST. PAULI, THE(1970, Ger.)
Gunther Stoll
CASTLE OF FU MANCHU, THE(1968, Ger./Span./Ital./Brit.); LAST MERCENARY, THE(1969, Ital./Span./Ger.); RETURN OF SABATA(1972, Ital./Fr./Ger.)
Misc. Talkies
IDEAL MARRIAGE, THE(1970)
Jack Stoll
DARWIN ADVENTURE, THE(1972, Brit.), art d
John Stoll
GREEN BUDDHA, THE(1954, Brit.), art d; SLEEPING TIGER, THE(1954, Brit.), art d; CROSS CHANNEL(1955, Brit.), art d; SECRET VENTURE(1955, Brit.), art d; PASSPORT TO TREASON(1956, Brit.), art d; TRACK THE MAN DOWN(1956, Brit.), art d; FIGHTING WILDCATS, THE(1957, Brit.), art d; OPERATION CON-SPIRACY(1957, Brit.), art d; WEAPON, THE(1957, Brit.), art d; MENACE IN THE NIGHT(1958, Brit.), art d; SNORKEL, THE(1958, Brit.), art d; STRANGE CASE OF DR. MANNING, THE(1958, Brit.), art d; NIGHT FIGHTERS, THE(1960), art d; SWORD OF SHERWOOD FOREST(1961, Brit.), art d; LAWRENCE OF ARABIA(1962, Brit.), art d; MILLION DOLLAR MANHUNT(1962, Brit.), art d; MAID FOR MURDER(1963, Brit.), art d; RUNNING MAN, THE(1963, Brit.), art d; PSYCHE 59(1964, Brit.), art d; SEVENTH DAWN, THE(1964), prod d; COLLECTOR, THE(1965), art d; HOW I WON THE WAR(1967, Brit.), art d; TWIST OF SAND, A(1968, Brit.), prod d; HANNIBAL BROOKS(1969, Brit.), prod d; CROMWELL(1970, Brit.), prod d; CREATURES THE WORLD FORGOT(1971, Brit.), prod d; LIVING FREE(1972, Brit.), prod d; SHAFT IN AFRICA(1973), prod d; BEAST MUST DIE, THE(1974, Brit.), art d; GOLDEN VOYAGE OF SINBAD, THE(1974, Brit.), prod d; SEVEN NIGHTS IN JAPAN(1976, Brit./Fr.), prod d
Dr. Josef Stoll
OPERATION DAYBREAK(1976, U.S./Brit./Czech.)
Nancy P. Stoll
MONDO TRASHO(1970)
Helen Stollaroff
WIFEMISTRESS(1979, Ital.)
Rudolf Stolle
DIAMONDS OF THE NIGHT(1968, Czech.)
Alvin Stoller
SUMMER LOVE(1958)
Mike Stoller
JAILHOUSE ROCK(1957)
David Stollery
PEGGY(1950); WHERE DANGER LIVES(1950); DARLING, HOW COULD YOU!(1951); TALES OF ROBIN HOOD(1951); JACK AND THE BEANSTALK(1952); HER TWELVE MEN(1954); STORM FEAR(1956); WESTWARD HO THE WA-GONS!(1956); DRANGO(1957); TEN WHO DARED(1960)
Victor Stolloff
DESERT DESPERADOES(1959), w
Ben Stoloff
BY WHOSE HAND?(1932), d; DESTRY RIDES AGAIN(1932), d; NIGHT MAYOR, THE(1932), d; SWELL-HEAD(1935), d; TO BEAT THE BAND(1935), d; DON'T TURN-'EM LOOSE(1936), d; FIGHT FOR YOUR LADY(1937), d; SEA DEVILS(1937), d; SUPER SLEUTH(1937), d; AFFAIRS OF ANNABEL(1938), d; RADIO CITY RE-

VELS(1938), d; LADY AND THE MOB, THE(1939), d; MARINES FLY HIGH, THE(1940), d; BODY DISAPPEARS, THE(1941), d; GREAT MR. NOBODY, THE(1941), d; LAW OF THE TROPICS(1941), p; THREE SONS O'GUNS(1941), d; YOU'RE IN THE ARMY NOW(1941), p; DANGEROUSLY THEY LIVE(1942), p; HIDDEN HAND, THE(1942), d; SECRET ENEMIES(1942), p; MYSTERIOUS DOCTOR, THE(1943), d; MAMA LOVES PAPA(1945), p; RADIO STARS ON PARADE(1945), p; TWO O'CLOCK COURAGE(1945), p; WHAT A BLONDE(1945), p; ZOMBIES ON BROADWAY(1945), p; JOHNNY COMES FLYING HOME(1946), d; BIG FIX, THE(1947), p; DEVIL ON WHEELS, THE(1947), p; HEARTACHES(1947), p; IT'S A JOKE, SON!(1947), d; RED STALLION, THE(1947), p; SPIRITUALIST, THE(1948), p
Silents
CIRCUS ACE, THE(1927), d; GAY RETREAT, THE(1927), d; SILVER VALLEY(1927), d
Benjamin Stoloff
GIRL FROM HAVANA, THE(1929), d; SPEAKEASY(1929), d; FOX MOVIETONE FOLLIES OF 1930(1930), d; HAPPY DAYS(1930), d; SOUP TO NUTS(1930), d; GOL-DIE(1931), d; THREE ROGUES(1931), d; DEVIL IS DRIVING, THE(1932), d; NO GREATER LOVE(1932), p; NIGHT OF TERROR(1933), d; OBEY THE LAW(1933), d; PALOOKA(1934), d; TRANSATLANTIC MERRY-GO-ROUND(1934), d; TWO IN THE DARK(1936), d; BERMUDA MYSTERY(1944), d
Silents
PROTECTION(1929), d
Misc. Silents
CANYON OF LIGHT, THE(1926), d; HORSEMAN OF THE PLAINS, A(1928), d; PLASTERED IN PARIS(1928), d
Jackie Stoloff
INTERNS, THE(1962)
M.W. Stoloff
3:10 TO YUMA(1957), md; I'LL TAKE ROMANCE(1937), md; ADVENTURE IN SAHARA(1938), md; HOLIDAY(1938), md; SHE MARRIED AN ARTIST(1938), md; BEWARE SPOOKS(1939), md; COAST GUARD(1939), m; FIRST OFFENDERS(1939), m; MAN THEY COULD NOT HANG, THE(1939), md; MISSING DAUGHTERS(1939), m; NORTH OF THE YUKON(1939), md; SMASHING THE SPY RING(1939), m; TEXAS STAMPEDE(1939), md; WOMAN IS THE JUDGE, A(1939), md; ARIZO-NA(1940), md; CONVICTED WOMAN(1940), md; ESCAPE TO GLORY(1940), md; FIVE LITTLE PEPPERS AT HOME(1940), md; GIRLS UNDER TWENTY-ONE(1940), m; HE STAYED FOR BREAKFAST(1940), md; ISLAND OF DOOMED MEN(1940), md; LADY IN QUESTION, THE(1940), md; MEN WITHOUT SOULS(1940), m; MUSIC IN MY HEART(1940), md; OUT WEST WITH THE PEPPERS(1940), md; SO YOU WON'T TALK(1940), md; THIS THING CALLED LOVE(1940), md; TOO MANY HUS-BANDS(1940), md; BLONDIE IN SOCIETY(1941), md; CONFESSIONS OF BOSTON BLACKIE(1941), md; FACE BEHIND THE MASK, THE(1941), md; GO WEST, YOUNG LADY(1941), md; HARMON OF MICHIGAN(1941), md; LADIES IN RETIRE-MENT(1941), md; OFFICER AND THE LADY, THE(1941), md; OUR WIFE(1941), md; PHANTOM SUBMARINE, THE(1941), md; RICHEST MAN IN TOWN(1941), m; SHE KNEW ALL THE ANSWERS(1941), md; SWEETHEART OF THE CAMPUS(1941), m; TEXAS(1941), md; TIME OUT FOR RHYTHM(1941), md; TWO IN A TAXI(1941), md; YOU BELONG TO ME(1941), md; ATLANTIC CONVOY(1942), m; BLONDIE GOES TO COLLEGE(1942), md; COMMANDOS STRIKE AT DAWN, THE(1942), md; FLIGHT LIEUTENANT(1942), md; HELLO ANNAPOLIS(1942), md; LUCKY LEGS(1942), md; MAN WHO RETURNED TO LIFE, THE(1942), md; MAN'S WORLD, A(1942), md; MEET THE STEWARTS(1942), md; PARACHUTE NURSE(1942), md; SABOTAGE SQUAD(1942), md; SPIRIT OF STANFORD, THE(1942), md; SWEETHEART OF THE FLEET(1942), md; WIFE TAKES A FLYER, THE(1942), md; AFTER MIDNIGHT WITH BOSTON BLACKIE(1943), m; DANGEROUS BLONDES(1943), md; DE-SPERADOES, THE(1943), md; DESTROYER(1943), md; DOUGHBOYS IN IRE-LAND(1943), md; FIRST COMES COURAGE(1943), md; FOOTLIGHT GLAMOUR(1943), md; IS EVERYBODY HAPPY?(1943), md; IT'S A GREAT LI-FE(1943), m; MURDER IN TIMES SQUARE(1943), md; MY KINGDOM FOR A COOK(1943), md; POWER OF THE PRESS(1943), md; SAHARA(1943), md; SHE HAS WHAT IT TAKES(1943), md; SOMETHING TO SHOUT ABOUT(1943), md; SWING OUT THE BLUES(1943), md; THERE'S SOMETHING ABOUT A SOLDIER(1943), md; TWO SENORITAS FROM CHICAGO(1943), md; WHAT'S BUZZIN COUSIN?(1943), md; ADDRESS UNKNOWN(1944), md; BEAUTIFUL BUT BROKE(1944), md; CAROLINA BLUES(1944), md; COVER GIRL(1944), md; GHOST THAT WALKS ALONE, THE(1944), md; GIRL IN THE CASE(1944), md; HEY, ROOKIE(1944), md; IMPATIENT YEARS, THE(1944), md; JAM SESSION(1944), md; KLONDIKE KA-TE(1944), md; MR. WINKLE GOES TO WAR(1944), md; ONCE UPON A TIME(1944), md; RACKET MAN, THE(1944), md; RETURN OF THE VAMPIRE, THE(1944), md; SAILOR'S HOLIDAY(1944), md; STRANGE AFFAIR(1944), md; TOGETHER AGAIN(1944), md; TWO-MAN SUBMARINE(1944), md; EADIE WAS A LADY(1945), md; FIGHTING GUARDSMAN, THE(1945), md; KISS AND TELL(1945), md; OVER 21(1945), md; SNAFU(1945), md; SONG TO REMEMBER, A(1945), md; GALLANT JOURNEY(1946), md; MEET ME ON BROADWAY(1946), md; MR. DISTRICT ATTOR-NEY(1946), md; PERILOUS HOLIDAY(1946), md; RENEGADES(1946), md; TARS AND SPARS(1946), md; WALLS CAME TUMBLING DOWN, THE(1946), md; DEAD RECKONING(1947), md; FRAMED(1947), md; HER HUSBAND'S AFFAIRS(1947), md; SWORDSMAN, THE(1947), md; DARK PAST, THE(1948), md; GALLANT BLADE, THE(1948), m; LOVES OF CARMEN, THE(1948), md; MATING OF MILLIE, THE(1948), md; RETURN OF OCTOBER, THE(1948), md; SIGN OF THE RAM, THE(1948), md; TO THE ENDS OF THE EARTH(1948), md; UNTAMED BREED, THE(1948), md; DOOLINS OF OKLAHOMA, THE(1949), m; MR. SOFT TOUCH(1949), m, md; SONG OF INDIA(1949), md; UNDERCOVER MAN, THE(1949), md; WE WERE STRANGERS(1949), md; MASK OF THE AVENGER(1951), md; SIROC-CO(1951), md; MISS SADIE THOMPSON(1953), md; WILD ONE, THE(1953), md; PUSHOVER(1954), md; REDHEAD FROM MANHATTAN(1954), md; FIVE AGAINST THE HOUSE(1955), md; IT HAPPENED TO JANE(1959), md; LAWRENCE OF ARABIA(1962, Brit.), md
Morris Stoloff
CORPSE CAME C.O.D., THE(, md; YOU CAN'T RUN AWAY FROM IT(1956), md; CRAIG'S WIFE(1936), md; MORE THAN A SECRETARY(1936), md; THEODORA GOES WILD(1936), md; AWFUL TRUTH, THE(1937), md; DEVIL IS DRIVING, THE(1937), md; DODGE CITY TRAIL(1937), md; GAME THAT KILLS, THE(1937), m; GIRLS CAN PLAY(1937), m; MURDER IN GREENWICH VILLAGE(1937), md; PAID TO DANCE(1937), md; RACKETEERS IN EXILE(1937), md; CALL OF THE ROCK-IES(1938), md; COLORADO TRAIL(1938), md; CONVICTED(1938), md; GIRLS' SCHOOL(1938), md; HOLLYWOOD ROUNDUP(1938), md; I AM THE LAW(1938), md; JUVENILE COURT(1938), md; LAW OF THE PLAINS(1938), md; NO TIME TO MARRY(1938), md; PENITENTIARY(1938), md; START CHEERING(1938), md; THERE'S ALWAYS A WOMAN(1938), md; YOU CAN'T TAKE IT WITH YOU(1938),

md; BLIND ALLEY(1939), m; BLONDIE BRINGS UP BABY(1939), md; HOMICIDE BUREAU(1939), md; MR. SMITH GOES TO WASHINGTON(1939), md; SPECIAL INSPECTOR(1939), md; SPOILERS OF THE RANGE(1939), md; ANGELS OVER BROADWAY(1940), md; BLONDIE ON A BUDGET(1940), md; CAFE HOSTESS(1940), md; DURANGO KID, THE(1940), md; LONE WOLF KEEPS A DATE, THE(1940), md; BLONDIE GOES LATIN(1941), md; PENNY SERENADE(1941), md; YOU'LL NEVER GET RICH(1941), md; BOSTON BLACKIE GOES HOLLYWOOD(1942), md; HARVARD, HERE I COME(1942), md; MY SISTER EILEEN(1942), md; NIGHT TO REMEMBER, A(1942), md; TALK OF THE TOWN(1942), md; NINE GIRLS(1944), md; SECRET COMMAND(1944), md; COUNTER-ATTACK(1945), md; SHE WOULDN'T SAY YES(1945), md; TONIGHT AND EVERY NIGHT(1945), md; BANDIT OF SHERWOOD FOREST, THE(1946), md; JOLSON STORY, THE(1946), md; JOHNNY O'CLOCK(1947), md; LADY FROM SHANGHAI, THE(1948), md; RELENTLESS(1948), md; JOHNNY ALLEGRO(1949), md; JOLSON SINGS AGAIN(1949), a, md; LUST FOR GOLD(1949), md; MISS GRANT TAKES RICHMOND(1949), md; RECKLESS MOMENTS, THE(1949), md; SHOCKPROOF(1949), md; SLIGHTLY FRENCH(1949), md; TELL IT TO THE JUDGE(1949), md; CARGO TO CAPETOWN(1950), md; CONVICTED(1950), md; EMERGENCY WEDDING(1950), md; FATHER IS A BACHELOR(1950), md; FORTUNES OF CAPTAIN BLOOD(1950), md; GOOD HUMOR MAN, THE(1950), md; KILL THE UMPIRE(1950), md; KILLER THAT STALKED NEW YORK, THE(1950), md; NEVADAN, THE(1950), md; NO SAD SONGS FOR ME(1950), md; PETTY GIRL, THE(1950), md; ROGUES OF SHERWOOD FOREST(1950), md; STAGE TO TUCSON(1950), md; WOMAN OF DISTINCTION, A(1950), md; BORN YESTERDAY(1951), md; FAMILY SECRET, THE(1951), md; HARLEM GLOBETROTTERS, THE(1951), md; HER FIRST ROMANCE(1951), md; LADY AND THE BANDIT, THE(1951), md; LORNA DOONE(1951), md; MOB, THE(1951), md; NEVER TRUST A GAMBLER(1951), md; SANTA FE(1951), md; SATURDAY'S HERO(1951), md; SON OF DR. JEKYLL, THE(1951), md; TEN TALL MEN(1951), md; TWO OF A KIND(1951), md; DEATH OF A SALESMAN(1952), md; EIGHT IRON MEN(1952), md; FIRST TIME, THE(1952), md; LAST OF THE COMANCHES(1952), md; MEMBER OF THE WEDDING, THE(1952), md; PAULA(1952), md; SCANDAL SHEET(1952), md; SNIPER, THE(1952), md; SOUND OFF(1952), md; ALL ASHORE(1953), md; FROM HERE TO ETERNITY(1953), md; JUGGLER, THE(1953), md; LET'S DO IT AGAIN(1953), md; 5,000 FINGERS OF DR. T. THE(1953), md; HUMAN DESIRE(1954), md; IT SHOULD HAPPEN TO YOU(1954), md; PHFFFT!(1954), m; BRING YOUR SMILE ALONG(1955), md; LAST FRONTIER, THE(1955), md; LONG GRAY LINE, THE(1955), m; MY SISTER EILEEN(1955), md; PICNIC(1955), md; QUEEN BEE(1955), md; THREE FOR THE SHOW(1955), md; THREE STRIPES IN THE SUN(1955), md; VIOLENT MEN, THE(1955), md; AUTUMN LEAVES(1956), md; EDDY DUCHIN STORY, THE(1956), md; NIGHTFALL(1956), md; JEANNE EAGELS(1957), md; PAL JOEY(1957), md; COWBOY(1958), md; GUNMAN'S WALK(1958), md; SENIOR PROM(1958), md; GIDGET(1959), m, md; 1001 ARABIAN NIGHTS(1959), md; MOUNTAIN ROAD, THE(1960), md; SONG WITHOUT END(1960), md; STRANGERS WHEN WE MEET(1960), md; FANNY(1961), md; NONE BUT THE BRAVE(1965, U.S./Jap.), md; NAKED RUNNER, THE(1967, Brit.), md

Morris W. Stoloff
IT'S ALL YOURS(1937), md; SHADOW, THE(1937), md; THERE'S THAT WOMAN AGAIN(1937), md; WEST OF CHEYENNE(1938), md; WHO KILLED GAIL PRESTON?(1938), md; AMAZING MR. WILLIAMS(1939), m; GOLDEN BOY(1939), md; GOOD GIRLS GO TO PARIS(1939), m; LET US LIVE(1939), md; LONE WOLF SPY HUNT, THE(1939), md; ONLY ANGELS HAVE WINGS(1939), m, md; BEFORE I HANG(1940), md; HIS GIRL FRIDAY(1940), m; MAN WITH NINE LIVES, THE(1940), md; HERE COMES MR. JORDAN(1941), m; SECRETS OF THE LONE WOLF(1941), md; STORK PAYS OFF, THE(1941), md; THEY DARE NOT LOVE(1941), md; THREE GIRLS ABOUT TOWN(1941), md; BOOGIE MAN WILL GET YOU, THE(1942), md; LADY IS WILLING, THE(1942), md; SHUT MY BIG MOUTH(1942), md; THEY ALL KISSED THE BRIDE(1942), md; MORE THE MERRIER, THE(1943), md; ONE DANGEROUS NIGHT(1943), md; PASSPORT TO SUEZ(1943), md; REVEILLE WITH BEVERLY(1943), md; WHAT A WOMAN!(1943), md; THOUSAND AND ONE NIGHTS, A(1945), md; SO DARK THE NIGHT(1946), m; DOWN TO EARTH(1947), md; GUILT OF JANET AMES, THE(1947), md; IT HAD TO BE YOU(1947), md; MAN FROM COLORADO, THE(1948), md; KNOCK ON ANY DOOR(1949), md; TOKYO JOE(1949), md; WALKING HILLS, THE(1949), md; FULLER BRUSH GIRL, THE(1950), md; HARRIET CRAIG(1950), md; IN A LONELY PLACE(1950), md; WHEN YOU'RE SMILING(1950), m; MARRYING KIND, THE(1952), md; SALOME(1953), md; MAN FROM LARAMIE, THE(1955), md; TIGHT SPOT(1955), md; FULL OF LIFE(1956), md; JUBAL(1956), md; OPERATION MAD BALL(1957), md; LAST ANGRY MAN, THE(1959), md; THEY CAME TO CORDURA(1959), md

Victor Stoloff
EGYPT BY THREE(1953), p&d; VOLCANO(1953, Ital.), w; SHE-GODS OF SHARK REEF(1958), w; OF LOVE AND DESIRE(1963), p, w; INTIMACY(1966), d; 300 YEAR WEEKEND(1971), p&d, w
Misc. Talkies
WASHINGTON AFFAIR, THE(1978), d

Alexander Stolper
ROAD TO LIFE(1932, USSR), w; LAD FROM OUR TOWN(1941, USSR), d; DAYS AND NIGHTS(1946, USSR), d

Robert Stolper
Misc. Talkies
MISSION TO DEATH(1966)

Sergei Stoltarov
LUCKY BRIDE, THE(1948, USSR)

Eric Stoltz
FAST TIMES AT RIDGEMONT HIGH(1982)
1984
HIGHWAY TO HELL(1984); RUNNING HOT(1984); SURF II(1984); WILD LIFE, THE(1984)

Barry Stoltze
Misc. Talkies
GRAD NIGHT(1980)

S.D. Stolyarov
HEROES OF THE SEA(1941)

Sergey Stolyarov
MAGIC VOYAGE OF SINBAD, THE(1962, USSR)

D. Stolyarskaya
ITALIANO BRAVA GENTE(1965, Ital./USSR); WHEN THE TREES WERE TALL(1965, USSR); MEET ME IN MOSCOW(1966, USSR)

Clarissa Stolz
LOCKER 69(1962, Brit.)

Milton Stolz
STATE FAIR(1962)

Robert Stolz
PRINCE OF ARCADIA(1933, Brit.), m; WHAT WOMEN DREAM(1933, Ger.), m; MY HEART IS CALLING(1935, Brit.), m; SPRING PARADE(1940), m; IT HAPPENED TOMORROW(1944), md

Mark Stolzenberg
LUGGAGE OF THE GODS(1983)

Z. Stomma
SECRET BRIGADE, THE(1951 USSR)

Stompie
PARDON MY GUN(1930)

Winston Stona
HARDER THEY COME, THE(1973, Jamaica)

A. Stone
NEVER PUT IT IN WRITING(1964), d&w

Al Stone
MILLION DOLLAR KID(1944)

Alan Stone
ONCE UPON A TIME(1944)

Albert Ray Hilda Stone
EVERYBODY'S BABY(1939), w

Alexandra Stone
DOUBLE-BARRELLED DETECTIVE STORY, THE(1965)

Allan Stone
DAVID AND BATHSHEBA(1951)

Alton Stone
Silents
BACK TRAIL, THE(1924)

Amelia Stone
MIRACLES FOR SALE(1939)

Andrew Stone
HI DIDDLE DIDDLE(1943), p&d; STORMY WEATHER(1943), d; BEDSIDE MANNER(1945), p&d; BACHELOR'S DAUGHTERS, THE(1946), p,d&w; HIGHWAY 301(1950), d&w; STEEL TRAP, THE(1952), d&w; BLUEPRINT FOR MURDER, A(1953), d&w; NIGHT HOLDS TERROR, THE(1955), p,d&w; CRY TERROR(1958), p, d&w; DECKS RAN RED, THE(1958), p, d&w; PASSWORD IS COURAGE, THE(1962, Brit.), p, d&w; FUN ON A WEEKEND(1979), p,d&w

Andrew L. Stone
HELL'S HEADQUARTERS(1932), d; GIRL SAID NO, THE(1937), w; SAY IT IN FRENCH(1938), p&d; STOLEN HEAVEN(1938), d, w; GREAT VICTOR HERBERT, THE(1939), p&d, w; THERE'S MAGIC IN MUSIC(1941), p&d, w; SENSATIONS OF 1945(1944), p&d, w; CONFIDENCE GIRL(1952), p,d&w; JULIE(1956), d&w; LAST VOYAGE, THE(1960), p, d&w; RING OF FIRE(1961), p, d&w; NEVER PUT IT IN WRITING(1964), d; SECRET OF MY SUCCESS, THE(1965, Brit.), p, d&w; SONG OF NORWAY(1970), w, p, d; GREAT WALTZ, THE(1972), p,d&w

Annette Stone
WHITE ZOMBIE(1932)

Arnold M. Stone
1984
SECRET HONOR(1984), w

Arthur Stone
FOX MOVIETONE FOLLIES(1929); FROZEN JUSTICE(1929); THRU DIFFERENT EYES(1929); ARIZONA KID, THE(1930); BAD MAN, THE(1930); GIRL OF THE GOLDEN WEST(1930); LASH, THE(1930); MAMBA(1930); ON THE LEVEL(1930); VAGABOND KING, THE(1930); BIG SHOT, THE(1931); CONQUERING HORDE, THE(1931); SECRET MENACE(1931); BROKEN WING, THE(1932); ROAR OF THE DRAGON(1932); SO BIG(1932); THAT'S MY BOY(1932); DEVIL'S BROTHER, THE(1933); I'LL TELL THE WORLD(1934); LOVE BIRDS(1934); SHE HAD TO CHOOSE(1934); BORDERTOWN(1935); CHARLIE CHAN IN EGYPT(1935); HOT TIP(1935); UNDER THE PAMPAS MOON(1935); FURY(1936); WESTBOUND MAIL(1937); GO CHASE YOURSELF(1938); RUTHLESS(1948); SPECIAL AGENT(1949)
Silents
IT MUST BE LOVE(1926); MISS NOBODY(1926); SILENT LOVER, THE(1926); AFFAIR OF THE FOLLIES, AN(1927); BABE COMES HOME(1927); SEA TIGER, THE(1927); RED WINE(1928); CAPTAIN LASH(1929); FAR CALL, THE(1929); FUGITIVES(1929); NEW YEAR'S EVE(1929)
Misc. Silents
HARD BOILED HAGGERTY(1927); VALLEY OF THE GIANTS, THE(1927); BURNING DAYLIGHT(1928); CHICKEN A LA KING(1928); FARMER'S DAUGHTER, THE(1928)

Barbara Stone
FORCE OF EVIL(1948); MILESTONES(1975), p

Ben Stone
SATAN IN HIGH HEELS(1962)

Bernard Stone
MAIN CHANCE, THE(1966, Brit.); SMASHING TIME(1967 Brit.); POOR COW(1968, Brit.); STRANGE AFFAIR, THE(1968, Brit.); STUD, THE(1979, Brit.)

Bob Stone
TRAIN TO ALCATRAZ(1948); STARK FEAR(1963); SUPER VAN(1977), m

Bobby Stone
GANGSTER'S BOY(1938); STREETS OF NEW YORK(1939); DOWN ARGENTINE WAY(1940); BOWERY BLITZKRIEG(1941); FLYING WILD(1941); PRIDE OF THE BOWERY(1941); JOAN OF OZARK(1942); LET'S GET TOUGH(1942); MR. WISE GUY(1942); 'NEATH BROOKLYN BRIDGE(1942); SONG OF THE ISLANDS(1942); GHOSTS ON THE LOOSE(1943); KID DYNAMITE(1943); MR. MUGGS STEPS OUT(1943); SECRETS OF THE UNDERGROUND(1943); FOLLOW THE LEADER(1944); MILLION DOLLAR KID(1944); I, JANE DOE(1948)

Brian Stone
TARGETS(1968), m

Butch Stone
SMART POLITICS(1948)

Caleb Stone
SATURDAY NIGHT AT THE BATHS(1975)

Carol Stone
FRECKLES(1935)

Cece Stone
HOOKED GENERATION, THE(1969)

Charles Stone
LORD RICHARD IN THE PANTRY(1930, Brit.); NO LADY(1931, Brit.); SKY'S THE LIMIT, THE(1937, Brit.)

Chris Stone
Misc. Talkies
WARHEAD(1974)

Christopher Stone
GRASSHOPPER, THE(1970); NOTORIOUS CLEOPATRA, THE(1970); LOVE ME DEADLY(1972); TREASURE OF JAMAICA REEF, THE(1976), m; HOWLING, THE(1981); JUNKMAN, THE(1982); CUJO(1983)

Christopher L. Stone
1984
COVERGIRL(1984, Can.), m; NADIA(1984, U.S./Yugo.), m

Cliffie Stone
SONG OF THE DRIFTER(1948)

Danny Stone
HALLUCINATION GENERATION(1966); DESPERATE ONES, THE(1968 U.S./Span.)
1984
GHOSTBUSTERS(1984)

Danton Stone
1984
JOY OF SEX(1984)

David Stone
HIDE AND SEEK(1964, Brit.), w; DOUBLE-BARRELLED DETECTIVE STORY, THE(1965), p; REPULSION(1965, Brit.), w; LONG SHOT(1981, Brit.)

David C. Stone
HALLELUJAH THE HILLS(1963), p; ICE(1970), p; MILESTONES(1975), a, p

Dick Stone
MURDER IN MISSISSIPPI(1965)

Doc Stone
POPPY(1936); SAN QUENTIN(1937), tech adv; KING OF THE UNDERWORLD(1939)
Silents
CIRCUS, THE(1928)

Doris Stone
DARK ANGEL, THE(1935); WITHOUT REGRET(1935); JOURNEY FOR MARGARET(1942); NOCTURNE(1946)
Silents
MOTHERS-IN-LAW(1923)

Dorothy Stone
REVOLT OF THE ZOMBIES(1936); I'LL BE SEEING YOU(1944)
Silents
BROADWAY AFTER DARK(1924)

Ed LeRoy Stone
Silents
FLOWING GOLD(1924), ed

Elly Stone
JACQUES BREL IS ALIVE AND WELL AND LIVING IN PARIS(1975)

Eric Stone
BLACK ZOO(1963)

Ethan Stone
TWILIGHT TIME(1983, U.S./Yugo.)

Ethel B. Stone
SCATTERGOOD MEETS BROADWAY(1941), w

Eugene C. Stone
MONEY MADNESS(1948), set d

Ezra Stone
THOSE WERE THE DAYS(1940); THIS IS THE ARMY(1943); TAMMY AND THE MILLIONAIRE(1967), d

Frank Stone
Silents
MY FOUR YEARS IN GERMANY(1918); ADORATION(1928), ed

Fred Stone
ALICE ADAMS(1935); FARMER IN THE DELL, THE(1936); GRAND JURY(1936); MY AMERICAN WIFE(1936); TRAIL OF THE LONESOME PINE, THE(1936); HIDEAWAY(1937); LIFE BEGINS IN COLLEGE(1937); QUICK MONEY(1938); KONGA, THE WILD STALLION(1939); NO PLACE TO GO(1939); WESTERNER, THE(1940); SHADOW OF THE CAT, THE(1961, Brit.); CASH ON DEMAND(1962, Brit.); WILD AFFAIR, THE(1966, Brit.)
Silents
JOHNNY GET YOUR GUN(1919); BILLY JIM(1922); BROADWAY AFTER DARK(1924)
Misc. Silents
GOAT, THE(1918); UNDER THE TOP(1919); DUKE OF CHIMNEY BUTTE, THE(1921)

Fredric Stone
THIEF(1981)

Gene Stone
SO THIS IS COLLEGE(1929); HOMICIDE BUREAU(1939); ISLE OF FORGOTTEN SINS(1943), spec eff; PASSPORT TO SUEZ(1943); OVERLAND RIDERS(1946), set d
Silents
FAIR CO-ED, THE(1927)
Misc. Silents
UNEASY PAYMENTS(1927)

Genie Stone
CALYPSO JOE(1957); PAL JOEY(1957)

George E. Stone
GIRL IN THE GLASS CAGE, THE(1929); MELODY LANE(1929); TWO MEN AND A MAID(1929); CIMARRON(1931); FIVE STAR FINAL(1931); FRONT PAGE, THE(1931); LITTLE CAESAR(1931); SOB SISTER(1931); SPIDER, THE(1931); FILE 113(1932); LAST MILE, THE(1932); PHANTOM OF CRESTWOOD, THE(1932); TAXI!(1932); WOMAN FROM MONTE CARLO, THE(1932); WORLD AND THE FLESH, THE(1932); BIG BRAIN, THE(1933); EMERGENCY CALL(1933); KING FOR A NIGHT(1933); LADIES MUST LOVE(1933); PENTHOUSE(1933); SAILOR BE GOOD(1933); SING SINNER, SING(1933); SONG OF THE EAGLE(1933); VAMPIRE BAT, THE(1933); WRECKER, THE(1933); 42ND STREET(1933); DRAGON MURDER CASE, THE(1934);

FRONTIER MARSHAL(1934); HE COULDN'T TAKE IT(1934); RETURN OF THE TERROR(1934); VIVA VILLA!(1934); FRISCO KID(1935); HOLD'EM YALE(1935); MAKE A MILLION(1935); MILLION DOLLAR BABY(1935); ONE HOUR LATE(1935); PUBLIC HERO NO. 1(1935); SECRET OF THE CHATEAU(1935); ANTHONY ADVERSE(1936); BULLETS OR BALLOTS(1936); FRESHMAN LOVE(1936); HERE COMES CARTER(1936); JAILBREAK(1936); KING OF HOCKEY(1936); MAN HUNT(1936); MOONLIGHT ON THE PRAIRIE(1936); POLO JOE(1936); RHYTHM ON THE RANGE(1936); ADVENTUROUS BLONDE(1937); ALCATRAZ ISLAND(1937); BACK IN CIRCULATION(1937); CLOTHES AND THE WOMAN(1937, Brit.); DON'T GET ME WRONG(1937, Brit.); MR. MOTO'S GAMBLE(1938); OVER THE WALL(1938); SLIGHT CASE OF MURDER, A(1938); SUBMARINE PATROL(1938); YOU AND ME(1938); HOUSEKEEPER'S DAUGHTER(1939); LONG SHOT, THE(1939); NIGHT OF NIGHTS, THE(1939); YOU CAN'T GET AWAY WITH MURDER(1939); CHEROKEE STRIP(1940); I TAKE THIS WOMAN(1940); ISLAND OF DOOMED MEN(1940); NORTHWEST MOUNTED POLICE(1940); SLIGHTLY TEMPTED(1940); BROADWAY LIMITED(1941); CONFESSIONS OF BOSTON BLACKIE(1941); FACE BEHIND THE MASK, THE(1941); LAST OF THE DUANES(1941); ROAD SHOW(1941); ALIAS BOSTON BLACKIE(1942); BOSTON BLACKIE GOES HOLLYWOOD(1942); DEVIL WITH HITLER, THE(1942); LITTLE TOKYO, U.S.A.(1942); LONE STAR RANGER(1942); AFTER MIDNIGHT WITH BOSTON BLACKIE(1943); CHANCE OF A LIFETIME, THE(1943); MY BUDDY(1944); ONE MYSTERIOUS NIGHT(1944); ROGER TOUHY, GANGSTER!(1944); TIMBER QUEEN(1944); BOSTON BLACKIE BOOKED ON SUSPICION(1945); BOSTON BLACKIE'S RENDEZVOUS(1945); DOLL FACE(1945); NOB HILL(1945); ONE EXCITING NIGHT(1945); SCARED STIFF(1945); ABIE'S IRISH ROSE(1946); BOSTON BLACKIE AND THE LAW(1946); CLOSE CALL FOR BOSTON BLACKIE, A(1946); PHANTOM THIEF, THE(1946); SENTIMENTAL JOURNEY(1946); SHOCK(1946); DAISY KENYON(1947); TRAPPED BY BOSTON BLACKIE(1948); UNTAMED BREED, THE(1948); DANCING IN THE DARK(1949); BLOODHOUNDS OF BROADWAY(1952); GIRL IN EVERY PORT, A(1952); COMBAT SQUAD(1953); PICKUP ON SOUTH STREET(1953); ROBE, THE(1953); BROKEN LANCE(1954); MIAMI STORY, THE(1954); STEEL CAGE, THE(1954); THREE RING CIRCUS(1954); WOMAN'S WORLD(1954); GUYS AND DOLLS(1955); MAN WITH THE GOLDEN ARM, THE(1955); SLIGHTLY SCARLET(1956); CALYPSO HEAT WAVE(1957); SIERRA STRANGER(1957); STORY OF MANKIND, THE(1957); TIJUANA STORY, THE(1957); ALIAS JESSE JAMES(1959); SOME CAME RUNNING(1959); SOME LIKE IT HOT(1959); OCEAN'S ELEVEN(1960); POCKETFUL OF MIRACLES(1961)
Misc. Talkies
JUNGLE HELL(1956)
Silents
BEAUTIFUL BUT DUMB(1928)
Misc. Silents
CLOTHES MAKE THE WOMAN(1928)

George Stone
STATE STREET SADIE(1928); REDEEMING SIN, THE(1929); WEARY RIVER(1929); EMBARRASSING MOMENTS(1934); SUSPENSE(1946); BABY FACE NELSON(1957)
Silents
GRETCHEN, THE GREENHORN(1916); LITTLE SCHOOL MA'AM, THE(1916); MARTHA'S VINDICATION(1916); PATRIOT, THE(1916); ALI BABA AND THE FORTY THIEVES(1918); JUNGLE TRAIL, THE(1919); SEVENTH HEAVEN(1927); RACKET, THE(1928); WALKING BACK(1928)
Misc. Silents
JIM BLUDSO(1917); JUST PALS(1920); JACKIE(1921); SAN FRANCISCO NIGHTS(1928); TURN BACK THE HOURS(1928)

Georgie Stone
TENDERLOIN(1928); SKIN DEEP(1929); MEDICINE MAN, THE(1930); UNDER A TEXAS MOON(1930); MAID TO ORDER(1932)
Silents
POPPY GIRL'S HUSBAND, THE(1919); WHITE AND UNMARRIED(1921); NAUGHTY BABY(1929)
Misc. Silents
RIO GRANDE(1920); DESPERATE TRAILS(1921); WHISTLE, THE(1921); BRASS KNUCKLES(1927)

Gloria Stone
PRODIGAL, THE(1955)

Gordon Stone
SHIRALEE, THE(1957, Brit.), ed; THIRD KEY, THE(1957, Brit.), ed; DUNKIRK(1958, Brit.), ed; KIDNAPPED(1960), ed; LONG AND THE SHORT AND THE TALL, THE(1961, Brit.), ed; SPARE THE ROD(1961, Brit.), ed; IN SEARCH OF THE CASTAWAYS(1962, Brit.), ed; THREE LIVES OF THOMASINA, THE(1963, U.S./Brit.), ed; MOON-SPINNERS, THE(1964), ed; THOSE MAGNIFICENT MEN IN THEIR FLYING MACHINES; OR HOW I FLEW FROM LONDON TO PARIS IN 25 HOURS AND 11 MINUTES(1965, Brit.), ed

Grace Zaring Stone
BITTER TEA OF GENERAL YEN, THE(1933), w

Gregory Stone
EASY TO TAKE(1936), m; HOLLYWOOD BOULEVARD(1936), m; INTERNES CAN'T TAKE MONEY(1937), m; GIRLS' SCHOOL(1938), m; HER JUNGLE LOVE(1938), m; JIVARO(1954), m

Hannah Stone
STARK FEAR(1963)

Harold Stone
SOUL OF NIGGER CHARLEY, THE(1973), w

Harold J. Stone
HARDER THEY FALL, THE(1956); SLANDER(1956); SOMEBODY UP THERE LIKES ME(1956); WRONG MAN, THE(1956); GARMENT JUNGLE, THE(1957); HOUSE OF NUMBERS(1957); INVISIBLE BOY, THE(1957); MAN AFRAID(1957); THESE THOUSAND HILLS(1959); SPARTACUS(1960); CHAPMAN REPORT, THE(1962); "X"–THE MAN WITH THE X-RAY EYES(1963); SHOWDOWN(1963); GIRL HAPPY(1965); GREATEST STORY EVER TOLD, THE(1965); BIG MOUTH, THE(1967); ST. VALENTINE'S DAY MASSACRE, THE(1967); WHICH WAY TO THE FRONT?(1970); SEVEN MINUTES, THE(1971); PICKUP ON 101(1972); MITCHELL(1975); WILD McCULLOCHS, THE(1975); HARDLY WORKING(1981)

Harry Stone
KILL, THE(1968)

Helen Stone
Silents
SALVAGE(1921)

Henry Stone
SARATOGA(1937)
Henry Lewis Stone
COURT JESTER, THE(1956)
Hilda Stone
PASSPORT HUSBAND(1938), w; PARDON OUR NERVE(1939), w; GIRL IN 313(1940), w
Irving Stone
ARKANSAS JUDGE(1941), w; MAGNIFICENT DOLL(1946), w; PRESIDENT'S LADY, THE(1953), w; LUST FOR LIFE(1956), w; AGONY AND THE ECSTASY, THE(1965), w
Ivory Stone
BLACKENSTEIN(1973)
Jack Stone
SALLY(1929), art d; LADY BY CHOICE(1934); MAN WITH THE GOLDEN ARM, THE(1955), makeup; YOUNG FURY(1965), makeup; THREE ON A COUCH(1966), makeup; TOO LATE THE HERO(1970), makeup; WHICH WAY TO THE FRONT?(1970), makeup
Silents
LILAC TIME(1928)
James Stone
GLASS WEB, THE(1953); HOW TO MARRY A MILLIONAIRE(1953); LAW AND ORDER(1953); FIVE GUNS WEST(1955); FIRST TRAVELING SALESLADY, THE(1956); RAINMAKER, THE(1956); TEENAGE REBEL(1956); KISS THEM FOR ME(1957); BAREFOOT IN THE PARK(1967)
James F. Stone
GUNSMOKE(1953); KID FROM LEFT FIELD, THE(1953); BLACK WIDOW(1954); BROKEN LANCE(1954); SIX BRIDGES TO CROSS(1955); SCARLET HOUR, THE(1956)
Jeff Stone
WHEN THE GIRLS TAKE OVER(1962)
Jeffery Stone
BIG BEAT, THE(1958)
Jeffrey Stone
TENDER HEARTS(1955); EDGE OF HELL(1956); GIRL IN THE KREMLIN, THE(1957); DAMN CITIZEN(1958); MONEY, WOMEN AND GUNS(1958); THING THAT COULDN'T DIE, THE(1958)
Jennifer Stone
LADYBUG, LADYBUG(1963); NEW LIFE STYLE, THE(1970, Ger.)
Jill Stone
ST. IVES(1976)
Joe Stone
MAGNIFICENT SEVEN RIDE, THE(1972), set d; PETE 'N' TILLIE(1972), set d; MIDNIGHT MAN, THE(1974), set d
John Stone
BLACK WATCH, THE(1929), w; GIRL FROM HAVANA, THE(1929), w; SALUTE(1929), w; WILD COMPANY(1930), w; BABY, TAKE A BOW(1934), p; CHARLIE CHAN IN LONDON(1934), p; SHE LEARNED ABOUT SAILORS(1934), p; THREE ON A HONEYMOON(1934), p; TWO AND ONE TWO(1934), p; BACHELOR OF ARTS(1935), p; CHARLIE CHAN IN SHANGHAI(1935), p; GREAT HOTEL MURDER(1935), p; MUSIC IS MAGIC(1935), p; SENORA CASADA NECEISITA MARIDO(1935), p; THUNDER IN THE NIGHT(1935), p; CHARLIE CHAN AT THE CIRCUS(1936), p; CHARLIE CHAN AT THE OPERA(1936), p; CHARLIE CHAN AT THE RACE TRACK(1936), p; CHARLIE CHAN'S SECRET(1936), p; FIRST BABY(1936), p; HERE COMES TROUBLE(1936), p; PEPPER(1936), p; UNDER YOUR SPELL(1936), p; ANGEL'S HOLIDAY(1937), p; CHARLIE CHAN AT MONTE CARLO(1937), p; CHARLIE CHAN AT THE OLYMPICS(1937), p; CHARLIE CHAN ON BROADWAY(1937), p; CHECKERS(1937), p; GREAT HOSPITAL MYSTERY, THE(1937), p; HOLY TERROR, THE(1937), p; STEP LIVELY, JEEVES(1937), p; WILD AND WOOLLY(1937), p; 45 FATHERS(1937), p; ALWAYS IN TROUBLE(1938), p; ARIZONA WILDCAT(1938), p; CHARLIE CHAN IN HONOLULU(1938), p; DOWN ON THE FARM(1938), p; KEEP SMILING(1938), p; MR. MOTO'S GAMBLE(1938), p; ONE WILD NIGHT(1938), p; RASCALS(1938), p; SAFETY IN NUMBERS(1938), p; BOY FRIEND(1939), p; CHARLIE CHAN IN RENO(1939), p; CHARLIE CHAN IN THE CITY OF DARKNESS(1939), p; CISCO KID AND THE LADY, THE(1939), p; EVERYBODY'S BABY(1939), p; JONES FAMILY IN HOLLYWOOD, THE(1939), p; MR. MOTO IN DANGER ISLAND(1939), p; QUICK MILLIONS(1939), p; TOO BUSY TO WORK(1939), p; SHOOTING HIGH(1940), p; YOUNG AS YOU FEEL(1940), p; PASSPORT TO SUEZ(1943), w; CLOSE CALL FOR BOSTON BLACKIE, A(1946), p; PHANTOM THIEF, THE(1946), p; HOLIDAY CAMP(1947, Brit.); UPTURNED GLASS, THE(1947, Brit.); COLONEL BOGEY(1948, Brit.); FIGHTING BACK(1948), w; WEAKER SEX, THE(1949, Brit.); OPERATION MURDER(1957, Brit.); THREE SUNDAYS TO LIVE(1957, Brit.); X THE UNKNOWN(1957, Brit.); MOMENT OF INDISCRETION(1958, Brit.); DEADLIER THAN THE MALE(1967, Brit.); ASSAULT(1971, Brit.); KILLING OF ANGEL STREET, THE(1983, Aus.)
Silents
GOLD AND THE GIRL(1925), w; LUCKY HORSESHOE, THE(1925), w; GREAT K & A TRAIN ROBBERY, THE(1926), w; MAN FOUR-SQUARE, A(1926), w; NO MAN'S GOLD(1926), w; ARIZONA BOUND(1927), w; ARIZONA WILDCAT(1927), w; AUCTIONEER, THE(1927), w; BRONCHO TWISTER(1927), w; LAST TRAIL, THE(1927), w; NEVADA(1927), w; DAREDEVIL'S REWARD(1928), w; HOMESICK(1928), w; PLAY GIRL, THE(1928), w; PREP AND PEP(1928), w; ROAD HOUSE(1928), w; CAPTAIN LASH(1929), w; FUGITIVES(1929), w
Jon Stone
WILD, FREE AND HUNGRY(1970)
Joseph Stone
WORLD IN MY CORNER(1956), w; WILD HERITAGE(1958), w; OPERATION PETTICOAT(1959), w
Joseph J. Stone
FASTEST GUITAR ALIVE, THE(1967), set d; WELCOME TO HARD TIMES(1967), set d; PROJECT X(1968), set d
Laurie Stone
1984
SECOND TIME LUCKY(1984, Aus./New Zealand), m
Leonard Stone
MUGGER, THE(1958); RETURN TO PEYTON PLACE(1961); SHOCK TREATMENT(1964); BIG MOUTH, THE(1967); MAN CALLED DAGGER, A(1967); ANGEL IN MY POCKET(1969); GETTING STRAIGHT(1970); I LOVE MY WIFE(1970); ZIG-ZAG(1970); WILLY WONKA AND THE CHOCOLATE FACTORY(1971); MAN, THE(1972); SOYLENT GREEN(1973); AMERICAN POP(1981); HARDLY WORKING(1981)

LeRoy Stone
TRUE TO LIFE(1943), ed; SHOW GIRL(1928), ed; PRISONERS(1929), ed; SALLY(1929), ed; TWIN BEDS(1929), ed; BRIDE OF THE REGIMENT(1930), ed; SUNNY(1930), ed; FINGER POINTS, THE(1931), ed; LADY WHO DARED, THE(1931), ed; PENROD AND SAM(1931), ed; MAKE ME A STAR(1932), ed; DUCK SOUP(1933), ed; BELLE OF THE NINETIES(1934), ed; SIX OF A KIND(1934), ed; GOIN' TO TOWN(1935), ed; MILKY WAY, THE(1936), ed; EBB TIDE(1937), ed; MAKE WAY FOR TOMORROW(1937), ed; COLLEGE SWING(1938), ed; SAY IT IN FRENCH(1938), ed; TEXANS, THE(1938), ed; MAN ABOUT TOWN(1939), ed; ADVENTURE IN DIAMONDS(1940), ed; BUCK BENNY RIDES AGAIN(1940), ed; I WANT A DIVORCE(1940), ed; LOVE THY NEIGHBOR(1940), ed; LOUISIANA PURCHASE(1941), ed; SKYLARK(1941), ed; ARE HUSBANDS NECESSARY?(1942), ed; WAKE ISLAND(1942), ed; RIDING HIGH(1943), ed; GOING MY WAY(1944), ed; HOLD THAT BLONDE(1945), ed; MURDER, HE SAYS(1945), ed; BLUE SKIES(1946), ed; VARIETY GIRL(1947), ed; ISN'T IT ROMANTIC?(1948), ed; MY OWN TRUE LOVE(1948), ed; CHICAGO DEADLINE(1949), ed; MY FRIEND IRMA(1949), ed; APPOINTMENT WITH DANGER(1951), ed
Silents
IF I MARRY AGAIN(1925), ed; HAROLD TEEN(1928), ed; NAUGHTY BABY(1929), ed
Lew Stone
UNDER YOUR HAT(1940, Brit.), m
Lewis Stone
YELLOW JACK(1938); PATRIOT, THE(1928); MADAME X(1929); THEIR OWN DESIRE(1929); TRIAL OF MARY DUGAN, THE(1929); WONDER OF WOMEN(1929); BIG HOUSE, THE(1930); OFFICE WIFE, THE(1930); PASSION FLOWER(1930); ROMANCE(1930); STRICTLY UNCONVENTIONAL(1930); ALWAYS GOODBYE(1931); BARGAIN, THE(1931); FATHER'S SON(1931); INSPIRATION(1931); MATA HARI(1931); MY PAST(1931); PHANTOM OF PARIS, THE(1931); SECRET SIX, THE(1931); SIN OF MADELON CLAUDET, THE(1931); STRICTLY DISHONORABLE(1931); DIVORCE IN THE FAMILY(1932); GRAND HOTEL(1932); LETTY LYNTON(1932); MASK OF FU MANCHU, THE(1932); NEW MORALS FOR OLD(1932); NIGHT COURT(1932); SON-DAUGHTER, THE(1932); UNASHAMED(1932); WET PARADE, THE(1932); BUREAU OF MISSING PERSONS(1933); LOOKING FORWARD(1933); MEN MUST FIGHT(1933); QUEEN CHRISTINA(1933); WHITE SISTER, THE(1933); GIRL FROM MISSOURI, THE(1934); MYSTERY OF MR. X, THE(1934); TREASURE ISLAND(1934); YOU CAN'T BUY EVERYTHING(1934); CHINA SEAS(1935); DAVID COPPERFIELD(1935); PUBLIC HERO NO. 1(1935); SHIPMATES FOREVER(1935); VANESSA, HER LOVE STORY(1935); WEST POINT OF THE AIR(1935); WOMAN WANTED(1935); DON'T TURN'EM LOOSE(1936); SMALL TOWN GIRL(1936); SUZY(1936); SWORN ENEMY(1936); THREE GODFATHERS(1936); UNGUARDED HOUR, THE(1936); MAN WHO CRIED WOLF, THE(1937); OUTCAST(1937); THIRTEENTH CHAIR, THE(1937); BAD MAN OF BRIMSTONE(1938); CHASER, THE(1938); JUDGE HARDY'S CHILDREN(1938); LOVE FINDS ANDY HARDY(1938); OUT WEST WITH THE HARDYS(1938); STOLEN HEAVEN(1938); YOU'RE ONLY YOUNG ONCE(1938); ANDY HARDY GETS SPRING FEVER(1939); HARDYS RIDE HIGH, THE(1939); ICE FOLLIES OF 1939(1939); JOE AND ETHEL TURP CALL ON THE PRESIDENT(1939); JUDGE HARDY AND SON(1939); ANDY HARDY MEETS DEBUTANTE(1940); SPORTING BLOOD(1940); ANDY HARDY'S PRIVATE SECRETARY(1941); BUGLE SOUNDS, THE(1941); LIFE BEGINS FOR ANDY HARDY(1941); ANDY HARDY'S DOUBLE LIFE(1942); COURTSHIP OF ANDY HARDY, THE(1942); ANDY HARDY'S BLONDE TROUBLE(1944); HOODLUM SAINT, THE(1946); LOVE LAUGHS AT ANDY HARDY(1946); THREE WISE FOOLS(1946); STATE OF THE UNION(1948); ANY NUMBER CAN PLAY(1949); SUN COMES UP, THE(1949); GROUNDS FOR MARRIAGE(1950); KEY TO THE CITY(1950); STARS IN MY CROWN(1950); ANGELS IN THE OUTFIELD(1951); BANNERLINE(1951); IT'S A BIG COUNTRY(1951); NIGHT INTO MORNING(1951); UNKNOWN MAN, THE(1951); JUST THIS ONCE(1952); PRISONER OF ZENDA, THE(1952); SCARAMOUCHE(1952); TALK ABOUT A STRANGER(1952); ALL THE BROTHERS WERE VALIANT(1953)
Silents
NOMADS OF THE NORTH(1920); DANGEROUS AGE, THE(1922); PRISONER OF ZENDA, THE(1922); SCARAMOUCHE(1923); CYTHEREA(1924); STRANGER, THE(1924); LOST WORLD, THE(1925); WHAT FOOLS MEN(1925); OLD LOVES AND NEW(1926); AFFAIR OF THE FOLLIES, AN(1927); NOTORIOUS LADY, THE(1927); FREEDOM OF THE PRESS(1928); WOMAN OF AFFAIRS, A(1928); WILD ORCHIDS(1929)
Misc. Silents
HELD BY THE ENEMY(1920); MILESTONES(1920); RIVER'S END, THE(1920); CHILD THOU GAVEST ME, THE(1921); GOLDEN SNARE, THE(1921); FOOL THERE WAS, A(1922); WORLD'S APPLAUSE, THE(1923); YOU CAN'T FOOL YOUR WIFE(1923); CYTHEREA(1924); WHY MEN LEAVE HOME(1924); CONFESSIONS OF A QUEEN(1925); FINE CLOTHES(1925); LADY WHO LIED, THE(1925); BLONDE SAINT, THE(1926); DON JUAN'S THREE NIGHTS(1926); GIRL FROM MONTMARTRE, THE(1926); MIDNIGHT LOVERS(1926); TOO MUCH MONEY(1926); LONESOME LADIES(1927); PRINCE OF HEADWAITERS, THE(1927); PRIVATE LIFE OF HELEN OF TROY, THE(1927); FOREIGN LEGION, THE(1928)
Lewis S. Stone
Silents
ACCORDING TO THE CODE(1916); INSIDE THE LINES(1918); BEAU REVEL(1921); HUSBANDS AND LOVERS(1924); INEZ FROM HOLLYWOOD(1924)
Misc. Silents
HAVOC, THE(1916); HONOR'S ALTAR(1916); MAN OF BRONZE, THE(1918); MAN'S DESIRE(1919); CONCERT, THE(1921); DON'T NEGLECT YOUR WIFE(1921); PILGRIMS OF THE NIGHT(1921); ROSARY, THE(1922); CHEAPER TO MARRY(1925); TALKER, THE(1925)
Lewis Stone, Sr.
RED HEADED WOMAN(1932)
Lou Stone
MURDER IN MISSISSIPPI(1965)
Malcolm Stone
DARK CRYSTAL, THE(1982, Brit.), art d
1984
WHERE IS PARSIFAL?(1984, Brit.), prod d
Marci Stone
FARMER'S OTHER DAUGHTER, THE(1965)
Marianne Stone
MISS PILGRIM'S PROGRESS(1950, Brit.); ISLAND RESCUE(1952, Brit.); MAGIC BOX, THE(1952, Brit.); DAY TO REMEMBER, A(1953, Brit.); PROJECT M7(1953, Brit.); SPACEWAYS(1953, Brit.); TERROR STREET(1953); TIME GENTLEMEN PLEASE!(1953, Brit.); DANCE LITTLE LADY(1954, Brit.); GOOD DIE YOUNG, THE(1954,

Brit.); MAD ABOUT MEN(1954, Brit.); RUNAWAY BUS, THE(1954, Brit.); YOU KNOW WHAT SAILORS ARE(1954, Brit.); FUN AT ST. FANNY'S(1956, Brit.); MURDER ON APPROVAL(1956, Brit.); PASSPORT TO TREASON(1956, Brit.); PRIVATE'S PROGRESS(1956, Brit.); SIMON AND LAURA(1956, Brit.); ENEMY FROM SPACE(1957, Brit.); GOOD COMPANIONS, THE(1957, Brit.); HIGH TERRACE(1957, Brit.); JUST MY LUCK(1957, Brit.); OPERATION CONSPIRACY(1957, Brit.); TEARS FOR SIMON(1957, Brit.); THUNDER OVER TANGIER(1957, Brit.); WOMEN IN A DRESSING GOWN(1957, Brit.); HELL DRIVERS(1958, Brit.); INBETWEEN AGE, THE(1958, Brit.); INNOCENT SINNERS(1958, Brit.); I'M ALL RIGHT, JACK(1959, Brit.); JACK THE RIPPER(1959, Brit.); MAN WHO LIKED FUNERALS, THE(1959, Brit.); TIGER BAY(1959, Brit.); PLEASE TURN OVER(1960, Brit.); DOUBLE BUNK(1961, Brit.); FIVE GOLDEN HOURS(1961, Brit.); FRIGHTENED CITY, THE(1961, Brit.); LOLITA(1962); NIGHT OF THE PROWLER(1962, Brit.); TWO AND TWO MAKE SIX(1962, Brit.); ECHO OF DIANA(1963, Brit.); OPERATION BULLSHINE(1963, Brit.); PARANOIAC(1963, Brit.); HARD DAY'S NIGHT, A(1964, Brit.); LADIES WHO DO(1964, Brit.); NO TREE IN THE STREET(1964, Brit.); WITCHCRAFT(1964, Brit.); YOUNG AND WILLING(1964, Brit.); ACT OF MURDER(1965, Brit.); CURSE OF THE MUMMY'S TOMB, THE(1965, Brit.); DEVILS OF DARKNESS, THE(1965, Brit.); HAVING A WILD WEEKEND(1965, Brit.); HYSTERIA(1965, Brit.); SPYLARKS(1965, Brit.); YOU MUST BE JOKING!(1965, Brit.); BEAUTY JUNGLE, THE(1966, Brit.); SPY WITH A COLD NOSE, THE(1966, Brit.); STRANGLER'S WEB(1966, Brit.); TRAITOR'S GATE(1966, Brit./Ger.); WRONG BOX, THE(1966, Brit.); BERSERK(1967, Brit.); DON'T LOSE YOUR HEAD(1967, Brit.); LONG DUEL, THE(1967, Brit.); TO SIR, WITH LOVE(1967, Brit.); OH! WHAT A LOVELY WAR(1969, Brit.); DOCTOR IN TROUBLE(1970, Brit.); SCROOGE(1970, Brit.); THERE'S A GIRL IN MY SOUP(1970, Brit.); ASSAULT(1971, Brit.); WHO SLEW AUNTIE ROO?(1971, U.S./Brit.); CRY OF THE PENGUINS(1972, Brit.); VAULT OF HORROR, THE(1973, Brit.); CONFESSIONS OF A WINDOW CLEANER(1974, Brit.); CRAZE(1974, Brit.); THAT LUCKY TOUCH(1975, Brit.); CLASS OF MISS MAC MICHAEL, THE(1978, Brit./U.S.); HUMAN FACTOR, THE(1979, Brit.); BEYOND THE FOG(1981, Brit.); FUNNY MONEY(1983, Brit.); WICKED LADY, THE(1983, Brit.)

Marjorie Stone
BRAINSTORM(1983), set d
Mark Stone
HAPPY DAYS ARE HERE AGAIN(1936, Brit.); PEARLS BRING TEARS(1937, Brit.); TALKING FEET(1937, Brit.); KATHLEEN(1938, Ireland); ON VELVET(1938, Brit.); QUIET WEDDING(1941, Brit.); UNEASY TERMS(1948, Brit.)
Marla Stone
1984
ALLEY CAT(1984)
Marshall Stone
COME SPY WITH ME(1967), d
Mary Stone
WHEN THE BOUGH BREAKS(1947, Brit.); IDOL OF PARIS(1948, Brit.)
Mary [Marianne] Stone
ESCAPE DANGEROUS(1947, Brit.); MARRY ME!(1949, Brit.)
Melville Stone
Silents
BREWSTER'S MILLIONS(1914), w
Merrill Stone
DRAGON'S GOLD(1954)
Merritt Stone
PORT SINISTER(1953); PROBLEM GIRLS(1953); SWORD OF VENUS(1953); SPIDER, THE(1958); TORMENTED(1960); MAGIC SWORD, THE(1962)
Michael Stone
WAITRESS(1982), w
Mike Stone
ENTER THE NINJA(1982), stunt
Milburn Stone
RENDEZVOUS(1935); CHINA CLIPPER(1936); MILKY WAY, THE(1936); MURDER WITH PICTURES(1936); PRINCESS COMES ACROSS, THE(1936); ROSE BOWL(1936); THREE MESQUITEERS, THE(1936); TWO IN A CROWD(1936); ATLANTIC FLIGHT(1937); BLAZING BARRIERS(1937); DOCTOR'S DIARY, A(1937); FEDERAL BULLETS(1937); MAN IN BLUE, THE(1937); MUSIC FOR MADAME(1937); SWING IT, PROFESSOR(1937); THIRTEENTH MAN, THE(1937); WINGS OVER HONOLULU(1937); YOU CAN'T BEAT LOVE(1937); YOUTH ON PAROLE(1937); CALIFORNIA FRONTIER(1938); CRIME SCHOOL(1938); MR. BOGGS STEPS OUT(1938); PAROLED FROM THE BIG HOUSE(1938); PORT OF MISSING GIRLS(1938); SINNERS IN PARADISE(1938); STORM, THE(1938); WIVES UNDER SUSPICION(1938); BLIND ALLEY(1939); CRASHING THRU(1939); DANGER FLIGHT(1939); FIGHTING MAD(1939); KING OF THE TURF(1939); MADE FOR EACH OTHER(1939); MYSTERY PLANE(1939); NICK CARTER, MASTER DETECTIVE(1939); SKY PATROL(1939); SOCIETY SMUGGLERS(1939); SPIRIT OF CULVER, THE(1939); STUNT PILOT(1939); TROPIC FURY(1939); WHEN TOMORROW COMES(1939); YOUNG MR. LINCOLN(1939); CHASING TROUBLE(1940); COLORADO(1940); ENEMY AGENT(1940); FRAMED(1940); GIVE US WINGS(1940); GREAT PLANE ROBBERY, THE(1940); JOHNNY APOLLO(1940); LILLIAN RUSSELL(1940); DEATH VALLEY OUTLAWS(1941); GREAT TRAIN ROBBERY, THE(1941); PHANTOM COWBOY, THE(1941); EYES IN THE NIGHT(1942); FRISCO LILL(1942); INVISIBLE AGENT(1942); PACIFIC RENDEZVOUS(1942); POLICE BULLETS(1942); REAP THE WILD WIND(1942); CAPTIVE WILD WOMAN(1943); CORVETTE K-225(1943); GET GOING(1943); GUNG HO!(1943); KEEP 'EM SLUGGING(1943); MAD GHOUL, THE(1943); SHERLOCK HOLMES FACES DEATH(1943); HAT CHECK HONEY(1944); HI, GOOD-LOOKIN'(1944); IMPOSTER, THE(1944); JUNGLE WOMAN(1944); MOON OVER LAS VEGAS(1944); PHANTOM LADY(1944); TWILIGHT ON THE PRAIRIE(1944); DALTONS RIDE AGAIN, THE(1945); FROZEN GHOST, THE(1945); I'LL REMEMBER APRIL(1945); ON STAGE EVERYBODY(1945); SHE GETS HER MAN(1945); STRANGE CONFESSION(1945); SWING OUT, SISTER(1945); BEAUTIFUL CHEAT, THE(1946); DANGER WOMAN(1946); HER ADVENTUROUS NIGHT(1946); INSIDE JOB(1946); LITTLE MISS BIG(1946); SMOOTH AS SILK(1946); SPIDER WOMAN STRIKES BACK, THE(1946); STRANGE CONQUEST(1946); CASS TIMBERLANE(1947); HEADING FOR HEAVEN(1947); KILLER DILL(1947); MICHIGAN KID, THE(1947); TRAIN TO ALCATRAZ(1948); CALAMITY JANE AND SAM BASS(1949); GREEN PROMISE, THE(1949); JUDGE, THE(1949); SKY DRAGON(1949); FIREBALL, THE(1950); NO MAN OF HER OWN(1950); SNOW DOG(1950); BRANDED(1951); OPERATION PACIFIC(1951); RACKET, THE(1951); ROADBLOCK(1951); ATOMIC CITY, THE(1952); ARROWHEAD(1953); INVADERS FROM MARS(1953); PICKUP ON SOUTH STREET(1953); SAVAGE, THE(1953); SECOND CHANCE(1953); SUN SHINES BRIGHT, THE(1953); SIEGE AT RED RIVER, THE(1954); BLACK TUESDAY(1955); LONG GRAY LINE, THE(1955); PRIVATE WAR OF MAJOR

BENSON, THE(1955); SMOKE SIGNAL(1955); WHITE FEATHER(1955); DRANGO(1957)
Misc. Talkies
PORT OF MISSING GIRLS(1938)
Mildred Stone
MISSISSIPPI(1935); THIRTEEN HOURS BY AIR(1936); SHOCKING MISS PILGRIM, THE(1947)
N. B. Stone, Jr.
MAN WITH THE GUN(1955), w; RIDE THE HIGH COUNTRY(1962), w
Najwa Stone
SEIZURE(1974), art d
Nancy Stone
IN LIKE FLINT(1967)
Noreen Stone
AMY(1981), w
Oliver Stone
SEIZURE(1974), d, w, ed; MIDNIGHT EXPRESS(1978, Brit.), w; HAND, THE(1981), a, d, w; CONAN THE BARBARIAN(1982), w; SCARFACE(1983), w
Paddy Stone
AS LONG AS THEY'RE HAPPY(1957, Brit.), ch; GOOD COMPANIONS, THE(1957, Brit.); VALUE FOR MONEY(1957, Brit.), a, ch; 6.5 SPECIAL(1958, Brit.), a, ch; GREAT CATHERINE(1968, Brit.), ch; SCROOGE(1970, Brit.); S.O.B.(1981), a, ch; VICTOR/VICTORIA(1982), ch
Paula Stone
HOPALONG CASSIDY(1935); CASE OF THE VELVET CLAWS, THE(1936); TRAILIN' WEST(1936); TREACHERY RIDES THE RANGE(1936); TWO AGAINST THE WORLD(1936); ATLANTIC FLIGHT(1937); GIRL SAID NO, THE(1937); RED LIGHTS AHEAD(1937); SWING IT, PROFESSOR(1937); CONVICTS AT LARGE(1938); IDIOT'S DELIGHT(1939); LAUGH IT OFF(1939)
Paulene Stone
DANDY IN ASPIC, A(1968, Brit.)
Peter Stone
TAKING OF PELHAM ONE, TWO, THREE, THE(1974), w; CHARADE(1963), w; FATHER GOOSE(1964), w; MIRAGE(1965), w; FAR FROM THE MADDING CROWD(1967, Brit.); JIGSAW(1968), w; SECRET WAR OF HARRY FRIGG, THE(1968), w; SWEET CHARITY(1969), w; 1776(1972), w; SILVER BEARS(1978), w; WHO IS KILLING THE GREAT CHEFS OF EUROPE?(1978, US/Ger.), w; WHY WOULD I LIE(1980), w
Phil Stone
DAMAGED GOODS(1937), d; POLTERGEIST(1982)
Silents
BACKSTAGE(1927), d
Misc. Silents
GIRL FROM GAY PAREE, THE(1927), d; ONCE AND FOREVER(1927), d; SNOWBOUND(1927), d; WILD GEESE(1927), d
Philip Stone
NEVER MENTION MURDER(1964, Brit.); UNEARTHLY STRANGER, THE(1964, Brit.); TWO GENTLEMEN SHARING(1969, Brit.); CARRY ON LOVING(1970, Brit.); MAN WHO HAD POWER OVER WOMEN, THE(1970, Brit.); CLOCKWORK ORANGE, A(1971, Brit.); FRAGMENT OF FEAR(1971, Brit.); HITLER: THE LAST TEN DAYS(1973, Brit./Ital.); O LUCKY MAN!(1973, Brit.); BARRY LYNDON(1975, Brit.); MEDUSA TOUCH, THE(1978, Brit.); ALL THINGS BRIGHT AND BEAUTIFUL(1979, Brit.); FLASH GORDON(1980); SHINING, THE(1980); GREEN ICE(1981, Brit.)
1984
INDIANA JONES AND THE TEMPLE OF DOOM(1984)
Reg Stone
SPLINTERS(1929, Brit.); SPLINTERS IN THE NAVY(1931, Brit.)
Rene Stone
NEW FACES OF 1937(1937); ROARING SIX GUNS(1937)
Ric Stone
GRENDEL GRENDEL GRENDEL(1981, Aus.)
Robert Stone
SOUTH OF PAGO PAGO(1940); KISSIN' COUSINS(1964); WHO'LL STOP THE RAIN?(1978), w
Robinson Stone
STALAG 17(1953)
Rose Stone
RACING FEVER(1964)
Roselle Stone
HOUSE BY THE LAKE, THE(1977, Can.)
Rosie Stone
Misc. Talkies
SCREAM IN THE STREETS, A(1972)
Roy Stone
MAN OUTSIDE, THE(1968, Brit.); BIG SWITCH, THE(1970, Brit.)
S. Stone
HOTEL RESERVE(1946, Brit.), ed
Sandra Stone
GUN STREET(1962)
Scott Stone
NIGHT IN HEAVEN, A(1983)
Sharon Stone
DEADLY BLESSING(1981)
1984
IRRECONCILABLE DIFFERENCES(1984)
Sid Stone
MY HEART GOES CRAZY(1953, Brit.), ed; GREEN SCARF, THE(1954, Brit.), ed; BE MY GUEST(1965, Brit.), ed
Sidney Stone
DEAR MR. PROHACK(1949, Brit.), ed; SLEEPING CAR TO TRIESTE(1949, Brit.), ed; NIGHT AND THE CITY(1950, Brit.), ed; DEVIL ON HORSEBACK(1954, Brit.), ed; HEART OF THE MATTER, THE(1954, Brit.), ed; MAKE MINE A DOUBLE(1962, Brit.), ed; GIRL HUNTERS, THE(1963, Brit.), ed; DATELINE DIAMONDS(1966, Brit.), ed; BATTLE BENEATH THE EARTH(1968, Brit.), ed
Sidney J. Stone
GREAT DAY(1945, Brit.), ed
Stan Stone
MITCHELL(1975)

Suzanne Stone
NASTY HABITS(1976, Brit.); SEDUCTION OF JOE TYNAN, THE(1979)
Sydney Stone
MARK OF CAIN, THE(1948, Brit.), ed; SATELLITE IN THE SKY(1956), ed
Tom Stone
Misc. Talkies
TINKER(1950, Brit.)
Uta Stone
HOW TO STUFF A WILD BIKINI(1965)
V. Stone
TREASURE OF JAMAICA REEF, THE(1976), d
Victor Stone
FAR FROM THE MADDING CROWD(1967, Brit.)
Virginia L. Stone
LAST VOYAGE, THE(1960), ed
Virginia Stone
CONFIDENCE GIRL(1952), ed; NIGHT HOLDS TERROR, THE(1955), ed; JU-
LIE(1956), ed; CRY TERROR(1958), p, ed; DECKS RAN RED, THE(1958), p, ed; LAST
VOYAGE, THE(1960), p; RING OF FIRE(1961), p, ed; PASSWORD IS COURAGE,
THE(1962, Brit.), p, ed; NEVER PUT IT IN WRITING(1964), p; SECRET OF MY
SUCCESS, THE(1965, Brit.), p; SONG OF NORWAY(1970), p; TREASURE OF JAMAI-
CA REEF, THE(1976), p
Virginia Lively Stone
SONG OF NORWAY(1970), ed
Walter Stone
GEORGE WHITE'S SCANDALS(1945)
Wayne Stone
1984
TERMINATOR, THE(1984)
Wes Stone
THUNDER IN CAROLINA(1960)
William C. Stone
CROOKED LADY, THE(1932, Brit.), w; THAT'S MY WIFE(1933, Brit.), w
William S. Stone
PAGAN LOVE SONG(1950), w
Stone Country
SKIDOO(1968)
Stone-Baron Puppeteers
ROAD TO RIO(1947)
Gail Stone-Stanton
1984
MAKING THE GRADE(1984)
Pamela Stonebrook
1984
BEST DEFENSE(1984)
Sam Stoneburger
1984
MOSCOW ON THE HUDSON(1984)
Sam Stoneburner
TOOTSIE(1982)
George Stonefish
WOLFEN(1981)
Stoneground
DRACULA A.D. 1972(1972, Brit.)
Charles Thurley Stoneham
KING OF THE JUNGLE(1933), w
John Stoneham
SHOOT(1976, Can.); HOUSE BY THE LAKE, THE(1977, Can.), stunts; PHOBIA(1980,
Can.); STRANGE BREW(1983)
Fred Stonehouse
Silents
SHATTERED REPUTATIONS(1923)
Marilyn Stonehouse
WELCOME TO BLOOD CITY(1977, Brit./Can.), p
Marsha Stonehouse
HIGH COUNTRY, THE(1981, Can.)
Ruth Stonehouse
Silents
ALSTER CASE, THE(1915); SLIM PRINCESS, THE(1915); KINKAID, GAM-
BLER(1916); FIGHTING FOR LOVE(1917); LOVE AFLAME(1917); ARE ALL MEN
ALIKE?(1920); DON'T CALL ME LITTLE GIRL(1921); LADYBIRD, THE(1927); APE,
THE(1928)
Misc. Silents
CRIMSON WING, THE(1915); LOVE NEVER DIES(1916); EDGE OF THE LAW(1917);
FOLLOW THE GIRL(1917); PHANTOM HUSBAND, A(1917); SAINTLY SINNER,
THE(1917); FOUR FLUSHER, THE(1919); RED VIPER, THE(1919); HOPE, THE(1920);
LAND OF JAZZ, THE(1920); PARLOR, BEDROOM AND BATH(1920); FLASH,
THE(1923); LIGHTS OUT(1923); WAY OF THE TRANSGRESSOR, THE(1923); ER-
MINE AND RHINESTONES(1925); FUGITIVE, THE(1925); STRAIGHT
THROUGH(1925); TWO-FISTED SHERIFF, A(1925); POOR GIRLS(1927); DEVIL'S
CAGE, THE(1928)
Robert Stoneman
HONKY TONK FREEWAY(1981)
The Stonemans
HELL ON WHEELS(1967)
Donald M. Stoner
PHANTOM EXPRESS, THE(1932), p
Joy Stoner
JEANNE EAGELS(1957); TIJUANA STORY, THE(1957); I WAS A TEENAGE
FRANKENSTEIN(1958)
Lynda Stoner
ESCAPE 2000(1983, Aus.)
Sherri Stoner
1984
IMPULSE(1984); LOVELINES(1984)
Susan L. Stoner
WEEKEND WITH THE BABYSITTER(1970)

Stuart Stones
BRONCO BULLFROG(1972, Brit.)
Walter Stones
SWISS FAMILY ROBINSON(1960), spec eff
Heather Stoney
DEATHLINE(1973, Brit.)
Jack Stoney
PIGSKIN PARADE(1936); MR. MOTO'S GAMBLE(1938); LAST OF THE DUA-
NES(1941); GIRL TROUBLE(1942); LADY BODYGUARD(1942); HELLO, FRISCO,
HELLO(1943); CRIME BY NIGHT(1944); ROAD TO UTOPIA(1945); THEY WERE
EXPENDABLE(1945); FALCON'S ALIBI, THE(1946); LADY LUCK(1946); BRASHER
DOUBLOON, THE(1947); SEA OF GRASS, THE(1947); KISS THE BLOOD OFF MY
HANDS(1948); STATION WEST(1948); MADAME BOVARY(1949); SET-UP, THE(1949);
GAMBLING HOUSE(1950); WOMAN ON PIER 13, THE(1950); FARMER TAKES A
WIFE, THE(1953); TARANTULA(1955)
Kevin Stoney
HOW TO MURDER A RICH UNCLE(1957, Brit.); PICKUP ALLEY(1957, Brit.); MAN
WHO WAS NOBODY, THE(1960, Brit.); SHADOW OF THE CAT, THE(1961, Brit.);
CASH ON DEMAND(1962, Brit.); RETURN OF A STRANGER(1962, Brit.); STRONG-
ROOM(1962, Brit.); MURDER AT THE GALLOP(1963, Brit.); BLOOD BEAST TERROR,
THE(1967, Brit.); ON THE RUN(1967, Brit.); GUNS IN THE HEATHER(1968, Brit.);
DRESSER, THE(1983)
1984
ORDEAL BY INNOCENCE(1984, Brit.)
Yvonne Stoney
HONEYBABY, HONEYBABY(1974), cos
Stoney Mountain Cloggers
COUNTRY BOY(1966); THAT TENNESSEE BEAT(1966)
Phil Stong
STRANGER'S RETURN(1933), w; VILLAGE TALE(1935), w; CAREER(1939), w;
STATE FAIR(1945), w
Philip Stong
STATE FAIR(1933), w; STATE FAIR(1962), w
Lee Stonsnider
PIT STOP(1969), p
Stooge
BORN TO BE WILD(1938)
The Three Stooges
IT'S A MAD, MAD, MAD, MAD WORLD(1963)
Ronald R. Stoops
FINAL COUNTDOWN, THE(1980)
Mieczyslaw Stoor
KNIGHTS OF THE TEUTONIC ORDER, THE(1962, Pol.)
A. P. Stootsberry
NOTORIOUS CLEOPATRA, THE(1970), p&d
Stop, Look and Listen
SWING IT SOLDIER(1941)
Stop, Look and Listen Trio
BABES ON BROADWAY(1941)
Harry C. Stopher
RAMPARTS WE WATCH, THE(1940)
Wallace Stopp
Silents
SHOOTING OF DAN MCGREW, THE(1915)
Paolo Stoppa
ADVENTURE OF SALVATOR ROSA, AN(1940, Ital.); ETERNAL MELODIES(1948,
Ital.); ROSSINI(1948, Ital.); RETURN OF THE BLACK EAGLE(1949, Ital.); MIRACLE
IN MILAN(1951, Ital.); BEAUTY AND THE DEVIL(1952, Fr./Ital.); LES BELLES-DE-
NUIT(1952, Fr.); RING AROUND THE CLOCK(1953, Ital.); SEVEN DEADLY SINS,
THE(1953, Fr./Ital.); TIMES GONE BY(1953, Ital.); DAUGHTERS OF DESTINY(1954,
Fr./Ital.); INDISCRETION OF AN AMERICAN WIFE(1954, U.S./Ital.); MY SEVEN
LITTLE SINS(1956, Fr./Ital.); GOLD OF NAPLES(1957, Ital.); MILLER'S WIFE,
THE(1957, Ital.); WHERE THE HOT WIND BLOWS(1960, Fr., Ital.); CARTHAGE IN
FLAMES(1961, Fr./Ital.); FROM A ROMAN BALCONY(1961, Fr./Ital.); NEOPOLITAN
CAROUSEL(1961, Ital.); ROCCO AND HIS BROTHERS(1961, Fr./Ital.); BOCCACCIO
'70(1962/Ital./Fr.); MOST WANTED MAN, THE(1962, Fr./Ital.); LEOPARD, THE(1963,
Ital.); BECKET(1964, Brit.); BEHOLD A PALE HORSE(1964); VISIT, THE(1964,
Ger./Fr./Ital./U.S.); MALE COMPANION(1965, Fr./Ital.); AFTER THE FOX(1966,
U.S./Brit./Ital.); DROP DEAD, MY LOVE(1968, Italy); ONCE UPON A TIME IN THE
WEST(1969, U.S./Ital.); ADVENTURES OF GERARD, THE(1970, Brit.)
Paul Stoppa
THIEF OF VENICE, THE(1952)
Tom Stoppard
ROMANTIC ENGLISHWOMAN, THE(1975, Brit./Fr.), w; DESPAIR(1978, Ger.), w;
HUMAN FACTOR, THE(1979, Brit.), w
Cheryl Stoppelmoor [Cheryl Ladd]
TREASURE OF JAMAICA REEF, THE(1976)
Franca Stoppi
1984
BURIED ALIVE(1984, Ital.)
Rudolf Stor
SLEEPING BEAUTY(1965, Ger.)
Bernard Stora
ADOPTION, THE(1978, Fr.), w
Jean-Pierre Stora
SECOND WIND, A(1978, Fr.), m
Vittorio Storaro
BIRD WITH THE CRYSTAL PLUMAGE, THE(1970, Ital./Ger.), ph; CONFORMIST,
THE(1971, Ital., Fr), ph; GIORDANO BRUNO(1973, Ital.), ph; 'TIS A PITY SHE'S A
WHORE(1973, Ital.), ph; MALICIOUS(1974, Ital.), ph; DRIVER'S SEAT, THE(1975,
Ital.), ph; 1900(1976, Ital.), ph; AGATHA(1979, Brit.), ph; APOCALYPSE NOW(1979),
ph; LUNA(1979, Ital.), ph; REDS(1981), ph; ONE FROM THE HEART(1982), ph;
WAGNER(1983, Brit./Hung./Aust.), ph
Arthur Storch
STRANGE ONE, THE(1957); MUGGER, THE(1958); GIRL OF THE NIGHT(1960);
LONNIE(1963); DEATH PLAY(1976), d
Gisela Storch
FITZCARRALDO(1982), cos

Gloria Storch
NOSFERATU, THE VAMPIRE(1979, Fr./Ger.), cos

Larry Storch
GUN FEVER(1958); LAST BLITZKRIEG, THE(1958); WHO WAS THAT LADY?(1960); FORTY POUNDS OF TROUBLE(1962); CAPTAIN NEWMAN, M.D.(1963); SEX AND THE SINGLE GIRL(1964); WILD AND WONDERFUL(1964); BUS RILEY'S BACK IN TOWN(1965); GREAT RACE, THE(1965); THAT FUNNY FEELING(1965); VERY SPECIAL FAVOR, A(1965); GREAT BANK ROBBERY, THE(1969); MONITORS, THE(1969); AIRPORT 1975(1974); JOURNEY BACK TO OZ(1974); RECORD CITY(1978); WITHOUT WARNING(1980); S.O.B.(1981); SWEET SIXTEEN(1983)

Helga Storck
ALL-AROUND REDUCED PERSONALITY–OUTTAKES, THE(1978, Ger.)

Jackie Storck
COOL AND THE CRAZY, THE(1958)

Shelby Storck
COOL AND THE CRAZY, THE(1958)

Axel Stordahl
SHIP AHOY(1942), m

William G. Storer
FLAMING SIGNAL(1933), w

J. Storer-Clouston
BIZARRE BIZARRE(1939, Fr.), w

Anthony Storey
ZULU DAWN(1980, Brit.), w

Cliff Storey
NORTHERN PURSUIT(1943); PLACE IN THE SUN, A(1951)

David Storey
THIS SPORTING LIFE(1963, Brit.), w; IN CELEBRATION(1975, Brit.), w

Edith Storey
Silents
CHRISTIAN, THE(1914); FLORIDA ENCHANTMENT, A(1914); ISLAND OF REGENERATION, THE(1915); ON HER WEDDING NIGHT(1915); PRICE FOR FOLLY, A(1915); TWO-EDGED SWORD, THE(1916); ALADDIN FROM BROADWAY(1917); CAPTAIN OF THE GRAY HORSE TROOP, THE(1917); MONEY MAGIC(1917); AS THE SUN WENT DOWN(1919); MOON MADNESS(1920)
Misc. Silents
CAPTAIN ALVAREZ(1914); DUST OF EGYPT, THE(1915); ENEMY TO THE KING, AN(1916); TARANTULA, THE(1916); WINIFRED THE SHOP GIRL(1916); CLAIM, THE(1918); DEMON, THE(1918); EYES OF MYSTERY, THE(1918); LEGION OF DEATH, THE(1918); REVENGE(1918); SILENT WOMAN, THE(1918); TREASURE OF THE SEA(1918); BEACH OF DREAMS(1921); GREATER PROFIT, THE(1921)

Fred Storey
Misc. Silents
FORGOTTEN(1914, Brit.)

Jack Storey
Silents
NIGHT OUT, A(1916)

June Storey
STUDENT TOUR(1934); I DREAM TOO MUCH(1935); CAREER WOMAN(1936); GIRLS' DORMITORY(1936); LOVE AND HISSES(1937); THIN ICE(1937); DOWN IN ARKANSAW(1938); IN OLD CHICAGO(1938); ISLAND IN THE SKY(1938); BLUE MONTANA SKIES(1939); COLORADO SUNSET(1939); FIRST LOVE(1939); HOME ON THE PRAIRIE(1939); IN OLD MONTEREY(1939); MICKEY, THE KID(1939); MOUNTAIN RHYTHM(1939); ORPHANS OF THE STREET(1939); SORORITY HOUSE(1939); SOUTH OF THE BORDER(1939); BARNYARD FOLLIES(1940); CAROLINA MOON(1940); GAUCHO SERENADE(1940); IN OLD MISSOURI(1940); RANCHO GRANDE(1940); RIDE, TENDERFOOT, RIDE(1940); DANCE HALL(1941); DANGEROUS LADY(1941); HELLO SUCKER(1941); LONE WOLF TAKES A CHANCE, THE(1941); GIRLS' TOWN(1942); END OF THE ROAD(1944); ROAD TO ALCATRAZ(1945); STRANGE WOMAN, THE(1946); KILLER McCOY(1947); CRY OF THE CITY(1948); MIRACULOUS JOURNEY(1948); SECRET SERVICE INVESTIGATOR(1948); SNAKE PIT, THE(1948); TRAIN TO ALCATRAZ(1948); MISS MINK OF 1949(1949); TOO LATE FOR TEARS(1949); TROUBLE PREFERRED(1949)
Misc. Talkies
SONG OF THE PRAIRIE(1945)

Lynne Storey
CHICAGO CONFIDENTIAL(1957)

Michael Storey
1984
ANOTHER COUNTRY(1984, Brit.), m; EVERY PICTURE TELLS A STORY(1984, Brit.), m

Ray Storey
IT CAME FROM BENEATH THE SEA(1955); TIME TRAVELERS, THE(1964), art d; FARMER'S OTHER DAUGHTER, THE(1965), set d; HOSTAGE, THE(1966), prod d; SPIDER BABY(1968), art d; HOUSE ON SKULL MOUNTAIN, THE(1974), p; MORE AMERICAN GRAFFITI(1979), art d

Robert Storey
LIGHT UP THE SKY(1960, Brit.), w

Ruth Storey
BLUE GARDENIA, THE(1953); SLAVES OF BABYLON(1953); I'LL CRY TOMORROW(1955); BELLS ARE RINGING(1960); SUBTERRANEANS, THE(1960); IN COLD BLOOD(1967)

Thomas Storey
TWO IN REVOLT(1936), w
Silents
GIRL OF THE GOLDEN WEST, THE(1923), ph

Roy Stork
VON RYAN'S EXPRESS(1965), makeup

Barry Storm
LUST FOR GOLD(1949), w

David Storm
GIDEON OF SCOTLAND YARD(1959, Brit.)

Debi Storm
PATCH OF BLUE, A(1965); EIGHT ON THE LAM(1967); FUN WITH DICK AND JANE(1977)

Douglas Storm
1984
DARK ENEMY(1984, Brit.)

Emy Storm
DEAR JOHN(1966, Swed.); RAVEN'S END(1970, Swed.)

Esben Storm
27A(1974, Aus.), d&w, ed; IN SEARCH OF ANNA(1978, Aus.), p,d,&w; MONKEY GRIP(1983, Aus.)

Florence Storm
RETURN OF THE FLY(1959)

Gail Storm
CITY OF MISSING GIRLS(1941)

Gale Storm
ONE CROWDED NIGHT(1940); TOM BROWN'S SCHOOL DAYS(1940); GAMBLING DAUGHTERS(1941); JESSE JAMES AT BAY(1941); LET'S GO COLLEGIATE(1941); RED RIVER VALLEY(1941); SADDLEMATES(1941); FOREIGN AGENT(1942); FRECKLES COMES HOME(1942); LURE OF THE ISLANDS(1942); MAN FROM CHEYENNE(1942); SMART ALECKS(1942); CAMPUS RHYTHM(1943); NEARLY EIGHTEEN(1943); REVENGE OF THE ZOMBIES(1943); RHYTHM PARADE(1943); WHERE ARE YOUR CHILDREN?(1943); FOREVER YOURS(1945); G.I. HONEYMOON(1945); SUNBONNET SUE(1945); SWING PARADE OF 1946(1946); IT HAPPENED ON 5TH AVENUE(1947); DUDE GOES WEST, THE(1948); ABANDONED(1949); STAMPEDE(1949); BETWEEN MIDNIGHT AND DAWN(1950); CURTAIN CALL AT CACTUS CREEK(1950); KID FROM TEXAS, THE(1950); WHIPPED, THE(1950); AL JENNINGS OF OKLAHOMA(1951); TEXAS RANGERS, THE(1951); WOMAN OF THE NORTH COUNTRY(1952)
Misc. Talkies
COSMO JONES, CRIME SMASHER(1943)

Gilda Storm
JENNIE GERHARDT(1933)

Howard Storm
TAKE THE MONEY AND RUN(1969); CHRISTIAN LICORICE STORE, THE(1971); STEELYARD BLUES(1973); MANCHU EAGLE MURDER CAPER MYSTERY, THE(1975); TUNNELVISION(1976); HOMEWORK(1982)
1984
BROADWAY DANNY ROSE(1984)

James Storm
NIGHT OF DARK SHADOWS(1971); WITHOUT A TRACE(1983)

Jane Storm
ADORABLE(1933), w; DR. BULL(1933), w; MY LIPS BETRAY(1933), w; MISS FANE'S BABY IS STOLEN(1934), w; MRS. WIGGS OF THE CABBAGE PATCH(1934), w; SUCH WOMEN ARE DANGEROUS(1934), w; MILLIONS IN THE AIR(1935), w; TWO FOR TONIGHT(1935), w; LOVE ON TOAST(1937), w; SANDY GETS HER MAN(1940), w; MRS. WIGGS OF THE CABBAGE PATCH(1942), w

Jerome Storm
COURTIN' WILDCATS(1929), d; SIGN OF THE CROSS, THE(1932); RACING STRAIN, THE(1933), d; LONE COWBOY(1934); MISSISSIPPI(1935); BEAU GESTE(1939)
Silents
CIVILIZATION(1916); CORNER IN COLLEENS, A(1916); PRIMAL LURE, THE(1916); BRIDE OF HATE, THE(1917); PINCH HITTER, THE(1917); NAUGHTY, NAUGHTY!(1918), d; ALARM CLOCK ANDY(1920), d; OLD FASHIONED BOY, AN(1920), d; PARIS GREEN(1920), d; RED HOT DOLLARS(1920), d; ARABIAN LOVE(1922), d; CALIFORNIA ROMANCE, A(1922), d; MADNESS OF YOUTH(1923), d; ST. ELMO(1923), d; GOLDFISH, THE(1924), d; SWEET ADELINE(1926), d; LADIES AT EASE(1927), d; RANGER OF THE NORTH(1927), d; CAPTAIN CARELESS(1928), d; DOG LAW(1928), d; FANGS OF THE WILD(1928), d
Misc. Silents
BIGGEST SHOW ON EARTH, THE(1918), d; DESERT WOOING, A(1918), d; KEYS OF THE RIGHTEOUS, THE(1918), d; VAMP, THE(1918), d; BILL HENRY(1919), d; BUSHER, THE(1919), d; EGG CRATE WALLOP, THE(1919), d; GIRL DODGER, THE(1919), d; GREASED LIGHTING(1919), d; HAY FOOT, STRAW FOOT(1919), d; HOMER COMES HOME(1920), d; PEACEFUL VALLEY(1920), d; VILLAGE SLEUTH, A(1920), d; HER SOCIAL VALUE(1921), d; HONOR FIRST(1922), d; ROSARY, THE(1922), d; CHILDREN OF JAZZ(1923), d; GOOD-BY GIRLS!(1923), d; TRUXTON KING(1923), d; BRASS BOWL, THE(1924), d; SIREN OF SEVILLE, THE(1924), d; SOME PUN'KINS(1925), d; SWIFT SHADOW, THE(1927), d; DOG JUSTICE(1928), d; LAW OF FEAR(1928), d; TRACKED(1928), d; YELLOWBACK, THE(1929), d

Jerry Storm
DIAMOND TRAIL(1933); RAINBOW RANCH(1933); HANDS ACROSS THE TABLE(1935); TOAST OF NEW YORK, THE(1937); MEN WITH WINGS(1938); FATHER TAKES A WIFE(1941)
Silents
ICED BULLET, THE(1917)

Joanna Storm
Misc. Talkies
IN LOVE(1983)

Lesley Storm
BANANA RIDGE(1941, Brit.), w; UNPUBLISHED STORY(1942, Brit.), w; FLIGHT FROM FOLLY(1945, Brit.), w; GREAT DAY(1945, Brit.), w; TONIGHT AND EVERY NIGHT(1945), w; HIGH FURY(1947, Brit.), w; MEET ME AT DAWN(1947, Brit.), w; FALLEN IDOL, THE(1949, Brit.), w; GOLDEN SALAMANDER(1950, Brit.), w; TONY DRAWS A HORSE(1951, Brit.), w; RINGER, THE(1953, Brit.), w; HEART OF THE MATTER, THE(1954, Brit.), w; PERSONAL AFFAIR(1954, Brit.), w; SPANISH GARDENER, THE(1957, Span.), w

Lorna Storm
MISTER CINDERS(1934, Brit.); WHAT HAPPENED THEN?(1934, Brit.)

Michael Storm
NEXT MAN, THE(1976)

Natalie Storm
MADAME SATAN(1930)

Olaf Storm
Silents
METROPOLIS(1927, Ger.)

Rafael Storm
LET'S GO NATIVE(1930); KISS AND MAKE UP(1934); ONE NIGHT OF LOVE(1934); GOIN' TO TOWN(1935); HERE COMES COOKIE(1935); IT HAPPENED IN NEW YORK(1935); LADY TUBBS(1935); RECKLESS(1935); RUGGLES OF RED GAP(1935); RUMBA(1935); UNDER THE PAMPAS MOON(1935); GOLDEN ARROW, THE(1936); HIS BROTHER'S WIFE(1936); HOUSE OF A THOUSAND CANDLES, THE(1936); BRIDE WORE RED, THE(1937); THANKS FOR LISTENING(1937); WISE GIRL(1937); STRAIGHT, PLACE AND SHOW(1938); ARISE, MY LOVE(1940); I TAKE THIS WOMAN(1940); MEXICAN SPITFIRE OUT WEST(1940); NEW MOON(1940); REPENT

Raphael Storm-

AT LEISURE(1941); TWO LATINS FROM MANHATTAN(1941); WHEN LADIES MEET(1941); I MARRIED AN ANGEL(1942); FOOTLIGHT GLAMOUR(1943); SUBMA-RINE BASE(1943); ACTION IN ARABIA(1944); TOGETHER AGAIN(1944); BULL-FIGHTERS, THE(1945)

Raphael Storm

FOUR JACKS AND A JILL(1941); POWERS GIRL, THE(1942); HAIRY APE, THE(1944)

Wayne Storm

TROUBLE MAN(1972); OKLAHOMA CRUDE(1973); SLITHER(1973); HEARTS OF THE WEST(1975); TIME AFTER TIME(1979, Brit.); FOXES(1980); PENNIES FROM HEAVEN(1981)

Kare Stormark

EDVARD MUNCH(1976, Norway/Swed.)

Sandra Storme

ARTISTS AND MODELS(1937); SOPHIE LANG GOES WEST(1937); SPOT OF BOTHER, A(1938, Brit.); CLOUDS OVER EUROPE(1939, Brit.); MURDER IN THE NIGHT(1940, Brit.)

Harald Stormeon

Misc. Silents

BRIDE OF GLOMDAL, THE(1925, Nor.)

Hans Stormoen

ONE DAY IN THE LIFE OF IVAN DENISOVICH(1971, U.S./Brit./Norway)

Kjell Stormoen

ONE DAY IN THE LIFE OF IVAN DENISOVICH(1971, U.S./Brit./Norway)

Paul Storob

PUTNEY SWOPE(1969)

James Storr

MY MAN(1928), w

Otto Storr

HEAD, THE(1961, Ger.); SPESSART INN, THE(1961, Ger.); PLAYGIRLS AND THE BELLBOY, THE(1962,Ger.); ISLE OF SIN(1963, Ger.)

Tim Storrier

STONE(1974, Aus.), art d

James J. Storrow, Jr.

KID RODELO(1966, U.S./Span.), p

Malcolm Storry

FIREFOX(1982)

Doc Stortt

DAYS OF WINE AND ROSES(1962); THX 1138(1971)

Alessandra Story

1984

BASILEUS QUARTET(1984, Ital.)

David Story

ICE HOUSE, THE(1969)

Elaine Story

WHEN YOU COMIN' BACK, RED RYDER?(1979)

Glen Story

KENTUCKY JUBILEE(1951)

Jack Trevor Story

DANGEROUS YOUTH(1958, Brit.), w; WONDERFUL THINGS!(1958, Brit.), w; HEART OF A MAN, THE(1959, Brit.), w; INVASION QUARTET(1961, Brit.), w; LIVE NOW–PAY LATER(1962, Brit.), w; MIX ME A PERSON(1962, Brit.), w; POSTMAN'S KNOCK(1962, Brit.), w

John Trevor Story

TROUBLE WITH HARRY, THE(1955), w

June Eve Story

NIGHT THEY RAIDED MINSKY'S, THE(1968)

Ralph Story

SEVEN MINUTES, THE(1971); FIVE DAYS FROM HOME(1978)

Robert Story

ICE HOUSE, THE(1969)

Tom Story

RECOMMENDATION FOR MERCY(1975, Can.)

E. Story-Gofton

Silents

OTHER PERSON, THE(1921, Brit.)

Johnstone Storyboard

FAIL SAFE(1964), cos

Lesley Storym

STRANGLER, THE(1941, Brit.), w

William Storz

MADE FOR EACH OTHER(1971), ph; HAIL(1973), ph

Ludwig Stossel

DEAD MAN'S SHOES(1939, Brit.); DANCE, GIRL, DANCE(1940); FLYING SQUAD, THE(1940, Brit.); FOUR SONS(1940); MAN I MARRIED, THE(1940); RETURN TO YESTERDAY(1940, Brit.); DOWN IN SAN DIEGO(1941); GREAT GUNS(1941); JEN-NIE(1941); MAN HUNT(1941); MARRY THE BOSS' DAUGHTER(1941); UNDER-GROUND(1941); ALL THROUGH THE NIGHT(1942); CASABLANCA(1942); GREAT IMPERSONATION, THE(1942); I MARRIED AN ANGEL(1942); ICELAND(1942); KING'S ROW(1942); PITTSBURGH(1942); PRIDE OF THE YANKEES, THE(1942); WHO DONE IT?(1942); WOMAN OF THE YEAR(1942); ABOVE SUSPICION(1943); ACTION IN THE NORTH ATLANTIC(1943); HERS TO HOLD(1943); HITLER'S MADMAN(1943); STRANGE DEATH OF ADOLF HITLER, THE(1943); TESTAMENT OF DR. MABUSE, THE(1943, Ger.); THEY CAME TO BLOW UP AMERICA(1943); BLUEBEARD(1944); CLIMAX, THE(1944); LAKE PLACID SERENADE(1944); DIL-LINGER(1945); HER HIGHNESS AND THE BELLBOY(1945); HOUSE OF DRACU-LA(1945); MISS SUSIE SLAGLE'S(1945); YOLANDA AND THE THIEF(1945); CLOAK AND DAGGER(1946); GIRL ON THE SPOT(1946); TEMPTATION(1946); BEGINNING OR THE END, THE(1947); ESCAPE ME NEVER(1947); SONG OF LOVE(1947); THIS TIME FOR KEEPS(1947); SONG IS BORN, A(1948); GREAT SINNER, THE(1949); AS YOUNG AS YOU FEEL(1951); CORKY OF GASOLINE ALLEY(1951); TOO YOUNG TO KISS(1951); MERRY WIDOW, THE(1952); NO TIME FOR FLOWERS(1952); SOME-BODY LOVES ME(1952); CALL ME MADAM(1953); GERALDINE(1953); SUN SHINES BRIGHT, THE(1953); WHITE GODDESS(1953); DEEP IN MY HEART(1954); FROM THE EARTH TO THE MOON(1958); ME AND THE COLONEL(1958); BLUE ANGEL, THE(1959)

Herbert Stothart

DYNAMITE(1930), m; LOTTERY BRIDE, THE(1930), w; SONG OF THE FLA-ME(1930), w; CUBAN LOVE SONG,THE(1931), m; PRODIGAL, THE(1931), m; SQUAW MAN, THE(1931), m; RASPUTIN AND THE EMPRESS(1932), m; SON-DAUGHTER, THE(1932), m; BARBARIAN, THE(1933), m; PEG O' MY HEART(1933), m; QUEEN CHRISTINA(1933), m; WHITE SISTER, THE(1933), m; CAT AND THE FIDDLE(1934), m;CHAINED(1934), m; LAUGHING BOY(1934), m; MERRY WIDOW, THE(1934), m; PAINTED VEIL, THE(1934), m; SEQUOIA(1934), m; TREASURE ISLAND(1934), m; VIVA VILLA!(1934), m; AH, WILDERNESS!(1935), m; ANNA KARENINA(1935), m; BIOGRAPHY OF A BACHELOR GIRL(1935), m; CHINA SEAS(1935), m; DAVID COPPERFIELD(1935), m; MUTINY ON THE BOUNTY(1935), m; NIGHT AT THE OPERA, A(1935), m; TALE OF TWO CITIES, A(1935), m; AFTER THE THIN MAN(1936), m; DEVIL IS A SISSY, THE(1936), m; GORGEOUS HUSSY, THE(1936), m; MOONLIGHT MURDER(1936), m; ROBIN HOOD OF EL DORA-DO(1936), m; ROMEO AND JULIET(1936), m; ROSE MARIE(1936), w, m, md; SAN FRANCISCO(1936), md; WIFE VERSUS SECRETARY(1936), m; CAMILLE(1937), m; CONQUEST(1937), m; FIREFLY, THE(1937), md; GOOD EARTH, THE(1937), m; MAYTIME(1937), md; ROSALIE(1937), md; GIRL OF THE GOLDEN WEST, THE(1938), m;MARIE ANTOINETTE(1938), m, m/1; OF HUMAN HEARTS(1938), m; SWEETHEARTS(1938), m; BALALAIKA(1939), m; IDIOT'S DELIGHT(1939), md; WIZARD OF OZ, THE(1939), m; BITTER SWEET(1940), md; EDISON, THE MAN(1940), m; NEW MOON(1940), md; NORTHWEST PASSAGE(1940), m; PRIDE AND PREJUDICE(1940), m; SUSAN AND GOD(1940), m; WATERLOO BRID-GE(1940), m; BLOSSOMS IN THE DUST(1941), m; COME LIVE WITH ME(1941), m; MEN OF BOYS TOWN(1941), m; SMILIN' THROUGH(1941), md; THEY MET IN BOMBAY(1941), m; ZIEGFELD GIRL(1941), m; CAIRO(1942), m; MRS. MINI-VER(1942), m; RANDOM HARVEST(1942), m; RIO RITA(1942), md; TENNESSEE JOHNSON(1942), m;GUY NAMED JOE, A(1943), m; HUMAN COMEDY, THE(1943), m; MADAME CURIE(1943), m; SONG OF RUSSIA(1943), m; THOUSANDS CHEER(1943), m, md;THREE HEARTS FOR JULIA(1943), m; DRAGON SEED(1944), m; KISMET(1944), m; NATIONAL VELVET(1944), m; THIRTY SECONDS OVER TOKYO(1944), m; WHITE CLIFFS OF DOVER, THE(1944), m; ADVENTURE(1945), m; PICTURE OF DORIAN GRAY, THE(1945), m; SON OF LASSIE(1945), m; THEY WERE EXPENDABLE(1945), m; VALLEY OF DECISION, THE(1945), m; GREEN YEARS, THE(1946), m; UNDERCURRENT(1946), m, md; YEARLING, THE(1946), m; DESIRE ME(1947), m; HIGH BARBAREE(1947), m; IF WINTER COMES(1947), m; SEA OF GRASS, THE(1947), m; UNFINISHED DANCE,THE(1947), m; HILLS OF HOME(1948), m; THREE MUSKETEERS, THE(1948), m; BIG JACK(1949), m; MINI-VER STORY, THE(1950, Brit./U.S.), m; ROSE MARIE(1954), w, m

Teddy Stotsek

APACHE GOLD(1965, Ger.)

Judith Stott

BURN WITCH BURN(1962)

Wally Stott

FOR BETTER FOR WORSE(1954, Brit.), m; WILL ANY GENTLEMAN?(1955, Brit.), m; IT'S NEVER TOO LATE(1958, Brit.), m; HEART OF A MAN, THE(1959, Brit.), m; LADY IS A SQUARE, THE(1959, Brit.), m; PEEPING TOM(1960, Brit.), m; CAPTAIN NEMO AND THE UNDERWATER CITY(1969, Brit.), m; LOOKING GLASS WAR, THE(1970, Brit.), m; WHEN EIGHT BELLS TOLL(1971, Brit.), m, md

Larry Stouffer

HORROR HIGH(1974), d

Vera Stough

UNDER THE YUM-YUM TREE(1963); FOOLS(1970)

Louis Clyde Stouman

OPERATION DAMES(1959), d, ed

Louis Clyde Stoumen

FIVE(1951), ph

Tina Stoumen

WINDFLOWERS(1968)

A. J. Stout

VARSITY(1928), ph; BENSON MURDER CASE, THE(1930), ph; DANGEROUS PARADISE(1930), ph; MANSLAUGHTER(1930), ph; MEN ARE LIKE THAT(1930), ph; RETURN OF DR. FU MANCHU, THE(1930), ph; CONQUERING HORDE, THE(1931), ph; OKLAHOMA JIM(1931), ph; MAN FROM UTAH, THE(1934), ph; CONFLICT(1937), ph; ANGEL AND THE BADMAN(1947), ph

Archibald Stout

Silents

TEN COMMANDMENTS, THE(1923), ph

Archie Stout

DARKENED ROOMS(1929), ph; DERELICT(1930), ph; HEADIN' NORTH(1930), ph; DUGAN OF THE BAD LANDS(1931), ph; GOD'S COUNTRY AND THE MAN(1931), ph; GUN SMOKE(1931), ph; IN THE LINE OF DUTY(1931), ph; LAW OF THE RIO GRANDE(1931), ph; MAN FROM DEATH VALLEY, THE(1931), ph; MONTANA KID, THE(1931), ph; MOTHER AND SON(1931), ph; NEAR THE TRAIL'S END(1931), ph; PARTNERS OF THE TRAIL(1931), ph; RIDER OF THE PLAINS(1931), ph; SHIPS OF HATE(1931), ph; SON OF THE PLAINS(1931), ph; SUNRISE TRAIL(1931), ph; COUN-TY FAIR, THE(1932), ph; FAME STREET(1932), ph; FORGOTTEN WOMEN(1932), ph; GALLOPING THRU(1932), ph; GHOST CITY(1932), ph; HONOR OF THE MOUNT-ED(1932), ph; LAND OF WANTED MEN(1932), ph; LAW OF THE NORTH(1932), ph; LAW OF THE SEA(1932), ph; MASON OF THE MOUNTED(1932), ph; RIDERS OF THE DESERT(1932), ph; SINGLE-HANDED SANDERS(1932), ph; SON OF OK-LAHOMA(1932), ph; FIGHTING CHAMP(1933), ph; FIGHTING TEXANS(1933), ph; FUGITIVE, THE(1933), ph; GALLOPING ROMEO(1933), ph; HERITAGE OF THE DESERT(1933), ph; LUCKY LARRIGAN(1933), ph; MY MOTHER(1933), ph; MYS-TERIOUS RIDER, THE(1933), ph; RAINBOW RANCH(1933), ph; RANGER'S CODE, THE(1933), ph; RIDERS OF DESTINY(1933), ph; SUNSET PASS(1933), ph; UNDER THE TONTO RIM(1933), ph; BLUE STEEL(1934), ph; HAPPY LANDING(1934), ph; HOUSE OF MYSTERY(1934), ph; LAST ROUND-UP, THE(1934), ph; 'NEATH THE ARIZONA SKIES(1934), ph; RANDY RIDES ALONE(1934), ph; SAGEBRUSH TRAIL(1934), ph; SIXTEEN FATHOMS DEEP(1934), ph; STAR PACKER, THE(1934), ph; TRAIL BEYOND, THE(1934), ph; DAWN RIDER(1935), ph; FLIRTING WITH DANGER(1935), ph; HOPALONG CASSIDY(1935), ph; LAWLESS FRONTIER, THE(1935), ph; LAWLESS RANGE(1935), ph; PARADISE CANYON(1935), ph; ROCKY MOUNTAIN MYSTERY(1935), ph; SING SING NIGHTS(1935), ph; TEXAS TERROR(1935), ph; BAR 20 RIDES AGAIN(1936), ph; CALL OF THE PRAIRIE(1936), ph; EAGLE'S BROOD(1936), ph; HOPALONG CASSIDY RETURNS(1936), ph; NEVADA(1936), ph; THREE ON THE TRAIL(1936), ph; TRAIL DUST(1936), ph; WESTWARD HO(1936), ph; BORDERLAND(1937), ph; HEART OF THE WEST(1937), ph; HILLS OF OLD WYOMING(1937), ph; PROFESSOR BEWARE(1938), ph; BEAU GESTE(1939), ph; MYSTERY PLANE(1939), ph; RULERS OF THE SEA(1939), ph;

TEXAS RANGERS RIDE AGAIN(1940), ph; WESTERNER, THE(1940), spec eff; ALASKA(1944), ph; DARK WATERS(1944), ph; IT HAPPENED TOMORROW(1944), ph; SUMMER STORM(1944), ph; CAPTAIN KIDD(1945), ph; TARZAN AND THE AMAZONS(1945), ph; TARZAN AND THE HUNTRESS(1947), ph; LUST FOR GOLD(1949), ph; NEVER FEAR(1950), ph; OUTRAGE(1950), ph; HARD, FAST, AND BEAUTIFUL(1951), ph; ON THE LOOSE(1951), ph; BIG JIM McLAIN(1952), ph; QUIET MAN, THE(1952), ph; HONDO(1953), ph; ISLAND IN THE SKY(1953), ph; TROUBLE ALONG THE WAY(1953), ph; HIGH AND THE MIGHTY, THE(1954), ph; PROFESSIONALS, THE(1966), ph

Archie J. Stout
SEA GOD, THE(1930), ph; YOUNG EAGLES(1930), ph; IT PAYS TO ADVERTISE(1931), ph; LUCKY TEXAN, THE(1934), ph; MYSTERY LINER(1934), ph; WEST OF THE DIVIDE(1934), ph; DESERT TRAIL(1935), ph; SEA SPOILERS, THE(1936), ph; ABILENE TOWN(1946), ph; FORT APACHE(1948), ph; SUN SHINES BRIGHT, THE(1953), ph

B. Stout
POCKET MONEY(1972)

Bill Stout
I WANT TO LIVE!(1958); UGLY AMERICAN, THE(1963); BEST MAN, THE(1964); CANDIDATE, THE(1972)

Budd Stout
VILLAIN, THE(1979)
1984
CANNONBALL RUN II(1984)

Don Stout
SHOCK WAVES(1977)

Dow Stout
SUPER FUZZ(1981)

George W. Stout
TUNDRA(1936), p; TARZAN AND THE GREEN GODDESS(1938), p

Jean Stout
YOUNG GIRLS OF ROCHEFORT, THE(1968, Fr.)

Naomi Stout
HERE COME THE CO-EDS(1945)

Paul Stout
1984
MEATBALLS PART II(1984)

Rex Stout
MEET NERO WOLFE(1936), w; LEAGUE OF FRIGHTENED MEN(1937), w

Royal G. Stout
ROYAL FAMILY OF BROADWAY, THE(1930)

Sara Stout
PAUL AND MICHELLE(1974, Fr./Brit.)

Scott Stout
1984
MEATBALLS PART II(1984)

Rene Stouthamer
LIFT, THE(1983, Neth.), spec eff

Hugh Stovall
SWING, SISTER, SWING(1938)

Myrtle Stovall
I'D CLIMB THE HIGHEST MOUNTAIN(1951)

Ted Stovall
BOY WHO CRIED WEREWOLF, THE(1973), m

Tom Stovall
FOOD OF THE GODS, THE(1976); SILKWOOD(1983)

George Stover
FIEND(; POLYESTER(1981); NIGHTBEAST(1982)
1984
ALIEN FACTOR, THE(1984)

Jerry Stovin
AFTER THE BALL(1957, Brit.); HELL DRIVERS(1958, Brit.); LOLITA(1962); WAR LOVER, THE(1962, U.S./Brit.); WHY BOTHER TO KNOCK(1964, Brit.); SOLO FOR SPARROW(1966, Brit.); PINK PANTHER STRIKES AGAIN, THE(1976, Brit.)

Hardy Stow
1984
STRIKEBOUND(1984, Aus.)

Bert Stowe
Silents
OLD CURIOSITY SHOP, THE(1913, Brit.)

Harriet Beecher Stowe
UNCLE TOM'S CABIN(1969, Fr./Ital./Ger./Yugo.), w
Silents
UNCLE TOM'S CABIN(1914), w

Leslie Stowe
MOTHER'S BOY(1929)
Silents
ADOPTED SON, THE(1917); NO TRESPASSING(1922); SEVENTH DAY, THE(1922); JAMESTOWN(1923); SECOND FIDDLE(1923)
Misc. Silents
CLOSED ROAD, THE(1916); LA VIE DE BOHEME(1916); SOCIAL QUICKSANDS(1918); BOLSHEVISM ON TRIAL(1919); GOOD-BAD WIFE, THE(1921); PEGGY PUTS IT OVER(1921); COLUMBUS(1923)

Leslie M. Stowe
Misc. Silents
DAWN OF LOVE, THE(1916)

Tiny Stowe
TALES OF ROBIN HOOD(1951)

Bruce Stowell
GIRL MOST LIKELY, THE(1957)

C.W. Stowell
RAMPARTS WE WATCH, THE(1940)

Dan Stowell
BOSTON BLACKIE BOOKED ON SUSPICION(1945); BOSTON BLACKIE'S RENDEZVOUS(1945); OVER 21(1945); BANDIT OF SHERWOOD FOREST, THE(1946); HER HUSBAND'S AFFAIRS(1947)

Don Stowell
REG'LAR FELLERS(1941); NIGHT IN PARADISE, A(1946)

Gene Stowell
BLACK ANGELS, THE(1970)

William Stowell
Silents
IMMEDIATE LEE(1916); OVERALLS(1916); FLASHLIGHT, THE(1917); RESCUE, THE(1917); RISKY ROAD, THE(1918)
Misc. Silents
BUZZARD'S SHADOW, THE(1915); END OF THE ROAD, THE(1915); LOVE HERMIT, THE(1916); MAN FROM MANHATTAN, THE(1916); OTHER SIDE OF THE DOOR, THE(1916); OVERCOAT, THE(1916); BONDAGE(1917); DOLL'S HOUSE, A(1917); FIGHTING MAD(1917); FIRES OF REBELLION(1917); GIRL IN THE CHECKERED COAT, THE(1917); HELL MORGAN'S GIRL(1917); PAY ME!(1917); PIPER'S PRICE, THE(1917); TRIUMPH(1917); BROADWAY LOVE(1918); GRAND PASSION, THE(1918); MORTGAGED WIFE, THE(1918); TALK OF THE TOWN(1918); DESTINY(1919); HEART OF HUMANITY, THE(1919); MAN IN THE MOONLIGHT, THE(1919); RIGHT TO HAPPINESS, THE(1919); WHEN A GIRL LOVES(1919)

Claude Stowers
I'D CLIMB THE HIGHEST MOUNTAIN(1951)

Fred Stowers
Silents
MOLLY O'(1921), w

Frederick Stowers
Silents
NINETEEN AND PHYLLIS(1920), w; AMERICAN VENUS, THE(1926), w; OLD SHOES(1927), d&w

Rita Stoya
NIGHTS OF SHAME(1961, Fr.)

Todor Stoyanov
DETOUR, THE(1968, Bulgarian), d, ph; PEACH THIEF, THE(1969, Bulgaria), ph

Mike Stoycoff
STAKEOUT ON DOPE STREET(1958)

Hans Straat
SMILES OF A SUMMER NIGHT(1957, Swed.); NO TIME TO KILL(1963, Brit./Swed./Ger.); PORT OF CALL(1963, Swed.); LOVING COUPLES(1966, Swed.); FANNY AND ALEXANDER(1983, Swed./Fr./Ger.)

Herbert Strabel
DUCK RINGS AT HALF PAST SEVEN, THE(1969, Ger./Ital.), set d; CABARET(1972), set d; FROM THE LIFE OF THE MARIONETTES(1980, Ger.), art d; NIGHT CROSSING(1982), art d
1984
NEVERENDING STORY, THE(1984, Ger.), art d

Thelma Strabel
FOREST RANGERS, THE(1942), w; REAP THE WILD WIND(1942), w; UNDERCURRENT(1946), w

Suzanne Stracey
WOMAN TO WOMAN(1946, Brit.)

Alan Strachan
GREEK TYCOON, THE(1978), ed; PASSAGE, THE(1979, Brit.), ed; FFOLKES(1980, Brit.), ed; FINAL CONFLICT, THE(1981), ed; SENDER, THE(1982, Brit.), ed
1984
SAHARA(1984), ed

Diane Strachan
AGE OF CONSENT(1969, Austral.)

Donald Strachan
I KNOW WHERE I'M GOING(1947, Brit.)

Alan Strachen
HUMAN FACTOR, THE(1975), ed

John Strachen
EL DORADO(1967)

Lytton Strachey
WHITE ANGEL, THE(1936), w

Janusz Strachocki
KNIGHTS OF THE TEUTONIC ORDER, THE(1962, Pol.)

Gunter Strack
TORN CURTAIN(1966); ODESSA FILE, THE(1974, Brit./Ger.)

Strad and His Newsboys
SATURDAY NIGHT REVUE(1937, Brit.)

Scott Strader
1984
KARATE KID, THE(1984)

Harry Stradling
LUCKY IN LOVE(1929), ph; MOTHER'S BOY(1929), ph; DIE MANNER UM LUCIE(1931), ph; CARNIVAL IN FLANDERS(1936, Fr.), ph; ACTION FOR SLANDER(1937, Brit.), ph; DARK JOURNEY(1937, Aust.), ph; EPISODE(1937, Aust.), ph; KNIGHT WITHOUT ARMOR(1937, Brit.), ph; CITADEL, THE(1938), ph; DIVORCE OF LADY X. THE(1938, Brit.), ph; PYGMALION(1938, Brit.), ph; SOUTH RIDING(1938, Brit.), ph; JAMAICA INN(1939, Brit.), ph; LION HAS WINGS, THE(1940, Brit.), ph; MY SON, MY SON!(1940), ph; OVER THE MOON(1940, Brit.), ph; THEY KNEW WHAT THEY WANTED(1940), ph; CORSICAN BROTHERS, THE(1941), ph; DEVIL AND MISS JONES, THE(1941), ph; MEN IN HER LIFE, THE(1941), ph; MR. AND MRS. NORTH(1941), ph; MR. AND MRS. SMITH(1941), ph; SUSPICION(1941), ph; FINGERS AT THE WINDOW(1942), ph; HER CARDBOARD LOVER(1942), ph; MAISIE GETS HER MAN(1942), ph; NAZI AGENT(1942), ph; WHITE CARGO(1942), ph; HUMAN COMEDY, THE(1943), ph; SONG OF RUSSIA(1943), ph; SWING SHIFT MAISIE(1943), ph; BATHING BEAUTY(1944), ph; HER HIGHNESS AND THE BELLBOY(1945), ph; PICTURE OF DORIAN GRAY, THE(1945), ph; THRILL OF A ROMANCE(1945), ph; EASY TO WED(1946), ph; HOLIDAY IN MEXICO(1946), ph; TILL THE CLOUDS ROLL BY(1946), ph; SEA OF GRASS, THE(1947), ph; SONG OF LOVE(1947), ph; PIRATE, THE(1948), ph; BARKLEYS OF BROADWAY, THE(1949), ph; IN THE GOOD OLD SUMMERTIME(1949), ph; TENSION(1949), ph; EDGE OF DOOM(1950), ph; YELLOW CAB MAN, THE(1950), ph; I WANT YOU(1951), ph; MILLIONAIRE FOR CHRISTY, A(1951), ph; STREETCAR NAMED DESIRE, A(1951), ph; VALENTINO(1951), ph; ANDROCLES AND THE LION(1952), ph; HANS CHRISTIAN ANDERSEN(1952), ph; ANGEL FACE(1953), ph; LION IS IN THE STREETS, A(1953), ph; HELEN OF TROY(1956, Ital.), ph; FACE IN THE CROWD, A(1957), ph; PAJAMA GAME, THE(1957), ph; MARJORIE MORNINGSTAR(1958), ph; SUMMER PLACE, A(1959), ph; WHO WAS THAT LADY?(1960), ph; ON THE DOUBLE(1961), ph; FIVE FINGER EXERCISE(1962), ph; MARY, MARY(1963), ph; HOW TO MUR-

DER YOUR WIFE(1965), ph; SYNANON(1965), ph; MOMENT TO MOMENT(1966), ph; PENELOPE(1966), ph; WALK, DON'T RUN(1966), ph; WHO'S AFRAID OF VIRGINIA WOOLF?(1966), ph; FUNNY GIRL(1968), ph; OWL AND THE PUSSYCAT, THE(1970), ph; MITCHELL(1975), ph; UP THE ACADEMY(1980), ph; PURSUIT OF D.B. COOPER, THE(1981), ph; S.O.B.(1981), ph; O'HARA'S WIFE(1983), ph

Silents
JIM THE PENMAN(1921), ph; SECRETS OF PARIS, THE(1922), ph; NEST, THE(1927), ph

Harry Stradling, Jr.
WAY WE WERE, THE(1973), ph; JOHNNY GUITAR(1954), ph; WELCOME TO HARD TIMES(1967), ph; WITH SIX YOU GET EGGROLL(1968), ph; GOOD GUYS AND THE BAD GUYS, THE(1969), ph; MAD ROOM, THE(1969), ph; SUPPORT YOUR LOCAL SHERIFF(1969), ph; YOUNG BILLY YOUNG(1969), ph; DIRTY DINGUS MAGEE(1970), ph; LITTLE BIG MAN(1970), ph; THERE WAS A CROOKED MAN(1970), ph; LATE LIZ, THE(1971), ph; SOMETHING BIG(1971), ph; SUPPORT YOUR LOCAL GUNFIGHTER(1971), ph; SKYJACKED(1972), ph; THUMB TRIPPING(1972), ph; 1776(1972), ph; MAN WHO LOVED CAT DANCING, THE(1973), ph; BANK SHOT(1974), ph; MC Q(1974), ph; BITE THE BULLET(1975), ph; ROOSTER COGBURN(1975), ph; BIG BUS, THE(1976), ph; MIDWAY(1976), ph; SPECIAL DELIVERY(1976), ph; DAMNATION ALLEY(1977), ph; GREATEST, THE(1977, U.S./Brit.), ph; BORN AGAIN(1978), ph; GO TELL THE SPARTANS(1978), ph; PROPHECY(1979), ph; CARNY(1980), ph; BUDDY BUDDY(1981), ph
1984
MICKI AND MAUDE(1984), ph

Henry Stradling
MY SON, JOHN(1952), ph

Walter Stradling
Silents
REBECCA OF SUNNYBROOK FARM(1917), ph; AMARILLY OF CLOTHESLINE ALLEY(1918), ph; M'LISS(1918), ph; OUT OF A CLEAR SKY(1918), ph; STELLA MARIS(1918), ph

Harry Stradling, Sr.
CLOUDS OVER EUROPE(1939, Brit.), ph; EASTER PARADE(1948), ph; FOREVER FEMALE(1953), ph; GUYS AND DOLLS(1955), ph; EDDY DUCHIN STORY, THE(1956), ph; AUNTIE MAME(1958), ph; YOUNG PHILADELPHIANS, THE(1959), ph; CROWDED SKY, THE(1960), ph; DARK AT THE TOP OF THE STAIRS, THE(1960), ph; MAJORITY OF ONE, A(1961), ph; PARRISH(1961), ph; GYPSY(1962), ph; ISLAND OF LOVE(1963), ph; HELLO, DOLLY!(1969), ph; ON A CLEAR DAY YOU CAN SEE FOREVER(1970), ph

Rose Stradner
LAST GANGSTER, THE(1937); BLIND ALLEY(1939); KEYS OF THE KINGDOM, THE(1944)

Nino Straesa
BUFFALO BILL, HERO OF THE FAR WEST(1962, Ital.), w

Ursula Straetz
EFFI BRIEST(1974, Ger.)

John Strahan
NEXT OF KIN(1983, Aus.)

Ruth P. Strahan
BODY HEAT(1981)

Erwin Strahl
FIVE BRANDED WOMEN(1960); ISLE OF SIN(1963, Ger.)

Franca Parisi Strahl
ATOM AGE VAMPIRE(1961, Ital.); FOREVER MY LOVE(1962); WHITE SLAVE SHIP(1962, Fr./Ital.)

Shirlee Strahm
SOLDIER IN THE RAIN(1963), cos; AUDREY ROSE(1977), cos

Shirley Strahm
FUNNY LADY(1975), cos; STAR IS BORN, A(1976), cos

Beatrice Straight
PHONE CALL FROM A STRANGER(1952); PATTERNS(1956); SILKEN AFFAIR, THE(1957, Brit.); NUN'S STORY, THE(1959); YOUNG LOVERS, THE(1964); NETWORK(1976); BLOODLINE(1979); PROMISE, THE(1979); FORMULA, THE(1980); ENDLESS LOVE(1981); POLTERGEIST(1982); TWO OF A KIND(1983)

Clarence Straight
MY LIFE WITH CAROLINE(1941); EAGLE SQUADRON(1942); MOONLIGHT IN HAVANA(1942); FLIGHT FOR FREEDOM(1943); GUY NAMED JOE, A(1943); NORTH STAR, THE(1943); YOU'RE A LUCKY FELLOW, MR. SMITH(1943); SEE HERE, PRIVATE HARGROVE(1944); SPELLBOUND(1945); SENATOR WAS INDISCREET, THE(1947); SMASH-UP, THE STORY OF A WOMAN(1947); ABBOTT AND COSTELLO MEET FRANKENSTEIN(1948); SAXON CHARM, THE(1948); CHICAGO DEADLINE(1949); FAR FRONTIER, THE(1949); GOLDEN STALLION, THE(1949); MRS. MIKE(1949); POWDER RIVER RUSTLERS(1949); PIONEER MARSHAL(1950); WHERE THE SIDEWALK ENDS(1950); ROADBLOCK(1951); COLORADO SUNDOWN(1952); FOUR GIRLS IN TOWN(1956); WRONG MAN, THE(1956); TATTERED DRESS, THE(1957); GUNMEN FROM LAREDO(1959); HANGING TREE, THE(1959)

Ken Strain
THING, THE(1982)

Sue Angelyn Strain
IN GOD WE TRUST(1980)

Bud Strait
HUNTING PARTY, THE(1977, Brit.)

Mark Strait
1984
FLAMINGO KID, THE(1984)

Paul Strait
DANGEROUS CHARTER(1962), w

Ralph Strait
SUPER COPS, THE(1974); BEASTMASTER, THE(1982); HALLOWEEN III: SEASON OF THE WITCH(1982)

Pauline Strake
Misc. Talkies
$20 A WEEK(1935)
Misc. Silents
IRISH EYES(1918)

Straker
GIRL STROKE BOY(1971, Brit.)

J.F. Straker
HELL IS EMPTY(1967, Brit./Ital), w

Avery Strakosch
SHE MARRIED AN ARTIST(1938), w

Ophelia Stral
MAGICIAN OF LUBLIN, THE(1979, Israel/Ger.)

R. James Straley
SILENT WITNESS, THE(1962)

Elzbieta Stralkowska
CONDUCTOR, THE(1981, Pol.)

Henry Stram
1984
VAMPING(1984)

Jimmy Strand
CLANCY STREET BOYS(1943); MR. MUGGS STEPS OUT(1943); BLOCK BUSTERS(1944); BOWERY CHAMPS(1944); FOLLOW THE LEADER(1944); MILLION DOLLAR KID(1944)

Joe Strand
DEER HUNTER, THE(1978)

Joseph Strand
1984
NATURAL, THE(1984)

Lee Strand
SQUEEZE, THE(1977, Brit.)

Maud Strand
SOMEWHERE IN TIME(1980)

Robert Strand
DREAMS OF GLASS(1969)

Sharon Strand
NARCOTICS STORY, THE(1958)

Walter Strand
TEXAN MEETS CALAMITY JANE, THE(1950)

Eva-Britt Strandberg
MASCULINE FEMININE(1966, Fr./Swed.)

Jon-Olof Strandberg
FLIGHT OF THE EAGLE(1983, Swed.)

Julius Strandberg
DAY THE EARTH FROZE, THE(1959, Fin./USSR), p

John L. Strandell
1984
STONE BOY, THE(1984)

Karin Strandjord
FRANCES(1982)

Erik Strandmark
NAKED NIGHT, THE(1956, Swed.); SEVENTH SEAL, THE(1958, Swed.); NO TIME TO KILL(1963, Brit./Swed./Ger.)

Chris Strang
VORTEX(1982)

Eric Strang
Silents
MR. NOBODY(1927, Brit.), w

Harry Strang
YELLOW JACK(1938); WITHOUT RESERVATIONS(1946); THEY WON'T BELIEVE ME(1947); SHADOW OF THE LAW(1930); HELL BOUND(1931); SUICIDE FLEET(1931); ALIAS MARY SMITH(1932); WIDOW IN SCARLET(1932); DEATH KISS, THE(1933); LADY KILLER(1933); MONKEY'S PAW, THE(1933); CAR 99(1935); CHARLIE CHAN IN SHANGHAI(1935); DANTE'S INFERNO(1935); GHOST WALKS, THE(1935); LITTLE COLONEL, THE(1935); DARK HOUR, THE(1936); GORGEOUS HUSSY, THE(1936); NAVY BORN(1936); PRISONER OF SHARK ISLAND, THE(1936); SAN FRANCISCO(1936); GAME THAT KILLS, THE(1937); PAID TO DANCE(1937); RANGER COURAGE(1937); SHADOW, THE(1937); STAGE DOOR(1937); COME ON, LEATHERNECKS(1938); FIRST 100 YEARS, THE(1938); GUNSMOKE TRAIL(1938); JUVENILE COURT(1938); MR. MOTO TAKES A VACATION(1938); PHANTOM RANGER(1938); PURPLE VIGILANTES, THE(1938); SQUADRON OF HONOR(1938); SUBMARINE PATROL(1938); ANGELS WASH THEIR FACES(1939); CONVICT'S CODE(1939); COWBOYS FROM TEXAS(1939); GONE WITH THE WIND(1939); IDIOT'S DELIGHT(1939); MR. MOTO IN DANGER ISLAND(1939); RETURN OF THE CISCO KID(1939); RIO GRANDE(1939); SERGEANT MADDEN(1939); SOCIETY LAWYER(1939); THUNDER AFLOAT(1939); ANGELS OVER BROADWAY(1940); CALLING PHILO VANCE(1940); CHARLIE CHAN'S MURDER CRUISE(1940); DANGER ON WHEELS(1940); DARK COMMAND(1940); GAUCHO SERENADE(1940); GRAPES OF WRATH(1940); I'M NOBODY'S SWEETHEART NOW(1940); INVISIBLE STRIPES(1940); ISLAND OF DOOMED MEN(1940); KIT CARSON(1940); LITTLE OLD NEW YORK(1940); LUCKY CISCO KID(1940); NEW MOON(1940); SAILOR'S LADY(1940); SANTA FE TRAIL(1940); TIN PAN ALLEY(1940); TRAIL BLAZERS, THE(1940); YOU'RE NOT SO TOUGH(1940); BUCK PRIVATES(1941); DEATH VALLEY OUTLAWS(1941); FACE BEHIND THE MASK, THE(1941); KEEP 'EM FLYING(1941); LOVE CRAZY(1941); MANPOWER(1941); MR. AND MRS. NORTH(1941); NAVY BLUES(1941); PHANTOM SUBMARINE, THE(1941); WESTERN UNION(1941); YOU'LL NEVER GET RICH(1941); BOMBAY CLIPPER(1942); I WAKE UP SCREAMING(1942); MY GAL SAL(1942); SABOTEUR(1942); SIN TOWN(1942); THEY ALL KISSED THE BRIDE(1942); THEY DIED WITH THEIR BOOTS ON(1942); THUNDER BIRDS(1942); TO THE SHORES OF TRIPOLI(1942); TORTILLA FLAT(1942); TRAMP, TRAMP, TRAMP(1942); WHO DONE IT?(1942); GOOD MORNING, JUDGE(1943); GUNG HO!(1943); HE'S MY GUY(1943); HI, BUDDY(1943); HIT THE ICE(1943); IT AIN'T HAY(1943); LONE STAR TRAIL, THE(1943); NORTH STAR, THE(1943); SO PROUDLY WE HAIL(1943); THOUSANDS CHEER(1943); TWO SENORITAS FROM CHICAGO(1943); DESTINY(1944); GYPSY WILDCAT(1944); LAURA(1944); MY BUDDY(1944); OLD TEXAS TRAIL, THE(1944); ONCE UPON A TIME(1944); SEE HERE, PRIVATE HARGROVE(1944); SULLIVANS, THE(1944); FALLEN ANGEL(1945); NOB HILL(1945); SWING OUT, SISTER(1945); WITHIN THESE WALLS(1945); CENTENNIAL SUMMER(1946); ROLL ON TEXAS MOON(1946); DEEP VALLEY(1947); DICK TRACY MEETS GRUESOME(1947); DICK TRACY'S DILEMMA(1947); FALL GUY(1947); FRAMED(1947); I, JANE DOE(1948); LADY FROM SHANGHAI, THE(1948); MICHAEL O'HALLORAN(1948); SILVER RIVER(1948); SINISTER JOURNEY(1948); SMART WOMAN(1948); EAST SIDE, WEST SIDE(1949); WHITE HEAT(1949); WHEN WILLIE COMES MARCHING HOME(1950); WOMAN OF DISTINCTION, A(1950); LET'S GO NAVY(1951); WAGONS WEST(1952); AT GUNPOINT(1955); LOOKING FOR DANGER(1957); TOUGHEST GUN IN TOMBSTONE(1958); NORTH BY NORTHWEST(1959)

Jack Strang
RING OF FEAR(1954)

Billy Strange
TROUBLE WITH GIRLS(AND HOW TO GET INTO IT), THE*1/2 (1969), m; LIVE A LITTLE, LOVE A LITTLE(1968), m; DE SADE(1969), m; BUNNY O'HARE(1971), m; COAL MINER'S DAUGHTER(1980)

Glenn Strange
BORDER LAW(1931); HARD HOMBRE(1931); RANGE FEUD, THE(1931); WILD HORSE(1931); MC KENNA OF THE MOUNTED(1932); STAR PACKER, THE(1934); GALLANT DEFENDER(1935); LAWLESS RANGE(1935); NEW FRONTIER, THE(1935); STORMY(1935); AVENGING WATERS(1936); CATTLE THIEF, THE(1936); FLASH GORDON(1936); FUGITIVE SHERIFF, THE(1936); MOONLIGHT ON THE PRAIRIE(1936); SONG OF THE GRINGO(1936); SUNSET OF POWER(1936); TRAILIN' WEST(1936); WESTWARD HO(1936); ADVENTURE'S END(1937); ARIZONA DAYS(1937); BLAZING SIXES(1937); CALIFORNIA MAIL, THE(1937); CHEROKEE STRIP(1937); DEVIL'S SADDLE LEGION, THE(1937); EMPTY HOLSTERS(1937); GUNS OF THE PECOS(1937); LAND BEYOND THE LAW(1937); SINGING OUTLAW(1937); TROUBLE IN TEXAS(1937); BLACK BANDIT(1938); BORDER WOLVES(1938); CALL OF THE ROCKIES(1938); DANGER VALLEY(1938); FORBIDDEN VALLEY(1938); GHOST TOWN RIDERS(1938); GUILTY TRAILS(1938); GUN PACKER(1938); GUNSMOKE TRAIL(1938); IN OLD MEXICO(1938); LAST STAND, THE(1938); MYSTERIOUS RIDER, THE(1938); PAINTED TRAIL, THE(1938); PRAIRIE JUSTICE(1938); PRIDE OF THE WEST(1938); PRISON BREAK(1938); SIX SHOOTIN' SHERIFF(1938); SPY RING, THE(1938); SUNSET TRAIL(1938); WHIRLWIND HORSEMAN(1938); ACROSS THE PLAINS(1939); ARIZONA LEGION(1939); BLUE MONTANA SKIES(1939); DAYS OF JESSE JAMES(1939); FIGHTING GRINGO, THE(1939); HONOR OF THE WEST(1939); LAW OF THE PAMPAS(1939); NIGHT RIDERS, THE(1939); OKLAHOMA TERROR(1939); OVERLAND MAIL(1939); PHANTOM STAGE, THE(1939); RANGE WAR(1939); ROUGH RIDERS' ROUNDUP(1939); COVERED WAGON TRAILS(1940); COWBOY FROM SUNDOWN(1940); DARK COMMAND, THE(1940); LAND OF THE SIX GUNS(1940); LLANO KID, THE(1940); PALS OF THE SILVER SAGE(1940); PIONEER DAYS(1940); RHYTHM OF THE RIO GRANDE(1940); STAGE TO CHINO(1940); THREE MEN FROM TEXAS(1940); TRIPLE JUSTICE(1940); WAGON TRAIN(1940); WYOMING(1940); ARIZONA CYCLONE(1941); BANDIT TRAIL, THE(1941); BILLY THE KID WANTED(1941); BILLY THE KID'S ROUNDUP(1941); DRIFTIN' KID, THE(1941); DUDE COWBOY(1941); FARGO KID, THE(1941); FORBIDDEN TRAILS(1941); FUGITIVE VALLEY(1941); IN OLD COLORADO(1941); KID'S LAST RIDE, THE(1941); SADDLEMATES(1941); SAN FRANCISCO DOCKS(1941); WIDE OPEN TOWN(1941); BANDIT RANGER(1942); BILLY THE KID TRAPPED(1942); COME ON DANGER(1942); DOWN TEXAS WAY(1942); JUKE GIRL(1942); LITTLE JOE, THE WRANGLER(1942); LONE RIDER AND THE BANDIT, THE(1942); LONE STAR LAW MEN(1942); MAD MONSTER, THE(1942); MUMMY'S TOMB, THE(1942); OVERLAND STAGECOACH(1942); RAIDERS OF THE WEST(1942); ROLLING DOWN THE GREAT DIVIDE(1942); ROMANCE ON THE RANGE(1942); STAGECOACH BUCKAROO(1942); SUNSET ON THE DESERT(1942); WESTERN MAIL(1942); ACTION IN THE NORTH ATLANTIC(1943); ARIZONA TRAIL(1943); BLACK MARKET RUSTLERS(1943); BLACK RAVEN, THE(1943); DESPERADOES, THE(1943); FALSE COLORS(1943); HAUNTED RANCH, THE(1943); KANSAN, THE(1943); KID RIDES AGAIN, THE(1943); MISSION TO MOSCOW(1943); RETURN OF THE RANGERS, THE(1943); WESTERN CYCLONE(1943); WILD HORSE STAMPEDE(1943); WOMAN OF THE TOWN, THE(1943); ALASKA(1944); CONTENDER, THE(1944); DEATH VALLEY RANGERS(1944); FORTY THIEVES(1944); HOUSE OF FRANKENSTEIN(1944); KNICKERBOCKER HOLIDAY(1944); MONSTER MAKER, THE(1944); SAN ANTONIO KID, THE(1944); SILVER CITY KID(1944); SONORA STAGECOACH(1944); TRAIL TO GUNSIGHT(1944); VALLEY OF VENGEANCE(1944); BAD MEN OF THE BORDER(1945); HOUSE OF DRACULA(1945); RENEGADES OF THE RIO GRANDE(1945); SARATOGA TRUNK(1945); BEAUTY AND THE BANDIT(1946); UP GOES MAISIE(1946); BRUTE FORCE(1947); FABULOUS TEXAN, THE(1947); SEA OF GRASS, THE(1947); SINBAD THE SAILOR(1947); WHITE STALLION(1947); WISTFUL WIDOW OF WAGON GAP, THE(1947); WYOMING(1947); ABBOTT AND COSTELLO MEET FRANKENSTEIN(1948); GALLANT LEGION, THE(1948); RED RIVER(1948); GAL WHO TOOK THE WEST, THE(1949); MASTER MINDS(1949); RIMFIRE(1949); ROLL, THUNDER, ROLL(1949); COMMANCHE TERRITORY(1950); DOUBLE CROSSBONES(1950); SURRENDER(1950); CALLAWAY WENT THATAWAY(1951); COMIN' ROUND THE MOUNTAIN(1951); RED BADGE OF COURAGE, THE(1951); TEXAS CARNIVAL(1951); VENGEANCE VALLEY(1951); LAWLESS BREED, THE(1952); LUSTY MEN, THE(1952); MONTANA BELLE(1952); WAGONS WEST(1952); BORN TO THE SADDLE(1953); DEVIL'S CANYON(1953); ESCAPE FROM FORT BRAVO(1953); GREAT SIOUX UPRISING, THE(1953); VEILS OF BAGDAD, THE(1953); JUBILEE TRAIL(1954); ROAD TO DENVER, THE(1955); VANISHING AMERICAN, THE(1955); FASTEST GUN ALIVE(1956); GUNFIRE AT INDIAN GAP(1957); HALLIDAY BRAND, THE(1957); JAILHOUSE ROCK(1957); LAST STAGECOACH WEST, THE(1957); QUANTRILL'S RAIDERS(1958); LAST TRAIN FROM GUN HILL(1959)
Misc. Talkies
BORDER VENGEANCE(1935); BOOT HILL BANDITS(1942); TEXAS TROUBLE SHOOTERS(1942)

Harry Strange
TWO-GUN JUSTICE(1938); DICK TRACY(1945)

Henry Strange
YELLOW CARGO(1936)

Hugh Stanislaus Strange
SEVENTEEN(1940), w

Julian Strange
VIOLENT STRANGER(1957, Brit.); SECOND BEST SECRET AGENT IN THE WHOLE WIDE WORLD, THE(1965, Brit.); MAIN CHANCE, THE(1966, Brit.)

Marc Strange
Misc. Talkies
PAPER PEOPLE, THE(1969)

Mark Strange
ISABEL(1968, Can.)

Melanie Strange
SPLIT IMAGE(1982)

Peewee "Glenn" Strange
TENDERFOOT GOES WEST, A(1937)

Philip Strange
BEHIND THAT CURTAIN(1929); UNHOLY NIGHT, THE(1929); WALL STREET(1929); NOTORIOUS AFFAIR, A(1930); VENGEANCE(1930); BRIGHT LIGHTS(1931); MONEY FOR NOTHING(1932, Brit.); RETURN OF RAFFLES, THE(1932, Brit.); MAYFAIR GIRL(1933, Brit.); BORROWED CLOTHES(1934, Brit.);

LOYALTIES(1934, Brit.); NO ESCAPE(1934, Brit.); ROMANCE IN RHYTHM(1934, Brit.); SCARLET PIMPERNEL, THE(1935, Brit.); JURY'S EVIDENCE(1936, Brit.); HIGH COMMAND(1938, Brit.)
Silents
NEVADA(1927); SPORTING GOODS(1928); RESCUE, THE(1929)
Misc. Silents
POPULAR SIN, THE(1926); BROADWAY NIGHTS(1927); MAN POWER(1927)

Phillip Strange
Silents
ACE OF CADS, THE(1926)

Robert Strange
CHEAT, THE(1931); SMILING LIEUTENANT, THE(1931); MISLEADING LADY, THE(1932); GAMBLING(1934); THESE THIRTY YEARS(1934); FRISCO KID(1935); I FOUND STELLA PARISH(1935); SPECIAL AGENT(1935); BELOVED ENEMY(1936); LEATHERNECKS HAVE LANDED, THE(1936); MURDER OF DR. HARRIGAN, THE(1936); STORY OF LOUIS PASTEUR, THE(1936); TRAPPED BY TELEVISION(1936); WALKING DEAD, THE(1936); JOHN MEADE'S WOMAN(1937); MARKED WOMAN(1937); STOLEN HOLIDAY(1937); I STAND ACCUSED(1938); SKY GIANT(1938); ANGELS WASH THEIR FACES(1939); HELL'S KITCHEN(1939); IN NAME ONLY(1939); MADE FOR EACH OTHER(1939); SAINT STRIKES BACK, THE(1939); SPELLBINDER, THE(1939); STORY OF VERNON AND IRENE CASTLE, THE(1939); THEY MADE ME A CRIMINAL(1939); YOU CAN'T GET AWAY WITH MURDER(1939); CASTLE ON THE HUDSON(1940); DR. EHRLICH'S MAGIC BULLET(1940); GAMBLING ON THE HIGH SEAS(1940); ARIZONA CYCLONE(1941); DESERT BANDIT(1941); DEVIL AND DANIEL WEBSTER, THE(1941); HIGH SIERRA(1941); MANPOWER(1941); PAPER BULLETS(1941); ROBIN HOOD OF THE PECOS(1941); MAD MONSTER, THE(1942); SOUTH OF SANTA FE(1942); DEAD MEN WALK(1943); MR. LUCKY(1943); THOROUGHBREDS(1945); TREE GROWS IN BROOKLYN, A(1945); SILVER TRAILS(1948); FAR FRONTIER, THE(1949)

Steve Strange
URBAN COWBOY(1980)

Walter Strange
APPOINTMENT WITH MURDER(1948), ph; DEVIL'S CARGO, THE(1948), ph

Wanda Strange
NIGHT THE LIGHTS WENT OUT IN GEORGIA, THE(1981); SHARKY'S MACHINE(1982)

William Strange
MUDLARK, THE(1950, Brit.); PICKWICK PAPERS, THE(1952, Brit.)

Elena Strangelo
BREAKDOWN(1953)

The Strangers
KILLERS THREE(1968); FROM NASHVILLE WITH MUSIC(1969)

Judy Stranges
DRAGON WELLS MASSACRE(1957)

Nigel Strangeways
NIGHT OF BLOODY HORROR zero(1969)

Frank Strangio
BMX BANDITS(1983), m

Judy Strangis
PAY OR DIE(1960)

Roselyn Strangis
LOVES OF CARMEN, THE(1948)

Frantisek Strangmuller
JOURNEY TO THE BEGINNING OF TIME(1966, Czech), m

Alan Stranks
DICK BARTON–SPECIAL AGENT(1948, Brit.), w; ADVENTURES OF PC 49, THE(1949, Brit.), w; CASE FOR PC 49, A(1951, Brit.), w

Susan Stranks
BLUE LAGOON, THE(1949, Brit.); MADELEINE(1950, Brit.)

John Strannage
PACIFIC ADVENTURE(1947, Aus.)

Carl Strano
1984
DREAMSCAPE(1984); FEAR CITY(1984); NADIA(1984, U.S./Yugo.)

Dino Strano
DIRTY OUTLAWS, THE(1971, Ital.)

Hope Stransbury
BLOOD(1974, Brit.)

Otto Stransky
AFTER THE BALL(1932, Brit.), m

Patrick Straram
TAKE IT ALL(1966, Can.)

Lee Strasberg
SOMEWHERE IN THE NIGHT(1946), w; GODFATHER, THE, PART II(1974); CASSANDRA CROSSING, THE(1977); THREE SISTERS, THE(1977), d; ...AND JUSTICE FOR ALL(1979); BOARDWALK(1979); GOING IN STYLE(1979)

Morris Strasberg
Silents
BROKEN HEARTS(1926)

Susan Strasberg
COBWEB, THE(1955); PICNIC(1955); STAGE STRUCK(1958); SCREAM OF FEAR(1961, Brit.); ADVENTURES OF A YOUNG MAN(1962); DISORDER(1964, Fr./Ital.); KAPO(1964, Ital./Fr./Yugo.); MC GUIRE, GO HOME!(1966, Brit.); TRIP, THE(1967); BROTHERHOOD, THE(1968); CHUBASCO(1968); NAME OF THE GAME IS KILL, THE(1968); PSYCH-OUT(1968); SWEET HUNTERS(1969, Panama); WHO FEARS THE DEVIL(1972); AND MILLIONS WILL DIE(1973); ROLLERCOASTER(1977); IN PRAISE OF OLDER WOMEN(1978, Can.); MANITOU, THE(1978); RETURNING, THE(1983); SWEET SIXTEEN(1983)
Misc. Talkies
PSYCHO SISTERS(1972); SAMMY SOMEBODY(1976); BLOODY BIRTHDAY(1980)

Ivan Strasburg
LONG SHOT(1981, Brit.), ph
1984
1919(1984, Brit.), ph

Jeanne Straser
LADY IN THE DARK(1944)

Max Strassberg
SHERLOCK HOLMES AND THE DEADLY NECKLACE(1962, Ger.); THREE PENNY OPERA(1963, Fr./Ger.)

Morris Strassberg
WHERE IS MY CHILD?(1937); TEVYA(1939); WAY WE LIVE NOW, THE(1970); KLUTE(1971)
Misc. Talkies
POWER OF LIFE, THE(1938)
Alfred Strasser
DOLLY GETS AHEAD(1931, Ger.), m
J. Strasser
SECRET AGENT, THE(1936, Brit.), cos
Jonathan Strasser
FAME(1980)
Maximillian Strasser
"RENT-A-GIRL"(1965), ph
Robin Strasser
BRIDE, THE(1973)
Shirley Strasser
HUNGRY WIVES(1973)
David Strassman
HUMANOIDS FROM THE DEEP(1980)
Marcia Strassman
CHANGES(1969); SOUP FOR ONE(1982)
Toni Strassmeir
SHOEMAKER AND THE ELVES, THE(1967, Ger.)
Fritz Strassner
SERPENT'S EGG, THE(1977, Ger./U.S.)
J. Strassner
39 STEPS, THE(1935, Brit.), cos
Joe Strassner
STORMY WEATHER(1935, Brit.), cos; RHODES(1936, Brit.), cos; WE'RE GOING TO BE RICH(1938, Brit.), cos; UNDER YOUR HAT(1940, Brit.), cos
Z. Straszewski
BARRIER(1966, Pol.), art d
Marta Straszna
BEADS OF ONE ROSARY, THE(1982, Pol.)
Teresa Stratas
CANADIANS, THE(1961, Brit.); LA TRAVIATA(1982)
Walter Strate
VIOLATED(1953), d
Burt Stratford
CLOWN AND THE KIDS, THE(1968, U.S./Bulgaria)
Cameron Stratford
Silents
RANK OUTSIDER(1920, Brit.)
Caroline Stratford
MELODY(1971, Brit.)
Gwen Stratford
Silents
RANK OUTSIDER(1920, Brit.)
James Stratford
1984
MAN OF FLOWERS(1984, Aus.)
Laurie Stratford
1984
FLAMINGO KID, THE(1984)
Nancy Stratford
Silents
FLAMES OF FEAR(1930, Brit.)
Peggy Stratford
LEAVENWORTH CASE, THE(1936); TRAPPED(1937); TWO GUN LAW(1937); WHEN YOU'RE IN LOVE(1937)
Peter Stratford
DAY AFTER HALLOWEEN, THE(1981, Aus.)
Tracy Stratford
MIRACLE OF THE HILLS, THE(1959); SECOND TIME AROUND, THE(1961); EVIL OF FRANKENSTEIN, THE(1964, Brit.)
Peter Stratful
DAY THE FISH CAME OUT, THE(1967. Brit./Gr.)
David Strathairn
RETURN OF THE SECAUCUS SEVEN(1980); LOVESICK(1983); SILKWOOD(1983)
1984
BROTHER FROM ANOTHER PLANET, THE(1984); ICEMAN(1984)
Frank Strather
Silents
LITTLE LORD FAUNTLEROY(1914, Brit.)
Harry Strathey
STUDENT TOUR(1934)
Stefanos Stratigos
ASTERO(1960, Gr.); AUNT FROM CHICAGO(1960, Gr.)
Jan Stration
1984
JOY OF SEX(1984)
Art Straton
Silents
WESTERN HEARTS(1921)
Dora Stratou
BOY ON A DOLPHIN(1957), ch; DAY THE FISH CAME OUT, THE(1967. Brit./Gr.)
Tony Stratta
WOLFEN(1981)
Christopher W. Strattan
KILL SQUAD(1982), ph
George Strattan
POINT BLANK(1967)
Dorothy Stratten
SKATETOWN, U.S.A.(1979); THEY ALL LAUGHED(1981)
Dorothy R. Stratten
GALAXINA(1980)
Arthur Stratton
WOULD YOU BELIEVE IT!(1930, Brit.); GABLES MYSTERY, THE(1931, Brit.); GLAMOUR(1931, Brit.); RINGER, THE(1932, Brit.); CRIME AT BLOSSOMS, THE(1933, Brit.); WIVES BEWARE(1933, Brit.)

Misc. Silents
WOULD YOU BELIEVE IT!(1929, Brit.)
Bob Stratton
TOWARD THE UNKNOWN(1956); NO TIME FOR SERGEANTS(1958); OPERATION PETTICOAT(1959)
Carmel Stratton
ONE MORE TIME(1970, Brit.)
Chester Stratton
JULIUS CAESAR(1953)
Chet Stratton
GO NAKED IN THE WORLD(1961); LOVER COME BACK(1961); ADVISE AND CONSENT(1962); THOSE CALLOWAYS(1964); BUS RILEY'S BACK IN TOWN(1965); GREATEST STORY EVER TOLD, THE(1965); IN HARM'S WAY(1965); TRACK OF THUNDER(1967); IF HE HOLLERS, LET HIM GO(1968); JOURNEY TO SHILOH(1968); MARLOWE(1969); SWEET CHARITY(1969)
Gil Stratton
GIRL CRAZY(1943); TUCSON(1949); ARMY BOUND(1952); HERE COME THE MARINES(1952); BUNDLE OF JOY(1956); CAT FROM OUTER SPACE, THE(1978); SEXTETTE(1978)
Gil Stratton, Jr.
DANGEROUS YEARS(1947); HALF PAST MIDNIGHT(1948); MR. BELVEDERE GOES TO COLLEGE(1949); HOT ROD(1950); BATTLE ZONE(1952); HOLD THAT LINE(1952); MONKEY BUSINESS(1952); STALAG 17(1953); WILD ONE, THE(1953)
Inger Stratton
PLAYGROUND, THE(1965); CHAMBER OF HORRORS(1966); NAKED RUNNER, THE(1967, Brit.); GREAT NORTHFIELD, MINNESOTA RAID, THE(1972)
Jan Stratton
MAN, WOMAN AND CHILD(1983)
Jean Stratton
LUSTY MEN, THE(1952)
John Stratton
CURE FOR LOVE, THE(1950, Brit.); ISLAND RESCUE(1952, Brit.); MR. LORD SAYS NO(1952, Brit.); CRUEL SEA, THE(1953); ABANDON SHIP(1957, Brit.); DECISION AGAINST TIME(1957, Brit.); THIRD KEY, THE(1957, Brit.); TERROR FROM THE YEAR 5,000(1958); IT TAKES A THIEF(1960, Brit.); STRANGLER'S WEB(1966, Brit.); FRANKENSTEIN AND THE MONSTER FROM HELL(1974, Brit.)
Julia Stratton
MAN WITH TWO HEADS, THE(1972)
Leopold Stratton
TALES OF ORDINARY MADNESS(1983, Ital.)
Mel Stratton
RED RUNS THE RIVER(1963)
Richard A. Stratton
Misc. Silents
WORLD OF TODAY, THE(1915)
Sarah Jane Stratton
INTERLUDE(1968, Brit.)
Walter Stratton
SWEET CHARITY(1969)
William Stratton
Silents
INVADERS, THE(1929), t; OKLAHOMA KID, THE(1929), t
Gene Stratton-Porter
FRECKLES(1935), w; LADDIE(1935), w; ANY MAN'S WIFE(1936), w; HARVESTER, THE(1936), w; MICHAEL O'HALLORAN(1937), w; LADDIE(1940), w; FRECKLES COMES HOME(1942), w; MICHAEL O'HALLORAN(1948), w; FRECKLES(1960), w
Ninon Straty
LITTLE BOY LOST(1953)
Ursula Stratz
FOX AND HIS FRIENDS(1976, Ger.)
Agnes Straub
DAUGHTER OF EVIL(1930, Ger.)
Daniele Straub
NOT RECONCILED, OR "ONLY VIOLENCE HELPS WHERE IT RULES"(1969, Ger.)
Jean Marie Straub
NOT RECONCILED, OR "ONLY VIOLENCE HELPS WHERE IT RULES"(1969, Ger.), w
Jean-Marie Straub
CHRONICLE OF ANNA MAGDALENA BACH(1968, Ital., Ger.), d, w; NOT RECONCILED, OR "ONLY VIOLENCE HELPS WHERE IT RULES"(1969, Ger.), p, d, ed; MOSES AND AARON(1975, Ger./Fr./Ital.), d&w, ed
John Straub
PROJECT MOONBASE(1953)
Jurgen Straub
EXPOSED(1983)
Peter Straub
GHOST STORY(1981), w; HAUNTING OF JULIA, THE(1981, Brit./Can.), w
Sue Straub
PEER GYNT(1965)
Richard Straubb
RUN FOR THE HILLS(1953), w
I. Strauch
Misc. Silents
FORTY-FIRST, THE(1927, USSR)
Joe Strauch
IF WINTER COMES(1947)
Joe Strauch, Jr.
UNDER FIESTA STARS(1941); BELLS OF CAPISTRANO(1942); CALL OF THE CANYON(1942); HEART OF THE RIO GRANDE(1942); HOME IN WYOMIN'(1942); THIS TIME FOR KEEPS(1942); BENEATH WESTERN SKIES(1944)
Jurgen Strauch
NAKED AMONG THE WOLVES(1967, Ger.)
Maxim Strauch
Misc. Silents
STRIKE(1925, USSR)
Leslie Straughn
NATIVE SON(1951, U.S., Arg.)

Christopher Strauli
RISING DAMP(1980, Brit.)
Charles Straumer
BADGE OF MARSHAL BRENNAN, THE(1957), ph; RAIDERS OF OLD CALI-
FORNIA(1957), ph; SCARFACE MOB, THE(1962), ph; JOHNNY TIGER(1966), ph
Barnard Straus
NIGHT WATCH(1973, Brit.), p
Charles Straus
HITLER(1962), w
E. Charles Straus
HITLER(1962), p
Oscar Straus
MARRIED IN HOLLYWOOD(1929), m; ONE HOUR WITH YOU(1932), m; FORBID-
DEN MUSIC(1936, Brit.), m; MAKE A WISH(1937), m; CHOCOLATE SOLDIER,
THE(1941), m; LA RONDE(1954, Fr.), m
Sylvie Straus
ACT ONE(1964); GOODBYE COLUMBUS(1969)
Alfred Strauss
SITTING BULL(1954), p; PHONY AMERICAN, THE(1964, Ger.), p
Audrey Strauss
STALAG 17(1953)
Charles Strauss
MALTESE BIPPY, THE(1969)
Eduard Strauss
STORY OF VICKIE, THE(1958, Aust.)
Eduard Strauss, Jr.
ETERNAL WALTZ, THE(1959, Ger.)
Helen M. Strauss
MR. QUILP(1975, Brit.), p; INCREDIBLE SARAH, THE(1976, Brit.), p
Jack Strauss
WHO SAYS I CAN'T RIDE A RAINBOW!(1971)
Jacques Strauss
SECRET WORLD(1969, Fr.), p
Jacques E. Strauss
SICILIAN CLAN, THE(1970, Fr.), p
Jacques-Eric Strauss
WITHOUT APPARENT MOTIVE(1972, Fr.), p
Jay Strauss
SWEETHEART OF THE NAVY(1937), w
Joanne Strauss
CALIFORNIA SPLIT(1974); BLACK OAK CONSPIRACY(1977)
Johann Strauss
WALTZ TIME(1933, Brit.), w; SOUTHERN ROSES(1936, Brit.), m; GREAT WALTZ,
THE(1938), m; RULES OF THE GAME, THE(1939, Fr.), m; OH ROSALINDA(1956,
Brit.), p,d&w, m; BOUDU SAVED FROM DROWNING(1967, Fr.), m; MY FATHER'S
MISTRESS(1970, Swed.), m
Johann Strauss, Jr.
GREAT WALTZ, THE(1972), m
Johann Strauss, Sr.
GREAT WALTZ, THE(1972), m
John Strauss
MIKEY AND NICKY(1976), m
1984
AMADEUS(1984), a, md
Josef Strauss
GREAT WALTZ, THE(1972), m
M. Strauss
Silents
AMERICAN BUDS(1918), w
Malcolm Strauss
Misc. Silents
SALOME(1923), d
Melanie Strauss
LITTLE SEX, A(1982)
Oscar Strauss
SMILING LIEUTENANT, THE(1931), m; RUNAWAY QUEEN, THE(1935, Brit.), w,
m; LAST WALTZ, THE(1936, Brit.), w
Peter Strauss
HAIL, HERO!(1969); SOLDIER BLUE(1970); TRIAL OF THE CATONSVILLE NINE,
THE(1972); LAST TYCOON, THE(1976); SECRET OF NIMH, THE(1982); SPACEHUNT-
ER: ADVENTURES IN THE FORBIDDEN ZONE(1983)
Ralph Strauss
Silents
MARRIED ALIVE(1927), w
Richard Strauss
SUNSET BOULEVARD(1950), m; CATCH-22(1970), m
1984
2010(1984), m
Robert Strauss
NATIVE LAND(1942); SLEEPING CITY, THE(1950); SAILOR BEWARE(1951);
JUMPING JACKS(1952); ACT OF LOVE(1953); HERE COME THE GIRLS(1953);
MONEY FROM HOME(1953); REDHEAD FROM WYOMING, THE(1953); STALAG
17(1953); ATOMIC KID, THE(1954); BRIDGES AT TOKO-RI, THE(1954); MAN WITH
THE GOLDEN ARM, THE(1955); SEVEN YEAR ITCH, THE(1955); ATTACK!(1956);
FRONTIER GUN(1958); I, MOBSTER(1959); INSIDE THE MAFIA(1959); LI'L AB-
NER(1959); 4D MAN(1959); SEPTEMBER STORM(1960); WAKE ME WHEN IT'S
OVER(1960); DONDI(1961); GEORGE RAFT STORY, THE(1961); LAST TIME I SAW
ARCHIE, THE(1961); TWENTY PLUS TWO(1961); GIRLS! GIRLS! GIRLS!(1962);
THRILL OF IT ALL, THE(1963); WHEELER DEALERS, THE(1963); STAGE TO
THUNDER ROCK(1964); FAMILY JEWELS, THE(1965); HARLOW(1965); THAT
FUNNY FEELING(1965); FRANKIE AND JOHNNY(1966); MOVIE STAR, AMERI-
CAN STYLE, OR, LSD I HATE YOU!(1966); FORT UTAH(1967)
Theodore Strauss
MISS SUSIE SLAGLE'S(1945), w; CALIFORNIA(1946), w; ISN'T IT ROMAN-
TIC?(1948), w; MOONRISE(1948), w; MY OWN TRUE LOVE(1948), w
Wally Strauss
JESUS TRIP, THE(1971); HOW TO SUCCEED IN BUSINESS WITHOUT REALLY
TRYING(1976)

William Strauss
SMILING IRISH EYES(1929); JAZZ CINDERELLA(1930); TEXAS RANGERS,
THE(1936)
Silents
LAW OF THE SNOW COUNTRY, THE(1926); PRIVATE IZZY MURPHY(1926);
ANKLES PREFERRED(1927); KING OF KINGS, THE(1927); SHOW GIRL, THE(1927)
William H. Strauss
PUBLIC ENEMY, THE(1931); HARD TO HANDLE(1933); ONE HOUR LATE(1935);
THERE'S ALWAYS A WOMAN(1938); GOLDEN BOY(1939)
Silents
NORTH WIND'S MALICE, THE(1920); SKINNER'S DRESS SUIT(1926); LADIES AT
EASE(1927); RAGTIME(1927); SALLY IN OUR ALLEY(1927); RAWHIDE KID,
THE(1928); SO THIS IS LOVE(1928)
Misc. Silents
BARRICADE, THE(1921); MAGIC CUP, THE(1921); SOLOMON IN SOCIETY(1922)
William K. Strauss
LUCKY BOY(1929)
The Strauss Dancers
SWEET SURRENDER(1935)
Johann Strauss the Elder
STRAUSS' GREAT WALTZ(1934, Brit.), m
Johann Strauss the Younger
STRAUSS' GREAT WALTZ(1934, Brit.), m
Herbert Stravel
LILI MARLEEN(1981, Ger.), art d
Frank Stravenger
GUNS AND GUITARS(1936)
Edward Straviak
1984
MEMOIRS(1984, Can.), m
I. Stravinskiy
LAST GAME, THE(1964, USSR)
Igor Stravinsky
FIREBIRD, THE(1934), m; FANTASIA(1940), w; TRUTH, THE(1961, Fr./Ital.), m;
BALCONY, THE(1963), m; SOLDIER'S TALE, THE(1964, Brit.), m; ALLEGRO NON
TROPPO(1977, Ital.), m
John Stravinsky
UNMARRIED WOMAN, AN(1978)
Jack Straw
PAJAMA GAME, THE(1957); BIG BEAT, THE(1958); THIRTY FOOT BRIDE OF
CANDY ROCK, THE(1959); DON'T GO NEAR THE WATER(1975)
Mary Strawberry
BLOOD AND LACE(1971)
The Strawberry Alarm Clock
PSYCH-OUT(1968)
Strawberry Roan the Heifer Calf
STRAWBERRY ROAN(1945, Brit.)
Larry Strawbridge
HAWMPS!(1976); TOM HORN(1980)
Arthur Strawn
BLACK ROOM, THE(1935), w; LADY FROM NOWHERE(1936), w; MAN WHO
LIVED TWICE(1936), w; ROAD AGENT(1941), w; EYES OF THE UNDER-
WORLD(1943), w; AFFAIRS OF GERALDINE(1946), w; BAD MEN OF TOMB-
STONE(1949), w; FLIGHT TO MARS(1951), w; HIAWATHA(1952), w
Frank Strayer
ACQUITTED(1929), d; FALL OF EVE, THE(1929), d; BORROWED WIVES(1930), d;
LET'S GO PLACES(1930), d; ANYBODY'S BLONDE(1931), d; CAUGHT CHEA-
TING(1931), d; SOUL OF THE SLUMS(1931), d; BEHIND STONE WALLS(1932), d;
CRUSADER, THE(1932), d; DRAGNET PATROL(1932), d; DYNAMITE DENNY(1932),
d; GORILLA SHIP, THE(1932), d; MANHATTAN TOWER(1932), d; BY APPOINT-
MENT ONLY(1933), d, w; DANCE, GIRL, DANCE(1933), d; CROSS STREETS(1934),
d; FUGITIVE ROAD(1934), d; IN THE MONEY(1934), d; TWIN HUSBANDS(1934), d;
CONDEMNED TO LIVE(1935), d; GHOST WALKS, THE(1935), d; ONE IN A MIL-
LION(1935), d; PORT OF LOST DREAMS(1935), d; SOCIETY FEVER(1935), d; SYM-
PHONY OF LIVING(1935), d; DEATH FROM A DISTANCE(1936), d; SEA SPOILERS,
THE(1936), d; BIG BUSINESS(1937), d; DARING YOUNG MAN, THE(1942), d;
MAMA LOVES PAPA(1945), d; SENORITA FROM THE WEST(1945), d; I RING
DOORBELLS(1946), d; MESSENGER OF PEACE(1950), d; SEEDS OF DESTRUC-
TION(1952), d
Misc. Talkies
LOVE IN HIGH GEAR(1932), d
Silents
MAN WHO, THE(1921); NOW WE'RE IN THE AIR(1927), d; ROUGH HOUSE
ROSIE(1927), d; JUST MARRIED(1928), d; PARTNERS IN CRIME(1928), d
Misc. Silents
STEPPIN' OUT(1925), d; PLEASURE BEFORE BUSINESS(1927), d; MORAN OF
THE MARINES(1928), d
Frank M. Strayer
TANGLED DESTINIES(1932), d
Frank R. Strayer
MURDER AT MIDNIGHT(1931), d, w; VAMPIRE BAT, THE(1933), d; FIFTEEN
WIVES(1934), d; IN LOVE WITH LIFE(1934), d; PUBLIC OPINION(1935), d; HITCH
HIKE TO HEAVEN(1936), d; MURDER AT GLEN ATHOL(1936), d; BIG TOWN
GIRL(1937), d; BORROWING TROUBLE(1937), d; HOT WATER(1937), d; LAUGHING
AT TROUBLE(1937), d; OFF TO THE RACES(1937), d; BLONDIE(1938), d; BLONDIE
BRINGS UP BABY(1939), d; BLONDIE MEETS THE BOSS(1939), d; BLONDIE
TAKES A VACATION(1939), d; BLONDIE HAS SERVANT TROUBLE(1940), d;
BLONDIE ON A BUDGET(1940), d; BLONDIE PLAYS CUPID(1940), d; BLONDIE
GOES LATIN(1941), d; BLONDIE IN SOCIETY(1941), d; GO WEST, YOUNG LA-
DY(1941), d; BLONDIE FOR VICTORY(1942), d; BLONDIE GOES TO COL-
LEGE(1942), d; BLONDIE'S BLESSED EVENT(1942), d; FOOTLIGHT
GLAMOUR(1943), p&d; IT'S A GREAT LIFE(1943), p&d
Misc. Talkies
SICKLE OR THE CROSS, THE(1951), d
Silents
ENEMY OF MEN, AN(1925), d; LURE OF THE WILD, THE(1925), d; WHEN THE
WIFE'S AWAY(1926), d; BACHELOR'S BABY, THE(1927), d
Misc. Silents
FATE OF A FLIRT, THE(1925), d; SWEET ROSIE O'GRADY(1926), d

Dan Strayhorn
1984
DESIREE(1984, Neth.)
Vice Adm. Bernard M. Strean, U.S.N.
MIDWAY(1976), tech adv
Noel Streatfield
WELCOME, MR. WASHINGTON(1944, Brit.), w; AUNT CLARA(1954, Brit.), w
Paul Streather
STORM OVER THE NILE(1955, Brit.)
Monica Strebel
WOMAN ON FIRE, A(1970, Ital.)
Karel Strebl
FANTASTIC PLANET(1973, Fr./Czech.), anim
Marianna Strebly
WISE GIRL(1937)
Josef Strecha
INTIMATE LIGHTING(1969, Czech.), ph
Coolidge W. Streeler
Silents
ANTICS OF ANN, THE(1917), w
Meryl Streep
JULIA(1977); DEER HUNTER, THE(1978); KRAMER VS. KRAMER(1979); MANHATTAN(1979); SEDUCTION OF JOE TYNAN, THE(1979); FRENCH LIEUTENANT'S WOMAN, THE(1981); SOPHIE'S CHOICE(1982); STILL OF THE NIGHT(1982); SILKWOOD(1983)
1984
FALLING IN LOVE(1984)
A.G. Street
STRAWBERRY ROAN(1945, Brit.), w
Al Street
SO LONG, BLUE BOY(1973), ed
Carol Street
SPEED LOVERS(1968)
Chuck Street
1984
BEST DEFENSE(1984), stunts
David Street
HONEYMOON LODGE(1943); WE'VE NEVER BEEN LICKED(1943); ANGEL COMES TO BROOKLYN, AN(1945); I SURRENDER DEAR(1948); MOONRISE(1948); HOLIDAY RHYTHM(1950)
Elliott Street
GRISSOM GANG, THE(1971); HONKY(1971); WELCOME HOME, SOLDIER BOYS(1972); HARRAD EXPERIMENT, THE(1973); RECORD CITY(1978)
George Street
NIGHT JOURNEY(1938, Brit.); WHAT WOULD YOU DO, CHUMS?(1939, Brit.); LADY FROM LISBON(1942, Brit.); PIMPERNEL SMITH(1942, Brit.); OLD MOTHER RILEY, DETECTIVE(1943, Brit.); DREAMING(1944, Brit.); ADVENTURE FOR TWO(1945, Brit.); UNEASY TERMS(1948, Brit.); GLORY AT SEA(1952, Brit.); ONCE A SINNER(1952, Brit.); DIPLOMATIC CORPSE, THE(1958, Brit.); JACK THE RIPPER(1959, Brit.); PLEASE TURN OVER(1960, Brit.); MANIA(1961, Brit.); SECRET OF MONTE CRISTO, THE(1961, Brit.); WATCH YOUR STERN(1961, Brit.)
Herbert Street
STALAG 17(1953)
James Street
BISCUIT EATER, THE(1940), w; TAP ROOTS(1948), w; LIVING IT UP(1954), w; GOODBYE, MY LADY(1956), w
James H. Street
NOTHING SACRED(1937), w
Juanita Street
SUNDOWN ON THE PRAIRIE(1939)
Julian Street
I'M FROM MISSOURI(1939), w
Julian Leonard Street
YOU'RE TELLING ME(1934), w
Nicola Street
GYPSY GIRL(1966, Brit.)
Peter Miller Street
SAN DEMETRIO, LONDON(1947, Brit.)
Robert Street
VALLEY OF THE DOLLS(1967)
Coolidge Streeter
Silents
MAN FROM BEYOND, THE(1922), w; RAMSHACKLE HOUSE(1924), w
Edward Streeter
FATHER OF THE BRIDE(1950), w; FATHER'S LITTLE DIVIDEND(1951), w; MR. HOBBS TAKES A VACATION(1962), w
Reggie Streeter
LAST GANGSTER, THE(1937); JUVENILE COURT(1938)
Reginald Streeter
CIMARRON(1931)
Sydney Streeter
QUILLER MEMORANDUM, THE(1966, Brit.), p; BATTLE OF BRITAIN, THE(1969, Brit.), prod d
Wendy Strehlow
HOODWINK(1981, Aus.)
Herb Streicher
FEMALE RESPONSE, THE(1972)
Gerard Streiff
THINGS OF LIFE, THE(1970, Fr./Ital./Switz.)
Judith Streiner
THERE'S ALWAYS VANILLA(1972)
Russell Streiner
NIGHT OF THE LIVING DEAD(1968), a, p
Russell W. Streiner
THERE'S ALWAYS VANILLA(1972), p
Barbara Streisand
OWL AND THE PUSSYCAT, THE(1970)

Barbra Streisand
WAY WE WERE, THE(1973); FUNNY GIRL(1968); HELLO, DOLLY!(1969); ON A CLEAR DAY YOU CAN SEE FOREVER(1970); UP THE SANDBOX(1972); WHAT'S UP, DOC?(1972); FUNNY LADY(1975); STAR IS BORN, A(1976); FOR PETE'S SAKE(1977); MAIN EVENT, THE(1979), a, p; ALL NIGHT LONG(1981); YENTL(1983), a, p, d, w
David Streit
PROWLER, THE(1981), p
Steve Strelich
GOODBYE BROADWAY(1938)
P. Strelin
IDIOT, THE(1960, USSR)
M. Strelkova
CAPTAIN GRANT'S CHILDREN(1939, USSR)
Maria Strelkova
Misc. Silents
RANKS AND PEOPLE(1929, USSR)
V. Strelnikov
DESTINY OF A MAN(1961, USSR)
A. Strelnikova
DIMKA(1964, USSR)
Judd Strelo
LIAR'S DICE(1980)
Dorothy Strelsin
GURU, THE(1969, U.S./India); CHAMP, THE(1979)
Gesine Strempel
ALL-AROUND REDUCED PERSONALITY–OUTTAKES, THE(1978, Ger.)
Walter Strenge
MOTHER'S BOY(1929), ph; TALK OF HOLLYWOOD, THE(1929), ph; LOVE KISS, THE(1930), ph; BEFORE MORNING(1933), ph; DRUMS O' VOODOO(1934), ph; BURNING CROSS, THE(1947), ph; LIGHTHOUSE(1947), ph; ROAD TO THE BIG HOUSE(1947), ph; MESSENGER OF PEACE(1950), ph; MILLION DOLLAR PURSUIT(1951), ph; RODEO KING AND THE SENORITA(1951), ph; SECRETS OF MONTE CARLO(1951), ph; MR. WALKIE TALKIE(1952), ph; STAGECOACH TO FURY(1956), ph; GOD IS MY PARTNER(1957), ph; HIT AND RUN(1957), ph; LURE OF THE SWAMP(1957), ph; ROCKABILLY BABY(1957), ph; CRY TERROR(1958), ph; FRONTIER GUN(1958), ph; LITTLEST HOBO, THE(1958), ph; OUTCASTS OF THE CITY(1958), ph; LONE TEXAN(1959), ph; OKLAHOMA TERRITORY(1960), ph; THIRTEEN FIGHTING MEN(1960), ph; GUN FIGHT(1961), ph; VALLEY OF MYSTERY(1967), ph; SERGEANT RYKER(1968), ph
Sara Strengell
HOUSE ON 92ND STREET, THE(1945)
Nino Stresa
GOLIATH AND THE BARBARIANS(1960, Ital.), w; CENTURION, THE(1962, Fr./Ital.), w
Joe Stressner
MY LIPS BETRAY(1933), cos
Reggie Strester
CAPTAINS COURAGEOUS(1937)
Stretch Cox Troupe
FIRE DOWN BELOW(1957, U.S./Brit.)
George Stretton
HAPPY FAMILY, THE(1936, Brit.), ph; IT'S YOU I WANT(1936, Brit.), ph; JURY'S EVIDENCE(1936, Brit.), ph; LEAVE IT TO ME(1937, Brit.), ph; LIVE WIRE, THE(1937, Brit.), ph; MELODY AND ROMANCE(1937, Brit.), ph; AROUND THE TOWN(1938, Brit.), ph; BLONDES FOR DANGER(1938, Brit.), ph; I'VE GOT A HORSE(1938, Brit.), ph; RETURN OF THE FROG, THE(1938, Brit.), ph; HOME FROM HOME(1939, Brit.), ph; MISSING PEOPLE, THE(1940, Brit.), ph; MYSTERIOUS MR. REEDER, THE(1940, Brit.), ph; FLOODTIDE(1949, Brit.), ph; POET'S PUB(1949, Brit.), ph; HA' PENNY BREEZE(1950, Brit.), ph; PRELUDE TO FAME(1950, Brit.), ph; BLACKMAILED(1951, Brit.), ph
George Dudgeon Stretton
WATCH BEVERLY(1932, Brit.), ph; HONEYMOON FOR THREE(1935, Brit.), ph; JIMMY BOY(1935, Brit.), ph; LIEUTENANT DARING, RN(1935, Brit.), ph; LINE ENGAGED(1935, Brit.), ph; ROLLING HOME(1935, Brit.), ph; PRISON BREAKER(1936, Brit.), ph; WARNING TO WANTONS, A(1949, Brit.), ph
Claus D. Streuber
1984
FLIGHT TO BERLIN(1984, Ger./Brit.)
S. Strezhnev
KATERINA IZMAILOVA(1969, USSR)
Melissa Stribling
CROW HOLLOW(1952, Brit.); WIDE BOY(1952, Brit.); DECAMERON NIGHTS(1953, Brit.); GHOST SHIP(1953, Brit.); NOOSE FOR A LADY(1953, Brit.); OUT OF THE CLOUDS(1957, Brit.); HORROR OF DRACULA, THE(1958, Brit.); MURDER REPORTED(1958, Brit.); SAFECRACKER, THE(1958, Brit.); LEAGUE OF GENTLEMEN, THE(1961, Brit.); SECRET PARTNER, THE(1961, Brit.); ONLY WHEN I LARF(1968, Brit.); CRUCIBLE OF TERROR(1971, Brit.); CONFESSIONS OF A WINDOW CLEANER(1974, Brit.)
Joseph Strick
SAVAGE EYE, THE(1960), p,d&w; BALCONY, THE(1963), p, d; ULYSSES(1967, U.S./Brit.), p&d, w; RING OF BRIGHT WATER(1969, Brit.), p; DARWIN ADVENTURE, THE(1972, Brit.), p; ROAD MOVIE(1974), p&d; PORTRAIT OF THE ARTIST AS A YOUNG MAN, A(1979, Ireland), d; NEVER CRY WOLF(1983), p
Terence Strick
PORTRAIT OF THE ARTIST AS A YOUNG MAN, A(1979, Ireland)
Flora Stricker
HILLS HAVE EYES, THE(1978)
Vera Stricker
OPERATION CAMEL(1961, Den.)
Kenneth Strickfaden
MASK OF FU MANCHU, THE(1932), spec eff; MURDER AT DAWN(1932), spec eff
Amzie Strickland
MAN WITH THE GUN(1955); CAPTAIN NEWMAN, M.D.(1963); PENELOPE(1966); HARPER VALLEY, P.T.A.(1978); ONE AND ONLY, THE(1978)
Connie Strickland
ROOMMATES, THE(1973); ACT OF VENGEANCE(1974); BLACK SAMSON(1974)
Misc. Talkies
BUMMER(1973)

Frank Strickland
DERELICT, THE(1937, Brit.)
Gail Strickland
DROWNING POOL, THE(1975); BITTERSWEET LOVE(1976); BOUND FOR GLO-RY(1976); ONE ON ONE(1977); WHO'LL STOP THE RAIN?(1978); NORMA RAE(1979); UNCOMMON VALOR(1983)
1984
LIES(1984, Brit.); OXFORD BLUES(1984)
Misc. Talkies
LIES(1983)
Gerald Strickland
DRIFTER(1975)
Helen Strickland
SCOUNDREL, THE(1935)
Silents
HOUSE OF THE LOST CORD, THE(1915); STEADFAST HEART, THE(1923)
Misc. Silents
DAUGHTER OF MARYLAND, A(1917); GHOST OF OLD MORRO, THE(1917); MASTER PASSION, THE(1917); PRIDE(1917)
Mable Strickland
ROUGH RIDING RANGER(1935)
Marion Strickland
DANTE'S INFERNO(1935)
Maurice Strickland
EXCUSE MY GLOVE(1936, Brit.)
Ray Strickland
DOGPOUND SHUFFLE(1975, Can.)
Robert Strickland
GOOD NEWS(1947); SONG OF THE THIN MAN(1947); THIS TIME FOR KEEPS(1947)
Robert E. Strickland
GIRL CRAZY(1943)
Dan Strickler
1984
COLD FEET(1984)
Sherwood Strickler
VELVET TRAP, THE(1966), ph
Dean Stricklin
WARM IN THE BUD(1970)
Ray Stricklyn
CATERED AFFAIR, THE(1956); CRIME IN THE STREETS(1956); LAST WAGON, THE(1956); PROUD AND THE PROFANE, THE(1956); RACK, THE(1956); SOMEBODY UP THERE LIKES ME(1956); RETURN OF DRACULA, THE(1958); 10 NORTH FREDERICK(1958); BIG FISHERMAN, THE(1959); REMARKABLE MR. PEN-NYPACKER, THE(1959); LOST WORLD, THE(1960); PLUNDERERS, THE(1960); YOUNG JESSE JAMES(1960); ARIZONA RAIDERS(1965); TRACK OF THUN-DER(1967)
April Stride
MASTER OF BANKDAM, THE(1947, Brit.); IDOL OF PARIS(1948, Brit.); SERE-NADE(1956)
John Stride
BITTER HARVEST(1963, Brit.); MACBETH(1971, Brit.); SOMETHING TO HI-DE(1972, Brit.); JUGGERNAUT(1974, Brit.); BRANNIGAN(1975, Brit.); OMEN, THE(1976); OH, HEAVENLY DOG!(1980)
Karen Stride
VAMPIRE HOOKERS, THE(1979, Phil.)
Virginia Stride
I WANT WHAT I WANT(1972, Brit.)
Jochen Striebeck
FRIENDS AND HUSBANDS(1983, Ger.)
Karl Striebeck
FRIENDS AND HUSBANDS(1983, Ger.)
Peter Striebeck
FRIENDS AND HUSBANDS(1983, Ger.)
Whitley Strieber
WOLFEN(1981), w; HUNGER, THE(1983), w
Mary Strieff
GREAT MUPPET CAPER, THE(1981), cos
Dan Striepeke
FOLLOW THAT DREAM(1962), makeup; MAGIC SWORD, THE(1962), makeup; TARAS BULBA(1962), makeup; PICTURE MOMMY DEAD(1966), makeup; LADY IN CEMENT(1968), makeup; PLANET OF THE APES(1968), makeup; SECRET LIFE OF AN AMERICAN WIFE, THE(1968), makeup; BUTCH CASSIDY AND THE SUN-DANCE KID(1969), makeup; HELLO, DOLLY!(1969), makeup; JUSTINE(1969), make-up; UNDEFEATED, THE(1969), makeup; M(1970), makeup; TORA! TORA! TORA!(1970, U.S./Jap.), makeup; ESCAPE FROM THE PLANET OF THE APES(1971), makeup; MEPHISTO WALTZ, THE(1971), makeup; SEVEN MINUTES(1971), makeup; THING WITH TWO HEADS, THE(1972), makeup; WELCOME HOME, SOLDIER BOYS(1972), makeup; WHEN THE LEGENDS DIE(1972), makeup; SSSSSSSS(1973), p, w; ISLAND OF DR. MOREAU, THE(1977), makeup
1984
CITY HEAT(1984), makeup
Daniel Striepke
MAGNIFICENT SEVEN, THE(1960), makeup
Bill Striglos
STRAWBERRY STATEMENT, THE(1970)
Wladimir Strijewski
CRIME AND PUNISHMENT(1935, Fr.), w
Fran Striker
HI-YO SILVER(1940), w
Joseph Striker
HOUSE OF SECRETS(1929)
Silents
SILVER WINGS(1922); WHAT FOOLS MEN ARE(1922); STEADFAST HEART, THE(1923); PAINTED PEOPLE(1924); ANNIE LAURIE(1927); KING OF KINGS, THE(1927); PARADISE(1928, Brit.)
Misc. Silents
BROMLEY CASE, THE(1920); HELP YOURSELF(1920); SCRAP OF PAPER, THE(1920); MATRIMONIAL WEB, THE(1921); BROADWAY PEACOCK, THE(1922); QUEEN OF THE MOULIN ROUGE(1922); WILDNESS OF YOUTH(1922); WRECKER,

THE(1928, Brit.)
Stephen Strimpell
FITZWILLY(1967); JENNY(1969); HESTER STREET(1975); DEATH PLAY(1976); STRANGER IS WATCHING, A(1982)
1984
ALMOST YOU(1984)
Anita Strinberg
WOMEN IN CELL BLOCK 7(1977, Ital./U.S.)
Alf Kare Strindberg
EDVARD MUNCH(1976, Norway/Swed.)
Anita Strindberg
ALMOST HUMAN(1974,Ital.); TEMPTER, THE(1978, Ital.); SALAMANDER, THE(1983, U.S./Ital./Brit.)
August Strindberg
DANCE OF DEATH, THE(1971, Brit.), w
Goeran Strindberg
RATS, THE(1955, Ger.), ph
Goram Strindberg
CRIME AND PUNISHMENT(1948, Swed.), ph
Goran Strindberg
KING IN SHADOW(1961, Ger.), ph; DEVIL'S WANTON, THE(1962, Swed.), ph; NIGHT IS MY FUTURE(1962, Swed.), ph
Johnny Strindley
LAST PICTURE SHOW, THE(1971), m
Arthur Stringer
PURCHASE PRICE, THE(1932), w; LADY FIGHTS BACK(1937), w; BUCK BENNY RIDES AGAIN(1940), w
Silents
BREAKER, THE(1916), w; ARE ALL MEN ALIKE?(1920), w; PRAIRIE WIFE, THE(1925), w; WOMANHANDLED(1925), w; WILDERNESS WOMAN, THE(1926), w; COWARD, THE(1927), w; GUN RUNNER, THE(1928), w; HALF A BRIDE(1928), w
Charles Stringer
STONE(1974, Aus.)
Clint Stringer
KILLERS THREE(1968)
David Stringer
NEARLY A NASTY ACCIDENT(1962, Brit.), w; LAST CHASE, THE(1981), spec eff
Kimberly Stringer
1984
THIS IS SPINAL TAP(1984)
Lewis Stringer
DESIGN FOR MURDER(1940, Brit.)
Michael Stringer
FOR BETTER FOR WORSE(1954, Brit.), art d; TARZAN'S GREATEST ADVEN-TURE(1959, Brit.), art d; SUNDOWNERS, THE(1960), art d; IN SEARCH OF THE CASTAWAYS(1962, Brit.), art d; THREE LIVES OF THOMASINA, THE(1963, U.S./ Brit.), art d; SHOT IN THE DARK, A(1964), prod d; SQUADRON 633(1964, U.S./Brit.), prod d; 633 SQUADRON(1964), prod d; RETURN FROM THE ASHES(1965, U.S./Brit.), prod d; YOUNG CASSIDY(1965, U.S./Brit.), art d; INSPECTOR CLOUSEAU(1968, Brit.), prod d; ALFRED THE GREAT(1969, Brit.), prod d; ANGELS DIE HARD(1970); TOOMORROW(1970, Brit.), prod d; FIDDLER ON THE ROOF(1971), art d; ALICE'S ADVENTURES IN WONDERLAND(1972, Brit.), set d; ONE OF OUR DINOSAURS IS MISSING(1975, Brit.), art d; KILLING OF A CHINESE BOOKIE, THE(1976), ph; ROBIN AND MARIAN(1976, Brit.), prod d; GULLIVER'S TRAVELS(1977, Brit., Bel.), prod d; GREEK TYCOON, THE(1978), prod d; ESCAPE TO ATHENA(1979, Brit.), prod d; AWAKENING, THE(1980), prod d; AMERICANA(1981), ph; HOUND OF THE BASKERVILLES, THE(1983, Brit.), prod d
Mike Stringer
GUN RUNNER(1969); HARD ROAD, THE(1970)
Nick Stringer
SHOUT, THE(1978, Brit.)
R. M. Stringer
DOUBLE EXPOSURE(1982), ph
R. Michael Stringer
MOONSHINE COUNTY EXPRESS(1977), ph
Robert Stringer
ST. BENNY THE DIP(1951), m
Robert W. Stringer
JIGSAW(1949), m; SO YOUNG, SO BAD(1950), m; DAREDEVIL, THE(1971), d
Sheila Stringer
LEGEND OF BLOOD MOUNTAIN, THE(1965)
Misc. Talkies
LEGEND OF BLOOD MOUNTAIN, THE(1965)
Jennie Stringfellow
GAL YOUNG UN(1979)
Jean Stringham
HARRY'S WAR(1981)
Gleb Strinzhenov
CHEREZ TERNII K SVEZDAM(1981 USSR)
Elaine Stritch
SCARLET HOUR, THE(1956); THREE VIOLENT PEOPLE(1956); FAREWELL TO ARMS, A(1957); PERFECT FURLOUGH, THE(1958); WHO KILLED TEDDY BEAR?(1965); TOO MANY THIEVES(1968); SIDELONG GLANCES OF A PIGEON KICKER, THE(1970); SPIRAL STAIRCASE, THE(1975, Brit.); PROVIDENCE(1977, Fr.)
Misc. Talkies
KISS HER GOODBYE(1959)
Oliver Stritzel
DAS BOOT(1982)
Jerry Strivelli
1984
ONCE UPON A TIME IN AMERICA(1984)
Gleb Strizhenov
LAST GAME, THE(1964, USSR); OPTIMISTIC TRAGEDY, THE(1964, USSR); RED AND THE WHITE, THE(1969, Hung./USSR)
Oleg Strizhenov
QUEEN OF SPADES(1961, USSR); DUEL, THE(1964, USSR); OPTIMISTIC TRAGE-DY, THE(1964, USSR); THEY CALL ME ROBERT(1967, USSR); THREE SISTERS, THE(1969, USSR)

M. Strizhenova
SOUND OF LIFE, THE(1962, USSR)
Marina Strizhenova
GORDEYEV FAMILY, THE(1961, U.S.S.R.)
Vladimir Strizhevsky
Misc. Silents
GRIFFON OF AN OLD WARRIOR(1916, USSR); REVOLUTIONIST(1917, USSR)
Ben Strobach
CALLAWAY WENT THATAWAY(1951)
Stanislava Strobachova
MEPHISTO(1981, Ger.)
John Strobel
FOG, THE(1980)
Axel Strobye
CRAZY PARADISE(1965, Den.); GERTRUD(1966, Den.)
Hebert L. Strock
Misc. Talkies
WITCHES' BREW(1980), d
Herbert L. Strock
DONOVAN'S BRAIN(1953), ed; MAGNETIC MONSTER, THE(1953), ed; GOG(1954), d, ed; RIDERS TO THE STARS(1954), ed; BATTLE TAXI(1955), d; HOW TO MAKE A MONSTER(1958), d; I WAS A TEENAGE FRANKENSTEIN(1958), d; DEVIL'S MESSENGER, THE(1962 U.S./Swed.), d; RIDER ON A DEAD HORSE(1962), d; SILENT WITNESS, THE(1962), ed; CRAWLING HAND, THE(1963), d, w, ed; MONSTER(1979), d
Misc. Talkies
BLACK JESUS(1971, Ital.); BROTHER ON THE RUN(1973), d
Otto Strode
DAY THE EARTH FROZE, THE(1959, Fin./USSR), m
Warren Strode
ABDUL THE DAMNED(1935, Brit.), w
Warren Chetham Strode
TWO WHO DARED(1937, Brit.), w; HONEYMOON MERRY-GO-ROUND(1939, Brit.), w; OUTSIDER, THE(1949, Brit.), w; LADY WITH A LAMP, THE(1951, Brit.), w; AFFAIR IN MONTE CARLO(1953, Brit.), w
Woody Strode
GENGHIS KHAN(U.S./Brit./Ger./Yugo); SUNDOWN(1941); STAR SPANGLED RHYTHM(1942); NO TIME FOR LOVE(1943); BRIDE OF THE GORILLA(1951); LION HUNTERS, THE(1951); AFRICAN TREASURE(1952); CARIBBEAN(1952); CITY BENEATH THE SEA(1953); DEMETRIUS AND THE GLADIATORS(1954); GAMBLER FROM NATCHEZ, THE(1954); JUNGLE GENTS(1954); SON OF SINBAD(1955); TEN COMMANDMENTS, THE(1956); TARZAN'S FIGHT FOR LIFE(1958); PORK CHOP HILL(1959); LAST VOYAGE, THE(1960); SERGEANT RUTLEDGE(1960); SINS OF RACHEL CADE, THE(1960); SPARTACUS(1960); TWO RODE TOGETHER(1961); MAN WHO SHOT LIBERTY VALANCE, THE(1962); TARZAN'S THREE CHALLENGES(1963); PROFESSIONALS, THE(1966); SEVEN WOMEN(1966); SEATED AT HIS RIGHT(1968, Ital.); SHALAKO(1968, Brit.); BOOT HILL(1969, Ital.); CHE!(1969); ONCE UPON A TIME IN THE WEST(1969, U.S./Ital.); UNHOLY FOUR, THE(1969, Ital.); TARZAN'S DEADLY SILENCE(1970); DESERTER, THE(1971 Ital./Yugo.); LAST REBEL, THE(1971); BLACK RODEO(1972); GATLING GUN, THE(1972); REVENGERS, THE(1972, U.S./Mex.); ITALIAN CONNECTION, THE(1972, U.S./Ital./Ger.); WINTERHAWK(1976); KINGDOM OF THE SPIDERS(1977); JAGUAR LIVES(1979); RAVAGERS, THE(1979); CUBA CROSSING(1980); BLACK STALLION RETURNS, THE(1983); VIGILANTE(1983)
1984
COTTON CLUB, THE(1984); JUNGLE WARRIORS(1984, U.S./Ger./Mex.)
Misc. Talkies
LOADED GUNS(1975); OIL(1977, Ital.)
Diane Stroebel
1984
ALLEY CAT(1984)
Constantin Stroesco
MILLION, THE(1931, Fr.)
Dale Stroever
VOICES(1979)
Yvan Strogoff
WALK WITH LOVE AND DEATH, A(1969)
Heidi Stroh
LET'S TALK ABOUT WOMEN(1964, Fr./Ital.)
Kandice Stroh
FOXES(1980)
Theodore Strohbach
SEA DEVILS(1931)
William Strohbach
MAN FROM HEADQUARTERS(1942), ph; MARKED TRAILS(1944), p; FASHION MODEL(1945), p; THERE GOES KELLY(1945), p
Dr. Egon Strohm
MARTIN LUTHER(1953)
Tara Strohmeier
GREAT TEXAS DYNAMITE CHASE, THE(1976); HOLLYWOOD BOULEVARD(1976); MALIBU BEACH(1978); VAN NUYS BLVD.(1979)
Tara Strohmeir
KENTUCKY FRIED MOVIE, THE(1977)
George H. Strohsahl, Jr.
FINAL COUNTDOWN, THE(1980)
Michael Stroka
KING RAT(1965); HOUSE OF DARK SHADOWS(1970)
Mike Stroka
36 HOURS(1965)
Ed Stroll
WILD AND THE INNOCENT, THE(1959)
Edson Stroll
SNOW WHITE AND THE THREE STOOGES(1961); THREE STOOGES IN ORBIT, THE(1962); MC HALE'S NAVY(1964); MC HALE'S NAVY JOINS THE AIR FORCE(1965)
John Stroll
LOST COMMAND, THE(1966), art d

Louis J. Stroller
EDDIE MACON'S RUN(1983), p
Bob Strom
DREAM ON(1981)
Carl Strom
INTERMEZZO(1937, Swed.); DOLLAR(1938, Swed.); NIGHT IN JUNE, A(1940, Swed.); OCEAN BREAKERS(1949, Swed.); ILLICIT INTERLUDE(1954, Swed.); SECRETS OF WOMEN(1961, Swed.)
Diane Strom
RED LINE 7000(1965); EL DORADO(1967)
Millie Strom
WILD STRAWBERRIES(1959, Swed.), cos
Olaf Strom
Silents
LAST LAUGH, THE(1924, Ger.)
Gary Stromberg
CARWASH(1976), p; FISH THAT SAVED PITTSBURGH, THE(1979), p, w
Hunt Stromberg
OUR MODERN MAIDENS(1929), p; RED DUST(1932), sup; WET PARADE, THE(1932), p; PENTHOUSE(1933), p; PRIZEFIGHTER AND THE LADY, THE(1933), p; STAGE MOTHER(1933), p; WHITE SISTER, THE(1933), p; CHAINED(1934), p; LAUGHING BOY(1934), p; PAINTED VEIL, THE(1934), p; THIN MAN, THE(1934), p; TREASURE ISLAND(1934), p; AH, WILDERNESS!(1935), p; NAUGHTY MARIETTA(1935), p; AFTER THE THIN MAN(1936), p; GREAT ZIEGFELD, THE(1936), p; ROSE MARIE(1936), p; SMALL TOWN GIRL(1936), p; WIFE VERSUS SECRETARY(1936), p; FIREFLY, THE(1937), p; MAYTIME(1937), p; NIGHT MUST FALL(1937), p; MARIE ANTOINETTE(1938), p; SWEETHEARTS(1938), p; ANOTHER THIN MAN(1939), p; IDIOT'S DELIGHT(1939), p; WOMEN, THE(1939), p; NORTHWEST PASSAGE(1940), p; PRIDE AND PREJUDICE(1940), p; SUSAN AND GOD(1940), p; SHADOW OF THE THIN MAN(1941), p; THEY MET IN BOMBAY(1941), p; I MARRIED AN ANGEL(1942), p; LADY OF BURLESQUE(1943), p; GUEST IN THE HOUSE(1944), p; YOUNG WIDOW(1946), p; TOO LATE FOR TEARS(1949), p; BETWEEN MIDNIGHT AND DAWN(1950), p; MASK OF THE AVENGER(1951), p
Silents
ROARING RAILS(1924), sup, w; CRIMSON RUNNER, THE(1925), sup; OFF THE HIGHWAY(1925), sup; OUR DANCING DAUGHTERS(1928), p; THUNDER(1929), sup
Misc. Silents
BREAKING INTO SOCIETY(1923), d; FIRE PATROL, THE(1924), d; PAINT AND POWDER(1925), d
Soren Stromberg
VENOM(1968, Den.)
William R. Stromberg
CRATER LAKE MONSTER, THE(1977), p&d, w
Vinette Strombergs
HARD PART BEGINS, THE(1973, Can.)
Stromboli
ELEPHANT MAN, THE(1980, Brit.)
Fred Stromscoe
WESTBOUND(1959)
Fred Stromsoe
SEA CHASE, THE(1955); JESSE JAMES MEETS FRANKENSTEIN'S DAUGHTER(1966); LOVE BUG, THE(1968); DIRTY HARRY(1971); WHAT'S UP, DOC?(1972)
Fred Stromsor
KARATE KILLERS, THE(1967)
Ulla Stromstedt
CATALINA CAPER, THE(1967); TARZAN'S JUNGLE REBELLION(1970)
Gunnar Stromvad
CRAZY PARADISE(1965, Den.); OPERATION LOVEBIRDS(1968, Den.)
Tami Stronach
1984
NEVERENDING STORY, THE(1984, Ger.)
Adele Strong
SMASHING TIME(1967 Brit.); O LUCKY MAN!(1973, Brit.)
Arnold Strong
LONG GOODBYE, THE(1973)
Arnold Strong [Arnold Schwarzenegger]
HERCULES IN NEW YORK(1970)
Austin Strong
ALONG CAME LOVE(1937), w; SEVENTH HEAVEN(1937), w; THREE WISE FOOLS(1946), w
Silents
GOOD LITTLE DEVIL, A(1914), w; THREE WISE FOOLS(1923), w; SEVENTH HEAVEN(1927), w
Bert Strong
Silents
ISLE OF HOPE, THE(1925)
Bob Strong
MY FOOLISH HEART(1949); HELL BOUND(1957)
Rev. David Strong
MC MASTERS, THE(1970)
Dennis Strong
LOST AND FOUND(1979); STONE COLD DEAD(1980, Can.); TITLE SHOT(1982, Can.)
Erica Strong
GREAT SINNER, THE(1949)
Eugene Strong
FRONT PAGE, THE(1931); MEN OF AMERICA(1933); LET 'EM HAVE IT(1935)
Silents
INFIDELITY(1917); TRAIL OF THE SHADOW, THE(1917); DROPKICK, THE(1927); WARNING, THE(1927); WEB OF FATE(1927)
Misc. Silents
BORDER LEGION, THE(1919); STITCH IN TIME, A(1919); HIS TEMPORARY WIFE(1920); BETTER WAY, THE(1926); NOT FOR PUBLICATION(1927); CONEY ISLAND(1928)
Frederick Strong
Silents
JAVA HEAD(1923)

Gene Strong
ST. LOUIS KID, THE(1934)
Gwyneth Strong
NOTHING BUT THE NIGHT(1975, Brit.)
Gwynneth Strong
BLOODY KIDS(1983, Brit.)
J. M. Strong
Silents
MAN WHO COULD NOT LOSE, THE(1914)
Janet Strong
SLITHER(1973), cos
Jay Strong
Silents
DOING THEIR BIT(1918)
Jeri Strong
G.I. JANE(1951)
John Strong
DOBERMAN GANG, THE(1972); EARTHLING, THE(1980), p
John C. Strong III
1984
SAVAGE STREETS(1984), p
John Mikale Strong
NO MORE WOMEN(1934), w
Johnny Strong
FIRST YANK INTO TOKYO(1945); THOSE ENDEARING YOUNG CHARMS(1945); FEAR(1946)
L.A.G. Strong
IRISH FOR LUCK(1936, Brit.), w; DR. O'DOWD(1940, Brit.), w; BROTHERS, THE(1948, Brit.), w; MR. PERRIN AND MR. TRAILL(1948, Brit.), w; TONIGHT'S THE NIGHT(1954, Brit.), w
Larry Strong
BATTLESTAR GALACTICA(1979), ed
Leonard Strong
LITTLE TOKYO, U.S.A.(1942); MANILA CALLING(1942); UNDERGROUND AGENT(1942); BEHIND THE RISING SUN(1943); BOMBARDIER(1943); JACK LONDON(1943); SALUTE TO THE MARINES(1943); DRAGON SEED(1944); KEYS OF THE KINGDOM, THE(1944); UP IN ARMS(1944); BACK TO BATAAN(1945); BLOOD ON THE SUN(1945); FIRST YANK INTO TOKYO(1945); ANNA AND THE KING OF SIAM(1946); DANGEROUS MILLIONS(1946); BACKLASH(1947); JEWELS OF BRANDENBURG(1947); SWORD OF THE AVENGER(1948); WE WERE STRANGERS(1949); BACKFIRE(1950); CARGO TO CAPETOWN(1950); MALAYA(1950); ATOMIC CITY, THE(1952); DESTINATION GOBI(1953); NAKED JUNGLE, THE(1953); SCARED STIFF(1953); SHANE(1953); HELL'S HALF ACRE(1954); PRISONER OF WAR(1954); CULT OF THE COBRA(1955); LOVE IS A MANY-SPLENDORED THING(1955); KING AND I, THE(1956); JET ATTACK(1958); ESCAPE FROM ZAHRAIN(1962)
Mark Strong
LAST OUTPOST, THE(1935); MARKED WOMAN(1937); PLAINSMAN, THE(1937); MISSION TO MOSCOW(1943); KISS TOMORROW GOODBYE(1950)
Silents
KING OF KINGS, THE(1927)
Michael Strong
SLEEPING CITY, THE(1950); DETECTIVE STORY(1951); DEAD HEAT ON A MERRY-GO-ROUND(1966); POINT BLANK(1967); SECRET CEREMONY(1968, Brit.); PATTON(1970)
Patrick Strong
PRIVATE PARTS(1972)
Percy Strong
DEVIL'S MAZE, THE(1929, Brit.), ph; ALF'S BUTTON(1930, Brit.), ph; LATIN LOVE(1930, Brit.), ph; EAST LYNNE ON THE WESTERN FRONT(1931, Brit.), ph; HAPPY ENDING, THE(1931, Brit.), ph; NO LADY(1931, Brit.), ph; AFTER THE BALL(1932, Brit.), ph; GIRL IN THE FLAT, THE(1934, Brit.), ph; SOMETHING ALWAYS HAPPENS(1934, Brit.), ph; WOMAN IN COMMAND, THE(1934 Brit.), ph; LAST JOURNEY, THE(1936, Brit.), ph
Phil Strong
THESE THIRTY YEARS(1934), w; FARMER IN THE DELL, THE(1936), w
Porter Strong
Silents
MARTHA'S VINDICATION(1916); I'LL GET HIM YET(1919); OUT OF LUCK(1919); ROMANCE OF HAPPY VALLEY, A(1919); FLYING PAT(1920); IDOL DANCER, THE(1920); WAY DOWN EAST(1920); DREAM STREET(1921); ONE EXCITING NIGHT(1922); WHITE ROSE, THE(1923)
Misc. Silents
TURNING THE TABLES(1919)
Robert Strong
YOUTH RUNS WILD(1944); SUDAN(1945); THEY WERE EXPENDABLE(1945); KID FROM BROOKLYN, THE(1946); FORCE OF EVIL(1948); MISS GRANT TAKES RICHMOND(1949); SCENE OF THE CRIME(1949); MYSTERY STREET(1950); ENFORCER, THE(1951); TOO YOUNG TO KISS(1951); IT GROWS ON TREES(1952); MISSISSIPPI GAMBLER, THE(1953); CAPTAIN NEWMAN, M.D.(1963); HELLCATS, THE(1968)
Sidney Strong
Misc. Silents
DEVIL'S PROFESSION, THE(1915, Brit.)
Steve Strong
LOOKER(1981)
Steven Strong
TARZAN, THE APE MAN(1981)
Ted Strong
HARLEM GLOBETROTTERS, THE(1951)
Veronica Strong
JOEY BOY(1965, Brit.)
Jules Strongbow
ROAD TO ZANZIBAR(1941)
Mildred Stronger
NAKED CITY, THE(1948)
Strongheart
Silents
SILENT CALL, THE(1921)
Misc. Silents
LOVE MASTER, THE(1924)

Nipo T. Strongheart
YOUNG DANIEL BOONE(1950); PONY SOLDIER(1952)
Dorothy Strongin
BASKET CASE(1982)
Mimi Strongin
SLEEPING CITY, THE(1950)
Cyrus Strongshield
NORSEMAN, THE(1978)
Tara Stronmeier
TRUCK TURNER(1974)
Gloria Stroock
DAY OF THE LOCUST, THE(1975); FUN WITH DICK AND JANE(1977); COMPETITION, THE(1980); SEED OF INNOCENCE(1980); UNCOMMON VALOR(1983)
Trey Strood
1984
INITIATION, THE(1984)
Shireen Strooker
STILL SMOKIN'(1983)
Daniel Stroppa
1984
RUSH(1984, Ital.)
Lee Strosnider
SKYDIVERS, THE(1963), ph
Robin Strosnider
BIRCH INTERVAL(1976)
Raymond Stross
REVERSE BE MY LOT, THE(1938, Brit.), d; HELL IS SOLD OUT(1951, Brit.), p; FRIGHTENED BRIDE, THE(1952, Brit.), p; SHOOT FIRST(1953, Brit.), p; JUMPING FOR JOY(1956, Brit.), p; STAR OF INDIA(1956, Brit.), p; TOUCH OF THE SUN, A(1956, Brit.), p; ALLIGATOR NAMED DAISY, AN(1957, Brit.), p; AS LONG AS THEY'RE HAPPY(1957, Brit.), p; FLESH IS WEAK, THE(1957, Brit.), p; ANGRY HILLS, THE(1959, Brit.), p; QUESTION OF ADULTERY, A(1959, Brit.), p; NIGHT FIGHTERS, THE(1960), p; MARK, THE(1961, Brit.), p; VERY EDGE, THE(1963, Brit.), p, w; BRAIN, THE(1965, Ger./Brit.), p; LEATHER BOYS, THE(1965, Brit.), p; 90 DEGREES IN THE SHADE(1966, Czech./Brit.), p; FOX, THE(1967), p; MIDAS RUN(1969), p; I WANT WHAT I WANT(1972, Brit.), p; GOOD LUCK, MISS WYCKOFF(1979), p
Bill Strother
Silents
SAFETY LAST(1923)
Fred Strother
1984
MOSCOW ON THE HUDSON(1984)
James Strother
HEROES DIE YOUNG(1960)
Sanford Strother
1001 ARABIAN NIGHTS(1959), anim
Fred Strothers
FORT APACHE, THE BRONX(1981)
Charles Stroud
ROOMMATES, THE(1973)
Chuck Stroud
ROOMMATES, THE(1973), p
Clarence Stroud
ACE OF ACES(1933)
Claude Stroud
ALL ABOUT EVE(1950); BORDER RANGERS(1950); GUNFIRE(1950); I SHOT BILLY THE KID(1950); JACKPOT, THE(1950); TRAIN TO TOMBSTONE(1950); INTERRUPTED MELODY(1955); LOVE ME OR LEAVE ME(1955); CRY BABY KILLER, THE(1958); ROOKIE, THE(1959); BREAKFAST AT TIFFANY'S(1961); MY SIX LOVES(1963); PROMISES, PROMISES(1963); MAN FROM GALVESTON, THE(1964); HOW TO SAVE A MARRIAGE-AND RUIN YOUR LIFE(1968); J.W. COOP(1971)
Colin Stroud
OUTSIDER, THE(1949, Brit.)
Don Stroud
GAMES(1967); BALLAD OF JOSIE(1968); COOGAN'S BLUFF(1968); JOURNEY TO SHILOH(1968); MADIGAN(1968); WHAT'S SO BAD ABOUT FEELING GOOD?(1968); EXPLOSION(1969, Can.); ANGEL UNCHAINED(1970); BLOODY MAMA(1970); ...TICK...TICK...TICK...(1970); VON RICHTHOFEN AND BROWN(1970); JOE KIDD(1972); SCALAWAG(1973, Yugo.); SLAUGHTER'S BIG RIP-OFF(1973); MURPH THE SURF(1974); KILLER INSIDE ME, THE(1976); CHOIRBOYS, THE(1977); HOUSE BY THE LAKE, THE(1977, Can.); BUDDY HOLLY STORY, THE(1978); AMITYVILLE HORROR, THE(1979); NIGHT THE LIGHTS WENT OUT IN GEORGIA, THE(1981); SEARCH AND DESTROY(1981); SWEET SIXTEEN(1983)
Misc. Talkies
HOLLYWOOD MAN, THE(1976); SUDDEN DEATH(1977); STRIKING BACK(1981)
Duke Stroud
LONG RIDERS, THE(1980); PENNIES FROM HEAVEN(1981); ZOOT SUIT(1981); MAX DUGAN RETURNS(1983)
1984
FLESHBURN(1984)
Greg Stroud
1984
MELVIN, SON OF ALVIN(1984, Aus.)
Gregory Stroud
MIKADO, THE(1939, Brit.)
John Stroud
TOWN THAT DREADED SUNDOWN, THE(1977)
Pam Stroud
ROOMMATES, THE(1973)
Pauline Stroud
ALF'S BABY(1953, Brit.); LADY GODIVA RIDES AGAIN(1955, Brit.); LIFE IN EMERGENCY WARD 10(1959, Brit.)
Robert Stroud
1984
INITIATION, THE(1984)
Sally Ann Stroud
FOXY DROWN(1974)

Walter Stroud
DOWNHILL RACER(1969)

Charles Strouse
BONNIE AND CLYDE(1967), m; NIGHT THEY RAIDED MINSKY'S, THE(1968), m; THERE WAS A CROOKED MAN(1970), m; JUST TELL ME WHAT YOU WANT(1980), m; ANNIE(1982), w

Georges Strouve
EASY LIFE, THE(1971, Fr.), ph

Stroux
M(1933, Ger.)

Annette Stroyberg
TESTAMENT OF ORPHEUS, THE(1962, Fr.); EYE OF THE NEEDLE, THE(1965, Ital./Fr.)

Carmilla Stroyberg
BLOOD AND ROSES(1961, Fr./Ital.)

A. Stroyev
OPTIMISTIC TRAGEDY, THE(1964, USSR)

V. Stroyeva
BORIS GODUNOV(1959, USSR), d, w

Ye. Stroyeva
WAR AND PEACE(1968, USSR)

Tito Stroza
CAVE OF THE LIVING DEAD(1966, Yugo./Ger.)

Kay Strozzi
CAPTAIN APPLEJACK(1931); EX-LADY(1933)

Stefano Strucchi
REVOLT OF THE SLAVES, THE(1961, Ital./Span./Ger.), w; WONDERS OF ALADDIN, THE(1961, Fr./Ital.), w; AND SUDDENLY IT'S MURDER!(1964, Ital.), w; MAGNIFICENT CUCKOLD, THE(1965, Fr./Ital.), w; MANDRAGOLA(1966 Fr./Ital.), w; MAIDEN FOR A PRINCE, A(1967, Fr./Ital.), w

Stefano Strucci
DROP DEAD, MY LOVE(1968, Italy), w

Ben Struckman
Silents
BRAVE AND BOLD(1918), ph

Debbie Strudas
NIGHT THE LIGHTS WENT OUT IN GEORGIA, THE(1981)

Joseph Struder
SWISS MISS(1938)

Louis Struder
SWISS MISS(1938)

Maud Strudthoff
MYSTERY OF THE BLACK JUNGLE(1955), cos

Jane Strudwick
CHEAPER TO KEEP HER(1980)

Peter Strudwick
TIME TRAVELERS, THE(1964)

Shepperd Strudwick
FAST COMPANY(1938); CONGO MAISIE(1940); DR. KILDARE'S STRANGE CASE(1940); FLIGHT COMMAND(1940); ENCHANTMENT(1948); FIGHTER SQUADRON(1948); JOAN OF ARC(1948); ALL THE KING'S MEN(1949); CHICAGO DEADLINE(1949); RECKLESS MOMENTS, THE(1949); RED PONY, THE(1949); KID FROM TEXAS, THE(1950); LET'S DANCE(1950); THREE HUSBANDS(1950); PLACE IN THE SUN, A(1951); UNDER THE GUN(1951); AUTUMN LEAVES(1956); BEYOND A REASONABLE DOUBT(1956); EDDY DUCHIN STORY, THE(1956); SAD SACK, THE(1957); THAT NIGHT(1957); PSYCHOMANIA(1964); DARING GAME(1968); MONITORS, THE(1969); SLAVES(1969); COPS AND ROBBERS(1973)

Katherine Strueby
DEATH DRIVES THROUGH(1935, Brit.), w; EXCUSE MY GLOVE(1936, Brit.), w; CAFE COLETTE(1937, Brit.), w; HIGH COMMAND(1938, Brit.), w; SPECIAL EDITION(1938, Brit.), w; MAXWELL ARCHER, DETECTIVE(1942, Brit.), w; CANDLELIGHT IN ALGERIA(1944, Brit.), w; FLIGHT FROM FOLLY(1945, Brit.), w; THEY WERE SISTERS(1945, Brit.), w; CODE OF SCOTLAND YARD(1948), w; SHOWTIME(1948, Brit.), w; FORBIDDEN(1949, Brit.), w; EIGHT O'CLOCK WALK(1954, Brit.), w

Kay Strueby
SPITFIRE(1943, Brit.), w

Arkady Strugatsky
DEAD MOUNTAINEER HOTEL, THE(1979, USSR), w; STALKER(1982, USSR), w

Boris Strugatsky
DEAD MOUNTAINEER HOTEL, THE(1979, USSR), w; STALKER(1982, USSR), w

John Struges
CAPTURE, THE(1950), d

Ralph Struh
GOIN' DOWN THE ROAD(1970, Can.)

Hanns Strum
Silents
GOLEM: HOW HE CAME INTO THE WORLD, THE(1920, Ger.)

Joe Strummer
RUDE BOY(1980, Brit.), m; KING OF COMEDY, THE(1983)

Jack Strumwasser
Silents
BAR NOTHIN'(1921), w; LIVE WIRES(1921), w; LITTLE MISS SMILES(1922), w; OATH-BOUND(1922), w; PARDON MY NERVE!(1922), w; INNOCENCE(1923), w; ROUGH SHOD(1925), w

Kay Strunk
1984
REVENGE OF THE NERDS(1984)

M. Strunova
HOUSE ON THE FRONT LINE, THE(1963, USSR)

Gunther Strupp
HANSEL AND GRETEL(1965, Ger.), art d; SNOW WHITE(1965, Ger.), art d

George Strus
SHAFT(1971)

Karl Struss
COQUETTE(1929), ph; LADY OF THE PAVEMENTS(1929), ph; TAMING OF THE SHREW, THE(1929), ph; ABRAHAM LINCOLN(1930), ph; BAD ONE, THE(1930), ph; BE YOURSELF(1930), ph; DANGER LIGHTS(1930), ph; LUMMOX(1930), ph; ONE ROMANTIC NIGHT(1930), ph; KIKI(1931), ph; MURDER BY THE CLOCK(1931), ph; ROAD TO RENO(1931), ph; SKIPPY(1931), ph; UP POPS THE DEVIL(1931), ph;

WOMEN LOVE ONCE(1931), ph; DANCERS IN THE DARK(1932), ph; DR. JEKYLL AND MR. HYDE(1932), ph; FORGOTTEN COMMANDMENTS(1932), ph; GUILTY AS HELL(1932), ph; MAN FROM YESTERDAY, THE(1932), ph; SIGN OF THE CROSS, THE(1932), ph; TWO KINDS OF WOMEN(1932), ph; WORLD AND THE FLESH, THE(1932), ph; DISGRACED(1933), ph; ISLAND OF LOST SOULS(1933), ph; STORY OF TEMPLE DRAKE, THE(1933), ph; TONIGHT IS OURS(1933), ph; TORCH SINGER(1933), ph; WOMAN ACCUSED(1933), ph; BELLE OF THE NINETIES(1934), ph; FOUR FRIGHTENED PEOPLE(1934), ph; HERE IS MY HEART(1934), ph; PURSUIT OF HAPPINESS, THE(1934), ph; GOIN' TO TOWN(1935), ph; TWO FOR TONIGHT(1935), ph; ANYTHING GOES(1936), ph; GO WEST, YOUNG MAN(1936), ph; HOLLYWOOD BOULEVARD(1936), ph; PREVIEW MURDER MYSTERY(1936), ph; RHYTHM ON THE RANGE(1936), ph; TOO MANY PARENTS(1936), ph; DOUBLE OR NOTHING(1937), ph; LET'S MAKE A MILLION(1937), ph; MOUNTAIN MUSIC(1937), ph; THUNDER TRAIL(1937), ph; WAIKIKI WEDDING(1937), ph; EVERY DAY'S A HOLIDAY(1938), ph; SING YOU SINNERS(1938), ph; THANKS FOR THE MEMORY(1938), ph; ISLAND OF LOST MEN(1939), ph; PARIS HONEYMOON(1939), ph; SOME LIKE IT HOT(1939), ph; STAR MAKER, THE(1939), ph; ZENOBIA(1939), ph; GREAT DICTATOR, THE(1940), ph; ALOMA OF THE SOUTH SEAS(1941), ph; CAUGHT IN THE DRAFT(1941), ph; JOURNEY INTO FEAR(1942), ph; HAPPY GO LUCKY(1943), ph; RIDING HIGH(1943), ph; AND THE ANGELS SING(1944), ph; RAINBOW ISLAND(1944), ph; BRING ON THE GIRLS(1945), ph; MR. ACE(1946), ph; SUSPENSE(1946), ph; TARZAN AND THE LEOPARD WOMAN(1946), ph; HEAVEN ONLY KNOWS(1947), ph; MACOMBER AFFAIR, THE(1947), ph; DUDE GOES WEST, THE(1948), ph; SIREN OF ATLANTIS(1948), ph; BAD BOY(1949), ph; TARZAN'S MAGIC FOUNTAIN(1949), ph; FATHER'S WILD GAME(1950), ph; IT'S A SMALL WORLD(1950), ph; RETURN OF JESSE JAMES, THE(1950), ph; ROCKETSHIP X-M(1950), ph; TEXAN MEETS CALAMITY JANE, THE(1950), ph; TARZAN'S PERIL(1951), ph; FACE TO FACE(1952), ph; LADY POSSESSED(1952), ph; LIMELIGHT(1952), ph; ROSE OF CIMARRON(1952), ph; TARZAN'S SAVAGE FURY(1952), ph; FATAL DESIRE(1953), ph; TARZAN AND THE SHE-DEVIL(1953), ph; TWO NIGHTS WITH CLEOPATRA(1953, Ital.), ph; MESA OF LOST WOMEN, THE(1956), ph; MOHAWK(1956), ph; DEERSLAYER, THE(1957), ph; SHE DEVIL(1957), ph; ATTILA(1958, Ital.), ph; FLY, THE(1958), ph; HOT ANGEL, THE(1958), ph; MACHETE(1958), ph; RAWHIDE TRAIL, THE(1958), ph; ALLIGATOR PEOPLE, THE(1959), ph; HERE COME THE JETS(1959), ph; REBEL SET, THE(1959), ph; SAD HORSE, THE(1959), ph

Silents
SOMETHING TO THINK ABOUT(1920), ph; AFFAIRS OF ANATOL, THE(1921), ph; RICH MEN'S WIVES(1922), ph; SATURDAY NIGHT(1922), ph; THORNS AND ORANGE BLOSSOMS(1922), ph; HERO, THE(1923), ph; MOTHERS-IN-LAW(1923), ph; POOR MEN'S WIVES(1923), ph; LEGEND OF HOLLYWOOD(1924), ph; BEN-HUR(1925), ph; WINDING STAIR, THE(1925), ph; FOREVER AFTER(1926), ph; SPARROWS(1926), ph; BABE COMES HOME(1927), ph; SUNRISE–A SONG OF TWO HUMANS(1927), ph; BATTLE OF THE SEXES, THE(1928), ph; NIGHT WATCH, THE(1928), ph

Kurt Struss
KRONOS(1957), ph

Jan Struther
MRS. MINIVER(1942), w; MINIVER STORY, THE(1950, Brit./U.S.), w

Ian Struthers
FIRE MAIDENS FROM OUTER SPACE(1956, Brit.), ph; GIRL IN THE PICTURE, THE(1956, Brit.), ph; LADY OF VENGEANCE(1957, Brit), ph; COME BACK PETER(1971, Brit.), ph

Sally Struthers
GETAWAY, THE(1972)

Sally Ann Struthers
FIVE EASY PIECES(1970); PHYNX, THE(1970)

Stuart Strutin
STUCK ON YOU(1983), w
1984
FIRST TURN-ON!, THE(1984), w; STUCK ON YOU(1984), w

Bill Strutton
ASSIGNMENT K(1968, Brit.), w

Ardy Struwer
VIBRATION(1969, Swed.), a, w

Carel Struycken
SGT. PEPPER'S LONELY HEARTS CLUB BAND(1978); DIE LAUGHING(1980)

Carl Struycken
1984
PREY, THE(1984)

Amy Stryker
WEDDING, A(1978); LONG RIDERS, THE(1980)
1984
IMPULSE(1984)

Jack Stryker
NORMA RAE(1979); SILENT SCREAM(1980)
1984
HARD TO HOLD(1984)

Johathan Stryker
CURTAINS(1983, Can.), d

Jacek Strzemzalski
CONSTANT FACTOR, THE(1980, Pol.)

Vladislav Strzhelchik
GARNET BRACELET, THE(1966, USSR); WAR AND PEACE(1968, USSR)

Wolfgang Stuadte
TALE OF FIVE WOMEN, A(1951, Brit.), d

Aimee Stuart
NINE TILL SIX(1932, Brit.), w; BORROWED CLOTHES(1934, Brit.), w; GIRL IN DISTRESS(1941, Brit.), w; GENTLE SEX, THE(1943, Brit.), w; WICKED LADY, THE(1946, Brit.), w; MAN OF EVIL(1948, Brit.), w; LET'S BE HAPPY(1957, Brit.), w

Alan Stuart
ROCK AROUND THE WORLD(1957, Brit.); SUPERMAN II(1980)
1984
COMFORT AND JOY(1984, Brit.)

Alexander Stuart
1984
ORDEAL BY INNOCENCE(1984, Brit.), w

Alexandra Stuart
Misc. Talkies
SLAP IN THE FACE(1974)
Allen Stuart
UNASHAMED(1938), d
Amy Stuart
HAIL, HERO!(1969)
Andy Stuart
I LOVE MY WIFE(1970)
Angela Stuart
NORTHWEST OUTPOST(1947), w
Anthony Stuart
DAY AND THE HOUR, THE(1963, Fr./ Ital.); LAFAYETTE(1963, Fr.); WEEKEND AT DUNKIRK(1966, Fr./Ital.); MAYERLING(1968, Brit./Fr.)
Arlen Stuart
TOP BANANA(1954); PILLOW TALK(1959); MAJORITY OF ONE, A(1961); KISS ME, STUPID(1964); KOTCH(1971); BEN(1972)
Arlene Stuart
HARPER VALLEY, P.T.A.(1978)
Barbara Stuart
MARINES, LET'S GO(1961); HELLFIGHTERS(1968); DREAMER(1979)
Billy Stuart
MR. H. C. ANDERSEN(1950, Brit.)
Binkie Stuart
LITTLE MISS SOMEBODY(1937, Brit.); SPLINTERS IN THE AIR(1937, Brit.); LITTLE DOLLY DAYDREAM(1938, Brit.); MOONLIGHT SONATA(1938, Brit.); ROSE OF TRALEE(1938, Ireland); TORPEDOED!(1939); LITTLE MISS MOLLY(1940)
Brian Stuart
SORCERESS(1983), d
Misc. Talkies
SORCERESS(1983), d
C.S. Stuart
ONCE MORE, WITH FEELING(1960)
Cassie Stuart
1984
ORDEAL BY INNOCENCE(1984, Brit.); SLAYGROUND(1984, Brit.)
Catherine Mary Stuart
APPLE, THE(1980 U.S./Ger.)
Chad Stuart
THREE IN THE ATTIC(1968), m
Charles Stuart
DARK ROAD, THE(1948, Brit.)
Clint Stuart
PASSAGE WEST(1951)
Dempsey Stuart
FALSE EVIDENCE(1937, Brit.); MURDER TOMORROW(1938, Brit.)
Dick Stuart
Misc. Talkies
IF YOU DON'T STOP IT, YOU'LL GO BLIND(1977)
Donald Stuart
INTERFERENCE(1928); DERELICT(1930); LONDON MELODY(1930, Brit.), p,d&w; SISTER TO ASSIST'ER, A(1930, Brit.); MAN FROM YESTERDAY, THE(1932); INVISIBLE MAN, THE(1933); MAN OUTSIDE, THE(1933, Brit.), w; WOMAN ACCUSED(1933); DANCING MAN(1934); RIP TIDE(1934); SHADOW, THE(1936, Brit.), w; FOREIGN CORRESPONDENT(1940); OLD BILL AND SON(1940, Brit.); YANK IN THE R.A.F., A(1941); DESTINATION UNKNOWN(1942); EAGLE SQUADRON(1942); UNDYING MONSTER, THE(1942); IMMORTAL SERGEANT, THE(1943); CANTERVILLE GHOST, THE(1944); HOUR BEFORE THE DAWN, THE(1944); LODGER, THE(1944); PASSAGE TO MARSEILLE(1944); SHERLOCK HOLMES AND THE SPIDER WOMAN(1944); DEVOTION(1946)
Silents
BEAU GESTE(1926); BRIDE OF THE STORM(1926); LONE EAGLE, THE(1927); OLYMPIC HERO, THE(1928)
Misc. Silents
NATURE GIRL, THE(1919)
Dorrell Stuart
HELLFIRE(1949), w
Douglas Stuart
SATURDAY NIGHT REVUE(1937, Brit.)
Silents
FORBIDDEN CARGOES(1925, Brit.), w
Eleanor Stuart
FORBIDDEN JOURNEY(1950, Can.); THIRTEENTH LETTER, THE(1951); OEDIPUS REX(1957, Can.)
Elizabeth Stuart
POLICEWOMAN(1974)
Emilia Stuart
SHARK(1970, U.S./Mex.)
Eric Stuart
OLD MOTHER RILEY'S GHOSTS(1941, Brit.)
Ethel Stuart
PRIMROSE PATH, THE(1934, Brit.)
Fiona Stuart
KEEP YOUR SEATS PLEASE(1936, Brit.)
Giacomo Rossi Stuart
FAREWELL TO ARMS, A(1957); DAY THE SKY EXPLODED, THE(1958, Fr./Ital.); HOUSE OF INTRIGUE, THE(1959, Ital.); FIVE BRANDED WOMEN(1960); AVENGER, THE(1962, Fr./Ital.); SODOM AND GOMORRAH(1962, U.S./Fr./Ital.); GRINGO(1963, Span./Ital.); INVASION 1700!(1965, Fr./Ital./Yugo.); REVENGE OF THE GLADIATORS(1965, Ital.) SEVEN SLAVES AGAINST THE WORLD(1965, Ital.); KILL BABY KILL(1966, Ital.); MYSTERY OF THUG ISLAND, THE(1966, Ital./Ger.); HORNET'S NEST(1970); WEEKEND MURDERS, THE(1972, Ital.); TO KILL OR TO DIE(1973, Ital.)
Gil Stuart
SCARLET COAT, THE(1955); DEVIL'S HAIRPIN, THE(1957); MORITURI(1965); SOUND OF MUSIC, THE(1965); HICKEY AND BOGGS(1972)
Gilchrist Stuart
CHARLEY'S AUNT(1941); YANK IN THE R.A.F., A(1941); FOREVER AMBER(1947); FIGHTER SQUADRON(1948); SWORD IN THE DESERT(1949); FANCY PANTS(1950); EAST OF SUMATRA(1953); KING OF THE KHYBER RIFLES(1953)

Gilcrist Stuart
ASSAULT ON A QUEEN(1966)
Gina Stuart
BIG DOLL HOUSE, THE(1971)
Glenn Stuart
Misc. Talkies
WEST OF DODGE CITY(1947)
Gloria Stuart
AIR MAIL(1932); ALL-AMERICAN, THE(1932); OLD DARK HOUSE, THE(1932); STREET OF WOMEN(1932); GIRL IN 419(1933); INVISIBLE MAN, THE(1933); IT'S GREAT TO BE ALIVE(1933); KISS BEFORE THE MIRROR, THE(1933); LAUGHTER IN HELL(1933); PRIVATE JONES(1933); ROMAN SCANDALS(1933); SECRET OF THE BLUE ROOM(1933); SWEEPINGS(1933); BELOVED(1934); GIFT OF GAB(1934); HERE COMES THE NAVY(1934); I LIKE IT THAT WAY(1934); I'LL TELL THE WORLD(1934); LOVE CAPTIVE, THE(1934); GOLD DIGGERS OF 1935(1935); LADDIE(1935); MAYBE IT'S LOVE(1935); CRIME OF DR. FORBES(1936); GIRL ON THE FRONT PAGE, THE(1936); POOR LITTLE RICH GIRL(1936); PRISONER OF SHARK ISLAND, THE(1936); PROFESSIONAL SOLDIER(1936); THIRTY SIX HOURS TO KILL(1936); WANTED: JANE TURNER(1936); GIRL OVERBOARD(1937); LADY ESCAPES, THE(1937); LIFE BEGINS IN COLLEGE(1937); CHANGE OF HEART(1938); ISLAND IN THE SKY(1938); KEEP SMILING(1938); LADY OBJECTS, THE(1938); REBECCA OF SUNNYBROOK FARM(1938); TIME OUT FOR MURDER(1938); IT COULD HAPPEN TO YOU(1939); THREE MUSKETEERS, THE(1939); WINNER TAKE ALL(1939); HERE COMES ELMER(1943); ENEMY OF WOMEN(1944); WHISTLER, THE(1944); SHE WROTE THE BOOK(1946)
1984
MASS APPEAL(1984)
Graham Stuart
GHOST SHIP(1953, Brit.); STRANGER FROM VENUS, THE(1954, Brit.); CONSTANT HUSBAND, THE(1955, Brit.); STOLEN ASSIGNMENT(1955, Brit.); WHAT A WHOPPER(1961, Brit.)
Greg Stuart
HELL SQUAD(1958)
Hardy Stuart
HORNET'S NEST(1970)
Helen Stuart
FORBIDDEN(1932)
Henry Stuart
Misc. Silents
SAJENKO THE SOVIET(1929, Ger.)
Ian Stuart
HAPPY GO LOVELY(1951, Brit.); LIMPING MAN, THE(1953, Brit.), w
Ian Stuart [Alistair MacLean]
SATAN BUG, THE(1965), w
Iris Stuart
Silents
CASEY AT THE BAT(1927); CHILDREN OF DIVORCE(1927); WEDDING BILL$(1927)
Misc. Silents
STRANDED IN PARIS(1926)
Jack Stuart
MYSTERY TRAIN(1931); OPERATION DISASTER(1951, Brit.); GLASS SPHINX, THE(1968, Egypt/Ital./Span.); FIVE MAN ARMY, THE(1970, Ital.)
Jack Stuart [Giacomo Rossi-Stuart]
LAST DAY OF THE WAR, THE(1969, U.S./Ital./Span.); WAR BETWEEN THE PLANETS(1971, Ital.)
Jade Stuart
MONSTER(1979)
James Stuart
NAVY BLUE AND GOLD(1937)
Jane Stuart
RAMPARTS WE WATCH, THE(1940)
Janet Stuart
YOICKS!(1932, Brit.)
Jean Stuart
KING OF PARIS, THE(1934, Brit.); BONNIE PRINCE CHARLIE(1948, Brit.); TWICE UPON A TIME(1953, Brit.)
Misc. Silents
RAINBOW, THE(1917)
Jeanne Stuart
LIMPING MAN, THE(1931, Brit.); MISCHIEF(1931, Brit.); SAFE AFFAIR, A(1931, Brit.); LEAP YEAR(1932, Brit.); LIFE GOES ON(1932, Brit.); MEDICINE MAN, THE(1933, Brit.); WHITE FACE(1933, Brit.); BELLA DONNA(1934, Brit.); GREAT DEFENDER, THE(1934, Brit.); MY HEART IS CALLING(1935, Brit.); MURDER ON THE SET(1936, Brit.); SHADOW, THE(1936, Brit.); FOREVER YOURS(1937, Brit.); BANK HOLIDAY(1938, Brit.); KATHLEEN(1938, Ireland); OLD MOTHER RILEY JOINS UP(1939, Brit.)
Jerry Stuart
SERVANTS' ENTRANCE(1934)
Jessica Stuart
DIRT GANG, THE(1972)
Joan Stuart
TIKI TIKI(1971, Can.); IN PRAISE OF OLDER WOMEN(1978, Can.)
John Stuart
ATLANTIC(1929 Brit.); HIGH SEAS(1929, Brit.); KITTY(1929, Brit.); TAXI FOR TWO(1929, Brit.); BRAT, THE(1930, Brit.); CHILDREN OF CHANCE(1930, Brit.); KISSING CUP'S RACE(1930, Brit.); NO EXIT(1930, Brit.); HINDLE WAKES(1931, Brit.); HOUND OF THE BASKERVILLES(1932, Brit.); MEN OF STEEL(1932, Brit.); MISTRESS OF ATLANTIS, THE(1932, Ger.); NUMBER SEVENTEEN(1932, Brit.); VERDICT OF THE SEA(1932, Brit.); ENEMY OF THE POLICE(1933, Brit.); HEAD OF THE FAMILY(1933, Brit.); HOME, SWEET HOME(1933, Brit.); HOUSE OF TRENT, THE(1933, Brit.); LOVE'S OLD SWEET SONG(1933, Brit.); MAYFAIR GIRL(1933, Brit.); MR. QUINCEY OF MONTE CARLO(1933, Brit.); NAUGHTY CINDERELLA(1933, Brit.); THIS WEEK OF GRACE(1933, Brit.); BELLA DONNA(1934, Brit.); BLACK ABBOT, THE(1934, Brit.); BLIND JUSTICE(1934, Brit.); BLUE SQUADRON, THE(1934, Brit.); FOUR MASKED MEN(1934, Brit.); GRAND PRIX(1934, Brit.); GREEN PACK, THE(1934, Brit.); POINTING FINGER, THE(1934, Brit.); ABDUL THE DAMNED(1935, Brit.); IN A MONASTERY GARDEN(1935, Brit.); LEND ME YOUR HUSBAND(1935, Brit.); ONCE A THIEF(1935, Brit.); REGAL CAVALCADE(1935, Brit.); WANDERING JEW, THE(1935, Brit.); REASONABLE DOUBT(1936, Brit.); SECRET

VOICE, THE(1936, Brit.); ELDER BROTHER, THE(1937, Brit.); LOST CHORD, THE(1937, Brit.); PEARLS BRING TEARS(1937, Brit.); SHOW GOES ON, THE(1937, Brit.); TALKING FEET(1937, Brit.); CLAYDON TREASURE MYSTERY, THE(1938, Brit.); CAPTAIN MOONLIGHT(1940, Brit.); OLD MOTHER RILEY IN SOCIETY(1940, Brit.); BANANA RIDGE(1941, Brit.); COURAGEOUS MR. PENN, THE(1941, Brit.); HARD STEEL(1941, Brit.); OLD MOTHER RILEY'S GHOSTS(1941, Brit.); SEVENTH SURVIVOR, THE(1941, Brit.); BIG BLOCKADE, THE(1942, Brit.); FLYING FOR-TRESS(1942, Brit.); MISSING MILLION, THE(1942, Brit.); SHIPS WITH WINGS(1942, Brit.); WOMEN AREN'T ANGELS(1942, Brit.); HEADLINE(1943, Brit.); CANDLES AT NINE(1944, Brit.); MADONNA OF THE SEVEN MOONS(1945, Brit.); HOUSE OF DARKNESS(1948, Brit.); MINE OWN EXECUTIONER(1948, Brit.); MAN FROM YESTERDAY, THE(1949, Brit.); MAN ON THE RUN(1949, Brit.); TEMPTRESS, THE(1949, Brit.); MRS. FITZHERBERT(1950, Brit.); THIRD TIME LUCKY(1950, Brit.); MAGIC BOX, THE(1952, Brit.); BOTH SIDES OF THE LAW(1953, Brit.); FOUR SIDED TRIANGLE(1953, Brit.); MR. DENNING DRIVES NORTH(1953, Brit.); RINGER, THE(1953, Brit.); WOMAN IN HIDING(1953, Brit.); GILDED CAGE, THE(1954, Brit.); ALIAS JOHN PRESTON(1956); EYEWITNESS(1956, Brit.); IT'S A GREAT DAY(1956, Brit.); JOHNNY, YOU'RE WANTED(1956, Brit.); TONS OF TROUBLE(1956, Brit.); ENEMY FROM SPACE(1957, Brit.); MEN OF SHERWOOD FOREST(1957, Brit.); BLOOD OF THE VAMPIRE(1958, Brit.); CHAIN OF EVENTS(1958, Brit.); FURTHER UP THE CREEK!(1958, Brit.); REVENGE OF FRANKENSTEIN, THE(1958, Brit.); SECRET MAN, THE(1958, Brit.); YOUR PAST IS SHOWING(1958, Brit.); MUMMY, THE(1959, Brit.); TOO MANY CROOKS(1959, Brit.); BOTTOMS UP(1960, Brit.); SINK THE BISMARCK!(1960, Brit.); VILLAGE OF THE DAMNED(1960, Brit.); PARA-NOIAC(1963, Brit.); YOUNG WINSTON(1972, Brit.); SUPERMAN(1978)

Silents

IF FOUR WALLS TOLD(1922, Brit.); ALLEY OF GOLDEN HEARTS, THE(1924, Brit.); DAUGHTER OF LOVE, A(1925, Brit.); PLEASURE GARDEN, THE(1925, Brit./Ger.); ROSES OF PICARDY(1927, Brit.); SMASHING THROUGH(1928, Brit.)

Misc. Silents

GREAT GAY ROAD, THE(1920, Brit.); LAND OF MY FATHERS(1921, Brit.); LITTLE MOTHER, THE(1922, Brit.); SINISTER STREET(1922, Brit.); SPORTING DOUBLE, A(1922, Brit.); LITTLE MISS NOBODY(1923, Brit.); LOVES OF MARY, QUEEN OF SCOTS, THE(1923); SCHOOL FOR SCANDAL, THE(1923, Brit.); THIS FREEDOM(1923, Brit.); GAYEST OF THE GAY, THE(1924, Brit.); HIS GRACE GIVES NOTICE(1924, Brit.); VENETIAN LOVERS(1925, Brit.); WE WOMEN(1925, Brit.); FANNY HAW-THORNE(1927, Brit.); FLIGHT COMMANDER, THE(1927); GLAD EYE, THE(1927, Brit.); WOMAN IN PAWN, A(1927, Brit.); SAILORS DON'T CARE(1928, Brit.); KITTY(1929, Brit.)

John Easton Stuart
MAN WITH TWO BRAINS, THE(1983)

John "Easton" Stuart
DEAD MEN DON'T WEAR PLAID(1982)

John Worthington Stuart
1984
CANNONBALL RUN II(1984)

Josephine Stuart
LOVES OF JOANNA GODDEN, THE(1947, Brit.); SILVER DARLINGS, THE(1947, Brit.); FLY AWAY PETER(1948, Brit.); MY BROTHER JONATHAN(1949, Brit.); OLIVER TWIST(1951, Brit.); STRAW MAN, THE(1953, Brit.); WEAK AND THE WICKED, THE(1954, Brit.); NO TIME FOR TEARS(1957, Brit.); NIGHT TRAIN FOR INVERNESS(1960, Brit.)

Julia Stuart
Silents
ARRIVAL OF PERPETUA, THE(1915); COTTON KING, THE(1915); LITTLE MISS BROWN(1915); BALLET GIRL, THE(1916); COMMON LAW, THE(1916); FRUITS OF DESIRE, THE(1916); LIFE'S WHIRLPOOL(1916); CRIMSON DOVE, THE(1917); NORTH WIND'S MALICE, THE(1920)

Misc. Silents
BOSS, THE(1915); BUTTERFLY, THE(1915); TRAVELING SALESMAN, THE(1916)

Katherine Stuart
Silents
TIMOTHY'S QUEST(1922), w

Kathleen Stuart
JUST WILLIAM'S LUCK(1948, Brit.); WILLIAM COMES TO TOWN(1948, Brit.)

Kathryn Stuart
Silents
ERSTWHILE SUSAN(1919), w; AWAY GOES PRUDENCE(1920), w

Leone Stuart
BLESS 'EM ALL(1949, Brit.), w; SKIMPY IN THE NAVY(1949, Brit.), w; FAREWELL PERFORMANCE(1963, Brit.), w

Leslie Stuart
Silents
MR. FIX-IT(1918); PRAIRIE WIFE, THE(1925)

Misc. Silents
DIPLOMATIC MISSION, A(1918); LORD AND LADY ALGY(1919); PROFITEERS, THE(1919)

Lillian Stuart
DAVID HARUM(1934)

Lily D. Stuart
SUCH WOMEN ARE DANGEROUS(1934)

Louise Stuart
PLAINSMAN, THE(1937)

Lowell Stuart
Misc. Silents
RUNAWAY WIFE, THE(1915)

Lynn Marie Stuart
CRACKING UP(1977)

Lynne Stuart
RAGGEDY ANN AND ANDY(1977)

Madge Stuart
Silents
ELUSIVE PIMPERNEL, THE(1919, Brit.); AMATEUR GENTLEMAN, THE(1920, Brit.); QUESTION OF TRUST, A(1920, Brit.); FRAILTY(1921, Brit.); GENERAL JOHN REGAN(1921, Brit.); INNOCENT(1921, Brit.); CRIMSON CIRCLE, THE(1922, Brit.); PASSIONATE FRIENDS, THE(1922, Brit.); POINTING FINGER, THE(1922, Brit.); RUNNING WATER(1922, Brit.); GAMBLE WITH HEARTS, A(1923, Brit.); UNINVIT-ED GUEST, THE(1923, Brit.); ONLY WAY, THE(1926, Brit.)

Misc. Silents
NATURE'S GENTLEMAN(1918, Brit.); BRANDED SOUL, THE(1920, Brit.); TAVERN KNIGHT, THE(1920, Brit.); GENTLEMAN OF FRANCE, A(1921, Brit.); GREAT-HEART(1921, Brit.); GWYNETH OF THE WELSH HILLS(1921, Brit.); CRIMSON CIRCLE, THE(1922, Brit.); FORTUNE'S FOOL(1922, Brit.); HIS WIFE'S HUS-BAND(1922, Brit.); KNIGHT ERRANT, THE(1922, Brit.); BELOVED VAGABOND, THE(1923, Brit.); WOMEN AND DIAMONDS(1924, Brit.)

Mae Stuart
Misc. Talkies
BEAST OF BORNEO(1935)

Malcolm Stuart
WAY...WAY OUT(1966), p; GREAT BANK ROBBERY, THE(1969), p; MASTER-MIND(1977), p

Margaret Stuart
DIGBY, THE BIGGEST DOG IN THE WORLD(1974, Brit.)

Marilyn Stuart
RECKLESS LIVING(1938)

Mark Stuart
PLEASE SIR(1971, Brit.), d

Martin Stuart
Misc. Silents
FORGOTTEN(1914, Brit.)

Marvin Stuart
SUPERFLY(1972), md

Mary Stuart
HITLER'S CHILDREN(1942); MEXICAN SPITFIRE'S ELEPHANT(1942); LADIES' DAY(1943); MR. LUCKY(1943); THIS LAND IS MINE(1943); THIS TIME FOR KEEPS(1947); BIG PUNCH, THE(1948); EMBRACEABLE YOU(1948); JUNE BRI-DE(1948); THUNDERHOOF(1948); TRIPLE THREAT(1948); ADVENTURES OF DON JUAN(1949); GIRL FROM JONES BEACH, THE(1949); HENRY, THE RAIN-MAKER(1949); LEAVE IT TO HENRY(1949); CARIBOO TRAIL, THE(1950); FATHER MAKES GOOD(1950)

Maxine Stuart
DAYS OF WINE AND ROSES(1962); KITTEN WITH A WHIP(1964); LOST MAN, THE(1969); WINNING(1969); SUPPOSE THEY GAVE A WAR AND NOBODY CA-ME?(1970); MAKING IT(1971); PRISONER OF SECOND AVENUE, THE(1975); FUN WITH DICK AND JANE(1977); COAST TO COAST(1980); PRIVATE BENJAMIN(1980)

Mel Stuart
IF IT'S TUESDAY, THIS MUST BE BELGIUM(1969), d; I LOVE MY WIFE(1970), d; WILLY WONKA AND THE CHOCOLATE FACTORY(1971), d; ONE IS A LONELY NUMBER(1972), d; MEAN DOG BLUES(1978), d

Misc. Talkies
WHITE LIONS(1981), d

Michael Stuart
THIS DAY AND AGE(1933)

Nellie Stuart
Silents
NELL GWYNNE(1914)

Nichola Stuart
GENTLE SEX, THE(1943, Brit.)

Nicholas Stuart
SECRET MISSION(1944, Brit.); TIME FLIES(1944, Brit.); JOHNNY IN THE CLOUDS(1945, Brit.); NIGHT BEAT(1948, Brit.); LOVE LOTTERY, THE(1954, Brit.); DIVIDED HEART, THE(1955, Brit.); JOE MACBETH(1955); NIGHT MY NUMBER CAME UP, THE(1955, Brit.); HIGH TIDE AT NOON(1957, Brit.); HIGH HELL(1958); SHERIFF OF FRACTURED JAW, THE(1958, Brit.); LONGEST DAY, THE(1962); WE JOINED THE NAVY(1962, Brit.); ADDING MACHINE, THE(1969)

Nick Stuart
WHY LEAVE HOME?(1929); FOURTH ALARM, THE(1930); HAPPY DAYS(1930); SWING HIGH(1930); SUNDOWN TRAIL(1931); TRAPPED(1931); POLICE CALL(1933); SECRET SINNERS(1933); DEMON FOR TROUBLE, A(1934); SECRETS OF CHINA-TOWN(1935); PUT ON THE SPOT(1936); RIO GRANDE ROMANCE(1936); FIGHTING PLAYBOY(1937); PRIDE OF THE BOWERY(1941); MR. MUGGS STEPS OUT(1943); JOURNEY TOGETHER(1946, Brit.); KILLER APE(1953); FRENCH LINE, THE(1954); IT'S A MAD, MAD, MAD, MAD WORLD(1963); THIS PROPERTY IS CONDEM-NED(1966)

Misc. Talkies
CHASING THROUGH EUROPE(1929); UNDERWORLD TERROR(1936); GUNS-MOKE(1947)

Silents
NEWS PARADE, THE(1928); GIRLS GONE WILD(1929); JOY STREET(1929)

Misc. Silents
HIGH SCHOOL HERO(1927)

Norman Stuart
ARNOLD(1973); BATTLESTAR GALACTICA(1979)

Patrick Stuart
CONQUEST OF THE EARTH(1980)

Peggy Stuart
SILKEN AFFAIR, THE(1957, Brit.), m

Peter Stuart
I LOVE MY WIFE(1970)

Philip Stuart
NINE TILL SIX(1932, Brit.), w; BORROWED CLOTHES(1934, Brit.), w

Randy Stuart
FOXES OF HARROW, THE(1947); APARTMENT FOR PEGGY(1948); SITTING PRETTY(1948); STREET WITH NO NAME, THE(1948); DANCING IN THE DARK(1949); I WAS A MALE WAR BRIDE(1949); WHIRLPOOL(1949); ALL ABOUT EVE(1950); STELLA(1950); I CAN GET IT FOR YOU WHOLESALE(1951); ROOM FOR ONE MORE(1952); STAR IN THE DUST(1956); INCREDIBLE SHRINKING MAN, THE(1957); MAN FROM GOD'S COUNTRY(1958)

Misc. Talkies
NEW DAY AT SUNDOWN(1957)

Robert Stuart
Silents
EVERYBODY'S GIRL(1918), ph; KING OF DIAMONDS, THE(1918), ph

Robert A. Stuart
Silents
NO TRESPASSING(1922), ph

Roy Stuart
LOVE GOD?, THE(1969)
Sheila Stuart
CAGED(1950)
Sir Simeon Stuart
Silents
AUCTION MART, THE(1920, Brit.); FACE AT THE WINDOW, THE(1920, Brit.);
TRUE TILDA(1920, Brit.); CREATION(1922, Brit.); CRIMSON CIRCLE, THE(1922,
Brit.); ROB ROY(1922, Brit.); PADDY, THE NEXT BEST THING(1923, Brit.); LIVING-
STONE(1925, Brit.); ONE OF THE BEST(1927, Brit.); VORTEX, THE(1927, Brit.)
Misc. Silents
LADY CLARE, THE(1919, Brit.); SNOW IN THE DESERT(1919, Brit.); INHERI-
TANCE(1920, Brit.); SHADOW BETWEEN, THE(1920, Brit.); IMPERFECT LOVER,
THE(1921, Brit.); SWORD OF FATE, THE(1921, Brit.); FORTUNE'S FOOL(1922, Brit.);
LOVE'S INFLUENCE(1922, Brit.); TEMPTATION OF CARLTON EARLYE, THE(1923,
Brit.); RECKLESS GAMBLE, A(1928, Brit.)
St. John Stuart
GAMMA PEOPLE, THE(1956)
Suzanne Stuart
SCREAM, BABY, SCREAM(1969)
Terence Stuart
MC VICAR(1982, Brit.)
V. Stuart
Silents
APARTMENT 29(1917)
Victoria Stuart
ONE NIGHT OF LOVE(1934)
Walker Stuart
MALATESTA'S CARNIVAL(1973), p; NEVER CRY WOLF(1983)
Wendy Stuart
OUTLAW'S SON(1957); PERSUADER, THE(1957); LITTLEST HOBO, THE(1958);
PANIC IN THE CITY(1968); WILD SCENE, THE(1970); WAITRESS(1982)
Bettina Stuart-Wortley
Silents
GREAT LOVE, THE(1918)
Mr. Stubbs
TOBY TYLER(1960)
Chuck Stubb
ANGELS WITH DIRTY FACES(1938)
Bruce Stubblefield
1984
SAVAGE STREETS(1984), ed
Sally Stubblefield
GREEN-EYED BLONDE, THE(1957), w
Stubby Stubblefield
CROWD ROARS, THE(1932)
Bill Stubbs
JOHNNY O'CLOCK(1947)
Billy Stubbs
UNDERCOVER MAN, THE(1949)
Chuck Stubbs
THEY SHALL HAVE MUSIC(1939); ONE MILLION B.C.(1940)
Harry Stubbs
ALIBI(1929); LOCKED DOOR, THE(1929); THREE LIVE GHOSTS(1929); BAD ONE,
THE(1930); LADIES MUST PLAY(1930); NIGHT RIDE(1930); TRUTH ABOUT YOUTH,
THE(1930); FANNY FOLEY HERSELF(1931); GANG BUSTER, THE(1931); HER
MAJESTY LOVE(1931); MILLIE(1931); MAN WHO PLAYED GOD, THE(1932); INVISI-
BLE MAN, THE(1933); MIND READER, THE(1933); WHEN STRANGERS MAR-
RY(1933); NOW AND FOREVER(1934); SPANISH CAPE MYSTERY(1935);
WEREWOLF OF LONDON, THE(1935); GIRL FROM MANDALAY(1936); IT HAD TO
HAPPEN(1936); MAN I MARRY, THE(1936); SUTTER'S GOLD(1936); LONDON BY
NIGHT(1937); LOVE AND HISSES(1937); ON THE AVENUE(1937); PLAINSMAN,
THE(1937); WAIKIKI WEDDING(1937); DR. RHYTHM(1938); I STAND AC-
CUSED(1938); IN OLD CHICAGO(1938); MARIE ANTOINETTE(1938); PECK'S BAD
BOY WITH THE CIRCUS(1938); HOUSE OF THE SEVEN GABLES, THE(1940);
INVISIBLE MAN RETURNS, THE(1940); MUMMY'S HAND, THE(1940); ZAN-
ZIBAR(1940); BURMA CONVOY(1941); SINGING HILL, THE(1941); WOLF MAN,
THE(1941); SHERLOCK HOLMES AND THE VOICE OF TERROR(1942); FLESH AND
FANTASY(1943); FRANKENSTEIN MEETS THE WOLF MAN(1943)
Imogen Stubbs
PRIVILEGED(1982, Brit.)
Jack Stubbs
DOLL FACE(1945), set d; DO YOU LOVE ME?(1946), set d; SUN ALSO RISES,
THE(1957), set d
Louise Stubbs
LANDLORD, THE(1970); BLACK GIRL(1972); WITHOUT A TRACE(1983)
Ray Stubbs
RAISIN IN THE SUN, A(1961)
Una Stubbs
SUMMER HOLIDAY(1963, Brit.); WEST 11(1963, Brit.); SWINGER'S PARADIS-
E(1965, Brit.); THREE HATS FOR LISA(1965, Brit.); MISTER TEN PERCENT(1967,
Brit.); ALF 'N' FAMILY(1968, Brit.)
William Stubbs
FRAMED(1947)
Alan Stubenrauch
INSIDE LOOKING OUT(1977, Aus.), art d
Solvi Stubing
SECRET AGENT SUPER DRAGON(1966, Fr./Ital./Ger./Monaco); TREASURE OF
SAN GENNARO(1968, Fr./Ital./Ger.); PUSSYCAT, PUSSYCAT, I LOVE YOU(1970);
BATTLE OF THE AMAZONS(1973, Ital./Span.)
Frank Stubock
NO DRUMS, NO BUGLES(1971)
Stephan Stucker
TRADING PLACES(1983)
Stephen Stucker
AIRPLANE!(1980); AIRPLANE II: THE SEQUEL(1982)
Misc. Talkies
CARNAL MADNESS(1975)

Steve Stucker
1984
BAD MANNERS(1984)
Steven Stucker
CRACKING UP(1977)
Scott Stuckman
FRATERNITY ROW(1977)
Erich Stuckmann
LAST TEN DAYS, THE(1956, Ger.)
Eugene Stuckmann
HOUSE ON 92ND STREET, THE(1945)
John Stuckmeyer
SWORD AND THE SORCERER, THE(1982), w
Murray Stuckoff
WHERE IS MY CHILD?(1937)
Victoria Studd
PRIVILEGED(1982, Brit.)
Grace Studdiford
Silents
BRANDED WOMAN, THE(1920)
Students of the Lodz Film School
KANAL(1961, Pol.)
Carl Studer
DAY AND THE HOUR, THE(1963, Fr./ Ital.); FINGERMAN, THE(1963, Fr.);
DOULOS-THE FINGER MAN(1964, Fr./Ital.); JOY HOUSE(1964, Fr.)
Karl Studer
TRIAL, THE(1963, Fr./Ital./Ger.); HAIL MAFIA(1965, Fr./Ital.); BLONDE FROM
PEKING, THE(1968, Fr.)
Kenny Studer
INDEPENDENCE DAY(1983)
Grace Studiford
Silents
NOBODY(1921)
Studio Film Service
PHANTOM PLANET, THE(1961), spec eff
Avala Studios
ONE-EYED SOLDIERS(1967, U.S./Brit./Yugo.), m
Allan Studley
APPLE DUMPLING GANG RIDES AGAIN, THE(1979)
Louise Studley
CAPTAIN LIGHTFOOT(1955)
Pat Studstill
PAPER LION(1968)
Harry Studt
MARKETA LAZAROVA(1968, Czech.)
Lomax Study
SAXON CHARM, THE(1948); STATION WEST(1948); FRENCH LINE, THE(1954);
MAN IN THE GREY FLANNEL SUIT, THE(1956); WRECK OF THE MARY DEAR,
THE(1959); NEW KIND OF LOVE, A(1963); BOEING BOEING(1965); MOMENT TO
MOMENT(1966); CAPER OF THE GOLDEN BULLS, THE(1967)
Carl Stueber
SHOEMAKER AND THE ELVES, THE(1967, Ger.), m
Hans Stuewe
BARBERINA(1932, Ger.); PRIVATE LIFE OF LOUIS XIV(1936, Ger.)
Daniel Stuffel
JONAH-WHO WILL BE 25 IN THE YEAR 2000(1976, Switz.)
Pamela Stufflebeam
VIEW FROM POMPEY'S HEAD, THE(1955)
Harry Stuhldreher
SPIRIT OF NOTRE DAME, THE(1931); BAND PLAYS ON, THE(1934), w
Dr. Johannes Stuhlmacher
MARTIN LUTHER(1953), cons
Jerzy Stuhr
WAR OF THE WORLDS-NEXT CENTURY, THE(1981, Pol.); CAMERA BUFF(1983,
Pol.), a, w
Robert Stull
DO NOT THROW CUSHIONS INTO THE RING(1970)
Charles Stumar
SHAKEDOWN, THE(1929), ph; HEAVEN ON EARTH(1931), ph; BILLION DOLLAR
SCANDAL(1932), ph; DOOMED BATTALION, THE(1932), ph; HEARTS OF HUMANI-
TY(1932), ph; HOUSE DIVIDED, A(1932), ph; MUMMY(1932), ph; NICE WOM-
AN(1932), ph; STEADY COMPANY(1932), ph; TOM BROWN OF CULVER(1932), ph;
BLACK BEAUTY(1933), ph; KING FOR A NIGHT(1933), ph; PRIVATE JONES(1933),
ph; SATURDAY'S MILLIONS(1933), ph; SECRET OF THE BLUE ROOM(1933), ph;
BOMBAY MAIL(1934), ph; COUNTESS OF MONTE CRISTO, THE(1934), ph; EMBAR-
RASSING MOMENTS(1934), ph; I LIKE IT THAT WAY(1934), ph; LET'S BE RIT-
ZY(1934), ph; LET'S TALK IT OVER(1934), ph; ROMANCE IN THE RAIN(1934), ph;
UNCERTAIN LADY(1934), ph; WAKE UP AND DREAM(1934), ph; MANHATTAN
MOON(1935), ph; RAVEN, THE(1935), ph; STORM OVER THE ANDES(1935), ph;
STRAIGHT FROM THE HEART(1935), ph; TRANSIENT LADY(1935), ph; WERE-
WOLF OF LONDON, THE(1935), ph; SPIRIT OF STANFORD, THE(1942), ph
Silents
PRISONER OF THE PINES(1918), ph; END OF THE GAME, THE(1919), ph; SAHA-
RA(1919), ph; SEX(1920), ph; LYING LIPS(1921), ph; SHAMS OF SOCIETY(1921), ph;
FRESHIE, THE(1922), ph; WHEN THE DEVIL DRIVES(1922), ph; ABYSMAL
BRUTE, THE(1923), ph; K-THE UNKNOWN(1924), ph; ROSE OF PARIS, THE(1924),
ph; RAFFLES, THE AMATEUR CRACKSMAN(1925), ph; COHENS AND KELLYS,
THE(1926), ph; COHENS AND THE KELLYS IN PARIS, THE(1928), ph; MICHIGAN
KID, THE(1928), ph; SLIM FINGERS(1929), ph
John Stumar
TIME, THE PLACE AND THE GIRL, THE(1929), ph; RECAPTURED LOVE(1930),
ph; SECOND CHOICE(1930), ph; FLOOD, THE(1931), ph; LEFTOVER LADIES(1931),
ph; CORNERED(1932), ph; LAUGHTER IN HELL(1933), ph; ABOVE THE
CLOUDS(1934), ph; BEFORE MIDNIGHT(1934), ph; FURY OF THE JUNGLE(1934),
ph; JEALOUSY(1934), ph; MOST PRECIOUS THING IN LIFE(1934), ph; NAME THE
WOMAN(1934), ph; ONCE TO EVERY WOMAN(1934), ph; ONE IS GUILTY(1934), ph;
VOICE IN THE NIGHT(1934), ph; YOUNG AND BEAUTIFUL(1934), ph; ATLANTIC
ADVENTURE(1935), ph; BEST MAN WINS, THE(1935), ph; ESCAPE FROM DEVIL'S
ISLAND(1935), ph; UNWELCOME STRANGER(1935), ph; COUNTERFEIT(1936), ph;
DEVIL'S SQUADRON(1936), ph; END OF THE TRAIL(1936), ph; IF YOU COULD

ONLY COOK(1936), ph; TWO-FISTED GENTLEMAN(1936), ph; INTIMATE RELATIONS(1937, Brit.), ph; ONE MAN JUSTICE(1937), ph; SOMETHING TO SING ABOUT(1937), ph; SONG OF THE ROAD(1937, Brit.), ph; HE LOVED AN ACTRESS(1938, Brit.), ph; MR. BOGGS STEPS OUT(1938), ph; LADY AND THE MOB, THE(1939), ph; MILL ON THE FLOSS(1939, Brit.), ph; PARENTS ON TRIAL(1939), ph; THOSE HIGH GREY WALLS(1939), ph; DURANGO KID, THE(1940), ph; MUSIC IN MY HEART(1940), ph; SECRET SEVEN, THE(1940), ph; HARMON OF MICHIGAN(1941), ph; I WAS A PRISONER ON DEVIL'S ISLAND(1941), ph; LONE WOLF TAKES A CHANCE, THE(1941), ph; NAVAL ACADEMY(1941), ph; TWO LATINS FROM MANHATTAN(1941), ph; UNDER AGE(1941), ph; TRAMP, TRAMP, TRAMP(1942), ph; POWER OF THE PRESS(1943), ph; KLONDIKE KATE(1944), ph; RETURN OF THE VAMPIRE, THE(1944), ph
Silents
NAUGHTY, NAUGHTY!(1918), ph; QUICKSANDS(1918), ph; DARK MIRROR, THE(1920), ph; DOLLAR DEVILS(1923), ph; TEMPORARY MARRIAGE(1923), ph; FAMILY SECRET, THE(1924), ph; DOWN THE STRETCH(1927), ph; IRRESISTIBLE LOVER, THE(1927), ph; RED LIPS(1928), ph; 13 WASHINGTON SQUARE(1928), ph
John S. Stumar
Silents
KAISER'S SHADOW, THE(1918), ph; EXTRAVAGANCE(1919), ph; ANNE OF LITTLE SMOKY(1921), ph; SHAMS OF SOCIETY(1921), ph; CARDIGAN(1922), ph; KINGDOM WITHIN, THE(1922), ph; SUPER-SEX, THE(1922), ph
Robert Stumm
SEVEN ALONE(1975), ph
Hans M. Stummer
OUR HITLER, A FILM FROM GERMANY(1980, Ger.), puppets
Cedar Stump
HOT STUFF(1979)
Mandy Stumpf
THOSE LIPS, THOSE EYES(1980)
Randy Stumpf
1984
SILENT NIGHT, DEADLY NIGHT(1984)
Wolfgang Stumpf
BRIDGE, THE(1961, Ger.); SIGNS OF LIFE(1981, Ger.)
Milton Stumph
MY NAME IS JULIA ROSS(1945), set d
Paul Stupin
MR. WINKLE GOES TO WAR(1944); O.S.S.(1946)
Svetozar Stur
ASSISTANT, THE(1982, Czech.), m
Carlin Sturdevant
SWAMP WOMAN(1941)
John Sturdevant
LAS VEGAS STORY, THE(1952), set d
Brian Sturdivant
VON RICHTHOFEN AND BROWN(1970)
Don Sturdy
CISCO PIKE(1971)
John Rhodes Sturdy
CORVETTE K-225(1943), w; CARIBOO TRAIL, THE(1950), w
Jennings Sturgeon
LOST BATTALION(1961, U.S./Phil.); RAIDERS OF LEYTE GULF(1963 U.S./Phil.); FLIGHT TO FURY(1966, U.S./Phil.)
John Sturgeon
Misc. Silents
TEST, THE(1915)
Rolin S. Sturgeon
Silents
AMERICAN CONSUL, THE(1917), d
Rollin Sturgeon
Silents
GILDED DREAM, THE(1920), d; ALL DOLLED UP(1921), d; MAD MARRIAGE, THE(1921), d; DAUGHTERS OF TODAY(1924), d
Misc. Silents
DANGER AHEAD(1921), d; WEST OF THE WATER TOWER(1924), d
Rollin S. Sturgeon
Silents
LITTLE ANGEL OF CANYON CREEK, THE(1914), d; IN FOLLY'S TRAIL(1920), d
Misc. Silents
CAPTAIN ALVAREZ(1914), d; CHALICE OF COURAGE, THE(1915), d; GOD'S COUNTRY AND THE WOMAN(1916), d; THROUGH THE WALL(1916), d; BETTY AND THE BUCCANEERS(1917), d; CALENDER GIRL, THE(1917), d; RAINBOW GIRL, THE(1917), d; SERPENT'S TOOTH, THE(1917), d; UPPER CRUST, THE(1917), d; WHOSE WIFE?(1917), d; HUGON THE MIGHTY(1918), d; PETTICOAT PILOT, A(1918), d; SHUTTLE, THE(1918), d; UNCLAIMED GOODS(1918), d; DESTINY(1919), d; PRETTY SMOOTH(1919), d; SUNDOWN TRAIL, THE(1919), d; BREATH OF THE GODS, THE(1920), d; GIRL IN THE RAIN, THE(1920), d
Eddie Sturges
JUNGLE PRINCESS, THE(1936)
Edwin Sturges
OUTSIDE THE LAW(1930)
Misc. Silents
MAN AND WOMAN(1921)
John Sturges
THEY KNEW WHAT THEY WANTED(1940), ed; SCATTERGOOD MEETS BROADWAY(1941), ed; TOM, DICK AND HARRY(1941), ed; SYNCOPATION(1942), ed; MAN WHO DARED, THE(1946), d; SHADOWED(1946), d; FOR THE LOVE OF RUSTY(1947), d; KEEPER OF THE BEES(1947), d; BEST MAN WINS(1948), d; SIGN OF THE RAM, THE(1948), d; WALKING HILLS, THE(1949), d; MAGNIFICENT YANKEE, THE(1950), d; MYSTERY STREET(1950), d; RIGHT CROSS(1950), d; IT'S A BIG COUNTRY(1951), d; KIND LADY(1951), d; PEOPLE AGAINST O'HARA, THE(1951), d; GIRL IN WHITE, THE(1952), d; ESCAPE FROM FORT BRAVO(1953), d; FAST COMPANY(1953), d; JEOPARDY(1953), d; BAD DAY AT BLACK ROCK(1955), d; SCARLET COAT, THE(1955), d; UNDERWATER!(1955), d; BACKLASH(1956), d; GUNFIGHT AT THE O.K. CORRAL(1957), d; LAW AND JAKE WADE, THE(1958), d; OLD MAN AND THE SEA, THE(1958), d; LAST TRAIN FROM GUN HILL(1959), d; NEVER SO FEW(1959), d; MAGNIFICENT SEVEN, THE(1960), p&d; BY LOVE POSSESSED(1961), d; GIRL NAMED TAMIKO, A(1962), d; SERGEANTS 3(1962), d; GREAT ESCAPE, THE(1963), p&d; HALLELUJAH TRAIL, THE(1965), p&d; SATAN

BUG, THE(1965), p&d; HOUR OF THE GUN(1967), p&d; ICE STATION ZEBRA(1968), d; MAROONED(1969), p, d; JOE KIDD(1972), d; MC Q(1974), d; CHINO(1976, Ital., Span., Fr.), d; EAGLE HAS LANDED, THE(1976, Brit.), d
Misc. Talkies
ALIAS MR. TWILIGHT(1946), d
Mark Sturges
SYNANON(1965); WILD, WILD WINTER(1966)
Preston Sturges
BIG POND, THE(1930), w; FAST AND LOOSE(1930), w; STRICTLY DISHONORABLE(1931), w; CHILD OF MANHATTAN(1933), w; POWER AND THE GLORY, THE(1933), w; THEY JUST HAD TO GET MARRIED(1933), w; THIRTY-DAY PRINCESS(1934), w; WE LIVE AGAIN(1934), w; DIAMOND JIM(1935), w; GOOD FAIRY, THE(1935), w; NEXT TIME WE LOVE(1936), w; EASY LIVING(1937), w; HOTEL HAYWIRE(1937), w; IF I WERE KING(1938), w; PORT OF SEVEN SEAS(1938), w; NEVER SAY DIE(1939), w; CHRISTMAS IN JULY(1940), a, d&w; GREAT McGINTY, THE(1940), d&w; REMEMBER THE NIGHT(1940), w; LADY EVE, THE(1941), d&w; SULLIVAN'S TRAVELS(1941), p; I MARRIED A WITCH(1942), p; PALM BEACH STORY, THE(1942), d&w; STAR SPANGLED RHYTHM(1942); GREAT MOMENT, THE(1944), p&d, w; HAIL THE CONQUERING HERO(1944), p,d&w; MIRACLE OF MORGAN'S CREEK, THE(1944), d&w; I'LL BE YOURS(1947), w; UNFAITHFULLY YOURS(1948), p,d,&w; BEAUTIFUL BLONDE FROM BASHFUL BEND, THE(1949), p,d&w; MAD WEDNESDAY(1950), p,d&w; VENDETTA(1950), p, d, w; STRICTLY DISHONORABLE(1951), w; FRENCH, THEY ARE A FUNNY RACE, THE(1956, Fr.), d&w; PARIS HOLIDAY(1958); ROCK-A-BYE BABY(1958), w; BIRDS AND THE BEES, THE(1965), w
1984
UNFAITHFULLY YOURS(1984), w
Ray Sturges
GENTLE SEX, THE(1943, Brit.), ph
Solomon Sturges
CHARRO(1969); WORKING GIRLS, THE(1973)
Olive Sturgess
LADY GODIVA(1955); KETTLES IN THE OZARKS, THE(1956); RAVEN, THE(1963); REQUIEM FOR A GUNFIGHTER(1965)
Phil Sturgess
MELODY OF MY HEART(1936, Brit.)
Ray Sturgess
TAWNY PIPIT(1947, Brit.), ph; SEVEN DAYS TO NOON(1950, Brit.), ph; WEDDING NIGHT(1970, Ireland), ph
Raymond Sturgess
HISTORY OF MR. POLLY, THE(1949, Brit.), ph; TOM BROWN'S SCHOOLDAYS(1951, Brit.), ph
Rosie Sturgess
THIRST(1979, Aus.)
Ann Sturgis
GREAT SINNER, THE(1949)
Eddie Sturgis
SHOOTING STRAIGHT(1930); SQUEALER, THE(1930); PHANTOM OF CRESTWOOD, THE(1932); YOUNG AMERICA(1932); HELL BENT FOR LOVE(1934); FRISCO KID(1935); MAN ON THE FLYING TRAPEZE, THE(1935); MISSISSIPPI(1935); RED HOT TIRES(1935); STOLEN HARMONY(1935); RIFF-RAFF(1936)
Silents
CASSIDY(1917); OAKDALE AFFAIR, THE(1919); AFTER MIDNIGHT(1927); BIG CITY, THE(1928)
Edward Sturgis
Silents
LOST BRIDEGROOM, THE(1916)
Edwin Sturgis
SOB SISTER(1931); HERE COMES THE GROOM(1934)
Silents
RAINBOW PRINCESS, THE(1916); DOING THEIR BIT(1918); JUST FOR TONIGHT(1918); PECK'S BAD GIRL(1918); MISS CRUSOE(1919); LEGALLY DEAD(1923); LET IT RAIN(1927); WOLF'S CLOTHING(1927)
Misc. Silents
GIRL LIKE THAT, A(1917); MAN AND WOMAN(1920)
Lawrence Sturhahn
THX 1138(1971), p
Dan Sturkie
THEY CALL ME TRINITY(1971, Ital.); DR. HECKYL AND MR. HYPE(1980); WOLFEN(1981)
Don Sturkie
CAST A GIANT SHADOW(1966)
Rose Sturlin
NIGHT OF THE BLOOD BEAST(1958)
Ross Sturlin
GAL YOUNG UN(1979)
Betty Sturm
WORLD'S GREATEST SINNER, THE(1962)
Dr. Friedrich Sturm
ZEPPELIN(1971, Brit.), tech adv
Hannes Sturm
Misc. Silents
LOST SHADOW, THE(1921, Ger.)
Hans Sturm
Misc. Silents
MONNA VANNA(1923, Ger.)
Peter Sturm
NAKED AMONG THE WOLVES(1967, Ger.)
Carl Sturmer
STUCK ON YOU(1983)
1984
STUCK ON YOU(1984)
Charles Sturridge
IF ...(1968, Brit.); RUNNERS(1983, Brit.), d
Dudley Sturrock
TROUBLE(1933, Brit.), w; RIVER OF UNREST(1937, Brit.), w; SWORD OF HONOUR(1938, Brit.), w; NOT WANTED ON VOYAGE(1957, Brit.), w

Lois Sturt
Silents
GLORIOUS ADVENTURE, THE(1922, U.S./Brit.)
Jimmy Sturtevant
COMPETITION, THE(1980); HELL NIGHT(1981)
John Sturtevant
BODY SNATCHER, THE(1945), set d; THOSE ENDEARING YOUNG CHARMS(1945), set d; BEDLAM(1946), set d; CROSSFIRE(1947), set d; UNDER THE TONTO RIM(1947), set d; WOMAN ON THE BEACH, THE(1947), set d; RACHEL AND THE STRANGER(1948), set d; WHERE DANGER LIVES(1950), set d; INVASION U.S.A.(1952), set d; CATTLE QUEEN OF MONTANA(1954), set d; PASSION(1954), set d; PETE KELLY'S BLUES(1955), set d; LOST WORLD, THE(1960), set d; LAST TIME I SAW ARCHIE, THE(1961), set d; VOYAGE TO THE BOTTOM OF THE SEA(1961), set d; MADISON AVENUE(1962), set d; SAND PEBBLES, THE(1966), set d; FLIM-FLAM MAN, THE(1967), set d; FORT UTAH(1967), set d
John Sturtivant
TRAIL STREET(1947), set d
Eugene Stutenroth
I RING DOORBELLS(1946)
Gene Stutenroth [Gene Roth]
STRANGE DEATH OF ADOLF HITLER, THE(1943); SULTAN'S DAUGHTER, THE(1943); CHARLIE CHAN IN THE SECRET SERVICE(1944); GIRL IN THE CASE(1944); LOUISIANA HAYRIDE(1944); SAN DIEGO, I LOVE YOU(1944); SHAKE HANDS WITH MURDER(1944); SHERLOCK HOLMES AND THE SPIDER WOMAN(1944); BAD MEN OF THE BORDER(1945); BEYOND THE PECOS(1945); GAME OF DEATH, A(1945); ROGUES GALLERY(1945); SHANGHAI COBRA, THE(1945); SUDAN(1945); BANDIT OF SHERWOOD FOREST, THE(1946); CANYON PASSAGE(1946); GIRL ON THE SPOT(1946); MR. HEX(1946); STRANGE JOURNEY(1946); BRUTE FORCE(1947); FRAMED(1947); HOMESTEADERS OF PARADISE VALLEY(1947); MARSHAL OF CRIPPLE CREEK, THE(1947); NEWS HOUNDS(1947); NIGHTMARE ALLEY(1947); SEA OF GRASS, THE(1947); FEUDIN', FUSSIN' AND A-FIGHTIN'(1948); GALLANT LEGION, THE(1948); OKLAHOMA BADLANDS(1948); SMUGGLERS' COVE(1948); BIG SOMBRERO, THE(1949)
Eugene Stutenroth [Gene Roth]
WHERE THERE'S LIFE(1947)
Fred Stuthman
W. W. AND THE DIXIE DANCEKINGS(1975); MARATHON MAN(1976); NETWORK(1976); ANOTHER MAN, ANOTHER CHANCE(1977 Fr/US); BAD NEWS BEARS IN BREAKING TRAINING, THE(1977); FOR PETE'S SAKE(1977); HEROES(1977); MAC ARTHUR(1977); RAGGEDY ANN AND ANDY(1977); SEMITOUGH(1977); SENTINEL, THE(1977); ESCAPE FROM ALCATRAZ(1979); FIREPOWER(1979, Brit.); CHEAPER TO KEEP HER(1980); PRIVATE EYES, THE(1980)
Frederick Stuthman
GROOVE TUBE, THE(1974)
Darlene Stuto
MS. 45(1981)
Kathy Stutsman
HITCHHIKERS, THE(1972)
Sophia Stutz
GOD'S LITTLE ACRE(1958), cos
Hans Stuwe
ECHO OF A DREAM(1930, Ger.)
Misc. Silents
CAGLIOSTRO(1928, Fr.)
Joris Stuyck
1984
RAZOR'S EDGE, THE(1984); SCANDALOUS(1984)
Pieter Stuyck
SUPERMAN(1978)
Amy Stuyvesant
1984
SILENT NIGHT, DEADLY NIGHT(1984)
Richard Stuyvesant [Mario Brega]
FISTFUL OF DOLLARS, A(1964, Ital./Ger./Span.)
Michael Style
VAMPIRE LOVERS, THE(1970, Brit.), p, w; FRIGHT(1971, Brit.), p; LUST FOR A VAMPIRE(1971, Brit.), p; TWINS OF EVIL(1971, Brit.), p
Beatrice Styler
Silents
ALSTER CASE, THE(1915)
Burt Styler
CALL ME MISTER(1951), w; DOWN AMONG THE SHELTERING PALMS(1953), w; BOY, DID I GET A WRONG NUMBER!(1966), w; EIGHT ON THE LAM(1967), w; WICKED DREAMS OF PAULA SCHULTZ, THE(1968), w
Bernie Styles
LAST OF THE RED HOT LOVERS(1972); ANNIE HALL(1977)
Edwin Styles
HELL BELOW(1933); ON THE AIR(1934, Brit.); ROAD HOUSE(1934, Brit.); FIVE POUND MAN, THE(1937, Brit.); PATRICIA GETS HER MAN(1937, Brit.); ADAM AND EVELYNE(1950, Brit.); LADY WITH A LAMP, THE(1951, Brit.); FOUR AGAINST FATE(1952, Brit.); ISN'T LIFE WONDERFUL!(1953, Brit.); MR. POTTS GOES TO MOSCOW(1953, Brit.); PENNY PRINCESS(1953, Brit.); FOR BETTER FOR WORSE(1954, Brit.); WEAK AND THE WICKED, THE(1954, Brit.); UP IN THE WORLD(1957, Brit.); STOP ME BEFORE I KILL!(1961, Brit.)
Gordon Styles
UNDER MILK WOOD(1973, Brit.)
Herkie Styles
BELLBOY, THE(1960)
Rick Styles
TERROR ON TOUR(1980)
Robert Styles
1984
SCANDALOUS(1984)
Eugene Stylianou
SHADOW OF FEAR(1963, Brit.)
Stymie
WINNER'S CIRCLE, THE(1948)

Jan Styne
SERGEANT RUTLEDGE(1960)
Jule Styne
HIT PARADE OF 1941(1940), m; HIT PARADE OF 1943(1943), md; TONIGHT AND EVERY NIGHT(1945), m; LADIES' MAN(1947), m; LIVING IT UP(1954), w; BELLS ARE RINGING(1960), w, m; FUNNY GIRL(1968), w; THIEVES(1977), m
Stanley Styne
JUKE BOX RHYTHM(1959), m
Jerry Styner
DEVIL'S ANGELS(1967), m/l Mike Curb; KILLERS THREE(1968), m; SAVAGE SEVEN, THE(1968), m; CYCLE SAVAGES(1969), m; SKI FEVER(1969, U.S./Aust./Czech.), m; MAGIC GARDEN OF STANLEY SWEETHART, THE(1970), m; ...TICK...TICK...TICK...(1970), m; CORKY(1972), m; BLACK JACK(1973), m; MITCHELL(1975), md
Jerry Stynerv
FIVE THE HARD WAY(1969), m
William Styron
SOPHIE'S CHOICE(1982), d&w
Jingmin Su
MARINE BATTLEGROUND(1966, U.S/S.K.), ph
Valentine Suard
1984
SUNDAY IN THE COUNTRY, A(1984, Fr.)
Bobby A. Suarez
BIONIC BOY, THE(1977, Hong Kong/Phil.), p; DYNAMITE JOHNSON(1978, Phil.), p&d
Carlos Suarez
MAN AND THE MONSTER, THE(1965, Mex.); VENGEANCE OF THE VAMPIRE WOMEN, THE(1969, Mex.)
Eunice Suarez
SHOOT THE MOON(1982)
Felix Suarez
FLAME OVER VIETNAM(1967, Span./Ger.), ed
Hilda Suarez
HAND IN THE TRAP, THE(1963, Arg./Span.)
Jose Suarez
MAIN STREET(1956, Span.); AVENGER, THE(1966, Ital.); SEVEN GOLDEN MEN(1969, Fr./Ital./Span.)
Misc. Talkies
SLAVE GIRLS OF SHEBA(1960)
Miguel Suarez
BANANAS(1971)
Miguelangel Suarez
STIR CRAZY(1980)
Norberto Suarez
TERRACE, THE(1964, Arg.)
Olga Suarez
WILD WOMEN OF WONGO, THE(1959), ch
Rafael Suarez
LITTLEST OUTLAW, THE(1955), set d; MAGNIFICENT SEVEN, THE(1960), set d
Ramon F. Suarez
DEATH OF A BUREAUCRAT(1979, Cuba), w, ph
Ricardo Suarez
DEATH OF A BUREAUCRAT(1979, Cuba)
Manley Suathojame
FOXFIRE(1955)
Ricardo Munoz Suay
DESERT WARRIOR(1961 Ital./Span.), d; VIRIDIANA(1962, Mex./Span.), p; HAND IN THE TRAP, THE(1963, Arg./Span.), w; MOMENT OF TRUTH, THE(1965, Ital./Span.), w; SAGA OF DRACULA, THE(1975, Span.), p
Cesar Suberi
TRUNK TO CAIRO(1966, Israel/Ger.)
Sidney Suberly
Misc. Silents
PAWNS OF PASSION(1929, Fr./USSR)
John "Bubbles" Sublett
CABIN IN THE SKY(1943)
Dick Subley
SUNBURN(1979)
Michel Subor
ANATOMY OF A MARRIAGE(MY DAYS WITH JEAN-MARC AND MY NIGHTS WITH FRANCOISE) (1964 Fr.); JULES AND JIM(1962, Fr.); PLEASE, NOT NOW!(1963, Fr./Ital.); LE PETIT SOLDAT(1965, Fr.); WHAT'S NEW, PUSSYCAT?(1965, U.S./Fr.); TOPAZ(1969, Brit.); NO TIME FOR BREAKFAST(1978, Fr.)
Milton Subotsky
ROCK, ROCK, ROCK!(1956), p, w, md; JAMBOREE(1957), p; LOST LAGOON(1958), w; LAST MILE, THE(1959), p, w; HORROR HOTEL(1960, Brit.), w; RING-A-DING RHYTHM(1962, Brit.); JUST FOR FUN(1963, Brit.), p, w; DR. TERROR'S HOUSE OF HORRORS(1965, Brit.), p, w; DR. WHO AND THE DALEKS(1965, Brit.), p, w; SKULL, THE(1965, Brit.), p, w; DALEKS–INVASION EARTH 2155 A.D.(1966, Brit.), p, w; PSYCHOPATH, THE(1966, Brit.), p; DEADLY BEES,THE(1967, Brit.), p; TERRORNAUTS, THE(1967, Brit.), p; THEY CAME FROM BEYOND SPACE(1967, Brit.), p, w; BIRTHDAY PARTY, THE(1968, Brit.), p; DANGER ROUTE(1968, Brit.), p; TORTURE GARDEN(1968, Brit.), p; THANK YOU ALL VERY MUCH(1969, Brit.), p; MIND OF MR. SOAMES, THE(1970, Brit.), p; SCREAM AND SCREAM AGAIN(1970, Brit.), p; HOUSE THAT DRIPPED BLOOD, THE(1971, Brit.), p; I, MONSTER(1971, Brit.), p, w; ASYLUM(1972, Brit.), p; TALES FROM THE CRYPT(1972, Brit.), p, w; WHAT BECAME OF JACK AND JILL?(1972, Brit.), p; AND NOW THE SCREAMING STARTS(1973, Brit.), p; VAULT OF HORROR, THE(1973, Brit.), p, w; BEAST MUST DIE, THE(1974, Brit.), p; FROM BEYOND THE GRAVE(1974, Brit.), p; MADHOUSE(1974, Brit.), p; AT THE EARTH'S CORE(1976, Brit.), w; DOMINIQUE(1978, Brit.), p; MONSTER CLUB, THE(1981, Brit.), p
Monika Subramaniam
SAINT JACK(1979)
Frank Sucack
PAT AND MIKE(1952)
John Suce
DANGEROUS LADY(1941)

Michel Such
QUARTET(1981, Brit./Fr.); INQUISITOR, THE(1982, Fr.)

Daniel Suchar
TATTOO(1981)

David Suchar
TATTOO(1981)

Henia Suchar
DAY AND THE HOUR, THE(1963, Fr./ Ital.); IS PARIS BURNING?(1966, U.S./Fr.);
25TH HOUR, THE(1967, Fr./Ital./Yugo.); WISE GUYS(1969, Fr./Ital.)

Harry Sucher
MUG TOWN(1943), w; FROZEN GHOST, THE(1945), w

Henry Sucher
MIRACLE KID(1942), w; MUMMY'S TOMB, THE(1942), w; CAPTIVE WILD WOM-
AN(1943), w; JUNGLE WOMAN(1944), w; MUMMY'S GHOST, THE(1944), w

Sherrie Sucher
GODSPELL(1973), cos

David Suchet
MISSIONARY, THE(1982); RED MONARCH(1983, Brit.); TRENCHCOAT(1983)
1984
GREYSTOKE: THE LEGEND OF TARZAN, LORD OF THE APES(1984); LITTLE
DRUMMER GIRL, THE(1984)

Wolfgang Suchitzky
THEATRE OF BLOOD(1973, Brit.), ph

Boris Suchow
NAKED AMONG THE WOLVES(1967, Ger.)

Arne Sucksdorff
GREAT ADVENTURE, THE(1955, Swed.), a, p,d,w,ph&ed; CRY OF THE PEN-
GUINS(1972, Brit.), ph

Kjell Sucksdorff
GREAT ADVENTURE, THE(1955, Swed.)

Anna Sudakevich
Misc. Silents
HEIR TO JENGHIS-KHAN, THE(1928, USSR); HOUSE ON TRUBNAYA SQUA-
RE(1928, USSR)

Phil Sudano
MOSS ROSE(1947)

Peter Sudarsky [Peter Skinner]
CHILD IS A WILD THING, A(1976), p,d,w&ph

Scott Sudden
CADDY SHACK(1980)

Sergei Sudeikin
WE LIVE AGAIN(1934), prod d

Hermann Sudermann
WONDER OF WOMEN(1929), w; SONG OF SONGS(1933), w
Silents
FLESH AND THE DEVIL(1926), w; SUNRISE–A SONG OF TWO HUMANS(1927), w

Caesare Sudero
Silents
ISN'T LIFE WONDERFUL(1924), m

Sudershan
SHAKESPEARE WALLAH(1966, India)

Pandit Sudershan
TIGER AND THE FLAME, THE(1955, India), w

Volodva Sudin
ADVENTURE IN ODESSA(1954, USSR)

A. Sudkaveich
Silents
STORM OVER ASIA(1929, USSR)

Joan Sudlow
QUEEN FOR A DAY(1951); PRIDE OF ST. LOUIS, THE(1952)

Lyle Sudrow
PRIZE, THE(1963)

Eugene Sue
Silents
SECRETS OF PARIS, THE(1922), w

Herbert Ah Sue
RETURN TO PARADISE(1953)

Julie Suedo
DANGEROUS SEAS(1931, Brit.); COMMISSIONAIRE(1933, Brit.); LOVE'S OLD
SWEET SONG(1933, Brit.); PARIS PLANE(1933, Brit.); NELL GWYN(1935, Brit.);
PLAY UP THE BAND(1935, Brit.); QUEEN OF HEARTS(1936, Brit.); DANCE OF
DEATH, THE(1938, Brit.); IF I WERE BOSS(1938, Brit.); NIGHT ALONE(1938, Brit.);
ON VELVET(1938, Brit.); VILLIERS DIAMOND, THE(1938, Brit.); IRELAND'S BOR-
DER LINE(1939, Ireland); TORPEDOED!(1939); HUMAN MONSTER, THE(1940, Brit.);
LILAC DOMINO, THE(1940, Brit.); SALOON BAR(1940, Brit.); KISS THE BRIDE
GOODBYE(1944, Brit.)
Silents
RAT, THE(1925, Brit.); ONE COLUMBO NIGHT(1926, Brit.); FAKE, THE(1927, Brit.);
ONE OF THE BEST(1927, Brit.); VORTEX, THE(1927, Brit.); AFTERWARDS(1928,
Brit.); PHYSICIAN, THE(1928, Brit.); SMASHING THROUGH(1928, Brit.)
Misc. Silents
TRIUMPH OF THE RAT, THE(1926, Brit.); VICTORY(1928, Brit.); WOMAN FROM
CHINA, THE(1930, Brit.)

Kathy Suergiu
EYES OF A STRANGER(1980); ABSENCE OF MALICE(1981)

Alan Sues
MOVE OVER, DARLING(1963); AMERICANIZATION OF EMILY, THE(1964);
RAGGEDY ANN AND ANDY(1977); OH, HEAVENLY DOG!(1980)

Leonard Sues
EBB TIDE(1937); THAT CERTAIN AGE(1938); MIDNIGHT(1939); WHAT A LI-
FE(1939); GHOST BREAKERS, THE(1940); LOVE, HONOR AND OH, BABY(1940);
STRIKE UP THE BAND(1940); LIFE BEGINS FOR ANDY HARDY(1941); WHERE
DID YOU GET THAT GIRL?(1941); ZIS BOOM BAH(1941); STRANGE CASE OF DR.
RX, THE(1942); SWEATER GIRL(1942); TUTTLES OF TAHITI(1942); HEAT'S ON,
THE(1943); MANHATTAN ANGEL(1948)

Maurie M. Suess
DESTINATION MURDER(1950), p; JACKIE ROBINSON STORY, THE(1950), ed

Pascale Sueur
1984
THREE CROWNS OF THE SAILOR(1984, Fr.), ed

Chan Suey
GENERAL DIED AT DAWN, THE(1936)

Suffel
COUNSEL FOR ROMANCE(1938, Fr.)

Madeleine Suffel
IT HAPPENED IN GIBRALTAR(1943, Fr.); CONFESSIONS OF A ROGUE(1948, Fr.)

Madeline Suffel
CONFLICT(1939, Fr.)

Norma Suffern
EAST OF KILIMANJARO(1962, Brit./Ital.), ed

Norman Suffern
MIGHTY JUNGLE, THE(1965, U.S./Mex.), ed

Fijio Suga
SOLDIER'S PRAYER, A(1970, Jap.)

Hidehisa Suga
WISER AGE(1962, Jap.), p

Takashi Suga
SONG FROM MY HEART, THE(1970, Jap.)

Toshiro Suga
MOONRAKER(1979, Brit.)

Tony Sugahara
KARATE, THE HAND OF DEATH(1961)

Ichiro Sugai
ODD OBSESSION(1961, Jap.); LIFE OF OHARU(1964, Jap.); GAMERA VERSUS
BARUGON(1966, Jap./U.S.); SANSHO THE BAILIFF(1969, Jap.); HARBOR LIGHT
YOKOHAMA(1970, Jap.); GEISHA, A(1978, Jap.)

Kin Sugai
ETERNITY OF LOVE(1961, Jap.); DODESKA-DEN(1970, Jap.)

Anna Sugano
CYCLE SAVAGES(1969)

Kanji Suganuma
BUDDHA(1965, Jap.), ed

Ted Sugar
GOIN' DOWN THE ROAD(1970, Can.)

Bert Sugarman
LAST FIGHT, THE(1983)

Sparky Sugarman
SUMMER CAMP(1979), m

Michiko Sugata
GAMERA THE INVINCIBLE(1966, Jap.)

Eizo Sugawa
CHALLENGE TO LIVE(1964, Jap.), d

Bunta Sugawara
MAN WHO STOLE THE SUN, THE(1980, Jap.)

Hideo Sugawara
Misc. Silents
I WAS BORN, BUT...(1932, Jap.)

Kenji Sugawara
GOLDEN DEMON(1956, Jap.)

Michisumi Sugawara
SNOW COUNTRY(1969, Jap.)

Mollie Sugden
Misc. Talkies
ARE YOU BEING SERVED?(1977)

Penny Sugg
COLOR ME DEAD(1969, Aus.); IT TAKES ALL KINDS(1969, U.S./Aus.); SQUEEZE
A FLOWER(1970, Aus.); NICHOLAS AND ALEXANDRA(1971, Brit.)

Michael Sugich
NIGHT GOD SCREAMED, THE(1975)

Toshio Sugie
DEATH ON THE MOUNTAIN(1961, Jap.), d; SAGA OF THE VAGABONDS(1964,
Jap.), d; THREE DOLLS FROM HONG KONG(1966, Jap.), d

Yoshi Sugihara
BALLAD OF NARAYAMA(1961, Jap.), ed; STRAY DOG(1963, Jap.), ed

Yuko Sugihara
SPACE AMOEBA, THE(1970, Jap.); YOG-MONSTER FROM SPACE(1970, Jap.)

Shojiro Sugimoto
WAYSIDE PEBBLE, THE(1962, Jap.), ph

Haruko Sugimura
EARLY AUTUMN(1962, Jap.); OHAYO(1962, Jap.); TILL TOMORROW COMES(1962,
Jap.); WISER AGE(1962, Jap.); SAMURAI ASSASSIN(1965, Jap.); RED BEARD(1966,
Jap.); DAPHNE, THE(1967); FLOATING WEEDS(1970, Jap.); TOKYO STORY(1972,
Jap.)

Yoshio Sugino
SEVEN SAMURAI, THE(1956, Jap.), stunts

Aguri Sugita
NUTCRACKER FANTASY(1979), ph

Rie Sugiura
KARATE, THE HAND OF DEATH(1961)

Kenji Sugiyama
ALAKAZAM THE GREAT!(1961, Jap.), ph

Kohei Sugiyama
GATE OF HELL(1954, Jap.), ph

Mitsuhiro Sugiyama
FLIGHT FROM ASHIYA(1964, U.S./Jap.)

Shosaku Sugiyama
ZATOICHI(1968, Jap.)

Suguru Sugiyama
SPACE FIREBIRD 2772(1979, Jap.), d&w

Taku Sugiyama
MAGIC BOY(1960, Jap.), anim; FOX WITH NINE TAILS, THE(1969, Jap.), anim

Lena Sugrobova
RESURRECTION(1963, USSR)

T. Sugunuma
ANATAHAN(1953, Jap.)

Homare Suguro
NONE BUT THE BRAVE(1965, U.S./Jap.); NO GREATER LOVE THAN THIS(1969, Jap.)

Yunsung Suh
YONGKARI MONSTER FROM THE DEEP(1967 S.K.), w

Dan Suhart
OUTSIDERS, THE(1983)

Robert Suhosky
HOUSE WHERE EVIL DWELLS, THE(1982), w

Alex Suhr
REPTILICUS(1962, U.S./Den.)

Dorien Suhr
MEDIUM COOL(1969)

Edward Suhr
TRUNKS OF MR. O.F., THE(1932, Ger.), cos

George Suhr
WEB OF DANGER, THE(1947), set d; WYOMING(1947), set d

Tim Suhrstedt
ANDROID(1982), ph; FORBIDDEN WORLD(1982), ph
1984
SUBURBIA(1984), ph

Timothy Suhrstedt
HOUSE ON SORORITY ROW, THE(1983), ph

Anna Sui
OFFENDERS, THE(1980)

Ray Suideau
VOICES(1979)

Gay Suilin
HONEYBABY, HONEYBABY(1974)

Ch. Suin
FRENCH TOUCH, THE(1954, Fr.), ph

Charles Suin
MR. PEEK-A-BOO(1951, Fr.), ph; PRIZE, THE(1952, Fr.), ph; MONTE CARLO BA-BY(1953, Fr.), ph; MY SEVEN LITTLE SINS(1956, Fr./Ital.), ph

B. Suiter
KISS THEM FOR ME(1957)

Bill Suiter
JEANNE EAGELS(1957)

Bobra Suiter
TRADING PLACES(1983)

Sujata
ALADDIN AND HIS LAMP(1952); MERRY WIDOW, THE(1952); DESERT LE-GION(1953); DIAMOND QUEEN, THE(1953); FAIR WIND TO JAVA(1953); FLAME OF CALCUTTA(1953); KING OF THE KHYBER RIFLES(1953); SALOME(1953); BENGAL BRIGADE(1954)

Li Hai Suk
SECRET, THE(1979, Hong Kong)

Gregory Suke
PURSUIT OF D.B. COOPER, THE(1981)

Ronald Sukenick
OUT(1982), w

P. Sukhanov
TIGER GIRL(1955, USSR)

Ludmilla Sukharevskaya
ROAD HOME, THE(1947, USSR)

Lev Sukhov
FATHER OF A SOLDIER(1966, USSR), ph

Radha Sukhu
HAIR(1979)

Somboon Sukinan
1 2 3 MONSTER EXPRESS(1977, Thai.)

Sukman
MAGIC FACE, THE(1951, Aust.)

Harry Sukman
GOG(1954), m; RIDERS TO THE STARS(1954), m; BULLET FOR JOEY, A(1955), m; PHENIX CITY STORY, THE(1955), m, md; SCREAMING EAGLES(1956), m, md; FORTY GUNS(1957), m; SABU AND THE MAGIC RING(1957), m; OUTCASTS OF THE CITY(1958), m, md; UNDERWATER WARRIOR(1958), m, md; CRIMSON KIMONO, THE(1959), m; HANGMAN, THE(1959), m; VERBOTEN!(1959), m; SONG WITHOUT END(1960), m; FANNY(1961), m; THUNDER OF DRUMS, A(1961), m; UNDERWORLD U.S.A.(1961), m; MADISON AVENUE(1962), m, md; GUNS OF DIA-BLO(1964), m; AROUND THE WORLD UNDER THE SEA(1966), m; SINGING NUN, THE(1966), m; NAKED RUNNER, THE(1967, Brit.), m; WELCOME TO HARD TI-MES(1967), m; IF HE HOLLERS, LET HIM GO(1968), m; PRIVATE NAVY OF SGT. O'FARRELL, THE(1968), m

Henry Sukman
FURY AT SHOWDOWN(1957), m

Herman Sukman
BATTLE TAXI(1955), m

Barbara Sukowa
GERMAN SISTERS, THE(1982, Ger.); LOLA(1982, Ger.)

Imamu Sukuma
FIVE ON THE BLACK HAND SIDE(1973)

Mme. Sul-Te-Wan
THOROUGHBRED, THE(1930); HEAVEN ON EARTH(1931); KING KONG(1933); IMITATION OF LIFE(1934); MAID OF SALEM(1937); IN OLD CHICAGO(1938); KENTUCKY(1938); TOY WIFE, THE(1938); TELL NO TALES(1939); TORCHY PLAYS WITH DYNAMITE(1939); SAFARI(1940); KING OF THE ZOMBIES(1941); SUL-LIVAN'S TRAVELS(1941); REVENGE OF THE ZOMBIES(1943); SOMETHING OF VALUE(1957)
Silents
NARROW STREET, THE(1924)

Ondrej Sulaj
ASSISTANT, THE(1982, Czech.), w

Jana Sulcova
MATTER OF DAYS, A(1969, Fr./Czech.)

Jitka Sulcova
DO YOU KEEP A LION AT HOME?(1966, Czech.), ed; LEMONADE JOE(1966, Czech.), ed

Jackie Sule
FAST BREAK(1979)

Omari Suleman
SYNDICATE, THE(1968, Brit.)

Vassily Sulich
MRS. POLLIFAX-SPY(1971)

Aldo Suligoi
WAKE UP AND DIE(1967, Fr./Ital.)

Boleslaw Sulik
DEEP END(1970 Ger./U.S.), w; MOONLIGHTING(1982, Brit.), w

Zygmunt Sulistrowski
MARIZINIA(1962, U.S./Braz.), a, p&d, w; KAREN, THE LOVEMAKER(1970), p&d, w, m, ed

Juris Sulit
AMBUSH BAY(1966)

Leo Sulkey
OUR RELATIONS(1936)

Leo Sulky
SONS O' GUNS(1936); REAP THE WILD WIND(1942); SHE COULDN'T SAY NO(1954)
Silents
BIG TOWN IDEAS(1921)

Margaret Sullavan
ONLY YESTERDAY(1933); LITTLE MAN, WHAT NOW?(1934); GOOD FAIRY, THE(1935); SO RED THE ROSE(1935); MOON'S OUR HOME, THE(1936); NEXT TIME WE LOVE(1936); SHINING HOUR, THE(1938); SHOPWORN ANGEL(1938); THREE COMRADES(1938); MORTAL STORM, THE(1940); SHOP AROUND THE CORNER, THE(1940); APPOINTMENT FOR LOVE(1941); BACK STREET(1941); SO ENDS OUR NIGHT(1941); CRY HAVOC(1943); NO SAD SONGS FOR ME(1950)

Francois Sullerot
AU HASARD, BALTHAZAR(1970, Fr.)

Frank Sulley
WILD HARVEST(1947)

Alan Sullivan
SILENT BARRIERS(1937, Brit.), w
Silents
GET YOUR MAN(1921), w

Ann Sullivan
FLAW, THE(1955, Brit.)

Arthur Sullivan
MIKADO, THE(1939, Brit.), w; SET-UP, THE(1949); GREAT GILBERT AND SUL-LIVAN, THE(1953, Brit.), m; STRANGER'S MEETING(1957, Brit.); COOL MIKADO, THE(1963, Brit.), w; MIKADO, THE(1967, Brit.), w; PIRATE MOVIE, THE(1982, Aus.), w; PIRATES OF PENZANCE, THE(1983), w, m

Artie Sullivan
WHIPLASH(1948)

Barry Sullivan
HIGH EXPLOSIVE(1943); WOMAN OF THE TOWN, THE(1943); AND NOW TOMOR-ROW(1944); LADY IN THE DARK(1944); RAINBOW ISLAND(1944); DUFFY'S TAV-ERN(1945); GETTING GERTIE'S GARTER(1945); SUSPENSE(1946); FRAMED(1947); GANGSTER, THE(1947); SMART WOMAN(1948); ANY NUMBER CAN PLAY(1949); BAD MEN OF TOMBSTONE(1949); GREAT GATSBY, THE(1949); TENSION(1949); GROUNDS FOR MARRIAGE(1950); LIFE OF HER OWN, A(1950); NANCY GOES TO RIO(1950); OUTRIDERS, THE(1950); CAUSE FOR ALARM(1951); I WAS A COMMU-NIST FOR THE F.B.I.(1951); INSIDE STRAIGHT(1951); MR. IMPERIUM(1951); NO QUESTIONS ASKED(1951); PAYMENT ON DEMAND(1951); THREE GUYS NAMED MIKE(1951); UNKNOWN MAN, THE(1951); BAD AND THE BEAUTIFUL, THE(1952); SKIRTS AHOY!(1952); CHINA VENTURE(1953); CRY OF THE HUNTED(1953); JEOPARDY(1953); HER TWELVE MEN(1954); LOOPHOLE(1954); MIAMI STORY, THE(1954); PLAYGIRL(1954); QUEEN BEE(1955); STRATEGIC AIR COM-MAND(1955); TEXAS LADY(1955); JULIE(1956); MAVERICK QUEEN, THE(1956); DRAGON WELLS MASSACRE(1957); FORTY GUNS(1957); WAY TO THE GOLD, THE(1957); ANOTHER TIME, ANOTHER PLACE(1958); WOLF LARSEN(1958); PUR-PLE GANG, THE(1960); SEVEN WAYS FROM SUNDOWN(1960); LIGHT IN THE PIAZZA(1962); GATHERING OF EAGLES, A(1963); MAN IN THE MIDDLE(1964, U.S./Brit.); PYRO(1964, U.S./Span.); STAGE TO THUNDER ROCK(1964); HAR-LOW(1965); MY BLOOD RUNS COLD(1965); PLANET OF THE VAMPIRES(1965, U.S./Ital./Span.); AMERICAN DREAM, AN(1966); INTIMACY(1966); POPPY IS ALSO A FLOWER, THE(1966); BUCKSKIN(1968); IT TAKES ALL KINDS(1969, U.S./Aus.); TELL THEM WILLIE BOY IS HERE(1969); THIS SAVAGE LAND(1969); SHARK(1970, U.S./Mex.); CANDIDATE, THE(1972); EARTHQUAKE(1974); HUMAN FACTOR, THE(1975); TAKE A HARD RIDE(1975, U.S./Ital.); SURVIVAL(1976); OH, GOD!(1977); CARAVANS(1978, U.S./Iranian); FRENCH QUARTER(1978)
Misc. Talkies
OUTRIDERS, THE(1950); UNDER THE SIGN OF CAPRICORN(1971); GRAND JURY(1977); WASHINGTON AFFAIR, THE(1978)

Bill Sullivan
MOONLIGHTING WIVES(1966); MITCHELL(1975)

Billy Sullivan
SWEEPSTAKES(1931)
Silents
GOAT GETTER(1925); BROADWAY BILLY(1926); GALLANT FOOL, THE(1926); HEART OF A COWARD, THE(1926); ONE PUNCH O'DAY(1926); SPEED COP(1926); SPEED CRAZED(1926); WHEN SECONDS COUNT(1927); WALKING BACK(1928)
Misc. Silents
WHAT BECOMES OF THE CHILDREN?(1918); SLANDERERS, THE(1924); FEAR FIGHTER, THE(1925); FIGHTING FATE(1925); RIDIN' PRETTY(1925); FIGHTING THOROBREDS(1926); PATENT LEATHER PUG, THE(1926); RAPID FIRE RO-MANCE(1926); STICK TO YOUR STORY(1926); WINDJAMMER, THE(1926); WIN-NER, THE(1926); CANCELLED DEBT, THE(1927); DARING DEEDS(1927); SMILING BILLY(1927); SPEEDY SMITH(1927)

Brad Sullivan
PARADES(1972); STING, THE(1973); SLAP SHOT(1977); WALK PROUD(1979); IS-LAND, THE(1980); GHOST STORY(1981); COLD RIVER(1982); LINE, THE(1982)
Misc. Talkies
PARADES(1972)

Brick Sullivan
YELLOW JACK(1938); SHE LOVED A FIREMAN(1937); PHANTOM SUBMARINE, THE(1941); WHISTLING IN THE DARK(1941); LUCKY LEGS(1942); NAZI AGENT(1942); SABOTAGE SQUAD(1942); DON JUAN QUILLIGAN(1945);

FEAR(1946); LADY LUCK(1946); POSTMAN ALWAYS RINGS TWICE, THE(1946); SECRET LIFE OF WALTER MITTY, THE(1947); TYCOON(1947); CANON CITY(1948); FORCE OF EVIL(1948); THREE DARING DAUGHTERS(1948); WALLS OF JERI-CHO(1948); JOHNNY ALLEGRO(1949); ENFORCER, THE(1951); PAINTING THE CLOUDS WITH SUNSHINE(1951); WHIP HAND, THE(1951); JUST FOR YOU(1952); KANSAS CITY CONFIDENTIAL(1952); MEET ME AT THE FAIR(1952); CLOWN, THE(1953); FROM HERE TO ETERNITY(1953); UNDERSEA GIRL(1957)

Bud Sullivan
WHERE THERE'S LIFE(1947)

Buddy Sullivan
SCARLET ANGEL(1952); TURNING POINT, THE(1952)

C. Gardener Sullivan
Silents
WRATH OF THE GODS, THE or THE DESTRUCTION OF SAKURA JIMA(1914), w

C. Gardner Sullivan
ALIBI(1929), w; LOCKED DOOR, THE(1929), w; CUBAN LOVE SONG,THE(1931), w; HUDDLE(1932), w; SKYSCRAPER SOULS(1932), w; STRANGE INTER-LUDE(1932), w; MEN MUST FIGHT(1933), w; CAR 99(1935), w; FATHER BROWN, DETECTIVE(1935), w; THREE LIVE GHOSTS(1935), w; UNION PACIFIC(1939), w; NORTHWEST MOUNTED POLICE(1940), w; JACKASS MAIL(1942), w; BUCCA-NEER, THE(1958), w

Silents
BATTLE OF GETTYSBURG(1914), w; EDGE OF THE ABYSS, THE(1915), w; ITALI-AN, THE(1915), w; PAINTED SOUL, THE(1915), w; REWARD, THE(1915), w; ARY-AN, THE(1916), w; CIVILIZATION(1916), w; CORNER IN COLLEENS, A(1916), w; DIVIDEND, THE(1916), w; EYE OF THE NIGHT, THE(1916), w; HELL'S HIN-GES(1916), w; HOME(1916), w; MARKET OF VAIN DESIRE, THE(1916), w; NOT MY SISTER(1916), w; PEGGY(1916), w; CRAB, THE(1917), w; HATER OF MEN(1917), w; ICED BULLET, THE(1917), w; PINCH HITTER, THE(1917), w; BRANDING BROAD-WAY(1918), w; NAUGHTY, NAUGHTY!(1918), w; WHEN DO WE EAT?(1918), w; POPPY GIRL'S HUSBAND, THE(1919), w; SAHARA(1919), w; HAIRPINS(1920), w; SEX(1920), w; WHITE HANDS(1922), w; DULCY(1923), w; LONG LIVE THE KING(1923), w; SOUL OF THE BEAST(1923), w; STRANGERS OF THE NIGHT(1923), w; GOLDFISH, THE(1924), w; HOUSE OF YOUTH, THE(1924), w; ONLY WOMAN, THE(1924), w; MONSTER, THE(1925), t; TUMBLEWEEDS(1925), w; CORPORAL KATE(1926), sup; SPARROWS(1926), w; VANITY(1927), sup; WHITE GOLD(1927), sup; YANKEE CLIPPER, THE(1927), sup; SADIE THOMPSON(1928), t, ed; TEM-PEST(1928), w

Cathy Sullivan
LIGHT FANTASTIC(1964)

Charles Sullivan
LOCKED DOOR, THE(1929); MAN I LOVE, THE(1929); NIGHT PARADE(1929, Brit.); FOR THE DEFENSE(1930); HIT THE DECK(1930); TRUE TO THE NAVY(1930); PUBLIC ENEMY, THE(1931); SUICIDE FLEET(1931); TIP-OFF, THE(1931); YOUNG DONOVAN'S KID(1931); BEAST OF THE CITY, THE(1932); CARNIVAL BOAT(1932); SCARFACE(1932); FOURTH HORSEMAN, THE(1933); KING KONG(1933); MAYOR OF HELL, THE(1933); LADY BY CHOICE(1934); STRAIGHTAWAY(1934); TWENTY MILLION SWEETHEARTS(1934); CAR 99(1935); SHE GETS HER MAN(1935); MR. DEEDS GOES TO TOWN(1936); SAN FRANCISCO(1936); WEDDING PRESENT(1936); GIRL WITH IDEAS, A(1937); OLD CORRAL, THE(1937); ANGELS WITH DIRTY FACES(1938); GOODBYE BROADWAY(1938); GOLDEN BOY(1939); HELL'S KITCH-EN(1939); I STOLE A MILLION(1939); ONE HOUR TO LIVE(1939); SERGEANT MADDEN(1939); TORCHY PLAYS WITH DYNAMITE(1939); ENEMY AGENT(1940); THEY DRIVE BY NIGHT(1940); HIT THE ROAD(1941); HONKY TONK(1941); IN THE NAVY(1941); MANPOWER(1941); PHANTOM SUBMARINE, THE(1941); SAN FRAN-CISCO DOCKS(1941); SEA WOLF, THE(1941); BOSTON BLACKIE GOES HOLLY-WOOD(1942); BROADWAY(1942); GLASS KEY, THE(1942); LARCENY, INC.(1942); LUCKY LEGS(1942); THEY ALL KISSED THE BRIDE(1942); WE WERE DAN-CING(1942); YOU'RE TELLING ME(1942); OLD ACQUAINTANCE(1943); SWING FEVER(1943); DESTINATION TOKYO(1944); LOUISIANA HAYRIDE(1944); MAN FROM FRISCO(1944); MARSHAL OF RENO(1944); DUFFY'S TAVERN(1945); HONEYMOON AHEAD(1945); JOHNNY ANGEL(1945); SHE GETS HER MAN(1945); THOROUGHBREDS(1945); COURAGE OF LASSIE(1946); EASY TO WED(1946); NO-BODY LIVES FOREVER(1946); TRAFFIC IN CRIME(1946); EASY COME, EASY GO(1947); LIKELY STORY, A(1947); SONG OF THE THIN MAN(1947); DAREDEVILS OF THE CLOUDS(1948); RIVER LADY(1948); WHIPLASH(1948); KNOCK ON ANY DOOR(1949); MISS GRANT TAKES RICHMOND(1949); SET-UP, THE(1949); TAKE ME OUT TO THE BALL GAME(1949); HOEDOWN(1950); DOUBLE DYNAMITE(1951); IRON MAN, THE(1951); KANSAS CITY CONFIDENTIAL(1952); THIS WOMAN IS DANGEROUS(1952); WOMAN IN THE DARK(1952); DREAM WIFE(1953); JUBILEE TRAIL(1954)

Silents
BEHIND THE FRONT(1926)

Charlie Sullivan
YELLOW JACK(1938); DANCING LADY(1933); DANTE'S INFERNO(1935); DR. SOCRATES(1935); RUMBA(1935); KID GALAHAD(1937); LAST GANGSTER, THE(1937); OH DOCTOR(1937); PERFECT SPECIMEN, THE(1937); PICK A STAR(1937); KING OF THE NEWSBOYS(1938); MIDNIGHT INTRUDER(1938); RECK-LESS LIVING(1938); TEST PILOT(1938); DEAD MAN'S GULCH(1943); MY BUD-DY(1944); EL PASO KID, THE(1946); LIVE WIRES(1946); OUT OF THE STORM(1948); SHANGHAI CHEST, THE(1948); FIGHTING FOOLS(1949); LAST HURRAH, THE(1958)

D.J. Sullivan
GOING APE!(1981)

Danny Sullivan
Silents
OTHER MAN'S WIFE, THE(1919)

David Sullivan
ADAM AT 6 A.M.(1970)

Didi Sullivan [Didi Perego]
CALTIKI, THE IMMORTAL MONSTER(1959, Ital.)

Don Sullivan
SEVEN GUNS TO MESA(1958); GIANT GILA MONSTER, THE(1959); MONSTER OF PIEDRAS BLANCAS, THE(1959); REBEL SET, THE(1959); TEENAGE ZOM-BIES(1960); PARADISE ALLEY(1962); DON IS DEAD, THE(1973), set d; MR. RIC-CO(1975), set d; SPECIAL DELIVERY(1976), set d; MEAN DOG BLUES(1978), set d; GREAT SANTINI, THE(1979), set d

Donald J. Sullivan
GRASSHOPPER, THE(1970), set d

Doug Sullivan
ONE ON ONE(1977)

E.P. Sullivan
Misc. Silents
EVANGELINE(1914, Can.), d; BLACK CROOK, THE(1916)

Ed Sullivan
THERE GOES MY HEART(1938), w; BIG TOWN CZAR(1939), a, w; MA, HE'S MAKING EYES AT ME(1940), w; SENIOR PROM(1958); BYE BYE BIRDIE(1963); LAST OF THE SECRET AGENTS?, THE(1966); SINGING NUN, THE(1966); PHYNX, THE(1970)

Edward Sullivan
MR. H. C. ANDERSEN(1950, Brit.)

Edward Dean Sullivan
HELL BOUND(1931), w; PEOPLE'S ENEMY, THE(1935), w

Edward P. Sullivan
Silents
GOVERNOR'S BOSS, THE(1915); HOW MOLLY MADE GOOD(1915)

Eileen Sullivan
YOU ONLY LIVE TWICE(1967, Brit.), cos

Elliott Sullivan
MR. DODD TAKES THE AIR(1937); THEY WON'T FORGET(1937); ACCIDENTS WILL HAPPEN(1938); ANGELS WITH DIRTY FACES(1938); FURY BELOW(1938); GANGS OF NEW YORK(1938); NEXT TIME I MARRY(1938); RACKET BUS-TERS(1938); EACH DAWN I DIE(1939); I AM NOT AFRAID(1939); KING OF THE UNDERWORLD(1939); OKLAHOMA KID, THE(1939); ROARING TWENTIES, THE(1939); SMASHING THE MONEY RING(1939); SPELLBINDER, THE(1939); THAT'S RIGHT-YOU'RE WRONG(1939); THEY MADE ME A CRIMINAL(1939); MAN WHO TALKED TOO MUCH, THE(1940); MILLIONAIRES IN PRISON(1940); SAINT'S DOUBLE TROUBLE, THE(1940); HONKY TONK(1941); KNOCKOUT(1941); MAN-POWER(1941); SIS HOPKINS(1941); ZIEGFELD GIRL(1941); IN THIS OUR LI-FE(1942); JOHNNY EAGER(1942); LUCKY JORDAN(1942); MAN WITH TWO LIVES, THE(1942); PHANTOM KILLER(1942); THIS GUN FOR HIRE(1942); WILD BILL HICKOK RIDES(1942); ACTION IN THE NORTH ATLANTIC(1943); GENTLE GANG-STER, A(1943); NAKED CITY, THE(1948); LADY GAMBLES, THE(1949); GUILTY BYSTANDER(1950); TAXI(1953); SERGEANT, THE(1968); ON HER MAJESTY'S SECRET SERVICE(1969, Brit.); FEAR IS THE KEY(1973); GREAT GATSBY, THE(1974); SPIKES GANG, THE(1974); VAMPYRES, DAUGHTERS OF DRACU-LA(1977, Brit.)

Erin Sullivan
BOY NAMED CHARLIE BROWN, A(1969)

Ernest Sullivan
DIE, MONSTER, DIE(1965, Brit.), spec eff

Ernie Sullivan
DAMN THE DEFIANT!(1962, Brit.), spec eff; MAROC 7(1967, Brit.), spec eff

Errol Sullivan
CATHY'S CHILD(1979, Aus.), p; CROSSTALK(1982, Aus.), p

Erroll Sullivan
HOODWINK(1981, Aus.), p

Eugene I. Sullivan
THX 1138(1971)

Everett Sullivan
IN OLD KENTUCKY(1935); FURY(1936)

Francis L. Sullivan
CHINESE PUZZLE, THE(1932, Brit.); MISSING REMBRANDT, THE(1932, Brit.); WHEN LONDON SLEEPS(1932, Brit.); CALLED BACK(1933, Brit.); FIRE RAISERS, THE(1933, Brit.); F.P. 1(1933, Brit.); RIGHT TO LIVE, THE(1933, Brit.); CHEATING CHEATERS(1934); CHU CHIN CHOW(1934, Brit.); GREAT EXPECTATIONS(1934); POWER(1934, Brit.); RETURN OF BULLDOG DRUMMOND, THE(1934, Brit.); WHAT HAPPENED THEN?(1934, Brit.); HER LAST AFFAIRE(1935, Brit.); MYSTERY OF EDWIN DROOD, THE(1935); PRINCESS CHARMING(1935, Brit.); STRANGE WI-VES(1935); WANDERING JEW, THE(1935, Brit.); INTERRUPTED HONEYMOON, THE(1936, Brit.); LIMPING MAN, THE(1936, Brit.); RED WAGON(1936); ACTION FOR SLANDER(1937, Brit.); DINNER AT THE RITZ(1937, Brit.); FINE FEATHERS(1937, Brit.); NON-STOP NEW YORK(1937, Brit.); TWO WHO DARED(1937, Brit.); CITADEL, THE(1938); CLIMBING HIGH(1938, Brit.); DRUMS(1938, Brit.); GABLES MYSTERY, THE(1938, Brit.); KATE PLUS TEN(1938, Brit.); SPY OF NAPOLEON(1939, Brit.); WARE CASE, THE(1939, Brit.); SECRET FOUR, THE(1940, Brit.); TWENTY-ONE DAYS TOGETHER(1940, Brit.); AVENGERS, THE(1942, Brit.); LADY FROM LIS-BON(1942, Brit.); PIMPERNEL SMITH(1942, Brit.); BUTLER'S DILEMMA, THE(1943, Brit.); YOUNG MAN'S FANCY(1943, Brit.); FIDDLERS THREE(1944, Brit.); CAESAR AND CLEOPATRA(1946, Brit.); GREAT EXPECTATIONS(1946, Brit.); BROKEN JOURNEY(1948, Brit.); JOAN OF ARC(1948); SMUGGLERS, THE(1948, Brit.); TAKE MY LIFE(1948, Brit.); CHRISTOPHER COLUMBUS(1949, Brit.); RED DANUBE, THE(1949); LAUGHING LADY, THE(1950, Brit.); NIGHT AND THE CITY(1950, Brit.); WINSLOW BOY, THE(1950); BEHAVE YOURSELF(1951); MY FAVORITE SPY(1951); OLIVER TWIST(1951, Brit.); CARIBBEAN(1952); PLUNDER OF THE SUN(1953); SANGAREE(1953); DRUMS OF TAHITI(1954); HELL'S ISLAND(1955); PRODIGAL, THE(1955)

Francis W. Sullivan
Silents
FLAMES OF CHANCE, THE(1918), w

Frank Sullivan
BELLAMY TRIAL, THE(1929), ed; SO THIS IS COLLEGE(1929), ed; GIRL SAID NO, THE(1930), ed; IT'S A GREAT LIFE(1930), ed; SINS OF THE CHILDREN(1930), ed; UNHOLY THREE, THE(1930), ed; WAY FOR A SAILOR(1930), ed; EASIEST WAY, THE(1931), ed; JUST A GIGOLO(1931), ed; MATA HARI(1931), ed; MEN CALL IT LOVE(1931), ed; NEW ADVENTURES OF GET-RICH-QUICK WALLINGFORD, THE(1931), ed; ARE YOU LISTENING?(1932), ed; PAYMENT DEFERRED(1932), ed; GOING HOLLYWOOD(1933), ed; HOLD YOUR MAN(1933), ed; NUISANCE, THE(1933), ed; SOLITAIRE MAN, THE(1933), ed; WHAT! NO BEER?(1933), ed; DEATH OF THE DIAMOND(1934), ed; GAY BRIDE, THE(1934); MEN IN WHI-TE(1934), ed; OPERATOR 13(1934), ed; O'SHAUGHNESSY'S BOY(1935), ed; PUBLIC HERO NO. 1(1935), ed; WEST POINT OF THE AIR(1935), ed; FURY(1936), ed; LOVE ON THE RUN(1936), ed; OLD HUTCH(1936), ed; RIFF-RAFF(1936), ed; THREE GOD-FATHERS(1936), ed; DOUBLE WEDDING(1937), ed; GOOD OLD SOAK, THE(1937), ed; LAST OF MRS. CHEYNEY, THE(1937), ed; BAD MAN OF BRIMSTONE(1938), ed; THREE COMRADES(1938), ed; TOO HOT TO HANDLE(1938), ed; BABES IN ARMS(1939), ed; BAD LITTLE ANGEL(1939), ed; STAND UP AND FIGHT(1939), ed;

TARZAN FINDS A SON!(1939), ed; PHILADELPHIA STORY, THE(1940), ed; SPORTING BLOOD(1940), ed; TWENTY MULE TEAM(1940), ed; SMILIN' THROUGH(1941), ed; WILD MAN OF BORNEO, THE(1941), ed; WOMAN'S FACE(1941), ed; APACHE TRAIL(1942), ed; MOKEY(1942), ed; WHISTLING IN DIXIE(1942), ed; WOMAN OF THE YEAR(1942), ed; ASSIGNMENT IN BRITTANY(1943), ed; GUY NAMED JOE, A(1943), ed; THIRTY SECONDS OVER TOKYO(1944), ed; ADVENTURE(1945), ed; WITHOUT LOVE(1945), ed; ZIEGFELD FOLLIES(1945), w; HUCKSTERS, THE(1947), ed; JOAN OF ARC(1948), ed; CROOKED WAY, THE(1949), ed; FIREBALL, THE(1950), ed; JOHNNY ONE-EYE(1950), ed; TERESA(1951), ed; MUTINY(1952), ed; TARZAN'S SAVAGE FURY(1952), ed; MY GUN IS QUICK(1957), ed; ROCK ALL NIGHT(1957), ed; UNDEAD, THE(1957), ed; I BURY THE LIVING(1958), ed; SHE-GODS OF SHARK REEF(1958), ed; SHOWDOWN AT BOOT HILL(1958), ed; TERROR IN A TEXAS TOWN(1958), ed

Silents
LOVE'S BLINDNESS(1926), ed; TORRENT, THE(1926), ed; SLIDE, KELLY, SLIDE(1927), ed; WEST POINT(1928), ed; DEVIL'S APPLE TREE(1929), ed; SPITE MARRIAGE(1929), ed

Fred Sullivan
EVENINGS FOR SALE(1932); BLIND ADVENTURE(1933); EARL OF CHICAGO, THE(1940), ed
Silents
TAILOR MADE MAN, A(1922)
Misc. Silents
SOLITARY SIN, THE(1919), d

Fred G. Sullivan
COLD RIVER(1982), p,d&w

Frederick Sullivan
BLACK WATCH, THE(1929); ONCE A GENTLEMAN(1930); PRINCE OF DIAMONDS(1930); MURDER BY THE CLOCK(1931)
Silents
COURTSHIP OF MILES STANDISH, THE(1923), d; BEGGAR ON HORSEBACK(1925)
Misc. Silents
DIVORCE AND THE DAUGHTER(1916), d; FUGITIVE, THE(1916), d; MASTER SHAKESPEARE, STROLLING PLAYER(1916), d; PILLORY, THE(1916), d; SAINT, DEVIL AND WOMAN(1916), d; HER LIFE AND HIS(1917), d; WHEN LOVE WAS BLIND(1917), d; COVE OF MISSING MEN(1918), d; FACE ON THE BARROOM FLOOR, THE(1923)

Gayne Sullivan
DEMENTIA(1955)

George Sullivan
REVENGE OF THE NINJA(1983)

Gerald Sullivan
THIS OTHER EDEN(1959, Brit.)

Gerry Sullivan
STORK TALK(1964, Brit.); UNDERGROUND(1970, Brit.); EDUCATING RITA(1983)

Haley Sullivan
LAST OF THE LONE WOLF(1930)

Helene Sullivan
Silents
JACK STRAW(1920); SIGN OF THE ROSE, THE(1922)

Henry Sullivan
PERFECT UNDERSTANDING(1933, Brit.), m

Herminie Sullivan
DRUMS O' VOODOO(1934)

Hugh Sullivan
PERSECUTION AND ASSASSINATION OF JEAN-PAUL MARAT AS PERFORMED BY THE INMATES OF THE ASYLUM OF CHARENTON UNDER THE DIRECTION OF THE MARQUIS DE SADE, THE(1967, Brit.); TELL ME LIES(1968, Brit.); MIDSUMMER NIGHT'S DREAM, A(1969, Brit.)

Hughie Sullivan
HOMER(1970)

Ian Sullivan
EASY MONEY(1983)

J. M. Sullivan
SILENCE(1931); MADE FOR EACH OTHER(1939); HEAVENLY DAYS(1944)

J. Maurice Sullivan
TRIAL OF VIVIENNE WARE, THE(1932); WALKING ON AIR(1936)

James Sullivan
IN THE NAVY(1941); HAIRY APE, THE(1944), art d; TOMORROW THE WORLD(1944), art d; BANDITS OF THE BADLANDS(1945), art d; MEXICANA(1945), art d; STORY OF G.I. JOE, THE(1945), art d; IN OLD SACRAMENTO(1946), art d; INVISIBLE INFORMER(1946), art d; PASSKEY TO DANGER(1946), md; SUN VALLEY CYCLONE(1946), art d; THAT BRENNAN GIRL(1946), art d; EXPOSED(1947), art d; PILGRIM LADY, THE(1947), art d; THAT'S MY MAN(1947), art d; WEB, THE(1947), art d; ANGEL ON THE AMAZON(1948), art d; I, JANE DOE(1948), art d; OLD LOS ANGELES(1948), art d; OUT OF THE STORM(1948), art d; SLIPPY MCGEE(1948), art d; SONS OF ADVENTURE(1948), art d; FIGHTING KENTUCKIAN, THE(1949), art d; HELLFIRE(1949), art d; SANDS OF IWO JIMA(1949), art d; TOO LATE FOR TEARS(1949), art d; WAKE OF THE RED WITCH(1949), art d; SURRENDER(1950), art d; BELLE LE GRAND(1951), art d; INVASION U.S.A.(1952), art d; KID MONK BARONI(1952), art d; WILD BLUE YONDER, THE(1952), art d; CITY THAT NEVER SLEEPS(1953), art d; FLIGHT NURSE(1953), art d; SWEETHEARTS ON PARADE(1953), art d; WOMAN THEY ALMOST LYNCHED, THE(1953), art d; JOHNNY GUITAR(1954), art d; MURDER IS MY BEAT(1955), art d; WORLD OF HENRY ORIENT, THE(1964), prod d; RAGE TO LIVE, A(1965), art d; HAWAII(1966), art d; ONE OF OUR SPIES IS MISSING(1966), art d; CHARRO(1969), art d; DADDY'S GONE A-HUNTING(1969), art d; LIMBO(1972), art d

James Brick Sullivan
NEVER GIVE A SUCKER AN EVEN BREAK(1941); WHERE DANGER LIVES(1950)

James M. Sullivan
UNKNOWN TERROR, THE(1957), art d

James R. Sullivan
Misc. Silents
VENUS OF THE SOUTH SEAS(1924), d

James W. Sullivan
FLYING LEATHERNECKS(1951), art d; AROUND THE WORLD IN 80 DAYS(1956), art d; BACK FROM THE DEAD(1957), art d; JOHNNY TROUBLE(1957), art d; RIDE A VIOLENT MILE(1957), art d; DESERT HELL(1958), art d; SPY IN THE GREEN HAT, THE(1966), art d; KARATE KILLERS, THE(1967), art d; IF HE HOLLERS, LET

HIM GO(1968), art d

Jay Sullivan
TO KILL A MOCKINGBIRD(1962)

Jean Sullivan
UNCERTAIN GLORY(1944); ESCAPE IN THE DESERT(1945); ROUGHLY SPEAKING(1945); SQUIRM(1976)

Jennie Sullivan
PLAZA SUITE(1971)

Jenny Sullivan
GETTING STRAIGHT(1970); CANDIDATE, THE(1972); OTHER, THE(1972); BREAKFAST IN BED(1978)

Jeremiah Sullivan
OPEN THE DOOR AND SEE ALL THE PEOPLE(1964); DOUBLE STOP(1968); SOMEBODY KILLED HER HUSBAND(1978); SOLDIER, THE(1982)

Jerry Sullivan
HEAVEN'S GATE(1980)

Jim Sullivan
QUICK, LET'S GET MARRIED(1965), art d; YETI(1977, Ital.)

Joe Sullivan
THRILL OF A ROMANCE(1945); WHISTLE AT EATON FALLS(1951); CAREER GIRL(1960)

John Sullivan
DANGEROUS AGE, A(1960, Can.); TARZAN THE MAGNIFICENT(1960, Brit.); SECRET OF MONTE CRISTO, THE(1961, Brit.); ZULU(1964, Brit.), a, stunts; NOBODY WAVED GOODBYE(1965, Can.); LAST VALLEY, THE(1971, Brit.), stunts; TAMARIND SEED, THE(1974, Brit.); BARRY LYNDON(1975, Brit.); PINK PANTHER STRIKES AGAIN, THE(1976, Brit.); CARAVANS(1978, U.S./Iranian), stunts; FLASH GORDON(1980)

John M. Sullivan
STRANGERS IN LOVE(1932); THREE-CORNERED MOON(1933); YOU'RE TELLING ME(1934); POSTMAN ALWAYS RINGS TWICE, THE(1946)

John Maurice Sullivan
TODAY(1930); MYSTERY LINER(1934); HIGH, WIDE AND HANDSOME(1937); TOAST OF NEW YORK, THE(1937); WE HAVE OUR MOMENTS(1937); GOOD GIRLS GO TO PARIS(1939)

Joseph Sullivan
VICE RAID(1959); GIRL ON THE RUN(1961); RANCHO DELUXE(1975); NUNZIO(1978); GOING IN STYLE(1979)
Silents
$5,000,000 COUNTERFEITING PLOT, THE(1914)
Misc. Silents
COQUETTE, THE(1915)

Judy Sullivan
1984
RECKLESS(1984)

Kate Sullivan
SHE KNOWS Y'KNOW(1962, Brit.), w; PULP(1972, Brit.)

Kathleen Sullivan
THIRTY-DAY PRINCESS(1934); YOU'RE TELLING ME(1934); MAN WHO BROKE THE BANK AT MONTE CARLO, THE(1935); MELVIN AND HOWARD(1980)

Kerry Sullivan
WRONG IS RIGHT(1982)

Kevin Sullivan
MORE AMERICAN GRAFFITI(1979); STAR TREK II: THE WRATH OF KHAN(1982)
1984
ADVENTURES OF BUCKAROO BANZAI: ACROSS THE 8TH DIMENSION, THE(1984)

Kevin R. Sullivan
NIGHT SHIFT(1982)

Kim Sullivan
MAD MAX(1979, Aus.)

Lee Sullivan
GREAT JOHN L. THE(1945)

Liam Sullivan
MAGIC SWORD, THE(1962); ONE MAN'S WAY(1964); THAT DARN CAT(1965)

Louis Sullivan
NO DEFENSE(1929), md

Margarto Sullivan
PRIZE, THE(1963)

Maxine Sullivan
GOING PLACES(1939); ST. LOUIS BLUES(1939)

Michael Sullivan
YOU'VE GOT TO WALK IT LIKE YOU TALK IT OR YOU'LL LOSE THAT BEAT(1971); GREASER'S PALACE(1972); CAN'T STOP THE MUSIC(1980), spec eff; MADMAN(1982)

Mike Sullivan
PIRANHA(1978)

Neil Sullivan
WHY RUSSIANS ARE REVOLTING(1970), a, p,d&w
Silents
SURE FIRE FLINT(1922), ph; LUCK(1923), ph; AVERAGE WOMAN, THE(1924), ph; LEND ME YOUR HUSBAND(1924), ph; EARLY BIRD, THE(1925), ph

Owen Sullivan
DAMIEN–OMEN II(1978); 10(1979)

Pat Sullivan
IT HAPPENED HERE(1966, Brit.); SQUEEZE A FLOWER(1970, Aus.); ABSENCE OF MALICE(1981)

Patrick Sullivan
LOVE CHILD(1982)

Paul Sullivan
1984
NATURAL, THE(1984)

Peter Sullivan
MOB TOWN(1941); SAN ANTONIO ROSE(1941); SWING IT SOLDIER(1941); WHERE DID YOU GET THAT GIRL?(1941); IT'S A SMALL WORLD(1950), ed

Robert Sullivan
SEXTETTE(1978), p

Ron Sullivan
PUT UP OR SHUT UP(1968, Arg.), p; PUTNEY SWOPE(1969), p
Ruth Sullivan
JAWS OF JUSTICE(1933); FEROCIOUS PAL(1934)
Silents
CHILD FOR SALE, A(1920); NO MOTHER TO GUIDE HER(1923)
Misc. Silents
CHILDREN NOT WANTED(1920)
Sean Sullivan
DURING ONE NIGHT(1962, Brit.); GANG WAR(1962, Brit.); WONDERFUL TO BE YOUNG!(1962, Brit.); ADULTEROUS AFFAIR(1966); 2001: A SPACE ODYSSEY(1968, U.S./Brit.); CHANGE OF MIND(1969); DR. FRANKENSTEIN ON CAMPUS(1970, Can.); WHY ROCK THE BOAT?(1974, Can.); ONE MAN(1979, Can.); ATLANTIC CITY(1981, U.S./Can.); SILENCE OF THE NORTH(1981, Can.); DEAD ZONE, THE(1983); GREY FOX, THE(1983, Can.)
1984
MRS. SOFFEL(1984)
Misc. Talkies
PINOCCHIO'S GREATEST ADVENTURE(1974)
Sheila Sullivan
NAME FOR EVIL, A(1970); HICKEY AND BOGGS(1972)
Susan Sullivan
Misc. Talkies
SPORTS KILLER, THE(1976); KILLER'S DELIGHT(1978)
Tim Sullivan
PRICE OF FEAR, THE(1956); TIN STAR, THE(1957); DON'T KNOCK THE TWIST(1962); WILD WESTERNERS, THE(1962); RUN HOME SLOW(1965), p&d; DEADLY SPAWN, THE(1983), d&w
Tom Sullivan
AIRPORT '77(1977); COCAINE COWBOYS(1979), a, w; IF YOU COULD SEE WHAT I HEAR(1982), w; EVIL DEAD, THE(1983), makeup
Wallace Sullivan
WALLS OF GOLD(1933), w; LAUGHING IRISH EYES(1936), w; LIBELED LADY(1936), w; RETURN OF JIMMY VALENTINE, THE(1936), w; FOUR'S A CROWD(1938), w; BIG GUY, THE(1939), w; SABOTAGE SQUAD(1942), w; I ESCAPED FROM THE GESTAPO(1943), w; SPY TRAIN(1943), w; BEHIND THE HIGH WALL(1956), w
Walter Sullivan
SCOBIE MALONE(1975, Aus.)
1984
TAIL OF THE TIGER(1984, Aus.)
Wayne R. Sullivan
PICNIC(1955)
William Sullivan
MURDER BY TELEVISION(1935)
Silents
COURTSHIP OF MILES STANDISH, THE(1923)
Bob Sully
GUY NAMED JOE, A(1943)
Eve Sully
KID MILLIONS(1934)
Francois [Francis L. Sullivan] Sully
SOMEWHERE IN FRANCE(1943, Brit.)
Frank Sully
YOU CAN'T RUN AWAY FROM IT(1956); 365 NIGHTS IN HOLLYWOOD(1934); ALIBI IKE(1935); MARY BURNS, FUGITIVE(1935); FURY(1936); POPPY(1936); SMALL TOWN GIRL(1936); THEODORA GOES WILD(1936); CAPTAINS COURAGEOUS(1937); CRIMINALS OF THE AIR(1937); DAUGHTER OF SHANGHAI(1937); HIGH, WIDE AND HANDSOME(1937); LIFE BEGINS IN COLLEGE(1937); LIVE, LOVE AND LEARN(1937); HIS EXCITING NIGHT(1938); HOLD THAT CO-ED(1938); TEST PILOT(1938); THANKS FOR EVERYTHING(1938); ANOTHER THIN MAN(1939); MIRACLES FOR SALE(1939); NEWSBOY'S HOME(1939); NIGHT OF NIGHTS, THE(1939); SOME LIKE IT HOT(1939); CROSS COUNTRY ROMANCE(1940); DOCTOR TAKES A WIFE(1940); DR. KILDARE'S CRISIS(1940); ESCAPE TO GLORY(1940); FIGHTING 69TH, THE(1940); GRAPES OF WRATH(1940); HE STAYED FOR BREAKFAST(1940); LILLIAN RUSSELL(1940); RETURN OF FRANK JAMES, THE(1940); YESTERDAY'S HEROES(1940); YOUNG PEOPLE(1940); DOUBLE DATE(1941); FLAME OF NEW ORLEANS, THE(1941); GIRL, A GUY AND A GOB, A(1941); LET'S GO COLLEGIATE(1941); MOUNTAIN MOONLIGHT(1941); PRIVATE NURSE(1941); SHE KNEW ALL THE ANSWERS(1941); YOU'LL NEVER GET RICH(1941); ALL THROUGH THE NIGHT(1942); BOOGIE MAN WILL GET YOU, THE(1942); INSIDE THE LAW(1942); MAN'S WORLD, A(1942); MY SISTER EILEEN(1942); PARACHUTE NURSE(1942); RINGS ON HER FINGERS(1942); SLEEPYTIME GAL(1942); TALK OF THE TOWN(1942); TO THE SHORES OF TRIPOLI(1942); TRUE TO THE ARMY(1942); TWO YANKS IN TRINIDAD(1942); DANGEROUS BLONDES(1943); GOOD LUCK, MR. YATES(1943); LAUGH YOUR BLUES AWAY(1943); MORE THE MERRIER, THE(1943); ONE DANGEROUS NIGHT(1943); POWER OF THE PRESS(1943); THERE'S SOMETHING ABOUT A SOLDIER(1943); THEY GOT ME COVERED(1943); THOUSANDS CHEER(1943); TWO SENORITAS FROM CHICAGO(1943); GHOST THAT WALKS ALONE, THE(1944); SECRET COMMAND(1944); TWO GIRLS AND A SAILOR(1944); ALONG CAME JONES(1945); BOSTON BLACKIE BOOKED ON SUSPICION(1945); BOSTON BLACKIE'S RENDEZVOUS(1945); I LOVE A BANDLEADER(1945); BOSTON BLACKIE AND THE LAW(1946); CLOSE CALL FOR BOSTON BLACKIE, A(1946); CRIME DOCTOR'S MAN HUNT(1946); DANGEROUS BUSINESS(1946); GENTLEMAN MISBEHAVES, THE(1946); IT'S GREAT TO BE YOUNG(1946); ONE WAY TO LOVE(1946); OUT OF THE DEPTHS(1946); PHANTOM THIEF, THE(1946); RENEGADES(1946); TALK ABOUT A LADY(1946); BLONDIE'S REWARD(1948); GUN SMUGGLERS(1948); LET'S LIVE A LITTLE(1948); TRAPPED BY BOSTON BLACKIE(1948); BOSTON BLACKIE'S CHINESE VENTURE(1949); JOE PALOOKA IN THE COUNTERPUNCH(1949); BEAUTY ON PARADE(1950); BLONDIE'S HERO(1950); BODYHOLD(1950); HUMPHREY TAKES A CHANCE(1950); JOE PALOOKA MEETS HUMPHREY(1950); KILLER SHARK(1950); ROOKIE FIREMAN(1950); SQUARE DANCE KATY(1950); FATHER'S LITTLE DIVIDEND(1951); I WANT YOU(1951); LET'S MAKE IT LEGAL(1951); MAN IN THE SADDLE(1951); PEOPLE AGAINST O'HARA(1951); PRAIRIE ROUNDUP(1951); RED BADGE OF COURAGE, THE(1951); NIGHT STAGE TO GALVESTON(1952); NO ROOM FOR THE GROOM(1952); SNIPER, THE(1952); WITH A SONG IN MY HEART(1952); NORTHERN PATROL(1953); TAKE ME TO TOWN(1953); BATTLE OF ROGUE RIVER(1954); LAW VS. BILLY THE KID, THE(1954); REDHEAD FROM MANHATTAN(1954); SILVER LODE(1954); JUNGLE MOON MEN(1955);

NAKED STREET, THE(1955); SPOILERS, THE(1955); TENDER TRAP, THE(1955); DESPERADOES ARE IN TOWN, THE(1956); FRONTIER GAMBLER(1956); BUCKSKIN LADY, THE(1957); PAL JOEY(1957); ROCKABILLY BABY(1957); LAST HURRAH, THE(1958); BYE BYE BIRDIE(1963)
Misc. Talkies
SOUTH OF THE CHISHOLM TRAIL(1947)
Janet Sully
Silents
PETAL ON THE CURRENT, THE(1919)
Joe Sully
EACH DAWN I DIE(1939); THEY KNEW WHAT THEY WANTED(1940)
Robert Sully
HEAVENLY BODY, THE(1943); MEET ME IN ST. LOUIS(1944); AFFAIRS OF SUSAN(1945); LOVE LETTERS(1945); YOU CAME ALONG(1945); WHEN WORLDS COLLIDE(1951)
Ronald Sully
DON'T CRY, IT'S ONLY THUNDER(1982)
Sandra Sully
GETTING OVER(1981)
Thomas Sully
KNOCK ON ANY DOOR(1949)
Walter Sully
ON OUR SELECTION(1930, Aus.), ph
Charles Suln
ANYTHING FOR A SONG(1947, Ital.), ph
Sulochana
JUNGLE, THE(1952); KENNER(1969)
Arne Sultan
BOYS' NIGHT OUT(1962), w; PROMISE HER ANYTHING(1966, Brit.), w; THREE ON A COUCH(1966), w; NUDE BOMB, THE(1980), w
Sultana
JOHN GOLDFARB, PLEASE COME HOME(1964)
Augustus Sultatos
SHAME, SHAME, EVERYBODY KNOWS HER NAME(1969)
Mme. Sultewan
MARYLAND(1940)
Max Sulz
WALK WITH LOVE AND DEATH, A(1969)
Cyrus L. Sulzberger
PLAYGROUND, THE(1965), w
William Sulzer
Silents
GOVERNOR'S BOSS, THE(1915)
Yma Sumac [Amy Camus]
SECRET OF THE INCAS(1954); OMAR KHAYYAM(1957)
Coco Sumaki
Misc. Talkies
BLUE SEXTET(1972)
Michael Suman
FAUST(1964), d&w
Sumant
CHAPTER TWO(1979)
A. Sumarokov
TRAIN GOES TO KIEV, THE(1961, USSR); FAREWELL, DOVES(1962, USSR)
Desiree Sumarra
SAFE AT HOME(1962)
Slim Sumerville
SHANNONS OF BROADWAY, THE(1929)
David Summer
YOUNG AND WILLING(1964, Brit.)
Donna Summer
THANK GOD IT'S FRIDAY(1978)
Frederick Summer
Misc. Silents
UPSTART, THE(1916)
Geoffrey Summer
DOG AND THE DIAMONDS, THE(1962, Brit.)
Laura Summer
1984
HARD TO HOLD(1984)
LeVerne Summer
Misc. Talkies
JOE'S BED-STUY BARBERSHOP: WE CUT HEADS(1983)
Kitty Summerall
SMITHEREENS(1982)
Pat Summerall
BLACK SUNDAY(1977)
Mike Summerbee
VICTORY(1981)
Helga Summerfeld
Misc. Talkies
MAN ON THE SPYING TRAPEZE(1965)
Diane Summerfield
Misc. Talkies
BLACK GODFATHER, THE(1974); GAME SHOW MODELS(1977)
Eleanor Summerfield
DULCIMER STREET(1948, Brit.); STORY OF SHIRLEY YORKE, THE(1948, Brit.); ALL OVER THE TOWN(1949, Brit.); MAN ON THE RUN(1949, Brit.); NO WAY BACK(1949, Brit.); WEAKER SEX, THE(1949, Brit.); LAUGHTER IN PARADISE(1951, Brit.); THIRD VISITOR, THE(1951, Brit.); CRASH OF SILENCE(1952, Brit.); MAN BAIT(1952, Brit.); BOTH SIDES OF THE LAW(1953, Brit.); ISN'T LIFE WONDERFUL(1953, Brit.); MR. POTTS GOES TO MOSCOW(1953, Brit.); BLACK GLOVE(1954, Brit.); BLACKOUT(1954, Brit.); FINAL APPOINTMENT(1954, Brit.); IT'S GREAT TO BE YOUNG(1956, Brit.); ODONGO(1956, Brit.); NO ROAD BACK(1957, Brit.); TEARS FOR SIMON(1957, Brit.); CRY FROM THE STREET, A(1959, Brit.); DENTIST IN THE CHAIR(1960, Brit.); MILLIONAIRESS, THE(1960, Brit.); PETTICOAT PIRATES(1961, Brit.); SPARE THE ROD(1961, Brit.); GUNS OF DARKNESS(1962, Brit.); ON THE BEAT(1962, Brit.); RUNNING MAN, THE(1963, Brit.); WHY BOTHER TO KNOCK(1964, Brit.); OPERATION SNAFU(1965, Brit.); YELLOW HAT, THE(1966, Brit.); SOME WILL, SOME WON'T(1970, Brit.); WATCHER IN THE WOODS,

THE(1980, Brit.)

Jennifer Summerfield
MAN WITH TWO HEADS, THE(1972)

Joan Summerfield
HIGH TREASON(1937, Brit.)

Mark Summerfield
DOLL'S HOUSE, A(1973)

Marvin Summerfield
ZIGZAG(1970), art d

Stefanie Summerfield
DOLL'S HOUSE, A(1973)

Sybil Summerfield
SAY IT WITH MUSIC(1932, Brit.)

Billy Summerford
TOMORROW(1972)

Augusta Summerland
AIRPORT 1975(1974)

Edgar Summerlin
WE SHALL RETURN(1963), m

Earl Summerline
SPRING FEVER(1983, Can.)

Capt. Summers
SUSPENSE(1946)

Ann Summers
MEXICAN SPITFIRE'S ELEPHANT(1942); AVENGING RIDER, THE(1943); FIGHTING FRONTIER(1943); FLIGHT FOR FREEDOM(1943); GILDERSLEEVE'S BAD DAY(1943); LADIES' DAY(1943); MEXICAN SPITFIRE'S BLESSED EVENT(1943); SEVENTH VICTIM, THE(1943); SKY'S THE LIMIT, THE(1943); GLASS HOUSES(1972)

Bill Summers
KID FROM CLEVELAND, THE(1949)

Bob Summers
IT'S A BIKINI WORLD(1967), m; LINCOLN CONSPIRACY, THE(1977), m; SIXTH AND MAIN(1977), m; BEYOND AND BACK(1978), m; GUYANA, CULT OF THE DAMNED(1980, Mex./Span./Panama), m; IN SEARCH OF HISTORIC JESUS(1980), m; BOOGENS, THE(1982), m; ONE DARK NIGHT(1983), m

Brian Summers
TOUCH OF THE SUN, A(1956, Brit.); STRANGE CASE OF DR. MANNING, THE(1958, Brit.)

Bunny Summers
FUZZ(1972); H.O.T.S.(1979); INDEPENDENCE DAY(1983)
1984
LAST STARFIGHTER, THE(1984); WEEKEND PASS(1984)

Deen Summers
PHANTOM OF THE PARADISE(1974)

Denise Summers
1984
LAUGHTER HOUSE(1984, Brit.)

Dolly Summers
FRENCH LINE, THE(1954)

Don Summers
WALK IN THE SUN, A(1945); THREE GODFATHERS, THE(1948); SHE WORE A YELLOW RIBBON(1949); TRIPOLI(1950); WAGONMASTER(1950); WHEN WILLIE COMES MARCHING HOME(1950)

Dorothy Summers
IT'S THAT MAN AGAIN(1943, Brit.); NO HAUNT FOR A GENTLEMAN(1952, Brit.)

Elizabeth Summers
HARRY AND WALTER GO TO NEW YORK(1976)

Esther Summers
CANON CITY(1948)

George Summers
EDGE OF THE WORLD, THE(1937, Brit.); U-BOAT 29(1939, Brit.)

Georgia Summers
NIGHT RIDERS, THE(1939)

Helen Debroy Summers
LONDON MELODY(1930, Brit.)

Hope Summers
ZERO HOUR!(1957); RETURN OF DRACULA, THE(1958); EDGE OF ETERNITY(1959); HOUND-DOG MAN(1959); INHERIT THE WIND(1960); CHILDREN'S HOUR, THE(1961); CLAUDELLE INGLISH(1961); HOMICIDAL(1961); PARRISH(1961); COUCH, THE(1962); SPENCER'S MOUNTAIN(1963); ONE MAN'S WAY(1964); HALLELUJAH TRAIL, THE(1965); GHOST AND MR. CHICKEN, THE(1966); FIVE CARD STUD(1968); ROSEMARY'S BABY(1968); SHAKIEST GUN IN THE WEST, THE(1968); LEARNING TREE, THE(1969); GET TO KNOW YOUR RABBIT(1972); WHERE DOES IT HURT?(1972); ACE ELI AND RODGER OF THE SKIES(1973); CHARLEY VARRICK(1973); OUR TIME(1974); FOUL PLAY(1978)

James Summers
PREHISTORIC WOMEN(1950); HANSEL AND GRETEL(1954), art d

Jaron Summers
PARALLELS(1980, Can.), w

Jason Summers
DETROIT 9000(1973)

Jeremy Summers
DEPTH CHARGE(1960, Brit.), d, w; PUNCH AND JUDY MAN, THE(1963, Brit.), d; CROOKS IN CLOISTERS(1964, Brit.), d; FERRY ACROSS THE MERSEY(1964, Brit.), d; SAN FERRY ANN(1965, Brit.), d; DATELINE DIAMONDS(1966, Brit.), d; FIVE GOLDEN DRAGONS(1967, Brit.), d; HOUSE OF 1,000 DOLLS(1967, Ger./Span./Brit.), d; EVE(1968, Brit./Span.), d; VENGEANCE OF FU MANCHU, THE(1968, Brit./Ger./Hong Kong/Ireland), d

Jerry Summers
LONE TEXAN(1959); LITTLE SHEPHERD OF KINGDOM COME(1961); PURPLE HILLS, THE(1961); FIREBRAND, THE(1962); YOUNG SWINGERS, THE(1963); LAW OF THE LAWLESS(1964); SURF PARTY(1964); YOUNG FURY(1965); KARATE KILLERS, THE(1967); COOGAN'S BLUFF(1968); HICKEY AND BOGGS(1972); WHAT'S UP, DOC?(1972); DILLINGER(1973); 99 AND 44/100% DEAD(1974)

Jill Summers
WHAT DO WE DO NOW?(1945, Brit.); AGATHA(1979, Brit.)

Jo Summers
LEFT-HANDED GUN, THE(1958); SPARTACUS(1960); MONEY TRAP, THE(1966)

John Summers
RAMPARTS WE WATCH, THE(1940)

Leslie Summers
DR. GOLDFOOT AND THE BIKINI MACHINE(1965); RED LINE 7000(1965); NEW YORK, NEW YORK(1977)

Lily Summers
DOWN OUR ALLEY(1939, Brit.)

Lorie Summers
"X"-THE MAN WITH THE X-RAY EYES(1963); MUSCLE BEACH PARTY(1964)

M. Summers
Misc. Talkies
FAT CHANCE(1982), d

Malcolm Summers
VICE VERSA(1948, Brit.)

Manuel Summers
FAT ANGELS(1980, U.S./Span.), d, w; THAT HOUSE IN THE OUTSKIRTS(1980, Span.), w

Neil Summers
LIFE AND TIMES OF JUDGE ROY BEAN, THE(1972); MY NAME IS NOBODY(1974, Ital./Fr./Ger.); MR. BILLION(1977)

Ray Summers
PURPLE HILLS, THE(1961), cos; FIREBRAND, THE(1962), cos; ZABRISKIE POINT(1970), cos; LE MANS(1971), cos; SOMETHING BIG(1971), cos; GETAWAY, THE(1972), cos; ULTIMATE THRILL, THE(1974), cos; PROPHECY(1979), cos; FINAL COUNTDOWN, THE(1980), cos; WRONG IS RIGHT(1982), cos
1984
ALL OF ME(1984), cos

Raymond H. Summers
TOGETHER BROTHERS(1974), cos

Richard Summers
SAN FRANCISCO STORY, THE(1952), w

Ricky Summers
RIOT(1969)

Robert Summers
GUARDIAN OF THE WILDERNESS(1977), m

Sean Summers
TOM SAWYER(1973)

Shannon Summers
HELLCATS, THE(1968)

Shari Summers
HAROLD AND MAUDE(1971); BAD NEWS BEARS, THE(1976); LAST MARRIED COUPLE IN AMERICA, THE(1980)

Tara Summers
BOLD AND THE BRAVE, THE(1956)

Virgil Summers
SABOTEUR(1942)

Walter Summers
FLAME OF LOVE, THE(1930, Brit.), d; RAISE THE ROOF(1930), p,d&w; SUSPENSE(1930, Brit.), p&d, w; FLYING FOOL, THE(1931, Brit.), d&w; HOUSE OPPOSITE, THE(1931, Brit.), p,d&w; MAN FROM CHICAGO, THE(1931, Brit.), d, w; TRAPPED IN A SUBMARINE(1931, Brit.), d, w; TIMBUCTOO(1933, Brit.), p, d, w; RETURN OF BULLDOG DRUMMOND, THE(1934, Brit.), d&w; WARREN CASE, THE(1934, Brit.), d&w; WHAT HAPPENED THEN?(1934, Brit.), d&w; HELL'S CARGO(1935, Brit.), d&w; MUSIC HATH CHARMS(1935, Brit.), d; REGAL CAVALCADE(1935, Brit.), d; LIMPING MAN, THE(1936, Brit.), p,d&w; LUCKY JADE(1937, Brit.), d&w; PRICE OF FOLLY, THE(1937, Brit.), p&d, w; BLACK LIMELIGHT(1938, Brit.), w; MUTINY OF THE ELSINORE, THE(1939, Brit.), w; HUMAN MONSTER, THE(1940, Brit.), d, w; ONE NIGHT IN PARIS(1940, Brit.), d; TORSO MURDER MYSTERY, THE(1940, Brit.), d, w; HOUSE OF MYSTERY(1941, Brit.), d; PIRATES OF THE SEVEN SEAS(1941, Brit.), w
Misc. Talkies
BUTTERFLY AFFAIR, THE(1934, Brit.), d
Silents
IF FOUR WALLS TOLD(1922, Brit.), w; KNOCKOUT, THE(1923, Brit.), w; UNWANTED, THE(1924, Brit.), d&w; NELSON(1926, Brit.), d&w; BATTLES OF THE CORONEL AND FALKLAND ISLANDS, THE(1928, Brit.), d; BOLIBAR(1928, Brit.), d&w; LOST PATROL, THE(1929, Brit.), d&w
Misc. Silents
AFTERGLOW(1923, Brit.), d; COST OF BEAUTY, THE(1924, Brit.), d; WHO IS THE MAN?(1924, Brit.), d; BATTLE OF MONS(1929), d; BETRAYAL, THE(1929), d; CHAMBER OF HORRORS(1929, Brit.), d

Frank Summerscales
CHILDREN OF THE DAMNED(1963, Brit.)

George Summerton
INGAGI(1931), ph

Peter Summerton
YOU CAN'T SEE 'ROUND CORNERS(1969, Aus.), p

Amelia Summerville
Silents
GETTING MARY MARRIED(1919); ROMOLA(1925)

Slim Summerville
LAST WARNING, THE(1929); ALL QUIET ON THE WESTERN FRONT(1930); FREE LOVE(1930); LITTLE ACCIDENT(1930); ONE HYSTERICAL NIGHT(1930); SEE AMERICA THIRST(1930); SPOILERS, THE(1930); TIGER ROSE(1930); TROOPERS THREE(1930); UNDER MONTANA SKIES(1930); BAD SISTER(1931); FRONT PAGE, THE(1931); HEAVEN ON EARTH(1931); LASCA OF THE RIO GRANDE(1931); MANY A SLIP(1931); RECKLESS LIVING(1931); AIR MAIL(1932); RACING YOUTH(1932); TOM BROWN OF CULVER(1932); UNEXPECTED FATHER(1932); HER FIRST MATE(1933); HORSEPLAY(1933); LOVE, HONOR, AND OH BABY!(1933); OUT ALL NIGHT(1933); THEY JUST HAD TO GET MARRIED(1933); LOVE BIRDS(1934); THEIR BIG MOMENT(1934); CAPTAIN JANUARY(1935); FARMER TAKES A WIFE, THE(1935); LIFE BEGINS AT 40(1935); WAY DOWN EAST(1935); CAN THIS BE DIXIE?(1936); COUNTRY DOCTOR, THE(1936); PEPPER(1936); REUNION(1936); WHITE FANG(1936); FIFTY ROADS TO TOWN(1937); LOVE IS NEWS(1937); OFF TO THE RACES(1937); ROAD BACK, THE(1937); FIVE OF A KIND(1938); KENTUCKY MOONSHINE(1938); REBECCA OF SUNNYBROOK FARM(1938); SUBMARINE PATROL(1938); UP THE RIVER(1938); CHARLIE CHAN IN RENO(1939); HENRY GOES ARIZONA(1939); JESSE JAMES(1939); WINNER TAKE ALL(1939); ANNE OF WINDY

POPLARS(1940); GOLD RUSH MAISIE(1940); HIGHWAY WEST(1941); PUDDIN' HEAD(1941); TOBACCO ROAD(1941); WESTERN UNION(1941); BRIDE BY MISTAKE(1944); I'M FROM ARKANSAS(1944); SWING IN THE SADDLE(1944); HOODLUM SAINT, THE(1946); MIGHTY MCGURK, THE(1946)
Misc. Talkies
SING ME A SONG OF TEXAS(1945)
Silents
TILLIE'S PUNCTURED ROMANCE(1914); BELOVED ROGUE, THE(1927); HEY! HEY! COWBOY(1927); PAINTED PONIES(1927); KING OF THE RODEO(1929); STRONG BOY(1929)
Misc. Silents
DENVER DUDE, THE(1927); RIDING FOR FAME(1928)
Cid Ricketts Sumner
PINKY(1949), w; TAMMY AND THE BACHELOR(1957), w; TAMMY, TELL ME TRUE(1961), w; TAMMY AND THE DOCTOR(1963), w; TAMMY AND THE MILLIONAIRE(1967), w
David Sumner
OUT OF THE FOG(1962, Brit.); TOUCH OF DEATH(1962, Brit.); FOLLOW THE BOYS(1963); WILD AFFAIR, THE(1966, Brit.); LONG DUEL, THE(1967, Brit.); 25TH HOUR, THE(1967, Fr./Ital./Yugo.); SUMARINE X-1(1969, Brit.)
Derek Sumner
DOUBLE, THE(1963, Brit)
Fred Sumner
HAPPINESS C.O.D.(1935)
Geoffrey Sumner
TOO MANY HUSBANDS(1938, Brit.); SHE COULDN'T SAY NO(1939, Brit.); LAW AND DISORDER(1940, Brit.); MURDER IN THE NIGHT(1940, Brit.); ONE NIGHT IN PARIS(1940, Brit.); DARK SECRET(1949, Brit.); HELTER SKELTER(1949, Brit.); WHILE THE SUN SHINES(1950, Brit.); DARK MAN, THE(1951, Brit.); TALE OF FIVE WOMEN, A(1951, Brit.); TRAVELLER'S JOY(1951, Brit.); ISLAND RESCUE(1952, Brit.); MR. LORD SAYS NO(1952, Brit.); THOSE PEOPLE NEXT DOOR(1952, Brit.); MR. POTTS GOES TO MOSCOW(1953, Brit.); ALWAYS A BRIDE(1954, Brit.); DOCTOR IN THE HOUSE(1954, Brit.); FLYING EYE, THE(1955, Brit.); SILKEN AFFAIR, THE(1957, Brit.); I ONLY ASKED!(1958, Brit.); BAND OF THIEVES(1962, Brit.); CUL-DE-SAC(1966, Brit.); THERE GOES THE BRIDE(1980, Brit.)
Graham Sumner
THIN RED LINE, THE(1964)
Jane Sumner
1984
SUPERGIRL(1984)
Misc. Talkies
HOT SUMMER IN BAREFOOT COUNTY(1974)
Josef Sumner
HIDE IN PLAIN SIGHT(1980)
Peter Sumner
COLOR ME DEAD(1969, Aus.); NED KELLY(1970, Brit.); AND MILLIONS WILL DIE(1973); MIDDLE AGE SPREAD(1979, New Zealand); CHANT OF JIMMIE BLACKSMITH, THE(1980, Aus.); SURVIVOR(1980, Aus.); BUSH CHRISTMAS(1983, Aus.)
Misc. Talkies
SPIRAL BUREAU, THE(1974)
Richard Sumner
TEXAS BAD MAN(1932)
Robin Sumner
YOUNG CASSIDY(1965, U.S./Brit.)
Will Sumner
PERSONALS, THE(1982), m
Donald Sumpter
LOST CONTINENT, THE(1968, Brit.); I AM A GROUPIE(1970, Brit.); NIGHT AFTER NIGHT AFTER NIGHT(1970, Brit.); WALKING STICK, THE(1970, Brit.); BLACK PANTHER, THE(1977, Brit.); MEETINGS WITH REMARKABLE MEN(1979, Brit.); CURSE OF THE PINK PANTHER(1983)
Ralph Sumpter
VAGABOND KING, THE(1956)
Irene Yah Ling Sun
HARPER VALLEY, P.T.A.(1978)
James Wong Sun
ENTER THE DRAGON(1973), art d
Leland Sun
JEKYLL AND HYDE...TOGETHER AGAIN(1982)
Li Sun
THREE CAME HOME(1950); I WAS AN AMERICAN SPY(1951); KOREA PATROL(1951)
Sabine Sun
WHAT'S NEW, PUSSYCAT?(1965, U.S./Fr.); FANTASTIC THREE, THE(1967, Ital./Ger./Fr./Yugo.); HARD CONTRACT(1969); MISTER FREEDOM(1970, Fr.); VALACHI PAPERS, THE(1972, Ital./Fr.); INCHON(1981)
Soo Hoo Sun
WELCOME DANGER(1929)
Abdullah Sunado
SAVAGE HARVEST(1981)
Abdulla Sunadu
WILBY CONSPIRACY, THE(1975, Brit.)
Sunanka
FLASH GORDON(1980)
Irving Sunasky
W.I.A.(WOUNDED IN ACTION)*1/2 (1966), p, d&w; WEDDINGS AND BABIES(1960), w; YEAR OF THE HORSE, THE(1966), d, w
Hideo Sunazuka
GODZILLA VERSUS THE SEA MONSTER(1966, Jap.)
Emily Sunbay
ONE LITTLE INDIAN(1973), cos
Emily Sunby
NOW YOU SEE HIM, NOW YOU DON'T(1972), cos
"Sunday"
ROUGH RIDING RANGER(1935)
Bert Sundberg
ELVIS! ELVIS!(1977, Swed.), p

Clinton Sundberg
LOVE LAUGHS AT ANDY HARDY(1946); MIGHTY MCGURK, THE(1946); UNDERCURRENT(1946); DESIRE ME(1947); GOOD NEWS(1947); HUCKSTERS, THE(1947); LIVING IN A BIG WAY(1947); SONG OF LOVE(1947); UNDERCOVER MAISIE(1947); COMMAND DECISION(1948); DATE WITH JUDY, A(1948); EASTER PARADE(1948); GOOD SAM(1948); KISSING BANDIT, THE(1948); MR. PEABODY AND THE MERMAID(1948); BARKLEYS OF BROADWAY, THE(1949); BIG JACK(1949); IN THE GOOD OLD SUMMERTIME(1949); ANNIE GET YOUR GUN(1950); DUCHESS OF IDAHO, THE(1950); FATHER IS A BACHELOR(1950); KEY TO THE CITY(1950); MRS. O'MALLEY AND MR. MALONE(1950); TOAST OF NEW ORLEANS, THE(1950); TWO WEEKS WITH LOVE(1950); AS YOUNG AS YOU FEEL(1951); FAT MAN, THE(1951); ON THE RIVERA(1951); BELLE OF NEW YORK, THE(1952); CADDY, THE(1953); GIRL NEXT DOOR, THE(1953); MAIN STREET TO BROADWAY(1953); SWEETHEARTS ON PARADE(1953); BACHELOR IN PARADISE(1961); HOW THE WEST WAS WON(1962); WONDERFUL WORLD OF THE BROTHERS ERIMM, THE(1962); BIRDS AND THE BEES, THE(1965); HOTEL(1967)
Hans Sundberg
LOVING COUPLES(1966, Swed.)
Par Sundberg
PIPPI IN THE SOUTH SEAS(1974, Swed./Ger.); PIPPI ON THE RUN(1977)
Clinton Sundburg
SONG OF THE THIN MAN(1947)
Emily Sundby
ONE AND ONLY GENUINE ORIGINAL FAMILY BAND, THE(1968), cos; SMITH(1969), cos; COMPUTER WORE TENNIS SHOES, THE(1970), cos; BAREFOOT EXECUTIVE, THE(1971), cos; SCANDALOUS JOHN(1971), cos; WILD COUNTRY, THE(1971), cos; $1,000,000 DUCK(1971), cos; NAPOLEON AND SAMANTHA(1972), cos; SNOWBALL EXPRESS(1972), cos; WORLD'S GREATEST ATHLETE, THE(1973), cos; CASTAWAY COWBOY, THE(1974), cos; HERBIE RIDES AGAIN(1974), cos; ESCAPE TO WITCH MOUNTAIN(1975), cos; SHAGGY D.A., THE(1976), cos; HERBIE GOES TO MONTE CARLO(1977), cos; NORTH AVENUE IRREGULARS, THE(1979), cos
Harry Sundby
TRUMAN CAPOTE'S TRILOGY(1969), ph
Mary Sunde
KID GALAHAD(1937)
Clinton Sundeen
PRINCE OF FOXES(1949)
Jean Sunderland
Silents
KAISER'S FINISH, THE(1918)
John Sunderland
1984
BLOODBATH AT THE HOUSE OF DEATH(1984, Brit.), art d
Misc. Silents
TO HELL WITH THE KAISER(1918)
Ninetta Sunderland
SWEEPINGS(1933)
Scott Sunderland
PYGMALION(1938, Brit.); GOODBYE MR. CHIPS(1939, Brit.)
Zoe Sunderland
KES(1970, Brit.)
Paul Sundfur
ATTACK OF THE KILLER TOMATOES(1978), m
Bill Sundholm
LAST MAN(1932); FEUDIN', FUSSIN' AND A-FIGHTIN'(1948)
Oscar W. Sundholm
ADVENTURE'S END(1937)
William Sundholm
LIFE BEGINS AT 40(1935); JOAN OF OZARK(1942); TRAIL TO VENGEANCE(1945); LOADED PISTOLS(1948)
Jere Sundin
Silents
CHORUS GIRL'S ROMANCE, A(1920)
Michael Sundin
1984
FOREVER YOUNG(1984, Brit.)
Per Olof Sundman
FLIGHT OF THE EAGLE(1983, Swed.), w
Folke Sundquist
BREAD OF LOVE, THE(1954, Swed.); WILD STRAWBERRIES(1959, Swed.); HOUR OF THE WOLF, THE(1968, Swed.); MY FATHER'S MISTRESS(1970, Swed.)
Gerry Sundquist
MEETINGS WITH REMARKABLE MEN(1979, Brit.); MUSIC MACHINE, THE(1979, Brit.)
1984
DON'T OPEN TILL CHRISTMAS(1984, Brit.)
Henry A. Sundquist
SAND CASTLE, THE(1961), ed; OPEN THE DOOR AND SEE ALL THE PEOPLE(1964), ed
Florence Sundstrom
ROSE TATTOO, THE(1955); VAGABOND KING, THE(1956); SPRING REUNION(1957); BACHELOR IN PARADISE(1961); LAST CHALLENGE, THE(1967); WORLD'S GREATEST LOVER, THE(1977)
Frank Sundstrom
SONG OF MY HEART(1947); NO TIME TO KILL(1963, Brit./Swed./Ger.); LOVING COUPLES(1966, Swed.); SHAME(1968, Swed.); STORY OF A WOMAN(1970, U.S./Ital.); GIRLS, THE(1972, Swed.)
Jacqueline Sundstrom
QUARE FELLOW, THE(1962, Brit.), w
Joan Sundstrom
FINNEY(1969)
Kurt Sundstrom
VALLEY OF EAGLES(1952, Brit.)
F. Sune
SOUTHERN STAR, THE(1969, Fr./Brit.), spec eff
Lia Siao Sung
BRUCE LEE–TRUE STORY(1976, Chi.)

Michael Sung
VARAN THE UNBELIEVABLE(1962, U.S./Jap.)
Ya Sing Sung
DESTINATION TOKYO(1944)
Yu Feng Sung
STORY OF DR. WASSELL, THE(1944)
Bruce Sunkees
NAKED ANGELS(1969)
J. Sunn
GOLDEN GATE GIRL(1941), ph
Brian Sunners
IT'S A WONDERFUL WORLD(1956, Brit.)
Jason Sunners
PUNISHMENT PARK(1971)
Eddie Sunrise
EXILES, THE(1966), m
Lee Sunrise
RIDE 'EM COWBOY(1942)
Riley Sunrise
ESCAPE TO BURMA(1955)
Bunny Sunshine
MR. SKEFFINGTON(1944); PILLOW TO POST(1945)
Clarence Sunshine
Silents
MAD DANCER(1925)
Jerry Sunshine
VALLEY OF THE DRAGONS(1961)
Mr. Sunshine
HONEYBABY HONEYBABY(1984)
The Sunshine Band
MISSISSIPPI RHYTHM(1949)
The Sunshine Boys
DRIFTIN' RIVER(1946); STARS OVER TEXAS(1946); TUMBLEWEED TRAIL(1946); RANGE BEYOND THE BLUE(1947); WILD COUNTRY(1947); SONG OF IDAHO(1948); WEST OF SONORA(1948); CHALLENGE OF THE RANGE(1949); QUICK ON THE TRIGGER(1949); PRAIRIE ROUNDUP(1951); JUNCTION CITY(1952)
The Sunshine Company
FOR SINGLES ONLY(1968)
Sunshine Girls
I'M FROM ARKANSAS(1944)
The Sunshine Girls
SONG OF IDAHO(1948)
The Sunshine Quartet
SCHLAGER-PARADE(1953)
Irene Sunters
WICKER MAN, THE(1974, Brit.)
Thach Suon
1984
KILLING FIELDS, THE(1984, Brit.)
Prabhakan Supare
GURU, THE(1969, U.S./India), ed
Branko Supek
RAMPAGE AT APACHE WELLS(1966, Ger./Yugo.)
Mark Supensky
FIEND(, set d, makeup
Glenn Super
1984
WHERE THE BOYS ARE '84(1984)
Ingrid Superstar
CHELSEA GIRLS, THE(1967)
Conchita Supervia
EVENSONG(1934, Brit.)
Ngamta Suphaphongs
BRIDGE ON THE RIVER KWAI, THE(1957)
Jerry Supiran
UNCOMMON VALOR(1983)
Ronald A. Suppa
PARADISE ALLEY(1978), p
Franz Suppe
STOLEN KISSES(1929), w
Walter Supper
BLACK ROSES(1936, Ger.), w
Cuyler Supplee
Silents
GEARED TO GO(1924); LIGHTNING ROMANCE(1924); LAST EDITION, THE(1925); LONE EAGLE, THE(1927); ONE GLORIOUS SCRAP(1927); ARIZONA CYCLONE(1928)
Misc. Silents
BRAND OF COWARDICE(1925)
Vincent Suprynowicz
CHILD IS A WILD THING, A(1976), ed
Antonin Sura
LEMONADE JOE(1966, Czech.)
Buz Suraci
MUPPET MOVIE, THE(1979)
Mark Suran
BLOOD AND BLACK LACE(1965, Ital.), ed
Valeska Suratt
Silents
IMMIGRANT, THE(1915); SOUL OF BROADWAY, THE(1915); NEW YORK PEACOCK, THE(1917)
Misc. Silents
JEALOUSY(1916); STRAIGHT WAY, THE(1916); VICTIM, THE(1916); RICH MAN'S PLAYTHING, A(1917); SHE(1917); SIREN, THE(1917); SLAVE, THE(1917); WIFE NUMBER TWO(1917)
Cholita Suray
TERROR IN THE JUNGLE(1968)

Yossif Surchadijev
WITH LOVE AND TENDERNESS(1978, Bulgaria)
George Arthur Surdez
DESERT LEGION(1953), w
Morris Surdin
HOSPITAL, THE(1971), m
Anna Maria Surdo
LEOPARD, THE(1963, Ital.)
Leyla Suren
YOU CAN'T WIN 'EM ALL(1970, Brit.), cos
Dmitriy Surenskiy
NIGHT BEFORE CHRISTMAS, A(1963, USSR), ph; MAGIC WEAVER, THE(1965, USSR), ph; JACK FROST(1966, USSR), ph
The Surftones
HELL'S PLAYGROUND(1967)
Alan M. Surgal
MICKEY ONE(1965), w
Tom Surgal
HOME MOVIES(1979), art d; VORTEX(1982), art d; FIRST TIME, THE(1983), art d
Helen Surgere
BRONTE SISTERS, THE(1979, Fr.)
Helene Surgere
BAROCCO(1976, Fr.)
Illia Surgutchoff
MAN WHO BROKE THE BANK AT MONTE CARLO, THE(1935), w
Ilya Surgutchoff
IF THIS BE SIN(1950, Brit.), w
Linda Surh
HAIR(1979)
Cristina Suriani
SAGA OF DRACULA, THE(1975, Span.)
Fred Surin
BRIDE IS MUCH TOO BEAUTIFUL, THE(1958, Fr.), d; VERY PRIVATE AFFAIR, A(1962, Fr./Ital.)
Daniela Surina
CHINA IS NEAR(1968, Ital.); DEAD ARE ALIVE, THE(1972, Yugo./Ger./Ital.)
Aida Suris
DOZENS, THE(1981)
Stephen Surjik
1984
RENO AND THE DOC(1984, Can.), prod d
Den Surles
HOSPITAL MASSACRE(1982); OSTERMAN WEEKEND, THE(1983)
1984
HOSPITAL MASSACRE(1984)
Nikolai Surorov
ISLAND OF DOOM(1933, USSR), set d
B. Surovtsev
MAGIC VOYAGE OF SINBAD, THE(1962, USSR)
Nicholas Surovy
FOR PETE'S SAKE!(1966); MAKE A FACE(1971); BANG THE DRUM SLOWLY(1973)
Nick Surovy
1984
ACT, THE(1984)
Alan Surtees
ADDING MACHINE, THE(1969); FRANKENSTEIN MUST BE DESTROYED!(1969, Brit.); EYE OF THE NEEDLE(1981)
Bruce Surtees
BEGUILED, THE(1971), ph; DIRTY HARRY(1971), ph; PLAY MISTY FOR ME(1971), ph; CONQUEST OF THE PLANET OF THE APES(1972), ph; GREAT NORTHFIELD, MINNESOTA RAID, THE(1972), ph; JOE KIDD(1972), ph; BLUME IN LOVE(1973), ph; HIGH PLAINS DRIFTER(1973), ph; OUTFIT, THE(1973), ph; LENNY(1974), ph; NIGHT MOVES(1975), ph; LEADBELLY(1976), ph; OUTLAW JOSEY WALES, THE(1976), ph; SHOOTIST, THE(1976), ph; SPARKLE(1976), ph; THREE WARRIORS(1977), ph; BIG WEDNESDAY(1978), ph; MOVIE MOVIE(1978), ph; DREAMER(1979), ph; ESCAPE FROM ALCATRAZ(1979), ph; INCHON(1981), ph; FIREFOX(1982), ph; HONKYTONK MAN(1982), ph; LADIES AND GENTLEMEN, THE FABULOUS STAINS(1982), ph; WHITE DOG(1982), ph; BAD BOYS(1983), ph; SUDDEN IMPACT(1983), ph
1984
BEVERLY HILLS COP(1984), ph; TIGHTROPE(1984), ph
Robert Surtees
LOST ANGEL(1944), ph; MEET THE PEOPLE(1944), ph; MUSIC FOR MILLIONS(1944), ph; THIRTY SECONDS OVER TOKYO(1944), ph; TWO GIRLS AND A SAILOR(1944), ph; OUR VINES HAVE TENDER GRAPES(1945), ph; STRANGE HOLIDAY(1945), ph; NO LEAVE, NO LOVE(1946), ph; TWO SISTERS FROM BOSTON(1946), ph; UNFINISHED DANCE,THE(1947), ph; BIG CITY(1948), ph; DATE WITH JUDY, A(1948), ph; KISSING BANDIT, THE(1948), ph; TENTH AVENUE ANGEL(1948), ph; ACT OF VIOLENCE(1949), ph; BIG JACK(1949), ph; INTRUDER IN THE DUST(1949), ph; THAT MIDNIGHT KISS(1949), ph; KING SOLOMON'S MINES(1950), ph; LIGHT TOUCH, THE(1951), ph; STRIP, THE(1951), ph; BAD AND THE BEAUTIFUL, THE(1952), ph; MERRY WIDOW, THE(1952), ph; WILD NORTH, THE(1952), ph; ESCAPE FROM FORT BRAVO(1953), ph; MOGAMBO(1953), ph; RIDE, VAQUERO!(1953), ph; LONG, LONG TRAILER, THE(1954), ph; VALLEY OF THE KINGS(1954), ph; OKLAHOMA(1955), ph; TRIAL(1955), ph; SWAN, THE(1956), ph; TRIBUTE TO A BADMAN(1956), ph; LES GIRLS(1957), ph; RAINTREE COUNTY(1957), ph; LAW AND JAKE WADE, THE(1958), ph; MERRY ANDREW(1958), ph; BEN HUR(1959), ph; CIMARRON(1960), ph; IT STARTED IN NAPLES(1960), ph; MUTINY ON THE BOUNTY(1962), ph; PT 109(1963), ph; KISSES FOR MY PRESIDENT(1964), ph; COLLECTOR, THE(1965), ph; HALLELUJAH TRAIL, THE(1965), ph; SATAN BUG, THE(1965), ph; THIRD DAY, THE(1965), ph; CHASE, THE(1966), ph; LOST COMMAND, THE(1966), ph; DOCTOR DOLITTLE(1967), ph; GRADUATE, THE(1967), ph; ARRANGEMENT, THE(1969), ph; SWEET CHARITY(1969), ph; LIBERATION OF L.B. JONES, THE(1970), ph; LAST PICTURE SHOW, THE(1971), ph; SUMMER OF '42(1971), ph; COWBOYS, THE(1972), ph; OTHER, THE(1972), ph; LOST HORIZON(1973), ph; OKLAHOMA CRUDE(1973), ph; STING, THE(1973), ph; GREAT WALDO PEPPER, THE(1975), ph; HINDENBURG, THE(1975), ph; STAR IS BORN, A(1976), ph; TURNING POINT, THE(1977), ph; BLOODBROTHERS(1978), ph; SAME TIME, NEXT YEAR(1978), ph

Sven Surtees
OCTOPUSSY(1983, Brit.)
The Surtees Twins
LORD OF THE FLIES(1963, Brit.)
Regis Survinski
NIGHT OF THE LIVING DEAD(1968), spec eff
Vincent Survinski
NIGHT OF THE LIVING DEAD(1968), prod d; THERE'S ALWAYS VANILLA(1972)
Bernard Sury
LIFE UPSIDE DOWN(1965, Fr.)
Arthur Sus
JULIUS CAESAR(1952)
Charlotte Susa
COPPER, THE(1930, Brit.); INHERITANCE IN PRETORIA(1936, Ger.); WATER FOR CANITOGA(1939, Ger.)
Misc. Silents
THOU SHALT NOT STEAL(1929, Ger.)
Katsuya Susaki
NONE BUT THE BRAVE(1965, U.S./Jap.), w
Black-Eyed Susan
KING OF THE GYPSIES(1978)
Julio Susana
LOVE IS A CAROUSEL(1970)
Patrick Susands
LOVE ON THE SPOT(1932, Brit.); DREAMS COME TRUE(1936, Brit.); SWORD OF HONOUR(1938, Brit.)
Silents
SAFETY FIRST(1926, Brit.); DAUGHTER IN REVOLT, A(1927, Brit.); MUMSIE(1927, Brit.)
Misc. Silents
HOUSE OF MARNEY(1926, Brit.)
Jacqueline Susann
VALLEY OF THE DOLLS(1967, a, w; LOVE MACHINE, THE,(1971), w; ONCE IS NOT ENOUGH(1975), w
Susanne
HOLLYWOOD HIGH(1977)
Peter Suschitzky
IT HAPPENED HERE(1966, Brit.), ph; VALENTINO(1977, Brit.), ph
Wolfgang Suschitzky
CAT AND MOUSE(1958, Brit), ph; LIVING FREE(1972, Brit.), ph
Peter Suschitzky
PRIVILEGE(1967, Brit.), ph; LOCK UP YOUR DAUGHTERS(1969, Brit.), ph; MIDSUMMER NIGHT'S DREAM, A(1969, Brit.), ph; GLADIATORS, THE(1970, Swed.), ph; LEO THE LAST(1970, Brit.), ph; MELODY(1971, Brit.), ph; HENRY VIII AND HIS SIX WIVES(1972, Brit.), ph; PIED PIPER, THE(1972, Brit.), ph; THAT'LL BE THE DAY(1974, Brit.), ph; ALL CREATURES GREAT AND SMALL(1975, Brit.), ph; LISZTOMANIA(1975, Brit.), ph; ROCKY HORROR PICTURE SHOW, THE(1975, Brit.), ph; EMPIRE STRIKES BACK, THE(1980), ph; KRULL(1983), ph
1984
FALLING IN LOVE(1984), ph
Peter Suschitzky II
THANK YOU ALL VERY MUCH(1969, Brit.), ph
Wolfgang Suschitzky
NO RESTING PLACE(1952, Brit.), ph; HORSE'S MOUTH, THE(1953, Brit.), ph; SMALL WORLD OF SAMMY LEE, THE(1963, Brit.), ph; SANDS OF BEERSHEBA(1966, U.S./Israel), ph; ULYSSES(1967, U.S./Brit.), ph; VENGEANCE OF SHE, THE(1968, Brit.), ph; RING OF BRIGHT WATER(1969, Brit.), ph; ENTERTAINING MR. SLOANE(1970, Brit.), ph; GET CARTER(1971, Brit.), ph; SOMETHING TO HIDE(1972, Brit.), ph; MOMENTS(1974, Brit.), ph; FALLING IN LOVE AGAIN(1980), ph
Boris Sushkevich
Misc. Silents
WHEN THE STRINGS OF THE HEART SOUND(1914, USSR), a, d; TSAR IVAN VASILYEVICH GROZNY(1915, USSR); FLOWERS ARE LATE, THE(1917, USSR), a, d; BREAD(1918, USSR), d
V. Sushkevich
RESURRECTION(1963, USSR)
Susi Bohm Dance School
SNOW WHITE(1965, Ger.)
Susie
FLIPPER'S NEW ADVENTURE(1964)
Marie Susini
MOUCHETTE(1970, Fr.)
Almanta Suska
1984
HUNTERS OF THE GOLDEN COBRA, THE(1984, Ital.)
Mitch Suskin
1984
SPLASH(1984), spec eff
Mitchell Suskin
E.T. THE EXTRA-TERRESTRIAL(1982)
Mikhail Suslov
1984
ON THE LINE(1984, Span.), ph; STRANGERS KISS(1984), ph
Judy Susman
ZOOT SUIT(1981)
Todd Susman
STAR SPANGLED GIRL(1971); LONERS, THE(1972); LITTLE CIGARS(1973); CALIFORNIA DREAMING(1979)
Henry Suso
DEATHSPORT(1978), d, w
Bernard Suss
READY FOR LOVE(1934); STRAIGHT FROM THE HEART(1935); ROSE BOWL(1936); CHAMPAGNE WALTZ(1937); EASY LIVING(1937); MAYTIME(1937); TRUE CONFESSION(1937); ACCIDENTS WILL HAPPEN(1938); IDIOT'S DELIGHT(1939); MOUNTAIN RHYTHM(1939); REMEMBER THE NIGHT(1940)
Bernie Suss
HE WALKED BY NIGHT(1948)

Herbert Sussan
NIGHTMARE IN WAX(1969), p
Deborah Sussel
TELL ME A RIDDLE(1980)
Arnim Sussenguth
COURT CONCERT, THE(1936, Ger.)
Walter Sussenguth
PILLARS OF SOCIETY(1936, Ger.)
Walther Sussenguth
CITY OF SECRETS(1963, Ger.)
Robert Sussfeld
ADVENTURES OF ARSENE LUPIN(1956, Fr./Ital.), p
David Susskind
EDGE OF THE CITY(1957), p; RAISIN IN THE SUN, A(1961), p; REQUIEM FOR A HEAVYWEIGHT(1962), p; ALL THE WAY HOME(1963), p; LOVERS AND OTHER STRANGERS(1970), p; PURSUIT OF HAPPINESS, THE(1971), p; ALICE DOESN'T LIVE HERE ANYMORE(1975), p; ALL CREATURES GREAT AND SMALL(1975, Brit.), p; SIMON(1980)
Steve Susskind
FRIDAY THE 13TH PART III(1982)
Barth Jules Sussman
BLOOD MONEY(1974, U.S./Hong Kong/Ital./Span.), w; NIGHT GAMES(1980), w
Joel Sussman
GUN RUNNER(1969), art d
Jiri Sust
CLOSELY WATCHED TRAINS(1967, Czech.), m; DAISIES(1967, Czech.), m; GIRL WITH THREE CAMELS, THE(1968, Czech.), m
F. Susui
WOMAN IN THE DUNES(1964, Jap.), ed
Akira Susuki
1984
ANTARCTICA(1984, Jap.), ed
Demmei Susuki
STOPOVER TOKYO(1957)
Tatsuo Susuki
DON'T RAISE THE BRIDGE, LOWER THE RIVER(1968, Brit.)
Jerzy Suszko
BOXER(1971, Pol.), w
Eddie Sutch
TOP OF THE FORM(1953, Brit.)
Herbert Sutch
Silents
HEARTS OF THE WORLD(1918); HUN WITHIN, THE(1918); SCARLET DAYS(1919); IDOL DANCER, THE(1920); ONE EXCITING NIGHT(1922); ORPHANS OF THE STORM(1922); WHITE ROSE, THE(1923)
Peter Sutchitsky
CHARLIE BUBBLES(1968, Brit.), ph
Rosemary Sutcliff
GHOST STORY(1974, Brit.), w
Clare Sutcliffe
I START COUNTING(1970, Brit.)
1984
PLOUGHMAN'S LUNCH, THE(1984, Brit.)
Olga Sutcliffe
WHERE LOVE HAS GONE(1964)
Marjorie Suter
NIGHT OF EVIL(1962)
A. Edward Sutherland
DANCE OF LIFE, THE(1929), a, d; FAST COMPANY(1929), d; SATURDAY NIGHT KID, THE(1929), d; POINTED HEELS(1930), d; SAP FROM SYRACUSE, THE(1930), d; SOCIAL LION, THE(1930), d; GANG BUSTER, THE(1931), d; JUNE MOON(1931), d; PALMY DAYS(1931), d; UP POPS THE DEVIL(1931), d; TOO MUCH HARMONY(1933), d; MISSISSIPPI(1935), d; POPPY(1936), d; CHAMPAGNE WALTZ(1937), d; EVERY DAY'S A HOLIDAY(1938), d; FLYING DEUCES, THE(1939), d; BEYOND TOMORROW(1940), d; ONE NIGHT IN THE TROPICS(1940), d; INVISIBLE WOMAN, THE(1941), d; NINE LIVES ARE NOT ENOUGH(1941), d; STEEL AGAINST THE SKY(1941), d; ARMY SURGEON(1942), d; NAVY COMES THROUGH, THE(1942), d; SING YOUR WORRIES AWAY(1942), d; DIXIE(1943), d; SECRET COMMAND(1944), d
A. Edward [Eddie] Sutherland
HAVING WONDERFUL CRIME(1945), d
Anne Sutherland
MY SIN(1931)
Misc. Silents
MOTHERHOOD(1917)
Claudette Sutherland
LITTLE ROMANCE, A(1979, U.S./Fr.)
Dan Sutherland
QUESTION OF ADULTERY, A(1959, Brit.), w
Delos Sutherland
Silents
SILK LEGS(1927), t; LADDIE BE GOOD(1928), t; MIDNIGHT LIFE(1928), t
Dick Sutherland
Silents
SAILOR-MADE MAN, A(1921); GRANDMA'S BOY(1922); RAGS TO RICHES(1922); RIP-TIDE, THE(1923); FIGHTER'S PARADISE(1924); JIMMIE'S MILLIONS(1925); BROKEN HEARTS OF HOLLYWOOD(1926); DON JUAN(1926); JAZZ GIRL, THE(1926); BELOVED ROGUE, THE(1927)
Misc. Silents
BATTLING MASON(1924); FIGHTING DEMON, THE(1925)
Donald Sutherland
CASTLE OF THE LIVING DEAD(1964, Ital./Fr.); BEDFORD INCIDENT, THE(1965, Brit.); DIE, DIE, MY DARLING(1965, Brit.); DR. TERROR'S HOUSE OF HORRORS(1965, Brit.); PROMISE HER ANYTHING(1966, Brit.); DIRTY DOZEN, THE(1967, Brit.); INTERLUDE(1968, Brit.); JOANNA(1968, Brit.); OEDIPUS THE KING(1968, Brit.); SEBASTIAN(1968, Brit.); SPLIT, THE(1968); ACT OF THE HEART(1970, Can.); ALEX IN WONDERLAND(1970); KELLY'S HEROES(1970, U.S./Yugo.); M(1970); START THE REVOLUTION WITHOUT ME(1970); JOHNNY GOT HIS GUN(1971); KLUTE(1971); LITTLE MURDERS(1971); DON'T LOOK NOW(1973, Brit./Ital.); LADY ICE(1973); STEELYARD BLUES(1973); S(1974); ALIEN THUNDER(1975,

US/Can.); DAY OF THE LOCUST, THE(1975); CASANOVA(1976, Ital.); EAGLE HAS LANDED, THE(1976, Brit.); 1900(1976, Ital.); KENTUCKY FRIED MOVIE, THE(1977); BLOOD RELATIVES(1978, Fr./Can.); INVASION OF THE BODY SNATCHERS(1978); NATIONAL LAMPOON'S ANIMAL HOUSE(1978); GREAT TRAIN ROBBERY, THE(1979, Brit.); MAN, A WOMAN, AND A BANK, A(1979, Can.); MURDER BY DECREE(1979, Brit.); BEAR ISLAND(1980, Brit.-Can.); NOTHING PERSONAL(1980, Can.); ORDINARY PEOPLE(1980); DISAPPEARANCE, THE(1981, Brit./Can.); EYE OF THE NEEDLE(1981); GAS(1981, Can.); MAX DUGAN RETURNS(1983); THRESHOLD(1983, Can.)
1984
CRACKERS(1984); ORDEAL BY INNOCENCE(1984, Brit.)
Misc. Talkies
BETHUNE(1977)

Duncan Sutherland
TERROR HOUSE(1942, Brit.), art d; NINE MEN(1943, Brit.), art d; FOR THOSE IN PERIL(1944, Brit.), art d; THUNDER ROCK(1944, Brit.), art d; UNDERGROUND GUERRILLAS(1944, Brit.), art d; JOHNNY FRENCHMAN(1946, Brit.), art d; LOVES OF JOANNA GODDEN, THE(1947, Brit.), art d; SAN DEMETRIO, LONDON(1947, Brit.), art d; HIDDEN ROOM, THE(1949, Brit.), art d; IT ALWAYS RAINS ON SUNDAY(1949, Brit.), art d; LAST HOLIDAY(1950, Brit.), art d; PINK STRING AND SEALING WAX(1950, Brit.), art d; DEAD MAN'S EVIDENCE(1962, Brit.), art d; MAKE MINE A DOUBLE(1962, Brit.), art d; STRONGROOM(1962, Brit.), art d; BAY OF SAINT MICHEL, THE(1963, Brit.), art d; FURY AT SMUGGLERS BAY(1963, Brit.), art d; JUNGLE STREET GIRLS(1963, Brit.), art d; PLEASURE LOVERS, THE(1964, Brit.), art d; PANIC(1966, Brit.), art d; VULTURE, THE(1967, U.S./Brit./Can.), art d

Ed Sutherland
COP HATER(1958), ed; LOST MISSILE, THE(1958, U.S./Can.), ed

Eddie Sutherland
GUN THE MAN DOWN(1957), ed
Silents
TILLIE'S PUNCTURED ROMANCE(1914); LOADED DOOR, THE(1922); SECOND HAND ROSE(1922); ABRAHAM LINCOLN(1924)
Misc. Silents
WHICH WOMAN?(1918); EVERYTHING FOR SALE(1921); JUST OUTSIDE THE DOOR(1921); WOMAN HE LOVED, THE(1922)

Edward Sutherland
CLOSE HARMONY(1929), d; BURNING UP(1930), d; MR. ROBINSON CRUSOE(1932), d; SECRETS OF THE FRENCH POLICE(1932), d; SKY DEVILS(1932), d, w; INTERNATIONAL HOUSE(1933), d; MURDERS IN THE ZOO(1933), d; DIAMOND JIM(1935), d; BOYS FROM SYRACUSE(1940), d; FOLLOW THE BOYS(1944), d; ABIE'S IRISH ROSE(1946), p&d; BERMUDA AFFAIR(1956, Brit.), d
Silents
ROUND UP, THE(1920); WITCHING HOUR, THE(1921); ELOPE IF YOU MUST(1922); NANCY FROM NOWHERE(1922); GIRL FROM THE WEST(1923); REGULAR FELLOW, A(1925), d; BEHIND THE FRONT(1926), d; IT'S THE OLD ARMY GAME(1926), p&d; FIREMAN, SAVE MY CHILD(1927), d; TILLIE'S PUNCTURED ROMANCE(1928), d; WHAT A NIGHT!(1928), d
Misc. Silents
LIGHT IN THE CLEARING, THE(1921); COMING THROUGH(1925), d; WILD, WILD SUSAN(1925), d; WE'RE IN THE NAVY NOW(1926), d; FIGURES DON'T LIE(1927), d; LOVE'S GREATEST MISTAKE(1927), d; BABY CYCLONE, THE(1928), d

Esther Sutherland
RIVERRUN(1968); BLACK BELT JONES(1974); TRUCK TURNER(1974); COMMITMENT, THE(1976); GOODBYE GIRL, THE(1977); NINE TO FIVE(1980); STIR CRAZY(1980); YOUNG DOCTORS IN LOVE(1982)

Ethel Sutherland
JUNE MOON(1931); COCK OF THE AIR(1932); STATE'S ATTORNEY(1932)

Evelyn Greenleaf Sutherland
Silents
MONSIEUR BEAUCAIRE(1924), w

Evelyn Sutherland
MONTE CARLO(1930), w

Everett Sutherland
MAN IN THE VAULT(1956), ed; SEVEN MEN FROM NOW(1956), ed; FOUR BOYS AND A GUN(1957), ed; STREET OF SINNERS(1957), ed; ISLAND WOMEN(1958), ed

Grant Sutherland
EDGE OF THE WORLD, THE(1937, Brit.); BREAKERS AHEAD(1938, Brit.); U-BOAT 29(1939, Brit.); PROUD VALLEY, THE(1941, Brit.); NINE MEN(1943, Brit.)

Hal Sutherland
JOURNEY BACK TO OZ(1974), d

Hamish Sutherland
EDGE OF THE WORLD, THE(1937, Brit.)

Hope Sutherland
TALK OF HOLLYWOOD, THE(1929)

Hugh Sutherland
Misc. Silents
TONGUES OF FLAME(1919)

Ian Sutherland
DEPUTY DRUMMER, THE(1935, Brit.), p; TRUST THE NAVY(1935, Brit.), p; HOT NEWS(1936, Brit.), p; VARIETY PARADE(1936, Brit.), p; CREEPER, THE(1980, Can.), w; IMPROPER CHANNELS(1981, Can.), w

James Sutherland
LITTLE KIDNAPPERS, THE(1954, Brit.); ROB ROY, THE HIGHLAND ROGUE(1954, Brit.)

John Sutherland
FLIGHT COMMAND(1940), w; BAMBI(1942); TOO MANY WINNERS(1947), p, w; LADY AT MIDNIGHT(1948), p; STRANGE MRS. CRANE, THE(1948), p

Keith Sutherland
HAPPY BIRTHDAY TO ME(1981)

Ken Sutherland
COOL WORLD, THE(1963); SAVANNAH SMILES(1983), m

Kiefer Sutherland
MAX DUGAN RETURNS(1983)
1984
BAY BOY(1984, Can.)

Lin Sutherland
WHOLE SHOOTIN' MATCH, THE(1979), p, w

Lynne Sutherland
1984
SACRED GROUND(1984), ed

Murray Sutherland
TOUGH ENOUGH(1983)

Nan Sutherland
UNCONQUERED(1947)

Ronald Sutherland
SUZANNE(1980, Can.), w

Sally Sutherland
HIS MAJESTY AND CO(1935, Brit.), w

Sid Sutherland
ADVENTURE'S END(1937), w

Sidney Sutherland
MATCH KING, THE(1932), w; I LOVED A WOMAN(1933), w; LADIES THEY TALK ABOUT(1933), w; FRIENDS OF MR. SWEENEY(1934), w; HI, NELLIE!(1934), w; I SELL ANYTHING(1934), w; I'VE GOT YOUR NUMBER(1934), w; LAUGHING IRISH EYES(1936), w; LEAVENWORTH CASE, THE(1936), w; SITTING ON THE MOON(1936), w; BOWERY BOY(1940), w; ALLOTMENT WIVES, INC.(1945), w; DIVORCE(1945), w; WIFE WANTED(1946), w

Taylor Sutherland
LAST CHASE, THE(1981), w

Victor Sutherland
HOUSE ON 92ND STREET, THE(1945); SLEEPING CITY, THE(1950); WHISTLE AT EATON FALLS(1951); CAPTIVE CITY(1952); LONE STAR(1952); WE'RE NOT MARRIED(1952); DONOVAN'S BRAIN(1953); POWDER RIVER(1953); THEM!(1954)
Silents
ONE DAY(1916); BAR SINISTER, THE(1917)
Misc. Silents
DANCER AND THE KING, THE(1914); THOSE WHO TOIL(1916); BUCHANAN'S WIFE(1918); FIREBRAND, THE(1918); HER PRICE(1918); LIAR, THE(1918); QUEEN OF HEARTS, THE(1918); SIGN INVISIBLE, THE(1918); VALLEY OF LOST SOULS, THE(1923); LOVE BANDIT, THE(1924)

Victor Sutherland, Sr.
PRIDE OF ST. LOUIS, THE(1952)

W. Macdonald Sutherland
GIVE HER A RING(1936, Brit.), art d

Yvonne Sutherland
CLAUDINE(1974)

Wayne Sutherlin
TELL THEM WILLIE BOY IS HERE(1969); 1,000 PLANE RAID, THE(1969); BLESS THE BEASTS AND CHILDREN(1971); CULPEPPER CATTLE COMPANY, THE(1972); GREAT NORTHFIELD, MINNESOTA RAID, THE(1972)

James Sutorius
CRUISING(1980); I'M DANCING AS FAST AS I CAN(1982)
1984
WINDY CITY(1984)

Alfred Sutro
LAUGHING LADY, THE(1930), w
Silents
JOHN GLAYDE'S HONOR(1915), w; SOCIETY SCANDAL, A(1924), w

John Sutro
INVADERS, THE,(1941), p; WAY AHEAD, THE(1945, Brit.), p; CARNIVAL(1946, Brit.), p; CHILDREN OF CHANCE(1949, Brit.), p; GLASS MOUNTAIN, THE(1950, Brit), p; TAMING OF DOROTHY, THE(1950, Brit.), p; CHEER THE BRAVE(1951, Brit.), p; HONEYMOON DEFERRED(1951, Brit.), p; KISENGA, MAN OF AFRICA(1952, Brit.), p

Grady Sutten
IN NAME ONLY(1939)

Larabie Sutter
WHITE SQUAW, THE(1956), w

Sonja Sutter
WILD DUCK, THE(1977, Ger./Aust.)

Joan Suttie
OLIVER TWIST(1951, Brit.), spec eff

Jennifer Suttles
1984
INITIATION, THE(1984)

Janine Sutto
KAMOURASKA(1973, Can./Fr.)

Arthur Sutton
1984
VIGIL(1984, New Zealand)

Brenda Sutton
FIVE ON THE BLACK HAND SIDE(1973); STUDENT TEACHERS, THE(1973)

Carol Sutton
SOUNDER, PART 2(1976)

Charles Sutton
Silents
GLADIOLA(1915); RAINBOW PRINCESS, THE(1916); PERSUASIVE PEGGY(1917); PAIR OF CUPIDS, A(1918); BEYOND PRICE(1921); AS A MAN LIVES(1923)
Misc. Silents
BLADE O' GRASS(1915); TEST, THE(1915); CELESTE OF THE AMBULANCE CORPS(1916); LAW OF THE NORTH(1917); PARDNERS(1917); ROYAL PAUPER, THE(1917); TELLTALE STEP, THE(1917); LOVE NET, THE(1918); HIT OR MISS(1919); GIRL OF THE GYPSY CAMP, THE(1925)

Charles W. Sutton
Misc. Silents
ETERNAL MOTHER, THE(1917)

Dolores Sutton
NINE MILES TO NOON(1963); TROUBLE WITH ANGELS, THE(1966); WHERE ANGELS GO...TROUBLE FOLLOWS(1968)

Dudley Sutton
BOYS, THE(1962, Brit.); LEATHER BOYS, THE(1965, Brit.); CROSSPLOT(1969, Brit.); ONE MORE TIME(1970, Brit.); WALKING STICK, THE(1970, Brit.); TOWN CALLED HELL, A(1971, Span./Brit.); CRY OF THE PENGUINS(1972, Brit.); PINK PANTHER STRIKES AGAIN, THE(1976, Brit.); VALENTINO(1977, Brit.); BIG SLEEP, THE½(1978, Brit.); ISLAND, THE(1980); BRIMSTONE AND TREACLE(1982, Brit.); TRAIL OF THE PINK PANTHER, THE(1982)

Misc. Talkies
DEVILS, THE(1971)
Ellen Sutton
YES SIR, MR. BONES(1951)
Emma Sutton
1984
SWORD OF THE VALIANT(1984, Brit.)
Frank Sutton
MARTY(1955); FOUR BOYS AND A GUN(1957); TOWN WITHOUT PITY(1961, Ger./Switz./U.S.); SATAN BUG, THE(1965)
Gertrude Sutton
BARNUM WAS RIGHT(1929); BIG NEWS(1929); ANYBODY'S WOMAN(1930); NAVY BLUES(1930); SOOKY(1931); EMERGENCY CALL(1933); SAILOR BE GOOD(1933); SON OF KONG(1933); WORKING MAN, THE(1933); PUBLIC OPINION(1935); TRAVELING SALESLADY, THE(1935); FURY(1936); LONGEST NIGHT, THE(1936); POPPY(1936); CAPTAINS COURAGEOUS(1937); EVER SINCE EVE(1937); SAY IT IN FRENCH(1938); SECOND FIDDLE(1939); TELL NO TALES(1939); DOCTOR TAKES A WIFE(1940)
Grady Sutton
LET'S GO NATIVE(1930); HOT SATURDAY(1932); MOVIE CRAZY(1932); PACK UP YOUR TROUBLES(1932); THIS RECKLESS AGE(1932); ONLY YESTERDAY(1933); STORY OF TEMPLE DRAKE, THE(1933); SWEETHEART OF SIGMA CHI(1933); BACHELOR BAIT(1934); ALICE ADAMS(1935); DR. SOCRATES(1935); GRIDIRON FLASH(1935); LADDIE(1935); MAN ON THE FLYING TRAPEZE, THE(1935); STONE OF SILVER CREEK(1935); KING OF THE ROYAL MOUNTED(1936); MY MAN GODFREY(1936); PALM SPRINGS(1936); PIGSKIN PARADE(1936); VALIANT IS THE WORD FOR CARRIE(1936); BEHIND THE MIKE(1937); DANGEROUS HOLIDAY(1937); LOVE TAKES FLIGHT(1937); SHE'S DANGEROUS(1937); STAGE DOOR(1937); TURN OFF THE MOON(1937); TWO MINUTES TO PLAY(1937); WAIKIKI WEDDING(1937); WE HAVE OUR MOMENTS(1937); ALEXANDER'S RAGTIME BAND(1938); HARD TO GET(1938); HAVING WONDERFUL TIME(1938); JOY OF LIVING(1938); MAD MISS MANTON, THE(1938); THREE LOVES HAS NANCY(1938); VIVACIOUS LADY(1938); ANGELS WASH THEIR FACES(1939); IT'S A WONDERFUL WORLD(1939); NAUGHTY BUT NICE(1939); THREE SONS(1939); YOU CAN'T CHEAT AN HONEST MAN(1939); BANK DICK, THE(1940); HE STAYED FOR BREAKFAST(1940); LUCKY PARTNERS(1940); SKY MURDER(1940); TOO MANY GIRLS(1940); TORRID ZONE(1940); WE WHO ARE YOUNG(1940); DOCTORS DON'T TELL(1941); FATHER TAKES A WIFE(1941); FLYING BLIND(1941); FOUR JACKS AND A JILL(1941); PENNY SERENADE(1941); SHE KNEW ALL THE ANSWERS(1941); YOU BELONG TO ME(1941); AFFAIRS OF MARTHA, THE(1942); BASHFUL BACHELOR, THE(1942); DUDES ARE PRETTY PEOPLE(1942); SOMEWHERE I'LL FIND YOU(1942); WHISPERING GHOSTS(1942); ALLERGIC TO LOVE(1943); LADY TAKES A CHANCE, A(1943); MORE THE MERRIER, THE(1943); WHAT A WOMAN!(1943); CASANOVA BROWN(1944); GOIN' TO TOWN(1944); GREAT MOMENT, THE(1944); HI BEAUTIFUL(1944); JOHNNY DOESN'T LIVE HERE ANY MORE(1944); NINE GIRLS(1944); SINCE YOU WENT AWAY(1944); WEEKEND PASS(1944); ANCHORS AWEIGH(1945); BELL FOR ADANO, A(1945); CAPTAIN EDDIE(1945); GRISSLY'S MILLIONS(1945); HER LUCKY NIGHT(1945); HIT THE HAY(1945); ON STAGE EVERYBODY(1945); PILLOW TO POST(1945); ROYAL SCANDAL, A(1945); STORK CLUB, THE(1945); THREE'S A CROWD(1945); DRAGONWYCH(1946); FABULOUS SUZANNE, THE(1946); IDEA GIRL(1946); IT'S GREAT TO BE YOUNG(1946); MAGNIFICENT ROGUE, THE(1946); NOBODY LIVES FOREVER(1946); PARTNERS IN TIME(1946); PLAINSMAN AND THE LADY(1946); SHOW-OFF, THE(1946); SUSIE STEPS OUT(1946); TWO SISTERS FROM BOSTON(1946); BEAT THE BAND(1947); DEAD RECKONING(1947); MY WILD IRISH ROSE(1947); PHILO VANCE'S GAMBLE(1947); LAST OF THE WILD HORSES(1948); MY DEAR SECRETARY(1948); ROMANCE ON THE HIGH SEAS(1948); AIR HOSTESS(1949); GRAND CANYON(1949); LIVING IT UP(1954); STAR IS BORN, A(1954); WHITE CHRISTMAS(1954); CHAPMAN REPORT, THE(1962); JUMBO(1962); MADISON AVENUE(1962); MY FAIR LADY(1964); BOUNTY KILLER, THE(1965); TICKLE ME(1965); CHASE, THE(1966); PARADISE, HAWAIIAN STYLE(1966); I LOVE YOU, ALICE B. TOKLAS!(1968); GREAT BANK ROBBERY, THE(1969); SUPPOSE THEY GAVE A WAR AND NOBODY CAME?(1970); SUPPORT YOUR LOCAL GUNFIGHTER(1971); ROCK 'N' ROLL HIGH SCHOOL(1979)
Silents
FRESHMAN, THE(1925); SKINNER'S DRESS SUIT(1926)
Hazel Sutton
SCOTLAND YARD INSPECTOR(1952, Brit.)
Henry Sutton
CHEAP DETECTIVE, THE(1978); CHAPTER TWO(1979); S.O.B.(1981)
James Sutton
ROLLOVER(1981)
Jan Sutton
STREET CORNER(1948)
Joana Sutton
DANTE'S INFERNO(1935)
John Sutton
BULLDOG DRUMMOND COMES BACK(1937); BLOND CHEAT(1938); BOOLOO(1938); DAWN PATROL, THE(1938); FOOLS FOR SCANDAL(1938); FOUR MEN AND A PRAYER(1938); ARREST BULLDOG DRUMMOND(1939, Brit.); BULLDOG DRUMMOND'S BRIDE(1939); CHARLIE MC CARTHY, DETECTIVE(1939); PRIVATE LIVES OF ELIZABETH AND ESSEX, THE(1939); SUSANNAH OF THE MOUNTIES(1939); TOWER OF LONDON(1939); ZAZA(1939); HUDSON'S BAY(1940); I CAN'T GIVE YOU ANYTHING BUT LOVE, BABY(1940); INVISIBLE MAN RETURNS, THE(1940); MURDER OVER NEW YORK(1940); SOUTH TO KARANGA(1940); MOON OVER HER SHOULDER(1941); VERY YOUNG LADY, A(1941); YANK IN THE R.A.F., A(1941); MY GAL SAL(1942); TEN GENTLEMEN FROM WEST POINT(1942); THUNDER BIRDS(1942); TONIGHT WE RAID CALAIS(1943); HOUR BEFORE THE DAWN, THE(1944); JANE EYRE(1944); CLAUDIA AND DAVID(1946); CAPTAIN FROM CASTILE(1947); ADVENTURES OF CASANOVA(1948); COUNTERFEITERS, THE(1948); MICKEY(1948); THREE MUSKETEERS, THE(1948); BAGDAD(1949); BRIDE OF VENGEANCE(1949); FAN, THE(1949); SECOND FACE, THE(1950); DAVID AND BATHSHEBA(1951); PAYMENT ON DEMAND(1951); SECOND WOMAN, THE(1951); CAPTAIN PIRATE(1952); FIVE FINGERS(1952); GOLDEN HAWK, THE(1952); LADY IN THE IRON MASK(1952); MY COUSIN RACHEL(1952); THIEF OF DAMASCUS(1952); EAST OF SUMATRA(1953); SANGAREE(1953); DEATH OF A SCOUNDREL(1956); BAT, THE(1959); BELOVED INFIDEL(1959); RETURN OF THE FLY(1959); CANADIANS, THE(1961, Brit.); MARIZINIA(1962, U.S./Braz.); SHADOW OF FEAR(1963, Brit.); OF HUMAN BONDAGE(1964, Brit.); DRUMS OF TABU, THE(1967, Ital./Span.); LAST SAFARI, THE(1967, Brit.)

Juana Sutton
MODERN TIMES(1936)
Julia Sutton
HALF A SIXPENCE(1967, Brit.)
Karen Sutton
GETTING OF WISDOM, THE(1977, Aus.)
Kay Sutton
OLD MAN RHYTHM(1935); RECKLESS(1935); ROBERTA(1935); FOLLOW THE FLEET(1936); CAREFREE(1938); HAVING WONDERFUL TIME(1938); I'M FROM THE CITY(1938); LAWLESS VALLEY(1938); MAD MISS MANTON, THE(1938); SAINT IN NEW YORK, THE(1938); SMASHING THE RACKETS(1938); THIS MARRIAGE BUSINESS(1938); VIVACIOUS LADY(1938); S.O.S. TIDAL WAVE(1939); STORY OF VERNON AND IRENE CASTLE, THE(1939); BANK DICK, THE(1940); LAUGHING AT DANGER(1940); LI'L ABNER(1940); MAN FROM MONTREAL, THE(1940); MAN WHO TALKED TOO MUCH, THE(1940); FLYING BLIND(1941); SERGEANT YORK(1941); TRIAL OF MARY DUGAN, THE(1941); YOU'RE OUT OF LUCK(1941); STATE FAIR(1962); PAJAMA PARTY(1964)
Kevin Sutton
JUST LIKE A WOMAN(1967, Brit.), m
Lisa Sutton
1984
RAW COURAGE(1984)
Lon Sutton
INVINCIBLE SIX, THE(1970, U.S./Iran)
Lori Sutton
HISTORY OF THE WORLD, PART 1(1981)
1984
NIGHT PATROL(1984); UP THE CREEK(1984)
Lorie Sutton
FAST TIMES AT RIDGEMONT HIGH(1982)
Mark Sutton
ROLLOVER(1981); WORLD ACCORDING TO GARP, The(1982)
Paul Sutton
FIREFLY, THE(1937); RIO GRANDE RANGER(1937); UNDER STRANGE FLAGS(1937); AIR DEVILS(1938); BAR 20 JUSTICE(1938); IN OLD MEXICO(1938); SHADOWS OVER SHANGHAI(1938); SPY RING, THE(1938); BALALAIKA(1939); GIRL AND THE GAMBLER, THE(1939); JESSE JAMES(1939); MIRACLES FOR SALE(1939); NORTH OF THE YUKON(1939); CHAD HANNA(1940); FOREIGN CORRESPONDENT(1940); GRAPES OF WRATH(1940); LITTLE OLD NEW YORK(1940); MARK OF ZORRO, THE(1940); NORTHWEST MOUNTED POLICE(1940); LAST OF THE DUANES(1941); NEW WINE(1941); PINTO KID, THE(1941); RIDE ON VAQUERO(1941); SUNSET MURDER CASE(1941); WILD GEESE CALLING(1941); IN OLD CALIFORNIA(1942); RIDERS OF THE NORTHLAND(1942); SUNDOWN JIM(1942); TOMBSTONE, THE TOWN TOO TOUGH TO DIE(1942); SILVER CITY RAIDERS(1943); ALONG CAME JONES(1945)
1984
PREPPIES(1984)
Prudence Sutton
Misc. Silents
PITFALLS OF PASSION(1927)
Raymond Sutton
DOGPOUND SHUFFLE(1975, Can.)
Robert Sutton
LOST COMMAND, THE(1966); SUDDEN IMPACT(1983)
Robert Ray Sutton
CHAMP, THE(1979)
Sharon Sutton
RAT FINK(1965)
Tom Sutton
STRANGE SHADOWS IN AN EMPTY ROOM(1977, Can./Ital.), stunts; RUN FOR THE ROSES(1978), stunts
Victor Sutton
MIDDLE AGE CRAZY(1980, Can.)
Betty Suttor
JEDDA, THE UNCIVILIZED(1956, Aus.)
V. Sutyrin
Misc. Silents
RED IMPS(1923, USSR)
Gus Suvall
Silents
WESTERN MUSKETEER, THE(1922)
M. Suvorov
MARRIAGE OF BALZAMINOV, THE(1966, USSR)
Nikolai Suvorov
THUNDERSTORM(1934, USSR), set d
Ikio Suwamura
GEISHA GIRL(1952)
Sulaliwan Suwanatat
1 2 3 MONSTER EXPRESS(1977, Thai.)
Robina Suwol
1984
LONELY GUY, THE(1984)
Han Suyin
LOVE IS A MANY-SPLENDORED THING(1955), w; YOUR SHADOW IS MINE(1963, Fr./Ital.), w
Katsuya Suzaki
MAN FROM THE EAST, THE(1961, Jap.), w; SIEGE OF FORT BISMARK(1968, Jap.), w; FALCON FIGHTERS, THE(1970, Jap.), w; WAY OUT, WAY IN(1970, Jap.), w
Allison Suzanne
1984
BODY ROCK(1984)
George Suzanne
SEVENTH CROSS, THE(1944); TO HAVE AND HAVE NOT(1944); NIGHT AND DAY(1946); JOAN OF ARC(1948); WHIPLASH(1948)
Janet Suzman
NICHOLAS AND ALEXANDRA(1971, Brit.); DAY IN THE DEATH OF JOE EGG, A(1972, Brit.); BLACK WINDMILL, THE(1974, Brit.); VOYAGE OF THE DAMNED(1976, Brit.); NIJINSKY(1980, Brit.); PRIEST OF LOVE(1981, Brit.); AND THE SHIP SAILS ON(1983, Ital./Fr.); DRAUGHTSMAN'S CONTRACT, THE(1983, Brit.)

T. Suzmk
ANATAHAN(1953, Jap.)
Akira Suzuki
WEIRD LOVE MAKERS, THE(1963, Jap.), ed; SAGA OF THE VAGABONDS(1964, Jap.), ph
Denmei Suzuki
Misc. Silents
SOULS ON THE ROAD(1921, Jap.)
Elizabeth Suzuki
GOLDEN APPLES OF THE SUN(1971, Can.); ONE MAN(1979, Can.)
Fukuo Suzuki
LAST UNICORN, THE(1982), anim
Hideaki Suzuki
RIFIFI IN TOKYO(1963, Fr./Ital.)
Hideo Suzuki
WALL-EYED NIPPON(1963, Jap.), d
Hisayuki Suzuki
DAY THE SUN ROSE, THE(1969, Jap.), w
Hiyoshi Suzuki
TIME SLIP(1981, Jap.), spec eff
Jun Suzuki
HARBOR LIGHT YOKOHAMA(1970, Jap.), m
Kazuo Suzuki
ANGRY ISLAND(1960, Jap.); WE WILL REMEMBER(1966, Jap.); DESTROY ALL MONSTERS(1969, Jap.)
Kensaku Suzuki
Misc. Silents
HUMAN SUFFERING(1923, Jap.), d
Nobuko Suzuki
PERFORMERS, THE(1970, Jap.); SONG FROM MY HEART, THE(1970, Jap.)
Pat Suzuki
SKULLDUGGERY(1970)
Richard Suzuki
CATHERINE & CO.(1976, Fr.), ph
Seijun Suzuki
GATE OF FLESH(1964, Jap.), d
Tatsuo Suzuki
LAKE, THE(1970, Jap.), ph; SILENCE HAS NO WINGS(1971, Jap.), ph; MAN WHO STOLE THE SUN, THE(1980, Jap.), ph
Toyoaki Suzuki
GODZILLA, RING OF THE MONSTERS(1956, Jap.)
Yasushi Suzuki
YOSAKOI JOURNEY(1970, Jap.)
Thomas Svanfeldt
TO LOVE(1964, Swed.)
Jan Svankmaier
ADELE HASN'T HAD HER SUPPER YET(1978, Czech.), spec eff
Bill Svanoe
UP IN THE CELLAR(1970); WALTZ ACROSS TEXAS(1982), w
S. Svashenko
DUEL, THE(1964, USSR); OPTIMISTIC TRAGEDY, THE(1964, USSR)
Seymon Svashenko
Silents
ARSENAL(1929, USSR)
Ada Svedin
Misc. Silents
BEYOND THE RIVER(1922, Ger.)
Ray Svedin
SCAVENGER HUNT(1979), spec eff
Doris Svedlund
DEVIL'S WANTON, THE(1962, Swed.)
Dick Svehla
NIGHTBEAST(1982)
Gary Svehla
NIGHTBEAST(1982)
Malene Sveinbjornsson
COCKTAIL MOLOTOV(1980, Fr.)
Steini Sveinbjornsson
EPILOGUE(1967, Den.), art d
Julius Svendsen
ONE HUNDRED AND ONE DALMATIANS(1961), anim; ARISTOCATS, THE(1970), w, anim
Sunja Svendsen
GREENWICH VILLAGE STORY(1963)
Tore Svennberg
WOMAN'S FACE, A(1939, Swed.); OCEAN BREAKERS(1949, Swed.)
Misc. Silents
PHANTOM CARRIAGE, THE(1921, Swed.)
Bo Svenson
BUTCHER BAKER(NIGHTMARE MAKER)* (1982); GREAT WALDO PEPPER, THE(1975); WALKING TALL, PART II(1975); BREAKING POINT(1976); SPECIAL DELIVERY(1976); FINAL CHAPTER–WALKING TALL zero(1977); NORTH DALLAS FORTY(1979); VIRUS(1980, Jap.); COUNTERFEIT COMMANDOS(1981, Ital.)
Misc. Talkies
MAURIE(1973); PORTRAIT OF A HITMAN(1984)
Gunnar Svensson
ADVENTURES OF PICASSO, THE(1980, Swed.), m
Allen Svensvold
HINDU, THE(1953, Brit.), ph
Nals Svenwall
ILLICIT INTERLUDE(1954, Swed.), set d
Nils Svenwall
SECRETS OF WOMEN(1961, Swed.), art d, set d; PORT OF CALL(1963, Swed.), art d
L. Sverdlin
UNIVERSITY OF LIFE(1941, USSR)
Lev Sverdlin
DEFENSE OF VOLOTCHAYEVSK, THE(1938, USSR); DAYS AND NIGHTS(1946, USSR)

Liubov Sveshnikova
COUNTRY BRIDE(1938, USSR)
Josef Svet
FIREMAN'S BALL, THE(1968, Czech.)
G. Svetlani
LAST GAME, THE(1964, USSR); SANDU FOLLOWS THE SUN(1965, USSR); WAR AND PEACE(1968, USSR)
G. Svetlani-Penkovskiy
SHE-WOLF, THE(1963, USSR)
Yevgeniy Svetlanov
TSAR'S BRIDE, THE(1966, USSR), md
S. Svetlichnaya
LULLABY(1961, USSR)
B. Svetlov
Misc. Silents
IN THE KINGDOM OF OIL AND MILLIONS(1916, USSR), d
Sviatoslav
MEN OF THE SEA(1938, USSR), ph
Svidetelev
CRANES ARE FLYING, THE(1960, USSR), set d
Anna Svierkier
DAY OF WRATH(1948, Den.)
Charles Svin
FERNANDEL THE DRESSMAKER(1957, Fr.), ph
Georgiy Sviridov
RESURRECTION(1963, USSR), m
Yuriy Svirin
LADY WITH THE DOG, THE(1962, USSR)
J. Svitak
ECSTACY OF YOUNG LOVE(1936, Czech.)
David Svoboda
CHRISTMAS STORY, A(1983)
Josef Svoboda
THREE SISTERS(1974, Brit.), prod d
1984
AMADEUS(1984), art d&set d
Miroslav Svoboda
SKELETON ON HORSEBACK(1940, Czech.); SWEET LIGHT IN A DARK ROOM(1966, Czech.); TRANSPORT FROM PARADISE(1967, Czech.)
V. Svoboda
Misc. Silents
ALARM, THE(1917, USSR)
N. Svobodin
RESURRECTION(1963, USSR)
Eva Svobodova
SKELETON ON HORSEBACK(1940, Czech.); 90 DEGREES IN THE SHADE(1966, Czech./Brit.); FIFTH HORSEMAN IS FEAR, THE(1968, Czech.)
Karlicka Svobodova
SWEET LIGHT IN A DARK ROOM(1966, Czech.)
Milena Svobodova
DIVINE EMMA, THE(1983, Czech,)
Petr Svojtka
MATTER OF DAYS, A(1969, Fr./Czech.)
Libuse Svormova
MURDER CZECH STYLE(1968, Czech.)
L. J. Swabacher
NORTHWEST TRAIL(1945), w
Arne Swabeck
REDS(1981)
E.W. Swackhamer
MAN AND BOY(1972), d
Misc. Talkies
LONGSHOT(1982), d
Elizabeth Swados
FOUR FRIENDS(1981), m, m
Jim Swados
AMITYVILLE HORROR, THE(1979), art d
Kim E. Swados
UNCLE VANYA(1958), art d
Kim Swados
GONE ARE THE DAYS(1963), prod d; DEER HUNTER, THE(1978), art d
Kim Edgar Swados
STAGE STRUCK(1958), art d
Geoffrey Swaffer
RIVER WOLVES, THE(1934, Brit.), w
Hannen Swaffer
DEATH AT A BROADCAST(1934, Brit.); LATE EXTRA(1935, Brit.); SPELL OF AMY NUGENT, THE(1945, Brit.)
Bob Swaim
LA BALANCE(1983, Fr.), d, w
Alan Swain
TRACK OF THE MOONBEAST(1976)
Caskey Swain
HEROES(1977)
Charles Swain
ANNA LUCASTA(1958)
David Swain
MUSIC MAN, THE(1962)
Doe Swain
LONE TEXAN(1959)
Dwight V. Swain
STARK FEAR(1963), p, w
Elaine Swain
GOODBYE COLUMBUS(1969)
Jack Swain
HEY! HEY! U.S.A.(1938, Brit.), w; SMOKY(1966), ph
Jeanne Swain
TRACK OF THE MOONBEAST(1976)

John D. Swain
IT'S GREAT TO BE ALIVE(1933), w
Silents
WHITE AND UNMARRIED(1921), w
Lucy Swain
TOMCAT, THE(1968, Brit.)
Mack Swain
CAUGHT IN THE FOG(1928); COHENS AND KELLYS IN ATLANTIC CITY, THE(1929); LAST WARNING, THE(1929); LOCKED DOOR, THE(1929); REDEMPTION(1930); SEA BAT, THE(1930); FINN AND HATTIE(1931); MIDNIGHT PATROL, THE(1932); DOWN MEMORY LANE(1949)
Silents
TILLIE'S PUNCTURED ROMANCE(1914); PILGRIM, THE(1923); GOLD RUSH, THE(1925); HANDS UP(1926); KIKI(1926); NERVOUS WRECK, THE(1926); SEA HORSES(1926); TORRENT, THE(1926); BELOVED ROGUE, THE(1927); FINNEGAN'S BALL(1927); MOCKERY(1927); MY BEST GIRL(1927); TEXAS STEER, A(1927); GENTLEMEN PREFER BLONDES(1928); TILLIE'S PUNCTURED ROMANCE(1928)
Misc. Silents
MODERN ENOCH ARDEN, A(1916); SEE YOU IN JAIL(1927); SHAMROCK AND THE ROSE, THE(1927); TIRED BUSINESS MAN, THE(1927)
Robert Swain
YEAR OF THE YAHOO(1971)
Frank Swales
SURRENDER(1931); TOAST OF NEW YORK, THE(1937); LUCKY LEGS(1942)
Frank Arthur Swales
UNDER YOUR SPELL(1936); MARIE ANTOINETTE(1938)
Swallow
Silents
ARYAN, THE(1916)
Darwyn Swalve
1984
CITY HEAT(1984)
Bob Swan
THUNDER OVER ARIZONA(1956); LAWLESS EIGHTIES, THE(1957); SPOILERS OF THE FOREST(1957); CROOKED CIRCLE, THE(1958)
1984
GRANDVIEW, U.S.A.(1984)
Buddy Swan
HAUNTED HOUSE, THE(1940); CITIZEN KANE(1941); SULLIVANS, THE(1944); SWEET AND LOWDOWN(1944); SCARED STIFF(1945); CENTENNIAL SUMMER(1946); GALLANT JOURNEY(1946); PREJUDICE(1949); ROARING WESTWARD(1949); SHOCKPROOF(1949); DESTINATION MURDER(1950); MILITARY ACADEMY WITH THAT TENTH AVENUE GANG(1950); ONE MINUTE TO ZERO(1952); MODERN MARRIAGE, A(1962)
Francis Swan
JUNGLE PATROL(1948), w; 711 OCEAN DRIVE(1950), w; BAREFOOT MAILMAN, THE(1951), w
Fred A. Swan
GHOSTS OF BERKELEY SQUARE(1947, Brit.), prod d
Giselle Swan
OLGA'S GIRLS(1964)
James Swan
FALLEN IDOL, THE(1949, Brit.)
Kathleen Swan
BEYOND THE REEF(1981)
Kitty Swan
HOUSE OF 1,000 DOLLS(1967, Ger./Span./Brit.); WILD, WILD PLANET, THE(1967, Ital.)
Marian Swan
SUMMER WISHES, WINTER DREAMS(1973); THREE DAYS OF THE CONDOR(1975)
Mark Swan
PARLOR, BEDROOM AND BATH(1931), w
Silents
LITTLE MADEMOISELLE, THE(1915), w; TILLIE WAKES UP(1917), w
Paul Swan
ILLIAC PASSION, THE(1968)
Robert Swan
MAVERICK QUEEN, THE(1956); FROM HELL IT CAME(1957); SPEED CRAZY(1959); HARD RIDE, THE(1971); FFOLKES(1980, Brit.); TAKE THIS JOB AND SHOVE IT(1981); DOCTOR DETROIT(1983)
Robert C. Swan
GUNFIGHT AT THE O.K. CORRAL(1957)
Tex Swan
CRACK-UP(1946); NOCTURNE(1946); WILD HARVEST(1947); KNOCK ON ANY DOOR(1949); WINDOW, THE(1949)
William Swan
MONSTER THAT CHALLENGED THE WORLD, THE(1957); LADY IN A CAGE(1964)
Don Swanagan
WARRIORS, THE(1979), art d
Alex Swanbeck
WALLS OF HELL, THE(1964, U.S./Phil.)
Lars Swanberg
HUGS AND KISSES(1968, Swed.), ph; DUET FOR CANNIBALS(1969, Swed.), ph
Don Swander
MOONLIGHT ON THE RANGE(1937), m; DEEP IN THE HEART OF TEXAS(1942), m/l Johnny Bond
Dale Swanepoel
KIMBERLEY JIM(1965, South Africa)
Johan Swanepoet
SPOTS ON MY LEOPARD, THE(1974, S. Africa)
Robert Swanger
I, THE JURY(1953)
Greg Swangon
MEATBALLS(1979, Can.)
Peter Swanick
AFRICAN QUEEN, THE(1951, U.S./Brit.); SECRETS OF A WINDMILL GIRL(1966, Brit.)

Robert Swank
LONG NIGHT, THE(1947), ed
Billy Swann
1984
SONGWRITER(1984)
Crist Swann
1984
DELIVERY BOYS(1984)
Ewa Swann
BYE BYE BARBARA(1969, Fr.); WINTER WIND(1970, Fr./Hung.)
Francis Swann
YOUNG AND WILLING(1943), w; MAKE YOUR OWN BED(1944), w; SHINE ON, HARVEST MOON(1944), w; TIME, THE PLACE AND THE GIRL, THE(1946), w; LOVE AND LEARN(1947), w; THAT WAY WITH WOMEN(1947), w; GAY INTRUDERS, THE(1948), w; COVER-UP(1949), w; BELLE OF OLD MEXICO(1950), w; TARZAN'S PERIL(1951), w; ONE BIG AFFAIR(1952), w; FORCE OF IMPULSE(1961), w
Frank Swann
YOUNG PEOPLE(1940)
Fred Swann
M'BLIMEY(1931, Brit.), w; DON GIOVANNI(1955, Brit.), p; TIME TO KILL, A(1955, Brit.), p
Frederick Albert Swann
MAN WHO BROKE THE BANK AT MONTE CARLO, THE(1935), w
Gabriel Swann
WHY WOULD I LIE(1980)
George Swann
Misc. Silents
PRINCE AND BETTY, THE(1919)
James Swann
CHARLEY-ONE-EYE(1973, Brit.), p
Robert Swann
IF ...(1968, Brit.); MUMSY, NANNY, SONNY, AND GIRLY(1970, Brit.)
Walt Swanner
HELLCATS, THE(1968)
Scott Swansom
1984
BIG MEAT EATER(1984, Can.)
Audrey Swanson
SOLID GOLD CADILLAC, THE(1956); THESE WILDER YEARS(1956); STRANGERS WHEN WE MEET(1960); UNDERWORLD U.S.A.(1961); EXPERIMENT IN TERROR(1962); NEW KIND OF LOVE, A(1963)
Barbara Swanson
SUSPENSE(1946)
Bernice Swanson
VIOLENT PLAYGROUND(1958, Brit.); LOOK BACK IN ANGER(1959); SO EVIL SO YOUNG(1961, Brit.); SHE ALWAYS GETS THEIR MAN(1962, Brit.)
Diane Swanson
SWINGIN' SUMMER, A(1965)
Donald Swanson
PENNYWHISTLE BLUES, THE(1952, South Africa), p&d, w
Forrest Swanson
TO ALL A GOODNIGHT(1980)
Gary Swanson
MAKING LOVE(1982); VICE SQUAD(1982)
Glenwood J. Swanson
BLACK GIRL(1972), ph
Gloria Swanson
TRESPASSER, THE(1929); WHAT A WIDOW(1930); INDISCREET(1931); TONIGHT OR NEVER(1931); PERFECT UNDERSTANDING(1933, Brit.), a, p; MUSIC IN THE AIR(1934); FATHER TAKES A WIFE(1941); DOWN MEMORY LANE(1949); SUNSET BOULEVARD(1950); THREE FOR BEDROOM C(1952), a, co; NERO'S MISTRESS(1962, Ital.); AIRPORT 1975(1974)
Silents
MALE AND FEMALE(1919); SOMETHING TO THINK ABOUT(1920); AFFAIRS OF ANATOL, THE(1921); DON'T TELL EVERYTHING(1921); BEYOND THE ROCKS(1922); HER GILDED CAGE(1922); IMPOSSIBLE MRS. BELLEW, THE(1922); MY AMERICAN WIFE(1923); SOCIETY SCANDAL, A(1924); FINE MANNERS(1926); UNTAMED LADY, THE(1926); SADIE THOMPSON(1928); QUEEN KELLY(1929)
Misc. Silents
EVERYWOMAN'S HUSBAND(1918); HER DECISION(1918); SECRET CODE, THE(1918); SHIFTING SANDS(1918); SOCIETY FOR SALE(1918); STATION CONTENT(1918); YOU CAN'T BELIEVE EVERYTHING(1918); DON'T CHANGE YOUR HUSBAND(1919); FOR BETTER, FOR WORSE(1919); WIFE OR COUNTRY(1919); WHY CHANGE YOUR WIFE?(1920); GREAT MOMENT, THE(1921); UNDER THE LASH(1921); HER HUSBAND'S TRADEMARK(1922); BLUEBEARD'S 8TH WIFE(1923); PRODIGAL DAUGHTERS(1923); ZAZA(1923); HER LOVE STORY(1924); HUMMING BIRD, THE(1924); MANHANDLED(1924); WAGES OF VIRTUE(1924); COAST OF FOLLY, THE(1925); MADAME SANS-GENE(1925); STAGE STRUCK(1925); LOVE OF SUNYA, THE(1927)
Greg Swanson
SHAPE OF THINGS TO COME, THE(1979, Can.); TERROR TRAIN(1980, Can.)
H.N. Swanson
HALF-NAKED TRUTH, THE(1932), w; PROFESSIONAL SWEETHEART(1933), p; HIPS, HIPS, HOORAY(1934), p; KENTUCKY KERNELS(1935), p
Harold N. Swanson
BIG BUSINESS GIRL(1931), w
John F. Swanson
ROLLERCOASTER(1977)
Karen Swanson
SCAVENGERS, THE(1969)
Karl Swanson
...TICK...TICK...TICK...(1970)
Larry Swanson
SCREAM, BABY, SCREAM(1969)
Len Swanson
WOMEN AND BLOODY TERROR(1970)
Lester A. Swanson
FIGHTER ATTACK(1953), ed

Logan Swanson
LAST MAN ON EARTH, THE(1964, U.S./Ital.), w
Mary Swanson
ELECTRIC HORSEMAN, THE(1979), set d; HIDE IN PLAIN SIGHT(1980), set d; UP THE ACADEMY(1980), set d
Mary Olivia Swanson
FORCED VENGEANCE(1982), set d
1984
FOOTLOOSE(1984), set d; PROTOCOL(1984), set d
Maura Swanson
HAPPY BIRTHDAY, GEMINI(1980)
Maureen Swanson
MOULIN ROUGE(1952); KNIGHTS OF THE ROUND TABLE(1953); MEN ARE CHILDREN TWICE(1953, Brit.); THREE CORNERED FATE(1954, Brit.); DEADLY GAME, THE(1955, Brit.); ONE JUST MAN(1955, Brit.); JACQUELINE(1956, Brit.); SPANISH GARDENER, THE(1957, Span.); UP IN THE WORLD(1957, Brit.); ROBBERY UNDER ARMS(1958, Brit.); TOWN LIKE ALICE, A(1958, Brit.); LOOK BACK IN ANGER(1959); ORDERS ARE ORDERS(1959, Brit.); MALPAS MYSTERY, THE(1967, Brit.)
Neil H. Swanson
UNCONQUERED(1947), w
Phillip Swanson
Misc. Talkies
ELMER(1977)
Robert Swanson
CARSON CITY(1952), ed; MARA MARU(1952), ed
Robert L. Swanson
SPRINGFIELD RIFLE(1952), ed; SCARFACE MOB, THE(1962), ed
Ruth Swanson
SO BIG(1953); CRY BABY KILLER, THE(1958)
Scott Swanson
BY DESIGN(1982)
Sterling Swanson
DOGS(1976); COMPETITION, THE(1980)
Tina Swanson
SATURDAY NIGHT OUT(1964, Brit.), cos
Carl Swanstrom
SILENT RAIDERS(1954)
Karin Swanstrom
SWEDENHIELMS(1935, Swed.); ON THE SUNNYSIDE(1936, Swed.); NIGHT IN JUNE, A(1940, Swed.)
Harold Swanton
APPOINTMENT WITH MURDER(1948), w; HELLIONS, THE(1962, Brit.), w; BALLAD OF JOSIE(1968), w; RASCAL(1969), w
Peter Swanwick
NO HAUNT FOR A GENTLEMAN(1952, Brit.); PRIVATE INFORMATION(1952, Brit.); SCOTLAND YARD INSPECTOR(1952, Brit.); ALBERT, R.N.(1953, Brit.); SLASHER, THE(1953, Brit.); TIME GENTLEMEN PLEASE!(1953, Brit.); CIRCUMSTANIAL EVIDENCE(1954, Brit.); DEVIL ON HORSEBACK(1954, Brit.); FUSS OVER FEATHERS(1954, Brit.); LOVE MATCH, THE(1955, Brit.); WINDFALL(1955, Brit.); MARCH HARE, THE(1956, Brit.); YOU PAY YOUR MONEY(1957, Brit.); DEATH OVER MY SHOULDER(1958, Brit.); KILL ME TOMORROW(1958, Brit.); MURDER REPORTED(1958, Brit.); DESPERATE MAN, THE(1959, Brit.); TWO-HEADED SPY, THE(1959, Brit.); CIRCUS OF HORRORS(1960, Brit.); DOUBLE BUNK(1961, Brit.); INVASION QUARTET(1961, Brit.); TRUNK, THE(1961, Brit.); MILLION DOLLAR MANHUNT(1962, Brit.); LIFE IN DANGER(1964, Brit.); LOOKING GLASS WAR, THE(1970, Brit.)
D.C. Swapp
STALLION CANYON(1949)
David Swapp
DALTON GIRLS, THE(1957)
David Swarbrick
FAR FROM THE MADDING CROWD(1967, Brit.)
J. Swarbrick
FREUD(1962)
Anne Sward
Misc. Talkies
CONVENTION GIRLS(1978)
Fred Swart
CREATURES THE WORLD FORGOT(1971, Brit.)
Robert Swarthe
STAR TREK: THE MOTION PICTURE(1979), spec eff; ONE FROM THE HEART(1982), spec eff
Gladys Swarthout
GIVE US THIS NIGHT(1936); ROSE OF THE RANCHO(1936); CHAMPAGNE WALTZ(1937); ROMANCE IN THE DARK(1938); AMBUSH(1939)
Glendon Swarthout
THEY CAME TO CORDURA(1959), w; WHERE THE BOYS ARE(1960), w; BLESS THE BEASTS AND CHILDREN(1971), w; SHOOTIST, THE(1976), w
1984
WHERE THE BOYS ARE '84(1984), w
Miles Hood Swarthout
SHOOTIST, THE(1976), w
Berman Swartz
JENNIFER(1953), p; DUFFY OF SAN QUENTIN(1954), p; NEW FACES(1954), p; STEEL CAGE, THE(1954), p, w
Aaron Swartz
LORDS OF DISCIPLINE, THE(1983)
Charles S. Swartz
IT'S A BIKINI WORLD(1967), p, w; STUDENT NURSES, THE(1970), p, w; VELVET VAMPIRE, THE(1971), p, w; SWEET SUGAR(1972), p; TERMINAL ISLAND(1973), p, w; WORKING GIRLS(1973), p
George Swartz
HANG'EM HIGH(1968), spec eff
Kelley Swartz
Misc. Talkies
HEADLESS EYES, THE(1983)

Ken Swartz
SENATOR WAS INDISCREET, THE(1947), set d
Kenneth Swartz
OUT OF THIS WORLD(1945), set d; WELL-GROOMED BRIDE, THE(1946), set d
Larry Swartz
BENJI(1974); HAWMPS!(1976)
Lester Swartz
THUNDER ROAD(1958), spec eff
Ralph Swartz
ICE STATION ZEBRA(1968), spec eff; SKYJACKED(1972), spec eff
Tony Swartz
BATTLESTAR GALACTICA(1979); SCHIZOID(1980)
W. Swaryczewska
PASSENGER, THE(1970, Pol.)
Walter Swash
I AM A GROUPIE(1970, Brit.)
Nikki Swassy
BODY AND SOUL(1981)
Martha Swatek
JAWS II(1978)
Ethel Sway
WOMAN OF DISTINCTION, A(1950); THIS EARTH IS MINE(1959)
Roger Swaybill
BREAKING POINT(1976), w; PORKY'S II: THE NEXT DAY(1983)
Roger E. Swaybill
PORKY'S II: THE NEXT DAY(1983), w
Daniel Swayne
INGAGI(1931)
Eleanor Swayne
ROCK, ROCK, ROCK!(1956)
Julia Swayne
Misc. Silents
MILLION BID, A(1914); ENEMY, THE(1916); BEHIND MASKS(1921); HEAVEN ON EARTH(1927)
Marian Swayne
Silents
ADVENTURES OF KITTY COBB, THE(1914); NET, THE(1916); TIE THAT BINDS, THE(1923)
Misc. Silents
FIGHT FOR MILLIONS, THE(1913); LOVE'S CROSS ROADS(1916); ADVENTURER, THE(1917); DEEMSTER, THE(1917); LITTLE MISS FORTUNE(1917); LITTLE SAMARITAN, THE(1917); ROAD BETWEEN, THE(1917); TRANSGRESSOR, THE(1918); CRIMSON CROSS, THE(1921); COUNTERFEIT LOVE(1923); MAN FROM GLENGARRY, THE(1923); HEART OF ALASKA(1924)
Viola Swayne
RIVALS(1972)
John Cameron Swayze
THE BOSTON STRANGLER, THE(1968)
Patrick Swayze
SKATETOWN, U.S.A.(1979); OUTSIDERS, THE(1983); UNCOMMON VALOR(1983)
1984
GRANDVIEW, U.S.A.(1984), a, ch; RED DAWN(1984)
Patsy Swayze
URBAN COWBOY(1980), ch
Margie Swearingen
JUST TELL ME WHAT YOU WANT(1980)
Willis P. Sweatnam
Silents
COUNTY CHAIRMAN, THE(1914)
A.W. Sweatt
NOTHING SACRED(1937); STAR IS BORN, A(1937); ANGELS WITH DIRTY FACES(1938)
The Sweaty Betty
I AM A GROUPIE(1970, Brit.)
Maurice Sweden
DREAMING(1944, Brit.)
Morris Sweden
DICK BARTON–SPECIAL AGENT(1948, Brit.); DICK BARTON STRIKES BACK(1949, Brit.); FAKE, THE(1953, Brit.)
Helen Swee
1984
NO SMALL AFFAIR(1984)
Bill Sweek
DRIVE, HE SAID(1971)
Al Sweeney
DAY OF THE BAD MAN(1958), art d
Alfred Sweeney
GREAT SIOUX UPRISING, THE(1953), art d; RICOCHET ROMANCE(1954), art d; LOOTERS, THE(1955), art d; REVENGE OF THE CREATURE(1955), art d; SPOILERS, THE(1955), art d; SQUARE JUNGLE, THE(1955), art d; TARANTULA(1955), art d; I'VE LIVED BEFORE(1956), art d; KETTLES IN THE OZARKS, THE(1956), art d; RAW EDGE(1956), art d; STAR IN THE DUST(1956), art d; UNGUARDED MOMENT, THE(1956), art d; GUN FOR A COWARD(1957), art d; JOE BUTTERFLY(1957), art d; MAN IN THE SHADOW(1957), art d; TARNISHED ANGELS, THE(1957), art d; TIME TO LOVE AND A TIME TO DIE, A(1958), art d; LAST SUNSET, THE(1961), art d; POSSE FROM HELL(1961), art d; TAMMY, TELL ME TRUE(1961), art d; CAPTAIN NEWMAN, M.D.(1963), art d; SHOWDOWN(1963), art d; UGLY AMERICAN, THE(1963), art d; LOVE HAS MANY FACES(1965), art d; SHENANDOAH(1965), art d; APPALOOSA, THE(1966), art d; HARPER(1966), art d; MOMENT TO MOMENT(1966), art d; WAR WAGON, THE(1967), art d; BRIDGE AT REMAGEN, THE(1969), art d; RABBIT, RUN(1970), art d; CISCO PIKE(1971), art d; FOOLS' PARADE(1971), art d; SOMETHING BIG(1971), art d; CAREY TREATMENT, THE(1972), art d; OKLAHOMA CRUDE(1973), prod d; TRAIN ROBBERS, THE(1973), art d; UPTOWN SATURDAY NIGHT(1974), prod d; LET'S DO IT AGAIN(1975), prod d; SILVER STREAK(1976), prod d; PIECE OF THE ACTION, A(1977), prod d; FOUL PLAY(1978), prod d; NORTH DALLAS FORTY(1979), prod d; UP FROM THE DEPTHS(1979, Phil.), w; BLACK MARBLE, THE(1980), prod d; STIR CRAZY(1980), prod d; TAPS(1981), art d; MR. MOM(1983), prod d; ROMANTIC COMEDY(1983), prod d

Alfred Sweeney, Jr.
BANDOLERO!(1968), art d; DEVIL'S BRIGADE, THE(1968), art d; THE RUNNER STUMBLES(1979), prod d

Anthony Sweeney
ROBBERY(1967, Brit.)

Augustin Sweeney
Misc. Silents
SANDRA(1924)

Aurelia Sweeney
GETTING OVER(1981)

Bob Sweeney
IT GROWS ON TREES(1952); MR. SCOUTMASTER(1953); LAST HURRAH, THE(1958); TOBY TYLER(1960); MOON PILOT(1962); SON OF FLUBBER(1963); MARNIE(1964); HOW TO SUCCEED IN BUSINESS WITHOUT REALLY TRYING(1976)

Carmelita Sweeney
Silents
DREAM MELODY, THE(1929), w, t

Cheryl Ivy Sweeney
1984
SIXTEEN CANDLES(1984)

Ed Sweeney
TWO RODE TOGETHER(1961)

Edward Sweeney
YOUNG LAND, THE(1959)

Ellen Sweeney
1984
CHATTANOOGA CHOO CHOO(1984)

Fred Sweeney
ANGELS OVER BROADWAY(1940)

George Sweeney
LION OF THE DESERT(1981, Libya/Brit.)

James Sweeney
LONE RIDER, THE(1930), ed; SHADOW RANCH(1930), ed; DAWN TRAIL, THE(1931), ed; LIGHTNING FLYER(1931), ed; DON'T GAMBLE WITH LOVE(1936), ed; LADY FROM NOWHERE(1936), ed; TRAPPED BY TELEVISION(1936), ed; TWO-FISTED GENTLEMAN(1936), ed; ALL-AMERICAN SWEETHEART(1937), ed; ACROSS THE SIERRAS(1941), ed; ADVENTURE IN WASHINGTON(1941), ed; BEYOND THE SACRAMENTO(1941), ed; MEET BOSTON BLACKIE(1941), ed; MYSTERY SHIP(1941), ed; PRAIRIE STRANGER(1941), ed; ROYAL MOUNTED PATROL, THE(1941), ed; ATLANTIC CONVOY(1942), ed; CANAL ZONE(1942), ed; SPIRIT OF STANFORD, THE(1942), ed; IS EVERYBODY HAPPY?(1943), ed; REVEILLE WITH BEVERLY(1943), ed; RIDERS OF THE NORTHWEST MOUNTED(1943), ed; WHAT'S BUZZIN COUSIN?(1943), ed; CAROLINA BLUES(1944), ed; HEY, ROOKIE(1944), ed; THEY LIVE IN FEAR(1944), ed; EADIE WAS A LADY(1945), ed; I LOVE A BAND-LEADER(1945), ed; MY NAME IS JULIA ROSS(1945), ed; TEN CENTS A DANCE(1945), ed; LANDRUSH(1946), ed; MEET ME ON BROADWAY(1946), ed; SHADOWED(1946), ed; TALK ABOUT A LADY(1946), ed; DEVIL SHIP(1947), ed; FOR THE LOVE OF RUSTY(1947), ed; KEEPER OF THE BEES(1947), ed; LAST OF THE REDMEN(1947), ed; BEST MAN WINS(1948), ed; BLACK EAGLE(1948), ed; PRINCE OF THIEVES, THE(1948), ed; RUSTY LEADS THE WAY(1948), ed; AIR HOSTESS(1949), ed; BARBARY PIRATE(1949), ed; LONE WOLF AND HIS LADY, THE(1949), ed; MARY RYAN, DETECTIVE(1949), ed; MUTINEERS, THE(1949), ed; PRISON WARDEN(1949), ed; RUSTY'S BIRTHDAY(1949), ed; SECRET OF ST. IVES, THE(1949), ed; BLAZING SUN, THE(1950), ed; BODYHOLD(1950), ed; INDIAN TERRITORY(1950), ed; MILITARY ACADEMY WITH THAT TENTH AVENUE GANG(1950), ed; STATE PENITENTIARY(1950), ed; GENE AUTRY AND THE MOUNTIES(1951), ed; HARLEM GLOBETROTTERS, THE(1951), ed; HILLS OF UTAH(1951), ed; SILVER CANYON(1951), ed; TEXANS NEVER CRY(1951), ed; VALLEY OF FIRE(1951), ed; APACHE COUNTRY(1952), ed; BARBED WIRE(1952), ed; BLUE CANADIAN ROCKIES(1952), ed; NIGHT STAGE TO GALVESTON(1952), ed; OLD WEST, THE(1952), ed; WAGON TEAM(1952), ed; GOLDTOWN GHOST RIDERS(1953), ed; GUN FURY(1953), ed; LAST OF THE PONY RIDERS(1953), ed; NEBRASKAN, THE(1953), ed; ON TOP OF OLD SMOKY(1953), ed; PACK TRAIN(1953), ed; SAGINAW TRAIL(1953), ed; STRANGER WORE A GUN, THE(1953), ed; WINNING OF THE WEST(1953), ed; REDHEAD FROM MANHATTAN(1954), ed; MAN BEAST(1956), ed; FLAME OF STAMBOUL(1957), ed; INCREDIBLE PETRIFIED WORLD, THE(1959), ed
Silents
CAMPUS KNIGHTS(1929), ed; JUST OFF BROADWAY(1929), ed; PEACOCK FAN(1929), ed

Joan Sweeney
1984
LONELY GUY, THE(1984)

Joseph Sweeney
SOAK THE RICH(1936); FASTEST GUN ALIVE(1956); MAN IN THE GREY FLANNEL SUIT, THE(1956); 12 ANGRY MEN(1957)

Keester Sweeney
LIVELY SET, THE(1964), makeup; MAN CALLED HORSE, A(1970), makeup

Lewis Sweeney
EXTRAORDINARY SEAMAN, THE(1969), makeup

Liam Sweeney
WHERE'S JACK?(1969, Brit.); QUACKSER FORTUNE HAS A COUSIN IN THE BRONX(1970)

Matt Sweeney
NINE TO FIVE(1980), spec eff

Maureen Sweeney
LAST DETAIL, THE(1973), makeup; RAINBOW BOYS, THE(1973, Can.), cos; INCUBUS, THE(1982, Can.), makeup

Pat Sweeney
HANDS ACROSS THE TABLE(1935)

Penny Sweeney
SON OF SINBAD(1955)

Robert Sweeney
SOUTH SEA WOMAN(1953)
Silents
DOG LAW(1928)

T. Bell Sweeney, Jr.
VIKING, THE(1931), w

Theodore C. Sweeney
COLD RIVER(1982)

Wendy Sweeney
FANDANGO(1970)

Ann Sweeny
INCREDIBLE MELTING MAN, THE(1978)

Ed Charles Sweeny
DESTINATION INNER SPACE(1966)

James Sweeny
BOSTON BLACKIE AND THE LAW(1946), ed

Alex Sweers
SPY IN THE SKY(1958)

Bettye Sweet
DARKTOWN STRUTTERS(1975)
Misc. Talkies
GET DOWN AND BOOGIE(1977)

Blance Sweet
Misc. Silents
BLACKLIST(1916)

Blanche Sweet
SHOW GIRL IN HOLLYWOOD(1930); SILVER HORDE, THE(1930); WOMAN RACKET, THE(1930)
Silents
AVENGING CONSCIENCE, THE(1914); CLASSMATES(1914); ESCAPE, THE(1914); HOME SWEET HOME(1914); JUDITH OF BETHULIA(1914); CAPTIVE, THE(1915); SECRET ORCHARD(1915); WARRENS OF VIRGINIA, THE(1915); DUPE, THE(1916); THOSE WITHOUT SIN(1917); HELP WANTED–MALE!(1920); ANNA CHRISTIE(1923); SOULS FOR SALE(1923); TESS OF THE D'URBERVILLES(1924); NEW COMMANDMENT, THE(1925); BLUEBEARD'S SEVEN WIVES(1926); FAR CRY, THE(1926); LADY FROM HELL, THE(1926); SINGED(1927)
Misc. Silents
CLUE, THE(1915); STOLEN GOODS(1915); PUBLIC OPINION(1916); SOWERS, THE(1916); STORM, THE(1916); THOUSAND DOLLAR HUSBAND, THE(1916); UNPROTECTED(1916); EVIL EYE, THE(1917); SILENT PARTNER, THE(1917); TIDES OF BARNEGAT, THE(1917); FIGHTING CRESSY(1919); UNPARDONABLE SIN, THE(1919); WOMAN OF PLEASURE, A(1919); DEADLIER SEX, THE(1920); GIRL IN THE WEB, THE(1920); HER UNWILLING HUSBAND(1920); HUSHED HOUR, THE(1920); SIMPLE SOULS(1920); THAT GIRL MONTANA(1921); QUINCY ADAMS SAWYER(1922); IN THE PALACE OF THE KING(1923); MEANEST MAN IN THE WORLD, THE(1923); THOSE WHO DANCE(1924); HIS SUPREME MOMENT(1925); SPORTING VENUS, THE(1925); WHY WOMEN LOVE(1925); DIPLOMACY(1926); WOMAN IN WHITE, THE(1929, Brit.)

Dolph Sweet
YOUNG DOCTORS, THE(1961); YOU'RE A BIG BOY NOW(1966); FINIAN'S RAINBOW(1968); LOVELY WAY TO DIE, A(1968); SWIMMER, THE(1968); COLOSSUS: THE FORBIN PROJECT(1969); LOST MAN, THE(1969); OUT OF TOWNERS, THE(1970); NEW CENTURIONS, THE(1972); FEAR IS THE KEY(1973); SISTERS(1973); AMAZING GRACE(1974); LORDS OF FLATBUSH, THE(1974); BAD NEWS BEARS IN BREAKING TRAINING, THE(1977); WHICH WAY IS UP?(1977); GO TELL THE SPARTANS(1978); HEAVEN CAN WAIT(1978); WANDERERS, THE(1979); BELOW THE BELT(1980); REDS(1981)

Freddy Sweet
FORCED ENTRY(1975), spec eff; STACY'S KNIGHTS(1983), p

Gary Sweet
Misc. Talkies
STAGEFRIGHT(1983)

Harry Sweet
HER MAN(1930); HIT THE DECK(1930); TRUE TO THE NAVY(1930); CARNIVAL BOAT(1932)
Silents
PLAY SAFE(1927), w; HOMESICK(1928)

Sgt. John Sweet
CANTERBURY TALE, A(1944, Brit.)

Katie Sweet
CRIMSON KIMONO, THE(1959); ROUSTABOUT(1964)

Kendrick Sweet
EDGE OF ETERNITY(1959), p

Marcia Sweet
STRIKE ME PINK(1936)

Sheila Sweet
FUSS OVER FEATHERS(1954, Brit.); MAN OF THE MOMENT(1955, Brit.); ANGEL WHO PAWNED HER HARP, THE(1956, Brit.); IT'S A GREAT DAY(1956, Brit.); LIFE IN EMERGENCY WARD 10(1959, Brit.)

Thomas A. Sweet
SNIPER'S RIDGE(1961)

Tom Sweet
SILENCERS, THE(1966)

The Sweet Gum Sisters and Brother
MOONSHINE MOUNTAIN(1964)

Sweet Inspirations
IDOLMAKER, THE(1980)

Cheryl Sweeten
PAJAMA PARTY(1964)

Tony Sweeting
BUS IS COMING, THE(1971)

Charles Sweetlove
FAR COUNTRY, THE(1955)

Henry Sweetman
MY FAIR LADY(1964)
Yvette Sweetman
CATTLE ANNIE AND LITTLE BRITCHES(1981)
Lisha Sweetnam
THIS IS ELVIS(1982)
Thomas Sweetwood
SCUM OF THE EARTH(1963)
Charles Sweigart
1984
HARD TO HOLD(1984)
Blanche Swell
Silents
FLYING FEET, THE(1929), ed
Arthur Swemmer
KIMBERLEY JIM(1965, South Africa); AFTER YOU, COMRADE(1967, S. Afr.)
William Swenning
BLACK SIX, THE(1974), ph, ed
Aida Swenson
EYE FOR AN EYE, AN(1966), cos
Albert Swenson
Misc. Silents
HYPOCRISY(1916)
Alfred Swenson
GREAT POWER, THE(1929)
Alice Swenson
TANGA-TIKA(1953)
Bo Swenson
MAURIE(1973)
Carin Swenson
OCEAN BREAKERS(1949, Swed.)
Charles Swenson
NAKED APE, THE(1973), anim; TWICE UPON A TIME(1983), d, w
Chuck Swenson
MOUSE AND HIS CHILD, THE(1977), d, anim
Inga Swenson
ADVISE AND CONSENT(1962); MIRACLE WORKER, THE(1962); LIPSTICK(1976); BETSY, THE(1978)
Karl Swenson
FOUR BOYS AND A GUN(1957); KINGS GO FORTH(1958); HANGING TREE, THE(1959); NO NAME ON THE BULLET(1959); FLAMING STAR(1960); GALLANT HOURS, THE(1960); ICE PALACE(1960); NORTH TO ALASKA(1960); ONE FOOT IN HELL(1960); JUDGMENT AT NUREMBERG(1961); HOW THE WEST WAS WON(1962); LONELY ARE THE BRAVE(1962); SPIRAL ROAD, THE(1962); WALK ON THE WILD SIDE(1962); PRIZE, THE(1963); SWORD IN THE STONE, THE(1963); MAN FROM GALVESTON, THE(1964); CINCINNATI KID, THE(1965); MAJOR DUNDEE(1965); SONS OF KATIE ELDER, THE(1965); SECONDS(1966); BRIGHTY OF THE GRAND CANYON(1967); HOUR OF THE GUN(1967); VANISHING POINT(1971); WILD COUNTRY, THE(1971); ULZANA'S RAID(1972)
Knut Swenson [Marion Hargrove]
EDGE OF ETERNITY(1959), w
Marcy Swenson
MOUSE AND HIS CHILD, THE(1977)
Swen Swenson
WHAT'S THE MATTER WITH HELEN?(1971)
George Swensson
OPERATION CAMEL(1961, Den.), m
Charles J. Swepeniser
LADY ICE(1973)
Arthur Swerdloff
ROADRACERS, THE(1959), d
Kevin Swerdlow
CLASS(1983)
Stanley Swerdlow
ZELIG(1983)
Tommy Swerdlow
1984
WILD LIFE, THE(1984)
Jo Swerling
KIBITZER, THE(1929), w; MELODY LANE(1929), w; HELL'S ISLAND(1930), w, ed; LADIES MUST PLAY(1930), w; LADIES OF LEISURE(1930), w; MADONNA OF THE STREETS(1930), w; RAIN OR SHINE(1930), w; SISTERS(1930), w; SQUEALER, THE(1930), w; DECEIVER, THE(1931), w; DIRIGIBLE(1931), w; GOOD BAD GIRL, THE(1931), w; MIRACLE WOMAN, THE(1931), w; PLATINUM BLONDE(1931), w; TEN CENTS A DANCE(1931), w; ATTORNEY FOR THE DEFENSE(1932), w; BEHIND THE MASK(1932), w; FORBIDDEN(1932), w; HOLLYWOOD SPEAKS(1932), w; LOVE AFFAIR(1932), w; MAN AGAINST WOMAN(1932), w; SHOPWORN(1932), w; WAR CORRESPONDENT(1932), w; WASHINGTON MERRY-GO-ROUND(1932), w; AS THE DEVIL COMMANDS(1933), w; BELOW THE SEA(1933), w; CIRCUS QUEEN MURDER, THE(1933), w; EAST OF FIFTH AVE.(1933), w; MAN'S CASTLE, A(1933), w; WRECKER, THE(1933), w; DEFENSE HESTS, THE(1934), w; LADY BY CHOICE(1934), w; NO GREATER GLORY(1934), w; ONCE TO EVERY WOMAN(1934), w; SISTERS UNDER THE SKIN(1934), w; LOVE ME FOREVER(1935), w; WHOLE TOWN'S TALKING, THE(1935), w; MUSIC GOES ROUND, THE(1936), w; PENNIES FROM HEAVEN(1936), w; DOUBLE WEDDING(1937), w; I AM THE LAW(1938), w; GONE WITH THE WIND(1939), w; MADE FOR EACH OTHER(1939), w; REAL GLORY, THE(1939), w; WESTERNER, THE(1940), w; BLOOD AND SAND(1941), w; CONFIRM OR DENY(1941), w; NEW YORK TOWN(1941), w; PRIDE OF THE YANKEES, THE(1942), w; CRASH DIVE(1943), w; LADY TAKES A CHANCE, A(1943), w; LIFEBOAT(1944), w; IT'S A WONDERFUL LIFE(1946), w; LEAVE HER TO HEAVEN(1946), w; THUNDER IN THE EAST(1953), w; GUYS AND DOLLS(1955), d&w; KING OF THE ROARING TWENTIES–THE STORY OF ARNOLD ROTHSTEIN(1961), w
Jo Swerling, Sr.
DR. RHYTHM(1938), w
Yetta Swerling
Misc. Talkies
MAZEL TOV, JEWS(1941)

William Swetland
1984
MIRRORS(1984)
Misc. Talkies
MIRRORS(1978)
T. L. P. Swicegood
MAN IN THE WATER, THE(1963), p, w; UNDERTAKER AND HIS PALS, THE(1966), w
Marly Swick
OFF THE WALL(1977), w
Charles Swickard
Silents
TYPHOON, THE(1914), w; FORBIDDEN ADVENTURE, THE(1915), d; CAPTIVE GOD, THE(1916), d; HELL'S HINGES(1916), d; ALMOST MARRIED(1919), d; ABABIAN KNIGHT, AN(1920), d; LAST STRAW, THE(1920), d&w
Misc. Silents
BEGGAR OF CAWNPORE, THE(1916), d; D'ARTAGNAN(1916), d; MIXED BLOOD(1916), d; RAIDERS, THE(1916), d; SIGN OF THE POPPY, THE(1916), d; GATES OF DOOM, THE(1917), d; LAIR OF THE WOLF, THE(1917), d; PHANTOM'S SECRET, THE(1917), d; PLOW WOMAN, THE(1917), d; SCARLET CRYSTAL, THE(1917), d; HITTING THE HIGH SPOTS(1918), d; LIGHT OF WESTERN STARS, THE(1918), d; FAITH(1919), d; SPENDER, THE(1919), d; BODY AND SOUL(1920), d; DEVIL'S CLAIM, THE(1920), d; THIRD WOMAN, THE(1920), d
Joe Swickard
Misc. Silents
TRICK OF FATE, A(1919)
Jose Swickard
PENITENTE MURDER CASE, THE(1936)
Josef Swickard
FROZEN RIVER(1929); VEILED WOMAN, THE(1929); DARKENED SKIES(1930); MAMBA(1930); PHANTOM OF THE DESERT(1930); SONG OF THE CABELLERO(1930); CROSS STREETS(1934); CRUSADES, THE(1935); BOSS RIDER OF GUN CREEK(1936); CARYL OF THE MOUNTAINS(1936); MILLIONAIRE KID(1936); UNDER YOUR SPELL(1936); GIRL SAID NO, THE(1937); SANDFLOW(1937); MEXICALI ROSE(1939); PAL FROM TEXAS, THE(1939)
Silents
TALE OF TWO CITIES, A(1917); MOON MADNESS(1920); CHEATED HEARTS(1921); FOUR HORSEMEN OF THE APOCALYPSE, THE(1921); ACROSS THE DEAD-LINE(1922); STORM, THE(1922); ETERNAL STRUGGLE, THE(1923); MOTHERS-IN-LAW(1923); MR. BILLINGS SPENDS HIS DIME(1923); MY AMERICAN WIFE(1923); DANTE'S INFERNO(1924); NORTH OF NEVADA(1924); NORTHERN CODE(1925); WIZARD OF OZ, THE(1925); DON JUAN(1926); KENTUCKY HANDICAP(1926); NIGHT PATROL, THE(1926); KING OF KINGS, THE(1927); OLD SAN FRANCISCO(1927); TIME TO LOVE(1927); SHARP SHOOTERS(1928); DEVIL'S CHAPLAIN(1929); ETERNAL WOMAN, THE(1929); PHANTOM OF THE NORTH(1929)
Misc. Silents
PAWNED(1922); CRICKET ON THE HEARTH, THE(1923); FORGIVE AND FORGET(1923); DEFYING THE LAW(1924); PAL O'MINE(1924); FIFTH AVENUE MODELS(1925); KEEPER OF THE BEES, THE(1925); BORDER WHIRLWIND, THE(1926); DEVIL'S DICE(1926); SENOR DAREDEVIL(1926); THREE PALS(1926); WHISPERING CANYON(1926); COMPASSION(1927); GET YOUR MAN(1927); SENORITA(1927)
Josef Swickard, Sr.
$1,000 A TOUCHDOWN(1939)
Joseph Swickard
TIMES SQUARE(1929); NARROW CORNER, THE(1933); DOG OF FLANDERS, A(1935); MAN WHO RECLAIMED HIS HEAD, THE(1935); SAY IT IN FRENCH(1938); YOU CAN'T TAKE IT WITH YOU(1938)
Silents
AMERICAN METHODS(1917); WHEN A WOMAN SINS(1918); NO WOMAN KNOWS(1921); GOLDEN GIFT, THE(1922); EASY MONEY(1925); OFF THE HIGHWAY(1925); OFFICER JIM(1926); UNKNOWN CAVALIER, THE(1926)
Misc. Silents
HIS MOTHER'S BOY(1917); KEYS OF THE RIGHTEOUS, THE(1918); LIGHT OF WESTERN STARS, THE(1918); TREASURE OF THE SEA(1918); GIRL IN BOHEMIA, A(1919); SNARES OF PARIS(1919); THIRD GENERATION, THE(1920); TRUMPET ISLAND(1920); OPENED SHUTTERS(1921); AGE OF DESIRE, THE(1923); MEN(1924); MYSTERIOUS STRANGER, THE(1925); FALSE MORALS(1927)
Jan Swiderski
EIGHTH DAY OF THE WEEK, THE(1959, Pol./Ger.)
Jerzy Swiech
CONTRACT, THE(1982, Pol.)
Allen Swift
MAD MONSTER PARTY(1967); RAGGEDY ANN AND ANDY(1977)
Misc. Talkies
ALICE OF WONDERLAND IN PARIS(1966)
Brent Swift
SEED OF INNOCENCE(1980), prod d; SPACEHUNTER: ADVENTURES IN THE FORBIDDEN ZONE(1983), art d
Bud Swift
RELUCTANT DRAGON, THE(1941), anim
Caroline Swift
OF HUMAN BONDAGE(1964, Brit.)
Clive Swift
HAVING A WILD WEEKEND(1965, Brit.); MIDSUMMER NIGHT'S DREAM, A(1969, Brit.); FRENZY(1972, Brit.); DEATHLINE(1973, Brit.); MAN AT THE TOP(1973, Brit.); NATIONAL HEALTH, OR NURSE NORTON'S AFFAIR, THE(1973, Brit.); SAILOR'S RETURN, THE(1978, Brit.); GREAT TRAIN ROBBERY, THE(1979, Brit.); EXCALIBUR(1981)
1984
MEMED MY HAWK(1984, Brit.); PASSAGE TO INDIA, A(1984, Brit.)
David Swift
POLLYANNA(1960), d&w; PARENT TRAP, THE(1961), d&w; INTERNS, THE(1962), d, w; LOVE IS A BALL(1963), d, w; UNDER THE YUM-YUM TREE(1963), d, w; GOOD NEIGHBOR SAM(1964), a, p&d, w; TRAVELS WITH MY AUNT(1972, Brit.); DAY OF THE JACKAL, THE(1973, Brit./Fr.); INTERNECINE PROJECT, THE(1974, Brit.); HOW TO SUCCEED IN BUSINESS WITHOUT REALLY TRYING(1976), a, p,d&w; BLACK PANTHER, THE(1977, Brit.); CANDLESHOE(1978), w; NO SEX PLEASE–WE'RE BRITISH(1979, Brit.); FOOLIN' AROUND(1980), w

Don Swift
THUNDER MOUNTAIN(1935), w; WHISPERING SMITH SPEAKS(1935), w; DAN MATTHEWS(1936), w; LET'S SING AGAIN(1936), w; MINE WITH THE IRON DOOR, THE(1936), w; WILD BRIAN KENT(1936), w

Howard Swift
FANTASIA(1940), anim; DUMBO(1941), anim

Jessica Swift
ZARDOZ(1974, Brit.)

Joan Swift
PATSY, THE(1964); BRAINSTORM(1965); DEADLY TRACKERS(1973)

John Swift
FOUR FAST GUNS(1959)

Jonathan Swift
GULLIVER'S TRAVELS(1939), w; THREE WORLDS OF GULLIVER, THE(1960, Brit.), w; GULLIVER'S TRAVELS(1977, Brit., Bel.), w

Jonathon Swift
GULLIVER'S TRAVELS BEYOND THE MOON(1966, Jap.), w

Kay Swift
NEVER A DULL MOMENT(1950), w

Milt Swift
MUSTANG(1959)

Paul Swift
FEMALE TROUBLE(1975)

Susan Swift
AUDREY ROSE(1977); HARPER VALLEY, P.T.A.(1978)
Misc. Talkies
COMING, THE(1983)

Howard Swiggett
POWER AND THE PRIZE, THE(1956), w

Saul Swimmer
FORCE OF IMPULSE(1961), d, w; WITHOUT EACH OTHER(1962), d, w; MRS. BROWN, YOU'VE GOT A LOVELY DAUGHTER(1968, Brit.), d; COMETOGETHER(1971), p&w, d; BLINDMAN(1972, Ital.), p
Misc. Talkies
BLACK PEARL, THE(1977), d

The Swimming Cherubs
JUPITER'S DARLING(1955)

Swinborne
M(1933, Ger.)

Lawrence Swinburne
Misc. Silents
MASTER SHAKESPEARE, STROLLING PLAYER(1916)

Mercia Swinburne
ALIBI(1931, Brit.); COMPULSORY WIFE, THE(1937, Brit.); SARABAND(1949, Brit.)

Nora Swinburne
ALF'S BUTTON(1930, Brit.); CASTE(1930, Brit.); HER STRANGE DESIRE(1931, Brit.); MAN OF MAYFAIR(1931, Brit.); THESE CHARMING PEOPLE(1931, Brit.); MAN WHO WON, THE(1933, Brit.); PERFECT UNDERSTANDING(1933, Brit.); TOO MANY WIVES(1933, Brit.); WHITE FACE(1933, Brit.); BOOMERANG(1934, Brit.); LEND ME YOUR HUSBAND(1935, Brit.); GAY ADVENTURE, THE(1936, Brit.); JURY'S EVIDENCE(1936, Brit.); DINNER AT THE RITZ(1937, Brit.); SCOTLAND YARD COMMANDS(1937, Brit.); CITADEL, THE(1938); LILY OF LAGUNA(1938, Brit.); FARMER'S WIFE, THE(1941, Brit.); IT HAPPENED TO ONE MAN(1941, Brit.); WINGS AND THE WOMAN(1942, Brit.); MAN IN GREY, THE(1943, Brit.); RANDOLPH FAMILY, THE(1945, Brit.); THEY KNEW MR. KNIGHT(1945, Brit.); BLIND GODDESS, THE(1948, Brit.); JASSY(1948, Brit.); MAN OF EVIL(1948, Brit.); BAD LORD BYRON, THE(1949, Brit.); CHRISTOPHER COLUMBUS(1949, Brit.); FOOLS RUSH IN(1949, Brit.); MARRY ME!(1949, Brit.); QUARTET(1949, Brit.); GOOD TIME GIRL(1950, Brit.); OPERATION X(1951, Brit.); QUO VADIS(1951); RIVER, THE(1951); LANDFALL(1953, Brit.); BETRAYED(1954); END OF THE AFFAIR, THE(1955, Brit.); HELEN OF TROY(1956, Ital); FEMALE FIENDS(1958, Brit.); THIRD MAN ON THE MOUNTAIN(1959); CONSPIRACY OF HEARTS(1960, Brit.); MAN COULD GET KILLED, A(1966, Brit.); INTERLUDE(1968, Brit.); ANNE OF THE THOUSAND DAYS(1969, Brit.)
Silents
AUTUMN OF PRIDE, THE(1921, Brit.); UNWANTED, THE(1924, Brit.); GIRL OF LONDON, A(1925, Brit.); ONE COLUMBO NIGHT(1926, Brit.)
Misc. Silents
BRANDED(1920, Brit.); SAVED FROM THE SEA(1920, Brit.); FORTUNE OF CHRISTINA MCNAB, THE(1921, Brit.); WEE MACGREGOR'S SWEETHEART, THE(1922, Brit.); HORNET'S NEST(1923, Brit.); RED TRAIL(1923); HIS GRACE GIVES NOTICE(1924, Brit.)

Simon Swindell
DINGAKA(1965, South Africa)

John Swindells
ASSAULT(1971, Brit.)

Buffalo Swing
1984
NATURAL, THE(1984)

Christina Swing
1984
FIRSTBORN(1984)

Santos Swing
TOY, THE(1982)

Willie Swing
TOY, THE(1982)

Ward Swingle
SWEET AND SOUR(1964, Fr./Ital.), m; TASTE FOR WOMEN, A(1966, Fr./Ital.), m; GATES TO PARADISE(1968, Brit./Ger.), m; SINGAPORE, SINGAPORE(1969, Fr./Ital.), m

Richard Swingler
E.T. THE EXTRA-TERRESTRIAL(1982); TWILIGHT ZONE–THE MOVIE(1983)

William Swingley
LUCK OF THE IRISH(1948)

Ralph Swink
CAPTIVE CITY(1952), ed

Robert Swink
ROMA RIVUOLE CESARE, ed; ACTION IN ARABIA(1944), ed; HEAVENLY DAYS(1944), ed; PASSPORT TO DESTINY(1944), ed; CRIMINAL COURT(1946), ed; STEP BY STEP(1946), ed; DEVIL THUMBS A RIDE, THE(1947), ed; I REMEMBER MAMA(1948), ed; ADVENTURE IN BALTIMORE(1949), ed; RIDERS OF THE RANGE(1949), ed; COMPANY SHE KEEPS, THE(1950), ed; DYNAMITE PASS(1950), ed; NEVER A DULL MOMENT(1950), ed; RIDER FROM TUCSON(1950), ed; STORM OVER WYOMING(1950), ed; DETECTIVE STORY(1951), ed; CARRIE(1952), ed; NARROW MARGIN, THE(1952), ed; WITNESS TO MURDER(1954), ed; CRASHOUT(1955), ed; DESPERATE HOURS, THE(1955), ed; FRIENDLY PERSUASION(1956), ed; YOUNG STRANGER, THE(1957), ed; DIARY OF ANNE FRANK, THE(1959), ed; CHILDREN'S HOUR, THE(1961), ed; YOUNG DOCTORS, THE(1961), ed; BEST MAN, THE(1964), ed; COLLECTOR, THE(1965), ed; HOW TO STEAL A MILLION(1966), ed; FLIM-FLAM MAN, THE(1967), ed; LIBERATION OF L.B. JONES, THE(1970), ed; CACTUS IN THE SNOW(1972), ed; COWBOYS, THE(1972), ed; SKYJACKED(1972), ed; LADY ICE(1973), ed; PAPILLON(1973), ed; THREE THE HARD WAY(1974), ed; ROOSTER COGBURN(1975), ed; MIDWAY(1976), ed; ISLANDS IN THE STREAM(1977), ed; GRAY LADY DOWN(1978), ed; GOING IN STYLE(1979), ed

Robert E. Swink
BOYS FROM BRAZIL, THE(1978), ed; IN-LAWS, THE(1979), ed; SPHINX(1981), ed

Ion Swinley
BARTON MYSTERY, THE(1932, Brit.)
Misc. Silents
TRILBY(1914, Brit.); HOW KITCHENER WAS BETRAYED(1921, Brit.)

Aida Swinson
1984
KARATE KID, THE(1984), cos

Joan Swinstead
WOLF'S CLOTHING(1936, Brit.); COLONEL BLIMP(1945, Brit.); ADAM AND EVELYNE(1950, Brit.); FINAL TEST, THE(1953, Brit.)

"Billy Boy" Swinton
Silents
BURN 'EM UP BARNES(1921)

Thomas H. Swinton
Misc. Silents
HOME-KEEPING HEARTS(1921)

Brad Swirnoff
TUNNELVISION(1976), d

Bradley R. Swirnoff
Misc. Talkies
AMERICAN RASPBERRY(1980), d

Loretta Swit
STAND UP AND BE COUNTED(1972); FREEBIE AND THE BEAN(1974); RACE WITH THE DEVIL(1975); S.O.B.(1981); DEADHEAD MILES(1982)

Willy Switkes
TOOTSIE(1982)

Carl Switzer
EASY TO TAKE(1936); GENERAL SPANKY(1937); ICE FOLLIES OF 1939(1939); WAR AGAINST MRS. HADLEY, THE(1942); LETTER TO THREE WIVES, A(1948); ON OUR MERRY WAY(1948); HERE COMES THE GROOM(1951); TWO DOLLAR BETTOR(1951); PAT AND MIKE(1952); WAC FROM WALLA WALLA, THE(1952); ISLAND IN THE SKY(1953); HIGH AND THE MIGHTY, THE(1954); THIS IS MY LOVE(1954); BETWEEN HEAVEN AND HELL(1956); DIG THAT URANIUM(1956); TEN COMMANDMENTS, THE(1956); MOTORCYCLE GANG(1957); DEFIANT ONES, THE(1958)

Carl "Alfalfa" Switzer
TOO MANY PARENTS(1936); WILD AND WOOLLY(1937); SCANDAL STREET(1938); BARNYARD FOLLIES(1940); I LOVE YOU AGAIN(1940); REG'LAR FELLERS(1941); HENRY AND DIZZY(1942); MRS. WIGGS OF THE CABBAGE PATCH(1942); MY FAVORITE BLONDE(1942); THERE'S ONE BORN EVERY MINUTE(1942); HUMAN COMEDY, THE(1943); JOHNNY DOUGHBOY(1943); SHANTYTOWN(1943); GOING MY WAY(1944); GREAT MIKE, THE(1944); ROSIE THE RIVETER(1944); TOGETHER AGAIN(1944); MAN ALIVE(1945); SHE WOULDN'T SAY YES(1945); BLUE SIERRA(1946); GAS HOUSE KIDS(1946); IT'S A WONDERFUL LIFE(1946); GAS HOUSE KIDS GO WEST(1947); GAS HOUSE KIDS IN HOLLYWOOD(1947); BIG TOWN SCANDAL(1948); STATE OF THE UNION(1948); REDWOOD FOREST TRAIL(1950); CAUSE FOR ALARM(1951); TRACK OF THE CAT(1954)

Carl Dean Switzer
I DREAM OF JEANIE(1952)

Robert Swiuk
DOUBLE DEAL(1950), ed

Leonid Swjetlow
NAKED AMONG THE WOLVES(1967, Ger.)

Ken Swofford
FATHER GOOSE(1964); FIRST TO FIGHT(1967); LAWYER, THE(1969); BLESS THE BEASTS AND CHILDREN(1971); SKYJACKED(1972); ONE LITTLE INDIAN(1973); BLACK BIRD, THE(1975); DOMINO PRINCIPLE, THE(1977); S.O.B.(1981); ANNIE(1982)

Harry Swoger
ANGEL BABY(1961); FATE IS THE HUNTER(1964); ROBIN AND THE SEVEN HOODS(1964)

John Swon
CHARLIE CHAN CARRIES ON(1931)

Herbert B. Swope, Jr.
HILDA CRANE(1956), p; THREE BRAVE MEN(1957), p; TRUE STORY OF JESSE JAMES, THE(1957), p; BRAVADOS, THE(1958), p; FIEND WHO WALKED THE WEST, THE(1958), p

Margaret Swope
LAST OUTPOST, THE(1935)

Marguerita Swope
MADAME SATAN(1930)

Mark Swope
WILD PARTY, THE(1975)

Rusty Swope
TEENAGE REBEL(1956); GOOD DAY FOR A HANGING(1958)

Topo Swope
GLORY BOY(1971); PRETTY MAIDS ALL IN A ROW(1971); HOT ROCK, THE(1972); TRACKS(1977)

Tracy Brooks Swope
1984
HARD TO HOLD(1984)

Bert Swor
WHY BRING THAT UP?(1929)

Bert Swor, Jr.
CARNATION KID(1929)
John Swor
UP THE RIVER(1930); QUICK MILLIONS(1931); HERE COMES THE NAVY(1934)
Jack Sword
WHAT'S UP FRONT(1964)
Travis Swords
DON'T CRY, IT'S ONLY THUNDER(1982)
Theodore Swystun
GIRL FROM POLTAVA(1937)
Mansour Sy
BROKEN ENGLISH(1981)
Feroza Syal
1984
MAJDHAR(1984, Brit.)
Amelie Syberberg
OUR HITLER, A FILM FROM GERMANY(1980, Ger.); PARSIFAL(1983, Fr.)
Hans-Jurgen Syberberg
OUR HITLER, A FILM FROM GERMANY(1980, Ger.), d&w; PARSIFAL(1983, Fr.), d
L. Sychova
Misc. Silents
TERCENTENARY OF THE ROMANOV DYNASTY'S ACCESSION TO THE THRONE(1913, USSR); DAYS OF OUR LIFE(1914, USSR); NEST OF NOBLEMEN, A(1915, USSR); TALE OF PRIEST PANKRATI(1918, USSR); MOTHER(1920, USSR)
Syd Dean and His Band
LADY GODIVA RIDES AGAIN(1955, Brit.)
Syd Seymour and His Mad Hatters
HAPPY DAYS ARE HERE AGAIN(1936, Brit.)
Syd Seymour's Mad Hatters
JUST FOR A SONG(1930, Brit.)
Anthony Sydes
CLAUDIA AND DAVID(1946); JOHNNY COMES FLYING HOME(1946); IT HAPPENED ON 5TH AVENUE(1947); MIRACLE ON 34TH STREET, THE(1947); SONG OF LOVE(1947); CANON CITY(1948); CHICKEN EVERY SUNDAY(1948); SITTING PRETTY(1948); CHEAPER BY THE DOZEN(1950); SHADOW ON THE WALL(1950); BELLES ON THEIR TOES(1952); GLENN MILLER STORY, THE(1953); LUST FOR LIFE(1956); GUNSMOKE IN TUCSON(1958)
Carol Sydes
GOOD MORNING, MISS DOVE(1955); CAPE FEAR(1962)
Deborah Sydes
GLENN MILLER STORY, THE(1953); GIRL RUSH, THE(1955)
Ann Sydney
Misc. Talkies
TREASURE OF THE AMAZON(1983)
Aurele Sydney
Silents
ANGEL ESQUIRE(1919, Brit.)
Misc. Silents
SALLY BISHOP(1916, Brit.); GREEN TERROR, THE(1919, Brit.)
Basil Sydney
MIDSHIPMAID GOB(1932, Brit.); DIRTY WORK(1934, Brit.); THIRD CLUE, THE(1934, Brit.); RIVERSIDE MURDER, THE(1935, Brit.); TRANSATLANTIC TUNNEL(1935, Brit.); WHITE LILAC(1935, Brit.); ACCUSED(1936, Brit.); AMATEUR GENTLEMAN(1936, Brit.); BLIND MAN'S BLUFF(1936, Brit.); CRIME OVER LONDON(1936, Brit.); RHODES(1936, Brit.); TALK OF THE DEVIL(1937, Brit.); SHADOWED EYES(1939, Brit.); SECRET FOUR, THE(1940, Brit.); BLACK SHEEP OF WHITEHALL, THE(1941 Brit.); FARMER'S WIFE, THE(1941, Brit.); SPRING MEETING(1941, Brit.); NEXT OF KIN(1942, Brit.); SHIPS WITH WINGS(1942, Brit.); 48 HOURS(1944, Brit.); CAESAR AND CLEOPATRA(1946, Brit.); MEET ME AT DAWN(1947, Brit.); HAMLET(1948, Brit.); JASSY(1948, Brit.); SMUGGLERS, THE(1948, Brit.); ANGEL WITH THE TRUMPET, THE(1950, Brit.); TREASURE ISLAND(1950, Brit.); IVANHOE(1952, Brit.); MAGIC BOX, THE(1952, Brit.); SALOME(1953); THREE'S COMPANY(1953, Brit.); HELL BELOW ZERO(1954, Brit.); DAM BUSTERS, THE(1955, Brit.); SIMBA(1955, Brit.); AROUND THE WORLD IN 80 DAYS(1956); STAR OF INDIA(1956, Brit.); ISLAND IN THE SUN(1957); SEA WIFE(1957, Brit.); DEVIL'S DISCIPLE, THE(1959); JOHN PAUL JONES(1959); QUESTION OF ADULTERY, A(1959, Brit.); STORY OF DAVID, A(1960, Brit.); THREE WORLDS OF GULLIVER, THE(1960, Brit.); HANDS OF ORLAC, THE(1964, Brit./Fr.)
Silents
RED HOT ROMANCE(1922)
Misc. Silents
ROMANCE(1920)
Denise Sydney
LOST ON THE WESTERN FRONT(1940, Brit.)
Derek Sydney
FIRE OVER AFRICA(1954, Brit.); GENTLEMEN MARRY BRUNETTES(1955); MAN OF THE MOMENT(1955, Brit.); WOMAN FOR JOE, THE(1955, Brit.); BLACK TENT, THE(1956, Brit.); KID FOR TWO FARTHINGS, A(1956, Brit.); PASSPORT TO TREASON(1956, Brit.); THUNDER OVER TANGIER(1957, Brit.); VIOLENT STRANGER(1957, Brit.); CRAWLING EYE, THE(1958, Brit.); WITNESS, THE(1959, Brit.); HAND IN HAND(1960, Brit.); MAKE MINE MINK(1960, Brit.); SANDS OF THE DESERT(1960, Brit.); HOT MONEY GIRL(1962, Brit./Ger.); CARRY ON SPYING(1964, Brit.)
Edward Sydney
Misc. Silents
WRECKER OF LIVES, THE(1914, Brit.)
Elizabeth Sydney
GREEN FOR DANGER(1946, Brit.); MY SISTER AND I(1948, Brit.)
Evelyn Sydney
Silents
BLIND BOY, THE(1917, Brit.)
Gloria Sydney
MAN OF EVIL(1948, Brit.)
Herbert Sydney
Misc. Silents
ANSWER THE CALL(1915, Brit.)
Lysbeth Sydney
GIVE US THE MOON(1944, Brit.)

R. Sydney
BLOOD RELATIVES(1978, Fr./Can.), w
Robert Sydney
EIGHT O'CLOCK WALK(1954, Brit.); CONSTANT HUSBAND, THE(1955, Brit.)
Susan Sydney
NO BLADE OF GRASS(1970, Brit.)
Susanne Sydney
GIRLS' TOWN(1959)
Suzanne Sydney
MOTORCYCLE GANG(1957); HIGH SCHOOL HELLCATS(1958)
Sylvia Sydney
GOOD DAME(1934); FURY(1936)
Sydney Baines and His Band
REGAL CAVALCADE(1935, Brit.)
Sydney Kyte and His Band
SATURDAY NIGHT REVUE(1937, Brit.)
Sydney Lipton and His Band
LET'S MAKE A NIGHT OF IT(1937, Brit.)
Sydney the Elephant
JUMBO(1962)
Dia Sydow
HOUSE OF THE LIVING DEAD(1973, S. Afr.)
Didi Sydow
DEADLIER THAN THE MALE(1967, Brit.)
Wulfhild Sydow
GERMAN SISTERS, THE(1982, Ger.)
F. Syemyannikov
SKY CALLS, THE(1959, USSR), spec eff
Elmer Syer
AIR FORCE(1943), ph
Thomas Syfan
I'D CLIMB THE HIGHEST MOUNTAIN(1951)
Tom Syie
Misc. Talkies
DEATH MAY BE YOUR SANTA CLAUS(1969)
Brenda Sykes
BABY MAKER, THE(1970); GETTING STRAIGHT(1970); LIBERATION OF L.B. JONES, THE(1970); HONKY(1971); PRETTY MAIDS ALL IN A ROW(1971); SKIN GAME(1971); BLACK GUNN(1972); CLEOPATRA JONES(1973); MANDINGO(1975); DRUM(1976)
Eric Sykes
COMING-OUT PARTY, A(; CHARLEY MOON(1956, Brit.); ROTTEN TO THE CORE(1956, Brit.); ORDERS ARE ORDERS(1959, Brit.), a, w; TOMMY THE TOREADOR(1960, Brit.); INVASION QUARTET(1961, Brit.); WATCH YOUR STERN(1961, Brit.); KILL OR CURE(1962, Brit.); VILLAGE OF DAUGHTERS(1962, Brit.); HEAVENS ABOVE!(1963, Brit.); BARGEE, THE(1964, Brit.); ONE WAY PENDULUM(1965, Brit.); THOSE MAGNIFICENT MEN IN THEIR FLYING MACHINES; OR HOW I FLEW FROM LONDON TO PARIS IN 25 HOURS AND 11 MINUTES(1965, Brit.); LIQUIDATOR, THE(1966, Brit.); SPY WITH A COLD NOSE, THE(1966, Brit.); PLANK, THE(1967, Brit.), a, d&w; SHALAKO(1968, Brit.); THOSE DARING YOUNG MEN IN THEIR JAUNTY JALOPIES(1969, Fr./Brit./ Ital.); THEATRE OF BLOOD(1973, Brit.)
Ethel Sykes
IT HAPPENED ONE NIGHT(1934); MAGNIFICENT OBSESSION(1935); GIVE ME YOUR HEART(1936); HITCH HIKE TO HEAVEN(1936)
Fairy Sykes
KILLERS THREE(1968)
H. Sykes
Silents
MUNITION GIRL'S ROMANCE, A(1917, Brit.)
Keith Sykes
SUMMER SOLDIERS(1972, Jap.)
Melissa Sykes
1984
FLASH OF GREEN, A(1984), set d
Peter Sykes
COMMITTEE, THE(1968, Brit.), d, w; DEMONS OF THE MIND(1972, Brit.), d; LEGEND OF SPIDER FOREST, THE(1976, Brit.), d; TO THE DEVIL A DAUGHTER(1976, Brit./Ger.), d; JESUS(1979), d
Rhona Sykes
SO WELL REMEMBERED(1947, Brit.)
Rupert Sykes
TABLE FOR FIVE(1983)
William R. Sykes
STRIPES(1981)
Jiri Sykora
MOST BEAUTIFUL AGE, THE(1970, Czech.)
Christina Sylba
TAKE ME AWAY, MY LOVE(1962, Gr.)
Charles Sylber
GUILTY AS HELL(1932)
Anthea Sylbert
TIGER MAKES OUT, THE(1967), cos; ROSEMARY'S BABY(1968), cos; ILLUSTRATED MAN, THE(1969), cos; JOHN AND MARY(1969), cos; SOME KIND OF A NUT(1969), cos; CARNAL KNOWLEDGE(1971), cos; NEW LEAF, A(1971), cos; STEAGLE, THE(1971), cos; COWBOYS, THE(1972), cos; HEARTBREAK KID, THE(1972), cos; DAY OF THE DOLPHIN, THE(1973), cos; CHINATOWN(1974), cos; SHAMPOO(1975), cos; KING KONG(1976), cos; JULIA(1977), cos; F.I.S.T.(1978), cos
1984
PROTOCOL(1984), p
Dick Sylbert
MURDER, INC.(1960), art d
Lulu Sylbert
STRANGE INVADERS(1983)
Paul Sylbert
WRONG MAN, THE(1956), art d; TEENAGE MILLIONAIRE(1961), art d; TIGER MAKES OUT, THE(1967), prod d; RIOT(1969), prod d &art d; STEAGLE, THE(1971), d, w; DROWNING POOL, THE(1975), prod d; ONE FLEW OVER THE CUCKOO'S NEST(1975), prod d; MIKEY AND NICKY(1976), prod d; HEAVEN CAN WAIT(1978), prod d; HARDCORE(1979), prod d; KRAMER VS. KRAMER(1979), prod d; RESURRECTION(1980), prod d; BLOW OUT(1981), prod d; NIGHTHAWKS(1981), w; WOLF-

Richard Sylbert-
EN(1981), prod d; GORKY PARK(1983), prod d; WITHOUT A TRACE(1983), prod d
1984
FIRSTBORN(1984), prod d; POPE OF GREENWICH VILLAGE, THE(1984), prod d

Richard Sylbert
PATTERNS(1956), art d; EDGE OF THE CITY(1957), art d; WIND ACROSS THE EVERGLADES(1958), art d; FUGITIVE KIND, THE(1960), art d; MAD DOG COLL(1961), art d; SPLENDOR IN THE GRASS(1961), art d; YOUNG DOCTORS, THE(1961), prod d; CONNECTION, THE(1962), prod d; LONG DAY'S JOURNEY INTO NIGHT(1962), prod d, art d; MANCHURIAN CANDIDATE, THE(1962), prod d, art d; WALK ON THE WILD SIDE(1962), art d; LILITH(1964), prod d; HOW TO MURDER YOUR WIFE, THE(1965), art d; PAWNBROKER, THE(1965), art d; GRAND PRIX(1966), prod d; WHO'S AFRAID OF VIRGINIA WOOLF?(1966), prod d; GRADUATE, THE(1967), prod d; ROSEMARY'S BABY(1968), prod d; APRIL FOOLS, THE(1969), prod d; CATCH-22(1970), prod d; CARNAL KNOWLEDGE(1971), prod d; FAT CITY(1972), prod d; HEARTBREAK KID, THE(1972), art d; DAY OF THE DOLPHIN, THE(1973), prod d; CHINATOWN(1974), prod d; FORTUNE, THE(1975), prod d; SHAMPOO(1975), prod d; PLAYERS(1979), prod d; REDS(1981), prod d; FRANCES(1982), prod d; PARTNERS(1982), prod d; BREATHLESS(1983), prod d
1984
COTTON CLUB, THE(1984), prod d

Frank Syles
C'MON, LET'S LIVE A LITTLE(1967), art d

Ken Sylk
HIDE IN PLAIN SIGHT(1980); AUTHOR! AUTHOR!(1982)

F. Frank Sylos
SO THIS IS NEW YORK(1948), art d

F. Paul Sylos
GLORY TRAIL, THE(1937), art d; HOLLYWOOD COWBOY(1937), art d; LOVE TAKES FLIGHT(1937), art d; WINDJAMMER(1937), art d; HOLLYWOOD ROUND-UP(1938), art d; OVERLAND EXPRESS, THE(1938), art d; MAD EMPRESS, THE(1940), art d; FORCED LANDING(1941), art d; POWER DIVE(1941), art d; I LIVE ON DANGER(1942), art d; ISLE OF MISSING MEN(1942), art d; MOON AND SIXPENCE, THE(1942), art d; WILDCAT(1942), art d; WRECKING CREW(1942), art d; HIGH EXPLOSIVE(1943), art d; MINESWEEPER(1943), art d; TORNADO(1943), art d; TWO WEEKS TO LIVE(1943), art d; DARK MOUNTAIN(1944), art d; DOUBLE EXPOSURE(1944), art d; GAMBLER'S CHOICE(1944), art d; I'M FROM ARKANSAS(1944), art d; NAVY WAY, THE(1944), art d; ONE BODY TOO MANY(1944), art d; TAKE IT BIG(1944), art d; TIMBER QUEEN(1944), art d; WHEN STRANGERS MARRY(1944), art d; FOLLOW THAT WOMAN(1945), art d; GREAT FLAMARION, THE(1945), art d; HIGH POWERED(1945), art d; PEOPLE ARE FUNNY(1945), art d; SCARED STIFF(1945), art d; TOKYO ROSE(1945), art d; HOT CARGO(1946), art d; SUSPENSE(1946), art d; SWAMP FIRE(1946), art d; THEY MADE ME A KILLER(1946), art d; DANGER STREET(1947), art d; FEAR IN THE NIGHT(1947), art d; GANGSTER, THE(1947), art d; GAS HOUSE KIDS IN HOLLYWOOD(1947), art d; I COVER BIG TOWN(1947), art d; JUNGLE FLIGHT(1947), art d; PRETENDER, THE(1947), art d; RETURN OF RIN TIN TIN, THE(1947), art d; SEVEN WERE SAVED(1947), art d; SHAGGY(1948), art d; SMART WOMAN(1948), art d; GRAND CANYON(1949), art d; RED LIGHT(1949), art d; RETURN OF JESSE JAMES, THE(1950), art d; DANGER ZONE(1951), art d; FBI GIRL(1951), art d; KENTUCKY JUBILEE(1951), art d; LITTLE BIG HORN(1951), art d; PIER 23(1951), art d; ROARING CITY(1951), art d; SAVAGE DRUMS(1951), art d; YES SIR, MR. BONES(1951), art d; SKY HIGH(1952), art d; SINS OF JEZEBEL(1953), art d

Frank Sylos
WESTERN GOLD(1937), art d; PRISON TRAIN(1938), art d; SOUTH OF PANAMA(1941), art d; SHE'S IN THE ARMY(1942), art d; DANGER! WOMEN AT WORK(1943), art d; GIRL FROM MONTEREY, THE(1943), art d; HARVEST MELODY(1943), art d; SUBMARINE BASE(1943), art d; THREE RUSSIAN GIRLS(1943), art d; JIVE JUNCTION(1944), art d; LADY IN THE DEATH HOUSE(1944), art d; MACHINE GUN MAMA(1944), art d; DIXIE JAMBOREE(1945), art d; ENCHANTED FOREST, THE(1945), art d; JEALOUSY(1945), art d; FABULOUS SUZANNE, THE(1946), art d; GAS HOUSE KIDS(1946), art d; LADY CHASER(1946), art d; SCANDAL IN PARIS, A(1946), art d; HEADING FOR HEAVEN(1947), art d; KILLER DILL(1947), art d; PRIVATE AFFAIRS OF BEL AMI, THE(1947), art d; RUTHLESS(1948), art d; I CHEATED THE LAW(1949), art d; SATAN'S CRADLE(1949), art d; STEEL LADY, THE(1953), art d; 99 RIVER STREET(1953), art d; MAD MAGICIAN, THE(1954), art d; SNOW CREATURE, THE(1954), art d; SUDDENLY(1954), art d; TOP GUN(1955), art d; NIGHTMARE(1956), art d; HELL ON DEVIL'S ISLAND(1957), art d; MEN IN WAR(1957), art d; SERGEANT WAS A LADY, THE(1961), art d; THEY SAVED HITLER'S BRAIN(1964), art d; BOY, DID I GET A WRONG NUMBER!(1966), art d; FLAREUP(1969), art d; HEAVEN WITH A GUN(1969), art d; CHRISTINE JORGENSEN STORY, THE(1970), art d; HONKY(1971), art d; NECROMANCY(1972), art d; RAGE(1972), art d; HEX(1973), art d; DRAGNET(1974), art d

Frank P. Sylos
CAUGHT(1949), art d; TOUGH ASSIGNMENT(1949), art d; MOTOR PATROL(1950), art d; MISS ROBIN CRUSOE(1954), art d; GREAT SIOUX MASSACRE, THE(1965), art d

Paul Sylos
ONE EXCITING NIGHT(1945), art d; BIG TOWN(1947), art d; BIG TOWN AFTER DARK(1947), art d; HE RIDES TALL(1964), art d; NIGHTMARE IN THE SUN(1964), art d; HUMAN DUPLICATORS, THE(1965), art d; MUTINY IN OUTER SPACE(1965), art d; BILLY THE KID VS. DRACULA(1966), art d; JESSE JAMES MEETS FRANKENSTEIN'S DAUGHTER(1966), art d; NAVY VS. THE NIGHT MONSTERS, THE(1966), art d; WOMEN OF THE PREHISTORIC PLANET(1966); art d; CASTLE OF EVIL(1967), art d; HILLBILLYS IN A HAUNTED HOUSE(1967), art d; 40 GUNS TO APACHE PASS(1967), art d; DESTRUCTORS, THE(1968), art d; MARYJANE(1968), art d; MONEY JUNGLE, THE(1968), art d; WILD IN THE STREETS(1968), art d; DEVIL'S 8, THE(1969), art d; GIRL WHO KNEW TOO MUCH, THE(1969), art d; RUN, ANGEL, RUN(1969), art d; DUNWICH HORROR, THE(1970), art d

Paul Sylos, Jr.
YOUNG AND THE BRAVE, THE(1963), art d; ARIZONA RAIDERS(1965), art d; CYBORG 2087(1966), art d; DESTINATION INNER SPACE(1966), art d; DIMENSION 5(1966), art d; VIOLENT ONES, THE(1967), art d; DAYTON'S DEVILS(1968), art d; PANIC IN THE CITY(1968), art d

Ralph Sylos
BAD MEN OF THE BORDER(1945), set d; SHADY LADY(1945), set d; INCIDENT AT PHANTOM HILL(1966), set d; PLAINSMAN, THE(1966), set d; RIDE TO HANGMAN'S TREE, THE(1967), set d; SULLIVAN'S EMPIRE(1967), set d; TAMMY AND THE MILLIONAIRE(1967), set d; YOUNG WARRIORS, THE(1967), set d; DID YOU HEAR THE ONE ABOUT THE TRAVELING SALESLADY?(1968), set d; FLAREUP(1969), set d; HEX(1973), set d

The Sylte Sisters
MADISON AVENUE(1962)

Ilena Sylva
GOOD TIME GIRL(1950, Brit.)

Margaret Sylva
LEOPARD MAN, THE(1943)

Marguerita Sylva
TO HAVE AND HAVE NOT(1944); GAY SENORITA, THE(1945)

Marguerite Sylva
SEVENTH VICTIM, THE(1943)
Misc. Silents
CARMEN(1917, Ital.); HONEY BEE, THE(1920)

Vesta Sylva
Silents
ARCADIANS, THE(1927, Brit.)
Misc. Silents
WHITE HEAT(1926, Brit.)

Sylvain
INNOCENTS IN PARIS(1955, Brit.); GATES OF PARIS(1958, Fr./Ital.); SOUTHERN STAR, THE(1969, Fr./Brit.)

Claude Sylvain
RIFIFI(1956, Fr.)

Jean Sylvain
KING OF HEARTS(1967, Fr./Ital.)

Jules Sylvain
COUNT OF THE MONK'S BRIDGE, THE(1934, Swed.), m; NIGHT IN JUNE, A(1940, Swed.), m; JUNGLE OF CHANG(1951), m

Marcel Sylvain
QUEBEC(1951)

June Sylvaine
ONE WILD OAT(1951, Brit.)

Sue Sylvaine
MAGNIFICENT TWO, THE(1967, Brit.)

Vernon Sylvaine
AREN'T MEN BEASTS?(1937, Brit.), w; MAKE IT THREE(1938, Brit.), w; SPOT OF BOTHER, A(1938, Brit.), w; WOMEN AREN'T ANGELS(1942, Brit.), w; WARN THAT MAN(1943, Brit.), w; MADAME LOUISE(1951, Brit.), w; ONE WILD OAT(1951, Brit.), w; MAN OF THE MOMENT(1955, Brit.), w; WILL ANY GENTLEMAN?(1955, Brit.), w; AS LONG AS THEY'RE HAPPY(1957, Brit.), w

Bonnie Sylvano
LORDS OF FLATBUSH, THE(1974)

Sam Sylvano
KONGA(1961, Brit.)

Jean Sylvere
FRENCH CANCAN(1956, Fr.); SEVENTH JUROR, THE(1964, Fr.); PARIS IN THE MONTH OF AUGUST(1968, Fr.)

The Sylvers
FISH THAT SAVED PITTSBURGH, THE(1979)

Sylvester
ROSE, THE(1979)

Bill [William] Sylvester
SALT TO THE DEVIL(1949, Brit.)

Charles Sylvester
Silents
THIEF OF BAGDAD, THE(1924)

Chris Sylvester
Misc. Silents
CASEY'S MILLIONS(1922, Brit.)

Denise Sylvester
LEAVE IT TO BLANCHE(1934, Brit.)

Harold Sylvester
SOUNDER, PART 2(1976); HERO AIN'T NOTHIN' BUT A SANDWICH, A(1977); FAST BREAK(1979); INSIDE MOVES(1980); OFFICER AND A GENTLEMAN, AN(1982); UNCOMMON VALOR(1983)

Henry Sylvester
SHE COULDN'T TAKE IT(1935); SHE MARRIED HER BOSS(1935); EAGLE'S BROOD, THE(1936); FAST COMPANY(1938); BEAU GESTE(1939); CAPTAIN IS A LADY, THE(1940); ONE MILLION B.C.(1940); TWENTY MULE TEAM(1940); HEAVENLY BODY, THE(1943); HOODLUM SAINT, THE(1946); HIGH BARBAREE(1947); HIGH WALL, THE(1947); LIFE WITH FATHER(1947); POSSESSED(1947); SEA OF GRASS, THE(1947); SONG OF THE THIN MAN(1947); NEPTUNE'S DAUGHTER(1949); SUN COMES UP, THE(1949); EMERGENCY WEDDING(1950); SUMMER STOCK(1950); IT'S A BIG COUNTRY(1951); DEEP IN MY HEART(1954)

John Sylvester
WORDS AND MUSIC(1929); I WANTED WINGS(1941); OBLIGING YOUNG LADY(1941); DESTINATION TOKYO(1944); SARATOGA TRUNK(1945); DESIRE IN THE DUST(1960), makeup; SILENT CALL, THE(1961), makeup
Silents
IS MONEY EVERYTHING?(1923)

John L. Sylvester
MEXICAN HAYRIDE(1948)

Lillian Sylvester
Silents
WATCH YOUR STEP(1922); MERRY-GO-ROUND(1923)

Maud Sylvester
Misc. Silents
ORPHAN SALLY(1922)

Rick Sylvester
FOR YOUR EYES ONLY(1981), stunts

Robert Sylvester
WE WERE STRANGERS(1949), w; JOE LOUIS STORY, THE(1953), w; BIG BOODLE, THE(1957), w

Vari Sylvester
MOON OVER THE ALLEY(1980, Brit.)

William Sylvester
ALBERT, R.N.(1953, Brit.); APPOINTMENT IN LONDON(1953, Brit.); HOUSE OF BLACKMAIL(1953, Brit.); YELLOW BALLOON, THE(1953, Brit.); UNHOLY FOUR, THE(1954, Brit.); WHAT EVERY WOMAN WANTS(1954, Brit.); POSTMARK FOR DANGER(1956, Brit.); HIGH TIDE AT NOON(1957, Brit.); DUBLIN NIGHTMARE(1958, Brit.); WHIRLPOOL(1959, Brit.); GORGO(1961, Brit.); OFFBEAT(1961,

Brit.); INFORMATION RECEIVED(1962, Brit.); MAN IN THE DARK(1963, Brit.); DEVIL DOLL(1964, Brit.); RING OF SPIES(1964, Brit.); DEVILS OF DARKNESS, THE(1965, Brit.); INCIDENT AT MIDNIGHT(1966, Brit.); HAND OF NIGHT, THE(1968, Brit.); SYNDICATE, THE(1968, Brit.); 2001: A SPACE ODYSSEY(1968, U.S./Brit.); LAWYER, THE(1969); BUSTING(1974); HINDENBURG, THE(1975); HEAVEN CAN WAIT(1978)
Misc. Talkies
KENYA–COUNTRY OF TREASURE(1964)
Sylvester and Nephew
DUMMY TALKS, THE(1943, Brit.)
Armando Sylvestre
HIAWATHA(1952)
Cleo Sylvestre
ALF 'N' FAMILY(1968, Brit.); MY LOVER, MY SON(1970, Brit.); TROG(1970, Brit.); SCHOOL FOR UNCLAIMED GIRLS(1973, Brit.)
Cleopatra Sylvestre
JOHNNY ON THE RUN(1953, Brit.)
Phil Sylvestre
HOUSE OF USHER(1960)
Philip Sylvestre
GENTLEMEN PREFER BLONDES(1953)
Simone Sylvestre
PARIS DOES STRANGE THINGS(1957, Fr./Ital.)
Franca Sylvi
LA TRAVIATA(1982), ed
Ilena Sylvia
IT'S IN THE AIR(1940, Brit.)
Melissa Sylvia
MOUNTAIN MEN, THE(1980)
Sylvia Kellaway and Leslie
GARRISON FOLLIES(1940, Brit.)
Rene Sylviano
FRUSTRATIONS(1967, Fr./Ital.), m
Sylvie
CRIME AND PUNISHMENT(1935, Fr.); UN CARNET DE BAL(1938, Fr.); IDIOT, THE(1948, Fr.); RAVEN, THE(1948, Fr.); ANGELS OF THE STREETS(1950, Fr.); LITTLE WORLD OF DON CAMILLO, THE(1953, Fr./Ital.); ULYSSES(1955, Ital.); ADULTERESS, THE(1959, Fr.); ANATOMY OF LOVE(1959, Ital.); FORBIDDEN FRUIT(1959, Fr.); MIRROR HAS TWO FACES, THE(1959, Fr.); MICHAEL STRO-GOFF(1960, Fr./Ital./Yugo.); FAMILY DIARY(1963 Ital.); NUTTY, NAUGHTY CHA-TEAU(1964, Fr./Ital.); SHAMELESS OLD LADY, THE(1966, Fr.)
Kari Sylwan
CRIES AND WHISPERS(1972, Swed.); FACE TO FACE(1976, Swed.)
Igo Sym
VIENNA, CITY OF SONGS(1931, Ger.)
Don Symington
DIARY OF A MAD HOUSEWIFE(1970)
Donald Symington
FROM THE MIXED-UP FILES OF MRS. BASIL E. FRANKWEILER(1973); TRICK BABY(1973); FRONT, THE(1976); ANNIE HALL(1977); WOLFEN(1981); HANKY-PANKY(1982); SPRING BREAK(1983)
John B. Symmes
MANHUNT IN THE JUNGLE(1958)
Margit Symo
CARMEN(1949, Span.)
Burk Symon
IN THIS CORNER(1948), w; BRIDE FOR SALE(1949); FIGHTING MAN OF THE PLAINS(1949); LEAVE IT TO HENRY(1949); BLACK HAND, THE(1950); SECRET FURY, THE(1950); YOUNG MAN WITH A HORN(1950)
Burke Symon
BIRTH OF A BABY(1938), w
Amanda Symonds
1984
SCRUBBERS(1984, Brit.)
Augustin Symonds
Silents
FOUR FEATHERS(1929)
David Symonds
SUDDEN TERROR(1970, Brit.), md
Henry R. Symonds
Silents
ONE PUNCH O'DAY(1926), w; LOST LIMITED, THE(1927), w
Henry Roberts Symonds
STREET ANGEL(1928), w; PACIFIC LINER(1939), w
Silents
GEARED TO GO(1924), w; KENTUCKY HANDICAP(1926), w; NIGHT OWL, THE(1926), w; RACING ROMANCE(1926), w
Julian Symonds
NARROWING CIRCLE, THE(1956, Brit.), w
Robert Symonds
GRAY LADY DOWN(1978); ...AND JUSTICE FOR ALL(1979)
1984
ICE PIRATES, THE(1984); MICKI AND MAUDE(1984)
Tom Symonds
VIOLENT STRANGER(1957, Brit.); SAIL A CROOKED SHIP(1961); NOTORIOUS LANDLADY, THE(1962)
Vic Symonds
LONG GOOD FRIDAY, THE(1982, Brit.), art d
George Symonette
ISLAND WOMEN(1958)
Fabienne Symons
ESCAPE FROM THE SEA(1968, Brit.)
Henry Symons
Misc. Silents
GO AND GET IT(1920), d
James Symons
ROCKY II(1979), ed
1984
OXFORD BLUES(1984), ed

Julian Symons
UNDERCOVER AGENT(1935, Brit.), w
Marylin Symons
TWO TICKETS TO BROADWAY(1951)
Red Symons
PURE S(1976, Aus.), m
Redmond Symons
CLINIC, THE(1983, Aus.), md
William Symons
HAPPIEST DAYS OF YOUR LIFE(1950, Brit.)
Tony Sympson
INDISCRETIONS OF EVE(1932, Brit.); SEXTON BLAKE AND THE BEARDED DOCTOR(1935, Brit.); SEXTON BLAKE AND THE MADEMOISELLE(1935, Brit.); RHYTHM IN THE AIR(1936, Brit.); SEXTON BLAKE AND THE HOODED TER-ROR(1938, Brit.); CHALLENGE, THE(1939, Brit.); MUTINY OF THE ELSINORE, THE(1939, Brit.); KEEP IT CLEAN(1956, Brit.); LOCK UP YOUR DAUGHTERS(1969, Brit.); HOUSE OF WHIPCORD(1974, Brit.); PINK PANTHER STRIKES AGAIN, THE(1976, Brit.); JABBERWOCKY(1977, Brit.); SHILLINGBURY BLOWERS, THE(1980, Brit.)
Sylvia Syms
BIRTHDAY PRESENT, THE(1957, Brit.); WOMEN IN A DRESSING GOWN(1957, Brit.); BACHELOR OF HEARTS(1958, Brit.); DESERT ATTACK(1958, Brit.); MOON-RAKER, THE(1958, Brit.); EXPRESSO BONGO(1959, Brit.); FERRY TO HONG KONG(1959, Brit.); TEENAGE BAD GIRL(1959, Brit.); CONSPIRACY OF HEARTS(1960, Brit.); WORLD OF SUZIE WONG, THE(1960, Brit.); FLAME IN THE STREETS(1961, Brit.); VICTIM(1961, Brit.); QUARE FELLOW, THE(1962, Brit.); PUNCH AND JUDY MAN, THE(1963, Brit.); EAST OF SUDAN(1964, Brit.); NO TREE IN THE STREET(1964, Brit.); BIG JOB, THE(1965, Brit.); OPERATION CROSS-BOW(1965, U.S./Ital.); PUSSYCAT ALLEY(1965, Brit.); DANGER ROUTE(1968, Brit.); DESPERADOS, THE(1969); RUN WILD, RUN FREE(1969, Brit.); BORN TO WIN(1971); ASYLUM(1972, Brit.); TAMARIND SEED, THE(1974, Brit.); THERE GOES THE BRIDE(1980, Brit.)
Syn Cat
INCREDIBLE JOURNEY, THE(1963)
Allan Synder
KING OF THE ROARING TWENTIES–THE STORY OF ARNOLD ROTH-STEIN(1961), makeup
Don Synder
INCREDIBLY STRANGE CREATURES WHO STOPPED LIVING AND BECAME CRAZY MIXED-UP ZOMBIES, THE(1965)
Drew Sylnder
DEATH WISH II(1982)
1984
FIRESTARTER(1984)
John Millington Synge
PLAYBOY OF THE WESTERN WORLD, THE(1963, Ireland), w
Derek Synney
CONSTANT HUSBAND, THE(1955, Brit.)
Anna Synodinou
300 SPARTANS, THE(1962)
Mary Synon
Silents
INNOCENT SINNER, THE(1917), w
Herbert Synott
Silents
AMATEUR GENTLEMAN, THE(1920, Brit.)
A. Syomin
WAR AND PEACE(1968, USSR)
Tamara Syomina
RESURRECTION(1963, USSR)
Eddie Syracuse
ANGELS WITH DIRTY FACES(1938)
William Syran
13 RUE MADELEINE(1946)
Netta Syrett
WOMAN REBELS, A(1936), w
Clancy Syrko
BLACK ANGELS, THE(1970), a, ed
Jan Syrovy
DIVINE EMMA, THE(1983, Czech,), p
Tony Syslo
DOUBLE NICKELS(1977), ph, ed; JUNKMAN, THE(1982), ph
Michael Syson
FEAR IN THE NIGHT(1972, Brit.), w; EAGLE'S WING(1979, Brit.), w
A. Sysoyev
Misc. Silents
STEPAN KHALTURIN(1925, USSR)
Vitya Sysoyev
GIRL AND THE BUGLER, THE(1967, USSR)
Albert Szabo
GIRL IN THE KREMLIN, THE(1957); HITLER(1962)
1984
LOVELINES(1984)
Bernard Szabo
1984
CHEECH AND CHONG'S THE CORSICAN BROTHERS(1984)
Erno Szabo
DIALOGUE(1967, Hung.)
Etienne Szabo
ASSOCIATE, THE(1982 Fr./Ger.), ph
Eva Szabo
ANGI VERA(1980, Hung.)
Gabor Szabo
1984
REVOLT OF JOB, THE(1984, Hung./Ger.), ph
Gyula Szabo
DIALOGUE(1967, Hung.)

Istvan Szabo
AGE OF ILLUSIONS(1967, Hung.), d&w; FATHER(1967, Hung.), d, w; CONFIDENCE(1980, Hung.), d&w; MEPHISTO(1981, Ger.), d, w

Laszlo Szabo
WEB OF PASSION(1961, Fr.); DOLL, THE(1962, Fr.); OPHELIA(1964, Fr.); ALPHAVILLE, A STRANGE CASE OF LEMMY CAUTION(1965, Fr.); LE PETIT SOLDAT(1965, Fr.); MADE IN U.S.A.(1966, Fr.); PIERROT LE FOU(1968, Fr./Ital.); WEEKEND(1968, Fr./Ital.); CONFESSION, THE(1970, Fr.); WINTER WIND(1970, Fr./Hung.); ZIG-ZAG(1975, Fr/Ital.), d&w; LAST METRO, THE(1981, Fr.); PASSION(1983, Fr./Switz.)
1984
FULL MOON IN PARIS(1984, Fr.); LOVE ON THE GROUND(1984,Fr.)

Lorinc G. Szabo
ROUND UP, THE(1969, Hung.)

Oscar Szabo
STORM IN A WATER GLASS(1931, Aust.)

Peter Szabo
JUKE BOX RACKET(1960)

Sandor Szabo
ONCE IN A BLUE MOON(1936); MISSION TO MOSCOW(1943); DREAMBOAT(1952); HELL'S ISLAND(1955); TOPAZ(1969, Brit.)

Valerie Szabo
JOY IN THE MORNING(1965)

Danuta Szaflarski
TONIGHT A TOWN DIES(1961, Pol.)

Szoeke Szakall [S. Z. "Cuddles" Sakall]
RENDEZ-VOUS(1932, Ger.); AFFAIRS OF MAUPASSANT(1938, Aust.)

Miklos Szakats
DIALOGUE(1967, Hung.)

Andrzej Szalawski
KNIGHTS OF THE TEUTONIC ORDER, THE(1962, Pol.)

Erika Szanto
CONFIDENCE(1980, Hung.), w

Szabo Szanto
CONFIDENCE(1980, Hung.), w

Szanto and Szecsen
AZURE EXPRESS(1938, Hung.), w

Keith Szarabajka
SIMON(1980); MISSING(1982)
1984
PROTOCOL(1984)

Al Szathmary
ROSEMARY'S BABY(1968)

Eugen Szatmari
TALES OF THE UNCANNY(1932, Ger.), w

Eugen Szatmary
TREMENDOUSLY RICH MAN, A(1932, Ger.), w

Jacek Szczek
IDENTIFICATION MARKS: NONE(1969, Pol.)

Jan Jozef Szczepanski
GUESTS ARE COMING(1965, Pol.), w

Andrzej Szczepkowski
YELLOW SLIPPERS, THE(1965, Pol.)

Marja Morozowiez Szczepokowska
DOCTOR MONICA(1934), w

Joanna Szczerbic
BARRIER(1966, Pol.)

Li Hua Sze
FISTS OF FURY(1973, Chi.)

Yang Sze
ENTER THE DRAGON(1973)

Hans Szekeley
EARLY TO BED(1933, Brit./Ger.), w; DESIRE(1936), w

Hans Szekely
DRAMATIC SCHOOL(1938), w

Istvan Szekely
HIPPOLYT, THE LACKEY(1932, Hung.), d

Istvan [Steve] Szekely
NO SURVIVORS, PLEASE(1963, Ger.), w

Michael Szekely
JOURNEY, THE(1959, U.S./Aust.)

Miklos B. Szekely
FORBIDDEN RELATIONS(1983, Hung.)

Stefan Szekely
GREAT YEARNING, THE(1930, Ger.), d; TREMENDOUSLY RICH MAN, A(1932, Ger.), d

Dr. Wilhelm Szekely
HIS MAJESTY, KING BALLYHOO(1931, Ger.), p

William Szekely
DECAMERON NIGHTS(1953, Brit.), p

Hans Szekley
FAREWELL TO LOVE(1931, Brit.), w

Zita Szeleczky
AZURE EXPRESS(1938, Hung.)

Lazlo Szemere
GOOD SOLDIER SCHWEIK, THE(1963, Ger.)

Mari Szemes
1984
DIARY FOR MY CHILDREN(1984, Hung.)

Andrzej Szenajch
YOUNG GIRLS OF WILKO, THE(1979, Pol./Fr.)

Fino Szenes
HIPPOLYT, THE LACKEY(1932, Hung.)

Jozsef Szentirmai
FATHER(1967, Hung.)

Henri Szeps
FATTY FINN(1980, Aus.); PLUMBER, THE(1980, Aus.)

George Szeptycki
CADDY SHACK(1980), art d

Gyula Szersen
ROUND UP, THE(1969, Hung.)

Janna Szerzerbic
1984
SUCCESS IS THE BEST REVENGE(1984, Brit.)

Jerzy Szeski
KANAL(1961, Pol.), cos

Eugeniusz Szewczyk
YELLOW SLIPPERS, THE(1965, Pol.)

Stefan Szezpanski
LOTNA(1966, Pol.), makeup

Cynthia Szigeti
YOU LIGHT UP MY LIFE(1977)
1984
JOHNNY DANGEROUSLY(1984)

Joseph Szigeti
HOLLYWOOD CANTEEN(1944)

Cynthia Szigetti
I NEVER PROMISED YOU A ROSE GARDEN(1977)

Tibor Szilagyi
ROUND UP, THE(1969, Hung.)

Sandor Szili
RED AND THE WHITE, THE(1969, Hung./USSR)

Miklos Szinetar
FORTRESS, THE(1979, Hung.), d, w

Adam Szirtes
DIALOGUE(1967, Hung.)

Richard E. Szlasa
1984
FIRSTBORN(1984)

Sandor Szlatloay
KIND STEPMOTHER(1936, Hung.), m

Diana Szlosberg
SHARKY'S MACHINE(1982)

Jerzy Szmidt
CONDUCTOR, THE(1981, Pol.)

Krystyna Sznerr
CONTRACT, THE(1982, Pol.)

Carl Szokoil
LAST TEN DAYS, THE(1956, Ger.), p

Carl Szokol
DOG EAT DOG(1963, U.S./Ger./Ital.), p

Carl Szokoll
AS THE SEA RAGES(1960 Ger.), p; SOME LIKE IT COOL(1979, Ger./Aust./Ital./Fr.), p

Bernard Szold
UNION STATION(1950); LEMON DROP KID, THE(1951); M(1951); QUEEN FOR A DAY(1951); SECRET OF CONVICT LAKE, THE(1951)

Bernadine Szold-Fritz
REDS(1981)

Andy Szolosi
DOMINO PRINCIPLE, THE(1977), set d

Szomahazy
OFFICE GIRL, THE(1932, Brit.), w

The Szonys
SO THIS IS LOVE(1953)

Julius Von Szoreghy
Misc. Silents
MODERN DU BARRY, A(1928, Ger.), d

Istvan Sztankai
DIALOGUE(1967, Hung.)

Laszlo Sztano
FATHER(1967, Hung.)

Shih Szu
DRACULA AND THE SEVEN GOLDEN VAMPIRES(1978, Brit./Chi.)

Steve Szucs
EASY MONEY(1983)

German Szulem
TERRACE, THE(1964, Arg.), p

Piotr Szulkin
GOLEM(1980, Pol.), d, w; WAR OF THE WORLDS–NEXT CENTURY, THE(1981, Pol.), d&w

Boris Szulzinger
MAMMA DRACULA(1980, Bel./Fr.), p&d, w
Misc. Talkies
SHAME OF THE JUNGLE(1980, Fr./Bel.), d

Denes Szunyogh
WINTER WIND(1970, Fr./Hung.)

Jeannot Szwarc
BUG(1975), d; JAWS II(1978), d; SOMEWHERE IN TIME(1980), d; ENIGMA(1983), d
1984
SUPERGIRL(1984), d
Misc. Talkies
EXTREME CLOSE-UP(1973), d

Karol Szymanowski
YOUNG GIRLS OF WILKO, THE(1979, Pol./Fr.), m

Zbigniew Szymborski
PASSENGER, THE(1970, Pol.)

Stanislaw Szymczyk
JOAN OF THE ANGELS(1962, Pol.)

Gloria Szymkovicz
DON'T GO IN THE HOUSE(1980)

T

Mr. T
PENITENTIARY II(1982); ROCKY III(1982); YOUNG DOCTORS IN LOVE(1982); D.C. CAB(1983)

T. J. and the Fourmations
COOL ONES THE(1967)

The T-Bones
NIGHTMARE IN WAX(1969)

T'ugaita
Misc. Silents
MOANA(1926)

Suzanne Ta Fel
SECURITY RISK(1954)

Ta-Tanisha
HALLS OF ANGER(1970); STING, THE(1973)

Ta'avale
Misc. Silents
MOANA(1926)

Alice Taaffe
Silents
NOT MY SISTER(1916); OLD WIVES FOR NEW(1918)

Alice Taaffe [Terry]
Silents
CORNER IN COLLEENS, A(1916)

Taao
NIKKI, WILD DOG OF THE NORTH(1961, U.S./Can.)

Dan Taba
GHOST OF THE CHINA SEA(1958)

Bernard Tabakin
WORLD FOR RANSOM(1954), p; FRESH FROM PARIS(1955), p; PARIS FOLLIES OF 1956(1955), p

Ralph Tabakin
DINER(1982)

Tari Tabakin
DEATHMASTER, THE(1972)

Oleg Tabakov
CLEAR SKIES(1963, USSR); WAR AND PEACE(1968, USSR); MOSCOW DOES NOT BELIEVE IN TEARS(1980, USSR)

Juan Tabar
FEMALE BUTCHER, THE(1972, Ital./Span.), w

Pierre Tabard
TRAPEZE(1956)

Guy Tabary
LONGEST DAY, THE(1962), ph; STOWAWAY IN THE SKY(1962, Fr.), ph; SKY ABOVE HEAVEN(1964, Fr./Ital.), ph; DARLING LILI(1970), ph

Khosrow Tabatabai
CARAVANS(1978, U.S./Iranian)

Mike Tabb
ROCKET ATTACK, U.S.A.(1961), ph

Diane Tabban
BLOB, THE(1958)

Christine Tabbott
HELL ON WHEELS(1967)

Ernst Tabe
TWO IN A SLEEPING BAG(1964, Ger.)

Richard Taber
LUCKY IN LOVE(1929); TWO FISTED(1935), w; KISS OF DEATH(1947); SLEEPING CITY, THE(1950); UNDER THE GUN(1951)
Silents
KICK IN(1917); MISS CRUSOE(1919); IS ZAT SO?(1927), w

Maj. W.H.M. Taberer
LION, THE(1962, Brit.), tech adv

Julio Perez Tabernero
MURIETA(1965, Span.); SON OF A GUNFIGHTER(1966, U.S./Span.); UP THE MACGREGORS(1967, Ital./Span.); SEVEN GUNS FOR THE MACGREGORS(1968, Ital./Span.)

Pablo Tabernero
AVENGERS, THE(1950), ph

Andre Tabet
FOLIES BERGERE(1958, Fr.), w; GIVE ME MY CHANCE(1958, Fr.), w; WOMAN OF SIN(1961, Fr.), w; LOVES OF SALAMMBO, THE(1962, Fr./Ital.), w; NIGHT THEY KILLED RASPUTIN, THE(1962, Fr./Ital.), w; RAVISHING IDIOT, A(1966, Ital./Fr.), w; SUCKER, THE(1966, Fr./Ital.), w; JOURNEY BENEATH THE DESERT(1967, Fr./Ital.), w; DON'T LOOK NOW(1969, Brit./Fr.), w; TIME OF THE WOLVES(1970, Fr.), w

Georges Tabet
AMAZING MONSIEUR FABRE, THE(1952, Fr.); GREEN GLOVE, THE(1952); FOLIES BERGERE(1958, Fr.), w; GIVE ME MY CHANCE(1958, Fr.), w; WOMAN OF SIN(1961, Fr.), w; PRICE OF FLESH, THE(1962, Fr.), w; RAVISHING IDIOT, A(1966, Ital./Fr.), w; SUCKER, THE(1966, Fr./Ital.), w; OLDEST PROFESSION, THE(1968, Fr./Ital./Ger.), w; DON'T LOOK NOW(1969, Brit./Fr.), w

Sylvio Tabet
BEASTMASTER, THE(1982), p; EVILSPEAK(1982), p

Tuvia Tabi
1984
SAHARA(1984)

Presco Tabios
CHAN IS MISSING(1982)

Dempsey Tabler
Silents
SPAWN OF THE DESERT(1923)
Misc. Silents
GAMBLE IN SOULS, A(1916); JUNGLE TRAIL OF THE SON OF TARZAN(1923)

P. D. Tabler
Silents
CAPTIVE GOD, THE(1916); PATRIOT, THE(1916)

P. Dempsey Tabler
Misc. Silents
GAMESTERS, THE(1920)

P.D. Tabler
Misc. Silents
PHANTOM, THE(1916)

Vic Tablian
RAIDERS OF THE LOST ARK(1981); SPHINX(1981); TRENCHCOAT(1983)

Carlos Enrique Taboada
ORLAK, THE HELL OF FRANKENSTEIN(1960, Mex.), w; WITCH'S MIRROR, THE(1960, Mex.), w

David Tabor
NESTING, THE(1981)

Eron Tabor
I SPIT ON YOUR GRAVE(1983)

Gunther Tabor
GREAT BRITISH TRAIN ROBBERY, THE(1967, Ger.)

Joan Tabor
TEENAGE MILLIONAIRE(1961)

Robert Tabor
Misc. Silents
HEART OF THE SUNSET(1918)

George Tabori
CRISIS(1950), d&w; I CONFESS(1953), w; THUNDER IN THE EAST(1953), w; CHANCE MEETING(1954, Brit.), w; JOURNEY, THE(1959, U.S./Aust.), w; NO EXIT(1962, U.S./Arg.), w; SECRET CEREMONY(1968, Brit.), w; LEO THE LAST(1970, Brit.), w; PARADES(1972), w

Kristoffer Tabori
JOHN AND MARY(1969); SIDELONG GLANCES OF A PIGEON KICKER, THE(1970); DIRTY HARRY(1971); MAKING IT(1971); JOURNEY THROUGH ROSEBUD(1972); GIRLFRIENDS(1978)

Lena Tabori
WEDDING PARTY, THE(1969)

Paul Tabori
VALLEY OF EAGLES(1952, Brit.), d&w; FOUR SIDED TRIANGLE(1953, Brit.), w; SPACEWAYS(1953, Brit.), w; WOMAN IN HIDING(1953, Brit.), w; DIPLOMATIC PASSPORT(1954, Brit.), w; PAID TO KILL(1954, Brit.), w; STAR OF MY NIGHT(1954, Brit.), w; TALE OF THREE WOMEN, A(1954, Brit.), w; THREE CORNERED FATE(1954, Brit.), w; COUNT OF TWELVE(1955, Brit.), w; FINAL COLUMN, THE(1955, Brit.), w; RACE FOR LIFE, A(1955, Brit.), w; ALIAS JOHN PRESTON(1956), w; STRANGE CASE OF DR. MANNING, THE(1958, Brit.), w; STRIP TEASE MURDER(1961, Brit.), w; DOOMSDAY AT ELEVEN(1963 Brit.), w; MALPAS MYSTERY, THE(1967, Brit.), w

Natalya Taborko
LITTLE HUMPBACKED HORSE, THE(1962, USSR)

Andre Tabot
DAUGHTERS OF DESTINY(1954, Fr./Ital.), w

Beatrice Tabourin
1984
L'ARGENT(1984, Fr./Switz.)

Mons. Tabourno
MOULIN ROUGE(1952)

Julio Tabuyo
CEREMONY, THE(1963, U.S./Span.)

Andrea Taccari
LA TRAVIATA(1968, Ital.), art d

Jean-Charles Tacchella
LAW IS THE LAW, THE(1959, Fr.), w; TIME BOMB(1961, Fr./Ital.), w; CRIME DOES NOT PAY(1962, Fr.), w; COUSIN, COUSINE(1976, Fr.), d, w; BLUE COUNTRY, THE(1977, Fr.), p,d&w

John Tacchi
FRONT LINE KIDS(1942, Brit.)

Kamiko Tachibana
THREE STRIPES IN THE SUN(1955)

Kimiko Tachibana
SANSHO THE BAILIFF(1969, Jap.)

Hiroshi Tachikawa
YOJIMBO(1961, Jap.); SANJURO(1962, Jap.); OUTPOST OF HELL(1966, Jap.)

Yoichi Tachikawa
THRONE OF BLOOD(1961, Jap.); I LIVE IN FEAR(1967, Jap.)

Bill Tackett
CASEY'S SHADOW(1978)

Steve Tackett
GUNS OF A STRANGER(1973)

Wesley Marie Tackitt
WILD AND THE INNOCENT, THE(1959)

Redge Tackley
SERPICO(1973), makeup

Reginald Tackley
NIGHT OF DARK SHADOWS(1971), makeup

Stanley Tackney
HOUSE ON 92ND STREET, THE(1945)

Gary Tacon
1984
ALPHABET CITY(1984); MUPPETS TAKE MANHATTAN, THE(1984)

Colette Taconnat
LIFE LOVE DEATH(1969, Fr./Ital.)

Sampa Tacorda
ONE MAN JURY(1978)

Kenzo Tadake
GODZILLA VS. THE THING(1964, Jap.)

Georgia Tadda
MEDIUM COOL(1969)

Ines Taddio
DOG EAT DOG(1963, U.S./Ger./Ital.)

Vladimir Tadej
DESPERADO TRAIL, THE(1965, Ger./Yugo.), art d; FRONTIER HELLCAT(1966, Fr./Ital./Ger./Yugo.), art d; LAST OF THE RENEGADES(1966, Fr./Ital./Ger./Yugo.), art d; FLAMING FRONTIER(1968, Ger./Yugo.), art d; KAYA, I'LL KILL YOU(1969, Yugo./Fr.), art d & cos

Vladmir Tadej
EAGLE IN A CAGE(1971, U.S./Yugo.), art d

Zenebech Tadesse
SHAFT IN AFRICA(1973)

Ljuba Tadic
STEPPE, THE(1963, Fr./Ital.); FRAGRANCE OF WILD FLOWERS, THE(1979, Yugo.)

Giovanni Tadini
HELL RAIDERS OF THE DEEP(1954, Ital.)

Monika Tadsen-Erfurth
GREAT BRITISH TRAIN ROBBERY, THE(1967, Ger.), ed

John Taea
HURRICANE(1979)

Ralph Taeger
X-15(1961); CARPETBAGGERS, THE(1964); HOUSE IS NOT A HOME, A(1964); STAGE TO THUNDER ROCK(1964); DELTA FACTOR, THE(1970)

Uta Taeger
GOODBYE AGAIN(1961); LIVE FOR LIFE(1967, Fr./Ital.)

G. Taffarel
SEVEN REVENGES, THE(1967, Ital.), w

Giuseppe Taffarel
GOLIATH AND THE BARBARIANS(1960, Ital.), w

Bess Taffel
TRUE TO LIFE(1943), w; BADMAN'S TERRITORY(1946), w; LIKELY STORY, A(1947), w; ELOPEMENT(1951), w

Al Taffet
PAPER LION(1968), ph

Toni Taffin
FIRE WITHIN, THE(1964, Fr./Ital.); IS PARIS BURNING?(1966, U.S./Fr.)

Taffy
TAFFY AND THE JUNGLE HUNTER(1965)

Jean Tafler
DEADLY SPAWN, THE(1983)

Jennifer Tafler
GIRL GETTERS, THE(1966, Brit.)

Jonathan Tafler
YENTL(1983)

Sidney Tafler
GALLOPING MAJOR, THE(1951, Brit.); SQUARE RING, THE(1955, Brit.); GUILTY?(1956, Brit.); SINK THE BISMARCK!(1960, Brit.); SEVENTH DAWN, THE(1964); SANDWICH MAN, THE(1966, Brit.); BERSERK(1967); SPY WHO LOVED ME, THE(1977, Brit.)

Sydney Tafler
YOUNG MR. PITT, THE(1942, Brit.); DULCIMER STREET(1948, Brit.); MONKEY'S PAW, THE(1948, Brit.); UNEASY TERMS(1948, Brit.); IT ALWAYS RAINS ON SUNDAY(1949, Brit.); PASSPORT TO PIMLICO(1949, Brit.); DANCE HALL(1950, Brit.); NO ROOM AT THE INN(1950, Brit.); ASSASSIN FOR HIRE(1951, Brit.); CHELSEA STORY(1951, Brit.); HOTEL SAHARA(1951, Brit.); LAVENDER HILL MOB, THE(1951, Brit.); LITTLE BALLERINA, THE(1951, Brit.); MYSTERY JUNCTION(1951, Brit.); SCARLET THREAD(1951, Brit.); BLIND MAN'S BLUFF(1952, Brit.); ONCE A SINNER(1952, Brit.); SECRET PEOPLE(1952, Brit.); WIDE BOY(1952, Brit.); ASSASSIN, THE(1953, Brit.); FLOATING DUTCHMAN, THE(1953, Brit.); JOHNNY ON THE RUN(1953, Brit.); OPERATION DIPLOMAT(1953, Brit.); THERE WAS A YOUNG LADY(1953, Brit.); TIME GENTLEMEN PLEASE!(1953, Brit.); CROWDED DAY, THE(1954, Brit.); SAINT'S GIRL FRIDAY, THE(1954, Brit.); COCKLESHELL HEROES, THE(1955); GLASS TOMB, THE(1955, Brit.); SEA SHALL NOT HAVE THEM, THE(1955, Brit.); WOMAN FOR JOE, THE(1955, Brit.); FIRE MAIDENS FROM OUTER SPACE(1956, Brit.); KID FOR TWO FARTHINGS, A(1956, Brit.); WAY OUT, THE(1956, Brit.); BOOBY TRAP(1957, Brit.); COUNTERFEIT PLAN, THE(1957, Brit.); PICKUP ALLEY(1957, Brit.); REACH FOR THE SKY(1957, Brit.); SURGEON'S KNIFE, THE(1957, Brit.); THIRD KEY, THE(1957, Brit.); BANK RAIDERS, THE(1958, Brit.); CARVE HER NAME WITH PRIDE(1958, Brit.); CROWNING TOUCH, THE(1959, Brit.); FOLLOW A STAR(1959, Brit.); TOO MANY CROOKS(1959, Brit.); BOTTOMS UP(1960, Brit.); LET'S GET MARRIED(1960, Brit.); LIGHT UP THE SKY(1960, Brit.); MAKE MINE MINK(1960, Brit.); BEWARE OF CHILDREN(1961, Brit.); CARRY ON REGARDLESS(1961, Brit.); FIVE GOLDEN HOURS(1961, Brit.); WEEKEND WITH LULU, A(1961, Brit.); RUNAWAY RAILWAY(1965, Brit.); ALFIE(1966, Brit.); PROMISE HER ANYTHING(1966, Brit.); BIRTHDAY PARTY, THE(1968, Brit.); ADVENTURERS, THE(1970)

Arnold Tafolla
SCARFACE(1983)

Al Tafoya
FADE TO BLACK(1980)

Ayesha Taft
WILD PARTY, THE(1975)

Billy Taft
GOOD NEWS(1930); FOOTLIGHT PARADE(1933); THIS SIDE OF HEAVEN(1934)

Gene Taft
HONEYSUCKLE ROSE(1980), p
1984
BLAME IT ON THE NIGHT(1984), p&d, w

Jerry Taft
IT'S ALIVE(1974); DUCHESS AND THE DIRTWATER FOX, THE(1976); STAR CHAMBER, THE(1983)

Joseph Taft
ONLY WAY HOME, THE(1972)

Lucille Taft
Silents
DRIFTER, THE(1916); IDOL OF THE STAGE, THE(1916)
Misc. Silents
QUALITY OF FAITH, THE(1916); QUEEN X(1917)

Mary Gordon Taft
ONLY WAY HOME, THE(1972)

Ron Taft
NIGHT OF THE WITCHES(1970)

Ronald Taft
BLOOD AND LACE(1971)

Sara Taft
BRIGHT VICTORY(1951); YOU NEVER CAN TELL(1951); KETTLES ON OLD MACDONALD'S FARM, THE(1957); VERTIGO(1958); STORY OF RUTH, THE(1960); PARRISH(1961); TOWER OF LONDON(1962); DONOVAN'S REEF(1963); DEATH OF A GUNFIGHTER(1969); REIVERS, THE(1969); MECHANIC, THE(1972)

Amid Taftazani
DRUMS(1938, Brit.); FOUR FEATHERS, THE(1939, Brit.)

Robert Tafur
FOR WHOM THE BELL TOLLS(1943); GOING MY WAY(1944); ONCE UPON A TIME(1944); GILDA(1946); WE WERE STRANGERS(1949); CRISIS(1950); HAREM GIRL(1952); SECRET OF THE INCAS(1954); GREEN FIRE(1955); THREE OUTLAWS, THE(1956); VIVA KNIEVEL!(1977)

Bernardo Tafuri
UNFAITHFULS, THE(1960, Ital.)

Sara Tafuri
CITY OF WOMEN(1980, Ital./Fr.); THREE BROTHERS(1982, Ital.)

Hidenori Taga
ALMOST TRANSPARENT BLUE(1980, Jap.), p; ALL RIGHT, MY FRIEND(1983, Japan), p

Kaori Tagasugi
ONIMASA(1983, Jap.)

Yoshita Tagawa
HOUSE ON 92ND STREET, THE(1945)

Brian Tagg
1984
BLOODBATH AT THE HOUSE OF DEATH(1984, Brit.), ed; CRIMES OF PASSION(1984), ed

Ben L. Taggart
Silents
SENTIMENTAL LADY, THE(1915)
Misc. Silents
HELLO BILL!(1915); SHE(1917)

Ben Taggart
KICK IN(1931); MONKEY BUSINESS(1931); SILENCE(1931); SMART MONEY(1931); HOLD'EM JAIL(1932); MILLION DOLLAR LEGS(1932); STRANGERS IN LOVE(1932); TAXI!(1932); MAYOR OF HELL, THE(1933); AMONG THE MISSING(1934); NOTORIOUS SOPHIE LANG, THE(1934); READY FOR LOVE(1934); SHOOT THE WORKS(1934); THIN MAN, THE(1934); MEN WITHOUT NAMES(1935); MURDER MAN(1935); STOLEN HARMONY(1935); UNKNOWN WOMAN(1935); WHOLE TOWN'S TALKING, THE(1935); I HAD TO HAPPEN(1936); SAN FRANCISCO(1936); MAN WHO CRIED WOLF, THE(1937); OH DOCTOR(1937); THIS IS MY AFFAIR(1937); KING OF THE NEWSBOYS(1938); LITTLE TOUGH GUY(1938); OVERLAND EXPRESS, THE(1938); I STOLE A MILLION(1939); TELL NO TALES(1939); BEFORE I HANG(1940); DURANGO KID, THE(1940); NOBODY'S CHILDREN(1940); FACE BEHIND THE MASK, THE(1941); HARD GUY(1941); I'LL SELL MY LIFE(1941); LONE WOLF TAKES A CHANCE, THE(1941); MAN MADE MONSTER(1941); MEDICO OF PAINTED SPRINGS, THE(1941); PENNY SERENADE(1941); THREE GIRLS ABOUT TOWN(1941); TWO IN A TAXI(1941); WILDCAT OF TUCSON(1941); ALIAS BOSTON BLACKIE(1942); ESCAPE FROM CRIME(1942); MIRACLE KID(1942); POLICE BULLETS(1942); REMARKABLE ANDREW, THE(1942); UNDERGROUND AGENT(1942); CHATTERBOX(1943); NO TIME FOR LOVE(1943); SECRETS OF THE UNDERGROUND(1943); JAM SESSION(1944); LOUISIANA HAYRIDE(1944); MAN FROM FRISCO(1944); MR. WINKLE GOES TO WAR(1944); ONE MYSTERIOUS NIGHT(1944)
Silents
OH, BOY!(1919)

Errol Taggart
SINNER TAKE ALL(1936), d; WOMEN ARE TROUBLE(1936), d; WOMEN MEN MARRY, THE(1937), d; STRANGE FACES(1938), d
Silents
AFTER BUSINESS HOURS(1925), ed; BLACK BIRD, THE(1926), ed; ROAD TO MANDALAY, THE(1926), ed; UNKNOWN, THE(1927), ed

George Taggart
NO GREATER SIN(1941)

Hal Taggart
UP IN CENTRAL PARK(1948); PUSHOVER(1954); FIRST TRAVELING SALESLADY, THE(1956); DESK SET(1957); GARMENT JUNGLE, THE(1957); GOOD NEIGHBOR SAM(1964)

James Taggart
FABULOUS DORSEYS, THE(1947); LAST FRONTIER UPRISING(1947); HOMECOMING(1948)

Rita Taggart
STRAIGHT TIME(1978); CHINA SYNDROME, THE(1979); 1941(1979); USED CARS(1980)
1984
TORCHLIGHT(1984)

Sharon Taggart
LAST PICTURE SHOW, THE(1971); HARRAD EXPERIMENT, THE(1973)

Tom Taggart
GOG(1954), w

Beverly Tagge
TOY, THE(1982)

Ben Taggert
FAITHLESS(1932); BIG SHAKEDOWN, THE(1934); SON OF ROARING DAN(1940)

Brian Taggert
VISITING HOURS(1982, Can.), w; OF UNKNOWN ORIGIN(1983, Can.), w

Errol Taggert
LONGEST NIGHT, THE(1936), d; SONG OF THE CITY(1937), d

Hal Taggert
HOLLYWOOD AND VINE(1945); MONSTER THAT CHALLENGED THE WORLD, THE(1957); OH, MEN! OH, WOMEN!(1957); CINCINNATI KID, THE(1965)

James Taggert
HELLDORADO(1946)

Rita Taggert
DIE LAUGHING(1980)
Andrea Tagliabue
SODOM AND GOMORRAH(1962, U.S./Fr./Ital.)
Carlo Tagliabue
NEOPOLITAN CAROUSEL(1961, Ital.)
P. Tagliaferri
KNIVES OF THE AVENGER(1967, Ital.), p
Patrick E. Tagliaferro
1984
BREAKIN' 2: ELECTRIC BOOGALOO(1984), art d
Renato Tagliani
THREE FACES OF A WOMAN(1965, Ital.); LOVE AND MARRIAGE(1966, Ital.)
Adriano Tagliavia
CAGLIOSTRO(1975, Ital.), ed
Ferruccio Tagliavini
ANYTHING FOR A SONG(1947, Ital.)
Ferrucio Tagliavini
BARBER OF SEVILLE, THE(1947, Ital.); LADY IS FICKLE, THE(1948, Ital.)
E. Benazzi Taglietti
JULIET OF THE SPIRITS(1965, Fr./Ital./W.Ger.), set d
Eddie Tagoe
WHO IS KILLING THE GREAT CHEFS OF EUROPE?(1978, US/Ger.); DOGS OF WAR, THE(1980, Brit.); RAIDERS OF THE LOST ARK(1981); PINK FLOYD–THE WALL(1982, Brit.)
1984
TOP SECRET!(1984)
Rabindranath Tagore
GODDESS, THE(1962, India), w; TWO DAUGHTERS(1963, India), w
1984
HOME AND THE WORLD, THE(1984, India), d&w
Sharmila Tagore
WORLD OF APU, THE(1960, India); GODDESS, THE(1962, India)
Roy Taguchi
WALK, DON'T RUN(1966)
Stephanie Tague
1984
LAUGHTER HOUSE(1984, Brit.)
Sami Tahasonee
CARAVANS(1978, U.S./Iranian)
Sami Tahasuni
MEETINGS WITH REMARKABLE MEN(1979, Brit.)
Jason Tahbo
WINDWALKER(1980)
Rama Tahe
TIMBUCTOO(1933, Brit.)
Moana Tahi
DR. GOLDFOOT AND THE GIRL BOMBS(1966, Ital.)
Moha Tahi
WILD, WILD PLANET, THE(1967, Ital.)
Daleep Tahil
GANDHI(1982)
Mahmed Tahir
CALCUTTA(1947)
Ursula Tahiri
1984
WOMAN IN FLAMES, A(1984, Ger.)
Katharina Tahlback
TIN DRUM, THE(1979, Ger./Fr./Yugo./Pol.)
Friedrich Tahler
PHONY AMERICAN, THE(1964, Ger.), art d
Ellen Tai
LIEUTENANT DARING, RN(1935, Brit.)
Grace Tai
LIEUTENANT DARING, RN(1935, Brit.)
Maria Tai
SO FINE(1981)
Lucien Tai Ten Quee
COUNTRYMAN(1982, Jamaica)
Kiwako Taichi
KUROENKO(1968, Jap); SCANDALOUS ADVENTURES OF BURAIKAN, THE(1970, Jap.)
Alex Taifer
IN SEARCH OF ANNA(1978, Aus.)
Jackson Tail
MAN CALLED HORSE, A(1970)
Fern Tailer
HAIR(1979)
Germaine Tailleferre
TIME OUT FOR LOVE(1963, Ital./Fr.), m
Gus Taillon
THIS LAND IS MINE(1943); TOP O' THE MORNING(1949); WAR OF THE WORLDS, THE(1953)
The Tailor Maids
COWBOY CANTEEN(1944); DOWN MISSOURI WAY(1946)
Hal Taines
1984
LOVELINES(1984), p
Lucien Tainguy
Silents
ALL MAN(1916), ph; MAN WHO FORGOT, THE(1917), ph; LEAP TO FAME(1918), ph; DAMSEL IN DISTRESS, A(1919), ph; LOVE IN A HURRY(1919), ph; IN WALKED MARY(1920), ph; NORTH WIND'S MALICE, THE(1920), ph; DIANE OF STAR HOLLOW(1921), ph
Andree Tainsy
END OF DESIRE(1962 Fr./Ital.); DIARY OF A CHAMBERMAID(1964, Fr./Ital.); FANTOMAS(1966, Fr./Ital.); Z(1969, Fr./Algeria); CLOCKMAKER, THE(1976, Fr.)

Rangapo A Taipoo
LAST OF THE PAGANS(1936)
Eddie Tair
ODE TO BILLY JOE(1976)
Ichiji Taira
MOTHRA(1962, Jap.), ed
Kanjiro Taira
ILLUSION OF BLOOD(1966, Jap.)
Kazuji Taira
BATTLE IN OUTER SPACE(1960), ed
Alexander Tairov
Misc. Silents
DEAD MAN, THE(1914, USSR), d
Don Tait
HELL'S ANGELS '69(1969), w; CHROME AND HOT LEATHER(1971), w; ONE MORE TRAIN TO ROB(1971), w; SNOWBALL EXPRESS(1972), w; CASTAWAY COWBOY, THE(1974), w; APPLE DUMPLING GANG, THE(1975), w; SHAGGY D.A., THE(1976), w; TREASURE OF MATECUMBE(1976), w; APPLE DUMPLING GANG RIDES AGAIN, THE(1979), w; NORTH AVENUE IRREGULARS, THE(1979), w; UNIDENTIFIED FLYING ODDBALL, THE(1979, Brit.), w; HERBIE GOES BANANAS(1980), w
Donald Tait
INCREDIBLE MR. LIMPET, THE(1964), ed; GIT!(1965), ed
Peter Tait
1984
WILD HORSES(1984, New Zealand)
Robert Tait
TREE GROWS IN BROOKLYN, A(1945)
Walter Tait
HALLELUJAH(1929)
O. Taito
GATES OF HELL, THE(1983, U.S./Ital.), art d
Taj Mahal
SOUNDER(1972), a, m; SOUNDER, PART 2(1976), a, m; BROTHERS(1977), m; SCOTT JOPLIN(1977)
Yoshibumi Tajima
RODAN(1958, Jap.); GODZILLA'S REVENGE(1969)
Yoshifumi Tajima
MOTHRA(1962, Jap.); DESTROY ALL MONSTERS(1969, Jap.)
Shinichi Tajiri
JOURNEYS FROM BERLIN–1971(1980), ph
Italo Tajo
BARBER OF SEVILLE, THE(1947, Ital.); THIS WINE OF LOVE(1948, Ital.)
Martha Taka
Misc. Silents
MYSTIC FACES(1918)
Miiko Taka
SAYONARA(1957); HELL TO ETERNITY(1960); CRY FOR HAPPY(1961); OPERATION BOTTLENECK(1961); GLOBAL AFFAIR, A(1964); ART OF LOVE, THE(1965); WALK, DON'T RUN(1966); POWER, THE(1968); LOST HORIZON(1973); PAPER TIGER(1975, Brit.); CHALLENGE, THE(1982)
Tetsuo Takaba
TORA-SAN PART 2(1970, Jap.), ph
Kenji Takabayashi
1984
DELIVERY BOYS(1984)
Hizuru Takachiho
TRAITORS(1957, Jap.); YOUTH IN FURY(1961, Jap.)
Maria Takacs
CITY OF FEAR(1965, Brit.)
Tibor Takacs
Misc. Talkies
METAL MESSIAH(1978), d; TOMORROW MAN, THE(1979), d
Akira Takada
PLEASURES OF THE FLESH, THE(1965), ph
Junko Takada
1984
BALLAD OF NARAYAMA, THE(1984, Jap.)
Koji Takada
VIRUS(1980, Jap.), w
Minoru Takada
BATTLE IN OUTER SPACE(1960)
Miwa Takada
MAJIN(1968, Jap.); ZATOICHI CHALLENGED(1970, Jap.)
Shinzo Takada
GEISHA GIRL(1952)
Shizuo Takada
TORA! TORA! TORA!(1970, U.S./Jap.), tech adv
Eiji Takaga
Misc. Silents
METROPOLITAN SYMPHONY(1929, Jap.)
Takagi
TOWN LIKE ALICE, A(1958, Brit.)
Kiyoshi Takagi
MADAME BUTTERFLY(1955 Ital./Jap.)
Masayuki Takagi
HARP OF BURMA(1967, Jap.), p
Nobuo Takagi
SONG FROM MY HEART, THE(1970, Jap.)
Shimpei Takagi
SEVEN SAMURAI, THE(1956, Jap.)
Tenji Takagi
SEA WIFE(1957, Brit.)
T. Takaha
TOPSY-TURVY JOURNEY(1970, Jap.), ph
Shuno Takahara
SEVEN SAMURAI, THE(1956, Jap.)

Takahashi
TOKYO STORY(1972, Jap.), art d

Atsuko Takahashi
SPACE AMOEBA, THE(1970, Jap.); YOG-MONSTER FROM SPACE(1970, Jap.)

Choei Takahashi
LAKE OF DRACULA(1973, Jap.)

Etsushi Takahashi
KILL(1968, Jap.); RED LION(1971, Jap.)

Fumi Takahashi
GAMERA THE INVINCIBLE(1966, Jap.), w; GAMERA VERSUS BARUGON(1966, Jap./U.S.), w; GAMERA VERSUS GAOS(1967, Jap.), w; GAMERA VERSUS GUI-RON(1969, Jap.), w; GAMERA VERSUS MONSTER K(1970, Jap.), w; GAMERA VERSUS ZIGRA(1971, Jap.), w

Genyo Takahashi
FAREWELL, MY BELOVED(1969, Jap.), w

Hideki Takahashi
FRIENDLY KILLER, THE(1970, Jap.)

Itsuo Takahashi
TOKYO STORY(1972, Jap.), prod d

Koichi Takahashi
FALCON FIGHTERS, THE(1970, Jap.), art d; GATEWAY TO GLORY(1970, Jap.), art d

Masay Takahashi
GOKE, BODYSNATCHER FROM HELL(1968, Jap.)

Michio Takahashi
GOLDEN DEMON(1956, Jap.), ph; HIROSHIMA, MON AMOUR(1959, Fr./Jap.), ph; GREAT WALL, THE(1965, Jap.), ph; GAMERA VERSUS BARUGON(1966, Jap./U.S.), ph

Mitsuko Takahashi
FIGHT FOR THE GLORY(1970, Jap.)

Tauenko Takahashi
NAVY WIFE(1956)

Teiji Takahashi
BALLAD OF NARAYAMA(1961, Jap.)

Toyoko Takahashi
OHAYO(1962, Jap.); TOKYO STORY(1972, Jap.)

Yoichiro Takahashi
EYES, THE SEA AND A BALL(1968 Jap.)

Fumi Takahaski
GAMERA VERSUS VIRAS(1968, Jap), w

Isao Takahata
1984
WARRIORS OF THE WIND(1984, Jap.), p

George Takai
HELL TO ETERNITY(1960)

Tan Takaiwa
MESSAGE FROM SPACE(1978, Jap.), p

Bo Takaki
HOTSPRINGS HOLIDAY(1970, Jap.)

Kenji Takaki
LONG AND THE SHORT AND THE TALL, THE(1961, Brit.); HIGH WIND IN JAMAICA, A(1965); LAST GRENADE, THE(1970, Brit.)

Masayuki Takaki
TEMPTRESS AND THE MONK, THE(1963, Jap.), p

Russell Takaki
STAR TREK II: THE WRATH OF KHAN(1982)

Kenji Takako
55 DAYS AT PEKING(1963)

Susumu Takaku
GOKE, BODYSNATCHER FROM HELL(1968, Jap.), w

Ken Takakura
TOO LATE THE HERO(1970)
1984
ANTARCTICA(1984, Jap.)

Tsutomo Takakuwa
GAMERA VERSUS MONSTER K(1970, Jap.)

Hideko Takamine
RICKSHAW MAN, THE(1960, Jap.); HAPPINESS OF US ALONE(1962, Jap.); WISER AGE(1962, Jap.); LONELY LANE(1963, Jap.); MY HOBO(1963, Jap.); WHEN A WOMAN ASCENDS THE STAIRS(1963, Jap.), a, cos; WOMAN'S LIFE, A(1964, Jap.); YEARNING(1964, Jap.); DEVIL'S TEMPLE(1969, Jap.); MOMENT OF TERROR(1969, Jap.); OUR SILENT LOVE(1969, Jap.); SOLDIER'S PRAYER, A(1970, Jap.)

Keishi Takamine
1984
BALLAD OF NARAYAMA, THE(1984, Jap.)

Mieko Takamine
LOVE UNDER THE CRUCIFIX(1965, Jap.); TUNNEL TO THE SUN(1968, Jap.); HINOTORI(1980, Jap.)

Ryoji Takamori
NUTCRACKER FANTASY(1979), ph

Iwao Takamoto
CHARLOTTE'S WEB(1973), d

Hiroshi Takamura
PORTRAIT OF CHIEKO(1968, Jap.), ph

Kurataro Takamura
GANGSTER VIP, THE(1968, Jap.), ph

Noboru Takanashi
MESSAGE FROM SPACE(1978, Jap.), spec eff

Noboru Takano
1984
WARRIORS OF THE WIND(1984, Jap.), anim

Shinji Takano
YOUTH IN FURY(1961, Jap.)

Mitsuko Takara
SODOM AND GOMORRAH(1962, U.S./Fr./Ital.)

Akira Takarada
HALF HUMAN(1955, Jap.); GODZILLA, RING OF THE MONSTERS(1956, Jap.); DANGEROUS KISS, THE(1961, Jap.); I BOMBED PEARL HARBOR(1961, Jap.); NIGHT IN HONG KONG, A(1961, Jap.); DIFFERENT SONS(1962, Jap.); EARLY AUTUMN(1962, Jap.); LAST WAR, THE(1962, Jap.); STAR OF HONG KONG(1962,

Jap.); WISER AGE(1962, Jap.); CHUSHINGURA(1963, Jap.); HONOLULU-TOKYO-HONG KONG(1963, Hong Kong/Jap.); LONELY LANE(1963, Jap.); WALL-EYED NIPPON(1963, Jap.); GODZILLA VS. THE THING(1964, Jap.); WOMAN'S LIFE, A(1964, Jap.); WHITE ROSE OF HONG KONG(1965, Jap.); GODZILLA VERSUS THE SEA MONSTER(1966, Jap.); DAPHNE, THE(1967); LET'S GO, YOUNG GUY!(1967, Jap.); KING KONG ESCAPES(1968, Jap.); LATITUDE ZERO(1969, U.S./Jap.); MONSTER ZERO(1970, Jap.)

Takarazuka Kabuki Ballet of Tokyo
MADAME BUTTERFLY(1955 Ital./Jap.)

Takase
WANDERING JEW, THE(1935, Brit.)

Hyoshi Takase
CHU CHIN CHOW(1934, Brit.)

Kenji Takase
STRANGLEHOLD(1931, Brit.); MISSING REMBRANDT, THE(1932, Brit.); INSIDE THE ROOM(1935, Brit.); WIFE OF GENERAL LING, THE(1938, Brit.)

Kiyoshi Takase
HIGH TREASON(1929, Brit.)

Yuri Takase
ALMOST TRANSPARENT BLUE(1980, Jap.)

Takashi
METAMORPHOSES(1978), p, d&w

Minoru Takashima
WAR OF THE MONSTERS(1972, Jap.)

Tadao Takashima
ETERNITY OF LOVE(1961, Jap.); KING KONG VERSUS GODZILLA(1963, Jap.); FRANKENSTEIN CONQUERS THE WORLD(1964, Jap./US); ATRAGON(1965, Jap.); SON OF GODZILLA(1967, Jap.)

Kaku Takashina
LAKE OF DRACULA(1973, Jap.)

May Takasugi
JAPANESE WAR BRIDE(1952); HOUSE OF BAMBOO(1955)

Gary Takata
"RENT-A-GIRL"(1965)

Koje Takata
ONIMASA(1983, Jap.), w

Toru Takatsuka
GAMERA VERSUS VIRAS(1968, Jap)

Yukiko Takayama
MONSTERS FROM THE UNKNOWN PLANET(1975, Jap.), w

S. Takayshvili
STEPCHILDREN(1962, USSR)

Toyoko Takechi
MANSTER, THE(1962, Jap.)

Izumo Takeda
CHUSHINGURA(1963, Jap.), w

Shichizo Takeda
TEAHOUSE OF THE AUGUST MOON, THE(1956); ONE-EYED JACKS(1961)

Ume Takeda
LATITUDE ZERO(1969, U.S./Jap.), ed

Yoshio Takee
GOLDEN DEMON(1956, Jap.)

George Takei
ICE PALACE(1960); MORITURI(1965); RED LINE 7000(1965); AMERICAN DREAM, AN(1966); WALK, DON'T RUN(1966); GREEN BERETS, THE(1968); WHICH WAY TO THE FRONT?(1970); STAR TREK: THE MOTION PICTURE(1979); STAR TREK II: THE WRATH OF KHAN(1982)
1984
STAR TREK III: THE SEARCH FOR SPOCK(1984)

Toru Takemitis
GLOWING AUTUMN(1981, Jap.), m

Tohru Takemitsu
ALONE ON THE PACIFIC(1964, Jap.), m

Toru Takemitsu
YOUTH IN FURY(1961, Jap.), m; HAHAKIRI(1963, Jap.), m; LOVE AT TWEN-TY(1963, Fr./Ital./Jap./Pol./Ger.), m; PRESSURE OF GUILT(1964, Jap.), m; TWIN SISTERS OF KYOTO(1964, Jap.), m; WOMAN IN THE DUNES(1964, Jap.), m; KWAIDAN(1965, Jap.), m; ILLUSION OF BLOOD(1966, Jap.), m; FACE OF ANOTH-ER, THE(1967, Jap.), m; REBELLION(1967, Jap.), m; SHE AND HE(1967, Jap.), m; ONCE A RAINY DAY(1968, Jap.), m; TWO IN THE SHADOW(1968, Jap.), m; DODE-SKA-DEN(1970, Jap.), m; DOUBLE SUICIDE(1970, Jap.), w, m; SUMMER SOL-DIERS(1972, Jap.), m; BANISHED(1978, Jap.), m

Hiroshi Takemura
THROUGH DAYS AND MONTHS(1969 Jap.), ph; SONG FROM MY HEART, THE(1970, Jap.), ph

Marvin Takes Horse
WINDWALKER(1980)

Takeshi
MERRY CHRISTMAS MR. LAWRENCE(1983, Jap./Brit.)

Don Keigo Takeuchi
TOKYO AFTER DARK(1959)

Kyoko Takeuchi
MY GEISHA(1962)

Ryo Takeuchi
HAHAKIRI(1963, Jap.)

Tack Takeuchi
JOURNEY TO SHILOH(1968), cos

Muga Takewaki
SONG FROM MY HEART, THE(1970, Jap.)

Michio Takeyama
HARP OF BURMA(1967, Jap.), w

Dakhin Mohan Takhur
MUSIC ROOM, THE(1963, India), m

Eiko Taki
FLIGHT FROM ASHIYA(1964, U.S./Jap.)

Yumi Takigawa
VIRUS(1980, Jap.)

Yasuhiko Takiguchi
REBELLION(1967, Jap.), w
H. Takima
Silents
DAWN OF THE EAST(1921)
K. Takimura
ANATAHAN(1953, Jap.), p
Kazuo Takimura
SAMURAI(PART III)** (1967, Jap.), p, p; SAMURAI(1955, Jap.), p
Yusuke Takita
WAYSIDE PEBBLE, THE(1962, Jap.); DOUBLE SUICIDE(1970, Jap.); TIDAL WA-VE(1975, U.S./Jap.)
Eisuke Takizawa
TEMPTRESS AND THE MONK, THE(1963, Jap.), d
Osamu Takizawa
FIRES ON THE PLAIN(1962, Jap.); LOVE UNDER THE CRUCIFIX(1965, Jap.); TUNNEL TO THE SUN(1968, Jap.); ZATOICHI MEETS YOJIMBO(1970, Jap.)
Elsa Maria Tako
SANTO Y BLUE DEMON CONTRA LOS MONSTRUOS(1968, Mex.)
Jim Taksas
PRIME CUT(1972)
Arthur Taksen
SALT TO THE DEVIL(1949, Brit.), set d; DOCTOR IN LOVE(1960, Brit.), set d; DOUBLE BUNK(1961, Brit.), set d; LEAGUE OF GENTLEMEN, THE(1961, Brit.), set d; NO LOVE FOR JOHNNIE(1961, Brit.), set d; SINGER NOT THE SONG, THE(1961, Brit.), set d; TIARA TAHITI(1962, Brit.), set d; DOCTOR IN DISTRESS(1963, Brit.), set d; IN THE DOGHOUSE(1964, Brit.), set d; NO, MY DARLING DAUGHTER(1964, Brit.), set d; YOUNG AND WILLING(1964, Brit.), set d; THOSE MAGNIFICENT MEN IN THEIR FLYING MACHINES; OR HOW I FLEW FROM LONDON TO PARIS IN 25 HOURS AND 11 MINUTES(1965, Brit.), set d; QUILLER MEMORANDUM, THE(1966, Brit.), set d; WALK IN THE SHADOW(1966, Brit.), set d; LONG DUEL, THE(1967, Brit.), set d; STITCH IN TIME, A(1967, Brit.), set d; THAT RIVIERA TOUCH(1968, Brit.), set d; WHERE EAGLES DARE(1968, Brit.), set d; CROMWELL(1970, Brit.), set d; SUDDEN TERROR(1970, Brit.), set d; KIDNAPPED(1971, Brit.), set d; ZEP-PELIN(1971, Brit.), set d; X Y & ZEE(1972, Brit.), set d
Tadao Takshima
DAPHNE, THE(1967)
May Taksugi
MACAO(1952)
Koji Taku
PRODIGAL SON, THE(1964, Jap.), m
Marie Takvam
1984
KAMILLA(1984, Norway)
Shmuel Tal
JESUS(1979)
Rene Tala
JAGUAR(1980, Phil.), ed
Shibley Talamas
GOLDEN MISTRESS, THE(1954)
Ros Talamini
STONE(1974, Aus.)
Gino Talamo
LAST OF THE VIKINGS, THE(1962, Fr./Ital.), ed; QUEEN OF THE NILE(1964, Ital.)
Misc. Silents
MESSALINA(1924, Ital.)
Roberto Talamo
PARIS OOH-LA-LA!(1963, U.S./Fr.)
Rinaldo Talamonti
SLAVERS(1977, Ger.)
Igor Talankin
SUMMER TO REMEMBER, A(1961, USSR), d, w
I. Talanov
Misc. Silents
BLOODY EAST, THE(1915, USSR); QUEEN'S SECRET, THE(1919, USSR); SPECTRE HAUNTS EUROPE, A(1923, USSR)
Vincenzo Talarico
SCANDAL IN SORRENTO(1957, Ital./Fr.), w; LOVE AND LARCENY(1963, Fr./Ital.); MORALIST, THE(1964, Ital.), w
Joe Talarowski
STUDENT BODIES(1981)
Frank Talavera
SALT OF THE EARTH(1954)
Meriam Talavera
ALSINO AND THE CONDOR(1983, Nicaragua), ed
Talazac
IT HAPPENED IN GIBRALTAR(1943, Fr.)
Odette Talazac
BLOOD OF A POET, THE(1930, Fr.); MILLION, THE(1931, Fr.); CRIME OF MON-SIEUR LANGE, THE(1936, Fr.); RULES OF THE GAME, THE(1939, Fr.); MURDERER LIVES AT NUMBER 21, THE(1947, Fr.)
Lina Talba
Silents
NERO(1922, U.S./Ital.)
Irving Talberg
Silents
MERRY WIDOW, THE(1925), p
Bob Talbert
SLAUGHTER IN SAN FRANCISCO(1981)
John Talbert
PSYCHO A GO-GO!(1965)
Brad Talbot
FINGER ON THE TRIGGER(1965, US/Span.)
Brud Talbot
FORCE OF IMPULSE(1961); WITHOUT EACH OTHER(1962)
Misc. Talkies
PITY ME NOT(1960)

Gloria Talbot
NORTHERN PATROL(1953); ALL THAT HEAVEN ALLOWS(1955); CRA-SHOUT(1955); DAUGHTER OF DR. JEKYLL(1957)
Hayden Talbot
Silents
TRUTH WAGON, THE(1914), w; IT IS THE LAW(1924), w
Helen Talbot
CANYON CITY(1943); PISTOL PACKIN' MAMA(1943); CALIFORNIA JOE(1944); FACES IN THE FOG(1944); OUTLAWS OF SANTA FE(1944); SAN FERNANDO VALLEY(1944); SONG OF NEVADA(1944); UP IN ARMS(1944); CORPUS CHRISTI BANDITS(1945); DON'T FENCE ME IN(1945); LONE TEXAS RANGER(1945); SWIN-GIN' ON A RAINBOW(1945); TRAIL OF KIT CARSON(1945)
Irvin Talbot
WOLF SONG(1929), md; UNION PACIFIC(1939), md; NIGHT AT EARL CAR-ROLL'S, A(1940), md; OUR TOWN(1940), md; REMEMBER THE NIGHT(1940), md; OUTLAWS OF THE DESERT(1941), md; PARSON OF PANAMINT, THE(1941), md; SECRETS OF THE WASTELANDS(1941), m; BORDER PATROL(1943), md; LEATH-ER BURNERS, THE(1943), md; RIDERS OF THE DEADLINE(1943), md; HENRY ALDRICH, BOY SCOUT(1944), md; HENRY ALDRICH PLAYS CUPID(1944), md; HENRY ALDRICH'S LITTLE SECRET(1944), md; MYSTERY MAN(1944), md; NA-TIONAL BARN DANCE(1944), m; YOU CAN'T RATION LOVE(1944), md; GANG-STER, THE(1947), md; LADIES' MAN(1947), md; WHERE THERE'S LIFE(1947), md; SUNDOWNERS, THE(1950), md; UNION STATION(1950), md; ALASKA SEAS(1954), md; LEATHER SAINT, THE(1956), m; SEARCH FOR BRIDEY MURPHY, THE(1956), md; SHORT CUT TO HELL(1957), m; PIGEON THAT TOOK ROME, THE(1962), md
Irving Talbot
NEW ORLEANS(1929), m; HIDDEN GOLD(1940), md; WIDE OPEN TOWN(1941), md; TURNING POINT, THE(1952), md
Irwin Talbot
HOPPY SERVES A WRIT(1943), md
Jay Slim Talbot
BIG COUNTRY, THE(1958)
Kathy Talbot
COMPETITION, THE(1980)
Kenneth [Ken] Talbot
OLD MOTHER RILEY, HEADMISTRESS(1950, Brit.), ph; ADVENTURE IN THE HOPFIELDS(1954, Brit.), ph; DESTINATION MILAN(1954, Brit.), ph; FOREVER MY HEART(1954, Brit.), ph; STRANGER FROM VENUS, THE(1954, Brit.), ph; TIME OF HIS LIFE, THE(1955, Brit.), ph; DOUBLE CROSS(1956, Brit.), ph; DEPTH CHAR-GE(1960, Brit.), w; GIRL HUNTERS, THE(1963, Brit.), ph; BORN FREE(1966), ph; MAROC 7(1967, Brit.), ph; BATTLE BENEATH THE EARTH(1968, Brit.), ph; HAM-MERHEAD(1968), ph; UNDERGROUND(1970, Brit.), ph; HANDS OF THE RIP-PER(1971, Brit.), ph; COUNTESS DRACULA(1972, Brit.), ph; DOOMWATCH(1972, Brit.), ph; CHARLEY-ONE-EYE(1973, Brit.), ph; PERSECUTION(1974, Brit.), ph; NOTHING BUT THE NIGHT(1975, Brit.), ph; DEVIL WITHIN HER, THE(1976, Brit.), ph
Lilian Talbot
STRANGE EXPERIMENT(1937, Brit.)
Lise Talbot
MY UNCLE ANTOINE(1971, Can.)
Lyle Talbot
BIG CITY BLUES(1932); KLONDIKE(1932); LOVE IS A RACKET(1932); MISS PINKERTON(1932); PURCHASE PRICE, THE(1932); STRANGER IN TOWN(1932); THIRTEENTH GUEST, THE(1932); THREE ON A MATCH(1932); UNHOLY LO-VE(1932); COLLEGE COACH(1933); GIRL MISSING(1933); HAVANA WIDOWS(1933); LADIES THEY TALK ABOUT(1933); LIFE OF JIMMY DOLAN, THE(1933); MARY STEVENS, M.D.(1933); NO MORE ORCHIDS(1933); SHE HAD TO SAY YES(1933); SHRIEK IN THE NIGHT, A(1933); 20,000 YEARS IN SING SING(1933); 42ND STREET(1933); DRAGON MURDER CASE, THE(1934); FOG OVER FRISCO(1934); HEAT LIGHTNING(1934); LOST LADY, A(1934); MANDALAY(1934); MURDER IN THE CLOUDS(1934); ONE NIGHT OF LOVE(1934); REGISTERED NURSE(1934); RETURN OF THE TERROR(1934); BROADWAY HOSTESS(1935); CASE OF THE LUCKY LEGS, THE(1935); CHINATOWN SQUAD(1935); IT HAPPENED IN NEW YORK(1935); OIL FOR THE LAMPS OF CHINA(1935); OUR LITTLE GIRL(1935); PAGE MISS GLORY(1935); RED HOT TIRES(1935); WHILE THE PATIENT SLEPT(1935); BOULDER DAM(1936); GO WEST, YOUNG MAN(1936); LAW IN HER HANDS, THE(1936); MURDER BY AN ARISTOCRAT(1936); SINGING KID, THE(1936); TRAPPED BY TELEVISION(1936); AFFAIRS OF CAPPY RICKS(1937); MIND YOUR OWN BUSINESS(1937); SECOND HONEYMOON(1937); THREE LE-GIONNAIRES(1937); WESTBOUND LIMITED(1937); WHAT PRICE VEN-GEANCE?(1937); ARKANSAS TRAVELER, THE(1938); CALL OF THE YUKON(1938); CHANGE OF HEART(1938); GATEWAY(1938); I STAND ACCUSED(1938); ONE WILD NIGHT(1938); FORGED PASSPORT(1939); SECOND FIDDLE(1939); THEY ASKED FOR IT(1939); TORTURE SHIP(1939); HE MARRIED HIS WIFE(1940); MIRACLE ON MAIN STREET, A(1940); PAROLE FIXER(1940); MEXICAN SPITFIRE'S ELE-PHANT(1942); NIGHT FOR CRIME, A(1942); SHE'S IN THE ARMY(1942); THEY RAID BY NIGHT(1942); MAN OF COURAGE(1943); ARE THESE OUR PA-RENTS?(1944); FALCON OUT WEST, THE(1944); GAMBLER'S CHOICE(1944); ONE BODY TOO MANY(1944); SENSATIONS OF 1945(1944); TRAIL TO GUNSIGHT(1944); UP IN ARMS(1944); DIXIE JAMBOREE(1945); GUN TOWN(1946); MURDER IS MY BUSINESS(1946); SONG OF ARIZONA(1946); STRANGE IMPERSONATION(1946); DANGER STREET(1947); APPOINTMENT WITH MURDER(1948); DEVIL'S CARGO, THE(1948); HIGHWAY 13(1948); JOE PALOOKA IN WINNER TAKE ALL(1948); VICIOUS CIRCLE, THE(1948); FIGHTING FOOLS(1949); JOE PALOOKA IN THE BIG FIGHT(1949); MISSISSIPPI RHYTHM(1949); MUTINEERS, THE(1949); PAROLE, INC.(1949); QUICK ON THE TRIGGER(1949); RINGSIDE(1949); SHEP COMES HO-ME(1949); SKY DRAGON(1949); THUNDER IN THE PINES(1949); WILD WEED(1949); BIG TIMBER(1950); BORDER RANGERS(1950); CHEROKEE UPRISING(1950); DAL-TON'S WOMEN, THE(1950); EVERYBODY'S DANCIN'(1950); FEDERAL MAN(1950); JACKPOT, THE(1950); LUCKY LOSERS(1950); ONE TOO MANY(1950); REVENUE AGENT(1950); TRIPLE TROUBLE(1950); ABILENE TRAIL(1951); BLUE BLOOD(1951); COLORADO AMBUSH(1951); FINGERPRINTS DON'T LIE(1951); FURY OF THE CONGO(1951); HURRICANE ISLAND(1951); JUNGLE MAN-HUNT(1951); MASK OF THE DRAGON(1951); OKLAHOMA JUSTICE(1951); PURPLE HEART DIARY(1951); SCARF, THE(1951); TEXAS LAWMEN(1951); AFRICAN TREASURE(1952); DESPERADOES OUTPOST(1952); FEUDIN' FOOLS(1952); GOLD RAIDERS(1952); KANSAS TERRITORY(1952); OLD WEST, THE(1952); OUT-LAW WOMEN(1952); SEA TIGER(1952); TEXAS CITY(1952); UNTAMED WO-MEN(1952); WITH A SONG IN MY HEART(1952); CLIPPED WINGS(1953); DOWN AMONG THE SHELTERING PALMS(1953); GLEN OR GLENDA(1953); STAR OF

TEXAS(1953); TUMBLEWEED(1953); WHITE LIGHTNING(1953); CAPTAIN KIDD AND THE SLAVE GIRL(1954); JAIL BAIT(1954); STEEL CAGE, THE(1954); THERE'S NO BUSINESS LIKE SHOW BUSINESS(1954); TOBOR THE GREAT(1954); JAIL BUSTERS(1955); SUDDEN DANGER(1955); CALLING HOMICIDE(1956); MESA OF LOST WOMEN, THE(1956); GREAT MAN, THE(1957); HIGH SCHOOL CONFIDENTIAL(1958); HOT ANGEL, THE(1958); NOTORIOUS MR. MONKS, THE(1958); CITY OF FEAR(1959); PLAN 9 FROM OUTER SPACE(1959); SUNRISE AT CAMPOBELLO(1960)
Misc. Talkies
MAN FROM SONORA(1951)
Mary Talbot
Silents
CUPID BY PROXY(1918)
Misc. Silents
CLEAN-UP, THE(1917); LIVE SPARKS(1920)
Michael Talbot
CARRIE(1976); NATIONAL LAMPOON'S VACATION(1983)
Michel Talbot
MY UNCLE ANTOINE(1971, Can.)
Mike Talbot
Misc. Talkies
REUNION, THE(1977), d
Monro Talbot
WHITE GORILLA(1947), w
Monroe Talbot
LAST OF THE CLINTONS, THE(1935), w; RUSTLER'S PARADISE(1935), w; WAGON TRAIL(1935), w; WILD MUSTANG(1935), w; ACES WILD(1937), w; GHOST TOWN(1937), w; LIGHTNING STRIKES WEST(1940), w
Munro Talbot
LURE OF THE WASTELAND(1939), w
Nina Talbot
THAT FUNNY FEELING(1965); CHAINED HEAT(1983 U.S./Ger.)
Nita Talbot
IT'S A GREAT FEELING(1949); CAGED(1950); MONTANA(1950); THIS SIDE OF THE LAW(1950); ON DANGEROUS GROUND(1951); BUNDLE OF JOY(1956); THIS COULD BE THE NIGHT(1957); I MARRIED A WOMAN(1958); ONCE UPON A HORSE(1958); WHO'S GOT THE ACTION?(1962); GIRL HAPPY(1965); VERY SPECIAL FAVOR, A(1965); COOL ONES THE(1967); BUCK AND THE PREACHER(1972); DAY OF THE LOCUST, THE(1975); MANCHU EAGLE MURDER CAPER MYSTERY, THE(1975); SWEET CREEK COUNTY WAR, THE(1979); SERIAL(1980); ISLAND CLAWS(1981); CONCRETE JUNGLE, THE(1982); NIGHT SHIFT(1982); FRIGHTMARE(1983)
Ogden Talbot
HOW SWEET IT IS(1968)
Robert W. Talbot
HOW TO BEAT THE HIGH COST OF LIVING(1980)
Roger Talbot
PLAYGROUND, THE(1965)
Rowland Talbot
Silents
IN THE HANDS OF THE LONDON CROOKS(1913, Brit.), w; LURE OF LONDON, THE(1914, Brit.), w; JACK TAR(1915, Brit.), w; ROGUES OF LONDON, THE(1915, Brit.), w; KENT, THE FIGHTING MAN(1916, Brit.), w; LOVE(1916, Brit.), w; PICTURE OF DORIAN GRAY, THE(1916, Brit.), w; HOLY ORDERS(1917, Brit.), w; ORA PRO NOBIS(1917, Brit.), w
Slim Talbot
TEXANS, THE(1938); GIANT(1956); HANGING TREE, THE(1959); MAN WHO SHOT LIBERTY VALANCE, THE(1962)
Stephen Talbot
BECAUSE THEY'RE YOUNG(1960)
Susan Talbot
WITCH WITHOUT A BROOM, A(1967, U.S./Span.)
Thomas Talbot
YOICKS!(1932, Brit.), w
Gloria Talbott
LUCY GALLANT(1955); WE'RE NO ANGELS(1955); STRANGE INTRUDER(1956); YOUNG GUNS, THE(1956); CYCLOPS(1957); KETTLES ON OLD MACDONALD'S FARM, THE(1957); OKLAHOMAN, THE(1957); TAMING SUTTON'S GAL(1957); I MARRIED A MONSTER FROM OUTER SPACE(1958); ALIAS JESSE JAMES(1959); GIRLS' TOWN(1959); OREGON TRAIL, THE(1959); LEECH WOMAN, THE(1960); OKLAHOMA TERRITORY(1960); ARIZONA RAIDERS(1965); EYE FOR AN EYE, AN(1966)
Misc. Talkies
BORDER CITY RUSTLERS(1953)
Glorta Talbott
CATTLE EMPIRE(1958)
Lori Talbott
HOLLYWOOD BARN DANCE(1947)
Michael Talbott
BIG BAD MAMA(1974); FOOLIN' AROUND(1980); USED CARS(1980); MOMMIE DEAREST(1981); FIRST BLOOD(1982)
1984
RACING WITH THE MOON(1984)
Vera Talchi
WALLS OF MALAPAGA, THE(1950, Fr./Ital.)
Abdelgassen Ben Taleb
Misc. Silents
GIRL FROM CARTHAGE, THE(1924, Tunisia)
Alberto Talegalli
TWO NIGHTS WITH CLEOPATRA(1953, Ital.)
Jane Talent
YOU CAN'T TAKE IT WITH YOU(1938)
Silents
LAST STRAW, THE(1920)
Ziggie Talent
MEET THE PEOPLE(1944)
Hira Talfrey
CURSE OF THE WEREWOLF, THE(1961); GYPSY GIRL(1966, Brit.); CONQUEROR WORM, THE(1968, Brit.); OBLONG BOX, THE(1969, Brit.)

Dean Taliaferro
PENNIES FROM HEAVEN(1981)
Edith Taliaferro
Misc. Silents
YOUNG ROMANCE(1915); WHO'S YOUR BROTHER?(1919)
Floyd Taliaferro
Silents
CROSSING TRAILS(1921); WESTERN HEARTS(1921)
Hal Taliaferro [Wally Wales]
UNKNOWN RANGER, THE(1936); GUN RANGER, THE(1937); HEART OF THE ROCKIES(1937); LAW OF THE RANGER(1937); ONE MAN JUSTICE(1937); RANGERS STEP IN, THE(1937); RIO GRANDE RANGER(1937); ROOTIN' TOOTIN' RHYTHM(1937); TRIGGER TRIO, THE(1937); BLACK BANDIT(1938); GUILTY TRAILS(1938); PHANTOM GOLD(1938); PIONEER TRAIL(1938); PRAIRIE JUSTICE(1938); SOUTH OF ARIZONA(1938); STAGECOACH DAYS(1938); WEST OF SANTA FE(1938); DAUGHTER OF THE TONG(1939); FRONTIERS OF '49(1939); NORTH OF THE YUKON(1939); OUTPOST OF THE MOUNTIES(1939); RIDERS OF THE FRONTIER(1939); RIO GRANDE(1939); SAGA OF DEATH VALLEY(1939); THUNDERING WEST, THE(1939); WESTERN CARAVANS(1939); BORDER LEGION, THE(1940); BULLETS FOR RUSTLERS(1940); CARSON CITY KID(1940); CHEROKEE STRIP(1940); COLORADO(1940); DARK COMMAND, THE(1940); HI-YO SILVER(1940); MAN WITH NINE LIVES, THE(1940); PIONEERS OF THE WEST(1940); STRANGER FROM TEXAS, THE(1940); TEXAS TERRORS(1940); TWO-FISTED RANGERS(1940); YOUNG BILL HICKOK(1940); ALONG THE RIO GRANDE(1941); BAD MAN OF DEADWOOD(1941); BORDER VIGILANTES(1941); GREAT TRAIN ROBBERY, THE(1941); IN OLD CHEYENNE(1941); JESSE JAMES AT BAY(1941); LAW OF THE RANGE(1941); RED RIVER VALLEY(1941); SHERIFF OF TOMBSTONE(1941); UNDER FIESTA STARS(1941); AMERICAN EMPIRE(1942); HEART OF THE GOLDEN WEST(1942); LITTLE JOE, THE WRANGLER(1942); RIDIN' DOWN THE CANYON(1942); ROMANCE ON THE RANGE(1942); SONS OF THE PIONEERS(1942); COWBOY IN THE CLOUDS(1943); FRONTIER LAW(1943); HOPPY SERVES A WRIT(1943); IDAHO(1943); LEATHER BURNERS, THE(1943); MAN FROM MUSIC MOUNTAIN(1943); SILVER SPURS(1943); SONG OF TEXAS(1943); WOMAN OF THE TOWN, THE(1943); COWBOY AND THE SENORITA(1944); LUMBERJACK(1944); VIGILANTES OF DODGE CITY(1944); YELLOW ROSE OF TEXAS, THE(1944); FALLEN ANGEL(1945); SAN ANTONIO(1945); UTAH(1945); IN OLD SACRAMENTO(1946); PLAINSMAN AND THE LADY(1946); RAMROD(1947); GALLANT LEGION, THE(1948); RED RIVER(1948); WEST OF SONORA(1948); BRIMSTONE(1949); COLT .45(1950); SAVAGE HORDE, THE(1950); SEA HORNET, THE(1951); JUNCTION CITY(1952)
Misc. Talkies
ROARING FRONTIERS(1941)
Mabel Taliaferro
MY LOVE CAME BACK(1940)
Silents
WHEN ROME RULED(1914); GOD'S HALF ACRE(1916)
Misc. Silents
THREE OF US, THE(1915); DAWN OF LOVE, THE(1916); HER GREAT PRICE(1916); SNOWBIRD, THE(1916); SUNBEAM, THE(1916); DRAFT 258(1917); JURY OF FATE, THE(1917); MAGDALENE OF THE HILLS, A(1917); PEGGY, THE WILL O' THE WISP(1917); KEEP TO THE RIGHT(1920); RICH SLAVE, THE(1921); SENTIMENTAL TOMMY(1921)
Tall Man's Boy
LAUGHING BOY(1934)
Alan Tall
1984
COMFORT AND JOY(1984, Brit.)
Don Tall
LITTLE AUSTRALIANS(1940, Aus.)
Greg Tallas
FLIGHT TO NOWHERE(1946), ed; ARGYLE SECRETS, THE(1948), ed
Misc. Talkies
CATACLYSM(1980), d
Gregg G. Tallas
SIREN OF ATLANTIS(1948), d, ed
Gregg Tallas
THREE RUSSIAN GIRLS(1943), ed; SUMMER STORM(1944), ed; SOUTHERNER, THE(1945), ed; WHISTLE STOP(1946), ed; WITHOUT HONOR(1949), ed; PREHISTORIC WOMEN(1950), d, w; BAREFOOT BATTALION, THE(1954, Gr.), d, w, ed
Misc. Talkies
BIKINI PARADISE(1967), d
Leigh G. Tallas
CAPTAIN APACHE(1971, Brit.), ed
Maria Tallchief
MILLION DOLLAR MERMAID(1952)
Marjorie Tallehief
NEOPOLITAN CAROUSEL(1961, Ital.)
James Tallent
JUMP(1971)
Jane Tallent
TREASURE ISLAND(1934); FRISCO KID(1935)
Guillermo Talles
RUN FOR THE SUN(1956)
Audrey Talley
FOUND ALIVE(1934)
Don Talley
1984
LAST HORROR FILM, THE(1984)
Marion Talley
FOLLOW YOUR HEART(1936)
Truman Talley
DEVIL TIGER(1934), ed
Silents
NEWS PARADE, THE(1928)
Carloni Talli
Silents
WHITE SISTER, THE(1923)

Hal Talliaferro
RIDERS OF THE TIMBERLINE(1941)
Margaret Tallichet
DESPERATE ADVENTURE, A(1938); GIRLS' SCHOOL(1938); STRANGER ON THE THIRD FLOOR(1940); DEVIL PAYS OFF, THE(1941); IT STARTED WITH EVE(1941)
Armand Tallier
Misc. Silents
MATER DOLOROSA(1917, Fr.); JOCELYN(1922, Fr.); LA BRIERE(1925, Fr.)
Nadine Tallier
PLEASE! MR. BALZAC(1957, Fr.); GIRLS AT SEA(1958, Brit.); GIVE ME MY CHANCE(1958, Fr.); HOT MONEY GIRL(1962, Brit./Ger.)
Kimi Tallmadge
SUNDAY BLOODY SUNDAY(1971, Brit.)
Chester Tallman
MEN AGAINST THE SKY(1940); MEXICAN SPITFIRE'S BABY(1941); SAINT IN PALM SPRINGS, THE(1941)
Frank Tallman
WRECKING CREW, THE(1968), ph; GREAT WALDO PEPPER, THE(1975), stunts
Pat Tallman
STUCK ON YOU(1983)
1984
STUCK ON YOU(1984)
Patricia Tallman
KNIGHTRIDERS(1981)
Robert Tallman
DEVIL'S CARGO, THE(1948), w; PRICE OF FEAR, THE(1956), w
Sara Jane Tallman
YOUNG GIRLS OF ROCHEFORT, THE(1968, Fr.)
Endre Tallos
ROUND UP, THE(1969, Hung.)
Luana Talltree
ANGELS FROM HELL(1968)
Zola Talma
Silents
ON WITH THE DANCE(1920)
Zolya Talma
ROSE TATTOO, THE(1955)
Constance Talmadge
Silents
MATRIMANIAC, THE(1916); GOOD NIGHT, PAUL(1918); PAIR OF SILK STOCKINGS, A(1918); ROMANCE AND ARABELLA(1919); IN SEARCH OF A SINNER(1920); LESSONS IN LOVE(1921); WOMAN'S PLACE(1921); EAST IS WEST(1922); DULCY(1923); GOLDFISH, THE(1924); IN HOLLYWOOD WITH POTASH AND PERLMUTTER(1924); LEARNING TO LOVE(1925)
Misc. Silents
MICROSCOPE MYSTERY, THE(1916); BETSY'S BURGLAR(1917); HONEYMOON, THE(1917); LESSON, THE(1917); SCANDAL(1917); LADY'S NAME, A(1918); MRS. LEFFINGWELL'S BOOTS(1918); SAUCE FOR THE GOOSE(1918); SHUTTLE, THE(1918); STUDIO GIRL, THE(1918); UP THE ROAD WITH SALLIE(1918); EXPERIMENTAL MARRIAGE(1919); HAPPINESS A LA MODE(1919); TEMPERAMENTAL WIFE, A(1919); VEILED ADVENTURE, THE(1919); VIRTUOUS VAMP, A(1919); WHO CARES?(1919); DANGEROUS BUSINESS(1920); GOOD REFERENCES(1920); LOVE EXPERT, THE(1920); PERFECT WOMAN, THE(1920); TWO WEEKS(1920); MAMA'S AFFAIR(1921); WEDDING BELLS(1921); POLLY OF THE FOLLIES(1922); PRIMITIVE LOVER, THE(1922); DANGEROUS MAID, THE(1923); HER NIGHT OF ROMANCE(1924); HER SISTER FROM PARIS(1925); DUCHESS OF BUFFALO, THE(1926); BREAKFAST AT SUNRISE(1927); VENUS OF VENICE(1927); VENUS(1929, Fr.)
Constance Talmadge
Misc. Silents
GIRL OF THE TIMBER CLAIMS, THE(1917)
Dick Talmadge
LUCKY LEGS(1942); HITLER'S MADMAN(1943)
Lulu Talmadge
MOVIE STAR, AMERICAN STYLE, OR, LSD I HATE YOU!(1966), w
Natalie Talmadge
Silents
ISLE OF CONQUEST(1919); OUR HOSPITALITY(1923)
Misc. Silents
LOVE EXPERT, THE(1920)
Norma Talmadge
NEW YORK NIGHTS(1929); DU BARRY, WOMAN OF PASSION(1930)
Silents
BATTLE CRY OF PEACE, THE(1915); MARTHA'S VINDICATION(1916); SOCIAL SECRETARY, THE(1916); ISLE OF CONQUEST(1919); NEW MOON, THE(1919); WAY OF A WOMAN(1919); BRANDED WOMAN, THE(1920); SHE LOVES AND LIES(1920); LOVE'S REDEMPTION(1921); ASHES OF VENGEANCE(1923); SONG OF LOVE, THE(1923); IN HOLLYWOOD WITH POTASH AND PERLMUTTER(1924); ONLY WOMAN, THE(1924); KIKI(1926); CAMILLE(1927); SHOW PEOPLE(1928)
Misc. Silents
(; CHILDREN IN THE HOUSE, THE(1916); CROWN PRINCE'S DOUBLE, THE(1916); DEVIL'S NEEDLE, THE(1916); FIFTY-FIFTY(1916); GOING STRAIGHT(1916); MISSING LINKS, THE(1916); LAW OF COMPENSATION, THE(1917); MOTH, THE(1917); PANTHEA(1917); POPPY(1917); SECRET OF THE STORM COUNTRY, THE(1917); BY RIGHT OF PURCHASE(1918); DELUXE ANNIE(1918); FORBIDDEN CITY, THE(1918); GHOSTS OF YESTERDAY(1918); HER ONLY WAY(1918); SAFETY CURTAIN, THE(1918); HEART OF WETONA, THE(1919); PROBATION WIFE, THE(1919); WOMAN GIVES, THE(1920); YES OR NO?(1920); PASSION FLOWER, THE(1921); SIGN ON THE DOOR, THE(1921); WONDERFUL THING, THE(1921); ETERNAL FLAME, THE(1922); SMILIN' THROUGH(1922); VOICE FROM THE MINARET, THE(1923); WITHIN THE LAW(1923); SECRETS(1924); GRAUSTARK(1925); LADY, THE(1925); DOVE, THE(1927); LAW OF COMPENSATION(1927); WOMAN DISPUTED, THE(1928)
Richard Talmadge
CAVALIER, THE(1928); DANCING DYNAMITE(1931), a, p; SCAREHEADS(1931), a, p; YANKEE DON(1931), a, p; GET THAT GIRL(1932); SPEED MADNESS(1932), a, p; SPEED REPORTER(1936); SOULS AT SEA(1937), w; BLACK EAGLE(1948); BORDER OUTLAWS(1950), p, d; PROJECT MOONBASE(1953), d; REDHEAD FROM MANHATTAN(1954); I KILLED WILD BILL HICKOK(1956), d

Misc. Talkies
FIGHTING PILOT, THE(1935); NEVER TOO LATE(1935); NOW OR NEVER(1935)
Silents
UNKNOWN, THE(1921); CUB REPORTER, THE(1922); PUTTING IT OVER(1922); TAKING CHANCES(1922); WATCH HIM STEP(1922); SPEED KING(1923); AMERICAN MANNERS(1924); IN FAST COMPANY(1924); LAUGHING AT DANGER(1924), a, stunts; ON TIME(1924); ISLE OF HOPE, THE(1925); JIMMIE'S MILLIONS(1925); BLUE STREAK, THE(1926); DOUBLING WITH DANGER(1926); NIGHT PATROL, THE(1926), a, p
Misc. Silents
LUCKY DAN(1922); WILDCAT JORDAN(1922); DANGER AHEAD(1923); LET'S GO(1923); THRU THE FLAMES(1923); HAIL THE HERO(1924); STEPPING LIVELY(1924); FIGHTING DEMON, THE(1925); MYSTERIOUS STRANGER, THE(1925); PRINCE OF PEP, THE(1925); TEARING THROUGH(1925); WALL STREET WHIZ, THE(1925); YOUTH AND ADVENTURE(1925); BETTER MAN, THE(1926); BROADWAY GALLANT, THE(1926); MERRY CAVALIER, THE(1926); CAVALIER, THE(1928); BACHELOR'S CLUB, THE(1929); POOR MILLIONAIRE, THE(1930)
Lloyd Talman
Silents
ROBIN HOOD(1922)
William Talman
RED, HOT AND BLUE(1949); ARMORED CAR ROBBERY(1950); KID FROM TEXAS, THE(1950); WOMAN ON PIER 13, THE(1950); RACKET, THE(1951); ONE MINUTE TO ZERO(1952); CITY THAT NEVER SLEEPS(1953); HITCH-HIKER, THE(1953); BIG HOUSE, U.S.A.(1955); CRASHOUT(1955); SMOKE SIGNAL(1955); I'VE LIVED BEFORE(1956), w; MAN IS ARMED, THE(1956); TWO-GUN LADY(1956); URANIUM BOOM(1956); HELL ON DEVIL'S ISLAND(1957); JOE DAKOTA(1957), w; PERSUADER, THE(1957); BALLAD OF JOSIE(1968)
Walter Talman-Gros
NOT RECONCILED, OR "ONLY VIOLENCE HELPS WHERE IT RULES"(1969, Ger.)
Akiva Talmi
TWO(1975), m
Shel Talmy
SCREAM AND SCREAM AGAIN(1970, Brit.), md
Akos Talnay
AVENGING HAND, THE(1936, Brit.), w
Sialofi Jerry Talo
DOWN AMONG THE SHELTERING PALMS(1953)
Hana Talpova
ASSISTANT, THE(1982, Czech.)
Vera Talqui
LITTLE WORLD OF DON CAMILLO, THE(1953, Fr./Ital.)
Ron Talsky
SUCH GOOD FRIENDS(1971), cos; SEPARATE PEACE, A(1972), cos; THREE MUSKETEERS, THE(1974, Panama), cos; 99 AND 44/100% DEAD(1974), cos; WILD PARTY, THE(1975), cos; DEEP, THE(1977), cos; HOT LEAD AND COLD FEET(1978), cos; JAGUAR LIVES(1979), cos; RAVAGERS, THE(1979), cos; INSIDE MOVES(1980), cos; CHU CHU AND THE PHILLY FLASH(1981), cos; DOUBLE EXPOSURE(1982), prod d; THAT CHAMPIONSHIP SEASON(1982), cos
1984
BEAR, THE(1984), cos
Ronald Talsky
TELL ME THAT YOU LOVE ME, JUNIE MOON(1970), cos; SPORTING CLUB, THE(1971), cos; KANSAS CITY BOMBER(1972), cos; SHEILA LEVINE IS DEAD AND LIVING IN NEW YORK(1975), cos
Alice Talton
DIVE BOMBER(1941); YOU'RE IN THE ARMY NOW(1941); HERS TO HOLD(1943); RANGER OF CHEROKEE STRIP(1949); GREAT JEWEL ROBBER, THE(1950); IN A LONELY PLACE(1950)
Alix Talton
MAN WHO CAME TO DINNER, THE(1942); SALLY AND SAINT ANNE(1952); STORY OF THREE LOVES, THE(1953); TANGIER INCIDENT(1953); CHA-CHA-CHA BOOM(1956); MAN WHO KNEW TOO MUCH, THE(1956); ROCK AROUND THE CLOCK(1956); DEADLY MANTIS, THE(1957); ROMANOFF AND JULIET(1961); WASTREL, THE(1963, Ital.)
Reedy Talton
DEAD TO THE WORLD(1961); RETURN TO PEYTON PLACE(1961)
Walter Talun
DAVID AND BATHSHEBA(1951)
Pamela Talus
STANLEY(1973)
Renato Talvacchia
DAISY MILLER(1974)
Olga Talyn
1984
MOSCOW ON THE HUDSON(1984)
N. Talyura
KIEV COMEDY, A(1963, USSR); MOTHER AND DAUGHTER(1965, USSR)
Teddy Talzlaff
LAST PARADE, THE(1931), ph
Simon Tam
KILLER ELITE, THE(1975)
Matahiarii Tama
MUTINY ON THE BOUNTY(1962)
Ryoichi Tamagawa
PLAY IT COOL(1970, Jap.)
Gino Tamagnini
1984
AFTER THE FALL OF NEW YORK(1984, Ital./Fr.), makeup
Masao Tamai
DIFFERENT SONS(1962, Jap.), ph; HAPPINESS OF US ALONE(1962, Jap.), ph
L Tamaki
THREE STRIPES IN THE SUN(1955)
Michiyo Tamaki
TWIN SISTERS OF KYOTO(1964, Jap.)
Sarah Tamakuni
CANDLESHOE(1978)

T. Tamamoto
Silents
INNOCENCE OF RUTH, THE(1916)
Misc. Silents
PAID IN FULL(1914)
Thomas Tamamoto
Misc. Silents
HER HUSBAND'S HONOR(1918)
Shuntaro Tamamura
EAST CHINA SEA(1969, Jap.)
Franca Tamantini
QUEEN OF SHEBA(1953, Ital.); MAN WHO WAGGED HIS TAIL, THE(1961, Ital./Span.)
Maria Tamar
FIVE WILD GIRLS(1966, Fr.)
Tamara
SWEET SURRENDER(1935); NO, NO NANETTE(1940); FUZZ(1972)
Misc. Silents
MIDSUMMER NIGHT'S DREAM, A(1928, Ger.)
Tom Tamarez
NIGHT WORLD(1932)
Boris Tamarin
Misc. Silents
DECEMBRISTS(1927, USSR); STATION MASTER, THE(1928, USSR)
Paul Tamarin
DR. STRANGELOVE: OR HOW I LEARNED TO STOP WORRYING AND LOVE THE BOMB(1964); GREAT GATSBY, THE(1974)
Dimitri Tamarov
KREMLIN LETTER, THE(1970)
M. Tamarov
Misc. Silents
ANNA KARENINA(1914, USSR); DAYS OF OUR LIFE(1914, USSR); NEST OF NOBLEMEN, A(1915, USSR)
Dunai Tamas
ANNA(1981, Fr./Hung.)
Zdenko Tamassy
MEPHISTO(1981, Ger.), m
Angela Tamayo
UNSATISFIED, THE(1964, Span.)
Manuel Tamayo y Baus
MAD QUEEN, THE(1950, Span.), w
Tamba
VOODOO TIGER(1952)
Tetsuro Tamba
DIPLOMAT'S MANSION, THE(1961, Jap.); HAHAKIRI(1963, Jap.); SAMURAI FROM NOWHERE(1964, Jap.); SEVENTH DAWN, THE(1964); KWAIDAN(1965, Jap.); YOU ONLY LIVE TWICE(1967, Brit.); PORTRAIT OF CHIEKO(1968, Jap.); GOYOKIN(1969, Jap.); FIVE MAN ARMY, THE(1970, Ital.); SCANDALOUS ADVENTURES OF BURAIKAN, THE(1970, Jap.); PROPHECIES OF NOSTRADAMUS(1974, Jap.); TIDAL WAVE(1975, U.S./Jap.); MESSAGE FROM SPACE(1978, Jap.); BUSHIDO BLADE, THE(1982 Brit./U.S.); ONIMASA(1983, Jap.)
Tetzuro Tamba
BRIDGE TO THE SUN(1961)
Tamba the Chimp
FORBIDDEN JUNGLE(1950); JUNGLE MANHUNT(1951); KILLER APE(1953); SAVAGE MUTINY(1953); VALLEY OF THE HEADHUNTERS(1953); JUNGLE MAN-EATERS(1954)
Jerry Tambasco
NUNZIO(1978)
Carlo Tamberlani
WALLS OF MALAPAGA, THE(1950, Fr./Ital.); ALONE IN THE STREETS(1956, Ital.); LAST DAYS OF POMPEII, THE(1960, Ital.); COLOSSUS OF RHODES, THE(1961, Ital., Fr., Span.); FURY OF HERCULES, THE(1961, Ital.); SAMSON(1961, Ital.); SON OF SAMSON(1962, Fr./Ital./Yugo.); TROJAN HORSE, THE(1962, Fr./Ital.); CAESAR THE CONQUEROR(1963, Ital.); FRIENDS FOR LIFE(1964, Ital.); SEVEN SLAVES AGAINST THE WORLD(1965, Ital.); DRUMS OF TABU, THE(1967, Ital./Span.); DIVINE NYMPH, THE(1979, Ital.)
Ferdinand Tamberlani
THIEF OF VENICE, THE(1952)
Nando Tamberlani
NIGHTS OF LUCRETIA BORGIA, THE(1960, Ital.); QUEEN OF THE PIRATES(1961, Ital./Ger.); CENTURION, THE(1962, Fr./Ital.); LAST OF THE VIKINGS, THE(1962, Fr./Ital.); PRISONER OF THE IRON MASK(1962, Fr./Ital.); TROJAN HORSE, THE(1962, Fr./Ital.); FALL OF ROME, THE(1963, Ital.); GLADIATOR OF ROME(1963, Ital.); SULEIMAN THE CONQUEROR(1963, Ital.); HERCULES AGAINST THE MOON MEN(1965, Fr./Ital.)
Elmer Tambert
FORBIDDEN VALLEY(1938), p
Charles Tamblyn [Carlo Tamberlani]
SABATA(1969, Ital.)
Eddie Tamblyn
FLOOD, THE(1931); FLYING DOWN TO RIO(1933); SWEETHEART OF SIGMA CHI(1933); HAROLD TEEN(1934); DANTE'S INFERNO(1935); IN OLD KENTUCKY(1935); SHOT IN THE DARK, A(1935); MOUNTAIN MUSIC(1937)
Edward Tamblyn
MONEY MEANS NOTHING(1934); MRS. WIGGS OF THE CABBAGE PATCH(1934)
Russ [Rusty] Tamblyn
BOY WITH THE GREEN HAIR, THE(1949); GUN CRAZY(1949); KID FROM CLEVELAND, THE(1949); SAMSON AND DELILAH(1949); CAPTAIN CAREY, U.S.A(1950); FATHER OF THE BRIDE(1950); VICIOUS YEARS, THE(1950); AS YOUNG AS YOU FEEL(1951); FATHER'S LITTLE DIVIDEND(1951); WINNING TEAM, THE(1952); TAKE THE HIGH GROUND(1953); DEEP IN MY HEART(1954); SEVEN BRIDES FOR SEVEN BROTHERS(1954); HIT THE DECK(1955); MANY RIVERS TO CROSS(1955); FASTEST GUN ALIVE(1956); LAST HUNT, THE(1956); YOUNG GUNS, THE(1956); PEYTON PLACE(1957); HIGH SCHOOL CONFIDENTIAL(1958); TOM THUMB(1958, Brit./U.S.); CIMARRON(1960); WEST SIDE STORY(1961); HOW THE WEST WAS WON(1962); WONDERFUL WORLD OF THE BROTHERS ERIMM, THE(1962); FOLLOW THE BOYS(1963); HAUNTING, THE(1963); LONG SHIPS, THE(1964, Brit./Yugo.); SON OF A GUNFIGHTER(1966, U.S./Span.); FEMALE BUNCH, THE(1969); FREE GRASS(1969); SATAN'S SADISTS(1969); WAR OF THE

GARGANTUAS, THE(1970, Jap.); LAST MOVIE, THE(1971); DON'T GO NEAR THE WATER(1975); WIN, PLACE, OR STEAL(1975); HUMAN HIGHWAY(1982), a, w
Misc. Talkies
BLACK HEAT(1976)
Jeffrey Tambor
...AND JUSTICE FOR ALL(1979); SATURDAY THE 14TH(1981); MAN WHO WASN'T THERE, THE(1983); MR. MOM(1983)
1984
NO SMALL AFFAIR(1984)
Jeff Tamborino
DEATH PLAY(1976), w
Paolo W. Tamburella
SHOE SHINE(1947, Ital.), p; RING AROUND THE CLOCK(1953, Ital.), p, d
Paolo William Tamburella
SEVEN DWARFS TO THE RESCUE, THE(1965, Ital.), p,d&w
Jenny Tamburi
FRANKENSTEIN-ITALIAN STYLE(1977, Ital.); WOMEN IN CELL BLOCK 7(1977, Ital./U.S.); PSYCHIC, THE(1979, Ital.)
Orfeo Tamburi
SEVEN DEADLY SINS, THE(1953, Fr./Ital.)
Dolores Tamburini
RAILROAD MAN, THE(1965, Ital.), ed
Richard Tamburino
MOONCHILD(1972), art d
Frank Tamburo
POLYESTER(1981)
Charles A. Tamburro
MITCHELL(1975); NICKELODEON(1976); NEW YORK, NEW YORK(1977); SCARFACE(1983)
1984
BIRDY(1984)
Chuck Tamburro
TWO-MINUTE WARNING(1976); STUNTS(1977); KING OF THE MOUNTAIN(1981); FIRST BLOOD(1982)
Nicola Tamburro
DILLINGER IS DEAD(1969, Ital.), art d; MEDEA(1971, Ital./Fr./Ger.), art d
Harry Tamekloe
UNCLE TOM'S CABIN(1969, Fr./Ital./Ger./Yugo.)
Val Tamelin
ANGEL BABY(1961), art d
Lion Tamer
PSYCHO-CIRCUS(1967, Brit.)
Tom Tamerez
CASBAH(1948)
Tom Tameriz
STUDENT TOUR(1934)
Carlo Tamerlani
MINOTAUR, THE(1961, Ital.)
Zoe Tamerlis
MS. 45(1981)
1984
SPECIAL EFFECTS(1984)
Masao Tami
WHEN A WOMAN ASCENDS THE STAIRS(1963, Jap.), ph
Pierre Tamin
IS PARIS BURNING?(1966, U.S./Fr.)
Helen Tamiris
UP IN CENTRAL PARK(1948), ch; JUST FOR YOU(1952), ch
Akim Tamiroff
OKAY AMERICA(1932); DEVIL'S IN LOVE, THE(1933); PROFESSIONAL SWEETHEART(1933); QUEEN CHRISTINA(1933); STORM AT DAYBREAK(1933); CAPTAIN HATES THE SEA, THE(1934); CHAINED(1934); FUGITIVE LOVERS(1934); GREAT FLIRTATION, THE(1934); HERE IS MY HEART(1934); MERRY WIDOW, THE(1934); NOW AND FOREVER(1934); SADIE MCKEE(1934); WHOM THE GODS DESTROY(1934); BIG BROADCAST OF 1936, THE(1935); BLACK FURY(1935); CHINA SEAS(1935); GAY DECEPTION, THE(1935); GO INTO YOUR DANCE(1935); LAST OUTPOST, THE(1935); LIVES OF A BENGAL LANCER(1935); NAUGHTY MARIETTA(1935); PARIS IN SPRING(1935); RECKLESS(1935); RUMBA(1935); TWO FISTED(1935); WINNING TICKET, THE(1935); ANTHONY ADVERSE(1936); DESIRE(1936); GENERAL DIED AT DAWN, THE(1936); JUNGLE PRINCESS, THE(1936); STORY OF LOUIS PASTEUR, THE(1936); WOMAN TRAP(1936); GREAT GAMBINI, THE(1937); HER HUSBAND LIES(1937); HIGH, WIDE AND HANDSOME(1937); KING OF GAMBLERS(1937); SOLDIER AND THE LADY, THE(1937); THIS WAY PLEASE(1937); BUCCANEER, THE(1938); DANGEROUS TO KNOW(1938); RIDE A CROOKED MILE(1938); SPAWN OF THE NORTH(1938); DISPUTED PASSAGE(1939); HONEYMOON IN BALI(1939); KING OF CHINATOWN(1939); MAGNIFICENT FRAUD, THE(1939); PARIS HONEYMOON(1939); UNION PACIFIC(1939); GREAT McGINTY, THE(1940); NORTHWEST MOUNTED POLICE(1940); TEXAS RANGERS RIDE AGAIN(1940); UNTAMED(1940); WAY OF ALL FLESH, THE(1940); CORSICAN BROTHERS, THE(1941); NEW YORK TOWN(1941); TORTILLA FLAT(1942); FIVE GRAVES TO CAIRO(1943); FOR WHOM THE BELL TOLLS(1943); HIS BUTLER'S SISTER(1943); BRIDGE OF SAN LUIS REY, THE(1944); CAN'T HELP SINGING(1944); DRAGON SEED(1944); MIRACLE OF MORGAN'S CREEK, THE(1944); PARDON MY PAST(1945); SCANDAL IN PARIS, A(1946); FIESTA(1947); GANGSTER, THE(1947); MY GIRL TISA(1948); RELENTLESS(1948); BLACK MAGIC(1949); OUTPOST IN MOROCCO(1949); DESERT LEGION(1953); THEY WHO DARE(1954, Brit.); YOU KNOW WHAT SAILORS ARE(1954, Brit.); ANASTASIA(1956); BATTLE HELL(1956, Brit.); BLACK SLEEP, THE(1956); CARTOUCHE(1957, Ital./US); ME AND THE COLONEL(1958); TOUCH OF EVIL(1958); DESERT DESPERADOES(1959); OCEAN'S ELEVEN(1960); ROMANOFF AND JULIET(1961); MR. ARKADIN(1962, Brit./Fr./Span.); RELUCTANT SAINT, THE(1962, U.S./Ital.); BACCHANTES, THE(1963, Fr./Ital.); TRIAL, THE(1963, Fr./Ital./Ger.); PANIC BUTTON(1964); TOPKAPI(1964); ALPHAVILLE, A STRANGE CASE OF LEMMY CAUTION(1965, Fr.); BAMBOLE!(1965, Ital.); INVASION 1700(1965, Fr./Ital./Yugo.); LORD JIM(1965, Brit.); AFTER THE FOX(1966, U.S./Brit./Ital.); HOTEL PARADISO(1966, U.S./Brit.); LIQUIDATOR, THE(1966, Brit.); LT. ROBIN CRUSOE, U.S.N.(1966); MARCO THE MAGNIFICENT(1966, Ital./Fr./Yugo./Egypt/Afghanistan); ROSE FOR EVERYONE, A(1967, Ital.); VULTURE, THE(1967, U.S./Brit./Can.); GREAT CATHERINE(1968, Brit.); GIRL WHO COULDN'T SAY NO, THE(1969, Ital.); GREAT BANK ROBBERY, THE(1969); JUSTINE(1969, Ital./Span.); SABRA(1970, Fr./Ital./

Israel)
Misc. Talkies
BLACK FOREST, THE(1954)
Jiro Tamiya
CREATURE CALLED MAN, THE(1970, Jap.); YELLOW DOG(1973, Brit.)
Gilles Tamiz
1984
CHEECH AND CHONG'S THE CORSICAN BROTHERS(1984)
David Tamkin
MAGNIFICENT DOLL(1946), md; SINGAPORE(1947), md; SLAVE GIRL(1947), md
Daniel Tamkus
WAY WE LIVE NOW, THE(1970), w, m; CLOUD DANCER(1980), w
Mary Tamm
TALES THAT WITNESS MADNESS(1973, Brit.); ODESSA FILE, THE(1974, Brit./Ger.); LIKELY LADS, THE(1976, Brit.)
P. Tamm
Misc. Silents
KATORGA(1928, USSR)
Peter Tammer
HOW WILLINGLY YOU SING(1975, Aus.), ph; INSIDE LOOKING OUT(1977, Aus.), ph
Diane Tammes
1984
SACRED HEARTS(1984, Brit.), ph
Tom V.V. Tammi
DINER(1982)
Harry Tampa
NOCTURNA(1979), d&w
Misc. Talkies
FAIRY TALES(1979), d
Irene Tams
Silents
OH, BOY!(1919)
Misc. Silents
WITHOUT A SOUL(1916); TAXI(1919); DETERMINATION(1922)
Robert Emmett Tamsey
PRAIRIE OUTLAWS(1948), p&d
Tamu
CLAUDINE(1974); SUPER COPS, THE(1974)
Kenzo Tamu
ETERNITY OF LOVE(1961, Jap.)
D. Tamura
ANATAHAN(1953, Jap.)
Masakazu Tamura
EAST CHINA SEA(1969, Jap.); UNDER THE BANNER OF SAMURAI(1969, Jap.)
Mayumi Tamura
WESTWARD DESPERADO(1961, Jap.)
Nami Tamura
LOVE AT TWENTY(1963, Fr./Ital./Jap./Pol./Ger.); OPERATION X(1963, Jap.); YOUNG SWORDSMAN(1964, Jap.); SAMURAI ASSASSIN(1965, Jap.); KILL(1968, Jap.)
Ryo Tamura
RISE AGAINST THE SWORD(1966, Jap.); MAD ATLANTIC, THE(1967, Jap.); ONCE A RAINY DAY(1968, Jap.); OUR SILENT LOVE(1969, Jap.)
Takahiro Tamura
SCARLET CAMELLIA, THE(1965, Jap.); DAY THE SUN ROSE, THE(1969, Jap.); TORA! TORA! TORA!(1970, U.S./Jap.); RED LION(1971, Jap.); MUDDY RIVER(1982, Jap.)
Takeshi Tamura
GOODBYE, MOSCOW(1968, Jap.), w
Tamutsu Tamura
WOMAN IN THE DUNES(1964, Jap.)
Tsutomo Tamura
DIARY OF A SHINJUKU BURGLAR(1969, Jap.), w
Don Tamuty
1984
PURPLE HEARTS(1984)
Jina Tan
MIXED COMPANY(1974)
John Tan
FIENDISH PLOT OF DR. FU MANCHU, THE(1980)
Laurence Tan
Misc. Talkies
HEROES THREE(1984)
Phil Tan
PRIVATES ON PARADE(1982)
1984
PRIVATES ON PARADE(1984, Brit.)
Philip Tan
FIENDISH PLOT OF DR. FU MANCHU, THE(1980)
Rolly Tan
RAW FORCE(1982)
Dan Tana
TWILIGHT TIME(1983, U.S./Yugo.), p, w
Leni Tana
SHE DEMONS(1958)
Temba Tana
GRASS IS SINGING, THE(1982, Brit./Swed.), m
1984
KILLING HEAT(1984), m
Goro Tanada
GATE OF FLESH(1964, Jap.), w
Bella Tanai
FORTRESS, THE(1979, Hung.)
Haruo Tanak
IKIRU(1960, Jap.)
Fumio Tanaka
SPACE AMOEBA, THE(1970, Jap.), p; YOG-MONSTER FROM SPACE(1970, Jap.), p; LAKE OF DRACULA(1973, Jap.), p; WAR OF THE PLANETS(1977, Jap.), p

Haruo Tanaka
RICKSHAW MAN, THE(1960, Jap.); LOWER DEPTHS, THE(1962, Jap.); OHAYO(1962, Jap.); FLOATING WEEDS(1970, Jap.); GEISHA, A(1978, Jap.)
Hiroshi Tanaka
RED SUN(1972, Fr./Ital./Span.)
Hoei Tanaka
LET'S GO, YOUNG GUY!(1967, Jap.)
Ken Tanaka
KARATE, THE HAND OF DEATH(1961), ed
Kinuyo Tanaka
UGETSU(1954, Jap.); WOMEN IN PRISON(1957, Jap.); BALLAD OF NARAYAMA(1961, Jap.); ETERNITY OF LOVE(1961, Jap.); LONELY LANE(1963, Jap.); ALONE ON THE PACIFIC(1964, Jap.); LIFE OF OHARU(1964, Jap.); LOVE UNDER THE CRUCIFIX(1965, Jap.), d; IT STARTED IN THE ALPS(1966, Jap.); RED BEARD(1966, Jap.); SANSHO THE BAILIFF(1969, Jap.)
Kunie Tanaka
ROAD TO ETERNITY(1962, Jap.); SANJURO(1962, Jap.); OPERATION X(1963, Jap.); RIVER OF FOREVER(1967, Jap.); GOYOKIN(1969, Jap.); YOUNG GUY GRADUATES(1969, Jap.); YOUNG GUY ON MT. COOK(1969, Jap.); DUEL AT EZO(1970, Jap.); LIVE YOUR OWN WAY(1970, Jap.); SILENCE HAS NO WINGS(1971, Jap.); SUMMER SOLDIERS(1972, Jap.)
Kunishige Tanaka
HELL IN THE PACIFIC(1968), spec eff
Michiko Tanaka
MADAME BUTTERFLY(1955 Ital./Jap.)
Nanette Tanaka
DEVIL AT FOUR O'CLOCK, THE(1961)
Osamu Tanaka
GREEN SLIME, THE(1969), ed; PROPHECIES OF NOSTRADAMUS(1974, Jap.), p
Shigeo Tanaka
GREAT WALL, THE(1965, Jap.), d; GAMERA VERSUS BARUGON(1966, Jap./U.S.), d
Shinji Tanaka
NAKED YOUTH(1961, Jap.); ISLAND, THE(1962, Jap.)
Sumie Tanaka
WOMEN IN PRISON(1957, Jap.), w; LONELY LANE(1963, Jap.), w
Tamoyuki Tanaka
MYSTERIANS, THE(1959, Jap.), p; SIEGE OF FORT BISMARK(1968, Jap.), p
Tokuzo Tanaka
SECRETS OF A WOMAN'S TEMPLE(1969, Jap.), d
Tomoyaki Tanaka
GODZILLA VERSUS THE SMOG MONSTER(1972, Jap.), p
Tomoyuki Tanaka
HALF HUMAN(1955, Jap.), p; GODZILLA, RING OF THE MONSTERS(1956, Jap.), p; RODAN(1958, Jap.), p; GIGANTIS(1959, Jap./U.S.), p; H-MAN, THE(1959, Jap.), p; I BOMBED PEARL HARBOR(1961, Jap.), p; LIFE OF A COUNTRY DOCTOR(1961, Jap.), p; SECRET OF THE TELEGIAN, THE(1961, Jap.), p; LAST WAR, THE(1962, Jap.), p; MOTHRA(1962, Jap.), p; SANJURO(1962, Jap.), p; HIGH AND LOW(1963, Jap.), p; KING KONG VERSUS GODZILLA(1963, Jap.), p; OPERATION X(1963, Jap.), p; WARRING CLANS(1963, Jap.), p; ATTACK OF THE MUSHROOM PEOPLE(1964, Jap.), p; BANDITS ON THE WIND(1964, Jap.), p; DAGORA THE SPACE MONSTER(1964, Jap.), p; FRANKENSTEIN CONQUERS THE WORLD(1964, Jap./US), p; GODZILLA VS. THE THING(1964, Jap.), p; HUMAN VAPOR, THE(1964, Jap.), p; YOUNG SWORDSMAN(1964, Jap.), p; GHIDRAH, THE THREE-HEADED MONSTER(1965, Jap.), p; RABBLE, THE(1965, Jap.), p; SAMURAI ASSASSIN(1965, Jap.), p; TIGER FLIGHT(1965, Jap.), p; FORT GRAVEYARD(1966, Jap.), p; GODZILLA VERSUS THE SEA MONSTER(1966, Jap.), p; RED BEARD(1966, Jap.), p; RISE AGAINST THE SWORD(1966, Jap.), p; MAD ATLANTIC, THE(1967, Jap.), p; REBELLION(1967, Jap.), p; SON OF GODZILLA(1967, Jap.), p; KING KONG ESCAPES(1968, Jap.), p; DESTROY ALL MONSTERS(1969, Jap.), p; GODZILLA'S REVENGE(1969), p; LATITUDE ZERO(1969, U.S./Jap.), p; PORTRAIT OF HELL(1969, Jap.), p; MONSTER ZERO(1970, Jap.), p; SPACE AMOEBA, THE(1970, Jap.), p; YOG-MONSTER FROM SPACE(1970, Jap.), p; WAR OF THE MONSTERS(1972, Jap.), p; GODZILLA VERSUS THE COSMIC MONSTER(1974, Jap.), p; PROPHECIES OF NOSTRADAMUS(1974, Jap.), p; MONSTERS FROM THE UNKNOWN PLANET(1975, Jap.), p; TIDAL WAVE(1975, U.S./Jap.), p; GODZILLA VS. MEGALON(1976, Jap.), p; WAR OF THE PLANETS(1977, Jap.), p
Toru Tanaka
EYE FOR AN EYE, AN(1981); REVENGE OF THE NINJA(1983)
Professor Toru Tanaka
1984
CHATTANOOGA CHOO CHOO(1984)
Yuko Tanaka
BATTLE IN OUTER SPACE(1960), p; ATRAGON(1965, Jap.), p; LOST WORLD OF SINBAD, THE(1965, Jap.), p
Yasuo Tanami
DON'T CALL ME A CON MAN(1966, Jap.), w; LET'S GO, YOUNG GUY!(1967, Jap.), w; LAS VEGAS FREE-FOR-ALL(1968, Jap.), w; COMPUTER FREE-FOR-ALL(1969, Jap.), w; YOUNG GUY GRADUATES(1969, Jap.), w; YOUNG GUY ON MT. COOK(1969, Jap.), w; HOTSPRINGS HOLIDAY(1970, Jap.), w
Yatsuko Tanami
IKIRU(1960, Jap.)
Paul Tanashian
YOUNG WARRIORS(1983)
Azumi Tanba
1984
BALLAD OF NARAYAMA, THE(1984, Jap.)
Nat Tanchuck
CHAINED FOR LIFE(1950), w; FEDERAL MAN(1950), w; I KILLED GERONIMO(1950), w; HOODLUM, THE(1951), w; BUFFALO BILL IN TOMAHAWK TERRITORY(1952), w; GARDEN OF EDEN(1954), w
Nathaniel Tanchuck
MARRIED TOO YOUNG(1962), w; SHUTTERED ROOM, THE(1968, Brit.), w
Anthony Tancred
AFFAIRS OF ADELAIDE(1949, U. S./Brit); RELUCTANT WIDOW, THE(1951, Brit.)
Mike Tancredi
JACKTOWN(1962)

Gerhard Tandar
SHOT AT DAWN, A(1934, Ger.)
Renee Tandil
Misc. Silents
L'ATRE(1923, Fr.)
Adolf Tandler
Silents
QUEEN KELLY(1929), m
Adolph Tandler
SCARFACE(1932), m
Lajos Tandor
WITNESS, THE(1982, Hung.)
Harald Tandrup
ONLY ONE NIGHT(1942, Swed.), w
Donald Tandy
HAND IN HAND(1960, Brit.); WRONG BOX, THE(1966, Brit.); 11 HARROW-HOUSE(1974, Brit.)
Gareth Tandy
CASH ON DEMAND(1962, Brit.); RESCUE SQUAD, THE(1963, Brit.)
Jessica Tandy
INDISCRETIONS OF EVE(1932, Brit.); MURDER IN THE FAMILY(1938, Brit.); SEVENTH CROSS, THE(1944); VALLEY OF DECISION, THE(1945); DRAGON-WYCH(1946); GREEN YEARS, THE(1946); FOREVER AMBER(1947); WOMAN'S VENGEANCE, A(1947); SEPTEMBER AFFAIR(1950); DESERT FOX, THE(1951); LIGHT IN THE FOREST, THE(1958); ADVENTURES OF A YOUNG MAN(1962); BIRDS, THE(1963); BUTLEY(1974, Brit.); HONKY TONK FREEWAY(1981); BEST FRIENDS(1982); STILL OF THE NIGHT(1982); WORLD ACCORDING TO GARP, The(1982)
1984
BOSTONIANS, THE(1984)
Victor Tandy
Silents
LITTLE DOOR INTO THE WORLD, THE(1923, Brit.)
A. Maana Tanelah
Misc. Talkies
SCREAM BLOODY MURDER(1973)
James Tanenbaum
GUN RUNNER(1969), p; COUNT YORGA, VAMPIRE(1970), spec eff
Ronald Tanet
MARDI GRAS MASSACRE(1978)
Misc. Talkies
CRYPT OF DARK SECRETS(1976)
Alan Tang
Misc. Talkies
DYNAMITE BROTHERS, THE(1974)
Frank Tang
GREAT DIVIDE, THE(1930); STUDENT TOUR(1934); LEATHERNECKS HAVE LANDED, THE(1936); WE'VE NEVER BEEN LICKED(1943); DESTINATION TO-KYO(1944); GOD IS MY CO-PILOT(1945); SOLDIER OF FORTUNE(1955); HUNTERS, THE(1958); LINEUP, THE(1958)
Kem Tang
TREASURE OF MONTE CRISTO(1949)
Tang-Hua-Ta
FIRST SPACESHIP ON VENUS(1960, Ger./Pol.)
Kiyoko Tange
FRIENDLY KILLER, THE(1970, Jap.)
Tangerine Dream
SORCERER(1977), m; SOLDIER, THE(1982), m; RISKY BUSINESS(1983), m
1984
FIRESTARTER(1984), m; FLASHPOINT(1984), m; HEARTBREAKERS(1984), m
Senkichi Tangiguchi
LOST WORLD OF SINBAD, THE(1965, Jap.), d
Mark Tangner
ON THE LOOSE(1951)
Robert L. Tangrea
ROCKY(1976)
Eva Tanguay
Misc. Silents
ENERGETIC EVA(1916); WILD GIRL, THE(1917)
Annick Tanguy
MY SEVEN LITTLE SINS(1956, Fr./Ital.)
Gerard Tanguy
SMUGGLERS, THE(1969, Fr.)
Yvan Tanguy
AND NOW MY LOVE(1975, Fr.)
Inspector Oliver Tangvay
I CONFESS(1953), police adv
Nigel Tangye
THINGS TO COME(1936, Brit.), tech adv
Akemi Tani
PHANTOM PLANET, THE(1961)
Akira Tani
SEVEN SAMURAI, THE(1956, Jap.); IKIRU(1960, Jap.)
Hank Tani
WILD ON THE BEACH(1965), w
Kei Tani
DON'T CALL ME A CON MAN(1966, Jap.); LAS VEGAS FREE-FOR-ALL(1968, Jap.); COMPUTER FREE-FOR-ALL(1969, Jap.)
Miki Tani
FOR LOVE AND MONEY(1967)
Yoko Tani
QUIET AMERICAN, THE(1958); WIND CANNOT READ, THE(1958, Brit.); FIRST SPACESHIP ON VENUS(1960, Ger./Pol.); PICCADILLY THIRD STOP(1960, Brit.); SAVAGE INNOCENTS, THE(1960, Brit.); MARCO POLO(1962, Fr./Ital.); MY GEI-SHA(1962); SAMSON AND THE SEVEN MIRACLES OF THE WORLD(1963, Fr./Ital.); WHO'S BEEN SLEEPING IN MY BED?(1963); DR. MABUSE'S RAYS OF DEATH(1964, Ger./Fr./Ital.); FIRE IN THE FLESH(1964, Fr.); INVASION(1965, Brit.); PARTNER, THE(1966, Brit.); WHITE, RED, YELLOW, PINK(1966, Ital.); LOVE FACTORY(1969, Ital.)

Misc. Talkies
TO CHASE A MILLION(1967)
Yuki Tani
WALK, DON'T RUN(1966)
Senkichi Taniguchi
MAN AGAINST MAN(1961, Jap.), d; OPERATION ENEMY FORT(1964, Jap.), p; GAMBLING SAMURAI, THE(1966, Jap.), d; OUTPOST OF HELL(1966, Jap.), d; WHAT'S UP, TIGER LILY?(1966), d; MAN IN THE STORM, THE(1969, Jap.), d, w
Shuntaro Tanikawa
HINOTORI(1980, Jap.), w
Masahiko Tanimura
NONE BUT THE BRAVE(1965, U.S./Jap.)
Pamela Tanimura
DIRTY HARRY(1971)
Eleanore Tanin
MIAMI EXPOSE(1956); WEREWOLF, THE(1956); FOOTSTEPS IN THE NIGHT(1957)
James Tanioka
UNHOLY ROLLERS(1972)
Junichiro Tanizaki
ODD OBSESSION(1961, Jap.), w; DEVIL'S TEMPLE(1969, Jap.), w
Dean Tanji
SKY RIDERS(1976, U.S./Gr.)
Mutsuo Tanji
INSECT WOMAN, THE(1964, Jap.), ed
Denis Tankard
THAT'S RIGHT-YOU'RE WRONG(1939); TOWER OF LONDON(1939); INVISIBLE MAN RETURNS, THE(1940)
J. B. Tanko
LOLLIPOP(1966, Braz.), d&w
Dan Tann
ENEMY BELOW, THE(1957)
Maureen Tann
REVENGE OF THE PINK PANTHER(1978)
Paul Tann
SECOND BEST SECRET AGENT IN THE WHOLE WIDE WORLD, THE(1965, Brit.)
Philip Tann
1984
INDIANA JONES AND THE TEMPLE OF DOOM(1984)
Tom Tann
SCOTLAND YARD DRAGNET(1957, Brit.)
Anette Tannader
GOLDENGIRL(1979)
Tsukasa Tannai
1984
WARRIORS OF THE WIND(1984, Jap.), anim
Nicholas Tannar
CONSTANT HUSBAND, THE(1955, Brit.)
Ron Tannas
SHAFT(1971); FUZZ(1972)
Jules Tannebaum
BLACK LIKE ME(1964), p
Myrtle Tannehill
Misc. Silents
BARNSTORMERS, THE(1915)
Bill Tannen
CONVICTED(1950); LAW AND ORDER(1953); CAPTAIN KIDD AND THE SLAVE GIRL(1954); SITTING BULL(1954); NOOSE FOR A GUNMAN(1960)
Charles Tannen
DARK ANGEL, THE(1935); EDUCATING FATHER(1936); LOVE BEFORE BREAK-FAST(1936); LOVE AND HISSES(1937); LOVE IS NEWS(1937); SECOND HONEY-MOON(1937); SING AND BE HAPPY(1937); ALEXANDER'S RAGTIME BAND(1938); MY LUCKY STAR(1938); SUBMARINE PATROL(1938); DRUMS ALONG THE MO-HAWK(1939); JESSE JAMES(1939); SECOND FIDDLE(1939); STORY OF ALEXAND-ER GRAHAM BELL, THE(1939); SWANEE RIVER(1939); YOUNG MR. LINCOLN(1939); GRAPES OF WRATH(1940); JOHNNY APOLLO(1940); LILLIAN RUSSELL(1940); RETURN OF FRANK JAMES, THE(1940); SAILOR'S LADY(1940); CADET GIRL(1941); GREAT AMERICAN BROADCAST, THE(1941); PERFECT SNOB, THE(1941); REMEMBER THE DAY(1941); CAREFUL, SOFT SHOULDERS(1942); FOOTLIGHT SERENADE(1942); LITTLE TOKYO, U.S.A.(1942); MANILA CAL-LING(1942); MY GAL SAL(1942); QUIET PLEASE, MURDER(1942); SUNDOWN JIM(1942); TALES OF MANHATTAN(1942); THUNDER BIRDS(1942); TO THE SHORES OF TRIPOLI(1942); CRASH DIVE(1943); THEY CAME TO BLOW UP AMERICA(1943); DOLL FACE(1945); SPIDER, THE(1945); BEHIND GREEN LIGHTS(1946); IF I'M LUCKY(1946); IT SHOULDN'T HAPPEN TO A DOG(1946); JOHNNY COMES FLYING HOME(1946); LEAVE HER TO HEAVEN(1946); SHOCK(1946); APARTMENT FOR PEGGY(1948); CRY OF THE CITY(1948); GREEN GRASS OF WYOMING(1948); SITTING PRETTY(1948); STREET WITH NO NAME, THE(1948); THAT WONDERFUL URGE(1948); UNFAITHFULLY YOURS(1948); WHEN MY BABY SMILES AT ME(1948); YOU WERE MEANT FOR ME(1948); DANCING IN THE DARK(1949); YOU'RE MY EVERYTHING(1949); I'LL GET BY(1950); JACKPOT, THE(1950); YOU'RE IN THE NAVY NOW(1951); NIGHT WITH-OUT SLEEP(1952); RED SKIES OF MONTANA(1952); WITHOUT WARNING(1952); CITY OF BAD MEN(1953); DANGEROUS CROSSING(1953); DOWN AMONG THE SHELTERING PALMS(1953); GENTLEMEN PREFER BLONDES(1953); KID FROM LEFT FIELD, THE(1953); BRIDGES AT TOKO-RI, THE(1954); COUNTRY GIRL, THE(1954); GORILLA AT LARGE(1954); STEEL CAGE(1954); GIRL IN THE RED VELVET SWING, THE(1955); I'LL CRY TOMORROW(1955); TRIAL(1955); FIRST TRAVELING SALESLADY, THE(1956); FOUR GIRLS IN TOWN(1956); HARDER THEY FALL, THE(1956); PROUD ONES, THE(1956); THESE WILDER YEARS(1956); MONSTER THAT CHALLENGED THE WORLD, THE(1957); FLY, THE(1958); MA BARKER'S KILLER BROOD(1960); VOYAGE TO THE BOTTOM OF THE SEA(1961); STAGECOACH TO DANCER'S PARK(1962)
Julian Tannen
GREAT MOMENT, THE(1944)
Julius Tannen
LADY BY CHOICE(1934); COLLEGIATE(1936); HALF ANGEL(1936); ONE IN A MILLION(1936); PIGSKIN PARADE(1936); REUNION(1936); ROAD TO GLORY, THE(1936); STOWAWAY(1936); THIRTY SIX HOURS TO KILL(1936); FAIR WARN-ING(1937); LOVE IS NEWS(1937); LOVE IS A HEADACHE(1938); MAMA RUNS WILD(1938); DANGER FLIGHT(1939); MAGNIFICENT FRAUD, THE(1939); CHRIST-

MAS IN JULY(1940); LADY IN QUESTION, THE(1940); MORTAL STORM, THE(1940); NO, NO NANETTE(1940); REMEMBER THE NIGHT(1940); CONFESSIONS OF BOSTON BLACKIE(1941); LADY EVE, THE(1941); SULLIVAN'S TRAVELS(1941); GHOST OF FRANKENSTEIN, THE(1942); HARVARD, HERE I COME(1942); PALM BEACH STORY, THE(1942); TWO YANKS IN TRINIDAD(1942); HOUSE OF FRANKENSTEIN(1944); MIRACLE OF MORGAN'S CREEK, THE(1944); NOB HILL(1945); UNFAITHFULLY YOURS(1948); MAD WEDNESDAY(1950); PEOPLE AGAINST O'HARA, THE(1951); CARRIE(1952); CLASH BY NIGHT(1952); SINGIN' IN THE RAIN(1952); LAST HURRAH, THE(1958)

Steve Tannen
LUNCH WAGON(1981)

Terrell Tannen
BOOGEY MAN, THE(1980), ed; TASTE OF SIN, A(1983), ed; YOUNG GIANTS(1983), d, w

William Tannen
BAND PLAYS ON, THE(1934); IT'S IN THE AIR(1935); SHE COULDN'T TAKE IT(1935); CRASH DONOVAN(1936); SPEED(1936); ROSALIE(1937); WHEN LOVE IS YOUNG(1937); ANOTHER THIN MAN(1939); STAND UP AND FIGHT(1939); FLIGHT COMMAND(1940); I LOVE YOU AGAIN(1940); NEW MOON(1940); SKY MURDER(1940); SPORTING BLOOD(1940); WYOMING(1940); BIG STORE, THE(1941); DOWN IN SAN DIEGO(1941); DR. JEKYLL AND MR. HYDE(1941); I'LL WAIT FOR YOU(1941); LOVE CRAZY(1941); TRIAL OF MARY DUGAN, THE(1941); TWO-FACED WOMAN(1941); WHISTLING IN THE DARK(1941); FINGERS AT THE WINDOW(1942); JOE SMITH, AMERICAN(1942); NAZI AGENT(1942); PACIFIC RENDEZVOUS(1942); SHIP AHOY(1942); STAND BY FOR ACTION(1942); WOMAN OF THE YEAR(1942); AIR RAID WARDENS(1943); PILOT NO. 5(1943); THOUSANDS CHEER(1943); THREE HEARTS FOR JULIA(1943); YOUNGEST PROFESSION, THE(1943); CANTERVILLE GHOST, THE(1944); MAISIE GOES TO RENO(1944); TWO SMART PEOPLE(1946); HIGH BARBAREE(1947); IT HAPPENED IN BROOKLYN(1947); THIS TIME FOR KEEPS(1947); DON'T TRUST YOUR HUSBAND(1948); HOMECOMING(1948); SOUTHERN YANKEE, A(1948); ALASKA PATROL(1949); GAL WHO TOOK THE WEST, THE(1949); MYSTERIOUS DESPERADO, THE(1949); RIDERS OF THE RANGE(1949); CHAIN GANG(1950); FATHER IS A BACHELOR(1950); PYGMY ISLAND(1950); THREE LITTLE WORDS(1950); FLAME OF ARABY(1951); I WAS AN AMERICAN SPY(1951); INSURANCE INVESTIGATOR(1951); NEW MEXICO(1951); ROARING CITY(1951); SANTA FE(1951); SHOW BOAT(1951); STRIP, THE(1951); YANK IN KOREA, A(1951); BAD AND THE BEAUTIFUL, THE(1952); JET JOB(1952); JUNGLE JIM IN THE FORBIDDEN LAND(1952); LOAN SHARK(1952); ROAD AGENT(1952); TALK ABOUT A STRANGER(1952); DANGEROUS CROSSING(1953); EL PASO STAMPEDE(1953); JACK MCCALL, DESPERADO(1953); RAIDERS OF THE SEVEN SEAS(1953); 99 RIVER STREET(1953); GOLDEN IDOL, THE(1954); JESSE JAMES VERSUS THE DALTONS(1954); LAW VS. BILLY THE KID, THE(1954); WOMAN'S WORLD(1954); DEVIL GODDESS(1955); JUPITER'S DARLING(1955); BLACKJACK KETCHUM, DESPERADO(1956); JAILHOUSE ROCK(1957); TIJUANA STORY, THE(1957); GREAT SIOUX MASSACRE, THE(1965); PANIC IN THE CITY(1968)
1984
FLASHPOINT(1984), d

William J. Tannen
LUST FOR GOLD(1949); SCENE OF THE CRIME(1949); SUNSET IN THE WEST(1950); BLUE BLOOD(1951); DIAL RED O(1955)

Yulius Tannen
DIMPLES(1936)

Farrel R. Tannenbaum
WANDERERS, THE(1979)

Jack Tannenbaum
INCREDIBLE INVASION, THE(1971, Mex./U.S.), spec eff

Alain Tanner
CHARLES, DEAD OR ALIVE(1972, Switz.), p; JONAH–WHO WILL BE 25 IN THE YEAR 2000(1976, Switz.), d, w; LIGHT YEARS AWAY(1982, Fr./Switz.), d&w; IN THE WHITE CITY(1983, Switz./Portugal), p, d&w

Cecile Tanner
EVERY MAN FOR HIMSELF(1980, Fr.)

Clay Tanner
MC HALE'S NAVY JOINS THE AIR FORCE(1965); ROSEMARY'S BABY(1968); HOW TO FRAME A FIGG(1971); LADY SINGS THE BLUES(1972); GRAVY TRAIN, THE(1974); RACE WITH THE DEVIL(1975); DRUM(1976); SMALL TOWN IN TEXAS, A(1976); W.C. FIELDS AND ME(1976); FINAL CHAPTER–WALKING TALL(1977)

David Tanner
SPLIT IMAGE(1982)

Fred Tanner
HEIDI(1954, Switz.); HEIDI AND PETER(1955, Switz.); SHADOWS GROW LONGER, THE(1962, Switz./Ger.)

Gita Tanner
CLASS(1983)

Gordon Tanner
YOU CAN'T BEAT THE IRISH(1952, Brit.); GAY ADVENTURE, THE(1953, Brit.); CAMPBELL'S KINGDOM(1957, Brit.); FIRE DOWN BELOW(1957, U.S./Brit.); TRIPLE DECEPTION(1957, Brit.); WOMAN OF MYSTERY, A(1957, Brit.); FLOODS OF FEAR(1958, Brit.); ON THE RUN(1958, Brit.); SHERIFF OF FRACTURED JAW, THE(1958, Brit.); CARRY ON SERGEANT(1959, Brit.); TIME LOCK(1959, Brit.); GREEN HELMET, THE(1961, Brit.); DR. STRANGELOVE: OR HOW I LEARNED TO STOP WORRYING AND LOVE THE BOMB(1964); RETURN OF MR. MOTO, THE(1965, Brit.); WHERE THE SPIES ARE(1965, Brit.); VULTURE, THE(1967, U.S./Brit./Can.)

Jack Tanner
Silents
JUST OFF BROADWAY(1929)

Jeffrey Tanner
IDOLMAKER, THE(1980)

Julius Tanner
LAST TRAIN FROM GUN HILL(1959)

Larry Tanner
MARS NEEDS WOMEN(1966)

Nicholas Tanner
ONE WAY OUT(1955, Brit.); UGLY DUCKLING, THE(1959, Brit.); FOLLOW THAT MAN(1961, Brit.); TRUNK, THE(1961, Brit.)

Paul Tanner
SUN VALLEY SERENADE(1941)

Peter Tanner
CROOKED ROAD, THE(, ed; KIND HEARTS AND CORONETS(1949, Brit.), ed; SCOTT OF THE ANTARCTIC(1949, Brit.). ed; BLUE LAMP, THE(1950, Brit.), ed; CAGE OF GOLD(1950, Brit.), ed; POOL OF LONDON(1951, Brit.), ed; GENTLE GUNMAN, THE(1952, Brit.), ed; SECRET PEOPLE(1952, Brit.), ed; CRUEL SEA, THE(1953), ed; I BELIEVE IN YOU(1953, Brit.), ed; HIGH AND DRY(1954, Brit.), ed; LEASE OF LIFE(1954, Brit.), ed; LIGHT TOUCH, THE(1955, Brit.), ed; NIGHT MY NUMBER CAME UP, THE(1955, Brit.), ed; WHO DONE IT?(1956, Brit.), ed; DECISION AGAINST TIME(1957, Brit.), ed; DAVY(1958, Brit.), ed; ANGRY HILLS, THE(1959, Brit.), ed; QUESTION OF ADULTERY, A(1959, Brit.), ed; HAND IN HAND(1960, Brit.), ed; LIGHT UP THE SKY(1960, Brit.), ed; NIGHT FIGHTERS, THE(1960), ed; GREYFRIARS BOBBY(1961, Brit.), ed; SODOM AND GOMORRAH(1962, U.S./Fr./Ital.), ed; JOLLY BAD FELLOW, A(1964, Brit.), ed; TAMAHINE(1964, Brit.), ed; DIAMONDS FOR BREAKFAST(1968, Brit.), ed; HUSBANDS(1970), ed; HOUSE THAT DRIPPED BLOOD, THE(1971, Brit.), ed; ASYLUM(1972, Brit.), ed; WHAT BECAME OF JACK AND JILL?(1972, Brit.), ed; AND NOW THE SCREAMING STARTS(1973, Brit.), ed; BEAST MUST DIE, THE(1974, Brit.), ed; HEDDA(1975, Brit.), ed; MAIDS, THE(1975, Brit.), ed; BELSTONE FOX, THE(1976, 1976), ed; NASTY HABITS(1976, Brit.), ed; STEVIE(1978, Brit.), ed; MONSTER CLUB, THE(1981, Brit.), ed

Ronny Tanner
ALL-AROUND REDUCED PERSONALITY–OUTTAKES, THE(1978, Ger.)

Sammy Tanner
CHANGES(1969)

Stella Tanner
MURDER MOST FOUL(1964, Brit.); OTLEY(1969, Brit.); 1,000 CONVICTS AND A WOMAN zero(1971, Brit.)

Tony Tanner
STRICTLY FOR THE BIRDS(1963, Brit.); PLEASURE GIRLS, THE(1966, Brit.); SANDWICH MAN, THE(1966, Brit.); STOP THE WORLD–I WANT TO GET OFF(1966, Brit.)

William Tanner
BADLANDS OF MONTANA(1957)

Michael Tannern
ONE-TRICK PONY(1980), p

Charles Tannes
DARK CORNER, THE(1946)

Elizabeth Tanney
THEY WERE SO YOUNG(1955)

Schweitzer Tanney
MAN WHO LOVED WOMEN, THE(1983)

Senilo Tanney
10(1979)

Sherloque Tanney
VICTOR/VICTORIA(1982)

Sidi Bin Tanney
CURSE OF THE PINK PANTHER(1983)

Stiffe Tanney
S.O.B.(1981)

Studs Tanney
WILD ROVERS(1971)

D.V. Tannlinger
LAW FOR TOMBSTONE(1937)

Louis Tanno
ONLY GOD KNOWS(1974, Can.)

Rita Marie Tanno
VAGABOND KING, THE(1956)

Rita Tanno
COUNTERPLOT(1959)

Mark Tannous
DEMON, THE(1981, S. Africa)

Philip Tannura
CIRCUS KID, THE(1928), ph; TAXI 13(1928), ph; LUCKY IN LOVE(1929), ph; COUNSEL'S OPINION(1933, Brit.), ph; CHANNEL CROSSING(1934, Brit.), ph; DIRTY WORK(1934, Brit.), ph; LADY IN DANGER(1934, Brit.), ph; CHARING CROSS ROAD(1935, Brit.), ph; FIGHTING STOCK(1935, Brit.), ph; STORMY WEATHER(1935, Brit.), ph; CRIMSON CIRCLE, THE(1936, Brit.), ph; DISHONOR BRIGHT(1936, Brit.), ph; I STAND CONDEMNED(1936, Brit.), ph; SOUTHERN ROSES(1936, Brit.), ph; DINNER AT THE RITZ(1937, Brit.), ph; LOVE FROM A STRANGER(1937, Brit.), ph; MAKE-UP(1937, Brit.), ph; BREAK THE NEWS(1938, Brit.), ph; DANGEROUS CARGO(1939, Brit.), ph; INSPECTOR HORNLEIGH(1939, Brit.), ph; SCHOOL FOR HUSBANDS(1939, Brit.), ph; DREAMING OUT LOUD(1940), ph; CONFESSIONS OF BOSTON BLACKIE(1941), ph; POISON PEN(1941, Brit.), ph; RETURN OF DANIEL BOONE, THE(1941), ph; SECRETS OF THE LONE WOLF(1941), ph; YOU'LL NEVER GET RICH(1941), ph; ALIAS BOSTON BLACKIE(1942), ph; COUNTER-ESPIONAGE(1942), ph; HELLO ANNAPOLIS(1942), ph; LUCKY LEGS(1942), ph; MAN WHO RETURNED TO LIFE, THE(1942), ph; PARACHUTE NURSE(1942), ph; SWEETHEART OF THE FLEET(1942), ph; DANGEROUS BLONDES(1943), ph; FOOTLIGHT GLAMOUR(1943), ph; GOOD LUCK, MR. YATES(1943), ph; LAUGH YOUR BLUES AWAY(1943), ph; REVEILLE WITH BEVERLY(1943), ph; THERE'S SOMETHING ABOUT A SOLDIER(1943), ph; KNICKERBOCKER HOLIDAY(1944), ph; PRISON SHIP(1945), ph; STRANGE ILLUSION(1945), ph; CRIME DOCTOR'S MAN HUNT(1946), ph; GENTLEMAN MISBEHAVES, THE(1946), ph; JUST BEFORE DAWN(1946), ph; MAN WHO DARED, THE(1946), ph; MYSTERIOUS INTRUDER(1946), ph; NIGHT EDITOR(1946), ph; OUT OF THE DEPTHS(1946), ph; CRIME DOCTOR'S GAMBLE(1947), ph; KEY WITNESS(1947), ph; KING OF THE WILD HORSES(1947), ph; MILLERSON CASE, THE(1947), ph; OLD-FASHIONED GIRL, AN(1948), ph; RETURN OF THE WHISTLER, THE(1948), ph; TRAPPED BY BOSTON BLACKIE(1948), ph; LONE WOLF AND HIS LADY, THE(1949), ph; SHAMROCK HILL(1949), ph; COUNTERSPY MEETS SCOTLAND YARD(1950), ph; CUSTOMS AGENT(1950), ph; FLYING SAUCER, THE(1950), ph; HI-JACKED(1950), ph; TOUGHER THEY COME, THE(1950), ph; CHAIN OF CIRCUMSTANCE(1951), ph; CHINA CORSAIR(1951), ph; CRIMINAL LAWYER(1951), ph; FLAME OF STAMBOUL(1957), ph
Silents
SWEET ADELINE(1926), ph; MAN IN THE ROUGH(1928), ph; MATINEE IDOL, THE(1928), ph; SALLY OF THE SCANDALS(1928), ph; SKINNER'S BIG IDEA(1928), ph

Phillip Tannura
MOTHER'S BOY(1929), ph; FOR VALOR(1937, Brit.), ph; STOLEN LIFE(1939, Brit.), ph; RICHEST MAN IN TOWN(1941), ph; TILLIE THE TOILER(1941), ph; TWO YANKS IN TRINIDAD(1942), ph; SHE HAS WHAT IT TAKES(1943), ph; TOWN WENT WILD, THE(1945), ph; BLONDIE KNOWS BEST(1946), ph; BABE RUTH STORY, THE(1948), ph; THERE'S A GIRL IN MY HEART(1949), ph; HARLEM GLOBETROTTERS, THE(1951), ph
Silents
JAKE THE PLUMBER(1927), ph; DEAD MAN'S CURVE(1928), ph
Armand Tanny
FRENCHMAN'S CREEK(1944); LADY IN THE DARK(1944); JET PILOT(1957)
Henry Tanous
SLEEPING BEAUTY(1959), anim
Tanry
CLEOPATRA JONES AND THE CASINO OF GOLD(1975 U. S. Hong Kong)
Julie Tanser
SUMMERDOG(1977), ed
Marilyn J. Tanser
GALAXINA(1980), p
Master Tansey
Silents
DESTRUCTION(1915)
Mrs. Tansey
Silents
JOAN OF THE WOODS(1918)
Derek Tansey
LAMP IN ASSASSIN MEWS, THE(1962, Brit.)
Emma Tansey
IF I HAD A MILLION(1932); GUN LORDS OF STIRRUP BASIN(1937); KNIGHT OF THE PLAINS(1939); LADY IN QUESTION, THE(1940); MEET JOHN DOE(1941); NEVER GIVE A SUCKER AN EVEN BREAK(1941)
John Tansey
Silents
BROKEN CHAINS(1916); LITTLE MISS HOOVER(1918); SKY RIDER, THE(1928)
Robert Tansey [Robert Emmett Tansey]
ARIZONA CYCLONE(1934), d, w; PARADISE CANYON(1935), w; PINTO RUS-TLERS(1937), w; GUN PACKER(1938), p; MAN'S COUNTRY(1938), p; MEXICALI KID, THE(1938), p; PAINTED TRAIL, THE(1938), p; OVERLAND MAIL(1939), p; TRIGGER SMITH(1939), p; WILD HORSE CANYON(1939), p; ARIZONA FRON-TIER(1940), w; DRIFTIN' KID, THE(1941), w; DYNAMITE CANYON(1941), p&d, w; RIDING THE SUNSET TRAIL(1941), p&d; WANDERERS OF THE WEST(1941), p; ARIZONA ROUNDUP(1942), p&d, w; LONE STAR LAW MEN(1942), p&d; TEXAS TO BATAAN(1942), p&d; TRAIL RIDERS(1942), d; WESTERN MAIL(1942), p&d; BLAZING GUNS(1943), p&d; HAUNTED RANCH, THE(1943), d; LAW RIDES AGAIN, THE(1943), p; TWO FISTED JUSTICE(1943), d; WILD HORSE STAMPEDE(1943), p; ARIZONA WHIRLWIND(1944), p&d; DEATH VALLEY RANGERS(1944), p&d; OUT-LAW TRAIL(1944), p&d; SONORA STAGECOACH(1944), p&d; WESTWARD BOUND(1944), p&d; WILDFIRE(1945), d; COLORADO SERENADE(1946), p&d; DRIFTIN' RIVER(1946), p&d; GOD'S COUNTRY(1946), p&d; STARS OVER TEX-AS(1946), p&d; TUMBLEWEED TRAIL(1946), p&d; WILD WEST(1946), p&d; EN-CHANTED VALLEY, THE(1948), d; SHAGGY(1948), d; RIDERS OF THE DUSK(1949), w; FEDERAL MAN(1950), d; FIGHTING STALLION, THE(1950), p, d; FORBIDDEN JUNGLE(1950), d; BADMAN'S GOLD(1951), p&d; CATTLE QUEEN(1951), d
Misc. Talkies
RIDERS OF RIO(1931), d; WHERE TRAILS END(1942), d
Sheridan Tansey
Silents
CONQUERED HEARTS(1918); OVER THE HILL TO THE POORHOUSE(1920)
Misc. Silents
FOOLISH VIRGIN, THE(1917)
Sherry Tansey
OPERATOR 13(1934); WAY OF THE WEST, THE(1934); NEW FRONTIER, THE(1935); RIDER OF THE LAW, THE(1935); GUNS AND GUITARS(1936); LAWLESS NINETIES, THE(1936); DOOMED AT SUNDOWN(1937); FIGHTING DEPUTY, THE(1937); GAMBLING TERROR, THE(1937); GUNS IN THE DARK(1937); HEADIN' FOR THE RIO GRANDE(1937); IDAHO KID, THE(1937); LAWMAN IS BORN, A(1937); LIGHTNIN' CRANDALL(1937); MOONLIGHT ON THE RANGE(1937); PINTO RUS-TLERS(1937); SILVER TRAIL, THE(1937); STARS OVER ARIZONA(1937); TRUSTED OUTLAW, THE(1937); WHISTLING BULLETS(1937); FEUD MAKER(1938); GUN PACKER(1938); GUNSMOKE TRAIL(1938); HEROES OF THE ALAMO(1938); IN EARLY ARIZONA(1938); MAN'S COUNTRY(1938); MEXICALI KID, THE(1938); PAROLED-TO DIE(1938); PHANTOM RANGER(1938); RANGER'S ROUNDUP, THE(1938); ROLLING CARAVANS(1938); STARLIGHT OVER TEXAS(1938); THUN-DER IN THE DESERT(1938); WEST OF RAINBOW'S END(1938); KNIGHT OF THE PLAINS(1939); LURE OF THE WASTELAND(1939); MAN FROM TEXAS, THE(1939); SILVER ON THE SAGE(1939); SIX-GUN RHYTHM(1939); TRIGGER SMITH(1939); WILD HORSE CANYON(1939); ARIZONA FRONTIER(1940); PHANTOM RAN-CHER(1940); DRIFTIN' KID, THE(1941); LONE RIDER CROSSES THE RIO, THE(1941); OUTLAWS OF THE RIO GRANDE(1941)
Misc. Talkies
RIDERS OF RIO(1931)
Silents
STEADFAST HEART, THE(1923); FIGHTING BOOB, THE(1926)
Misc. Silents
OBLIGIN' BUCKAROO, THE(1927)
Bob Tansill
DOWN THE STRETCH(1936); RACING BLOOD(1938)
Natasa Tanska
KRAKATIT(1948, Czech.)
Derek Tansley
DON'T SAY DIE(1950, Brit.); HORSE'S MOUTH, THE(1953, Brit.); KNIGHTS OF THE ROUND TABLE(1953); HIDE AND SEEK(1964, Brit.); SERVANT, THE(1964, Brit.); CRIMSON CULT, THE(1970, Brit.)
Alexander Tansman
PARIS UNDERGROUND(1945), m, md; SISTER KENNY(1946), m
Alexandre Tansman
POIL DE CAROTTE(1932, Fr.), m; FLESH AND FANTASY(1943), m

Savior Tanti
TRENCHCOAT(1983)
Saskia Cohen Tanugi
NEVER SAY NEVER AGAIN(1983)
Philip Tanura
REDHEAD FROM MANHATTAN(1954), ph
Tanya
PRAISE MARX AND PASS THE AMMUNITION(1970, Brit.)
Igor and Tanya
ROSE OF WASHINGTON SQUARE(1939)
Mark M. Tanz
INSIDE MOVES(1980), p
Warhawk Tanzania
DEVIL'S EXPRESS(1975)
Misc. Talkies
FORCE FOUR(1975)
Mrs. B. Tanzey
Silents
LONE HORSEMAN, THE(1929)
Lia Tanzi
CLARETTA AND BEN(1983, Ital., Fr.)
Mario Tanzi
ON THE RIGHT TRACK(1981)
Ricki Tanzi
JANIE(1944)
Josiane Tanzilli
PUSSYCAT, PUSSYCAT, I LOVE YOU(1970); AMARCORD(1974, Ital.)
Dario Tanzini
ROMEO AND JULIET(1968, Brit./Ital.)
Franz Tanzler
NOUS IRONS A PARIS(1949, Fr.), w
Hans Tanzler
WATCH ON THE RHINE(1943); RENDEZVOUS 24(1946); DESIRE ME(1947)
Jeanne Tanzy
RIVALS(1972)
Ho Chung Tao
BRUCE LEE-TRUE STORY(1976, Chi.)
Loh Ming Tao
LOVERS' ROCK(1966, Taiwan), m
Winiata Tapa
PICTURES(1982, New Zealand)
George Tapare
BEYOND THE REEF(1981)
Geo Taparelli
BELLISSIMA(1952, Ital.)
Robert G. Tapert
EVIL DEAD, THE(1983), p
Miguel Tapia
WITHOUT RESERVATIONS(1946); RIDE THE PINK HORSE(1947)
Jose Maria Tapiador
SON OF A GUNFIGHTER(1966, U.S./Span.), set d; GUNS OF THE MAGNIFICENT SEVEN(1969), art d; CANNON FOR CORDOBA(1970), art d; LAST RUN, THE(1971), art d; VALDEZ IS COMING(1971), art d; MAN CALLED NOON, THE(1973, Brit.), art d; SHAFT IN AFRICA(1973), art d; TEN LITTLE INDIANS(1975, Ital./Fr./Span./Ger.), set d; MARCH OR DIE(1977, Brit.), art d
Josefina Tapias
DAY THE HOTLINE GOT HOT, THE(1968, Fr./Span.)
Martin Tapin [Martin Tapak]
VOYAGE TO THE END OF THE UNIVERSE(1963, Czech.)
Sydney Tapler
HUNDRED HOUR HUNT(1953, Brit.)
Colin Tapley
DOUBLE DOOR(1934); LIMEHOUSE BLUES(1934); MURDER AT THE VANI-TIES(1934); PURSUIT OF HAPPINESS, THE(1934); BECKY SHARP(1935); BLACK ROOM, THE(1935); CRUSADES, THE(1935); LAST OUTPOST, THE(1935); LIVES OF A BENGAL LANCER(1935); PETER IBBETSON(1935); WITHOUT REGRET(1935); EAR-LY TO BED(1936); MY MARRIAGE(1936); RETURN OF SOPHIE LANG, THE(1936); SKY PARADE(1936); THANK YOU, JEEVES(1936); TILL WE MEET AGAIN(1936); TOO MANY PARENTS(1936); BULLDOG DRUMMOND ESCAPES(1937); CRIME NOBOBY SAW, THE(1937); HOTEL HAYWIRE(1937); KING OF GAMBLERS(1937); MAID OF SALEM(1937); NIGHT OF MYSTERY(1937); WILD MONEY(1937); BOO-LOO(1938); IF I WERE KING(1938); STORM OVER BENGAL(1938); LIGHT THAT FAILED, THE(1939); ARIZONA(1940); WOMEN IN WAR(1940); SAMSON AND DELI-LAH(1949); CLOUDBURST(1952, Brit.); DEAD ON COURSE(1952, Brit.); WIDE BOY(1952, Brit.); NOOSE FOR A LADY(1953, Brit.); STEEL KEY, THE(1953, Brit.); WHITE FIRE(1953, Brit.); DIAMOND WIZARD, THE(1954, Brit.); CASE OF THE RED MONKEY(1955, Brit.); DAM BUSTERS, THE(1955, Brit.); MURDER ON AP-PROVAL(1956, Brit.); STRANGER IN TOWN(1957, Brit.); BLOOD OF THE VAM-PIRE(1958, Brit.); SAFECRACKER, THE(1958, Brit.); HIGH JUMP(1959, Brit.); HONOURABLE MURDER, AN(1959, Brit.); INNOCENT MEETING(1959, Brit.); MAN ACCUSED(1959); COMPELLED(1960, Brit.); NIGHT TRAIN FOR INVERNESS(1960, Brit.); SO EVIL SO YOUNG(1961, Brit.); EMERGENCY(1962, Brit.); GANG WAR(1962, Brit.); LAMP IN ASSASSIN MEWS, THE(1962, Brit.); STRONGROOM(1962, Brit.); PARANOIAC(1963, Brit.); SHADOW OF FEAR(1963, Brit.); FRAULEIN DOK-TOR(1969, Ital./Yugo.)
Rose Tapley
CHARLATAN, THE(1929); HIS FIRST COMMAND(1929); RESURRECTION(1931)
Silents
CHRISTIAN, THE(1914); EVE'S DAUGHTER(1918); JAVA HEAD(1923); PONY EXPRESS, THE(1925); REDEEMING SIN, THE(1925); PRINCE OF PILSEN, THE(1926); IT(1927); OUT OF THE PAST(1927)
Misc. Silents
MY OFFICIAL WIFE(1914); WHO KILLED JOE MERRION?(1915); CHATTEL, THE(1916); SHADOWS OF THE PAST(1919); HER MAJESTY(1922)
Jonathan Taplin
UNDER FIRE(1983), p
Jonathan T. Taplin
MEAN STREETS(1973), p; GRAVY TRAIN, THE(1974), p

Terence Taplin
ALFIE DARLING(1975, Brit.)
Gordie Tapp
Misc. Talkies
SWEET COUNTRY ROAD(1981)
James Tapp
STRANGE SHADOWS IN AN EMPTY ROOM(1977, Can./Ital.)
Jimmy Tapp
OF UNKNOWN ORIGIN(1983, Can.)
Tony Tapp
MANGANINNIE(1982, Aus.)
Shane Tapper
NORMAN LOVES ROSE(1982, Aus.)
Horst Tappert
GREAT BRITISH TRAIN ROBBERY, THE(1967, Ger.); NEW LIFE STYLE, THE(1970, Ger.)
George Tapps
SPLENDOR IN THE GRASS(1961), ch; ANGEL IN MY POCKET(1969)
Georgie Tapps
VOGUES OF 1938(1937); 52ND STREET(1937)
Jonie Taps
WHEN YOU'RE SMILING(1950), p; SUNNY SIDE OF THE STREET(1951), p; RAINBOW 'ROUND MY SHOULDER(1952), p; SOUND OFF(1952), p; ALL ASHORE(1953), p; CRUISIN' DOWN THE RIVER(1953), p; DRIVE A CROOKED ROAD(1954), p; BRING YOUR SMILE ALONG(1955), p; THREE FOR THE SHOW(1955), p; HE LAUGHED LAST(1956), p; SHADOW ON THE WINDOW, THE(1957), p
Horace Tapscott
SWEET JESUS, PREACHER MAN(1973), m
Kay Tapscott
LADIES MAN, THE(1961)
Mark Tapscott
LATE LIZ, THE(1971); BLACK GUNN(1972)
Mario Taquibulos
ONCE BEFORE I DIE(1967, U.S./Phil.)
Tar
SABOTEUR(1942)
Tara Irish Dancers
KATHLEEN(1938, Ireland)
Daniel Taradash
FOR LOVE OR MONEY(1939), w; GOLDEN BOY(1939), w; LITTLE BIT OF HEAVEN, A(1940), w; KNOCK ON ANY DOOR(1949), w; DON'T BOTHER TO KNOCK(1952), w; RANCHO NOTORIOUS(1952), w; FROM HERE TO ETERNITY(1953), w; DESIREE(1954), w; PICNIC(1955), w; STORM CENTER(1956), d, w; BELL, BOOK AND CANDLE(1958), w; MORITURI(1965), w; HAWAII(1966), w; CASTLE KEEP(1969), w; DOCTORS' WIVES(1971), w; OTHER SIDE OF MIDNIGHT, THE(1977), w
Rajen Tarafder
RIVER, THE(1961, India), w&d
Anna Tarallo
JOAN AT THE STAKE(1954, Ital./Fr.)
Armando Tarallo
LOVE AND MARRIAGE(1966, Ital.)
Giovanni Tarallo
FOR A FEW DOLLARS MORE(1967, Ital./Ger./Span.); HAWKS AND THE SPARROWS, THE(1967, Ital.); MORE THAN A MIRACLE(1967, Ital./Fr.)
George Taran
FABULOUS WORLD OF JULES VERNE, THE(1961, Czech.), ph, spec eff
Anya Taranda
MURDER AT THE VANITIES(1934); MAN WHO BROKE THE BANK AT MONTE CARLO, THE(1935); STRIKE ME PINK(1936); THESE THREE(1936); ZIEGFELD GIRL(1941)
John Tarangelo
PUSHOVER(1954); RETURN FROM THE SEA(1954); RIOT IN CELL BLOCK 11(1954)
Johnny Tarangelo
WILD ONE, THE(1953); JEANNE EAGELS(1957)
Jiri Tarantik
BARON MUNCHAUSEN(1962, Czech.), ph; LAST ACT OF MARTIN WESTON, THE(1970, Can./Czech.), ph
Brian Tarantina
1984
COTTON CLUB, THE(1984)
Nino Taranto
TWO COLONELS, THE(1963, Ital.)
Martin B. Taras
WIZARDS(1977), anim
Enzo Tarascio
CONFORMIST, THE(1971, Ital., Fr); TRINITY IS STILL MY NAME(1971, Ital.); DEAD ARE ALIVE, THE(1972, Yugo./Ger./Ital.)
D. Tarasov
WINGS OF VICTORY(1941, USSR), w; HOUSE WITH AN ATTIC, THE(1964, USSR)
Pavel Tarasov
GORDEYEV FAMILY, THE(1961, U.S.S.R.)
Alla Tarasova
THUNDERSTORM(1934, USSR)
Zenia Tarasova
WINGS OF VICTORY(1941, USSR)
Georgi Taratorkin
CRIME AND PUNISHMENT(1975, USSR)
Tarbaby the Horse
LAST OUTPOST, THE(1951)
Lorna Tarbat
HEADLINE(1943, Brit.)
Jean-Jacques Tarbe
BANZAI(1983, Fr.), ph
J.J. Tarbes
BLACKOUT(1978, Fr./Can.), ph
Jean-Jacques Tarbes
FAREWELL, FRIEND(1968, Fr./Ital.), ph; BORSALINO(1970, Fr.), ph; POPSY POP(1971, Fr.), ph; TWO MEN IN TOWN(1973, Fr.), ph; BORSALINO AND CO.(1974, Fr.), ph

1984
MY NEW PARTNER(1984, Fr.), ph
Monique Tarbes
MAGNIFICENT ONE, THE(1974, Fr./Ital.); LUMIERE(1976, Fr.)
Jimmy Tarbuck
PLANK, THE(1967, Brit.); LOLA(1971, Brit./Ital.)
Mary Tarcai
HALF ANGEL(1951)
Mary Tarcal
ARGYLE SECRETS, THE(1948)
M.N. Tarchanov
HOUSE OF GREED(1934, USSR)
Iginio Ugo Tarchetti
PASSION OF LOVE(1982, Ital./Fr.), w
Mario Tarchetti
8 ½(1963, Ital.)
Graham Tardif
1984
TAIL OF THE TIGER(1984, Aus.), m
Sergio Tardioli
IDENTIFICATION OF A WOMAN(1983, Ital.)
Harry Tardios
MOON-SPINNERS, THE(1964)
Bruno Tardon
1984
PAR OU T'ES RENTRE? ON T'A PAS VUE SORTIR(1984, Fr./Tunisia), w
Henri Tarerna
MAGNIFICENT SINNER(1963, Fr.), ed
Le Tari
FAST BREAK(1979); ONION FIELD, THE(1979)
Yuri Tarich
Misc. Silents
WINGS OF A SERF(1926, USSR), d
Sameen Tarighati
ONE-TRICK PONY(1980)
Javier Torres Tarija
PEARL, THE(1948, U.S./Mex.), art d
Tarita
MUTINY ON THE BOUNTY(1962)
Mikhail Tariverdiyev
SANDU FOLLOWS THE SUN(1965, USSR), m; WELCOME KOSTYA!(1965, USSR), m
Gyoergy Tarjan
FORTRESS, THE(1979, Hung.)
Fran Tarkenton
M(1970)
M.M. Tarkhanov
DIARY OF A REVOLUTIONIST(1932, USSR); THUNDERSTORM(1934, USSR)
Mikhail Tarkhanov
Misc. Silents
RANKS AND PEOPLE(1929, USSR)
Z. Tarkhovskaya
Misc. Silents
ADVENTURES OF AN OCTOBERITE, THE(1924, USSR)
Booth Tarkington
GERALDINE(1929), w; MISTER ANTONIO(1929), w; RIVER OF ROMANCE(1929), w; CAMEO KIRBY(1930), w; MONTE CARLO(1930), w; BAD SISTER(1931), w; FATHER'S SON(1931), w; MILLIONAIRE, THE(1931), w; PENROD AND SAM(1931), w; BUSINESS AND PLEASURE(1932), w; ALICE ADAMS(1935), w; MISSISSIPPI(1935), w; GENTLE JULIA(1936), w; CLARENCE(1937), w; PENROD AND SAM(1937), w; PENROD AND HIS TWIN BROTHER(1938), w; PENROD'S DOUBLE TROUBLE(1938), w; LITTLE ORVIE(1940), w; SEVENTEEN(1940), w; FATHER'S SON(1941), w; MAGNIFICENT AMBERSONS, THE(1942), w; PRESENTING LILY MARS(1943), w; MONSIEUR BEAUCAIRE(1946), w; ON MOONLIGHT BAY(1951), w; BY THE LIGHT OF THE SILVERY MOON(1953), w
Silents
MAN FROM HOME, THE(1914), w; SPRINGTIME(1915), w; FLIRT, THE(1922), w; PENROD(1922), w; ALICE ADAMS(1923), w; BOY OF MINE(1923), w; GENTLE JULIA(1923), w; PENROD AND SAM(1923), w; FIGHTING COWARD, THE(1924), w; MONSIEUR BEAUCAIRE(1924), w
Rockne Tarkington
SOLDIER IN THE RAIN(1963); CLARENCE, THE CROSS-EYED LION(1965); TELL ME IN THE SUNLIGHT(1967); GREAT WHITE HOPE, THE(1970); MELINDA(1972); BLACK SAMSON(1974); NO MERCY MAN, THE(1975); GREAT GUNDOWN, THE(1977); BALTIMORE BULLET, THE(1980)
1984
ICE PIRATES, THE(1984)
Misc. Talkies
BLACK STARLET(1974); ZEBRA FORCE(1977)
Andrey Tarkovskiy
VIOLIN AND ROLLER(1962, USSR), d, w
Andrei Tarkovsky
MY NAME IS IVAN(1963, USSR), d; SOLARIS(1972, USSR), d, w; ANDREI ROUBLOV(1973, USSR), d, w; STALKER(1982, USSR), d, prod d
1984
NOSTALGHIA(1984, USSR/Ital.), d, w
I. Tarkovsky
MY NAME IS IVAN(1963, USSR)
Michal Tarkowski
MAN OF MARBLE(1979, Pol.)
Sadik Tarlan
FIVE FINGERS(1952)
Harriette Tarler
JOKER IS WILD, THE(1957)
Frank Tarloff
CAMPUS RHYTHM(1943), w; BEHAVE YOURSELF(1951), w; FATHER GOOSE(1964), w; DOUBLE MAN, THE(1967), w; GUIDE FOR THE MARRIED MAN, A(1967), w; SECRET WAR OF HARRY FRIGG, THE(1968), w; ONCE YOU KISS A STRANGER(1969), w

Florence Tarlow
WHERE'S POPPA?(1970); GANG THAT COULDN'T SHOOT STRAIGHT, THE(1971); PANIC IN NEEDLE PARK(1971); HAPPY HOOKER, THE(1975); ARTHUR(1981)

Alan Tarlton
MEN AGAINST THE SUN(1953, Brit.); ESCAPE IN THE SUN(1956, Brit.); WHITE HUNTRESS(1957, Brit.); MANSTER, THE(1962, Jap.)

Michael Tarn
CLOCKWORK ORANGE, A(1971, Brit.)

Aulekki Tarnanen
MAKE LIKE A THIEF(1966, Fin.)

Toby Tarnow
ONE PLUS ONE(1961, Can.); NOBODY WAVED GOODBYE(1965, Can.); ONLY GOD KNOWS(1974, Can.); UTILITIES(1983, Can.)

Mary Jo Tarola
AFFAIR WITH A STRANGER(1953)

Giovanni Tarollo
GHOSTS, ITALIAN STYLE(1969, Ital./Fr.)

Shaul Taron
1984
SAHARA(1984)

Didier Tarot
LE GENDARME ET LES EXTRATERRESTRES(1978, Fr.), ph

M. Tarov
Misc. Silents
BLOODY EAST, THE(1915, USSR)

Lotte Tarp
CASE OF THE 44'S, THE(1964 Brit./Den.); WEEKEND(1964, Den.); CRAZY PARADISE(1965, Den.); JOKERS, THE(1967, Brit.); MAN WHO THOUGHT LIFE, THE(1969, Den.); PEOPLE MEET AND SWEET MUSIC FILLS THE HEART(1969, Den./Swed.)

Svend Erik Tarp
GOLDEN MOUNTAINS(1958, Den.), m

Tom Tarpey
FM(1978); NINE TO FIVE(1980)

Candece Tarpley
GANJA AND HESS(1973)
Misc. Talkies
BLOOD COUPLE(1974)

Sam Tarpley
FORTY ACRE FEUD(1965); THAT TENNESSEE BEAT(1966); TRACK OF THUNDER(1967)

Eschilo Tarquini
WAR AND PEACE(1956, Ital./U.S.)

Cynthia Tarr
1984
OH GOD! YOU DEVIL(1984)

Justin Tarr
BULLITT(1968)

Renata Tarrago
DEADFALL(1968, Brit.)

Jerry Tarrant
BEFORE WINTER COMES(1969, Brit.)

John Tarrant
LUGGAGE OF THE GODS(1983)

Manville Tarrant
DULCIMER STREET(1948, Brit.); GUNMAN HAS ESCAPED, A(1948, Brit.); VENGEANCE IS MINE(1948, Brit.); CHEER THE BRAVE(1951, Brit.)

Carmen Tarrazo
LOST COMMAND, THE(1966); SON OF A GUNFIGHTER(1966, U.S./Span.)

Troy Tarrell
BADMAN'S GOLD(1951)

Suzette Tarri
SOMEWHERE IN CIVVIES(1943, Brit.)

Abel Tarride
ENTENTE CORDIALE(1939, Fr.)

Jacques Tarride
NANA(1957, Fr./Ital.)

Jaques Tarride
AMOUR, AMOUR(1937, Fr.)

The Tarriers
CALYPSO HEAT WAVE(1957)

Elsie Tarron
Silents
CYCLONE OF THE RANGE(1927); SKY-HIGH SAUNDERS(1927)

Antonio Tarruella
LAST RUN, THE(1971)

Tony Tarruella
1984
YELLOW HAIR AND THE FORTRESS OF GOLD(1984)

Lillian Tarry
SWEET JESUS, PREACHER MAN(1973)

Bernhard Tarschys
DEVIL, THE(1963)

Jay Tarses
UP THE ACADEMY(1980), w; GREAT MUPPET CAPER, THE(1981), w
1984
MUPPETS TAKE MANHATTAN, THE(1984), w

Micheal Tarshanoff
Misc. Silents
CRIME AND PUNISHMENT(1929, Ger.)

Harold Tarshis
CONCENTRATIN' KID, THE(1930), w; TRAILING TROUBLE(1930), w; CARNIVAL LADY(1933), w; DECEPTION(1933), w; FAST COMPANY(1938), w; JONES FAMILY IN HOLLYWOOD, THE(1939), w; STOP, LOOK, AND LOVE(1939), w; WHISPERING ENEMIES(1939), w; HIGH SCHOOL(1940), w; JAIL HOUSE BLUES(1942), w; MUG TOWN(1943), w; ADVENTURES OF DON COYOTE(1947), w
Silents
CLEARING THE TRAIL(1928), t; KING OF THE RODEO(1929), t; LARIAT KID, THE(1929), t; POINTS WEST(1929), t

Ignacio Lopez Tarso
LA CUCARACHA(1961, Mex.); EMPTY STAR, THE(1962, Mex.); NAZARIN(1968, Mex.)
1984
UNDER THE VOLCANO(1984)

Alex Tartaglia
PRINCE AND THE PAUPER, THE(1969), w

James Tartan
MARIGOLD MAN(1970)

Mara Tartar
MUMMY'S HAND, THE(1940)

Clara Tarte
NAMU, THE KILLER WHALE(1966)

Henry Tarvainen
WINTER KEPT US WARM(1968, Can.)

Jim G. Tarver
Silents
JACK AND THE BEANSTALK(1917)

Leonard Tarver
BEAST WITH A MILLION EYES, THE(1956)

Tony Tarver
HAMLET(1948, Brit.)

Tarzan
PARADE OF THE WEST(1930); RANGE LAW(1931); COME ON TARZAN(1933); KING OF THE ARENA(1933); LONE AVENGER, THE(1933); INSIDE INFORMATION(1934); WESTERN COURAGE(1935); WESTERN FRONTIER(1935); DEATH RIDES THE RANGE(1940)

Tarzan the Horse
SENOR AMERICANO(1929); FIGHTING LEGION, THE(1930); MOUNTAIN JUSTICE(1930); SONG OF THE CABELLERO(1930); SONS OF THE SADDLE(1930); FIGHTING THRU(1931); TWO GUN MAN, THE(1931); DYNAMITE RANCH(1932); HELL FIRE AUSTIN(1932); POCATELLO KID(1932); SUNSET TRAIL(1932); TOMBSTONE CANYON(1932); WHISTLIN' DAN(1932); PHANTOM THUNDERBOLT, THE(1933); FIDDLIN' BUCKAROO, THE(1934); HONOR OF THE RANGE(1934); SMOKING GUNS(1934); TRAIL DRIVE, THE(1934); WHEELS OF DESTINY(1934); IN OLD SANTA FE(1935); FUGITIVE SHERIFF, THE(1936); HEIR TO TROUBLE(1936); HEROES OF THE RANGE(1936); LAWLESS RIDERS(1936); TRAILING TROUBLE(1937); SIX SHOOTIN' SHERIFF(1938); WHIRLWIND HORSEMAN(1938); LIGHTNING STRIKES WEST(1940); PHANTOM RANCHER(1940)
Silents
HAUNTED RANGE, THE(1926); UNKNOWN CAVALIER, THE(1926); SOMEWHERE IN SONORA(1927); LAWLESS LEGION, THE(1929); ROYAL RIDER, THE(1929)

Tarzan the Police Dog
Misc. Talkies
MILLION DOLLAR HAUL(1935)

Herman Tarzana
BLOOD AND BLACK LACE(1965, Ital.), ph

John Tarzenberger
VALENTINO(1977, Brit.)

Erol Tas [Errol Tash]
DRY SUMMER(1967, Turkey)

Kei Tasaka
GOYOKIN(1969, Jap.), w

Jun Tasaki
SEVEN SAMURAI, THE(1956, Jap.)

Alessandro Tasca
NEVER TAKE NO FOR AN ANSWER(1952, Brit./Ital.); GOSPEL ACCORDING TO ST. MATTHEW, THE(1966, Fr., Ital.)

Herbert Taschner
CROSS OF IRON(1977, Brit., Ger.), ed

Ingeborg Taschner
DUCK RINGS AT HALF PAST SEVEN, THE(1969, Ger./Ital.), ed

Rai Tasco
BLACK GESTAPO, THE(1975)

Bill Tasgal
I SPIT ON YOUR GRAVE(1983)

Steven Tash
CHRISTINE(1983)
1984
GHOSTBUSTERS(1984)

Kikue Tashiro
1984
MOSCOW ON THE HUDSON(1984)

Frank Tashlin
DELIGHTFULLY DANGEROUS(1945), w; VARIETY GIRL(1947), w; FULLER BRUSH MAN(1948), w; ONE TOUCH OF VENUS(1948), w; PALEFACE, THE(1948), w; LOVE HAPPY(1949), w; MISS GRANT TAKES RICHMOND(1949), w; FULLER BRUSH GIRL, THE(1950), w; GOOD HUMOR MAN, THE(1950), w; KILL THE UMPIRE(1950), w; WOMAN OF DISTINCTION, A(1950), w; LEMON DROP KID, THE(1951), w; FIRST TIME, THE(1952), d, w; SON OF PALEFACE(1952), d, w; MARRY ME AGAIN(1953), d&w; SUSAN SLEPT HERE(1954), d; ARTISTS AND MODELS(1955), d, w; GIRL CAN'T HELP IT, THE(1956), p&d; HOLLYWOOD OR BUST(1956), d; LIEUTENANT WORE SKIRTS, THE(1956), d, w; SCARLET HOUR, THE(1956), w; WILL SUCCESS SPOIL ROCK HUNTER?(1957), p,d&w; GEISHA BOY, THE(1958), d&w; ROCK-A-BYE BABY(1958), d&w; SAY ONE FOR ME(1959), p&d; CINDERFELLA(1960), d&w; BACHELOR FLAT(1962), d, w; IT'S ONLY MONEY(1962), d; MAN FROM THE DINERS' CLUB, THE(1963), d; WHO'S MINDING THE STORE?(1963), d, w; DISORDERLY ORDERLY, THE(1964), d, w; ALPHABET MURDERS, THE(1966), d; GLASS BOTTOM BOAT, THE(1966), d; CAPRICE(1967), d, w; PRIVATE NAVY OF SGT. O'FARRELL, THE(1968), d, w; SHAKIEST GUN IN THE WEST, THE(1968), w

Lilyan Tashman
MANHATTAN COCKTAIL(1928); BULLDOG DRUMMOND(1929); GOLD DIGGERS OF BROADWAY(1929); LONE WOLF'S DAUGHTER, THE(1929); MARRIAGE PLAYGROUND, THE(1929); NEW YORK NIGHTS(1929); TRIAL OF MARY DUGAN, THE(1929); CAT CREEPS, THE(1930); LEATHERNECKING(1930); MATRIMONIAL BED, THE(1930); NO, NO NANETTE(1930); ON THE LEVEL(1930); PUTTIN' ON THE RITZ(1930); FINN AND HATTIE(1931); GIRLS ABOUT TOWN(1931); MAD PARADE, THE(1931); MILLIE(1931); MURDER BY THE CLOCK(1931); ONE HEAVENLY

NIGHT(1931); ROAD TO RENO(1931); UP POPS THE DEVIL(1931); SCARLET DAWN(1932); THOSE WE LOVE(1932); WISER SEX, THE(1932); MAMA LOVES PAPA(1933); TOO MUCH HARMONY(1933); RIP TIDE(1934); WINE, WOMEN, AND SONG(1934); FRANKIE AND JOHNNY(1936)
Silents
IS LOVE EVERYTHING?(1924); NELLIE, THE BEAUTIFUL CLOAK MODEL(1924); BRIGHT LIGHTS(1925); GIRL WHO WOULDN'T WORK, THE(1925); PORTS OF CALL(1925); PRETTY LADIES(1925); LOVE'S BLINDNESS(1926); SIBERIA(1926); SKYROCKET, THE(1926); SO THIS IS PARIS(1926); WHISPERING SMITH(1926); CAMILLE(1927); FRENCH DRESSING(1927); STOLEN BRIDE, THE(1927); TEXAS STEER, A(1927); WOMAN WHO DID NOT CARE, THE(1927); CRAIG'S WIFE(1928); PHYLLIS OF THE FOLLIES(1928); TAKE ME HOME(1928); HARDBOILED(1929)
Misc. Silents
MANHANDLED(1924); WINNER TAKE ALL(1924); I'LL SHOW YOU THE TOWN(1925); SEVEN DAYS(1925); FOR ALIMONY ONLY(1926); ROCKING MOON(1926); DON'T TELL THE WIFE(1927); PRINCE OF HEADWAITERS, THE(1927); LADY RAFFLES(1928)

Piero Tasi
WHITE NIGHTS(1961, Ital./Fr.), cos

Zara Tasil
SCREAM IN THE NIGHT(1943)

Maggie Task
STRANGER IS WATCHING, A(1982); VERDICT, THE(1982); LIANNA(1983)

Harold Tasker
JULIUS CAESAR(1952)

Robert Tasker
DOCTOR X(1932), w; HELL'S HIGHWAY(1932), w; SECRETS OF THE FRENCH POLICE(1932), w; HERE COMES TROUBLE(1936), w; JOHN MEADE'S WO-MAN(1937), w; SAN QUENTIN(1937), w; BACK DOOR TO HEAVEN(1939), w; SE-CRET SEVEN, THE(1940), w, w; HOME IN WYOMIN'(1942), w; SECRETS OF THE UNDERGROUND(1943), w

Tiger Tasker
TROUBLE BREWING(1939, Brit.)

Taskin
ENEMIES OF PROGRESS(1934, USSR); HOUSE OF GREED(1934, USSR)

Eric Taslitz
AMERICAN POP(1981)

Alain Tasma
LAST METRO, THE(1981, Fr.)

Charles Tasman
MASSACRE HILL(1949, Brit.); GLENROWAN AFFAIR, THE(1951, Aus.); SMILEY GETS A GUN(1959, Brit.)

Rolf Tasna
TWO NIGHTS WITH CLEOPATRA(1953, Ital.); DEVIL IS A WOMAN, THE(1975, Brit./Ital.)

Maria Tasnady-Fekete
KIND STEPMOTHER(1936, Hung.)

Riccardo Tassani
LOYALTY OF LOVE(1937, Ital.)

Aldo Tassara
YOUNG GIANTS(1983)

Francois Tasse
TAKE IT ALL(1966, Can.); WAITING FOR CAROLINE(1969, Can.)

Gustave Tassell
PLAY IT AS IT LAYS(1972), cos

Reba Tassell
GOOD MORNING, MISS DOVE(1955); BRASS LEGEND, THE(1956)

Franz Tassie
LITTLE MELODY FROM VIENNA(1948, Aust.), w; ANGEL WITH THE TRUMPET, THE(1950, Brit.), w

Torquato Tasso
MIGHTY CRUSADERS, THE(1961, Ital.), w

Christian Tassou
NIGHTS OF CABIRIA(1957, Ital.)

Vasilia Tastaman
FANTASTIC COMEDY, A(1975, Rum.)

Joe E. Tata
UNHOLY ROLLERS(1972)

Joe Tata
HICKEY AND BOGGS(1972)

Ben Tatar
THIN RED LINE, THE(1964); CRACK IN THE WORLD(1965); LONG DUEL, THE(1967, Brit.); LAND RAIDERS(1969); WIND AND THE LION, THE(1975)

George Tatar
RICH, YOUNG AND PRETTY(1951)

Katrin Tatar
RICH, YOUNG AND PRETTY(1951)

Jun Tatara
RICKSHAW MAN, THE(1960, Jap.); HAPPINESS OF US ALONE(1962, Jap.); ROAD TO ETERNITY(1962, Jap.)

Tom Tataranowicz
HEY, GOOD LOOKIN'(1982), anim

Maria Tatarczuk
CHRONOPOLIS(1982, Fr.), anim

Jun Tatari
SEVEN SAMURAI, THE(1956, Jap.)

V. Tatarinov
MARRIAGE OF BALZAMINOV, THE(1966, USSR)

Cullen Tate
Silents
SIXTY CENTS AN HOUR(1923); CARNIVAL GIRL, THE(1926), d
Misc. Silents
TRY AND GET IT(1924), d

Dennis Tate
SHAFT(1971); NO PLACE TO HIDE(1975)

Ernie Tate
LANDSLIDE(1937, Brit.); FLASHDANCE(1983)

Harry Tate
HER FIRST AFFAIRE(1932, Brit.); COUNSEL'S OPINION(1933, Brit.); I SPY(1933, Brit.); MY LUCKY STAR(1933, Brit.); HAPPY(1934, Brit.); HYDE PARK COR-NER(1935, Brit.); LOOK UP AND LAUGH(1935, Brit.); REGAL CAVALCADE(1935, Brit.); KEEP YOUR SEATS PLEASE(1936, Brit.); VARIETY PARADE(1936, Brit.); SAM SMALL LEAVES TOWN(1937, Brit.); TAKE A CHANCE(1937, Brit.); WINGS OF THE MORNING(1937, Brit.); MEN OF THE SEA(1951, Brit.)
Silents
MOTORING(1927, Brit.), a, w

John Tate
SMITHY(1946, Aus.); PACIFIC ADVENTURE(1947, Aus.); ON THE BEACH(1959); SMILEY GETS A GUN(1959, Brit.); DREAM MAKER, THE(1963, Brit.); JULIUS CAESAR(1970, Brit.)

Julie Tate
GUIDE FOR THE MARRIED MAN, A(1967)

Kevin Tate
BULLET FOR A BADMAN(1964); SEVEN FACES OF DR. LAO(1964); YOUR CHEATIN' HEART(1964); FIRECREEK(1968)

Lincoln Tate
BATTLE OF THE AMAZONS(1973, Ital./Span.); LEGEND OF THE LONE RANGER, THE(1981)
Misc. Talkies
FULLER REPORT, THE(1966)

Lola Tate
Misc. Talkies
GIRL TROUBLE(1933)

Michael Tate
IF YOU COULD SEE WHAT I HEAR(1982)

Nicholas Tate
SUMARINE X-1(1969, Brit.)

Nick Tate
DEVIL'S PLAYGROUND, THE(1976, Aus.); SUMMERFIELD(1977, Aus.)
Misc. Talkies
LICENSED TO LOVE AND KILL(1979, Brit.)

Norman Tate
FANTASIA(1940), anim; PINOCCHIO(1940), anim

Patricia Tate
UNEXPECTED GUEST(1946); DANGEROUS VENTURE(1947)

Reginald Tate
TANGLED EVIDENCE(1934, Brit.); WHISPERING TONGUES(1934, Brit.); PHAN-TOM LIGHT, THE(1935, Brit.); RIVERSIDE MURDER, THE(1935, Brit.); MAN BE-HIND THE MASK, THE(1936, Brit.); DARK JOURNEY(1937, Brit.); FOR VALOR(1937, Brit.); TOO DANGEROUS TO LIVE(1939, Brit.); IT HAPPENED TO ONE MAN(1941, Brit.); POISON PEN(1941, Brit.); NEXT OF KIN(1942, Brit.); COLONEL BLIMP(1945, Brit.); MADONNA OF THE SEVEN MOONS(1945, Brit.); WAY AHEAD, THE(1945, Brit.); MAN FROM MOROCCO, THE(1946, Brit.); SO WELL REMEMBERED(1947, Brit.); DIAMOND CITY(1949, Brit.); SILK NOOSE, THE(1950, Brit.); INHERITANCE, THE(1951, Brit.); MIDNIGHT EPISODE(1951, Brit.); SECRET PEOPLE(1952, Brit.); STORY OF ROBIN HOOD, THE(1952, Brit.); I'LL GET YOU(1953, Brit.); MALTA STORY(1954, Brit.); KING'S RHAPSODY(1955, Brit.)

Richard Tate
WILD SCENE, THE(1970)

Ronald Tate
VARIETY PARADE(1936, Brit.)

Ronnie Tate
Silents
MOTORING(1927, Brit.)

Sharon Tate
DON'T MAKE WAVES(1967); EYE OF THE DEVIL(1967, Brit.); FEARLESS VAM-PIRE KILLERS, OR PARDON ME BUT YOUR TEETH ARE IN MY NECK, THE(1967); VALLEY OF THE DOLLS(1967); WRECKING CREW, THE(1968); TWELVE PLUS ONE(1970, Fr./Ital.)

Sylvia Tate
WOMAN ON THE RUN(1950), w; FUZZY PINK NIGHTGOWN, THE(1957), w

Tiffany Tate
GENERAL MASSACRE(1973, U.S./Bel.)

John Tateham
WRONG BOX, THE(1966, Brit.)

Hiroshi Tatehara
YOSAKOI JOURNEY(1970, Jap.)

Harry Tatelman
UNDERWATER!(1955), p; HOT BLOOD(1956), p; RUN FOR THE SUN(1956), p; INCIDENT AT PHANTOM HILL(1966), p, w; VALLEY OF MYSTERY(1967), p; COUNTERFEIT KILLER, THE(1968), p; RAID ON ROMMEL(1971), p

Jacques Tati
DEVIL IN THE FLESH, THE(1949, Fr.); SYLVIA AND THE PHANTOM(1950, Fr.); JOUR DE FETE(1952, Fr.), a, d, w; MR. HULOT'S HOLIDAY(1954, Fr.), a, p, d, w; MY UNCLE(1958, Fr.), a, p&d, w; TRAFFIC(1972, Fr.), a, d, w; PLAYTIME(1973, Fr.), a, d, w

Branco Tatic
WITNESS OUT OF HELL(1967, Ger./Yugo.)

Branko Tatic
NINTH CIRCLE, THE(1961, Yugo.)

Josif Tatic
HOROSCOPE(1950, Yugo.)

Sophie Tatischeff "Tati"
TRAFFIC(1972, Fr.), ed; POURQUOI PAS!(1979, Fr.), ed

Tatjana Gsovsky and Her Dancers
SCHLAGER-PARADE(1953)

Michele Tatosian
SLEEPAWAY CAMP(1983), p

Ryutaro Tatsumi
TUNNEL TO THE SUN(1968, Jap.); GIRL I ABANDONED, THE(1970, Jap.)
1984
BALLAD OF NARAYAMA, THE(1984, Jap.)

Pietro Tattanelli
CONJUGAL BED, THE(1963, Ital.)

LY YEARS(1982, U.S./Fr.), ed
Joost Taverne
SPLITTING UP(1981, Neth.), p
Albert Tavernier
Silents
MAN FROM BEYOND, THE(1922)
Misc. Silents
STOP THIEF(1915); BETTY OF GRAYSTONE(1916); FLOWER OF FAITH, THE(1916); SAINTS AND SINNERS(1916); GOD'S MAN(1917)
B. Tavernier
QUESTION, THE(1977, Fr.), p
Bertrand Tavernier
CLOCKMAKER, THE(1976, Fr.), d; LET JOY REIGN SUPREME(1977, Fr.), d, w; JUDGE AND THE ASSASSIN, THE(1979, Fr.), d, w; DEATHWATCH(1980, Fr./Ger.), d, w; COUP DE TORCHON(1981, Fr.), d, w
1984
SUNDAY IN THE COUNTRY, A(1984, Fr.), d, w
Colo Tavernier
1984
SUNDAY IN THE COUNTRY, A(1984, Fr.), w
Niels Tavernier
ENTRE NOUS(1983, Fr.)
Tuvia Tavi
DREAMER, THE(1970, Israel); PARADISE(1982)
Franco Brogi Taviani
MASOCH(1980, Ital.), p, d&w
Lina Nerli Taviani
1984
NOSTALGHIA(1984, USSR/Ital.), cos
Lina Taviani
LUNA(1979, Ital.), cos; TRAGEDY OF A RIDICULOUS MAN, THE(1982, Ital.), cos
Paolo Vittorio Taviani
SUBVERSIVES, THE(1967, Ital.), d&w; PADRE PADRONE(1977, Ital.), d&w; NIGHT OF THE SHOOTING STARS, THE(1982, Ital.), d
Vittorio Taviani
SUBVERSIVES, THE(1967, Ital.), d&w; PADRE PADRONE(1977, Ital.), titles; NIGHT OF THE SHOOTING STARS, THE(1982, Ital.), d
Tavianis
NIGHT OF THE SHOOTING STARS, THE(1982, Ital.), w
Reginald Taviner
CRIME RING(1938), w; BUNCO SQUAD(1950), w
Norman Tavis
OH, HEAVENLY DOG!(1980)
Norman Taviss
SINS OF THE FATHERS(1948, Can.); APPRENTICESHIP OF DUDDY KRAVITZ, THE(1974, Can.); MOURNING SUIT, THE(1975, Can.)
Jacques Tavoli
GENERALS WITHOUT BUTTONS(1938, Fr.)
Lucianno Tavoli
BYE BYE MONKEY(1978, Ital/Fr.), ph
Luciano Tavoli
DESERT OF THE TARTARS, THE(1976 Fr./Ital./Iranian), ph
Michael Tavon
DEATH WISH II(1982)
Eli Tavor
EVERY BASTARD A KING(1968, Israel), w
Dean Tavoularis
INSIDE DAISY CLOVER(1965), art d; BONNIE AND CLYDE(1967), art d; CANDY(1968, Ital./Fr.), art d; PETULIA(1968, U.S./Brit.), art d; LITTLE BIG MAN(1970), prod d; ZABRISKIE POINT(1970), prod d; GODFATHER, THE(1972), prod d; CONVERSATION, THE(1974), prod d; GODFATHER, THE, PART II(1974), prod d; FAREWELL, MY LOVELY(1975), prod d; APOCALYPSE NOW(1979), prod d; ESCAPE ARTIST, THE(1982), prod d; HAMMETT(1982), prod d; ONE FROM THE HEART(1982), prod d; OUTSIDERS, THE(1983), prod d; RUMBLE FISH(1983), prod d
Y. Tavrov
NIGHT BEFORE CHRISTMAS, A(1963, USSR)
George Tawde
Silents
FANCY DRESS(1919, Brit.); JOYOUS ADVENTURES OF ARISTIDE PUJOL, THE(1920, Brit.)
D.J. Tawe-Jones
THREE WEIRD SISTERS, THE(1948, Brit.)
Dave Tawil
Misc. Talkies
AMERICAN GAME, THE(1979)
Jan Tax
GIRL WITH THE RED HAIR, THE(1983, Neth.), cos
Yan Tax
SPETTERS(1983, Holland), cos
Taxi the Dog
Silents
JACQUELINE, OR BLAZING BARRIERS(1923)
Arthur Taxier
LOOKER(1981); MOMMIE DEAREST(1981); MAKING LOVE(1982)
1984
NO SMALL AFFAIR(1984)
Peter Tay
SAINT JACK(1979)
Christopher Tayback
WIZARDS(1977)
Victor [Vic] Tayback
FIVE MINUTES TO LIVE(1961); SURFTIDE 77(1962); LOVE WITH THE PROPER STRANGER(1963); BULLITT(1968); WITH SIX YOU GET EGGROLL(1968); BLOOD AND LACE(1971); DON IS DEAD, THE(1973); EMPEROR OF THE NORTH POLE(1973); PAPILLON(1973); GAMBLER, THE(1974); THUNDERBOLT AND LIGHTFOOT(1974); ALICE DOESN'T LIVE HERE ANYMORE(1975); LEPKE(1975, U.S./Israel); REPORT TO THE COMMISSIONER(1975); BIG BUS, THE(1976); MANSION OF THE DOOMED(1976); NO DEPOSIT, NO RETURN(1976); SHAGGY D.A., THE(1976); SPECIAL DELIVERY(1976); CHOIRBOYS, THE(1977); CHEAP DETECTIVE, THE(1978)

Tayeb
ANOTHER SKY(1960 Brit.)
N. Tayenko
SONG OF THE FOREST(1963, USSR)
Andre Tayir
WEST SIDE STORY(1961); LAST OF THE SECRET AGENTS?, THE(1966), ch; GOOD TIMES(1967), ch; SWINGING BARMAIDS, THE(1976)
Clarice Tayler
FIVE ON THE BLACK HAND SIDE(1973)
Kim Taylforth
REMEMBRANCE(1982, Brit.); BLOODY KIDS(1983, Brit.)
Taylor
HANDS OF ORLAC, THE(1964, Brit./Fr.), w
A.J.P. Taylor
MAD LITTLE ISLAND(1958, Brit.)
Al Taylor
AVENGER, THE(1931); GHOST VALLEY(1932); LAW AND LAWLESS(1932); SADDLE BUSTER, THE(1932); COME ON TARZAN(1933); CATTLE THIEF, THE(1936); FUGITIVE SHERIFF, THE(1936); GUNS AND GUITARS(1936); LAWLESS NINETIES, THE(1936); ROARIN' GUNS(1936); COME ON, COWBOYS(1937); GIT ALONG, LITTLE DOGIES(1937); RANGE DEFENDERS(1937); RECKLESS RANGER(1937); RIO GRANDE RANGER(1937); YODELIN' KID FROM PINE RIDGE(1937); GOLD MINE IN THE SKY(1938); MAN FROM MUSIC MOUNTAIN(1938); RED RIVER RANGE(1938); COME ON RANGERS(1939); MEXICALI ROSE(1939); WYOMING OUTLAW(1939); CARSON CITY KID(1940); DARK COMMAND, THE(1940); GHOST VALLEY RAIDERS(1940); HEROES OF THE SADDLE(1940); GANGS OF SONORA(1941); OUTLAWS OF THE CHEROKEE TRAIL(1941); CODE OF THE OUTLAW(1942); MAN FROM CHEYENNE(1942); OUTLAWS OF PINE RIDGE(1942); PHANTOM PLAINSMEN, THE(1942); PRAIRIE PALS(1942); RAIDERS OF THE RANGE(1942); WESTWARD HO(1942); BLACK HILLS EXPRESS(1943); DEAD MAN'S GULCH(1943); DEATH VALLEY MANHUNT(1943); MAN FROM THUNDER RIVER, THE(1943); RAIDERS OF SUNSET PASS(1943); SANTA FE SCOUTS(1943); THUNDERING TRAILS(1943); MARSHAL OF RENO(1944); DUEL IN THE SUN(1946); RIO GRANDE RAIDERS(1946)
1984
NIGHT SHADOWS(1984), ph
Silents
FIGHTING CHEAT, THE(1926)
Misc. Silents
RAWHIDE(1926); BETWEEN DANGERS(1927); INTERFERIN' GENT, THE(1927)
Albert Taylor
ACCENT ON YOUTH(1935); MAN ON THE FLYING TRAPEZE, THE(1935); FURY(1936); NEVADA(1936); DESERT RATS, THE(1953)
Alfred Taylor
TELL NO TALES(1939), w; BEACH BALL(1965), ph; BLOOD BATH(1966), ph; SOFI(1967), ph; SPIDER BABY(1968), ph
Alma Taylor
DEADLOCK(1931, Brit.); BACHELOR'S BABY(1932, Brit.); THINGS ARE LOOKING UP(1934, Brit.); EVERYBODY DANCE(1936, Brit.); LET'S MAKE UP(1955, Brit.); STOCK CAR(1955, Brit.); MAN WHO KNEW TOO MUCH, THE(1956); TEARS FOR SIMON(1957, Brit.); BLUE MURDER AT ST. TRINIAN'S(1958, Brit.)
Misc. Talkies
HOUSE OF DREAMS(1933)
Silents
OLD CURIOSITY SHOP, THE(1913, Brit.); JUSTICE(1914, Brit.); IRIS(1915, Brit.); MOLLY BAWN(1916, Brit.); NATURE OF THE BEAST, THE(1919, Brit.); ALF'S BUTTON(1920, Brit.); ANNA THE ADVENTURESS(1920, Brit.); NARROW VALLEY, THE(1921, Brit.); PIPES OF PAN, THE(1923, Brit.); SHADOW OF EGYPT, THE(1924, Brit.)
Misc. Silents
CLOISTER AND THE HEARTH, THE(1913, Brit.); DAVID COPPERFIELD(1913, Brit.); HEART OF MIDLOTHIAN, THE(1914, Brit.); IN THE SHADOW OF BIG BEN(1914, Brit.); JUSTICE(1914, Brit.); LANCASHIRE LASS, A(1915, Brit.); MAN WHO STAYED AT HOME, THE(1915, Brit.); SWEET LAVENDER(1915, Brit.); ANNIE LAURIE(1916, Brit.); COMIN' THRO' THE RYE(1916, Brit.); MARRIAGE OF WILLIAM ASHE, THE(1916, Brit.); SOWING THE WIND(1916, Brit.); TRELAWNEY OF THE WELLS(1916, Brit.); COBWEB, THE(1917, Brit.); MERELY MRS. STUBBS(1917, Brit.); NEARER MY GOD TO THEE(1917, Brit.); BOUNDARY HOUSE(1918, Brit.); TOUCH OF A CHILD, THE(1918, Brit.); FOREST ON THE HILL, THE(1919, Brit.); SHEBA(1919, Brit.); SUNKEN ROCKS(1919, Brit.); HELEN OF FOUR GATES(1920, Brit.); DOLLARS IN SURREY(1921, Brit.); TANSY(1921, Brit.); TINTED VENUS, THE(1921, Brit.); COMIN' THRO' THE RYE(1923, Brit.); MIST IN THE VALLEY(1923, Brit.); STRANGLING THREADS(1923, Brit.); HOUSE OF MARNEY(1926, Brit.); TWO LITTLE DRUMMER BOYS(1928, Brit.)
Anita Taylor
STUDENT BODIES(1981)
Ann Taylor
WEB OF SUSPICION(1959, Brit.); YOU'VE GOT TO WALK IT LIKE YOU TALK IT OR YOU'LL LOSE THAT BEAT(1971)
Anna Taylor
1984
ALPHABET CITY(1984), cos
Anthony M. Taylor
INCUBUS(1966), p
Arch Taylor
WATCH YOUR STERN(1961, Brit.)
Austen Taylor
1984
CENSUS TAKER, THE(1984)
Avonne Taylor
HONOR AMONG LOVERS(1931)
Silents
MY BEST GIRL(1927)
B.T. Taylor
EDUCATION OF SONNY CARSON, THE(1974)
Barbi Taylor
ROAD GAMES(1981, Aus.), p

Ben Taylor
SUPER FUZZ(1981)
Benedict Taylor
WATCHER IN THE WOODS, THE(1980, Brit.)
Bernard Taylor
LOVE AND DEATH(1975); MR. QUILP(1975, Brit.); GODSEND, THE(1980, Can.), w
Beryl Taylor
DEVIL'S SISTERS, THE(1966)
Beth Taylor
MIRACLE OF THE BELLS, THE(1948); PRAIRIE, THE(1948)
Betty Taylor
VENGEANCE IS MINE(1948, Brit.); EAST SIDE, WEST SIDE(1949); KNOCK ON ANY DOOR(1949)
Beverly Taylor
...TICK...TICK...TICK...(1970)
Bill Taylor
DARK STAR(1975), spec eff
Bill Taylor
FOG, THE(1980)
Billy Taylor
HEADS UP(1930)
Blanche Taylor
HIRED WIFE(1934); RAZOR'S EDGE, THE(1946); ROAD HOUSE(1948); I'VE LIVED BEFORE(1956)
Bob Taylor
BLAST OF SILENCE(1961)
Bobby Taylor
OKLAHOMA ANNIE(1952)
Bockie Taylor
THOSE DARING YOUNG MEN IN THEIR JAUNTY JALOPIES(1969, Fr./Brit./ Ital.)
Brad Taylor
ATLANTIC CITY(1944); SING, NEIGHBOR, SING(1944); HITCHHIKE TO HAPPINESS(1945); SWINGIN' ON A RAINBOW(1945)
Brian Taylor
COMPELLED(1960, Brit.), p; ESCORT FOR HIRE(1960, Brit.), p; FEET OF CLAY(1960, Brit.), p; TASTE OF MONEY, A(1960, Brit.), p; COURT MARTIAL OF MAJOR KELLER, THE(1961, Brit.), p; MIDDLE COURSE, THE(1961, Brit.), p; PART-TIME WIFE(1961, Brit.), p; SO EVIL SO YOUNG(1961, Brit.), p; TARNISHED HEROES(1961, Brit.), p; TRANSATLANTIC(1961, Brit.), p; TWO WIVES AT ONE WEDDING(1961, Brit.), p; FATE TAKES A HAND(1962, Brit.), p; GENTLE TERROR, THE(1962, Brit.), p; LAMP IN ASSASSIN MEWS, THE(1962, Brit.), p; RETURN OF A STRANGER(1962, Brit.), p; SPANISH SWORD, THE(1962, Brit.), p; WHAT EVERY WOMAN WANTS(1962, Brit.), p; TRYGON FACTOR, THE(1969, Brit.), p; WARRIORS, THE(1979)
Buck Taylor
AND NOW MIGUEL(1966); WILD ANGELS, THE(1966); DEVIL'S ANGELS(1967); PONY EXPRESS RIDER(1976); CATTLE ANNIE AND LITTLE BRITCHES(1981); LEGEND OF THE LONE RANGER, THE(1981); TRIUMPHS OF A MAN CALLED HORSE(1983, US/Mex.)
Misc. Talkies
BEARTOOTH(1978); DOC HOOKER'S BUNCH(1978)
Bud Taylor
RANGERS RIDE, THE(1948)
Burt Taylor
BIRDS DO IT(1966)
C.B. Taylor
THUNDER AT THE BORDER(1966, Ger./Yugo.), w
C.D. Taylor
TUNNELVISION(1976), a, art d; CRACKING UP(1977), p, art d
Carli Taylor
LIVES OF A BENGAL LANCER(1935)
Carlie Taylor
YOU CAN'T TAKE IT WITH YOU(1938); GUY NAMED JOE, A(1943)
Carlie Taylor
NUN AND THE SERGEANT, THE(1962), makeup
Carly Taylor
THUNDER ROAD(1958), makeup
Cathie Taylor
HOOTENANNY HOOT(1963)
Charles Taylor
Misc. Silents
THRU THE EYES OF MEN(1920), d
Charles A. Taylor
Silents
OLD AGE HANDICAP(1928), w
Misc. Silents
HALF BREED, THE(1922), d
Chip Taylor
CATAMOUNT KILLING, THE(1975, Ger.); MELVIN AND HOWARD(1980)
Cindy Taylor
GNOME-MOBILE, THE(1967)
Clarice Taylor
PLAY MISTY FOR ME(1971); SUCH GOOD FRIENDS(1971)
1984
NOTHING LASTS FOREVER(1984)
Clarisse Taylor
CHANGE OF MIND(1969); TELL ME THAT YOU LOVE ME, JUNIE MOON(1970)
Clark Taylor
1984
BIRDY(1984)
Cliff Taylor
DEAD MAN'S GOLD(1948); FRONTIER REVENGE(1948); MARK OF THE LASH(1948); DALTON GANG, THE(1949); RIMFIRE(1949); SON OF BILLY THE KID(1949); SQUARE DANCE JUBILEE(1949); CROOKED RIVER(1950); DALTON'S WOMEN, THE(1950); FAST ON THE DRAW(1950); HOSTILE COUNTRY(1950); KING OF THE BULLWHIP(1950); MARSHAL OF HELDORADO(1950); KENTUCKY JUBILEE, THE(1951); THUNDERING TRAIL, THE(1951); VANISHING OUTPOST(1951); YES SIR, MR. BONES(1951); FRONTIER PHANTOM, THE(1952); WILD NORTH, THE(1952)

Clifford Taylor
DEATH DRIVES THROUGH(1935, Brit.), p
Colin Taylor
FLASH GORDON(1980)
Curtis Brown Taylor
LIKE A CROW ON A JUNE BUG(1972), w
Curtis Taylor
ONCE UPON A COFFEE HOUSE(1965); MR. SYCAMORE(1975)
1984
CHATTANOOGA CHOO CHOO(1984)
"Daddy" Taylor
Silents
GOLD RUSH, THE(1925)
Dan Taylor
1984
NIGHT PATROL(1984)
Dave Taylor
STIR(1980, Aus.)
David Taylor
LAST ESCAPE, THE(1970, Brit.); HANKY-PANKY(1982), w; GET CRAZY(1983), w
1984
LASSITER(1984), w
Deborah Taylor
LIANNA(1983)
1984
BROTHER FROM ANOTHER PLANET, THE(1984)
Deems Taylor
FANTASIA(1940); THERE'S MAGIC IN MUSIC(1941); BARBER OF SEVILLE, THE(1947, Ital.), w
Silents
JANICE MEREDITH(1924), m
Delores Taylor
BORN LOSERS(1967), p; BILLY JACK(1971); TRIAL OF BILLY JACK, THE(1974); BILLY JACK GOES TO WASHINGTON(1977)
Dennis Taylor
BANK RAIDERS, THE(1958, Brit.)
Diane Taylor
PURSUIT(1975)
Dick Taylor
FAR COUNTRY, THE(1955)
Don Taylor
GIRL CRAZY(1943); HUMAN COMEDY, THE(1943); THOUSANDS CHEER(1943); SONG OF THE THIN MAN(1947); FOR THE LOVE OF MARY(1948); NAKED CITY, THE(1948); BATTLEGROUND(1949); AMBUSH(1950); FATHER OF THE BRIDE(1950); BLUE VEIL, THE(1951); FATHER'S LITTLE DIVIDEND(1951); FLYING LEATHERNECKS(1951); SUBMARINE COMMAND(1951); TARGET UNKNOWN(1951); JAPANESE WAR BRIDE(1952); DESTINATION GOBI(1953); GIRLS OF PLEASURE ISLAND, THE(1953); STALAG 17(1953); JOHNNY DARK(1954); I'LL CRY TOMORROW(1955); BOLD AND THE BRAVE, THE(1956); RIDE THE HIGH IRON(1956); LOVE SLAVES OF THE AMAZONS(1957); MEN OF SHERWOOD FOREST(1957, Brit.); EVERYTHING'S DUCKY(1961), d; SAVAGE GUNS, THE(1962, U.S./Span.); RIDE THE WILD SURF(1964), d; JACK OF DIAMONDS(1967, U.S./Ger.), d; FIVE MAN ARMY, THE(1970, Ital.), d; ESCAPE FROM THE PLANET OF THE APES(1971), d; TOM SAWYER(1973), d; ECHOES OF A SUMMER(1976), d; GREAT SCOUT AND CATHOUSE THURSDAY, THE(1976), d; ISLAND OF DR. MOREAU, THE(1977), d; DAMIEN–OMEN II(1978), d; FINAL COUNTDOWN, THE(1980), d
Cpl. Don Taylor
WINGED VICTORY(1944)
Donald Dexter Taylor
RED DRAGON, THE(1946)
Donald F. Taylor
PROMISES, PROMISES(1963), p
Donald Taylor
BATTLE FOR MUSIC(1943, Brit.), p&d; MAN IN THE DINGHY, THE(1951, Brit.), w; STRAW MAN, THE(1953, Brit.), p,d&w; NIGHT OF THE FULL MOON, THE(1954, Brit.), p&d, w; DOUBLE CROSS(1956, Brit.), p; ORDERS ARE ORDERS(1959, Brit.), p, w; FOXHOLE IN CAIRO(1960, Brit.), p, w; HORROR HOTEL(1960, Brit.), p; DEVIL'S DAFFODIL, THE(1961, Brit./Ger.), p, w; SPARROWS CAN'T SING(1963, Brit.), p; HANDS OF ORLAC, THE(1964, Brit./Fr.), p; JOLLY BAD FELLOW, A(1964, Brit.), p, w
Dorothy [Totti] Truman Taylor
WOMAN IN THE HALL, THE(1949, Brit.)
Dub [Cannonball] Taylor
YOU CAN'T RUN AWAY FROM IT(1956); YOU CAN'T TAKE IT WITH YOU(1938); MR. SMITH GOES TO WASHINGTON(1939); TAMING OF THE WEST, THE(1939); MAN FROM TUMBLEWEEDS, THE(1940); ONE MAN'S LAW(1940); PIONEERS OF THE FRONTIER(1940); PRAIRIE SCHOONERS(1940); RETURN OF WILD BILL, THE(1940); ACROSS THE SIERRAS(1941); BEYOND THE SACRAMENTO(1941); KING OF DODGE CITY(1941); NORTH FROM LONE STAR(1941); RETURN OF DANIEL BOONE, THE(1941); SON OF DAVY CROCKETT, THE(1941); WILDCAT OF TUCSON(1941); LONE PRAIRIE, THE(1942); COWBOY IN THE CLOUDS(1943); RIDERS OF THE NORTHWEST MOUNTED(1943); SILVER CITY RAIDERS(1943); WHAT'S BUZZIN' COUSIN?(1943); COWBOY CANTEEN(1944); COWBOY FROM LONESOME RIVER(1944); CYCLONE PRAIRIE RANGERS(1944); LAST HORSEMAN, THE(1944); SUNDOWN VALLEY(1944); OUTLAWS OF THE ROCKIES(1945); LAWLESS EMPIRE(1946); RIDIN' DOWN THE TRAIL(1947); COURTIN' TROUBLE(1948); COWBOY CAVALIER(1948); OKLAHOMA BLUES(1948); OUTLAW BRAND(1948); PARTNERS OF THE SUNSET(1948); RANGE RENEGADES(1948); RANGERS RIDE, THE(1948); SILVER TRAILS(1948); SONG OF THE DRIFTER(1948); ACROSS THE RIO GRANDE(1949); BRAND OF FEAR(1949); GUN LAW JUSTICE(1949); GUN RUNNER(1949); LAWLESS CODE(1949); ROARING WESTWARD(1949); RIDING HIGH(1950); STORY OF WILL ROGERS, THE(1952); CHARGE AT FEATHER RIVER, THE(1953); BOUNTY HUNTER, THE(1954); CRIME WAVE(1954); RIDING SHOTGUN(1954); STAR IS BORN, A(1954); THEM!(1954); I DIED A THOUSAND TIMES(1955); TALL MAN RIDING(1955); FASTEST GUN ALIVE(1956); HOT ROD GANG(1958); NO TIME FOR SERGEANTS(1958); STREET OF DARKNESS(1958); HOLE IN THE HEAD, A(1959); HOME FROM THE HILL(1960); PARRISH(1961); SWEET BIRD OF YOUTH(1962); BLACK GOLD(1963); SPENCER'S MOUNTAIN(1963); CINCINNATI KID, THE(1965); HALLELUJAH TRAIL, THE(1965); MAJOR DUNDEE(1965); ADVENTURES OF BULLWHIP GRIFFIN, THE(1967); BON-

NIE AND CLYDE(1967); DON'T MAKE WAVES(1967); BANDOLERO!(1968); MONEY JUNGLE, THE(1968); SHAKIEST GUN IN THE WEST, THE(1968); THREE GUNS FOR TEXAS(1968); DEATH OF A GUNFIGHTER(1969); LEARNING TREE, THE(1969); REIVERS, THE(1969); UNDEFEATED, THE(1969); WILD BUNCH, THE(1969); LIBERATION OF L.B. JONES, THE(1970); MAN CALLED HORSE, A(1970); ...TICK...TICK...TICK...(1970); EVEL KNIEVEL(1971); SUPPORT YOUR LOCAL GUNFIGHTER(1971); WILD COUNTRY, THE(1971); GETAWAY, THE(1972); JUNIOR BONNER(1972); MAN AND BOY(1972); BLACK JACK(1973); PAT GARRETT AND BILLY THE KID(1973); THIS IS A HIJACK(1973); TOM SAWYER(1973); THUNDERBOLT AND LIGHTFOOT(1974); FORTUNE, THE(1975); HEARTS OF THE WEST(1975); BURNT OFFERINGS(1976); CREATURE FROM BLACK LAKE, THE(1976); FLASH AND THE FIRECAT(1976); GATOR(1976); PONY EXPRESS RIDER(1976); TREASURE OF MATECUMBE(1976); MOONSHINE COUNTY EXPRESS(1977); RESCUERS, THE(1977); THEY WENT THAT-A-WAY AND THAT-A-WAY(1978); 1941(1979); USED CARS(1980); SOGGY BOTTOM U.S.A.(1982)
1984
CANNONBALL RUN II(1984)
Misc. Talkies
HANDS ACROSS THE ROCKIES(1941); TORNADO IN THE SADDLE, A(1942); SADDLES AND SAGEBRUSH(1943); SADDLE LEATHER LAW(1944); VIGILANTES RIDE, THE(1944); WYOMING HURRICANE(1944); BLAZING THE WESTERN TRAIL(1945); BOTH BARRELS BLAZING(1945); ROUGH RIDIN' JUSTICE(1945); RUSTLERS OF THE BADLANDS(1945); SAGEBRUSH HEROES(1945); TEXAS PANHANDLE(1945); FRONTIER GUNLAW(1946); COUNTRY BLUE(1975); POOR PRETTY EDDIE(1975); WINDS OF AUTUMN, THE(1976); BEARTOOTH(1978); DOC HOOKER'S BUNCH(1978); HEARTBREAK MOTEL(1978)

Duke Taylor
OUTLAWS OF PINE RIDGE(1942); TWO YANKS IN TRINIDAD(1942); ANGEL ON MY SHOULDER(1946); RACKET, THE(1951)

Duncan Taylor
WHAT'S GOOD FOR THE GOOSE(1969, Brit.)

Dwight Taylor
NUMBERED MEN(1930), w; SECRETS OF A SECRETARY(1931), w; ARE YOU LISTENING?(1932), w; IF I WERE FREE(1933), w; TODAY WE LIVE(1933), w; GAY DIVORCEE, THE(1934), w; LADY BY CHOICE(1934), w; LONG LOST FATHER(1934), w; PARIS IN SPRING(1935), w; TOP HAT(1935), w; FOLLOW THE FLEET(1936), w; GANGWAY(1937, Brit.), w; HEAD OVER HEELS IN LOVE(1937, Brit.), w; AMAZING MR. WILLIAMS(1939), w; WHEN TOMORROW COMES(1939), w; RHYTHM ON THE RIVER(1940), w; KISS THE BOYS GOODBYE(1941), w; I WAKE UP SCREAMING(1942), w; NIGHTMARE(1942), p; THIN MAN GOES HOME, THE(1944), w; CONFLICT(1945), w; SOMETHING TO LIVE FOR(1952), w; WE'RE NOT MARRIED(1952), w; PICKUP ON SOUTH STREET(1953), w; VICKI(1953), w; SPECIAL DELIVERY(1955, Ger.), w; BOY ON A DOLPHIN(1957), w; INTERLUDE(1957), w

E. Forrest Taylor
Misc. Silents
ABANDONMENT, THE(1916); APRIL(1916); TRUE NOBILITY(1916); WHITE ROSETTE, THE(1916)

Ed Taylor
1984
BIRDY(1984)

Eddie Taylor
RIDERS OF THE DAWN(1945)

Edna Taylor
DON'T KNOCK THE TWIST(1962), cos; SHOOTIST, THE(1976), cos; TELEFON(1977), cos

Edward C. Taylor
Misc. Silents
HAND OF THE LAW, THE(1915), d

Elaine Taylor
ANNIVERSARY, THE(1968, Brit.); DIAMONDS FOR BREAKFAST(1968, Brit.); LOCK UP YOUR DAUGHTERS(1969, Brit.); ALL THE WAY UP(1970, Brit.); GAMES, THE(1970)

Eleanor Taylor
THIS LOVE OF OURS(1945)

Elisabeth Taylor
ASH WEDNESDAY(1973)

Elizabeth Taylor
THERE'S ONE BORN EVERY MINUTE(1942); LASSIE, COME HOME(1943); JANE EYRE(1944); NATIONAL VELVET(1944); WHITE CLIFFS OF DOVER, THE(1944); BLUE SIERRA(1946); COURAGE OF LASSIE(1946); CYNTHIA(1947); LIFE WITH FATHER(1947); DATE WITH JUDY, A(1948); JULIA MISBEHAVES(1948); CONSPIRATOR(1949, Brit.); LITTLE WOMEN(1949); BIG HANGOVER, THE(1950); FATHER OF THE BRIDE(1950); CALLAWAY WENT THATAWAY(1951); FATHER'S LITTLE DIVIDEND(1951); PLACE IN THE SUN, A(1951); QUO VADIS(1951); IVANHOE(1952, Brit.); LOVE IS BETTER THAN EVER(1952); GIRL WHO HAD EVERYTHING, THE(1953); BEAU BRUMMELL(1954); ELEPHANT WALK(1954); LAST TIME I SAW PARIS, THE(1954); RHAPSODY(1954); GIANT(1956); RAINTREE COUNTY(1957); CAT ON A HOT TIN ROOF(1958); SUDDENLY, LAST SUMMER(1959, Brit.); BUTTERFIELD 8(1960); SCENT OF MYSTERY(1960); CLEOPATRA(1963); V.I.P.s, THE(1963, Brit.); SANDPIPER, THE(1965); WHO'S AFRAID OF VIRGINIA WOOLF?(1966); COMEDIANS, THE(1967); DOCTOR FAUSTUS(1967, Brit.); REFLECTIONS IN A GOLDEN EYE(1967); TAMING OF THE SHREW, THE(1967, U.S./Ital.), a, p; BOOM!(1968); SECRET CEREMONY(1968, Brit.); ONLY GAME IN TOWN, THE(1970); HAMMERSMITH IS OUT(1972); X Y & ZEE(1972, Brit.); NIGHT WATCH(1973, Brit.); UNDER MILK WOOD(1973, Brit.); DRIVER'S SEAT, THE(1975, Ital.); BLUE BIRD, THE(1976); LITTLE NIGHT MUSIC, A(1977, Aust./U.S./Ger.); WINTER KILLS(1979); MIRROR CRACK'D, THE(1980, Brit.)
Misc. Silents
WHOSE WIFE?(1917)

Eloise Taylor
CONVICT'S CODE(1930); DAMAGED LOVE(1931)

Elsie Taylor
MACBETH(1971, Brit.)

Enid Stamp Taylor
FARMER'S WIFE, THE(1941, Brit.); CANDLELIGHT IN ALGERIA(1944, Brit.)
Silents
LAND OF HOPE AND GLORY(1927, Brit.)
Misc. Silents
REMEMBRANCE(1927, Brit.)

Eric Taylor
HAPPY-GO-LUCKY(1937), w; NAVY BLUES(1937), w; WRONG ROAD, THE(1937), w; LADY IN THE MORGUE(1938), w; ROMANCE ON THE RUN(1938), w; FUGITIVE AT LARGE(1939), w; ORPHANS OF THE STREET(1939), w; TRAPPED IN THE SKY(1939), w; BLACK FRIDAY(1940), w; ELLERY QUEEN. MASTER DETECTIVE(1940), w; OUTSIDE THE 3-MILE LIMIT(1940), w; BLACK CAT, THE(1941), w; ELLERY QUEEN AND THE MURDER RING(1941), w; ELLERY QUEEN AND THE PERFECT CRIME(1941), w; ELLERY QUEEN'S PENTHOUSE MYSTERY(1941), w; GREAT SWINDLE, THE(1941), w; CLOSE CALL FOR ELLERY QUEEN, A(1942), w; DESPERATE CHANCE FOR ELLERY QUEEN, A(1942), w; ENEMY AGENTS MEET ELLERY QUEEN(1942), w; GHOST OF FRANKENSTEIN, THE(1942), w; CRIME DOCTOR'S STRANGEST CASE(1943), w; NO PLACE FOR A LADY(1943), w; PHANTOM OF THE OPERA(1943), w; SON OF DRACULA(1943), w; SHADOWS IN THE NIGHT(1944), w; WHISTLER, THE(1944), w; CRIME DOCTOR'S COURAGE, THE(1945), w; CRIME DOCTOR'S WARNING(1945), w; DICK TRACY(1945), w; CRIME DOCTOR'S MAN HUNT(1946), w; JUST BEFORE DAWN(1946), w; MYSTERIOUS INTRUDER(1946), w; SPIDER WOMAN STRIKES BACK, THE(1946), w; TRUTH ABOUT MURDER, THE(1946), w; DICK TRACY MEETS GRUESOME(1947), w; DEVIL'S HENCHMEN, THE(1949), w; PRISON WARDEN(1949), w; SECRET OF ST. IVES, THE(1949), w; DESTINATION BIG HOUSE(1950), w; HEART OF THE ROCKIES(1951), w; SOUTH OF CALIENTE(1951), w; BIG JIM McLAIN(1952), w; COLORADO SUNDOWN(1952), w; PALS OF THE GOLDEN WEST(1952), w; WHITE GODDESS(1953), w

Ernest Taylor
FRIEDA(1947, Brit.), makeup; NICHOLAS NICKLEBY(1947, Brit.), makeup; IT ALWAYS RAINS ON SUNDAY(1949, Brit.), makeup; SCOTT OF THE ANTARCTIC(1949, Brit.), makeup; MAN IN THE WHITE SUIT, THE(1952), makeup

Ernest Taylor III
STRAIGHT TIME(1978)

Estelle Taylor
LILIOM(1930); CIMARRON(1931); STREET SCENE(1931); UNHOLY GARDEN, THE(1931); CALL HER SAVAGE(1932); WESTERN LIMITED(1932); SOUTHERNER, THE(1945)
Silents
WHILE NEW YORK SLEEPS(1920); CALIFORNIA ROMANCE, A(1922); ONLY A SHOP GIRL(1922); THORNS AND ORANGE BLOSSOMS(1922); TEN COMMANDMENTS, THE(1923); ALASKAN, THE(1924); PLAYTHINGS OF DESIRE(1924); DON JUAN(1926); NEW YORK(1927); SHOW PEOPLE(1928); WHIP WOMAN, THE(1928); WHERE EAST IS EAST(1929)
Misc. Silents
GOLDEN SHOWER, THE(1919); ADVENTURER, THE(1920); BLIND WIVES(1920); RETURN OF TARZAN, THE(1920); FOOTFALLS(1921); FOOL THERE WAS, A(1922); LIGHTS OF NEW YORK, THE(1922); MONTE CRISTO(1922); BAVU(1923); DESIRE(1923); FORGIVE AND FORGET(1923); PASSION'S PATHWAY(1924); TIGER LOVE(1924); MANHATTAN MADNESS(1925); WANDERING FOOTSTEPS(1925); HONOR BOUND(1928); LADY RAFFLES(1928), a, d; SINGAPORE MUTINY, THE(1928)

Eva Taylor
Silents
NIGHT OUT, A(1916)

Evelyn Taylor
OKLAHOMA(1955)

Femi Taylor
RETURN OF THE JEDI(1983)

Ferris Taylor
LADIES THEY TALK ABOUT(1933); TILLIE AND GUS(1933); EVER SINCE EVE(1937); LUCK OF ROARING CAMP, THE(1937); MR. DODD TAKES THE AIR(1937); WRONG ROAD, THE(1937); DAREDEVIL DRIVERS(1938); FORBIDDEN VALLEY(1938); HE COULDN'T SAY NO(1938); JURY'S SECRET(1938); KING OF THE NEWSBOYS(1938); RACKET BUSTERS(1938); RECKLESS LIVING(1938); SANTA FE STAMPEDE(1938); YOUNG FUGITIVES(1938); FRONTIER MARSHAL(1939); MAIN STREET LAWYER(1939); MAN OF CONQUEST(1939); MOUNTAIN RHYTHM(1939); MR. SMITH GOES TO WASHINGTON(1939); SOCIETY LAWYER(1939); S.O.S. TIDAL WAVE(1939); YOU CAN'T CHEAT AN HONEST MAN(1939); ZERO HOUR, THE(1939); ALWAYS A BRIDE(1940); CHIP OF THE FLYING U(1940); DARK COMMAND, THE(1940); DIAMOND FRONTIER(1940); FLIGHT ANGELS(1940); FOREIGN CORRESPONDENT(1940); GRAND OLE OPRY(1940); LADIES MUST LIVE(1940); MEXICAN SPITFIRE OUT WEST(1940); ONE CROWDED NIGHT(1940); RANCHO GRANDE(1940); COUNTRY FAIR(1941); DEVIL AND DANIEL WEBSTER, THE(1941); MAN BETRAYED, A(1941); RICHEST MAN IN TOWN(1941); RIDIN' ON A RAINBOW(1941); SAINT IN PALM SPRINGS, THE(1941); SAN ANTONIO ROSE(1941); SHE COULDN'T SAY NO(1941); HELLO ANNAPOLIS(1942); MAN'S WORLD, A(1942); MEXICAN SPITFIRE AT SEA(1942); HAPPY LAND(1943); HENRY ALDRICH HAUNTS A HOUSE(1943); HOOSIER HOLIDAY(1943); SKY'S THE LIMIT, THE(1943); BEAUTIFUL BUT BROKE(1944); END OF THE ROAD(1944); HENRY ALDRICH PLAYS CUPID(1944); ROGER TOUHY, GANGSTER!(1944); TOGETHER AGAIN(1944); WILSON(1944); COLONEL EFFINGHAM'S RAID(1945); I'LL TELL THE WORLD(1945); TOWN WENT WILD, THE(1945); BRINGING UP FATHER(1946); CENTENNIAL SUMMER(1946); DECOY(1946); DON'T GAMBLE WITH STRANGERS(1946); IDEA GIRL(1946); MAGNIFICENT DOLL(1946); MAN FROM RAINBOW VALLEY, THE(1946); RENDEZVOUS 24(1946); DOCKS OF NEW ORLEANS(1948); GALLANT LEGION, THE(1948); MY DOG RUSTY(1948); LAWTON STORY, THE(1949); GUNFIGHTER, THE(1950); TWO FLAGS WEST(1950); MR. BELVEDERE RINGS THE BELL(1951); PRINCE OF PEACE, THE(1951); HANNAH LEE(1953); SIEGE AT RED RIVER, THE(1954)

Floyd Taylor
FATHER OF THE BRIDE(1950); PEGGY(1950)

Forest Taylor
PRAIRIE JUSTICE(1938); FBI STORY, THE(1959)

Forrest Taylor
DEATH KISS, THE(1933); RIDERS OF DESTINY(1933); COURAGEOUS AVENGER, THE(1935); MISSISSIPPI(1935); RIDER OF THE LAW, THE(1935); TRAIL OF TERROR(1935); FACE IN THE FOG, A(1936); KELLY OF THE SECRET SERVICE(1936); MEN OF THE PLAINS(1936); PRISON SHADOWS(1936); PUT ON THE SPOT(1936); RIO GRANDE ROMANCE(1936); RIP ROARIN' BUCKAROO(1936); SONG OF THE GRINGO(1936); TOO MUCH BEEF(1936); VALLEY OF THE LAWLESS(1936); WEST OF NEVADA(1936); ARIZONA DAYS(1937); DESERT PHANTOM(1937); HEADIN' FOR THE RIO GRANDE(1937); ISLAND CAPTIVES(1937); LOST RANCH(1937); MOONLIGHT ON THE RANGE(1937); MYSTERY OF THE HOODED HORSEMEN, THE(1937); RED ROPE, THE(1937); RIDERS OF THE DAWN(1937); ROAMING

COWBOY, THE(1937); ROGUE OF THE RANGE(1937); STARS OVER ARIZONA(1937); TEX RIDES WITH THE BOY SCOUTS(1937); TWO MINUTES TO PLAY(1937); WHERE TRAILS DIVIDE(1937); BLACK BANDIT(1938); DESERT PATROL(1938); DURANGO VALLEY RAIDERS(1938); FEUD MAKER(1938); FRONTIER TOWN(1938); GHOST TOWN RIDERS(1938); GUILTY TRAILS(1938); GUN PACKER(1938); HEROES OF THE HILLS(1938); LAST STAND, THE(1938); LAW OF THE TEXAN(1938); MAN'S COUNTRY(1938); ORPHAN OF THE PECOS(1938); OUTLAW EXPRESS(1938); PAINTED TRAIL, THE(1938); PHANTOM OF THE RANGE, THE(1938); SPY RING, THE(1938); WESTERN TRAILS(1938); CODE OF THE CACTUS(1939); FIGHTING GRINGO, THE(1939); FIGHTING RENEGADE(1939); HONOR OF THE WEST(1939); LAW COMES TO TEXAS, THE(1939); OUTLAW'S PARADISE(1939); PHANTOM STAGE, THE(1939); RIDERS OF BLACK RIVER(1939); RIDERS OF THE FRONTIER(1939); RIO GRANDE(1939); ROVIN' TUMBLEWEEDS(1939); TEXAS WILDCATS(1939); TRIGGER FINGERS ½(1939); TRIGGER SMITH(1939); ARIZONA GANGBUSTERS(1940); CHEYENNE KID, THE(1940); CHIP OF THE FLYING U(1940); DURANGO KID, THE(1940); FRONTIER CRUSADER(1940); GOLDEN TRAIL, THE(1940); KID FROM SANTA FE, THE(1940); MY SON IS GUILTY(1940); RHYTHM OF THE RIO GRANDE(1940); SAGEBRUSH FAMILY TRAILS WEST, THE(1940); STRAIGHT SHOOTER(1940); TRAILING DOUBLE TROUBLE(1940); WEST OF ABILENE(1940); BILLY THE KID'S FIGHTING PALS(1941); FLYING WILD(1941); KANSAS CYCLONE(1941); PALS OF THE PECOS(1941); RIDIN' ON A RAINBOW(1941); RIDING THE CHEROKEE TRAIL(1941); UNDERGROUND RUSTLERS(1941); WILDCAT OF TUCSON(1941); WRANGLER'S ROOST(1941); CODE OF THE OUTLAW(1942); COWBOY SERENADE(1942); DOWN RIO GRANDE WAY(1942); HOME IN WYOMIN'(1942); IN OLD CALIFORNIA(1942); JUKE GIRL(1942); KING OF THE STALLIONS(1942); LONE STAR VIGILANTES, THE(1942); NIGHT FOR CRIME, A(1942); OUTLAWS OF PINE RIDGE(1942); RANGERS TAKE OVER, THE(1942); RIDIN' DOWN THE CANYON(1942); SONS OF THE PIONEERS(1942); SPOILERS, THE(1942); SUNSET ON THE DESERT(1942); TRAIL RIDERS(1942); YANKS ARE COMING, THE(1942); AIR RAID WARDENS(1943); FIGHTING BUCKAROO, THE(1943); KING OF THE COWBOYS(1943); LAND OF HUNTED MEN(1943); MAN OF COURAGE(1943); PAYOFF, THE(1943); SILVER SPURS(1943); SLEEPY LAGOON(1943); SONG OF TEXAS(1943); THUNDERING TRAILS(1943); WILD HORSE STAMPEDE(1943); CHEYENNE WILDCAT(1944); CYCLONE PRAIRIE RANGERS(1944); DEATH VALLEY RANGERS(1944); LADY IN THE DEATH HOUSE(1944); LAST HORSEMAN, THE(1944); MOJAVE FIREBRAND(1944); MYSTERY MAN(1944); OUTLAWS OF SANTA FE(1944); RANGE LAW(1944); SHAKE HANDS WITH MURDER(1944); SONG OF NEVADA(1944); SONORA STAGECOACH(1944); SUNDOWN VALLEY(1944); THREE LITTLE SISTERS(1944); TRAIL TO GUNSIGHT(1944); BANDITS OF THE BADLANDS(1945); BEYOND THE PECOS(1945); DANGEROUS INTRUDER(1945); IDENTITY UNKNOWN(1945); ROCKIN' IN THE ROCKIES(1945); STRANGE VOYAGE(1945); CARAVAN TRAIL, THE(1946); COLORADO SERENADE(1946); DRIFTIN' RIVER(1946); GIRL ON THE SPOT(1946); GLASS ALIBI, THE(1946); LADY LUCK(1946); LAWLESS EMPIRE(1946); ROMANCE OF THE WEST(1946); SANTA FE UPRISING(1946); STAGECOACH TO DENVER(1946); PRETENDER, THE(1947); RUSTLERS OF DEVIL'S CANYON(1947); SEA OF GRASS, THE(1947); TRAIL STREET(1947); YANKEE FAKIR(1947); BUCKAROO FROM POWDER RIVER(1948); CORONER CREEK(1948); FOUR FACES WEST(1948); MYSTERY OF THE GOLDEN EYE, THE(1948); RETURN OF THE BADMEN(1948); DEATH VALLEY GUNFIGHTER(1949); DEPUTY MARSHAL(1949); GAL WHO TOOK THE WEST, THE(1949); LAWTON STORY, THE(1949); NAVAJO TRAIL RAIDERS(1949); SCENE OF THE CRIME(1949); STALLION CANYON(1949); CHEROKEE UPRISING(1950); CODE OF THE SILVER SAGE(1950); COWBOY AND THE PRIZEFIGHTER(1950); FIGHTING REDHEAD, THE(1950); FIGHTING STALLION, THE(1950); FORBIDDEN JUNGLE(1950); MONTANA(1950); RUSTLERS ON HORSEBACK(1950); WINCHESTER '73(1950); PRAIRIE ROUNDUP(1951); PRINCE OF PEACE, THE(1951); WELLS FARGO GUNMASTER(1951); BORDER SADDLEMATES(1952); NIGHT RAIDERS(1952); PARK ROW(1952); SMOKY CANYON(1952); SOUTH PACIFIC TRAIL(1952); IRON MOUNTAIN TRAIL(1953); MARSHAL'S DAUGHTER, THE(1953); BITTER CREEK(1954); DAWN AT SOCORRO(1954)
Misc. Talkies
BULLETS FOR BANDITS(1942); TEXAS PANHANDLE(1945)
Silents
NO MAN'S GOLD(1926)
Frank Taylor
WEE GEORDIE(1956, Brit.); SMASH PALACE(1982, New Zealand)
1984
RIVER, THE(1984)
Frank E. Taylor
MYSTERY STREET(1950), p; MISFITS, THE(1961), p
Frank Wilson Taylor
MYSTERY SUBMARINE(1963, Brit.); TRAITORS, THE(1963, Brit.)
Fred Taylor
ROSE TATTOO, THE(1955); TERROR FROM THE YEAR 5,000(1958)
Gene Taylor
1984
STREETS OF FIRE(1984)
Geoffrey Taylor
RACE FOR LIFE, A(1955, Brit.)
George Taylor
ANGEL'S HOLIDAY(1937); MARRIED BEFORE BREAKFAST(1937); NANCY STEELE IS MISSING(1937); ANGELS WITH DIRTY FACES(1938); INVISIBLE STRIPES(1940); O.S.S.(1946); WINTER MEETING(1948); WHITE HEAT(1949); TREASURE OF LOST CANYON, THE(1952); REDHEAD FROM WYOMING, THE(1953); ROGUE COP(1954); BADLANDS OF MONTANA(1957); SUMMER PLACE, A(1959); RISE AND FALL OF LEGS DIAMOND, THE(1960); TARZAN THE MAGNIFICENT(1960, Brit.)
Misc. Talkies
BATTLE OF THE EAGLES(1981)
George F. Taylor
JACKTOWN(1962)
Gerald Taylor
CHITTY CHITTY BANG BANG(1968, Brit.)
Geretta Taylor
GUN RUNNER(1969); DARK SIDE OF TOMORROW, THE(1970)
Gil Taylor
BEDFORD INCIDENT, THE(1965, Brit.), ph; CUL-DE-SAC(1966, Brit.), ph; MAN OUTSIDE, THE(1968, Brit.), ph; NICE GIRL LIKE ME, A(1969, Brit.), ph; DAY AT THE BEACH, A(1970, Brit.), ph; FRENZY(1972, Brit.), ph; UNDERCOVERS HERO(1975, Brit.), ph; ESCAPE TO ATHENA(1979, Brit.), ph; FLASH GORDON(1980), ph; LOSIN'

IT(1983), ph
1984
LASSITER(1984), ph
Gilbert Taylor
BRIGHTON ROCK(1947, Brit.), ph; OUTSIDER, THE(1949, Brit.), ph; SEVEN DAYS TO NOON(1950, Brit.), ph; HIGH TREASON(1951, Brit.), ph; SAILOR OF THE KING(1953, Brit.), ph; YELLOW BALLOON, THE(1953, Brit.), ph; CREST OF THE WAVE(1954, Brit.), ph; FRONT PAGE STORY(1954, Brit.), ph; WEAK AND THE WICKED, THE(1954, Brit.), ph; DAM BUSTERS, THE(1955, Brit.), spec eff; JOSEPHINE AND MEN(1955, Brit.), ph; BLONDE SINNER(1956, Brit.), ph; IT'S GREAT TO BE YOUNG(1956, Brit.), ph; AS LONG AS THEY'RE HAPPY(1957, Brit.), ph; GOOD COMPANIONS, THE(1957, Brit.), ph; NO TIME FOR TEARS(1957, Brit.), ph; SILKEN AFFAIR, THE(1957, Brit.), ph; WOMEN IN A DRESSING GOWN(1957, Brit.), ph; DESERT ATTACK(1958, Brit.), ph; BOTTOMS UP(1960, Brit.), ph; SANDS OF THE DESERT(1960, Brit.), ph; TOMMY THE TOREADOR(1960, Brit.), ph; CALL ME GENIUS(1961, Brit.), ph; PETTICOAT PIRATES(1961, Brit.), ph; STOP ME BEFORE I KILL!(1961, Brit.), ph; OPERATION BULLSHINE(1963, Brit.), ph; PUNCH AND JUDY MAN, THE(1963, Brit.), ph; FERRY ACROSS THE MERSEY(1964, Brit.), ph; HARD DAY'S NIGHT, A(1964, Brit.), ph; HIDE AND SEEK(1964, Brit.), ph; NO TREE IN THE STREET(1964, Brit.), ph; REPULSION(1965, Brit.), ph; THEATRE OF DEATH(1967, Brit.), ph; WORK IS A FOUR LETTER WORD(1968, Brit.), ph; BEFORE WINTER COMES(1969, Brit.), ph; QUACKSER FORTUNE HAS A COUSIN IN THE BRONX(1970), ph; MACBETH(1971, Brit.), ph; OMEN, THE(1976), ph; STAR WARS(1977), ph; DRACULA(1979); MEETINGS WITH REMARKABLE MEN(1979, Brit.), ph; GREEN ICE(1981, Brit.), ph; VENOM(1982, Brit.), ph
Gilbert W. Taylor
DR. FRANKENSTEIN ON CAMPUS(1970, Can.), d, w; KLONDIKE FEVER(1980), p
Gillian Taylor
ADULTEROUS AFFAIR(1966)
Grant Taylor
TERROR TRAIL(1933), w; FORTY THOUSAND HORSEMEN(1941, Aus.); KANGAROO KID, THE(1950, Aus./U.S.); RATS OF TOBRUK(1951, Aus.); HIS MAJESTY O'KEEFE(1953, Aus.); LONG JOHN SILVER(1954, Aus.); ON THE BEACH(1959); SMILEY GETS A GUN(1959, Brit.); FOUR DESPERATE MEN(1960, Brit.); CALAMITY THE COW(1967, Brit.); FIVE MILLION YEARS TO EARTH(1968, Brit.)
Gregg Taylor
1984
REPO MAN(1984)
Grigor Taylor
HIGH ROLLING(1977, Aus.)
Gwen Taylor
MONTY PYTHON'S LIFE OF BRIAN(1979, Brit.); RICHARD'S THINGS(1981, Brit.)
H. Grenville Taylor
Silents
POTTER'S CLAY(1922, Brit.), d
H. Taylor
ZONTAR, THE THING FROM VENUS(1966), w
Harold Vaughn Taylor
MAGIC CHRISTMAS TREE(1964), w; PRINCESS AND THE MAGIC FROG, THE(1965), w
Harry Taylor
CAMPUS SLEUTH(1948)
Helen Taylor
EVERY NIGHT AT EIGHT(1935), cos; MARY BURNS, FUGITIVE(1935), cos; BIG BROWN EYES(1936), cos; PALM SPRINGS(1936), cos; STAND-IN(1937), cos; VOGUES OF 1938(1937), cos; TRADE WINDS(1938), cos
Henrietta Taylor
LADY TAKES A SAILOR, THE(1949); SHE'S WORKING HER WAY THROUGH COLLEGE(1952)
Henry Taylor
CANYON HAWKS(1930), w; FIREBRAND JORDAN(1930), p; TRAILS OF DANGER(1930), d&w; RED FORK RANGE(1931), w; EVERY NIGHT AT EIGHT(1935); DOUBLE WEDDING(1937); HATS OFF(1937); MARRIED BEFORE BREAKFAST(1937); YOU ONLY LIVE ONCE(1937); JUVENILE COURT(1938), w; WHO KILLED GAIL PRESTON?(1938), w
Hilary Taylor
FEMALE TROUBLE(1975)
Holland Taylor
NEXT MAN, THE(1976)
1984
ROMANCING THE STONE(1984)
Homer Taylor
MAN, WOMAN AND CHILD(1983)
Howard Taylor
NATIONAL VELVET(1944); BOOM!(1968); OUT OF THE BLUE(1982)
1984
BIG MEAT EATER(1984, Can.)
Irma Whelpley Taylor
Silents
OTHER MAN, THE(1918), w
J. O. Taylor
SONG O' MY HEART(1930), ph; SOLDIER'S PLAYTHING, A(1931), ph; KING KONG(1933), ph; MONKEY'S PAW, THE(1933), ph; SON OF KONG(1933), ph
Silents
GRIM GAME, THE(1919), ph; BLIND HEARTS(1921), ph; PRIVATE SCANDAL, A(1921), ph; SEA LION, THE(1921), ph; SCARS OF JEALOUSY(1923), ph; HOUSE OF YOUTH, THE(1924), ph; AFRAID TO LOVE(1927), ph; ALIAS THE LONE WOLF(1927), ph; BACHELOR'S BABY, THE(1927), ph; BY WHOSE HAND?(1927), ph; KID SISTER, THE(1927), ph; SALLY IN OUR ALLEY(1927), ph; STOLEN PLEASURES(1927), ph; WANDERING GIRLS(1927), ph; CHICAGO AFTER MIDNIGHT(1928), ph; SMOKE BELLEW(1929), ph
J.G. Taylor
SILVER RIVER(1948), tech adv
Jack Taylor
STORY OF ROBIN HOOD, THE(1952, Brit.); MASTER OF BALLANTRAE, THE(1953, U.S./Brit.); UNHOLY FOUR, THE(1954, Brit.); SEA SHALL NOT HAVE THEM, THE(1955, Brit.); SHADOW OF A MAN(1955, Brit.); HIDEOUT, THE(1956, Brit.);

FIGHTING MAD(1957, Brit.); YOU PAY YOUR MONEY(1957, Brit.); MAN WITH A GUN(1958, Brit.); STORMY CROSSING(1958, Brit.); ACTION STATIONS(1959, Brit.); SEA FURY(1959, Brit.); SON OF ROBIN HOOD(1959, Brit.); OPERATION CUPID(1960, Brit.), w; SENTENCED FOR LIFE(1960, Brit.); SHAKEDOWN, THE(1960, Brit.); PARANOIAC(1963, Brit.); SHADOW OF FEAR(1963, Brit.); CARRY ON SPYING(1964, Brit.); CHRISTMAS KID, THE(1968, U.S., Span.); COUNT DRACULA(1971, Sp., Ital., Ger., Brit.); DR. JEKYLL AND THE WOLFMAN(1971, Span.); VAMPIRE'S NIGHT ORGY, THE(1973, Span./Ital.); HORROR OF THE ZOMBIES(1974, Span.); CONAN THE BARBARIAN(1982); PIECES(1983, Span./Puerto Rico)

Misc. Talkies
SIGMA III(1966); NIGHT OF THE SORCERORS(1970)

Jack Taylor
NATIONAL LAMPOON'S CLASS REUNION(1982), set d; NIGHTMARES(1983), art d

Jack G. Taylor ,Jr.
STAR 80(1983), art d; UNCOMMON VALOR(1983), art d

Jack Gammon Taylor, Jr.
NINE TO FIVE(1980), art d

Jackie Taylor
DEVIL'S BROTHER, THE(1933); MADE FOR EACH OTHER(1939); FEMALE BUNCH, THE(1969); SATAN'S SADISTS(1969); COOLEY HIGH(1975)

Jacqueline Taylor
KID MILLIONS(1934); LITTLE MEN(1935); OF HUMAN BONDAGE(1964, Brit.)

James A. Taylor
LAST EMBRACE(1979), art d

James Taylor
TWO-LANE BLACKTOP(1971)

Jana Taylor
COLD WIND IN AUGUST(1961); JUDGMENT AT NUREMBERG(1961); HELL'S ANGELS ON WHEELS(1967)
1984
DREAMSCAPE(1984)

Jane Taylor
JACK THE RIPPER(1959, Brit.); YOUNG SINNER, THE(1965)

Janet Taylor
PROMISES IN THE DARK(1979)

Jean Taylor
FIVE ON THE BLACK HAND SIDE(1973)
Silents
JUST JIM(1915)

Jeanette Taylor
FAT SPY(1966)

Jeanne Taylor
ERRAND BOY, THE(1961)

Jeannine Taylor
FRIDAY THE 13TH(1980)

Jeffrey Taylor
SONG OF NORWAY(1970)

Jerry Taylor
CYCLE SAVAGES(1969); MACHO CALLAHAN(1970), ed

Jimmy Taylor
MARLOWE(1969), cos

Jo Taylor
Misc. Silents
MAN FROM MANHATTAN, THE(1916)

Joan Taylor
FIGHTING MAN OF THE PLAINS(1949); OFF LIMITS(1953); SAVAGE, THE(1953); WAR PAINT(1953); ROSE MARIE(1954); APACHE WOMAN(1955); FORT YUMA(1955); EARTH VS. THE FLYING SAUCERS(1956); GIRLS IN PRISON(1956); OMAR KHAYYAM(1957); WAR DRUMS(1957); 20 MILLION MILES TO EARTH(1957)

Joe Taylor
SOME OF MY BEST FRIENDS ARE...(1971)

John Taylor
MANY HAPPY RETURNS(1934); SOLDIER, SAILOR(1944, Brit.), p; ON DANGEROUS GROUND(1951); LAST RHINO, THE(1961, Brit.); ANGELS HARD AS THEY COME(1971); UNHOLY ROLLERS(1972); ON THE YARD(1978); FIENDISH PLOT OF DR. FU MANCHU, THE(1980); TAPS(1981)
Misc. Talkies
FOX STYLE(1973)

John Raymond Taylor
PEACE KILLERS, THE(1971)

Johnny Taylor
DUKE IS THE TOPS, THE(1938)

Jonathan Taylor
TOM SAWYER(1973)

Josh Taylor
SEPARATE WAYS(1981); WALTZ ACROSS TEXAS(1982)

Joyce Taylor
BEYOND A REASONABLE DOUBT(1956); FBI STORY, THE(1959); ATLANTIS, THE LOST CONTINENT(1961); RING OF FIRE(1961); BEAUTY AND THE BEAST(1963); THIRTEEN FRIGHTENED GIRLS(1963); TWICE TOLD TALES(1963); WINDSPLITTER, THE(1971)

Jud Taylor
INTERNS, THE(1962); GREAT ESCAPE, THE(1963)

Judson Taylor
GARMENT JUNGLE, THE(1957)

Juretta Taylor
GAS-S-S-S!(1970)

Kate Taylor
TRADING PLACES(1983)

Katherine Haviland Taylor
ONE MAN'S JOURNEY(1933), w

Kay Taylor
HIGH YELLOW(1965); PICNIC AT HANGING ROCK(1975, Aus.)
Misc. Talkies
NIGHT NURSE, THE(1977)

Keith Taylor
BOY, DID I GET A WRONG NUMBER!(1966); FOLLOW ME, BOYS!(1966); PERILS OF PAULINE, THE(1967); BORN WILD(1968); YOUNG RUNAWAYS, THE(1968)

Ken Taylor
LET'S GET MARRIED(1960, Brit.), w; ALFRED THE GREAT(1969, Brit.), w
1984
BEAR, THE(1984)

Kenneth Taylor
BEYOND THIS PLACE(1959, Brit.), w

Kent Taylor
HUSBAND'S HOLIDAY(1931); BLONDE VENUS(1932); DANCERS IN THE DARK(1932); DEVIL AND THE DEEP(1932); FORGOTTEN COMMANDMENTS(1932); IF I HAD A MILLION(1932); MERRILY WE GO TO HELL(1932); SIGN OF THE CROSS, THE(1932); TWO KINDS OF WOMEN(1932); CRADLE SONG(1933); I'M NO ANGEL(1933); LADY'S PROFESSION, A(1933); MYSTERIOUS RIDER, THE(1933); STORY OF TEMPLE DRAKE, THE(1933); SUNSET PASS(1933); UNDER THE TONTO RIM(1933); WHITE WOMAN(1933); DAVID HARUM(1934); DEATH TAKES A HOLIDAY(1934); DOUBLE DOOR(1934); LIMEHOUSE BLUES(1934); MANY HAPPY RETURNS(1934); MRS. WIGGS OF THE CABBAGE PATCH(1934); COLLEGE SCANDAL(1935); COUNTY CHAIRMAN, THE(1935); SMART GIRL(1935); TWO FISTED(1935); WITHOUT REGRET(1935); ACCUSING FINGER, THE(1936); FLORIDA SPECIAL(1936); MY MARRIAGE(1936); RAMONA(1936); SKY PARADE(1936); GIRL WITH IDEAS, A(1937); LADY FIGHTS BACK(1937); LOVE IN A BUNGALOW(1937); PRESCRIPTION FOR ROMANCE(1937); WHEN LOVE IS YOUNG(1937); WINGS OVER HONOLULU(1937); JURY'S SECRET, THE(1938); LAST EXPRESS, THE(1938); ESCAPE TO PARADISE(1939); FIVE CAME BACK(1939); FOUR GIRLS IN WHITE(1939); GRACIE ALLEN MURDER CASE(1939); PIRATES OF THE SKIES(1939); THREE SONS(1939); GIRL FROM AVENUE A(1940); GIRL IN 313(1940); I TAKE THIS WOMAN(1940); I'M STILL ALIVE(1940); MEN AGAINST THE SKY(1940); SUED FOR LIBEL(1940); TWO GIRLS ON BROADWAY(1940); REPENT AT LEISURE(1941); WASHINGTON MELODRAMA(1941); ARMY SURGEON(1942); FRISCO LILL(1942); HALF WAY TO SHANGHAI(1942); MISSISSIPPI GAMBLER(1942); TOMBSTONE, THE TOWN TOO TOUGH TO DIE(1942); BOMBER'S MOON(1943); ALASKA(1944); ROGER TOUHY, GANGSTER!(1944); DALTONS RIDE AGAIN, THE(1945); DANGEROUS MILLIONS(1946); DEADLINE FOR MURDER(1946); SMOOTH AS SILK(1946); TANGIER(1946); YOUNG WIDOW(1946); CRIMSON KEY, THE(1947); SECOND CHANCE(1947); HALF PAST MIDNIGHT(1948); FEDERAL AGENT AT LARGE(1950); TRIAL WITHOUT JURY(1950); WESTERN PACIFIC AGENT(1950); PAYMENT ON DEMAND(1951); SEEDS OF DESTRUCTION(1952); PLAYGIRL(1954); SECRET VENTURE(1955, Brit.); FRONTIER GAMBLER(1956); GHOST TOWN(1956); PHANTOM FROM 10,000 LEAGUES, THE(1956); SLIGHTLY SCARLET(1956); TRACK THE MAN DOWN(1956, Brit.); IRON SHERIFF, THE(1957); FORT BOWIE(1958); GANG WAR(1958); WALK TALL(1960); PURPLE HILLS, THE(1961); BROKEN LAND, THE(1962); FIREBRAND, THE(1962); CRAWLING HAND, THE(1963); DAY MARS INVADED EARTH, THE(1963); HARBOR LIGHTS(1963); LAW OF THE LAWLESS(1964); FORT COURAGEOUS(1965); BRIDES OF BLOOD(1968, US/Phil.); MIGHTY GORGA, THE(1969); SATAN'S SADISTS(1969); HELL'S BLOODY DEVILS(1970); BRAIN OF BLOOD(1971, Phil.)
Misc. Talkies
ANGELS' WILD WOMEN(1972); GIRLS FOR RENT(1974)

Kit Taylor
LONG JOHN SILVER(1954, Aus.); ASSAULT(1971, Brit.); DON'S PARTY(1976, Aus.); WEEKEND OF SHADOWS(1978, Aus.)

Kressman Taylor
ADDRESS UNKNOWN(1944), w

Kurt Taylor
TUNNELVISION(1976); CRACKING UP(1977)

Lance Taylor
THREE THE HARD WAY(1974)

Lance Taylor, Sr.
BLACULA(1972); FROGS(1972); HUGO THE HIPPO(1976, Hung./U.S.)

Larry [Laurence] Taylor
TAKE A POWDER(1953, Brit.); ALEXANDER THE GREAT(1956); PORT AFRIQUE(1956, Brit.); YOU PAY YOUR MONEY(1957, Brit.); GYPSY AND THE GENTLEMAN, THE(1958, Brit.); ROBBERY UNDER ARMS(1958, Brit.); SHERIFF OF FRACTURED JAW, THE(1958, Brit.); BANDIT OF ZHOBE, THE(1959); FIRST MAN INTO SPACE(1959, Brit.); MAN WHO LIKED FUNERALS, THE(1959, Brit.); SHAKEDOWN, THE(1960, Brit.); SWISS FAMILY ROBINSON(1960); TOO HOT TO HANDLE(1961, Brit.); TWO-WAY STRETCH(1961, Brit.); CONCRETE JUNGLE, THE(1962, Brit.); CROSSTRAP(1962, Brit.); INFORMATION RECEIVED(1962, Brit.); GIRL HUNTERS, THE(1963, Brit.); KING AND COUNTRY(1964, Brit.); ZULU(1964, Brit.); KALEIDOSCOPE(1966, Brit.); FOLLOW THAT CAMEL(1967, Brit.); NEVER BACK LOSERS(1967, Brit.); CHITTY CHITTY BANG BANG(1968, Brit.); SWAPPERS, THE(1970, Brit.); THIS, THAT AND THE OTHER(1970, Brit.); LAST VALLEY, THE(1971, Brit.); S(1974); GET CHARLIE TULLY(1976, Brit.); SLAVERS(1977, Ger.)

Lauren-Marie Taylor
FRIDAY THE 13TH PART II(1981); NEIGHBORS(1981)
1984
FRIDAY THE 13TH-THE FINAL CHAPTER(1984); GIRLS NIGHT OUT(1984)

Laurette Taylor
Misc. Silents
PEG O' MY HEART(1922); HAPPINESS(1924); ONE NIGHT IN ROME(1924)

Laurie Taylor
DICK BARTON STRIKES BACK(1949, Brit.); GAMBLER AND THE LADY, THE(1952, Brit.); SCOTLAND YARD INSPECTOR(1952, Brit.); SEA DEVILS(1953); WHITE FIRE(1953, Brit.)

Lawrence Taylor
INNER CIRCLE, THE(1946), w; JACKIE ROBINSON STORY, THE(1950), w; LADY WITHOUT PASSPORT, A(1950), w; SKIN GAME, THE(1965, Brit.)

Lawrence Edmund Taylor
UNDERDOG, THE(1943), w; DIXIE JAMBOREE(1945), w; DEVIL SHIP(1947), w; PHILO VANCE'S GAMBLE(1947), w; PHILO VANCE'S SECRET MISSION(1947), w

Lee Taylor
WOLFPEN PRINCIPLE, THE(1974, Can.)

Leigh Taylor
SUBWAY RIDERS(1981)

Lelah Taylor
FAIR WARNING(1937); BABES IN ARMS(1939)

Leon Taylor
PEOPLE WILL TALK(1951)

LeRoy Taylor
OVER 21(1945)
Les Taylor
DOUBLE NICKELS(1977)
Libby Taylor
I'M NO ANGEL(1933); BELLE OF THE NINETIES(1934); WHEN A MAN SEES RED(1934); MISSISSIPPI(1935); RECKLESS(1935); RUGGLES OF RED GAP(1935); SHANGHAI(1935); STREAMLINE EXPRESS(1935); DANGEROUS(1936); LIBELED LADY(1936); STAGE STRUCK(1936); FURY AND THE WOMAN(1937); HOLLYWOOD HOTEL(1937); MYSTERIOUS CROSSING(1937); AMAZING DR. CLITTERHOUSE, THE(1938); TOY WIFE, THE(1938); ICE FOLLIES OF 1939(1939); GREAT McGINTY, THE(1940); HOWARDS OF VIRGINIA, THE(1940); SANTA FE TRAIL(1940); FLIGHT FROM DESTINY(1941); MY GAL SAL(1942); AND THE ANGELS SING(1944); HOME IN INDIANA(1944); SARATOGA TRUNK(1945); TOMORROW IS FOREVER(1946); FOXES OF HARROW, THE(1947); ANOTHER PART OF THE FOREST(1948); YOU'RE MY EVERYTHING(1949); TWO TICKETS TO BROADWAY(1951)
Linda Taylor
GROOVE TUBE, THE(1974), anim; CRACKING UP(1977), anim
1984
SAM'S SON(1984), cos
Lisa Taylor
EYES OF LAURA MARS(1978); WHERE THE BUFFALO ROAM(1980)
1984
WINDY CITY(1984)
Lori Taylor
MARK OF THE WITCH(1970)
Lynn Taylor
1984
HEY BABE!(1984, Can.), ch
Lynne Taylor
WALK IN THE SHADOW(1966, Brit.)
Malcolm Taylor
ROBBERY(1967, Brit.)
Margaret Taylor
Misc. Talkies
OLD TESTAMENT(1963, Ital.)
Marian Taylor
DOZENS, THE(1981), a, w
Marilyn Taylor
TRIUMPHS OF A MAN CALLED HORSE(1983, US/Mex.), art d
Marjorie Taylor
CRIMES OF STEPHEN HAWKE, THE(1936, Brit.); HEIRLOOM MYSTERY, THE(1936, Brit.); NOTHING LIKE PUBLICITY(1936, Brit.); REASONABLE DOUBT(1936, Brit.); WELL DONE, HENRY(1936, Brit.); ELDER BROTHER, THE(1937, Brit.); IT'S NEVER TOO LATE TO MEND(1937, Brit.); RACING ROMANCE(1937, Brit.); TICKET OF LEAVE MAN, THE(1937, Brit.); EASY RICHES(1938, Brit.); MIRACLES DO HAPPEN(1938, Brit.); PAID IN ERROR(1938, Brit.); SILVER TOP(1938, Brit.); FACE AT THE WINDOW, THE(1939, Brit.); THREE SILENT MEN(1940, Brit.)
Mark Taylor
SERIAL(1980)
Mark L. Taylor
DAMNATION ALLEY(1977); RAISE THE TITANIC(1980, Brit.)
Mary Taylor
SOAK THE RICH(1936); LADY OF THE TROPICS(1939)
Mary Imlay Taylor
CONQUEST(1929), w
Mathew Taylor
NIGHT CROSSING(1982)
Matt Taylor
RED HOT SPEED ½(1929), w; SKINNER STEPS OUT(1929), w; TONIGHT AT TWELVE(1929), w; DAMES AHOY(1930), w; HIDE-OUT, THE(1930), w; YOUNG DESIRE(1930), w; LION AND THE LAMB(1931), w; MORE THAN A SECRETARY(1936), w; WOMEN MEN MARRY, THE(1937), w; HERO FOR A DAY(1939), w; ROAD TO HAPPINESS(1942), w
Silents
STEPPING ALONG(1926), w; ALL ABOARD(1927), w; SKINNER'S BIG IDEA(1928), w; EXALTED FLAPPER, THE(1929), w
Matthew Taylor
CATTLE ANNIE AND LITTLE BRITCHES(1981)
Maxie Taylor
WOMAN TO WOMAN(1946, Brit.)
Maxine Taylor
DARK ROAD, THE(1948, Brit.)
Megan Taylor
ICE-CAPADES(1941)
Merle Ann Taylor
DR. HECKYL AND MR. HYPE(1980)
Meshach Taylor
DAMIEN–OMEN II(1978); BEAST WITHIN, THE(1982)
Michael Taylor
HONEYMOON HOTEL(1946, Brit.); LAST EMBRACE(1979), p; FOXES(1980); PURSUIT OF D.B. COOPER, THE(1981), p
Michelle Taylor
1984
SUPERGIRL(1984)
Mike Taylor
QUADROPHENIA(1979, Brit.), ed; LONG GOOD FRIDAY, THE(1982, Brit.), ed
Minnie Taylor
CRUCIFIX, THE(1934, Brit.)
Monica Taylor
Misc. Talkies
BIG BUST-OUT, THE(1973)
Morgan Taylor
ICE-CAPADES REVUE(1942)
Morton Taylor
LILITH(1964)
Nan Taylor
SMITHY(1946, Aus.); PACIFIC ADVENTURE(1947, Aus.)

Nathaniel Taylor
PASSING THROUGH(1977); HUNTER, THE(1980)
Nel Taylor
STRANGER FROM VENUS, THE(1954, Brit.), makeup
Nell Taylor
UPTURNED GLASS, THE(1947, Brit.), makeup
Noel Taylor
GENERATION(1969), cos; MRS. POLLIFAX-SPY(1971), cos; ONCE UPON A SCOUNDREL(1973), cos; RHINOCEROS(1974), cos; ENEMY OF THE PEOPLE, AN(1978), cos; LEGEND OF THE LONE RANGER, THE(1981), cos
Norma Taylor
GIRL HABIT(1931); TUMBLING TUMBLEWEEDS(1935); WATERFRONT LADY(1935); I DEMAND PAYMENT(1938)
Opal Taylor
ROBIN OF TEXAS(1947)
Otis Taylor
RED, WHITE AND BLACK, THE(1970)
Capt. P.G. Taylor
SMITHY(1946, Aus.); PACIFIC ADVENTURE(1947, Aus.)
Patrick Taylor
ENDLESS LOVE(1981)
Patti Taylor
GOG(1954)
Pauline Taylor
HOW I WON THE WAR(1967, Brit.); CLOCKWORK ORANGE, A(1971, Brit.)
"Peanuts" Taylor
ISLAND WOMEN(1958)
Peggy Ann Taylor
THREE MEN IN A BOAT(1958, Brit.)
Peter Taylor
CAIRO ROAD(1950, Brit.), ed; DEVIL GIRL FROM MARS(1954, Brit.), ed; FOR BETTER FOR WORSE(1954, Brit.), ed; HOBSON'S CHOICE(1954, Brit.), ed; MAN OF THE MOMENT(1955, Brit.); SUMMERTIME(1955), ed; TECKMAN MYSTERY, THE(1955, Brit); KID FOR TWO FARTHINGS, A(1956, Brit.); LAST MAN TO HANG, THE(1956, Brit.), ed; POSTMARK FOR DANGER(1956, Brit.), ed; BRIDGE ON THE RIVER KWAI, THE(1957, Brit.), ed; SEA WIFE(1957, Brit.), ed; DEVIL'S DAFFODIL, THE(1961, Brit./Ger.), ed; MARK, THE(1961, Brit.), ed; TWO AND TWO MAKE SIX(1962, Brit.), ed; WALTZ OF THE TOREADORS(1962, Brit.), ed; THIS SPORTING LIFE(1963, Brit.), ed; JUDITH(1965), ed; ONE WAY PENDULUM(1965, Brit.), ed; SANDWICH MAN, THE(1966, Brit.), ed; TAMING OF THE SHREW, THE(1967, U.S./Ital.), ed; ANZIO(1968, Ital.), ed; THOSE DARING YOUNG MEN IN THEIR JAUNTY JALOPIES(1969, Fr./Brit./ Ital.), ed; TEMPTER, THE(1974, Ital./Brit.), ed; DEVIL IS A WOMAN, THE(1975, Brit./Ital.), ed; MATTER OF TIME, A(1976, Ital./U.S.), ed; LA TRAVIATA(1982), ed
Phil Taylor
HOWARDS OF VIRGINIA, THE(1940); ICE-CAPADES(1941); ICE-CAPADES REVUE(1942); INTRIGUE(1947)
Phoebe Taylor
CARNY(1980), w
Ray Taylor
ONE WAY TRAIL, THE(1931), d; FIGHTING TROOPER, THE(1935), d; IVORY-HANDLED GUN(1935), d; OUTLAWED GUNS(1935), d; THROWBACK, THE(1935), d; COWBOY AND THE KID,THE(1936), d; SILVER SPURS(1936), d; SUNSET OF POWER(1936), d; THREE MESQUITEERS, THE(1936), d; BOSS OF LONELY VALLEY(1937), d; MYSTERY OF THE HOODED HORSEMEN, THE(1937), d; RAW TIMBER(1937), d; TEX RIDES WITH THE BOY SCOUTS(1937), d; FRONTIER TOWN(1938), d; HAWAIIAN BUCKAROO(1938), d; PANAMINT'S BAD MAN(1938), d; RAWHIDE(1938), d; SUDDEN BILL DORN(1938), d; BAD MAN FROM RED BUTTE(1940), d; LAW AND ORDER(1940), d; PONY POST(1940), d; RAGTIME COWBOY JOE(1940), d; RIDERS OF PASCO BASIN(1940), d; WEST OF CARSON CITY(1940), d; BOSS OF BULLION CITY(1941), d; BURY ME NOT ON THE LONE PRAIRIE(1941), d; LAW OF THE RANGE(1941), d; MAN FROM MONTANA(1941), d; RAWHIDE RANGERS(1941), d; DESTINATION UNKNOWN(1942), d; FIGHTING BILL FARGO(1942), d; STAGECOACH BUCKAROO(1942), d; TREAT EM' ROUGH(1942), d; CHEYENNE ROUNDUP(1943), d; LONE STAR TRAIL, THE(1943), d; MUG TOWN(1943), d; DALTONS RIDE AGAIN, THE(1945), d; BORDER FEUD(1947), d; CHEYENNE TAKES OVER(1947), d; FIGHTING VIGILANTES, THE(1947), d; GHOST TOWN RENEGADES(1947), d; LAW OF THE LASH(1947), d; MICHIGAN KID, THE(1947), d; PIONEER JUSTICE(1947), d; RANGE BEYOND THE BLUE(1947), d; RETURN OF THE LASH(1947), d; SHADOW VALLEY(1947), d; STAGE TO MESA CITY(1947), d; VIGILANTES RETURN, THE(1947), d; WEST TO GLORY(1947), d; WILD COUNTRY(1947), d; BLACK HILLS(1948), d; CHECK YOUR GUNS(1948), d; DEAD MAN'S GOLD(1948), d; FRONTIER REVENGE(1948), d&w; GUNNING FOR JUSTICE(1948), d; HAWK OF POWDER RIVER, THE(1948), d; MARK OF THE LASH(1948), d; RETURN OF WILDFIRE, THE(1948), d; TIOGA KID, THE(1948), d; TORNADO RANGE(1948), d; WESTWARD TRAIL, THE(1948), d; CRASHING THRU(1949), d; HIDDEN DANGER(1949), d; LAW OF THE WEST(1949), d; OUTLAW COUNTRY(1949), d; RANGE JUSTICE(1949), d; SHADOWS OF THE WEST(1949), d; SON OF A BADMAN(1949), d; SON OF BILLY THE KID(1949), d; WEST OF EL DORADO(1949), d
Misc. Talkies
BOSS OF BOOMTOWN(1944), d; JUNGLE QUEEN(1946), d
Silents
AVENGING SHADOW, THE(1928), d; BEAUTY AND BULLETS(1928), d; EYES OF THE UNDERWORLD(1929), d
Misc. Silents
CLEAN-UP MAN, THE(1928), d; CRIMSON CANYON, THE(1928), d; GREASED LIGHTING(1928), d; QUICK TRIGGER(1928); BORDER WILDCAT, THE(1929), d; RIDIN' DEMON, THE(1929), d
Reeve Taylor
MIDNIGHT EPISODE(1951, Brit.), w
Regina Taylor
Misc. Silents
LURE OF A WOMAN, THE(1921)
Renee Taylor
ERRAND BOY, THE(1961); FINE MADNESS, A(1966); PRODUCERS, THE(1967); DETECTIVE, THE(1968); LOVERS AND OTHER STRANGERS(1970), w; JENNIFER ON MY MIND(1971); MADE FOR EACH OTHER(1971), a, w; NEW LEAF, A(1971); LAST OF THE RED HOT LOVERS(1972); LOVESICK(1983)

Rex Taylor
UNDER THE GREENWOOD TREE(1930, Brit.), w; SIT TIGHT(1931), w; VAGA-BOND QUEEN, THE(1931, Brit.), w; HIGH GEAR(1933), w; HELLDORADO(1935), w; SITTING ON THE MOON(1936), w; MANDARIN MYSTERY, THE(1937), w; DAY-TIME WIFE(1939), w; REDHEAD FROM MANHATTAN(1954), w
Silents
LOVE SWINDLE(1918), w; OTHER MAN, THE(1918), w; CABARET GIRL, THE(1919), w; TWIN BEDS(1920), w; WAY OF A MAID, THE(1921), w; SEEING'S BELIEVING(1922), w; NOISE IN NEWBORO, A(1923), w; SOCIAL CODE, THE(1923), w; JACK O' CLUBS(1924), w; RECKLESS AGE, THE(1924), w; HIGH AND HAND-SOME(1925), w; IRENE(1926), w; ROLLING HOME(1926), w; SKINNER'S DRESS SUIT(1926), w; HONEYMOON AHEAD(1927, Brit.), w; SMILE, BROTHER, SMI-LE(1927), w; SO THIS IS LOVE(1928), w; WEEKEND WIVES(1928, Brit.), w
Rheet Taylor
SUPER SPOOK(1975), m
Richard Taylor
JOHNNY BELINDA(1948); MOTHER IS A FRESHMAN(1949); KILL THE UM-PIRE(1950); JOE MACBETH(1955), m, md; DEADLIEST SIN, THE(1956, Brit.), m; FINGER OF GUILT(1956, Brit.), md; SPIN A DARK WEB(1956, Brit.), m; WAY OUT, THE(1956, Brit.), md; COUNTERFEIT PLAN, THE(1957, Brit.), m; LONG HAUL, THE(1957, Brit.), md; SCOTLAND YARD DRAGNET(1957, Brit.), md; ELECTRONIC MONSTER. THE(1960, Brit.), m; THUNDER IN CAROLINA(1960); TERMINAL IS-LAND(1973); NIGHTHAWKS(1978, Brit.), ed; STINGRAY(1978), d&w; TRON(1982), spec eff
1984
DREAMSCAPE(1984), spec eff
Richard G. Taylor
GOG(1954), w; AMBUSH AT CIMARRON PASS(1958), w
Rip Taylor
THINGS ARE TOUGH ALL OVER(1982); I'D RATHER BE RICH(1964); GONG SHOW MOVIE, THE(1980)
Robert Taylor
HANDY ANDY(1934); WICKED WOMAN, A(1934); BROADWAY MELODY OF 1936(1935); MAGNIFICENT OBSESSION(1935); MURDER IN THE FLEET(1935); SOCIETY DOCTOR(1935); TIMES SQUARE LADY(1935); WEST POINT OF THE AIR(1935); GORGEOUS HUSSY, THE(1936); HIS BROTHER'S WIFE(1936); PRIVATE NUMBER(1936); SMALL TOWN GIRL(1936); BROADWAY MELODY OF '38(1937); CAMILLE(1937); PERSONAL PROPERTY(1937); THIS IS MY AFFAIR(1937); CROWD ROARS, THE(1938); THREE COMRADES(1938); YANK AT OXFORD, A(1938); LADY OF THE TROPICS(1939); LUCKY NIGHT(1939); REMEMBER?(1939); STAND UP AND FIGHT(1939); ESCAPE(1940); FLIGHT COMMAND(1940); WATERLOO BRIDGE(1940); BILLY THE KID(1941); WHEN LADIES MEET(1941); HER CARD-BOARD LOVER(1942); JOHNNY EAGER(1942); STAND BY FOR ACTION(1942); BATAAN(1943); SONG OF RUSSIA(1943); YOUNGEST PROFESSION, THE(1943); UNDERCURRENT(1946); HIGH WALL, THE(1947); BRIBE, THE(1949); CONSPIRA-TOR(1949, Brit.); AMBUSH(1950); DEVIL'S DOORWAY(1950); QUO VADIS(1951); WESTWARD THE WOMEN(1951); IVANHOE(1952, Brit.); ABOVE AND BEYOND(1953); ALL THE BROTHERS WERE VALIANT(1953); I LOVE MEL-VIN(1953); KNIGHTS OF THE ROUND TABLE(1953); RIDE, VAQUERO!(1953); ROGUE COP(1954); VALLEY OF THE KINGS(1954); MANY RIVERS TO CROSS(1955); QUENTIN DURWARD(1955); D-DAY, THE SIXTH OF JUNE(1956); LAST HUNT, THE(1956); POWER AND THE PRIZE, THE(1956); TIP ON A DEAD JOCKEY(1957); LAW AND JAKE WADE, THE(1958); PARTY GIRL(1958); SADDLE THE WIND(1958); HANGMAN, THE(1959); HOUSE OF THE SEVEN HAWKS, THE(1959); KILLERS OF KILIMANJARO(1960, Brit.); CATTLE KING(1963); MIRACLE OF THE WHITE STAL-LIONS(1963); HOUSE IS NOT A HOME, A(1964); NIGHT WALKER, THE(1964); JOHNNY TIGER(1966); SAVAGE PAMPAS(1967, Span./Arg.); DAY THE HOTLINE GOT HOT, THE(1968, Fr./Span.); GLASS SPHINX, THE(1968, Egypt/Ital./Span.); WHERE ANGELS GO...TROUBLE FOLLOWS(1968); WIZARDS(1977), anim; HEIDI'S SONG(1982), d, w; HEY, GOOD LOOKIN'(1982), anim
1984
BAY BOY(1984, Can.); BEAT STREET(1984)
Misc. Talkies
NINE LIVES OF FRITZ THE CAT, THE(1974), d
Misc. Silents
GLORIOUS LADY, THE(1919)
Robert Lewis Taylor
SILKEN AFFAIR, THE(1957, Brit.), w; GUNS OF DIABLO(1964), w; TREASURE OF MATECUMBE(1976), w
Rocky Taylor
LAST RUN, THE(1971); SLIPPER AND THE ROSE, THE(1976, Brit.); RAIDERS OF THE LOST ARK(1981)
1984
SAHARA(1984)
Rocky Taylor [Omar Sharif]
PINK PANTHER STRIKES AGAIN, THE(1976, Brit.)
Rod Taylor
TOP GUN(1955); VIRGIN QUEEN, THE(1955); CATERED AFFAIR, THE(1956); GIANT(1956); KING OF THE CORAL SEA(1956, Aus.); RACK, THE(1956); WORLD WITHOUT END(1956); RAINTREE COUNTY(1957); SEPARATE TABLES(1958); STEP DOWN TO TERROR(1958); ASK ANY GIRL(1959); TIME MACHINE, THE(1960, Brit./U.S.); ONE HUNDRED AND ONE DALMATIANS(1961); BIRDS, THE(1963); GATHERING OF EAGLES, A(1963); SEVEN SEAS TO CALAIS(1963, Ital.); SUNDAY IN NEW YORK(1963); V.I.P.s, THE(1963, Brit.); FATE IS THE HUNTER(1964); DO NOT DISTURB(1965); YOUNG CASSIDY(1965, U.S./Brit.); 36 HOURS(1965); GLASS BOT-TOM BOAT, THE(1966); LIQUIDATOR, THE(1966, Brit.); CHUKA(1967), a, p; HO-TEL(1967); DARK OF THE SUN(1968, Brit.); HELL WITH HEROES, THE(1968); HIGH COMMISSIONER, THE(1968, U.S./Brit.); DARKER THAN AMBER(1970); MAN WHO HAD POWER OVER WOMEN, THE(1970, Brit.); ZABRISKIE POINT(1970); DEADLY TRACKERS(1973); TRADER HORN(1973); TRAIN ROBBERS, THE(1973); PICTURE SHOW MAN, THE(1980, Aus.); ON THE RUN(1983, Aus.); TIME TO DIE, A(1983)
Misc. Talkies
COLOSSUS AND THE AMAZONS(1960); JAMAICAN GOLD(1971); HEROES, THE(1975); HELL RIVER(1977)
Roderick Taylor
STAR CHAMBER, THE(1983), w
Rodney [Rod] Taylor
HELL ON FRISCO BAY(1956)

Rodney [Rod] Taylor
LONG JOHN SILVER(1954, Aus.)
Ron Taylor
TWO AND TWO MAKE SIX(1962, Brit.), ph; NOBODY WAVED GOODBYE(1965, Can.); HOFFMAN(1970, Brit.); JAWS(1975), ph; LONG SHOT(1981, Brit.); TRADING PLACES(1983)
1984
EXTERMINATOR 2(1984); SILENT ONE, THE(1984, New Zealand), ph
Ronald Taylor
BLOODY BROOD, THE(1959, Can.)
Ronnie Taylor
TOMMY(1975, Brit.), ph; CIRCLE OF IRON(1979, Brit.), ph; SAVAGE HAR-VEST(1981), ph; GANDHI(1982), ph; HIGH ROAD TO CHINA(1983), ph; HOUND OF THE BASKERVILLES, THE(1983, Brit.), ph
1984
CHAMPIONS(1984), ph; SPLITZ(1984), ph
Roosevelt Taylor
MACK, THE(1973)
Rosamund Taylor
VACATION FROM MARRIAGE(1945, Brit.)
Rosemary Taylor
CHICKEN EVERY SUNDAY(1948), w; PETER RABBIT AND TALES OF BEATRIX POTTER(1971, Brit.)
Ross Taylor
I'VE GOTTA HORSE(1965, Brit.), ch
Roy Taylor
COME ACROSS(1929), d
Ruth Taylor
COLLEGE COQUETTE, THE(1929); THIS THING CALLED LOVE(1929); HERE'S GEORGE(1932, Brit.); NEW HOTEL, THE(1932, Brit.); EXCESS BAGGAGE(1933, Brit.); DOUBLE EVENT, THE(1934, Brit.); IT'S A GRAND LIFE(1953, Brit.)
Silents
JACK SPURLOCK, PRODIGAL(1918); WILD HONEY(1919); GENTLEMEN PREFER BLONDES(1928); JUST MARRIED(1928)
S.E.V. Taylor
Silents
GREAT LOVE, THE(1918), w; GREATEST THING IN LIFE, THE(1918), w; GIRL WHO STAYED AT HOME, THE(1919), w; ROMANCE OF HAPPY VALLEY, A(1919), w; SCARLET DAYS(1919), w; GREATEST QUESTION, THE(1920), w; IDOL DANCER, THE(1920), w; ROULETTE(1924), d; BREED OF THE SUNSETS(1928), w; DOG LAW(1928), w
Misc. Silents
VOW, THE(1915), d; RISE OF SUSAN, THE(1916), d; PUBLIC BE DAMNED(1917), d; MOHICAN'S DAUGHTER, THE(1922), d; LONE WOLF, THE(1924), d; MIRACLE OF LIFE, THE(1926), d
Sam Taylor
COQUETTE(1929), d, w; LADY OF THE PAVEMENTS(1929), w; DU BARRY, WOM-AN OF PASSION(1930), d&w; AMBASSADOR BILL(1931), d; KIKI(1931), d&w; SKY-LINE(1931), d; DEVIL'S LOTTERY(1932), d; OUT ALL NIGHT(1933), d; CAT'S PAW, THE(1934), d&w; VAGABOND LADY(1935), p&d; NOTHING BUT TROUBLE(1944), d
Silents
SAILOR-MADE MAN, A(1921), w; DOCTOR JACK(1922), w; GRANDMA'S BOY(1922), w; SAFETY LAST(1923), d, w; WHY WORRY(1923), d, w; GIRL SHY(1924), d, w; HOT WATER(1924), d, w; FRESHMAN, THE(1925), d, w; EXIT SMILING(1926), d, w; FOR HEAVEN'S SAKE(1926), d; MY BEST GIRL(1927), d; TEMPEST(1928), d
Samuel Taylor
TAMING OF THE SHREW, THE(1929), d, w; SABRINA(1954), w; EDDY DUCHIN STORY, THE(1956), w; VERTIGO(1958), w; GOODBYE AGAIN(1961), w; PLEASURE OF HIS COMPANY, THE(1961), w; THREE ON A COUCH(1966), w; ROSIE!(1967), w; TOPAZ(1969, Brit.), w; PROMISE AT DAWN(1970, U.S./Fr.), w; LOVE MACHINE, THE,(1971), w; AVANTI!(1972), w
Samuel A. Taylor
MONTE CARLO STORY, THE(1957, Ital.), d, w
Samuel W. Taylor
MAN WHO RETURNED TO LIFE, THE(1942), w; MAN WITH MY FACE, THE(1951), w; BAIT(1954), w; ABSENT-MINDED PROFESSOR, THE(1961), w; SON OF FLUB-BER(1963), w
Scott Taylor
JIGGS AND MAGGIE IN SOCIETY(1948)
Sharon Taylor
ATTACK OF THE KILLER TOMATOES(1978)
Shirin Taylor
NANA(1983, Ital.)
Siobhan Taylor
THESE ARE THE DAMNED(1965, Brit.); THIS, THAT AND THE OTHER(1970, Brit.)
Siobhan Taylor
DOG OF FLANDERS, A(1959)
Slats Taylor
FORCE OF ARMS(1951)
Stan Taylor
MR. AND MRS. SMITH(1941)
Stanley Taylor
HOME TOWNERS, THE(1928); GLAD RAG DOLL(1929); HOTTENTOT, THE(1929); CODE OF HONOR(1930); MANHATTAN MELODRAMA(1934); THIS SIDE OF HEAVEN(1934); MEN OF THE HOUR(1935); HOLY TERROR, THE(1937); WHEN TOMORROW COMES(1939)
Silents
ANCIENT HIGHWAY, THE(1925); BANDIT'S SON, THE(1927); WAR HORSE, THE(1927); RED LIPS(1928)
Misc. Silents
GUILTY ONE, THE(1924); RED HOT HOOFS(1926); ROMANTIC AGE, THE(1927)
Stanley E.V. Taylor
Misc. Silents
SIGHT UNSEEN, A(1914), d
Stanner E.V. Taylor
Misc. Silents
HER GREAT HOUR(1916), d; PASSERS-BY(1916), d

Stephen Taylor
MAN WHO WOULD NOT DIE, THE(1975), w; SCARECROW, THE(1982, New Zealand)
1984
CONSTANCE(1984, New Zealand)
Steve Taylor
KID FROM BOOKLYN, THE(1946); LIVE WIRES(1946)
Stuart Taylor
MALIBU HIGH(1979)
Susan Taylor
JOHN AND MARY(1969)
Suzette Taylor
1984
AMERICAN TABOO(1984)
Sydney Taylor
BULLDOG BREED, THE(1960, Brit.)
Tammy Taylor
MALIBU HIGH(1979); SECOND THOUGHTS(1983)
1984
LOVELINES(1984); MEATBALLS PART II(1984)
Ted Taylor
COUNTERFEIT TRAITOR, THE(1962)
Teddy Taylor
Misc. Silents
NEARER MY GOD TO THEE(1917, Brit.)
Teri Taylor
EMMA MAE(1976)
Terri Taylor
Misc. Talkies
GREAT SKYCOPTER RESCUE, THE(1982)
Tex Taylor
PRACTICALLY YOURS(1944)
Theodore Taylor
SHOWDOWN(1973), w
Tim Brooke Taylor
TWELVE PLUS ONE(1970, Fr./Ital.)
Tina Taylor
SILENT SCREAM(1980)
Tom Taylor
PEG OF OLD DRURY(1936, Brit.), w; TICKET OF LEAVE MAN, THE(1937, Brit.), w; RESURRECTION(1980)
Silents
STILL WATERS RUN DEEP(1916, Brit.), w
Tony Taylor
BABE RUTH STORY, THE(1948); THREE LITTLE WORDS(1950); WINCHESTER '73(1950); IT'S A BIG COUNTRY(1951); ROOM FOR ONE MORE(1952); SCANDAL AT SCOURIE(1953)
Totti Truman Taylor
EIGHT O'CLOCK WALK(1954, Brit.); FRENCH, THEY ARE A FUNNY RACE, THE(1956, Fr.); NOT SO DUSTY(1956, Brit.); PORTRAIT IN SMOKE(1957, Brit.); TOWN ON TRIAL(1957, Brit.); UNDERCOVER GIRL(1957, Brit.); LINKS OF JUSTICE(1958); MOMENT OF INDISCRETION(1958, Brit.); RX MURDER(1958, Brit.); WOMAN POSSESSED, A(1958, Brit.); TOP FLOOR GIRL(1959, Brit.); DATE AT MIDNIGHT(1960, Brit.); PRESS FOR TIME(1966, Brit.); CHITTY CHITTY BANG BANG(1968, Brit.); CONFESSIONS OF A WINDOW CLEANER(1974, Brit.)
Twyla Taylor
EVICTORS, THE(1979)
Valerie Taylor
BERKELEY SQUARE(1933); DESIGNING WOMEN(1934, Brit.); 48 HOURS(1944, Brit.); TAKE MY LIFE(1948, Brit.), w; FACES IN THE DARK(1960, Brit.); WHAT A CARVE UP!(1962, Brit.); IN THE COOL OF THE DAY(1963); MACBETH(1963); REPULSION(1965, Brit.); JAWS(1975), ph
1984
SILENT ONE, THE(1984, New Zealand), ph
Vashti Taylor
SMITH'S WIVES(1935, Brit.); WHITE LILAC(1935, Brit.)
Vaughn Taylor
LAWYER MAN(1933); PICTURE SNATCHER(1933); FRANCIS GOES TO THE RACES(1951); UP FRONT(1951); BACK AT THE FRONT(1952); MEET DANNY WILSON(1952); IT SHOULD HAPPEN TO YOU(1954); DECISION AT SUNDOWN(1957); JAILHOUSE ROCK(1957); THIS COULD BE THE NIGHT(1957); ANDY HARDY COMES HOME(1958); CAT ON A HOT TIN ROOF(1958); COWBOY(1958); GUNSMOKE IN TUCSON(1958); LINEUP, THE(1958); PARTY GIRL(1958); SCREAMING MIMI(1958); YOUNG LIONS, THE(1958); BLUE DENIM(1959); WARLOCK(1959); GALLANT HOURS, THE(1960); PLUNDERERS, THE(1960); PSYCHO(1960); WIZARD OF BAGHDAD, THE(1960); DIAMOND HEAD(1962); TWILIGHT OF HONOR(1963); WHEELER DEALERS, THE(1963); CARPETBAGGERS, THE(1964); FBI CODE 98(1964); UNSINKABLE MOLLY BROWN, THE(1964); DARK INTRUDER(1965); ZEBRA IN THE KITCHEN(1965); PROFESSIONALS, THE(1966); RUSSIANS ARE COMING, THE RUSSIANS ARE COMING, THE(1966); IN COLD BLOOD(1967); FEVER HEAT(1968); POWER, THE(1968); SHAKIEST GUN IN THE WEST, THE(1968); BALLAD OF CABLE HOGUE, THE(1970); $1,000,000 DUCK(1971); GUMBALL RALLY, THE(1976)
Vern Taylor
BUSTIN' LOOSE(1981); FRANCES(1982); OFFICER AND A GENTLEMAN, AN(1982)
Victor Taylor
MEN OF IRELAND(1938, Ireland), p
Vida Taylor
GOD TOLD ME TO(1976); CLASH OF THE TITANS(1981)
Vin Taylor
HARLEM RIDES THE RANGE(1939), art d; GHOST GUNS(1944), set d; NAVAJO TRAIL, THE(1945), set d; SHANGHAI COBRA, THE(1945), art d; STRANGE MR. GREGORY, THE(1945), set d; THERE GOES KELLY(1945), set d; FEAR(1946), set d; GENTLEMAN FROM TEXAS(1946), art d; WEST OF THE ALAMO(1946), set d; FALL GUY(1947), set d; RAIDERS OF THE SOUTH(1947), set d; SIX GUN SERENADE(1947), set d; SONG OF THE DRIFTER(1948), art d; STAMPEDE(1949), set d
Vincent Taylor
MARK OF THE LASH(1948), art d

Vincent A. Taylor
YANKEE FAKIR(1947), set d
Virgil "Slats" Taylor
COMIN' ROUND THE MOUNTAIN(1951); STORY OF WILL ROGERS, THE(1952)
Wade Taylor
LILITH(1964)
Wally Taylor
COOL BREEZE(1972); SHAFT'S BIG SCORE(1972); HANGUP(1974); LORD SHANGO(1975); GUMBALL RALLY, THE(1976); WHEN A STRANGER CALLS(1979); ROCKY III(1982)
Walter Taylor
OUR RELATIONS(1936); LURE OF THE WILDERNESS(1952)
Wayne Taylor
OPERATION SECRET(1952); CHARGE AT FEATHER RIVER, THE(1953); THREE SAILORS AND A GIRL(1953); FRENCH LINE, THE(1954); CELL 2455, DEATH ROW(1955); SCREAMING EAGLES(1956); MOTORCYCLE GANG(1957); REFORM SCHOOL GIRL(1957); UNTAMED YOUTH(1957); TOUCH OF EVIL(1958); J.W. COOP(1971)
Wendy E. Taylor
FIRST MONDAY IN OCTOBER(1981)
Wesley Taylor
MC CABE AND MRS. MILLER(1971)
Wilda Taylor
HOUSE IS NOT A HOME, A(1964); ROUSTABOUT(1964); HARUM SCARUM(1965); FRANKIE AND JOHNNY(1966); HOLD ON(1966), ch; FASTEST GUITAR ALIVE, THE(1967); ANGEL, ANGEL, DOWN WE GO(1969), ch; LOVE GOD?, THE(1969), ch
William H. Taylor
PHONY AMERICAN, THE(1964, Ger.)
William B. Taylor
TWILIGHT ZONE–THE MOVIE(1983)
William D. Taylor
Silents
LAST CHAPTER, THE(1915), d
Misc. Silents
CAPTAIN ALVAREZ(1914); EYE FOR AN EYE, AN(1915), d; HIGH HAND, THE(1915), d; LONESOME HEART(1915), d; AMERICAN BEAUTY, THE(1916), d; BEN BLAIR(1916), d; HE FELL IN LOVE WITH HIS WIFE(1916), d; HER FATHER'S SON(1916), d; HOUSE OF LIES, THE(1916), d; BIG TIMBER(1917), d; HAPPINESS OF THREE WOMEN, THE(1917), d; HIS MAJESTY BUNKER BEAN(1918), d; HOW COULD YOU, JEAN?(1918), d; FURNANCE, THE(1920), d; GREEN TEMPTATION, THE(1922), d
William Desmond Taylor
Silents
CAPRICES OF KITTY, THE(1915), d; NEARLY A LADY(1915), d; PARSON OF PANAMINT, THE(1916), d; JACK AND JILL(1917), d; HUCK AND TOM(1918), d; ANNE OF GREEN GABLES(1919), d; HUCKLEBERRY FINN(1920), d; JENNY BE GOOD(1920), d; JUDY OF ROGUES' HARBOUR(1920), d; NURSE MARJORIE(1920), d; SOUL OF YOUTH, THE(1920), d; BEYOND(1921), d; MORALS(1921), d; WEALTH(1921), d; WITCHING HOUR, THE(1921), d; TOP OF NEW YORK, THE(1925), d
Misc. Silents
DAVY CROCKETT(1916), d; PASQUALE(1916), d; NORTH OF FIFTY-THREE(1917), d; OUT OF THE WRECK(1917), d; REDEEMING LOVE, THE(1917), d; TOM SAWYER(1917), d; VARMINT, THE(1917), d; WORLD APART, THE(1917), d; JOHANNA ENLISTS(1918), d; MILE-A-MINUTE KENDALL(1918), d; SPIRIT OF '17, THE(1918), d; UP THE ROAD WITH SALLIE(1918), d; CAPTAIN KIDD, JR.(1919), d; SACRED AND PROFANE LOVE(1921), d
William Taylor
MY FAIR LADY(1964)
Wilton Taylor
Silents
ALIAS JIMMY VALENTINE(1920); TREASURE ISLAND(1920); GASOLINE GUS(1921); LITTLE CLOWN, THE(1921); OUTSIDE THE LAW(1921); SHERLOCK BROWN(1921); RIDIN' WILD(1922); MADNESS OF YOUTH(1923)
Misc. Silents
GIRL FROM THE OUTSIDE, THE(1919); CAVE GIRL, THE(1921); TRAVELING SALESMAN, THE(1921); LANE THAT HAD NO TURNING, THE(1922); DRIVIN' FOOL, THE(1923)
Zack Taylor
YOUNG NURSES, THE(1973)
Misc. Talkies
GROUP MARRIAGE(1972)
Jack Taylor, Jr.
LOOKER(1981), art d
Lee Taylor-Allen
ALONE IN THE DARK(1982)
Lynne Taylor-Corbett
1984
FOOTLOOSE(1984), ch
Jean Taylor-Smith
DOCTOR IN THE HOUSE(1954, Brit.); WEAK AND THE WICKED, THE(1954, Brit.); RING OF BRIGHT WATER(1969, Brit.); MY CHILDHOOD(1972, Brit.); MY AIN FOLK(1974, Brit.)
Leigh Taylor-Young
I LOVE YOU, ALICE B. TOKLAS!(1968); BIG BOUNCE, THE(1969); ADVENTURERS, THE(1970); GAMES, THE(1970); BUTTERCUP CHAIN, THE(1971, Brit.); GANG THAT COULDN'T SHOOT STRAIGHT, THE(1971); HORSEMEN, THE(1971); SOYLENT GREEN(1973); CAN'T STOP THE MUSIC(1980); LOOKER(1981)
Robert Tayman
MOON ZERO TWO(1970, Brit.); VAMPIRE CIRCUS(1972, Brit.); HOUSE OF WHIPCORD(1974, Brit.); INTERNECINE PROJECT, THE(1974, Brit.); STUD, THE(1979, Brit.)
Hisa Tayo
BORN IN FLAMES(1983), w
Jun Tazaki
TOKYO FILE 212(1951); GATE OF HELL(1954, Jap.); I BOMBED PEARL HARBOR(1961, Jap.); MAN AGAINST MAN(1961, Jap.); TATSU(1962, Jap.); GODZILLA VS. THE THING(1964, Jap.); GORATH(1964, Jap.); OPERATION ENEMY FORT(1964, Jap.); ATRAGON(1965, Jap.); LOST WORLD OF SINBAD, THE(1965, Jap.); GODZILLA VERSUS THE SEA MONSTER(1966, Jap.); EMPEROR AND A GENERAL, THE(1968,

Jap.); DAREDEVIL IN THE CASTLE(1969, Jap.); DESTROY ALL MONSTERS(1969, Jap.); MAN IN THE STORM, THE(1969, Jap.); MONSTER ZERO(1970, Jap.); WAR OF THE GARGANTUAS, THE(1970, Jap.)

Zara Tazil
CYCLONE RANGER(1935); LAWLESS BORDER(1935), w

Ladislav Tazky
DESERTER AND THE NOMADS, THE(1969, Czech./Ital.), w

Rolf Tbiele
DAY WILL COME, A(1960, Ger.), p

Peter Ilich Tchaikovsky
SCARLET EMPRESS, THE(1934), m; FANTASIA(1940), w; SONG OF MY HEART(1947), m; UNFAITHFULLY YOURS(1948), m; ILLICIT INTERLUDE(1954, Swed.), m; RHAPSODY(1954), m; QUEEN OF SPADES(1961, USSR), w; TWICE A MAN(1964), m; YOLANTA(1964, USSR), m; SLEEPING BEAUTY, THE(1966, USSR), m; WEEKEND MURDERS, THE(1972, Ital.), m
1984
UNFAITHFULLY YOURS(1984), m

Peter Illych Tchaikovsky
NUTCRACKER FANTASY(1979), m

Peter Ilyich Tchaikovsky
TAXI TO HEAVEN(1944, USSR), m; SECOND WOMAN, THE(1951), m; SWAN LAKE, THE(1967), w, m; ROMEO AND JULIET(1968, Ital./Span.), m; MUSIC LOVERS, THE(1971, Brit.), m

Petr Ilich Tchaikovsky
ISADORA(1968, Brit.), m; WOMEN IN LOVE(1969, Brit.), m

Petr Illich Tchaikovsky
DRACULA(1931), m; FINAL CHORD, THE(1936, Ger.), m; SLEEPING BEAUTY(1959), m

Petr Ilyich Tchaikovsky
POCKETFUL OF MIRACLES(1961), m

Ludmilla Tchakalova
STOLEN PLANS, THE(1962, Brit.)

Emil Tchakarov
EXPOSED(1983)

Raffi Tchalikian
DEAD ZONE, THE(1983)

Giacomo Tchang
SAMSON AND THE SEVEN MIRACLES OF THE WORLD(1963, Fr./Ital.)

Leon Tchaso
FAT ANGELS(1980, U.S./Span.), w

Ivan Tchenko
ISADORA(1968, Brit.)

Katia Tchenko
1984
AMERICAN DREAMER(1984)

Ludmilla Tcherina
RED SHOES, THE(1948, Brit.); TALES OF HOFFMANN, THE(1951, Brit.); MATA HARI'S DAUGHTER(1954, Fr./Ital), a, ch; SIGN OF THE PAGAN(1954); OH ROSALINDA(1956, Brit.); LOVERS OF TERUEL, THE(1962, Fr.)

Alexis Tcherkassky
COSSACKS IN EXILE(1939, Ukrainian)

Marianna Tcherkassky
TURNING POINT, THE(1977)

Pierre Tchernia
LA BELLE AMERICAINE(1961, Fr.), a, w; WAR OF THE BUTTONS(1963 Fr.); COUNTERFEIT CONSTABLE, THE(1966, Fr.), a, w; LUCKY LUKE(1971, Fr./Bel.), w

Sophico Tchiaourelli
COLOR OF POMEGRANATES, THE(1980, Armenian)

Kostia Tchikime
JOHNNY THE GIANT KILLER(1953, Fr.), ph

Boris Tchirkof
DEFENSE OF VOLOTCHAYEVSK, THE(1938, USSR)

A. Tchistiakov
Silents
STORM OVER ASIA(1929, USSR)

D. Tchitorina
Misc. Silents
SNOW MAIDEN, THE(1914, USSR)

Stephane Tcholdieff
DEVIL PROBABLY, THE(1977, FR.), p

Ludmilla Tchor
GIRL GRABBERS, THE(1968)

Mme. Sul Te Wan
Silents
QUEEN KELLY(1929)

Beryl Te Wiata
DEAD KIDS(1981 Aus./New Zealand)
1984
CONSTANCE(1984, New Zealand)

Inia Te Wiata
LAND OF FURY(1955 Brit.); MAN OF THE MOMENT(1955, Brit.); SANDS OF THE DESERT(1960, Brit.)

Teachers and Children of the Pestalozzi Village, Switzerland
VILLAGE, THE(1953, Brit./Switz.)

Paul Tead
SIX OF A KIND(1934)

Phil Tead
FRONT PAGE, THE(1931); GUILTY GENERATION, THE(1931); KIKI(1931); VICE SQUAD, THE(1931); FAITHLESS(1932); FINAL EDITION(1932); ME AND MY GAL(1932); TRIAL OF VIVIENNE WARE, THE(1932); WINNER TAKE ALL(1932); BOWERY, THE(1933); BROADWAY BAD(1933); LADY KILLER(1933); PICTURE SNATCHER(1933); SITTING PRETTY(1933); DAMES(1934); EVELYN PRENTICE(1934); STAND UP AND CHEER(1934 80m FOX bw); THIN MAN, THE(1934); THIS SIDE OF HEAVEN(1934); DARING YOUNG MAN, THE(1935); IT HAPPENED IN NEW YORK(1935); MARY BURNS, FUGITIVE(1935); MEN WITHOUT NAMES(1935); ONE HOUR LATE(1935); PAGE MISS GLORY(1935); STRAIGHT FROM THE HEART(1935); WINGS IN THE DARK(1935); GREAT ZIEGFELD, THE(1936); HOLLYWOOD BOULEVARD(1936); MILKY WAY, THE(1936); MURDER WITH PICTURES(1936); PRINCESS COMES ACROSS, THE(1936); I STOLE A MILLION(1939); STRONGER THAN DESIRE(1939); TELL NO TALES(1939); JOHNNY APOLLO(1940);

MUSIC IN MY HEART(1940); SUSAN AND GOD(1940); WESTERNER, THE(1940); PACIFIC RENDEZVOUS(1942); RIGHT TO THE HEART(1942); RINGS ON HER FINGERS(1942); THIS GUN FOR HIRE(1942); YOU'RE TELLING ME(1942); CASANOVA BROWN(1944); COLONEL EFFINGHAM'S RAID(1945); GOODBYE, MY FANCY(1951); UNKNOWN MAN, THE(1951); ARCTIC FLIGHT(1952); KANSAS CITY CONFIDENTIAL(1952); CONFIDENTIAL CONNIE(1953); FANGS OF THE ARCTIC(1953); FANGS OF THE WILD(1954); WIRETAPPERS(1956); ROCKABILLY BABY(1957)

Philip Tead
LIGHTNIN'(1930)

Phillips Tead
Silents
SHE LOVES AND LIES(1920); WHISPERS(1920)

John K. Teaford
ACCOMPLICE(1946), p

Jack Teagarden
BIRTH OF THE BLUES(1941); STRIP, THE(1951); GLORY ALLEY(1952); GLASS WALL, THE(1953)

Phyllis Teagardin
CABINET OF CALIGARI, THE(1962)

A. Guy Teague
CATTLE TOWN(1952); WYOMING RENEGADES(1955)

Anthony Teague
TROUBLE WITH GIRLS(AND HOW TO GET INTO IT), THE*1/2 (1969); BAREFOOT EXECUTIVE, THE(1971); HOW TO SUCCEED IN BUSINESS WITHOUT REALLY TRYING(1976)

Christina Teague
THIRD FINGER, LEFT HAND(1940)

Frances Teague
Silents
IRON HORSE, THE(1924); LAST EDITION, THE(1925)
Misc. Silents
WILD JUSTICE(1925)

Gary Teague
GAL WHO TOOK THE WEST, THE(1949)

George Teague
PHILO VANCE'S SECRET MISSION(1947), spec eff

George J. Teague
OUT OF THE BLUE(1947), spec eff; T-MEN(1947), spec eff; BEHIND LOCKED DOORS(1948), spec eff; HE WALKED BY NIGHT(1948), spec eff; HOLLOW TRIUMPH(1948), spec eff; LET'S LIVE A LITTLE(1948), spec eff; RAW DEAL(1948), spec eff

Guy Teague
SHOWDOWN, THE(1950); VIGILANTE HIDEOUT(1950); KID FROM AMARILLO, THE(1951); BATTLES OF CHIEF PONTIAC(1952); HAREM GIRL(1952); STRANGER WORE A GUN, THE(1953); OUTLAW STALLION, THE(1954); LAWLESS STREET, A(1955); FURY AT GUNSIGHT PASS(1956); GIANT(1956); WHITE SQUAW, THE(1956)

Jim Teague
SHEPHERD OF THE HILLS, THE(1964)

Lewis Teague
HARD ROAD, THE(1970); DIRTY O'NEIL(1974), d; SUMMER RUN(1974), ed; BORN TO KILL(1975), ed; CRAZY MAMA(1975), ed; AVALANCHE(1978), spec eff; LADY IN RED, THE(1979), d, ed; ALLIGATOR(1980), d; DEATH VENGEANCE(1982), d; CUJO(1983), d

Louis Teague
DO NOT THROW CUSHIONS INTO THE RING(1970), a, ph

Scooter Teague
WEST SIDE STORY(1961)

Mary Teahan
NIGHT IN HEAVEN, A(1983)

Spencer Teakle
ANOTHER DAWN(1937); SHALL WE DANCE(1937); FIRST MAN INTO SPACE(1959, Brit.); COVER GIRL KILLER(1960, Brit.); GENTLE TRAP, THE(1960, Brit.)

Phil Teal
WHAT PRICE HOLLYWOOD?(1932)

Ray Teal
WESTERN JAMBOREE(1938); CHEROKEE STRIP(1940); I LOVE YOU AGAIN(1940); KITTY FOYLE(1940); NEW MOON(1940); NORTHWEST PASSAGE(1940); PONY POST(1940); PRAIRIE SCHOONERS(1940); STRANGE CARGO(1940); THIRD FINGER, LEFT HAND(1940); HONKY TONK(1941); OUTLAWS OF THE PANHANDLE(1941); SERGEANT YORK(1941); SHADOW OF THE THIN MAN(1941); ZIEGFELD GIRL(1941); APACHE TRAIL(1942); JUKE GIRL(1942); NAZI AGENT(1942); SECRET ENEMIES(1942); THEY DIED WITH THEIR BOOTS ON(1942); WILD BILL HICKOK RIDES(1942); WOMAN OF THE YEAR(1942); GENTLE GANGSTER, A(1943); MADAME CURIE(1943); NORTH STAR, THE(1943); SHE HAS WHAT IT TAKES(1943); SLIGHTLY DANGEROUS(1943); THOUSANDS CHEER(1943); YOUNGEST PROFESSION, THE(1943); GENTLE ANNIE(1944); HOLLYWOOD CANTEEN(1944); NONE SHALL ESCAPE(1944); NOTHING BUT TROUBLE(1944); ONCE UPON A TIME(1944); PRINCESS AND THE PIRATE, THE(1944); STRANGE AFFAIR(1944); THIN MAN GOES HOME, THE(1944); WING AND A PRAYER(1944); ALONG CAME JONES(1945); ANCHORS AWEIGH(1945); BACK TO BATAAN(1945); CAPTAIN KIDD(1945); CIRCUMSTANTIAL EVIDENCE(1945); FIGHTING GUARDSMAN, THE(1945); KEEP YOUR POWDER DRY(1945); STRANGE VOYAGE(1945); SUDAN(1945); WONDER MAN(1945); ZIEGFELD FOLLIES(1945); BANDIT OF SHERWOOD FOREST, THE(1946); BEST YEARS OF OUR LIVES, THE(1946); CANYON PASSAGE(1946); DEADLINE FOR MURDER(1946); DECOY(1946); HARVEY GIRLS, THE(1946); MISSING LADY, THE(1946); TILL THE CLOUDS ROLL BY(1946); BRUTE FORCE(1947); CHEYENNE(1947); DEAD RECKONING(1947); DEEP VALLEY(1947); DESERT FURY(1947); DRIFTWOOD(1947); FABULOUS TEXAN, THE(1947); HIGH WALL, THE(1947); LONG NIGHT, THE(1947); MICHIGAN KID, THE(1947); MY FAVORITE BRUNETTE(1947); NORTHWEST OUTPOST(1947); PURSUED(1947); RAMROD(1947); ROAD TO RIO(1947); SEA OF GRASS, THE(1947); UNCONQUERED(1947); ACT OF MURDER, AN(1948); COUNTESS OF MONTE CRISTO, THE(1948); DAREDEVILS OF THE CLOUDS(1948); FURY AT FURNACE CREEK(1948); I WOULDN'T BE IN YOUR SHOES(1948); JOAN OF ARC(1948); MIRACLE OF THE BELLS, THE(1948); ONE SUNDAY AFTERNOON(1948); ROAD HOUSE(1948); WALK A CROOKED MILE(1948); WHISPERING SMITH(1948); BLONDIE HITS THE JACKPOT(1949); IT HAPPENS EVERY SPRING(1949); KAZAN(1949); ONCE MORE, MY DARLING(1949); RUSTY'S BIRTHDAY(1949); SCENE OF THE CRIME(1949); STREETS OF LAREDO(1949); AM-

BUSH(1950); CONVICTED(1950); DAVY CROCKETT, INDIAN SCOUT(1950); EDGE OF DOOM(1950); HARBOR OF MISSING MEN(1950); KID FROM TEXAS, THE(1950); MEN, THE(1950); NO WAY OUT(1950); OUR VERY OWN(1950); PETTY GIRL, THE(1950); REDHEAD AND THE COWBOY, THE(1950); WHEN YOU'RE SMILING(1950); WHERE DANGER LIVES(1950); WINCHESTER '73(1950); ALONG THE GREAT DIVIDE(1951); BIG CARNIVAL, THE(1951); DISTANT DRUMS(1951); FLAMING FEATHER(1951); FORT WORTH(1951); LORNA DOONE(1951); SECRET OF CONVICT LAKE, THE(1951); TOMORROW IS ANOTHER DAY(1951); CAPTIVE CITY(1952); CARRIE(1952); CATTLE TOWN(1952); HANGMAN'S KNOT(1952); JUMPING JACKS(1952); LION AND THE HORSE, THE(1952); MONTANA BELLE(1952); TURNING POINT, THE(1952); WILD NORTH, THE(1952); AMBUSH AT TOMAHAWK GAP(1953); WILD ONE, THE(1953); ABOUT MRS. LESLIE(1954); COMMAND, THE(1954); LUCKY ME(1954); ROGUE COP(1954); APACHE AMBUSH(1955); DESPERATE HOURS, THE(1955); INDIAN FIGHTER, THE(1955); MAN FROM BITTER RIDGE, THE(1955); RAGE AT DAWN(1955); RUN FOR COVER(1955); BURNING HILLS, THE(1956); BAND OF ANGELS(1957); DECISION AT SUNDOWN(1957); GUNS OF FORT PETTICOAT, THE(1957); OKLAHOMAN, THE(1957); PHANTOM STAGECOACH, THE(1957); TALL STRANGER, THE(1957); UTAH BLAINE(1957); WAYWARD GIRL, THE(1957); GUNMAN'S WALK(1958); SADDLE THE WIND(1958); HOME FROM THE HILL(1960); INHERIT THE WIND(1960); JUDGMENT AT NUREMBERG(1961); ONE-EYED JACKS(1961); POSSE FROM HELL(1961); GIRL NAMED TAMIRO, A(1962); CATTLE KING(1963); TAGGART(1964); CHISUM(1970); LIBERATION OF L.B. JONES, THE(1970)

Sonne Teal
DOLL, THE(1962, Fr.)

Cynthia Teale
MADNESS OF THE HEART(1949, Brit.)

Leonard Teale
SMILEY GETS A GUN(1959, Brit.); SUNDOWNERS, THE(1960)

Ken Tealor
TRIAL OF BILLY JACK, THE(1974)

Monica Teama
HISTORY OF THE WORLD, PART 1(1981)

Miss Sam Teardrop
DIRTYMOUTH(1970)

Ethel Teare
Silents
WOMAN WHO SINNED, A(1925)

Conway Tearle
EVIDENCE(1929); GOLD DIGGERS OF BROADWAY(1929); LOST ZEPPELIN(1930); TRUTH ABOUT YOUTH, THE(1930); CAPTIVATION(1931, Brit); LADY WHO DARED, THE(1931); MORALS FOR WOMEN(1931); FALSE MADONNA(1932); HER MAD NIGHT(1932); KING MURDER, THE(1932); MAN ABOUT TOWN(1932); VANITY FAIR(1932); DAY OF RECKONING(1933); PLEASURE(1933); SHOULD LADIES BEHAVE?(1933); FIFTEEN WIVES(1934); STINGAREE(1934); HEADLINE WOMAN, THE(1935); SING SING NIGHTS(1935); DESERT GUNS(1936); KLONDIKE ANNIE(1936); PREVIEW MURDER MYSTERY(1936); ROMEO AND JULIET(1936)
Misc. Talkies
JUDGMENT BOOK, THE(1935); TRAIL'S END(1935); SENOR JIM(1936)
Silents
NIGHTINGALE, THE(1914); SEVEN SISTERS, THE(1915); COMMON LAW, THE(1916); STELLA MARIS(1918); WAY OF A WOMAN(1919); FORBIDDEN WOMAN, THE(1920); SHE LOVES AND LIES(1920); AFTER MIDNIGHT(1921); FIGHTER, THE(1921); SOCIETY SNOBS(1921), a, w; ONE WEEK OF LOVE(1922); REFEREE, THE(1922); SHADOWS OF THE SEA(1922); WIDE-OPEN TOWN, A(1922); ASHES OF VENGEANCE(1923); COMMON LAW, THE(1923); JUST A WOMAN(1925); DANCING MOTHERS(1926); ALTARS OF DESIRE(1927); ISLE OF FORGOTTEN WOMEN(1927); SMOKE BELLEW(1929)
Misc. Silents
SHORE ACRES(1914); HELENE OF THE NORTH(1915); POOR SCHMALTZ(1915); HEART OF THE HILLS, THE(1916); FOOLISH VIRGIN, THE(1917); JUDGEMENT HOUSE, THE(1917); WORLD FOR SALE, THE(1918); HER GAME(1919); HUMAN DESIRE, THE(1919); MIND THE PAINT GIRL(1919); VIRTUOUS VAMP, A(1919); VIRTUOUS WIVES(1919); ATONEMENT(1920); MAROONED HEARTS(1920); ROAD OF AMBITION, THE(1920); TWO WEEKS(1920); WHISPERING DEVILS(1920); BUCKING THE TIGER(1921); MAN OF STONE, THE(1921); OATH, THE(1921); ETERNAL FLAME, THE(1922); LOVE'S MASQUERADE(1922); BELLA DONNA(1923); DANGEROUS MAID, THE(1923); RUSTLE OF SILK, THE(1923); BLACK OXEN(1924); FLIRTING WITH LOVE(1924); LILLIES OF THE FIELD(1924); NEXT CORNER, THE(1924); WHITE MOTH, THE(1924); BAD COMPANY(1925); GREAT DIVIDE, THE(1925); HEART OF A SIREN(1925); MORALS FOR MEN(1925); MYSTIC, THE(1925); SCHOOL FOR WIVES(1925); DANCER OF PARIS, THE(1926); GREATER GLORY, THE(1926); MY OFFICIAL WIFE(1926); SPORTING LOVER, THE(1926); MOULDERS OF MEN(1927); LOST ZEPPELIN, THE(1929)

David Tearle
GREEN GODDESS, THE(1930)

Godfrey Tearle
THESE CHARMING PEOPLE(1931, Brit.); SHADOW BETWEEN, THE(1932, Brit.); WOLVES OF THE UNDERWORLD(1935, Brit.); 39 STEPS, THE(1935, Brit.); EAST MEETS WEST(1936, Brit.); LAST JOURNEY, THE(1936, Brit.); TOMORROW WE LIVE(1936, Brit.); ONE OF OUR AIRCRAFT IS MISSING(1942, Brit.); AT DAWN WE DIE(1943, Brit.); LAMP STILL BURNS, THE(1943, Brit.); UNDERGROUND GUERRILLAS(1944, Brit.); NOTORIOUS GENTLEMAN(1945, Brit.); GAY INTRUDERS, THE(1946, Brit.); BEGINNING OR THE END, THE(1947); PRIVATE ANGELO(1949, Brit.); CRASH OF SILENCE(1952, Brit.); WHITE CORRIDORS(1952, Brit.); DECAMERON NIGHTS(1953, Brit.); I BELIEVE IN YOU(1953, Brit.); TITFIELD THUNDERBOLT, THE(1953, Brit.)
Silents
FANCY DRESS(1919, Brit.); MARCH HARE, THE(1919, Brit.); NOBODY'S CHILD(1919, Brit.); QUEEN'S EVIDENCE(1919, Brit.); IF YOUTH BUT KNEW(1926, Brit.); ONE COLUMBO NIGHT(1926, Brit.)
Misc. Silents
MIDNIGHT GAMBOLS(1919, Brit.); SALOME OF THE TENEMENTS(1925)

Malcolm Tearle
HER REPUTATION(1931, Brit.)

Noel Tearle
Silents
OVER THE HILL TO THE POORHOUSE(1920); STARDUST(1921); SPLENDID LIE, THE(1922)

Audrey Teasdale
LIFE IN HER HANDS(1951, Brit.)

Ralph Teasdale
TO CATCH A THIEF(1936, Brit.)

Verree Teasdale
SYNCOPATION(1929); SAP FROM SYRACUSE, THE(1930); PAYMENT DEFERRED(1932); SKYSCRAPER SOULS(1932); LOVE, HONOR, AND OH BABY!(1933); LUXURY LINER(1933); ROMAN SCANDALS(1933); TERROR ABOARD(1933); THEY JUST HAD TO GET MARRIED(1933); DESIRABLE(1934); DOCTOR MONICA(1934); FASHIONS OF 1934(1934); FIREBIRD, THE(1934); GOODBYE LOVE(1934); MADAME DU BARRY(1934); MODERN HERO, A(1934); MIDSUMMER'S NIGHT'S DREAM, A(1935); MILKY WAY, THE(1936); FIRST LADY(1937); FIFTH AVENUE GIRL(1939); TOPPER TAKES A TRIP(1939); I TAKE THIS WOMAN(1940); LOVE THY NEIGHBOR(1940); TURNABOUT(1940); COME LIVE WITH ME(1941)

Earl Teass
MR. DISTRICT ATTORNEY(1946), set d; CIGARETTE GIRL(1947), set d

Ida Teater
TEMPORARY WIDOW, THE(1930, Ger./Brit.)

Teatro Real Dell Opera Di Roma
MADAME BUTTERFLY(1955 Ital./Jap.)

Juan Tebar
HOUSE THAT SCREAMED, THE(1970, Span.), w

Oscar Tebar
1984
THREE CROWNS OF THE SAILOR(1984, Fr.)

Susan Tebbs
LITTLEST HORSE THIEVES, THE(1977)

William R. Tebbs
GOING HOME(1971)

Frank Tebeck
COOL AND THE CRAZY, THE(1958)

John-Michael Tebelak
GODSPELL(1973), w

Michael Teboul
ONCE IN PARIS(1978)

Nicole Teboul
ONCE IN PARIS(1978)

Philippe Teboul
FIRST TIME, THE(1978, Fr.)

Robert Tebow
YOUNG GIRLS OF ROCHEFORT, THE(1968, Fr.)

Tec-Art Studios
TEN NIGHTS IN A BARROOM(1931), set d
Silents
TIMOTHY'S QUEST(1922), set d; SUCCESS(1923), set d; EARLY BIRD, THE(1925), set d; MAD DANCER(1925), set d; SHORE LEAVE(1925), set d; JUST SUPPOSE(1926), ed

Jacopo Tecchi
SEVEN SEAS TO CALAIS(1963, Ital.)

A. Techihaya
Misc. Silents
SLUMS OF TOKYO(1930, Jap.)

Andre Techine
BAROCCO(1976, Fr.), d, w; BRONTE SISTERS, THE(1979, Fr.), d, w

Technical Film Studios
MURDER IN MISSISSIPPI(1965), spec eff

Alfred Technik
DEVIL'S TRAP, THE(1964, Czech.), w

Theo Tecklenburg
EFFI BRIEST(1974, Ger.)

Ted
FLOWER THIEF, THE(1962)

Ted Dawson Orchestra
HIGH HAT(1937)

Ted Fio Rito and Band
BROADWAY GONDOLIER(1935)

Ted Fio Rito and His Orchestra
MELODY PARADE(1943); SILVER SKATES(1943)

Ted Fio Rito's Orchestra
RHYTHM PARADE(1943)

Ted Fio-Rito and His Orchestra
SWEETHEART OF SIGMA CHI(1933)

Ted Fiorito and His Band
TWENTY MILLION SWEETHEARTS(1934)

Ted Heath and His Music
DANCE HALL(1950, Brit.)

Ted Heath and His Orchestra
JAZZ BOAT(1960, Brit.)

Ted Heath's Kenny Baker Swing Group
HOUR OF GLORY(1949, Brit.)

Ted Lewis and His Band
FOLLOW THE BOYS(1944)

Ted Lewis and his Orchestra
HOLD THAT GHOST(1941)

Ted Mapes and The Sons of the Pioneers
RED RIVER VALLEY(1941)

Ted Weems and his Orchestra
HAT CHECK HONEY(1944)

Ted Weems Orchestra
SWING, SISTER, SWING(1938)

Teddy
JAWS OF JUSTICE(1933)
Silents
STELLA MARIS(1918)

Teddy Buckner and His All Stars
FOUR FOR TEXAS(1963)

Teddy Buckner and His All-Stars
HUSH... HUSH, SWEET CHARLOTTE(1964)

Teddy Foster and his Band
LANDFALL(1953, Brit.)
Teddy Joyce and his Band
RADIO FOLLIES(1935, Brit.); HEARTS OF HUMANITY(1936, Brit.)
Teddy Kennedy Group
INBETWEEN AGE, THE(1958, Brit.)
Teddy Powell Orchestra
JAM SESSION(1944)
Teddy Wilson and His Band
SOMETHING TO SHOUT ABOUT(1943)
Alberto Tedecco
REVOLT OF THE MERCENARIES(1964, Ital./Span.)
Sylvia Tedemar
GOOD MORNING... AND GOODBYE(1967)
Nico Tedenco
BANG BANG KID, THE(1968 U.S./Span./Ital.), m
Giannco Tedeschi
DROP DEAD, MY LOVE(1968, Italy)
Gianrico Tedeschi
CARTHAGE IN FLAMES(1961, Fr./Ital.); MADAME(1963, Fr./Ital./Span.); THREE FABLES OF LOVE(1963, Fr./Ital./Span.); FASCIST, THE(1965, Ital.); LOVE A LA CARTE(1965, Ital.); FRANKENSTEIN-ITALIAN STYLE(1977, Ital.)
Giorgio Tedeschi
ENGAGEMENT ITALIANO(1966, Fr./Ital.)
Maria Tedeschi
8 ½(1963, Ital.)
Guy J. Tedesco
REQUIEM FOR A GUNFIGHTER(1965), w
Paola Tedesco
GOSPEL ACCORDING TO ST. MATTHEW, THE(1966, Fr., Ital.); BATTLE OF THE AMAZONS(1973, Ital./Span.); CRIME BOSS(1976, Ital.); I HATE BLONDES(1981, Ital.)
Charles L. Tedford
WAKAMBA!(1955), w
Charles Tedford
HERE COMES HAPPINESS(1941), w; TANGA-TIKA(1953), w
Charlotte Tedlie
EARLY BIRD, THE(1936, Brit.); LUCK OF THE IRISH, THE(1937, Ireland)
William Tedmarsh
Misc. Silents
LONESOME TOWN(1916); SEQUEL TO THE DIAMOND FROM THE SKY(1916); FATE AND THE CHILD(1917); GYPSY'S TRUST, THE(1917)
Irene Tedrow
UNCLE HARRY(1945); THEY WON'T BELIEVE ME(1947); MOON AND SIXPENCE, THE(1942); SONG OF THE OPEN ROAD(1944); JUST BEFORE DAWN(1946); AIR HOSTESS(1949); THIEVES' HIGHWAY(1949); COMPANY SHE KEEPS, THE(1950); LION IS IN THE STREETS, A(1953); SANTA FE PASSAGE(1955); TEN COMMANDMENTS, THE(1956); LOVING YOU(1957); HOT SPELL(1958); SADDLE THE WIND(1958); PLEASE DON'T EAT THE DAISIES(1960); THUNDER OF DRUMS, A(1961); DEADLY DUO(1962); CINCINNATI KID, THE(1965); FOR PETE'S SAKE!(1966); GETTING STRAIGHT(1970); MANDINGO(1975); EMPIRE OF THE ANTS(1977); FOUL PLAY(1978); MIDNIGHT MADNESS(1980)
Elsa Tee
HEAVEN IS ROUND THE CORNER(1944, Brit.); TWILIGHT HOUR(1944, Brit.); HERE COMES THE SUN(1945, Brit.); SCHOOL FOR RANDLE(1949, Brit.)
Richard Tee
ONE-TRICK PONY(1980)
G.H. Teed
SEXTON BLAKE AND THE MADEMOISELLE(1935, Brit.), w
John Teed
YOUNG WOODLEY(1930, Brit.); BYPASS TO HAPPINESS(1934, Brit.); HOUSE OF DARKNESS(1948, Brit.)
Phil Teed
GLAMOUR(1934)
Maureen Teefy
SCAVENGER HUNT(1979); FAME(1980); GREASE 2(1982)
1984
SUPERGIRL(1984)
Jim Teegarden
MOTEL HELL(1980), set d
William J. Teegarden
TWILIGHT ZONE–THE MOVIE(1983), set d
William Teegarden
E.T. THE EXTRA-TERRESTRIAL(1982), set
Joachim Teege
MERRY WIVES OF WINDSOR, THE(1952, Ger.); THOSE FANTASTIC FLYING FOOLS(1967, Brit); HOW TO SEDUCE A PLAYBOY(1968, Aust./Fr./Ital.)
Margaret Teele
SILENCERS, THE(; MOTHER GOOSE A GO-GO(1966)
Ann Teeman
JOE AND ETHEL TURP CALL ON THE PRESIDENT(1939)
Anne Teeman
Silents
KING OF KINGS, THE(1927)
Van Teen
SHE FREAK(1967)
The Teen-Agers
ONE EXCITING WEEK(1946)
Perc Teeple
POLO JOE(1936); CONFESSION(1937); EVER SINCE EVE(1937)
Barbara Ann Teer
SLAVES(1969); ANGEL LEVINE, THE(1970)
Carol Teesdale
1984
RUNAWAY(1984)
Susan Teesdale
1984
WHERE THE BOYS ARE '84(1984)

Al Teeter
SWEET SUZY(1973), m
Asa Teeter
EAGLE HAS LANDED, THE(1976, Brit.)
Myrl Teeter
TOWN THAT DREADED SUNDOWN, THE(1977), art d
Rita Teeter
NIGHT THE LIGHTS WENT OUT IN GEORGIA, THE(1981)
Roger Teeter
NIGHT THE LIGHTS WENT OUT IN GEORGIA, THE(1981)
Teeto
JAWS OF THE JUNGLE(1936)
Maureen Teety
1941(1979)
Horst Teetzmann
PILLARS OF SOCIETY(1936, Ger.)
Simplet Tefane
HURRICANE(1979)
Mondial Tefi
DEAD ARE ALIVE, THE(1972, Yugo./Ger./Ital.), p
Members of the Tefik Tribes
SANDERS OF THE RIVER(1935, Brit.)
Shirley Tegge
WHERE THE SIDEWALK ENDS(1950); GUY WHO CAME BACK, THE(1951); STRANGERS ON A TRAIN(1951); TAKE CARE OF MY LITTLE GIRL(1951); TWO TICKETS TO BROADWAY(1951); LAS VEGAS STORY, THE(1952); FRENCH LINE, THE(1954)
Bruce Tegner
MARRIAGE-GO-ROUND, THE(1960); GOOD TIMES(1967)
Jon Tegner
MY FAVORITE SPY(1951)
Richard Tegstrom
CROWNING EXPERIENCE, THE(1960), ph; VOICE OF THE HURRICANE(1964), ph
Tehen-You-Lin
ROMEO AND JULIET(1955, USSR), ph
Safai Teherani
BURNING YEARS, THE(1979, Ital.), ph
Tora Tehje
Misc. Silents
EROTIKON(1920, Swed.)
Frank Teichman
FANDANGO(1970)
Karen Teichman
HELLCATS, THE(1968), art d
Howard Teichmann
SOLID GOLD CADILLAC, THE(1956), w; LONELYHEARTS(1958), w
Lotte Teig
EDVARD MUNCH(1976, Norway/Swed.)
Jan Teige
HARPER VALLEY, P.T.A.(1978)
Laura Teige
HARPER VALLEY, P.T.A.(1978)
Lila Teigh
THUNDERBOLT AND LIGHTFOOT(1974); BLOODBROTHERS(1978)
Olive Teil
RIGHT OF WAY, THE(1931)
Darwin L. Teilhet
THEY WANTED TO MARRY(1937), w; NO ROOM FOR THE GROOM(1952), w; FEARMAKERS, THE(1958), w; MACABRE(1958), w
Irving Teiltelbaum
LOOKS AND SMILES(1982, Brit.), p
Thomas Teily
BIG LAND, THE(1957), ed
Harry Teinowitz
UP THE ACADEMY(1980)
Monique Teisseire
LOLA(1961, Fr./Ital.), ed
Elisabeth Teissier
TENDER SCOUNDREL(1967, Fr./Ital.)
Elizabeth Teissier
CASTLE KEEP(1969)
Carol Teitel
HAMLET(1964)
Abraham Teitelbaum
WANDERING JEW, THE(1933); TWO SISTERS(1938)
Misc. Talkies
ABRAHAM OUR PATRIARCH(1933)
Carl Teitelbaum
JOURNEYS FROM BERLIN–1971(1980), ph
John Teitsort
ECHOES(1983)
Virgilio Teixeira
SEVENTH VOYAGE OF SINBAD, THE(1958); REDEEMER, THE(1965, Span.); MAN COULD GET KILLED, A(1966); SAUL AND DAVID(1968, Ital./Span.)
Tore Teja
Misc. Silents
KARIN, INGMAR'S DAUGHTER(1920, Swed.)
Celia Tejada
MACARIO(1961, Mex.)
Luis Tejada
DESPERATE ONES, THE(1968 U.S./Span.)
Miguel Tejada-Flores
1984
REVENGE OF THE NERDS(1984), w
Herrera Tejedde
Misc. Silents
GOWN OF DESTINY, THE(1918)

Prince Tui Teka
NATE AND HAYES(1983, U.S./New Zealand)
Kyoshi Tekase
DEADLOCK(1931, Brit.)
Silents
QUALIFIED ADVENTURER, THE(1925, Brit.); RED PEARLS(1930, Brit.)
Sondra Teke
NEW KIND OF LOVE, A(1963)
Katarina Tekelova
DESERTER AND THE NOMADS, THE(1969, Czech./Ital.)
Sumru Tekin
DOZENS, THE(1981)
Saliha Tekneci
DIARY OF A BACHELOR(1964)
Ariirau Tekurarere
HURRICANE(1979)
Kris Tel
MADAME X(1966)
Tela-Tchai
ROBBER SYMPHONY, THE(1937, Brit.)
Bill Telaak
BOY MEETS GIRL(1938); HONKY TONK(1941)
William Telaak
PHANTOM PLANET, THE(1961), w
William Telark
CASTLE ON THE HUDSON(1940)
Jose Telavera
RETURN OF THE SEVEN(1966, Span.)
Ken Telbot
RED DRESS, THE(1954, Brit.), ph
Tele
MARGIN, THE,(1969, Braz.)
Tele-Visual Aids Inc.
HONEYMOON OF HORROR(1964), ed
Raymond Telega
PROUD RIDER, THE(1971, Can.), art d
V. Telegina
CITY OF YOUTH(1938, USSR); NEW TEACHER, THE(1941, USSR)
Valentina Telegina
FAREWELL, DOVES(1962, USSR); RESURRECTION(1963, USSR); SANDU FOLLOWS THE SUN(1965, USSR)
Belle Teleone
MY THIRD WIFE GEORGE(1968)
The Television Toppers
MAKE MINE A MILLION(1965, Brit.)
Isabella Telezynska
LUDWIG(1973, Ital./Ger./Fr.); TO THE DEVIL A DAUGHTER(1976, Brit./Ger.)
Izabella Telezynska
MUSIC LOVERS, THE(1971, Brit.); PANDEMONIUM(1982)
Dariel Telfer
CARETAKERS, THE(1963), w
Jay Telfer
KID VENGEANCE(1977), w
Frank Telford
BAMBOO SAUCER, THE(1968), d&w; SERGEANT RYKER(1968), p; HELLO DOWN THERE(1969), w
Robert Telford
WHERE THE RED FERN GROWS(1974); WHOSE LIFE IS IT ANYWAY?(1981)
A. Sanchez Telio
RANCHO GRANDE(1938, Mex.)
Alma Tell
SATURDAY'S CHILDREN(1929); LOVE COMES ALONG(1930); IMITATION OF LIFE(1934)
Silents
SIMON THE JESTER(1915); ON WITH THE DANCE(1920); BROADWAY ROSE(1922); SILENT COMMAND, THE(1923)
Misc. Silents
NEARLY MARRIED(1917); IRON TRAIL, THE(1921); PAYING THE PIPER(1921)
Nick Tell
URANIUM BOOM(1956)
Olive Tell
HEARTS IN EXILE(1929); TRIAL OF MARY DUGAN, THE(1929); VERY IDEA, THE(1929); COCK O' THE WALK(1930); LAWFUL LARCENY(1930); DELICIOUS(1931); DEVOTION(1931); LADIES' MAN(1931); WOMAN HUNGRY(1931); STRICTLY PERSONAL(1933); BABY, TAKE A BOW(1934); PRIVATE SCANDAL(1934); SCARLET EMPRESS, THE(1934); WITCHING HOUR, THE(1934); FOUR HOURS TO KILL(1935); SHANGHAI(1935); BRILLIANT MARRIAGE(1936); IN HIS STEPS(1936); POLO JOE(1936); YOURS FOR THE ASKING(1936); ZAZA(1939)
Silents
WOMAN'S BUSINESS, A(1920); WOMANHANDLED(1925); SUMMER BACHELORS(1926); SLAVES OF BEAUTY(1927)
Misc. Silents
HER SISTER(1917); SILENT MASTER, THE(1917); UNFORSEEN, THE(1917); GIRL AND THE JUDGE, THE(1918); SECRET STRINGS(1918); TO HELL WITH THE KAISER(1918); TRAP, THE(1919); CLOTHES(1920); LOVE WITHOUT QUESTION(1920); WRONG WOMAN, THE(1920); WORLDS APART(1921)
Tove Tellback
Misc. Silents
BRIDE OF GLOMDAL, THE(1925, Nor.)
Mike Tellegan
KIM(1950)
Paul Tellegan
Misc. Silents
SCULPTOR'S DREAM(1929)
Eve Tellegen
ONCE UPON A COFFEE HOUSE(1965)
Lou Tellegen
ENEMIES OF THE LAW(1931); TOGETHER WE LIVE(1935)

Silents
QUEEN ELIZABETH(1912, Fr.); AFTER BUSINESS HOURS(1925); BORROWED FINERY(1925); FAIR PLAY(1925); REDEEMING SIN, THE(1925); OUTSIDER, THE(1926); SIBERIA(1926); WOMANPOWER(1926); MARRIED ALIVE(1927); PRINCESS FROM HOBOKEN, THE(1927); STAGE MADNESS(1927); NO OTHER WOMAN(1928), d
Misc. Silents
UNKNOWN, THE(1915); VICTORIA CROSS, THE(1916); VICTORY OF CONSCIENCE, THE(1916); BLACK WOLF, THE(1917); LONG TRAIL, THE(1917); WHAT MONEY CAN'T BUY(1917), d; FLAME OF THE DESERT(1919); WORLD AND ITS WOMAN, THE(1919); WOMAN AND THE PUPPET, THE(1920); BETWEEN FRIENDS(1924); GREATER THAN MARRIAGE(1924); LET NO MAN PUT ASUNDER(1924); THOSE WHO JUDGE(1924); EAST LYNNE(1925); PARISIAN NIGHTS(1925); SPORTING CHANCE, THE(1925); VERDICT, THE(1925); WITH THIS RING(1925); THREE BAD MEN(1926); LITTLE FIREBRAND, THE(1927)
Michael Tellegen
Silents
RED WINE(1928)
Mike Tellegen
ROBERTA(1935); DOWN TO THE SEA(1936); KID NIGHTINGALE(1939)
Lou Tellegren
Misc. Silents
THINGS WE LOVE, THE(1918), d
Francis Kee Teller
NAVAJO(1952)
Ira Teller
SILENT NIGHT, BLOODY NIGHT(1974), w
Iza Teller
ISADORA(1968, Brit.)
Mrs. Teller
NAVAJO(1952)
Nadja Teller
LA BABY SITTER(1975, Fr./Ital./Ger.)
Zon Teller
HOT ANGEL, THE(1958)
Isabel Telleria
SPIRIT OF THE BEEHIVE, THE(1976, Span.)
Michael Tellering
MAGIC FACE, THE(1951, Aust.); DEVIL MAKES THREE, THE(1952); FIDELIO(1961, Aust.); MIRACLE OF THE WHITE STALLIONS(1963); GREAT WALTZ, THE(1972)
Nadine Tellier
TONIGHT THE SKIRTS FLY(1956, Fr.)
Tellini
DONATELLA(1956, Ital.), w
P. Tellini
UTOPIA(1952, Fr./Ital.), w
Piero Tellini
TO LIVE IN PEACE(1947, Ital.), w; ANGELINA(1948, Ital.), w; CHILDREN OF CHANCE(1949, Brit.), w; CHILDREN OF CHANCE(1950, Ital.), w; TALE OF FIVE WOMEN, A(1951, Brit.), w; WHITE LINE, THE(1952, Ital.), w; VOLCANO(1953, Ital.), w
Constance Tellissier
GREAT GARRICK, THE(1937)
Alfonso Sanchez Tello
BANDIDO(1956)
Ding Tello
NO MAN IS AN ISLAND(1962)
Enrique Tello
SCALPHUNTERS, THE(1968)
Luis Sanchez Tello
LITTLEST OUTLAW, THE(1955), prod d
Rita Tellone
EYES OF LAURA MARS(1978); NIGHTHAWKS(1981)
Basil Tellou
CASBAH(1948); SAXON CHARM, THE(1948); MRS. O'MALLEY AND MR. MALONE(1950)
Michael Telmont
1984
FOOTLOOSE(1984)
Teddy Telzlaff
GOOD BAD GIRL, THE(1931), ph
Muzaffer Tema
CERTAIN SMILE, A(1958)
Irving Temaner
LAST ESCAPE, THE(1970, Brit.), p
Elza Temary
RASPUTIN(1932, Ger.)
Misc. Silents
DANGERS OF THE ENGAGEMENT PERIOD(1929, Ger.)
Telo A. Tematua
LAST OF THE PAGANS(1936)
Albertina Temba
CRY, THE BELOVED COUNTRY(1952, Brit.)
Jack Temchin
HOME MOVIES(1979), p
Vladimir Temelianov
STORM PLANET(1962, USSR)
A. Temerin
DAY THE WAR ENDED, THE(1961, USSR)
Temerson
DEVIL IS AN EMPRESS, THE(1939, Fr.); PERSONAL COLUMN(1939, Fr.); FLESH AND THE WOMAN(1954, Fr./Ital.)
Jean Temerson
VOLPONE(1947, Fr.); DIABOLIQUE(1955, Fr.)
Hedi Temessy
MEPHISTO(1981, Ger.)
1984
REVOLT OF JOB, THE(1984, Hung./Ger.)

Alvina Temin
EVERY GIRL SHOULD BE MARRIED(1948)

Okay Temiz
1984
HORSE, THE(1984, Turk.), m

Jeff Temkin
CHAMP, THE(1979); BALTIMORE BULLET, THE(1980); ROCKY III(1982)

Serge Temoff
WE LIVE AGAIN(1934)
Misc. Silents
DEVIL DANCER, THE(1927)

Vincenzo Tempera
NEST OF VIPERS(1979, Ital.), m

The Temperance Seven
RING-A-DING RHYTHM(1962, Brit. 73m Amicus/COL bw (G.B: IT'S TRAD, DAD!); WRONG BOX, THE(1966, Brit.)

Stephen Temperley
SPY WHO LOVED ME, THE(1977, Brit.)

Nicky Temperton
YOUNG GIRLS OF ROCHEFORT, THE(1968, Fr.)

Maire Tempest
Misc. Silents
MRS. PLUM'S PUDDING(1915)

Marie Tempest
MOONLIGHT SONATA(1938, Brit.); YELLOW SANDS(1938, Brit.)

Tom Tempest
Silents
TOLL OF MAMON(1914)
Misc. Silents
WHEN FATE LEADS TRUMP(1914); THOSE WHO TOIL(1916)

M. Tempesta
MAN COULD GET KILLED, A(1966)

Giotto Tempestini
ATLAS AGAINST THE CYCLOPS(1963, Ital.)

Fabrizio Tempio
HORNET'S NEST(1970)

Maurizio Tempio
HORNET'S NEST(1970)

Alvina Temple
MY FAVORITE SPY(1951)

Brooke Temple
SIX GUN MAN(1946)

Brooks Temple
RIDERS OF THE DAWN(1945)

Eileen Temple
Silents
MESSAGE FROM MARS, A(1913, Brit.)

Fay Temple
Silents
MOTHERHOOD(1915, Brit.)
Misc. Silents
HEARTS THAT ARE HUMAN(1915, Brit.); MYSTERY OF A HANSOM CAB, THE(1915, Brit.); SCORPION'S STING, THE(1915, Brit.); SHADOWS(1915, Brit.); WILD OATS(1915, Brit.); CHANCE OF A LIFETIME, THE(1916, Brit.)

George Temple
ALIAS THE CHAMP(1949)

Joan Temple
PRIMROSE PATH, THE(1934, Brit.), w; NO ROOM AT THE INN(1950, Brit.), w

Loretta Temple
BOY WHO CRIED WEREWOLF, THE(1973)

Louise Temple
ANTI-CLOCK(1980)

Marjory Temple
Misc. Silents
WOLF WOMAN, THE(1916)

Mary Jane Temple
PALM SPRINGS(1936); WOMEN OF GLAMOUR(1937)
Misc. Silents
COWBOY KID, THE(1928)

Ralph Temple
OLD MOTHER RILEY AT HOME(1945, Brit.), w

Renny Temple
1984
BEST DEFENSE(1984)

Richard Temple
Silents
EVIDENCE(1915)

Shirley Temple [Shirley Jane Temple]
RED-HAIRED ALIBI, THE(1932); OUT ALL NIGHT(1933); TO THE LAST MAN(1933); BABY, TAKE A BOW(1934); BRIGHT EYES(1934); CAROLINA(1934); CHANGE OF HEART(1934); LITTLE MISS MARKER(1934); MANDALAY(1934); NOW AND FOREVER(1934); NOW I'LL TELL(1934); STAND UP AND CHEER(1934 80m FOX bw); CAPTAIN JANUARY(1935); CURLY TOP(1935); LITTLE COLONEL, THE(1935); LITTLEST REBEL, THE(1935); OUR LITTLE GIRL(1935); DIMPLES(1936); POOR LITTLE RICH GIRL(1936); STOWAWAY(1936); HEIDI(1937); WEE WILLIE WINKIE(1937); JUST AROUND THE CORNER(1938); LITTLE MISS BROADWAY(1938); REBECCA OF SUNNYBROOK FARM(1938); LITTLE PRINCESS, THE(1939); SUSANNAH OF THE MOUNTIES(1939); BLUE BIRD, THE(1940); YOUNG PEOPLE(1940); KATHLEEN(1941); MISS ANNIE ROONEY(1942); I'LL BE SEEING YOU(1944); SINCE YOU WENT AWAY(1944); KISS AND TELL(1945); BACHELOR AND THE BOBBY-SOXER, THE(1947); HONEYMOON(1947); THAT HAGEN GIRL(1947); FORT APACHE(1948); ADVENTURE IN BALTIMORE(1949); KISS FOR CORLISS, A(1949); MR. BELVEDERE GOES TO COLLEGE(1949); STORY OF SEABISCUIT, THE(1949)

Sy Temple
HORSEMEN, THE(1971)

Wilfred Temple
SPLINTERS(1929, Brit.); NOT SO QUIET ON THE WESTERN FRONT(1930, Brit.); YELLOW MASK, THE(1930, Brit.); SPLINTERS IN THE NAVY(1931, Brit.)

William T. Temple
FOUR SIDED TRIANGLE(1953, Brit.), w

John Temple-Smith
HOME TO DANGER(1951, Brit.), w; GIRL ON THE PIER, THE(1953, Brit.), p; PROFILE(1954, Brit.), p, w; ONE WAY OUT(1955, Brit.), p, w; FIND THE LADY(1956, Brit.), p; HIDEOUT, THE(1956, Brit.), p; ACCOUNT RENDERED(1957, Brit.), p; BIG CHANCE, THE(1957, Brit.), p; SUBWAY IN THE SKY(1959, Brit.), p; IT TAKES A THIEF(1960, Brit.), p; NIGHT CREATURES(1962, Brit.), p; VIKING QUEEN, THE(1967, Brit.), p, w; ISLAND OF DR. MOREAU, THE(1977), p

Harcourt Templeman
DARK RED ROSES(1930, Brit.), w; BELLS, THE(1931, Brit.), d; MONEY MEANS NOTHING(1932, Brit.), d, w; HYDE PARK CORNER(1935, Brit.), p; GAY ADVENTURE, THE(1936, Brit.), p; BOMBS OVER LONDON(1937, Brit.), p; COMMAND PERFORMANCE(1937, Brit.), p; TAKE A CHANCE(1937, Brit.), p; FOLLOW YOUR STAR(1938, Brit.),

Beatrix Templeton
Silents
PRINCESS OF HAPPY CHANCE, THE(1916, Brit.)

Bob Templeton
LOCKET, THE(1946); O.S.S.(1946); FLIGHT TO TANGIER(1953); PONY EXPRESS(1953); STALAG 17(1953); NIGHT MOVES(1975)

Charles Templeton
KIDNAPPING OF THE PRESIDENT, THE(1980, Can.), w

Dink Templeton
MAKE ME A STAR(1932); NIGHT AFTER NIGHT(1932); THIN MAN, THE(1934)

Fay Templeton
BROADWAY TO HOLLYWOOD(1933)

George Templeton
TOO MANY PARENTS(1936), w; SATURDAY'S HEROES(1937), w; ON THE SUNNY SIDE(1942), w; HIGH LONESOME(1950), p; SUNDOWNERS, THE(1950), d; QUEBEC(1951), d
Misc. Talkies
GIFT FOR HEIDI, A(1958), d

Harry Templeton
THIS RECKLESS AGE(1932); TIP-OFF GIRLS(1938); GERONIMO(1939); $1,000 A TOUCHDOWN(1939); FOREST RANGERS, THE(1942); FILE ON THELMA JORDAN, THE(1950)

Joyce Templeton
Misc. Silents
JADE HEART, THE(1915, Brit.); TOM BROWN'S SCHOOLDAYS(1916, Brit.)

Olive Templeton
Silents
DAMAGED GOODS(1915)

Pat Templeton
VARIETY GIRL(1947)

Robert Templeton
MR. MAJESTYK(1974)

W.F. Templeton
TAMING OF DOROTHY, THE(1950, Brit.), w

William Templeton
FALLEN IDOL, THE(1949, Brit.), w; MIDNIGHT EPISODE(1951, Brit.), w; DOUBLE CONFESSION(1953, Brit.), w; NAKED WORLD OF HARRISON MARKS, THE(1967, Brit.), w

William P. Templeton
1984
1984(1956, Brit.), w

Marguerite Templey
COUNSEL FOR ROMANCE(1938, Fr.)

Dan M. Templin
BOULDER DAM(1936), w

Nino Tempo
GEORGE WHITE'S SCANDALS(1945); RED PONY, THE(1949); GLENN MILLER STORY, THE(1953); GIRL CAN'T HELP IT, THE(1956); JOHNNY TROUBLE(1957); OPERATION PETTICOAT(1959)

Paul Temps
LOWER DEPTHS, THE(1937, Fr.); JOHNNY BANCO(1969, Fr./Ital./Ger.), p; JUST BEFORE NIGHTFALL(1975, Fr./Ital.)

Corrie ten Boom
HIDING PLACE, THE(1975), w

Ten Master Singers
CALLING ALL CROOKS(1938, Brit.)

Arend J. Ten Pas
RED RUNS THE RIVER(1963)

Jose Tasso Tena
NIGHT HEAVEN FELL, THE(1958, Fr.)

Joseph Tenaglio
1984
RECKLESS(1984)

Tenaya
MANITOU, THE(1978)

Harry Tenbrook
SEVEN FOOTPRINTS TO SATAN(1929); MEN WITHOUT WOMEN(1930); ON THE LEVEL(1930); RUNAWAY BRIDE(1930); SEA WOLF, THE(1930); SEAS BENEATH, THE(1931); SUICIDE FLEET(1931); YOUNG DONOVAN'S KID(1931); COME ON DANGER!(1932); SCARFACE(1932); TAXI!(1932); THIRTEENTH GUEST, THE(1932); BOWERY, THE(1933); FOURTH HORSEMAN, THE(1933); KING KONG(1933); LITTLE GIANT, THE(1933); SON OF KONG(1933); TERROR TRAIL(1933); CAT'S PAW, THE(1934); JUDGE PRIEST(1934); LADY BY CHOICE(1934); THIN MAN, THE(1934); FRISCO KID(1935); MILLIONS IN THE AIR(1935); NAUGHTY MARIETTA(1935); GREAT GUY(1936); HIT THE SADDLE(1937); MUSIC FOR MADAME(1937); ROARIN' LEAD(1937); PROFESSOR BEWARE(1938); RACKET BUSTERS(1938); RAWHIDE(1938); SLIGHT CASE OF MURDER, A(1938); YOU AND ME(1938); DESTRY RIDES AGAIN(1939); HOTEL IMPERIAL(1939); LADY'S FROM KENTUCKY, THE(1939); LET FREEDOM RING(1939); OKLAHOMA FRONTIER(1939); OUR LEADING CITIZEN(1939); STAGECOACH(1939); CHIP OF THE FLYING U(1940); GRAPES OF WRATH(1940); LONG VOYAGE HOME, THE(1940); RAGTIME COWBOY JOE(1940); FIGHTING BILL FARGO(1942); LUCKY LEGS(1942); STAGECOACH BUCKAROO(1942); GOVERNMENT GIRL(1943); MAN FROM FRISCO(1944); THEY WERE EXPENDABLE(1945); HOODLUM SAINT, THE(1946); FORT APACHE(1948); PINKY(1949); WHEN WILLIE COMES MARCHING HOME(1950); SANTA FE(1951); QUIET MAN, THE(1952); MISTER ROBERTS(1955); LAST HURRAH, THE(1958)

Silents
KINDLED COURAGE(1923); MEASURE OF A MAN, THE(1924); OUTLAW DOG, THE(1927); PLAY GIRL, THE(1928); EYES OF THE UNDERWORLD(1929)
Misc. Silents
SPEEDY SMITH(1927)
Jim Tenbrooke
Silents
CLAY DOLLARS(1921)
Kay Tendeter
FALL OF THE HOUSE OF USHER, THE(1952, Brit.)
Stacey Tendeter
TWO ENGLISH GIRLS(1972, Fr.)
Mark Tendler
HERCULES IN NEW YORK(1970); BADGE 373(1973)
V. Tendryakov
FORTY-NINE DAYS(1964, USSR), w
Arthur Tenen
PORTRAIT OF A MOBSTER(1961)
Peter Tenen
CHILDISH THINGS(1969)
Pat Tenerelli
GIRL, THE BODY, AND THE PILL, THE(1967)
Guido Tenesi
SLAP SHOT(1977)
Taiji Teneyama
BANISHED(1978, Jap.)
Lillian Teneycke
GOOD GIRLS GO TO PARIS(1939)
Ma Teng
FLYING GUILLOTINE, THE(1975, Chi.)
Gustaf Tenggren
SNOW WHITE AND THE SEVEN DWARFS(1937), art d
Boris Tenin
Misc. Silents
LACE(1928, USSR)
Ziro Tenkai
NAVY WIFE(1956)
Andy Tennant
1941(1979)
Barbara Tennant
Silents
DOLLAR MARK, THE(1914); WHEN BROADWAY WAS A TRAIL(1914); SHADOWS OF CONSCIENCE(1921); BULLDOG COURAGE(1922); DESERTED AT THE AL-TAR(1922); LOVE GAMBLER, THE(1922); THELMA(1922); CIRCUS DAYS(1923); DRUG TRAFFIC, THE(1923); CAPTAIN JANUARY(1924); HOUSE OF YOUTH, THE(1924); BORROWED FINERY(1925); CLOWN, THE(1927); KING OF KINGS, THE(1927); YOUR WIFE AND MINE(1927)
Misc. Silents
ACROSS THE PACIFIC(1914); MARKED WOMAN, THE(1914); BUTTERFLY, THE(1915); M'LISS(1915); CLOSED ROAD, THE(1916); PRICE OF MALICE, THE(1916); WHEN A MAN LOVES(1920); WHAT LOVE WILL DO(1921); YOU CAN'T GET AWAY WITH IT(1923); STREET OF TEARS, THE(1924); HEARTS AND SPAN-GLES(1926); HIDDEN ACES(1927)
Dorothy Tennant
MEN WITH WINGS(1938); RICH MAN, POOR GIRL(1938)
Frank Tennant
Silents
FLYING FROM JUSTICE(1915, Brit.); LOVE(1916, Brit.); OLD ARM CHAIR, THE(1920, Brit.); WON BY A HEAD(1920, Brit.)
Misc. Silents
HARPER MYSTERY, THE(1913, Brit.); MURDOCK TRIAL, THE(1914, Brit.); COAL KING, THE(1915, Brit.); MARRIED FOR MONEY(1915, Brit.); ROGUE'S WIFE, A(1915, Brit.); ROMANY RYE, THE(1915, Brit.); ROYAL LOVE(1915, Brit.); WHAT'S BRED..-.COMES OUT IN THE FLESH(1916, Brit.); STORY OF THE ROSARY, THE(1920, Brit.)
Pauline Tennant
GREAT DAY(1945, Brit.); QUEEN OF SPADES(1948, Brit.)
Victoria Tennant
RAGMAN'S DAUGHTER, THE(1974, Brit.); DOGS OF WAR, THE(1980, Brit.); HORROR PLANET(1982, Brit.)
1984
ALL OF ME(1984); STRANGERS KISS(1984)
William Tennant
CLEOPATRA JONES(1973), p; CLEOPATRA JONES AND THE CASINO OF GOLD(1975 U. S. Hong Kong), p, w; HOLLYWOOD KNIGHTS, THE(1980), w
Jean-Marc Tennberg
FANFAN THE TULIP(1952, Fr.); ADORABLE CREATURES(1956, Fr.); FRENCH CANCAN(1956, Fr.); SEVEN CAPITAL SINS(1962, Fr./Ital.); LOVE ON A PIL-LOW(1963, Fr./Ital.); RAVISHING IDIOT, A(1966, Ital./Fr.); FRUSTRATIONS(1967, Fr./Ital.)
Lisa Tennele
WANDERLOVE(1970)
Arthur Tennen
HEROES DIE YOUNG(1960)
Monica Tenner
MORE AMERICAN GRAFFITI(1979)
The Tennessee Ramblers
YODELIN' KID FROM PINE RIDGE(1937); RIDING THE CHEROKEE TRAIL(1941); O, MY DARLING CLEMENTINE(1943); SWING YOUR PARTNER(1943)
Beth Tenney
Misc. Silents
SINS OF THE CHILDREN(1918)
Christopher Tenney
FIRST MONDAY IN OCTOBER(1981)
Del Tenney
SATAN IN HIGH HEELS(1962); CURSE OF THE LIVING CORPSE, THE(1964), p,d&w; HORROR OF PARTY BEACH, THE(1964), p&d; PSYCHOMANIA(1964), p; I EAT YOUR SKIN(1971), p

Mike Tennis
Misc. Talkies
CRUISIN' 57(1975)
Phillip Tenny
NAVY BLUE AND GOLD(1937)
Alfred Tennyson
PRICE OF THINGS, THE(1930, Brit.)
Alfred Lord Tennyson
Silents
NAKED HEARTS(1916), w
Gladys Tennyson
Silents
BROADWAY AFTER DARK(1924)
Misc. Silents
LAST MAN ON EARTH, THE(1924)
Pen Tennyson
CONVOY(1940), d, w
Penrose Tennyson
THERE AIN'T NO JUSTICE(1939, Brit.), d, w; PROUD VALLEY, THE(1941, Brit.), d, w
Walter Tennyson
PRICE OF THINGS, THE(1930, Brit.); TROUBLE(1933, Brit.), w; ALIBI INN(1935, Brit.), p&d; ANNIE LAURIE(1936, Brit.), d, p; KING OF HEARTS(1936, Brit.), p,d&w; LITTLE MISS SOMEBODY(1937, Brit.), p, d, w; FATHER O'FLYNN(1938, Irish), d
Silents
CALL OF THE EAST, THE(1922, Brit.); MUTINY(1925, Brit.); BRIDE OF THE STORM(1926); DRESS PARADE(1927)
Misc. Silents
HIS SUPREME SACRIFICE(1922, Brit.); VIRGIN QUEEN, THE(1923, Brit.); INFA-MOUS LADY, THE(1928, Brit.)
John Tenorio
Misc. Talkies
GRAD NIGHT(1980), d
Aldo Tenossi
JOAN AT THE STAKE(1954, Ital./Fr.)
Marilyn J. Tenser
MALIBU BEACH(1978), p; VAN NUYS BLVD.(1979), p; BEACH GIRLS(1982), p; MY TUTOR(1983), p
1984
WEEKEND PASS(1984), p
Mark Tenser
COACH(1978), p; HEARSE, THE(1980), p; MY TUTOR(1983), w
1984
WEEKEND PASS(1984), w
Tony Tenser
BLACK TORMENT, THE(1965, Brit.), p; CUL-DE-SAC(1966, Brit.), p; BLOOD BEAST TERROR, THE(1967, Brit.), p; SORCERERS, THE(1967, Brit.), p; TOMCAT, THE(1968, Brit.), p, w; BODY STEALERS, THE(1969), p; WHAT'S GOOD FOR THE GOOSE(1969, Brit.), p; HORROR HOUSE(1970, Brit.), p; DOOMWATCH(1972, Brit.), p
Francesco Tensi
ANGELA(1955, Ital.); COME SEPTEMBER(1961); SODOM AND GOMORRAH(1962, U.S./Fr./Ital.); CONQUERED CITY(1966, Ital.); OPERATION KID BROTHER(1967, Ital.); UP THE MACGREGORS(1967, Ital./Span.); GHOSTS, ITALIAN STYLE(1969, Ital./Fr.); DORIAN GRAY(1970, Ital./Brit./Ger./Liechtenstein)
Bert Tenzer
2000 YEARS LATER(1969), a, p,d&w
Misc. Talkies
TWO THOUSAND YEARS LATER(1969), d
Ion Teodorescu
FOUL PLAY(1978); BLACK MARBLE, THE(1980); WHOLLY MOSES(1980)
Ovidiu Teodorescu
STEPS TO THE MOON(1963, Rum.)
Oded Teomi
THEY WERE TEN(1961, Israel); MY MARGO(1969, Israel); OPERATION THUNDER-BOLT(1978, ISRAEL)
Noel Teparii
HURRICANE(1979)
Taia Tepava
TAHITIAN, THE(1956)
Waldemar Tepel
ORDERED TO LOVE(1963, Ger.)
Greg Tepper
WE OF THE NEVER NEVER(1983, Aus.), p
William Tepper
DRIVE, HE SAID(1971); BREATHLESS(1983)
Joy Tepperman
WINTER KEPT US WARM(1968, Can.)
Angel Ter
SUPERSONIC MAN(1979, Span.)
Rouben Ter-Arutunian
LOVED ONE, THE(1965), prod d, cos; SUCH GOOD FRIENDS(1971), prod d
D. Ter-Tatevosyan
NINE DAYS OF ONE YEAR(1964, USSR), m
Chikao Tera
MAGIC BOY(1960, Jap.), anim
S.H. Terac
NAKED WOMAN, THE(1950, Fr.), w
Makoto Terada
OUTPOST OF HELL(1966, Jap.)
No Terada
RED LION(1971, Jap.)
Tadahiro Teramoto
EARLY AUTUMN(1962, Jap.), p; LONELY LANE(1963, Jap.), p
Massimo Terano
BARBER OF SEVILLE, THE(1947, Ital.), ph
Gwen Terasaki
BRIDGE TO THE SUN(1961), w

Shuji Terayama
YOUTH IN FURY(1961, Jap.), w; SCANDALOUS ADVENTURES OF BURAIKAN, THE(1970, Jap.), w
James Terbell
Silents
SONNY(1922)
Phoebe Terbell
VIVACIOUS LADY(1938)
Gilberte Terbois
ANGELS OF THE STREETS(1950, Fr.)
Jounnu Terbush
BLACK GESTAPO, THE(1975), ed
Alain Tercinet
JE T'AIME, JE T'AIME(1972, Fr./Swed.)
Margareta Terechova
BLUE BIRD, THE(1976)
V. Terentiev
ON HIS OWN(1939, USSR)
Levit Tereria
SAVAGE HARVEST(1981)
Max Tereshkovich
Misc. Silents
ELDER VASILI GRYAZNOV(1924, USSR)
Rene Tereusa
FRUIT IS RIPE, THE(1961, Fr./Ital.)
John Terhaak
PUPPET ON A CHAIN(1971, Brit.), stunts
Albert Payson Terhune
WHOM THE GODS DESTROY(1934), w; MIGHTY TREVE, THE(1937), w; LAD: A DOG(1962), w
Silents
FIGHTER, THE(1921), w
Bob Terhune
RIO BRAVO(1959); WELCOME TO HARD TIMES(1967); ST. IVES(1976); WHICH WAY IS UP?(1977); PROPHECY(1979); GOING APE!(1981); SIX PACK(1982)
1984
CITY HEAT(1984); DREAMSCAPE(1984)
Charles Terhune
WILD SCENE, THE(1970)
Max Terhune
RIDE, RANGER, RIDE(1936); BIG SHOW, THE(1937); COME ON, COWBOYS(1937); GHOST TOWN GOLD(1937); GUNSMOKE RANCH(1937); HEART OF THE ROCK-IES(1937); HIT PARADE, THE(1937); HIT THE SADDLE(1937); MANHATTAN MER-RY-GO-ROUND(1937); RANGE DEFENDERS(1937); RIDERS OF THE WHISTLING SKULL(1937); ROARIN' LEAD(1937); TRIGGER TRIO, THE(1937); CALL THE MES-QUITEERS(1938); HEROES OF THE HILLS(1938); LADIES IN DISTRESS(1938); MAMA RUNS WILD(1938); OUTLAWS OF SONORA(1938); OVERLAND STAGE RAIDERS(1938); PALS OF THE SADDLE(1938); PURPLE VIGILANTES, THE(1938); RED RIVER RANGE(1938); RIDERS OF THE BLACK HILLS(1938); SANTA FE STAMPEDE(1938); WILD HORSE RODEO(1938); MAN OF CONQUEST(1939); NIGHT RIDERS, THE(1939); THREE TEXAS STEERS(1939); RANGE BUSTERS, THE(1940); TRAILING DOUBLE TROUBLE(1940); WEST OF PINTO BASIN(1940); FUGITIVE VALLEY(1941); KID'S LAST RIDE, THE(1941); SADDLE MOUNTAIN ROUN-DUP(1941); TONTO BASIN OUTLAWS(1941); TRAIL OF THE SILVER SPURS(1941); TUMBLEDOWN RANCH IN ARIZONA(1941); UNDERGROUND RUSTLERS(1941); WRANGLER'S ROOST(1941); ARIZONA STAGECOACH(1942); ROCK RIVER RENE-GADES(1942); TEXAS TO BATAAN(1942); THUNDER RIVER FEUD(1942); TRAIL RIDERS(1942); BLACK MARKET RUSTLERS(1943); COWBOY COMMANDOS(1943); HAUNTED RANCH, THE(1943); LAND OF HUNTED MEN(1943); TWO FISTED JUSTICE(1943); COWBOY CANTEEN(1944); SHERIFF OF SUNDOWN(1944); ALONG THE OREGON TRAIL(1947); WHITE STALLION(1947); GUNNING FOR JUS-TICE(1948); HIDDEN DANGER(1949); LAW OF THE WEST(1949); RANGE JUS-TICE(1949); SQUARE DANCE JUBILEE(1949); TRAIL'S END(1949); WEST OF EL DORADO(1949); WESTERN RENEGADES(1949); RAWHIDE(1951); GIANT(1956)
Misc. Talkies
BOOT HILL BANDITS(1942); TEXAS TROUBLE SHOOTERS(1942); BULLETS AND SADDLES(1943); SWING, COWBOY, SWING(1944); SHERIFF OF MEDICINE BOW, THE(1948)
Pete Terhune
CARNY(1980)
Robert Terhune
SMOKY(1966); KING'S PIRATE(1967)
William Terhune
DEVIL'S BROTHER, THE(1933), ed; BABES IN TOYLAND(1934), ed; KELLY THE SECOND(1936), w; PICK A STAR(1937), ed; TOPPER(1937), ed; MERRILY WE LI-VE(1938), ed; THERE GOES MY HEART(1938), ed; AT THE CIRCUS(1939), ed; TOPPER TAKES A TRIP(1939), ed; GHOST COMES HOME, THE(1940), ed; SUSAN AND GOD(1940), ed
Arpad Teri
BOYS OF PAUL STREET, THE(1969, Hung./US)
Linda Terito
NEW YEAR'S EVIL(1980)
Louis Terkel
RAISIN IN THE SUN, A(1961)
G. Terkhov
1812(1944, USSR)
Carla Terlizzi
CITY OF WOMEN(1980, Ital./Fr.)
Lenka Termer
MATTER OF DAYS, A(1969, Fr./Czech.)
Mike Termini
1984
SAM'S SON(1984), cos
Tony Termini
FOXES(1980)
Anna Terminiello
SILHOUETTES(1982)

Leonard Termo
HEART LIKE A WHEEL(1983)
1984
COTTON CLUB, THE(1984); JOHNNY DANGEROUSLY(1984); POPE OF GREEN-WICH VILLAGE, THE(1984)
Al Terr
BULLWHIP(1958)
Michael Terr
TWO LOST WORLDS(1950), m; RED SNOW(1952), md; MOVIE STUNTMEN(1953), m; TOWN ON TRIAL(1957, Brit.), md; UNEARTHLY, THE(1957), md
Mischa Terr
KING DINOSAUR(1955), m; NASTY RABBIT, THE(1964)
Renato Terra
DAVID AND GOLIATH(1961, Ital.); WHITE NIGHTS(1961, Ital./Fr.); TARTARS, THE(1962, Ital./Yugo.); FALL OF ROME, THE(1963, Ital.); CAVERN, THE(1965, Ital./Ger.); FACTS OF MURDER, THE(1965, Ital.); MYTH, THE(1965, Ital.); GOSPEL ACCORDING TO ST. MATTHEW, THE(1966, Fr., Ital.); THE DIRTY GAME(1966, Fr./Ital./Ger.); VERY HANDY MAN, A(1966, Fr./Ital.); DRUMS OF TABU, THE(1967, Ital./Span.); KISS THE GIRLS AND MAKE THEM DIE(1967, U.S./Ital.); KNIVES OF THE AVENGER(1967, Ital.); SEVEN GOLDEN MEN(1969, Fr./Ital./Span.)
Stefano Terra
WHITE LINE, THE(1952, Ital.), w; LEGIONS OF THE NILE(1960, Ital.)
Charlotte Terrabust
BOY ON A DOLPHIN(1957)
Linda Terrace
CALYPSO JOE(1957)
John Terrade
Misc. Talkies
I AM FRIGID...WHY?(1973)
Lucienne Terrades
OLIVE TREES OF JUSTICE, THE(1967, Fr.)
Molly Terraine
TWICE UPON A TIME(1953, Brit.)
Silents
FIRM OF GIRDLESTONE, THE(1915, Brit.)
John Terrano
JOHNNY O'CLOCK(1947)
Dino Terranoua
WRONG MAN, THE(1956)
Dan Terranova
BLACKBOARD JUNGLE, THE(1955); RUMBLE ON THE DOCKS(1956); BABY FACE NELSON(1957); YOUNG DILLINGER(1965)
Daniel Terranova
CRIME IN THE STREETS(1956)
Giuseppe Terranova
BLACK VEIL FOR LISA, A(1969 Ital./Ger.); INVESTIGATION OF A CITIZEN ABOVE SUSPICION(1970, Ital.)
Don Terranove
SIDE STREET(1950)
Michel Terrazon
ME(1970, Fr.)
Ernest Terrazzas
THREE CABALLEROS, THE(1944), w
Tromp Terre'Blanche
KIMBERLEY JIM(1965, South Africa)
Tromp Terreblanche
Misc. Talkies
STRANGERS AT SUNRISE(1969)
Rosa Terregrosa
EVERY DAY IS A HOLIDAY(1966, Span.), ed
Ken Terrel
BOLD FRONTIERSMAN, THE(1948)
Bill Terrell
SKIN GAME(1971)
Dan Terrell
STATE FAIR(1962)
Ken Terrell
COWBOY SERENADE(1942); OUTLAWS OF PINE RIDGE(1942); RAIDERS OF THE RANGE(1942); MAN FROM THE RIO GRANDE, THE(1943); CODE OF THE PRAI-RIE(1944); DESTINY(1944); GIRL RUSH(1944); MARSHAL OF RENO(1944); MAR-SHAL OF LAREDO(1945); MISSING CORPSE, THE(1945); ROBIN OF TEXAS(1947); GAY RANCHERO, THE(1948); GRAND CANYON TRAIL(1948); DANGEROUS PROFESSION, A(1949); WINDOW, THE(1949); ON DANGEROUS GROUND(1951); LYDIA BAILEY(1952); PALS OF THE GOLDEN WEST(1952); JEOPARDY(1953); MA AND PA KETTLE ON VACATION(1953); PORT SINISTER(1953); DRUMS ACROSS THE RIVER(1954); MA AND PA KETTLE AT HOME(1954); RETURN TO TREASURE ISLAND(1954); PROUD ONES, THE(1956); ATTACK OF THE 50 FOOT WOMAN(1958); PIER 5, HAVANA(1959); SPARTACUS(1960); MASTER OF THE WORLD(1961)
Kenneth Terrell
LIVING ON LOVE(1937); IN OLD NEW MEXICO(1945); LAST TRAIN FROM BOMBAY(1952); INDESTRUCTIBLE MAN, THE(1956); SABU AND THE MAGIC RING(1957); BRAIN FROM THE PLANET AROUS, THE(1958)
Steve Terrell
DRAGSTRIP GIRL(1957); INVASION OF THE SAUCER MEN(1957)
Steven Terrell
NAKED HILLS, THE(1956); TEA AND SYMPATHY(1956); MOTORCYCLE GANG(1957); RUNAWAY DAUGHTERS(1957)
Yolande Terrell
BUCKET OF BLOOD(1934, Brit.); NIGHT JOURNEY(1938, Brit.); THEY DRIVE BY NIGHT(1938, Brit.)
P. Terreno
GREEN TREE, THE(1965, Ital.)
Patrizia Terreno
1984
NOSTALGHIA(1984, USSR/Ital.)
Renee Terres
CAPTAIN BLOOD(1935)

Michael Terresco
SWAMP COUNTRY(1966), m
Courtenay Terrett
RECKLESS LIVING(1931), w; MADE ON BROADWAY(1933), w
Courteney Terrett
CASTLE ON THE HUDSON(1940), w
Courtey Terrett
HUSH MONEY(1931), w; QUICK MILLIONS(1931), w; DARK HORSE, THE(1932), w; FAMOUS FERGUSON CASE, THE(1932), w; LOVE IS A RACKET(1932), w; 20,000 YEARS IN SING SING(1933), w; MUSIC HATH CHARMS(1935, Brit.), w
Pia Terri
FOR BETTER FOR WORSE(1954, Brit.)
Anita Terrian
GOIN' SOUTH(1978)
Luigi Terribile
TWO WOMEN(1961, Ital./Fr.)
Giovanna Terribili
Misc. Silents
MESSALINA(1924, Ital.)
Terrible Tom
MACK, THE(1973)
Evelyn Terrill
Silents
LIGHT AT DUSK, THE(1916)
Howard Terrill
MOVING VIOLATION(1976), ed; PARADISE(1982), ed
Richard Terrill
1984
PHAR LAP(1984, Aus.)
Terry Terrill
MY SIX LOVES(1963)
Terrill Cowboys
BIG COUNTRY, THE(1958)
Kit Terrington
ESCAPADE(1955, Brit.); SECRET OF THE FOREST, THE(1955, Brit.); TWO GROOMS FOR A BRIDE(1957)
Deney Terrio
IDOLMAKER, THE(1980), a, ch; NIGHT IN HEAVEN, A(1983), a, ch
Malcolm Terris
OTHELLO(1965, Brit.); GREAT TRAIN ROBBERY, THE(1979, Brit.); MC VI-CAR(1982, Brit.)
1984
BOUNTY, THE(1984); PLAGUE DOGS, THE(1984, U.S./Brit.); SLAYGROUND(1984, Brit.)
Milly Terris
Misc. Silents
CHIMES, THE(1914)
Norma Terris
MARRIED IN HOLLYWOOD(1929); CAMEO KIRBY(1930)
Tom Terris
CIRCUMSTANTIAL EVIDENCE(1935), w
Silents
CAPTAIN'S CAPTAIN, THE(1919), w
Elaine Terriss
Misc. Silents
SOCIETY WOLVES(1916)
Ellaline Terriss
ATLANTIC(1929 Brit.); GLAMOUR(1931, Brit.); MAN OF MAYFAIR(1931, Brit.); IRON DUKE, THE(1935, Brit.); REGAL CAVALCADE(1935, Brit.); SECRET FOUR, THE(1940, Brit.)
Silents
LAND OF HOPE AND GLORY(1927, Brit.)
Misc. Silents
BLIGHTY(1927, Brit.)
Tom Terriss
Silents
EVERYBODY'S GIRL(1918), d; CAPTAIN'S CAPTAIN, THE(1919), d; CLIMBERS, THE(1919), d; HEART OF MARYLAND, THE(1921), d; FIRES OF FATE(1923, Brit.), d; GIRL FROM RIO, THE(1927), d, w
Misc. Silents
CHIMES, THE(1914), d; MYSTERY OF EDWIN DROOD, THE(1914), a, d; FLAME OF PASSION, THE(1915), a, d; PEARL OF ANTILLES, THE(1915), a, d; MY COUNTRY FIRST(1916), a, d; SOCIETY WOLVES(1916), d; FETTERED WOMAN, THE(1917), d; BUSINESS OF LIFE(1918), d; FIND THE WOMAN(1918), d; SONG OF THE SOUL, THE(1918), d; TO THE HIGHEST BIDDER(1918), d; TRIUMPH OF THE WEAK, THE(1918), d; WOMAN BETWEEN FRIENDS, THE(1918), d; BRAMBLE BUSH, THE(1919), d; CAMBRIC MASK, THE(1919), d; LION AND THE MOUSE, THE(1919), d; SPARK DIVINE, THE(1919), d; THIRD DEGREE, THE(1919), d; VENGEANCE OF DURAND, THE(1919), d; CAPTAIN SWIFT(1920), d; DEAD MEN TELL NO TALES(1920), d; FORTUNE HUNTER, THE(1920), d; TOWER OF JEWELS, THE(1920), d; TRUMPET ISLAND(1920), d; BOOMERANG BILL(1922), d; CHALLENGE, THE(1922), d; FIND THE WOMAN(1922), d; HARBOUR LIGHTS, THE(1923, Brit.), d; BANDOLERO, THE(1924), d; DESERT SHEIK, THE(1924), d; HIS BUDDY'S WIFE(1925), d; ROMANCE OF A MILLION DOLLARS, THE(1926), d; TEMPTATIONS OF A SHOP GIRL(1927), d; BEYOND LONDON LIGHTS(1928), d; CLOTHES MAKE THE WOMAN(1928), d; NAUGHTY DUCHESS, THE(1928), d
Salvado Terroba
GARDEN OF EVIL(1954)
Charles Terrot
ANGEL WHO PAWNED HER HARP, THE(1956, Brit.), w
Terry the Dog
WIZARD OF OZ, THE(1939)
Terry the Tramp
HELL'S ANGELS '69(1969)
Terry Twins
Misc. Silents
FOOLISH TWINS, THE(1923)

The Terry Twins
Misc. Silents
FORDINGTON TWINS, THE(1920, Brit.)
Al Terry
DEADLINE(1948); BATTLING MARSHAL(1950)
Misc. Talkies
FIGHTING MUSTANG(1948); SUNSET CARSON RIDES AGAIN(1948)
Albert Terry
MAN FROM MUSIC MOUNTAIN(1938)
Alice Terry
LOVE IN MOROCCO(1933, Fr.), d
Silents
CONQUERING POWER, THE(1921); FOUR HORSEMEN OF THE APOCALYPSE, THE(1921); PRISONER OF ZENDA, THE(1922); SCARAMOUCHE(1923); ARAB, THE(1924); ANY WOMAN(1925); MARE NOSTRUM(1926)
Misc. Silents
BACHELOR'S CHILDREN, A(1918); HEARTS ARE TRUMPS(1920); TURN TO THE RIGHT(1922); WHERE THE PAVEMENT ENDS(1923); CONFESSIONS OF A QUEEN(1925); GREAT DIVIDE, THE(1925); SACKCLOTH AND SCARLET(1925); MAGICIAN, THE(1926); GARDEN OF ALLAH, THE(1927); LOVERS?(1927); THREE PASSIONS, THE(1928, Brit.)
Alix Terry
GASLIGHT(1944)
Allen Terry
SAVANNAH SMILES(1983), art d
Baby Terry
SHE SHALL HAVE MUSIC(1935, Brit.)
Ben Terry
GOING HOME(1971)
Bob Terry
$1,000,000 RACKET(1937); BROTHERS OF THE WEST(1938); SIX SHOOTIN' SHERIFF(1938); STARLIGHT OVER TEXAS(1938); STRANGER FROM ARIZONA, THE(1938); WHERE THE BUFFALO ROAM(1938); CODE OF THE CACTUS(1939); DOWN THE WYOMING TRAIL(1939); FLAMING LEAD(1939); OUTLAW'S PARADISE(1939); SMOKY TRAILS(1939); SONG OF THE BUCKAROO(1939); SUNDOWN ON THE PRAIRIE(1939); TEXAS WILDCATS(1939); DANGER AHEAD(1940); SKY BANDITS, THE(1940); YUKON FLIGHT(1940); NOCTURNE(1946)
Misc. Talkies
LIGHTNING CARSON RIDES AGAIN(1938)
Carol Terry
DOLL SQUAD, THE(1973)
Denine Terry
NO DRUMS, NO BUGLES(1971)
Dick Terry
COWBOY STAR, THE(1936); CAUGHT IN THE ACT(1941); LUCKY DEVILS(1941)
Don Terry
UNTAMED(1929); VALIANT, THE(1929); BORDER ROMANCE(1930); LADY WITH A PAST(1932); WHISTLIN' DAN(1932); DANGEROUS ADVENTURE, A(1937); FIGHT TO THE FINISH, A(1937); PAID TO DANCE(1937); SQUADRON OF HONOR(1938); WHEN G-MEN STEP IN(1938); WHO KILLED GAIL PRESTON?(1938); YOU CAN'T CHEAT AN HONEST MAN(1939); BARNACLE BILL(1941); HOLD THAT GHOST(1941); IN THE NAVY(1941); MUTINY IN THE ARCTIC(1941); DANGER IN THE PACIFIC(1942); DRUMS OF THE CONGO(1942); ESCAPE FROM HONG KONG(1942); MOONLIGHT IN HAVANA(1942); TOP SERGEANT(1942); UNSEEN ENEMY(1942); VALLEY OF THE SUN(1942); SHERLOCK HOLMES IN WASHINGTON(1943); WHITE SAVAGE(1943)
Silents
FUGITIVES(1929)
Misc. Silents
ME, GANGSTER(1928)
Edward Terry
CHILDREN, THE(1980), a, w
Edwin Terry
Silents
CALIFORNIA(1927)
Misc. Silents
WOLF'S TRAIL(1927)
Eliza Terry
I AM A GROUPIE(1970, Brit.)
Ellen Terry
Silents
POTTER'S CLAY(1922, Brit.)
Misc. Silents
HER GREATEST PERFORMANCE(1916, Brit.); DENNY FROM IRELAND(1918); VICTORY AND PEACE(1918, Brit.); PILLARS OF SOCIETY(1920, Brit.); BOHEMIAN GIRL, THE(1922, Brit.)
Ethel Grey Terry
Silents
APARTMENT 29(1917); ARSENE LUPIN(1917); DOLL'S HOUSE, A(1918); JUST FOR TONIGHT(1918); FOOD FOR SCANDAL(1920); PENALTY, THE(1920); BREAKING POINT, THE(1921); KICK BACK, THE(1922); OATH-BOUND(1922); SHATTERED IDOLS(1922); TOO MUCH BUSINESS(1922); TRAVELIN' ON(1922); GARRISON'S FINISH(1923); WHAT WIVES WANT(1923); WHAT FOOLS MEN(1925); LOVE TOY, THE(1926); OLD SHOES(1927); SKINNER'S BIG IDEA(1928); OBJECT-ALIMONY(1929)
Misc. Silents
HAWK, THE(1917); SNAIL, THE(1918); MYSTERY OF THE YELLOW ROOM, THE(1919); THOUSAND TO ONE, A(1920); SUSPICIOUS WIVES(1921); CROSSROADS OF NEW YORK, THE(1922); SELF-MADE WIFE, THE(1923); WHY WOMEN REMARRY(1923); WILD BILL HICKOK(1923); FAST WORKER, THE(1924); CONFESSIONS OF A WIFE(1928); MODERN MOTHERS(1928)
Ethelind Terry
LORD BYRON OF BROADWAY(1930); ARIZONA DAYS(1937)
Evelyn Terry
GOLDWYN FOLLIES, THE(1938)
Frank Terry
SEVEN DAYS LEAVE(1930), m; GREAT IMPERSONATION, THE(1935); OLD MOTHER RILEY IN PARIS(1938, Brit.)

Fred Terry
Misc. Silents
WITH WINGS OUTSPREAD(1922)
Gordon Terry
HIDDEN GUNS(1956); HONKYTONK MAN(1982)
Harry Terry
AMERICAN PRISONER, THE(1929 Brit.); RETURN OF THE RAT, THE(1929, Brit.); LORD RICHARD IN THE PANTRY(1930, Brit.); NIGHT BIRDS(1931, Brit.); SHERLOCK HOLMES' FATAL HOUR(1931, Brit.); THIRD TIME LUCKY(1931, Brit.); VAGABOND QUEEN, THE(1931, Brit.); PICCADILLY(1932, Brit.); REUNION(1932, Brit.); I'M AN EXPLOSIVE(1933, Brit.); LOVE WAGER, THE(1933, Brit.); BROKEN MELODY, THE(1934, Brit.); MASTER AND MAN(1934, Brit.); UNHOLY QUEST, THE(1934, Brit.); SCARLET PIMPERNEL, THE(1935, Brit.); PENNY POOL, THE(1937, Brit.); ALMOST A GENTLEMAN(1938, Brit.); FACE AT THE WINDOW, THE(1939, Brit.); JAILBIRDS(1939, Brit.); FUGITIVE, THE(1940, Brit.); OLD MOTHER RILEY, DETECTIVE(1943, Brit.); YOUNG MAN'S FANCY(1943, Brit.); HERE COMES THE SUN(1945, Brit.); LAUGHING LADY, THE(1950, Brit.)
Silents
RING, THE(1927, Brit.); MANXMAN, THE(1929, Brit.)
Hazel Terry
MISSING, BELIEVED MARRIED(1937, Brit.); SWEET DEVIL(1937, Brit.); PRISONER OF CORBAL(1939, Brit.); TORPEDOED!(1939); KILL OR CURE(1962, Brit.); SERVANT, THE(1964, Brit.)
Iris Terry
SCHOONER GANG, THE(1937, Brit.), a, w; DANCE OF DEATH, THE(1938, Brit.)
J. E. Howard Terry
Silents
GENERAL POST(1920, Brit.), w
Jack Terry
Silents
OLD HOME WEEK(1925)
Jessie Terry
Misc. Silents
HEARTACHES(1915)
Joe Terry
FIRST MONDAY IN OCTOBER(1981); CANNERY ROW(1982)
Misc. Talkies
I'M GOING TO BE FAMOUS(1981)
John Terry
HAWK THE SLAYER(1980, Brit.); THERE GOES THE BRIDE(1980, Brit.); SPRING BREAK(1983)
Misc. Talkies
JEKYLL AND HYDE PORTFOLIO, THE(1972); HOTWIRE(1980)
Silents
FAIR PRETENDER, THE(1918)
Misc. Silents
HIS BONDED WIFE(1918)
Jon Terry
CUTTER AND BONE(1981); HALLOWEEN III: SEASON OF THE WITCH(1982)
Jonathan Terry
1984
AGAINST ALL ODDS(1984)
Joy Terry
NAKED STREET, THE(1955)
Joyce Terry
NEANDERTHAL MAN, THE(1953); SNOW QUEEN, THE(1959, USSR); BEATNIKS, THE(1960)
June Ellen Terry
Silents
JANE EYRE(1921)
June Terry
THIS IS MY AFFAIR(1937)
Karen Terry
NO BLADE OF GRASS(1970, Brit.)
Kathleen Terry
O.S.S.(1946)
Kim Terry
SECOND THOUGHTS(1983)
Linda Terry
MAD MISS MANTON, THE(1938); PARENTS ON TRIAL(1939)
Lynn Terry
GOING HOME(1971)
Madge Terry
ALL THIS AND HEAVEN TOO(1940)
Martin Terry
WRONG BOX, THE(1966, Brit.); SORCERERS, THE(1967, Brit.); BATTLE BENEATH THE EARTH(1968, Brit.); CONQUEROR WORM, THE(1968, Brit.); MAN OUTSIDE, THE(1968, Brit.); OBLONG BOX, THE(1969, Brit.)
Nigel Terry
LION IN WINTER, THE(1968, Brit.); EXCALIBUR(1981)
Norbert Terry
LOVERS OF TERUEL, THE(1962, Fr.), titles; LAFAYETTE(1963, Fr.), titles; WHAT'S NEW, PUSSYCAT?(1965, U.S./Fr.)
Paula Terry
ALOMA OF THE SOUTH SEAS(1941)
Peggy Terry
BELOVED(1934); AIR HAWKS(1935)
Phil Terry
TORPEDO BOAT(1942); DEADLINE–U.S.A.(1952)
Philip Terry
HOLD THAT KISS(1938); GEORGE WHITE'S SCANDALS(1945)
Phillip Terry
YELLOW JACK(1938); LAST GANGSTER, THE(1937); MANNEQUIN(1937); ROSALIE(1937); MARIE ANTOINETTE(1938); OF HUMAN HEARTS(1938); TEST PILOT(1938); YOUNG DR. KILDARE(1938); BALALAIKA(1939); FOUR GIRLS IN WHITE(1939); MIRACLES FOR SALE(1939); ON BORROWED TIME(1939); THUNDER AFLOAT(1939); DANCING ON A DIME(1940); FUGITIVE FROM A PRISON CAMP(1940); NORTHWEST MOUNTED POLICE(1940); THOSE WERE THE DAYS(1940); I WANTED WINGS(1941); MONSTER AND THE GIRL, THE(1941); PARSON OF PANAMINT, THE(1941); PUBLIC ENEMIES(1941); ARE HUSBANDS

NECESSARY?(1942); SWEATER GIRL(1942); WAKE ISLAND(1942); BATAAN(1943); DOUBLE EXPOSURE(1944); LADIES COURAGEOUS(1944); MUSIC IN MANHATTAN(1944); LOST WEEKEND, THE(1945); PAN-AMERICANA(1945); DARK HORSE, THE(1946); TO EACH HIS OWN(1946); BEAT THE BAND(1947); BORN TO KILL(1947); SEVEN KEYS TO BALDPATE(1947); MAN FROM GOD'S COUNTRY(1958); MONEY, WOMEN AND GUNS(1958); LEECH WOMAN, THE(1960); EXPLOSIVE GENERATION, THE(1961); NAVY VS. THE NIGHT MONSTERS, THE(1966)
Phyllis Neilson Terry
Misc. Silents
L'APPEL DU SANG(1920, Fr.)
Phyllis Neilsson Terry
Silents
TRILBY(1915)
Richard R. Terry
THAT GANG OF MINE(1940)
Richard Terry
BIG RACE, THE(1934); JUNGLE PRINCESS, THE(1936); GIRLS CAN PLAY(1937); KING OF GAMBLERS(1937); MOTOR MADNESS(1937); CITY GIRL(1938); NICK CARTER, MASTER DETECTIVE(1939); BLONDE FROM SINGAPORE, THE(1941); BORROWED HERO(1941); UNDER AGE(1941); THIS TIME FOR KEEPS(1947)
Richard Terry [Jack Perrin]
JAWS OF JUSTICE(1933)
Robert A. Terry
COSMIC MAN, THE(1959), p
Robert Terry
RENFREW OF THE ROYAL MOUNTED(1937); SANDFLOW(1937); ON THE GREAT WHITE TRAIL(1938); LIGHTNING STRIKES WEST(1940); DESERT RAVEN, THE(1965); MURDERERS' ROW(1966); VELVET TRAP, THE(1966); PANIC IN THE CITY(1968); SWEET CHARITY(1969)
Ruth Terry
LOVE AND HISSES(1937); ALEXANDER'S RAGTIME BAND(1938); HOLD THAT CO-ED(1938); INTERNATIONAL SETTLEMENT(1938); HOTEL FOR WOMEN(1939); WIFE, HUSBAND AND FRIEND(1939); ANGEL FROM TEXAS, AN(1940); SING, DANCE, PLENTY HOT(1940); SLIGHTLY HONORABLE(1940); APPOINTMENT FOR LOVE(1941); BLONDIE GOES LATIN(1941); ROOKIES ON PARADE(1941); CALL OF THE CANYON(1942); HEART OF THE GOLDEN WEST(1942); SLEEPYTIME GAL(1942); HANDS ACROSS THE BORDER(1943); MAN FROM MUSIC MOUNTAIN(1943); MYSTERY BROADCAST(1943); PISTOL PACKIN' MAMA(1943); YOUTH ON PARADE(1943); GOODNIGHT SWEETHEART(1944); JAMBOREE(1944); LAKE PLACID SERENADE(1944); MY BUDDY(1944); SING, NEIGHBOR, SING(1944); THREE LITTLE SISTERS(1944); CHEATERS, THE(1945); STEPPIN' IN SOCIETY(1945); TELL IT TO A STAR(1945); HAND OF DEATH(1962)
Misc. Talkies
SMOKY RIVER SERENADE(1947)
Sheila Terry
BIG CITY BLUES(1932); CROONER(1932); HAUNTED GOLD(1932); I AM A FUGITIVE FROM A CHAIN GANG(1932); MADAME BUTTERFLY(1932); SCARLET DAWN(1932); THREE ON A MATCH(1932); WEEK-END MARRIAGE(1932); YOU SAID A MOUTHFUL(1932); HOUSE ON 56TH STREET, THE(1933); LAWYER MAN(1933); MAYOR OF HELL, THE(1933); PARACHUTE JUMPER(1933); PRIVATE DETECTIVE 62(1933); SILK EXPRESS, THE(1933); SON OF A SAILOR(1933); SPHINX, THE(1933); 20,000 YEARS IN SING SING(1933); 'NEATH THE ARIZONA SKIES(1934); ROCKY RHODES(1934); TAKE THE STAND(1934); WHEN STRANGERS MEET(1934); LAWLESS FRONTIER, THE(1935); RESCUE SQUAD(1935); SOCIETY FEVER(1935); BARS OF HATE(1936); MURDER ON A BRIDLE PATH(1936); SPECIAL INVESTIGATOR(1936); FURY BELOW(1938); I DEMAND PAYMENT(1938); SCREAM IN THE NIGHT(1943)
Misc. Talkies
GO-GET-'EM HAINES(1936)
Sherrill Terry
WILL SUCCESS SPOIL ROCK HUNTER?(1957)
Sonny Terry
JERK, THE(1979)
Susan Terry
MISSION BLOODY MARY(1967, Fr./Ital./Span.)
Tex Terry
HEROES OF THE SADDLE(1940); PIONEERS OF THE WEST(1940); BOSS OF BULLION CITY(1941); KANSAS CYCLONE(1941); RAWHIDE RANGERS(1941); SUNSET IN WYOMING(1942); OUTLAWS OF PINE RIDGE(1942); SAN ANTONIO KID, THE(1944); MAN FROM OKLAHOMA, THE(1945); OREGON TRAIL(1945); ROUGH RIDERS OF CHEYENNE(1945); SUNSET IN EL DORADO(1945); ALIAS BILLY THE KID(1946); EL PASO KID, THE(1946); PLAINSMAN AND THE LADY(1946); RED RIVER RENEGADES(1946); RIO GRANDE RAIDERS(1946); SIOUX CITY SUE(1946); APACHE ROSE(1947); TWILIGHT ON THE RIO GRANDE(1947); WYOMING(1947); GALLANT LEGION, THE(1948); LAST BANDIT, THE(1949); SURRENDER(1950); OLD WEST, THE(1952); PACK TRAIN(1953); SWEETHEARTS ON PARADE(1953); JUBILEE TRAIL(1954); ROAD TO DENVER, THE(1955); TIMBERJACK(1955); TOUGHEST GUN IN TOMBSTONE(1958); OREGON TRAIL, THE(1959)
Tony Terry
BURNING HILLS, THE(1956)
Valya Terry
MISSION TO MOSCOW(1943)
W. Benson Terry
WHERE'S POPPA?(1970)
Walter Terry
TORTURE DUNGEON(1970), makeup
William Terry
GANGWAY FOR TOMORROW(1943); STAGE DOOR CANTEEN(1943); JOHNNY DOESN'T LIVE HERE ANY MORE(1944); STRANGERS IN THE NIGHT(1944); THREE LITTLE SISTERS(1944); 3 IS A FAMILY(1944); BEHIND CITY LIGHTS(1945); IT'S IN THE BAG(1945)
William W. Terry
MEN IN HER DIARY(1945)
Terry Lightfoot and His New Orleans Jazz Band
RING-A-DING RHYTHM(1962, Brit. 73m Amicus/COL bw (G.B: IT'S TRAD, DAD!)
Terry-David
SIEGE(1983, Can.)

Mabel Terry-Lewis
CASTE(1930, Brit.); THIRD CLUE, THE(1934, Brit.); SCARLET PIMPERNEL, THE(1935, Brit.); DISHONOR BRIGHT(1936, Brit.); MURDER ON DIAMOND ROW(1937, Brit.); STOLEN LIFE(1939, Brit.); THEY CAME TO A CITY(1944, Brit.)

Terry-Thomas
IT'S LOVE AGAIN(1936, Brit.); DATE WITH A DREAM, A(1948, Brit.); HELTER SKELTER(1949, Brit.); MELODY CLUB(1949, Brit.); LUCKY MASCOT, THE(1951, Brit.); PRIVATE'S PROGRESS(1956, Brit.); GREEN MAN, THE(1957, Brit.); LUCKY JIM(1957, Brit.); BLUE MURDER AT ST. TRINIAN'S(1958, Brit.); HAPPY IS THE BRIDE(1958, Brit.); TOM THUMB(1958, Brit./U.S.); YOUR PAST IS SHOWING(1958, Brit.); I'M ALL RIGHT, JACK(1959, Brit.); TOO MANY CROOKS(1959, Brit.); MAKE MINE MINK(1960, Brit.); MAN IN A COCKED HAT(1960, Bri.); SCHOOL FOR SCOUNDRELS(1960, Brit.); HIS AND HERS(1961, Brit.); BACHELOR FLAT(1962); KILL OR CURE(1962, Brit.); MATTER OF WHO, A(1962, Brit.); OPERATION SNATCH(1962, Brit.); WONDERFUL WORLD OF THE BROTHERS ERIMM, THE(1962); IT'S A MAD, MAD, MAD, MAD WORLD(1963); MOUSE ON THE MOON, THE(1963, Brit.); HOW TO MURDER YOUR WIFE(1965); STRANGE BEDFEL-LOWS(1965); THOSE MAGNIFICENT MEN IN THEIR FLYING MACHINES; OR HOW I FLEWFROM LONDON TO PARIS IN 25 HOURS AND 11 MINUTES(1965, Brit.); BANG, BANG, YOU'RE DEAD(1966); DAYDREAMER, THE(1966); MUNSTER, GO HOME(1966); SANDWICH MAN, THE(1966, Brit.); WILD AFFAIR, THE(1966, Brit.); GUIDE FOR THE MARRIED MAN, A(1967); KARATE KILLERS(1967); KISS THE GIRLS AND MAKE THEM DIE(1967, U.S./Ital.); PERILS OF PAULINE, THE(1967); DANGER: DIABOLIK(1968, Ital./Fr.); DON'T RAISE THE BRIDGE, LOWER THE RIVER(1968, Brit.); HOW SWEET IT IS(1968); WHERE WERE YOU WHEN THE LIGHTS WENT OUT?(1968); ARABELLA(1969, U.S./Ital.); DON'T LOOK NOW(1969, Brit./Fr.); THOSE DARING YOUNG MEN IN THEIR JAUNTY JALO-PIES(1969, Fr./Brit./ Ital.); 2000 YEARS LATER(1969); TWELVE PLUS ONE(1970, Fr./Ital.); ABOMINABLE DR. PHIBES, THE(1971, Brit.); DOCTOR PHIBES RISES AGAIN(1972, Brit.); ROBIN HOOD(1973); VAULT OF HORROR, THE(1973, Brit.); SPANISH FLY(1975, Brit.); MYSTERIOUS HOUSE OF DR. C., THE(1976); LAST REMAKE OF BEAU GESTE, THE(1977); HOUND OF THE BASKERVILLES, THE(1980, Brit.)
Misc. Talkies
TWO THOUSAND YEARS LATER(1969); ARTHUR!! ARTHUR?(1970); SEVEN TIMES SEVEN(1973, Ital.); HEROES, THE(1975)

Pat Terry-Thomas
MISS TULIP STAYS THE NIGHT(1955, Brit.)

Terry's Juveniles
AROUND THE TOWN(1938, Brit.); CHIPS(1938. Brit.)

Ferdinand Terschack
GLASS MOUNTAIN, THE(1950, Brit)

Marilyn Terschluse
STUCKEY'S LAST STAND(1980)

Gijsbert Tersteeg
LAST BLITZKRIEG, THE(1958); DOG OF FLANDERS, A(1959)

Zh. Terteryan
GARNET BRACELET, THE(1966, USSR)

Edith Tertza
CLEO FROM 5 TO 7(1961, Fr.), prod d

Juhni Tervataa
FARMER'S DAUGHTER, THE(1947), w

George Terwilliger
AFTER THE FOG(1930), w; OUANGA(1936, Brit.), p,d&w; POCOMANIA(1939), w
Silents
DAUGHTERS OF MEN(1914), d; WHAT FOOLS MEN ARE(1922), d; DAUGHTERS WHO PAY(1925), d
Misc. Silents
CIPHER KEY, THE(1915), d; DESTINY'S SKEIN(1915), d; LASH OF DESTINY, THE(1916), d; PRICE WOMAN PAYS, THE(1919), d; DOLLARS AND THE WO-MAN(1920), d; SLAVES OF PRIDE(1920), d; SPORTING DUCHESS, THE(1920), d; LITTLE ITALY(1921), d; BIG SHOW, THE(1926), d; MARRIED?(1926), d

George W. Terwilliger
Silents
NATION'S PERIL, THE(1915), d, w
Misc. Silents
REGENERATING LOVE, THE(1915), d; RINGTAILED RHINOCEROS, THE(1915), d; CITY OF FAILING LIGHT, THE(1916), d; RACE SUICIDE(1916), d; FATAL HOUR, THE(1920), d; BRIDE'S PLAY, THE(1922), d; WIFE IN NAME ONLY(1923), d; HIGH-BINDERS, THE(1926), d

Marcelle Tery
GERVAISE(1956, Fr.)

Ubaldo Terzano
BLACK SUNDAY(1961, Ital.), ph; BLACK SABBATH(1963, Ital.), ph; ERIK THE CONQUEROR(1963, Fr./Ital.), ph

Laurent Terzieff
CHEATERS, THE(1961, Fr./Ital.); LA NOTTE BRAVA(1962, Fr./Ital.); SEVEN CAPITAL SINS(1962, Fr./Ital.); KAPO(1964, Ital./Fr./Yugo.); IMMORAL MOMENT, THE(1967, Fr.); TWO WEEKS IN SEPTEMBER(1967, Fr./Brit.); LA PRISONNIERE(1969, Fr./Ital.); MILKY WAY, THE(1969, Fr./Ital.); MEDEA(1971, Ital./Fr./Ger.); DESERT OF THE TARTARS, THE(1976 Fr./Ital./Iranian); MOSES(1976, Brit./Ital.)
Misc. Talkies
BROTHER CARL(1972)

Nino Terzo
TWO COLONELS, THE(1963, Ital.); BETTER A WIDOW(1969, Ital.)

Lorenzo Terzon
LADY HAMILTON(1969, Ger./Ital./Fr.); NUN AT THE CROSSROADS, A(1970, Ital./Span.)

Jan Tesarz
MAN OF IRON(1981, Pol.)

Don Tescher
MEMENTO MEI(1963)

Prof. Teschner
Misc. Silents
MYSTIC MIRROR, THE(1928, Ger.), d

Hiroshi Teshigahara
WOMAN IN THE DUNES(1964, Jap.), d; FACE OF ANOTHER, THE(1967, Jap.), d; SUMMER SOLDIERS(1972, Jap.), d, ph

Jovan Tesic
GENGHIS KHAN(U.S./Brit./Ger./Yugo)

Steve Tesich
BREAKING AWAY(1979), w; EYEWITNESS(1981), w; FOUR FRIENDS(1981), w, w; WORLD ACCORDING TO GARP, The(1982), w

Charles Teske
EASY TO LOOK AT(1945); MASQUERADE IN MEXICO(1945); ON STAGE EVERY-BODY(1945); WONDER MAN(1945)

Jack Tesler
ABBOTT AND COSTELLO GO TO MARS(1953); BAND WAGON, THE(1953); STORY OF THREE LOVES, THE(1953); THUNDER BAY(1953); CAGE OF EVIL(1960); LEP-KE(1975, U.S./Israel)

Jeanne Teslof
WACKY WORLD OF DR. MORGUS, THE(1962)

V. Teslya
FAREWELL, DOVES(1962, USSR)

Tessa
FLASH GORDON(1980)

Duccio Tessari
ALWAYS VICTORIOUS(1960, Ital.), w; LAST DAYS OF POMPEII, THE(1960, Ital.), w; CARTHAGE IN FLAMES(1961, Fr./Ital.), w; COLOSSUS OF RHODES, THE(1961, Ital., Fr., Span.), w; REVOLT OF THE SLAVES, THE(1961, Ital./Span./Ger.), w; WONDERS OF ALADDIN, THE(1961, Fr./Ital.), w; MARCO POLO(1962, Fr./Ital.), w; DUEL OF THE TITANS(1963, Ital.), w; MY SON, THE HERO(1963, Ital./Fr.), d, w; SAMSON AND THE SEVEN MIRACLES OF THE WORLD(1963, Fr./Ital.), w; FIST-FUL OF DOLLARS, A(1964, Ital./Ger./Span.), w; GOLIATH AND THE VAM-PIRES(1964, Ital.), w; HERCULES IN THE HAUNTED WORLD(1964, Ital.), w; PISTOL FOR RINGO, A(1966, Ital./Span.), d&w; RETURN OF RINGO, THE(1966, Ital./Span.), d, w; SEVEN GUNS FOR THE MACGREGORS(1968, Ital./Span.), w; BETTER A WIDOW(1969, Ital.), d, w; SONS OF SATAN(1969, Ital./Fr./Ger.), d, w; DEATH TOOK PLACE LAST NIGHT(1970, Ital./Ger.), d, w; DON'T TURN THE OTHER CHEEK(1974, Ital./Ger./Span.), d; THREE TOUGH GUYS(1974, U.S./Ital.), d; NO WAY OUT(1975, Ital./Fr.), d
Misc. Talkies
HEROES, THE(1975), d

Horace Tesseron
Misc. Silents
TOILERS OF THE SEA(1923 US/Ital.)

Tessie
ESCAPE TO BURMA(1955)

Bob Tessier
HOW COME NOBODY'S ON OUR SIDE?(1975); CANNONBALL RUN, THE(1981)

Diane Tessier
FIVE THE HARD WAY(1969)

Elisabeth Tessier
BLOOD ROSE, THE(1970, Fr.)

Jack Tessier
Silents
JACK TAR(1915, Brit.)
Misc. Silents
BY THE SHORTEST OF HEADS(1915, Brit.)

Jacques Tessier
SUNDAYS AND CYBELE(1962, Fr.)

Joey Tessier
FIVE THE HARD WAY(1969)

Laurence Tessier
Silents
MARY LATIMER, NUN(1920, Brit.)
Misc. Silents
GRIP OF IRON, THE(1920, Brit.)

Pierre Tessier
1984
L'ARGENT(1984, Fr./Switz.)

R. Tessier
DOUBLE EXPOSURE(1982)

Robert Tessier
BORN LOSERS(1967); GLORY STOMPERS, THE(1967); FIVE THE HARD WAY(1969); CRY BLOOD, APACHE(1970); HARD RIDE, THE(1971); JESUS TRIP, THE(1971); LONGEST YARD, THE(1974); DOC SAVAGE... THE MAN OF BRON-ZE(1975); HARD TIMES(1975); BREAKHEART PASS(1976); DEEP, THE(1977); HOOP-ER(1978); STARCRASH(1979); VILLAIN, THE(1979); STEEL(1980); SWORD AND THE SORCERER, THE(1982)
Misc. Talkies
BABYSITTER, THE(1969)

Valentine Tessier
ABUSED CONFIDENCE(1938, Fr. ABUS DE CONFIANCE); LUCRECE BOR-GIA(1953, Ital./Fr.); FRENCH CANCAN(1956, Fr.); HUNCHBACK OF NOTRE DAME, THE(1957, Fr.); EGLANTINE(1972, Fr.)

Nella Tessieri-Frediani
SHE AND HE(1969, Ital.)

Anna Mae Tessle
TOO MANY GIRLS(1940)

Gary Tessler
ULTIMATE THRILL, THE(1974)

Sheela Tessler
BILLION DOLLAR HOBO, THE(1977)

Charles W. Tessmer
TRIAL OF LEE HARVEY OSWALD, THE(1964)

Alberto Testa
LA TRAVIATA(1982), ch

Alfred Testa
Silents
LITTLE MISS SMILES(1922)

Donna Testa
SHE-DEVILS ON WHEELS(1968)

M.W. Testa
Misc. Silents
EDGE OF THE LAW(1917)

Mary Testa
GOING IN STYLE(1979)
Desmond Tester
LATE EXTRA(1935, Brit.); BELOVED VAGABOND, THE(1936, Brit.); LADY JANE GREY(1936, Brit.); NON-STOP NEW YORK(1937, Brit.); SABOTAGE(1937, Brit.); DRUMS(1938, Brit.); MAD MEN OF EUROPE(1940, Brit.); STARS LOOK DOWN, THE(1940, Brit.); TURNERS OF PROSPECT ROAD, THE(1947, Brit.); MEN OF THE SEA(1951, Brit.)
1984
BROTHERS(1984, Aus.)
Edward Tester
BOY TEN FEET TALL, A(1965, Brit.), art d
Ted Tester
NEGATIVES(1968, Brit.), art d; RUN WILD, RUN FREE(1969, Brit.), art d; FIGURES IN A LANDSCAPE(1970, Brit.), art d; DAY IN THE DEATH OF JOE EGG, A(1972, Brit.), art d; CONDUCT UNBECOMING(1975, Brit.), art d; HEDDA(1975, Brit.), art d; CARAVANS(1978, U.S./Iranian), art d; LOST AND FOUND(1979), art d; SUN-BURN(1979), prod d; PRIEST OF LOVE(1981, Brit.), prod d
Fabio Testi
'TIS A PITY SHE'S A WHORE(1973, Ital.); NADA GANG, THE(1974, Fr./Ital.); BLOOD IN THE STREETS(1975, Ital./Fr.); MAIN THING IS TO LOVE, THE(1975, Ital./Fr.); GARDEN OF THE FINZI-CONTINIS, THE(1976, Ital./Ger.); STATELINE MOTEL(1976, Ital.); CHINA 9, LIBERTY 37(1978, Ital.); INHERITANCE, THE(1978, Ital.)
1984
AMBASSADOR, THE(1984)
Giovanni Testori
ROCCO AND HIS BROTHERS(1961, Fr./Ital.), w
Sergei Testori
WATERLOO(1970, Ital./USSR)
Francois Testory
1984
MIDSUMMER NIGHT'S DREAM, A(1984, Brit./Span.)
Adeline Tetahaimuai
TANGA-TIKA(1953)
Jack Teter
IN THE HEAT OF THE NIGHT(1967)
E. Teterin
OTHELLO(1960, U.S.S.R.)
Yevgeniy Teterin
DESTINY OF A MAN(1961, USSR); LULLABY(1961, USSR); MUMU(1961, USSR), a, d; NINE DAYS OF ONE YEAR(1964, USSR)
Verne Teters
BADMAN'S GOLD(1951); CATTLE QUEEN(1951); SON OF THE RENEGADE(1953)
Charles Tetford
VALLEY OF HUNTED MEN(1942), w
Ann Tetheradge
WILD HEART, THE(1952, Brit.)
Federico Teti
AIDA(1954, Ital.), p; HERCULES(1959, Ital.), p; LOST SOULS(1961, Ital.), p
Giuseppe Teti
SALVATORE GIULIANO(1966, Ital.)
Jaroslav Tetiva
LEMONADE JOE(1966, Czech.)
Dorothy Tetley
BLARNEY KISS(1933, Brit.)
Graeme Tetley
1984
VIGIL(1984, New Zealand), w
Walter Tetley
BOY SLAVES(1938); LORD JEFF(1938); PRAIRIE MOON(1938); SPIRIT OF CULVER, THE(1939); THEY SHALL HAVE MUSIC(1939); TOWER OF LONDON(1939); YOU CAN'T CHEAT AN HONEST MAN(1939); EMERGENCY SQUAD(1940); LET'S MAKE MUSIC(1940); MILITARY ACADEMY(1940); UNDER TEXAS SKIES(1940); BROAD-WAY(1942); EYES IN THE NIGHT(1942); GORILLA MAN(1942); INVISIBLE AGENT(1942); MOONLIGHT IN HAVANA(1942); THUNDER BIRDS(1942); WHO DONE IT?(1942); FOLLOW THE BOYS(1944); LODGER, THE(1944); PIN UP GIRL(1944); MOLLY AND ME(1945)
Teton
SAVAGE WILD, THE(1970)
Charles Tetoni
ONE DARK NIGHT(1983), ed; STAR CHAMBER, THE(1983), ed
Jean Rosario Tetreault
SLAP SHOT(1977)
Bob Tetrick
SPIDER, THE(1958); SUICIDE BATTALION(1958); NOOSE FOR A GUNMAN(1960)
Ted Tetrick
THREE STOOGES IN ORBIT, THE(1962), cos; THREE STOOGES GO AROUND THE WORLD IN A DAZE, THE(1963), cos; DIAMONDS ARE FOREVER(1971, Brit.), cos
Rene Tetro
HAIL, HERO!(1969)
John Tettemer
LEOPARD MAN, THE(1943)
John Tettener
LOST HORIZON(1937)
Taeve Tetuamia
HURRICANE(1979)
Ted Tetzaff
LOVE THY NEIGHBOR(1940), ph
Joan Tetzel
DUEL IN THE SUN(1946); PARADINE CASE, THE(1947); FILE ON THELMA JORDAN, THE(1950); HELL BELOW ZERO(1954, Brit.); RED DRESS, THE(1954, Brit.); JOY IN THE MORNING(1965)
Ted Tetzlaff
ACQUITTED(1929), ph; DONOVAN AFFAIR, THE(1929), ph; FALL OF EVE, THE(1929), ph; FATHER AND SON(1929), ph; LIGHT FINGERS(1929), ph; MEX-ICALI ROSE(1929), ph; WALL STREET(1929), ph; YOUNGER GENERATION(1929), ph; FOR THE LOVE O'LIL(1930), ph; GUILTY?(1930), ph; HELL'S ISLAND(1930), ph; MELODY MAN(1930), ph; PERSONALITY(1930), ph; PRINCE OF DIAMONDS(1930), ph; ROYAL ROMANCE, A(1930), ph; SISTERS(1930), ph; SOLDIERS AND WO-

MEN(1930), ph; SQUEALER, THE(1930), ph; TOL'ABLE DAVID(1930), ph; DANGER-OUS AFFAIR, A(1931), ph; FIGHTING SHERIFF, THE(1931), ph; LIGHTNING FLY-ER(1931), ph; MEN ARE LIKE THAT(1931), ph; MEN IN HER LIFE(1931), ph; SHANGHAIED LOVE(1931), ph; TEXAS RANGER, THE(1931), ph; ATTORNEY FOR THE DEFENSE(1932), ph; BEHIND THE MASK(1932), ph; BY WHOSE HAND?(1932), ph; HIGH SPEED(1932), ph; HOLLYWOOD SPEAKS(1932), ph; LOVE AF-FAIR(1932), ph; MAN AGAINST WOMAN(1932), ph; NIGHT CLUB LADY(1932), ph; NIGHT MAYOR, THE(1932), ph; THIS SPORTING AGE(1932), ph; THREE WISE GIRLS(1932), ph; WASHINGTON MERRY-GO-ROUND(1932), ph; ANN CARVER'S PROFESSION(1933), ph; BRIEF MOMENT(1933), ph; CHILD OF MANHAT-TAN(1933), ph; DAY OF RECKONING(1933), ph; SHOULD LADIES BEHAVE?(1933), ph; SOLDIERS OF THE STORM(1933), ph; THRILL HUNTER, THE(1933), ph; COLLEGE RHYTHM(1934), ph; FUGITIVE LOVERS(1934), ph; HIS GREATEST GAMBLE(1934), ph; LADY BY CHOICE(1934), ph; TRANSATLANTIC MERRY-GO-ROUND(1934), ph; ANNAPOLIS FAREWELL(1935), ph; HANDS ACROSS THE TA-BLE(1935), ph; PARIS IN SPRING(1935), ph; RUMBA(1935), ph; LADY OF SE-CRETS(1936), ph; LOVE BEFORE BREAKFAST(1936), ph; MURDER WITH PICTURES(1936), ph; MY MAN GODFREY(1936), ph; PRINCESS COMES ACROSS, THE(1936), ph; EASY LIVING(1937), ph; SOPHIE LANG GOES WEST(1937), ph; SWING HIGH, SWING LOW(1937), ph; TRUE CONFESSION(1937), ph; TURN OFF THE MOON(1937), ph; ARTISTS AND MODELS ABROAD(1938), ph; FOOLS FOR SCANDAL(1938), ph; ARREST BULLDOG DRUMMOND(1939, Brit.), ph; CAFE SO-CIETY(1939), ph; HONEYMOON IN BALI(1939), ph; MAN ABOUT TOWN(1939), ph; TOM SAWYER, DETECTIVE(1939), ph; I WANT A DIVORCE(1940), ph; REMEMBER THE NIGHT(1940), ph; RHYTHM ON THE RIVER(1940), ph; SAFARI(1940), ph; KISS THE BOYS GOODBYE(1941), ph; MAD DOCTOR, THE(1941), ph; ROAD TO ZANZI-BAR(1941), ph; YOU'RE THE ONE(1941), ph; I MARRIED A WITCH(1942), ph; LADY IS WILLING, THE(1942), ph; TALK OF THE TOWN(1942), ph; YOU WERE NEVER LOVELIER(1942), ph; MORE THE MERRIER, THE(1943), ph; ENCHANTED COT-TAGE, THE(1945), ph; THOSE ENDEARING YOUNG CHARMS(1945), ph; NOTORI-OUS(1946), ph; RIFFRAFF(1947), d; FIGHTING FATHER DUNNE(1948), d; DANGEROUS PROFESSION, A(1949), d; JOHNNY ALLEGRO(1949), d; WINDOW, THE(1949), d; GAMBLING HOUSE(1950), d; WHITE TOWER, THE(1950), d; UNDER THE GUN(1951), d; TREASURE OF LOST CANYON, THE(1952), d; TERROR ON A TRAIN(1953), d; SON OF SINBAD(1955), d; YOUNG LAND, THE(1959), d
Silents
ATTA BOY!(1926), ph; EAGER LIPS(1927), ph; LADYBIRD, THE(1927), ph; RAG-TIME(1927), ph; APACHE, THE(1928), ph; INTO NO MAN'S LAND(1928), ph; MASKED ANGEL(1928), ph; POWER OF THE PRESS, THE(1928), ph

Toni Tetzlaff
COURT CONCERT, THE(1936, Ger.)
Tony Tetzlaff
PILLARS OF SOCIETY(1936, Ger.)
Misc. Silents
HER GREATEST BLUFF(1927, Ger.)

Ted Tetzlatt
WORLD PREMIERE(1941), d
Andreas Teuber
DOCTOR FAUSTUS(1967, Brit.)
Karl-Heinz Teuber
1984
AMADEUS(1984)
Monica Teuber
DUCK RINGS AT HALF PAST SEVEN, THE(1969, Ger./Ital.)
Tumata Teuiau
MAEVA(1961)
Jan Teulings
BEAUTIFUL SWINDLERS, THE(1967, Fr./Ital./Jap./Neth.)
Rangitoheriri Teupokopakari
1984
VIGIL(1984, New Zealand)
Pamela Teves
1984
FOURTH MAN, THE(1984, Neth.)
Thierry Tevini
COUSINS IN LOVE(1982)
Carol Tevis
ONCE IN A LIFETIME(1932); FLYING DOWN TO RIO(1933); GIRL FROM MIS-SOURI, THE(1934); SWEEPSTAKE ANNIE(1935); SING, BABY, SING(1936); LOVE IS NEWS(1937); LOVE TAKES FLIGHT(1937); THREE LOVES HAS NANCY(1938); UNFINISHED BUSINESS(1941)
Walter Tevis
HUSTLER, THE(1961), w; MAN WHO FELL TO EARTH, THE(1976, Brit.), w
C.J. Tevlin
BAT, THE(1959), p
Eugene Tevlin
BENGAZI(1955), p
Herbert Tevos
MESA OF LOST WOMEN, THE(1956), d, w
Graham Tew
GAMEKEEPER, THE(1980, Brit.), art d
Lauren Tewes
EYES OF A STRANGER(1980)
Joan Tewkesbury
MAN'S FAVORITE SPORT(?)(1964); THIEVES LIKE US(1974), a, w; NASHVIL-LE(1975), w; OLD BOYFRIENDS(1979), d; NIGHT IN HEAVEN, A(1983), w
Peter Tewksbury
TROUBLE WITH GIRLS(AND HOW TO GET INTO IT), THE*1/2 (1969), d; SUNDAY IN NEW YORK(1963), d; EMIL AND THE DETECTIVES(1964), d; DOCTOR, YOU'VE GOT TO BE KIDDING(1967), d; STAY AWAY, JOE(1968), d
Josephine Tewson
TROUBLESOME DOUBLE, THE(1971, Brit.)
Tex
BORN LOSERS(1967)
Tex Ritter's Tornadoes
HITTIN' THE TRAIL(1937)

Temple Texas
KISS OF DEATH(1947)
Texas Jim Lewis and His Lone Star Cowboys
PARDON MY GUN(1942)
Texas Kid
Silents
ONE-ROUND HOGAN(1927)
The Texas Rangers
OKLAHOMA FRONTIER(1939); RAGTIME COWBOY JOE(1940); SON OF ROARING DAN(1940); RAWHIDE RANGERS(1941); LAST ROUND UP(1947)
Students of the Texas State College for Women
WE'VE NEVER BEEN LICKED(1943)
The Texas Tornados
RIDERS OF THE ROCKIES(1937); TROUBLE IN TEXAS(1937)
Texas Wanderers
VILLAGE BARN DANCE(1940)
Denise Texeira
1984
SPLATTER UNIVERSITY(1984)
Virgilio Texeira
ALEXANDER THE GREAT(1956); FACE OF TERROR(1964, Span.); DOCTOR ZHIVAGO(1965); RETURN OF THE SEVEN(1966, Span.); MAGNIFICENT TWO, THE(1967, Brit.)
Virgilio Texera
BOY WHO STOLE A MILLION, THE(1960, Brit.); TOMMY THE TOREADOR(1960, Brit.); HAPPY THIEVES, THE(1962); FALL OF THE ROMAN EMPIRE, THE(1964)
Jacob Texiere
Misc. Silents
LEAVES FROM SATAN'S BOOK(1921, Den.)
Gilda Texter
ANGELS HARD AS THEY COME(1971); VANISHING POINT(1971); WHERE THE BUFFALO ROAM(1980), cos
Misc. Talkies
RUNAWAY(1971)
Beverly Tey
Misc. Talkies
MAN OUTSIDE(1965)
Josephine Tey
YOUNG AND INNOCENT(1938, Brit.), w; FRANCHISE AFFAIR, THE(1952, Brit.), w
T. Teykh
OVERCOAT, THE(1965, USSR)
Maurice Teynac
NIGHT WITHOUT STARS(1953, Brit.); BEDEVILLED(1955); NAPOLEON(1955, Fr.); PARIS HOLIDAY(1958); CRACK IN THE MIRROR(1960); DEVIL AND THE TEN COMMANDMENTS, THE(1962, Fr.); PASSION OF SLOW FIRE, THE(1962, Fr.); IN THE FRENCH STYLE(1963, U.S./Fr.); TRIAL, THE(1963, Fr./Ital./Ger.); MAYERLING(1968, Brit./Fr.); THERESE AND ISABELLE(1968, U.S./Ger.); UNINHIBITED, THE(1968, Fr./Ital./Span.); ASH WEDNESDAY(1973); DAY OF THE JACKAL, THE(1973, Brit./Fr.); STATE OF SIEGE(1973, Fr./U.S./Ital./Ger.)
Mike Tezcan
VICTOR/VICTORIA(1982)
Osamu Tezuka
ALAKAZAM THE GREAT!(1961, Jap.), w; HINOTORI(1980, Jap.), w
Shigeo Tezuka
ANGRY ISLAND(1960, Jap.)
Osamu Tezuku
SPACE FIREBIRD 2772(1979, Jap.), d&w
Lt. Comdr. John S. Thach
WE'VE NEVER BEEN LICKED(1943), tech adv
Russell Thacher
SOYLENT GREEN(1973), p; LAST HARD MEN, THE(1976), p
Clive Thacker
O LUCKY MAN!(1973, Brit.)
Russ Thacker
PARADES(1972); SAVAGES(1972); LINE, THE(1982)
Misc. Talkies
PARADES(1972); AWOL(1973)
Tab Thacker
1984
CITY HEAT(1984)
Tom Thacker
VANISHING POINT(1971), m
Bud Thackeray
BANDITS OF THE BADLANDS(1945), ph; ALIAS BILLY THE KID(1946), ph
Phyllis Thackeray
EVERYTHING IS RHYTHM(1940, Brit.)
Sue Thackeray
EIGHT O'CLOCK WALK(1954, Brit.)
William Makepeace Thackeray
VANITY FAIR(1932), w; BECKY SHARP(1935), w; BARRY LYNDON(1975, Brit.), w
Ellis Thackerey
VAMPIRE'S GHOST, THE(1945), ph
Bud Thackery
GANGS OF SONORA(1941), ph; GAY VAGABOND, THE(1941), ph; CYCLONE KID, THE(1942), ph; GIRL FROM ALASKA(1942), ph; OUTLAWS OF PINE RIDGE(1942), ph; PHANTOM PLAINSMEN, THE(1942), ph; SONS OF THE PIONEERS(1942), ph; STARDUST ON THE SAGE(1942), ph; SUNSET SERENADE(1942), ph; TRAITOR WITHIN, THE(1942), ph; VALLEY OF HUNTED MEN(1942), ph; BEYOND THE LAST FRONTIER(1943), ph; HEADIN' FOR GOD'S COUNTRY(1943), ph; HERE COMES ELMER(1943), ph; MAN FROM THUNDER RIVER, THE(1943), ph; O, MY DARLING CLEMENTINE(1943), ph; SLEEPY LAGOON(1943), ph; SWING YOUR PARTNER(1943), ph; CHEYENNE WILDCAT(1944), ph; CODE OF THE PRAIRIE(1944), ph; FIREBRANDS OF ARIZONA(1944), ph; GIRL WHO DARED, THE(1944), ph; GOODNIGHT SWEETHEART(1944), ph; SHERIFF OF SUNDOWN(1944), ph; CORPUS CHRISTI BANDITS(1945), ph; FATAL WITNESS, THE(1945), ph; GREAT STAGECOACH ROBBERY(1945), ph; LONE TEXAS RANGER(1945), ph; MARSHAL OF LAREDO(1945), ph; OREGON TRAIL(1945), ph; SHERIFF OF CIMARRON(1945), ph; TOPEKA TERROR(1945), ph; TRAIL OF KIT CARSON(1945), ph; CYCLOTRODE X(1946), ph; MAN FROM RAINBOW VALLEY,

THE(1946), ph; OUT CALIFORNIA WAY(1946), ph; SANTA FE UPRISING(1946), ph; SUN VALLEY CYCLONE(1946), ph; TRAFFIC IN CRIME(1946), ph; UNDERCOVER WOMAN, THE(1946), ph; LAST FRONTIER UPRISING(1947), ph; SADDLE PALS(1947), ph; THAT'S MY GAL(1947), ph; OUTCASTS OF THE TRAIL(1949), ph; PRINCE OF THE PLAINS(1949), ph; BLACK HILLS AMBUSH(1952), ph; LEADVILLE GUNSLINGER(1952), ph; BANDITS OF THE WEST(1953), ph; IRON MOUNTAIN TRAIL(1953), ph; RED RIVER SHORE(1953), ph; SAVAGE FRONTIER(1953), ph; SHADOWS OF TOMBSTONE(1953), ph; PHANTOM STALLION, THE(1954), ph; FIGHTING CHANCE, THE(1955), ph; FLAME OF THE ISLANDS(1955), ph; NO MAN'S WOMAN(1955), ph; SANTA FE PASSAGE(1955), ph; TWINKLE IN GOD'S EYE, THE(1955), ph; ACCUSED OF MURDER(1956), ph; JAGUAR(1956), ph; MAN IS ARMED, THE(1956), ph; STRANGE ADVENTURE, A(1956), ph; STRANGER AT MY DOOR(1956), ph; TERROR AT MIDNIGHT(1956), ph; THUNDER OVER ARIZONA(1956), ph; RAIDERS, THE(1964), ph; BEAU GESTE(1966), ph; PLAINSMAN, THE(1966), ph; TAMMY AND THE MILLIONAIRE(1967), ph; COOGAN'S BLUFF(1968), ph; DID YOU HEAR THE ONE ABOUT THE TRAVELING SALESLADY?(1968), ph; HELL WITH HEROES, THE(1968), ph; STRATEGY OF TERROR(1969), ph
Ellis F. Thackery
SEA HORNET, THE(1951), ph; WILD BLUE YONDER, THE(1952), spec eff
Ellis Thackery
HOUSE OF A THOUSAND CANDLES, THE(1936), spec eff; LARAMIE TRAIL, THE(1944), ph
Eugene Thackery
UNFINISHED BUSINESS(1941), w
Frank Thackery
MISSION GALACTICA: THE CYLON ATTACK(1979), ph
Gene Thackery
ARTISTS AND MODELS(1937), w
Patricia Thackray
RAGGEDY ANN AND ANDY(1977), w
Eugene Thackrey
BED OF ROSES(1933), w; LADY IN A JAM(1942), w
Arthur Thahasso
AIR POLICE(1931)
Moa Thai
BLOODY PIT OF HORROR, THE(1965, Ital.)
Arthur Thalasso
VIVA VILLA!(1934); CHARGE OF THE LIGHT BRIGADE, THE(1936); MILLIONAIRE KID(1936); QUIET PLEASE, MURDER(1942); NOB HILL(1945)
Silents
CHILDREN OF THE NIGHT(1921); LITTLE LORD FAUNTLEROY(1921); SIGN OF THE ROSE, THE(1922); STRONG MAN, THE(1926); THREE'S A CROWD(1927); AVENGING RIDER, THE(1928); INTO THE NIGHT(1928); OUT WITH THE TIDE(1928)
Katharina Thalbach
SOPHIE'S CHOICE(1982)
Deborah Thalberg
CLASS(1983)
Irving Thalberg [Bernard Hyman]
LAST OF MRS. CHEYNEY, THE(1929), p; GUARDSMAN, THE(1931), p; MATA HARI(1931), p; MASK OF FU MANCHU, THE(1932), p; TARZAN, THE APE MAN(1932), p; BARRETTS OF WIMPOLE STREET, THE(1934), p; MERRY WIDOW, THE(1934), p; RIP TIDE(1934), p; BIOGRAPHY OF A BACHELOR GIRL(1935), p; CHINA SEAS(1935), p; MUTINY ON THE BOUNTY(1935), p; NIGHT AT THE OPERA, A(1935), p; NO MORE LADIES(1935), p; RIFF-RAFF(1936), p; ROMEO AND JULIET(1936), p; GOOD EARTH, THE(1937), p
Silents
MERRY-GO-ROUND(1923), p
Sylvia Thalberg
UNTAMED(1929), w; MONTANA MOON(1930), w; NEW MOON(1930), w; STRICTLY UNCONVENTIONAL(1930), w; THOSE THREE FRENCH GIRLS(1930), w; THIS MODERN AGE(1931), w; FELLER NEEDS A FRIEND(1932), w; PROSPERITY(1932), w; CHRISTOPHER BEAN(1933), w; SON COMES HOME, A(1936), w
Silents
BABY MINE(1928), w
Friedrich Thaler
SERPENT'S EGG, THE(1977, Ger./U.S.), art d
Sylvia Thalliery
NOW AND FOREVER(1934), w
Bent Thalmay
CHRISTINE KEELER AFFAIR, THE(1964, Brit.)
Dora Thalmer
EIGHT GIRLS IN A BOAT(1932, Ger.)
Tilda Thamar
MASTER PLAN, THE(1955, Brit.); FRIENDS AND NEIGHBORS(1963, Brit.)
Bjorn Thambert
SHAME(1968, Swed.); MY FATHER'S MISTRESS(1970, Swed.)
Byron Thames
HEART LIKE A WHEEL(1983)
1984
BLAME IT ON THE NIGHT(1984); JOHNNY DANGEROUSLY(1984)
Joseph Than
NONE SHALL ESCAPE(1944), w; DECEPTION(1946), w; PIRATE, THE(1948), w
Win Min Than
PURPLE PLAIN, THE(1954, Brit.)
Thanasis
CANNON AND THE NIGHTINGALE, THE(1969, Gr.)
Thandi
DINGAKA(1965, South Africa)
Dick Thane
WEST OF PINTO BASIN(1940)
Dirk Thane
OVERLAND STAGE RAIDERS(1938); WOLVES OF THE SEA(1938); DAUGHTER OF THE TONG(1939); RIDERS OF BLACK MOUNTAIN(1941); TWO GUN SHERIFF(1941); LOUISIANA HAYRIDE(1944)
Bui Thi Thanh
HOA-BINH(1971, Fr.)

Jennifer Thanisch
DARK PLACES(1974, Brit.)
Romesh Thappar
HOUSEHOLDER, THE(1963, US/India)
Fredrik Tharaldsen
HAGBARD AND SIGNE(1968, Den./Iceland/Swed.)
Kunchuck Tharching
1984
RAZOR'S EDGE, THE(1984)
Grahame Tharp
VIRGIN ISLAND(1960, Brit.), p
Norman Tharp
Silents
MASQUERADERS, THE(1915)
Misc. Silents
LAND OF MYSTERY, THE(1920, Brit.)
Twyla Tharp
HAIR(1979), ch; RAGTIME(1981), ch
1984
AMADEUS(1984), ch
A. Thatcher
KILL OR CURE(1962, Brit.), set d
Barbara Thatcher
TWO TICKETS TO BROADWAY(1951); BAD AND THE BEAUTIFUL, THE(1952);
LAS VEGAS STORY, THE(1952)
Billy Thatcher
VACATION FROM MARRIAGE(1945, Brit.); WALKING ON AIR(1946, Brit.); FOR-
TUNE LANE(1947, Brit.); NO PLACE FOR JENNIFER(1950, Brit.)
Bob Thatcher
HAVING WONDERFUL TIME(1938)
Eva Thatcher
Silents
FRIENDLY HUSBAND, A(1923); LAW FORBIDS, THE(1924); KNOCKOUT KID,
THE(1925); BLAZING DAYS(1927)
Evelyn Thatcher
Misc. Silents
FLASH O'LIGHTING(1925); RANCHERS AND RASCALS(1925); TROUBLE BUST-
ER, THE(1925)
Fred Thatcher
Misc. Silents
FLAME, THE(1920, Brit.); SCALLYWAG, THE(1921, Brit.); WOMAN OF HIS
DREAM, THE(1921, Brit.)
Heather Thatcher
PLAYTHING, THE(1929, Brit.); WARM CORNER, A(1930, Brit.); BUT THE FLESH IS
WEAK(1932); IT'S A BOY(1934, Brit.); LOYALTIES(1934, Brit.); PRIVATE LIFE OF
DON JUAN, THE(1934, Brit.); DICTATOR, THE(1935, Brit./Ger.); MAMA STEPS
OUT(1937); THIRTEENTH CHAIR, THE(1937); TOVARICH(1937); FOOLS FOR SCAN-
DAL(1938); GIRLS' SCHOOL(1938); IF I WERE KING(1938); BEAU GESTE(1939); MAN
HUNT(1941); JOURNEY FOR MARGARET(1942); MOON AND SIXPENCE,
THE(1942); SON OF FURY(1942); THIS ABOVE ALL(1942); UNDYING MONSTER,
THE(1942); WE WERE DANCING(1942); FLESH AND FANTASY(1943); GAS-
LIGHT(1944); ANNA KARENINA(1948, Brit.); DEAR MR. PROHACK(1949, Brit.); GAY
LADY, THE(1949, Brit.); ENCORE(1951, Brit.); FATHER'S DOING FINE(1952, Brit.);
HOUR OF THIRTEEN, THE(1952); DUEL IN THE JUNGLE(1954, Brit.); DEEP BLUE
SEA, THE(1955, Brit.); JOSEPHINE AND MEN(1955, Brit.); WILL ANY GENTLE-
MAN?(1955, Brit.)
Silents
ALTAR CHAINS(1916, Brit.)
Misc. Silents
KEY OF THE WORLD, THE(1918, Brit.); FIRST MEN IN THE MOON, THE(1919,
Brit.); GREEN TERROR, THE(1919, Brit.); PALLARD THE PUNTER(1919, Brit.);
LITTLE HOUR OF PETER WELLS, THE(1920, Brit.)
Leora Thatcher
THEODORA GOES WILD(1936); DIARY OF A BACHELOR(1964)
Mary Thatcher
HITCHHIKERS, THE(1972)
Phyllis Thatcher
Silents
JIMMY(1916, Brit.)
Torin Thatcher [Torren Thatcher]
NORAH O'NEALE(1934, Brit.); SCHOOL FOR STARS(1935, Brit.); RED WA-
GON(1936, Brit.); WELL DONE, HENRY(1936, Brit.); KNIGHT WITHOUT ARMOR(1937,
Brit.); MAN WHO COULD WORK MIRACLES, THE(1937, Brit.); SABOTAGE(1937,
Brit.); CLIMBING HIGH(1938, Brit.); RETURN OF THE SCARLET PIMPERNEL(1938,
Brit.); YOUNG AND INNOCENT(1938, Brit.); OLD MOTHER RILEY MP(1939, Brit.);
TOO DANGEROUS TO LIVE(1939, Brit.); U-BOAT 29(1939, Brit.); CASE OF THE
FRIGHTENED LADY, THE(1940. Brit.); GASBAGS(1940, Brit.); LAW AND DISORD-
ER(1940, Brit.); LET GEORGE DO IT(1940, Brit.); LION HAS WINGS(1940, Brit.);
NIGHT TRAIN(1940, Brit.); SALOON BAR(1940, Brit.); MAJOR BARBARA(1941, Brit.);
NEXT OF KIN(1942, Brit.); SABOTEUR(1942); ADVENTURESS, THE(1946, Brit.);
GREAT EXPECTATIONS(1946, Brit.); END OF THE RIVER, THE(1947, Brit.); WHEN
THE BOUGH BREAKS(1947, Brit.); JASSY(1948, Brit.); SMUGGLERS, THE(1948,
Brit.); FALLEN IDOL, THE(1949, Brit.); AFFAIR IN TRINIDAD(1952); BLACKBEARD
THE PIRATE(1952); CRIMSON PIRATE, THE(1952); SNOWS OF KILIMANJARO,
THE(1952); DESERT RATS, THE(1953); HOUDINI(1953); ROBE, THE(1953); BENGAL
BRIGADE(1954); BLACK SHIELD OF FALWORTH, THE(1954); KNOCK ON
WOOD(1954); DIANE(1955); LADY GODIVA(1955); LOVE IS A MANY-SPLENDORED
THING(1955); HELEN OF TROY(1956, Ital); BAND OF ANGELS(1957); ISTAN-
BUL(1957); WITNESS FOR THE PROSECUTION(1957); DARBY'S RANGERS(1958);
SEVENTH VOYAGE OF SINBAD, THE(1958); MIRACLE, THE(1959); CANADIANS,
THE(1961, Brit.); JACK THE GIANT KILLER(1962); MUTINY ON THE BOUN-
TY(1962); DRUMS OF AFRICA(1963); SANDPIPER, THE(1965); HAWAII(1966);
KING'S PIRATE(1967)
Wendy Thatcher
STONE COLD DEAD(1980, Can.)
Hilmar Thate
VERONIKA VOSS(1982, Ger.)

Leon Thau
GREAT ST. TRINIAN'S TRAIN ROBBERY, THE(1966, Brit.); CARRY ON, UP THE
KHYBER(1968, Brit.); MAGIC CHRISTIAN, THE(1970, Brit.)
Evelyn Nesbit Thaw
Misc. Silents
THREADS OF DESTINY(1914)
John Thaw
LONELINESS OF THE LONG DISTANCE RUNNER, THE(1962, Brit.); FIVE TO
ONE(1963, Brit.); DEAD MAN'S CHEST(1965, Brit.); BOFORS GUN, THE(1968, Brit.);
LAST GRENADE, THE(1970, Brit.); PRAISE MARX AND PASS THE AMMUNI-
TION(1970, Brit.); DOCTOR PHIBES RISES AGAIN(1972, Brit.); SWEENEY(1977,
Brit.); SWEENEY 2(1978, Brit.); GRASS IS SINGING, THE(1982, Brit./Swed.)
1984
KILLING HEAT(1984)
Russell Thaw
Silents
I WANT TO FORGET(1918)
Misc. Silents
REDEMPTION(1917); WOMAN WHO GAVE, THE(1918)
Russell William Thaw
Misc. Silents
THREADS OF DESTINY(1914)
Teresa Thaw
CAIN'S WAY(1969)
Tony Thawnton
WOMAN POSSESSED, A(1958, Brit.); FOLLOW THAT HORSE!(1960, Brit.); MARY
HAD A LITTLE(1961, Brit.); SECRET OF MONTE CRISTO, THE(1961, Brit.); DESERT
PATROL(1962, Brit.); CURSE OF THE VOODOO(1965, Brit.); WRONG BOX, THE(1966,
Brit.); OH! WHAT A LOVELY WAR(1969, Brit.); 10 RILLINGTON PLACE(1971, Brit.)
Tony Thawton
OBLONG BOX, THE(1969, Brit.)
Phyllis Thaxter
THIRTY SECONDS OVER TOKYO(1944); BEWITCHED(1945); WEEKEND AT THE
WALDORF(1945); LIVING IN A BIG WAY(1947); SEA OF GRASS, THE(1947); BLOOD
ON THE MOON(1948); SIGN OF THE RAM, THE(1948); TENTH AVENUE AN-
GEL(1948); ACT OF VIOLENCE(1949); BREAKING POINT, THE(1950); NO MAN OF
HER OWN(1950); COME FILL THE CUP(1951); FORT WORTH(1951); JIM THORPE-
ALL AMERICAN(1951); OPERATION SECRET(1952); SHE'S WORKING HER WAY
THROUGH COLLEGE(1952); SPRINGFIELD RIFLE(1952); WOMEN'S PRISON(1955);
MAN AFRAID(1957); WORLD OF HENRY ORIENT, THE(1964); SUPERMAN(1978)
Lee Thaxton
VALDEZ IS COMING(1971)
Lloyd Thaxton
PATSY, THE(1964)
Robin Thaxton
VALDEZ IS COMING(1971)
Carl Thayer
ABDUCTORS, THE(1957)
Edna Thayer
GIRL FEVER(1961)
Ernest Thayer
Silents
CASEY AT THE BAT(1927), w
Guy Thayer
WALLABY JIM OF THE ISLANDS(1937), ed; RIDE 'EM COWGIRL(1939), ed;
FEDERAL FUGITIVES(1941), ed; BROADWAY BIG SHOT(1942), ed
Ivy Thayer
WILD HARVEST(1962); LITTLE LAURA AND BIG JOHN(1973)
Julia Thayer
GUNSMOKE RANCH(1937)
Lorna Thayer
LUSTY MEN, THE(1952); TEXAS CITY(1952); JENNIFER(1953); WOMEN'S PRIS-
ON(1955); BEAST WITH A MILLION EYES, THE(1956); I'VE LIVED BEFORE(1956);
WOMEN OF PITCAIRN ISLAND, THE(1957); I WANT TO LIVE!(1958); FRECK-
LES(1960); POLICE NURSE(1963); FIVE EASY PIECES(1970); TRAVELING EXECU-
TIONER, THE(1970); CISCO PIKE(1971); GLASS HOUSES(1972); SKYJACKED(1972);
GRAVY TRAIN, THE(1974); RHINOCEROS(1974); SMOKE IN THE WIND(1975)
Max Thayer
1984
HOT AND DEADLY(1984)
Meriwyn Thayer
Silents
MERRY WIDOW, THE(1925)
Michael Thayer
PLANET OF DINOSAURS(1978)
Misc. Talkies
ILSA, HAREM KEEPER OF THE OIL SHEIKS(1976)
Otis B. Thayer
Misc. Silents
MYSTERY OF NO. 47, THE(1917), d; MISS ARIZONA(1919), d; DESERT SCORPION,
THE(1920), d; WOLVES OF THE STREET(1920), d; FINDERS KEEPERS(1921), d;
OUT OF THE DEPTHS(1921), d; RIDERS OF THE RANGE(1923), d; TRACY THE
OUTLAW(1928), d
Otis Thayer
Misc. Silents
AWAKENING OF BESS MORTON, THE(1916), d; DESERT SCORPION, THE(1920)
Tiffany Thayer
CALL HER SAVAGE(1932), w; IF I HAD A MILLION(1932), w; STRANGERS OF
THE EVENING(1932), w; THIRTEEN WOMEN(1932), w; DEVIL ON HORSEBACK,
THE(1936); KING OF GAMBLERS(1937), w; CHICAGO DEADLINE(1949), w
Tina Thayer
GIRLS UNDER TWENTY-ONE(1940); MEET JOHN DOE(1941); SECRETS OF A
CO-ED(1942); YANK AT ETON, A(1942); PAYOFF, THE(1943); HENRY ALDRICH'S
LITTLE SECRET(1944); JIVE JUNCTION(1944)
Guy V. Thayer, Jr.
SINGING COWGIRL, THE(1939), ed; WATER RUSTLERS(1939), ed; MURDER ON
THE YUKON(1940), ed; DUKE OF THE NAVY(1942), ed; MIRACLE KID(1942), ed

Carl Thayler
LAST ROUND-UP, THE(1947); MAN FROM DEL RIO(1956); TRUE STORY OF JESSE JAMES, THE(1957); HIGH SCHOOL CONFIDENTIAL(1958); PARTY GIRL(1958)
Anna Thea
NICKELODEON(1976)
Ralph Theadore
DANCE OF LIFE, THE(1929); CONFESSIONS OF BOSTON BLACKIE(1941)
George Theakos
BLACK SIX, THE(1974), w
David Theakston
BROTHERS AND SISTERS(1980, Brit.)
Sam Theard
STING II, THE(1983)
Mlle. Theaudiere
WILD CHILD, THE(1970, Fr.)
Philippe Theaudiere
SMUGGLERS, THE(1969, Fr.), ph
Marion Thebaud
CATHERINE & CO.(1976, Fr.)
Tina Theberge
VALLEY GIRL(1983)
1984
MICKI AND MAUDE(1984)
Blanche Thebom
IRISH EYES ARE SMILING(1944); GREAT CARUSO, THE(1951)
Rosemary Theby
MIDNIGHT DADDIES(1929); TEN NIGHTS IN A BARROOM(1931); MAN ON THE FLYING TRAPEZE, THE(1935); HIS BROTHER'S WIFE(1936); OUR RELATIONS(1936); SAN FRANCISCO(1936); YOURS FOR THE ASKING(1936); MAKE WAY FOR TOMORROW(1937); VOGUES OF 1938(1937); YOU CAN'T TAKE IT WITH YOU(1938); ONE MILLION B.C.(1940)
Silents
EARL OF PAWTUCKET, THE(1915); GREAT LOVE, THE(1918); MIDNIGHT PATROL, THE(1918); AMATEUR ADVENTURESS, THE(1919); ARE YOU LEGALLY MARRIED?(1919); KISMET(1920); CONNECTICUT YANKEE AT KING ARTHUR'S COURT, A(1921); LAST TRAIL(1921); SHAME(1921); RICH MEN'S WIVES(1922); GIRL OF THE GOLDEN WEST, THE(1923); IN SEARCH OF A THRILL(1923); LONG LIVE THE KING(1923); RIP-TIDE, THE(1923); SLANDER THE WOMAN(1923); SO BIG(1924); AS MAN DESIRES(1925); ONE YEAR TO LIVE(1925); BOWERY CINDERELLA(1927); DREAM MELODY, THE(1929); GIRLS WHO DARE(1929); PEACOCK FAN(1929)
Misc. Silents
MAN OF SHAME, THE(1915); WINGED MYSTERY, THE(1917); LOVE'S PAY DAY(1918); FAITH(1919); PEGGY DOES HER DARNDEST(1919); UPSTAIRS AND DOWN(1919); WHEN A WOMAN STRIKES(1919); DICE OF DESTINY(1920); LITTLE GREY MOUSE, THE(1920); RIO GRANDE(1920); SPLENDID HAZARD, A(1920); TERROR ISLAND(1920); WHISPERING DEVILS(1920); ACROSS THE DIVIDE(1921); FIGHTIN' MAD(1921); GOOD WOMEN(1921); HICKVILLE TO BROADWAY(1921); PARTNERS OF FATE(1921); I AM THE LAW(1922); MORE TO BE PITIED THAN SCORNED(1922); YELLOW MEN AND GOLD(1922); TEA-WITH A KICK(1923); YOUR FRIEND AND MINE(1923); SON OF THE SAHARA, A(1924); WRECKAGE(1925); RIDING TO FAME(1927); MONTMARTE ROSE(1929)
Lynn Theel
HUMANOIDS FROM THE DEEP(1980); WITHOUT WARNING(1980)
Misc. Talkies
FYRE(1979)
Cyrus Theibeault
REVENGE OF THE NINJA(1983)
Sid Theil
MAVERICK, THE(1952), w; HOMESTEADERS, THE(1953), w; VIGILANTE TERROR(1953), w
Sidney Theil
REBEL CITY(1953), w
Nina Theilade
MIDSUMMER'S NIGHT'S DREAM, A(1935), ch
Nini Theilade
MIDSUMMER'S NIGHT'S DREAM, A(1935)
Colin Theile
BLUE FIN(1978, Aus.), w
William Theile
WALTZ TIME(1933, Brit.), d; BRIDAL SUITE(1939), d
Herbert Theis
MISSION BATANGAS(1968), ph; KAREN, THE LOVEMAKER(1970), ph; NIGHT OF THE WITCHES(1970), ph
Joe Theismann
MAN WITH BOGART'S FACE, THE(1980)
1984
CANNONBALL RUN II(1984)
Bill Theiss
HAROLD AND MAUDE(1971), cos
Herbert V. Theiss
KILLER FISH(1979, Ital./Braz.), d
Manuella Theiss
BARN OF THE NAKED DEAD(1976)
Ursula Theiss
BENGAL BRIGADE(1954)
Misc. Talkies
LEFT HAND OF GEMINI, THE(1972)
William Theiss
BUTCH AND SUNDANCE: THE EARLY DAYS(1979), cos
William Ware Theiss
PRETTY MAIDS ALL IN A ROW(1971), cos; GOIN' SOUTH(1978), cos; HEART LIKE A WHEEL(1983), cos
1984
KIDCO(1984), cos
Barbara Theitelbaum
COME BACK BABY(1968)

Norma Thelan
REUNION IN FRANCE(1942)
Claes Thelander
MATTER OF MORALS, A(1961, U.S./Swed.); LOVING COUPLES(1966, Swed.)
Jenny Thelen
NIGHT CROSSING(1982)
Jodi Thelen
FOUR FRIENDS(1981); BLACK STALLION RETURNS, THE(1983); TWILIGHT TIME(1983, U.S./Yugo.)
Leonie Thelen
EAGLE HAS LANDED, THE(1976, Brit.)
Eje Thelin
TO LOVE(1964, Swed.), md
Peter Thelin
SWEDISH WEDDING NIGHT(1965, Swed.)
Erikav Thellmann
TOXI(1952, Ger.)
Antonio Thellung
SIGN OF THE GLADIATOR(1959, Fr./Ger./Ital.), w
Francesco Thellung
WARRIOR AND THE SLAVE GIRL, THE(1959, Ital.), w; PRISONER OF THE IRON MASK(1962, Fr./Ital.), p; INVINCIBLE GLADIATOR, THE(1963, c.u. Ital./Span.), w
Jose Thelman
UNSATISFIED, THE(1964, Span.)
Thembi
DINGAKA(1965, South Africa)
Paris Themmen
WILLY WONKA AND THE CHOCOLATE FACTORY(1971)
Kostas Themos
OEDIPUS THE KING(1968, Brit.)
Genevieve Thenier
YOUNG GIRLS OF ROCHEFORT, THE(1968, Fr.); TIME OF THE WOLVES(1970, Fr.)
Roland Thenot
MISSISSIPPI MERMAID(1970, Fr./Ital.); LOVE ON THE RUN(1980, Fr.); CONFIDENTIALLY YOURS(1983, Fr.)
Terence Theobald
KING'S RHAPSODY(1955, Brit.)
George Theobold
1984
HOT DOG...THE MOVIE(1984)
Kyveli Theochari
POLICEMAN OF THE 16TH PRECINCT, THE(1963, Gr.)
Kyvell Theochari
GIRL OF THE MOUNTAINS(1958, Gr.)
Mikis Theodorakis
BAREFOOT BATTALION, THE(1954, Gr.), m; NIGHT AMBUSH(1958, Brit.), m; SHADOW OF THE CAT, THE(1961, Brit.), m; ELECTRA(1962, Gr.), m; LOVERS OF TERUEL, THE(1962, Fr.), m; PHAEDRA(1962, U.S./Gr./Fr.), m; FIVE MILES TO MIDNIGHT(1963, U.S./Fr./Ital.), m; ZORBA THE GREEK(1964, U.S./Gr.), m&md; DAY THE FISH CAME OUT, THE(1967. Brit./Gr.), m; Z(1969, Fr./Algeria), m; TROJAN WOMEN, THE(1971), m; SERPICO(1973), m; STATE OF SIEGE(1973, Fr./U.S./Ital./Ger.), m; IPHIGENIA(1977, Gr.), m
Brother Theodore
NOCTURNA(1979)
Misc. Talkies
GUMS(1976)
Karl Theodore
BIG SCORE, THE(1983)
Katherine Theodore
DREAM OF KINGS, A(1969)
Lee Theodore
HONEY POT, THE(1967, Brit.), ch; SONG OF NORWAY(1970), ch
Mike Theodore
MARDI GRAS MASSACRE(1978), m
Pete Theodore
SHALL WE DANCE(1937); MAYOR OF 44TH STREET, THE(1942)
Ralph Theodore
LIGHT FINGERS(1929); LAST MILE, THE(1932); ANGELS OVER BROADWAY(1940)
Misc. Talkies
BULLETS FOR BANDITS(1942)
Sondra Theodore
SKATEBOARD(1978); STINGRAY(1978)
Stag Theodore
FOR YOUR EYES ONLY(1981)
The Theodores
SITTING ON THE MOON(1936); EVER SINCE EVE(1937)
Nelle Theodorou
STEFANIA(1968, Gr.), w
Tsilka Theodorou
1984
A NOS AMOURS(1984, Fr.)
Vanghel Theodorou
1984
A NOS AMOURS(1984, Fr.)
Dimos Theos
THANOS AND DESPINA(1970, Fr./Gr.), p
Julia Theresa
Misc. Silents
BODY AND SOUL(1925)
Al Theriot
PANIC IN THE STREETS(1950)
Sven Thermaenius
BREAD OF LOVE, THE(1954, Swed.), ph
Bjorn Thermenius
WILD STRAWBERRIES(1959, Swed.), ph
Paul Theroux
SAINT JACK(1979), w

Jacques Thery
ROYAL DIVORCE, A(1938, Brit.), w; ARISE, MY LOVE(1940), w; RHYTHM ON THE RIVER(1940), w; BETWEEN US GIRLS(1942), w; JOAN OF PARIS(1942), w; SPRING-TIME IN THE ROCKIES(1942), w; HEAVENLY BODY, THE(1943), w; YOLANDA AND THE THIEF(1945), w; TO EACH HIS OWN(1946), w

Ernest Thesiger
VAGABOND QUEEN, THE(1931, Brit.); OLD DARK HOUSE, THE(1932); EMPRESS AND I, THE(1933, Ger.); HEART SONG(1933, Brit.); GHOUL, THE(1934, Brit.); NIGHT OF THE PARTY, THE(1934, Brit.); MY HEART IS CALLING(1935, Brit.); MAN WHO COULD WORK MIRACLES, THE(1937, Brit.); LIGHTNING CONDUCTOR(1938, Brit.); THEY DRIVE BY NIGHT(1938, Brit.); WARE CASE, THE(1939, Brit.); LAMP STILL BURNS, THE(1943, Brit.); MY LEARNED FRIEND(1943, Brit.); DON'T TAKE IT TO HEART(1944, Brit.); PLACE OF ONE'S OWN, A(1945, Brit.); BEWARE OF PITY(1946, Brit.); CAESAR AND CLEOPATRA(1946, Brit.); HENRY V(1946, Brit.); GHOSTS OF BERKELEY SQUARE(1947, Brit.); GIRL IN THE PAINTING, THE(1948, Brit.); JASSY(1948, Brit.); SMUGGLERS, THE(1948, Brit.); BAD LORD BYRON, THE(1949, Brit.); QUARTET(1949, Brit.); LAST HOLIDAY(1950, Brit.); WINSLOW BOY, THE(1950); CHRISTMAS CAROL(1951, Brit.); LAUGHTER IN PARADISE(1951, Brit.); LUCKY MASCOT, THE(1951, Brit.); MAGIC BOX, THE(1952, Brit.); MAN IN THE WHITE SUIT, THE(1952); MEET MR. LUCIFER(1953, Brit.); ROBE, THE(1953); DETECTIVE, THE(1954, Qit.); MAKE ME AN OFFER(1954, Brit.); MAN WITH A MILLION(1954, Brit.); WOMAN'S ANGLE, THE(1954, Brit.); WHO DONE IT?(1956, Brit.); ALLIGATOR NAMED DAISY, AN(1957, Brit.); DOCTOR AT LARGE(1957, Brit.); VALUE FOR MONEY(1957, Brit.); HORSE'S MOUTH, THE(1958, Brit.); THREE MEN IN A BOAT(1958, Brit.); TRUTH ABOUT WOMEN, THE(1958, Brit.); BATTLE OF THE SEXES, THE(1960, Brit.); SONS AND LOVERS(1960, Brit.); INVITATION TO MURDER(1962, Brit.)
Silents
NELSON(1918, Brit.); ADVENTURES OF MR. PICKWICK, THE(1921, Brit.); BACHELORS' CLUB, THE(1921, Brit.); WEEKEND WIVES(1928, Brit.)
Misc. Silents
LIFE STORY OF DAVID LLOYD GEORGE, THE(1918, Brit.); LITTLE BIT OF FLUFF, A(1919, Brit.)

Bob Thessier
VELVET VAMPIRE, THE(1971)

Bertrand Theubet
PASSION(1983, Fr./Switz.)

Thomas Theuerkauf
LADY IN THE LAKE(1947), set d

A. Theurer
BLUE VEIL, THE(1947, Fr.), m

Pierre Thevenet
STOWAWAY IN THE SKY(1962, Fr.), art d; WAR OF THE BUTTONS(1963 Fr.), art d; WEB OF FEAR(1966, Fr./Span.), art d; SOUTHERN STAR, THE(1969, Fr./Brit.), set d; HORSEMEN, THE(1971), prod d
1984
BIZET'S CARMEN(1984, Fr./Ital.), set d

Pierre-Louis Thevenet
PATTON(1970), set d

Rene Thevenet
FRUIT IS RIPE, THE(1961, Fr./Ital.), p; SECRET OF MAGIC ISLAND, THE(1964, Fr./Ital.), art d; SOFT SKIN ON BLACK SILK(1964, Fr./Span.), p; KILLING GAME, THE(1968, Fr.), p

Virginia Thevenet
LIKE A TURTLE ON ITS BACK(1981, Fr.)
1984
FULL MOON IN PARIS(1984, Fr.)

Virginie Thevenet
SOPHIE'S WAYS(1970, Fr.); SMALL CHANGE(1976, Fr.); QUARTET(1981, Brit./Fr.); LE BEAU MARIAGE(1982, Fr.)

Patrick Thevenon
MALE HUNT(1965, Fr./Ital.)

Danielle Thevenot
TIGHT SKIRTS, LOOSE PLEASURES(1966, Fr.), makeup

Francoise Thevenot
ONE SINGS, THE OTHER DOESN'T(1977, Fr.), ed

Rene Thevent
DANIELLA BY NIGHT(1962, Fr/Ger.), p

Sir Frederick Theves
Silents
GREAT LOVE, THE(1918)

Harry Thew
OPERATOR 13(1934), w

Harvey Thew
ARGYLE CASE, THE(1929), w; BLOCKADE(1929), w; GIVE AND TARE(1929), w; HOTTENTOT, THE(1929), w; LOVE IN THE DESERT(1929), w, w; SACRED FLAME, THE(1929), w; DUMBBELLS IN ERMINE(1930), w; MAN FROM BLANKLEY'S, THE(1930), w; MATRIMONIAL BED, THE(1930), w; SHE COULDN'T SAY NO(1930), w; SHOW GIRL IN HOLLYWOOD(1930), w; SINNER'S HOLIDAY(1930), w; SONG OF THE WEST(1930), w; TIGER ROSE(1930), w; DIVORCE AMONG FRIENDS(1931), w; EXPENSIVE WOMEN(1931), w; ILLICIT(1931), w; MAD GENIUS, THE(1931), w; PUBLIC ENEMY, THE(1931), w; FAMOUS FERGUSON CASE, THE(1932), w; SILVER DOLLAR(1932), w; STRANGER IN TOWN(1932), W; TWO SECONDS(1932), w; WOMAN FROM MONTE CARLO, THE(1932), w; SHE DONE HIM WRONG(1933), w; SUPERNATURAL(1933), w; TERROR ABOARD(1933), w; BEDSIDE(1934), w; DEATH OF THE DIAMOND(1934), w; TRANSIENT LADY(1935), w; TRAIL OF THE LONESOME PINE, THE(1936), w
Silents
PLOW GIRL, THE(1916), w; AMERICAN CONSUL, THE(1917), w; HOMESPUN VAMP, A(1922), w; ENEMY SEX, THE(1924), w; FLAMING BARRIERS(1924), w; OH, DOCTOR(1924), w; RAFFLES, THE AMATEUR CRACKSMAN(1925), w; TAKE IT FROM ME(1926), w; OUT ALL NIGHT(1927), w; HEAD MAN, THE(1928), w

Harvey F. Thew
Silents
THOSE WITHOUT SIN(1917), w; JULES OF THE STRONG HEART(1918), ph; HEARTS OF MEN(1919), w

Manora Thew
Silents
ARSENE LUPIN(1916, Brit.); NEW CLOWN, THE(1916, Brit.); GRIT OF A JEW, THE(1917, Brit.); MAN AND THE MOMENT, THE(1918, Brit.); ONCE UPON A TIME(1918, Brit.); POLAR STAR, THE(1919, Brit.); AT THE VILLA ROSE(1920, Brit.); OLD ARM CHAIR, THE(1920, Brit.)
Misc. Silents
MR. LYNDON AT LIBERTY(1915, Brit.); SHULMATE, THE(1915); BROKEN MELODY, THE(1916, Brit.); FOLLY OF DESIRE, THE OR THE SHULAMITE(1916); HIS DAUGHTER'S DILEMMA(1916, Brit.); HONOUR IN PAWN(1916, Brit.); SMITH(1917, Brit.); NOT NEGOTIABLE(1918, Brit.); FETTERED(1919, Brit.); HOMEMAKER, THE(1919, Brit.); SPLENDID FOLLY(1919, Brit.); TOILERS, THE(1919, Brit.); WHEN IT WAS DARK(1919, Brit.); ROMANCE OF OLD BAGDAD, A(1922, Brit.)

Harvey Thews
FOUR DAYS WONDER(1936), w

Helen Thibault
TRIAL, THE(1963, Fr./Ital./Ger.), cos

Henry Thibault
DEMONIAQUE(1958, Fr.), ph

Jean Marc Thibault
LA BELLE AMERICAINE(1961, Fr.)

Olivette Thibault
MY UNCLE ANTOINE(1971, Can.); KAMOURASKA(1973, Can./Fr.)

Jack Thibeau
APOCALYPSE NOW(1979); ESCAPE FROM ALCATRAZ(1979); 1941(1979); HONKY TONK FREEWAY(1981); MS. 45(1981); TEX(1982); 48 HOURS(1982); SUDDEN IMPACT(1983)
1984
CITY HEAT(1984)

Jerome Thibergien
STRANGE SHADOWS IN AN EMPTY ROOM(1977, Can./Ital.)

Valerie Thibodeaux
1984
TIGHTROPE(1984)

Klaus-Dieter Thiedemann
PINOCCHIO(1969, E. Ger.)

Jacqueline Thiedot
COUNTERFEITERS OF PARIS, THE(1962, Fr., Ital.), ed; MAGNIFICENT TRAMP, THE(1962, Fr./Ital.), ed; BEAR, THE(1963, Fr.), ed; TAXI FOR TOBRUK(1965, Fr./Span./Ger.), ed; MARCO THE MAGNIFICENT(1966, Ital./Fr./Yugo./Egypt/Afghanistan), ed; THINGS OF LIFE, THE(1970, Fr./Ital./Switz.), ed

Rita Thiel
SILENCERS, THE(

Roy Thiel
DEVIL'S ANGELS(1967)

Walter Thiel
FIRST COMES COURAGE(1943)

Annabelle Thiele
SON OF SINBAD(1955)

Colin Thiele
STORM BOY(1976, Aus.), w; FIRE IN THE STONE, THE(1983, Aus.), w

Hertha Thiele
MAEDCHEN IN UNIFORM(1932, Ger.)

Leonard Thiele
THREE IN ONE(1956, Aus.)

Rolf Thiele
ROSEMARY(1960, Ger.), d, w; LULU(1962, Aus.), d&w; TONIO KROGER(1968, Fr./Ger.), d; DUCK RINGS AT HALF PAST SEVEN, THE(1969, Ger./Ital.), d; JUST A GIGOLO(1979, Ger.), p

Walter Thiele
BEASTS OF BERLIN(1939); THUNDER AFLOAT(1939); THIS LAND IS MINE(1943)

Wilhelm Thiele
LOVE WALTZ, THE(1930, Ger.), d

William Thiele
MARRY ME(1932, Brit.), d; LOTTERY LOVER(1935), d; DON'T GET PERSONAL(1936), w; JUNGLE PRINCESS, THE(1936), d; BEG, BORROW OR STEAL(1937), d; LONDON BY NIGHT(1937), d; STABLEMATES(1938), w; BAD LITTLE ANGEL(1939), d; GHOST COMES HOME, THE(1940), d; TARZAN TRIUMPHS(1943), d; TARZAN'S DESERT MYSTERY(1943), d; SHE WOULDN'T SAY YES(1945), w; FACE OF MARBLE, THE(1946), w; MADONNA'S SECRET, THE(1946), d, w

Uwe Thielisch
PINOCCHIO(1969, E. Ger.)

Gary Thieltges
EATING RAOUL(1982), ph

Shirley Thieman
SECRET MAN, THE(1958, Brit.)

Lisa Thiemann
RUMPELSTILTSKIN(1965, Ger.), ed

Herman Thieme
GEORGE(1973, U.S./Switz.), m, md

Thien-Huong
GAME OF TRUTH, THE(1961, Fr.); MARCO POLO(1962, Fr./Ital.)

Maurice Thieret
THEY ARE NOT ANGELS(1948, Fr.), m

Eric Thiermann
RENEGADE GIRLS(1974), art d

Jean-Baptiste Thierree
MURIEL(1963, Fr./Ital.); SWEET AND SOUR(1964, Fr./Ital.)

Franz Thierry
LAST TOMAHAWK, THE(1965, Ger./Ital./Span.), p

Marie-Louise Thierry
ME(1970, Fr.)

Paul Thierry
ISTANBUL(1957); OPERATION EICHMANN(1961)

Richard Thierry [Riccardo Pallottini]
SECRET AGENT FIREBALL(1965, Fr./Ital.), ph

Rene Thierry
ME(1970, Fr.)

Roland Thierry
PICNIC ON THE GRASS(1960, Fr.)

Rose Thierry
BEAU PERE(1981, Fr.); LAST METRO, THE(1981, Fr.); RETURN OF MARTIN GUERRE, THE(1983, Fr.)
Fritz Thiery
F.P. 1(1933, Brit.), ph
Dorothea Thies
GIRL FROM THE MARSH CROFT, THE(1935, Ger.)
Richard Thies
TALISMAN, THE(1966)
Bill Thiese
HICKEY AND BOGGS(1972), cos
Dorothea Thiess
MOSCOW SHANGHAI(1936, Ger.)
Manuela Thiess
CHANGES(1969)
Richard Thiess
J-MEN FOREVER(1980), m
Ursula Thiess
MONSOON(1953); IRON GLOVE, THE(1954); AMERICANO, THE(1955); BANDIDO(1956)
Corbett H. Thigpen, M.D.
THREE FACES OF EVE, THE(1957), p,d&w
Helen Thigpen
PORGY AND BESS(1959)
Lynne Thigpen
GODSPELL(1973); WARRIORS, THE(1979); TOOTSIE(1982)
1984
STREETS OF FIRE(1984)
Edward Thilby
Misc. Silents
HEART OF A ROSE, THE(1919, Brit.)
Georges Thill
LOUISE(1940, Fr.)
Peter Thillaye
WHY SHOOT THE TEACHER(1977, Can.), ed
Hans Thimig
MONEY ON THE STREET(1930, Aust.); STORY OF VICKIE, THE(1958, Aust.); GOOD SOLDIER SCHWEIK, THE(1963, Ger.)
Helen Thimig
HITLER GANG, THE(1944); STRANGERS IN THE NIGHT(1944); THIS LOVE OF OURS(1945)
Helene Thimig
GAY SISTERS, THE(1942); EDGE OF DARKNESS(1943); MOON IS DOWN, THE(1943); NONE BUT THE LONELY HEART(1944); HOTEL BERLIN(1945); ISLE OF THE DEAD(1945); ROUGHLY SPEAKING(1945); CLOAK AND DAGGER(1946); LOCKET, THE(1946); CRY WOLF(1947); ESCAPE ME NEVER(1947); HIGH CONQUEST(1947); DECISION BEFORE DAWN(1951)
Herman Thimig
THREEPENNY OPERA, THE(1931, Ger./U.S.); DREAM OF SCHONBRUNN(1933, Aus.); TRIAL, THE(1948, Aust.); ETERNAL WALTZ, THE(1959, Ger.)
Misc. Silents
CINDERELLA(1926, Ger.)
Hugo Thimig
MONEY ON THE STREET(1930, Aust.)
Justin Thin Elk
MAN CALLED HORSE, A(1970)
Armando Thine
MAFIOSO(1962, Ital.)
Roy Thinnes
JOURNEY TO THE FAR SIDE OF THE SUN(1969, Brit.); CHARLEY-ONE-EYE(1973, Brit.); AIRPORT 1975(1974); HINDENBURG, THE(1975)
Thirard
DARK EYES(1938, Fr.), ph
A. Thirard
HEART OF PARIS(1939, Fr.), ph
Armand Thirard
DAVID GOLDER(1932, Fr.), ph; POIL DE CAROTTE(1932, Fr.), ph; MAYERLING(1937, Fr.), ph; FRIC FRAC(1939, FR.), ph; LIVING CORPSE, THE(1940, Fr.), ph; STORMY WATERS(1946, Fr.), ph; MAN ABOUT TOWN(1947, Fr.), ph; MURDERER LIVES AT NUMBER 21, THE(1947, Fr.), ph; JENNY LAMOUR(1948, Fr.), ph; SYMPHONIE PASTORALE(1948, Fr.), ph; DEVIL'S DAUGHTER(1949, Fr.), ph; MANON(1950, Fr.), ph; LES BELLES-DE-NUIT(1952, Fr./Ital.), ph; ACT OF LOVE(1953), ph; DIABOLIQUE(1955, Fr.), ph; NAKED HEART, THE(1955, Brit.), ph; WAGES OF FEAR, THE(1955, Fr./Ital.), ph; AND GOD CREATED WOMAN(1957, Fr.), ph; DEADLIER THAN THE MALE(1957, Fr.), ph; NIGHT HEAVEN FELL, THE(1958, Fr.), ph; BABETTE GOES TO WAR(1960, Fr.), ph; PORT OF DESIRE(1960, Fr.), ph; GOODBYE AGAIN(1961), ph; TIME BOMB(1961, Fr./Ital.), ph; TRUTH, THE(1961, Fr./Ital.), ph; MOST WANTED MAN, THE(1962, Fr./Ital.), ph; TALES OF PARIS(1962, Fr./Ital.), ph; LOVE ON A PILLOW(1963, Fr./Ital.), ph; THREE FABLES OF LOVE(1963, Fr./Ital./Span.), ph; DON'T TEMPT THE DEVIL(1964, Fr./Ital.), ph; LIARS, THE(1964, Fr.), ph; MODERATO CANTABILE(1964, Fr./Ital.), ph; NUTTY, NAUGHTY CHATEAU(1964, Fr./Ital.), ph; MARCO THE MAGNIFICENT(1966, Ital./Fr./Yugo./Egypt/Afghanistan), ph; GUNS FOR SAN SEBASTIAN(1968, U.S./Fr./Mex./Ital.), ph; BRAIN, THE(1969, Fr./US) ph
Thiraud and Nee
WITH A SMILE(1939, Fr.), ph
Bud Third
ROAD TO FORT ALAMO, THE(1966, Fr./Ital.), ph
The Third Ear Band
MACBETH(1971, Brit.), m
Maurice Thiriet
WOMAN I LOVE, THE(1937), m; CHILDREN OF PARADISE(1945, Fr.), m; ETERNAL HUSBAND, THE(1946, Fr.), m; DEVIL'S ENVOYS, THE(1947, Fr.), m; IDIOT, THE(1948, Fr.), m; FANFAN THE TULIP(1952, Fr.), m; LUCRECE BORGIA(1953, Ital./Fr.), m; FLESH AND THE WOMAN(1954, Fr./Ital.), m; BERNADETTE OF LOURDES(1962, Fr.), m
Monique Thiriet
SMUGGLERS, THE(1969, Fr.)

George Thirlwell
LYONS MAIL, THE(1931, Brit.); FIRE OVER ENGLAND(1937, Brit.)
Silents
CHINESE BUNGALOW, THE(1926, Brit.)
Thirteenth Committee
WILD WHEELS(1969)
30 Gypsy Revelers
CALLING ALL CROOKS(1938, Brit.)
Wayne Thistleton
MELODY(1971, Brit.)
Thomas Thiteley
PLEASURE(1933), w
Aida Carange Thivat
DEADLY TRAP, THE(1972, Fr./Ital.), makeup
Christian Thivat
MISTER FREEDOM(1970, Fr.), p
Aida Thivat-Carange
JOY(1983, Fr./Can.), makeup
Cocky Thlothlalemaje
KILLER FORCE(1975, Switz./Ireland)
Joe Thoben
I MET HIM IN PARIS(1937)
Sharon Thober
HELL'S BELLES(1969), cos
Henry Thody
LA DOLCE VITA(1961, Ital./Fr.)
Peter Thoemke
PURPLE HAZE(1982), a, ch
Robert Thoeren
HOTEL IMPERIAL(1939), w; RAGE IN HEAVEN(1941), w; MRS. PARKINGTON(1944), w; SUMMER STORM(1944), w; TEMPTATION(1946), w; SINGAPORE(1947), w; ACT OF MURDER, AN(1948), w; BIG JACK(1949), w; FIGHTING O'FLYNN, THE(1949), w; CAPTAIN CAREY, U.S.A(1950), w; SEPTEMBER AFFAIR(1950), w; OPERATION X(1951, Brit.), w; PROWLER, THE(1951), w; CONFESSIONS OF FELIX KRULL, THE(1957, Ger.), w; SOME LIKE IT HOT(1959), w; BETWEEN TIME AND ETERNITY(1960, Ger.), w
Lotte Tholander
Z.P.G.(1972)
Verner Tholsgaard
GOLDEN MOUNTAINS(1958, Den.)
Ninja Tholstrup
LURE OF THE JUNGLE, THE(1970, Den.)
Bob Thom
THEY WON'T BELIEVE ME(1947); LOVE .BEFORE BREAKFAST(1936); IRON MAJOR, THE(1943); THEY WERE EXPENDABLE(1945); HOODLUM SAINT, THE(1946); JOAN OF ARC(1948); NEVER A DULL MOMENT(1950); TWO TICKETS TO BROADWAY(1951)
Peter Thom
JUDGE AND THE SINNER, THE(1964, Ger.)
Robert Thom
WHIP HAND, THE(1951); ALL THE FINE YOUNG CANNIBALS(1960), w; SUBTERRANEANS, THE(1960), w; LEGEND OF LYLAH CLARE, THE(1968), w; WILD IN THE STREETS(1968), w; ANGEL, ANGEL, DOWN WE GO(1969), d&w; BLOODY MAMA(1970), w; CRAZY MAMA(1975), w; DEATH RACE 2000(1975), w; THIRD WALKER, THE(1978, Can.), w
Ruth Thom
BODY HEAT(1981)
Michael Thoma
WINTER KILLS(1979)
Anna Thomaidou
DREAM OF PASSION, A(1978, Gr.)
Guy Thomajan
BOOMERANG(1947); MIRACLE ON 34TH STREET, THE(1947); BREAKING POINT, THE(1950); PANIC IN THE STREETS(1950); VIVA ZAPATA!(1952); PINK PANTHER, THE(1964)
Thomas
COMPLIMENTS OF MR. FLOW(1941, Fr.), ph
A. E. Thomas
BIG POND, THE(1930), w; HONEY(1930), w; BODY AND SOUL(1931), w; GIRL HABIT(1931), w; NO MORE LADIES(1935), w; EVERYBODY'S OLD MAN(1936), w; GOOD OLD SOAR, THE(1937), w
Silents
THIRTY DAYS(1922), w; WORLD'S CHAMPION, THE(1922), w; ONLY 38(1923), w; JUST SUPPOSE(1926), w
A. Leslie Thomas
THRILL OF BRAZIL, THE(1946), art d; WALLS CAME TUMBLING DOWN, THE(1946), art d; SWORDSMAN, THE(1947), art d; WHEN A GIRL'S BEAUTIFUL(1947), art d; BLACK ARROW(1948), art d; MAN FROM COLORADO, THE(1948), art d; RETURN OF JACK SLADE, THE(1955), art d
Al Franklin Thomas
Silents
CONQUERED HEARTS(1918)
Al Thomas
MASSACRE HILL(1949, Brit.); LONG JOHN SILVER(1954, Aus.); SEASON OF PASSION(1961, Aus./Brit.); SHOES OF THE FISHERMAN, THE(1968); OUTBACK(1971, Aus.)
Alfred Thomas
TARZANA, THE WILD GIRL(1973); ROLLERBALL(1975)
Amy Brandon Thomas
MURDER(1930, Brit.); MYSTERY AT THE VILLA ROSE(1930, Brit.); JAVA HEAD(1935, Brit.); VINTAGE WINE(1935, Brit.)
Silents
PROFLIGATE, THE(1917, Brit.)
Misc. Silents
CRY FOR JUSTICE, THE(1919, Brit.)
Andre Thomas
LA FERME DU PENDU(1946, Fr.), ph; CORRIDOR OF MIRRORS(1948, Brit.), ph; ONE NIGHT WITH YOU(1948, Brit), ph; WOMAN HATER(1949, Brit.), ph; SEVEN DEADLY SINS, THE(1953, Fr./Ital.), ph

Angelika Thomas
1984
  GERMANY PALE MOTHER(1984, Ger.)
Ann Thomas
  DUFFY'S TAVERN(1945); WALK EAST ON BEACON(1952); ME, NATALIE(1969); MIDNIGHT COWBOY(1969); GOING HOME(1971); KING OF MARVIN GARDENS, THE(1972)
Anna Thomas
  CONFESSIONS OF AMANS, THE(1977), w; HAUNTING OF M, THE(1979), p,d&w, ed; END OF AUGUST, THE(1982), w
1984
  EL NORTE(1984), p, w
Anne Marie Thomas
1984
  IRRECONCILABLE DIFFERENCES(1984), cos
Anthony Thomas
  WILD SEASON(1968, South Africa)
1984
  BROTHER FROM ANOTHER PLANET, THE(1984)
Arlette Thomas
  NAKED HEARTS(1970, Fr.)
Augustus Thomas
  MEN ARE LIKE THAT(1931), w; WITCHING HOUR, THE(1934), w
Silents
  JUNGLE, THE(1914), d; NIGHTINGALE, THE(1914), d&w; EARL OF PAWTUCKET, THE(1915), w; ARIZONA(1918), w; ON THE QUIET(1918), w; WITCHING HOUR, THE(1921), w
Misc. Silents
  PAID IN FULL(1914), d; SOLDIERS OF FORTUNE(1914), d; GARDEN OF LIES, THE(1915), d
Auld Thomas
Silents
  SOULS FOR SALE(1923)
B. J. Thomas
  JORY(1972)
Basil Thomas
  STOP PRESS GIRL(1949, Brit.), w; GREAT GAME, THE(1953, Brit.), w; RAMSBOTTOM RIDES AGAIN(1956, Brit.), w; PLEASE TURN OVER(1960, Brit.), w; NIGHT WE GOT THE BIRD, THE(1961, Brit.), w
Belle Thomas
  DELINQUENT DAUGHTERS(1944)
Benny Thomas
  TOOMORROW(1970, Brit.)
Bernard B. Thomas
  FOLLOW THE BOYS(1944); PILLOW OF DEATH(1945)
Bernard Thomas
  HAPPY LAND(1943); GUNMAN'S CODE(1946)
Bernie Thomas
  STAKEOUT!(1962)
Betty Thomas
  WARNING TO WANTONS, A(1949, Brit.); JACKSON COUNTY JAIL(1976); LAST AFFAIR, THE(1976); TUNNELVISION(1976); USED CARS(1980); HOMEWORK(1982)
Beverly Thomas
  TWO TICKETS TO BROADWAY(1951); LAS VEGAS STORY, THE(1952)
Bili Thomas
  FOXFIRE(1955), cos
Bill Thomas
  TROUBLE WITH GIRLS(AND HOW TO GET INTO IT), THE (1969), cos; THIS WAY PLEASE(1937), w; ALASKA HIGHWAY(1943), p; NEVER A DULL MOMENT(1943), cos; MYSTERY SUBMARINE(1950), cos; SPY HUNT(1950), cos; UNDERCOVER GIRL(1950), cos; WYOMING MAIL(1950), cos; IRON MAN, THE(1951), cos; LADY PAYS OFF, THE(1951), cos; RAGING TIDE, THE(1951), cos; SMUGGLER'S ISLAND(1951), cos; THUNDER ON THE HILL(1951), cos; WEEKEND WITH FATHER(1951), cos; YOU NEVER CAN TELL(1951), cos; MEET DANNY WILSON(1952), cos; NO ROOM FOR THE GROOM(1952), cos; RAIDERS, THE(1952), cos; STEEL TOWN(1952), cos; UNTAMED FRONTIER(1952), cos; WORLD IN HIS ARMS, THE(1952), cos; MAN FROM THE ALAMO, THE(1953), cos; MISSISSIPPI GAMBLER, THE(1953), cos; STAND AT APACHE RIVER, THE(1953), cos; TAKE ME TO TOWN(1953), cos; WINGS OF THE HAWK(1953), cos; MAGNIFICENT OBSESSION(1954), cos; SASKATCHEWAN(1954), cos; SIGN OF THE PAGAN(1954), cos; YELLOW MOUNTAIN, THE(1954), cos; ALL THAT HEAVEN ALLOWS(1955), cos; CAPTAIN LIGHTFOOT(1955), cos; ONE DESIRE(1955), cos; PURPLE MASK, THE(1955), cos; RUNNING WILD(1955), cos; SMOKE SIGNAL(1955), cos; SPOILERS, THE(1955), cos; BEHIND THE HIGH WALL(1956), cos; BENNY GOODMAN STORY, THE(1956), cos; I'VE LIVED BEFORE(1956), cos; NEVER SAY GOODBYE(1956), cos; RAW EDGE(1956), cos; RAWHIDE YEARS, THE(1956), cos; WALK THE PROUD LAND(1956), cos; WORLD IN MY CORNER(1956), cos; WRITTEN ON THE WIND(1956), cos; BATTLE HYMN(1957), cos; GIRL IN THE KREMLIN, THE(1957), cos; GREAT MAN, THE(1957), cos; MAN AFRAID(1957), cos; MAN IN THE SHADOW(1957), cos; MAN OF A THOUSAND FACES(1957), cos; MISTER CORY(1957), cos; MY MAN GODFREY(1957), cos; NIGHT PASSAGE(1957), cos; SLAUGHTER ON TENTH AVENUE(1957), cos; SLIM CARTER(1957), cos; TAMMY AND THE BACHELOR(1957), cos; TARNISHED ANGELS, THE(1957), cos; FEMALE ANIMAL, THE(1958), cos; FLOOD TIDE(1958), cos; KATHY O'(1958), cos; LADY TAKES A FLYER, THE(1958), cos; LIVE FAST, DIE YOUNG(1958), cos; MONSTER ON THE CAMPUS(1958), cos; ONCE UPON A HORSE(1958), cos; PERFECT FURLOUGH, THE(1958), cos; RIDE A CROOKED TRAIL(1958), cos; SAGA OF HEMP BROWN, THE(1958), cos; THING THAT COULDN'T DIE, THE(1958), cos; TIME TO LOVE AND A TIME TO DIE, A(1958), cos; TOUCH OF EVIL(1958), cos; TWILIGHT FOR THE GODS(1958), cos; VOICE IN THE MIRROR(1958), cos; CURSE OF THE UNDEAD(1959), cos; IMITATION OF LIFE(1959), cos; NEVER STEAL ANYTHING SMALL(1959), cos; NO NAME ON THE BULLET(1959), cos; OPERATION PETTICOAT(1959), cos; PILLOW TALK(1959), cos; RABBIT TRAP, THE(1959), cos; STRANGER IN MY ARMS(1959), cos; TAKE A GIANT STEP(1959), cos; THIS EARTH IS MINE(1959), cos; HIGH TIME(1960), cos; LEECH WOMAN, THE(1960), cos; NORTH TO ALASKA(1960), cos; SEVEN THIEVES(1960), cos; SPARTACUS(1960), cos; WAKE ME WHEN IT'S OVER(1960), cos; BABES IN TOYLAND(1961), cos; BY LOVE POSSESSED(1961), cos; PARENT TRAP, THE(1961), cos; ROMANOFF AND JULIET(1961), cos; MOON PILOT(1962), cos; IT'S A MAD, MAD, MAD, MAD WORLD(1963), cos; SON OF FLUBBER(1963), cos; SUMMER MAGIC(1963), cos;

TOYS IN THE ATTIC(1963), cos; AMERICANIZATION OF EMILY, THE(1964), cos; GLOBAL AFFAIR, A(1964), cos; HONEYMOON HOTEL(1964), cos; KISS ME, STUPID(1964), cos; THOSE CALLOWAYS(1964), cos; CAT BALLOU(1965), cos; INSIDE DAISY CLOVER(1965), cos; SHIP OF FOOLS(1965), cos; THAT DARN CAT(1965), cos; FOLLOW ME, BOYS!(1966), cos; IT HAPPENED HERE(1966, Brit.); LT. ROBIN CRUSOE, U.S.N.(1966), cos; ADVENTURES OF BULLWHIP GRIFFIN, THE(1967), cos; GNOME-MOBILE, THE(1967), cos; HAPPIEST MILLIONAIRE, THE(1967), cos; MONKEYS, GO HOME!(1967), cos; BLACKBEARD'S GHOST(1968), cos; HORSE IN THE GRAY FLANNEL SUIT, THE(1968), cos; LOVE BUG, THE(1968), cos; NEVER A DULL MOMENT(1968), cos; ONE AND ONLY GENUINE ORIGINAL FAMILY BAND, THE(1968), cos; GYPSY MOTHS, THE(1969), cos; UNDEFEATED, THE(1969), cos; HAWAIIANS, THE(1970), cos; BEDKNOBS AND BROOMSTICKS(1971), cos; SEVEN MINUTES, THE(1971), cos; OKLAHOMA CRUDE(1973), cos; ISLAND AT THE TOP OF THE WORLD, THE(1974), cos; LOGAN'S RUN(1976), cos; PETE'S DRAGON(1977), cos; BLACK HOLE, THE(1979), cos; FORMULA, THE(1980), cos
Billie Thomas
  GENERAL SPANKY(1937)
Bob Thomas
  SAGA OF DEATH VALLEY(1939); MARRY ME AGAIN(1953)
Bonita Thomas
  VILLAIN(1971, Brit.)
Brad Thomas
Misc. Talkies
  MARK OF THE GUN(1969)
Brandon Thomas
  CHARLEY'S(BIG-HEARTED) AUNT*1/2 (1940), w; CHARLEY'S AUNT(1930), w; CHARLEY'S AUNT(1941), w; WHERE'S CHARLEY?(1952, Brit.), w
Brenda Thomas
  WITHOUT A TRACE(1983)
Bruce Thomas
  SAFECRACKER, THE(1958, Brit.), w
Bryan V. Thomas
  LAST DAYS OF DOLWYN, THE(1949, Brit.)
Brynmore Thomas
  UNDERGROUND GUERRILLAS(1944, Brit.)
Buckwheat Thomas
  COLORADO PIONEERS(1945)
Calvin Thomas
Misc. Silents
  MONEY MASTER, THE(1915)
Cameron Thomas
  NETWORK(1976)
Carmen Thomas
1984
  BEAR, THE(1984)
Charles Thomas
  TULSA KID, THE(1940); JOHNNY EAGER(1942)
Charles Bob Thomas
  TWO GUN SHERIFF(1941)
Charles D. Thomas
  SUPER FUZZ(1981)
Chet Thomas
Silents
  WARMING UP(1928)
Christine Thomas
  EAGLE ROCK(1964, Brit.); WEDDING IN WHITE(1972, Can.)
Christopher Thomas
1984
  MAKING THE GRADE(1984); SPLASH(1984)
Clarence Thomas
  LENNY(1974); NOBODY'S PERFEKT zero(1981)
Misc. Talkies
  CONVENTION GIRLS(1978)
Claude Thomas
  CLAY(1964 Aus.)
Cliff Thomas
Silents
  FREE LIPS(1928), ph
Craig Thomas
  FIREFOX(1982), w; SPRING FEVER(1983, Can.)
Daisy Thomas
  ROYAL DIVORCE, A(1938, Brit.)
Damien Thomas
  JULIUS CAESAR(1970, Brit.); TWINS OF EVIL(1971, Brit.); HENRY VIII AND HIS SIX WIVES(1972, Brit.); MOHAMMAD, MESSENGER OF GOD(1976, Lebanon/Brit.); SINBAD AND THE EYE OF THE TIGER(1977, U.S./Brit.)
Danny Thomas
  UNFINISHED DANCE,THE(1947); BIG CITY(1948); CALL ME MISTER(1951); I'LL SEE YOU IN MY DREAMS(1951); JAZZ SINGER, THE(1953); LOOKING FOR LOVE(1964); DON'T WORRY, WE'LL THINK OF A TITLE(1966); JOURNEY BACK TO OZ(1974)
Misc. Talkies
  CRICKET OF THE HEARTH, THE(1968)
Dave Thomas
  STRIPES(1981); STRANGE BREW(1983), a, d, w
David Thomas
  RAINBOW BOYS, THE(1973, Can.); SUMMER WISHES, WINTER DREAMS(1973); TRICK BABY(1973); ROSELAND(1977); COLD RIVER(1982)
Silents
  SMOKE BELLEW(1929), sup
David M. Thomas
  CONVENTION GIRL(1935), p
David O. Thomas
  MAN, WOMAN AND CHILD(1983)
Daxson Thomas
  FEVER HEAT(1968)
Della Thomas
  SWEET JESUS, PREACHER MAN(1973); DARKTOWN STRUTTERS(1975)

Delmar Thomas
CRAZY OVER HORSES(1951)
Derek Thomas
VOYAGE TO THE PLANET OF PREHISTORIC WOMEN(1966), d
Diane Thomas
1984
ROMANCING THE STONE(1984), w
Dietrich Thomas
SNOW WHITE(1965, Ger.)
Dilys Thomas
PROUD VALLEY, THE(1941, Brit.)
Dog Thomas
LUGGAGE OF THE GODS(1983)
Duane Thomas
DR. HECKYL AND MR. HYPE(1980)
Dylan Thomas
THREE WEIRD SISTERS, THE(1948, Brit.), w; NO ROOM AT THE INN(1950, Brit.), w; UNDER MILK WOOD(1973, Brit.), w; MOUSE AND THE WOMAN, THE(1981, Brit.), w
E. Leslie Thomas
BRAIN FROM THE PLANET AROUS, THE(1958)
Ed Thomas
I AM THE LAW(1938); YOU CAN'T CHEAT AN HONEST MAN(1939); NOBODY'S CHILDREN(1940); DESIGN FOR SCANDAL(1941); SAINT IN PALM SPRINGS, THE(1941); MEET THE STEWARTS(1942); SEVEN DAYS LEAVE(1942); SEVENTH VICTIM, THE(1943); ETERNAL SUMMER(1961)
Eddie Thomas
BULLET FOR PRETTY BOY, A(1970)
Edmond Thomas
UNDER MILK WOOD(1973, Brit.)
Edna Thomas
STREETCAR NAMED DESIRE, A(1951)
Edward Thomas
Silents
TEA FOR THREE(1927)
Elton Thomas [Douglas Fairbanks]
IRON MASK, THE(1929), w; MR. ROBINSON CRUSOE(1932), w
Silents
MARK OF ZORRO(1920), w; NUT, THE(1921), w; ROBIN HOOD(1922), w; THIEF OF BAGDAD, THE(1924), w; BLACK PIRATE, THE(1926), w; GAUCHO, THE(1928), w
Emanuel Thomas
LAST OF THE SECRET AGENTS?, THE(1966)
Evan Thomas
INSIDE THE LINES(1930); ASK BECCLES(1933, Brit.); MRS. DANE'S DEFENCE(1933, Brit.); LEND ME YOUR HUSBAND(1935, Brit.); GIRL FROM MAXIM'S, THE(1936, Brit.); FOR VALOR(1937, Brit.); BULLDOG DRUMMOND IN AFRICA(1938); ARREST BULLDOG DRUMMOND(1939, Brit.); HOUND OF THE BASKERVILLES, THE(1939); LITTLE PRINCESS, THE(1939); NORTHWEST MOUNTED POLICE(1940); ONE NIGHT IN LISBON(1941); ROYAL MOUNTED PATROL, THE(1941); FIRST COMES COURAGE(1943); FRENCHMAN'S CREEK(1944); OUR HEARTS WERE YOUNG AND GAY(1944); UNINVITED, THE(1944); DOLLY SISTERS, THE(1945); MY NAME IS JULIA ROSS(1945); RENDEZVOUS 24(1946); TOMORROW IS FOREVER(1946)
Silents
STARTING POINT, THE(1919, Brit.); ONCE ABOARD THE LUGGER(1920, Brit.)
Misc. Silents
LOVE OF AN ACTRESS, THE(1914, Brit.); NON-CONFORMIST PARSON, A(1919, Brit.); WISP O' THE WOODS(1919, Brit.); WARNED OFF(1928, Brit.)
Faith Thomas
RED HOT SPEED ½(1929), w; I CAN'T ESCAPE(1934), w; HOLLYWOOD BOULEVARD(1936), w; CONSPIRACY(1939), w; ROCK RIVER RENEGADES(1942), w
Silents
SILKS AND SADDLES(1929), w
Fat Thomas
STILETTO(1969)
Fats Thomas
NIGHT THEY RAIDED MINSKY'S, THE(1968)
Fay Thomas
PRIDE OF THE YANKEES, THE(1942)
Frank M. Thomas
BIG GAME, THE(1936); DON'T TURN 'EM LOOSE(1936); EX-MRS. BRADFORD, THE(1936); GRAND JURY(1936); M'LISS(1936); MUMMY'S BOYS(1936); WANTED: JANE TURNER(1936); WITHOUT ORDERS(1936); BEHIND THE HEADLINES(1937); BIG SHOT, THE(1937); BREAKFAST FOR TWO(1937); CHINA PASSAGE(1937); CRASHING HOLLYWOOD(1937); CRIMINAL LAWYER(1937); DANGER PATROL(1937); FORTY NAUGHTY GIRLS(1937); MAN WHO FOUND HIMSELF, THE(1937); MEET THE MISSUS(1937); OUTCASTS OF POKER FLAT, THE(1937); RACING LADY(1937); THEY WANTED TO MARRY(1937); WE WHO ARE ABOUT TO DIE(1937); WE'RE ON THE JURY(1937); YOU CAN'T BEAT LOVE(1937); YOU CAN'T BUY LUCK(1937); BLIND ALIBI(1938); BRINGING UP BABY(1938); CRIME RING(1938); EVERYBODY'S DOING IT(1938); GO CHASE YOURSELF(1938); JOY OF LIVING(1938); LAW OF THE UNDERWORLD(1938); MAID'S NIGHT OUT(1938); MAN TO REMEMBER, A(1938); MR. DOODLE KICKS OFF(1938); NIGHT SPOT(1938); QUICK MONEY(1938); SAINT IN NEW YORK, THE(1938); SMASHING THE RACKETS(1938); STRANGE FACES(1938); THIS MARRIAGE BUSINESS(1938); VIVACIOUS LADY(1938); BACHELOR MOTHER(1939); BURN 'EM UP O'CONNER(1939); DEATH OF A CHAMPION(1939); DISBARRED(1939); GERONIMO(1939); GRAND JURY SECRETS(1939); IDIOT'S DELIGHT(1939); MYSTERIOUS MISS X, THE(1939); ROOKIE COP, THE(1939); SAGA OF DEATH VALLEY(1939); SECRET SERVICE OF THE AIR(1939); SOCIETY LAWYER(1939); THEY ALL COME OUT(1939); THEY MADE HER A SPY(1939); $1,000 A TOUCHDOWN(1939); QUEEN OF THE MOB(1940); SCANDAL SHEET(1940); SHOOTING HIGH(1940); AMONG THE LIVING(1941); ARKANSAS JUDGE(1941); LIFE WITH HENRY(1941); MONSTER AND THE GIRL, THE(1941); OBLIGING YOUNG LADY(1941); SHOT IN THE DARK, THE(1941); SIERRA SUE(1941); THREE SONS O'GUNS(1941); WYOMING WILDCAT(1941); APACHE TRAIL(1942); DANGEROUSLY THEY LIVE(1942); GREAT MAN'S LADY, THE(1942); MOUNTAIN RHYTHM(1942); POSTMAN DIDN'T RING, THE(1942); REAP THE WILD WIND(1942); SUNSET ON THE DESERT(1942); SUNSET SERENADE(1942); TALK OF THE TOWN(1942); SLEEPING CITY, THE(1950)

Frank Thomas
SNOW WHITE AND THE SEVEN DWARFS(1937), anim; BRIGHAM YOUNG-FRONTIERSMAN(1940); CHAD HANNA(1940); LILLIAN RUSSELL(1940); MARYLAND(1940); DESPERATE CHANCE FOR ELLERY QUEEN, A(1942); EYES IN THE NIGHT(1942); HELLO, FRISCO, HELLO(1943); NO PLACE FOR A LADY(1943); KILLING OF A CHINESE BOOKIE, THE(1976)
Misc. Silents
NEARLY MARRIED(1917); DEADLINE AT ELEVEN(1920)
Frank Thomas, Jr.
NANCY DREW-REPORTER(1939)
Frank M. Thomas, Sr.
LAST OUTLAW, THE(1936)
Frankie Thomas
WEDNESDAY'S CHILD(1934); DOG OF FLANDERS, A(1935); BOYS TOWN(1938); LITTLE TOUGH GUYS IN SOCIETY(1938); NANCY DREW-DETECTIVE(1938); ANGELS WASH THEIR FACES(1939); CODE OF THE STREETS(1939); DEAD END KIDS ON DRESS PARADE(1939); NANCY DREW AND THE HIDDEN STAIRCASE(1939); NANCY DREW, TROUBLE SHOOTER(1939); INVISIBLE STRIPES(1940); FLYING CADETS(1941); ONE FOOT IN HEAVEN(1941); ALWAYS IN MY HEART(1942); MAJOR AND THE MINOR, THE(1942)
Franklin Thomas [Frank Thomas]
SNOW WHITE AND THE SEVEN DWARFS(1937), anim; PINOCCHIO(1940), anim d; BAMBI(1942), anim; THREE CABALLEROS, THE(1944), anim; ALICE IN WONDERLAND(1951), anim; PETER PAN(1953), anim; LADY AND THE TRAMP(1955), anim d; ONE HUNDRED AND ONE DALMATIANS(1961), anim; SWORD IN THE STONE, THE(1963), anim; MARY POPPINS(1964), anim; JUNGLE BOOK, THE(1967), anim d; ARISTOCATS, THE(1970), anim d, w; ROBIN HOOD(1973), anim d; RESCUERS, THE(1977), w, anim d
G. Thomas
WINDJAMMER, THE(1931, Brit.)
Gaklen Thomas
1941(1979)
Georg Thomas
ISLE OF SIN(1963, Ger.)
George Thomas
WICKED DIE SLOW, THE(1968), ed
Gerald Thomas
TONY DRAWS A HORSE(1951, Brit.), ed; ISLAND RESCUE(1952, Brit.), ed; DAY TO REMEMBER, A(1953, Brit.), ed; SWORD AND THE ROSE, THE(1953), ed; DOCTOR IN THE HOUSE(1954, Brit.), ed; MAD ABOUT MEN(1954, Brit.), ed; ABOVE US THE WAVES(1956, Brit.), ed; NOVEL AFFAIR, A(1957, Brit.), p; CHAIN OF EVENTS(1958, Brit.), d; DUKE WORE JEANS, THE(1958, Brit.), d; SOLITARY CHILD, THE(1958, Brit.), d; CARRY ON NURSE(1959, Brit.), d; CARRY ON SERGEANT(1959, Brit.), d; CIRCLE, THE(1959, Brit.), d; TIME LOCK(1959, Brit.), d; CARRY ON CONSTABLE(1960, Brit.), d; PLEASE TURN OVER(1960, Brit.), d; BEWARE OF CHILDREN(1961, Brit.), d; WATCH YOUR STERN(1961, Brit.), d; CARRY ON CRUISING(1962, Brit.), d; CARRY ON TEACHER(1962, Brit.), d; CIRCUS FRIENDS(1962, Brit.), d; ROOMMATES(1962, Brit.), d; TWICE AROUND THE DAFFODILS(1962, Brit.), d; CARRY ON CABBIE(1963, Brit.), d; CARRY ON JACK(1963, Brit.), d; SWINGIN' MAIDEN, THE(1963, Brit.), d; CARRY ON CLEO(1964, Brit.), d; CARRY ON SPYING(1964, Brit.), d; NURSE ON WHEELS(1964, Brit.), d; BIG JOB, THE(1965, Brit.), d; CARRY ON COWBOY(1966, Brit.), d; CARRY ON SCREAMING(1966, Brit.), d; FOLLOW THAT CAMEL(1967, Brit.), d; CARRY ON DOCTOR(1968, Brit.), d; CARRY ON, UP THE KHYBER(1968, Brit.), d; CARRY ON AGAIN, DOCTOR(1969, Brit.), d; CARRY ON CAMPING(1969, Brit.), d; CARRY ON HENRY VIII(1970, Brit.), d; CARRY ON LOVING(1970, Brit.), d; CARRY ON UP THE JUNGLE(1970, Brit.), d; CARRY ON ENGLAND(1976, Brit.), d; CARRY ON EMANUELLE(1978, Brit.), d
Misc. Talkies
BLESS THIS HOUSE(1972, Brit.), d; CARRY ON MATRON(1973, Brit.), d; CARRY ON ABROAD(1974, Brit.), d; CARRY ON BEHIND(1975, Brit.), d; CARRY ON DICK(1975, Brit.), d
Gilbert Thomas, Jr.
ESCAPE FROM ALCATRAZ(1979)
Gilbert Travers Thomas
S.O.S. PACIFIC(1960, Brit.), w
Gordon Thomas
VOYAGE OF THE DAMNED(1976, Brit.), w; WHEN TIME RAN OUT(1980), w
Gretchen Thomas
SPRING IS HERE(1930); YOUNG DESIRE(1930); DAMAGED GOODS(1937); I WAS A TEENAGE FRANKENSTEIN(1958)
Gus Thomas
Silents
ALIAS JULIUS CAESAR(1922)
Guy Thomas
WHOLLY MOSES(1980), w
Gwen Thomas
PHOBIA(1980, Can.)
Gwydion Thomas
DOCTOR FAUSTUS(1967, Brit.)
Harding Thomas
Silents
ORA PRO NOBIS(1917, Brit.); ST. ELMO(1923, Brit.)
Harold Thomas
Silents
NUMBER 17(1920)
Harry Thomas
PARIS MODEL(1953), makeup; KILLERS FROM SPACE(1954), makeup; NEW YORK CONFIDENTIAL(1955), makeup; FRANKENSTEIN'S DAUGHTER(1958), makeup; MISSILE TO THE MOON(1959), makeup; FLIGHT THAT DISAPPEARED, THE(1961), makeup; GUN FIGHT(1961), makeup; WHEN THE CLOCK STRIKES(1961), makeup; YOU HAVE TO RUN FAST(1961), makeup; INCIDENT IN AN ALLEY(1962), makeup; WOMAN HUNT(1962), makeup; TERRIFIED!(1963), makeup; NAKED KISS, THE(1964), makeup; RAIDERS FROM BENEATH THE SEA(1964), makeup; NAVY VS. THE NIGHT MONSTERS, THE(1966), makeup; SHE FREAK(1967), makeup; SOFI(1967), makeup; RUN, ANGEL, RUN(1969), makeup
Heather Thomas
ZAPPED!(1982)

Helen Thomas
CARRY ON CABBIE(1963, Brit.), set d; NOTHING BUT THE BEST(1964, Brit.), set d; BERSERK(1967), set d; TROG(1970, Brit.), set d; DANCE OF DEATH, THE(1971, Brit.), set d; TALES FROM THE CRYPT(1972, Brit.), set d; WHAT BECAME OF JACK AND JILL?(1972, Brit.), set d

Helga Thomas
Misc. Silents
CINDERELLA(1926, Ger.); RICHTOFEN(1932, Ger.)

Henry Thomas
TOY WIFE, THE(1938); LITTLE FOXES, THE(1941); RAGGEDY MAN(1981); E.T. THE EXTRA-TERRESTRIAL(1982)
1984
CLOAK AND DAGGER(1984); MISUNDERSTOOD(1984)

Herbert Thomas
JOHNNY FRENCHMAN(1946, Brit.)

Hilary Thomas
FURY, THE(1978)

Howard Thomas
WE'LL MEET AGAIN(1942, Brit.), w; HEIGHTS OF DANGER(1962, Brit.), p; STOLEN AIRLINER, THE(1962, Brit.), p

Hugh Thomas
IF ...(1968, Brit.); O LUCKY MAN!(1973, Brit.); BREAKING GLASS(1980, Brit.); ROUGH CUT(1980, Brit.)
Silents
COWARD, THE(1927)

Huw Thomas
FIRST MEN IN THE MOON(1964, Brit.)

Irene Thomas
I'LL REMEMBER APRIL(1945); SWING OUT, SISTER(1945)

Isa Thomas
1984
FLASH OF GREEN, A(1984)

Ivan Thomas
GETAWAY, THE(1972)

Jack Thomas
OLD MAN RHYTHM(1935); LONE TEXAN(1959), w; THIRTEEN FIGHTING MEN(1960), w; FRANCIS OF ASSISI(1961), w; 20,000 EYES(1961), w

Jack W. Thomas
EMBRYO(1976), w

Jacqueline Thomas
STAGE STRUCK(1948)
Misc. Talkies
HOME IN SAN ANTONE(1949)

James Thomas
Silents
FARMER'S WIFE, THE(1928, Brit.)

Jameson Thomas
FEATHER, THE(1929, Brit.); HIGH TREASON(1929, Brit.); TESHA(1929, Brit.); EXTRAVAGANCE(1930); HATE SHIP, THE(1930, Brit.); CONVICTED(1931); LOVER COME BACK(1931); NIGHT BIRDS(1931, Brit.); NIGHT LIFE IN RENO(1931); DEVIL PAYS, THE(1932); ESCAPADE(1932); PHANTOM PRESIDENT, THE(1932); PICCADILLY(1932, Brit.); THREE WISE GIRLS(1932); TRIAL OF VIVIENNE WARE, THE(1932); BRIEF MOMENT(1933); INVISIBLE MAN, THE(1933); MY MOTHER(1933); NO MORE ORCHIDS(1933); BEGGARS IN ERMINE(1934); IT HAPPENED ONE NIGHT(1934); LOST LADY, A(1934); MOONSTONE, THE(1934); NOW AND FOREVER(1934); SCARLET EMPRESS, THE(1934); STOLEN SWEETS(1934); SUCCESSFUL FAILURE, A(1934); CHARLIE CHAN IN EGYPT(1935); CORONADO(1935); CURTAIN FALLS, THE(1935); JANE EYRE(1935); LADY IN SCARLET, THE(1935); LAST OUTPOST, THE(1935); LIVES OF A BENGAL LANCER(1935); MAN WHO RECLAIMED HIS HEAD, THE(1935); MR. DYNAMITE(1935); RUMBA(1935); SING SING NIGHTS(1935); WORLD ACCUSES, THE(1935); LADY LUCK(1936); MR. DEEDS GOES TO TOWN(1936); GIRL LOVES BOY(1937); HOUSE OF SECRETS, THE(1937); LEAGUE OF FRIGHTENED MEN(1937); MAN WHO CRIED WOLF, THE(1937); 100 MEN AND A GIRL(1937); DEATH GOES NORTH(1939)
Misc. Talkies
WOMAN'S MAN, A(1934)
Silents
DECAMERON NIGHTS(1924, Brit.); AFRAID OF LOVE(1925, Brit.); APACHE, THE(1925, Brit.); DAUGHTER OF LOVE, A(1925, Brit.); JUNGLE WOMAN, THE(1926, Brit.); PEARL OF THE SOUTH SEAS(1927, Brit.); POPPIES OF FLANDERS(1927, Brit.); ROSES OF PICARDY(1927, Brit.); WEEKEND WIVES(1928, Brit.); POWER OVER MEN(1929, Brit.)
Misc. Silents
GOLD CURE, THE(1925); BLIGHTY(1927, Brit.); RISING GENERATION, THE(1928, Brit.); WHITE SHEIK, THE(1928, Brit.)

Jane Thomas
Silents
SECRETS OF PARIS, THE(1922); SILVER WINGS(1922); EXCITERS, THE(1923); WHITE ROSE, THE(1923); ADORABLE DECEIVER, THE(1926); LAW OF THE SNOW COUNTRY, THE(1926)
Misc. Silents
RECKLESS WIVES(1921); TOWN THAT FORGOT GOD, THE(1922); LOST IN A BIG CITY(1923); FLOODGATES(1924); HOOSIER SCHOOLMASTER, THE(1924); LIFE'S GREATEST GAME(1924); GETTING 'EM RIGHT(1925); BIG SHOW, THE(1926); IN SEARCH OF A HERO(1926); ROARING ROAD(1926)

Janet Thomas
VARIETY GIRL(1947); CARNY(1980)

Jay Thomas
1984
C.H.U.D.(1984)

Jean-Paul Thomas
THUNDER IN THE BLOOD(1962, Fr.)

Jeanine Thomas
NEW ORLEANS AFTER DARK(1958)

Jeffrey Douglas Thomas
NINE TO FIVE(1980)

Jeremy Thomas
MAD DOG MORGAN(1976,Aus.), p; SHOUT, THE(1978, Brit.), p; EUREKA(1983, Brit.), p; MERRY CHRISTMAS MR. LAWRENCE(1983, Jap./Brit.), p

Jerome Thomas
DANGEROUS BLONDES(1943), ed; RIDING WEST(1944), ed; COWBOY BLUES(1946), ed; PYGMY ISLAND(1950), ed; CORKY OF GASOLINE ALLEY(1951), ed; GUN FURY(1953), ed; CHA-CHA-CHA BOOM(1956), ed; CRASH LANDING(1958), ed; GUNMAN'S WALK(1958), ed; BOY AND THE PIRATES, THE(1960), ed

Jerry Thomas
BORDER FEUD(1947), p; CHEYENNE TAKES OVER(1947), p; FIGHTING VIGILANTES, THE(1947), p; GHOST TOWN RENEGADES(1947), p; LAW OF THE LASH(1947), p; PIONEER JUSTICE(1947), p; RANGE BEYOND THE BLUE(1947), p; RETURN OF THE LASH(1947), p; SHADOW VALLEY(1947), p; STAGE TO MESA CITY(1947), p; WEST TO GLORY(1947), p; WILD COUNTRY(1947), p; BLACK HILLS(1948), p; CHECK YOUR GUNS(1948), p; HAWK OF POWDER RIVER, THE(1948), p; TIOGA KID, THE(1948), p; TORNADO RANGE(1948), p; WESTWARD TRAIL, THE(1948), p; RIDE, RYDER, RIDE!(1949), p; ROLL, THUNDER, ROLL!(1949), p; COWBOY AND THE PRIZEFIGHTER(1950), p, w; FIGHTING REDHEAD, THE(1950), p, w; LAW OF THE PANHANDLE(1950), p; FEUDIN' FOOLS(1952), p; HERE COME THE MARINES(1952), p; HOLD THAT LINE(1952), p; NO HOLDS BARRED(1952), p; COMBAT SQUAD(1953), p; AFRICAN MANHUNT(1955), p; TRUE STORY OF ESKIMO NELL, THE(1975, Aus.)

Jess Thomas
WAGNER(1983, Brit./Hung./Aust.)

Jiri Thomas
BLACK SUN, THE(1979, Czech.)

Joe Joe Thomas
Misc. Talkies
PARADISE IN HARLEM(1939)

Joe Thomas
WILD GUITAR(1962), w

Joel Thomas
DEAD TO THE WORLD(1961)

John Thomas
SANDERS OF THE RIVER(1935, Brit.); LONE WOLF RETURNS, THE(1936); HARLEM RIDES THE RANGE(1939); ONE DARK NIGHT(1939); FOOD OF THE GODS, THE(1976), spec eff; ANGELA(1977, Can.), spec eff; DAYS OF HEAVEN(1978), spec eff; QUINTET(1979), spec eff; KLONDIKE FEVER(1980), spec eff; NEVER CRY WOLF(1983), spec eff

John Charles Thomas
Silents
UNDER THE RED ROBE(1923)

John G. Thomas
TIN MAN(1983), p&d

Johnny Thomas
GANG WAR(1940)

Jon Thomas
ZOOT SUIT(1981)

Judy Thomas
WEDDING PARTY, THE(1969)

Karen Thomas
Misc. Talkies
PERILOUS JOURNEY(1983)

Kelvin Thomas
DOGS OF WAR, THE(1980, Brit.)

Kertia Thomas
STRAWBERRY STATEMENT, THE(1970)

Larri Thomas
SILENCERS, THE(; GUYS AND DOLLS(1955); LOVE ME OR LEAVE ME(1955); CURUCU, BEAST OF THE AMAZON(1956); ISLAND OF LOVE(1963); FRANKIE AND JOHNNY(1966); IN GOD WE TRUST(1980)

Leslie Thomas
THREE CAME HOME(1950); KILLER IS LOOSE, THE(1956), art d; SEVEN MEN FROM NOW(1956), art d; CRIME OF PASSION(1957), art d; FURY AT SHOWDOWN(1957), art d; I WAS A TEENAGE FRANKENSTEIN(1958), art d; VIRGIN SOLDIERS, THE(1970, Brit.), w; TIME FOR DYING, A(1971), art d; SPOOK WHO SAT BY THE DOOR, THE(1973), art d; STAND UP VIRGIN SOLDIERS(1977, Brit.), w; DANGEROUS DAVIES–THE LAST DETECTIVE(1981, Brit.), w

Lida Thomas
HOW TO MARRY A MILLIONAIRE(1953); GIRL MOST LIKELY, THE(1957)

Linda Thomas
HALLS OF ANGER(1970)

Lisa Thomas
ONE MILLION YEARS B.C.(1967, Brit./U.S.)

Llewellyn Thomas
BOOGEYMAN II(1983)

Lonnie Thomas
MR. BELVEDERE GOES TO COLLEGE(1949); RETURN OF THE TEXAN(1952)

Louis Thomas
DIABOLICALLY YOURS(1968, Fr.), w

Lowell Thomas
LION HAS WINGS, THE(1940, Brit.); PATTON(1970)

Loyette Thomas
FEAR IN THE NIGHT(1947)

Lyn Thomas
BLACK MIDNIGHT(1949); BIG TIMBER(1950); COVERED WAGON RAID(1950); MISSOURIANS, THE(1950); PETTY GIRL, THE(1950); TRIPLE TROUBLE(1950); BLADES OF THE MUSKETEERS(1953); RED RIVER SHORE(1953); WITNESS TO MURDER(1954); FRONTIER GUN(1958); SPACE MASTER X-7(1958); ALASKA PASSAGE(1959); ARSON FOR HIRE(1959); HERE COME THE JETS(1959); NOOSE FOR A GUNMAN(1960); THREE CAME TO KILL(1960)

Madeleine Thomas
NO TRACE(1950, Brit.)

Madoline Thomas
GIRL ON THE CANAL, THE(1947, Brit.); BLUE SCAR(1949, Brit.); LAST DAYS OF DOLWYN, THE(1949, Brit.); GHOST SHIP(1953, Brit.); MEN ARE CHILDREN TWICE(1953, Brit.); SQUARE RING, THE(1955, Brit.); ROGUE'S YARN(1956, Brit.); SECOND FIDDLE(1957, Brit.); SUSPENDED ALIBI(1957, Brit.)

Marci Thomas
PENITENTIARY II(1982)

Margot Thomas
KNACK ... AND HOW TO GET IT, THE(1965, Brit.)
Marie Thomas
NIGHT HAS A THOUSAND EYES(1948); STATION WEST(1948); RED, HOT AND BLUE(1949); WHERE DANGER LIVES(1950); MY FAVORITE SPY(1951); TWO TICKETS TO BROADWAY(1951)
Marjorie Thomas
GREAT GILBERT AND SULLIVAN, THE(1953, Brit.)
Mark Thomas
DIRTY HARRY(1971); WORKING GIRLS, THE(1973); ST. IVES(1976); ROLLERCOASTER(1977); 9/30/55(1977); FINAL COUNTDOWN, THE(1980)
Dr. Mark Thomas
KONA COAST(1968)
Marlo Thomas
JENNY(1969); THIEVES(1977)
Misc. Talkies
CRICKET OF THE HEARTH, THE(1968)
Mary Thomas
OUR NEIGHBORS–THE CARTERS(1939); GREAT McGINTY, THE(1940); GAY SISTERS, THE(1942); KING'S ROW(1942); MRS. WIGGS OF THE CABBAGE PATCH(1942); WAKE ISLAND(1942); 'TILL WE MEET AGAIN(1944); TAKE CARE OF MY LITTLE GIRL(1951); PROUD ONES, THE(1956)
Melody Thomas
BEGUILED, THE(1971); DIRTY HARRY(1971); POSSE(1975); SHOOTIST, THE(1976); CAR, THE(1977); FURY, THE(1978); PIRANHA(1978)
Michael Thomas
COUNTRYMAN(1982, Jamaica), w; HUNGER, THE(1983), w
Misc. Talkies
YOUNG SEDUCERS, THE(1974), d
Michel Thomas
TRAPEZE(1956); JULIE THE REDHEAD(1963, Fr.)
Mike Thomas
Misc. Talkies
BROTHERHOOD OF DEATH(1976)
Nicole Thomas
1984
EVIL THAT MEN DO, THE(1984)
Nina Thomas
FLAME(1975, Brit.)
Misc. Talkies
DEAD CERT(1974, Brit.)
Nona Thomas
Silents
APOSTLE OF VENGEANCE, THE(1916); PEGGY(1916)
Misc. Silents
DARKENING TRAIL, THE(1915)
Olive Thomas
Silents
FOLLIES GIRL, THE(1919); DARLING MINE(1920); EVERYBODY'S SWEETHEART(1920); FLAPPER, THE(1920); OUT YONDER(1920)
Misc. Silents
BROADWAY ARIZONA(1917); EVEN BREAK, AN(1917); INDISCREET CORINNE(1917); MADCAP MADGE(1917); BETTY TAKES A HAND(1918); HEIRESS FOR A DAY(1918); LIMOUSINE LIFE(1918); GLORIOUS LADY, THE(1919); LOVE'S PRISONER(1919); PRUDENCE ON BROADWAY(1919); SPITE BRIDE, THE(1919); TOTON(1919); UPSTAIRS AND DOWN(1919); FOOTLIGHTS AND SHADOWS(1920); YOUTHFUL FOLLY(1920)
Orlanders Thomas
SPOOK WHO SAT BY THE DOOR, THE(1973)
Pascal Thomas
DON'T CRY WITH YOUR MOUTH FULL(1974, Fr.), d, w
Patricia Thomas
HOUSE IS NOT A HOME, A(1964)
Patty Thomas
YOU CAN'T TAKE IT WITH YOU(1938); LADIES MAN, THE(1961)
Paul Thomas
DEFECTOR, THE(1966, Ger./Fr.), w
Peggy Thomas
LOOK OUT SISTER(1948)
Perry Thomas
SPOOK WHO SAT BY THE DOOR, THE(1973)
Peter Thomas
ESCAPE TO BERLIN(1962, U.S./Switz./Ger.), m; ENDLESS NIGHT, THE(1963, Ger.), m; I, TOO, AM ONLY A WOMAN(1963, Ger.), m; ENCOUNTERS IN SALZBURG(1964, Ger.), m; STOP TRAIN 349(1964, Fr./Ital./Ger.), m; LITTLE ONES, THE(1965, Brit.); MOONWOLF(1966, Fin./Ger.), m; ONLY A WOMAN(1966, Ger.), m; SOLO FOR SPARROW(1966, Brit.); TRAITOR'S GATE(1966, Brit./Ger.), m; BLOOD DEMON(1967, Ger.), m; JACK OF DIAMONDS(1967, U.S./Ger.), m, md; CONQUEROR WORM, THE(1968, Brit.); SEPARATION(1968, Brit.); THAT WOMAN(1968, Ger.), m; TRYGON FACTOR, THE(1969, Brit.), m; UNCLE TOM'S CABIN(1969, Fr./Ital./Ger./Yugo.), m; FROGS(1972), p; TALES FROM THE CRYPT(1972, Brit.); BREAKTHROUGH(1978, Ger.), m
Peter Evan Thomas
TIN GODS(1932, Brit.); WOMEN WHO PLAY(1932, Brit.); SCARLET PIMPERNEL, THE(1935, Brit.); KNIGHT WITHOUT ARMOR(1937, Brit.); YOU'RE IN THE ARMY NOW(1937, Brit.); CHILDREN GALORE(1954, Brit.)
Phil Thomas
BELOVED IMPOSTER(1936, Brit.); JENIFER HALE(1937, Brit.); SONG OF THE ROAD(1937, Brit.); SCHOOL FOR HUSBANDS(1939, Brit.); WINGS OVER AFRICA(1939)
Philip Michael Thomas
Misc. Talkies
BLACK FIST(1977)
Philip Thomas
BOOK OF NUMBERS(1973); MR. RICCO(1975)
Philip Thomas
MC CABE AND MRS. MILLER(1971), art d; AVALANCHE(1978), art d; LADY IN RED, THE(1979), art d

1984
CHATTANOOGA CHOO CHOO(1984), art d; ON THE LINE(1984, Span.), set d
Philip M. Thomas
STIGMA(1972); COONSKIN(1975); SPARKLE(1976); HEY, GOOD LOOKIN'(1982)
Philip-Michael Thomas
MUSHROOM EATER, THE(1976, Mex.)
Powys Thomas
SHOOT FIRST(1953, Brit.); LUCK OF GINGER COFFEY, THE(1964, U.S./Can.)
Queenie Thomas
Silents
MAN THE ARMY MADE, A(1917, Brit.); IT'S HAPPINESS THAT COUNTS(1918, Brit.); ALLEY OF GOLDEN HEARTS, THE(1924, Brit.); LAST WITNESS, THE(1925, Brit.); SAFETY FIRST(1926, Brit.)
Misc. Silents
INFELICE(1915, Brit.); CHANCE OF A LIFETIME, THE(1916, Brit.); MEG O' THE WOODS(1918, Brit.); ROCK OF AGES(1918, Brit.); WHAT WOULD A GENTLEMAN DO?(1918, Brit.); LITTLE CHILD SHALL LEAD THEM, A(1919, Brit.); TROUSERS(1920, Brit.); SCHOOL FOR SCANDAL, THE(1923, Brit.); GAYEST OF THE GAY, THE(1924, Brit.); STRAWS IN THE WIND(1924, Brit.); GOLD CURE, THE(1925); WARNED OFF(1928, Brit.)
R. Thomas
WIFE OF GENERAL LING, THE(1938, Brit.), ed
R.J. Thomas
I KILLED WILD BILL HICKOK(1956)
Rachel Thomas
PROUD VALLEY, THE(1941, Brit.); UNDERGROUND GUERRILLAS(1944, Brit.); HALF-WAY HOUSE, THE(1945, Brit.); CAPTIVE HEART, THE(1948, Brit.); BLUE SCAR(1949, Brit.); MEN ARE CHILDREN TWICE(1953, Brit.); TIGER BAY(1959, Brit.); WOMAN WHO WOULDN'T DIE, THE(1965, Brit.); GYPSY GIRL(1966, Brit.); HAPPY AS THE GRASS WAS GREEN(1973); UNDER MILK WOOD(1973, Brit.); HAZEL'S PEOPLE(1978)
Ralph L. Thomas
TICKET TO HEAVEN(1981), d, w
Ralph Thomas
HELTER SKELTER(1949, Brit.), d; ONCE UPON A DREAM(1949, Brit.), d; CLOUDED YELLOW, THE(1950, Brit.), d; TRAVELLER'S JOY(1951, Brit.), d; ISLAND RESCUE(1952, Brit.), d; ASSASSIN, THE(1953, Brit.), d; DAY TO REMEMBER, A(1953, Brit.), d; DOCTOR IN THE HOUSE(1954, Brit.), d; MAD ABOUT MEN(1954, Brit.), d; DOCTOR AT SEA(1955, Brit.), d; ABOVE US THE WAVES(1956, Brit.), d; IRON PETTICOAT, THE(1956, Brit.), d; CAMPBELL'S KINGDOM(1957, Brit.), d; CHECKPOINT(1957, Brit.), d; DOCTOR AT LARGE(1957, Brit.), d; TALE OF TWO CITIES, A(1958, Brit.), d; WIND CANNOT READ, THE(1958, Brit.), d; CONSPIRACY OF HEARTS(1960, Brit.), p, d; DOCTOR IN LOVE(1960, Brit.), p, d; THIRTY NINE STEPS, THE(1960, Brit.), d; NO LOVE FOR JOHNNIE(1961, Brit.), d; UPSTAIRS AND DOWNSTAIRS(1961, Brit.), d; DOG AND THE DIAMONDS, THE(1962, Brit.), d; AGENT 8 3/4(1963, Brit.), d; DOCTOR IN DISTRESS(1963, Brit.), p, d; PAIR OF BRIEFS, A(1963, Brit.), d; FATE IS THE HUNTER(1964); NO, MY DARLING DAUGHTER(1964, Brit.), d; STARFIGHTERS, THE(1964); YOUNG AND WILLING(1964, Brit.), d; MC GUIRE, GO HOME!(1966, Brit.), d; CARNABY, M.D.(1967, Brit.), d; DEADLIER THAN THE MALE(1967, Brit.), d; HIGH COMMISSIONER, THE(1968, U.S./Brit.), d; LAWYER, THE(1969, Brit.), d; SOME GIRLS DO(1969, Brit.), d; DOCTOR IN TROUBLE(1970, Brit.), p, d; PERCY(1971, Brit.), d; QUEST FOR LOVE(1971, Brit.), d; IT'S A 2"6" ABOVE THE GROUND WORLD(1972, Brit.), p, d; IT'S NOT THE SIZE THAT COUNTS(1979, Brit.), d
Misc. Talkies
NIGHTINGALE SANG IN BERKELEY SQUARE, A(1979), d
Ray Thomas
GUN FURY(1953)
Richard Thomas
BRIEF ENCOUNTER(1945, Brit.); LAST SUMMER(1969); WINNING(1969); RED SKY AT MORNING(1971); TODD KILLINGS, THE(1971); CACTUS IN THE SNOW(1972); YOU'LL LIKE MY MOTHER(1972); 9/30/55(1977); BATTLE BEYOND THE STARS(1980); BLOODY KIDS(1983, Brit.)
Misc. Silents
LOVE PIRATE, THE(1923), d; PHANTOM JUSTICE(1924), d; TRUTHFUL SEX, THE(1926), d; WOMAN WHO WAS FORGOTTEN, THE(1930), d
Richard H. Thomas
SLEEPING BEAUTY(1959), art d
Rob Thomas
PUBERTY BLUES(1983, Aus.)
Robert Thomas
RIDE, RANGER, RIDE(1936); LA BONNE SOUPE(1964, Fr./Ital.), d&w; FRIEND OF THE FAMILY(1965, Fr./Ital.), d&w
1984
HOTEL NEW HAMPSHIRE, THE(1984)
Robert C. Thomas
GHOST TOWN GOLD(1937)
Ron Thomas
1984
KARATE KID, THE(1984)
Ronnie Thomas
FIRST MONDAY IN OCTOBER(1981)
Ross Thomas
HAMMETT(1982), w
Roy Thomas
NONE BUT THE LONELY HEART(1944); THEY WERE EXPENDABLE(1945); FIRE AND ICE(1983), w
1984
CONAN THE DESTROYER(1984), w
Ruth Thomas
CRASH DIVE(1943)
Sabine Thomas
1984
LIFE IS A BED OF ROSES(1984, Fr.)
Scott Thomas
KONA COAST(1968); GUNS OF THE MAGNIFICENT SEVEN(1969); 1,000 PLANE RAID, THE(1969)
1984
ADERYN PAPUR(1984, Brit.), ed

Shari Thomas
UNCLE SCAM(1981)
Sharon Thomas
9/30/55(1977), set d
1984
FLAMINGO KID, THE(1984); STAR TREK III: THE SEARCH FOR SPOCK(1984); STONE BOY, THE(1984)
Misc. Talkies
GRAND JURY(1977)
Shirley Thomas
OVER-EXPOSED(1956)
Sonny Thomas
WALKING ON AIR(1946, Brit.)
Talfryn Thomas
UNDER MILK WOOD(1973, Brit.)
Ted Thomas
OUT OF THE DEPTHS(1946), w; TALK ABOUT A LADY(1946), w; KING OF THE WILD HORSES(1947), w; GALLANT BLADE, THE(1948), w; NIGHTMARE IN THE SUN(1964), w
1984
PURPLE HEARTS(1984)
Terry Thomas
BROTHERS IN LAW(1957, Brit.); YOU MUST BE JOKING!(1965, Brit.); THOSE FANTASTIC FLYING FOOLS(1967, Brit); BAWDY ADVENTURES OF TOM JONES, THE(1976, Brit.)
Theodora Thomas
MELVIN AND HOWARD(1980)
Thomas Thomas
MY SIX LOVES(1963); FRATERNITY ROW(1977)
Tim Thomas
CRY OF THE BANSHEE(1970, Brit.)
Tina Thomas
FLASH GORDON(1980)
Tony Thomas
1984
FIRSTBORN(1984), p
Towyna Thomas
NOTORIOUS LANDLADY, THE(1962); ADVANCE TO THE REAR(1964); STERILE CUCKOO, THE(1969)
Trevor Thomas
BLACK JOY(1977, Brit.); YESTERDAY'S HERO(1979, Brit.); HORROR PLA-NET(1982, Brit.)
1984
SHEENA(1984)
Varley Thomas
GOLDFINGER(1964, Brit.)
Vincent Thomas
ROAD TO FORT ALAMO, THE(1966, Fr./Ital.), w
Vincent P. Thomas
STRANGE SHADOWS IN AN EMPTY ROOM(1977, Can./Ital.), ed
Virginia Thomas
WILD PARTY, THE(1929)
W. Morgan Thomas
1984
SHEENA(1984), w
W. Thomas
Silents
IVANHOE(1913)
Wally Thomas
HEART WITHIN, THE(1957, Brit.)
Wayne Thomas
ZEBRA IN THE KITCHEN(1965)
Whitey Thomas
MARK OF THE WITCH(1970), m
William Thomas
YOU'RE A SWEETHEART(1937), w; TORPEDO BOAT(1942), p. William Pine; WRECKING CREW(1942), p; COWBOY IN MANHATTTAN(1943), w; MINESWEEP-ER(1943), p; SUBMARINE ALERT(1943), p; DARK MOUNTAIN(1944), p; GAM-BLER'S CHOICE(1944), p; NAVY WAY, THE(1944), p; ONE BODY TOO MANY(1944), p; TIMBER QUEEN(1944), p; FOLLOW THAT WOMAN(1945), p; HIGH POWERED(1945), p; SCARED STIFF(1945), p; HOT CARGO(1946), p; SWAMP FI-RE(1946), p; ADVENTURE ISLAND(1947), p; DANGER STREET(1947), p; I COVER BIG TOWN(1947), p; JUNGLE FLIGHT(1947), p; SEVEN WERE SAVED(1947), p; ALBUQUERQUE(1948), p; CAGED FURY(1948), p. William Pine; DISASTER(1948), p; DYNAMITE(1948), p; MR. RECKLESS(1948), p; SHAGGY(1948), p; SPEED TO SPARE(1948), p; WATERFRONT AT MIDNIGHT(1948), p; EL PASO(1949), p;CROSS-WINDS(1951), p; PASSAGE WEST(1951), p; CARIBBEAN(1952), p; BAILOUT AT 43,000(1957), p; BIG CAPER, THE(1957), p; ISTANBUL(1957), cos; CASEY'S SHAD-OW(1978)
William Thomas, Jr.
KING OF THE GYPSIES(1978)
William "Buckwheat" Thomas
MOKEY(1942)
William C. Thomas
ILLEGAL TRAFFIC(1938), w; KING OF ALCATRAZ(1938), p; SOME LIKE IT HOT(1939), p; SUDDEN MONEY(1939), p; $1,000 A TOUCHDOWN(1939), p; FARM-ER'S DAUGHTER, THE(1940), p; FLYING BLIND(1941), p; FORCED LAND-ING(1941), p; NO HANDS ON THE CLOCK(1941), p; POWER DIVE(1941), p; I LIVE ON DANGER(1942), p; WILDCAT(1942), p; TORNADO(1943), p; DOUBLE EXPO-SURE(1944), p; TAKE IT BIG(1944), p; ONE EXCITING NIGHT(1945), d; TOKYO ROSE(1945), p; THEY MADE ME A KILLER(1946), p, d; BIG TOWN(1947), p, d; BIG TOWN AFTER DARK(1947), p, d; FEAR IN THE NIGHT(1947), p; I COVER BIG TOWN(1947), d; BIG TOWN SCANDAL(1948), p, d; CAPTAIN CHINA(1949), p; MAN-HANDLED(1949), p; SPECIAL AGENT(1949), p, d; EAGLE AND THE HAWK, THE(1950), p; LAWLESS, THE(1950), p; TRIPOLI(1950), p; HONG KONG(1951), p; LAST OUTPOST, THE(1951), p; BLAZING FOREST, THE(1952), p; JAMAICA RUN(1953), p; SANGAREE(1953), p; THOSE REDHEADS FROM SEATTLE(1953), p; TROPIC ZONE(1953), p; VANQUISHED, THE(1953), p; JIVARO(1954), p; FAR HORI-ZONS, THE(1955), p; HELL'S ISLAND(1955), p; LUCY GALLANT(1955), p; RUN FOR COVER(1955), p; NIGHTMARE(1956), p; ASTOUNDING SHE-MONSTER, THE(1958),

ph; CAT MURKIL AND THE SILKS(1976), p, w
Willie Thomas
HONEYMOON LODGE(1943)
Wynford Vaughan Thomas
JOHN AND JULIE(1957, Brit.)
Wynn Thomas
1984
BEAT STREET(1984), art d
Yvonne Thomas
Silents
OWD BOB(1924, Brit.)
Misc. Silents
LAND OF MY FATHERS(1921, Brit.); UNTO EACH OTHER(1929, Brit.)
Anna Thomashefsky
Misc. Talkies
LOVE AND SACRIFICE(1936)
Boris Thomashefsky
Misc. Talkies
BAR MITSVE(1935)
Harry Thomashefsky
Misc. Talkies
JEWISH KING LEAR(1935), d
Thomasina the Cat
THREE LIVES OF THOMASINA, THE(1963, U.S./Brit.)
Larry Thomasof
TERROR ON TOUR(1980)
Alan Thomason
LITTLE MISS MARKER(1980)
Harry Thomason
ENCOUNTER WITH THE UNKNOWN(1973), d; So SAD ABOUT GLORIA(1973), p&d
Misc. Talkies
GREAT LESTER BOGGS, THE(1975), d
Jimmy Thomason
LOUISIANA(1947)
Nick Thomason
GIRL OF THE GOLDEN WEST, THE(1938)
Stan Thomason
IT'S A WONDERFUL WORLD(1956, Brit.)
William Thomason
DEVIL'S SLEEP, THE(1951)
Balthasar Thomass
PARSIFAL(1983, Fr.)
Harry Thomasson
EVICTORS, THE(1979)
Harry Z. Thomazon
Misc. Talkies
DAY IT CAME TO EARTH, THE(1979), d
Rudolf Thome
NOT RECONCILED, OR "ONLY VIOLENCE HELPS WHERE IT RULES"(1969, Ger.)
Tim Thomerson
CARNY(1980); FADE TO BLACK(1980); ST. HELENS(1981); TAKE THIS JOB AND SHOVE IT(1981); HONKYTONK MAN(1982); JEKYLL AND HYDE...TOGETHER AGAIN(1982); SOME KIND OF HERO(1982); METALSTORM: THE DESTRUCTION OF JARED-SYN(1983); OSTERMAN WEEKEND, THE(1983); UNCOMMON VA-LOR(1983)
1984
RHINESTONE(1984)
Timothy Thomerson
CARWASH(1976); WHICH WAY IS UP?(1977); RECORD CITY(1978); REMEMBER MY NAME(1978); WEDDING, A(1978)
Thommeray
CESAR(1936, Fr.)
Connie Thompkin
MISS SUSIE SLAGLE'S(1945)
Anthony Thompkins
D.C. CAB(1983)
Bea Thompkins
NEW CENTURIONS, THE(1972)
Joe J. Thompkins
WHEN YOU COMIN' BACK, RED RYDER?(1979), cos
Dennis Thompsett
POWERFORCE(1983), w
Derek Thompsn
BREAKING GLASS(1980, Brit.)
Thompson
RED RIVER RENEGADES(1946), ed
Al Thompson
SONS OF THE DESERT(1933); FALSE PRETENSES(1935); SONS OF STEEL(1935); LITTLE ACCIDENT(1939); LUCKY NIGHT(1939); FOREST RANGERS, THE(1942); IN SOCIETY(1944); HOODLUM SAINT, THE(1946); STREET WITH NO NAME, THE(1948); RIDERS OF THE WHISTLING PINES(1949); FATHER IS A BA-CHELOR(1950); TOUGHER THEY COME, THE(1950); LURE OF THE WILDER-NESS(1952)
Albert Thompson
LOVES OF JOANNA GODDEN, THE(1947, Brit.)
Alex Thompson
RISE AND RISE OF MICHAEL RIMMER, THE(1970, Brit.), ph; CAT AND THE CANARY, THE(1979, Brit.), ph
Silents
ARCADIANS, THE(1927, Brit.), w
Allan Thompson
FOR THE SERVICE(1936), ph; SILVER SPURS(1936), ph; EMPTY SADDLES(1937), ph
Silents
RACING FOR LIFE(1924), ph; RANGER OF THE BIG PINES(1925), ph; FIGHTING EDGE(1926), ph

Allen Thompson
MANHATTAN MELODRAMA(1934); OUTLAWED GUNS(1935), ph; THROWBACK, THE(1935), ph; BOSS RIDER OF GUN CREEK(1936), ph; COWBOY AND THE KID,THE(1936), ph; RIDE 'EM COWBOY(1936), ph; SUNSET OF POWER(1936), ph; BLACK ACES(1937), ph; BOSS OF LONELY VALLEY(1937), ph; HEADIN' EAST(1937), ph; LAW FOR TOMBSTONE(1937), ph; LEFT-HANDED LAW(1937), ph; SANDFLOW(1937), ph; SMOKE TREE RANGE(1937), ph; HAWAIIAN BUCK-AROO(1938), ph; PANAMINT'S BAD MAN(1938), ph; SUDDEN BILL DORN(1938), ph
Silents
FEARLESS LOVER, THE(1925), ph
Allen G. Thompson
HOLLYWOOD ROUNDUP(1938), ph
Allen Q. Thompson
OVERLAND EXPRESS, THE(1938), ph; RAWHIDE(1938), ph
Andrew Thompson
CLINIC, THE(1983, Aus.)
Anita Thompson
GOLD DIGGERS OF 1933(1933)
Misc. Silents
BY RIGHT OF BIRTH(1921)
Anne Thompson
LOCAL HERO(1983, Brit.)
Art Thompson
UP IN CENTRAL PARK(1948)
1984
PURPLE HEARTS(1984)
Arthur Thompson
DRAGONWYCH(1946)
Beatrix Thompson
OLD CURIOSITY SHOP, THE(1935, Brit.)
Bennett Thompson
WHEN THE LEGENDS DIE(1972)
Benny Thompson
ULZANA'S RAID(1972)
Beverly Thompson
DUFFY'S TAVERN(1945); BLUE DAHLIA, THE(1946); TO EACH HIS OWN(1946); LIFE OF HER OWN, A(1950); FATHER'S LITTLE DIVIDEND(1951); I CAN GET IT FOR YOU WHOLESALE(1951); LET'S MAKE IT LEGAL(1951); O. HENRY'S FULL HOUSE(1952); WITH A SONG IN MY HEART(1952); GIRL NEXT DOOR, THE(1953); FRENCH LINE, THE(1954); WOMAN'S WORLD(1954)
Bill Thompson
COMIN' ROUND THE MOUNTAIN(1940); LOOK WHO'S LAUGHING(1941); HERE WE GO AGAIN(1942); ALICE IN WONDERLAND(1951); PETER PAN(1953); JAIL BAIT(1954), ph; LADY AND THE TRAMP(1955); SLEEPING BEAUTY(1959); HELL'S BELLES(1969); ARISTOCATS, THE(1970)
Blanche Thompson
Misc. Silents
AS THE WORLD ROLLS ON(1921)
Bob Thompson
GIANT GILA MONSTER, THE(1959); MY DOG, BUDDY(1960); THUMB TRIP-PING(1972), m
Bob Thompson, Jr.
SWEET CHARITY(1969)
Brad Thompson
SMILE(1975)
Brian Thompson
1984
TERMINATOR, THE(1984)
Carl Thompson
TOO LATE FOR TEARS(1949); WAKE OF THE RED WITCH(1949); WOMAN IN THE DARK(1952)
Carlos Thompson
FORT ALGIERS(1953); FLAME AND THE FLESH(1954); VALLEY OF THE KINGS(1954); MAGIC FIRE(1956); THUNDERSTORM(1956); RAW WIND IN EDEN(1958); MISTRESS OF THE WORLD(1959, Ital./Fr./Ger.); BETWEEN TIME AND ETERNITY(1960, Ger.); LAST REBEL, THE(1961, Mex.); SPESSART INN, THE(1961, Ger.); END OF MRS. CHENEY(1963, Ger.); LA VIE DE CHATEAU(1967, Fr.)
Misc. Talkies
OUR MAN IN THE CARIBBEAN(1962)
Carol Jean Thompson
CURIOUS FEMALE, THE(1969)
Carol-Jean Thompson
FLAREUP(1969); MALTESE BIPPY, THE(1969)
Charles P. Thompson
TROUBLE WITH GIRLS(AND HOW TO GET INTO IT), THE*1/2 (1969); NAKED CITY, THE(1948); TEENAGE CAVEMAN(1958); HOT RODS TO HELL(1967)
Charles S. Thompson
INCREDIBLE JOURNEY, THE(1963), set d; LOOKING FOR LOVE(1964), set d; PATCH OF BLUE, A(1965), set d; ONE OF OUR SPIES IS MISSING(1966), set d; DOCTOR, YOU'VE GOT TO BE KIDDING(1967), set d; DON'T MAKE WAVES(1967), set d; HOW SWEET IT IS(1968), set d; TIME TO SING, A(1968), set d; JOE KIDD(1972), set d
Charles Thompson
DESTINATION TOKYO(1944); PHANTOM OF THE PLAINS(1945), set d; SPORTING CHANCE, A(1945), set d; STRANGE MR. GREGORY, THE(1945), set d; TOPEKA TERROR, THE(1945), set d; FEAR(1946), set d; LIVE WIRES(1946), set d; PILGRIM LADY, THE(1947), set d; I, JANE DOE(1948), set d; OLD LOS ANGELES(1948), set d; SECRET SERVICE INVESTIGATOR(1948), set d; SLIPPY MCGEE(1948), set d; SUN-DOWN IN SANTA FE(1948), set d; TIMBER TRAIL, THE(1948), set d; SHERIFF OF WICHITA(1949), set d; STREETS OF SAN FRANCISCO(1949), set d; TOO LATE FOR TEARS(1949), set d; WYOMING BANDIT, THE(1949), set d; HOUSE BY THE RI-VER(1950), set d; RIO GRANDE(1950), set d; SURRENDER(1950), set d; QUIET MAN, THE(1952), set d; WILD BLUE YONDER, THE(1952), set d; WOMAN OF THE NORTH COUNTRY(1952), set d; CITY THAT NEVER SLEEPS(1953), set d; LONE RANGER AND THE LOST CITY OF GOLD, THE(1958), set d; PORTRAIT IN BLACK(1960), set d; FOR LOVE OR MONEY(1963), set d; SHOCK CORRIDOR(1963), set d; TWICE TOLD TA-LES(1963), set d; GLOBAL AFFAIR, A(1964), set d; CHARRO(1969), set d; DADDY'S GONE A-HUNTING(1969), set d; DREAMS OF GLASS(1969), set d; SAM WHISKEY(1969), set d; ONE MORE TRAIN TO ROB(1971), set d

Charlotte Thompson
REBECCA OF SUNNYBROOK FARM(1932), w; REBECCA OF SUNNYBROOK FARM(1938), w
Silents
REBECCA OF SUNNYBROOK FARM(1917), w; IN SEARCH OF A SINNER(1920), w
Clarence Thompson
LOVE TRAP, THE(1929), w; CLIMAX, THE(1930), w
Silents
SENSATION SEEKERS(1927)
Cliff Thompson
MURDER IN THE PRIVATE CAR(1934); TWENTIETH CENTURY(1934)
Cotton Thompson
SONG OF THE WASTELAND(1947)
Creighton Thompson
MIRACLE IN HARLEM(1948)
D.J. Thompson
ONCE MORE, MY DARLING(1949); TROOPER HOOK(1957)
Dale G. Thompson
WOMEN AND BLOODY TERROR(1970)
Daniele Thompson
BRAIN, THE(1969, Fr./US), w; DON'T LOOK NOW(1969, Brit./Fr.), a, w; ADVEN-TURES OF RABBI JACOB, THE(1973, Fr.), w; ACE OF ACES(1982, Fr./Ger.), w; LA BOUM(1983, Fr.), w
Danielle Thompson
DELUSIONS OF GRANDEUR(1971 Fr.), w; COUSIN, COUSINE(1976, Fr.), w
Dave Thompson
HARDCORE(1979); TERROR ON TOUR(1980)
David Thompson
Misc. Silents
LIFE'S SHADOWS(1916), d; STOLEN TRIUMPH, THE(1916), d; SUNBEAM, THE(1916)
Dee J. Thompson
IT GROWS ON TREES(1952); KILLER IS LOOSE, THE(1956); LADY TAKES A FLYER, THE(1958); LOVE IN A GOLDFISH BOWL(1961); GLASS BOTTOM BOAT, THE(1966)
Derek Thompson
YANKS(1979); PATERNITY(1981); LONG GOOD FRIDAY, THE(1982, Brit.)
Don Thompson
BATTLE BEYOND THE STARS(1980)
Donald G. Thompson
PROJECT: KILL(1976), w; EVIL, THE(1978), w
Dorothy Thompson
MAN ON THE FLYING TRAPEZE, THE(1935); TWO FOR TONIGHT(1935); MUR-DER WITH PICTURES(1936); EVER SINCE EVE(1937)
Duane Thompson
VOICE OF THE CITY(1929); HOLLYWOOD HOTEL(1937)
Silents
APRIL FOOL(1926); COLLEGE DAYS(1926); LODGE IN THE WILDERNESS, THE(1926); HUSBAND HUNTERS(1927); ONE HOUR OF LOVE(1927); BEAUTY AND BULLETS(1928); DESERT PIRATE, THE(1928); PHANTOM OF THE RANGE(1928); PHYLLIS OF THE FOLLIES(1928); SLIM FINGERS(1929)
Misc. Silents
SOME PUN'KINS(1925); FALSE MORALS(1927); SILENT AVENGER, THE(1927); FIGHTIN' REDHEAD, THE(1928); HER SUMMER HERO(1928); PRICE OF FEAR, THE(1928); WIZARD OF THE SADDLE(1928); BORN TO THE SADDLE(1929); TIP-OFF, THE(1929)
E. Thompson
Silents
ALIAS MARY BROWN(1918)
Eddie Thompson
AM I GUILTY?(1940)
Misc. Talkies
DOUBLE DEAL(1939)
Edward Thompson
DUKE IS THE TOPS, THE(1938); REFORM SCHOOL(1939); GOLDEN GIRL(1951), w; FABIAN OF THE YARD(1954, Brit.), d; FIREBALL JUNGLE(1968)
Misc. Talkies
GUN MOLL(1938); LIFE GOES ON(1938); MYSTERY IN SWING(1940)
Misc. Silents
SPIDER'S WEB, THE(1927)
Elaine Thompson
1984
BIG MEAT EATER(1984, Can.)
Eleanor Thompson
Misc. Silents
RAVEN, THE(1915)
Elisabeth Thompson
FREE GRASS(1969)
Elizabeth Thompson
YOUNG SWINGERS, THE(1963); MAGNIFICENT SEVEN RIDE, THE(1972); W.C. FIELDS AND ME(1976); CAR, THE(1977)
Eric Thompson
TALL TIMBERS(1937, Aus.), set d; LOVERS AND LUGGERS(1938, Aus.), art d; FORTY THOUSAND HORSEMEN(1941, Aus.), set d; BARBER OF STAMFORD HILL, THE(1963, Brit.); PRIVATE POTTER(1963, Brit.); JOKERS, THE(1967, Brit.); ONE DAY IN THE LIFE OF IVAN DENISOVICH(1971, U.S./Brit./Norway)
Ernest Thompson
ON GOLDEN POND(1981), w; STAR 80(1983)
Eunice Thompson
MAN, A WOMAN, AND A BANK, A(1979, Can.)
Evan Thompson
CHAPMAN REPORT, THE(1962)
F.A. Thompson
Misc. Silents
EYE OF ENVY, THE(1917)
F. Martin Thompson
Misc. Silents
LAMP IN THE DESERT(1922, Brit.), d

Francis Thompson
SAND CASTLE, THE(1961), spec eff

Frank Thompson
WIND ACROSS THE EVERGLADES(1958), cos; LAST MILE, THE(1959), cos; FUGITIVE KIND, THE(1960), cos; LOVE IS A BALL(1963), cos; TRUMAN CAPOTE'S TRILOGY(1969), cos; MAGIC GARDEN OF STANLEY SWEETHART, THE(1970), cos; HOSPITAL, THE(1971), cos; POSSESSION OF JOEL DELANEY, THE(1972), cos; MAN WHO LOVED CAT DANCING, THE(1973), cos; SHAMUS(1973), cos; PARALLAX VIEW, THE(1974), cos; FOR PETE'S SAKE(1977), cos
Misc. Silents
PECK O' PICKLES(1916); LOOT(1919); HELLHOUNDS OF THE WEST(1922)

Frank L. Thompson
GODDESS, THE(1958), cos; MIDDLE OF THE NIGHT(1959), cos

Franklin Thompson
FORCED VENGEANCE(1982), w

Fred Thompson
RIO RITA(1929), w; BRIDEGROOM FOR TWO(1932, Brit.), w; CHARMING DECEIVER, THE(1933, Brit.), w; I SPY(1933, Brit.), w; THOSE WERE THE DAYS(1934, Brit.), w; NO LIMIT(1935, Brit.), w; 18 MINUTES(1935, Brit.), w; SHE KNEW WHAT SHE WANTED(1936, Brit.), w; SONS O' GUNS(1936), w; TROUBLE AHEAD(1936, Brit.), w; HEAD OVER HEELS IN LOVE(1937, Brit.), w; SHE COULDN'T SAY NO(1939, Brit.), w; FIVE WILD GIRLS(1966, Fr.)
Silents
GOOSE GIRL, THE(1915), d; GALLOPING GALLAGHER(1924); HANDS ACROSS THE BORDER(1926); DON MIKE(1927); LADY BE GOOD(1928), w
Misc. Silents
CHATTEL, THE(1916), d; FEUD GIRL, THE(1916), d; MAN OF MYSTERY, THE(1917), d; WILD PRIMROSE(1918), d; FIGHTING SAP, THE(1924); ALL AROUND FRYING PAN(1925); BANDIT'S BABY, THE(1925); LONE HAND SAUNDERS(1926); ARIZONA NIGHTS(1927)

Fred A. Thompson
Misc. Silents
NYMPH OF THE FOOTHILLS, A(1918), d

Freda Thompson
NAKED PREY, THE(1966, U.S./South Africa), cos

Frederick Thompson
Silents
CHRISTIAN, THE(1914), d; NEARLY A KING(1916), d; TAILOR MADE MAN, A(1922)
Misc. Silents
AFTER DARK(1915), d; HER MOTHER'S SECRET(1915), d; WONDERFUL ADVENTURE, THE(1915), d; SALESLADY, THE(1916), d; HOW COULD YOU, CAROLINE?(1918), d; MATING, THE(1918), d

Frederick A. Thompson
Silents
POWER OF THE PRESS, THE(1928), w
Misc. Silents
PARISIAN ROMANCE, A(1916), d; DANGER TRAIL, THE(1917), d; MARRIAGE PIT, THE(1920), d; HEART LINE, THE(1921), d

Galen Thompson
PROJECT: KILL(1976); EVIL, THE(1978)

Garfield Thompson
Silents
PLUNDERER, THE(1915), w; PRINCE IN A PAWNSHOP, A(1916), w; ARSENE LUPIN(1917), w; BY RIGHT OF POSSESSION(1917), w; IN THE BALANCE(1917), w; ALL MAN(1918), w

Garth Thompson
MOVIE MOVIE(1978)

Gene Thompson
KID FROM LEFT FIELD, THE(1953)

George Thompson
WHY BRING THAT UP?(1929); CHARRO(1969), spec eff

George A. Thompson
BIG HOUSE, U.S.A.(1955), cos

George C. Thompson
NEVADA SMITH(1966), spec eff

Gib Thompson
LOUISIANA(1947)

Gladys Thompson
Silents
IRON RING, THE(1917)

Glen Thompson
KILLER AT LARGE(1947), art d; KNOCK ON ANY DOOR(1949); MISS GRANT TAKES RICHMOND(1949); UNDERCOVER MAN, THE(1949)

Glenn Thompson
SILENCERS, THE(; PANAMA PATROL(1939), set d; PEOPLE ARE FUNNY(1945), set d; TOKYO ROSE(1945), set d; THEY MADE ME A KILLER(1946), set d; BIG TOWN AFTER DARK(1947), set d; BIG TOWN SCANDAL(1948), set d; RECKLESS MOMENTS, THE(1949); DALLAS(1950); KILL THE UMPIRE(1950); LORNA DOONE(1951); PRAIRIE ROUNDUP(1951); KETTLES ON OLD MACDONALD'S FARM, THE(1957)

Glenn P. Thompson
DETOUR(1945), set d; SHADOW OF TERROR(1945), set d; STRANGLER OF THE SWAMP(1945), set d; WHY GIRLS LEAVE HOME(1945), set d; BLACK BEAUTY(1946), set d; DEVIL BAT'S DAUGHTER, THE(1946), set d; WIFE OF MONTE CRISTO, THE(1946), set d

Glenn T. Thompson
THEY RAID BY NIGHT(1942), art d; LIGHTHOUSE(1947), ed; WINTER WONDERLAND(1947), set d

Gordon Thompson
SUZANNE(1980, Can.)

Grace Thompson
Silents
SCARLET SIN, THE(1915)
Misc. Silents
GRIP OF JEALOUSY, THE(1916)

Graham Thompson
GREGORY'S GIRL(1982, Brit.)

H. W. Thompson
Silents
ALL ROADS LEAD TO CALVARY(1921, Brit.), p; NO. 5 JOHN STREET(1921, Brit.), p
Misc. Silents
STREET OF ADVENTURE, THE(1921, Brit.), d

Hal Thompson
ANIMAL CRACKERS(1930); LASSIE FROM LANCASHIRE(1938, Brit.); PLAYBOY, THE(1942, Brit.); FOLLIES GIRL(1943)
Silents
COMING AN' GOING(1926)
Misc. Silents
WHO'S YOUR FRIEND(1925)

Hamilton Thompson
Silents
ROWDY, THE(1921), w

Hank Thompson
LAST PICTURE SHOW, THE(1971), m

Harlan Thompson
GHOST TALKS, THE(1929), w; MARRIED IN HOLLYWOOD(1929), w; ARE YOU THERE?(1930), w; BIG PARTY, THE(1930), w; WOMEN EVERYWHERE(1930), w; GIRLS DEMAND EXCITEMENT(1931), w; PHANTOM PRESIDENT, THE(1932), w; HE LEARNED ABOUT WOMEN(1933), w; I'M NO ANGEL(1933), w; PAST OF MARY HOLMES, THE(1933), d; HERE IS MY HEART(1934), w; KISS AND MAKE UP(1934), d, w; RUGGLES OF RED GAP(1935), w; SHIP CAFE(1935), w; COLLEGE HOLIDAY(1936), p; EARLY TO BED(1936), p; IT'S A GREAT LIFE(1936), w; ROSE OF THE RANCHO(1936), w; WIVES NEVER KNOW(1936), p; BIG BROADCAST OF 1938, THE(1937), p; CHAMPAGNE WALTZ(1937), p; ROMANCE IN THE DARK(1938), p; DISPUTED PASSAGE(1939), p; MAGNIFICENT FRAUD, THE(1939), p; PARIS HONEYMOON(1939), p; EAST OF THE RIVER(1940), p; ROAD TO SINGAPORE(1940), p; BAD MEN OF MISSOURI(1941), p; KISSES FOR BREAKFAST(1941), p; SINGAPORE WOMAN(1941), p; WAGONS ROLL AT NIGHT, THE(1941), p; HOW TO BE VERY, VERY, POPULAR(1955), w
Silents
HOT NEWS(1928), w; TAKE ME HOME(1928), w

Harriet Thompson
Silents
CAPRICE OF THE MOUNTAINS(1916)

Harry Thompson
EGYPTIAN. THE(1954)

Helen Thompson
MISSION BATANGAS(1968)
Misc. Talkies
BLOODLESS VAMPIRE, THE(1965)

Henry Thompson
Silents
STARTING POINT, THE(1919, Brit.); AFTER MANY YEARS(1930, Brit.)
Misc. Silents
SECRET OF THE MOOR, THE(1919, Brit.)

Herbert Thompson
Silents
APACHE, THE(1925, Brit.), p

Hilarie Thompson
HOW SWEET IT IS(1968); MARYJANE(1968); WHERE ANGELS GO...TROUBLE FOLLOWS(1968); MODEL SHOP, THE(1969); GETTING STRAIGHT(1970); HEX(1973); NIGHTHAWKS(1981)

Hilary Thompson
IF IT'S TUESDAY, THIS MUST BE BELGIUM(1969)

Hilda Offley Thompson
SEPIA CINDERELLA(1947)

Honey Thompson
PICTURES(1982, New Zealand)

Howard Thompson
GLITTERBALL, THE(1977, Brit), w

Hugh Thompson
Silents
LOVE AUCTION, THE(1919); WHAT HAPPENED TO ROSA?(1921); ALTAR STAIRS, THE(1922)
Misc. Silents
LITTLE MISS FORTUNE(1917); QUEEN X(1917); DAUGHTER OF FRANCE, A(1918); FORBIDDEN PATH, THE(1918); HOUSE OF GOLD, THE(1918); KEY TO POWER, THE(1918); QUEEN OF THE SEA(1918); SECRET STRINGS(1918); SOUL OF BUDDHA, THE(1918); STREET OF SEVEN STARS, THE(1918); FALSE GODS(1919); PHIL-FOR-SHORT(1919); SOMEONE MUST PAY(1919); WOMAN UNDER OATH, THE(1919); CYNTHIA-OF-THE-MINUTE(1920); HUSBANDS AND WIVES(1920); SLIM PRINCESS, THE(1920); WIT WINS(1920); HALF BREED, THE(1922); HEAD OVER HEELS(1922); GRUB STAKE(1923); REFUGE(1923); MEDDLING WOMEN(1924); GOLDEN YUKON, THE(1927)

Hunter S. Thompson
WHERE THE BUFFALO ROAM(1980), w

Ian Thompson
TOUCH OF CLASS, A(1973, Brit.); MADHOUSE(1974, Brit.); CLASS OF MISS MAC MICHAEL, THE(1978, Brit./U.S.)

Irene Thompson
LADY BY CHOICE(1934); TWENTIETH CENTURY(1934); RECKLESS(1935); TWO FOR TONIGHT(1935)

J. Lee Thompson
STRANGLER, THE(1941, Brit.), w; YELLOW BALLOON, THE(1953, Brit.), d, w; FOR BETTER FOR WORSE(1954, Brit.), d, w; WEAK AND THE WICKED, THE(1954, Brit.), d, w; BLONDE SINNER(1956, Brit.), d; ALLIGATOR NAMED DAISY, AN(1957, Brit.), d; AS LONG AS THEY'RE HAPPY(1957, Brit.), d; WOMEN IN A DRESSING GOWN(1957, Brit.), p; TIGER BAY(1959, Brit.), d; FLAME OVER INDIA(1960, Brit.), d; I AIM AT THE STARS(1960), d; GUNS OF NAVARONE, THE(1961), d; CAPE FEAR(1962), d; TARAS BULBA(1962), d; KINGS OF THE SUN(1963), d; JOHN GOLDFARB, PLEASE COME HOME(1964), d; NO TREE IN THE STREET(1964, Brit.), d; WHAT A WAY TO GO(1964), d; RETURN FROM THE ASHES(1965, U.S./Brit.), p, d; EYE OF THE DEVIL(1967, Brit.), d; BEFORE WINTER COMES(1969, Brit.), d; CHAIRMAN, THE(1969), d; MACKENNA'S GOLD(1969), d; BROTHERLY LOVE(1970, Brit.), d; CONQUEST OF THE PLANET OF THE APES(1972), d; BATTLE FOR THE PLANET OF THE APES(1973), d; HUCKLEBERRY FINN(1974), d; REIN-

CARNATION OF PETER PROUD, THE(1975), d; ST. IVES(1976), d; WHITE BUF-FALO, THE(1977), d; GREEK TYCOON, THE(1978), d; PASSAGE, THE(1979, Brit.), d; CABOBLANCO(1981), d; HAPPY BIRTHDAY TO ME(1981), d; 10 TO MID-NIGHT(1983), d

1984
AMBASSADOR, THE(1984), d; EVIL THAT MEN DO, THE(1984), d

J. Reilly Thompson
JAM SESSION(1944)

Jack Thompson
FEVER HEAT(1968); OUTBACK(1971, Aus.); PETERSEN(1974, Aus.); SCOBIE MA-LONE(1975, Aus.); SUNDAY TOO FAR AWAY(1975, Aus.); CADDIE(1976, Aus.); MAD DOG MORGAN(1976,Aus.); BREAKER MORANT(1980, Aus.); CHANT OF JIMMIE BLACKSMITH, THE(1980, Aus.); CLUB, THE(1980, Aus.); EARTHLING, THE(1980); MAN FROM SNOWY RIVER, THE(1983, Aus.); MERRY CHRISTMAS MR. LAW-RENCE(1983, Jap./Brit.)

James Thompson
Misc. Silents
YOUTH'S GAMBLE(1925)

James E. Thompson
1984
NADIA(1984, U.S./Yugo.), p

James "Slim" Thompson
RHYTHM ON THE RANGE(1936)

Jan Thompson
FINNEGANS WAKE(1965)

Janice Thompson
SINGING VAGABOND, THE(1935); LIAR'S MOON(1982), w

Jay Thompson
THOROUGHLY MODERN MILLIE(1967); HARRY AND WALTER GO TO NEW YORK(1976)

Jeanne Thompson
MISSISSIPPI GAMBLER, THE(1953)

Jeff Thompson
DAVY CROCKETT, KING OF THE WILD FRONTIER(1955); LAWYER, THE(1969); ALL-AMERICAN BOY, THE(1973)

Jeffery Thompson
WOLFEN(1981)

Jenn Thompson
LITTLE DARLINGS(1980); HONKY TONK FREEWAY(1981)

Jerry Thompson
HOT ROD(1950), p

Jim Thompson
KILLING, THE(1956), w; PATHS OF GLORY(1957), w; GETAWAY, THE(1972), w; FAREWELL, MY LOVELY(1975); KILLER INSIDE ME, THE(1976), w; COUP DE TORCHON(1981, Fr.), w

Jimmie Thompson
SINGIN' IN THE RAIN(1952); BAND WAGON, THE(1953); CLOWN, THE(1953)

Jimmy Thompson
SUMMER STOCK(1950); BRIGADOON(1954); FORBIDDEN PLANET(1956); WHOLE TRUTH, THE(1958, Brit.); MAN WHO LIKED FUNERALS, THE(1959, Brit.); CARRY ON REGARDLESS(1961, Brit.); BAND OF THIEVES(1962, Brit.); CARRY ON CRUIS-ING(1962, Brit.); ROOMMATES(1962, Brit.); CARRY ON JACK(1963, Brit.); THOSE MAGNIFICENT MEN IN THEIR FLYING MACHINES; OR HOW I FLEWFROM LONDON TO PARIS IN 25 HOURS AND 11 MINUTES(1965, Brit.); HOT MIL-LIONS(1968, Brit.)

John Thompson
THESE ARE THE DAMNED(1965, Brit.); YOUNG NURSES, THE(1973); EAT MY DUST!(1976); BLUE FIN(1978, Aus.); SCAVENGER HUNT(1979), w; SERIAL(1980); LUNCH WAGON(1981); TIME TO DIE, A(1983), art d
Silents
CROSSING TRAILS(1921), ph; MY DAD(1922), ph

Joy Thompson
PROM NIGHT(1980)
Misc. Talkies
TRAPPED(1982)

Judith Thompson
1984
CITY GIRL, THE(1984), w

Julian Thompson
WARRIOR'S HUSBAND, THE(1933), w

June Thompson
SINGING VAGABOND, THE(1935)

Kate Thompson
CRIMINAL CONVERSATION(1980, Ireland)

Katheryn Thompson
CHALLENGE(1974)

Kay Thompson
ZIEGFELD FOLLIES(1945), w; KID FROM BOOKLYN, THE(1946); FUNNY FA-CE(1957); TELL ME THAT YOU LOVE ME, JUNIE MOON(1970)

Keane Thompson
AS THE DEVIL COMMANDS(1933), d

Keene Thompson
ACQUITTED(1929), w; VIRGINIAN, THE(1929), w; WOLF SONG(1929), w; LOVE AMONG THE MILLIONAIRES(1930), w; ONLY THE BRAVE(1930), w; TRUE TO THE NAVY(1930), w; CAUGHT(1931), w; FIGHTING CARAVANS(1931), w; JUNE MOON(1931), w; PALMY DAYS(1931), w; SIN SHIP(1931), w; LAST MAN(1932), w; MAN AGAINST WOMAN(1932), w; WAR CORRESPONDENT(1932), w; AIR HOST-ESS(1933), w; MAMA LOVES PAPA(1933), w; NO MORE ORCHIDS(1933), w; MANY HAPPY RETURNS(1934), w; SIX OF A KIND(1934), w; SPRINGTIME FOR HEN-RY(1934), w; LOVE IN BLOOM(1935), w; PARIS IN SPRING(1935); WIVES NEV-ER KNOW(1936), w
Silents
REACHING FOR THE MOON(1917); PREPARED TO DIE(1923), w; BORDER WOM-EN(1924), w; NIGHT CLUB, THE(1925), w; PATHS TO PARADISE(1925), w; REGU-LAR FELLOW, A(1925), w; NOW WE'RE IN THE AIR(1927), w; ROUGH RIDERS, THE(1927), w; WEDDING BILL$(1927), w; TILLIE'S PUNCTURED ROMANCE(1928), w

Kenneth Thompson
BROADWAY MELODY, THE(1929); CARELESS AGE(1929); CHILDREN OF PLEAS-URE(1930); RENO(1930); BAD COMPANY(1931); UP FOR MURDER(1931); BY WHOSE HAND?(1932); MANY HAPPY RETURNS(1934); BLACKMAILER(1936); FALL OF THE HOUSE OF USHER, THE(1952, Brit.), w
Silents
CORPORAL KATE(1926)

Kevin Thompson
BLADE RUNNER(1982); RETURN OF THE JEDI(1983)

Knud Leif Thompson
VENOM(1968, Den.), p, d&w

Larry Thompson
DOUGHBOYS IN IRELAND(1943); GUADALCANAL DIARY(1943); HAPPY LAND(1943); HEY, ROOKIE(1944); MR. WINKLE GOES TO WAR(1944); PRACTICAL-LY YOURS(1944); RAINBOW ISLAND(1944); SUNDAY DINNER FOR A SOL-DIER(1944); WHEN THE LIGHTS GO ON AGAIN(1944); WING AND A PRAYER(1944); DAKOTA(1945); TOO YOUNG TO KNOW(1945); WHERE DO WE GO FROM HERE?(1945); CROSS MY HEART(1946); DEADLINE AT DAWN(1946); WELL-GROOMED BRIDE, THE(1946); GANGSTER, THE(1947); JOHNNY ALLEGRO(1949); WHERE THE SIDEWALK ENDS(1950)

Lea Thompson
ALL THE RIGHT MOVES(1983); JAWS 3-D(1983)
1984
RED DAWN(1984); WILD LIFE, THE(1984)

Lee Thompson
WOMEN IN A DRESSING GOWN(1957, Brit.), d

Leslie Thompson
ARNOLD(1973); TERROR IN THE WAX MUSEUM(1973)

Linda Thompson
THIS IS ELVIS(1982)

Lorraine Thompson
Silents
TESS OF THE STORM COUNTRY(1914)

Lotus Thompson
MADAME SATAN(1930); I FOUND STELLA PARISH(1935); FOOLS FOR SCAN-DAL(1938); JOURNEY FOR MARGARET(1942); RED DANUBE, THE(1949)
Silents
NEW CHAMPION(1925); YELLOW BACK, THE(1926); CASEY AT THE BAT(1927); FRECKLED RASCAL, THE(1929); PHANTOM RIDER, THE(1929)
Misc. Silents
FLASHING FANGS(1926); DESERT DUST(1927); CRIMSON CANYON, THE(1928)

Lucille Thompson
BORN TO THE SADDLE(1953)

Mae Thompson
Misc. Silents
BLACK CROOK, THE(1916)

Maravene Thompson
Silents
PERSUASIVE PEGGY(1917), w; NEIGHBORS(1918), w; NET, THE(1923), w

Marc Thompson
DRAGSTRIP RIOT(1958)

Margaret Thompson
CHILD'S PLAY(1954, Brit.), d
Silents
REWARD, THE(1915); DIVIDEND, THE(1916); ICED BULLET, THE(1917); WOODEN SHOES(1917)
Misc. Silents
ALOHA OE(1915); HONORABLE ALGY, THE(1916); SIN YE DO, THE(1916); STEP-PING STONE, THE(1916); THOROUGHBRED, THE(1916); BACK OF THE MAN(1917); EVEN BREAK, AN(1917); FLAME OF THE YUKON, THE(1917)

Marian Thompson
SHAKE HANDS WITH THE DEVIL(1959, Ireland), w

Marion Thompson
PHANTOM PLANET, THE(1961)

Marjorie Thompson
FLASH THE SHEEPDOG(1967, Brit.)

Mark Thompson
INVASION OF THE STAR CREATURES(1962)

Marshall Thompson
BLONDE FEVER(1944); PURPLE HEART, THE(1944); RECKLESS AGE(1944); CLOCK, THE(1945); THEY WERE EXPENDABLE(1945); TWICE BLESSED(1945); VALLEY OF DECISION, THE(1945); BAD BASCOMB(1946); COCKEYED MIRACLE, THE(1946); GALLANT BESS(1946); SECRET HEART, THE(1946); SHOW-OFF, THE(1946); ROMANCE OF ROSY RIDGE, THE(1947); B. F.'S DAUGHTER(1948); COMMAND DECISION(1948); HOMECOMING(1948); BATTLEGROUND(1949); RO-SEANNA McCOY(1949); DEVIL'S DOORWAY(1950); DIAL 1119(1950); MYSTERY STREET(1950); STARS IN MY CROWN(1950); BASKETBALL FIX, THE(1951); TALL TARGET, THE(1951); MY SIX CONVICTS(1952); ROSE BOWL STORY, THE(1952); CADDY, THE(1953); BATTLE TAXI(1955); CRASHOUT(1955); CULT OF THE CO-BRA(1955); GOOD MORNING, MISS DOVE(1955); PORT OF HELL(1955); TO HELL AND BACK(1955); LURE OF THE SWAMP(1957); FIEND WITHOUT A FACE(1958); IT! THE TERROR FROM BEYOND SPACE(1958); SECRET MAN, THE(1958, Brit.); FIRST MAN INTO SPACE(1959, Brit.); FLIGHT OF THE LOST BALLOON(1961); EAST OF KILIMANJARO(1962, Brit./Ital.); NO MAN IS AN ISLAND(1962); YANK IN VIET-NAM, A(1964), a, d; CLARENCE, THE CROSS-EYED LION(1965), a, w; MIGHTY JUNGLE, THE(1965, U.S./Mex.); AROUND THE WORLD UNDER THE SEA(1966); TO THE SHORES OF HELL(1966); GEORGE(1973, U.S./Switz.), a, p, w; TURNING POINT, THE(1977); FORMULA, THE(1980); WHITE DOG(1982)
Misc. Talkies
RIDE THE TIGER(1971)

Marvin C. Thompson
STAR IS BORN, A(1976), makeup

Mary Agnes Thompson
LOVING YOU(1957), w

Mary Ann Thompson
FRATERNITY ROW(1977)

Maurice Thompson
Misc. Silents
CHILDREN OF COURAGE(1921, Brit.); FIFTH FORM AT ST. DOMINIC'S, THE(1921, Brit.); SOUL'S AWAKENING, A(1922, Brit.)

Melvin Thompson
SUDDEN IMPACT(1983)
Michael Thompson
DREAM MAKER, THE(1963, Brit.)
Mickey Thompson
LIVELY SET, THE(1964)
Mort Thompson
NIGHT RIDERS OF MONTANA(1951)
Misc. Silents
CHILD OF THE PRAIRIE, A(1925)
Morton Thompson
TWO IN A TAXI(1941), w; MY BROTHER TALKS TO HORSES(1946), w; NOT AS A STRANGER(1955), w
Morton C. Thompson
WAR OF THE WORLDS, THE(1953); WHAT'S UP, DOC?(1972)
Myrna Thompson
Silents
WEST OF THE LAW(1926)
N.J. Thompson
Misc. Silents
WOMAN'S POWER, A(1916)
Natalie Thompson
MARRIED BACHELOR(1941); RINGSIDE MAISIE(1941); UNHOLY PARTNERS(1941); VANISHING VIRGINIAN, THE(1941); SHIP AHOY(1942)
Neil Thompson
KENTUCKY FRIED MOVIE, THE(1977); MODERN PROBLEMS(1981)
Nein Thompson
MAD MAX(1979, Aus.)
Neville C. Thompson
MISSIONARY, THE(1982), p
Nick Thompson
GENERAL CRACK(1929); TONIGHT AT TWELVE(1929); STORM, THE(1930); THOSE WHO DANCE(1930); CITY STREETS(1931); DEFENDERS OF THE LAW(1931); MAKE ME A STAR(1932); THREE-CORNERED MOON(1933); TOP HAT(1935); UNDER THE PAMPAS MOON(1935); LIBELED LADY(1936); WOMAN REBELS, A(1936); TOAST OF NEW YORK, THE(1937); WALLABY JIM OF THE ISLANDS(1937); BLOCKADE(1938); IN OLD CHEYENNE(1941); PHANTOM COWBOY, THE(1941); SON OF DAVY CROCKETT, THE(1941); TUMBLEDOWN RANCH IN ARIZONA(1941); LAWLESS PLAINSMEN(1942); PASSPORT TO SUEZ(1943); BUFFALO BILL(1944); LAST HORSEMAN, THE(1944); LOST IN A HAREM(1944); MASK OF DIMITRIOS, THE(1944); WONDER MAN(1945); LOCKET, THE(1946); RENEGADE GIRL(1946); SINGIN' IN THE CORN(1946); TEMPTATION(1946); SINBAD THE SAILOR(1947); FAMILY HONEYMOON(1948); KISSING BANDIT, THE(1948); TOAST OF NEW ORLEANS, THE(1950); TRAVELING SALESWOMAN(1950); VICIOUS YEARS, THE(1950); SAVAGE DRUMS(1951); HAREM GIRL(1952); STORY OF THREE LOVES, THE(1953); APACHE WARRIOR(1957)
Silents
PUPPETS(1926)
Misc. Silents
SNOW BRIDE, THE(1923)
Palmer Thompson
FIVE MINUTES TO LIVE(1961), w; MAKE LIKE A THIEF(1966, Fin.), a, p, d, w
Pamela D'On Thompson
PONY EXPRESS RIDER(1976)
Pat Thompson
1984
PHAR LAP(1984, Aus.)
Patsy Ann Thompson
TOMORROW THE WORLD(1944)
Paul Thompson
THIS'LL MAKE YOU WHISTLE(1938, Brit.), w; SNOWS OF KILIMANJARO, THE(1952); VALLEY OF THE HEADHUNTERS(1953); WHITE WITCH DOCTOR(1953); JUNGLE MAN-EATERS(1954); UNTAMED(1955); DISEMBODIED, THE(1957); SOMETHING OF VALUE(1957); WATUSI(1959)
Peggy Thompson
KING OF THE NEWSBOYS(1938), w; MEN OF THE SEA(1951, Brit.), w
Peter Thompson
BUCK PRIVATES COME HOME(1947); DOUBLE LIFE, A(1947); WISTFUL WIDOW OF WAGON GAP, THE(1947); EAST SIDE, WEST SIDE(1949); FATHER OF THE BRIDE(1950); HAPPY YEARS, THE(1950); LIFE OF HER OWN, A(1950); MYSTERY STREET(1950); SIDE STREET(1950); FORT SAVAGE RAIDERS(1951); HARLEM GLOBETROTTERS, THE(1951); INDIAN UPRISING(1951); RIDIN' THE OUTLAW TRAIL(1951); SANTA FE(1951); SATURDAY'S HERO(1951); SMUGGLER'S GOLD(1951); ONE MINUTE TO ZERO(1952); FURY IN PARADISE(1955, U.S./Mex.); YANK IN ERMINE, A(1955, Brit.); WHISPERERS, THE(1967, Brit.); TWINS OF EVIL(1971, Brit.); MANGANINNIE(1982, Aus.)
Peter J. Thompson
NOT NOW DARLING(1975, Brit.), p
Peter Lee Thompson
10 TO MIDNIGHT(1983), ed
R.H. Thompson
TICKET TO HEAVEN(1981)
R.P. Thompson
Misc. Silents
PHANTOM BUCCANEER, THE(1916)
Ray Thompson
Silents
GO WEST(1925); ENCHANTED HILL, THE(1926)
Misc. Silents
HEART OF A CHILD, THE(1920)
Raymond Thompson
SUPERMAN(1978)
Rex Thompson
YOUNG BESS(1953); HER TWELVE MEN(1954); EDDY DUCHIN STORY, THE(1956); KING AND I, THE(1956); ALL MINE TO GIVE(1957)
Richard Thompson
BOY NAMED CHARLIE BROWN, A(1969), anim; PHANTOM TOLLBOOTH, THE(1970), anim; CASEY'S SHADOW(1978)

Riley Thompson
FANTASIA(1940), anim
Rob Thompson
HEARTS OF THE WEST(1975), w
Robert Thompson
RAIDERS OF SAN JOAQUIN(1943); WEST SIDE STORY(1961); PATRICK(1979, Aus.); THIRST(1979, Aus.); ROAD GAMES(1981, Aus.)
Robert C. Thompson
PAPER CHASE, THE(1973), p
Robert E. Thompson
THEY SHOOT HORSES, DON'T THEY?(1969), w
Ron Thompson
WHITE BUFFALO, THE(1977); AMERICAN POP(1981)
Ronnie Thompson
Misc. Talkies
BRIDGES TO HEAVEN(1975)
Ross Thompson
TORPEDO ALLEY(1953); NICKEL QUEEN, THE(1971, Aus.); TRESPASSERS, THE(1976, Aus.); CHAIN REACTION(1980, Aus.)
Roy Thompson
SUNSET BOULEVARD(1950)
Russell Thompson
PERFECT WOMAN, THE(1950, Brit.), ph
Sada Thompson
DESPERATE CHARACTERS(1971); PURSUIT OF HAPPINESS, THE(1971); ENTERTAINER, THE(1975)
Sandra Thompson
ROOM AT THE TOP(1959, Brit.)
Scott Thompson
1984
POLICE ACADEMY(1984)
Slim Thompson
GREEN PASTURES(1936); PETRIFIED FOREST, THE(1936)
Sophie Thompson
MISSIONARY, THE(1982)
Stewart Thompson
ON THIN ICE(1933, Brit.)
Stuart Thompson
DEATH OF A CHAMPION(1939), ph; EMERGENCY SQUAD(1940), ph; YOU CAN'T RATION LOVE(1944), ph; OUT OF THIS WORLD(1945), ph; BRIDE WORE BOOTS, THE(1946), ph; CROSS MY HEART(1946), ph; OUR HEARTS WERE GROWING UP(1946), ph; LADIES' MAN(1947), ph; VARIETY GIRL(1947), ph; DEAR WIFE(1949), ph; AT WAR WITH THE ARMY(1950), ph; CALYPSO JOE(1957), ph
Susanne Thompson
FINISHING SCHOOL(1934); STUDENT TOUR(1934)
Ted Thompson
WEDDING PRESENT(1936); THAT CERTAIN WOMAN(1937); TOAST OF NEW YORK, THE(1937); LET FREEDOM RING(1939); MILLION DOLLAR BABY(1941)
Misc. Silents
FAR WESTERN TRAILS(1929)
Ted A. Thompson
POLO JOE(1936)
Terry Thompson
YOUNG SINNER, THE(1965); TOMB OF TORTURE(1966, Ital.); LADY LIBERTY(1972, Ital./Fr.)
Theresa Thompson
STACY'S KNIGHTS(1983)
Thomas Thompson
PENNY PARADISE(1938, Brit.), w; SHOOT TO KILL(1947), set d; SADDLE THE WIND(1958), w; CATTLE KING(1963), w
Tiger Thompson
OVER THE EDGE(1979); EARTHBOUND(1981)
Tina Thompson
BELLES ON THEIR TOES(1952); MR. SCOUTMASTER(1953); UNTAMED(1955)
Tommy Thompson
RANGERS STEP IN, THE(1937)
Tommy Thompson
SPY FOR A DAY(1939, Brit.), w
Tommy Thompson
TOO MANY WINNERS(1947), art d
Tommy Thompson
BETRAYED WOMEN(1955), cos; LAS VEGAS SHAKEDOWN(1955), cos; FLIGHT TO HONG KONG(1956), cos
Tommy Thompson
IMAGES(1972, Ireland), p
Tommy Thompson
NASHVILLE(1975), makeup
Traftin E. Thompson
1984
SOLDIER'S STORY, A(1984)
Trey Thompson
1984
OH GOD! YOU DEVIL(1984)
Victoria Thompson
HARRAD EXPERIMENT, THE(1973); HARRAD SUMMER, THE(1974)
Viola Thompson
KISENGA, MAN OF AFRICA(1952, Brit.); TO KILL A MOCKINGBIRD(1962), cos
Virgil Thompson
GODDESS, THE(1958), m
W. C. Thompson
Silents
SEALED VALLEY, THE(1915), ph
W. H. Thompson
Silents
DAMSEL IN DISTRESS, A(1919); OH, BOY!(1919)
Walker Thompson
Misc. Silents
SYMBOL OF THE UNCONQUERED(1921)

Walter Thompson
PARTNERS(1932), ed; UNDER SECRET ORDERS(1933), ed; TUNDRA(1936), ed; SECOND HONEYMOON(1937), ed; WEE WILLIE WINKIE(1937), ed; WIFE, DOCTOR AND NURSE(1937), ed; LITTLE MISS BROADWAY(1938), ed; SALLY, IRENE AND MARY(1938), ed; EVERYTHING HAPPENS AT NIGHT(1939), ed; HOLLYWOOD CAVALCADE(1939), ed; STORY OF ALEXANDER GRAHAM BELL, THE(1939), ed; WIFE, HUSBAND AND FRIEND(1939), ed; YOUNG MR. LINCOLN(1939), ed; LILLIAN RUSSELL(1940), ed; RETURN OF FRANK JAMES, THE(1940), ed; TIN PAN ALLEY(1940), ed; MOON OVER MIAMI(1941), ed; SWAMP WATER(1941), ed; THAT NIGHT IN RIO(1941), ed; WILD GEESE CALLING(1941), ed; SON OF FURY(1942), ed; THIS ABOVE ALL(1942), ed; THUNDER BIRDS(1942), ed; CRASH DIVE(1943), ed; JANE EYRE(1944), ed; GANGSTER, THE(1947), ed; OTHER LOVE, THE(1947), ed; FORCE OF EVIL(1948), ed; PITFALL(1948), ed; SO THIS IS NEW YORK(1948), ed; BIG WHEEL, THE(1949), ed; GUILTY OF TREASON(1950), ed; QUICKSAND(1950), ed; SECOND WOMAN, THE(1951), ed; NUN'S STORY, THE(1959), ed; SAMAR(1962), ed; WONDERFUL WORLD OF THE BROTHERS GRIMM, THE(1962), ed; BEHOLD A PALE HORSE(1964), ed; KING RAT(1965), ed; MURDERERS' ROW(1966), ed; RAGE(1966, U.S./Mex.), ed; WALK, DON'T RUN(1966), ed; FLEA IN HER EAR, A(1968, Fr.), ed; MAROONED(1969), ed; MODEL SHOP, THE(1969), ed; BABY MAKER, THE(1970), ed; SKIN GAME(1971), ed; TODD KILLINGS, THE(1971), ed; MAGNIFICENT SEVEN RIDE, THE(1972), ed; BAD CHARLESTON CHARLIE(1973), ed; PAPER CHASE, THE(1973), ed; SHAMUS(1973), ed; MIXED COMPANY(1974), ed; BLACK BIRD, THE(1975), ed; FAREWELL, MY LOVELY(1975), ed; RAFFERTY AND THE GOLD DUST TWINS(1975), ed

Wanda Lee Thompson
GIANT(1956)
Wendy Thompson
GREEN FOR DANGER(1946, Brit.); MY BROTHER JONATHAN(1949, Brit.)
William Thompson
NO GREATER LOVE(1932), ph; RIDERS OF THE GOLDEN GULCH(1932), ph; DEMON FOR TROUBLE, A(1934), ph; FOUND ALIVE(1934), ph; MANIAC(1934), ph; GIGOLETTE(1935), ed; HIGH SCHOOL GIRL(1935), ph; PEOPLE'S ENEMY, THE(1935), ed; THREE MESQUITEERS, THE(1936), ed; ROARIN' LEAD(1937), ed; TULSA KID, THE(1940), ed; RED RIVER VALLEY(1941), ed; JESSE JAMES, JR.(1942), ed; MAN FROM CHEYENNE(1942), ed; MISSOURI OUTLAW, A(1942), ed; OUTLAWS OF PINE RIDGE(1942), ed; PHANTOM PLAINSMEN, THE(1942), ed; SHADOWS ON THE SAGE(1942), ed; SOMBRERO KID, THE(1942), ed; SOUTH OF SANTA FE(1942), ed; STAGECOACH EXPRESS(1942), ed; SUNDOWN KID, THE(1942), ed; VALLEY OF HUNTED MEN(1942), ed; WESTWARD HO(1942), ed; DRUMS OF FU MANCHU(1943), ed; THUNDERING TRAILS(1943), ed; SPOILERS OF THE NORTH(1947), ed; WEB OF DANGER, THE(1947), ed; PROJECT MOONBASE(1953), ph; DEMENTIA(1955), ed; TOO SOON TO LOVE(1960), ph; TENDER WARRIOR, THE(1971), p
1984
LOVE STREAMS(1984)
Silents
AS THE SUN WENT DOWN(1919), ph; ENEMIES OF WOMEN, THE(1923)
Misc. Silents
MOHICAN'S DAUGHTER, THE(1922)
William C. Thompson
ARCTIC FURY(1949), ph; GLEN OR GLENDA(1953), ph; GOLDEN MISTRESS, THE(1954), ph; LAWLESS RIDER, THE(1954), ph; BRIDE OF THE MONSTER(1955), ph; JOURNEY TO FREEDOM(1957), ph; MUSTANG(1959), ph; PLAN 9 FROM OUTER SPACE(1959), ph
William H. Thompson
Silents
DIVIDEND, THE(1916); EYE OF THE NIGHT, THE(1916); PEGGY(1916)
Misc. Silents
CIVILIZATION'S CHILD(1916)
Mayor William Hale Thompson
Silents
IS YOUR DAUGHTER SAFE?(1927)
William L. Thompson
Misc. Talkies
IRISH GRINGO, THE(1935), d
William P. Thompson
CRIME OF THE CENTURY(1946), ed; EL PASO KID, THE(1946), ed; ONE EXCITING WEEK(1946), ed; RIO GRANDE RAIDERS(1946), ed; SANTA FE UPRISING(1946), ed; VALLEY OF THE ZOMBIES(1946), ed; VIGILANTES OF BOOMTOWN(1947), ed
Ernest Thompson-Seton
LEGEND OF LOBO, THE(1962), w
Albie Thoms
PALM BEACH(1979, Aus.), p,d&w, ed
Dietrich Thoms
MAN WHO WALKED THROUGH THE WALL, THE(1964, Ger.)
Gerald Thoms
DON'T LOSE YOUR HEAD(1967, Brit.), d
Jerome Thoms
CORPSE CAME C.O.D., THE(, ed; KING OF DODGE CITY(1941), ed; CHANCE OF A LIFETIME, THE(1943), ed; LAW OF THE NORTHWEST(1943), ed; ROBIN HOOD OF THE RANGE(1943), ed; SILVER CITY RAIDERS(1943), ed; SWING OUT THE BLUES(1943), ed; TWO SENORITAS FROM CHICAGO(1943), ed; GHOST THAT WALKS ALONE, THE(1944), ed; LAST HORSEMAN, THE(1944), ed; MEET MISS BOBBY SOCKS(1944), ed; STARS ON PARADE(1944), ed; TWO-MAN SUBMARINE(1944), ed; WHISTLER, THE(1944), ed; BLONDE FROM BROOKLYN(1945), ed; ESCAPE IN THE FOG(1945), ed; EVE KNEW HER APPLES(1945), ed; TAHITI NIGHTS(1945), ed; CLOSE CALL FOR BOSTON BLACKIE, A(1946), ed; DEVIL'S MASK, THE(1946), ed; LIFE WITH BLONDIE(1946), ed; SO DARK THE NIGHT(1946), ed; BLONDIE'S BIG MOMENT(1947), ed; BLONDIE'S HOLIDAY(1947), ed; CIGARETTE GIRL(1947), ed; TWO BLONDES AND A REDHEAD(1947), ed; WHEN A GIRL'S BEAUTIFUL(1947), ed; BLACK ARROW(1948), ed; MY DOG RUSTY(1948), ed; THUNDERHOOF(1948), ed; TRIPLE THREAT(1948), ed; UNTAMED BREED, THE(1948), ed; WEST OF SONORA(1948), ed; CRIME DOCTOR'S DIARY, THE(1949), ed; JOHNNY ALLEGRO(1949), ed; MAKE BELIEVE BALLROOM(1949), ed; MISS GRANT TAKES RICHMOND(1949), ed; FATHER IS A BACHELOR(1950), ed; GOOD HUMOR MAN, THE(1950), ed; KILLER THAT STALKED NEW YORK, THE(1950), ed; HER FIRST ROMANCE(1951), ed; MASK OF THE AVENGER(1951), ed; SUNNY SIDE OF THE STREET(1951), ed; BRIGAND, THE(1952), ed; OKINAWA(1952), ed; PATHFINDER, THE(1952), ed; SCANDAL SHEET(1952), ed; CHINA VEN-

TURE(1953), ed; CRUISIN' DOWN THE RIVER(1953), ed; FLAME OF CALCUTTA(1953), ed; FORT ALGIERS(1953), ed; PRINCE OF PIRATES(1953), ed; SIREN OF BAGDAD(1953), ed; DRIVE A CROOKED ROAD(1954), ed; DRUMS OF TAHITI(1954), ed; PUSHOVER(1954), ed; APACHE AMBUSH(1955), ed; FIVE AGAINST THE HOUSE(1955), ed; IT CAME FROM BENEATH THE SEA(1955), ed; SEMINOLE UPRISING(1955), ed; TEEN-AGE CRIME WAVE(1955), ed; VIOLENT MEN, THE(1955), ed; BATTLE STATIONS(1956), ed; HARDER THEY FALL, THE(1956), ed; REPRISAL(1956), ed; RUMBLE ON THE DOCKS(1956), ed; HELLCATS OF THE NAVY(1957), ed; JEANNE EAGELS(1957), ed; NO TIME TO BE YOUNG(1957), ed; PAL JOEY(1957), ed; 27TH DAY, THE(1957), ed; GOOD DAY FOR A HANGING(1958), ed; SCREAMING MIMI(1958), ed; SEVENTH VOYAGE OF SINBAD, THE(1958), ed; TARAWA BEACHHEAD(1958), ed; CRIMSON KIMONO, THE(1959), ed; EDGE OF ETERNITY(1959), ed; FACE OF A FUGITIVE(1959), ed; FORBIDDEN ISLAND(1959), ed; RIDE LONESOME(1959), ed; TWIST AROUND THE CLOCK(1961), ed; UNDERWORLD U.S.A.(1961), ed; DON'T KNOCK THE TWIST(1962), ed; INTERNS, THE(1962), ed; WILD WESTERNERS, THE(1962), ed; SHOCK CORRIDOR(1963), ed; SHOWDOWN(1963), ed; NAKED KISS, THE(1964), ed

Jerry Thoms
SEA BAT, THE(1930), ed; WAY OUT WEST(1930), ed
Konrad Thoms
EMIL AND THE DETECTIVES(1964); STOP TRAIN 349(1964, Fr./Ital./Ger.)
Anne Werner Thomsen
OPERATION LOVEBIRDS(1968, Den.)
Kathie Thomsen
SISTERS, OR THE BALANCE OF HAPPINESS(1982, Ger.)
Poul Thomsen
REPTILICUS(1962, U.S./Den.)
Richard Thomsen
1984
BEAT STREET(1984)
Robert Thomsen
UNKNOWN MAN, THE(1951), p
Sally Thomsett
SEVENTY DEADLY PILLS(1964, Brit.); RAILWAY CHILDREN, THE(1971, Brit.); STRAW DOGS(1971, Brit.); BAXTER(1973, Brit.)
Misc. Talkies
MAN ABOUT THE HOUSE(1974, Brit.)
Alex Thomson
HERE WE GO ROUND THE MULBERRY BUSH(1968, Brit.), ph; STRANGE AFFAIR, THE(1968, Brit.), ph; ALFRED THE GREAT(1969, Brit.), ph; BEST HOUSE IN LONDON, THE(1969, Brit.), ph; I START COUNTING(1970, Brit.), ph; NIGHT DIGGER, THE(1971, Brit.), ph; DOCTOR PHIBES RISES AGAIN(1972, Brit.), ph; FEAR IS THE KEY(1973), ph; CLASS OF MISS MAC MICHAEL, THE(1978, Brit./U.S.), ph; EXCALIBUR(1981), ph; BULLSHOT(1983), ph; EUREKA(1983, Brit.), ph; KEEP, THE(1983), ph
1984
ELECTRIC DREAMS(1984), ph
Alice Thomson
Silents
SCANDAL(1915)
Amy Thomson
DEATH OF A GUNFIGHTER(1969); MOVE(1970); UP YOUR TEDDY BEAR(1970)
Beatrix Thomson
DREYFUS CASE, THE(1931, Brit.); CROWN VS STEVENS(1936); STORY OF SHIRLEY YORKE, THE(1948, Brit.)
Bobbie Thomson
KENTUCKY(1938)
Boxcar Bertha Thomson
BOXCAR BERTHA(1972), w
Brian Thomson
ROCKY HORROR PICTURE SHOW, THE(1975, Brit.), prod d; SHOCK TREATMENT(1981), w, prod d; STARSTRUCK(1982, Aus.), prod d
David Thomson
MURIETA(1965, Span.); SPIKES GANG, THE(1974)
Dorri Thomson
CHESTY ANDERSON, U.S. NAVY(1976)
Fred Thomson
Silents
JUST AROUND THE CORNER(1921); LOVE LIGHT, THE(1921); OATHBOUND(1922); PENROD(1922); NORTH OF NEVADA(1924); RIDIN' THE WIND(1925); REGULAR SCOUT, A(1926); JESSE JAMES(1927); SILVER COMES THROUGH(1927); KIT CARSON(1928); PIONEER SCOUT, THE(1928); SUNSET LEGION, THE(1928)
Misc. Silents
DANGEROUS COWARD, THE(1924); MASK OF LOPEZ, THE(1924); SILENT STRANGER, THE(1924); THUNDERING HOOFS(1924); THAT DEVIL QUEMADO(1925); WILD BULL'S LAIR, THE(1925); TOUGH GUY, THE(1926); TWO-GUN MAN, THE(1926)
Frederick Thomson
Misc. Silents
COUNTRY BOY, THE(1915), d; ENEMY TO THE KING, AN(1916), d
Gail Thomson
FINAL ASSIGNMENT(1980, Can.), p
Gordon Thomson
EXPLOSION(1969, Can.); LEOPARD IN THE SNOW(1979, Brit./Can.); LOVE(1982, Can.)
H.A.R. Thomson
NAKED PREY, THE(1966, U.S./South Africa), ph; NO BLADE OF GRASS(1970, Brit.), ph
Dr. Hans Thomson
HOUSE ON 92ND STREET, THE(1945)
Ian Thomson
BAXTER(1973, Brit.)
Jill Thomson
CONQUEROR WORM, THE(1968, Brit.), cos
Jimmy Thomson
CADDY, THE(1953)
Kenneth Thomson
BELLAMY TRIAL, THE(1929); GIRL FROM HAVANA, THE(1929); LETTER, THE(1929); VEILED WOMAN, THE(1929); DOORWAY TO HELL(1930); JUST IMAGINE(1930); LAWFUL LARCENY(1930); NOTORIOUS AFFAIR, A(1930); OTHER TO-

MORROW, THE(1930); SWEET MAMA(1930); SWEETHEARTS ON PARADE(1930); WILD COMPANY(1930); MURDER AT MIDNIGHT(1931); WOMAN HUNGRY(1931); FAMOUS FERGUSON CASE, THE(1932); FAST LIFE(1932); HER MAD NIGHT(1932); MAN WANTED(1932); MOVIE CRAZY(1932); THIRTEEN WOMEN(1932); 70,000 WITNESSES(1932); DARING DAUGHTERS(1933); FEMALE(1933); FROM HEAD-QUARTERS(1933); HOLD ME TIGHT(1933); JUNGLE BRIDE(1933); LAWYER MAN(1933); LITTLE GIANT, THE(1933); SITTING PRETTY(1933); SON OF A SAILOR(1933); CHANGE OF HEART(1934); CROSS STREETS(1934); BEHIND GREEN LIGHTS(1935); BEHOLD MY WIFE(1935); HOPALONG CASSIDY(1935); IN OLD SANTA FE(1935); WHISPERING SMITH SPEAKS(1935); JIM HANVEY, DETECTIVE(1937)
Misc. Talkies
MANHATTAN BUTTERFLY(1935)
Silents
MAN BAIT(1926); KING OF KINGS, THE(1927); WHITE GOLD(1927); SECRET HOUR, THE(1928)
Misc. Silents
RISKY BUSINESS(1926); ALMOST HUMAN(1927); TURKISH DELIGHT(1927); STREET OF ILLUSION, THE(1928)

Kim Thomson
LORDS OF DISCIPLINE, THE(1983); PARTY PARTY(1983, Brit.)
Marjorie Thomson
GORBALS STORY, THE(1950, Brit.)
Marsh Thomson
OPERATION CIA(1965)
Monica Thomson
TWICE UPON A TIME(1953, Brit.)
Neil Thomson
MOUSE AND THE WOMAN, THE(1981, Brit.), ed; GIRO CITY(1982, Brit.), ed
Norman Thomson
LADY FROM SHANGHAI, THE(1948); BARBARIAN AND THE GEISHA, THE(1958)
Paul Thomson
CAN YOU HEAR ME MOTHER?(1935, Brit.), a, w
R. Scott Thomson
FOXES(1980)
R.H. Thomson
FOND MEMORIES(1982, Can.); IF YOU COULD SEE WHAT I HEAR(1982)
Russel Thomson
CARDBOARD CAVALIER, THE(1949, Brit.), ph
Scott Thomson
TIME OF THEIR LIVES, THE(1946); FAST TIMES AT RIDGEMONT HIGH(1982); FRIGHTMARE(1983)
1984
JOHNNY DANGEROUSLY(1984)
Sybil Thomson
GORBALS STORY, THE(1950, Brit.)
Ted Thomson
I LOVE YOU AGAIN(1940)
Virgil Thomson
LOUISIANA STORY(1948), m
William Thomson
SON OF THE RENEGADE(1953), ph
Allen Thomspon
IVORY-HANDLED GUN(1935), ph
Jerry Thompson
RIOT(1969)
Rip Thonger
FLY NOW, PAY LATER(1969)
Gerard Thoolen
LIFT, THE(1983, Neth.)
Dr. George Thooris
TAHITIAN, THE(1956)
Jerome Thor
RIOT IN JUVENILE PRISON(1959); 55 DAYS AT PEKING(1963); MR. SYCAMORE(1975); ST. IVES(1976); 10 TO MIDNIGHT(1983)
Larry Thor
PRIDE OF ST. LOUIS, THE(1952); KID FROM LEFT FIELD, THE(1953); MISSISSIPPI GAMBLER, THE(1953); FAST AND THE FURIOUS, THE(1954); FIVE GUNS WEST(1955); AMAZING COLOSSAL MAN, THE(1957); HELL BOUND(1957); PORTLAND EXPOSE(1957); ZERO HOUR!(1957); HUNTERS, THE(1958); LITTLEST HOBO, THE(1958); MACHINE GUN KELLY(1958); TARAWA BEACHHEAD(1958); BATTLE OF THE CORAL SEA(1959); LET'S MAKE LOVE(1960); COMPANY OF KILLERS(1970); PHANTOM TOLLBOOTH, THE(1970)
Billy Thorburn
TALKING FEET(1937, Brit.); STEPPING TOES(1938, Brit.)
June Thorburn
PICKWICK PAPERS, THE(1952, Brit.); CRUEL SEA, THE(1953); CHILDREN GALORE(1954, Brit.); DEATH OF MICHAEL TURBIN, THE(1954, Brit.); DELAYED ACTION(1954, Brit.); FAST AND LOOSE(1954, Brit.); HORNET'S NEST, THE(1955, Brit.); LIGHT TOUCH, THE(1955, Brit.); TRUE AS A TURTLE(1957, Brit.); ROONEY(1958, Brit.); TOM THUMB(1958, Brit./U.S.); BROTH OF A BOY(1959, Brit.); ORDERS ARE ORDERS(1959, Brit.); ESCORT FOR HIRE(1960, Brit.); PRICE OF SILENCE, THE(1960, Brit.); THREE WORLDS OF GULLIVER, THE(1960, Brit.); TRANSATLANTIC(1961, Brit.); DESIGN FOR LOVING(1962, Brit.); SPANISH SWORD, THE(1962, Brit.); FURY AT SMUGGLERS BAY(1963, Brit.); CRIMSON BLADE, THE(1964, Brit.); MASTER SPY(1964, Brit.); WHY BOTHER TO KNOCK(1964, Brit.)
Margaret Thorburn
WOMAN HATER(1949, Brit.)
Sybil Thordike
Misc. Silents
MOTH AND RUST(1921, Brit.)
Kelly Thordsen
DESPERADOES ARE IN TOWN, THE(1956); INVASION OF THE SAUCER MEN(1957); FEARMAKERS, THE(1958); MONEY, WOMEN AND GUNS(1958); CITY OF FEAR(1959); DESIRE IN THE DUST(1960); SWEET BIRD OF YOUTH(1962); TO KILL A MOCKINGBIRD(1962); MISADVENTURES OF MERLIN JONES, THE(1964); SHENANDOAH(1965); BOY, DID I GET A WRONG NUMBER!(1966); GUNPOINT(1966); TEXAS ACROSS THE RIVER(1966); UGLY DACHSHUND, THE(1966); GOOD TIMES(1967); DID YOU HEAR THE ONE ABOUT THE TRAVELING SALES-

LADY?(1968); BOATNIKS, THE(1970); NOW YOU SEE HIM, NOW YOU DON'T(1972); BAD CHARLESTON CHARLIE(1973); CHARLEY AND THE ANGEL(1973)
Misc. Talkies
PUSHING UP DAISIES(1971)
Terese Thoreaux
PROMISE AT DAWN(1970, U.S./Fr.)
Renee Thorel
LE CIEL EST A VOUS(1957, Fr.)
Hallvar Thorensen
VICTORY(1981)
Andre Thorent
PARIS BELONGS TO US(1962, Fr.); LIFE UPSIDE DOWN(1965, Fr.); CLOPORTES(1966, Fr., Ital.); SHAMELESS OLD LADY, THE(1966, Fr.); SICILIAN CLAN, THE(1970, Fr.); GODSON, THE(1972, Ital./Fr.); CATHERINE & CO.(1976, Fr.)
Ed Thorgersen
HIT PARADE, THE(1937); MARYLAND(1940)
Edward Thorgersen
LIFE BEGINS IN COLLEGE(1937)
Donald Thorin
THIEF(1981), ph; OFFICER AND A GENTLEMAN, AN(1982), ph; BAD BOYS(1983), ph
1984
AGAINST ALL ODDS(1984), ph; PURPLE RAIN(1984), ph
Thorleifsson
1984
KAMILLA(1984, Norway)
Victor Thorley
KISS OF DEATH(1947); YOUNG DON'T CRY, THE(1957)
Gundel Thormann
TWO IN A SLEEPING BAG(1964, Ger.)
Bert Thorn
TAXI(1953)
Maj. Britt Thorn
PIMPERNEL SVENSSON(1953, Swed.)
Christin Thorn
Misc. Talkies
BIG BUST-OUT, THE(1973)
Mike Thorn
MEMOIRS OF A SURVIVOR(1981, Brit.), m
Ray Thorn
INCREDIBLE TWO-HEADED TRANSPLANT, THE(1971)
Ronald Scott Thorn
STOP ME BEFORE I KILL!(1961, Brit.), w; DOCTOR IN DISTRESS(1963, Brit.), w
William Thorn
LOVE TAKES FLIGHT(1937)
Randy Thornally
STRAWBERRY STATEMENT, THE(1970)
Maiken Thornberg
PRIZE, THE(1963)
Patrick Thornberry
SUNDAY BLOODY SUNDAY(1971, Brit.)
Lee Thornburg
1984
HOLLYWOOD HIGH PART II(1984), d
Misc. Talkies
LONE STAR COUNTRY(1983), d
Newton Thornburg
CUTTER AND BONE(1981), w
Bill Thornbury
SUMMER SCHOOL TEACHERS(1977); PHANTASM(1979)
Robert Thornby
TODAY(1930)
Silents
BROKEN CHAINS(1916), d; KISS FOR SUSIE, A(1917), d; MOLLY ENTANGLED(1917), d; CAROLYN OF THE CORNERS(1919), d; BLAZING TRAIL, THE(1921), d; KICK BACK, THE(1922), ph; TRAP, THE(1922), d; STORM-SWEPT(1923), p&d
Misc. Silents
ALMIGHTY DOLLAR, THE(1916), d; CRUCIAL TEST, THE(1916), d; HER MATERNAL RIGHT(1916), d; FAIR BARBARIAN, THE(1917), d; HOSTAGE, THE(1917), d; LITTLE MISS OPTIMIST(1917), d; ON DANGEROUS GROUND(1917), d; FALLEN ANGEL, THE(1918), d; HER INSPIRATION(1918), d; LAWLESS LOVE(1918), d; PRINCE AND BETTY, THE(1919), d; ROSE OF THE RIVER(1919), d; WHEN MY SHIP COMES IN(1919), d; DEADLIER SEX, THE(1920), d; FELIX O'DAY(1920), d; GIRL IN THE WEB, THE(1920), d; HALF A CHANCE(1920), d; SIMPLE SOULS(1920), d; FOX, THE(1921), d; MAGNIFICENT BRUTE, THE(1921), d; THAT GIRL MONTANA(1921), d; SPEEDING VENUS, THE(1926), d; WEST OF BROADWAY(1926), d
Robert S. Thornby
Misc. Silents
FORBIDDEN PATHS(1917), d
Robert T. Thornby
Silents
ARE YOU LEGALLY MARRIED?(1919), d; GOLD MADNESS(1923), d
Misc. Silents
LITTLE SISTER OF EVERYBODY, A(1918), d; FIGHTING CRESSY(1919), d; SAGEBRUSH TRAIL, THE(1922), d; DRIVIN' FOOL, THE(1923), d
Robert W. Thornby
Misc. Silents
WOMAN'S POWER, A(1916), d
Eileen Thorndike
HEART OF THE MATTER, THE(1954, Brit.)
Oliver Thorndike
STORY OF DR. WASSELL, THE(1944); UNCONQUERED(1947)
Russell Thorndike
ROOF, THE(1933, Brit.); SHOT IN THE DARK, A(1933, Brit.); WHISPERING TONGUES(1934, Brit.); WOLVES OF THE UNDERWORLD(1935, Brit.); FAME(1936, Brit.); DOCTOR SYN(1937, Brit.), w; FIDDLERS THREE(1944, Brit.); HENRY V(1946, Brit.); HAMLET(1948, Brit.); RICHARD III(1956, Brit.); NIGHT CREATURES(1962, Brit.), w; DR. SYN, ALIAS THE SCARECROW(1975), w

Silents
AUDACIOUS MR. SQUIRE, THE(1923, Brit.); HEARTSTRINGS(1923, Brit.); HUMAN DESIRES(1924, Brit.); MIRIAM ROZELLA(1924, Brit.)
Misc. Silents
FAIR MAID OF PERTH, THE(1923, Brit.)
Sybil Thorndike
TO WHAT RED HELL(1929, Brit.); GENTLEMAN OF PARIS, A(1931); HINDLE WAKES(1931, Brit.); LADY JANE GREY(1936, Brit.); MAJOR BARBARA(1941, Brit.); NICHOLAS NICKLEBY(1947, Brit.); MAGIC BOX, THE(1952, Brit.); MELBA(1953, Brit.); WEAK AND THE WICKED, THE(1954, Brit.); PRINCE AND THE SHOWGIRL, THE(1957, Brit.); SHAKE HANDS WITH THE DEVIL(1959, Ireland); SMILEY GETS A GUN(1959, Brit.); HAND IN HAND(1960, Brit.); JET STORM(1961, Brit.); ALIVE AND KICKING(1962, Brit.); UNCLE VANYA(1977, Brit.)
Silents
DAWN(1928, Brit.)
Misc. Silents
BLEAK HOUSE(1922, Brit.)
Dame Sybil Thorndike
AFFAIRS OF ADELAIDE(1949, U. S./Brit.); STAGE FRIGHT(1950, Brit.); LADY WITH A LAMP, THE(1951, Brit.)
Dame Sybil Thorndyke
BIG GAMBLE, THE(1961)
Russell Thorndyke
CAESAR AND CLEOPATRA(1946, Brit.)
Sybil Thorndyke
WILD HEART, THE(1952, Brit.)
Angela Thorne
OH! WHAT A LOVELY WAR(1969, Brit.); HUMAN FACTOR, THE(1979, Brit.); FFOLKES(1980, Brit.)
Anthony Thorne
BAD LORD BYRON, THE(1949, Brit.), w; SO LONG AT THE FAIR(1951, Brit.), w; BABY AND THE BATTLESHIP, THE(1957, Brit.), w
Bill Thorne
DRAKE CASE, THE(1929)
Dennis Thorne
CONQUEROR WORM, THE(1968, Brit.)
Dick Thorne
EVE KNEW HER APPLES(1945); THEY WERE EXPENDABLE(1945)
Dyanne Thorne
POINT OF TERROR(1971); SWINGING BARMAIDS, THE(1976)
Misc. Talkies
ILSA, SHE WOLF OF THE SS(1975); ILSA, HAREM KEEPER OF THE OIL SHEIKS(1976)
E.P. Thorne
THREE SILENT MEN(1940, Brit.), w
Edward Thorne
TORRID ZONE(1940), set d
Silents
ETERNAL SIN, THE(1917)
Frank Thorne
Silents
RED LANE, THE(1920); SECRET OF THE HILLS, THE(1921); BILLY JIM(1922)
Misc. Silents
GREY PARASOL, THE(1918)
Garry Thorne
HIGH TIDE AT NOON(1957, Brit.)
Gary Thorne
THUNDERSTORM(1956); DEPRAVED, THE(1957, Brit.)
George Thorne
CONSTANT HUSBAND, THE(1955, Brit.)
Harold Thorne
PAY BOX ADVENTURE(1936, Brit.)
Ian Thorne
HENRY VIII AND HIS SIX WIVES(1972, Brit.), w
Jim Thorne
DIRTYMOUTH(1970)
Ken Thorne
DEAD MAN'S EVIDENCE(1962, Brit.), m; RING-A-DING RHYTHM(1962, Brit. 73m Amicus/COL bw (G.B: IT'S TRAD, DAD!), m; MASTER SPY(1964, Brit.), m; HELP!(1965, Brit.), m, md; HOW I WON THE WAR(1967, Brit.), m; HEAD(1968), m; INSPECTOR CLOUSEAU(1968, Brit.), m; SINFUL DAVEY(1969, Brit.), m, md; MAGIC CHRISTIAN, THE(1970, Brit.), m, md; HANNIE CALDER(1971, Brit.), m; MURPHY'S WAR(1971, Brit.), m; WELCOME TO THE CLUB(1971), m; BROTHER SUN, SISTER MOON(1973, Brit./Ital.), md; JUGGERNAUT(1974, Brit.), m; ROYAL FLASH(1975, Brit.), m; ASSAULT ON AGATHON(1976, Brit./Gr.), m; RITZ, THE(1976), m; ARABIAN ADVENTURE(1979, Brit.), m; SUPERMAN II(1980), m; HOUSE WHERE EVIL DWELLS, THE(1982), m; SUPERMAN III(1983), m
1984
EVIL THAT MEN DO, THE(1984), m; FINDERS KEEPERS(1984), m; LASSITER(1984), m
Lizette Thorne
Silents
BROKEN DOLL, A(1921)
Misc. Silents
BRUISER, THE(1916); DREAM OR TWO AGO, A(1916); FAITH(1916); THOROUGHBRED, THE(1916); TRUE NOBILITY(1916)
Lois Thorne
ODDS AGAINST TOMORROW(1959)
Nancy Thorne
ROSE BOWL STORY, THE(1952)
Raymond Thorne
JUST TELL ME WHAT YOU WANT(1980)
Regina Thorne
BIG CUBE, THE(1969)
Richard Thorne
HEAVENLY DAYS(1944); MRS. PARKINGTON(1944); RETURN OF THE BADMEN(1948); FOR HEAVEN'S SAKE(1950)

Robert Thorne
Silents
JANICE MEREDITH(1924)
Ronald Thorne
WALK THE ANGRY BEACH(1961), ed
Ronald Scott Thorne
UPSTAIRS AND DOWNSTAIRS(1961, Brit.), w
Stephen Thorne
1984
RUNAWAY(1984)
Teresa Thorne
JOE MACBETH(1955)
Vick Thorne
HAREM BUNCH; OR WAR AND PIECE, THE(1969)
Victor Thorne
Silents
ANNE AGAINST THE WORLD(1929), w
W. L. Thorne
ABRAHAM LINCOLN(1930); PEACOCK ALLEY(1930); MONTANA KID, THE(1931); RAINBOW TRAIL(1932); GOLD RACKET, THE(1937)
Silents
KICK-OFF, THE(1926)
William Thorne
BANK ALARM(1937); FORGOTTEN WOMAN, THE(1939)
William L. Thorne
THUNDERBOLT(1929); FIGHTING THRU(1931); SHE-WOLF, THE(1931); LAW OF THE NORTH(1932); NEVADA(1936)
Misc. Talkies
VANISHING MEN(1932)
Hans Thorner
KISS THE GIRLS AND MAKE THEM DIE(1967, U.S./Ital.); SONS OF SATAN(1969, Ital./Fr./Ger.)
Sally Thorner
1984
PROTOCOL(1984)
Alan Thornhill
CROWNING EXPERIENCE, THE(1960), w; VOICE OF THE HURRICANE(1964), w
James Thornhill
POOR COW(1968, Brit.); LIMBO LINE, THE(1969, Brit.)
Michael Thornhill
SUMMER OF SECRETS(1976, Aus.), p; F.J. HOLDEN, THE(1977, Aus.), p&d
Steven Thornley
HANGAR 18(1980), w
William Thornley
Silents
DOLLY'S VACATION(1918), ph; DEVIL'S TRAIL, THE(1919), ph; MAN TO MAN(1922), ph; CRASHIN' THRU(1923), ph; NEAR LADY, THE(1923), ph; DARK STAIRWAYS(1924), ph; JACK O' CLUBS(1924), ph; GREY DEVIL, THE(1926), ph; WEST OF THE RAINBOW'S END(1926), ph; PHANTOM OF THE NORTH(1929), ph
Conchita Thornston
PUNISHMENT PARK(1971)
Ann Thornton
EUREKA(1983, Brit.)
Bernard Thornton
Misc. Silents
CAMOUFLAGE KISS, A(1918); HEART OF ROMANCE, THE(1918); OH MARY BE CAREFUL(1921)
Cherokee Thornton
DRUMS O' VOODOO(1934)
Claudette Thornton
TWO TICKETS TO BROADWAY(1951); REDHEAD FROM WYOMING, THE(1953); MA AND PA KETTLE AT WAIKIKI(1955)
Cyril Thornton
THIN MAN, THE(1934); BARBARY COAST(1935); FOLIES DERGERE(1935); PRISONER OF SHARK ISLAND, THE(1936); EMPEROR'S CANDLESTICKS, THE(1937); SERGEANT MURPHY(1938); MAN ABOUT TOWN(1939); WE ARE NOT ALONE(1939); CASE OF THE BLACK PARROT, THE(1941); INTERNATIONAL SQUADRON(1941); MEET JOHN DOE(1941); THIS ABOVE ALL(1942); GLASS ALIBI, THE(1946); IF WINTER COMES(1947); JULIA MISBEHAVES(1948)
Drake Thornton
AND THE ANGELS SING(1944)
Edith Thornton
MYSTIC HOUR, THE(1934)
Silents
ON PROBATION(1924); POISON(1924); SURGING SEAS(1924); FAIR PLAY(1925); WAS IT BIGAMY?(1925)
Misc. Silents
BETTER WOMAN, THE(1915); FIFTH COMMANDMENT, THE(1915); HURRICANE HUTCH IN MANY ADVENTURES(1924, Brit.); HUTCH OF THE U.S.A.(1924); VIRTUE'S REVOLT(1924); LITTLE FIREBRAND, THE(1927); DANGER MAN, THE(1930)
Evans Thornton
NIGHT OF THE LEPUS(1972); TRIAL OF BILLY JACK, THE(1974)
F. Martin Thornton
Silents
LITTLE LORD FAUNTLEROY(1914, Brit.), d; IF THOU WERT BLIND(1917, Brit.), d; LOVE'S OLD SWEET SONG(1917, Brit.), d; MAN THE ARMY MADE, A(1917, Brit.), w; KNAVE OF HEARTS, THE(1919, Brit.), d; POWER OF RIGHT, THE(1919, Brit.), d; FRAILTY(1921, Brit.), d; MUTINY(1925, Brit.), d
Misc. Silents
WORLD, THE FLESH AND THE DEVIL, THE(1914, Brit.), d; FAITH OF A CHILD, THE(1915, Brit.), d; STRIFE ETERNAL, THE(1915, Brit.), d; DIANA AND DESTINY(1916, Brit.), d; MAN WHO BOUGHT LONDON, THE(1916, Brit.), d; HAPPY WARRIOR, THE(1917, Brit.), d; GREAT IMPOSTER, THE(1918, Brit.), d; NATURE'S GENTLEMAN(1918, Brit.), d; RILKA(1918, Brit.), d; SPLENDID COWARD, THE(1918, Brit.), d; MAN WHO FORGOT, THE(1919, Brit.), d; WARRIOR STRAIN, THE(1919, Brit.), d; BARS OF IRON(1920, Brit.), d; BRANDED SOUL, THE(1920, Brit.), d; FLAME, THE(1920, Brit.), d; GWYNETH OF THE WELSH HILLS(1921, Brit.), d; MY LORD CONCEIT(1921, Brit.), d; PREY OF THE DRAGON, THE(1921, Brit.), d; RIVER OF STARS, THE(1921, Brit.), d; BELONGING(1922, Brit.), d; LITTLE BROTHER OF GOD(1922, Brit.), d; SAILOR TRAMP, A(1922, Brit.), d; ROMANY, THE(1923, Brit.), d;

WOMEN AND DIAMONDS(1924, Brit.), d

Frank Thornton
CRACKED NUTS(1931); GAMBLING LADY(1934); MAN WHO BROKE THE BANK AT MONTE CARLO, THE(1935); SECRET OF THE CHATEAU(1935); RADIO CAB MURDER(1954, Brit.); STOCK CAR(1955, Brit.); OPERATION CONSPIRACY(1957, Brit.); RING-A-DING RHYTHM(1962, Brit. 73m Amicus/COL bw (G.B: IT'S TRAD, DAD!); TELL-TALE HEART, THE(1962, Brit.); TRIAL AND ERROR(1962, Brit.); EARLY BIRD, THE(1965, Brit.); GONKS GO BEAT(1965, Brit.); TOMB OF LIGEIA, THE(1965, Brit.); CARRY ON SCREAMING(1966, Brit.); FUNNY THING HAPPENED ON THE WAY TO THE FORUM, A(1966); MURDER GAME, THE(1966, Brit.); WILD AFFAIR, THE(1966, Brit.); ALF 'N' FAMILY(1968, Brit.); FLEA IN HER EAR, A(1968, Fr.); 30 IS A DANGEROUS AGE, CYNTHIA(1968, Brit.); ASSASSINATION BUREAU, THE(1969, Brit.); BED SITTING ROOM, THE(1969, Brit.); MAGIC CHRISTIAN, THE(1970, Brit.); PRIVATE LIFE OF SHERLOCK HOLMES, THE(1970, Brit.); RISE AND RISE OF MICHAEL RIMMER, THE(1970, Brit.); SOPHIE'S PLACE(1970); DIGBY, THE BIGGEST DOG IN THE WORLD(1974, Brit.); OLD DRACULA(1975, Brit.); SPANISH FLY(1975, Brit.); BAWDY ADVENTURES OF TOM JONES, THE(1976, Brit.)
Misc. Talkies
ARE YOU BEING SERVED?(1977)

Gladys Thornton
IF A MAN ANSWERS(1962)

James Thornton
METALSTORM: THE DESTRUCTION OF JARED-SYN(1983), set d

Joan Thornton
ROUND TRIP(1967)

Kathi Thornton
HOT ANGEL, THE(1958)

Martin Thornton
RISING OF THE MOON, THE(1957, Ireland)

Capt. Milton M. Thornton
STORY OF G.I. JOE, THE(1945), tech adv

Peter Thornton
MAN WITH A GUN(1958, Brit.); BUNNY LAKE IS MISSING(1965), ed; POPPY IS ALSO A FLOWER, THE(1966), ed; ROVER, THE(1967, Ital.), ed; TO SIR, WITH LOVE(1967, Brit.), ed; MY SIDE OF THE MOUNTAIN(1969), ed; WHERE'S JACK?(1969, Brit.), ed; LADY IN THE CAR WITH GLASSES AND A GUN, THE(1970, U.S./Fr.), ed; MAN OF VIOLENCE(1970, Brit.); I WANT WHAT I WANT(1972, Brit.), ed; THEATRE OF BLOOD(1973, Brit.); ROSEBUD(1975), ed; KILL AND KILL AGAIN(1981), ed

Philip Thornton
GHOST SHIP(1953, Brit.), w

Ralph Thornton
BLOOD OF DRACULA(1957), w; I WAS A TEENAGE WEREWOLF(1957), w

Richard Thornton
Misc. Silents
DUBARRY(1915)

Scoody Thornton
BAD NEWS BEARS GO TO JAPAN, THE(1978)

Sigrid Thornton
GETTING OF WISDOM, THE(1977, Aus.); DAY AFTER HALLOWEEN, THE(1981, Aus.); DUET FOR FOUR(1982, Aus.); MAN FROM SNOWY RIVER, THE(1983, Aus.)

Madeleine Thornton-Sherwood
CHANGELING, THE(1980, Can.); RESURRECTION(1980)

Adelaide Thornveit
NORTHERN LIGHTS(1978)

Frank Thornwald
Silents
ACROSS THE DEAD-LINE(1922)

Christian Thorogood
OH! WHAT A LOVELY WAR(1969, Brit.)

John Thorp
SEVEN(1979)

Molly Thorp
ADVENTURE IN THE HOPFIELDS(1954, Brit.), w

Nola Thorp
DONDI(1961)

Norman Thorp
Misc. Silents
ROMANTIC JOURNEY, THE(1916)

Raymond W. Thorp
JEREMIAH JOHNSON(1972), w

Richard Thorp
MELODY IN THE DARK(1948, Brit.); GOOD COMPANIONS, THE(1957, Brit.); THERE'S ALWAYS A THURSDAY(1957, Brit.); BITTER HARVEST(1963, Brit.); MYSTERY SUBMARINE(1963, Brit.); SWINGIN' MAIDEN, THE(1963, Brit.); 20,000 POUNDS KISS, THE(1964, Brit.)

Roderick Thorp
DETECTIVE, THE(1968), w

Ruth Thorp
Misc. Silents
BLUE STREAK, THE(1917)

Bill Thorpe
RHUBARB(1951)

Buddy Thorpe
FIXED BAYONETS(1951); JOE LOUIS STORY, THE(1953)

George Thorpe
UNPUBLISHED STORY(1942, Brit.); YELLOW CANARY, THE(1944, Brit.); ADVENTURE FOR TWO(1945, Brit.); MEET ME AT DAWN(1947, Brit.); DAUGHTER OF DARKNESS(1948, Brit.); GIRL IN THE PAINTING, THE(1948, Brit.); QUIET WEEKEND(1948, Brit.); MAN ON THE EIFFEL TOWER, THE(1949); QUARTET(1949, Brit.); OPERATION DISASTER(1951, Brit.); RELUCTANT WIDOW, THE(1951, Brit.); FATHER'S DOING FINE(1952, Brit.); RAINBOW JACKET, THE(1954, Brit.)

Gordon Thorpe
BRIDGE OF SAN LUIS REY, THE(1929); IRON MASK, THE(1929); ABRAHAM LINCOLN(1930); SINS OF THE CHILDREN(1930); DAWN PATROL, THE(1938)
Silents
WAY OF ALL FLESH, THE(1927)

Harriet Thorpe
1984
GREYSTOKE: THE LEGEND OF TARZAN, LORD OF THE APES(1984)

Harry Thorpe
Silents
MAN FROM PAINTED POST, THE(1917), ph; MODERN MUSKETEER, A(1917), ph; REACHING FOR THE MOON(1917), ph; HEADIN' SOUTH(1918), ph; MARK OF ZORRO(1920), ph; MOLLYCODDLE, THE(1920), ph; WHEN THE CLOUDS ROLL BY(1920), ph; NUT, THE(1921), ph; WILD HONEY(1922), ph; RUPERT OF HENTZAU(1923), ph; WEDDING MARCH, THE(1927), ph

Herbert Thorpe
IRISH AND PROUD OF IT(1938, Ireland); MY AIN FOLK(1944, Brit.)

J. A. Thorpe
MANY WATERS(1931, Brit.), p

James Thorpe
JIM THORPE–ALL AMERICAN(1951), w, tech adv

Jerry Thorpe
VENETIAN AFFAIR, THE(1967), p, d; DAY OF THE EVIL GUN(1968), p&d; COMPANY OF KILLERS(1970), p, d

Jim Thorpe
TOUCHDOWN!(1931); AIR MAIL(1932); MY PAL, THE KING(1932); WHITE EAGLE(1932); WILD HORSE MESA(1932); KING KONG(1933); BARBARY COAST(1935); BEHOLD MY WIFE(1935); CODE OF THE MOUNTED(1935); FARMER TAKES A WIFE, THE(1935); SHE(1935); WANDERER OF THE WASTELAND(1935); SUTTER'S GOLD(1936); TRAILIN' WEST(1936); TREACHERY RIDES THE RANGE(1936); WILDCAT TROOPER(1936); BIG CITY(1937); GREEN LIGHT(1937); HENRY GOES ARIZONA(1939); ARIZONA FRONTIER(1940); PRAIRIE SCHOONERS(1940); OUTLAW TRAIL(1944); BEYOND THE PECOS(1945); ROAD TO UTOPIA(1945); WHITE HEAT(1949); WAGONMASTER(1950)

Morgan Thorpe
Silents
KATHLEEN MAVOURNEEN(1919); FREEDOM OF THE PRESS(1928)
Misc. Silents
HOUSE OF THE TOLLING BELLS, THE(1920)

Norman Thorpe
Silents
KIPPS(1921, Brit.)

Phil Thorpe
KNUTE ROCKNE–ALL AMERICAN(1940)

Richard Thorpe
BACHELOR GIRL, THE(1929), d; BORDER ROMANCE(1930), d; DUDE WRANGLER, THE(1930), d; THOROUGHBRED, THE(1930), d; UNDER MONTANA SKIES(1930), d; UTAH KID, THE(1930), d; WINGS OF ADVENTURE(1930), d; GRIEF STREET(1931), d&ed; LADY FROM NOWHERE(1931), d, ed; LAWLESS WOMAN, THE(1931), d, w; NECK AND NECK(1931), d; SKY SPIDER, THE(1931), d; WILD HORSE(1931), d; BEAUTY PARLOR(1932), d; CROSS-EXAMINATION(1932), d; DEVIL PAYS, THE(1932), d; ESCAPADE(1932), d; FORBIDDEN COMPANY(1932), d; FORGOTTEN WOMEN(1932), d; KING MURDER, THE(1932), d; MIDNIGHT LADY(1932), d; MURDER AT DAWN(1932), d; PROBATION(1932), d, ed; SECRETS OF WU SIN(1932), d; THRILL OF YOUTH(1932), d; FORGOTTEN(1933), d; I HAVE LIVED(1933), d; LOVE IS LIKE THAT(1933), d; MAN OF SENTIMENT, A(1933), d; RAINBOW OVER BROADWAY(1933), d; SLIGHTLY MARRIED(1933), d; STRANGE PEOPLE(1933), d; WOMEN WON'T TELL(1933), d; CHEATING CHEATERS(1934), d; CITY PARK(1934), d; GREEN EYES(1934), d; MURDER ON THE CAMPUS(1934), d; NOTORIOUS BUT NICE(1934), d; QUITTERS, THE(1934), d; STOLEN SWEETS(1934), d; SECRET OF THE CHATEAU(1935), d; STRANGE WIVES(1935), d; LAST OF THE PAGANS(1936), d; TARZAN ESCAPES(1936), d; VOICE OF BUGLE ANN(1936), d; DOUBLE WEDDING(1937), d; NIGHT MUST FALL(1937), d; CROWD ROARS, THE(1938), d; FIRST 100 YEARS, THE(1938), d; LOVE IS A HEADACHE(1938), d; MAN-PROOF(1938), d; THREE LOVES HAS NANCY(1938), d; TOY WIFE, THE(1938), d; HUCKLEBERRY FINN(1939), d; TARZAN FINDS A SON!(1939), d; EARL OF CHICAGO, THE(1940), d; TWENTY MULE TEAM(1940), d; WYOMING(1940), d; BAD MAN, THE(1941), d; BARNACLE BILL(1941), d; TARZAN'S SECRET TREASURE(1941), d; APACHE TRAIL(1942), d; JOE SMITH, AMERICAN(1942), d; TARZAN'S NEW YORK ADVENTURE(1942), d; WHITE CARGO(1942), d; ABOVE SUSPICION(1943), d; CRY HAVOC(1943), d; THREE HEARTS FOR JULIA(1943), d; THIN MAN GOES HOME, THE(1944), d; TWO GIRLS AND A SAILOR(1944), d; HER HIGHNESS AND THE BELLBOY(1945), d; THRILL OF A ROMANCE(1945), d; WHAT NEXT, CORPORAL HARGROVE?(1945), d; FIESTA(1947), d; THIS TIME FOR KEEPS(1947), d; DATE WITH JUDY, A(1948), d; ON AN ISLAND WITH YOU(1948), d; BIG JACK(1949), d; CHALLENGE TO LASSIE(1949), d; SUN COMES UP, THE(1949), d; BLACK HAND, THE(1950), d; MALAYA(1950), d; THREE LITTLE WORDS(1950), d; GREAT CARUSO, THE(1951), d; UNKNOWN MAN, THE(1951), d; VENGEANCE VALLEY(1951), d; CARBINE WILLIAMS(1952), d; IVANHOE(1952, Brit.), d; PRISONER OF ZENDA, THE(1952), d; ALL THE BROTHERS WERE VALIANT(1953), d; GIRL WHO HAD EVERYTHING, THE(1953), d; KNIGHTS OF THE ROUND TABLE(1953), d; ATHENA(1954), d; STUDENT PRINCE, THE(1954), d; PRODIGAL, THE(1955), d; QUENTIN DURWARD(1955), d; BARRETTS OF WIMPOLE STREET, THE(1957), d; JAILHOUSE ROCK(1957), d; TEN THOUSAND BEDROOMS(1957), d; TIP ON A DEAD JOCKEY(1957), d; HOUSE OF THE SEVEN HAWKS, THE(1959), d; KILLERS OF KILIMANJARO(1960, Brit.), d; HONEYMOON MACHINE, THE(1961), d; HORIZONTAL LIEUTENANT, THE(1962), d; HOW THE WEST WAS WON(1962), d; TARTARS, THE(1962, Ital./Yugo.), d; FOLLOW THE BOYS(1963), d; FUN IN ACAPULCO(1963), d; SWORD OF LANCELOT(1963, Brit.); GOLDEN HEAD, THE(1965, Hung., U.S.), d; THAT FUNNY FEELING(1965), d; TRUTH ABOUT SPRING, THE(1965, Brit.), d; LAST CHALLENGE, THE(1967), p&d; SUBURBAN WIVES(1973, Brit.)
Silents
BURN 'EM UP BARNES(1921); WALLOPING WALLACE(1924), d; ON THE GO(1925), d; QUICKER'N LIGHTNIN'(1925), d; COLLEGE DAYS(1926), d; COMING AN' GOING(1926), d; FIGHTING CHEAT, THE(1926), d; JOSSELYN'S WIFE(1926), d; GALLOPING GOBS, THE(1927), d
Misc. Silents
BATTLING BUDDY(; THREE O'CLOCK IN THE MORNING(1923); (1924), d; BRINGIN' HOME THE BACON(1924), d; FAST AND FEARLESS(1924), d; FLAMES OF DESIRE(1924), d; HARD HITTIN' HAMILTON(1924), d; RARIN' TO GO(1924), d; RIP ROARIN' ROBERTS(1924), d; ROUGH RIDIN'(1924), a, d; THUNDERING ROMANCE(1924), d; DESERT DEMON, THE(1925), d; DOUBLE ACTION DANIELS(1925), d; FAST FIGHTIN'(1925), d; FULL SPEED(1925), d; GALLOPING ON(1925), d; GOLD AND GRIT(1925), d; SADDLE CYCLONE(1925), d; STREAK OF

LUCK, A(1925), d; TEARIN' LOOSE(1925), d; BANDIT BUSTER, THE(1926), d; BONANZA BUCKAROO, THE(1926), d; DANGEROUS DUB, THE(1926), d; DEUCE HIGH(1926), d; DOUBLE DARING(1926), d; EASY GOING(1926), d; RAWHIDE(1926), d; RIDING RIVALS(1926), d; ROARING RIDER(1926), d; SPEEDY SPURS(1926), d; TRUMPIN' TROUBLE(1926), d; TWIN TRIGGERS(1926), d; TWISTED TRIGGERS(1926), d; BETWEEN DANGERS(1927), d; CYCLONE COWBOY, THE(1927), d; DESERT OF THE LOST, THE(1927), d; FIRST NIGHT, THE(1927), d; INTERFERIN' GENT, THE(1927), d; MEDDLIN' STRANGER, THE(1927), d; OBLIGIN' BUCKAROO, THE(1927), d; PALS IN PERIL(1927), d; RIDE 'EM HIGH(1927), d; RIDIN' ROWDY, THE(1927), d; ROARIN' BRONCS(1927), d; SKEDADDLE GOLD(1927), d; SODA WATER COWBOY(1927), d; TEARIN' INTO TROUBLE(1927), d; WHITE PEBBLES(1927), d; BALLYHOO BUSTER, THE(1928), d; COWBOY CAVALIER, THE(1928), d; DESPERATE COURAGE(1928), d; FLYING BUCKAROO, THE(1928), d; SADDLE MATES(1928), d; VALLEY OF HUNTED MEN, THE(1928), d

Richard L. Thorpe
SHADY LADY, THE(1929), w
Simon Thorpe
CLINIC, THE(1983, Aus.); NEXT OF KIN(1983, Aus.)
1984
SQUIZZY TAYLOR(1984, Aus.)
Ted Thorpe
HERE COMES THE GROOM(1951); FLAME OF CALCUTTA(1953); SAVAGE MUTINY(1953); IT SHOULD HAPPEN TO YOU(1954); PHFFFT!(1954); WITNESS TO MURDER(1954); MACHINE GUN KELLY(1958); BACK STREET(1961); IF A MAN ANSWERS(1962); HANG'EM HIGH(1968)
Virginia Thorpe
KID FROM BOOKLYN, THE(1946)
Peggy Thorpe-Bates
IN THE DOGHOUSE(1964, Brit.); GEORGY GIRL(1966, Brit.); THANK YOU ALL VERY MUCH(1969, Brit.); MOSQUITO SQUADRON(1970, Brit.)
Richard Thorps
DANGEROUS NUMBER(1937), d
Kelly Thorsden
PARALLAX VIEW, THE(1974)
Karen Thorsell
ONCE UPON A COFFEE HOUSE(1965)
Duane Thorsen
JACK SLADE(1953); SEMINOLE(1953); BLACK WHIP, THE(1956)
Jean Thorsen
HOODLUM SAINT, THE(1946)
Joan Thorsen
GUY NAMED JOE, A(1943); HEAT'S ON, THE(1943); TWO GIRLS AND A SAILOR(1944); UNDERCURRENT(1946)
Mel Thorsen
STRANGER FROM TEXAS, THE(1940), ed; MEDICO OF PAINTED SPRINGS, THE(1941), ed; NORTH FROM LONE STAR(1941), ed; PINTO KID, THE(1941), ed; RETURN OF DANIEL BOONE, THE(1941), ed; SON OF DAVY CROCKETT, THE(1941), ed; DOWN RIO GRANDE WAY(1942), ed; LONE STAR VIGILANTES, THE(1942), ed; PARACHUTE NURSE(1942), ed; PARDON MY GUN(1942), ed; WEST OF TOMBSTONE(1942), ed; DOUGHBOYS IN IRELAND(1943), ed; JUNIOR ARMY(1943), ed; PASSPORT TO SUEZ(1943), ed; POWER OF THE PRESS(1943), ed; KLONDIKE KATE(1944), ed; SWORD OF THE AVENGER(1948), ed
Rex Thorsen
FEMALE JUNGLE, THE(1955)
Russ Thorsen
UNDERSEA GIRL(1957)
Russell Thorsen
HALF HUMAN(1955, Jap.); TARAWA BEACHHEAD(1958)
Sven Ole Thorsen
CONAN THE BARBARIAN(1982)
1984
CONAN THE DESTROYER(1984)
Barbara Thorson
GEORGE WHITE'S SCANDALS(1945)
Joan Thorson
HARVEY GIRLS, THE(1946)
Linda Thorson
VALENTINO(1977, Brit.); GREEK TYCOON, THE(1978); CURTAINS(1983, Can.)
Marilyn Thorson
SMALL HOURS, THE(1962)
Ralph Thorson
HUNTER, THE(1980), a, w
Russ Thorson
EASY LIVING(1949); DOUBLE DYNAMITE(1951); DANGEROUS MISSION(1954); HOT ROD GIRL(1956); PLEASE MURDER ME(1956); DESTINATION 60,000(1957)
Russell Thorson
ZERO HOUR!(1957); GOOD DAY FOR A HANGING(1958); GUN FEVER(1958); I WANT TO LIVE!(1958); GUNFIGHTERS OF ABILENE(1960); MY BLOOD RUNS COLD(1965); TWO ON A GUILLOTINE(1965); 36 HOURS(1965); COVENANT WITH DEATH, A(1966); HANG'EM HIGH(1968); LEARNING TREE, THE(1969); STALKING MOON, THE(1969); WALKING TALL(1973)
Drake Thorton
HIGHER AND HIGHER(1943)
Einar Thorvaldson
MATCH KING, THE(1932), w
Bruno Thost
COUP DE GRACE(1978, Ger./Fr.); TIN DRUM, THE(1979, Ger./Fr./Yugo./Pol.)
1984
SWANN IN LOVE(1984, Fr.Ger.)
Lise Thouin
VISITING HOURS(1982, Can.), ed
William Thourlby
MANCHURIAN CANDIDATE, THE(1962); CREEPING TERROR, THE(1964); VENGEANCE(1964), a, p; DESTINATION INNER SPACE(1966); CASTLE OF EVIL(1967)
Misc. Talkies
SHOCK HILL(1966)
Adolfo Thous
TOWN CALLED HELL, A(1971, Span./Brit.); MAN CALLED NOON, THE(1973, Brit.); CHINO(1976, Ital., Span., Fr.)

Adolpho Thous
SPIKES GANG, THE(1974)
Jean Thrall
Misc. Silents
IL TROVATORE(1914)
Edith Thrane
ORDET(1957, Den.)
Leslie Thrasher
FOR THE LOVE O'LIL(1930), w
Kenneth Threadgill
HONEYSUCKLE ROSE(1980)
Elizabeth Threatt
BIG SKY, THE(1952)
Three Brian Sisters
THANKS FOR LISTENING(1937)
The Three Brian Sisters
SING WHILE YOU'RE ABLE(1937)
Three Brown Sisters
FOOLS FOR SCANDAL(1938)
Three Cheers
SWING IT SOLDIER(1941); HIT PARADE OF 1943(1943)
The Three Cheers
OKAY AMERICA(1932)
Three Chocolateers
NEW FACES OF 1937(1937)
The Three Chocolateers
MOONLIGHT MASQUERADE(1942)
The Three Degrees
FRENCH CONNECTION, THE(1971)
Three Diamond Brothers
FRESHMAN YEAR(1938)
The Three Diamond Brothers
KNIGHTS FOR A DAY(1937, Brit.)
The Three Dots
STEPPING TOES(1938, Brit.)
The Three Dunhills
MY WILD IRISH ROSE(1947)
Three Ginx
HELLO SWEETHEART(1935, Brit.)
THREE HILLBILLIES
AROUND THE TOWN(1938$c Brit.)
Three Hits and a Miss
TOPPER(1937)
The Three Jokers
MUSIC HALL PARADE(1939, Brit.)
The Three Maxwells
LAUGH IT OFF(1940, Brit.)
The Three Midshipmen
SWEETHEART OF SIGMA CHI(1933)
Three Murtagh Sisters
FRESHMAN YEAR(1938)
The Three Nagels
VARIETY PARADE(1936, Brit.)
The Three Nelsons
KEEP SMILING(1938)
The Three Normans
NIGHT AT EARL CARROLL'S, A(1940)
Three of August
WILD WHEELS(1969)
The Three Peppers
LADY TAKES A CHANCE, A(1943)
The Three Radio Rogues
GOING HOLLYWOOD(1933); TWENTY MILLION SWEETHEARTS(1934)
The Three Rhythm Sisters
FEATHER YOUR NEST(1937, Brit.)
Three Sailors
RADIO FOLLIES(1935, Brit.)
The Three Sailors
TOP OF THE TOWN(1937)
The Three Sea Hawks
Silents
FLYING FEET, THE(1929)
The Three Sisters
IN SOCIETY(1944)
The Three Stooges
START CHEERING(1938); TIME OUT FOR RHYTHM(1941); MY SISTER EILEEN(1942); SWING PARADE OF 1946(1946); SNOW WHITE AND THE THREE STOOGES(1961); FOUR FOR TEXAS(1963)
The Three Suns
TWO GALS AND A GUY(1951)
The Three Swifts
NOB HILL(1945)
Papa Threecards
COUNTRYMAN(1982, Jamaica)
Gail Threlkeld
BADLANDS(1974)
Ken Thret
WARRIORS, THE(1979)
Maggie Thrett
DIMENSION 5(1966); OUT OF SIGHT(1966); THREE IN THE ATTIC(1968)
Meggie Thrett
COVER ME BABE(1970)
R. B. Thrift
LONG RIDERS, THE(1980)
F.W. Thring
HIS ROYAL HIGHNESS(1932, Aus.), p&d; SENTIMENTAL BLOKE(1932, Aus.), p; HARMONY ROW(1933, Aus.), d

Frank Thring
VIKINGS, THE(1958); BEN HUR(1959); QUESTION OF ADULTERY, A(1959, Brit.); EL CID(1961, U.S./Ital.); KING OF KINGS(1961); AGE OF CONSENT(1969, Austral.); NED KELLY(1970, Brit.); ALVIN RIDES AGAIN(1974, Aus.); MAN FROM HONG KONG(1975); MAD DOG MORGAN(1976,Aus.)

Malachi Throne
YOUNG LOVERS, THE(1964); BEAU GESTE(1966); FRASIER, THE SENSUOUS LION(1973); GREATEST, THE(1977, U.S./Brit.); STUNTS(1977)

Harmon Thronebury
TURN ON TO LOVE(1969), m

Margaret Throsby
STIR(1980, Aus.)

Maxie Thrower
MY FRIEND IRMA GOES WEST(1950); STREETCAR NAMED DESIRE, A(1951); SHE COULDN'T SAY NO(1954)

Dave Thrusby
RULERS OF THE SEA(1939)

Turk Thrust [Bryan Forbes]
SHOT IN THE DARK, A(1964)

Jean Thuiller
MAN ESCAPED, A(1957, Fr.), p

Jean Thuillier
FRANTIC(1961, Fr.), p; TESTAMENT OF ORPHEUS, THE(1962, Fr.), p; NAKED AUTUMN(1963, Fr.), p

Bjorn Thulin
GYPSY FURY(1950, Fr.), art d; SCENES FROM A MARRIAGE(1974, Swed.), set d

Ingrid Thulin
MAGICIAN, THE(1959, Swed.); WILD STRAWBERRIES(1959, Swed.); BRINK OF LIFE(1960, Swed.); FOUR HORSEMEN OF THE APOCALYPSE, THE(1962); WINTER LIGHT, THE(1963, Swed.); SILENCE, THE(1964, Swed.); RETURN FROM THE ASHES(1965, U.S./Brit.); NIGHT GAMES(1966, Swed.); LA GUERRE EST FINIE(1967, Fr./Swed.); HOUR OF THE WOLF, THE(1968, Swed.); FINO A FARTI MALE(1969, Fr./Ital.); RITUAL, THE(1970, Swed.); N. P.(1971, Ital.); CRIES AND WHISPERS(1972, Swed.); LA CAGE(1975, Fr.); MOSES(1976, Brit./Ital.); CASSANDRA CROSSING, THE(1977)
1984
AFTER THE REHEARSAL(1984, Swed.)

Ron Thulin
TEX(1982)

Betty Thumling
TWO HEARTS IN HARMONY(1935, Brit.)

Leonora Thuna
HOW TO BEAT THE HIGH COST OF LIVING(1980), w

Olof Thunberg
WINTER LIGHT, THE(1963, Swed.)

Thunder the Dog
Silents
HIS MASTER'S VOICE(1925); WINGS OF THE STORM(1926)

Thunder the Wonder Horse
SILVER STALLION(1941)

Thunder
Misc. Silents
WOLF FANGS(1927)

Rino Thunder
WOLFEN(1981)

Rolling Thunder
TRIAL OF BILLY JACK, THE(1974)

Richard Thunder-Sky
PONY SOLDIER(1952)

Chief Thundercloud
ANNIE OAKLEY(1935); FARMER TAKES A WIFE, THE(1935); WAGON TRAIL(1935); RIDE, RANGER, RIDE(1936); GERONIMO(1939); UNCONQUERED(1941); AMBUSH(1950)

John Thundercloud
MELVIN AND HOWARD(1980)

Thunderhoof the Horse
THUNDERHOOF(1948)

Bill Thunhurst
HUNGRY WIVES(1973)

W. L. Thunhurst, Jr.
THE CRAZIES(1973)

Will Thunis
OUR HEARTS WERE YOUNG AND GAY(1944); O.S.S.(1946)

Thomas Thurban
SPLINTERS IN THE NAVY(1931, Brit.)

James Thurber
RISE AND SHINE(1941), w; MALE ANIMAL, THE(1942), w; SECRET LIFE OF WALTER MITTY, THE(1947), w; SHE'S WORKING HER WAY THROUGH COLLEGE(1952), w; BATTLE OF THE SEXES, THE(1960, Brit.), d; WAR BETWEEN MEN AND WOMEN, THE(1972), w

Kent Thurber
PRISONER OF JAPAN(1942)

Debbie Thureson
1984
PREY, THE(1984)

Francoise Thuries
QUESTION, THE(1977, Fr.)

Martin C. Thurley
SECRETS(1971)

Cecille Thurlow
THREE LOVES HAS NANCY(1938)

Gretl Urban Thurlow
Silents
WHEN KNIGHTHOOD WAS IN FLOWER(1922), cos; JANICE MEREDITH(1924), cos

Leavitt Thurlow, Jr.
ROSE BOWL(1936)

Betsy Thurman
GANJA AND HESS(1973)

Beverly Thurman
GIANT GILA MONSTER, THE(1959)

Bill Thurman
HIGH YELLOW(1965); CURSE OF THE SWAMP CREATURE(1966); IN THE YEAR 2889(1966); MARS NEEDS WOMEN(1966); ZONTAR, THE THING FROM VENUS(1966); BULLET FOR PRETTY BOY, A(1970); LAST PICTURE SHOW, THE(1971); GATOR BAIT(1974); SUGARLAND EXPRESS, THE(1974); WHERE THE RED FERN GROWS(1974); CREATURE FROM BLACK LAKE, THE(1976); SLUMBER PARTY '57(1977); CHARGE OF THE MODEL-T'S(1979); EVICTORS, THE(1979); KEEP MY GRAVE OPEN(1980); TOM HORN(1980); RAGGEDY MAN(1981)
1984
PLACES IN THE HEART(1984)

Billy Thurman
IT'S ALIVE(1968)

Diane Thurman
RAVAGER, THE(1970)

Homer Thurman
RUN, ANGEL, RUN(1969)

Lawrence Thurman
FIRST LOVE(1977), p

Mary Thurman
Silents
THIS HERO STUFF(1919); SAND(1920); BROKEN DOLL, A(1921); SIN OF MARTHA QUEED, THE(1921); BRIDE FOR A NIGHT, A(1923); PLAYTHINGS OF DESIRE(1924); DOWN UPON THE SUWANNEE RIVER(1925); NECESSARY EVIL, THE(1925)
Misc. Silents
PRINCE AND BETTY, THE(1919); SPOTLIGHT SADIE(1919); IN THE HEART OF A FOOL(1920); SCOFFER, THE(1920); VALLEY OF TOMORROW, THE(1920); BARE KNUCKLES(1921); LADY FROM LONGACRE, THE(1921); PRIMAL LAW, THE(1921); TENTS OF ALLAH, THE(1923); WIFE IN NAME ONLY(1923); FOR ANOTHER WOMAN(1924); LAW AND THE LADY, THE(1924); LOVE OF WOMEN(1924); THOSE WHO JUDGE(1924); TROUPING WITH ELLEN(1924); TRUTH ABOUT WOMEN, THE(1924); BACK TO LIFE(1925); LITTLE GIRL IN A BIG CITY, A(1925)

Sammy Thurman
IN COLD BLOOD(1967)

Theodora Thurman
JAIL BAIT(1954)

Wallace Thurman
HIGH SCHOOL GIRL(1935), w

Lin Thurmond
SANTA CLAUS CONQUERS THE MARTIANS(1964)

Nate Thurmond
TROIKA(1969)

Alexis Thurn-Taxis
NIGHT FOR CRIME, A(1942), d; YANKS ARE COMING, THE(1942), d; MAN OF COURAGE(1943), d; SLIGHTLY TERRIFIC(1944), p; BOSTON BLACKIE'S RENDEZVOUS(1945), p; GIRL OF THE LIMBERLOST, THE(1945), p; HOLLYWOOD AND VINE(1945), d; PRISON SHIP(1945), p; ROUGH, TOUGH AND READY(1945), p; GENTLEMAN MISBEHAVES, THE(1946), p

Dave Thursby
SMILING IRISH EYES(1929); CAPTAINS COURAGEOUS(1937); LANCER SPY(1937); BULLDOG DRUMMOND'S PERIL(1938); SERGEANT MURPHY(1938); TOWER OF LONDON(1939); INVISIBLE MAN RETURNS, THE(1940); RAGE IN HEAVEN(1941); SCOTLAND YARD(1941); MRS. MINIVER(1942); UNDYING MONSTER, THE(1942); GANGWAY FOR TOMORROW(1943); LODGER, THE(1944); LOCKET, THE(1946); IVY(1947); JULIA MISBEHAVES(1948); SEALED CARGO(1951)

David Thursby
UNTIL THEY SAIL(1957); KEY, THE(1934); CAPTAIN BLOOD(1935); GILDED LILY, THE(1935); MUTINY ON THE BOUNTY(1935); NO MORE LADIES(1935); WEREWOLF OF LONDON, THE(1935); CHARGE OF THE LIGHT BRIGADE, THE(1936); RETURN OF SOPHIE LANG, THE(1936); SAN FRANCISCO(1936); HOUSE OF SECRETS, THE(1937); RAFFLES(1939); SEA HAWK, THE(1940); INTERNATIONAL SQUADRON(1941); STRAWBERRY BLONDE, THE(1941); THEY MET IN BOMBAY(1941); BLACK SWAN, THE(1942); GHOST AND MRS. MUIR, THE(1942); JOURNEY FOR MARGARET(1942); IMMORTAL SERGEANT, THE(1943); THANK YOUR LUCKY STARS(1943); FRENCHMAN'S CREEK(1944); MUSIC IN MANHATTAN(1944); NONE BUT THE LONELY HEART(1944); TONIGHT AND EVERY NIGHT(1945); DEVOTION(1946); MOTHER WORE TIGHTS(1947); HILLS OF HOME(1948); MY OWN TRUE LOVE(1948); THAT WONDERFUL URGE(1948); HEIRESS, THE(1949); ROPE OF SAND(1949); TITANIC(1953); VIRGIN QUEEN, THE(1955); ZERO HOUR!(1957); TWELVE HOURS TO KILL(1960)

Betty Thurston
PRINCESS AND THE PIRATE, THE(1944)

C.E. Thurston
Silents
DOUBLING FOR ROMEO(1921); ROLLING HOME(1926)

Carol Thurston
CONSPIRATORS, THE(1944); STORY OF DR. WASSELL, THE(1944); CHINA SKY(1945); SWAMP FIRE(1946); JEWELS OF BRANDENBURG(1947); LAST ROUNDUP, THE(1947); ROGUES' REGIMENT(1948); APACHE CHIEF(1949); ARCTIC MANHUNT(1949); FLAMING FEATHER(1951); ARCTIC FLIGHT(1952); CONQUEST OF COCHISE(1953); KILLER APE(1953); YUKON VENGEANCE(1954); PEARL OF THE SOUTH PACIFIC(1955); WOMEN OF PITCAIRN ISLAND, THE(1957); THE HYPNOTIC EYE(1960); SHOWDOWN(1963)

Charles Thurston
UNKNOWN VALLEY(1933)
Silents
RIDGEWAY OF MONTANA(1924); IS THAT NICE?(1926); CHASER, THE(1928)

E. Temple Thurston
DISCORD(1933, Brit.), w; ONE PRECIOUS YEAR(1933, Brit.), d&w; CITY OF BEAUTIFUL NONSENSE, THE(1935, Brit.), w; WANDERING JEW, THE(1935, Brit.), w
Silents
GREATEST WISH IN THE WORLD, THE(1918, Brit.), w; GARDEN OF RESURRECTION, THE(1919, Brit.), Guy Newall; NATURE OF THE BEAST, THE(1919, Brit.), w; DAVID AND JONATHAN(1920, Brit.), w; ENCHANTMENT(1920, Brit.), w; MIRAGE, THE(1920, Brit.), w

Ellen Thurston
SCORCHY(1976)
H.M. Thurston
Silents
ANTHING ONCE(1917)
Harry Thurston
AND THEN THERE WERE NONE(1945)
Helen Thurston
PRINCESS AND THE PIRATE, THE(1944); MADAME BOVARY(1949)
Katherine Cecil Thurston
MASQUERADER, THE(1933), w
Robert Thurston
Misc. Silents
STACKED CARDS(1926)
Ted Thurston
LI'L ABNER(1959)
Temple Thurston
SALLY BISHOP(1932, Brit.), w
Thu Thuy
DON'T CRY, IT'S ONLY THUNDER(1982)
F.W. Thwaites
BROKEN MELODY(1938, Aus.), w
Alexander Thynne
BLUE BLOOD(1973, Brit.), d&w
Michael Thys
1984
GODS MUST BE CRAZY, THE(1984, Botswana)
Herman Thyson
RAVAGER, THE(1970), set d
Greta Thyssen
ACCUSED OF MURDER(1956); BUS STOP(1956); BEAST OF BUDAPEST, THE(1958);
TERROR IS A MAN(1959, U.S./Phil.); SHADOWS(1960); THREE BLONDES IN HIS
LIFE(1961); JOURNEY TO THE SEVENTH PLANET(1962, U.S./Swed.); DOUBLE-
BARRELLED DETECTIVE STORY, THE(1965); COTTONPICKIN' CHICKENPICK-
ERS(1967)
Misc. Talkies
CATCH ME IF YOU CAN(1959)
Chin Ti
RETURN OF THE DRAGON(1974, Chin.)
Tiana
KILLER ELITE, THE(1975)
Lou Tiano
WORKING GIRLS, THE(1973)
1984
SPLASH(1984)
Luigi Tiano
CONCRETE JUNGLE, THE(1962, Brit.)
Elena Tiapkina
RAINBOW, THE(1944, USSR)
Patricia Tiara
KITTEN WITH A WHIP(1964)
Lawrence Tibbett
NEW MOON(1930); ROGUE SONG, THE(1930); CUBAN LOVE SONG,THE(1931);
PRODIGAL, THE(1931); METROPOLITAN(1935); UNDER YOUR SPELL(1936);
HOUSE OF STRANGERS(1949)
Lawrence Tibbett, Jr.
EL PASO(1949)
Martha Tibbetts
CEILNG ZERO(1935); SPECIAL AGENT(1935); MEET NERO WOLFE(1936); UN-
KNOWN RANGER, THE(1936); CRIMINALS OF THE AIR(1937); RANGER COUR-
AGE(1937); FEMALE FUGITIVE(1938)
George Tibbles
MUNSTER, GO HOME(1966), w; TAMMY AND THE MILLIONAIRE(1967), w; HOW
TO FRAME A FIGG(1971), w
Casey Tibbs
BRONCO BUSTER(1952); WILD HERITAGE(1958); THUNDER OF DRUMS, A(1961);
TOMBOY AND THE CHAMP(1961); ROUNDERS, THE(1965); JUNIOR BON-
NER(1972); BREAKHEART PASS(1976)
Cleo Tibbs
MONEY TRAP, THE(1966)
Gary Tibbs
BREAKING GLASS(1980, Brit.)
Tibby
FASHIONS OF 1934(1934)
Jerome Tiberghien
RABID(1976, Can.); TOMORROW NEVER COMES(1978, Brit./Can.), stunts; CITY ON
FIRE(1979 Can.); ONE MAN(1979, Can.); OH, HEAVENLY DOG!(1980); HAPPY
BIRTHDAY TO ME(1981); JOY(1983, Fr./Can.)
1984
HOTEL NEW HAMPSHIRE, THE(1984)
Laura Tiberti
LADY WITHOUT CAMELLIAS, THE(1981, Ital.)
Vanda Tibursi
VERY HANDY MAN, A(1966, Fr./Ital.)
Vittorio Tiburz
THEY ALL LAUGHED(1981)
Dave Tice
WINDFLOWERS(1968)
Jan Tice
MIDNIGHT COWBOY(1969); MELINDA(1972)
Stephan Tice
YOU LIGHT UP MY LIFE(1977)
Vera Tichankova
SWEET LIGHT IN A DARK ROOM(1966, Czech.); 90 DEGREES IN THE SHA-
DE(1966, Czech./Brit.)
Leo Tichat
EGON SCHIELE–EXCESS AND PUNISHMENT(1981, Ger.), w

Edna Tichenor
Silents
GOLD DIGGERS, THE(1923); MERRY WIDOW, THE(1925); LONDON AFTER
MIDNIGHT(1927)
Gerard Tichy
FIRE OVER AFRICA(1954, Brit.); EL CID(1961, U.S./Ital.); KING OF KINGS(1961);
HAPPY THIEVES, THE(1962); FACE OF TERROR(1964, Span.); DOCTOR ZHIVA-
GO(1965); GUNMEN OF THE RIO GRANDE(1965, Fr./Ital./Span.); PLACE CALLED
GLORY, A(1966, Span./Ger.); SECRET SEVEN, THE(1966, Ital./Span.); SUPERARGO
VERSUS DIABOLICUS(1966, Ital./Span.); TEXICAN, THE(1966, U.S./Span.); THAT
MAN IN ISTANBUL(1966, Fr./Ital./Span.); SEA PIRATE, THE(1967, Fr./Span./Ital.);
DAY THE HOTLINE GOT HOT, THE(1968, Fr./Span.); HATCHET FOR A HONEY-
MOON(1969, Span./Ital.); LAST DAY OF THE WAR, THE(1969, U.S./Ital./Span.);
THEY CAME TO ROB LAS VEGAS(1969, Fr./Ital./Span./Ger.); MADIGAN'S MIL-
LIONS(1970, Span./Ital); MYSTERIOUS ISLAND OF CAPTAIN NEMO, THE(1973,
Fr./Ital. 87m Span./Cameroon); MONSTER ISLAND(1981, Span./U.S.); PIECES(1983,
Span./Puerto Rico)
Misc. Talkies
BEHIND THE SHUTTERS(1976, Span.)
Jerrard Tickell
ODETTE(1951, Brit.), w; ISLAND RESCUE(1952, Brit.), w; DAY TO REMEMBER,
A(1953, Brit.), w
Phil Ticker
NUDE BOMB, THE(1980), ed
Frank Tickle
BANK MESSENGER MYSTERY, THE(1936, Brit.); TWO ON A DOORSTEP(1936,
Brit.); TWIN FACES(1937, Brit.); LION HAS WINGS, THE(1940, Brit.); ATLANTIC
FERRY(1941, Brit.); FIDDLERS THREE(1944, Brit.); HENRY V(1946, Brit.); ANNA
KARENINA(1948, Brit.); ESCAPE(1948, Brit.); VICE VERSA(1948, Brit.); CHILDREN
OF CHANCE(1949, Brit.); WINSLOW BOY, THE(1950); LONG DARK HALL, THE(1951,
Brit.); BRANDY FOR THE PARSON(1952, Brit.); DEATH OF AN ANGEL(1952, Brit.);
IT STARTED IN PARADISE(1952, Brit.); QUENTIN DURWARD(1955)
Boyston Tickner
GOODBYE MR. CHIPS(1969, U.S./Brit.)
Clive Tickner
ASCENDANCY(1983, Brit.), ph
1984
LAUGHTER HOUSE(1984, Brit.), ph; LOOSE CONNECTIONS(1984, Brit.), ph;
PLOUGHMAN'S LUNCH, THE(1984, Brit.), ph
Royston Tickner
WORK IS A FOUR LETTER WORD(1968, Brit.); KEEP, THE(1983)
Tanya Ticktin
LOCAL HERO(1983, Brit.)
Alcide Tico
ROMAN HOLIDAY(1953)
Rachel Ticotin
FORT APACHE, THE BRONX(1981)
Inga Tidblad
INTERMEZZO(1937, Swed.); FOREIGN INTRIGUE(1956)
Don Tidbury
BELLES OF ST. CLEMENTS, THE(1936, Brit.)
Eldred Tidbury
WAGON WHEELS(1934); RUMBA(1935)
Kerstin Tidelius
ADALEN 31(1969, Swed.); FANNY AND ALEXANDER(1983, Swed./Fr./Ger.)
Selma Tiden
Silents
OLD HOME WEEK(1925)
Monica Tidewell
Misc. Talkies
ASTROLOGER, THE(1979)
E.V. Tidmarsh
IS YOUR HONEYMOON REALLY NECESSARY?(1953, Brit.), w
Ferdinand Tidmarsh
Silents
FORTUNE HUNTER, THE(1914); CLIMBERS, THE(1915)
Misc. Silents
WOLF, THE(1914); WORLD'S GREAT SNARE, THE(1916)
Fred Tidmarsh
Silents
DIMPLES(1916)
Vivian Tidmarsh
CHIPS(1938. Brit.), w
Bob Tidwell
GOOD SAM(1948)
John Tidwell
1984
SIGNAL 7(1984)
Monica Tidwell
NOCTURNA(1979)
Misc. Talkies
ROBIN(1979)
Robert Tidwell
SITTING PRETTY(1948)
Frank Tidy
DUELLISTS, THE(1977, Brit.), ph; LUCKY STAR, THE(1980, Can.), ph; GREY FOX,
THE(1983, Can.), ph; SPACEHUNTER: ADVENTURES IN THE FORBIDDEN ZO-
NE(1983), ph
Ernest Tidyman
FRENCH CONNECTION, THE(1971), w; SHAFT(1971), w; SHAFT'S BIG SCO-
RE(1972), p, w; HIGH PLAINS DRIFTER(1973), w; SHAFT IN AFRICA(1973), w;
REPORT TO THE COMMISSIONER(1975), w; STREET PEOPLE(1976, U.S./Ital.), w;
FORCE OF ONE, A(1979), w
Ludwig Tieck
LEONOR(1977, Fr./Span./Ital.), w
Herbert Tiede
COURT MARTIAL(1962, Ger.); DIE FASTNACHTSBEICHTE(1962, Ger.); FOUN-
TAIN OF LOVE, THE(1968, Aust.)

Trisha Tiedemann
CARNY(1980)
Jakob Tiedtke
LIFE BEGINS ANEW(1938, Ger.)
Silents
ONE ARABIAN NIGHT(1921, Ger.)
Misc. Silents
PIED PIPER OF HAMELIN, THE(1917, Ger.); LITTLE NAPOLEON, THE(1923, Ger.)
Gregory Tiefer
AMSTERDAM KILL, THE(1978, Hong Kong), w
Bill Tiegs
1984
OH GOD! YOU DEVIL(1984), cos
Vick Tiel
WHAT'S NEW, PUSSYCAT?(1965, U.S./Fr.), cos
Vicki Tiel
ONLY GAME IN TOWN, THE(1970), cos; WALKING STICK, THE(1970, Brit.), cos
Vicky Tiel
CANDY(1968, Ital./Fr.), cos; BLUEBEARD(1972), cos
Jean Baptiste Tiemele
PASSENGER, THE(1975, Ital.)
Hans Tiemeyer
SPY IN THE SKY(1958)
Miao Tien
DRAGON INN(1968, Chi.)
Paul Tien
FISTS OF FURY(1973, Chi.)
Tien
Misc. Talkies
KUNG FU HALLOWEEN(1981)
Hsieh Tien-fu
FLYING GUILLOTINE, THE(1975, Chi.)
Juan Garcia Tienda
VIRIDIANA(1962, Mex./Span.)
Vanda Tierendelli
Silents
MAN WORTH WHILE, THE(1921)
Aroldo Tieri
SINGING TAXI DRIVER(1953, Ital.); MAN WHO WAGGED HIS TAIL, THE(1961, Ital./Span.); 00-2 MOST SECRET AGENTS(1965, Ital.)
Lawrence Tiernan
KISS OF DEATH(1947)
Pat Tiernan
WALK ON THE WILD SIDE(1962)
Patricia Tiernan
APACHE WAR SMOKE(1952); BATTLE CIRCUS(1953); DREAM WIFE(1953); SCANDAL AT SCOURIE(1953)
Edward Tierney
HOODLUM, THE(1951)
Gene Tierney
TOYS IN THE ATTIC(1963); HUDSON'S BAY(1940); RETURN OF FRANK JAMES, THE(1940); BELLE STARR(1941); SHANGHAI GESTURE, THE(1941); SUNDOWN(1941); TOBACCO ROAD(1941); CHINA GIRL(1942); GHOST AND MRS. MUIR, THE(1942); RINGS ON HER FINGERS(1942); SON OF FURY(1942); THUNDER BIRDS(1942); HEAVEN CAN WAIT(1943); LAURA(1944); BELL FOR ADANO, A(1945); DRAGONWYCH(1946); LEAVE HER TO HEAVEN(1946); RAZOR'S EDGE, THE(1946); IRON CURTAIN, THE(1948); THAT WONDERFUL URGE(1948); WHIRLPOOL(1949); NIGHT AND THE CITY(1950, Brit.); WHERE THE SIDEWALK ENDS(1950); CLOSE TO MY HEART(1951); MATING SEASON, THE(1951); ON THE RIVERA(1951); SECRET OF CONVICT LAKE, THE(1951); PLYMOUTH ADVENTURE(1952); WAY OF A GAUCHO(1952); NEVER LET ME GO(1953, U.S./Brit.); BLACK WIDOW(1954); EGYPTIAN. THE(1954); PERSONAL AFFAIR(1954, Brit.); LEFT HAND OF GOD, THE(1955); ADVISE AND CONSENT(1962); PLEASURE SEEKERS, THE(1964)
Harry Tierney
RIO RITA(1929), m; DIXIANA(1930), m; ONE BRIEF SUMMER(1971, Brit.), w
Silents
IRENE(1926), m
Joy Tierney
MY FAIR LADY(1964)
Lawrence Tierney
GHOST SHIP, THE(1943); GOVERNMENT GIRL(1943); FALCON OUT WEST, THE(1944); YOUTH RUNS WILD(1944); BACK TO BATAAN(1945); DILLINGER(1945); MAMA LOVES PAPA(1945); THOSE ENDEARING YOUNG CHARMS(1945); BADMAN'S TERRITORY(1946); SAN QUENTIN(1946); STEP BY STEP(1946); BORN TO KILL(1947); DEVIL THUMBS A RIDE, THE(1947); BODYGUARD(1948); KILL OR BE KILLED(1950); SHAKEDOWN(1950); BEST OF THE BADMEN(1951); HOODLUM, THE(1951); BUSHWHACKERS, THE(1952); GREATEST SHOW ON EARTH, THE(1952); STEEL CAGE, THE(1954); FEMALE JUNGLE, THE(1955); SINGING IN THE DARK(1956); CHILD IS WAITING, A(1963); CUSTER OF THE WEST(1968, U.S., Span.); SUCH GOOD FRIENDS(1971); ABDUCTION(1975); KIRLIAN WITNESS, THE(1978); ARTHUR(1981); PROWLER, THE(1981); MIDNIGHT(1983)
Malcolm Tierney
FAMILY LIFE(1971, Brit.); MEDUSA TOUCH, THE(1978, Brit.); MC VICAR(1982, Brit.)
Jonathan Tierston
SLEEPAWAY CAMP(1983)
Richard Tietjen
JOYRIDE(1977)
Augusto Tiezzi
DISHONORED(1950, Ital.), ph; JOURNEY TO LOVE(1953, Ital.), ph; MONSTER OF THE ISLAND(1953, Ital.), ph; PIRATE AND THE SLAVE GIRL, THE(1961, Fr./Ital.), ph; SAMSON AND THE SLAVE QUEEN(1963, Ital.), ph; CONQUEST OF MYCENE(1965, Ital., Fr.), ph; GUILT IS NOT MINE(1968, Ital.), ph
Milan Tiff
PERSONAL BEST(1982)
Lylah Tiffany
ALL THE WAY HOME(1963)

Stanley Tiffany
PLASTIC DOME OF NORMA JEAN, THE(1966)
Trevor Tiffany
PLEDGEMASTERS, THE(1971)
Pamela Tiffin
ONE, TWO, THREE(1961); SUMMER AND SMOKE(1961); STATE FAIR(1962); COME FLY WITH ME(1963); FOR THOSE WHO THINK YOUNG(1964); LIVELY SET, THE(1964); PLEASURE SEEKERS, THE(1964); HALLELUJAH TRAIL, THE(1965); HARPER(1966); KISS THE OTHER SHEIK(1968, Fr./Ital.); VIVA MAX!(1969); DEAF SMITH AND JOHNNY EARS(1973, Ital.)
Misc. Talkies
PRELUDE TO TAURUS(1972); EVIL FINGERS(1975)
Tigano
LAST OF THE VIKINGS, THE(1962, Fr./Ital.), cos
Kenneth Tigar
HAPPY HOOKER, THE(1975)
Tiger
LOVE IN A GOLDFISH BOWL(1961); BOY AND HIS DOG, A(1975)
J. G. Tiger
ROCK BABY, ROCK IT(1957), p
Vernon Tiger
PORKY'S II: THE NEXT DAY(1983)
Gary Tigerman
HELLO DOWN THERE(1969); HALLS OF ANGER(1970); PRETTY MAIDS ALL IN A ROW(1971)
Jacob Tigerskiold
FANNY AND ALEXANDER(1983, Swed./Fr./Ger.), set d
Eileen Tighe
JUNE BRIDE(1948), w
Gertrude Tighe
NO WAY OUT(1950)
Gwynneth Tighe
LADY IS A SQUARE, THE(1959, Brit.)
Harry Tighe
Silents
WIDE-OPEN TOWN, A(1922)
Karen Tighe
DEADLY SPAWN, THE(1983)
Madeleine Tighe
Misc. Silents
POTTERY GIRL'S ROMANCE, A(1918, Brit.)
Tammie M. Tignor
STUDENT BODIES(1981)
Betty Loh Tih
LOVE ETERNE, THE(1964, Hong Kong); ENCHANTING SHADOW, THE(1965, Hong Kong); SONS OF GOOD EARTH(1967, Hong Kong)
David Tihmar
FIREFLY, THE(1937)
Tik
XTRO(1983, Brit.)
Roman Tikhomirov
QUEEN OF SPADES(1961, USSR), d, w; MORNING STAR(1962, USSR), d, w
Vyacheslav Tikhonav
HOUSE ON THE FRONT LINE, THE(1963, USSR)
Nicolai Tikhonov
Misc. Silents
REVOLT IN THE DESERT(1932, USSR), d
Vyacheslav Tikhonov
OPTIMISTIC TRAGEDY, THE(1964, USSR); WAR AND PEACE(1968, USSR)
S. Tikhonravov
CHILDHOOD OF MAXIM GORKY(1938, Russ.); RESURRECTION(1963, USSR)
Roger Til
TWELVE TO THE MOON(1960); VALLEY OF THE DRAGONS(1961); SWEET CHARITY(1969); TOPAZ(1969, Brit.); HARRY AND WALTER GO TO NEW YORK(1976); OTHER SIDE OF MIDNIGHT, THE(1977)
1984
PROTOCOL(1984)
Eldred Tilbury
FATHER BROWN, DETECTIVE(1935)
Jessie Tilbury
Misc. Silents
BLIND MAN'S LUCK(1917)
Peter Tilbury
BREAKING GLASS(1980, Brit.)
Zeffie Tilbury
SHIP FROM SHANGHAI, THE(1930); MYSTERY LINER(1934); ALICE ADAMS(1935); FARMER TAKES A WIFE, THE(1935); LAST DAYS OF POMPEII, THE(1935); MARK OF THE VAMPIRE(1935); MYSTERY OF EDWIN DROOD, THE(1935); PUBLIC HERO NO. 1(1935); STRANDED(1935); WEREWOLF OF LONDON, THE(1935); WOMEN MUST DRESS(1935); AFTER THE THIN MAN(1936); BOHEMIAN GIRL, THE(1936); DESIRE(1936); GIVE ME YOUR HEART(1936); GORGEOUS HUSSY, THE(1936); OLD HUTCH(1936); PAROLE(1936); BULLDOG DRUMMOND COMES BACK(1937); BULLDOG DRUMMOND ESCAPES(1937); FEDERAL BULLETS(1937); IT HAPPENED IN HOLLYWOOD(1937); LIVE, LOVE AND LEARN(1937); MAID OF SALEM(1937); RHYTHM IN THE CLOUDS(1937); UNDER COVER OF NIGHT(1937); BULLDOG DRUMMOND'S PERIL(1938); HUNTED MEN(1938); JOSETTE(1938); MARIE ANTOINETTE(1938); WOMAN AGAINST WOMAN(1938); ARREST BULLDOG DRUMMOND(1939, Brit.); BALALAIKA(1939); BOY TROUBLE(1939); LADY OF THE TROPICS(1939); STORY OF ALEXANDER GRAHAM BELL, THE(1939); TELL NO TALES(1939); COMIN' ROUND THE MOUNTAIN(1940); EARL OF CHICAGO, THE(1940); EMERGENCY SQUAD(1940); GRAPES OF WRATH(1940); SHE COULDN'T SAY NO(1941); SHERIFF OF TOMBSTONE(1941); TOBACCO ROAD(1941)
Silents
AVALANCHE, THE(1919); MARRIAGE OF WILLIAM ASHE, THE(1921); ANOTHER SCANDAL(1924); SINGLE STANDARD, THE(1929)
Beau Tilden
BUTTERFIELD 8(1960)

Fred Tilden
Misc. Silents
SMALL TOWN GUY, THE(1917)
Jane Tilden
EMBEZZLED HEAVEN(1959,Ger.); GOOD SOLDIER SCHWEIK, THE(1963, Ger.)
William T. Tilden
Misc. Silents
HIGHBINDERS, THE(1926)
Scott Tiler
1984
ONCE UPON A TIME IN AMERICA(1984)
Alan Tilern
STICK UP, THE(1978, Brit.)
Lottie Tilford
Misc. Silents
HUMAN PASSIONS(1919)
Walter F. Tilford
THANK YOUR LUCKY STARS(1943), set d; CONSPIRATORS, THE(1944), set d; DESTINATION TOKYO(1944), set d; MASK OF DIMITRIOS, THE(1944), set d; UNCERTAIN GLORY(1944), set d; PILLOW TO POST(1945), set d; CLOAK AND DAGGER(1946), set d; NORA PRENTISS(1947), set d
Bert Dawley Tilford Cinema Studios
Silents
HAS THE WORLD GONE MAD!(1923), ph
Oliver T. Marsh Tilford Cinema Studios
Silents
SCHOOL DAYS(1921), ph; BROADWAY ROSE(1922), ph
Robin Tilghman
HE KNOWS YOU'RE ALONE(1980)
William Tilghman
Misc. Silents
PASSING OF THE OKLAHOMA OUTLAWS, THE(1915), d
Eric Till
GREAT BIG THING, A(1968, U.S./Can.), d; HOT MILLIONS(1968, Brit.), d; WALKING STICK, THE(1970, Brit.), d; FAN'S NOTES, A(1972, Can.), d; ALL THINGS BRIGHT AND BEAUTIFUL(1979, Brit.), d; WILD HORSE HANK(1979, Can.), d; IMPROPER CHANNELS(1981, Can.), d; IF YOU COULD SEE WHAT I HEAR(1982), p, d
Misc. Talkies
BETHUNE(1977), d
Jenny Till
HELP!(1965, Brit.); THEATRE OF DEATH(1967, Brit.); CHALLENGE FOR ROBIN HOOD, A(1968, Brit.); GREAT TRAIN ROBBERY, THE(1979, Brit.)
Tilde Till
TERROR-CREATURES FROM THE GRAVE(1967, U.S./Ital.)
Elfi Tillack
1984
GERMANY PALE MOTHER(1984, Ger.), ed
Jack K. Tillar
1984
MYSTERY MANSION(1984), m
Eris Tillare
SIMON, KING OF THE WITCHES(1971)
Zeffie Tillbury
Misc. Silents
CAMILLE(1921)
Jodie Lynn Tillen
CITIZENS BAND(1977), cos; LOOKING FOR MR. GOODBAR(1977), cos
Jodie Tillen
BEST FRIENDS(1975), art d; LEPKE(1975, U.S./Israel), cos
John Tillenger
DIARY OF A MAD HOUSEWIFE(1970)
Antoin Tiller
Misc. Silents
GOOD AND EVIL(1921)
Luch Tiller
DOC(1971)
Nadja Tiller
SCHLAGER-PARADE(1953); LIFE AND LOVES OF MOZART, THE(1959, Ger.); ROSEMARY(1960, Ger.); NIGHT AFFAIR(1961, Fr.); PORTRAIT OF A SINNER(1961, Brit.); LULU(1962, Aus.); RIFF RAFF GIRLS(1962, Fr./Ital.); WORLD IN MY POCKET, THE(1962, Fr./Ital./Ger.); AND SO TO BED(1965, Ger.); POPPY IS ALSO A FLOWER, THE(1966); TENDER SCOUNDREL(1967, Fr./Ital.); UPPER HAND, THE(1967, Fr./Ital./Ger.); TONIO KROGER(1968, Fr./Ger.); LADY HAMILTON(1969, Ger./Ital./Fr.); DEAD ARE ALIVE, THE(1972, Yugo./Ger./Ital.)
Tiller Girls
Silents
ARCADIANS, THE(1927, Brit.)
The Tiller Sunshine Girls
HALF SHOT AT SUNRISE(1930)
Mangan Tillerettes
JUST FOR A SONG(1930, Brit.)
Gary Tilles
STACY'S KNIGHTS(1983)
Ken Tilles
DREAMS OF GLASS(1969)
Paul Tillett
ROMANCE IN RHYTHM(1934, Brit.)
Brick Tilley
OSTERMAN WEEKEND, THE(1983)
Colin Tilley
NED KELLY(1970, Brit.)
David Tilley
CIRCUS FRIENDS(1962, Brit.)
Frank A. Tilley
Misc. Silents
VENETIAN LOVERS(1925, Brit.), d

Katie Tilley
NIGHT OF THE STRANGLER(1975)
Patric Tilley
LEGACY, THE(1979, Brit.), w
Patrick Tilley
WUTHERING HEIGHTS(1970, Brit.), w; PEOPLE THAT TIME FORGOT, THE(1977, Brit.), w
Sherri Tilley
MACHISMO–40 GRAVES FOR 40 GUNS(1970), cos
Vesta Tilley
Silents
GIRL WHO LOVES A SOLDIER, THE(1916, Brit.)
John Tillinger
RESURRECTION(1980); LITTLE SEX, A(1982); LOVESICK(1983)
Mel Tillis
COTTONPICKIN' CHICKENPICKERS(1967); W. W. AND THE DIXIE DANCEKINGS(1975); VILLAIN, THE(1979); SMOKEY AND THE BANDIT II(1980); CANNONBALL RUN, THE(1981)
1984
CANNONBALL RUN II(1984)
A.C. Tillman
ALL THE KING'S MEN(1949)
Edwin Tillman
NAVY VS. THE NIGHT MONSTERS, THE(1966), spec eff
Fritz Tillman
CONFESS DR. CORDA(1960, Ger.); MONSTER OF LONDON CITY, THE(1967, Ger.)
Harrell Tillman
Misc. Talkies
FIGHT NEVER ENDS, THE(1947)
Hazel Tillman
Misc. Talkies
THAT MAN OF MINE(1947)
Luke Tillman
PUFNSTUF(1970), spec eff
Fritz Tillmann
KING IN SHADOW(1961, Ger.); DIE GANS VON SEDAN(1962, Fr/Ger.)
David Leo Tillotson
THEY JUST HAD TO GET MARRIED(1933); LAST GANGSTER, THE(1937)
David Tillotson
SUSAN AND GOD(1940); 'TIL WE MEET AGAIN(1940)
Johnny Tillotson
JUST FOR FUN(1963, Brit.); FAT SPY(1966)
Grant Tilly
SKIN DEEP(1978, New Zealand); MIDDLE AGE SPREAD(1979, New Zealand); BEYOND REASONABLE DOUBT(1980, New Zeal.); NATE AND HAYES(1983, U.S./New Zealand)
1984
TREASURE OF THE YANKEE ZEPHYR(1984)
Jennifer Tilly
1984
NO SMALL AFFAIR(1984)
Meg Tilly
TEX(1982); BIG CHILL, THE(1983); ONE DARK NIGHT(1983); PSYCHO II(1983)
1984
IMPULSE(1984)
Frank Tilsley
DAMN THE DEFIANT!(1962, Brit.), w
Reg Tilsley
WHAT'S GOOD FOR THE GOOSE(1969, Brit.), m; HORROR HOUSE(1970, Brit.), m
C. Tilson-Chowne
Silents
GAME OF LIFE, THE(1922, Brit.)
Misc. Silents
FOUR JUST MEN, THE(1921, Brit.)
Charles Tilson-Chowne
Misc. Silents
MARRIAGE LINES, THE(1921, Brit.)
Zeffie Tiltbury
CHARLIE CHAN CARRIES ON(1931)
Bill Tilton
LOOSE ENDS(1975)
Charlene Tilton
FREAKY FRIDAY(1976); FALL OF THE HOUSE OF USHER, THE(1980)
Connie Tilton
GORGO(1961, Brit.); WHEN DINOSAURS RULED THE EARTH(1971, Brit.)
E.B. Tilton
Misc. Silents
CUPID'S ROUND-UP(1918); SHUTTLE, THE(1918); WEB OF CHANCE, THE(1919)
Edward Tilton
Silents
MIDNIGHT ROMANCE, A(1919)
Edwin B. Tilton
Silents
FAITH(1920); HUNGRY HEARTS(1922)
Misc. Silents
UNDER THE YOKE(1918); MERRY-GO ROUND, THE(1919); CURTAIN(1920); BUCKING THE LINE(1921); LOVETIME(1921); WINNING WITH WITS(1922)
Edwin Booth Tilton
Silents
SPLENDID SIN, THE(1919); CHILDREN OF THE NIGHT(1921); LAMPLIGHTER, THE(1921); CUB REPORTER, THE(1922); GLEAM O'DAWN(1922); HOUSE OF YOUTH, THE(1924); MIDNIGHT EXPRESS, THE(1924); RACING FOR LIFE(1924)
Misc. Silents
IRON HEART, THE(1920); LITTLE WANDERER, THE(1920); LOVE'S HARVEST(1920); MOTHER HEART, THE(1921); WHILE THE DEVIL LAUGHS(1921); THUNDERGATE(1923); LONE CHANCE, THE(1924); TAMING OF THE WEST, THE(1925)

Francis Tilton
TOAST OF NEW YORK, THE(1937)
Francis Palmer Tilton
EASIEST WAY, THE(1931); DARK ANGEL, THE(1935)
Frank Tilton
LOVE UP THE POLE(1936, Brit.); SONG OF THE FORGE(1937, Brit.)
George Tilton
SOLDIERS AND WOMEN(1930), w
James Tilton
DEAR, DEAD DELILAH(1972), art d
Capt. James A. Tilton
Silents
DOWN TO THE SEA IN SHIPS(1923)
Martha Tilton
IRENE(1940); SUNNY(1941); YOU'LL NEVER GET RICH(1941); STRICTLY IN THE GROOVE(1942); SWING HOSTESS(1944); CRIME, INC.(1945); BENNY GOODMAN STORY, THE(1956)
Alan Tilvern
HIDEOUT(1948, Brit.); KNIGHTS OF THE ROUND TABLE(1953); MASTER PLAN, THE(1955, Brit.); BHOWANI JUNCTION(1956); TRIPLE DECEPTION(1957, Brit.); CHASE A CROOKED SHADOW(1958, Brit.); TANK FORCE(1958, Brit.); DESERT MICE(1960, Brit.); FOUR DESPERATE MEN(1960, Brit.); SANDS OF THE DESERT(1960, Brit.); DANGER BY MY SIDE(1962, Brit.); SHADOW OF FEAR(1963, Brit.); KHARTOUM(1966, Brit.); RASPUTIN–THE MAD MONK(1966, Brit.); FROZEN DEAD, THE(1967, Brit.); MALPAS MYSTERY, THE(1967, Brit.); REVOLUTIONARY, THE(1970, Brit.); LOVE AND DEATH(1975); SUPERMAN(1978); MEETINGS WITH REMARKABLE MEN(1979, Brit.); FIREFOX(1982)
1984
1919(1984, Brit.)
Tany Tim
CROCODILE(1979, Thai./Hong Kong)
Jacob Timan
DREAMER, THE(1970, Israel)
John Timanus
LOVE BUG, THE(1968)
Stephen Timar
MASK, THE(1961, Can.), ed
Anders Timberg
2,000 WOMEN(1944, Brit.); ECHO MURDERS, THE(1945, Brit.); TROJAN BROTHERS, THE(1946)
Dee Timberlake
WHO KILLED MARY WHAT'SER NAME?(1971); UP THE SANDBOX(1972)
Charles Timblin
LARCENY ON THE AIR(1937); MOUNTAIN MUSIC(1937)
Tiny Timbrell
WHEN MY BABY SMILES AT ME(1948); YOU WERE MEANT FOR ME(1948); LOVE THAT BRUTE(1950)
N. Timchenko
1812(1944, USSR)
Paul Timcho
NO RETURN ADDRESS(1961)
Tom Timcho
1984
RECKLESS(1984)
Evelyn Times
Silents
DAUGHTER PAYS, THE(1920)
Jim Timiaough
SAVAGE WILD, THE(1970)
Johnny Timko
PROPHECY(1979)
1984
HOT MOVES(1984)
Bruno Timm
STORM IN A WATER GLASS(1931, Aust.), ph
Reinhold Timm
NEW LIFE STYLE, THE(1970, Ger.)
Y. Timme
Misc. Silents
COWARD, THE(1914, USSR)
Chad Timmermans
BLUE LAGOON, THE(1980)
Cali Timmins
SPACEHUNTER: ADVENTURES IN THE FORBIDDEN ZONE(1983)
1984
HOTEL NEW HAMPSHIRE, THE(1984)
Cori Timmons
HAPPY BIRTHDAY TO ME(1981)
Lee Timmons
SWEET SURRENDER(1935)
Misc. Silents
MASKED LOVER, THE(1928)
Sally Timmons
DRUMS O' VOODOO(1934)
E. Timms
UNCIVILISED(1937, Aus.), w
Stanley Timms
WARRIORS, THE(1979)
Walter Timms
Misc. Silents
LITTLE CHILD SHALL LEAD THEM, A(1919, Brit.)
N. Timofeev
DREAM COME TRUE, A(1963, USSR)
Nikolai Timofeev
CHEREZ TERNII K SVEZDAM(1981 USSR)
Nikolay Timofeyev
LULLABY(1961, USSR); PEACE TO HIM WHO ENTERS(1963, USSR); TSAR'S BRIDE, THE(1966, USSR)

M. Timofeyeva
CLEAR SKIES(1963, USSR), ed
S.D. Timokhin
HEROES OF THE SEA(1941)
A. Timontayev
ON HIS OWN(1939, USSR); GORDEYEV FAMILY, THE(1961, U.S.S.R.); JACK FROST(1966, USSR)
Semen Timoshenko
ISLAND OF DOOM(1933, USSR), d&w
A. Timotayev
DIARY OF A REVOLUTIONIST(1932, USSR)
Andrew Timothy
DOWN AMONG THE Z MEN(1952, Brit.)
Christopher Timothy
OTHELLO(1965, Brit.); HERE WE GO ROUND THE MULBERRY BUSH(1968, Brit.); ALFRED THE GREAT(1969, Brit.); SPRING AND PORT WINE(1970, Brit.); VIRGIN SOLDIERS, THE(1970, Brit.)
Megan Timothy
GOOD MORNING... AND GOODBYE(1967); HELL'S CHOSEN FEW(1968); MIGHTY GORGA, THE(1969)
Theodore W. Timreck
GOOD DISSONANCE LIKE A MAN, A(1977), p&d
Kosta Timvios
DAY THE FISH CAME OUT, THE(1967. Brit./Gr.)
Lee Tin
MERRY WIDOW, THE(1934)
My Tin
YANK IN VIET-NAM, A(1964)
Tin Pan Alley Trio
AROUND THE TOWN(1938, Brit.)
Frank Tinajero
ONE MILLION B.C.(1940)
Daniel Tinayre
GAMES MEN PLAY, THE(1968, Arg.), d
Fay Tincher
Silents
BATTLE OF THE SEXES, THE(1914); HOME SWEET HOME(1914); EXCITEMENT(1924)
Misc. Silents
DON QUIXOTE(1916); MR. GOODE, THE SAMARITAN(1916); SUNSHINE DAD(1916)
Pam Tindal
NIGHT IN HEAVEN, A(1983)
Hilary Tindall
TOP FLOOR GIRL(1959, Brit.)
Loren Tindall
SHE'S A SWEETHEART(1944); GIRL OF THE LIMBERLOST, THE(1945); OVER 21(1945); POWER OF THE WHISTLER, THE(1945); ROUGH, TOUGH AND READY(1945); SERGEANT MIKE(1945); GALLANT JOURNEY(1946); MEET ME ON BROADWAY(1946); OUT OF THE DEPTHS(1946); TILL THE END OF TIME(1946); GOOD NEWS(1947); FRANCIS(1949); MISS GRANT TAKES RICHMOND(1949)
Marilyn Tindall
SILENCERS, THE(; MURDERERS' ROW(1966)
Tom Tiner
MISSOURI TRAVELER, THE(1958); YOUNG LAND, THE(1959)
Dennis Tinerino
HERCULES IN NEW YORK(1970)
Guy Tiney
Silents
AFRAID TO FIGHT(1922)
Li Ting
GRAND SUBSTITUTION, THE(1965, Hong Kong); SHEPHERD GIRL, THE(1965, Hong Kong)
Kuo Ting-Hung
TRIPLE IRONS(1973, Hong Kong), ed
Cynthia Tingey
GENGHIS KHAN(U.S./Brit./Ger./Yugo), cos; PORTRAIT IN SMOKE(1957, Brit.), cos; DOUBLE BUNK(1961, Brit.), cos; SWINGER'S PARADISE(1965, Brit.), cos; DEADLY AFFAIR, THE(1967, Brit.), cos; SALT & PEPPER(1968, Brit.), cos; SHALAKO(1968, Brit.), cos; WHERE'S JACK?(1969, Brit.), cos; SINBAD AND THE EYE OF THE TIGER(1977, U.S./Brit.), cos
Faith Tingle
1984
SCRUBBERS(1984, Brit.)
Sig Tinglof
BAKER'S HAWK(1976), set d; JUST YOU AND ME, KID(1979), art d
Charles "Bud" Tingwell
ALWAYS ANOTHER DAWN(1948, Aus.); BITTER SPRINGS(1950, Aus.); INTO THE STRAIGHT(1950, Aus.); KANGAROO(1952); DESERT RATS, THE(1953); KING OF THE CORAL SEA(1956, Aus.); SHIRALEE, THE(1957, Brit.); SMILEY(1957, Brit.); BOBBIKINS(1959, Brit.); LIFE IN EMERGENCY WARD 10(1959, Brit.); TARZAN THE MAGNIFICENT(1960, Brit.); MURDER SHE SAID(1961, Brit.); TROUBLE IN THE SKY(1961, Brit.); MURDER AT THE GALLOP(1963, Brit.); MURDER AHOY(1964, Brit.); MURDER MOST FOUL(1964, Brit.); SECRET OF BLOOD ISLAND, THE(1965, Brit.); DRACULA–PRINCE OF DARKNESS(1966, Brit.); HIGH COMMISSIONER, THE(1968, U.S./Brit.); THUNDERBIRDS ARE GO(1968, Brit.); PETERSEN(1974, Aus.); END PLAY(1975, Aus.); ELIZA FRASER(1976, Aus.); SUMMERFIELD(1977, Aus.); MONEY MOVERS(1978, Aus.); BREAKER MORANT(1980, Aus.); PUBERTY BLUES(1983, Aus.)
Misc. Talkies
GONE TO GROUND(1976)
Virginia Tingwell
DEVIL'S WIDOW, THE(1972, Brit.)
Cynthia Tingye
FINDERS KEEPERS(1966, Brit.), cos
Tommy Tinirau
SLEEPING DOGS(1977, New Zealand)

James S. Tinling
SECOND CHANCE(1947), d
James Tinling
WORDS AND MUSIC(1929), d, d; FOR THE LOVE O'LIL(1930), d; FLOOD, THE(1931), d; ARIZONA TO BROADWAY(1933), d; JIMMY AND SALLY(1933), d; CALL IT LUCK(1934), d; LAST TRAIL, THE(1934), d; LOVE TIME(1934), d; THREE ON A HONEYMOON(1934), d; CHARLIE CHAN IN SHANGHAI(1935), d; SENORA CASADA NECEISITA MARIDO(1935), d; UNDER THE PAMPAS MOON(1935), d; WELCOME HOME(1935), d; YOUR UNCLE DUDLEY(1935), d; BACK TO NATU-RE(1936), d; CHAMPAGNE CHARLIE(1936), d; EDUCATING FATHER(1936), d; EV-ERY SATURDAY NIGHT(1936), d; PEPPER(1936), d; ANGEL'S HOLIDAY(1937), d; GREAT HOSPITAL MYSTERY, THE(1937), d; HOLY TERROR, THE(1937), d; SING AND BE HAPPY(1937), d; 45 FATHERS(1937), d; CHANGE OF HEART(1938), d; MR. MOTO'S GAMBLE(1938), d; PASSPORT HUSBAND(1938), d; SHARPSHOOT-ERS(1938), d; BOY FRIEND(1939), d; LAST OF THE DUANES(1941), d; RIDERS OF THE PURPLE SAGE(1941), d; LONE STAR RANGER(1942), d; SUNDOWN JIM(1942), d; DANGEROUS MILLIONS(1946), d; DEADLINE FOR MURDER(1946), d; RENDEZVOUS 24(1946), d; STRANGE JOURNEY(1946), d; ROSES ARE RED(1947), d; NIGHT WIND(1948), d; TROUBLE PREFERRED(1949), d; TALES OF ROBIN HOOD(1951), d
Misc. Talkies
COSMO JONES, CRIME SMASHER(1943), d
Silents
DON'T MARRY(1928), d; EXALTED FLAPPER, THE(1929), d
Misc. Silents
VERY CONFIDENTIAL(1927), d; SOFT LIVING(1928), d; TRUE HEAVEN(1929), d
John A. Tinn
MARK OF THE HAWK, THE(1958); WINDOM'S WAY(1958, Brit.); 55 DAYS AT PEKING(1963); REVENGE OF THE PINK PANTHER(1978)
John Tinn
PURPLE PLAIN, THE(1954, Brit.); WOMAN EATER, THE(1959, Brit.)
Lee Tinn
MAN FROM NEW MEXICO, THE(1932)
Alex Tinne
HANG YOUR HAT ON THE WIND(1969); SCANDALOUS JOHN(1971); HERO-ES(1977); HERBIE GOES BANANAS(1980)
Cal Tinney
MISSOURI TRAVELER, THE(1958)
Clark Tinney
Misc. Talkies
NAUGHTY NYMPHS(1974)
Claus Tinney
TERROR OF DR. MABUSE, THE(1965, Ger.)
Frank Tinney
Silents
GOVERNOR'S BOSS, THE(1915); BROADWAY AFTER DARK(1924)
Eva Tinschmann
FINAL CHORD, THE(1936, Ger.)
Denis Tinsley
HOUSE OF WHIPCORD(1974, Brit.)
Louis Tinsley
MAN WHO WON, THE(1933, Brit.)
Louise Tinsley
CAPTIVATION(1931, Brit)
Theodore Tinsley
MANHATTAN SHAKEDOWN(1939), w
Theordore A. Tinsley
MURDER IS NEWS(1939), w
Francine Tint
DEATH PLAY(1976), cos
Gabriele Tinti
ESTHER AND THE KING(1960, U.S./Ital.); HEAVEN ON EARTH(1960, Ital./U.S.); DAVID AND GOLIATH(1961, Ital.); LOST SOULS(1961, Ital.); SODOM AND GOMOR-RAH(1962, U.S./Fr./Ital.); TORPEDO BAY(1964, Ital./Fr.); FLIGHT OF THE PHO-ENIX, THE(1965); GENDARME OF ST. TROPEZ, THE(1966, Fr./Ital.); JOURNEY BENEATH THE DESERT(1967, Fr./Ital.); LEGEND OF LYLAH CLARE, THE(1968); OLDEST PROFESSION, THE(1968, Fr./Ital./Ger.); WILD EYE, THE(1968, Ital.); SEVEN GOLDEN MEN(1969, Fr./Ital./Span.); CANNON FOR CORDOBA(1970); DEATH TOOK PLACE LAST NIGHT(1970, Ital./Ger.); RIDER ON THE RAIN(1970, Fr./Ital.); DELUSIONS OF GRANDEUR(1971 Fr.); MYSTERIOUS ISLAND OF CAP-TAIN NEMO, THE(1973, Fr./Ital. 87m Span./Cameroon); AND NOW MY LOVE(1975, Fr.); CHILDREN OF RAGE(1975, Brit.-Israeli); HOUSE OF EXORCISM, THE(1976, Ital.); TORMENTED, THE(1978, Ital.)
1984
CAGED WOMEN(1984, Ital./Fr.)
Alberto Tintini
HOUSE OF EXORCISM, THE(1976, Ital.), w
David Tintle
JAWS II(1978)
Peter Tinturin
CARSON CITY KID(1940), m
Tiny Tim
ONE-TRICK PONY(1980)
Dimitri Tiomkin
ROGUE SONG, THE(1930), m; RESURRECTION(1931), m; I LIVE MY LIFE(1935), m; MAD LOVE(1935), m; LOST HORIZON(1937), m; ROAD BACK,THE(1937), m; SPAWN OF THE NORTH(1938), m; YOU CAN'T TAKE IT WITH YOU(1938), m; MR. SMITH GOES TO WASHINGTON(1939), m; ONLY ANGELS HAVE WINGS(1939), m; LUCKY PARTNERS(1940), m; WESTERNER, THE(1940), m; FORCED LAND-ING(1941), md; MEET JOHN DOE(1941), m; GENTLEMAN AFTER DARK, A(1942), m; TWIN BEDS(1942), m; SHADOW OF A DOUBT(1943), m; UNKNOWN GUEST, THE(1943), m; IMPOSTER, THE(1944), m&md; WHEN STRANGERS MARRY(1944), m; DILLINGER(1945), m; DUEL IN THE SUN(1946), m, md; WHISTLE STOP(1946), m, md; DUDE GOES WEST, THE(1948), m, md; RED RIVER(1948), m; SO THIS IS NEW YORK(1948), m; TARZAN AND THE MERMAIDS(1948), m, md; CANADIAN PACIFIC(1949), m; CHAMPION(1949), m; PORTRAIT OF JENNIE(1949), m, md; RED LIGHT(1949), m; CHAMPAGNE FOR CAESAR(1950), m; CYRANO DE BER-GERAC(1950), m; GUILTY BYSTANDER(1950), m; MEN, THE(1950), m, md; DRUMS IN THE DEEP SOUTH(1951), m; MR. UNIVERSE(1951), m, md; PEKING EX-PRESS(1951), m; STRANGERS ON A TRAIN(1951), m; THING, THE(1951), m, md;

WELL, THE(1951), m; LADY IN THE IRON MASK(1952), m; MUTINY(1952), m, md; MY SIX CONVICTS(1952), m; STEEL TRAP, THE(1952), m, md; I CONFESS(1953), m; JEOPARDY(1953), md; RETURN TO PARADISE(1953), m; TAKE THE HIGH GROUND(1953), m; COMMAND, THE(1954), m; DIAL M FOR MURDER(1954), m; COURT-MARTIAL OF BILLY MITCHELL, THE(1955), m; LAND OF THE PHA-RAOHS(1955), m; TENSION AT TABLE ROCK(1956), m, md; NIGHT PASS-AGE(1957), m; WILD IS THE WIND(1957), m; OLD MAN AND THE SEA, THE(1958), m, md; LAST TRAIN FROM GUN HILL(1959), m, md; RIO BRAVO(1959), m, md; YOUNG LAND, THE(1959), m&md; SUNDOWNERS, THE(1960), m; UNFOR-GIVEN, THE(1960), m, md; TOWN WITHOUT PITY(1961, Ger./Switz./U.S.), m; WITHOUT EACH OTHER(1962), m; 55 DAYS AT PEKING(1963), m, md; FALL OF THE ROMAN EMPIRE, THE(1964), m; 36 HOURS(1965), m; WAR WAGON, THE(1967), m; MACKENNA'S GOLD(1969), p
Dmitri Tiomkin
ALICE IN WONDERLAND(1933), m; GREAT WALTZ, THE(1938), m; FLYING BLIND(1941), m; MOON AND SIXPENCE, THE(1942), m; BRIDGE OF SAN LUIS REY, THE(1944), md; PARDON MY PAST(1945), m, md; ANGEL ON MY SHOUL-DER(1946), m; BLACK BEAUTY(1946), m; DARK MIRROR, THE(1946), m; IT'S A WONDERFUL LIFE(1946), m, md; LONG NIGHT, THE(1947), m, md; HOME OF THE BRAVE(1949), m, md; DAKOTA LIL(1950), m; D.O.A.(1950), m; BIG SKY, THE(1952), m; BUGLES IN THE AFTERNOON(1952), m; FOUR POSTER, THE(1952), m, md; HAPPY TIME, THE(1952), m; HIGH NOON(1952), m; ANGEL FACE(1953), m; BLOWING WILD(1953), m; HIS MAJESTY O'KEEFE(1953), m, md; ADVENTURES OF HAJJI BABA(1954), m; BULLET IS WAITING, A(1954), m; HIGH AND THE MIGHTY, THE(1954), m; STRANGE LADY IN TOWN(1955), m; FRIENDLY PERSUA-SION(1956), m; GIANT(1956), m, md; ALAMO, THE(1960), m; GUNS OF NAVA-RONE, THE(1961), m, md; GREAT CATHERINE(1968, Brit.), m
Dimitri Tiornkin
CIRCUS WORLD(1964), m
Tip, Tap and Toe
YOU CAN'T HAVE EVERYTHING(1937); ALL BY MYSELF(1943); HONEYMOON LODGE(1943); HI, GOOD-LOOKIN'(1944)
Bernard Tiphaine
DEAD RUN(1961, Fr./Ital./Ger.); FIRE WITHIN, THE(1964, Fr./Ital.)
Tipica Orchestra
SONG OF MEXICO(1945)
Lee Tiplitsky
HAWMPS!(1976)
Clark Tippet
TURNING POINT, THE(1977)
Jimmy Tippet
1984
NUMBER ONE(1984, Brit.)
Philip Tippet
STAR WARS(1977), anim
Phil Tippett
RETURN OF THE JEDI(1983), spec eff
Reginald Tippett
INQUEST(1931, Brit.)
Wayne Tippett
TELL ME THAT YOU LOVE ME, JUNIE MOON(1970); TAPS(1981)
Corey Tippin
L'AMOUR(1973)
Brian Tipping
KING AND COUNTRY(1964, Brit.); OH! WHAT A LOVELY WAR(1969, Brit.); DAVID COPPERFIELD(1970, Brit.); ROUGH CUT(1980, Brit.)
Richard Tipping
Misc. Talkies
SWEET DREAMERS(1981)
Tania Tipping
WOMAN IN THE HALL, THE(1949, Brit.)
Sherill Tippins
RENT CONTROL(1981), w
Wayne Tippit
PIPE DREAMS(1976); ROLLERCOASTER(1977)
Patti Tippo
10 TO MIDNIGHT(1983)
George Aliceson Tipton
PHANTOM OF THE PARADISE(1974), m
George Tipton
SKIDOO(1968), md; BADLANDS(1974), m
Henri Tiquet
COUNTERFEIT CONSTABLE, THE(1966, Fr.), ph
Romualdo Tirado
TEXAN, THE(1930); SENORA CASADA NECEISITA MARIDO(1935); STORM OVER THE ANDES(1935)
Ann Tirard
STOP ME BEFORE I KILL!(1961, Brit.); FROZEN DEAD, THE(1967, Brit.); CON-QUEROR WORM, THE(1968, Brit.); PERFECT FRIDAY(1970, Brit.); MEMOIRS OF A SURVIVOR(1981, Brit.); MOONLIGHTING(1982, Brit.)
Eduardo Tirella
DON'T MAKE WAVES(1967)
Jaime Tirelli
MARATHON MAN(1976); FORT APACHE, THE BRONX(1981); AUTHOR! AU-THOR!(1982); SOUP FOR ONE(1982)
1984
BROTHER FROM ANOTHER PLANET, THE(1984)
Theresa Tirelli
GODFATHER, THE, PART II(1974)
Tirentev
AMPHIBIOUS MAN, THE(1961, USSR), m
Ion Tiriac
PLAYERS(1979)
Anthony Tirico
WANDERERS, THE(1979)
George Tirl
1984
ELLIE(1984), ph; INITIATION, THE(1984), ph; NOT FOR PUBLICATION(1984), ph

Bogdan Tirnanic
EARLY WORKS(1970, Yugo.)
James Tiroff
Misc. Talkies
BRIG, THE(1965)
Saggitario Tirso
ALL THE OTHER GIRLS DO!(1967, Ital.), p
Kostia Tirtov
BALLAD OF COSSACK GLOOTA(1938, USSR)
Steve Tisch
OUTLAW BLUES(1977), p; RISKY BUSINESS(1983), p
Bernd Tischer
YOUNG TORLESS(1968, Fr./Ger.)
Bill Tischer
SCARLET HOUR, THE(1956)
Stanford Tischler
BIGAMIST,THE(1953), ed; PRIVATE HELL 36(1954), ed; CASE OF PATTY SMITH, THE(1962), ed
John Tisdale
THINGS ARE TOUGH ALL OVER(1982)
Comdr. M.S. Tisdale, U.S.N.
SHIPMATES FOREVER(1935), tech adv
Billy Tisdall
MAD MAX(1979, Aus.)
Steve Tish
COAST TO COAST(1980), p
Tuvia Tishler
RABBI AND THE SHIKSE, THE(1976, Israel)
T. Tishura
WHEN THE TREES WERE TALL(1965, USSR)
Henri Tisot
WOULD-BE GENTLEMAN, THE(1960, Fr.); DEVIL AND THE TEN COMMAND-MENTS, THE(1962, Fr.); TALES OF PARIS(1962, Fr./Ital.); LAFAYETTE(1963, Fr.); MARRIAGE OF FIGARO, THE(1963, Fr.)
Edouard Tisse
MAN OF MUSIC(1953, USSR), ph; SILVER DUST(1953, USSR), ph
Eduard Tisse
Silents
TEN DAYS THAT SHOOK THE WORLD(1927, USSR), a, ph
Edward Tisse
IVAN THE TERRIBLE(Part I, 1947, USSR), ph; ALEXANDER NEVSKY(1939), ph; IMMORTAL GARRISON, THE(1957, USSR), d, ph
Silents
BATTLESHIP POTEMKIN, THE(1925, USSR), ph
K. Tisse
SEEDS OF FREEDOM(1943, USSR), ph
Berthe Tissen
LADY CHATTERLEY'S LOVER(1959, Fr.)
Alain Tissier
OLD SHATTERHAND(1968, Ger./Yugo./Fr./Ital.)
Barbara Tissier
PASSION(1983, Fr./Switz.)
Jean Tissier
SLIPPER EPISODE, THE(1938, Fr); WHIRLWIND OF PARIS(1946, Fr.); HER FIRST AFFAIR(1947, Fr.); MURDERER LIVES AT NUMBER 21, THE(1947, Fr.); STRAN-GERS IN THE HOUSE(1949, Fr.); DANGER IS A WOMAN(1952, Fr.); FATHER'S DILEMMA(1952, Ital.); FRENCH WAY, THE(1952, Fr.); JUPITER(1952, Fr.); MESSA-LINE(1952, Fr./Ital.); AFFAIRS OF MESSALINA, THE(1954, Ital.); SPICE OF LI-FE(1954, Fr.); IF PARIS WERE TOLD TO US(1956, Fr.); AND GOD CREATED WOMAN(1957, Fr.); HUNCHBACK OF NOTRE DAME, THE(1957, Fr.); ROYAL AFFAIRS IN VERSAILLES(1957, Fr.); MARIE OF THE ISLES(1960, Fr.); DEAD RUN(1961, Fr./Ital./Ger.); MAIDEN, THE(1961, Fr.); PALACE OF NUDES(1961, Fr./Ital.); CANDIDE(1962, Fr./Ital.); PLEASE, NOT NOW!(1963, Fr./Ital.); SWEET SKIN(1965, Fr./Ital.); THANK HEAVEN FOR SMALL FAVORS(1965, Fr./Ital.); WHITE VOICES(1965, Fr./Ital.)
J. Tissler
CROSSROADS(1938, Fr.)
Jean Tissler
COURIER OF LYONS(1938, Fr.)
Alice Tissot
LA MATERNELLE(1933, Fr.); GLORY OF FAITH, THE(1938, Fr.); GATES OF PARIS(1958, Fr./Ital.); LONGEST DAY, THE(1962)
Silents
ITALIAN STRAW HAT, AN(1927, Fr.)
Henri Tissot
CHARLES AND LUCIE(1982, Fr.)
Tisui
BRUCE LEE–TRUE STORY(1976, Chi.)
Karl-Heinz Titelbach
TIN DRUM, THE(1979, Ger./Fr./Yugo./Pol.)
Dion Titheradge
HER FIRST AFFAIRE(1932, Brit.), w; SHADOW BETWEEN, THE(1932, Brit.), w; FORTUNATE FOOL, THE(1933, Brit.), w; MAN WHO WON, THE(1933, Brit.), w; DANGEROUS GROUND(1934, Brit.), w; LILIES OF THE FIELD(1934, Brit.), w
Silents
CRIMSON DOVE, THE(1917); HER STORY(1920, Brit.), w
Misc. Silents
SUNSHINE ALLEY(1917)
Madge Titheradge
Silents
DAVID AND JONATHAN(1920, Brit.); HER STORY(1920, Brit.)
Misc. Silents
BRIGADIER GERARD(1915, Brit.); FAIR IMPOSTER, A(1916, Brit.); WOMAN WHO WAS NOTHING, THE(1917, Brit.); GAMBLERS ALL(1919, Brit.); HUSBAND HUNT-ER, THE(1920, Brit.); LOVE IN THE WILDERNESS(1920, Brit.); TEMPORARY GENTLEMAN, A(1920, Brit.); HER STORY(1922)
Dion Titherage
CROOKED BILLET, THE(1930, Brit.), w; LOOSE ENDS(1930, Brit.), w; FIRES OF FATE(1932, Brit.), w

Madge Titherage
Misc. Silents
GOD BLESS OUR RED, WHITE AND BLUE(1918, Brit.)
Franco Titi
WHITE SHEIK, THE(1956, Ital.), makeup
Pacific Title
HOW SWEET IT IS(1968), spec eff
Phylis Titmuss
Misc. Silents
BELOVED VAGABOND, THE(1923, Brit.)
Phyllis Titmuss
Misc. Silents
RECOIL, THE(1922, Brit.)
A. Titov
HOUSE ON THE FRONT LINE, THE(1963, USSR); SHE-WOLF, THE(1963, USSR)
I. Titova
MEET ME IN MOSCOW(1966, USSR)
V. Titova
KATERINA IZMAILOVA(1969, USSR)
Valentina Titova
STAR INSPECTOR, THE(1980, USSR)
Fanny Tittell-Brune
Silents
IRON JUSTICE(1915, Brit.)
Misc. Silents
ESTHER REDEEMED(1915, Brit.); TEMPTATION'S HOUR(1916, Brit.)
Frank Titterton
WALTZ TIME(1933, Brit.); SONG AT EVENTIDE(1934, Brit.); BARNACLE BILL(1935, Brit.)
Gregg Tittinger
NURSE SHERRI(1978), w
Frank Titus
WHITE HEAT(1934), ph
Harold Titus
GREAT MR. NOBODY, THE(1941), w
Silents
LAST STRAW, THE(1920), w
Lydia Titus
Silents
BEAU REVEL(1921); NOBODY'S FOOL(1921); QUEENIE(1921)
Lydia Yeamans Titus
SHANGHAI LADY(1929); LUMMOX(1930)
Silents
JUDGE NOT OR THE WOMAN OF MONA DIGGINGS(1915); TONGUES OF MEN, THE(1916); HIGH SPEED(1917); ALL NIGHT(1918); ROMANCE OF HAPPY VALLEY, A(1919); NURSE MARJORIE(1920); PRINCE OF AVENUE A., THE(1920); ALL DOLLED UP(1921); BEATING THE GAME(1921); INVISIBLE POWER, THE(1921); MAD MARRIAGE, THE(1921); MARRIAGE OF WILLIAM ASHE(1921); MIS-TRESS OF SHENSTONE, THE(1921); LAVENDER BATH LADY, THE(1922); SCARA-MOUCHE(1923); WANTERS, THE(1923); CYTHEREA(1924); IN FAST COMPANY(1924); LULLABY, THE(1924); RAG MAN, THE(1925); IRENE(1926); NIGHT LIFE(1927); SWEET SIXTEEN(1928); TWO LOVERS(1928); WHILE THE CITY SLEEPS(1928)
Misc. Silents
HE FELL IN LOVE WITH HIS WIFE(1916); EDGE OF THE LAW(1917); CALL OF THE SOUL, THE(1919); PEACE OF ROARING RIVER, THE(1919); STRICTLY CONFI-DENTIAL(1919)
Mickey Titus
JUNIOR MISS(1945)
Russ Titus
VICTORS, THE(1963)
Alexander Tiu
GIRLS! GIRLS! GIRLS!(1962)
Elizabeth Tiu
GIRLS! GIRLS! GIRLS!(1962)
Ginny Tiu
GIRLS! GIRLS! GIRLS!(1962)
Vicky Tiu
IT HAPPENED AT THE WORLD'S FAIR(1963)
Tiziani
BOOM!(1968), cos
Tiziani of Rome
COMEDIANS, THE(1967), set d
Herbert Tjadens
HELP I'M INVISIBLE(1952, Ger.), w
Cal Tjader
HOT CAR GIRL(1958), m, md; FOR SINGLES ONLY(1968)
Ove Tjernberg
SWEDISH WEDDING NIGHT(1965, Swed.)
R. Tkachuk
KATERINA IZMAILOVA(1969, USSR)
Yegor Tkachuk
LAST HILL, THE(1945, USSR)
Konstantin Tkaczenko
GIRL IN ROOM 13(1961, U.S./Braz.), ph
Cocky Tlhotlhalemji
DINGAKA(1965, South Africa)
Hisao Toake
TORA! TORA! TORA!(1970, U.S./Jap.); TOKYO STORY(1972, Jap.)
Yukie Toake
ZATOICHI'S CONSPIRACY(1974, Jap.)
Maureen Toal
ROONEY(1958, Brit.); GUY CALLED CAESAR, A(1962, Brit.); ULYSSES(1967, U.S./Brit.); OTLEY(1969, Brit.); PADDY(1970, Irish)
James Toback
GAMBLER, THE(1974), w; FINGERS(1978), d&w; LOVE AND MONEY(1982), p,d,&w; EXPOSED(1983), a, p,d&w

Norman Toback
CODE OF SILENCE(1960), w

Carlos Tobalina
Misc. Talkies
DOUBLE INITIATION(1970), a, d; LAST TANGO IN ACAPULCO, THE(1975), d

Linda Tobalina
Misc. Talkies
LAST TANGO IN ACAPULCO, THE(1975)

Alfredo Tobares
TERRACE, THE(1964, Arg.)

Maria Tober
ESCAPE FROM EAST BERLIN(1962)

Ralph Tobert
HAMMERHEAD(1968), ch

Dan Tobey
MILKY WAY, THE(1936); HOLLYWOOD STADIUM MYSTERY(1938); PITTS-BURGH KID, THE(1941); SHADOW OF THE THIN MAN(1941); HARVARD, HERE I COME(1942); SWING FEVER(1943); DUKE OF CHICAGO(1949)

Kenneth [Ken] Tobey
THIS TIME FOR KEEPS(1947); HE WALKED BY NIGHT(1948); FREE FOR ALL(1949); GREAT SINNER, THE(1949); I WAS A MALE WAR BRIDE(1949); ILLE-GAL ENTRY(1949); STRATTON STORY, THE(1949); TASK FORCE(1949); TWELVE O'CLOCK HIGH(1949); FILE ON THELMA JORDAN, THE(1950); FLYING MIS-SILE(1950); GUNFIGHTER, THE(1950); KISS TOMORROW GOODBYE(1950); MY FRIEND IRMA GOES WEST(1950); RIGHT CROSS(1950); WHEN WILLIE COMES MARCHING HOME(1950); RAWHIDE(1951); THING, THE(1951); ANGEL FACE(1953); BEAST FROM 20,000 FATHOMS, THE(1953); BIGAMIST,THE(1953); FIGHTER AT-TACK(1953); DOWN THREE DARK STREETS(1954); RING OF FEAR(1954); STEEL CAGE, THE(1954); DAVY CROCKETT, KING OF THE WILD FRONTIER(1955); IT CAME FROM BENEATH THE SEA(1955); RAGE AT DAWN(1955); DAVY CROCKETT AND THE RIVER PIRATES(1956); GREAT LOCOMOTIVE CHASE, THE(1956); MAN IN THE GREY FLANNEL SUIT, THE(1956); SEARCH FOR BRIDEY MURPHY, THE(1956); STEEL JUNGLE, THE(1956); GUNFIGHT AT THE O.K. CORRAL(1957); JET PILOT(1957); VAMPIRE, THE(1957); WINGS OF EAGLES, THE(1957); CRY TERROR(1958); SEVEN WAYS FROM SUNDOWN(1960); X-15(1961); STARK FEAR(1963); MAN CALLED ADAM, A(1966); TIME FOR KILLING, A(1967); 40 GUNS TO APACHE PASS(1967); MARLOWE(1969); BILLY JACK(1971); BEN(1972); CANDI-DATE, THE(1972); RAGE(1972); WALKING TALL(1973); DIRTY MARY, CRAZY LARRY(1974); HOMEBODIES(1974); BABY BLUE MARINE(1976); W.C. FIELDS AND ME(1976); MAC ARTHUR(1977); AIRPLANE!(1980); HERO AT LARGE(1980); HOWL-ING, THE(1981); STRANGE INVADERS(1983)

Robert Tobey
SPACE MONSTER(1965), ph

Ruth Tobey
AND ONE WAS BEAUTIFUL(1940); OUR TOWN(1940); ZIEGFELD GIRL(1941); CALLING DR. GILLESPIE(1942); JANIE(1944); KNICKERBOCKER HOLIDAY(1944); DELIGHTFULLY DANGEROUS(1945); JANIE GETS MARRIED(1946); I REMEMBER MAMA(1948); MOTHER IS A FRESHMAN(1949); MR. BELVEDERE GOES TO COLLEGE(1949)

Tobi
CHILDREN OF BABYLON(1980, Jamaica)

Victoria Tobian
HARD TRAIL(1969)

Billy Tobias
Misc. Talkies
DUNCAN'S WORLD(1977)

Frances Tobias
ONE PLUS ONE(1961, Can.)

George Tobias
BALALAIKA(1939); MAISIE(1939); NINOTCHKA(1939); THEY ALL COME OUT(1939); CALLING ALL HUSBANDS(1940); EAST OF THE RIVER(1940); MAN WHO TALKED TOO MUCH, THE(1940); MUSIC IN MY HEART(1940); RIVER'S END(1940); SATURDAY'S CHILDREN(1940); SOUTH OF SUEZ(1940); THEY DRIVE BY NIGHT(1940); TORRID ZONE(1940); AFFECTIONATELY YOURS(1941); BRIDE CAME C.O.D., THE(1941); CITY, FOR CONQUEST(1941); OUT OF THE FOG(1941); SERGEANT YORK(1941); STRAWBERRY BLONDE, THE(1941); CAPTAINS OF THE CLOUDS(1942); JUKE GIRL(1942); MY SISTER EILEEN(1942); WINGS FOR THE EAGLE(1942); YANKEE DOODLE DANDY(1942); AIR FORCE(1943); MISSION TO MOSCOW(1943); THANK YOUR LUCKY STARS(1943); THIS IS THE ARMY(1943); BETWEEN TWO WORLDS(1944); MAKE YOUR OWN BED(1944); MASK OF DI-MITRIOS, THE(1944); PASSAGE TO MARSEILLE(1944); MILDRED PIERCE(1945); OBJECTIVE, BURMA!(1945); GALLANT BESS(1946); HER KIND OF MAN(1946); NOBODY LIVES FOREVER(1946); MY WILD IRISH ROSE(1947); SINBAD THE SAILOR(1947); ADVENTURES OF CASANOVA(1948); EVERYBODY DOES IT(1949); JUDGE STEPS OUT, THE(1949); SET-UP, THE(1949); SOUTHSIDE 1-1000(1950); MAGIC CARPET, THE(1951); MARK OF THE RENEGADE(1951); RAWHIDE(1951); TEN TALL MEN(1951); DESERT PURSUIT(1952); GLENN MILLER STORY, THE(1953); SEVEN LITTLE FOYS, THE(1955); SILK STOCKINGS(1957); TATTERED DRESS, THE(1957); MARJORIE MORNINGSTAR(1958); NEW KIND OF LOVE, A(1963); BULLET FOR A BADMAN(1964); NIGHTMARE IN THE SUN(1964); GLASS BOTTOM BOAT, THE(1966); PHYNX, THE(1970)

Hank Tobias
I'LL BE SEEING YOU(1944)

Harry Tobias
CRIMINAL LAWYER(1937), m

Larry Tobias
Misc. Talkies
DUNCAN'S WORLD(1977)

Myron Tobias
MEET ME IN ST. LOUIS(1944); MRS. PARKINGTON(1944)

Oliver Tobias
ROMANCE OF A HORSE THIEF(1971); 'TIS A PITY SHE'S A WHORE(1973, Ital.); ARABIAN ADVENTURE(1979, Brit.); STUD, THE(1979, Brit.); WICKED LADY, THE(1983, Brit.)
Misc. Talkies
NIGHTINGALE SANG IN BERKELEY SQUARE, A(1979)

Sarett Tobias
SHE WOULDN'T SAY YES(1945), w; TARS AND SPARS(1946), w

Walter Tobias
TWO ON A DOORSTEP(1936, Brit.); MOUNTAINS O'MOURNE(1938, Brit.)

Ellen Tobie
1984
PROTOCOL(1984)

Alan Tobin
SQUEEZE A FLOWER(1970, Aus.)

Bill Tobin
JACK AND THE BEANSTALK(1970), ph; THUMBELINA(1970), ph

Dan Tobin
BLACK LIMELIGHT(1938, Brit.); WOMAN OF THE YEAR(1942); UNDERCUR-RENT(1946); BACHELOR AND THE BOBBY-SOXER, THE(1947); LIKELY STORY, A(1947); BIG CLOCK, THE(1948); MISS TATLOCK'S MILLIONS(1948); MR. BLAND-INGS BUILDS HIS DREAM HOUSE(1948); SEALED VERDICT(1948); VELVET TOUCH, THE(1948); SONG OF SURRENDER(1949); MAGNIFICENT YANKEE, THE(1950); QUEEN FOR A DAY(1951); DREAM WIFE(1953); CATERED AFFAIR, THE(1956); LAST ANGRY MAN, THE(1959); WHO'S GOT THE ACTION?(1962); HERBIE RIDES AGAIN(1974); HOW TO SUCCEED IN BUSINESS WITHOUT REAL-LY TRYING(1976)

Darra Lyn Tobin
BUNNY O'HARE(1971)

Don Tobin
FANTASIA(1940), anim; PINOCCHIO(1940), anim

Ethel Tobin
MAISIE GOES TO RENO(1944); HOODLUM SAINT, THE(1946)

Frances Tobin
STERILE CUCKOO, THE(1969)

Genevieve Tobin
FREE LOVE(1930); LADY SURRENDERS, A(1930); GAY DIPLOMAT, THE(1931); SEED(1931); UP FOR MURDER(1931); HOLLYWOOD SPEAKS(1932); ONE HOUR WITH YOU(1932); GOLDEN HARVEST(1933); GOODBYE AGAIN(1933); I LOVED A WOMAN(1933); INFERNAL MACHINE(1933); PERFECT UNDERSTANDING(1933, Brit.); PLEASURE CRUISE(1933); WRECKER, THE(1933); DARK HAZARD(1934); EASY TO LOVE(1934); KISS AND MAKE UP(1934); NINTH GUEST, THE(1934); SUCCESS AT ANY PRICE(1934); UNCERTAIN LADY(1934); BROADWAY HOS-TESS(1935); BY YOUR LEAVE(1935); CASE OF THE LUCKY LEGS, THE(1935); GOOSE AND THE GANDER, THE(1935); HERE'S TO ROMANCE(1935); WOMAN IN RED, THE(1935); MAN IN THE MIRROR, THE(1936, Brit.); PETRIFIED FOREST, THE(1936); SNOWED UNDER(1936); DUKE COMES BACK, THE(1937); GREAT GAMBINI, THE(1937); DRAMATIC SCHOOL(1938); KATE PLUS TEN(1938, Brit.); OUR NEIGHBORS—THE CARTERS(1939); YES, MY DARLING DAUGHTER(1939); ZAZA(1939); NO TIME FOR COMEDY(1940)
Misc. Talkies
WOMAN PURSUED(1931)
Silents
NO MOTHER TO GUIDE HER(1923)

George Tobin
LIFE AND TIMES OF CHESTER-ANGUS RAMSGOOD, THE(1971, Can.)

Grace Tobin
42ND STREET(1933)

Joseph Tobin
SOPHIE'S CHOICE(1982)

Joy Tobin
C'MON, LET'S LIVE A LITTLE(1967)

Lawrence Tobin
SHANTY TRAMP(1967); TASTE OF BLOOD, A(1967)

Lu Tobin
D.I., THE(1957)

Mark Tobin
MAN FROM THE DINERS' CLUB, THE(1963)

Matthew Tobin
FRONT, THE(1976); REAL LIFE(1979); VAN NUYS BLVD.(1979); FORCE: FI-VE(1981)

Michele Tobin
YOURS, MINE AND OURS(1968); 80 STEPS TO JONAH(1969); DIRTY HARRY(1971); WACKO(1983)

Niall Tobin
1984
REFLECTIONS(1984, Brit.)

Norm Tobin
THIEF(1981)

Pat Tobin
POSSE(1975)

Peter Tobin
MY WAY(1974, South Africa)

Rita Tobin
WRONG BOX, THE(1966, Brit.)

Thomas J. Tobin
FRATERNITY ROW(1977), d

Vivian Tobin
SIGN OF THE CROSS, THE(1932); IF I WERE FREE(1933); THIS MAN IS MI-NE(1934); BORDERTOWN(1935); WORLD ACCUSES, THE(1935)

Tobin Mathews and the All Stars
TWIST ALL NIGHT(1961)

Mario Tobino
DOWN THE ANCIENT STAIRCASE(1975, Ital.), w

Lotte Tobisch
DON JUAN(1956, Aust.); LAST TEN DAYS, THE(1956, Ger.)

Stephen Tobolowsky
KEEP MY GRAVE OPEN(1980)
1984
PHILADELPHIA EXPERIMENT, THE(1984); SWING SHIFT(1984)

Alexander Tobuloff
EVERY NIGHT AT EIGHT(1935), art d

Dan Toby
MAN-PROOF(1938); BIG SHOW-OFF, THE(1945); RINGSIDE(1949)

Doug Toby
1984
RED DAWN(1984)

Kenneth Toby
CREATURE WASN'T NICE,THE(1981)
Mark Toby
COURTSHIP OF EDDY'S FATHER, THE(1963), John Gay
John Tobyansen
WHEN A STRANGER CALLS(1979)
Bruno Tocci
CAESAR THE CONQUEROR(1963, Ital.)
James E. Tocci
DEAD AND BURIED(1981), set d
Jim Tocci
HUNTER, THE(1980), set d
Vincenzo Tocci
FACTS OF MURDER, THE(1965, Ital.)
Dr. Ernest Toch
CAT AND THE CANARY, THE(1939), m
Ernest Toch
PRIVATE LIFE OF DON JUAN, THE(1934, Brit.), m; NONE SHALL ESCAPE(1944), m
Ernst Toch
PETER IBBETSON(1935), m; ON SUCH A NIGHT(1937), m; DR. CYCLOPS(1940), m; GHOST BREAKERS, THE(1940), m; LADIES IN RETIREMENT(1941), m; FIRST COMES COURAGE(1943), m; ADDRESS UNKNOWN(1944), m; UNSEEN, THE(1945), m
Brian Tochi
OMEGA MAN, THE(1971)
1984
REVENGE OF THE NERDS(1984)
Wendy Tochi
DIRTY HARRY(1971)
Jane Tochihara
WALK, DON'T RUN(1966)
Jodee Tochihara
WALK, DON'T RUN(1966)
Wendee Tochihara
WALK, DON'T RUN(1966)
Masao Tochizaga
1984
BALLAD OF NARAYAMA, THE(1984, Jap.), ph
Masao Tochizawa
KURAGEJIMA-LEGENDS FROM A SOUTHERN ISLAND(1970, Jap.), ph
Marija Tocinowsky
SUBVERSIVES, THE(1967, Ital.); DIARY OF A SCHIZOPHRENIC GIRL(1970, Ital.)
Louis Tock [Lubor Tokos]
FABULOUS WORLD OF JULES VERNE, THE(1961, Czech.)
Malcolm Tod
LOVE'S OLD SWEET SONG(1933, Brit.); NINE FORTY-FIVE(1934, Brit.)
Silents
CRIMSON CIRCLE, THE(1922, Brit.); AUDACIOUS MR. SQUIRE, THE(1923, Brit.); HUTCH STIRS 'EM UP(1923, Brit.); CHINESE BUNGALOW, THE(1926, Brit.); WOMAN TEMPTED, THE(1928, Brit.); AFTER THE VERDICT(1929, Brit.)
Misc. Silents
BACHELOR'S BABY, A(1922, Brit.); HURRICANE HUTCH IN MANY ADVENTURES(1924, Brit.)
Pacita Tod-Tod
THEY WERE EXPENDABLE(1945)
Shigemasa Toda
HAHAKIRI(1963, Jap.), art d; KWAIDAN(1965, Jap.), art d; SCANDALOUS ADVENTURES OF BURAIKAN, THE(1970, Jap.), art d; MERRY CHRISTMAS MR. LAWRENCE(1983, Jap./Brit.), prod d
Toshi Toda
IT'S MY TURN(1980)
Al Todd
MARSHAL OF GUNSMOKE(1944), ed
Alvin Todd
ARIZONA TRAIL(1943), ed
Ann E. Todd
BRIGHAM YOUNG–FRONTIERSMAN(1940); BLOOD AND SAND(1941); JOLSON STORY, THE(1946); DANGEROUS YEARS(1947); ARTHUR TAKES OVER(1948); THREE DARING DAUGHTERS(1948); COVER-UP(1949)
Ann Todd
KEEPERS OF YOUTH(1931, Brit.); THESE CHARMING PEOPLE(1931, Brit.); WATER GYPSIES, THE(1932, Brit.); GHOST TRAIN, THE(1933, Brit.); RETURN OF BULLDOG DRUMMOND, THE(1934, Brit.); THINGS TO COME(1936, Brit.); ACTION FOR SLANDER(1937, Brit.); MURDER ON DIAMOND ROW(1937, Brit.); SOUTH RIDING(1938, Brit.); BAD LITTLE ANGEL(1939); CALLING DR. KILDARE(1939); DESTRY RIDES AGAIN(1939); INTERMEZZO: A LOVE STORY(1939); STRONGER THAN DESIRE(1939); TOWER OF LONDON(1939); ZAZA(1939); ZERO HOUR, THE(1939); ALL THIS AND HEAVEN TOO(1940); DR. EHRLICH'S MAGIC BULLET(1940); GRANNY GET YOUR GUN(1940); LITTLE ORVIE(1940); BAD MEN OF MISSOURI(1941); DANNY BOY(1941, Brit.); HOW GREEN WAS MY VALLEY(1941); MEN IN HER LIFE, THE(1941); POISON PEN(1941, Brit.); PRIVATE NURSE(1941); REMEMBER THE DAY(1941); BEYOND THE BLUE HORIZON(1942); KING'S ROW(1942); ON THE SUNNY SIDE(1942); SHIPS WITH WINGS(1942, Brit.); DIXIE DUGAN(1943); ROUGHLY SPEAKING(1945); VACATION FROM MARRIAGE(1945, Brit.); MARGIE(1946); MY REPUTATION(1946); SEVENTH VEIL, THE(1946, Brit.); HOMESTEADERS OF PARADISE VALLEY(1947); PARADINE CASE, THE(1947); DAYDREAK(1948, Brit.); SHOWTIME(1948, Brit.); SO EVIL MY LOVE(1948, Brit.); ONE WOMAN'S STORY(1949, Brit.); MADELEINE(1950, Brit.); LION HUNTERS, THE(1951); BREAKING THE SOUND BARRIER(1952); GREEN SCARF, THE(1954, Brit.); TIME WITHOUT PITY(1957, Brit.); SCREAM OF FEAR(1961, Brit.); SON OF CAPTAIN BLOOD, THE(1964, U.S./Ital./Span.); 90 DEGREES IN THE SHADE(1966, Czech./Brit.); HUMAN FACTOR, THE(1979, Brit.)
Misc. Talkies
FIEND, THE(1971, Brit.); BEWARE MY BRETHREN(1972, Brit.)
Arthur Todd
CLEAR THE DECKS(1929), ph; FORWARD PASS, THE(1929), ph; HIS LUCKY DAY(1929), ph; RED HOT SPEED ½(1929), ph; DEVIL WITH WOMEN, A(1930), ph; EMBARRASSING MOMENTS(1930), ph; LOOSE ANKLES(1930), ph; ONE HYSTERICAL NIGHT(1930), ph; WHAT A MAN(1930), ph; LAWYER'S SECRET, THE(1931),

ph; MONKEY BUSINESS(1931), ph; SOOKY(1931), ph; TOUCHDOWN!(1931), ph; MILLION DOLLAR LEGS(1932), ph; WILD HORSE MESA(1932), ph; COLLEGE COACH(1933), ph; ELMER THE GREAT(1933), ph; EVER IN MY HEART(1933), ph; GIRL MISSING(1933), ph; SHE HAD TO SAY YES(1933), ph; WILD BOYS OF THE ROAD(1933), ph; BABBITT(1934), ph; BIG HEARTED HERBERT(1934), ph; HAROLD TEEN(1934), ph; I'VE GOT YOUR NUMBER(1934), ph; RETURN OF THE TERROR(1934), ph; ALIBI IKE(1935), ph; BROADWAY HOSTESS(1935), ph; FLORENTINE DAGGER, THE(1935), ph; MISS PACIFIC FLEET(1935), ph; PAYOFF, THE(1935), ph; RED HOT TIRES(1935), ph; WE'RE IN THE MONEY(1935), ph; BOULDER DAM(1936), ph; DOWN THE STRETCH(1936), ph; EARTHWORM TRACTORS(1936), ph; HERE COMES CARTER(1936), ph; JAILBREAK(1936), ph; MURDER BY AN ARISTOCRAT(1936), ph; MURDER OF DR. HARRIGAN, THE(1936), ph; SING ME A LOVE SONG(1936), ph; SNOWED UNDER(1936), ph; ADVENTUROUS BLONDE(1937), ph; BACK IN CIRCULATION(1937), ph; HER HUSBAND'S SECRETARY(1937), ph; MARRY THE GIRL(1937), ph; MELODY FOR TWO(1937), ph; MEN IN EXILE(1937), ph; SH! THE OCTOPUS(1937), ph; CRIME SCHOOL(1938), ph; GIRLS ON PROBATION(1938), ph; HE COULDN'T SAY NO(1938), ph; PENROD AND HIS TWIN BROTHER(1938), ph; PENROD'S DOUBLE TROUBLE(1938), ph; TORCHY GETS HER MAN(1938), ph; AMAZING MR. WILLIAMS(1939), ph; I AM NOT AFRAID(1939), ph; SOUTH OF SUEZ(1940), ph; GREAT MR. NOBODY, THE(1941), ph; SMILING GHOST, THE(1941), ph; THREE SONS O'GUNS(1941), ph; YOU'RE IN THE ARMY NOW(1941), ph; LADY GANGSTER(1942), ph
Silents
CHALLENGE OF CHANCE, THE(1919), ph; LORD LOVES THE IRISH, THE(1919), ph; DEVIL TO PAY, THE(1920), ph; GREEN FLAME, THE(1920), ph; ACCORDING TO HOYLE(1922), ph; ISLE OF LOST SHIPS, THE(1923), ph; SPEED KING(1923), ph; ROLLING HOME(1926), ph; SKINNER'S DRESS SUIT(1926), ph; TAKE IT FROM ME(1926), ph; WHAT HAPPENED TO JONES(1926), ph; LONE EAGLE, THE(1927), ph; OUT ALL NIGHT(1927), ph; THANKS FOR THE BUGGY RIDE(1928), ph
Arthur L. Todd
DANCERS, THE(1930), ph; ONCE A SINNER(1931), ph; HOT SATURDAY(1932), ph; SINGING MARINE, THE(1937), ph; ANGELS WASH THEIR FACES(1939), ph; DEAD END KIDS ON DRESS PARADE(1939), ph; GOING PLACES(1939), ph; MAN WHO DARED, THE(1939), ph; NAUGHTY BUT NICE(1939), ph; TORCHY PLAYS WITH DYNAMITE(1939), ph; ANGEL FROM TEXAS, AN(1940), ph; FUGITIVE FROM JUSTICE, A(1940), ph; RIVER'S END(1940), ph; BAD MEN OF MISSOURI(1941), ph
Silents
IN EVERY WOMAN'S LIFE(1924), ph; TORMENT(1924), ph; JUST A WOMAN(1925), ph; ONE YEAR TO LIVE(1925), ph; WATCH YOUR WIFE(1926), ph
Beverly Todd
LOST MAN, THE(1969); THEY CALL ME MISTER TIBBS(1970); BROTHER JOHN(1971); HOMEWORK(1982); VICE SQUAD(1982)
Bob Todd
POSTMAN'S KNOCK(1962, Brit.); SMELL OF HONEY, A SWALLOW OF BRINE! A(1966); HOT MILLIONS(1968, Brit.); SCARS OF DRACULA, THE(1970, Brit.); DIGBY, THE BIGGEST DOG IN THE WORLD(1974, Brit.); FLYING SORCERER, THE(1974, Brit.); CONFESSIONS OF A POP PERFORMER(1975, Brit.); SUPERMAN III(1983)
Bobby Todd
GLASS OF WATER, A(1962, Cgr.); SHOEMAKER AND THE ELVES, THE(1967, Ger.)
Burt Todd
HER SPLENDID FOLLY(1933)
Charles Todd
BIG BOODLE, THE(1957)
Christine Todd
LADY IN CEMENT(1968)
Dana Todd
Silents
KISSES(1922); WALL FLOWER, THE(1922)
Diane Todd
6.5 SPECIAL(1958, Brit.)
Donna Todd
THAT LUCKY TOUCH(1975, Brit.)
Edward Todd
HI-YO SILVER(1940), ed; DRUMS OF FU MANCHU(1943), ed
Eleanor Todd
LUSTY MEN, THE(1952); SHE COULDN'T SAY NO(1954)
Emily Todd
UNASHAMED(1938)
Eula Guy Todd
SOCIETY GIRL(1932)
Floyd E. Todd
BREAKING AWAY(1979)
Gary Todd
Misc. Talkies
MODERN DAY HOUDINI(1983)
George Todd
CHILDREN OF PLEASURE(1930), ed; FREE AND EASY(1930), ed; CREATURE OF THE WALKING DEAD(1960, Mex.); WILD, FREE AND HUNGRY(1970)
Hallie Todd
1984
SAM'S SON(1984)
Harry Todd
RIVER WOMAN, THE(1928); COURTIN' WILDCATS(1929); ONE STOLEN NIGHT(1929); BORROWED WIVES(1930); FIGHTING LEGION, THE(1930); LAST DANCE, THE(1930); SONS OF THE SADDLE(1930); UNDER MONTANA SKIES(1930); IN OLD CHEYENNE(1931); LAW OF THE RIO GRANDE(1931); MIRACLE WOMAN, THE(1931); TEN CENTS A DANCE(1931); TEN NIGHTS IN A BARROOM(1931); TEXAS RANGER, THE(1931); DEADLINE(1932); FIGHTING FOOL, THE(1932); FIGHTING MARSHAL, THE(1932); GOLD(1932); LONE TRAIL, THE(1932); ONE-MAN LAW(1932); GUN LAW(1933); HER SPLENDID FOLLY(1933); SUNDOWN RIDER, THE(1933); THRILL HUNTER, THE(1933); IT HAPPENED ONE NIGHT(1934); LAW BEYOND THE RANGE(1935); VAGABOND LADY(1935); PRESCOTT KID, THE(1936); WESTERNER, THE(1936)
Misc. Talkies
WYOMING WHIRLWIND(1932); TROUBLE BUSTERS(1933)
Silents
FICKLE WOMEN(1920); HER ELEPHANT MAN(1920); JACK KNIFE MAN, THE(1920); GIRLS DON'T GAMBLE(1921); KEEPING UP WITH LIZZIE(1921); PATSY(1921); SKY PILOT, THE(1921); ACCORDING TO HOYLE(1922); DANGER POINT, THE(1922); PENROD(1922); RIDE FOR YOUR LIFE(1924); SAWDUST

TRAIL(1924); HURRICANE KID, THE(1925); OUTLAW'S DAUGHTER, THE(1925); QUICKER'N LIGHTNIN'(1925); COMING AN' GOING(1926); THIRD DEGREE, THE(1926); RAWHIDE KID, THE(1928); KING OF THE RODEO(1929)

Misc. Silents

PLEASE GET MARRIED(1919); TASTE OF LIFE, A(1919); BELLS OF SAN JUAN(1922); HORSESHOE LUCK(1924); THUNDERING ROMANCE(1924); DESERT DEMON, THE(1925); TWO-FISTED JONES(1925); BONANZA BUCKAROO, THE(1926); BUCKAROO KID, THE(1926); PRISONERS OF THE STORM(1926); INTERFERIN' GENT, THE(1927); OBLIGIN' BUCKAROO, THE(1927); ONE MAN GAME, A(1927); RIDIN' ROWDY, THE(1927); ROARIN' BRONCS(1927); FLYIN' COWBOY, THE(1928); RIVER WOMAN(1929); LUCKY LARKIN(1930)

Holbrook N. Todd

JAWS OF THE JUNGLE(1936), ed; LOST RANCH(1937), ed; NATION AFLAME(1937), ed; RENFREW OF THE ROYAL MOUNTED(1937), ed; TENDERFOOT GOES WEST, A(1937), ed; STRANGER FROM ARIZONA, THE(1938), ed; UNASHAMED(1938), ed; BURIED ALIVE(1939), ed; TEXAS WILDCATS(1939), ed; TORTURE SHIP(1939), ed; TRIGGER FINGERS ½(1939), ed; ARIZONA GANGBUSTERS(1940), ed; BILLY THE KID IN TEXAS(1940), ed; FRONTIER CRUSADER(1940), ed; GUN CODE(1940), ed; INVISIBLE KILLER, THE(1940), ed; MARKED MEN(1940), ed; MERCY PLANE(1940), ed; STRAIGHT SHOOTER(1940), ed; BILLY THE KID IN SANTA FE(1941), ed; BILLY THE KID WANTED(1941), ed; BILLY THE KID'S FIGHTING PALS(1941), ed; BLONDE COMET(1941), ed; JUNGLE MAN(1941), ed; LONE RIDER AMBUSHED, THE(1941), ed; LONE RIDER CROSSES THE RIO, THE(1941), ed; LONE RIDER FIGHTS BACK, THE(1941), ed; LONE RIDER IN GHOST TOWN, THE(1941), ed; OUTLAWS OF THE RIO GRANDE(1941), ed; TEXAS MARSHAL, THE(1941), ed; BILLY THE KID TRAPPED(1942), ed; JUNGLE SIREN(1942), ed; LAW AND ORDER(1942), ed; LONE RIDER AND THE BANDIT, THE(1942), ed; MAD MONSTER, THE(1942), ed; MYSTERIOUS RIDER, THE(1942), ed; PRAIRIE PALS(1942), ed; QUEEN OF BROADWAY(1942), ed; RAIDERS OF THE WEST(1942), ed; ROLLING DOWN THE GREAT DIVIDE(1942), ed; SHERIFF OF SAGE VALLEY(1942), ed; TEXAS MAN HUNT(1942), ed; BEHIND PRISON WALLS(1943), ed; BLACK RAVEN, THE(1943), ed; DEAD MEN WALK(1943), ed; HARVEST MELODY(1943), ed; KID RIDES AGAIN, THE(1943), ed; SUBMARINE BASE(1943), ed; WESTERN CYCLONE(1943), ed; WILD HORSE RUSTLERS(1943), ed; WOLVES OF THE RANGE(1943), ed; BLAZING FRONTIER(1944), ed; CONTENDER, THE(1944), ed; DRIFTER, THE(1944), ed; FRONTIER OUTLAWS(1944), ed; FUZZY SETTLES DOWN(1944), ed; LAW OF THE SADDLE(1944), ed; MONSTER MAKER, THE(1944), ed; NABONGA(1944), ed; RAIDERS OF RED GAP(1944), ed; RUSTLER'S HIDEOUT(1944), ed; SWING HOSTESS(1944), ed; THUNDERING GUN SLINGERS(1944), ed; VALLEY OF VENGEANCE(1944), ed; VOICE IN THE WIND(1944), ed; WILD HORSE PHANTOM(1944), ed; APOLOGY FOR MURDER(1945), ed; BORDER BADMEN(1945), ed; FIGHTING BILL CARSON(1945), ed; FLAMING BULLETS(1945), ed; FRONTIER FUGITIVES(1945), ed; HIS BROTHER'S GHOST(1945), ed; KID SISTER, THE(1945), ed; LIGHTNING RAIDERS(1945), ed; MARKED FOR MURDER(1945), ed; PRAIRIE RUSTLERS(1945), ed; SHADOWS OF DEATH(1945), ed; STAGECOACH OUTLAWS(1945), ed; THREE IN THE SADDLE(1945), ed; WHITE PONGO(1945), ed; BLONDE FOR A DAY(1946), ed; FLYING SERPENT, THE(1946), ed; GAS HOUSE KIDS(1946), ed; GENTLEMEN WITH GUNS(1946), ed; GHOST OF HIDDEN VALLEY(1946), ed; LADY CHASER(1946), ed; LARCENY IN HER HEART(1946), ed; MURDER IS MY BUSINESS(1946), ed; OUTLAW OF THE PLAINS(1946), ed; OVERLAND RIDERS(1946), ed; PRAIRIE BADMEN(1946), ed; TERRORS ON HORSEBACK(1946), ed; THREE ON A TICKET(1947), ed; MIRACULOUS JOURNEY(1948), ed; MONEY MADNESS(1948), ed; STATE DEPARTMENT–FILE 649(1949), ed; DAUGHTER OF DR. JEKYLL(1957), ed

Holbrook Todd

COWBOY HOLIDAY(1934), ed; DAMAGED GOODS(1937), ed; $1,000,000 RACKET(1937), ed; BROTHERS OF THE WEST(1938), ed; FEUD OF THE TRAIL(1938), ed; ORPHAN OF THE PECOS(1938), ed; BEASTS OF BERLIN(1939), ed; DOWN THE WYOMING TRAIL(1939), ed; FIGHTING RENEGADE(1939), ed; FLAMING LEAD(1939), ed; HEADLEYS AT HOME, THE(1939), ed; OUTLAW'S PARADISE(1939), ed; DEATH RIDES THE RANGE(1940), ed; HOLD THAT WOMAN(1940), ed; I TAKE THIS OATH(1940), ed; DEVIL BAT, THE(1941), ed; RIDERS OF BLACK MOUNTAIN(1941), ed; PRISONER OF JAPAN(1942), ed; CATTLE STAMPEDE(1943), ed; DEATH RIDES THE PLAINS(1944), ed; ARSON SQUAD(1945), ed; ENEMY OF THE LAW(1945), ed; LADY CONFESSES, THE(1945), ed; BEAST OF HOLLOW MOUNTAIN, THE(1956), ed; LAST OF THE DESPERADOES(1956), ed

Misc. Talkies

SECRETS OF HOLLYWOOD(1933), d

J. Hunter Todd

GOLD GUITAR, THE(1966), d

James Todd

UNTIL THEY SAIL(1957); RIDERS OF THE PURPLE SAGE(1931); CARELESS LADY(1932); CHARLIE CHAN'S CHANCE(1932); DISORDERLY CONDUCT(1932); FOR THE LOVE OF MARY(1948); LUCK OF THE IRISH(1948); VELVET TOUCH, THE(1948); FIGHTING MAN OF THE PLAINS(1949); FRANCIS(1949); GAL WHO TOOK THE WEST, THE(1949); LONE WOLF AND HIS LADY, THE(1949); TRAPPED(1949); MALAYA(1950); PEGGY(1950); BIGAMIST,THE(1953); TITANIC(1953); TORCH SONG(1953); TRIAL(1955); SCARLET HOUR, THE(1956); SOMEBODY UP THERE LIKES ME(1956); THIS COULD BE THE NIGHT(1957); WINGS OF EAGLES, THE(1957); BUCCANEER, THE(1958); HIGH SCHOOL CONFIDENTIAL(1958)

Jerry Todd

FIVE GUNS TO TOMBSTONE(1961); POLICE DOG STORY, THE(1961)

Joy Todd

1984

MOSCOW ON THE HUDSON(1984)

Judson Todd

LOVE MERCHANT, THE(1966)

Misc. Talkies

RED ROSES OF PASSION(1967)

Kay Todd

SEDUCTION OF JOE TYNAN, THE(1979)

Lina Todd

IMPOSTORS(1979)

Lisa Todd

GIRL WHO KNEW TOO MUCH, THE(1969); DIRTY DINGUS MAGEE(1970); DOLL SQUAD, THE(1973); DEVIL'S RAIN, THE(1975, U.S./Mex.); WOMAN HUNT, THE(1975, U.S./Phil.)

Lola Todd

Silents

DARK STAIRWAYS(1924); WAR HORSE, THE(1927)

Misc. Silents

DEMON, THE(1926); FIGHTING PEACEMAKER, THE(1926); REMEMBER(1926); TOUGH GUY, THE(1926); TAKING A CHANCE(1928)

Lucas Todd

FURY AT SHOWDOWN(1957), w

Mabel Todd

HOLLYWOOD HOTEL(1937); OVER THE GOAL(1937); VARSITY SHOW(1937); COWBOY AND THE LADY, THE(1938); GARDEN OF THE MOON(1938); GOLD DIGGERS IN PARIS(1938); MYSTERIOUS MISS X, THE(1939); MYSTERY OF THE WHITE ROOM(1939); STREET OF MISSING MEN(1939); TALK OF THE TOWN(1942); TRAMP, TRAMP, TRAMP(1942); GHOST AND THE GUEST(1943); IN SOCIETY(1944); DOWN MISSOURI WAY(1946); WIFE WANTED(1946)

Madeleine Todd

PRIEST OF LOVE(1981, Brit.)

Malcolm Todd

Silents

POPPIES OF FLANDERS(1927, Brit.)

Misc. Silents

EXPIATION(1922, Brit.)

Maria Todd

ENDLESS LOVE(1981)

Mel Todd

VILLAIN, THE(1979)

Melvin Todd

WANDA NEVADA(1979)

Michael Todd

AROUND THE WORLD IN 80 DAYS(1956), p; RIDE THE HIGH WIND(1967, South Africa)

Michael Todd, Jr.

SCENT OF MYSTERY(1960), p; BELL JAR, THE(1979), p

Paul Todd

GET YOURSELF A COLLEGE GIRL(1964); MONEY TRAP, THE(1966)

Quentin Todd

AMATEUR GENTLEMAN(1936, Brit.), ch

Richard Todd

FOR THEM THAT TRESPASS(1949, Brit.); HASTY HEART, THE(1949); INTERRUPTED JOURNEY, THE(1949, Brit.); STAGE FRIGHT(1950, Brit.); FLESH AND BLOOD(1951, Brit.); LIGHTNING STRIKES TWICE(1951); PORTRAIT OF CLARE(1951, Brit.); STORY OF ROBIN HOOD, THE(1952, Brit.); AFFAIR IN MONTE CARLO(1953, Brit.); ASSASSIN, THE(1953, Brit.); SWORD AND THE ROSE, THE(1953); ROB ROY, THE HIGHLAND ROGUE(1954, Brit.); SECRETS D'ALCOVE(1954, Fr./Ital.); DAM BUSTERS, THE(1955, Brit.); MAN CALLED PETER, THE(1955); VIRGIN QUEEN, THE(1955); BATTLE HELL(1956, Brit.); D-DAY, THE SIXTH OF JUNE(1956); SAINT JOAN(1957); CHASE A CROOKED SHADOW(1958, Brit.); INTENT TO KILL(1958, Brit.); NAKED EARTH, THE(1958, Brit.); BREAKOUT(1960, Brit.); NEVER LET GO(1960, Brit.); LONG AND THE SHORT AND THE TALL, THE(1961, Brit.); BOYS, THE(1962, Brit.); CRIME DOES NOT PAY(1962, Fr.); HELLIONS, THE(1962, Brit.); LONGEST DAY, THE(1962); SANDERS(1963, Brit.); VERY EDGE, THE(1963, Brit.); WHY BOTHER TO KNOCK(1964, Brit.), a, p; BATTLE OF THE VILLA FIORITA, THE(1965, Brit.); COAST OF SKELETONS(1965, Brit.); OPERATION CROSSBOW(1965, U.S./Ital.); LOVE-INS, THE(1967); SUBTERFUGE(1969, US/Brit.); DORIAN GRAY(1970, Ital./Brit./Ger./Liechtenstein); ASYLUM(1972, Brit.); BIG SLEEP, THE½(1978, Brit.); HOUSE OF LONG SHADOWS, THE(1983, Brit.)

Misc. Talkies

AQUARIAN, THE(1972)

Russell Todd

HE KNOWS YOU'RE ALONE(1980); FRIDAY THE 13TH PART II(1981)

1984

FRIDAY THE 13TH–THE FINAL CHAPTER(1984); WHERE THE BOYS ARE '84(1984)

Ruth Todd

CORNERED(1932), w

Silents

TERROR OF BAR X, THE(1927), t; LINDA(1929), t

Sally Jo Todd

REVOLT OF MAMIE STOVER, THE(1956)

Sally Todd

UNEARTHLY, THE(1957); FRANKENSTEIN'S DAUGHTER(1958)

Sherman Todd

PALMY DAYS(1931), ed; CARDINAL RICHELIEU(1935), ed; DARK ANGEL, THE(1935), ed; FOLIES DERGERE(1935), ed; BELOVED ENEMY(1936), ed; STRIKE ME PINK(1936), ed; STELLA DALLAS(1937), ed; COWBOY AND THE LADY, THE(1938), ed; GOLDWYN FOLLIES, THE(1938), ed; RAFFLES(1939), ed; THEY SHALL HAVE MUSIC(1939), ed; LONG VOYAGE HOME, THE(1940), ed; OUR TOWN(1940), ed; DEVIL AND MISS JONES, THE(1941), ed; LOOK WHO'S LAUGHING(1941), ed; JOAN OF PARIS(1942), ed; FOR WHOM THE BELL TOLLS(1943), ed; SKY'S THE LIMIT, THE(1943), p; MAGIC TOWN(1947), ed; SINBAD THE SAILOR(1947), ed; BERLIN EXPRESS(1948), ed; THEY LIVE BY NIGHT(1949), ed; WOMAN'S SECRET, A(1949), ed; OUR VERY OWN(1950), ed; SUN SETS AT DAWN, THE(1950), ed; FLYING LEATHERNECKS(1951), ed; RACKET, THE(1951), ed; BACKLASH(1956), ed; CONGO CROSSING(1956), ed; DAY OF FURY, A(1956), ed; EVERYTHING BUT THE TRUTH(1956), ed; GIRL IN THE KREMLIN(1957), ed; GREAT MAN, THE(1957), ed; ISTANBUL(1957), ed; NIGHT PASSAGE(1957), ed; DAY OF THE BAD MAN(1958), ed; LADY TAKES A FLYER, THE(1958), ed

Sherman A. Todd

WALK THE PROUD LAND(1956), ed

Stendal Todd

DEVIL'S ROCK(1938, Brit.)

Thelma Todd

HAUNTED HOUSE, THE(1928); BACHELOR GIRL, THE(1929); CAREERS(1929); HER PRIVATE LIFE(1929); HOUSE OF HORROR(1929); SEVEN FOOTPRINTS TO SATAN(1929); FOLLOW THRU(1930); HER MAN(1930); ALOHA(1931); BROADMINDED(1931); COMMAND PERFORMANCE(1931); HOT HEIRESS(1931); MALTESE FALCON, THE(1931); MONKEY BUSINESS(1931); CALL HER SAVAGE(1932); HORSE FEATHERS(1932); KLONDIKE(1932); SPEAK EASILY(1932); THIS IS THE NIGHT(1932); AIR HOSTESS(1933); CHEATING BLONDES(1933); COUNSELLOR-AT-

LAW(1933); DECEPTION(1933); DEVIL'S BROTHER, THE(1933); MARY STEVENS, M.D.(1933); SITTING PRETTY(1933); BOTTOMS UP(1934); COCKEYED CAVALIERS(1934); HIPS, HIPS, HOORAY(1934); PALOOKA(1934); POOR RICH, THE(1934); TAKE THE STAND(1934); YOU MADE ME LOVE YOU(1934, Brit.); AFTER THE DANCE(1935); LIGHTNING STRIKES TWICE(1935); TWO FOR TONIGHT(1935); BOHEMIAN GIRL, THE(1936)
Misc. Talkies
SWANEE RIVER(1931); BIG TIMER(1932)
Silents
NEVADA(1927); SHIELD OF HONOR, THE(1927); NOOSE, THE(1928); VAMPING VENUS(1928); NAUGHTY BABY(1929)
Misc. Silents
GAY DEFENDER, THE(1927); RUBBER HEELS(1927); CRASH, THE(1928); HAUNTED HOUSE, THE(1928); SEVEN FOOTPRINTS TO SATAN(1929); TRAIL MARRIAGE(1929)

Thelma Todd [Alison Loyd]
SON OF A SAILOR(1933)

Toni Todd
PHILO VANCE'S GAMBLE(1947); PHILO VANCE'S SECRET MISSION(1947)

William Todd
HER SPLENDID FOLLY(1933)

Doris Toddings
WONDER MAN(1945)

Guerrino Todero
MOSES AND AARON(1975, Ger./Fr./Ital.), cos

Anita Todesco
MORGAN THE PIRATE(1961, Fr./Ital.); PHAROAH'S WOMAN, THE(1961, Ital.); THIEF OF BAGHDAD, THE(1961, Ital./Fr.); EMBALMER, THE(1966, Ital.)

Mario Todisco
1984
HOME FREE ALL(1984)

Bora Todorovic
MONTENEGRO(1981, Brit./Swed.); TWILIGHT TIME(1983, U.S./Yugo.)

Karin Toeche-Mittler
LAST YEAR AT MARIENBAD(1962, Fr./Ital.)

Anya Toelle
PARSIFAL(1983, Fr.)

Claire Toeman
SHOCK TREATMENT(1981); MOONLIGHTING(1982, Brit.)

Ludovico Toeplitz
PRIVATE LIFE OF HENRY VIII, THE(1933), p; DICTATOR, THE(1935, Brit./Ger.), p; BELOVED VAGABOND, THE(1936, Brit.), p; GIRL FROM MAXIM'S, THE(1936, Brit.), p; CHILDREN OF CHANCE(1949, Brit.), p

Arnaoldo Toeri
LOST HAPPINESS(1948, Ital.)

Jenoe Toerzs
MISS PRESIDENT(1935, Hung.)

Blossom Toes
LA COLLECTIONNEUSE(1971, Fr.), m

Malcolm Toes
NO BLADE OF GRASS(1970, Brit.)

Arturo Tofanelli
COMMANDO(1962, Ital., Span., Bel., Ger.), w

Gilberto Tofano
WAR AND PEACE(1956, Ital./U.S.)

Sergio Tofano
DREAMS IN A DRAWER(1957, Fr./Ital.); HEAD OF THE FAMILY(1967, Ital./Fr.); GUILT IS NOT MINE(1968, Ital.)

Andre Toffel
ON THE RIVERA(1951); DOGS OF WAR, THE(1980, Brit.)

Lino Toffolo
WHEN WOMEN HAD TAILS(1970, Ital.)

Jotaro Togami
SECRET SCROLLS(PART I)**1/2 (1968, Jap.); KOJIRO(1967, Jap.)

Seuko Togami
FRANKENSTEIN CONQUERS THE WORLD(1964, Jap./US)

Yoshiko Togawa
TOKYO STORY(1972, Jap.)

Chotaro Togin
GODZILLA'S REVENGE(1969); YOG-MONSTER FROM SPACE(1970, Jap.)

Chutaro Togin
WE WILL REMEMBER(1966, Jap.)

Rick Tognazzi
OPIATE '67(1967, Fr./Ital.)

Riki Tognazzi
TRAGEDY OF A RIDICULOUS MAN, THE(1982, Ital.)

Ugo Tognazzi
TOTO IN THE MOON(1957, Ital./Span.); PSYCOSISSIMO(1962, Ital.); CONJUGAL BED, THE(1963, Ital.); APE WOMAN, THE(1964, Ital.); CRAZY DESIRE(1964, Ital.); LOVE, THE ITALIAN WAY(1964, Ital.); AMERICAN WIFE, AN(1965, Ital.); FASCIST, THE(1965, Ital.); HOURS OF LOVE, THE(1965, Ital.); MAGNIFICENT CUCKOLD, THE(1965, Fr./Ital.); RUN FOR YOUR WIFE(1966, Fr./Ital.); VERY HANDY MAN, A(1966, Fr./Ital.); CLIMAX, THE(1967, Fr., Ital.); HEAD OF THE FAMILY(1967, Ital./Fr.); OPIATE '67(1967, Fr./Ital.); BARBARELLA(1968, Fr./Ital.); MAN WITH THE BALLOONS, THE(1968, Ital./Fr.); MAN WHO CAME FOR COFFEE, THE(1970, Ital.); LA GRANDE BOUFFE(1973, Fr.); DON'T TOUCH WHITE WOMEN!(1974, Fr.); DUCH IN ORANGE SAUCE(1976, Ital.); GOODNIGHT, LADIES AND GENTLEMEN(1977, Ital.); VIVA ITALIA(1978, Ital.); LA CAGE AUX FOLLES(1979, Fr./Ital.); LA CAGE AUX FOLLES II(1981, Ital./Fr.); TRAGEDY OF A RIDICULOUS MAN, THE(1982, Ital.); CLARETTA AND BEN(1983, Ital., Fr.)
1984
JOKE OF DESTINY LYING IN WAIT AROUND THE CORNER LIKE A STREET-BANDIT, A(1984, Ital.)

Alex Togni
LOVES AND TIMES OF SCARAMOUCHE, THE(1976, Ital.)

Togo
SIGN OF FOUR, THE(1932, Brit.)

Haruko Togo
DANGEROUS KISS, THE(1961, Jap.); EARLY AUTUMN(1962, Jap.); HONOLULU-TOKYO-HONG KONG(1963, Hong Kong/Jap.); I LIVE IN FEAR(1967, Jap.)

Kazuo Togo
DELICATE DELINQUENT, THE(1957)

David Toguri
DEVIL'S BRIDE, THE(1968, Brit.), ch; WELCOME TO THE CLUB(1971); ROCKY HORROR PICTURE SHOW, THE(1975, Brit.), ch
1984
GIVE MY REGARDS TO BROAD STREET(1984, Brit.), ch

Maria Toho
PICTURES(1982, New Zealand)

Niall Toibin
GUNS IN THE HEATHER(1968, Brit.); RYAN'S DAUGHTER(1970, Brit.); POITIN(1979, Irish); OUTSIDER, THE(1980); WAGNER(1983, Brit./Hung./Aust.)

A. Toidze
DRAGONFLY, THE(1955 USSR)

Paul Toien
FOLIES DERGERE(1935)

Teresa Toigo
1984
CHILDREN OF THE CORN(1984)

Akos Toinay
DRAKE THE PIRATE(1935, Brit.), w

Annie Toinon
WAYS OF LOVE(1950, Ital./Fr.)

Mme. Toinon
ANGELE(1934 Fr.)

Koji Toita
PRODIGAL SON, THE(1964, Jap.), p

Tok
XTRO(1983, Brit.)

Frank Tokanaga
Silents
GIRL IN THE DARK, THE(1918)

Norman Tokar
BIG RED(1962), d; SAVAGE SAM(1963), d; THOSE CALLOWAYS(1964), d; TIGER WALKS, A(1964), d; FOLLOW ME, BOYS!(1966), d; UGLY DACHSHUND, THE(1966), d; HAPPIEST MILLIONAIRE, THE(1967), d; HORSE IN THE GRAY FLANNEL SUIT, THE(1968), d; RASCAL(1969), d; BOATNIKS, THE(1970), d; SNOWBALL EXPRESS(1972), d; WHERE THE RED FERN GROWS(1974), d; APPLE DUMPLING GANG, THE(1975), d; NO DEPOSIT, NO RETURN(1976), d; CANDLESHOE(1978), d; CAT FROM OUTER SPACE, THE(1978), p, d

Tokatoo
Misc. Silents
KIVALINA OF THE ICE LANDS(1925)

Leon Tokatyan
WHO KILLED TEDDY BEAR?(1965), w

Lana Tokel
UNION CITY(1980), ed

Yoji Toki
SONG FROM MY HEART, THE(1970, Jap.)

Jerry Tokofsky
WHERE'S POPPA?(1970), p
1984
DREAMSCAPE(1984), p; FEAR CITY(1984), p

Claus Toksvig
REPTILICUS(1962, U.S./Den.)

Hiroshi Tokuda
1984
ANTARCTICA(1984, Jap.), prod d

Marilyn Tokuda
XANADU(1980); MY TUTOR(1983)
1984
ALL OF ME(1984)

Yoshiyuki Tokumasa
YOG-MONSTER FROM SPACE(1970, Jap.), ph

Frank Tokunaga
TEAHOUSE OF THE AUGUST MOON, THE(1956); ESCAPADE IN JAPAN(1957)
Silents
ANTHING ONCE(1917)

Narumi Tokura
ALMOST TRANSPARENT BLUE(1980, Jap.)

Henriette Tol
1984
QUESTION OF SILENCE(1984, Neth.)

Johnny Tolan
TO PLEASE A LADY(1950)

Kathleen Tolan
DEATH WISH(1974); LINE, THE(1982)

Larry Tolan
SAVAGE, THE(1953)

Lawrence Tolan
ENFORCER, THE(1951); FORT WORTH(1951); INSIDE THE WALLS OF FOLSOM PRISON(1951); PEOPLE AGAINST O'HARA, THE(1951)

Michael Tolan
HIAWATHA(1952); SECOND CHANCE(1953); GREATEST STORY EVER TOLD, THE(1965); HOUR OF THE GUN(1967); JOURNEY INTO DARKNESS(1968, Brit.); JOHN AND MARY(1969); LOST MAN, THE(1969); 300 YEAR WEEKEND(1971); FIVE ON THE BLACK HAND SIDE(1973), p; ALL THAT JAZZ(1979)

Richard Tolan
1984
SECRETS(1984, Brit.)
Misc. Talkies
DOLL'S EYE(1982)

Thomas M. Tolan
KING OF COMEDY, THE(1983)

Gregg Toland
BULLDOG DRUMMOND(1929), ph; CONDEMNED(1929), ph; THIS IS HEA-
VEN(1929), ph; TRESPASSER, THE(1929), ph; DEVIL TO PAY, THE(1930), ph; RAF-
FLES(1930), ph; WHOOPEE(1930), ph; INDISCREET(1931), ph; ONE HEAVENLY
NIGHT(1931), ph; PALMY DAYS(1931), ph; TONIGHT OR NEVER(1931), ph; UNHO-
LY GARDEN, THE(1931), ph; KID FROM SPAIN, THE(1932), ph; MAN WAN-
TED(1932), ph; PLAY GIRL(1932), ph; TENDERFOOT, THE(1932), ph;
WASHINGTON MASQUERADE(1932), ph; MASQUERADER, THE(1933), ph; NUI-
SANCE, THE(1933), ph; ROMAN SCANDALS(1933), ph; TUGBOAT ANNIE(1933), ph;
LAZY RIVER(1934), ph; NANA(1934), ph; WE LIVE AGAIN(1934), ph; DARK AN-
GEL, THE(1935), ph; FORSAKING ALL OTHERS(1935), ph; LES MISERA-
BLES(1935), ph; MAD LOVE(1935), ph; PUBLIC HERO NO. 1(1935), ph;
SPLENDOR(1935), ph; WEDDING NIGHT, THE(1935), ph; BELOVED ENEMY(1936),
ph; COME AND GET IT(1936), ph; ROAD TO GLORY, THE(1936), ph; STRIKE ME
PINK(1936), ph; THESE THREE(1936), ph; DEAD END(1937), ph; HISTORY IS
MADE AT NIGHT(1937), ph; WOMAN CHASES MAN(1937), ph; COWBOY AND THE
LADY, THE(1938), ph; GOLDWYN FOLLIES, THE(1938), ph; KIDNAPPED(1938), ph;
INTERMEZZO: A LOVE STORY(1939), ph; RAFFLES(1939), ph; THEY SHALL HAVE
MUSIC(1939), ph; WUTHERING HEIGHTS(1939), ph; GRAPES OF WRATH(1940),
ph; LONG VOYAGE HOME, THE(1940), ph; WESTERNER, THE(1940), ph; BALL OF
FIRE(1941), ph; CITIZEN KANE(1941), ph; LITTLE FOXES, THE(1941), ph; OUT-
LAW, THE(1943), ph; BEST YEARS OF OUR LIVES, THE(1946), ph; KID FROM
BOOKLYN, THE(1946), ph; SONG OF THE SOUTH(1946), ph; BISHOP'S WIFE,
THE(1947), ph; ENCHANTMENT(1948), ph; SONG IS BORN, A(1948), ph
Silents
QUEEN KELLY(1929), ph
John Toland
LIFE STUDY(1973)
Virginia Toland
LET'S DANCE(1950); GASOLINE ALLEY(1951)
Gene Tolar
FEROCIOUS PAL(1934)
R. L. Tolbert
LEGEND OF THE LONE RANGER, THE(1981)
John S. Toldy
ARISE, MY LOVE(1940), w; PARIS CALLING(1941), w
William Tole
NEW YORK, NEW YORK(1977)
Philippe Toledano
FAR FROM DALLAS(1972, Fr.), d, w
Daniel Toledo
RAT FINK(1965), art d
Joe Toledo
BOBBIE JO AND THE OUTLAW(1976)
Jose Toledo
NIGHTWING(1979)
Rodolfo Toledo
SCALPHUNTERS, THE(1968)
Lito Tolentino
YEAR OF LIVING DANGEROUSLY, THE(1982, Aus.)
Narciso Tolentino
DANCE OF THE DWARFS(1983, U.S., Phil.), spec eff
Hooper Toler
Silents
GIRL OF MY HEART(1920)
Pauline Toler
Silents
SEVEN CHANCES(1925)
Ron Toler
NOCTURNA(1979)
Sidney Toler
MADAME X(1929); STRICTLY DISHONORABLE(1931); WHITE SHOULDERS(1931);
BILLION DOLLAR SCANDAL(1932); BLONDE VENUS(1932); BLONDIE OF THE
FOLLIES(1932); IS MY FACE RED?(1932); PHANTOM PRESIDENT, THE(1932);
RADIO PATROL(1932); SPEAK EASILY(1932); STRANGERS IN LOVE(1932); TOM
BROWN OF CULVER(1932); HE LEARNED ABOUT WOMEN(1933); KING OF THE
JUNGLE(1933); NARROW CORNER, THE(1933); WAY TO LOVE, THE(1933); WORLD
CHANGES, THE(1933); DARK HAZARD(1934); HERE COMES THE GROOM(1934);
MASSACRE(1934); OPERATOR 13(1934); REGISTERED NURSE(1934); SPIT-
FIRE(1934); TRUMPET BLOWS, THE(1934); UPPER WORLD(1934); CALL OF THE
WILD(1935); CHAMPAGNE FOR BREAKFAST(1935); DARING YOUNG MAN,
THE(1935); ORCHIDS TO YOU(1935); ROMANCE IN MANHATTAN(1935); THIS IS
THE LIFE(1935); GIVE US THIS NIGHT(1936); GORGEOUS HUSSY, THE(1936);
LONGEST NIGHT, THE(1936); OUR RELATIONS(1936); THREE GODFA-
THERS(1936); DOUBLE WEDDING(1937); THAT CERTAIN WOMAN(1937); CHARL-
IE CHAN IN HONOLULU(1938); GOLD IS WHERE YOU FIND IT(1938); IF I WERE
KING(1938); MYSTERIOUS RIDER, THE(1938); ONE WILD NIGHT(1938); UP THE
RIVER(1938); WIDE OPEN FACES(1938); CHARLIE CHAN AT TREASURE IS-
LAND(1939); CHARLIE CHAN IN RENO(1939); CHARLIE CHAN IN THE CITY OF
DARKNESS(1939); DISBARRED(1939); HERITAGE OF THE DESERT(1939); KID
FROM KOKOMO, THE(1939); KING OF CHINATOWN(1939); LAW OF THE PAM-
PAS(1939); CHARLIE CHAN AT THE WAX MUSEUM(1940); CHARLIE CHAN IN
PANAMA(1940); CHARLIE CHAN'S MURDER CRUISE(1940); MURDER OVER NEW
YORK(1940); CHARLIE CHAN IN RIO(1941); DEAD MEN TELL(1941); CASTLE IN
THE DESERT(1942); NIGHT TO REMEMBER, A(1942); ISLE OF FORGOTTEN
SINS(1943); WHITE SAVAGE(1943); CHARLIE CHAN IN BLACK MAGIC(1944);
CHARLIE CHAN IN THE SECRET SERVICE(1944); CHINESE CAT, THE(1944); IT'S
IN THE BAG(1945); JADE MASK, THE(1945); SCARLET CLUE, THE(1945); SHANG-
HAI COBRA, THE(1945); DANGEROUS MONEY(1946); DARK ALIBI(1946); RED
DRAGON, THE(1946); SHADOWS OVER CHINATOWN(1946); TRAP, THE(1947)
Silents
BAIT, THE(1921), w
Jackie Toles
CARWASH(1976)
Raffaello Tolfo
WHITE SHEIK, THE(1956, Ital.), art d
Louis H. Tolhurst
MYSTERIOUS ISLAND(1929), spec eff

Robin Tolhurst
STRANGE AFFAIR, THE(1968, Brit.)
Stan Tolhurst
OVERLANDERS, THE(1946, Brit./Aus.); BUSH CHRISTMAS(1947, Brit.); KAN-
GAROO(1952)
N. Tolkachyov
WAR AND PEACE(1968, USSR)
James Tolkan
STILETTO(1969); THEY MIGHT BE GIANTS(1971); FRIENDS OF EDDIE COYLE,
THE(1973); LOVE AND DEATH(1975); PRINCE OF THE CITY(1981); WOLFEN(1981);
AUTHOR! AUTHOR!(1982); HANKY-PANKY(1982); NIGHTMARES(1983); WAR-
GAMES(1983)
1984
ICEMAN(1984); RIVER, THE(1984)
J.R.R. Tolkien
LORD OF THE RINGS, THE(1978), w
James Tolkin
SERPICO(1973)
Mel Tolkin
LAST OF THE SECRET AGENTS?, THE(1966), w
Stacy Heather Tolkin
CONCORDE, THE–AIRPORT '79(
Betsy Toll
LOVE LETTERS(1983)
Gerry Toll
BLOODSUCKING FREAKS(1982), ph
John Toll
YOUNG GRADUATES, THE(1971), ph; HOAX, THE(1972), ph
Lionel J. Toll
BLONDE SAVAGE(1947), p
Pamela Toll
RASCAL(1969); TUNNELVISION(1976); HOUSE CALLS(1978)
August Tollaire
HIS CAPTIVE WOMAN(1929); HOT FOR PARIS(1930); PASSIONATE PLUM-
BER(1932); GIRL WITHOUT A ROOM(1933)
Silents
WHAT PRICE GLORY(1926); MONKEY TALKS, THE(1927); TENDER HOUR,
THE(1927); FOUR SONS(1928); WIFE SAVERS(1928)
Auguste Tollaire
WEDDING NIGHT, THE(1935)
Gerry Tolland
PLUMBER, THE(1980, Aus.), m
Helga Tolle
DIE FASTNACHTSBEICHTE(1962, Ger.)
H.V. Tollemach
Misc. Silents
STREET OF ADVENTURE, THE(1921, Brit.)
Ernst Toller
PASTOR HALL(1940, Brit.), w
Gene Toller
JAWS OF JUSTICE(1933)
Jean Tolley
Silents
TAKE IT FROM ME(1926)
Misc. Silents
UNINVITED GUEST, THE(1924)
June Tolley
GARMENT JUNGLE, THE(1957)
Paul Tolley
1984
BROTHERS(1984, Aus.), art d
Nat Tolmach
LOVED ONE, THE(1965), cos; POCKET MONEY(1972), cos
Daniel Day Tolman
PLAINSMAN AND THE LADY(1946)
Jennifer Tolman
SAILOR WHO FELL FROM GRACE WITH THE SEA, THE(1976, Brit.)
Kenneth Tolman
GIT!(1965), set d
Akos Tolnay
ELEPHANT BOY(1937, Brit.), w; SECOND BUREAU(1937, Brit.), w; THUNDER IN
THE CITY(1937, Brit.), p, w; WIFE OF GENERAL LING, THE(1938, Brit.), w; WINGS
OVER AFRICA(1939), w; FACE BEHIND THE SCAR(1940, Brit.), w; OPEN CITY(1946,
Ital.); CALL OF THE BLOOD(1948, Brit.), w; DISILLUSION(1949, Ital.), w
Askos Tolnay
GOLDEN MADONNA, THE(1949, Brit.), w
Klari Tolnay
AZURE EXPRESS(1938, Hung.); FATHER(1967, Hung.)
Akos Tolney
WHITE WARRIOR, THE(1961, Ital./Yugo.), w. Gino
Alfred Tolney
BALL AT SAVOY(1936, Brit.), w
Marilu Tolo
MARRIAGE–ITALIAN STYLE(1964, Fr./Ital.); HERCULES VS THE GIANT WARRI-
ORS(1965 Fr./Ital.); SCHEHERAZADE(1965, Fr./Ital./Span.); KISS THE GIRLS AND
MAKE THEM DIE(1967, U.S./Ital.); CANDY(1968, Ital./Fr.); OLDEST PROFESSION,
THE(1968, Fr./Ital./Ger.); WITCHES, THE(1969, Fr./Ital.); CONFESSIONS OF A
POLICE CAPTAIN(1971, Ital.); ROMANCE OF A HORSE THIEF(1971); BLUE-
BEARD(1972); DON'T TURN THE OTHER CHEEK(1974, Ital./Ger./Span.); BEYOND
FEAR(1977, Fr.); GREEK TYCOON, THE(1978)
Susan Tolsky
PRETTY MAIDS ALL IN A ROW(1971); CHARLEY AND THE ANGEL(1973);
RECORD CITY(1978); HOW TO BEAT THE HIGH COST OF LIVING(1980)
Arnold Tolson
Silents
MEG(1926, Brit.), w
Pearl Tolson
JOAN OF OZARK(1942)

Jeffrey Tolstad
FRATERNITY ROW(1977)
Scott Tolstad
FRATERNITY ROW(1977)
Alexei Tolstoy
HYPERBOLOID OF ENGINEER GARIN, THE(1965, USSR), w
Leo Tolstoy
REDEMPTION(1930), w; RESURRECTION(1931), w; WE LIVE AGAIN(1934), w; LIVING CORPSE, THE(1940, Fr.), w; WAR AND PEACE(1956, Ital./U.S.), w; WHITE WARRIOR, THE(1961, Ital./Yugo.), w. Gino; BLACK SABBATH(1963, Ital.), w; RESURRECTION(1963, USSR), w; WAR AND PEACE(1968, USSR), w
1984
L'ARGENT(1984, Fr./Switz.), w
Count Leo Tolstoy
ANNA KARENINA(1935), w; ANNA KARENINA(1948, Brit.), w
Leo Nikolayevich Tolstoy
Silents
LOVE(1927), w
Serge Tolstoy
LONGEST DAY, THE(1962)
Julia Tolsva
Silents
ANY WIFE(1922), w
Marilu Tolu
POPPY IS ALSO A FLOWER, THE(1966); DJANGO KILL(1967, Ital./Span.)
Yuriy Tolubeyeu
OVERCOAT, THE(1965, USSR)
Y. Tolubeyev
NEW HORIZONS(1939, USSR)
Yuri Tolubeyev
DON QUIXOTE(1961, USSR); HAMLET(1966, USSR); THEY CALL ME RO-BERT(1967, USSR)
Alexander Toluboff
RASPUTIN AND THE EMPRESS(1932), art d; QUEEN CHRISTINA(1933), art d; CHAINED(1934), art d; RIP TIDE(1934), art d; BIG BROWN EYES(1936), art d; SPENDTHRIFT(1936), art d; STAND-IN(1937), art d; VOGUES OF 1938(1937), art d; YOU ONLY LIVE ONCE(1937), art d; ALGIERS(1938), art d; BLOCKADE(1938), art d; TRADE WINDS(1938), art d; STAGECOACH(1939), art d
Silents
LOVE(1927), set d; LOVELORN, THE(1927), set d; MOCKERY(1927), set d; ADVEN-TURER, THE(1928), set d
Theodore Toluboff
CAT AND THE FIDDLE(1934), art d
Anna Tom
NIGHT HAS A THOUSAND EYES(1948)
Carl Tom
QUILLER MEMORANDUM, THE(1966, Brit.), cos
Connie Tom
KING OF GAMBLERS(1937)
Conrad Tom
PRIVATE ANGELO(1949, Brit.)
Frank Tom
ROAR(1981)
Konrad Tom
YIDDLE WITH HIS FIDDLE(1937, Pol.), w
Lauren Tom
1984
NOTHING LASTS FOREVER(1984)
Layne Tom, Jr.
CHARLIE CHAN AT THE OLYMPICS(1937); DAUGHTER OF SHANGHAI(1937); HURRICANE, THE(1937); CHARLIE CHAN IN HONOLULU(1938); CHARLIE CHAN'S MURDER CRUISE(1940); CHINA SKY(1945)
Paul Tom
GENERAL DIED AT DAWN, THE(1936)
Christian Toma
FANTOMAS(1966, Fr./Ital.)
Dave Tomack
UNDER FIRE(1957)
David Tomack
HE LAUGHED LAST(1956); SPIDER, THE(1958); IMITATION OF LIFE(1959); PURPLE GANG, THE(1960); EXPERIMENT IN TERROR(1962)
Michael Tomack
THIS IS ELVIS(1982)
Sid Tomack
THRILL OF BRAZIL, THE(1946); BLONDIE'S HOLIDAY(1947); DOUBLE LIFE, A(1947); FOR THE LOVE OF RUSTY(1947); FRAMED(1947); I LOVE TROUBLE(1947); FORCE OF EVIL(1948); HOLLOW TRIUMPH(1948); HOMICIDE FOR THREE(1948); MY GIRL TISA(1948); ABANDONED(1949); BOSTON BLACKIE'S CHINESE VEN-TURE(1949); CRIME DOCTOR'S DIARY, THE(1949); HOUSE OF STRANGERS(1949); KNOCK ON ANY DOOR(1949); MAKE BELIEVE BALLROOM(1949); SORROWFUL JONES(1949); FULLER BRUSH GIRL, THE(1950); LOVE THAT BRUTE(1950); SIDE STREET(1950); JOE PALOOKA IN TRIPLE CROSS(1951); NEVER TRUST A GAM-BLER(1951); TWO TICKETS TO BROADWAY(1951); HOODLUM EMPIRE(1952); SOMEBODY LOVES ME(1952); LIVING IT UP(1954); GIRL RUSH, THE(1955); KETTLES IN THE OZARKS, THE(1956); THAT CERTAIN FEELING(1956); THESE WILDER YEARS(1956); SPRING REUNION(1957); TOO MUCH, TOO SOON(1958); LAST TRAIN FROM GUN HILL(1959); SAIL A CROOKED SHIP(1961)
Misc. Talkies
BLIND SPOT(1947)
Tullio Tomadoni
BARABBAS(1962, Ital.)
Tomahawks
EDUCATION OF SONNY CARSON, THE(1974)
Titti Tomaino
EVIL EYE(1964 Ital.)
Joe Tomal
KANGAROO(1952)

O'Brian Tomalin
DOGS(1976), w; ACAPULCO GOLD(1978), w
David Tomaras
SMALL CIRCLE OF FRIENDS, A(1980)
Ludovico Tomarchio
SWISS MISS(1938)
Jason Tomarken
STAR CHAMBER, THE(1983)
Peter Tomarken
HEAVEN CAN WAIT(1978)
Tomas
NEST, THE(1982, Span.)
Milagros Tomas
VIRIDIANA(1962, Mex./Span.)
Sharon Tomas
SIXTH AND MAIN(1977)
Vincente Tomas
SCAVENGERS, THE(1959, U.S./Phil.), art d
Joachim Tomaschewsky
NAKED AMONG THE WOLVES(1967, Ger.)
Frank Tomasello
FLASHDANCE(1983)
Andre Tomasi
MY WIFE'S HUSBAND(1965, Fr./Ital.)
Henri Tomasi
LETTERS FROM MY WINDMILL(1955, Fr.), m
Vincenzo Tomasi
FROM HELL TO VICTORY(1979, Fr./Ital./Span.), ed
Jenny Tomasin
ADVENTURES OF BARRY McKENZIE(1972, Austral.); MR. QUILP(1975, Brit.)
Jeana Tomasina
BEACH GIRLS(1982); 10 TO MIDNIGHT(1983)
1984
UP THE CREEK(1984)
George Tomasine
WILD HARVEST(1947), ed
George Tomasini
TURNING POINT, THE(1952), ed; HOUDINI(1953), ed; STALAG 17(1953), ed; ELE-PHANT WALK(1954), ed; REAR WINDOW(1954), ed; TO CATCH A THIEF(1955), ed; MAN WHO KNEW TOO MUCH, THE(1956), ed; WRONG MAN, THE(1956), ed; HEAR ME GOOD(1957), ed; I MARRIED A MONSTER FROM OUTER SPACE(1958), ed; VERTIGO(1958), ed; PSYCHO(1960), ed; TIME MACHINE, THE(1960; Brit./U.S.), ed; MISFITS, THE(1961), ed; CAPE FEAR(1962), ed; BIRDS, THE(1963), ed; WHO'S BEEN SLEEPING IN MY BED?(1963), ed; MARNIE(1964), ed; SEVEN FACES OF DR. LAO(1964), ed; IN HARM'S WAY(1965), ed
Giulio Tomasini
VERY HANDY MAN, A(1966, Fr./Ital.)
Jeana Tomasino
HISTORY OF THE WORLD, PART 1(1981); LOOKER(1981); OFF THE WALL(1983)
Jan Tomaskovic
MAN WHO LIES, THE(1970, Czech./Fr.), p
Vincenzo Tomassi
WEEKEND MURDERS, THE(1972, Ital.), ed; TEMPTER, THE(1978, Ital.), ed; ZOM-BIE(1980, Ital.), ed
1984
BLACK CAT, THE(1984, Ital./Brit.), ed; HOUSE BY THE CEMETERY, THE(1984, Ital.), ed, cos; RUSH(1984, Ital.), ed
Vincerzo Tomassi
CHOSEN, THE(1978, Brit./Ital.), ed
Christa Tomasulo
1984
MUPPETS TAKE MANHATTAN, THE(1984)
Teresa Tomaszewska
PASSENGER, THE(1970, Pol.), makeup
Bohdan Tomaszewski
BOXER(1971, Pol.), w
Henry Tomaszewski
BILLY IN THE LOWLANDS(1979); DARK END OF THE STREET, THE(1981)
Giovanni Tomatis
Silents
CABIRIA(1914, Ital.), ph
T. Tomatis
LOVE IN MOROCCO(1933, Fr.), ph
Julio Tomaz
MR. MAJESTYK(1974)
Despina Tomazani
THEY CALL HER ONE EYE(1974, Swed.)
Andrew Tombee
CHARTER PILOT(1940)
Andrew Tombes
BOWERY, THE(1933); BORN TO BE BAD(1934); MOULIN ROUGE(1934); DOUBT-ING THOMAS(1935); HERE COMES COOKIE(1935); MUSIC IS MAGIC(1935); THANKS A MILLION(1935); HERE COMES TROUBLE(1936); HOT MONEY(1936); IT HAD TO HAPPEN(1936); KING OF BURLESQUE(1936); STAGE STRUCK(1936); TICKET TO PARADISE(1936); BORROWING TROUBLE(1937); CHARLIE CHAN AT THE OLYMPICS(1937); CHECKERS(1937); EASY LIVING(1937); FAIR WAR-NING(1937); HOLY TERROR, THE(1937); MEET THE BOY FRIEND(1937); RIDING ON AIR(1937); SING AND BE HAPPY(1937); TIME OUT FOR ROMANCE(1937); TURN OFF THE MOON(1937); 45 FATHERS(1937); ALWAYS IN TROUBLE(1938); BATTLE OF BROADWAY(1938); DESPERATE ADVENTURE, A(1938); FIVE OF A KIND(1938); ONE WILD NIGHT(1938); ROMANCE ON THE RUN(1938); SALLY, IRENE AND MARY(1938); THANKS FOR EVERYTHING(1938); VACATION FROM LOVE(1938); BOY TROUBLE(1939); TOO BUSY TO WORK(1939); WHAT A LIFE(1939); CAPTAIN CAUTION(1940); IN OLD MISSOURI(1940); MONEY TO BURN(1940); THIRD FIN-GER, LEFT HAND(1940); VILLAGE BARN DANCE(1940); WOLF OF NEW YORK(1940); CAUGHT IN THE DRAFT(1941); DON'T GET PERSONAL(1941); DOU-BLE DATE(1941); DOWN MEXICO WAY(1941); GIRL, A GUY AND A GOB, A(1941); HELLZAPOPPIN'(1941); LADY SCARFACE(1941); LAST OF THE DUANES(1941); LOUISIANA PURCHASE(1941); MEET JOHN DOE(1941); MEET THE CHUMP(1941); MELODY FOR THREE(1941); MOUNTAIN MOONLIGHT(1941); OBLIGING YOUNG

Andrew J. Tombes- (continued)

LADY(1941); SIS HOPKINS(1941); TEXAS(1941); WILD MAN OF BORNEO, THE(1941); WORLD PREMIERE(1941); BEDTIME STORY(1942); BETWEEN US GIRLS(1942); BLONDIE GOES TO COLLEGE(1942); CLOSE CALL FOR ELLERY QUEEN, A(1942); LARCENY, INC.(1942); MY GAL SAL(1942); ROAD TO MOROC-CO(1942); THEY ALL KISSED THE BRIDE(1942); CONEY ISLAND(1943); CRAZY HOUSE(1943); DU BARRY WAS A LADY(1943); HI DIDDLE DIDDLE(1943); HIS BUTLER'S SISTER(1943); HI'YA, CHUM(1943); HONEYMOON LODGE(1943); I DOOD IT(1943); IT AIN'T HAY(1943); LET'S FACE IT(1943); MAD GHOUL, THE(1943); MEANEST MAN IN THE WORLD, THE(1943); MY KINGDOM FOR A COOK(1943); REVEILLE WITH BEVERLY(1943); RIDING HIGH(1943); STRANGER IN TOWN, A(1943); SWING FEVER(1943); CAN'T HELP SINGING(1944); GOIN' TO TOWN(1944); LAKE PLACID SERENADE(1944); NIGHT CLUB GIRL(1944); PHANTOM LA-DY(1944); RECKLESS AGE(1944); SAN FERNANDO VALLEY(1944); SINGING SHE-RIFF, THE(1944); SOMETHING FOR THE BOYS(1944); WEEKEND PASS(1944); BRING ON THE GIRLS(1945); DON'T FENCE ME IN(1945); FRONTIER GAL(1945); G.I. HONEYMOON(1945); INCENDIARY BLONDE(1945); PATRICK THE GREAT(1945); RHAPSODY IN BLUE(1945); YOU CAME ALONG(1945); BADMAN'S TERRITORY(1946); SING WHILE YOU DANCE(1946); BEAT THE BAND(1947); CHRISTMAS EVE(1947); DEVIL THUMBS A RIDE, THE(1947); FABULOUS DOR-SEYS, THE(1947); HOPPY'S HOLIDAY(1947); MY WILD IRISH ROSE(1947); TWO GUYS FROM TEXAS(1948); OH, YOU BEAUTIFUL DOLL(1949); HUMPHREY TAKES A CHANCE(1950); JACKPOT, THE(1950); I DREAM OF JEANIE(1952); OKLAHOMA ANNIE(1952); HOW TO BE VERY, VERY, POPULAR(1955)

Andrew J. Tombes
BIG CITY(1937)

Richard Tombleson
IF ...(1968, Brit.)

Maurice Tombragel
LEGION OF LOST FLYERS(1939), w; TROPIC FURY(1939), w; DANGER ON WHEELS(1940), w; HOT STEEL(1940), w; ZANZIBAR(1940), w; HORROR IS-LAND(1941), w; MEN OF THE TIMBERLAND(1941), w; MUTINY IN THE ARC-TIC(1941), w; RAIDERS OF THE DESERT(1941), w; ROAD AGENT(1941), w; DANGER IN THE PACIFIC(1942), w; SWEETHEART OF THE FLEET(1942), w; TWO SENORITAS FROM CHICAGO(1943), w; MUSIC IN MANHATTAN(1944), w; LONE WOLF IN MEXICO, THE(1947), w; CREEPER, THE(1948), w; HIGHWAY 13(1948), w; PRINCE OF THIEVES, THE(1948), w; RETURN OF THE WHISTLER, THE(1948), w; TRAPPED BY BOSTON BLACKIE(1948), w; ARSON, INC.(1949), w; BOSTON BLACK-IE'S CHINESE VENTURE(1949), w; SKY LINER(1949), w; THUNDER IN THE PINES(1949), w; COLORADO RANGER(1950), w; CROOKED RIVER(1950), w; DAL-TON'S WOMEN, THE(1950), w; FAST ON THE DRAW(1950), w; HOSTILE COUN-TRY(1950), w; MARSHAL OF HELDORADO(1950), w; MOTOR PATROL(1950), w; WEST OF THE BRAZOS(1950), w; KENTUCKY JUBILEE(1951), w; FRONTIER PHANTOM, THE(1952), w; LAWLESS COWBOYS(1952), w; NIGHT RAIDERS(1952), w; DALTON GIRLS, THE(1957), w; FORT BOWIE(1958), w; STREET OF DARK-NESS(1958), w; MOON PILOT(1962), w; MONKEYS, GO HOME!(1967), w

John Tomecko
PROJECT MOONBASE(1953)

Louis Tomei
CHARGE AT FEATHER RIVER, THE(1953); JALOPY(1953); JEOPARDY(1953)

Marisa Tomei
1984
FLAMINGO KID, THE(1984)

Louis Tomel
ARMY BOUND(1952)

Frances Tomelty
ROMANTIC ENGLISHWOMAN, THE(1975, Brit./Fr.); MEDUSA TOUCH, THE(1978, Brit.)

Francis Tomelty
BULLSHOT(1983)

Joseph Tomelty
ODD MAN OUT(1947, Brit.); BREAKING THE SOUND BARRIER(1952); GENTLE GUNMAN, THE(1952, Brit.); TREASURE HUNT(1952, Brit.); YOU'RE ONLY YOUNG TWICE(1952, Brit.); HORSE'S MOUTH, THE(1953, Brit.); MEET MR. LUCIFER(1953, Brit.); MELBA(1953, Brit.); CHANCE MEETING(1954, Brit.); DEATH OF MICHAEL TURBIN, THE(1954, Brit.); DEVIL GIRL FROM MARS(1954, Brit.); FRONT PAGE STORY(1954, Brit.); HELL BELOW ZERO(1954, Brit.); HOBSON'S CHOICE(1954, Brit.); TONIGHT'S THE NIGHT(1954, Brit.); ATOMIC MAN, THE(1955, Brit.); BEDEVIL-LED(1955); PRIZE OF GOLD, A(1955); SIMBA(1955, Brit.); KID FOR TWO FARTH-INGS, A(1956, Brit.); MOBY DICK(1956, Brit.); JOHN AND JULIE(1957, Brit.); NIGHT TO REMEMBER, A(1958, Brit.); TREAD SOFTLY STRANGER(1959, Brit.); CAPTAIN'S TABLE, THE(1960, Brit.); DAY THEY ROBBED THE BANK OF ENGLAND, THE(1960, Brit.); HELL IS A CITY(1960, Brit.); UPSTAIRS AND DOWNSTAIRS(1961, Brit.); LIFE IS A CIRCUS(1962, Brit.); SWORD OF LANCELOT(1963, Brit.); BLACK TORMENT, THE(1965, Brit.)

John Tomerlin
OPERATION BIKINI(1963), w

Mariza Tomic
BIG SHOW, THE(1961)

Mica Tomic
THREE(1967, Yugo.)

Xica Tomic
FRAGRANCE OF WILD FLOWERS, THE(1979, Yugo.)

Frank Tomick
HELL'S ANGELS(1930); CEILNG ZERO(1935)
Silents
AIR HAWK, THE(1924); AIR PATROL, THE(1928)

Nakajiro Tomida
EAST CHINA SEA(1969, Jap.)

Massahiro Tomikawa
SHOGUN ASSASSIN(1980, Jap.)

Alvena Tomin
BAILOUT AT 43,000(1957), cos

Misako Tominaga
GATE OF FLESH(1964, Jap.)

Yuki Tominaga
NAKED YOUTH(1961, Jap.); YOUTH IN FURY(1961, Jap.)

V. Tomingas
LAST GAME, THE(1964, USSR)

Arthur Tomioka
NUTCRACKER FANTASY(1979), p

Mike Tomioka
WAR OF THE WIZARDS(1983, Taiwan), ph

Mototaka Tomioka
GODZILLA'S REVENGE(1969), ph

Motoyoshi Tomioka
GODZILLA VS. THE THING(1964, Jap.), spec eff; MONSTERS FROM THE UN-KNOWN PLANET(1975, Jap.), ph

Taeko Tomioka
DOUBLE SUICIDE(1970, Jap.), w

Gualtiero Tomiselli
HEART AND SOUL(1950, Ital.)

Laura Tomiselli
DIVORCE, ITALIAN STYLE(1962, Ital.)

Kotaro Tomita
GODZILLA VS. MEGALON(1976, Jap.)

Nakajiro Tomita
HARBOR LIGHT YOKOHAMA(1970, Jap.)

Tsuneo Tomita
JUDO SHOWDOWN(1966, Jap.), w

Yoski Tomita
BLACKBOARD JUNGLE, THE(1955)

Yukio Tomizawa
SUMMER SOLDIERS(1972, Jap.), p

Alan Tomkins
MACKINTOSH MAN, THE(1973, Brit.), art; ABDICATION, THE(1974, Brit.), art d; JUGGERNAUT(1974, Brit.), art d; GREAT EXPECTATIONS(1975, Brit.), art d; ROY-AL FLASH(1975, Brit.), art d; EMPIRE STRIKES BACK, THE(1980), art d; GREEN ICE(1981, Brit.), art d; TRAIL OF THE PINK PANTHER, THE(1982), art d; CURSE OF THE PINK PANTHER(1983), art d; KEEP, THE(1983), art d
1984
LASSITER(1984), art d

Brian Tomkins
WHAT'S NEXT?(1975, Brit.), ed

Darlene Tomkins
FUN IN ACAPULCO(1963)

Don Tomkins
FOLLOW THRU(1930)

F. Tomkins
Silents
LITTLE LORD FAUNTLEROY(1914, Brit.)

Les Tomkins
SHINING, THE(1980), art d

Leslie Tomkins
GREEN ICE(1981, Brit.), art d; YENTL(1983), art d
1984
PASSAGE TO INDIA, A(1984, Brit.), art d

Henen Tomko
DEER HUNTER, THE(1978)

Eric Tomlin
SKYDIVERS, THE(1963); HELLCATS, THE(1968)

Herman Tomlin
HELLCATS, THE(1968), p

Lily Tomlin
NASHVILLE(1975); LATE SHOW, THE(1977); MOMENT BY MOMENT(1978); NINE TO FIVE(1980); INCREDIBLE SHRINKING WOMAN, THE(1981)
1984
ALL OF ME(1984)

Pinky Tomlin
KING SOLOMON OF BROADWAY(1935); PADDY O'DAY(1935); SMART GIRL(1935); TIMES SQUARE LADY(1935); DON'T GET PERSONAL(1936), a, m; SING WHILE YOU'RE ABLE(1937); SWING IT, PROFESSOR(1937); THANKS FOR LISTENING(1937); WITH LOVE AND KISSES(1937); DOWN IN ARKANSAW(1938); HERE COMES ELMER(1943); STORY OF WILL ROGERS, THE(1952); SHE COULDN'T SAY NO(1954)
Misc. Talkies
SING ME A SONG OF TEXAS(1945)

Willie Tomlin
PIE IN THE SKY(1964)

Charles D. Tomlinson
RUBY(1977), set d

Charles Tomlinson
RIVALS(1972), cos

Daniel G. Tomlinson
Silents
CROWD, THE(1928); CAPTAIN LASH(1929), w

David Tomlinson
GARRISON FOLLIES(1940, Brit.); MY WIFE'S FAMILY(1941, Brit.); QUIET WED-DING(1941, Brit.); PIMPERNEL SMITH(1942, Brit.); JOHNNY IN THE CLOUDS(1945, Brit.); ADVENTURESS, THE(1946, Brit.); SCHOOL FOR SECRETS(1946, Brit.); FAME IS THE SPUR(1947, Brit.); MASTER OF BANKDAM, THE(1947, Brit.); BROKEN JOURNEY(1948, Brit.); EASY MONEY(1948, Brit.); HERE COME THE HUG-GETTS(1948, Brit.); LOVE IN WAITING(1948, Brit.); VOTE FOR HUGGETT(1948, Brit.); AMAZING MR. BEECHAM, THE(1949, Brit.); HELTER SKELTER(1949, Brit.); MARRY ME!(1949, Brit.); MIRANDA(1949, Brit.); MY BROTHER'S KEEPER(1949, Brit.); SLEEPING CAR TO TRIESTE(1949, Brit.); WARNING TO WANTONS, A(1949, Brit.); CALLING BULLDOG DRUMMOND(1951, Brit.); HOTEL SAHARA(1951, Brit.); SO LONG AT THE FAIR(1951, Brit.); WOODEN HORSE, THE(1951); CASTLE IN THE AIR(1952, Brit.); MADE IN HEAVEN(1952, Brit.); MAGIC BOX, THE(1952, Brit.); IS YOUR HONEYMOON REALLY NECESSARY?(1953, Brit.); LANDFALL(1953, Brit.); ALL FOR MARY(1956, Brit.); CARRY ON ADMIRAL(1957, Brit.); FURTHER UP THE CREEK!(1958, Brit.); THREE MEN IN A BOAT(1958, Brit.); UP THE CREEK(1958, Brit.); FOLLOW THAT HORSE!(1960, Brit.); TOM JONES(1963, Brit.); MARY POP-PINS(1964); CITY UNDER THE SEA(1965, Brit.); TRUTH ABOUT SPRING, THE(1965, Brit.); LIQUIDATOR, THE(1966, Brit.); LOVE BUG, THE(1968); BEDKNOBS AND BROOMSTICKS(1971); WOMBLING FREE(1977, Brit.); DOMINIQUE(1978, Brit.); WATER BABIES, THE(1979, Brit.); FIENDISH PLOT OF DR. FU MANCHU, THE(1980)

Flying Officer David Tomlinson
JOURNEY TOGETHER(1946, Brit.)
Lionel Tomlinson
HIDDEN MENACE, THE(1940, Brit.), ed; ONE NIGHT IN PARIS(1940, Brit.), ed; FALSE RAPTURE(1941), ed; TERROR, THE(1941, Brit.), ed; MY HANDS ARE CLAY(1948, Irish), d; TAKE A POWDER(1953, Brit.), p, d; WHO KILLED VAN LOON?(1984, Brit.), d
Martin Tomlinson
REACH FOR GLORY(1963, Brit.)
Tommy Tomlinson
NO MORE LADIES(1935); FURY(1936); JOURNEY TOGETHER(1946, Brit.)
Amedeo Tommasi
THIS MAN CAN'T DIE(1970, Ital.), m
Andrea Tommasi
ULYSSES(1955, Ital.), set d
Tony Tommy
Silents
CLASSMATES(1924)
Tommy Boy the Horse
SPORTING BLOOD(1931)
Tommy Christian and His Band
Misc. Talkies
HOWDY BROADWAY(1929)
Tommy Devel and Partner
FAREWELL PERFORMANCE(1963, Brit.)
Tommy Dorsey & His Band
DU BARRY WAS A LADY(1943)
Tommy Dorsey and His Band
GIRL CRAZY(1943)
Tommy Dorsey and His Orchestra
LAS VEGAS NIGHTS(1941); SHIP AHOY(1942); PRESENTING LILY MARS(1943); BROADWAY RHYTHM(1944)
Tommy Dorsey and His Orchestras
THRILL OF A ROMANCE(1945)
Tommy Dorsey and Orchestra
SONG IS BORN, A(1948)
Tommy Dorsey's Orchestra
FABULOUS DORSEYS, THE(1947)
Tommy Duncan and his Western All Stars
SOUTH OF DEATH VALLEY(1949)
Tommy Eytle's Calypso Band
ROCK AROUND THE WORLD(1957, Brit.)
Jiro Tomoda
1984
BALLAD OF NARAYAMA, THE(1984, Jap.), p
Hiroshi Tomono
BRIDGE TO THE SUN(1961)
Kasai Tomoo
YAKUZA, THE(1975, U.S./Jap.), spec eff
The Tomorrow
SMASHING TIME(1967 Brit.)
George Tomosini
NORTH BY NORTHWEST(1959), ed
Alan Tompkins
TOUCH OF CLASS, A(1973, Brit.), art d
Andrew Tompkins
WICKER MAN, THE(1974, Brit.)
Angel Tompkins
HANG YOUR HAT ON THE WIND(1969); I LOVE MY WIFE(1970); PRIME CUT(1972); DON IS DEAD, THE(1973); LITTLE CIGARS(1973); HOW TO SEDUCE A WOMAN(1974); TEACHER, THE(1974); WALKING TALL, PART II(1975); FARMER, THE(1977); BEES, THE(1978); ONE MAN JURY(1978); ALLIGATOR(1980)
Bee Tompkins
PANIC IN THE CITY(1968); HEAVEN WITH A GUN(1969); THAT TENDER TOUCH(1969)
Connie Tompkins
MIRACLE OF MORGAN'S CREEK, THE(1944)
Darlene Tompkins
BEYOND THE TIME BARRIER(1960); BLUE HAWAII(1961); MY SIX LOVES(1963)
Joan Tompkins
POPI(1969); CHRISTINE JORGENSEN STORY, THE(1970); I LOVE MY WIFE(1970); ZIGZAG(1970)
Joe Tompkins
FOOLIN' AROUND(1980), cos; MISSING(1982)
Joe I. Tompkins
COAL MINER'S DAUGHTER(1980), cos; RAGGEDY MAN(1981), cos; TRUE CONFESSIONS(1981), cos; MISSING(1982), cos; CROSS CREEK(1983), cos; ROMANTIC COMEDY(1983), cos
1984
IRRECONCILABLE DIFFERENCES(1984), cos; RIVER, THE(1984), cos; SWING SHIFT(1984), cos
Juliet Wilbur Tompkins
FANNY FOLEY HERSELF(1931), w; MISBEHAVING LADIES(1931), w
Silents
LITTLE COMRADE(1919), w
Rex Tompkins
Silents
GREYHOUND, THE(1914)
Troy Tompkins
1984
SAVAGE STREETS(1984)
Dr. Ross Tompson
RAZOR'S EDGE, THE(1946); STRANGE FASCINATION(1952)
Bernard Toms
STRANGE AFFAIR, THE(1968, Brit.), w
Carl Toms
SHE(1965, Brit.), cos; ONE MILLION YEARS B.C.(1967, Brit./U.S.), cos; PREHISTORIC WOMEN(1967, Brit.), cos; THOSE FANTASTIC FLYING FOOLS(1967, Brit), cos; LOST CONTINENT, THE(1968, Brit.), cos; VENGEANCE OF SHE, THE(1968, Brit.), cos; WINTER'S TALE, THE(1968, Brit.), prod d; MOON ZERO TWO(1970,

Brit.), cos; WHEN DINOSAURS RULED THE EARTH(1971, Brit.), cos
Jaroslav Tomsa
LEMONADE JOE(1966, Czech.)
Alex Tomson
DEATHLINE(1973, Brit.), ph
Tomoyuki Tonaka
MAN IN THE STORM, THE(1969, Jap.), p
Kate Toncray
Silents
LAMB, THE(1915); REBECCA OF SUNNYBROOK FARM(1917); CHARM SCHOOL, THE(1921); PRISONERS OF LOVE(1921); COUNTRY KID, THE(1923); LOVER'S LANE(1924); NARROW STREET, THE(1924)
Misc. Silents
CASEY AT THE BAT(1916); LITTLE YANK, THE(1917); STAGE STRUCK(1917); UP THE ROAD WITH SALLIE(1918); VIVIETTE(1918); BING BANG BOOM(1922)
Kate V. Toncray
Silents
OUT OF LUCK(1919)
Tondeleyo
SEPIA CINDERELLA(1947)
Gianrico Tondinelli
LA CAGE AUX FOLLES II(1981, Ital./Fr.)
Franchot Tone
TRUE TO LIFE(1943); WISER SEX, THE(1932); BOMBSHELL(1933); DANCING LADY(1933); GABRIEL OVER THE WHITE HOUSE(1933); MIDNIGHT MARY(1933); STAGE MOTHER(1933); STRANGER'S RETURN(1933); TODAY WE LIVE(1933); GENTLEMEN ARE BORN(1934); GIRL FROM MISSOURI, THE(1934); MOULIN ROUGE(1934); SADIE MCKEE(1934); STRAIGHT IS THE WAY(1934); WORLD MOVES ON, THE(1934); LIVES OF A BENGAL LANCER(1935); MUTINY ON THE BOUNTY(1935); NO MORE LADIES(1935); ONE NEW YORK NIGHT(1935); RECKLESS(1935); DANGEROUS(1936); EXCLUSIVE STORY(1936); GORGEOUS HUSSY, THE(1936); KING STEPS OUT, THE(1936); LOVE ON THE RUN(1936); SUZY(1936); UNGUARDED HOUR, THE(1936); BETWEEN TWO WOMEN(1937); BRIDE WORE RED, THE(1937); QUALITY STREET(1937); THEY GAVE HIM A GUN(1937); GIRL DOWNSTAIRS, THE(1938); LOVE IS A HEADACHE(1938); MAN-PROOF(1938); THREE COMRADES(1938); THREE LOVES HAS NANCY(1938); FAST AND FURIOUS(1939); TRAIL OF THE VIGILANTES(1940); NICE GIRL?(1941); SHE KNEW ALL THE ANSWERS(1941); THIS WOMAN IS MINE(1941); STAR SPANGLED RHYTHM(1942); WIFE TAKES A FLYER, THE(1942); FIVE GRAVES TO CAIRO(1943); HIS BUTLER'S SISTER(1943); PILOT NO. 5(1943); DARK WATERS(1944); HOUR BEFORE THE DAWN, THE(1944); PHANTOM LADY(1944); THAT NIGHT WITH YOU(1945); BECAUSE OF HIM(1946); HER HUSBAND'S AFFAIRS(1947); HONEYMOON(1947); I LOVE TROUBLE(1947); LOST HONEYMOON(1947); EVERY GIRL SHOULD BE MARRIED(1948); JIGSAW(1949); MAN ON THE EIFFEL TOWER, THE(1949); WITHOUT HONOR(1949); HERE COMES THE GROOM(1951); UNCLE VANYA(1958), a, p, d; ADVISE AND CONSENT(1962); LA BONNE SOUPE(1964, Fr./Ital.); IN HARM'S WAY(1965); MICKEY ONE(1965); HIGH COMMISSIONER, THE(1968, U.S./Brit.)
Richard Tone
VAGABOND KING, THE(1956)
Davide Tonelli
ADIEU PHILLIPINE(1962, Fr./Ital.)
Elvira Tonelli
IT HAPPENED IN ROME(1959, Ital.); ORGANIZER, THE(1964, Fr./Ital./Yugo.)
Pat Tonema
LADY IN RED, THE(1979), cos
Anthony Toner
SOMEWHERE IN CAMP(1942, Brit.), w; SOMEWHERE ON LEAVE(1942, Brit.), w; DEMOBBED(1944, Brit.), w; HOME SWEET HOME(1945, Brit.), w; HONEYMOON HOTEL(1946, Brit.), w; CUP-TIE HONEYMOON(1948, Brit.), w; HOLIDAYS WITH PAY(1948, Brit.), w; SCHOOL FOR RANDLE(1949, Brit.), w; WHAT A CARRY ON!(1949, Brit.), w; OVER THE GARDEN WALL(1950, Brit.), w; STICK 'EM UP(1950, Brit.), w
Bessie Toner
Silents
ROMANCE OF TARZAN, THE(1918); TARZAN OF THE APES(1918)
Claire Toner
Silents
AMERICAN LIVE WIRE, AN(1918)
Thomas Toner
ON THE YARD(1978)
Tom Toner
MIDNIGHT LACE(1960); CAPER OF THE GOLDEN BULLS, THE(1967); I LOVE MY WIFE(1970); RETURN OF COUNT YORGA, THE(1971); GLASS HOUSES(1972)
1984
SPLASH(1984)
Tom Tonery
TOOTSIE(1982), set d
Jim Toney
IT'S IN THE AIR(1935); LONELY TRAIL, THE(1936); RHYTHM ON THE RANGE(1936); FIFTY ROADS TO TOWN(1937); LEFT-HANDED LAW(1937); MOUNTAIN JUSTICE(1937); TRUE CONFESSION(1937); CASSIDY OF BAR 20(1938); PRIDE OF THE WEST(1938); SUNSET TRAIL(1938); LADY AND THE MOB, THE(1939); DEVIL AND DANIEL WEBSTER, THE(1941); GHOST AND THE GUEST(1943); HARRIGAN'S KID(1943); COLONEL EFFINGHAM'S RAID(1945); HOLD THAT BLONDE(1945); FORCE OF EVIL(1948); LADY GAMBLES, THE(1949); ONCE MORE, MY DARLING(1949); TAKE ONE FALSE STEP(1949); WHITE HEAT(1949); NO WAY OUT(1950); PEOPLE AGAINST O'HARA, THE(1951)
T. Toney
DOLEMITE(1975), p
Theadore Toney
PETEY WHEATSTRAW(1978), p
Arthur Tong
PANIC IN THE STREETS(1950)
Carolyn Tong
MISTER ROBERTS(1955)
Harold Tong
GENERAL DIED AT DAWN, THE(1936)

Kaem Tong
SALUTE TO THE MARINES(1943)

Kaity Tong
1984
MOSCOW ON THE HUDSON(1984)

Kam Tong
GENERAL DIED AT DAWN, THE(1936); REAL GLORY, THE(1939); ACROSS THE PACIFIC(1942); CHINA GIRL(1942); HIDDEN HAND, THE(1942); JOAN OF OZARK(1942); LURE OF THE ISLANDS(1942); RUBBER RACKETEERS(1942); THEY GOT ME COVERED(1943); TARGET HONG KONG(1952); THIS IS MY LOVE(1954); LOVE IS A MANY-SPLENDORED THING(1955); SOLDIER OF FORTUNE(1955); HUNTERS, THE(1958); WHO WAS THAT LADY?(1960); FLOWER DRUM SONG(1961); IT HAPPENED AT THE WORLD'S FAIR(1963); DIMENSION 5(1966); MISTER BUDDWING(1966); KILL A DRAGON(1967)

Sammee [Sam] Tong
LOVE BEFORE BREAKFAST(1936); GOOD EARTH, THE(1937); ONLY ANGELS HAVE WINGS(1939); OUT OF THIS WORLD(1945); HELL BOUND(1957); SUICIDE BATTALION(1958); IT'S A MAD, MAD, MAD, MAD WORLD(1963); FOR THOSE WHO THINK YOUNG(1964); FLUFFY(1965)

Kathy Tongay
SKIRTS AHOY!(1952)

Russell "Bubba" Tongay
SKIRTS AHOY!(1952)

Lillian B. Tonge
LAUGHING LADY, THE(1930)

Philip Tonge
LOVE FROM A STRANGER(1947); MIRACLE ON 34TH STREET, THE(1947); HANS CHRISTIAN ANDERSEN(1952); O. HENRY'S FULL HOUSE(1952); HOUSE OF WAX(1953); SCANDAL AT SCOURIE(1953); SMALL TOWN GIRL(1953); ELEPHANT WALK(1954); KHYBER PATROL(1954); TRACK OF THE CAT(1954); DESERT SANDS(1955); PRODIGAL, THE(1955); PARDNERS(1956); PEACEMAKER, THE(1956); LES GIRLS(1957); WITNESS FOR THE PROSECUTION(1957); DARBY'S RANGERS(1958); MACABRE(1958); INVISIBLE INVADERS(1959); THIS EARTH IS MINE(1959)

Phillip Tonge
HIS DOUBLE LIFE(1933); RICOCHET ROMANCE(1954); SILVER CHALICE, THE(1954)
Silents
STILL WATERS(1915)

Tongolee
SNAKE PEOPLE, THE(1968, Mex./U.S.)

Aldo Toni
DAMON AND PYTHIAS(1962), ph; CATCH AS CATCH CAN(1968, Ital.), ph; WOMAN AT HER WINDOW, A(1978, Fr./Ital./Ger.), ph

Viviana Toni
EYES, THE MOUTH, THE(1982, Ital./Fr.)

Anne Tonietti
JOKER, THE(1961, Fr.); TWO ARE GUILTY(1964, Fr.); SPIRITS OF THE DEAD(1969, Fr./Ital.)

Edoardo Toniolo
RAGE OF THE BUCCANEERS(1963, Ital.); GLADIATORS 7(1964, Span./Ital.)

Edoardo Toniono
ANGELO IN THE CROWD(1952, Ital.)

Alfred Tonkel
CRASHING LAS VEGAS(1956); OH, MEN! OH, WOMEN!(1957); PEYTON PLACE(1957); MARDI GRAS(1958); YOUNG LIONS, THE(1958); HELLER IN PINK TIGHTS(1960)

Phil Tonkin
SECRET OF MAGIC ISLAND, THE(1964, Fr./Ital.)

Gertrude Tonkonogy
THREE-CORNERED MOON(1933), w

David Tonnelli
TOMORROW IS MY TURN(1962, Fr./Ital./Ger.)

Eijiro Tono
SAMURAI(PART II)** (1967, Jap.); SECRET SCROLLS(PART I)**1/2 (1968, Jap.); SEVEN SAMURAI, THE(1956, Jap.); YOJIMBO(1961, Jap.); LOWER DEPTHS, THE(1962, Jap.); OHAYO(1962, Jap.); TWILIGHT STORY, THE(1962, Jap.); NAKED GENERAL, THE(1964, Jap.); THIS MADDING CROWD(1964, Jap.); GREAT WALL, THE(1965, Jap.); RED BEARD(1966, Jap.); I LIVE IN FEAR(1967, Jap.); KILL(1968, Jap.); LOST SEX(1968, Jap.); TORA-SAN PART 2(1970, Jap.); TORA! TORA! TORA!(1970, U.S./Jap.); TOKYO STORY(1972, Jap.); AFFAIR AT AKITSU(1980, Jap.)

Taiji Tonomura
ONIBABA(1965, Jap.)

Toshiyuki Tonomura
DODESKA-DEN(1970, Jap.)

Hatsue Tonooka
FRIENDLY KILLER, THE(1970, Jap.)

Taiji Tonoyama
ISLAND, THE(1962, Jap.); INSECT WOMAN, THE(1964, Jap.); KUROENKO(1968, Jap); EAST CHINA SEA(1969, Jap.); KURAGEJIMA–LEGENDS FROM A SOUTHERN ISLAND(1970, Jap.); AFFAIR AT AKITSU(1980, Jap.); MUDDY RIVER(1982, Jap.)
1984
BALLAD OF NARAYAMA, THE(1984, Jap.)

Adam Tonsberg
1984
ZAPPA(1984, Den.)

Joan Tontaine
CONSTANT NYMPH, THE(1943)

Aldo Tonti
BANDIT, THE(1949, Ital.), ph; MERCHANT OF SLAVES(1949, Ital.), ph; OUTCRY(1949, Ital.), ph; PEDDLIN' IN SOCIETY(1949, Ital.), ph; WITHOUT PITY(1949, Ital.), ph; CENTO ANNI D'AMORE(1954, Ital.), ph; GREATEST LOVE, THE(1954, Ital.), ph; HELLO, ELEPHANT(1954, Ital.), ph; SENSUALITA(1954, Ital.), ph; WAR AND PEACE(1956, Ital./U.S.), ph; NIGHTS OF CABIRIA(1957, Ital.), ph; ATTILA(1958, Ital.), ph; TEMPEST(1958, Ital./Yugo./Fr.), ph; FOR THE FIRST TIME(1959, U.S./Ger./Ital.), ph; IT HAPPENED IN ROME(1959, Ital.), ph; OSSESSIONE(1959, Ital.), ph; SAVAGE INNOCENTS, THE(1960, Brit.), ph; UNDER TEN FLAGS(1960, U.S./Ital.), ph; UNFAITHFULS, THE(1960, Ital.), ph; LOST SOULS(1961, Ital.), ph; AGOSTINO(1962, Ital.), ph; BARABBAS(1962, Ital.), ph; DEVIL, THE(1963), ph; HUNCHBACK OF ROME, THE(1963, Ital.), ph; SHIP OF CONDEMNED WOMEN, THE(1963, ITAL.), ph; APE WOMAN, THE(1964, Ital.), ph; CASANOVA '70(1965, Ital.), ph; CAST A GIANT SHADOW(1966), ph; KISS THE GIRLS AND MAKE THEM DIE(1967, U.S./Ital.), ph; REFLECTIONS IN A GOLDEN EYE(1967), ph; DEVIL IN LOVE, THE(1968, Ital.), ph; MAN WITH THE BALLOONS, THE(1968, Ital./Fr.), ph; TREASURE OF SAN GENNARO(1968, Fr./Ital./Ger.), ph; BIG AND THE BAD, THE(1971, Ital./Fr./Span.), ph; DESERTER, THE(1971 Ital./Yugo.), ph; VALACHI PAPERS, THE(1972, Ital./Fr.), ph; CRAZY JOE(1974), ph; FAMILY, THE(1974, Fr./Ital.), ph; THREE TOUGH GUYS(1974, U.S./Ital.), ph; COUNT OF MONTE CRISTO(1976, Brit.), ph; ASHANTI(1979), ph

Giorgio Tonti
IN SEARCH OF GREGORY(1970, Brit./Ital.), ph

Edmund Tontini
WILD ONES ON WHEELS(1967)

Renato Tontini
DEVIL'S COMMANDMENT, THE zero(1956, Ital.); WOMAN OF ROME(1956, Ital.)

G. Tonunts
SKY CALLS, THE(1959, USSR)

Tony
NEST, THE(1982, Span.)
Silents
TONY RUNS WILD(1926); YANKEE SENOR, THE(1926); LAST TRAIL, THE(1927); DAREDEVIL'S REWARD(1928)

Tony the Horse
Silents
CYCLONE, THE(1920); JUST TONY(1922); STEPPING FAST(1923); OH, YOU TONY!(1924); GREAT K & A TRAIN ROBBERY, THE(1926); NO MAN'S GOLD(1926); ARIZONA WILDCAT(1927); BRONCHO TWISTER(1927); CIRCUS ACE, THE(1927); TUMBLING RIVER(1927)

Tony the Wonder Horse
DESTRY RIDES AGAIN(1932); MY PAL, THE KING(1932); RIDER OF DEATH VALLEY(1932); TEXAS BAD MAN(1932); FLAMING GUNS(1933); HIDDEN GOLD(1933); RUSTLERS' ROUNDUP(1933); TERROR TRAIL(1933)

Edward Tony
REFORM SCHOOL(1939)

Victor Tony
RIDERS OF THE TIMBERLINE(1941)

Tony Coca Cola and the Roosters
DRILLER KILLER(1979)

Tony Crombie and His Rockets
ROCK YOU SINNERS(1957, Brit.)

Tony Kinsey Bands
WEST 11(1963, Brit.)

Tony Martinez and His Band
ROCK AROUND THE CLOCK(1956)

Tony Pastor and His Orchestra
TWO BLONDES AND A REDHEAD(1947)

Rita Toofy
Misc. Silents
GODS OF FATE, THE(1916)

Nora Toohey
NEXT OF KIN(1983, Aus.)

Barry Took
THINK DIRTY(1970, Brit.), w

Arim Tooker
Silents
SPRINGTIME(1915)

W. H. Tooker
Silents
DAUGHTER OF THE SEA, A(1915); DEVIL'S PLAYGROUND, THE(1918); GREATER THAN FAME(1920)

William Tooker
WOMAN OF EXPERIENCE, A(1931); IT'S A GIFT(1934); MURDER BY TELEVISION(1935)
Silents
CHILD FOR SALE, A(1920); WOMAN'S MAN(1920); PEACOCK ALLEY(1922); AVERAGE WOMAN, THE(1924); LADIES MUST DRESS(1927); NIGHT OF LOVE, THE(1927); NIGHT WATCH, THE(1928)
Misc. Silents
LIGHT IN DARKNESS(1917); WOMAN THE GERMANS SHOT(1918); MY FRIEND, THE DEVIL(1922)

William H. Tooker
LOVE IN THE DESERT(1929); SOUP TO NUTS(1930)
Silents
CAPTAIN SWIFT(1914); GREYHOUND, THE(1914); ORDEAL, THE(1914); HOW MOLLY MADE GOOD(1915); SPRINGTIME(1915); AMBITION(1916); EAST LYNNE(1916); ALIAS MRS. JESSOP(1917); CRADLE BUSTER(1922); BRIDE FOR A NIGHT, A(1923); NET, THE(1923); SCARLET LETTER, THE(1926); WHITE BLACK SHEEP, THE(1926); JAKE THE PLUMBER(1927); SWEET SIXTEEN(1928); PROTECTION(1929)
Misc. Silents
BANKER'S DAUGHTER, THE(1914); NORTHERN LIGHTS(1914); AVALANCHE, THE(1915); MODERN MAGDALEN, A(1915); UNBROKEN ROAD, THE(1915); FOOL'S REVENGE, THE(1916); HERE SURRENDER(1916); MODERN THELMA, A(1916); BITTER TRUTH(1917); RED, WHITE AND BLUE BLOOD(1918); WOMAN! WOMAN!(1919); STEALERS, THE(1920); GOD'S COUNTRY AND THE LAW(1921); POWER WITHIN, THE(1921); WORLDS APART(1921); SINNER OR SAINT(1923); WOMAN IN CHAINS, THE(1923); MERRY CAVALIER, THE(1926); LOOK OUT GIRL, THE(1928)

William H. Tooker, Sr.
NO DEFENSE(1929)

George A. Tooks
STILL OF THE NIGHT(1982)

Alan Toomayan
EATING RAOUL(1982), ed
1984
NOT FOR PUBLICATION(1984), ed

Andrew Toombes
COUNTRY BEYOND, THE(1936); DANGEROUS GAME, A(1941); MURDER IN THE BLUE ROOM(1944)

Alfred Toombs
RAISING A RIOT(1957, Brit.), w

Harvey Toombs
FANTASIA(1940), anim; DUMBO(1941), anim; RELUCTANT DRAGON, THE(1941), anim; THREE CABALLEROS, THE(1944), anim; MAKE MINE MUSIC(1946), anim; SONG OF THE SOUTH(1946), anim; MELODY TIME(1948), animators; CINDEREL-LA(1950), anim; ALICE IN WONDERLAND(1951), anim; PETER PAN(1953), anim; LADY AND THE TRAMP(1955), anim; SLEEPING BEAUTY(1959), anim; 1001 ARABIAN NIGHTS(1959), anim; GAY PURR-EE(1962), anim

Bill Toomey
WORLD'S GREATEST ATHLETE, THE(1973)

Brandon Toomey
HELL BELOW ZERO(1954, Brit.)

Brendan Toomey
BOTANY BAY(1953)

Gerald Toomey
KNACK ... AND HOW TO GET IT, THE(1965, Brit.)

Jerry Toomey
SWARM, THE(1978)

Kelly Toomey
1984
RIVER, THE(1984)

Regis Toomey
MAN'S FAVORITE SPORT(?) (1964); ALIBI(1929); ILLUSION(1929); RICH PEO-PLE(1929); WHEEL OF LIFE, THE(1929); CRAZY THAT WAY(1930); FRAMED(1930); GOOD INTENTIONS(1930); LIGHT OF WESTERN STARS, THE(1930); MAN FROM WYOMING, A(1930); SHADOW OF THE LAW(1930); STREET OF CHANCE(1930); FINGER POINTS, THE(1931); FINN AND HATTIE(1931); GRAFT(1931); KICK IN(1931); MURDER BY THE CLOCK(1931); OTHER MEN'S WOMEN(1931); SCANDAL SHEET(1931); TOUCHDOWN!(1931); 24 HOURS(1931); CROWD ROARS, THE(1932); MIDNIGHT PATROL, THE(1932); SHOPWORN(1932); STRANGE ADVEN-TURE(1932); THEY NEVER COME BACK(1932); UNDER EIGHTEEN(1932); LAUGH-ING AT LIFE(1933); PENAL CODE, THE(1933); SHE HAD TO SAY YES(1933); SOLDIERS OF THE STORM(1933); STATE TROOPER(1933); BIG TIME OR BUST(1934); MURDER ON THE BLACKBOARD(1934); PICTURE BRIDES(1934); RED HEAD(1934); SHE HAD TO CHOOSE(1934); WHAT'S YOUR RACKET?(1934); G-MEN(1935); GREAT GOD GOLD(1935); MANHATTAN MOON(1935); ONE FRIGHT-ENED NIGHT(1935); RECKLESS ROADS(1935); RED MORNING(1935); SHADOW OF A DOUBT(1935); BARS OF HATE(1936); BULLDOG EDITION(1936); BACK IN CIRCU-LATION(1937); BIG CITY(1937); MIDNIGHT TAXI(1937); SHADOWS OF THE ORI-ENT(1937); SUBMARINE D-1(1937); HIS EXCITING NIGHT(1938); HUNTED MEN(1938); ILLEGAL TRAFFIC(1938); INVISIBLE MENACE, THE(1938); SKULL AND CROWN(1938); HIDDEN POWER(1939); INDIANAPOLIS SPEEDWAY(1939); MYSTERIOUS MISS X, THE(1939); PIRATES OF THE SKIES(1939); SMASHING THE SPY RING(1939); SOCIETY SMUGGLERS(1939); STREET OF MISSING MEN(1939); THUNDER AFLOAT(1939); TRAPPED IN THE SKY(1939); UNION PACIFIC(1939); WINGS OF THE NAVY(1939); ARIZONA(1940); HIS GIRL FRIDAY(1940); NORTH-WEST MOUNTED POLICE(1940); NORTHWEST PASSAGE(1940); 'TIL WE MEET AGAIN(1940); DEVIL AND MISS JONES, THE(1941); DIVE BOMBER(1941); LAW OF THE TROPICS(1941); LONE WOLF TAKES A CHANCE, THE(1941); MEET JOHN DOE(1941); NURSE'S SECRET, THE(1941); REACHING FOR THE SUN(1941); SHOT IN THE DARK, THE(1941); YOU'RE IN THE ARMY NOW(1941); BULLET SCARS(1942); FOREST RANGERS, THE(1942); I WAS FRAMED(1942); TENNESSEE JOHNSON(1942); THEY DIED WITH THEIR BOOTS ON(1942); DESTROYER(1943); JACK LONDON(1943); DARK MOUNTAIN(1944); DOUGHGIRLS, THE(1944); FOL-LOW THE BOYS(1944); MURDER IN THE BLUE ROOM(1944); PHANTOM LA-DY(1944); SONG OF THE OPEN ROAD(1944); WHEN THE LIGHTS GO ON AGAIN(1944); BETRAYAL FROM THE EAST(1945); FOLLOW THAT WOMAN(1945); SPELLBOUND(1945); STRANGE ILLUSION(1945); BIG SLEEP, THE(1946); CHILD OF DIVORCE(1946); HER SISTER'S SECRET(1946); MYSTERIOUS INTRUDER(1946); SISTER KENNY(1946); BIG FIX, THE(1947); BISHOP'S WIFE, THE(1947); GUILTY, THE(1947); HIGH TIDE(1947); MAGIC TOWN(1947); 13TH HOUR, THE(1947); I WOULDN'T BE IN YOUR SHOES(1948); STATION WEST(1948); BEYOND THE FOREST(1949); BOY WITH THE GREEN HAIR, THE(1949); COME TO THE STA-BLE(1949); DEVIL'S HENCHMEN, THE(1949); MIGHTY JOE YOUNG(1949); DYNA-MITE PASS(1950); FRENCHIE(1950); MRS. O'MALLEY AND MR. MALONE(1950); UNDERCOVER GIRL(1950); CRY DANGER(1951); NAVY BOUND(1951); PEOPLE AGAINST O'HARA, THE(1951); SHOW BOAT(1951); TALL TARGET, THE(1951); TOMAHAWK(1951); BATTLE AT APACHE PASS, THE(1952); JUST FOR YOU(1952); MY PAL GUS(1952); MY SIX CONVICTS(1952); NEVER WAVE AT A WAC(1952); ISLAND IN THE SKY(1953); IT HAPPENS EVERY THURSDAY(1953); NEBRASKAN, THE(1953); SON OF BELLE STARR(1953); TAKE THE HIGH GROUND(1953); DRUMS ACROSS THE RIVER(1954); HIGH AND THE MIGHTY, THE(1954); HUMAN JUN-GLE, THE(1954); GUYS AND DOLLS(1955); TOP GUN(1955); DAKOTA IN-CIDENT(1956); GREAT DAY IN THE MORNING(1956); THREE FOR JAMIE DAWN(1956); CURFEW BREAKERS(1957); JOY RIDE(1958); SING, BOY, SING(1958); WARLOCK(1959); GUNS OF THE TIMBERLAND(1960); KING OF THE ROARING TWENTIES–THE STORY OF ARNOLD ROTHSTEIN(1961); LAST SUNSET, THE(1961); VOYAGE TO THE BOTTOM OF THE SEA(1961); NIGHT OF THE GRIZZLY, THE(1966); GUNN(1967); CHANGE OF HABIT(1969); COVER ME BA-BE(1970); CAREY TREATMENT, THE(1972); WON TON TON, THE DOG WHO SAVED HOLLYWOOD(1976); C.H.O.M.P.S.(1979)
Misc. Talkies
GOD BLESS DR. SHAGETZ(1977)

Susie Toomey
1984
RIVER, THE(1984)

Melissa Toomin
1984
INITIATION, THE(1984)

Geoffrey Toone
NIGHT JOURNEY(1938, Brit.); SWORD OF HONOUR(1938, Brit.); NORTH SEA PATROL(1939, Brit.); MAD MEN OF EUROPE(1940, Brit.); PIRATES OF THE SEVEN SEAS(1941, Brit.); POISON PEN(1941, Brit.); GREAT GAME, THE(1953, Brit.); MAN BETWEEN, THE(1953, Brit.); WOMAN'S ANGLE, THE(1954, Brit.); CAPTAIN LIGHT-FOOT(1955); DIANE(1955); KING AND I, THE(1956); JOHNNY TREMAIN(1957); ZERO HOUR!(1957); MURDER AT SITE THREE(1959, Brit.); ENTERTAINER, THE(1960, Brit.); ONCE MORE, WITH FEELING(1960); TERROR OF THE TONGS, THE(1961, Brit.); BLAZE OF GLORY(1963, Brit.); CAPTAIN SINDBAD(1963); DR. CRIPPEN(1963, Brit.); ECHO OF DIANA(1963, Brit.); DR. WHO AND THE DA-

LEKS(1965, Brit.)

Jim Toone
FINAL COUNTDOWN, THE(1980)

Fred S. Toones
DEATH VALLEY OUTLAWS(1941); BELLS OF SAN ANGELO(1947)

Fred "Snowflake" Toones
SHANGHAIED LOVE(1931); HAT CHECK GIRL(1932); HUMAN TARGETS(1932); OUT OF SINGAPORE(1932); SINGLE-HANDED SANDERS(1932); GOLD DIGGERS OF 1933(1933); DAMES(1934); GAY BRIDE, THE(1934); HERE COMES THE GROOM(1934); HERE COMES THE NAVY(1934); IMITATION OF LIFE(1934); LADY BY CHOICE(1934); PALOOKA(1934); TWENTIETH CENTURY(1934); ALIBI IKE(1935); HANDS ACROSS THE TABLE(1935); MISSISSIPPI(1935); STOLEN HAR-MONY(1935); COLLEGE HOLIDAY(1936); DESERT JUSTICE(1936); GOLD DIGGERS OF 1937(1936); GORGEOUS HUSSY, THE(1936); PALM SPRINGS(1936); GUNSMOKE RANCH(1937); OFF TO THE RACES(1937); OH, SUSANNA(1937); RANGE DEFEND-ERS(1937); SARATOGA(1937); SHE LOVED A FIREMAN(1937); SMART BLON-DE(1937); STAR IS BORN, A(1937); WAY OUT WEST(1937); GOLD MINE IN THE SKY(1938); HAWAIIAN BUCKAROO(1938); RED RIVER RANGE(1938); UNDER THE BIG TOP(1938); WILD HORSE RODEO(1938); FRONTIER VENGEANCE(1939); MEX-ICALI ROSE(1939); MR. SMITH GOES TO WASHINGTON(1939); ROVIN' TUM-BLEWEEDS(1939); GAUCHO SERENADE(1940); I WANT A DIVORCE(1940); ONE MAN'S LAW(1940); REMEMBER THE NIGHT(1940); RIDE, TENDERFOOT, RI-DE(1940); SEVENTEEN(1940); SPEED LIMITED(1940); TEXAS TERRORS(1940); TUL-SA KID, THE(1940); APACHE KID, THE(1941); OBLIGING YOUNG LADY(1941); PENNY SERENADE(1941); REPENT AT LEISURE(1941); SUN VALLEY SERENA-DE(1941); TWO GUN SHERIFF(1941); GIVE OUT, SISTERS(1942); GREAT MAN'S LADY, THE(1942); MISSOURI OUTLAW, A(1942); PALM BEACH STORY, THE(1942); QUEEN OF BROADWAY(1942); RAIDERS OF THE WEST(1942); SILVER QUEEN(1942); HAUNTED RANCH, THE(1943); LAND OF HUNTED MEN(1943); SPY TRAIN(1943); FIREBRANDS OF ARIZONA(1944); HIDDEN VALLEY OUT-LAWS(1944); MEET THE PEOPLE(1944); LOST WEEKEND, THE(1945); CENTENNI-AL SUMMER(1946); FOOL'S GOLD(1946); HOODLUM SAINT, THE(1946); TWO SMART PEOPLE(1946)
Misc. Talkies
HAIR-TRIGGER CASEY(1936); WILDCAT SAUNDERS(1936)

Michael Toost
ETERNAL WALTZ, THE(1959, Ger.)

Paul Toothill
CARRY ON ENGLAND(1976, Brit.)

Gordon Tootoosie
MARIE-ANN(1978, Can.)

George Tootoosis
ALIEN THUNDER(1975, US/Can.)

Tootsie
W. W. AND THE DIXIE DANCEKINGS(1975)

Fred Tooze
NOVEL AFFAIR, A(1957, Brit.)

John Topa
RED PLANET MARS(1952)

Jean Topart
LEATHER AND NYLON(1969, Fr./Ital.); COLD SWEAT(1974, Ital., Fr.)

Robert Topart
FIVE WILD GIRLS(1966, Fr.), w

Ahmet Danyal Topatan
TOPKAPI(1964)

Lamont Topaum
Misc. Talkies
CRY TO THE WIND(1979)

Manat Topayat
1 2 3 MONSTER EXPRESS(1977, Thai.), ed

Roland Toper
1984
SWANN IN LOVE(1984, Fr.Ger.)

Byron Topetchy
GOOD MORNING, JUDGE(1943)

Jesus Topete
TROPIC HOLIDAY(1938); ARISE, MY LOVE(1940); RANGERS OF FORTUNE(1940); HOLD BACK THE DAWN(1941)

Frank Topham
RAGING BULL(1980)

Chris Tophe
MARRIED WOMAN, THE(1965, Fr.)

Katharine Topkins
KOTCH(1971), w

Murray Hill Topman
HEAVEN ON EARTH(1960, Ital./U.S.), w

Topol
SALLAH(1965, Israel); CAST A GIANT SHADOW(1966); BEFORE WINTER CO-MES(1969, Brit.); PUBLIC EYE, THE(1972, Brit.); GALILEO(1975, Brit.); FLASH GORDON(1980); FOR YOUR EYES ONLY(1981)

Chaim Topol
FIDDLER ON THE ROOF(1971)

Haim Topol
EVERY BASTARD A KING(1968, Israel), p

Robert Topol
JAWS OF SATAN(1980), art d

Roland Topor
FANTASTIC PLANET(1973, Fr./Czech.), w; TENANT, THE(1976, Fr.), w; DIE HAM-BURGER KRANKHEIT(1979, Ger./Fr.), w; NOSFERATU, THE VAMPIRE(1979, Fr./Ger.); RATATAPLAN(1979, Ital.)

Toporcoff
DRAGNET NIGHT(1931, Fr.), ph

Nicolas Toporkoff
ETERNAL HUSBAND, THE(1946, Fr.), ph; FANNY(1948, Fr.), ph

V. Toporkov
DEVOTION(1955, USSR)

Vasili Toporkov
Misc. Silents
FATHER FROST(1924, USSR)

Roman Toporow
BERLIN EXPRESS(1948); RED DANUBE, THE(1949); KIM(1950)

Burt Topper
HELL SQUAD(1958), p,d&w; NO PLACE TO LAND(1958); DIARY OF A HIGH SCHOOL BRIDE(1959), p&d, w; PLUNDERERS OF PAINTED FLATS(1959); TANK COMMANDOS(1959), p,d&w; STRANGLER, THE(1964), d; WAR IS HELL(1964), a, p, d&w; SPACE MONSTER(1965), p; FIREBALL 590(1966), p; DEVIL'S ANGELS(1967), p; THUNDER ALLEY(1967), p; DEVIL'S 8, THE(1969), p&d; HARD RIDE, THE(1971), d&w
Misc. Talkies
DAY THE LORD GOT BUSTED, THE(1976), d

Topper the Horse
SILVER ON THE SAGE(1939)

Television Toppers
DOWN AMONG THE Z MEN(1952, Brit.)

Michael Tor
DEPORTED(1950); FUGITIVE LADY(1951); WAR AND PEACE(1956, Ital./U.S.)

Sigfrid Tor
LADY HAS PLANS, THE(1942); THEY RAID BY NIGHT(1942); 27TH DAY, THE(1957)

Sigfried Tor
DESPERATE JOURNEY(1942); PRIZE, THE(1963)

Sigurd Tor
CAREFUL, SOFT SHOULDERS(1942); THEY CAME TO BLOW UP AMERICA(1943)

Lia Tora
MAKING THE GRADE(1929); VEILED WOMAN, THE(1929), a, w

Frederick Torberg
VOICE IN THE WIND(1944), w

Bruce Torbet
MURDER A LA MOD(1968), ph; MISSISSIPPI SUMMER(1971), ph; BASKET CASE(1982), ph

Thierry Torchet
ATTENTION, THE KIDS ARE WATCHING(1978, Fr.)

Mimi Torchin
DOUBLE STOP(1968)

Zina Torchina
MISSION TO MOSCOW(1943); UNCERTAIN GLORY(1944)

Teri Tordai
ANNA(1981, Fr./Hung.); MEPHISTO(1981, Ger.)

Jesus Tordesilla
HORSEMEN, THE(1971)

Jesus Tordesillas
MAD QUEEN, THE(1950, Span.); SPANISH AFFAIR(1958, Span.)

Pietro Tordi
QUO VADIS(1951); CROSSED SWORDS(1954); BEN HUR(1959); DIVORCE, ITALIAN STYLE(1962, Ital.); HUNS, THE(1962, Fr./Ital.); HERCULES, SAMSON & ULYSSES(1964, Ital.); ARIZONA COLT(1965, It./Fr./Span.); FACTS OF MURDER, THE(1965, Ital.); SEVEN DWARFS TO THE RESCUE, THE(1965, Ital.); WITCHES, THE(1969, Fr./Ital.); LION OF THE DESERT(1981, Libya/Brit.)

Fabian Tordjinann
MACHO CALLAHAN(1970), ed

Fabien Tordjman
RETURN OF COUNT YORGA, THE(1971), ed; VAN, THE(1977), ed

Fabian Tordjmann
SCREAM BLACULA SCREAM(1973), ed

Fabien Dahlen Tordjmann
MARVIN AND TIGE(1983), ed

Fabien Tordjmann
ANOTHER MAN, ANOTHER CHANCE(1977 Fr/US), ed; PRIZE FIGHTER, THE(1979), ed; PRIVATE EYES, THE(1980), ed

John Tordoff
STORIES FROM A FLYING TRUNK(1979, Brit.)

Geza Tordy
ROUND UP, THE(1969, Hung.)

Lydia Torea
SHIP OF FOOLS(1965)

Edith Toreg
1984
KAMILLA(1984, Norway), ed

Erina Torelli
VERY HANDY MAN, A(1966, Fr./Ital.)

Giuseppe Torelli
RAVEN'S END(1970, Swed.), m

Heller Toren
FIVE TO ONE(1963, Brit.)

Marta Toren
CASBAH(1948); ROGUES' REGIMENT(1948); ILLEGAL ENTRY(1949); SWORD IN THE DESERT(1949); DEPORTED(1950); MYSTERY SUBMARINE(1950); ONE WAY STREET(1950); SPY HUNT(1950); SIROCCO(1951); ASSIGNMENT–PARIS(1952); PARIS EXPRESS, THE(1953, Brit.)

Juan Torena
GAY CABALLERO, THE(1932); NADA MAS QUE UNA MUJER(1934); CAPTAIN CALAMITY(1936); EAGLE'S BROOD, THE(1936); MESSAGE TO GARCIA, A(1936); ESPIONAGE(1937); LOVE UNDER FIRE(1937); WALLABY JIM OF THE ISLANDS(1937); HOMESTRETCH, THE(1947); AMERICAN GUERRILLA IN THE PHILIPPINES, AN(1950); MY MAN AND I(1952); JEOPARDY(1953)

Lyllah Torena
Misc. Talkies
FLY ME(1973)

Juan Toreno
MEET NERO WOLFE(1936)

Mario Torero
HEARTBREAKER(1983), art d

Krist Toresen
NORTHERN LIGHTS(1978)

Ludmila Toretzka
MEN IN HER LIFE, THE(1941)

Hal Torey
CRASH LANDING(1958); SPIDER, THE(1958); INSIDE THE MAFIA(1959); INVISIBLE INVADERS(1959); VALLEY OF THE REDWOODS(1960); CAT BURGLAR, THE(1961); SERGEANT WAS A LADY, THE(1961)

Alex Torffey
45 FATHERS(1937), ed

Edwin Dial Torgenson
ONE WILD NIGHT(1938), w

Sonia Torgenson
TEENAGERS FROM OUTER SPACE(1959)

Edwin Dial Torgerson
SPEED TO BURN(1938), w

Skip Torgerson
MR. SCOUTMASTER(1953); RAIDERS OF THE SEVEN SEAS(1953); PARTY CRASHERS, THE(1958)

Skippy Torgerson
BOY FROM OKLAHOMA, THE(1954)

Sonia Torgeson
DADDY-O(1959)

Albert Torgessen
TWICE A MAN(1964)

Mark Torgl
1984
FIRST TURN-ON!, THE(1984), a, w

Sarah Torgov
MEATBALLS(1979, Can.); IF YOU COULD SEE WHAT I HEAR(1982)

Lauri Torhonen
GORKY PARK(1983)

Reggie Torian
THREE THE HARD WAY(1974)

Caprice Toriel
MURDER BY CONTRACT(1958)

Javier T. Torija
DEADLY TRACKERS(1973), art d

Javier Torres Torija
WITCH'S MIRROR, THE(1960, Mex.), art d; CURSE OF THE AZTEC MUMMY, THE(1965, Mex.), art d; ROBOT VS. THE AZTEC MUMMY, THE(1965, Mex.), art d; NIGHT OF THE BLOODY APES(1968, Mex.), spec eff

Joe Torilla
STRICTLY DISHONORABLE(1931)

Cosimo Torino
SALVATORE GIULIANO(1966, Ital.)

Boaz Torjemann
1984
DRIFTING(1984, Israel)

Peter Tork
HEAD(1968)

Sofia Torkeli
LAST MAN, THE(1968, Fr.)

Sophia Torkeli
TWO FOR THE ROAD(1967, Brit.)

Leigh Torlage
1984
WHERE THE BOYS ARE '84(1984)

Flaminia Torlonia
8 ½(1963, Ital.)

Mel Torme
HIGHER AND HIGHER(1943); GHOST CATCHERS(1944); PARDON MY RHYTHM(1944); JUNIOR MISS(1945); LET'S GO STEADY(1945); JANIE GETS MARRIED(1946); GOOD NEWS(1947); DUCHESS OF IDAHO, THE(1950); FEARMAKERS, THE(1958); BIG OPERATOR, THE(1959); GIRLS' TOWN(1959); WALK LIKE A DRAGON(1960); PRIVATE LIVES OF ADAM AND EVE, THE(1961); PATSY, THE(1964); MAN CALLED ADAM, A(1966); LAND OF NO RETURN, THE(1981)

Melissa Torme-March
CAREY TREATMENT, THE(1972)

Danae Torn
MAIDSTONE(1970)

Rip Torn
TIME LIMIT(1957); PORK CHOP HILL(1959); KING OF KINGS(1961); HERO'S ISLAND(1962); SWEET BIRD OF YOUTH(1962); CRITIC'S CHOICE(1963); CINCINNATI KID, THE(1965); ONE SPY TOO MANY(1966); YOU'RE A BIG BOY NOW(1966); BEACH RED(1967); BEYOND THE LAW(1968); SOL MADRID(1968); MAIDSTONE(1970); PAYDAY(1972); SLAUGHTER(1972); CRAZY JOE(1974); BIRCH INTERVAL(1976); MAN WHO FELL TO EARTH, THE(1976, Brit.); NASTY HABITS(1976, Brit.); COMA(1978); PRIVATE FILES OF J. EDGAR HOOVER, THE(1978); SEDUCTION OF JOE TYNAN, THE(1979); FIRST FAMILY(1980); HEARTLAND(1980); ONE-TRICK PONY(1980); AIRPLANE II: THE SEQUEL(1982); BEASTMASTER, THE(1982); JINXED!(1982); SCARAB(1982, U.S./Span.); STRANGER IS WATCHING, A(1982); CROSS CREEK(1983)
1984
CITY HEAT(1984); FLASHPOINT(1984); MISUNDERSTOOD(1984); SONGWRITER(1984)
Misc. Talkies
COMING APART(1969); COTTER(1972)

Pierre Tornade
DEVIL BY THE TAIL, THE(1969, Fr./Ital.)

Tony Tornado
PIXOTE(1981, Braz.)

The Tornadoes
FAREWELL PERFORMANCE(1963, Brit.)

The Tornados
JUST FOR FUN(1963, Brit.)

Joe Tornatore
TOP OF THE HEAP(1972); STING, THE(1973); SWEET JESUS, PREACHER MAN(1973); BLACK SAMSON(1974); MC Q(1974); FORTUNE, THE(1975); TRACKDOWN(1976); CHAMP, THE(1979)
1984
CHATTANOOGA CHOO CHOO(1984)

Misc. Talkies
ZEBRA FORCE(1977), d
Joseph A. Tornatore
CLEOPATRA JONES(1973)
Joseph Tornatore
MACHISMO–40 GRAVES FOR 40 GUNS(1970), a, stunts ch
Joe Tornatori
GAY DECEIVERS, THE(1969)
Kay A. Tornberg
FOXES(1980)
Stig Tornblom
HERE'S YOUR LIFE(1968, Swed.)
Kay Tornburg
WHO?(1975, Brit./Ger.)
Regina Torne
MADAME DEATH(1968, Mex.)
Frank Toro
1984
KARATE KID, THE(1984), spec eff
Jorge Luis Toro
1984
C.H.U.D.(1984), art d
Mari Torocsik
DIALOGUE(1967, Hung.); BOYS OF PAUL STREET, THE(1969, Hung./US); LO-VE(1972, Hung.); FORBIDDEN RELATIONS(1983, Hung.)
Peter Torquill
RICOCHET(1966, Brit.)
Achille Filo Della Torre
EYE OF THE NEEDLE, THE(1965, Ital./Fr.), p
Javier Torre
MAFIA, THE(1972, Arg.), w, w
Leopoldo Torre-Nilsson
SUMMERSKIN(1962, Arg.), p&d, w; HAND IN THE TRAP, THE(1963, Arg./Span.), d, w; MONDAY'S CHILD(1967, U.S., Arg.), d, w; MAFIA, THE(1972, Arg.), p&d
Gabrielle Torrei
CRAZY JOE(1974)
Juan Ramon Torremocha
EVERY DAY IS A HOLIDAY(1966, Span.)
David Torrence
CAVALIER, THE(1928); BLACK WATCH, THE(1929); DISRAELI(1929); HEARTS IN EXILE(1929); CITY GIRL(1930); DEVIL TO PAY, THE(1930); RAFFLES(1930); SCOTLAND YARD(1930); BACHELOR FATHER(1931); EAST LYNNE(1931); FIVE STAR FINAL(1931); RIVER'S END(1931); MASK OF FU MANCHU, THE(1932); SMILIN' THROUGH(1932); SUCCESSFUL CALAMITY, A(1932); BERKELEY SQUARE(1933); HORSEPLAY(1933); MASQUERADER, THE(1933); QUEEN CHRISTINA(1933); VOLTAIRE(1933); CHARLIE CHAN IN LONDON(1934); MANDALAY(1934); WHAT EVERY WOMAN KNOWS(1934); BLACK SHEEP(1935); BONNIE SCOTLAND(1935); CAPTAIN BLOOD(1935); DARK ANGEL, THE(1935); HARMONY LANE(1935); JANE EYRE(1935); MUTINY ON THE BOUNTY(1935); BELOVED ENEMY(1936); COUNTRY DOCTOR, THE(1936); MARY OF SCOTLAND(1936); EBB TIDE(1937); FIVE OF A KIND(1938); RULERS OF THE SEA(1939); STANLEY AND LIVINGSTONE(1939)
Silents
SHERLOCK HOLMES(1922); TESS OF THE STORM COUNTRY(1922); ABYSMAL BRUTE, THE(1923); RAILROADED(1923); LOVE'S WILDERNESS(1924); SAWDUST TRAIL(1924); SURGING SEAS(1924); RECKLESS SEX, THE(1925); TOWER OF LIES, THE(1925); WHAT FOOLS MEN(1925); AUCTION BLOCK, THE(1926); BROWN OF HARVARD(1926); FOREVER AFTER(1926); ISLE OF RETRIBUTION, THE(1926); KING OF THE TURF, THE(1926); OH, WHAT A NURSE!(1926); SANDY(1926); THIRD DEGREE, THE(1926); UNKNOWN CAVALIER, THE(1926); ANNIE LAURIE(1927); HAZARDOUS VALLEY(1927); MIDNIGHT WATCH, THE(1927); ROLLED STOCKINGS(1927); SILKS AND SADDLES(1929); STRONG BOY(1929)
Misc. Silents
INSIDE OF THE CUP, THE(1921); POWER OF A LIE, THE(1922); RECEIVED PAYMENT(1922); VIRGIN'S SACRIFICE, A(1922); DRUMS OF JEOPARDY, THE(1923); LIGHT THAT FAILED, THE(1923); MAN NEXT DOOR, THE(1923); DAWN OF A TOMORROW, THE(1924); WHICH SHALL IT BE?(1924); FIGHTING THE FLAMES(1925); HE WHO LAUGHS LAST(1925); HER HUSBAND'S SECRET(1925); OTHER WOMAN'S STORY, THE(1925); MAN IN THE SHADOW, THE(1926); RACE WILD(1926); MYSTERIOUS RIDER, THE(1927); ON THE STROKE OF TWELVE(1927); CAVALIER, THE(1928); CITY OF PURPLE DREAMS(1928); UNDRESSED(1928); UNTAMED JUSTICE(1929)
Ernest Torrence
BRIDGE OF SAN LUIS REY, THE(1929); UNHOLY NIGHT, THE(1929); UNTAMED(1929); CALL OF THE FLESH(1930); OFFICER O'BRIEN(1930); STRICTLY UNCONVENTIONAL(1930); SWEET KITTY BELLAIRS(1930); CUBAN LOVE SONG, THE(1931); FIGHTING CARAVANS(1931); GREAT LOVER, THE(1931); NEW ADVENTURES OF GET-RICH-QUICK WALLINGFORD, THE(1931); SHIPMATES(1931); SPORTING BLOOD(1931); SHERLOCK HOLMES(1932); HYPNOTIZED(1933); I COVER THE WATERFRONT(1933)
Silents
TOL'ABLE DAVID(1921); KINGDOM WITHIN, THE(1922); SINGED WINGS(1922); COVERED WAGON, THE(1923); HUNCHBACK OF NOTRE DAME, THE(1923); RUGGLES OF RED GAP(1923); FIGHTING COWARD(1924); NORTH OF 36(1924); PETER PAN(1924); SIDESHOW OF LIFE, THE(1924); NIGHT LIFE OF NEW YORK(1925); PONY EXPRESS, THE(1925); AMERICAN VENUS, THE(1926); BLIND GODDESS, THE(1926); RAINMAKER, THE(1926); CAPTAIN SALVATION(1927); KING OF KINGS, THE(1927); TWELVE MILES OUT(1927); ACROSS THE SINGAPORE(1928); STEAMBOAT BILL, JR.(1928)
Misc. Silents
BROKEN CHAINS(1922); PRODIGAL JUDGE, THE(1922); BRASS BOTTLE, THE(1923); TRAIL OF THE LONESOME, THE(1923); HERITAGE OF THE DESERT, THE(1924); WEST OF THE WATER TOWER(1924); DRESSMAKER FROM PARIS, THE(1925); LADY OF THE HAREM, THE(1926); MANTRAP(1926); WANDERER, THE(1926); COSSACKS, THE(1928); DESERT NIGHTS(1929); SPEEDWAY(1929)
Lena Torrence
LYDIA BAILEY(1952)
Richard Torrence
WACKIEST SHIP IN THE ARMY, THE(1961)

Pip Torrens
1984
OXFORD BLUES(1984)
Tania Torrens
SMALL CHANGE(1976, Fr.)
Agnes Torrent
JOY(1983, Fr./Can.)
Ana Torrent
SPIRIT OF THE BEEHIVE, THE(1976, Span.); NEST, THE(1982, Span.)
Ugo Torrente
DIVORCE, ITALIAN STYLE(1962, Ital.); SALVATORE GIULIANO(1966, Ital.)
Carlos Torres
GIVEN WORD, THE(1964, Braz.)
Cesar Torres
MILKY WAY, THE(1969, Fr./Ital.)
Claudio Torres
WAY OF A GAUCHO(1952)
Don Torres
FUNNY LADY(1975)
Enoch Torres
GIVEN WORD, THE(1964, Braz.)
Flavio Torres
GIRL IN ROOM 13(1961, U.S./Braz.), makeup
Gabriel Torres
TARZAN'S DEADLY SILENCE(1970), ed; TARZAN'S JUNGLE REBELLION(1970), ed; REVENGERS, THE(1972, U.S./Mex.), ph; DEADLY TRACKERS(1973), ph; CHOSEN SURVIVORS(1974 U.S.-Mex.), ph
Henry Torres
TESTAMENT OF ORPHEUS, THE(1962, Fr.)
Ignacio Lopez Torres
MACARIO(1961, Mex.)
Irma Torres
PORTRAIT OF MARIA(1946, Mex.); LITTLE RED RIDING HOOD(1963, Mex.)
Joan Torres
BLACULA(1972), w; SCREAM BLACULA SCREAM(1973), w
Jose Torres
BIG GUNDOWN, THE(1968, Ital.); WILD 90(1968); DEATH RIDES A HORSE(1969, Ital.); FIVE MAN ARMY, THE(1970, Ital.); MAIDSTONE(1970)
Jose "Chegui" Torres
LAST FIGHT, THE(1983)
Jose L. Torres
OLIVER'S STORY(1978)
Juan Antonio Ortiz Torres
1984
ERENDIRA(1984, Mex./Fr./Ger.)
Juan Carlos Torres
TEXICAN, THE(1966, U.S./Span.)
Liz Torres
YOU'VE GOT TO WALK IT LIKE YOU TALK IT OR YOU'LL LOSE THAT BEAT(1971); SCAVENGER HUNT(1979)
Louis Torres, Jr.
MAN CALLED PETER, THE(1955)
Luis Torres
FOLLOW THE BOYS(1944); PARTNERS(1982)
Marina Torres
QUEEN'S SWORDSMEN, THE(1963, Mex.)
Miguel C. Torres
MAD EMPRESS, THE(1940), p&d, w
Misc. Silents
EL RELICARIO(1926)
Miguel Contreras Torres
PANCHO VILLA RETURNS(1950, Mex.), p,d,&w; LAST REBEL, THE(1961, Mex.), p&d, w
Ramona Torres
WILD 90(1968)
Raquel Torres
WHITE SHADOWS IN THE SOUTH SEAS(1928); SEA BAT, THE(1930); UNDER A TEXAS MOON(1930); ALOHA(1931); DUCK SOUP(1933); SO THIS IS AFRICA(1933); WOMAN I STOLE, THE(1933); RED WAGON(1936)
Silents
DESERT RIDER, THE(1929)
Russel Torres
FIEND OF DOPE ISLAND(1961)
Stanley Torres
TELL THEM WILLIE BOY IS HERE(1969)
Stuart Torres
MILLION DOLLAR MERMAID(1952)
Tomas Torres
LA DOLCE VITA(1961, Ital./Fr.); LAST MERCENARY, THE(1969, Ital./Span./Ger.)
Victor Torres
SALT OF THE EARTH(1954)
Yvette Torres
FAME(1980)
Mrs. James Torrey
HUCKLEBERRY FINN(1974)
Len Torrey
RIDERS OF THE WHISTLING PINES(1949)
Mary Torrey
FM(1978)
Roger Torrey
PLUNDERERS, THE(1960); NUN AND THE SERGEANT, THE(1962); TOWN TAMER(1965)
Pier Luigi Torri
YOUNG REBEL, THE(1969, Fr./Ital./Span.), p
Rosemary Torri
DARK ODYSSEY(1961)
Aimee Torriani
TO CATCH A THIEF(1955)

Edoardo Torricella
JULIET OF THE SPIRITS(1965, Fr./Ital./W.Ger.)
Al Torrieri
SWING OUT THE BLUES(1943)
Francesco Torrisi
00-2 MOST SECRET AGENTS(1965, Ital.)
Piero Torrisi
WITCHES, THE(1969, Fr./Ital.)
Piertro Torrisi
ARENA, THE(1973)
Dr. Rafael Torrobo
NIGHT HEAVEN FELL, THE(1958, Fr.)
Miguel Torruco
MASSACRE(1956)
Victor Torruella
SWORD OF EL CID, THE(1965, Span./Ital.), w
Hal Torry
TWIST ALL NIGHT(1961)
David Tors
Misc. Talkies
ESCAPE FROM ANGOLA(1976)
Ivan Tors
SONG OF LOVE(1947), w; IN THE GOOD OLD SUMMERTIME(1949), w; THAT FORSYTE WOMAN(1949), w; WATCH THE BIRDIE(1950), w; STORM OVER TIBET(1952), p, w; FORTY-NINTH MAN, THE(1953), w; GLASS WALL, THE(1953), p, w; MAGNETIC MONSTER, THE(1953), p, w; GOG(1954), p, w; RIDERS TO THE STARS(1954), p; BATTLE TAXI(1955), p; UNDERWATER WARRIOR(1958), p; FLIPPER(1963), p; FLIPPER'S NEW ADVENTURE(1964), p, w; RHINO(1964), d; ZEBRA IN THE KITCHEN(1965), p&d; BIRDS DO IT(1966), p; AFRICA–TEXAS STYLE!(1967 U.S./Brit.), p; GENTLE GIANT(1967), p; DARING GAME(1968), p; HELLO DOWN THERE(1969), w
Misc. Talkies
ESCAPE FROM ANGOLA(1976)
Peter Tors
SPRING BREAK(1983), stunts
Misc. Talkies
ESCAPE FROM ANGOLA(1976)
Gilda Torterello
1984
BROADWAY DANNY ROSE(1984)
Robert Torti
1984
ALLEY CAT(1984)
Oz Tortora
LAST MARRIED COUPLE IN AMERICA, THE(1980)
Ozzie Tortora
PRISM(1971)
Misc. Talkies
PRISM(1971)
Jose Luis Tortosa
TANGO BAR(1935); MESSAGE TO GARCIA, A(1936); CODE OF THE SECRET SERVICE(1939); DOOMED CARAVAN(1941)
Jose Tortosa
LAW OF THE TEXAN(1938); SIX LESSONS FROM MADAME LA ZONGA(1941); FOR WHOM THE BELL TOLLS(1943)
Silvia Tortosa
HORROR EXPRESS(1972, Span./Brit.)
Joe Torvay
SERENADE(1956)
Jose Torvay
MYSTERY IN MEXICO(1948); SOFIA(1948); TREASURE OF THE SIERRA MADRE, THE(1948); BORDER INCIDENT(1949); BORDERLINE(1950); BRAVE BULLS, THE(1951); MY BROTHER, THE OUTLAW(1951); MY MAN AND I(1952); ONE BIG AFFAIR(1952); HITCH-HIKER, THE(1953); GREEN FIRE(1955); LIFE IN THE BALANCE, A(1955); LITTLEST OUTLAW, THE(1955); STRANGE LADY IN TOWN(1955); WOMAN'S DEVOTION, A(1956); FROM HELL TO TEXAS(1958); LAST SUNSET, THE(1961); TWO MULES FOR SISTER SARA(1970); KID BLUE(1973)
Jose I. Torvay
FUGITIVE, THE(1947); TORCH, THE(1950); BANDIDO(1956)
Geoffrey Tory
1984
SWANN IN LOVE(1984, Fr.Ger.)
Hal Tory
EARTH VS. THE SPIDER(1958)
Tass Tory
LAST GUNFIGHTER, THE(1961, Can.)
Mario Toscana
FANDANGO(1970), m; KINFOLK(1970), m
Jean Toscane
LETTERS FROM MY WINDMILL(1955, Fr.)
Toscano
AND GOD CREATED WOMAN(1957, Fr.)
Laura Toscano
I HATE BLONDES(1981, Ital.), w; BINGO BONGO(1983, Ital.), w
Sol Tosco
MY THIRD WIFE GEORGE(1968), m
Piero Tose
INNOCENT, THE(1979, Ital.), cos
Peter Tosh
ROCKERS(1980)
Tosi
NIGHT HEAVEN FELL, THE(1958, Fr.)
Adele Tosi
SEVEN SEAS TO CALAIS(1963, Ital.), set d
Arturo Tosi
SEVEN DWARFS TO THE RESCUE, THE(1965, Ital.)
Domenico Tosi
SEVEN DWARFS TO THE RESCUE, THE(1965, Ital.)

Giuseppe Tosi
LA VIACCIA(1962, Fr./Ital.)
Luigi Tosi
EARTH CRIES OUT, THE(1949, Ital.); CITY OF PAIN(1951, Ital.); UTOPIA(1952, Fr./Ital.); STRANGE DECEPTION(1953, Ital.); MYSTERY OF THE BLACK JUNGLE(1955); GODDESS OF LOVE, THE(1960, Ital./Fr.); HEAD OF A TYRANT(1960, Fr./Ital.); DAVID AND GOLIATH(1961, Ital.); PIRATE AND THE SLAVE GIRL, THE(1961, Fr./Ital.); WONDERS OF ALADDIN, THE(1961, Fr./Ital.); SHIP OF CONDEMNED WOMEN, THE(1963, ITAL.); FRIENDS FOR LIFE(1964, Ital.)
Mario Tosi
THIEF OF VENICE, THE(1952); SWAMP COUNTRY(1966), ph; TERROR IN THE JUNGLE(1968), ph; FROGS(1972), ph; OUTSIDE IN(1972), ph; HEARTS OF THE WEST(1975), ph; REPORT TO THE COMMISSIONER(1975), ph; SMOKE IN THE WIND(1975), ph; CARRIE(1976), ph; MAC ARTHUR(1977), ph; BETSY, THE(1978), ph; MAIN EVENT, THE(1979), ph; COAST TO COAST(1980), ph; RESURRECTION(1980), ph; STUNT MAN, THE(1980), ph; WHOSE LIFE IS IT ANYWAY?(1981), ph; SIX PACK(1982), ph
Piero Tosi
ROCCO AND HIS BROTHERS(1961, Fr./Ital.), cos; BELL' ANTONIO(1962, Ital.), art d; LA VIACCIA(1962, Fr./Ital.), set d, cos; LEOPARD, THE(1963, Ital.), cos; APE WOMAN, THE(1964, Ital.), cos; MARRIAGE–ITALIAN STYLE(1964, Fr./Ital.), cos; ORGANIZER, THE(1964, Fr./Ital./Yugo.), cos; YESTERDAY, TODAY, AND TOMORROW(1964, Ital./Fr.), cos; THREE FACES OF A WOMAN(1965, Ital.); AFTER THE FOX(1966, U.S./Brit./Ital.), cos; MATCHLESS(1967, Ital.), cos; STRANGER, THE(1967, Algeria/Fr./Ital.), cos; SENSO(1968, Ital.), cos; GHOSTS, ITALIAN STYLE(1969, Ital./Fr.), cos; SPIRITS OF THE DEAD(1969, Fr./Ital.), art d, cos; WITCHES, THE(1969, Fr./Ital.), cos; DEATH IN VENICE(1971, Ital./Fr.), cos; MEDEA(1971, Ital./Fr./Ger.), cos; LUDWIG(1973, Ital./Ger./Fr.), cos; NIGHT PORTER, THE(1974, Ital./U.S.), cos; LA CAGE AUX FOLLES(1979, Fr./Ital.), cos; LA TRAVIATA(1982), cos
Virgilio Tosi
PHAROAH'S WOMAN, THE(1961, Ital.), w
Otello Toso
DISHONORED(1950, Ital.); VERGINITA(1953, Ital.); AGE OF INFIDELITY(1958, Span.)
Othelo Toso
DESERT DESPERADOES(1959)
Ottello Toso
PLANETS AGAINST US, THE(1961, Ital./Fr.)
Dino Tosques
GAS(1981, Can.)
Mario Tossi
GLORY STOMPERS, THE(1967), ph; SOME CALL IT LOVING(1973), ph
Helene Tossy
GAME OF LOVE, THE(1954, Fr.); GERVAISE(1956, Fr.); FRUIT IS RIPE, THE(1961, Fr./Ital.); TWO FOR THE ROAD(1967, Brit.)
Father Frank Toste
OLIVER'S STORY(1978)
Americo Tot
LISTEN, LET'S MAKE LOVE(1969, Fr./Ital.)
Amerigo Tot
PULP(1972, Brit.); GODFATHER, THE, PART II(1974)
Stacey Toten
1984
LOVELINES(1984)
Alex Toth
PROJECT X(1968), prod d
Frank Toth
HOT ROD HULLABALOO(1966), ed; E.T. THE EXTRA-TERRESTRIAL(1982); TWILIGHT ZONE–THE MOVIE(1983)
George Toth
SEA GYPSIES, THE(1978), animal t
Janos Toth
LOVE(1972, Hung.), ph
Jozsef Toth
FORBIDDEN RELATIONS(1983, Hung.)
Lilliam Toth
T.R. BASKIN(1971), makeup
Nick Toth
STRIPES(1981)
Tamas Toth
1984
DIARY FOR MY CHILDREN(1984, Hung.)
Tibor Kovacs Toth
FATHER(1967, Hung.)
Tibor Toth
WINTER WIND(1970, Fr./Hung.)
Dan Totheroh
RIVER OF ROMANCE(1929), w; DAWN PATROL, THE(1930), w; SEVEN DAYS LEAVE(1930), w; ZOO IN BUDAPEST(1933), w; TWO ALONE(1934), w; REMEMBER LAST NIGHT(1935), w; YELLOW DUST(1936), w; DAWN PATROL, THE(1938), w; DEVIL AND DANIEL WEBSTER, THE(1941), w; DEEP VALLEY(1947), w; ROOGIE'S BUMP(1954), w
Roland H. Totheroh
Silents
KID, THE(1921), ph; CIRCUS, THE(1928), ph
Roland Totheroh
MODERN TIMES(1936), ph; GREAT DICTATOR, THE(1940), ph; MONSIEUR VERDOUX(1947), ph; SONG OF MY HEART(1947), ph
Silents
GOLD RUSH, THE(1925), ph; CITY LIGHTS(1931), ph
Rollie Totheroh
Silents
PILGRIM, THE(1923), ph; WOMAN OF PARIS, A(1923), ph
W. Totman
ALOHA(1931), w
Weilyn Totman
CONFIDENTIAL(1935), w

Wellyn Totman
GOD'S COUNTRY AND THE MAN(1931), w; MOTHER AND SON(1931), w; RIDER OF THE PLAINS(1931), w; SHIPS OF HATE(1931), w; SUNRISE TRAIL(1931), w; BROADWAY TO CHEYENNE(1932), w; FORGOTTEN WOMEN(1932), w; GALLOPING THRU(1932), w; HIDDEN VALLEY(1932), w; RIDERS OF THE DESERT(1932), w; SON OF OKLAHOMA(1932), w; TEXAS PIONEERS(1932), w; YOUNG BLOOD(1932), w; CARNIVAL LADY(1933), w; CRASHING BROADWAY(1933), w; FIGHTING CHAMP(1933), w; FIGHTING TEXANS(1933), w; LUCKY LARRIGAN(1933), w; SON OF THE BORDER(1933), w; MYSTERY LINER(1934), w; LADIES CRAVE EXCITEMENT(1935), w; ONE FRIGHTENED NIGHT(1935), w; WATERFRONT LADY(1935), w; DANCING FEET(1936), w; DOWN TO THE SEA(1936), w; GIRL FROM MANDALAY(1936), w; LEATHERNECKS HAVE LANDED, THE(1936), w; EXILED TO SHANGHAI(1937), w; HAPPY-GO-LUCKY(1937), w; GANGS OF NEW YORK(1938), w; WANTED BY THE POLICE(1938), w; BOY'S REFORMATORY(1939), w; FIGHTING THOROUGHBREDS(1939), w; TOUGH KID(1939), w; DEADLY GAME, THE(1941), w; THOROUGHBREDS(1945), w
Silents
ALBANY NIGHT BOAT, THE(1928), w; ETERNAL WOMAN, THE(1929), w

Toto
GOLD OF NAPLES(1957, Ital.); TOTO IN THE MOON(1957, Ital./Span.); ANATOMY OF LOVE(1959, Ital.); LAW IS THE LAW, THE(1959, Fr.); BIG DEAL ON MADONNA STREET, THE(1960); LADY DOCTOR, THE(1963, Fr./Ital./Span.); PASSIONATE THIEF, THE(1963, Ital.); TWO COLONELS, THE(1963, Ital.); MANDRAGOLA(1966 Fr./Ital.); HAWKS AND THE SPARROWS, THE(1967, Ital.); TREASURE OF SAN GENNARO(1968, Fr./Ital./Ger.); WITCHES, THE(1969, Fr./Ital.)
1984
DUNE(1984), m

Chiyo Toto
CRIMSON KIMONO, THE(1959)

Ecce Homo Toto
KING SOLOMON'S MINES(1937, Brit.)

Yennis Totsicas
RECONSTRUCTION OF A CRIME(1970, Ger.)

Edyth Totten
Silents
FACTORY MAGDALEN, A(1914), a, w

Joseph Byron Totten
Misc. Silents
BLINDNESS OF VIRTUE, THE(1915), d; CALL OF THE SEA, THE(1915), d; VILLAGE HOMESTEAD, THE(1915), a, d

O.R.C. Totten
QUICK AND THE DEAD, THE(1963), art d

Priscilla Totten
DRAMATIC SCHOOL(1938)

Robert Totten
TRAUMA(1962); QUICK AND THE DEAD, THE(1963), d, w; RIDE A NORTHBOUND HORSE(1969), d; WILD COUNTRY, THE(1971), d; PONY EXPRESS RIDER(1976), w; APPLE DUMPLING GANG RIDES AGAIN, THE(1979)

Jack Tottenham
THIRD TIME LUCKY(1950, Brit.)

Loftus Tottenham
Silents
ADVENTUROUS YOUTH(1928, Brit.)

Merle Tottenham
DOWN OUR STREET(1932, Brit.); HERE'S GEORGE(1932, Brit.); BONDAGE(1933); CAVALCADE(1933); INVISIBLE MAN, THE(1933); PADDY, THE NEXT BEST THING(1933); NIGHT CLUB QUEEN(1934, Brit.); YOUTHFUL FOLLY(1934, Brit.); CHICK(1936, Brit.); NIGHT MUST FALL(1937); BANK HOLIDAY(1938, Brit.); DEAD MEN ARE DANGEROUS(1939, Brit.); GIRL MUST LIVE, A(1941, Brit.); POISON PEN(1941, Brit.); YOUNG MR. PITT, THE(1942, Brit.); HEADLINE(1943, Brit.); WE DIVE AT DAWN(1943, Brit.); THIS HAPPY BREED(1944, Brit.); I DIDN'T DO IT(1945, Brit.); CARAVAN(1946, Brit.); MY BROTHER JONATHAN(1949, Brit.); ROOM TO LET(1949, Brit.); SLEEPING CAR TO TRIESTE(1949, Brit.); WEAKER SEX, THE(1949, Brit.); FIVE ANGLES ON MURDER(1950, Brit.); TWENTY QUESTIONS MURDER MYSTERY, THE(1950, Brit.)

Aubrey Totter
ADVENTURE(1945)

Audrey Totter
MAIN STREET AFTER DARK(1944); BEWITCHED(1945); DANGEROUS PARTNERS(1945); HER HIGHNESS AND THE BELLBOY(1945); ZIEGFELD FOLLIES(1945); COCKEYED MIRACLE, THE(1946); POSTMAN ALWAYS RINGS TWICE, THE(1946); SAILOR TAKES A WIFE, THE(1946); SECRET HEART, THE(1946); BEGINNING OR THE END, THE(1947); HIGH WALL, THE(1947); LADY IN THE LAKE(1947); UNSUSPECTED, THE(1947); SAXON CHARM, THE(1948); ALIAS NICK BEAL(1949); ANY NUMBER CAN PLAY(1949); SET-UP, THE(1949); TENSION(1949); BLUE VEIL, THE(1951); FBI GIRL(1951); SELLOUT, THE(1951); UNDER THE GUN(1951); ASSIGNMENT-PARIS(1952); MY PAL GUS(1952); CHAMP FOR A DAY(1953); CRUISIN' DOWN THE RIVER(1953); MAN IN THE DARK(1953); MISSION OVER KOREA(1953); WOMAN THEY ALMOST LYNCHED, THE(1953); MASSACRE CANYON(1954); BULLET FOR JOEY, A(1955); VANISHING AMERICAN, THE(1955); WOMEN'S PRISON(1955); GHOST DIVER(1957); JET ATTACK(1958); MAN OR GUN(1958); CARPETBAGGERS, THE(1964); HARLOW(1965); CHUBASCO(1968); APPLE DUMPLING GANG RIDES AGAIN, THE(1979)

Jayne Tottman
SUPERMAN(1978)

Michel Toty
1984
LE BAL(1984, Fr./Ital./Algeria)

Ruth Totz
THREE STEPS NORTH(1951), ed

Bernard Toublanc-Michel
SINGAPORE, SINGAPORE(1969, Fr./Ital.), d, w

Philip Toubus
JESUS CHRIST, SUPERSTAR(1973)

Enrique Touceda
BULLET FOR PRETTY BOY, A(1970), w

Touch
JAGUAR(1956)

Georges Toudouze
WOLVES(1930, Brit.), w

Michael Tough
PROM NIGHT(1980)
Misc. Talkies
PHANTOM KID, THE(1983)

George Toulatos
FIREBIRD 2015 AD(1981)

George Touliatos
ONLY GOD KNOWS(1974, Can.); POWER PLAY(1978, Brit./Can.); FIREPOWER(1979, Brit.); PROM NIGHT(1980); STONE COLD DEAD(1980, Can.); AGENCY(1981, Can.); HEARTACHES(1981, Can.); LAST CHASE, THE(1981)
Misc. Talkies
FALCON'S GOLD(1982)

Jean Toulot
Misc. Silents
LA FETE ESPAGNOLE(1919, Fr.)

Jean Toulout
ENTENTE CORDIALE(1939, Fr.); NAKED WOMAN, THE(1950, Fr.); EDWARD AND CAROLINE(1952, Fr.)
Misc. Silents
LA DIXIEME SYMPHONIE(1918, Fr.); LE ROI DE CAMARGUE(1921, Fr.); DIAMANT NOIR(1922, Fr.); NOTRE DAME D'AMOUR(1922, Fr.)

Vincent Touly
SMALL CHANGE(1976, Fr.)

Tamara Toumanova
DAYS OF GLORY(1944); TONIGHT WE SING(1953); DEEP IN MY HEART(1954); INVITATION TO THE DANCE(1956); TORN CURTAIN(1966); PRIVATE LIFE OF SHERLOCK HOLMES, THE(1970, Brit.)

Patricia Toun
SNIPER, THE(1952)

Larbi Tounsi
DAUGHTER OF THE SANDS(1952, Fr.)

Georges Toupin
NOW THAT APRIL'S HERE(1958, Can.)

Robert Toupin
1984
C.H.U.D.(1984)

Mitsuhiro Toura
PLEASURES OF THE FLESH, THE(1965)

Rokko Toura
EMPEROR AND A GENERAL, THE(1968, Jap.); KUROENKO(1968, Jap); MERRY CHRISTMAS MR. LAWRENCE(1983, Jap./Brit.)

Jean Tourane
SECRET OF MAGIC ISLAND, THE(1964, Fr./Ital.), w, d

Aboutbaker Toure
BLACK AND WHITE IN COLOR(1976, Fr.)

Bachir Toure
ROOTS OF HEAVEN, THE(1958)

Moustapha Toure
MANDABI(1970, Fr./Senegal)

Askina Touree
1984
DESIREE(1984, Neth.)

Marion Toures
MONSEIGNEUR(1950, Fr.)

Lambros Touris
1984
VAMPING(1984)

V. Tourjanski
DEAD MELODY(1938, Ger.), d

V. Tourjansky
DARK EYES(1938, Fr.), d, w

Viachetslav Tourjansky
Silents
ADVENTURER, THE(1928), d

Viatcheslaw Tourjansky
Misc. Silents
L'ORDONNANCE(1921, Fr.), d; LA RIPOSTE(1922, Fr.), d; LE 15E PRELUDE DE CHOPIN(1922, Fr.), d; LES CONTES LES MILLES ET UNE NUITS(1922, Fr.), d; LES NUITS DE CARNAVAL(1922, Fr.), d; UNE AVENTURE(1922, Fr.), d; CALVAIRE D'AMOUR(1923, Fr.), d; LE CHANT DE L'AMOUR TRIOMPHANT(1923, Fr.), d; CE COCHON DE MORIN(1924, Fr.), d; LA DAME MASQUEE(1924, Fr.), d; LE PRINCE CHARMANT(1925, Fr.), d; MICHEL STROGOFF(1926, Fr.), d

W. Tourjansky
COSSACKS, THE(1960, It.), p; HEROD THE GREAT(1960, Ital.), p, w; PRISONER OF THE VOLGA(1960, Fr./Ital.), d

Wenceslav Tourjansky
PHARAOH'S WOMAN, THE(1961, Ital.), d

Francoise Tournafond
LAFAYETTE(1963, Fr.), cos; MILKY WAY, THE(1969, Fr./Ital.), cos
1984
LE BAL(1984, Fr./Ital./Algeria), cos

Andree Tourner
Misc. Silents
DESERT'S CRUCIBLE, THE(1922); CUPID'S KNOCKOUT(1926)

Maurice Tourner
Misc. Silents
EXILE(1917), d; COUNTY FAIR, THE(1920), d; BRASS BOTTLE, THE(1923), d; CHRISTIAN, THE(1923), d

Andree Tourneur
Silents
CONQUERING POWER, THE(1921); UNKNOWN, THE(1921); LIGHTS OF THE DESERT(1922); MARSHAL OF MONEYMINT, THE(1922); GILDED HIGHWAY, THE(1926); SPEED CRAZED(1926); ACTRESS, THE(1928)
Misc. Silents
FACE BETWEEN, THE(1922); TRAIL OF HATE(1922); SACRIFICE(1929, Brit.)

Christiana Tourneur
PARIS AFTER DARK(1943)

Jacques Tourneur
TALE OF TWO CITIES, A(1935), staging; NICK CARTER, MASTER DETECTIVE(1939), d; THEY ALL COME OUT(1939), d; PHANTOM RAIDERS(1940), d; DOCTORS DON'T TELL(1941), d; CAT PEOPLE(1942), d; I WALKED WITH A ZOMBIE(1943), d; LEOPARD MAN, THE(1943), d; DAYS OF GLORY(1944), d; EXPERIMENT PERILOUS(1944), d; CANYON PASSAGE(1946), d; OUT OF THE PAST(1947), d; BERLIN EXPRESS(1948), d; EASY LIVING(1949), d; FLAME AND THE ARROW, THE(1950), d; STARS IN MY CROWN(1950), d; ANNE OF THE INDIES(1951), d; CIRCLE OF DANGER(1951, Brit.), d; WAY OF A GAUCHO(1952), d; APPOINTMENT IN HONDURAS(1953), d; STRANGER ON HORSEBACK(1955), d; WICHITA(1955), d; GREAT DAY IN THE MORNING(1956), d; NIGHTFALL(1956), d; CURSE OF THE DEMON(1958), d; FEARMAKERS, THE(1958), d; TIMBUKTU(1959), d; GIANT OF MARATHON, THE(1960, Ital.), d; COMEDY OF TERRORS, THE(1964), d; CITY UNDER THE SEA(1965, Brit.), d

Maurice Tourneur
MYSTERIOUS ISLAND(1929), d; ACCUSED—STAND UP(1930, Fr.), d; KOENIGSMARK(1935, Fr.), d; WITH A SMILE(1939, Fr.), p&d; CARNIVAL OF SINNERS(1947, Fr.), p&d; VOLPONE(1947, Fr.), d; APRES L'AMOUR(1948, Fr.), d
Silents
MOTHER(1914), d&w; WISHING RING, THE(1914), d&w; CUB, THE(1915), d&w; IVORY SNUFF BOX, THE(1915), d; TRILBY(1915), d; GIRL'S FOLLY, A(1917), d&w; LAW OF THE LAND, THE(1917), d; POOR LITTLE RICH GIRL, A(1917), d; PRIDE OF THE CLAN, THE(1917), d; RISE OF JENNIE CUSHING, THE(1917), d; DOLL'S HOUSE, A(1918), d; PRUNELLA(1918), d; ROSE OF THE WORLD(1918), d; LAST OF THE MOHICANS, THE(1920), d; TREASURE ISLAND(1920), d; BAIT, THE(1921), d; ISLE OF LOST SHIPS, THE(1923), d; JEALOUS HUSBANDS(1923), d; TORMENT(1924), d; CLOTHES MAKE THE PIRATE(1925), d; NEVER THE TWAIN SHALL MEET(1925), d; ALOMA OF THE SOUTH SEAS(1926), d; OLD LOVES AND NEW(1926), d; LORNA DOONE(1927), p&d, w
Misc. Silents
ALIAS JIMMY VALENTINE(1915), d; PIT, THE(1915), d; CLOSED ROAD, THE(1916), d; HAND OF PERIL, THE(1916), d; PAWN OF FATE, THE(1916), d; RAIL RIDER, THE(1916), d; VELVET PAW, THE(1916), d; BARBARY SHEEP(1917), d; UNDYING FLAME, THE(1917), d; WHIP, THE(1917), d; BLUEBIRD, THE(1918), d; SPORTING LIFE(1918), d; BROKEN BUTTERFLY, THE(1919), d; LIFE LINE, THE(1919), d; VICTORY(1919), d; WHITE HEATHER, THE(1919), d; WOMAN(1919), d; DEEP WATERS(1920), d; MY LADY'S GARTER(1920), d; WHITE CIRCLE, THE(1920), d; FOOLISH MATRONS, THE(1921), d; WHILE PARIS SLEEPS(1923), d; WHITE MOTH, THE(1924), d; SPORTING LIFE(1925), d; SHIP OF LOST MEN, THE(1929, Ger.), d

Germaine Tournier
LAST CHANCE, THE(1945, Switz.)

Jean Tournier
AMELIE OR THE TIME TO LOVE(1961, Fr.), ph; TRAIN, THE(1965, Fr./Ital./U.S.), ph; COUNTERFEIT CONSTABLE, THE(1966, Fr.), ph; SLEEPING CAR MURDER, THE(1966, Fr.), ph; SHOCK TROOPS(1968, Ital./Fr.), ph; START THE REVOLUTION WITHOUT ME(1970), ph; DAY OF THE JACKAL, THE(1973, Brit./Fr.), ph; MOONRAKER(1979, Brit.), ph; FIENDISH PLOT OF DR. FU MANCHU, THE(1980), ph; THREE MEN TO DESTROY(1980, Fr.), ph; MAN, WOMAN AND CHILD(1983), ph

Raymond Tournon
YO YO(1967, Fr.), art d

Georges Tourreil
MISTRESS OF ATLANTIS, THE(1932, Ger.); TESTAMENT OF DR. MABUSE, THE(1943, Ger.)

Georges Tourrell
BELLMAN, THE(1947, Fr.)

Frank Tours
GLORIFYING THE AMERICAN GIRL(1930), ch; ONE HEAVENLY NIGHT(1931), md; EMPEROR JONES, THE(1933), md; SCOUNDREL, THE(1935), md; FIGHT FOR YOUR LADY(1937), md; EVERYBODY'S DOING IT(1938), md; JOY OF LIVING(1938), md; MOTHER CAREY'S CHICKENS(1938), md; TARNISHED ANGEL(1938), md; CONSPIRACY(1939), m; MEN AGAINST THE SKY(1940), md; VILLAIN STILL PURSUED HER, THE(1940), md

Joan Tours
JOAN OF OZARK(1942); SO PROUDLY WE HAIL(1943)

Allen Toussaint
BLACK SAMSON(1974), m

Olivier Toussaint
1984
IRRECONCILABLE DIFFERENCES(1984), m

Reginal M. Toussaint
CHAMP, THE(1979)

Yolande Toussaint
FOR LOVE OF IVY(1968)

Roland Toutain
LILIOM(1935, Fr.); SACRIFICE OF HONOR(1938, Fr.); RULES OF THE GAME, THE(1939, Fr.); ETERNAL RETURN, THE(1943, Fr.); MASK OF KOREA(1950, Fr.)

Maurice Touze
Misc. Silents
LA BELLE NIVERNAISE(1923, Fr.); LA FILLE DE L'EAU(1924, Fr.); PEAU DE PECHE(1929, Fr.)

Houshang Touzie
1984
MISSION, THE(1984)

Lupita Tova
OLD SPANISH CUSTOM, AN(1936, Brit.)

Teresa Tova
CURTAINS(1983, Can.)

Luciano Tovali
BREAD AND CHOCOLATE(1978, Ital.), ph

Jesus Tovar
JETLAG(1981, U.S./Span.)

Leo Tovar
F MAN(1936), ph; FLORIDA SPECIAL(1936), ph; NIGHT OF NIGHTS, THE(1939), ph; NIGHT AT EARL CARROLL'S, A(1940), ph; QUARTERBACK, THE(1940), ph; BLUE DENIM(1959), ph

Loretta Tovar
OPEN SEASON(1974, U.S./Span.)

Lupila Tovar
CRIME DOCTOR'S COURAGE, THE(1945)

Lupita Tovar
VEILED WOMAN, THE(1929); BORDER LAW(1931); EAST OF BORNEO(1931); YANKEE DON(1931); SANTA(1932, Mex.); STORM OVER THE ANDES(1935); BLOCKADE(1938); FIGHTING GRINGO, THE(1939); SOUTH OF THE BORDER(1939); TROPIC FURY(1939); GREEN HELL(1940); WESTERNER, THE(1940); TWO GUN SHERIFF(1941)

Marisa Tovar
HUNTING PARTY, THE(1977, Brit.)

Pattick Tovatt
ON THE NICKEL(1980)

Arthur Tovay
MAN CALLED PETER, THE(1955)

Birthe Tove
Z.P.G.(1972)

Lee Tover
STREET GIRL(1929), ph

Leo Tover
TANNED LEGS(1929), ph; VAGABOND LOVER(1929), ph; VERY IDEA, THE(1929), ph; FALL GUY, THE(1930), ph; FRAMED(1930), ph; RUNAWAY BRIDE(1930), ph; SHE'S MY WEAKNESS(1930), ph; SILVER HORDE, THE(1930), ph; ARE THESE OUR CHILDREN?(1931), ph; BACHELOR APARTMENT(1931), ph; GAY DIPLOMAT, THE(1931), ph; LADY REFUSES, THE(1931), ph; ROYAL BED, THE(1931), ph; TRANSGRESSION(1931), ph; TRAVELING HUSBANDS(1931), ph; FLAG LIEUTENANT, THE(1932, Brit.), w; GIRL OF THE RIO(1932), ph; IS MY FACE RED?(1932), ph; STATE'S ATTORNEY(1932), ph; SYMPHONY OF SIX MILLION(1932), ph; THIRTEEN WOMEN(1932), ph; COLLEGE HUMOR(1933), ph; GIRL WITHOUT A ROOM(1933), ph; I'M NO ANGEL(1933), ph; MONKEY'S PAW, THE(1933), ph; NO MAN OF HER OWN(1933), ph; BOLERO(1934), ph; COLLEGE RHYTHM(1934), ph; MURDER AT THE VANITIES(1934), ph; SHOOT THE WORKS(1934), ph; YOU BELONG TO ME(1934), ph; BIG BROADCAST OF 1936, THE(1935), ph; LOVE IN BLOOM(1935), ph; ARIZONA RAIDERS, THE(1936), ph; BRIDE COMES HOME(1936), ph; ROSE OF THE RANCHO(1936), ph; VALIANT IS THE WORD FOR CARRIE(1936), ph; EBB TIDE(1937), ph; I MET HIM IN PARIS(1937), ph; MAID OF SALEM(1937), ph; NIGHT CLUB SCANDAL(1937), ph; ARKANSAS TRAVELER, THE(1938), ph; BLUEBEARD'S EIGHTH WIFE(1938), ph; COCOANUT GROVE(1938), ph; INVITATION TO HAPPINESS(1939), ph; KING OF CHINATOWN(1939), ph; NEVER SAY DIE(1939), ph; BISCUIT EATER, THE(1940), ph; FARMER'S DAUGHTER, THE(1940), ph; UNTAMED(1940), ph; VICTORY(1940), ph; BAHAMA PASSAGE(1941), ph; HOLD BACK THE DAWN(1941), ph; I WANTED WINGS(1941), ph; LIFE WITH HENRY(1941), ph; MAJOR AND THE MINOR, THE(1942), ph; MRS. WIGGS OF THE CABBAGE PATCH(1942), ph; NIGHT IN NEW ORLEANS, A(1942), ph; STAR SPANGLED RHYTHM(1942), ph; CHINA(1943), ph; CRYSTAL BALL, THE(1943), ph; YOUNG AND WILLING(1943), ph; DEAD RECKONING(1947), ph; WOMAN ON THE BEACH, THE(1947), ph; I WALK ALONE(1948), ph; SEALED VERDICT(1948), ph; SNAKE PIT, THE(1948), ph; HEIRESS, THE(1949), ph; MY FRIEND IRMA(1949), ph; PAID IN FULL(1950), ph; SECRET FURY, THE(1950), ph; WHEN WILLIE COMES MARCHING HOME(1950), ph; DAY THE EARTH STOOD STILL, THE(1951), ph; FOLLOW THE SUN(1951), ph; PAYMENT ON DEMAND(1951), ph; SECRET OF CONVICT LAKE, THE(1951), ph; MY PAL GUS(1952), ph; MY WIFE'S BEST FRIEND(1952), ph; PRIDE OF ST. LOUIS, THE(1952), ph; WE'RE NOT MARRIED(1952), ph; BLUEPRINT FOR MURDER, A(1953), ph; MAN IN THE ATTIC(1953), ph; PRESIDENT'S LADY, THE(1953), ph; SOLDIER OF FORTUNE(1955), ph; TALL MEN, THE(1955), ph; UNTAMED(1955), ph; BETWEEN HEAVEN AND HELL(1956), ph; CONQUEROR, THE(1956), ph; LIEUTENANT WORE SKIRTS, THE(1956), ph; LOVE ME TENDER(1956), ph; REVOLT OF MAMIE STOVER, THE(1956), ph; SUN ALSO RISES, THE(1957), ph; WAY TO THE GOLD, THE(1957), ph; FRAULEIN(1958), ph; IN LOVE AND WAR(1958), ph; MAN IN THE ATTIC(1953), ph; NICE LITTLE BANK THAT SHOULD BE ROBBED, A(1958), ph; JOURNEY TO THE CENTER OF THE EARTH(1959), ph; SAY ONE FOR ME(1959), ph; FROM THE TERRACE(1960), ph; MARRIAGE-GO-ROUND, THE(1960), ph; ALL HANDS ON DECK(1961), ph; MISTY(1961), ph; FOLLOW THAT DREAM(1962), ph; SUNDAY IN NEW YORK(1963), ph; ISLAND OF THE BLUE DOLPHINS(1964), ph; STRANGE BEDFELLOWS(1965), ph; VERY SPECIAL FAVOR, A(1965), ph
Silents
FLAG LIEUTENANT, THE(1919, Brit.), w; FLAG LIEUTENANT, THE(1926, Brit.), w; GREAT GATSBY, THE(1926), ph; TELEPHONE GIRL, THE(1927), ph

Leon Tover
GIRL OF THE PORT(1930), ph

Arthur Tovey
SOMETHING TO LIVE FOR(1952); TATTERED DRESS, THE(1957); WILLARD(1971)

George Tovey
STRANGER'S MEETING(1957, Brit.); LIFE IN EMERGENCY WARD 10(1959, Brit.); SECRET PARTNER, THE(1961, Brit.); NEVER BACK LOSERS(1967, Brit.); VULTURE, THE(1967, U.S./Brit./Can.); POOR COW(1968, Brit.); BAXTER(1973, Brit.)

Roberta Tovey
PIPER'S TUNE, THE(1962, Brit.); TOUCH OF DEATH(1962, Brit.); DR. WHO AND THE DALEKS(1965, Brit.); HIGH WIND IN JAMAICA, A(1965); RUNAWAY RAILWAY(1965, Brit.); DALEKS—INVASION EARTH 2155 A.D.(1966, Brit.); OPERATION THIRD FORM(1966, Brit.)

Lucian Tovoli
SUSPIRIA(1977, Ital.), ph

Luciano Tovoli
PASSENGER, THE(1975, Ital.), ph; LEONOR(1977, Fr./Span./Ital.), ph; ADOPTION, THE(1978, Fr.), ph

Harry Towb
QUIET WOMAN, THE(1951, Brit.); GLORY AT SEA(1952, Brit.); JOHN WESLEY(1954, Brit.); SLEEPING TIGER, THE(1954, Brit.); LOVERS, HAPPY LOVERS!(1954, Brit.); PRIZE OF GOLD, A(1955, Brit.); ABOVE US THE WAVES(1956, Brit.); DOUBLE CROSS(1956, Brit.); MURDER AT SITE THREE(1959, Brit.); ALL NIGHT LONG(1961, Brit.); CRIMSON BLADE, THE(1964, Brit.); BLUE MAX, THE(1966); PRUDENCE AND THE PILL(1968, Brit.); 30 IS A DANGEROUS AGE, CYNTHIA(1968, Brit.); ALL NEAT IN BLACK STOCKINGS(1969, Brit.); DIGBY, THE BIGGEST DOG IN THE WORLD(1974, Brit.); GIRL FROM PETROVKA, THE(1974); BARRY LYNDON(1975, Brit.)

1984
LASSITER(1984)
David Towbin
STREET IS MY BEAT, THE(1966), art d
Halsey H. Tower
Misc. Silents
MAN'S FATE(1917)
Richard Tower
DOCTOR X(1932), ph
Whitney Tower
WILD PARTY, THE(1975)
Angela Towers
WOMEN OF DESIRE(1968)
Constance Towers
BRING YOUR SMILE ALONG(1955); HORSE SOLDIERS, THE(1959); SERGEANT RUTLEDGE(1960); SHOCK CORRIDOR(1963); FATE IS THE HUNTER(1964); NAKED KISS, THE(1964)
Donald Towers
NO DOWN PAYMENT(1957); MA BARKER'S KILLER BROOD(1960)
Harry Alan Towers
INVITATION TO MURDER(1962, Brit.), p; SANDERS(1963, Brit.), p, w; CODE 7, VICTIM 5(1964, Brit.), p; CITY OF FEAR(1965, Brit.), p; COAST OF SKELETONS(1965, Brit.), p; FACE OF FU MANCHU, THE(1965, Brit.), p; BANG, BANG, YOU'RE DEAD(1966), p; BRIDES OF FU MANCHU, THE(1966, Brit.), p; MOZAMBIQUE(1966, Brit.), p; 24 HOURS TO KILL(1966, Brit.), p; FIVE GOLDEN DRAGONS(1967, Brit.), p; HOUSE OF 1,000 DOLLS(1967, Ger./Span./Brit.), p; MILLION EYES OF SU-MURU, THE(1967, Brit.), p; PSYCHO-CIRCUS(1967, Brit.), p; THOSE FANTASTIC FLYING FOOLS(1967, Brit), p; BLOOD OF FU MANCHU, THE(1968, Brit.), p; CASTLE OF FU MANCHU, THE(1968, Ger./Span./Ital./Brit.), p; EVE(1968, Brit./Span.), p; VENGEANCE OF FU MANCHU, THE(1968, Brit./Ger./Hong Kong/Ireland), p; SANDY THE SEAL(1969, Brit.), p; VENUS IN FURS(1970, Ital./Brit./Ger.), p; COUNT DRACULA(1971, Sp., Ital., Ger., Brit.), p, w; TREASURE ISLAND(1972, Brit./Span./Fr./Ger.), p; TEN LITTLE INDIANS(1975, Ital./Fr./Span./Ger.), p
Harry Allan Towers
RIO 70(1970, U.S./Ger./Span.), p, w
Helen Towers
WHITE TRAP, THE(1959, Brit.)
Jim Towers
SCARFACE(1983)
Katie Towers
SQUATTER'S DAUGHTER(1933, Aus.); FLYING DOCTOR, THE(1936, Aus.)
Louis Towers
THESE WILDER YEARS(1956); RIDE BACK, THE(1957); TRUE STORY OF LYNN STUART, THE(1958)
Richard Towers
YOU SAID A MOUTHFUL(1932), ph
Robert Towers
TERRIFIED!(1963)
Tracee Towers
LILITH(1964)
Glen Towery
GRAND THEFT AUTO(1977)
Julia Kaye Towery
1984
BREAKIN'(1984), set d; WEEKEND PASS(1984), set d
Julie Kaye Towery
NEW YEAR'S EVIL(1980)
Ted Towey
MAVERICK QUEEN, THE(1956), cos
The Town Criers
COWBOY BLUES(1946)
Aline Towne
HARBOR OF MISSING MEN(1950); HIGHWAY 301(1950); VANISHING WESTERNER, THE(1950); I CAN GET IT FOR YOU WHOLESALE(1951); PURPLE HEART DIARY(1951); ROUGH RIDERS OF DURANGO(1951); CONFIDENCE GIRL(1952); STEEL TRAP, THE(1952); BLUEPRINT FOR MURDER, A(1953); GOG(1954); JULIE(1956); SATAN'S SATELLITES(1958); BRASS BOTTLE, THE(1964); SEND ME NO FLOWERS(1964); GUIDE FOR THE MARRIED MAN, A(1967); SONG OF NORWAY(1970)
Misc. Talkies
COMMANDO CODY(1953)
Brad Towne
THEY WERE EXPENDABLE(1945)
Earle Towne
HEROES(1977)
Elaine Towne
WOMAN OF DISTINCTION, A(1950)
Silents
OUT WITH THE TIDE(1928), w
Gene Towne
DRAG(1929), w; CZAR OF BRODWAY, THE(1930), w; LITTLE ACCIDENT(1930), w; LOOSE ANKLES(1930), w; STRICTLY MODERN(1930), w, titles; GOLDIE(1931), w; BILLION DOLLAR SCANDAL(1932), w; BUSINESS AND PLEASURE(1932), w; BROADWAY THROUGH A KEYHOLE(1933), w; HYPNOTIZED(1933), w; I LOVE THAT MAN(1933), w; SONG OF THE EAGLE(1933), w; PERSONALITY KID, THE(1934), w; EVERY NIGHT AT EIGHT(1935), w; GIRL FRIEND, THE(1935), w; GRAND EXIT(1935), w; MARY BURNS, FUGITIVE(1935), w; SHANGHAI(1935), w; SHE COULDN'T TAKE IT(1935), w; THIS IS THE LIFE(1935), w; CASE AGAINST MRS. AMES, THE(1936), w; ALI BABA GOES TO TOWN(1937), w; HISTORY IS MADE AT NIGHT(1937), w; STAND-IN(1937), w; YOU ONLY LIVE ONCE(1937), w; JOY OF LIVING(1938), w; ETERNALLY YOURS(1939), w; LITTLE MEN(1940), p; SWISS FAMILY ROBINSON(1940), p, w; TOM BROWN'S SCHOOL DAYS(1940), p, w; TOP BANANA(1954), w
Silents
DO YOUR DUTY(1928), t; FLYING ROMEOS(1928), t; LADY BE GOOD(1928), t; OUTCAST(1928), t
Kathryn Towne
DARLING, HOW COULD YOU!(1951)

Lester Towne
DUKE OF THE NAVY(1942)
Linda Towne
ADVENTURERS, THE(1970); THEY CALL ME MISTER TIBBS(1970); YOUNG NURSES, THE(1973)
Michael Towne
CORPSE CAME C.O.D., THE(; WE'VE NEVER BEEN LICKED(1943); GALLANT JOURNEY(1946); FRAMED(1947); IT HAD TO BE YOU(1947); 13TH HOUR, THE(1947); YOU WERE MEANT FOR ME(1948); SLIGHTLY FRENCH(1949)
Morris Towne
FLY NOW, PAY LATER(1969)
Robert Towne
TOMB OF LIGEIA, THE(1965, Brit.), w; VILLA RIDES(1968), w; DRIVE, HE SAID(1971); LAST DETAIL, THE(1973), w; CHINATOWN(1974), w; SHAMPOO(1975), w; YAKUZA, THE(1975, U.S./Jap.), w; PERSONAL BEST(1982), p,d&w
Roger Towne
1984
NATURAL, THE(1984), w
Rosella Towne
IT'S LOVE I'M AFTER(1937); BLONDES AT WORK(1938); BOY MEETS GIRL(1938); COWBOY FROM BROOKLYN(1938); FOOLS FOR SCANDAL(1938); PATIENT IN ROOM 18, THE(1938); SERGEANT MURPHY(1938); SISTERS, THE(1938); ADVENTURES OF JANE ARDEN(1939); CODE OF THE SECRET SERVICE(1939); DARK VICTORY(1939); GOING PLACES(1939); PRIVATE LIVES OF ELIZABETH AND ESSEX, THE(1939); SECRET SERVICE OF THE AIR(1939); WOMEN IN THE WIND(1939); FLIGHT ANGELS(1940); NO, NO NANETTE(1940); ROCKY MOUNTAIN RANGERS(1940); THERE'S MAGIC IN MUSIC(1941); GENTLE GANGSTER, A(1943)
Spencer Towne
PRISON TRAIN(1938), w
W. Townend
WISHBONE, THE(1933, Brit.), w
Herb Towner
THAT'S THE WAY OF THE WORLD(1975)
J.B. Towner
WHAT AM I BID?(1967)
Robert Towner
FAUST(1964)
Wesley Towner
MAD MARTINDALES, THE(1942), w
Anthony T. Townes
SMOKEY AND THE BANDIT II(1980)
Carol Lynn Townes
1984
BREAKIN' 2: ELECTRIC BOOGALOO(1984)
Christopher Townes
Misc. Talkies
TOUGH(1974)
Harry Townes
OPERATION MANHUNT(1954); MOUNTAIN, THE(1956); BROTHERS KARAMAZOV, THE(1958); SCREAMING MIMI(1958); CRY TOUGH(1959); SANCTUARY(1961); FITZWILLY(1967); IN ENEMY COUNTRY(1968); HEAVEN WITH A GUN(1969); STRATEGY OF TERROR(1969); HAWAIIANS, THE(1970); SANTEE(1973)
Barry Townley
ENEMIES OF THE LAW(1931)
Jack Townley
BACHELOR GIRL, THE(1929), w; COHENS AND KELLYS IN ATLANTIC CITY, THE(1929), w; LAST DANCE, THE(1930), d; AVENGER, THE(1931), w; DIVORCE AMONG FRIENDS(1931), w; STRANGE PEOPLE(1933), w; GUILTY PARENTS(1934), d&w; LAST OUTLAW, THE(1936), w; MUMMY'S BOYS(1936), w; PLOT THICKENS, THE(1936), w; SILLY BILLIES(1936), w; ALL OVER TOWN(1937), w; MEET THE MISSUS(1937), w; GANGS OF NEW YORK(1938), w; HIGGINS FAMILY, THE(1938), w; ROMANCE ON THE RUN(1938), w; COVERED TRAILER, THE(1939), w; HOME ON THE PRAIRIE(1939), d; MY WIFE'S RELATIVES(1939), w; ORPHANS OF THE STREET(1939), w; SHOULD HUSBANDS WORK?(1939), w; GRANDPA GOES TO TOWN(1940), w; MEXICAN SPITFIRE OUT WEST(1940), w; MONEY TO BURN(1940), w; SCATTERBRAIN(1940), w; ICE-CAPADES(1941), w; PITTSBURGH KID, THE(1941), d; PUDDIN' HEAD(1941), w; ROOKIES ON PARADE(1941), w; SIS HOPKINS(1941), w; GREAT GILDERSLEEVE, THE(1942), w; JOAN OF OZARK(1942), w; TRAITOR WITHIN, THE(1942), w; ALLERGIC TO LOVE(1943), w; GILDERSLEEVE'S BAD DAY(1943), w; HERE COMES ELMER(1943), w; PETTICOAT LARCENY(1943), w; FACES IN THE FOG(1944), w; GOODNIGHT SWEETHEART(1944), w; JAMBOREE(1944), w; ROSIE THE RIVETER(1944), w; YELLOW ROSE OF TEXAS, THE(1944), w; BELLS OF ROSARITA(1945), w; CHICAGO KID, THE(1945), w; HITCHHIKE TO HAPPINESS(1945), w; UTAH(1945), w; MY PAL TRIGGER(1946), w; ONE EXCITING WEEK(1946), w; LAST ROUND-UP, THE(1947), w; RIDERS OF THE WHISTLING PINES(1949), w; BLAZING SUN, THE(1950), w; CUBAN FIREBALL(1951), w; HAVANA ROSE(1951), w; HONEYCHILE(1951), w; FABULOUS SENORITA, THE(1952), w; OKLAHOMA ANNIE(1952), w; UNTAMED HEIRESS(1954), w; CRASHING LAS VEGAS(1956), w; HOT SHOTS(1956), w; DISEMBODIED, THE(1957), w; UP IN SMOKE(1957), w; CROOKED CIRCLE, THE(1958), w; IN THE MONEY(1958), w
Robert H. Townley
Misc. Silents
WEST OF THE RIO GRANDE(1921), d; PARTNERS OF THE SUNSET(1922), d; WELCOME TO OUR CITY(1922), d
Robin H. Townley
Misc. Silents
PROFITEER, THE(1919)
Robin Townley
Misc. Silents
HUNS WIHIN OUR GATES(1918); HONEYMOON RANCH(1920), d
Toke Townley
TREASURE HUNT(1952, Brit.); MEET MR. LUCIFER(1953, Brit.); TIME GENTLEMEN PLEASE!(1953, Brit.); BANG! YOU'RE DEAD(1954, Brit.); FAST AND LOOSE(1954, Brit.); RUNAWAY BUS, THE(1954, Brit.); DOCTOR AT SEA(1955, Brit.); INNOCENTS IN PARIS(1955, Brit.); LADY GODIVA RIDES AGAIN(1955, Brit.); ADMIRABLE CRICHTON, THE(1957, Brit.); CARRY ON ADMIRAL(1957, Brit.); MEN OF SHERWOOD FOREST(1957, Brit.); THREE MEN IN A BOAT(1958, Brit.); CRY FROM THE STREET, A(1959, Brit.); LOOK BACK IN ANGER(1959); MISSING NOTE, THE(1961, Brit.); DAMN THE DEFIANT!(1962, Brit.); CHALK GARDEN, THE(1964,

Brit.); SCARS OF DRACULA, THE(1970, Brit.)
Colin Towns
FULL CIRCLE(1977, Brit./Can.), m; HAUNTING OF JULIA, THE(1981, Brit./Can.), m
1984
SLAYGROUND(1984, Brit.), m
Herman Townsely
RING OF FIRE(1961), spec eff
Anna Townsend
Silents
DOCTOR JACK(1922); GRANDMA'S BOY(1922); DADDY(1923); SAFETY LAST(1923)
Bill Townsend
PURSUIT OF D.B. COOPER, THE(1981)
Billy Townsend
RANGERS STEP IN, THE(1937)
Bud Townsend
NIGHTMARE IN WAX(1969), d; TERROR HOUSE(1972), d; COACH(1978), d; HIGH COUNTRY, THE(1981, Can.), w
Candy Townsend
Misc. Talkies
BOSS LADY(1982)
Casey Townsend
SYNANON(1965); WHO KILLED TEDDY BEAR?(1965)
Charles Townsend
FIREFLY, THE(1937)
Colleen Townsend
HOLLYWOOD CANTEEN(1944); JANIE(1944); CHICKEN EVERY SUNDAY(1948); SCUDDA-HOO! SCUDDA-HAY!(1948); WALLS OF JERICHO(1948); WHEN WILLIE COMES MARCHING HOME(1950)
Dale Townsend
1984
HARD TO HOLD(1984)
David Townsend
SHOW-OFF, THE(1934), art d; THIN MAN, THE(1934), art d; CHINA SEAS(1935), art d
Silents
CALLAHANS AND THE MURPHYS, THE(1927), set d; FOREIGN DEVILS(1927), art d; SLIDE, KELLY, SLIDE(1927), set d; TAXI DANCER, THE(1927), set d; TILLIE THE TOILER(1927), art d
E. W. Townsend
Silents
CHIMMIE FADDEN(1915), w; CHIMMIE FADDEN OUT WEST(1915), w
Ed Townsend
ULTIMATE THRILL, THE(1974), m
Franklin Townsend
COVER ME BABE(1970)
Genevieve Townsend
Silents
GIRL OF LONDON, A(1925, Brit.); QUALIFIED ADVENTURER, THE(1925, Brit.); CHINESE BUNGALOW, THE(1926, Brit.)
Misc. Silents
BEYOND THE VEIL(1925, Brit.); CHINESE BUNGALOW, THE(1926, Brit.)
Genvieve Townsend
Misc. Silents
WAY OF A WOMAN, THE(1925, Brit.)
J. Townsend
VISITOR, THE(1980, Ital./U.S.)
Jeffrey Townsend
BABY, IT'S YOU(1983), prod d
1984
OLD ENOUGH(1984), prod d; RECKLESS(1984), prod d
Jill Townsend
SPIRIT IS WILLING, THE(1967); SITTING TARGET(1972, Brit.); ALFIE DARLING(1975, Brit.); SEVEN-PER-CENT SOLUTION, THE(1977, Brit.); AWAKENING, THE(1980)
Julian C. Townsend
CROSS AND THE SWITCHBLADE, THE(1970), ph
Julian Townsend
DIARY OF A BACHELOR(1964), ph; GAMERA THE INVINCIBLE(1966, Jap.), ph
K.C. Townsend
HUSBANDS(1970); BELOW THE BELT(1980)
Kathleen Townsend
Misc. Silents
PRINCESS' NECKLACE, THE(1917)
Leo Townsend
IT STARTED WITH EVE(1941), w; SEVEN SWEETHEARTS(1942), w; AMAZING MRS. HOLLIDAY(1943), w; CHIP OFF THE OLD BLOCK(1944), w; NIGHT AND DAY(1946), w; THAT WAY WITH WOMEN(1947), w; PORT OF NEW YORK(1949), w; BLACK HAND, THE(1950), w; SOUTHSIDE 1-1000(1950), w; ONE BIG AFFAIR(1952), w; DANGEROUS CROSSING(1953), w; VICKI(1953), w; LIFE IN THE BALANCE, A(1955), w; RUNNING WILD(1955), w; WHITE FEATHER(1955), w; FLIGHT TO HONG KONG(1956), w; FOUR BOYS AND A GUN(1957), w; SHADOW ON THE WINDOW, THE(1957), w; FRAULEIN(1958), w; STRANGE CASE OF DR. MANNING, THE(1958, Brit.), w; BIKINI BEACH(1964), w; I'D RATHER BE RICH(1964), w; BEACH BLANKET BINGO(1965), w; HOW TO STUFF A WILD BIKINI(1965), w; FIREBALL 590(1966), w
Leonard Townsend
HELLFIRE CLUB, THE(1963, Brit.), set d; SWORD OF LANCELOT(1963, Brit.), set d
Margaret Townsend
Misc. Silents
SONG OF SIXPENCE, A(1917)
Martyn Townsend
1984
ORDEAL BY INNOCENCE(1984, Brit.)
Mary Townsend
RIDE A VIOLENT MILE(1957); UNDER FIRE(1957)

Merry Townsend
HOUSE OF WAX(1953); REVOLT OF MAMIE STOVER, THE(1956)
Pat Townsend
BEACH GIRLS(1982), d
Patrice Townsend
SITTING DUCKS(1979)
Primi Townsend
SCHIZO(1977, Brit.)
Robert Townsend
WILLIE AND PHIL(1980)
1984
SOLDIER'S STORY, A(1984); STREETS OF FIRE(1984)
Roy L. Townsend
HAIL(1973), p
Roy Townsend
SOAPBOX DERBY(1958, Brit.)
Sher Townsend
BEACH BLANKET BINGO(1965), w
Vince Townsend
COUNT THREE AND PRAY(1955); TRIAL(1955)
Vince Townsend, Jr.
NEVER WAVE AT A WAC(1952); CAT ON A HOT TIN ROOF(1958); ALLIGATOR PEOPLE, THE(1959); MIRACLE OF THE HILLS, THE(1959); PORGY AND BESS(1959); FOR LOVE OR MONEY(1963)
Vince M. Townsend, Jr.
FOREVER FEMALE(1953); VALLEY OF THE HEADHUNTERS(1953); JUNGLE MAN-EATERS(1954); DUEL ON THE MISSISSIPPI(1955)
Vince Monroe Townsend, Jr.
20,000 EYES(1961)
William E. Townsend
WHOSE LIFE IS IT ANYWAY?(1981)
Pete Townshend
QUADROPHENIA(1979, Brit.), w, md
Peter Townshend
TOMMY(1975, Brit.), a, w, m, md
Roy Townshend
MADE FOR EACH OTHER(1971), p
Don Townsley
FANTASIA(1940), anim
Herman Townsley
MASK, THE(1961, Can.), spec eff; LORD LOVE A DUCK(1966), spec eff; HELLFIGHTERS(1968), spec eff; SCALPHUNTERS, THE(1968), spec eff; MC MASTERS, THE(1970), spec eff; SOLDIER BLUE(1970), spec eff; SLAUGHTER(1972), spec eff
Don Towsley
PINOCCHIO(1940), anim; DUMBO(1941), anim
Candy Toxton
MOONRISE(1948)
Alan Toy
1984
SWING SHIFT(1984)
Barbara Toy
MONKEY'S PAW, THE(1948, Brit.), w
Diane Toy
NEW FACES OF 1937(1937); ADVENTURES OF MARCO POLO, THE(1938)
Mary Mon Toy
YEAR OF THE HORSE, THE(1966)
Noel Toy
HOW TO BE VERY, VERY, POPULAR(1955); LEFT HAND OF GOD, THE(1955); SOLDIER OF FORTUNE(1955); S.O.B.(1981)
Peggy Toy
MISTER BROWN(1972)
Teri Toy
SINBAD THE SAILOR(1947)
Toy and Wing
NO ORCHIDS FOR MISS BLANDISH(1948, Brit.)
Haruko Toyama
SEVEN SAMURAI, THE(1956, Jap.)
Masayuki Toyama
PLAY IT COOL(1970, Jap.), w
Geoffrey Toye
REMBRANDT(1936, Brit.), m; MEN ARE NOT GODS(1937, Brit.), m; MIKADO, THE(1939, Brit.), p, w
Terry Toye
UNDERGROUND U.S.A.(1980)
Wendy Toye
INVITATION TO THE WALTZ(1935, Brit.); I'LL BE YOUR SWEETHEART(1945, Brit.); TECKMAN MYSTERY, THE(1955, Brit), d; THREE CASES OF MURDER(1955, Brit.), d; ALL FOR MARY(1956, Brit.), d; RAISING A RIOT(1957, Brit.), d; TRUE AS A TURTLE(1957, Brit.), d; WE JOINED THE NAVY(1962, Brit.), d
Toyia
SATURDAY NIGHT AT THE BATHS(1975)
Christopher Toyne
CHILD IN THE HOUSE(1956, Brit.)
Gabriel Toyne
MURDER AT MONTE CARLO(1935, Brit.); CURSE OF THE WRAYDONS, THE(1946, Brit.)
Shiro Toyoda
DIPLOMAT'S MANSION, THE(1961, Jap.), d; TILL TOMORROW COMES(1962, Jap.), d; TWILIGHT STORY, THE(1962, Jap.), d; MADAME AKI(1963, Jap.), d; ILLUSION OF BLOOD(1966, Jap.), d; RIVER OF FOREVER(1967, Jap.), d; PORTRAIT OF HELL(1969, Jap.), d
Victor Toyota
MODERN ROMANCE(1981)
Esko Toyri
MOONWOLF(1966, Fin./Ger.), ph
The Toys
IT'S A BIKINI WORLD(1967)

Geoffrey Tozer
JIG SAW(1965, Brit.), art d; GIRL GETTERS, THE(1966, Brit.), art d; TROG(1970, Brit.), art d; PUPPET ON A CHAIN(1971, Brit.), art d; UNDER MILK WOOD(1973, Brit.), art d; DARK PLACES(1974, Brit.), art d; GET CHARLIE TULLY(1976, Brit.), art d; DANGEROUS DAVIES–THE LAST DETECTIVE(1981, Brit.), art d
1984
LITTLE DRUMMER GIRL, THE(1984), art d
J. R. Tozer
YELLOW STOCKINGS(1930, Brit.); ANOTHER DAWN(1937); MAID OF SA-LEM(1937)
Silents
HARD WAY, THE(1916, Brit.); MERCHANT OF VENICE, THE(1916, Brit.); OLD WIVES' TALE, THE(1921, Brit.); POINTING FINGER, THE(1922, Brit.); PASSIONATE ADVENTURE, THE(1924, Brit.); AFTERWARDS(1928, Brit.); ZERO(1928, Brit.)
Misc. Silents
BURNT WINGS(1916, Brit.); BARS OF IRON(1920, Brit.); DIANA OF THE CROSS-WAYS(1922, Brit.); FORTUNE'S FOOL(1922, Brit.); LAMP IN THE DESERT(1922, Brit.); SPORTING INSTINCT, THE(1922, Brit.)
Joe E. Tozer
ANNA KARENINA(1935)
Joseph Tozer
CLIVE OF INDIA(1935); HANDS ACROSS THE TABLE(1935); LADY ESCAPES, THE(1937)
Joseph E. Tozer
DRACULA'S DAUGHTER(1936)
Joseph R. Tozer
CARDINAL RICHELIEU(1935); RETURN OF SOPHIE LANG, THE(1936); SU-ZY(1936)
Stephen Tozer
1984
UTU(1984, New Zealand)
Steven Tozer
GOODBYE PORK PIE(1981, New Zealand)
T.R. Tozer
Silents
ANSWER, THE(1916, Brit.)
Fred Tozere
CONFESSIONS OF A NAZI SPY(1939); HELL'S KITCHEN(1939); I AM NOT AFRAID(1939); MAN WHO DARED, THE(1939); NANCY DREW AND THE HIDDEN STAIRCASE(1939); PRIDE OF THE BLUEGRASS(1939)
Frederic Tozere
COWBOY QUARTERBACK(1939); EVERYBODY'S HOBBY(1939); ACT OF MUR-DER, AN(1948); IRON CURTAIN, THE(1948); RETURN OF OCTOBER, THE(1948); MADAME BOVARY(1949); FATHER IS A BACHELOR(1950)
Fausto Tozzi
UNDER THE SUN OF ROME(1949, Ital.), w; FOUR WAYS OUT(1954, Ital.); EL CID(1961, U.S./Ital.); RED CLOAK, THE(1961, Ital./Fr.); RETURN OF DR. MABUSE, THE(1961, Ger./Fr./Ital.); WONDERS OF ALADDIN, THE(1961, Fr./Ital.); COMMAN-DO(1962, Ital., Span., Bel., Ger.); CONSTANTINE AND THE CROSS(1962, Ital.); EAST OF KILIMANJARO(1962, Brit./Ital.); SWORDSMAN OF SIENA, THE(1962, Fr./Ital.); VISIT, THE(1964, Ger./Fr./Ital./U.S.); AGONY AND THE ECSTASY, THE(1965); SCHEHERAZADE(1965, Fr./Ital./Span.); KNIVES OF THE AVENGER(1967, Ital.); MAN WHO KILLED BILLY THE KID, THE(1967, Span./Ital.); SAILOR FROM GIBRALTAR, THE(1967, Brit.); FEW BULLETS MORE, A(1968, Ital./Span.); APPOINT-MENT, THE(1969); DESERTER, THE(1971 Ital./Yugo.); MAN CALLED SLEDGE, A(1971, Ital.); VALACHI PAPERS, THE(1972, Ital./Fr.); CRAZY JOE(1974); CHI-NO(1976, Ital., Span., Fr.); STREET PEOPLE(1976, U.S./Ital.); SICILIAN CONNEC-TION, THE(1977); BLACK STALLION, THE(1979)
Ferruccio Tozzi
UNDER THE SUN OF ROME(1949, Ital.)
Georgio Tozzi
SHAMUS(1973)
Maria Tozzi
UNDER THE SUN OF ROME(1949, Ital.)
Pierre Trabaud
ANTOINE ET ANTOINETTE(1947 Fr.); WAR OF THE BUTTONS(1963 Fr.)
Johnny Traber
MOONRAKER(1979, Brit.)
Tony Trabert
OUTFIT, THE(1973)
Candy Trabuco
LOVE CHILD(1982)
Brigitte Trace
DOCTOR ZHIVAGO(1965)
Christopher Trace
WRONG NUMBER(1959, Brit.); URGE TO KILL(1960, Brit.)
Doreen Tracey
WESTWARD HO THE WAGONS!(1956)
Ella Tracey
DEVIL DOLL(1964, Brit.)
Gloria Tracey
LADIES MAN, THE(1961)
Harry Tracey
Silents
SKID PROOF(1923); OUT ALL NIGHT(1927)
Ian Tracey
KEEPER, THE(1976, Can.); IN PRAISE OF OLDER WOMEN(1978, Can.); EURE-KA(1983, Brit.)
Lynn Tracey
MIRACLE IN SOHO(1957, Brit.)
Ray Tracey
JOE PANTHER(1976); SEEMS LIKE OLD TIMES(1980)
Tabbetha Tracey
EYES OF A STRANGER(1980)
Thomas Tracey
Silents
MAN HATER, THE(1917)

Tracey and Haye
Silents
ARCADIANS, THE(1927, Brit.)
Amy Trachtenberg
STUDENT TEACHERS, THE(1973)
Bud Trackery
SAN ANTONE(1953), ph
Tracy
SIDEWINDER ONE(1977), art d
Adele Tracy
Misc. Talkies
WYOMING WHIRLWIND(1932)
Arthur Tracy
BACKSTAGE(1937, Brit.); COMMAND PERFORMANCE(1937, Brit.); STREET SING-ER, THE(1937, Brit.); FOLLOW YOUR STAR(1938, Brit.), a, w
Bert Tracy
BOOTS! BOOTS!(1934, Brit.), d; HOLIDAYS WITH PAY(1948, Brit.)
Silents
KENTUCKY DERBY, THE(1922)
Bill Tracy
HERE COMES TROUBLE(1948)
Bobby Tracy
NOTHING SACRED(1937); MEN WITH WINGS(1938)
Clyde Tracy
Misc. Silents
RUMPELSTILSKIN(1915)
Don Tracy
CRISS CROSS(1949), w
Ed Tracy
MEN OF THE FIGHTING LADY(1954)
Edward Tracy
GENTLEMEN MARRY BRUNETTES(1955)
Emerson Tracy
CHAMPAGNE FOR BREAKFAST(1935)
Harry Tracy
LOVE BEFORE BREAKFAST(1936); NEXT TIME WE LOVE(1936)
Helen Tracy
Silents
ROMEO AND JULIET(1916); NET, THE(1923)
Misc. Silents
LAND OF PROMISE, THE(1917); BLUE-EYED MARY(1918); SUNSHINE NAN(1918)
Jack Tracy
ROBBER SYMPHONY, THE(1937, Brit.)
Jim Tracy
PERSONAL BEST(1982)
John Tracy
DRIFTER, THE(1966); MISTER BUDDWING(1966); DIRTY HARRY(1971)
Kim Tracy
KONGA(1961, Brit.); PETTICOAT PIRATES(1961, Brit.); GIRL HUNTERS, THE(1963, Brit.)
Lee Tracy
BIG TIME(1929); SALUTE(1929); BORN RECKLESS(1930); GOT WHAT SHE WANT-ED(1930); LILIOM(1930); SHE GOT WHAT SHE WANTED(1930); BLESSED EVENT(1932); DOCTOR X(1932); HALF-NAKED TRUTH, THE(1932); NIGHT MAYOR, THE(1932); STRANGE LOVE OF MOLLY LOUVAIN, THE(1932); WASHINGTON MERRY-GO-ROUND(1932); ADVICE TO THE LOVELORN(1933); BOMBSHELL(1933); CLEAR ALL WIRES(1933); DINNER AT EIGHT(1933); NUISANCE, THE(1933); PRIVATE JONES(1933); TURN BACK THE CLOCK(1933); I'LL TELL THE WORLD(1934); LEMON DROP KID, THE(1934); YOU BELONG TO ME(1934); CARNI-VAL(1935); TWO FISTED(1935); SUTTER'S GOLD(1936); WANTED: JANE TUR-NER(1936); BEHIND THE HEADLINES(1937); CRASHING HOLLYWOOD(1937); CRIMINAL LAWYER(1937); FIXER DUGAN(1939); SPELLBINDER, THE(1939); MIL-LIONAIRES IN PRISON(1940); PAYOFF, THE(1943); POWER OF THE PRESS(1943); BETRAYAL FROM THE EAST(1945); I'LL TELL THE WORLD(1945); HIGH TI-DE(1947); BEST MAN, THE(1964)
Louis Tracy
Silents
NUMBER 17(1920), w
Lynn Tracy
CURSE OF THE DEMON(1958)
Margaret Tracy
SIGN OF THE RAM, THE(1948); SMART WOMAN(1948)
Marlene Tracy
PICTURE MOMMY DEAD(1966); I DISMEMBER MAMA(1974); WOMAN INSIDE, THE(1981)
Spencer Tracy
UP THE RIVER(1930); GOLDIE(1931); QUICK MILLIONS(1931); SIX CYLINDER LOVE(1931); DISORDERLY CONDUCT(1932); ME AND MY GAL(1932); PAINTED WOMAN(1932); SHE WANTED A MILLIONAIRE(1932); SKY DEVILS(1932); SOCIE-TY GIRL(1932); YOUNG AMERICA(1932); FACE IN THE SKY(1933); MAD GAME, THE(1933); MAN'S CASTLE, A(1933); POWER AND THE GLORY, THE(1933); SHANG-HAI MADNESS(1933); 20,000 YEARS IN SING SING(1933); BOTTOMS UP(1934); LOOKING FOR TROUBLE(1934); MARIE GALANTE(1934); NOW I'LL TELL(1934); SHOW-OFF, THE(1934); DANTE'S INFERNO(1935); IT'S A SMALL WORLD(1935); MURDER MAN(1935); FURY(1936); LIBELED LADY(1936); RIFF-RAFF(1936); SAN FRANCISCO(1936); WHIPSAW(1936); BIG CITY(1937); CAPTAINS COURA-GEOUS(1937); MANNEQUIN(1937); THEY GAVE HIM A GUN(1937); BOYS TOWN(1938); TEST PILOT(1938); STANLEY AND LIVINGSTONE(1939); BOOM TOWN(1940); EDISON, THE MAN(1940); I TAKE THIS WOMAN(1940); NORTHWEST PASSAGE(1940); DR. JEKYLL AND MR. HYDE(1941); MEN OF BOYS TOWN(1941); KEEPER OF THE FLAME(1942); TORTILLA FLAT(1942); WOMAN OF THE YEAR(1942); GUY NAMED JOE, A(1943); SEVENTH CROSS(1944); THIRTY SECONDS OVER TOKYO(1944); WITHOUT LOVE(1945); CASS TIMBERLANE(1947); SEA OF GRASS, THE(1947); STATE OF THE UNION(1948); ADAM'S RIB(1949); EDWARD, MY SON(1949, U.S./Brit.); FATHER OF THE BRIDE(1950); MA-LAYA(1950); FATHER'S LITTLE DIVIDEND(1951); PEOPLE AGAINST O'HARA, THE(1951); PAT AND MIKE(1952); PLYMOUTH ADVENTURE(1952); ACTRESS, THE(1953); BROKEN LANCE(1954); BAD DAY AT BLACK ROCK(1955); MOUNTAIN, THE(1956); DESK SET(1957); LAST HURRAH, THE(1958); OLD MAN AND THE SEA, THE(1958); INHERIT THE WIND(1960); DEVIL AT FOUR O'CLOCK, THE(1961);

JUDGMENT AT NUREMBERG(1961); HOW THE WEST WAS WON(1962); IT'S A MAD, MAD, MAD, MAD WORLD(1963); GUESS WHO'S COMING TO DINNER(1967)

Steve Tracy
NATIONAL LAMPOON'S CLASS REUNION(1982)

Thomas Tracy
Silents
SENATOR, THE(1915)

Virginia Tracy
Silents
QUEEN OF SHEBA, THE(1921), w; NERO(1922, U.S./Ital.), w

William Tracy
ANGELS WITH DIRTY FACES(1938); BROTHER RAT(1938); JONES FAMILY IN HOLLYWOOD, THE(1939); MILLION DOLLAR LEGS(1939); GALLANT SONS(1940); SHOP AROUND THE CORNER, THE(1940); STRIKE UP THE BAND(1940); HER FIRST BEAU(1941); MR. AND MRS. SMITH(1941); SHE KNEW ALL THE ANSWERS(1941); TANKS A MILLION(1941); TILLIE THE TOILER(1941); TOBACCO ROAD(1941); ABOUT FACE(1942); GEORGE WASHINGTON SLEPT HERE(1942); HAY FOOT(1942); TO THE SHORES OF TRIPOLI(1942); YOUNG AMERICA(1942); YANKS AHOY(1943); WALLS OF JERICHO(1948); HENRY, THE RAINMAKER(1949); ONE TOO MANY(1950); AS YOU WERE(1951); SUNNY SIDE OF THE STREET(1951); MR. WALKIE TALKIE(1952); WINGS OF EAGLES, THE(1957)

Tracy and Elwood
LOVE AT FIRST SIGHT(1930)

George Henry Trader
Misc. Silents
WHOSO TAKETH A WIFE(1916)

Larry Trader
1984
SONGWRITER(1984)

Marie Trado
Misc. Silents
FOLKS FROM WAY DOWN EAST(1924)

Evelyn Traeger
Misc. Talkies
YOUNG SEDUCERS, THE(1974)

Rick Traeger
HITLER(1962); MORITURI(1965); KARATE KILLERS, THE(1967); DESTRUCTORS, THE(1968); BEDKNOBS AND BROOMSTICKS(1971); LEGEND OF THE LONE RANGER, THE(1981)

Paul Trafas
1984
GHOSTBUSTERS(1984)

Traffic
HERE WE GO ROUND THE MULBERRY BUSH(1968, Brit.), m

Judith Trafford
LOVABLE CHEAT, THE(1949)

Frank Tragear
HOT MILLIONS(1968, Brit.)

Paul Trahair
1984
SQUIZZY TAYLOR(1984, Aus.)

Jane Trahey
TROUBLE WITH ANGELS, THE(1966), w; WHERE ANGELS GO...TROUBLE FOLLOWS(1968), w

Madalyn Trahey
PARSON AND THE OUTLAW, THE(1957); MUSTANG(1959)

Piero Traiannoni
ORGANIZER, THE(1964, Fr./Ital./Yugo.)

Dieter Traier
WAR AND PEACE(1983, Ger.)

Armitage Trail
SCARFACE(1932), w; THIRTEENTH GUEST, THE(1932), w; MYSTERY OF THE 13TH GUEST, THE(1943), w

Dorothy Trail
SING FOR YOUR SUPPER(1941); PARACHUTE NURSE(1942)

George Traill
Silents
ANGEL ESQUIRE(1919, Brit.)

Ken Traill
THIS SPORTING LIFE(1963, Brit.)

Mavis Traill
VALUE FOR MONEY(1957, Brit.)

Arthur Chesney Train
ILLUSION(1929), w
Silents
BLIND GODDESS, THE(1926), w

Dean Train
TALL TEXAN, THE(1953)

Jack Train
KING ARTHUR WAS A GENTLEMAN(1942, Brit.); IT'S THAT MAN AGAIN(1943, Brit.); MISS LONDON LTD.(1943, Brit.); COLONEL BOGEY(1948, Brit.); SHOWTIME(1948, Brit.); TWENTY QUESTIONS MURDER MYSTERY, THE(1950, Brit.); WOMAN WHO WOULDN'T DIE, THE(1965, Brit.)

Teal Traina
MINX, THE(1969)

Bennett Trainer
1984
KIDCO(1984), w

Len Trainer
LIFE BEGINS AT 40(1935)

Leonard Trainer
TERROR TRAIL(1933); WATER RUSTLERS(1939)

Susan Trainer
1984
CONSTANCE(1984, New Zealand)

Tommy Trainer
DOWN OUR ALLEY(1939, Brit.)

Leonard Trainor
STAGECOACH(1939)
Misc. Silents
HI-JACKING RUSTLERS(1926)

Mary Ellen Trainor
1984
ROMANCING THE STONE(1984); STONE BOY, THE(1984)

Vaclav Trajan
EMPEROR AND THE NIGHTINGALE, THE(1949, Czech.), m

Trakhtina
ENEMIES OF PROGRESS(1934, USSR)

E. Traktovenko
MAGIC WEAVER, THE(1965, USSR)

Johnny Trama
TOP BANANA(1954)

Tramel
BARRANCO(1932, Fr.); COGNASSE(1932, Fr.); WELL-DIGGER'S DAUGHTER, THE(1946, Fr.)

Felicien Tramel
IDIOT, THE(1948, Fr.)

Lucien Tramel
Misc. Silents
LE CRIME DU BOUIF(1921, Fr.); LA RESURRECTION DU BOUIF(1922, Fr.)

Peter Tramm
1984
FOOTLOOSE(1984)

Col. Charles M. Trammel, Jr.
RACK, THE(1956), tech adv

Jean-Claude Tramont
ASH WEDNESDAY(1973), w; ALL NIGHT LONG(1981), d

Sergio Tramonti
INVESTIGATION OF A CITIZEN ABOVE SUSPICION(1970, Ital.)

The Tramp Band
STORMY WEATHER(1943)

Ray Trampe
BOY'S REFORMATORY(1939), w

Walter Trampler
OF STARS AND MEN(1961), md

Hout Ming Tran
1984
KILLING FIELDS, THE(1984, Brit.)

Franco Tranchina
WE STILL KILL THE OLD WAY(1967, Ital.)

Vincenzo Tranchina
L'AVVENTURA(1960, Ital.)

Reuben Trane
SHOCK WAVES(1977), p, ph

Eligio Trani
NIGHTS OF CABIRIA(1957, Ital.), makeup

Emilio Trani
JULIET OF THE SPIRITS(1965, Fr./Ital./W.Ger.), makeup

Maurizio Trani
DR. BUTCHER, M.D.(1982, Ital.), spec eff; 1990: THE BRONX WARRIORS(1983, Ital.), makeup
1984
HOUSE BY THE CEMETERY, THE(1984, Ital.), makeup

Silvano Tranquilli
SHOOT LOUD, LOUDER... I DON'T UNDERSTAND(1966, Ital.); SUNFLOWER(1970, Fr./Ital.); BLACK BELLY OF THE TARANTULA, THE(1972, Ital.); DIARY OF AN ITALIAN(1972, Ital.); NO WAY OUT(1975, Ital./Fr.)

Trans Love Airways
CAPTAIN MILKSHAKE(1970)

Flo Transfield
DIARY OF A MAD HOUSEWIFE(1970), cos

Giuseppe Transocchi
SUSPIRIA(1977, Ital.)

Bert Transwell
SUMMERSPELL(1983)

Joseph H. Trant
Silents
ACCORDING TO LAW(1916), w

Florence Tranter
GIRLS IN THE STREET(1937, Brit.), w; GIRL IN THE STREET(1938, Brit.), w; SUICIDE LEGION(1940, Brit.), w; COURTNEY AFFAIR, THE(1947, Brit.), w; PICCADILLY INCIDENT(1948, Brit.), w

Nigel Tranter
BRIDAL PATH, THE(1959, Brit.), w

Cordula Trantow
BRIDGE, THE(1961, Ger.); HITLER(1962); TOMORROW IS MY TURN(1962, Fr./Ital./Ger.); CASTLE, THE(1969, Ger.)

Herbert Trantow
AFFAIR BLUM, THE(1949, Ger.), m; WOZZECK(1962, E. Ger.), m; CASTLE, THE(1969, Ger.), m

Cesare Trapani
STRANGER ON THE PROWL(1953, Ital.)

Enzo Trapani
BRIEF RAPTURE(1952, Ital.), d, w

Coles Trapnell
WITHIN THESE WALLS(1945), w

Roger Trapp
SUNDAYS AND CYBELE(1962, Fr.); HOW NOT TO ROB A DEPARTMENT STORE(1965, Fr./Ital.); LADY L(1965, Fr./Ital.); STOLEN KISSES(1969, Fr.); LE PETIT THEATRE DE JEAN RENOIR(1974, Fr.); LA NUIT DE VARENNES(1983, Fr./Ital.)

Mildred Trares
PENDULUM(1969)

Luciano Trasatti
VITELLONI(1956, Ital./Fr.), ph; SIGN OF THE GLADIATOR(1959, Fr./Ger./Ital.), ph; RICE GIRL(1963, Fr./Ital.), ph; BLOODY PIT OF HORROR, THE(1965, Ital.), ph; LOVE AND MARRIAGE(1966, Ital.), ph; TAMING OF THE SHREW, THE(1967, U.S./Ital.), ph; PSYCHOUT FOR MURDER(1971, Arg./Ital.), ph

Kathryn Trask
SHOOT THE MOON(1982)
Nina Trask
Silents
GOLD RUSH, THE(1925)
Walter Trask
WAY OUT WEST(1937)
Robert Trasker
NOTORIOUS GENTLEMAN, A(1935), w; ACCUSING FINGER, THE(1936), w; GIRL OF THE OZARKS(1936), w
Lydia Trasmonte
PASSIONATE STRANGERS, THE(1968, Phil.)
Ami Traub
1984
DRIFTING(1984, Israel)
Joe Traub
MERRY WIVES OF RENO, THE(1934), w
Silents
INTO THE NIGHT(1928), t
Toe Traub
EARTHWORM TRACTORS(1936), w
Shepard Traube
BRIDE WORE CRUTCHES, THE(1940), d; STREET OF MEMORIES(1940), d; FOR BEAUTY'S SAKE(1941), d
Shephard Traube
BEASTS OF BERLIN(1939), w
Shepherd Traube
ONCE UPON A COFFEE HOUSE(1965), d
Helen Traubel
DEEP IN MY HEART(1954); LADIES MAN, THE(1961); GUNN(1967)
Illya Trauberg
SON OF MONGOLIA(1936, USSR), d
Ilya Trauberg
Misc. Silents
BLUE EXPRESS(1929, USSR), d
Leonid Trauberg
NEW HORIZONS(1939, USSR), d&w
Misc. Silents
ADVENTURES OF AN OCTOBERITE, THE(1924, USSR), d; CLUB OF THE BIG DEED, THE(1927, USSR), d; NEW BABYLON, THE(1929, USSR), d
Alex Trauner
ONCE MORE, WITH FEELING(1960), prod d; FIENDISH PLOT OF DR. FU MAN-CHU, THE(1980), prod d
Alexander Trauner
CHILDREN OF PARADISE(1945, Fr.), art d; STORMY WATERS(1946, Fr.), art d; GREEN GLOVE, THE(1952), art d; LOVE IN THE AFTERNOON(1957), a, art d; NUN'S STORY, THE(1959), art d; APARTMENT, THE(1960), art d; ONE, TWO, THREE(1961), art d; PARIS BLUES(1961), art d; ROMANOFF AND JULIET(1961), art d; FIVE MILES TO MIDNIGHT(1963, U.S./Fr./Ital.), art d; IRMA LA DOU-CE(1963), art d; KISS ME, STUPID(1964), prod d; HOW TO STEAL A MILLION(1966), prod d; NIGHT OF THE GENERALS, THE(1967, Brit./Fr.), prod d; FLEA IN HER EAR, A(1968, Fr.), prod d; PRIVATE LIFE OF SHERLOCK HOLMES, THE(1970, Brit.), prod d; MAN WHO WOULD BE KING, THE(1975, Brit.), prod d; MR. KLEIN(1976, Fr.), art d; FIRST TIME, THE(1978, Fr.), art d; ONE-TRICK PONY(1980), art d
Alexandre Trauner
PORT OF SHADOWS(1938, Fr.), prod d; DAYBREAK(1940, Fr.), set d; GATES OF THE NIGHT(1950, Fr.), prod d; LAND OF THE PHARAOHS(1955), art d; OTHEL-LO(1955, U.S./Fr./Ital.), art d; HAPPY ROAD, THE(1957), art d; LIGHT ACROSSS THE STREET, THE(1957, Fr.), art d; WITNESS FOR THE PROSECUTION(1957), art d; GOODBYE AGAIN(1961), art d; UPTIGHT(1968), prod d; PROMISE AT DAWN(1970, U.S./Fr.), prod d; IMPOSSIBLE OBJECT(1973, Fr.), art d; DON GIOVAN-NI(1979, Fr./Ital./Ger.), art d; COUP DE TORCHON(1981, Fr.), prod d; TROUT, THE(1982, Fr.), prod d
Ilse Trautschold
POSSESSION(1981, Fr./Ger.)
Armando Travajoi
LA NUIT DE VARENNES(1983, Fr./Ital.), m
Fred Travalena
BUDDY HOLLY STORY, THE(1978)
Daniel J. Travanti
ST. IVES(1976)
Dan Travanty
WHO KILLED TEDDY BEAR?(1965); ORGANIZATION, THE(1971)
Noel Travarthen
TO HAVE AND TO HOLD(1963, Brit.)
George Traveil
CONVICTS AT LARGE(1938)
Richard Traveis
SPEED TO SPARE(1948)
George Travell
DRAMATIC SCHOOL(1938); FOREIGN AGENT(1942); REUNION IN FRANCE(1942); HIGH BARBAREE(1947); LADY IN THE LAKE(1947)
B. Traven [Berwick Traven Torsvan]
TREASURE OF THE SIERRA MADRE, THE(1948), d&w; REBELLION OF THE HANGED, THE(1954, Mex.), w
Bruno Traven
MACARIO(1961, Mex.), w
Alfred Travers
MEET THE NAVY(1946, Brit.), d; DUAL ALIBI(1947, Brit.), d, w; YOU CAN'T FOOL AN IRISHMAN(1950, Ireland), d, w; SOLUTION BY PHONE(1954, Brit.), d; DON GIOVANNI(1955, Brit.), d; ALIVE ON SATURDAY(1957, Brit.), d; GIRLS OF LATIN QUARTER(1960, Brit.), d, w; PRIMITIVES, THE(1962, Brit.), d, w
Alma Travers
FLYING DOWN TO RIO(1933)
Alred Travers
GIRLS OF LATIN QUARTER(1960, Brit.), w
Beatie Olna Travers
Silents
OLD CURIOSITY SHOP, THE(1921, Brit.)

Ben Travers
ONE EMBARRASSING NIGHT(1930, Brit.), w; CHANCE OF A NIGHT-TIME, THE(1931, Brit), w; MISCHIEF(1931, Brit.), w; PLUNDER(1931, Brit.), w; NIGHT LIKE THIS, A(1932, Brit.), w; THARK(1932, Brit.), w; CUCKOO IN THE NEST, THE(1933, Brit.), w; JUST MY LUCK(1933, Brit.), w; TURKEY TIME(1933, Brit.), w; UP TO THE NECK(1933, Brit.), w; CUP OF KINDNESS, A(1934, Brit.), w; DIRTY WORK(1934, Brit.), w; LADY IN DANGER(1934, Brit.), w; FIGHTING STOCK(1935, Brit.), w; FOREIGN AFFAIRES(1935, Brit.), w; STORMY WEATHER(1935, Brit.), w; DISHONOR BRIGHT(1936, Brit.), w; POT LUCK(1936, Brit.), w; FOR VALOR(1937, Brit.), w; SECOND BEST BED(1937, Brit.), w; OLD IRON(1938, Brit.), w; SO THIS IS LONDON(1940, Brit.), w; BANANA RIDGE(1941, Brit.), w; INHERITANCE, THE(1951, Brit.), w; FAST AND LOOSE(1954, Brit.), w
Beverly Travers
Silents
WIFE'S AWAKENING, A(1921); MISSING MILLIONS(1922)
Bill Linden Travers
TRIO(1950, Brit.)
Bill Travers
UNDERCOVER AGENT(1935, Brit.); BROWNING VERSION, THE(1951, Brit.); WOODEN HORSE, THE(1951); HOLIDAY WEEK(1952, Brit.); IT STARTED IN PARADISE(1952, Brit.); OUTPOST IN MALAYA(1952, Brit.); STORY OF ROBIN HOOD, THE(1952, Brit.); GENIE, THE(1953, Brit.); SHADOW MAN(1953, Brit.); WOMAN IN HIDING(1953, Brit.); ROMEO AND JULIET(1954, Brit.); FOOTSTEPS IN THE FOG(1955, Brit.); SQUARE RING, THE(1955, Brit.); BHOWANI JUNCTION(1956); WEE GEORDIE(1956, Brit.); BARRETTS OF WIMPOLE STREET, THE(1957); SEV-ENTH SIN, THE(1957); SMALLEST SHOW ON EARTH, THE(1957, Brit.); BRIDAL PATH, THE(1959, Brit.); PASSIONATE SUMMER(1959, Brit.); GORGO(1961, Brit.); GREEN HELMET, THE(1961, Brit.); INVASION QUARTET(1961, Brit.); TWO LIVING, ONE DEAD(1964, Brit./Swed.); BORN FREE(1966); DUEL AT DIABLO(1966); MID-SUMMER NIGHT'S DREAM, A(1969, Brit.); RING OF BRIGHT WATER(1969, Brit.), a, w; ELEPHANT CALLED SLOWLY, AN(1970, Brit.), a, p&w; BELSTONE FOX, THE(1976, 1976); CHRISTIAN THE LION(1976, Brit.), a, p,d&w
Celia Travers
SKY MURDER(1940); WHISTLING IN DIXIE(1942); HITLER'S MADMAN(1943); SWING SHIFT MAISIE(1943); MEET THE PEOPLE(1944); MRS. PARKINGTON(1944); EASY TO WED(1946); LITTLE MISTER JIM(1946); HIGH WALL, THE(1947); UNDER-COVER MAISIE(1947)
Constance Travers
WHITE LILAC(1935, Brit.)
Douglas Travers
MAN TO REMEMBER, A(1938), spec eff; STORY OF VERNON AND IRENE CASTLE, THE(1939), spec eff; LOUISIANA TERRITORY(1953), p
Esther Travers
NAKED WITCH, THE(1964)
George Travers
Silents
ALL ROADS LEAD TO CALVARY(1921, Brit.)
Henry Travers
ANOTHER LANGUAGE(1933); INVISIBLE MAN, THE(1933); MY WEAK-NESS(1933); REUNION IN VIENNA(1933); BORN TO BE BAD(1934); DEATH TAKES A HOLIDAY(1934); PARTY'S OVER, THE(1934); READY FOR LOVE(1934); AFTER OFFICE HOURS(1935); CAPTAIN HURRICANE(1935); ESCAPADE(1935); FOUR HOURS TO KILL(1935); MAYBE IT'S LOVE(1935); PURSUIT(1935); SEVEN KEYS TO BALDPATE(1935); TOO MANY PARENTS(1936); SISTERS, THE(1938); DARK VICTO-RY(1939); DODGE CITY(1939); ON BORROWED TIME(1939); RAINS CAME, THE(1939); REMEMBER?(1939); STANLEY AND LIVINGSTONE(1939); YOU CAN'T GET AWAY WITH MURDER(1939); ANNE OF WINDY POPLARS(1940); EDISON, THE MAN(1940); PRIMROSE PATH(1940); WYOMING(1940); BAD MAN, THE(1941); BALL OF FIRE(1941); GIRL, A GUY AND A GOB, A(1941); HIGH SIERRA(1941); I'LL WAIT FOR YOU(1941); MRS. MINIVER(1942); PIERRE OF THE PLAINS(1942); RANDOM HARVEST(1942); MADAME CURIE(1943); MOON IS DOWN, THE(1943); SHADOW OF A DOUBT(1943); DRAGON SEED(1944); NONE SHALL ESCAPE(1944); VERY THOUGHT OF YOU, THE(1944); BELLS OF ST. MARY'S, THE(1945); NAUGHTY NINETIES, THE(1945); THRILL OF A ROMANCE(1945); GALLANT JOURNEY(1946); IT'S A WONDERFUL LIFE(1946); YEARLING, THE(1946); BEYOND GLORY(1948); FLAME, THE(1948); GIRL FROM JONES BEACH, THE(1949)
Ian Travers
GALILEO(1975, Brit.)
Lans Travers
DEADLY FEMALES, THE(1976, Brit.)
Linden Travers
CHILDREN OF THE FOG(1935, Brit.); WEDNESDAY'S LUCK(1936, Brit.); AGAINST THE TIDE(1937, Brit.); BRIEF ECSTASY(1937, Brit.); LAST ADVENTURERS, THE(1937, Brit); ALMOST A HONEYMOON(1938, Brit.); BANK HOLIDAY(1938, Brit.); DANGEROUS SECRETS(1938, Brit.); LADY VANISHES, THE(1938, Brit.); INSPEC-TOR HORNLEIGH ON HOLIDAY(1939, Brit.); STARS LOOK DOWN, THE(1940, Brit.); GHOST TRAIN, THE(1941, Brit.); SEVENTH SURVIVOR, THE(1941, Brit.); SOUTH AMERICAN GEORGE(1941, Brit.); TERROR, THE(1941, Brit.); MISSING MILLION, THE(1942, Brit.); BEWARE OF PITY(1946, Brit.); MASTER OF BANKDAM, THE(1947, Brit.); JASSY(1948, Brit.); NO ORCHIDS FOR MISS BLANDISH(1948, Brit.); BAD LORD BYRON, THE(1949, Brit.); CHRISTOPHER COLUMBUS(1949, Brit.); DON'T EVER LEAVE ME(1949, Brit.); QUARTET(1949, Brit.)
Madalaine Travers
Silents
PENALTY, THE(1920)
Madlaine Travers
Misc. Silents
CAILLAUX CASE, THE(1918); ROSE OF THE WEST(1919); WHAT WOULD YOU DO?(1920)
P. L. Travers
MARY POPPINS(1964), w
Patricia Travers
THERE'S MAGIC IN MUSIC(1941)
Peter Travers
WEREWOLF IN A GIRL'S DORMITORY(1961, Ital./Aust.), art d
Phil Travers
HERCULES(1983), spec eff

Richard C. Travers
Misc. Silents
IN THE PALACE OF THE KING(1915); MAN TRAIL, THE(1915); WHITE SISTER, THE(1915); CAPTAIN JINKS OF THE HORSE MARINES(1916); LITTLE SHEPHERD OF BARGIAN ROW, THE(1916); PHANTOM BUCCANEER, THE(1916); TRUFFLERS, THE(1917); WHITE MOLL, THE(1920); MOUNTAIN WOMAN, THE(1921); DAWN OF REVENGE(1922); BROAD ROAD, THE(1923); STILL ALARM, THE(1926)

Richard Travers
BLACK WATCH, THE(1929); UNHOLY NIGHT, THE(1929); WOMAN RACKET, THE(1930)
Silents
SINGLE TRACK, THE(1921); NOTORIETY(1922); ACQUITTAL, THE(1923); RENDEZVOUS, THE(1923); HOUSE OF YOUTH, THE(1924)
Misc. Silents
HOUSE WITHOUT CHILDREN, THE(1919); RIDER OF THE KING LOG, THE(1921); LOVE NEST, THE(1922); WHITE HELL(1922); HEAD WINDS(1925)

Roy Travers
BLOCKADE(1928, Brit.); KISS ME, SERGEANT(1930, Brit.); ROMANY LOVE(1931, Brit.); WINDJAMMER, THE(1931, Brit.)
Silents
EAST LYNNE(1913, Brit.); IN THE HANDS OF THE LONDON CROOKS(1913, Brit.); ROGUES OF LONDON, THE(1915, Brit.); AULD LANG SYNE(1917, Brit.); AVE MARIA(1918, Brit.); ALL ROADS LEAD TO CALVARY(1921, Brit.); NO. 5 JOHN STREET(1921, Brit.); INDIAN LOVE LYRICS, THE(1923, Brit.); MOTORING(1927, Brit.)
Misc. Silents
STRIFE ETERNAL, THE(1915, Brit.); DIANA AND DESTINY(1916, Brit.); MAN WHO BOUGHT LONDON, THE(1916, Brit.); SPLENDID COWARD, THE(1918, Brit.); LACKEY AND THE LADY, THE(1919, Brit.); CHERRY RIPE(1921, Brit.); DOUBLE EVENT, THE(1921, Brit.); HOUSE OF PERIL, THE(1922, Brit.); ROMANCE OF OLD BAGDAD, A(1922, Brit.); FOR VALOUR(1928, Brit.); DOWN CHANNEL(1929, Brit.)

Sally Travers
NEXT TO NO TIME(1960, Brit.); ISADORA(1968, Brit.)

Susan Travers
DUKE WORE JEANS, THE(1958, Brit.); PEEPING TOM(1960, Brit.); SONS AND LOVERS(1960, Brit.); SNAKE WOMAN, THE(1961, Brit.); HOT MONEY GIRL(1962, Brit./Ger.); OUT OF THE FOG(1962, Brit.); ABOMINABLE DR. PHIBES, THE(1971, Brit.); STATUE, THE(1971, Brit.); DARWIN ADVENTURE, THE(1972, Brit.); HAPPINESS CAGE, THE(1972)

Sy Travers
MIKEY AND NICKY(1976)

Tom Travers
CLINIC, THE(1983, Aus.)

Tony Travers
SEA CHASE, THE(1955)

Vic Travers
IT HAPPENED ON 5TH AVENUE(1947)

Vicky Travers
ENTERTAINER, THE(1960, Brit.)

Victor Travers
YOU CAN'T TAKE IT WITH YOU(1938); ONLY ANGELS HAVE WINGS(1939); MY SON IS GUILTY(1940); FACE BEHIND THE MASK, THE(1941); TALK OF THE TOWN(1942); COVER GIRL(1944); JAM SESSION(1944); STORM OVER LISBON(1944); HIT THE HAY(1945); TONIGHT AND EVERY NIGHT(1945); HER HUSBAND'S AFFAIRS(1947); IT HAD TO BE YOU(1947); JOAN OF ARC(1948)

Claire Travers-Deacon
FRENCH LIEUTENANT'S WOMAN, THE(1981)

Fabio Traversari
HERCULES(1983), spec eff

Beverly Traverse
Misc. Silents
ILLUSTRIOUS PRINCE, THE(1919)

Claude Traverse
LOVIN' MOLLY(1974)

Lyn Traverse
PLAINSONG(1982)

Madaline Traverse
Silents
FRUITS OF DESIRE, THE(1916)

Madeline Traverse
Silents
POOR LITTLE RICH GIRL, A(1917)
Misc. Silents
CLOSING NET, THE(1915)

Madlaine Traverse
Silents
GAMBLING IN SOULS(1919); SPLENDID SIN, THE(1919)
Misc. Silents
DANGER ZONE, THE(1918); LOST MONEY(1919); LOVE THAT DARES, THE(1919); SNARES OF PARIS(1919); WHEN FATE DECIDES(1919); HELL SHIP, THE(1920); IRON HEART, THE(1920); SPIRIT OF GOOD, THE(1920); TATTLERS, THE(1920)

Fabio Traversi
BURNING YEARS, THE(1979, Ital.)

Marisa Traversi
SUNFLOWER(1970, Fr./Ital.)

Rafael Garcia Traversi
SANTO CONTRA LA INVASION DE LOS MARCIANOS(1966, Mex.), w; SANTO CONTRA BLUE DEMON EN LA ATLANTIDA(1968, Mex.), w; SANTO Y BLUE DEMON CONTRA LOS MONSTRUOS(1968, Mex.), w

Alfredo Traverso
PUT UP OR SHUT UP(1968, Arg.), ph

Antonio Traverso
BICYCLE THIEF, THE(1949, Ital.), art d

Rafael Garcia Travesi
LITTLE RED RIDING HOOD(1963, Mex.), w; SPIRITISM(1965, Mex.), w

Travilla
NIGHT AND DAY(1946), cos; ALWAYS TOGETHER(1947), cos; CRY WOLF(1947), cos; ESCAPE ME NEVER(1947), cos; NORA PRENTISS(1947), cos; THAT HAGEN GIRL(1947), cos; FLAMINGO ROAD(1949), cos; AMERICAN GUERRILLA IN THE PHILIPPINES, AN(1950), cos; PANIC IN THE STREETS(1950), cos; RAWHIDE(1951),

cos; BLOODHOUNDS OF BROADWAY(1952), cos; DREAMBOAT(1952), cos; MONKEY BUSINESS(1952), cos; GENTLEMEN PREFER BLONDES(1953), cos; KING OF THE KHYBER RIFLES(1953), cos; PICKUP ON SOUTH STREET(1953), cos; BROKEN LANCE(1954), cos; GARDEN OF EVIL(1954), cos; HELL AND HIGH WATER(1954), cos; RIVER OF NO RETURN(1954), cos; THREE YOUNG TEXANS(1954), cos; GENTLEMEN MARRY BRUNETTES(1955), cos; HOW TO BE VERY, VERY, POPULAR(1955), cos; LEFT HAND OF GOD, THE(1955), cos; RAINS OF RANCHIPUR, THE(1955), cos; TALL MEN, THE(1955), cos; PROUD ONES, THE(1956), cos; REVOLT OF MAMIE STOVER, THE(1956), cos; 23 PACES TO BAKER STREET(1956), cos; FROM THE TERRACE(1960), cos; MARY, MARY(1963), cos; STRIPPER, THE(1963), cos; TAKE HER, SHE'S MINE(1963), cos; SIGNPOST TO MURDER(1964), cos; VALLEY OF THE DOLLS(1967), cos; SECRET LIFE OF AN AMERICAN WIFE, THE(1968), cos; THE BOSTON STRANGLER, THE(1968), cos; DADDY'S GONE A-HUNTING(1969), cos

Billy Travilla
FUZZY PINK NIGHTGOWN, THE(1957), cos

William Travilla
TWO YANKS IN TRINIDAD(1942), cos; TWO SENORITAS FROM CHICAGO(1943), cos; SILVER RIVER(1948), cos; DANCING IN THE DARK(1949), cos; NO WAY OUT(1950), cos; WOMAN ON THE RUN(1950), cos; TAKE CARE OF MY LITTLE GIRL(1951), cos; PRINCESS OF THE NILE(1954), cos; SEVEN YEAR ITCH, THE(1955), cos; WHITE FEATHER(1955), cos

B. Travis
INVASION OF THE BEE GIRLS(1973), ed

Bernie Travis
DIRTYMOUTH(1970)

Charles Travis
Silents
SPRINGTIME(1915)

Charles W. Travis
Silents
ACCORDING TO LAW(1916); AS A WOMAN SOWS(1916); IDOL OF THE STAGE, THE(1916)
Misc. Silents
QUALITY OF FAITH, THE(1916)

Deborah Travis
RIOT ON SUNSET STRIP(1967)

Dianne Turley Travis
COME BACK TO THE 5 & DIME, JIMMY DEAN, JIMMY DEAN(1982)

Douglas Travis
TWO(1975)

George Travis
INDEPENDENCE DAY(1976)

Greg Travis
HUMANOIDS FROM THE DEEP(1980)

Henry Travis
BRAIN FROM THE PLANET AROUS, THE(1958)

James Travis
SWINGING BARMAIDS, THE(1976)

June Travis
BROADWAY GONDOLIER(1935); CEILNG ZERO(1935); DR. SOCRATES(1935); STRANDED(1935); BENGAL TIGER(1936); BIG GAME, THE(1936); CASE OF THE BLACK CAT, THE(1936); EARTHWORM TRACTORS(1936); JAILBREAK(1936); TIMES SQUARE PLAYBOY(1936); CIRCUS GIRL(1937); EXILED TO SHANGHAI(1937); JOIN THE MARINES(1937); KID COMES BACK, THE(1937); LOVE IS ON THE AIR(1937); MEN IN EXILE(1937); OVER THE GOAL(1937); GLADIATOR, THE(1938); GO CHASE YOURSELF(1938); LITTLE ORPHAN ANNIE(1938); MARINES ARE HERE, THE(1938); MR. DOODLE KICKS OFF(1938); NIGHT HAWK, THE(1938); OVER THE WALL(1938); FEDERAL MAN-HUNT(1939); STAR, THE(1953); MONSTER A GO-GO(1965)

Len Travis
PRIVATE PARTS(1972)

Mark Travis
SAMMY STOPS THE WORLD zero(1978), p

Merle Travis
OLD TEXAS TRAIL, THE(1944); FROM HERE TO ETERNITY(1953); FIVE MINUTES TO LIVE(1961); THAT TENNESSEE BEAT(1966); HONKYTONK MAN(1982)

Michael Travis
NORMAN...IS THAT YOU?(1976), cos

Mike Travis
MOONCHILD(1972); HAWMPS!(1976)

Neal Travis
JAWS II(1978), ed

Neil Travis
TRAVELING EXECUTIONER, THE(1970), ed; COWBOYS, THE(1972), ed; HOT STUFF(1979), ed; DIE LAUGHING(1980), ed; IDOLMAKER, THE(1980), ed; NOBODY'S PERFEKT(1981), ed; CUJO(1983), ed; SECOND THOUGHTS(1983), ed

R. Travis
INVASION OF THE BEE GIRLS(1973), ed

Richard [Dick] Travis
BRIDE CAME C.O.D., THE(1941); DIVE BOMBER(1941); INTERNATIONAL SQUADRON(1941); NAVY BLUES(1941); BIG SHOT, THE(1942); BUSSES ROAR(1942); ESCAPE FROM CRIME(1942); MAN WHO CAME TO DINNER, THE(1942); POSTMAN DIDN'T RING, THE(1942); MISSION TO MOSCOW(1943); SPY TRAIN(1943); TRUCK BUSTERS(1943); LAST RIDE, THE(1944); BACKLASH(1947); BIG TOWN AFTER DARK(1947); JEWELS OF BRANDENBURG(1947); OUT OF THE STORM(1948); WATERFRONT AT MIDNIGHT(1948); ALASKA PATROL(1949); SKY LINER(1949); LONELY HEARTS BANDITS(1950); MOTOR PATROL(1950); ONE TOO MANY(1950); OPERATION HAYLIFT(1950); DANGER ZONE(1951); FINGERPRINTS DON'T LIE(1951); MASK OF THE DRAGON(1951); PASSAGE WEST(1951); PIER 23(1951); ROARING CITY(1951); CITY OF SHADOWS(1955); GIRL IN THE RED VELVET SWING, THE(1955); BLONDE BAIT(1956, U.S./Brit.); MESA OF LOST WOMEN, THE(1956); MISSILE TO THE MOON(1959)

Ron Travis
OUTLAND(1981)
1984
SCANDALOUS(1984); SUPERGIRL(1984)

Tony Travis
JAMBOREE(1957); BEATNIKS, THE(1960); LOVING COUPLES(1980)

William Travis
LINCOLN CONSPIRACY, THE(1977)

Boris Travkin
ITALIANO BRAVA GENTE(1965, Ital./USSR), spec eff; PORTRAIT OF LENIN(1967, Pol./USSR), spec eff

Ann Travolta
SATURDAY NIGHT FEVER(1977); URBAN COWBOY(1980); TWO OF A KIND(1983)

Ellen Travolta
GREASE(1978); HUMAN EXPERIMENTS(1980)

Helen Travolta
SATURDAY NIGHT FEVER(1977)

Joey Travolta
SUNNYSIDE(1979)
1984
PRODIGAL, THE(1984)

John Travolta
DEVIL'S RAIN, THE(1975, U.S./Mex.); CARRIE(1976); SATURDAY NIGHT FEVER(1977); GREASE(1978); MOMENT BY MOMENT(1978); URBAN COWBOY(1980); BLOW OUT(1981); STAYING ALIVE(1983); TWO OF A KIND(1983)

Ernest Traxler
Misc. Silents
CALEB PIPER'S GIRL(1919), d; GO GET 'EM GARRINGER(1919), d

Stephen Traxler
SLITHIS(1978), p, d&w

Michael Traxon
SONG OF THE LOON(1970)

John Trayhorn
HOVERBUG(1970, Brit.)

Darvy Traylor
GONG SHOW MOVIE, THE(1980)

William Traylor
LAST FRONTIER, THE(1955); ONE PLUS ONE(1961, Can.); DIARY OF A BACHELOR(1964); WINDFLOWERS(1968); CISCO PIKE(1971); WHO FEARS THE DEVIL(1972); SMILE(1975); LONG RIDERS, THE(1980); POSTMAN ALWAYS RINGS TWICE, THE(1981); MAN WITH TWO BRAINS, THE(1983)
1984
ADVENTURES OF BUCKAROO BANZAI: ACROSS THE 8TH DIMENSION, THE(1984); FLETCH(1984)

John Traynor
MEN OF TOMORROW(1935, Brit.)

John F. Traynor
VIPER, THE(1938, Brit.)

Peter Traynor
DEATH GAME(1977), p, d
Misc. Talkies
GOD BLESS DR. SHAGETZ(1977), d

Peter S. Traynor
STEEL ARENA(1973), p; ULTIMATE THRILL, THE(1974), p

Robert Traynor
BODY HEAT(1981); PSYCHO II(1983)
1984
CLOAK AND DAGGER(1984)

Adrienne Trazillo
HOODLUM SAINT, THE(1946)

Edmund Trczinski
STALAG 17(1953)

Arthur Treacher
BATTLE OF PARIS, THE(1929); CAPTAIN HATES THE SEA, THE(1934); DESIRABLE(1934); FASHIONS OF 1934(1934); GAMBLING LADY(1934); HERE COMES THE GROOM(1934); HOLLYWOOD PARTY(1934); KEY, THE(1934); MADAME DU BARRY(1934); RIP TIDE(1934); VIVA VILLA!(1934); BORDERTOWN(1935); BRIGHT LIGHTS(1935); CURLY TOP(1935); DARING YOUNG MAN, THE(1935); DAVID COPPERFIELD(1935); FORSAKING ALL OTHERS(1935); GOING HIGHBROW(1935); I LIVE MY LIFE(1935); LET'S LIVE TONIGHT(1935); MAGNIFICENT OBSESSION(1935); MIDSUMMER'S NIGHT DREAM, A(1935); NO MORE LADIES(1935); ORCHIDS TO YOU(1935); PERSONAL MAID'S SECRET(1935); REMEMBER LAST NIGHT(1935); SPLENDOR(1935); WOMAN IN RED, THE(1935); ANYTHING GOES(1936); CASE AGAINST MRS. AMES, THE(1936); HEARTS DIVIDED(1936); HITCH HIKE LADY(1936); MISTER CINDERELLA(1936); SATAN MET A LADY(1936); STOWAWAY(1936); THANK YOU, JEEVES(1936); UNDER YOUR SPELL(1936); HEIDI(1937); SHE HAD TO EAT(1937); STEP LIVELY, JEEVES(1937); THIN ICE(1937); YOU CAN'T HAVE EVERYTHING(1937); ALWAYS IN TROUBLE(1938); MAD ABOUT MUSIC(1938); MY LUCKY STAR(1938); UP THE RIVER(1938); BARRICADE(1939); BRIDAL SUITE(1939); LITTLE PRINCESS, THE(1939); BROTHER RAT AND A BABY(1940); IRENE(1940); STAR SPANGLED RHYTHM(1942); AMAZING MRS. HOLLIDAY(1943); FOREVER AND A DAY(1943); CHIP OFF THE OLD BLOCK(1944); IN SOCIETY(1944); NATIONAL VELVET(1944); DELIGHTFULLY DANGEROUS(1945); SWING OUT, SISTER(1945); THAT'S THE SPIRIT(1945); SLAVE GIRL(1947); COUNTESS OF MONTE CRISTO, THE(1948); THAT MIDNIGHT KISS(1949); LOVE THAT BRUTE(1950); MARY POPPINS(1964); FUN ON A WEEK-END(1979)

Treacherous Three
1984
BEAT STREET(1984)

Emerson Treacy
ONCE A GENTLEMAN(1930); GIRLS DEMAND EXCITEMENT(1931); MOUTHPIECE, THE(1932); OKAY AMERICA(1932); NEIGHBORS' WIVES(1933); TWO ALONE(1934); DR. SOCRATES(1935); MAN WHO RECLAIMED HIS HEAD, THE(1935); CALIFORNIA STRAIGHT AHEAD(1937); GIVE ME A SAILOR(1938); GONE WITH THE WIND(1939); INVITATION TO HAPPINESS(1939); LONG SHOT, THE(1939); ADAM'S RIB(1949); WYOMING MAIL(1950); FORT WORTH(1951); PROWLER, THE(1951); MUTINY(1952); STAR IS BORN, A(1954); RUN FOR COVER(1955); WRONG MAN, THE(1956); PRIVATE'S AFFAIR, A(1959); DARK AT THE TOP OF THE STAIRS, THE(1960); RETURN TO PEYTON PLACE(1961)

Jack Treacy
CAPTURE THAT CAPSULE(1961)

Bette Treadville
DAY OF THE NIGHTMARE(1965)

Betty Treadville
ONE DARK NIGHT(1939)

Charlotte Treadway
DEAD END(1937); SHEIK STEPS OUT, THE(1937); FEMALE FUGITIVE(1938); GOING PLACES(1939); WOMEN, THE(1939); DOCTOR TAKES A WIFE(1940); LIFE WITH HENRY(1941); MISBEHAVING HUSBANDS(1941); ONE FOOT IN HEAVEN(1941); SHADOW OF SUSPICION(1944); SONG OF THE OPEN ROAD(1944); BOY, A GIRL, AND A DOG, A(1946)

Wayne Treadway
DOUBLE LIFE, A(1947); SECRET BEYOND THE DOOR, THE(1948); SINISTER JOURNEY(1948); CALLAWAY WENT THATAWAY(1951)

Alan Treadwell
HOUSE ON SORORITY ROW, THE(1983)

Gary Treadwell
GAS-S-S-S!(1970)

Laura Treadwell
FASHIONS OF 1934(1934); GAMBLING LADY(1934); WOMAN UNAFRAID(1934); ACCENT ON YOUTH(1935); GET THAT MAN(1935); GOIN' TO TOWN(1935); SHE GETS HER MAN(1935); FATAL LADY(1936); THEODORA GOES WILD(1936); EASY LIVING(1937); NOBODY'S BABY(1937); HAWAIIAN BUCKAROO(1938); MANPROOF(1938); YOU CAN'T TAKE IT WITH YOU(1938); DANCING CO-ED(1939); MR. SMITH GOES TO WASHINGTON(1939); NIGHT OF NIGHTS, THE(1939); FIVE LITTLE PEPPERS AT HOME(1940); QUEEN OF THE MOB(1940); JOAN OF OZARK(1942); BRINGING UP FATHER(1946); NIGHT AND DAY(1946); UNDERCURRENT(1946); LADY IN THE LAKE(1947); LIFE WITH FATHER(1947); NIGHTMARE ALLEY(1947); SEA OF GRASS, THE(1947); B. F.'S DAUGHTER(1948); I WOULDN'T BE IN YOUR SHOES(1948); KING OF THE BANDITS(1948); WINTER MEETING(1948); BARKLEYS OF BROADWAY, THE(1949); TASK FORCE(1949); STRANGERS ON A TRAIN(1951)

Liz Treadwell
ADIOS AMIGO(1975)

Mickey Treanor
1984
NATURAL, THE(1984)

Terri Treas
HEADIN' FOR BROADWAY(1980)

Many Treaties
DEERSLAYER(1943)

Major C. Court Treatt
Misc. Silents
STAMPEDE(1930, Sudan), d

John Trebach
KILLERS, THE(1946); ANGEL ON THE AMAZON(1948); FLAME, THE(1948); WHIRLPOOL(1949); WHERE THE SIDEWALK ENDS(1950); FOLLOW THE SUN(1951)

Johnny Trebach
DUCHESS OF IDAHO, THE(1950)

Edouard Trebaol
Silents
PENALTY, THE(1920); OLIVER TWIST(1922)

Francis Trebaol
Misc. Silents
BREAKING INTO SOCIETY(1923)

Gyula Trebitsch
DEVIL'S GENERAL, THE(1957, Ger.), p; GIRL OF THE MOORS, THE(1961, Ger.), p

Fred Treble
TRAIN TO TOMBSTONE(1950), art d

Robert Trebor
GORP(1980); FIRST TIME, THE(1983)

Marie Treboul
Silents
TILLIE(1922)

Fabrizio Trifone Trecca
TO KILL OR TO DIE(1973, Ital.), w

Pirmin Trecu
WHY BOTHER TO KNOCK(1964, Brit.)

Wayne Tredway
UP IN CENTRAL PARK(1948); LADY WANTS MINK, THE(1953); DINOSAURUS(1960)

Chief Big Tree
DRUMS ALONG THE MOHAWK(1939)

Cindy Tree
Misc. Talkies
PELVIS(1977)

David Tree
KNIGHT WITHOUT ARMOR(1937, Brit.); DRUMS(1938, Brit.); GAIETY GIRLS, THE(1938, Brit.); OLD IRON(1938, Brit.); PYGMALION(1938, Brit.); RETURN OF THE SCARLET PIMPERNEL(1938, Brit.); CLOUDS OVER EUROPE(1939, Brit.); FRENCH WITHOUT TEARS(1939, Brit.); GOODBYE MR. CHIPS(1939, Brit.); JUST WILLIAM(1939, Brit.); OVER THE MOON(1940, Brit.); RETURN TO YESTERDAY(1940, Brit.); MAJOR BARBARA(1941, Brit.); DON'T LOOK NOW(1973, Brit./Ital.)

Dolly Tree
Silents
LOVE IN A WOOD(1915, Brit.)
Misc. Silents
TWO LANCASHIRE LASSES IN LONDON(1916, Brit.)

Dolly [Dorothy] Tree
JUST IMAGINE(1930), cos; WICKED(1931), cos; STEPPING SISTERS(1932), cos; GAY BRIDE, THE(1934), cos; MANHATTAN MELODRAMA(1934), cos; STAMBOUL QUEST(1934), cos; STRAIGHT IS THE WAY(1934), cos; THIN MAN, THE(1934), cos; VIVA VILLA!(1934), cos; DAVID COPPERFIELD(1935), cos; NIGHT AT THE OPERA, A(1935), cos; NIGHT IS YOUNG, THE(1935), cos; TALE OF TWO CITIES, A(1935), cos; THREE LIVE GHOSTS(1935), cos; VANESSA, HER LOVE STORY(1935), cos; WEST POINT OF THE AIR(1935), cos; FURY(1936), cos; HIS BROTHER'S WIFE(1936), cos; LIBELED LADY(1936), cos; RIFF-RAFF(1936), cos; ROBIN HOOD OF EL DORADO(1936), cos; SINNER TAKE ALL(1936), cos; SUZY(1936), cos; THREE GODFATHERS(1936), cos; THREE WISE GUYS, THE(1936), cos; VOICE OF BUGLE ANN(1936), cos; WE WENT TO COLLEGE(1936), cos; WHIPSAW(1936), cos; GOOD

EARTH, THE(1937), cos; NAVY BLUE AND GOLD(1937), cos; PERSONAL PROPERTY(1937), cos; ROSALIE(1937), cos; SARATOGA(1937), cos; THOROUGHBREDS DON'T CRY(1937), cos; RICH MAN, POOR GIRL(1938), cos; TEST PILOT(1938), cos; TOO HOT TO HANDLE(1938), cos; WOMAN AGAINST WOMAN(1938), cos; BABES IN ARMS(1939), cos; DANCING CO-ED(1939), cos; LET FREEDOM RING(1939), cos; MAISIE(1939), cos; MIRACLES FOR SALE(1939), cos; SOCIETY LAWYER(1939), cos; STAND UP AND FIGHT(1939), cos; THESE GLAMOUR GIRLS(1939), cos; THUNDER AFLOAT(1939), cos; EDISON, THE MAN(1940), cos; FLIGHT COMMAND(1940), cos; LITTLE NELLIE KELLY(1940), cos; MAN FROM DAKOTA, THE(1940), cos; SPORTING BLOOD(1940), cos; STRIKE UP THE BAND(1940), cos; TWENTY MULE TEAM(1940), cos; TWO GIRLS ON BROADWAY(1940), cos; WE WHO ARE YOUNG(1940), cos; YOUNG TOM EDISON(1940), cos; TRIAL OF MARY DUGAN, THE(1941), cos; WILD MAN OF BORNEO, THE(1941), cos; PIED PIPER, THE(1942), cos; TALES OF MANHATTAN(1942), cos; THUNDER BIRDS(1942), cos; TOO HOT TO HANDLE(1961, Brit.), cos; NIGHT MUST FALL(1964, Brit.), cos

Dorothy Tree
HUSBAND'S HOLIDAY(1931); LIFE BEGINS(1932); EAST OF FIFTH AVE.(1933); CASE OF THE HOWLING DOG, THE(1934); DRAGON MURDER CASE, THE(1934); FIREBIRD, THE(1934); FRIENDS OF MR. SWEENEY(1934); HERE COMES THE NAVY(1934); MADAME DU BARRY(1934); MAN WITH TWO FACES, THE(1934); SIDE STREETS(1934); FOUR HOURS TO KILL(1935); NIGHT AT THE RITZ, A(1935); WHILE THE PATIENT SLEPT(1935); WOMAN IN RED, THE(1935); BRIDGE OF SIGHS(1936); NAVY BORN(1936); THREE GODFATHERS(1936); GREAT GARRICK, THE(1937); HAVING WONDERFUL TIME(1938); TRADE WINDS(1938); CAFE SOCIETY(1939); CHARLIE CHAN IN THE CITY OF DARKNESS(1939); CONFESSIONS OF A NAZI SPY(1939); MYSTERIOUS MISS X, THE(1939); MYSTERY OF MR. WONG, THE(1939); TELEVISION SPY(1939); ZAZA(1939); ABE LINCOLN IN ILLINOIS(1940); KNUTE ROCKNE--ALL AMERICAN(1940); LITTLE ORVIE(1940); SKY MURDER(1940); HIGHWAY WEST(1941); MAN WHO LOST HIMSELF, THE(1941); SINGAPORE WOMAN(1941); HITLER--DEAD OR ALIVE(1942); NAZI AGENT(1942); CRIME DOCTOR(1943); EDGE OF DARKNESS(1943); CASANOVA BROWN(1944); ASPHALT JUNGLE, THE(1950); LIFE OF HER OWN, A(1950); MEN, THE(1950); NO SAD SONGS FOR ME(1950); FAMILY SECRET, THE(1951)

Earl Tree
WHAT PRICE CRIME?(1935)

Sir Herbert Beerbohm Tree
Silents
OLD FOLKS AT HOME, THE(1916)

Sir Herbert Beerbom Tree
Misc. Silents
MACBETH(1916)

Sir Herbert Tree
Misc. Silents
TRILBY(1914, Brit.)

Iris Tree
MOBY DICK(1956, Brit.); LA DOLCE VITA(1961, Ital./Fr.)

Joan Tree
MAD ABOUT MUSIC(1938)

Joanne Tree
GIRLS' SCHOOL(1938); GIRLS UNDER TWENTY-ONE(1940); PROJECT X(1949); SUMMER STOCK(1950)

Lady Tree
SUCH IS THE LAW(1930, Brit.); WEDDING REHEARSAL(1932, Brit.); EARLY TO BED(1933, Brit./Ger.); HER IMAGINARY LOVER(1933, Brit.); PRIVATE LIFE OF HENRY VIII, THE(1933); GIRL FROM MAXIM'S, THE(1936, Brit.); MAN WHO COULD WORK MIRACLES, THE(1937, Brit.)
Silents
STILL WATERS RUN DEEP(1916, Brit.)
Misc. Silents
LITTLE DORRIT(1920, Brit.)

Madge Tree
Silents
HARD TIMES(1915, Brit.); GARDEN OF RESURRECTION, THE(1919, Brit.); TATTERLY(1919, Brit.); HOUSE ON THE MARSH, THE(1920, Brit.); WON BY A HEAD(1920, Brit.); FIRES OF INNOCENCE(1922, Brit.); ST. ELMO(1923, Brit.); DAUGHTER OF LOVE, A(1925, Brit.)
Misc. Silents
SILVER BRIDGE, THE(1920, Brit.)

Marietta Tree
MISFITS, THE(1961)

Vera Tree
WYOMING(1940), cos

Viola Tree
DANCERS, THE(1930), w; FOR THE LOVE OF MIKE(1933, Brit.); HEART'S DESIRE(1937, Brit.); PYGMALION(1938, Brit.)

Mary Lou Treen
BRIDES ARE LIKE THAT(1936); THEY GAVE HIM A GUN(1937); ROOM FOR ONE MORE(1952)

Mary Louise Treen
HAPPINESS AHEAD(1934)

Mary Treen
BABBITT(1934); ST. LOUIS KID, THE(1934); BROADWAY GONDOLIER(1935); CASE OF THE LUCKY LEGS, THE(1935); DON'T BET ON BLONDES(1935); FRONT PAGE WOMAN(1935); G-MEN(1935); GIRL FROM TENTH AVENUE, THE(1935); I FOUND STELLA PARISH(1935); I LIVE FOR LOVE(1935); NIGHT AT THE RITZ, A(1935); PAGE MISS GLORY(1935); RED HOT TIRES(1935); SHIPMATES FOREVER(1935); SWEET ADELINE(1935); SWEET MUSIC(1935); TRAVELING SALESLADY, THE(1935); COLLEEN(1936); DANGEROUS(1936); DOWN THE STRETCH(1936); FRESHMAN LOVE(1936); GOLDEN ARROW(1936); JAILBREAK(1936); LOVE BEGINS AT TWENTY(1936); MURDER BY AN ARISTOCRAT(1936); MURDER OF DR. HARRIGAN, THE(1936); SNOWED UNDER(1936); STAGE STRUCK(1936); CAPTAIN'S KID, THE(1937); DANCE, CHARLIE, DANCE(1937); EVER SINCE EVE(1937); FUGITIVE IN THE SKY(1937); GO-GETTER, THE(1937); GOD'S COUNTRY AND THE WOMAN(1937); MAID OF SALEM(1937); SECOND HONEYMOON(1937); SWING IT SAILOR(1937); TALENT SCOUT(1937); KENTUCKY MOONSHINE(1938); SALLY, IRENE AND MARY(1938); STRANGE FACES(1938); YOUNG FUGITIVES(1938); FIRST LOVE(1939); FOR LOVE OR MONEY(1939); WHEN TOMORROW COMES(1939); BLACK DIAMONDS(1940); DANGER ON WHEELS(1940); DOUBLE ALIBI(1940); GIRL IN 313(1940); KITTY FOYLE(1940); QUEEN OF THE MOB(1940); TOO MANY HUSBANDS(1940); FATHER

TAKES A WIFE(1941); FLAME OF NEW ORLEANS, THE(1941); MIDNIGHT ANGEL(1941); TALL, DARK AND HANDSOME(1941); YOU BELONG TO ME(1941); BETWEEN US GIRLS(1942); GREAT MAN'S LADY, THE(1942); LADY BODYGUARD(1942); NIGHT BEFORE THE DIVORCE, THE(1942); PACIFIC BLACKOUT(1942); POWERS GIRL, THE(1942); RINGS ON HER FINGERS(1942); ROXIE HART(1942); SHIP AHOY(1942); THEY ALL KISSED THE BRIDE(1942); TRUE TO THE ARMY(1942); FLIGHT FOR FREEDOM(1943); HANDS ACROSS THE BORDER(1943); HIT PARADE OF 1943(1943); MORE THE MERRIER, THE(1943); MYSTERY BROADCAST(1943); SO PROUDLY WE HAIL(1943); THANK YOUR LUCKY STARS(1943); THEY GOT ME COVERED(1943); CASANOVA BROWN(1944); I LOVE A SOLDIER(1944); NAVY WAY, THE(1944); SWING IN THE SADDLE(1944); BLONDE FROM BROOKLYN(1945); DON JUAN QUILLIGAN(1945); HIGH POWERED(1945); TAHITI NIGHTS(1945); FROM THIS DAY FORWARD(1946); GUY COULD CHANGE, A(1946); IT'S A WONDERFUL LIFE(1946); ONE EXCITING WEEK(1946); STRANGE IMPERSONATION(1946); SWING PARADE OF 1946(1946); LIKELY STORY, A(1947); LET'S LIVE A LITTLE(1948); SNAKE PIT, THE(1948); TEXAS, BROOKLYN AND HEAVEN(1948); YOUNG DANIEL BOONE(1950); SAILOR BEWARE(1951); DREAMBOAT(1952); CLIPPED WINGS(1953); GREAT JESSE JAMES RAID, THE(1953); LET'S DO IT AGAIN(1953); BUNDLE OF JOY(1956); WHEN GANGLAND STRIKES(1956); GUN DUEL IN DURANGO(1957); JOKER IS WILD, THE(1957); SAD SACK, THE(1957); I MARRIED A MONSTER FROM OUTER SPACE(1958); CAREER(1959); ADA(1961); ALL IN A NIGHT'S WORK(1961); ERRAND BOY, THE(1961); WHO'S MINDING THE STORE?(1963); BIRDS AND THE BEES, THE(1965); PARADISE, HAWAIIAN STYLE(1966)

Mark Trefethen
SEPARATE PEACE, A(1972)

Alice Treff
CANARIS(1955, Ger.); TIME TO LOVE AND A TIME TO DIE, A(1958); GIRL OF THE MOORS, THE(1961, Ger.); YOUNG GO WILD, THE(1962, Ger.); WITNESS OUT OF HELL(1967, Ger./Yugo.)

Bobbe Trefts
HERO FOR A DAY(1939); LITTLE ACCIDENT(1939); WHEN TOMORROW COMES(1939)

Jeannette Tregarthan
HOLIDAY CAMP(1947, Brit.)

Jeanette Tregarthen
MEET SIMON CHERRY(1949, Brit.)

Richard Tregaskis
GUADALCANAL DIARY(1943), w; FORCE OF ARMS(1951), w; WILD BLUE YONDER, THE(1952), w; FAIR WIND TO JAVA(1953), w; MISSION OVER KOREA(1953), w

Joe Treggonino
SILVER BEARS(1978)

T. Tregl
INSPECTOR GENERAL, THE(1937, Czech.)

Ann Trego
GREED OF WILLIAM HART, THE(1948, Brit.)

William Tregoe
GONG SHOW MOVIE, THE(1980)

Joseph Tregonino
INADMISSIBLE EVIDENCE(1968, Brit.)

I. Tregubova
KIEV COMEDY, A(1963, USSR), spec eff; MOTHER AND DAUGHTER(1965, USSR), spec eff

Roger Treherne
MAN ESCAPED, A(1957, Fr.)

Count Treiberg
GERMANY, YEAR ZERO(1949, Ger.)

Wilhelm M. Treichlinger
HEIDI(1954, Switz.), w

Seymour Treitman
So SAD ABOUT GLORIA(1973)

Georg Friedrich Treitschke
FIDELIO(1970, Ger.), w

Guy Trejan
CHECKERBOARD(1969, Fr.); BEAST, THE(1975, Fr.); PIAF--THE EARLY YEARS(1982, U.S./Fr.)

Guy Trejean
LA PARISIENNE(1958, Fr./Ital.); SKY ABOVE HEAVEN(1964, Fr./Ital.); SERPENT, THE(1973, Fr./Ital./Ger.)

Paul Trejo
HOUSE ON SORORITY ROW, THE(1983), ed

Jerzy Trela
MAN OF IRON(1981, Pol.)

Max Trell
LAWYER MAN(1933), w; SIXTEEN FATHOMS DEEP(1948), w; NEW MEXICO(1951), w; JUST THIS ONCE(1952), w; HELL BELOW ZERO(1954, Brit.), w; LAST MAN TO HANG, THE(1956, Brit.), w

Jerzy Trella
DANTON(1983)

Norma Trelvar
NATION AFLAME(1937)

Frances Tremaine
YOUNG GRADUATES, THE(1971)

Kathleen Tremaine
UMBRELLA, THE(1933, Brit.); LADY VANISHES, THE(1938, Brit.)

Paul Tremaine
RIDE THE WILD SURF(1964)

Sydney Tremaine
Silents
AUCTION MART, THE(1920, Brit.), w

Trevor Tremaine
MIGHTY MCGURK, THE(1946)

Vernon Tremaine
Silents
ON THE HIGH SEAS(1922)

W.L. Tremaine
Misc. Silents
LONELY TRAIL, THE(1922)

Leonard Tremayne
Misc. Silents
ISLAND OF ROMANCE, THE(1922, Brit.)
Les Tremayne
BLUE VEIL, THE(1951); RACKET, THE(1951); FRANCIS GOES TO WEST POINT(1952); IT GROWS ON TREES(1952); DREAM WIFE(1953); I LOVE MELVIN(1953); WAR OF THE WORLDS, THE(1953); SUSAN SLEPT HERE(1954); MAN CALLED PETER, THE(1955); EVERYTHING BUT THE TRUTH(1956); LIEUTENANT WORE SKIRTS, THE(1956); UNGUARDED MOMENT, THE(1956); MONOLITH MONSTERS, THE(1957); PERFECT FURLOUGH, THE(1958); ANGRY RED PLANET, THE(1959); MONSTER OF PIEDRAS BLANCAS, THE(1959); NORTH BY NORTHWEST(1959); SAY ONE FOR ME(1959); GALLANT HOURS, THE(1960); STORY OF RUTH, THE(1960); SHOOT OUT AT BIG SAG(1962); SLIME PEOPLE, THE(1963); FORTUNE COOKIE, THE(1966); MR. MAGOO'S HOLIDAY FESTIVAL(1970); PHANTOM TOLLBOOTH, THE(1970); DAFFY DUCK'S MOVIE: FANTASTIC ISLAND(1983)
Misc. Talkies
CREATURE OF DESTRUCTION(1967); FANGS(1974)
Herni Tremblay
TROUBLE-FETE(1964, Can.)
Bonnie Tremenal
TRADING PLACES(1983)
Doug Tremlett
CLINIC, THE(1983, Aus.)
Mrs. Horace Tremlett
KNIGHT IN LONDON, A(1930, Brit./Ger.), w
Mike Tremont
1984
CORRUPT(1984, Ital.)
Michael Tremor
PLEDGEMASTERS, THE(1971)
Will Tremper
ESCAPE TO BERLIN(1962, U.S./Switz./Ger.), d,w&ed; ENDLESS NIGHT, THE(1963, Ger.), p,d&w; STOP TRAIN 349(1964, Fr./Ital./Ger.), w; THAT WOMAN(1968, Ger.), p,d&w; UNWILLING AGENT(1968, Ger.), w
John Trenaman
DAYLIGHT ROBBERY(1964, Brit.); HOW I WON THE WAR(1967, Brit.); CHARGE OF THE LIGHT BRIGADE, THE(1968, Brit.); CONQUEROR WORM, THE(1968, Brit.); CRY WOLF(1968, Brit.); DECLINE AND FALL... OF A BIRD WATCHER(1969, Brit.); HAMLET(1969, Brit.)
Brian Trenchard-Smith
BMX BANDITS(1983), d; ESCAPE 2000(1983, Aus.), d
Jean Trend
STRICTLY CONFIDENTIAL(1959, Brit.)
Jack Trendall
ROBBER SYMPHONY, THE(1937, Brit.), w
George W. Trendle
LEGEND OF THE LONE RANGER, THE(1981), w
N. Treneva
MAN OF MUSIC(1953, USSR), w
Helen Trenholme
CASE OF THE HOWLING DOG, THE(1934); FIREBIRD, THE(1934)
The Treniers
DON'T KNOCK THE ROCK(1956); GIRL CAN'T HELP IT, THE(1956); CALYPSO HEAT WAVE(1957); JUKE BOX RHYTHM(1959)
William Trenk
CORPSE CAME C.O.D., THE(; STRANGE DEATH OF ADOLF HITLER, THE(1943); SEARCHING WIND, THE(1946); WHITE TIE AND TAILS(1946); EXILE, THE(1947); GUILT OF JANET AMES, THE(1947); I'LL BE YOURS(1947); LETTER FROM AN UNKNOWN WOMAN(1948)
Willy Trenk
HITCHHIKE TO HAPPINESS(1945)
William Trenk-Trebitsch
THEY WERE SO YOUNG(1955)
Willy Trenk-Trebitsch
RASPUTIN(1932, Ger.); ETERNAL WALTZ, THE(1959, Ger.); QUESTION 7(1961, U.S./Ger.); HELDINNEN(1962, Ger.)
Louis Trenker
Misc. Silents
PEAKS OF DESTINY(1927, Ger.)
Luis Trenker
DOOMED BATTALION, THE(1932), a, w; REBEL, THE(1933, Ger.), a, d&w; PRODIGAL SON, THE(1935), a, d&w; CHALLENGE, THE(1939, Brit.), a, d
Freddie Trenkler
COUNTESS OF MONTE CRISTO, THE(1948)
Anthony Trent
TOMCAT, THE(1968, Brit.); MC VICAR(1982, Brit.)
1984
WINTER FLIGHT(1984, Brit.)
Bruce Trent
BAND WAGGON(1940, Brit.)
George Trent
EARTH CRIES OUT, THE(1949, Ital.)
Hilary Trent
FLAMINGO AFFAIR, THE(1948, Brit.)
Jack Trent
HALF-MARRIAGE(1929); SPOILERS, THE(1930); DEVIL PAYS, THE(1932); DISCARDED LOVERS(1932); PHANTOM EXPRESS, THE(1932); OUTLAW JUSTICE(1933); STICK TO YOUR GUNS(1941); THEY WERE EXPENDABLE(1945); HURRICANE SMITH(1952)
Silents
LOVE AND LEARN(1928)
Jean Trent
ARABIAN NIGHTS(1942); SABOTEUR(1942); SIN TOWN(1942); WESTERN MAIL(1942); FRONTIER GAL(1945); LADY ON A TRAIN(1945); SALOME, WHERE SHE DANCED(1945); THIS LOVE OF OURS(1945); NIGHT IN PARADISE, A(1946)
Jerry Trent
SWEET CHARITY(1969); XANADU(1980), ch

John Trent
SKY SPIDER, THE(1931); BADGE OF HONOR(1934); BLOSSOMS ON BROADWAY(1937); DOCTOR'S DIARY, A(1937); GREAT GAMBINI, THE(1937); JOHN MEADE'S WOMAN(1937); SHE'S NO LADY(1937); DANGER FLIGHT(1939); MYSTERY PLANE(1939); SKY PATROL(1939); STUNT PILOT(1939); I WANTED WINGS(1941); BUSHBABY, THE(1970), p, d; HOMER(1970), d; IT SEEMED LIKE A GOOD IDEA AT THE TIME(1975, Can.), d, w; SUNDAY IN THE COUNTRY(1975, Can.), d, w; MIDDLE AGE CRAZY(1980, Can.), d
Misc. Talkies
ONLY WAY OUT IS DEAD, THE(1970), d
Karen Sue Trent
GARDEN OF EDEN(1954)
Karen Trent
FIDDLER ON THE ROOF(1971)
Lee Trent
LADY OF BURLESQUE(1943); FALCON OUT WEST, THE(1944); HAVING WONDERFUL CRIME(1945); NEW YORK CONFIDENTIAL(1955); JEANNE EAGELS(1957)
Paul Trent
Silents
WHEN GREEK MEETS GREEK(1922, Brit.), w
Peter Trent
BLACK MAGIC(1949); DEAD WOMAN'S KISS, A(1951, Ital.); QUIET AMERICAN, THE(1958)
Philip Trent
FLIRTING WITH FATE(1938); LETTER OF INTRODUCTION(1938); SPY RING, THE(1938); GONE WITH THE WIND(1939); LET US LIVE(1939); PIRATES OF THE SKIES(1939); WHEN TOMORROW COMES(1939); MURDER BY INVITATION(1941); OUTLAWS OF THE CHEROKEE TRAIL(1941); PAPER BULLETS(1941); BOMBAY CLIPPER(1942)
Russell Trent
STRIP, THE(1951); WELL, THE(1951); SHORT CUT TO HELL(1957); THIRTY FOOT BRIDE OF CANDY ROCK, THE(1959)
Ruth Trent
WEEKEND OF FEAR(1966)
Barbara Trentham
POSSESSION OF JOEL DELANEY, THE(1972); ROLLERBALL(1975); SKY RIDERS(1976, U.S./Gr.)
Brian Trentham
SKY PIRATE, THE(1970), m, spec eff
Margherita Trentini
DEAF SMITH AND JOHNNY EARS(1973, Ital.)
Peggy Trentini
1984
UP THE CREEK(1984)
Guido Trento
STREET ANGEL(1928); PARDON US(1931); SECRETS OF THE FRENCH POLICE(1932)
Silents
NERO(1922, U.S./Ital.); IT IS THE LAW(1924)
Misc. Silents
CHARGE OF THE GAUCHOS, THE(1928); STREET ANGEL(1928)
Cecil Trenton
GHOST OF HIDDEN VALLEY(1946)
James Davis Trenton
1984
LOVELINES(1984)
Pell Trenton
Silents
JOYOUS LIAR, THE(1919); NEW DISCIPLE, THE(1921)
Misc. Silents
ADVENTURER, THE(1917); STRANDED IN ARCADY(1917); CAMOUFLAGE KISS, A(1918); HOUSE OF GLASS, THE(1918); FAIR AND WARMER(1919); FIGHTING CRESSY(1919); REBELLIOUS BRIDE, THE(1919); UPLIFTERS, THE(1919); BEAUTIFULLY TRIMMED(1920); BLUE MOON, THE(1920); HOUSE OF TOYS, THE(1920); WILLOW TREE, THE(1920); GREATER PROFIT, THE(1921)
Cheryl Trepton
MANTIS IN LACE(1968)
Gunther Treptow
YOUNG LORD, THE(1970, Ger.)
Los Tres Ases
LOS AUTOMATAS DE LA MUERTE(1960, Mex.); NEUTRON CONTRA EL DR. CARONTE(1962, Mex.); NEUTRON EL ENMASCARADO NEGRO(1962, Mex.)
Ivan Tresault
MISSION TO MOSCOW(1943)
Vladimir Treschalov
DIMKA(1964, USSR)
Al Trescony
DOWN IN SAN DIEGO(1941)
Ivy Tresmand
DARK STAIRWAY, THE(1938, Brit.)
Nina Tresoff
LIMIT, THE(1972)
David Tress
1984
MISSING IN ACTION(1984)
Dieter Tressier
BARON BLOOD(1972, Ital.)
Dieter Tressler
WALK WITH LOVE AND DEATH, A(1969)
George Tressler
MERRY WIVES OF WINDSOR, THE(1966, Aust.), d
Hans Jurgel Tressler
EPISODE(1937, Aust.)
Otto Tressler
STORM IN A WATER GLASS(1931, Aust.); COURT CONCERT, THE(1936, Ger.); EPISODE(1937, Aust.); ONE APRIL 2000(1952, Aust.); STORY OF VICKIE, THE(1958, Aust.); FOREVER MY LOVE(1962)

Wolf Dieter Tressler
EPISODE(1937, Aust.)
Giorgio Trestini
DON'T LOOK NOW(1973, Brit./Ital.)
Rosemary Treston
WOMAN HATER(1949, Brit.)
Andre Treton
WAR OF THE BUTTONS(1963 Fr.)
Annika Tretow
NAKED NIGHT, THE(1956, Swed.)
Richard Tretter
SILENCERS, THE(; WINGS OF CHANCE(1961, Can.); CATTLE KING(1963);
MADAME X(1966); ON HER BED OF ROSES(1966)
Henry Trettin
CRY OF THE PENGUINS(1972, Brit.), p
Olga Tretyakov
Misc. Silents
BEAUTY AND THE BOLSHEVIK(1923, USSR)
V. Tretyakov
KATERINA IZMAILOVA(1969, USSR)
Olga Tretyakova
Misc. Silents
FIGHT FOR THE 'ULTIMATUM' FACTORY(1923, USSR); FROM SPARKS–
FLAMES(1924, USSR); THREE FRIENDS AND AN INVENTION(1928, USSR)
Wolfgang Treu
CASTLE, THE(1969, Ger.), ph; SALZBURG CONNECTION, THE(1972), ph; PEDE-
STRIAN, THE(1974, Ger.), ph; DISORDER AND EARLY TORMENT(1977, Ger.), ph;
NIGHT OF THE ASKARI(1978, Ger./South African), ph
1984
LITTLE DRUMMER GIRL, THE(1984), ph
Franz Graf Treuberg
FEAR(1956, Ger.), w
John Treul
STREET CORNER(1948)
Johnny Treul
ROUGHLY SPEAKING(1945)
Battista Trevaini
TREE OF WOODEN CLOGS, THE(1979, Ital.)
Jack Trevan
GIGI(1958)
Trevanian
EIGER SANCTION, THE(1975), w
Noel Trevarthan
ESCORT FOR HIRE(1960, Brit.)
Noel Trevarthen
WITNESS IN THE DARK(1959, Brit.); BACKFIRE!(1961, Brit.); FATE TAKES A
HAND(1962, Brit.); YOUR MONEY OR YOUR WIFE(1965, Brit.); IT!(1967, Brit.);
CORRUPTION(1968, Brit.); VENGEANCE OF FU MANCHU, THE(1968, Brit./Ger./
Hong Kong/Ireland); ABDICATION, THE(1974, Brit.)
Michael Trevellyan
LEND ME YOUR HUSBAND(1935, Brit.), w
H. B. Trevelyan
Silents
DARK ANGEL, THE(1925), w
Hilda Trevelyan
COLONEL BLOOD(1934, Brit.); TRANSATLANTIC TUNNEL(1935, Brit.)
Silents
WHAT EVERY WOMAN KNOWS(1917, Brit.)
Misc. Silents
SALLY IN OUR ALLEY(1916, Brit.); ANOTHER MAN'S SHOES(1922)
Michael Trevelyan
DARING DANGER(1932), w
Una Trevelyan
Silents
DEVIL'S PASSKEY, THE(1920)
Hilda Trevelyn
TRANSATLANTIC TUNNEL(1935, Brit.)
David Trevena
MAHLER(1974, Brit.)
1984
1984(1984, Brit.)
Davie Trevena
ONE MORE TIME(1970, Brit.)
Frederick Treves
HIGH TERRACE(1957, Brit.); MARK OF THE HAWK, THE(1958); ELEPHANT MAN,
THE(1980, Brit.); NIGHTHAWKS(1981)
Sir Frederick Treves
ELEPHANT MAN, THE(1980, Brit.), w
George Treville
Misc. Silents
MARRIED LIFE(1921, Brit.), d
Georges Treville
Silents
ALL SORTS AND CONDITIONS OF MEN(1921, Brit.), d; MOULIN ROUGE(1928,
Brit.)
Roger Treville
PARISIAN, THE(1931, Fr.); RUNAWAY LADIES(1935, Brit.); SLIPPER EPISODE,
THE(1938, Fr); MR. PEEK-A-BOO(1951, Fr.); GREEN GLOVE, THE(1952); HAPPY
ROAD, THE(1957); BRIDE IS MUCH TOO BEAUTIFUL, THE(1958, Fr.); PARIS
HOLIDAY(1958); DEAD RUN(1961, Fr./Ital./Ger.); HOW TO STEAL A MIL-
LION(1966); PONTIUS PILATE(1967, Fr./Ital.)
Misc. Silents
MARRIED LIFE(1921, Brit.)
Antonio Trevino
HERBIE GOES BANANAS(1980)
Carmen Trevino
1984
FOOTLOOSE(1984)

George Trevino
CAPTAIN SCARLETT(1953); BRAVE ONE, THE(1956); BLACK PATCH(1957);
GHOST DIVER(1957); RIDE BACK, THE(1957); THIRD VOICE, THE(1960)
Jorge Trevino
PANCHO VILLA RETURNS(1950, Mex.); SOMBRERO(1953); WHITE ORCHID,
THE(1954); LIFE IN THE BALANCE, A(1955); BEAST OF HOLLOW MOUNTAIN,
THE(1956); LAST OF THE FAST GUNS, THE(1958); VILLA!(1958)
Nacho Trevino
MAGNIFICENT MATADOR, THE(1955)
Di Trevis
HANOVER STREET(1979, Brit.)
Franco Trevisi
TRAGEDY OF A RIDICULOUS MAN, THE(1982, Ital.)
John Trevlac [Calvert]
DARK VENTURE(1956)
Ann Trevor
MURDER IN THE OLD RED BARN(1936, Brit.)
Silents
ROGUE IN LOVE, A(1922, Brit.)
Misc. Silents
BUILD THY HOUSE(1920, Brit.); DANIEL DERONDA(1921, Brit.)
Anne Trevor
Misc. Silents
WUTHERING HEIGHTS(1920, Brit.)
Austin Trevor
ESCAPE(1930, Brit.); MYSTERY AT THE VILLA ROSE(1930, Brit.); "W" PLAN,
THE(1931, Brit.); ALIBI(1931, Brit.); BLACK COFFEE(1931, Brit.); MAN FROM
CHICAGO, THE(1931, Brit.); NIGHT IN MONTMARTE, A(1931, Brit.); CHINESE
PUZZLE, THE(1932, Brit.); CROOKED LADY, THE(1932, Brit.); SECRET AGENT(1933,
Brit.); BROKEN MELODY, THE(1934, Brit.); DEATH AT A BROADCAST(1934, Brit.);
LORD EDGEWARE DIES(1934, Brit.); INSIDE THE ROOM(1935, Brit.); MIMI(1935,
Brit.); REGAL CAVALCADE(1935, Brit.); SILENT PASSENGER, THE(1935, Brit.); AS
YOU LIKE IT(1936, Brit.); BELOVED VAGABOND, THE(1936, Brit.); REM-
BRANDT(1936, Brit.); DARK JOURNEY(1937, Brit.); KNIGHT WITHOUT AR-
MOR(1937, Brit.); SABOTAGE(1937, Brit.); HIDEOUT IN THE ALPS(1938, Brit.);
GOODBYE MR. CHIPS(1939, Brit.); BRIGGS FAMILY, THE(1940, Brit.); LAW AND
DISORDER(1940, Brit.); LION HAS WINGS, THE(1940, Brit.); NIGHT TRAIN(1940,
Brit.); UNDER YOUR HAT(1940, Brit.); SEVENTH SURVIVOR, THE(1941, Brit.); BIG
BLOCKADE, THE(1942, Brit.); YOUNG MR. PITT, THE(1942, Brit.); CHAMPAGNE
CHARLIE(1944, Brit.); LISBON STORY, THE(1946, Brit.); ANNA KARENINA(1948,
Brit.); RED SHOES, THE(1948, Brit.); SO LONG AT THE FAIR(1951, Brit.); DETEC-
TIVE, THE(1954, Qit.); TO PARIS WITH LOVE(1955, Brit.); TONS OF TROUBLE(1956,
Brit.); ABANDON SHIP(1957, Brit.); DANGEROUS EXILE(1958, Brit.); HORRORS OF
THE BLACK MUSEUM(1959, U.S./Brit.); COURT MARTIAL OF MAJOR KELLER,
THE(1961, Brit.); DAY THE EARTH CAUGHT FIRE, THE(1961, Brit.); KONGA(1961,
Brit.); ALPHABET MURDERS, THE(1966); NEVER BACK LOSERS(1967, Brit.)
Claire Trevor
TWO WEEKS IN ANOTHER TOWN(1962); JIMMY AND SALLY(1933); LIFE IN THE
RAW(1933); MAD GAME, THE(1933); BABY, TAKE A BOW(1934); HOLD THAT
GIRL(1934); LAST TRAIL, THE(1934); WILD GOLD(1934); BLACK SHEEP(1935);
DANTE'S INFERNO(1935); ELINOR NORTON(1935); SPRING TONIC(1935); CAREER
WOMAN(1936); FIFTEEN MAIDEN LANE(1936); HUMAN CARGO(1936); MY MAR-
RIAGE(1936); NAVY WIFE(1936); SONG AND DANCE MAN, THE(1936); STAR FOR
A NIGHT(1936); TO MARY–WITH LOVE(1936); BIG TOWN GIRL(1937); DEAD
END(1937); KING OF GAMBLERS(1937); ONE MILE FROM HEAVEN(1937); SECOND
HONEYMOON(1937); TIME OUT FOR ROMANCE(1937); AMAZING DR. CLITTER-
HOUSE, THE(1938); FIVE OF A KIND(1938); VALLEY OF THE GIANTS(1938);
WALKING DOWN BROADWAY(1938); ALLEGHENY UPRISING(1939); I STOLE A
MILLION(1939); STAGECOACH(1939); DARK COMMAND, THE(1940); HONKY
TONK(1941); TEXAS(1941); ADVENTURES OF MARTIN EDEN, THE(1942); CROSS-
ROADS(1942); STREET OF CHANCE(1942); DESPERADOES, THE(1943); GOOD
LUCK, MR. YATES(1943); WOMAN OF THE TOWN, THE(1943); JOHNNY AN-
GEL(1945); MURDER, MY SWEET(1945); BACHELOR'S DAUGHTERS, THE(1946);
CRACK-UP(1946); BORN TO KILL(1947); BABE RUTH STORY, THE(1948); KEY
LARGO(1948); RAW DEAL(1948); VELVET TOUCH, THE(1948); LUCKY STIFF,
THE(1949); BORDERLINE(1950); BEST OF THE BADMEN(1951); HARD, FAST, AND
BEAUTIFUL(1951); HOODLUM EMPIRE(1952); MY MAN AND I(1952); STOP,
YOU'RE KILLING ME(1952); STRANGER WORE A GUN, THE(1953); HIGH AND
THE MIGHTY, THE(1954); LUCY GALLANT(1955); MAN WITHOUT A STAR(1955);
MOUNTAIN, THE(1956); MARJORIE MORNINGSTAR(1958); STRIPPER, THE(1963);
HOW TO MURDER YOUR WIFE(1965); CAPETOWN AFFAIR(1967, U.S./South Afr.);
KISS ME GOODBYE(1982)
Edward Trevor
WAY DOWN EAST(1935); CHARLIE CHAN'S SECRET(1936)
Elleston Trevor
DEAD ON COURSE(1952, Brit.), w; WOMAN IN HIDING(1953, Brit.), w; DUN-
KIRK(1958, Brit.), w; 80,000 SUSPECTS(1963, Brit.), w; FLIGHT OF THE PHOENIX,
THE(1965), w
Evelyn Trevor
Misc. Silents
GATES OF DUTY(1919, Brit.)
George Trevor
Silents
WAY OF A WOMAN(1919)
Howard Trevor
MUMSY, NANNY, SONNY, AND GIRLY(1970, Brit.)
Hugh Trevor
TAXI 13(1928); LOVE IN THE DESERT(1929); NIGHT PARADE(1929, Brit.); VERY
IDEA, THE(1929); CONSPIRACY(1930); CUCKOOS, THE(1930); HALF SHOT AT
SUNRISE(1930); MIDNIGHT MYSTERY(1930); PAY OFF, THE(1930); ROYAL BED,
THE(1931)
Silents
RANGER OF THE NORTH(1927); HEY RUBE!(1928); RED LIPS(1928); SKINNER'S
BIG IDEA(1928)
Misc. Silents
BEAU BROADWAY(1928); HER SUMMER HERO(1928); WALLFLOWERS(1928)
Jack Trevor
TWO WORLD(1930, Brit.); LILY CHRISTINE(1932, Brit.)

Silents
PAGES OF LIFE(1922, Brit.); NOT FOR SALE(1924, Brit.); CHAMPAGNE(1928, Brit.); ALLEY CAT, THE(1929, Brit.)
Misc. Silents
PETTICOAT LOOSE(1922, Brit.); SECRETS OF A SOUL(1925, Ger.); RASPUTIN(1930)
John Trevor
STEEL BAYONET, THE(1958, Brit.)
Norman Trevor
LOVE TRAP, THE(1929); TONIGHT AT TWELVE(1929)
Silents
IVORY SNUFF BOX, THE(1915); DAUGHTER PAYS, THE(1920); JANE EYRE(1921); ROULETTE(1924); ACE OF CADS, THE(1926); BEAU GESTE(1926); DANCING MOTHERS(1926); AFRAID TO LOVE(1927); CHILDREN OF DIVORCE(1927); NEW YORK(1927); WARNING, THE(1927)
Misc. Silents
RUNAWAY, THE(1917); DAREDEVIL, THE(1918); ROMANCE(1920); BLACK PANTHER'S CUB, THE(1921); WAGES OF VIRTUE(1924); SONG AND DANCE MAN, THE(1926); MUSIC MASTER, THE(1927); SIREN, THE(1927); RESTLESS YOUTH(1928)
Olive Trevor
Silents
OTHER MAN'S WIFE, THE(1919); DOWN BY THE RIO GRANDE(1924)
Richard Trevor
HUMAN FACTOR, THE(1979, Brit.), ed
Simon Trevor
ELEPHANT CALLED SLOWLY, AN(1970, Brit.), ph; CHRISTIAN THE LION(1976, Brit.), ph
Spencer Trevor
CONGRESS DANCES(1932, Ger.); LOVE CONTRACT, THE(1932, Brit.); LUCKY GIRL(1932, Brit.); WIVES BEWARE(1933, Brit.); PRIVATE LIFE OF DON JUAN, THE(1934, Brit.); RETURN OF BULLDOG DRUMMOND, THE(1934, Brit.); APRIL BLOSSOMS(1937, Brit.); LET THE PEOPLE SING(1942, Brit.); COLONEL BLIMP(1945, Brit.)
John Trevor-Davis
ROBBERY WITH VIOLENCE(1958, Brit.)
Maurice Trewern
1984
VIGIL(1984, New Zealand)
Ralph Trewhela
PENNYWHISTLE BLUES, THE(1952, South Africa), m
Anita Treyens
ROAD TO SHAME, THE(1962, Fr.)
Albert M. Treynor
Silents
FLASHLIGHT, THE(1917), w
Albert Treynor
IT'S A SMALL WORLD(1935), w; RAINMAKERS, THE(1935), w; ALWAYS IN TROUBLE(1938), w; DANCING CO-ED(1939), w
Eva Treytnorova
WHAT WOULD YOU SAY TO SOME SPINACH(1976, Czech.)
E. Treyvas
SPRINGTIME ON THE VOLGA(1961, USSR); SONG OVER MOSCOW(1964, USSR)
Antonio Triama
GAY SENORITA, THE(1945)
Antonio Triana
GAY SENORITA, THE(1945), ch; STRANGE LADY IN TOWN(1955)
Louisa Triana
LES GIRLS(1957)
Luisa Triana
STRANGE LADY IN TOWN(1955); COMANCHEROS, THE(1961)
Lusite Triana
GAY SENORITA, THE(1945)
The Trianas
STRANGE LADY IN TOWN(1955)
Niki Triandafylidou
CANNON AND THE NIGHTINGALE, THE(1969, Gr.)
Antonio Triano
LADY AND THE MONSTER, THE(1944); SERENADE(1956)
Nancy Tribush
OH! CALCUTTA!(1972)
Ron Trice
YOUNGBLOOD(1978); KING OF THE MOUNTAIN(1981)
Bernard Triche
GOIN' HOME(1976)
Marie Trichet
MOUCHETTE(1970, Fr.)
Tommy Trick
FAT SPY(1966)
David Trickett
SHIPBUILDERS, THE(1943, Brit.); GIVE ME THE STARS(1944, Brit.); GAY INTRUDERS, THE(1946, Brit.)
Vicki Trickett
PEPE(1960); GIDGET GOES HAWAIIAN(1961); CABINET OF CALIGARI, THE(1962); THREE STOOGES MEET HERCULES, THE(1962)
Tricoche
MARATHON MAN(1976)
Carlo Tricoli
BLACK HAND, THE(1950); CRISIS(1950); LADY WITHOUT PASSPORT, A(1950); SPY HUNT(1950); VICIOUS YEARS, THE(1950); MASK OF THE AVENGER(1951); TEN TALL MEN(1951); OPERATION SECRET(1952); WAGON TEAM(1952); SALOME(1953); PAY OR DIE(1960)
Elena Tricoli
ASH WEDNESDAY(1973)
L. Tridenskaya
Misc. Silents
CHRISTMAS EVE(1913, USSR)
Martin Trieb
NOT RECONCILED, OR "ONLY VIOLENCE HELPS WHERE IT RULES"(1969, Ger.)

Augie Triebach
GROUND ZERO(1973)
A. Trielli
SOUTHERN STAR, THE(1969, Fr./Brit.), spec eff
Andre Trielli
CIRCLE OF DECEIT(1982, Fr./Ger.), spec eff
Paul Trielli
CIRCLE OF DECEIT(1982, Fr./Ger.), spec eff
Ivan Triesault
STRANGE DEATH OF ADOLF HITLER, THE(1943); BLACK PARACHUTE, THE(1944); CRY OF THE WEREWOLF(1944); DAYS OF GLORY(1944); HITLER GANG, THE(1944); IN OUR TIME(1944); MUMMY'S GHOST, THE(1944); UNCERTAIN GLORY(1944); COUNTER-ATTACK(1945); ESCAPE IN THE FOG(1945); SONG TO REMEMBER, A(1945); CRIME DOCTOR'S MAN HUNT(1946); NOTORIOUS(1946); RETURN OF MONTE CRISTO, THE(1946); CRIMSON KEY, THE(1947); ESCAPE ME NEVER(1947); GOLDEN EARRINGS(1947); TO THE ENDS OF THE EARTH(1948); WOMAN FROM TANGIER, THE(1948); JOHNNY ALLEGRO(1949); KIM(1950); SPY HUNT(1950); DESERT FOX, THE(1951); LADY AND THE BANDIT, THE(1951); MY FAVORITE SPY(1951); MY TRUE STORY(1951); BAD AND THE BEAUTIFUL, THE(1952); FIVE FINGERS(1952); BACK TO GOD'S COUNTRY(1953); CHARGE OF THE LANCERS(1953); DESERT LEGION(1953); HOW TO MARRY A MILLIONAIRE(1953); MA AND PA KETTLE ON VACATION(1953); SCANDAL AT SCOURIE(1953); YOUNG BESS(1953); BORDER RIVER(1954); GAMBLER FROM NATCHEZ, THE(1954); HER TWELVE MEN(1954); GIRL IN THE RED VELVET SWING, THE(1955); BUSTER KEATON STORY, THE(1957); JET PILOT(1957); SILK STOCKINGS(1957); TOP SECRET AFFAIR(1957); FRAULEIN(1958); YOUNG LIONS, THE(1958); AMAZING TRANSPARENT MAN, THE(1960); CIMARRON(1960); BARABBAS(1962, Ital.); IT HAPPENED IN ATHENS(1962); 300 SPARTANS, THE(1962); PRIZE, THE(1963); VIVA LAS VEGAS(1964); MORITURI(1965); VON RYAN'S EXPRESS(1965)
Charles Trieschmann
TWO(1975), p,d&w
Frank Triest
LIAR'S DICE(1980)
1984
SIGNAL 7(1984)
Leopoldo Trieste
SKY IS RED, THE(1952, Ital.), w; COUNTERFEITERS, THE(1953, Ital.), w; VITELLONI(1956, Ital./Fr.); WHITE SHEIK, THE(1956, Ital.); FAREWELL TO ARMS, A(1957); DIVORCE, ITALIAN STYLE(1962, Ital.); MORALIST, THE(1964, Ital.); SEDUCED AND ABANDONED(1964, Fr./Ital.); DAY IN COURT, A(1965, Ital.); EYE OF THE NEEDLE, THE(1965, Ital./Fr.); WHITE VOICES(1965, Fr./Ital.); SHOOT LOUD, LOUDER... I DON'T UNDERSTAND(1966, Ital.); MAIDEN FOR A PRINCE, A(1967, Fr./Ital.); WE STILL KILL THE OLD WAY(1967, Ital.); WEEKEND, ITALIAN STYLE(1967, Fr./Ital./Span.); CHASTITY BELT, THE(1968, Ital.); SHOES OF THE FISHERMAN, THE(1968); LOVE FACTORY(1969, Ital.); SECRET OF SANTA VITTORIA, THE(1969); PUSSYCAT, PUSSYCAT, I LOVE YOU(1970); SICILIAN CLAN, THE(1970, Fr.); VACATION, THE(1971, Ital.); EVERY LITTLE CROOK AND NANNY(1972); PULP(1972, Brit.); DON'T LOOK NOW(1973, Brit./Ital.); GODFATHER, THE, PART II(1974); TRENCHCOAT(1983)
Tamara Trifflex
STORY WITHOUT WORDS(1981, Ital.)
Kathy Triffon
MAN WHO WOULD NOT DIE, THE(1975)
Neil Trifunovich
FIREBIRD 2015 AD(1981), spec eff
1984
MRS. SOFFEL(1984), spec eff
Derek Trigg
1984
JIGSAW MAN, THE(1984, Brit.), ed
Earle Trigg
PAYDAY(1972)
Toekie Trigg
GIVE ME YOUR HEART(1936)
Ian Trigger
DIAMONDS FOR BREAKFAST(1968, Brit.); PUSSYCAT, PUSSYCAT, I LOVE YOU(1970); UP POMPEII(1971, Brit.)
John Trigger
OH! WHAT A LOVELY WAR(1969, Brit.)
Trigger the Horse
SHINE ON, HARVEST MOON(1938); UNDER WESTERN STARS(1938); COME ON RANGERS(1939); DAYS OF JESSE JAMES(1939); FRONTIER PONY EXPRESS(1939); IN OLD CALIENTE(1939); ROUGH RIDERS' ROUNDUP(1939); SAGA OF DEATH VALLEY(1939); SOUTHWARD HO!(1939); WALL STREET COWBOY(1939); RANGER AND THE LADY, THE(1940); YOUNG BILL HICKOK(1940); YOUNG BUFFALO BILL(1940); IN OLD CHEYENNE(1941); JESSE JAMES AT BAY(1941); NEVADA CITY(1941); RED RIVER VALLEY(1941); ROBIN HOOD OF THE PECOS(1941); SHERIFF OF TOMBSTONE(1941); HEART OF THE GOLDEN WEST(1942); MAN FROM CHEYENNE(1942); RIDIN' DOWN THE CANYON(1942); ROMANCE ON THE RANGE(1942); SONS OF THE PIONEERS(1942); SOUTH OF SANTA FE(1942); SUNSET ON THE DESERT(1942); SUNSET SERENADE(1942); HANDS ACROSS THE BORDER(1943); IDAHO(1943); KING OF THE COWBOYS(1943); MAN FROM MUSIC MOUNTAIN(1943); SILVER SPURS(1943); SONG OF TEXAS(1943); HOLLYWOOD CANTEEN(1944); LIGHTS OF OLD SANTA FE(1944); SAN FERNANDO VALLEY(1944); SONG OF NEVADA(1944); YELLOW ROSE OF TEXAS, THE(1944); DON'T FENCE ME IN(1945); MAN FROM OKLAHOMA, THE(1945); SUNSET IN EL DORADO(1945); UTAH(1945); HELLDORADO(1946); HOME IN OKLAHOMA(1946); MY PAL TRIGGER(1946); OUT CALIFORNIA WAY(1946); RAINBOW OVER TEXAS(1946); ROLL ON TEXAS MOON(1946); SONG OF ARIZONA(1946); UNDER NEVADA SKIES(1946); APACHE ROSE(1947); HIT PARADE OF 1947(1947); SPRINGTIME IN THE SIERRAS(1947); GAY RANCHERO, THE(1948); GRAND CANYON TRAIL(1948); NIGHT TIME IN NEVADA(1948); UNDER CALIFORNIA STARS(1948); FAR FRONTIER, THE(1949); GOLDEN STALLION, THE(1949); SUSANNA PASS(1949); NORTH OF THE GREAT DIVIDE(1950); SUNSET IN THE WEST(1950); TRAIL OF ROBIN HOOD(1950); TRIGGER, JR.(1950); TWILIGHT IN THE SIERRAS(1950); HEART OF THE ROCKIES(1951); IN OLD AMARILLO(1951); SOUTH OF CALIENTE(1951); SPOILERS OF THE PLAINS(1951); PALS OF THE GOLDEN WEST(1952)

Trigger, the Smartest Horse in the Movies
BELLS OF CORONADO(1950)
Raffaele Triggia
SACCO AND VANZETTI(1971, Ital./Fr.)
John Trigonis
TANK BATTALION(1958)
Elli Trigonopoulou
ELECTRA(1962, Gr.)
Michael Trikilis
SIX PACK(1982), p
Sasha Trikojus
FIRM MAN, THE(1975, Aus.), ph
Gina Trikonis
WEST SIDE STORY(1961); THIRTEEN FRIGHTENED GIRLS(1963)
Gus Trikonis
WEST SIDE STORY(1961); PAJAMA PARTY(1964); UNSINKABLE MOLLY BROWN, THE(1964); SAND PEBBLES, THE(1966); ST. VALENTINE'S DAY MASSACRE, THE(1967); HELLCATS, THE(1968); FIVE THE HARD WAY(1969), d; STUDENT BODY, THE(1976), d; SWINGING BARMAIDS, THE(1976), d; MOONSHINE COUNTY EXPRESS(1977), d; NEW GIRL IN TOWN(1977), d; EVIL, THE(1978), d; TOUCHED BY LOVE(1980), d; TAKE THIS JOB AND SHOVE IT(1981), d; DANCE OF THE DWARFS(1983, U.S., Phil.), d
Misc. Talkies
SUPERCOCK(1975), d
Armand Triller
Silents
GOLD RUSH, THE(1925)
Amedeo Trilli
MINOTAUR, THE(1961, Ital.); SEVEN TASKS OF ALI BABA, THE(1963, Ital.); SULEIMAN THE CONQUEROR(1963, Ital.); RAILROAD MAN, THE(1965, Ital.); SEVEN DWARFS TO THE RESCUE, THE(1965, Ital.); GUILT IS NOT MINE(1968, Ital.); SERAFINO(1970, Fr./Ital.)
Brenda Trillo
HEAT(1970, Arg.)
Michele Trimarchi
SANDRA(1966, Ital.), makeup; MINUTE TO PRAY, A SECOND TO DIE, A(1968, Ital.), makeup; SEVEN GOLDEN MEN(1969, Fr./Ital./Span.), makeup; MACHINE GUN McCAIN(1970, Ital.), makeup
Rose Trimarco
SO FINE(1981), cos
A.A. Trimble
GREAT ZIEGFELD, THE(1936)
Andrew A. Trimble
YOU'RE A SWEETHEART(1937)
David Trimble
SCREAM, BABY, SCREAM(1969), set d
Elliott Trimble
HUCKLEBERRY FINN(1974)
George S. Trimble
Silents
ARMS AND THE GIRL(1917); DEVIL'S PLAYGROUND, THE(1918)
George Trimble
Silents
HOUSE NEXT DOOR, THE(1914); POLLY OF THE CIRCUS(1917); OUR MRS. McCHESNEY(1918); DAMSEL IN DISTRESS, A(1919)
Misc. Silents
MAN WHO STOOD STILL, THE(1916)
Larry Trimble
Silents
ALONE IN LONDON(1915, Brit.), d; FAR FROM THE MADDING CROWD(1915, Brit.), d&w; GREAT ADVENTURE, THE(1915, Brit.), d; MY OLD DUTCH(1915, Brit.), d; DOORSTEPS(1916, Brit.), w; PLACE IN THE SUN, A(1916, Brit.), d&w; SPREADING DAWN, THE(1917), d
Misc. Silents
HARPER MYSTERY, THE(1913, Brit.), d; FOR HER PEOPLE(1914, Brit.), d; MURDOCK TRIAL, THE(1914, Brit.), d; SHEPHERD LASSIE OF ARGYLE, THE(1914, Brit.), d; SHOPGIRLS; OR, THE GREAT QUESTION(1914, Brit.), d; THROUGH THE VALLEY OF SHADOWS(1914, Brit.), d; LOST AND WON(1915, Brit.), d; REDEEMED(1915, Brit.), d; GRIM JUSTICE(1916, Brit.), d; SALLY IN OUR ALLEY(1916, Brit.), d; CASTLE(1917, Brit.), d; LIGHT WITHIN, THE(1918), d; WOMAN GOD SENT, THE(1920), d
Laurence Trimble
Misc. Silents
BRAWN OF THE NORTH(1922), d; LOVE MASTER, THE(1924), d; SUNDOWN(1924), d
Lawrence Trimble
BLANCHE(1971, Fr.); SUPERMAN(1978)
Silents
AUCTION BLOCK, THE(1917), d; DARLING MINE(1920), d, w; SILENT CALL, THE(1921), d
Misc. Silents
MINE OF MISSING MEN(1917), d; FOOL'S GOLD(1919), d; SPOTLIGHT SADIE(1919), d; WHITE FANG(1925), d; MY OLD DUTCH(1926), d
Terry Trimble
1984
SQUIZZY TAYLOR(1984, Aus.)
Heinrich Trimbur
5 SINNERS(1961, Ger.)
Ernest A. Trimingham
Silents
JACK, SAM AND PETE(1919, Brit.)
Romano Trina
BETTER A WIDOW(1969, Ital.), ed
Americo Trindade
VOYAGE OF SILENCE(1968, Fr.)
Tommy Trinder
ALMOST A HONEYMOON(1938, Brit.); SAVE A LITTLE SUNSHINE(1938, Brit.); SHE COULDN'T SAY NO(1939, Brit.); LAUGH IT OFF(1940, Brit.); THREE COCKEYED SAILORS(1940, Brit.); BELLS GO DOWN, THE(1943, Brit.); SOMEWHERE IN FRANCE(1943, Brit.); CHAMPAGNE CHARLIE(1944, Brit.); FIDDLERS THREE(1944,

Brit.); BITTER SPRINGS(1950, Aus.); YOU LUCKY PEOPLE(1955, Brit.), a, w; MAKE MINE A MILLION(1965, Brit.); THESE ARE THE DAMNED(1965, Brit.); BEAUTY JUNGLE, THE(1966, Brit.); BARRY MC KENZIE HOLDS HIS OWN(1975, Aus.)
John Trinian
ANY NUMBER CAN WIN(1963 Fr.), w
Arsenio Trinidad
COAST TO COAST(1980)
Jose Trinidad
CEREMONY, THE(1963, U.S./Span.)
Koko Trinidad
1984
PURPLE HEARTS(1984)
Solano Trinidade
MACUMBA LOVE(1960), ch
Hans Trinkaus
SOMEWHERE IN BERLIN(1949, E. Ger.)
Amanda Trinkle
Misc. Silents
MOTHER MACHREE(1922)
Victor Trinkler
SONG OF LIFE, THE(1931, Ger.), ph
Mabel Trinnear
Silents
SALAMANDER, THE(1915)
Jean-Louis Trintignant
AND GOD CREATED WOMAN(1957, Fr.); GAME OF TRUTH, THE(1961, Fr.); LES LIAISONS DANGEREUSES(1961, Fr./Ital.); VIOLENT SUMMER(1961, Fr./Ital.); SEVEN CAPITAL SINS(1962, Fr./Ital.); EASY LIFE, THE(1963, Ital.); FRENCH GAME, THE(1963, Fr.); NUTTY, NAUGHTY CHATEAU(1964, Fr./Ital.); MATA HARI(1965, Fr./Ital.); IS PARIS BURNING?(1966, U.S./Fr.); MAN AND A WOMAN, A(1966, Fr.); SLEEPING CAR MURDER THE(1966, Fr.); JOURNEY BENEATH THE DESERT(1967, Fr./Ital.); LES BICHES(1968, Fr.); TRANS-EUROP-EXPRESS(1968, Fr.); PLUCKED(1969, Fr./Ital.); Z(1969, Fr./Algeria); MAN WHO LIES, THE(1970, Czech./Fr.); MY NIGHT AT MAUD'S(1970, Fr.); CONFORMIST, THE(1971, Ital., Fr.); CROOK, THE(1971, Fr.); AND HOPE TO DIE(1972 Fr/US); WITHOUT APPARENT MOTIVE(1972, Fr.); FRENCH CONSPIRACY, THE(1973, Fr.); OUTSIDE MAN, THE(1973, U.S./FR.); FRENCH WAY, THE(1975, Fr.); DESERT OF THE TARTARS(1976 Fr./Ital./Iranian); MALEVIL(1981, Fr./Ger.); PASSION OF LOVE(1982, Ital./Fr.); BLOW TO THE HEART(1983, Ital.); CONFIDENTIALLY YOURS(1983, Fr.); LA NUIT DE VARENNES(1983, Fr./Ital.); UNDER FIRE(1983)
1984
LE BON PLAISIR(1984, Fr.)
Marie Trintignant
IT ONLY HAPPENS TO OTHERS(1971, Fr./Ital.)
Nadine Trintignant
OF FLESH AND BLOOD(1964, Fr./Ital.), ed; IT ONLY HAPPENS TO OTHERS(1971, Fr./Ital.), d&w
Trio Ascencio Del Rio
GUADALAJARA(1943, Mex.)
Trio Calaveras
THREE CABALLEROS, THE(1944); LEGEND OF A BANDIT, THE(1945, Mex.), m
Trio Calaveros
GUADALAJARA(1943, Mex.)
Trio Los Diamantes
LOS AUTOMATAS DE LA MUERTE(1960, Mex.); NEUTRON CONTRA EL DR. CARONTE(1962, Mex.); NEUTRON EL ENMASCARADO NEGRO(1962, Mex.)
Ann Triola
MOON OVER LAS VEGAS(1944)
Anne Triola
WITHOUT RESERVATIONS(1946); SLEEP, MY LOVE(1948); LULLABY OF BROADWAY, THE(1951)
Claudio Trionfi
DIRTY OUTLAWS, THE(1971, Ital.)
Claudio Trionfo
CHINA IS NEAR(1968, Ital.)
K. S. Tripathi
TARZAN GOES TO INDIA(1962, U.S./Brit./Switz.)
Joseph Tripi
NUNZIO(1978)
Irene Tripod
FEATHER, THE(1929, Brit.)
Silents
JOYOUS ADVENTURES OF ARISTIDE PUJOL, THE(1920, Brit.); SQUIBS, MP(1923, Brit.); SQUIBS' HONEYMOON(1926, Brit.)
Anthony Tripoli
INTERLUDE(1957)
Brick Tripp
EDDIE MACON'S RUN(1983)
Freddie Tripp
HOT ICE(1952, Brit.)
John Tripp
1984
ACT, THE(1984)
Paul Tripp
HANSEL AND GRETEL(1965, Ger.); SLEEPING BEAUTY(1965, Ger.); SNOW WHITE(1965, Ger.); CHRISMAS THAT ALMOST WASN'T. THE(1966, Ital.), a, w; SNOW WHITE AND ROSE RED(1966, Ger.)
Misc. Talkies
BIG BAD WOLF, THE(1968)
Paul Trippe
MY HANDS ARE CLAY(1948, Irish), w
Richard Tripper
GOOD NEWS(1947)
Charles Trippi
TRIPLE THREAT(1948)
Gaby Triquet
LES MISERABLES(1936, Fr.)

A. Trirard
APRES L'AMOUR(1948, Fr.), ph
George Trirogoff
UNHOLY ROLLERS(1972), ed; BUTCH AND SUNDANCE: THE EARLY DAYS(1979), ed; SATAN'S MISTRESS(1982), ed
Filomena Triscari
BODY HEAT(1981)
Jan Triska
DEATH OF TARZAN, THE(1968, Czech); REDS(1981); AMATEUR, THE(1982); OSTERMAN WEEKEND, THE(1983); UNCOMMON VALOR(1983)
1984
NOTHING LASTS FOREVER(1984); UNFAITHFULLY YOURS(1984); 2010(1984)
Elisabeth Trissenaar
MARRIAGE OF MARIA BRAUN, THE(1979, Ger.); IN A YEAR OF THIRTEEN MOONS(1980, Ger.)
1984
LOVE IN GERMANY, A(1984, Fr./Ger.)
Dorothy Tristan
KLUTE(1971); SCARECROW(1973); MAN ON A SWING(1974); SWASHBUCK-LER(1976); ROLLERCOASTER(1977); JAWS II(1978), w; CALIFORNIA DREAMING(1979)
Misc. Talkies
TRUCKIN'(1975)
Jean-Louis Tristan
MICHELLE(1970, Fr.); LE PETIT THEATRE DE JEAN RENOIR(1974, Fr.)
Jean-Louise Tristan
FRUSTRATIONS(1967, Fr./Ital.)
Una Tristram
Misc. Silents
WRECKER OF LIVES, THE(1914, Brit.)
Conrad Tritschler
WHITE ZOMBIE(1932), set d
Carlo Tritto
OPERATION KID BROTHER(1967, Ital.), w
Victor Trivas
KARAMAZOV(1931, Ger.), w, set d; SONG OF LIFE, THE(1931, Ger.), w; HELL ON EARTH(1934, Ger.), d; SONG OF RUSSIA(1943), w; THREE RUSSIAN GIRLS(1943), w; STRANGER THE(1946), w; WHERE THE SIDEWALK ENDS(1950), w; SECRET OF CONVICT LAKE, THE(1951), w; HEAD, THE(1961, Ger.), d&w
Barry Trivers
ROMANCE IN THE RAIN(1934), w; BABY FACE HARRINGTON(1935), w; LADY TUBBS(1935), w; MANHATTAN MOON(1935), w; NIGHT LIFE OF THE GODS(1935), w; STRANGE WIVES(1935), w; THREE KIDS AND A QUEEN(1935), w; BIG BROAD-CAST OF 1937, THE(1936), w; HERE COMES TROUBLE(1936), w; THREE CHEERS FOR LOVE(1936), w; BEHIND THE MIKE(1937), w; THAT'S MY STORY(1937), w; ARIZONA WILDCAT(1938), w; ARMY GIRL(1938), w; DESPERATE ADVENTURE, A(1938), w; BOY FRIEND(1939), w; CITY OF CHANCE(1940), w; DREAMING OUT LOUD(1940), w; GIRL IN 313(1940), w; RIVER'S END(1940), w; SOUTH OF SUEZ(1940), w; FLIGHT FROM DESTINY(1941), w; INTERNATIONAL SQUAD-RON(1941), w; WAGONS ROLL AT NIGHT, THE(1941), w; ARMY SURGEON(1942), w; FLYING TIGERS(1942), w; THERE'S SOMETHING ABOUT A SOLDIER(1943), w; WHAT A WOMAN!(1943), w; TALK ABOUT A LADY(1946), w; TARS AND SPARS(1946), w; INTRIGUE(1947), w; HONEYCHILE(1951), w; FLOOD TIDE(1958), w; LAST ESCAPE, THE(1970, Brit.), w
Paul Trivers
MEN IN HER LIFE, THE(1941), w
Thomas Trivier
CITY NEWS(1983)
Trixie
MY GAL LOVES MUSIC(1944)
Trixie the Dog
Silents
LONE EAGLE, THE(1927)
Jiri Trnka
EMPEROR AND THE NIGHTINGALE, THE(1949, Czech.), d, w; EMPEROR AND THE GOLEM, THE(1955, Czech.), cos; MIDSUMMERS NIGHT'S DREAM, A(1961, Czech.), p, d, w, art d
George Troast
LEGION OF THE DOOMED(1958), art d; SEVEN GUNS TO MESA(1958), art d; BUFFALO GUN(1961), art d; LASSIE'S GREAT ADVENTURE(1963), art d
George W. Troast
TRIAL OF BILLY JACK, THE(1974), art d
The Trocadero Girls
PRICE OF FOLLY, THE(1937, Brit.)
Bob Trocolor
BIG LEAGUER(1953)
Kenith Trodd
1984
FOUR DAYS IN JULY(1984), p
Kenneth Trodd
BRIMSTONE AND TREACLE(1982, Brit.), p
Troell
NEW LAND, THE(1973, Swed.), ph
Jan Troell
HERE'S YOUR LIFE(1968, Swed.), d, w, ph, ed; EMIGRANTS, THE(1972, Swed.), d, w, ph, ed; NEW LAND, THE(1973, Swed.), d, w, ed; ZANDY'S BRIDE(1974), d; HURRICANE(1979), d; FLIGHT OF THE EAGLE(1983, Swed.), d, ph, ed
Klaus Rifbjerg Troell
FLIGHT OF THE EAGLE(1983, Swed.), w
Al Troffey
DEVIL ON WHEELS, THE(1947), ed
Alex Troffey
SALUTE(1929), ed; CAMEO KIRBY(1930), ed; CISCO KID(1931), ed; GOLDIE(1931), ed; GOOD SPORT(1931), ed; CARELESS LADY(1932), ed; CHARLIE CHAN'S CHANCE(1932), ed; PAINTED WOMAN(1932), ed; CHARLIE CHAN'S GREATEST CASE(1933), ed; MY LIPS BETRAY(1933), ed; PLEASURE CRUISE(1933), ed; SECOND HAND WIFE(1933), ed; LOVE TIME(1934), ed; THREE ON A HONEY-MOON(1934), ed; CHARLIE CHAN AT THE CIRCUS(1936), ed; CHARLIE CHAN AT THE OPERA(1936), ed; CRIME OF DR. FORBES(1936), ed; FIFTEEN MAIDEN LANE(1936), ed; MY MARRIAGE(1936), ed; STAR FOR A NIGHT(1936), ed; BORN

RECKLESS(1937), ed; OFF TO THE RACES(1937), ed; THINK FAST, MR. MO-TO(1937), ed
Silents
RECOIL, THE(1924), ed; NONE BUT THE BRAVE(1928), ed; RILEY THE COP(1928), ed
Alexander Troffey
BLACK WATCH, THE(1929), ed; DANCERS, THE(1930), ed; NOT DAMAGED(1930), ed; TOO BUSY TO WORK(1932), ed; LIFE BEGINS AT 40(1935), ed; MUSIC IS MAGIC(1935), ed; DR. RHYTHM(1938), ed; MAN WHO WOULDN'T TALK, THE(1940), ed; MANHATTAN HEARTBEAT(1940), ed; CHARLIE CHAN IN RI-O(1941), ed; SMALL TOWN DEB(1941), ed; THEY MEET AGAIN(1941), ed; MAN IN THE TRUNK, THE(1942), ed; WHISPERING GHOSTS(1942), ed; MEET THE PEO-PLE(1944), ed
Nickolay Trofimov
WAR AND PEACE(1968, USSR)
Pier Luigi Troglio
FIST IN HIS POCKET(1968, Ital.)
Stefania Troglio
FIST IN HIS POCKET(1968, Ital.)
Jean Trognon
LAST ADVENTURE, THE(1968, Fr./Ital.)
Ray Troha
RETURN TO CAMPUS(1975)
Amalia Troiani
SANDRA(1966, Ital.); THAT SPLENDID NOVEMBER(1971, Ital./Fr.)
Obadan Troiani
OTHELLO(1955, U.S./Fr./Ital.), ph
Linda Troiano
LORDS OF FLATBUSH, THE(1974)
William G. Troiano
HORROR OF THE BLOOD MONSTERS zero(1970, U.S./Phil.), ph
William Troiano
DRACULA(THE DIRTY OLD MAN) (1969), ph; DEVIL'S MESSENGER, THE(1962 U.S./Swed.), ph; SLIME PEOPLE, THE(1963), ph; HANDLE WITH CARE(1964), ph; SHE FREAK(1967), ph
Troise and His Mandoliers
SUNSHINE AHEAD(1936, Brit.)
Dante Troisi
EYE OF THE NEEDLE, THE(1965, Ital./Fr.), w
Lino Troisi
ROME WANTS ANOTHER CAESAR(1974, Ital.); NO WAY OUT(1975, Ital./Fr.); STORY WITHOUT WORDS(1981, Ital.)
Antonio Troisio
MAGNIFICENT BANDITS, THE(1969, Ital./Span.), w
L. Troitskiy
MAGIC WEAVER, THE(1965, USSR)
S. Troitskiy
GORDEYEV FAMILY, THE(1961, U.S.S.R.); SANDU FOLLOWS THE SUN(1965, USSR)
S. Troitsky
OTHELLO(1960, U.S.S.R.)
Vaclav Trojan
MIDSUMMERS NIGHT'S DREAM, A(1961, Czech), m
Oberdan Trojani
HERCULES AGAINST THE MOON MEN(1965, Fr./Ital.), ph; NARCO MEN, THE(1969, Span./Ital.), ph
Jan Trojanswoki
ELISABETH OF AUSTRIA(1931, Ger.), ch
Susan Troldmyr
EDVARD MUNCH(1976, Norway/Swed.)
The Troles
GONKS GO BEAT(1965, Brit.)
Max Troll
HIGH CONQUEST(1947), w
Carola Trolle
Misc. Silents
FOUR AROUND THE WOMAN(1921, Ger.)
Leonard Trolley
PRELUDE TO FAME(1950, Brit.); COUNTESS FROM HONG KONG, A(1967, Brit.); MOHAMMAD, MESSENGER OF GOD(1976, Lebanon/Brit.); STUD, THE(1979, Brit.); AMIN-THE RISE AND FALL(1982, Kenya)
1984
CHAMPIONS(1984)
Anthony Trollope
MALACHI'S COVE(1973, Brit.), d&w
Sheldon Tromberg
REDEEMER, THE(1978), p
Giorgio Trombetti
MEDEA(1971, Ital./Fr./Ger.)
Marie Trombetti
BARBER OF SEVILLE, THE(1947, Ital.), p
Ugo Trombetti
BARBER OF SEVILLE, THE(1947, Ital.), p
Elia Trombly
Silents
ANTON THE TERRIBLE(1916)
Ilse Tromm
SONG OF NORWAY(1970)
James Tromp
Silents
ARIZONA KID, THE(1929)
Marilee Troncone
LEGACY OF BLOOD(1978)
Misc. Talkies
LEGACY OF HORROR(1978)
Bernard Tronczyk
LOULOU(1980, Fr.)

Barik Trone
LOVED ONE, THE(1965)
Bud Trone
ADAM AT 6 A.M.(1970)
Michael Tronick
1984
STREETS OF FIRE(1984), ed
Robert Tronson
MAN AT THE CARLTON TOWER(1961, Brit.), d; MAN DETAINED(1961, Brit.), d; NUMBER SIX(1962, Brit.), d; FAREWELL PERFORMANCE(1963, Brit.), d; TRAITORS, THE(1963, Brit.), d; RING OF SPIES(1964, Brit.), d; NEVER BACK LOSERS(1967, Brit.), d; ON THE RUN(1967, Brit.), d
Eugene Troobnick
CALIFORNIA SPLIT(1974); PATERNITY(1981)
Gene Troobnick
HARVEY MIDDLEMAN, FIREMAN(1965); FUNNY LADY(1975)
Margot Trooger
CITY OF SECRETS(1963, Ger.); HYPNOSIS(1966, Ger./Sp./Ital.); TRAITOR'S GATE(1966, Brit./Ger.); FEMMINA(1968 Fr./Ital./Ger.); HEIDI(1968, Aust.)
U.S. Army Parachute Troops
OBJECTIVE, BURMA!(1945), tech adv
Lester Troos
LITTLE FUGITIVE, THE(1953), ed
Jack Dunn Trop
ORDERED TO LOVE(1963, Ger.), w; PLEASE, NOT NOW!(1963, Fr./Ital.), w; SECRET OF MAGIC ISLAND, THE(1964, Fr./Ital.), p, w
Shelley Trope
WILD SEASON(1968, South Africa)
Tripi Trope
Misc. Talkies
TELL ME THAT YOU LOVE ME(1983), d
Ferdinando Tropea
SCHOOLGIRL DIARY(1947, Ital.), ed
Paul Tropea
SAILOR WHO FELL FROM GRACE WITH THE SEA, THE(1976, Brit.)
Astri Trorvik
HIGH(1968, Can.)
Guy Trosper
I'LL WAIT FOR YOU(1941), w; CROSSROADS(1942), w; EYES IN THE NIGHT(1942), w; GIRL TROUBLE(1942), w; STRATTON STORY, THE(1949), w; DEVIL'S DOORWAY(1950), w; INSIDE STRAIGHT(1951), w; PRIDE OF ST. LOUIS, THE(1952), w; STEEL CAGE, THE(1954), w; AMERICANO, THE(1955), w; MANY RIVERS TO CROSS(1955), w; GIRL HE LEFT BEHIND, THE(1956), w; JAILHOUSE ROCK(1957), w; DARBY'S RANGERS(1958), w; THUNDER IN THE SUN(1959), w; ONE-EYED JACKS(1961), w; BIRDMAN OF ALCATRAZ(1962), p, w; SPY WHO CAME IN FROM THE COLD, THE(1965, Brit.), w
Carol Trost
WHICH WAY IS UP?(1977)
Ed Trostle
Misc. Talkies
MARK TWAIN, AMERICAN(1976)
James Trotman
1984
GOODBYE PEOPLE, THE(1984)
William Trotman
FIREPOWER(1979, Brit.)
Karen Trott
RETURN OF THE SECAUCUS SEVEN(1980)
Lamar Trott
GENTLE JULIA(1936), w
Walter Trott
$(DOLLARS)(1971)
Charles I. Trotter
STUDENT BODIES(1981)
John Scott Trotter
RHYTHM ON THE RIVER(1940); KISS THE BOYS GOODBYE(1941); ABIE'S IRISH ROSE(1946), m
Kate Trotter
THRESHOLD(1983, Can.)
Laura Trotter
CITY OF THE WALKING DEAD(1983, Span./Ital.)
1984
RUSH(1984, Ital.)
Lamar Trotti
MAN WHO DARED, THE(1933), w; CALL IT LUCK(1934), w; HOLD THAT GIRL(1934), w; JUDGE PRIEST(1934), w; WILD GOLD(1934), w; YOU CAN'T BUY EVERYTHING(1934), w; BACHELOR OF ARTS(1935), w; LIFE BEGINS AT 40(1935), w; STEAMBOAT ROUND THE BEND(1935), w; THIS IS THE LIFE(1935), w; $10 RAISE(1935), w; CAN THIS BE DIXIE?(1936), w; CAREER WOMAN(1936), w; COUNTRY BEYOND, THE(1936), w; FIRST BABY(1936), w; PEPPER(1936), w; RAMONA(1936), w; SLAVE SHIP(1937), w; THIS IS MY AFFAIR(1937), w; WIFE, DOCTOR AND NURSE(1937), w; ALEXANDER'S RAGTIME BAND(1938), w; BARONESS AND THE BUTLER, THE(1938), w; GATEWAY(1938), w; IN OLD CHICAGO(1938), w; KENTUCKY(1938), w; DRUMS ALONG THE MOHAWK(1939), w; STORY OF ALEXANDER GRAHAM BELL, THE(1939), w; YOUNG MR. LINCOLN(1939), w; BRIGHAM YOUNG–FRONTIERSMAN(1940), w; HUDSON'S BAY(1940), w; BELLE STARR(1941), w; TALES OF MANHATTAN(1942), w; THUNDER BIRDS(1942), p, w; TO THE SHORES OF TRIPOLI(1942), w; GUADALCANAL DIARY(1943), w; IMMORTAL SERGEANT, THE(1943), p, w; OX-BOW INCIDENT, THE(1943), p, w; WILSON(1944), w; BELL FOR ADANO, A(1945), p, w; COLONEL EFFINGHAM'S RAID(1945), p; RAZOR'S EDGE, THE(1946), w; CAPTAIN FROM CASTILE(1947), p, w; MOTHER WORE TIGHTS(1947), p, w; WALLS OF JERICHO(1948), p, w; WHEN MY BABY SMILES AT ME(1948), w; YELLOW SKY(1948), p, w; YOU'RE MY EVERYTHING(1949), p, w; AMERICAN GUERRILLA IN THE PHILIPPINES, AN(1950), p, w; CHEAPER BY THE DOZEN(1950), p, w; MY BLUE HEAVEN(1950), w; AS YOUNG AS YOU FEEL(1951), p, w; I'D CLIMB THE HIGHEST MOUNTAIN(1951), p, w; O. HENRY'S FULL HOUSE(1952), w; STARS AND STRIPES FOREVER(1952), p, w; WITH A SONG IN MY HEART(1952), p, w; THERE'S NO BUSINESS LIKE SHOW BUSINESS(1954), w; JACKALS, THE(1967, South Africa), w

Adolf Trotz
ELISABETH OF AUSTRIA(1931, Ger.), d; RASPUTIN(1932, Ger.), d
Troubetskoy
SAVAGE BRIGADE(1948, Fr.)
Maria Troubetskoy
MERRY WIDOW, THE(1934)
Youcca Troubetskoy
MADAME SATAN(1930)
M. Troubetsky
WORDS AND MUSIC(1929)
Youcca Troubetzkoy
HIS GLORIOUS NIGHT(1929); CHASING RAINBOWS(1930); VIRTUOUS SIN, THE(1930)
Silents
BEAUTIFUL CHEAT, THE(1926)
Misc. Silents
FLOWER OF NIGHT(1925)
Andrea Troubridge
THIS ENGLAND(1941, Brit.); TIME OF HIS LIFE, THE(1955, Brit.); HOUSE IN THE WOODS, THE(1957, Brit.)
Adolfo Trouche
Silents
NERO(1922, U.S./Ital.)
John Troughton
TALK OF HOLLYWOOD, THE(1929)
Patrick Troughton
ESCAPE(1948, Brit.); HAMLET(1948, Brit.); CHANCE OF A LIFETIME(1950, Brit.); TREASURE ISLAND(1950, Brit.); HER PANELLED DOOR(1951, Brit.); FRANCHISE AFFAIR, THE(1952, Brit.); WHITE CORRIDORS(1952, Brit.); BLACK KNIGHT, THE(1954); RICHARD III(1956, Brit.); CURSE OF FRANKENSTEIN, THE(1957, Brit.); MOONRAKER, THE(1958, Brit.); PHANTOM OF THE OPERA, THE(1962, Brit.); JASON AND THE ARGONAUTS(1963, Brit.); GORGON, THE(1964, Brit.); BLACK TORMENT, THE(1965, Brit.); VIKING QUEEN, THE(1967, Brit.); SCARS OF DRACULA, THE(1970, Brit.); FRANKENSTEIN AND THE MONSTER FROM HELL(1974, Brit.); OMEN, THE(1976); SINBAD AND THE EYE OF THE TIGER(1977, U.S./Brit.); HITCH IN TIME, A(1978, Brit.)
Clovis Trouille
OH! CALCUTTA!(1972), w
Cecil Trouncer
PYGMALION(1938, Brit.); DULCIMER STREET(1948, Brit.); OUTSIDER, THE(1949, Brit.); SARABAND(1949, Brit.); WHILE THE SUN SHINES(1950, Brit.); LADY WITH A LAMP, THE(1951, Brit.); MAGIC BOX, THE(1952, Brit.); PICKWICK PAPERS, THE(1952, Brit.); ISN'T LIFE WONDERFUL!(1953, Brit.); WEAK AND THE WICKED, THE(1954, Brit.)
Ruth Trouncer
NO SMOKING(1955, Brit.); SMALL HOTEL(1957, Brit.); FAMILY WAY, THE(1966, Brit.); MAN WHO HAD POWER OVER WOMEN, THE(1970, Brit.); MAN WHO HAUNTED HIMSELF, THE(1970, Brit.); THERE'S A GIRL IN MY SOUP(1970, Brit.)
Bobby Troup
SMART POLITICS(1948), m/l; MR. IMPERIUM(1951); HIGH COST OF LOVING, THE(1958); FIVE PENNIES, THE(1959); GENE KRUPA STORY, THE(1959); FIRST TO FIGHT(1967); NUMBER ONE(1969); M(1970)
Ronne Troup
TROUBLE WITH ANGELS, THE(1966)
Al Troupe
MICROWAVE MASSACRE(1983)
Pina Troupe
MAN ABOUT TOWN(1939)
Su Yee Troupe
LIEUTENANT DARING, RN(1935, Brit.)
Thomas Troupe
BIG FISHERMAN, THE(1959)
Tom Troupe
SOFI(1967), a, w; DEVIL'S BRIGADE, THE(1968); CHE!(1969); KELLY'S HEROES(1970, U.S./Yugo.); MAKING IT(1971)
Dink Trout
UNDER YOUR SPELL(1936); CINDERELLA SWINGS IT(1942); GILDERSLEEVE'S BAD DAY(1943); DOUGHGIRLS, THE(1944); SUDAN(1945); NOTORIOUS(1946); ALICE IN WONDERLAND(1951)
Francis "Dink" Trout
SCATTERGOOD BAINES(1941); SCATTERGOOD PULLS THE STRINGS(1941)
Jimi Trout
LADY AND THE TRAMP(1955), art d
Tom Trout
BETWEEN TWO WOMEN(1944); MAIN STREET AFTER DARK(1944); ANCHORS AWEIGH(1945); HER HIGHNESS AND THE BELLBOY(1945); MERTON OF THE MOVIES(1947); SONG OF THE THIN MAN(1947); TENTH AVENUE ANGEL(1948); KID FROM TEXAS, THE(1950); PALOMINO, THE(1950)
Skip Troutman
HAMMER(1972), art d
Armando Trovaioli
WOMAN OF THE RIVER(1954, Fr./Ital.), m; LET'S TALK ABOUT WOMEN(1964, Fr./Ital.), m; DEVIL IN LOVE, THE(1968, Ital.), m; DROP DEAD, MY LOVE(1968, Italy), m; PIZZA TRIANGLE, THE(1970, Ital./Span.), m; PRIEST'S WIFE, THE(1971, Ital./Fr.), m; MOST WONDERFUL EVENING OF MY LIFE, THE(1972, Ital./Fr.), m; ITALIAN CONNECTION, THE(1973, U.S./Ital./Ger.), m; ROCCO PAPALEO(1974, Ital./Fr.), m; DUCH IN ORANGE SAUCE(1976, Ital.), m; SCENT OF A WOMAN(1976, Ital.), m; SPECIAL DAY, A(1977, Ital./Can.), m
Trovajoli
UNFAITHFULS, THE(1960, Ital.), m; SEVEN GOLDEN MEN(1969, Fr./Ital./Span.), md
Armando Trovajoli
TWO NIGHTS WITH CLEOPATRA(1953, Ital.), m; HERCULES' PILLS(1960, Ital.), m; ATOM AGE VAMPIRE(1961, Ital.), m; MAGIC WORLD OF TOPO GIGIO, THE(1961, Ital.), m; TWO WOMEN(1961, Ital./Fr.), m; BOCCACCIO '70(1962/Ital./Fr.), m; WARRIORS FIVE(1962), m; GIANT OF METROPOLIS, THE(1963, Ital.), m; HERCULES AND THE CAPTIVE WOMEN(1963, Fr./Ital.), m; HERCULES IN THE HAUNTED WORLD(1964, Ital.), m; MARRIAGE–ITALIAN STYLE(1964, Fr./Ital.), m; YESTERDAY, TODAY, AND TOMORROW(1964, Ital./Fr.), a, m; CASANOVA '70(1965, Ital.), m; DAY IN COURT, A(1965, Ital.), m; HIGH INFIDELITY(1965, Fr./Ital.), m; ITALIA-

NO BRAVA GENTE(1965, Ital./USSR), m; MAGNIFICENT CUCKOLD, THE(1965, Fr./Ital.), m; MYTH, THE(1965, Ital.), m; ENGAGEMENT ITALIANO(1966, Fr./Ital.), m; LA VISITA(1966, Ital./Fr.), m; OPIATE '67(1967, Fr./Ital.), m; ANYONE CAN PLAY(1968, Ital.), m; TREASURE OF SAN GENNARO(1968, Fr./Ital./Ger.), m; SEVEN GOLDEN MEN(1969, Fr./Ital./Span.), m; MOTIVE WAS JEALOUSY, THE(1970 Ital./Span.), m; STRANGE SHADOWS IN AN EMPTY ROOM(1977, Can./Ital.), m; VIVA ITALIA(1978, Ital.), m; WIFEMISTRESS(1979, Ital.), m; PASSION OF LOVE(1982, Ital./Fr.), m

Leo Trover
LOST SQUADRON, THE(1932), ph

Bob Trow
HUNGRY WIVES(1973)

Buster Trow
Silents
WHAT HAPPENED TO ROSA?(1921)

George Swift Trow
SAVAGES(1972), w

Karinne Trow
COUSINS IN LOVE(1982), m

Robert Trow
THERE'S ALWAYS VANILLA(1972)

Tony Trow
BY DESIGN(1982), ed

Andrea Trowbridge
PRIME MINISTER, THE(1941, Brit.)

Charles Trowbridge
DAMAGED LOVE(1931); I TAKE THIS WOMAN(1931); SECRET CALL, THE(1931); SILENCE(1931); CALM YOURSELF(1935); IT'S IN THE AIR(1935); MAD LOVE(1935); MURDER MAN(1935); RENDEZVOUS(1935); AFTER THE THIN MAN(1936); EXCLUSIVE STORY(1936); GARDEN MURDER CASE, THE(1936); GORGEOUS HUSSY, THE(1936); GREAT ZIEGFELD, THE(1936); LIBELED LADY(1936); LOVE ON THE RUN(1936); MOONLIGHT MURDER(1936); ROBIN HOOD OF EL DORADO(1936); SPEED(1936); WE WENT TO COLLEGE(1936); WIFE VERSUS SECRETARY(1936); ALCATRAZ ISLAND(1937); CAPTAINS COURAGEOUS(1937); DANGEROUS NUMBER(1937); DAY AT THE RACES, A(1937); ESPIONAGE(1937); EVER SINCE EVE(1937); EXILED TO SHANGHAI(1937); FIT FOR A KING(1937); SATURDAY'S HEROES(1937); SEA RACKETEERS(1937); THAT CERTAIN WOMAN(1937); THAT'S MY STORY(1937); THEY GAVE HIM A GUN(1937); THIRTEENTH CHAIR, THE(1937); ANGELS WITH DIRTY FACES(1938); CITY GIRL(1938); COLLEGE SWING(1938); CRIME RING(1938); CRIME SCHOOL(1938); FOUR'S A CROWD(1938); GANG BULLETS(1938); GANGS OF NEW YORK(1938); HOLIDAY(1938); INVISIBLE MENACE, THE(1938); KENTUCKY(1938); LAST EXPRESS, THE(1938); LITTLE TOUGH GUY(1938); MAD MISS MANTON, THE(1938); MEN WITH WINGS(1938); NANCY DREW-DETECTIVE(1938); PATIENT IN ROOM 18, THE(1938); RACKET BUSTERS(1938); SUBMARINE PATROL(1938); THANKS FOR EVERYTHING(1938); BOY TROUBLE(1939); CAFE SOCIETY(1939); CONFESSIONS OF A NAZI SPY(1939); DISPUTED PASSAGE(1939); EACH DAWN I DIE(1939); HOMICIDE BUREAU(1939); JOE AND ETHEL TURP CALL ON THE PRESIDENT(1939); KING OF CHINATOWN(1939); KING OF THE UNDERWORLD(1939); LADY OF THE TROPICS(1939); LADY'S FROM KENTUCKY, THE(1939); LET US LIVE(1939); MAN THEY COULD NOT HANG, THE(1939); MUTINY ON THE BLACKHAWK(1939); ON TRIAL(1939); PRIDE OF THE NAVY(1939); RISKY BUSINESS(1939); SERGEANT MADDEN(1939); STORY OF ALEXANDER GRAHAM BELL, THE(1939); SWANEE RIVER(1939); TROPIC FURY(1939); CHARLIE CHAN AT THE WAX MUSEUM(1940); CHEROKEE STRIP(1940); DR. KILDARE GOES HOME(1940); EDISON, THE MAN(1940); FATAL HOUR, THE(1940); FIGHTING 69TH, THE(1940); HOUSE OF THE SEVEN GABLES, THE(1940); I TAKE THIS WOMAN(1940); JOHNNY APOLLO(1940); KNUTE ROCKNE-ALL AMERICAN(1940); MAN WITH NINE LIVES, THE(1940); MUMMY'S HAND, THE(1940); MY LOVE CAME BACK(1940); OUR TOWN(1940); SAILOR'S LADY(1940); SON OF MONTE CRISTO(1940); TRAIL OF THE VIGILANTES(1940); VIRGINIA CITY(1940); BELLE STARR(1941); BLUE, WHITE, AND PERFECT(1941); DRESSED TO KILL(1941); GREAT GUNS(1941); GREAT LIE, THE(1941); GREAT MR. NOBODY, THE(1941); MEET JOHN DOE(1941); NURSE'S SECRET, THE(1941); RAGS TO RICHES(1941); SERGEANT YORK(1941); STRANGE ALIBI(1941); TOO MANY BLONDES(1941); WE GO FAST(1941); HURRICANE SMITH(1942); OVER MY DEAD BODY(1942); SWEETHEART OF THE FLEET(1942); TEN GENTLEMEN FROM WEST POINT(1942); TENNESSEE JOHNSON(1942); THAT OTHER WOMAN(1942); WAKE ISLAND(1942); WHO IS HOPE SCHUYLER?(1942); MADAME CURIE(1943); MISSION TO MOSCOW(1943); SALUTE TO THE MARINES(1943); SHE'S FOR ME(1943); SWEET ROSIE O'GRADY(1943); WINTERTIME(1943); FACES IN THE FOG(1944); HEAVENLY DAYS(1944); HEY, ROOKIE(1944); STORY OF DR. WASSELL, THE(1944); SUMMER STORM(1944); WING AND A PRAYER(1944); COLONEL EFFINGHAM'S RAID(1945); MILDRED PIERCE(1945); THEY WERE EXPENDABLE(1945); DON'T GAMBLE WITH STRANGERS(1946); HOODLUM SAINT, THE(1946); MR. DISTRICT ATTORNEY(1946); RED DRAGON, THE(1946); SECRET OF THE WHISTLER(1946); SHOCK(1946); SMOOTH AS SILK(1946); UNDERCURRENT(1946); VALLEY OF THE ZOMBIES(1946); BLACK GOLD(1947); HER HUSBAND'S AFFAIRS(1947); HONEYMOON(1947); KEY WITNESS(1947); PRIVATE AFFAIRS OF BEL AMI, THE(1947); SEA OF GRASS, THE(1947); SECRET LIFE OF WALTER MITTY, THE(1947); SONG OF MY HEART(1947); TARZAN AND THE HUNTRESS(1947); TYCOON(1947); HOLLOW TRIUMPH(1948); PALEFACE, THE(1948); STAGE STRUCK(1948); BAD BOY(1949); MR. SOFT TOUCH(1949); SUN COMES UP, THE(1949); PEGGY(1950); UNMASKED(1950); WHEN WILLIE COMES MARCHING HOME(1950); WOMAN OF DISTINCTION, A(1950); BUSHWHACKERS, THE(1952); HOODLUM EMPIRE(1952); WINGS OF EAGLES, THE(1957); LAST HURRAH, THE(1958)
Silents
PROHIBITION(1915); ETERNAL MAGDALENE, THE(1919)
Misc. Silents
FIGHT, THE(1915); ISLAND WIVES(1922)

Deborah Trowbridge
VERY NATURAL THING, A(1974)

Douglas Trowbridge
SHOOT TO KILL(1947)

Fred Trowbridge
PLAYMATES(1941); GILDERSLEEVE'S BAD DAY(1943)

Jean Trowbridge
ZELIG(1983)

Jesse Trowbridge
VERY NATURAL THING, A(1974)

Lady Trowbridge
GOLDEN CAGE, THE(1933, Brit.), w; HIS GRACE GIVES NOTICE(1933, Brit.), w

Gisela Trowe
AFFAIR BLUM, THE(1949, Ger.); LOST ONE, THE(1951, Ger.)

Jose Chavez Trowe
RUN FOR THE SUN(1956); LAST OF THE FAST GUNS, THE(1958)

Jose Trowe
SIERRA BARON(1958); VILLA!(1958)

Stanford Trowell
PERSECUTION AND ASSASSINATION OF JEAN-PAUL MARAT AS PERFORMED BY THE INMATES OF THE ASYLUM OF CHARENTON UNDER THE DIRECTION OF THE MARQUIS DE SADE, THE(1967, Brit.)

Chad Trower
SERGEANT MURPHY(1938)

Bill Troy
ADVANCE TO THE REAR(1964)

Doris Troy
THAT'S THE WAY OF THE WORLD(1975)

Eleanor Troy
NOTHING SACRED(1937)

Elinor Troy
FLEET'S IN, THE(1942); LADY OF BURLESQUE(1943); LET'S FACE IT(1943); LOST IN A HAREM(1944)

Elizabeth Troy
LOVE, HONOR AND OH, BABY(1940), w

Hector Troy
BADGE 373(1973); BANG THE DRUM SLOWLY(1973); SUPER COPS, THE(1974); EYES OF LAURA MARS(1978); ON THE YARD(1978); PATERNITY(1981)
1984
MUPPETS TAKE MANHATTAN, THE(1984)

Helen Troy
HUMAN CARGO(1936); SONG AND DANCE MAN, THE(1936); BETWEEN TWO WOMEN(1937); BIG CITY(1937); BROADWAY MELODY OF '38(1937); MANNEQUIN(1937); THOROUGHBREDS DON'T CRY(1937); KID NIGHTINGALE(1939); VILLAGE BARN DANCE(1940)

Louise Troy
ROOGIE'S BUMP(1954); SWIMMER, THE(1968); YOURS, MINE AND OURS(1968)

Sid Troy
SHE GETS HER MAN(1945)

Una Troy
SHE DIDN'T SAY NO!(1962, Brit.), w

Helen Troya
CRY OF THE CITY(1948)

Mark Troyanovskiy
DAY THE EARTH FROZE, THE(1959, Fin./USSR); LULLABY(1961, USSR); MAGIC VOYAGE OF SINBAD, THE(1962, USSR); HOUSE ON THE FRONT LINE, THE(1963, USSR); NIGHT BEFORE CHRISTMAS, A(1963, USSR)

M. G. Troyanovsky
CHILDHOOD OF MAXIM GORKY(1938, Russ.)

M. Troyanovsky
ON HIS OWN(1939, USSR); OTHELLO(1960, U.S.S.R.)

Henri Troyat
MOUNTAIN, THE(1956), w; BIG CHIEF, THE(1960, Fr.), w

Henry Troyat
FIRE IN THE STRAW(1943), w

Debra Troyer
1984
ICE PIRATES, THE(1984); PHILADELPHIA EXPERIMENT, THE(1984)

Gabi Trsek
ILLUMINATIONS(1976, Aus.)

Vane Truant
Misc. Silents
FIGHTING FOR JUSTICE(1924)

Jimmie Truax
Silents
TIPPED OFF(1923)

John Truax
HE LAUGHED LAST(1956); WRONG MAN, THE(1956); FUZZY PINK NIGHTGOWN, THE(1957); CURSE OF THE UNDEAD(1959); GREAT RACE, THE(1965)

Maud Truax
MAN OF THE WORLD(1931)

Maude Truax
TWO AGAINST THE WORLD(1932); I HAVE LIVED(1933); DANCING MAN(1934); FUGITIVE LADY(1934); DANTE'S INFERNO(1935); LONE WOLF RETURNS, THE(1936)
Silents
MANHATTAN KNIGHTS(1928)
Misc. Silents
TEN MODERN COMMANDMENTS(1927)

Sarah Truax
Silents
JORDAN IS A HARD ROAD(1915)

Michael Trubshawe
DANCE HALL(1950, Brit.); ENCORE(1951, Brit.); LAVENDER HILL MOB, THE(1951, Brit.); THEY WERE NOT DIVIDED(1951, Brit.); BRANDY FOR THE PARSON(1952, Brit.); MAGIC BOX, THE(1952, Brit.); PROMOTER, THE(1952, Brit.); SOMETHING MONEY CAN'T BUY(1952, Brit.); TITFIELD THUNDERBOLT, THE(1953, Brit.); TONIGHT AT 8:30(1953, Brit.); RAINBOW JACKET, THE(1954, Brit.); YOU LUCKY PEOPLE(1955, Brit.); PRIVATE'S PROGRESS(1956, Brit.); 23 PACES TO BAKER STREET(1956); DOCTOR AT LARGE(1957, Brit.); NOVEL AFFAIR, A(1957, Brit.); RISING OF THE MOON, THE(1957, Ireland); I ACCUSE!(1958, Brit.); LAW AND DISORDER(1958, Brit.); GIDEON OF SCOTLAND YARD(1959, Brit.); ORDERS ARE ORDERS(1959, Brit.); SCENT OF MYSTERY(1960); GUNS OF NAVARONE, THE(1961); BEST OF ENEMIES, THE(1962); OPERATION SNATCH(1962, Brit.); MOUSE ON THE MOON, THE(1963, Brit.); REACH FOR GLORY(1963, Brit.); HARD DAY'S NIGHT, A(1964, Brit.); PINK PANTHER, THE(1964); RUNAWAY(1964, Brit.); AMOROUS ADVENTURES OF MOLL FLANDERS, THE(1965); THOSE MAGNIFICENT MEN IN THEIR FLYING MACHINES; OR HOW I FLEW FROM LONDON

TO PARIS IN 25 HOURS AND 11 MINUTES(1965, Brit.); SPY WITH A COLD NOSE, THE(1966, Brit.); BEDAZZLED(1967, Brit.); DANDY IN ASPIC, A(1968, Brit.); SALT & PEPPER(1968, Brit.); THOSE DARING YOUNG MEN IN THEIR JAUNTY JALOPIES(1969, Fr./Brit./ Ital.); MAGIC CHRISTIAN, THE(1970, Brit.); RISE AND RISE OF MICHAEL RIMMER, THE(1970, Brit.)

A. Truby
VIENNA WALTZES(1961, Aust.)

Albert Truby
TRIAL, THE(1948, Aust.)

Gondrano Trucchi
VITELLONI(1956, Ital./Fr.)

Orestes Trucco
VIOLATED LOVE(1966, Arg.), p; CURIOUS DR. HUMPP(1967, Arg.), p

Jose Truchado
GLASS SPHINX, THE(1968, Egypt/Ital./Span.)

Jose Truchado, Jr.
1984
YELLOW HAIR AND THE FORTRESS OF GOLD(1984)

Alex Truchy
LA MARSEILLAISE(1938, Fr.)

Margaret Trudeau
1984
KINGS AND DESPERATE MEN(1984, Brit.)

Alice True
Silents
PEACOCK FAN(1929)

Bess True
Misc. Silents
HEARTBOUND(1925)

Garrison True
DAY OF THE ANIMALS(1977)

Pauline True
DESIRABLE(1934); DOCTOR MONICA(1934); HERE COMES THE NAVY(1934)

Christofer Trueblood
Misc. Talkies
CANDY SNATCHERS, THE(1974)

Guerdon Trueblood
DAY THE HOTLINE GOT HOT, THE(1968, Fr./Span.), w; LAST HARD MEN, THE(1976), w; JAWS 3-D(1983), w
Misc. Talkies
CANDY SNATCHERS, THE(1974), d

John Truel
MOONLIGHT IN VERMONT(1943); PATRICK THE GREAT(1945)

John Trueman
YOUNG BESS(1953)

Paula Trueman
CRIME WITHOUT PASSION(1934); ONE FOOT IN HEAVEN(1941); PAINT YOUR WAGON(1969); ANDERSON TAPES, THE(1971); HOMEBODIES(1974); STEPFORD WIVES, THE(1975); OUTLAW JOSEY WALES, THE(1976); ANNIE HALL(1977); CAN'T STOP THE MUSIC(1980); ZELIG(1983)
1984
MRS. SOFFEL(1984); ULTIMATE SOLUTION OF GRACE QUIGLEY, THE(1984)

Fred Truesdale
Silents
ARRIVAL OF PERPETUA, THE(1915)

Howard Truesdale
LONG, LONG TRAIL, THE(1929)
Silents
EMBARRASSMENT OF RICHES, THE(1918); NO TRESPASSING(1922); GO WEST(1925); JAZZ GIRL, THE(1926); SINGED(1927)
Misc. Silents
SUSPENCE(1919); WHAT WOMEN WANT(1920); WONDERFUL THING, THE(1921); FRENCH HEELS(1922)

Frank Truesdell
Misc. Silents
AGE OF DESIRE, THE(1923)

Fred C. Truesdell
Misc. Silents
GREAT VICTORY, WILSON OR THE KAISER?, THE(1918); WHY GERMANY MUST PAY(1919)

Fred Truesdell
Silents
COTTON KING, THE(1915); OUTWITTED(1917)
Misc. Silents
SHADOWS(1919)

Frederick Truesdell
Silents
PLEASURE MAD(1923)
Misc. Silents
MARRIAGE MARKET, THE(1917); HEARTS OF LOVE(1918); MAN'S WORLD, A(1918)

Frederick C. Truesdell
Silents
MAN WHO FORGOT, THE(1917)

Howard Truesdell
PAINTED FACES(1929)
Silents
PRETENDERS, THE(1916); ASHES OF VENGEANCE(1923); OUT OF LUCK(1923); RIDE FOR YOUR LIFE(1924); DUDE COWBOY, THE(1926); LAWLESS LEGION, THE(1929)
Misc. Silents
COME-BACK, THE(1916); CORNER IN COTTON, A(1916), a, d; PURPLE LADY, THE(1916); BOLSHEVISM ON TRIAL(1919); COLUMBUS(1923); NIGHT MESSAGE, THE(1924); STRONGER WILL, THE(1928)

June Truesdell
ACCUSED, THE(1949), w

Barry Truex
BENNY GOODMAN STORY, THE(1956); ROCKABILLY BABY(1957); DRAGSTRIP RIOT(1958)

Ernest Truex
TRUE TO LIFE(1943); IF I HAD A MILLION(1932); WARRIOR'S HUSBAND, THE(1933); WHISTLING IN THE DARK(1933); EVERYBODY DANCE(1936, Brit.); ADVENTURES OF MARCO POLO, THE(1938); FRESHMAN YEAR(1938); MAMA RUNS WILD(1938); START CHEERING(1938); SWING, SISTER, SWING(1938); SWING THAT CHEER(1938); AMBUSH(1939); BACHELOR MOTHER(1939); ISLAND OF LOST MEN(1939); IT'S A WONDERFUL WORLD(1939); LITTLE ACCIDENT(1939); THESE GLAMOUR GIRLS(1939); UNDER-PUP, THE(1939); ADVENTURE IN DIAMONDS(1940); CALLING ALL HUSBANDS(1940); CHRISTMAS IN JULY(1940); DANCE, GIRL, DANCE(1940); HIS GIRL FRIDAY(1940); LILLIAN RUSSELL(1940); LITTLE ORVIE(1940); SLIGHTLY HONORABLE(1940); DON'T GET PERSONAL(1941); GAY VAGABOND, THE(1941); TILLIE THE TOILER(1941); UNEXPECTED UNCLE(1941); WE GO FAST(1941); AFFAIRS OF MARTHA, THE(1942); PRIVATE BUCKAROO(1942); STAR SPANGLED RHYTHM(1942); TWIN BEDS(1942); YOU'RE TELLING ME(1942); CRYSTAL BALL, THE(1943); FIRED WIFE(1943); RHYTHM OF THE ISLANDS(1943); SLEEPY LAGOON(1943); THIS IS THE ARMY(1943); CHIP OFF THE OLD BLOCK(1944); HER PRIMITIVE MAN(1944); MEN IN HER DIARY(1945); PAN-AMERICANA(1945); CLUB HAVANA(1946); LIFE WITH BLONDIE(1946); NIGHT IN PARADISE, A(1946); ALWAYS TOGETHER(1947); GIRL FROM MANHATTAN(1948); LEATHER SAINT, THE(1956); ALL MINE TO GIVE(1957); TWILIGHT FOR THE GODS(1958); FLUFFY(1965)
Silents
GOOD LITTLE DEVIL, A(1914); WHEN ROME RULED(1914); ARTIE, THE MILLIONAIRE KID(1916); GOOD-BYE, BILL(1919)
Misc. Silents
CAPRICE(1913); QUEST OF THE SACRED GEM, THE(1914); COME ON IN(1918); OH, YOU WOMEN!(1919); SIX CYLINDER LOVE(1923)

Lizanne Truex
OKLAHOMA(1955)

Philip Truex
THIS IS THE ARMY(1943); TROUBLE WITH HARRY, THE(1955)

Eva Truffaut
WILD CHILD, THE(1970, Fr.); TWO ENGLISH GIRLS(1972, Fr.); SMALL CHANGE(1976, Fr.)

Francois Truffaut
FOUR HUNDRED BLOWS, THE(1959), p&d, w; JULES AND JIM(1962, Fr.), d, w; SHOOT THE PIANO PLAYER(1962, Fr.), d, w; ARMY GAME, THE(1963, Fr.), a, p, w; LOVE AT TWENTY(1963, Fr./Ital./Jap./Pol./Ger.), d&w; SOFT SKIN, THE(1964, Fr.), d, w; MATA HARI(1965, Fr./Ital.), w; FAHRENHEIT 451(1966, Brit.), d, w; BRIDE WORE BLACK, THE(1968, Fr./Ital.), d, w; STOLEN KISSES(1969, Fr.), d, w; ME(1970, Fr.), p; MISSISSIPPI MERMAID(1970, Fr./Ital.), w; WILD CHILD, THE(1970, Fr.), a, d, w; BED AND BOARD(1971, Fr.), p&d, w; TWO ENGLISH GIRLS(1972, Fr.), a, d, w; DAY FOR NIGHT(1973, Fr.), a, d, w; SUCH A GORGEOUS KID LIKE ME(1973, Fr.), d, w; STORY OF ADELE H., THE(1975, Fr.), a, d, w; SMALL CHANGE(1976, Fr.), a, d, w; CLOSE ENCOUNTERS OF THE THIRD KIND(1977); MAN WHO LOVED WOMEN, THE(1977, Fr.), d, w; GREEN ROOM, THE(1979, Fr.), a, d, w; LOVE ON THE RUN(1980, Fr.), d&w; LAST METRO, THE(1981, Fr.), d, w; WOMAN NEXT DOOR, THE(1981, Fr.), d, w; BREATHLESS(1983), w; CONFIDENTIALLY YOURS(1983, Fr.), d, w; MAN WHO LOVED WOMEN, THE(1983), w

Laura Truffaut
WILD CHILD, THE(1970, Fr.); TWO ENGLISH GIRLS(1972, Fr.); SMALL CHANGE(1976, Fr.)

Charlie Truhan
SLOW DANCING IN THE BIG CITY(1978), set d

Daniel Truhitte
SOUND OF MUSIC, THE(1965)

Rosa Truich
EL DORADO(1967)

Sadie Truitt
IN COLD BLOOD(1967)

James Truitte
SINS OF RACHEL CADE, THE(1960), ch

Anthony T. Trujillio
1984
TERMINATOR, THE(1984)

Julia Trujillo
1984
IT'S NEVER TOO LATE(1984, Span.)

Margaret Trujillo
GIANT(1956)

Roberto Trujillo
HOUSE CALLS(1978)

Ronald Trujillo
OUTSIDER, THE(1962)

Suzanna Trujillo
MOUNTAIN MEN, THE(1980)

Valentin Trujillo
RAGE(1966, U.S./Mex.)

Bud Truland
LILITH(1964)

Bess Truman
EXTRAORDINARY SEAMAN, THE(1969)

Bruce Truman
Silents
JAZZ GIRL, THE(1926), w

California Truman
Misc. Silents
WHO CARES?(1919)

Jeff Truman
WILD DUCK, THE(1983, Aus.)

Michael Truman
THEY CAME TO A CITY(1944, Brit.), ed; JOHNNY FRENCHMAN(1946, Brit.), ed; LOVES OF JOANNA GODDEN, THE(1947, Brit.), ed; IT ALWAYS RAINS ON SUNDAY(1949, Brit.), ed; PASSPORT TO PIMLICO(1949, Brit.), ed; SARABAND(1949, Brit.), ed; PINK STRING AND SEALING WAX(1950, Brit.), ed; RUN FOR YOUR MONEY, A(1950, Brit.), ed; HIS EXCELLENCY(1952, Brit.), p; TITFIELD THUNDERBOLT, THE(1953, Brit.), p; HIGH AND DRY(1954, Brit.), p; DIVIDED HEART, THE(1955, Brit.), p; LIGHT TOUCH, THE(1955, Brit.), d; GO TO BLAZES(1962, Brit.), d; DAYLIGHT ROBBERY(1964, Brit.), d; MODEL MURDER CASE, THE(1964,

Brit.), d; CRY WOLF(1968, Brit.), p

Ralph Truman
BELLS, THE(1931, Brit.); PERFECT FLAW, THE(1934, Brit.); CAPTAIN BILL(1935, Brit.); CASE OF GABRIEL PERRY, THE(1935, Brit.); JUBILEE WINDOW(1935, Brit.); LAD, THE(1935, Brit.); LATE EXTRA(1935, Brit.); LIEUTENANT DARING, RN(1935, Brit.); SILENT PASSENGER, THE(1935, Brit.); THAT'S MY UNCLE(1935, Brit.); THREE WITNESSES(1935, Brit.); CRIMSON CIRCLE, THE(1936, Brit.); EAST MEETS WEST(1936, Brit.); GAY ADVENTURE, THE(1936, Brit.); MR. COHEN TAKES A WALK(1936, Brit.); CHANGE FOR A SOVEREIGN(1937, Brit.); DINNER AT THE RITZ(1937, Brit.); IT'S A GRAND OLD WORLD(1937, Brit.); UNDER THE RED ROBE(1937, Brit.); FATHER O'FLYNN(1938, Irish); MANY TANKS MR. ATKINS(1938, Brit.); SOUTH RIDING(1938, Brit.); ANYTHING TO DECLARE?(1939, Brit.); CHALLENGE, THE(1939, Brit.); JUST LIKE A WOMAN(1939, Brit.); PRISONER OF CORBAL(1939, Brit.); SAINT IN LONDON, THE(1939, Brit.); OUTSIDER, THE(1940, Brit.); MURDER AT THE BASKERVILLES(1941, Brit.); SEVENTH SURVIVOR, THE(1941, Brit.); SABOTAGE AT SEA(1942, Brit.); BUTLER'S DILEMMA, THE(1943, Brit.); HENRY V(1946, Brit.); LISBON STORY, THE(1946, Brit.); WOMAN TO WO-MAN(1946, Brit.); MR. PERRIN AND MR. TRAILL(1948, Brit.); SMUGGLERS, THE(1948, Brit.); CHRISTOPHER COLUMBUS(1949, Brit.); INTERRUPTED JOURNEY, THE(1949, Brit.); MASSACRE HILL(1949, Brit.); LAUGHING LADY, THE(1950, Brit.); MRS. FITZHERBERT(1950, Brit.); TREASURE ISLAND(1950, Brit.); OLIVER TWIST(1951, Brit.); QUO VADIS(1951); RELUCTANT WIDOW, THE(1951, Brit.); GOLDEN COACH, THE(1953, Fr./Ital.); MASTER OF BALLANTRAE, THE(1953, U.S./Brit.); BEAU BRUMMELL(1954); MALTA STORY(1954, Brit.); NIGHT MY NUM-BER CAME UP, THE(1955, Brit.); BLACK TENT, THE(1956, Brit.); MAN WHO KNEW TOO MUCH, THE(1956); SHIP THAT DIED OF SHAME, THE(1956, Brit.); TONS OF TROUBLE(1956, Brit.); GOOD COMPANIONS, THE(1957, Brit.); PORTRAIT IN SMOKE(1957, Brit.); SILKEN AFFAIR, THE(1957, Brit.); THIRD KEY, THE(1957, Brit.); SPANIARD'S CURSE, THE(1958, Brit.); BEN HUR(1959); BEYOND THIS PLACE(1959, Brit.); EXODUS(1960); UNDER TEN FLAGS(1960, U.S./Ital.); EL CID(1961, U.S./Ital.); NICHOLAS AND ALEXANDRA(1971, Brit.); LADY CAROLINE LAMB(1972, Brit./Ital.)

Totti Truman-Taylor
THERE WAS A CROOKED MAN(1962, Brit.); TAKE ME OVER(1963, Brit.); WRONG BOX, THE(1966, Brit.); MINI-AFFAIR, THE(1968, Brit.); NICE GIRL LIKE ME, A(1969, Brit.)

Brad Trumball
PARATROOP COMMAND(1959)

Christopher Trumbo
DON IS DEAD, THE(1973), w; BRANNIGAN(1975, Brit.), w

Dalton Trumbo
LOVE BEGINS AT TWENTY(1936), w; ROAD GANG(1936), w; DEVIL'S PLAY-GROUND(1937), w; FUGITIVES FOR A NIGHT(1938), w; MAN TO REMEMBER, A(1938), w; CAREER(1939), w; FIVE CAME BACK(1939), w; FLYING IRISHMAN, THE(1939), w; HEAVEN WITH A BARBED WIRE FENCE(1939), w; KID FROM KOKOMO, THE(1939), w; SORORITY HOUSE(1939), w; BILL OF DIVOR-CEMENT(1940), w; CURTAIN CALL(1940), w; HALF A SINNER(1940), w; KITTY FOYLE(1940), w; LONE WOLF STRIKES, THE(1940), w; WE WHO ARE YOUNG(1940), w; ACCENT ON LOVE(1941), w; YOU BELONG TO ME(1941), w; I MARRIED A WITCH(1942), w; REMARKABLE ANDREW, THE(1942), w; GUY NAMED JOE, A(1943), w; TENDER COMRADE(1943), w; THIRTY SECONDS OVER TOKYO(1944), w; JEALOUSY(1945), w; OUR VINES HAVE TENDER GRAPES(1945), w; EMERGENCY WEDDING(1950), w; PROWLER, THE(1951), w; EXODUS(1960), w; SPARTACUS(1960), w; LAST SUNSET, THE(1961), w; LONELY ARE THE BRA-VE(1962), w; SANDPIPER, THE(1965), w; HAWAII(1966), w; FIXER, THE(1968), w; HORSEMEN, THE(1971), w; JOHNNY GOT HIS GUN(1971), d&w; EXECUTIVE ACTION(1973), w; PAPILLON(1973), a, w

Brad Trumbull
WITNESS TO MURDER(1954); EDDY DUCHIN STORY, THE(1956); CRIME OF PASSION(1957); FIVE GUNS TO TOMBSTONE(1961); FLIGHT THAT DISAP-PEARED, THE(1961); GAMBLER WORE A GUN, THE(1961); POLICE DOG STORY, THE(1961); YOU HAVE TO RUN FAST(1961); INCIDENT IN AN ALLEY(1962); MOVE OVER, DARLING(1963); RIGHT HAND OF THE DEVIL, THE(1963); PATER-NITY(1981)

Brian Trumbull
1984
RACING WITH THE MOON(1984)

Clyde Trumbull
PRIDE OF ST. LOUIS, THE(1952)

Douglas Trumbull
CANDY(1968, Ital./Fr.), spec eff; 2001: A SPACE ODYSSEY(1968, U.S./Brit.), spec eff; SILENT RUNNING(1972), d, spec eff; CLOSE ENCOUNTERS OF THE THIRD KIND(1977), spec eff; STAR TREK: THE MOTION PICTURE(1979), spec eff; BLADE RUNNER(1982), spec eff; BRAINSTORM(1983), p&d

John Trumbull
CONQUEST OF THE AIR(1940)

Leonard Trumm
SO EVIL MY LOVE(1948, Brit.), ed

Herbert Trumper
Misc. Silents
ANGEL OF THE WARD, THE(1915, Brit.)

John Trumper
BRANDY FOR THE PARSON(1952, Brit.), ed; BACKGROUND(1953, Brit.), ed; LIT-TLE KIDNAPPERS, THE(1954, Brit.), ed; ESCAPADE(1955, Brit.), ed; PACIFIC DES-TINY(1956, Brit.), ed; MAN UPSTAIRS, THE(1959, Brit.), ed; TIME LOCK(1959, Brit.), ed; STRONGROOM(1962, Brit.), ed; WEBSTER BOY, THE(1962, Brit.), ed; CROOKS ANONYMOUS(1963, Brit.), ed; MAN IN THE DARK(1963, Brit.), ed; MUR-DER CAN BE DEADLY(1963, Brit.), ed; CODE 7, VICTIM 5(1964, Brit.), ed; LIFE IN DANGER(1964, Brit.), ed; SING AND SWING(1964, Brit.), ed; TOMORROW AT TEN(1964, Brit.), ed; COAST OF SKELETONS(1965, Brit.), ed; DEVILS OF DARK-NESS, THE(1965, Brit.), ed; FACE OF FU MANCHU, THE(1965, Brit.), ed; 24 HOURS TO KILL(1966, Brit.), ed; PENTHOUSE, THE(1967, Brit.), ed; PRIVILEGE(1967, Brit.), ed; PSYCHO-CIRCUS(1967, Brit.), ed; LONG DAY'S DYING, THE(1968, Brit.), ed; UP THE JUNCTION(1968, Brit.), ed; ITALIAN JOB, THE(1969, Brit.), ed; ENTERTAIN-ING MR. SLOANE(1970, Brit.), ed; GET CARTER(1971, Brit.), ed; PIED PIPER, THE(1972, Brit.), ed; ALFIE DARLING(1975, Brit.), ed; TEN LITTLE INDIANS(1975, Ital./Fr./Span./Ger.), ed; TO THE DEVIL A DAUGHTER(1976, Brit./Ger.), ed

Ruth Trumpp
DECISION BEFORE DAWN(1951)

Natalie Trundy
CARELESS YEARS, THE(1957); MONTE CARLO STORY, THE(1957, Ital.); WALK LIKE A DRAGON(1960); MR. HOBBS TAKES A VACATION(1962); BENEATH THE PLANET OF THE APES(1970); ESCAPE FROM THE PLANET OF THE APES(1971); CONQUEST OF THE PLANET OF THE APES(1972); BATTLE FOR THE PLANET OF THE APES(1973); HUCKLEBERRY FINN(1974)

Curt Truninger
BLACK SPIDER, THE(1983, Swit.)

Mabel Trunnelle
Silents
EUGENE ARAM(1915); RANSON'S FOLLY(1915); SINGED WINGS(1922)
Misc. Silents
GREAT PHYSCIAN, THE(1913); DESTROYING ANGEL, THE(1915); MAGIC SKIN, THE(1915); OUT OF THE RUINS(1915); SHADOWS FROM THE PAST(1915); TRAGE-DIES OF THE CRYSTAL GLOBE, THE(1915); HEART OF THE HILLS, THE(1916); MARTYRDOM OF PHILLIP STRONG, THE(1916); MESSAGE TO GARCIA, A(1916); MASTER PASSION, THE(1917)

Helmut Trunz
BENJAMIN(1973, Ger.), a, ph

Joe Trunzo
ONE DOWN TWO TO GO(1982), m

Victor Truro
MANHATTAN(1979); REACHING OUT(1983)

Alice Truscott
1984
BIRDY(1984)

John Truscott
CAMELOT(1967), cos; PAINT YOUR WAGON(1969), prod d, cos; SPY WHO LOVED ME, THE(1977, Brit.)

Lenore Truscott
1984
CONSTANCE(1984, New Zealand)

Sara Truslow
JUST TELL ME WHAT YOU WANT(1980)

A. Trusov
HOUSE ON THE FRONT LINE, THE(1963, USSR)

V. Trusov
WHEN THE TREES WERE TALL(1965, USSR)

Seldon Truss
LONG KNIFE, THE(1958, Brit.), w

Hal Trussel
ONE DARK NIGHT(1983), ph

Christopher Trussell
HOT POTATO(1976), m

George M. Trussell
DAMN CITIZEN(1958)

Alan R. Trustman
BULLITT(1968), w; THOMAS CROWN AFFAIR, THE(1968), w; THEY CALL ME MISTER TIBBS(1970), w; HIT(1973), w

Alan Trustman
LADY ICE(1973), w; NEXT MAN, THE(1976), w

Susan Trustman
STAY AWAY, JOE(1968)

Trutz
M(1933, Ger.)

John Truwe
SUNDAY IN NEW YORK(1963), makeup; POINT BLANK(1967), makeup

George Truzzi
KING IN NEW YORK, A(1957, Brit.)

Doreen Tryden
SALOME, WHERE SHE DANCED(1945)

Brandon Trynan
GIRL OF THE GOLDEN WEST, THE(1938)

William Tryoler
PHANTOM OF THE OPERA, THE(1929)
Silents
PHANTOM OF THE OPERA, THE(1925)

Glen Tryon
BROADWAY(1929); NECK AND NECK(1931)

Glenn Tryon
LONESOME(1928); BARNUM WAS RIGHT(1929); IT CAN BE DONE(1929); SKIN-NER STEPS OUT(1929); DAMES AHOY(1930); IT'S A DEAL(1930); DAYBREAK(1931); MIDNIGHT SPECIAL(1931); SECRET MENACE(1931); SKY SPIDER, THE(1931); DRAGNET PATROL(1932); PRIDE OF THE LEGION, THE(1932); TANGLED DESTI-NIES(1932); WIDOW IN SCARLET(1932); BIG PAYOFF, THE(1933); RAFTER RO-MANCE(1934), w; DARING YOUNG MAN, THE(1935), w; GRIDIRON FLASH(1935), d, w; ROBERTA(1935), w; EASY TO TAKE(1936), d; TWO IN RE-VOLT(1936), d; SMALL TOWN BOY(1937), d&w; LAW WEST OF TOMBSTONE, THE(1938), d; BEAUTY FOR THE ASKING(1939), d; HIRED WIFE(1940), p; PRI-VATE AFFAIRS(1940), p; DOUBLE DATE(1941), p; KEEP 'EM FLYING(1941), p; DEVIL WITH HITLER, THE(1942), p; THAT NAZTY NUISANCE(1943), p&d; LAW MEN(1944), w; MEET MISS BOBBY SOCKS(1944), d; GEORGE WHITE'S SCAN-DALS(1945); VARIETY GIRL(1947); MISS MINK OF 1949(1949), d; MESSENGER OF PEACE(1950), w; HOME TOWN STORY(1951)
Silents
PAINTING THE TOWN(1927); GATE CRASHER, THE(1928); THANKS FOR THE BUGGY RIDE(1928); KID'S CLEVER, THE(1929)
Misc. Silents
BATTLING ORIOLES, THE(1924); WHITE SHEEP, THE(1924); HERO FOR A NIGHT, A(1927); 2 GIRLS WANTED(1927); HOT HEELS(1928); HOW TO HANDLE WOMEN(1928)

Helen Tryon
WOLFMAN(1979)

Johnny Tryon
MAYOR OF 44TH STREET, THE(1942)

Thomas Tryon
OTHER, THE(1972), w; FEDORA(1978, Ger./Fr.), w
Tom Tryon
SCARLET HOUR, THE(1956); SCREAMING EAGLES(1956); THREE VIOLENT PEOPLE(1956); UNHOLY WIFE, THE(1957); I MARRIED A MONSTER FROM OUTER SPACE(1958); STORY OF RUTH, THE(1960); MARINES, LET'S GO(1961); LONGEST DAY, THE(1962); MOON PILOT(1962); CARDINAL, THE(1963); GLORY GUYS, THE(1965); IN HARM'S WAY(1965); COLOR ME DEAD(1969, Aus.); NARCO MEN, THE(1969, Span./Ital.)
Georg Tryphon
1984
WOMAN IN FLAMES, A(1984, Ger.)
W.L. Trytel
JUGGERNAUT(1937, Brit.), m; MAXWELL ARCHER, DETECTIVE(1942, Brit.), md; SISTER TO ASSIST'ER, A(1948, Brit.), p
William Trytel
IS YOUR HONEYMOON REALLY NECESSARY?(1953, Brit.), m
W. L. Trytell
BRIDE OF THE LAKE(1934, Brit.), md
Andrzej Trzaskowski
WALKOVER(1969, Pol.), m
1984
SHIVERS(1984, Pol.), m
Edmund Trzcinski
STALAG 17(1953), w
Frantiszek Trzeciak
MAN OF IRON(1981, Pol.)
Manolis Tsafos
Misc. Talkies
RIP OFF(1977), d
C. Tsagarell
THEY WANTED PEACE(1940, USSR), d&w
Nikos Tsahiridas
SKY RIDERS(1976, U.S./Gr.)
Tsai
GENERAL MASSACRE(1973, U.S./Bel.)
Chin Tsai-feng
DREAM OF THE RED CHAMBER, THE(1966, Chi.)
Chris Tsalikis
CLAY(1964 Aus.)
Kenneth Tsang
DEMONSTRATOR(1971, Aus.)
Yu Tsang-shan
GRAND SUBSTITUTION, THE(1965, Hong Kong), ph
Christopher Tsangarides
MEMOIRS OF A SURVIVOR(1981, Brit.)
Christos Tsangas
IPHIGENIA(1977, Gr.)
Lambros Tsangas
THANOS AND DESPINA(1970, Fr./Gr.)
Tsanusdi
TRADER HORNEE(1970), d
Johnson Tsao
CLEOPATRA JONES AND THE CASINO OF GOLD(1975 U. S. Hong Kong), art d; DRACULA AND THE SEVEN GOLDEN VAMPIRES(1978, Brit./Chi.), art d
Teresa Tsao
LA DOLCE VITA(1961, Ital./Fr.)
George Tsaoulis
YOUNG APHRODITES(1966, Gr.), ed
Zoras Tsapelis
RAPE, THE(1965, Gr.)
B. Tsaryov
SOUND OF LIFE, THE(1962, USSR), art d; LAST GAME, THE(1964, USSR), art d
Slava Tsaryov
WELCOME KOSTYA!(1965, USSR)
Olga Tscechova
Misc. Silents
HAUNTED CASTLE, THE(1921, Ger.)
Olga Tschechowa
WORLD WITHOUT A MASK, THE(1934, Ger.); BURG THEATRE(1936, Ger.); ETERNAL MASK, THE(1937, Swiss); U-47 LT. COMMANDER PRIEN(1967, Ger.)
Silents
MOULIN ROUGE(1928, Brit.); AFTER THE VERDICT(1929, Brit.)
Vera Tschechowa
FREDDY UNTER FREMDEN STERNEN(1962, Ger.); LOVE AT TWENTY(1963, Fr./Ital./Jap./Pol./Ger.)
Olga Tschekowa
Silents
ITALIAN STRAW HAT, AN(1927, Fr.)
Hubert Tscheppe
LITTLE NIGHT MUSIC, A(1977, Aust./U.S./Ger.)
Jeny Tschernichin
Misc. Silents
KISS OF DEATH(1916, Swed.)
Jenny Tschernichin-Larsson
Misc. Silents
LOVE AND JOURNALISM(1916, Swed.)
Sergei Tschernisch
COLOSSUS: THE FORBIN PROJECT(1969)
A. Tschernow
THREE DAYS OF VIKTOR TSCHERNIKOFF(1968, USSR)
Valentin Tschernych
MOSCOW DOES NOT BELIEVE IN TEARS(1980, USSR), w
Konstantin Tschet
BOMBARDMENT OF MONTE CARLO, THE(1931, Ger.), ph; HAPPY EVER AFTER(1932, Ger./Brit.), ph; F.P. 1 DOESN'T ANSWER(1933, Ger.), ph; SHOT AT DAWN, A(1934, Ger.), ph

Konstantin Tschetwerikoff
Silents
WOMAN ON THE MOON, THE(1929, Ger.), spec eff
Konstantin Tschetwerikow
F.P. 1 DOESN'T ANSWER(1933, Ger.), spec eff
Klaus Tschichan
$(DOLLARS) (1971)
Olaf Tschierschke
MIRACLE OF THE WHITE STALLIONS(1963)
I.P. Tschouvelev
THUNDERSTORM(1934, USSR)
Michael Tschudin
HONEYBABY, HONEYBABY(1974), m
D. Tschukowski
THREE DAYS OF VIKTOR TSCHERNIKOFF(1968, USSR)
Eddie Tse
REVENGE OF THE NINJA(1983)
Mariko Tse
CANNERY ROW(1982)
Yang Tse-ching
GRAND SUBSTITUTION, THE(1965, Hong Kong); MERMAID, THE(1966, Hong Kong)
G. Tsekaviy
DAY THE EARTH FROZE, THE(1959, Fin./USSR), ph
Tsekhanskaya
Misc. Silents
FIGHT FOR THE 'ULTIMATUM' FACTORY(1923, USSR)
Ludmila Tselikovskaya
IVAN THE TERRIBLE(Part I, 1947, USSR); TAXI TO HEAVEN(1944, USSR)
Jane Tsentas
HAREM BUNCH; OR WAR AND PIECE, THE(1969); WILD, FREE AND HUNGRY(1970)
Nikolai Tseretelli
Misc. Silents
GREEN SPIDER, THE(1916, USSR); CIGARETTE GIRL FROM MOSSELPROM(1924, USSR)
Emma Tsessatskaya
Misc. Silents
WOMEN OF RYAZAN(1927, USSR)
Daniel Tshabalala
ZULU(1964, Brit.)
H.T. Tsiang
BEHIND THE RISING SUN(1943); KEYS OF THE KINGDOM, THE(1944); PURPLE HEART, THE(1944); CHINA SKY(1945); CHINA'S LITTLE DEVILS(1945); TOKYO ROSE(1945); IN OLD SACRAMENTO(1946); BLACK GOLD(1947); SINGAPORE(1947); CHICKEN EVERY SUNDAY(1948); STATE DEPARTMENT–FILE 649(1949); PANIC IN THE STREETS(1950); SMUGGLER'S ISLAND(1951); OCEAN'S ELEVEN(1960); WINTER A GO-GO(1965)
M. Tsibulsky
Misc. Silents
SOLD APPETITE, THE(1928, USSR)
Mari Tsien
27TH DAY, THE(1957)
Maria Tsien
ALL THE YOUNG MEN(1960)
Marie Tsien
LEFT HAND OF GOD, THE(1955); LOVE IS A MANY-SPLENDORED THING(1955)
Tami Tsifroni
EVERY BASTARD A KING(1968, Israel)
Millie Tsigonoff
ANGELO MY LOVE(1983)
Steve "Patalay" Tsigonoff
ANGELO MY LOVE(1983)
1984
STONE BOY, THE(1984)
A. Tsinman
GORDEYEV FAMILY, THE(1961, U.S.S.R.)
Sulkhan Tsintsadze
FATHER OF A SOLDIER(1966, USSR), m
Elena Tsiplakova
1984
JAZZMAN(1984, USSR)
V. Tsirlina
MOTHER AND DAUGHTER(1965, USSR), set d
Tsitsino Tsitsishvili
STEPCHILDREN(1962, USSR)
Irene Tso
CHINA(1943)
Geoffrey Tsobe
DIAMOND SAFARI(1958)
S. Tsomayev
DON QUIXOTE(1961, USSR)
Corinna Tsopei
VALLEY OF THE DOLLS(1967); SWEET RIDE, THE(1968); MAN CALLED HORSE, A(1970)
V. Tsoppi
Misc. Silents
HEIR TO JENGHIS-KHAN, THE(1928, USSR)
Irene Tsu
TAKE HER, SHE'S MINE(1963); UNDER THE YUM-YUM TREE(1963); JOHN GOLDFARB, PLEASE COME HOME(1964); HOW TO STUFF A WILD BIKINI(1965); SWORD OF ALI BABA, THE(1965); PARADISE, HAWAIIAN STYLE(1966); SEVEN WOMEN(1966); WOMEN OF THE PREHISTORIC PLANET(1966); CAPRICE(1967); KARATE KILLERS, THE(1967); GREEN BERETS, THE(1968); AIRPORT 1975(1974); THREE THE HARD WAY(1974); PAPER TIGER(1975, Brit.); HOT POTATO(1976)
Misc. Talkies
DAMIEN'S ISLAND(1976)

Takashi Tsuboshima
LAS VEGAS FREE-FOR-ALL(1968, Jap.), d
David Tsubouchi
VIDEODROME(1983, Can.)
Mikiko Tsubouchi
ZATOICHI CHALLENGED(1970, Jap.); GAMERA VERSUS ZIGRA(1971, Jap.)
Eii Tsuburaya
GODZILLA'S REVENGE(1969), spec eff
Eiji Tsuburaya
GODZILLA, RING OF THE MONSTERS(1956, Jap.), spec eff; RODAN(1958, Jap.), spec eff; GIGANTIS(1959, Jap./U.S.), spec eff; H-MAN, THE(1959, Jap.), spec eff; MYSTERIANS, THE(1959, Jap.), spec eff; BATTLE IN OUTER SPACE(1960), spec eff; I BOMBED PEARL HARBOR(1961, Jap.), spec eff; SECRET OF THE TELEGIAN, THE(1961, Jap.), spec eff; LAST WAR, THE(1962, Jap.), spec eff; MOTHRA(1962, Jap.), spec eff; VARAN THE UNBELIEVABLE(1962, U.S./Jap.), spec eff; KING KONG VERSUS GODZILLA(1963, Jap.), sp eff; YOUTH AND HIS AMULET, THE(1963, Jap.), spec eff; ATTACK OF THE MUSHROOM PEOPLE(1964, Jap.), spec eff; DAGORA THE SPACE MONSTER(1964, Jap.), ed; GODZILLA VS. THE THING(1964, Jap.), spec eff; GORATH(1964, Jap.), spec eff; HUMAN VAPOR, THE(1964, Jap.), spec eff; ATRAGON(1965, Jap.), spec eff; GHIDRAH, THE THREE-HEADED MONSTER(1965, Jap.), spec eff; LOST WORLD OF SINBAD, THE(1965, Jap.), spec eff; NONE BUT THE BRAVE(1965, U.S./Jap.), spec eff; GODZILLA VERSUS THE SEA MONSTER(1966, Jap.), spec eff; SON OF GODZILLA(1967, Jap.), spec eff; KING KONG ESCAPES(1968, Jap.), spec eff; SIEGE OF FORT BISMARK(1968, Jap.), spec eff; WHIRLWIND(1968, Jap.), spec eff; DAREDEVIL IN THE CASTLE(1969, Jap.), spec eff; DESTROY ALL MONSTERS(1969, Jap.), spec eff; LATITUDE ZERO(1969, U.S./Jap.), spec eff; MONSTER ZERO(1970, Jap.), spec eff; WAR OF THE GARGANTUAS, THE(1970, Jap.), spec eff
Kichijiro Tsuchida
UGETSU(1954, Jap.)
Nobu Tsuchiya
TWO IN THE SHADOW(1968, Jap.)
Toshio Tsuchiya
HIGH AND LOW(1963, Jap.); SPACE AMOEBA, THE(1970, Jap.)
Yasuo Tsuchiya
ANGRY ISLAND(1960, Jap.)
Yoshio Tsuchiya
SEVEN SAMURAI, THE(1956, Jap.); BATTLE IN OUTER SPACE(1960); DEATH ON THE MOUNTAIN(1961, Jap.); SECRET OF THE TELEGIAN, THE(1961, Jap.); YOJIMBO(1961, Jap.); SANJURO(1962, Jap.); TATSU(1962, Jap.); ATTACK OF THE MUSHROOM PEOPLE(1964, Jap.); FRANKENSTEIN CONQUERS THE WORLD(1964, Jap./US); HUMAN VAPOR, THE(1964, Jap.); RED BEARD(1966, Jap.); KOJIRO(1967, Jap.); SON OF GODZILLA(1967, Jap.); EMPEROR AND A GENERAL, THE(1968, Jap.); KILL(1968, Jap.); DESTROY ALL MONSTERS(1969, Jap.); MONSTER ZERO(1970, Jap.); YOG-MONSTER FROM SPACE(1970, Jap.)
Akiko Tsuda
MY GEISHA(1962)
Hiro Tsugawa
METAMORPHOSES(1978), p
Masashiko Tsugawa
SANSHO THE BAILIFF(1969, Jap.)
Shintaro Tsuji
NUTCRACKER FANTASY(1979), w
Masanori Tsujii
TEMPTRESS AND THE MONK, THE(1963, Jap.), ed; HARP OF BURMA(1967, Jap.), ed
Junichi Tsujita
1984
FAMILY GAME, THE(1984, Jap.)
Takamitsu Tsukahara
PANDA AND THE MAGIC SERPENT(1961, Jap.), ph
Raynum K. Tsukamoto
TEAHOUSE OF THE AUGUST MOON, THE(1956); OPERATION BIKINI(1963)
Raynum Tsukamoto
MANCHURIAN CANDIDATE, THE(1962)
Hiroaki Tsukasa
TORA-SAN PART 2(1970, Jap.)
Toko Tsukasa
LONELY LANE(1963, Jap.)
Yoko Tsukasa
NIGHT IN HONG KONG, A(1961, Jap.); YOJIMBO(1961, Jap.); EARLY AUTUMN(1962, Jap.); WISER AGE(1962, Jap.); CHUSHINGURA(1963, Jap.); CHALLENGE TO LIVE(1964, Jap.); SAGA OF THE VAGABONDS(1964, Jap.); TWILIGHT PATH(1965, Jap.); DAPHNE, THE(1967); KOJIRO(1967, Jap.); REBELLION(1967, Jap.); TWO IN THE SHADOW(1968, Jap.); GOYOKIN(1969, Jap.); MOMENT OF TERROR(1969, Jap.); LATE AUTUMN(1973, Jap.); PROPHECIES OF NOSTRADAMUS(1974, Jap.)
Slava Tsukerman
LIQUID SKY(1982), p&d, w, m
Masaya Tsukida
FIRES ON THE PLAIN(1962, Jap.)
Ryunosuke Tsukigata
YOUNG SWORDSMAN(1964, Jap.)
Yonesaburo Tsukiji
GAMERA THE INVINCIBLE(1966, Jap.), spec eff
Sennosuke Tsukimori
LOVE UNDER THE CRUCIFIX(1965, Jap.), p
Yumeji Tsukioka
TEMPTRESS AND THE MONK, THE(1963, Jap.); LOVE UNDER THE CRUCIFIX(1965, Jap.)
Fugio Tsumeda
1984
BALLAD OF NARAYAMA, THE(1984, Jap.)
Hsang Tsung-hsin
LOVERS' ROCK(1966, Taiwan)
Ken-ichiro Tsunoda
HAPPINESS OF US ALONE(1962, Jap.), p; TILL TOMORROW COMES(1962, Jap.), p; KOJIRO(1967, Jap.), p

Kenichiro Tsunoda
OPERATION X(1963, Jap.), p
Rin Tsuong
STAR OF HONG KONG(1962, Jap.)
Yu. Tsupko
TRAIN GOES TO KIEV, THE(1961, USSR)
Joji Tsurumi
BUDDHA(1965, Jap.)
Koji Tsuruta
SAMURAI(PART III) (1967, Jap.); SECRET SCROLLS(PART I) (1968, Jap.); I BOMBED PEARL HARBOR(1961, Jap.); SECRET OF THE TELEGIAN, THE(1961, Jap.); SAGA OF THE VAGABONDS(1964, Jap.); TEA AND RICE(1964, Jap.)
Koyu Tsuruta
SONG FROM MY HEART, THE(1970, Jap.)
Yosan Tsuruta
TOKYO JOE(1949)
Namboku Tsuruya
ILLUSION OF BLOOD(1966, Jap.), w
Keiko Tsushima
SEVEN SAMURAI, THE(1956, Jap.); TEA AND RICE(1964, Jap.)
Toshiaki Tsushima
GREEN SLIME, THE(1969), m
Yasuhisa Tsutsumi
SEVEN SAMURAI, THE(1956, Jap.); GODZILLA VS. THE THING(1964, Jap.)
Shigeru Tsuyuguchi
UNHOLY DESIRE(1964, Jap.); HIKEN YABURI(1969, Jap.); GIRL I ABANDONED, THE(1970, Jap.); LAKE, THE(1970, Jap.)
Shoichi Tsuyuguchi
INSECT WOMAN, THE(1964, Jap.)
Francesca Tu
DIAMONDS FOR BREAKFAST(1968, Brit.); WELCOME TO THE CLUB(1971)
Francisca Tu
DON'T RAISE THE BRIDGE, LOWER THE RIVER(1968, Brit.); SALT & PEPPER(1968, Brit.); CHAIRMAN, THE(1969); HUNTING PARTY, THE(1977, Brit.)
L. Tu
FIGHT TO THE LAST(1938, Chi.)
Lou Tu
SOD SISTERS(1969)
Tua
RANGO(1931)
Roland Tual
ANGELS OF THE STREETS(1950, Fr.), p
Anh Tuan
HOA-BINH(1971, Fr.)
Le Tuan
UNCOMMON VALOR(1983)
Vu Ngoc Tuan
TOWN LIKE ALICE, A(1958, Brit.)
Ivan Tubau
GUNFIGHTERS OF CASA GRANDE(1965, U.S./Span.)
Dick Tubb
OLD CURIOSITY SHOP, THE(1935, Brit.); FOLLOW YOUR STAR(1938, Brit.)
Ernest Tubb
FIGHTING BUCKAROO, THE(1943); RIDING WEST(1944); HOLLYWOOD BARN DANCE(1947); COAL MINER'S DAUGHTER(1980)
Bill Tubbs
PAISAN(1948, Ital.)
William C. Tubbs
PRIVATE ANGELO(1949, Brit.); THREE STEPS NORTH(1951); SINGING TAXI DRIVER(1953, Ital.)
William Tubbs
PIRATES OF CAPRI, THE(1949); QUO VADIS(1951); EDWARD AND CAROLINE(1952, Fr.); GOLDEN COACH, THE(1953, Fr./Ital.); GREATEST LOVE, THE(1954, Ital.); WAGES OF FEAR, THE(1955, Fr./Ital.)
Tubby Hayes Quintet
DR. TERROR'S HOUSE OF HORRORS(1965, Brit.)
Sandy Tube
Misc. Talkies
BOESMAN AND LENA(1976)
Joel Tuber
GREAT WALL OF CHINA, THE(1970, Brit.), d&w, ed
The Tubes
CRACKING UP(1977), m; J-MEN FOREVER(1980), m
Mort Tubor
CAT BURGLAR, THE(1961), ed; BLOOD BATH(1966), ed; RED, WHITE AND BLACK, THE(1970), ed; BEES, THE(1978), ed
Morton Tubor
GIRLS ON THE BEACH(1965), ed; SKI PARTY(1965), ed; COOL BREEZE(1972), ed; HIT MAN(1972), ed; PRIVATE PARTS(1972), ed; SLAMS, THE(1973), ed; DARKTOWN STRUTTERS(1975), ed; CANNONBALL(1976, U.S./Hong Kong), ed; VIGILANTE FORCE(1976), ed; BIG RED ONE, THE(1980), ed
Sam Tubuo
ON AN ISLAND WITH YOU(1948)
Giorgio Tucci
ZOMBIE(1980, Ital.), m
Maria Tucci
ME AND MY BROTHER(1969); DANIEL(1983)
Michael Tucci
GREASE(1978); SUNNYSIDE(1979); LUNCH WAGON(1981)
Mike Tucci
NIGHT THEY ROBBED BIG BERTHA'S, THE(1975)
Reig Tucci
TANGO BAR(1935), md
Ugo Tucci
ZOMBIE(1980, Ital.), p; GREAT WHITE, THE(1982, Ital.), p
Fred Tuch
SPEED LOVERS(1968), w, prod d; AVALANCHE EXPRESS(1979), prod d; PENNIES FROM HEAVEN(1981), art d

Walter Tuch
FIDELIO(1961, Aust.), ph; 5 SINNERS(1961, Ger.), ph; TURKISH CUCUMBER, THE(1963, Ger.), ph; $100 A NIGHT(1968, Ger.), ph

Eugene Tucherer
CAT, THE(1959, Fr.), p

Bruno Tuchetto
ADIOS GRINGO(1967, Ital./Fr./Span.), p

Michael Tuchner
VILLAIN(1971, Brit.), d; FEAR IS THE KEY(1973, Brit.), d; MR. QUILP(1975, Brit.), d; LIKELY LADS, THE(1976, Brit.), d; TRENCHCOAT(1983), d

Wanda Tuchock
HALLELUJAH(1929), w; BILLY THE KID(1930), w; NOT SO DUMB(1930), w; SPORTING BLOOD(1931), w; SUSAN LENOX–HER FALL AND RISE(1931), w; BIRD OF PARADISE(1932), w; LETTY LYNTON(1932), w; LITTLE ORPHAN ANNIE(1932), w; NEW MORALS FOR OLD(1932), w; BED OF ROSES(1933), w; NO OTHER WOMAN(1933), w; FINISHING SCHOOL(1934), d, w; GRAND OLD GIRL(1935), w; O'SHAUGHNESSY'S BOY(1935), w; HAWAII CALLS(1938), w; LLANO KID, THE(1940), w; YOUTH WILL BE SERVED(1940), w; FOR BEAUTY'S SAKE(1941), w; LADIES OF WASHINGTON(1944), w; SUNDAY DINNER FOR A SOLDIER(1944), w; THIS IS THE LIFE(1944), w; NOB HILL(1945), w; WITHIN THESE WALLS(1945), w; FOXES OF HARROW, THE(1947), w; HOMESTRETCH, THE(1947), w
Silents
SHOW PEOPLE(1928), w

Marta Tuck
VALDEZ IS COMING(1971)

Martha Tuck
MAN IN THE WILDERNESS(1971, U.S./Span.)

Mel Tuck
QUIET DAY IN BELFAST, A(1974, Can.); GREY FOX, THE(1983, Can.)

Alan Tucker
BURKE AND HARE(1972, Brit.)

Augusta Tucker
MISS SUSIE SLAGLE'S(1945), w

Brian Tucker
TOO HOT TO HANDLE(1961, Brit.)

Burnell Tucker
DEVILS OF DARKNESS, THE(1965, Brit.); DATELINE DIAMONDS(1966, Brit.); FINDERS KEEPERS(1966, Brit.); COUNTESS FROM HONG KONG, A(1967, Brit.); SOME MAY LIVE(1967, Brit.); CRY OF THE PENGUINS(1972, Brit.); ROLLERBALL(1975); SUPERMAN(1978); EMPIRE STRIKES BACK, THE(1980); FLASH GORDON(1980); SHINING, THE(1980); PRIEST OF LOVE(1981, Brit.)
1984
SCREAM FOR HELP(1984)

Christopher Tucker
QUEST FOR FIRE(1982, Fr./Can.), makeup

Danny Tucker
MELVIN AND HOWARD(1980); WHERE THE BUFFALO ROAM(1980); LOOKIN' TO GET OUT(1982)

David Tucker
WE SHALL RETURN(1963), ed
Misc. Talkies
CAIO(1967), d

Dean Tucker
Misc. Talkies
VALLEY OF BLOOD(1973), d

Debie Tucker
URBAN COWBOY(1980)

Duane Tucker
CHARLIE CHAN AND THE CURSE OF THE DRAGON QUEEN(1981); FAST TIMES AT RIDGEMONT HIGH(1982)

Edward Tucker
VAMPIRE, THE(1968, Mex.)

Ellen Tucker
EVEL KNIEVEL(1971)

Forrest Tucker
WESTERNER, THE(1940); EMERGENCY LANDING(1941); HONOLULU LU(1941); NEW WINE(1941); BOSTON BLACKIE GOES HOLLYWOOD(1942); CANAL ZONE(1942); COUNTER-ESPIONAGE(1942); KEEPER OF THE FLAME(1942); MY SISTER EILEEN(1942); PARACHUTE NURSE(1942); SHUT MY BIG MOUTH(1942); SPIRIT OF STANFORD, THE(1942); SUBMARINE RAIDER(1942); TRAMP, TRAMP, TRAMP(1942); DANGEROUS BUSINESS(1946); MAN WHO DARED, THE(1946); NEVER SAY GOODBYE(1946); RENEGADES(1946); TALK ABOUT A LADY(1946); YEARLING, THE(1946); GUNFIGHTERS, THE(1947); ADVENTURES IN SILVERADO(1948); CORONER CREEK(1948); PLUNDERERS, THE(1948); TWO GUYS FROM TEXAS(1948); BIG CAT, THE(1949); BRIMSTONE(1949); HELLFIRE(1949); LAST BANDIT, THE(1949); SANDS OF IWO JIMA(1949); CALIFORNIA PASSAGE(1950); NEVADAN, THE(1950); ROCK ISLAND TRAIL(1950); CROSSWINDS(1951); FIGHTING COAST GUARD(1951); FLAMING FEATHER(1951); OH! SUSANNA(1951); WARPATH(1951); BUGLES IN THE AFTERNOON(1952); HOODLUM EMPIRE(1952); HURRICANE SMITH(1952); MONTANA BELLE(1952); RIDE THE MAN DOWN(1952); WILD BLUE YONDER, THE(1952); FLIGHT NURSE(1953); PONY EXPRESS(1953); SAN ANTONE(1953); JUBILEE TRAIL(1954); LAUGHING ANNE(1954, Brit./U.S.); TROUBLE IN THE GLEN(1954, Brit.); FINGER MAN(1955); FRESH FROM PARIS(1955); NIGHT FREIGHT(1955); PARIS FOLLIES OF 1956(1955); RAGE AT DAWN(1955); VANISHING AMERICAN, THE(1955); STAGECOACH TO FURY(1956); THREE VIOLENT PEOPLE(1956); ABOMINABLE SNOWMAN OF THE HIMALAYAS, THE(1957, Brit.); BREAK IN THE CIRCLE, THE(1957, Brit.); DEERSLAYER, THE(1957); QUIET GUN, THE(1957); AUNTIE MAME(1958); COSMIC MONSTERS(1958, Brit.); CRAWLING EYE, THE(1958, Brit.); FORT MASSACRE(1958); GIRL IN THE WOODS(1958); GUNSMOKE IN TUCSON(1958); COUNTERPLOT(1959); DON'T WORRY, WE'LL THINK OF A TITLE(1966); NIGHT THEY RAIDED MINSKY'S, THE(1968); BARQUERO(1970); CHISUM(1970); CANCEL MY RESERVATION(1972); WILD McCULLOCHS, THE(1975); WACKIEST WAGON TRAIN IN THE WEST, THE(1976); FINAL CHAPTER–WALKING TALL zero(1977)
1984
RARE BREED(1984)
Misc. Talkies
CRAWLING TERROR, THE(1958, Brit.)

GeorgeDe Normand Tucker
OVER THE BORDER(1950)

George L. Tucker
Silents
ARSENE LUPIN(1916, Brit.), d
Misc. Silents
CALLED BACK(1914, Brit.), d; I BELIEVE(1916, Brit.), d; MANXMAN, THE(1916, Brit.), d; MOTHER OF DARTMOOR, THE(1916, Brit.), d

George Loane Tucker
Silents
TRAFFIC IN SOULS(1913), d, w; PRISONER OF ZENDA, THE(1915, Brit.), d; RUPERT OF HENTZAU(1915, Brit.), d; JOAN OF PLATTSBURG(1918), d, w; MIRACLE MAN, THE(1919), d&w
Misc. Silents
SHE STOOPS TO CONQUER(1914, Brit.), d; CHRISTIAN, THE(1915, Brit.), d; MAN OF HIS WORD, A(1915, Brit.), d; MIDDLEMAN, THE(1915, Brit.), d; SHULMATE, THE(1915), d; SONS OF SATAN, THE(1915, Brit.), d; 1914(1915, Brit.), d; FOLLY OF DESIRE, THE OR THE SHULAMITE(1916), d; MORALS OF WEYBURY, THE(1916, Brit.), d; UNDER SUSPICION(1916, Brit.), d; CINDERELLA MAN, THE(1918), d; DODGING A MILLION(1918), d; VIRTUOUS WIVES(1919), d; LADIES MUST LIVE(1921), d

Gerald Tucker
1984
MRS. SOFFEL(1984)

Gil Tucker
MAD MAX(1979, Aus.)

Glenn Tucker
VIVA MAX!(1969)

Gloria Tucker
KEEPER OF THE FLAME(1942); YOUNGEST PROFESSION, THE(1943)

Harlan Tucker
KING FOR A NIGHT(1933); PHANTOM BROADCAST, THE(1933); ONCE A DOCTOR(1937); RACING LADY(1937); ROAD TO HAPPINESS(1942); MAGNIFICENT DOLL(1946); WHERE THERE'S LIFE(1947)
Silents
BEAU REVEL(1921); ADORABLE DECEIVER, THE(1926); STOLEN PLEASURES(1927)

Harland Tucker
CHINA CLIPPER(1936); KID GALAHAD(1937); MISSING WITNESSES(1937); SLIM(1937); INVISIBLE MENACE, THE(1938); PATIENT IN ROOM 18, THE(1938); KING OF THE UNDERWORLD(1939); LONE WOLF STRIKES, THE(1940); ROAR OF THE PRESS(1941); DESERT FURY(1947); HIT PARADE OF 1947(1947); MY FAVORITE BRUNETTE(1947); BEYOND GLORY(1948); FOREIGN AFFAIR, A(1948); NIGHT HAS A THOUSAND EYES(1948); YOU GOTTA STAY HAPPY(1948); DEAR WIFE(1949); RED, HOT AND BLUE(1949); TAKE ONE FALSE STEP(1949)
Silents
SWAMP, THE(1921)
Misc. Silents
SAUCE FOR THE GOOSE(1918); SHAMEFUL BEHAVIOR?(1926)

Ian Tucker
GYPSY(1962)

Jack Tucker
PETEY WHEATSTRAW(1978), ed
1984
SIGNAL 7(1984); THEY'RE PLAYING WITH FIRE(1984), ed

Jerry Tucker
PROSPERITY(1932); HELLO, EVERYBODY(1933); SITTING PRETTY(1933); CAPTAIN JANUARY(1935); ANYTHING GOES(1936); CAVALCADE OF THE WEST(1936); LOVE IN A BUNGALOW(1937); LOVE IS ON THE AIR(1937); PENROD AND SAM(1937); TOVARICH(1937); PENROD AND HIS TWIN BROTHER(1938); RECKLESS LIVING(1938); FEDERAL MAN-HUNT(1939)

John Bartholomew Tucker
ABDUCTION(1975)

John Tucker
1984
BEDROOM EYES(1984, Can.), m

Joyce Tucker
GREAT MR. NOBODY, THE(1941); NORTH STAR, THE(1943); ADVENTURES OF MARK TWAIN, THE(1944); UNCERTAIN GLORY(1944); TREE GROWS IN BROOKLYN, A(1945)

Larry Tucker
BLAST OF SILENCE(1961); SHOCK CORRIDOR(1963); I LOVE YOU, ALICE B. TOKLAS!(1968), w; BOB AND CAROL AND TED AND ALICE(1969), p, w; ALEX IN WONDERLAND(1970), p, w; ANGELS HARD AS THEY COME(1971)

Lee Tucker
1984
VARIETY(1984)

Len Tucker
BLACK KING(1932)

Lillian Tucker
Silents
EVIDENCE(1915); RED WIDOW, THE(1916); WHAT EVERY WOMAN KNOWS(1921)
Misc. Silents
MUMMY AND THE HUMMINGBIRD, THE(1915); LIGHT THAT FAILED, THE(1916); MARRIAGE PIT, THE(1920)

Lorenzo Tucker
TEMPTATION(1936)
Misc. Talkies
WAGES OF SIN, THE(1929); DAUGHTER OF THE CONGO, A(1930); EASY STREET(1930); VEILED ARISTOCRATS(1932); HARLEM AFTER MIDNIGHT(1934); REET, PETITE AND GONE(1947)

Martin Tucker
Misc. Talkies
DEATH SCREAMS(1982)

Mary Tucker
DEAD DON'T DREAM, THE(1948)

Maxine Tucker
CHAD HANNA(1940); REMEMBER THE DAY(1941)
Melville Tucker
ALONG THE OREGON TRAIL(1947), p; UNDER COLORADO SKIES(1947), p; CALIFORNIA FIREBRAND(1948), p; SON OF GOD'S COUNTRY(1948), p; SUNDOWN IN SANTA FE(1948), p; TIMBER TRAIL, THE(1948), p; LAW OF THE GOLDEN WEST(1949), p; OUTCASTS OF THE TRAIL(1949), p; PRINCE OF THE PLAINS(1949), p; RANGER OF CHEROKEE STRIP(1949), p; SAN ANTONE AMBUSH(1949), p; SOUTH OF RIO(1949), p; MISSOURIANS, THE(1950), p; OLD FRONTIER, THE(1950), p; PIONEER MARSHAL(1950), p; SINGING GUNS(1950), p; UNDER MEXICALI STARS(1950), p; VANISHING WESTERNER, THE(1950), p; RODEO KING AND THE SENORITA(1951), p; SILVER CITY BONANZA(1951), p; THUNDER IN GOD'S COUNTRY(1951), p; UTAH WAGON TRAIN(1951), p; BLACK SHIELD OF FALWORTH, THE(1954), p; DRUMS ACROSS THE RIVER(1954), p; LOST MAN, THE(1969), p; WARM DECEMBER, A(1973, Brit.), p; UPTOWN SATURDAY NIGHT(1974), p; LET'S DO IT AGAIN(1975), p; PIECE OF THE ACTION, A(1977), p
Michael Tucker
END OF THE WORLD(in Our Usual Bed In a Night Full of Rain), THE (1978, Ital.); EYES OF LAURA MARS(1978); UNMARRIED WOMAN, AN(1978); DINER(1982)
1984
GOODBYE PEOPLE, THE(1984)
Nana Tucker
SENTINEL, THE(1977)
Norman Tucker
URBAN COWBOY(1980)
Orrin Tucker
YOU'RE THE ONE(1941); TENDER IS THE NIGHT(1961)
Paul Tucker
NEVER SAY NEVER AGAIN(1983)
Phil Tucker
ROBOT MONSTER(1953), p&d; CAPE CANAVERAL MONSTERS(1960), d&w; CHARLIE CHAN AND THE CURSE OF THE DRAGON QUEEN(1981), ed
Misc. Talkies
DANCE HALL RACKET(1956), d
Richard Tucker
JAZZ SINGER, THE(1927); MY MAN(1928); ON TRIAL(1928); SHOW GIRL(1928); DUMMY, THE(1929); HALF-MARRIAGE(1929); PAINTED FACES(1929); SQUALL, THE(1929); THIS IS HEAVEN(1929); UNHOLY NIGHT, THE(1929); BAT WHISPERS, THE(1930); BENSON MURDER CASE, THE(1930); BROTHERS(1930); COLLEGE LOVERS(1930); COURAGE(1930); MADONNA OF THE STREETS(1930); MANSLAUGHTER(1930); PEACOCK ALLEY(1930); PUTTIN' ON THE RITZ(1930); RECAPTURED LOVE(1930); SAFETY IN NUMBERS(1930); SHADOW OF THE LAW(1930); BLACK CAMEL, THE(1931); CONVICTED(1931); DECEIVER, THE(1931); GRAFT(1931); HELL BOUND(1931); HOLY TERROR, A(1931); INSPIRATION(1931); MAKER OF MEN(1931); SEED(1931); TOO YOUNG TO MARRY(1931); UP FOR MURDER(1931); CARELESS LADY(1932); DEVIL PAYS, THE(1932); FLAMES(1932); GUILTY AS HELL(1932); HAT CHECK GIRL(1932); PACK UP YOUR TROUBLES(1932); STOKER, THE(1932); SUCCESSFUL CALAMITY, A(1932); THE CRASH(1932); WEEK-END MARRIAGE(1932); DARING DAUGHTERS(1933); HER RESALE VALUE(1933); IRON MASTER, THE(1933); ONLY YESTERDAY(1933); SATURDAY'S MILLIONS(1933); WORKING MAN, THE(1933); WORLD GONE MAD, THE(1933); BABY, TAKE A BOW(1934); COUNTESS OF MONTE CRISTO, THE(1934); EVELYN PRENTICE(1934); GIRL FROM MISSOURI, THE(1934); HANDY ANDY(1934); MODERN HERO, A(1934); MONEY MEANS NOTHING(1934); OPERATOR 13(1934); PARIS INTERLUDE(1934); ROAD TO RUIN(1934); SHOW-OFF, THE(1934); SUCCESSFUL FAILURE, A(1934); TAKE THE STAND(1934); THIS SIDE OF HEAVEN(1934); CALM YOURSELF(1935); DANTE'S INFERNO(1935); DIAMOND JIM(1935); MURDER IN THE FLEET(1935); PUBLIC STENOGRAPHER(1935); SHADOW OF A DOUBT(1935); SING SING NIGHTS(1935); SYMPHONY OF LIVING(1935); WEST POINT OF THE AIR(1935); FLASH GORDON(1936); FLYING HOSTESS(1936); GREAT ZIEGFELD, THE(1936); LIBELED LADY(1936); PLOT THICKENS, THE(1936); RING AROUND THE MOON(1936); ARMORED CAR(1937); GIRL SAID NO, THE(1937); HEADLINE CRASHER(1937); I COVER THE WAR(1937); MAKE A WISH(1937); ROSALIE(1937); SHE'S DANGEROUS(1937); SOMETHING TO SING ABOUT(1937); SPECIAL AGENT K-7(1937); TRAPPED BY G-MEN(1937); TWO MINUTES TO PLAY(1937); DELINQUENT PARENTS(1938); GIRL OF THE GOLDEN WEST, THE(1938); HIGGINS FAMILY, THE(1938); LETTER OF INTRODUCTION(1938); ON THE GREAT WHITE TRAIL(1938); SHE'S GOT EVERYTHING(1938); SONS OF THE LEGION(1938); SWEETHEARTS(1938); TEST PILOT(1938); TEXANS, THE(1938); TRADE WINDS(1938); COVERED TRAILER, THE(1939); GIRL FROM RIO, THE(1939); GREAT VICTOR HERBERT, THE(1939); RISKY BUSINESS(1939); SUDDEN MONEY(1939); ROAD TO SINGAPORE(1940); SPORTING BLOOD(1940)
Misc. Talkies
BROKEN DISHES(1930); CROOKED ROAD(1932)
Silents
BABBLING TONGUES(1917); POWER OF DECISION, THE(1917); BRANDING IRON, THE(1920); DARLING MINE(1920); DOLLARS AND SENSE(1920); VOICE IN THE DARK(1921); DANGEROUS AGE, THE(1922); RAGS TO RICHES(1922); WHEN THE DEVIL DRIVES(1922); ELEVENTH HOUR, THE(1923); IS DIVORCE A FAILURE?(1923); POOR MEN'S WIVES(1923); BEAU BRUMMEL(1924); HELEN'S BABIES(1924); AIR MAIL, THE(1925); LURE OF THE WILD, THE(1925); BLIND GODDESS, THE(1926); THAT'S MY BABY(1926); GIRL FROM RIO, THE(1927); MATINEE LADIES(1927); WINGS(1927); CRIMSON CITY, THE(1928); GRAIN OF DUST, THE(1928); THANKS FOR THE BUGGY RIDE(1928)
Misc. Silents
CHILD IN JUDGEMENT, A(1915); COSSACK WHIP, THE(1916); WHEN LOVE IS KING(1916); BEHIND THE MASK(1917); LAW OF THE NORTH, THE(1917); LITTLE CHEVALIER, THE(1917); PARDNERS(1917); ROYAL PAUPER, THE(1917); THINK IT OVER(1917); THREADS OF FATE(1917); ROADS OF DESTINY(1921); GRAND LARCENY(1922); STRANGE IDOLS(1922); WORLDLY MADONNA, THE(1922); HER ACCIDENTAL HUSBAND(1923); LOVEBOUND(1923); STAR DUST TRAIL, THE(1924); TORNADO, THE(1924); 40-HORSE HAWKINS(1924); BRIDGE OF SIGHS, THE(1925); MAN WITHOUT A COUNTRY, THE(1925); DEVIL'S ISLAND(1926); GOLDEN COCOON, THE(1926); SHAMEFUL BEHAVIOR?(1926); WORLD AT HER FEET, THE(1927); BORDER PATROL, THE(1928); CAPTAIN SWAGGER(1928); LOVE OVER NIGHT(1928); LOVES OF AN ACTRESS(1928); DAUGHTERS OF DESIRE(1929)
Robert Tucker
STREETS OF NEW YORK(1939); STARS IN MY CROWN(1950), m; GYPSY(1962), ch; UNDER THE YUM-YUM TREE(1963), ch; FOR THOSE WHO THINK YOUNG(1964), ch; YOU'RE A BIG BOY NOW(1966), ch

Sophie Tucker
HONKY TONK(1929); GAY LOVE(1936, Brit.); BROADWAY MELODY OF '38(1937); THOROUGHBREDS DON'T CRY(1937); FOLLOW THE BOYS(1944); SENSATIONS OF 1945(1944); JOKER IS WILD, THE(1957)
Steve Tucker
ON THE NICKEL(1980)
Tanya Tucker
HARD COUNTRY(1981)
Teddy Tucker
DEEP, THE(1977)
Tomas Tucker
1984
SIGNAL 7(1984), ph
Tommy Tucker
TEST PILOT(1938)
William Tucker
STREETS OF NEW YORK(1939)
Misc. Silents
WIFE IN NAME ONLY(1923)
Garth Tuckett
GOLD(1974, Brit.)
Rita Tuckett
LOVE(1982, Can.)
Antoine Tudal
MODIGLIANI OF MONTPARNASSE(1961, Fr./Ital.); SUNDAYS AND CYBELE(1962, Fr.), a, w
Enrique Torres Tudela
TERROR IN THE JUNGLE(1968), p, w
Robert Tudewali
JEDDA, THE UNCIVILIZED(1956, Aus.)
Federico Martinez Tudo
SOFT SKIN ON BLACK SILK(1964, Fr./Span.), m
F.C.S. Tudor
Misc. Silents
DEVIL'S PROFESSION, THE(1915, Brit.), d
Fred Tudor
LAST GUNFIGHTER, THE(1961, Can.), m
Jennifer Tudor
PERSECUTION AND ASSASSINATION OF JEAN-PAUL MARAT AS PERFORMED BY THE INMATES OF THE ASYLUM OF CHARENTON UNDER THE DIRECTION OF THE MARQUIS DE SADE, THE(1967, Brit.); HAMLET(1969, Brit.)
Pamela Tudor
DOLLARS FOR A FAST GUN(1969, Ital./Span.); ONE STEP TO HELL(1969, U.S./Ital./Span.)
Misc. Talkies
REVOLT IN CANADA(1964); MAN ON THE SPYING TRAPEZE(1965)
Ray Tudor
FLESH EATERS, THE(1964)
Theresa Tudor
SEA CHASE, THE(1955)
Maurice Tuech
1984
UNTIL SEPTEMBER(1984)
John Tuell
OPENING NIGHT(1977)
Abisag Tuellmann
ALL-AROUND REDUCED PERSONALITY–OUTTAKES, THE(1978, Ger.)
Marina Tuerke
YOUNG LORD, THE(1970, Ger.)
Paul Tuerpe
SUPERMAN(1978); RAISE THE TITANIC(1980, Brit.); TOY, THE(1982)
William Tuers
Silents
ONE MILLION IN JEWELS(1923), ph; DIXIE FLYER, THE(1926), ph; NIGHT OWL, THE(1926), ph; RACING ROMANCE(1926), ph
Philip Tuersky
CHAMP, THE(1979)
Peter Tuesday
CHASE, THE(1946), cos
Ruby Tuesday
SHE-DEVILS ON WHEELS(1968); LOOSE ENDS(1975)
Bert Tuey
Silents
ALL FOR A GIRL(1915); GOVERNOR'S BOSS, THE(1915)
Brian Tufano
BIG SWITCH, THE(1970, Brit.), ph; QUADROPHENIA(1979, Brit.), ph; LORDS OF DISCIPLINE, THE(1983), ph
1984
DREAMSCAPE(1984), ph
Dennis Tufano
1984
BLAME IT ON THE NIGHT(1984)
Tuff de Lyle the Dog
UNDER PROOF(1936, Brit.); PIONEER TRAIL(1938)
Tuffy the Dog
TRAIL OF THE LONESOME PINE, THE(1936); MIGHTY TREVE, THE(1937); PHANTOM GOLD(1938); ROLLING CARAVANS(1938); STAGECOACH DAYS(1938)
Foale and Tuffin
TWO FOR THE ROAD(1967, Brit.), cos
Sally Tuffin
KALEIDOSCOPE(1966, Brit.), cos
Rich Tufo
TO ALL A GOODNIGHT(1980), m
Richard Tufo
THREE THE HARD WAY(1974), m; DEMENTED(1980), m
Hartley Tufts
AMBUSH(1939)

Sonny Tufts
GOVERNMENT GIRL(1943); SO PROUDLY WE HAIL(1943); HERE COME THE WAVES(1944); I LOVE A SOLDIER(1944); BRING ON THE GIRLS(1945); DUFFY'S TAVERN(1945); MISS SUSIE SLAGLE'S(1945); CROSS MY HEART(1946); SWELL GUY(1946); VIRGINIAN, THE(1946); WELL-GROOMED BRIDE, THE(1946); BLAZE OF NOON(1947); EASY COME, EASY GO(1947); VARIETY GIRL(1947); UNTAMED BREED, THE(1948); CROOKED WAY, THE(1949); EASY LIVING(1949); GLORY AT SEA(1952, Brit.); CAT WOMEN OF THE MOON(1953); NO ESCAPE(1953); RUN FOR THE HILLS(1953); SERPENT ISLAND(1954); SEVEN YEAR ITCH, THE(1955); COME NEXT SPRING(1956); PARSON AND THE OUTLAW, THE(1957); TOWN TAMER(1965); COTTONPICKIN' CHICKENPICKERS(1967)

T. Tugarinova
TSAR'S BRIDE, THE(1966, USSR)

Nikolay Tugelov
MORNING STAR(1962, USSR), a, w

Harry Tugend
TRUE TO LIFE(1943), w; CAPTAIN JANUARY(1935), w; LITTLEST REBEL, THE(1935), w; KING OF BURLESQUE(1936), w; PIGSKIN PARADE(1936), w; POOR LITTLE RICH GIRL(1936), w; SING, BABY, SING(1936), w; ALI BABA GOES TO TOWN(1937), w; LOVE IS NEWS(1937), w; WAKE UP AND LIVE(1937), w; YOU CAN'T HAVE EVERYTHING(1937), w; LITTLE MISS BROADWAY(1938), w; MY LUCKY STAR(1938), w; SALLY, IRENE AND MARY(1938), w; THANKS FOR EVERYTHING(1938), w; SECOND FIDDLE(1939), w; LITTLE OLD NEW YORK(1940), w; SEVEN SINNERS(1940), w; BIRTH OF THE BLUES(1941), w; CAUGHT IN THE DRAFT(1941), w; KISS THE BOYS GOODBYE(1941), w; POT O' GOLD(1941), w; LADY HAS PLANS, THE(1942), w; STAR SPANGLED RHYTHM(1942), w; LET'S FACE IT(1943), w; CROSS MY HEART(1946), p, w; GOLDEN EARRINGS(1947), p; TROUBLE WITH WOMEN, THE(1947), p; SONG IS BORN, A(1948), w; SOUTHERN YANKEE, A(1948), w; TAKE ME OUT TO THE BALL GAME(1949), w; WABASH AVENUE(1950), w; DARLING, HOW COULD YOU!(1951), p; ROAD TO BALI(1952), p, w; OFF LIMITS(1953), p; PUBLIC PIGEON NO. 1(1957), p, w; POCKETFUL OF MIRACLES(1961), w; WHO'S MINDING THE STORE?(1963), w

Richard Tuggle
ESCAPE FROM ALCATRAZ(1979), w
1984
TIGHTROPE(1984), d&w

Chief Elmer Tugsmith
NICKELODEON(1976)

Marita Tuhkunen
MAKE LIKE A THIEF(1966, Fin.)

Tuiletefuga
PACIFIC DESTINY(1956, Brit.)

Vladimiro Tuilovich
HERCULES, SAMSON & ULYSSES(1964, Ital.)

Peter Tuinman
GIRL WITH THE RED HAIR, THE(1983, Neth.); SPETTERS(1983, Holland)

Timothy Tuinstra
GUNFIGHT, A(1971)

Tino Tuiolosega
SEVEN(1979)

Kuka L. Tuitama
ROAD TO BALI(1952)

Kuka Tuitama
WAKE OF THE RED WITCH(1949); ESCAPE TO BURMA(1955)

Sam K. Tuiteleapaga
PARADISE ISLE(1937), m

Vladimir Tukan
1984
MOSCOW ON THE HUDSON(1984)

Paul Tuke
LOOKS AND SMILES(1982, Brit.)

Ziona Tukterman
SINAI COMMANDOS: THE STORY OF THE SIX DAY WAR(1968, Israel/Ger.)

Tula
FOR YOUR EYES ONLY(1981)

Ingrid Tulean [Thulin]
FOREIGN INTRIGUE(1956)

Mark Tulin
DEFIANCE(1980), w

Debbie Tull
HAPPY BIRTHDAY TO ME(1981)

John Tull
DOBERMAN GANG, THE(1972)
Misc. Talkies
COUNTRY CUZZINS(1972); MIDNIGHT PLOWBOY(1973)

Paul Tulley
METEOR(1979)
1984
JOY OF SEX(1984)
Misc. Talkies
KID FROM NOT SO BIG, THE(1978)

Marco Tulli
BEAT THE DEVIL(1953); ROMAN HOLIDAY(1953); MONTE CARLO STORY, THE(1957, Ital.); SEVEN HILLS OF ROME, THE(1958); FAST AND SEXY(1960, Fr./Ital.); NIGHTS OF LUCRETIA BORGIA, THE(1960, Ital.); WONDERS OF ALADDIN, THE(1961, Fr./Ital.); PRISONER OF THE IRON MASK(1962, Fr./Ital.); THREE FACES OF SIN(1963, Fr./Ital.); LET'S TALK ABOUT WOMEN(1964, Fr./Ital.); REVOLT OF THE MERCENARIES(1964, Ital./Span.); VARIETY LIGHTS(1965, Ital.); SECRET OF SANTA VITTORIA, THE(1969); STATUE, THE(1971, Brit.); MR. BILLION(1977)

Tullia
EYE OF THE CAT(1969)

Mike Tulligan
MISSION TO MOSCOW(1943)

Christian Tullio
WIND FROM THE EAST(1970, Fr./Ital./Ger.)

Chris Tullio-Altan
CELINE AND JULIE GO BOATING(1974, Fr.), ed

Edward Tullis
TOMAHAWK(1951)

Jerry Tullis [Jiri Vrstala]
VOYAGE TO THE END OF THE UNIVERSE(1963, Czech.)

Jerry Tullos
RISKY BUSINESS(1983)

Amanda Jane Tully
Misc. Talkies
JOHNSTOWN MONSTER, THE(1971)

Brian Tully
INTERNECINE PROJECT, THE(1974, Brit.)

Caroline Tully
QUACKSER FORTUNE HAS A COUSIN IN THE BRONX(1970)

Colin Tully
THAT SINKING FEELING(1979, Brit.), m; GREGORY'S GIRL(1982, Brit.), m

Ethel Tully
Misc. Silents
FLAMES OF JOHANNIS, THE(1916); IGNORANCE(1916)

Frank Tully
BAD FOR EACH OTHER(1954)

George Tully
Silents
JIMMY(1916, Brit.)
Misc. Silents
WOMAN WHO WAS NOTHING, THE(1917, Brit.); DIVINE GIFT, THE(1918, Brit.)

Jim Tully
BEGGARS OF LIFE(1928), w, ed; WAY FOR A SAILOR(1930); LAUGHTER IN HELL(1933), w

John Tully
DUBLIN NIGHTMARE(1958, Brit.), w; FACES IN THE DARK(1960, Brit.), w; IN THE WAKE OF A STRANGER(1960, Brit.), w
Silents
GOLD RUSH, THE(1925)

May Tully
Silents
KISSES(1922), w
Misc. Silents
OLD OAKEN BUCKET, THE(1921), d; THAT OLD GANG OF MINE(1925), d

Montgomery Tully
FOR YOU ALONE(1945, Brit.), w; QUERY(1945, Brit.), d&w; MURDER IN REVERSE(1946, Brit.), d&w; WALTZ TIME(1946, Brit.), w; SPRINGTIME(1948, Brit.), d, w; BOYS IN BROWN(1949, Brit.), d&w; MRS. FITZHERBERT(1950, Brit.), d, w; TALE OF FIVE WOMEN, A(1951, Brit.), d; GIRDLE OF GOLD(1952, Brit.), d; SMALL TOWN STORY(1953, Brit.), d; TERROR STREET(1953), d; DEVIL'S HARBOR(1954, Brit.), d; DIAMOND WIZARD, THE(1954, Brit.), d; PAID TO KILL(1954, Brit.), d; GLASS TOMB, THE(1955, Brit.), d; WAY OUT, THE(1956, Brit.), d&w; COUNTERFEIT PLAN, THE(1957, Brit.), d; KEY MAN, THE(1957, Brit.), d; NO ROAD BACK(1957, Brit.), d, w; SCOTLAND YARD DRAGNET(1957, Brit.), d&w; VIOLENT STRANGER(1957, Brit.), d; DIPLOMATIC CORPSE, THE(1958, Brit.), d; FEMALE FIENDS(1958, Brit.), d; I ONLY ASKED!(1958, Brit.), d; LONG KNIFE, THE(1958, Brit.), d; MAN WITH A GUN(1958, Brit.), d; MAN ACCUSED(1959), d; DEAD LUCKY(1960, Brit.), d; ELECTRONIC MONSTER. THE(1960, Brit.), d; HOUSE IN MARSH ROAD, THE(1960, Brit.), d; JACKPOT(1960, Brit.), d, w; MAN WHO WAS NOBODY, THE(1960, Brit.), d; PRICE OF SILENCE, THE(1960, Brit.), d; MIDDLE COURSE, THE(1961, Brit.), d; THIRD ALIBI, THE(1961, Brit.), d; TWO WIVES AT ONE WEDDING(1961, Brit.), d; OUT OF THE FOG(1962, Brit.), d&w; SHE KNOWS Y'KNOW(1962, Brit.), d, w; MASTER SPY(1964, Brit.), d, w; ESCAPE BY NIGHT(1965, Brit.), d, w; WHO KILLED THE CAT?(1966, Brit.), d, w; TERRORNAUTS, THE(1967, Brit.), d; BATTLE BENEATH THE EARTH(1968, Brit.), d

Phil Tully
DARK PAST, THE(1948); FORCE OF EVIL(1948); ALL THE KING'S MEN(1949); HOUSE OF STRANGERS(1949); OH, YOU BEAUTIFUL DOLL(1949); LOVE THAT BRUTE(1950); NO WAY OUT(1950); WHERE THE SIDEWALK ENDS(1950); I WAS A COMMUNIST FOR THE F.B.I.(1951); AGAINST ALL FLAGS(1952); O. HENRY'S FULL HOUSE(1952); STRANGER WORE A GUN, THE(1953); KNOCK ON WOOD(1954)

Philip Tully
LIVE, LOVE AND LEARN(1937)

Phillip Tully
NO MAN OF HER OWN(1950)

Richard Walton Tully
BIRD OF PARADISE(1932), w; ROSE OF THE RANCHO(1936), w; BIRD OF PARADISE(1951), w
Silents
ROSE OF THE RANCHO(1914), w; FLOWING GOLD(1924), w

Simon Tully
Misc. Talkies
JOHNSTOWN MONSTER, THE(1971)

Susan Tully
TO FIND A MAN(1972)

Tom Tully
CAREFREE(1938); MISSION TO MOSCOW(1943); NORTHERN PURSUIT(1943); DESTINATION TOKYO(1944); I'LL BE SEEING YOU(1944); SECRET COMMAND(1944); ADVENTURE(1945); KISS AND TELL(1945); TOWN WENT WILD, THE(1945); UNSEEN, THE(1945); TILL THE END OF TIME(1946); VIRGINIAN, THE(1946); INTRIGUE(1947); KILLER McCOY(1947); LADY IN THE LAKE(1947); BLOOD ON THE MOON(1948); JUNE BRIDE(1948); RACHEL AND THE STRANGER(1948); SCUDDA-HOO! SCUDDA-HAY!(1948); ILLEGAL ENTRY(1949); KISS FOR CORLISS, A(1949); LADY TAKES A SAILOR, THE(1949); WHERE THE SIDEWALK ENDS(1950); BRANDED(1951); LADY AND THE BANDIT, THE(1951); TEXAS CARNIVAL(1951); TOMAHAWK(1951); LOVE IS BETTER THAN EVER(1952); LURE OF THE WILDERNESS(1952); RETURN OF THE TEXAN(1952); RUBY GENTRY(1952); TURNING POINT, THE(1952); JAZZ SINGER, THE(1953); MOON IS BLUE, THE(1953); SEA OF LOST SHIPS(1953); TROUBLE ALONG THE WAY(1953); ARROW IN THE DUST(1954); CAINE MUTINY, THE(1954); LOVE ME OR LEAVE ME(1955); SOLDIER OF FORTUNE(1955); BEHIND THE HIGH WALL(1956); 10 NORTH FREDERICK(1958); WACKIEST SHIP IN THE ARMY, THE(1961); CARPETBAGGERS, THE(1964); MC HALE'S NAVY JOINS THE AIR FORCE(1965); COOGAN'S BLUFF(1968); CHARLEY VARRICK(1973); PORKY'S II: THE NEXT DAY(1983)

Tumaatura
TANGA-TIKA(1953)
Y. Tumanskaya
Misc. Silents
MIRACLE-MAKER(1922, USSR)
Carlo Tumberlani
BURIED ALIVE(1951, Ital.)
Tumbleweed Tumblers
SQUARE DANCE JUBILEE(1949)
Gualtiero Tumiati
DEVOTION(1953, Ital.); STRANGE DECEPTION(1953, Ital.); ULYSSES(1955, Ital.); WAR AND PEACE(1956, Ital./U.S.); SHIP OF CONDEMNED WOMEN, THE(1963, ITAL.)
Helen Tumpson
THERE'S ALWAYS VANILLA(1972)
Tun Tun
CHAMBER OF HORRORS(1966)
Charlie Tuna
ROLLERCOASTER(1977)
Karl Tunberg
LIFE BEGINS IN COLLEGE(1937), w; YOU CAN'T HAVE EVERYTHING(1937), w; HOLD THAT CO-ED(1938), w; MY LUCKY STAR(1938), w; REBECCA OF SUNNY-BROOK FARM(1938), w; SALLY, IRENE AND MARY(1938), w; DOWN ARGENTINE WAY(1940), w; I WAS AN ADVENTURESS(1940), w; PUBLIC DEB NO. 1(1940), w; SHIPYARD SALLY(1940, Brit.), w; TALL, DARK AND HANDSOME(1941), w; WEEK-END IN HAVANA(1941), w; YANK IN THE R.A.F., A(1941), w; LUCKY JOR-DAN(1942), w; MY GAL SAL(1942), w; ORCHESTRA WIVES(1942), w; STANDING ROOM ONLY(1944), w; BRING ON THE GIRLS(1945), w; KITTY(1945), p, w; MAS-QUERADE IN MEXICO(1945), p, w; IMPERFECT LADY, THE(1947), p, w; UP IN CENTRAL PARK(1948), p, w; YOU GOTTA STAY HAPPY(1948), p, w; LOVE THAT BRUTE(1950), w; LAW AND THE LADY, THE(1951), w; NIGHT INTO MOR-NING(1951), w; BECAUSE YOU'RE MINE(1952), w; SCANDAL AT SCOURIE(1953), w; BEAU BRUMMELL(1954), w; VALLEY OF THE KINGS(1954), w; SCARLET COAT, THE(1955), w; SEVENTH SIN, THE(1957), w; BEN HUR(1959), w; COUNT YOUR BLESSINGS(1959), p, w; LIBEL(1959, Brit.), w; I THANK A FOOL(1962, Brit.), w; TARAS BULBA(1962), w; SEVENTH DAWN, THE(1964), w; HARLOW(1965), w; WHERE WERE YOU WHEN THE LIGHTS WENT OUT?(1968), w; HOW DO I LOVE THEE?(1970), w
William Tunberg
THAT'S MY BABY(1944), w; WAR PAINT(1953), w; GARDEN OF EVIL(1954), w; MASSACRE(1956), w; OLD YELLER(1957), w; SAVAGE SAM(1963), w
Graham Tunbridge
OLD MOTHER RILEY, HEADMISTRESS(1950, Brit.); INTRUDER, THE(1955, Brit.)
Irene Tunc
PARIS HOLIDAY(1958); LIVE FOR LIFE(1967, Fr./Ital.); LAST ADVENTURE, THE(1968, Fr./Ital.); JE T'AIME, JE T'AIME(1972, Fr./Swed.); TWO ENGLISH GIRLS(1972, Fr.)
V. Gareth Tundrey
JOURNEY'S END(1930), w
Russell Tune
MASSACRE AT CENTRAL HIGH(1976), art d
Tommy Tune
HELLO, DOLLY!(1969); BOY FRIEND, THE(1971, Brit.)
The Tune Twisters
SWEET SURRENDER(1935)
Zeki Tuney
DRY SUMMER(1967, Turkey)
Al Tung
BLOOD MONEY(1974, U.S./Hong Kong/Ital./Span.)
Harry Tung
SHE LEARNED ABOUT SAILORS(1934)
Sandy Tung
SUPER SPOOK(1975), ed; MARRIAGE, A(1983), d&w
Yau Shan Tung
DON'T WORRY, WE'LL THINK OF A TITLE(1966)
Lee Tung-Foo
FLIGHT COMMAND(1940); THEY KNEW WHAT THEY WANTED(1940); INVISI-BLE AGENT(1942); MRS. PARKINGTON(1944); PURPLE HEART, THE(1944)
Irv Tunick
MURDER, INC.(1960), w
Irve Tunick
LADY OF VENGEANCE(1957, Brit), w; HIGH HELL(1958), w
Jonathan Tunick
TWELVE CHAIRS, THE(1970), md; LITTLE NIGHT MUSIC, A(1977, Aust./U.S./Ger.); ENDLESS LOVE(1981), m; FORT APACHE, THE BRONX(1981), m; I AM THE CHEESE(1983), m
John R. Tunis
HARD, FAST, AND BEAUTIFUL(1951), w
Earl Tunner
FIRETRAP, THE(1935), ed
Gene Tunney
Misc. Silents
FIGHTING MARINE, THE(1926)
Sen. John V Tunney
CANDIDATE, THE(1972)
G. Tunney-Smith
PLUMBER, THE(1980, Aus.), ed
Reg Tunnicliffe
RAINBOW BOYS, THE(1973, Can.), set d
Bill Tuntke
SON OF FLUBBER(1963), art d
William H. Tuntke
TIMETABLE(1956), art d; MARY POPPINS(1964), art d; MONKEY'S UNCLE, THE(1965), art d; THAT DARN CAT(1965), art d; GNOME-MOBILE, THE(1967), art d
William Tuntke
MISADVENTURES OF MERLIN JONES, THE(1964), art d; ANDROMEDA STRAIN, THE(1971), art d; GRAY LADY DOWN(1978), prod d; NUDE BOMB, THE(1980), prod d

1984
CLOAK AND DAGGER(1984), prod d
Dorothy Tuomi
NIGHT IN PARADISE, A(1946)
Olavi Tuomi
PRELUDE TO ECSTASY(1963, Fin.), ph
Arto Tuominen
TIME OF ROSES(1970, Fin.)
Oleg Tupine
LOOK FOR THE SILVER LINING(1949)
Manu Tupou
HAWAII(1966); EXTRAORDINARY SEAMAN, THE(1969); MAN CALLED HORSE, A(1970); CASTAWAY COWBOY, THE(1974); HURRICANE(1979)
Loretta Tupper
ANNIE HALL(1977); SOMETHING SHORT OF PARADISE(1979); HONKY TONK FREEWAY(1981); KING OF COMEDY, THE(1983)
Madelon Tupper
WHAT'S THE MATTER WITH HELEN?(1971)
Pearl Tupper
Silents
HUNCHBACK OF NOTRE DAME, THE(1923)
Tristam Tupper
KLONDIKE(1932), w; PHANTOM BROADCAST, THE(1933), w; KLONDIKE FU-RY(1942), w
Tristram Tupper
RIVER, THE(1928), w; CHRISTINA(1929), w; LUCKY STAR(1929), w; SALU-TE(1929), w; AVENGER, THE(1933), w; MY MOTHER(1933), w; BEGGARS IN ER-MINE(1934), w; LOST IN THE STRATOSPHERE(1935), w; RED HOT TIRES(1935), w; GIRL OVERBOARD(1937), w; NIGHT KEY(1937), w
Leonid Tur
MILITARY SECRET(1945, USSR), w
Peter Tur
MILITARY SECRET(1945, USSR), w
Teddy Turai-Rossi
BIG SHOW, THE(1961), cos
Ben Turbett
Misc. Silents
WHEN LOVE IS KING(1916), d; BUILDERS OF CASTLES(1917), d; COURAGE OF THE COMMONPLACE(1917), d; CY WHITTAKER'S WARD(1917), d; LADY OF THE PHOTOGRAPH, THE(1917), d; LAST SENTENCE, THE(1917), d; ROYAL PAUPER, THE(1917), d
James Turbin
Silents
BAR SINISTER, THE(1917)
Sylvia Turbova
MAN WHO LIES, THE(1970, Czech./Fr.)
A. Turcewicz
WALKOVER(1969, Pol.)
Felipe Turch
BEAUTY AND THE BANDIT(1946)
I. Turchenkov
WAR AND PEACE(1968, USSR)
Bruno Turchetto
CONQUEST OF MYCENE(1965, Ital., Fr.), p; CONFESSIONS OF A POLICE CAP-TAIN(1971, Ital.), p
Guido Turchi
STEPPE, THE(1963, Fr./Ital.), m
Enzo Turchini
WHITE SISTER(1973, Ital./Span./Fr.)
Annabella Turco
1984
MOSCOW ON THE HUDSON(1984)
Enzo Turco
FOUR DAYS OF NAPLES, THE(1963, US/Ital.); ANZIO(1968, Ital.)
Paolo Turco
THAT SPLENDID NOVEMBER(1971, Ital./Fr.); BREAD AND CHOCOLATE(1978, Ital.)
Tony Turco
PRINCE OF THE CITY(1981)
1984
BROADWAY DANNY ROSE(1984)
Umberto Turco
CONFESSIONS OF A POLICE CAPTAIN(1971, Ital.), art d&cos; TEMPTER, THE(1974, Ital./Brit.), art d
Zigmund Turcoff
VILNA LEGEND, A(1949, U.S./Pol.)
Andree Turcy
OF FLESH AND BLOOD(1964, Fr./Ital.)
Michel Tureau
ANATOMY OF A MARRIAGE(MY DAYS WITH JEAN-MARC AND MY NIGHTS WITH FRANCOISE) (1964 Fr.)
Ludwig Turek
OUR DAILY BREAD(1950, Ger.), w
Louis Turenne
HAPPY BIRTHDAY, WANDA JUNE(1971); MANDINGO(1975); GOOD DISSO-NANCE LIKE A MAN, A(1977); OLIVER'S STORY(1978); POSTMAN ALWAYS RINGS TWICE, THE(1981)
Blanche Turer
WIRE SERVICE(1942)
James Turfler
Silents
DOWN TO THE SEA IN SHIPS(1923); WARRENS OF VIRGINIA, THE(1924)
Ivan Turgenev
FATHERS AND SONS(1960, USSR), w; FIRST LOVE(1970, Ger./Switz.), w
Ivan Sergeyevich Turgenev
MUMU(1961, USSR), w
Peter Turgeon
DEAR HEART(1964); MUSCLE BEACH PARTY(1964); WHAT'S SO BAD ABOUT FEELING GOOD?(1968); LAST SUMMER(1969); ME, NATALIE(1969); SOME KIND OF A NUT(1969); AIRPORT(1970); POSSESSION OF JOEL DELANEY, THE(1972);

FROM THE MIXED-UP FILES OF MRS. BASIL E. FRANKWEILER(1973); AMERICAN GIGOLO(1980)

Turi
DIFFICULT YEARS(1950, Ital.)

Felipe Turich
BELLS OF SAN FERNANDO(1947); MEXICAN HAYRIDE(1948); TO THE VICTOR(1948); SON OF BILLY THE KID(1949); WE WERE STRANGERS(1949); BANDIT QUEEN(1950); CAPTURE, THE(1950); CRISIS(1950); LAWLESS, THE(1950); SHORT GRASS(1950); WYOMING MAIL(1950); MY FAVORITE SPY(1951); RANCHO NOTORIOUS(1952); HITCH-HIKER, THE(1953); JEOPARDY(1953); JUBILEE TRAIL(1954); THREE HOURS TO KILL(1954); GIANT(1956); ONE-EYED JACKS(1961); JESSE JAMES MEETS FRANKENSTEIN'S DAUGHTER(1966); HOOK, LINE AND SINKER(1969); FUZZ(1972); WALK PROUD(1979)

Phillip Turich
LONE RIDER CROSSES THE RIO, THE(1941)

Phillips Turich
OUTLAWS OF THE RIO GRANDE(1941)

Rosa Turich
STARLIGHT OVER TEXAS(1938); RANGERS OF FORTUNE(1940); SIX LESSONS FROM MADAME LA ZONGA(1941); BOWERY BUCKAROOS(1947); LOVES OF CARMEN, THE(1948); SON OF BILLY THE KID(1949); DAKOTA LIL(1950); KID FROM TEXAS, THE(1950); ON THE ISLE OF SAMOA(1950); TRIPOLI(1950); CUBAN FIREBALL(1951); HAVANA ROSE(1951); JIVARO(1954); JUBILEE TRAIL(1954); PASSION(1954); PHANTOM STALLION, THE(1954); MOVE OVER, DARLING(1963); JESSE JAMES MEETS FRANKENSTEIN'S DAUGHTER(1966)

Rose Turich
ROSE OF THE RIO GRANDE(1938); DRIFTING WESTWARD(1939); HITCH-HIKER, THE(1953)

Marcello Turilli
MODESTY BLAISE(1966, Brit.)

Max Turilli
HORNET'S NEST(1970)

Julie Turin
CHARLES AND LUCIE(1982, Fr.)

Victor Turin
Misc. Silents
TURKSIB(1930, USSR), d

Luciana Turina
SERAFINO(1970, Fr./Ital.)

Danilo Turk
CAVE OF THE LIVING DEAD(1966, Yugo./Ger.)

Dave Turk
LOVES OF JOANNA GODDEN, THE(1947, Brit.)

John Turk
ROUSTABOUT(1964)

Jonathan Turk
MY BODYGUARD(1980)

Marcus Turk
SOUTHERN YANKEE, A(1948)

Marion Turk
I WONDER WHO'S KISSING HER NOW(1947), w; DANCING IN THE DARK(1949), w

Turk Murphy Jazz Band
Misc. Talkies
ALABAMA'S GHOST(1972)

Ann Turkel
PAPER LION(1968); 99 AND 44/100% DEAD(1974); CASSANDRA CROSSING, THE(1977); GOLDEN RENDEZVOUS(1977); RAVAGERS, THE(1979); HUMANOIDS FROM THE DEEP(1980)
Misc. Talkies
PORTRAIT OF A HITMAN(1984)

Joe Turkel
STARLIFT(1951); MAN CRAZY(1953); SLIGHT CASE OF LARCENY, A(1953); NAKED STREET, THE(1955); FRIENDLY PERSUASION(1956); WARLOCK(1959); SHINING, THE(1980); BLADE RUNNER(1982)

Joseph Turkel
ANGELS IN DISGUISE(1949); CITY ACROSS THE RIVER(1949); SWORD IN THE DESERT(1949); FEDERAL MAN(1950); LUCKY LOSERS(1950); TRIPLE TROUBLE(1950); GLASS WALL, THE(1953); DUFFY OF SAN QUENTIN(1954); INSIDE DETROIT(1955); MAD AT THE WORLD(1955); KILLING, THE(1956); HELLCATS OF THE NAVY(1957); JEANNE EAGELS(1957); PATHS OF GLORY(1957); BEAST OF BUDAPEST, THE(1958); BONNIE PARKER STORY, THE(1958); CASE AGAINST BROOKLYN, THE(1958); HERE COME THE JETS(1959); VERBOTEN!(1959); PURPLE GANG, THE(1960); TORMENTED(1960); PORTRAIT OF A MOBSTER(1961); YELLOW CANARY, THE(1963); CARPETBAGGERS, THE(1964); KING RAT(1965); VILLAGE OF THE GIANTS(1965); SAND PEBBLES, THE(1966); ST. VALENTINE'S DAY MASSACRE, THE(1967); DEVIL'S 8, THE(1969); ANIMALS, THE(1971); BLACK JACK(1973); HINDENBURG, THE(1975); SAVAGE ABDUCTION(1975); COMMITMENT, THE(1976); WHICH WAY IS UP?(1977)

Greta Turken
SOPHIE'S CHOICE(1982)

Mikandr Turkin
Misc. Silents
DAREDEVIL(1919, USSR), d

Nikandr Turkin
Misc. Silents
SHACKLED BY FILM(1918, USSR), d

Clifford Turknett
DUCHESS AND THE DIRTWATER FOX, THE(1976)

Marie Turko
1984
SCARRED(1984), p, d&w, ed

Burton Turkus
MURDER, INC.(1960), w

Veronica Turleigh
KING ARTHUR WAS A GENTLEMAN(1942, Brit.); PROMOTER, THE(1952, Brit.); HORSE'S MOUTH, THE(1958, Brit.)

Diane Turley
M(1970)
Misc. Talkies
END OF AUGUST(1974)

Dianne Turley
ANGELS DIE HARD(1970); BURY ME AN ANGEL(1972)

George Turley
STORY ON PAGE ONE, THE(1959)

Jack Turley
EMPIRE OF THE ANTS(1977), w

Linda Turley
DEAD AND BURIED(1981)

Tom Turlley
GALAXINA(1980), prod d

Philippe Turlure
MURMUR OF THE HEART(1971, Fr./Ital./Ger.), art d

Robert Turlure
FANNY(1961), set d; CHRISTMAS TREE, THE(1969, Fr.), set d

Glynn Turman
FIVE ON THE BLACK HAND SIDE(1973); THOMASINE AND BUSHROD(1974); TOGETHER BROTHERS(1974); COOLEY HIGH(1975); J.D.'S REVENGE(1976); HERO AIN'T NOTHIN' BUT A SANDWICH, A(1977); SERPENT'S EGG, THE(1977, Ger./U.S.); PENITENTIARY II(1982)
1984
GREMLINS(1984)
Misc. Talkies
AWOL(1973)

Lawrence Turman
YOUNG DOCTORS, THE(1961), p; I COULD GO ON SINGING(1963), p; BEST MAN, THE(1964), p; FLIM-FLAM MAN, THE(1967), p; GRADUATE, THE(1967), p; GREAT WHITE HOPE, THE(1970), p; MARRIAGE OF A YOUNG STOCKBROKER, THE(1971), p&d; DROWNING POOL, THE(1975), p; HEROES(1977), p; WALK PROUD(1979), p; CAVEMAN(1981), p; THING, THE(1982), p; SECOND THOUGHTS(1983), p, d
1984
MASS APPEAL(1984), p

Shila Turna
BUSTIN' LOOSE(1981)

Bob Turnbull
DRAGSTRIP RIOT(1958)

David Turnbull
2,000 WEEKS(1970, Aus.)

Debbie Turnbull
HOMER(1970)

Deborah Turnbull
RED DRESS, THE(1954, Brit.); THRESHOLD(1983, Can.)

Glen Turnbull
MODEL WIFE(1941); WEST POINT STORY, THE(1950); SHE'S WORKING HER WAY THROUGH COLLEGE(1952); WINNING TEAM, THE(1952)

Glenn Turnbull
RICHEST MAN IN TOWN(1941); TRAMP, TRAMP, TRAMP(1942); HOLIDAY RHYTHM(1950); I DREAM OF JEANIE(1952)

Hector Turnbull
DUMMY, THE(1929), p; WHY BRING THAT UP?(1929), w; ANYBODY'S WAR(1930), w; MOROCCO(1930), p; CHEAT, THE(1931), w
Silents
MARRIAGE OF KITTY, THE(1915), w; TEMPTATION(1915), w; ALIEN SOULS(1916), w; DUPE, THE(1916), w; RACE, THE(1916), w; CLEVER MRS. CARFAX, THE(1917), w; PRIVATE SCANDAL, A(1921), w; HOMESPUN VAMP, A(1922), w; MY AMERICAN WIFE(1923), w; CASEY AT THE BAT(1927), p, w; UNDERWORLD(1927), p

John Turnbull
GABLES MYSTERY, THE(1931, Brit.); KEEPERS OF YOUTH(1931, Brit.); TONS OF MONEY(1931, Brit.); WICKHAM MYSTERY, THE(1931, Brit.); 77 PARK LANE(1931, Brit.); MURDER ON THE SECOND FLOOR(1932, Brit.); ASK BECCLES(1933, Brit.); IRON STAIR, THE(1933, Brit.); MAN OUTSIDE, THE(1933, Brit.); MEDICINE MAN, THE(1933, Brit.); PRIVATE LIFE OF HENRY VIII, THE(1933); TOO MANY WIVES(1933, Brit.); UMBRELLA, THE(1933, Brit.); BADGER'S GREEN(1934, Brit.); BLACK ABBOT, THE(1934, Brit.); CASE FOR THE CROWN, THE(1934, Brit.); GIRL IN THE FLAT, THE(1934, Brit.); IT'S A COP(1934, Brit.); LADY IS WILLING, THE(1934, Brit.); LORD EDGEWARE DIES(1934, Brit.); NIGHT OF THE PARTY, THE(1934, Brit.); PASSING SHADOWS(1934, Brit.); TANGLED EVIDENCE(1934, Brit.); WARN LONDON!(1934, Brit.); WHAT HAPPENED TO HARKNESS(1934, Brit.); BLACK MASK(1935, Brit.); LAD, THE(1935, Brit.); LINE ENGAGED(1935, Brit.); MUSIC HATH CHARMS(1935, Brit.); ONCE IN A NEW MOON(1935, Brit.); RADIO PIRATES(1935, Brit.); REAL BLOKE, A(1935, Brit.); SCARLET PIMPERNEL, THE(1935, Brit.); SEXTON BLAKE AND THE BEARDED DOCTOR(1935, Brit.); WOLVES OF THE UNDERWORLD(1935, Brit.); HEARTS OF HUMANITY(1936, Brit.); LADY JANE GREY(1936, Brit.); LIMPING MAN, THE(1936, Brit.); PASSING OF THE THIRD FLOOR BACK, THE(1936, Brit.); REMBRANDT(1936, Brit.); SHADOW, THE(1936, Brit.); SHIPMATES O' MINE(1936, Brit.); WHERE THERE'S A WILL(1936, Brit); DEATH CROONS THE BLUES(1937, Brit.); IT'S A GRAND OLD WORLD(1937, Brit.); MAKE-UP(1937, Brit.); MAN OF AFFAIRS(1937, Brit.); ROMANCE AND RICHES(1937, Brit.); SATURDAY NIGHT REVUE(1937, Brit.); SONG OF THE ROAD(1937, Brit.); TALKING FEET(1937, Brit.); WHO KILLED FEN MARKHAM?(1937, Brit.); NIGHT ALONE(1938, Brit.); STEPPING TOES(1938, Brit.); STRANGE BOARDERS(1938, Brit.); DEAD MEN ARE DANGEROUS(1939, Brit.); INSPECTOR HORNLEIGH ON HOLIDAY(1939, Brit.); HIDDEN MENACE, THE(1940, Brit.); RETURN TO YESTERDAY(1940, Brit.); SPARE A COPPER(1940, Brit.); SPIES OF THE AIR(1940, Brit.); THREE SILENT MEN(1940, Brit.); HARD STEEL(1941, Brit.); MURDER AT THE BASKERVILLES(1941, Brit.); OLD MOTHER RILEY'S CIRCUS(1941, Brit.); TERROR, THE(1941, Brit.); SHIPBUILDERS, THE(1943, Brit.); DON'T TAKE IT TO HEART(1944, Brit.); PLACE OF ONE'S OWN, A(1945, Brit.); HANGMAN WAITS, THE(1947, Brit.); SO WELL REMEMBERED(1947, Brit.); DAYDREAK(1948, Brit.); MAN OF EVIL(1948, Brit.); HAPPIEST DAYS OF YOUR LIFE(1950, Brit.)

Lee Turnbull
I WANT YOU(1951); DREAMBOAT(1952); NO ROOM FOR THE GROOM(1952); FARMER TAKES A WIFE, THE(1953); COME ON, THE(1956)

Margaret Turnbull
BAD LITTLE ANGEL(1939), w
Silents
CLASSMATES(1914), w; ARMSTRONG'S WIFE(1915), w; ALIEN SOULS(1916), w; DUPE, THE(1916), w; JACK AND JILL(1917), w; EVE'S DAUGHTER(1918), w; MY COUSIN(1918), w; THOU ART THE MAN(1920), w; APPEARANCES(1921), w; ANNA ASCENDS(1922), w; CLASSMATES(1924), w
Patrick Turnbull
Silents
ARTISTIC TEMPERAMENT, THE(1919, Brit.)
Stanley Turnbull
Silents
AS HE WAS BORN(1919, Brit.)
Dee Turnell
EASTER PARADE(1948); BARKLEYS OF BROADWAY, THE(1949); ROYAL WEDDING(1951); STRIP, THE(1951); BAD AND THE BEAUTIFUL, THE(1952); BAND WAGON, THE(1953); GIRL WHO HAD EVERYTHING, THE(1953); BRIGADOON(1954); DEEP IN MY HEART(1954)
Mrs. Turner
Silents
PAIR OF CUPIDS, A(1918)
Alfred Turner
Silents
MISSING THE TIDE(1918, Brit.), w
Alicia Turner
Silents
WET GOLD(1921)
Anita Turner
STRANGE MR. GREGORY, THE(1945); GANGSTER, THE(1947); RIVER LADY(1948)
Anna Turner
FLOATING DUTCHMAN, THE(1953, Brit.); WOMAN IN HIDING(1953, Brit.); DELAVINE AFFAIR, THE(1954, Brit.); EYEWITNESS(1956, Brit.); LAST MAN TO HANG, THE(1956, Brit.); GOOD COMPANIONS, THE(1957, Brit.); TEARS FOR SIMON(1957, Brit.); URGE TO KILL(1960, Brit.); HOT MONEY GIRL(1962, Brit./Ger.); STRONGROOM(1962, Brit.); ISLAND OF THE BURNING DAMNED(1971, Brit.)
Arnold Turner
VICE SQUAD(1982)
1984
FLETCH(1984)
Arnold F. Turner
DIRTY HARRY(1971)
B.J. Turner
1984
SAM'S SON(1984)
B.M. Turner
Misc. Silents
HELL ROARIN' REFORM(1919)
Baby Turner
Silents
SINGER JIM MCKEE(1924)
Barbara Turner
TWO-GUN LADY(1956); MONSTER FROM THE GREEN HELL(1958); WINK OF AN EYE(1958); OPERATION EICHMANN(1961); DEATHWATCH(1966), w; PETULIA(1968, U.S./Brit.), w; SOLDIER BLUE(1970)
Betty Turner
O LUCKY MAN!(1973, Brit.); VISITOR, THE(1980, Ital./U.S.)
Bill Turner
INCREDIBLY STRANGE CREATURES WHO STOPPED LIVING AND BECAME CRAZY MIXED-UP ZOMBIES, THE(1965), ch; SAND PEBBLES, THE(1966), makeup; WHAT EVER HAPPENED TO AUNT ALICE?(1969), makeup
Bjaye Turner
48 HOURS(1982)
Bowd "Smoke" Turner
Silents
ARE ALL MEN ALIKE?(1920)
Bowditch Turner
Silents
FOUR HORSEMEN OF THE APOCALYPSE, THE(1921); SCARAMOUCHE(1923); VOLCANO(1926)
Bridget Turner
WALKING STICK, THE(1970, Brit.); CATCH ME A SPY(1971, Brit./Fr.); UNDER MILK WOOD(1973, Brit.); RUNNERS(1983, Brit.)
Brookes Turner
WE'LL SMILE AGAIN(1942, Brit.); GIVE ME THE STARS(1944, Brit.); MEET SEXTON BLAKE(1944, Brit.); GREEN FINGERS(1947); STOLEN FACE(1952, Brit.)
Brooks Turner
TIME FLIES(1944, Brit.)
Charles Turner
SUPER COPS, THE(1974)
Claramae Turner
CAROUSEL(1956)
Clifford Turner
HOUR OF GLORY(1949, Brit.), ed
Colin Turner
KING SOLOMON'S TREASURE(1978, Can.), w
Curtis Turner
THUNDER IN CAROLINA(1960)
D.H. Turner
STORY OF VERNON AND IRENE CASTLE, THE(1939)
Misc. Silents
HER AMERICAN PRINCE(1916), d
Dave Turner
CHARRIOTS OF FIRE(1981, Brit.)
David Turner
ALL THE WAY UP(1970, Brit.), w
Dean Turner
EMBASSY(1972, Brit.)

Debbie Turner
SOUND OF MUSIC, THE(1965)
Diane Turner
FRANCHETTE; LES INTRIGUES(1969)
Don Turner
DEVIL DOGS OF THE AIR(1935); SONS O' GUNS(1936); EVER SINCE EVE(1937); SUBMARINE D-1(1937); COWBOY QUARTERBACK(1939); HELL'S KITCHEN(1939); SECRET SERVICE OF THE AIR(1939); SMASHING THE MONEY RING(1939); THEY DRIVE BY NIGHT(1940); TUGBOAT ANNIE SAILS AGAIN(1940); DIVE BOMBER(1941); MEET JOHN DOE(1941); BULLET SCARS(1942); CLOAK AND DAGGER(1946); HUMORESQUE(1946); SLAVE GIRL(1947); SERENADE(1956); WRONG MAN, THE(1956); BIG FISHERMAN, THE(1959)
Doreen Turner
Silents
LOVE GAMBLER, THE(1922); ROSITA(1923); DARING CHANCES(1924); ROSE OF PARIS, THE(1924); WESTERN VENGEANCE(1924)
Misc. Silents
TOP O' THE MORNING, THE(1922); LORRAINE OF THE LIONS(1925)
E. Turner
BRANDED MEN(1931), ed; MAIL TRAIN(1941, Brit.)
E.A. Turner
Silents
MYSTERY OF THE POISON POOL, THE(1914); AS THE SUN WENT DOWN(1919)
Earl Turner
IN OLD CALIFORNIA(1929), ed; FIGHTING THRU(1931), ed; RANGE LAW(1931), ed; LOST JUNGLE, THE(1934), ed; FACE IN THE FOG, A(1936), ed; CRUSADE AGAINST RACKETS(1937), ed; TAMING THE WILD(1937), ed; EAST SIDE KIDS(1940), ed
Silents
SOULS AFLAME(1928), ed; CAMPUS KNIGHTS(1929), ed
Earl C. Turner
Silents
PEACEFUL PETERS(1922), ed; RANGE RIDERS, THE(1927), a, t, ed; OLD CODE, THE(1928), ed
Elaine Turner
SECRET EVIDENCE(1941), ed
Elizabeth Turner
BEYOND THE DOOR(1975, Ital./U.S.); CANNIBALS IN THE STREETS(1982, Ital./Span.)
Misc. Talkies
INVASION OF THE FLESH HUNTERS(1981)
Emanuel A. Turner
Silents
ARE ALL MEN ALIKE?(1920)
Misc. Silents
REDEMPTION OF DAVE DARCEY, THE(1916)
Emanuel Turner
Silents
LOVE SWINDLE(1918)
Ethel Turner
ONE-WAY TICKET(1935), w; LITTLE AUSTRALIANS(1940, Aus.), w
Eugene Turner
ICELAND(1942); SILVER SKATES(1943)
Eve Turner
LOVE TEST, THE(1935, Brit.)
Evelyn Turner
HOW DO I LOVE THEE?(1970)
F. A. Turner
Silents
HOME SWEET HOME(1914); PENITENTES, THE(1915); ACQUITTED(1916); LOVE SWINDLE(1918); MIRACLE MAN, THE(1919)
Misc. Silents
LOST HOUSE, THE(1915); DEVIL'S NEEDLE, THE(1916); HER OFFICAL FATHERS(1917)
Florence Turner
RAMPANT AGE, THE(1930); SIGN OF THE CROSS, THE(1932); ONE RAINY AFTERNOON(1936); THOUSANDS CHEER(1943)
Misc. Talkies
RIDIN' FOOL, THE(1931)
Silents
ALONE IN LONDON(1915, Brit.); FAR FROM THE MADDING CROWD(1915, Brit.); MY OLD DUTCH(1915, Brit.); WELSH SINGER, A(1915, Brit.); DOORSTEPS(1916, Brit.); EAST IS EAST(1916, Brit.); ALL DOLLED UP(1921); OLD WIVES' TALE, THE(1921, Brit.); DARK ANGEL, THE(1925); NEVER THE TWAIN SHALL MEET(1925); GILDED HIGHWAY, THE(1926); LAST ALARM, THE(1926); COLLEGE(1927); SALLY IN OUR ALLEY(1927); STRANDED(1927); JAZZLAND(1928); MARRY THE GIRL(1928); WALKING BACK(1928); KID'S CLEVER, THE(1929)
Misc. Silents
HARPER MYSTERY, THE(1913, Brit.); FOR HER PEOPLE(1914, Brit.); MURDOCK TRIAL, THE(1914, Brit.); SHEPHERD LASSIE OF ARGYLE, THE(1914, Brit.); SHOPGIRLS; OR, THE GREAT QUESTION(1914, Brit.); THROUGH THE VALLEY OF SHADOWS(1914, Brit.); LOST AND WON(1915, Brit.); REDEEMED(1915, Brit.); GRIM JUSTICE(1916, Brit.); FOOL'S GOLD(1919); BRAND OF LOPEZ, THE(1920); UGLY DUCKLING, THE(1920, Brit.); LITTLE MOTHER, THE(1922, Brit.); WAS SHE JUSTIFIED?(1922, Brit.); HORNET'S NEST(1923, Brit.); SALLY BISHOP(1923, Brit.); WOMEN AND DIAMONDS(1924, Brit.); PRICE OF SUCCESS, THE(1925); BROKEN GATE, THE(1927); CANCELLED DEBT, THE(1927); CHINESE PARROT, THE(1927); PACE THAT KILLS, THE(1928); ROAD TO RUIN, THE(1928)
Frank Turner
PSYCHO-CIRCUS(1967, Brit.), makeup; SILENCE OF THE NORTH(1981, Can.); GREY FOX, THE(1983, Can.)
Silents
REBECCA OF SUNNYBROOK FARM(1917)
Frantz Turner
GOING BERSERK(1983)
1984
GHOSTBUSTERS(1984)

Fred Turner
Silents
INTOLERANCE(1916); EYES OF THE HEART(1920); JACK KNIFE MAN, THE(1920); WITCHING HOUR, THE(1921)
Misc. Silents
LOVE SUBLIME, A(1917); VELVET HAND, THE(1918); TROPICAL LOVE(1921)

Fred A. Turner
Silents
ESCAPE, THE(1914); ATTA BOY'S LAST RACE(1916)
Misc. Silents
MICROSCOPE MYSTERY, THE(1916); SUSAN ROCKS THE BOAT(1916)

Gail Turner
DON'T GO IN THE HOUSE(1980); FIST OF FEAR, TOUCH OF DEATH(1980)

George Turner
BLOCKADE(1928, Brit.); WHITE CARGO(1930, Brit.); SAFE AFFAIR, A(1931, Brit.); BRITANNIA OF BILLINGSGATE(1933, Brit.); MAN FROM TORONTO, THE(1933, Brit.); TROUBLE(1933, Brit.); CAFE MASCOT(1936, Brit.); FULL SPEED AHEAD(1936, Brit.); PAY BOX ADVENTURE(1936, Brit.); MISSING, BELIEVED MARRIED(1937, Brit.); TWIN FACES(1937, Brit.); I AM THE LAW(1938); THERE'S THAT WOMAN AGAIN(1938); LADY'S FROM KENTUCKY, THE(1939); HENRY STEPS OUT(1940, Brit.); TWO SMART MEN(1940, Brit.); I WANTED WINGS(1941); FOREST RANGERS, THE(1942); GLASS KEY, THE(1942); MY FAVORITE BLONDE(1942); TRAMP, TRAMP, TRAMP(1942); TRUE TO THE ARMY(1942); WIFE TAKES A FLYER, THE(1942); CONTENDER, THE(1944); HERE COME THE WAVES(1944); HOLLYWOOD CANTEEN(1944); OLD TEXAS TRAIL, THE(1944); PRACTICALLY YOURS(1944); DUFFY'S TAVERN(1945); WALK IN THE SUN, A(1945); WELL-GROOMED BRIDE, THE(1946); CROSSFIRE(1947); RANGE BEYOND THE BLUE(1947); VIGILANTES OF BOOMTOWN(1947); CALL NORTHSIDE 777(1948); RACE STREET(1948)
Silents
RUNNING WATER(1922, Brit.); GAY CORINTHIAN, THE(1924); NETS OF DESTINY(1924, Brit.)

George Kibbe Turner
GIRL IN THE GLASS CAGE, THE(1929), w; HALF-MARRIAGE(1929), w; THOSE WHO DANCE(1930), w; TIP-OFF, THE(1931), w; ROAR OF THE DRAGON(1932), w
Silents
WALKING BACK(1928), w

Geraldine Turner
BREAK OF DAY(1977, Aus.); SUMMERFIELD(1977, Aus.)
1984
CAREFUL, HE MIGHT HEAR YOU(1984, Aus.)

Gil Turner
1001 ARABIAN NIGHTS(1959), d

Glynn Turner
RIVER NIGER, THE(1976)

Grant Turner
COAL MINER'S DAUGHTER(1980)

Helene Turner
LADY LIES, THE(1929), ed; DANGEROUS NAN McGREW(1930), ed; LAUGHTER(1930), ed; ROADHOUSE NIGHTS(1930), ed; SAP FROM SYRACUSE, THE(1930), ed; HONOR AMONG LOVERS(1931), ed; SECRETS OF A SECRETARY(1931), ed; HIRED WIFE(1934), ed; RETURN OF SHERLOCK HOLMES(1936), ed; CARSON CITY KID(1940), ed; HI-YO SILVER(1940), ed; HUK(1956), ed; DELINQUENTS, THE(1957), ed; COOL AND THE CRAZY, THE(1958), ed; HONG KONG AFFAIR(1958), w, ed; COSMIC MAN, THE(1959), ed

Holt Turner
MUSIC MAKER, THE(1936, Brit.), p

Ike Turner
TAKING OFF(1971)

J.T. Turner
RUMBLE FISH(1983)

Jack Turner
ENTER THE NINJA(1982); REVENGE OF THE NINJA(1983)

James Turner
CANDLELIGHT IN ALGERIA(1944, Brit.), m

James D. Turner
TRADING PLACES(1983)

Janine Turner
YOUNG DOCTORS IN LOVE(1982)

Jay Turner
Silents
FRIENDLY HUSBAND, A(1923), ph

Jesse Turner
Misc. Talkies
SMOKEY AND THE GOODTIME OUTLAWS(1978)

Joe Turner
SHAKE, RATTLE, AND ROCK!(1957); MC VICAR(1982, Brit.)

John Turner
MY AIN FOLK(1944, Brit.); BEHEMOTH, THE SEA MONSTER(1959, Brit.); NOWHERE TO GO(1959, Brit.); PETTICOAT PIRATES(1961, Brit.); VAMPIRE AND THE BALLERINA, THE(1962, Ital.); STORK TALK(1964, Brit.); BLACK TORMENT, THE(1965, Brit.); BOY TEN FEET TALL, A(1965, Brit.); CAPTAIN NEMO AND THE UNDERWATER CITY(1969, Brit.); SLIPPER AND THE ROSE, THE(1976, Brit.)
Misc. Talkies
BLACK TORMENT(1984)

John Hastings Turner
BLIND SPOT(1932, Brit.), w; HELP YOURSELF(1932, Brit.), w; ILLEGAL(1932, Brit.), w; LORD OF THE MANOR(1933, Brit.), w; GHOUL, THE(1934, Brit.), w; GREAT DEFENDER, THE(1934, Brit.), w; LILIES OF THE FIELD(1934, Brit.), w; NIGHT OF THE PARTY, THE(1934, Brit.), w; SONG AT EVENTIDE(1934, Brit.), w; MURDER AT MONTE CARLO(1935, Brit.), w; IT HAPPENED TO ONE MAN(1941, Brit.), w

Johnny Turner
RAGING BULL(1980)

June Turner
DEATHLINE(1973, Brit.)

Kathalyn Turner
GRASSHOPPER, THE(1970)

Kathleen Turner
BODY HEAT(1981); MAN WITH TWO BRAINS, THE(1983)
1984
BREED APART, A(1984); CRIMES OF PASSION(1984); ROMANCING THE STONE(1984)

Kathy Turner
CONRACK(1974)

Kay Turner
MADIGAN(1968); WHAT'S SO BAD ABOUT FEELING GOOD?(1968)

Kedaki Turner
FOR LOVE OF IVY(1968)

Kenneth Turner
Misc. Talkies
LOVE PILL, THE(1971), d

Lana Turner
GREAT GARRICK, THE(1937); STAR IS BORN, A(1937); THEY WON'T FORGET(1937); ADVENTURES OF MARCO POLO, THE(1938); CHASER, THE(1938); DRAMATIC SCHOOL(1938); LOVE FINDS ANDY HARDY(1938); RICH MAN, POOR GIRL(1938); CALLING DR. KILDARE(1939); DANCING CO-ED(1939); THESE GLAMOUR GIRLS(1939); TWO GIRLS ON BROADWAY(1940); WE WHO ARE YOUNG(1940); DR. JEKYLL AND MR. HYDE(1941); HONKY TONK(1941); ZIEGFELD GIRL(1941); JOHNNY EAGER(1942); SOMEWHERE I'LL FIND YOU(1942); DU BARRY WAS A LADY(1943); SLIGHTLY DANGEROUS(1943); YOUNGEST PROFESSION, THE(1943); MARRIAGE IS A PRIVATE AFFAIR(1944); KEEP YOUR POWDER DRY(1945); WEEKEND AT THE WALDORF(1945); POSTMAN ALWAYS RINGS TWICE, THE(1946); CASS TIMBERLANE(1947); GREEN DOLPHIN STREET(1947); HOMECOMING(1948); THREE MUSKETEERS, THE(1948); LIFE OF HER OWN, A(1950); MR. IMPERIUM(1951); BAD AND THE BEAUTIFUL, THE(1952); MERRY WIDOW, THE(1952); LATIN LOVERS(1953); BETRAYED(1954); FLAME AND THE FLESH(1954); DIANE(1955); PRODIGAL, THE(1955); RAINS OF RANCHIPUR, THE(1955); SEA CHASE, THE(1955); PEYTON PLACE(1957); ANOTHER TIME, ANOTHER PLACE(1958); LADY TAKES A FLYER, THE(1958); IMITATION OF LIFE(1959); PORTRAIT IN BLACK(1960); BACHELOR IN PARADISE(1961); BY LOVE POSSESSED(1961); WHO'S GOT THE ACTION?(1962); LOVE HAS MANY FACES(1965); MADAME X(1966); BIG CUBE, THE(1969); PERSECUTION(1974, Brit.); BITTERSWEET LOVE(1976)
Misc. Talkies
WITCHES' BREW(1980)

Larry Turner
PIT AND THE PENDULUM, THE(1961)

Leslie Turner
MARY LOU(1948); JOURNEY INTO LIGHT(1951)

Lewis M. Turner
SOURDOUGH(1977), w

Mable Turner
Misc. Silents
PAIR OF HELLIONS, A(1924)

Mae Turner
SPIRIT OF YOUTH(1937); AM I GUILTY?(1940)

Maidel Turner
ANOTHER LANGUAGE(1933); WORST WOMAN IN PARIS(1933); FUGITIVE LADY(1934); IT HAPPENED ONE NIGHT(1934); LIFE OF VERGIE WINTERS, THE(1934); MEN OF THE NIGHT(1934); MERRY FRINKS, THE(1934); MODERN HERO, A(1934); MONEY MEANS NOTHING(1934); OLSEN'S BIG MOMENT(1934); SHE HAD TO CHOOSE(1934); UNKNOWN BLONDE(1934); WHOM THE GODS DESTROY(1934); DANTE'S INFERNO(1935); DIAMOND JIM(1935); DR. SOCRATES(1935); MUTINY AHEAD(1935); RAVEN, THE(1935); SOCIETY FEVER(1935); SPLENDOR(1935); AND SUDDEN DEATH(1936); KLONDIKE ANNIE(1936); MAKE WAY FOR A LADY(1936); PALM SPRINGS(1936); LOVE IS NEWS(1937); MR. DODD TAKES THE AIR(1937); SHE'S DANGEROUS(1937); SLIM(1937); LIFE RETURNS(1939); STATE OF THE UNION(1948); HERE COMES THE GROOM(1951)

Maria Turner
TAXI DRIVER(1976)

Martin Turner
OPERATOR 13(1934); SMOKING GUNS(1934); LAST GANGSTER, THE(1937); SMART BLONDE(1937); WINGS OVER HONOLULU(1937); GHOST TOWN RIDERS(1938); WINTER CARNIVAL(1939); WE WERE DANCING(1942)
Silents
FAMILY SECRET, THE(1924); RAINBOW RANGERS(1924); WESTERN VENGEANCE(1924); KNOCKOUT KID, THE(1925)
Misc. Silents
THEY'RE OFF(1922); SELL 'EM COWBOY(1924); GHOST RIDER, THE(1925); ROPIN' RIDIN' FOOL, A(1925); SILENT SHELDON(1925); LOST EXPRESS, THE(1926); THREE PALS(1926)

Mary Turner
THUNDERBIRDS ARE GO(1968, Brit.), puppeteer

Maude Turner
Misc. Silents
PRICE OF POSSESSION, THE(1921)

Mercia Turner
ENTERTAINER, THE(1960, Brit.)

Michael Turner
OTHELLO(1965, Brit.)

Moira Turner
TWO FOR THE SEESAW(1962)

Moria Turner
TABLE FOR FIVE(1983)

Muriel Godfrey Turner
Silents
ALL DOLLED UP(1921)
Misc. Silents
DESPERATE YOUTH(1921)

Nicki Turner
LITTLE JUNGLE BOY(1969, Aus.)

Otis Turner
Silents
DAMON AND PYTHIAS(1914), d; NEPTUNE'S DAUGHTER(1914), d; OPENED SHUTTERS, THE(1914), d; SCARLET SIN, THE(1915), d; MEDIATOR, THE(1916), d, w

Misc. Silents
CALLED BACK(1914), d; SPY, THE(1914), d; BUSINESS IS BUSINESS(1915), d; FRAME-UP, THE(1915), d; LITTLE BROTHER OF THE RICH, A(1915), d; GAY LORD WARING, THE(1916), d; LANDON'S LEGACY(1916), d; POOL OF FLAME, THE(1916), d; SEEKERS, THE(1916), d; SON OF THE IMMORTALS, A(1916), d; WHIRLPOOL OF DESTINY, THE(1916), d; YOUTH OF FORTUNE, A(1916), d; BOOK AGENT, THE(1917), d; HIGH FINANCE(1917), d; ISLAND OF DESIRE, THE(1917), d; MELTING MILLIONS(1917), d; SOME BOY(1917), d; SOUL OF SATAN, THE(1917), d; TO HONOR AND OBEY(1917), d

Paulette Turner
HORIZONS WEST(1952)

Peter Turner
COMEBACK, THE(1982, Brit.); RUNNERS(1983, Brit.)

Ray Turner
KING KONG(1933); EAST OF JAVA(1935); DARKEST AFRICA(1936); EXCLUSIVE(1937); SHE'S DANGEROUS(1937); TENDERFOOT GOES WEST, A(1937); WINGS OVER HONOLULU(1937); PROFESSOR BEWARE(1938); CHARLIE MC CARTHY, DETECTIVE(1939); GOOD GIRLS GO TO PARIS(1939); LITTLE ACCIDENT(1939); BLONDIE HAS SERVANT TROUBLE(1940); GRANDPA GOES TO TOWN(1940); LITTLE ORVIE(1940); TURNABOUT(1940); THEY GOT ME COVERED(1943); DUFFY'S TAVERN(1945)

Raymond Turner
WEARY RIVER(1929); YOUNG NOWHERES(1929); LITTLE JOHNNY JONES(1930); SHE COULDN'T TAKE IT(1935); IT HAD TO HAPPEN(1936); GUN PACKER(1938); JOSETTE(1938)
Silents
NO-GUN MAN, THE(1924); HEADS UP(1925); SMILIN' AT TROUBLE(1925); KIT CARSON(1928)
Misc. Silents
LOVE MART, THE(1927)

Ric Turner
SERGEANT WAS A LADY, THE(1961)

Richard Turner
TWILIGHT HOUR(1944, Brit.); STRAWBERRY ROAN(1945, Brit.); WHILE THE SUN SHINES(1950, Brit.); DOWN AMONG THE Z MEN(1952, Brit.); INBETWEEN AGE, THE(1958, Brit.)
Silents
CONQUERED HEARTS(1918); PAGES OF LIFE(1922, Brit.)
Misc. Silents
COMBAT, THE(1916); DESTROYERS, THE(1916); TROUBLEMAKERS(1917); WEB OF DESIRE, THE(1917)

Rita Turner
CHAMP, THE(1979)

Robert Brookes Turner
GREAT GILBERT AND SULLIVAN, THE(1953, Brit.)

Robert Brooks Turner
BREAKING THE SOUND BARRIER(1952)

Robin Turner
VICTORY(1981)

Roscoe Turner
HELL'S ANGELS(1930)

Col. Roscoe Turner
FLIGHT AT MIDNIGHT(1939)

Scott Turner
PUNISHMENT PARK(1971)
Misc. Silents
SEALED LIPS(1925)

Simon Turner
BIG SLEEP, THE½(1978, Brit.)

Smoke Turner
Silents
OFF THE HIGHWAY(1925)

"Smoke" Turner
Silents
SHARK MASTER, THE(1921)

Snow Turner
1984
VIGIL(1984, New Zealand)

Stephen Turner
FINAL CONFLICT, THE(1981)

Sydney Turner
GREEN HELMET, THE(1961, Brit.), makeup; GIRL HUNTERS, THE(1963, Brit.), makeup; MAN IN THE MIDDLE(1964, U.S./Brit.), makeup

Ted Turner
TOWN WITHOUT PITY(1961, Ger./Switz./U.S.); NO SURVIVORS, PLEASE(1963, Ger.); STOP TRAIN 349(1964, Fr./Ital./Ger.); IMPROPER CHANNELS(1981, Can.)

Teddy Turner
DRACULA(1979)

Terry Turner
SHOULD A GIRL MARRY?(1929), w

Tierre Turner
BUCKTOWN(1975); CORNBREAD, EARL AND ME(1975); FRIDAY FOSTER(1975)

Tim Turner
GLORY AT SEA(1952, Brit.); HOLIDAY WEEK(1952, Brit.); MOULIN ROUGE(1952); MR. POTTS GOES TO MOSCOW(1953, Brit.); COMPANIONS IN CRIME(1954, Brit.); NIGHT OF THE FULL MOON, THE(1954, Brit.); PARATROOPER(1954, Brit.); POLICE DOG(1955, Brit.); RACE FOR LIFE, A(1955, Brit.); HAUNTED STRANGLER, THE(1958, Brit.); NIGHT TO REMEMBER, A(1958, Brit.); TOWN LIKE ALICE, A(1958, Brit.); JACKPOT(1960, Brit.); NOT A HOPE IN HELL(1960, Brit.); OPERATION AMSTERDAM(1960, Brit.)

Tina Turner
TAKING OFF(1971); TOMMY(1975, Brit.); SGT. PEPPER'S LONELY HEARTS CLUB BAND(1978)

Tom Turner
SHOOT IT: BLACK, SHOOT IT: BLUE(1974)

Toni Turner
FAT SPY(1966)
Misc. Talkies
LUST TO KILL(1960)

Vickery Turner
PRUDENCE AND THE PILL(1968, Brit.); MIND OF MR. SOAMES, THE(1970, Brit.); SOPHIE'S PLACE(1970); RETURN OF THE SOLDIER, THE(1983, Brit.)

Wally Turner
Misc. Talkies
GIRL TROUBLE(1933)

Wendy Turner
SPIDER'S WEB, THE(1960, Brit.); SUMMER MAGIC(1963)

William Turner
MR. BUG GOES TO TOWN(1941), w; SCREAM OF THE BUTTERFLY(1965); STAR!(1968), makeup; TOO LATE THE HERO(1970), makeup; BREAKOUT(1975), w
Silents
TRAFFIC IN SOULS(1913); AMERICAN MANNERS(1924); MEASURE OF A MAN, THE(1924); PONY EXPRESS, THE(1925)
Misc. Silents
FAST AND FEARLESS(1924)

William H. Turner
LAST PERFORMANCE, THE(1929); LOVE ME TONIGHT(1932); LAUGHTER IN HELL(1933)
Silents
NATION'S PERIL, THE(1915); LOVE'S TOLL(1916); ENEMY SEX, THE(1924); DRIFTIN' SANDS(1928)
Misc. Silents
DARKNESS BEFORE DAWN, THE(1915); CITY OF FAILING LIGHT, THE(1916); HER GOOD NAME(1917); GOLD AND GRIT(1925); WHITE THUNDER(1925); THREE PALS(1926)

Winki Turner
SOMEWHERE IN ENGLAND(1940, Brit.)

Wyetta Turner
KING OF MARVIN GARDENS, THE(1972); JESUS CHRIST, SUPERSTAR(1973)

Yolanda Turner
COME BACK PETER(1971, Brit.)

Yolande Turner
I THANK A FOOL(1962, Brit.); FIVE MILES TO MIDNIGHT(1963, U.S./Fr./Ital.); GIRL WITH GREEN EYES(1964, Brit.); LIMBO LINE, THE(1969, Brit.)

Catherine Turney
MAN I LOVE, THE(1946), w; MY REPUTATION(1946), w; OF HUMAN BONDAGE(1946), w; ONE MORE TOMORROW(1946), w; STOLEN LIFE, A(1946), w; CRY WOLF(1947), w; WINTER MEETING(1948), w; NO MAN OF HER OWN(1950), w; JAPANESE WAR BRIDE(1952), w; BACK FROM THE DEAD(1957), w

Gladys Turney
SILVER RIVER(1948)

Kieran Turney
SPRING MEETING(1941, Brit.)

Nadyne Turney
AROUSERS, THE(1973)

Tallulah Turney
GIRO CITY(1982, Brit.)

Turney-Smith
CONSTANT HUSBAND, THE(1955, Brit.), ed

G. Turney-Smith
IF THIS BE SIN(1950, Brit.), ed; FLESH AND BLOOD(1951, Brit.), ed; SMILEY GETS A GUN(1959, Brit.), ed; PRIVATE COLLECTION(1972, Aus.), ed; STORM BOY(1976, Aus.), ed

Gerald Turney-Smith
BOND STREET(1948, Brit.), ed; NOW BARABBAS WAS A ROBBER(1949, Brit.), ed; WINSLOW BOY, THE(1950), ed; PASSIONATE SENTRY, THE(1952, Brit.), ed; CAPTAIN'S PARADISE, THE(1953, Brit.), ed; GAY ADVENTURE, THE(1953, Brit.), ed; GREAT GILBERT AND SULLIVAN, THE(1953, Brit.), ed; MR. DENNING DRIVES NORTH(1953, Brit.), ed; THREE CASES OF MURDER(1955, Brit.), ed; FOLLOW THAT HORSE!(1960, Brit.), ed; MALAGA(1962, Brit.), ed; THEY'RE A WEIRD MOB(1966, Aus.), ed

Frances Turnham
GARDEN OF ALLAH, THE(1936)

Francis Turnham
Misc. Talkies
BARGAIN WITH BULLETS(1937)

Ardene Turning Bear
MAN CALLED HORSE, A(1970)

Cole Turnley
CLAY(1964 Aus.)

W. Turowski
EVE WANTS TO SLEEP(1961, Pol.)

Ben Turpin
LOVE PARADE, THE(1929); SWING HIGH(1930); AMBASSADOR BILL(1931); CRACKED NUTS(1931); MAKE ME A STAR(1932); MILLION DOLLAR LEGS(1932); HOLLYWOOD CAVALCADE(1939); SAPS AT SEA(1940); DOWN MEMORY LANE(1949)
Silents
SMALL TOWN IDOL, A(1921)
Misc. Silents
MARRIED LIFE(1920); HOME TALENT(1921); SHRIEK OF ARABY, THE(1923); COLLEGE HERO, THE(1927); WIFE'S RELATIONS, THE(1928)

Gerald Turpin
QUEEN'S GUARDS, THE(1963, Brit.), ph

Gerry Turpin
SEANCE ON A WET AFTERNOON(1964 Brit.), ph; DUTCHMAN(1966, Brit.), ph; MORGAN!(1966, Brit.), ph; WRONG BOX, THE(1966, Brit.), ph; BOBO, THE(1967, Brit.), ph; WHISPERERS, THE(1967, Brit.), ph; DEADFALL(1968, Brit.), ph; DIAMONDS FOR BREAKFAST(1968, Brit.), ph; OH! WHAT A LOVELY WAR(1969, Brit.), ph; HOFFMAN(1970, Brit.), ph; MAN WHO HAD POWER OVER WOMEN, THE(1970, Brit.), ph; I WANT WHAT I WANT(1972, Brit.), ph; WHAT BECAME OF JACK AND JILL?(1972, Brit.), ph; YOUNG WINSTON(1972, Brit.), ph; LAST OF SHEILA, THE(1973), ph

Helen Turpin
OH, MEN! OH, WOMEN!(1957), hairstyles; SNOW WHITE AND THE THREE STOOGES(1961), makeup

Turk Turpin
COTTON COMES TO HARLEM(1970)
Dean Turpitt
CASEY'S SHADOW(1978)
Todd Turquand
BURNT OFFERINGS(1976)
Jac Turrell
WHEN THE LIGHTS GO ON AGAIN(1944)
Tomas Perez Turrent
ALSINO AND THE CONDOR(1983, Nicaragua), w
Donatella Turri
LA FEMME INFIDELE(1969, Fr./Ital.)
Bozidara Turronovova
DIVINE EMMA, THE(1983, Czech,)
Leon G. Turrou
CONFESSIONS OF A NAZI SPY(1939), tech adv
Leon Turrou
CONFESSIONS OF A NAZI SPY(1939), w
Zbigniew Turski
YELLOW SLIPPERS, THE(1965, Pol.), m
Claude Turtin
FORTY THOUSAND HORSEMEN(1941, Aus.)
The Turtles
OUT OF SIGHT(1966)
Stuart Craig Turton
NIGHTHAWKS(1978, Brit.)
Stuart Turton
VICTOR/VICTORIA(1982)
Robert Turturice
1984
UP THE CREEK(1984), cos
Sam Turturici
HOMER(1970)
Vincent Turturici
GROUND ZERO(1973)
John Turturro
1984
EXTERMINATOR 2(1984); FLAMINGO KID, THE(1984)
Turzhansky
Misc. Silents
GREAT MAGARAZ, THE(1915, USSR)
V. Turzhansky
Misc. Silents
TERRIBLE REVENGE, A(1913, USSR); SYMPHONY OF LOVE AND DEATH(1914, USSR), d; WANDERER BEYOND THE GRAVE(1915, USSR), a, d; ISLE OF OBLIVION(1917, USSR)
Vyacheslav Turzhansky
Misc. Silents
GREAT MAGARAZ, THE(1915, USSR), d; ISLE OF OBLIVION(1917, USSR), d; PARADISE WITHOUT ADAM(1918, USSR), d
Tusa
PACIFIC DESTINY(1956, Brit.)
Jean Tuscano
LOVE ON A PILLOW(1963, Fr./Ital.)
Eugen Tuscherer
KARAMAZOV(1931, Ger.), p
Eugene Tuscherer
GIRL IN THE TAXI(1937, Brit.), p; CROSSROADS(1938, Fr.), p; BACK STREETS OF PARIS(1962, Fr.), p
Felix Tusell
EYEBALL(1978, Ital.), w
Betty Tusher
PSYCH-OUT(1968), w
Will Tusher
MAN WITH BOGART'S FACE, THE(1980)
Rita Tushingham
TASTE OF HONEY, A(1962, Brit.); GIRL WITH GREEN EYES(1964, Brit.); PLACE TO GO, A(1964, Brit.); DOCTOR ZHIVAGO(1965); KNACK ... AND HOW TO GET IT, THE(1965, Brit.); LEATHER BOYS, THE(1965, Brit.); SMASHING TIME(1967 Brit.); TRAP, THE(1967, Can./Brit.); DIAMONDS FOR BREAKFAST(1968, Brit.); BED SITTING ROOM, THE(1969, Brit.); GURU, THE(1969, U.S./India); STRAIGHT ON TILL MORNING(1974, Brit.); HUMAN FACTOR, THE(1975); MYSTERIES(1979, Neth.)
Misc. Talkies
INSTANT COFFEE(1974); RACHEL'S MAN(1974); SLAUGHTERDAY(1981)
Tusk the Elephant
TUSK(1980, Fr.)
Tuskegee Institute Choir
GEORGE WASHINGTON CARVER(1940)
Thelma Tuson
CHU CHIN CHOW(1934, Brit.)
Georgiy Tusuzov
SPRINGTIME ON THE VOLGA(1961, USSR)
Teresa Tuszynska
NIGHTS OF PRAGUE, THE(1968, Czech.)
Juliana Tutak
HEART BEAT(1979)
Warren Tute
JOURNEY AHEAD(1947, Brit.), w
Frederic Tuten
POSSESSION(1981, Fr./Ger.), w
Jacqueline Tuteur
LOOKING UP(1977)
Kula Tutiama
MALAYA(1950)
Dorothy Tutin
IMPORTANCE OF BEING EARNEST, THE(1952, Brit.); BEGGAR'S OPERA, THE(1953); TALE OF TWO CITIES, A(1958, Brit.); CROMWELL(1970, Brit.); SAVAGE MESSIAH(1972, Brit.)

Andrei Tutishkin
MILITARY SECRET(1945, USSR)
J. Homer Tutt
Misc. Silents
BIRTHRIGHT(1924); BROKEN VIOLIN, THE(1927)
Bertram Tuttle
KING RICHARD AND THE CRUSADERS(1954), art d
Bud Tuttle
UNDERGROUND RUSTLERS(1941), w
Burl Tuttle
SON OF OKLAHOMA(1932), w; 'NEATH THE ARIZONA SKIES(1934), w
Burl R. Tuttle
CIRCLE CANYON(1934), w
C. Tuttle
CHEYENNE KID, THE(1933), w
Day Tuttle
OPEN THE DOOR AND SEE ALL THE PEOPLE(1964); PSYCHOMANIA(1964)
Dorothy Tuttle
HARVEY GIRLS, THE(1946); JOAN OF ARC(1948); SUMMER STOCK(1950); ROYAL WEDDING(1951)
Frank Tuttle
VARSITY(1928), d; GREENE MURDER CASE, THE(1929), d; STUDIO MURDER MYSTERY, THE(1929), d, w; SWEETIE(1929), d; BENSON MURDER CASE, THE(1930), d; HER WEDDING NIGHT(1930), d; LOVE AMONG THE MILLIONAIRES(1930), d; MEN ARE LIKE THAT(1930), d; ONLY THE BRAVE(1930), d; TRUE TO THE NAVY(1930), d; DUDE RANCH(1931), d; IT PAYS TO ADVERTISE(1931), d; NO LIMIT(1931), d; BIG BROADCAST, THE(1932), d; THIS IS THE NIGHT(1932), d; THIS RECKLESS AGE(1932), d, w; DANGEROUSLY YOURS(1933), d; PLEASURE CRUISE(1933), d; ROMAN SCANDALS(1933), d; HERE IS MY HEART(1934), d; LADIES SHOULD LISTEN(1934), d; SPRINGTIME FOR HENRY(1934), d, w; ALL THE KING'S HORSES(1935), d, w; GLASS KEY, THE(1935), d; TWO FOR TONIGHT(1935), d; COLLEGE HOLIDAY(1936), d; WAIKIKI WEDDING(1937), d; DR. RHYTHM(1938), d; CHARLIE MC CARTHY, DETECTIVE(1939), p&d; I STOLE A MILLION(1939), d; PARIS HONEYMOON(1939), d; LUCKY JORDAN(1942), d; THIS GUN FOR HIRE(1942), d; YOU WERE NEVER LOVELIER(1942), set d; HOSTAGES(1943), d; HOUR BEFORE THE DAWN, THE(1944), d; DON JUAN QUILLIGAN(1945), d; GREAT JOHN L. THE(1945), d; SONG TO REMEMBER, A(1945), set d; THOUSAND AND ONE NIGHTS, A(1945), set d; TONIGHT AND EVERY NIGHT(1945), set d; PERILOUS HOLIDAY(1946), set d; SUSPENSE(1946), d; SWELL GUY(1946), d; GUILT OF JANET AMES, THE(1947), set d; DARK PAST, THE(1948), set d; JOHNNY ALLEGRO(1949), set d; MAGIC FACE, THE(1951, Aust.), d; MOB, THE(1951), set d; HANGMAN'S KNOT(1952), set d; JUNCTION CITY(1952), set d; LAST OF THE COMANCHES(1952), set d; MEMBER OF THE WEDDING, THE(1952), set d; FROM HERE TO ETERNITY(1953), set d; FIVE AGAINST THE HOUSE(1955), set d; LONG GRAY LINE, THE(1955), set d; CRY IN THE NIGHT, A(1956), d; HELL ON FRISCO BAY(1956), d; STORM CENTER(1956), set d; HITLER(1962), set d; CARETAKERS, THE(1963), set d; QUICK GUN, THE(1964), set d; STRAIT-JACKET(1964), set d; BABY, THE RAIN MUST FALL(1965), set d; I'LL TAKE SWEDEN(1965), set d; KING RAT(1965), set d; CHASE, THE(1966), set d; DEAD HEAT ON A MERRY-GO-ROUND(1966), set d; PROFESSIONALS, THE(1966), set d; BIG MOUTH, THE(1967), set d; DIVORCE AMERICAN STYLE(1967), set d; GUESS WHO'S COMING TO DINNER(1967), set d; LUV(1967), set d; WHERE ANGELS GO...TROUBLE FOLLOWS(1968), set d; WRECKING CREW, THE(1968), set d; HOOK, LINE AND SINKER(1969), set d; MAROONED(1969), set d; STALKING MOON, THE(1969), set d; LIBERATION OF L.B. JONES, THE(1970), set d
Silents
CRADLE BUSTER, THE(1922), p, d&w; SECOND FIDDLE(1923), d, w; GRIT(1924), d; KISS IN THE DARK, A(1925), d; MISS BLUEBEARD(1925), d; AMERICAN VENUS, THE(1926), d; KID BOOTS(1926), d; UNTAMED LADY, THE(1926), d; BLIND ALLEYS(1927), d; ONE WOMAN TO ANOTHER(1927), d; TIME TO LOVE(1927), d; EASY COME, EASY GO(1928), d; LOVE AND LEARN(1928), d
Misc. Silents
PURITAN PASSIONS(1923), d; YOUTHFUL CHEATERS(1923), d; DANGEROUS MONEY(1924), d; LOVERS IN QUARANTINE(1925), d; LUCKY DEVIL(1925), d; MANICURE GIRL, THE(1925), d; LOVE 'EM AND LEAVE 'EM(1926), d; SPOTLIGHT, THE(1927), d; HIS PRIVATE LIFE(1928), d; SOMETHING ALWAYS HAPPENS(1928), d; VARSITY(1928), d; MARQUIS PREFERRED(1929), d
Frank A. Tuttle
GARMENT JUNGLE, THE(1957), set d; GUNMAN'S WALK(1958), set d; EDGE OF ETERNITY(1959), set d; RIDE LONESOME(1959), set d; THEY CAME TO CORDURA(1959), set d
Frank W. Tuttle
ISLAND OF LOST WOMEN(1959), d
Silents
KENTUCKIANS, THE(1921), w; MANHATTAN(1924), w
Gene Tuttle
RODEO RHYTHM(1941), w
Lan Nam Tuttle
OPERATION BIKINI(1963)
Laurene Tuttle
GIVE A GIRL A BREAK(1953); CRITIC'S CHOICE(1963)
Lurene Tuttle
STAND UP AND CHEER(1934 80m FOX bw); TOM, DICK AND HARRY(1941); HEAVEN ONLY KNOWS(1947); HOMECOMING(1948); MACBETH(1948); MR. BLANDINGS BUILDS HIS DREAM HOUSE(1948); GOODBYE, MY FANCY(1951); TOMORROW IS ANOTHER DAY(1951); WHIP HAND, THE(1951); DON'T BOTHER TO KNOCK(1952); NEVER WAVE AT A WAC(1952); ROOM FOR ONE MORE(1952); AFFAIRS OF DOBIE GILLIS, THE(1953); NIAGARA(1953); GLASS SLIPPER, THE(1955); SINCERELY YOURS(1955); SLANDER(1956); SWEET SMELL OF SUCCESS(1957); UNTAMED YOUTH(1957); MA BARKER'S KILLER BROOD(1960); PSYCHO(1960); NIGHTMARE IN THE SUN(1964); RESTLESS ONES, THE(1965); FORTUNE COOKIE, THE(1966); GHOST AND MR. CHICKEN, THE(1966); HORSE IN THE GRAY FLANNEL SUIT, THE(1968); WALKING TALL(1973); WALKING TALL, PART II(1975); FINAL CHAPTER–WALKING TALL zero(1977); MANITOU, THE(1978); CLONUS HORROR, THE(1979); NUTCRACKER FANTASY(1979); TESTAMENT(1983)
Margaretta Tuttle
Silents
UNGUARDED HOUR, THE(1925), w

Thomas Tuttle
CAPE FEAR(1962), makeup
Tom Tuttle
RAILROADED(1947), makeup; CALL NORTHSIDE 777(1948), makeup; ROAD HOUSE(1948), makeup; SOME KIND OF A NUT(1969), makeup; SUPPORT YOUR LOCAL GUNFIGHTER(1971), makeup; WILD ROVERS(1971), makeup; GREATEST, THE(1977, U.S./Brit.), makeup
Tommy Tuttle
STREET WITH NO NAME, THE(1948), makeup
W.C. Tuttle
ROCKY RHODES(1934), w; LAWLESS VALLEY(1938), w; HENRY GOES ARIZONA(1939), w; FARGO KID, THE(1941), w
Silents
SPAWN OF THE DESERT(1923), w; RUSTLER'S RANCH(1926), w; DRIFTIN' SANDS(1928), w; MAN IN THE ROUGH(1928), w
Wilbur C. Tuttle
Silents
FOOLS OF FORTUNE(1922), w; PEACEFUL PETERS(1922), w
William Tuttle
TWO WEEKS IN ANOTHER TOWN(1962), makeup; TROUBLE WITH GIRLS(AND HOW TO GET INTO IT), THE (1969), makeup; KIM(1950), makeup; LIFE OF HER OWN, A(1950), makeup; TWO WEEKS WITH LOVE(1950), makeup; MAN WITH A CLOAK, THE(1951), makeup; MR. IMPERIUM(1951), makeup; PEOPLE AGAINST O'HARA, THE(1951), makeup; STRICTLY DISHONORABLE(1951), makeup; STRIP, THE(1951), makeup; TEXAS CARNIVAL(1951), makeup; BAD AND THE BEAUTIFUL, THE(1952), makeup; MERRY WIDOW, THE(1952), makeup; PAT AND MIKE(1952), makeup; SCARAMOUCHE(1952), makeup; JULIUS CAESAR(1953), makeup; LILI(1953), makeup; SMALL TOWN GIRL(1953), makeup; EXECUTIVE SUITE(1954), makeup; RHAPSODY(1954), makeup; ROGUE COP(1954), makeup; DIANE(1955), makeup; GREEN FIRE(1955), makeup; IT'S ALWAYS FAIR WEATHER(1955), makeup; PRODIGAL, THE(1955), makeup; TENDER TRAP, THE(1955), makeup; FORBIDDEN PLANET(1956), makeup; GREAT AMERICAN PASTIME, THE(1956), makeup; HIGH SOCIETY(1956), makeup; MEET ME IN LAS VEGAS(1956), makeup; OPPOSITE SEX, THE(1956), makeup; RACK, THE(1956), makeup; THESE WILDER YEARS(1956), makeup; TRIBUTE TO A BADMAN(1956), makeup; JAILHOUSE ROCK(1957), makeup; RAINTREE COUNTY(1957), makeup; SILK STOCKINGS(1957), makeup; WINGS OF EAGLES, THE(1957), makeup; CAT ON A HOT TIN ROOF(1958), makeup; GIGI(1958), makeup; HIGH SCHOOL CONFIDENTIAL(1958), makeup; LAW AND JAKE WADE, THE(1958), makeup; PARTY GIRL(1958), makeup; SHEEPMAN, THE(1958), makeup; NEVER SO FEW(1959), makeup; NORTH BY NORTHWEST(1959), makeup; SOME CAME RUNNING(1959), makeup; WRECK OF THE MARY DEAR, THE(1959), makeup; PLEASE DON'T EAT THE DAISIES(1960), makeup; SUBTERRANEANS, THE(1960), makeup; TIME MACHINE, THE(1960; Brit./U.S.), makeup; GO NAKED IN THE WORLD(1961), makeup; HONEYMOON MACHINE, THE(1961), makeup; TWO LOVES(1961), makeup; HOOK, THE(1962), makeup; HOW THE WEST WAS WON(1962), makeup; JUMBO(1962), makeup; MUTINY ON THE BOUNTY(1962), makeup; PERIOD OF ADJUSTMENT(1962), makeup; RIDE THE HIGH COUNTRY(1962), makeup; SWEET BIRD OF YOUTH(1962), makeup; WONDERFUL WORLD OF THE BROTHERS GRIMM, THE(1962), makeup; PRIZE, THE(1963), makeup; SUNDAY IN NEW YORK(1963), makeup; TWILIGHT OF HONOR(1963), makeup; WHEELER DEALERS, THE(1963), makeup; GLOBAL AFFAIR, A(1964), makeup; HONEYMOON HOTEL(1964), makeup; KISSIN' COUSINS(1964), makeup; LOOKING FOR LOVE(1964), makeup; MAIL ORDER BRIDE(1964), makeup; OUTRAGE, THE(1964), makeup; QUICK, BEFORE IT MELTS(1964), makeup; SEVEN FACES OF DR. LAO(1964), makeup; SIGNPOST TO MURDER(1964), makeup; UNSINKABLE MOLLY BROWN, THE(1964), makeup; VIVA LAS VEGAS(1964), makeup; YOUR CHEATIN' HEART(1964), makeup; GIRL HAPPY(1965), makeup; HARUM SCARUM(1965), makeup; JOY IN THE MORNING(1965), makeup; LADY L(1965, Fr./Ital.), makeup; ONCE A THIEF(1965), makeup; PATCH OF BLUE, A(1965), makeup; ROUNDERS, THE(1965), makeup; SANDPIPER, THE(1965), makeup; WHEN THE BOYS MEET THE GIRLS(1965), makeup; ZEBRA IN THE KITCHEN(1965), makeup; 36 HOURS(1965), makeup; GLASS BOTTOM BOAT, THE(1966), makeup; MISTER BUDDWING(1966), makeup; MONEY TRAP, THE(1966), makeup; PENELOPE(1966), makeup; SEVEN WOMEN(1966), makeup; SINGING NUN, THE(1966), makeup; SPINOUT(1966), makeup; DON'T MAKE WAVES(1967), makeup; DOUBLE TROUBLE(1967), makeup; HOT RODS TO HELL(1967), makeup; LAST CHALLENGE, THE(1967), makeup; LOVE-INS, THE(1967), makeup; POINT BLANK(1967), makeup; RIOT ON SUNSET STRIP(1967), makeup; VENETIAN AFFAIR, THE(1967), makeup; WELCOME TO HARD TIMES(1967), makeup; IMPOSSIBLE YEARS, THE(1968), makeup; LEGEND OF LYLAH CLARE, THE(1968), makeup; LIVE A LITTLE, LOVE A LITTLE(1968), makeup; POWER, THE(1968), makeup; SOL MADRID(1968), makeup; SPEEDWAY(1968), makeup; SPLIT, THE(1968), makeup; STAY AWAY, JOE(1968), makeup; TIME TO SING, A(1968), makeup; WHERE WERE YOU WHEN THE LIGHTS WENT OUT?(1968), makeup; YOUNG RUNAWAYS, THE(1968), makeup; EXTRAORDINARY SEAMAN, THE(1969), makeup; GYPSY MOTHS, THE(1969), makeup; MALTESE BIPPY, THE(1969), makeup; MOONSHINE WAR, THE(1970), makeup; WHAT'S THE MATTER WITH HELEN?(1971), makeup; LIFE AND TIMES OF JUDGE ROY BEAN, THE(1972), makeup; NECROMANCY(1972), makeup; WHAT'S UP, DOC?(1972), makeup; YOUNG FRANKENSTEIN(1974), makeup; SILENT MOVIE(1976), makeup; SILVER STREAK(1976), makeup; GREATEST, THE(1977, U.S./Brit.), makeup; FURY, THE(1978), makeup; SAME TIME, NEXT YEAR(1978), makeup
William C. Tuttle
WILDFIRE(1945), w
William J. Tuttle
PAGAN LOVE SONG(1950), makeup; TO PLEASE A LADY(1950), makeup; WATCH THE BIRDIE(1950), makeup; ROYAL WEDDING(1951), makeup; SHOW BOAT(1951), makeup
Randy Tutton
1984
STARMAN(1984)
Thomas Tutweiler
BRIDGES AT TOKO-RI, THE(1954), ph
Thomas Tutwiler
BLAZE OF NOON(1947), ph
Tom Tutwiler
HUNTERS, THE(1958), ph; OLD MAN AND THE SEA, THE(1958), ph

A. Tutyshkin
GROWN-UP CHILDREN(1963, USSR)
Sissel Tuul
PASSIONATE DEMONS, THE(1962, Norway)
Eya Tuuli
CASTLE KEEP(1969)
Betty Tuven
JUST ONCE MORE(1963, Swed.)
Erik Tuxen
TORMENT(1947, Swed.), md
Jaroslav Tuzar
BORDER STREET(1950, Pol.), ph
Ferit Tuzun
DRY SUMMER(1967, Turkey), md
V. Tvoruzhek
FAREWELL, DOVES(1962, USSR)
Ali Twaha
AFRICA–TEXAS STYLE!(1967 U.S./Brit.); ELEPHANT CALLED SLOWLY, AN(1970, Brit.)
Mark Twain
TOM SAWYER(1930), w; CONNECTICUT YANKEE, A(1931), w; PRINCE AND THE PAUPER, THE(1937), w; ADVENTURES OF TOM SAWYER, THE(1938), w; HUCKLEBERRY FINN(1939), w; TOM SAWYER, DETECTIVE(1939), w; BEST MAN WINS(1948), w; CONNECTICUT YANKEE IN KING ARTHUR'S COURT, A(1949), w; MAN WITH A MILLION(1954, Brit.), w; ADVENTURES OF HUCKLEBERRY FINN, THE(1960), w; DOUBLE-BARRELLED DETECTIVE STORY, THE(1965), w; PRINCE AND THE PAUPER, THE(1969), w; TOM SAWYER(1973), w; HUCKLEBERRY FINN(1974), w; CROSSED SWORDS(1978), w; UNIDENTIFIED FLYING ODDBALL, THE(1979, Brit.), w
Silents
PRINCE AND THE PAUPER, THE(1915), w; HUCK AND TOM(1918), w; HUCKLEBERRY FINN(1920), w; CONNECTICUT YANKEE AT KING ARTHUR'S COURT, A(1921), w
Frank Tweddell
CLAUDIA(1943); CLAUDIA AND DAVID(1946); UNDERCOVER MAN, THE(1949); SLEEPING CITY, THE(1950); TATTOOED STRANGER, THE(1950); I'D CLIMB THE HIGHEST MOUNTAIN(1951); CAROUSEL(1956); DIARY OF ANNE FRANK, THE(1959)
George R. Tweed
NO MAN IS AN ISLAND(1962), w
Shannon Tweed
OF UNKNOWN ORIGIN(1983, Can.)
1984
HOT DOG...THE MOVIE(1984); SURROGATE, THE(1984, Can.)
T.F. Tweed
GABRIEL OVER THE WHITE HOUSE(1933), w
Terry Tweed
REINCARNATE, THE(1971, Can.)
Tommy Tweed
INCREDIBLE JOURNEY, THE(1963)
Carolyn Tweedle
SCREWBALLS(1983)
Molly Tweedlie
MUTATIONS, THE(1974, Brit.)
Don Tweedy
STEEL ARENA(1973), m
12 Arcadian Nymphs
Silents
ARCADIANS, THE(1927, Brit.)
12 Hippodrome Girls
SHOW GOES ON, THE(1938, Brit.)
Helen Twelvetrees
GHOST TALKS, THE(1929); WORDS AND MUSIC(1929); CAT CREEPS, THE(1930); GRAND PARADE, THE(1930); HER MAN(1930); SWING HIGH(1930); BAD COMPANY(1931); MILLIE(1931); PAINTED DESERT, THE(1931); WOMAN OF EXPERIENCE, A(1931); IS MY FACE RED?(1932); PANAMA FLO(1932); STATE'S ATTORNEY(1932); UNASHAMED(1932); YOUNG BRIDE(1932); BEDTIME STORY, A(1933); DISGRACED(1933); KING FOR A NIGHT(1933); MY WOMAN(1933); ALL MEN ARE ENEMIES(1934); NOW I'LL TELL(1934); SHE WAS A LADY(1934); FRISCO WATERFRONT(1935); ONE HOUR LATE(1935); SHE GETS HER MAN(1935); SPANISH CAPE MYSTERY(1935); TIMES SQUARE LADY(1935); THOROUGHBRED(1936, Aus.); HOLLYWOOD ROUNDUP(1938); PERSONS IN HIDING(1939); UNMARRIED(1939)
Misc. Talkies
BROKEN HEARTS(1933)
Misc. Silents
BLUE SKIES(1929)
Mabel Twemlow
HAWLEY'S OF HIGH STREET(1933, Brit.); MELODY OF MY HEART(1936, Brit.); MERRY COMES TO STAY(1937, Brit.); MINSTREL BOY, THE(1937, Brit.); SPECIAL EDITION(1938, Brit.); MAN WITH THE MAGNETIC EYES, THE(1945, Brit.)
Zehava Twena
WANTED(1937, Brit.)
1984
SAHARA(1984)
Twenty Tiny Tappers
CHIPS(1938. Brit.)
Joe Twerp
GAY BRIDE, THE(1934); MARY BURNS, FUGITIVE(1935); ALL-AMERICAN SWEETHEART(1937); WOMAN I LOVE, THE(1937); KENTUCKY MOONSHINE(1938)
Curley Twiford
ENCHANTED VALLEY, THE(1948), animalt
Twiggy [Leslie Hornby]
BOY FRIEND, THE(1971, Brit.); W(1974); BLUES BROTHERS, THE(1980); THERE GOES THE BRIDE(1980, Brit.)
The Twilight Blondes
OFF THE DOLE(1935, Brit.)
Chris Twinn
DRAGONSLAYER(1981)

FINGER, LEFT HAND(1940); YOUNG PEOPLE(1940); BEHIND THE NEWS(1941); REMEMBER THE DAY(1941); RICHEST MAN IN TOWN(1941); SULLIVAN'S TRAVELS(1941); TILLIE THE TOILER(1941); TOBACCO ROAD(1941); BROADWAY(1942); I MARRIED A WITCH(1942); LADY BODYGUARD(1942); MEXICAN SPITFIRE SEES A GHOST(1942); PALM BEACH STORY, THE(1942); STREET OF CHANCE(1942); DANCING MASTERS, THE(1943); IRON MAJOR, THE(1943); SHE HAS WHAT IT TAKES(1943); WHAT'S BUZZIN COUSIN?(1943); ADVENTURES OF MARK TWAIN, THE(1944); ATLANTIC CITY(1944); CASANOVA IN BURLESQUE(1944); DOUGHGIRLS, THE(1944); MRS. PARKINGTON(1944); SAN DIEGO, I LOVE YOU(1944); SEE HERE, PRIVATE HARGROVE(1944); WILSON(1944); ABBOTT AND COSTELLO IN HOLLYWOOD(1945); DUFFY'S TAVERN(1945); IDENTITY UNKNOWN(1945); I'LL TELL THE WORLD(1945); WOMAN WHO CAME BACK(1945); BLUE DAHLIA, THE(1946); DECOY(1946); FABULOUS SUZANNE, THE(1946); I RING DOORBELLS(1946); JOHNNY COMES FLYING HOME(1946); MIGHTY MCGURK, THE(1946); NIGHT EDITOR(1946); SLIGHTLY SCANDALOUS(1946); SOMEWHERE IN THE NIGHT(1946); HEADING FOR HEAVEN(1947); HIGH BARBAREE(1947); SARGE GOES TO COLLEGE(1947); THIS TIME FOR KEEPS(1947); WINTER WONDERLAND(1947); WOMAN ON THE BEACH, THE(1947); DEEP WATERS(1948); SMART POLITICS(1948); STRIKE IT RICH(1948); THAT WONDERFUL URGE(1948); UNTAMED BREED, THE(1948); AIR HOSTESS(1949); BEAUTIFUL BLONDE FROM BASHFUL BEND, THE(1949); HELLFIRE(1949); MA AND PA KETTLE(1949); MASTER MINDS(1949); SORROWFUL JONES(1949); LUCKY LOSERS(1950); NEVER A DULL MOMENT(1950); RIDER FROM TUCSON(1950); TRAVELING SALESWOMAN(1950); WOMAN OF DISTINCTION, A(1950); BEDTIME FOR BONZO(1951); CORKY OF GASOLINE ALLEY(1951); FAT MAN, THE(1951); SANTA FE(1951); TEXANS NEVER CRY(1951); DEADLINE–U.S.A.(1952); QUIET MAN, THE(1952); THIS WOMAN IS DANGEROUS(1952); WAGONS WEST(1952); PERILOUS JOURNEY, A(1953); SHE'S BACK ON BROADWAY(1953); THEM!(1954); WITNESS TO MURDER(1954); ABBOTT AND COSTELLO MEET THE KEYSTONE KOPS(1955); GLORY(1955); GUYS AND DOLLS(1955); LAWLESS STREET, A(1955); TEXAS LADY(1955); DAY OF FURY, A(1956); THESE WILDER YEARS(1956); FOOTSTEPS IN THE NIGHT(1957); PLUNDER ROAD(1957); LAST HURRAH, THE(1958); PILLOW TALK(1959)

Harry O. Tyler
HEAT'S ON, THE(1943); GLASS WEB, THE(1953); NAKED STREET, THE(1955)

Henry Tyler
JAIL BUSTERS(1955)

Ian Tyler
LORDS OF DISCIPLINE, THE(1983)

Jeff Tyler
1984
BEAR, THE(1984)

Joan Tyler
FIRST TRAVELING SALESLADY, THE(1956)

Joyce Tyler
MANIACS ON WHEELS(1951, Brit.)

Judy Tyler
JAILHOUSE ROCK(1957)

Lela Tyler
CHARLIE CHAN IN THE SECRET SERVICE(1944); FIGHTING BACK(1948)

Lelah Tyler
SHE HAD TO EAT(1937); TIME OUT FOR ROMANCE(1937); EAST SIDE OF HEAVEN(1939); HONEYMOON'S OVER, THE(1939); DR. CHRISTIAN MEETS THE WOMEN(1940); TALK OF THE TOWN(1942); CASANOVA BROWN(1944); MR. SKEFFINGTON(1944); PILLOW TO POST(1945); ARSON, INC.(1949); RUSTY'S BIRTHDAY(1949); FULLER BRUSH GIRL, THE(1950); ONE TOO MANY(1950); WOMAN OF DISTINCTION, A(1950); MODERN MARRIAGE, A(1962)

Leon Tyler
MELODY FOR THREE(1941); THEY MEET AGAIN(1941); WHISTLING IN THE DARK(1941); LOVES OF EDGAR ALLAN POE, THE(1942); ON THE SUNNY SIDE(1942); GREAT MIKE, THE(1944); MAISIE GOES TO RENO(1944); SULLIVANS, THE(1944); GREAT STAGECOACH ROBBERY(1945); SON OF LASSIE(1945); THIS LOVE OF OURS(1945); MICKEY(1948); DEAR WIFE(1949); MR. SOFT TOUCH(1949); MILITARY ACADEMY WITH THAT TENTH AVENUE GANG(1950); CARRIE(1952); HAS ANYBODY SEEN MY GAL?(1952); JUST FOR YOU(1952); SWEETHEARTS ON PARADE(1953); PRISONER OF WAR(1954); LAY THAT RIFLE DOWN(1955); ACCUSED OF MURDER(1956); THESE WILDER YEARS(1956); DRAGSTRIP GIRL(1957); JEANNE EAGELS(1957); SHAKE, RATTLE, AND ROCK!(1957); SPRING REUNION(1957); JUVENILE JUNGLE(1958); OUTCASTS OF THE CITY(1958); GHOST OF DRAGSTRIP HOLLOW(1959); SUBMARINE SEAHAWK(1959); MY SIX LOVES(1963); SON OF FLUBBER(1963); MONKEY'S UNCLE, THE(1965)

Leyla Tyler
YOU CAN'T CHEAT AN HONEST MAN(1939)

Nelson Tyler
TOBRUK(1966), ph; ICE STATION ZEBRA(1968), ph; PAINT YOUR WAGON(1969), ph; CATCH-22(1970), ph; STUNT MAN, THE(1980)

Poyntz Tyler
FITZWILLY(1967), w

R.E. Tyler
BEYOND THE ROCKIES(1932), art d

Richard Tyler
SPIRAL STAIRCASE, THE(1946); FATHER WAS A FULLBACK(1949); TRIAL(1955); TEA AND SYMPATHY(1956); BLUE ANGEL, THE(1959); ATOMIC SUBMARINE, THE(1960); WAKE ME WHEN IT'S OVER(1960); HOOPER(1978); PROPERTY(1979), a, m
Misc. Talkies
TRAIL BLAZERS(1953)

Robert Tyler
1984
SOLDIER'S STORY, A(1984)

Ronnie Tyler
PERFECT STRANGERS(1950)

T. Texas Tyler
HORSEMEN OF THE SIERRAS(1950)

Tom Tyler
CANYON OF MISSING MEN, THE(1930); GOD'S COUNTRY AND THE MAN(1931); MAN FROM DEATH VALLEY, THE(1931); PARTNERS OF THE TRAIL(1931); RIDER OF THE PLAINS(1931); TWO-FISTED JUSTICE(1931); WEST OF CHEYENNE(1931); 99 WOUNDS(1931); FORTY-NINERS, THE(1932); GALLOPING THRU(1932); HONOR OF THE MOUNTED(1932); MAN FROM NEW MEXICO, THE(1932); SINGLE-HAND-

ED SANDERS(1932); DEADWOOD PASS(1933); WAR OF THE RANGE(1933); WHEN A MAN RIDES ALONE(1933); FIGHTING HERO(1934); COYOTE TRAILS(1935); POWDERSMOKE RANGE(1935); FAST BULLETS(1936); LAST OUTLAW, THE(1936); RIP ROARIN' BUCKAROO(1936); CHEYENNE RIDES AGAIN(1937); LOST RANCH(1937); MYSTERY RANGE(1937); PINTO RUSTLERS(1937); RIDING ON(1937); SANTA FE BOUND(1937); BROTHERS OF THE WEST(1938); FEUD OF THE TRAIL(1938); KING OF ALCATRAZ(1938); ORPHAN OF THE PECOS(1938); PHANTOM OF THE RANGE, THE(1938); DRUMS ALONG THE MOHAWK(1939); FRONTIER MARSHAL(1939); NIGHT RIDERS, THE(1939); STAGECOACH(1939); BROTHER ORCHID(1940); CHEROKEE STRIP(1940); GRAPES OF WRATH(1940); LIGHT OF WESTERN STARS, THE(1940); MUMMY'S HAND, THE(1940); TEXAS RANGERS RIDE AGAIN(1940); WESTERNER, THE(1940); BORDER VIGILANTES(1941); BUCK PRIVATES(1941); GAUCHOS OF EL DORADO(1941); OUTLAWS OF THE CHEROKEE TRAIL(1941); RIDERS OF THE TIMBERLINE(1941); WEST OF CIMARRON(1942); CODE OF THE OUTLAW(1942); PHANTOM PLAINSMEN, THE(1942); RAIDERS OF THE RANGE(1942); SHADOWS ON THE SAGE(1942); TALK OF THE TOWN(1942); VALLEY OF HUNTED MEN(1942); VALLEY OF THE SUN(1942); WESTWARD HO(1942); RIDERS OF THE RIO GRANDE(1943); SANTA FE SCOUTS(1943); THUNDERING TRAILS(1943); WAGON TRACKS WEST(1943); PRINCESS AND THE PIRATE, THE(1944); SAN ANTONIO(1945); THEY WERE EXPENDABLE(1945); BADMAN'S TERRITORY(1946); NEVER SAY GOODBYE(1946); CHEYENNE(1947); BLOOD ON THE MOON(1948); DUDE GOES WEST, THE(1948); MYSTERY OF THE GOLDEN EYE, THE(1948); RED RIVER(1948); RETURN OF THE BADMEN(1948); THREE MUSKETEERS, THE(1948); I SHOT JESSE JAMES(1949); LUST FOR GOLD(1949); MASKED RAIDERS(1949); RIDERS OF THE RANGE(1949); SAMSON AND DELILAH(1949); SHE WORE A YELLOW RIBBON(1949); SQUARE DANCE JUBILEE(1949); YOUNGER BROTHERS, THE(1949); COLORADO RANGER(1950); CROOKED RIVER(1950); DALTON'S WOMEN, THE(1950); FAST ON THE DRAW(1950); GREAT MISSOURI RAID, THE(1950); HOSTILE COUNTRY(1950); MARSHAL OF HELDORADO(1950); RIO GRANDE PATROL(1950); TRAIL OF ROBIN HOOD(1950); WEST OF THE BRAZOS(1950); BEST OF THE BADMEN(1951); LION AND THE HORSE, THE(1952); ROAD AGENT(1952); WHAT PRICE GLORY?(1952); COW COUNTRY(1953)
Misc. Talkies
VANISHING MEN(1932); MYSTERY RANCH(1934); TERROR OF THE PLAINS(1934); BORN TO BATTLE(1935); LARAMIE KID, THE(1935); RIDIN' THRU(1935); RIO RATTLER(1935); SILVER BULLET, THE(1935); TRACY RIDES(1935); TRIGGER TOM(1935); UNCONQUERED BANDIT(1935); RIDIN' ON(1936); ROAMIN' WILD(1936); BLOCKED TRAIL, THE(1943); BOSS OF BOOMTOWN(1944); SING ME A SONG OF TEXAS(1945)
Silents
OUT OF THE WEST(1926); TOM AND HIS PALS(1926); CYCLONE OF THE RANGE(1927); LIGHTNING LARIATS(1927); SONORA KID, THE(1927); SPLITTING THE BREEZE(1927); AVENGING RIDER, THE(1928); DESERT PIRATE, THE(1928); PHANTOM OF THE RANGE(1928); GUN LAW(1929); IDAHO RED(1929); LONE HORSEMAN, THE(1929); PHANTOM RIDER, THE(1929)
Misc. Silents
COWBOY MUSKETEER, THE(1925); LET'S GO GALLAGHER(1925); WYOMING WILDCAT, THE(1925); ARIZONA STREAK, THE(1926); BORN TO BATTLE(1926); COWBOY COP, THE(1926); MASQUERADE BANDIT, THE(1926); RED HOT HOOFS(1926); WILD TO GO(1926); CHEROKEE KID, THE(1927); FLYING U RANCH, THE(1927); TOM'S GANG(1927); TERROR(1928); TERROR MOUNTAIN(1928); TEXAS TORNADO, THE(1928); TYRANT OF RED GULCH(1928); WHEN THE LAW RIDES(1928); LAW OF THE PLAINS(1929); MAN FROM NEVADA, THE(1929); 'NEATH WESTERN SKIES(1929); PIONEERS OF THE WEST(1929); TRAIL OF THE HORSE THIEVES, THE(1929); CALL OF THE DESERT(1930); CANYON OF MISSING MEN, THE(1930)

Walter Tyler
ROMA RIVUOLE CESARE(, art d; HENRY ALDRICH, BOY SCOUT(1944), art d; MAN IN HALF-MOON STREET, THE(1944), art d; YOU CAN'T RATION LOVE(1944), art d; HOLD THAT BLONDE(1945), art d; KITTY(1945), art d; BLUE DAHLIA, THE(1946), art d; LADIES' MAN(1947), art d; UNCONQUERED(1947), art d; FOREIGN AFFAIR, A(1948), art d; WHISPERING SMITH(1948), art d; SAMSON AND DELILAH(1949), art d; RIDING HIGH(1950), art d; PLACE IN THE SUN, A(1951), art d; GREATEST SHOW ON EARTH, THE(1952), art d; HURRICANE SMITH(1952), art d; SOMETHING TO LIVE FOR(1952), art d; OFF LIMITS(1953), art d; SHANE(1953), art d; SABRINA(1954), art d; RAINMAKER, THE(1956), art d; TEN COMMANDMENTS, THE(1956), art d; GUNFIGHT AT THE O.K. CORRAL(1957), art d; DON'T GIVE UP THE SHIP(1959), art d; LAST TRAIN FROM GUN HILL(1959), art d; G.I. BLUES(1960), art d; VISIT TO A SMALL PLANET(1960), art d; ALL IN A NIGHT'S WORK(1961), art d; SUMMER AND SMOKE(1961), art d; GIRL NAMED TAMIRO, A(1962), art d; GIRLS! GIRLS! GIRLS!(1962), art d; FUN IN ACAPULCO(1963), art d; NUTTY PROFESSOR, THE(1963), art d; WIVES AND LOVERS(1963), art d; CARPETBAGGERS, THE(1964), art d; ROUSTABOUT(1964), art d; WHERE LOVE HAS GONE(1964), art d; BOEING BOEING(1965), art d; SONS OF KATIE ELDER, THE(1965), art d; PARADISE, HAWAIIAN STYLE(1966), art d; SWINGER, THE(1966), art d; EASY COME, EASY GO(1967), art d; SPIRIT IS WILLING, THE(1967), art d; FIVE CARD STUD(1968), prod d; ODD COUPLE, THE(1968), art d; PROJECT X(1968), art d; TRUE GRIT(1969), prod d; NORWOOD(1970), art d; OUT OF TOWNERS, THE(1970), art d; RED SKY AT MORNING(1971), art d; SHOOT OUT(1971), art d; NOW YOU SEE HIM, NOW YOU DON'T(1972), art d; SNOWBALL EXPRESS(1972), art d; WORLD'S GREATEST ATHLETE, THE(1973), art d; HERBIE RIDES AGAIN(1974), art d; ISLAND AT THE TOP OF THE WORLD, THE(1974), art d; APPLE DUMPLING GANG, THE(1975), art d; MIDWAY(1976), art d

William Tyler
MARINES, LET'S GO(1961)

Willie Tyler
COMING HOME(1978)

Michael Tylo
DETROIT 9000(1973)

Odette Tylor
Silents
SAPHEAD, THE(1921)

S. Tym
WALKOVER(1969, Pol.)

Brandon Tyman
LUCKY PARTNERS(1940)

George Tyme
NOT WITH MY WIFE, YOU DON'T!(1966)
Andrzej Tymowski
1984
FAR FROM POLAND(1984), p&d
Brandon Tynan
PARNELL(1937); SH! THE OCTOPUS(1937); WELLS FARGO(1937); NANCY DREW–DETECTIVE(1938); YOUTH TAKES A FLING(1938); ALMOST A GENTLEMAN(1939); GREAT MAN VOTES, THE(1939); LADY AND THE MOB, THE(1939); LONE WOLF SPY HUNT, THE(1939); I WANT A DIVORCE(1940); IT ALL CAME TRUE(1940); MY FAVORITE WIFE(1940); RANGERS OF FORTUNE(1940); VIRGINIA CITY(1940); MARRY THE BOSS' DAUGHTER(1941)
Silents
LOYAL LIVES(1923); SUCCESS(1923)
Misc. Silents
UNRESTRAINED YOUTH(1925)
James Tynan
OLSEN'S BIG MOMENT(1934), w
James J. Tynan
Silents
HIS MASTER'S VOICE(1925), w; ONE OF THE BRAVEST(1925), w; OVERLAND LIMITED, THE(1925), w; SILENT POWER, THE(1926), w; IRRESISTIBLE LOVER, THE(1927), w
John Tynan
LADY CHATTERLEY'S LOVER(1981, Fr./Brit.)
Kathleen Tynan
AGATHA(1979, Brit.), w
Kenneth Tynan
NOWHERE TO GO(1959, Brit.), d; MACBETH(1971, Brit.), w; OH! CALCUTTA!(1972), w
Tracy Tynan
1984
CHOOSE ME(1984), cos; STRANGERS KISS(1984), cos
Wanda Tynan
CAGED(1950)
Kate Tyndale
Silents
MESSAGE FROM MARS, A(1913, Brit.)
Elliott Tyne
REBEL ANGEL(1962), w
George Tyne [Buddy Yarus]
THEY WON'T BELIEVE ME(1947); DANCING MASTERS, THE(1943); OBJECTIVE, BURMA!(1945); WALK IN THE SUN, A(1945); DEADLINE AT DAWN(1946); LIFE WITH BLONDIE(1946); CALL NORTHSIDE 777(1948); OPEN SECRET(1948); LONE WOLF AND HIS LADY, THE(1949); RED PONY, THE(1949); SANDS OF IWO JIMA(1949); SWORD IN THE DESERT(1949); THIEVES' HIGHWAY(1949); NO WAY OUT(1950); SIDE STREET(1950); DECISION BEFORE DAWN(1951); DON'T MAKE WAVES(1967); VALLEY OF MYSTERY(1967); COUNTERFEIT KILLER, THE(1968); LOST MAN, THE(1969); MARLOWE(1969); TELL THEM WILLIE BOY IS HERE(1969); SKIN GAME(1971); MR. RICCO(1975); I WILL ...I WILL ...FOR NOW(1976); ROMANTIC COMEDY(1983)
Charles Tyner
LILITH(1964); COOL HAND LUKE(1967); GAILY, GAILY(1969); REIVERS, THE(1969); STALKING MOON, THE(1969); CHEYENNE SOCIAL CLUB, THE(1970); MONTE WALSH(1970); MOONSHINE WAR, THE(1970); TRAVELING EXECUTIONER, THE(1970); HAROLD AND MAUDE(1971); LAWMAN(1971); SOMETIMES A GREAT NOTION(1971); BAD COMPANY(1972); COWBOYS, THE(1972); FUZZ(1972); JEREMIAH JOHNSON(1972); EMPEROR OF THE NORTH POLE(1973); STONE KILLER, THE(1973); LONGEST YARD, THE(1974); MIDNIGHT MAN, THE(1974); FAMILY PLOT(1976); PETE'S DRAGON(1977); EVILSPEAK(1982)
Paul Tyner
SHOOT IT: BLACK, SHOOT IT: BLUE(1974), w
Jim Tynes
DEMENTED(1980), ph
Tom Tyon
MAN CALLED HORSE, A(1970)
Dan Tyra
KRAMER VS. KRAMER(1979)
Tyrand
WAYS OF LOVE(1950, Ital./Fr.)
Betty Tyree
UNWRITTEN LAW, THE(1932)
Owen Tyree
DARK CITY(1950)
Betty Tyrel
Silents
IN AGAIN-OUT AGAIN(1917)
Ann Tyrell
CAGED(1950); FATHER'S WILD GAME(1950); MY TRUE STORY(1951); SELLOUT, THE(1951); LOVE IS BETTER THAN EVER(1952); JULIUS CAESAR(1953); TAKE ME TO TOWN(1953); EXECUTIVE SUITE(1954); GOOD MORNING, MISS DOVE(1955)
David Tyrell
LOVE BEFORE BREAKFAST(1936); SAINTLY SINNERS(1962)
Elizabeth Tyrell
DAY IN THE DEATH OF JOE EGG, A(1972, Brit.)
Gerrard Tyrell
HER LAST AFFAIRE(1935, Brit.); MURDER IN THE OLD RED BARN(1936, Brit.)
John Tyrell
LADY FROM NOWHERE(1936); LEGION OF TERROR(1936); COUNTERFEIT LADY(1937); GAME THAT KILLS, THE(1937); JUVENILE COURT(1938); LAW OF THE PLAINS(1938); FIRST OFFENDERS(1939); MY SON IS A CRIMINAL(1939); RIO GRANDE(1939); TAMING OF THE WEST, THE(1939); BLAZING SIX SHOOTERS(1940); DURANGO KID, THE(1940); GIRLS UNDER TWENTY-ONE(1940); FACE BEHIND THE MASK, THE(1941); MYSTERY SHIP(1941); PHANTOM SUBMARINE, THE(1941); SON OF DAVY CROCKETT, THE(1941); LUCKY LEGS(1942); PARACHUTE NURSE(1942); SHUT MY BIG MOUTH(1942); SPIRIT OF STANFORD, THE(1942); SWEETHEART OF THE FLEET(1942); LAUGH YOUR BLUES AWAY(1943); ONE DANGEROUS NIGHT(1943); SILVER CITY RAIDERS(1943); COWBOY FROM LONESOME RIVER(1944); CYCLONE PRAIRIE RANGERS(1944); ONE MYSTERIOUS NIGHT(1944); ESCAPE IN THE FOG(1945); NIGHT EDI-

TOR(1946)
Susan Tyrell
BEEN DOWN SO LONG IT LOOKS LIKE UP TO ME(1977); RACQUET(1979)
Tom Tyrell
Misc. Talkies
BLAST-OFF GIRLS(1967)
Bertram Tyrer
STOLEN AIRLINER, THE(1962, Brit.), art d
Jacques Tyrol
Misc. Silents
HUMAN PASSIONS(1919), d; RED VIPER, THE(1919), d
Glenn Tyron
BACHELOR BAIT(1934), w
Misc. Talkies
WIDOW IN SCARLET(1932)
Max Tyron
Silents
GREED(1925)
Kathleen Tyrone
ROSE OF TRALEE(1938, Ireland), d&w
Madge Tyrone
Silents
ONE CLEAR CALL(1922), ed; HUSBANDS AND LOVERS(1924), t
Misc. Silents
HOUSE OF TEARS, THE(1915)
The Tyrones
LET'S ROCK(1958)
John Tyrrel
PASSPORT TO SUEZ(1943)
Alice Tyrrell
ANGEL COMES TO BROOKLYN, AN(1945); CALIFORNIA FIREBRAND(1948); I SURRENDER DEAR(1948); MANHATTAN ANGEL(1948)
Andrew Tyrrell
HAVING A WILD WEEKEND(1965, Brit.)
Ann Tyrrell
BRIDE FOR SALE(1949); EMERGENCY WEDDING(1950); GLASS MENAGERIE, THE(1950); KISS TOMORROW GOODBYE(1950); MOTHER DIDN'T TELL ME(1950); NO WAY OUT(1950); ONCE A THIEF(1950); BEDTIME FOR BONZO(1951); GIRL IN WHITE, THE(1952); PAULA(1952); YOUNG BESS(1953); LUCKY ME(1954); SEVEN ANGRY MEN(1955)
Geoffrey Tyrrell
NIGHT MY NUMBER CAME UP, THE(1955, Brit.); CAT GIRL(1957); DEADLY RECORD(1959, Brit.); MANIA(1961, Brit.)
Gerard Tyrrell
ESTHER WATERS(1948, Brit.), w
John Tyrrell
AWFUL TRUTH, THE(1937); FRAME-UP THE(1937); GIRLS CAN PLAY(1937); MOTOR MADNESS(1937); SHADOW, THE(1937); CALL OF THE ROCKIES(1938); MAIN EVENT, THE(1938); SOUTH OF ARIZONA(1938); WEST OF CHEYENNE(1938); WOMEN IN PRISON(1938); YOU CAN'T TAKE IT WITH YOU(1938); HOMICIDE BUREAU(1939); LONE WOLF SPY RING, THE(1939); MAN THEY COULD NOT HANG, THE(1939); SMASHING THE SPY RING(1939); ISLAND OF DOOMED MEN(1940); MAN FROM TUMBLEWEEDS, THE(1940); MY SON IS GUILTY(1940); THUNDERING FRONTIER(1940); HONOLULU LU(1941); I WAS A PRISONER ON DEVIL'S ISLAND(1941); MEET BOSTON BLACKIE(1941); PENNY SERENADE(1941); RICHEST MAN IN TOWN(1941); THREE GIRLS ABOUT TOWN(1941); BOSTON BLACKIE GOES HOLLYWOOD(1942); CANAL ZONE(1942); HARVARD, HERE I COME(1942); SABOTAGE SQUAD(1942); TALK OF THE TOWN(1942); TRAMP, TRAMP, TRAMP(1942); COWBOY IN THE CLOUDS(1943); IS EVERYBODY HAPPY?(1943); WHAT'S BUZZIN COUSIN?(1943); COVER GIRL(1944); CRY OF THE WEREWOLF(1944); GHOST THAT WALKS ALONE, THE(1944); JAM SESSION(1944); ONCE UPON A TIME(1944); BOSTON BLACKIE'S RENDEZVOUS(1945); EVE KNEW HER APPLES(1945); ROUGH, TOUGH AND READY(1945); SERGEANT MIKE(1945); SHE WOULDN'T SAY YES(1945); GILDA(1946); OUT OF THE DEPTHS(1946); MY FAVORITE BRUNETTE(1947); SECRET LIFE OF WALTER MITTY, THE(1947)
Johnny Tyrrell
CRIMINALS OF THE AIR(1937); GOOD GIRLS GO TO PARIS(1939); UNDERGROUND AGENT(1942)
Susan Tyrrell
BUTCHER BAKER(NIGHTMARE MAKER)* (1982); SHOOT OUT(1971); STEAGLE, THE(1971); FAT CITY(1972); CATCH MY SOUL(1974); ZANDY'S BRIDE(1974); KILLER INSIDE ME, THE(1976); ANOTHER MAN, ANOTHER CHANCE(1977 Fr/US); I NEVER PROMISED YOU A ROSE GARDEN(1977); ISLANDS IN THE STREAM(1977); 9/30/55(1977); FORBIDDEN ZONE(1980); LOOSE SHOES(1980); SUBWAY RIDERS(1981); FAST-WALKING(1982); LIAR'S MOON(1982); FIRE AND ICE(1983); TALES OF ORDINARY MADNESS(1983, Ital.)
1984
ANGEL(1984); KILLERS, THE(1984)
Joan Tysen
PILGRIMAGE(1972)
Sallie Tysha
Silents
SHAMS OF SOCIETY(1921)
V. Tyshkovets
MOTHER AND DAUGHTER(1965, USSR), ph
Sylvia Tysick
NICE GIRL LIKE ME, A(1969, Brit.)
Cicely Tyson
LAST ANGRY MAN, THE(1959); ODDS AGAINST TOMORROW(1959); MAN CALLED ADAM, A(1966); COMEDIANS, THE(1967); HEART IS A LONELY HUNTER, THE(1968); SOUNDER(1972); BLUE BIRD, THE(1976); RIVER NIGER, THE(1976); HERO AIN'T NOTHIN' BUT A SANDWICH, A(1977); CONCORDE, THE–AIRPORT '79(1979); BUSTIN' LOOSE(1981)
Emma Tyson
AND NOW MIGUEL(1966)
George Tyson
BASHFUL ELEPHANT, THE(1962, Aust.), ph

Hylda Tyson
  JANE EYRE(1935)
James Tyson
1984
  TANK(1984), cos
Jim Tyson
1984
  FLETCH(1984), cos
Beata Tysziewicz
  CONTRACT, THE(1982, Pol.)
Beata Tyszkiewicz
  TONIGHT A TOWN DIES(1961, Pol.); WINDOWS OF TIME, THE(1969, Hung.); SARAGOSSA MANUSCRIPT, THE(1972, Pol.)
1984
  EDITH AND MARCEL(1984, Fr.)
Vladimir Tytla
  SNOW WHITE AND THE SEVEN DWARFS(1937), anim; FANTASIA(1940), anim; PINOCCHIO(1940), anim d; DUMBO(1941), anim d; INCREDIBLE MR. LIMPET, THE(1964), spec eff
Jim D. Tytler
  SHAKESPEARE WALLAH(1966, India)
Sh. Tyumenbayev
  HUNTING IN SIBERIA(1962, USSR)
Joseph Tyzack
  LITTLE LORD FAUNTLEROY(1936)
Margaret Tyzack
  BEHIND THE MASK(1958, Brit.); ROOM 43(1959, Brit.); HIGHWAY TO BATTLE(1961, Brit.); RING OF SPIES(1964, Brit.); WHISPERERS, THE(1967, Brit.); 2001: A SPACE ODYSSEY(1968, U.S./Brit.); THANK YOU ALL VERY MUCH(1969, Brit.); CLOCKWORK ORANGE, A(1971, Brit.); LEGACY, THE(1979, Brit.); QUATERMASS CONCLUSION(1980, Brit.)
Ziporah Tzabari
1984
  BEST DEFENSE(1984)
Christ Tzagneas
  WE HAVE ONLY ONE LIFE(1963, Gr.)
George Tzavellas
  GROUCH, THE(1961, Gr.), d&w; ANTIGONE(1962 Gr.), d&w; WE HAVE ONLY ONE LIFE(1963, Gr.), d&w
Anna Tzelniker
  YENTL(1983)
Meier Tzelniker
  MR. EMMANUEL(1945, Brit.); IT ALWAYS RAINS ON SUNDAY(1949, Brit.); LAST HOLIDAY(1950, Brit.); MAKE ME AN OFFER(1954, Brit.); TECKMAN MYSTERY, THE(1955, Brit); WOMAN FOR JOE, THE(1955, Brit.); EXTRA DAY, THE(1956, Brit.); STARS IN YOUR EYES(1956, Brit.); LONG HAUL, THE(1957, Brit.); NIGHT TO REMEMBER, A(1958, Brit.); EXPRESSO BONGO(1959, Brit.); LET'S GET MARRIED(1960, Brit.); CIRCLE OF DECEPTON(1961, Brit.); HIS AND HERS(1961, Brit.); JUNGLE STREET GIRLS(1963, Brit.); SORCERERS, THE(1967, Brit.); 25TH HOUR, THE(1967, Fr./Ital./Yugo.)
S. Tzintzadze
  DRAGONFLY, THE(1955 USSR), m
Yannis Tziotis
  APOLLO GOES ON HOLIDAY(1968, Ger./Swed.), w
Georges Tzipine
  MYSTERY OF THE BLACK JUNGLE(1955), m
T. Tzitzishvill
  DRAGONFLY, THE(1955 USSR)
Nikos Tzoyias
  PHAEDRA(1962, U.S./Gr./Fr.)
T. Tzutzunava
  DRAGONFLY, THE(1955 USSR)

U

The U.F.O.'s
LOVE-INS, THE(1967)

Norma Uatuhan
YEAR OF LIVING DANGEROUSLY, THE(1982, Aus.)
Giorgio Ubaldi
INVINCIBLE GLADIATOR, THE(1963, c.u. Ital./Span.)
Pino Ubaldo
IT HAPPENED IN CANADA(1962, Can.)
Mark Ubell
SUMMER CAMP(1979), ed
Steve Ubels
ESCAPE TO ATHENA(1979, Brit.); DRAUGHTSMAN'S CONTRACT, THE(1983, Brit.)
1984
TOP SECRET!(1984)

Anny Delli Uberti
HORROR CASTLE(1965, Ital.)
Toshio Ubukata
IDIOT, THE(1963, Jap.), ph; SCANDAL(1964, Jap.), ph
Semra Ucar
YOL(1982, Turkey)
Paul Uccello
CASEY'S SHADOW(1978)
Toni Ucci
ASSASSIN, THE(1961, Ital./Fr.); PASSIONATE THIEF, THE(1963, Ital.); TWO COLONELS, THE(1963, Ital.); FACTS OF MURDER, THE(1965, Ital.)

Ugo Ucellini
Silents
ROMOLA(1925)
Asao Uchida
TORA! TORA! TORA!(1970, U.S./Jap.)
Christine Uchida
HAIR(1979)
Katsumasu Uchida
MONSTERS FROM THE UNKNOWN PLANET(1975, Jap.)
Ryohei Uchida
JUDO SHOWDOWN(1966, Jap.); EAST CHINA SEA(1969, Jap.); HARBOR LIGHT YOKOHAMA(1970, Jap.)
Takako Uchida
HOUSE OF STRANGE LOVES, THE(1969, Jap.)

Yoshiro Uchida
GAMERA THE INVINCIBLE(1966, Jap.)
Yuya Uchida
MERRY CHRISTMAS MR. LAWRENCE(1983, Jap./Brit.)
Seiichiro Uchikawa
SAMURAI FROM NOWHERE(1964, Jap.), d; JUDO SAGA(1965, Jap.), d
Barbara Uchiyamada
HOUSE OF BAMBOO(1955)
Gustav Ucicky
TEMPORARY WIDOW, THE(1930, Ger./Brit.), d; IMMORTAL VAGABOND(1931, Ger.), d; GIRL OF THE MOORS, THE(1961, Ger.), d
Misc. Silents
CAFE ELECTRIC(1927, Aust.), d

Hatsuo Uda
DIFFERENT STORY, A(1978)
Vicky Udall
HUMAN FACTOR, THE(1979, Brit.)
Charles Uday
VIOLATED(1953)
Bill Udell
WITHOUT RESERVATIONS(1946)
George Udell
POLYESTER(1981)
Peggy Udell
Misc. Silents
RIDIN' STREAK, THE(1925)
Ernst Udet
S.O.S. ICEBERG(1933)
Chris Udvarnoky
OTHER, THE(1972)
Martin Udvarnoky
OTHER, THE(1972)
Claudia Udy
JOY(1983, Fr./Can.)
1984
AMERICAN NIGHTMARE(1984); SAVAGE DAWN(1984)
Helen Udy
DEAD ZONE, THE(1983)
Helene Udy
MY BLOODY VALENTINE(1981, Can.); PICK-UP SUMMER(1981)
Ueda
WELCOME TO THE CLUB(1971)
Akinari Ueda
UGETSU(1954, Jap.), w
Hirochi Ueda
SECRET SCROLLS(PART I)**1/2 (1968, Jap.), art d
Hiroshi Ueda
SECRET SCROLLS(PART II)**1/2 (1968, Jap.), art d; KOJIRO(1967, Jap.), art d; UNDER THE BANNER OF SAMURAI(1969, Jap.), art d; RED LION(1971, Jap.), art d

Kichijiro Ueda
RASHOMON(1951, Jap.); SEVEN SAMURAI, THE(1956, Jap.); HIDDEN FORTRESS, THE(1959, Jap.); DANGEROUS KISS, THE(1961, Jap.); LOWER DEPTHS, THE(1962, Jap.); GAMERA VERSUS GAOS(1967, Jap.); I LIVE IN FEAR(1967, Jap.)
Shoji Ueda
KAGEMUSHA(1980, Jap.), ph; BUSHIDO BLADE, THE(1982 Brit./U.S.), ph
Keinosuke Uegusa
DRUNKEN ANGEL(1948, Jap.), w
Akira Uehara
GAMERA VERSUS GAOS(1967, Jap.), ph; GATEWAY TO GLORY(1970, Jap.), ph; GAMERA VERSUS ZIGRA(1971, Jap.), ph
Ken Uehara
NIGHT IN HONG KONG, A(1961, Jap.); MOTHRA(1962, Jap.); HONOLULU-TOKYO-HONG KONG(1963, Hong Kong/Jap.); ATRAGON(1965, Jap.)
Misa Uehara
HIDDEN FORTRESS, THE(1959, Jap.); I BOMBED PEARL HARBOR(1961, Jap.); SAGA OF THE VAGABONDS(1964, Jap.)
Shin Uehara
PANDA AND THE MAGIC SERPENT(1961, Jap.), w
Mitzi Uehlein
HOUSE ACROSS THE BAY, THE(1940)
Mitzie Uehlein
EASY TO WED(1946); SHOW BOAT(1951)
Hetoshi Ueki
DON'T CALL ME A CON MAN(1966, Jap.)
Hitoshi Ueki
LAS VEGAS FREE-FOR-ALL(1968, Jap.); COMPUTER FREE-FOR-ALL(1969, Jap.)
Erica Ueland
DEVONSVILLE TERROR, THE(1983), makeup
Banjiro Uemura
MESSAGE FROM SPACE(1978, Jap.), p
Kenjiro Uemura
GATE OF HELL(1954, Jap.)
Nobuko Uenishi
FOR LOVE OF IVY(1968)
Yoshio Ueno
BUDDHA(1965, Jap.), cos
Kelsey Ufford
ICE CASTLES(1978)
Claire Ufland
AMOROUS ADVENTURES OF MOLL FLANDERS, THE(1965)
Harry Ufland
KING OF COMEDY, THE(1983)
Julian Ugarte
PRIDE AND THE PASSION, THE(1957); FRANKENSTEIN'S BLOODY TERROR(1968, Span.); MALENKA, THE VAMPIRE(1972, Span./Ital.); MAN CALLED NOON, THE(1973, Brit.); BLOOD MONEY(1974, U.S./Hong Kong/Ital./Span.)
Salvadore Ugarte
Misc. Talkies
MISS LESLIE'S DOLLS(1972)
Alan Uger
BLAZING SADDLES(1974), w
Leslie Uggams
TWO WEEKS IN ANOTHER TOWN(1962); BLACK GIRL(1972); SKYJACKED(1972)
Misc. Talkies
POOR PRETTY EDDIE(1975); HEARTBREAK MOTEL(1978)
Fernande Ugi
PICNIC ON THE GRASS(1960, Fr.), makeup
Rudy Ugland
VALDEZ IS COMING(1971); CHATO'S LAND(1972)
Anthony Ugrin
WAY OF A GAUCHO(1952)
Genia Ugrinsky
DANCING HEART, THE(1959, Ger.)
Ali Ugur
DRY SUMMER(1967, Turkey), ph
Milan Uhde
SIGN OF THE VIRGIN(1969, Czech.), w
Vance Uhden
DEVIL'S JEST, THE(1954, Brit.), w
Annely Uherek
1984
STRANGERS KISS(1984)
Alfred Uhl
DON JUAN(1956, Aust.), w
Tommy Uhlar
LADY IN CEMENT(1968)
Gisela Uhlen
MARRIAGE OF MARIA BRAUN, THE(1979, Ger.)
Michael Uhlenkot
1984
MIKE'S MURDER(1984)
Eric Uhler
GOODBYE GIRL, THE(1977)
Laurent Uhler
IN THE WHITE CITY(1983, Switz./Portugal), ed
Karel Uhlik
INTIMATE LIGHTING(1969, Czech.)
Jane Uhrig
CAT ATE THE PARAKEET, THE(1972)
Ghislain Uhry
VIVA MARIA(1965, Fr./Ital.), cos; THIEF OF PARIS, THE(1967, Fr./Ital.), cos; SPIRITS OF THE DEAD(1969, Fr./Ital.), art d, cos; LACOMBE, LUCIEN(1974), art d; BLACK MOON(1975, Fr.), w; MALEVIL(1981, Fr./Ger.), cos
Betty Uitti
HANS CHRISTIAN ANDERSEN(1952); SEVEN LITTLE FOYS, THE(1955); THIS COULD BE THE NIGHT(1957)

Matthias Uitz
WATERMELON MAN(1970)
Shinko Ujiie
NAKED YOUTH(1961, Jap.)
Karoly Ujlaky
MEPHISTO(1981, Ger.)
Emery J. Ujvari
DARK OF THE SUN(1968, Brit.)
Ky Huot Uk
ODYSSEY OF THE PACIFIC(1983, Can./Fr.)
Gabriel Ukaegbu
WHITE WITCH DOCTOR(1953)
Vsevolod Ukhov
SLEEPING BEAUTY, THE(1966, USSR)
Saburo Ukida
ANGRY ISLAND(1960, Jap.)
Bruno Ukmar
SEVEN SEAS TO CALAIS(1963, Ital.); SABATA(1969, Ital.)
Franco Ukmar
SEVEN SEAS TO CALAIS(1963, Ital.); SABATA(1969, Ital.)
A.E. Ukonu
DISEMBODIED, THE(1957)
Ukonu and his Afro-Calypsonians
PANAMA SAL(1957)
Richard Ulacia
1984
MIXED BLOOD(1984)
Orest Ulan
HAPPY MOTHER'S DAY... LOVE, GEORGE(1973)
Finn Ulbach
THREE LEGIONNAIRES, THE(1937), ed
Finn Ulback
CORRUPTION(1933), ed; DRUMS OF DESTINY(1937), ed; BAREFOOT BOY(1938), ed; MY OLD KENTUCKY HOME(1938), ed
Walter Ulbrich
SINS OF ROSE BERND, THE(1959, Ger.), w; AS THE SEA RAGES(1960 Ger.), w
Anthony Ulc
1984
HOTEL NEW HAMPSHIRE, THE(1984)
Frantisek Uldrich
WHAT WOULD YOU SAY TO SOME SPINACH(1976, Czech.), ph
Frantisek Uldrych
NIGHTS OF PRAGUE, THE(1968, Czech.), ph
Detlef Ule
SONS OF SATAN(1969, Ital./Fr./Ger.)
Vera Ulesova
SECRET MISSION(1949, USSR)
Ulhas
TIGER AND THE FLAME, THE(1955, India)
Judy Ulian
SON OF SINBAD(1955)
V. Ulitko
SLEEPING BEAUTY, THE(1966, USSR), art d
Betty Ulius
PSYCH-OUT(1968), w
Olga Uljanovskaja
MISSION TO MOSCOW(1943)
Ullas
GUIDE, THE(1965, U.S./India); MAYA(1966)
Lurline Uller
HOUSE ACROSS THE BAY, THE(1940)
Carl Ullman
Silents
LITTLE BROTHER, THE(1917)
Misc. Silents
WOLF LOWRY(1917); WHAT WOMEN LOVE(1920)
Dan Ullman
CHEROKEE UPRISING(1950), w; HOT ROD(1950), w; OUTLAWS OF TEXAS(1950), w; SILVER RAIDERS(1950), w; CAVALRY SCOUT(1951), w; LONGHORN, THE(1951), w; MONTANA DESPERADO(1951), w; FORT OSAGE(1952), w; HIAWATHA(1952), w; KANSAS TERRITORY(1952), w; WACO(1952), w; WAGONS WEST(1952), w; WILD STALLION(1952), w; FIGHTING LAWMAN, THE(1953), w; FORT VENGEANCE(1953), w; KANSAS PACIFIC(1953), w; MARKSMAN, THE(1953), w; MAZE, THE(1953), w; ROYAL AFRICAN RIFLES, THE(1953), w; STAR OF TEXAS(1953), w; FORTYNINERS, THE(1954), w; TWO GUNS AND A BADGE(1954), w; ANNAPOLIS STORY, AN(1955), w
Dan B. Ullman
SQUARE DANCE JUBILEE(1949), w
Daniel Ullman
BIG GUSHER, THE(1951), w; SMUGGLER'S GOLD(1951), w; WICHITA(1955), w; BATTLE OF THE CORAL SEA(1959), w; MYSTERIOUS ISLAND(1961, U.S./Brit.), w
Daniel B. Ullman
RED DESERT(1949), w; RINGSIDE(1949), w; UNDER THE GUN(1951), w; AT GUNPOINT(1955), w; BOBBY WARE IS MISSING(1955), w; DIAL RED O(1955), d&w; SEVEN ANGRY MEN(1955), w; SUDDEN DANGER(1955), w; WARRIORS, THE(1955), w; CANYON RIVER(1956), w; FIRST TEXAN, THE(1956), w; BADLANDS OF MONTANA(1957), p,d&w; FLAME OF STAMBOUL(1957), w; LAST OF THE BADMEN(1957), w; MAN AFRAID(1957), w; OKLAHOMAN, THE(1957), w; CASE AGAINST BROOKLYN, THE(1958), w; CATTLE EMPIRE(1958), w; GOOD DAY FOR A HANGING(1959), w; FACE OF A FUGITIVE(1959), w; GUNFIGHT AT DODGE CITY, THE(1959), w
Ellwood Ullman
PUBLIC STENOGRAPHER(1935), w; MEN IN HER DIARY(1945), w; IDEA GIRL(1946), w; PRIVATE EYES(1953), w
Elwood Ullman
HONEYMOON AHEAD(1945), w; SUSIE STEPS OUT(1946), w; GOLD RAIDERS, THE(1952), w; HAREM GIRL(1952), w; LOST IN ALASKA(1952), w; STOOGE, THE(1952), w; CLIPPED WINGS(1953), w; HOT NEWS(1953), w; LOOSE IN LONDON(1953), w; BOWERY BOYS MEET THE MONSTERS, THE(1954), w; JUNGLE GENTS(1954), w; PARIS PLAYBOYS(1954), w; BOWERY TO BAGDAD(1955), w;

HIGH SOCIETY(1955), w; JAIL BUSTERS(1955), w; MA AND PA KETTLE AT WAIKIKI(1955), w; SUDDEN DANGER(1955), w; DIG THAT URANIUM(1956), w; HOT SHOTS(1956), w; CHAIN OF EVIDENCE(1957), w; FOOTSTEPS IN THE NIGHT(1957), w; LOOKING FOR DANGER(1957), w; SPOOK CHASERS(1957), w; UP IN SMOKE(1957), w; IN THE MONEY(1958), w; BATTLE CRY(1959), w; BLOODY BROOD, THE(1959, Can.), w; SNOW WHITE AND THE THREE STOOGES(1961), w; THREE STOOGES IN ORBIT, THE(1962), w; THREE STOOGES MEET HERCULES, THE(1962), w; THREE STOOGES GO AROUND THE WORLD IN A DAZE, THE(1963), w; DR. GOLDFOOT AND THE BIKINI MACHINE(1965), w; TICKLE ME(1965), w; GHOST IN THE INVISIBLE BIKINI(1966), w
Esther Ullman
SINAI COMMANDOS: THE STORY OF THE SIX DAY WAR(1968, Israel/Ger.)
William A. Ullman, Jr.
DOWN TO THE SEA(1936), w; BURIED ALIVE(1939), w; THOSE HIGH GREY WALLS(1939), w; I TAKE THIS OATH(1940), w
Ethel Ullman
Silents
CIVILIZATION(1916); DIVIDEND, THE(1916)
Frederic Ullman, Jr.
I'M STILL ALIVE(1940), p; WINDOW, THE(1949), p
James Ramsay Ullman
WHITE TOWER, THE(1950), w
James Ramsey Ullman
HIGH CONQUEST(1947), w; WINDOM'S WAY(1958, Brit.), w; THIRD MAN ON THE MOUNTAIN(1959), w
Jeffrey Ullman
MY DINNER WITH ANDRE(1981), cos
1984
HARD CHOICES(1984), cos
Karrie Ullman
1984
NADIA(1984, U.S./Yugo.)
Liv Ullman
ABDICATION, THE(1974, Brit.); COLD SWEAT(1974, Ital., Fr.)
Robert Ullman
LUMMOX(1930)
Sidney Ullman
LOST PATROL, THE,(1934), art d
Silents
BIG GAME(1921), art d; SCARLET LETTER, THE(1926), set d
Tracey Ullman
1984
GIVE MY REGARDS TO BROAD STREET(1984, Brit.)
William A. Ullman
SERGEANT MADDEN(1939), w
Greta Ullman
GOLDEN EARRINGS(1947)
James Ramsey Ullmann
THIRD MAN ON THE MOUNTAIN(1959)
Linn Ullmann
EMIGRANTS, THE(1972, Swed.); AUTUMN SONATA(1978, Swed.)
Liv Ullmann
PERSONA(1967, Swed.); HOUR OF THE WOLF, THE(1968, Swed.); SHAME(1968, Swed.); SHORT IS THE SUMMER(1968, Swed.); NIGHT VISITOR, THE(1970, Swed./U.S.); PASSION OF ANNA, THE(1970, Swed.); CRIES AND WHISPERS(1972, Swed.); EMIGRANTS, THE(1972, Swed.); POPE JOAN(1972, Brit.); FORTY CARATS(1973); LOST HORIZON(1973); NEW LAND, THE(1973, Swed.); SCENES FROM A MARRIAGE(1974, Swed.); ZANDY'S BRIDE(1974); FACE TO FACE(1976, Swed.); BRIDGE TOO FAR, A(1977, Brit.); LEONOR(1977, Fr./Span./Ital.); SERPENT'S EGG, THE(1977, Ger./U.S.); AUTUMN SONATA(1978, Swed.); RICHARD'S THINGS(1981, Brit.); LOVE(1982$c Can.), d, w; WILD DUCK, THE(1983, Aus.)
1984
BAY BOY(1984, Can.)
Alejandre Ulloa
OPERATION KID BROTHER(1967, Ital.), ph
Alejandro Ulloa
GOLIATH AGAINST THE GIANTS(1963, Ital./Span.), ph; SON OF CAPTAIN BLOOD, THE(1964, U.S./Ital./Span.), ph; DIABOLICAL DR. Z, THE(1966 Span./Fr.), ph; HATE FOR HATE(1967, Ital.), ph; SEVEN GUNS FOR THE MACGREGORS(1968, Ital./Span.), ph; MAGNIFICENT BANDITS, THE(1969, Ital./Span.), ph; COMPANEROS(1970 Ital./Span./Ger.), ph; KILL THEM ALL AND COME BACK ALONE(1970, Ital./Span.), ph; MERCENARY, THE(1970, Ital./Span.), ph; HORROR EXPRESS(1972, Span./Brit.), ph; EAGLE OVER LONDON(1973, Ital.), ph; BLOOD MONEY(1975, U.S./Hong Kong/Ital./Span.), ph; PANCHO VILLA(1975, Span.), ph
Alexander Ulloa [Alejandro Ulloa]
UP THE MACGREGORS(1967, Ital./Span.), ph; BAD MAN'S RIVER(1972, Span.), ph
Allejandro Ulloa
MR. SUPERINVISIBLE(1974, Ital./Span./Ger.), ph
Luise Ullrich
DAY AFTER THE DIVORCE, THE(1940, Ger.)
Edward Ulman
Silents
PENROD AND SAM(1923), ph; PROWLERS OF THE NIGHT(1926), ph
Elwood Ulman
FIGHTING TROUBLE(1956), w
Ernest Ulman
HOTEL RESERVE(1946, Brit.)
Ernst Ulman
WEDDING OF LILLI MARLENE, THE(1953, Brit.); INVASION QUARTET(1961, Brit.)
W.A. Ulman, Jr.
BEHIND PRISON WALLS(1943), w
E.G. Ulmer
GIRL FROM POLTAVA(1937), d; COSSACKS IN EXILE(1939, Ukrainian), d
Edgar Ulmer
CORREGIDOR(1943), w; STRANGE WOMAN, THE(1946), d; LOVES OF THREE QUEENS, THE(1954, Ital./Fr.), d
Silents
SUNRISE-A SONG OF TWO HUMANS(1927), art d

Edgar G. Ulmer
BLACK CAT, THE(1934), d, w; DAMAGED LIVES(1937), d, w; GREEN FIELDS(1937), d; SINGING BLACKSMITH(1938), d; PRISONER OF JAPAN(1942), w; TOMORROW WE LIVE(1942), d; DANGER! WOMEN AT WORK(1943), w; GIRLS IN CHAINS(1943), d, w; ISLE OF FORGOTTEN SINS(1943), d, w; MY SON, THE HERO(1943), d, w; BLUEBEARD(1944), d; JIVE JUNCTION(1944), d; MINSTREL MAN(1944), prod d; DETOUR(1945), d; STRANGE ILLUSION(1945), d; CLUB HAVANA(1946), d; HER SISTER'S SECRET(1946), d; WIFE OF MONTE CRISTO, THE(1946), d, w; CARNEGIE HALL(1947), d; RUTHLESS(1948), d; PIRATES OF CAPRI, THE(1949), d; MAN FROM PLANET X, THE(1951), d; ST. BENNY THE DIP(1951), d; BABES IN BAGDAD(1952), d; MURDER IS MY BEAT(1955), d; NAKED DAWN, THE(1955), d; DAUGHTER OF DR. JEKYLL(1957), d; AMAZING TRANSPARENT MAN, THE(1960), d; BEYOND THE TIME BARRIER(1960), d; HANNIBAL(1960, Ital.), d; CAVERN, THE(1965, Ital./Ger.), p&d; JOURNEY BENEATH THE DESERT(1967, Fr./Ital.), d, prod d
Misc. Talkies
AMERICAN MATCHMAKER(1940), d; DOBBIN, THE(1939), d; MOON OVER HARLEM(1939), d
Misc. Silents
PEOPLE ON SUNDAY(1929, Ger.), d

Jonathan Ulmer
STRANGE INVADERS(1983)

Terri Gay Ulmer
1984
FOOTLOOSE(1984)

Lenore Ulric
FROZEN JUSTICE(1929); SOUTH SEA ROSE(1929); CAMILLE(1937); TEMPTATION(1946); TWO SMART PEOPLE(1946); NORTHWEST OUTPOST(1947)
Misc. Silents
TIGER ROSE(1923)

Barbara Ulrich
CAT IN THE SACK, THE(1967, Can.); DUCHESS AND THE DIRTWATER FOX, THE(1976)

Florence Ulrich
Misc. Silents
FALSE FRIENDS(1926); MELODIES(1926)

Kurt Ulrich
ROSES FOR THE PROSECUTOR(1961, Ger.), p; THREE PENNY OPERA(1963, Fr./Ger.), p; JUDGE AND THE SINNER, THE(1964, Ger.), p; MAN WHO WALKED THROUGH THE WALL, THE(1964, Ger.), p

Lenore Ulrich
Misc. Silents
BETTER WOMAN, THE(1915); HEART OF PAULA, THE(1916); INTRIGUE(1916); ROAD TO LOVE, THE(1916); HER OWN PEOPLE(1917)

Leonore Ulrich
Silents
KILMENY(1915)

Luise Ulrich
SHADOWS GROW LONGER, THE(1962, Switz./Ger.)

Ronald Ulrich
MADELEINE IS(1971, Can.); CANNIBAL GIRLS(1973)

Trude Ulrich
MAD EXECUTIONERS, THE(1965, Ger.), cos; MONSTER OF LONDON CITY, THE(1967, Ger.), cos

Rebecca Ulrick
LAST PICTURE SHOW, THE(1971)

Ultra Violet
MIDNIGHT COWBOY(1969); BELIEVE IN ME(1971)

L. Ulyanenko
ITALIANO BRAVA GENTE(1965, Ital./USSR)

Ilya Nikolayevich Ulyanov
SONS AND MOTHERS(1967, USSR)

Mariya Aleksandrovna Ulyanova
SONS AND MOTHERS(1967, USSR)

Jamie Ulys
DINGAKA(1965, South Africa), p,d&w

Fred Ulysse
MOON IN THE GUTTER, THE(1983, Fr./Ital.)

Jean-Paul Ulysse
RELUCTANT DEBUTANTE, THE(1958), makeup; LOVE IS A BALL(1963), makeup

Resti Umali
HOT BOX, THE(1972, U.S./Phil.), m

Restie Umali
CRY FREEDOM(1961, Phil.), m; NO MAN IS AN ISLAND(1962), m

Mauritz Umansky
DAYS AND NIGHTS(1946, USSR), art d

Margaret Umbers
SMASH PALACE(1982, New Zealand)

Werner Umburg
MURDERS IN THE RUE MORGUE(1971)

Jolanta Umecka
KNIFE IN THE WATER(1963, Pol.)

Chiyoo Umeda
SCARLET CAMELLIA, THE(1965, Jap.), art d; FIGHT FOR THE GLORY(1970, Jap.), art d; HOTSPRINGS HOLIDAY(1970, Jap.), art d; SONG FROM MY HEART, THE(1970, Jap.), art d

Tomoko Umeda
WAR OF THE MONSTERS(1972, Jap.)

Miyoshi Umeki
SAYONARA(1957); CRY FOR HAPPY(1961); FLOWER DRUM SONG(1961); GIRL NAMED TAMIRO, A(1962); HORIZONTAL LIEUTENANT, THE(1962)

Tatsuo Umemiya
FINAL WAR, THE(1960, Jap.); SPOILS OF THE NIGHT(1969, Jap.)

Yoko Umemura
Misc. Silents
PAPER DOLL'S WHISPER OF SPRING, A(1926, Jap.); WOMAN WHO TOUCHED THE LEGS, THE(1926, Jap.)

Meijiro Umezu
HARBOR LIGHT YOKOHAMA(1970, Jap.), d

Sakae Umezu
LAKE, THE(1970, Jap.)

Fritz Umgelter
PLAYGIRLS AND THE BELLBOY, THE(1962,Ger.), d

Piero Umiliani
FIASCO IN MILAN(1963, Fr./Ital.), m; OF WAYWARD LOVE(1964, Ital./Ger.), m; RED LIPS(1964, Fr./Ital.), m; 00-2 MOST SECRET AGENTS(1965, Ital.), m; BEAUTIFUL SWINDLERS, THE(1967, Fr./Ital./Jap./Neth.), m; WAR ITALIAN STYLE(1967, Ital.), m; LOVE FACTORY(1969, Ital.), m; I HATE BLONDES(1981, Ital.), m

Klaus Umjo
IT HAPPENED HERE(1966, Brit.)

Ellen Umlaud
MARK OF THE DEVIL II(1975, Ger./Brit.)

Ellen Umlauf
DIE FLEDERMAUS(1964, Aust.); FOUNTAIN OF LOVE, THE(1968, Aust.); SERPENT'S EGG, THE(1977, Ger./U.S.)
1984
FLIGHT TO BERLIN(1984, Ger./Brit.)

Piero Umliani
WHITE, RED, YELLOW, PINK(1966, Ital.), m

Leo Umyssa
HIPPODROME(1961, Aust./Ger.), makeup; DIE FLEDERMAUS(1964, Aust.), makeup

Sieg un Jager
DAVID(1979, Ger.), ed

Hiroshi Unayama
HIGH AND LOW(1963, Jap.)

Uncle Dave Macon and Dorris
GRAND OLE OPRY(1940)

Emilia Unda
MAEDCHEN IN UNIFORM(1932, Ger.); BARCAROLE(1935, Ger.)

The Undeads
PHANTOM OF THE PARADISE(1974)

Stephanie Underdorn
PARIS OOH-LA-LA!(1963, U.S./Fr.)

Edward Underdown
GIRLS PLEASE!(1934, Brit.); WARREN CASE, THE(1934, Brit.); ANNIE, LEAVE THE ROOM(1935, Brit.); INSPECTOR HORNLEIGH(1939, Brit.); MAIL TRAIN(1941, Brit.); OCTOBER MAN, THE(1948, Brit.); MAN ON THE RUN(1949, Brit.); WOMAN IN THE HALL, THE(1949, Brit.); DARK MAN, THE(1951, Brit.); HER PANELLED DOOR(1951, Brit.); LUCKY MASCOT, THE(1951, Brit.); THEY WERE NOT DIVIDED(1951, Brit.); BEAT THE DEVIL(1953); MURDER WILL OUT(1953, Brit.); RECOIL(1953); SHADOW MAN(1953, Brit.); RAINBOW JACKET, THE(1954, Brit.); WOMAN'S ANGLE, THE(1954, Brit.); CAMP ON BLOOD ISLAND, THE(1958, Brit.); TWO-HEADED SPY, THE(1959, Brit.); DAY THE EARTH CAUGHT FIRE, THE(1961, Brit.); THIRD ALIBI, THE(1961, Brit.); INFORMATION RECEIVED(1962, Brit.); LOCKER 69(1962, Brit.); BAY OF SAINT MICHEL, THE(1963, Brit.); DR. CRIPPEN(1963, Brit.); MAN IN THE MIDDLE(1964, U.S./Brit.); WOMAN OF STRAW(1964, Brit.); DR. TERROR'S HOUSE OF HORRORS(1965, Brit.); THUNDERBALL(1965, Brit.); KHARTOUM(1966, Brit.); TRAITOR'S GATE(1966, Brit./Ger.); GREAT PONY RAID, THE(1968, Brit.); HAND OF NIGHT, THE(1968, Brit.); MAGIC CHRISTIAN, THE(1970, Brit.); LAST VALLEY, THE(1971, Brit.); RUNNING SCARED(1972, Brit.); ABDICATION, THE(1974, Brit.); DIGBY, THE BIGGEST DOG IN THE WORLD(1974, Brit.)

Teddy Underdown
WINGS OF THE MORNING(1937, Brit.)

John Underhill
Silents
JOYOUS TROUBLEMAKERS, THE(1920)

Betty Underwood
DANGEROUS PROFESSION, A(1949); GIRL FROM JONES BEACH, THE(1949); STORM OVER WYOMING(1950)

David Underwood
1984
ANGEL(1984)

Doug Underwood
NATCHEZ TRACE(1960)

Edward Underwood
NO DRUMS, NO BUGLES(1971)

Evelyn Underwood
KNOCK ON ANY DOOR(1949); WOMAN'S SECRET, A(1949); IN A LONELY PLACE(1950)

Franklin Underwood
Silents
NEWS PARADE, THE(1928)

Lawrence Underwood
Silents
PASSIONATE YOUTH(1925)
Misc. Silents
THAT SOMETHING(1921), d

Loyal Underwood
PALEFACE, THE(1948); MY FAVORITE SPY(1951)
Silents
MY AMERICAN WIFE(1923); PILGRIM, THE(1923); SHOOTIN' IRONS(1927)

Monica Underwood
SECRET LIFE OF WALTER MITTY, THE(1947), ed

Ray Underwood
JENNIFER(1978)

Robert Underwood
SMALL CIRCLE OF FRIENDS, A(1980)

Roy Underwood
MASSACRE AT CENTRAL HIGH(1976)

Ruth Underwood
TWO HUNDRED MOTELS(1971, Brit.)

Sam H. Underwood
LADY IN A JAM(1942)

Sophie Kerr Underwood
FATHER IS A PRINCE(1940), w
Susan Underwood
FIRST NUDIE MUSICAL, THE(1976)
Tod Underwood
Silents
OLD AGE HANDICAP(1928), w
Richard Unekis
DIRTY MARY, CRAZY LARRY(1974), w
Lawrence Ung
THUNDER BIRDS(1942); THIS EARTH IS MINE(1959)
Richard Ung
SPAWN OF THE NORTH(1938); GAY PURR-EE(1962), prod d; MR. MAGOO'S
HOLIDAY FESTIVAL(1970), prod d
Tom Ung
GENERAL DIED AT DAWN, THE(1936); FORLORN RIVER(1937)
Enzo Ungari
DESIRE, THE INTERIOR LIFE(1980, Ital./Ger.), w
Nestore Ungaro
TENTACLES(1977, Ital.), ph
Anthony Unger
UNSEEN, THE(1981), p
Anthony B. Unger
PROMISE, THE(1969, Brit.), p; FORCE 10 FROM NAVARONE(1978, Brit.), p; SI-
LENT RAGE(1982), p
Becky Gardiner Unger
COMING OUT PARTY(1934), w
Bertel Unger
DOLL SQUAD, THE(1973)
Bertil Unger
LOVE IS BETTER THAN EVER(1952); NICKELODEON(1976); TABLE FOR FI-
VE(1983)
David Andre Unger
SILENT RAGE(1982)
Freddy Unger
SECRET AGENT FIREBALL(1965, Fr./Ital.); WILD, WILD PLANET, THE(1967, Ital.);
VENGEANCE(1968, Ital./Ger.); CANNIBALS IN THE STREETS(1982, Ital./Span.),
stunts; TREASURE OF THE FOUR CROWNS(1983, Span./U.S.), spec eff
Fredy Unger
COMIN' AT YA!(1981), spec eff
Gladys Unger
MARIANNE(1929), w; DYNAMITE(1930), John Howard Lawson; MADAME SA-
TAN(1930), w; WAYWARD(1932), w; CHEATING CHEATERS(1934), w; COMING
OUT PARTY(1934), w; EMBARRASSING MOMENTS(1934), w; GLAMOUR(1934), w;
GREAT EXPECTATIONS(1934), w; ROMANCE IN THE RAIN(1934), w; ALIAS
MARY DOW(1935), w; MUSIC IS MAGIC(1935), w; MYSTERY OF EDWIN DROOD,
THE(1935), w; PRIVATE WORLDS(1935), w; RENDEZVOUS AT MIDNIGHT(1935),
w; STRANGE WIVES(1935), w; SYLVIA SCARLETT(1936), w; DAUGHTER OF
SHANGHAI(1937), w; NIGHT OF MYSTERY(1937), w
Silents
LONDON PRIDE(1920, Brit.), w; GOLDFISH, THE(1924), w; DIVINE WOMAN,
THE(1928), w
Goffredo Unger
HERCULES AGAINST THE MOON MEN(1965, Fr./Ital.)
Guspave Unger
DOLL SQUAD, THE(1973)
Gustaf Unger
WORLD'S GREATEST LOVER, THE(1977); TABLE FOR FIVE(1983)
Gustar Unger
NICKELODEON(1976)
Jerry Unger
HERCULES(1983), spec eff
Joe Unger
GO TELL THE SPARTANS(1978)
1984
JOY OF SEX(1984); NIGHTMARE ON ELM STREET, A(1984)
Kurt Unger
JUDITH(1965), p; BEST HOUSE IN LONDON, THE(1969, Brit.), p; PUPPET ON A
CHAIN(1971, Brit.), p; POPE JOAN(1972, Brit.), p
Leanne Unger
TIMES SQUARE(1980), w
Oliver Unger
FACE OF FU MANCHU, THE(1965, Brit.), p; SANDY THE SEAL(1969, Brit.), p
Oliver A. Unger
COAST OF SKELETONS(1965, Brit.), p; TEN LITTLE INDIANS(1965, Brit.), p;
BRIDES OF FU MANCHU, THE(1966, Brit.), p; FORCE 10 FROM NAVARONE(1978,
Brit.), p
Patti Unger
"EQUUS"(1977), cos
1984
HIGHPOINT(1984, Can.), cos
Patty Unger
WEDDING IN WHITE(1972, Can.), cos
1984
MRS. SOFFEL(1984), cos
Paul Unger
RIDING HIGH(1943)
Sherry Unger
WHEN YOU COMIN' BACK, RED RYDER?(1979)
1984
JOY OF SEX(1984)
Lilith Ungerer
WHY DOES HERR R. RUN AMOK?(1977, Ger.)
R. Ungern
Misc. Silents
COWARD, THE(1914, USSR), d
I. Unguryanu
SANDU FOLLOWS THE SUN(1965, USSR)

George Unholz
HYPNOTIZED(1933), ph
John Unicombe
RUGGED O'RIORDANS, THE(1949, Aus.)
Morris Unicombe
BUSH CHRISTMAS(1947, Brit.)
Little Unicorn
RETURN OF THE DRAGON(1974, Chin.)
Germaine Unikovsky
NOT MINE TO LOVE(1969, Israel); FLYING MATCHMAKER, THE(1970, Israel)
Jermain Unikovsky
TWO KOUNEY LEMELS(1966, Israel)
Johnny Unitas
GUS(1976)
The United States Air Force
OPERATION HAYLIFT(1950)
United States Army
JOURNEY TOGETHER(1946, Brit.)
Universal Ranch Riders
Silents
CLEARING THE TRAIL(1928)
University of Arizona Glee Club
TUMBLEDOWN RANCH IN ARIZONA(1941)
Students of University of Djakarta
SKULLDUGGERY(1970)
University of Southern California Baseball Team
Silents
COLLEGE(1927)
University of Southern California Polo Team
FLIRTATION WALK(1934)
Petr Unkel
GREH(1962, Ger./Yugo.)
Rolf Unkel
HAMLET(1962, Ger.), m
Earl Unkraut
BOOTS MALONE(1952)
EFX Unlimited
WHY RUSSIANS ARE REVOLTING(1970), spec eff
Uno
TEN GENTLEMEN FROM WEST POINT(1942)
Akira Uno
METAMORPHOSES(1978), prod d
Jinkichi Uno
AFFAIR AT AKITSU(1980, Jap.)
Joji Uno
GODZILLA VS. THE THING(1964, Jap.)
Jukichi Uno
LIFE OF OHARU(1964, Jap.); ONIBABA(1965, Jap.); TUNNEL TO THE SUN(1968,
Jap.); NO GREATER LOVE THAN THIS(1969, Jap.)
Koji Uno
NAKED YOUTH(1961, Jap.), art d
Seiichiro Uno
WORLD OF HANS CHRISTIAN ANDERSEN, THE(1971, Jap.), m
Shinsaku Uno
WHITE ROSE OF HONG KONG(1965, Jap.), ph; YOUNG GUY ON MT. COOK(1969,
Jap.), ph
Erika Unruh
Misc. Silents
MASTER OF LOVE, THE(1919, Ger.)
Jesse M. Unruh
CANDIDATE, THE(1972)
Joyce Unruh
KENTUCKY FRIED MOVIE, THE(1977), cos
Jose Maria Fernandez Unsain
LA NAVE DE LOS MONSTRUOS(1959, Mex.), w; CREATURE OF THE WALKING
DEAD(1960, Mex.), w
Eve Unsel
Silents
PRODIGAL WIFE, THE(1918), w; YANKEE SENOR, THE(1926), w
Eva Unsell
MEDICINE MAN, THE(1930), w
Eve Unsell
CONQUEST(1929), w; SECRET CALL, THE(1931), w; UNFAITHFUL(1931), w; UP
POPS THE DEVIL(1931), w
Silents
ONE OF OUR GIRLS(1914), w; RANSOM, THE(1916), w; ETERNAL TEMPTRESS,
THE(1917), w; MARRIAGE PRICE(1919), w; OUT OF THE SHADOW(1919), w; CALL
OF YOUTH, THE(1920, Brit.), w; PRIVATE SCANDAL, A(1921), w; SHADOWS(1922),
w; THORNS AND ORANGE BLOSSOMS(1922), ed; ARE YOU A FAILURE?(1923), w;
CIRCUS DAYS(1923), t; HERO, THE(1923), w; LONELY ROAD, THE(1923), ed; LONG
LIVE THE KING(1923), w; POOR MEN'S WIVES(1923), t; SCARLET LILY,
THE(1923), ed; CAPTAIN JANUARY(1924), w; LOVE'S WILDERNESS(1924), w; AN-
CIENT HIGHWAY, THE(1925), w; ANCIENT MARINER, THE(1925), w; NECES-
SARY EVIL, THE(1925), w; PLASTIC AGE, THE(1925), w; WHAT FOOLS
MEN(1925), w; SANDY(1926), w; SIBERIA(1926), w; YELLOW FINGERS(1926), w
Bobby Unser
WINNING(1969)
Joe Unsinn
1984
CITY HEAT(1984), spec eff; REVENGE OF THE NERDS(1984), spec eff
Vic Unson
TWILIGHT PEOPLE(1972, Phil.)
Geoffrey Unsworth
ZARDOZ(, ph; GENGHIS KHAN(U.S./Brit./Ger./Yugo), ph; DRUMS(1938, Brit.),
ph; BLANCHE FURY(1948, Brit.), ph; JASSY(1948, Brit.), ph; SMUGGLERS,
THE(1948, Brit.), ph; BLUE LAGOON, THE(1949, Brit.), ph; FOOLS RUSH IN(1949,
Brit.), ph; SCOTT OF THE ANTARCTIC(1949, Brit.), ph; CLOUDED YELLOW,
THE(1950, Brit.), ph; LAUGHING LADY, THE(1950, Brit.), ph; TRIO(1950, Brit.), ph;
IVORY HUNTER(1952, Brit.), ph; MADE IN HEAVEN(1952, Brit.), ph; OUTPOST IN
MALAYA(1952, Brit.), ph; SPIDER AND THE FLY, THE(1952, Brit.), ph; DOUBLE

CONFESSION(1953, Brit.), ph; PENNY PRINCESS(1953, Brit.), ph; SWORD AND THE ROSE, THE(1953), ph; MAN WITH A MILLION(1954, Brit.), ph; PURPLE PLAIN, THE(1954, Brit.), ph; TURN THE KEY SOFTLY(1954, Brit.), ph; LAND OF FURY(1955 Brit.), ph; PASSAGE HOME(1955, Brit.), ph; SIMBA(1955, Brit.), ph; JACQUELINE(1956, Brit.), ph; TIGER IN THE SMOKE(1956, Brit.), ph; VALUE FOR MONEY(1957, Brit.), ph; BACHELOR OF HEARTS(1958, Brit.), ph; DANGEROUS EXILE(1958, Brit.), ph; HELL DRIVERS(1958, Brit.), ph; NIGHT TO REMEMBER, A(1958, Brit.), ph; TOWN LIKE ALICE, A(1958, Brit.), ph; WHIRLPOOL(1959, Brit.), ph; FLAME OVER INDIA(1960, Brit.), ph; WORLD OF SUZIE WONG, THE(1960), ph; ON THE DOUBLE(1961), ph; MAIN ATTRACTION, THE(1962, Brit.), ph; 300 SPARTANS, THE(1962), ph; PLAYBOY OF THE WESTERN WORLD, THE(1963, Ireland), ph; BECKET(1964, Brit.), ph; TAMAHINE(1964, Brit.), ph; WHY BOTHER TO KNOCK(1964, Brit.), ph; OTHELLO(1965, Brit.), ph; YOU MUST BE JOKING!(1965, Brit.), ph; HALF A SIXPENCE(1967, Brit.), ph; OH DAD, POOR DAD, MAMA'S HUNG YOU IN THE CLOSET AND I'M FEELIN' SO SAD(1967), ph; BLISS OF MRS. BLOSSOM, THE(1968, Brit.), ph; 2001: A SPACE ODYSSEY(1968, U.S./Brit.), ph; ASSASSINATION BUREAU, THE(1969, Brit.), ph; CROMWELL(1970, Brit.), ph; GOODBYE GEMINI(1970, Brit.), ph; MAGIC CHRISTIAN, THE(1970, Brit.), ph; DANCE OF DEATH, THE(1971, Brit.), ph; RECKONING, THE(1971, Brit.), ph; SAY HELLO TO YESTERDAY(1971, Brit.), ph; UNMAN, WITTERING AND ZIGO(1971, Brit.), ph; ALICE'S ADVENTURES IN WONDERLAND(1972, Brit.), ph; CABARET(1972), ph; BAXTER(1973, Brit.), ph; DON QUIXOTE(1973, Aus.), ph; LOVE AND PAIN AND THE WHOLE DAMN THING(1973), ph; VOICES(1973, Brit.), ph; ABDICATION, THE(1974, Brit.), ph; INTERNECINE PROJECT, THE(1974, Brit.), ph; MURDER ON THE ORIENT EXPRESS(1974, Brit.), ph; THREE SISTERS(1974, Brit.), ph; LUCKY LADY(1975), ph; RETURN OF THE PINK PANTHER, THE(1975, Brit.), ph; ROYAL FLASH(1975, Brit.), ph; MATTER OF TIME, A(1976, Ital./U.S.), ph; BRIDGE TOO FAR, A(1977, Brit.), ph; SUPERMAN(1978), ph; GREAT TRAIN ROBBERY, THE(1979, Brit.), ph; SUPERMAN II(1980), ph; TESS(1980, Fr./Brit.), ph

Margaret Unsworth
OTHELLO(1965, Brit.), w

Hans Unterkirchen
Silents
LAST LAUGH, THE(1924, Ger.)

Hans Unterkirchner
SONG WITHOUT END(1960)

J. Untershalk
Misc. Silents
SEEDS OF FREEDOM(1929, USSR)

The Untouchables
1984
REPO MAN(1984)

Stanley Unwin
FUN AT ST. FANNY'S(1956, Brit.); INN FOR TROUBLE(1960, Brit.); CARRY ON REGARDLESS(1961, Brit.); HAIR OF THE DOG(1962, Brit.); PRESS FOR TIME(1966, Brit.); CHITTY CHITTY BANG BANG(1968, Brit.)

Paul Uny
GOODBYE AGAIN(1961)

Paul C. Uogel
HAPPY YEARS, THE(1950), ph

Remegio Uoung
WARKILL(1968, U.S./Phil.), ph

Peter Upcher
Silents
PRODIGAL SON, THE(1923, Brit.)
Misc. Silents
DEFINITE OBJECT, THE(1920, Brit.); MR. GILFIL'S LOVE STORY(1920, Brit.); RIGHT TO LIVE, THE(1921, Brit.)

Allan Eugene Updegraff
Silents
SECOND YOUTH(1924), w

John Updike
RABBIT, RUN(1970), w

Randall Updyke III
MEN, THE(1950)

S. Lee Upgostin
GOLDEN NEEDLES(1974), w

Mike Upmalis
RECOMMENDATION FOR MERCY(1975, Can.)

John Uppman
TEN NIGHTS IN A BARROOM(1931)

Ake Uppstrom
WALPURGIS NIGHT(1941, Swed.)

Blance Upright
Silents
YOUR WIFE AND MINE(1927)

Blanche Upright
Silents
PLEASURE MAD(1923), w

Kim Upshur
1984
PURPLE RAIN(1984)

Denise Upson
Misc. Talkies
CHEERLEADERS BEACH PARTY(1978)

William Hazlett Upson
EARTHWORM TRACTORS(1936), w

Adrienne Upton
NEW YEAR'S EVIL(1980)

Bill Upton
SUDDEN IMPACT(1983)

Elizabeth Upton
Misc. Talkies
BRASS RING, THE(1975); MANHUNTER(1983)

Frances Upton
NIGHT WORK(1930)

Gabrielle Upton
GIDGET(1959), w; ESCAPE FROM EAST BERLIN(1962), w

Julian Upton
MARSHAL'S DAUGHTER, THE(1953); TO HELL AND BACK(1955); SHADOW ON THE WINDOW, THE(1957); QUICK, LET'S GET MARRIED(1965)

Morgan Upton
TROIKA(1969); CANDIDATE, THE(1972); ONE IS A LONELY NUMBER(1972); STEELYARD BLUES(1973); KLANSMAN, THE(1974); BUCKTOWN(1975); NIGHTMARE IN BLOOD(1978); MORE AMERICAN GRAFFITI(1979); DIE LAUGHING(1980); CHU CHU AND THE PHILLY FLASH(1981); SHOOT THE MOON(1982); SUDDEN IMPACT(1983); SURVIVORS, THE(1983)
1984
NO SMALL AFFAIR(1984)

Kumeko Urabe
GOLDEN DEMON(1956, Jap.); IKIRU(1960, Jap.); YEARNING(1964, Jap.); EYES, THE SEA AND A BALL(1968 Jap.)

Yoko Uraji
ENJO(1959, Jap.)

I. Uralov
Misc. Silents
COWARD, THE(1914, USSR)

S. Uralov
LAD FROM OUR TOWN(1941, USSR), ph

V. Uralski
MEN OF THE SEA(1938, USSR)

V. Uralskiy
DAY THE EARTH FROZE, THE(1959, Fin./USSR); WELCOME KOSTYA!(1965, USSR); FATHER OF A SOLDIER(1966, USSR)

A. Uralsky
Misc. Silents
1812(1912, USSR), d; TERCENTENARY OF THE ROMANOV DYNASTY'S ACCESSION TO THE THRONE(1913, USSR), d; YEKATERINA IVANOVNA(1915, USSR), d

Viktor Uralsky
MOSCOW DOES NOT BELIEVE IN TEARS(1980, USSR)

Vadim Uraneff
MEDICINE MAN, THE(1930)
Silents
SEA BEAST, THE(1926); SIBERIA(1926); SILENT POWER, THE(1926); MIDNIGHT MADNESS(1928)

Vadim Uraneffy
Misc. Silents
FAZIL(1928)

Martha Jane Urann
D.C. CAB(1983)

Keichi Uraoka
NAKED YOUTH(1961, Jap.), ed

Keiichi Uraoka
HUMAN CONDITION, THE(1959, Jap.), ed; YOUTH IN FURY(1961, Jap.), ed; ROAD TO ETERNITY(1962, Jap.), ed; SOLDIER'S PRAYER, A(1970, Jap.), ed; VENGEANCE IS MINE(1980, Jap.), ed; GLOWING AUTUMN(1981, Jap.), ed

Kirio Urayama
GIRL I ABANDONED, THE(1970, Jap.), d

Ulvi Uraz
L'IMMORTELLE(1969, Fr./Ital./Turkey)

James Urbain
MAYERLING(1968, Brit./Fr.)

Gretl Urban
Silents
UNDER THE RED ROBE(1923), cos; ZANDER THE GREAT(1925), set d

Jane Urban
Silents
LAST EGYPTIAN, THE(1914)

Joseph Urban
EAST LYNNE(1931), set d; MAN WHO CAME BACK, THE(1931), set d
Silents
BURIED TREASURE(1921), set d; JUST AROUND THE CORNER(1921), set d; WOMAN GOD CHANGED, THE(1921), set d; SISTERS(1922), set d; WHEN KNIGHTHOOD WAS IN FLOWER(1922), set d; ADAM AND EVA(1923), set d; ENEMIES OF WOMEN, THE(1923), set d; UNDER THE RED ROBE(1923), set d; JANICE MEREDITH(1924), set d; NEVER THE TWAIN SHALL MEET(1925), set d; ZANDER THE GREAT(1925), set d

Klaus Urban
NAKED AMONG THE WOLVES(1967, Ger.)

Maria Urban
JOURNEY, THE(1959, U.S./Aust.)

Marisa Urban
WILD PACK, THE(1972)

Maurice Urban
MAN WITH THE TRANSPLANTED BRAIN, THE(1972, Fr./Ital./Ger.), p

Sheila Urban
CURFEW BREAKERS(1957)

Luigi Urbani
BLACK BELLY OF THE TARANTULA, THE(1972, Ital.), set d; STREET PEOPLE(1976, U.S./Ital.), set d

Elisabeth Urbanic
SPESSART INN, THE(1961, Ger.), cos

Ernest Urbank
SCHOOL FOR SECRETS(1946, Brit.)

Carl Urbano
PROJECT X(1968), prod d

Evgeni Urbanski
BALLAD OF A SOLDIER(1960, USSR)

Yevgeniy Urbanskiy
LETTER THAT WAS NEVER SENT, THE(1962, USSR); CLEAR SKIES(1963, USSR)

Phillip A. Urbansky
STRIPES(1981)

Jacques Urbant
TOYS ARE NOT FOR CHILDREN(1972), md

Peter Urbe
IT HAPPENED HERE(1966, Brit.)

Luis Urbina
LAST TIME I SAW PARIS, THE(1954)
Luigi Urbini
MEDEA(1971, Ital./Fr./Ger.)
Pierluigi Urbini
WHITE WARRIOR, THE(1961, Ital./Yugo.), md; TARTARS, THE(1962, Ital./Yugo.), md; SLAVE, THE(1963, Ital.), md; ORGANIZER, THE(1964, Fr./Ital./Yugo.), md; PLAYGIRLS AND THE VAMPIRE(1964, Ital.), md; SEDUCED AND ABAN-DONED(1964, Fr./Ital.), md; PONTIUS PILATE(1967, Fr./Ital.), md
Vanna Urbino
JULES AND JIM(1962, Fr.)
Serse Urbisaglia
SODOM AND GOMORRAH(1962, U.S./Fr./Ital.), spec eff; FOUR DAYS OF NAPLES, THE(1963, US/Ital.), spec eff; WITCH'S CURSE, THE(1963, Ital.), spec eff
Peter Martin Urcel
TO COMMIT A MURDER(1970, Fr./Ital./Ger.)
Tony Urchal
SUEZ(1938)
George Urchel
NORTHERN PURSUIT(1943)
Tony Urchel
UNION PACIFIC(1939)
George Urchell
RAINBOW ISLAND(1944)
Tony Urchell
HER JUNGLE LOVE(1938)
Margaret Ure
STONE(1974, Aus.)
Mary Ure
STORM OVER THE NILE(1955, Brit.); WINDOM'S WAY(1958, Brit.); LOOK BACK IN ANGER(1959); SONS AND LOVERS(1960, Brit.); MIND BENDERS, THE(1963, Brit.); LUCK OF GINGER COFFEY, THE(1964, U.S./Can.); CUSTER OF THE WEST(1968, U.S., Span.); WHERE EAGLES DARE(1968, Brit.); REFLECTION OF FEAR, A(1973)
Minerva Urecal
WITHOUT RESERVATIONS(1946); SADIE MCKEE(1934); STUDENT TOUR(1934); BONNIE SCOTLAND(1935); MAN ON THE FLYING TRAPEZE, THE(1935); FU-RY(1936); LOVE ON A BET(1936); EVER SINCE EVE(1937); EXILED TO SHANG-HAI(1937); GO-GETTER, THE(1937); GOD'S COUNTRY AND THE WOMAN(1937); HER HUSBAND'S SECRETARY(1937); LIFE BEGINS WITH LOVE(1937); LIVE, LOVE AND LEARN(1937); LOVE IN A BUNGALOW(1937); MOUNTAIN JUS-TICE(1937); OH DOCTOR(1937); SHE LOVED A FIREMAN(1937); AIR DEVILS(1938); DRAMATIC SCHOOL(1938); IN OLD CHICAGO(1938); PRISON NURSE(1938); START CHEERING(1938); WIVES UNDER SUSPICION(1938); DANCING CO-ED(1939); DES-TRY RIDES AGAIN(1939); FRONTIER SCOUT(1939); GOLDEN BOY(1939); LITTLE ACCIDENT(1939); SECOND FIDDLE(1939); YOU CAN'T CHEAT AN HONEST MAN(1939); BOYS OF THE CITY(1940); NO, NO NANETTE(1940); SAGEBRUSH FAMILY TRAILS WEST, THE(1940); YOU CAN'T FOOL YOUR WIFE(1940); ACCENT ON LOVE(1941); ARKANSAS JUDGE(1941); COWBOY AND THE BLONDE, THE(1941); LADY FOR A NIGHT(1941); MAN AT LARGE(1941); MURDER BY INVITATION(1941); NEVER GIVE A SUCKER AN EVEN BREAK(1941); SAN FRAN-CISCO DOCKS(1941); SIX LESSONS FROM MADAME LA ZONGA(1941); SKY-LARK(1941); TRIAL OF MARY DUGAN, THE(1941); CORPSE VANISHES, THE(1942); DARING YOUNG MAN, THE(1942); HENRY AND DIZZY(1942); IN OLD CALI-FORNIA(1942); LIVING GHOST, THE(1942); MY FAVORITE BLONDE(1942); POW-ERS GIRL, THE(1942); QUIET PLEASE, MURDER(1942); SONS OF THE PIONEERS(1942); SWEATER GIRL(1942); THAT OTHER WOMAN(1942); THEY DIED WITH THEIR BOOTS ON(1942); APE MAN, THE(1943); GHOSTS ON THE LOO-SE(1943); HIT THE ICE(1943); KEEP 'EM SLUGGING(1943); KID DYNAMITE(1943); SHADOW OF A DOUBT(1943); SO THIS IS WASHINGTON(1943); SONG OF BER-NADETTE, THE(1943); WAGON TRACKS WEST(1943); WHITE SAVAGE(1943); BLOCK BUSTERS(1944); BRIDGE OF SAN LUIS REY, THE(1944); CRAZY KNIGHTS(1944); DOUGHGIRLS, THE(1944); IRISH EYES ARE SMILING(1944); KISMET(1944); LOUISIANA HAYRIDE(1944); MAN FROM FRISCO(1944); MOON-LIGHT AND CACTUS(1944); MUSIC IN MANHATTAN(1944); WHEN STRANGERS MARRY(1944); BELLS OF ST. MARY'S, THE(1945); COLONEL EFFINGHAM'S RAID(1945); GEORGE WHITE'S SCANDALS(1945); KID SISTER, THE(1945); MEDAL FOR BENNY, A(1945); MEN IN HER DIARY(1945); MR. MUGGS RIDES AGAIN(1945); SENSATION HUNTERS(1945); STATE FAIR(1945); WANDERER OF THE WASTE-LAND(1945); BRIDE WORE BOOTS, THE(1946); CALIFORNIA(1946); DARK COR-NER, THE(1946); LITTLE MISS BIG(1946); RAINBOW OVER TEXAS(1946); SIOUX CITY SUE(1946); WAKE UP AND DREAM(1946); WELL-GROOMED BRIDE, THE(1946); APACHE ROSE(1947); BOWERY BUCKAROOS(1947); HIGH CON-QUEST(1947); LOST MOMENT, THE(1947); SADDLE PALS(1947); SECRET LIFE OF WALTER MITTY, THE(1947); TRAP, THE(1947); FAMILY HONEYMOON(1948); FURY AT FURNACE CREEK(1948); GOOD SAM(1948); JOAN OF ARC(1948); MAR-SHAL OF AMARILLO(1948); NIGHT HAS A THOUSAND EYES(1948); NOOSE HANGS HIGH, THE(1948); SECRET SERVICE INVESTIGATOR(1948); SITTING PRETTY(1948); SNAKE PIT, THE(1948); SUNDOWN IN SANTA FE(1948); HOLIDAY IN HAVANA(1949); LOVABLE CHEAT, THE(1949); MASTER MINDS(1949); OUT-CASTS OF THE TRAIL(1949); SCENE OF THE CRIME(1949); TAKE ONE FALSE STEP(1949); ARIZONA COWBOY, THE(1950); HARVEY(1950); JACKPOT, THE(1950); MILKMAN, THE(1950); MISTER 880(1950); MY BLUE HEAVEN(1950); QUICK-SAND(1950); SIDE STREET(1950); TRAVELING SALESWOMAN(1950); MASK OF THE AVENGER(1951); STOP THAT CAB(1951); TEXANS NEVER CRY(1951); AARON SLICK FROM PUNKIN CRICK(1952); GOBS AND GALS(1952); HAREM GIRL(1952); LOST IN ALASKA(1952); OKLAHOMA ANNIE(1952); NIAGARA(1953); SHE'S BACK ON BROADWAY(1953); WOMAN THEY ALMOST LYNCHED, THE(1953); MAN ALONE, A(1955); SUDDEN DANGER(1955); CRASHING LAS VEGAS(1956); MIRA-CLE IN THE RAIN(1956); MR. HOBBS TAKES A VACATION(1962); SEVEN FACES OF DR. LAO(1964); THAT FUNNY FEELING(1965)
Minerval Urecal
CHARLIE CHAN AT THE OLYMPICS(1937); MAN BETRAYED, A(1941); MR. SKEFFINGTON(1944)
Alice Uretta
HOUSE OF EVIL(1968, U.S./Mex.), m; SNAKE PEOPLE, THE(1968, Mex./U.S.), m; INCREDIBLE INVASION, THE(1971, Mex./U.S.), m
Lisa Urette
REAL LIFE(1979)

N. Urgant
TIGER GIRL(1955, USSR); OVERCOAT, THE(1965, USSR)
Freddy Urger
WAR BETWEEN THE PLANETS(1971, Ital.)
Adriano Uriani
HOUSE OF INTRIGUE, THE(1959, Ital.)
Alfredo Uriba
VAMPIRES, THE(1969, Mex.), ph
Alfredo Uribe
BLUE DEMON VERSUS THE INFERNAL BRAINS(1967, Mex.), ph
Ernesto Uribe
PROUD AND THE DAMNED, THE(1972)
Imanol Uribe
1984
ESCAPE FROM SEGOVIA(1984, Span.), d, w
Justa Uribe
Silents
ARAB, THE(1924)
Robert Urich
MAGNUM FORCE(1973); ENDANGERED SPECIES(1982)
1984
ICE PIRATES, THE(1984)
Robert Uricola
WHO'S THAT KNOCKING AT MY DOOR?(1968)
J.I. Urinov
DIARY OF A REVOLUTIONIST(1932, USSR), d, w
Frank Urioste
WHAT EVER HAPPENED TO AUNT ALICE?(1969), ed; GET TO KNOW YOUR RABBIT(1972), ed; HOAX, THE(1972), ed; LOVING COUPLES(1980), ed
Frank J. Urioste
SPIKES GANG, THE(1974), ed; MIDWAY(1976), ed; DAMNATION ALLEY(1977), ed; BOYS IN COMPANY C, THE(1978, U.S./Hong Kong), ed; FAST BREAK(1979), ed; JAZZ SINGER, THE(1980), ed; ENTITY, THE(1982), ed; AMITYVILLE 3-D(1983), ed; TRENCHCOAT(1983), ed
1984
CONAN THE DESTROYER(1984), ed
Leon Uris
GUNFIGHT AT THE O.K. CORRAL(1957), w; ANGRY HILLS, THE(1959, Brit.), w; EXODUS(1960), w; TOPAZ(1969, Brit.), w
Leon W. Uris
BATTLE FLAME(1955), w
Michael Uris
HAPPY GO LUCKY(1943), w; IN THE MEANTIME, DARLING(1944), w; PLAINS-MAN AND THE LADY(1946), w
Michael H. Uris
FOUR DAYS WONDER(1936), w
J.T. Urishin
SOD SISTERS(1969), p, ed
Mark Urman
1984
HOME FREE ALL(1984)
Molly Urquart
DIGBY, THE BIGGEST DOG IN THE WORLD(1974, Brit.)
Dresden Urquhart
JAWS 3-D(1983), cos
Gordon Urquhart
FEMALE JUNGLE, THE(1955); BRAIN EATERS, THE(1958), w
Mollie Urquhart
BEHOLD A PALE HORSE(1964)
Molly Urquhart
FLOODTIDE(1949, Brit.); HAPPY GO LOVELY(1951, Brit.); PORTRAIT OF CLA-RE(1951, Brit.); STRANGER IN BETWEEN, THE(1952, Brit.); YOU'RE ONLY YOUNG TWICE(1952, Brit.); BLONDE SINNER(1956, Brit.); CHILD IN THE HOUSE(1956, Brit.); WEE GEORDIE(1956, Brit.); DOCTOR AT LARGE(1957, Brit.); DEVIL'S BAIT(1959, Brit.); NUN'S STORY, THE(1959); BIG DAY, THE(1960, Brit.); SUNDOWN-ERS, THE(1960); HOUSE OF MYSTERY(1961, Brit.); MAN FOR ALL SEASONS, A(1966, Brit.); JULIA(1977)
Robert Urquhart
PAUL TEMPLE RETURNS(1952, Brit.); TREAD SOFTLY(1952, Brit.); YOU'RE ONLY YOUNG TWICE(1952, Brit.); HOUSE OF THE ARROW, THE(1953, Brit.); ISN'T LIFE WONDERFUL!(1953, Brit.); KNIGHTS OF THE ROUND TABLE(1953); TONIGHT'S THE NIGHT(1954, Brit.); WARRIORS, THE(1955); YOU CAN'T ESCAPE(1955, Brit.); BATTLE HELL(1956, Brit.); CURSE OF FRANKENSTEIN, THE(1957, Brit.); WHITE HUNTRESS(1957, Brit.); DUNKIRK(1958, Brit.); BULLDOG BREED, THE(1960, Brit.); DANGER TOMORROW(1960, Brit.); FOXHOLE IN CAIRO(1960, Brit.); BREAK, THE(1962, Brit.); MURDER AT THE GALLOP(1963, Brit.); 55 DAYS AT PEKING(1963); IN TROUBLE WITH EVE(1964, Brit.); SYNDICATE, THE(1968, Brit.); LIMBO LINE, THE(1969, Brit.); BROTHERLY LOVE(1970, Brit.); LOOKING GLASS WAR, THE(1970, Brit.); MOSQUITO SQUADRON(1970, Brit.); DOGS OF WAR, THE(1980, Brit.)
1984
KIPPERBANG(1984, Brit.)
Benny "The Jet" Urquidez
FORCE: FIVE(1981)
Dylan Urquidi
BUTTERFLY(1982)
J. Gomez Urquiza
LIFE IN THE BALANCE, A(1955), ph
Manuel Gomez Urquiza
LOS ASTRONAUTAS(1960, Mex.), ph
Tom Urray
CLOWN, THE(1953)
Cid Urrutia
RUBY(1977), makeup
David Ursin
1984
BODY DOUBLE(1984)
Susan Ursitti
ZAPPED!(1982)

Frank Urson
Silents
  NINA, THE FLOWER GIRL(1917), ph; ADVENTURE IN HEARTS, AN(1919), ph; ALIAS MIKE MORAN(1919), ph; HAWTHORNE OF THE U.S.A.(1919), ph; ROARING ROAD, THE(1919), ph; EXIT THE VAMP(1921), d; TOO MUCH SPEED(1921), d; SOUTH OF SUVA(1922), d; STRANGER'S BANQUET(1922), w; TILLIE(1922), d; ETERNAL THREE, THE(1923), d; FORTY WINKS(1925), d; NIGHT CLUB, THE(1925), d; CHICAGO(1928), d
Misc. Silents
  HELL DIGGERS, THE(1921), d; LOVE SPECIAL, THE(1921), d; HEART SPECIALIST, THE(1922), d; MINNIE(1922), d; TILLIE, A MENONITE MAID(1922), d; CHANGING HUSBANDS(1924), d; HER MAN O'WAR(1926), d; ALMOST HUMAN(1927), d

Martin Urtel
  DECISION BEFORE DAWN(1951)

Peter Martin Urtel
  DEEP END(1970 Ger./U.S.); CIRCLE OF DECEIT(1982, Fr./Ger.)

Hector Urtiaga
  SALOME(1953)

Rene Urtreger
  FIRST TIME, THE(1978, Fr.), m

Chano Urueta
  GUADALAJARA(1943, Mex.), w, d; DOCTOR CRIMEN(1953, Mex.), d, w; WITCH'S MIRROR, THE(1960, Mex.), d, w; BLUE DEMON VERSUS THE INFERNAL BRAINS(1967, Mex.), d; GUNS FOR SAN SEBASTIAN(1968, U.S./Fr./Mex./Ital.); WILD BUNCH, THE(1969); BRING ME THE HEAD OF ALFREDO GARCIA(1974)

Chanto Urueta
  LIVING HEAD, THE(1969, Mex.), d

George Uruf
  GREEN SLIME, THE(1969)

Sergey Urusevskiy
  LETTER THAT WAS NEVER SENT, THE(1962, USSR), ph

S. Urusevsky
  DREAM OF A COSSACK(1982, USSR), ph

Sergei Uruseysky
  MILITARY SECRET(1945, USSR), ph

Sergei Urussevsky
  CRANES ARE FLYING, THE(1960, USSR), ph

Leo Urvantzov
  HER PRIVATE AFFAIR(1930), w

Chano Urveta
  WRATH OF GOD, THE(1972)

Rosetta Urzi
  SEDUCED AND ABANDONED(1964, Fr./Ital.)

Saro Urzi
  BEAT THE DEVIL(1953); COUNTERFEITERS, THE(1953, Ital.); FRUIT IS RIPE, THE(1961, Fr./Ital.); SON OF THE RED CORSAIR(1963, Ital.); SEDUCED AND ABANDONED(1964, Fr./Ital.); FACTS OF MURDER, THE(1965, Ital.); RAILROAD MAN, THE(1965, Ital.); MODESTY BLAISE(1966, Brit.); SUCKER, THE(1966, Fr./Ital.); SELLERS OF GIRLS(1967, Fr.); SERAFINO(1970, Fr./Ital.); WHO'S GOT THE BLACK BOX?(1970, Fr./Gr./Ital.); GODFATHER, THE(1972); VALACHI PAPERS, THE(1972, Ital./Fr.); ALFREDO, ALFREDO(1973, Ital.)

Us Girls
1984
  BEAT STREET(1984)

Gino Usai
  INVESTIGATION OF A CITIZEN ABOVE SUSPICION(1970, Ital.)

Remo Usai
  TRAIN ROBBERY CONFIDENTIAL(1965, Braz.), m

Junya Usami
  MAN IN THE MOONLIGHT MASK, THE(1958, Jap.); TORA! TORA! TORA!(1970, U.S./Jap.)

Florence Useem
  ARSON FOR HIRE(1959)

Heinz Usener
  SIGNS OF LIFE(1981, Ger.)

Ted Usetti
  CENTO ANNI D'AMORE(1954, Ital.), m

Valentina Ushajova
  YOLANTA(1964, USSR)

S. Ushakov
  GROWN-UP CHILDREN(1963, USSR), art d

Vladimir Ushakov
  BRIDE WITH A DOWRY(1954, USSR)

Valentina Ushakova
  MOSCOW DOES NOT BELIEVE IN TEARS(1980, USSR)

Billy Usher
  ON STAGE EVERYBODY(1945)

Bob Usher
  SHE DONE HIM WRONG(1933), art d

Cary Usher
  GIRLS ON THE BEACH(1965), m

Gary Usher
  MUSCLE BEACH PARTY(1964); SKI PARTY(1965), m

Geoff Usher
  TIM(1981, Aus.)

Guy Usher
  PENGUIN POOL MURDER, THE(1932); CLEAR ALL WIRES(1933); FACE IN THE SKY(1933); FAST WORKERS(1933); HEROES FOR SALE(1933); LITTLE GIANT, THE(1933); THIS DAY AND AGE(1933); TUGBOAT ANNIE(1933); ALL OF ME(1934); BORN TO BE BAD(1934); GOOD DAME(1934); HELL BENT FOR LOVE(1934); HELL CAT, THE(1934); IT'S A GIFT(1934); KID MILLIONS(1934); MAN WITH TWO FACES, THE(1934); ST. LOUIS KID, THE(1934); STAND UP AND CHEER(1934 80m FOX bw); UPPER WORLD(1934); VOICE IN THE NIGHT(1934); CRUSADES, THE(1935); ELINOR NORTON(1935); FLIRTING WITH DANGER(1935); GOOSE AND THE GANDER, THE(1935); GRAND EXIT(1935); HOLD'EM YALE(1935); IT HAPPENED IN NEW YORK(1935); JUSTICE OF THE RANGE(1935); LAW BEYOND THE RANGE(1935); LIFE BEGINS AT 40(1935); LITTLE BIG SHOT(1935); MYSTERY MAN, THE(1935); NAUGHTY MARIETTA(1935); RENDEZVOUS(1935); SHIPMATES FOREVER(1935); SPANISH CAPE MYSTERY(1935); TWO FOR TONIGHT(1935); AFTER THE THIN MAN(1936); CASE OF THE BLACK CAT, THE(1936); CHARLIE CHAN AT THE OPERA(1936); DANGEROUS WATERS(1936); FURY(1936); KING OF HOCKEY(1936); PAROLE(1936); POSTAL INSPECTOR(1936); PRESIDENT'S MYSTERY, THE(1936); RETURN OF SOPHIE LANG, THE(1936); SPENDTHRIFT(1936); BOOTS AND SADDLES(1937); BOY OF THE STREETS(1937); HOTEL HAYWIRE(1937); MARKED WOMAN(1937); MICHAEL O'HALLORAN(1937); MIGHTY TREVE, THE(1937); NANCY STEELE IS MISSING(1937); OLD WYOMING TRAIL, THE(1937); ONCE A DOCTOR(1937); SOPHIE LANG GOES WEST(1937); TIME OUT FOR ROMANCE(1937); CRASHIN' THRU DANGER(1938); LITTLE MISS ROUGHNECK(1938); MIDNIGHT INTRUDER(1938); RENEGADE RANGER(1938); ROMANCE OF THE LIMBERLOST(1938); SPAWN OF THE NORTH(1938); STATE POLICE(1938); UNDER WESTERN STARS(1938); DISBARRED(1939); INVITATION TO HAPPINESS(1939); KING OF CHINATOWN(1939); MR. WONG IN CHINATOWN(1939); OFF THE RECORD(1939); PIRATES OF THE SKIES(1939); ROUGH RIDERS' ROUNDUP(1939); ROVIN' TUMBLEWEEDS(1939); TIMBER STAMPEDE(1939); UNION PACIFIC(1939); WOLF CALL(1939); DANGER AHEAD(1940); DOOMED TO DIE(1940); HOLD THAT WOMAN(1940); I TAKE THIS OATH(1940); LAUGHING AT DANGER(1940); ONE MAN'S LAW(1940); PASSPORT TO ALCATRAZ(1940); QUEEN OF THE YUKON(1940); BANDIT TRAIL, THE(1941); BORROWED HERO(1941); BUY ME THAT TOWN(1941); DEVIL BAT, THE(1941); GREAT TRAIN ROBBERY, THE(1941); KANSAS CYCLONE(1941); KID FROM KANSAS, THE(1941); KING OF DODGE CITY(1941); KING OF THE ZOMBIES(1941); LADY FOR A NIGHT(1941); MEET JOHN DOE(1941); NO GREATER SIN(1941); PUBLIC ENEMIES(1941); RIDIN' ON A RAINBOW(1941); WEST OF CIMARRON(1941); BAD MEN OF THE HILLS(1942); I WAS FRAMED(1942); IN OLD CALIFORNIA(1942); PARDON MY GUN(1942); SHEPHERD OF THE OZARKS(1942); SIN TOWN(1942); LOST CANYON(1943)

James Usher
  CHARRIOTS OF FIRE(1981, Brit.)

Madeleine Usher
  KIMBERLEY JIM(1965, South Africa); MY WAY(1974, South Africa)

Richard Usher
  LANDLORD, THE(1970)

Robert Usher
  NOW AND FOREVER(1934), art d; SHOOT THE WORKS(1934), art d; GOIN' TO TOWN(1935), art d; PETER IBBETSON(1935), art d; RUMBA(1935), art d; BRIDE COMES HOME(1936), art d; DESIRE(1936), art d; RHYTHM ON THE RANGE(1936), art d; ANGEL(1937), art d; TRUE CONFESSION(1937), art d; CAT AND THE CANARY, THE(1939), art d; MAN ABOUT TOWN(1939), art d; STAR MAKER, THE(1939), art d; ZAZA(1939), art d; ARISE, MY LOVE(1940), art d; GHOST BREAKERS, THE(1940), art d; RANGERS OF FORTUNE(1940), art d; THOSE WERE THE DAYS(1940), art d; VICTORY(1940), art d; HOLD BACK THE DAWN(1941), art d; I WANTED WINGS(1941), art d; LOUISIANA PURCHASE(1941), art d; NOTHING BUT THE TRUTH(1941), art d; ROAD TO ZANZIBAR(1941), art d; MY FAVORITE BLONDE(1942), art d; ROAD TO MOROCCO(1942), art d; NO TIME FOR LOVE(1943), art d; PRACTICALLY YOURS(1944), art d; 'TILL WE MEET AGAIN(1944), art d; CHASE, THE(1946), art d; MAD WEDNESDAY(1950), art d; VENDETTA(1950), art d

Kasuo Ushida
  KARATE, THE HAND OF DEATH(1961)

Mantaro Ushio
  ODD OBSESSION(1961, Jap.); FIRES ON THE PLAIN(1962, Jap.); FLOATING WEEDS(1970, Jap.)

John Ushler
  STORM RIDER, THE(1957), art d

Rodolfo Usigli
  CRIMINAL LIFE OF ARCHIBALDO DE LA CRUZ, THE(1962, Mex.), w

Michael E. Uslan
  SWAMP THING(1982), p

Jerry Uslander
  MORO WITCH DOCTOR(1964, U.S./Phil.)

Maria Uspenskaya
Misc. Silents
  FLOWERS ARE LATE, THE(1917, USSR)

S. Uspenskaya
  WAR AND PEACE(1968, USSR)

Vladimir Ussachevsky
  NO EXIT(1962, U.S./Arg.), m

Natalie Usselmann
  MARRIAGE OF FIGARO, THE(1970, Ger.)

Olaf Ussing
  DAY OF WRATH(1948, Den.); SCANDAL IN DENMARK(1970, Den.)

Pavla Ustinov
  CHARLIE CHAN AND THE CURSE OF THE DRAGON QUEEN(1981)

Peter Ustinov
  MEIN KAMPF-MY CRIMES(1940, Brit.); GOOSE STEPS OUT, THE(1942, Brit.); ONE OF OUR AIRCRAFT IS MISSING(1942, Brit.); WAY AHEAD, THE(1945, Brit.), a, w; CARNIVAL(1946, Brit.), w; SCHOOL FOR SECRETS(1946, Brit.), p, d&w; VICE VERSA(1948, Brit.), p, d&w; PRIVATE ANGELO(1949, Brit.), a, p, d, w; HOTEL SAHARA(1951, Brit.); ODETTE(1951, Brit.); QUO VADIS(1951); MAGIC BOX, THE(1952, Brit.); BEAU BRUMMELL(1954); EGYPTIAN. THE(1954); LOLA MONTES(1955, Fr./Ger.); WE'RE NO ANGELS(1955); SCHOOL FOR SCOUNDRELS(1960, Brit.), w; SPARTACUS(1960); SUNDOWNERS, THE(1960); MAN WHO WAGGED HIS TAIL, THE(1961, Ital./Span.); ROMANOFF AND JULIET(1961), a, p,d&w; BILLY BUDD(1962), a, p&d, w; JOHN GOLDFARB, PLEASE COME HOME(1964); TOPKAPI(1964); LADY L(1965, Fr./Ital.), a, d&w; COMEDIANS, THE(1967); BLACKBEARD'S GHOST(1968); HOT MILLIONS(1968, Brit.), a, w; VIVA MAX!(1969); HAMMERSMITH IS OUT(1972, Brit.); ONE OF OUR DINOSAURS IS MISSING(1975, Brit.); LOGAN'S RUN(1976); TREASURE OF MATECUMBE(1976); LAST REMAKE OF BEAU GESTE, THE(1977); MOUSE AND HIS CHILD, THE(1977); PURPLE TAXI, THE(1977, Fr./Ital./Ireland); DEATH ON THE NILE(1978, Brit.); ASHANTI(1979); WE'LL GROW THIN TOGETHER(1979, Fr.); CHARLIE CHAN AND THE CURSE OF THE DRAGON QUEEN(1981); GREAT MUPPET CAPER, THE(1981); GRENDEL GRENDEL GRENDEL(1981, Aus.); EVIL UNDER THE SUN(1982, Brit.)
1984
  MEMED MY HAWK(1984, Brit.), a, d&w

Tamara Ustinov
  BLOOD ON SATAN'S CLAW, THE(1970, Brit.); BLOOD FROM THE MUMMY'S TOMB(1972, Brit.)

Tec Usuelli
DILLINGER IS DEAD(1969, Ital.), m
Teo Usuelli
CONJUGAL BED, THE(1963, Ital.), m; APE WOMAN, THE(1964, Ital.), m; MAN
WITH THE BALLOONS, THE(1968, Ital./Fr.), m; SAUL AND DAVID(1968, Ital./
Span.), m; SEED OF MAN, THE(1970, Ital.), m
Matyas Usztics
WAGNER(1983, Brit./Hung./Aust.)
1984
BRADY'S ESCAPE(1984, U.S./Hung.)
Utah
TYPHOON TREASURE(1939, Brit.)
Valentina Utchakova
SILVER DUST(1953, USSR)
Siegfried Utecht
SOMEWHERE IN BERLIN(1949, E. Ger.)
Yuri Utekin
ISLAND OF DOOM(1933, USSR), ph
Utz Utermann
TRAPP FAMILY, THE(1961, Ger.), p
Betty Utey
PAL JOEY(1957); TARNISHED ANGELS, THE(1957); PARTY GIRL(1958); KING OF
KINGS(1961), ch
A. Utkin
MAN OF MUSIC(1953, USSR), set d
Byron Utley
HAIR(1979)
Ken Utsui
GREAT WALL, THE(1965, Jap.); FALCON FIGHTERS, THE(1970, Jap.); GATEWAY
TO GLORY(1970, Jap.)
Midori Utsumi
YOUNG GUY ON MT. COOK(1969, Jap.)
Shoji Utsumi [Masaharu Utsumi]
LAS VEGAS FREE-FOR-ALL(1968, Jap.), ph
Kenneth Utt
STAR 80(1983), p
Robin Utt
TAXI DRIVER(1976)
Kari Uusitalo
MAKE LIKE A THIEF(1966, Fin.), ed
V. Uvarov
WAR AND PEACE(1968, USSR), set d
Y. Uvarova
Misc. Silents
NEST OF NOBLEMEN, A(1915, USSR)
Martin Uvince
LIGHT AT THE EDGE OF THE WORLD, THE(1971, U.S./Span./Lichtenstein)
Yoshijiro Uyeda
HOTSPRINGS HOLIDAY(1970, Jap.)
Jamie Uys
HELLIONS, THE(1962, Brit.); AFTER YOU, COMRADE(1967, S. Afr.), a, p,d&w
1984
GODS MUST BE CRAZY, THE(1984, Botswana), a, p,d&w, ph, ed
Jaqueline Uytenbogaart
COME BACK BABY(1968)
Peter Uytterhoeven
LIFE LOVE DEATH(1969, Fr./Ital.), w
Pierre Uytterhoeven
MAN AND A WOMAN, A(1966, Fr.), w; LIVE FOR LIFE(1967, Fr./Ital.), w; TO BE A
CROOK(1967, Fr.), w; LOVE IS A FUNNY THING(1970, Fr./Ital.), w; CROOK,
THE(1971, Fr.), w; AND NOW MY LOVE(1975, Fr.), w
1984
EDITH AND MARCEL(1984, Fr.), w
Vera Uzelacova
90 DEGREES IN THE SHADE(1966, Czech./Brit.); MURDER CZECH STYLE(1968,
Czech.)
Natasha Uzhvey
RAINBOW, THE(1944, USSR)
N. Uzhvi
NEW HORIZONS(1939, USSR)
Moshe Uziel
JESUS CHRIST, SUPERSTAR(1973)
Brian Uzzell
CAYMAN TRIANGLE, THE(1977)
Corene Uzzell
Silents
ON TRIAL(1917); OAKDALE AFFAIR, THE(1919)
Misc. Silents
SEVEN KEYS TO BALDPATE(1917); CLOUDED NAME, THE(1919)
Corinne Uzzell
Silents
CONQUERED HEARTS(1918); LUCK AND PLUCK(1919)
Misc. Silents
DETERMINATION(1922); MR. POTTER OF TEXAS(1922)
Thomas H. Uzzell
Silents
ANTON THE TERRIBLE(1916), w

Ron Vaad
ROLLOVER(1981)
Erica Vaal
THUNDERSTORM(1956); JOURNEY, THE(1959, U.S./Aust.)
A. Vabnik
Misc. Silents
BENNIE THE HOWL(1927, USSR)
Jost Vacano
LOST HONOR OF KATHARINA BLUM, THE(1975, Ger.), ph; SOLDIER OF ORANGE(1979, Dutch), ph; DAS BOOT(1982), ph; SPETTERS(1983, Holland), ph
1984
NEVERENDING STORY, THE(1984, Ger.), ph
Milan Vacca
FABULOUS WORLD OF JULES VERNE, THE(1961, Czech.), w
Andrea Vaccarello
1984
INITIATION, THE(1984)
Paola Vaccari
EMBALMER, THE(1966, Ital.)
Brenda Vaccaro
MIDNIGHT COWBOY(1969); WHERE IT'S AT(1969); I LOVE MY WIFE(1970); GOING HOME(1971); SUMMERTREE(1971); ONCE IS NOT ENOUGH(1975); AIRPORT '77(1977); HOUSE BY THE LAKE, THE(1977, Can.); CAPRICORN ONE(1978); FAST CHARLIE... THE MOONBEAM RIDER(1979); FIRST DEADLY SIN, THE(1980); CHANEL SOLITAIRE(1981); ZORRO, THE GAY BLADE(1981)
1984
SUPERGIRL(1984)
Tracy Vaccaro
MAN WHO LOVED WOMEN, THE(1983)
1984
RARE BREED(1984)
Franz Vacek
IN A YEAR OF THIRTEEN MOONS(1980, Ger.), prod d
Jack Vacek
DOUBLE NICKELS(1977), a, p&d, w, ed
John Vacek
GONE IN 60 SECONDS(1974), ph
Zlatomir Vacek
DEVIL'S TRAP, THE(1964, Czech.); TRANSPORT FROM PARADISE(1967, Czech.)
Sandra Vacey
GLORY BOY(1971); HAZING, THE(1978)
Fernand Vacha
LEMONADE JOE(1966, Czech.), cos
H.A. Vachell
STORY OF SHIRLEY YORKE, THE(1948, Brit.), w
Horace Annesley Vachell
LORD CAMBER'S LADIES(1932, Brit.), w; IF I WERE RICH(1936), w
Vasil Vachev
PEACH THIEF, THE(1969, Bulgaria)
Deni Vachlioti
NEVER ON SUNDAY(1960, Gr.), cos
Denny Vachlioti
PHAEDRA(1962, U.S./Gr./Fr.), cos; TOPKAPI(1964), cos; OEDIPUS THE KING(1968, Brit.), cos
Nata Vachnadze
Misc. Silents
IN THE PILLORY(1924, USSR); GIULLI(1927, USSR); LIVING CORPSE, A(1931, USSR)
Jean Vachon
LES MISERABLES(1952); LADY WANTS MINK, THE(1953); JEANNE EAGELS(1957); MARJORIE MORNINGSTAR(1958)
"Mad Dog" Vachon
Misc. Talkies
WRESTLING QUEEN, THE(1975)
Vivian Vachon
Misc. Talkies
WRESTLING QUEEN, THE(1975)
Vera Vachova
SWEET LIGHT IN A DARK ROOM(1966, Czech.)
Nativadid Vacio
GIANT(1956)
Natividad Vacio
HITCH-HIKER, THE(1953); JEOPARDY(1953); GREEN FIRE(1955); ESCAPE FROM RED ROCK(1958); GUN HAWK, THE(1963); CASTLE OF EVIL(1967); PINK JUNGLE, THE(1968); MAN WITH TWO BRAINS, THE(1983)
The Vacqueros
GONKS GO BEAT(1965, Brit.)
Tibor Vadas
SHOP ON MAIN STREET, THE(1966, Czech.)
Zotland Vadasz
1984
BRADY'S ESCAPE(1984, U.S./Hung.)
Zsolt Vadaszffy
IPCRESS FILE, THE(1965, Brit.)
Bernard Lamarche Vadel
1984
L'ARGENT(1984, Fr./Switz.)

Michel Vadet
PERFECTIONIST, THE(1952, Fr.); LE PLAISIR(1954, Fr.)
Annette Vadim
BLOOD AND ROSES(1961, Fr./Ital.); LES LIAISONS DANGEREUSES(1961, Fr./Ital.)
Christian Vadim
1984
FULL MOON IN PARIS(1984, Fr.)
Roger Vadim
BLACKMAILED(1951, Brit.), w; NAKED HEART, THE(1955, Brit.), w; AND GOD CREATED WOMAN(1957, Fr.), d, w; PLEASE! MR. BALZAC(1957, Fr.), w; NIGHT HEAVEN FELL, THE(1958, Fr.), d, w; BLOOD AND ROSES(1961, Fr./Ital.), d&w; LES LIAISONS DANGEREUSES(1961, Fr./Ital.), d, w; SEVEN CAPITAL SINS(1962, Fr./Ital.), d, w; TALES OF PARIS(1962, Fr./Ital.), w; TESTAMENT OF ORPHEUS, THE(1962, Fr.); LOVE ON A PILLOW(1963, Fr./Ital.), d, w; PLEASE, NOT NOW!(1963, Fr./Ital.), d; NUTTY, NAUGHTY CHATEAU(1964, Fr./Ital.), d, w; SWEET AND SOUR(1964, Fr./Ital.); CIRCLE OF LOVE(1965, Fr.), d; VICE AND VIRTUE(1965, Fr./Ital.), p&d, w; GAME IS OVER, THE(1967, Fr.), p&d, w; BARBARELLA(1968, Fr./Ital.), d, w; SPIRITS OF THE DEAD(1969, Fr./Ital.), d, w; PRETTY MAIDS ALL IN A ROW(1971), d; CIAO MANHATTAN(1973); NIGHT GAMES(1980), d; RICH AND FAMOUS(1981)
Dan Vadis
REBEL GLADIATORS, THE(1963, Ital.); HERCULES VS THE GIANT WARRIORS(1965 Fr./Ital.); SHOOT FIRST, LAUGH LAST(1967, Ital./Ger./U.S.); SCALPHUNTERS, THE(1968); STRANGER RETURNS, THE(1968, U.S./Ital./Ger./Span.); CAHILL, UNITED STATES MARSHAL(1973); HIGH PLAINS DRIFTER(1973); GAUNTLET, THE(1977); WHITE BUFFALO, THE(1977); ANY WHICH WAY YOU CAN(1980); BRONCO BILLY(1980)
Misc. Talkies
TEN GLADIATORS, THE(1960); HERCULES THE INVINCIBLE(1963)
Ernest Vadja
SON OF INDIA(1931), w; GREAT GARRICK, THE(1937), w
Silents
CAT'S PAJAMAS, THE(1926), w
Ernst Vadja
DRAMATIC SCHOOL(1938), w
L. Vadja
LOVE ON SKIS(1933, Brit.), d
Ladislaus Vadnai
JOSETTE(1938), w
Laszlo Vadnai
TALES OF MANHATTAN(1942), w
Laslo Vadnay
SEVEN SINNERS(1940), w; FLESH AND FANTASY(1943), w; COPACABANA(1947), w; GREAT RUPERT, THE(1950), w; SOUTH SEA SINNER(1950), w; NO TIME FOR FLOWERS(1952), w; EASY TO LOVE(1953), w; GREAT DIAMOND ROBBERY(1953), w; I LOVE MELVIN(1953), w; TEN THOUSAND BEDROOMS(1957), w; IT HAPPENED IN ATHENS(1962), w; DIME WITH A HALO(1963), p, w; WAY...WAY OUT(1966), w
Laszlo Vadnay
GIRL RUSH(1944), w; UNCERTAIN GLORY(1944), w
Leslie Vadney
BIG SHOW-OFF, THE(1945), w
Eric Vaesser
Misc. Talkies
APE CREATURE(1968, Ger.)
Wally Vaevers
THINGS TO COME(1936, Brit.), spec eff
The Vagabonds
SOMETHING TO SING ABOUT(1937); SHE HAS WHAT IT TAKES(1943); HEY, ROOKIE(1944); PEOPLE ARE FUNNY(1945); TAHITI NIGHTS(1945)
The Vagabonds
IT AIN'T HAY(1943)
Students of the Vaganova Dancing School
SLEEPING BEAUTY, THE(1966, USSR)
Helen Vager
GUNS(1980, Fr.), p
V. Vagina
WAR AND PEACE(1968, USSR)
Winie Vagliani
LA DOLCE VITA(1961, Ital./Fr.)
V. Vaglini
GREEN TREE, THE(1965, Ital.)
Gino Vagniluca
JOHNNY HAMLET(1972, Ital.), spec eff
Steven Vagnino
Misc. Talkies
PLEASURE DOING BUSINESS, A(1979), d
Eugene Vagnone
UNDER FIRE(1983)
Vera Vague
DESIGN FOR SCANDAL(1941); HI, NEIGHBOR(1942); PRIORITIES ON PARADE(1942); GET GOING(1943); SWING YOUR PARTNER(1943); GIRL RUSH(1944); HENRY ALDRICH PLAYS CUPID(1944); ROSIE THE RIVETER(1944); EARL CARROLL SKETCHBOOK(1946); BORN TO BE LOVED(1959)
Vera Vague [Barbara Jo Allen]
WOMEN, THE(1939); MRS. WIGGS OF THE CABBAGE PATCH(1942); COWBOY CANTEEN(1944); MOON OVER LAS VEGAS(1944); SNAFU(1945); SQUARE DANCE KATY(1950); MOHAWK(1956)
Anna Vaguena
MATCHMAKING OF ANNA, THE(1972, Gr.)
Marc Vahanian
BLESS THE BEASTS AND CHILDREN(1971); KING OF THE GYPSIES(1978)
1984
EXTERMINATOR 2(1984)
Mark Vahanian
UP THE SANDBOX(1972)

Vahio
TAHITIAN, THE(1956)
Henry Vahl
MAN WHO WALKED THROUGH THE WALL, THE(1964, Ger.)
Uolevi Vahteristo
MAKE LIKE A THIEF(1966, Fin.)
Litsa Vaidou
DREAM OF PASSION, A(1978, Gr.)
Jadine Vaighn
COVENANT WITH DEATH, A(1966)
Bill Vail
MAUSOLEUM(1983)
Leslie Vail
CONSOLATION MARRIAGE(1931)
Lester Vail
BEAU IDEAL(1931); DANCE, FOOLS, DANCE(1931); I TAKE THIS WOMAN(1931);
IT'S A WISE CHILD(1931); MURDER BY THE CLOCK(1931); WOMAN BET-
WEEN(1931); BIG TOWN(1932)
Mabel Vail
Silents
JOY STREET(1929)
Myrtle Vail
MYRT AND MARGE(1934); LITTLE SHOP OF HORRORS(1961)
Steven A. Vail
SCAVENGER HUNT(1979), p, w
William Vail
TEXAS CHAIN SAW MASSACRE, THE(1974); POLTERGEIST(1982)
Bruno Vailati
GIANT OF MARATHON, THE(1960, Ital.), p, w; HERCULES UNCHAINED(1960,
Ital./Fr.), p; THIEF OF BAGHDAD, THE(1961, Ital./Fr.), p, w; GOLDEN ARROW,
THE(1964, Ital.), w; TORPEDO BAY(1964, Ital./Fr.), p, d, w
David Vaile
STRATEGIC AIR COMMAND(1955); SIMON, KING OF THE WITCHES(1971)
Eleanor Vaill
GIRL, THE BODY, AND THE PILL, THE(1967); TASTE OF BLOOD, A(1967)
Roger Vailland
WHERE THE HOT WIND BLOWS(1960, Fr., Ital.), w; BLOOD AND ROSES(1961,
Fr./Ital.), d&w; LES LIAISONS DANGEREUSES(1961, Fr./Ital.), w; DAY AND THE
HOUR, THE(1963, Fr./Ital.), w; NAKED AUTUMN(1963, Fr.), w; RITA(1963, Fr./Ital.),
w; VICE AND VIRTUE(1965, Fr./Ital.), w; TROUT, THE(1982, Fr.), w
Pierre-Jean Vaillard
LOVE AND THE FRENCHWOMAN(1961, Fr.); THUNDER IN THE BLOOD(1962, Fr.)
Earlise Vails
HAIR(1979)
M. Vainberg
CRANES ARE FLYING, THE(1960, USSR), m
Vladimir Vainstok
ARMED AND DANGEROUS(1977, USSR), p&d
Ernest Vaio
PRINCESS AND THE MAGIC FROG, THE(1965)
A. Vaisfeld
OTHELLO(1960, U.S.S.R.), art d
Eva Vaiti
DISORDER AND EARLY TORMENT(1977, Ger.)
Eva Vaitl
BRIDGE, THE(1961, Ger.)
Ernest Vajda
MANHATTAN COCKTAIL(1928), w; INNOCENTS OF PARIS(1929), w; MONTE
CARLO(1930), w; SUCH MEN ARE DANGEROUS(1930), w; SMILING LIEUTENANT,
THE(1931), w; TONIGHT OR NEVER(1931), w; BROKEN LULLABY(1932), w; PAY-
MENT DEFERRED(1932), w; SMILIN' THROUGH(1932), w; REUNION IN VIEN-
NA(1933), w; BARRETTS OF WIMPOLE STREET, THE(1934), w; MERRY WIDOW,
THE(1934), w; WOMAN REBELS, A(1936), w; PERSONAL PROPERTY(1937), w;
MARIE ANTOINETTE(1938), w; HE STAYED FOR BREAKFAST(1940), w; CHOCO-
LATE SOLDIER, THE(1941), w; THEY DARE NOT LOVE(1941), w; STARS AND
STRIPES FOREVER(1952), w
Silents
MANHATTAN COWBOY(1928), w; NIGHT OF MYSTERY, A(1928), w
Erno Vajda
Silents
WOMAN ON TRIAL, THE(1927), w
Ernst Vajda
LOVE PARADE, THE(1929), w; GUARDSMAN, THE(1931), w; RESERVED FOR
LADIES(1932, Brit.), w
Ladislao Vajda
IT HAPPENED IN BROAD DAYLIGHT(1960, Ger./Switz.), d, w; MAN WHO
WAGGED HIS TAIL, THE(1961, Ital./Span.), d, w; SHADOWS GROW LONGER,
THE(1962, Switz./Ger.), d, w; MAN WHO WALKED THROUGH THE WALL,
THE(1964, Ger.), d
Ladislas Vajda
WIFE OF GENERAL LING, THE(1938, Brit.), d; CALL OF THE BLOOD(1948,
Brit.), d; GOLDEN MADONNA, THE(1949, Brit.), d; HER PANELLED DOOR(1951,
Brit.), d, w; STORY OF THREE LOVES, THE(1953), w
Ladislaus Vajda
THREEPENNY OPERA, THE(1931, Ger./U.S.), w; MISTRESS OF ATLANTIS,
THE(1932, Ger.), w; WINGS OVER AFRICA(1939), d
Silents
PANDORA'S BOX(1929, Ger.), w
Laszlo Vajda
WHERE IS THIS LADY?(1932, Brit.), d
Vajira
EAST OF ELEPHANT ROCK(1976, Brit.)
Andrew G. Vajna
DEADLY CHINA DOLL(1973, Hong Kong), p
Yevgeni Vakhtangov
Misc. Silents
WHEN THE STRINGS OF THE HEART SOUND(1914, USSR); GREAT MAGARAZ,
THE(1915, USSR); BREAD(1918, USSR)

Jean Val
13 RUE MADELEINE(1946)
Maria Val
PETULIA(1968, U.S./Brit.); JOE KIDD(1972)
Percy Val
NEW HOTEL, THE(1932, Brit.)
Robert Val
GOLDEN EARRINGS(1947)
William Val
KID FROM GOWER GULCH, THE(1949); HARVEY(1950)
Dennis Val Norton
GARRISON FOLLIES(1940, Brit.)
Denys Val Norton
STOP PRESS GIRL(1949, Brit.); SHE SHALL HAVE MURDER(1950, Brit.)
Jiri Vala
LOST FACE, THE(1965, Czech.)
Gustav Valach
ADRIFT(1971, Czech.)
Jece Valadao
PRETTY BUT WICKED(1965, Braz.), a, p, w; LOLLIPOP(1966, Braz.)
Enrique Valades
RIDE THE PINK HORSE(1947)
Enrique Valadez
MASQUERADE IN MEXICO(1945)
Josette Valague
PASSION IN THE SUN(1964)
V. Valaitis
YOLANTA(1964, USSR)
Antigoni Valakou
GIRL OF THE MOUNTAINS(1958, Gr.)
N. Valandina
SOUND OF LIFE, THE(1962, USSR)
Mary Valange
MYSTERY AT THE BURLESQUE(1950, Brit.)
Lee Valanios
HEROES OF THE ALAMO(1938)
Teresa Valarde
1984
CHOOSE ME(1984)
Martha Valardi
ONE STEP TO HELL(1969, U.S./Ital./Span.)
Andre Valardy
1984
AMERICAN DREAMER(1984)
Betty Valassi
DREAM OF PASSION, A(1978, Gr.)
Maurice Valay
RISE OF LOUIS XIV, THE(1970, Fr.), art d
Robert Valbar
Misc. Silents
RASPUTIN(1929, Ger.)
Marc Valbel
TAKE ME TO PARIS(1951, Brit.)
Birgitta Valberg
SMILES OF A SUMMER NIGHT(1957, Swed.); VIRGIN SPRING, THE(1960, Swed.);
PORT OF CALL(1963, Swed.); SWEDISH MISTRESS, THE(1964, Swed.); SHAME(1968,
Swed.); STORY OF A WOMAN(1970, U.S./Ital.); TIME IN THE SUN, A(1970, Swed.)
N. Valbert
UNIVERSITY OF LIFE(1941, USSR)
John Valby
LOSIN' IT(1983)
Armando Valcauda
STARCRASH(1979), spec eff; HERCULES(1983), spec eff
Serge-Henri Valcke
LIFT, THE(1983, Neth.)
Armando Valcuada
HUMANOID, THE(1979, Ital.), spec eff
A. Valdarnini
DIVINE NYMPH, THE(1979, Ital.), w
Alfio Valdarnini
'TIS A PITY SHE'S A WHORE(1973, Ital.), w
Leona Valde
WOMEN OF GLAMOUR(1937)
Cardona Valdemar
GUYANA, CULT OF THE DAMNED(1980, Mex./Span./Panama), w
Carlos Valdemar
GUYANA, CULT OF THE DAMNED(1980, Mex./Span./Panama), w
Thais Valdemar
Silents
AGAINST ALL ODDS(1924)
Misc. Silents
RANGE TERROR, THE(1925)
Mario Valdemarin
GREAT WAR, THE(1961, Fr., Ital.); HERCULES AND THE CAPTIVE WOMEN(1963,
Fr./Ital.); SANDOKAN THE GREAT(1964, Fr./Ital./Span.); SPY IN YOUR EYE(1966,
Ital.)
Bernard Valdeneige
JE T'AIME, JE T'AIME(1972, Fr./Swed.)
Giuseppe Valdengo
GREAT CARUSO, THE(1951)
Xenia Valderi
CENTO ANNI D'AMORE(1954, Ital.); WOMAN OF ROME(1956, Ital.); VIOLENT
SUMMER(1961, Fr./Ital.); SWINDLE, THE(1962, Fr./Ital.); RED DESERT(1965, Fr./
Ital.)
E. F. Valderrama
1984
NO SMALL AFFAIR(1984)

Joan Valderrama
1984
  NO SMALL AFFAIR(1984)
David Valdes
1984
  TIGHTROPE(1984)
German "Tin Tan" Valdes
  FACE OF THE SCREAMING WEREWOLF(1959, Mex.)
Manuel Loco Valdes
  FRANKENSTEIN, THE VAMPIRE AND CO.(1961, Mex.)
Manuel Valdes
  LITTLE RED RIDING HOOD(1963, Mex.); LITTLE RED RIDING HOOD AND HER
  FRIENDS(1964, Mex.); LITTLE RED RIDING HOOD AND THE MONSTERS(1965,
  Mex.)
Miguelito Valdes
  PAN-AMERICANA(1945)
Paloma Valdes
  NUN AT THE CROSSROADS, A(1970, Ital./Span.)
Alberto Valdespino
  TREASURE OF THE SIERRA MADRE, THE(1948)
Valdesta
  DRIVE-IN MASSACRE(1976); SUMMER CAMP(1979)
Misc. Talkies
  C.B. HUSTLERS(1978)
Antoinette Valdez
  ONE NIGHT IN LISBON(1941)
Carlos Valdez
  SUDDEN BILL DORN(1938)
Corinne Valdez
  LADY FOR A NIGHT(1941); COWBOY AND THE SENORITA(1944)
Daniel Valdez
  CHINA SYNDROME, THE(1979); ZOOT SUIT(1981), a, m
Danny Valdez
  WHICH WAY IS UP?(1977)
Eric Valdez
  UNDER FIRE(1983)
Esteban Valdez
  CAVEMAN(1981)
Jorge Valdez
  BUGSY MALONE(1976, Brit.)
Luis Valdez
  WHICH WAY IS UP?(1977); ZOOT SUIT(1981), d&w
Luz Valdez
  MERRILL'S MARAUDERS(1962)
Mario Valdez
  HIGH RISK(1981); MISSING(1982)
Miguelito Valdez
  SUSPENSE(1946)
Ray Valdez
  TIMERIDER(1983)
Ronaldo Valdez
  MAD DOCTOR OF BLOOD ISLAND, THE(1969, Phil./U.S.)
Socorro Valdez
  ZOOT SUIT(1981)
1984
  PARIS, TEXAS(1984, Ger./Fr.)
Tere Valdez
  INCREDIBLE INVASION, THE(1971, Mex./U.S.)
Tito Valdez
  COWBOY AND THE SENORITA(1944)
Vera Valdez
  FIRE WITHIN, THE(1964, Fr./Ital.)
Norma Valdi
  SERENITY(1962)
Ramon Valdiosera
  LIVING IDOL, THE(1957), cos
Sigrid Valdis
  MARRIAGE ON THE ROCKS(1965); OUR MAN FLINT(1966)
Valdy
  SALLY FIELDGOOD & CO.(1975, Can.), m
Christina Vale
  VICIOUS CIRCLE, THE(1948)
Diedra Vale
  DR. CHRISTIAN MEETS THE WOMEN(1940); PARACHUTE NURSE(1942); NONE
  BUT THE LONELY HEART(1944)
Edith Vale
  FINISHING SCHOOL(1934)
Eugene Vale
  SECOND FACE, THE(1950), w; FRANCIS OF ASSISI(1961), w; GLOBAL AFFAIR,
  A(1964), w
Leslie Vale
  LINDA BE GOOD(1947), w
Louise Vale
Silents
  JOAN OF THE WOODS(1918), w; JOURNEY'S END(1918)
Misc. Silents
  SEX LURE, THE(1916); EASY MONEY(1917); VENGEANCE(1918)
Martin Vale
  TWO MRS. CARROLLS, THE(1947), w
Michael Vale
  GUERRILLA GIRL(1953); MARATHON MAN(1976); LOOKING UP(1977)
Nina Vale
  CORNERED(1945); MYSTERIOUS INTRUDER(1946)
Quentin Vale
  CANDIDATE, THE(1964), w
Rita Vale
  THIEF, THE(1952)

Travers Vale
Silents
  HEART OF THE BLUE RIDGE, THE(1915), w; MEN SHE MARRIED, THE(1916), d;
  TANGLED FATES(1916), d; DANCER'S PERIL, THE(1917), d; DIVORCE GAME,
  THE(1917), d; JOAN OF THE WOODS(1918), d; JOURNEY'S END(1918), d; JUST
  SYLVIA(1918), d; MAN HUNT, THE(1918), d; BARRIERS OF THE LAW(1925), w
Misc. Silents
  WHAT HAPPENED TO JONES(1915), d; MADNESS OF HELEN, THE(1916), d;
  SALLY IN OUR ALLEY(1916), d; SCARLET OATH, THE(1916), d; BETSY ROSS(1917),
  d; BONDAGE OF FEAR, THE(1917), d; DARKEST RUSSIA(1917), d; DORMANT
  POWER, THE(1917), d; EASY MONEY(1917), d; MAN'S WOMAN(1917), d; SELF
  MADE WIDOW(1917), d; WOMAN BENEATH, THE(1917), d; SOUL WITHOUT WIN-
  DOWS, A(1918), d; SPURS OF SYBIL, THE(1918), d; STOLEN HOURS(1918), d;
  VENGEANCE(1918), d; WHIMS OF SOCIETY, THE(1918), d; WITCH WOMAN,
  THE(1918), d; WOMAN OF REDEMPTION, A(1918), d; BLUFFER, THE(1919), d;
  HEART OF GOLD(1919), d; MORAL DEADLINE, THE(1919), d; QUICKENING
  FLAME, THE(1919), d; LIFE(1920), d; PASTEBOARD CROWN, A(1922), d; STREET
  OF TEARS, THE(1924), d; WESTERN PLUCK(1926), d
Viola Vale
Silents
  EACH TO HIS KIND(1917)
Virginia Vale
  COCOANUT GROVE(1938); HER JUNGLE LOVE(1938); DISBARRED(1939); MAR-
  SHAL OF MESA CITY, THE(1939); BULLET CODE(1940); LEGION OF THE LAW-
  LESS(1940); MILLIONAIRES IN PRISON(1940); PRAIRIE LAW(1940); STAGE TO
  CHINO(1940); TRIPLE JUSTICE(1940); YOU CAN'T FOOL YOUR WIFE(1940);
  BLONDE COMET(1941); GAY FALCON, THE(1941); REPENT AT LEISURE(1941);
  ROBBERS OF THE RANGE(1941); SOUTH OF PANAMA(1941); BROADWAY BIG
  SHOT(1942); CRIME, INC.(1945)
Silents
  IN EVERY WOMAN'S LIFE(1924)
Virginia Vale [Dorothy Howe]
  THREE SONS(1939)
Vola Vale
Silents
  ALIAS JIMMY VALENTINE(1920); MASTER STROKE, A(1920); OVERLAND
  RED(1920); PURPLE CIPHER, THE(1920); SINGING RIVER(1921); WHITE
  OAK(1921); CRASHIN' THRU(1923); MOTHERS-IN-LAW(1923); SOUL OF THE
  BEAST(1923); LITTLE ANNIE ROONEY(1925)
Misc. Silents
  LADY IN THE LIBRARY, THE(1917); MENTIONED IN CONFIDENCE(1917); SE-
  CRET OF BLACK MOUNTAIN, THE(1917); SILENT MAN, THE(1917); SON OF HIS
  FATHER, THE(1917); LOCKED HEART, THE(1918); WOLVES OF THE RAIL(1918);
  HEART IN PAWN, A(1919); HEARTS ASLEEP(1919); HORNET'S NEST, THE(1919);
  SIX FEET FOUR(1919); COMMON SENSE(1920); IRON RIDER, THE(1920); SOME-
  ONE IN THE HOUSE(1920); DUKE OF CHIMNEY BUTTE, THE(1921); GOOD MEN
  AND TRUE(1922); MAN BETWEEN, THE(1923); MIRAGE, THE(1924); HEARTLESS
  HUSBANDS(1925); HER BIG ADVENTURE(1926); SKY PIRATE, THE(1926); BLACK
  TEARS(1927)
Z. Valecskaya
Misc. Silents
  ON THE WARSAW HIGHROAD(1916, USSR)
Kieri Valee
  HARRY'S WAR(1981)
Dorothy Valegra
Misc. Silents
  LIFE'S GREATEST QUESTION(1921)
Jaroslav Valek
  ROCKET TO NOWHERE(1962, Czech.)
Maria Valence
  SOFT SKIN ON BLACK SILK(1964, Fr./Span.)
E. Valencia
Silents
  RAMONA(1916)
Edward Valencia
  LORD OF THE FLIES(1963, Brit.)
Manuel Valencia
  UNDER THE PAMPAS MOON(1935); TROPIC HOLIDAY(1938)
Ralph Valencia
  TIJUANA STORY, THE(1957)
The Valencia Trio
  GAMBLER AND THE LADY, THE(1952, Brit.)
Maurice Valency
  VISIT, THE(1964, Ger./Fr./Ital./U.S.), w
E. G. Valens
  OTHER SIDE OF THE MOUNTAIN, THE(1975), w
Ritchie Valens
  GO, JOHNNY, GO!(1959)
Paula Valenska
  BOND STREET(1948, Brit.); GAY ADVENTURE, THE(1953, Brit.)
Jiri Valenta
  DO YOU KEEP A LION AT HOME?(1966, Czech.)
Vladimir Valenta
  CLOSELY WATCHED TRAINS(1967, Czech.); END OF A PRIEST(1970, Czech.);
  WOLFPEN PRINCIPLE, THE(1974, Can.); SUNDAY IN THE COUNTRY(1975, Can.);
  AMATEUR, THE(1982)
Antonio Valente
  STRANGER ON THE PROWL(1953, Ital.), art d
Caterina Valente
  CASINO DE PARIS(1957, Fr./Ger.)
Danilo Valente
  NEPTUNE'S DAUGHTER(1949)
Melu Valente
  AVANTI!(1972)
Michael Valente
  DIAMONDS ARE FOREVER(1971, Brit.)
Renee Valente
  LOVING COUPLES(1980), p

Rian Valente
BIG SOMBRERO, THE(1949)
Danilo Valenti
CRISIS(1950)
Gino Valenti
1984
ALLEY CAT(1984)
Lili Valenti
HARRAD SUMMER, THE(1974)
Osvaldo Valenti
ADVENTURE OF SALVATOR ROSA, AN(1940, Ital.); FEDORA(1946, Ital.)
Roman Valenti
BARN OF THE NAKED DEAD(1976), w
Diana Valentien
SQUEEZE PLAY(1981)
Albert Valentin
AMPHYTRYON(1937, Ger.), w; AFFAIRS OF MESSALINA, THE(1954, Ital.), p,d&w; MADAME DU BARRY(1954 Fr./Ital.), w; LE CIEL EST A VOUS(1957, Fr.), w; NANA(1957, Fr./Ital.), w; FEMALE, THE(1960, Fr.), w; MAGNIFICENT TRAMP, THE(1962, Fr./Ital.), w; MAXIME(1962, Fr.), w; MURDER AT 45 R.P.M.(1965, Fr.), w; 24 HOURS IN A WOMAN'S LIFE(1968, Fr./Ger.), w
Angel Valentin
1984
DELIVERY BOYS(1984)
Barbara Valentin
HEAD, THE(1961, Ger.); IT'S HOT IN PARADISE(1962, Ger./Yugo.); THERE IS STILL ROOM IN HELL(1963, Ger.); KING, QUEEN, KNAVE(1972, Ger./U.S.); EFFI BRIEST(1974, Ger.); FEAR EATS THE SOUL(1974, Ger.); FOX AND HIS FRIENDS(1976, Ger.); LILI MARLEEN(1981, Ger.)
Hermann Valentin
Silents
SPIES(1929, Ger.)
Maurice Valentin
Silents
POLLY OF THE STORM COUNTRY(1920)
Mirko Valentin
HILLS RUN RED, THE(1967, Ital.); ROVER, THE(1967, Ital.)
Anna Valentina
NEVER LET ME GO(1953, U.S./Brit.)
Valentine
MAN WHO CAME FOR COFFEE, THE(1970, Ital.); WHITE SISTER(1973, Ital./Span./Fr.)
A.J. Valentine
FLIGHT OF THE LOST BALLOON(1961)
Annette Valentine
LOLLIPOP COVER, THE(1965)
Anthony Valentine
GIRL ON THE PIER, THE(1953, Brit.); BRAIN MACHINE, THE(1955, Brit.); THESE ARE THE DAMNED(1965, Brit.); TO THE DEVIL A DAUGHTER(1976, Brit./Ger.); ESCAPE TO ATHENA(1979, Brit.); BEYOND THE FOG(1981, Brit.); MONSTER CLUB, THE(1981, Brit.)
1984
PLAGUE DOGS, THE(1984, U.S./Brit.)
Arthur Valentine
TONS OF MONEY(1931, Brit.), w; TWILIGHT HOUR(1944, Brit.), w
B. Valentine
Misc. Talkies
LOVE, VAMPIRE STYLE(1971)
Barbara Valentine
CARMEN, BABY(1967, Yugo./Ger.)
Bobby Valentine
DANNY BOY(1946); STALLION ROAD(1947)
Diane Valentine
ROAD TO HONG KONG, THE(1962, U.S./Brit.)
Dick Valentine
1984
ANGEL(1984)
Dickie Valentine
6.5 SPECIAL(1958, Brit.)
E.G. Valentine
SHOW GOES ON, THE(1937, Brit.), w
Elizabeth Valentine
I WANT A DIVORCE(1940); KING'S ROW(1942); GUY NAMED JOE, A(1943); SANTA FE SCOUTS(1943); UNDERDOG, THE(1943); APOLOGY FOR MURDER(1945); NIGHT AND DAY(1946); KISS OF EVIL(1963, Brit.)
Elmer Valentine
CHASTITY(1969)
Gilliat Valentine
BELLES OF ST. TRINIAN'S, THE(1954, Brit.), w
Grace Valentine
PHANTOM IN THE HOUSE, THE(1929); SILVER LINING(1932)
Silents
BRAND OF COWARDICE, THE(1916); BABBLING TONGUES(1917); MAN'S HOME, A(1921)
Misc. Silents
BLACK FEAR(1915); NEW ADAM AND EVE, THE(1915); BLINDNESS OF LOVE, THE(1916); DORIAN'S DIVORCE(1916); EVIL THEREOF, THE(1916)
J. Valentine
STRONGER SEX, THE(1931, Brit.), w
James Valentine
STOLEN FACE(1952, Brit.)
Jimmy Valentine
PRIDE OF THE YANKEES, THE(1942)
Joe Valentine
TOP OF THE TOWN(1937), ph; THREE SMART GIRLS GROW UP(1939), ph; BOYS FROM SYRACUSE(1940), ph; BETWEEN US GIRLS(1942), ph
John Valentine
AMERICAN PRISONER, THE(1929 Brit.); DELINQUENT DAUGHTERS(1944); DANGEROUS PARTNERS(1945); FASHION MODEL(1945); G.I. HONEYMOON(1945); ROGUES GALLERY(1945); EASY TO WED(1946); HOODLUM SAINT, THE(1946);

SENATOR WAS INDISCREET, THE(1947); ONE TOUCH OF VENUS(1948)
1984
SOLDIER'S STORY, A(1984)
Silents
LOST PATROL, THE(1929, Brit.)
Joseph Valentine
ARE YOU THERE?(1930), ph; CRAZY THAT WAY(1930), ph; SOUP TO NUTS(1930), ph; JIMMY AND SALLY(1933), ph; MAN HUNT(1933), ph; NIGHT OF TERROR(1933), ph; OBEY THE LAW(1933), ph; CALL IT LUCK(1934), ph; STUDENT TOUR(1934), ph; THREE ON A HONEYMOON(1934), ph; WILD GOLD(1934), ph; ALIAS MARY DOW(1935), ph; DOUBTING THOMAS(1935), ph; GAY DECEPTION, THE(1935), ph; MAN I MARRY, THE(1936), ph; MOON'S OUR HOME, THE(1936), ph; NEXT TIME WE LOVE(1936), ph; TWO IN A CROWD(1936), ph; MERRY-GO-ROUND OF 1938(1937), ph; THREE SMART GIRLS(1937), ph; WINGS OVER HONOLULU(1937), ph; 100 MEN AND A GIRL(1937), ph; MAD ABOUT MUSIC(1938), ph; RAGE OF PARIS, THE(1938), ph; THAT CERTAIN AGE(1938), ph; FIRST LOVE(1939), ph; IT'S A DATE(1940), ph; MY LITTLE CHICKADEE(1940), ph; ONE NIGHT IN THE TROPICS(1940), ph; SPRING PARADE(1940), ph; TRAIL OF THE VIGILANTES(1940), ph; APPOINTMENT FOR LOVE(1941), ph; HOLD THAT GHOST(1941), ph; IN THE NAVY(1941), ph; KEEP 'EM FLYING(1941), ph; NICE GIRL?(1941), ph; UNFINISHED BUSINESS(1941), ph; WOLF MAN, THE(1941), ph; SABOTEUR(1942), ph; SHADOW OF A DOUBT(1943), ph; GUEST WIFE(1945), ph; HEARTBEAT(1946), ph; LOVER COME BACK(1946), ph; MAGNIFICENT DOLL(1946), ph; SO GOES MY LOVE(1946), ph; TOMORROW IS FOREVER(1946), ph; POSSESSED(1947), ph; JOAN OF ARC(1948), ph; ROPE(1948), ph; SLEEP, MY LOVE(1948), ph; BRIDE FOR SALE(1949), ph
Silents
MY HUSBAND'S WIVES(1924), ph; PREP AND PEP(1928), ph; PROTECTION(1929), ph
Joseph A. Valentine
SPEAKEASY(1929), ph; WHAT PRICE INNOCENCE?(1933), ph; MYRT AND MARGE(1934), ph; REMEMBER LAST NIGHT(1935), ph; SWELL-HEAD(1935), ph
Silents
NEWS PARADE, THE(1928), ph
June Valentine
WRITTEN ON THE WIND(1956)
Karen Valentine
FOREVER YOUNG, FOREVER FREE(1976, South Afr.); HOT LEAD AND COLD FEET(1978); NORTH AVENUE IRREGULARS, THE(1979)
Leila Valentine
Misc. Silents
PASSERS-BY(1920)
Lew Valentine
SWING IT SOLDIER(1941)
Louiszita Valentine
Misc. Silents
GAUNTLET, THE(1920); MR. POTTER OF TEXAS(1922)
Louizetta Valentine
Misc. Silents
MYSTERY OF NO. 47, THE(1917)
Nancy Valentine
GIRL FROM JONES BEACH, THE(1949); WHIRLPOOL(1949); FATHER OF THE BRIDE(1950); FATHER'S LITTLE DIVIDEND(1951); BLACK CASTLE, THE(1952); SMALL TOWN GIRL(1953); –30–(1959); TESS OF THE STORM COUNTRY(1961)
Paul Valentine
OUT OF THE PAST(1947); HOUSE OF STRANGERS(1949); LOVE HAPPY(1949); SPECIAL AGENT(1949); LOVE ISLAND(1952); SOMETHING TO LIVE FOR(1952); PENNIES FROM HEAVEN(1981); TRUE CONFESSIONS(1981)
1984
AGAINST ALL ODDS(1984); LOVELINES(1984)
Richard Valentine
GIT!(1965)
Val Valentine
ALF'S CARPET(1929, Brit.), w; COMPULSORY HUSBAND, THE(1930, Brit.), w; KISS ME, SERGEANT(1930, Brit.), w; SONG OF SOHO(1930, Brit.), w; WHY SAILORS LEAVE HOME(1930, Brit.), w; YELLOW MASK, THE(1930, Brit.), w; COMPROMISED!(1931, Brit.), w; LOVE HABIT, THE(1931, Brit.), w; OLD SOLDIERS NEVER DIE(1931, Brit.), w; POOR OLD BILL(1931, Brit.), w; VAGABOND QUEEN, THE(1931, Brit.), w; MY WIFE'S FAMILY(1932, Brit.), w; RICH AND STRANGE(1932, Brit.), w; CAPTAIN BILL(1935, Brit.), w; EXCUSE MY GLOVE(1936, Brit.), w; CAFE COLETTE(1937, Brit.), w; GIRL IN THE TAXI(1937, Brit.), w; HIGH COMMAND(1938, Brit.), w; SMILING ALONG(1938, Brit.), w; COME ON GEORGE(1939, Brit.), w; GASBAGS(1940, Brit.), w; SHIPYARD SALLY(1940, Brit.), w; BALLOON GOES UP, THE(1942, Brit.), w; UP WITH THE LARK(1943, Brit.), w; WE DIVE AT DAWN(1943, Brit.), w; I'LL BE YOUR SWEETHEART(1945, Brit.), w; NOTORIOUS GENTLEMAN(1945, Brit.), w; THIS MAN IS MINE(1946 Brit.), w; FORBIDDEN(1949, Brit.), w; THIS WAS A WOMAN(1949, Brit.), w; WATERLOO ROAD(1949, Brit.), w; OLD MOTHER RILEY'S JUNGLE TREASURE(1951, Brit.), w; MISS ROBIN HOOD(1952, Brit.), w; RINGER, THE(1953, Brit.), w; BELLES OF ST. TRINIAN'S, THE(1954, Brit.), w; CONSTANT HUSBAND, THE(1955, Brit.), w; LADY GODIVA RIDES AGAIN(1955, Brit.), w; SEE HOW THEY RUN(1955, Brit.), w; THEY CAN'T HANG ME(1955, Brit.), w; WICKED WIFE(1955, Brit.), w; SHE PLAYED WITH FIRE(1957, Brit.), w; BLUE MURDER AT ST. TRINIAN'S(1958, Brit.), w; LEFT, RIGHT AND CENTRE(1959), w; PURE HELL OF ST. TRINIAN'S, THE(1961, Brit.), w; WEEKEND WITH LULU, A(1961, Brit.), w; FRIENDS AND NEIGHBORS(1963, Brit.), w; MY SON, THE VAMPIRE(1963, Brit.), w
Vangie Valentine
Misc. Silents
WHEN BEARCAT WENT DRY(1919)
Giorgio Valentini
ALLEGRO NON TROPPO(1977, Ital.), anim
Vincent Valentini
CONVICT'S CODE(1930), w; WAR IS A RACKET(1934), w; BOY! WHAT A GIRL!(1947), w; SEPIA CINDERELLA(1947), w; MIRACLE IN HARLEM(1948), w
Valentino
MAFIA, THE(1972, Arg.), makeup; NIGHT WATCH(1973, Brit.), cos; LITTLE GIRL WHO LIVES DOWN THE LANE, THE(1977, Can.), cos

Albert Valentino
Misc. Silents
CHINA SLAVER(1929)
Alfred Valentino
ONE RAINY AFTERNOON(1936)
Hugo Valentino
TABLE FOR FIVE(1983)
Jean Acker Valentino
SOMETHING TO LIVE FOR(1952)
Pat Valentino
GLORY ALLEY(1952)
Patrick Valentino
ESCAPE FROM ALCATRAZ(1979)
Pedro Valentino
SATURDAY NIGHT AT THE BATHS(1975)
Rudolph Valentino
Silents
ALL NIGHT(1918); OUT OF LUCK(1919); CONQUERING POWER, THE(1921); FOUR HORSEMEN OF THE APOCALYPSE, THE(1921); SHEIK, THE(1921); BEYOND THE ROCKS(1922); BLOOD AND SAND(1922); MORAN OF THE LADY LETTY(1922); MONSIEUR BEAUCAIRE(1924); SAINTED DEVIL, A(1924); COBRA(1925); EAGLE, THE(1925); SON OF THE SHEIK(1926)
Misc. Silents
SOCIETY SENSATION, A(1918); BIG LITTLE PERSON, THE(1919); DELICIOUS LITTLE DEVIL, THE(1919); STOLEN MOMENTS(1920); WONDERFUL CHANCE, THE(1920); CAMILLE(1921); UNCHARTED SEAS(1921); ISLE OF LOVE, THE(1922); YOUNG RAHAH, THE(1922)
Thomas J. Valentino
SATAN'S BED(1965), m
Lili Valenty
WILD IS THE WIND(1957); IN LOVE AND WAR(1958); SPARTACUS(1960); STORY OF RUTH, THE(1960); GIRLS! GIRLS! GIRLS!(1962); IT HAPPENED IN ATHENS(1962); ROME ADVENTURE(1962); BABY MAKER, THE(1970); TELL ME A RIDDLE(1980)
David Valenza
1984
FOOTLOOSE(1984)
Tasia Valenza
1984
CRACKERS(1984)
Carlo Valenzano
LEOPARD, THE(1963, Ital.)
Mariano Valenzuala
UNDER THE PAMPAS MOON(1935)
Rose Marie Valenzuea
GIRL ON THE BRIDGE, THE(1951)
Albert Valenzuela
ONCE UPON A SCOUNDREL(1973), ed
Albert E. Valenzuela
LITTLE SAVAGE, THE(1959), ed
Alberto Valenzuela
ADVENTURES OF ROBINSON CRUSOE, THE(1954), ed; SEPTEMBER STORM(1960), ed; GINA(1961, Fr./Mex.), ed
Laura Valenzuela
MADAME(1963, Fr./Ital./Span.)
M. Valerbe
MOULIN ROUGE(1952)
Jean Valere
TIME OUT FOR LOVE(1963, Ital./Fr.), d, w
Simone Valere
BEAUTY AND THE DEVIL(1952, Fr./Ital.); GRAND MANEUVER, THE(1956, Fr.); GERMINAL(1963, Fr.); ASSASSINATION OF TROTSKY, THE(1972 Fr./Ital.); COP, A(1973, Fr.); DIRTY MONEY(1977, Fr.)
Franca Valeri
SIGN OF VENUS, THE(1955, Ital.), a, w; LOVE SPECIALIST, THE(1959, Ital.); ROCCO AND HIS BROTHERS(1961, Fr./Ital.); AND SUDDENLY IT'S MURDER!(1964, Ital.); MORALIST, THE(1964, Ital.); VARIETY LIGHTS(1965, Ital.); LISTEN, LET'S MAKE LOVE(1969, Fr./Ital.), a, w
Marcella Valeri
FROM A ROMAN BALCONY(1961, Fr./Ital.); LA NOTTE BRAVA(1962, Fr./Ital.); LA VIACCIA(1962, Fr./Ital.); ANZIO(1968, Ital.)
Valerio Valeri
KILL BABY KILL(1966, Ital.)
Babs Valerie
MAN IN GREY, THE(1943, Brit.); HONEYMOON HOTEL(1946, Brit.)
Gertrude Valerie
DEAD END(1937); LIFE WITH FATHER(1947); UNCONQUERED(1947)
Gladys Valerie
Misc. Silents
MRS. WIGGS OF THE CABBAGE PATCH(1919); HIDDEN LIGHT(1920); PASTE-BOARD CROWN, A(1922)
Jeanne Valerie
HERCULES' PILLS(1960, Ital.); FROM A ROMAN BALCONY(1961, Fr./Ital.); GAME OF TRUTH, THE(1961, Fr.); LES LIAISONS DANGEREUSES(1961, Fr./Ital.); WEB OF PASSION(1961, Fr.); LOVES OF SALAMMBO, THE(1962, Fr./Ital.); ADORABLE JULIA(1964, Fr./Aust.); LET'S TALK ABOUT WOMEN(1964, Fr./Ital.); RED LIPS(1964, Fr./Ital.); WHITE VOICES(1965, Fr./Ital.); HIRED KILLER, THE(1967, Fr./Ital.)
Joan Valerie
KENTUCKY(1938); ROAD DEMON(1938); SUBMARINE PATROL(1938); TRIP TO PARIS, A(1938); DAY-TIME WIFE(1939); TAIL SPIN(1939); CHARLIE CHAN AT THE WAX MUSEUM(1940); FREE, BLONDE AND 21(1940); GIRL IN 313(1940); GREAT PROFILE, THE(1940); KILLERS OF THE WILD(1940); LILLIAN RUSSELL(1940); MAN WHO WOULDN'T TALK, THE(1940); MICHAEL SHAYNE, PRIVATE DETECTIVE(1940); MURDER OVER NEW YORK(1940); PIER 13(1940); YOUNG AS YOU FEEL(1940); JENNIE(1941); JUST OFF BROADWAY(1942); RIO RITA(1942); WHO IS HOPE SCHUYLER?(1942); AROUND THE WORLD(1943); GOVERNMENT GIRL(1943); HUCKSTERS, THE(1947); THREE DARING DAUGHTERS(1948); MISTER 880(1950); FATHER TAKES THE AIR(1951); ROARING CITY(1951); GIRL IN WHITE, THE(1952)

Olive Valerie
Silents
RED HOT ROMANCE(1922)
Simone Valerie
GAME IS OVER, THE(1967, Fr.)
Joan Valeries
LIFE OF HER OWN, A(1950)
Tonino Valerii
PRICE OF POWER, THE(1969, Ital./Span.), d; DAY OF ANGER(1970, Ital./Ger.), d, w; MY NAME IS NOBODY(1974, Ital./Fr./Ger.), d; REASON TO LIVE, A REASON TO DIE, A(1974, Ital./Fr./Ger./Span.), d, w
Albano Valerio
PAN-AMERICANA(1945)
Silents
LOVES OF RICARDO, THE(1926)
Francesca Valerio
1984
HOME FREE ALL(1984)
Joe Valerio
TOWN WITHOUT PITY(1961, Ger./Switz./U.S.)
Jean-Louis Valero
PAULINE AT THE BEACH(1983, Fr.), m
Jose Valero
TOMMY THE TOREADOR(1960, Brit.)
Lucia Valero
LT. ROBIN CRUSOE, U.S.N.(1966)
Maria Jose Valero
HOUSE THAT SCREAMED, THE(1970, Span.)
Valerskaya
Misc. Silents
KIRA KIRALINA(1927, USSR)
Valery
PARISIAN, THE(1931, Fr.)
Ann Valery
MARRY ME!(1949, Brit.); STOP PRESS GIRL(1949, Brit.); KING OF THE UNDER-WORLD(1952, Brit.)
Anne Valery
KIND HEARTS AND CORONETS(1949, Brit.); WHAT THE BUTLER SAW(1950, Brit.); ONE WAY OUT(1955, Brit.)
Jean Valery
Misc. Talkies
NO DIAMONDS FOR URSULA(1967)
Olga Valery
ANASTASIA(1956); LOVE IN THE AFTERNOON(1957); PARIS DOES STRANGE THINGS(1957, Fr./Ital.); LOVE IS A BALL(1963); ONLY GAME IN TOWN, THE(1970)
Vales
LET FREEDOM RING(1939), cos
Lizalotta Valesca
THIS ISLAND EARTH(1955)
Palace Valet
STORY OF VICKIE, THE(1958, Aust.)
Rosa Valette
BLUE ANGEL, THE(1930, Ger.)
Lisl Valetti
I MARRIED AN ANGEL(1942); ABOVE SUSPICION(1943)
Rosa Valetti
BARBERINA(1932, Ger.); M(1933, Ger.); LILIOM(1935, Fr.)
Z. Valevskaya
Misc. Silents
CURSED MILLIONS(1917, USSR)
Kippee Valez
BRUTE FORCE(1947); MEXICAN HAYRIDE(1948); CRISS CROSS(1949); DARING CABALLERO, THE(1949); MILKMAN, THE(1950); SOUTHSIDE 1-1000(1950)
Lupe Valez
MEXICAN SPITFIRE'S ELEPHANT(1942)
Martin Valez
SONG OF THE LOON(1970)
Mario Valgoi
MAN CALLED SLEDGE, A(1971, Ital.)
Robert Valgova
DRIVE-IN(1976)
Valia
Silents
GREEN CARAVAN, THE(1922, Brit.); PASSIONATE FRIENDS, THE(1922, Brit.); AUDACIOUS MR. SQUIRE, THE(1923, Brit.); GAMBLE WITH HEARTS, A(1923, Brit.); IN THE BLOOD(1923, Brit.); SLAVES OF DESTINY(1924, Brit.)
Misc. Silents
FRUITFUL VINE, THE(1921, Brit.); LITTLE BROTHER OF GOD(1922, Brit.); SHIFTING SANDS(1922, Brit.); STARLIT GARDEN, THE(1923, Brit.); WOMAN WHO OBEYED, THE(1923, Brit.); GREAT PRINCE SHAN, THE(1924, Brit.)
Ladislaus Valicek
SEVEN DARING GIRLS(1962, Ger.), makeup
Jacques Valin
MAN WHO LOVED WOMEN, THE(1983), set d
Joe Valino
COMMITMENT, THE(1976)
Andre Valio-Cavaglione
FANTASTIC PLANET(1973, Fr./Czech.), p
Andre Valiquette
1984
MISUNDERSTOOD(1984)
Jean Valjean
SPANISH MAIN, THE(1945)
Frederick Valk
GASBAGS(1940, Brit.); NEUTRAL PORT(1941, Brit.); SUICIDE SQUADRON(1942, Brit.); YOUNG MR. PITT, THE(1942, Brit.); THUNDER ROCK(1944, Brit.); DEAD OF NIGHT(1946, Brit.); FRENZY(1946, Brit.); HOTEL RESERVE(1946, Brit.); PATIENT VANISHES, THE(1947, Brit.); DEAR MR. PROHACK(1949, Brit.); SARABAND(1949, Brit.); MRS. FITZHERBERT(1950, Brit.); OUTCAST OF THE ISLANDS(1952, Brit.); ALBERT, R.N.(1953, Brit.); BAD BLONDE(1953, Brit.); MR. POTTS GOES TO MOS-

COW(1953, Brit.); NEVER LET ME GO(1953, U.S./Brit.); COLDITZ STORY, THE(1955, Brit.); I AM A CAMERA(1955, Brit.); SECRET VENTURE(1955, Brit.); MAGIC FIRE(1956); ZARAK(1956, Brit.); PORTRAIT IN SMOKE(1957, Brit.)

Frederick [Fritz] Valk
NIGHT TRAIN(1940, Brit.)

Fritz [Frederick] Valk
TORSO MURDER MYSTERY, THE(1940, Brit.)

Yvonne Valkenberg
SPETTERS(1983, Holland)

Nicholas Valkenburg
LORD OF THE FLIES(1963, Brit.)

Patrick Valkenburg
LORD OF THE FLIES(1963, Brit.)

Helen Valkis
BLAZING SIXES(1937); CHEROKEE STRIP(1937); CONFESSION(1937); GO-GETTER, THE(1937); IT'S LOVE I'M AFTER(1937); PRINCE AND THE PAUPER, THE(1937); TALENT SCOUT(1937); OLD BARN DANCE, THE(1938); SERGEANT MURPHY(1938)

Valkyra
Misc. Talkies
NOT TONIGHT HENRY(1961)

Valkyrien
Misc. Silents
IMAGE MAKER, THE(1917)

Miss Valkyrien
Misc. Silents
UNWELCOME MOTHER, THE(1916)

Mme. Valkyrien [Baroness Dewitz]
Misc. Silents
HIDDEN VALLEY, THE(1916)

Valda Valkyrien
Misc. Silents
MAGDA(1917); HUNS WIHIN OUR GATES(1918)

Bengt V. Vall
VIBRATION(1969, Swed.), w

David Valla
INADMISSIBLE EVIDENCE(1968, Brit.)

Kitty Vallacher
GRAVE OF THE VAMPIRE(1972)
Misc. Talkies
TO HELL YOU PREACH(1972); LEGEND OF FRANK WOODS, THE(1977)

Richard Valladeres
KING OF THE GYPSIES(1978)

Louise Vallance
Misc. Talkies
FALCON'S GOLD(1982)

Rose Valland
TRAIN, THE(1965, Fr./Ital./U.S.), w

Saverio Vallane
GRIM REAPER, THE(1981, Ital.)

Mary Vallange
WILLIAM COMES TO TOWN(1948, Brit.); MISS PILGRIM'S PROGRESS(1950, Brit.)

David Vallard
COLONEL EFFINGHAM'S RAID(1945)

Andre Vallardy
DON'T PLAY WITH MARTIANS(1967, Fr.)

Vic Vallaro
SHAME, SHAME, EVERYBODY KNOWS HER NAME(1969); FORTUNE, THE(1975)

Valle
BASHFUL ELEPHANT, THE(1962, Aust.)

Alfonso Castro Valle
1984
UNDER THE VOLCANO(1984)

Brad Della Valle
SONG OF THE LOON(1970)

Felix Valle
Silents
PLASTIC AGE, THE(1925); GIRL IN EVERY PORT, A(1928)

Jack Valle
HARD ROAD, THE(1970)

Marcel Valle
CAFE DE PARIS(1938, Fr.)

Mary Jane Valle
HONEYSUCKLE ROSE(1980)

Ricardo Valle
ALEXANDER THE GREAT(1956); AWFUL DR. ORLOFF, THE(1964, Span./Fr.); HERCULES AGAINST THE SONS OF THE SUN(1964, Span./Ital.); ISLAND OF THE DOOMED(1968, Span./Ger.)

Riccardo Valle
HEAD OF A TYRANT(1960, Fr./Ital.)

Sandra Della Valle
HILDUR AND THE MAGICIAN(1969)

Fred Valleca
VALACHI PAPERS, THE(1972, Ital./Fr.)

Maine Vallee
JOUR DE FETE(1952, Fr.)

Marcel Vallee
TOPAZE(1935, Fr.); CINDERELLA(1937, Fr.); FRIC FRAC(1939, FR.); WITH A SMILE(1939, Fr.); HONEYMOON HOTEL(1946, Brit.); MONSIEUR VINCENT(1949, Fr.)
Misc. Silents
PARIS QUI DORT(1924, Fr.)

Mary Vallee
YOUNGEST PROFESSION, THE(1943)

Rudy Vallee
VAGABOND LOVER(1929); INTERNATIONAL HOUSE(1933); GEORGE WHITE'S SCANDALS(1934); SWEET MUSIC(1935); GOLD DIGGERS IN PARIS(1938); SECOND FIDDLE(1939); TIME OUT FOR RHYTHM(1941); TOO MANY BLONDES(1941); PALM BEACH STORY, THE(1942); HAPPY GO LUCKY(1943); IT'S IN THE BAG(1945); MAN ALIVE(1945); PEOPLE ARE FUNNY(1945); FABULOUS SUZANNE, THE(1946);

BACHELOR AND THE BOBBY-SOXER, THE(1947); I REMEMBER MAMA(1948); MY DEAR SECRETARY(1948); SO THIS IS NEW YORK(1948); UNFAITHFULLY YOURS(1948); BEAUTIFUL BLONDE FROM BASHFUL BEND, THE(1949); FATHER WAS A FULLBACK(1949); MOTHER IS A FRESHMAN(1949); ADMIRAL WAS A LADY, THE(1950); MAD WEDNESDAY(1950); RICOCHET ROMANCE(1954); GENTLEMEN MARRY BRUNETTES(1955); HELEN MORGAN STORY, THE(1959); LIVE A LITTLE, LOVE A LITTLE(1968); NIGHT THEY RAIDED MINSKY'S, THE(1968); PHYNX, THE(1970); HOW TO SUCCEED IN BUSINESS WITHOUT REALLY TRYING(1976); WON TON TON, THE DOG WHO SAVED HOLLYWOOD(1976)
Misc. Talkies
SUNBURST(1975)

Augie Vallejo
J.W. COOP(1971)

E. J. Vallejo
Silents
MILLIONAIRE, THE(1921), ph; DON Q, SON OF ZORRO(1925), ph

Enrico Vallejo
Silents
RAMONA(1916), ph

Harry Vallejo
Silents
ROMANCE OF TARZAN, THE(1918), ph; TARZAN OF THE APES(1918), ph; RIDERS OF THE DAWN(1920), ph; KILLER, THE(1921), ph; RAGE OF PARIS, THE(1921), ph

Jim Vallely
1984
ROSEBUD BEACH HOTEL(1984)

Hermann Vallentin
CAPTAIN FROM KOEPENICK(1933, Ger.)

Valles
LADY OF THE TROPICS(1939), cos; MAISIE(1939), cos; STAND UP AND FIGHT(1939), cos; THUNDER AFLOAT(1939), cos; WYOMING(1940), cos; HER HIGHNESS AND THE BELLBOY(1945), cos; HARVEY GIRLS, THE(1946), cos; HOODLUM SAINT, THE(1946), cos; THREE WISE FOOLS(1946), cos; TILL THE CLOUDS ROLL BY(1946), cos; TWO SMART PEOPLE(1946), cos; GOOD NEWS(1947), cos; GREEN DOLPHIN STREET(1947), cos; SONG OF LOVE(1947), cos; SOUTHERN YANKEE, A(1948), cos; TAKE ME OUT TO THE BALL GAME(1949), cos; THAT FORSYTE WOMAN(1949), cos; KIM(1950), cos; MALAYA(1950), cos

Arlington Valles
ADVENTURES OF CAPTAIN FABIAN(1951), cos

Carlos Valles
HONEY POT, THE(1967, Brit.); IDENTIFICATION OF A WOMAN(1983, Ital.)

Dave Valles
HOT FOR PARIS(1930)

F. Arlington Valles
SWORD AND THE ROSE, THE(1953), cos

Irene Valles
DRAGON SEED(1944), cos; EASTER PARADE(1948), cos; GREAT SINNER, THE(1949), cos

J. Arlington Valles
SPARTACUS(1960), cos

Al Valletta
1984
ALLEY CAT(1984), d

Valli
MIRACLE OF THE BELLS, THE(1948); SUBSTITUTION(1970), makeup

Alida Valli
BALL AT THE CASTLE(1939, Ital.); SCHOOLGIRL DIARY(1947, Ital.); LAUGH PAGLIACCI(1948, Ital.); THIRD MAN, THE(1950, Brit.); LOVERS OF TOLEDO, THE(1954, Fr./Span./Ital.); STRANGER'S HAND, THE(1955, Brit.); NIGHT HEAVEN FELL, THE(1958, Fr.); THIS ANGRY AGE(1958, Ital./Fr.); HAPPY THIEVES, THE(1962); HORROR CHAMBER OF DR. FAUSTUS, THE(1962, Fr./Ital.); IL GRIDO(1962, U.S./Ital.); LONG ABSENCE, THE(1962, Fr./Ital.); CASTILIAN, THE(1963, Span./U.S.); DISORDER(1964, Fr./Ital.); OPHELIA(1964, Fr.); SENSO(1968, Ital.); DIARY OF AN ITALIAN(1972, Ital.); HOUSE OF EXORCISM, THE(1976, Ital.); 1900(1976, Ital.); CASSANDRA CROSSING, THE(1977); SUSPIRIA(1977, Ital.); TEMPTER, THE(1978, Ital.); LUNA(1979, Ital.); INFERNO(1980, Ital.); THAT HOUSE IN THE OUTSKIRTS(1980, Span.)

[Alida] Valli
PARADINE CASE, THE(1947); WALK SOFTLY, STRANGER(1950); WHITE TOWER, THE(1950)

Federico Valli
JULIET OF THE SPIRITS(1965, Fr./Ital./W.Ger.)

Frankie Valli
SGT. PEPPER'S LONELY HEARTS CLUB BAND(1978)

Joe Valli
HERITAGE(1935, Aus.); FLYING DOCTOR, THE(1936, Aus.); ORPHAN OF THE WILDERNESS(1937, Aus.); TALL TIMBERS(1937, Aus.); WILD INNOCENCE(1937, Aus.); TYPHOON TREASURE(1939, Brit.); FORTY THOUSAND HORSEMEN(1941, Aus.); SMITHY(1946, Aus.)
Misc. Talkies
LET GEORGE DO IT(1938, Aus.)

Marie Valli
MADAME SATAN(1930)

Roberta Valli
8 ½(1963, Ital.)

Romolo Valli
FIVE BRANDED WOMEN(1960); GIRL WITH A SUITCASE(1961, Fr./Ital.); GREAT WAR, THE(1961, Fr., Ital.); BOCCACCIO '70(1962/Ital./Fr.); LA VIACCIA(1962, Fr./Ital.); LEOPARD, THE(1963, Ital.); SWEET AND SOUR(1964, Fr./Ital.); VISIT, THE(1964, Ger./Fr./Ital./U.S.); MANDRAGOLA(1966 Fr./Ital.); BOOM!(1968); DROP DEAD, MY LOVE(1968, Italy); DEATH IN VENICE(1971, Ital./Fr.); DUCK, YOU SUCKER!(1972, Ital.); CHE?(1973, Ital./Fr./Ger.); GARDEN OF THE FINZI-CONTINIS, THE(1976, Ital./Ger.); 1900(1976, Ital.); BOBBY DEERFIELD(1977); CHOSEN, THE(1978, Brit./Ital.); WOMANLIGHT(1979, Fr./Ger./Ital.); CLAIR DE FEMME(1980,Fr.)

Valli Valli
Misc. Silents
HIGH ROAD, THE(1915); WOMAN PAYS, THE(1915); HER DEBT OF HONOR(1916); TURMOIL, THE(1916)

Virginia Valli
ISLE OF LOST SHIPS(1929); MISTER ANTONIO(1929); GUILTY?(1930); LOST ZEPPELIN(1930); NIGHT LIFE IN RENO(1931)
Silents
EFFICIENCY EDGAR'S COURTSHIP(1917); IDLE RICH, THE(1921); LOVE'S PENALTY(1921); MAN WHO, THE(1921); SILVER LINING, THE(1921); RIGHT THAT FAILED, THE(1922); STORM, THE(1922); TRACKED TO EARTH(1922); SHOCK, THE(1923); K–THE UNKNOWN(1924); SIGNAL TOWER, THE(1924); PLEASURE GARDEN, THE(1925, Brit./Ger.); WATCH YOUR WIFE(1926); EVENING CLOTHES(1927); JUDGMENT OF THE HILLS(1927); LADIES MUST DRESS(1927); STAGE MADNESS(1927); ESCAPE, THE(1928)
Misc. Silents
FIBBERS, THE(1917); GOLDEN IDIOT, THE(1917); RUGGLES OF RED GAP(1918); UNEASY MONEY(1918); BLACK CIRCLE, THE(1919); COMMON SIN, THE(1920); PLUNGER, THE(1920); VERY IDEA, THE(1920); DEVIL WITHIN, THE(1921); TRIP TO PARADISE, A(1921); BLACK BAG, THE(1922); HIS BACK AGAINST THE WALL(1922); VILLAGE BLACKSMITH, THE(1922); CONFIDENCE MAN, THE(1924); LADY OF QUALITY, A(1924); WILD ORANGES(1924); LADY WHO LIED, THE(1925); MAN WHO FOUND HIMSELF, THE(1925); PRICE OF PLEASURE, THE(1925); SIEGE(1925); UP THE LADDER(1925); FAMILY UPSTAIRS, THE(1926); FLAMES(1926); EAST SIDE, WEST SIDE(1927); MARRIAGE(1927); PAID TO LOVE(1927); STREET OF ILLUSION, THE(1928); BEHIND CLOSED DOORS(1929); LOST ZEPPELIN, THE(1929)

Sonny Vallie
THREE RING CIRCUS(1954)

Helen Vallier
LOVE AND DEATH(1975)

Helene Vallier
SAADIA(1953); CHANEL SOLITAIRE(1981)

Xavier Vallier
GIRL IN THE BIKINI, THE(1958, Fr.), w; GIRL CAN'T STOP, THE(1966, Fr./Gr.), w

Archie Valliere
JAWS 3-D(1983)

Renee Valliers
DON QUIXOTE(1935, Fr.)

Katherine Vallin
1984
HIGHWAY TO HELL(1984), prod d; RUNNING HOT(1984), prod d

Michael Vallin
DAWN EXPRESS, THE(1942)

Ric Vallin
SLEEPYTIME GAL(1942); YOUTH ON PARADE(1943); RAIDERS OF OLD CALIFORNIA(1957); TIJUANA STORY, THE(1957)

Rick Vallin
DRAMATIC SCHOOL(1938); KING OF THE STALLIONS(1942); SECRETS OF A CO-ED(1942); CLANCY STREET BOYS(1943); CORREGIDOR(1943); GHOSTS ON THE LOOSE(1943); ISLE OF FORGOTTEN SINS(1943); LADY FROM CHUNGKING(1943); NEARLY EIGHTEEN(1943); RIDERS OF THE RIO GRANDE(1943); SMART GUY(1943); WAGON TRACKS WEST(1943); ARMY WIVES(1944); DANGEROUS MONEY(1946); SECRETS OF A SORORITY GIRL(1946); LAST OF THE REDMEN(1947); NORTHWEST OUTPOST(1947); TWO BLONDES AND A REDHEAD(1947); JUNGLE JIM(1948); SHAMROCK HILL(1949); TUNA CLIPPER(1949); CAPTIVE GIRL(1950); COMMANCHE TERRITORY(1950); COUNTERSPY MEETS SCOTLAND YARD(1950); KILLER SHARK(1950); REVENUE AGENT(1950); RIO GRANDE PATROL(1950); SNOW DOG(1950); STATE PENITENTIARY(1950); HURRICANE ISLAND(1951); JUNGLE MANHUNT(1951); MAGIC CARPET, THE(1951); WHEN THE REDSKINS RODE(1951); ALADDIN AND HIS LAMP(1952); STRANGE FASCINATION(1952); VOODOO TIGER(1952); WOMAN IN THE DARK(1952); FIGHTING LAWMAN, THE(1953); HOMESTEADERS, THE(1953); MARKSMAN, THE(1953); SALOME(1953); STAR OF TEXAS(1953); TOPEKA(1953); GOLDEN IDOL, THE(1954); MA AND PA KETTLE AT HOME(1954); THUNDER PASS(1954); AT GUNPOINT(1955); BOWERY TO BAGDAD(1955); DIAL RED O(1955); SCARLET COAT, THE(1955); TREASURE OF RUBY HILLS(1955); FIGHTING TROUBLE(1956); FRONTIER GAMBLER(1956); NAKED GUN, THE(1956); STORM RIDER, THE(1957); BULLWHIP(1958); ESCAPE FROM RED ROCK(1958); PIER 5, HAVANA(1959)

Ricki Vallin
NIGHT FOR CRIME, A(1942); PANTHER'S CLAW, THE(1942)

Bob Vallis
Silents
PLACE OF HONOUR, THE(1921, Brit.); FORBIDDEN CARGOES(1925, Brit.)
Misc. Silents
PEACEMAKER, THE(1922, Brit.)

Jane Vallis
PICNIC AT HANGING ROCK(1975, Aus.)

Robert Vallis
Silents
KILTIES THREE(1918, Brit.); AMAZING PARTNERSHIP, THE(1921, Brit.); GENERAL JOHN REGAN(1921, Brit.); BEAUTIFUL KITTY(1923, Brit.); NOT FOR SALE(1924, Brit.); SQUIBS' HONEYMOON(1926, Brit.)

Kay Vallon
DOWN TO EARTH(1947)

Lilya Vallon
HOTEL VARIETY(1933)

Michael Vallon
DEATH RIDES THE RANGE(1940); BOSS OF BULLION CITY(1941); BOSS OF HANGTOWN MESA(1942); LITTLE JOE, THE WRANGLER(1942); SILVER BULLET, THE(1942); BAD MEN OF THUNDER GAP(1943); BORDER BUCKAROOS(1943); HI'YA, CHUM(1943); LONE STAR TRAIL, THE(1943); OLD CHISHOLM TRAIL(1943); RAIDERS OF SAN JOAQUIN(1943); GIRL RUSH(1944); GUNSMOKE MESA(1944); MARSHAL OF GUNSMOKE(1944); TRIGGER TRAIL(1944); GANGSTER, THE(1947); TREASURE OF MONTE CRISTO(1949); TUNA CLIPPER(1949); TARNISHED(1950); SWORD OF MONTE CRISTO, THE(1951); BARBED WIRE(1952); CONFIDENCE GIRL(1952); PRISONER OF ZENDA, THE(1952); REBEL CITY(1953); TOPEKA(1953); BLACK WIDOW(1954); ABBOTT AND COSTELLO MEET THE MUMMY(1955); GUN BATTLE AT MONTEREY(1957); LOOKING FOR DANGER(1957); PURPLE GANG, THE(1960)

Mike Vallon
FRONTIER LAW(1943); JOHNNY DOESN'T LIVE HERE ANY MORE(1944); SNOW-FIRE(1958)

Nanette Vallon
WITHOUT RESERVATIONS(1946); BROTHER ORCHID(1940); MY LOVE CAME BACK(1940); THEY MET IN BOMBAY(1941); MAN WHO CAME TO DINNER, THE(1942); THIS LOVE OF OURS(1945); THREE'S A CROWD(1945); DRAGONWYCH(1946); GAS HOUSE KIDS(1946); SMASH-UP, THE STORY OF A WOMAN(1947)
Misc. Talkies
LOVE IN HIGH GEAR(1932)

Nenette Vallon
LOVES OF CARMEN, THE(1948)

John Vallone
STAR TREK: THE MOTION PICTURE(1979), art d; SOUTHERN COMFORT(1981), prod d; 48 HOURS(1982), prod d; BRAINSTORM(1983), prod d
1984
STREETS OF FIRE(1984), prod d

Raf Vallone
BITTER RICE(1950, Ital.); ANNA(1951, Ital.); WHITE LINE, THE(1952, Ital.); STRANGE DECEPTION(1953, Ital.); ANITA GARIBALDI(1954, Ital.); DAUGHTERS OF DESTINY(1954, Fr./Ital.); OBSESSION(1954, Fr./Ital.); SIGN OF VENUS, THE(1955, Ital.); ADULTERESS, THE(1959, Fr.); SINS OF ROSE BERND, THE(1959, Ger.); EL CID(1961, U.S./Ital.); TWO WOMEN(1961, Ital./Fr.); PHAEDRA(1962, U.S./Gr./Fr.); VIEW FROM THE BRIDGE, A(1962, Fr./Ital.); CARDINAL, THE(1963); SECRET INVASION, THE(1964); HARLOW(1965); NEVADA SMITH(1966); KISS THE GIRLS AND MAKE THEM DIE(1967, U.S./Ital.); DESPERATE ONES, THE(1968 U.S./Span.); ITALIAN JOB, THE(1969, Brit.); CANNON FOR CORDOBA(1970); DEATH TOOK PLACE LAST NIGHT(1970, Ital./Ger.); KREMLIN LETTER, THE(1970); GUNFIGHT, A(1971); SUMMERTIME KILLER(1973); HUMAN FACTOR, THE(1975); ROSEBUD(1975); THAT LUCKY TOUCH(1975, Brit.); OTHER SIDE OF MIDNIGHT, THE(1977); GREEK TYCOON, THE(1978); ALMOST PERFECT AFFAIR, AN(1979); LION OF THE DESERT(1981, Libya/Brit.); TIME TO DIE, A(1983)

Saverio Vallone
PASSION OF LOVE(1982, Ital./Fr.)

Paul Vally
ZAZIE(1961, Fr.); THIEF OF PARIS, THE(1967, Fr./Ital.)

Valma
DIARY OF A MAD HOUSEWIFE(1970)

Lillian Valmar
MASTER OF HORROR(1965, Arg.)

Valme and Terzolli
GIFT, THE(1983, Fr./Ital.), w

Jean Valmence
CATHERINE & CO.(1976, Fr.)

Jean Valmont
IS PARIS BURNING?(1966, U.S./Fr.); HORNET'S NEST(1970); CHANEL SOLITAIRE(1981)

Vera Valmont
CASINO DE PARIS(1957, Fr./Ger.); SEPTEMBER STORM(1960)

Andre Valmy
MANON(1950, Fr.); SECRET DOCUMENT – VIENNA(1954, Fr.); SLEEPING CAR MURDER THE(1966, Fr.)

Roger Valmy
TO HAVE AND HAVE NOT(1944); RAZOR'S EDGE, THE(1946); JUMP INTO HELL(1955)

Ruth Valmy
PRINCESS AND THE PIRATE, THE(1944); SHOW BUSINESS(1944); SINCE YOU WENT AWAY(1944); UP IN ARMS(1944); WOMAN IN THE WINDOW, THE(1945); WONDER MAN(1945); KID FROM BOOKLYN, THE(1946); NIGHT IN PARADISE, A(1946)

Karel Valnoha
FIREMAN'S BALL, THE(1968, Czech.)

Lucy Valnor
ETERNAL HUSBAND, THE(1946, Fr.)

Fernand Valois
BRAIN, THE(1969, Fr./US)

Nanette Valone
Silents
LOST LADY, A(1924)

Lina Valonghi
KISS THE OTHER SHEIK(1968, Fr./Ital.)

Francois Valorbe
CLOPORTES(1966, Fr., Ital.); MARCH OR DIE(1977, Brit.)

Bice Valori
ALL THE OTHER GIRLS DO!(1967, Ital.); TAMING OF THE SHREW, THE(1967, U.S./Ital.)

Nora Valsami
STEFANIA(1968, Gr.)

Seven Valsecchi
Misc. Talkies
DAY SANTA CLAUS CRIED, THE(1980)

John Valtenburgs
KEEP MY GRAVE OPEN(1980), ph

Thanassis Valtinas
RECONSTRUCTION OF A CRIME(1970, Ger.), w

Ginette Valton
LOLA(1961, Fr./Ital.)

Pat Valturri
YOUNG, THE EVIL AND THE SAVAGE, THE(1968, Ital.)

Patrizia Valturri
SECRET OF SANTA VITTORIA, THE(1969)

Josef Valusiak
ADRIFT(1971, Czech.), ed

Vladimir Valutski
TEST OF PILOT PIRX, THE(1978, Pol./USSR), w

John Valva
CLEOPATRA(1963)

Rafael Valverda
QUANDO EL AMOR RIE(1933)

Rafael Justo Valverde
ALL NUDITY SHALL BE PUNISHED(1974, Brazil), ed

Marcello Valvestito
DEVIL IN LOVE, THE(1968, Ital.), ed
Valy
TOGETHER(1956, Brit.)
Rose Valyda
EAST SIDE OF HEAVEN(1939)
Vampira
BEAT GENERATION, THE(1959); SEX KITTENS GO TO COLLEGE(1960)
Vampira [Maila Nurmi]
PLAN 9 FROM OUTER SPACE(1959)
Albert Van
Misc. Silents
JUST A WIFE(1920)
Allen Van
MACK, THE(1973)
Beatrice Van
MODERN LOVE(1929), w; NO, NO NANETTE(1930), w; TAKE THE HEIR(1930), w; NIGHT OF TERROR(1933), w
Silents
GIRL FROM HIS TOWN, THE(1915); GOOD NIGHT, PAUL(1918); CRASHIN' THRU(1923), w; ANY WOMAN(1925), w; IRRESISTIBLE LOVER, THE(1927), w; SINNER'S PARADE(1928), w; THANKS FOR THE BUGGY RIDE(1928), w
Misc. Silents
PEARL OF PARADISE, THE(1916); HANDS UP(1917); TOLD AT THE TWILIGHT(1917); WHO WAS THE OTHER MAN?(1917); MY UNMARRIED WIFE(1918); DANGEROUS TALENT, THE(1920)
Billy B. Van
Misc. Silents
BEAUTY SHOP, THE(1922)
Bobby Van
BECAUSE YOU'RE MINE(1952); SKIRTS AHOY!(1952); AFFAIRS OF DOBIE GILLIS, THE(1953); KISS ME KATE(1953); SMALL TOWN GIRL(1953); LADIES MAN, THE(1961), ch; IT'S ONLY MONEY(1962), ch; NAVY VS. THE NIGHT MONSTERS, THE(1966); DOOMSDAY MACHINE(1967); LOST HORIZON(1973)
Connie Van
NEVER A DULL MOMENT(1950); SECRET FURY, THE(1950); LONG, LONG TRAILER, THE(1954); FAR COUNTRY, THE(1955)
Frankie Van
KID NIGHTINGALE(1939); LADY'S FROM KENTUCKY, THE(1939); FOOTLIGHT SERENADE(1942); THERE'S ONE BORN EVERY MINUTE(1942); ABBOTT AND COSTELLO MEET THE KILLER, BORIS KARLOFF(1949); DUKE OF CHICAGO(1949); RINGSIDE(1949); ABBOTT AND COSTELLO MEET THE INVISIBLE MAN(1951); SCARLET ANGEL(1952); SQUARE JUNGLE, THE(1955); CURSE OF THE UNDEAD(1959); ROCKY(1976)
Gus Van
THEY LEARNED ABOUT WOMEN(1930); ATLANTIC CITY(1944)
Jean Van
DARK HORSE, THE(1946); LITTLE MISTER JIM(1946); FIESTA(1947); SADDLE PALS(1947)
Le Van
YANK IN VIET-NAM, A(1964)
Paul Van
PROMISES IN THE DARK(1979)
Wally Van
Silents
MAN BEHIND THE DOOR, THE(1914), a, d; COMMON LAW, THE(1923); EAST SIDE-WEST SIDE(1923); SLAVE OF DESIRE(1923)
Misc. Silents
WIN(K)SOME WIDOW, THE (1914); FALSE GODS(1919), d; DRIVIN' FOOL, THE(1923); ROUGH GOING(1925), d
Wilfried van Aacken
BATTLE OF BRITAIN, THE(1969, Brit.)
Robert van Ackeren
JIMMY ORPHEUS(1966, Ger.), ph; QUERELLE(1983, Ger./Fr.)
1984
WOMAN IN FLAMES, A(1984, Ger.), p&d, w
Marlies van Alcmaer
BRIDGE TOO FAR, A(1977, Brit.)
Betty Van Allen
BELOVED BACHELOR, THE(1931)
Egbert Van Alstyne
WAY OUT WEST(1937), m
Fred Van Amburg
RACE FOR YOUR LIFE, CHARLIE BROWN(1977)
Willeke Van Ammelrooy
LIFT, THE(1983, Neth.); OUTSIDER IN AMSTERDAM(1983, Neth.)
Carla Van Amstel
STILL SMOKIN'(1983)
Albert Van Antwerp
JACK LONDON(1943); MASK OF DIMITRIOS, THE(1944); UNCERTAIN GLORY(1944); O.S.S.(1946)
Misc. Silents
CHECHAHCOS, THE(1924)
Joan Van Ark
FROGS(1972)
Butch Van Artsdalen
MUSCLE BEACH PARTY(1964)
Bob van Aspern
CHRONICLE OF ANNA MAGDALENA BACH(1968, Ital., Ger.)
Lee Van Atta
SECOND WIFE(1936); CAPTAINS COURAGEOUS(1937); AFFAIRS OF ANNABEL(1938)
Winfred Van Atta
SHOCK TREATMENT(1964), w
Betty Van Auken
GARDEN OF ALLAH, THE(1936)
Gary Van Auken
ABSENCE OF MALICE(1981)

C.A. Van Auker
Misc. Silents
JACQUES OF THE SILVER NORTH(1919)
Cecil Van Auker
Silents
GIRL OF MY HEART(1920); RAGGED HEIRESS, THE(1922)
Misc. Silents
INTRIGUE(1916); FLAME OF YOUTH(1920); LITTLE WANDERER, THE(1920); CINDERELLA OF THE HILLS(1921); MOTHER HEART, THE(1921); PAYMENT GUARANTEED(1921); UP AND GOING(1922); YOUTH MUST HAVE LOVE(1922)
Billie Van Avery
GODLESS GIRL, THE(1929)
Nico van Baarle
LAST BLITZKRIEG, THE(1958), art d; SPY IN THE SKY(1958), art d
Polly Van Bailey
EGG AND I, THE(1947)
Hans van Beek
SPLITTING UP(1981, Neth.), ed
Tom Van Beek
HIDING PLACE, THE(1975)
Stanley Van Beer
STRANGER FROM VENUS, THE(1954, Brit.)
Anna van Beers
1984
QUESTION OF SILENCE(1984, Neth.)
Stanley Van Beers
VICE VERSA(1948, Brit.); CRY, THE BELOVED COUNTRY(1952, Brit.); FAKE, THE(1953, Brit.); SO LITTLE TIME(1953, Brit.); TERROR SHIP(1954, Brit.); DAM BUSTERS, THE(1955, Brit.); SHADOW OF FEAR(1956, Brit.); THE CREEPING UNKNOWN(1956, Brit.); MAN WITHOUT A BODY, THE(1957, Brit.); ANGRY HILLS, THE(1959, Brit.); LOOK BACK IN ANGER(1959)
Ludwig van Beethoven
FINAL CHORD, THE(1936, Ger.), m; LIFE AND LOVES OF BEETHOVEN, THE(1937, Fr.), m; I'VE ALWAYS LOVED YOU(1946), m; GREAT DAWN, THE(1947, Ital.), m; INTERLUDE(1957), m; ONCE MORE, WITH FEELING(1960), m; FIDELIO(1961, Aust.), w, m; TRUTH, THE(1961, Fr./Ital.), m; WOMAN OF STRAW(1964, Brit.), m; ISADORA(1968, Brit.), m; FIDELIO(1970, Ger.), w, m; TWO OR THREE THINGS I KNOW ABOUT HER(1970, Fr.), m
Ludwig van Beethoven Amilcare Ponchielli
FANTASIA(1940), w
Ingrid van Bergen
ARENT WE WONDERFUL?(1959, Ger.); DEVIL'S DAFFODIL, THE(1961, Brit./Ger.); ROSES FOR THE PROSECUTOR(1961, Ger.); TOWN WITHOUT PITY(1961, Ger./Switz./U.S.); ESCAPE FROM EAST BERLIN(1962); I, TOO, AM ONLY A WOMAN(1963, Ger.); ONLY A WOMAN(1966, Ger.)
Lewis van Bergen
PASSOVER PLOT, THE(1976, Israel); HARD COUNTRY(1981); DEATH VENGEANCE(1982)
R. Van Boolen
13 MEN AND A GUN(1938, Brit.)
Peter Van Boorn
MOVIE STAR, AMERICAN STYLE, OR, LSD I HATE YOU!(1966)
Jane Van Boskirk
HOW TO BEAT THE HIGH COST OF LIVING(1980)
E. Van Bousen
Misc. Silents
FOOTLIGHTS AND SHADOWS(1920)
Henry Van Bousen
Silents
AMERICA(1924)
Misc. Silents
BEWARE OF THE LAW(1922); LONESOME CORNERS(1922)
Steve Van Brandenberg
LAST BLITZKRIEG, THE(1958)
Tony van Bridge
OEDIPUS REX(1957, Can.); IF YOU COULD SEE WHAT I HEAR(1982)
Norman Van Brocklin
LONG GRAY LINE, THE(1955)
lp: Myron Van Brundt
Misc. Talkies
APOCALYPSE 3:16(1964)
Tad Van Brunt
DREAM GIRL(1947); ROAD TO RIO(1947); BIG CLOCK, THE(1948)
A. Van Buren
Silents
CAPTAIN OF THE GRAY HORSE TROOP, THE(1917), w
A.H. Van Buren
PRINCE OF DIAMONDS(1930), d
Misc. Silents
DISTRICT ATTORNEY, THE(1915); VIXEN, THE(1916)
Catherine Van Buren
Misc. Silents
TWO-GUN BETTY(1918)
J. K. Van Buren
Silents
RAIDERS, THE(1921)
Kate Van Buren
Misc. Silents
DOLLAR FOR DOLLAR(1920); SMOULDERING EMBERS(1920)
Kristian Van Buren
HELL'S BELLES(1969)
Kristin Van Buren
STRAWBERRY STATEMENT, THE(1970)
Mabel Van Buren
HIS FIRST COMMAND(1929); NEIGHBORS' WIVES(1933); MISSISSIPPI(1935)
Silents
BREWSTER'S MILLIONS(1914); CIRCUS MAN, THE(1914); DISHONORED MEDAL, THE(1914); MAN FROM HOME, THE(1914); MASTER MIND, THE(1914); GIRL OF THE GOLDEN WEST, THE(1915); SHOULD A WIFE FORGIVE?(1915); WARRENS OF VIRGINIA, THE(1915); WOMAN, THE(1915); RAMONA(1916); THOSE WITHOUT

SIN(1917); HEARTS OF MEN(1919); SINS OF ROZANNE(1920); BIG GAME(1921); FOUR HORSEMEN OF THE APOCALYPSE, THE(1921); WISE FOOL, A(1921); WHILE SATAN SLEEPS(1922); WOMAN WHO WALKED ALONE, THE(1922); YOUTH TO YOUTH(1922); IN SEARCH OF A THRILL(1923); HIS SECRETARY(1925); KING OF KINGS, THE(1927); CRAIG'S WIFE(1928)
Misc. Silents
LOST PARADISE, THE(1914); SOWERS, THE(1916); LOST AND WON(1917); SCHOOL FOR HUSBANDS, A(1917); RIDERS OF THE NIGHT(1918); WINDING TRAIL, THE(1918); CONRAD IN QUEST OF HIS YOUTH(1920); WANDERING DAUGHTERS(1923); MEDDLIN' STRANGER, THE(1927)

Mable Van Buren
Silents
BEYOND THE ROCKS(1922)

Mildred Van Buren
CRUSADES, THE(1935)

Ned Van Buren
Silents
ASHES OF EMBERS(1916), ph; WILD HONEY(1919), ph; SIN THAT WAS HIS, THE(1920), ph; BURN 'EM UP BARNES(1921), ph; CARDIGAN(1922), ph; HAS THE WORLD GONE MAD!(1923), ph

Steve Van Buren
TRIPLE THREAT(1948)

H. Van Busen
Silents
EASY TO GET(1920)

Robert Van Campbell
ROCKERS(1980)

Christian Van Cau
MILKY WAY, THE(1969, Fr./Ital.)

Ben Van Cauwenbergh
NIJINSKY(1980, Brit.)

Catherine van Cauwenberghe
PASSION(1983, Fr./Switz.)

I. Van Charles
WINDSPLITTER, THE(1971)

Nathan Van Cleave
ROBINSON CRUSOE ON MARS(1964), m; PROJECT X(1968), m

Lee Van Cleef
HIGH NOON(1952); KANSAS CITY CONFIDENTIAL(1952); LAWLESS BREED, THE(1952); UNTAMED FRONTIER(1952); ARENA(1953); BANDITS OF CORSICA, THE(1953); BEAST FROM 20,000 FATHOMS, THE(1953); JACK SLADE(1953); NEBRASKAN, THE(1953); PRIVATE EYES(1953); TUMBLEWEED(1953); VICE SQUAD(1953); WHITE LIGHTNING(1953); ARROW IN THE DUST(1954); DAWN AT SOCORRO(1954); DESPERADO, THE(1954); GYPSY COLT(1954); PRINCESS OF THE NILE(1954); RAILS INTO LARAMIE(1954); YELLOW TOMAHAWK, THE(1954); BIG COMBO, THE(1955); I COVER THE UNDERWORLD(1955); MAN ALONE, A(1955); ROAD TO DENVER, THE(1955); TEN WANTED MEN(1955); TREASURE OF RUBY HILLS(1955); VANISHING AMERICAN, THE(1955); ACCUSED OF MURDER(1956); CONQUEROR, THE(1956); IT CONQUERED THE WORLD(1956); PARDNERS(1956); TRIBUTE TO A BADMAN(1956); BADGE OF MARSHAL BRENNAN, THE(1957); CHINA GATE(1957); GUN BATTLE AT MONTEREY(1957); GUNFIGHT AT THE O.K. CORRAL(1957); JOE DAKOTA(1957); LAST STAGECOACH WEST, THE(1957); LONELY MAN, THE(1957); QUIET GUN, THE(1957); RAIDERS OF OLD CALIFORNIA(1957); TIN STAR, THE(1957); BRAVADOS, THE(1958); DAY OF THE BAD MAN(1958); GUNS, GIRLS AND GANGSTERS(1958); MACHETE(1958); YOUNG LIONS, THE(1958); RIDE LONESOME(1959); POSSE FROM HELL(1961); HOW THE WEST WAS WON(1962); MAN WHO SHOT LIBERTY VALANCE, THE(1962); BEYOND THE LAW(1967, Ital.); FOR A FEW DOLLARS MORE(1967, Ital./Ger./Span.); GOOD, THE BAD, AND THE UGLY, THE(1967, Ital./Span.); BIG GUNDOWN, THE(1968, Ital.); DEATH RIDES A HORSE(1969, Ital.); SABATA(1969, Ital.); BARQUERO(1970); DAY OF ANGER(1970, Ital./Ger.); EL CONDOR(1970); CAPTAIN APACHE(1971, Brit.); BAD MAN'S RIVER(1972, Span.); MAGNIFICENT SEVEN RIDE, THE(1972); RETURN OF SABATA(1972, Ital./Fr./Ger.); BLOOD MONEY(1974, U.S./Hong Kong/Ital./Span.); TAKE A HARD RIDE(1975, U.S./Ital.); CRIME BOSS(1976, Ital.); MEAN FRANK AND CRAZY TONY(1976, Ital.); GOD'S GUN(1977); KID VENGEANCE(1977); OCTAGON, THE(1980); SQUEEZE, THE(1980, Ital.); ESCAPE FROM NEW YORK(1981)
Misc. Talkies
PERFECT KILLER, THE(1977, Span.); HARD WAY, THE(1980, Brit.)

Richard Van Cleemput
DESIREE(1954)

Cheryl Van Cleve
1984
NINJA III—THE DOMINATION(1984)

Edith Van Cleve
AGE OF INNOCENCE(1934); HAT, COAT AND GLOVE(1934)

Ron Van Clief
FIST OF FEAR, TOUCH OF DEATH(1980)
Misc. Talkies
SUPER WEAPON, THE(1976)

Charles Van Courtlandt
Silents
INTOLERANCE(1916)

Robert Van Daalen
BLACK VEIL FOR LISA, A(1969 Ital./Ger.)

Edmond van Daele
LA MATERNELLE(1933, Fr.)
Silents
NAPOLEON(1927, Fr.)
Misc. Silents
COEUR FIDELE(1923, Fr.); 6 ½ X 11(1927, Fr.)

Pamela van Dale
HIGH JINKS IN SOCIETY(1949, Brit.)

Josine Van Dalsum
LIFT, THE(1983, Neth.)

Gwen Van Dam
LILITH(1964); HUSBANDS(1970); SECOND-HAND HEARTS(1981); TRUE CONFESSIONS(1981); SECOND THOUGHTS(1983)

Misc. Talkies
CALLIOPE(1971)

Jose Van Dam
DON GIOVANNI(1979, Fr./Ital./Ger.)

Charles Van Damme
BENVENUTA(1983, Fr.), ph

Charlie Van Damme
ONE SINGS, THE OTHER DOESN'T(1977, Fr.), ph

Lt. Van Dapperen
SILVER FLEET, THE(1945, Brit.)

Theo Van De Sande
GIRL WITH THE RED HAIR, THE(1983, Neth.), ph

Monique van de Ven
SPLITTING UP(1981, Neth.)

Werner Van Deeg
COUNTERFEIT TRAITOR, THE(1962)

Madam van Deerbeck
MR. H. C. ANDERSEN(1950, Brit.)

Albert Van Dekker [Dekker]
EXTORTION(1938); LONE WOLF IN PARIS, THE(1938); SHE MARRIED AN ARTIST(1938)

Lex Van Delden
HIDING PLACE, THE(1975); SOLDIER OF ORANGE(1979, Dutch)

Hennie Van Den Akker
GIRL WITH THE RED HAIR, THE(1983, Neth.)

Brahm van den Berg
SAMSON AND DELILAH(1949)

Caspar van den Berg
INDECENT(1962, Ger.), ed

Gert van den Berg
NAKED PREY, THE(1966, U.S./South Africa); SANDY THE SEAL(1969, Brit.)

Hans Bentz van den Berg
LAST BLITZKRIEG, THE(1958)

Robert Van Den Berg
SCARFACE(1983)

Gert van den Bergh
DIAMOND SAFARI(1958); HELLIONS, THE(1962, Brit.); CODE 7, VICTIM 5(1964, Brit.); ZULU(1964, Brit.); MOZAMBIQUE(1966, Brit.); RIDER IN THE NIGHT, THE(1968, South Africa); SEVEN AGAINST THE SUN(1968, South Africa); WILD SEASON(1968, South Africa)

John van den Broek
Silents
MOTHER(1914), ph; WISHING RING, THE(1914), ph

Louis Van Den Ecker
RENEGADES(1930), tech adv; ARTISTS AND MODELS ABROAD(1938)

Sylvie van den Elsen
1984
L'ARGENT(1984, Fr./Switz.)

Joop Van Den Ende
SPETTERS(1983, Holland), p

Edouard van den Enden
TRAFFIC(1972, Fr.), ph

Ton Van Den Heurel
LITTLE ARK, THE(1972), makeup

Debbie Van Den Houten
WHAT'S THE MATTER WITH HELEN?(1971)

John van der Broek
Silents
POOR LITTLE RICH GIRL, A(1917), ph; PRIDE OF THE CLAN, THE(1917), ph; PRUNELLA(1918), ph

Margot van der Burgh
MAN WHO COULDN'T WALK, THE(1964, Brit.)

Louis Van Der Ecker
BEAU GESTE(1939), tech ad

Eddy Van Der Eden
LIFESPAN(1975, U.S./Brit./Neth.), ph

Eddy van der Enden
BUTTERFLY(1982), ph; TIME TO DIE, A(1983), ph

Edward Van Der Enden
DAUGHTERS OF DARKNESS(1971, Bel./ Fr./ Ger./ Ital.), ph

Dora Van Der Groen
MALPERTIUS(1972, Bel./Fr.)

Anna Van Der Heida
LILITH(1964)

Anna Van Der Heide
LIST OF ADRIAN MESSENGER, THE(1963)

Victoria Van Der Kloot
THEY ALL LAUGHED(1981)

Hendrick J. Van Der Kolk
OUTRAGEOUS!(1977, Can.), p

Henk Van Der Kolk
WILD HORSE HANK(1979, Can.), p; CIRCLE OF TWO(1980, Can.), p; HANK WILLIAMS: THE SHOW HE NEVER GAVE(1982, Can.), p

William Van Der Leer
CRAWLING HAND, THE(1963), ph

Fred Van der Linde
TRUE STORY OF ESKIMO NELL, THE(1975, Aus.)

Dorus Van Der Linden
GIRL WITH THE RED HAIR, THE(1983, Neth.), art d

Paul van der Linden
HIGH(1968, Can.), ph; MERRY WIVES OF TOBIAS ROUKE, THE(1972, Can.), ph; ELIZA'S HOROSCOPE(1975, Can.), ph; LIES MY FATHER TOLD ME(1975, Can.), ph; KING SOLOMON'S TREASURE(1978, Can.), ph; LAST CHASE, THE(1981), ph
1984
KINGS AND DESPERATE MEN(1984, Brit.), ph

Sandy van der Linden
Misc. Talkies
LOVE COMES QUIETLY(1974)

Guus van der Made
1984
FOURTH MAN, THE(1984, Neth.)
Gabrielle Van Der Mal
NUN'S STORY, THE(1959)
Frank Van Der Meer
KING KONG(1976), spec eff
Maxence van der Meersch
TWO WOMEN(1940, Fr.), w
Maxene Van Der Meersch
DOCTOR AND THE GIRL, THE(1949), w
Hendrik Van Der Merwe
HELLIONS, THE(1962, Brit.)
Marc Antony Van Der Nagel
RABBIT, RUN(1970)
Carl van der Plas
1984
QUESTION OF SILENCE(1984, Neth.)
Laurens Van Der Post
MERRY CHRISTMAS MR. LAWRENCE(1983, Jap./Brit.), w
Peter Van Der Sloot
HERCULES AND THE CAPTIVE WOMEN(1963, Fr./Ital.), ch
Pieter Van Der Sloot
LEGIONS OF THE NILE(1960, Ital.), ch
Jace Van Der Veen
CHRISTINA(1974, Can.)
Ellinor Van Der Veer
PACK UP YOUR TROUBLES(1932)
Frank Van Der Veer
LOGAN'S RUN(1976), spec eff
Gregory Van Der Veer
METALSTORM: THE DESTRUCTION OF JARED-SYN(1983), spec eff
Van Der Veer Photo Effects
DARLING LILI(1970), spec eff; VIVA KNIEVEL!(1977), spec eff; SWARM, THE(1978), spec eff
Nadine Van Der Velde
PRIVATE SCHOOL(1983)
Diana Van Der Vlis
"X"–THE MAN WITH THE X-RAY EYES(1963); INCIDENT, THE(1967); SWIMMER, THE(1968)
Bram van der Vlugt
1984
QUESTION OF SILENCE(1984, Neth.)
Dawid Van Der Walt
KIMBERLEY JIM(1965, South Africa)
Keith Van Der Wat
Misc. Talkies
THREE BULLETS FOR A LONG GUN(1973)
Erik van der Wurff
SPLITTING UP(1981, Neth.), m
Richard Van Der Wyk
SKATEBOARD(1978)
Vola Van Dere
QUESTION OF ADULTERY, A(1959, Brit.)
Carol Van Derman
BUT NOT IN VAIN(1948, Brit.); SILK NOOSE, THE(1950, Brit.)
Tonia Van Deter
HOW TO STUFF A WILD BIKINI(1965)
Cortland Van Deusen
Misc. Silents
SHARE AND SHARE ALIKE(1925)
Courtlandt J. Van Deusen
Misc. Silents
MAN BEHIND THE CURTAIN, THE(1916), d
Trish Van Devere
LANDLORD, THE(1970); WHERE'S POPPA?(1970); LAST RUN, THE(1971); ONE IS A LONELY NUMBER(1972); DAY OF THE DOLPHIN, THE(1973); HARRY IN YOUR POCKET(1973); SAVAGE IS LOOSE, THE(1974); MOVIE MOVIE(1978); CHANGELING, THE(1980, Can.); HEARSE, THE(1980)
Selma Van Dias
ONE OF OUR AIRCRAFT IS MISSING(1942, Brit.)
Ruud Van Dijk
STILL SMOKIN'(1983), art d
S.S. Van Dine
CANARY MURDER CASE, THE(1929), w; GREENE MURDER CASE, THE(1929), w; BENSON MURDER CASE, THE(1930), w; BISHOP MURDER CASE, THE(1930), w; KENNEL MURDER CASE, THE(1933), w; DRAGON MURDER CASE, THE(1934), w; CASINO MURDER CASE, THE(1935), w; GARDEN MURDER CASE, THE(1936), w; PRESIDENT'S MYSTERY, THE(1936), w; SCARAB MURDER CASE, THE(1936, Brit.), w; NIGHT OF MYSTERY(1937), w; GRACIE ALLEN MURDER CASE(1939), w; CALLING PHILO VANCE(1940), w
Peter Van Dissel
DUFFY(1968, Brit.)
Peter Van Dissell
KILLER FORCE(1975, Switz./Ireland)
Foy Van Dolsen
TOAST OF NEW YORK, THE(1937); SWING YOUR LADY(1938); NEVER SAY DIE(1939)
Foy Van Dolson
TOM SAWYER, DETECTIVE(1939); HORROR ISLAND(1941)
Hans Van Dongen
LIFT, THE(1983, Neth.), ed
1984
QUESTION OF SILENCE(1984, Neth.), ed
Trudy van Doorn
QUEST FOR LOVE(1971, Brit.)
Bethan Van Doorninck
1984
DARK ENEMY(1984, Brit.)

Cerian Van Doorninck
1984
DARK ENEMY(1984, Brit.)
Mamie Van Doren
HIS KIND OF WOMAN(1951); ALL-AMERICAN, THE(1953); FORBIDDEN(1953); FRANCIS JOINS THE WACS(1954); YANKEE PASHA(1954); AIN'T MISBEHAVIN'(1955); RUNNING WILD(1955); SECOND GREATEST SEX, THE(1955); STAR IN THE DUST(1956); GIRL IN BLACK STOCKINGS(1957); JET PILOT(1957); UNTAMED YOUTH(1957); GUNS, GIRLS AND GANGSTERS(1958); HIGH SCHOOL CONFIDENTIAL(1958); TEACHER'S PET(1958); BEAT GENERATION, THE(1959); BIG OPERATOR, THE(1959); BORN RECKLESS(1959); GIRLS' TOWN(1959); VICE RAID(1959); COLLEGE CONFIDENTIAL(1960); SEX KITTENS GO TO COLLEGE(1960); PRIVATE LIVES OF ADAM AND EVE, THE(1961); CANDIDATE, THE(1964); THREE NUTS IN SEARCH OF A BOLT(1964); LAS VEGAS HILLBILLYS(1966); NAVY VS. THE NIGHT MONSTERS, THE(1966); VOYAGE TO THE PLANET OF PREHISTORIC WOMEN(1966); YOU'VE GOT TO BE SMART(1967)
Trudi Van Doren
NOT NOW DARLING(1975, Brit.)
Philip Van Doren Stern
IT'S A WONDERFUL LIFE(1946), w
Mildred Van Dorn
HOLD YOUR MAN(1929); LILIOM(1930); SON OF THE GODS(1930); WILD COMPANY(1930); I TAKE THIS WOMAN(1931); IRON MAN, THE(1931)
Cortland Van Dousen
Silents
FLORIDA ENCHANTMENT, A(1914)
John Van Dreelan
BIG GAME, THE(1972); LOST HORIZON(1973)
John Van Dreelen
TIME TO LOVE AND A TIME TO DIE, A(1958); FLYING FONTAINES, THE(1959); BEYOND THE TIME BARRIER(1960); ENEMY GENERAL, THE(1960); LEECH WOMAN, THE(1960); THIRTEEN GHOSTS(1960); WIZARD OF BAGHDAD, THE(1960); VON RYAN'S EXPRESS(1965); I DEAL IN DANGER(1966); MADAME X(1966); DUCK RINGS AT HALF PAST SEVEN, THE(1969, Ger./Ital.); TOPAZ(1969, Brit.); FORMULA, THE(1980)
John Van Druten
CARELESS AGE(1929), w; YOUNG WOODLEY(1930, Brit.), w; UNFAITHFUL(1931), w; AFTER OFFICE HOURS(1932, Brit.), w; NEW MORALS FOR OLD(1932), w; IF I WERE FREE(1933), w; KING OF PARIS, THE(1934, Brit.), w; NIGHT MUST FALL(1937), w; PARNELL(1937), w; GONE WITH THE WIND(1939), w; RAFFLES(1939), w; LUCKY PARTNERS(1940), w; MY LIFE WITH CAROLINE(1941), w; ONE NIGHT IN LISBON(1941), w; FOREVER AND A DAY(1943), w; JOHNNY COME LATELY(1943), w; OLD ACQUAINTANCE(1943), w; GASLIGHT(1944), w; VOICE OF THE TURTLE, THE(1947), w; I REMEMBER MAMA(1948), w; MAIN STREET TO BROADWAY(1953); I AM A CAMERA(1955, Brit.), w; BELL, BOOK AND CANDLE(1958), w; CABARET(1972), w; RICH AND FAMOUS(1981), w
Boris van Dueren
MONTENEGRO(1981, Brit./Swed.), ch
Peter Van Duinen
GIRLS IN CHAINS(1943), p
Peter R. Van Duinen
ISLE OF FORGOTTEN SINS(1943), p; MY SON, THE HERO(1943), p
Ton Van Duinhoven
LAST BLITZKRIEG, THE(1958)
Ernest Van Duren
Misc. Silents
LA PRINCESSE MANDANE(1928, Fr.)
Bruce van Dusen
1984
COLD FEET(1984), d&w
Granville Van Dusen
STATUE, THE(1971, Brit.); IT AIN'T EASY(1972)
Ricki Van Dusen
UP IN ARMS(1944); T-MEN(1947)
H. Jane Van Duser
P.J.(1968)
Jane Van Duser
IT HAPPENS EVERY SPRING(1949); WHIRLPOOL(1949)
Winifred Van Duzer
GOOD BAD GIRL, THE(1931), w
Tom Van Dycke
ALIBI FOR MURDER(1936), w; MAN WHO LIVED TWICE(1936), w; TWO-FISTED GENTLEMAN(1936), w; COUNTERFEIT LADY(1937), w; MAN IN THE DARK(1953), w
James J. Van Dyk
SLEEPING CITY, THE(1950)
Allison Van Dyke
FASCINATION(1931, Brit.)
Barry Van Dyke
CONQUEST OF THE EARTH(1980)
Bonnie Van Dyke
BAT PEOPLE, THE(1974)
Carol Van Dyke
TWO FOR THE ROAD(1967, Brit.)
Conny Van Dyke
YOUNG SINNER, THE(1965); HELL'S ANGELS '69(1969); FRAMED(1975); W. W. AND THE DIXIE DANCEKINGS(1975)
Dick Van Dyke
BYE BYE BIRDIE(1963); MARY POPPINS(1964); WHAT A WAY TO GO(1964); ART OF LOVE, THE(1965); LT. ROBIN CRUSOE, U.S.N.(1966); DIVORCE AMERICAN STYLE(1967); FITZWILLY(1967); CHITTY CHITTY BANG BANG(1968, Brit.); NEVER A DULL MOMENT(1968); COMIC, THE(1969); SOME KIND OF A NUT(1969); COLD TURKEY(1971); THE RUNNER STUMBLES(1979)
Edmay Van Dyke
IF A MAN ANSWERS(1962)
Jerry Van Dyke
COURTSHIP OF EDDY'S FATHER, THE(1963); MC LINTOCK!(1963); PALM SPRINGS WEEKEND(1963); LOVE AND KISSES(1965); ANGEL IN MY POCKET(1969)

LeRoy Van Dyke
WHAT AM I BID?(1967)
Marcia Van Dyke
IN THE GOOD OLD SUMMERTIME(1949); SHADOW ON THE WALL(1950)
Tom Van Dyke
MURDER AT MONTE CARLO(1935, Brit.), w; WILDCATTER, THE(1937), w
Truman Van Dyke
JANIE(1944)
Misc. Talkies
RIDERS OF THE PONY EXPRESS(1949)
Silents
MAD MARRIAGE, THE(1921); TWO MINUTES TO GO(1921); DAUGHTERS OF TODAY(1924)
Misc. Silents
MIDLANDERS, THE(1920); STAR REPORTER, THE(1921); DUSK TO DAWN(1922)
W.S. Van Dyke
PAGAN, THE(1929), d; CUBAN LOVE SONG,THE(1931), d; NEVER THE TWAIN SHALL MEET(1931), d; NIGHT COURT(1932), d; TARZAN, THE APE MAN(1932), d; PENTHOUSE(1933), d; PRIZEFIGHTER AND THE LADY, THE(1933), d; LAUGHING BOY(1934), d; THIN MAN, THE(1934), d; FORSAKING ALL OTHERS(1935), d; I LIVE MY LIFE(1935), d; AFTER THE THIN MAN(1936), d; DEVIL IS A SISSY, THE(1936), d; HIS BROTHER'S WIFE(1936), d; PRISONER OF ZENDA, THE(1937), d; ROSALIE(1937), d; ANOTHER THIN MAN(1939), p; I TAKE THIS WOMAN(1940), d
Silents
OLIVER TWIST(1916); ACCORDING TO HOYLE(1922), d; MIRACLE MAKERS, THE(1923), d; DESERT'S PRICE, THE(1926), d; WAR PAINT(1926), d; CALIFORNIA(1927), d; FOREIGN DEVILS(1927), d
Misc. Silents
GIFT O' GAB(1917), d; LAND OF LONG SHADOWS(1917), d; MEN OF THE DESERT(1917), d; OPEN PLACES(1917), d; RANGE BOSS, THE(1917), d; SADIE GOES TO HEAVEN(1917), d; BOSS OF CAMP 4, THE(1922), d; FORGET-ME-NOT(1922), d; DESTROYING ANGEL, THE(1923), d; LITTLE GIRL NEXT DOOR, THE(1923), d; BATTLING FOOL, THE(1924), d; BEAUTIFUL SINNER, THE(1924), d; LOVING LIES(1924), d; BARRIERS BURNED AWAY(1925), d; EYES OF THE TOTEM(1927), d; SPOILERS OF THE WEST(1927), d; WINNERS OF THE WILDERNESS(1927), d; UNDER THE BLACK EAGLE(1928), d; WYOMING(1928), d; PAGAN, THE(1929), d
W S Van Dyke II
GUILTY HANDS(1931), d; TRADER HORN(1931), d; HIDE-OUT(1934), d; MANHATTAN MELODRAMA(1934), d; NAUGHTY MARIETTA(1935), d; LOVE ON THE RUN(1936), d; ROSE MARIE(1936), d; SAN FRANCISCO(1936), d; PERSONAL PROPERTY(1937), d; THEY GAVE HIM A GUN(1937), d; MARIE ANTOINETTE(1938), d; SWEETHEARTS(1938), d; ANDY HARDY GETS SPRING FEVER(1939), d; IT'S A WONDERFUL WORLD(1939), d; STAND UP AND FIGHT(1939), d; BITTER SWEET(1940), d; I LOVE YOU AGAIN(1940), d; DR. KILDARE'S VICTORY(1941), d; FEMININE TOUCH, THE(1941), d; RAGE IN HEAVEN(1941), d; SHADOW OF THE THIN MAN(1941), d; CAIRO(1942), d; JOURNEY FOR MARGARET(1942), d
Maj. W.S. Van Dyke II
I MARRIED AN ANGEL(1942), d
William S. Van Dyke
Silents
RANGER OF THE BIG PINES(1925), d
Misc. Silents
LADY OF THE DUGOUT(1918), d; GOLD HEELS(1924), d; HALF-A-DOLLAR BILL(1924), d; WINNER TAKE ALL(1924), d; HEARTS AND SPURS(1925), d; TIMBER WOLF(1925), d; TRAIL RIDER, THE(1925), d; GENTLE CYCLONE, THE(1926), d
Woodbridge S. Van Dyke
WHITE SHADOWS IN THE SOUTH SEAS(1928), d
Annie van Ees
BOEFJE(1939, Ger.)
Ben Van Eeslyn
BUT NOT IN VAIN(1948, Brit.), w
Bertrand van Effenterre
MAIS OU ET DONC ORNICAR(1979, Fr.), p, d, w; BIQUEFARRE(1983, Fr.), p
Joele van Effenterre
MAIS OU ET DONC ORNICAR(1979, Fr.), ed; LIKE A TURTLE ON ITS BACK(1981, Fr.), ed; GIRL FROM LORRAINE, A(1982, Fr./Switz.), ed; DEATH OF MARIO RICCI, THE(1983, Ital.), ed; ENTRE NOUS(1984), ed
Joelle van Effenterre
INVITATION, THE(1975, Fr./Switz.), ed; LACEMAKER, THE(1977, Fr.), ed; ONE SINGS, THE OTHER DOESN'T(1977, Fr.), ed; PEPPERMINT SODA(1979, Fr.), ed
1984
HEAT OF DESIRE(1984, Fr.), ed
Joelle Van Effentree
COCKTAIL MOLOTOV(1980, Fr.), ed
Willard Van Elger
PURSUED(1947), spec eff
Theodore Van Eltz
OLD SWIMMIN' HOLE, THE(1941); DEVIL'S CARGO, THE(1948)
Charles Van Eman
1984
JOY OF SEX(1984)
William Van Engen
I WAS A SPY(1934, Brit.), ph
Bick Van Enger, Jr.
FINAL COMEDOWN, THE(1972), ed
Charles Van Enger
FOX MOVIETONE FOLLIES(1929), ph; MARRIED IN HOLLYWOOD(1929), ph; PHANTOM OF THE OPERA, THE(1929), ph; WORDS AND MUSIC(1929), ph, ph; HIGH SOCIETY BLUES(1930), ph; HOT FOR PARIS(1930), ph; ONE MAD KISS(1930), ph; AVENGER, THE(1931), ph; MAD PARADE, THE(1931), ph; MEET THE WIFE(1931), ph; TURKEY TIME(1933, Brit.), ph; ALONG CAME SALLY(1934, Brit.), ph; FRIDAY THE 13TH(1934, Brit.), ph; CAPTAIN BILL(1935, Brit.), ph; ME AND MARLBOROUGH(1935, Brit.), ph; MY SONG FOR YOU(1935, Brit.), ph; STOKER, THE(1935, Brit.), ph; BOYS WILL BE BOYS(1936, Brit.), ph; WHERE THERE'S A WILL(1936, Brit), ph; TWO OF US, THE(1938, Brit.), ph; HALF A SINNER(1940), ph; SLIGHTLY TEMPTED(1940), ph; ARIZONA CYCLONE(1941), ph; CRACKED NUTS(1941), ph; HELLO SUCKER(1941), ph; LAW OF THE RANGE(1941), ph; LUCKY DEVILS(1941), ph; MAN FROM MONTANA(1941), ph; MASKED RIDER, THE(1941), ph; NEVER GIVE A SUCKER AN EVEN BREAK(1941), ph; RAWHIDE RANGERS(1941), ph; BOSS OF HANGTOWN MESA(1942), ph; FIGHTING BILL FARGO(1942), ph; FRISCO LILL(1942), ph; MOONLIGHT IN HAVANA(1942), ph; NIGHT MONSTER(1942), ph; NORTH TO THE KLONDIKE(1942), ph; SILVER BULLET, THE(1942), ph; WHO DONE IT?(1942), ph; CRAZY HOUSE(1943), ph; HIT THE ICE(1943), ph; HI'YA, CHUM(1943), ph; IT AIN'T HAY(1943), ph; NEVER A DULL MOMENT(1943), ph; SHERLOCK HOLMES FACES DEATH(1943), ph; BOWERY TO BROADWAY(1944), ph; CHIP OFF THE OLD BLOCK(1944), ph; GHOST CATCHERS(1944), ph; HER PRIMITIVE MAN(1944), ph; MERRY MONAHANS, THE(1944), ph; NIGHT CLUB GIRL(1944), ph; SHERLOCK HOLMES AND THE SPIDER WOMAN(1944), ph; SINGING SHERIFF, THE(1944), ph; DALTONS RIDE AGAIN, THE(1945), ph; FRISCO SAL(1945), ph; ON STAGE EVERYBODY(1945), ph; THAT'S THE SPIRIT(1945), ph; UNDER WESTERN SKIES(1945), ph; LITTLE GIANT(1946), ph; STRANGE CONQUEST(1946), ph; TIME OF THEIR LIVES, THE(1946), ph; WHITE TIE AND TAILS(1946), ph; BUCK PRIVATES COME HOME(1947), ph; WISTFUL WIDOW OF WAGON GAP, THE(1947), ph; ABBOTT AND COSTELLO MEET FRANKENSTEIN(1948), ph; MEXICAN HAYRIDE(1948), ph; NOOSE HANGS HIGH, THE(1948), ph; ABBOTT AND COSTELLO MEET THE KILLER, BORIS KARLOFF(1949), ph; AFRICA SCREAMS(1949), ph; KID FROM TEXAS, THE(1950), ph; MA AND PA KETTLE GO TO TOWN(1950), ph, art d; BRIDE OF THE GORILLA(1951), ph; LORNA DOONE(1951), ph; MA AND PA KETTLE BACK ON THE FARM(1951), ph; TWO DOLLAR BETTOR(1951), ph; BATTLES OF CHIEF PONTIAC(1952), ph; BELA LUGOSI MEETS A BROOKLYN GORILLA(1952), ph; KID MONK BARONI(1952), ph; COMBAT SQUAD(1953), ph; MAGNETIC MONSTER, THE(1953), ph; SABRE JET(1953), ph; KHYBER PATROL(1954), ph; SITTING BULL(1954), ph; BRASS LEGEND, THE(1956), ph; MAGNIFICENT ROUGHNECKS(1956), ph; TIMETABLE(1956), ph; GUN FEVER(1958), ph
Silents
LAST OF THE MOHICANS, THE(1920), ph; KINDRED OF THE DUST(1922), ph; SALOME(1922), ph; THREE WISE FOOLS(1923), ph; BROADWAY AFTER DARK(1924), ph; FORBIDDEN PARADISE(1924), ph; LOVER'S LANE(1924), ph; MARRIAGE CIRCLE, THE(1924), ph; KISS ME AGAIN(1925), ph; LADY WINDERMERE'S FAN(1925), ph; PARADISE(1926), ph; PUPPETS(1926), ph; EASY PICKINGS(1927), ph; SEA TIGER, THE(1927), ph; SMILE, BROTHER, SMILE(1927), ph; HEAD OF THE FAMILY, THE(1928), ph; HOMESICK(1928), ph; NONE BUT THE BRAVE(1928), ph
Charles J. Van Enger
Silents
DARING YOUTH(1924), ph; PHANTOM OF THE OPERA, THE(1925), ph
Charles L. Van Enger
THAT NIGHT WITH YOU(1945), ph
Richard Van Enger
HEART OF THE GOLDEN WEST(1942), ed; MOUNTAIN RHYTHM(1942), ed; BORDERTOWN GUNFIGHTERS(1943), ed; FUGITIVE FROM SONORA(1943), ed; HERE COMES ELMER(1943), ed; SLEEPY LAGOON(1943), ed; SWING YOUR PARTNER(1943), ed; TAHITI HONEY(1943), ed; CALL OF THE SOUTH SEAS(1944), ed; FIGHTING SEABEES, THE(1944), ed; JAMBOREE(1944), ed; PORT OF 40 THIEVES, THE(1944), ed; ROAD TO ALCATRAZ(1945), ed; SITTING BULL(1954), ed; ROAD TO DENVER, THE(1955), ed; BLACK SCORPION, THE(1957), ed
Richard L. Van Enger
MOON AND SIXPENCE, THE(1942), ed; ATLANTIC CITY(1944), ed; CHEATERS, THE(1945), ed; EARL CARROLL'S VANITIES(1945), ed; FLAME OF THE BARBARY COAST(1945), ed; LOVE, HONOR AND GOODBYE(1945), ed; OREGON TRAIL(1945), ed; EARL CARROLL SKETCHBOOK(1946), ed; INVISIBLE INFORMER(1946), ed; I'VE ALWAYS LOVED YOU(1946), ed; MAGNIFICENT ROGUE, THE(1946), ed; MYSTERIOUS MR. VALENTINE, THE(1946), ed; FABULOUS TEXAN, THE(1947), ed; THAT'S MY MAN(1947), ed; ANGEL ON THE AMAZON(1948), ed; DAREDEVILS OF THE CLOUDS(1948), ed; FLAME, THE(1948), ed; I, JANE DOE(1948), ed; OLD LOS ANGELES(1948), ed; OUT OF THE STORM(1948), ed; FIGHTING KENTUCKIAN, THE(1949), ed; HIDEOUT(1949), ed; LAW OF THE GOLDEN WEST(1949), ed; PRINCE OF THE PLAINS(1949), ed; SANDS OF IWO JIMA(1949), ed; WAKE OF THE RED WITCH(1949), ed; SALT LAKE RAIDERS(1950), ed; SINGING GUNS(1950), ed; SURRENDER(1950), ed; VANISHING WESTERNER, THE(1950), ed; BULLFIGHTER AND THE LADY(1951), ed; HONEYCHILE(1951), ed; HOODLUM EMPIRE(1952), ed; OKLAHOMA ANNIE(1952), ed; THUNDERBIRDS(1952), ed; TOUGHEST MAN IN ARIZONA(1952), ed; WILD BLUE YONDER, THE(1952), ed; WOMAN OF THE NORTH COUNTRY(1952), ed; FAIR WIND TO JAVA(1953), ed; PERILOUS JOURNEY, A(1953), ed; SEA OF LOST SHIPS(1953), ed; SHADOWS OF TOMBSTONE(1953), ed; JOHNNY GUITAR(1954), ed; JUBILEE TRAIL(1954), ed; FLAME OF THE ISLANDS(1955), ed; HELL'S OUTPOST(1955), ed; MAN ALONE, A(1955), ed; TIMBERJACK(1955), ed; VANISHING AMERICAN, THE(1955), ed; LISBON(1956), ed; MAVERICK QUEEN, THE(1956), ed; WOMAN'S DEVOTION, A(1956), ed; DUEL AT APACHE WELLS(1957), ed; SPOILERS OF THE FOREST(1957), ed
Willard Van Enger
ISLE OF FURY(1936), spec eff; PETRIFIED FOREST, THE(1936), spec eff; GREEN LIGHT(1937), spec eff; PRINCE AND THE PAUPER, THE(1937), spec eff; FLOWING GOLD(1940), spec eff; ACROSS THE PACIFIC(1942), spec eff; CASABLANCA(1942), spec eff; HARD WAY, THE(1942), spec eff; WILD BILL HICKOK RIDES(1942), spec eff; BACKGROUND TO DANGER(1943), spec eff; CONSPIRATORS, THE(1944), spec eff; DESTINATION TOKYO(1944), spec eff; MAKE YOUR OWN BED(1944), spec eff; ESCAPE IN THE DESERT(1945), spec eff; MILDRED PIERCE(1945), spec eff; SAN ANTONIO(1945), spec eff; NEVER SAY GOODBYE(1946), spec eff; STOLEN LIFE, A(1946), spec eff; ESCAPE ME NEVER(1947), spec eff
Silents
LITTLE IRISH GIRL, THE(1926), ph; WHAT HAPPENED TO FATHER(1927), ph
William Van Enger
ILLEGAL(1932, Brit.), ph; NOBODY LIVES FOREVER(1946), spec eff
Dorothy Van Engle
Misc. Talkies
BRAND OF CAIN, THE(1935); SWING(1938)
Harry van Engle
DRAUGHTSMAN'S CONTRACT, THE(1983, Brit.)
George Van Eps
PETE KELLY'S BLUES(1955)
Robert Van Eps
MAN FROM BUTTON WILLOW, THE(1965), m
Connie Van Ess
STIGMA(1972)

Ben Van Esselstyn [Eeslyn]
BUT NOT IN VAIN(1948, Brit.)

Lis Van Essen
ETERNAL WALTZ, THE(1959, Ger.)

Kristina van Euck
EGON SCHIELE–EXCESS AND PUNISHMENT(1981, Ger.)

Jack Van Evera
KING OF THE GRIZZLIES(1970); MY BLOODY VALENTINE(1981, Can.)
1984
HIGHPOINT(1984, Can.)

Warren Van Evera
1984
MRS. SOFFEL(1984)

Maria Van Everett
ECHOES OF SILENCE(1966)

Billie Van Every
MONTE CARLO NIGHTS(1934); SHE MARRIED HER BOSS(1935); NAVY BORN(1936)

Dale Van Every
MARIANNE(1929), w; NAVY BLUES(1930), w; THOSE THREE FRENCH GIRLS(1930), w; EAST OF BORNEO(1931), w; EX-BAD BOY(1931), w; SPIRIT OF NOTRE DAME, THE(1931), w; TRADER HORN(1931), w; VIRTUOUS HUSBAND(1931), w; AIR MAIL(1932), w; ALL-AMERICAN, THE(1932), w; HOUSE DIVIDED, A(1932), w; MURDERS IN THE RUE MORGUE(1932), w; TOM BROWN OF CULVER(1932), w; UNEXPECTED FATHER(1932), w; HORSEPLAY(1933), w; NAGANA(1933), w; SATURDAY'S MILLIONS(1933), w; I'LL TELL THE WORLD(1934), w; LOVE BIRDS(1934), w; POOR RICH, THE(1934), w; UNCERTAIN LADY(1934), p; AFTER OFFICE HOURS(1935), w; ANNAPOLIS FAREWELL(1935), w; MEN WITHOUT NAMES(1935), w; WINGS IN THE DARK(1935), w; MORE THAN A SECRETARY(1936), w; CAPTAINS COURAGEOUS(1937), w; SOULS AT SEA(1937), w; SPAWN OF THE NORTH(1938), w; DR. CYCLOPS(1940), p; RANGERS OF FORTUNE(1940), p; TALK OF THE TOWN(1942), w; SEALED CARGO(1951), w
Silents
ACQUITTAL, THE(1923), w; TELLING THE WORLD(1928), w; DUKE STEPS OUT, THE(1929), w

Edward Van Every
SWEET ROSIE O'GRADY(1943), w

Goetz Van Eyck
HITLER'S CHILDREN(1942)

John Van Eyck
SPLENDOR(1935); THREE HEARTS FOR JULIA(1943)

Peter Van Eyck
EDGE OF DARKNESS(1943); FIVE GRAVES TO CAIRO(1943); MOON IS DOWN, THE(1943); ADDRESS UNKNOWN(1944); IMPOSTER, THE(1944); SAILOR OF THE KING(1953, Brit.); ALERT IN THE SOUTH(1954, Fr.); FLESH AND THE WOMAN(1954, Fr./Ital.); NIGHT PEOPLE(1954); BULLET FOR JOEY, A(1955); JUMP INTO HELL(1955); TARZAN'S HIDDEN JUNGLE(1955); WAGES OF FEAR, THE(1955, Fr./Ital.); ATTACK!(1956); RAWHIDE YEARS, THE(1956); RUN FOR THE SUN(1956); SNORKEL, THE(1958, Brit.); GLASS TOWER, THE(1959, Ger.); FOXHOLE IN CAIRO(1960, Brit.); REST IS SILENCE, THE(1960, Ger.); ROSEMARY(1960, Ger.); THOUSAND EYES OF DR. MABUSE, THE(1960, Fr./Ital./Ger.); DEVIL'S AGENT, THE(1962, Brit.); INDECENT(1962, Ger.); LONGEST DAY, THE(1962); MR. ARKADIN(1962, Brit./Fr./Span.); WORLD IN MY POCKET, THE(1962, Fr./Ital./Ger.); YOUNG GO WILD, THE(1962, Ger.); NO TIME FOR ECSTASY(1963, Fr.); SCOTLAND YARD HUNTS DR. MABUSE(1963, Ger.); DR. MABUSE'S RAYS OF DEATH(1964, Ger./Fr./Ital.); STATION SIX-SAHARA(1964, Brit./Ger.); AND SO TO BED(1965, Ger.); BRAIN, THE(1965, Ger./Brit.); SPY WHO CAME IN FROM THE COLD, THE(1965, Brit.); MYSTERY OF THUG ISLAND, THE(1966, Ital./Ger.); REQUIEM FOR A SECRET AGENT(1966, Ital.); THE DIRTY GAME(1966, Fr./Ital./Ger.); SEDUCTION BY THE SEA(1967, Ger./Yugo.); ASSIGNMENT TO KILL(1968); SHALAKO(1968, Brit.); BRIDGE AT REMAGEN, THE(1969)

Osso Van Eyes
BIG JACK(1949), w

Edgar Van Eyss
I WAS A PRISONER ON DEVIL'S ISLAND(1941), w

Otto Van Eyss
I WAS A PRISONER ON DEVIL'S ISLAND(1941), w

John Van Eyssen
FOUR SIDED TRIANGLE(1953, Brit.); THREE STEPS IN THE DARK(1953, Brit.); COCKLESHELL HEROES, THE(1955); ACCOUNT RENDERED(1957, Brit.); ENEMY FROM SPACE(1957, Brit.); MEN OF SHERWOOD FOREST(1957, Brit.); ACCURSED, THE(1958, Brit.); HORROR OF DRACULA, THE(1958, Brit.); MOMENT OF INDISCRETION(1958, Brit.); ONE THAT GOT AWAY, THE(1958, Brit.); WHOLE TRUTH, THE(1958, Brit.); CARRY ON NURSE(1959, Brit.); I'M ALL RIGHT, JACK(1959, Brit.); CHANCE MEETING(1960, Brit.); MAN IN A COCKED HAT(1960, Bri.); STORY OF DAVID, A(1960, Brit.); CONCRETE JUNGLE, THE(1962, Brit.); MARRIAGE OF CONVENIENCE(1970, Brit.)
Misc. Talkies
PARTNERS IN CRIME(1961, Brit.)

Glenn Van Fleet
LUGGAGE OF THE GODS(1983), spec eff

Jo Van Fleet
EAST OF EDEN(1955); I'LL CRY TOMORROW(1955); ROSE TATTOO, THE(1955); KING AND FOUR QUEENS, THE(1956); GUNFIGHT AT THE O.K. CORRAL(1957); THIS ANGRY AGE(1958, Ital./Fr.); WILD RIVER(1960); COOL HAND LUKE(1967); I LOVE YOU, ALICE B. TOKLAS!(1968); 80 STEPS TO JONAH(1969); GANG THAT COULDN'T SHOOT STRAIGHT, THE(1971)

Richard Van Fleet
ANGEL IN MY POCKET(1969); BEN(1972)

Priscilla Van Gorder
DEVONSVILLE TERROR, THE(1983), set d

Peter Van Greenaway
MEDUSA TOUCH, THE(1978, Brit.), w

Isaac Van Grove
I'LL TAKE ROMANCE(1937), md

Eddy Van Guyse
BREAKING AWAY(1979)

Andre Van Gysegham
SURGEON'S KNIFE, THE(1957, Brit.); MENACE IN THE NIGHT(1958, Brit.)

Andre Van Gyseghem
CANDLES AT NINE(1944, Brit.); WARNING TO WANTONS, A(1949, Brit.); LIMPING MAN, THE(1953, Brit.); HOUSE OF THE SEVEN HAWKS, THE(1959); PIED PIPER, THE(1972, Brit.)

Anders Van Haden
CHEATERS AT PLAY(1932); BEST OF ENEMIES(1933); SECRET OF THE BLUE ROOM(1933); MADAME SPY(1934); WE LIVE AGAIN(1934); BARBARY COAST(1935); FOLIES DERGERE(1935)

Edward Van Halen
1984
WILD LIFE, THE(1984), m

Martine Van Hamel
TURNING POINT, THE(1977)

Jean Van Hamme
DIVA(1982, Fr.), w

Chuck Van Haren
OPERATION DAMES(1959)

Lo Van Hartingsveld
NOSFERATU, THE VAMPIRE(1979, Fr./Ger.)

Norman Van Hawley
MANSTER, THE(1962, Jap.)

Anders Van Hayden
PASSPORT TO HELL(1932)

J. Van Hearn
ETERNAL SUMMER(1961), p, w

Johan Van Heerdan
RIDER IN THE NIGHT, THE(1968, South Africa)

Matthijs Van Heijningen
LIFT, THE(1983, Neth.), p
1984
QUESTION OF SILENCE(1984, Neth.), p

Lo Van Hensbergen
AMSTERDAM AFFAIR, THE(1968 Brit.); LITTLE ARK, THE(1972); MALOU(1983)

Kevin Van Hentenryck
BASKET CASE(1982)

Lo van Hernsbergen
DOG OF FLANDERS, A(1959)

Carol Van Herwijen
STILL SMOKIN'(1983)

Jean Van Herzeele
LOULOU(1980, Fr.)

Fay W. Van Hessen
LOST LAGOON(1958), art d

James Van Heusen
DIXIE(1943), m; OSCAR, THE(1966), m/l Ralph Rainger

Jimmy Van Heusen
MY HEART GOES CRAZY(1953, Brit.), m

Matthijs Van Heyningen
MYSTERIES(1979, Neth.), p

Anita Van Hezewyck
"EQUUS"(1977)

Paul Van Himst
VICTORY(1981)

Brant Van Hoffman
1984
POLICE ACADEMY(1984)

Eleanore van Hoogstraten
TOWN WITHOUT PITY(1961, Ger./Switz./U.S.)

Roger Van Hool
WOMAN NEXT DOOR, THE(1981, Fr.)

Teresa Van Hoorn
MIND BENDERS, THE(1963, Brit.)

B. Van Horn
YELLOWBEARD(1983), stunts

Buddy Van Horn
TWO MULES FOR SISTER SARA(1970), stunts; JOE KIDD(1972), stunts; HIGH PLAINS DRIFTER(1973), a, stunts; THUNDERBOLT AND LIGHTFOOT(1974), stunts; SWASHBUCKLER(1976), stunts; LAST REMAKE OF BEAU GESTE, THE(1977), stunts; ANY WHICH WAY YOU CAN(1980), d

Emil Van Horn
KEEP 'EM FLYING(1941); NEVER GIVE A SUCKER AN EVEN BREAK(1941); ICE-CAPADES REVUE(1942); APE MAN, THE(1943); SLEEPY LAGOON(1943)

James Van Horn
FAST ON THE DRAW(1950); HOSTILE COUNTRY(1950); MARSHAL OF HELDORADO(1950); SILVER CITY(1951); SON OF PALEFACE(1952); TAZA, SON OF COCHISE(1954)

Jimmy Van Horn
CAVE OF OUTLAWS(1951); GUNSMOKE(1953)

Kelly Van Horn
LAST RITES(1980), p
1984
SPLITZ(1984), p, w

Maya Van Horn
DRAGONWYCH(1946); SNOWS OF KILIMANJARO, THE(1952); MISSISSIPPI GAMBLER, THE(1953); LADY GODIVA(1955); NIGHTFALL(1956); LES GIRLS(1957)

Nya Van Horn
UNTAMED(1955)

Wayne Van Horn
ESCAPE TO BURMA(1955); SPARTACUS(1960); DIRTY HARRY(1971); ENFORCER, THE(1976), stunts; GAUNTLET, THE(1977), stunts; EVERY WHICH WAY BUT LOOSE(1978), stunt
1984
CITY HEAT(1984), a, stunts; TIGHTROPE(1984), stunts

Andreas Van Horne
Misc. Silents
HOUND OF THE BASKERVILLES, THE(1914, Ger.)

Jimmy Van Horne
ESCAPE TO BURMA(1955)
Job Van Huelsen
CROSSROADS OF PASSION(1951, Fr.)
Joop Van Hulsen
FUGITIVE LADY(1951); WAR AND PEACE(1956, Ital./U.S.)
Giovanni Van Hulzen
BLACK MAGIC(1949)
Joop Van Hulzen
OPEN CITY(1946, Ital.); PRINCE OF FOXES(1949); NEVER TAKE NO FOR AN ANSWER(1952, Brit./Ital.)
Dan Van Husen
EL CONDOR(1970); CAPTAIN APACHE(1971, Brit.); DOC(1971); NOSFERATU, THE VAMPIRE(1979, Fr./Ger.); SEA WOLVES, THE(1981, Brit.)
Don Van Husen
DON'T TURN THE OTHER CHEEK(1974, Ital./Ger./Span.)
Hans Van In't Veld
STILL SMOKIN'(1983)
Sharon Van Ivan
OPENING NIGHT(1977)
Michael van Joseph
1984
RENO AND THE DOC(1984, Can.)
Merete Van Kamp
OSTERMAN WEEKEND, THE(1983)
Tran Van Khe
TOWN LIKE ALICE, A(1958, Brit.)
Doug Van Koss
MORE AMERICAN GRAFFITI(1979), set d
Therese Van Kye
GREAT MANHUNT, THE(1951, Brit.)
Anthony Van Laast
OUTLAND(1981), ch; FINAL OPTION, THE(1983, Brit.), ch; NEVER SAY NEVER AGAIN(1983)
Jay Van Leer
CLAUDINE(1974)
Gertrude Van Lent
BIG TRAIL, THE(1930)
Lucille Van Lent
BIG TRAIL, THE(1930)
Silents
WEDDING MARCH, THE(1927); QUEEN KELLY(1929)
Chako van Leuwen
PIRANHA II: THE SPAWNING(1981, Neth.), p
Tran Van Lich
HOA-BINH(1971, Fr.)
Erland Van Lidth
ALONE IN THE DARK(1982)
Corinne Van Lissel
ROSEANNA McCOY(1949)
H.H. Van Loan
MISSISSIPPI GAMBLER(1929), w; RUNAWAY BRIDE(1930), w; DOCKS OF SAN FRANCISCO(1932), w; I'D GIVE MY LIFE(1936), w
Silents
NEW MOON, THE(1919), w; BREAKING POINT, THE(1921), w; CLEAN UP, THE(1923), w; FOG, THE(1923), w; STORMSWEPT(1923), w; NELLIE, THE BEAUTIFUL CLOAK MODEL(1924), w; FLATTERY(1925), w; DIXIE FLYER, THE(1926), w; KICK-OFF, THE(1926), w; MIDNIGHT MESSAGE, THE(1926), w; SHOW GIRL, THE(1927), w; NOOSE, THE(1928), w
Philip Van Loan
Silents
KAISER'S FINISH, THE(1918); LEAP TO FAME(1918)
Misc. Silents
FORBIDDEN LOVE(1921), d; JESUS OF NAZARETH(1928)
Jan van Loewen
HEAVEN IS ROUND THE CORNER(1944, Brit.); COLONEL BLIMP(1945, Brit.); NOTORIOUS GENTLEMAN(1945, Brit.); LISBON STORY, THE(1946, Brit.); MAN FROM MOROCCO, THE(1946, Brit.); CODE OF SCOTLAND YARD)(1948)
Hendrik Willem Van Loon
STORY OF MANKIND, THE(1957), w
Larry van Loon
SCALPS(1983), ph
Robert Van Loon
PAISAN(1948, Ital.)
Joachim van Ludwig
JULIE DARLING(1982, Can./Ger.), m
Jan Van Lusil
TORSO MURDER MYSTERY, THE(1940, Brit.), w
Henry van Lyck
24-HOUR LOVER(1970, Ger.); EVERY MAN FOR HIMSELF AND GOD AGAINST ALL(1975, Ger.); COUP DE GRACE(1978, Ger./Fr.); SIGNS OF LIFE(1981, Ger.)
Vincent Van Lynn
SILENCERS, THE(1966); WRECKING CREW, THE(1968); MAROONED(1969); DOCTORS' WIVES(1971); FUZZ(1972); REPORT TO THE COMMISSIONER(1975)
Kathy Van Lypps
ASH WEDNESDAY(1973)
Hans Van Manen
BLACK TIGHTS(1962, Fr.)
George Van Marta
SLAUGHTER TRAIL(1951), art d
George Van Martar
CHAMPAGNE FOR CAESAR(1950), art d
George Van Marten
CRIME DOCTOR'S STRANGEST CASE(1943), art d; MAGNETIC MONSTER, THE(1953), prod d
G.C. Van Marter
MR. WISE GUY(1942), art d

George Van Marter
WHISTLER, THE(1944), art d; HOLLYWOOD AND VINE(1945), art d; TOWN WENT WILD, THE(1945), art d; LITTLE IODINE(1946), art d; SUSIE STEPS OUT(1946), art d; WHISTLE STOP(1946), art d; GUNFIGHTERS, THE(1947), art d; HALF PAST MIDNIGHT(1948), art d; NIGHT WIND(1948), art d; OPEN SECRET(1948), art d; DAUGHTER OF THE WEST(1949), art d; FIGHTING MAN OF THE PLAINS(1949), art d; FOUR GUNS TO THE BORDER(1954), w; THUNDER PASS(1954), w; DRANGO(1957), art d; FIERCEST HEART, THE(1961), art d; PIRATES OF TORTUGA(1961), art d; TWIST AROUND THE CLOCK(1961), art d; SWINGIN' ALONG(1962), art d
George C. Van Marter
SPIRIT OF WEST POINT, THE(1947), art d
Harry Van Meter
Silents
KAISER, BEAST OF BERLIN, THE(1918); CHALLENGE OF CHANCE, THE(1919); LONE HAND, THE(1920); BEAUTIFUL GAMBLER, THE(1921); REPUTATION(1921); PUTTING IT OVER(1922); HUNCHBACK OF NOTRE DAME, THE(1923); NOBODY'S BRIDE(1923); SPEED KING(1923)
Misc. Silents
BUZZARD'S SHADOW, THE(1915); CAPTAIN KIDDO(1917); DREAM LADY, THE(1918); MIDNIGHT MADNESS(1918); DAY SHE PAID, THE(1919); GUN-FIGHTIN' GENTLEMAN, A(1919); ALIAS MISS DODD(1920); CHEATER, THE(1920); DOLLAR FOR DOLLAR(1920); UNDER CRIMSON SKIES(1920); UNFORTUNATE SEX, THE(1920); GUILTY CONSCIENCE, A(1921); BROADWAY MADONNA, THE(1922); WHEN ROMANCE RIDES(1922); WILDCAT JORDAN(1922)
Robert Van Meter
LIBERATION OF L.B. JONES, THE(1970)
Heleen Van Meurs
LITTLE ARK, THE(1972)
Hubert Van Meyerinck
ONE, TWO, THREE(1961)
To Van Minh
GLADIATORS, THE(1970, Swed.)
Eunice Van Moore
Silents
HUCKLEBERRY FINN(1920)
Burt Van Munster
MASSACRE AT CENTRAL HIGH(1976), ph
John Van Ness
POSTMAN ALWAYS RINGS TWICE, THE(1981)
Jon Van Ness
TOURIST TRAP, THE(1979); BRUBAKER(1980); RUCKUS(1981); HOSPITAL MASSACRE(1982); SOME KIND OF HERO(1982)
1984
HOSPITAL MASSACRE(1984); NATURAL, THE(1984)
John Van Ness Philip
1984
BOSTONIANS, THE(1984)
Franz van Norde
MC KENZIE BREAK, THE(1970)
Peter Van Norden
SQUEEZE PLAY(1981)
1984
HARD TO HOLD(1984); ROADHOUSE 66(1984)
Ed Van Nordic
HOWZER(1973)
George Van Noy
GAS-S-S-S!(1970), ed; VON RICHTHOFEN AND BROWN(1970), ed; STUDENT TEACHERS, THE(1973), ed; MR. SYCAMORE(1975), ed; FREEWHEELIN'(1976), w, ed
Rik Van Nutter
THUNDERBALL(1965, Brit.)
Dorothy Van Nuys
ZIEGFELD FOLLIES(1945); HARVEY GIRLS, THE(1946)
Ed Van Nuys
WILLIE AND PHIL(1980)
1984
SILENT MADNESS(1984); UNFAITHFULLY YOURS(1984)
Laura Bower Van Nuys
ONE AND ONLY GENUINE ORIGINAL FAMILY BAND, THE(1968), w
Jaspar Von Oertzer
ONE, TWO, THREE(1961)
Debbie van Orden
SEVEN ALONE(1975)
Robert Van Orden
CARBINE WILLIAMS(1952)
Valerie Van Ost
CARRY ON DOCTOR(1968, Brit.); CORRUPTION(1968, Brit.); COUNT DRACULA AND HIS VAMPIRE BRIDE(1978, Brit.)
Rogier Van Otterloo
SOLDIER OF ORANGE(1979, Dutch), m; OUTSIDER IN AMSTERDAM(1983, Neth.), m
Anita Van Ow
IT HAPPENED IN BROAD DAYLIGHT(1960, Ger./Switz.)
Pierre Van Paassen
J'ACCUSE(1939, Fr.), titles
Frederick Van Pallandt
HU-MAN(1975, Fr.)
Nina van Pallandt
LONG GOODBYE, THE(1973); ASSAULT ON AGATHON(1976, Brit./Gr.); WEDDING, A(1978); QUINTET(1979); AMERICAN GIGOLO(1980); CLOUD DANCER(1980); CUTTER AND BONE(1981); SWORD AND THE SORCERER, THE(1982)
1984
JUNGLE WARRIORS(1984, U.S./Ger./Mex.)
Georges Van Parys
MILLION, THE(1931, Fr.), m; ABUSED CONFIDENCE(1938, Fr. ABUS DE CONFIANCE), m; COUNSEL FOR ROMANCE(1938, Fr.), m; MAN ABOUT TOWN(1947, Fr.), md; MR. PEEK-A-BOO(1951, Fr.), m; FANFAN THE TULIP(1952, Fr.), m; JUPITER(1952, Fr.), m; LES BELLES-DE-NUIT(1952, Fr.), m; EARRINGS OF MADAME DE..., THE(1954, Fr.), m; FLESH AND THE WOMAN(1954, Fr./Ital.), m; SECRETS D'ALCOVE(1954, Fr./Ital.), m; DIABOLIQUE(1955, Fr.), m; CASQUE D'OR(1956, Fr.),

m; FRENCH CANCAN(1956, Fr.), m; GRAND MANEUVER, THE(1956, Fr.), m; HAPPY ROAD, THE(1957), m; NANA(1957, Fr./Ital.), m; MILLIONAIRESS, THE(1960, Brit.), m; NATHALIE, AGENT SECRET(1960, Fr.), m; MODIGLIANI OF MONTPARNASSE(1961, Fr./Ital.), m; I LIKE MONEY(1962, Brit.), m; MAXIME(1962, Fr.), m; DOUBLE DECEPTION(1963, Fr.), m

Dick Van Patten
CHARLY(1968); MAKING IT(1971); ZACHARIAH(1971); DIRTY LITTLE BILLY(1972); JOE KIDD(1972); SNOWBALL EXPRESS(1972); SOYLENT GREEN(1973); WESTWORLD(1973); SUPERDAD(1974); STRONGEST MAN IN THE WORLD, THE(1975); FREAKY FRIDAY(1976); GUS(1976); SHAGGY D.A., THE(1976); TREASURE OF MATECUMBE(1976); HIGH ANXIETY(1977); NUTCRACKER FANTASY(1979)

James Van Patten
YOUNG WARRIORS(1983)

Jimmie Van Patten
LUNCH WAGON(1981)

Jimmy Van Patten
FREAKY FRIDAY(1976); HOT LEAD AND COLD FEET(1978); APPLE DUMPLING GANG RIDES AGAIN, THE(1979); CALIFORNIA DREAMING(1979); ROLLER BOOGIE(1979)

Joyce Van Patten
TROUBLE WITH GIRLS(AND HOW TO GET INTO IT), THE*1/2(1969); FOURTEEN HOURS(1951); GODDESS, THE(1958); I LOVE YOU, ALICE B. TOKLAS!(1968); PUSSYCAT, PUSSYCAT, I LOVE YOU(1970); MAKING IT(1971); SOMETHING BIG(1971); THUMB TRIPPING(1972); MAME(1974); MANCHU EAGLE MURDER CAPER MYSTERY, THE(1975); BAD NEWS BEARS, THE(1976); MIKEY AND NICKY(1976)
Misc. Talkies
BONE(1972)

Nels Van Patten
LUNCH WAGON(1981); YOUNG WARRIORS(1983)

Patricia Van Patten
HERBIE GOES BANANAS(1980)

Richard [Dick] Van Patten
PSYCHOMANIA(1964)

Timothy Van Patten
CLASS OF 1984(1982, Can.)
Misc. Talkies
ESCAPE FROM EL DIABLO(1983, U.S./Brit./Span.)

Vince Van Patten
YESTERDAY(1980, Can.)

Vincent Van Patten
CHARLEY AND THE ANGEL(1973); CHINO(1976, Ital., Span., Fr.); ROCK 'N' ROLL HIGH SCHOOL(1979); SURVIVAL RUN(1980); HELL NIGHT(1981)
Misc. Talkies
THIS TIME FOREVER(1981)

Mario Van Peebles
1984
DELIVERY BOYS(1984); EXTERMINATOR 2(1984)

Melvin Van Peebles
STORY OF A THREE DAY PASS, THE(1968, Fr.), d&w, m; WATERMELON MAN(1970), d, m; GREASED LIGHTNING(1977), w
Misc. Talkies
DON'T PLAY US CHEAP(1973), d

Ernest Van Pelt
I LIVE FOR LOVE(1935)
Silents
BRING HIM IN(1921); AVENGING FANGS(1927), d

John Van Pelt
CROOKED TRAIL, THE(1936); SINGING COWBOY, THE(1936); RIDERS OF THE WHISTLING SKULL(1937)

Stacey A. Van Petten
Silents
ENEMIES OF YOUTH(1925), w

Tom Van Plack
Misc. Silents
GOLDEN ROSARY, THE(1917), d

Uors van Planta
MAN WHO WALKED THROUGH THE WALL, THE(1964, Ger.), prod d

Ruth Van Poons
BELL JAR, THE(1979)

Lionel Van Praag
MONEY FOR SPEED(1933, Brit.)

Van Van Praag
MEN IN WAR(1957), w

Dianne Van Proosdy
DETECTIVE, THE(1954, Qit.)

Joanne Van Raaphorst
TENTACLES(1977, Ital.)

William Van Raaphorst
TENTACLES(1977, Ital.)

Dorothy Van Raven
Misc. Silents
BATTLE OF BALLOTS, THE(1915)

Apollonia van Ravenstein
1984
NOTHING LASTS FOREVER(1984)

Jan Van Reenen
PERSONAL BEST(1982)

Tim Van Rellim
NED KELLY(1970, Brit.); EUREKA(1983, Brit.)

Willie Van Rensburg
RIDER IN THE NIGHT, THE(1968, South Africa)

Frederic Van Rensselear Dey
Silents
MASTER STROKE, A(1920), w

Deborah Van Rhyn
Misc. Talkies
GOIN' ALL THE WAY(1982)

Greg Van Riel
RABID(1976, Can.)

Mario Van Riel
KING OF KINGS(1961), makeup; MORE THAN A MIRACLE(1967, Ital./Fr.), makeup; PLACE FOR LOVERS, A(1969, Ital./Fr.), makeup; SWEET BODY OF DEBORAH, THE(1969, Ital./Fr.), makeup

Raimondo Van Riel
BEN HUR(1959)

Cor Van Rijn
TIME TO DIE, A(1983)

Kay Van Riper
FAMILY AFFAIR, A(1937), w; JUDGE HARDY'S CHILDREN(1938), w; OUT WEST WITH THE HARDYS(1938), w; YOU'RE ONLY YOUNG ONCE(1938), w; ANDY HARDY GETS SPRING FEVER(1939), w; BABES IN ARMS(1939), w; BLONDIE MEETS THE BOSS(1939), w; HARDYS RIDE HIGH, THE(1939), w; STRIKE UP THE BAND(1940), w; KATHLEEN(1941), w; LADY BE GOOD(1941), w

Joe Van Rogers
BRAIN OF BLOOD(1971, Phil.), w

Jo Van Ronkel
CONVICTED(1931), w

Rip van Ronkel
DESTINATION MOON(1950), w; BEAUTIFUL STRANGER(1954, Brit.), w; HIGH COST OF LOVING, THE(1958), w; ONCE UPON A SCOUNDREL(1973), w

Luis Van Rooten
HITLER GANG, THE(1944); TWO YEARS BEFORE THE MAST(1946); BEYOND GLORY(1948); BIG CLOCK, THE(1948); GENTLEMAN FROM NOWHERE, THE(1948); NIGHT HAS A THOUSAND EYES(1948); SAIGON(1948); TO THE ENDS OF THE EARTH(1948); TO THE VICTOR(1948); BOSTON BLACKIE'S CHINESE VENTURE(1949); CHAMPION(1949); CITY ACROSS THE RIVER(1949); SECRET OF ST. IVES, THE(1949); CINDERELLA(1950); DETECTIVE STORY(1951); MY FAVORITE SPY(1951); LYDIA BAILEY(1952); SEA CHASE, THE(1955); UNHOLY WIFE, THE(1957); CURSE OF THE FACELESS MAN(1958); FRAULEIN(1958); OPERATION EICHMANN(1961)

Alex Van Rooyen
Misc. Talkies
BECAUSE OF THE CATS(1974)

DeWet Van Rooyen
WILD GEESE, THE(1978, Brit.)

Laurens Van Rooyen
MYSTERIES(1979, Neth.), m

Robert Van Rosen
CANTOR'S SON, THE(1937), art d

Felicity Van Runkle
ACE ELI AND RODGER OF THE SKIES(1973)

Theadora Van Runkle
I LOVE YOU, ALICE B. TOKLAS!(1968), cos; THOMAS CROWN AFFAIR, THE(1968), cos; PLACE FOR LOVERS, A(1969, Ital./Fr.), cos; REIVERS, THE(1969), cos; MAME(1974), cos; NICKELODEON(1976), cos; NEW YORK, NEW YORK(1977), cos; SAME TIME, NEXT YEAR(1978), cos; HEARTBEEPS(1981), cos; S.O.B.(1981), cos
1984
RHINESTONE(1984), cos

Theodora Van Runkle
BONNIE AND CLYDE(1967), cos; BULLITT(1968), cos; ACE ELI AND RODGER OF THE SKIES(1973), cos; KID BLUE(1973), cos; GODFATHER, THE, PART II(1974), cos; HEAVEN CAN WAIT(1978), cos; JERK, THE(1979), cos; BEST LITTLE WHOREHOUSE IN TEXAS, THE(1982), cos

Glory Van Scott
WIZ, THE(1978)

Chris Van Scoyk
REMARKABLE MR. PENNYPACKER, THE(1959)

Jon Van Scoyk
REMARKABLE MR. PENNYPACKER, THE(1959)

Robert A. Van Senus
1984
SUBURBIA(1984)

Dale Van Sickel
RICHEST GIRL IN THE WORLD, THE(1934); STUDENT TOUR(1934); ROBERTA(1935); DODSWORTH(1936); MR. DEEDS GOES TO TOWN(1936); SWING TIME(1936); THIS IS MY AFFAIR(1937); KING OF THE NEWSBOYS(1938); RACKET BUSTERS(1938); SECOND FIDDLE(1939); SERGEANT MADDEN(1939); YOU CAN'T CHEAT AN HONEST MAN(1939); RETURN OF FRANK JAMES, THE(1940); HELLZAPOPPIN'(1941); LAW OF THE TROPICS(1941); IT HAPPENED IN FLATBUSH(1942); REAP THE WILD WIND(1942); SABOTEUR(1942); SPIRIT OF STANFORD, THE(1942); THEY ALL KISSED THE BRIDE(1942); DESTROYER(1943); DESTINY(1944); GIRL RUSH(1944); KISMET(1944); LONE TEXAS RANGER(1945); STOLEN LIFE, A(1946); WELL-GROOMED BRIDE, THE(1946); TRESPASSER, THE(1947); CARSON CITY RAIDERS(1948); DESPERADOES OF DODGE CITY(1948); LIGHTNIN' IN THE FOREST(1948); OKLAHOMA BADLANDS(1948); RENEGADES OF SONORA(1948); DUKE OF CHICAGO(1949); GOLDEN STALLION, THE(1949); MIGHTY JOE YOUNG(1949); DESERT HAWK, THE(1950); SIDESHOW(1950); STORM WARNING(1950); HE RAN ALL THE WAY(1951); ROUGH RIDERS OF DURANGO(1951); DEAD MAN'S TRAIL(1952); GREATEST SHOW ON EARTH, THE(1952); SCARLET ANGEL(1952); HERE COME THE GIRLS(1953); MISSISSIPPI GAMBLER, THE(1953); NORTHERN PATROL(1953); THUNDER BAY(1953); TOPEKA(1953); VEILS OF BAGDAD, THE(1953); WAR OF THE WORLDS, THE(1953), a, stunts; ROGUE COP(1954); LOVE ME OR LEAVE ME(1955); BEHIND THE HIGH WALL(1956); HE LAUGHED LAST(1956); SEARCHERS, THE(1956); TEA AND SYMPATHY(1956); GARMENT JUNGLE, THE(1957); GIRL IN THE KREMLIN, THE(1957); NIGHT RUNNER, THE(1957); OMAR KHAYYAM(1957); SHOOT-OUT AT MEDICINE BEND(1957); 20 MILLION MILES TO EARTH(1957); ENCHANTED ISLAND(1958); SATAN'S SATELLITES(1958); GHOST OF ZORRO(1959); NORTH BY NORTHWEST(1959); SPARTACUS(1960); SIX BLACK HORSES(1962); REQUIEM FOR A GUNFIGHTER(1965); TOWN TAMER(1965); CYBORG 2087(1966); GNOME-MOBILE, THE(1967); GUIDE FOR THE MARRIED MAN, A(1967); ST. VALENTINE'S DAY MASSACRE, THE(1967); LOVE BUG, THE(1968)

Dan Van Sickel
COBRA WOMAN(1944)

Don Van Sickel
IT'S A MAD, MAD, MAD, MAD WORLD(1963)
Dale Van Sickle
GOD IS MY CO-PILOT(1945); LAST ROUND-UP, THE(1947); ARCTIC FLIGHT(1952); SEVEN WAYS FROM SUNDOWN(1960); JOHNNY RENO(1966)
E.L. Van Sickle
Misc. Silents
BETTER MAN WINS, THE(1922)
Edward Van Sickle
GODFATHER, THE, PART II(1974)
Joe Van Sickle
ROCK 'N' ROLL HIGH SCHOOL(1979)
Ken Van Sickle
MAKE A FACE(1971), ph
Kenneth Van Sickle
HESTER STREET(1975), ph; BETWEEN THE LINES(1977), ph
Raymond Van Sickle
NADA MAS QUE UNA MUJER(1934), w; THREE ON A HONEYMOON(1934), w
Willard Van Simons
WONDER MAN(1945)
Bill Van Sleet
LORDS OF FLATBUSH, THE(1974)
Edward Van Sloan
DRACULA(1931); FRANKENSTEIN(1931); MANHATTAN PARADE(1931); BEHIND THE MASK(1932); FORGOTTEN COMMANDMENTS(1932); MAN WANTED(1932); MUMMY, THE(1932); PLAY GIRL(1932); THUNDER BELOW(1932); DEATH KISS, THE(1933); DELUGE(1933); INFERNAL MACHINE(1933); IT'S GREAT TO BE ALIVE(1933); SILK EXPRESS, THE(1933); TRICK FOR TRICK(1933); WORKING MAN, THE(1933); CROSBY CASE, THE(1934); DEATH TAKES A HOLIDAY(1934); I'LL FIX IT(1934); LIFE OF VERGIE WINTERS, THE(1934); MANHATTAN MELODRAMA(1934); MURDER ON THE CAMPUS(1934); SCARLET EMPRESS, THE(1934); AIR HAWKS(1935); BLACK ROOM, THE(1935); GRAND EXIT(1935); GRAND OLD GIRL(1935); LAST DAYS OF POMPEII, THE(1935); MAN WHO RECLAIMED HIS HEAD, THE(1935); MILLS OF THE GODS(1935); SHOT IN THE DARK, A(1935); WOMAN IN RED, THE(1935); DRACULA'S DAUGHTER(1936); FATAL LADY(1936); ROAD GANG(1936); SINS OF MAN(1936); STORY OF LOUIS PASTEUR, THE(1936); MAN WHO FOUND HIMSELF, THE(1937); ROAD BACK,THE(1937); DANGER ON THE AIR(1938); PENITENTIARY(1938); STORM OVER BENGAL(1938); HONEYMOON IN BALI(1939); BEFORE I HANG(1940); DOCTOR TAKES A WIFE(1940); SECRET SEVEN, THE(1940); LOVE CRAZY(1941); MONSTER AND THE GIRL, THE(1941); VIRGINIA(1941); DESTINATION UNKNOWN(1942); HITLER'S CHILDREN(1942); MAN'S WORLD, A(1942); VALLEY OF HUNTED MEN(1942); MISSION TO MOSCOW(1943); RIDERS OF THE RIO GRANDE(1943); SONG OF BERNADETTE, THE(1943); END OF THE ROAD(1944); WING AND A PRAYER(1944); BETTY CO-ED(1946); MASK OF DIIJON, THE(1946); SEALED VERDICT(1948)
Misc. Silents
SLANDER(1916)
Arthur Van Slyke
LAW FOR TOMBSTONE(1937); SANDFLOW(1937); BLACK BANDIT(1938); BORDER WOLVES(1938); OUTLAW EXPRESS(1938)
Perry Van Soest
1984
JOY OF SEX(1984)
Michel Van Speybroeck
1984
LE BAL(1984, Fr./Ital./Algeria)
Marcel van Steenhuyse
1984
SMURFS AND THE MAGIC FLUTE, THE(1984, Fr./Belg.), ph
Doorn Van Steyn
TROJAN BROTHERS, THE(1946); MADAME LOUISE(1951, Brit.)
Gilda Doorn Van Steyn
TEL AVIV TAXI(1957, Israel)
Anton Van Stralen
JAILBREAKERS, THE(1960); HONEYMOON OF TERROR(1961); SNIPER'S RIDGE(1961); INVASION OF THE STAR CREATURES(1962)
Van Straten's Piccadilly Dance Band
UP WITH THE LARK(1943, Brit.)
Robert Van Strawder
SINGLE ROOM FURNISHED(1968)
Leontine Van Strein
LA DOLCE VITA(1961, Ital./Fr.)
Jan Van Tamelen
TRADER HORN(1973), art d
Marie Van Tassell
Misc. Silents
DULCIE'S ADVENTURE(1916); HIGHEST BID, THE(1916)
B. Van Thal
THE BEACHCOMBER(1938, Brit.), w
Ernt Van Theumer
JULIE DARLING(1982, Can./Ger.), p
Friedrich Van Thun
PRAYING MANTIS(1982, Brit.)
Hans Van Tongeren
SUMMER LOVERS(1982); SPETTERS(1983, Holland)
J. C. Van Trees
Silents
NURSE MARJORIE(1920), ph; SOUL OF YOUTH, THE(1920), ph
J.G. Van Trees
ARGYLE CASE, THE(1929), ph
James Van Trees
LONE WOLF'S DAUGHTER, THE(1929), ph; SACRED FLAME, THE(1929), ph; SO LONG LETTY(1929), ph; GREEN GODDESS, THE(1930), ph; MAN FROM BLANKLEY'S, THE(1930), ph; MAN HUNTER, THE(1930), ph; OLD ENGLISH(1930), ph; SHE COULDN'T SAY NO(1930), ph; VIENNESE NIGHTS(1930), ph; ALEXANDER HAMILTON(1931), ph; CAPTAIN THUNDER(1931), ph; CHILDREN OF DREAMS(1931), ph; GOLD DUST GERTIE(1931), ph; MILLIONAIRE, THE(1931), ph; RECKLESS HOUR, THE(1931), ph; STAR WITNESS(1931), ph; BIG CITY BLUES(1932), ph; HEART OF NEW YORK(1932), ph; LIFE BEGINS(1932), ph; MAN WHO PLAYED GOD, THE(1932), ph; SILVER DOLLAR(1932), ph; SUCCESSFUL

CALAMITY, A(1932), ph; TAXI!(1932), ph; THEY CALL IT SIN(1932), ph; BABY FACE(1933), ph; BLOOD MONEY(1933), ph; HEROES FOR SALE(1933), ph; I LOVED A WOMAN(1933), ph; KING'S VACATION, THE(1933), ph; MIDNIGHT MARY(1933), ph; PARACHUTE JUMPER(1933), ph; AGE OF INNOCENCE(1934), ph; GENTLEMEN ARE BORN(1934), ph; LOOKING FOR TROUBLE(1934), ph; MURDER IN THE PRIVATE CAR(1934), ph; EVERY NIGHT AT EIGHT(1935), ph; GIRL FROM TENTH AVENUE, THE(1935), ph; NIGHT AT THE RITZ, A(1935), ph; SHANGHAI(1935), ph; SWEET MUSIC(1935), ph; WEST OF THE PECOS(1935), ph; CAREER WOMAN(1936), ph; FLYING HOSTESS(1936), ph; HER MASTER'S VOICE(1936), ph; MAN WHO LIVED TWICE(1936), ph; PALM SPRINGS(1936), ph; THEY MET IN A TAXI(1936), ph; UNGUARDED HOUR, THE(1936), ph; EXPENSIVE HUSBANDS(1937), ph; IT'S LOVE I'M AFTER(1937), ph; LET THEM LIVE(1937), ph; LOVE IS ON THE AIR(1937), ph; OVER THE WALL(1938), ph; PATIENT IN ROOM 18, THE(1938), ph; SMASHING THE MONEY RING(1939), ph; WATERFRONT(1939), ph; FLIGHT FROM DESTINY(1941), ph; HERE COMES HAPPINESS(1941), ph; INTERNATIONAL SQUADRON(1941), ph; NURSE'S SECRET, THE(1941), ph; SHOT IN THE DARK, THE(1941), ph; STEEL AGAINST THE SKY(1941), ph; BUSSES ROAR(1942), ph; ESCAPE FROM CRIME(1942), ph; GORILLA MAN(1942), ph; SECRET ENEMIES(1942), ph; YOU CAN'T ESCAPE FOREVER(1942), ph; ADVENTURES IN IRAQ(1943), ph; FIND THE BLACKMAILER(1943), ph; LAST RIDE, THE(1944), ph; NINE GIRLS(1944), ph; TWO-MAN SUBMARINE(1944), ph; BEDSIDE MANNER(1945), ph; GREAT JOHN L. THE(1945), ph; HIT THE HAY(1945), ph; ANGEL ON MY SHOULDER(1946), ph; NIGHT IN CASABLANCA, A(1946), ph; FABULOUS DORSEYS, THE(1947), ph
Silents
WITCHING HOUR, THE(1921), ph; WHITE FLOWER, THE(1923), ph; TOP OF NEW YORK, THE(1925), ph; CRYSTAL CUP, THE(1927), ph; MAN CRAZY(1927), ph; HEART OF A FOLLIES GIRL, THE(1928), ph; SCARLET LADY, THE(1928), ph; SINNER'S PARADE(1928), ph
James Van Trees, Sr.
ADVICE TO THE LOVELORN(1933), ph; WINE, WOMEN AND HORSES(1937), ph
James C. Van Trees
Silents
GOOD NIGHT, PAUL(1918), ph; PAIR OF SILK STOCKINGS, A(1918), ph; ROMANCE AND ARABELLA(1919), ph; JENNY BE GOOD(1920), ph; JUDY OF ROGUES' HARBOUR(1920), ph; MORALS(1921), ph; WEALTH(1921), ph; HUNTRESS, THE(1923), ph; IF I MARRY AGAIN(1925), ph; PRINCE OF PILSEN, THE(1926), ph; TWINKLETOES(1926), ph; NOOSE, THE(1928), ph
James Van Tress
STINGAREE(1934), ph
Jessalyn Van Trump
Misc. Silents
GIRL IN THE RAIN, THE(1920)
Helen Van Tuyl
DADDY LONG LEGS(1955)
Helen Marr Van Tuyl
JEANNE EAGELS(1957)
Hellen Van Tuyl
CONFIDENCE GIRL(1952); STARS AND STRIPES FOREVER(1952); TITANIC(1953); GIRL IN THE RED VELVET SWING, THE(1955)
Bert Van Tuyle
Misc. Silents
GRUB STAKE, THE(1923), d
Hans Van Twardowski
JOAN OF OZARK(1942)
Helen Van Upp
Silents
WOLVERINE, THE(1921), w
Virginia Van Upp
PURSUIT OF HAPPINESS, THE(1934), w; EASY TO TAKE(1936), w; MY AMERICAN WIFE(1936), w; POPPY(1936), w; TIMOTHY'S QUEST(1936), w; TOO MANY PARENTS(1936), w; SWING HIGH, SWING LOW(1937), w; YOU AND ME(1938), w; CAFE SOCIETY(1939), w; HONEYMOON IN BALI(1939), w; ST. LOUIS BLUES(1939), w; BAHAMA PASSAGE(1941), w; COME LIVE WITH ME(1941), w; ONE NIGHT IN LISBON(1941), w; VIRGINIA(1941), w; CRYSTAL BALL, THE(1943), w; YOUNG AND WILLING(1943), w; COVER GIRL(1944), w; IMPATIENT YEARS, THE(1944), w; TOGETHER AGAIN(1944), p, w; SHE WOULDN'T SAY YES(1945), p, w; GILDA(1946), p; HERE COMES THE GROOM(1951), w; AFFAIR IN TRINIDAD(1952), w
Freddie Van Urk
WILD SEASON(1968, South Africa)
Gerrit Van Urk
WILD SEASON(1968, South Africa)
Diane Van Valin
GIRL WHO KNEW TOO MUCH, THE(1969)
Eric Van Valkenburg
FAN, THE(1981); EASY MONEY(1983)
Richard Van Valkenburg
EASY MONEY(1983)
Deborah Van Valkenburgh
WARRIORS, THE(1979); KING OF THE MOUNTAIN(1981)
1984
STREETS OF FIRE(1984)
Herman van Veen
SPLITTING UP(1981, Neth.), a, d&w
Bill Van Vleck
SEA OF GRASS, THE(1947)
Gohr Van Vleck
MYSTERY SEA RAIDER(1940); JOHNNY EAGER(1942); LUCKY LEGS(1942); ONCE UPON A HONEYMOON(1942); WIFE TAKES A FLYER, THE(1942)
William Van Vleck
OUT OF THE PAST(1947)
Silents
RANGER OF THE NORTH(1927)
Jean Van Vliet
Silents
LADIES AT EASE(1927)
John Van Vliet
RAIDERS OF THE LOST ARK(1981), anim

Monique Van Vooren
TARZAN AND THE SHE-DEVIL(1953); TEN THOUSAND BEDROOMS(1957); GIGI(1958); HAPPY ANNIVERSARY(1959); FEARLESS FRANK(1967); ASH WEDNESDAY(1973)
Misc. Talkies
ANDY WARHOL'S FRANKENSTEIN(1974)

Yvette Van Voorhees
XANADU(1980)

Westbrook Van Voorhis
RAMPARTS WE WATCH, THE(1940); LADIES MAN, THE(1961)

Marie Van Vorst
Silents
GIRL FROM HIS TOWN, THE(1915), w; BIG TREMAINE(1916), w

Peter Van Weigen
MILL OF THE STONE WOMEN(1963, Fr./Ital.), w

Carola Gijbers Van Wijk
LIFT, THE(1983, Neth.)

Joseph Van Winkle
GATLING GUN, THE(1972), w; DARK PLACES(1974, Brit.), w; WOMAN INSIDE, THE(1981), d&w

Judy Van Wormer
GNOME-MOBILE, THE(1967); 1941(1979), ch

Edwin Van Wyk
1984
SUPERGIRL(1984)

Billy Van Zandt
JAWS II(1978); STAR TREK: THE MOTION PICTURE(1979); TAPS(1981)

Jack Van Zandt
RIVER LADY(1948)

Julie Van Zandt
BEST THINGS IN LIFE ARE FREE, THE(1956)

Phil Van Zandt
AIR RAID WARDENS(1943); DEERSLAYER(1943); HANGMEN ALSO DIE(1943); TARZAN'S DESERT MYSTERY(1943); BIG NOISE, THE(1944); CALL OF THE JUNGLE(1944); UNWRITTEN CODE, THE(1944); BOSTON BLACKIE'S RENDEZVOUS(1945); SUDAN(1945); DECOY(1946); DON'T GAMBLE WITH STRANGERS(1946); GILDA(1946); SOMEWHERE IN THE NIGHT(1946); LIFE WITH FATHER(1947); LADY FROM SHANGHAI, THE(1948); ALIAS NICK BEAL(1949); LADY GAMBLES, THE(1949); PRIDE OF ST. LOUIS, THE(1952); VIVA ZAPATA!(1952); THREE SAILORS AND A GIRL(1953); THREE RING CIRCUS(1954); MAN OF A THOUSAND FACES(1957); 27TH DAY, THE(1957)

Philip Van Zandt
CITIZEN KANE(1941); CITY OF MISSING GIRLS(1941); IN OLD COLORADO(1941); PARIS CALLING(1941); SO ENDS OUR NIGHT(1941); COMMANDOS STRIKE AT DAWN, THE(1942); DARING YOUNG MAN, THE(1942); INVISIBLE AGENT(1942); NAZI AGENT(1942); REUNION IN FRANCE(1942); WAKE ISLAND(1942); ALWAYS A BRIDESMAID(1943); HOSTAGES(1943); MURDER ON THE WATERFRONT(1943); OLD ACQUAINTANCE(1943); TARZAN TRIUMPHS(1943); DRAGON SEED(1944); 'TILL WE MEET AGAIN(1944); COUNTER-ATTACK(1945); I LOVE A BANDLEADER(1945); OUTLAWS OF THE ROCKIES(1945); THOUSAND AND ONE NIGHTS, A(1945); AVALANCHE(1946); BANDIT OF SHERWOOD FOREST, THE(1946); BELOW THE DEADLINE(1946); CALIFORNIA(1946); JOE PALOOKA, CHAMP(1946); MONSIEUR BEAUCAIRE(1946); LAST FRONTIER UPRISING(1947); SLAVE GIRL(1947); BIG CLOCK, THE(1948); EMBRACEABLE YOU(1948); LOVES OF CARMEN, THE(1948); NIGHT HAS A THOUSAND EYES(1948); SAXON CHARM, THE(1948); SHANGHAI CHEST, THE(1948); STREET WITH NO NAME, THE(1948); VICIOUS CIRCLE, THE(1948); WALK A CROOKED MILE(1948); LONE WOLF AND HIS LADY, THE(1949); RED, HOT AND BLUE(1949); TENSION(1949); BETWEEN MIDNIGHT AND DAWN(1950); BLONDE BANDIT, THE(1950); CYRANO DE BERGERAC(1950); INDIAN TERRITORY(1950); JACKPOT, THE(1950); PETTY GIRL, THE(1950); WHERE DANGER LIVES(1950); DESERT FOX, THE(1951); GHOST CHASERS(1951); HIS KIND OF WOMAN(1951); MASK OF THE AVENGER(1951); SUBMARINE COMMAND(1951); TEN TALL MEN(1951); MACAO(1952); SON OF ALI BABA(1952); THIEF OF DAMASCUS(1952); YUKON GOLD(1952); CLIPPED WINGS(1953); GIRL WHO HAD EVERYTHING, THE(1953); PERILOUS JOURNEY, A(1953); PRISONERS OF THE CASBAH(1953); RIDE, VAQUERO!(1953); DRAGON'S GOLD(1954); GOG(1954); HIGH AND THE MIGHTY, THE(1954); KNOCK ON WOOD(1954); PLAYGIRL(1954); YANKEE PASHA(1954); BIG COMBO, THE(1955); I COVER THE UNDERWORLD(1955); TO CATCH A THIEF(1955); UNTAMED(1955); OUR MISS BROOKS(1956); URANIUM BOOM(1956); LONELY MAN, THE(1957); PRIDE AND THE PASSION, THE(1957); SHOOT-OUT AT MEDICINE BEND(1957); CROOKED CIRCLE, THE(1958)

Phillip Van Zandt
SHERLOCK HOLMES AND THE SECRET WEAPON(1942); GUY NAMED JOE, A(1943); APRIL SHOWERS(1948); COPPER CANYON(1950); TWO DOLLAR BETTOR(1951)

Philp Van Zandt
HOUSE OF FRANKENSTEIN(1944)

Martin Van Zundert
Misc. Talkies
BECAUSE OF THE CATS(1974)

Josef Vana
FANTASTIC PLANET(1973, Fr./Czech.), anim

Jack Vanair
SYLVIA SCARLETT(1936)

Jacques Vanair
LOVE ON THE RUN(1936)

Jacques Vanaire
FASHIONS IN LOVE(1929); BEHIND THE MAKEUP(1930); JEWEL ROBBERY(1932); MAN WHO BROKE THE BANK AT MONTE CARLO, THE(1935); UNDER THE PAMPAS MOON(1935); ROAD TO GLORY, THE(1936); EBB TIDE(1937); ESPIONAGE(1937); I MET HIM IN PARIS(1937); ARSENE LUPIN RETURNS(1938); ARTISTS AND MODELS ABROAD(1938); JEZEBEL(1938); SHINING HOUR, THE(1938); SUEZ(1938); SWISS MISS(1938); ARISE, MY LOVE(1940); TOO MANY HUSBANDS(1940); PARIS CALLING(1941); PHANTOM SUBMARINE, THE(1941); PLAYMATES(1941); UNFINISHED BUSINESS(1941); I MARRIED AN ANGEL(1942); ONCE UPON A HONEYMOON(1942); WE WERE DANCING(1942)

Varick Vanardy
Silents
ALIAS THE NIGHT WIND(1923), w

Mario Vanarelli
NO EXIT(1962, U.S./Arg.), art d; MASTER OF HORROR(1965, Arg.), art d

Paul Vanase
SATURDAY NIGHT AT THE BATHS(1975)

Irene Vanbrugh
HEAD OF THE FAMILY(1933, Brit.); CATHERINE THE GREAT(1934, Brit.); GIRLS WILL BE BOYS(1934, Brit.); WAY OF YOUTH, THE(1934, Brit.); YOUTHFUL FOLLY(1934, Brit.); ESCAPE ME NEVER(1935, Brit.); KNIGHT WITHOUT ARMOR(1937, Brit.); WINGS OF THE MORNING(1937, Brit.); IT HAPPENED ONE SUNDAY(1944, Brit.); YANK IN LONDON, A(1946, Brit.)
Silents
GAY LORD QUEX, THE(1917, Brit.)
Misc. Silents
MASKS AND FACES(1917, Brit.)

John Vanbrugh
LOCK UP YOUR DAUGHTERS(1969, Brit.), w

Prudence Vanbrugh
Silents
KING OF THE CASTLE(1925, Brit.)

Violet Vanbrugh
JOY RIDE(1935, Brit.); PYGMALION(1938, Brit.); YOUNG MAN'S FANCY(1943, Brit.)
Misc. Silents
MACBETH(1916, Ger.)

Louis Joseph Vanca
COUNTER-ESPIONAGE(1942), w

Colin Vancao
CHARGE OF THE LIGHT BRIGADE, THE(1968, Brit.); ROAD GAMES(1981, Aus.)

Vance
WITNESS IN THE DARK(1959, Brit.), w

Byron Vance
SAGEBRUSH FAMILY TRAILS WEST, THE(1940); LONE RIDER IN GHOST TOWN, THE(1941); TEXAS MARSHAL, THE(1941)

Charles Vance
STRANGER AT MY DOOR(1950, Brit.)

Clarice Vance
Silents
DOWN TO THE SEA IN SHIPS(1923)

Dana Vance
TERMS OF ENDEARMENT(1983)

Daniel Vance
NO MERCY MAN, THE(1975), d, w

Denis Vance
WARNING TO WANTONS, A(1949, Brit.)

Dennis Vance
TROUBLE IN THE AIR(1948, Brit.); CHRISTOPHER COLUMBUS(1949, Brit.); DIAMOND CITY(1949, Brit.); SCOTT OF THE ANTARCTIC(1949, Brit.); SING ALONG WITH ME(1952, Brit.), a, w; LANDFALL(1953, Brit.); SHADOW OF THE EAGLE(1955, Brit.)

Diana Vance
FIRST NUDIE MUSICAL, THE(1976)

Don Vance
GROUNDSTAR CONSPIRACY, THE(1972, Can.)

Dorothy Vance
NIGHT OF THE IGUANA, THE(1964)

Ethel Vance
ESCAPE(1940), w; WINTER MEETING(1948), w

Gayle Vance
ON THE NICKEL(1980)

Jack Vance
CRIMINAL CODE(1931)

James Vance
MONSTER THAT CHALLENGED THE WORLD, THE(1957), art d; VAMPIRE, THE(1957), art d; FLAME BARRIER, THE(1958), art d; RETURN OF DRACULA, THE(1958), art d; GRISSOM GANG, THE(1971), art d; ULZANA'S RAID(1972), art d; MURPH THE SURF(1974), prod d; NIGHTWING(1979), prod d

James D. Vance
LONE RANGER AND THE LOST CITY OF GOLD, THE(1958), art d; MIDNIGHT MAN, THE(1974), prod d; THREE WOMEN(1977), art d; MAKING LOVE(1982), prod d
1984
LONELY GUY, THE(1984), prod d

James Dowell Vance
TOO LATE THE HERO(1970), art d

James S. Vance
LONGEST YARD, THE(1974), prod d

Jim Vance
SCREAM, BABY, SCREAM(1969)
Misc. Talkies
HOW TO MAKE A DOLL(1967)

Kenny Vance
MANHATTAN(1979); EDDIE AND THE CRUISERS(1983)

Leigh Vance
FLESH IS WEAK, THE(1957, Brit.), w; HEART OF A CHILD(1958, Brit.), w; AND WOMEN SHALL WEEP(1960, Brit.), w; PICCADILLY THIRD STOP(1960, Brit.), w; SHAKEDOWN, THE(1960, Brit.), w; FRIGHTENED CITY, THE(1961, Brit.), p, w; DR. CRIPPEN(1963, Brit.), w; DREAM MAKER, THE(1963, Brit.), w; CURSE OF THE VOODOO(1965, Brit.), w; CROSSPLOT(1969, Brit.), w; BLACK WINDMILL, THE(1974, Brit.), w

Louis Joseph Vance
MASQUERADE(1929), w; LAST OF THE LONE WOLF(1930), w; CHEATERS AT PLAY(1932), w; LONE WOLF RETURNS, THE(1936), w; LONE WOLF IN PARIS, THE(1938), w; LONE WOLF SPY HUNT, THE(1939), w; SECRETS OF THE LONE WOLF(1941), w; ONE DANGEROUS NIGHT(1943), w; LONE WOLF IN MEXICO, THE(1947), w

Silents
DAY OF DAYS, THE(1914), w; FALSE FACES(1919), w; WILD HONEY(1919), w; DARK MIRROR, THE(1920), w; BEAU REVEL(1921), w; BRONZE BELL, THE(1921), w; MARRIED FLIRTS(1924), w; KING OF THE TURF, THE(1926), w; ALIAS THE LONE WOLF(1927), w

Lucile Vance
UNSUSPECTED, THE(1947)

Lucille Vance
BOWERY AT MIDNIGHT(1942); BAD MEN OF THUNDER GAP(1943); BOSS OF THE RAWHIDE(1944); IDEA GIRL(1946)

Luis H. Vance
36 HOURS(1965), d&w

Marc Vance
1984
HOT DOG...THE MOVIE(1984)

Marilyn Vance
1984
ROMANCING THE STONE(1984), cos; STREETS OF FIRE(1984), cos; WILD LIFE, THE(1984), cos

Marilyn Kay Vance
JEKYLL AND HYDE...TOGETHER AGAIN(1982), cos; 48 HOURS(1982), cos

Norma Vance
DESTINATION MURDER(1950)

Pam Vance
UNDER THE RAINBOW(1981)

Tommy Vance
FLAME(1975, Brit.)

Tracy Vance
FAT SPY(1966)

Vera Vance
Silents
UNHOLY THREE, THE(1925)

Virginia Vance
Silents
GOAT GETTER(1925); NEW YEAR'S EVE(1929)
Misc. Silents
FIGHTING MARINE, THE(1926)

Vivian Vance
SECRET FURY, THE(1950); BLUE VEIL, THE(1951); GREAT RACE, THE(1965)

Florestano Vancini
WOMAN OF THE RIVER(1954, Fr./Ital.), w

Vladislav Vancura
MARKETA LAZAROVA(1968, Czech.), w

Vanda
HEART OF A MAN, THE(1959, Brit.)

Marcel Vandal
Misc. Silents
GRAZIELLA(1926, Fr.), d; FLEUR D'AMOUR(1927, Fr.), d; LE SOUS MARIN DE CRISTAL(1928, Fr.), d

Raoul Vandamme
1984
LIFE IS A BED OF ROSES(1984, Fr.)

Monte Vandegrift
KENNEL MURDER CASE, THE(1933); G-MEN(1935); ONE HOUR LATE(1935); SMART GIRL(1935); TWO FOR TONIGHT(1935); MOON'S OUR HOME, THE(1936); MANDARIN MYSTERY, THE(1937); WESTBOUND LIMITED(1937); MIRACLES FOR SALE(1939); SMASHING THE MONEY RING(1939); TELEVISION SPY(1939)

Monty Vandegrift
HOLLYWOOD BOULEVARD(1936)

Iris Vandeleur
GERT AND DAISY'S WEEKEND(1941, Brit.); OLD MOTHER RILEY'S CIRCUS(1941, Brit.); GERT AND DAISY CLEAN UP(1942, Brit.); ROSE OF TRALEE(1942, Brit.); HOME SWEET HOME(1945, Brit.); LOVE ON THE DOLE(1945, Brit.); SILVER DARLINGS, THE(1947, Brit.); GOOD TIME GIRL(1950, Brit.); LOVE MATCH, THE(1955, Brit.); TRACK THE MAN DOWN(1956, Brit.); IN TROUBLE WITH EVE(1964, Brit.)

Gerard Vandenberg
ZERO IN THE UNIVERSE(1966), ph

Paul Vandenberghe
WOMAN OF SIN(1961, Fr.)

Henry Vandenbroek
HARDCORE(1979)

Craig Vandenburgh
HANKY-PANKY(1982)
1984
BROADWAY DANNY ROSE(1984)

Beau Vandenecker
HARUM SCARUM(1965), cos

Anne Vandenne
LE CIEL EST A VOUS(1957, Fr.)

Jean Vander Pyl
DEEP IN MY HEART(1954); MAN CALLED FLINTSTONE, THE(1966)

Gerard Vanderberg
DREAM TOWN(1973, Ger.), ph

Romano Vanderbes
1984
NEW YORK NIGHTS(1984), p, w

Cornelius Vanderbilt, Jr.
RENO(1930), w

Gloria Vanderbilt
YOUNG DOCTORS, THE(1961)

William "Dutch" Vanderbyl
NECROMANCY(1972), spec eff

John W. Vandercook
MURDER IN TRINIDAD(1934), w; MR. MOTO IN DANGER ISLAND(1939), w; CARIBBEAN MYSTERY, THE(1945), w

Don Vandergriff
WORLD IS JUST A 'B' MOVIE, THE(1971)

Dan Vandergrift
BREAKER! BREAKER!(1977)

Doug Vandergrift
IN SEARCH OF HISTORIC JESUS(1980), art d

Monte Vandergrift
SHOTGUN PASS(1932); SHOOT THE WORKS(1934); ST. LOUIS KID, THE(1934); UPPER WORLD(1934); PRIVATE WORLDS(1935); RENDEZVOUS(1935); SEVEN KEYS TO BALDPATE(1935); EASY MONEY(1936); LONE WOLF RETURNS, THE(1936); RETURN OF SOPHIE LANG, THE(1936); STRIKE ME PINK(1936); SUNSET OF POWER(1936); BREAKFAST FOR TWO(1937); CAPTAINS COURAGEOUS(1937); GIRL WITH IDEAS, A(1937); THIS IS MY AFFAIR(1937); TRUE CONFESSION(1937); COWBOY FROM BROOKLYN(1938); FIRST 100 YEARS, THE(1938); LET US LIVE(1939); TELL NO TALES(1939)

Monty Vandergrift
CALIFORNIA STRAIGHT AHEAD(1937)

Myrtle Vandergrift
ACCIDENTS WILL HAPPEN(1938)

J. Emanuel Vanderhauf
THRILL OF BRAZIL, THE(1946)

A. Vanderhyde
FREUD(1962)

Victoria Vanderkloot
WARRIORS, THE(1979); TIMES SQUARE(1980); FAN, THE(1981); LITTLE SEX, A(1982)
1984
MRS. SOFFEL(1984); OH GOD! YOU DEVIL(1984)

Tom Vanderlaan
NATE AND HAYES(1983, U.S./New Zealand)

George Vanderlip
Silents
PRINCE OF AVENUE A., THE(1920)

Lisa Vanderpump
TOUCH OF CLASS, A(1973, Brit.)

William Vanderpuye
MELODY(1971, Brit.)

Jean Vanderpyl
SANTA AND THE THREE BEARS(1970)

Bill Vanders
STATUE, THE(1971, Brit.)

Warren Vanders
ROUGH NIGHT IN JERICHO(1967); SPLIT, THE(1968); STAY AWAY, JOE(1968); PRICE OF POWER, THE(1969, Ital./Span.); REVENGERS, THE(1972, U.S./Mex.); ROOSTER COGBURN(1975); HOT LEAD AND COLD FEET(1978)

Joyce Vanderveen
TEN COMMANDMENTS, THE(1956); SINGING NUN, THE(1966)

Elinor Vanderveer
NOTORIOUS AFFAIR, A(1930); MOVIE CRAZY(1932)

Leo Vandervelde
HOMECOMING(1948)

Diana Vandervlis
GIRL IN BLACK STOCKINGS(1957)

Phil Vandervort
MARYJANE(1968); BLACK JACK(1973)

Jean Vanderwilt [Bunny Sunshine]
SOUTHERNER, THE(1945)

Mike Vandever
MAN-TRAP(1961); INCIDENT IN AN ALLEY(1962); NEW INTERNS, THE(1964)

Tito Vandis
HARRAD SUMMER, THE(1974)

Titos Vandis
ASTERO(1960, Gr.); NEVER ON SUNDAY(1960, Gr.); IT HAPPENED IN ATHENS(1962); ISLAND OF LOVE(1963); TOPKAPI(1964); STILETTO(1969); EVERYTHING YOU ALWAYS WANTED TO KNOW ABOUT SEX, BUT WE'RE AFRAID TO ASK(1972); EXORCIST, THE(1973); ONCE UPON A SCOUNDREL(1973); BLACK SAMSON(1974); NEWMAN'S LAW(1974); THUNDERBOLT AND LIGHTFOOT(1974); SMILE(1975); OH, GOD!(1977); OTHER SIDE OF MIDNIGHT, THE(1977); PIECE OF THE ACTION, A(1977); BETSY, THE(1978); PERFECT COUPLE, A(1979); YOUNG DOCTORS IN LOVE(1982)

Jerry Vandiver
I'D CLIMB THE HIGHEST MOUNTAIN(1951)

Elinor Vandivere
NINOTCHKA(1939)

Elinore Vandivere
EXILE, THE(1947)

John Vandom
BLOOD OF FRANKENSTEIN(1970), p

Ivan Vandor
SEATED AT HIS RIGHT(1968, Ital.), m; DIARY OF A SCHIZOPHRENIC GIRL(1970, Ital.), m

Nelson Vandor
DON QUIXOTE(1935, Fr.), p

Monte Vandrgrift
WOMAN CHASES MAN(1937)

Charles Vane
Silents
KENT, THE FIGHTING MAN(1916, Brit.); SOLDIER AND A MAN, A(1916, Brit.); QUEEN OF MY HEART(1917, Brit.); MAN AND THE MOMENT, THE(1918, Brit.); NOT GUILTY(1919, Brit.); POLAR STAR, THE(1919, Brit.)
Misc. Silents
SECRET SEVEN, THE(1915, Brit.); TRAFFIC(1915, Brit.); BOYS OF THE OLD BRIGADE, THE(1916, Brit.); WHEEL OF DEATH, THE(1916, Brit.); IT'S NEVER TOO LATE TO MEND(1917, Brit.); SLAVE, THE(1918, Brit.); FETTERED(1919, Brit.); SPLENDID FOLLY(1919, Brit.); WHEN IT WAS DARK(1919, Brit.); LADDIE(1920, Brit.); STORY OF THE ROSARY, THE(1920, Brit.); WAY OF THE WORLD, THE(1920, Brit.); STELLA(1921)

Denton Vane
Silents
ON HER WEDDING NIGHT(1915); APARTMENT 29(1917); IN THE BALANCE(1917); FORTUNE'S CHILD(1919)

Misc. Silents
NAN WHO COULDN'T BEAT GOD, THE(1915); ORDEAL OF ELIZABETH, THE(1916); GLORY OF YOLANDA, THE(1917); GRELL MYSTERY, THE(1917); HAWK, THE(1917); MAELSTROM, THE(1917); STOLEN TREATY, THE(1917); BACHELOR'S CHILDREN, A(1918); BELOVED IMPOSTER, THE(1918); GAME WITH FATE, A(1918); LOVE WATCHES(1918); MISS AMBITION(1918); MOTHER'S SIN, A(1918); BEAUTY PROOF(1919); GIRL AT BAY, A(1919); FLESH AND SPIRIT(1922)

Derek Vane
Silents
MODERN MARRIAGE(1923), w

Gerald Vane
LITTLE DOLLY DAYDREAM(1938, Brit.)

Kenny Vane
AMERICAN HOT WAX(1978)

Myrtle Vane
Silents
APRIL SHOWERS(1923); ARE YOU A FAILURE?(1923); K-THE UNKNOWN(1924)

Norman Thaddeus Vane
CONSCIENCE BAY(1960, Brit.), p, d&w; FLEDGLINGS(1965, Brit), p,d&w; LOLA(1971, Brit./Ital.), w; SHADOW OF THE HAWK(1976, Can.), w; FRIGHTMARE(1983), d&w
1984
BLACK ROOM, THE(1984), d, w
Misc. Talkies
BLACK ROOM, THE(1983), d

Sutton Vane
OUTWARD BOUND(1930), w; BETWEEN TWO WORLDS(1944), w

Thaddeus Vane
MRS. BROWN, YOU'VE GOT A LOVELY DAUGHTER(1968, Brit.), w

James Vaneck
WEEKEND OF FEAR(1966)

Pierre Vaneck
WOMAN OF SIN(1961, Fr.); SEASON FOR LOVE, THE(1963, Fr.); IS PARIS BURNING?(1966, U.S./Fr.)
1984
ERENDIRA(1984, Mex./Fr./Ger.)

Charles Vanel
ACCUSED–STAND UP(1930, Fr.); LES MISERABLES(1936, Fr.); COURRIER SUD(1937, Fr.); ABUSED CONFIDENCE(1938, Fr. ABUS DE CONFIANCE); CROSSROADS(1938, Fr.); THEY WERE FIVE(1938, Fr.); LA FERME DU PENDU(1946, Fr.); SAVAGE BRIGADE(1948, Fr.); WOMAN WHO DARED(1949, Fr.); DIABOLIQUE(1955, Fr.); TO CATCH A THIEF(1955); WAGES OF FEAR, THE(1955, Fr./Ital.); DEFEND MY LOVE(1956, Ital.); LE CIEL EST A VOUS(1957, Fr.); ROYAL AFFAIRS IN VERSAILLES(1957, Fr.); GORILLA GREETS YOU, THE(1958, Fr.); PRISONER OF THE VOLGA(1960, Fr./Ital.); GINA(1961, Fr./Mex.); TRUTH, THE(1961, Fr./Ital.); RIFIFI IN TOKYO(1963, Fr./Ital.); STEPPE, THE(1963, Fr./Ital.); SYMPHONY FOR A MASSACRE(1965, Fr./Ital.); SHOCK TROOPS(1968, Ital./Fr.); LA PRISONNIERE(1969, Fr./Ital.); MOST WONDERFUL EVENING OF MY LIFE, THE(1972, Ital./Fr.); ALICE, OR THE LAST ESCAPADE(1977, Fr.); DEATH IN THE GARDEN(1977, Fr./Mex.); THREE BROTHERS(1982, Ital.)
Misc. Silents
GYPSY PASSION(1922, Fr.); L'ATRE(1923, Fr.); IN THE SPIDER'S WEB(1924); PECHEUR D'ISLANDE(1924, Fr.); LA PROIE DU VENT(1927, Fr.); WHITE SLAVE, THE(1929)

Willard Vanenger
RHAPSODY IN BLUE(1945), spec eff

Clo Vanesco
TRANS-EUROP-EXPRESS(1968, Fr.)

Connie Vaness
MUGGER, THE(1958)

Miss Vanessi
MIN AND BILL(1930)

X.O. Vangam
DRACULA(THE DIRTY OLD MAN) (1969), art d

Vangelis
BLADE RUNNER(1982), m; MISSING(1982), m
1984
ANTARCTICA(1984, Jap.), m; BOUNTY, THE(1984), m

Wanda Vangen
END OF THE WORLD, THE(1930, Fr.)

Ves Vanghielova
PRINCE OF FOXES(1949)

Eva Vanicek
LUXURY GIRLS(1953, Ital.)

Ivan Vanicek
DESERTER AND THE NOMADS, THE(1969, Czech./Ital.), art d

Gianni Vanicola
DESERTER, THE(1971 Ital./Yugo.)

A. Vanin
SPRINGTIME ON THE VOLGA(1961, USSR)

V. Vanin
CONCENTRATION CAMP(1939, USSR)

Vasili Vanin
WINGS OF VICTORY(1941, USSR)

Vassili Vanin
ROAD HOME, THE(1947, USSR)

Ralph Vanio
LOST ON THE WESTERN FRONT(1940, Brit.), w

Yelena Vanke
WAR AND PEACE(1968, USSR)

Jim Vanko
FIRST MONDAY IN OCTOBER(1981)

I. Vankov
OPTIMISTIC TRAGEDY, THE(1964, USSR)

Monty Vanks
WHAT A NIGHT!(1931, Brit.), p&d

Simone Vanlancker
LOVE IN THE AFTERNOON(1957)

Derek Vanlint
ALIEN(1979), ph; DRAGONSLAYER(1981), ph

Rolfe E. Vanlo
INFORMER, THE(1929, Brit.), w

Frankie Vann
CRAIG'S WIFE(1936)

Howard Vann
S.O.B.(1981); SECOND THOUGHTS(1983)

Jay Vann
TARZAN'S REVENGE(1938), w

Polly Vann
MIDNIGHT INTRUDER(1938)

Ruth Vann
WOMEN'S PRISON(1955)

Teddy Vann
MOVING FINGER, THE(1963), m

Virginia Vann
LOVES OF CARMEN, THE(1948)

Nina Vanna
SHOW GOES ON, THE(1937, Brit.)
Silents
MAN WITHOUT DESIRE, THE(1923, Brit.); MONEY HABIT, THE(1924, Brit.); WOMAN TEMPTED, THE(1928, Brit.)
Misc. Silents
GUY FAWKES(1923, Brit.); WE WOMEN(1925, Brit.); TRIUMPH OF THE RAT, THE(1926, Brit.)

Marda Vanne
STRANGE BOARDERS(1938, Brit.); JOANNA(1968, Brit.)

Pamela Vanneck
FIRE IN THE STONE, THE(1983, Aus.), p

Louis Vanner [Luigi Vannucchi]
JOHNNY YUMA(1967, Ital.)

Sue Vanner
SPY WHO LOVED ME, THE(1977, Brit.)

Susan Vanner
NIGHTHAWKS(1981)

Bob Vanni
PSYCHOTRONIC MAN, THE(1980), spec eff

Massimo Vanni
LOVES AND TIMES OF SCARAMOUCHE, THE(1976, Ital.); 1990: THE BRONX WARRIORS(1983, Ital.)
1984
LAST HUNTER, THE(1984, Ital.); WARRIORS OF THE WASTELAND(1984, Ital.)

Renata Vanni
STOP THAT CAB(1951); WESTWARD THE WOMEN(1951); TROUBLE ALONG THE WAY(1953); COMMAND, THE(1954); THREE COINS IN THE FOUNTAIN(1954); SEVEN LITTLE FOYS, THE(1955); FOUR GIRLS IN TOWN(1956); HELL ON FRISCO BAY(1956); HARD MAN, THE(1957); PAY OR DIE(1960); FRONTIER UPRISING(1961); GREATEST STORY EVER TOLD, THE(1965); PATCH OF BLUE, A(1965); ONCE IS NOT ENOUGH(1975)

Renati Vanni
DREAM OF KINGS, A(1969)

Renato Vanni
MAN IN THE GREY FLANNEL SUIT, THE(1956)

Emma Vannoni
TRAMPLERS, THE(1966, Ital.)

Luigi Vannucchi
TIGER AND THE PUSSYCAT, THE(1967, U.S., Ital.); DEVIL IN LOVE, THE(1968, Ital.); ASSASSINATION OF TROTSKY, THE(1972 Fr./Ital.); YEAR ONE(1974, Ital.)

Sabina Vannucchi
NIGHT OF THE SHOOTING STARS, THE(1982, Ital.)

Luigi Vannuchi
RED TENT, THE(1971, Ital./USSR)

Ruos Vanny
YOUR SHADOW IS MINE(1963, Fr./Ital.)

Sander Vanocour
GANG THAT COULDN'T SHOOT STRAIGHT, THE(1971)

Sander Vanocur
RAISE THE TITANIC(1980, Brit.)

Arnelia Vanoni
DUEL OF THE TITANS(1963, Ital.)

Cesar Vanoni
TEXAN, THE(1930)

Ornella Vanoni
INVASION 1700(1965, Fr./Ital./Yugo.)

Franco Vanorio
1984
BASILEUS QUARTET(1984, Ital.), set d

Gene Vans
MAGIC OF LASSIE, THE(1978)

Gerald Vansier
MY BLOODY VALENTINE(1981, Can.), ed

Robert Vansittart
SIXTY GLORIOUS YEARS(1938, Brit.), w

Bob Vanstone
FLAMING FRONTIER(1958, Can.)

Richard Vanstone
STRANGE AFFAIR, THE(1968, Brit.); TWO A PENNY(1968, Brit.); MADE(1972, Brit.)

Terry Vantell
BRUTE AND THE BEAST, THE(1968, Ital.), d

Freda T. Vanterpool
DEATHMASTER, THE(1972)

Lola Vanti
FOREVER AND A DAY(1943)

Reinder Vantil
HARDCORE(1979)

Richard Vanture
AIRPORT '77(1977)

Luigi Vanucchi
SAVAGE, THE(1975, Fr.)
Vanya
FOR YOUR EYES ONLY(1981)
V. Vanyshev
RESURRECTION(1963, USSR)
Manolo Vaquero
CEREMONY, THE(1963, U.S./Span.), spec eff
Rafael Vaquero
DJANGO(1966 Ital./Span.); HELLBENDERS, THE(1967, U.S./Ital./Span.); UGLY ONES, THE(1968, Ital./Span.)
Maria Var
MASTER OF BANKDAM, THE(1947, Brit.); SILENT DUST(1949, Brit.)
Sarita Vara
CHE!(1969)
Brian Varaday
KILL OR BE KILLED(1980), ed
Jean Varas
MR. ORCHID(1948, Fr.); DEVIL IN THE FLESH, THE(1949, Fr.)
Yvan Varco
PIAF–THE EARLY YEARS(1982, U.S./Fr.)
Victor Varconi
BLACK CAMEL, THE(1931); CAPTAIN THUNDER(1931); DOCTORS' WIVES(1931); MEN IN HER LIFE(1931); SAFE IN HELL(1931); DOOMED BATTALION, THE(1932); REBEL, THE(1933, Ger.); SONG YOU GAVE ME, THE(1934, Brit.); WHEN LONDON SLEEPS(1934, Brit.), a, w; FEATHER IN HER HAT, A(1935); MR. DYNAMITE(1935); ROBERTA(1935); DANCING PIRATE(1936); BIG CITY(1937); MEN IN EXILE(1937); PLAINSMAN, THE(1937); TROUBLE IN MOROCCO(1937); KING OF THE NEWS-BOYS(1938); MR. MOTO TAKES A VACATION(1938); SUBMARINE PATROL(1938); SUEZ(1938); DISPUTED PASSAGE(1939); EVERYTHING HAPPENS AT NIGHT(1939); STORY OF VERNON AND IRENE CASTLE, THE(1939); SEA HAWK, THE(1940); STRANGE CARGO(1940); FEDERAL FUGITIVES(1941); FORCED LAND-ING(1941); MY FAVORITE BLONDE(1942); REAP THE WILD WIND(1942); THEY RAID BY NIGHT(1942); FOR WHOM THE BELL TOLLS(1943); HITLER GANG, THE(1944); STORY OF DR. WASSELL, THE(1944); DAKOTA(1945); SCOTLAND YARD INVESTIGATOR(1945, Brit.); PIRATES OF MONTEREY(1947); UNCON-QUERED(1947); WHERE THERE'S LIFE(1947); SAMSON AND DELILAH(1949); MAN WHO TURNED TO STONE, THE(1957); ATOMIC SUBMARINE, THE(1960)
Misc. Talkies
DIVINE LADY, THE(1929)
Silents
VOLGA BOATMAN, THE(1926); ANGEL OF BROADWAY, THE(1927); KING OF KINGS, THE(1927); CHICAGO(1928); SINNER'S PARADE(1928); ETERNAL LO-VE(1929)
Misc. Silents
CHANGING HUSBANDS(1924); TRIUMPH(1924); WORLDLY GOODS(1924); FOR WIVES ONLY(1926); SILKEN SHACKLES(1926); FIGHTING LOVE(1927); TENTH AVENUE(1928)
Agnes Varda
CLEO FROM 5 TO 7(1961, Fr.), d&w; LE BONHEUR(1966, Fr.), d&w; YOUNG GIRLS OF ROCHEFORT, THE(1968, Fr.), d&w; LES CREATURES(1969, Fr./Swed.), d&w; LIONS LOVE(1969), a, p,d&w; ONE SINGS, THE OTHER DOESN'T(1977, Fr.), d&w
Valerie Varda
MR. HOBBS TAKES A VACATION(1962); NEW KIND OF LOVE, A(1963)
Misc. Talkies
GUERILLAS IN PINK LACE(1964)
Gyula Vardai
RED AND THE WHITE, THE(1969, Hung./USSR), cos
Arlyne Varden
LADY IN THE DARK(1944)
Dorothy Varden
THEY MADE ME A CRIMINAL(1939)
Evelyn Varden
PINKY(1949); CHEAPER BY THE DOZEN(1950); STELLA(1950); WHEN WILLIE COMES MARCHING HOME(1950); ELOPEMENT(1951); FINDERS KEEPERS(1951); PHONE CALL FROM A STRANGER(1952); ATHENA(1954); DESIREE(1954); STU-DENT PRINCE, THE(1954); NIGHT OF THE HUNTER, THE(1955); BAD SEED, THE(1956); HILDA CRANE(1956); TEN THOUSAND BEDROOMS(1957)
Norma Varden
NIGHT LIKE THIS, A(1932, Brit.); TURKEY TIME(1933, Brit.); HAPPY(1934, Brit.); FOREIGN AFFAIRES(1935, Brit.); GET OFF MY FOOT(1935, Brit.); IRON DUKE, THE(1935, Brit.); MUSIC HATH CHARMS(1935, Brit.); BOYS WILL BE BOYS(1936, Brit.); EAST MEETS WEST(1936, Brit.); STUDENT'S ROMANCE, THE(1936, Brit.); WHERE THERE'S A WILL(1936, Brit); MAKE-UP(1937, Brit.); RHYTHM RACK-ETEER(1937, Brit.); STRANGE ADVENTURES OF MR. SMITH, THE(1937, Brit.); WANTED(1937, Brit.); WINDBAG THE SAILOR(1937, Brit.); EVERYTHING HAP-PENS TO ME(1938, Brit.); FOOLS FOR SCANDAL(1938); YOU'RE THE DOCTOR(1938, Brit.); HOME FROM HOME(1939, Brit.); EARL OF CHICAGO, THE(1940); SHIPYARD SALLY(1940, Brit.); WATERLOO BRIDGE(1940); GLAMOUR BOY(1941); ROAD TO ZANZIBAR(1941); SCOTLAND YARD(1941); CASABLANCA(1942); FLYING WITH MUSIC(1942); GLASS KEY, THE(1942); MAJOR AND THE MINOR, THE(1942); RANDOM HARVEST(1942); WE WERE DANCING(1942); DIXIE(1943); GOOD FEL-LOWS, THE(1943); SHERLOCK HOLMES FACES DEATH(1943); SLIGHTLY DAN-GEROUS(1943); WHAT A WOMAN!(1943); MADEMOISELLE FIFI(1944); NATIONAL VELVET(1944); WHITE CLIFFS OF DOVER, THE(1944); BRING ON THE GIRLS(1945); CHEATERS, THE(1945); GIRLS OF THE BIG HOUSE(1945); HOLD THAT BLONDE(1945); THOSE ENDEARING YOUNG CHARMS(1945); GREEN YEARS, THE(1946); FOREVER AMBER(1947); IVY(1947); MILLIE'S DAUGHT-ER(1947); SENATOR WAS INDISCREET, THE(1947); TROUBLE WITH WOMEN, THE(1947); WHERE THERE'S LIFE(1947); HOLLOW TRIUMPH(1948); LET'S LIVE A LITTLE(1948); MY OWN TRUE LOVE(1948); ADVENTURE IN BALTIMORE(1949); SECRET GARDEN, THE(1949); FANCY PANTS(1950); STRANGERS ON A TRAIN(1951); THUNDER ON THE HILL(1951); LES MISERABLES(1952); SOME-THING FOR THE BIRDS(1952); GENTLEMEN PREFER BLONDES(1953); LOOSE IN LONDON(1953); YOUNG BESS(1953); ELEPHANT WALK(1954); THREE COINS IN THE FOUNTAIN(1954); JUPITER'S DARLING(1955); WITNESS FOR THE PROSECU-TION(1957); IN THE MONEY(1958); FIVE MINUTES TO LIVE(1961); ISLAND OF LOVE(1963); THIRTEEN FRIGHTENED GIRLS(1963); SOUND OF MUSIC, THE(1965); VERY SPECIAL FAVOR, A(1965); DOCTOR DOLITTLE(1967)

Norman Varden
SEARCHING WIND, THE(1946)
M. Vardeshvili
Misc. Silents
GIULLI(1927, USSR)
David Vardi
TEL AVIV TAXI(1957, Israel)
Emanuel Vardi
ONCE BEFORE I DIE(1967, U.S./Phil.), m, md; LIFE STUDY(1973), m
Manny Vardi
DIRTYMOUTH(1970), m
Mirella Vardi
1984
BLIND DATE(1984)
Sara Vardi
BLUE(1968)
Josette Vardier
DEVIL AND THE TEN COMMANDMENTS, THE(1962, Fr.)
Ring Vardner, Jr.
FOUR DAYS LEAVE(1950, Switz.), w
Irene Vardoulaki
SISTERS, THE(1969, Gr.), w
Mike Vardy
MAN AT THE TOP(1973, Brit.), d
Alfredo Varela, Jr.
LA NAVE DE LOS MONSTRUOS(1959, Mex.), w; CREATURE OF THE WALKING DEAD(1960, Mex.), w; CHIQUTTO PERO PICOSO(1967, Mex.)
Alvaro Varela
CEREMONY, THE(1963, U.S./Span.)
Amanda Varela
FALCON'S BROTHER, THE(1942)
Misc. Talkies
PAPA SOLTERO(1939)
Ann Varela
TERROR IN A TEXAS TOWN(1958)
Gloria Varela
JUBILEE TRAIL(1954)
Jay Varela
UNHOLY ROLLERS(1972); KID BLUE(1973); MAN WHO LOVED CAT DANCING, THE(1973)
Migdia Varela
1984
SPLASH(1984)
Nina Varela
VIVA ZAPATA!(1952); NIAGARA(1953); PRESIDENT'S LADY, THE(1953); WOMAN THEY ALMOST LYNCHED, THE(1953); JUBILEE TRAIL(1954); LOVE WITH THE PROPER STRANGER(1963); MADIGAN(1968); CHRISTIAN LICORICE STORE, THE(1971)
Rosarita Varela
PEOPLE ARE FUNNY(1945)
Trina Varela
BANDIT QUEEN(1950); CRISIS(1950)
Trini Varela
FOR WHOM THE BELL TOLLS(1943)
Uvaldo Varela
ARIZONA(1940)
Jose Varella
LES GAULOISES BLEUES(1969, Fr.); WIND FROM THE EAST(1970, Fr./Ital./Ger.)
Marion Varella
EXPOSED(1983)
Rosa Rita Varella
LEOPARD MAN, THE(1943)
Trina Varella
LOCKET, THE(1946)
Alfredo Varelli
QUO VADIS(1951); MAN FROM CAIRO, THE(1953); STRANGER ON THE PROWL(1953, Ital.); SIGN OF THE GLADIATOR(1959, Fr./Ger./Ital.); SIEGE OF SYRACUSE(1962, Fr./Ital.); DUEL OF CHAMPIONS(1964 Ital./Span.); CAVERN, THE(1965, Ital./Ger.); EYE OF THE NEEDLE, THE(1965, Ital./Fr.); PONTIUS PILA-TE(1967, Fr./Ital.)
Jacques Varenne
CAROLINE CHERIE(1951, Fr.)
Andre Varennes
CARNIVAL OF SINNERS(1947, Fr.)
Jacques Varennes
PERSONAL COLUMN(1939, Fr.); HONEYMOON HOTEL(1946, Brit.); EAGLE WITH TWO HEADS(1948, Fr.); ORPHEUS(1950, Fr.); RED AND THE BLACK, THE(1954, Fr./Ital.); DIABOLIQUE(1955, Fr.); ROYAL AFFAIRS IN VERSAILLES(1957, Fr.)
Michel Varesano
JULES AND JIM(1962, Fr.)
Gilda Varesi
Silents
ENTER MADAME(1922), w
Vilda Varesi
Misc. Silents
MAN OF MYSTERY, THE(1917)
Bill Varga
PIER 23(1951)
Billy Varga
ALIAS THE CHAMP(1949); BODYHOLD(1950); MISS SADIE THOMPSON(1953); TWENTY PLUS TWO(1961); CONVICTS FOUR(1962); OKLAHOMA CRUDE(1973)
Carol Varga
BRIDE OF THE GORILLA(1951); PRINCE WHO WAS A THIEF, THE(1951); LIVE FAST, DIE YOUNG(1958); SPACE MASTER X-7(1958); KIDNAPPERS, THE(1964, U.S./Phil.); SECRET OF THE SACRED FOREST, THE(1970)
Daniele Varga
GIANT OF MARATHON, THE(1960, Ital.)

Gyozo Varga
WINTER WIND(1970, Fr./Hung.)
Joe Varga
MAGNIFICENT BRUTE, THE(1936)
Karen Varga
GOLDEN HORDE, THE(1951)
Vargas
WORLD WITHOUT END(1956), cos
Aurora Vargas
1984
BIZET'S CARMEN(1984, Fr./Ital.)
Carmen Vargas
1984
BIZET'S CARMEN(1984, Fr./Ital.)
Christopher Vargas
PERSONAL BEST(1982)
Concha Vargas
1984
BIZET'S CARMEN(1984, Fr./Ital.)
Daniel Vargas
ARENA, THE(1973); THOSE DIRTY DOGS(1974, U.S./Ital./Span.)
Daniele Vargas
PIRATE AND THE SLAVE GIRL, THE(1961, Fr./Ital.); THIEF OF BAGHDAD,
THE(1961, Ital./Fr.); SODOM AND GOMORRAH(1962, U.S./Fr./Ital.); FURY OF THE
PAGANS(1963, Ital.); TORPEDO BAY(1964, Ital./Fr.); REVENGE OF THE GLADIA-
TORS(1965, Ital.); AFTER THE FOX(1966, U.S./Brit./Ital.); MAN COULD GET
KILLED, A(1966); WEB OF VIOLENCE(1966, Ital./Span.); OPIATE '67(1967, Fr./Ital.);
SHOOT FIRST, LAUGH LAST(1967, Ital./Ger./U.S.); TERROR OF THE BLACK
MASK(1967, Fr./Ital.); STRANGER RETURNS, THE(1968, U.S./Ital./Ger./Span.);
SPIRITS OF THE DEAD(1969, Fr./Ital.)
Don Vargas
1984
CANNONBALL RUN II(1984), cos
Edmund Vargas
TWO LOVES(1961)
Eleonora Vargas
GLADIATOR OF ROME(1963, Ital.); INVASION 1700(1965, Fr./Ital./Yugo.)
Eleonore Vargas
DYNAMITE JACK(1961, Fr.)
Gaby Vargas
SEASIDE SWINGERS(1965, Brit.)
Jean Vargas
SLUMBER PARTY MASSACRE, THE(1982)
John Vargas
STAR TREK II: THE WRATH OF KHAN(1982); MY TUTOR(1983)
1984
MASS APPEAL(1984)
Jon Vargas
ONLY WHEN I LAUGH(1981)
Luis Vargas
Misc. Talkies
DOUBLE INITIATION(1970)
Manuela Vargas
1984
MIDSUMMER NIGHT'S DREAM, A(1984, Brit./Span.)
Martin Vargas
MARACAIBO(1958)
Olga Vargas
HOW DO I LOVE THEE?(1970)
Paul Vargas
1984
DELIVERY BOYS(1984)
Pedrito Vargas
LITTLEST OUTLAW, THE(1955)
Purita Vargas
SPANISH AFFAIR(1958, Span.)
Victoria Vargas
SHADOWS(1960)
Matyas Vargha
FATHER(1967, Hung.)
Mark Vargo
1984
GHOSTBUSTERS(1984), spec eff
Michael C. Varhol
LAST WORD, THE(1979), p, w
Giovanni Vari
SWORD OF THE CONQUEROR(1962, Ital.)
Giuseppe Vari
SWINDLE, THE(1962, Fr./Ital.), ed; SEVEN DWARFS TO THE RESCUE, THE(1965,
Ital.), ed; WAR OF THE ZOMBIES, THE(1965 Ital.), d, ed
John Vari
LAST MILE, THE(1959)
Rita Varian
TWILIGHT HOUR(1944, Brit.); TEMPTRESS, THE(1949, Brit.)
Giovanni Variano
YOUNG APHRODITES(1966, Gr.), ph
Rita Varien
GEORGE IN CIVVY STREET(1946, Brit.)
The Variety Proteges
TALKING FEET(1937, Brit.)
Carlo Varini
1984
LE DERNIER COMBAT(1984, Fr.), ph
Kelly Varis
GAMERA VERSUS MONSTER K(1970, Jap.)
Zas Varka
GEORGE WHITE'S SCANDALS(1945)

Landa Varle
FACE OF THE SCREAMING WEREWOLF(1959, Mex.)
Ann Varley
FOLLY TO BE WISE(1953); NESTING, THE(1981)
Beatrice Varley
YOUNG AND INNOCENT(1938, Brit.); POISON PEN(1941, Brit.); SOUTH AMERI-
CAN GEORGE(1941, Brit.); REMARKABLE MR. KIPPS(1942, Brit.); TALK ABOUT
JACQUELINE(1942, Brit.); BELLS GO DOWN, THE(1943, Brit.); I'LL WALK BESIDE
YOU(1943, Brit.); MAN IN GREY, THE(1943, Brit.); MILLIONS LIKE US(1943, Brit.);
SQUADRON LEADER X(1943, Brit.); WE DIVE AT DAWN(1943, Brit.); BEES IN
PARADISE(1944, Brit.); SECRET MISSION(1944, Brit.); WELCOME, MR. WASHING-
TON(1944, Brit.); GREAT DAY(1945, Brit.); BEDELIA(1946, Brit.); JOHNNY FRENCH-
MAN(1946, Brit.); SEND FOR PAUL TEMPLE(1946, Brit.); SEVENTH VEIL, THE(1946,
Brit.); WICKED LADY, THE(1946, Brit.); HOLIDAY CAMP(1947, Brit.); LADY SUR-
RENDERS, A(1947, Brit.); MASTER OF BANKDAM, THE(1947, Brit.); UPTURNED
GLASS, THE(1947, Brit.); HATTER'S CASTLE(1948, Brit.); JASSY(1948, Brit.); AGITA-
TOR, THE(1949); MARRY ME!(1949, Brit.); MY BROTHER JONATHAN(1949, Brit.);
MY BROTHER'S KEEPER(1949, Brit.); WATERLOO ROAD(1949, Brit.); ADAM AND
EVELYNE(1950, Brit.); GOOD TIME GIRL(1950, Brit.); NO ROOM AT THE INN(1950,
Brit.); SHE SHALL HAVE MURDER(1950, Brit.); LITTLE BALLERINA, THE(1951,
Brit.); PAUL TEMPLE'S TRIUMPH(1951, Brit.); HOLIDAY WEEK(1952, Brit.); WILD
HEART, THE(1952, Brit.); DEATM GOES TO SCHOOL(1953, Brit.); MELBA(1953, Brit.);
BANG! YOU'RE DEAD(1954, Brit.); BLACK RIDER, THE(1954, Brit.); GENTLE
TOUCH, THE(1956, Brit.); JUMPING FOR JOY(1956, Brit.); TIGER IN THE SMO-
KE(1956, Brit.); GOOD COMPANIONS, THE(1957, Brit.); SEA WIFE(1957, Brit.);
SURGEON'S KNIFE, THE(1957, Brit.); BACHELOR OF HEARTS(1958, Brit.); HELL
DRIVERS(1958, Brit.); HORRORS OF THE BLACK MUSEUM(1959, U.S./Brit.); ROOM
AT THE TOP(1959, Brit.); IDENTITY UNKNOWN(1960, Brit.); ECHO OF BAR-
BARA(1961, Brit.); PORTRAIT OF A SINNER(1961, Brit.); NIGHT WITHOUT PI-
TY(1962, Brit.)
John Varley
PLEASURE(1933), w; ENLIGHTEN THY DAUGHTER(1934), d; YANK AT OX-
FORD, A(1938); NINE MEN(1943, Brit.); MEET SEXTON BLAKE(1944, Brit.)
Sarah Jane Varley
MR. QUILP(1975, Brit.); AND THE SHIP SAILS ON(1983, Ital./Fr.)
Mayrita Varna
TOP OF THE HEAP(1972)
Sandorne Varnagy
FATHER(1967, Hung.)
Christine Varnai
WILLIE AND PHIL(1980)
Wendy Varnals
RUNAWAY, THE(1964, Brit.); CORRUPTION(1968, Brit.)
Valerie Varnam
LEATHER BOYS, THE(1965, Brit.)
Martin Varnaud
NIGHTMARE IN WAX(1969), makeup
Marcel Varnel
ALMOST MARRIED(1932), d; CHANDU THE MAGICIAN(1932), d; SILENT WIT-
NESS, THE(1932), d; INFERNAL MACHINE(1933), d; FREEDOM OF THE
SEAS(1934, Brit.), d; GIRLS WILL BE BOYS(1934, Brit.), d; DANCE BAND(1935,
Brit.), d; NO MONKEY BUSINESS(1935, Brit.), d; REGAL CAVALCADE(1935, Brit.),
d; ALL IN(1936, Brit.), d; PUBLIC NUISANCE NO. 1(1936, Brit.), d; OH, MR.
PORTER!(1937, Brit.), d; OKAY FOR SOUND(1937, Brit.), d; WHERE THERE'S A
WILL(1937, Brit.), d; ALF'S BUTTON AFLOAT(1938, Brit.), d; CONVICT 99(1938,
Brit.), d; HEY! HEY! U.S.A.(1938, Brit.), d; LOVES OF MADAME DUBARRY,
THE(1938, Brit.), d; OLD BONES OF THE RIVER(1938, Brit.), d; ASK A POLICE-
MAN(1939, Brit.), d; FROZEN LIMITS, THE(1939, Brit.), d; WHERE'S THAT FI-
RE?(1939, Brit.), d; BAND WAGGON(1940, Brit.), d; GASBAGS(1940, Brit.), d; LET
GEORGE DO IT(1940, Brit.), d; GHOST OF ST. MICHAEL'S. THE(1941, Brit.), d; HI,
GANG!(1941, Brit.), d; I THANK YOU(1941, Brit.), d; NEUTRAL PORT(1941, Brit.), d;
SOUTH AMERICAN GEORGE(1941, Brit.), d; TURNED OUT NICE AGAIN(1941,
Brit.), d; KING ARTHUR WAS A GENTLEMAN(1942, Brit.), d; MUCH TOO SHY(1942,
Brit.), d; BELL-BOTTOM GEORGE(1943, Brit.), d; GET CRACKING(1943, Brit.), d; HE
SNOOPS TO CONQUER(1944, Brit.), p, d; I DIDN'T DO IT(1945, Brit.), p, d; GEORGE
IN CIVVY STREET(1946, Brit.), p, d; THIS MAN IS MINE(1946 Brit.), p&d
Max Varnel
HOW TO MURDER A RICH UNCLE(1957, Brit.), d; LINKS OF JUSTICE(1958), d;
MOMENT OF INDISCRETION(1958, Brit.), d; WOMAN POSSESSED, A(1958, Brit.), d;
CHILD AND THE KILLER, THE(1959, Brit.), d; CRASH DRIVE(1959, Brit.), d; NO
SAFETY AHEAD(1959, Brit.), d; TOP FLOOR GIRL(1959, Brit.), d; WEB OF SUSPI-
CION(1959, Brit.), d; SENTENCED FOR LIFE(1960, Brit.), d; TASTE OF MONEY,
A(1960, Brit.), d; ENTER INSPECTOR DUVAL(1961, Brit.), d; PART-TIME WIFE(1961,
Brit.), d; QUESTION OF SUSPENSE, A(1961, Brit.), d; FATE TAKES A HAND(1962,
Brit.), d; MRS. GIBBONS' BOYS(1962, Brit.), d, w; MURDER IN EDEN(1962, Brit.), d;
RETURN OF A STRANGER(1962, Brit.), d; SILENT INVASION, THE(1962, Brit.), d;
GREAT VAN ROBBERY, THE(1963, Brit.), d; RIVALS, THE(1963, Brit.), d
Carl Varnell
GUNG HO!(1943)
Patricia Varner
ROMAN HOLIDAY(1953)
Russell Varner
COAL MINER'S DAUGHTER(1980)
Arthur Varney
ROAD TO FORTUNE, THE(1930, Brit.), p&d; ETERNAL FEMININE, THE(1931,
Brit.), a, p&d, w
Misc. Silents
WINDS OF THE PAMPAS(1927), d
Ginger Varney
ROADIE(1980)
Harold "Hal" Varney
MOVIE CRAZY(1932)
Peter Varney
THIRTY SECONDS OVER TOKYO(1944); TILL THE END OF TIME(1946); SONG OF
SCHEHERAZADE(1947)
Reg Varney
MISS ROBIN HOOD(1952, Brit.); JOEY BOY(1965, Brit.); GREAT ST. TRINIAN'S
TRAIN ROBBERY, THE(1966, Brit.); ON THE BUSES(1972, Brit.)

Misc. Talkies
DOUBLE TAKE(1972, Brit.); GO FOR A TAKE(1972, Brit.); HOLIDAY ON THE BUSES(1974, Brit.)
Robert Varney
SWARM, THE(1978)
Giuseppe Varni
RIGOLETTO(1949); SINGING TAXI DRIVER(1953, Ital.); AFFAIRS OF MESSALINA, THE(1954, Ital.)
Guiseppe Varni
BEFORE HIM ALL ROME TREMBLED(1947, Ital.); BLACK MAGIC(1949)
Neil P. Varnick
DANGER IN THE PACIFIC(1942), w; MUMMY'S TOMB, THE(1942), w
Martin Varno
NIGHT OF THE BLOOD BEAST(1958), w
Roland Varno
AS YOU DESIRE ME(1932); PRIVATE JONES(1933); CONQUEST(1937); EMPEROR'S CANDLESTICKS, THE(1937); QUALITY STREET(1937); BALALAIKA(1939); GUNGA DIN(1939); FIGHTING 69TH, THE(1940); MYSTERY SEA RAIDER(1940); THREE FACES WEST(1940); DEVIL PAYS OFF, THE(1941); PARIS CALLING(1941); UNDERGROUND(1941); DESPERATE JOURNEY(1942); HITLER'S CHILDREN(1942); NAZI AGENT(1942); TO BE OR NOT TO BE(1942); VALLEY OF HUNTED MEN(1942); HOSTAGES(1943); WOMEN IN BONDAGE(1943); OUR HEARTS WERE YOUNG AND GAY(1944); RETURN OF THE VAMPIRE, THE(1944); UNWRITTEN CODE, THE(1944); BETRAYAL FROM THE EAST(1945); MY NAME IS JULIA ROSS(1945); PARIS UNDERGROUND(1945); THREE'S A CROWD(1945); FLIGHT TO NOWHERE(1946); SCARED TO DEATH(1947); LETTER FROM AN UNKNOWN WOMAN(1948); ISTANBUL(1957)
John Varnum
Misc. Talkies
DANGEROUS RELATIONS(1973)
Andre Varonne
COLONEL CHABERT(1947, Fr.)
Gabriel Varriale
LUXURY GIRLS(1953, Ital.), ed
Gabriele Varriale
ANNA(1951, Ital.), ed; ANGELS OF DARKNESS(1956, Ital.), ed; CONSTANTINE AND THE CROSS(1962, Ital.), ed; WARRIORS FIVE(1962), ed
Emilio Varriano
BARON BLOOD(1972, Ital.), ph
Juan Varro
MR. LUCKY(1943); TAMPICO(1944); BUNGALOW 13(1948)
Micki Varro
CHAMP, THE(1979)
Paul Varro
LILITH(1964)
Allegra Varron
RIDING SHOTGUN(1954); ROUNDERS, THE(1965)
Henry Vars
MAN IN THE VAULT(1956), m; SEVEN MEN FROM NOW(1956), m; GUN THE MAN DOWN(1957), m; UNEARTHLY, THE(1957), md; CHINA DOLL(1958), m; ESCORT WEST(1959), m; FRECKLES(1960), m; BATTLE AT BLOODY BEACH(1961), m; LITTLE SHEPHERD OF KINGDOM COME(1961), m, md; TWO LITTLE BEARS, THE(1961), m; WOMAN HUNT(1962), m&md; FLIPPER(1963), m; HOUSE OF THE DAMNED(1963), m; FLIPPER'S NEW ADVENTURE(1964), m; FOOLS' PARADE(1971), m
Henry Varse
TOWN ON TRIAL(1957, Brit.), md
Michael Varshaviak
JESUS(1979)
Annette Varsi
RAW WEEKEND(1964)
Diane Varsi
PEYTON PLACE(1957); FROM HELL TO TEXAS(1958); 10 NORTH FREDERICK(1958); COMPULSION(1959); SWEET LOVE, BITTER(1967); KILLERS THREE(1968); WILD IN THE STREETS(1968); BLOODY MAMA(1970); JOHNNY GOT HIS GUN(1971); I NEVER PROMISED YOU A ROSE GARDEN(1977)
Henry Vart
JUDGE AND THE ASSASSIN, THE(1979, Fr.)
Sylvie Vartan
FRIEND OF THE FAMILY(1965, Fr./Ital.); MALPERTIUS(1972, Bel./Fr.)
Rosy Varte
PLEASURES AND VICES(1962, Fr.); LOVE AT TWENTY(1963, Fr./Ital./Jap./Pol./Ger.); MALE COMPANION(1965, Fr./Ital.); MAN WITH CONNECTIONS, THE(1970, Fr.); LOVE ON THE RUN(1980, Fr.)
Thomas Vartian
HAPPY DAYS(1930)
Buddy Varus
IRON MAJOR, THE(1943)
Pearl Varvalle
DEADLINE AT DAWN(1946)
Pearl Varvell
LOVE IN THE DESERT(1929); MYSTERY OF MR. X, THE(1934); YOU CAN'T TAKE IT WITH YOU(1938)
Pearl Varvelle
SMART WOMAN(1931)
Otakar Varvra
BLACK SUN, THE(1979, Czech.), d, w
Doreen Varwithen
BREAK IN THE CIRCLE, THE(1957, Brit.), m
Barbara Vary
WINDFLOWERS(1968)
Margaret Vary
WINDFLOWERS(1968)
Elena Varzi
STRANGE DECEPTION(1953, Ital.)
Steven Vas
CRYSTAL BALL, THE(1943), w; TWO SENORITAS FROM CHICAGO(1943), w

Zelma Vas Dias
LADY VANISHES, THE(1938, Brit.)
Josef Vasa
ON HER MAJESTY'S SECRET SERVICE(1969, Brit.)
Irina Vasailchikoff
GIDGET GOES TO ROME(1963)
Carlos Vasallo
1984
CONQUEST(1984, Ital./Span./Mex.), w
Magda Vasarykova
ON THE COMET(1970, Czech.)
Magda Vasaryova
MARKETA LAZAROVA(1968, Czech.); DESERTER AND THE NOMADS, THE(1969, Czech./Ital.); BLACK SUN, THE(1979, Czech.)
Emilie Vasayova
VOYAGE TO THE END OF THE UNIVERSE(1963, Czech.)
Miguel Vascez
RETURN OF SABATA(1972, Ital./Fr./Ger.)
Aldo Vasco
LA DOLCE VITA(1961, Ital./Fr.)
Benito Vasconi
RETURN OF SABATA(1972, Ital./Fr./Ger.)
Jose-Luis Vasconselos
1984
THREE CROWNS OF THE SAILOR(1984, Fr.), p
Julius Vasek
MAN WHO LIES, THE(1970, Czech./Fr.)
Paul Vasel
Silents
AWAKENING, THE(1928)
Renata Vaselle
SWEET CHARITY(1969)
Vittorio Vaser
MINOTAUR, THE(1961, Ital.); SWORD OF THE CONQUEROR(1962, Ital.)
James Vasevi
WUTHERING HEIGHTS(1939), art d
Ed Vasgersian
ESCAPE FROM ALCATRAZ(1979)
Karl Vash
M(1933, Ger.), w; TESTAMENT OF DR. MABUSE, THE(1943, Ger.), ph; M(1951), w
R. Vashadze
FATHER OF A SOLDIER(1966, USSR), spec eff
Vera Vashilieva
BRIDE WITH A DOWRY(1954, USSR)
Lyda Vashkulat
STALAG 17(1953)
Leonard Vasian
IT HAPPENED IN BROOKLYN(1947), art d
Leonid Vasian
JACKASS MAIL(1942), art d; GENTLE ANNIE(1944), art d; SEVENTH CROSS, THE(1944), art d; KEEP YOUR POWDER DRY(1945), art d; WHAT NEXT, CORPORAL HARGROVE?(1945), art d; MY BROTHER TALKS TO HORSES(1946), art d; HIGH WALL, THE(1947), art d; SCENE OF THE CRIME(1949), art d; TENSION(1949), art d; DEVIL'S DOORWAY(1950), art d; FATHER OF THE BRIDE(1950), art d; FATHER'S LITTLE DIVIDEND(1951), art d; PAINTED HILLS, THE(1951), art d; STRIP, THE(1951), art d; GIRL IN WHITE, THE(1952), art d; SKY FULL OF MOON(1952), art d; FAST COMPANY(1953), art d
Art Vasil
FOR THE LOVE OF BENJI(1977)
Nadia Vasil
EROTIQUE(1969, Fr.)
Vasilchikov
Misc. Silents
YOUR ACQUAINTANCE(1927, USSR)
Juri Vasile
BEYOND THE DOOR II(1979, Ital.), p
Paolo Vasile
SQUEEZE, THE(1980, Ital.), m
Turi Vasile
VERGINITA(1953, Ital.), w; HEAD OF THE FAMILY(1967, Ital./Fr.), p; OPERATION ST. PETER'S(1968, Ital.), p; TREASURE OF SAN GENNARO(1968, Fr./Ital./Ger.), p; BETTER A WIDOW(1969, Ital.), p; SONS OF SATAN(1969, Ital./Fr./Ger.), p; ANONYMOUS VENETIAN, THE(1971), p; ROMA(1972, Ital./Fr.), p; SQUEEZE, THE(1980, Ital.), p
I. Vasilenko
WAR AND PEACE(1968, USSR)
Lucia Vasilico
LA DOLCE VITA(1961, Ital./Fr.)
Georgi Vasiliev
DEFENSE OF VOLOTCHAYEVSK, THE(1938, USSR), d&w
Georgy Vasiliev
QUEEN OF SPADES(1961, USSR), w
Kostya Vasiliev
Misc. Silents
OLD AND NEW(1930, USSR)
Sergei Vasiliev
DEFENSE OF VOLOTCHAYEVSK, THE(1938, USSR), d&w
Grigori Vasiliu-Birlic
STEPS TO THE MOON(1963, Rum.)
T. Vasilkovskaya
SLEEPING BEAUTY, THE(1966, USSR), art d
Monica Vasilliou
SUNDAY BLOODY SUNDAY(1971, Brit.)
Yuri Vasilyer
MOSCOW DOES NOT BELIEVE IN TEARS(1980, USSR)
A. Vasilyev
DAY THE WAR ENDED, THE(1961, USSR)

M. Vasilyev
NIGHT BEFORE CHRISTMAS, A(1963, USSR)
Serge Vasilyev
QUEEN OF SPADES(1961, USSR), w
Vladimir Vasilyev
DON QUIXOTE(1961, USSR); LITTLE HUMPBACKED HORSE, THE(1962, USSR); SONG OVER MOSCOW(1964, USSR)
V. Vasilyeva
MEET ME IN MOSCOW(1966, USSR)
Marie Vasova
BOHEMIAN RAPTURE(1948, Czech); EMPEROR AND THE GOLEM, THE(1955, Czech.); LOST FACE, THE(1965, Czech.)
Lee Vasque
RIDE BEYOND VENGEANCE(1966), spec eff; SPIRIT IS WILLING, THE(1967), spec eff; CATCH-22(1970), spec eff
Alberto Vasques-Figueroa
ASHANTI(1979), w
David Vasquez
EASY MONEY(1983)
Esperanza Vasquez
ONLY ONCE IN A LIFETIME(1979), ed
Isabel Vasquez
1984
UNDER THE VOLCANO(1984)
Jose Luis Vasquez
BRAVE BULLS, THE(1951)
Jose-Luis Lopez Vasquez
1984
HEAT OF DESIRE(1984, Fr.)
Juan Vasquez
HIGH RISK(1981)
Lita Vasquez
1984
ALLEY CAT(1984), stunts
Luz Vasquez
PAN-AMERICANA(1945)
Marie Castro Vasquez
TROUT, THE(1982, Fr.), ed
Nelso Vasquez
1984
DELIVERY BOYS(1984), ch
Nelson Vasquez
1984
DELIVERY BOYS(1984)
Pablo Vasquez
1984
DELIVERY BOYS(1984)
Rey Vasquez
ADVENTURERS, THE(1970); PROUD AND THE DAMNED, THE(1972)
Romeo Vasquez
CURSE OF THE VAMPIRES(1970, Phil., U.S.)
The Vass Family
COUNTRY FAIR(1941)
E. Vassal-Vaughn
Misc. Silents
GREEN ORCHARD, THE(1916, Brit.)
Charles Vassar
SATAN BUG, THE(1965), set d
Queenie Vassar
PRIMROSE PATH(1940); LADY IN A JAM(1942); NONE BUT THE LONELY HEART(1944)
Vittorio Vassarotti
CROSSED SWORDS(1954), p
Didier Vasseur
BLACKOUT(1978, Fr./Can.), m
Jean-Marc Vasseur
HOUSE ON SORORITY ROW, THE(1983), ed
Leonid Vassian
YOUNG IDEAS(1943), art d
Karis Vassili
RETURN OF SABATA(1972, Ital./Fr./Ger.)
Georgia Vassiliadou
ASTERO(1960, Gr.); AUNT FROM CHICAGO(1960, Gr.); FORTUNE TELLER, THE(1961, Gr.); GROUCH, THE(1961, Gr.); MIDWIFE, THE(1961, Greece)
Vera Vassilieva
SYMPHONY OF LIFE(1949, USSR)
Vassili Vassilikos
Z(1969, Fr./Algeria), w
Vassilis Vassilikos
YOUNG APHRODITES(1966, Gr.), w
Spyros Vassiliou
DAY THE FISH CAME OUT, THE(1967. Brit./Gr.), art d
Vladimir Vassiljev
LA TRAVIATA(1982)
D.I. Vassilev
ALEXANDER NEVSKY(1939), d
Spyros Vassilou
ELECTRA(1962, Gr.), art d
Dimitri Vassiloupoulos
ZELIG(1983)
Pierre Vassilu
TO BE A CROOK(1967, Fr.), m; FINO A FARTI MALE(1969, Fr./Ital.), m
Cecile Vassort
INVITATION, THE(1975, Fr./Switz.); CLOCKMAKER, THE(1976, Fr.); JUDGE AND THE ASSASSIN, THE(1979, Fr.)
1984
ONE DEADLY SUMMER(1984, Fr.)

Vassy
MARIUS(1933, Fr.)
Gilles Vaster
DANTON(1983), art d
Gillian Vastlake
FLY NOW, PAY LATER(1969), w
Nick Vasu
BON VOYAGE, CHARLIE BROWN(AND DON'T COME BACK)*** (1980), ph; BOY NAMED CHARLIE BROWN, A(1969), ph; SNOOPY, COME HOME(1972), ph; BUGS BUNNY'S THIRD MOVIE–1001 RABBIT TALES(1982), ph
Piroska Vaszary
KIND STEPMOTHER(1936, Hung.)
B. Vatayev
HOUSE ON THE FRONT LINE, THE(1963, USSR)
Francoise Vatel
SMUGGLERS, THE(1969, Fr.)
Martine Vatel
MURIEL(1963, Fr./Ital.); LA GUERRE EST FINIE(1967, Fr./Swed.)
Erwin Vater
Silents
METROPOLIS(1927, Ger.)
Richard Vath
WHEN WORLDS COLLIDE(1951); RED SNOW(1952); CREATION OF THE HUMAN-OIDS(1962)
Bjorg Vatle
SHORT IS THE SUMMER(1968, Swed.)
Zeni Vatori
MAGNIFICENT BRUTE, THE(1936); FIREFLY, THE(1937)
Zeni Vatoria
PUBLIC WEDDING(1937)
Robert Vattier
MARIUS(1933, Fr.); CESAR(1936, Fr.); BAKER'S WIFE, THE(1940, Fr.); FANNY(1948, Fr.); ROYAL AFFAIR, A(1950); UTOPIA(1952, Fr./Ital.); LA RONDE(1954, Fr.); LETTERS FROM MY WINDMILL(1955, Fr.); FAR FROM DALLAS(1972, Fr.)
Robert Vattler
CARNIVAL OF SINNERS(1947, Fr.)
Jean-Marie Vauclin
JOY(1983, Fr./Can.)
Maurice Vaudaux
VIOLETTE(1978, Fr.)
Monte Vaudergrift
RACKET BUSTERS(1938)
E. Vaudray
Silents
ROAD TO RUIN, THE(1913, Brit.)
Simone Vaudry
MYSTERY OF THE PINK VILLA, THE(1930, Fr.)
Alberta Vaugh
Silents
BACKSTAGE(1927)
Alberta Vaughan
Silents
ADORABLE DECEIVER, THE(1926)
Bernard Vaughan
Misc. Silents
CINEMA GIRL'S ROMANCE, A(1915, Brit.); ROCK OF AGES(1918, Brit.); TROUSERS(1920, Brit.)
Beryl Vaughan
GIRLS UNDER TWENTY-ONE(1940)
Billy Vaughan
DEADLY COMPANIONS, THE(1961)
Brian Vaughan
MAN IN THE MIDDLE(1964, U.S./Brit.)
Clifford Vaughan
OLD YELLER(1957), md
Cyril Vaughan
Misc. Silents
BARNABY(1919, Brit.)
Darryl Vaughan
DON'T WORRY, WE'LL THINK OF A TITLE(1966); WILD, WILD WINTER(1966)
David Vaughan
KILLER'S KISS(1955), a, ch
Dorothy Vaughan
MARY BURNS, FUGITIVE(1935); LOVE BEGINS AT TWENTY(1936); TIMES SQUARE PLAYBOY(1936); BLACK LEGION, THE(1937); MICHAEL O'HAL-LORAN(1937); SLIM(1937); STELLA DALLAS(1937); THAT MAN'S HERE AGAIN(1937); COWBOY FROM BROOKLYN(1938); MAN-PROOF(1938); QUICK MONEY(1938); TEST PILOT(1938); ESPIONAGE AGENT(1939); FIRST LOVE(1939); MAN IN THE IRON MASK, THE(1939); STAR MAKER, THE(1939); YOUNG MR. LINCOLN(1939); APE, THE(1940); DIAMOND FRONTIER(1940); FOREIGN CORRESPONDENT(1940); KITTY FOYLE(1940); THEY DRIVE BY NIGHT(1940); BAD MEN OF MISSOURI(1941); MANPOWER(1941); MOB TOWN(1941); ONE FOOT IN HEAVEN(1941); SECRET EVIDENCE(1941); STRAWBERRY BLONDE, THE(1941); THREE GIRLS ABOUT TOWN(1941); UNFINISHED BUSINESS(1941); LADY GANGSTER(1942); NOW, VOYAGER(1942); PRIDE OF THE YANKEES, THE(1942); DOUGHBOYS IN IRELAND(1943); KEEP 'EM SLUGGING(1943); MOONLIGHT IN VERMONT(1943); ADVENTURES OF MARK TWAIN, THE(1944); SWEET AND LOWDOWN(1944); DANCING IN MANHATTAN(1945); WHAT A BLONDE(1945); BAMBOO BLONDE, THE(1946); CROSS MY HEART(1946); RIVERBOAT RHYTHM(1946); THAT BRENNAN GIRL(1946); EGG AND I, THE(1947); LURED(1947); ROBIN OF TEXAS(1947); SEA OF GRASS, THE(1947); TRAIL TO SAN ANTONE(1947); LADY FROM SHANGHAI, THE(1948); MANHATTAN ANGEL(1948); FIGHTING FOOLS(1949); TAKE ONE FALSE STEP(1949); CHAIN GANG(1950); RIDER FROM TUCSON(1950); SQUARE DANCE KATY(1950)
Elizabeth Vaughan
HAWLEY'S OF HIGH STREET(1933, Brit.); GIRL IN THE CROWD, THE(1934, Brit.); HAPPY(1934, Brit.); JIMMY BOY(1935, Brit.); VICTOR/VICTORIA(1982)

Frankie Vaughan
ESCAPE IN THE SUN(1956, Brit.); RAMSBOTTOM RIDES AGAIN(1956, Brit.); DANGEROUS YOUTH(1958, Brit.); WONDERFUL THINGS!(1958, Brit.); HEART OF A MAN, THE(1959, Brit.); LADY IS A SQUARE, THE(1959, Brit.); LET'S MAKE LOVE(1960); RIGHT APPROACH, THE(1961); IT'S ALL OVER TOWN(1963, Brit.)

Gillian Vaughan
BACHELOR OF HEARTS(1958, Brit.); MOONRAKER, THE(1958, Brit.); DEVIL'S BAIT(1959, Brit.); WHITE TRAP, THE(1959, Brit.); AND WOMEN SHALL WEEP(1960, Brit.)

Gwyneth Vaughan
THINGS HAPPEN AT NIGHT(1948, Brit.); BLUE SCAR(1949, Brit.); INTERRUPTED JOURNEY, THE(1949, Brit.); MAN FROM YESTERDAY, THE(1949, Brit.); MELODY CLUB(1949, Brit.); HA' PENNY BREEZE(1950, Brit.)

Jane Vaughan
OTHER WOMAN, THE(1931, Brit.)

Jimmy Vaughan
WOMAN EATER, THE(1959, Brit.)

Kathleen Vaughan
LAST HOUR, THE(1930, Brit.)
Silents
HANDY ANDY(1921, Brit.); OLD COUNTRY, THE(1921, Brit.); CRIMSON CIRCLE, THE(1922, Brit.)
Misc. Silents
SINGLE LIFE(1921, Brit.)

Lloyd Vaughan
PHANTOM TOLLBOOTH, THE(1970), anim

Margaret Vaughan
Silents
GIRL WITHOUT A SOUL, THE(1917)

Martin Vaughan
PICNIC AT HANGING ROCK(1975, Aus.); JUST OUT OF REACH(1979, Aus.); WE OF THE NEVER NEVER(1983, Aus.)
1984
CONSTANCE(1984, New Zealand); PHAR LAP(1984, Aus.)

Michael Vaughan
HE SNOOPS TO CONQUER(1944, Brit.), w; I DIDN'T DO IT(1945, Brit.), w

Norman Vaughan
CARNABY, M.D.(1967, Brit.); LOLA(1971, Brit./Ital.)

Peter Vaughan
ROTTEN TO THE CORE(1956, Brit.); VILLAGE OF THE DAMNED(1960, Brit.); DEVIL'S AGENT, THE(1962, Brit.); PUNCH AND JUDY MAN, THE(1963, Brit.); VICTORS, THE(1963); SMOKESCREEN(1964, Brit.); TWO LIVING, ONE DEAD(1964, Brit./Swed.); DIE, DIE, MY DARLING(1965, Brit.); NAKED RUNNER, THE(1967, Brit.); HAMMERHEAD(1968); MAN OUTSIDE, THE(1968, Brit.); TWIST OF SAND, A(1968, Brit.); ALFRED THE GREAT(1969, Brit.); TASTE OF EXCITEMENT(1969, Brit.); SUDDEN TERROR(1970, Brit.); STRAW DOGS(1971, Brit.); SAVAGE MESSIAH(1972, Brit.); MACKINTOSH MAN, THE(1973, Brit.); BLOCKHOUSE, THE(1974, Brit.); 11 HARROWHOUSE(1974, Brit.); SYMPTOMS(1976, Brit.); VALENTINO(1977, Brit.); DOING TIME(1979, Brit.); ZULU DAWN(1980, Brit.); FRENCH LIEUTENANT'S WOMAN, THE(1981); TIME BANDITS(1981, Brit.); MISSIONARY, THE(1982)
1984
RAZOR'S EDGE, THE(1984)
Misc. Talkies
CZECH MATE(1984, Brit.)

Robert Vaughan
TO TRAP A SPY(1966); HELICOPTER SPIES, THE(1968)

Sarah Vaughan
DISC JOCKEY(1951)

Silvia Vaughan
DARK ANGEL, THE(1935)

Steven Vaughan
HOWZER(1973)

Tony Vaughan
DISCOVERIES(1939, Brit.)

Virginia Vaughan
BIG BUSINESS(1930, Brit.)

Walter Vaughan
C-MAN(1949)

William Vaughan
AMBUSH AT CIMARRON PASS(1958)

Wynford Vaughan-Thomas
ANZIO(1968, Ital.), w

James T. Vaughin
DOUBLE DEAL(1950), p

Ada Mae Vaughn
Silents
LAST EDITION, THE(1925)
Misc. Silents
ARIZONA STREAK, THE(1926)

Albert Vaughn
ALIMONY MADNESS(1933)

Alberta Vaughn
MOLLY AND ME(1929); NOISY NEIGHBORS(1929); WILD HORSE(1931); WORKING GIRLS(1931); DANCERS IN THE DARK(1932); DARING DANGER(1932); MIDNIGHT MORALS(1932); DANCE MALL HOSTESS(1933); EMERGENCY CALL(1933); RANDY RIDES ALONE(1934)
Misc. Talkies
LOVE IN HIGH GEAR(1932); LARAMIE KID, THE(1935)
Silents
FRIENDLY HUSBAND, A(1923); AIN'T LOVE FUNNY?(1927); DROPKICK, THE(1927); OLD AGE HANDICAP(1928); POINTS WEST(1929)
Misc. Silents
COLLEGIATE(1926); ROMANTIC AGE, THE(1927); SINEWS OF STEEL(1927); UNEASY PAYMENTS(1927); SKYSCRAPER(1928)

Ben Vaughn
BENJI(1974)

Bernard Vaughn
Silents
LITTLE LORD FAUNTLEROY(1914, Brit.); ALLEY OF GOLDEN HEARTS, THE(1924, Brit.)

Misc. Silents
DAWN OF THE TRUTH, THE(1920, Brit.)

Beryl Vaughn
PENNY SERENADE(1941)

Dorothy Vaughn
AFTER THE THIN MAN(1936); HERE'S FLASH CASEY(1937); THERE GOES MY GIRL(1937); LITTLE MISS THOROUGHBRED(1938); LITTLE ORPHAN ANNIE(1938); SLANDER HOUSE(1938); TELEPHONE OPERATOR(1938); GAMBLING SHIP(1939); UNEXPECTED FATHER(1939); HOUSE ACROSS THE BAY, THE(1940); OLD SWIMMIN' HOLE, THE(1941); GENTLEMAN JIM(1942); MAGNIFICENT AMBERSONS, THE(1942); HIT THE ICE(1943); IRON MAJOR, THE(1943); DESTINY(1944); HENRY ALDRICH'S LITTLE SECRET(1944); MUMMY'S GHOST, THE(1944); THOSE ENDEARING YOUNG CHARMS(1945); TOWN WENT WILD, THE(1945); HIGH WALL, THE(1947); I WOULDN'T BE IN YOUR SHOES(1948); SONG OF IDAHO(1948); TELL IT TO THE JUDGE(1949); EMERGENCY WEDDING(1950); PETTY GIRL, THE(1950); THREE HUSBANDS(1950)

Elizabeth Vaughn
HOUND OF THE BASKERVILLES(1932, Brit.)

Gillian Vaughn
HORSE'S MOUTH, THE(1958, Brit.)

Heidi Vaughn
NO MERCY MAN, THE(1975)

Henry Vaughn
THAT SPLENDID NOVEMBER(1971, Ital./Fr.), w

Hilda Vaughn
THREE LIVE GHOSTS(1929); MANSLAUGHTER(1930); IT'S A WISE CHILD(1931); SUSAN LENOX-HER FALL AND RISE(1931); LADIES OF THE BIG HOUSE(1932); PHANTOM OF CRESTWOOD, THE(1932); DINNER AT EIGHT(1933); NO MARRIAGE TIES(1933); NO OTHER WOMAN(1933); TODAY WE LIVE(1933); ANNE OF GREEN GABLES(1934); I LIVE MY LIFE(1935); MEN WITHOUT NAMES(1935); STRAIGHT FROM THE HEART(1935); WEDDING NIGHT, THE(1935); ACCUSING FINGER, THE(1936); BANJO ON MY KNEE(1936); EVERYBODY'S OLD MAN(1936); HALF ANGEL(1936); TRAIL OF THE LONESOME PINE, THE(1936); WITNESS CHAIR, THE(1936); DANGER-LOVE AT WORK(1937); MAID'S NIGHT OUT(1938); CHARLIE CHAN AT THE WAX MUSEUM(1940)

Jean Vaughn
MANCHURIAN CANDIDATE, THE(1962)

Jeanne Vaughn
PRINCESS OF THE NILE(1954)

Jerry Vaughn
1984
LIES(1984, Brit.)

Jimmy Vaughn
KING OF CHINATOWN(1939)

Judson Vaughn
BEACH GIRLS(1982)

Kathleen Vaughn
Silents
FACE AT THE WINDOW, THE(1920, Brit.); ADVENTURES OF MR. PICKWICK, THE(1921, Brit.); PRINCE AND THE BEGGARMAID, THE(1921, Brit.)
Misc. Silents
BELPHEGOR THE MOUNTEBANK(1921, Brit.); CORINTHIAN JACK(1921, Brit.)

Kerry Vaughn
FRONTIER GAL(1945); HAVING WONDERFUL CRIME(1945); SALOME, WHERE SHE DANCED(1945); SCARLET STREET(1945); THIS LOVE OF OURS(1945); NIGHT IN PARADISE, A(1946); PREHISTORIC WOMEN(1950); SOMETHING TO LIVE FOR(1952)

Laura Vaughn
TALES OF MANHATTAN(1942)

LeRoy Vaughn
SHOOT IT: BLACK, SHOOT IT: BLUE(1974)

Linda Vaughn
STROKER ACE(1983)

Michael Vaughn
1984
NO SMALL AFFAIR(1984)

Mina Vaughn
LOVER COME BACK(1961)

Norman Vaughn
YOU MUST BE JOKING!(1965, Brit.)

Peter Vaughn
PIED PIPER, THE(1972, Brit.)

Ray Vaughn
SQUARE DANCE JUBILEE(1949)

Rees Vaughn
PLAYGROUND, THE(1965)

Robert Vaughn
TEN COMMANDMENTS, THE(1956); HELL'S CROSSROADS(1957); NO TIME TO BE YOUNG(1957); GOOD DAY FOR A HANGING(1958); TEENAGE CAVEMAN(1958); UNWED MOTHER(1958); YOUNG PHILADELPHIANS, THE(1959); MAGNIFICENT SEVEN, THE(1960); BIG SHOW, THE(1961); CARETAKERS, THE(1963); GLASS BOTTOM BOAT, THE(1966); ONE OF OUR SPIES IS MISSING(1966); ONE SPY TOO MANY(1966); SPY IN THE GREEN HAT, THE(1966); SPY WITH MY FACE, THE(1966); KARATE KILLERS, THE(1967); VENETIAN AFFAIR, THE(1967); BULLITT(1968); BRIDGE AT REMAGEN, THE(1969); IF IT'S TUESDAY, THIS MUST BE BELGIUM(1969); JULIUS CAESAR(1970, Brit.); MIND OF MR. SOAMES, THE(1970, Brit.); CLAY PIGEON(1971); STATUE, THE(1971, Brit.); TOWERING INFERNO, THE(1974); LA BABY SITTER(1975, Fr./Ital./Ger.); DEMON SEED(1977); BRASS TARGET(1978); STARSHIP INVASIONS(1978, Can.); GOOD LUCK, MISS WYCKOFF(1979); BATTLE BEYOND THE STARS(1980); CUBA CROSSING(1980); HANGAR 18(1980); VIRUS(1980, Jap.); S.O.B.(1981); SUPERMAN III(1983)
Misc. Talkies
LUCIFER COMPLEX, THE(1978)
Silents
STILL WATERS(1915)
Misc. Silents
MOTHER'S HEART, A(1914); MASTER SHAKESPEARE, STROLLING PLAYER(1916); UNDER FALSE COLORS(1917); FOLKS FROM WAY DOWN EAST(1924)

Sammy Vaughn
BORN WILD(1968); CHANGES(1969)
Sarah Vaughn
MURDER, INC.(1960)
Sharon Vaughn
FUNNY GIRL(1968)
Skeeter Vaughn
Misc. Talkies
ADVENTURES OF STAR BIRD(1978)
Tina Vaughn
1984
POPE OF GREENWICH VILLAGE, THE(1984)
Tyra Vaughn
KID FROM BOOKLYN, THE(1946); SHADOWS OVER CHINATOWN(1946)
Ven Vaughn
FOR THE LOVE OF BENJI(1977), p, w
Walter Vaughn
JIGSAW(1949)
William Vaughn
CONDEMNED(1929); DEADLY GAME, THE(1941); MAN HUNT(1941); JOAN OF OZARK(1942); MISS V FROM MOSCOW(1942); ONCE UPON A HONEYMOON(1942); YANK IN LIBYA, A(1942); BACKGROUND TO DANGER(1943); PURPLE V, THE(1943)
William Vaughn [Von Brincken]
CONFESSIONS OF A NAZI SPY(1939)
Vaughn Monroe and his Orchestra
MEET THE PEOPLE(1944)
Vaughn Monroe Orchestra
CARNEGIE HALL(1947)
Gerald Vaughn-Hughes
SEBASTIAN(1968, Brit.), w; DUELLISTS, THE(1977, Brit.), w
Georges Vaultier
Misc. Silents
LE FANTOME DU MOULIN ROUGE(1925, Fr.)
Georges Vaur
BIRD WATCH, THE(1983, Fr.)
Genevieve Vaury
NIGHT WATCH, THE(1964, Fr./Ital.), ed; DE L'AMOUR(1968, Fr./Ital.), ed
Genia Vaury
LA MARSEILLAISE(1938, Fr.)
Germaine Vaury
PARIS PICK-UP(1963, Fr./Ital.), ed
Jim Vaus
WIRETAPPERS(1956), p, w
Jean Vauthier
LES ABYSSES(1964, Fr.), w; THANOS AND DESPINA(1970, Fr./Gr.), w
Nicole Vauthier
WOMAN NEXT DOOR, THE(1981, Fr.)
Elmire Vautier
STORY OF A CHEAT, THE(1938, Fr.)
Sydney Vautier
Silents
BID FOR FORTUNE, A(1917, Brit.)
Misc. Silents
AVENGING HAND, THE(1915, Brit.); THIRD GENERATION, THE(1915, Brit.); 1914(1915, Brit.); DERELICTS(1917, Brit.)
Marc Vautour
SIEGE(1983, Can.), w
Yvonne Vautrot
BELL FOR ADANO, A(1945)
Anton Vaverka
LOVE PARADE, THE(1929); PHANTOM OF THE OPERA, THE(1929); MELODY MAN(1930)
Silents
MERRY-GO-ROUND(1923); PHANTOM OF THE OPERA, THE(1925); ROLLING HOME(1926); ON ZE BOULEVARD(1927); WEDDING MARCH, THE(1927); THREE SINNERS(1928)
Natalya Vavilova
MOSCOW DOES NOT BELIEVE IN TEARS(1980, USSR)
Michael Vavitch
BRIDGE OF SAN LUIS REY, THE(1929); WOLF SONG(1929); BIG HOUSE, THE(1930); DEVIL WITH WOMEN, A(1930); WAR NURSE(1930)
Silents
THIRD DEGREE, THE(1926); GAUCHO, THE(1928)
Misc. Silents
TWO ARABIAN KNIGHTS(1927)
Rudi Vavpotic
SERGEANT JIM(1962, Yugo.), ph
Josef Vavra
QUERELLE(1983, Ger./Fr.), ph
Otakar Vavra
MERRY WIVES, THE(1940, Czech.), d&w; KRAKATIT(1948, Czech.), d, w
Karel Vavrik
DO YOU KEEP A LION AT HOME?(1966, Czech.)
Tafana Vavrincova
90 DEGREES IN THE SHADE(1966, Czech./Brit.)
Milos Vavruska
LEMONADE JOE(1966, Czech.)
Kazimierz Vavrzyniak
GREAT BIG WORLD AND LITTLE CHILDREN, THE(1962, Pol.), ph
Nancy Vawter
SECOND THOUGHTS(1983)
Ron Vawter
BORN IN FLAMES(1983); KING BLANK(1983)
Misc. Talkies
STRONG MEDICINE(1981)
Armando Vay
Misc. Silents
AFTER SIX DAYS(1922), d

Tomas Vayer
BLUEBEARD(1972), art d
Vanessa Vaylor
TENANT, THE(1976, Fr.)
Vasiliy Ivanovich Vaynonen
LITTLE HUMPBACKED HORSE, THE(1962, USSR), w
Arnold Vaysfeld
MUMU(1961, USSR), art d; FORTY-NINE DAYS(1964, USSR), art d
Selma Vaz Dias
POWER(1934, Brit.); BAD BLONDE(1953, Brit.); YOUNG WIVES' TALE(1954, Brit.); CAT GIRL(1957); PORTRAIT IN SMOKE(1957, Brit.); STRANGER'S MEETING(1957, Brit.); ORDERS TO KILL(1958, Brit.); SINGER NOT THE SONG, THE(1961, Brit.); TELL-TALE HEART, THE(1962, Brit.)
Akaki Vazadze
Misc. Silents
IN THE PILLORY(1924, USSR)
P.H. Vazak "Robert Towne"
1984
GREYSTOKE: THE LEGEND OF TARZAN, LORD OF THE APES(1984), w
Susan Vaziri
CARAVANS(1978, U.S./Iranian)
Alberto Vazquez
DEFIANCE(1980)
Jose Luis Lopez Vazquez
NOT ON YOUR LIFE(1965, Ital./Span.); OPERATION DELILAH(1966, U.S./Span.); TRAVELS WITH MY AUNT(1972, Brit.)
Juan Vazquez
MISSING(1982)
Julio Cesar Vazquez
UNDER FIRE(1983)
Lopez Vazquez
GIRL FROM VALLADOLIO(1958, Span.)
Luis Vazquez
GOD FORGIVES–I DON'T!(1969, Ital./Span.), art d; MERCENARY, THE(1970, Ital./Span.), art d
Ricardo Vazquez
CANNON FOR CORDOBA(1970), makeup; STRANGE VENGEANCE OF ROSALIE, THE(1972), makeup
Roland Vazquez
MIDSUMMER NIGHT'S DREAM, A(1966)
Vazquez Brothers
FEW BULLETS MORE, A(1968, Ital./Span.), set d
Carlos Lenin Vazuez
UNDER FIRE(1983)
Cookie Vazzana
WHY RUSSIANS ARE REVOLTING(1970)
Elsa Vazzoler
GREAT WAR, THE(1961, Fr., Ital.); RITA(1963, Fr./Ital.); FASCIST, THE(1965, Ital.); HEAD OF THE FAMILY(1967, Ital./Fr.); ROMEO AND JULIET(1968, Ital./Span.); STORY OF A WOMAN(1970, U.S./Ital.)
Bruno Ve Sota
LONG WAIT, THE(1954); TENNESSEE CHAMP(1954); DEMENTIA(1955); FEMALE JUNGLE, THE(1955), a, d, w; GUNSLINGER(1956); TEENAGE DOLL(1957); HOT CAR GIRL(1958); ATTACK OF THE GIANT LEECHES(1959); WASP WOMAN, THE(1959); CODE OF SILENCE(1960); CREATURE OF THE WALKING DEAD(1960, Mex.); VALLEY OF THE REDWOODS(1960); CAT BURGLAR, THE(1961); CHOPPERS, THE(1961); 20,000 EYES(1961); CASE OF PATTY SMITH, THE(1962); INVASION OF THE STAR CREATURES(1962), d; ATTACK OF THE MAYAN MUMMY(1963, U.S./Mex.); HAUNTED PALACE, THE(1963); NIGHT TIDE(1963); GIRLS ON THE BEACH(1965); HELL'S ANGELS ON WHEELS(1967); MAN CALLED DAGGER, A(1967); SINGLE ROOM FURNISHED(1968)
Jebbie Ve Sota
DEMENTIA(1955)
Bruno Ve Soto
UNDEAD, THE(1957); BRAIN EATERS, THE(1958), d
Katena Vea [Katherine Victor]
MESA OF LOST WOMEN, THE(1956)
Smaro Veaki
MATCHMAKING OF ANNA, THE(1972, Gr.)
Bob Veal
GETAWAY, THE(1972)
John Veale
PURPLE PLAIN, THE(1954, Brit.), m; POSTMARK FOR DANGER(1956, Brit.), m; HIGH TIDE AT NOON(1957, Brit.), m; NO ROAD BACK(1957, Brit.), m; SPANISH GARDENER, THE(1957, Span.), m; ESCAPE BY NIGHT(1965, Brit.), m
Clark Veater
STALLION CANYON(1949)
Carol Veazie
CATERED AFFAIR, THE(1956); CRY IN THE NIGHT, A(1956); NAVY WIFE(1956); DESIGNING WOMAN(1957); AUNTIE MAME(1958); RETURN TO PEYTON PLACE(1961); TENDER IS THE NIGHT(1961); SIGNPOST TO MURDER(1964); BABY, THE RAIN MUST FALL(1965); CAT BALLOU(1965)
Etienne Veazie
JOHNNY GOT HIS GUN(1971)
Francis Veber
TALL BLOND MAN WITH ONE BLACK SHOE, THE(1973, Fr.), w; MAGNIFICENT ONE, THE(1974, Fr./Ital.), w; LA CAGE AUX FOLLES(1979, Fr./Ital.), w; SUNDAY LOVERS(1980, Ital./Fr.), w; BUDDY BUDDY(1981), w; LA CAGE AUX FOLLES II(1981, Ital./Fr.), w; PARTNERS(1982), w; TOY, THE(1982), w
1984
LES COMPERES(1984, Fr.), d&w
Serge Veber
NOUS IRONS A PARIS(1949, Fr.), w; FRENCH TOUCH, THE(1954, Fr.), w; MY SEVEN LITTLE SINS(1956, Fr./Ital.), w; FERNANDEL THE DRESSMAKER(1957, Fr.), w
Sal Vecchio
RUBY(1977)

Mario Vecci
ON THE BEACH(1959)

S. Vecheslov
LOSS OF FEELING(1935, USSR)

Alberto Vechietti
MONSTER OF THE ISLAND(1953, Ital.), w

Isabel Vecki
MEN OF THE NIGHT(1934)

Isabelle Vecki
STRANGE ADVENTURE(1932)

Stephen Vecoe
CONSTANT HUSBAND, THE(1955, Brit.)

Ferenc Vecsey
COURT CONCERT, THE(1936, Ger.), m

Claire Vedara
MARK OF THE VAMPIRE(1935)

Edward Vedder
MOZART STORY, THE(1948, Aust.)

Liell K. Vedder
WELCOME DANGER(1929), art d
Silents
FRESHMAN, THE(1925), art d; FOR HEAVEN'S SAKE(1926), art d

Will Vedder
YOU NEVER CAN TELL(1951)

William Vedder
BRIDE FOR SALE(1949); LEAVE IT TO HENRY(1949); ONCE MORE, MY DAR-LING(1949); UNDERCOVER MAN, THE(1949); CONVICTED(1950); GUNFIGHTER, THE(1950); PAINTING THE CLOUDS WITH SUNSHINE(1951); O. HENRY'S FULL HOUSE(1952); PAULA(1952); STARS AND STRIPES FOREVER(1952); DREAM WI-FE(1953); MISSISSIPPI GAMBLER, THE(1953); WORLD WITHOUT END(1956)

William H. Vedder
SENATOR WAS INDISCREET, THE(1947); JINX MONEY(1948)

Yvette Vedder
SUNSET BOULEVARD(1950)

Jack Vedders
Silents
GOLD RUSH, THE(1925)

Clare Vedera
ANOTHER DAWN(1937)

A. Vedernikov
TSAR'S BRIDE, THE(1966, USSR); KATERINA IZMAILOVA(1969, USSR)

Slobodan Vedernjak
RAMPAGE AT APACHE WELLS(1966, Ger./Yugo.)

Julian Vedey
ROMANCE IN RHYTHM(1934, Brit.); CAFE MASCOT(1936, Brit.); YOU'RE THE DOCTOR(1938, Brit.); BLACKOUT(1940, Brit.); WE'LL SMILE AGAIN(1942, Brit.); GREEN COCKATOO, THE(1947, Brit.)

Julien Vedey
FULL SPEED AHEAD(1936, Brit.); STRANGE CARGO(1936, Brit.); BITER BIT, THE(1937, Brit.); COMMAND PERFORMANCE(1937, Brit.); MELODY AND RO-MANCE(1937, Brit.); MISSING, BELIEVED MARRIED(1937, Brit.); NIGHT RI-DE(1937, Brit.), a, w; SATURDAY NIGHT REVUE(1937, Brit.); SPOT OF BOTHER, A(1938, Brit.); DISCOVERIES(1939, Brit.); WHAT WOULD YOU DO, CHUMS?(1939, Brit.); THREE COCKEYED SAILORS(1940, Brit.); PLAYBOY, THE(1942, Brit.); BELLS GO DOWN, THE(1943, Brit.); TAKE A POWDER(1953, Brit.), a, d, w

Jesus Velazquez
CURSE OF THE AZTEC MUMMY, THE(1965, Mex.); ROBOT VS. THE AZTEC MUMMY, THE(1965, Mex.)

Luciana Vedovelli
GUN, THE(1978, Ital.), art d

Nicole Vedres
LIFE BEGINS TOMORROW(1952, Fr.), d&w

Bobby Vee
SWINGIN' ALONG(1962); JUST FOR FUN(1963, Brit.); PLAY IT COOL(1963, Brit.); C'MON, LET'S LIVE A LITTLE(1967)

Bill Veeck
KID FROM CLEVELAND, THE(1949)

Jace Vander Veen
MC CABE AND MRS. MILLER(1971)

John Veenenbos
WALK WITH LOVE AND DEATH, A(1969)

Hans Veerman
LIFT, THE(1983, Neth.); SPETTERS(1983, Holland)
1984
FOURTH MAN, THE(1984, Neth.)

Wally Veevers
RICHARD III(1956, Brit.), spec eff; ROTTEN TO THE CORE(1956, Brit.), spec eff; SATELLITE IN THE SKY(1956), spec eff; GUNS OF NAVARONE, THE(1961), art d; PURE HELL OF ST. TRINIAN'S, THE(1961, Brit.), spec eff; NEARLY A NASTY ACCIDENT(1962, Brit.), spec eff; ROAD TO HONG KONG, THE(1962, U.S./Brit.), spec eff; SODOM AND GOMORRAH(1962, U.S./Fr./Ital.), spec eff; VALIANT, THE(1962, Brit./Ital.), spec eff; WAR LOVER, THE(1962, U.S./Brit.), spec eff; DAY OF THE TRIFFIDS, THE(1963), spec eff; MYSTERY SUBMARINE(1963, Brit.), spec eff; VIC-TORS, THE(1963), spec eff; DR. STRANGELOVE: OR HOW I LEARNED TO STOP WORRYING AND LOVE THE BOMB(1964), spec eff; DIE, MONSTER, DIE(1965, Brit.), spec eff; STUDY IN TERROR, A(1966, Brit./Ger.), spec eff; 2001: A SPACE ODYSSEY(1968, U.S./Brit.), spec eff; MAGIC CHRISTIAN, THE(1970, Brit.), spec eff; PRIVATE LIFE OF SHERLOCK HOLMES, THE(1970, Brit.), spec eff; SCROOGE(1970, Brit.), spec eff; DIAMONDS ARE FOREVER(1971, Brit.), spec eff; ROCKY HORROR PICTURE SHOW, THE(1975, Brit.), spec eff; KEEP, THE(1983, Brit.), spec eff; LOCAL HERO(1983, Brit.), spec eff

Claude Vega
BED AND BOARD(1971, Fr.)

Gonzalo Vega
SURVIVAL RUN(1980)

Ildefonso Vega
TREASURE OF THE SIERRA MADRE, THE(1948)

Isala Vega
RAGE(1966, U.S./Mex.)

Isela Vega
MADAME DEATH(1968, Mex.); POR MIS PISTOLAS(1969, Mex.); DEADLY TRACK-ERS(1973); BRING ME THE HEAD OF ALFREDO GARCIA(1974); DRUM(1976); JOSHUA(1976); MUSHROOM EATER, THE(1976, Mex.); BARBAROSA(1982)

June Vega
OLGA'S GIRLS(1964)

Marlina Vega
OTHER SIDE OF THE MOUNTAIN–PART 2, THE(1978)

Rosa Vega
Silents
LOVES OF RICARDO, THE(1926)

Fernando Vegal
TERRACE, THE(1964, Arg.)

Lolly Vegas
NASTY RABBIT, THE(1964)

Pat Vegas
NASTY RABBIT, THE(1964)

Ray Vegas
NASTY RABBIT, THE(1964); DEADWOOD'76(1965); VELVET TRAP, THE(1966)

Serge Veher
AMPHYTRYON(1937, Ger.), w

Bill Vehr
LUPE(1967)

Nicholas Vehr
ABOVE SUSPICION(1943); THREE HEARTS FOR JULIA(1943)

Nick Vehr
FOREST RANGERS, THE(1942); THIS LAND IS MINE(1943)

John Veich
RIVER OF NO RETURN(1954)

Conrad Veidt
LAST PERFORMANCE, THE(1929); CONGRESS DANCES(1932, Ger.); RAS-PUTIN(1932, Ger.); EMPRESS AND I, THE(1933, Ger.); F.P. 1(1933, Brit.); ROME EXPRESS(1933, Brit.); BELLA DONNA(1934, Brit.); I WAS A SPY(1934, Brit.); POWER(1934, Brit.); WANDERING JEW, THE(1935, Brit.); KING OF THE DAM-NED(1936, Brit.); PASSING OF THE THIRD FLOOR BACK, THE(1936, Brit.); DARK JOURNEY(1937, Brit.); UNDER THE RED ROBE(1937, Brit.); DEVIL IS AN EMPRESS, THE(1939, Fr.); U-BOAT 29(1939, Brit.); BLACKOUT(1940, Brit.); ESCAPE(1940); THIEF OF BAGHDAD, THE(1940, Brit.); MEN IN HER LIFE, THE(1941); WHISTLING IN THE DARK(1941); WOMAN'S FACE(1941); ALL THROUGH THE NIGHT(1942); CASABLANCA(1942); NAZI AGENT(1942); ABOVE SUSPICION(1943)
Silents
CABINET OF DR. CALIGARI, THE(1921, Ger.); BELOVED ROGUE, THE(1927); MAN WHO LAUGHS, THE(1927); STUDENT OF PRAGUE, THE(1927, Ger.)
Misc. Silents
FIVE SINISTER STORIES(1919, Ger.); SATANAS(1919, Ger.); CAGLIOSTRO(1920, Ger.); HEAD OF JANUS, THE(1920, Ger.); HUNCHBACK AND THE DANCER, THE(1920, Ger.); ALL FOR A WOMAN(1921, Ger.); MYSTERIES OF INDIA(1922, Ger.); WAXWORKS(1924, Ger.); HANDS OF ORLAC, THE(1925, Aust.); MAN'S PAST, A(1927)

Dianora Veiga
ROMAN HOLIDAY(1953)

Joel Veiga
BADGE 373(1973)

Lud Veigel
DESERT HELL(1958)

Joel Veigg
SUCH GOOD FRIENDS(1971)

Anna Veigl
LITTLE NIGHT MUSIC, A(1977, Aust./U.S./Ger.)

Anthony Veiler
WINTERSET(1936), w

Anthony Veiller
MENACE(1934), w; WITCHING HOUR, THE(1934), w; BREAK OF HEARTS(1935), w; JALNA(1935), w; SEVEN KEYS TO BALDPATE(1935), w; STAR OF MID-NIGHT(1935), w; EX-MRS. BRADFORD, THE(1936), w; LADY CONSENTS, THE(1936), w; WOMAN REBELS, A(1936), w; SOLDIER AND THE LADY, THE(1937), w; STAGE DOOR(1937), w; RADIO CITY REVELS(1938), w; DISPUTED PASS-AGE(1939), w; LET US LIVE(1939), w; THEY SHALL HAVE MUSIC(1939), w; MOON OVER BURMA(1940), p; QUARTERBACK, THE(1940), p; TY-PHOON(1940), p; VICTORY(1940), p; NEW YORK TOWN(1941), p; BREACH OF PROMISE(1942, Brit.), w; HER CARDBOARD LOVER(1942), w; ASSIGNMENT IN BRITTANY(1943), w; KILLERS, THE(1946), w; STRANGER(1946), w; STATE OF THE UNION(1948), w; COLORADO TERRITORY(1949), p; BACKFIRE(1950), p; CHAIN LIGHTNING(1950), p; DALLAS(1950), p; ALONG THE GREAT DIVIDE(1951), p; FORCE OF ARMS(1951), p; FORT WORTH(1951), p; MOULIN ROUGE(1952), w; RED PLANET MARS(1952), p, w; THAT LADY(1955, Brit.), w; SAFARI(1956), w; MONKEY ON MY BACK(1957), w; TIMBUKTU(1959), w; LIST OF ADRIAN MESS-ENGER, THE(1963), w; NIGHT OF THE IGUANA, THE(1964), w
Silents
ACQUITTAL, THE(1923), w

Bayard Veiller
TRIAL OF MARY DUGAN, THE(1929), d, w; ALIAS FRENCH GERTIE(1930), w; PAID(1930), w; THIRTEENTH CHAIR, THE(1930), w; GUILTY HANDS(1931), w; ARSENE LUPIN(1932), w; NIGHT COURT(1932), w; UNASHAMED(1932), w; DIS-GRACED(1933), p; WOMAN ACCUSED(1933), w; NOTORIOUS SOPHIE LANG, THE(1934), p, w; WITCHING HOUR, THE(1934), p; CAR 99(1935), p; THIRTEENTH CHAIR, THE(1937), w; WITHIN THE LAW(1939), w
Silents
LURE OF YOUTH, THE(1921), p; MARRIAGE OF WILLIAM ASHE, THE(1921), sup; SHERLOCK BROWN(1921), d, w; RIGHT THAT FAILED, THE(1922), d; UNDER THE RED ROBE(1923), w; HELD BY THE LAW(1927), w
Misc. Silents
LADYFINGERS(1921), d; LAST CARD, THE(1921), d; THERE ARE NO VIL-LAINS(1921), d; FACE BETWEEN, THE(1922), d

Jim Veillieux
STAR TREK II: THE WRATH OF KHAN(1982), spec eff

Claude Veillor
GREED IN THE SUN(1965, Fr./ Ital.), w
Claude Veillot
QUESTION, THE(1977, Fr.), w
Anthony Scott Veitch
KANGAROO KID, THE(1950, Aus./U.S.), w; COAST OF SKELETONS(1965, Brit.), w
John D. Veitch
FROM HERE TO ETERNITY(1953)
John P. Veitch
STALAG 17(1953)
Jonna Veitch
SKATETOWN, U.S.A.(1979)
Ronald McCleod Veitch
1984
COMFORT AND JOY(1984, Brit.)
Chico Vejar
WORLD IN MY CORNER(1956); MIDNIGHT STORY, THE(1957)
Harry Vejar
MEXICALI ROSE(1929); STOKER, THE(1932); MIRACLES FOR SALE(1939); WEST TO GLORY(1947); TREASURE OF THE SIERRA MADRE, THE(1948); TOO LATE FOR TEARS(1949); WAKE OF THE RED WITCH(1949); WE WERE STRANGERS(1949); CRISIS(1950)
Harry J. Vejar
SCARFACE(1932); RIDE THE PINK HORSE(1947); INVASION OF THE BODY SNATCHERS(1956)
Laurie Vejar
DR. GILLESPIE'S CRIMINAL CASE(1943), ed
Michael Vejar
SPEEDTRAP(1978), ed
Mike Vejar
JOE PANTHER(1976), ed
Bent Vejlby
REPTILICUS(1962, U.S./Den.)
Vitezslav Vejrazka
DEVIL'S TRAP, THE(1964, Czech.)
Perry Vekroff
BIG BOY(1930), w; SOLDIER'S PLAYTHING, A(1931), w
Silents
DUST OF DESIRE(1919), d
Misc. Silents
BRIDGES BURNED(1917), d; CYNTHIA-OF-THE-MINUTE(1920), d
Perry N. Vekroff
Silents
WHAT WIVES WANT(1923), w
Misc. Silents
HEARTS OF MEN(1915), d; THREE WEEKS(1915), d; WHEN IT STRIKES HOME(1915), d; HER SECRET(1917), d; MORE EXCELLENT WAY, THE(1917), d; QUESTION, THE(1917), d; RICHARD THE BRAZEN(1917), d; SECRET OF EVE, THE(1917), d; WOMAN'S EXPERIENCE, A(1918), d; WHAT LOVE FORGIVES(1919), d
Reginald Vel Johnson
WOLFEN(1981)
Maricarmen Vela
MAN AND THE MONSTER, THE(1965, Mex.)
Pilar Vela
TRISTANA(1970, Span./Ital./Fr.)
Roseanne Vela
HEAVEN'S GATE(1980)
Andrew Velajquez
ONE BIG AFFAIR(1952)
Meta Velander
LOVING COUPLES(1966, Swed.)
Louis Velarde
LIGHT TOUCH, THE(1951)
Mike Velarde
BACK DOOR TO HELL(1964), m; HORROR OF THE BLOOD MONSTERS(1970, U.S./Phil.), m
Antonio Velart
NIGHT OF THE ZOMBIES(1983, Span./Ital.), prod d
Adela Velasco
WIDOWS' NEST(1977, U.S./Span.), cos
Chuck Velasco
1984
SOLDIER'S STORY, A(1984), cos
Conchita Velasco
ERNESTO(1979, Ital.)
Fred Velasco
STARLIGHT OVER TEXAS(1938); GREAT FLAMARION, THE(1945)
Jerry Velasco
TELL THEM WILLIE BOY IS HERE(1969)
Maria Velasco
ALL NIGHT LONG(1961, Brit.); OPERATION CAMEL(1961, Den.); PARIS BLUES(1961)
Maria Helena Velasco
1984
BLAME IT ON RIO(1984)
Nemia Velasco
MORO WITCH DOCTOR(1964, U.S./Phil.)
Noela Velasco
ANGELS BRIGADE(1980)
Velasco and Lenee
PENTHOUSE RHYTHM(1945)
The Velascos
GAUCHO SERENADE(1940)
Andres Velasquez
LITTLEST OUTLAW, THE(1955)
Antonio Velasquez
MAGNIFICENT MATADOR, THE(1955)

Ernest Velasquez
SALT OF THE EARTH(1954)
Jesus Velasquez
RAGE(1966, U.S./Mex.), w
Jose Velasquez
MY BROTHER, THE OUTLAW(1951)
Emil Velazco
STALLION CANYON(1949), md; STRANGE WORLD(1952), m
Cuco Velazquez
SCALPHUNTERS, THE(1968)
Jesus Murcielago Velazquez
AZTEC MUMMY, THE(1957, Mex.); PEARL OF TLAYUCAN, THE(1964, Mex.), w
Lorena Velazquez
LA NAVE DE LOS MONSTRUOS(1959, Mex.); DOCTOR OF DOOM(1962, Mex.)
Teresa Velazquez
CASTILIAN, THE(1963, Span./U.S.)
Alex Velcoff
D.I., THE(1957), cos
Olbdrich Velen
90 DEGREES IN THE SHADE(1966, Czech./Brit.)
Istvan Velenczei
ROUND UP, THE(1969, Hung.)
Ellen Velero
FANNY HILL: MEMOIRS OF A WOMAN OF PLEASURE zero(1965)
Reina Veles
PANAMA FLO(1932)
Senka Veletanlic-Petrovic
THREE(1967, Yugo.)
Eddie Velez
1984
REPO MAN(1984)
Gladys Velez
POPI(1969)
Jorge Velez
GUADALAJARA(1943, Mex.)
Josephine Velez
DRACULA(1931)
Misc. Talkies
RIDIN' FOOL, THE(1931)
Lupe Velez
LADY OF THE PAVEMENTS(1929); WOLF SONG(1929); EAST IS WEST(1930); HELL HARBOR(1930); STORM, THE(1930); TIGER ROSE(1930); CUBAN LOVE SONG,THE(1931); RESURRECTION(1931); SQUAW MAN, THE(1931); BROKEN WING, THE(1932); HALF-NAKED TRUTH, THE(1932); KONGO(1932); HOT PEPPER(1933); HOLLYWOOD PARTY(1934); LAUGHING BOY(1934); PALOOKA(1934); STRICTLY DYNAMITE(1934); GYPSY MELODY(1936, Brit.); MORALS OF MARCUS, THE(1936, Brit.); HIGH FLYERS(1937); HE LOVED AN ACTRESS(1938, Brit.); GIRL FROM MEXICO, THE(1939); MEXICAN SPITFIRE(1939); MEXICAN SPITFIRE OUT WEST(1940); HONOLULU LU(1941); MEXICAN SPITFIRE'S BABY(1941); PLAYMATES(1941); SIX LESSONS FROM MADAME LA ZONGA(1941); MEXICAN SPITFIRE AT SEA(1942); MEXICAN SPITFIRE SEES A GHOST(1942); LADIES' DAY(1943); MEXICAN SPITFIRE'S BLESSED EVENT(1943); REDHEAD FROM MANHATTAN(1954)
Silents
GAUCHO, THE(1928); STAND AND DELIVER(1928); WHERE EAST IS EAST(1929)
Olga Velez
TIGER BY THE TAIL(1970)
Richard Velez
MAD DOG COLL(1961); YOUNG SAVAGES, THE(1961)
Wanda Velez
AARON LOVES ANGELA(1975)
Robert Velguth
1984
PLAGUE DOGS, THE(1984, U.S./Brit.), ph
Tania Velia
QUEEN OF OUTER SPACE(1958); MISSILE TO THE MOON(1959); FIEND OF DOPE ISLAND(1961)
Marco Veliante
WOMAN ON FIRE, A(1970, Ital.)
M. Velich
PUT UP OR SHUT UP(1968, Arg.)
V. Velichko
SKI BATTALION(1938, USSR), ph
Frantisek Velicky
MARKETA LAZAROVA(1968, Czech.)
Lester Velie
GARMENT JUNGLE, THE(1957), w
Joe Velitch
MELODY OF MY HEART(1936, Brit.)
Jesse Veliz
WINTER KILLS(1979)
Helen Velkovorska
CABARET(1972)
Carol Vell
LEATHER AND NYLON(1969, Fr./Ital.)
John Vella
RACING FEVER(1964); STING OF DEATH(1966); WILD REBELS, THE(1967); MORE AMERICAN GRAFFITI(1979)
Fred Vellaca
MAYERLING(1968, Brit./Fr.)
Zul Vellani
SIDDHARTHA(1972)
G. Vellchko
SEVEN BRAVE MEN(1936, USSR), ph
Louis Velle
MY SEVEN LITTLE SINS(1956, Fr./Ital.); FRONTIER HELLCAT(1966, Fr./Ital./Ger./Yugo.)

Rafael Velledde
PRETTY BUT WICKED(1965, Braz.), ed
Lucio Vellegas
MARK OF ZORRO, THE(1940)
Bayard Veller
TRIAL OF MARY DUGAN, THE(1941), w
Bayard Vellier
RED PLANET MARS(1952)
Kevin Velligan
1984
ALLEY CAT(1984)
Roberto Veloccia
MACHINE GUN McCAIN(1970, Ital.), set d
Segundo Veloria
NO MAN IS AN ISLAND(1962)
Harriet Veloshin
HOW DO I LOVE THEE?(1970)
Thanas Veloudios
SERENITY(1962)
Frank Veloz
THEY MET IN ARGENTINA(1941), ch; LATIN LOVERS(1953), ch
Veloz & Yolanda
CHAMPAGNE WALTZ(1937)
Veloz and Yolanda
UNDER THE PAMPAS MOON(1935); PRIDE OF THE YANKEES, THE(1942); HONEYMOON LODGE(1943); BRAZIL(1944); THRILL OF BRAZIL, THE(1946)
Marc Velperlaan
OUTSIDER IN AMSTERDAM(1983, Neth.), ph
Paul Velsa
FIRST OFFENCE(1936, Brit.)
Phillipp Velt
INHERITANCE IN PRETORIA(1936, Ger.)
Orlando Veltran
HITCH-HIKER, THE(1953)
International Velvet
CHELSEA GIRLS, THE(1967)
The Velvet Underground
CHELSEA GIRLS, THE(1967), m
Richard L. Ven Enger
ACCUSED OF MURDER(1956), ed
Evelyn Venable
CRADLE SONG(1933); DAVID HARUM(1934); DEATH TAKES A HOLIDAY(1934); DOUBLE DOOR(1934); MRS. WIGGS OF THE CABBAGE PATCH(1934); ALICE ADAMS(1935); COUNTY CHAIRMAN, THE(1935); HARMONY LANE(1935); LITTLE COLONEL, THE(1935); STREAMLINE EXPRESS(1935); VAGABOND LADY(1935); STAR FOR A NIGHT(1936); HAPPY-GO-LUCKY(1937); NORTH OF NOME(1937); RACKETEERS IN EXILE(1937); FEMALE FUGITIVE(1938); FRONTIERSMAN, THE(1938); HOLLYWOOD STADIUM MYSTERY(1938); MY OLD KENTUCKY HOME(1938); HEADLEYS AT HOME, THE(1939); HERITAGE OF THE DESERT(1939); LUCKY CISCO KID(1940); PINOCCHIO(1940); HE HIRED THE BOSS(1943)
Sarah Venable
TWO(1975); MARTIN(1979)
Ted Venables
HE SNOOPS TO CONQUER(1944, Brit.)
Jacques Venaire
PRINCESS COMES ACROSS, THE(1936)
Vanantino Venantini
AGONY AND THE ECSTASY, THE(1965)
Venantino Venantini
NUDE ODYSSEY(1962, Fr./Ital.); WARRIORS FIVE(1962); CONQUERED CITY(1966, Ital.); GALIA(1966, Fr./Ital.); SUCKER, THE(1966, Fr./Ital.); ROUND TRIP(1967); ANZIO(1968, Ital.); FEMMINA(1968 Fr./Ital./Ger.); PRIEST'S WIFE, THE(1971, Ital./Fr.); AND NOW MY LOVE(1975, Fr.); GATES OF HELL, THE(1983, U.S./Ital.)
1984
WARRIORS OF THE WASTELAND(1984, Ital.)
Shirley Venard
Misc. Talkies
JACKPOT(1982)
Venatino Venatini
BANDIDOS(1967, Ital.)
Veronique Vendell
BECKET(1964, Brit.); CODE 7, VICTIM 5(1964, Brit.); NIGHT OF THE GENERALS, THE(1967, Brit./Fr.); WEEKEND, ITALIAN STYLE(1967, Fr./Ital./Span.); MAYERLING(1968, Brit./Fr.); WITCHES, THE(1969, Fr./Ital.); CROSS OF IRON(1977, Brit., Ger.); BREAKTHROUGH(1978, Ger.)
Misc. Talkies
WOMEN FOR SALE(1975)
The Vendells
PSYCHO A GO-GO!(1965)
Magali Vendeuil
LES BELLES-DE-NUIT(1952, Fr.)
Ida Vendicktow
HANSEL AND GRETEL(1954), cos
Herb Vendig
CHECKERED FLAG, THE(1963), p
Peggy Vendig
CHECKERED FLAG, THE(1963)
Antonello Venditti
GOODNIGHT, LADIES AND GENTLEMEN(1977, Ital.), m
News Vendor
NEVER LET GO(1960, Brit.)
Mike Vendrell
UNDER FIRE(1983)
Henry Vendresse
LUCREZIA BORGIA(1937, Fr.), w
Ferenc Vendrey
AZURE EXPRESS(1938, Hung.)

Sue Veneer
HOLLYWOOD BOULEVARD(1976)
Charles A. Venegas
LITTLE MISS MARKER(1980)
Jose Bronco Venegas
LOS PLATILLOS VOLADORES(1955, Mex.)
Ernie Veneri
SKY HIGH(1952)
Amy Venesa
GOOD TIME GIRL(1950, Brit.)
Amy Veness
HOBSON'S CHOICE(1931, Brit.); LET ME EXPLAIN, DEAR(1932); MARRIAGE BOND, THE(1932, Brit.); MONEY FOR NOTHING(1932, Brit.); MURDER ON THE SECOND FLOOR(1932, Brit.); MY WIFE'S FAMILY(1932, Brit.); SELF-MADE LADY(1932, Brit.); TONIGHT'S THE NIGHT(1932, Brit.); HAWLEY'S OF HIGH STREET(1933, Brit.); LOVE NEST, THE(1933, Brit.); SOUTHERN MAID, A(1933, Brit.); THEIR NIGHT OUT(1933, Brit.); BREWSTER'S MILLIONS(1935, Brit.); DRAKE THE PIRATE(1935, Brit.); JOY RIDE(1935, Brit.); LORNA DOONE(1935, Brit.); OLD CURIOSITY SHOP, THE(1935, Brit.); PLAY UP THE BAND(1935, Brit.); REGAL CAVALCADE(1935, Brit.); BLACK ROSES(1936, Ger.); KING OF HEARTS(1936, Brit.); RED WAGON(1936); SKYLARKS(1936, Brit.); AREN'T MEN BEASTS?(1937, Brit.); SHOW GOES ON, THE(1937, Brit.); WHO KILLED FEN MARKHAM?(1937, Brit.); WINDBAG THE SAILOR(1937, Brit.); THISTLEDOWN(1938, Brit.); YELLOW SANDS(1938, Brit.); FLYING FIFTY-FIVE(1939, Brit.); JUST WILLIAM(1939, Brit.); MILL ON THE FLOSS(1939, Brit.); MAN IN GREY, THE(1943, Brit.); MILLIONS LIKE US(1943, Brit.); SAINT MEETS THE TIGER, THE(1943, Brit.); DON'T TAKE IT TO HEART(1944, Brit.); THIS HAPPY BREED(1944, Brit.); WORLD OWES ME A LIVING, THE(1944, Brit.); DON CHICAGO(1945, Brit.); MADONNA OF THE SEVEN MOONS(1945, Brit.); THEY WERE SISTERS(1945, Brit.); CARNIVAL(1946, Brit.); TURNERS OF PROSPECT ROAD, THE(1947, Brit.); BLANCHE FURY(1948, Brit.); HERE COME THE HUGGETTS(1948, Brit.); MAN OF EVIL(1948, Brit.); VOTE FOR HUGGETT(1948, Brit.); BOY, A GIRL AND A BIKE, A(1949 Brit.); HUGGETTS ABROAD, THE(1949, Brit.); MY BROTHER'S KEEPER(1949, Brit.); ASTONISHED HEART, THE(1950, Brit.); CHANCE OF A LIFETIME(1950, Brit.); MADELEINE(1950, Brit.); CAPTAIN HORATIO HORNBLOWER(1951, Brit.); HER PANELLED DOOR(1951, Brit.); OLIVER TWIST(1951, Brit.); PORTRAIT OF CLARE(1951, Brit.); TOM BROWN'S SCHOOLDAYS(1951, Brit.); ANGELS ONE FIVE(1954, Brit.); DOCTOR IN THE HOUSE(1954, Brit.); WOMAN FOR JOE, THE(1955, Brit.)
Silents
BRAT, THE(1919)
Nick Venet
OUT OF SIGHT(1966), m
Philippe Venet
IN THE FRENCH STYLE(1963, U.S./Fr.), cos
Anna Veneti
RAPE, THE(1965, Gr.)
Warner Venetz
WALKING TALL(1973)
Howard Venezia
OPERATION PETTICOAT(1959)
Sandy Veneziano
EYE FOR AN EYE, AN(1981), prod d; SIX WEEKS(1982), prod d; TERMS OF ENDEARMENT(1983), set d
Karin Vengay
FLIGHT TO TANGIER(1953); LITTLE BOY LOST(1953)
Anita Venge
SUMMER STORM(1944)
Thanassis Vengos
POLICEMAN OF THE 16TH PRECINCT, THE(1963, Gr.); MADALENA(1965, Gr.)
Jeanne Veniat
PRIZE, THE(1952, Fr.)
Venice Opera House Orchestra and Chorus
GLASS MOUNTAIN, THE(1950, Brit)
Mara Venier
DIARY OF AN ITALIAN(1972, Ital.)
Kathalina Veniero
KILLING OF A CHINESE BOOKIE, THE(1976); STING II, THE(1983)
Valia Venitskaya
Misc. Silents
ROMANCE OF WASTDALE, A(1921, Brit.)
Daniel Venn
FLASH GORDON(1980)
John Venn
LETTER TO THREE WIVES, A(1948)
Anne-Marie Vennel
DANTON(1983)
Chick Vennera
THANK GOD IT'S FRIDAY(1978); YANKS(1979); HIGH RISK(1981)
Ernie Venneri
MOB, THE(1951)
Ina Venning
HIDE AND SEEK(1964, Brit.)
Una Venning
PORTRAIT OF CLARE(1951, Brit.)
Silents
WELSH SINGER, A(1915, Brit.)
Johnny Venocur
1984
SAVAGE STREETS(1984)
Albert Venohr
Silents
NOSFERATU, THE VAMPIRE(1922, Ger.)
Edoardo Venola
WORLD IN MY POCKET, THE(1962, Fr./Ital./Ger.)
Diane Venora
WOLFEN(1981)
1984
COTTON CLUB, THE(1984)

Frank Venorio
VISITOR, THE(1980, Ital./U.S.), art d
Venrey
BLUE IDOL, THE(1931, Hung.)
John Ventantonio
PRIVATE PARTS(1972)
Lorenzo Ventavoli
RIDER ON THE RAIN(1970, Fr./Ital.), w; SOMEONE BEHIND THE DOOR(1971, Fr./Brit.), w
Pearl Venters
DISCOVERIES(1939, Brit.)
Peter Ventham
PASSAGE HOME(1955, Brit.)
Wanda Ventham
NAVY LARK, THE(1959, Brit.); TEENAGE BAD GIRL(1959, Brit.); CRACKSMAN, THE(1963, Brit.); KNACK ... AND HOW TO GET IT, THE(1965, Brit.); SPY WITH A COLD NOSE, THE(1966, Brit.); BLOOD BEAST TERROR, THE(1967, Brit.); LOVE IS A WOMAN(1967, Brit.); MISTER TEN PERCENT(1967, Brit.); CARRY ON, UP THE KHYBER(1968, Brit.); CAPTAIN KRONOS: VAMPIRE HUNTER(1974, Brit.)
Baron [Giovanni] Ventigmilia
Silents
PLEASURE GARDEN, THE(1925, Brit./Ger.), ph; FEAR O' GOD(1926, Brit./Ger.), ph; LODGER, THE(1926, Brit.), ph
Carlos Ventigmilia
20 MILLION MILES TO EARTH(1957), ph
Baron Ventimiglia
Silents
PHYSICIAN, THE(1928, Brit.), ph
Giovanni Ventimiglia
JOURNEY BENEATH THE DESERT(1967, Fr./Ital.), spec eff
Eugene Ventresca
JACK AND THE BEANSTALK(1970), m
Beverly Ventriss
EMMA MAE(1976), cos
Ray Ventura
AMERICAN LOVE(1932, Fr.), m
Angelo Ventura
TWILIGHT PEOPLE(1972, Phil.)
Claudio Ventura
WE'LL GROW THIN TOGETHER(1979, Fr.), ed
1984
JUST THE WAY YOU ARE(1984), ed
Clyde Ventura
BURY ME AN ANGEL(1972); TERMINAL ISLAND(1973); GATOR BAIT(1974); SERIAL(1980)
Jacqueline Ventura
AND GOD CREATED WOMAN(1957, Fr.)
Jan Ventura
1984
BREAKIN' 2: ELECTRIC BOOGALOO(1984), w
Lino Ventura
GORILLA GREETS YOU, THE(1958, Fr.); MISTRESS OF THE WORLD(1959, Ital./Fr./Ger.); FRANTIC(1961, Fr.); MODIGLIANI OF MONTPARNASSE(1961, Fr./Ital.); DEVIL AND THE TEN COMMANDMENTS, THE(1962, Fr.); THREE PENNY OPERA(1963, Fr./Ger.); GREED IN THE SUN(1965, Fr./ Ital.); TAXI FOR TOBRUK(1965, Fr./Span./Ger.); CLOPORTES(1966, Fr., Ital.); GREAT SPY CHASE, THE(1966, Fr.); LAST ADVENTURE, THE(1968, Fr./Ital.); L'ARMEE DES OMBRES(1969, Fr./Ital.); WISE GUYS(1969, Fr./Ital.); SICILIAN CLAN, THE(1970, Fr.); VALACHI PAPERS, THE(1972, Ital./Fr.); THREE TOUGH GUYS(1974, U.S./Ital.); LA CAGE(1975, Fr.); BUTTERFLY ON THE SHOULDER, A(1978, Fr.); MEDUSA TOUCH, THE(1978, Brit.); ANGRY MAN, THE(1979 Fr./Can.); SUNDAY LOVERS(1980, Ital./Fr.); INQUISITOR, THE(1982, Fr.); LES MISERABLES(1982, Fr.)
Misc. Talkies
JIG SAW(1979)
Mary Ann Ventura
BIRD OF PARADISE(1951)
Michael Ventura
ROADIE(1980), w
Misraki Ventura
AMERICAN LOVE(1932, Fr.), m
Ray Ventura
WHIRLWIND OF PARIS(1946, Fr.); MONTE CARLO BABY(1953, Fr.), p; STOP TRAIN 349(1964, Fr./Ital./Ger.), p
Renato Ventura
GUN, THE(1978, Ital.), art d
Riccardo Ventura
SACCO AND VANZETTI(1971, Ital./Fr.)
Viviane Ventura
HIGH WIND IN JAMAICA, A(1965); RETURN FROM THE ASHES(1965, U.S./Brit.); BATTLE BENEATH THE EARTH(1968, Brit.)
Vivienne Ventura
PROMISE HER ANYTHING(1966, Brit.)
Vivlane Ventura
FINDERS KEEPERS(1966, Brit.)
Richard Venture
DARK INTRUDER(1965); EFFECT OF GAMMA RAYS ON MAN-IN-THE-MOON MARIGOLDS, THE(1972); MAN ON A SWING(1974); GREATEST, THE(1977, U.S./Brit.); BETSY, THE(1978); BEING THERE(1979); LAST WORD, THE(1979); ONION FIELD, THE(1979); HUNTER, THE(1980); LOOKER(1981); MISSING(1982)
Silvana Venturelli
CAMILLE 2000(1969); LONG RIDE FROM HELL, A(1970, Ital.)
Annibal Venturi
RETURN OF SABATA(1972, Ital./Fr./Ger.)
Tom Venturi
ILLIAC PASSION, THE(1968)
Edward Venturini
LLANO KID, THE(1940), d
Misc. Silents
HEADLESS HORSEMAN, THE(1922), d; OLD FOOL, THE(1923), d

Edward T. Venturini
IN OLD MEXICO(1938), d
Georges Venturini
MYSTERY OF THE BLACK JUNGLE(1955), p
Giorgio Venturini
PHAROAH'S WOMAN, THE(1961, Ital.), p; AVENGER, THE(1962, Fr./Ital.), p; BLACK VEIL FOR LISA, A(1969 Ital./Ger.), p; DEAD OF SUMMER(1970 Ital./Fr.), p; HUMANOID, THE(1979, Ital.), p
Livia Venturini
LA STRADA(1956, Ital.)
Vittorio Venturoli
ROVER, THE(1967, Ital.)
Sam Ventury
MEDIUM COOL(1969)
Brenda Venus
PSYCHOPATH, THE(1973); EIGER SANCTION, THE(1975); JOSHUA(1976); DEATHSPORT(1978); FM(1978); 48 HOURS(1982)
Benay Venuta
REPEAT PERFORMANCE(1947); EASTER PARADE(1948); I, JANE DOE(1948); ANNIE GET YOUR GUN(1950); CALL ME MISTER(1951); STARS AND STRIPES FOREVER(1952); RICOCHET ROMANCE(1954)
Renay Venuta
FUZZY PINK NIGHTGOWN, THE(1957)
Joe Venuti
SYNCOPATION(1942); SARGE GOES TO COLLEGE(1947); BELLE OF OLD MEXICO(1950); DISC JOCKEY(1951); PETE KELLY'S BLUES(1955)
Stefano Venzina
APPOINTMENT FOR MURDER(1954, Ital.), w
Carl Veo
THOSE DIRTY DOGS(1974, U.S./Ital./Span.), w
Carlo Veo
FEW BULLETS MORE, A(1968, Ital./Span.), w
Fritz Vepper
BRIDGE, THE(1961, Ger.)
C.J. Ver Halen, Jr.
HIDDEN GUNS(1956), p
Darleem Ver Jean
WORDS AND MUSIC(1929)
Darleen Ver Jean
WORDS AND MUSIC(1929)
Billy Vera
1984
ADVENTURES OF BUCKAROO BANZAI: ACROSS THE 8TH DIMENSION, THE(1984)
Carlos Vera
TEN WANTED MEN(1955)
Connie Vera
WITHOUT WARNING(1952)
Herman Vera
RANCHO GRANDE(1938, Mex.); TOAST TO LOVE(1951, Mex.)
Memo Vera
1984
THIS IS SPINAL TAP(1984)
Richard Vera
SECOND CHANCE(1953)
Ricky Vera
LEATHER SAINT, THE(1956)
Vera-Ellen
WONDER MAN(1945); KID FROM BOOKLYN, THE(1946); THREE LITTLE GIRLS IN BLUE(1946); CARNIVAL IN COSTA RICA(1947); LOVE HAPPY(1949); ON THE TOWN(1949); THREE LITTLE WORDS(1950); HAPPY GO LOVELY(1951, Brit.); BELLE OF NEW YORK, THE(1952); BIG LEAGUER(1953); CALL ME MADAM(1953); WHITE CHRISTMAS(1954)
Louis Enrique Veragara
FEAR CHAMBER, THE(1968, US/Mex.), p
Cecilia Verandi
VIGILANTE(1983), makeup
Linda Veras
GENERALE DELLA ROVERE(1960, Ital./Fr.); CONTEMPT(1963, Fr./Ital.); PLAYMATES(1969, Fr./Ital.); SABATA(1969, Ital.); MICHELLE(1970, Fr.); ROMANCE OF A HORSE THIEF(1971)
Robert Verberkmoes
I EAT YOUR SKIN(1971), art d
Robert Verberkmoss
CURSE OF THE LIVING CORPSE, THE(1964), art d; HORROR OF PARTY BEACH, THE(1964), art d
Erno Verbes
ALIAS NICK BEAL(1949)
Gisela Verbisek
DARK CORNER, THE(1946)
Helen Verbit
LITTLE BIG MAN(1970); MADE FOR EACH OTHER(1971); HOW TO SUCCEED IN BUSINESS WITHOUT REALLY TRYING(1976); I NEVER PROMISED YOU A ROSE GARDEN(1977)
1984
LONELY GUY, THE(1984)
Y. Verbitskaya
YOLANTA(1964, USSR)
Jack Verbois
WHAT'S UP, DOC?(1972); NICKELODEON(1976); HALLOWEEN II(1981)
Verbong
GIRL WITH THE RED HAIR, THE(1983, Neth.), w
Ben Verbong
GIRL WITH THE RED HAIR, THE(1983, Neth.), d
Jacques Verbrugge
HUNTED IN HOLLAND(1961, Brit.)
Roger Vercel
STORMY WATERS(1946, Fr.), w

Elios Vercelloni
RED CLOAK, THE(1961, Ital./Fr.), p; TARTARS, THE(1962, Ital./Yugo.), ph
Stephen Vercoe
KNIGHTS OF THE ROUND TABLE(1953); MASTER OF BALLANTRAE, THE(1953, U.S./Brit.); TERROR STREET(1953); FRONT PAGE STORY(1954, Brit.); LES GIRLS(1957); ORDERS ARE ORDERS(1959, Brit.)
Vercors [Jean "Marcel" Brewer]
SKULLDUGGERY(1970), w
Marcel Vercoutere
SUPPORT YOUR LOCAL SHERIFF(1969), spec eff; DIRTY DINGUS MAGEE(1970), spec eff; MC CABE AND MRS. MILLER(1971), spec eff; DELIVERANCE(1972), spec eff; NIGHT MOVES(1975), spec eff
Robert Verdaine
LOST MOMENT, THE(1947); SMASH-UP, THE STORY OF A WOMAN(1947); ROGUES' REGIMENT(1948)
Violette Verday
BALLERINA(1950, Fr.)
Dino Verde
DIRTY HEROES(1971, Ital./Fr./Ger.), w
Paul Verden
SILENCE OF THE NORTH(1981, Can.)
Claire Verdera
NONE BUT THE LONELY HEART(1944)
Clara Verdera
Silents
ERSTWHILE SUSAN(1919)
Clare Verdera
DARK ANGEL, THE(1935); ANNABEL TAKES A TOUR(1938); RULERS OF THE SEA(1939); LADY FROM CHEYENNE(1941); SHINING VICTORY(1941); THIS ABOVE ALL(1942)
Francis M. Verdi
HOUSE OF SECRETS(1929)
Freddie Verdi
Misc. Silents
PRIMA DONNA'S HUSBAND, THE(1916); LITTLE CHEVALIER, THE(1917)
Giuseppe Verdi
MAMMY(1930), m; MOONLIGHT MURDER(1936), m; KING'S JESTER, THE(1947, Ital.), w; RIGOLETTO(1949), m; AIDA(1954, Ital.), w; LEOPARD, THE(1963, Ital.), m; LA TRAVIATA(1968, Ital.), m; SENSO(1968, Ital.), m; TRANS-EUROP-EXPRESS(1968, Fr.), m; BITTER TEARS OF PETRA VON KANT, THE(1972, Ger.), m; LUNA(1979, Ital.), m
1984
EL NORTE(1984), m
Guiseppe Verdi
LOST WEEKEND, THE(1945), m; LA TRAVIATA(1982), m
Joe Verdi
CRIME OF DR. CRESPI, THE(1936); SIDE STREET(1950); VINTAGE, THE(1957)
Ed Verdier
BRIDE WORE CRUTCHES, THE(1940), w
Edward Verdier
SEVEN DAYS ASHORE(1944), w; SONG OF THE OPEN ROAD(1944), w; DELIGHTFULLY DANGEROUS(1945), w
Julien Verdier
TAMANGO(1959, Fr.); MURIEL(1963, Fr./Ital.); MURDER AT 45 R.P.M.(1965, Fr.); WEEKEND AT DUNKIRK(1966, Fr./Ital.)
Nadine Verdier
TRANS-EUROP-EXPRESS(1968, Fr.)
Paul Verdier
RUSSIANS ARE COMING, THE RUSSIANS ARE COMING, THE(1966); THOMAS CROWN AFFAIR, THE(1968)
Bliss Verdon
KING OF THE GYPSIES(1978)
Gwen Verdon
MEET ME AFTER THE SHOW(1951), a, ch; DREAMBOAT(1952); MERRY WIDOW, THE(1952); FARMER TAKES A WIFE, THE(1953); MISSISSIPPI GAMBLER, THE(1953), a, ch; DAMN YANKEES(1958)
1984
COTTON CLUB, THE(1984)
Gwyneth Verdon
DAVID AND BATHSHEBA(1951)
Gwyneth [Gwen] Verdon
ON THE RIVERA(1951); I DON'T CARE GIRL, THE(1952)
Mario Verdon
TWO FOR THE ROAD(1967, Brit.)
Carlo Verdone
LUNA(1979, Ital.)
Ann Verdugo
GREAT SCOUT AND CATHOUSE THURSDAY, THE(1976)
Elena Verdugo
THERE'S MAGIC IN MUSIC(1941); MOON AND SIXPENCE, THE(1942); TO THE SHORES OF TRIPOLI(1942); HOUSE OF FRANKENSTEIN(1944); RAINBOW ISLAND(1944); FROZEN GHOST, THE(1945); STRANGE VOYAGE(1945); LITTLE GIANT(1946); SONG OF SCHEHERAZADE(1947); BIG SOMBRERO, THE(1949); EL DORADO PASS(1949); LOST TRIBE, THE(1949); SKY DRAGON(1949); TUNA CLIPPER(1949); CYRANO DE BERGERAC(1950); LOST VOLCANO, THE(1950); SNOW DOG(1950); GENE AUTRY AND THE MOUNTIES(1951); JET JOB(1952); PATHFINDER, THE(1952); THIEF OF DAMASCUS(1952); MARKSMAN, THE(1953); PANAMA SAL(1957); DAY OF THE NIGHTMARE(1965); HOW SWEET IT IS(1968); ANGEL IN MY POCKET(1969)
Henri Verdun
MONSEIGNEUR(1950, Fr.), m
Henry Verdun
J'ACCUSE(1939, Fr.), m; THREE HOURS(1944, Fr.), m
Christine Verdy
FIRST TASTE OF LOVE(1962, Fr.)
Irene Vere
THIS'LL MAKE YOU WHISTLE(1938, Brit.)

John Vere
IT ALWAYS RAINS ON SUNDAY(1949, Brit.); FLESH AND BLOOD(1951, Brit.); LADY WITH A LAMP, THE(1951, Brit.); PICKWICK PAPERS, THE(1952, Brit.); SWORD AND THE ROSE, THE(1953); TOUCH OF THE SUN, A(1956, Brit.)
Peter Vere-Jones
PICTURES(1982, New Zealand)
Lisette Verea
NIGHT IN CASABLANCA, A(1946)
Ernest Verebes
MAGNIFICENT FRAUD, THE(1939)
Silents
GHOST TRAIN, THE(1927, Brit.)
Erno Verebes
DESPERATE ADVENTURE, A(1938); DANCE, GIRL, DANCE(1940); NEW WINE(1941); UNDERGROUND(1941); MOONLIGHT MASQUERADE(1942); TO BE OR NOT TO BE(1942); STRANGE DEATH OF ADOLF HITLER, THE(1943); CLIMAX, THE(1944); SHADY LADY(1945); GILDA(1946); TANGIER(1946); CALCUTTA(1947); NORTHWEST OUTPOST(1947); WHERE THERE'S LIFE(1947); BIG CLOCK, THE(1948); MY OWN TRUE LOVE(1948); GREAT SINNER, THE(1949); MY FRIEND IRMA(1949); OUTPOST IN MOROCCO(1949); RED, HOT AND BLUE(1949); COPPER CANYON(1950); GOLDBERGS, THE(1950); WHERE DANGER LIVES(1950); HIS KIND OF WOMAN(1951); TOO YOUNG TO KISS(1951); O. HENRY'S FULL HOUSE(1952); STARS AND STRIPES FOREVER(1952); CALL ME MADAM(1953); HOUDINI(1953); REMAINS TO BE SEEN(1953)
Misc. Silents
PAUL STREET BOYS(1929)
Ernst Verebes
DREAM OF SCHONBRUNN(1933, Aus.); HOTEL IMPERIAL(1939); HITLER GANG, THE(1944)
Ran Vered
1984
AMBASSADOR, THE(1984); SAHARA(1984)
Ben Vereen
SWEET CHARITY(1969); GAS-S-S-S!(1970); FUNNY LADY(1975); ALL THAT JAZZ(1979)
Nina Verella
YOU'RE A BIG BOY NOW(1966)
Yvan Verella
BOLDEST JOB IN THE WEST, THE(1971, Ital.)
Michele Verez
MARTIAN IN PARIS, A(1961, Fr.); CANDIDE(1962, Fr.); SEASON FOR LOVE, THE(1963, Fr.)
Carlos Vereza
1984
MEMOIRS OF PRISON(1984, Braz.)
Giovanni Verga
LA TERRA TREMA(1947, Ital.), w; FATAL DESIRE(1953), w
Aldo Vergano
OUTCRY(1949, Ital.), d, w
Serena Vergano
FAMILY DIARY(1963 Ital.); MATHIAS SANDORF(1963, Fr.)
Alfredo Vergara
LITTLE RED RIDING HOOD AND HER FRIENDS(1964, Mex.)
Enrique Vergara
HOUSE OF EVIL(1968, U.S./Mex.), p, d
Louis Enrique Vergara
INCREDIBLE INVASION, THE(1971, Mex./U.S.), p
Louis Enriquez Vergara
INCREDIBLE INVASION, THE(1971, Mex./U.S.), w
Luis Enrique Vergara
CEREBROS DIABOLICOS(1966, Mex.), p; MADAME DEATH(1968, Mex.), p; VAMPIRES, THE(1969, Mex.), p
Luis Enrique Vergara [Henry Verg]
SNAKE PEOPLE, THE(1968, Mex./U.S.), p
Manuel Vergara
LAST SUNSET, THE(1961)
Daniele Vergas
VOYAGE, THE(1974, Ital.)
Alicia Vergel
CAVALRY COMMAND(1963, U.S./Phil.)
Fiamma Verges
HUMAN FACTOR, THE(1975)
Jeannine Vergne
JACQUES BREL IS ALIVE AND WELL AND LIVING IN PARIS(1975), cos
Marie-Blanche Vergne
JE T'AIME, JE T'AIME(1972, Fr./Swed.)
Marie-Blanche Vergnes
I SPIT ON YOUR GRAVE(1962, Fr.)
Ray Verhaege
JE T'AIME, JE T'AIME(1972, Fr./Swed.)
Joseph Verhauz
1984
BEAT STREET(1984)
Guy Verhille
COMIC, THE(1969), cos; WHICH WAY TO THE FRONT?(1970), cos; GOING HOME(1971), cos; NEW CENTURIONS, THE(1972), cos; SHANKS(1974), cos; BUG(1975), cos; DREAMER(1979), cos; WHOLLY MOSES(1980), cos
Guy C. Verhille
FOOLS' PARADE(1971), cos
Michael Verhoeven
JUDGE AND THE SINNER, THE(1964, Ger.)
Paul Verhoeven
COURT CONCERT, THE(1936, Ger.), w; DAY AFTER THE DIVORCE, THE(1940, Ger.), d; ETERNAL WALTZ, THE(1959, Ger.), d; HAMLET(1962, Ger.); JUDGE AND THE SINNER, THE(1964, Ger.), d; UNWILLING AGENT(1968, Ger.); SOLDIER OF ORANGE(1979, Dutch), d, w; SPETTERS(1983, Holland), d
1984
FOURTH MAN, THE(1984, Neth.), d

Daniel Verite
BURGLARS, THE(1972, Fr./Ital.); AFRICAN, THE(1983, Fr.), stunts

Amy Verity
Misc. Silents
SINISTER STREET(1922, Brit.)

Erwin Verity
RELUCTANT DRAGON, THE(1941), cartoon d

Terence Verity
HASTY HEART, THE(1949), art d; GLASS MOUNTAIN, THE(1950, Brit.), art d; STAGE FRIGHT(1950, Brit.), set d; YOUNG WIVES' TALE(1954, Brit.), art d; WARRIORS, THE(1955), art d; 1984(1956, Brit.), art d; LET'S BE HAPPY(1957, Brit.), art d; MARK OF THE HAWK, THE(1958), art d; NAKED EARTH, THE(1958, Brit.), art d; SCHOOL FOR SCOUNDRELS(1960, Brit.), art d; LONG AND THE SHORT AND THE TALL, THE(1961, Brit.), art d

Terrence Verity
NO PLACE FOR JENNIFER(1950, Brit.), set d; DEVIL'S DISCIPLE, THE(1959), art d

Tom Verity
ONE NIGHT WITH YOU(1948, Brit), art d

Dennis Verkler
BURNT OFFERINGS(1976), ed

Jan Verkoren
LAST BLITZKRIEG, THE(1958)

Gisele Verlaine
SOUTH SEA WOMAN(1953); FOUR GIRLS IN TOWN(1956); NEVER SAY GOOD-BYE(1956)

Renaud Verlay
HOW NOT TO ROB A DEPARTMENT STORE(1965, Fr./Ital.)

Nikos Verlekis
LAND OF THE MINOTAUR(1976, Gr.)

Beatrice Verley
SO WELL REMEMBERED(1947, Brit.)

Bernard Verley
MILKY WAY, THE(1969, Fr./Ital.); CHLOE IN THE AFTERNOON(1972, Fr.); PHANTOM OF LIBERTY, THE(1974, Fr.)

Francoise Verley
CHLOE IN THE AFTERNOON(1972, Fr.)

Renaud Verley
UNINHIBITED, THE(1968, Fr./Ital./Span.)

Jacques Verlier
GIRL WITH THE GOLDEN EYES, THE(1962, Fr.)

Melanie Verlin
MIDNIGHT(1983)

Catherine Verlor
COUSIN, COUSINE(1976, Fr.); JUDGE AND THE ASSASSIN, THE(1979, Fr.)

Michele Verly
Misc. Silents
SOUL OF FRANCE(1929, Fr.)

Rani Verma
NINE HOURS TO RAMA(1963, U.S./Brit.)

Monique Vermeer
GUNS AND THE FURY, THE(1983)

Harold Vermilyea
O.S.S.(1946); GENTLEMAN'S AGREEMENT(1947); BEYOND GLORY(1948); BIG CLOCK, THE(1948); EMPEROR WALTZ, THE(1948); MIRACLE OF THE BELLS, THE(1948); SAINTED SISTERS, THE(1948); SORRY, WRONG NUMBER(1948); CHICAGO DEADLINE(1949); MANHANDLED(1949); BORN TO BE BAD(1950); EDGE OF DOOM(1950); KATIE DID IT(1951)

Lester J. Vermilyea
Silents
FINE FEATHERS(1921), art d

W. Vermilyea
Silents
JUNGLE, THE(1914)

John Vermont
RED SUN(1972, Fr./Ital./Span.)

Monique Vermont
MUSIC MAN, THE(1962)

S. Vermont
SUBWAY RIDERS(1981)

Claude Vermorel
LOVERS OF TOLEDO, THE(1954, Fr./Span./Ital.), w

Jean Vermorel
JOHNNY BANCO(1969, Fr./Ital./Ger.), w

Paul Vermoyal
Silents
ARAB, THE(1924)
Misc. Silents
LE DROIT A LA VIE(1917, Fr.)

Frederick Vern
MASSACRE HILL(1949, Brit.)

Denise Vernac
MASK OF DIIJON, THE(1946); CHEATERS, THE(1961, Fr.); MODIGLIANI OF MONTPARNASSE(1961, Fr./Ital.)

Maguy Vernadet
JUDEX(1966, Fr./Ital.), makeup; FRIENDS(1971, Brit.), makeup

Ron Vernan
ESCAPE FROM ALCATRAZ(1979)

Denise Vernanc
ALRAUNE(1952, Ger.)

Annie Vernay
BETRAYAL(1939, Fr.)

Paula Vernay
SON OF SINBAD(1955)

Raymonde Vernay
LE CIEL EST A VOUS(1957, Fr.)

Robert Vernay
PEPE LE MOKO(1937, Fr.), set d; COUNT OF MONTE-CRISTO(1955, Fr., Ital.), d, w

Andra Verne
VARIETY GIRL(1947); SAIGON(1948)

Ernest Verne
NIGHT INVADER, THE(1943, Brit)

Jules Verne
MYSTERIOUS ISLAND(1929), w; SOLDIER AND THE LADY, THE(1937), w; CAPTAIN GRANT'S CHILDREN(1939, USSR), w; MYSTERIOUS ISLAND(1941, USSR), w; 20,000 LEAGUES UNDER THE SEA(1954), w; AROUND THE WORLD IN 80 DAYS(1956), w; FROM THE EARTH TO THE MOON(1958), w; JOURNEY TO THE CENTER OF THE EARTH(1959), w; MICHAEL STROGOFF(1960, Fr./Ital./Yugo.), w; FABULOUS WORLD OF JULES VERNE, THE(1961, Czech.), w; MASTER OF THE WORLD(1961), w; MYSTERIOUS ISLAND(1961, U.S./Brit.), w; VALLEY OF THE DRAGONS(1961), w, d&w; FIVE WEEKS IN A BALLOON(1962), w; IN SEARCH OF THE CASTAWAYS(1962, Brit.), w; MATHIAS SANDORF(1963, Fr.), w; UP TO HIS EARS(1966, Fr./Ital.), w; THOSE FANTASTIC FLYING FOOLS(1967, Brit), w; SOUTHERN STAR, THE(1969, Fr./Brit.), w; STRANGE HOLIDAY(1969, Aus.), w; ON THE COMET(1970, Czech.), w; LIGHT AT THE EDGE OF THE WORLD, THE(1971, U.S./Span./Lichtenstein), w; MYSTERIOUS ISLAND OF CAPTAIN NEMO, THE(1973, Fr./Ital. 87m Span./Cameroon), w; MONSTER ISLAND(1981, Span./Cameroon), w
1984
DREAM ONE(1984, Brit./Fr.), w
Silents
20,000 LEAGUES UNDER THE SEA(1916), w

Kaaren Verne
UNDERGROUND(1941); ALL THROUGH THE NIGHT(1942); GREAT IMPERSONATION, THE(1942); KING'S ROW(1942); SHERLOCK HOLMES AND THE SECRET WEAPON(1942); SEVENTH CROSS, THE(1944); MADAME X(1966)

Karen Verne
SKY MURDER(1940); MISSING TEN DAYS(1941, Brit.); WILD MAN OF BORNEO, THE(1941); BAD AND THE BEAUTIFUL, THE(1952); STORY OF THREE LOVES, THE(1953); BULLET FOR JOEY, A(1955); OUTSIDE THE LAW(1956); SHIP OF FOOLS(1965)

Janine Verneau
CLEO FROM 5 TO 7(1961, Fr.), ed; LOVERS ON A TIGHTROPE(1962, Fr.), ed; LE BONHEUR(1966, Fr.), ed; LES CREATURES(1969, Fr./Swed.), ed
1984
THREE CROWNS OF THE SAILOR(1984, Fr.), ed

Louis Verneuil
CROSS MY HEART(1946), w

Carl Vernell
FLESH AND FANTASY(1943); FOLLOW THE BOYS(1944); FAMILY HONEYMOON(1948); CHICAGO CALLING(1951); GLENN MILLER STORY, THE(1953)

Anthony Verner
TREAD SOFTLY(1952, Brit.); AT THE EARTH'S CORE(1976, Brit.)

Gerald Verner
TREAD SOFTLY(1952, Brit.), w; NOOSE FOR A LADY(1953, Brit.), w; MEET MR. CALLAGHAN(1954, Brit.), w

Hans Verner
JUDITH(1965); NIGHT OF LUST(1965, Fr.); RAVISHING IDIOT, A(1966, Ital./Fr.); ROSEBUD(1975); JULIA(1977)

Jean Verner
UTOPIA(1952, Fr./Ital.); FOUR BAGS FULL(1957, Fr./Ital.); DIE GANS VON SEDAN(1962, Fr/Ger.)

Lois Verner
STEAMBOAT ROUND THE BEND(1935); SHOW BOAT(1936); ROMANCE IN THE DARK(1938); NANCY DREW-REPORTER(1939); GIRLS UNDER TWENTY-ONE(1940)

Pierre Vernet
MAYERLING(1968, Brit./Fr.)

Tevaite Vernette
1984
BOUNTY, THE(1984)

Henri Verneuil
CARNIVAL(1953, Fr.), d; LOVER'S NET(1957, Fr.), d; FORBIDDEN FRUIT(1959, Fr.), d, w; BIG CHIEF, THE(1960, Fr.), d, w; COW AND I, THE(1961, Fr., Ital., Ger.), d, w; MAXIME(1962, Fr.), w; MONKEY IN WINTER, A(1962, Fr.), d; MOST WANTED MAN, THE(1962, Fr./Ital.), d; ANY NUMBER CAN WIN(1963 Fr.), d, w; GREED IN THE SUN(1965, Fr./ Ital.), d; 25TH HOUR, THE(1967, Fr./Ital./Yugo.), d, w; GUNS FOR SAN SEBASTIAN(1968, U.S./Fr./Mex./Ital.), d; SICILIAN CLAN, THE(1970, Fr.), d, w; BURGLARS, THE(1972, Fr./Ital./Ger.), p&d, w; SERPENT, THE(1973, Fr./Ital./Ger.), d, w

Henry Verneuil
WEEKEND AT DUNKIRK(1966, Fr./Ital.), d

Juliette Verneuil
GOLGOTHA(1937, Fr.)

Louis Verneuil
JEALOUSY(1929), w; LOVE HABIT, THE(1931, Brit.), w; GET YOUR MAN(1934, Brit.), w; LADY IS WILLING, THE(1934, Brit.), w; TRUE CONFESSION(1937), w; WITH A SMILE(1939, Fr.), w; MY LIFE WITH CAROLINE(1941), w; DECEPTION(1946), w

Rene Verneuil
AZAIS(1931, Fr.), d

Anthony Verney
LIMPING MAN, THE(1953, Brit.), w; YOU LUCKY PEOPLE(1955, Brit.), w

Antony Verney
FUN AT ST. FANNY'S(1956, Brit.), w

Guy Verney
THIS HAPPY BREED(1944, Brit.); FAME IS THE SPUR(1947, Brit.); ANNA KARENINA(1948, Brit.); FOOLS RUSH IN(1949, Brit.); HELD IN TRUST(1949, Brit.); TRAIN OF EVENTS(1952, Brit.); FLOATING DUTCHMAN, THE(1953, Brit.); MARTIN LUTHER(1953); FUSS OVER FEATHERS(1954, Brit.); MAN WHO KNEW TOO MUCH, THE(1956)

William Vernick
REDEEMER, THE(1978), w

Richard Vernie
COUNTERPLOT(1959)

Claude Vernier
CONFESSION, THE(1970, Fr.); LADY IN THE CAR WITH GLASSES AND A GUN, THE(1970, U.S./Fr.)

Jean-Pierre Vernier
COUSINS IN LOVE(1982)
Pierre Vernier
OPHELIA(1964, Fr.); WEEKEND AT DUNKIRK(1966, Fr./Ital.); GIRL FROM LORRAINE, A(1982, Fr./Switz.); PIAF–THE EARLY YEARS(1982, U.S./Fr.)
Francette Vernillat
SEVEN DEADLY SINS, THE(1953, Fr./Ital.)
Jerry Verno
BEGGAR STUDENT, THE(1931,Brit.); MY FRIEND THE KING(1931, Brit.); HIS LORDSHIP(1932, Brit.); HIS WIFE'S MOTHER(1932, Brit.); HOTEL SPLENDIDE(1932, Brit.); THERE GOES THE BRIDE(1933, Brit.); LIFE OF THE PARTY(1934, Brit.); LIEUTENANT DARING, RN(1935, Brit.); REGAL CAVALCADE(1935, Brit.); BROKEN BLOSSOMS(1936, Brit.); CLOWN MUST LAUGH, A(1936, Brit.); GYPSY MELODY(1936, Brit.); SENSATION(1936, Brit.); NON-STOP NEW YORK(1937, Brit.); RIVER OF UNREST(1937, Brit.); GABLES MYSTERY, THE(1938, Brit.); MOUNTAINS O'-MOURNE(1938, Brit.); OH BOY!(1938, Brit.); OLD MOTHER RILEY IN PARIS(1938, Brit.); TROOPSHIP(1938, Brit.); YOUNG AND INNOCENT(1938, Brit.); DEMON BARBER OF FLEET STREET, THE(1939, Brit.); CHINESE DEN, THE(1940, Brit.); SIDEWALKS OF LONDON(1940, Brit.); COMMON TOUCH, THE(1941, Brit.); PIRATES OF THE SEVEN SEAS(1941, Brit.); RED SHOES, THE(1948, Brit.); DEAR MR. PROHACK(1949, Brit.); AFTER THE BALL(1957, Brit.); PLACE TO GO, A(1964, Brit.); PLAGUE OF THE ZOMBIES, THE(1966, Brit.)
Agnes Vernon
Misc. Silents
STRANGER FROM SOMEWHERE, A(1916); TANGLED HEARTS(1916); CLOCK, THE(1917); MAN WHO TOOK A CHANCE, THE(1917); BARE-FISTED GALLAGHER(1919)
Agnes "Brownie" Vernon
Misc. Silents
BRINGING HOME FATHER(1917); STORMY KNIGHT, A(1917)
Anne Vernon
WARNING TO WANTONS, A(1949, Brit.); SHAKEDOWN(1950); TALE OF FIVE WOMEN, A(1951, Brit.); EDWARD AND CAROLINE(1952, Fr.); BACHELOR IN PARIS(1953, Brit.); TERROR ON A TRAIN(1953); LOVE LOTTERY, THE(1954, Brit.); TONIGHT THE SKIRTS FLY(1956, Fr.); DIARY OF A BAD GIRL(1958, Fr.); GENERALE DELLA ROVERE(1960, Ital./Fr.); UMBRELLAS OF CHERBOURG, THE(1964, Fr./Ger.); FRIEND OF THE FAMILY(1965, Fr./Ital.); THERESE AND ISABELLE(1968, U.S./Ger.)
Anthony Vernon
ARENA, THE(1973)
Billy Vernon
MURDER IN THE MUSIC HALL(1946); JET PILOT(1957)
Bobby Vernon
MAKE ME A STAR(1932); LONE COWBOY(1934), w; MAN ON THE FLYING TRAPEZE, THE(1935), w
Brownie Vernon
Misc. Silents
CAR OF CHANCE, THE(1917); CLEAN-UP, THE(1917); FEAR NOT(1917); FLIRTING WITH DEATH(1917); HIGH SIGN, THE(1917); WIDOW BY PROXY(1919); BETTER MAN, THE(1921); SHADOW OF LIGHTING RIDGE, THE(1921); QUEEN O' TURF(1922)
Diane Vernon
DISCREET CHARM OF THE BOURGEOISIE, THE(1972, Fr.)
Dick Vernon
CONQUEST OF THE AIR(1940)
Don Vernon
HALF A SIXPENCE(1967, Brit.); MACBETH(1971, Brit.)
Doremy Vernon
MADE(1972, Brit.)
Dorothy Vernon
TENDERLOIN(1928); SHOULD A GIRL MARRY?(1929); CLEANING UP(1933, Brit.); POLITICAL PARTY, A(1933, Brit.); PUBLIC LIFE OF HENRY THE NINTH, THE(1934, Brit.); ALL AT SEA(1935, Brit.); FIND THE LADY(1936, Brit.); MELODY OF MY HEART(1936, Brit.); THEODORA GOES WILD(1936, Brit.); AGAINST THE TIDE(1937, Brit.); MINSTREL BOY, THE(1937, Brit.); OLD MOTHER RILEY(1937, Brit.); ALMOST A GENTLEMAN(1938, Brit.); FATHER O'FLYNN(1938, Irish); JUVENILE COURT(1938); ROSE OF TRALEE(1938, Ireland); SISTER TO ASSIST'ER, A(1938, Brit.); YOU CAN'T TAKE IT WITH YOU(1938); MY LITTLE CHICKADEE(1940); RIDERS FROM NOWHERE(1940); THIRD FINGER, LEFT HAND(1940); FATHER TAKES A WIFE(1941); RICHEST MAN IN TOWN(1941); YOU'LL NEVER GET RICH(1941); GREAT MR. HANDEL, THE(1942, Brit.); PRAIRIE RUSTLERS(1945); MONSIEUR BEAUCAIRE(1946); KNOCK ON ANY DOOR(1949); MY BROTHER'S KEEPER(1949, Brit.); GOOD TIME GIRL(1950, Brit.); EASY TO LOVE(1953); WAR OF THE WORLDS, THE(1953)
Silents
LOVER'S LANE(1924); MANHATTAN COWBOY(1928); HEADIN' WESTWARD(1929)
Misc. Silents
CIGARETTE MAKER'S ROMANCE, A(1920, Brit.); RIDERS OF THE STORM(1929)
Dorothy D. Vernon
STRAIGHT FROM THE HEART(1935)
Elmo Vernon
THOROUGHBREDS DON'T CRY(1937), ed; BOYS TOWN(1938), ed; GIRL DOWNSTAIRS, THE(1938), ed; TOY WIFE, THE(1938), ed; FAST AND FURIOUS(1939), ed; LADY OF THE TROPICS(1939), ed; LUCKY NIGHT(1939), ed; MORTAL STORM, THE(1940), ed; ANDY HARDY'S PRIVATE SECRETARY(1941), ed; COURTSHIP OF ANDY HARDY, THE(1942), ed
Gabor Vernon
DRACULA(1979); JOURNEYS FROM BERLIN–1971(1980); OCTOPUSSY(1983, Brit.)
Glen Vernon
BEDLAM(1946); HEART OF VIRGINIA(1948); LUCKY LOSERS(1950); BELLE LE GRAND(1951); WILD BLUE YONDER, THE(1952)
Glenn Vernon
DAYS OF GLORY(1944); YOUTH RUNS WILD(1944); SING YOUR WAY HOME(1945); THOSE ENDEARING YOUNG CHARMS(1945); BAMBOO BLONDE, THE(1946); DING DONG WILLIAMS(1946); RIVERBOAT RHYTHM(1946); DEVIL THUMBS A RIDE, THE(1947); WOMAN ON THE BEACH, THE(1947); IMPACT(1949); I BURY THE LIVING(1958)

Harry Maurice Vernon
Silents
MR. WU(1919, Brit.), w; MR. WU(1927), w
Harvey Vernon
MAC ARTHUR(1977)
1984
ALL OF ME(1984)
Howard Vernon
ADVENTURES OF CAPTAIN FABIAN(1951); SECRET DOCUMENT – VIENNA(1954, Fr.); ROYAL AFFAIRS IN VERSAILLES(1957, Fr.); GIRL IN THE BIKINI, THE(1958, Fr.); THOUSAND EYES OF DR. MABUSE, THE(1960, Fr./Ital./Ger.); SECRET WAYS, THE(1961); AWFUL DR. ORLOFF, THE(1964, Span./Fr.); ALPHAVILLE, A STRANGE CASE OF LEMMY CAUTION(1965, Fr.); TRAIN, THE(1965, Fr./Ital./U.S.); VICE AND VIRTUE(1965, Fr./Ital.); WHAT'S NEW, PUSSYCAT?(1965, U.S./Fr.); DIABOLICAL DR. Z, THE(1966 Span./Fr.); POPPY IS ALSO A FLOWER, THE(1966); GAME IS OVER, THE(1967, Fr.); TRIPLE CROSS(1967, Fr./Brit.); UNKNOWN MAN OF SHANDIGOR, THE(1967, Switz.); MAYERLING(1968, Brit./Fr.); BLOOD ROSE, THE(1970, Fr.); DRACULA VERSUS FRANKENSTEIN(1972, Span.); LOVE AND DEATH(1975)
Irene Vernon
SECRET LIFE OF WALTER MITTY, THE(1947); SONG IS BORN, A(1948); SOUND OF FURY, THE(1950); DEADLINE–U.S.A.(1952)
Misc. Silents
MYSTERY OF THE OLD MILL, THE(1914, Brit.)
Isabel Vernon
Silents
POLLY OF THE CIRCUS(1917); RISE OF JENNIE CUSHING, THE(1917); JOAN OF PLATTSBURG(1918)
Misc. Silents
AMATEUR ORPHAN, AN(1917)
Isabelle Vernon
Silents
TAILOR MADE MAN, A(1922)
Misc. Silents
STRUGGLE, THE(1916)
Jack Vernon
Misc. Silents
BORDER INTRIGUE(1925)
Jackie Vernon
MONITORS, THE(1969); GANG THAT COULDN'T SHOOT STRAIGHT, THE(1971); MICROWAVE MASSACRE(1983)
James M. Vernon
1984
TAIL OF THE TIGER(1984, Aus.), p
Janet Vernon
DON QUIXOTE(1973, Aus.)
Jerry Vernon
39 STEPS, THE(1935, Brit.)
John Vernon
NOBODY WAVED GOODBYE(1965, Can.); POINT BLANK(1967); JUSTINE(1969); TELL THEM WILLIE BOY IS HERE(1969); TOPAZ(1969, Brit.); DIRTY HARRY(1971); ONE MORE TRAIN TO ROB(1971); CHARLEY VARRICK(1973); FEAR IS THE KEY(1973); BLACK WINDMILL, THE(1974, Brit.); W(1974); BRANNIGAN(1975, Brit.); OUTLAW JOSEY WALES, THE(1976); ANGELA(1977, Can.); GOLDEN RENDEZVOUS(1977); JOURNEY(1977, Can.); SPECIAL DAY, A(1977, Ital./Can.); UNCANNY, THE(1977, Brit./Can.); NATIONAL LAMPOON'S ANIMAL HOUSE(1978); FANTASTICA(1980, Can./Fr.); HERBIE GOES BANANAS(1980); HEAVY METAL(1981, Can.); AIRPLANE II: THE SEQUEL(1982); CHAINED HEAT(1983 U.S./Ger.); CURTAINS(1983, Can.)
1984
JUNGLE WARRIORS(1984, U.S./Ger./Mex.); SAVAGE STREETS(1984)
Misc. Talkies
CRUNCH(1975,Brit.)
Kate Vernon
1984
ALPHABET CITY(1984); ROADHOUSE 66(1984)
Libby Vernon
SON OF SINBAD(1955)
Lou Vernon
EXILE, THE(1931); HIS ROYAL HIGHNESS(1932, Aus.); ANTS IN HIS PANTS(1940, Aus.); THAT CERTAIN SOMETHING(1941, Aus.); BETRAYAL, THE(1948); ON THE BEACH(1959)
Marilyn Vernon
RADIO CITY REVELS(1938)
Mickey Vernon
KID FROM CLEVELAND, THE(1949)
Miss Vernon
MADAME SATAN(1930)
Richard Vernon
COURAGEOUS MR. PENN, THE(1941, Brit.), p; THOSE KIDS FROM TOWN(1942, Brit.), p; KISS THE BLOOD OFF MY HANDS(1948), p; STOP PRESS GIRL(1949, Brit.); SHADOW MAN(1953, Brit.), d&w; INDISCREET(1958); FOUR DESPERATE MEN(1960, Brit.); FOXHOLE IN CAIRO(1960, Brit.); VILLAGE OF THE DAMNED(1960, Brit.); CASH ON DEMAND(1962, Brit.); ACCIDENTAL DEATH(1963, Brit.); AGENT 8 3/4(1963, Brit.); JUST FOR FUN(1963, Brit.); REACH FOR GLORY(1963, Brit.); GOLDFINGER(1964, Brit.); HARD DAY'S NIGHT, A(1964, Brit.); SERVANT, THE(1964, Brit.); EARLY BIRD, THE(1965, Brit.); SECRET OF MY SUCCESS, THE(1965, Brit.); SPYLARKS(1965, Brit.); TOMB OF LIGEIA, THE(1965, Brit.); YELLOW ROLLS-ROYCE, THE(1965, Brit.); COUNTERFEIT CONSTABLE, THE(1966, Brit.); SHARE OUT, THE(1966, Brit.); CLUE OF THE TWISTED CANDLE(1968, Brit.); SONG OF NORWAY(1970); ONE BRIEF SUMMER(1971, Brit.); PINK PANTHER STRIKES AGAIN, THE(1976, Brit.); COUNT DRACULA AND HIS VAMPIRE BRIDE(1978, Brit.); HUMAN FACTOR, THE(1979, Brit.); OH, HEAVENLY DOG!(1980); EVIL UNDER THE SUN(1982, Brit.); GANDHI(1982); LA TRAVIATA(1982)
Misc. Talkies
SHE'LL FOLLOW YOU ANYWHERE(1971)
Sherri Vernon
10 VIOLENT WOMEN(1982)

Susy Vernon
Misc. Silents
SAJENKO THE SOVIET(1929, Ger.)
Suzy Vernon
Silents
NAPOLEON(1927, Fr.)
Misc. Silents
LA VIERGE FOLLE(1929, Fr.); PARIS GIRLS(1929, Fr.)
Valerie Vernon
SHE'S WORKING HER WAY THROUGH COLLEGE(1952); SON OF PALEFA-CE(1952); ESCAPE FROM FORT BRAVO(1953); DELAVINE AFFAIR, THE(1954, Brit.); GOG(1954); GLASS TOMB, THE(1955, Brit.)
Veronique Vernon
PEPPERMINT SODA(1979, Fr.)
Virginia Vernon
RANDOLPH FAMILY, THE(1945, Brit.); MILLIONAIRESS, THE(1960, Brit.); NURSE ON WHEELS(1964, Brit.)
Wally Vernon
MOUNTAIN MUSIC(1937); THIS WAY PLEASE(1937); YOU CAN'T HAVE EVERY-THING(1937); ALEXANDER'S RAGTIME BAND(1938); HAPPY LANDING(1938); KENTUCKY MOONSHINE(1938); MEET THE GIRLS(1938); SHARPSHOOT-ERS(1938); BROADWAY SERENADE(1939); CHARLIE CHAN AT TREASURE IS-LAND(1939); CHASING DANGER(1939); GORILLA, THE(1939); TAIL SPIN(1939); MARGIE(1940); SAILOR'S LADY(1940); SANDY GETS HER MAN(1940); BLACK HILLS EXPRESS(1943); CANYON CITY(1943); FUGITIVE FROM SONORA(1943); GET GOING(1943); HERE COMES ELMER(1943); MAN FROM THE RIO GRANDE, THE(1943); PISTOL PACKIN' MAMA(1943); REVEILLE WITH BEVERLY(1943); SCREAM IN THE DARK, A(1943); TAHITI HONEY(1943); CALIFORNIA JOE(1944); CALL OF THE SOUTH SEAS(1944); OUTLAWS OF SANTA FE(1944); SILENT PARTNER(1944); SILVER CITY KID(1944); STAGECOACH TO MONTEREY(1944); FIGHTING MAD(1948); HE WALKED BY NIGHT(1948); JOE PALOOKA IN WINNER TAKE ALL(1948); KING OF THE GAMBLERS(1948); ALWAYS LEAVE THEM LAUGHING(1949); SQUARE DANCE JUBILEE(1949); BEAUTY ON PARADE(1950); BORDER RANGERS(1950); GUNFIRE(1950); HOLIDAY RHYTHM(1950); I SHOT BILLY THE KID(1950); TRAIN TO TOMBSTONE(1950); BLOODHOUNDS OF BROAD-WAY(1952); WHAT PRICE GLORY?(1952); AFFAIR WITH A STRANGER(1953); FURY AT GUNSIGHT PASS(1956); WHITE SQUAW, THE(1956); WHAT A WAY TO GO(1964)
Whit Vernon
DETROIT 9000(1973)
Vernon and Draper
SAN FERNANDO VALLEY(1944)
The Vernon Girls
JUST FOR FUN(1963, Brit.)
Henry J. Vernot
Misc. Silents
DEAD ALIVE, THE(1916), d; FEATHERTOP(1916), d
Henry Vernot
Misc. Silents
SPORT OF THE GODS, THE(1921), d
Gennadi Vernov
STORM PLANET(1962, USSR)
Gianni Vernuccio
DESERT WARRIOR(1961 Ital./Span.), d; LOVE NOW...PAY LATER(1966, Ital.), p
Dennis Vero
1984
SIXTEEN CANDLES(1984)
Elmo Veron
CAPTAINS COURAGEOUS(1937), ed; SARATOGA(1937), ed; PARADISE FOR THREE(1938), ed; YOUNG DR. KILDARE(1938), ed; FAST AND LOOSE(1939), ed; NICK CARTER, MASTER DETECTIVE(1939), ed; THIRD FINGER, LEFT HAND(1940), ed; YOUNG TOM EDISON(1940), ed; DESIGN FOR SCANDAL(1941), ed; I'LL WAIT FOR YOU(1941), ed; KEEPING COMPANY(1941), ed; LIFE BEGINS FOR ANDY HARDY(1941), ed; CALLING DR. GILLESPIE(1942), ed; JOE SMITH, AMERICAN(1942), ed; REUNION IN FRANCE(1942), ed; WAR AGAINST MRS. HADLEY, THE(1942), ed; STRANGER IN TOWN, A(1943), ed; SWING SHIFT MAI-SIE(1943), ed; 'TILL WE MEET AGAIN(1944), ed; CRY VENGEANCE(1954), ed
Irene Veron
TILL THE CLOUDS ROLL BY(1946)
Michael Ross Verona
MOVING VIOLATION(1976); I WANNA HOLD YOUR HAND(1978)
Stephen F. Verona
LORDS OF FLATBUSH, THE(1974), p, d, w
Stephen Verona
PIPE DREAMS(1976), p,d&w; BOARDWALK(1979), d, w
Gigi Verone
PARADISE, HAWAIIAN STYLE(1966)
Vera Veronia
Silents
HUNTINGTOWER(1927, Brit.)
Countessa Veronica
VACATION, THE(1971, Ital.)
Chet Verovan
FIRST YANK INTO TOKYO(1945)
Framl Verpillat
BEAUTIFUL PRISONER, THE(1983, Fr.), w
Cec Verrell
1984
RUNAWAY(1984)
George Verrell
Misc. Silents
SOCIETY SECRETS(1921)
Roquell Verria
LONE RIDER CROSSES THE RIO, THE(1941)
Virginia Verrill
VOGUES OF 1938(1937)
Vivian Verrilli
SERENITY(1962)

Harold Verrnilyea
FINDERS KEEPERS(1951)
Frank Verroca
I WANNA HOLD YOUR HAND(1978); 1941(1979)
John Verros
GLASS WEB, THE(1953); GLORY BRIGADE, THE(1953); DESERT HELL(1958); POCKET MONEY(1972); OUTLAW JOSEY WALES, THE(1976)
John J. Verros
LOVES OF CARMEN, THE(1948)
Fred Versacci
THAT'S THE WAY OF THE WORLD(1975)
Jeffrey B. Versalle
ENDLESS LOVE(1981)
Ben Verschieiser
BREACH OF PROMISE(1942, Brit.), w
Ben Verschleiser
DEVIL'S MATE(1933), p; MONEY MEANS NOTHING(1934), p; JANE EYRE(1935), p; MILLION DOLLAR BABY(1935), p; THREE KIDS AND A QUEEN(1935), p
Gust Verschueren
DAUGHTERS OF DARKNESS(1971, Bel./ Fr./ Ger./ Ital.), ed
Andre Versein
UN CARNET DE BAL(1938, Fr.), ed
Ida Versenyi
MEPHISTO(1981, Ger.)
Irving Vershal
I'M FROM ARKANSAS(1944), p
Boris Vershilov
Misc. Silents
DELUGE, THE(1925, USSR), d
Ilya Vershinin
COUNTER-ATTACK(1945), w
Andre Versini
CAT, THE(1959, Fr.); I SPIT ON YOUR GRAVE(1962, Fr.)
Marie Versini
TALE OF TWO CITIES, A(1958, Brit.); PARIS BLUES(1961); YOUNG RACERS, THE(1963); APACHE GOLD(1965, Ger.); BRIDES OF FU MANCHU, THE(1966, Brit.); IS PARIS BURNING?(1966, U.S./Fr.); THUNDER AT THE BORDER(1966, Ger./Yugo.)
Karoly Versits
FATHER(1967, Hung.)
Alberto Verso
LA TRAVIATA(1968, Ital.), set d
Eddie Verso
WEST SIDE STORY(1961) ·
Odile Versois
LES DERNIERES VACANCES(1947, Fr.); MAN IN THE DINGHY, THE(1951, Brit.); DAY TO REMEMBER, A(1953, Brit.); CHANCE MEETING(1954, Brit.); TO PARIS WITH LOVE(1955, Brit.); CHECKPOINT(1957, Brit.); ROOM 43(1959, Brit.); NUDE IN A WHITE CAR(1960, Fr.); KING IN SHADOW(1961, Ger.); CARTOUCHE(1962, Fr./Ital.); BENJAMIN(1968, Fr.); EGLANTINE(1972, Fr.)
1984
LE CRABE TAMBOUR(1984, Fr.)
Wim Verstappen
OUTSIDER IN AMSTERDAM(1983, Neth.), d, w
Guus Verstraete
LITTLE ARK, THE(1972)
Marcel Vertes
MIKADO, THE(1939, Brit.), cos; THIEF OF BAGHDAD, THE(1940, Brit.), cos; LYDIA(1941), cos; TONIGHT AND EVERY NIGHT(1945), cos; MOULIN ROU-GE(1952), cos
Anastasia Vertinskaya
HAMLET(1966, USSR); WAR AND PEACE(1968, USSR)
L. Vertinskaya
DON QUIXOTE(1961, USSR); MAGIC VOYAGE OF SINBAD, THE(1962, USSR)
Marianna Vertinskaya
THEY CALL ME ROBERT(1967, USSR)
A. Vertinsky
ANNA CROSS, THE(1954, USSR)
Steve Vertlieb
FIEND(
Dziga Vertov
Misc. Silents
SIXTH OF THE WORLD, A(1926, USSR), d; ELEVENTH [YEAR], THE(1928, USSR), d
Beryl Vertue
PLANK, THE(1967, Brit.), p; ALF 'N' FAMILY(1968, Brit.), p; ENTERTAINER, THE(1975), p
Alberto Verucci
DIRTY HEROES(1971, Ital./Fr./Ger.), w
Franco Verucci
DETECTIVE BELLI(1970, Ital.), w; NO WAY OUT(1975, Ital./Fr.), w
Nicole Vervil
CONFESSION, THE(1970, Fr.)
Robert Vervoordt
NIGHT THEY ROBBED BIG BERTHA'S, THE(1975), w
Helene Vervors
BLIND DESIRE(1948, Fr.)
Percy Verwagen
STRAIGHT TO HEAVEN(1939)
Percy Verwayen
SEPIA CINDERELLA(1947)
Misc. Silents
BURDEN OF RACE, THE(1921); SECRET SORROW(1921); CONJURE WOMAN, THE(1926), Evelyn Preer
Louw Verwey
1984
GODS MUST BE CRAZY, THE(1984, Botswana)
Linda Very
IMPROPER CHANNELS(1981, Can.)

Pierre Very
IT HAPPENED AT THE INN(1945, Fr.), w; ROOM UPSTAIRS, THE(1948, Fr.), w; GYPSY FURY(1950, Fr.), w; PERFECTIONIST, THE(1952, Fr.), w

Nora Veryan
FRANKENSTEIN, THE VAMPIRE AND CO.(1961, Mex.)

Z. Veryovkina
SUN SHINES FOR ALL, THE(1961, USSR), ed

Rene Verzier
LOVE IN A FOUR LETTER WORLD(1970, Can.), ph; PYX, THE(1973, Can.), ph; JE T'AIME(1974, Can.), ph; JACQUES BREL IS ALIVE AND WELL AND LIVING IN PARIS(1975), ph; RABID(1976, Can.), ph; LITTLE GIRL WHO LIVES DOWN THE LANE, THE(1977, Can.), ph; HIGH-BALLIN'(1978), ph; TWO SOLITUDES(1978, Can.), ph; CITY ON FIRE(1979 Can.), ph; DEATH SHIP(1980, Can.), ph; DOUBLE NEGATIVE(1980, Can.), ph; HOG WILD(1980, Can.), ph; TERROR TRAIN(1980, Can.), ph; FISH HAWK(1981, Can.), ph; GAS(1981, Can.), ph; SEARCH AND DESTROY(1981), ph; DEADLY EYES(1982), ph; FUNNY FARM, THE(1982, Can.), ph; VISITING HOURS(1982, Can.), ph; CROSS COUNTRY(1983, Can.), ph; JOY(1983, Fr./Can.), ph; OF UNKNOWN ORIGIN(1983, Can.), ph
1984
COVERGIRL(1984, Can.), ph

Matteo Verzini
STARCRASH(1979), spec eff

George Vescey
COAL MINER'S DAUGHTER(1980), w

Lene Vesegaard
Z.P.G.(1972)

Jarmila Vesela
LEMONADE JOE(1966, Czech.)

Branka Veselinovic
TWELVE CHAIRS, THE(1970)

Mladja Veselinovic
TWELVE CHAIRS, THE(1970)

Herbert Vesely
EGON SCHIELE–EXCESS AND PUNISHMENT(1981, Ger.), d, w

Karin Vesely
SUITOR, THE(1963, Fr.)

M. Vesely
MOST BEAUTIFUL AGE, THE(1970, Czech.)

Vladimir Veshnovsky
ROAD TO LIFE(1932, USSR)

P. Vesklyarov
FAREWELL, DOVES(1962, USSR); SONG OF THE FOREST(1963, USSR)

E. Vesnik
OTHELLO(1960, U.S.S.R.)

Bruno VeSota
SYSTEM, THE(1953); BAIT(1954); FAST AND THE FURIOUS, THE(1954); JUPITER'S DARLING(1955); ROCK ALL NIGHT(1957); DADDY-O(1959); WILD ROVERS(1971)

Bruno VeSoto
WILD ONE, THE(1953)

Chico Vespa
Misc. Talkies
ACID EATERS, THE(1968)

Ritva Vespa
TIME OF ROSES(1970, Fin.)

Edith Vesperini
HANNAH K.(1983, Fr.), cos

Gerd Vesperman
BIG SHOW, THE(1961)

Kurt Vesperman
Misc. Silents
TRAGEDY OF LOVE(1923, Ger.)

Gerd Vespermann
QUESTION 7(1961, U.S./Ger.); TOWN WITHOUT PITY(1961, Ger./Switz./U.S.); CABARET(1972)

Gert Vespermann
LAST ESCAPE, THE(1970, Brit.)

Kurt Vespermann
BEAUTIFUL ADVENTURE(1932, Ger.); SHOT AT DAWN, A(1934, Ger.); WORLD WITHOUT A MASK, THE(1934, Ger.); INHERITANCE IN PRETORIA(1936, Ger.)

Renzo Vespignani
ASSASSIN, THE(1961, Ital./Fr.), art d

Christophe Vesque
DAY FOR NIGHT(1973, Fr.)

Karl Vess
FOREST RANGERS, THE(1942)

LaVerne Vess
ROAD TO ZANZIBAR(1941)

Edy Vessel
THIEF OF BAGHDAD, THE(1961, Ital./Fr.); PSYCOSISSIMO(1962, Ital.); SWORD OF THE CONQUEROR(1962, Ital.); PASSIONATE THIEF, THE(1963, Ital.)

Hedy Vessel
TROJAN HORSE, THE(1962, Fr./Ital.); SEVEN SEAS TO CALAIS(1963, Ital.); 8 ½(1963, Ital.)

George Vessey
Misc. Talkies
BIRTHRIGHT(1939)

Bud Vest
SWEET CHARITY(1969)

Sunny Vest
DELIRIUM(1979), p

Ray Vestal
Misc. Talkies
HEAT(1972)

Max Vesterhalt
FOR YOUR EYES ONLY(1981)

Virginia Vestoff
SUCH GOOD FRIENDS(1971); 1776(1972); WEDDING, A(1978)

Endre Veszi
ANGI VERA(1980, Hung.), w

Margit Veszi
ALL IN A NIGHT'S WORK(1961), w

Alexander Vetchinski
DOCTOR SYN(1937, Brit.), set d

Vetchinsky
NIGHT TRAIN(1940, Brit.), art d; ESCAPE(1948, Brit.), art d; MARK OF CAIN, THE(1948, Brit.), art d; NIGHT WITHOUT STARS(1953, Brit.), art d; JANE EYRE(1971, Brit.), art d

A. Vetchinsky
HUNGRY HILL(1947, Brit.), art d

Alec Vetchinsky
DON'T TAKE IT TO HEART(1944, Brit.), art d; SAILOR OF THE KING(1953, Brit.), art d; GOLD(1974, Brit.), prod d

Alex Vetchinsky
LUCKY NUMBER, THE(1933, Brit.), art d; WOMAN IN COMMAND, THE(1934 Brit.), art d; PHANTOM LIGHT, THE(1935, Brit.), art d; MAN WHO LIVED AGAIN, THE(1936, Brit.), art d; WHERE THERE'S A WILL(1936, Brit), art d; WINDBAG THE SAILOR(1937, Brit.), art d; LADY VANISHES, THE(1938, Brit.), set d; YOUNG MR. PITT, THE(1942, Brit.), art d; UNCENSORED(1944, Brit.), art d; TAWNY PIPIT(1947, Brit.), art d; SALT TO THE DEVIL(1949, Brit.), art d; WATERLOO ROAD(1949, Brit.), art d; WEAKER SEX, THE(1949, Brit.), art d; HIGH TREASON(1951, Brit.), set d; OPERATION DISASTER(1951, Brit.), art d; SOMETHING MONEY CAN'T BUY(1952, Brit.), art d; STRANGER IN BETWEEN, THE(1952, Brit.), art d; WATERFRONT WOMEN(1952, Brit.), set d; TROUBLE IN STORE(1955, Brit.), art d; ROTTEN TO THE CORE(1956, Brit.), art d; TRIPLE DECEPTION(1957, Brit.), art d; VALUE FOR MONEY(1957, Brit.), art d; NIGHT AMBUSH(1958, Brit.), art d; NIGHT TO REMEMBER, A(1958, Brit.), art d; ROBBERY UNDER ARMS(1958, Brit.), art d; TOWN LIKE ALICE, A(1958, Brit.), art d; OPERATION AMSTERDAM(1960, Brit.), art d; FLAME IN THE STREETS(1961, Brit.), art d; SINGER NOT THE SONG, THE(1961, Brit.), art d; VICTIM(1961, Brit.), art d; CARRY ON TEACHER(1962, Brit.), art d; TIARA TAHITI(1962, Brit.), art d; DOCTOR IN DISTRESS(1963, Brit.), art d; CARRY ON SPYING(1964, Brit.), art d; YOUNG AND WILLING(1964, Brit.), art d; UNDERWORLD INFORMERS(1965, Brit.), art d; STUDY IN TERROR, A(1966, Brit./Ger.), prod d; WALK IN THE SHADOW(1966, Brit.), art d; CARNABY, M.D.(1967, Brit.), art d; LONG DUEL, THE(1967, Brit.), art d; CARRY ON, UP THE KHYBER(1968, Brit.), art d; CARRY ON UP THE JUNGLE(1970, Brit.), art d; DAVID COPPERFIELD(1970, Brit.), art d; SOPHIE'S PLACE(1970), art d; ISLAND OF THE BURNING DAMNED(1971, Brit.), art d; KIDNAPPED(1971, Brit.), art d

Alexander Vetchinsky
OCTOBER MAN, THE(1948, Brit.), art d; MADNESS OF THE HEART(1949, Brit.), art d

Richard Vetere
VIGILANTE(1983), w; WAR OF THE WIZARDS(1983, Taiwan), w

Voldemar Vetluguin
EAST SIDE, WEST SIDE(1949), p; LIFE OF HER OWN, A(1950), p

Victoria Vetri
WHEN DINOSAURS RULED THE EARTH(1971, Brit.); INVASION OF THE BEE GIRLS(1973)
Misc. Talkies
GROUP MARRIAGE(1972)

Yu. Vetrov
WAR AND PEACE(1968, USSR)

Josef Vetrovec
STOLEN DIRIGIBLE, THE(1966, Czech.); ON THE COMET(1970, Czech.)

Charles Vetter
CORRIDORS OF BLOOD(1962, Brit.), p; BATTLE BENEATH THE EARTH(1968, Brit.), p

Charles Francis Vetter
GREEN HELMET, THE(1961, Brit.), p

Charles F. Vetter, Jr.
FIRST MAN INTO SPACE(1959, Brit.), p

Dmitri Vetter
NOT SO QUIET ON THE WESTERN FRONT(1930, Brit.); WHY SAILORS LEAVE HOME(1930, Brit.)

Beatrice Vetterly
1984
BLIND DATE(1984)

Giovanni Vettorazzo
LA CAGE AUX FOLLES II(1981, Ital./Fr.)

Victoria Vettri
KINGS OF THE SUN(1963)

Nora Veyran
SPIRITISM(1965, Mex.); TOM THUMB(1967, Mex.); CURSE OF THE DOLL PEOPLE, THE(1968, Mex.)

Pavel Veysbrem
QUEEN OF SPADES(1961, USSR), w

Semyon Veyts
STRIPES(1981)

L. Veytsler
GIRL AND THE BUGLER, THE(1967, USSR)

Ross Vezarian
KEEPER, THE(1976, Can.)

Bernhard Vezat
MOON IN THE GUTTER, THE(1983, Fr./Ital.), prod d

Manfred Vezie
TOUCHDOWN!(1931)

Arthur Vezin
Silents
SHIPS THAT PASS IN THE NIGHT(1921, Brit.)

Philip Vezina
1984
MEMOIRS(1984, Can.), m

Mario Via
SUNSCORCHED(1966, Span./Ger.)

Mario Viadiano
BRUCE LEE–TRUE STORY(1976, Chi.)

Laura Viala
Misc. Talkies
THAT GIRL IS A TRAMP(1974)
Michel Viala
INVITATION, THE(1975, Fr./Switz.), w
A. Vialla
RED, INN, THE(1954, Fr.)
Abraham Vialla
TARZAN'S DEADLY SILENCE(1970), ph; TARZAN'S JUNGLE REBELLION(1970), ph
Boris Vian
HUNCHBACK OF NOTRE DAME, THE(1957, Fr.); LES LIAISONS DANGEREUSES(1961, Fr./Ital.)
Ursula Vian
SEASON FOR LOVE, THE(1963, Fr.)
Wilson Viana
CURUCU, BEAST OF THE AMAZON(1956)
Zelito Viana
EARTH ENTRANCED(1970, Braz.), p
Adrian Vianello
CENTURION, THE(1962, Fr./Ital.)
Maria Teresa Vianello
LA DOLCE VITA(1961, Ital./Fr.)
Raimondo Vianello
PSYCOSISSIMO(1962, Ital.); MY WIFE'S ENEMY(1967, Ital.); KISS THE OTHER SHEIK(1968, Fr./Ital.)
Vera Vianna
LOLLIPOP(1966, Braz.)
Wilson Vianna
LOVE SLAVES OF THE AMAZONS(1957)
Boris Vians
I SPIT ON YOUR GRAVE(1962, Fr.), w
Gerard Viard
FRENCH CONNECTION 11(1975), art d
1984
TO CATCH A COP(1984, Fr.), art d
Lucien Viard
NIGHT AFFAIR(1961, Fr.), p
Enrico Viarisio
FATHER'S DILEMMA(1952, Ital.); INDISCRETION OF AN AMERICAN WIFE(1954, U.S./Ital.); VITELLONI(1956, Ital./Fr.); LOVE SPECIALIST, THE(1959, Ital.); NEOPOLITAN CAROUSEL(1961, Ital.)
Brian Viary
THREE IN ONE(1956, Aus.)
June Viasek
CHANDU THE MAGICIAN(1932)
Francois Viaur
PLAYTIME(1973, Fr.); TENANT, THE(1976, Fr.); QUARTET(1981, Brit./Fr.)
1984
AMERICAN DREAMER(1984)
Nikolai Viazemsky
DARK IS THE NIGHT(1946, USSR)
Henry Vibart
HIGH TREASON(1929, Brit.); SCHOOL FOR SCANDAL, THE(1930, Brit.); STRANGLEHOLD(1931, Brit.)
Silents
MOLLY BAWN(1916, Brit.); GOD AND THE MAN(1918, Brit.); AYLWIN(1920, Brit.); ENCHANTMENT(1920, Brit.); JUDGE NOT(1920, Brit.); MR. JUSTICE RAFFLES(1921, Brit.); CRIMSON CIRCLE, THE(1922, Brit.); FLAMES OF PASSION(1922, Brit.); WEAVERS OF FORTUNE(1922, Brit.); PRUDES FALL, THE(1924, Brit.); JUST SUPPOSE(1926); KISS FOR CINDERELLA, A(1926); WILDERNESS WOMAN, THE(1926); LAND OF HOPE AND GLORY(1927, Brit.); POPPIES OF FLANDERS(1927, Brit.); PHYSICIAN, THE(1928, Brit.)
Misc. Silents
IN THE SHADOW OF BIG BEN(1914, Brit.); CITY OF BEAUTIFUL NONSENSE, THE(1919, Brit.); BURNT IN(1920, Brit.); FOUR FEATHERS, THE(1921, Brit.); BODEN'S BOY(1923, Brit.); SHOULD A DOCTOR TELL?(1923, Brit.); DANCER OF PARIS, THE(1926); LOVE'S OPTION(1928, Brit.); BONDMAN, THE(1929, Brit.)
Myrtle Vibart
Silents
WEAVERS OF FORTUNE(1922, Brit.)
Bo A. Vibenius
THEY CALL HER ONE EYE(1974, Swed.), p, w
Celia Viberos
SANTO CONTRA EL CEREBRO DIABOLICO zero(1962, Mex.)
Francois Vibert
VERY HAPPY ALEXANDER(1969, Fr.); VERDICT(1975, Fr./Ital.)
Marcel Vibert
Silents
CHAMPAGNE(1928, Brit.); LIFE(1928, Brit.); MOULIN ROUGE(1928, Brit.)
Misc. Silents
VISAGES VIOLES...AMES CLOSES(1921, Fr.); GARDEN OF ALLAH, THE(1927)
Bu Vibulnan
1 2 3 MONSTER EXPRESS(1977, Thai.)
Captain Vic
Misc. Silents
LAUGHING AT DEATH(1929)
Vaclav Vic
SKY IS RED, THE(1952, Ital.), ph
Antonio Vica
FISTFUL OF DOLLARS, A(1964, Ital./Ger./Span.)
Clem Vicari
MOTHER'S DAY(1980), m
Marco Vicario
APPOINTMENT FOR MURDER(1954, Ital.); ALONE IN THE STREETS(1956, Ital.); ALONE AGAINST ROME(1963, Ital.), p; FALL OF ROME, THE(1963, Ital.), p; NAKED HOURS, THE(1964, Ital.), p&d, w; SEVEN GOLDEN MEN(1969, Fr./Ital./Span.), p&d, w; MACHINE GUN McCAIN(1970, Ital.), p; WIFEMISTRESS(1979, Ital.), d

Mario Vicario
WONDERS OF ALADDIN, THE(1961, Fr./Ital.), w; HORROR CASTLE(1965, Ital.), p
Renata Vicario
MONSTER OF THE ISLAND(1953, Ital.)
Anthony Vicars
DEVIL'S HARBOR(1954, Brit.)
Antony Vicars
MACKINTOSH MAN, THE(1973, Brit.)
Mike Vicars
AT THE EARTH'S CORE(1976, Brit.), m
Victor Vicas
WAYWARD BUS, THE(1957), d; COUNT FIVE AND DIE(1958, Brit.), d; STOP TRAIN 349(1964, Fr./Ital./Ger.), w; MAN WITH THE TRANSPLANTED BRAIN, THE(1972, Fr./Ital./Ger.), w
Gladys Vicat
Silents
LA POUPEE(1920, Brit.)
Philip Viccars
STOLEN FACE(1952, Brit.)
Giovanni Viccola
Silents
WHITE SISTER, THE(1923)
Joana Vicente
IN THE WHITE CITY(1983, Switz./Portugal)
Luciano Vicenzoni
DUCK, YOU SUCKER!(1972, Ital.), w
Vaclav Vich
GOLEM, THE(1937, Czech./Fr.), ph; NIGHT BEAT(1948, Brit.), ph; WANDERING JEW, THE(1948, Ital.), ph; LOST ONE, THE(1951, Ger.), ph; DEVIL MAKES THREE, THE(1952), ph; WORLD IN MY POCKET, THE(1962, Fr./Ital./Ger.), ph; JOURNEY INTO NOWHERE(1963, Brit.), ph
Valcav Vich
BALL AT THE CASTLE(1939, Ital.), ph
Gerry Vichi
WINDOWS(1980)
Shlomo Vichinsky
TRUNK TO CAIRO(1966, Israel/Ger.)
Jeni Vici
1984
PARIS, TEXAS(1984, Ger./Fr.)
Elena Vicini
QUIET PLACE IN THE COUNTRY, A(1970, Ital./Fr.)
Helen Vick
NATIONAL LAMPOON'S ANIMAL HOUSE(1978)
John Allen Vick
WHAT'S UP, DOC?(1972); PROMISE, THE(1979)
John F. Vick
DIRTY HARRY(1971)
John Vick
LAUGHING POLICEMAN, THE(1973); MACK, THE(1973); FOG, THE(1980)
Angus Vicker
FEVER HEAT(1968), w
Scott Vickerey
1984
MIXED BLOOD(1984), ed
Harold Vickers
Silents
MEN SHE MARRIED, THE(1916), w
Howie Vickers
SUPREME KID, THE(1976, Can.), m
James Warry Vickers
Misc. Silents
LADY JENNIFER(1915, Brit.), d
Martha Vickers
WOLF MAN, THE(1941); FRANKENSTEIN MEETS THE WOLF MAN(1943); HI' YA, SAILOR(1943); TOP MAN(1943); MUMMY'S GHOST, THE(1944); THIS IS THE LIFE(1944); BIG SLEEP, THE(1946); MAN I LOVE, THE(1946); TIME, THE PLACE AND THE GIRL, THE(1946); LOVE AND LEARN(1947); THAT WAY WITH WOMEN(1947); RUTHLESS(1948); ALIMONY(1949); BAD BOY(1949); DAUGHTER OF THE WEST(1949); BIG BLUFF, THE(1955); BURGLAR, THE(1956); FOUR FAST GUNS(1959)
Michael Vickers
DRACULA A.D. 1972(1972, Brit.), m
Mike Vickers
PRESS FOR TIME(1966, Brit.), m; SANDWICH MAN, THE(1966, Brit.), m; MY LOVER, MY SON(1970, Brit.), m, md; PLEASE SIR(1971, Brit.), m; WARLORDS OF ATLANTIS(1978, Brit.), m
Patricia Vickers
VISITOR, THE(1973, Can.)
Philip Vickers
NO HIGHWAY IN THE SKY(1951, Brit.); JOE MACBETH(1955); NIGHT MY NUMBER CAME UP, THE(1955, Brit.); WHOLE TRUTH, THE(1958, Brit.)
Phillip Vickers
MARK OF THE HAWK, THE(1958)
Roy Vickers
FALSE EVIDENCE(1937, Brit.), d&w; GIRL IN THE NEWS, THE(1941, Brit.), w; QUESTION OF SUSPENSE, A(1961, Brit.), w
Steven Vickers
LOVE IN A TAXI(1980), art d
Sunny Vickers
RIDIN' THE OUTLAW TRAIL(1951); YANK IN KOREA, A(1951)
Yvette Vickers
REFORM SCHOOL GIRL(1957); SAD SACK, THE(1957); SHORT CUT TO HELL(1957); ATTACK OF THE 50 FOOT WOMAN(1958); SAGA OF HEMP BROWN, THE(1958); ATTACK OF THE GIANT LEECHES(1959); I, MOBSTER(1959); PRESSURE POINT(1962); BEACH PARTY(1963); HUD(1963); WHAT'S THE MATTER WITH HELEN?(1971)

Jose S. Vicuna
OPEN SEASON(1974, U.S./Span.), p
Zsuzsa Vicze
ROUND UP, THE(1969, Hung.), cos
Zuzsa Vicze
WINTER WIND(1970, Fr./Hung.), cos
Jeff Vida
GOING BERSERK(1983)
Piero Vida
GALILEO(1968, Ital./Bul.); PAYMENT IN BLOOD(1968, Ital.); NIGHT PORTER, THE(1974, Ital./U.S.)
Irvine Vidacovich
PANIC IN THE STREETS(1950)
Vidal
Silents
NAPOLEON(1927, Fr.)
Annie Vidal
CHAMPAGNE MURDERS, THE(1968, Fr.)
Antonio Vidal
WHEN YOU'RE IN LOVE(1937); FOR WHOM THE BELL TOLLS(1943)
Celso Vidal
PUT UP OR SHUT UP(1968, Arg.)
Darryl Vidal
1984
KARATE KID, THE(1984)
Gil Vidal
SCHEHERAZADE(1965, Fr./Ital./Span.)
Gore Vidal
CATERED AFFAIR, THE(1956), w; I ACCUSE(1958, Brit.), w; LEFT-HANDED GUN, THE(1958), w; SCAPEGOAT, THE(1959, Brit.), w; SUDDENLY, LAST SUMMER(1959, Brit.), w; VISIT TO A SMALL PLANET(1960), w; BEST MAN, THE(1964), w; IS PARIS BURNING?(1966, U.S./Fr.), w; ROMA(1972, Ital./Fr.)
Henri Vidal
DAMNED, THE(1948, Fr.); FABIOLA(1951, Ital.); DANGER IS A WOMAN(1952, Fr.); IT HAPPENED IN PARIS(1953, Fr.); DESPERATE DECISION(1954, Fr.); ATTILA(1958, Ital.); GATES OF PARIS(1958, Fr./Ital.); LA PARISIENNE(1958, Fr./Ital.); COME DANCE WITH ME(1960, Fr.); WICKED GO TO HELL, THE(1961, Fr.)
Lisa Vidal
1984
DELIVERY BOYS(1984)
Luisi Vidal
NAPOLEON(1955, Fr.)
Pedro Vidal
FOUR RODE OUT(1969, US/Span.), p
Pianing Vidal
NO PLACE TO HIDE(1956)
Valeria Vidal
MARGIN, THE,(1969, Braz.)
Albert Vidalie
NIGHT HEAVEN FELL, THE(1958, Fr.), w
Robert Vidalin
LES MISERABLES(1936, Fr.); SACRIFICE OF HONOR(1938, Fr.); DON'T TEMPT THE DEVIL(1964, Fr./Ital.)
Silents
NAPOLEON(1927, Fr.)
Pat Vidan
WINNING(1969)
King Vidar
HALLELUJAH(1929), w
Raanhild Vidar
PRIZE, THE(1963)
Walter Vidarie
ALIAS BIG SHOT(1962, Argen.)
L. Vidavskiy
WAR AND PEACE(1968, USSR)
Vidette
DOOMSDAY VOYAGE(1972), d&w
John Vidette
WEDDING IN WHITE(1972, Can.), p
Linda Videtti
COLD RIVER(1982)
Charles Vidiac
MAN OF THE HOUR, THE(1940, Fr.), w
Robert Vidmark
BATTLE OF THE AMAZONS(1973, Ital./Span.)
Mareo Vido
I'LL TAKE ROMANCE(1937)
Francois Eugene Vidocq
SCANDAL IN PARIS, A(1946), w
Rocco Vidolazzi
ROCCO AND HIS BROTHERS(1961, Fr./Ital.)
Henry Vidom
MISSILE FROM HELL(1960, Brit.)
Henri Vidon
GREAT HOPE, THE(1954, Ital.); MISTRESS FOR THE SUMMER, A(1964, Fr./Ital.); ARRIVEDERCI, BABY!(1966, Brit.)
Henry Vidon
KEY MAN, THE(1957, Brit.); BLOOD OF THE VAMPIRE(1958, Brit.); SAFECRACKER, THE(1958, Brit.); SNORKEL, THE(1958, Brit.); BEHEMOTH, THE SEA MONSTER(1959, Brit.)
Charles Vidor
DOUBLE DOOR(1934), d; SENSATION HUNTERS(1934), d; ARIZONIAN, THE(1935), d; STRANGERS ALL(1935), d; HIS FAMILY TREE(1936), d; MUSS 'EM UP(1936), d; DOCTOR'S DIARY, A(1937), d; GREAT GAMBINI, THE(1937), d; SHE'S NO LADY(1937), d; BLIND ALLEY(1939), d; ROMANCE OF THE REDWOODS(1939), d; THOSE HIGH GREY WALLS(1939), d; LADY IN QUESTION, THE(1940), d; MY SON, MY SON!(1940), d; LADIES IN RETIREMENT(1941), d; NEW YORK TOWN(1941), d; TUTTLES OF TAHITI(1942), d; DESPERADOES, THE(1943), d; COVER GIRL(1944), d; TOGETHER AGAIN(1944), d; OVER 21(1945), d; SONG TO REMEMBER, A(1945), d; GILDA(1946), d; LOVES OF CARMEN, THE(1948), p&d;

EDGE OF DOOM(1950), d; HANS CHRISTIAN ANDERSEN(1952), d; THUNDER IN THE EAST(1953), d; RHAPSODY(1954), d; LOVE ME OR LEAVE ME(1955), d; SWAN, THE(1956), d; FAREWELL TO ARMS, A(1957), d; JOKER IS WILD, THE(1957), d; SONG WITHOUT END(1960), d
Elizabeth Hill Vidor
TEXAS RANGERS, THE(1936), w
Florence Vidor
PATRIOT, THE(1928); CHINATOWN NIGHTS(1929)
Silents
AMERICAN METHODS(1917); SECRET GAME, THE(1917); TALE OF TWO CITIES, A(1917); BRAVEST WAY, THE(1918); OLD WIVES FOR NEW(1918); POOR RELATIONS(1919); JACK KNIFE MAN, THE(1920); BEAU REVEL(1921); LYING LIPS(1921); REAL ADVENTURE, THE(1922); ALICE ADAMS(1923); SOULS FOR SALE(1923); VIRGINIAN, THE(1923); HUSBANDS AND LOVERS(1924); MARRIAGE CIRCLE, THE(1924); WELCOME STRANGER(1924); ARE PARENTS PEOPLE?(1925); ENCHANTED HILL, THE(1926); GRAND DUCHESS AND THE WAITER, THE(1926); SEA HORSES(1926); AFRAID TO LOVE(1927); ONE WOMAN TO ANOTHER(1927); MAGNIFICENT FLIRT, THE(1928)
Misc. Silents
COOK OF CANYON CAMP, THE(1917); COUNTESS CHARMING, THE(1917); HIDDEN PEARLS(1918); HONOR OF HIS HOUSE, THE(1918); 'TILL I COME BACK TO YOU(1918); WHITE MAN'S LAW, THE(1918); WIDOW'S MIGHT, THE(1918); OTHER HALF, THE(1919); FAMILY HONOR, THE(1920); HAIL THE WOMAN(1921); CONQUERING THE WOMAN(1922); DUSK TO DAWN(1922); SKIN DEEP(1922); WOMAN, WAKE UP!(1922); MAIN STREET(1923); BARBARA FRIETCHIE(1924); BORROWED HUSBANDS(1924); CHRISTINE OF THE HUNGRY HEART(1924); MIRAGE, THE(1924); GIRL OF GOLD, THE(1925); GROUNDS FOR DIVORCE(1925); MARRY ME(1925); TROUBLE WITH WIVES, THE(1925); EAGLE OF THE SEA, THE(1926); POPULAR SIN, THE(1926); YOU NEVER KNOW WOMEN(1926); HONEYMOON HATE(1927); WORLD AT HER FEET, THE(1927); DOOMSDAY(1928)
King Vidor
HALLELUJAH(1929), p&d; BILLY THE KID(1930), d; NOT SO DUMB(1930), d; CHAMP, THE(1931), d; STREET SCENE(1931), d; BIRD OF PARADISE(1932), d; CYNARA(1932), d; MASK OF FU MANCHU, THE(1932), d; STRANGER'S RETURN(1933), d; OUR DAILY BREAD(1934), p&d, w; SO RED THE ROSE(1935), d; WEDDING NIGHT, THE(1935), d; TEXAS RANGERS, THE(1936), p&d, w; STELLA DALLAS(1937), d; CITADEL, THE(1938), d; WIZARD OF OZ, THE(1939), d; COMRADE X(1940), d; NORTHWEST PASSAGE(1940), d; H.M. PULHAM, ESQ.(1941), p&d, w; AMERICAN ROMANCE, AN(1944), p&d, w; ON OUR MERRY WAY(1948), d; BEYOND THE FOREST(1949), d; FOUNTAINHEAD, THE(1949), d; IT'S A GREAT FEELING(1949); LIGHTNING STRIKES TWICE(1951), d; JAPANESE WAR BRIDE(1952), d; RUBY GENTRY(1952), p, d; MAN WITHOUT A STAR(1955), d; WAR AND PEACE(1956, Ital./U.S.), d, w; LOVE AND MONEY(1982)
Silents
POOR RELATIONS(1919), d&w; JACK KNIFE MAN, THE(1920), d, w; SKY PILOT, THE(1921), d; REAL ADVENTURE, THE(1922), d; SOULS FOR SALE(1923); THREE WISE FOOLS(1923), d, w; HIS HOUR(1924), d, t; BIG PARADE, THE(1925), d; PROUD FLESH(1925), d; CROWD, THE(1928), p&d, w; SHOW PEOPLE(1928), d
Misc. Silents
OTHER HALF, THE(1919), d; TURN IN THE ROAD, THE(1919), d; FAMILY HONOR, THE(1920), d; LOVE NEVER DIES(1921), d; CONQUERING THE WOMAN(1922), d; DUSK TO DAWN(1922), d; PEG O' MY HEART(1922), d; WOMAN OF BRONZE, THE(1923), d; HAPPINESS(1924), d; WIFE OF THE CENTAUR(1924), d; WILD ORANGES(1924), d; WINE OF YOUTH(1924), d; BARDELYS THE MAGNIFICENT(1926), d; LA BOHEME(1926), d; PATSY, THE(1928), d
King W. Vidor
Misc. Silents
BETTER TIMES(1919), d
Leslie Vidor
CATTLE EMPIRE(1958), ed
Charles Vidor
IT'S A BIG COUNTRY(1951), d
Rex Vidor
HORROR CASTLE(1965, Ital.)
Zoli Vidor
COME SPY WITH ME(1967), ph; SAVAGE WEEKEND(1983), ph
Oleg Vidov
HAGBARD AND SIGNE(1968, Den./Iceland/Swed.); WATERLOO(1970, Ital./USSR); BATTLE OF THE NERETVA(1971, Yugo./Ital./Ger.)
Ivica Vidovic
RAT SAVIOUR, THE(1977, Yugo.)
Julian Vidrie
VALDEZ IS COMING(1971)
Manolin Vidrie
VALDEZ IS COMING(1971)
Florence Vie
LOVE RACE, THE(1931, Brit.); JOSSER JOINS THE NAVY(1932, Brit.); MY OLD DUCHESS(1933, Brit.); TO BE A LADY(1934, Brit.); CHANGE FOR A SOVEREIGN(1937, Brit.)
Steve Viedor
Misc. Talkies
KEEP IT UP, JACK!(1975)
Pierre Viel-Lescu
HAIL MAFIA(1965, Fr./Ital.), w
Margaret Vieler
GUTTER GIRLS(1964, Brit.)
Pierre Vielhescazes
CONFESSION, THE(1970, Fr.)
Eric Viellard
1984
A NOS AMOURS(1984, Fr.)
Dominique Vielleville
LES GAULOISES BLEUES(1969, Fr.)
Louise Vienna
FORTUNE COOKIE, THE(1966)
Vienna Boy's Choir
UNFINISHED SYMPHONY, THE(1953, Aust./Brit.)

Vienna Boys Choir
  BIG BROADCAST OF 1936, THE(1935)
the Vienna Boys Choir
  ALMOST ANGELS(1962)
the Vienna Boys' Choir
  MAD ABOUT MUSIC(1938)
Vienna Opera Choir
  UNFINISHED SYMPHONY, THE(1953, Aust./Brit.)
Vienna Philharmonic Orchestra
  UNFINISHED SYMPHONY, THE(1953, Aust./Brit.); LIFE AND LOVES OF MO-
ZART, THE(1959, Ger.)
Vienna State Ballet
  DIE FLEDERMAUS(1964, Aust.)
The Vienna State Opera Ballet
  SWAN LAKE, THE(1967)
Vienna State Opera Chorus
  FIDELIO(1961, Aust.)
Vienna Volksopera Ballet
  DIE FLEDERMAUS(1964, Aust.)
Valerie Vienne
  MATTER OF DAYS, A(1969, Fr./Czech.)
Jimmy Vientola
  TAMING OF DOROTHY, THE(1950, Brit.)
Viera
  WAR LOVER, THE(1962, U.S./Brit.)
Eddie Viera
  THIRTEEN WOMEN(1932)
Joey Viera
  EVEL KNIEVEL(1971)
Max Vierlinger
  COURT CONCERT, THE(1936, Ger.)
Jean-Jacques Vierne
  NO TIME FOR ECSTASY(1963, Fr.), d, w
Sacha Vierny
  HIROSHIMA, MON AMOUR(1959, Fr./Jap.), ph; LAST YEAR AT MARIEN-
BAD(1962, Fr./Ital.), ph; MURIEL(1963, Fr./Ital.), ph; SEASON FOR LOVE, THE(1963,
Fr.), ph; TASTE FOR WOMEN, A(1966, Fr./Ital.), ph; LA GUERRE EST FINIE(1967,
Fr./Swed.), ph; BELLE DE JOUR(1968, Fr.), ph; CAROLINE CHERIE(1968, Fr.), ph;
STAVISKY(1974, Fr.), ph; MON ONCLE D'AMERIQUE(1980, Fr.), ph; BEAU PE-
RE(1981, Fr.), ph
1984
  THREE CROWNS OF THE SAILOR(1984, Fr.), ph
Frithjof Vierock
  PHONY AMERICAN, THE(1964, Ger.)
Frank Vierra
  GROUND ZERO(1973), m
Berthold Viertel
  FOUR DEVILS(1929), w; SEVEN FACES(1929), d; CITY GIRL(1930), w; MAN TROU-
BLE(1930), d; GOD IS MY WITNESS(1931), p&d; MAGNIFICENT LIE(1931), d; MAN
FROM YESTERDAY, THE(1932), d; WISER SEX, THE(1932), d; LITTLE
FRIEND(1934, Brit.), d, w; PASSING OF THE THIRD FLOOR BACK, THE(1936,
Brit.), d; RHODES(1936, Brit.), d
Misc. Talkies
  SPY, THE(1931), d
Misc. Silents
  ONE WOMAN IDEA, THE(1929), d
Jack Viertel
1984
  HOUSE WHERE DEATH LIVES, THE(1984), w
Peter Viertel
  HARD WAY, THE(1942), w; SABOTEUR(1942), w; ROUGHSHOD(1949), w; WE
WERE STRANGERS(1949), w; DECISION BEFORE DAWN(1951), w; SUN ALSO
RISES, THE(1957), w; OLD MAN AND THE SEA, THE(1958), w; FIVE MILES TO
MIDNIGHT(1963, U.S./Fr./Ital.), w
Salka Viertel
  QUEEN CHRISTINA(1933), w; PAINTED VEIL, THE(1934), w; ANNA KARENI-
NA(1935), w; CONQUEST(1937), w; TWO-FACED WOMAN(1941), w; DEEP VAL-
LEY(1947), w; LOVES OF THREE QUEENS, THE(1954, Ital./Fr.), w; PRISONER OF
THE VOLGA(1960, Fr./Ital.), w
Manuel Viescas
  BORDER, THE(1982)
Alex Viespi [Alex Cord]
  CHAPMAN REPORT, THE(1962)
Howard Viet
  HIGH SCHOOL BIG SHOT(1959); WITCHMAKER, THE(1969)
The Viewers
  MONSTER CLUB, THE(1981, Brit.)
Emilio Vieyra
  VIOLATED LOVE(1966, Arg.), d; CURIOUS DR. HUMPP(1967, Arg.), d&w
Adolphe Viezzi
  COUP DE TORCHON(1981, Fr.), p
Tommy Vig
  FORCED ENTRY(1975), m; THEY CALL ME BRUCE(1982), m; SWEET SIX-
TEEN(1983), m
Le Vigan
  HARVEST(1939, Fr.); LOUISE(1940, Fr.)
Kristen Vigard
  BLACK STALLION, THE(1979); SURVIVORS, THE(1983)
Drew Vigen
  HOUSE OF WOMEN(1962)
Gregor Vigen
  FOLLOW ME, BOYS!(1966)
Viki Vigen
  ROSEMARY'S BABY(1968)
Vittorio Vighi
  00-2 MOST SECRET AGENTS(1965, Ital.), w
Lucienne Vigier
  CHILDREN OF PARADISE(1945, Fr.)

Eldred Vigil, Jr.
  WHEN THE LEGENDS DIE(1972)
Gerardo Vigil
  MISSING(1982)
The Vigilantes
  HARVEST MELODY(1943)
Aldo Vigliarolo
  JETLAG(1981, U.S./Span.), w
Katina Viglietti
  GARDEN OF THE FINZI-CONTINIS, THE(1976, Ital./Ger.)
Kim Vignal
1984
  WILD LIFE, THE(1984)
Pascale Vignal
1984
  SUNDAY IN THE COUNTRY, A(1984, Fr.)
Raymond Vignale
  ASH WEDNESDAY(1973)
Pedro Juan Vignalle
  VIOLENT AND THE DAMNED, THE(1962, Braz.), w
Angelo Vignari
  NOCTURNA(1979); NIGHT SHIFT(1982)
Steve Vignari
1984
  COTTON CLUB, THE(1984)
Steven Vignari
  SHAMUS(1973)
Jean-Daniel Vignat
  SLOGAN(1970, Fr.), art d
Benno Vignay
  LOVE IN MOROCCO(1933, Fr.), w
Daniel Vigne
  RETURN OF MARTIN GUERRE, THE(1983, Fr.), p&d, w
Odette Vigne
  SPIDER, THE(1945)
Gilles Vigneault
  ACT OF THE HEART(1970, Can.)
Raoul Vignerte
  KOENIGSMARK(1935, Fr.)
Robert Vignola
  BROKEN DREAMS(1933), d; GIRL FROM SCOTLAND YARD, THE(1937), d
Silents
  FROM THE MANGER TO THE CROSS(1913); AUDREY(1916), d; SPIDER,
THE(1916), d
Misc. Silents
  DON CAESAR DE BAZAN(1915), d; PRETENDERS, THE(1915), d; VANDERHOFF
AFFAIR, THE(1915), d; BLACK CROOK, THE(1916), d; EVIL THEREOF, THE(1916),
d; MOMENT BEFORE, THE(1916), d; UNDER COVER(1916), d; HER BETTER
SELF(1917), d; DECLASSE(1925), d; TROPIC MADNESS(1928), d
Robert G. Vignola
  SCARLET LETTER, THE(1934), d; PERFECT CLUE, THE(1935), d
Silents
  GREAT EXPECTATIONS(1917), d; KNIFE, THE(1918), d; LOUISIANA(1919), d; EN-
CHANTMENT(1921), d; STRAIGHT IS THE WAY(1921), d; WOMAN GOD
CHANGED, THE(1921), d; WHEN KNIGHTHOOD WAS IN FLOWER(1922), d; ADAM
AND EVA(1923), d; MARRIED FLIRTS(1924), d
Misc. Silents
  REWARD OF PATIENCE, THE(1916), d; SEVENTEEN(1916), d; DOUBLE
CROSSED(1917), d; FORTUNES OF FIFI, THE(1917), d; HUNGRY HEART,
THE(1917), d; LOVE THAT LIVES, THE(1917), d; CLAW, THE(1918), d; GIRL WHO
CAME BACK, THE(1918), d; MADAME JEALOUSY(1918), d; REASON WHY,
THE(1918), d; WOMAN'S WEAPONS(1918), d; EXPERIMENTAL MARRIAGE(1919),
d; HIS OFFICIAL FIANCEE(1919), d; HOME TOWN GIRL, THE(1919), d; INNOCENT
ADVENTURESS, AN(1919), d; MORE DEADLY THAN THE MALE(1919), d; THIRD
KISS, THE(1919), d; VICKY VAN(1919), d; WINNING GIRL, THE(1919), d; YOU
NEVER SAID SUCH A GIRL(1919), d; HEART OF YOUTH, THE(1920), d; WORLD
AND HIS WIFE, THE(1920), d; 13TH COMMANDMENT, THE(1920), d; PASSIONATE
PILGRIM, THE(1921), d; BEAUTY'S WORTH(1922), d; YOUNG DIANA, THE(1922),
d; WAY OF A GIRL, THE(1925), d; FIFTH AVENUE(1926), d; CABARET(1927), d;
RED SWORD, THE(1929), d
Jean-Paul Vignon
  DEVIL'S BRIGADE, THE(1968)
Virginie Vignon
  TRANS-EUROP-EXPRESS(1968, Fr.); WEEKEND(1968, Fr./Ital.)
1984
  ONE DEADLY SUMMER(1984, Fr.)
Benno Vigny
  MOROCCO(1930), w; DIE MANNER UM LUCIE(1931), w; LOST ONE, THE(1951,
Ger.), w; VIENNA WALTZES(1961, Aust.), w
Aurike Vigo
  LOLA(1982, Ger.)
David Vigo
  RUNAWAY, THE(1964, Brit.), p
Jean Vigo
  L'ATALANTE(1947, Fr.), d, w
Abe Vigoda
  GODFATHER, THE(1972); DON IS DEAD, THE(1973); GODFATHER, THE, PART
II(1974); NEWMAN'S LAW(1974); CHEAP DETECTIVE, THE(1978)
1984
  CANNONBALL RUN II(1984)
Aldo Vigorelli
  VIOLENT FOUR, THE(1968, Ital.)
Herb Vigran
  YOU CAN'T RUN AWAY FROM IT(1956); MONSIEUR VERDOUX(1947); FIGHTING
MAD(1948); NOOSE HANGS HIGH, THE(1948); TEXAS, BROOKLYN AND HEA-
VEN(1948); JUDGE, THE(1949); NIGHT INTO MORNING(1951); RACKET, THE(1951);
OKLAHOMA ANNIE(1952); ROSE BOWL STORY, THE(1952); BAND WAGON,
THE(1953); LET'S DO IT AGAIN(1953); DRAGNET(1954); LONG, LONG TRAILER,
THE(1954); LUCKY ME(1954); SUSAN SLEPT HERE(1954); WHITE CHRIST-
MAS(1954); 20,000 LEAGUES UNDER THE SEA(1954); I DIED A THOUSAND

TIMES(1955); ILLEGAL(1955); CALLING HOMICIDE(1956); CRY IN THE NIGHT, A(1956); OUR MISS BROOKS(1956); THESE WILDER YEARS(1956); THREE FOR JAMIE DAWN(1956); GUNSIGHT RIDGE(1957); PUBLIC PIGEON NO. 1(1957); VAMPIRE, THE(1957); CASE AGAINST BROOKLYN, THE(1958); GO, JOHNNY, GO!(1959); PLUNDERERS OF PAINTED FLATS(1959); ERRAND BOY, THE(1961); BRASS BOTTLE, THE(1964); CANDIDATE, THE(1964); SEND ME NO FLOWERS(1964); UNSINKABLE MOLLY BROWN, THE(1964); THAT FUNNY FEELING(1965); DID YOU HEAR THE ONE ABOUT THE TRAVELING SALESLADY?(1968); SUPPORT YOUR LOCAL GUNFIGHTER(1971); CANCEL MY RESERVATION(1972); CHARLOTTE'S WEB(1973); BENJI(1974); HOW TO SEDUCE A WOMAN(1974); MURPH THE SURF(1974); HAWMPS!(1976); SHAGGY D.A., THE(1976); FIRST MONDAY IN OCTOBER(1981)

Herbert Vigran
DEATH FROM A DISTANCE(1936); IT ALL CAME TRUE(1940); STRANGER ON THE THIRD FLOOR(1940); MILLION DOLLAR BABY(1941); MURDER BY INVITATION(1941); REG'LAR FELLERS(1941); SECRETS OF A CO-ED(1942); GHOST SHIP, THE(1943); IT AIN'T HAY(1943); SECRETS OF THE UNDERGROUND(1943); SWEET ROSIE O'GRADY(1943); HER ADVENTUROUS NIGHT(1946); ALL MY SONS(1948); HOUSE OF STRANGERS(1949); TELL IT TO THE JUDGE(1949); LET'S DANCE(1950); MISTER 880(1950); MRS. O'MALLEY AND MR. MALONE(1950); SIDE STREET(1950); ABBOTT AND COSTELLO MEET THE INVISIBLE MAN(1951); BEDTIME FOR BONZO(1951); HALF ANGEL(1951); IRON MAN, THE(1951); JUST ACROSS THE STREET(1952); JUST FOR YOU(1952); SOMEBODY LOVES ME(1952); GIRL NEXT DOOR, THE(1953); THAT CERTAIN FEELING(1956); MIDNIGHT STORY, THE(1957)

Herbert "Herb" Vigran
VAGABOND LADY(1935)

Juan Viguie
SECRET OF THE PURPLE REEF, THE(1960), art d

Larry Vigus
1984
FLESHBURN(1984)

Robert Viharo
VALLEY OF THE DOLLS(1967); VILLA RIDES(1968); RETURN TO MACON COUNTY(1975); I NEVER PROMISED YOU A ROSE GARDEN(1977); OVER-UNDER, SIDEWAYS-DOWN(1977); BARE KNUCKLES(1978); EVIL, THE(1978); HAPPY BIRTHDAY, GEMINI(1980); HIDE IN PLAIN SIGHT(1980)
Misc. Talkies
BARE KNUCKLES(1977); KID FROM NOT SO BIG, THE(1978)

Titus Vihe-Mueller
WHALERS, THE(1942, Swed.)

Judex C. Vijoen
DINGAKA(1965, South Africa), ph

O. Vikland
DON QUIXOTE(1961, USSR); KIEV COMEDY, A(1963, USSR)

O. Viklandt
MAGIC VOYAGE OF SINBAD, THE(1962, USSR)

Richard Viktorov
MOSCOW–CASSIOPEIA(1974, USSR), d; TEENAGERS IN SPACE(1975, USSR), d; CHEREZ TERNII K SVEZDAM(1981 USSR), d, w

Vladamir Vikulin
Misc. Silents
SON OF THE LAND(1931, USSR)

Alberto Vila
THEY MET IN ARGENTINA(1941)

Janine Vila
FRUIT IS RIPE, THE(1961, Fr./Ital.); OLIVE TREES OF JUSTICE, THE(1967, Fr.)

Vilallonga
BREAKFAST AT TIFFANY'S(1961)

Jose-Luis Vilallonga
BEHOLD A PALE HORSE(1964)

Jimmy Vilan
CORREGIDOR(1943)

Bruce Vilanch
MAHOGANY(1975)
1984
ICE PIRATES, THE(1984)

Victor Vilanova
TEXICAN, THE(1966, U.S./Span.)

Antonio Vilar
DISHONORED(1950, Ital.); FEMALE, THE(1960, Fr.); REDEEMER, THE(1965, Span.); SCHEHERAZADE(1965, Fr./Ital./Span.)

Jean Vilar
GATES OF THE NIGHT(1950, Fr.)

Leonardo Vilar
GIVEN WORD, THE(1964, Braz.)

Tom Vilard
FORCE: FIVE(1981)

Robert Vilardi
SONG OF THE LOON(1970)

Henry Vilardo
WALLS OF JERICHO(1948), makeup; SECOND WOMAN, THE(1951), makeup

Felix Vilars
DEVIL WOMAN(1976, Phil.), d

Guillermo Vilas
PLAYERS(1979)

L. Vilasenor
WOMAN WITH RED BOOTS, THE(1977, Fr./Span.), ph

Vilbert
PRIZE, THE(1952, Fr.)

Henri Vilbert
MANON(1950, Fr.); ALI BABA(1954, Fr.); LETTERS FROM MY WINDMILL(1955, Fr.); LOVE IN A HOT CLIMATE(1959, Fr./Span.); GUINGUETTE(1959, Fr.); MARTIAN IN PARIS, A(1961, Fr.); DEVIL AND THE TEN COMMANDMENTS, THE(1962, Fr.); STORY OF THE COUNT OF MONTE CRISTO, THE(1962, Fr./Ital.); TWO ARE GUILTY(1964, Fr.); MY WIFE'S HUSBAND(1965, Fr./Ital.); ATTENTION, THE KIDS ARE WATCHING(1978, Fr.)

Veronique Vilbert
CAT IN THE SACK, THE(1967, Can.)

Enrique Vilches
HAND IN THE TRAP, THE(1963, Arg./Span.)

Humberto Vilches
UNDER FIRE(1983)

Franck Vilcour
GENDARME OF ST. TROPEZ, THE(1966, Fr./Ital.)

Roland Vildo
ROSE TATTOO, THE(1955)

Vania Vilers
JE T'AIME, JE T'AIME(1972, Fr./Swed.); CARAVAN TO VACCARES(1974, Brit./Fr)

Vilfrid
MARTIAN IN PARIS, A(1961, Fr.), w

Jacques Vilfrid
MARTIAN IN PARIS, A(1961, Fr.), p; GENDARME OF ST. TROPEZ, THE(1966, Fr./Ital.), w; BLONDE FROM PEKING, THE(1968, Fr.), w; LE GENDARME ET LES EXTRATERRESTRES(1978, Fr.), w

Eric Vilgertshofer
GERMANY IN AUTUMN(1978, Ger.)

Arthur T. Viliesid
CAT GANG, THE(1959, Brit.), p

Judex C. Viljoen
KIMBERLEY JIM(1965, South Africa), ph

Ed. E. Villa
DANDY, THE ALL AMERICAN GIRL(1976)

Edmund Villa
ON THE NICKEL(1980)

Francesca Villa
TREE OF WOODEN CLOGS, THE(1979, Ital.)

Franco Villa
MYTH, THE(1965, Ital.), ph; MY NAME IS PECOS(1966, Ital.), ph; NO ROOM TO DIE(1969, Ital.), ph; WOMAN ON FIRE, A(1970, Ital.), ph; ITALIAN CONNECTION, THE(1973, U.S./Ital./Ger.), ph

Jose Trinidad Villa
WAR WAGON, THE(1967)

Miguel Villa
SUPERSONIC MAN(1979, Span.), spec eff

Robert Villa
OPERATION X(1951, Brit.)

Roberto Villa
DISILLUSION(1949, Ital.)

Hector Villa-Lobos
GREEN MANSIONS(1959), m

Teddy Villaba
WITCH WITHOUT A BROOM, A(1967, U.S./Span.), art d

Ignacio Villabajo
TREASURE OF THE SIERRA MADRE, THE(1948)

the Villagers of Chinchero
LAST MOVIE, THE(1971), m

Paolo Villaggio
GOODNIGHT, LADIES AND GENTLEMEN(1977, Ital.)

Paolo Villagio
DON'T TOUCH WHITE WOMEN!(1974, Fr.)

Teddy Villalba
ROMEO AND JULIET(1968, Ital./Span.), art d

Francisco Villalobos
GIANT(1956); RETURN OF THE FLY(1959)

Ray Villalobos
URBAN COWBOY(1980), ph; BALLAD OF GREGORIO CORTEZ, THE(1983), ph

Reynaldo Villalobos
NINE TO FIVE(1980), ph; RISKY BUSINESS(1983), ph
1984
BLAME IT ON RIO(1984), ph; GRANDVIEW, U.S.A.(1984), ph; MIKE'S MURDER(1984), ph; WINDY CITY(1984), ph

Marthe Villalonga
BIG RED ONE, THE(1980); BANZAI(1983, Fr.)
1984
PAR OU T'ES RENTRE? ON T'A PAS VUE SORTIR(1984, Fr./Tunisia)

David Villalpando
1984
EL NORTE(1984)

Nora Villamayor
1984
BONA(1984, Phil.), p

Ricardo Villamin
LOSERS, THE(1970), makeup

Totoy Villamin
IMPASSE(1969), makeup

Fred Villani
PAJAMA GAME, THE(1957)

Ludwick Villani
ON THE YARD(1978)

Luigi Villani
TRUE STORY OF ESKIMO NELL, THE(1975, Aus.)

Michael Villani
1984
PHILADELPHIA EXPERIMENT, THE(1984)

Carlos Villanos
CALIFORNIA FRONTIER(1938)

Carlos Villar
CALIFORNIA TRAIL, THE(1933); BORDERTOWN(1935)

Pancho Villar
EXCUSE MY GLOVE(1936, Brit.)

Andre Villard
BEAR, THE(1963, Fr.), ph; BIQUEFARRE(1983, Fr.), ph

Dimitri Villard
TIME WALKER(1982), p

Franck Villard
GIGOT(1962)

Frank Villard
CHEAT, THE(1950, Fr.); SEVEN DEADLY SINS, THE(1953, Fr./Ital.); SECRET DOCUMENT – VIENNA(1954, Fr.); GUILTY?(1956, Brit.); COUNTERFEITERS OF PARIS, THE(1962, Fr., Ital.); CRIME DOES NOT PAY(1962, Fr.); PRICE OF FLESH, THE(1962, Fr.); MATA HARI(1965, Fr./Ital.)

Jean Villard
LE MONDE TREMBLERA(1939, Fr.), w

Juliette Villard
WANDERER, THE(1969, Fr.)

Marc Villard
SNOW(1983, Fr.), w

Richard Villard
GRASS EATER, THE(1961)

Tom Villard
PARASITE(1982)
1984
SURF II(1984)

Maria Vico Villardo
CON MEN, THE(1973, Ital.,Span.)

Julio Villareal
TORCH, THE(1950); PLUNDER OF THE SUN(1953); SEVEN CITIES OF GOLD(1955); BEAST OF HOLLOW MOUNTAIN, THE(1956)

Julio Villareale
HONEYMOON(1947)

Carlos Villarias
QUANDO EL AMOR RIE(1933); STARLIGHT OVER TEXAS(1938); TROPIC HOLIDAY(1938); FRONTIERS OF '49(1939); HOLD BACK THE DAWN(1941)
Misc. Talkies
PAPA SOLTERO(1939)

Anthony Villaroel
TO SIR, WITH LOVE(1967, Brit.); PRAISE MARX AND PASS THE AMMUNITION(1970, Brit.)

Julio Villarreal
MADCAP OF THE HOUSE(1950, Mex.)

Helena Villarroya
DR. COPPELIUS(1968, U.S./Span.)

Juan Villasana
PANIC IN THE STREETS(1950)

Jose Villasante
SPIRIT OF THE BEEHIVE, THE(1976, Span.)

George C. Villasenor
1984
LOVE STREAMS(1984), ed

Leopoldo Villasenor
WEREWOLF VS. THE VAMPIRE WOMAN, THE(1970, Span./Ger.), ph; GUYANA, CULT OF THE DAMNED(1980, Mex./Span./Panama), ph

Victor Villasenor
BALLAD OF GREGORIO CORTEZ, THE(1983), w

John Villasin
REAL GLORY, THE(1939)

Astrid Villaume
VENOM(1968, Den.); SCANDAL IN DENMARK(1970, Den.)

E. Villavicencio
UNDER FIRE(1983)

Paul Ville
LOVE AND THE FRENCHWOMAN(1961, Fr.); WILD CHILD, THE(1970, Fr.)

Victoria Ville
ONCE IN PARIS(1978)

Herve Villechaize
GANG THAT COULDN'T SHOOT STRAIGHT, THE(1971); GREASER'S PALACE(1972); MALATESTA'S CARNIVAL(1973); CRAZY JOE(1974); MAN WITH THE GOLDEN GUN, THE(1974, Brit.); SEIZURE(1974); HOT TOMORROWS(1978); ONE AND ONLY, THE(1978); FORBIDDEN ZONE(1980)

Lucio Villegas
YELLOW JACK(1938); NADA MAS QUE UNA MUJER(1934); NOTORIOUS SOPHIE LANG, THE(1934); GOIN' TO TOWN(1935); STORM OVER THE ANDES(1935); UNDER THE PAMPAS MOON(1935); MESSAGE TO GARCIA, A(1936); I'LL TAKE ROMANCE(1937); RENEGADE RANGER(1938); FIGHTING GRINGO, THE(1939); ONLY ANGELS HAVE WINGS(1939); REAL GLORY, THE(1939); LIGHT OF WESTERN STARS, THE(1940); THREE MEN FROM TEXAS(1940); BORDER BANDITS(1946); TYCOON(1947); SECRET BEYOND THE DOOR, THE(1948)

Lucius Villegas
PIRATES OF MONTEREY(1947)

Michael Villela
SLUMBER PARTY MASSACRE, THE(1982)

Edward Villella
MIDSUMMER NIGHT'S DREAM, A(1966)

Villena
MARCH OR DIE(1977, Brit.)

Carmen Villena
BLOOD WEDDING(1981, Sp.)

Fernando Villena
GUNFIGHTERS OF CASA GRANDE(1965, U.S./Span.); MURIETA(1965, Span.); PLANET OF THE VAMPIRES(1965, U.S./Ital./Span.); ONE STEP TO HELL(1969, U.S./Ital./Span.); MERCENARY, THE(1970, Ital./Span.)

Francisco Villena
TREASURE OF THE FOUR CROWNS(1983, Span./U.S.)

Lionel Villeneauve
MY UNCLE ANTOINE(1971, Can.)

Clifford Villeneuve
TWO(1975)

Lionel Villeneuve
JE T'AIME(1974, Can.)

Jacques Villeret
MY FIRST LOVE(1978, Fr.); MALEVIL(1981, Fr./Ger.); BOLERO(1982, Fr.); DANTON(1983)
1984
EDITH AND MARCEL(1984, Fr.); FIRST NAME: CARMEN(1984, Fr.)

Carlos Villerias
FLIRTING WITH FATE(1938)

Daniel Villerois
NUDE IN HIS POCKET(1962, Fr.), art d

Michele Villerot
ADIOS GRINGO(1967, Ital./Fr./Span.), w

Claude Villers
LA BALANCE(1983, Fr.)

James Villers
WRONG BOX, THE(1966, Brit.)

Marjorie Villers
Misc. Silents
ONE MOMENT'S TEMPTATION(1922); MEN WHO FORGET(1923)

Mavis Villers
MAD MEN OF EUROPE(1940, Brit.)

Eddie Villery
SUNSHINE BOYS, THE(1975); GOODBYE GIRL, THE(1977); CALIFORNIA SUITE(1978)

Raymond Villette
Misc. Silents
GULLIVER IN LILLIPUT(1923, Fr.), d

Stephane Villette
1984
L'ARGENT(1984, Fr./Switz.)

Olga Villi
BIRDS, THE BEES AND THE ITALIANS, THE(1967); QUEENS, THE(1968, Ital./Fr.)

A. J. Villiers
WINDJAMMER, THE(1931, Brit.), w, ph

Charles Villiers
SCHLOCK(1973)
Misc. Silents
BETTER MAN, THE(1921)

Christopher Villiers
1984
TOP SECRET!(1984)

David Villiers
CANDIDATE FOR MURDER(1966, Brit.), d

Francois Villiers
WEB OF FEAR(1966, Fr./Span.), d

Francoise Villiers
THREE FACES OF SIN(1963, Fr./Ital.), d, w

James Villiers
CLUE OF THE NEW PIN, THE(1961, Brit.); EVA(1962, Fr./Ital.); OPERATION SNATCH(1962, Brit.); MURDER AT THE GALLOP(1963, Brit.); DAYLIGHT ROBBERY(1964, Brit.); FATHER CAME TOO(1964, Brit.); KING AND COUNTRY(1964, Brit.); MODEL MURDER CASE, THE(1964, Brit.); NOTHING BUT THE BEST(1964, Brit.); NANNY, THE(1965, Brit.); REPULSION(1965, Brit.); THESE ARE THE DAMNED(1965, Brit.); YOU MUST BE JOKING!(1965, Brit.); ALPHABET MURDERS, THE(1966); HALF A SIXPENCE(1967, Brit.); NICE GIRL LIKE ME, A(1969, Brit.); OTLEY(1969, Brit.); SOME GIRLS DO(1969, Brit.); ASYLUM(1972, Brit.); BLOOD FROM THE MUMMY'S TOMB(1972, Brit.); RULING CLASS, THE(1972, Brit.); AMAZING MR. BLUNDEN, THE(1973, Brit.); SEVEN NIGHTS IN JAPAN(1976, Brit./Fr.); JOSEPH ANDREWS(1977, Brit.); SAINT JACK(1979); FOR YOUR EYES ONLY(1981)
1984
UNDER THE VOLCANO(1984)

Kenneth Villiers
WHITE ENSIGN(1934, Brit.); MR. COHEN TAKES A WALK(1936, Brit.); THEY DIDN'T KNOW(1936, Brit.); THINGS TO COME(1936, Brit.); YANK AT OXFORD, A(1938)

Mavin Villiers
CORRIDOR OF MIRRORS(1948, Brit.)

Mavis Villiers
LADY'S MORALS, A(1930); KING OF THE CASTLE(1936, Brit.); NURSEMAID WHO DISAPPEARED, THE(1939, Brit.); SAILOR'S DON'T CARE(1940, Brit.); SALOON BAR(1940, Brit.); HI, GANG!(1941, Brit.); SOUTH AMERICAN GEORGE(1941, Brit.); YOU CAN'T DO WITHOUT LOVE(1946, Brit.); CHEER THE BRAVE(1951, Brit.); POOL OF LONDON(1951, Brit.); TIME IS MY ENEMY(1957, Brit.); MOUSE THAT ROARED, THE(1959, Brit.); SUDDENLY, LAST SUMMER(1959, Brit.); ROMAN SPRING OF MRS. STONE, THE(1961, U.S./Brit.); VICTIM(1961, Brit.); HAUNTING, THE(1963); PROMISE HER ANYTHING(1966, Brit.)
Silents
OLD AGE HANDICAP(1928)

Patrick Villiers
JOHN PAUL JONES(1959)

Arthur Villiesid
Misc. Silents
WOODPIGEON PATROL, THE(1930, Brit.)

Gina Villines
KONA COAST(1968)

Andre Villion
PRETTY BUT WICKED(1965, Braz.)

Marjorie Villis
Silents
BRENDA OF THE BARGE(1920, Brit.)

Marjorie Villis
Silents
POWER OF RIGHT, THE(1919, Brit.); STARTING POINT, THE(1919, Brit.); EDUCATION OF NICKY, THE(1921, Brit.)
Misc. Silents
FIGHTING COBBLER, THE(1915, Brit.); TRAFFIC(1915, Brit.); SALLY BISHOP(1916, Brit.); RILKA(1918, Brit.); RUGGED PATH, THE(1918, Brit.); FURTHER EXPLOITS OF SEXTON BLAKE, THE - MYSTERY OF THE S.S. OLYMPIC, THE(1919, Brit.); MAN WHO FORGOT, THE(1919, Brit.); SILVER GREYHOUND, THE(1919, Brit.); LOVE IN THE WELSH HILLS(1921, Brit.)

Jorge Villoldo
AVENGERS, THE(1950); WAY OF A GAUCHO(1952)

Andre Villon
SO THIS IS PARIS(1954)

Angela Villroel
MALOU(1983)
Vladimir Vilner
Misc. Silents
BENNIE THE HOWL(1927, USSR), d; SIMPLE TAILOR, THE(1934, USSR), d
Orlando Vilone
VIOLATED LOVE(1966, Arg.), makeup
Opal Vils
MAN FROM DEL RIO(1956), cos
Stanley Vilven
CHELSEA LIFE(1933, Brit.); MOUNTAINS O'MOURNE(1938, Brit.); OLD MOTHER
RILEY IN PARIS(1938, Brit.); DARK SECRET(1949, Brit.); SOMETHING IN THE
CITY(1950, Brit.)
Nina Vilvovskaya
DUEL, THE(1964, USSR); SONS AND MOTHERS(1967, USSR)
Babette Vimenet
CHRONOPOLIS(1982, Fr.), anim
Catherine Vimenet
TWO OR THREE THINGS I KNOW ABOUT HER(1970, Fr.), d&w
Jean Vimenet
MOUCHETTE(1970, Fr.)
Victor Vina
Misc. Silents
VISAGE D'ENFANTS(1926, Fr.); CARMEN(1928, Fr.)
Bob Vinas
TOO YOUNG, TOO IMMORAL!(1962), m
Pedro Vinas
MESSAGE TO GARCIA, A(1936)
Luciano Vincanzoni
BIRDS, THE BEES AND THE ITALIANS, THE(1967), w
Barrie Vince
NEGATIVES(1968, Brit.), ed; DEEP END(1970 Ger./U.S.), ed; HOFFMAN(1970,
Brit.), ed; TRIPLE ECHO, THE(1973, Brit.), ed; LAST DAYS OF MAN ON EARTH,
THE(1975, Brit.), ed; ODD JOB, THE(1978, Brit.), ed; SHOUT, THE(1978, Brit.), ed
1984
SUCCESS IS THE BEST REVENGE(1984, Brit.), ed
Barry Vince
CURSE OF THE VOODOO(1965, Brit.), ed; NAKED RUNNER, THE(1967, Brit.), ed;
SMASHING TIME(1967 Brit.), ed; MOONLIGHTING(1982, Brit.), w, ed
Charles Vince
PROFESSIONALS, THE(1960, Brit.)
Eugene Vince
GREEN SLIME, THE(1969)
Louis Vincenot
INTERNATIONAL HOUSE(1933); LIMEHOUSE BLUES(1934); SHE GETS HER
MAN(1935); WEREWOLF OF LONDON, THE(1935); LEATHERNECKS HAVE LAND-
ED, THE(1936); THIRTEENTH CHAIR, THE(1937); WEE WILLIE WINKIE(1937);
SUEZ(1938)
Allan Vincent
MOTHER'S BOY(1929)
Allen Vincent
CROONER(1932); STREET OF WOMEN(1932); THIS RECKLESS AGE(1932);
THRILL OF YOUTH(1932); TWO AGAINST THE WORLD(1932); BROADWAY
BAD(1933); CARNIVAL LADY(1933); DARING DAUGHTERS(1933); I HAVE LI-
VED(1933); MYSTERY OF THE WAX MUSEUM, THE(1933); NO MORE OR-
CHIDS(1933); HI, NELLIE!(1934); SUCCESS AT ANY PRICE(1934); BAD BOY(1935);
IT'S A BET(1935, Brit.); RETURN OF PETER GRIMM, THE(1935); CHATTER-
BOX(1936); EASY MONEY(1936); SUTTER'S GOLD(1936); FAMILY AFFAIR, A(1937);
ARMY GIRL(1938); LADIES IN DISTRESS(1938); FACE BEHIND THE MASK,
THE(1941), w; SONG OF LOVE(1947), w; JOHNNY BELINDA(1948), w; GIRL IN
WHITE, THE(1952), w
Anna Vincent
MIKADO, THE(1967, Brit.)
Billy Vincent
SUBMARINE D-1(1937); SAN ANTONIO KID, THE(1944); SANTA FE SADDLE-
MATES(1945); TRAIL STREET(1947); RETURN OF THE BADMEN(1948); FULLER
BRUSH GIRL, THE(1950); MONTANA(1950); MAN BEHIND THE GUN, THE(1952);
STEEL JUNGLE, THE(1956); AFFAIR IN RENO(1957)
"Billy" Vincent
PEOPLE AGAINST O'HARA, THE(1951)
Charles Vincent
LOVABLE CHEAT, THE(1949); DOBERMAN GANG, THE(1972)
Chuck Vincent
SUMMER CAMP(1979), d
1984
HOLLYWOOD HOT TUBS(1984), d; PREPPIES(1984), p&d, w
Misc. Talkies
BLUE SUMMER(1973), d; MATTER OF LOVE, A(1979), d; HOT T-SHIRTS(1980), d;
C.O.D.(1983), d; IN LOVE(1983), d
Claude Vincent
1984
OVER THE BROOKLYN BRIDGE(1984); POPE OF GREENWICH VILLAGE,
THE(1984)
Dan Vincent
BATTLE BEYOND THE STARS(1980)
Diane Vincent
COMMITMENT, THE(1976)
Dominique Vincent
RISE OF LOUIS XIV, THE(1970, Fr.)
Don Vincent
HAPPY MOTHER'S DAY... LOVE, GEORGE(1973), m
Donald Vincent
SQUARES(1972), m
Elmore Vincent
GOOD MORNING, MISS DOVE(1955)
Frank Vincent
DEATH COLLECTOR(1976); RAGING BULL(1980); BABY, IT'S YOU(1983); DEAR
MR. WONDERFUL(1983, Ger.)

1984
POPE OF GREENWICH VILLAGE, THE(1984)
Frankie Vincent
KENTUCKY JUBILEE(1951)
Fred Vincent
WHO?(1975, Brit./Ger.)
Gene Vincent
HOT ROD GANG(1958); RING-A-DING RHYTHM(1962, Brit. 73m Amicus/COL bw
(G.B: IT'S TRAD, DAD!); SING AND SWING(1964, Brit.)
Henrietta Vincent
BRIEF ENCOUNTER(1945, Brit.)
Hilda Vincent
DANGER PATROL(1937), w; YOUTH WILL BE SERVED(1940), w
Jack Vincent
Misc. Silents
WITH ALL HER HEART(1920, Brit.)
James Vincent
EMPEROR WALTZ, THE(1948); PRINCE WHO WAS A THIEF, THE(1951)
Silents
AMBITION(1916), d; BATTLE OF LIFE, THE(1916), d
Misc. Silents
NAN O' THE BACKWOODS(1915); GOLD AND THE WOMAN(1916), d; LOVE AND
HATE(1916), d; SINS OF MEN(1916), d; UNWELCOME MOTHER, THE(1916), d;
ROYAL ROMANCE(1917), d; SISTER AGAINST SISTER(1917), d; WRATH OF LO-
VE(1917), d; STOLEN MOMENTS(1920), d
Jan Michael Vincent
DEFIANCE(1980)
Jan-Michael Vincent
UNDEFEATED, THE(1969); TRIBES(1970); GOING HOME(1971); MECHANIC,
THE(1972); WORLD'S GREATEST ATHLETE, THE(1973); BITE THE BULLET(1975);
WHITE LINE FEVER(1975, Can.); BABY BLUE MARINE(1976); SHADOW OF THE
HAWK(1976, Can.); VIGILANTE FORCE(1976); DAMNATION ALLEY(1977); BIG
WEDNESDAY(1978); HOOPER(1978); RETURN, THE(1980); HARD COUNTRY(1981)
Misc. Talkies
BUSTER AND BILLIE(1974); ALIEN'S RETURN, THE(1980); LAST PLANE
OUT(1983)
Julie Vincent
FOND MEMORIES(1982, Can.)
June Vincent
HONEYMOON LODGE(1943); SING A JINGLE(1943); CAN'T HELP SINGING(1944);
CLIMAX, THE(1944); LADIES COURAGEOUS(1944); HERE COME THE CO-
EDS(1945); THAT'S THE SPIRIT(1945); BLACK ANGEL(1946); CHALLENGE,
THE(1948); CREEPER, THE(1948); SHED NO TEARS(1948); SONG OF IDAHO(1948);
TRAPPED BY BOSTON BLACKIE(1948); LONE WOLF AND HIS LADY, THE(1949);
MARY RYAN, DETECTIVE(1949); ZAMBA(1949); COUNTERSPY MEETS SCOTLAND
YARD(1950); IN A LONELY PLACE(1950); SECRETS OF MONTE CARLO(1951);
COLORADO SUNDOWN(1952); NIGHT WITHOUT SLEEP(1952); WAC FROM WALLA
WALLA, THE(1952); CLIPPED WINGS(1953); MARRY ME AGAIN(1953); CITY OF
SHADOWS(1955); MIRACLE OF THE HILLS, THE(1959)
Keith Vincent
LIEUTENANT WORE SKIRTS, THE(1956); THREE BRAVE MEN(1957)
Larry Vincent
WITCHMAKER, THE(1969); INCREDIBLE TWO-HEADED TRANSPLANT,
THE(1971); DOCTOR DEATH: SEEKER OF SOULS(1973)
Leslie Vincent
THEY MET IN BOMBAY(1941); MRS. MINIVER(1942); GUY NAMED JOE, A(1943);
IMMORTAL SERGEANT, THE(1943); TONIGHT WE RAID CALAIS(1943); JANE
EYRE(1944); SECRETS OF SCOTLAND YARD(1944); CORN IS GREEN, THE(1945);
PARIS UNDERGROUND(1945); PURSUIT TO ALGIERS(1945); DEADLINE FOR
MURDER(1946)
Louise Vincent
SPARTACUS(1960); LUDWIG(1973, Ital./Ger./Fr.); CHANEL SOLITAIRE(1981)
Maria Vincent
PRICE OF FLESH, THE(1962, Fr.); THERE IS STILL ROOM IN HELL(1963, Ger.)
May Vincent
NIGHT IS OURS(1930, Fr.)
Meredith Vincent
OUT OF TOWNERS, THE(1970)
Michael Vincent
JOURNEY TO SHILOH(1968)
Mike Vincent
NORSEMAN, THE(1978)
Mildred Vincent
UP THE RIVER(1930)
Millard Vincent
I AM NOT AFRAID(1939); TORCHY RUNS FOR MAYOR(1939); OUT WEST WITH
THE PEPPERS(1940)
Pamela Vincent
TAKE ALL OF ME(1978, Ital.)
Patrick Vincent
DEADLY TRAP, THE(1972, Fr./Ital.)
Paul Vincent
SCREAM BLOODY MURDER(1972); ARTHUR(1981)
Misc. Talkies
WILLIE AND SCRATCH(1975)
Robbie Vincent
SOMEWHERE IN ENGLAND(1940, Brit.); SOMEWHERE IN CAMP(1942, Brit.);
SOMEWHERE ON LEAVE(1942, Brit.); HAPPIDROME(1943, Brit.)
Roger Vincent
CAGE OF NIGHTINGALES, A(1947, Fr.)
Romo Vincent
MUSIC FOR MADAME(1937); THIS WAY PLEASE(1937); TURN OFF THE
MOON(1937); START CHEERING(1938); LUXURY LINER(1948); SCENE OF THE
CRIME(1949); TOAST OF NEW ORLEANS, THE(1950); HURRICANE ISLAND(1951);
STARS AND STRIPES FOREVER(1952); CADDY, THE(1953); MONEY FROM HO-
ME(1953); NAKED JUNGLE, THE(1953); CASANOVA'S BIG NIGHT(1954); FEMALE
ON THE BEACH(1955); YOU'RE NEVER TOO YOUNG(1955); BLUEPRINT FOR
ROBBERY(1961); POCKETFUL OF MIRACLES(1961); COME BLOW YOUR
HORN(1963); LAW OF THE LAWLESS(1964); SERGEANT DEADHEAD(1965); WHEN
THE BOYS MEET THE GIRLS(1965); MISTER BUDDWING(1966); SWINGER,

THE(1966); WARNING SHOT(1967); YOUNG RUNAWAYS, THE(1968); ANGEL, ANGEL, DOWN WE GO(1969); WON TON TON, THE DOG WHO SAVED HOLLYWOOD(1976)

Ron Vincent
AMERICAN GRAFFITI(1973)

Russ Vincent
GILDA(1946); JOE PALOOKA, CHAMP(1946); APACHE ROSE(1947); HEADING FOR HEAVEN(1947); LAST ROUND-UP, THE(1947); SONG OF SCHEHERAZADE(1947); PRAIRIE, THE(1948); BLONDE ICE(1949); TWILIGHT IN THE SIERRAS(1950); CUBAN FIREBALL(1951)

Russel Vincent
THAT TENDER TOUCH(1969), p,d&w

Sailor Vincent
MAN I LOVE, THE(1929); SPEAKEASY(1929); BOWERY, THE(1933); PERSONALITY KID, THE(1934); FOLIES DERGERE(1935); IRISH IN US, THE(1935); SWING TIME(1936); SHADOW OF THE THIN MAN(1941); YANKEE DOODLE DANDY(1942); WHIPLASH(1948); MADAME BOVARY(1949); ESCAPE FROM RED ROCK(1958); ADVANCE TO THE REAR(1964); YOUNG FURY(1965)

"Sailor" Vincent
DESTINATION TOKYO(1944)

Stan Vincent
FOREPLAY(1975), m

Steve Vincent
MANTIS IN LACE(1968); GOLDEN BOX, THE(1970); WILD RIDERS(1971); LOOKIN' TO GET OUT(1982)
Misc. Talkies
ALL MEN ARE APES(1965); DANDY(1973)

Virginia Vincent
TAXI(1953); I WANT TO LIVE!(1958); RETURN OF DRACULA, THE(1958); HELEN MORGAN STORY, THE(1959); NEVER STEAL ANYTHING SMALL(1959); LOVE WITH THE PROPER STRANGER(1963); NAVAJO RUN(1966); TONY ROME(1967); SWEET NOVEMBER(1968); CHANGE OF HABIT(1969); RABBIT, RUN(1970); $1,000,000 DUCK(1971); TREASURE OF MATECUMBE(1976); HILLS HAVE EYES, THE(1978); AMY(1981)

William Vincent
HOT ROD(1950); LET'S GO NAVY(1951)

William "Sailor Billy" Vincent
WOMAN TRAP(1929)

Yves Vincent
ANATOMY OF A MARRIAGE(MY DAYS WITH JEAN-MARC AND MY NIGHTS WITH FRANCOISE)**1/2 (1964 Fr.); NAKED WOMAN, THE(1950, Fr.); BABETTE GOES TO WAR(1960, Fr.); MURIEL(1963, Fr./Ital.)

Zachary Vincent
RETURN, THE(1980)

Larry Vincente
KILL, THE(1968)

Roy Vincente
MONSTER OF HIGHGATE PONDS, THE(1961, Brit.)

Paul Vincenti
VEILED WOMAN, THE(1929)

Luciana Vincenzi
SEVEN SLAVES AGAINST THE WORLD(1965, Ital.); OPIATE '67(1967, Fr./Ital.); COBRA, THE(1968); JOHNNY BANCO(1969, Fr./Ital./Ger.)

Luciano Vincenzoni
GREAT WAR, THE(1961, Fr., Ital.), w; BEST OF ENEMIES, THE(1962), w; HUNCHBACK OF ROME, THE(1963, Ital.), w; DUEL OF CHAMPIONS(1964 Ital./Span.), w; REVOLT OF THE MERCENARIES(1964, Ital./Span.), w; RAILROAD MAN, THE(1965, Ital.), w; FOR A FEW DOLLARS MORE(1967, Ital./Ger./Span.), w; GOOD, THE BAD, AND THE UGLY, THE(1967, Ital./Span.), w; ROVER, THE(1967, Ital.), w; GIRL GAME(1968, Braz./Fr./Ital.), w; DEATH RIDES A HORSE(1969, Ital.), w; MERCENARY, THE(1970, Ital./Span.), w; QUIET PLACE IN THE COUNTRY, A(1970, Ital./Fr.), w; THREE TOUGH GUYS(1974, U.S./Ital.), w; ORCA(1977), p, w

Carlo Vinci
MAN CALLED FLINTSTONE, THE(1966), anim

Jean Vinci
DON JUAN(1956, Aust.); HEAT OF MIDNIGHT(1966, Fr.)

Herman Vinck
1984
QUESTION OF SILENCE(1984, Neth.)

Ivo Vinco
LA BOHEME(1965, Ital.)

Ernest Vincze
ROSELAND(1977), ph; WINSTANLEY(1979, Brit.), ph
1984
SCRUBBERS(1984, Brit.), ph

Ernst Vincze
JANE AUSTEN IN MANHATTAN(1980), ph

Imre Vincze
DIALOGUE(1967, Hung.), m

Billy Vine
LUCKY STIFF, THE(1949); VAGABOND KING, THE(1956)

Douglas Vine
FATAL HOUR, THE(1937, Brit.)

Harriet Vine
DARK INTRUDER(1965)

Harryette Vine
KEEP 'EM SLUGGING(1943)

John Vine
RICHARD'S THINGS(1981, Brit.); GANDHI(1982); EUREKA(1983, Brit.); KEEP, THE(1983)

Stanley Vine
MAN WHO CHANGED HIS NAME, THE(1934, Brit.); SONG OF THE FORGE(1937, Brit.)

William Vine
I ESCAPED FROM THE GESTAPO(1943)

Edward Viner
Silents
LITTLE LORD FAUNTLEROY(1914, Brit.); LURE OF LONDON, THE(1914, Brit.)

Michael Viner
THING WITH TWO HEADS, THE(1972); TOUCHED BY LOVE(1980), p; DANCE OF THE DWARFS(1983, U.S., Phil.), p, w

Margaret Vines
FRAIL WOMEN(1932, Brit.); OPEN ALL NIGHT(1934, Brit.); VICAR OF BRAY, THE(1937, Brit.); SARABAND(1949, Brit.)

William Vines
1984
WINDY CITY(1984)

Vinette
ROBBER SYMPHONY, THE(1937, Brit.)

I. R. Ving
Silents
DON'T GET PERSONAL(1922), w

Lee Ving
FLASHDANCE(1983); GET CRAZY(1983)
1984
STREETS OF FIRE(1984); WILD LIFE, THE(1984)

Nino Vingelli
WHERE THE HOT WIND BLOWS(1960, Fr., Ital.); CONJUGAL BED, THE(1963, Ital.); ITALIANO BRAVA GENTE(1965, Ital./USSR); DEATH RIDES A HORSE(1969, Ital.); BLACK BELLY OF THE TARANTULA, THE(1972, Ital.)

Marcos Vinicius
BYE-BYE BRASIL(1980, Braz.)

Marcus Vinicius
XICA(1982, Braz.)

Laurie Vining
THUNDER BAY(1953)

David Vinitskiy
LETTER THAT WAS NEVER SENT, THE(1962, USSR), art d; RESURRECTION(1963, USSR), art d; ITALIANO BRAVA GENTE(1965, Ital./USSR), art d

David Vinitskj
SUNFLOWER(1970, Fr./Ital.), art d

David Vinitsky
RED TENT, THE(1971, Ital./USSR), art d

Josef Vinklar
TRANSPORT FROM PARADISE(1967, Czech.); FIFTH HORSEMAN IS FEAR, THE(1968, Czech.)

Carter Vinnegar
LEARNING TREE, THE(1969)

P. Vinnik
SUMMER TO REMEMBER, A(1961, USSR); HOUSE ON THE FRONT LINE, THE(1963, USSR); RESURRECTION(1963, USSR); DUEL, THE(1964, USSR); THREE SISTERS, THE(1969, USSR)

P. Vinnikov
DESTINY OF A MAN(1961, USSR)

Valeriy Vinogradov
DAY THE WAR ENDED, THE(1961, USSR)

Vitya Vinogradov
RAINBOW, THE(1944, USSR)

B. Vinogradova
MAN OF MUSIC(1953, USSR)

M. Vinogradova
RESURRECTION(1963, USSR)

N. Vinogradova
MEET ME IN MOSCOW(1966, USSR)

A. Vinokurov
RESURRECTION(1963, USSR), spec eff

Yu. Vinokurova
SUN SHINES FOR ALL, THE(1961, USSR), w

Mother Vinot
Silents
KID, THE(1921)

Stephen Vinovich
MECHANIC, THE(1972)

Steve Vinovich
WEEKEND WITH THE BABYSITTER(1970); JENNIFER ON MY MIND(1971)

Gary Vinson
ROCKABILLY BABY(1957); YOUNG STRANGER, THE(1957); YELLOWSTONE KELLY(1959); HIGH SCHOOL CAESAR(1960); MAJORITY OF ONE, A(1961); MC HALE'S NAVY(1964); MC HALE'S NAVY JOINS THE AIR FORCE(1965); NOBODY'S PERFECT(1968)

Helen Vinson
IT'S A DEAL(1930); I AM A FUGITIVE FROM A CHAIN GANG(1932); JEWEL ROBBERY(1932); THE CRASH(1932); THEY CALL IT SIN(1932); TWO AGAINST THE WORLD(1932); GRAND SLAM(1933); KENNEL MURDER CASE, THE(1933); LAWYER MAN(1933); LITTLE GIANT, THE(1933); MIDNIGHT CLUB(1933); POWER AND THE GLORY, THE(1933); SECOND HAND WIFE(1933); AS HUSBANDS GO(1934); BROADWAY BILL(1934); CAPTAIN HATES THE SEA, THE(1934); GIFT OF GAB(1934); LET'S TRY AGAIN(1934); LIFE OF VERGIE WINTERS, THE(1934); AGE OF INDISCRETION(1935); NOTORIOUS GENTLEMAN, A(1935); PRIVATE WORLDS(1935); TRANSATLANTIC TUNNEL(1935, Brit.); WEDDING NIGHT, THE(1935); KING OF THE DAMNED(1936, Brit.); LOVE IN EXILE(1936, Brit.); REUNION(1936); LIVE, LOVE AND LEARN(1937); VOGUES OF 1938(1937); IN NAME ONLY(1939); BEYOND TOMORROW(1940); WELCOME HOME, SOLDIER BOYS(1972); BOWERY BOY(1940); CURTAIN CALL(1940); ENEMY AGENT(1940); MARRIED AND IN LOVE(1940); TORRID ZONE(1940); NOTHING BUT THE TRUTH(1941); ARE THESE OUR PARENTS?(1944); CHIP OFF THE OLD BLOCK(1944); LADY AND THE MONSTER, THE(1944); THIN MAN GOES HOME, THE(1944)

Robert Vinson
PIRANHA(1978)

Alan Vint
MC MASTERS, THE(1970); PANIC IN NEEDLE PARK(1971); TWO-LANE BLACKTOP(1971); UNHOLY ROLLERS(1972); WELCOME HOME, SOLDIER BOYS(1972); BADLANDS(1974); EARTHQUAKE(1974); MACON COUNTY LINE(1974); BREAKOUT(1975); CHECKERED FLAG OR CRASH(1978); LADY IN RED, THE(1979); BALLAD OF GREGORIO CORTEZ, THE(1983)

Bill Vint
SUMMERTREE(1971); OTHER SIDE OF THE MOUNTAIN, THE(1975); SIDEWIND-ER ONE(1977)
Jesse Vint
LITTLE BIG MAN(1970); SILENT RUNNING(1972); CHINATOWN(1974); EARTH-QUAKE(1974); MACON COUNTY LINE(1974); BUG(1975); BOBBIE JO AND THE OUTLAW(1976); TENDER FLESH(1976); BLACK OAK CONSPIRACY(1977), a, p, w; DEATHSPORT(1978); FAST CHARLIE... THE MOONBEAM RIDER(1979); HOME-TOWN U.S.A.(1979), p, w; FORBIDDEN WORLD(1982)
1984
DADDY'S DEADLY DARLING(1984); ON THE LINE(1984, Span.)
Jesse Vint III
HOMETOWN U.S.A.(1979)
William M. Vint
BALTIMORE BULLET, THE(1980)
Wyndham T. Vint
TRIAL OF MADAM X, THE(1948, Brit.), p
Gustav Vintas
1984
MICKI AND MAUDE(1984)
Ivor Vintnor
VARIETY PARADE(1936, Brit.)
Arthur Vinton
VIKING, THE(1931); HANDLE WITH CARE(1932); MAN AGAINST WOMAN(1932); WASHINGTON MERRY-GO-ROUND(1932); AVENGER, THE(1933); BLONDIE JOHN-SON(1933); CENTRAL AIRPORT(1933); GAMBLING SHIP(1933); HEROES FOR SALE(1933); LAUGHTER IN HELL(1933); LILLY TURNER(1933); MAN HUNT(1933); PICTURE SNATCHER(1933); SKYWAY(1933); SON OF A SAILOR(1933); THIS DAY AND AGE(1933); WHEN STRANGERS MARRY(1933); CROSS COUNTRY CRUI-SE(1934); DAMES(1934); GAMBLING LADY(1934); JEALOUSY(1934); MAN TRAIL-ER, THE(1934); PERSONALITY KID, THE(1934); STAND UP AND CHEER(1934 80m FOX bw); VERY HONORABLE GUY, A(1934); CIRCUMSTANTIAL EVIDENCE(1935); KING SOLOMON OF BROADWAY(1935); LITTLE BIG SHOT(1935); RED SALU-TE(1935); RENDEZVOUS AT MIDNIGHT(1935); UNKNOWN WOMAN(1935)
Misc. Talkies
MAN TRAILER, THE(1934)
Bobby Vinton
SURF PARTY(1964); BIG JAKE(1971); TRAIN ROBBERS, THE(1973)
Horace Vinton
Misc. Silents
OTHER GIRL, THE(1916); NIGHT IN NEW ARABIA, A(1917)
Victoria Vinton
MADAME DU BARRY(1934); ST. LOUIS KID, THE(1934); CHEYENNE TOR-NADO(1935); AMBUSH VALLEY(1936); BULLETS OR BALLOTS(1936); POLO JO-E(1936); SINGING BUCKAROO, THE(1937); HOUSE ACROSS THE BAY, THE(1940)
Misc. Talkies
VENGEANCE OF RANNAH(1936)
Ivor Vintor
Silents
ARCADIANS, THE(1927, Brit.)
F.A. Vinyals
TROUBLE IN THE GLEN(1954, Brit.)
I. Vinyar-Kagur
Misc. Silents
MABUL(1927, USSR)
Viola
BULLDOG DRUMMOND(1929), ed
Al Viola
SOME CAME RUNNING(1959); CRY OF THE PENGUINS(1972, Brit.), d; THIE-VES(1977), d
Albert T. Viola
PREACHERMAN(1971), p&d, w; NIGHT THEY ROBBED BIG BERTHA'S, THE(1975), w
Misc. Talkies
INTERPLAY(1970), d; PREACHERMAN MEETS WIDDERWOMAN(1973), d
Cesare G. Viola
LITTLE MARTYR, THE(1947, Ital.), w
Cesare Giulio Viola
SHOE SHINE(1947, Ital.), w
Cesare Viola
LAUGH PAGLIACCI(1948, Ital.), w
Gail Viola
HAPPY HOOKER GOES TO WASHINGTON, THE(1977), cos
1984
STONE BOY, THE(1984), cos
Jeff Viola
STRIPES(1981)
Joe Viola
ANGELS HARD AS THEY COME(1971), d, w; HOT BOX, THE(1972, U.S./Phil.), d, w; RENEGADE GIRLS(1974)
Joseph Viola
BLACK MAMA, WHITE MAMA(1973), w
Viola Brothers Shore
HUSBAND'S HOLIDAY(1931), w; CHICKEN WAGON FAMILY(1939), w
E.E. Violet
Misc. Silents
DANGER LINE, THE(1924), d
Edouard Violet
Misc. Silents
FANTAISIE DE MILLARDAIRE(1919, Fr.), d; L'ACCUSATEUR(1920, Fr.), d; LES MAINS FLETRIES(1920, Fr.), d; LI-HANG LE CRUEL(1920, Fr.), d; PAPILLON(1920, Fr.), d; L'EPINGLE ROUGE(1921, Fr.), d; LA RUSE(1922, Fr.), d; LA BATAILLE(1923, Fr.), d; LE ROI DE CIRQUE(1925, Fr.), d
Louise Violet
GIRL GRABBERS, THE(1968); EVENTS(1970)
Mme. Violet
Silents
SUZANNA(1922), cos

Ultra Violet
MAIDSTONE(1970); PHYNX, THE(1970); SIMON, KING OF THE WITCHES(1971); TAKING OFF(1971); SAVAGES(1972); UNMARRIED WOMAN, AN(1978)
Violetta the Donkey
NEVER TAKE NO FOR AN ANSWER(1952, Brit./Ital.)
Joy Violette
SIN OF MONA KENT, THE(1961)
Mina Violetto
Misc. Silents
TOILER, THE(1932, Ital.)
Alexander Violmov
NO GREATER LOVE(1944, USSR)
Cesare Viori
ROMAN HOLIDAY(1953)
Jacques Viot
DAYBREAK(1940, Fr.), w; PORTRAIT OF A WOMAN(1946, Fr.), w; LONG NIGHT, THE(1947), w; BLACK ORPHEUS(1959 Fr./Ital./Braz.), w; BACK STREETS OF PA-RIS(1962, Fr.), w; DRAGON SKY(1964, Fr.), w
G. Vipin
TWELFTH NIGHT(1956, USSR)
Neil Vipond
HARD PART BEGINS, THE(1973, Can.); PHOBIA(1980, Can.); PARADISE(1982)
1984
KINGS AND DESPERATE MEN(1984, Brit.)
Fiddle Viracola
EASY MONEY(1983)
A. Virago
DARK RED ROSES(1930, Brit.), ph
Fred Viray
SECRET OF THE SACRED FOREST, THE(1970)
Robert Virchall
BUCKTOWN(1975), ph
Louis Viret
PLEASURES AND VICES(1962, Fr.); SUCKER, THE(1966, Fr./Ital.)
Hellmuch, Virgien & Friends
NINE TO FIVE(1980), anim
Helen Virgil
GOOD NEWS(1930)
Jack Virgil
GAY BRIDE, THE(1934), m; STUDENT TOUR(1934), md
Elisabetta Virgili
GREAT ADVENTURE, THE(1976, Span./Ital.)
Virginia
Silents
NET, THE(1923), w
Harriet Virginia
Silents
ADVENTUROUS SOUL, THE(1927), sup; AIR MAIL PILOT, THE(1928), w
Virginie
CHEATERS, THE(1961, Fr.), cos
Yossi Virginsky
1984
AMBASSADOR, THE(1984)
Peter Virgo
TWO SMART PEOPLE(1946); BODY AND SOUL(1947); BRUTE FORCE(1947); ARCH OF TRIUMPH(1948); LOVES OF CARMEN, THE(1948); SMART WOMAN(1948); SONG IS BORN, A(1948); TO THE ENDS OF THE EARTH(1948); KNOCK ON ANY DOOR(1949); UNDERCOVER MAN, THE(1949); WE WERE STRANGERS(1949); WITHOUT HONOR(1949); CONVICTED(1950); KILLER THAT STALKED NEW YORK, THE(1950); SHAKEDOWN(1950); HARLEM GLOBETROTTERS, THE(1951); MOB, THE(1951); SATURDAY'S HERO(1951); HAREM GIRL(1952); MY SIX CON-VICTS(1952); NARROW MARGIN, THE(1952); SAN FRANCISCO STORY, THE(1952); SCANDAL SHEET(1952)
Peter Virgo, Jr.
EXPLOSIVE GENERATION, THE(1961); FEAR NO MORE(1961); WHATEVER HAPPENED TO BABY JANE?(1962); JOHNNY GOT HIS GUN(1971)
Peter Virgo, Sr.
EXPLOSIVE GENERATION, THE(1961)
Herb Virgran
GOOD MORNING, MISS DOVE(1955)
Renaldo Viri
SNIPER, THE(1952)
Henri Virjoleux
MADWOMAN OF CHAILLOT, THE(1969)
Dennis Virkler
CHOSEN SURVIVORS(1974 U.S.-Mex.), ed; XANADU(1980), ed; CONTINENTAL DIVIDE(1981), ed; AIRPLANE II: THE SEQUEL(1982), ed; GORKY PARK(1983), ed; INDEPENDENCE DAY(1983), ed
1984
RIVER RAT, THE(1984), ed
Henri Virlogeux
LOVERS ON A TIGHTROPE(1962, Fr.); DAY AND THE HOUR, THE(1963, Fr./Ital.); VICE AND VIRTUE(1965, Fr./Ital.); SUCKER, THE(1966, Fr./Ital.); LIGHT YEARS AWAY(1982, Fr./Switz.)
Henri Virlojeux
FOUR HUNDRED BLOWS, THE(1959); SEVEN CAPITAL SINS(1962, Fr./Ital.); ANY NUMBER CAN WIN(1963 Fr.); FRIEND OF THE FAMILY(1965, Fr./Ital.); WOMEN AND WAR(1965, Fr.); SHADOW OF EVIL(1967, Fr./Ital.)
Gami Virray
SECRET OF THE SACRED FOREST, THE(1970)
Solomon Virsaladze
HAMLET(1966, USSR), cos
Tom Virtue
TEX(1982)
A. Virubov
Misc. Silents
FLOOD(1915, USSR); WANDERER BEYOND THE GRAVE(1915, USSR)

Eleanor Virzie
ROAD DEMON(1938)

M. Virzinskaya
AMPHIBIOUS MAN, THE(1961, USSR)

Eleanor Virzle
WINNER TAKE ALL(1939)

Michael Visaroff
DISRAELI(1929); FOUR DEVILS(1929); ILLUSION(1929); MOROCCO(1930); ARIZONA TERROR(1931); DRACULA(1931); MATA HARI(1931); FREAKS(1932); MAN WHO PLAYED GOD, THE(1932); KING OF THE ARENA(1933); STRANGE PEOPLE(1933); CAT'S PAW, THE(1934); FUGITIVE ROAD(1934); MERRY FRINKS, THE(1934); PICTURE BRIDES(1934); VIVA VILLA!(1934); MARINES ARE COMING, THE(1935); MARK OF THE VAMPIRE(1935); ONE MORE SPRING(1935); GAY DESPERADO, THE(1936); CHAMPAGNE WALTZ(1937); SOLDIER AND THE LADY, THE(1937); AIR DEVILS(1938); SUEZ(1938); TROPIC HOLIDAY(1938); EVERYTHING HAPPENS AT NIGHT(1939); FLYING DEUCES, THE(1939); MIDNIGHT(1939); PARIS HONEYMOON(1939); CHARLIE CHAN AT THE WAX MUSEUM(1940); FOUR SONS(1940); MAD EMPRESS, THE(1940); SECOND CHORUS(1940); SON OF MONTE CRISTO(1940); NEVER GIVE A SUCKER AN EVEN BREAK(1941); INVISIBLE AGENT(1942); PACIFIC RENDEZVOUS(1942); REUNION IN FRANCE(1942); WOMAN OF THE YEAR(1942); FOR WHOM THE BELL TOLLS(1943); HOSTAGES(1943); MADAME CURIE(1943); MISSION TO MOSCOW(1943); PARIS AFTER DARK(1943); EXPERIMENT PERILOUS(1944); IN OUR TIME(1944); MASK OF DIMITRIOS, THE(1944); DAKOTA(1945); OUT OF THIS WORLD(1945); ROYAL SCANDAL, A(1945); SONG TO REMEMBER, A(1945); YOLANDA AND THE THIEF(1945); DON RICARDO RETURNS(1946); FLIGHT TO NOWHERE(1946); DESPERATE(1947); INTRIGUE(1947); NORTHWEST OUTPOST(1947); MACAO(1952)
Silents
CAMILLE(1927); SUNSET DERBY, THE(1927); ADVENTURER, THE(1928); LAST COMMAND, THE(1928); RAMONA(1928); TEMPEST(1928); EXALTED FLAPPER, THE(1929)
Misc. Silents
PARIS(1926)

Michael S. Visaroff
WAGON WHEELS(1934); WE LIVE AGAIN(1934); ESCAPADE(1935); MAN ON THE FLYING TRAPEZE, THE(1935); PADDY O'DAY(1935); SYLVIA SCARLETT(1936); ANGEL(1937); ESPIONAGE(1937); LANCER SPY(1937)

Nina Visaroff
PADDY O'DAY(1935)

Natalie Visart
MADAME SATAN(1930); PLAINSMAN, THE(1937), cos; UNION PACIFIC(1939), cos; NORTHWEST MOUNTED POLICE(1940), cos; MEET JOHN DOE(1941), cos; LADY OF BURLESQUE(1943), cos; STORY OF DR. WASSELL, THE(1944), cos; STRANGE WOMAN, THE(1946), cos

Blanca Vischer
WITHOUT RESERVATIONS(1946); WILD GOLD(1934); UNDER THE PAMPAS MOON(1935); MESSAGE TO GARCIA, A(1936); STRIKE ME PINK(1936); SWING TIME(1936); DAUGHTER OF SHANGHAI(1937); TROPIC HOLIDAY(1938); YOU AND ME(1938); GHOST BREAKERS, THE(1940); TYCOON(1947); FURY OF THE CONGO(1951)

Tony Viscont
BREAKING GLASS(1980, Brit.), m

Eriprando Visconti
LADY OF MONZA, THE(1970, Ital.), d, w

Luchino Visconti
LA TERRA TREMA(1947, Ital.), a, d&w; BELLISSIMA(1952, Ital.), d; OSSESSIONE(1959, Ital.), d; ROCCO AND HIS BROTHERS(1961, Fr./Ital.), d, w; WHITE NIGHTS(1961, Ital./Fr.), d, w; BOCCACCIO '70(1962/Ital./Fr.), d, w; LEOPARD, THE(1963, Ital.), d, w; SANDRA(1966, Ital.), d, w; STRANGER, THE(1967, Algeria/Fr./Ital.), d, w; SENSO(1968, Ital.), d, w; WITCHES, THE(1969, Fr./Ital.), d; DEATH IN VENICE(1971, Ital./Fr.), p&d, w; LUDWIG(1973, Ital./Ger./Fr.), d&w; CONVERSATION PIECE(1976, Ital., Fr.), d, w; INNOCENT, THE(1979, Ital.), d, w

Luigi Visconti
THIEF OF BAGHDAD, THE(1961, Ital./Fr.); ROMMEL'S TREASURE(1962, Ital.); SON OF THE RED CORSAIR(1963, Ital.); TORPEDO BAY(1964, Ital./Fr.)

Marco Visconti
FROM A ROMAN BALCONY(1961, Fr./Ital.), w

Vera Visconti
FAMILY HONOR(1973)

Michael Viscroff
CHINATOWN AFTER DARK(1931)

Sal Viscuso
WORLD'S GREATEST LOVER, THE(1977); FATSO(1980); MAX DUGAN RETURNS(1983)

Sheila Viseltear
WOMAN UNDER THE INFLUENCE, A(1974), ed

Shlomo Vishinsky
FLYING MATCHMAKER, THE(1970, Israel); OPERATION THUNDERBOLT(1978, ISRAEL)

Sofia Vishnevetskaya
OPTIMISTIC TRAGEDY, THE(1964, USSR), w

Galina Vishnevskaya
KATERINA IZMAILOVA(1969, USSR)

N. Vishnyak
Misc. Silents
IN THE WHIRLWIND OF REVOLUTION(1922, USSR)

Robert Viskin
DR. TARR'S TORTURE DUNGEON(1972, Mex.), p

Roberto Viskin
EL TOPO(1971, Mex.), p

Vyacheslav Viskovksy
Misc. Silents
WOMAN WHO INVENTED LOVE, THE(1918, USSR), d

Vyacheslav Viskovsky
Misc. Silents
HIS EYES(1916, USSR), d; NINTH OF JANUARY(1925, USSR), d

Ye. Vislotskaya
SONG OF THE FOREST(1963, USSR), ch

Vsevolod Vitaliyevich Visnevskiy
OPTIMISTIC TRAGEDY, THE(1964, USSR), w

Juraj Visny
WHO KILLED JESSIE?(1965, Czech.)

Antonio Visone
CENTURION, THE(1962, Fr./Ital.), spec eff; LIGHTNING BOLT(1967, Ital./Sp.), art d; YOUNG, THE EVIL AND THE SAVAGE, THE(1968, Ital.), art d; NEW BARBARIANS, THE(1983, Ital.), prod d
1984
WARRIORS OF THE WASTELAND(1984, Ital.), prod d

Mikhail Visotsky
TARAS FAMILY, THE(1946, USSR)

Gino Vissentini
BELL' ANTONIO(1962, Ital.), w

Lucie Visser
TIME TO DIE, A(1983)

Charles Vissiere
LE PLAISIR(1954, Fr.)

Charles Vissieres
DEVIL IN THE FLESH, THE(1949, Fr.); LITTLE WORLD OF DON CAMILLO, THE(1953, Fr./Ital.)

William Visteen
CLASS(1983)

Agatha Visviki
1984
BLIND DATE(1984)

N. Viswanathan
KANCHENJUNGHA(1966, India)

Norbert Viszlay
FIXER, THE(1968)

Adriano Vita
SEVEN SLAVES AGAINST THE WORLD(1965, Ital.)

Alfio Vita
BOCCACCIO '70(1962/Ital./Fr.)

Helen Vita
ROSEMARY(1960, Ger.); CABARET(1972); DREAM TOWN(1973, Ger.); LILI MARLEEN(1981, Ger.)

Johnny Vita
HEY, GOOD LOOKIN'(1982), art d

Monique Vita
ROAD TO SHAME, THE(1962, Fr.); BEBO'S GIRL(1964, Ital.)

Perlo Vita [Jules Dassin]
RIFIFI(1956, Fr.); PROMISE AT DAWN(1970, U.S./Fr.)

Joe Vitagliano
DOZENS, THE(1981), ph

Vital
DOUBLE CRIME IN THE MAGINOT LINE(1939, Fr.)

Gaby Vital
TOMB OF TORTURE(1966, Ital.), ed

Geymond Vital
DOCTEUR LAENNEC(1949, Fr.); DIARY OF A CHAMBERMAID(1964, Fr./Ital.)
Misc. Silents
GARDIENS DE PHARE(1929, Fr.)

Jean-Jacques Vital
SPUTNIK(1960, Fr.), w; STORY OF THE COUNT OF MONTE CRISTO, THE(1962, Fr./Ital.), p; POSTMAN GOES TO WAR, THE(1968, Fr.), p

Adriano Vitale
MINOTAUR, THE(1961, Ital.), ch; PHAROAH'S WOMAN, THE(1961, Ital.), ch; SEVEN SEAS TO CALAIS(1963, Ital.); QUEEN OF THE NILE(1964, Ital.); BETTER A WIDOW(1969, Ital.)

Anthony Vitale
NORSEMAN, THE(1978)

Enzo Vitale
SEVEN BEAUTIES(1976, Ital.)

Frank Vitale
JOE(1970); BATTLE OF LOVE'S RETURN, THE(1971), p, ph; MONTREAL MAIN(1974, Can.), a, p, d, ed; RUBBER GUN, THE(1977, Can.), ph

Joe Vitale
STOP, YOU'RE KILLING ME(1952); NEW YORK CONFIDENTIAL(1955); RACERS, THE(1955); HONG KONG CONFIDENTIAL(1958); ALIAS JESSE JAMES(1959)

John Vitale
NO RETURN ADDRESS(1961)

Joseph Vitale
DAYS OF GLORY(1944); FALCON IN MEXICO, THE(1944); GILDERSLEEVE'S GHOST(1944); NONE BUT THE LONELY HEART(1944); PASSPORT TO DESTINY(1944); SHOW BUSINESS(1944); ZOMBIES ON BROADWAY(1945); LADY LUCK(1946); DANGEROUS YEARS(1947); ROAD TO RIO(1947); WHERE THERE'S LIFE(1947); PALEFACE, THE(1948); CONNECTICUT YANKEE IN KING ARTHUR'S COURT, A(1949); ILLEGAL ENTRY(1949); LOST TRIBE, THE(1949); RED, HOT AND BLUE(1949); FANCY PANTS(1950); MY FRIEND IRMA GOES WEST(1950); MR. IMPERIUM(1951); MY FAVORITE SPY(1951); YANKEE BUCCANEER(1952); STRANGER WORE A GUN, THE(1953); BULLET FOR JOEY, A(1955); SQUARE JUNGLE, THE(1955); RUMBLE ON THE DOCKS(1956); SERENADE(1956); DEERSLAYER, THE(1957); WILD IS THE WIND(1957); WHO'S GOT THE ACTION?(1962)

Joseph A. Vitale
APACHE RIFLES(1964)

Mario Vitale
STROMBOLI(1950, Ital.)

Millie Vitale
GUTS IN THE SUN(1959, Fr.); CHECKERBOARD(1969, Fr.)

Milly Vitale
DIFFICULT YEARS(1950, Ital.); BURIED ALIVE(1951, Ital.); JUGGLER, THE(1953); MATA HARI'S DAUGHTER(1954, Fr./Ital.); RASPOUTINE(1954, Fr.); SEVEN LITTLE FOYS, THE(1955); WAR AND PEACE(1956, Ital./U.S.); FLESH IS WEAK, THE(1957, Brit.); BREATH OF SCANDAL, A(1960); HANNIBAL(1960, Ital.); MISSILE FROM HELL(1960, Brit.)

Sam Vitale
WHEN A STRANGER CALLS(1979), ed

1984
HADLEY'S REBELLION(1984), ed
Alvaro Vitali
ROMA(1972, Ital./Fr.); AMARCORD(1974, Ital.)
Keith Vitali
REVENGE OF THE NINJA(1983)
Leon Vitali
BARRY LYNDON(1975, Brit.); VICTOR FRANKENSTEIN(1975, Swed./Ireland)
Nadia Vitali
TIKO AND THE SHARK(1966, U.S./Ital./Fr.), cos
Piccini Vitali
MATA HARI'S DAUGHTER(1954, Fr./Ital), w
Alberico Vitalini
EAST OF KILIMANJARO(1962, Brit./Ital.), m
Alberto Vitalini
HEAVEN ON EARTH(1960, Ital./U.S.), m
Georges Vitaly
NIGHT ENCOUNTER(1963, Fr./Ital.)
A.G. Vitanza
HIGH-POWERED RIFLE, THE(1960)
Vitaphone
Silents
LILAC TIME(1928), s eff
Vitaphone Orchestra
DARK STREETS(1929), m
Eddie Vitch
GOOD BEGINNING, THE(1953, Brit.)
N.M. Viteftof
HOUSE OF DEATH(1932, USSR)
Berta Vitek
HIPPODROME(1961, Aust./Ger.)
K. Vitek
LEMONADE JOE(1966, Czech.)
Lorelei Vitek
THERE'S ALWAYS TOMORROW(1956); STUDS LONIGAN(1960)
Loreli Vitek
WOMAN'S SECRET, A(1949)
Sel Vitella
KING OF COMEDY, THE(1983)
Stella Vitelleschi
BEN HUR(1959); NAKED MAJA, THE(1959, Ital./U.S.); COME SEPTEMBER(1961)
Art Vitello
RAGGEDY ANN AND ANDY(1977), anim
Arthur Vitello
WIZARDS(1977), anim
Patricia Viterbo
YOU MUST BE JOKING!(1965, Brit.); HELL IS EMPTY(1967, Brit./Ital); TWO FOR THE ROAD(1967, Brit.)
Antoine Vitez
LA GUERRE EST FINIE(1967, Fr./Swed.); CONFESSION, THE(1970, Fr.); MY NIGHT AT MAUD'S(1970, Fr.); GREEN ROOM, THE(1979, Fr.)
Miklos Vitez
MISS PRESIDENT(1935, Hung.), w
Dolores Vitina
ER LOVE A STRANGER(1958)
Hana Vitkova
END OF AUGUST AT THE HOTEL OZONE, THE(1967, Czech.)
Viktor Vitkovich
DAY THE EARTH FROZE, THE(1959, Fin./USSR), w
Fernanda Vitobello
CATCH-22(1970)
Famie Kaufman Vitola
LOS PLATILLOS VOLADORES(1955, Mex.)
Michel Vitold
MESSALINE(1952, Fr./Ital.); AFFAIRS OF MESSALINA, THE(1954, Ital.); ADORABLE LIAR(1962, Fr.); RIFIFI IN TOKYO(1963, Fr./Ital.); JUDEX(1966, Fr./Ital.); CONFESSION, THE(1970, Fr.); LA NUIT DE VARENNES(1983, Fr./Ital.)
1984
BASILEUS QUARTET(1984, Ital.)
Beatrice Vitoldi
Silents
BATTLESHIP POTEMKIN, THE(1925, USSR)
Frank X. Vitolo
FAME(1980)
Rocco Vitolozzi
GOLIATH AND THE VAMPIRES(1964, Ital.)
Emmanuil Vitorgan
STAR INSPECTOR, THE(1980, USSR)
Sasha Vitoslavskiy
VIOLIN AND ROLLER(1962, USSR)
Alexander Vitov
FATHERS AND SONS(1960, USSR), w
Hana Vitova
MERRY WIVES, THE(1940, Czech.)
Jean-Louis Vitrac
DIVA(1982, Fr.)
Roger Vitrac
MASK OF KOREA(1950, Fr.), w
Lionel Vitrant
BORSALINO(1970, Fr.); OUTSIDE MAN, THE(1973, U.S./FR.)
Georges Vitray
MONSIEUR VINCENT(1949, Fr.); LE PLAISIR(1954, Fr.)
Anna Vitre
CROSS COUNTRY(1983, Can.)
Jacques Vitry
DOUBLE CRIME IN THE MAGINOT LINE(1939, Fr.)
G. Vitsin
DON QUIXOTE(1961, USSR)

Georgiy Vitsin
MARRIAGE OF BALZAMINOV, THE(1966, USSR)
Gueorgui Vitsine
THREE TALES OF CHEKHOV(1961, USSR)
Ray Vitte
UP IN SMOKE(1978); CARWASH(1976); THANK GOD IT'S FRIDAY(1978); FORCE OF ONE, A(1979); HEART BEAT(1979); NINE TO FIVE(1980)
Lou Vittes
HERE COME THE JETS(1959), w; REBEL SET, THE(1959), w
Louis Vittes
BENGAZI(1955), w; PAWNEE(1957), w; GANG WAR(1958), w; I MARRIED A MONSTER FROM OUTER SPACE(1958), w; MONSTER FROM THE GREEN HELL(1958), w; SHOWDOWN AT BOOT HILL(1958), w; VILLA!(1958), w; OREGON TRAIL, THE(1959), w; EYES OF ANNIE JONES, THE(1963, Brit.), w
Monica Vitti
L'AVVENTURA(1960, Ital.); LA NOTTE(1961, Fr./Ital.); ECLIPSE(1962, Fr./Ital.); THREE FABLES OF LOVE(1963, Fr./Ital./Span.); FLYING SAUCER, THE(1964, Ital.); NUTTY, NAUGHTY CHATEAU(1964, Fr./Ital.); SWEET AND SOUR(1964, Fr./Ital.); BAMBOLE!(1965, Ital.); RED DESERT(1965, Fr./Ital.); MODESTY BLAISE(1966, Brit.); CHASTITY BELT, THE(1968, Ital.); GIRL WITH A PISTOL, THE(1968, Ital.); QUEENS, THE(1968, Ital./Fr.); MOTIVE WAS JEALOUSY, THE(1970 Ital./Span.); PIZZA TRIANGLE, THE(1970, Ital./Span.); PHANTOM OF LIBERTY, THE(1974, Fr.); MIDNIGHT PLEASURES(1975, Ital.); DUCH IN ORANGE SAUCE(1976, Ital.); ALMOST PERFECT AFFAIR, AN(1979); IMMORTAL BACHELOR, THE(1980, Ital.)
Ralph Vitti [Michael Dante]
SOMEBODY UP THERE LIKES ME(1956); RAINTREE COUNTY(1957)
Luciano Vittori
CAT O'NINE TAILS(1971, Ital./Ger./Fr.), spec eff
Vittorio Vittori
HAWKS AND THE SPARROWS, THE(1967, Ital.); FELLINI SATYRICON(1969, Fr./Ital.)
Vittoria
CHILDREN OF CHANCE(1949, Brit.)
George Vitzin
BLUE BIRD, THE(1976)
Carlos Viudes
WEB OF VIOLENCE(1966, Ital./Span.), art d
Viva
LONESOME COWBOYS(1968); LIONS LOVE(1969); MIDNIGHT COWBOY(1969); CISCO PIKE(1971); SAM'S SONG(1971); PLAY IT AGAIN, SAM(1972); CIAO MANHATTAN(1973); FLASH GORDON(1980); FORBIDDEN ZONE(1980); FOR YOUR EYES ONLY(1981)
Vivaldi
ALLEGRO NON TROPPO(1977, Ital.), m
Antonio Vivaldi
LES ENFANTS TERRIBLES(1952, Fr.), m; GOLDEN COACH, THE(1953, Fr./Ital.), m; CAT IN THE SACK, THE(1967, Can.), m; PIERROT LE FOU(1968, Fr./Ital.), m; WILD CHILD, THE(1970, Fr.), m; KRAMER VS. KRAMER(1979), m; FOUR SEASONS, THE(1981), m; LONG SHOT(1981, Brit.), m
Giana Vivaldi
KILL BABY KILL(1966, Ital.)
Laura Vivaldi
LIPSTICK(1965, Fr./Ital.)
Dominique Vivant
LOVERS, THE(1959, Fr.), w
Eva Vivar
ONCE BEFORE I DIE(1967, U.S./Phil.)
L. Viven
MEN OF THE SEA(1938, USSR)
Jean-Pierre Vivet
MIDNIGHT MEETING(1962, Fr.), w
L. Vivet
JULIE THE REDHEAD(1963, Fr.)
Vivi
LAST PARADE, THE(1931)
April Vivian
KENTUCKY MINSTRELS(1934, Brit.); BREAKERS AHEAD(1935, Brit.); VARIETY(1935, Brit.)
Bette Vivian
INTRUDER, THE(1955, Brit.); OH! WHAT A LOVELY WAR(1969, Brit.)
Jack Vivian
DEAD MEN TELL NO TALES(1939, Brit.)
James Vivian
UNDERCOVER AGENT(1935, Brit.)
Monique Vivian
PALACE OF NUDES(1961, Fr./Ital.)
Percival Vivian
KNICKERBOCKER HOLIDAY(1944); KITTY(1945); LETTER FOR EVIE, A(1945); WOMAN IN GREEN, THE(1945); SUSIE STEPS OUT(1946); DOUBLE LIFE, A(1947); KISS IN THE DARK, A(1949); HOLD THAT LINE(1952); PRINCE VALIANT(1954); DADDY LONG LEGS(1955); PRINCE OF PLAYERS(1955); SPIRIT OF ST. LOUIS, THE(1957)
Robert Vivian
BACK DOOR TO HEAVEN(1939)
Silents
CAPRICE OF THE MOUNTAINS(1916); ARGYLE CASE, THE(1917); LAW OF THE LAND, THE(1917); MAN HATER, THE(1917); JACK SPURLOCK, PRODIGAL(1918); OUT OF A CLEAR SKY(1918); COUNTERFEIT(1919)
Misc. Silents
WAR BRIDE'S SECRET, THE(1916)
Ruth Vivian
MAN WHO CAME TO DINNER, THE(1942); LETTER TO THREE WIVES, A(1948)
Sidney Vivian
WHISPERING SMITH VERSUS SCOTLAND YARD(1952, Brit.); DOUBLE CONFESSION(1953, Brit.); LADY GODIVA RIDES AGAIN(1955, Brit.); KEY, THE(1958, Brit.); STRANGE AFFECTION(1959, Brit.); MARY HAD A LITTLE(1961, Brit.); KILL OR CURE(1962, Brit.); DAY OF THE TRIFFIDS, THE(1963); SUBTERFUGE(1969, US/Brit.)

Sydney Vivian
DICK BARTON STRIKES BACK(1949, Brit.); GREAT GAME, THE(1953, Brit.); SECRET PARTNER, THE(1961, Brit.); HIDE AND SEEK(1964, Brit.)

Percival Vivien
JOAN OF ARC(1948)

Diane Vivienne
MOONLIGHTING WIVES(1966)

Huguette Vivier
MURDERER LIVES AT NUMBER 21, THE(1947, Fr.)

Karl-Wilhelm Vivier
BRIDGE, THE(1961, Ger.), w

Linda Vivitello
CANNONBALL(1976, U.S./Hong Kong)

Lea Vivot
Misc. Talkies
ROAD OF DEATH(1977)

John Vivyan
WRONG MAN, THE(1956); IMITATION OF LIFE(1959); THREE ON A SPREE(1961, Brit.); TWO-WAY STRETCH(1961, Brit.); RIDER ON A DEAD HORSE(1962)

Harold Vizard
Silents
FLYING PAT(1920)

Juri Vizbor
RED TENT, THE(1971, Ital./USSR)

Leandro Vizcaino
SHAME OF THE SABINE WOMEN, THE(1962, Mex.)

Tom Vize
QUICK, BEFORE IT MELTS(1964)

Norm Vizents
STRANGER IN HOLLYWOOD(1968), ed

Gyorgy Vizi
BOYS OF PAUL STREET, THE(1969, Hung./US)

Stephen Vizinczey
IN PRAISE OF OLDER WOMEN(1978, Can.), w

Maria Rosa Vizzina
EMBALMER, THE(1966, Ital.)

Aris Vlachopoulos
NAKED BRIGADE, THE(1965, U.S./Gr.)

Anestis Vlachos
YOUNG APHRODITES(1966, Gr.); FEAR, THE(1967, Gr.)

Stefanos Vlachos
DREAM OF PASSION, A(1978, Gr.)

Frantisek Vlacil
DEVIL'S TRAP, THE(1964, Czech.), d; MARKETA LAZAROVA(1968, Czech.), d, w

Alessandro Vlad
LUNA(1979, Ital.)

Roman Vlad
WALLS OF MALAPAGA, THE(1950, Fr./Ital.), m; THREE STEPS NORTH(1951), md; BEAUTY AND THE DEVIL(1952, Fr./Ital.), m; ROMEO AND JULIET(1954, Brit.), m; LOVERS, HAPPY LOVERS!(1955, Brit.), m; DREAMS IN A DRAWER(1957, Fr./Ital.), m; WHERE THE HOT WIND BLOWS(1960, Fr., Ital.), m; AND THE WILD, WILD WOMEN(1961, Ital.), m; END OF DESIRE(1962 Fr./Ital.), m; MIGHTY URSUS(1962, Ital./Span.), m; SON OF THE RED CORSAIR(1963, Ital.), m; HORRIBLE DR. HICHCOCK, THE(1964, Ital.), m; HYPNOSIS(1966, Ger./Sp./Ital.), m

Dimitri Vladimiroff
MEET ME AT DAWN(1947, Brit.), ch

Vladimir Vladimirov
ARMED AND DANGEROUS(1977, USSR), w

V. Vladimirova
RESURRECTION(1963, USSR); GIRL AND THE BUGLER, THE(1967, USSR)

Vladimir Vladislavsky
ADMIRAL NAKHIMOV(1948, USSR)

Marina Vlady
LUXURY GIRLS(1953, Ital.); NUDE IN A WHITE CAR(1960, Fr.); UNFAITHFULS, THE(1960, Ital.); WICKED GO TO HELL, THE(1961, Fr.); ADORABLE LIAR(1962, Fr.); CONJUGAL BED, THE(1963, Ital.); NIGHT ENCOUNTER(1963, Fr./Ital.); STEPPE, THE(1963, Fr./Ital.); DON'T TEMPT THE DEVIL(1964, Fr./Ital.); SWEET AND SOUR(1964, Fr./Ital.); AMERICAN WIFE, AN(1965, Ital.); ENOUGH ROPE(1966, Fr./Ital./Ger.); RUN FOR YOUR WIFE(1966, Fr./Ital.); CHIMES AT MIDNIGHT(1967, Span.,Switz.); TWO OR THREE THINGS I KNOW ABOUT HER(1970, Fr.); WINTER WIND(1970, Fr./Hung.); LET JOY REIGN SUPREME(1977, Fr.)

John Vlahos
TONTO BASIN OUTLAWS(1941), w; UNDERGROUND RUSTLERS(1941), w; WRANGLER'S ROOST(1941), w; PRIDE OF THE ARMY(1942), w; ROCK RIVER RENEGADES(1942), w; THUNDER RIVER FEUD(1942), w; WAR DOGS(1942), w; MAN OF COURAGE(1943), w; LET'S LIVE AGAIN(1948), w

Persa Vlahos
ANNA OF RHODES(1950, Gr.)

James Vlamos
DARK ODYSSEY(1961), w

John Vlamos
FUGITIVE VALLEY(1941), d

June Vlasek
MAN WHO DARED, THE(1933)

June Vlasek "Lang"
SHE LEARNED ABOUT SAILORS(1934)

J. Vlaskin
MAN WHO BROKE THE BANK AT MONTE CARLO, THE(1935)

Jack Vlaskin
I MARRIED AN ANGEL(1942); NORTH STAR, THE(1943)

Marie Vlaskin
NORTH STAR, THE(1943)

A. Vlasov
MARRIAGE OF BALZAMINOV, THE(1966, USSR)

V. Vlasov
QUEEN OF SPADES(1961, USSR); YOLANTA(1964, USSR)

N. Vlassov
BRIDE WITH A DOWRY(1954, USSR), ph

Vlastimila Vlkova
INTIMATE LIGHTING(1969, Czech.)

Ben Vlok
SPOTS ON MY LEOPARD, THE(1974, S. Africa), p; KINGFISH CAPER, THE(1976, South Africa), p

Peter Vob
SERGEANT BERRY(1938, Ger.)

Nicolas Vobel
DAY OF THE JACKAL, THE(1973, Brit./Fr.)

Borya Voblyy
SONG OF THE FOREST(1963, USSR)

Thomas Voborka
1984
WOMAN IN FLAMES, A(1984, Ger.)

Frank Vobs
ANNIE HALL(1977)

Goff Vockler
LET THE BALLOON GO(1977, Aus.)

Michael Vocoret
HEAT OF MIDNIGHT(1966, Fr.)

Michel Vocoret
HOT HOURS(1963, Fr.); WE'LL GROW THIN TOGETHER(1979, Fr.), d&w

Stelios Vocovits
PHAEDRA(1962, U.S./Gr./Fr.)

Anton Vodak
Misc. Talkies
ATOMIC WAR BRIDE(1966)

Mathew Vodiany
GIRL FROM POLTAVA(1937)

Max Vodnoy
GREEN FIELDS(1937); SINGING BLACKSMITH(1938)

Frano Vodopivec
WHITE WARRIOR, THE(1961, Ital./Yugo.), ph; KAYA, I'LL KILL YOU(1969, Yugo./Fr.), ph; EVENT, AN(1970, Yugo.), ph; EAGLE IN A CAGE(1971, U.S./Yugo.), ph

Marie Voe
WOMAN ON PIER 13, THE(1950)

Sandra Voe
LOCAL HERO(1983, Brit.)
1984
PLOUGHMAN'S LUNCH, THE(1984, Brit.)

Walt Voegeler
DARK ANGEL, THE(1935)

Petra Voelffen
FROM THE LIFE OF THE MARIONETTES(1980, Ger.), ed

Elda Voelkel
ONLY THE BRAVE(1930); VAGABOND KING, THE(1930)

Georg Voelmmer
COUNTERFEIT TRAITOR, THE(1962)

Niels Voersel
1984
ELEMENT OF CRIME, THE(1984, Den.), w

Emmet Vogan
LIVING ON VELVET(1935); ADVENTURE IN MANHATTAN(1936); COLLEEN(1936); GENTLEMAN JIM(1942); KING OF THE COWBOYS(1943); COVER-UP(1949)

Emmett Vogan
FLIRTATION WALK(1934); JEALOUSY(1934); LOVE BIRDS(1934); MANHATTAN MELODRAMA(1934); G-MEN(1935); I FOUND STELLA PARISH(1935); I LIVE FOR LOVE(1935); IRISH IN US, THE(1935); MISS PACIFIC FLEET(1935); PAGE MISS GLORY(1935); SECRET BRIDE, THE(1935); SHE COULDN'T TAKE IT(1935); SHE GETS HER MAN(1935); SHIPMATES FOREVER(1935); SPECIAL AGENT(1935); STARS OVER BROADWAY(1935); STRANDED(1935); SWEET ADELINE(1935); THREE KIDS AND A QUEEN(1935); WHOLE TOWN'S TALKING, THE(1935); CHARLIE CHAN AT THE OPERA(1936); CHINA CLIPPER(1936); IT HAD TO HAPPEN(1936); NEXT TIME WE LOVE(1936); PUBLIC ENEMY'S WIFE(1936); RHYTHM ON THE RANGE(1936); SING ME A LOVE SONG(1936); TWO IN REVOLT(1936); ANGEL'S HOLIDAY(1937); CHARLIE CHAN AT THE OLYMPICS(1937); EMPTY HOLSTERS(1937); FLY-AWAY BABY(1937); HOLY TERROR, THE(1937); KID GALAHAD(1937); LET'S GET MARRIED(1937); LOVE IS NEWS(1937); MARKED WOMAN(1937); SAN QUENTIN(1937); SLIM(1937); THAT CERTAIN WOMAN(1937); THIS IS MY AFFAIR(1937); BELOVED BRAT(1938); CITY GIRL(1938); COMET OVER BROADWAY(1938); COWBOY FROM BROOKLYN(1938); FEMALE FUGITIVE(1938); KING OF THE NEWSBOYS(1938); MEET THE GIRLS(1938); MR. MOTO'S GAMBLE(1938); RHYTHM OF THE SADDLE(1938); SECRETS OF AN ACTRESS(1938); SERGEANT MURPHY(1938); SWING, SISTER, SWING(1938); YOUNG DR. KILDARE(1938); CONFESSIONS OF A NAZI SPY(1939); EACH DAWN I DIE(1939); GREAT VICTOR HERBERT, THE(1939); I AM NOT AFRAID(1939); I STOLE A MILLION(1939); KID FROM KOKOMO, THE(1939); LET US LIVE(1939); MAISIE(1939); MAN WHO DARED, THE(1939); OFF THE RECORD(1939); ST. LOUIS BLUES(1939); STANLEY AND LIVINGSTONE(1939); THEY SHALL HAVE MUSIC(1939); THOU SHALT NOT KILL(1939); WHEN TOMORROW COMES(1939); WINGS OF THE NAVY(1939); WOMEN IN THE WIND(1939); $1,000 A TOUCHDOWN(1939); BANK DICK, THE(1940); CHARLIE CHAN AT THE WAX MUSEUM(1940); CHARLIE CHAN'S MURDER CRUISE(1940); EDISON, THE MAN(1940); FIGHTING 69TH, THE(1940); GHOST BREAKERS, THE(1940); HONEYMOON DEFERRED(1940); HOUSE ACROSS THE BAY, THE(1940); HOWARDS OF VIRGINIA, THE(1940); JOHNNY APOLLO(1940); MANHATTAN HEARTBEAT(1940); MARGIE(1940); SAILOR'S LADY(1940); BLUE, WHITE, AND PERFECT(1941); CRACKED NUTS(1941); CRIMINALS WITHIN(1941); DANGEROUS LADY(1941); EMERGENCY LANDING(1941); HORROR ISLAND(1941); LADY FROM CHEYENNE(1941); LOVE CRAZY(1941); MONSTER AND THE GIRL, THE(1941); NAVY BLUES(1941); NEVER GIVE A SUCKER AN EVEN BREAK(1941); PETTICOAT POLITICS(1941); THERE'S MAGIC IN MUSIC(1941); WHISTLING IN THE DARK(1941); YOU'LL NEVER GET RICH(1941); CALLING DR. GILLESPIE(1942); CAPTAINS OF THE CLOUDS(1942); GIVE OUT, SISTERS(1942); HURRICANE SMITH(1942); LADY BODYGUARD(1942); MUMMY'S TOMB, THE(1942); STARDUST ON THE SAGE(1942); TENNESSEE JOHNSON(1942); THIS GUN FOR HIRE(1942); TOP SERGEANT(1942); TORTILLA FLAT(1942); TRAITOR WITHIN, THE(1942); WE WERE DANCING(1942); WHISTLING IN DIXIE(1942); YOKEL BOY(1942); CANYON CITY(1943); CHATTERBOX(1943); DIXIE DUGAN(1943); HANGMEN ALSO DIE(1943); HE HIRED THE

BOSS(1943); HERE COMES KELLY(1943); HI, BUDDY(1943); HONEYMOON LODGE(1943); IN OLD OKLAHOMA(1943); MARGIN FOR ERROR(1943); MR. MUGGS STEPS OUT(1943); MYSTERY BROADCAST(1943); O, MY DARLING CLEMENTINE(1943); SALUTE FOR THREE(1943); SO'S YOUR UNCLE(1943); YOU'RE A LUCKY FELLOW, MR. SMITH(1943); ARE THESE OUR PARENTS?(1944); BEAUTIFUL BUT BROKE(1944); END OF THE ROAD(1944); FACES IN THE FOG(1944); FOLLOW THE BOYS(1944); HAT CHECK HONEY(1944); HI, GOOD-LOOKIN'(1944); IRISH EYES ARE SMILING(1944); LADY IN THE DARK(1944); LADY, LET'S DANCE(1944); MR. WINKLE GOES TO WAR(1944); MUMMY'S GHOST, THE(1944); MURDER IN THE BLUE ROOM(1944); MY BUDDY(1944); NIGHT CLUB GIRL(1944); ONCE UPON A TIME(1944); SONG OF NEVADA(1944); SWINGTIME JOHNNY(1944); TROCADERO(1944); YELLOW ROSE OF TEXAS, THE(1944); ALONG THE NAVAJO TRAIL(1945); BEHIND CITY LIGHTS(1945); BLOOD ON THE SUN(1945); BULLFIGHTERS, THE(1945); COLORADO PIONEERS(1945); CONFLICT(1945); CORPUS CHRISTI BANDITS(1945); DON JUAN QUILLIGAN(1945); DUFFY'S TAVERN(1945); FLAME OF THE BARBARY COAST(1945); INCENDIARY BLONDE(1945); LADY CONFESSES, THE(1945); LOST WEEKEND, THE(1945); NAUGHTY NINETIES, THE(1945); ON STAGE EVERYBODY(1945); PATRICK THE GREAT(1945); ROUGHLY SPEAKING(1945); SCARLET STREET(1945); SENORITA FROM THE WEST(1945); SHE GETS HER MAN(1945); THEY WERE EXPENDABLE(1945); UTAH(1945); VAMPIRE'S GHOST, THE(1945); WOMAN WHO CAME BACK(1945); BIG SLEEP, THE(1946); BOWERY BOMBSHELL(1946); CLOSE CALL FOR BOSTON BLACKIE, A(1946); DANGEROUS MONEY(1946); FREDDIE STEPS OUT(1946); FRENCH KEY, THE(1946); GAY BLADES(1946); JOLSON STORY, THE(1946); MAGNIFICENT DOLL(1946); NIGHT EDITOR(1946); NOTORIOUS(1946); RENDEZVOUS 24(1946); SECRETS OF A SORORITY GIRL(1946); SHADOW RETURNS, THE(1946); SUSIE STEPS OUT(1946); CASS TIMBERLANE(1947); CIGARETTE GIRL(1947); HER HUSBAND'S AFFAIRS(1947); HOMESTEADERS OF PARADISE VALLEY(1947); I WONDER WHO'S KISSING HER NOW(1947); JEWELS OF BRANDENBURG(1947); LAST OF THE REDMEN(1947); LIKELY STORY, A(1947); MAGIC TOWN(1947); MY WILD IRISH ROSE(1947); NEWS HOUNDS(1947); DENVER KID, THE(1948); DOCKS OF NEW ORLEANS(1948); FIGHTING FATHER DUNNE(1948); GALLANT LEGION, THE(1948); LADIES OF THE CHORUS(1948); MARY LOU(1948); ONE SUNDAY AFTERNOON(1948); SMUGGLERS' COVE(1948); ALIAS THE CHAMP(1949); ARSON, INC.(1949); BROTHERS IN THE SADDLE(1949); DOWN DAKOTA WAY(1949); HOLD THAT BABY!(1949); POST OFFICE INVESTIGATOR(1949); RIDERS OF THE WHISTLING PINES(1949); RUSTY SAVES A LIFE(1949); SKY DRAGON(1949); SORROWFUL JONES(1949); SOUTH OF RIO(1949); FATHER'S WILD GAME(1950); BIG GUSHER, THE(1951); FOLLOW THE SUN(1951); MILLIONAIRE FOR CHRISTY, A(1951); PRIDE OF MARYLAND(1951); STREET BANDITS(1951); UNKNOWN MAN, THE(1951); DON'T BOTHER TO KNOCK(1952); MY WIFE'S BEST FRIEND(1952); PALS OF THE GOLDEN WEST(1952); SOMETHING FOR THE BIRDS(1952); WITH A SONG IN MY HEART(1952); CITY THAT NEVER SLEEPS(1953); HOW TO MARRY A MILLIONAIRE(1953); RED RIVER SHORE(1953); LONG, LONG TRAILER, THE(1954); SABRINA(1954); TOBOR THE GREAT(1954); THESE WILDER YEARS(1956)

Emmett Vogan, Jr.
SWEETHEART OF SIGMA CHI(1946); NEWS HOUNDS(1947); SONG OF SCHEHERAZADE(1947)

Rich Vogan
IT FELL FROM THE SKY(1980)

Emmett Vogar
SANTA FE TRAIL(1940)

Gunther Vogdt
JAZZBAND FIVE, THE(1932, Ger,)

Fred Vogeding
CRIMSON ROMANCE(1934); BEASTS OF BERLIN(1939); ESPIONAGE AGENT(1939); KNUTE ROCKNE–ALL AMERICAN(1940); PARIS CALLING(1941); GREAT IMPERSONATION, THE(1942)

Frederick Vogeding
ONE NIGHT OF LOVE(1934); BLACK ROOM, THE(1935); MESSAGE TO GARCIA, A(1936); LAST GANGSTER(1937); THINK FAST, MR. MOTO(1937); COWBOY AND THE LADY, THE(1938); CONFESSIONS OF A NAZI SPY(1939); BRITISH INTELLIGENCE(1940); I MARRIED AN ANGEL(1942)
Silents
HIGH HEELS(1921)
Misc. Silents
BEHIND MASKS(1921)

Frederik Vogeding
WHARF ANGEL(1934)

Fredrik Vogeding
BELOW THE SEA(1933); FURY OF THE JUNGLE(1934); MURDER ON THE BLACKBOARD(1934); ORIENT EXPRESS(1934); BARBARY COAST(1935); CHARLIE CHAN IN SHANGHAI(1935); MAGNIFICENT OBSESSION(1935); MILLS OF THE GODS(1935); WOMAN IN RED, THE(1935); DANGEROUS INTRIGUE(1936); HOUSE OF A THOUSAND CANDLES, THE(1936); HUMAN CARGO(1936); CAFE METROPOLE(1937); CHARLIE CHAN AT THE OLYMPICS(1937); LANCER SPY(1937); MAN WHO CRIED WOLF, THE(1937); MR. MOTO TAKES A CHANCE(1938); MYSTERIOUS MR. MOTO(1938); CHARLIE CHAN IN THE CITY OF DARKNESS(1939); THREE MUSKETEERS(1939); FOUR SONS(1940); MAN I MARRIED, THE(1940); SAFARI(1940); DOWN IN SAN DIEGO(1941); MAN HUNT(1941); SO ENDS OUR NIGHT(1941); THAT NIGHT IN RIO(1941)

Henry Frederick Vogeding
MEET JOHN DOE(1941)

Vogel
FREUD(1962)

Carine Vogel
PAUL AND MICHELLE(1974, Fr./Brit.)

Carol Vogel
GHASTLY ONES, THE(1968); HI, MOM!(1970)

Daniel Vogel
DAYDREAMER, THE(1975, Fr.), ph

Debbie Vogel
FIEND(

Egon Vogel
EMIL AND THE DETECTIVES(1964); STOP TRAIN 349(1964, Fr./Ital./Ger.)

Eleanor Vogel
THEY WERE EXPENDABLE(1945)

Eleanore Vogel
NIGHT HAS A THOUSAND EYES(1948); GOOD MORNING, MISS DOVE(1955)

Jesse Vogel
CARMEN, BABY(1967, Yugo./Ger.), w; THERESE AND ISABELLE(1968, U.S./Ger.), w
Misc. Talkies
ADVENTURES OF PINOCCHIO, THE(1978), d

Klaus Vogel
VIRGIN WITCH, THE(1973, Brit.), w

Lisa Vogel
1984
ELECTRIC DREAMS(1984)

Matt Vogel
MS. 45(1981), spec eff; NESTING, THE(1981), spec eff

Mitch Vogel
YOURS, MINE AND OURS(1968); REIVERS, THE(1969)
Misc. Talkies
TEXAS DETOUR(1978)

Nadine Vogel
BIZARRE BIZARRE(1939, Fr.)

Nic Vogel
THEY ARE NOT ANGELS(1948, Fr.)

Nicolas Vogel
DESPERATE DECISION(1954, Fr.); LES LIAISONS DANGEREUSES(1961, Fr./Ital.); FIVE MILES TO MIDNIGHT(1963, U.S./Fr./Ital.)

Paul C. Vogel
WIDE OPEN FACES(1938), ph; THEY ALL COME OUT(1939), ph; PILOT NO. 5(1943), ph; LADY IN THE LAKE(1947), ph; MERTON OF THE MOVIES(1947), ph; BATTLEGROUND(1949), ph; SCENE OF THE CRIME(1949), ph; BLACK HAND, THE(1950), ph; DIAL 1119(1950), ph; LADY WITHOUT PASSPORT, A(1950), ph; WATCH THE BIRDIE(1950), ph; ANGELS IN THE OUTFIELD(1951), ph; GO FOR BROKE(1951), ph; TALL TARGET, THE(1951), ph; THREE GUYS NAMED MIKE(1951), ph; GIRL IN WHITE, THE(1952), ph; ROGUE'S MARCH(1952), ph; YOU FOR ME(1952), ph; ARENA(1953), ph; STUDENT PRINCE, THE(1954), ph; BAR SINISTER, THE(1955), ph; INTERRUPTED MELODY(1955), ph; JUPITER'S DARLING(1955), ph; SCARLET COAT, THE(1955), ph; TENDER TRAP, THE(1955), ph; HIGH SOCIETY(1956), ph; ROCK, THE(1956), ph; PUBLIC PIGEON NO. 1(1957), ph; WINGS OF EAGLES, THE(1957), ph; GAZEBO, THE(1959), ph; TARZAN, THE APE MAN(1959), ph; TIME MACHINE, THE(1960; Brit./U.S.), ph; MAGIC SWORD, THE(1962), ph; PERIOD OF ADJUSTMENT(1962), ph; WONDERFUL WORLD OF THE BROTHERS ERIMM, THE(1962), ph; DRUMS OF AFRICA(1963), ph; GUN HAWK, THE(1963), ph; MAIL ORDER BRIDE(1964), ph; SIGNPOST TO MURDER(1964), ph; ROUNDERS, THE(1965), ph; WHEN THE BOYS MEET THE GIRLS(1965), ph; HOLD ON(1966), ph; MONEY TRAP, THE(1966), ph; RETURN OF THE SEVEN(1966, Span.), ph; RIOT ON SUNSET STRIP(1967), ph

Paul G. Vogel
SELLOUT, THE(1951), ph

Paul Vogel
FIT FOR A KING(1937), ph; EVERYBODY'S DOING IT(1938), ph; DOWN IN SAN DIEGO(1941), ph; KID GLOVE KILLER(1942), ph; PACIFIC RENDEZVOUS(1942), ph; SUNDAY PUNCH(1942), ph; TISH(1942), ph; HIGH WALL, THE(1947), ph; HOLIDAY FOR SINNERS(1952), ph; CLOWN, THE(1953), ph; GIRL WHO HAD EVERYTHING, THE(1953), ph; HALF A HERO(1953), ph; ROSE MARIE(1954), ph; GREEN FIRE(1955), ph; BERNARDINE(1957), ph
Silents
POTTERS, THE(1927), ph

Peter Vogel
MAN WHO WALKED THROUGH THE WALL, THE(1964, Ger.); PHANTOM OF SOHO, THE(1967, Ger.)

Robert Vogel
BASKET CASE(1982)

Rudolf Vogel
CASINO DE PARIS(1957, Fr./Ger.); BEGGAR STUDENT, THE(1958, Ger.); STORY OF VICKIE, THE(1958, Aust.); EMBEZZLED HEAVEN(1959,Ger.); MRS. WARREN'S PROFESSION(1960, Ger.); SPESSART INN, THE(1961, Ger.); MAN WHO WALKED THROUGH THE WALL, THE(1964, Ger.); GIRL AND THE LEGEND, THE(1966, Ger.); HEIDI(1968, Aust.)

Stanley Vogel
FIRST TIME, THE(1983), ed

Tony Vogel
ISADORA(1968, Brit.); OH! WHAT A LOVELY WAR(1969, Brit.); CAPTAIN APACHE(1971, Brit.); LAST VALLEY, THE(1971, Brit.); HUMAN FACTOR, THE(1979, Brit.); MEETINGS WITH REMARKABLE MEN(1979, Brit.); FINAL CONFLICT, THE(1981); RAIDERS OF THE LOST ARK(1981)

Virgil Vogel
MYSTERY SUBMARINE(1950), ed; ABBOTT AND COSTELLO MEET THE INVISIBLE MAN(1951), ed; HOLLYWOOD STORY(1951), ed; LADY FROM TEXAS, THE(1951), ed; REUNION IN RENO(1951), ed; UNDER THE GUN(1951), ed; BECAUSE OF YOU(1952), ed; FLESH AND FURY(1952), ed; JUST ACROSS THE STREET(1952), ed; MEET DANNY WILSON(1952), ed; SON OF ALI BABA(1952), ed; UNTAMED FRONTIER(1952), ed; EAST OF SUMATRA(1953), ed; MAN FROM THE ALAMO, THE(1953), ed; SEMINOLE(1953), ed; TUMBLEWEED(1953), ed; DRUMS ACROSS THE RIVER(1954), ed; PLAYGIRL(1954), ed; SO THIS IS PARIS(1954), ed; YANKEE PASHA(1954), ed; MA AND PA KETTLE AT WAIKIKI(1955), ed; MAN WITHOUT A STAR(1955), ed; THIS ISLAND EARTH(1955), ed; MOLE PEOPLE, THE(1957), d; KETTLES ON OLD MACDONALD'S FARM, THE(1957), d; LAND UNKNOWN, THE(1957), d

Virgil W. Vogel
TOUCH OF EVIL(1958), ed; INVASION OF THE ANIMAL PEOPLE(1962, U.S./Swed.), d; SWORD OF ALI BABA, THE(1965), d

Joy Michael Vogelbacher
NIGHT SHIFT(1982)

Theodor Vogeler
SLEEPING BEAUTY(1965, Ger.); GOOSE GIRL, THE(1967, Ger.)

Willy Schulte Vogelheim
CONGRESS DANCES(1957, Ger.), ch

Paul C. Vogell
VILLAGE OF THE GIANTS(1965), ph

Karlheinz Vogelmann
MISSION STARDUST(1968, Ital./Span./Ger.), w
Anne Vogler
NIGHT OF THE FOLLOWING DAY, THE(1969, Brit.), ed
Karl Michael Vogler
HAMLET(1962, Ger.); MAN WHO WALKED THROUGH THE WALL, THE(1964, Ger.); THOSE MAGNIFICENT MEN IN THEIR FLYING MACHINES; OR HOW I FLEWFROM LONDON TO PARIS IN 25 HOURS AND 11 MINUTES(1965, Brit.); BLUE MAX, THE(1966); HOW I WON THE WAR(1967, Brit.); DOWNHILL RACER(1969); DEEP END(1970 Ger./U.S.); PATTON(1970); SHOUT AT THE DEVIL(1976, Brit.)
Rudiger Vogler
ALICE IN THE CITIES(1974, W. Ger.); KINGS OF THE ROAD(1976, Ger.); LEFT-HANDED WOMAN, THE(1980, Ger.); GERMAN SISTERS, THE(1982, Ger.)
Jack Voglin
FOREIGN CORRESPONDENT(1940); UNFINISHED BUSINESS(1941)
Yannis Voglis
DREAM OF PASSION, A(1978, Gr.)
Carl de Vogt
Misc. Silents
SPIDERS, THE(1919, Ger.)
Charles Vogt
Misc. Silents
MASTER OF BEASTS, THE(1922)
Paul Vogt
LADY LIBERTY(1972, Ital./Fr.), set d; LAW AND DISORDER(1974), set d
Peter Vogt
GOODBYE GIRL, THE(1977)
1984
HOT DOG...THE MOVIE(1984)
Alfred Vohrer
DARK EYES OF LONDON(1961, Ger.), d; YOUNG GO WILD, THE(1962, Ger.), d; AMONG VULTURES(1964, Ger./Ital./Fr./Yugo.), d; FRONTIER HELLCAT(1966, Fr./Ital./Ger./Yugo.), d; THUNDER AT THE BORDER(1966, Ger./Yugo.), d; FLAMING FRONTIER(1968, Ger./Yugo.), d; CREATURE WITH THE BLUE HAND(1971, Ger.), d
Misc. Talkies
APE CREATURE(1968, Ger.), d
Joan Vohs
GIRL FROM JONES BEACH, THE(1949); IT'S A GREAT FEELING(1949); MY DREAM IS YOURS(1949); YES SIR, THAT'S MY BABY(1949); COUNTY FAIR(1950); GIRLS' SCHOOL(1950); AS YOU WERE(1951); ROYAL WEDDING(1951); CRAZYLEGS, ALL AMERICAN(1953); FORT TI(1953); VICE SQUAD(1953); CRY VENGEANCE(1954); SABRINA(1954); FORT YUMA(1955); TERROR AT MIDNIGHT(1956); LURE OF THE SWAMP(1957)
Voice of Experience
HIT PARADE, THE(1937)
V. Tsitta voices
QUEEN OF SPADES(1961, USSR)
Angelina Jolie Voight
LOOKIN' TO GET OUT(1982)
Ed Voight
CAGED(1950), makeup
Jill Voight
FRIDAY THE 13TH PART II(1981)
John Voight
BEASTS OF BERLIN(1939); CONFESSIONS OF A NAZI SPY(1939)
Jon Voight
FEARLESS FRANK(1967); HOUR OF THE GUN(1967); MIDNIGHT COWBOY(1969); OUT OF IT(1969); CATCH-22(1970); REVOLUTIONARY, THE(1970, Brit.); DELIVERANCE(1972); ALL-AMERICAN BOY, THE(1973); CONRACK(1974); ODESSA FILE, THE(1974, Brit./Ger.); END OF THE GAME(1976, Ger./Ital.); COMING HOME(1978); CHAMP, THE(1979); LOOKIN' TO GET OUT(1982), a, w; TABLE FOR FIVE(1983)
Voigt
FREUD(1962)
Jill Voigt
Misc. Talkies
TRIP WITH THE TEACHER(1975)
Ted Voigtlander
NIGHT OF THE LEPUS(1972), ph
1984
SAM'S SON(1984), ph
Konstantin Voinov
SUN SHINES FOR ALL, THE(1961, USSR), d; MARRIAGE OF BALZAMINOV, THE(1966, USSR), d&w
R. Voinquel
PERSONAL COLUMN(1939, Fr.), ph
Ada Voisik
Misc. Silents
FORTY-FIRST, THE(1927, USSR)
Simone Voisin
UTOPIA(1952, Fr./Ital.)
Mieczyslaw Voit
JOAN OF THE ANGELS(1962, Pol.); KNIGHTS OF THE TEUTONIC ORDER, THE(1962, Pol.)
Ada Voitsik
IVAN THE TERRIBLE(Part I, 1947, USSR)
Jar Vojta
ECSTACY OF YOUNG LOVE(1936, Czech.)
Jaroslav Vojta
SKELETON ON HORSEBACK(1940, Czech.)
Jiri Vojta
MIDSUMMERS NIGHT'S DREAM, A(1961, Czech.), ph; LOST FACE, THE(1965, Czech.), ph; DO YOU KEEP A LION AT HOME?(1966, Czech.), ph
Elda Vokel
FIRST YEAR, THE(1932)
May Vokes
Silents
JANICE MEREDITH(1924)

Twyla-Dawn Vokins
Misc. Talkies
KELLY(1981, Can.)
Jiri Vokoum
FANTASTIC PLANET(1973, Fr./Czech.), anim
De Vol
HAPPENING, THE(1967), m
Herb Voland
NORTH AVENUE IRREGULARS, THE(1979)
Herbert Voland
DON'T JUST STAND THERE(1968); SHAKIEST GUN IN THE WEST, THE(1968); WITH SIX YOU GET EGGROLL(1968); LOVE GOD?, THE(1969)
Vicki Volante
BLOOD OF DRACULA'S CASTLE(1967); GUN RIDERS, THE(1969); HELL'S BLOODY DEVILS(1970); HORROR OF THE BLOOD MONSTERS(1970, U.S./Phil.); BRAIN OF BLOOD(1971, Phil.)
Misc. Talkies
ANGELS' WILD WOMEN(1972)
Lorena Volare
Misc. Silents
HIS GREATEST SACRIFICE(1921)
Lorna Volare
Silents
MAN AND THE WOMAN, A(1917)
Volcano
HIT THE SADDLE(1937)
Boris Volchek
THIRTEEN, THE(1937, USSR), ph
G. Volchek
DON QUIXOTE(1961, USSR); UNCOMMON THIEF, AN(1967, USSR)
George Volck
JULIA MISBEHAVES(1948)
Doug Vold
WHEN THE LEGENDS DIE(1972)
Betty Lou Volder
RAZOR'S EDGE, THE(1946)
Gary Voldseth
HEARTLAND(1980)
John Voldstad
STRIPES(1981); JOYSTICKS(1983)
Nathan W. Volfovitz
DREAMER, THE(1970, Israel)
M. Volgina
LOSS OF FEELING(1935, USSR)
Mario Volgoi
ITALIAN JOB, THE(1969, Brit.)
Ben Volk
KILL OR BE KILLED(1980), p
George Volk
NIGHT AND DAY(1946); TO THE ENDS OF THE EARTH(1948); HOODLUM EMPIRE(1952)
Ralph Volke
SET-UP, THE(1949); BIG KNIFE, THE(1955)
Wilhelm Volker
Misc. Silents
MAN BY THE ROADSIDE, THE(1923, Ger.)
S. Volkhovskaya
Misc. Silents
WHEN WILL WE DEAD AWAKEN?(1918, USSR)
Ralph Volkie
EAST OF THE RIVER(1940); TALK OF THE TOWN(1942); JOHNNY O'CLOCK(1947); LEATHER GLOVES(1948); SOUTHERN YANKEE, A(1948); WHIPLASH(1948); DANGEROUS PROFESSION, A(1949); KNOCK ON ANY DOOR(1949); UNDERCOVER MAN, THE(1949); NEW MEXICO(1951); SLAUGHTER TRAIL(1951); TEN TALL MEN(1951); BLOODHOUNDS OF BROADWAY(1952); BOOTS MALONE(1952); LUSTY MEN, THE(1952); SCANDAL SHEET(1952); SNIPER, THE(1952); DANGEROUS MISSION(1954); FRENCH LINE, THE(1954); AUTUMN LEAVES(1956); SERENADE(1956); CHICAGO CONFIDENTIAL(1957); PAJAMA GAME, THE(1957); MAN WHO SHOT LIBERTY VALANCE, THE(1962); DONOVAN'S REEF(1963); FOUR FOR TEXAS(1963); MC LINTOCK!(1963); SONS OF KATIE ELDER, THE(1965); EL DORADO(1967); CHISUM(1970)
Twyla Volkins
TOUCHED BY LOVE(1980)
Elisabeth Volkman
LOVE FEAST, THE(1966, Ger.)
Ivan Volkman
HOW TO SUCCEED IN BUSINESS WITHOUT REALLY TRYING(1976)
Nancy Volkman
PRISM(1971)
Misc. Talkies
PRISM(1971)
Carol Volkmann
ROCK, PRETTY BABY(1956)
Caryl Volkmann
ROCKABILLY BABY(1957)
Elisabeth Volkmann
LILI MARLEEN(1981, Ger.); LOLA(1982, Ger.); VERONIKA VOSS(1982, Ger.)
Martin Volkmann
PUSS 'N' BOOTS(1967, Ger.)
Susan Volkmann
ROCK, PRETTY BABY(1956); ROCKABILLY BABY(1957)
Ulrich Volkmar
DECISION BEFORE DAWN(1951)
Waldemar Volkmer
SLEEPING BEAUTY(1965, Ger.), art d
Alexandre Volkoff
Misc. Silents
KEAN(1924, Fr.), d; LES OMBRES QUI PASSANT(1924, Fr.), d; CASANOVA(1927, Fr.), d

Nicole Volkoff
VICE SQUAD(1982)
A. Volkonskiy
MAGIC WEAVER, THE(1965, USSR), m
Alexander Volkov
Misc. Silents
GREEN SPIDER, THE(1916, USSR), d; LE BRASIER ARDENT(1923, Fr.), d
B. Volkov
LITTLE HUMPBACKED HORSE, THE(1962, USSR), art d
F. Volkov
SKI BATTALION(1938, USSR)
N. Volkov
DREAM COME TRUE, A(1963, USSR); SANDU FOLLOWS THE SUN(1965, USSR)
P. Volkov
CITY OF YOUTH(1938, USSR)
Pavel Volkov
NEW TEACHER, THE(1941, USSR); SON OF THE REGIMENT(1948, USSR); DESTI-
NY OF A MAN(1961, USSR)
S. Volkov
IDIOT, THE(1960, USSR), ed
V. Volkov
MEET ME IN MOSCOW(1966, USSR)
Yu Volkov
THERE WAS AN OLD COUPLE(1967, USSR)
Yu. Volkov
LAST GAME, THE(1964, USSR)
Lida Volkova
WELCOME KOSTYA!(1965, USSR)
Hendrik Vollaerts
BOP GIRL GOES CALYPSO(1957), w
George Vollaire
ROAD TO FORTUNE, THE(1930, Brit.)
Karl Vollbrecht
M(1933, Ger.), prod d, art d; TESTAMENT OF DR. MABUSE, THE(1943, Ger.), prod
d, art d
Silents
KRIEMHILD'S REVENGE(1924, Ger.), art d; SIEGFRIED(1924, Ger.), art d; MET-
ROPOLIS(1927, Ger.), art d; SPIES(1929, Ger.), art d; WOMAN ON THE MOON,
THE(1929, Ger.), art d
Danielle Volle
LA BONNE SOUPE(1964, Fr./Ital.); SICILIAN CLAN, THE(1970, Fr.)
Ida Vollmar
VOGUES OF 1938(1937)
Lula Vollmer
SPITFIRE(1934), w
Joseph Vollmert
NOT RECONCILED, OR "ONLY VIOLENCE HELPS WHERE IT RULES"(1969, Ger.)
Karl Vollmoeller
SHANGHAI GESTURE, THE(1941), w; BLUE ANGEL, THE(1959), w; MIRACLE,
THE(1959), w
Karl Gustav Vollmoeller
LADY OF THE PAVEMENTS(1929), w
Karl Vollmoller
BLUE ANGEL, THE(1930, Ger.), w
Fern Vollner
THREE IN THE ATTIC(1968), cos
Helmut Volmer
COURT MARTIAL(1962, Ger.), p
Ruth Volner
ANNIE HALL(1977)
Aleksandr Volodin
AUTUMN MARATHON(1982, USSR), w
Alexander Volodin
GIRL AND THE BUGLER, THE(1967, USSR), w
V. Volodin
QUEEN OF SPADES(1961, USSR)
Margarita Volodina
OPTIMISTIC TRAGEDY, THE(1964, USSR); THREE SISTERS, THE(1969, USSR)
Gian Maria Volonte
UNDER TEN FLAGS(1960, U.S./Ital.); FOUR DAYS OF NAPLES, THE(1963, US/
Ital.); HERCULES AND THE CAPTIVE WOMEN(1963, Fr./Ital.); MAGNIFICENT
CUCKOLD, THE(1965, Fr./Ital.); BULLET FOR THE GENERAL, A(1967, Ital.); FOR A
FEW DOLLARS MORE(1967, Ital./Ger./Span.); JOURNEY BENEATH THE DE-
SERT(1967, Fr./Ital.); WAKE UP AND DIE(1967, Fr./Ital.); WE STILL KILL THE OLD
WAY(1967, Ital.); VIOLENT FOUR, THE(1968, Ital.); WITCH, THE(1969, Ital.); INVES-
TIGATION OF A CITIZEN ABOVE SUSPICION(1970, Ital.); WIND FROM THE
EAST(1970, Fr./Ital./Ger.); SACCO AND VANZETTI(1971, Ital./Fr.); FRENCH CON-
SPIRACY, THE(1973, Fr.); GIORDANO BRUNO(1973, Ital.); RE: LUCKY LUCIA-
NO(1974, Fr./Ital.); EBOLI(1980, Ital.)
Gian-Maria Volonte
FACE TO FACE(1967, Ital.)
Gian-Marie Volonte
DEATH OF MARIO RICCI, THE(1983, Ital.)
Gian Maria Volonte [Carlo Hintermann]
GIRL WITH A SUITCASE(1961, Fr./Ital.)
Claudio Volonto
TWITCH OF THE DEATH NERVE(1973, Ital.)
Alex Voloshin
DESTRY RIDES AGAIN(1939)
Julian Voloshin
BIRDS DO IT(1966)
P. Voloshin
RESURRECTION(1963, USSR)
Luciano Volpato
LE AMICHE(1962, Ital.)
Flora Volpe
LOVE AND MARRIAGE(1966, Ital.)

Fred Volpe
LORD RICHARD IN THE PANTRY(1930, Brit.); MIDDLE WATCH, THE(1930, Brit.)
Silents
ALTAR CHAINS(1916, Brit.); LABOUR LEADER, THE(1917, Brit.); PROFLIGATE,
THE(1917, Brit.); ONCE UPON A TIME(1918, Brit.); ADVENTURES OF MR. PICK-
WICK, THE(1921, Brit.)
Frederick Volpe
BED AND BREAKFAST(1930, Brit.); CAPTIVATION(1931, Brit)
Lenore Volpe
NUNZIO(1978)
Nick Volpe
FORTUNES OF CAPTAIN BLOOD(1950)
Roger Volper
IS PARIS BURNING?(1966, U.S./Fr.), set d; TWO FOR THE ROAD(1967, Brit.), set
d
Franco Volpi
DUEL OF THE TITANS(1963, Ital.)
Mikhail Volpin
JACK FROST(1966, USSR), w
L. Volskaya
MUMU(1961, USSR)
Ye. Volskaya
RESURRECTION(1963, USSR)
John Volstadt
1941(1979)
Voltaire
CANDIDE(1962, Fr.), w
Joe Volti
PACIFIC ADVENTURE(1947, Aus.)
Frederick Voltz
O.S.S.(1946)
Eros Volusia
RIO RITA(1942)
Alexander Volz
FRIENDS AND HUSBANDS(1983, Ger.)
Benjamin Volz
MARTYR, THE(1976, Ger./Israel)
Nedra Volz
YOUR THREE MINUTES ARE UP(1973); 10(1979); LITTLE MISS MARKER(1980)
Wolfgang Volz
EMIL AND THE DETECTIVES(1964); FUNERAL IN BERLIN(1966, Brit.); PIPPI IN
THE SOUTH SEAS(1974, Swed./Ger.)
Reinhardt Vom Bauer
MALOU(1983)
Ronald Von
AGENT FOR H.A.R.M.(1966)
Vyola Von
Misc. Talkies
TIMBERESQUE(1937)
Ralph von Albertson
SUMMER CAMP(1979)
Ferdinand von Alten
1914(1932, Ger.)
Silents
STUDENT OF PRAGUE, THE(1927, Ger.)
Jurgen Von Alten
1984
LOVE IN GERMANY, A(1984, Fr./Ger.)
Theo Von Alten
Silents
CHAMPAGNE(1928, Brit.)
Axel Von Ambesser
GOOD SOLDIER SCHWEIK, THE(1963, Ger.), d
Albert Von Antwerp
NOBODY LIVES FOREVER(1946)
Rainer von Artenfels
OUR HITLER, A FILM FROM GERMANY(1980, Ger.)
Peter von Bagh
TIME OF ROSES(1970, Fin.), w
Josef Von Baky
CITY OF TORMENT(1950, Ger.), d; DREADING LIPS(1958, Ger.), d; CONFESS DR.
CORDA(1960, Ger.), d; GIRL AND THE LEGEND, THE(1966, Ger.), d
Joseph von Baky
INTERMEZZO(1937, Ger.), d
Victoria von Ballasko
OUR DAILY BREAD(1950, Ger.)
Ludwig von Beethoven
VERBOTEN!(1959), m; GARNET BRACELET, THE(1966, USSR), m; MADE IN
U.S.A.(1966, Fr.), m; JAIL BAIT(1977, Ger.), m
1984
BASILEUS QUARTET(1984, Ital.), m; FIRST NAME: CARMEN(1984, Fr.), m; NOS-
TALGHIA(1984, USSR/Ital.), m
Brad Von Beltz
Misc. Talkies
KILL THE GOLDEN GOOSE(1979)
George Von Benko
FISH THAT SAVED PITTSBURGH, THE(1979)
Gregory von Berblinger
SWEET CREEK COUNTY WAR, THE(1979), ph
Mark Von Berblinger
SADIST, THE(1963), art d
Tilo von Berlepsch
ROSEMARY(1960, Ger.)
Fred Von Bernewitz
CHAFED ELBOWS(1967), ed
Tosca von Bissing
BELLES OF ST. CLEMENTS, THE(1936, Brit.)

Toska von Bissing
LORNA DOONE(1935, Brit.); MAD HATTERS, THE(1935, Brit.)
Christiane Von Blank
DEAD ARE ALIVE, THE(1972, Yugo./Ger./Ital.)
Wolfram Von Bock
THUNDER AFLOAT(1939)
Lucy Von Boden
SONG TO REMEMBER, A(1945)
Thekla von Bodo
TWO WORLD(1930, Brit.), w
Geza von Bolvary
VAGABOND QUEEN, THE(1931, Brit.), d; WHAT WOMEN DREAM(1933, Ger.), d
Gerd von Bonin
BRIDGE, THE(1961, Ger.), ph; ESCAPE TO BERLIN(1962, U.S./Switz./Ger.), ph
Claus Von Boro
SPESSART INN, THE(1961, Ger.), ed; HELDINNEN(1962, Ger.), ed; GIRL AND THE LEGEND, THE(1966, Ger.), ed; UNWILLING AGENT(1968, Ger.), ed; YOUNG TORLESS(1968, Fr./Ger.), ed; DEGREE OF MURDER, A(1969, Ger.), ed
Hilwa von Boro
KING IN SHADOW(1961, Ger.), ed; TWO IN A SLEEPING BAG(1964, Ger.), ed
Hans von Borsody
DON JUAN(1956, Aust.); COMMANDO(1962, Ital., Span., Bel., Ger.); INVISIBLE MAN, THE(1963, Ger.); CAVERN, THE(1965, Ital./Ger.); TRUNK TO CAIRO(1966, Israel/Ger.)
Julius von Borsody
HIS MAJESTY, KING BALLYHOO(1931, Ger.), art d; WHITE DEMON, THE(1932, Ger.), art d
Paul Von Brack
COOLEY HIGH(1975), ph
Kim von Brandenstein
LITTLE SEX, A(1982)
Patricia von Brandenstein
TOUCHED(1983), prod d
Patrizia von Brandenstein
CANDIDATE, THE(1972), set d; BETWEEN THE LINES(1977), cos; SATURDAY NIGHT FEVER(1977), cos; GIRLFRIENDS(1978), art d; TELL ME A RIDDLE(1980), prod d; RAGTIME(1981), art d; LITTLE SEX, A(1982), cos; SILKWOOD(1983), prod d
1984
AMADEUS(1984), prod d; BEAT STREET(1984), prod d
William von Brincken
GENERAL CRACK(1929); HELL'S ANGELS(1930); INSIDE THE LINES(1930); LONESOME TRAIL, THE(1930); MAMBA(1930); THREE FACES EAST(1930); COMMAND PERFORMANCE(1931); SURRENDER(1931); UNHOLY GARDEN, THE(1931); NIGHT CLUB LADY(1932); PASSPORT TO HELL(1932); SIX HOURS TO LIVE(1932); SHANGHAI MADNESS(1933); CRIMSON ROMANCE(1934); GAY BRIDE, THE(1934); I'LL TELL THE WORLD(1934); KING KELLY OF THE U.S.A(1934); VIVA VILLA!(1934); FLIRTING WITH DANGER(1935); MELODY LINGERS ON, THE(1935); DRACULA'S DAUGHTER(1936); ESPIONAGE(1937); LIFE OF EMILE ZOLA, THE(1937); PRISONER OF ZENDA, THE(1937); THANK YOU, MR. MOTO(1937); WALLABY JIM OF THE ISLANDS(1937); BULLDOG DRUMMOND IN AFRICA(1938); INTERNATIONAL CRIME(1938); CONSPIRACY(1939); NAVY SECRETS(1939); PACK UP YOUR TROUBLES(1939); PANAMA PATROL(1939); FOUR SONS(1940); HIDDEN ENEMY(1940); SO ENDS OUR NIGHT(1941); UNDERGROUND(1941); ACTION IN THE NORTH ATLANTIC(1943)
Silents
MERRY WIDOW, THE(1925); PRINCE OF PILSEN, THE(1926); WEDDING MARCH, THE(1927); QUEEN KELLY(1929)
Baron William Von Brinken
LEATHERNECKING(1930); MEXICALI KID, THE(1938)
Margaret Von Brockdorff
TRENCHCOAT(1983)
Roni von Bukovics
SERGEANT BERRY(1938, Ger.)
Viktoria von Campe
WILLY(1963, U.S./Ger.)
Irma Von Cube
BE MINE TONIGHT(1933, Brit.), w; MY SONG FOR YOU(1935, Brit.), w; MAYERLING(1937, Fr.), w; UNDER SECRET ORDERS(1943, Brit.), w
Irmgard von Cube
THEY SHALL HAVE MUSIC(1939), w; SONG OF LOVE(1947), w; JOHNNY BELINDA(1948), w; GIRL IN WHITE, THE(1952), w
Geza von Cziffra
TALE OF FIVE WOMEN, A(1951, Brit.), d; DIE FLEDERMAUS(1964, Aust.), d, w
Albert von Dalsum
BOEFJE(1939, Ger.)
Doris von Danwitz
MARK OF THE DEVIL(1970, Ger./Brit.)
Wilhelm von Deek
LAST YEAR AT MARIENBAD(1962, Fr./Ital.)
Diane Von den Ecker
ANNA AND THE KING OF SIAM(1946)
Barbara von der Heyde
SONG OF NORWAY(1970)
Peter Von Dissel
FUNERAL FOR AN ASSASSIN(1977)
Baron von Dobeneck
Silents
TILLIE'S PUNCTURED ROMANCE(1928)
Bob Von Dobeneck
FOLIES DERGERE(1935)
Lenny Von Dohlen
TENDER MERCIES(1982)
1984
ELECTRIC DREAMS(1984)
Christoph von Dohnanyi
YOUNG LORD, THE(1970, Ger.), md
Peter von Dongen
DREADING LIPS(1958, Ger.)

Helen Von Dongren
LOUISIANA STORY(1948), ed
Shoto von Douglas
BOOGEYMAN II(1983)
Baron A. Von Dungern
Misc. Silents
PORI(1930, Ger.), d
Milena von Eckardt
DIE FASTNACHTSBEICHTE(1962, Ger.)
Theodore Von Eltz
AWFUL TRUTH, THE(1929); VERY IDEA, THE(1929); ARIZONA KID, THE(1930); CAT CREEPS, THE(1930); FURIES, THE(1930); KISMET(1930); LOVE AMONG THE MILLIONAIRES(1930); BEYOND VICTORY(1931); ONCE A LADY(1931); PRODIGAL, THE(1931); SECRET SIX, THE(1931); SUSAN LENOX–HER FALL AND RISE(1931); UP POPS THE DEVIL(1931); WICKED(1931); DRIFTING(1932); HOTEL CONTINENTAL(1932); LADIES OF THE BIG HOUSE(1932); MIDNIGHT LADY(1932); PRIVATE SCANDAL, A(1932); RED-HAIRED ALIBI, THE(1932); SCARLET WEEKEND, A(1932); STRANGERS OF THE EVENING(1932); UNWRITTEN LAW, THE(1932); ARIZONA TO BROADWAY(1933); DANCE, GIRL, DANCE(1933); ELEVENTH COMMANDMENT(1933); GIGOLETTES OF PARIS(1933); HER SPLENDID FOLLY(1933); HIGH GEAR(1933); JENNIE GERHARDT(1933); LUXURY LINER(1933); MASTER OF MEN(1933); MY MOTHER(1933); NO OTHER WOMAN(1933); PLEASURE CRUISE(1933); SECRETS(1933); BRIGHT EYES(1934); CALL IT LUCK(1934); CHANGE OF HEART(1934); LOVE PAST THIRTY(1934); THIS SIDE OF HEAVEN(1934); BEHIND GREEN LIGHTS(1935); CONFIDENTIAL(1935); ELINOR NORTON(1935); GRAND OLD GIRL(1935); HEADLINE WOMAN, THE(1935); HIS NIGHT OUT(1935); MAGNIFICENT OBSESSION(1935); MURDER MAN(1935); PRIVATE WORLDS(1935); RENDEZVOUS(1935); SILVER STREAK, THE(1935); SMART GIRL(1935); STREAMLINE EXPRESS(1935); TRAILS OF THE WILD(1935); BELOVED ENEMY(1936); BELOW THE DEADLINE(1936); HIGH TENSION(1936); LOVE BEFORE BREAKFAST(1936); ROAD TO GLORY, THE(1936); SINNER TAKE ALL(1936); SUZY(1936); TICKET TO PARADISE(1936); UNDER YOUR SPELL(1936); CALIFORNIA STRAIGHT AHEAD(1937); CLARENCE(1937); EMPEROR'S CANDLESTICKS, THE(1937); FIREFLY, THE(1937); JIM HANVEY, DETECTIVE(1937); MAN BETRAYED, A(1937); MIND YOUR OWN BUSINESS(1937); STAGE DOOR(1937); TOPPER(1937); UNDER COVER OF NIGHT(1937); WESTLAND CASE, THE(1937); YOUTH ON PAROLE(1937); ADVENTURES OF MARCO POLO, THE(1938); BLONDES AT WORK(1938); DELINQUENT PARENTS(1938); I AM THE LAW(1938); I COVER CHINATOWN(1938); LETTER OF INTRODUCTION(1938); MARIE ANTOINETTE(1938); SMASHING THE RACKETS(1938); FIFTH AVENUE GIRL(1939); INSIDE STORY(1939); LEGION OF LOST FLYERS(1939); NIGHT OF NIGHTS, THE(1939); PARDON OUR NERVE(1939); STORY OF VERNON AND IRENE CASTLE, THE(1939); SUN NEVER SETS, THE(1939); THEY MADE HER A SPY(1939); DISPATCH FROM REUTERS, A(1940); DR. EHRLICH'S MAGIC BULLET(1940); GREAT PLANE ROBBERY, THE(1940); KITTY FOYLE(1940); LITTLE OLD NEW YORK(1940); SAINT TAKES OVER, THE(1940); SON OF MONTE CRISTO(1940); ELLERY QUEEN'S PENTHOUSE MYSTERY(1941); I'LL WAIT FOR YOU(1941); LIFE WITH HENRY(1941); SERGEANT YORK(1941); SHOT IN THE DARK, THE(1941); BREACH OF PROMISE(1942, Brit.); GREAT MAN'S LADY, THE(1942); MAN IN THE TRUNK, THE(1942); QUIET PLEASE, MURDER(1942); AIR FORCE(1943); FLIGHT FOR FREEDOM(1943); BERMUDA MYSTERY(1944); FOLLOW THE BOYS(1944); HOLLYWOOD CANTEEN(1944); SINCE YOU WENT AWAY(1944); RHAPSODY IN BLUE(1945); SARATOGA TRUNK(1945); BIG SLEEP, THE(1946); TRIAL WITHOUT JURY(1950)
Misc. Talkies
DRIFTING SOULS(1932); SELF DEFENSE(1933)
Silents
TRAFFIC COP, THE(1916); SHERLOCK BROWN(1921); SPEED GIRL, THE(1921); BREAKING POINT, THE(1924); HEARTS OF OAK(1924); ON THIN ICE(1925); LAST ALARM, THE(1926); QUEEN O' DIAMONDS(1926); REDHEADS PREFERRED(1926); GREAT MAIL ROBBERY, THE(1927); NO MAN'S LAW(1927); ONE WOMAN TO ANOTHER(1927); NOTHING TO WEAR(1928); WAY OF THE STRONG, THE(1928); FOUR FEATHERS(1929); RESCUE, THE(1929)
Misc. Silents
EXTRAVAGANCE(1921); FOURTEENTH LOVER, THE(1922); LIGHTS OUT(1923); WOMAN WITH FOUR FACES, THE(1923); THAT FRENCH LADY(1924); TURMOIL, THE(1924); BROADWAY LADY(1925); LOCKED DOORS(1925); PAINT AND POWDER(1925); SPORTING CHANCE, THE(1925); THOROUGHBRED, THE(1925); WHITE FANG(1925); DESPERATE MOMENT, A(1926); FOOLS OF FASHION(1926); HIS NEW YORK WIFE(1926); LADDIE(1926); SEA WOLF, THE(1926); PERCH OF THE DEVIL(1927); LIFE'S MOCKERY(1928); VOICE OF THE STORM, THE(1929); SWEEPING AGAINST THE WINDS(1930)
Theodore von Eltz [Frederick]
Silents
RED KIMONO(1925)
Andre von Engleman
Silents
MARE NOSTRUM(1926)
Alexandra von Engstroen
RENDEZ-VOUS(1932, Ger.)
Desiree Von Essen
FREEWHEELIN'(1976)
Geza von Foldessy
LA HABANERA(1937, Ger.)
Hardy von Francois
Silents
NOSFERATU, THE VAMPIRE(1922, Ger.); SIEGFRIED(1924, Ger.)
Fritz von Friedl
LONE CLIMBER, THE(1950, Brit./Aust.)
Loni von Friedl
5 SINNERS(1961, Ger.); SHADOWS GROW LONGER, THE(1962, Switz./Ger.); BLUE MAX, THE(1966); JOURNEY TO THE FAR SIDE OF THE SUN(1969, Brit.)
Kort von Fuberg
MAD EMPRESS, THE(1940)
Ira von Furstenberg
DEAD RUN(1961, Fr./Ital./Ger.); MATCHLESS(1967, Ital.)
Veith von Furstenberg
Misc. Talkies
FIRE AND SWORD(1982, Brit.), d

Mogens von Gadow
SOMETHING FOR EVERYONE(1970); KING, QUEEN, KNAVE(1972, Ger./U.S.)

Baron von Genin
HOUSE ON 92ND STREET, THE(1945)

Arthur Von Gerlach
Misc. Silents
VANINA(1922, Ger.), d; CHRONICLES OF THE GRAY HOUSE, THE(1923, Ger.), d

Henning von Gierke
GERMANY IN AUTUMN(1978, Ger.), set d; NOSFERATU, THE VAMPIRE(1979, Fr./Ger.), prod d, art d; FITZCARRALDO(1982), art d

Johann Wolfgang von Goethe
FAUST(1963, Ger.), w
Silents
FAUST(1926, Ger.), w

A.P. Von Gontard
Misc. Silents
PORI(1930, Ger.)

Wolff von Gordon
MERRY WIVES OF WINDSOR, THE(1952, Ger.), w

Ermin Von Gross
PERMISSION TO KILL(1975, U.S./Aust.)

Carl von Haartman
HELL'S ANGELS(1930)

Anders Von Haden
STAMBOUL QUEST(1934)

Egon von Hagen
Misc. Silents
LITTLE NAPOLEON, THE(1923, Ger.)

Ruth von Hagen
WHITE SLAVE SHIP(1962, Fr./Ital.)

Victor von Halem
NOT RECONCILED, OR "ONLY VIOLENCE HELPS WHERE IT RULES"(1969, Ger.)

Eva Von Hanno
FANNY AND ALEXANDER(1983, Swed./Fr./Ger.); FLIGHT OF THE EAGLE(1983, Swed.)

Thea von Harbou
M(1933, Ger.), w; TESTAMENT OF DR. MABUSE, THE(1943, Ger.), w; KOLBERG(1945, Ger.), w; M(1951), w; AFFAIRS OF DR. HOLL(1954, Ger.), w; JOURNEY TO THE LOST CITY(1960, Ger./Fr./Ital.), w; TERROR OF DR. MABUSE, THE(1965, Ger.), w
Silents
KRIEMHILD'S REVENGE(1924, Ger.), w; SIEGFRIED(1924, Ger.), w; METROPOLIS(1927, Ger.), w; SPIES(1929, Ger.), w; WOMAN ON THE MOON, THE(1929, Ger.), w

William Von Hardenburg
LOVE PARADE, THE(1929)
Silents
SLAVE OF DESIRE(1923); ABRAHAM LINCOLN(1924); PRINCE OF PILSEN, THE(1926); THREE SINNERS(1928)

Capt. Peter von Hartman
Silents
WEDDING MARCH, THE(1927)

Carl von Hartmann
Silents
WINGS(1927)

Ila Von Hasperg
CHINESE ROULETTE(1977, Ger.), ed
1984
VARIETY(1984), ed

Abi von Hasse
ONE, TWO, THREE(1961)

Karl Heinz von Hassel
LILI MARLEEN(1981, Ger.); QUERELLE(1983, Ger./Fr.)

Karl-Heinz von Hassel
MARRIAGE OF MARIA BRAUN, THE(1979, Ger.); LOLA(1982, Ger.); VERONIKA VOSS(1982, Ger.)

Paul Von Hausen
DEMONS OF LUDLOW, THE(1983)

Ted Von Hemert
WOMAN IN GREEN, THE(1945), set d; SMOOTH AS SILK(1946), set d; TANGIER(1946), set d

Paul von Henreid [Paul Henreid]
VICTORIA THE GREAT(1937, Brit.); MAD MEN OF EUROPE(1940, Brit.)

Hubert Von Herkomer
Misc. Silents
OLD WOOD CARVER, THE(1913, Brit.), d

Paul [Henreid] von Hernreid
NIGHT TRAIN(1940, Brit.)

Frouwke von Herwynen
NOT RECONCILED, OR "ONLY VIOLENCE HELPS WHERE IT RULES"(1969, Ger.)

Baron von Hesse
PRISONERS(1929)

Cornelia B. von Hessert
COVER GIRL(1944)

Jerry Von Hoeltke
MOVIE MOVIE(1978)

Mildred Von Hollen
KITTEN WITH A WHIP(1964)

Renate von Holt
THOSE FANTASTIC FLYING FOOLS(1967, Brit); NEW LIFE STYLE, THE(1970, Ger.)

Wilhelm Von Homburg
MORITURI(1965); LAST OF THE SECRET AGENTS?, THE(1966); HELL WITH HEROES, THE(1968); WRECKING CREW, THE(1968)

Joop Von Hulzen
BEFORE HIM ALL ROME TREMBLED(1947, Ital.)

Maria von Ilosvay
MARRIAGE OF FIGARO, THE(1970, Ger.)

Tibor von Janny
Silents
FOUR SONS(1928)

Egon Von Jordan
STOLEN IDENTITY(1953); FOREVER MY LOVE(1962); GOOD SOLDIER SCHWEIK, THE(1963, Ger.)

Herbert von Karajan
LA BOHEME(1965, Ital.), p

Carola von Kayser
COURT MARTIAL(1962, Ger.)

Georg von Kieseritzky
GERMAN SISTERS, THE(1982, Ger.), art d

George von Kieseritzky
LADY VANISHES, THE(1980, Brit.), art d

Ron Von Klausen
RACING FEVER(1964), stunts

Urban von Klebelsberg
PARSIFAL(1983, Fr.)

Erland von Koch
DEVIL'S WANTON, THE(1962, Swed.), m; NIGHT IS MY FUTURE(1962, Swed.), m; PORT OF CALL(1963, Swed.), m

Elsie von Koczain
Silents
WOMAN ON TRIAL, THE(1927), w

Johanna von Koczian
ARENT WE WONDERFUL?(1959, Ger.); FOR THE FIRST TIME(1959, U.S./Ger./Ital.); HELDINNEN(1962, Ger.); UNWILLING AGENT(1968, Ger.)

Leo Von Kokorny
WAKE UP FAMOUS(1937, Brit.)

Louise Von Kories
SON OF SINBAD(1955)

Yvette von Koris
CUBAN PETE(1946)

Doug Von Koss
PLAY IT AGAIN, SAM(1972), set d; LAUGHING POLICEMAN, THE(1973), set d; CONVERSATION, THE(1974), set d; DIE LAUGHING(1980), set d

John Van Kotze
SCENT OF MYSTERY(1960), ph; BANG, BANG, YOU'RE DEAD(1966), ph; HE WHO RIDES A TIGER(1966, Brit.), ph; FIVE GOLDEN DRAGONS(1967, Brit.), ph; VENGEANCE OF FU MANCHU, THE(1968, Brit./Ger./Hong Kong/Ireland), ph

Richard von Krafft-Ebing
ON HER BED OF ROSES(1966), w

Britta von Krogh
STOPOVER FOREVER(1964, Brit.)

Agnes von Krusenstjerna
LOVING COUPLES(1966, Swed.), w

Ingeborg von Kusserow
COURT CONCERT, THE(1936, Ger.)

Ver von Langen
DEAD MELODY(1938, Ger.)

Leopold Von Ledebour
HIS MAJESTY, KING BALLYHOO(1931, Ger.)
Misc. Silents
LAST PAYMENT(1921, Ger.)

Frederick von Ledebur
BREATH OF SCANDAL, A(1960)

Friedrich von Ledebur
ASSIGNMENT K(1968, Brit.)

Leopold von Ledebur
BLONDE NIGHTINGALE(1931, Ger.)

Hunter Von Leer
UNHOLY ROLLERS(1972); CAHILL, UNITED STATES MARSHAL(1973); EXECUTIVE ACTION(1973); FRAMED(1975); MISSOURI BREAKS, THE(1976); STEEL(1980); HALLOWEEN 11(1981); HISTORY OF THE WORLD, PART 1(1981)

Angela von Leitner
SLEEPING BEAUTY(1965, Ger.)

Lea Von Lenkeffy
Misc. Silents
OTHELLO(1922, Ger.)

Lucille von Lent
Silents
MERRY WIDOW, THE(1925)

Margo Von Leu
RED DANUBE, THE(1949)

Liv Von Linden
EVEL KNIEVEL(1971); SAVE THE TIGER(1973); WIN, PLACE, OR STEAL(1975)

Erich von Loewis
ROSEMARY(1960, Ger.)

Erik von Loewis
RESTLESS NIGHT, THE(1964, Ger.)

Mme. Von Major
WOLF'S CLOTHING(1936, Brit.)

Felix von Manteuffel
FRIENDS AND HUSBANDS(1983, Ger.)

Lena von Martens
FALL OF THE ROMAN EMPIRE, THE(1964); VICE AND VIRTUE(1965, Fr./Ital.)

Sabine von Maydell
DISORDER AND EARLY TORMENT(1977, Ger.)

Caroline von Mayrhauser
COOL AND THE CRAZY, THE(1958)

Barbara Von Meck
MUSIC LOVERS, THE(1971, Brit.), w

Galina Von Meck
REDS(1981)

Harry von Meter
BORDER ROMANCE(1930)
Silents
MY DAD(1922); KID BOOTS(1926)

Misc. Silents
ABANDONMENT, THE(1916); APRIL(1916); DUST(1916); LONE STAR(1916); LOVE HERMIT, THE(1916); OTHER SIDE OF THE DOOR, THE(1916); WHITE ROSETTE, THE(1916); YOUTH'S ENDEARING CHARM(1916); WHOSE WIFE?(1917); LURE OF LUXURY, THE(1918); MAN OF BRONZE, THE(1918); HEART OF THE NORTH, THE(1921); LIFE'S GREATEST QUESTION(1921); GREAT DIAMOND MYSTERY, THE(1924); SAGEBRUSH GOSPEL(1924); CLOUD RIDER, THE(1925); TEXAS BEAR-CAT, THE(1925); TRIPLE ACTION(1925); HOUR OF RECKONING, THE(1927)

Irene von Meyendorf
MOZART STORY, THE(1948, Aust.)

Irene von Meyendorff
FILM WITHOUT A NAME(1950, Ger.); HELL IS EMPTY(1967, Brit./Ital); MAYERLING(1968, Brit./Fr.)

Hubert von Meyerinck
WHITE DEMON, THE(1932, Ger.); MANULESCU(1933, Ger.); WORLD WITHOUT A MASK, THE(1934, Ger.); BARCAROLE(1935, Ger.); ROSEMARY(1960, Ger.); SECRET WAYS, THE(1961); SPESSART INN, THE(1961, Ger.); TURKISH CUCUMBER, THE(1963, Ger.); MAN WHO WALKED THROUGH THE WALL, THE(1964, Ger.)
Misc. Talkies
APE CREATURE(1968, Ger.)

Don Von Mizener
Misc. Talkies
WEST IS STILL WILD, THE(1977), d

Beate von Molo
IS PARIS BURNING?(1966, U.S./Fr.), w

Conrad von Molo
AMATEUR GENTLEMAN(1936, Brit.), ed; WHEN THIEF MEETS THIEF(1937, Brit.), ed

Curt von Molo
TRUNKS OF MR. O.F., THE(1932, Ger.), ed

Elisabeth Von Molo
SITUATION HOPELESS--BUT NOT SERIOUS(1965)

Trude von Molo
WHITE DEMON, THE(1932, Ger.)

Hans von Morehart
BEASTS OF BERLIN(1939)

Erich Von Morhardt
PARIS UNDERGROUND(1945)

Hans von Morhart
UNDER TWO FLAGS(1936); PURSUIT OF HAPPINESS, THE(1934); GENERAL DIED AT DAWN, THE(1936); FOREIGN CORRESPONDENT(1940); MAN I MARRIED, THE(1940); SAFARI(1940); DEADLY GAME, THE(1941); DOWN IN SAN DIEGO(1941); PARIS CALLING(1941); UNDERGROUND(1941); YANK IN THE R.A.F., A(1941); BERLIN CORRESPONDENT(1942); DAWN EXPRESS, THE(1942); GREAT IMPERSONATION, THE(1942); LADY HAS PLANS, THE(1942); PACIFIC RENDEZVOUS(1942); PIED PIPER, THE(1942); ABOVE SUSPICION(1943); FIRST COMES COURAGE(1943); IMMORTAL SERGEANT, THE(1943); STRANGE DEATH OF ADOLF HITLER, THE(1943); THIS LAND IS MINE(1943); THREE HEARTS FOR JULIA(1943); WATCH ON THE RHINE(1943); TAMPICO(1944); WHERE DO WE GO FROM HERE?(1945); GOLDEN EARRINGS(1947); WHERE THERE'S LIFE(1947)

Menrad von Mulldorfer
KRONOS(1957), spec eff

Helen von Munchhofen
Silents
METROPOLIS(1927, Ger.)

Kaethe von Nagy
BEAUTIFUL ADVENTURE(1932, Ger.)

Rolf von Nauckhoff
MAGIC FOUNTAIN, THE(1961)

Rolf von Naucskhoff
QUESTION 7(1961, U.S./Ger.)

Rolf von Naukhaff
NO SURVIVORS, PLEASE(1963, Ger.)

Rolf von Naukoff
ISLAND OF THE DOOMED(1968, Span./Ger.)

G. von Nazzani
MADDEST CAR IN THE WORLD, THE(1974, Ger.), w

Russ Von Neida
SHINBONE ALLEY(1971), anim

Dagmar von Netzer
NOT RECONCILED, OR "ONLY VIOLENCE HELPS WHERE IT RULES"(1969, Ger.)

Michael von Newlinski
TESTAMENT OF DR. MABUSE, THE(1943, Ger.)

Michael von Newlinsky
Silents
PANDORA'S BOX(1929, Ger.)

Margarethe Schell von Noe
PEDESTRIAN, THE(1974, Ger.); END OF THE GAME(1976, Ger./Ital.)

Magdalene von Nussbaum
SOMEWHERE IN BERLIN(1949, E. Ger.)

Rik von Nutter
ASSIGNMENT OUTER SPACE(1960, Ital.); ROMANOFF AND JULIET(1961); PASSIONATE THIEF, THE(1963, Ital.)

Petra Von Oelffen
SERPENT'S EGG, THE(1977, Ger./U.S.), ed

Petra Von Oelfen
DEAD KIDS(1981 Aus./New Zealand), ed

Jasper Von Oertzen
MAGIC FACE, THE(1951, Aust.); RIVER CHANGES, THE(1956)

Manuella Von Oppen
MADWOMAN OF CHAILLOT, THE(1969)

Eddison von Ottenfeld
SWORD OF THE AVENGER(1948), m

Lenora Von Ottinger
Misc. Silents
NARROW PATH, THE(1916)

Margut Von Oven
GEORGE(1973, U.S./Switz.), ed

Anita von Ow
MAN WHO WALKED THROUGH THE WALL, THE(1964, Ger.)

Aldo von Pinelli
SCHLAGER-PARADE(1953), w; FREDDY UNTER FREMDEN STERNEN(1962, Ger.), w; UNCLE TOM'S CABIN(1969, Fr./Ital./Ger./Yugo.), p

Flockina von Platen
COURT CONCERT, THE(1936, Ger.)

Victor Baron Von Plessan
WAJAN(1938, South Bali), p

Leo von Pokorny
DREAMS COME TRUE(1936, Brit.)

Leo [Pokorny] von Pokorny
STRANGE BOARDERS(1938, Brit.)

Leo Von Porkony
SECOND BUREAU(1937, Brit.)

Leon von Porkorny
YOU'RE IN THE ARMY NOW(1937, Brit.)

Evelyn von Rabenau
BLACK SPIDER, THE(1983, Swit.), ed

Geza von Radvanyi
UNCLE TOM'S CABIN(1969, Fr./Ital./Ger./Yugo.), d, w

Akos von Rathony
MRS. WARREN'S PROFESSION(1960, Ger.), d; PHONY AMERICAN, THE(1964, Ger.), d; CAVE OF THE LIVING DEAD(1966, Yugo./Ger.), p&d, w

Klaus von Rautenfeld
SINS OF ROSE BERND, THE(1959, Ger.), ph; ROSEMARY(1960, Ger.), w; TWO IN A SLEEPING BAG(1964, Ger.), ph; TERROR AFTER MIDNIGHT(1965, Ger.), ph; GIRL FROM HONG KONG(1966, Ger.), ph

Gregor von Rezzori
VERY PRIVATE AFFAIR, A(1962, Fr./Ital.); VIVA MARIA(1965, Fr./Ital.); DEGREE OF MURDER, A(1969, Ger.), w

Sigrid Von Richthofen
CABARET(1972)

Erich von Ritzau
Silents
GREED(1925); PRAIRIE WIFE, THE(1925)

Gunther von Ritzau
Silents
INTOLERANCE(1916)

C. Von Rock
CAVE OF THE LIVING DEAD(1966, Yugo./Ger.), w

Laci von Ronay
LITTLE NIGHT MUSIC, A(1977, Aust./U.S./Ger.), prod d

Jo Von Ronbeo
SEA GHOST, THE(1931), w

Jo von Ronkel
PLEASURE(1933), w

Rip Von Ronkel
SCARLET HOUR, THE(1956), w; BAMBOO SAUCER, THE(1968), w

Rip Von Ronkle
HANNAH LEE(1953), w

Anna von Rosen
TOUCH, THE(1971, U.S./Swed.)

Irmgard von Rottenhal
Misc. Silents
MIDNIGHT AT MAXIM'S(1915)

Rita von Royen
BEAUTIFUL SWINDLERS, THE(1967, Fr./Ital./Jap./Neth.), ed

Greta von Rue
LOCKED DOOR, THE(1929)
Misc. Silents
HER HONOR THE GOVERNOR(1926); HIS FOREIGN WIFE(1927)

Kurt Von Ruffin
ROYAL WALTZ, THE(1936)

Leopold von Sacher-Masoch
VENUS IN FURS(1970, Ital./Brit./Ger.), w

Suzanne von Schaack
TOOTSIE(1982)

Deidi Von Schaewen
INJUN FENDER(1973), ph

Catherina von Schell
TRAITOR'S GATE(1966, Brit./Ger.); ASSIGNMENT K(1968, Brit.); ON HER MAJESTY'S SECRET SERVICE(1969, Brit.); MOON ZERO TWO(1970, Brit.)

Catherine von Schell
HELL IS EMPTY(1967, Brit./Ital); AMSTERDAM AFFAIR, THE(1968 Brit.)

Sasha Von Scherler
NETWORK(1976); LAST EMBRACE(1979)

Hans Adalbert von Schetlow
Misc. Silents
LAST WALTZ, THE(1927, Ger.)

Carl von Schiller
Silents
CAPTAIN COURTESY(1915); SAVING THE FAMILY NAME(1916)
Misc. Silents
LAW UNTO HIMSELF, A(1916); SINS OF HER PARENT(1916); VENGEANCE IS MINE!(1916)

Erich Von Schilling
EXILE, THE(1947)

Margot von Schleffen
TRAPP FAMILY, THE(1961, Ger.), ed

A.W. von Schlegel
HAMLET(1962, Ger.), d&w

Hans von Schlettow
Silents
ISN'T LIFE WONDERFUL(1924)

Hans Adalbert von Schlettow
Silents
KRIEMHILD'S REVENGE(1924, Ger.); SIEGFRIED(1924, Ger.)

Hans-Adalbert von Schlettow
Misc. Silents
 THERESE RAQUIN(1928, Fr./Ger.)
Margot von Schlieffen
 CORPSE OF BEVERLY HILLS, THE(1965, Ger.), ed; SERENADE FOR TWO
 SPIES(1966, Ital./Ger.), ed; HOW TO SEDUCE A PLAYBOY(1968, Aust./Fr./Ital.), ed
Paul von Schreiber
 ALL HANDS ON DECK(1961); RIGHT APPROACH, THE(1961)
Shawn von Schreiber
 STRANGER IS WATCHING, A(1982)
Roland von Schulze
1984
 WOMAN IN FLAMES, A(1984, Ger.)
Augustus Von Schumacher
 WON TON TON, THE DOG WHO SAVED HOLLYWOOD(1976)
Wolfgang Von Schwind
 HIS MAJESTY, KING BALLYHOO(1931, Ger.)
Wolfgang von Schwindt
 1914(1932, Ger.)
Gustav von Seffertitz
Misc. Silents
 UNSEEING EYES(1923)
Edith von Seydewitz
 HYPNOSIS(1966, Ger./Sp./Ital.), ed
Gustave von Seyferttitz
 NURSE EDITH CAVELL(1939)
Gustav von Seyfferitz
 CASE OF SERGEANT GRISCHA, THE(1930)
Misc. Silents
 BELLS, THE(1926)
Gustav Von Seyffertitz
 CANARY MURDER CASE, THE(1929); HIS GLORIOUS NIGHT(1929); SEVEN
 FACES(1929); ARE YOU THERE?(1930); BAT WHISPERS, THE(1930); DANGEROUS
 PARADISE(1930); AMBASSADOR BILL(1931); DISHONORED(1931); SAFE IN
 HELL(1931); AFRAID TO TALK(1932); PENGUIN POOL MURDER, THE(1932);
 ROADHOUSE MURDER, THE(1932); SHANGHAI EXPRESS(1932); QUEEN CHRIS-
 TINA(1933); SILVER CORD(1933); WHEN STRANGERS MARRY(1933); CHANGE OF
 HEART(1934); MOONSTONE, THE(1934); MURDER ON THE BLACKBOARD(1934);
 MYSTERY LINER(1934); LITTLE MEN(1935); REMEMBER LAST NIGHT(1935);
 SHE(1935); MAD HOLIDAY(1936); MR. DEEDS GOES TO TOWN(1936); MURDER ON
 A BRIDLE PATH(1936); CIPHER BUREAU(1938); IN OLD CHICAGO(1938); KING OF
 ALCATRAZ(1938); MARIE ANTOINETTE(1938); PARADISE FOR THREE(1938);
 SWISS MISS(1938); HOTEL IMPERIAL(1939); NEVER SAY DIE(1939); SON OF
 FRANKENSTEIN(1939); MAD EMPRESS, THE(1940)
Misc. Talkies
 CHASING THROUGH EUROPE(1929)
Silents
 OLD WIVES FOR NEW(1918); MADONNAS AND MEN(1920); AMAZING LO-
 VERS(1921); INNER MAN, THE(1922); SHERLOCK HOLMES(1922); WHEN KNIGHT-
 HOOD WAS IN FLOWER(1922); UNDER THE RED ROBE(1923); EAGLE, THE(1925);
 GOOSE WOMAN, THE(1925); REGULAR FELLOW, A(1925); DON JUAN(1926);
 PRIVATE IZZY MURPHY(1926); RED DICE(1926); SPARROWS(1926); BARBED
 WIRE(1927); GAUCHO, THE(1928); MYSTERIOUS LADY, THE(1928); RED MARK,
 THE(1928); VAMPING VENUS(1928)
Misc. Silents
 LESS THAN KIN(1918); WIDOW'S MIGHT, THE(1918); VENGEANCE OF DURAND,
 THE(1919); DEAD MEN TELL NO TALES(1920); SPORTING DUCHESS, THE(1920);
 MARK OF THE BEAST(1923); BANDOLERO, THE(1924); DANGER GIRL, THE(1926);
 GOING CROOKED(1926); LONE WOLF RETURNS, THE(1926); BIRDS OF
 PREY(1927); DICE WOMAN, THE(1927); MAGIC FLAME, THE(1927); PRICE OF
 HONOR, THE(1927); STUDENT PRINCE IN OLD HEIDELBERG, THE(1927); WIZ-
 ARD, THE(1927); YELLOW LILY, THE(1928); CASE OF LENA SMITH, THE(1929)
Gustave Von Seyffertitz
 DOOMED BATTALION, THE(1932)
Silents
 DOWN TO EARTH(1917)
Gustov Von Seyffertitz
 RASPUTIN AND THE EMPRESS(1932)
Henry von Seyfried
 GUN RUNNER(1969)
H. von Sickle
Silents
 RIDING WITH DEATH(1921)
Sue Kiss von Soly
 LONG WEEKEND(1978, Aus.)
Reudiger von Sperl
 MAYA(1966), makeup
Rudiger Von Sperle
 KENNER(1969), makeup
Josef von Sternberg
 THUNDERBOLT(1929), d; BLUE ANGEL, THE(1930, Ger.), d; AMERICAN TRAGE-
 DY, AN(1931), d; DISHONORED(1931), d, w, m; BLONDE VENUS(1932), d, w;
 SHANGHAI EXPRESS(1932), p; SCARLET EMPRESS, THE(1934), d, m, ed; CRIME
 AND PUNISHMENT(1935), d; DEVIL IS A WOMAN, THE(1935), d, ph; KING STEPS
 OUT, THE(1936), d; GREAT WALTZ, THE(1938), d; SERGEANT MADDEN(1939), d; I
 TAKE THIS WOMAN(1940), d; SHANGHAI GESTURE, THE(1941), d, w; MA-
 CAO(1952), d; JET PILOT(1957), d
Silents
 SALVATION HUNTERS, THE(1925), d&w; UNDERWORLD(1927), d; WEDDING
 MARCH, THE(1927), ed; LAST COMMAND, THE(1928), d; STREET OF SIN,
 THE(1928), d, w
Misc. Silents
 WOMAN OF THE SEA, A(1926), d; DOCKS OF NEW YORK, THE(1928), d; CASE OF
 LENA SMITH, THE(1929), d
Joseph von Sternberg
 MOROCCO(1930), d; ANATAHAN(1953, Jap.), d&ph
Silents
 EXQUISITE SINNER, THE(1926), d, w; IT(1927), d; DRAGNET, THE(1928), d

Nicholas Von Sternberg
 TOURIST TRAP, THE(1979), ph; HOSPITAL MASSACRE(1982), ph; JOYS-
 TICKS(1983), ph; WACKO(1983), ph
1984
 HOSPITAL MASSACRE(1984), ph; JUNGLE WARRIORS(1984, U.S./Ger./Mex.), ph;
 ON THE LINE(1984, Span.), ph
Nicholas J. von Sternberg
 PINK MOTEL(1983), ph
Nicholas Josef von Sternberg
 DOLEMITE(1975), ph; MISTRESS OF THE APES(1981), ph
Nickolas Von Sternberg
 PETEY WHEATSTRAW(1978), ph
Erich Von Stoheim
Misc. Silents
 HIS ROYAL HIGHNESS(1918)
Hilde von Stolz
 MY HEART IS CALLING(1935, Brit.); DREAMER, THE(1936, Ger.); LIFE BEGINS
 ANEW(1938, Ger.); TRAPP FAMILY, THE(1961, Ger.)
Anton von Stralen
 MANCHURIAN CANDIDATE, THE(1962)
Erich Von Stroheim
 GREAT GABBO, THE(1929); THREE FACES EAST(1930); FRIENDS AND LO-
 VERS(1931); AS YOU DESIRE ME(1932); LOST SQUADRON, THE(1932); HELLO
 SISTER!(1933), d, w; CRIMSON ROMANCE(1934); FUGITIVE ROAD(1934); CRIME
 OF DR. CRESPI, THE(1936); DEVIL DOLL, THE(1936), w; SAN FRANCISCO(1936), w;
 BETWEEN TWO WOMEN(1937), w; GRAND ILLUSION(1938, Fr.); ALIBI, THE(1939,
 Fr.); LE MONDE TREMBLERA(1939, Fr.); PERSONAL COLUMN(1939, Fr.); I WAS AN
 ADVENTURESS(1940); ULTIMATUM(1940, Fr.); SO ENDS OUR NIGHT(1941); FIVE
 GRAVES TO CAIRO(1943); IT HAPPENED IN GIBRALTAR(1943, Fr.); NORTH STAR,
 THE(1943); UNDER SECRET ORDERS(1943, Brit.); LADY AND THE MONSTER,
 THE(1944); STORM OVER LISBON(1944); GREAT FLAMARION, THE(1945); SCOT-
 LAND YARD INVESTIGATOR(1945, Brit.); MASK OF DIIJON, THE(1946); MASK OF
 KOREA(1950, Fr.); SUNSET BOULEVARD(1950); ALRAUNE(1952, Ger.); ALERT IN
 THE SOUTH(1954, Fr.); NAPOLEON(1955, Fr.)
Silents
 BIRTH OF A NATION, THE(1915); INTOLERANCE(1916); SOCIAL SECRETARY,
 THE(1916); IN AGAIN-OUT AGAIN(1917), a, art d; REACHING FOR THE
 MOON(1917); HEARTS OF THE WORLD(1918); HUN WITHIN, THE(1918); BLIND
 HUSBANDS(1919), a, d&w&art d; DEVIL'S PASSKEY, THE(1920), d&w, w, ed, art
 d; FOOLISH WIVES(1920), a, d&w; MERRY-GO-ROUND(1923), a, d&w, t; SOULS FOR
 SALE(1923); GREED(1925), p, d, w, t, prod d; MERRY WIDOW, THE(1925), d, w,
 cos; WEDDING MARCH, THE(1927), a, d, w, art d; QUEEN KELLY(1929), d&w, art
 d
Misc. Silents
 CAPTAIN MACKLIN(1915); OLD HEIDELBERG(1915); HEART OF HUMANITY,
 THE(1919)
Erich Von Stroheim, Jr.
 TWO WEEKS IN ANOTHER TOWN(1962); SQUARE SHOULDERS(1929); OLD MAN
 RHYTHM(1935); PARTY GIRL(1958)
Franz von Suppe
 WAY OUT WEST(1937), m
Clas S. Von Sydow
 HAWAII(1966)
Henrik Von Sydow
 HAWAII(1966)
Max von Sydow
 SEVENTH SEAL, THE(1958, Swed.); MAGICIAN, THE(1959, Swed.); WILD STRAWB-
 ERRIES(1959, Swed.); BRINK OF LIFE(1960, Swed.); VIRGIN SPRING, THE(1960,
 Swed.); THROUGH A GLASS DARKLY(1962, Swed.); WINTER LIGHT, THE(1963,
 Swed.); SWEDISH MISTRESS, THE(1964, Swed.); GREATEST STORY EVER TOLD,
 THE(1965); REWARD, THE(1965); HAWAII(1966); QUILLER MEMORANDUM,
 THE(1966, Brit.); HERE'S YOUR LIFE(1968, Swed.); HOUR OF THE WOLF, THE(1968,
 Swed.); SHAME(1968, Swed.); KREMLIN LETTER, THE(1970); NIGHT VISITOR,
 THE(1970, Swed./U.S.); PASSION OF ANNA, THE(1970, Swed.); TOUCH, THE(1971,
 U.S./Swed.); EMBASSY(1972, Brit.); EMIGRANTS, THE(1972, Swed.); EXORCIST,
 THE(1973); NEW LAND, THE(1973, Swed.); STEPPENWOLF(1974); THREE DAYS OF
 THE CONDOR(1975); ULTIMATE WARRIOR, THE(1975); DESERT OF THE TAR-
 TARS, THE(1976 Fr./Ital./Iranian); VOYAGE OF THE DAMNED(1976, Brit.); EXOR-
 CIST II: THE HERETIC(1977); FOXTROT(1977, Mex./Swiss); MARCH OR DIE(1977,
 Brit.); BRASS TARGET(1978); HURRICANE(1979); DEATHWATCH(1980, Fr./Ger.);
 FLASH GORDON(1980); SHE DANCES ALONE(1981, Aust./U.S.); VICTORY(1981);
 CONAN THE BARBARIAN(1982); FLIGHT OF THE EAGLE(1983, Swed.); NEVER
 SAY NEVER AGAIN(1983); STRANGE BREW(1983)
1984
 DREAMSCAPE(1984); DUNE(1984)
Maria von Tasnady
 FINAL CHORD, THE(1936, Ger.)
Hantz Von Teuffen
 FLYING SAUCER, THE(1950)
Erika von Thellmann
 GOOD SOLDIER SCHWEIK, THE(1963, Ger.); UNCLE TOM'S CABIN(1969, Fr./Ital./
 Ger./Yugo.)
E. Von Theumer
 MISSION STARDUST(1968, Ital./Span./Ger.), p
Ernst R. von Theumer
1984
 JUNGLE WARRIORS(1984, U.S./Ger./Mex.), p&d, w
Ernst Ritter von Theumer
 THERE IS STILL ROOM IN HELL(1963, Ger.), p&d; ISLAND OF THE DOO-
 MED(1968, Span./Ger.), w
Brit von Thiesenhausen
 SHADOWS GROW LONGER, THE(1962, Switz./Ger.)
Friedrich von Thun
 ASSIGNMENT K(1968, Brit.)
Ulrich von Thuna
 NOT RECONCILED, OR "ONLY VIOLENCE HELPS WHERE IT RULES"(1969, Ger.)
Albert Von Tilzer
 RAINBOW OVER BROADWAY(1933), m

Slavo Vorkapich
MARIE ANTOINETTE(1938), spec eff
Stavko Vorkapich
CRIME WITHOUT PASSION(1934), spec eff; CROWD ROARS, THE(1938), ph
Slavko Vorkapitch
Silents
SCARAMOUCHE(1923)
Zandor Vorkov
BLOOD OF FRANKENSTEIN(1970); BRAIN OF BLOOD(1971, Phil.)
Z. Vorkul
JACK FROST(1966, USSR)
Vorlicek
SIR, YOU ARE A WIDOWER(1971, Czech.), w
Vaclav Vorlicek
WHO KILLED JESSIE?(1965, Czech.), d; SIR, YOU ARE A WIDOWER(1971, Czech.), d; WHAT WOULD YOU SAY TO SOME SPINACH(1976, Czech.), d&w
Anthony Vorno
WALK THE ANGRY BEACH(1961)
M. Vorobyev
TRAIN GOES EAST, THE(1949, USSR)
M. Vorobyov
WAR AND PEACE(1968, USSR)
Vasya Vorokhobko
LITTLE HUMPBACKED HORSE, THE(1962, USSR)
Vera Voronina
PATRIOT, THE(1928)
Silents
TIME TO LOVE(1927)
Misc. Silents
WHIRLPOOL OF YOUTH, THE(1927)
Arthur Voronka
LOVE IN A FOUR LETTER WORLD(1970, Can.), p, w
1984
HEY BABE!(1984, Can.), p
Sergev Voronkov
OPTIMISTIC TRAGEDY, THE(1964, USSR), art d
Sergey Voronkov
THREE SISTERS, THE(1969, USSR), art d
Sergy Voronkov
DESTINY OF A MAN(1961, USSR), art d
I. Voronov
DAY THE EARTH FROZE, THE(1959, Fin./USSR)
G. Voropayev
OVERCOAT, THE(1965, USSR)
Heaton Vorse
REDS(1981)
Mary Heaton Vorse
Silents
SEA TIGER, THE(1927), w
Gordon Vorster
DIAMOND SAFARI(1958), art d; GUEST AT STEENKAMPSKRAAL, THE(1977, South Africa)
1984
GUEST, THE(1984, Brit.)
Wilhelm Vorwerg
WORLD IN MY POCKET, THE(1962, Fr./Ital./Ger.), art d
Marik Vos
VIRGIN SPRING, THE(1960, Swed.), cos; FANNY AND ALEXANDER(1983, Swed./Fr./Ger.), cos
Victor Vos
LEAP OF FAITH(1931, Brit.)
Marik Vos-Lundh
SILENCE, THE(1964, Swed.), cos; HOUR OF THE WOLF, THE(1968, Swed.), art d & set d
J. Vosalik
MOST BEAUTIFUL AGE, THE(1970, Czech.)
Jose Vosalik
INSPECTOR GENERAL, THE(1937, Czech.)
John Vosberg
HEARTS OF HUMANITY(1932)
John Vosburg
CONVICTED(1931)
Alfred Vosburgh
Misc. Silents
HER FATHER'S SON(1916); DIVORCEE, THE(1917); MONEY MADNESS(1917); PRINCESS OF THE DARK, A(1917); SHACKLES OF TRUTH(1917)
Dick Vosburgh
GIRLS OF LATIN QUARTER(1960, Brit.), w
Harold Vosburgh
Silents
IF WOMEN ONLY KNEW(1921)
Misc. Silents
SMUGGLERS, THE(1916)
Jack Vosburgh
Misc. Silents
LADY IN THE LIBRARY, THE(1917); MY FIGHTING GENTLEMAN(1917); SOUTHERN PRIDE(1917)
John Vosburgh
RED-HAIRED ALIBI, THE(1932); WESTERN LIMITED(1932)
Marcy Vosburgh
STAR TREK II: THE WRATH OF KHAN(1982)
Tilly Vosburgh
MISSIONARY, THE(1982); PIRATES OF PENZANCE, THE(1983)
Carl Voscherau
FILM WITHOUT A NAME(1950, Ger.)
Kenneth Vose
GREASED LIGHTNING(1977), w

Judith Voselli
ROGUE SONG, THE(1930); SECOND FLOOR MYSTERY, THE(1930)
Karl Heinz Vosgerau
LOST HONOR OF KATHARINA BLUM, THE(1975, Ger.)
John M. Voshell
Silents
ENEMIES OF CHILDREN(1923), d&w
Vaclav Voska
BOHEMIAN RAPTURE(1948, Czech.); MURDER CZECH STYLE(1968, Czech.)
Robert Voskanian
CHILD, THE(1977), d
George Voskovec
AFFAIR IN TRINIDAD(1952); IRON MISTRESS, THE(1952); 27TH DAY, THE(1957); BRAVADOS, THE(1958); UNCLE VANYA(1958); WIND ACROSS THE EVERGLADES(1958); BUTTERFIELD 8(1960); HAMLET(1964); SPY WHO CAME IN FROM THE COLD, THE(1965, Brit.); MISTER BUDDWING(1966); DESPERATE ONES, THE(1968 U.S./Span.); THE BOSTON STRANGLER, THE(1968); ICEMAN COMETH, THE(1973); MAN ON A SWING(1974); SOMEWHERE IN TIME(1980); BARBAROSA(1982)
Jiri Voskovec
GOLEM, THE(1937, Czech./Fr.), w
George Voskovek
12 ANGRY MEN(1957)
Zoya Voskresenskaya
SONS AND MOTHERS(1967, USSR), w
G. Voskresensky
Misc. Silents
DEAD MAN, THE(1914, USSR)
Behrooz Vosoughi
CARAVANS(1978, U.S./Iranian)
Edgar Vosper
YOUNG MR. PITT, THE(1942, Brit.)
Frank Vosper
LAST POST, THE(1929, Brit.); MURDER ON THE SECOND FLOOR(1932, Brit.), w; DICK TURPIN(1933, Brit.); ROME EXPRESS(1933, Brit.), a, d; SECRET AGENT(1933, Brit.), w; STRANGE EVIDENCE(1933, Brit.); BLIND JUSTICE(1934, Brit.); NO FUNNY BUSINESS(1934, Brit.), w; OPEN ALL NIGHT(1934, Brit.); POWER(1934, Brit.); STRAUSS' GREAT WALTZ(1934, Brit.); STRIKE!(1934, Brit.); KOENIGSMARK(1935, Fr.); MAN WHO KNEW TOO MUCH, THE(1935, Brit.); REGAL CAVALCADE(1935, Brit.); SECRET OF STAMBOUL, THE(1936, Brit.); HEART'S DESIRE(1937, Brit.); LOVE FROM A STRANGER(1937, Brit.), w; SPY OF NAPOLEON(1939, Brit.); SHADOWS ON THE STAIRS(1941), w; LOVE FROM A STRANGER(1947), w
John Vosper
MISS V FROM MOSCOW(1942); UNDERCOVER MAN(1942); WIFE TAKES A FLYER, THE(1942); DEAD MAN'S GULCH(1943); MR. SKEFFINGTON(1944); THOSE ENDEARING YOUNG CHARMS(1945); BOY, A GIRL, AND A DOG, A(1946); MAN I LOVE, THE(1946); NIGHT AND DAY(1946); NOTORIOUS(1946); PERFECT MARRIAGE(1946); HIGH CONQUEST(1947); HOMESTRETCH(1947); SEA OF GRASS, THE(1947); JUNE BRIDE(1948); DESERT FOX, THE(1951); TALES OF ROBIN HOOD(1951); BLACK HILLS AMBUSH(1952); BREAKDOWN(1953); MAGNETIC MONSTER, THE(1953); NO ESCAPE(1953); TENDER HEARTS(1955); EDGE OF HELL(1956)
Anne Voss
TOM SAWYER(1973)
Carl Voss
BEAU GESTE(1939); LIGHT THAT FAILED, THE(1939); TWO YEARS BEFORE THE MAST(1946)
Carol Voss
DARK ANGEL, THE(1935)
Peter Voss
WATER FOR CANITOGA(1939, Ger.)
Philip Voss
FRANKENSTEIN AND THE MONSTER FROM HELL(1974, Brit.); HOPSCOTCH(1980); OCTOPUSSY(1983, Brit.)
Ursula Voss
DECISION BEFORE DAWN(1951)
V.I. Voss
VOODOO WOMAN(1957), w
Judith Vosselli
AWFUL TRUTH, THE(1929); LADY'S MORALS, A(1930); RENO(1930); SUNNY(1930); TODAY(1930); INSPIRATION(1931); KISS ME AGAIN(1931); LADY WHO DARED, THE(1931); MADAME BUTTERFLY(1932); UNDER EIGHTEEN(1932); LOVE IS LIKE THAT(1933); CITY PARK(1934); GREAT FLIRTATION, THE(1934); MODERN HERO, A(1934); STAMBOUL QUEST(1934); ROBERTA(1935)
Bob Vossler
LOVE MATCH, THE(1955, Brit.)
Robert Vossler
MURDER REPORTED(1958, Brit.)
Vostorgov
Misc. Silents
STORY OF SEVEN WHO WERE HANGED(1920, USSR)
Alena Vostra
MATTER OF DAYS, A(1969, Fr./Czech.), w
Jan Vostrcil
LOVES OF A BLONDE(1966, Czech.); FIREMAN'S BALL, THE(1968, Czech.); INTIMATE LIGHTING(1969, Czech.)
Behrooz Vosugi
INVINCIBLE SIX, THE(1970, U.S./Iran)
Jack Votion
DREAMING OUT LOUD(1940), p
Jack William Votion
GOIN' TO TOWN(1944), p
Jack Williams Votion
BASHFUL BACHELOR, THE(1942), p
Peter Votrian
ASSIGNMENT-PARIS(1952); HANS CHRISTIAN ANDERSEN(1952); PRISONER OF ZENDA, THE(1952); HER TWELVE MEN(1954); BIG HOUSE, U.S.A.(1955); MAN CALLED PETER, THE(1955); CRIME IN THE STREETS(1956); HELL ON FRISCO BAY(1956); OKLAHOMAN, THE(1957)

Peter J. Votrian
FEAR STRIKES OUT(1957)
Ralph Votrian
UNTIL THEY SAIL(1957); CORKY OF GASOLINE ALLEY(1951); BOLD AND THE BRAVE, THE(1956); SCREAMING EAGLES(1956); TEA AND SYMPATHY(1956); INVISIBLE BOY, THE(1957); IMITATION GENERAL(1958)
Ralph J. Votrian
PILLARS OF THE SKY(1956)
Antonios Voulgaris
BAREFOOT BATTALION, THE(1954, Gr.)
Pantelis Voulgaris
MATCHMAKING OF ANNA, THE(1972, Gr.), d, w
Lefteris Vournas
RAPE, THE(1965, Gr.); STEFANIA(1968, Gr.)
Georges Vourvahakis
IPHIGENIA(1977, Gr.)
Val Vousden
Misc. Talkies
UNCLE NICK(1938)
Andreas Voutsinas
PRODUCERS, THE(1967); FRAULEIN DOKTOR(1969, Ital./Yugo.); SPIRITS OF THE DEAD(1969, Fr./Ital.); TWELVE CHAIRS, THE(1970); DREAM OF PASSION, A(1978, Gr.); HISTORY OF THE WORLD, PART 1(1981)
Aliki Vouyouklaki
ASTERO(1960, Gr.); MADALENA(1965, Gr.)
Misc. Talkies
ALIKI-MY LOVE(1963, U.S./Gr.)
A. Vovsi
DAY THE WAR ENDED, THE(1961, USSR)
Donald Vowles
DELAYED ACTION(1954, Brit.)
Hilliard Vox
THIRTEENTH CANDLE, THE(1933, Brit.)
George [Yorgo] Voyadjis
ZORBA THE GREEK(1964, U.S./Gr.)
Yorgo Voyagis
ADVENTURERS, THE(1970); LOVE PROBLEMS(1970, Ital.); LAST VALLEY, THE(1971, Brit.)
1984
LITTLE DRUMMER GIRL, THE(1984)
John Voyantiz
GUIDE, THE(1965, U.S./India)
Boris Voyetekho
LAST HILL, THE(1945, USSR), w
Zina Voynow
JEREMY(1973), ed
Ada Voyst Voystik
ONCE THERE WAS A GIRL(1945, USSR)
Steven Voyt
LUM AND ABNER ABROAD(1956)
Voytek
1984
SUCCESS IS THE BEST REVENGE(1984, Brit.), prod d
Ada Voytsik
DAY THE EARTH FROZE, THE(1959, Fin./USSR); LULLABY(1961, USSR); NINE DAYS OF ONE YEAR(1964, USSR)
Elly Vozikiadou
ELECTRA(1962, Gr.)
Lorimme Vozoff
1984
IRRECONCILABLE DIFFERENCES(1984)
Lorinne Vozoff
1984
IMPULSE(1984); IRRECONCILABLE DIFFERENCES(1984)
Arnost Vrana
FIFTH HORSEMAN IS FEAR, THE(1968, Czech.)
Frantisek Vrana
DIAMONDS OF THE NIGHT(1968, Czech.)
Vlasta Vrana
RABID(1976, Can.); ONE MAN(1979, Can.); GAS(1981, Can.); HAPPY BIRTHDAY TO ME(1981)
1984
HEY BABE!(1984, Can.)
Bedrich Vrbsky
KRAKATIT(1948, Czech.)
R. Vrchota
BORDER STREET(1950, Pol.)
Anton Vrdoljak
RAT(1960, Yugo.)
Helen Vreeland
DANGER PATROL(1937), w
Richard Vreeland
MELODY FOR TWO(1937), ch
Robert Vreeland
CITY, FOR CONQUEST(1941), ch; FOOTSTEPS IN THE DARK(1941), ch
Cornelis Vreswijk
FLIGHT OF THE EAGLE(1983, Swed.)
Janez Vrhovec
TEMPEST(1958, Ital./Yugo./Fr.); FRAULEIN DOKTOR(1969, Ital./Yugo.)
Janez Vrhovic
RAT(1960, Yugo.)
Alfredo Vribe
CEREBROS DIABOLICOS(1966, Mex.), ph
Irena Vrkljan
DAVID(1979, Ger.)
Peter Vrocco
ONE AND ONLY, THE(1978)

Elizabeth Vroman
BRIGHT ROAD(1953), w
Olga Vronska
DESERTER AND THE NOMADS, THE(1969, Czech./Ital.)
Vronsky
Misc. Silents
CRIME AND PUNISHMENT(1913, USSR)
I. Vronsky
Misc. Silents
CRIME AND PUNISHMENT(1913, USSR), d; HE WHO GETS SLAPPED(1916, USSR)
Sergei Vronsky
AUTUMN MARATHON(1982, USSR), ph
Albert Vroom
Silents
SONG OF THE WAGE SLAVE, THE(1915)
Edward Vroom
Silents
FAITH HEALER, THE(1921)
Fred Vroom
Silents
MILLIONAIRE, THE(1921); WHITE AND UNMARRIED(1921)
Frederick Vroom
Silents
JUNGLE CHILD, THE(1916); I LOVE YOU(1918); ISLAND OF INTRIGUE, THE(1919); PRINCE OF AVENUE A., THE(1920); FAITH HEALER, THE(1921); TAILOR MADE MAN, A(1922); WOMAN WHO WALKED ALONE, THE(1922); ACQUITTAL, THE(1923); TIGER'S CLAW, THE(1923); HIS HOUR(1924); NAVIGATOR, THE(1924); RECKLESS AGE, THE(1924); EYES RIGHT(1926); GENERAL, THE(1927)
Misc. Silents
BETTY TAKES A HAND(1918); LITTLE RED DECIDES(1918); SHE HIRED A HUSBAND(1919); WHERE THE WEST BEGINS(1919); KENTUCKY COLONEL, THE(1920); MARRIAGE PIT, THE(1920); MISFIT WIFE, THE(1921); HEART LINE, THE(1921); PHANTOM JUSTICE(1924); SPORTING YOUTH(1924); POOR MILLIONAIRE, THE(1930)
Henry Vroom
WITHOUT RESERVATIONS(1946); O.S.S.(1946); GOLDEN EARRINGS(1947); WHIPLASH(1948)
Judith Ann Vroom
LOVE THAT BRUTE(1950)
Siem Vroom
BRIDGE TOO FAR, A(1977, Brit.); LIFT, THE(1983, Neth.)
Jiri Vrstala
ROCKET TO NOWHERE(1962, Czech.); DEVIL'S TRAP, THE(1964, Czech.); TRANSPORT FROM PARADISE(1967, Czech.); FIFTH HORSEMAN IS FEAR, THE(1968, Czech.)
Iris Vrus
SEVENTH CONTINENT, THE(1968, Czech./Yugo.)
Ivo Vrzal
1984
MOSCOW ON THE HUDSON(1984)
V. Vsevolodov
HOME FOR TANYA, A(1961, USSR)
Rene G. Vuattoux
RIFIFI(1956, Fr.), p
Branko Vucicevic
EARLY WORKS(1970, Yugo.), w; MONTENEGRO(1981, Brit./Swed.), w
Aljosa Vuckovic
ROMANCE OF A HORSE THIEF(1971)
Olivera Vuco
I EVEN MET HAPPY GYPSIES(1968, Yugo.); FRAULEIN DOKTOR(1969, Ital./Yugo.); MARK OF THE DEVIL(1970, Ger./Brit.)
Milena Vucotich
JULIET OF THE SPIRITS(1965, Fr./Ital./W.Ger.); MADE IN ITALY(1967, Fr./Ital.); TAMING OF THE SHREW, THE(1967, U.S./Ital.)
Popol Vuh
AGUIRRE, THE WRATH OF GOD(1977, W. Ger.), m; NOSFERATU, THE VAMPIRE(1979, Fr./Ger.), m; FITZCARRALDO(1982), m
George-Alain Vuille
ASHANTI(1979), p
Georges Alain Vuille
CLAIR DE FEMME(1980,Fr.), p
Georges-Alain Vuille
WOMANLIGHT(1979, Fr./Ger./Ital.), p
Pierre Vuilleumier
TRON(1982)
Milja Vujanovic
EARLY WORKS(1970, Yugo.)
Stevo Vujatovic
EVENT, AN(1970, Yugo.)
D. Sztojan Vujicsics
WINTER WIND(1970, Fr./Hung.)
Tihamer Vujicsics
WINTER WIND(1970, Fr./Hung.), a, m
Dusan Vujisic
GENGHIS KHAN(U.S./Brit./Ger./Yugo); DESPERADO TRAIL, THE(1965, Ger./Yugo.)
Pavle Vujisic
HOROSCOPE(1950, Yugo.); STEPPE, THE(1963, Fr./Ital.); EVENT, AN(1970, Yugo.); TWILIGHT TIME(1983, U.S./Yugo.)
Ivanka Vukasovic
INNOCENCE UNPROTECTED(1971, Yugo.), ed
Zeno Vukelich
PLACE FOR LOVERS, A(1969, Ital./Fr.), md
Bisera Vukotic
CASTLE KEEP(1969)
Dusan Vukotic
SEVENTH CONTINENT, THE(1968, Czech./Yugo.), d, w; VISITORS FROM THE GALAXY(1981, Yugo.), d, w

Melina Vukotic
GIDGET GOES TO ROME(1963)
Milena Vukotic
COME SEPTEMBER(1961); CENTURION, THE(1962, Fr./Ital.); INVASION 1700(1965, Fr./Ital./Yugo.); ADVENTURERS, THE(1970); MAN WHO CAME FOR COFFEE, THE(1970, Ital.); DISCREET CHARM OF THE BOURGEOISIE, THE(1972, Fr.); PHANTOM OF LIBERTY, THE(1974, Fr.); THAT OBSCURE OBJECT OF DESIRE(1977, Fr./Span.); MONSIGNOR(1982); MOON IN THE GUTTER, THE(1983, Fr./Ital.)
1984
NOSTALGHIA(1984, USSR/Ital.)
Tom Vukusic
1984
NADIA(1984, U.S./Yugo.)
The Vulcanes
I'LL TAKE SWEDEN(1965)
Rangel Vulchanov
WITH LOVE AND TENDERNESS(1978, Bulgaria), d
C.E. Vulliamy
COURAGEOUS MR. PENN, THE(1941, Brit.), w; JOLLY BAD FELLOW, A(1964, Brit.), w
Mario Vulpiani
DILLINGER IS DEAD(1969, Ital.), ph; SEED OF MAN, THE(1970, Ital.), ph; WIND FROM THE EAST(1970, Fr./Ital./Ger.), ph; LA GRANDE BOUFFE(1973, Fr.), ph; TEMPTER, THE(1974, Ital./Brit.), ph; DEVIL IS A WOMAN, THE(1975, Brit./Ital.), ph; CLARETTA AND BEN(1983, Ital., Fr.), ph
Mario Vulpiano
LIZA(1976, Fr./Ital.), ph
Paul Vulpius
TWO OF US, THE(1938, Brit.), w
Ka Vundia
AMIN–THE RISE AND FALL(1982, Kenya)
Tito Vuolo
SHADOW OF THE THIN MAN(1941); BISHOP'S WIFE, THE(1947); DAISY KEN-YON(1947); KISS OF DEATH(1947); MOURNING BECOMES ELECTRA(1947); T-MEN(1947); WEB, THE(1947); CRY OF THE CITY(1948); I WOULDN'T BE IN YOUR SHOES(1948); LUCK OF THE IRISH(1948); MR. BLANDINGS BUILDS HIS DREAM HOUSE(1948); SORRY, WRONG NUMBER(1948); EVERYBODY DOES IT(1949); FLAMINGO ROAD(1949); FOUNTAINHEAD, THE(1949); GREAT GATSBY, THE(1949); HOUSE OF STRANGERS(1949); RED DANUBE, THE(1949); BETWEEN MIDNIGHT AND DAWN(1950); DEPORTED(1950); ENFORCER, THE(1951); MAN WHO CHEATED HIMSELF, THE(1951); MATING SEASON, THE(1951); RACKET, THE(1951); RAGING TIDE, THE(1951); SATURDAY'S HERO(1951); UP FRONT(1951); SIX BRIDGES TO CROSS(1955); YOUNG AT HEART(1955); EMERGENCY HOSPI-TAL(1956); KILLING, THE(1956); DRAGSTRIP GIRL(1957); MIDNIGHT STORY, THE(1957); 20 MILLION MILES TO EARTH(1957)
I. Vuskovich
SON OF MONGOLIA(1936, USSR), art d; QUEEN OF SPADES(1961, USSR), art d
Lydia Vuynovich
FIEND(
Vaclav Vydra
MERRY WIVES, THE(1940, Czech.); SKELETON ON HORSEBACK(1940, Czech.)
John Vye
NUTCRACKER(1982, Brit.)
Murvyn Vye
GOLDEN EARRINGS(1947); WHISPERING SMITH(1948); CONNECTICUT YAN-KEE IN KING ARTHUR'S COURT, A(1949); ROAD TO BALI(1952); DESTINATION GOBI(1953); PICKUP ON SOUTH STREET(1953); BLACK HORSE CANYON(1954); RIVER OF NO RETURN(1954); ESCAPE TO BURMA(1955); GREEN FIRE(1955); PEARL OF THE SOUTH PACIFIC(1955); BEST THINGS IN LIFE ARE FREE, THE(1956); SHORT CUT TO HELL(1957); THIS COULD BE THE NIGHT(1957); VOODOO ISLAND(1957); GIRL IN THE WOODS(1958); IN LOVE AND WAR(1958); RALLY 'ROUND THE FLAG, BOYS!(1958); AL CAPONE(1959); BOY AND THE PIRATES, THE(1960); GEORGE RAFT STORY, THE(1961); KING OF THE ROARING TWENTIES–THE STORY OF ARNOLD ROTHSTEIN(1961); ANDY(1965)
I. Vykhodtseva
FATHER OF A SOLDIER(1966, USSR)
Sergei Vykulov
SLEEPING BEAUTY, THE(1966, USSR)
C. Vylars
FRENZY(1946, Brit.), w; HOUSE OF MYSTERY(1961, Brit.), w
Margaret Vyner
FLYING DOCTOR, THE(1936, Aus.); SENSATION(1936, Brit.); BOMBS OVER LON-DON(1937, Brit.); CAVALIER OF THE STREETS, THE(1937, Brit.); INCIDENT IN SHANGHAI(1937, Brit.); CLIMBING HIGH(1938, Brit.); SAILING ALONG(1938, Brit.); YOUNG MR. PITT, THE(1942, Brit.); LAMP STILL BURNS, THE(1943, Brit.); GIVE ME THE STARS(1944, Brit.); TWILIGHT HOUR(1944, Brit.); MR. EMMANUEL(1945, Brit.); PATIENT VANISHES, THE(1947, Brit.); ENCORE(1951, Brit.); SOMETHING MONEY CAN'T BUY(1952, Brit.)
Kosmo Vynil
KING OF COMEDY, THE(1983)
V. Vyshkovskiy
THERE WAS AN OLD COUPLE(1967, USSR)
Ivan Vyskocil
REPORT ON THE PARTY AND THE GUESTS, A(1968, Czech.); SIGN OF THE VIRGIN(1969, Czech.)
Jack Vyvian
YOUNG AND INNOCENT(1938, Brit.)
Jack Vyvyan
THAT'S MY WIFE(1933, Brit.); HOWARD CASE, THE(1936, Brit.); UNDER A CLOUD(1937, Brit.); I SEE ICE(1938); MAN WITH 100 FACES, THE(1938, Brit.); MERELY MR. HAWKINS(1938, Brit.); YOU'RE THE DOCTOR(1938, Brit.); HOME FROM HOME(1939, Brit.); THIS MAN IS NEWS(1939, Brit.); THREE SILENT MEN(1940, Brit.); FACING THE MUSIC(1941, Brit.); SHEEPDOG OF THE HILLS(1941, Brit.); GET CRACKING(1943, Brit.); IT'S IN THE BAG(1943, Brit.); MILLIONS LIKE US(1943, Brit.); OLD MOTHER RILEY, DETECTIVE(1943, Brit.); OLD MOTHER RILEY OVERSEAS(1943, Brit.); HE SNOOPS TO CONQUER(1944, Brit.); MEET SEXTON BLAKE(1944, Brit.); NOTORIOUS GENTLEMAN(1945, Brit.); RANDOLPH FAMILY, THE(1945, Brit.); I'LL TURN TO YOU(1946, Brit.); MY SISTER AND I(1948, Brit.); INTERRUPTED JOURNEY, THE(1949, Brit.); RELUCTANT WIDOW,

THE(1951, Brit.)
Jennifer Vyvyan
GREAT GILBERT AND SULLIVAN, THE(1953, Brit.)
Jimmy Vyvyan
JOHNNY, YOU'RE WANTED(1956, Brit.)
John H. Vyvyan
MRS. DANE'S DEFENCE(1933, Brit.)
Jack Vyvyian
GARRISON FOLLIES(1940, Brit.)
Pat Vyvyvan
YOU'RE IN THE ARMY NOW(1937, Brit.)

W

Miriam W'Abdullah
UP THE SANDBOX(1972)
Hanna Waag
KARAMAZOV(1931, Ger.)
Sam Waagenaar
FIVE GRAVES TO CAIRO(1943); HITLER'S MADMAN(1943); IMMORTAL SER-GEANT, THE(1943); NORTHERN PURSUIT(1943)
George Waaka
1984
UTU(1984, New Zealand)
Konrad Waalkes
ENTER THE NINJA(1982)
Emil Wabschke
CAPTAIN FROM KOEPENICK(1933, Ger.)
Valerie Waburton
THREE CARD MONTE(1978, Can.)
Nat Wachberger
THAT MAN IN ISTANBUL(1966, Fr./Ital./Span.), w
Chaim Wachgold
DREAM NO MORE(1950, Palestine)
Sophie Wachner
BIG TIME(1929), cos; MARRIED IN HOLLYWOOD(1929), cos; NIX ON DA-MES(1929), cos; PLEASURE CRAZED(1929), cos; ROMANCE OF THE RIO GRAN-DE(1929), cos; SEVEN FACES(1929), cos; SONG OF KENTUCKY(1929), cos; SOUTH SEA ROSE(1929), cos; SPEAKEASY(1929), cos; SUNNY SIDE UP(1929), cos; THEY HAD TO SEE PARIS(1929), cos; THRU DIFFERENT EYES(1929), cos; WORDS AND MUSIC(1929), cos, cos; ARE YOU THERE?(1930), cos; ARIZONA KID, THE(1930), cos; CRAZY THAT WAY(1930), cos; HAPPY DAYS(1930), cos; HIGH SOCIETY BLUES(1930), cos; JUST IMAGINE(1930), cos; LAST OF THE DUANES(1930), cos; LIGHTNIN'(1930), cos; LILIOM(1930), cos; MAN TROUBLE(1930), cos; OH, FOR A MAN!(1930), cos; ON THE LEVEL(1930), cos; ON YOUR BACK(1930), cos; PRINCESS AND THE PLUMBER, THE(1930), cos; RENEGADES(1930), cos; SCOTLAND YARD(1930), cos; SO THIS IS LONDON(1930), cos; SONG O' MY HEART(1930), cos; SUCH MEN ARE DANGEROUS(1930), cos; WILD COMPANY(1930), cos; WOMEN EVERYWHERE(1930), cos; ANNABELLE'S AFFAIRS(1931), cos; QUICK MIL-LIONS(1931), cos; UP THE RIVER(1938), cos; QUICK MILLIONS(1939), cos
Silents
SNOB, THE(1924), cos; RED WINE(1928), cos
A. Wachnickie
YOUNG GIRLS OF WILKO, THE(1979, Pol./Fr.)
M. Wachnickie
YOUNG GIRLS OF WILKO, THE(1979, Pol./Fr.)
Jutta Wachowiak
FLOWERS FOR THE MAN IN THE MOON(1975, Ger.)
Maria Wachowiak
PARTINGS(1962, Pol.)
Nat Wachsberger
QUEEN OF BABYLON, THE(1956, Ital.), p; VISCOUNT, THE(1967, Fr./Span./Ital./Ger.), p; THEY CAME TO ROB LAS VEGAS(1969, Fr./Ital./Span./Ger.), p; KILLER FORCE(1975, Switz./Ireland), p; STARCRASH(1979), p, w
Patrick Wachsberger
KILLER FORCE(1975, Switz./Ireland), p; STARCRASH(1979), p
Franz Wachsmann [Franz Waxman]
EMPRESS AND I, THE(1933, Ger.), m
Teresa Wachter
1984
UNDER THE VOLCANO(1984), set d
Lee Wackerhagen
RAGGEDY MAN(1981)
Erika Wackernagel
1984
LOVE IN GERMANY, A(1984, Fr./Ger.)
Erika Wackernager
DEEP END(1970 Ger./U.S.)
Jonathan Wacks
1984
REPO MAN(1984), p
Peter Wacks
1984
REPO MAN(1984)
Emi Wada
MARCO(1973), cos
Eriko Wada
SONG FROM MY HEART, THE(1970, Jap.)
Hiroshi Wada
HARBOR LIGHT YOKOHAMA(1970, Jap.); ALMOST TRANSPARENT BLUE(1980, Jap.), art d
Koji Wada
GAPPA THE TRIFIBIAN MONSTER(1967, Jap.)
Natto Wada
ENJO(1959, Jap.), w; ODD OBSESSION(1961, Jap.), w; FIRES ON THE PLAIN(1962, Jap.), w; ACTOR'S REVENGE, AN(1963, Jap.), w; ALONE ON THE PACIFIC(1964, Jap.), w; HARP OF BURMA(1967, Jap.), w
Sanzo Wada
GATE OF HELL(1954, Jap.), cos
Takashi Wada
DEATH ON THE MOUNTAIN(1961, Jap.)
Yoichi Wada
KARATE, THE HAND OF DEATH(1961)
C. C. Wadde
Silents
SO THIS IS ARIZONA(1922), w

Gary Waddell
PURE S(1976, Aus.); F.J. HOLDEN, THE(1977, Aus.); 20TH CENTURY OZ(1977, Aus.); IN SEARCH OF ANNA(1978, Aus.); STIR(1980, Aus.); MONKEY GRIP(1983, Aus.)
Joan Waddell
NEW KIND OF LOVE, A(1963)
Lt. Joseph Waddell
Silents
OFF-SHORE PIRATE, THE(1921), ph
Martin Waddell
OTLEY(1969, Brit.), w
Carol Wadder
CRY DR. CHICAGO(1971)
Philip Waddilove
CONQUEROR WORM, THE(1968, Brit.); BUTTERCUP CHAIN, THE(1971, Brit.), p
Patrick Waddington
LOYALTIES(1934, Brit.); BLACK TULIP, THE(1937, Brit.); LOVES OF MADAME DUBARRY, THE(1938, Brit.); JOURNEY TOGETHER(1946, Brit.); SCHOOL FOR SECRETS(1946, Brit.); CLOUDED CRYSTAL, THE(1948, Brit.); SHOWTIME(1948, Brit.); IT'S NOT CRICKET(1949, Brit.); STOP PRESS GIRL(1949, Brit.); IF THIS BE SIN(1950, Brit.); WOODEN HORSE, THE(1951, Brit.); MOONRAKER, THE(1958, Brit.); NIGHT TO REMEMBER, A(1958, Brit.); RX MURDER(1958, Brit.)
Silents
IF YOUTH BUT KNEW(1926, Brit.)
Russell Waddle
WRECKER, THE(1933)
Edward Waddy
HOSTILE WITNESS(1968, Brit.)
Gyle Waddy
WIZ, THE(1978)
Adam Wade
WANDERLOVE(1970); SHAFT(1971); COME BACK CIHARLESTON BLUE(1972); GORDON'S WAR(1973); CLAUDINE(1974); CRAZY JOE(1974); PHANTOM OF THE PARADISE(1974); KISS ME GOODBYE(1982)
Bess Wade
MILLIONS IN THE AIR(1935); LET US LIVE(1939); STRANGER ON THE THIRD FLOOR(1940)
Besse Wade
STREET OF CHANCE(1942); CROSS MY HEART(1946); VELVET TOUCH, THE(1948)
Bessie Wade
SISTERS, THE(1938); YOU CAN'T TAKE IT WITH YOU(1938); FIVE LITTLE PEPPERS AND HOW THEY GREW(1939); MY SON IS GUILTY(1940); FACE BEHIND THE MASK, THE(1941); MEET JOHN DOE(1941); HITLER'S CHILDREN(1942); MISTER 880(1950); SEALED CARGO(1951)
Bob Wade
IMMORAL MOMENT, THE(1967, Fr.), ed; TRANS-EUROP-EXPRESS(1968, Fr.), ed; L'IMMORTELLE(1969, Fr./Ital./Turkey), ed; MAN WHO LIES, THE(1970, Czech./Fr.), ed; ONE NIGHT STAND(1976, Fr.), ed; BEAUTIFUL PRISONER, THE(1983, Fr.), ed
Charles Wade
KISSING CUP'S RACE(1930, Brit.); THANK EVANS(1938, Brit.); SEND FOR PAUL TEMPLE(1946, Brit.); MARCH HARE, THE(1956, Brit.); FROZEN DEAD, THE(1967, Brit.)
Clessia Wade
THREE PENNY OPERA(1963, Fr./Ger.)
David Wade
KNUTE ROCKNE–ALL AMERICAN(1940)
Ernest Wade
Silents
KINGDOM OF LOVE, THE(1918)
Ernestine Wade
GIRL HE LEFT BEHIND, THE(1956); THREE VIOLENT PEOPLE(1956); BERNAR-DINE(1957); GUNS OF FORT PETTICOAT, THE(1957); CRITIC'S CHOICE(1963)
Eugene Wade
HUMAN FACTOR, THE(1975)
Frank Wade
LEFT HAND OF GOD, THE(1955), set d; YOUNG LOVERS, THE(1964), set d; THAT COLD DAY IN THE PARK(1969, U.S./Can.)
Geoffrey Wade
THIRD MAN, THE(1950, Brit.)
J.P. Wade
MANIAC(1934)
Misc. Silents
BIT OF KINDLING, A(1917)
Jack Wade
WORDS AND MUSIC(1929)
Joanne Wade
ZERO HOUR!(1957)
John Wade
HEROES OF THE HILLS(1938)
John Wade
Misc. Talkies
SUNDANCE CASSIDY AND BUTCH THE KID(1975)
John P. Wade
Silents
WIDE-OPEN TOWN, A(1922)
Misc. Silents
OPEN DOOR, THE(1919); WAKEFIELD CASE, THE(1921)
Johnny Wade
CUP FEVER(1965, Brit.); STICK UP, THE(1978, Brit.); FUNNY MONEY(1983, Brit.)
Kevin Wade
SCENIC ROUTE, THE(1978); IMPOSTORS(1979)
Lindy Wade
DEVIL AND DANIEL WEBSTER, THE(1941); SYNCOPATION(1942)
Margaret Wade
UNSUITABLE JOB FOR A WOMAN, AN(1982, Brit.)
1984
REFLECTIONS(1984, Brit.)

Mark Anthony Wade
1984
HARRY AND SON(1984)
Mary Louise Wade
THIEF(1981)
Mary Ruth Wade
PLUNDERERS, THE(1948)
Michael Wade
LONG HAUL, THE(1957, Brit.); THEM NICE AMERICANS(1958, Brit.); MONSTER OF HIGHGATE PONDS, THE(1961, Brit.)
Monroe Wade
HORROR OF PARTY BEACH, THE(1964)
Philip Wade
WRATH OF JEALOUSY(1936, Brit.), w; DREAMING(1944, Brit.)
Ron Wade
HARD TRAIL(1969)
Roy Wade
HEY THERE, IT'S YOGI BEAR(1964), ph; MAN CALLED FLINTSTONE, THE(1966), ph; CHARLOTTE'S WEB(1973), ph
Russell Wade
FLYING HOSTESS(1936); POSTAL INSPECTOR(1936); THESE GLAMOUR GIRLS(1939); YOU CAN'T CHEAT AN HONEST MAN(1939); ARMY SURGEON(1942); BANDIT RANGER(1942); PIRATES OF THE PRAIRIE(1942); BOMBARDIER(1943); FALCON IN DANGER, THE(1943); FALLEN SPARROW, THE(1943); FIGHTING FRONTIER(1943); GHOST SHIP, THE(1943); GILDERSLEEVE'S BAD DAY(1943); IRON MAJOR, THE(1943); LADIES' DAY(1943); LEOPARD MAN, THE(1943); RED RIVER ROBIN HOOD(1943); MARINE RAIDERS(1944); TALL IN THE SADDLE(1944); BODY SNATCHER, THE(1945); GAME OF DEATH, A(1945); BAMBOO BLONDE, THE(1946); RENEGADE GIRL(1946); SHOOT TO KILL(1947); BEYOND GLORY(1948); SUNDOWN RIDERS(1948)
Scott Wade
1984
HEARTBREAKERS(1984)
Stuart Wade
MONSTER FROM THE OCEAN FLOOR, THE(1954); TARANTULA(1955); TEENAGE MONSTER(1958); I'D RATHER BE RICH(1964)
Tom Wade
CHICAGO CONFIDENTIAL(1957)
Tony Wade
VICE GIRLS, LTD.(1964)
Vanita Wade
WHEN MY BABY SMILES AT ME(1948)
Vera Wade
THRILL OF YOUTH(1932), ed
Warren Wade
HELLER IN PINK TIGHTS(1960)
Tommy Wadelton
LITTLE MISTER JIM(1946), w
Annette Wademant
EDWARD AND CAROLINE(1952, Fr.), w; EARRINGS OF MADAME DE..., THE(1954, Fr.), w; LOLA MONTES(1955, Fr./Ger.), w; LA PARISIENNE(1958, Fr./Ital.), w; COME DANCE WITH ME(1960, Fr.), w; LOVE AND THE FRENCH-WOMAN(1961, Fr.), w; TALES OF PARIS(1962, Fr./Ital.), w
Joe Wadham
END OF THE LINE, THE(1959, Brit.); HIDDEN HOMICIDE(1959, Brit.); GREAT ARMORED CAR SWINDLE, THE(1964); SALT & PEPPER(1968, Brit.); THOSE DARING YOUNG MEN IN THEIR JAUNTY JALOPIES(1969, Fr./Brit./ Ital.); SUN-DAY BLOODY SUNDAY(1971, Brit.)
John Wadham
FAKE, THE(1953, Brit.)
Agnes Wadleigh
Silents
LIGHTS OF NEW YORK, THE(1916)
Michael Wadleigh
DAVID HOLZMAN'S DIARY(1968), ph; WHO'S THAT KNOCKING AT MY DOOR?(1968), ph; WOLFEN(1981), a, d, w
Wilbert Wadleigh
Silents
KING OF KINGS, THE(1927)
George Wadmore
DENTIST IN THE CHAIR(1960, Brit.), w
Gunnel Wadner
PIMPERNEL SVENSSON(1953, Swed.)
Ben Ayassa Wadrassi
ARABIAN NIGHTS(1942)
Richard H. Wadsack
SCREAMS OF A WINTER NIGHT(1979), p, w
Olive Wadsley
Silents
POSSESSION(1919, Brit.), w; FRAILTY(1921, Brit.), w
Derek Wadsworth
CHILD IS A WILD THING, A(1976), m
Frances Wadsworth
Misc. Silents
LITTLE FOOL, THE(1921)
George Wadsworth
JACK AND THE BEANSTALK(1970)
Henry Wadsworth
APPLAUSE(1929); FAST AND LOOSE(1930); SLIGHTLY SCARLET(1930); HOLD THE PRESS(1933); LUXURY LINER(1933); SOLDIERS OF THE STORM(1933); EVE-LYN PRENTICE(1934); IT HAPPENED ONE NIGHT(1934); OPERATOR 13(1934); SHOW-OFF, THE(1934); THIN MAN, THE(1934); THIS SIDE OF HEAVEN(1934); BIG BROADCAST OF 1936, THE(1935); CEILNG ZERO(1935); DANGEROUS COR-NER(1935); MARK OF THE VAMPIRE(1935); WEST POINT OF THE AIR(1935); SITTING ON THE MOON(1936); VOICE OF BUGLE ANN(1936); DR. RHYTHM(1938); DR. KILDARE GOES HOME(1940); SILVER SKATES(1943)
Sally Wadsworth
MEXICAN SPITFIRE SEES A GHOST(1942); LADIES' DAY(1943)

William Wadsworth
Silents
ENVY(1917); KIDNAPPED(1917)
Misc. Silents
COHEN'S LUCK(1915); VANITY FAIR(1915); CATSPAW, THE(1916); MATCH-MAK-ERS, THE(1916); BILLY AND THE BIG STICK(1917); BUILDERS OF CASTLES(1917); CY WHITTAKER'S WARD(1917); PUTTING THE BEE IN HERBERT(1917); SALT OF THE EARTH(1917); YOUNG AMERICA(1918)
Eberhard Waechter
HOUSE OF THE THREE GIRLS, THE(1961, Aust.)
Eva Waegner
PARADISIO(1962, Brit.)
Elisabeth Waelchli
YOL(1982, Turkey), ed
Aribert Waescher
MAN BETWEEN, THE(1953, Brit.)
Aribert Waesher
MASTER OF THE WORLD(1935, Ger.)
Waffles
GO WEST, YOUNG LADY(1941)
Wim Wagenaar
PUPPET ON A CHAIN(1971, Brit.), stunts
Hilde Wagener
STORY OF VICKIE, THE(1958, Aust.); FOREVER MY LOVE(1962)
Charles Wagenheim
SMILING LIEUTENANT, THE(1931); JEZEBEL(1938); CHARLIE CHAN AT THE WAX MUSEUM(1940); FOREIGN CORRESPONDENT(1940); HE STAYED FOR BREAKFAST(1940); I LOVE YOU AGAIN(1940); SPORTING BLOOD(1940); TWO GIRLS ON BROADWAY(1940); GET-AWAY, THE(1941); MEET BOSTON BLACK-IE(1941); PARIS CALLING(1941); BLONDIE FOR VICTORY(1942); DR. RENAULT'S SECRET(1942); FINGERS AT THE WINDOW(1942); HALF WAY TO SHANG-HAI(1942); MYSTERY OF MARIE ROGET, THE(1942); SIN TOWN(1942); CALLING DR. DEATH(1943); FRONTIER BADMEN(1943); I ESCAPED FROM THE GES-TAPO(1943); SONG OF BERNADETTE, THE(1943); BLACK PARACHUTE, THE(1944); STORM OVER LISBON(1944); SUMMER STORM(1944); COLONEL EFFINGHAM'S RAID(1945); DANGEROUS PARTNERS(1945); EASY TO LOOK AT(1945); HOUSE ON 92ND STREET, THE(1945); JUNGLE CAPTIVE(1945); SALOME, WHERE SHE DANCED(1945); SERGEANT MIKE(1945); SONG TO REMEMBER, A(1945); WITHIN THESE WALLS(1945); DARK CORNER, THE(1946); FROM THIS DAY FOR-WARD(1946); HOODLUM SAINT, THE(1946); NIGHT EDITOR(1946); SPIRAL STAIR-CASE, THE(1946); TANGIER(1946); LIGHTHOUSE(1947); MONSIEUR VERDOUX(1947); PIRATES OF MONTEREY(1947); CRY OF THE CITY(1948); JOAN OF ARC(1948); MAN-EATER OF KUMAON(1948); RIVER LADY(1948); SCUDDA-HOO! SCUDDA-HAY!(1948); SIREN OF ATLANTIS(1948); CRISS CROSS(1949); GREAT SINNER, THE(1949); I CHEATED THE LAW(1949); SCENE OF THE CRI-ME(1949); SET-UP, THE(1949); WOMAN'S SECRET, A(1949); LADY WITHOUT PASS-PORT, A(1950); MOTOR PATROL(1950); MYSTERY STREET(1950); THREE LITTLE WORDS(1950); HOUSE ON TELEGRAPH HILL(1951); PIER 23(1951); STREET BAN-DITS(1951); STREETCAR NAMED DESIRE, A(1951); BENEATH THE 12-MILE REEF(1953); GIRL NEXT DOOR, THE(1953); LOOSE IN LONDON(1953); SALO-ME(1953); VEILS OF BAGDAD, THE(1953); VICKI(1953); EXECUTIVE SUITE(1954); PRODIGAL, THE(1955); BLACKJACK KETCHUM, DESPERADO(1956); LONELY-HEARTS(1958); TOUGHEST GUN IN TOMBSTONE(1958); TUNNEL OF LOVE, THE(1958); DIARY OF ANNE FRANK, THE(1959); STORY OF RUTH, THE(1960); CAT BALLOU(1965); CINCINNATI KID, THE(1965); HAIL, HERO!(1969); MISSOURI BREAKS, THE(1976)
Charlie Wagenheim
BABY MAKER, THE(1970)
Wagenia Tribe of Belgian Congo
MOGAMBO(1953)
Anthony Wager
GREAT EXPECTATIONS(1946, Brit.); FAME IS THE SPUR(1947, Brit.); HUNGRY HILL(1947, Brit.); NO PLACE FOR JENNIFER(1950, Brit.); ABOVE US THE WA-VES(1956, Brit.); WIND CANNOT READ, THE(1958, Brit.); NIGHT OF THE PROWL-ER(1962, Brit.); HI-JACKERS, THE(1963, Brit.); SHADOW OF FEAR(1963, Brit.); BLOOD BEAST FROM OUTER SPACE(1965, Brit.); LITTLE ONES, THE(1965, Brit.)
Diane Wager
WHOLLY MOSES(1980), set d; ANNIE(1982), art d; TWO OF A KIND(1983), set d
Dianne Wager
SLEEPER(1973), art d
1984
RHINESTONE(1984), set d
Dianne I. Wager
MAN WHO LOVED WOMEN, THE(1983), set d
Michael Wager
HILL 24 DOESN'T ANSWER(1955, Israel); EXODUS(1960); KING OF KINGS(1961); JANE AUSTEN IN MANHATTAN(1980)
Tony Wager
BE MY GUEST(1965, Brit.); AND MILLIONS WILL DIE(1973); STIR(1980, Aus.)
Walter Wager
TELEFON(1977), w; TWILIGHT'S LAST GLEAMING(1977, U.S./Ger.), w
Seth Wagerman
1984
BAD MANNERS(1984); CRIMES OF PASSION(1984)
Dave Wages
DIRTY LITTLE BILLY(1972), ed
David Wages
HIDDEN FEAR(1957), ed; MARY, MARY(1963), ed; SPENCER'S MOUNTAIN(1963), ed; DISTANT TRUMPET, A(1964), ed; SEX AND THE SINGLE GIRL(1964), ed; HOW TO MURDER YOUR WIFE(1965), ed; SYNANON(1965), ed; CHAMBER OF HOR-RORS(1966), ed; OH DAD, POOR DAD, MAMA'S HUNG YOU IN THE CLOSET AND I'M FEELIN' SO SAD(1967), ed
Jeremy Wagg
SQUADRON 633(1964, U.S./Brit.); 633 SQUADRON(1964)
Gloria Jewel Waggener
BUSTIN' LOOSE(1981)
Charles Waggenheim
CAPTIVE CITY(1952); SUDDENLY(1954); CANYON CROSSROADS(1955); POLICE DOG STORY, THE(1961); BEAUTY AND THE BEAST(1963)

Fernando Waggner
MY BROTHER, THE OUTLAW(1951)

George Waggner
OH, YEAH!(1929), m; SWEETHEART OF SIGMA CHI(1933), w; CITY LIMITS(1934), w; LINEUP, THE(1934), w; ONCE TO EVERY BACHELOR(1934), w; CAPPY RICKS RETURNS(1935), w; CHAMPAGNE FOR BREAKFAST(1935), w; COWBOY MILLIONAIRE(1935), w; GIRL O' MY DREAMS(1935), w, m; HEALER, THE(1935), w; KEEPER OF THE BEES(1935), w; NUT FARM, THE(1935), w; CHEERS OF THE CROWD(1936), w; DIZZY DAMES(1936), w; DON'T GET PERSONAL(1936), w; SEA SPOILERS, THE(1936), w; I COVER THE WAR(1937), w; IDOL OF THE CROWDS(1937), w; THREE LEGIONNAIRES, THE(1937), w; AIR DEVILS(1938), w; BLACK BANDIT(1938), d; GHOST TOWN RIDERS(1938), d; GUILTY TRAILS(1938), d; MIDNIGHT INTRUDER(1938), w; OUTLAW EXPRESS(1938), d; PRAIRIE JUSTICE(1938), d; SPY RING, THE(1938), w; STATE POLICE(1938), w; WESTERN TRAILS(1938), d; HONOR OF THE WEST(1939), d; MYSTERY PLANE(1939), d; PHANTOM STAGE, THE(1939), d; STUNT PILOT(1939), d; WOLF CALL(1939), d; DRUMS OF THE DESERT(1940), d; BADLANDS OF DAKOTA(1941), p; HORROR ISLAND(1941), d; MAN MADE MONSTER(1941), d; SEALED LIPS(1941), d&w; SOUTH OF TAHITI(1941), p&d; WOLF MAN, THE(1941), p&d; GHOST OF FRANKENSTEIN, THE(1942), p; MEN OF TEXAS(1942), p; SIN TOWN(1942), p; FRANKENSTEIN MEETS THE WOLF MAN(1943), p; PHANTOM OF THE OPERA(1943), p, m; WHITE SAVAGE(1943), p; CLIMAX, THE(1944), p&d; COBRA WOMAN(1944), p; GYPSY WILDCAT(1944), p; FRISCO SAL(1945), p&d; SHADY LADY(1945), p&d; SWEETHEART OF SIGMA CHI(1946), w; TANGIER(1946), d; GUNFIGHTERS, THE(1947), d; FIGHTING KENTUCKIAN, THE(1949), d&w; OPERATION PACIFIC(1951), d&w; BITTER CREEK(1954), w; RETURN FROM THE SEA(1954), w; DESTINATION 60,000(1957), d&w; PAWNEE(1957), d, w; MAN FROM GOD'S COUNTRY(1958), w
Silents
SHEIK, THE(1921); LOVE'S BLINDNESS(1926)
Misc. Silents
DESERT DRIVEN(1923)

Leah Waggner
MY FAVORITE SPY(1951); HOODLUM EMPIRE(1952)

Lia Waggner
INCIDENT IN AN ALLEY(1962)

Shy Waggner
FIGHTING KENTUCKIAN, THE(1949)

Dolores Waggoner
1984
ALLEY CAT(1984)

George Waggoner
HE COULDN'T TAKE IT(1934), w
Silents
HIS HOUR(1924)
Misc. Silents
BRANDED MAN(1922)

Lyle Waggoner
SWAMP COUNTRY(1966); WOMEN OF THE PREHISTORIC PLANET(1966); CATALINA CAPER, THE(1967); JOURNEY TO THE CENTER OF TIME(1967); LOVE ME DEADLY(1972)
1984
SURF II(1984)

Mabel Wagnalls
Silents
REVELATION(1924), w

Wagner
PEOPLE WILL TALK(1951), m; L'AGE D'OR(1979, Fr.), m

Captain Wagner
Misc. Talkies
ADVENTURE GIRL(1934)

Adeline Wagner
THREE PENNY OPERA(1963, Fr./Ger.); LOVE FEAST, THE(1966, Ger.); TONIO KROGER(1968, Fr./Ger.)

Bernd Wagner
NOT RECONCILED, OR "ONLY VIOLENCE HELPS WHERE IT RULES"(1969, Ger.)

Billie Wagner
Silents
KAISER'S FINISH, THE(1918)

Blake Wagner
Silents
ATTA BOY!(1926), ph; FINNEGAN'S BALL(1927), ph; PLAY SAFE(1927), ph

Bo Wagner
GYPSY(1962)

Bob Wagner
NO DRUMS, NO BUGLES(1971)

Carlyn Wagner
Misc. Silents
SPREADING EVIL, THE(1919); OUTLAWED(1921)

Carolyn Wagner
Silents
DEVIL DODGER, THE(1917)

Christiane Wagner
JULES AND JIM(1962, Fr.)

Christie Wagner
SHE-DEVILS ON WHEELS(1968)

Danny Wagner
1984
SILENT NIGHT, DEADLY NIGHT(1984)

Daphne Wagner
WAGNER(1983, Brit./Hung./Aust.)

David Wagner
1984
MYSTERY MANSION(1984)

Dru Wagner
HOW TO BEAT THE HIGH COST OF LIVING(1980)

Ed Wagner
MURDER, INC.(1960); KING OF THE GYPSIES(1978)

Elsa Wagner
BARCAROLE(1935, Ger.); CITY OF TORMENT(1950, Ger.); EMIL AND THE DETECTIVES(1964); MONSTER OF LONDON CITY, THE(1967, Ger.); PEDESTRIAN, THE(1974, Ger.)

Fernando Wagner
PEARL, THE(1948, U.S./Mex.); SOFIA(1948); TARZAN AND THE MERMAIDS(1948); DOCTOR CRIMEN(1953, Mex.); GARDEN OF EVIL(1954); SEVEN CITIES OF GOLD(1955); SIERRA BARON(1958); VIRGIN SACRIFICE(1959), a, d; VIVA MARIA(1965, Fr./Ital.); WILD BUNCH, THE(1969)

Florence Wagner
AMONG THE MISSING(1934), w

Fritz Arne Wagner
DOLLY GETS AHEAD(1931, Ger.), ph

Fritz Arno Wagner
THREEPENNY OPERA, THE(1931, Ger./U.S.), ph; BEAUTIFUL ADVENTURE(1932, Ger.), ph; BE MINE TONIGHT(1933, Brit.), ph; M(1933, Ger.), ph; GLAMOROUS NIGHT(1937, Brit.), ph; TESTAMENT OF DR. MABUSE, THE(1943, Ger.), ph; ONE APRIL 2000(1952, Aust.), ph; APRIL 1, 2000(1953, Aust.), ph; ETERNAL LOVE(1960, Ger.), ph
Silents
NOSFERATU, THE VAMPIRE(1922, Ger.), ph; SPIES(1929, Ger.), ph

Fritz Wagner
FILM WITHOUT A NAME(1950, Ger.)

George Wagner
GORILLA SHIP, THE(1932), w; CANNONBALL(1976, U.S./Hong Kong); HOLLYWOOD BOULEVARD(1976); GRAND THEFT AUTO(1977)
Silents
IRON HORSE, THE(1924)

Guyri Wagner
ODETTE(1951, Brit.)

Harold Wagner
PAISAN(1948, Ital.)

Harry Wagner
POPPY(1936)

Jack Wagner
CLANCY IN WALL STREET(1930), w; LITTLE MINISTER, THE(1934), w; DANCING PIRATE(1936), w; ANGELS WASH THEIR FACES(1939); NANCY DREW–REPORTER(1939); JIVE JUNCTION(1944); MEDAL FOR BENNY, A(1945), w; PEARL, THE(1948, U.S./Mex.), w
Silents
FIGHTING EDGE(1926), w; SYNCOPATING SUE(1926), w; WHAT EVERY GIRL SHOULD KNOW(1927), w; LADY BE GOOD(1928), w

Jane Wagner
MOMENT BY MOMENT(1978), d&w; INCREDIBLE SHRINKING WOMAN, THE(1981), w

Kid Wagner
STREET WITH NO NAME, THE(1948)
Silents
ABYSMAL BRUTE, THE(1923)

Lee Wagner
1984
KILLPOINT(1984)

Leon Wagner
WOMAN UNDER THE INFLUENCE, A(1974); BINGO LONG TRAVELING ALL-STARS AND MOTOR KINGS, THE(1976)

Lindsay Wagner
PAPER CHASE, THE(1973); TWO PEOPLE(1973); SECOND WIND(1976, Can.); HIGH RISK(1981); NIGHTHAWKS(1981)

Lou Wagner
PLANET OF THE APES(1968); HELLO DOWN THERE(1969); AIRPORT(1970); BENEATH THE PLANET OF THE APES(1970); PUFNSTUF(1970); CONQUEST OF THE PLANET OF THE APES(1972); GORP(1980)
1984
MIRRORS(1984)

Mamie Wagner
Silents
CALL OF THE NORTH, THE(1914), ed; SQUAW MAN, THE(1914), ed

Max Wagner
RENEGADES OF THE WEST(1932); WORLD AND THE FLESH, THE(1932); ARIZONA TO BROADWAY(1933); SONS OF THE DESERT(1933); DEATH OF THE DIAMOND(1934); HELL BENT FOR LOVE(1934); LOST JUNGLE, THE(1934); WHARF ANGEL(1934); CHARLIE CHAN IN SHANGHAI(1935); LADIES CRAVE EXCITEMENT(1935); MARY BURNS, FUGITIVE(1935); UNDER THE PAMPAS MOON(1935); BULLETS OR BALLOTS(1936); CASE AGAINST MRS. AMES, THE(1936); CRIME PATROL, THE(1936); DANCING PIRATE(1936); HOUSE OF A THOUSAND CANDLES, THE(1936); LOVE BEGINS AT TWENTY(1936); MOON'S OUR HOME, THE(1936); SONS O' GUNS(1936); TWO IN REVOLT(1936); BORDER CAFE(1937); GOD'S COUNTRY AND THE WOMAN(1937); GREAT O'MALLEY, THE(1937); SAN QUENTIN(1937); SLIM(1937); SMART BLONDE(1937); STEP LIVELY, JEEVES(1937); TOAST OF NEW YORK, THE(1937); WINGS OVER HONOLULU(1937); ACCIDENTS WILL HAPPEN(1938); COCOANUT GROVE(1938); PAINTED DESERT, THE(1938); PENROD AND HIS TWIN BROTHER(1938); PROFESSOR BEWARE(1938); CAFE SOCIETY(1939); FIFTH AVENUE GIRL(1939); STAR MAKER, THE(1939); WINGS OF THE NAVY(1939); GHOST BREAKERS, THE(1940); HOUSE ACROSS THE BAY, THE(1940); I'M NOBODY'S SWEETHEART NOW(1940); MEN AGAINST THE SKY(1940); POP ALWAYS PAYS(1940); THEY DRIVE BY NIGHT(1940); TRAIL OF THE VIGILANTES(1940); YOU CAN'T FOOL YOUR WIFE(1940); CYCLONE ON HORSEBACK(1941); MEXICAN SPITFIRE'S BABY(1941); OBLIGING YOUNG LADY(1941); SAN FRANCISCO DOCKS(1941); MEXICAN SPITFIRE'S ELEPHANT(1942); MY FAVORITE BLONDE(1942); PALM BEACH STORY, THE(1942); PANAMA HATTIE(1942); SABOTAGE SQUAD(1942); SEVEN DAYS LEAVE(1942); TALK OF THE TOWN(1942); WIFE TAKES A FLYER, THE(1942); SECRETS OF THE UNDERGROUND(1943); BULLFIGHTERS, THE(1945); FALLEN ANGEL(1945); I'LL TELL THE WORLD(1945); MEDAL FOR BENNY, A(1945); RADIO STARS ON PARADE(1945); SHE GETS HER MAN(1945); SPANISH MAIN, THE(1945); WHERE DO WE GO FROM HERE?(1945); WITHIN THESE WALLS(1945); SMOKY(1946); STRANGE LOVE OF MARTHA IVERS, THE(1946); POSSESSED(1947); SINBAD THE SAILOR(1947); TYCOON(1947); FORCE OF EVIL(1948); MIRACLE OF THE BELLS, THE(1948); ON OUR MERRY WAY(1948); SAINTED SISTERS, THE(1948); RED PONY, THE(1949); MAD WEDNESDAY(1950); BANDITS OF EL DORADO(1951);

Mike Wagner
MEET ME AFTER THE SHOW(1951); RACKET, THE(1951); SECRET OF CONVICT LAKE, THE(1951); BIG SKY, THE(1952); BLAZING FOREST, THE(1952); MEET ME AT THE FAIR(1952); FARMER TAKES A WIFE, THE(1953); INVADERS FROM MARS(1953); LADY WANTS MINK, THE(1953); SECOND CHANCE(1953); COUNTRY GIRL, THE(1954); COURT-MARTIAL OF BILLY MITCHELL, THE(1955); GIRL IN THE RED VELVET SWING, THE(1955); ILLEGAL(1955); LUCY GALLANT(1955); SON OF SINBAD(1955); UNDERWATER!(1955)

Mike Wagner
TROUBLE WITH GIRLS(AND HOW TO GET INTO IT), THE*1/2 (1969); BUSYBODY, THE(1967); DIRTY DINGUS MAGEE(1970); SUPPORT YOUR LOCAL GUNFIGHTER(1971)

Paul Wagner
UNFINISHED SYMPHONY, THE(1953, Aust./Brit.); FRENCH, THEY ARE A FUNNY RACE, THE(1956, Fr.), p

Pauline Wagner
MR. DEEDS GOES TO TOWN(1936)

Ray Wagner
BOYS IN COMPANY C, THE(1978, U.S./Hong Kong)

Raymond Wagner
PETULIA(1968, U.S./Brit.), p

Richard Wagner
DRACULA(1931), m; SCARLET EMPRESS, THE(1934), m; I'VE ALWAYS LOVED YOU(1946), m; UNFAITHFULLY YOURS(1948), m; PANDORA AND THE FLYING DUTCHMAN(1951, Brit.), d&w; MAGIC FIRE(1956), m; INTERLUDE(1957), m; VERBOTEN!(1959), m; ONCE MORE, WITH FEELING(1960), m; TESTAMENT OF ORPHEUS, THE(1962, Fr.), m; DUET FOR CANNIBALS(1969, Swed.), m; LUDWIG(1973, Ital./Ger./Fr.), m; LISZTOMANIA(1975, Brit.), m; NOSFERATU, THE VAMPIRE(1979, Fr./Ger.), m; OUR HITLER, A FILM FROM GERMANY(1980, Ger.), m; PARSIFAL(1983, Fr.), m; WAGNER(1983, Brit./Hung./Aust.), m

Rob Wagner
Silents
HEADS UP(1925), w; SMILIN' AT TROUBLE(1925), w; LADIES AT EASE(1927), w
Misc. Silents
FAIR WEEK(1924), d

Robert Wagner
CONCORDE, THE–AIRPORT '79(; FROGMEN, THE(1951); HALLS OF MONTEZUMA(1951); LET'S MAKE IT LEGAL(1951); STARS AND STRIPES FOREVER(1952); WHAT PRICE GLORY?(1952); WITH A SONG IN MY HEART(1952); BENEATH THE 12-MILE REEF(1953); SILVER WHIP, THE(1953); TITANIC(1953); BROKEN LANCE(1954); PRINCE VALIANT(1954); WHITE FEATHER(1955); BETWEEN HEAVEN AND HELL(1956); KISS BEFORE DYING, A(1956); MOUNTAIN, THE(1956); STOPOVER TOKYO(1957); TRUE STORY OF JESSE JAMES, THE(1957); HUNTERS, THE(1958); IN LOVE AND WAR(1958); MARDI GRAS(1958); SAY ONE FOR ME(1959); ALL THE FINE YOUNG CANNIBALS(1960); SAIL A CROOKED SHIP(1961); LONGEST DAY, THE(1962); WAR LOVER, THE(1962, U.S./Brit.); CONDEMNED OF ALTONA, THE(1963); PINK PANTHER, THE(1964); HARPER(1966); BANNING(1967); BIGGEST BUNDLE OF THEM ALL, THE(1968); DON'T JUST STAND THERE(1968); WINNING(1969); JOURNEY THROUGH ROSEBUD(1972); TOWERING INFERNO, THE(1974); MIDWAY(1976); CURSE OF THE PINK PANTHER(1983); I AM THE CHEESE(1983)

Robin Wagner
GLORY BOY(1971), art d

Roger Wagner
GALLANT HOURS, THE(1960), m; PAINT YOUR WAGON(1969), md

Shooki Wagner
JESUS CHRIST, SUPERSTAR(1973)

Sid Wagner
FIGHTING RANGER, THE(1934), ph

Sidney Wagner
UNDER TWO FLAGS(1936), ph; HIDE-OUT(1934), ph; PURSUIT(1935), ph; SINS OF MAN(1936), ph; TO MARY–WITH LOVE(1936), ph; UNDER YOUR SPELL(1936), ph; FAIR WARNING(1937), ph; ONE MILE FROM HEAVEN(1937), ph; BOYS TOWN(1938), ph; CHRISTMAS CAROL, A(1938), ph; HENRY GOES ARIZONA(1939), ph; KID FROM TEXAS, THE(1939), ph; LET FREEDOM RING(1939), ph; ANDY HARDY MEETS DEBUTANTE(1940), ph; GALLANT SONS(1940), ph; NORTHWEST PASSAGE(1940), ph; SPORTING BLOOD(1940), ph; YOUNG TOM EDISON(1940), ph; BLONDE INSPIRATION(1941), ph; GET-AWAY, THE(1941), ph; I'LL WAIT FOR YOU(1941), ph; KATHLEEN(1941), ph; WHISTLING IN THE DARK(1941), ph; APACHE TRAIL(1942), ph; BORN TO SING(1942), ph; OMAHA TRAIL, THE(1942), ph; TARZAN'S NEW YORK ADVENTURE(1942), ph; BATAAN(1943), ph; CABIN IN THE SKY(1943), ph; CROSS OF LORRAINE, THE(1943), ph; MAN FROM DOWN UNDER, THE(1943), ph; STRANGER IN TOWN, A(1943), ph; DRAGON SEED(1944), ph; RATIONING(1944), ph; THIS MAN'S NAVY(1945), ph; POSTMAN ALWAYS RINGS TWICE, THE(1946), ph; SAILOR TAKES A WIFE, THE(1946), ph; FIESTA(1947), ph; HIGH BARBAREE(1947), ph; ROMANCE OF ROSY RIDGE, THE(1947), ph
Silents
GAY RETREAT, THE(1927), ph; NEWS PARADE, THE(1928), ph; PREP AND PEP(1928), ph; WOMAN WISE(1928), ph; MASKED EMOTIONS(1929), ph

Starke Wagner
Silents
ARIZONA EXPRESS, THE(1924), ph

Wende Wagner
RIO CONCHOS(1964); COVENANT WITH DEATH, A(1966); OUT OF SIGHT(1966); GUNS OF THE MAGNIFICENT SEVEN(1969)

Wendy Wagner
DESTINATION INNER SPACE(1966); ROSEMARY'S BABY(1968)

William Wagner
ROMAN SCANDALS(1933); RUSTLERS' ROUNDUP(1933); FRISCO KID(1935); JANE EYRE(1935); NO MORE LADIES(1935); ONE MORE SPRING(1935); LLOYDS OF LONDON(1936); MORE THAN A SECRETARY(1936); WHIPSAW(1936); EASY LIVING(1937); MAID OF SALEM(1937); SECOND HONEYMOON(1937); PROFESSOR BEWARE(1938); REBECCA OF SUNNYBROOK FARM(1938); STORY OF ALEXANDER GRAHAM BELL, THE(1939); GLASS KEY, THE(1942); JOAN OF ARC(1948)
Silents
PRETENDERS, THE(1916), ph; WHISPERS(1920), ph; WAY OF A MAID, THE(1921), ph; REFEREE, THE(1922), ph; WIDE-OPEN TOWN, A(1922), ph

Terry Wagner-Otis
1984
JOY OF SEX(1984)

David Wagoner
ESCAPE ARTIST, THE(1982), w

Porter Wagoner
NASHVILLE REBEL(1966); HONKYTONK MAN(1982)

Herb Wagreitch
1984
GHOSTBUSTERS(1984), ph; SLAYGROUND(1984, Brit.), ph

Alfred Wagstaff
RUSTLER'S ROUNDUP(1946)

Elsie Wagstaff
MEET SEXTON BLAKE(1944, Brit.); MY BROTHER JONATHAN(1949, Brit.); GOLDEN LINK, THE(1954, Brit.); END OF THE AFFAIR, THE(1955, Brit.); YOU PAY YOUR MONEY(1957, Brit.); SATURDAY NIGHT AND SUNDAY MORNING(1961, Brit.); SNAKE WOMAN, THE(1961, Brit.); WHISTLE DOWN THE WIND(1961, Brit.); HEAVENS ABOVE!(1963, Brit.)

Joseph Wagstaff
SONG OF KENTUCKY(1929); LET'S GO PLACES(1930)

Keith Wagstaff
MAN FROM SNOWY RIVER, THE(1983, Aus.), ph

Stuart Wagstaff
SUNSTRUCK(1973, Aus.)

Elsie Wagstaffe
SHOW GOES ON, THE(1937, Brit.); JOHN HALIFAX–GENTLEMAN(1938, Brit.); LASSIE FROM LANCASHIRE(1938, Brit.); BALLOON GOES UP, THE(1942, Brit.); DARK TOWER, THE(1943, Brit.); WELCOME, MR. WASHINGTON(1944, Brit.); APPOINTMENT WITH CRIME(1945, Brit.); OLD MOTHER RILEY AT HOME(1945, Brit.); CELIA(1949, Brit.); INTERRUPTED JOURNEY, THE(1949, Brit.)

George Wong Wah
GENERAL DIED AT DAWN, THE(1936)

Abdul Wahab
CAESAR AND CLEOPATRA(1946, Brit.)

Adiel F. Wahl
TOMAHAWK(1951)

Bric Wahl
Misc. Talkies
ACID EATERS, THE(1968)

Chuck Wahl
PORKY'S II: THE NEXT DAY(1983)

Evelyn Wahl
JUNGLE SIREN(1942); PARACHUTE NURSE(1942)

Ken Wahl
WANDERERS, THE(1979); FORT APACHE, THE BRONX(1981); JINXED!(1982); SOLDIER, THE(1982)
1984
PURPLE HEARTS(1984); TREASURE OF THE YANKEE ZEPHYR(1984)
Misc. Talkies
RUNNING SCARED(1980)

Marjorie Wahl
LIMBO(1972), cos; LONG GOODBYE, THE(1973), cos

Sharon Wahl
1984
BIG MEAT EATER(1984, Can.)

Walter Dare Wahl
TOP BANANA(1954)

Wolfgang Wahl
THREE MOVES TO FREEDOM(1960, Ger.); BRAINWASHED(1961, Ger.); ROSES FOR THE PROSECUTOR(1961, Ger.)

Mimmi Wahlander
TOUCH, THE(1971, U.S./Swed.)

Evelyn Wahle
HERS TO HOLD(1943)

Nicholas Wahler
Misc. Talkies
PLACE WITHOUT PARENTS, A(1974); TRUCKIN'(1975)

Robert Wahler
OUR WINNING SEASON(1978); LAST MARRIED COUPLE IN AMERICA, THE(1980)

Ivar Wahlgren
PIMPERNEL SVENSSON(1953, Swed.)

Per Wahloo
LAUGHING POLICEMAN, THE(1973), w; KAMIKAZE '89(1983, Ger.), w

Bo Wahlstrom
DEAR JOHN(1966, Swed.); HERE'S YOUR LIFE(1968, Swed.)

Torsten Wahlund
JUST ONCE MORE(1963, Swed.); ISLAND AT THE TOP OF THE WORLD, THE(1974)
Misc. Talkies
BROTHER CARL(1972)

Tim Wahrer
TAPS(1981)

Timothy Wahrer
PROWLER, THE(1981)

Diane Wahrman
TERROR IN THE WAX MUSEUM(1973)

Edward Wahrman
SUNSET BOULEVARD(1950); WAR OF THE WORLDS, THE(1953)

Lillian Wai
OUT OF THE TIGER'S MOUTH(1962)

Hui Wai-hon
1984
AH YING(1984, Hong Kong)

Pat Waid
Misc. Talkies
KAHUNA!(1981)

Bynn Wailer
ROCKERS(1980)

Ann Wain
PURE HELL OF ST. TRINIAN'S, THE(1961, Brit.)

Barbara Wain
HORSEMEN, THE(1971)
Charles Wain
LAST WAVE, THE(1978, Aus.), m
Edward Wain
LAST WOMAN ON EARTH, THE(1960); CREATURE FROM THE HAUNTED SEA(1961)
Gill Wain
MELODY(1971, Brit.)
Kit Wain
TOM BROWN OF CULVER(1932)
Roy Wain
MELODY(1971, Brit.)
Gordon Waine
DEAD MAN'S EVIDENCE(1962, Brit.); DREAM MAKER, THE(1963, Brit.)
Cherry Wainer
GIRLS OF LATIN QUARTER(1960, Brit.)
Lee Wainer
ANGEL COMES TO BROOKLYN, AN(1945), w; KILROY WAS HERE(1947), w; HOLIDAY RHYTHM(1950), w; DEVIL'S ANGELS(1967)
Leland Wainscott
BLOOD ON THE ARROW(1964)
Earl Wainwright
MY THIRD WIFE GEORGE(1968), ed
James Wainwright
JOE KIDD(1972); MEAN DOG BLUES(1978); PRIVATE FILES OF J. EDGAR HOOVER, THE(1978); BATTLETRUCK(1982); SURVIVORS, THE(1983)
John Wainwright
INQUISITOR, THE(1982, Fr.), w
Marie Wainwright
Misc. Silents
POLLY WITH A PAST(1920)
Michael Wainwright
ZAPPED!(1982)
Richard Wainwright
CRIMSON CIRCLE, THE(1936, Brit.), p; SECRET OF STAMBOUL, THE(1936, Brit.), p, w; WOLF'S CLOTHING(1936, Brit.), p; EMIL(1938, Brit.), p; FORBIDDEN TERRITORY(1938, Brit.), p; KATE PLUS TEN(1938, Brit.), p; SCHOOL FOR HUSBANDS(1939, Brit.), p; MADNESS OF THE HEART(1949, Brit.), p
Rupert Wainwright
1984
ANOTHER COUNTRY(1984, Brit.)
George Waiss
SHINBONE ALLEY(1971), anim
Melissa Ann Wait
NORMA RAE(1979)
Christopher Waite
LE MANS(1971)
Eric Waite
ICE-CAPADES REVUE(1942)
Genevieve Waite
JOANNA(1968, Brit.); MOVE(1970)
Glenn Waite
Misc. Silents
SACRED RUBY, THE(1920), d
John Waite
TRIAL AND ERROR(1962, Brit.)
Kerry Shear Waite
ON THE NICKEL(1980)
Malcolm Waite
NOAH'S ARK(1928); VAGABOND LOVER(1929); 24 HOURS(1931); KID MILLIONS(1934); POPPY(1936); HONKY TONK(1941); JACKASS MAIL(1942)
Silents
GOLD RUSH, THE(1925); GREAT LOVE, THE(1925); LUCKY HORSESHOE, THE(1925); KID BOOTS(1926); NO MAN'S GOLD(1926); BRONCHO TWISTER(1927); MONKEY TALKS, THE(1927); NOW WE'RE IN THE AIR(1927)
Misc. Silents
DURAND OF THE BAD LANDS(1925); KENTUCKY PRIDE(1925); BLARNEY(1926); DESERT VALLEY(1926)
Murray Waite
SHAMROCK HILL(1949), set d
Ralph Waite
COOL HAND LUKE(1967); LOVELY WAY TO DIE, A(1968); LAST SUMMER(1969); FIVE EASY PIECES(1970); GRISSOM GANG, THE(1971); LAWMAN(1971); PURSUIT OF HAPPINESS, THE(1971); SPORTING CLUB, THE(1971); CHATO'S LAND(1972); MAGNIFICENT SEVEN RIDE, THE(1972); TROUBLE MAN(1972); HOT SUMMER WEEK(1973, Can.); KID BLUE(1973); STONE KILLER, THE(1973); ON THE NICKEL(1980), a, p,d&w
Ric Waite
OTHER SIDE OF THE MOUNTAIN–PART 2, THE(1978), ph; DEFIANCE(1980), ph; LONG RIDERS, THE(1980), ph; ON THE NICKEL(1980), ph; BORDER, THE(1982), ph; TEX(1982), ph; 48 HOURS(1982), ph; CLASS(1983), ph; UNCOMMON VALOR(1983), ph
1984
FOOTLOOSE(1984), ph; RED DAWN(1984), ph
the Waiter
NO ESCAPE(1953)
Cyril Waites
I BELIEVE IN YOU(1953, Brit.)
Thomas Waites
ON THE YARD(1978); ...AND JUSTICE FOR ALL(1979); WARRIORS, THE(1979); THING, THE(1982)
Herbert Waithe
Silents
ROBINSON CRUSOE(1927, Brit.)
Mary Waits
THIEVES LIKE US(1974)

Tom Waits
PARADISE ALLEY(1978); ONE FROM THE HEART(1982), m; OUTSIDERS, THE(1983); RUMBLE FISH(1983)
1984
COTTON CLUB, THE(1984)
Adolfo Waitzmann
OPERATION DELILAH(1966, U.S./Span.), m
Kurt Waitzmann
ESCAPE FROM EAST BERLIN(1962)
Max Waizman
WOMAN OF EXPERIENCE, A(1931)
Wajan
WAJAN(1938, South Bali)
Andrzej Wajda
ASHES AND DIAMONDS(1961, Pol.), d, w; KANAL(1961, Pol.), d; LOVE AT TWENTY(1963, Fr./Ital./Jap./Pol./Ger.), d; LOTNA(1966, Pol.), d, w; GATES TO PARADISE(1968, Brit./Ger.), d; MAN OF MARBLE(1979, Pol.), p&d; YOUNG GIRLS OF WILKO, THE(1979, Pol./Fr.), d; CONDUCTOR, THE(1981, Pol.), d; MAN OF IRON(1981, Pol.), d; DANTON(1983), d, w
1984
LOVE IN GERMANY, A(1984, Fr./Ger.), w
Alexander Wajnberg
MAMMA DRACULA(1980, Bel./Fr.)
Marc-Henri Wajnberg
MAMMA DRACULA(1980, Bel./Fr.), a, w
Akiko Wakabayashi
WALL-EYED NIPPON(1963, Jap.); BANDITS ON THE WIND(1964, Jap.); DAGORA THE SPACE MONSTER(1964, Jap.); GHIDRAH, THE THREE-HEADED MONSTER(1965, Jap.); IT STARTED IN THE ALPS(1966, Jap.); WHAT'S UP, TIGER LILY?(1966); THIN LINE, THE(1967, Jap.); YOU ONLY LIVE TWICE(1967, Brit.)
Eiko Wakabayashi
LOST WORLD OF SINBAD, THE(1965, Jap.)
Eiko Wakabayshi
KING KONG VERSUS GODZILLA(1963, Jap.)
Tamami Wakahara
LOVE ROBOTS, THE(1965, Jap.)
Koji Wakamatsu
LOVE ROBOTS, THE(1965, Jap.), p&d
Yaeko Wakamizu
MAN IN THE MOONLIGHT MASK, THE(1958, Jap.)
Ayako Wakao
ACTOR'S REVENGE, AN(1963, Jap.); GREAT WALL, THE(1965, Jap.); PASSION(1968, Jap.); THOUSAND CRANES(1969, Jap.); FLOATING WEEDS(1970, Jap.); ZATOICHI MEETS YOJIMBO(1970, Jap.); GEISHA, A(1978, Jap.)
Tokuhei Wakao
SAMURAI(PART III) (1967, Jap.), w; SECRET SCROLLS(PART II) (1968, Jap.), w; SAMURAI(1955, Jap.), w
Keiko Wakasa
ALMOST TRANSPARENT BLUE(1980, Jap.)
Akihito Wakatsuki
NUTCRACKER FANTASY(1979), m
Shigeru Wakatsuki
HUMAN CONDITION, THE(1959, Jap.), p; KWAIDAN(1965, Jap.), p; LOVE UNDER THE CRUCIFIX(1965, Jap.), p; SOLDIER'S PRAYER, A(1970, Jap.), p
Setsuko Wakayama
GIGANTIS(1959, Jap./U.S.)
Tomisaburo Wakayama
BAD NEWS BEARS GO TO JAPAN, THE(1978); HINOTORI(1980, Jap.); SHOGUN ASSASSIN(1980, Jap.)
Joanna Wake
SERVANT, THE(1964, Brit.); ONE MORE TIME(1970, Brit.)
Agnes Wakefield
Silents
OUT OF THE SHADOW(1919)
Ann Wakefield
UNTIL THEY SAIL(1957); WHEN HELL BROKE LOOSE(1958); SINGING NUN, THE(1966)
Anne Wakefield
300 SPARTANS, THE(1962)
C.T Wakefield
CROSS CREEK(1983)
Dan Wakefield
STARTING OVER(1979), w
David Wakefield
1984
SAM'S SON(1984)
Douglas Wakefield
THIS WEEK OF GRACE(1933, Brit.); LOOK UP AND LAUGH(1935, Brit.)
Duggie Wakefield
PENNY POOL, THE(1937, Brit.); CALLING ALL CROOKS(1938, Brit.); SPY FOR A DAY(1939, Brit.)
Foster Wakefield
SATURDAY NIGHT IN APPLE VALLEY(1965), m
G. E. Wakefield
SALLY BISHOP(1932, Brit.), w
Gilbert Wakefield
ARENT WE ALL?(1932, Brit.), w; LORD CAMBER'S LADIES(1932, Brit.), w; WOMEN WHO PLAY(1932, Brit.), w; COUNSEL'S OPINION(1933, Brit.), w; DIVORCE OF LADY X. THE(1938, Brit.), w; ROOM FOR TWO(1940, Brit.), w
Hugh Wakefield
FAREWELL TO LOVE(1931, Brit.); SPORT OF KINGS, THE(1931, Brit.); ARENT WE ALL?(1932, Brit.); LIFE GOES ON(1932, Brit.); CRIME AT BLOSSOMS, THE(1933, Brit.); FORTUNATE FOOL, THE(1933, Brit.); KING OF THE RITZ(1933, Brit.); MAN THEY COULDN'T ARREST, THE(1933, Brit.); LADY IN DANGER(1934, Brit.); LUCK OF A SAILOR, THE(1934, Brit.); MAN WHO KNEW TOO MUCH, THE(1935, Brit.); MARRY THE GIRL(1935, Brit.); MY HEART IS CALLING(1935, Brit.); NO MONKEY BUSINESS(1935, Brit.); RUNAWAY LADIES(1935, Brit.); 18 MINUTES(1935, Brit.); CRIMSON CIRCLE, THE(1936, Brit.); DREAMS COME TRUE(1936, Brit.); IMPROPER DUCHESS, THE(1936, Brit.); INTERRUPTED HONEYMOON, THE(1936, Brit.); IT'S YOU I WANT(1936, Brit.); LIMPING MAN, THE(1936, Brit.); DEATH CROONS THE

BLUES(1937, Brit.); FOREVER YOURS(1937, Brit.); LIVE WIRE, THE(1937, Brit.); STREET SINGER, THE(1937, Brit.); MAKE IT THREE(1938, Brit.); BLITHE SPIRIT(1945, Brit.); ONE NIGHT WITH YOU(1948, Brit); NO HIGHWAY IN THE SKY(1951, Brit.); CARETAKERS DAUGHTER, THE(1952, Brit.), a, w; MAN WITH A MILLION(1954, Brit.)

Squadron Leader Hugh Wakefield
JOURNEY TOGETHER(1946, Brit.)

J.H. Wakefield
ROAD TO FORTUNE, THE(1930, Brit.)

Jack Wakefield
VIVA MAX!(1969); HARDLY WORKING(1981)

Jim Wakefield
SUPERDAD(1974)

Oliver Wakefield
FRENCH LEAVE(1937, Brit.); LET'S MAKE A NIGHT OF IT(1937, Brit.); THERE WAS A YOUNG MAN(1937, Brit.); BRIGGS FAMILY, THE(1940, Brit.); GEORGE AND MARGARET(1940, Brit.); SHIPYARD SALLY(1940, Brit.); LET THE PEOPLE SING(1942, Brit.); PETERVILLE DIAMOND, THE(1942, Brit.)

Simon Wakefield
FRENZY(1972, Brit.), set d; FROM BEYOND THE GRAVE(1974, Brit.), set d; HENNESSY(1975, Brit.), set d; PEOPLE THAT TIME FORGOT, THE(1977, Brit.), set d; FFOLKES(1980, Brit.), set d
1984
SLAYGROUND(1984, Brit.), set d

Kent L. Wakeford
ALICE DOESN'T LIVE HERE ANYMORE(1975), ph

Kent Wakeford
DOCTOR DEATH: SEEKER OF SOULS(1973), ph; MEAN STREETS(1973), ph; BLACK BELT JONES(1974), ph

Deborah Wakeham
MIDDLE AGE CRAZY(1980, Can.)
1984
COVERGIRL(1984, Can.)

Steven Wakelam
1984
ELEMENT OF CRIME, THE(1984, Den.), w

Gwen Wakeling
PARIS BOUND(1929), cos; RICH PEOPLE(1929), cos; THIS THING CALLED LOVE(1929), cos; BIG MONEY(1930), cos; HOLIDAY(1930), cos; OFFICER O'BRIEN(1930), cos; RED HOT RHYTHM(1930), cos; SIN TAKES A HOLIDAY(1930), cos; SWING HIGH(1930), cos; SUICIDE FLEET(1931), cos; TIP-OFF, THE(1931), cos; CARNIVAL BOAT(1932), cos; WOMAN COMMANDS, A(1932), cos; TRANSATLANTIC MERRY-GO-ROUND(1934), cos; LITTLEST REBEL, THE(1935), cos; BANJO ON MY KNEE(1936), cos; GIRLS' DORMITORY(1936), cos; HUMAN CARGO(1936), cos; KING OF BURLESQUE(1936), cos; LADIES IN LOVE(1936), cos; PIGSKIN PARADE(1936), cos; POOR LITTLE RICH GIRL(1936), cos; PRISONER OF SHARK ISLAND, THE(1936), cos; ROAD TO GLORY, THE(1936), cos; ALI BABA GOES TO TOWN(1937), cos; NANCY STEELE IS MISSING(1937), cos; ON THE AVENUE(1937), cos; SECOND HONEYMOON(1937), cos; SEVENTH HEAVEN(1937), cos; WAKE UP AND LIVE(1937), cos; WEE WILLIE WINKIE(1937), cos; ALEXANDER'S RAGTIME BAND(1938), cos; SALLY, IRENE AND MARY(1938), cos; STRAIGHT, PLACE AND SHOW(1938), cos; SUBMARINE PATROL(1938), cos; THREE BLIND MICE(1938), cos; DRUMS ALONG THE MOHAWK(1939), cos; HOUND OF THE BASKERVILLES, THE(1939), cos; RAINS CAME, THE(1939), cos; RETURN OF THE CISCO KID(1939), cos; TAIL SPIN(1939), cos; BRIGHAM YOUNG–FRONTIERSMAN(1940), cos; JOHNNY APOLLO(1940), cos; STAR DUST(1940), cos; YOUNG PEOPLE(1940), cos; HOW GREEN WAS MY VALLEY(1941), cos; INTERNATIONAL LADY(1941), cos; RISE AND SHINE(1941), cos; SWAMP WATER(1941), cos; WEEKEND IN HAVANA(1941), cos; MY GAL SAL(1942), cos; RINGS ON HER FINGERS(1942), cos; ROXIE HART(1942), cos; SON OF FURY(1942), cos; TALES OF MANHATTAN(1942), cos; THIS ABOVE ALL(1942), cos; TO THE SHORES OF TRIPOLI(1942), cos; UNCONQUERED(1947), cos; SAMSON AND DELILAH(1949), cos; HIGH AND THE MIGHTY, THE(1954), cos; PASSION(1954), cos; TRACK OF THE CAT(1954), cos; BLOOD ALLEY(1955), cos; ESCAPE TO BURMA(1955), cos; TENNESSEE'S PARTNER(1955), cos; GREAT DAY IN THE MORNING(1956), cos; JOHNNY CONCHO(1956), cos; RIVER'S EDGE, THE(1957), cos; MOST DANGEROUS MAN ALIVE(1961), cos

Jimmy Wakely
SAGA OF DEATH VALLEY(1939); SIX LESSONS FROM MADAME LA ZONGA(1941); STICK TO YOUR GUNS(1941); COWBOY IN THE CLOUDS(1943); OLD CHISHOLM TRAIL(1943); COWBOY FROM LONESOME RIVER(1944); I'M FROM ARKANSAS(1944); RIDERS OF THE DAWN(1945); SONG OF THE SIERRAS(1946); WEST OF THE ALAMO(1946); RAINBOW OVER THE ROCKIES(1947); RIDIN' DOWN THE TRAIL(1947); SIX GUN SERENADE(1947); SONG OF THE WASTELAND(1947); COWBOY CAVALIER(1948); OKLAHOMA BLUES(1948); OUTLAW BRAND(1948); PARTNERS OF THE SUNSET(1948); RANGE RENEGADES(1948); RANGERS RIDE, THE(1948); SILVER TRAILS(1948); SONG OF THE DRIFTER(1949); ACROSS THE RIO GRANDE(1949); BRAND OF FEAR(1949); DESERT VIGILANTE(1949); GUN LAW JUSTICE(1949); GUN RUNNER(1949); LAWLESS CODE(1949); ROARING WESTWARD(1949); MARSHAL'S DAUGHTER, THE(1953); ARROW IN THE DUST(1954), a,

Misc. Talkies
SONG OF THE RANGE(1944); LONESOME TRAIL(1945); SADDLE SERENADE(1945); SPRINGTIME IN TEXAS(1945); MOON OVER MONTANA(1946); TRAIL TO MEXICO(1946)

Frederic Wakeman
HUCKSTERS, THE(1947), w; KISS THEM FOR ME(1957), w; WASTREL, THE(1963, Ital.), w

Rick Wakeman
LISZTOMANIA(1975, Brit.), m, md; BURNING, THE(1981), m
1984
CRIMES OF PASSION(1984), m

George Wakhevitch
PERSONAL COLUMN(1939, Fr.), art d&set d; DEVIL'S ENVOYS, THE(1947, Fr.), art d; ROOM UPSTAIRS, THE(1948, Fr.), art d; DEDEE(1949, Fr.), set d; ME AND THE COLONEL(1958), art d; MEETINGS WITH REMARKABLE MEN(1979, Brit.), prod d

Georges Wakhevitch
LA MARSEILLAISE(1938, Fr.), set d; ETERNAL RETURN, THE(1943, Fr.), set d; MEDIUM, THE(1951), art d; PARIS HOLIDAY(1958), prod d; KING OF KINGS(1961), set d&cos; CRIME DOES NOT PAY(1962, Fr.), set d & cos; DIARY OF A CHAMBERMAID(1964, Fr./Ital.), art d, set d, cos; SCHEHERAZADE(1965, Fr./Ital./Span.), art

d, cos; TENDER SCOUNDREL(1967, Fr./Ital.), art d; MAYERLING(1968, Brit./Fr.), prod d; DELUSIONS OF GRANDEUR(1971 Fr.), art d; KING LEAR(1971, Brit./Den.), prod d

Kayoka Wakita
REVOLT OF MAMIE STOVER, THE(1956)

Nathan Waks
REMOVALISTS, THE(1975, Aus.), md; MY BRILLIANT CAREER(1980, Aus.), m

Wal-Berg
GENERALS WITHOUT BUTTONS(1938, Fr.), m; AFFAIR LAFONT, THE(1939, Fr.), m; FRENCH WAY, THE(1952, Fr.), m

Hana Walachova
MIDSUMMERS NIGHT'S DREAM, A(1961, Czech), ed

Adam Walacinski
JOAN OF THE ANGELS(1962, Pol.), m; PORTRAIT OF LENIN(1967, Pol./USSR), m

Chris Walas
SCANNERS(1981, Can.), spec eff
1984
GREMLINS(1984), spec eff

Betty Walberg
FUNNY LADY(1975), ch

Bobby Walberg
ADAM HAD FOUR SONS(1941); UNCERTAIN GLORY(1944)

Gargy Walberg
CHARRO(1969)

Garry Walberg
MALTESE BIPPY, THE(1969); TELL THEM WILLIE BOY IS HERE(1969); THEY CALL ME MISTER TIBBS(1970); ORGANIZATION, THE(1971); WHEN THE LEGENDS DIE(1972); TWO-MINUTE WARNING(1976)

Gary Walberg
MAN, THE(1972); REVENGE OF THE CHEERLEADERS(1976); MAC ARTHUR(1977)

John Walbridge
FANTASIA(1940), art d; PINOCCHIO(1940), art d; DUMBO(1941), art d; MELODY TIME(1948), w; ALICE IN WONDERLAND(1951), w

Anton Walbrook
VICTORIA THE GREAT(1937, Brit.); SOLDIER AND THE LADY, THE(1937); RAT, THE(1938, Brit.); SIXTY GLORIOUS YEARS(1938, Brit.); GASLIGHT(1940); INVADERS, THE(1941); SUICIDE SQUADRON(1942, Brit.); COLONEL BLIMP(1945, Brit.); MAN FROM MOROCCO, THE(1946, Brit.); QUEEN OF SPADES(1948, Brit.); RED SHOES, THE(1948, Brit.); LA RONDE(1954, Fr.); LE PLAISIR(1954, Fr.); LOLA MONTES(1955, Fr./Ger.); OH ROSALINDA(1956, Brit.); SAINT JOAN(1957); I ACCUSE(1958, Brit.); VIENNA WALTZES(1961, Aust.)

Ernst Walbrunn
TURKISH CUCUMBER, THE(1963, Ger.)

Otto Walburg
CROSSROADS(1938, Fr.)

Ben Walburn
1984
TANK(1984)

Fred Walburn
SHADOW OF THE THIN MAN(1941); EYES IN THE NIGHT(1942); LARCENY, INC.(1942); THIS GUN FOR HIRE(1942); GANG'S ALL HERE, THE(1943)

Freddie Walburn
GLASS KEY, THE(1942); ON THE SUNNY SIDE(1942); LADY OF BURLESQUE(1943)

Freddy Walburn
WAGONS ROLL AT NIGHT, THE(1941)

Raymond Walburn
LAUGHING LADY, THE(1930); BROADWAY BILL(1934); COUNT OF MONTE CRISTO, THE(1934); DEFENSE HESTS(1934); GREAT FLIRTATION, THE(1934); JEALOUSY(1934); LADY BY CHOICE(1934); DEATH FLIES EAST(1935); IT'S A SMALL WORLD(1935); MILLS OF THE GODS(1935); REDHEADS ON PARADE(1935); SHE MARRIED HER BOSS(1935); SOCIETY DOCTOR(1935); THANKS A MILLION(1935); WELCOME HOME(1935); ABSOLUTE QUIET(1936); BORN TO DANCE(1936); CRAIG'S WIFE(1936); GREAT ZIEGFELD, THE(1936); KING STEPS OUT, THE(1936); LONE WOLF RETURNS, THE(1936); MISTER CINDERELLA(1936); MR. DEEDS GOES TO TOWN(1936); THEY MET IN A TAXI(1936); THREE WISE GUYS, THE(1936); BREEZING HOME(1937); BROADWAY MELODY OF '38(1937); HIGH, WIDE AND HANDSOME(1937); IT CAN'T LAST FOREVER(1937); LET'S GET MARRIED(1937); MURDER IN GREENWICH VILLAGE(1937); THIN ICE(1937); BATTLE OF BROADWAY(1938); GATEWAY(1938); PROFESSOR BEWARE(1938); START CHEERING(1938); SWEETHEARTS(1938); ETERNALLY YOURS(1939); HEAVEN WITH A BARBED WIRE FENCE(1939); IT COULD HAPPEN TO YOU(1939); LET FREEDOM RING(1939); UNDER-PUP, THE(1939); CHRISTMAS IN JULY(1940); DARK COMMAND, THE(1940); FLOWING GOLD(1940); MILLIONAIRES IN PRISON(1940); THIRD FINGER, LEFT HAND(1940); BACHELOR DADDY(1941); CONFIRM OR DENY(1941); KISS THE BOYS GOODBYE(1941); LOUISIANA PURCHASE(1941); RISE AND SHINE(1941); SAN FRANCISCO DOCKS(1941); LADY BODYGUARD(1942); MAN IN THE TRUNK, THE(1942); DESPERADOES, THE(1943); DIXIE(1943); DIXIE DUGAN(1943); LET'S FACE IT(1943); AND THE ANGELS SING(1944); HAIL THE CONQUERING HERO(1944); HEAVENLY DAYS(1944); MUSIC IN MANHATTAN(1944); CHEATERS, THE(1945); HONEYMOON AHEAD(1945); I'LL TELL THE WORLD(1945); AFFAIRS OF GERALDINE(1946); LOVER COME BACK(1946); PLAINSMAN AND THE LADY(1946); RENDEZVOUS WITH ANNIE(1946); STATE OF THE UNION(1948); HENRY, THE RAINMAKER(1949); LEAVE IT TO HENRY(1949); RED, HOT AND BLUE(1949); FATHER MAKES GOOD(1950); FATHER'S WILD GAME(1950); KEY TO THE CITY(1950); MAD WEDNESDAY(1950); RIDING HIGH(1950); SHORT GRASS(1950); EXCUSE MY DUST(1951); FATHER TAKES THE AIR(1951); GOLDEN GIRL(1951); SHE COULDN'T SAY NO(1954); SPOILERS, THE(1955)

Raymond Walburn, Sr.
PUDDIN' HEAD(1941)

Marie Walcamp
Silents
HOP, THE DEVIL'S BREW(1916); JOHN NEEDHAM'S DOUBLE(1916); BLOT, THE(1921); WESTERN VENGEANCE(1924)
Misc. Silents
CORAL(1915); FLIRT, THE(1916); WHERE ARE MY CHILDREN?(1916); TONGUES OF FLAME(1919); DESPERATE ADVENTURE, A(1924); TREASURE CANYON(1924); IN A MOMENT OF TEMPTATION(1927)

Morek Walcewski
WAR OF THE WORLDS–NEXT CENTURY, THE(1981, Pol.)

Ernest Walch
CURSE OF THE STONE HAND(1965, Mex/Chile)

Sean Walch
STOOLIE, THE(1972)

Ezra Walck
Silents
$5,000,000 COUNTERFEITING PLOT, THE(1914); FRUITS OF DESIRE, THE(1916)

Arthur Walcott
Silents
SOLDIER AND A MAN, A(1916, Brit.); UNDER SUSPICION(1919, Brit.); KISSING CUP'S RACE(1920, Brit.); AMAZING PARTNERSHIP, THE(1921, Brit.); OTHER PERSON, THE(1921, Brit.); WHEN GREEK MEETS GREEK(1922, Brit.); BEAUTIFUL KITTY(1923, Brit.); IN THE BLOOD(1923, Brit.); UNINVITED GUEST, THE(1923, Brit.); SHADOW OF EGYPT, THE(1924, Brit.); DAUGHTER OF LOVE, A(1925, Brit.)
Misc. Silents
MYSTERY OF A HANSOM CAB, THE(1915, Brit.); KISSING CUP'S RACE(1920, Brit.); SON OF DAVID, A(1920, Brit.); SCARLET LADY, THE(1922, Brit.); SON OF KISSING CUP(1922, Brit.); WAS SHE JUSTIFIED?(1922, Brit.); LADY OWNER, THE(1923, Brit.)

Charles Walcott
Misc. Silents
PHIL-FOR-SHORT(1919)

Donald Walcott
Silents
IF YOUTH BUT KNEW(1926, Brit.)

George Walcott
FURY(1936); BORROWING TROUBLE(1937); GREAT HOSPITAL MYSTERY, THE(1937); MANDARIN MYSTERY, THE(1937); STELLA DALLAS(1937); COCOANUT GROVE(1938); WESTERN JAMBOREE(1938); FORGOTTEN WOMAN, THE(1939); QUIET PLEASE, MURDER(1942); BATTLE FLAME(1955)

Greg Walcott
TEXAS LADY(1955)

Gregory Walcott
ABOVE AND BEYOND(1953); COURT-MARTIAL OF BILLY MITCHELL, THE(1955); MC CONNELL STORY, THE(1955); MISTER ROBERTS(1955); STRANGE LADY IN TOWN(1955); LIEUTENANT WORE SKIRTS, THE(1956); STEEL JUNGLE, THE(1956); THUNDER OVER ARIZONA(1956); PERSUADER, THE(1957); JET ATTACK(1958); PLAN 9 FROM OUTER SPACE(1959); ON THE DOUBLE(1961); OUTSIDER, THE(1962); CAPTAIN NEWMAN, M.D.(1963); JOE KIDD(1972); PRIME CUT(1972); LAST AMERICAN HERO, THE(1973); MAN FROM THE EAST, A(1974, Ital./Fr.); SUGARLAND EXPRESS, THE(1974); THUNDERBOLT AND LIGHTFOOT(1974); EIGER SANCTION, THE(1975); MIDWAY(1976); NORMA RAE(1979); TILT(1979)

Hubert Walcott
Misc. Silents
NOT NEGOTIABLE(1918, Brit.)

Jacqueline Walcott
SHADOWS(1960)

Jersey Joe Walcott
HARDER THEY FALL, THE(1956)

Julia Walcott
Silents
LITTLE GRAY LADY, THE(1914)

William Walcott
Silents
DOWN TO THE SEA IN SHIPS(1923)
Misc. Silents
GIRL WITH A JAZZ HEART, THE(1920); GIRL WITH THE JAZZ HEART, THE(1920)

William S. Walcott
Misc. Silents
MYSTERY OF THE YELLOW ROOM, THE(1919)

John Walcutt
1984
SAM'S SON(1984)

Marek Walczewski
PASSENGER, THE(1970, Pol.); GOLEM(1980, Pol.)

Wald
NAVY BLUES(1941), w

Jane Wald
THREE STOOGES IN ORBIT, THE(1962); UNDER THE YUM-YUM TREE(1963); JOHN GOLDFARB, PLEASE COME HOME(1964); WHAT A WAY TO GO(1964); DEAR BRIGETTE(1965); HELL'S BLOODY DEVILS(1970)

Jarry Wald
OUT OF THE FOG(1941), w

Jeff Wald
PARADISE ALLEY(1978)

Jerry Wald
GIFT OF GAB(1934), w; TWENTY MILLION SWEETHEARTS(1934), w; BROADWAY GONDOLIER(1935), w; I LIVE FOR LOVE(1935), w; IN CALIENTE(1935), w; LITTLE BIG SHOT(1935), w; LIVING ON VELVET(1935), w; MAYBE IT'S LOVE(1935), w; STARS OVER BROADWAY(1935), w; SWEET MUSIC(1935), w; SING ME A LOVE SONG(1936), w; SONS O' GUNS(1936), w; HOLLYWOOD HOTEL(1937), w; READY, WILLING AND ABLE(1937), w; VARSITY SHOW(1937), w; BROTHER RAT(1938), w; GARDEN OF THE MOON(1938), w; GOLD DIGGERS IN PARIS(1938), w; HARD TO GET(1938), w; GOING PLACES(1939), w; KID FROM KOKOMO, THE(1939), w; NAUGHTY BUT NICE(1939), w; ON YOUR TOES(1939), w; ROARING TWENTIES, THE(1939), w; BROTHER RAT AND A BABY(1940), w; FLIGHT ANGELS(1940), w; THEY DRIVE BY NIGHT(1940), w; THREE CHEERS FOR THE IRISH(1940), w; TORRID ZONE(1940), w; MANPOWER(1941), w; MILLION DOLLAR BABY(1941), w; ACROSS THE PACIFIC(1942), p; GEORGE WASHINGTON SLEPT HERE(1942), p; HARD WAY, THE(1942), p, w; LARCENY, INC.(1942), p; MAN WHO CAME TO DINNER, THE(1942), p; ACTION IN THE NORTH ATLANTIC(1943), p; BACKGROUND TO DANGER(1943), p; DESTINATION TOKYO(1943), p; IN OUR TIME(1944), p; VERY THOUGHT OF YOU, THE(1944), p; MILDRED PIERCE(1945), p; OBJECTIVE, BURMA!(1945), p; PRIDE OF THE MARINES(1945), p; HUMORESQUE(1946), p; DARK PASSAGE(1947), p; POSSESSED(1947), p; SARGE GOES TO COLLEGE(1947); UNFAITHFUL, THE(1947), p; VACATION DAYS(1947); JOHNNY BELINDA(1948), p; KEY LARGO(1948), p; ONE SUNDAY AFTERNOON(1948), p; TO THE VICTOR(1948), p; ADVENTURES OF DON JUAN(1949), p; ALWAYS LEAVE

THEM LAUGHING(1949), p; FLAMINGO ROAD(1949), p; INSPECTOR GENERAL, THE(1949), p; JOHN LOVES MARY(1949), p; MY DREAM IS YOURS(1949), w; TASK FORCE(1949), p; BREAKING POINT, THE(1950), p; CAGED(1950), p; DAMNED DON'T CRY, THE(1950), p; GLASS MENAGERIE, THE(1950), p; PERFECT STRANGERS(1950), p; STORM WARNING(1950), p; YOUNG MAN WITH A HORN(1950), p; BEHAVE YOURSELF!(1951), p; BLUE VEIL, THE(1951), p; TWO TICKETS TO BROADWAY(1951), p; LUSTY MEN, THE(1952), p; MISS SADIE THOMPSON(1953), p; QUEEN BEE(1955), p; EDDY DUCHIN STORY, THE(1956), p; AFFAIR TO REMEMBER, AN(1957), p; KISS THEM FOR ME(1957), p; NO DOWN PAYMENT(1957), p; PEYTON PLACE(1957), p; IN LOVE AND WAR(1958), p; LONG, HOT SUMMER, THE(1958), p; MARDI GRAS(1958), p; BELOVED INFIDEL(1959), p; BEST OF EVERYTHING, THE(1959), p; HOUND-DOG MAN(1959), p; SOUND AND THE FURY, THE(1959), p; STORY ON PAGE ONE, THE(1959), p; LET'S MAKE LOVE(1960), p; SONS AND LOVERS(1960, Brit.), p; RETURN TO PEYTON PLACE(1961), p; WILD IN THE COUNTRY(1961), p; ADVENTURES OF A YOUNG MAN(1962), p; MR. HOBBS TAKES A VACATION(1962), p; STRIPPER, THE(1963), p

John Wald
WHISTLING IN THE DARK(1941); DIXIE DUGAN(1943); GANGWAY FOR TOMORROW(1943); MARGIN FOR ERROR(1943); PRACTICALLY YOURS(1944); HER ADVENTUROUS NIGHT(1946); MURDER IN THE MUSIC HALL(1946); LOST HONEYMOON(1947); NIGHTMARE ALLEY(1947); CANON CITY(1948); UNDER CALIFORNIA STARS(1948); ALIAS THE CHAMP(1949); MA AND PA KETTLE(1949); SLATTERY'S HURRICANE(1949); PEGGY(1950); PRIDE OF ST. LOUIS, THE(1952)

John R. Wald
SENATOR WAS INDISCREET, THE(1947)

Karl Wald
BEACH BALL(1965), ed

Malvin Wald
TWO IN A TAXI(1941), w; POWERS GIRL, THE(1942), w; TEN GENTLEMEN FROM WEST POINT(1942), w; UNDERDOG, THE(1943), w; JIVE JUNCTION(1944), w; BEHIND LOCKED DOORS(1948), w; DARK PAST, THE(1948), w; NAKED CITY, THE(1948), w; NOT WANTED(1949), w; UNDERCOVER MAN, THE(1949), w; OUTRAGE(1950), w; ON THE LOOSE(1951), w; BATTLE TAXI(1955), w; MAN ON FIRE(1957), w; STREET OF DARKNESS(1958), w; STEEL CLAW, THE(1961), w; VENUS IN FURS(1970, Ital./Brit./Ger.), w; IN SEARCH OF HISTORIC JESUS(1980), w

Marvin Wald
AL CAPONE(1959), w

Pavel Wald
CRAZY QUILT, THE(1966)

Robert Wald
SUMMER CAMP(1979)
1984
PREY, THE(1984)

Gustav Waldau
AFFAIRS OF DR. HOLL(1954, Ger.)

Ernest Waldbaum
TRIAL, THE(1948, Aust.)

Eddie Waldburger
DOWNHILL RACER(1969)

Rune Waldekranz
NAKED NIGHT, THE(1956, Swed.), p; MAKE WAY FOR LILA(1962, Swed./Ger.), p; TO LOVE(1964, Swed.), p; LOVING COUPLES(1966, Swed.), p; SHORT IS THE SUMMER(1968, Swed.), p

Barbara Walden
PRIVATE LIVES OF ADAM AND EVE, THE(1961); FREAKY FRIDAY(1976)

Charles Walden
HELL'S CHOSEN FEW(1968), m; MIGHTY GORGA, THE(1969), m

Diana Walden
PHANTOM OF THE PARADISE(1974)

Harold Walden
CUP-TIE HONEYMOON(1948, Brit.)
Silents
WINNING GOAL, THE(1929, Brit.)

Jerzy Walden
JOAN OF THE ANGELS(1962, Pol.)

Jill Walden
TELL ME IN THE SUNLIGHT(1967)

Lois Walden
MEAN STREETS(1973)

Louis Walden
LONESOME COWBOYS(1968); VIRGIN PRESIDENT, THE(1968); FEEDBACK(1979)

Lynette Walden
SPLIT IMAGE(1982)

Mary Walden
DEVONSVILLE TERROR, THE(1983)

Regina Walden
1984
ELECTRIC DREAMS(1984)

Robert Walden
BLOODY MAMA(1970); OUT OF TOWNERS, THE(1970); SIDELONG GLANCES OF A PIGEON KICKER, THE(1970); HOSPITAL, THE(1971); EVERYTHING YOU ALWAYS WANTED TO KNOW ABOUT SEX, BUT WE'RE AFRAID TO ASK(1972); RAGE(1972); OUR TIME(1974); ALL THE PRESIDENT'S MEN(1976); AUDREY ROSE(1977); BLUE SUNSHINE(1978); CAPRICORN ONE(1978)

Sandra Walden
NEXT TO NO TIME(1960, Brit.)

Susan Walden
WINTER KILLS(1979)

Sylvia Walden
HARRAD SUMMER, THE(1974); RESURRECTION(1980)

Tom Walden
1984
BOSTONIANS, THE(1984), art d

Ernest Walder
SAFECRACKER, THE(1958, Brit.); TANK FORCE(1958, Brit.); JOEY BOY(1965, Brit.)

Ernst Walder
HELL, HEAVEN OR HOBOKEN(1958, Brit.); WEEKEND WITH LULU, A(1961, Brit.); DARLING(1965, Brit.); QUILLER MEMORANDUM, THE(1966, Brit.); DOUBLE MAN, THE(1967); GUNS IN THE HEATHER(1968, Brit.); WHERE EAGLES DARE(1968,

Brit.); LOOKING GLASS WAR, THE(1970, Brit.)

Gertrude Walder
RAILROADED(1947), w

Theodore Waldeyer
PROJECT X(1949), ed

Paul Waldherr
MIRACLE OF THE WHITE STALLIONS(1963), spec eff

Gary Waldhorn
ZEPPELIN(1971, Brit.); HANOVER STREET(1979, Brit.); VICTORY(1981)

Congressman Jerry Waldie
CANDIDATE, THE(1972)

May Walding
EXODUS(1960), cos; JET STORM(1961, Brit.), cos

Otto Waldis
M(1933, Ger.); EXILE, THE(1947); BERLIN EXPRESS(1948); CALL NORTHSIDE 777(1948); LETTER FROM AN UNKNOWN WOMAN(1948); BAGDAD(1949); BORDER INCIDENT(1949); FIGHTING O'FLYNN, THE(1949); LOVABLE CHEAT, THE(1949); DARK CITY(1950); SPY HUNT(1950); WOMAN FROM HEADQUARTERS(1950); BIRD OF PARADISE(1951); NIGHT INTO MORNING(1951); SECRETS OF MONTE CARLO(1951); UNKNOWN WORLD(1951); WHIP HAND, THE(1951); ANYTHING CAN HAPPEN(1952); BLACK CASTLE, THE(1952); FIVE FINGERS(1952); ROGUE'S MARCH(1952); FLIGHT TO TANGIER(1953); REBEL CITY(1953); IRON GLOVE, THE(1954); KNOCK ON WOOD(1954); PRINCE VALIANT(1954); DESERT SANDS(1955); PORT OF HELL(1955); RUNNING WILD(1955); SINCERELY YOURS(1955); MAN FROM DEL RIO(1956); RIDE THE HIGH IRON(1956); ATTACK OF THE 50 FOOT WOMAN(1958); PIER 5, HAVANA(1959); JUDGMENT AT NUREMBERG(1961); PHANTOM OF SOHO, THE(1967, Ger.)

Luggi Waldleitner
BOOMERANG(1960, Ger.), p; ROSEMARY(1960, Ger.), p; THREE MOVES TO FREEDOM(1960, Ger.), p; BRAINWASHED(1961, Ger.), p; END OF MRS. CHENEY(1963, Ger.), p; DUCK RINGS AT HALF PAST SEVEN, THE(1969, Ger./Ital.), p; LILI MARLEEN(1981, Ger.), p

Cantor Leible Waldman
MOTEL, THE OPERATOR(1940)

Dan Waldman
Misc. Talkies
GOIN' ALL THE WAY(1982)

Frank Waldman
BATHING BEAUTY(1944), w; OUR HEARTS WERE GROWING UP(1946), w; HIGH TIME(1960), w; LOVE IS A BALL(1963), w; INSPECTOR CLOUSEAU(1968, Brit.), w; PARTY, THE(1968), w; DIRTY DINGUS MAGEE(1970), w; RETURN OF THE PINK PANTHER, THE(1975, Brit.), w; PINK PANTHER STRIKES AGAIN, THE(1976, Brit.), w; REVENGE OF THE PINK PANTHER(1978), w; TRAIL OF THE PINK PANTHER, THE(1982), w

Harvey Waldman
OFF THE WALL(1977), a, w
1984
ALMOST YOU(1984)

Herman Waldman
VICIOUS CIRCLE, THE(1948)

Jack Waldman
MARRIAGE, A(1983), m

Jenny Waldman
PRIVILEGED(1982, Brit.)

Leibele Waldman
Misc. Talkies
ABRAHAM OUR PATRIARCH(1933); LOVE AND SACRIFICE(1936); I WANT TO BE A MOTHER(1937); KOL NIDRE(1939); MAZEL TOV, JEWS(1941)

Mable Waldman
O'SHAUGHNESSY'S BOY(1935)

Marian Waldman
BLACK CHRISTMAS(1974, Can.); PHOBIA(1980, Can.)

Marion Waldman
CLASS OF '44(1973); DERANGED(1974, Can.)

Max Waldman
CODE OF THE OUTLAW(1942)

Ronnie Waldman
MAN OF THE MOMENT(1955, Brit.)

Tom Waldman
HIGH TIME(1960), w; LOVE IS A BALL(1963), w; INSPECTOR CLOUSEAU(1968, Brit.), w; PARTY, THE(1968), w; DIRTY DINGUS MAGEE(1970), w; TRAIL OF THE PINK PANTHER, THE(1982), w

Lizzi Waldmueller
CASE VAN GELDERN(1932, Ger.)

Waldo
DEATH OF A SCOUNDREL(1956), cos

Charles Waldo
EIGER SANCTION, THE(1975), cos

Elizabeth Waldo
SONG OF MEXICO(1945)

Janet Waldo
COCOANUT GROVE(1938); HUNTED MEN(1938); CAFE SOCIETY(1939); HONEYMOON IN BALI(1939); OUR NEIGHBORS–THE CARTERS(1939); STAR MAKER, THE(1939); TOM SAWYER, DETECTIVE(1939); WHAT A LIFE(1939); ZAZA(1939); FARMER'S DAUGHTER, THE(1940); ONE MAN'S LAW(1940); THOSE WERE THE DAYS(1940); WATERLOO BRIDGE(1940); BANDIT TRAIL(1941); LAND OF THE OPEN RANGE(1941); SILVER STALLION(1941); MAN CALLED FLINTSTONE, THE(1966); FANTASTIC PLANET(1973, Fr./Czech.); HEIDI'S SONG(1982)

Kip Waldo
1984
HARDBODIES(1984); NIGHT PATROL(1984); STREETS OF FIRE(1984)

Ralph Waldo
CAIN'S WAY(1969), ph; WILD WHEELS(1969), ph

Denis Waldock
DANCE BAND(1935, Brit.), w; MIMI(1935, Brit.), w; MARRY ME!(1949, Brit.), w; MIRANDA(1949, Brit.), w; FUN AT ST. FANNY'S(1956, Brit.), w

John Waldon
HYPNOTIZED(1933), w

Louis Waldon
DOUBLE-BARRELLED DETECTIVE STORY, THE(1965); ME AND MY BROTHER(1969); DREAM TOWN(1973, Ger.)

Marion Waldon
WORDS AND MUSIC(1929)

Regina Waldon
FOG, THE(1980)

Robert Waldon
STRANGER ON THE THIRD FLOOR(1940)

David Waldor
PLUNDERERS OF PAINTED FLATS(1959)

Dolly Waldorf
SOMETHING TO SING ABOUT(1937)

Sven Olaf Waldorf
GEORGIA, GEORGIA(1972), m

Gustav Waldou
LOLA MONTES(1955, Fr./Ger.)

Ernst Waldow
BOCCACCIO(1936, Ger.); COURT CONCERT, THE(1936, Ger.); DREAMER, THE(1936, Ger.); TOXI(1952, Ger.)

Charles D. Waldren
THRU DIFFERENT EYES(1942)

Harold Waldridge
FIVE STAR FINAL(1931); JUNE MOON(1931); MANHATTAN PARADE(1931); SOB SISTER(1931); ALIAS THE DOCTOR(1932); FALSE FACES(1932); HEART OF NEW YORK(1932); HIGH PRESSURE(1932); JEWEL ROBBERY(1932); PLAY GIRL(1932); STRANGE LOVE OF MOLLY LOUVAIN, THE(1932); STRANGERS OF THE EVENING(1932); DEATH KISS, THE(1933); DEVIL'S MATE(1933); LADY KILLER(1933); SHE HAD TO SAY YES(1933); EASY TO LOVE(1934); IN THE MONEY(1934); MANHATTAN LOVE SONG(1934); PRIVATE SCANDAL(1934); GIGOLETTE(1935); DANCING PIRATE(1936); HITCH HIKE LADY(1936); YOU BELONG TO ME(1941)
Silents
RULING PASSION, THE(1922)

Harold Waldrige
ALL-AMERICAN, THE(1932)

Bella Waldritter
TINDER BOX, THE(1968, E. Ger.)

Andrew Waldron
Silents
HILLS OF MISSING MEN(1922); PUTTING IT OVER(1922); WHEN EAST COMES WEST(1922); BAFFLED(1924); DOWN BY THE RIO GRANDE(1924); FIGHTER'S PARADISE(1924); WILD GIRL, THE(1925); RECKLESS CHANCES(5 reels)
Misc. Silents
GUN SHY(1922); WOLVES OF THE BORDER(1923); PALS(1925); ACE OF CLUBS, THE(1926)

Arthur Waldron, Jr.
GIVE MY REGARDS TO BROADWAY(1948)

Andy Waldron
Silents
GREY DEVIL, THE(1926); CLEARING THE TRAIL(1928); LARIAT KID, THE(1929)
Misc. Silents
DISCONTENTED WIVES(1921)

Bhetty Waldron
HIT MAN(1972)

Charles Waldron
CRIME AND PUNISHMENT(1935); GREAT IMPERSONATION, THE(1935); MARY BURNS, FUGITIVE(1935); GARDEN OF ALLAH, THE(1936); RAMONA(1936); DOCTOR'S DIARY, A(1937); EMPEROR'S CANDLESTICKS, THE(1937); ESCAPE BY NIGHT(1937); IT'S ALL YOURS(1937); MY DEAR MISS ALDRICH(1937); NAVY BLUE AND GOLD(1937); KENTUCKY(1938); LITTLE ADVENTURESS, THE(1938); MARIE ANTOINETTE(1938); ON BORROWED TIME(1939); REAL GLORY, THE(1939); THOU SHALT NOT KILL(1939); AND ONE WAS BEAUTIFUL(1940); DR. KILDARE'S STRANGE CASE(1940); EDISON, THE MAN(1940); REMEMBER THE NIGHT(1940); SON OF MONTE CRISTO(1940); STRANGER ON THE THIRD FLOOR(1940); STREET OF MEMORIES(1940); THREE FACES WEST(1940); UNTAMED(1940); DEVIL AND MISS JONES, THE(1941); RISE AND SHINE(1941); RANDOM HARVEST(1942); SONG OF BERNADETTE, THE(1943); ADVENTURES OF MARK TWAIN, THE(1944); BLACK PARACHUTE, THE(1944); MADEMOISELLE FIFI(1944); ONCE UPON A TIME(1944); WING AND A PRAYER(1944); FIGHTING GUARDSMAN, THE(1945); BIG SLEEP, THE(1946); DRAGONWYCH(1946)
Silents
ESMERALDA(1915); AUDREY(1916); MICE AND MEN(1916); EVERYMAN'S PRICE(1921)
Misc. Silents
AT BAY(1915); WHEN WE WERE TWENTY-ONE(1915); THIEF, THE(1920)

Charles Waldron, Jr.
TEST PILOT(1938); FOR YOU I DIE(1947); OPEN SECRET(1948); TASK FORCE(1949)

Charles D. Waldron
DOCTOR'S DIARY, A(1937); CASE OF THE BLACK PARROT, THE(1941); I WANTED WINGS(1941); NURSE'S SECRET, THE(1941); THREE SONS O'GUNS(1941); GAY SISTERS, THE(1942)

Charles Waldron, Sr.
WANDERER OF THE WASTELAND(1935); CAREER WOMAN(1936)

Dee Waldron
1984
SUBURBIA(1984)

Edna Waldron
MERRY WIDOW, THE(1934); RECKLESS(1935)

Gy Waldron
MOONRUNNERS(1975), d&w

Jack Waldron
PAJAMA GAME, THE(1957)

Jackee Waldron
TARZAN AND THE SLAVE GIRL(1950)

John A. Waldron
MIDNIGHT DADDIES(1929), w

Mal Waldron
COOL WORLD, THE(1963), m; SWEET LOVE, BITTER(1967), m

Philip Waldron
KID GALAHAD(1937); THAT CERTAIN WOMAN(1937)
Regina Waldron
TIME AFTER TIME(1979, Brit.)
Robert Waldron
FLYING DOCTOR, THE(1936, Aus.), w
Tom Waldron
STRANGE CASE OF DR. MANNING, THE(1958, Brit.), w
Wendy Waldron
DESERT HAWK, THE(1950); FATHER OF THE BRIDE(1950); LUCKY LO-
SERS(1950); SHAKEDOWN(1950); FATHER'S LITTLE DIVIDEND(1951); NAVY
BOUND(1951); TRAIL GUIDE(1952)
Misc. Talkies
TRAIL OF THE ARROW(1952)
Nils Waldt
SILENCE, THE(1964, Swed.)
Nils Janette Walen
WILD DUCK, THE(1977, Ger./Aust.), m
Anna Walentynowicz
MAN OF IRON(1981, Pol.)
Mavis Waler
CONDUCTOR, THE(1981, Pol.)
Gregorio Walerstein
LIVING IDOL, THE(1957), p
Betty Wales
Silents
KING SPRUCE(1920)
Ethel Wales
PERFECT CRIME, THE(1928); TAXI 13(1928); DOCTOR'S SECRET(1929); DONOVAN
AFFAIR, THE(1929); GIRL IN THE SHOW, THE(1929); SATURDAY NIGHT KID,
THE(1929); DUDE WRANGLER, THE(1930); LOOSE ANKLES(1930); TOM SA-
WYER(1930); UNDER MONTANA SKIES(1930); CRIMINAL CODE(1931); FLOOD,
THE(1931); HONEYMOON LANE(1931); MAKER OF MEN(1931); SUBWAY EX-
PRESS(1931); FIGHTING FOOL, THE(1932); KLONDIKE(1932); LOVE ME TO-
NIGHT(1932); MAN'S LAND, A(1932); SIGN OF THE CROSS, THE(1932); TANGLED
DESTINIES(1932); THIRTEENTH GUEST, THE(1932); TRIAL OF VIVIENNE WARE,
THE(1932); EASY MILLIONS(1933); ELEVENTH COMMANDMENT(1933); EVER IN
MY HEART(1933); FIGHTING PARSON, THE(1933); IMPORTANT WITNESS,
THE(1933); RACING STRAIN, THE(1933); CRIME DOCTOR, THE(1934); MERRY
FRINKS, THE(1934); MIGHTY BARNUM, THE(1934); ANOTHER FACE(1935); BAR-
BARY COAST(1935); BAR 20 RIDES AGAIN(1936); SMALL TOWN GIRL(1936);
GLADIATOR, THE(1938); DAYS OF JESSE JAMES(1939); FRONTIER PONY EX-
PRESS(1939); IN OLD CALIENTE(1939); SUDDEN MONEY(1939); HIDDEN
GOLD(1940); KNIGHTS OF THE RANGE(1940); WYOMING(1940); YOUNG BILL
HICKOK(1940); BORDER VIGILANTES(1941); LUMBERJACK(1944); IN OLD SAC-
RAMENTO(1946); SMASH-UP, THE STORY OF A WOMAN(1947); UNCON-
QUERED(1947); WELCOME STRANGER(1947); FANCY PANTS(1950);
TARNISHED(1950)
Misc. Talkies
LOVE IN HIGH GEAR(1932)
Silents
MIDSUMMER MADNESS(1920); AFTER THE SHOW(1921); NICE PEOPLE(1922);
OUR LEADING CITIZEN(1922); COVERED WAGON, THE(1923); FOG, THE(1923);
STEPPING FAST(1923); BEDROOM WINDOW, THE(1924); ICEBOUND(1924); LOV-
ER'S LANE(1924); REVELATION(1924); MONSTER, THE(1925); OVERLAND LIMIT-
ED, THE(1925); WEDDING SONG, THE(1925); LADIES AT PLAY(1926); TAKE IT
FROM ME(1926); BERTHA, THE SEWING MACHINE GIRL(1927); STAGE KIS-
SES(1927); CRAIG'S WIFE(1928); ON TO RENO(1928)
Misc. Silents
WHICH SHALL IT BE?(1924); GO STRAIGHT(1925); LET WOMEN ALONE(1925);
SHATTERED LIVES(1925); WHEN HUSBANDS FLIRT(1925); MADE FOR LO-
VE(1926); CRADLE SNATCHERS, THE(1927); MY FRIEND FROM INDIA(1927);
BLUE SKIES(1929)
Henry Wales
YOU MAY BE NEXT(1936), w; CONFIRM OR DENY(1941), w
Jonathan Wales
DEADLY AFFAIR, THE(1967, Brit.)
Judee Wales
NIGHTHAWKS(1981)
Ken Wales
OPERATION BOTTLENECK(1961); EXPERIMENT IN TERROR(1962); ADVANCE
TO THE REAR(1964); GREAT RACE, THE(1965); WHAT DID YOU DO IN THE WAR,
DADDY?(1966); GUNN(1967); PARTY, THE(1968); WILD ROVERS(1971), p; TAMA-
RIND SEED, THE(1974, Brit.), p
1984
DOOR TO DOOR(1984), p; PRODIGAL, THE(1984), a, p
Pauline Wales
MIKADO, THE(1967, Brit.)
Ricky Wales
MELODY(1971, Brit.)
Robert Ellis Wales
Silents
PENITENTES, THE(1915), w
Victoria Wales
TO BE FREE(1972)
Misc. Talkies
IMAGO(1970)
Wally [Hal Taliaferro] Wales
LUCKY TERROR(1936)
William Wales
AMITYVILLE 3-D(1983), w
Wally Wales [Hal Taliaferro]
OVERLAND BOUND(1929); BAR L RANCH(1930); CANYON HAWKS(1930); TRAILS
OF DANGER(1930); RED FORK RANGE(1931); RIDERS OF THE CACTUS(1931); 99
WOUNDS(1931); LAW AND LAWLESS(1932); DEADWOOD PASS(1933); FIGHTING
TEXANS(1933); ARIZONA CYCLONE(1934); HONOR OF THE RANGE(1934); LOST
JUNGLE, THE(1934); SAGEBRUSH TRAIL(1934); SMOKING GUNS(1934); TRAIL
DRIVE, THE(1934); WAY OF THE WEST, THE(1934); WHEELS OF DESTINY(1934);
COWBOY AND THE BANDIT, THE(1935); DANGER TRAILS(1935); FIGHTING
CABALLERO(1935); POWDERSMOKE RANGE(1935); STRANDED(1935); AMBUSH

VALLEY(1936); AVENGING WATERS(1936); GUN PLAY(1936); HEIR TO TROU-
BLE(1936); HEROES OF THE RANGE(1936); LAWLESS RIDERS(1936); SWIF-
TY(1936); TRAITOR, THE(1936); LAW AND LEAD(1937); LAW OF THE
LAWLESS(1964)
Misc. Talkies
BREED OF THE WEST(1930); RIDIN' KID(1930); FLYING LARIATS(1931); HELL'S
VALLEY(1931); SECRETS OF HOLLYWOOD(1933); LONE BANDIT, THE(1934);
LONE RIDER, THE(1934); POTLUCK PARDS(1934); RANGE WARFARE(1935); SIX
GUN JUSTICE(1935); VANISHING RIDERS(1935); WESTERN RACKETEERS(1935);
HAIR-TRIGGER CASEY(1936); SUNDOWN TRAIL, THE(1975)
Silents
ACE OF ACTION(1926); FIGHTING CHEAT, THE(1926); VANISHING HOOFS(1926)
Misc. Silents
GALLOPING ON(1925); HURRICANE HORSEMAN(1925); TEARIN' LOOSE(1925);
DOUBLE DARING(1926); RIDING RIVALS(1926); ROARING RIDER(1926); TWISTED
TRIGGERS(1926); CYCLONE COWBOY, THE(1927); DESERT OF THE LOST,
THE(1927); MEDDLIN' STRANGER, THE(1927); SKEDADDLE GOLD(1927); SODA
WATER COWBOY(1927); TEARIN' INTO TROUBLE(1927); WHITE PEBBLES(1927);
DESPERATE COURAGE(1928); FLYING BUCKAROO, THE(1928); SADDLE MA-
TES(1928)
Lech Walesa
MAN OF IRON(1981, Pol.)
Blanka Waleska
DISTANT JOURNEY(1950, Czech.)
Ian Walfe
PEARL OF DEATH, THE(1944)
Ann Walford
GOLD EXPRESS, THE(1955, Brit.); ORDERS TO KILL(1958, Brit.)
Arthur Walge
MEET ME AFTER THE SHOW(1951); QUO VADIS(1951)
Cecily Walger
TWICE UPON A TIME(1953, Brit.)
Monona Wali
1984
REPO MAN(1984)
Charles Walke
GOIN' COCONUTS(1978)
Charles Edmund Walk
Silents
GIRL IN THE DARK, THE(1918), w
Byrl Walkeley
HIS ROYAL HIGHNESS(1932, Aus.)
Christopher Walken
ME AND MY BROTHER(1969); ANDERSON TAPES, THE(1971); HAPPINESS CAGE,
THE(1972); NEXT STOP, GREENWICH VILLAGE(1976); ANNIE HALL(1977); ROSE-
LAND(1977); SENTINEL, THE(1977); DEER HUNTER, THE(1978); LAST EM-
BRACE(1979); DOGS OF WAR, THE(1980, Brit.); HEAVEN'S GATE(1980); PENNIES
FROM HEAVEN(1981); BRAINSTORM(1983); DEAD ZONE, THE(1983)
Misc. Talkies
SHOOT THE SUN DOWN(1981)
Georgianne Walken
BRAINSTORM(1983)
Glenn Walken
GOING HOME(1971); APOCALYPSE NOW(1979)
Ken Walken
BLUE ANGEL, THE(1959)
Walker
TOP HAT(1935), spec eff
A. E. J. Walker
LIEUTENANT DARING, RN(1935, Brit.)
Mrs. Walker
Silents
WANTED FOR MURDER(1919)
Alan Walker
1984
TANK(1984)
Mrs. Allen Walker
Silents
NEPTUNE'S DAUGHTER(1914)
Amanda Walker
DEADLY AFFAIR, THE(1967, Brit.); RICHARD'S THINGS(1981, Brit.); HEAT AND
DUST(1983, Brit.)
Antoinette Walker
Misc. Silents
STING OF VICTORY, THE(1916)
April Walker
PINK PANTHER STRIKES AGAIN, THE(1976, Brit.)
Art Walker
Silents
GOLD RUSH, THE(1925)
Misc. Silents
TWO-FISTED SHERIFF, A(1925)
Arthur Walker
I WALKED WITH A ZOMBIE(1943)
Aurora Walker
EL(1955, Mex.)
Barbara Walker
MY THIRD WIFE GEORGE(1968)
Basil Walker
CADET GIRL(1941); CHARLEY'S AUNT(1941); I WAKE UP SCREAMING(1942); TO
THE SHORES OF TRIPOLI(1942); MARGIE(1946); MIRACLE ON 34TH STREET,
THE(1947); MOSS ROSE(1947)
Ben Walker
Silents
PIRATES OF THE SKY(1927)
Misc. Silents
WINNER, THE(1926); TRUNK MYSTERY, THE(1927)

Betty Walker
OUT OF THIS WORLD(1945); GOLDBERGS, THE(1950); MIDDLE OF THE NIGHT(1959); EXODUS(1960); WHO IS HARRY KELLERMAN AND WHY IS HE SAYING THOSE TERRIBLE THINGS ABOUT ME?(1971)

Beverly Walker
NOSFERATU, THE VAMPIRE(1979, Fr./Ger.)

Bill Walker
YOU CAN'T RUN AWAY FROM IT(1956); NORTH STAR, THE(1943); WE'VE NEVER BEEN LICKED(1943); KILLERS, THE(1946); CANON CITY(1948); I WOULDN'T BE IN YOUR SHOES(1948); LARCENY(1948); MYSTERY OF THE GOLDEN EYE, THE(1948); BAD BOY(1949); FREE FOR ALL(1949); NO WAY OUT(1950); PEGGY(1950); YOUNG MAN WITH A HORN(1950); FAMILY SECRET, THE(1951); FRANCIS GOES TO THE RACES(1951); HARLEM GLOBETROTTERS, THE(1951); WELL, THE(1951); BLOODHOUNDS OF BROADWAY(1952); BOMBA AND THE JUNGLE GIRL(1952); NIGHT WITHOUT SLEEP(1952); MISSISSIPPI GAMBLER, THE(1953); REBEL CITY(1953); KILLER LEOPARD(1954); OUTCAST, THE(1954); BIG KNIFE, THE(1955); FAR HORIZONS, THE(1955); GOOD MORNING, MISS DOVE(1955); QUEEN BEE(1955); VIEW FROM POMPEY'S HEAD, THE(1955); EVERYTHING BUT THE TRUTH(1956); KISS BEFORE DYING, A(1956); RAINTREE COUNTY(1957); HOT SPELL(1958); RIDE A CROOKED TRAIL(1958); MASK, THE(1961, Can.); TO KILL A MOCKINGBIRD(1962); WALK ON THE WILD SIDE(1962); WALL OF NOISE(1963); KISSES FOR MY PRESIDENT(1964); THIRD DAY, THE(1965); DIMENSION 5(1966); LAST CHALLENGE, THE(1967); DREAM OF KINGS, A(1969); RIOT(1969); GREAT WHITE HOPE, THE(1970); ...TICK...TICK...TICK...(1970); GOING HOME(1971), m; LITTLE LAURA AND BIG JOHN(1973), m; MAURIE(1973); TWILIGHT'S LAST GLEAMING(1977, U.S./Ger.); SCARECROW, THE(1982, New Zealand)
Misc. Talkies
SUN TAN RANCH(1948)

Billy Walker
HOLE IN THE HEAD, A(1959); KIMBERLEY JIM(1965, South Africa), m; SECOND FIDDLE TO A STEEL GUITAR(1965); FAT CITY(1972)

Blanche Walker
Silents
ROYAL OAK, THE(1923, Brit.)

Bob Walker
FIGHTING LEGION, THE(1930); MARY BURNS, FUGITIVE(1935); OUTLAWED GUNS(1935); THROWBACK, THE(1935); FAST BULLETS(1936); SPEED REPORTER(1936); GUNSMOKE RANCH(1937)
Silents
ISOBEL(1920); DRUG TRAFFIC, THE(1923)
Misc. Silents
RIDIN' COMET(1925)

Bonnie Walker
KILL, THE(1968)

Brian Walker
1984
BLIND DATE(1984)
Misc. Talkies
AMERICAN GAME, THE(1979)

Brian Walker
BELLS(1981, Can.), p
1984
BLIND DATE(1984)

Brittain Saine Walker
1984
SCREAM FOR HELP(1984)

Bruce Walker
DICK BARTON STRIKES BACK(1949, Brit.); DR. MORELLE–THE CASE OF THE MISSING HEIRESS(1949, Brit.); MAN'S AFFAIR, A(1949, Brit.); THIRD TIME LUCKY(1950, Brit.); SLASHER, THE(1953, Brit.), w

Carl Walker
BLOOD ALLEY(1955), cos; DAVY CROCKETT AND THE RIVER PIRATES(1956), cos; GOODBYE, MY LADY(1956), cos; SEVEN MEN FROM NOW(1956), cos

Carol Walker
LA FUGA(1966, Ital.)

Carole Walker
HALF A SIXPENCE(1967, Brit.)

Carolyn Walker
WHAT'S UP FRONT(1964)

Charles Walker
SHEILA LEVINE IS DEAD AND LIVING IN NEW YORK(1975); DR. BLACK AND MR. HYDE(1976), p; MEAN JOHNNY BARROWS(1976), w
1984
SPLASH(1984)

Charlotte Walker
PARIS BOUND(1929); SOUTH SEA ROSE(1929); DOUBLE CROSS ROADS(1930); LIGHTNIN'(1930); SCARLET PAGES(1930); THREE FACES EAST(1930); MILLIE(1931); SCATTERGOOD NELL(1931); HOTEL VARIETY(1933); SCATTERGOOD MEETS BROADWAY(1941)
Silents
KINDLING(1915); CLASSMATES(1924); CLOWN, THE(1927); ANNAPOLIS(1928)
Misc. Silents
TRAIL OF THE LONESOME PINE, THE(1916); MARY LAWSON'S SECRET(1917); PARDNERS(1917); SLOTH(1917); EVE IN EXILE(1919); EVERY MOTHER'S SON(1919); SIXTH COMMANDMENT, THE(1924); MIDNIGHT GIRL, THE(1925)

Cheryl Walker
COCOANUT GROVE(1938); IF I WERE KING(1938); MEN WITH WINGS(1938); TIP-OFF GIRLS(1938); YOU AND ME(1938); $1,000 A TOUCHDOWN(1939); CHASING TROUBLE(1940); SHADOWS ON THE SAGE(1942); STAGE DOOR CANTEEN(1943); YOUNG AND WILLING(1943); THREE LITTLE SISTERS(1944); 3 IS A FAMILY(1944); IDENTITY UNKNOWN(1945); IT'S A PLEASURE(1945); SONG FOR MISS JULIE, A(1945); HOW DO YOU DO?(1946); LARCENY IN HER HEART(1946); MURDER IS MY BUSINESS(1946); THREE ON A TICKET(1947); WATERFRONT AT MIDNIGHT(1948)
Misc. Talkies
RHYTHM ROUND-UP(1945)

Chris Walker
Silents
MAN WITHOUT DESIRE, THE(1923, Brit.)

Cindy Walker
FRONTIER VENGEANCE(1939); RIDE, TENDERFOOT, RIDE(1940)

Clarence Walker
NIGHT TRAIN TO MUNDO FINE(1966)

Clint Walker
TEN COMMANDMENTS, THE(1956); FORT DOBBS(1958); YELLOWSTONE KELLY(1959); GOLD OF THE SEVEN SAINTS(1961); SEND ME NO FLOWERS(1964); NONE BUT THE BRAVE(1965, U.S./Jap.); MAYA(1966); NIGHT OF THE GRIZZLY, THE(1966); DIRTY DOZEN, THE(1967, Brit.); MORE DEAD THAN ALIVE(1968); GREAT BANK ROBBERY, THE(1969); SAM WHISKEY(1969); PHYNX, THE(1970); PANCHO VILLA(1975, Span.); BAKER'S HAWK(1976); WHITE BUFFALO, THE(1977); HYSTERICAL(1983)
Misc. Talkies
DEADLY HARVEST(1972)

Danvers Walker
COP-OUT(1967, Brit.)

David Walker
WEE GEORDIE(1956, Brit.), w; HARRY BLACK AND THE TIGER(1958, Brit.), w; CHARGE OF THE LIGHT BRIGADE, THE(1968, Brit.), cos; SONG OF NORWAY(1970), cos; EAGLE IN A CAGE(1971, U.S./Yugo.), cos; GREAT WALTZ, THE(1972), cos; LADY CAROLINE LAMB(1972, Brit./Ital.), cos; HOUSE OF WHIPCORD(1974, Brit.), p&d

David E. Walker
OPERATION AMSTERDAM(1960, Brit.), w

David Esdaile Walker
MAN COULD GET KILLED, A(1966), w

Del Walker
BRONCO BULLFROG(1972, Brit.)

Dolores Walker
RECESS(1967), w

Don Walker
JULIUS CAESAR(1952); THOUSAND CLOWNS, A(1965), m

Dorian Walker
1984
MAKING THE GRADE(1984), d

Drake Walker
BUCK AND THE PREACHER(1972), a, w

Dusty Walker
FORT SAVAGE RAIDERS(1951); TAKE ME TO TOWN(1953)

Earl Walker
Silents
BACKSTAGE(1927), ph

Eddy C. Walker
SIX GUN GOLD(1941)

Eddy Walker
OKLAHOMA BADLANDS(1948)

Edith Cambell Walker
Misc. Silents
WOMAN'S WAY, A(1916)

Eileen Walker
Silents
CONQUERED HEARTS(1918)

Elaine Walker
STUDS LONIGAN(1960); SECRET OF DEEP HARBOR(1961)

Elizabeth Walker
"RENT-A-GIRL"(1965)

Elizabeth "Tippy" Walker
JESUS TRIP, THE(1971)

Ellie Walker
EASY RIDER(1969)

Ellie Wood Walker
TARGETS(1968)

Elsa Walker
CASBAH(1948)

Engineer Walker
FOR FREEDOM(1940, Brit.)

Ernest Walker
LET'S GET MARRIED(1960, Brit.), ed; GREAT WALTZ, THE(1972), ed

Fiona Walker
FAR FROM THE MADDING CROWD(1967, Brit.); ASPHYX, THE(1972, Brit.)

Francis Walker
WAGON TRAIL(1935); WILD MUSTANG(1935); LONELY TRAIL, THE(1936); RIDING AVENGER, THE(1936); CHEYENNE RIDES AGAIN(1937); GALLOPING DYNAMITE(1937); GUNS IN THE DARK(1937); LAW FOR TOMBSTONE(1937); RANGERS STEP IN, THE(1937); TRAIL OF VENGEANCE(1937); FEUD OF THE TRAIL(1938); ROLLING CARAVANS(1938); NIGHT RIDERS, THE(1939); BLAZING SIX SHOOTERS(1940); BULLETS FOR RUSTLERS(1940); DURANGO KID, THE(1940); MAN FROM TUMBLEWEEDS, THE(1940); RETURN OF WILD BILL, THE(1940); TEXAS STAGECOACH(1940); THUNDERING FRONTIER(1940); TWO-FISTED RANGERS(1940); WEST OF ABILENE(1940); KING OF DODGE CITY(1941); PINTO KID, THE(1941); PRAIRIE STRANGER(1941); RETURN OF DANIEL BOONE, THE(1941); RIDERS OF THE BADLANDS(1941); WILDCAT OF TUCSON(1941); RIDERS OF THE NORTHLAND(1942); WEST OF TOMBSTONE(1942)

Frank Walker
OPERATION KID BROTHER(1967, Ital.), w; WHY RUSSIANS ARE REVOLTING(1970); HEIDI'S SONG(1982)
Silents
JOHNNY RING AND THE CAPTAIN'S SWORD(1921)

Fred Walker
Silents
KING OF KINGS, THE(1927)

Gene Walker
CASBAH(1948); LIZZIE(1957); UNDER FIRE(1983)

Gerald Walker
CRUISING(1980), w

Gertrude Walker
MARY BURNS, FUGITIVE(1935); DANGER! WOMEN AT WORK(1943), w; MYSTERY BROADCAST(1943), w; WHISPERING FOOTSTEPS(1943), w; END OF THE ROAD(1944), w; SILENT PARTNER(1944), w; CRIME OF THE CENTURY(1946), w; DAMNED DON'T CRY, THE(1950), w; INSURANCE INVESTIGATOR(1951), w

Gilmore Walker
LONG, LONG TRAIL, THE(1929), ed; MOUNTED STRANGER, THE(1930), ed; ROARING RANCH(1930), ed; TRAILING TROUBLE(1930), ed; TRIGGER TRICKS(1930), ed
Silents
CLEARING THE TRAIL(1928), ed; KING OF THE RODEO(1929), ed; LARIAT KID, THE(1929), ed

Glen Walker
LAST SUMMER(1969)

Grace Walker
SUMMERFIELD(1977, Aus.), art d; JUST OUT OF REACH(1979, Aus.), art d

Graham Walker
IRISHMAN, THE(1978, Aus.), art d; CHAIN REACTION(1980, Aus.), art d; ROAD WARRIOR, THE(1982, Aus.), art d

Granville Walker
BARRICADE(1939), w

Greg Walker
LEGEND OF THE LONE RANGER, THE(1981)
1984
CHOOSE ME(1984)

H.M. Walker
PARDON US(1931), w; PACK UP YOUR TROUBLES(1932), w; HER FIRST MATE(1933), w; HORSEPLAY(1933), w; SON OF A SAILOR(1933), w; THEY JUST HAD TO GET MARRIED(1933), w; AFFAIR OF SUSAN(1935), w
Silents
SAILOR-MADE MAN, A(1921), t; GRANDMA'S BOY(1922), t; BLACK CYCLONE(1925), t

Hal Walker
DUFFY'S TAVERN(1945), d; OUT OF THIS WORLD(1945), d; ROAD TO UTOPIA(1945), d; STORK CLUB, THE(1945), d; AT WAR WITH THE ARMY(1950), d; MY FRIEND IRMA GOES WEST(1950), d; SAILOR BEWARE(1951), d; THAT'S MY BOY(1951), d; ROAD TO BALI(1952), d

Harry Walker
FOR THE DEFENSE(1930); SONG OF THE EAGLE(1933); RADIO STARS ON PARADE(1945), ph
Silents
MY BEST GIRL(1927)

Helen Walker
LUCKY JORDAN(1942); GOOD FELLOWS, THE(1943); ABROAD WITH TWO YANKS(1944); MAN IN HALF-MOON STREET, THE(1944); BREWSTER'S MILLIONS(1945); DUFFY'S TAVERN(1945); MURDER, HE SAYS(1945); PEOPLE ARE FUNNY(1945); CLUNY BROWN(1946); HER ADVENTUROUS NIGHT(1946); MURDER IN THE MUSIC HALL(1946); HOMESTRETCH, THE(1947); NIGHTMARE ALLEY(1947); CALL NORTHSIDE 777(1948); MY DEAR SECRETARY(1948); IMPACT(1949); MY TRUE STORY(1951); PROBLEM GIRLS(1953); BIG COMBO, THE(1955)

Horace Walker
SUNDOWN(1941)

Hugh Walker
CRIMINAL CODE(1931); FAR FROM THE MADDING CROWD(1967, Brit.)

Ian Walker
LILY OF LAGUNA(1938, Brit.), w; LITTLE DOLLY DAYDREAM(1938, Brit.), d&w; ROSE OF TRALEE(1938, Ireland), d&w; LITTLE MISS MOLLY(1940), w; ROSE OF TRALEE(1942, Brit.), w

Jack Walker
SOUTH OF SONORA(1930)
Silents
RIDIN' WILD(1922)

Jack David Walker
COACH(1978)

James Walker
1984
1984(1984, Brit.)

Mayor James Walker
GLORIFYING THE AMERICAN GIRL(1930)

Mrs. James Walker
GLORIFYING THE AMERICAN GIRL(1930)

James "Chuckles" Walker
SOMETHING TO SHOUT ABOUT(1943)

Jason Walker
Misc. Talkies
FIRST TIME ROUND(1972)

Jay Walker
1984
ALLEY CAT(1984)

Jean Walker
Misc. Talkies
CRUNCH(1975,Brit.)

Jeff Walker
JOHNNY GOT HIS GUN(1971)

Jennifer Walker
SAFE PLACE, A(1971)

Jessica Walker
1984
SECRET PLACES(1984, Brit.)

Jewel Walker
SMALL HOURS, THE(1962)

Jim Walker
ELECTRA GLIDE IN BLUE(1973), set d; SUPER SPOOK(1975), ph

Jimmie Walker
CONCORDE, THE–AIRPORT '79(; LET'S DO IT AGAIN(1975); AIRPLANE!(1980)

Jimmy Walker
COURTIN' TROUBLE(1948); RABBIT TEST(1978)

Joe Walker
BROADWAY HOOFER, THE(1929), ph; MURDER ON THE ROOF(1930), ph; HERE COMES MR. JORDAN(1941), ph
Silents
AFLAME IN THE SKY(1927), ph; GREAT MAIL ROBBERY, THE(1927), ph; OUTLAW DOG, THE(1927), ph; AFTER THE STORM(1928), ph

John Walker
HANGMAN'S WHARF(1950, Brit.); MR. MAGOO'S HOLIDAY FESTIVAL(1970), anim
Silents
IMPOSSIBLE CATHERINE(1919); GREATER THAN FAME(1920)

John E. Walker, Sr.
HEY, GOOD LOOKIN'(1982), anim

Johnnie Walker
LADIES OF LEISURE(1930)
Silents
KNIFE, THE(1918); JOLT, THE(1921); LIVE WIRES(1921); MY DAD(1922); THIRD ALARM, THE(1922); KNOCK ON THE DOOR, THE(1923), p; MAILMAN, THE(1923); RED LIGHTS(1923); SHATTERED REPUTATIONS(1923); RECKLESS SEX, THE(1925); CROSS BREED(1927); HELD BY THE LAW(1927); SWELL-HEAD, THE(1927); MATINEE IDOL, THE(1928); SO THIS IS LOVE(1928)
Misc. Silents
PLAY SQUARE(1921); WHAT LOVE WILL DO(1921); CAPTAIN FLY-BY-NIGHT(1922); EXTRA! EXTRA!(1922); BROKEN HEARTS OF BROADWAY, THE(1923); CHILDREN OF DUST(1923); FASHIONABLE FAKERS(1923); FOURTH MUSKETEER, THE(1923); GIRLS MEN FORGET(1924); LIFE'S GREATEST GAME(1924); SLANDERERS, THE(1924); SPIRIT OF THE U.S.A., THE(1924); LILLIES OF THE STREETS(1925); HONESTY-THE BEST POLICY(1926); MORGANSON'S FINISH(1926); TRANSCONTINENTAL LIMITED(1926); SNARL OF HATE, THE(1927); WHERE TRAILS BEGIN(1927); WOLVES OF THE AIR(1927); BARE KNEES(1928)

Johnny Walker
GIRL OF THE GOLDEN WEST(1930); LADIES IN LOVE(1930); MELODY MAN(1930); SWELLHEAD, THE(1930); UP THE RIVER(1930); ENEMIES OF THE LAW(1931)
1984
ALIEN FACTOR, THE(1984)
Silents
OVER THE HILL TO THE POORHOUSE(1920); SOULS FOR SALE(1923); MAD DANCER(1925); FANGS OF JUSTICE(1926); LIGHTNING REPORTER(1926); OLD IRONSIDES(1926); CLOWN, THE(1927); PRETTY CLOTHES(1927)
Misc. Silents
BACHELOR APARTMENTS(1920), d; SAGEBRUSH TRAIL, THE(1922); SOILED(1924); CHILDREN OF THE WHIRLWIND(1925); LENA RIVERS(1925); SCARLET WEST, THE(1925); BOY OF THE STREETS, A(1927); PRINCESS OF BROADWAY, THE(1927); ROSE OF THE BOWERY(1927)

Joseph Walker
BACHELOR GIRL, THE(1929), ph; FLIGHT(1929), ph; SONG OF LOVE, THE(1929), ph; LADIES MUST PLAY(1930), ph; LADIES OF LEISURE(1930), ph; MIDNIGHT MYSTERY(1930), ph; RAIN OR SHINE(1930), ph; DECEIVER, THE(1931), ph; FIFTY FATHOMS DEEP(1931), ph; LOVER COME BACK(1931), ph; MIRACLE WOMAN, THE(1931), ph; PLATINUM BLONDE(1931), ph; SUBWAY EXPRESS(1931), ph; AMERICAN MADNESS(1932), ph; BY WHOSE HAND?(1932), ph; FORBIDDEN(1932), ph; SHOPWORN(1932), ph; VIRTUE(1932), ph; AIR HOSTESS(1933), ph; BELOW THE SEA(1933), ph; BITTER TEA OF GENERAL YEN, THE(1933), ph; LADY FOR A DAY(1933), ph; BROADWAY BILL(1934), ph; IT HAPPENED ONE NIGHT(1934), ph; LADY IS WILLING, THE(1934, Brit.), ph; ONE NIGHT OF LOVE(1934), ph; FEATHER IN HER HAT, A(1935), ph; GIRL FRIEND, THE(1935), ph; LET'S LIVE TONIGHT(1935), ph; LOVE ME FOREVER(1935), ph; MR. DEEDS GOES TO TOWN(1936), ph; MUSIC GOES ROUND, THE(1936), ph; THEODORA GOES WILD(1936), ph; AWFUL TRUTH, THE(1937), ph; IT HAPPENED IN HOLLYWOOD(1937), ph; LOST HORIZON(1937), ph; WHEN YOU'RE IN LOVE(1937), ph; JOY OF LIVING(1938), ph; START CHEERING(1938), ph; THERE'S THAT WOMAN AGAIN(1938), ph; YOU CAN'T TAKE IT WITH YOU(1938), ph; MR. SMITH GOES TO WASHINGTON(1939), ph; ONLY ANGELS HAVE WINGS(1939), ph; ARIZONA(1940), ph; HE STAYED FOR BREAKFAST(1940), ph; HIS GIRL FRIDAY(1940), ph; THIS THING CALLED LOVE(1940), ph; TOO MANY HUSBANDS(1940), ph; PENNY SERENADE(1941), ph; YOU BELONG TO ME(1941), ph; BEDTIME STORY(1942), ph; MY SISTER EILEEN(1942), ph; NIGHT TO REMEMBER, A(1942), ph; TALES OF MANHATTAN(1942), ph; THEY ALL KISSED THE BRIDE(1942), ph; FIRST COMES COURAGE(1943), ph; WHAT A WOMAN!(1943), ph; WHAT'S BUZZIN COUSIN?(1943), ph; MR. WINKLE GOES TO WAR(1944), ph; TOGETHER AGAIN(1944), ph; ROUGHLY SPEAKING(1945), ph; SHE WOULDN'T SAY YES(1945), ph; IT'S A WONDERFUL LIFE(1946), ph; JOLSON STORY, THE(1946), ph; TARS AND SPARS(1946), ph; GUILT OF JANET AMES, THE(1947), ph; DARK PAST, THE(1948), ph; MATING OF MILLIE, THE(1948), ph; VELVET TOUCH, THE(1948), ph; MR. SOFT TOUCH(1949), ph; TELL IT TO THE JUDGE(1949), ph; HARRIET CRAIG(1950), ph; NEVER A DULL MOMENT(1950), ph; NO SAD SONGS FOR ME(1950), ph; WOMAN OF DISTINCTION, A(1950), ph; BORN YESTERDAY(1951), ph; MOB, THE(1951), ph; AFFAIR IN TRINIDAD(1952), ph; MARRYING KIND, THE(1952), ph
Silents
GIRL ON THE STAIRS, THE(1924), ph; DIXIE FLYER, THE(1926), ph; ISLE OF FORGOTTEN WOMEN(1927), ph; STAGE KISSES(1927), ph; NOTHING TO WEAR(1928), ph; RANSOM(1928), ph; ETERNAL WOMAN, THE(1929), ph; OBJECT-ALIMONY(1929), ph

Joseph A. Walker
RIVER NIGER, THE(1976), w

Joyce Walker
SHAFT'S BIG SCORE(1972); WILLIE DYNAMITE(1973); EDUCATION OF SONNY CARSON, THE(1974)

June Walker
WAR NURSE(1930); THRU DIFFERENT EYES(1942); UNFORGIVEN, THE(1960); CHILD IS WAITING, A(1963)
Misc. Silents
COINCIDENCE(1921)

Kathryn Walker
BLADE(1973); SLAP SHOT(1977); GIRLFRIENDS(1978); RICH KIDS(1979); NEIGHBORS(1981)

Keith Walker
TILL DEATH(1978)
Ken Walker
DEADLY SPAWN, THE(1983), m
Kenneth Walker
1984
ALIEN FACTOR, THE(1984), m
Kerry Walker
NIGHT OF THE PROWLER, THE(1979, Aus.)
Laura Walker
Silents
EXPERIMENT, THE(1922, Brit.); NETS OF DESTINY(1924, Brit.)
Leonard Walker
FOLIES DERGERE(1935); LLOYDS OF LONDON(1936); MEET ME IN ST. LOUIS(1944)
Dr. Leonard Walker
STAR IS BORN, A(1937)
Lesley Walker
EAGLE'S WING(1979, Brit.), ed; LOVE AND BULLETS(1979, Brit.), ed; PORTRAIT OF THE ARTIST AS A YOUNG MAN, A(1979, Ireland), ed; RICHARD'S THINGS(1981, Brit.), ed
1984
WINTER FLIGHT(1984, Brit.), ed
Lew Walker
VISITOR, THE(1980, Ital./U.S.)
Lewis Walker
NIGHT ANGEL, THE(1931)
Lilian Walker
Misc. Silents
WOMAN OF NO IMPORTANCE, A(1921, Brit.)
Lillian Walker
ENLIGHTEN THY DAUGHTER(1934)
Silents
KID, THE(1916); EMBARRASSMENT OF RICHES, THE(1918); JOYOUS LIAR, THE(1919); WOMAN GOD CHANGED, THE(1921)
Misc. Silents
HEARTS AND THE HIGHWAY(1915); BLUE ENVELOPE MYSTERY, THE(1916); DOLLAR AND THE LAW, THE(1916); GREEN STOCKINGS(1916); HESPER OF THE MOUNTAINS(1916); MAN BEHIND THE CURTAIN, THE(1916); ORDEAL OF ELIZABETH, THE(1916); INDISCRETION(1917); KITTY MACKAY(1917); LUST OF THE AGES, THE(1917); PRINCESS OF PARK ROW, THE(1917); SALLY IN A HURRY(1917); LOVE HUNGER, THE(1919)
Lillias Walker
MR. BROWN COMES DOWN THE HILL(1966, Brit.); WHAT BECAME OF JACK AND JILL?(1972, Brit.); HIDING PLACE, THE(1975); ROMANTIC ENGLISHWOMAN, THE(1975, Brit./Fr.)
Lynn Walker
SO PROUDLY WE HAIL(1943); SECRET LIFE OF WALTER MITTY, THE(1947)
Marjorie Walker
EVERY GIRL SHOULD BE MARRIED(1948)
Mark Walker
NEPTUNE FACTOR, THE(1973, Can.); SUNDAY IN THE COUNTRY(1975, Can.); RABID(1976, Can.)
Martin Walker
FLYING FOOL, THE(1931, Brit.); HELP YOURSELF(1932, Brit.); RIVER WOLVES, THE(1934, Brit.); ANYTHING MIGHT HAPPEN(1935, Brit.); LIEUTENANT DARING, RN(1935, Brit.); MIMI(1935, Brit.); OH, WHAT A NIGHT(1935); SANDERS OF THE RIVER(1935, Brit.); SENSATION(1936, Brit.); VICAR OF BRAY, THE(1937, Brit.); DRUMS(1938, Brit.); DANGEROUS CARGO(1939, Brit.); MURDER IN THE NIGHT(1940, Brit.); OUTSIDER, THE(1940, Brit.); MURDER AT THE BASKERVILLES(1941, Brit.); THIS ENGLAND(1941, Brit.); NIGHT INVADER, THE(1943, Brit); LOVE ON THE DOLE(1945, Brit.); LISBON STORY, THE(1946, Brit.); WOMAN IN THE HALL, THE(1949, Brit.); BLACK 13(1954, Brit.)
Mary Walker
FEVER HEAT(1968)
Mary Kathleen Walker
STAGECOACH(1939)
Michael Walker
DARING GAME(1968); HELL'S BELLES(1969)
Michelle Walker
HALLOWEEN III: SEASON OF THE WITCH(1982)
Nancy Walker
BEST FOOT FORWARD(1943); GIRL CRAZY(1943); BROADWAY RHYTHM(1944); LUCKY ME(1954); STAND UP AND BE COUNTED(1972); FORTY CARATS(1973); WORLD'S GREATEST ATHLETE, THE(1973); MURDER BY DEATH(1976); WON TON TON, THE DOG WHO SAVED HOLLYWOOD(1976); CAN'T STOP THE MUSIC(1980), d
Natalie Walker
HEY, LET'S TWIST!(1961), cos; TWO TICKETS TO PARIS(1962), cos
Nella Walker
TANNED LEGS(1929); VAGABOND LOVER(1929); EXTRAVAGANCE(1930); SEVEN KEYS TO BALDPATE(1930); WHAT A WIDOW(1930); DAUGHTER OF THE DRAGON(1931); HOT HEIRESS(1931); HUSH MONEY(1931); INDISCREET(1931); PUBLIC DEFENDER, THE(1931); LADY WITH A PAST(1932); THEY CALL IT SIN(1932); TROUBLE IN PARADISE(1932); DANGEROUSLY YOURS(1933); EVER IN MY HEART(1933); HOUSE ON 56TH STREET, THE(1933); HUMANITY(1933); REUNION IN VIENNA(1933); SECOND HAND WIFE(1933); THIS DAY AND AGE(1933); 20,000 YEARS IN SING SING(1933); ALL OF ME(1934); BIG HEARTED HERBERT(1934); CHANGE OF HEART(1934); ELMER AND ELSIE(1934); FASHIONS OF 1934(1934); FOUR FRIGHTENED PEOPLE(1934); FUGITIVE LADY(1934); MADAME DU BARRY(1934); NINTH GUEST, THE(1934); SENSATION HUNTERS(1934); BEHOLD MY WIFE(1935); CAPTAIN JANUARY(1935); CORONADO(1935); DANTE'S INFERNO(1935); DOG OF FLANDERS, A(1935); GOING HIGHBROW(1935); I LIVE MY LIFE(1935); MC FADDEN'S FLATS(1935); RIGHT TO LIVE, THE(1935); WOMAN IN RED, THE(1935); DON'T TURN'EM LOOSE(1936); KLONDIKE ANNIE(1936); SMALL TOWN GIRL(1936); STELLA DALLAS(1937); THREE SMART GIRLS(1937); 45 FATHERS(1937); CRIME OF DR. HALLET(1938); HARD TO GET(1938); PROFESSOR BEWARE(1938); RAGE OF PARIS, THE(1938); YOUNG DR. KILDARE(1938); ESPIONAGE AGENT(1939); IN NAME ONLY(1939); MADE FOR EACH OTHER(1939); SAINT STRIKES BACK, THE(1939); SWANEE RIVER(1939);

THESE GLAMOUR GIRLS(1939); THREE SMART GIRLS GROW UP(1939); WHEN TOMORROW COMES(1939); CHILD IS BORN, A(1940); I LOVE YOU AGAIN(1940); IRENE(1940); KITTY FOYLE(1940); NO TIME FOR COMEDY(1940); SAINT TAKES OVER, THE(1940); BACK STREET(1941); BUCK PRIVATES(1941); GIRL, A GUY AND A GOB, A(1941); HELLZAPOPPIN'(1941); KATHLEEN(1941); MANPOWER(1941); REACHING FOR THE SUN(1941); REPENT AT LEISURE(1941); KID GLOVE KILLER(1942); WE WERE DANCING(1942); AIR RAID WARDENS(1943); HERS TO HOLD(1943); WINTERTIME(1943); IN SOCIETY(1944); LADIES OF WASHINGTON(1944); MURDER IN THE BLUE ROOM(1944); TAKE IT OR LEAVE IT(1944); GUY, A GAL AND A PAL, A(1945); LOCKET, THE(1946); TWO SISTERS FROM BOSTON(1946); THAT HAGEN GIRL(1947); THIS TIME FOR KEEPS(1947); UNDERCOVER MAISIE(1947); VARIETY GIRL(1947); NANCY GOES TO RIO(1950); FLESH AND FURY(1952); SABRINA(1954)
Nina Walker
MISLEADING LADY, THE(1932)
Noreen Walker
SOMEWHERE IN TIME(1980)
Norman Walker
ROMANCE OF SEVILLE, A(1929, Brit.), d; HATE SHIP, THE(1930, Brit.), d; LOOSE ENDS(1930, Brit.), d, w; MIDDLE WATCH, THE(1930, Brit.), d, w; GREAT, MEADOW, THE(1931), d; UNEASY VIRTUE(1931, Brit.), d&w; FIRES OF FATE(1932, Brit.), p&d; SHADOW BETWEEN, THE(1932, Brit.), d, w; FLAW, THE(1933, Brit.), d; FORTUNATE FOOL, THE(1933, Brit.), d; HOUSE OF TRENT, THE(1933, Brit.), d; MAN WHO WON, THE(1933, Brit.), p&d; DANGEROUS GROUND(1934, Brit.), d; LILIES OF THE FIELD(1934, Brit.), d; SING AS WE GO(1934, Brit.), d; WAY OF YOUTH, THE(1934, Brit.), p&d; KEY TO HARMONY(1935, Brit.), d; LOOK UP AND LAUGH(1935, Brit.); TURN OF THE TIDE(1935, Brit.), d; DEBT OF HONOR(1936, Brit.), d; TORPEDOED!(1939), d; MOZART(1940, Brit.), d; SUICIDE LEGION(1940, Brit.), d; HARD STEEL(1941, Brit.), d; GREAT MR. HANDEL, THE(1942, Brit.), d; THEY KNEW MR. KNIGHT(1945, Brit.), d, w; WAY AHEAD, THE(1945, Brit.), p; MEN OF THE SEA(1951, Brit.); JOHN WESLEY(1954, Brit.), d; SHIELD OF FAITH, THE(1956, Brit.), d; SUPREME SECRET, THE(1958, Brit.), d; CROWNING GIFT, THE(1967, Brit.), d
Silents
FLATTERY(1925), sup
Misc. Silents
TOMMY ATKINS(1928, Brit.), d; WIDECOMBE FAIR(1928, Brit.), d
Ollie Walker
Misc. Silents
ORDEAL OF ELIZABETH, THE(1916)
Pat Walker
G.I. WAR BRIDES(1946); LARCENY(1948); SONG IS BORN, A(1948)
Patricia Walker
JULIA MISBEHAVES(1948); FAN, THE(1949); DEATH OF A SALESMAN(1952); ALL ASHORE(1953); YOUR THREE MINUTES ARE UP(1973)
Pax Walker
SUSPICION(1941); NIGHTMARE(1942); RANDOM HARVEST(1942); FOREVER AND A DAY(1943)
Pete Walker
SCHOOL FOR SEX(1969, Brit.), p,d&w; BIG SWITCH, THE(1970, Brit.), p,d&w; DIE SCREAMING, MARIANNE(1970, Brit.), p&d; FLESH AND BLOOD SHOW, THE(1974, Brit.), p&d; HOUSE OF WHIPCORD(1974, Brit.); TIFFANY JONES(1976), p&d; COMEBACK, THE(1982, Brit.), p&d
Misc. Talkies
DIE, BEAUTIFUL MARYANNE(1969), d; DIRTIEST GIRL I EVER MET, THE(1973), d; THREE DIMENSIONS OF GRETA(1973), d
Peter Walker
UNDER FIRE(1957); VALERIE(1957); WAYWARD GIRL, THE(1957); GREAT ARMORED CAR SWINDLE, THE(1964); COOL IT, CAROL!(1970, Brit.), p&d; MAN OF VIOLENCE(1970, Brit.), p&d, w; FRIGHTMARE(1974, Brit.), p&d, w; W(1974); CONFESSIONAL, THE(1977, Brit.), p&d; SCHIZO(1977, Brit.), p&d; HOUSE OF LONG SHADOWS, THE(1983, Brit.), d
Polly Walker
HIT THE DECK(1930); SLEEPLESS NIGHTS(1933, Brit.)
R. J. Walker
WINDJAMMER, THE(1931, Brit.), ph
Ray Walker
DEVIL'S MATE(1933); SKYWAY(1933); BABY, TAKE A BOW(1934); CITY LIMITS(1934); GOODBYE LOVE(1934); HAPPY LANDING(1934); HE COULDN'T TAKE IT(1934); LOUDSPEAKER, THE(1934); THIRTY-DAY PRINCESS(1934); WHEN STRANGERS MEET(1934); CAPPY RICKS RETURNS(1935); GIRL FRIEND, THE(1935); LADIES LOVE DANGER(1935); MILLION DOLLAR BABY(1935); MUSIC IS MAGIC(1935); ONE HOUR LATE(1935); $10 RAISE(1935); BRILLIANT MARRIAGE(1936); BULLDOG EDITION(1936); CRIME PATROL, THE(1936); DARK HOUR, THE(1936); LAUGHING IRISH EYES(1936); ANGEL'S HOLIDAY(1937); HIDEAWAY GIRL(1937); ONE MILE FROM HEAVEN(1937); OUTLAWS OF THE ORIENT(1937); CRASHIN' THRU DANGER(1938); LETTER OF INTRODUCTION(1938); MARINES ARE HERE, THE(1938); TEST PILOT(1938); FORGOTTEN WOMAN, THE(1939); LET US LIVE(1939); MISSING EVIDENCE(1939); PIRATES OF THE SKIES(1939); TELL NO TALES(1939); NIGHT AT EARL CARROLL'S, A(1940); DON'T GET PERSONAL(1941); THREE GIRLS ABOUT TOWN(1941); ALMOST MARRIED(1942); CAPTAINS OF THE CLOUDS(1942); HOUSE OF ERRORS(1942); PITTSBURGH(1942); SPIRIT OF STANFORD, THE(1942); DIXIE DUGAN(1943); GOVERNMENT GIRL(1943); HENRY ALDRICH HAUNTS A HOUSE(1943); HI'YA, CHUM(1943); IS EVERYBODY HAPPY?(1943); IT'S A GREAT LIFE(1943); MISSION TO MOSCOW(1943); PRINCESS O'ROURKE(1943); UNKNOWN GUEST, THE(1943); HAT CHECK HONEY(1944); IRISH EYES ARE SMILING(1944); JAM SESSION(1944); MAN FROM FRISCO(1944); MY BUDDY(1944); SILENT PARTNER(1944); SOUTH OF DIXIE(1944); STARS ON PARADE(1944); SWINGTIME JOHNNY(1944); EVE KNEW HER APPLES(1945); INCENDIARY BLONDE(1945); PATRICK THE GREAT(1945); ROGUES GALLERY(1945); BEAST WITH FIVE FINGERS, THE(1946); CRIME OF THE CENTURY(1946); DARK ALIBI(1946); GAY BLADES(1946); GIRL ON THE SPOT(1946); IT'S A WONDERFUL LIFE(1946); LIFE WITH BLONDIE(1946); SECRET OF THE WHISTLER(1946); SECRETS OF A SORORITY GIRL(1946); STEP BY STEP(1946); TARS AND SPARS(1946); GUILT OF JANET AMES, THE(1947); PILGRIM LADY, THE(1947); ROBIN OF TEXAS(1947); THAT'S MY GAL(1947); UNSUSPECTED, THE(1947); APRIL SHOWERS(1948); BLACK BART(1948); RETURN OF OCTOBER, THE(1948); SAINTED SISTERS, THE(1948); ADAM'S RIB(1949); ANGELS IN DISGUISE(1949); BLONDIE'S BIG DEAL(1949); CHINATOWN AT MIDNIGHT(1949); GREAT GATSBY, THE(1949); HOLIDAY IN HAVANA(1949); OH, YOU BEAUTIFUL

DOLL(1949); SONG OF SURRENDER(1949); BODYHOLD(1950); HOEDOWN(1950); JOE PALOOKA MEETS HUMPHREY(1950); NO MAN OF HER OWN(1950); PIONEER MARSHAL(1950); REVENUE AGENT(1950); SIDESHOW(1950); SQUARE DANCE KATY(1950); UNDER MEXICALI STARS(1950); HARLEM GLOBETROTTERS, THE(1951); LET'S GO NAVY(1951); SKIPALONG ROSENBLOOM(1951); SUPERMAN AND THE MOLE MEN(1951); TOO YOUNG TO KISS(1951); NO HOLDS BARRED(1952); BLUE GARDENIA, THE(1953); CLIPPED WINGS(1953); HOMESTEADERS, THE(1953); MARRY ME AGAIN(1953); REBEL CITY(1953); ROAR OF THE CROWD(1953); SHE'S BACK ON BROADWAY(1953); PRIDE OF THE BLUE GRASS(1954); EVERYTHING BUT THE TRUTH(1956); HOT SHOTS(1956); SOMEBODY UP THERE LIKES ME(1956); YAQUI DRUMS(1956); IRON SHERIFF, THE(1957); SPIRIT OF ST. LOUIS, THE(1957); PEPE(1960); TEN WHO DARED(1960); WALK ON THE WILD SIDE(1962)
Misc. Talkies
LAST ASSIGNMENT, THE(1936)
Raymond Walker
NEW MOON(1940)
Rex Walker
AWAKENING, THE(1938, Brit.)
Rhod Walker
STONE(1974, Aus.)
Rickey Walker
CONRACK(1974)
Robert Walker
BAR L RANCH(1930); CANYON HAWKS(1930); PHANTOM OF THE DESERT(1930); RIDIN' LAW(1930); HEADIN' FOR TROUBLE(1931); KID FROM ARIZONA, THE(1931), a, w; WEST OF CHEYENNE(1931); WESTWARD BOUND(1931); LONE TRAIL, THE(1932); MAN FROM NEW MEXICO, THE(1932); SCARLET BRAND(1932); TEX TAKES A HOLIDAY(1932), w; COME ON TARZAN(1933); JAWS OF JUSTICE(1933); KING OF THE ARENA(1933); STRAWBERRY ROAN(1933); FOG OVER FRISCO(1934); COYOTE TRAILS(1935); CRIMSON TRAIL, THE(1935); FIGHTING CABALLERO(1935); ROUGH RIDING RANGER(1935); CARYL OF THE MOUNTAINS(1936); TWO-FISTED SHERIFF(1937); SKULL AND CROWN(1938); DANCING CO-ED(1939); EL DIABLO RIDES(1939); PAL FROM TEXAS, THE(1939); WINTER CARNIVAL(1939); PIONEER DAYS(1940); I'LL SELL MY LIFE(1941); TALK OF THE TOWN(1942); BATAAN(1943); MADAME CURIE(1943); SEE HERE, PRIVATE HARGROVE(1944); SINCE YOU WENT AWAY(1944); THIRTY SECONDS OVER TOKYO(1944); CLOCK, THE(1945); HER HIGHNESS AND THE BELLBOY(1945); WHAT NEXT, CORPORAL HARGROVE?(1945); SAILOR TAKES A WIFE, THE(1946); TILL THE CLOUDS ROLL BY(1946); BEGINNING OR THE END, THE(1947); LAST ROUND-UP, THE(1947); SEA OF GRASS, THE(1947); SONG OF LOVE(1947); ANNA KARENINA(1948, Brit.), ph; ONE TOUCH OF VENUS(1948); ELIZABETH OF LADYMEAD(1949, Brit.), ph; RIDERS IN THE SKY(1949); PLEASE BELIEVE ME(1950); SKIPPER SURPRISED HIS WIFE, THE(1950); STRANGERS ON A TRAIN(1951); VENGEANCE VALLEY(1951); MY SON, JOHN(1952); STREET OF DARKNESS(1958), d; CEREMONY, THE(1963, U.S./Span.); BEWARE! THE BLOB(1972); THREE SISTERS(1974, Brit.); PASSOVER PLOT, THE(1976, Israel); MC VICAR(1982, Brit.); TASTE OF SIN, A(1983)
1984
HAMBONE AND HILLIE(1984)
Misc. Talkies
POTLUCK PARDS(1934); CAPTURED IN CHINATOWN(1935); NOW OR NEVER(1935); TEXAS JACK(1935); PRELUDE TO TAURUS(1972)
Silents
ALADDIN'S OTHER LAMP(1917); GIRL WITHOUT A SOUL, THE(1917); FAIR PRETENDER, THE(1918); WHITE OAK(1921); OUTLAW'S DAUGHTER, THE(1925); GALLANT FOOL, THE(1926); WESTERN COURAGE(1927); DREAM MELODY, THE(1929); RECKLESS CHANCES(5 reels)
Misc. Silents
WAY BACK, THE(1915); COSSACK WHIP, THE(1916); GATES OF EDEN, THE(1916); LIGHT OF HAPPINESS, THE(1916); BLUE JEANS(1917); GOD'S LAW AND MAN'S(1917); LADY BARNACLE(1917); MORTAL SIN, THE(1917); AT THE MERCY OF MEN(1918); MISS INNOCENCE(1918); WOMAN BETWEEN FRIENDS, THE(1918); WOMAN WHO GAVE, THE(1918); BURGLAR BY PROXY(1919); LIGHT, THE(1919); ROGUE AND RICHES(1920); SHORE ACRES(1920); DANCING CHEAT, THE(1924); DAUGHTER OF THE SIOUX, A(1925); DRUG STORE COWBOY(1925); RIP SNORTER, THE(1925); WARRIOR GAP(1925); DEUCE HIGH(1926)
Robert D. Walker
Silents
CAPRICE OF THE MOUNTAINS(1916)
Misc. Silents
DON CAESAR DE BAZAN(1915)
Robert S. Walker
BATTLE OF LOVE'S RETURN, THE(1971)
Robert V. Walker
WANDA NEVADA(1979)
Robert Walker, Jr.
HOOK, THE(1962); ENSIGN PULVER(1964); HAPPENING, THE(1967); WAR WAGON, THE(1967); EVE(1968, Brit./Span.); KILLERS THREE(1968); SAVAGE SEVEN, THE(1968); EASY RIDER(1969); YOUNG BILLY YOUNG(1969); MAN FROM O.R.G.Y., THE(1970); ROAD TO SALINA(1971, Fr./Ital.); HEX(1973); SPECTRE OF EDGAR ALLAN POE, THE(1974); DEVONSVILLE TERROR, THE(1983)
Misc. Talkies
SPECTRE OF EDGAR ALLAN POE(1973); GONE WITH THE WEST(1976)
Rock Walker
ELECTRA GLIDE IN BLUE(1973); BLACK OAK CONSPIRACY(1977); THING, THE(1982)
1984
STREETS OF FIRE(1984)
Rock A. Walker
48 HOURS(1982)
Roy Walker
RYAN'S DAUGHTER(1970, Brit.), art d; LAST RUN, THE(1971), art d; STRANGE VENEGEANCE OF ROSALIE, THE(1972), art d; HITLER: THE LAST TEN DAYS(1973, Brit./Ital.), art d; TALES THAT WITNESS MADNESS(1973, Brit.), art d; BARRY LYNDON(1975, Brit.), art d; RUSSIAN ROULETTE(1975), art d; SORCERER(1977), art d; SHINING, THE(1980), prod d; YENTL(1983), prod d
1984
KILLING FIELDS, THE(1984, Brit.), prod d

Rudolph Walker
DRUMS O' VOODOO(1934); GIRL STROKE BOY(1971, Brit.); UNIVERSAL SOLDIER(1971, Brit.); 10 RILLINGTON PLACE(1971, Brit.)
Misc. Talkies
LOVE THY NEIGHBOUR(1973)
Sandra Walker
FOUL PLAY(1978)
Sarah Walker
1984
MAN OF FLOWERS(1984, Aus.)
Scott Walker
DIRTY LITTLE BILLY(1972); HIGH PLAINS DRIFTER(1973); DOC SAVAGE... THE MAN OF BRONZE(1975); HINDENBURG, THE(1975); ORCA(1977); WHITE BUFFALO, THE(1977); BORN AGAIN(1978); MUPPET MOVIE, THE(1979)
Sebastian Walker
DOCTOR FAUSTUS(1967, Brit.)
Shirley Walker
END OF AUGUST, THE(1982), m; TOUCHED(1983), m
Sid Walker
GIFT OF GAB(1934)
Simon Walker
WILD DUCK, THE(1983, Aus.), m
Stacey Walker
SMELL OF HONEY, A SWALLOW OF BRINE! A(1966)
Stuart Walker
SECRET CALL, THE(1931), d; EVENINGS FOR SALE(1932), d; FALSE MADONNA(1932), d; MISLEADING LADY, THE(1932), d; EAGLE AND THE HAWK, THE(1933), d; TONIGHT IS OURS(1933), d; WHITE WOMAN(1933), d; GREAT EXPECTATIONS(1934), d; ROMANCE IN THE RAIN(1934), d; MANHATTAN MOON(1935), d; MYSTERY OF EDWIN DROOD, THE(1935), d; WEREWOLF OF LONDON, THE(1935), d; SONS OF THE LEGION(1938), p; ARREST BULLDOG DRUMMOND(1939, Brit.), p; BULLDOG DRUMMOND'S BRIDE(1939), p; DISBARRED(1939), p; EMERGENCY SQUAD(1940), p; OPENED BY MISTAKE(1940), p; SEVENTEEN(1940), p, w
Syd Walker
REGAL CAVALCADE(1935, Brit.); LET'S MAKE A NIGHT OF IT(1937, Brit.); OVER SHE GOES(1937, Brit.); SWEET DEVIL(1937, Brit.); HOLD MY HAND(1938, Brit.); OH BOY!(1938, Brit.); WHAT WOULD YOU DO, CHUMS?(1939, Brit.); WHO IS GUILTY?(1940, Brit.); AMAZING MR. FORREST, THE(1943, Brit.)
Silents
OLD BILL THROUGH THE AGES(1924, Brit.)
Sydney Walker
LOVELY WAY TO DIE, A(1968); LOVE STORY(1970); PUZZLE OF A DOWNFALL CHILD(1970); WAY WE LIVE NOW, THE(1970)
Tammy Walker
BROTHERS AND SISTERS(1980, Brit.), w
Terry Walker
AND SUDDEN DEATH(1936); BLONDE TROUBLE(1937); FEDERAL BULLETS(1937); MOUNTAIN MUSIC(1937); 23 ½ HOURS LEAVE(1937); DELINQUENT PARENTS(1938); ON THE GREAT WHITE TRAIL(1938); BILLY THE KID IN TEXAS(1940); DANGEROUS LADY(1941); INVISIBLE GHOST, THE(1941); MEDICO OF PAINTED SPRINGS, THE(1941); VOODOO MAN(1944)
Misc. Talkies
TAKE ME BACK TO OKLAHOMA(1940)
Tippy Walker
WORLD OF HENRY ORIENT, THE(1964); JENNIFER ON MY MIND(1971)
Tom Walker
GREAT JESSE JAMES RAID, THE(1953); BIG CHASE, THE(1954)
Tommy Walker
TASK FORCE(1949); TENSION(1949); STORM WARNING(1950); YOU FOR ME(1952); HELL AND HIGH WATER(1954)
Tracey Walker
RAGGEDY MAN(1981)
Turnley Walker
WOLF LARSEN(1958), w
Vern Walker
FLYING DOWN TO RIO(1933), spec eff
Verne L. Walker
TEN NIGHTS IN A BARROOM(1931), ph
Vernon L. Walker
WITHOUT RESERVATIONS(1946), spec eff; KING KONG(1933), ph; MONKEY'S PAW, THE(1933), spec eff; STINGAREE(1934), spec eff; THREE MUSKETEERS, THE(1935), spec eff; TOP HAT(1935), ph; MARY OF SCOTLAND(1936), spec eff; CRASHING HOLLYWOOD(1937), spec eff; DAMSEL IN DISTRESS, A(1937), spec eff; FLIGHT FROM GLORY(1937), spec eff; HIGH FLYERS(1937), spec eff; LIFE OF THE PARTY, THE(1937), spec eff; MAN WHO FOUND HIMSELF, THE(1937), spec eff; MUSIC FOR MADAME(1937), spec eff; NEW FACES OF 1937(1937), spec eff; SEA DEVILS(1937), spec eff; SUPER SLEUTH(1937), spec eff; THERE GOES MY GIRL(1937), spec eff; TOAST OF NEW YORK, THE(1937), spec eff; BRINGING UP BABY(1938), spec eff; GO CHASE YOURSELF(1938), spec eff; HAVING WONDERFUL TIME(1938), spec eff; I'M FROM THE CITY(1938), spec eff; JOY OF LIVING(1938), spec eff; RADIO CITY REVELS(1938), spec eff; FLYING IRISHMAN, THE(1939), spec eff; GUNGA DIN(1939), spec eff; HUNCHBACK OF NOTRE DAME, THE(1939), spec eff; IN NAME ONLY(1939), spec eff; LOVE AFFAIR(1939), spec eff; NURSE EDITH CAVELL(1939), spec eff; PANAMA LADY(1939), spec eff; STORY OF VERNON AND IRENE CASTLE, THE(1939), spec eff; THAT'S RIGHT-YOU'RE WRONG(1939), spec eff; WAY DOWN SOUTH(1939), spec eff; DANCE, GIRL, DANCE(1940), spec eff; I'M STILL ALIVE(1940), spec eff; KITTY FOYLE(1940), spec eff; LADDIE(1940), spec eff; LUCKY PARTNERS(1940), spec eff; MEN AGAINST THE SKY(1940), spec eff; MEXICAN SPITFIRE OUT WEST(1940), spec eff; MILLIONAIRE PLAYBOY(1940), spec eff; MILLIONAIRES IN PRISON(1940), spec eff; PRIMROSE PATH(1940), spec eff; STRANGER ON THE THIRD FLOOR(1940), spec eff; SWISS FAMILY ROBINSON(1940), spec eff; THEY KNEW WHAT THEY WANTED(1940), spec eff; TOM BROWN'S SCHOOL DAYS(1940), spec eff; TOO MANY GIRLS(1940), spec eff; WILDCAT BUS(1940), spec eff; YOU'LL FIND OUT(1940), spec eff; CITIZEN KANE(1941), spec eff; DEVIL AND DANIEL WEBSTER, THE(1941), spec eff; DEVIL AND MISS JONES, THE(1941), spec eff; FOUR JACKS AND A JILL(1941), spec eff; GIRL, A GUY AND A GOB, A(1941), spec eff; LOOK WHO'S LAUGHING(1941), spec eff; MR. AND MRS. SMITH(1941), spec eff; REPENT AT LEISURE(1941), spec eff; SUNNY(1941), spec eff; SUSPICION(1941), spec eff; THEY MET IN ARGEN-

TINA(1941), spec eff; TOM, DICK AND HARRY(1941), spec eff; BIG STREET, THE(1942), spec eff; CALL OUT THE MARINES(1942), spec eff; HITLER'S CHILDREN(1942), spec eff; JOURNEY INTO FEAR(1942), spec eff; MAGNIFICENT AMBERSONS, THE(1942), spec eff; MY FAVORITE SPY(1942), spec eff; NAVY COMES THROUGH, THE(1942), spec eff; ONCE UPON A HONEYMOON(1942), spec eff; POWDER TOWN(1942), spec eff; SEVEN DAYS LEAVE(1942), spec eff; TUTTLES OF TAHITI(1942), spec eff; VALLEY OF THE SUN(1942), spec eff; BEHIND THE RISING SUN(1943), spec eff; FALCON AND THE CO-EDS, THE(1943), spec eff; FALLEN SPARROW, THE(1943), spec eff; FLIGHT FOR FREEDOM(1943), spec eff; FOREVER AND A DAY(1943), spec eff; GANGWAY FOR TOMORROW(1943), spec eff; GHOST SHIP, THE(1943), spec eff; LADY TAKES A CHANCE, A(1943), spec eff; MR. LUCKY(1943), spec eff; SKY'S THE LIMIT, THE(1943), spec eff; TENDER COMRADE(1943), spec eff; THIS LAND IS MINE(1943), spec eff; ACTION IN ARABIA(1944), spec eff; EXPERIMENT PERILOUS(1944), spec eff; FALCON IN MEXICO, THE(1944), spec eff; GILDERSLEEVE'S GHOST(1944), spec eff; GIRL RUSH(1944), spec eff; HEAVENLY DAYS(1944), spec eff; MADEMOISELLE FIFI(1944), spec. eff; MARINE RAIDERS(1944), spec eff; MY PAL, WOLF(1944), spec eff; NONE BUT THE LONELY HEART(1944), spec eff; PASSPORT TO DESTINY(1944), spec eff; SEVEN DAYS ASHORE(1944), spec eff; TALL IN THE SADDLE(1944), spec eff; YOUTH RUNS WILD(1944), spec eff; BACK TO BATAAN(1945), spec. eff.; BETRAYAL FROM THE EAST(1945), spec eff; BRIGHTON STRANGLER, THE(1945), spec eff; CHINA SKY(1945), spec eff; ENCHANTED COTTAGE, THE(1945), spec eff; GEORGE WHITE'S SCANDALS(1945), spec eff; HAVING WONDERFUL CRIME(1945), spec eff; JOHNNY ANGEL(1945), spec eff; MAN ALIVE(1945), spec eff; MURDER, MY SWEET(1945), spec eff; RADIO STARS ON PARADE(1945), spec eff; SPANISH MAIN, THE(1945), spec eff; THOSE ENDEARING YOUNG CHARMS(1945), spec eff; TWO O'CLOCK COURAGE(1945), spec eff; BEDLAM(1946), spec eff; DEADLINE AT DAWN(1946), spec eff; FROM THIS DAY FORWARD(1946), spec eff; GENIUS AT WORK(1946), ph; NOTORIOUS(1946), spec eff; SISTER KENNY(1946), spec eff; SPIRAL STAIRCASE, THE(1946), spec eff; MOURNING BECOMES ELECTRA(1947), spec eff; SINBAD THE SAILOR(1947), spec eff; TYCOON(1947), spec eff

Vernon Walker
CHRISTOPHER STRONG(1933), spec eff; SON OF KONG(1933), ph; DOWN TO THEIR LAST YACHT(1934), ph; GAY DIVORCEE, THE(1934), spec eff; LITTLE MINISTER, THE(1934), spec eff; BY YOUR LEAVE(1935), ph; LAST DAYS OF POMPEII, THE(1935), spec eff; MURDER ON A HONEYMOON(1935), spec eff; ROMANCE IN MANHATTAN(1935), spec eff; SHE(1935), spec eff; SILVER STREAK, THE(1935), ph; FOLLOW THE FLEET(1936), spec eff; GRAND JURY(1936), ph; MUMMY'S BOYS(1936), ph; SWING TIME(1936), spec eff; WINTERSET(1936), spec eff; WITHOUT ORDERS(1936), ph; DON'T TELL THE WIFE(1937), spec eff; SHALL WE DANCE(1937), spec eff; WOMAN I LOVE, THE(1937), spec eff; CAREFREE(1938), spec eff; SKY GIANT(1938), spec eff; BACHELOR MOTHER(1939), spec eff; IRENE(1940), spec eff; SAINT'S DOUBLE TROUBLE, THE(1940), spec eff; WOMAN IN THE WINDOW, THE(1945), spec eff
Silents
LAST STRAW, THE(1920), ph; FRONT PAGE STORY, A(1922), ph; MAN FROM HARDPAN, THE(1927), ph

Victoria Rae Walker
1984
HOT DOG...THE MOVIE(1984)

Virginia Walker
BRINGING UP BABY(1938); CARIBBEAN MYSTERY, THE(1945); NOB HILL(1945); ROYAL SCANDAL, A(1945)

W.F. Walker
STREET MUSIC(1982)

Wade Walker
MOONLIGHT ON THE RANGE(1937); SIX-GUN RHYTHM(1939)

Wally Walker
PLAYMATES(1941); DESTINATION TOKYO(1944); FALL GUY(1947); GINGER(1947); DOCKS OF NEW ORLEANS(1948); I WOULDN'T BE IN YOUR SHOES(1948); SMART WOMAN(1948); TRAIL OF THE YUKON(1949); DESERT HAWK, THE(1950); MILKMAN, THE(1950); JUST ACROSS THE STREET(1952); HOUSEBOAT(1958)

Walter Walker
GREAT POWER, THE(1929); ANNABELLE'S AFFAIRS(1931); COMMON LAW, THE(1931); NEW ADVENTURES OF GET-RICH-QUICK WALLINGFORD, THE(1931); REACHING FOR THE MOON(1931); REBOUND(1931); TAILOR MADE MAN, A(1931); AMERICAN MADNESS(1932); CONQUERORS, THE(1932); KID FROM SPAIN, THE(1932); LAST MILE, THE(1932); LETTY LYNTON(1932); LIFE BEGINS(1932); MADAME RACKETEER(1932); MOUTHPIECE, THE(1932); RICH ARE ALWAYS WITH US, THE(1932); TOMORROW AND TOMORROW(1932); TWO AGAINST THE WORLD(1932); WOMAN IN ROOM 13, THE(1932); YOU SAID A MOUTHFUL(1932); FEMALE(1933); FLYING DOWN TO RIO(1933); FROM HELL TO HEAVEN(1933); GREAT JASPER, THE(1933); HARD TO HANDLE(1933); HELLO SISTER!(1933); HOUSE ON 56TH STREET, THE(1933); I LOVE THAT MAN(1933); I LOVED A WOMAN(1933); I'M NO ANGEL(1933); JENNIE GERHARDT(1933); MARY STEVENS, M.D.(1933); NO MAN OF HER OWN(1933); OUR BETTERS(1933); SITTING PRETTY(1933); BELLE OF THE NINETIES(1934); COUNT OF MONTE CRISTO, THE(1934); GAY BRIDE, THE(1934); IMITATION OF LIFE(1934); LOST LADY, A(1934); MRS. WIGGS OF THE CABBAGE PATCH(1934); YOU CAN'T BUY EVERYTHING(1934); FRONT PAGE WOMAN(1935); MAGNIFICENT OBSESSION(1935); MAN WHO RECLAIMED HIS HEAD, THE(1935); NO MORE LADIES(1935); SHE COULDN'T TAKE IT(1935); SONS OF STEEL(1935); STRANGE WIVES(1935); WHILE THE PATIENT SLEPT(1935); DANGEROUS(1936); EVERYBODY'S OLD MAN(1936); GO WEST, YOUNG MAN(1936); YOURS FOR THE ASKING(1936); COWBOY AND THE LADY, THE(1938); MARIE ANTOINETTE(1938); YOU CAN'T TAKE IT WITH YOU(1938)
Silents
IN AGAIN-OUT AGAIN(1917); DARLING OF THE RICH, THE(1923)
Misc. Silents
AMERICA - THAT'S ALL(1917)

Whimsical Walker
Silents
STARTING POINT, THE(1919, Brit.)

Will Walker
WHITE BUFFALO, THE(1977); DEATHSPORT(1978); DRIVER, THE(1978); SUNSET COVE(1978); HARDCORE(1979)

William Walker
BRIGHT LEAF(1950); ANNE OF THE INDIES(1951); FOLLOW THE SUN(1951); LYDIA BAILEY(1952); WAIT 'TIL THE SUN SHINES, NELLIE(1952); GIRL WHO HAD EVERYTHING, THE(1953); JAMAICA RUN(1953); PRESIDENT'S LADY, THE(1953); SANGAREE(1953); MAN CALLED PETER, THE(1955); PRINCE OF PLAYERS(1955); LONG, HOT SUMMER, THE(1958); PORGY AND BESS(1959); BOY WHO CAUGHT A CROOK(1961); HUSH... HUSH, SWEET CHARLOTTE(1964); OUR MAN FLINT(1966); BIG JAKE(1971)

William "Bill" Walker
SAND(1949)

Zena Walker
DANGER TOMORROW(1960, Brit.); SNOWBALL(1960, Brit.); EMERGENCY(1962, Brit.); HELLIONS, THE(1962, Brit.); MARKED ONE, THE(1963, Brit.); TRAITORS, THE(1963, Brit.); DAYLIGHT ROBBERY(1964, Brit.); MODEL MURDER CASE, THE(1964, Brit.); BOY TEN FEET TALL, A(1965, Brit.); CHANGE PARTNERS(1965, Brit.); LAST SHOT YOU HEAR, THE(1969, Brit.); CROMWELL(1970, Brit.); RECKONING, THE(1971, Brit.); LIKELY LADS, THE(1976, Brit.); DRESSER, THE(1983)
Misc. Talkies
TROUBLED WATERS(1964, Brit.); ONE OF THOSE THINGS(1974, Brit.)

Clark Walkington
1984
TREASURE OF THE YANKEE ZEPHYR(1984)

Hugh Walkinshaw
OUTSIDERS, THE(1983)

Beryl Walkley
SECOND MATE, THE(1950, Brit.)

Barbara Walkowna
PASSENGER, THE(1970, Pol.)

Bruce Walkup
WINNING(1969); SPECIAL DELIVERY(1976), cos
1984
MASS APPEAL(1984), cos

Anita Wall
SCENES FROM A MARRIAGE(1974, Swed.)

Bob Wall
ENTER THE DRAGON(1973)

Boots Wall
Silents
UNCLE TOM'S CABIN(1914)

Dave Wall
Silents
DAY OF DAYS, THE(1914); PORT OF MISSING MEN(1914)
Misc. Silents
LADY OF QUALITY, A(1913); PORT OF DOOM, THE(1913); PRICE OF HAPPINESS, THE(1916)

David Wall
Silents
CAPTAIN SWIFT(1914); GREYHOUND, THE(1914); PROHIBITION(1915)
Misc. Silents
BANKER'S DAUGHTER, THE(1914); NORTHERN LIGHTS(1914); TIME LOCK NO. 776(1915); WALL STREET MYSTERY, THE(1920)

David V. Wall
Misc. Silents
IN THE BISHOP'S CARRIAGE(1913)

Estelle Wall
ROWDYMAN, THE(1973, Can.)

Evelyn Wall
SOMETHING WILD(1961)

Fay Wall
SEVENTH CROSS, THE(1944); YOUNG BESS(1953)

Faye Wall
HITLER–DEAD OR ALIVE(1942)

Geraldine Wall
REMEMBER THE DAY(1941); SONG OF BERNADETTE, THE(1943); CHARLIE CHAN IN BLACK MAGIC(1944); IN THE MEANTIME, DARLING(1944); WINGED VICTORY(1944); GIRLS OF THE BIG HOUSE(1945); KEEP YOUR POWDER DRY(1945); VALLEY OF DECISION, THE(1945); BOYS' RANCH(1946); JANIE GETS MARRIED(1946); LOVE LAUGHS AT ANDY HARDY(1946); MADONNA'S SECRET, THE(1946); BORN TO SPEED(1947); DARK DELUSION(1947); HIGH BARBAREE(1947); BEYOND GLORY(1948); GREEN GRASS OF WYOMING(1948); HOMECOMING(1948); SCUDDA-HOO! SCUDDA-HAY!(1948); ALIAS NICK BEAL(1949); EVERYBODY DOES IT(1949); FOUNTAINHEAD, THE(1949); GREEN PROMISE, THE(1949); FILE ON THELMA JORDAN(1950); LIFE OF HER OWN, A(1950); MISTER 880(1950); PAID IN FULL(1950); WHERE DANGER LIVES(1950); APPOINTMENT WITH DANGER(1951); BY THE LIGHT OF THE SILVERY MOON(1953); BLACK WIDOW(1954); MAN IN THE GREY FLANNEL SUIT, THE(1956); AFFAIR TO REMEMBER, AN(1957); CRIME OF PASSION(1957); MARDI GRAS(1958); PARTY GIRL(1958); SOME CAME RUNNING(1959); THIS EARTH IS MINE(1959); HELLER IN PINK TIGHTS(1960); LET'S MAKE LOVE(1960); PLEASE DON'T EAT THE DAISIES(1960); ONE MAN'S WAY(1964)

Jean Wall
FIRST OFFENCE(1936, Brit.); BLIND DESIRE(1948, Fr.); THEY ARE NOT ANGELS(1948, Fr.); JUST ME(1950, Fr.); ROYAL AFFAIR, A(1950); CROSSROADS OF PASSION(1951, Fr.); IT HAPPENED IN PARIS(1953, Fr.); FROU-FROU(1955, Fr.); FRANTIC(1961, Fr.)

Kendra Wall
RETURN OF THE JEDI(1983)

Lyle S. Wall
Misc. Talkies
THURSDAY MORNING MURDERS, THE(1976)

Max Wall
ON THE AIR(1934, Brit.); SAVE A LITTLE SUNSHINE(1938, Brit.); COME DANCE WITH ME(1950, Brit.); CHITTY CHITTY BANG BANG(1968, Brit.); JABBERWOCKY(1977, Brit.); HANOVER STREET(1979, Brit.); HOUND OF THE BASKERVILLES, THE(1980, Brit.)

Mildred Wall
SIDE STREET(1950)

Robert Wall
RETURN OF THE DRAGON(1974, Chin.); GAME OF DEATH, THE(1979)

Toff Wall
Misc. Silents
LAST CHALLENGE, THE(1916, Brit.)

Tony Wall
DOUBLE, THE(1963, Brit); SECOND BEST SECRET AGENT IN THE WHOLE WIDE WORLD, THE(1965, Brit.); TALES FROM THE CRYPT(1972, Brit.)

Marilyn Wall-Asse
1984
FLASH OF GREEN, A(1984), cos

Walla
JAWS OF THE JUNGLE(1936)

Marianne Walla
DIVIDED HEART, THE(1955, Brit.)

Alice Wallace
SHOW BUSINESS(1944); UP IN ARMS(1944); HOODLUM SAINT, THE(1946); TILL THE CLOUDS ROLL BY(1946); SONG IS BORN, A(1948); GIRL FROM JONES BEACH, THE(1949); LIFE OF HER OWN, A(1950)

Andy Wallace
2001: A SPACE ODYSSEY(1968, U.S./Brit.)

Anthony Wallace
RIGHT STUFF, THE(1983)

Anzac Wallace
1984
SILENT ONE, THE(1984, New Zealand); UTU(1984, New Zealand)

Art Wallace
WELCOME TO THE CLUB(1971)

Babe Wallace
STORMY WEATHER(1943)

Beryl Wallace
MURDER AT THE VANITIES(1934); ROUGH RIDIN' RHYTHM(1937); THANKS FOR LISTENING(1937); AIR DEVILS(1938); DRAMATIC SCHOOL(1938); ROMANCE OF THE ROCKIES(1938); TRADE WINDS(1938); YOU CAN'T CHEAT AN HONEST MAN(1939); NIGHT AT EARL CARROLL'S, A(1940); I MARRIED AN ANGEL(1942); JOHNNY EAGER(1942); SUNSET ON THE DESERT(1942); KANSAN(1943); WOMAN OF THE TOWN, THE(1943); ENEMY OF WOMEN(1944)

Bill Wallace
DESPERATE(1947); GUILT OF JANET AMES, THE(1947); HER HUSBAND'S AFFAIRS(1947); JOHNNY O'CLOCK(1947); LIKELY STORY, A(1947); OUT OF THE PAST(1947); WILD HARVEST(1947); FORCE OF ONE, A(1979)

Bob Wallace
WITHOUT RESERVATIONS(1946); TOWING(1978)

Brad Wallace
1984
FLASH OF GREEN, A(1984)

Brian Wallace
PEEPING TOM(1960, Brit.)

Brown Wallace
END OF AUGUST, THE(1982)

Bryan Wallace
MY OLD DUTCH(1934, Brit.), w; MURDER ON DIAMOND ROW(1937, Brit.), w; STRANGERS ON A HONEYMOON(1937, Brit.), w; INSPECTOR HORNLEIGH(1939, Brit.), w; MYSTERIOUS MR. REEDER, THE(1940, Brit.), w

Bryan Edgar Wallace
FLYING SQUAD, THE(1932, Brit.), w; WHITE FACE(1933, Brit.), w; CLAIRVOYANT, THE(1935, Brit.), w; YOU'RE IN THE ARMY NOW(1937, Brit.), w; MAD EXECUTIONERS, THE(1965, Ger.), w; MONSTER OF LONDON CITY, THE(1967, Ger.), w; PHANTOM OF SOHO, THE(1967, Ger.), w

Major C. Wallace
SANDERS OF THE RIVER(1935, Brit.), tech adv

C. R. Wallace
Silents
CONNECTICUT YANKEE AT KING ARTHUR'S COURT, A(1921), ed; MAID OF THE WEST(1921), d; WHATEVER SHE WANTS(1921), d; ELOPE IF YOU MUST(1922), d; WEST OF CHICAGO(1922), d; LITTLE CHURCH AROUND THE CORNER(1923), ed

Carl Wallace
PLASTIC DOME OF NORMA JEAN, THE(1966)

Catherine Wallace
ILLUSION(1929); WHEN YOU'RE IN LOVE(1937); MOON OVER BURMA(1940); WEST POINT WIDOW(1941); THOSE ENDEARING YOUNG CHARMS(1945)
Silents
JENNY BE GOOD(1920); DARING CHANCES(1924)

Charles A. Wallace
STAGE TO THUNDER ROCK(1964), w; CASTLE OF EVIL(1967), w; MONEY JUNGLE, THE(1968), w; GIRL WHO KNEW TOO MUCH, THE(1969), w; TIGER BY THE TAIL(1970), w

Chris Wallace
DON'T ANSWER THE PHONE(1980); NEW YEAR'S EVIL(1980)

Maj. Claude Wallace
SONG OF FREEDOM(1938, Brit.), w

Coley Wallace
JOE LOUIS STORY, THE(1953)

Connie Wallace
RAVEN, THE(1963)

Dan Wallace
JANE EYRE(1944); BIG SLEEP, THE(1946)

David Wallace
HUMONGOUS(1982, Can.); SPLIT IMAGE(1982); MORTUARY(1983)
Misc. Talkies
MONEY TO BURN(1981)
Misc. Silents
KINGDOM OF TWILIGHT, THE(1929, Brit.)

Dee Wallace
HILLS HAVE EYES, THE(1978); 10(1979); HOWLING, THE(1981); E.T. THE EXTRA-TERRESTRIAL(1982); JIMMY THE KID(1982); CUJO(1983)

Dennis Wallace
DEATH HUNT(1981)

Dick Wallace
HEARTS OF HUMANITY(1932)

Donald K. Wallace
NIGHT OF THE ZOMBIES(1981)

Dorothy Wallace
Silents
OCCASIONALLY YOURS(1920); WHAT NO MAN KNOWS(1921); MERRY-GO-ROUND(1923)

Earle Wallace
RECAPTURED LOVE(1930)

Edgar Wallace
TERROR, THE(1928), w; CLUE OF THE NEW PIN, THE(1929, Brit.), w; CRIMSON CIRCLE, THE(1930, Brit.), w; SQUEAKER, THE(1930, Brit.), d&w; CALENDAR, THE(1931, Brit.), w; SHOULD A DOCTOR TELL?(1931, Brit.), w; TO OBLIGE A LADY(1931, Brit.), w; CRIMINAL AT LARGE(1932, Brit.), w; FLYING SQUAD, THE(1932, Brit.), w; HOUND OF THE BASKERVILLES(1932, Brit.), w; MENACE, THE(1932), w; OLD MAN, THE(1932, Brit.), w; RINGER, THE(1932, Brit.), w; BEFORE DAWN(1933), w; PRISON BREAKER(1936, Brit.), w; JEWEL, THE(1933, Brit.), w; KING KONG(1933), w; WHITE FACE(1933, Brit.), w; FEATHERED SERPENT, THE(1934, Brit.), w; GREEN PACK, THE(1934, Brit.), w; MAN WHO CHANGED HIS NAME, THE(1934, Brit.), w; MYSTERY LINER(1934), w; RETURN OF THE TERROR(1934), w; BORN TO GAMBLE(1935), w; LAD, THE(1935, Brit.), w; SANDERS OF THE RIVER(1935, Brit.), w; CHICK(1936, Brit.), w; CRIMSON CIRCLE, THE(1936, Brit.), w; EDUCATED EVANS(1936, Brit.), w; PRISON BREAKER(1936, Brit.), w; FROG, THE(1937, Brit.), w; MURDER ON DIAMOND ROW(1937, Brit.), w; STRANGERS ON A HONEYMOON(1937, Brit.), w; DANGEROUS TO KNOW(1938), w; KATE PLUS TEN(1938, Brit.), w; OLD BONES OF THE RIVER(1938, Brit.), w; RETURN OF THE FROG, THE(1938, Brit.), w; THANK EVANS(1938, Brit.), w; FLYING FIFTY-FIVE(1939, Brit.), w; PHANTOM STRIKES, THE(1939, Brit.), w; CASE OF THE FRIGHTENED LADY, THE(1940, Brit.), w; FLYING SQUAD, THE(1940, Brit.), w; HUMAN MONSTER, THE(1940, Brit.), w; MISSING PEOPLE, THE(1940, Brit.), w; MYSTERIOUS MR. REEDER, THE(1940, Brit.), w; SECRET FOUR, THE(1940, Brit.), w; CHAMBER OF HORRORS(1941, Brit.), w; MYSTERY OF ROOM 13(1941, Brit.), w; TERROR, THE(1941, Brit.), w; MISSING MILLION, THE(1942, Brit.), w; CALENDAR, THE(1948, Brit.), w; RINGER, THE(1953, Brit.), w; MAN WHO WAS NOBODY, THE(1960, Brit.), w; ATTEMPT TO KILL(1961, Brit.), w; BACKFIRE!(1961, Brit.), w; CLUE OF THE NEW PIN, THE(1961, Brit.), w; CLUE OF THE SILVER KEY, THE(1961, Brit.), w; DARK EYES OF LONDON(1961, Ger.), w; DEVIL'S DAFFODIL, THE(1961, Brit./Ger.), w; FOURTH SQUARE, THE(1961, Brit.), w; MAN AT THE CARLTON TOWER(1961, Brit.), w; MAN DETAINED(1961), w; MAN IN THE BACK SEAT, THE(1961, Brit.), w; DEATH TRAP(1962, Brit.), w; FLAT TWO(1962, Brit.), w; LOCKER 69(1962, Brit.), w; NUMBER SIX(1962, Brit.), w; PLAYBACK(1962, Brit.), w; TIME TO REMEMBER(1962, Brit.), w; ACCIDENTAL DEATH(1963, Brit.), w; DOUBLE, THE(1963, Brit), w; FIVE TO ONE(1963, Brit.), w; RETURN TO SENDER(1963, Brit.), w; RIVALS, THE(1963, Brit.), w; SANDERS(1963, Brit.), w; SET-UP, THE(1963, Brit.), w; TO HAVE AND TO HOLD(1963, Brit.), w; DOWNFALL(1964, Brit.), w; FACE OF A STRANGER(1964, Brit.), w; NEVER MENTION MURDER(1964, Brit.), w; VERDICT, THE(1964, Brit.), w; WE SHALL SEE(1964, Brit.), w; WHO WAS MADDOX?(1964, Brit.), w; 20,000 POUNDS KISS, THE(1964, Brit.), w; COAST OF SKELETONS(1965, Brit.), w; SINISTER MAN, THE(1965, Brit.), w; CANDIDATE FOR MURDER(1966, Brit.), w; INCIDENT AT MIDNIGHT(1966, Brit.), w; MAIN CHANCE, THE(1966, Brit.), w; PARTNER, THE(1966, Brit.), w; RICOCHET(1966, Brit.), w; SHARE OUT, THE(1966, Brit.), w; SOLO FOR SPARROW(1966, Brit.), w; TRAITOR'S GATE(1966, Brit./Ger.), w; MALPAS MYSTERY, THE(1967, Brit.), w; NEVER BACK LOSERS(1967, Brit.), w; ON THE RUN(1967, Brit.), w; PSYCHO-CIRCUS(1967, Brit.), w; CLUE OF THE TWISTED CANDLE(1968, Brit.), w; MARRIAGE OF CONVENIENCE(1970, Brit.), w; CREATURE WITH THE BLUE HAND(1971, Ger.), w
Silents
ANGEL ESQUIRE(1919, Brit.), w; CRIMSON CIRCLE, THE(1922, Brit.), w; FLYING FIFTY-FIVE, THE(1924, Brit.), w; MAN WHO CHANGED HIS NAME, THE(1928, Brit.), w; RINGER, THE(1928, Brit.), w
Misc. Silents
RED ACES(1929, Brit.), d

Elizabeth Wallace
DEATH OF MICHAEL TURBIN, THE(1954, Brit.); NIGHT OF THE FULL MOON, THE(1954, Brit.)

Emmett "Babe" Wallace
POCOMANIA(1939)
Misc. Talkies
FIGHT NEVER ENDS, THE(1947)

Enrique Wallace
AZTEC MUMMY, THE(1957, Mex.), ph; FRANKENSTEIN, THE VAMPIRE AND CO.(1961, Mex.), ph; DOCTOR OF DOOM(1962, Mex.), ph; CURSE OF THE AZTEC MUMMY, THE(1965, Mex.), ph; ROBOT VS. THE AZTEC MUMMY, THE(1965, Mex.), ph; SPIRITISM(1965, Mex.), ph; CURSE OF THE DOLL PEOPLE, THE(1968, Mex.), ph

Ernest Wallace
Silents
FLAG LIEUTENANT, THE(1919, Brit.)

Fay Wallace
Misc. Silents
CAVEMAN, THE(1915)

Francis Wallace
TOUCHDOWN!(1931), w; HUDDLE(1932), w; THAT'S MY BOY(1932), w; BIG GAME, THE(1936), w; ROSE BOWL(1936), w; KID GALAHAD(1937), w; WAGONS ROLL AT NIGHT, THE(1941), w; KID GALAHAD(1962), w

Frank Wallace [Franco Mannino]
GHOST, THE(1965, Ital.), m

Fred Wallace
SEA GOD, THE(1930); WHITE PARADE, THE(1934); DOUBTING THOMAS(1935); EVERY SATURDAY NIGHT(1936)

Frederick Wallace
LADY AND GENT(1932)

Frederick William Wallace
Silents
CAPTAIN SALVATION(1927), w

Geoffrey Wallace
THEY CAME FROM BEYOND SPACE(1967, Brit.); TORTURE GARDEN(1968, Brit.)

George Wallace
THINGS ARE TOUGH ALL OVER(1982); HIS ROYAL HIGHNESS(1932, Aus.), w; HARMONY ROW(1933, Aus.), a, w; GONE TO THE DOGS(1939, Aus.), a, w; FAT MAN, THE(1951); RATS OF TOBRUK(1951, Aus.); SUBMARINE COMMAND(1951); BIG SKY, THE(1952); JAPANESE WAR BRIDE(1952); KANSAS CITY CONFIDENTIAL(1952); LAWLESS BREED, THE(1952); MILLION DOLLAR MERMAID(1952);

ARENA(1953); HOMESTEADERS, THE(1953); STAR OF TEXAS(1953); VIGILANTE TERROR(1953); WHEREVER SHE GOES(1953, Aus.); BORDER RIVER(1954); DESTRY(1954); DRUMS ACROSS THE RIVER(1954); FRENCH LINE, THE(1954); HUMAN JUNGLE, THE(1954); MAN WITHOUT A STAR(1955); SECOND GREATEST SEX, THE(1955); SOLDIER OF FORTUNE(1955); STRANGE LADY IN TOWN(1955); FORBIDDEN PLANET(1956); SIX BLACK HORSES(1962); DEAD HEAT ON A MERRY-GO-ROUND(1966); TEXAS ACROSS THE RIVER(1966); SKIN GAME(1971)
Misc. Talkies
LET GEORGE DO IT(1938, Aus.)

George D. Wallace
STUNT MAN, THE(1980)
1984
PROTOCOL(1984)

Gill Wallace
VELVET TOUCH, THE(1948)

Gloria Wallace
TOP BANANA(1954)

Grace Wallace
NIX ON DAMES(1929); WALL STREET(1929)

Griselda Wallace
1984
DARK ENEMY(1984, Brit.), cos, makeup

Harry Wallace
STREET SCENE(1931); NIGHT AFTER NIGHT(1932); SHE DONE HIM WRONG(1933); JIMMY THE GENT(1934); MURDER WITH PICTURES(1936)

Hedgar Wallace
PASSPORT TO CHINA(1961, Brit.)

Hedger Wallace
INTENT TO KILL(1958, Brit.); WITNESS, THE(1959, Brit.); DOUBLE BUNK(1961, Brit.); TROUBLE IN THE SKY(1961, Brit.); MYSTERY SUBMARINE(1963, Brit.); NIGHTMARE(1963, Brit.); DR. TERROR'S HOUSE OF HORRORS(1965, Brit.); TRAITOR'S GATE(1966, Brit./Ger.); TORTURE GARDEN(1968, Brit.); OBLONG BOX, THE(1969, Brit.); TALES FROM THE CRYPT(1972, Brit.)

Helen Wallace
SIOUX CITY SUE(1946); MARSHAL OF CRIPPLE CREEK, THE(1947); THAT HAGEN GIRL(1947); VOICE OF THE TURTLE, THE(1947); MOONRISE(1948); OUT OF THE STORM(1948); UNDERCOVER MAN, THE(1949); CHAIN OF CIRCUMSTANCE(1951); STREET BANDITS(1951); HAS ANYBODY SEEN MY GAL?(1952); RAINBOW 'ROUND MY SHOULDER(1952); GLASS WEB, THE(1953); LAST POSSE, THE(1953); THREE YOUNG TEXANS(1954); CULT OF THE COBRA(1955); FAR HORIZONS, THE(1955); TIGHT SPOT(1955); FRANCIS IN THE HAUNTED HOUSE(1956); NEVER SAY GOODBYE(1956); BACK FROM THE DEAD(1957); DRANGO(1957); MIDNIGHT STORY, THE(1957); REFORM SCHOOL GIRL(1957); RIDE A VIOLENT MILE(1957); SPOILERS OF THE FOREST(1957); LONG, HOT SUMMER, THE(1958); 10 NORTH FREDERICK(1958); ASK ANY GIRL(1959); SUMMER PLACE, A(1959); DARK AT THE TOP OF THE STAIRS, THE(1960); PSYCHO(1960); JACK THE GIANT KILLER(1962)

Helene Wallace
Misc. Silents
GRANDEE'S RING, THE(1915)

Ian Wallace
FLOODTIDE(1949, Brit.); ASSASSIN FOR HIRE(1951, Brit.); GREAT GILBERT AND SULLIVAN, THE(1953, Brit.); NOOSE FOR A LADY(1953, Brit.); TOM THUMB(1958, Brit./U.S.); DENTIST IN THE CHAIR(1960, Brit.)

Inez Wallace
I WALKED WITH A ZOMBIE(1943), w

Irene Wallace
Silents
TRAFFIC IN SOULS(1913)

Irving Wallace
JIVE JUNCTION(1944), w; THAT'S MY BABY(1944), w; WEST POINT STORY, THE(1950), w; MEET ME AT THE FAIR(1952), w; DESERT LEGION(1953), w; GUN FURY(1953), w; SPLIT SECOND(1953), w; BAD FOR EACH OTHER(1954), w; GAMBLER FROM NATCHEZ, THE(1954), w; JUMP INTO HELL(1955), w; SINCERELY YOURS(1955), w; BURNING HILLS, THE(1956), w; BOMBERS B-52(1957), w; BIG CIRCUS, THE(1959), w; CHAPMAN REPORT, THE(1962), w; PRIZE, THE(1963), w; SEVEN MINUTES, THE(1971), w; MAN, THE(1972), w

Jack Wallace
UNDER PRESSURE(1935); KLONDIKE ANNIE(1936); ASSIGNMENT OUTER SPACE(1960, Ital.); DEATH WISH(1974); LAST AFFAIR, THE(1976)

Jacque Wallace
NIGHT MOVES(1975)

Jean Wallace
LOUISIANA PURCHASE(1941); ZIEGFELD GIRL(1941); YOU CAN'T RATION LOVE(1944); IT SHOULDN'T HAPPEN TO A DOG(1946); BLAZE OF NOON(1947); WHEN MY BABY SMILES AT ME(1948); JIGSAW(1949); MAN ON THE EIFFEL TOWER, THE(1949); GOOD HUMOR MAN, THE(1950); NATIVE SON(1951, U.S., Arg.); BIG COMBO, THE(1955); STAR OF INDIA(1956, Brit.); STORM FEAR(1956); DEVIL'S HAIRPIN, THE(1957); MARACAIBO(1958); SWORD OF LANCELOT(1963, Brit.); BEACH RED(1967); NO BLADE OF GRASS(1970, Brit.)

Jennifer Wallace
KITCHEN, THE(1961, Brit.)
1984
BEST DEFENSE(1984)

Jerry Wallace
FRIDAY THE 13TH PART II(1981)

Jo Wallace
NICE WOMAN(1932)

Joe Wallace
NIGHT WORLD(1932)

John Wallace
DONOVAN AFFAIR, THE(1929); FIGHTING RANGER, THE(1934); LIFE BEGINS AT 40(1935); STEAMBOAT ROUND THE BEND(1935); LUCK OF ROARING CAMP, THE(1937); BLOOD AND SAND(1941); WALLFLOWER(1948), makeup; FOUNTAINHEAD, THE(1949), makeup; FERRY TO HONG KONG(1959, Brit.); SCAVENGERS, THE(1959, U.S./Phil.)
Silents
GOLD RUSH, THE(1925); BLACK PIRATE, THE(1926); YELLOW FINGERS(1926)

Judy Wallace
DARKER THAN AMBER(1970); HOW DO I LOVE THEE?(1970)

Karl Wallace
Misc. Talkies
INVASION FROM INNER EARTH(1977)

Katherine Wallace
STRANGER ON THE THIRD FLOOR(1940)

Lee Wallace
TAKING OF PELHAM ONE, TWO, THREE, THE(1974); KLUTE(1971); HOT ROCK, THE(1972); HAPPY HOOKER, THE(1975); THIEVES(1977); PRIVATE BENJAMIN(1980)

Leroy Wallace
ROCKERS(1980)

Lew Wallace
BEN HUR(1959), w
Silents
PRINCE OF INDIA, A(1914), w

Lewis Wallace
Silents
BEN-HUR(1925), w

Linda Wallace
CHARLIE, THE LONESOME COUGAR(1967)

Mark Wallace
1984
DARK ENEMY(1984, Brit.)

Marquerita Wallace
48 HOURS(1982)

Mary Jane Wallace
PRECIOUS JEWELS(1969)

Mary Wallace
COLLEGE RHYTHM(1934); DIAMOND JIM(1935); LADY TUBBS(1935); RIFF-RAFF(1936)

Maude Wallace
ELOPEMENT(1951); LOVE NEST(1951); PEOPLE WILL TALK(1951); SCARLET ANGEL(1952); STARS AND STRIPES FOREVER(1952); TALK ABOUT A STRANGER(1952); WE'RE NOT MARRIED(1952); WITH A SONG IN MY HEART(1952)

May Wallace
PAINTED FACES(1929); WHAT'S YOUR RACKET?(1934); INTERNES CAN'T TAKE MONEY(1937); MIDNIGHT MADONNA(1937); PICK A STAR(1937); WAY OUT WEST(1937); WHEN YOU'RE IN LOVE(1937); SMASHING THE SPY RING(1939)
Silents
DOLLAR DEVILS(1923); GIMMIE(1923); OH, YOU TONY!(1924); RECKLESS AGE, THE(1924)

Maybelle Wallace
RUMBLE FISH(1983)

Michael Wallace
GOLD DIGGERS OF 1937(1936), w; RACE STREET(1948)

Milton Wallace
KISS AND MAKE UP(1934); MIGHTY BARNUM, THE(1934); NONE BUT THE LONELY HEART(1944); SEVEN DOORS TO DEATH(1944); CORNERED(1945); LOST WEEKEND, THE(1945); KILLERS, THE(1946)

Morgan Wallace
BIG MONEY(1930); SISTERS(1930); UP THE RIVER(1930); ALEXANDER HAMILTON(1931); EXPENSIVE WOMEN(1931); IT PAYS TO ADVERTISE(1931); SAFE IN HELL(1931); SMART MONEY(1931); UNHOLY GARDEN, THE(1931); BEAST OF THE CITY, THE(1932); BLONDE VENUS(1932); CENTRAL PARK(1932); FINAL EDITION(1932); GRAND HOTEL(1932); HELL'S HOUSE(1932); IF I HAD A MILLION(1932); LADY AND GENT(1932); MOUTHPIECE, THE(1932); STEADY COMPANY(1932); WILD GIRL(1932); JENNIE GERHARDT(1933); MAMA LOVES PAPA(1933); PRIZEFIGHTER AND THE LADY, THE(1933); SONG OF SONGS(1933); TERROR ABOARD(1933); ABOVE THE CLOUDS(1934); CHEATING CHEATERS(1934); I BELIEVED IN YOU(1934); IT'S A GIFT(1934); MANY HAPPY RETURNS(1934); MEANEST GAL IN TOWN, THE(1934); MERRY WIDOW, THE(1934); TRUMPET BLOWS, THE(1934); WE LIVE AGAIN(1934); CONFIDENTIAL(1935); DANTE'S INFERNO(1935); DEVIL IS A WOMAN, THE(1935); GOIN' TO TOWN(1935); HEADLINE WOMAN, THE(1935); MARY BURNS, FUGITIVE(1935); MURDER ON A HONEYMOON(1935); RENDEZVOUS(1935); THUNDER MOUNTAIN(1935); $1,000 A MINUTE(1935); FURY(1936); GORGEOUS HUSSY, THE(1936); HUMAN CARGO(1936); LOVE ON A BET(1936); MISTER CINDERELLA(1936); SUTTER'S GOLD(1936); CALIFORNIAN, THE(1937); CHARLIE CHAN AT THE OLYMPICS(1937); HOUSE OF SECRETS, THE(1937); UNDER SUSPICION(1937); BILLY THE KID RETURNS(1938); DELINQUENT PARENTS(1938); GANG BULLETS(1938); LADY IN THE MORGUE(1938); LETTER OF INTRODUCTION(1938); MR. MOTO TAKES A VACATION(1938); OF HUMAN HEARTS(1938); THREE COMRADES(1938); WOMAN AGAINST WOMAN(1938); MYSTERY OF MR. WONG, THE(1939); STAR MAKER, THE(1939); STAR REPORTER(1939); TIMBER STAMPEDE(1939); UNION PACIFIC(1939); ELLERY QUEEN. MASTER DETECTIVE(1940); I LOVE YOU AGAIN(1940); MY LITTLE CHICKADEE(1940); PAROLE FIXER(1940); THREE MEN FROM TEXAS(1940); HONKY TONK(1941); IN OLD COLORADO(1941); SCATTERGOOD MEETS BROADWAY(1941); KISMET(1944); DICK TRACY(1945); I'LL REMEMBER APRIL(1945); SONG OF THE SARONG(1945); FALCON'S ALIBI, THE(1946)
Silents
FLYING PAT(1920); DREAM STREET(1921); ONE EXCITING NIGHT(1922); ORPHANS OF THE STORM(1922); HOTEL MOUSE, THE(1923, Brit.); RECKLESS ROMANCE(1924); TORMENT(1924); WOMAN WHO SINNED, A(1925)
Misc. Silents
DANGEROUS MAID, THE(1923); FIGHTING BLADE, THE(1923)

Nellie Wallace
WISHBONE, THE(1933, Brit.); RADIO FOLLIES(1935, Brit.); VARIETY(1935, Brit.); BOYS WILL BE GIRLS(1937, Brit.)

Oliver Wallace
MURDER BY TELEVISION(1935), m; FUN AND FANCY FREE(1947), m; ADVENTURES OF ICHABOD AND MR. TOAD(1949), md; CINDERELLA(1950), m, md; ALICE IN WONDERLAND(1951), m; PETER PAN(1953), m; LADY AND THE TRAMP(1955), m; OLD YELLER(1957), m; TONKA(1958), m; DARBY O'GILL AND THE LITTLE PEOPLE(1959), m; TEN WHO DARED(1960), m; NIKKI, WILD DOG OF THE NORTH(1961, U.S./Can.), m; LEGEND OF LOBO, THE(1962), m; INCREDIBLE JOURNEY, THE(1963), m; SAVAGE SAM(1963), m

Ollie Wallace
TOBY TYLER(1960)
Parnham Wallace
OUR MOTHER'S HOUSE(1967, Brit.)
Patricia Wallace
TOO LATE FOR TEARS(1949)
Paul Wallace
JOHNNY TROUBLE(1957); GYPSY(1962)
Ramsay Wallace
Misc. Silents
WOMAN AND THE LAW(1918)
Ramsaye Wallace
Silents
AMAZING LOVERS(1921)
Misc. Silents
EVEN AS EVE(1920)
Ramsey Wallace
Silents
RAGE OF PARIS, THE(1921); VOICE IN THE DARK(1921); LITTLE WILDCAT(1922);
EXTRA GIRL, THE(1923); EMPTY HANDS(1924)
Misc. Silents
HER ONLY WAY(1918); HER BELOVED VILLIAN(1920); HER HONOR THE
MAYOR(1920); WOMAN IN HIS HOUSE, THE(1920); LURING LIPS(1921); CALL OF
HOME, THE(1922); GIRL I LOVED, THE(1923); GOSSIP(1923); BROKEN LAWS(1924);
CHALK MARKS(1924)
Ratch Wallace
OFFERING, THE(1966, Can.); ISABEL(1968, Can.); ACT OF THE HEART(1970, Can.);
MERRY WIVES OF TOBIAS ROUKE, THE(1972, Can.); SUNDAY IN THE COUN-
TRY(1975, Can.); AGE OF INNOCENCE(1977, Can.), w
Regina Wallace
ADVENTURES OF MARTIN EDEN, THE(1942); MALE ANIMAL, THE(1942); SCAT-
TERGOOD RIDES HIGH(1942); THIS TIME FOR KEEPS(1942); BEHIND PRISON
WALLS(1943); CRYSTAL BALL, THE(1943); MR. SKEFFINGTON(1944); STANDING
ROOM ONLY(1944); BLONDE FROM BROOKLYN(1945); PILLOW TO POST(1945);
AVALANCHE(1946); BAMBOO BLONDE, THE(1946); BECAUSE OF HIM(1946);
DARK CORNER, THE(1946); NIGHT AND DAY(1946); PERSONALITY KID(1946);
SMOOTH AS SILK(1946); HIGH CONQUEST(1947); TWO BLONDES AND A RED-
HEAD(1947); I SURRENDER DEAR(1948); LET'S LIVE A LITTLE(1948); MIRACLE
OF THE BELLS, THE(1948); NIGHT HAS A THOUSAND EYES(1948); RACHEL AND
THE STRANGER(1948); TRIPLE THREAT(1948); MY FOOLISH HEART(1949)
Misc. Talkies
SWING THE WESTERN WAY(1947)
Richard Wallace
SHOPWORN ANGEL, THE(1928), d; INNOCENTS OF PARIS(1929), d; RIVER OF
ROMANCE(1929), d; ANYBODY'S WAR(1930), d; SEVEN DAYS LEAVE(1930), d;
KICK IN(1931), d; MAN OF THE WORLD(1931), d; RIGHT TO LOVE, THE(1931), d;
ROAD TO RENO(1931), d; DIVORCE IN THE FAMILY(1932); THUNDER BE-
LOW(1932), d; TOMORROW AND TOMORROW(1932), d; MASQUERADER,
THE(1933), d; EIGHT GIRLS IN A BOAT(1934), d; LITTLE MINISTER, THE(1934), d;
WEDDING PRESENT(1936), d; BLOSSOMS ON BROADWAY(1937), d; JOHN
MEADE'S WOMAN(1937), d; YOUNG IN HEART, THE(1938), d; UNDER-PUP,
THE(1939), d; CAPTAIN CAUTION(1940), d; GIRL, A GUY AND A GOB, A(1941), d;
OBLIGING YOUNG LADY(1941), d; SHE KNEW ALL THE ANSWERS(1941), d;
NIGHT TO REMEMBER, A(1942), d; WIFE TAKES A FLYER, THE(1942), d; BOM-
BARDIER(1943), d; FALLEN SPARROW, THE(1943), d; MY KINGDOM FOR A
COOK(1943), d; BRIDE BY MISTAKE(1944), d; IT'S IN THE BAG(1945), d; KISS AND
TELL(1945), d; BECAUSE OF HIM(1946), d; FRAMED(1947), d; SINBAD THE SAIL-
OR(1947), d; TYCOON(1947), d; LET'S LIVE A LITTLE(1948), d; ADVENTURE IN
BALTIMORE(1949), d; KISS FOR CORLISS, A(1949), d; CREATURE OF THE WALK-
ING DEAD(1960, Mex.), ph; WEEKEND OF SHADOWS(1978, Aus.), ph
Misc. Talkies
ANYBODY'S WAR(1930), d
Silents
SYNCOPATING SUE(1926), d; AMERICAN BEAUTY(1927), d; TEXAS STEER,
A(1927), d; LADY BE GOOD(1928), d
Misc. Silents
MCFADDEN FLATS(1927), d; POOR NUT, THE(1927), d; BUTTER AND EGG MAN,
THE(1928), d
Rit Wallace
1984
SURROGATE, THE(1984, Can.), ed
Rob Wallace
CHILD, THE(1977), m
Robert Wallace
THAT NIGHT(1957), w; DEVIL'S RAIN, THE(1975, U.S./Mex.)
Rowena Wallace
YOU CAN'T SEE 'ROUND CORNERS(1969, Aus.); SQUEEZE A FLOWER(1970, Aus.);
PUBERTY BLUES(1983, Aus.)
Royce Wallace
TAKE A GIANT STEP(1959); GOODBYE COLUMBUS(1969); COOL BREEZE(1972);
WILLIE DYNAMITE(1973); FUNNY LADY(1975)
Scott Wallace
SAVAGE HARVEST(1981), ed
Shani Wallace
KING IN NEW YORK, A(1957, Brit.)
Stephen Wallace
STIR(1980, Aus.), d
Misc. Talkies
LOVELETTERS FROM TERALBA ROAD(1977), d
Sue Wallace
EXPERIENCE PREFERRED... BUT NOT ESSENTIAL(1983, Brit.)
Tim Wallace
NOOSE HANGS HIGH, THE(1948); GOING HOME(1971)
Toby Wallace
LIVING LEGEND(1980)
Tommy Wallace
ASSAULT ON PRECINCT 13(1976), art d; FOG, THE(1980), a, ed, prod d; CHRIST-
MAS STORY, A(1983)

Tommy Lee Wallace
HALLOWEEN(1978), ed, prod d; AMITYVILLE II: THE POSSESSION(1982), w;
HALLOWEEN III: SEASON OF THE WITCH(1982), d&w
Tony Wallace
VICTORS, THE(1963)
Trevor Wallace
SUBTERFUGE(1969, US/Brit.), p; GROUNDSTAR CONSPIRACY, THE(1972, Can.),
p; CHRISTINA(1974, Can.), p, w; JOURNEY INTO FEAR(1976, Can), p, w
Virginia J. Wallace
FINNEGANS WAKE(1965)
W. David Edgar Wallace
YELLOW MASK, THE(1930, Brit.), w
William Wallace
BLUE SIERRA(1946); UNFAITHFUL, THE(1947), set d; BIG PUNCH, THE(1948), set
d; JOHNNY BELINDA(1948), set d; JUNE BRIDE(1948), set d; SMART GIRLS DON'T
TALK(1948), set d; CHAIN LIGHTNING(1950), set d; YOUNG MAN WITH A
HORN(1950), set d; DISTANT DRUMS(1951), set d; JIM THORPE–ALL AMERI-
CAN(1951), set d; ON MOONLIGHT BAY(1951), set d; LUCKY ME(1954), set d;
REBEL WITHOUT A CAUSE(1955), prod d; SEA CHASE, THE(1955), set d; YOUNG
AT HEART(1955), set d; SERENADE(1956), set d; TOP SECRET AFFAIR(1957), set d;
TWO ON A GUILLOTINE(1965), set d
1984
BEVERLY HILLS COP(1984)
William G. Wallace
SILVER RIVER(1948), set d
Wallace Reid and Family
Silents
NIGHT LIFE IN HOLLYWOOD(1922)
Eli Wallach
GENGHIS KHAN(U.S./Brit./Ger./Yugo); BABY DOLL(1956); LINEUP, THE(1958);
MAGNIFICENT SEVEN, THE(1960); SEVEN THIEVES(1960); MISFITS, THE(1961);
ADVENTURES OF A YOUNG MAN(1962); HOW THE WEST WAS WON(1962);
VICTORS, THE(1963); ACT ONE(1964); KISSES FOR MY PRESIDENT(1964); MOON-
SPINNERS, THE(1964); LORD JIM(1965, Brit.); HOW TO STEAL A MILLION(1966);
POPPY IS ALSO A FLOWER, THE(1966); GOOD, THE BAD, AND THE UGLY,
THE(1967, Ital./Span.); TIGER MAKES OUT, THE(1967); HOW TO SAVE A MAR-
RIAGE–AND RUIN YOUR LIFE(1968); LOVELY WAY TO DIE, A(1968); REVENGE
AT EL PASO(1968, Ital.); ACE HIGH(1969, Ital.); BRAIN, THE(1969, Fr./US); MACK-
ENNA'S GOLD(1969); ADVENTURES OF GERARD, THE(1970, Brit.); ANGEL LE-
VINE, THE(1970); PEOPLE NEXT DOOR, THE(1970); ZIGZAG(1970); ROMANCE OF
A HORSE THIEF(1971); CINDERELLA LIBERTY(1973); CRAZY JOE(1974); DON'T
TURN THE OTHER CHEEK(1974, Ital./Ger./Span.); NASTY HABITS(1976, Brit.);
STATELINE MOTEL(1976, Ital.); DEEP, THE(1977); DOMINO PRINCIPLE, THE(1977);
SENTINEL, THE(1977); GIRLFRIENDS(1978); MOVIE MOVIE(1978); CIRCLE OF
IRON(1979, Brit.); FIREPOWER(1979, Brit.); WINTER KILLS(1979); HUNTER,
THE(1980); SALAMANDER, THE(1983, U.S./Ital./Brit.)
1984
SAM'S SON(1984)
Ira Wallach
BOYS' NIGHT OUT(1962), w; WHEELER DEALERS, THE(1963), w; DON'T MAKE
WAVES(1967), w; HOT MILLIONS(1968, Brit.), w
Katherine Wallach
KING OF COMEDY, THE(1983)
Lewis Wallach
UP THE DOWN STAIRCASE(1967)
Peter Wallach
DEEP, THE(1977)
Roberta Wallach
EFFECT OF GAMMA RAYS ON MAN-IN-THE-MOON MARIGOLDS, THE(1972);
FM(1978)
Siegfried Wallach
EIGER SANCTION, THE(1975)
E. N. Wallack
Silents
FAME AND FORTUNE(1918); JOHNNY-ON-THE-SPOT(1919)
Roy Holmer Wallack
FAST TIMES AT RIDGEMONT HIGH(1982)
Edward Lewis Wallant
PAWNBROKER, THE(1965), w
Derek Wallbank
HAMLET(1976, Brit.), ed
Garrett Wallberg
GANGSTER STORY(1959)
Hasse Wallbom
VIBRATION(1969, Swed.)
David Wallbridge
NOTORIOUS GENTLEMAN(1945, Brit.); TAKE MY LIFE(1948, Brit.); PINK STRING
AND SEALING WAX(1950, Brit.)
Otto Wallburg
BOMBARDMENT OF MONTE CARLO, THE(1931, Ger.); BEAUTIFUL ADVEN-
TURE(1932, Ger.); TRAPEZE(1932, Ger.); WHAT WOMEN DREAM(1933, Ger.)
Otto Walldurg
CRIMSON CIRCLE, THE(1930, Brit.)
Lennart Wallen
FOREIGN INTRIGUE(1956), ed; SEVENTH SEAL, THE(1958, Swed.), ed; DEVIL'S
WANTON, THE(1962, Swed.), ed; MAKE WAY FOR LILA(1962, Swed./Ger.), ed;
NIGHT IS MY FUTURE(1962, Swed.), ed; NO TIME TO KILL(1963, Brit./Swed./Ger.),
ed; SWEDISH MISTRESS, THE(1964, Swed.), ed; TO LOVE(1964, Swed.), ed; DEAR
JOHN(1966, Swed.), ed; LOVE MATES(1967, Swed.), ed; SHORT IS THE SUM-
MER(1968, Swed.), ed
Sigurd Wallen
COUNT OF THE MONK'S BRIDGE, THE(1934, Swed.), a, d; SWEDEN-
HIELMS(1935, Swed.); WOMAN'S FACE, A(1939, Swed.); NIGHT IN JUNE, A(1940,
Swed.); JOHANSSON GETS SCOLDED(1945, Swed.), a, d; CRIME AND PUNISH-
MENT(1948, Swed.)
Jose Wallenstein
IN THE WHITE CITY(1983, Switz./Portugal)

Alfred Waller
OLD MOTHER RILEY, HEADMISTRESS(1950, Brit.)
Brad Alan Waller
TAKE THIS JOB AND SHOVE IT(1981)
David Waller
WORK IS A FOUR LETTER WORD(1968, Brit.); PERFECT FRIDAY(1970, Brit.)
E. Lewis Waller
Silents
RUNNING WATER(1922, Brit.)
Ed Waller
CINDERELLA SWINGS IT(1942); LADY ON A TRAIN(1945)
Eddie Waller
RETURN OF THE CISCO KID(1939); BANDIT TRAIL, THE(1941); UP IN ARMS(1944); ABILENE TOWN(1946)
Eddie C. Waller
POPPY(1936); GRAPES OF WRATH(1940)
Eddy Waller
BANJO ON MY KNEE(1936); MEET NERO WOLFE(1936); RHYTHM ON THE RANGE(1936); CALL THE MESQUITEERS(1938); STATE POLICE(1938); STRANGE FACES(1938); JESSE JAMES(1939); KONGA, THE WILD STALLION(1939); LEGION OF LOST FLYERS(1939); MUTINY ON THE BLACKHAWK(1939); NEW FRONTIER(1939); ROUGH RIDERS' ROUNDUP(1939); STAND UP AND FIGHT(1939); DEVIL'S PIPELINE, THE(1940); ENEMY AGENT(1940); GOLD RUSH MAISIE(1940); LEGION OF THE LAWLESS(1940); LOVE, HONOR AND OH, BABY(1940); SANTA FE TRAIL(1940); STAGECOACH WAR(1940); TEXAS TERRORS(1940); TWENTY MULE TEAM(1940); YOU'RE NOT SO TOUGH(1940); DON'T GET PERSONAL(1941); DOUBLE DATE(1941); HONKY TONK(1941); IN OLD COLORADO(1941); PUBLIC ENEMIES(1941); SON OF DAVY CROCKETT, THE(1941); WESTERN UNION(1941); JUKE GIRL(1942); MY GAL SAL(1942); NIGHT MONSTER(1942); SCATTERGOOD SURVIVES A MURDER(1942); SHUT MY BIG MOUTH(1942); SIN TOWN(1942); SUNDOWN JIM(1942); DESTROYER(1943); FRONTIER BADMEN(1943); HANGMEN ALSO DIE(1943); HEADIN' FOR GOD'S COUNTRY(1943); KANSAN, THE(1943); LADY TAKES A CHANCE, A(1943); MY KINGDOM FOR A COOK(1943); SILVER SPURS(1943); HOME IN INDIANA(1944); MAN FROM FRISCO(1944); MUMMY'S GHOST, THE(1944); RATIONING(1944); TALL IN THE SADDLE(1944); DAKOTA(1945); MAN WHO WALKED ALONE, THE(1945); MISSING CORPSE, THE(1945); ROUGH RIDERS OF CHEYENNE(1945); SAN ANTONIO(1945); UNDER WESTERN SKIES(1945); AVALANCHE(1946); IN OLD SACRAMENTO(1946); LITTLE GIANT(1946); LOVER COME BACK(1946); MAGNIFICENT DOLL(1946); PLAINSMAN AND THE LADY(1946); RENEGADES(1946); RUSTLER'S ROUNDUP(1946); SING WHILE YOU DANCE(1946); SUN VALLEY CYCLONE(1946); BANDITS OF DARK CANYON(1947); LOUISIANA(1947); MAGIC TOWN(1947); MILLERSON CASE, THE(1947); NIGHTMARE ALLEY(1947); PURSUED(1947); SEA OF GRASS, THE(1947); WILD FRONTIER, THE(1947); WYOMING(1947); BOLD FRONTIERSMAN, THE(1948); CARSON CITY RAIDERS(1948); DENVER KID, THE(1948); DESPERADOES OF DODGE CITY(1948); GIRL FROM MANHATTAN(1948); MARSHAL OF AMARILLO(1948); RENEGADES OF SONORA(1948); RETURN OF THE WHISTLER, THE(1948); STRAWBERRY ROAN, THE(1948); SUNDOWN IN SANTA FE(1948); WHISPERING SMITH(1948); BANDIT KING OF TEXAS(1949); DEATH VALLEY GUNFIGHTER(1949); FRONTIER INVESTIGATOR(1949); LUST FOR GOLD(1949); MASSACRE RIVER(1949); NAVAJO TRAIL RAIDERS(1949); POWDER RIVER RUSTLERS(1949); SHERIFF OF WICHITA(1949); WYOMING BANDIT, THE(1949); CALIFORNIA PASSAGE(1950); CODE OF THE SILVER SAGE(1950); COVERED WAGON RAID(1950); FATHER IS A BACHELOR(1950); FRISCO TORNADO(1950); GUNMEN OF ABILENE(1950); HE'S A COCKEYED WONDER(1950); RUSTLERS ON HORSEBACK(1950); SALT LAKE RAIDERS(1950); TRAVELING SALESWOMAN(1950); VIGILANTE HIDEOUT(1950); CAVALRY SCOUT(1951); INDIAN UPRISING(1951); BLACK HILLS AMBUSH(1952); DESPERADOES OUTPOST(1952); LEADVILLE GUNSLINGER(1952); MONTANA TERRITORY(1952); THUNDERING CARAVANS(1952); BANDITS OF THE WEST(1953); CHAMP FOR A DAY(1953); EL PASO STAMPEDE(1953); IT HAPPENS EVERY THURSDAY(1953); LAST POSSE, THE(1953); MARSHAL OF CEDAR ROCK(1953); SAVAGE FRONTIER(1953); 99 RIVER STREET(1953); MAKE HASTE TO LIVE(1954); FOXFIRE(1955); MAN FROM LARAMIE, THE(1955); PHANTOM STAGECOACH, THE(1957); RESTLESS BREED, THE(1957); DAY OF THE BAD MAN(1958)
Eddy C. Waller
TWO BRIGHT BOYS(1939); MAN FROM MONTREAL, THE(1940); LONE STAR RANGER(1942); MICHIGAN KID, THE(1947); WILD HARVEST(1947); BLACK BART(1948); RIVER LADY(1948); SECRET BEYOND THE DOOR, THE(1948); MA AND PA KETTLE(1949); FURIES, THE(1950); FAR COUNTRY, THE(1955); MAN WITHOUT A STAR(1955); NIGHT RUNNER, THE(1957)
Edward Waller
SMALL TOWN BOY(1937); SWEETHEART OF THE NAVY(1937); CURTAIN CALL AT CACTUS CREEK(1950)
Elizabeth Waller
FOR YOUR EYES ONLY(1981), cos
Elsie Waller
HOT SPELL(1958)
Fats Waller
HOORAY FOR LOVE(1935); KING OF BURLESQUE(1936); STORMY WEATHER(1943); ERASERHEAD(1978), m
Fred Waller
Silents
GRIT(1924), ph
Fred Waller, Jr.
Silents
CRADLE BUSTER, THE(1922), p, ph; SECOND FIDDLE(1923), ph
Garry Waller
RAIDERS OF THE LOST ARK(1981), anim
Gerard Waller
TASK FORCE(1949)
Gordon Waller
LOLA(1971, Brit./Ital.)
J. Wallett Waller
Silents
MESSAGE FROM MARS, A(1913, Brit.), d&w
Kenneth Waller
ROOM AT THE TOP(1959, Brit.); CHITTY CHITTY BANG BANG(1968, Brit.)

Misc. Talkies
LOVE PILL, THE(1971)
Leslie Waller
HIDE IN PLAIN SIGHT(1980), w
Lewis Waller
Silents
FIRES OF FATE(1923, Brit.), w
Misc. Silents
BRIGADIER GERARD(1915, Brit.)
Louis Waller
Silents
MONSIEUR BEAUCAIRE(1924)
Marianne Waller
ODETTE(1951, Brit.)
Nancy Lewis Waller
Misc. Silents
MILL-OWNER'S DAUGHTER, THE(1916, Brit.)
Ossie Waller
DYNAMITERS, THE(1956, Brit.)
Peggy Waller
VOICES(1979)
Rani Waller
MIXED DOUBLES(1933, Brit.); THIRD CLUE, THE(1934, Brit.); CHILDREN OF THE FOG(1935, Brit.); FLAME IN THE HEATHER(1935, Brit.); BEHIND YOUR BACK(1937, Brit.); FIRST NIGHT(1937, Brit.); MURDER IN THE FAMILY(1938, Brit.); MURDER TOMORROW(1938, Brit.)
Tod Waller
FIND THE LADY(1936, Brit.), w; UNDER PROOF(1936, Brit.), w
Wallett Waller
Misc. Silents
VAGABOND'S REVENGE, A(1915, Brit.), d
Gregory Wallerstein
VIOLENT AND THE DAMNED, THE(1962, Braz.), p
Norman Wallerstein
DR. MINX(1975), ed
Rose Wallerstein
CANTOR'S SON, THE(1937)
Adrian Wallet
MARK OF CAIN, THE(1948, Brit.)
Jacques Wallet
LA GUERRE EST FINIE(1967, Fr./Swed.)
Deborah Walley
GIDGET GOES HAWAIIAN(1961); BON VOYAGE(1962); SUMMER MAGIC(1963); YOUNG LOVERS, THE(1964); BEACH BLANKET BINGO(1965); DR. GOLDFOOT AND THE BIKINI MACHINE(1965); SKI PARTY(1965); GHOST IN THE INVISIBLE BIKINI(1966); SPINOUT(1966); BUBBLE, THE(1967); IT'S A BIKINI WORLD(1967); BENJI(1974)
Misc. Talkies
CRAWLING ARM, THE(1973); SEVERED ARM(1973)
Moira Walley
1984
RUNAWAY(1984)
Norma Walley
Silents
CRIMSON CIRCLE, THE(1922, Brit.)
Gann Wallgren
CRIME AND PUNISHMENT(1948, Swed.)
Gunn Wallgren
FANNY AND ALEXANDER(1983, Swed./Fr./Ger.)
Pernilla Wallgren
FANNY AND ALEXANDER(1983, Swed./Fr./Ger.)
Marco Walli
DOWNHILL RACER(1969)
Joseph Wallikas
WAVELENGTH(1983), spec eff
Arne Wallin
DEAR JOHN(1966, Swed.), m
Seppo Wallin
MAKE LIKE A THIEF(1966, Fin.)
Jonathan Walling
STUDENT BODIES(1981)
Mike Walling
PIRATES OF PENZANCE, THE(1983)
1984
SCANDALOUS(1984)
Richard Walling
Silents
'MARRIAGE LICENSE?'(1926); RETURN OF PETER GRIMM, THE(1926); SLAVES OF BEAUTY(1927); STAGE MADNESS(1927); HEAD OF THE FAMILY, THE(1928); WALKING BACK(1928); SILKS AND SADDLES(1929)
Misc. Silents
MIDNIGHT KISS, THE(1926); SHANGHAI ROSE(1929)
Will Walling
JAZZ SINGER, THE(1927); DARK STREETS(1929); KISMET(1930); PAINTED DESERT, THE(1931)
Silents
KILLER, THE(1921); SIREN CALL, THE(1922); NORTH OF HUDSON BAY(1923); IRON HORSE, THE(1924); NELLIE, THE BEAUTIFUL CLOAK MODEL(1924); HIS MASTER'S VOICE(1925); RANGER OF THE BIG PINES(1925); WHISPERING SMITH(1926); KING OF KINGS(1927)
Misc. Silents
HIS BACK AGAINST THE WALL(1922); LITTLE ROBINSON CRUSOE(1924); GENTLE CYCLONE, THE(1926); DEVIL'S SADDLE, THE(1927)
Will R. Walling
Silents
CRIMSON CHALLENGE, THE(1922); NORTH OF THE RIO GRANDE(1922); WHILE SATAN SLEEPS(1922); ABYSMAL BRUTE, THE(1923); NOBODY'S MONEY(1923); PRINCESS FROM HOBOKEN, THE(1927)

Misc. Silents
HARVESTER, THE(1927)
William Walling
WELCOME DANGER(1929); DERELICT(1930); MOBY DICK(1930); RANGE FEUD, THE(1931); RIDERS OF THE NORTH(1931); TWO-FISTED JUSTICE(1931); HIGH SPEED(1932); RIDIN' FOR JUSTICE(1932)
Silents
MAKING THE GRADE(1921); GREAT K & A TRAIN ROBBERY, THE(1926); WOMANPOWER(1926); NOOSE, THE(1928)
Misc. Silents
VILLAGE BLACKSMITH, THE(1922); TEMPLE OF VENUS, THE(1923); SIR LUMBERJACK(1926)
Jimmy Wallington
HOLLYWOOD STADIUM MYSTERY(1938); START CHEERING(1938); JOE PALOOKA IN TRIPLE CROSS(1951)
Bertram Wallis
WANDERING JEW, THE(1935, Brit.); CHIPS(1938. Brit.); SHIPBUILDERS, THE(1943, Brit.); TWILIGHT HOUR(1944, Brit.)
Bill Wallis
ROMANTIC ENGLISHWOMAN, THE(1975, Brit./Fr.)
Edwin B. Wallis
CRISIS(1950), set d
Erwin B. Wallis
DR. JEKYLL AND MR. HYDE(1941), set d
Hal Wallis
LITTLE CAESAR(1931), p; I AM A FUGITIVE FROM A CHAIN GANG(1932), p; MAN WANTED(1932), p; MATCH KING, THE(1932), p; MISS PINKERTON(1932), p; ONE WAY PASSAGE(1932), p; STRANGE LOVE OF MOLLY LOUVAIN, THE(1932), p; THEY CALL IT SIN(1932), p; TWO SECONDS(1932), p; GRAND SLAM(1933), p; KEYHOLE, THE(1933), p; LAWYER MAN(1933), p; MIND READER, THE(1933), p; NARROW CORNER, THE(1933), p; CONFESSION(1937), p; BROTHER ORCHID(1940), p; MALTESE FALCON, THE(1941), p; IN THIS OUR LIFE(1942), p; AFFAIRS OF SUSAN(1945), p; MY FRIEND IRMA(1949), p; MY FRIEND IRMA GOES WEST(1950), p; SCARED STIFF(1953), p; HOLLYWOOD OR BUST(1956), p; DON'T GIVE UP THE SHIP(1959), p; G.I. BLUES(1960), p; FUN IN ACAPULCO(1963), p; PARADISE, HAWAIIAN STYLE(1966), p; BAREFOOT IN THE PARK(1967), p
Hal B. Wallis
SCARLET DAWN(1932), p; STREET OF WOMEN(1932), p; CAPTURED(1933), p; CENTRAL AIRPORT(1933), p; MARY STEVENS, M.D.(1933), p; CAPTAIN BLOOD(1935), p; GOLD DIGGERS OF 1937(1936), p; ANOTHER DAWN(1937), p; BACK IN CIRCULATION(1937), p; CALL IT A DAY(1937), p; EVER SINCE EVE(1937), p; FIRST LADY(1937), p; GO-GETTER, THE(1937), p; GOD'S COUNTRY AND THE WOMAN(1937), p; GREEN LIGHT(1937), p; HOLLYWOOD HOTEL(1937), p; IT'S LOVE I'M AFTER(1937), p; KID GALAHAD(1937), p; LIFE OF EMILE ZOLA, THE(1937), p; MARRY THE GIRL(1937), p; PERFECT SPECIMEN, THE(1937), p; PRINCE AND THE PAUPER, THE(1937), p; SLIM(1937), p; STOLEN HOLIDAY(1937), p; ADVENTURES OF ROBIN HOOD, THE(1938), p; BOY MEETS GIRL(1938), p; DAWN PATROL, THE(1938), p; FOUR DAUGHTERS(1938), p; FOUR'S A CROWD(1938), p; GOLD IS WHERE YOU FIND IT(1938), p; HARD TO GET(1938), p; JEZEBEL(1938), p; LOVE, HONOR AND BEHAVE(1938), p; SISTERS, THE(1938), p; SLIGHT CASE OF MURDER, A(1938), p; SWING YOUR LADY(1938), p; WHITE BANNERS(1938), p; DARK VICTORY(1939), p; DAUGHTERS COURAGEOUS(1939), p; FOUR WIVES(1939), p; GOING PLACES(1939), p; JUAREZ(1939), p; OLD MAID, THE(1939), p; PRIVATE LIVES OF ELIZABETH AND ESSEX, THE(1939), p; ROARING TWENTIES, THE(1939), p; THEY MADE ME A CRIMINAL(1939), p; YES, MY DARLING DAUGHTER(1939), p; ALL THIS AND HEAVEN TOO(1940), p; DISPATCH FROM REUTERS, A(1940), p; DR. EHRLICH'S MAGIC BULLET(1940), p; KNUTE ROCKNE–ALL AMERICAN(1940), p; NO TIME FOR COMEDY(1940), p; SANTA FE TRAIL(1940), p; SATURDAY'S CHILDREN(1940), p; SEA HAWK, THE(1940), p; 'TIL WE MEET AGAIN(1940), p; AFFECTIONATELY YOURS(1941), p; BRIDE CAME C.O.D., THE(1941), p; DIVE BOMBER(1941), p; GREAT LIE, THE(1941), p; MILLION DOLLAR BABY(1941), p; NAVY BLUES(1941), p; ONE FOOT IN HEAVEN(1941), p; OUT OF THE FOG(1941), p; SEA WOLF, THE(1941), p; STRAWBERRY BLONDE, THE(1941), p; UNDERGROUND(1941), p; ALL THROUGH THE NIGHT(1942), p; CAPTAINS OF THE CLOUDS(1942), p; CASABLANCA(1942), p; DESPERATE JOURNEY(1942), p; JUKE GIRL(1942), p; KING'S ROW(1942), p; LARCENY, INC.(1942), p; MALE ANIMAL, THE(1942), p; MAN WHO CAME TO DINNER, THE(1942), p; NOW, VOYAGER(1942), p; THEY DIED WITH THEIR BOOTS ON(1942), p; YANKEE DOODLE DANDY(1942), p; AIR FORCE(1943), p; PRINCESS O'ROURKE(1943), p; THIS IS THE ARMY(1943), p; WATCH ON THE RHINE(1943), p; PASSAGE TO MARSEILLE(1944), p; LOVE LETTERS(1945), p; SARATOGA TRUNK(1945), p; YOU CAME ALONG(1945), p; PERFECT MARRIAGE, THE(1946), p; SEARCHING WIND, THE(1946), p; STRANGE LOVE OF MARTHA IVERS, THE(1946), p; DESERT FURY(1947), p; I WALK ALONE(1948), p; SO EVIL MY LOVE(1948, Brit.), p; SORRY, WRONG NUMBER(1948), p; ACCUSED, THE(1949), p; ROPE OF SAND(1949), p; DARK CITY(1950), p; FILE ON THELMA JORDAN, THE(1950), p; FURIES, THE(1950), p; PAID IN FULL(1950), p; SEPTEMBER AFFAIR(1950), p; PEKING EXPRESS(1951), p; RED MOUNTAIN(1951), p; SAILOR BEWARE(1951), p; THAT'S MY BOY(1951), p; COME BACK LITTLE SHEBA(1952), p; JUMPING JACKS(1952), p; STOOGE, THE(1952), p; MONEY FROM HOME(1953), p; ABOUT MRS. LESLIE(1954), p; THREE RING CIRCUS(1954), p; ARTISTS AND MODELS(1955), p; ROSE TATTOO, THE(1955), p; RAINMAKER, THE(1956), p; GUNFIGHT AT THE O.K. CORRAL(1957), p; LOVING YOU(1957), p; SAD SACK, THE(1957), p; WILD IS THE WIND(1957), p; HOT SPELL(1958), p; KING CREOLE(1958), p; LAST TRAIN FROM GUN HILL(1959), p; VISIT TO A SMALL PLANET(1960), p; ALL IN A NIGHT'S WORK(1961), p; BLUE HAWAII(1961), p; SUMMER AND SMOKE(1961), p; GIRLS! GIRLS! GIRLS!(1962), p; WIVES AND LOVERS(1963), p; BECKET(1964, Brit.), p; ROUSTABOUT(1964), p; BOEING BOEING(1965), p; SONS OF KATIE ELDER, THE(1965), p; EASY COME, EASY GO(1967), p; FIVE CARD STUD(1968), p; ANNE OF THE THOUSAND DAYS(1969, Brit.), p; TRUE GRIT(1969), p; NORWOOD(1970), p; MARY, QUEEN OF SCOTS(1971, Brit.), p; RED SKY AT MORNING(1971), p; SHOOT OUT(1971), p; PUBLIC EYE, THE(1972, Brit.), p; DON IS DEAD, THE(1973), p; NELSON AFFAIR, THE(1973, Brit.), p; ROOSTER COGBURN(1975), p
J.H. Wallis
WOMAN IN THE WINDOW, THE(1945), w; STRANGE BARGAIN(1949), w
Jack Wallis
GET CARTER(1971, Brit.), spec eff

Jacqueline Wallis
KISS OF EVIL(1963, Brit.); BEAUTY JUNGLE, THE(1966, Brit.)
Kit Wallis
MY BLOODY VALENTINE(1981, Can.), ed
Milton Wallis
CHEATING BLONDES(1933)
Pat Wallis
BLACK JACK(1979, Brit.)
Peter Wallis
DRACULA(1979)
Ray Wallis
OUT OF THE BLUE(1982)
Rodger Wallis
LOVING COUPLES(1966, Swed.), m
Shani Wallis
EXTRA DAY, THE(1956, Brit.); RAMSBOTTOM RIDES AGAIN(1956, Brit.); OLIVER!(1968, Brit.); ARNOLD(1973); TERROR IN THE WAX MUSEUM(1973)
Margherita Wallman
AIDA(1954, Ital.), ch
Marguerite Wallmann
ANNA KARENINA(1935), ch
Hans Wallner
JOHNNY STEALS EUROPE(1932, Ger.)
Herman Wallner
KISS OF THE TARANTULA(1975)
Martha Wallner
CASTLE, THE(1969, Ger.)
Max Wallner
LAST WALTZ, THE(1936, Brit.), w; ONE NIGHT IN PARIS(1940, Brit.), w
Franz Wallner-Baste
COURT CONCERT, THE(1936, Ger.), w
Rev. A. Mark Wallock
LAWTON STORY, THE(1949), w; PRINCE OF PEACE, THE(1951), w
Edwin Wallock
Silents
PRICE MARK, THE(1917); GREEN FLAME, THE(1920); ACE OF HEARTS, THE(1921); STRUGGLE, THE(1921); HUNCHBACK OF NOTRE DAME, THE(1923)
Misc. Silents
BING BANG BOOM(1922)
Michael Wallon
LIGHTNING STRIKES WEST(1940)
Douglas Wallop
DAMN YANKEES(1958), w
Marvin Wallowitz
HELL SQUAD(1958), ed; TRUCK STOP WOMEN(1974), ed; BELL JAR, THE(1979), ed
Blanche Walls
Misc. Silents
RESURRECTION(1912)
Bud Walls
HONKERS, THE(1972); WHAT'S UP, DOC?(1972)
Byron Walls
1984
STARMAN(1984)
Joe Walls
ABBOTT AND COSTELLO MEET FRANKENSTEIN(1948)
Thomas Walls
WELCOME TO L.A.(1976), ed; REMEMBER MY NAME(1978), ed
Tom Walls
CANARIES SOMETIMES SING(1930, Brit.), a, d; ON APPROVAL(1930, Brit.), a, d; ONE EMBARRASSING NIGHT(1930, Brit.), a, d; PLUNDER(1931, Brit.), a, d; TONS OF MONEY(1931, Brit.), d; LEAP YEAR(1932, Brit.), a, d; NIGHT LIKE THIS, A(1932, Brit.), a, d, w; THARK(1932, Brit.), a, d; BLARNEY KISS(1933, Brit.), a, d; CUCKOO IN THE NEST, THE(1933, Brit.), a, d; TURKEY TIME(1933, Brit.), a, d; CUP OF KINDNESS, A(1934, Brit.), a, d; DIRTY WORK(1934, Brit.), a, d; LADY IN DANGER(1934, Brit.), a, d; LEAVE IT TO SMITH(1934), a, d; FIGHTING STOCK(1935, Brit.), a, d; FOREIGN AFFAIRES(1935, Brit.), a, d; ME AND MARLBOROUGH(1935, Brit.); STORMY WEATHER(1935, Brit.), a, d; DISHONOR BRIGHT(1936, Brit.), a, d; POT LUCK(1936, Brit.), a, d; FOR VALOR(1937, Brit.), a, d; SECOND BEST BED(1937, Brit.), a, d; MAN WITH 100 FACES, THE(1938, Brit.); OLD IRON(1938, Brit.), a, p&d; STRANGE BOARDERS(1938, Brit.); UNDERGROUND GUERRILLAS(1944, Brit.); HALF-WAY HOUSE, THE(1945, Brit.); THEY MET IN THE DARK(1945, Brit.); JOHNNY FRENCHMAN(1946, Brit.); THIS MAN IS MINE(1946 Brit.); LADY SURRENDERS, A(1947, Brit.); MASTER OF BANKDAM, THE(1947, Brit.); WHILE I LIVE(1947, Brit.); INTERRUPTED JOURNEY, THE(1949, Brit.); SPRING IN PARK LANE(1949, Brit.); MAYTIME IN MAYFAIR(1952, Brit.); SKID KIDS(1953, Brit.); I ESCAPED FROM DEVIL'S ISLAND(1973), ed; ROADIE(1980), ed; ENDANGERED SPECIES(1982), ed; T.A.G.: THE ASSASSINATION GAME(1982), ed
1984
GIMME AN 'F'(1984), ed; ICE PIRATES, THE(1984), ed
Tom Walls, Jr.
GHOSTS OF BERKELEY SQUARE(1947, Brit.); SPRING IN PARK LANE(1949, Brit.); GALLOPING MAJOR, THE(1951, Brit.); FOUR AGAINST FATE(1952, Brit.); MAYTIME IN MAYFAIR(1952, Brit.); HIGH RISK(1981), ed
Will Walls
THIRTY SECONDS OVER TOKYO(1944)
Robert Wallsten
SOAK THE RICH(1936)
Clara Wallucks
Silents
MERRY WIDOW, THE(1925)
John Wallwork
GUNFIGHT, A(1971)
William Wally
Silents
CAPPY RICKS(1921)
Leo Walmesley
BREAKERS AHEAD(1938, Brit.), w

Luis Walmo
TERRACE, THE(1964, Arg.)
Anna Walmsley
REVENGE OF FRANKENSTEIN, THE(1958, Brit.)
Bryce Walmsley
1984
RAZORBACK(1984, Aus.), prod d
Fred Walmsley
DODGING THE DOLE(1936, Brit.)
John Walmsley
ONE AND ONLY GENUINE ORIGINAL FAMILY BAND, THE(1968)
Leo Walmsley
TURN OF THE TIDE(1935, Brit.), w
Peter Walmsley
1984
PLOUGHMAN'S LUNCH, THE(1984, Brit.)
Dustin Waln
GAS(1981, Can.); VISITING HOURS(1982, Can.)
Sven Walnum
YOUNG SINNER, THE(1965), ph; BURY ME AN ANGEL(1972), ph
Marvin Walowitz
BROTHERHOOD OF SATAN, THE(1971), ed
Cecily Walper
NAUGHTY ARLETTE(1951, Brit.); FOUR AGAINST FATE(1952, Brit.)
Cicely Walper
NOTORIOUS LANDLADY, THE(1962)
Hugh Walpole
DAVID COPPERFIELD(1935), a, w; KIND LADY(1935), w; VANESSA, HER LOVE STORY(1935), w; LITTLE LORD FAUNTLEROY(1936), w; MR. PERRIN AND MR. TRAILL(1948, Brit.), w; KIND LADY(1951), w
Irene Walpole
YOU'RE NEVER TOO YOUNG(1955)
Stanley Walpole
Silents
OTHER MAN, THE(1918); FORTUNE'S CHILD(1919); IN WALKED MARY(1920); WOMAN'S BUSINESS, A(1920); DEVIL'S PARTNER, THE(1923)
Misc. Silents
GIRL WHO DIDN'T THINK, THE(1917); LIAR, THE(1918); TRAIL OF THE CIGARETTE, THE(1920)
Ranson Walrod
DEATH WISH II(1982)
Helen Walron
Silents
HUNTRESS, THE(1923)
Holga Walrow
THIRD MAN, THE(1950, Brit.)
Franz Walsch
WHY DOES HERR R. RUN AMOK?(1977, Ger.), ed; DESPAIR(1978, Ger.), ed; LILI MARLEEN(1981, Ger.), ed; QUERELLE(1983, Ger./Fr.), ed
Franz Walsch [Fassbinder]
MARRIAGE OF MARIA BRAUN, THE(1979, Ger.), ed
John Walsch
SIEGE(1983, Can.), p
Franzisca Walser
GERMANY IN AUTUMN(1978, Ger.)
Adam Walsh
SPIRIT OF NOTRE DAME, THE(1931)
Anitra Walsh
MARK OF THE WITCH(1970); DEALING: OR THE BERKELEY-TO-BOSTON FORTY-BRICK LOST-BAG BLUES(1971)
Anthony Walsh
DOUBLE STOP(1968)
Arthur Walsh
BLONDE FEVER(1944); TWO GIRLS AND A SAILOR(1944); THEY WERE EXPENDABLE(1945); THIS MAN'S NAVY(1945); TWICE BLESSED(1945), ch; WHAT NEXT, CORPORAL HARGROVE?(1945); ZIEGFELD FOLLIES(1945); COURAGE OF LASSIE(1946); MY DARLING CLEMENTINE(1946); NO LEAVE, NO LOVE(1946); SARGE GOES TO COLLEGE(1947); ON AN ISLAND WITH YOU(1948); YOU GOTTA STAY HAPPY(1948); FLAME OF YOUTH(1949); LITTLE WOMEN(1949); GUNMEN OF ABILENE(1950); MR. IMPERIUM(1951); STREET BANDITS(1951); LADY WANTS MINK, THE(1953); THREE SAILORS AND A GIRL(1953); LAST HURRAH, THE(1958); BATTLE CRY(1959)
Bailie Walsh
1984
SUPERGIRL(1984)
Bill Walsh
DAVY CROCKETT, KING OF THE WILD FRONTIER(1955), p; LITTLEST OUTLAW, THE(1955), w; DAVY CROCKETT AND THE RIVER PIRATES(1956), p; WESTWARD HO THE WAGONS!(1956), p; FLAMING FRONTIER(1958, Can.); SHAGGY DOG, THE(1959), p, w; TOBY TYLER(1960), p, w; ABSENT-MINDED PROFESSOR, THE(1961), w; BON VOYAGE(1962), w; SON OF FLUBBER(1963), p, w; MARY POPPINS(1964), p, w; MISADVENTURES OF MERLIN JONES, THE(1964), w; MONKEY'S UNCLE, THE(1965), w; THAT DARN CAT(1965), p, w; LT. ROBIN CRUSOE, U.S.N.(1966), p, w; BLACKBEARD'S GHOST(1968), p, w; LOVE BUG, THE(1968), p, w; BEDKNOBS AND BROOMSTICKS(1971), p, w; SCANDALOUS JOHN(1971), p, w; WORLD'S GREATEST ATHLETE, THE(1973), p; HERBIE RIDES AGAIN(1974), p, w; ONE OF OUR DINOSAURS IS MISSING(1975, Brit.), p, w
Brian Walsh
WONDERWALL(1969, Brit.)
Christy Walsh
SPIRIT OF NOTRE DAME, THE(1931), w
Chuck Walsh
FOUL PLAY(1978)
Dale Walsh
NEW ADVENTURES OF TARZAN(1935); TARZAN AND THE GREEN GODDESS(1938)
David Walsh
LORD OF THE FLIES(1963, Brit.); EVEL KNIEVEL(1971), ph; CORKY(1972), ph; CLEOPATRA JONES(1973), ph; LAUGHING POLICEMAN, THE(1973), ph; WHIFFS(1975), ph; JUST YOU AND ME, KID(1979), ph

David M. Walsh
I WALK THE LINE(1970), ph; MONTE WALSH(1970), ph; GUNFIGHT, A(1971), ph; EVERYTHING YOU ALWAYS WANTED TO KNOW ABOUT SEX, BUT WE'RE AFRAID TO ASK(1972), ph; ACE ELI AND RODGER OF THE SKIES(1973), ph; SLEEPER(1973), ph; CRAZY WORLD OF JULIUS VROODER, THE(1974), ph; OTHER SIDE OF THE MOUNTAIN, THE(1975), ph; SUNSHINE BOYS, THE(1975), ph; MURDER BY DEATH(1976), ph; SILVER STREAK(1976), ph; W.C. FIELDS AND ME(1976), ph; GOODBYE GIRL, THE(1977), ph; ROLLERCOASTER(1977), ph; SCOTT JOPLIN(1977), ph; CALIFORNIA SUITE(1978), ph; FOUL PLAY(1978), ph; HOUSE CALLS(1978), ph; CHAPTER TWO(1979), ph; IN-LAWS, THE(1979), ph; HERO AT LARGE(1980), ph; PRIVATE BENJAMIN(1980), ph; SEEMS LIKE OLD TIMES(1980), ph; ONLY WHEN I LAUGH(1981), ph; I OUGHT TO BE IN PICTURES(1982), ph; MAKING LOVE(1982), ph; MAX DUGAN RETURNS(1983), ph; ROMANTIC COMEDY(1983), ph
1984
COUNTRY(1984), ph; JOHNNY DANGEROUSLY(1984), ph; TEACHERS(1984), ph; UNFAITHFULLY YOURS(1984), ph
Dermot Walsh
UNDERCOVER AGENT(1935, Brit.); HUNGRY HILL(1947, Brit.); JASSY(1948, Brit.); MARK OF CAIN, THE(1948, Brit.); MY SISTER AND I(1948, Brit.); PAPER GALLOWS(1950, Brit.); THIRD TIME LUCKY(1950, Brit.); FRIGHTENED MAN, THE(1952, Brit.); BLUE PARROT, THE(1953, Brit.); FLOATING DUTCHMAN, THE(1953, Brit.); GHOST SHIP(1953, Brit.); STRAW MAN, THE(1953, Brit.); NIGHT OF THE FULL MOON, THE(1954, Brit.); BOND OF FEAR(1956, Brit.); HIDEOUT, THE(1956, Brit.); AT THE STROKE OF NINE(1957, Brit.); WOMAN OF MYSTERY, A(1957, Brit.); CHAIN OF EVENTS(1958, Brit.); BANDIT OF ZHOBE, THE(1959); CRASH DRIVE(1959, Brit.); CROWNING TOUCH, THE(1959, Brit.); SEA FURY(1959, Brit.); WITNESS, THE(1959, Brit.); IT TAKES A THIEF(1960, Brit.); BREAKING POINT, THE(1961, Brit.); MANIA(1961, Brit.); SHOOT TO KILL(1961, Brit.); TARNISHED HEROES(1961, Brit.); TRUNK, THE(1961, Brit.); DESERT PATROL(1962, Brit.); EMERGENCY(1962, Brit.); TELL-TALE HEART, THE(1962, Brit.); COOL MIKADO, THE(1963, Brit.); MURDER ON THE CAMPUS(1963, Brit.); SWITCH, THE(1963, Brit.); GREAT ARMORED CAR SWINDLE, THE(1964); MAKE MINE A MILLION(1965, Brit.); WICKED LADY, THE(1983, Brit.)
Dick Walsh
UNFAITHFUL, THE(1947); UNSUSPECTED, THE(1947); HELL SQUAD(1958)
Dickie Walsh
1984
RUNNING HOT(1984)
Edward Walsh
COUNT YORGA, VAMPIRE(1970); WHY RUSSIANS ARE REVOLTING(1970); RETURN OF COUNT YORGA, THE(1971); CALIFORNIA SPLIT(1974); HARD TIMES(1975)
Eugene Walsh
LAUGH YOUR BLUES AWAY(1943)
Frank Walsh
LOCAL HERO(1983, Brit.), art d
Silents
AMERICA(1924); JOY GIRL, THE(1927)
Gabriel Walsh
QUACKSER FORTUNE HAS A COUSIN IN THE BRONX(1970), w; NIGHT FLOWERS(1979), a, w; HEAVEN'S GATE(1980); RETURNING, THE(1983)
Dr. Darrell Walsh
THRESHOLD(1983, Can.)
Gene Walsh
Silents
SUPREME TEST, THE(1923)
George Walsh
ME AND MY GAL(1932); OUT OF SINGAPORE(1932); BLACK BEAUTY(1933); BOWERY, THE(1933); RETURN OF CASEY JONES(1933); BELLE OF THE NINETIES(1934); UNDER PRESSURE(1935); KLONDIKE ANNIE(1936); PUT ON THE SPOT(1936); RIO GRANDE ROMANCE(1936); PINTO RUSTLERS(1937)
Silents
INTOLERANCE(1916); MEDIATOR, THE(1916); SERPENT, THE(1916), a, w; HONOR SYSTEM, THE(1917); BRAVE AND BOLD(1918); JACK SPURLOCK, PRODIGAL(1918); LUCK AND PLUCK(1919); NEVER SAY QUIT(1919); WINNING STROKE, THE(1919); NUMBER 17(1920); MIRACLE MAKERS, THE(1923); RENO(1923); ROSITA(1923); SLAVE OF DESIRE(1923); SOULS FOR SALE(1923); BLUE BLOOD(1925); KICK-OFF, THE(1926); STRIVING FOR FORTUNE(1926)
Misc. Silents
BEAST, THE(1916); BLUE BLOOD AND RED(1916); BOOK AGENT, THE(1917); HIGH FINANCE(1917); ISLAND OF DESIRE, THE(1917); MELTING MILLIONS(1917); PRIDE OF NEW YORK, THE(1917); SOME BOY(1917); THIS IS THE LIFE(1917); YANKEE WAY, THE(1917); I'LL SAY SO(1918); KID IS CLEVER, THE(1918); ON THE JUMP(1918); HELP! HELP! POLICE!(1919); PUTTING ONE OVER(1919); DEAD LINE, THE(1920); FROM NOW ON(1920); MANHATTAN KNIGHT, A(1920); PLUNGER, THE(1920); SHARK, THE(1920); DYNAMITE ALLEN(1921); SERENADE(1921); VANITY FAIR(1923); AMERICAN PLUCK(1925); COUNT OF LUXEMBOURG, THE(1926); MAN OF QUALITY, A(1926); PRINCE OF BROADWAY, THE(1926); TEST OF DONALD NORTON, THE(1926); BACK TO LIBERTY(1927); BROADWAY DRIFTER, THE(1927); COMBAT(1927); HIS RISE TO FAME(1927); WINNING OAR, THE(1927); INSPIRATION(1928)
Gordon Walsh
SCREAM, BABY, SCREAM(1969)
Harry Walsh
WILD REBELS, THE(1967), ph
J. D. Walsh
Silents
MAN WHO PLAYED GOD, THE(1922); NO MOTHER TO GUIDE HER(1923)
J.T. Walsh
EDDIE MACON'S RUN(1983)
1984
HARD CHOICES(1984)
Jack Walsh
STORY OF ALEXANDER GRAHAM BELL, THE(1939); MONDO TRASHO(1970); EDUCATING RITA(1983)
James Walsh
DOUBLE-BARRELLED DETECTIVE STORY, THE(1965)

Jane Walsh
MAN WHO FOUND HIMSELF, THE(1937); ON AGAIN–OFF AGAIN(1937)

Jean Walsh
Silents
WEB OF THE LAW, THE(1923)
Misc. Silents
BELL BOY 13(1923)

Jessie May Walsh
Silents
PATCHWORK GIRL OF OZ, THE(1914)

Jim Walsh
STONE(1974, Aus.)

Jody Walsh
SECOND CHANCE(1953)

Joe Walsh
FAST TIMES AT RIDGEMONT HIGH(1982), m

Joey Walsh
JUGGLER, THE(1953); CAPTAIN NEWMAN, M.D.(1963); DRIVE, HE SAID(1971)

Joey [Joseph] Walsh
HANS CHRISTIAN ANDERSEN(1952)

John Walsh
PHANTOM OF THE OPERA(1943); DOUGHGIRLS, THE(1944); LOVE LAUGHS AT ANDY HARDY(1946); YOUNG SAVAGES, THE(1961); LORD OF THE FLIES(1963, Brit.); WARM IN THE BUD(1970), ph
1984
FRIDAY THE 13TH–THE FINAL CHAPTER(1984)

Johnny Walsh
KEEP 'EM SLUGGING(1943); MUG TOWN(1943); SLEEPY LAGOON(1943); YOUTH RUNS WILD(1944); MILDRED PIERCE(1945); LAWLESS EMPIRE(1946); WILD WOMEN OF WONGO, THE(1959)

Joseph Walsh
ANZIO(1968, Ital.); CALIFORNIA SPLIT(1974), a, p, w; DRIVER, THE(1978)

Joseph R. Walsh
POLTERGEIST(1982)

Judy Walsh
TAKE CARE OF MY LITTLE GIRL(1951); HALF-BREED, THE(1952); CAT WOMEN OF THE MOON(1953); CANNIBAL ATTACK(1954)

Katherine Walsh
CHASE, THE(1966); TRIP, THE(1967)

Kay Walsh
GET YOUR MAN(1934, Brit.); SMITH'S WIVES(1935, Brit.); ALL THAT GLITTERS(1936, Brit.); IF I WERE RICH(1936); SECRET OF STAMBOUL, THE(1936, Brit.); KEEP FIT(1937, Brit.); LAST ADVENTURERS, THE(1937, Brit.); LUCK OF THE IRISH, THE(1937, Ireland); I SEE ICE(1938); MEET MR. PENNY(1938, Brit.); ALL AT SEA(1939, Brit.); MIDDLE WATCH, THE(1939, Brit.); SONS OF THE SEA(1939, Brit.); CHINESE DEN, THE(1940, Brit.); MISSING PEOPLE, THE(1940, Brit.); MYSTERIOUS MR. REEDER, THE(1940, Brit.); SECOND MR. BUSH, THE(1940, Brit.); IN WHICH WE SERVE(1942, Brit.); THIS HAPPY BREED(1944, Brit.); GREAT EXPECTATIONS(1946, Brit.), w; OCTOBER MAN, THE(1948, Brit.); VICE VERSA(1948, Brit.); LAST HOLIDAY(1950, Brit.); MAGNET, THE(1950, Brit.); STAGE FRIGHT(1950, Brit.); OLIVER TWIST(1951, Brit.); MAGIC BOX, THE(1952, Brit.); STRANGER IN BETWEEN, THE(1952, Brit.); TONIGHT AT 8:30(1953, Brit.); YOUNG BESS(1953); LEASE OF LIFE(1954, Brit.); RAINBOW JACKET, THE(1954, Brit.); NOW AND FOREVER(1956, Brit.); CAST A DARK SHADOW(1958, Brit.); HORSE'S MOUTH, THE(1958, Brit.); TUNES OF GLORY(1960, Brit.); GREYFRIARS BOBBY(1961, Brit.); L-SHAPED ROOM, THE(1962, Brit.); LUNCH HOUR(1962, Brit.); REACH FOR GLORY(1963, Brit.); 80,000 SUSPECTS(1963, Brit.); CIRCUS WORLD(1964); BEAUTY JUNGLE, THE(1966, Brit.); HE WHO RIDES A TIGER(1966, Brit.); STUDY IN TERROR, A(1966, Brit./Ger.); DEVIL'S OWN, THE(1967, Brit.); TASTE OF EXCITEMENT(1969, Brit.); SCROOGE(1970, Brit.); VIRGIN AND THE GYPSY, THE(1970, Brit.); CONNECTING ROOMS(1971, Brit.); RULING CLASS, THE(1972, Brit.); DR. SYN, ALIAS THE SCARECROW(1975); NIGHT CROSSING(1982)
Misc. Talkies
BIKINI PARADISE(1967)

Lelia Walsh
MARA OF THE WILDERNESS(1966)

Leonard Walsh
BATTLE IN OUTER SPACE(1960)

M. Walsh
WILD WOMEN OF WONGO, THE(1959), ph

M. Emmet Walsh
ALICE'S RESTAURANT(1969); LITTLE BIG MAN(1970); TRAVELING EXECUTIONER, THE(1970); COLD TURKEY(1971); ESCAPE FROM THE PLANET OF THE APES(1971); THEY MIGHT BE GIANTS(1971); GET TO KNOW YOUR RABBIT(1972); WHAT'S UP, DOC?(1972); KID BLUE(1973); SERPICO(1973); GAMBLER, THE(1974); AT LONG LAST LOVE(1975); MIKEY AND NICKY(1976); NICKELODEON(1976); AIRPORT '77(1977); SLAP SHOT(1977); STRAIGHT TIME(1978); FISH THAT SAVED PITTSBURGH, THE(1979); JERK, THE(1979); ORDINARY PEOPLE(1980); RAISE THE TITANIC(1980, Brit.); BACK ROADS(1981); REDS(1981); BLADE RUNNER(1982); CANNERY ROW(1982); ESCAPE ARTIST, THE(1982); FAST-WALKING(1982); SILKWOOD(1983)
1984
BLOOD SIMPLE(1984); FLETCH(1984); GRANDVIEW, U.S.A.(1984); MISSING IN ACTION(1984); POPE OF GREENWICH VILLAGE, THE(1984); RAW COURAGE(1984); SCANDALOUS(1984)

Martin Walsh
1984
SACRED HEARTS(1984, Brit.), ed

Mary Joyce Walsh
THAT NIGHT IN RIO(1941)

Maurice Walsh
QUIET MAN, THE(1952), w; TROUBLE IN THE GLEN(1954, Brit.), w

Myonne Walsh
MR. SMITH GOES TO WASHINGTON(1939)

Neil Walsh
CHICAGO 70(1970)

Pat Walsh
WIZARD OF OZ, THE(1939); MY BLOODY VALENTINE(1981, Can.)

Paul Walsh
Misc. Talkies
REDNECK MILLER(1977)

Percy Walsh
BOAT FROM SHANGHAI(1931, Brit.), w; DIPLOMATIC LOVER, THE(1934, Brit.); GREEN PACK, THE(1934, Brit.); POWER(1934, Brit.); ADMIRALS ALL(1935, Brit.); BORN FOR GLORY(1935, Brit.); CASE OF GABRIEL PERRY, THE(1935, Brit.); CHECKMATE(1935, Brit.); DEATH DRIVES THROUGH(1935, Brit.); ME AND MARLBOROUGH(1935, Brit.); RIVER HOUSE MYSTERY, THE(1935, Brit.); ANNIE LAURIE(1936, Brit.); BOYS WILL BE BOYS(1936, Brit.); EDUCATED EVANS(1936, Brit.); KING OF THE DAMNED(1936, Brit.); DARK JOURNEY(1937, Brit.); KNIGHTS FOR A DAY(1937, Brit.); OH, MR. PORTER!(1937, Brit.); TAKE A CHANCE(1937, Brit.); GANG, THE(1938, Brit.); IT'S IN THE BLOOD(1938, Brit.); PRISONER OF CORBAL(1939, Brit.); LET GEORGE DO IT(1940, Brit.); OLD BILL AND SON(1940, Brit.); PASTOR HALL(1940, Brit.); SECRET FOUR, THE(1940, Brit.); TORSO MURDER MYSTERY, THE(1940, Brit.); COMMON TOUCH, THE(1941, Brit.); GIRL IN DISTRESS(1941, Brit.); MAIL TRAIN(1941, Brit.); MISSING TEN DAYS(1941, Brit.); PIMPERNEL SMITH(1942, Brit.); TALK ABOUT JACQUELINE(1942, Brit.); ADVENTURE IN BLACKMAIL(1943, Brit.); ADVENTURES OF TARTU(1943, Brit.); THURSDAY'S CHILD(1943, Brit.); SECRET MISSION(1944, Brit.); YANK IN LONDON, A(1946, Brit.); COURTNEY AFFAIR, THE(1947, Brit.); FAME IS THE SPUR(1947, Brit.); MEET ME AT DAWN(1947, Brit.); NOW BARABBAS WAS A ROBBER(1949, Brit.); OUTSIDER, THE(1949, Brit.); SCOTT OF THE ANTARCTIC(1949, Brit.); STOP PRESS GIRL(1949, Brit.); THIS WAS A WOMAN(1949, Brit.); DICK BARTON AT BAY(1950, Brit.); GOLDEN SALAMANDER(1950, Brit.); HAPPIEST DAYS OF YOUR LIFE(1950, Brit.); TRAIN OF EVENTS(1952, Brit.)

R.A. [Raoul] Walsh
Silents
KINDRED OF THE DUST(1922), d
Misc. Silents
CONQUEROR, THE(1917), d; LOST AND FOUND ON A SOUTH SEA ISLAND(1923), d

Raoul A. Walsh
Silents
HONOR SYSTEM, THE(1917), d&w; INNOCENT SINNER, THE(1917), d&w
Misc. Silents
THIS IS THE LIFE(1917), d

Raoul Walsh
COCK-EYED WORLD, THE(1929), d, w; IN OLD ARIZONA(1929), d; BIG TRAIL, THE(1930), d, w; HOT FOR PARIS(1930), d, w; MAN WHO CAME BACK, THE(1931), d; WOMEN OF ALL NATIONS(1931), d; YELLOW TICKET, THE(1931), d; ME AND MY GAL(1932), d; WILD GIRL(1932), d; BOWERY, THE(1933), d; SAILOR'S LUCK(1933), d; BABY FACE HARRINGTON(1935), d; EVERY NIGHT AT EIGHT(1935), d; UNDER PRESSURE(1935), d; BIG BROWN EYES(1936), d, w; KLONDIKE ANNIE(1936), d; SPENDTHRIFT(1936), d; ARTISTS AND MODELS(1937), d; HITTING A NEW HIGH(1937), d; WHEN THIEF MEETS THIEF(1937, Brit.), d; YOU'RE IN THE ARMY NOW(1937, Brit.), d; COLLEGE SWING(1938), d; ROARING TWENTIES, THE(1939), d; ST. LOUIS BLUES(1939), d; DARK COMMAND, THE(1940), d; THEY DRIVE BY NIGHT(1940), d; HIGH SIERRA(1941), d; MANPOWER(1941), d; STRAWBERRY BLONDE, THE(1941), d; DESPERATE JOURNEY(1942), d; GENTLEMAN JIM(1942), d; THEY DIED WITH THEIR BOOTS ON(1942), d; BACKGROUND TO DANGER(1943), d; NORTHERN PURSUIT(1943), d; UNCERTAIN GLORY(1944), d; HORN BLOWS AT MIDNIGHT, THE(1945), d; OBJECTIVE, BURMA!(1945), d; SALTY O'ROURKE(1945), d; MAN I LOVE, THE(1946), d; CHEYENNE(1947), d; PURSUED(1947), d; STALLION ROAD(1947), d; FIGHTER SQUADRON(1948), d; ONE SUNDAY AFTERNOON(1948), d; SILVER RIVER(1948), d; COLORADO TERRITORY(1949), d; IT'S A GREAT FEELING(1949); WHITE HEAT(1949), d; ALONG THE GREAT DIVIDE(1951), d; CAPTAIN HORATIO HORNBLOWER(1951, Brit.), d; DISTANT DRUMS(1951), d; ENFORCER, THE(1951), d; BLACKBEARD THE PIRATE(1952), d; GLORY ALLEY(1952), d; LAWLESS BREED, THE(1952), d; WORLD IN HIS ARMS, THE(1952), d; GUN FURY(1953), d; LION IS IN THE STREETS, A(1953), d; SEA DEVILS(1953), d; SASKATCHEWAN(1954), d; BATTLE FLAME(1955), p; TALL MEN, THE(1955), d; KING AND FOUR QUEENS, THE(1956), d; REVOLT OF MAMIE STOVER, THE(1956), d; BAND OF ANGELS(1957), d; NAKED AND THE DEAD, THE(1958), d; SHERIFF OF FRACTURED JAW, THE(1958, Brit.), d; PRIVATE'S AFFAIR, A(1959), d; ESTHER AND THE KING(1960, U.S./Ital.), p&d, w; MARINES, LET'S GO(1961), p&d, w; DISTANT TRUMPET, A(1964), d
Silents
DISHONORED MEDAL, THE(1914); GREAT LEAP, THE(1914); BIRTH OF A NATION, THE(1915); SERPENT, THE(1916), d, w; THIEF OF BAGDAD, THE(1924), d; EAST OF SUEZ(1925), d; WHAT PRICE GLORY(1926), d; MONKEY TALKS, THE(1927), d; SADIE THOMPSON(1928), a, d&w
Misc. Silents
LIFE OF GENERAL VILLA, THE(1914), d; CARMEN(1915), d; REGENERATION, THE(1915), d; BLUE BLOOD AND RED(1916), d; PILLARS OF SOCIETY(1916), d; PRIDE OF NEW YORK, THE(1917), d; SILENT LIE, THE(1917), d; I'LL SAY SO(1918), d; ON THE JUMP(1918), d; PRUSSIAN CUR, THE(1918), d; WOMAN AND THE LAW(1918), d; EVANGELINE(1919), d; EVERY MOTHER'S SON(1919), d; SHOULD A HUSBAND FORGIVE?(1919), d; DEEP PURPLE, THE(1920), d; FROM NOW ON(1920), d; STRONGEST, THE(1920), d; OATH, THE(1921), d; SERENADE(1921), d; SPANIARD, THE(1925), d; LADY OF THE HAREM, THE(1926), d; LUCKY LADY, THE(1926), d; WANDERER, THE(1926), d; LOVES OF CARMEN(1927), d; ME, GANGSTER(1928), d; RED DANCE, THE(1928), d

Raymond J. Walsh
THX 1138(1971)

Richard Walsh
DECEPTION(1946); HUMORESQUE(1946); DARK PASSAGE(1947); NORA PRENTISS(1947); POSSESSED(1947); JOHNNY BELINDA(1948); SMART GIRLS DON'T TALK(1948); WHIPLASH(1948); ISLAND IN THE SKY(1953); NORTHERN PATROL(1953); EDDY DUCHIN STORY, THE(1956); FATE IS THE HUNTER(1964); SMOKEY AND THE BANDIT–PART 3(1983)
1984
HIGHWAY TO HELL(1984)

Rob Walsh
BUGS BUNNY'S THIRD MOVIE–1001 RABBIT TALES(1982), m; NIGHTBEAST(1982), m; REVENGE OF THE SHOGUN WOMEN(1982, Taiwan), m; HEARTBREAKER(1983), m; REVENGE OF THE NINJA(1983), m; YOUNG WARRIORS(1983), m

Robert Walsh
VON RICHTHOFEN AND BROWN(1970)
Robin Walsh
MIDNIGHT(1983)
Ronald Walsh
SHAKE HANDS WITH THE DEVIL(1959, Ireland); MURDER IN EDEN(1962, Brit.)
Ronnie Walsh
FLIGHT OF THE DOVES(1971)
Ruth Walsh
HOUSE ON SORORITY ROW, THE(1983)
Sally Walsh
CURSE OF FRANKENSTEIN, THE(1957, Brit.)
Sharon Walsh
INCREDIBLY STRANGE CREATURES WHO STOPPED LIVING AND BECAME CRAZY MIXED-UP ZOMBIES, THE(1965)
Sheila Walsh
Silents
ONLY A MILL GIRL(1919, Brit.), d
Sidney Walsh
SWEETHEARTS ON PARADE(1930), ed
Stephen Walsh
PARALLELS(1980, Can.)
Stuart Walsh
DESERT RAVEN, THE(1965); MARA OF THE WILDERNESS(1966)
Susan Walsh
PAN-AMERICANA(1945); FEMALE TROUBLE(1975)
Thomas Walsh
DON'T TURN'EM LOOSE(1936), w; WE'RE ONLY HUMAN(1936), w; UNION STATION(1950), w; PUSHOVER(1954), w; GLORY BOY(1971), cos
Thomas B. Walsh
Silents
SHAMS OF SOCIETY(1921), d
Thommie Walsh
JESUS CHRIST, SUPERSTAR(1973)
Tom Walsh
Silents
DANGER SIGNAL, THE(1915)
Tricia Walsh
TERROR(1979, Brit.)
Valerie Walsh
STRICTLY FOR THE BIRDS(1963, Brit.)
W. R. Walsh
MANHATTAN MELODRAMA(1934)
Walter Walsh
GOING HOLLYWOOD(1933), p&d
Evelyn Walsh-Hall
MRS. DANE'S DEFENCE(1933, Brit.)
Douglas Walshe
Silents
GIRL OF LONDON, A(1925, Brit.), w
Pat Walshe
ROSEANNA McCOY(1949); PANIC IN THE STREETS(1950)
Gana Walska
Misc. Silents
CHILD OF DESTINY, THE(1916)
Harry Walston
Misc. Silents
POLITICIANS, THE(1915)
Ray Walston
KISS THEM FOR ME(1957); DAMN YANKEES(1958); SOUTH PACIFIC(1958); SAY ONE FOR ME(1959); APARTMENT, THE(1960); PORTRAIT IN BLACK(1960); TALL STORY(1960); CONVICTS FOUR(1962); WHO'S MINDING THE STORE?(1963); WIVES AND LOVERS(1963); KISS ME, STUPID(1964); CAPRICE(1967); PAINT YOUR WAGON(1969); STING, THE(1973); SILVER STREAK(1976); HAPPY HOOKER GOES TO WASHINGTON, THE(1977); FALL OF THE HOUSE OF USHER, THE(1980); POPEYE(1980); GALAXY OF TERROR(1981); FAST TIMES AT RIDGEMONT HIGH(1982); O'HARA'S WIFE(1983); PRIVATE SCHOOL(1983)
1984
JOHNNY DANGEROUSLY(1984)
Wade Walston
1984
SUBURBIA(1984)
Bill Walstrom
MURDER, INC.(1960), cos; PRETTY BOY FLOYD(1960), cos; MAD DOG COLL(1961), cos
Members of the Staff at Walt Disney Studios
RELUCTANT DRAGON, THE(1941)
Walt Shrum and the Colorado Hillbillies
BLUE MONTANA SKIES(1939); DESERT HORSEMAN, THE(1946)
Mike Waltari
EGYPTIAN. THE(1954), w
Jack Waltemeyer
Silents
CARMEN OF THE KLONDIKE(1918); DYNAMITE DAN(1924)
Misc. Silents
MONTANA BILL(1921); WILDCAT JORDAN(1922)
Rafal Waltenberger
CAMERA BUFF(1983, Pol.), art d
Alphonse Walter
1984
MIKE'S MURDER(1984)
Bruno Walter
CARNEGIE HALL(1947)
C. Jervis Walter
Misc. Silents
LADDIE(1920, Brit.)
Christa Walter
FOXTROT(1977, Mex./Swiss)

Cyril Jervis Walter
CAESAR AND CLEOPATRA(1946, Brit.)
Eddie Walter
MRS. O'MALLEY AND MR. MALONE(1950)
Ernest Walter
QUENTIN DURWARD(1955), ed; BEYOND MOMBASA(1957), ed; LITTLE HUT, THE(1957), ed; INN OF THE SIXTH HAPPINESS, THE(1958), ed; SAFECRACKER, THE(1958, Brit.), ed BEYOND THIS PLACE(1959, Brit.), ed; HOUSE OF THE SEVEN HAWKS, THE(1959), ed; INVASION QUARTET(1961, Brit.), ed; MURDER SHE SAID(1961, Brit.), ed; LISA(1962, Brit.), ed; HAUNTING, THE(1963), ed; NINE HOURS TO RAMA(1963, U.S./Brit.), ed; MURDER AHOY(1964, Brit.), ed; MURDER MOST FOUL(1964, Brit.), ed; OPERATION CROSSBOW(1965, U.S./Ital.), ed; LIQUIDATOR, THE(1966, Brit.), ed; COP-OUT(1967, Brit.), ed; EYE OF THE DEVIL(1967, Brit.), ed; DARK OF THE SUN(1968, Brit.), ed; SHOES OF THE FISHERMAN, THE(1968), ed; PRIVATE LIFE OF SHERLOCK HOLMES, THE(1970, Brit.), ed; NICHOLAS AND ALEXANDRA(1971, Brit.), ed; 10 RILLINGTON PLACE(1971, Brit.), ed; TAMARIND SEED, THE(1974, Brit.), ed; PERMISSION TO KILL(1975, U.S./Aust.), ed; WILBY CONSPIRACY, THE(1975, Brit.), ed; BLUE BIRD, THE(1976), ed; CROSSED SWORDS(1978), ed
Ernie Walter
CHILDREN OF THE DAMNED(1963, Brit.), ed; CIRCLE OF IRON(1979, Brit.), ed
Eugene Walter
MOTHER KNOWS BEST(1928), w; JEALOUSY(1929), w; SIDE STREET(1929), w; EASIEST WAY, THE(1931), w; WOMAN TRAP(1936), w; 8 ½(1963, Ital.); BLACK BELLY OF THE TARANTULA, THE(1972, Ital.)
Silents
TESS OF THE STORM COUNTRY(1914); FINE FEATHERS(1915), w; KNIFE, THE(1918), w; WAY OF A WOMAN(1919), w; LOVE, HONOR AND OBEY(1920), w; FINE FEATHERS(1921), w; WHAT FOOLS MEN ARE(1922), w; JUST A WOMAN(1925), w
George Walter
DANGEROUS SECRETS(1938, Brit.), md
Georges Walter
JE T'AIME, JE T'AIME(1972, Fr./Swed.)
Harriet Walter
FRENCH LIEUTENANT'S WOMAN, THE(1981)
1984
REFLECTIONS(1984, Brit.)
Harry Walter
AND NOW MY LOVE(1975, Fr.)
Misc. Silents
BLACK TULIP, THE(1921, Brit.)
Herbert David Walter
Silents
DRESS PARADE(1927), w
Jerry Walter
NIGHTMARE IN BLOOD(1978); PROMISE, THE(1979)
Jessica Walter
LILITH(1964); GRAND PRIX(1966); GROUP, THE(1966); BYE BYE BRAVERMAN(1968); NUMBER ONE(1969); PLAY MISTY FOR ME(1971); GOING APE!(1981); SPRING FEVER(1983, Can.)
1984
FLAMINGO KID, THE(1984)
Karl Walter
SCHLAGER-PARADE(1953), set d
Len Walter
THUNDERBIRDS ARE GO(1968, Brit.), ed; JOURNEY TO THE FAR SIDE OF THE SUN(1969, Brit.), ed
Linda Lee Walter
MANIAC(1980)
Luana Walter
END OF THE TRAIL(1932); MISS PINKERTON(1932)
Lucien Walter
CHILDREN OF PARADISE(1945, Fr.)
Luke Walter
NIGHTHAWKS(1981)
Marcia Walter
CLOSE-UP(1948)
Margot Walter
COPPER, THE(1930, Brit.); BARBERINA(1932, Ger.)
Mariane Walter
TOOLBOX MURDERS, THE(1978)
Mary Walter
CURSE OF THE VAMPIRES(1970, Phil., U.S.)
Maurice Walter
Misc. Silents
WOODPIGEON PATROL, THE(1930, Brit.)
Mike Walter
METALSTORM: THE DESTRUCTION OF JARED-SYN(1983)
Misc. Talkies
STARK RAVING MAD(1983)
Olive Walter
MEET SEXTON BLAKE(1944, Brit.); ECHO MURDERS, THE(1945, Brit.); FOR YOU ALONE(1945, Brit.); STOP PRESS GIRL(1949, Brit.)
Pat Walter
HAREM GIRL(1952); GLASS HOUSES(1972)
Perla Walter
WAR WAGON, THE(1967); FRIDAY THE 13TH PART III(1982); MAN WITH TWO BRAINS, THE(1983)
Perle Walter
1984
SAVAGE STREETS(1984)
Pietro Walter
EMBALMER, THE(1966, Ital.)
Polly Walter
EXPENSIVE WOMEN(1931)
Richard Walter
FRIENDS AND NEIGHBORS(1963, Brit.)

Rosa Walter
Silents
GHOST TRAIN, THE(1927, Brit.)
Tracey Walter
GOIN' SOUTH(1978); HARDCORE(1979); HUNTER, THE(1980); HAND, THE(1981); HONKYTONK MAN(1982); RUMBLE FISH(1983); TIMERIDER(1983)
1984
CONAN THE DESTROYER(1984); REPO MAN(1984)
Tracy Walter
BADGE 373(1973)
W. Walter
BORDER STREET(1950, Pol.)
Wilfred Walter
TO THE VICTOR(1938, Brit.); LADY IN DISTRESS(1942, Brit.); CAESAR AND CLEOPATRA(1946, Brit.)
Wilfrid Walter
OLD ROSES(1935, Brit.); HEARTS OF HUMANITY(1936, Brit.); CONVICT 99(1938, Brit.); HUMAN MONSTER, THE(1940, Brit.); NIGHT TRAIN(1940, Brit.); NO HIGHWAY IN THE SKY(1951, Brit.); JUDGMENT DEFERRED(1952, Brit.); CLUE OF THE MISSING APE, THE(1953, Brit.)
Wilmer Walter
Silents
FAIR PRETENDER, THE(1918)
Wladyslaw Walter
FIRST START(1953, Pol.)
Walter Dare Wahl and Company
STAR SPANGLED RHYTHM(1942)
Walter Fuller's Orchestra
SEPIA CINDERELLA(1947)
Walter Saull's Scotia Singers
COMIN' THRU' THE RYE(1947, Brit.)
Walter Shrum and His Colorado Hillbillies
OLD BARN DANCE, THE(1938)
Walter Wanderly Trio with Talya Ferro
FOR SINGLES ONLY(1968)
Desmond Walter-Ellis
DON'T SAY DIE(1950, Brit.); RUN FOR YOUR MONEY, A(1950, Brit.); MAYTIME IN MAYFAIR(1952, Brit.); PENNY PRINCESS(1953, Brit.); RISE AND RISE OF MICHAEL RIMMER, THE(1970, Brit.); STATUE, THE(1971, Brit.)
Andre Walters
1984
SCARRED(1984)
Barbara Ann Walters
CRAZY MAMA(1975); GOIN' SOUTH(1978); ROCK 'N' ROLL HIGH SCHOOL(1979); IN GOD WE TRUST(1980)
Bette Lou Walters
MARSHAL'S DAUGHTER, THE(1953)
Bob Walters
Misc. Talkies
GIRLS OF 42ND STREET(1974)
Casey Walters
KATHY O'(1958); TRUE STORY OF LYNN STUART, THE(1958)
Charles Walters
SEVEN DAYS LEAVE(1942), ch; DU BARRY WAS A LADY(1943), ch; GIRL CRAZY(1943), ch; MEET ME IN ST. LOUIS(1944), ch; MEET THE PEOPLE(1944), ch; SINCE YOU WENT AWAY(1944), ch; ABBOTT AND COSTELLO IN HOLLYWOOD(1945), ch; HER HIGHNESS AND THE BELLBOY(1945), ch; WEEKEND AT THE WALDORF(1945), ch; ZIEGFELD FOLLIES(1945), d, w; GOOD NEWS(1947), d; EASTER PARADE(1948), d; SUMMER HOLIDAY(1948), ch; BARKLEYS OF BROADWAY, THE(1949), d; SUMMER STOCK(1950), d, ch; TEXAS CARNIVAL(1951), d; THREE GUYS NAMED MIKE(1951), d; BELLE OF NEW YORK, THE(1952), d; DANGEROUS WHEN WET(1953), d; EASY TO LOVE(1953), d, ch; LILI(1953), d, ch; TORCH SONG(1953), a, d, ch; GLASS SLIPPER, THE(1955), d; TENDER TRAP, THE(1955), d; HIGH SOCIETY(1956), d, ch; ASK ANY GIRL(1959), d; PLEASE DON'T EAT THE DAISIES(1960), d; TWO LOVES(1961), d; JUMBO(1962), d; UNSINKABLE MOLLY BROWN, THE(1964), d; WALK, DON'T RUN(1966), d; DON'T GO NEAR THE WATER(1975), d
Cherie Walters
FLY NOW, PAY LATER(1969)
Christa Walters
SUNBURN(1979)
Dickie Walters
CARNIVAL(1935); EASY MONEY(1936); STAR FOR A NIGHT(1936)
Donald Walters
Misc. Talkies
CAREER BED(1972)
Dorothy Walters
QUEEN HIGH(1930)
Silents
LITTLE MISS HOOVER(1918); AWAY GOES PRUDENCE(1920); FLYING PAT(1920); BEYOND PRICE(1921); LIGHT IN THE DARK, THE(1922); KISS FOR CINDERELLA, A(1926)
Misc. Silents
VEILED MARRIAGE, THE(1920)
Easter Walters
Misc. Silents
COMMON CLAY(1919)
Elizabeth Walters
BILL AND COO(1947)
Silents
KINDRED OF THE DUST(1922)
Ermadean Walters
SONG OF BERNADETTE, THE(1943)
Floyd Walters
TIME OF YOUR LIFE, THE(1948)
Fred Walters
Silents
OUR MRS. McCHESNEY(1918)

Glen Walters
SHE GOES TO WAR(1929); STAND UP AND CHEER(1934 80m FOX bw); LITTLE SHEPHERD OF KINGDOM COME(1961); SPIRAL ROAD, THE(1962)
Hal Walters
OLD SPANISH CUSTOMERS(1932, Brit.); RIVER HOUSE GHOST, THE(1932, Brit.); TONIGHT'S THE NIGHT(1932, Brit.); VERDICT OF THE SEA(1932, Brit.); ENEMY OF THE POLICE(1933, Brit.); GOING STRAIGHT(1933, Brit.); GREAT STUFF(1933, Brit.); I'LL STICK TO YOU(1933, Brit.); MAROONED(1933, Brit.); STRIKE IT RICH(1933, Brit.); THAT'S MY WIFE(1933, Brit.); BIG BUSINESS(1934, Brit.); CRAZY PEOPLE(1934, Brit.); MAN I WANT, THE(1934, Brit.); PERFECT FLAW, THE(1934, Brit.); VIRGINIA'S HUSBAND(1934, Brit.); BLUE SMOKE(1935, Brit.); DEPARTMENT STORE(1935, Brit.); FIRE HAS BEEN ARRANGED, A(1935, Brit.); RIGHT AGE TO MARRY, THE(1935, Brit.); DON'T RUSH ME(1936, Brit.); EDUCATED EVANS(1936, Brit.); INTERRUPTED HONEYMOON, THE(1936, Brit.); MURDER ON THE SET(1936, Brit.); THEY DIDN'T KNOW(1936, Brit.); WHERE THERE'S A WILL(1936, Brit); KEEP FIT(1937, Brit.); LITTLE MISS SOMEBODY(1937, Brit.); NON-STOP NEW YORK(1937, Brit.); PEARLS BRING TEARS(1937, Brit.); SONG OF THE FORGE(1937, Brit.); STRANGE ADVENTURES OF MR. SMITH, THE(1937, Brit.); TELEVISION TALENT(1937, Brit.); VULTURE, THE(1937, Brit.); DOUBLE OR QUITS(1938, Brit.); EVERYTHING HAPPENS TO ME(1938, Brit.); MAN WITH 100 FACES, THE(1938, Brit.); MEET MR. PENNY(1938, Brit.); THANK EVANS(1938, Brit.); VIPER, THE(1938, Brit.); FOUR FEATHERS, THE(1939, Brit.); GOOD OLD DAYS, THE(1939, Brit.); HOOTS MON!(1939, Brit.); SECOND MR. BUSH, THE(1940, Brit.); THAT'S THE TICKET(1940, Brit.); THEY CAME BY NIGHT(1940, Brit.)
Silents
WEST OF THE LAW(1926)
Misc. Silents
MISTAKEN ORDERS(1926); RIDING FOR LIFE(1926)
Hugh Walters
HAVING A WILD WEEKEND(1965, Brit.); ALFIE DARLING(1975, Brit.); MISSIONARY, THE(1982)
1984
1984(1984, Brit.)
Ingram P. Walters
CASE OF PATTY SMITH, THE(1962), m
J. Walters
PRIME MINISTER, THE(1941, Brit.)
Jack Walters
ISLAND OF LOST SOULS(1933); FRONTIERS OF '49(1939)
Silents
GALLOPING KID, THE(1922)
Misc. Silents
DAUGHTER OF THE LAW, A(1921); HEADIN' NORTH(1921); BETTER MAN WINS, THE(1922)
James M. Walters
TO EACH HIS OWN(1946), set d; IMPERFECT LADY, THE(1947), set d; JOURNEY TO SHILOH(1968), set d
James M. Walters, Sr.
TAGGART(1964), set d; THREE GUNS FOR TEXAS(1968), set d; HOW TO FRAME A FIGG(1971), set d
Jayne Walters
1984
WILD LIFE, THE(1984)
Jean Walters
WOMAN'S WORLD(1954); HOW TO BE VERY, VERY, POPULAR(1955)
Jerrie Walters
SMALL TOWN DEB(1941), w
Jimmy Walters
BLUE DAHLIA, THE(1946), set d
John Walters
SUMMERFIELD(1977, Aus.)
Joseph Walters
Silents
SMOKE BELLEW(1929), ph
Julie Walters
EDUCATING RITA(1983)
June Walters
Misc. Talkies
SECRETS OF HOLLYWOOD(1933)
Justin Walters
CURSE OF THE WEREWOLF, THE(1961)
Laurie Walters
HARRAD EXPERIMENT, THE(1973); HARRAD SUMMER, THE(1974)
Luana Walters
TWO SECONDS(1932); FIGHTING TEXANS(1933); MERRY WIDOW, THE(1934); ACES AND EIGHTS(1936); RIDE 'EM COWBOY(1936); SPEED REPORTER(1936); SUZY(1936); SOULS AT SEA(1937); UNDER STRANGE FLAGS(1937); ALGIERS(1938); MARIE ANTOINETTE(1938); SAY IT IN FRENCH(1938); WHERE THE WEST BEGINS(1938); CAFE SOCIETY(1939); ETERNALLY YOURS(1939); HONEYMOON IN BALI(1939); HOTEL IMPERIAL(1939); MEXICALI ROSE(1939); PARIS HONEYMOON(1939); BLONDIE PLAYS CUPID(1940); DURANGO KID, THE(1940); RANGE BUSTERS, THE(1940); RETURN OF WILD BILL, THE(1940); TULSA KID, THE(1940); ACROSS THE SIERRAS(1941); ARIZONA BOUND(1941); KID'S LAST RIDE, THE(1941); MISBEHAVING HUSBANDS(1941); NO GREATER SIN(1941); THUNDERING HOOFS(1941); BAD MEN OF THE HILLS(1942); CORPSE VANISHES, THE(1942); DOWN TEXAS WAY(1942); LAWLESS PLAINSMEN(1942); LONE STAR VIGILANTES, THE(1942); DRUMS OF FU MANCHU(1943); GIRLS IN PRISON(1956)
Misc. Talkies
LAW OF THE WILD(1941)
Luane Walters
ROAD AGENT(1941)
Luanna Walters
INSIDE THE LAW(1942)
Mariann Walters
T.R. BASKIN(1971)
Marilyn Walters
MOONSHINE MOUNTAIN(1964)

Marrian Walters
MEDIUM COOL(1969)
Marvin Walters
SHAFT'S BIG SCORE(1972), stunts; RIVER NIGER, THE(1976), stunts
Marvin James Walters
WHAT'S UP, DOC?(1972)
Matthew Walters
FEARLESS VAMPIRE KILLERS, OR PARDON ME BUT YOUR TEETH ARE IN MY NECK, THE(1967)
Michael Walters
HAVE A NICE WEEKEND(1975), d, w
Monica Walters
ONE PLUS ONE(1969, Brit.)
Nancy Walters
MONSTER ON THE CAMPUS(1958); BELLS ARE RINGING(1960); BLUE HAWAII(1961); GREEN HELMET, THE(1961, Brit.); SINGING NUN, THE(1966)
Olive Walters
GREEN FINGERS(1947)
Patricia Walters
RIVER, THE(1951)
Peanuts Walters
JOAN OF OZARK(1942)
Peppy Walters
JOAN OF OZARK(1942)
Polly Walters
BLONDE CRAZY(1931); FIVE STAR FINAL(1931); MANHATTAN PARADE(1931); SMART MONEY(1931); BEAUTY AND THE BOSS(1932); HIGH PRESSURE(1932); MAKE ME A STAR(1932); MOUTHPIECE, THE(1932); PLAY GIRL(1932); TAXI!(1932); UNION DEPOT(1932); YOUNG BRIDE(1932)
R. Martin Walters
MARIE-ANN(1978, Can.), d
Ray Walters
Misc. Silents
SHIELD OF SILENCE, THE(1925)
Renee Walters
IT HAPPENED IN CANADA(1962, Can.)
Richard Walters
SON OF ROBIN HOOD(1959, Brit.)
Robert Walters
Silents
SUZANNA(1922), ph
Ron Walters
POINT BLANK(1967)
Ronald Walters
MINSTREL BOY, THE(1937, Brit.)
Rupert Walters
PRIVILEGED(1982, Brit.), w
Russell Walters
BRAVE DON'T CRY, THE(1952, Brit.)
Scott Walters
MALIBU HIGH(1979)
Selene Walters
SENIOR PROM(1958); JET OVER THE ATLANTIC(1960)
Serge Walters
GAY SENORITA, THE(1945), m/l "Buenos Noches," Don George
Susan Walters
SHOOT TO KILL(1947); TRIP, THE(1967)
Suzy Walters
ANGELS FROM HELL(1968)
Thorley Walters
ONCE IN A NEW MOON(1935, Brit.); AMONG HUMAN WOLVES(1940 Brit.); DESIGN FOR MURDER(1940, Brit.); IT HAPPENED TO ONE MAN(1941, Brit.); THEY WERE SISTERS(1945, Brit.); GAY INTRUDERS, THE(1946, Brit.); WALTZ TIME(1946, Brit.); JOSEPHINE AND MEN(1955, Brit.); YOU CAN'T ESCAPE(1955, Brit.); PRIVATE'S PROGRESS(1956, Brit.); ROTTEN TO THE CORE(1956, Brit.); WHO DONE IT?(1956, Brit.); BIRTHDAY PRESENT, THE(1957, Brit.); NOVEL AFFAIR, A(1957, Brit.); SECOND FIDDLE(1957, Brit.); BLUE MURDER AT ST. TRINIAN'S(1958, Brit.); HAPPY IS THE BRIDE(1958, Brit.); LADY MISLAID, A(1958, Brit.); TRUTH ABOUT WOMEN, THE(1958, Brit.); DON'T PANIC CHAPS!(1959, Brit.); FRENCH MISTRESS(1960, Brit.); MAN IN A COCKED HAT(1960, Bri.); INVASION QUARTET(1961, Brit.); MURDER SHE SAID(1961, Brit.); PETTICOAT PIRATES(1961, Brit.); PURE HELL OF ST. TRINIAN'S, THE(1961, Brit.); RISK, THE(1961, Brit.); TWO-WAY STRETCH(1961, Brit.); PHANTOM OF THE OPERA, THE(1962, Brit.); SHERLOCK HOLMES AND THE DEADLY NECKLACE(1962, Ger.); HEAVENS ABOVE!(1963, Brit.); EARTH DIES SCREAMING, THE(1964, Brit.); RING OF SPIES(1964, Brit.); FRANKENSTEIN CREATED WOMAN(1965, Brit.); JOEY BOY(1965, Brit.); DRACULA—PRINCE OF DARKNESS(1966, Brit.); FAMILY WAY, THE(1966, Brit.); PSYCHOPATH, THE(1966, Brit.); WRONG BOX, THE(1966, Brit.); FRANKENSTEIN MUST BE DESTROYED!(1969, Brit.); LAST SHOT YOU HEAR, THE(1969, Brit.); OH! WHAT A LOVELY WAR(1969, Brit.); TWISTED NERVE(1969, Brit.); BARTLEBY(1970, Brit.); MAN WHO HAUNTED HIMSELF, THE(1970, Brit.); SOPHIE'S PLACE(1970); THERE'S A GIRL IN MY SOUP(1970, Brit.); TROG(1970, Brit.); CRY OF THE PENGUINS(1972, Brit.); VAMPIRE CIRCUS(1972, Brit.); YOUNG WINSTON(1972, Brit.); ADVENTURES OF SHERLOCK HOLMES' SMARTER BROTHER, THE(1975, Brit.); PEOPLE THAT TIME FORGOT, THE(1977, Brit.); WILDCATS OF ST. TRINIAN'S, THE(1980, Brit.); SIGN OF FOUR, THE(1983, Brit.)
1984
LITTLE DRUMMER GIRL, THE(1984)
W. R. Walters
Silents
TESS OF THE STORM COUNTRY(1914)
Walth
M(1933, Ger.)
Anna May Walthall
Silents
HEARTS OF THE WORLD(1918); AS MAN DESIRES(1925); DESERT FLOWER, THE(1925)
Misc. Silents
TRUANT SOUL, THE(1917)

Henry Walthall
ANYBODY'S BLONDE(1931)
Misc. Silents
PARTED CURTAINS(1921); GOLDEN BED, THE(1925); THREE FACES EAST(1926)
H. B. Walthall
BEGGARS IN ERMINE(1934); GIRL OF THE LIMBERLOST(1934)
Silents
GIMMIE(1923)
Henry B. Walthall
BRIDGE OF SAN LUIS REY, THE(1929); FROM HEADQUARTERS(1929); IN OLD CALIFORNIA(1929); JAZZ AGE, THE(1929); RIVER OF ROMANCE(1929); SPEAK-EASY(1929); STARK MAD(1929); TRESPASSER, THE(1929); ABRAHAM LINCOLN(1930); BLAZE O' GLORY(1930); LOVE TRADER(1930); TEMPLE TOWER(1930); TOL'ABLE DAVID(1930); IS THERE JUSTICE?(1931); ALIAS MARY SMITH(1932); CABIN IN THE COTTON(1932); CENTRAL PARK(1932); CHANDU THE MAGICIAN(1932); FAME STREET(1932); HOTEL CONTINENTAL(1932); KLONDIKE(1932); ME AND MY GAL(1932); RIDE HIM, COWBOY(1932); STRANGE INTERLUDE(1932); FLAMING SIGNAL(1933); HEADLINE SHOOTER(1933); HER FORGOTTEN PAST(1933); LAUGHING AT LIFE(1933); MY MOTHER(1933); SIN OF NORA MORAN(1933); SOMEWHERE IN SONORA(1933); 42ND STREET(1933); CITY PARK(1934); DARK HAZARD(1934); JUDGE PRIEST(1934); LEMON DROP KID, THE(1934); LOVE TIME(1934); MEN IN WHITE(1934); MURDER IN THE MUSEUM(1934); SCARLET LETTER, THE(1934); VIVA VILLA!(1934); BACHELOR OF ARTS(1935); DANTE'S INFERNO(1935); HELLDORADO(1935); CITY OF TWO CITIES, A(1935); CHINA CLIPPER(1936); DEVIL DOLL, THE(1936); GARDEN MURDER CASE, THE(1936); HEARTS IN BONDAGE(1936); LAST OUTLAW, THE(1936); MINE WITH THE IRON DOOR, THE(1936)
Silents
AVENGING CONSCIENCE, THE(1914); CLASSMATES(1914); FLOOR ABOVE, THE(1914); GANGSTERS OF NEW YORK, THE(1914); HOME SWEET HOME(1914); JUDITH OF BETHULIA(1914); MOUNTAIN RAT, THE(1914); BIRTH OF A NATION, THE(1915); AND A STILL, SMALL VOICE(1918); GREAT LOVE, THE(1918); HIS ROBE OF HONOR(1918); FALSE FACES(1919); ABLEMINDED LADY, THE(1922); KICK BACK, THE(1922); LONG CHANCE, THE(1922); ONE CLEAR CALL(1922); BOY OF MINE(1923); GIRL WHO WOULDN'T WORK, THE(1925); PLASTIC AGE, THE(1925); BARRIER, THE(1926); ROAD TO MANDALAY, THE(1926); SCARLET LETTER, THE(1926); ENCHANTED ISLAND, THE(1927); LIGHT IN THE WINDOW, THE(1927); LONDON AFTER MIDNIGHT(1927); WINGS(1927); FREEDOM OF THE PRESS(1928); LOVE ME AND THE WORLD IS MINE(1928)
Misc. Silents
LORD CHUMLEY(1914); BEULAH(1915); GHOSTS(1915); RAVEN, THE(1915); BIRTH OF A MAN, THE(1916); MISLEADING LADY, THE(1916); PILLARS OF SOCIETY(1916); STING OF VICTORY, THE(1916); BURNING THE CANDLE(1917); LITTLE SHOES(1917); SAINT'S ADVENTURE, THE(1917); TRUANT SOUL, THE(1917); HUMDRUM BROWN(1918); BOOMERANG, THE(1919); LONG ARM OF MANNISTER, THE(1919); LONG LANE'S TURNING, THE(1919); MODERN HUSBANDS(1919); CONFESSION, THE(1920); SPLENDID HAZARD, A(1920); FLOWER OF THE NORTH(1921); MARRIAGE CHANCE, THE(1922); FACE ON THE BARROOM FLOOR, THE(1923); UNKNOWN PURPLE, THE(1923); BOWERY BISHOP, THE(1924); DOLLAR DOWN(1925); KENTUCKY PRIDE(1925); KIT CARSON OVER THE GREAT DIVIDE(1925); ON THE THRESHOLD(1925); SIMON THE JESTER(1925); UNKNOWN SOLDIER, THE(1926); FIGHTING LOVE(1927); ROSE OF KILDARE, THE(1927); BLACK MAGIC(1929)
Henry E. Walthall
PHANTOM IN THE HOUSE, THE(1929)
Pat Walthall
EMPTY HOLSTERS(1937)
Patricia Walthall
IT'S LOVE I'M AFTER(1937)
Gretchen Walther
LANDLORD, THE(1970)
Jorg Walther
TASTE OF SIN, A(1983), ph
Leon Walther
EARRINGS OF MADAME DE..., THE(1954, Fr.)
Rudolf Walther-Fein
BECAUSE I LOVED YOU(1930, Ger.), d
Jurg Walthers
1984
NIGHT PATROL(1984), ph
Bill Waltho
DR. FRANKENSTEIN ON CAMPUS(1970, Can.)
Linda Waltman
PERSONAL BEST(1982)
Al Walton
CORNERED(1945)
Charles Walton
Misc. Silents
STITCH IN TIME, A(1919)
Douglas Walton
OVER THE HILL(1931); DR. JEKYLL AND MR. HYDE(1932); LOOKING FORWARD(1933); SECRET OF MADAME BLANCHE, THE(1933); CHARLIE CHAN IN LONDON(1934); COUNT OF MONTE CRISTO, THE(1934); LOST PATROL, THE,(1934); MADAME SPY(1934); MURDER IN TRINIDAD(1934); CAPTAIN HURRICANE(1935); DARK ANGEL, THE(1935); MUTINY ON THE BOUNTY(1935); GARDEN MURDER CASE, THE(1936); I CONQUER THE SEA(1936); MARY OF SCOTLAND(1936); THANK YOU, JEEVES(1936); CAMILLE(1937); DAMAGED GOODS(1937); FLIGHT FROM GLORY(1937); NATION AFLAME(1937); WALLABY JIM OF THE ISLANDS(1937); STORM OVER BENGAL(1938); BAD LANDS(1939); RAFFLES(1939); STORY OF VERNON AND IRENE CASTLE, THE(1939); SUN NEVER SETS, THE(1939); LETTER, THE(1940); LONG VOYAGE HOME, THE(1940); NORTHWEST PASSAGE(1940); TOO MANY GIRLS(1940); HURRY, CHARLIE, HURRY(1941); ONE NIGHT IN LISBON(1941); SINGAPORE WOMAN(1941); DESPERATE JOURNEY(1942); JESSE JAMES, JR.(1942); KITTY(1945); MURDER, MY SWEET(1945); PICTURE OF DORIAN GRAY, THE(1945); CLOAK AND DAGGER(1946); OUR HEARTS WERE GROWING UP(1946); GREEN DOLPHIN STREET(1947); HIGH CONQUEST(1947); HIGH TIDE(1947); SECRET OF ST. IVES, THE(1949); THREE CAME HOME(1950)

Edward Walton
Silents
$5,000,000 COUNTERFEITING PLOT, THE(1914)
Emma Walton
CURSE OF THE PINK PANTHER(1983)
1984
MICKI AND MAUDE(1984)
Florence Walton
Silents
QUEST OF LIFE, THE(1916)
Francis Walton
WOMEN IN THE WIND(1939), w
Fred Walton
DYNAMITE(1930); LAST DANCE, THE(1930); SIN TAKES A HOLIDAY(1930); BIG GAMBLE, THE(1931); KIKI(1931); BRITISH AGENT(1934); CAT'S PAW, THE(1934); IT HAPPENED ONE NIGHT(1934); MOONSTONE, THE(1934); DRACULA'S DAUGHTER(1936); FORBIDDEN HEAVEN(1936); HOUSE OF A THOUSAND CANDLES, THE(1936); LITTLE LORD FAUNTLEROY(1936); STORY OF LOUIS PASTEUR, THE(1936); TORTURE SHIP(1939); LILI(1953); WHEN A STRANGER CALLS(1979), d, w
1984
HADLEY'S REBELLION(1984), d&w
Silents
NEW BROOMS(1925)
Misc. Silents
WISE WIFE, THE(1927)
Col. George Walton
DEVIL'S BRIGADE, THE(1968), w
Gladys Walton
Silents
PINK TIGHTS(1920); ALL DOLLED UP(1921); HIGH HEELS(1921); ROWDY, THE(1921); LAVENDER BATH LADY, THE(1922); SECOND HAND ROSE(1922); LOVE LETTER, THE(1923); NEAR LADY, THE(1923); SAWDUST(1923); TOWN SCANDAL, THE(1923); ANYTHING ONCE(1925); EASY MONEY(1925); ENEMIES OF YOUTH(1925); APE, THE(1928)
Misc. Silents
LA LA LUCILLE(1920); RISKY BUSINESS(1920); SECRET GIFT, THE(1920); DESPERATE YOUTH(1921); MAN TAMER, THE(1921); PLAYING WITH FIRE(1921); RICH GIRL, POOR GIRL(1921); SHORT SKIRTS(1921); DANGEROUS GAME, A(1922); GIRL WHO RAN WILD, THE(1922); GUTTERSNIPE, THE(1922); TOP O' THE MORNING, THE(1922); TROUPER, THE(1922); WISE KID, THE(1922); CROSSED WIRES(1923); GOSSIP(1923); UNTAMEABLE, THE(1923); WILD PARTY, THE(1923); LITTLE GIRL IN A BIG CITY, A(1925); SKY RAIDER, THE(1925)
Henry Walton
Silents
LIVINGSTONE(1925, Brit.)
Herbert Walton
TAKE MY LIFE(1948, Brit.); AFFAIRS OF ADELAIDE(1949, U.S./Brit); MR. DENNING DRIVES NORTH(1953, Brit.)
Herbert C. Walton
MARRY ME!(1949, Brit.); WARNING TO WANTONS, A(1949, Brit.); LITTLE BALLERINA, THE(1951, Brit.); ISLAND RESCUE(1952, Brit.); JUDGMENT DEFERRED(1952, Brit.); CRUEL SEA, THE(1953); MEET MR. LUCIFER(1953, Brit.); TERROR ON A TRAIN(1953, Brit.); TITFIELD THUNDERBOLT, THE(1953, Brit.); END OF THE ROAD, THE(1954, Brit.); HOBSON'S CHOICE(1954, Brit.); RAINBOW JACKET, THE(1954, Brit.)
Herbert L. Walton
I BELIEVE IN YOU(1953, Brit.)
Jennie Walton
SONG OF NORWAY(1970)
Jess Walton
STRAWBERRY STATEMENT, THE(1970); PEACE KILLERS, THE(1971)
[Joseph Losey] Joseph Walton
FINGER OF GUILT(1956, Brit.), d
Judy Walton
1984
SAVAGE STREETS(1984)
Kent Walton
SMALL TOWN STORY(1953, Brit.); HEART OF A MAN, THE(1959, Brit.)
Lee-Max Walton
1984
MRS. SOFFEL(1984)
Maurice Walton
Silents
QUEST OF LIFE, THE(1916)
Nancy Walton
STEEL ARENA(1973)
Mrs. O. F. Walton
Silents
PEEP BEHIND THE SCENES, A(1918, Brit.), w; OLD ARM CHAIR, THE(1920, Brit.), w; PEEP BEHIND THE SCENES, A(1929, Brit.), w
Patrick Walton
HORROR CASTLE(1965, Ital.)
Peggy Walton
WHAT'S THE MATTER WITH HELEN?(1971)
Peter Walton
MELODY(1971, Brit.)
Misc. Silents
OUR MUTUAL FRIEND(1921, Swed.)
Todd Walton
INSIDE MOVES(1980), w
Tom Walton
THUNDERING JETS(1958)
Tony Walton
WIZ, THE(1978), prod d; MARY POPPINS(1964), cos; FAHRENHEIT 451(1966, Brit.), prod d, cos; FUNNY THING HAPPENED ON THE WAY TO THE FORUM, A(1966), prod d, cos; PETULIA(1968, U.S./Brit.), prod d, cos; SEA GULL, THE(1968), prod d, cos; BOY FRIEND, THE(1971, Brit.), set d; MURDER ON THE ORIENT EXPRESS(1974, Brit.), prod d, cos; "EQUUS"(1977), prod d, cos; JUST TELL ME WHAT YOU WANT(1980), prod d, cos; PRINCE OF THE CITY(1981), prod d; DEATH-

TRAP(1982), prod d, cos
1984
GOODBYE PEOPLE, THE(1984), prod d, cos
William Walton
ESCAPE ME NEVER(1935, Brit.), m; AS YOU LIKE IT(1936, Brit.), md; MAJOR BARBARA(1941, Brit.), m; NEXT OF KIN(1942, Brit.), m; SOMEWHERE IN FRANCE(1943, Brit.), m; SPITFIRE(1943, Brit.), m; 48 HOURS(1944, Brit.), m; HENRY V(1946, Brit.), m; HAMLET(1948, Brit.), m; WAGNER(1983, Brit./Hung./Aust.)
Sir William Walton
RICHARD III(1956, Brit.), m; BATTLE OF BRITAIN, THE(1969, Brit.), m; THREE SISTERS(1974, Brit.), m
Peggy Walton-Walker
BEST FRIENDS(1982)
Edward Waltyre
Misc. Silents
THEN YOU'LL REMEMBER ME(1918, Brit.), d
Christoph Waltz
Misc. Talkies
FIRE AND SWORD(1982, Brit.)
Pat Waltz
UNTIL THEY SAIL(1957); HUMAN JUNGLE, THE(1954)
Patrick Waltz
QUEEN OF OUTER SPACE(1958); LASSIE'S GREAT ADVENTURE(1963); GOOD NEIGHBOR SAM(1964); SILENCERS, THE(1966)
Jack Waltzer
WEREWOLF OF WASHINGTON(1973); FARMER, THE(1977)
Kent Walwin
MALACHI'S COVE(1973, Brit.), p
Katschi Walzel
CARMEN, BABY(1967, Yugo./Ger.), makeup
Max Walzman
GUN MAN FROM BODIE, THE(1941); RAIDERS OF THE RANGE(1942)
Honey Wamala
AFRICA–TEXAS STYLE!(1967 U.S./Brit.)
Joseph Wambaugh
NEW CENTURIONS, THE(1972), w; CHOIRBOYS, THE(1977), w; ONION FIELD, THE(1979), w; BLACK MARBLE, THE(1980), w
Sacha Wamberg
LURE OF THE JUNGLE, THE(1970, Den.)
Oke Wambu
HUNGER, THE(1983)
Stanley Wamerton
Misc. Silents
BROADWAY BUBBLE, THE(1920)
Wamni-Omni-Ska-Romideau
WINDWALKER(1980)
the Wampas Baby Stars of 1934
KISS AND MAKE UP(1934)
Sul Te Wan
Silents
BIRTH OF A NATION, THE(1915)
Wan-chu
FLYING GUILLOTINE, THE(1975, Chi.)
Sam Wanamaker
MY GIRL TISA(1948); SALT TO THE DEVIL(1949, Brit.); MR. DENNING DRIVES NORTH(1953, Brit.); SECRET, THE(1955, Brit.); BATTLE OF THE SEXES, THE(1960, Brit.); CONCRETE JUNGLE, THE(1962, Brit.); TARAS BULBA(1962); MAN IN THE MIDDLE(1964, U.S./Brit.); SPY WHO CAME IN FROM THE COLD, THE(1965, Brit.); THOSE MAGNIFICENT MEN IN THEIR FLYING MACHINES; OR HOW I FLEW FROM LONDON TO PARIS IN 25 HOURS AND 11 MINUTES(1965, Brit.); DAY THE FISH CAME OUT, THE(1967. Brit./Gr.); WARNING SHOT(1967); DANGER ROUTE(1968, Brit.); FILE OF THE GOLDEN GOOSE, THE(1969, Brit.), d; EXECUTIONER, THE(1970, Brit.), d; CATLOW(1971, Span.), d; SPIRAL STAIRCASE, THE(1975, Brit.); SELL OUT, THE(1976); VOYAGE OF THE DAMNED(1976); BILLY JACK GOES TO WASHINGTON(1977); SINBAD AND THE EYE OF THE TIGER(1977, U.S./Brit.), d; DEATH ON THE NILE(1978, Brit.); FROM HELL TO VICTORY(1979, Fr./Ital./Span.); COMPETITION, THE(1980); PRIVATE BENJAMIN(1980)
1984
IRRECONCILABLE DIFFERENCES(1984)
Wanani
BURN(1970)
Warren D. Wandberg
SIERRA PASSAGE(1951), w; YELLOW FIN(1951), w
Ray Wander
ABDUCTORS, THE(1957), p, w
Skippy Wanders
LOVES OF EDGAR ALLAN POE, THE(1942)
Tony Wane
SANDERS OF THE RIVER(1935, Brit.)
Len Wanetik
COME BACK BABY(1968)
Chang Wang
Misc. Talkies
KUNG FU HALLOWEEN(1981)
George Wang
TENTH VICTIM, THE(1965, Fr./Ital.); SPY IN YOUR EYE(1966, Ital.); BIG GAME, THE(1972); SUPERFLY T.N.T.(1973)
Misc. Talkies
TRINITY(1975)
Henry Wang
SAND PEBBLES, THE(1966)
James Wang
CHARLIE CHAN'S COURAGE(1934); MEN OF THE NIGHT(1934); PAINTED VEIL, THE(1934)
Silents
HILLS OF MISSING MEN(1922); TIPPED OFF(1923); FIGHTING AMERICAN, THE(1924); NEVER THE TWAIN SHALL MEET(1925); SINGED(1927); YANKEE CLIPPER, THE(1927)

Jim Wang
Silents
EAST IS WEST(1922); EAGLE'S FEATHER, THE(1923)
Jimmy Wang
WELCOME DANGER(1929); ARE THESE OUR CHILDREN?(1931); LAST MAN(1932); ROAR OF THE DRAGON(1932); SECRETS OF WU SIN(1932)
K. Wang
KISS THE GIRLS AND MAKE THEM DIE(1967, U.S./Ital.)
Pay Ling Wang
BANZAI(1983, Fr.), art d
Peter Wang
CHAN IS MISSING(1982)
1984
AH YING(1984, Hong Kong), a, w
Richard Wang
KEYS OF THE KINGDOM, THE(1944); FIRST YANK INTO TOKYO(1945); DECEPTION(1946); CHINESE RING, THE(1947)
Robert Wang
IMPASSE(1969)
Tuen Wang
MONGOLS, THE(1966, Fr./Ital.)
Wayne Wang
MAN, A WOMAN AND A KILLER, A(1975), d, w; CHAN IS MISSING(1982), p&d, w, ed
Wu Wang-sheng
GOLIATHON(1979, Hong Kong)
Niels Wangberg
HAGBARD AND SIGNE(1968, Den./Iceland/Swed.), art d
Willy Bruno Wange
NOT RECONCILED, OR "ONLY VIOLENCE HELPS WHERE IT RULES"(1969, Ger.)
Richard Wangemann
Misc. Silents
THROUGH FIRE TO FORTUNE OR THE SUNKEN VILLAGE(1914); WEAKNESS OF MAN, THE(1916); INDISCRETION(1917)
Walter Wanger
TARNISHED LADY(1931), p; ANOTHER LANGUAGE(1933), p; BITTER TEA OF GENERAL YEN, THE(1933), p; GABRIEL OVER THE WHITE HOUSE(1933), p; QUEEN CHRISTINA(1933), p; PRESIDENT VANISHES, THE(1934), p; EVERY NIGHT AT EIGHT(1935), p; MARY BURNS, FUGITIVE(1935), p; PRIVATE WORLDS(1935), p; SHANGHAI(1935), p; SMART GIRL(1935), p; BIG BROWN EYES(1936), p; CASE AGAINST MRS. AMES, THE(1936), p; FATAL LADY(1936), p; HER MASTER'S VOICE(1936), p; MOON'S OUR HOME, THE(1936), p; PALM SPRINGS(1936), p; SPENDTHRIFT(1936), p; TRAIL OF THE LONESOME PINE, THE(1936), p; HISTORY IS MADE AT NIGHT(1937), p; STAND-IN(1937), p; VOGUES OF 1938(1937), p; YOU ONLY LIVE ONCE(1937), p; 52ND STREET(1937), p; ALGIERS(1938), p; BLOCKADE(1938), p; I MET MY LOVE AGAIN(1938), p; TRADE WINDS(1938), p; ETERNALLY YOURS(1939), p; STAGECOACH(1939), p; WINTER CARNIVAL(1939), p; FOREIGN CORRESPONDENT(1940), p; HOUSE ACROSS THE BAY, THE(1940), p; LONG VOYAGE HOME, THE(1940), p; SUNDOWN(1941), p; ARABIAN NIGHTS(1942), p; EAGLE SQUADRON(1942), p; GUNG HO!(1943), p; WE'VE NEVER BEEN LICKED(1943), p; LADIES COURAGEOUS(1944), p; CANYON PASSAGE(1946), p; NIGHT IN PARADISE, A(1946), p; LOST MOMENT, THE(1947), p; SMASH-UP, THE STORY OF A WOMAN(1947), p; JOAN OF ARC(1948), p; TAP ROOTS(1948), p; TULSA(1949), p; ALADDIN AND HIS LAMP(1952), p; LADY IN THE IRON MASK(1952), p; FORT VENGEANCE(1953), p; KANSAS PACIFIC(1953), p; ADVENTURES OF HAJJI BABA(1954), p; RIOT IN CELL BLOCK 11(1954), p; INVASION OF THE BODY SNATCHERS(1956), p; NAVY WIFE(1956), p; I WANT TO LIVE!(1958), p; CLEOPATRA(1963), p
Hans Wangraf
CONVOY(1940)
Kathy Waniata
THREE NUTS IN SEARCH OF A BOLT(1964)
Edward Wanisko
WILD REBELS, THE(1967)
Iwa Wanja
COURT CONCERT, THE(1936, Ger.); LIFE BEGINS ANEW(1938, Ger.)
Lia Wanjtal
MURMUR OF THE HEART(1971, Fr./Ital./Ger.)
Wanka
M(1933, Ger.)
R. Wanka
MAGIC FACE, THE(1951, Aust.)
Rolf Wanka
CAPTAIN SINDBAD(1963)
Josef Wanke
EMIL AND THE DETECTIVES(1964), cos; GREAT WALTZ, THE(1972), cos
Peppi Wanke
PERMISSION TO KILL(1975, U.S./Aust.), cos
Thomas P. Wann
1984
TANK(1984)
Ken Wannberg
HUCKLEBERRY FINN(1974); LEPKE(1975, U.S./Israel), m; BITTERSWEET LOVE(1976), m; LATE SHOW, THE(1977), m; AMATEUR, THE(1982), m; MOTHER LODE(1982), m, md; LOSIN' IT(1983), m; OF UNKNOWN ORIGIN(1983, Can.), m
1984
BLAME IT ON RIO(1984), m; PHILADELPHIA EXPERIMENT, THE(1984), m
Kenn Wannberg
TRIBUTE(1980, Can.), m
Kenneth Wannberg
PEACE KILLERS, THE(1971), m; TENDER WARRIOR, THE(1971), m
Wannemann
M(1933, Ger.)
Hughes Wanner
FOUR BAGS FULL(1957, Fr./Ital.); NIGHT OF THE FOLLOWING DAY, THE(1969, Brit.)
Hugues Wanner
DAY AND THE HOUR, THE(1963, Fr./ Ital.); FANTOMAS(1966, Fr./Ital.)

Galbert Wanoskia
CASEY'S SHADOW(1978)
Walter Wanper
RECKLESS MOMENTS, THE(1949), p
Norman Wanstall
JOANNA(1968, Brit.), ed; LOLA(1971, Brit./Ital.), ed; JERUSALEM FILE, THE(1972, U.S./Israel), ed; NEITHER THE SEA NOR THE SAND(1974, Brit.), ed; WHO?(1975, Brit./Ger.), ed
Wayne Want
DARK SIDE OF TOMORROW, THE(1970)
Misc. Talkies
JUST THE TWO OF US(1975)
Norman Wanvick
CREEPING FLESH,THE(1973, Brit.), ph
Arthur Wanzer
SOLDIERS OF THE STORM(1933); UNKNOWN VALLEY(1933); MADAME SPY(1934); STUDENT TOUR(1934); HIGH SCHOOL GIRL(1935); GENTLEMAN FROM LOUISIANA(1936); HEARTS IN BONDAGE(1936); MY MAN GODFREY(1936)
Arthur G. Wanzer
LAW AND ORDER(1932); SHE MARRIED HER BOSS(1935)
Orville Wanzer
DEVIL'S MISTRESS, THE(1968), d&w
War
RIVER NIGER, THE(1976), m; YOUNGBLOOD(1978), m
War Admiral
WINNER'S CIRCLE, THE(1948)
John War Eagle
GOLDEN WEST, THE(1932); BROKEN ARROW(1950); TICKET TO TOMAHAWK(1950); LAST OUTPOST, THE(1951); BUGLES IN THE AFTERNOON(1952); LARAMIE MOUNTAINS(1952); LAST OF THE COMANCHES(1952); PONY SOLDIER(1952); BLACK DAKOTAS, THE(1954); THEY RODE WEST(1954); WESTWARD HO THE WAGONS!(1956); OUTSIDER, THE(1962); FLAP(1970)
Percy Waram
MUTINY ON THE BOUNTY(1935); ONE THIRD OF A NATION(1939); MINISTRY OF FEAR(1945); IT HAD TO BE YOU(1947); LATE GEORGE APLEY, THE(1947); BIG HANGOVER, THE(1950); FACE IN THE CROWD, A(1957)
David Warbeck
MY LOVER, MY SON(1970, Brit.); TROG(1970, Brit.); TWINS OF EVIL(1971, Brit.); SWEET SUZY(1973); CRAZE(1974, Brit.)
1984
BLACK CAT, THE(1984, Ital./Brit.); HUNTERS OF THE GOLDEN COBRA, THE(1984, Ital.); LASSITER(1984); LAST HUNTER, THE(1984, Ital.)
Misc. Talkies
BLACKSNAKE(1973); SEVEN DOORS OF DEATH(1983)
Christopher Warbey
END OF THE AFFAIR, THE(1955, Brit.); PERIL FOR THE GUY(1956, Brit.); SAFARI(1956); DEVIL'S PASS, THE(1957, Brit.); SALVAGE GANG, THE(1958, Brit.)
Dorothy Warboys
Misc. Silents
FLOTSAM(1921)
Jack Warboys
Misc. Silents
FLOTSAM(1921)
Ani Warbrick
Misc. Silents
DEVIL'S PIT, THE(1930)
Patiti Warbrick
Misc. Silents
DEVIL'S PIT, THE(1930)
Patrick Warbrick
LAND OF FURY(1955 Brit.)
Bertram Warburgh
LOST WEEKEND, THE(1945)
Cotton Warburton
BIG CITY(1937); CALLAWAY WENT THATAWAY(1951), ed; STRICTLY DISHONORABLE(1951), ed; SKIRTS AHOY!(1952), ed; ABOVE AND BEYOND(1953), ed; ARENA(1953), ed; CRAZYLEGS, ALL AMERICAN(1953), ed; REMAINS TO BE SEEN(1953), ed; SOMBRERO(1953), ed; UNCHAINED(1955), ed; WESTWARD HO THE WAGONS!(1956), ed; SIGN OF ZORRO, THE(1960), ed; TEN WHO DARED(1960), ed; ABSENT-MINDED PROFESSOR, THE(1961), ed; BON VOYAGE(1962), ed; MOON PILOT(1962), ed; MIRACLE OF THE WHITE STALLIONS(1963), ed; SON OF FLUBBER(1963), ed; EMIL AND THE DETECTIVES(1964), ed; MARY POPPINS(1964), ed; MISADVENTURES OF MERLIN JONES, THE(1964), ed; MONKEY'S UNCLE, THE(1965), ed; THAT DARN CAT(1965), ed; LT. ROBIN CRUSOE, U.S.N.(1966), ed; HAPPIEST MILLIONAIRE, THE(1967), ed; LOVE BUG, THE(1968), ed; ONE AND ONLY GENUINE ORIGINAL FAMILY BAND, THE(1968), ed; BOATNIKS, THE(1970), ed; COMPUTER WORE TENNIS SHOES, THE(1970), ed; BEDKNOBS AND BROOMSTICKS(1971), ed; SCANDALOUS JOHN(1971), ed; NOW YOU SEE HIM, NOW YOU DON'T(1972), ed; WORLD'S GREATEST ATHLETE, THE(1973), ed; CASTAWAY COWBOY, THE(1974), ed; HERBIE RIDES AGAIN(1974), ed; STRONGEST MAN IN THE WORLD, THE(1975), ed; FREAKY FRIDAY(1976), ed; NO DEPOSIT, NO RETURN(1976), ed; TREASURE OF MATECUMBE(1976), ed; HERBIE GOES TO MONTE CARLO(1977), ed; CAT FROM OUTER SPACE, THE(1978), ed
Doreen Warburton
THEY'RE A WEIRD MOB(1966, Aus.); NED KELLY(1970, Brit.); DEMONSTRATOR(1971, Aus.); NICKEL QUEEN, THE(1971, Aus.); ADAM'S WOMAN(1972, Austral.)
Irvine Warburton
AIR RAID WARDENS(1943), ed; THREE HEARTS FOR JULIA(1943), ed; THIS MAN'S NAVY(1945), ed; FAITHFUL IN MY FASHION(1946), ed; LOVE LAUGHS AT ANDY HARDY(1946), ed; SAILOR TAKES A WIFE, THE(1946), ed; UP GOES MAISIE(1946), ed; CYNTHIA(1947), ed; SUN COMES UP, THE(1949), ed; SHADOW ON THE WALL(1950), ed; SKIPPER SURPRISED HIS WIFE, THE(1950), ed; TWO WEEKS WITH LOVE(1950), ed; EXCUSE MY DUST(1951), ed; THREE GUYS NAMED MIKE(1951), ed
Irving Warburton
NEPTUNE'S DAUGHTER(1949), ed; BLACK HAND, THE(1950), ed

John Warburton
SECRETS OF THE FRENCH POLICE(1932); SILVER LINING(1932); BLIND ADVENTURE(1933); CAVALCADE(1933); CHARLIE CHAN'S GREATEST CASE(1933); LOVE IS LIKE THAT(1933); STUDY IN SCARLET, A(1933); LET'S TALK IT OVER(1934); DIZZY DAMES(1936); PARTNERS OF THE PLAINS(1938); SISTERS, THE(1938); CAPTAIN FURY(1939); MARRIAGE IS A PRIVATE AFFAIR(1944); NOTHING BUT TROUBLE(1944); WHITE CLIFFS OF DOVER, THE(1944); CONFIDENTIAL AGENT(1945); DANGEROUS PARTNERS(1945); SARATOGA TRUNK(1945); VALLEY OF DECISION, THE(1945); LIVING IN A BIG WAY(1947); TARZAN AND THE HUNTRESS(1947); CITY BENEATH THE SEA(1953); EAST OF SUMATRA(1953); ROYAL AFRICAN RIFLES, THE(1953); HEADLINE HUNTERS(1955); SECRET FILE: HOLLYWOOD(1962); KING RAT(1965); ASSAULT ON A QUEEN(1966)

Andrzej Warchol
CAMERA BUFF(1983, Pol.)

Suni Warcloud
JIM THORPE–ALL AMERICAN(1951)

Abril Ward
DREAM MAKER, THE(1963, Brit.)

Al Ward
FANTASM(1976, Aus.)

Al C. Ward
BLACK PIRATES, THE(1954, Mex.), w; PLEASE MURDER ME(1956), w

Alan Ward
EXPERIMENT PERILOUS(1944); MADEMOISELLE FIFI(1944); MY PAL, WOLF(1944); NEVADA(1944); BANDITS OF THE BADLANDS(1945); DEADLINE AT DAWN(1946); FRENCH KEY, THE(1946); MY REPUTATION(1946); NOTORIOUS(1946)

Albert Ward
LUCKY MASCOT, THE(1951, Brit.)
Silents
PHANTOM PICTURE, THE(1916, Brit.), d&w; PLEYDELL MYSTERY, THE(1916, Brit.), d&w; QUEEN OF THE WICKED(1916, Brit.), d&w; QUEEN OF MY HEART(1917, Brit.), d; AUNT RACHEL(1920, Brit.), d; LAST ROSE OF SUMMER, THE(1920, Brit.), d; PRIDE OF THE FANCY, THE(1920, Brit.), d
Misc. Silents
LOVES AND ADVENTURES IN THE LIFE OF SHAKESPEARE(1914, Brit.); FEMALE SWINDLER, THE(1916, Brit.), d; GIRL WHO WRECKED HIS HOME, THE(1916, Brit.), d; WHEN WOMAN HATES(1916, Brit.), d; LINKED BY FATE(1919, Brit.), d; MEMBER OF THE TATTERSALL'S, A(1919, Brit.), d; NANCE(1920, Brit.), d; MR. PIM PASSES BY(1921, Brit.), d; BROKEN SHADOWS(1922), d; STABLE COMPANIONS(1922, Brit.), d

Alcardo Ward
SPIRITS OF THE DEAD(1969, Fr./Ital.)

Alice Ward
SKYLINE(1931); FACE ON THE BARROOM FLOOR, THE(1932); RAINBOW TRAIL(1932); CROSSROADS(1942)
Silents
PORTS OF CALL(1925)

Alonzo Ward
JAWS 3-D(1983)

Amelia Ward
COME OUT FIGHTING(1945)

Amelita Ward
FALCON AND THE CO-EDS, THE(1943); FALCON IN DANGER, THE(1943); GANGWAY FOR TOMORROW(1943); SKY'S THE LIMIT, THE(1943); GILDERSLEEVE'S GHOST(1944); SEVEN DAYS ASHORE(1944); JUNGLE CAPTIVE(1945); ROUGH, TOUGH AND READY(1945); SWINGIN' ON A RAINBOW(1945); DARK MIRROR, THE(1946); WHEN A GIRL'S BEAUTIFUL(1947); SMUGGLERS' COVE(1948); RIM OF THE CANYON(1949); SLATTERY'S HURRICANE(1949)

Amlita Ward
CLANCY STREET BOYS(1943)

Andrew Ward
MACK, THE(1973)

Anthony Ward
PARIS UNDERGROUND(1945); STORM WARNING(1950)

Arch Ward
GOLDEN GLOVES STORY, THE(1950)

Autry Ward
MACKINTOSH & T.J.(1975)

B. A. Ward
LORD SHANGO(1975)

B.J. Ward
TOM HORN(1980); GALAXY EXPRESS(1982, Jap.)

Baby Ivy Ward
Misc. Silents
CYCLONE HIGGINS, D.D.(1918); HEADS WIN(1919); TEN NIGHTS IN A BAR ROOM(1921); LOST IN A BIG CITY(1923); FLOODGATES(1924)

Beatrice Ward
NOTHING BUT THE NIGHT(1975, Brit.)

Bernard Ward
300 YEAR WEEKEND(1971)

Bill Ward
AMAZING MRS. HOLLIDAY(1943); TO EACH HIS OWN(1946); GOLD RAIDERS, THE(1952); SON OF THE RENEGADE(1953); WAR ARROW(1953); BLACK WHIP, THE(1956); HIDDEN GUNS(1956); NAKED GUN, THE(1956); NO PLACE TO LAND(1958); BALLAD OF A GUNFIGHTER(1964), p,d&w; INCREDIBLY STRANGE CREATURES WHO STOPPED LIVING AND BECAME CRAZY MIXED-UP ZOMBIES, THE(1965); ALF 'N' FAMILY(1968, Brit.)
1984
SECRET PLACES(1984, Brit.)

Billy Ward
EXPERIMENT PERILOUS(1944); THIS LOVE OF OURS(1945)

Black-Jack Ward
FIGHTING MARSHAL, THE(1932)

Blackjack Ward
RANGE LAW(1931); WHEELS OF DESTINY(1934); GHOST RIDER, THE(1935); END OF THE TRAIL(1936); FUGITIVE SHERIFF, THE(1936); O'MALLEY OF THE MOUNTED(1936); TOLL OF THE DESERT(1936); HOPALONG RIDES AGAIN(1937); PLAINSMAN, THE(1937); FRONTIERSMAN, THE(1938); GUNSMOKE TRAIL(1938); STAGECOACH DAYS(1938); TEXAS STAMPEDE(1939); TEXAS TERRORS(1940);

WESTERNER, THE(1940); RIDERS OF THE NORTHLAND(1942); SHUT MY BIG MOUTH(1942)

Bobbie Ward
CATHY'S CHILD(1979, Aus.)

Bobby Ward
MY BRILLIANT CAREER(1980, Aus.)

Brad Ward
LAWLESS STREET, A(1955), w

Brain Ward
GOODBYE PORK PIE(1981, New Zealand)

Brendan Ward
TAPS(1981)

Burt Ward
BATMAN(1966)

Carrie Clark Ward
Silents
HONOR SYSTEM, THE(1917); OUT OF THE STORM(1920); BOB HAMPTON OF PLACER(1921); HER WINNING WAY(1921); LOVE CHARM, THE(1921); ONE WILD WEEK(1921); SHAM(1921); PENROD(1922); SCARAMOUCHE(1923); SOUL OF THE BEAST(1923); HIS HOUR(1924); EAGLE, THE(1925); ROSE OF THE WORLD(1925); TOP OF NEW YORK, THE(1925)
Misc. Silents
OLD LADY 31(1920); BREAKING INTO SOCIETY(1923)

Carrie Clarke Ward
Silents
AWFUL TRUTH, THE(1925)

Catherine Clare Ward
WHITE LIES(1935)

Chance Ward
BAT WHISPERS, THE(1930)
Silents
ISLAND OF INTRIGUE, THE(1919); ROLLED STOCKINGS(1927)

Charles Ward
TURNING POINT, THE(1977); STAYING ALIVE(1983)

Clara Ward
TIME TO SING, A(1968)

Colin Ward
JACKPOT, THE(1950)

Colleen Ward
ZAZA(1939)

Craig Ward
Silents
OUR HOSPITALITY(1923)
Misc. Silents
CUSTOMARY TWO WEEKS, THE(1917); HEARTS AFLAME(1923)

D.J. Ward
THE BEACHCOMBER(1938, Brit.)

David Ward
ONE OF OUR AIRCRAFT IS MISSING(1942, Brit.); TWILIGHT HOUR(1944, Brit.); YELLOW CANARY, THE(1944, Brit.); COLONEL BLIMP(1945, Brit.); GREAT DAY(1945, Brit.); NOTORIOUS GENTLEMAN(1945, Brit.); ADVENTURESS, THE(1946, Brit.); HOTEL RESERVE(1946, Brit.); MY BROTHER JONATHAN(1949, Brit.); MURDER IN THE CATHEDRAL(1952, Brit.)

David S. Ward
STEELYARD BLUES(1973), w; STING, THE(1973), w; CANNERY ROW(1982), d&w; STING II, THE(1983), w

Dervis Ward
PRIVATE ANGELO(1949, Brit.); SHADOW OF THE PAST(1950, Brit.); LONG HAUL, THE(1957, Brit.); BEN HUR(1959); GIDEON OF SCOTLAND YARD(1959, Brit.); GORGO(1961, Brit.); LONELINESS OF THE LONG DISTANCE RUNNER, THE(1962, Brit.); DEADLIER THAN THE MALE(1967, Brit.); TO SIR, WITH LOVE(1967, Brit.); VENGEANCE OF SHE, THE(1968, Brit.)

Diana Ward
SHE SHALL HAVE MUSIC(1935, Brit.); ELIZA COMES TO STAY(1936, Brit.); MURDER IN THE NIGHT(1940, Brit.)

Dick Ward
COPS AND ROBBERS(1973)

Don Ward
MORGAN'S MARAUDERS(1929)

Dorothea Ward
ROYAL WEDDING(1951)

Dorothy Ward
WORDS AND MUSIC(1929); COURAGE(1930); GOLDEN WEST, THE(1932)
Silents
JOY STREET(1929); PROTECTION(1929)
Misc. Silents
WALLOPING KID(1926)

Doublas Turner Ward
MAN AND BOY(1972)

Eddie Ward
BRIDE OF THE REGIMENT(1930), m; TRAPEZE(1956)

Edmund Ward
YANK AT OXFORD, A(1938), m; AMSTERDAM AFFAIR, THE(1968 Brit.), w; VIOLENT ENEMY, THE(1969, Brit.), w; GOODBYE GEMINI(1970, Brit.), w
1984
KINGS AND DESPERATE MEN(1984, Brit.), w

Edward Ward
BISHOP MISBEHAVES, THE(1933), m; GIFT OF GAB(1934), md; GIRL O' MY DREAMS(1935), m; HERE COMES THE BAND(1935), m; KIND LADY(1935), m; MYSTERY OF EDWIN DROOD, THE(1935), m; NO MORE LADIES(1935), m; PUBLIC HERO NO. 1(1935), m; MOONLIGHT MURDER(1936), m; RIFF-RAFF(1936), m; SAN FRANCISCO(1936), m; SINNER TAKE ALL(1936), m; SWORN ENEMY(1936), m; WOMEN ARE TROUBLE(1936), m; BAD GUY(1937), m; DOUBLE WEDDING(1937), m; GOOD OLD SOAK, THE(1937), m; MAN OF THE PEOPLE(1937), m; MANNEQUIN(1937), m; NAVY BLUE AND GOLD(1937), m; NIGHT MUST FALL(1937), m; SARATOGA(1937), m; WOMEN MEN MARRY, THE(1937), m; BOYS TOWN(1938), m; CROWD ROARS, THE(1938), m; HOLD THAT KISS(1938), m; LORD JEFF(1938), m; LOVE IS A HEADACHE(1938), m; MEET THE MAYOR(1938), m; PARADISE FOR THREE(1938), m; SHOPWORN ANGEL(1938), m; STABLEMATES(1938), m; TOY WIFE, THE(1938), m; VACATION FROM LOVE(1938), m/l; ANOTHER THIN

MAN(1939), m; BAD LITTLE ANGEL(1939), m; DANCING CO-ED(1939), m; REMEMBER?(1939), m; SOCIETY LAWYER(1939), m; THESE GLAMOUR GIRLS(1939), m; THUNDER AFLOAT(1939), m; WOMEN, THE(1939), m; CONGO MAISIE(1940), m; DANCE, GIRL, DANCE(1940), m; KIT CARSON(1940), m, md; MY SON, MY SON!(1940), md; SON OF MONTE CRISTO(1940), m; SOUTH OF PAGO PAGO(1940), md; YOUNG TOM EDISON(1940), m; MR. AND MRS. SMITH(1941), m; TANKS A MILLION(1941), md; DUDES ARE PRETTY PEOPLE(1942), m; FLYING WITH MUSIC(1942), m; HAY FOOT(1942), m; MOONLIGHT IN VERMONT(1943), m; PHANTOM OF THE OPERA(1943), m, md; THAT NAZTY NUISANCE(1943), m; ALI BABA AND THE FORTY THIEVES(1944), m; BOWERY TO BROADWAY(1944), m&md; CLIMAX, THE(1944), md; COBRA WOMAN(1944), m; GHOST CATCHERS(1944), m; GYPSY WILDCAT(1944), m&md; HER PRIMITIVE MAN(1944), md; FRISCO SAL(1945), md; SALOME, WHERE SHE DANCED(1945), m, md; SONG OF THE SARONG(1945), m; IT HAPPENED ON 5TH AVENUE(1947), m; BABE RUTH STORY, THE(1948), m

Eileen Ward
1984
WHERE THE BOYS ARE '84(1984)

Evelyn Ward
Misc. Silents
BRAND OF LOPEZ, THE(1920)

Fannie Ward
Silents
EACH PEARL A TEAR(1916); TENNESSEE'S PARDNER(1916); INNOCENT(1918); NARROW PATH, THE(1918)
Misc. Silents
CHEAT, THE(1915); FOR THE DEFENCE(1916); GUTTER MAGDALENE, THE(1916); WITCHCRAFT(1916); YEARS OF THE LOCUST, THE(1916); BETTY TO THE RESCUE(1917); CRYSTAL GAZER, THE(1917); HER STRANGE WEDDING(1917); ON THE LEVEL(1917); SCHOOL FOR HUSBANDS, A(1917); UNCONQUERED(1917); WINNING OF SALLY TEMPLE, THE(1917); JAPANESE NIGHTINGALE, A(1918); YELLOW TICKET, THE(1918); COMMON CLAY(1919); CRY OF THE WEAK, THE(1919); OUR BETTER SELVES(1919); PROFITEERS, THE(1919)

Fanny Ward
Silents
MARRIAGE OF KITTY, THE(1915)
Misc. Silents
LA RAFALE(1920, Fr.); LE SECRET DU 'LONE STAR'(1920, Fr.)

Fleming Ward
Misc. Silents
WHEN MEN DESIRE(1919); INVISIBLE BOND, THE(1920)

Frances Ward
OLD ACQUAINTANCE(1943); FLASH GORDON(1980)

Francis L. Ward
OPERATION PETTICOAT(1959)

Frank Ward
OUTLAW, THE(1943); MACK, THE(1973)

Fred Ward
ESCAPE FROM ALCATRAZ(1979); CARNY(1980); SOUTHERN COMFORT(1981); RIGHT STUFF, THE(1983); SILKWOOD(1983); TIMERIDER(1983); UNCOMMON VALOR(1983)
1984
SWING SHIFT(1984)
Misc. Silents
CRICKET, THE(1917)

Fuzzy Ward
GOLD RAIDERS, THE(1952)

G. H. Ward
MURDER AT MONTE CARLO(1935, Brit.), art d

George Ward
THEIR OWN DESIRE(1929), m; TURNERS OF PROSPECT ROAD, THE(1947, Brit.), art d

Georgina Ward
MAN WHO FINALLY DIED, THE(1967, Brit.); TWO WEEKS IN SEPTEMBER(1967, Fr./Brit.)

Gerald Ward
Silents
CAPTIVE, THE(1915); WARRENS OF VIRGINIA, THE(1915)
Misc. Silents
FIGHTING HOPE, THE(1915)

Gil Ward
Misc. Talkies
1ST NOTCH, THE(1977), d

Guy Ward
STUD, THE(1979, Brit.)

Hap Ward
Silents
FUGITIVES(1929)

Ivy Ward
Silents
NEIGHBORS(1918); GUILTY OF LOVE(1920); NEGLECTED WIVES(1920)

Jack Ward
ONE WAY TRAIL, THE(1931); TWO GUN MAN, THE(1931); HELL FIRE AUSTIN(1932); POCATELLO KID(1932); TEXAS GUN FIGHTER(1932); COME ON TARZAN(1933); LONE AVENGER, THE(1933); GUN JUSTICE(1934); HONOR OF THE RANGE(1934); SMOKING GUNS(1934); HEIR TO TROUBLE(1936)

Jackie Ward
STRAIGHT TO HEAVEN(1939); YOUNG GIRLS OF ROCHEFORT, THE(1968, Fr.)

James Ward
KISS ME, STUPID(1964); KITTEN WITH A WHIP(1964); NIGHT OF THE IGUANA, THE(1964); RED LINE 7000(1965); RUN WITH THE WIND(1966, Brit.), p

Janet Ward
FAIL SAFE(1964); ANDERSON TAPES, THE(1971); NIGHT MOVES(1975)

Jason Ward
Misc. Talkies
1ST NOTCH, THE(1977)

Jay Ward
REDUCING(1931); GOODBYE AGAIN(1933); MAN WHO DARED, THE(1933); PILGRIMAGE(1933); TO THE LAST MAN(1933); AS HUSBANDS GO(1934); BIG HEARTED HERBERT(1934); HOLD THAT GIRL(1934); CAPTAINS COURAGEOUS(1937);

Jay Walter Ward
STOP, LOOK, AND LOVE(1939); STRANGE CASE OF DR. MEADE(1939); EDISON, THE MAN(1940); POT O' GOLD(1941); KEEPER OF THE FLAME(1942); HARRIGAN'S KID(1943); HUMAN COMEDY, THE(1943); DESTINATION TOKYO(1944); WING AND A PRAYER(1944)

Jay Walter Ward
IN SPITE OF DANGER(1935)

Jerome Ward
HEROES OF THE RANGE(1936); OLD WYOMING TRAIL, THE(1937)

Joan Ward
NO BLADE OF GRASS(1970, Brit.)

John Ward
BOOTS AND SADDLES(1937); BULLDOG DRUMMOND COMES BACK(1937); GALLOPING DYNAMITE(1937); HEADLINE CRASHER(1937); RIDERS OF THE WHISTLING DYNAMITE(1938); PROFESSOR BEWARE(1938); SWING, SISTER, SWING(1938); TWO-GUN TROUBADOR(1939); GUNSMOKE IN TUCSON(1958); SPACE MASTER X-7(1958); PT 109(1963); LOVELY WAY TO DIE, A(1968), set d
Misc. Talkies
RIDIN' THE TRAIL(1940)

Jomarie Ward
PRETTY MAIDS ALL IN A ROW(1971)

Jon Ward
THX 1138(1971), stunts

Jon Parker Ward
SCAVENGER HUNT(1979), stunts

Jonas Ward
BUCHANAN RIDES ALONE(1958), w

Joni Lynn Ward
PRIVATE SCHOOL(1983)

Julia Ward
TERROR SHIP(1954, Brit.), w

Julie Ward
Misc. Talkies
1ST NOTCH, THE(1977)

Katherin Clare Ward
STRICTLY MODERN(1930)

Katherine Ward
DRAG(1929); ISLE OF LOST SHIPS(1929); MIDNIGHT DADDIES(1929); AIR EAGLES(1932); SON OF KONG(1933)

Katherine C. Ward
THREE WISE GIRLS(1932)

Katherine Claire Ward
MAN AGAINST WOMAN(1932); LILLY TURNER(1933)

Katherine Clare Ward
LET 'EM HAVE IT(1935); LIFE BEGINS AT 40(1935); SECRET BRIDE, THE(1935)

Kathrin Claire Ward
VANITY STREET(1932)

Kathrin Clare Ward
CONQUERING HORDE, THE(1931); TEN NIGHTS IN A BARROOM(1931); THREE GIRLS LOST(1931); JEALOUSY(1934); KEY, THE(1934); ONCE TO EVERY WOMAN(1934); PUBLIC ENEMY'S WIFE(1936); STAGE STRUCK(1936); WHITE ANGEL, THE(1936); SHE LOVED A FIREMAN(1937)
Misc. Talkies
CALL OF THE WEST(1930)

Kelly Ward
GREASE(1978); BIG RED ONE, THE(1980); ZOOT SUIT(1981)

Lalla Ward
VAMPIRE CIRCUS(1972, Brit.); GOT IT MADE(1974, Brit.); ROSEBUD(1975); CROSSED SWORDS(1978)

Lancer Ward
SONG OF THE LOON(1970)

Larry Ward
DISTANT TRUMPET, A(1964); HOMBRE(1967)
Misc. Talkies
DEATHHEAD VIRGIN, THE(1974)

Lawrence Ward
LUXURY GIRLS(1953, Ital.); MAD ABOUT MEN(1954, Brit.)

Leah Ward
TOGETHER BROTHERS(1974)

Les Ward
LUCKY MASCOT, THE(1951, Brit.)

Lesley Ward
HANOVER STREET(1979, Brit.)

Lillian Ward
Misc. Silents
DEVIL'S CONFESSION, THE(1921)

Lita Ward
AERIAL GUNNER(1943)

Luci Ward
LAW IN HER HANDS, THE(1936), w; MURDER BY AN ARISTOCRAT(1936), w; CHEROKEE STRIP(1937), w; LAND BEYOND THE LAW(1937), w; MELODY FOR TWO(1937), w; MOUNTAIN JUSTICE(1937), w; CALL THE MESQUITEERS(1938), w; MAN FROM MUSIC MOUNTAIN(1938), w; OVERLAND STAGE RAIDERS(1938), w; PANAMINT'S BAD MAN(1938), w; RED RIVER RANGE(1938), w; SANTA FE STAMPEDE(1938), w; ARIZONA KID, THE(1939), w; COLORADO SUNSET(1939), w; KANSAS TERRORS, THE(1939), w; MEXICALI ROSE(1939), w; NEW FRONTIER(1939), w; BEYOND THE SACRAMENTO(1941), w; BAD MEN OF THE HILLS(1942), w; LAWLESS PLAINSMEN(1942), w; LONE STAR VIGILANTES, THE(1942), w; CALLING WILD BILL ELLIOTT(1943), w; FIGHTING BUCKAROO, THE(1943), w; LAW OF THE NORTHWEST(1943), w; COWBOY FROM LONESOME RIVER(1944), w; RIDING WEST(1944), w; SUNDOWN VALLEY(1944), w; FROZEN GHOST, THE(1945), w; BADMAN'S TERRITORY(1946), w; DICK TRACY VS. CUEBALL(1946), w; BLACK BART(1948), w; RETURN OF THE BADMEN(1948), w; LAST BANDIT, THE(1949), w; RUSTLERS(1949), w; BLACKJACK KETCHUM, DESPERADO(1956), w; NIGHT THE WORLD EXPLODED, THE(1957), w; RIDE TO HANGMAN'S TREE, THE(1967), w

Lucille Ward
WHAT A MAN(1930); SIDE SHOW(1931); PURCHASE PRICE, THE(1932); REBECCA OF SUNNYBROOK FARM(1932); LILLY TURNER(1933); MAN OF SENTIMENT, A(1933); ZOO IN BUDAPEST(1933); LITTLE MISS MARKER(1934); MARRIAGE ON APPROVAL(1934); DR. SOCRATES(1935); SPECIAL AGENT(1935); WAY DOWN

EAST(1935); FATAL LADY(1936); HARVESTER, THE(1936); NAVY BORN(1936); RETURN OF JIMMY VALENTINE, THE(1936); WIFE VERSUS SECRETARY(1936); WHEN YOU'RE IN LOVE(1937); MOTHER CAREY'S CHICKENS(1938); SONS OF THE LEGION(1938); FIRST LOVE(1939); CHRISTMAS IN JULY(1940); SONG OF BERNADETTE, THE(1943); HENRY ALDRICH'S LITTLE SECRET(1944)

Silents

GIRL FROM HIS TOWN, THE(1915); INFATUATION(1915); FRAME UP, THE(1917); IN BAD(1918); AMATEUR ADVENTURESS, THE(1919); EAST SIDE—WEST SIDE(1923); SIXTY CENTS AN HOUR(1923); OH, DOCTOR(1924); SKINNER'S DRESS SUIT(1926)

Misc. Silents

LONESOME HEART(1915); MIRACLE OF LIFE, THE(1915); HOUSE OF LIES, THE(1916); ROAD TO LOVE, THE(1916); GIRL IN THE LIMOUSINE, THE(1924)

Mrs. Lucille Ward

Silents

ISLAND OF INTRIGUE, THE(1919)

Lyman Ward

WHOSE LIFE IS IT ANYWAY?(1981)

1984

MOSCOW ON THE HUDSON(1984); PROTOCOL(1984)

Mackenzie Ward

LUCKY IN LOVE(1929); SYNCOPATION(1929); LADY OF SCANDAL, THE(1930); SUNNY(1930); GOLDEN CAGE, THE(1933, Brit.); WHILE PARENTS SLEEP(1935, Brit.); AS YOU LIKE IT(1936, Brit.); STUDENT'S ROMANCE, THE(1936, Brit.); GIRL IN THE TAXI(1937, Brit.); SONS OF THE SEA(1939, Brit.); OVER THE MOON(1940, Brit.); TURNED OUT NICE AGAIN(1941, Brit.); REMARKABLE MR. KIPPS(1942, Brit.); WORLD OWES ME A LIVING, THE(1944, Brit.); CAESAR AND CLEOPATRA(1946, Brit.); CARNIVAL(1946, Brit.); DARK ROAD, THE(1948, Brit.); MONKEY'S PAW, THE(1948, Brit.); DARK SECRET(1949, Brit.); RUN FOR YOUR MONEY, A(1950, Brit.); SOMETHING IN THE CITY(1950, Brit.); LAUGHTER IN PARADISE(1951, Brit.); MADAME LOUISE(1951, Brit.)

Margaret Ward

RING OF SPIES(1964, Brit.); HENRY VIII AND HIS SIX WIVES(1972, Brit.)

Marion Ward

HIGH WIND IN JAMAICA, A(1965)

Silents

MAN WHO LAUGHS, THE(1927), w

Mark Ward

ATTACK ON THE IRON COAST(1968, U.S./Brit.)

Marshall Ward

OWL AND THE PUSSYCAT, THE(1970)

Mary Augusta Ward

Silents

MARRIAGE OF WILLIAM ASHE, THE(1921), w

Mary Jane Ward

SNAKE PIT, THE(1948), w

May Ward

Misc. Silents

CONTINENTAL GIRL, A(1915); WHERE IS MY FATHER?(1916)

Michael Ward

TOMORROW IS FOREVER(1946); IDEAL HUSBAND, AN(1948, Brit.); HIGH JINKS IN SOCIETY(1949, Brit.); SLEEPING CAR TO TRIESTE(1949, Brit.); STOP PRESS GIRL(1949, Brit.); NO TRACE(1950, Brit.); TRIO(1950, Brit.); WHAT THE BUTLER SAW(1950, Brit.); CHEER THE BRAVE(1951, Brit.); CHELSEA STORY(1951, Brit.); GALLOPING MAJOR, THE(1951, Brit.); LILLI MARLENE(1951, Brit.); POOL OF LONDON(1951, Brit.); TOM BROWN'S SCHOOLDAYS(1951, Brit.); TONY DRAWS A HORSE(1951, Brit.); FRIGHTENED BRIDE, THE(1952, Brit.); FRIGHTENED MAN, THE(1952, Brit.); ISLAND RESCUE(1952, Brit.); MR. LORD SAYS NO(1952, Brit.); TREAD SOFTLY(1952, Brit.); WHISPERING SMITH VERSUS SCOTLAND YARD(1952, Brit.); 13 EAST STREET(1952, Brit.); FAKE, THE(1953, Brit.); LOVE LOTTERY, THE(1954, Brit.); MAN OF THE MOMENT(1955, Brit.); TROUBLE IN STORE(1955, Brit.); FINGER OF GUILT(1956, Brit.); JUMPING FOR JOY(1956, Brit.); PRIVATE'S PROGRESS(1956, Brit.); JUST MY LUCK(1957, Brit.); TEARS FOR SIMON(1957, Brit.); UP IN THE WORLD(1957, Brit.); I'M ALL RIGHT, JACK(1959, Brit.); UGLY DUCKLING, THE(1959, Brit.); DOCTOR IN LOVE(1960, Brit.); MAN IN A COCKED HAT(1960, Bri.); CARRY ON REGARDLESS(1961, Brit.); MARY HAD A LITTLE(1961, Brit.); PORTRAIT OF A SINNER(1961, Brit.); CARRY ON CABBIE(1963, Brit.); CARRY ON CLEO(1964, Brit.); WHERE THE BULLETS FLY(1966, Brit.); DON'T LOSE YOUR HEAD(1967, Brit.); SMASHING TIME(1967 Brit.); REVENGE OF THE PINK PANTHER(1978)

Michael Joseph Ward

RIDERS OF THE DAWN(1945)

Mike Ward

TEARS FOR SIMON(1957, Brit.)

Norman Ward

Misc. Silents

MODERN CAIN, A(1925)

Paddy Ward

RAILWAY CHILDREN, THE(1971, Brit.); VICTOR/VICTORIA(1982)

Patrick Ward

MONKEY'S PAW, THE(1948, Brit.); ISN'T LIFE WONDERFUL!(1953, Brit.), p; STONE(1974, Aus.); SIDECAR RACERS(1975, Aus.); CHAIN REACTION(1980, Aus.)

Peggy Ward

TICKLE ME(1965)

Penelope Ward

HER MAN GILBEY(1949, Brit.)

Penelope Dudley Ward

I STAND CONDEMNED(1936, Brit.); CITADEL, THE(1938); DANGEROUS CARGO(1939, Brit.); CASE OF THE FRIGHTENED LADY, THE(1940. Brit.); CONVOY(1940); MAJOR BARBARA(1941, Brit.); IN WHICH WE SERVE(1942, Brit.); ADVENTURE FOR TWO(1945, Brit.)

Perry "Bill" Ward

FOREVER AMBER(1947)

Perry William Ward

FOXES OF HARROW, THE(1947)

Phil Ward

STREAMERS(1983)

Polly Ward

ALF'S BUTTON(1930, Brit.); HARMONY HEAVEN(1930, Brit.); HIS LORDSHIP(1932, Brit.); KENTUCKY MINSTRELS(1934, Brit.); IT'S A BET(1935, Brit.); OLD CURIOSITY SHOP, THE(1935, Brit.); ANNIE LAURIE(1936, Brit.); SHIPMATES O' MINE(1936, Brit.); SHOW FLAT(1936, Brit.); FEATHER YOUR NEST(1937, Brit.); TELEVISION TALENT(1937, Brit.); HOLD MY HAND(1938, Brit.); THANK EVANS(1938, Brit.); BULLDOG SEES IT THROUGH(1940, Brit.); IT'S IN THE AIR(1940, Brit.); SIDEWALKS OF LONDON(1940, Brit.); WOMEN AREN'T ANGELS(1942, Brit.); NEW FACES(1954)

Silents

THIS MARRIAGE BUSINESS(1927, Brit.)

Rachel Ward

NIGHT SCHOOL(1981); TERROR EYES(1981); DEAD MEN DON'T WEAR PLAID(1982); SHARKY'S MACHINE(1982); FINAL TERROR, THE(1983)

1984

AGAINST ALL ODDS(1984)

Misc. Talkies

CAMPSITE MASSACRE(1981)

Ralph Ward

WOODEN HORSE, THE(1951)

Raymond Ward

OLIVER!(1968, Brit.)

Rhett Ward

THREE MEN IN A BOAT(1958, Brit.)

Richard Ward

COOL WORLD, THE(1963); BLACK LIKE ME(1964); NOTHING BUT A MAN(1964); LEARNING TREE, THE(1969); BROTHER JOHN(1971); ACROSS 110TH STREET(1972); MANDINGO(1975); FOR PETE'S SAKE(1977); JERK, THE(1979); BRUBAKER(1980)

Robert Ward

STRAIT-JACKET(1964); DESERT RAVEN, THE(1965); SILENCERS, THE(1966)

Misc. Talkies

TIME OF FURY(1968)

Robert Ward

CATTLE ANNIE AND LITTLE BRITCHES(1981), w

Roberta Ward

GREAT MUPPET CAPER, THE(1981)

Robin Ward

EXPLOSION(1969, Can.); DR. FRANKENSTEIN ON CAMPUS(1970, Can.); SUDDEN FURY(1975, Can.)

Roger Ward

SET, THE(1970, Aus.), w; SQUEEZE A FLOWER(1970, Aus.); STONE(1974, Aus.); MAN FROM HONG KONG(1975); DEATHCHEATERS(1976, Aus.); HIGH ROLLING(1977, Aus.); IRISHMAN, THE(1978, Aus.); MAD MAX(1979, Aus.); LADY, STAY DEAD(1982, Aus.); PIRATE MOVIE, THE(1982, Aus.); ESCAPE 2000(1983, Aus.)

1984

BROTHERS(1984, Aus.), a, p,d&w

Rollo Ward

RAINBOW'S END(1935), w

Ronald Ward

ALIBI(1931, Brit.); LOVE'S OLD SWEET SONG(1933, Brit.); BRIDES TO BE(1934, Brit.); BROKEN ROSARY, THE(1934, Brit.); GIRLS WILL BE BOYS(1934, Brit.); EAST MEETS WEST(1936, Brit.); MAN BEHIND THE MASK, THE(1936, Brit.); PASSING OF THE THIRD FLOOR BACK, THE(1936, Brit.); SPLINTERS IN THE AIR(1937, Brit.); STRANGE EXPERIMENT(1937, Brit.); HE LOVED AN ACTRESS(1938, Brit.); CONFIDENTIAL LADY(1939, Brit.); GOODBYE MR. CHIPS(1939, Brit.); SIDEWALKS OF LONDON(1940, Brit.); THIS ENGLAND(1941, Brit.); TURNED OUT NICE AGAIN(1941, Brit.); WE'LL MEET AGAIN(1942, Brit.); ESCAPE TO DANGER(1943, Brit.); THEY MET IN THE DARK(1945, Brit.); CARNIVAL(1946, Brit.); OPERATION X(1951, Brit.); SECOND MRS. TANQUERAY, THE(1952, Brit.); STRAW MAN, THE(1953, Brit.); AUNT CLARA(1954, Brit.); RAINBOW JACKET, THE(1954, Brit.); TEARS FOR SIMON(1957, Brit.)

Roscoe Ward

Silents

WEST OF ZANZIBAR(1928)

S.J.H. "James" Ward

WHERE THE BULLETS FLY(1966, Brit.), p

S.J.H. Ward

SECOND BEST SECRET AGENT IN THE WHOLE WIDE WORLD, THE(1965, Brit.), p

Sally Ward

EVERYBODY'S DOING IT(1938)

Sandy Ward

VELVET VAMPIRE, THE(1971); EXECUTIVE ACTION(1973); TERMINAL ISLAND(1973); HINDENBURG, THE(1975); BEING THERE(1979); ROSE, THE(1979); WHOLLY MOSES(1980); FAST-WALKING(1982); SOME KIND OF HERO(1982); CUJO(1983)

1984

TANK(1984)

Sela Ward

MAN WHO LOVED WOMEN, THE(1983)

Sheila Ward

SAINTS AND SINNERS(1949, Brit.)

Shela Ward

END OF THE AFFAIR, THE(1955, Brit.)

Simon Ward

FRANKENSTEIN MUST BE DESTROYED!(1969, Brit.); I START COUNTING(1970, Brit.); YOUNG WINSTON(1972, Brit.); HITLER: THE LAST TEN DAYS(1973, Brit./Ital.); DEADLY STRANGERS(1974, Brit.); THREE MUSKETEERS, THE(1974, Panama); ALL CREATURES GREAT AND SMALL(1975, Brit.); CHILDREN OF RAGE(1975, Brit.-Israeli); FOUR MUSKETEERS, THE(1975); ACES HIGH(1977, Brit.); CHOSEN, THE(1978, Brit./Ital.); DOMINIQUE(1978, Brit.); SABINA, THE(1979, Span./Swed.); ZULU DAWN(1980, Brit.); MONSTER CLUB, THE(1981, Brit.)

1984

SUPERGIRL(1984)

Skip Ward

ROADRACERS, THE(1959); VOYAGE TO THE BOTTOM OF THE SEA(1961); NUTTY PROFESSOR, THE(1963); IS PARIS BURNING?(1966, U.S./Fr.); EASY COME, EASY GO(1967); HOMBRE(1967); MAD ROOM, THE(1969)

Solly Ward
DANGER PATROL(1937); FLIGHT FROM GLORY(1937); LIVING ON LOVE(1937); BLIND ALIBI(1938); MAID'S NIGHT OUT(1938); SHE'S GOT EVERYTHING(1938); SUED FOR LIBEL(1940)
Sophie Ward
FULL CIRCLE(1977, Brit./Can.); HAUNTING OF JULIA, THE(1981, Brit./Can.); HUNGER, THE(1983); LORDS OF DISCIPLINE, THE(1983)
Steve Ward
BOOTLEGGERS(1974); MACKINTOSH & T.J.(1975); TOUGH ENOUGH(1983)
Ted Ward
MACK, THE(1973)
Tiny Ward
Silents
WANING SEX, THE(1926)
Tom Ward
GREASED LIGHTNING(1977), spec eff
Tony Ward [Anthony Warde]
GHOST AND THE GUEST(1943); RIDERS OF THE DEADLINE(1943)
Tony Ward
COLOR ME DEAD(1969, Aus.)
Trevor Ward
FAN, THE(1949); ROPE OF SAND(1949); DESERT FOX, THE(1951); LORNA DOONE(1951); MY COUSIN RACHEL(1952); SALOME(1953); THUNDER IN THE EAST(1953); COURT JESTER, THE(1956); FLASH GORDON(1980)
Troy Ward
MACKINTOSH & T.J.(1975)
Valerie Ward
DEAR MURDERER(1947, Brit.)
Victoria Ward
D-DAY, THE SIXTH OF JUNE(1956)
Vincent Ward
1984
VIGIL(1984, New Zealand), d, w
W. Bradley Ward
Silents
SHADOWS OF CONSCIENCE(1921)
Walter Ward
BOY SLAVES(1938)
Warwick Ward
INFORMER, THE(1929, Brit.); WAY OF LOST SOULS, THE(1929, Brit.); WOMAN HE SCORNED, THE(1930, Brit.); YELLOW MASK, THE(1930, Brit.); DEADLOCK(1931, Brit.); GABLES MYSTERY, THE(1931, Brit.), p; MAN OF MAYFAIR(1931, Brit.); PERFECT ALIBI, THE(1931, Brit.); STAMBOUL(1931, Brit.); TO OBLIGE A LADY(1931, Brit.); BLIND SPOT(1932, Brit.); CALLBOX MYSTERY, THE(1932, Brit.); LIFE GOES ON(1932, Brit.); F.P. 1(1933, Brit.); FRENCH LEAVE(1937, Brit.), p; LAST CHANCE, THE(1937, Brit.), p; SATURDAY NIGHT REVUE(1937, Brit.), p; ALMOST A HONEYMOON(1938, Brit.), p; GABLES MYSTERY, THE(1938, Brit.), p; NIGHT ALONE(1938, Brit.), p; SAVE A LITTLE SUNSHINE(1938, Brit.), p; DEAD MEN ARE DANGEROUS(1939, Brit.), p; ME AND MY PAL(1939, Brit.), p; WOMEN AREN'T ANGELS(1942, Brit.), p; SUSPECTED PERSON(1943, Brit.), p; WARN THAT MAN(1943, Brit.), p; MAN FROM MOROCCO, THE(1946, Brit.), p, w; QUIET WEEKEND(1948, Brit.), p, w; MY BROTHER JONATHAN(1949, Brit.), p; DANCING YEARS, THE(1950, Brit.), p&w; YOUNG AND THE GUILTY, THE(1958, Brit.), p
Silents
MANCHESTER MAN, THE(1920, Brit.); MARY LATIMER, NUN(1920, Brit.); DIAMOND NECKLACE, THE(1921, Brit.); HANDY ANDY(1921, Brit.); CALL OF THE EAST, THE(1922, Brit.); BULLDOG DRUMMOND(1923, Brit.); HUMAN DESIRES(1924, Brit.); MONEY HABIT, THE(1924, Brit.); PRUDES FALL, THE(1924, Brit.); WOMAN'S SECRET, A(1924, Brit.); VARIETY(1925, Ger.); WOMAN TEMPTED, THE(1928, Brit.); AFTER THE VERDICT(1929, Brit.)
Misc. Silents
SILVER LINING, THE(1919, Brit.); BUILD THY HOUSE(1920, Brit.); CALL OF THE ROAD, THE(1920, Brit.); WUTHERING HEIGHTS(1920, Brit.); BELPHEGOR THE MOUNTEBANK(1921, Brit.); CORINTHIAN JACK(1921, Brit.); GOLDEN DAWN, THE(1921, Brit.); LITTLE MEG'S CHILDREN(1921, Brit.); MAYOR OF CASTERBRIDGE, THE(1921, Brit.); WHY MEN FORGET(1921, Brit.); HIS SUPREME SACRIFICE(1922, Brit.); LILAC SUNBONNET, THE(1922, Brit.); PETTICOAT LOOSE(1922, Brit.); LADY OWNER, THE(1923, Brit.); GREAT TURF MYSTERY, THE(1924, Brit.); HURRICANE HUTCH IN MANY ADVENTURES(1924, Brit.); MARIA MARTEN(1928, Brit.); WHITE SHEIK, THE(1928, Brit.); THREE KINGS, THE(1929, Brit.); STRANGE CASE OF DISTRICT ATTORNEY M.(1930)
William Ward
LOVERS AND LOLLIPOPS(1956)
Willie Ward
MACK, THE(1973)
Woodrow Ward
DAYTON'S DEVILS(1968), spec eff; CHARRO(1969), spec eff
Zack Ward
CHRISTMAS STORY, A(1983)
Tim Ward-Booth
1984
SHEENA(1984)
Cassandra Ward-Freeman
1984
FIRESTARTER(1984)
Anthony Warde
ESCAPE BY NIGHT(1937); GIRL WITH IDEAS, A(1937); AFFAIRS OF ANNABEL(1938); COME ON, LEATHERNECKS(1938); LAW OF THE UNDERWORLD(1938); MARIE ANTOINETTE(1938); MR. MOTO TAKES A VACATION(1938); NEWSBOY'S HOME(1939); OKLAHOMA FRONTIER(1939); TELL NO TALES(1939); CHIP OF THE FLYING U(1940); EARL OF CHICAGO, THE(1940); SO YOU WON'T TALK(1940); DOWN IN SAN DIEGO(1941); RIDIN' ON A RAINBOW(1941); BROADWAY(1942); JOHNNY EAGER(1942); MAN WITH TWO LIVES, THE(1942); GENTLE GANGSTER, A(1943); I ESCAPED FROM THE GESTAPO(1943); KEEP 'EM SLUGGING(1943); SO'S YOUR UNCLE(1943); THREE HEARTS FOR JULIA(1943); WHERE ARE YOUR CHILDREN?(1943); WHITE SAVAGE(1943); ARE THESE OUR PARENTS?(1944); CHINESE CAT, THE(1944); FOLLOW THE BOYS(1944); MACHINE GUN MAMA(1944); MUMMY'S GHOST, THE(1944); SENSATIONS OF 1945(1944); SHADOW OF SUSPICION(1944); THIN MAN GOES HOME, THE(1944); ALLOTMENT WIVES, INC.(1945); CAPTAIN TUGBOAT ANNIE(1945); CISCO KID RETURNS, THE(1945); HERE COME THE CO-EDS(1945); THERE GOES KELLY(1945); DARK ALIBI(1946); DON RICARDO RETURNS(1946); MISSING LADY, THE(1946); SECRETS OF A SORORITY GIRL(1946); WIFE OF MONTE CRISTO, THE(1946); WIFE WANTED(1946); BELLS OF SAN FERNANDO(1947); DEVIL SHIP(1947); HIGH TIDE(1947); KILLER DILL(1947); THAT HAGEN GIRL(1947); 13TH HOUR, THE(1947); KING OF THE BANDITS(1948); STAGE STRUCK(1948); FIGHTING FOOLS(1949); TRAIL OF THE YUKON(1949); ROARING CITY(1951); ATOMIC CITY, THE(1952); HURRICANE SMITH(1952); GIRL WHO HAD EVERYTHING, THE(1953); HOUDINI(1953); RAIDERS OF THE SEVEN SEAS(1953); WAR OF THE WORLDS, THE(1953); DAY OF TRIUMPH(1954); REAR WINDOW(1954); STRATEGIC AIR COMMAND(1955); MAN WHO KNEW TOO MUCH, THE(1956); CARPETBAGGERS, THE(1964)
Beatrice Warde
OUTRAGE(1950)
Bobby Warde
FABULOUS DORSEYS, THE(1947)
Carrie Clarke Warde
Silents
DADDY LONG LEGS(1919)
Cecil Warde
Misc. Silents
USURPER, THE(1919, Brit.)
Ernest Warde
Silents
KING LEAR(1916), a, d
Misc. Silents
HIDDEN VALLEY, THE(1916), a, d; SILAS MARNER(1916), d; HER BELOVED ENEMY(1917), d; HINTON'S DOUBLE(1917), d; VICAR OF WAKEFIELD, THE(1917), d
Ernest C. Warde
Silents
MORE TROUBLE(1918), d; PRISONER OF THE PINES(1918), d; JOYOUS LIAR, THE(1919), d; LORD LOVES THE IRISH, THE(1919), d; MAN IN THE OPEN, A(1919), d; DEVIL TO PAY, THE(1920), d; GREEN FLAME, THE(1920), d; TRAIL OF THE AXE, THE(1922), d
Misc. Silents
MAN WITHOUT A COUNTRY, THE(1917), d; WAR AND THE WOMAN(1917), a, d; WOMAN AND THE BEAST, THE(1917), d; WOMAN IN WHITE, THE(1917), d; BELLS, THE(1918), d; RULER OF THE ROAD(1918), d; THREE X GORDON(1918), d; FALSE CODE, THE(1919), d; GATES OF BRASS(1919), d; MASTER MAN, THE(1919), d; MIDNIGHT STAGE, THE(1919), d; WORLD AFLAME, THE(1919), d; COAST OF OPPORTUNITY, THE(1920), d; DREAM CHEATER, THE(1920), d; HOUSE OF WHISPERS, THE(1920), d; LIVE SPARKS(1920), d; NO.99(1920), d; $30,000(1920), d
Francesca Warde
Silents
MICE AND MEN(1916)
Frederick Warde
Silents
KING LEAR(1916); LOVER'S OATH, A(1925)
Misc. Silents
RICHARD III(1913), a, d; SILAS MARNER(1916); FIRES OF YOUTH(1917); HEART OF EZRA GREER, THE(1917); HINTON'S DOUBLE(1917); UNDER FALSE COLORS(1917); VICAR OF WAKEFIELD, THE(1917); RICH MAN, POOR MAN(1918); UNVEILING HAND, THE(1919)
George Warde
Silents
AMERICAN MANNERS(1924)
Harlan Warde
I WANTED WINGS(1941); O.S.S.(1946); IT HAD TO BE YOU(1947); HE WALKED BY NIGHT(1948); LADY AT MIDNIGHT(1948); MONEY MADNESS(1948); FOUNTAINHEAD, THE(1949); IT'S A GREAT FEELING(1949); JOHNNY ALLEGRO(1949); PRISON WARDEN(1949); STATE DEPARTMENT-FILE 649(1949); TASK FORCE(1949); TELL IT TO THE JUDGE(1949); UNDERCOVER MAN, THE(1949); WAKE OF THE RED WITCH(1949); CAGED(1950); CUSTOMS AGENT(1950); DAVID HARDING, COUNTERSPY(1950); MAGNIFICENT YANKEE, THE(1950); NO SAD SONGS FOR ME(1950); CRIMINAL LAWYER(1951); FLYING LEATHERNECKS(1951); HER FIRST ROMANCE(1951); MAN WHO CHEATED HIMSELF, THE(1951); SMUGGLER'S GOLD(1951); BOOTS MALONE(1952); LOAN SHARK(1952); OPERATION SECRET(1952); WITHOUT WARNING(1952); ABOVE AND BEYOND(1953); DONOVAN'S BRAIN(1953); DOWN THREE DARK STREETS(1954); DRAGNET(1954); HELL AND HIGH WATER(1954); I'LL CRY TOMORROW(1955); SCARLET COAT, THE(1955); STRATEGIC AIR COMMAND(1955); JULIE(1956); CHICAGO CONFIDENTIAL(1957); LAST OF THE BADMEN(1957); MONSTER THAT CHALLENGED THE WORLD, THE(1957); SAYONARA(1957); SPIRIT OF ST. LOUIS, THE(1957); WINGS OF EAGLES, THE(1957); CRY TERROR(1958); DECKS RAN RED, THE(1958); HOT SPELL(1958); CRY FOR HAPPY(1961); INCIDENT IN AN ALLEY(1962); ADVANCE TO THE REAR(1964); BILLIE(1965)
Harland Warde
SNIPER, THE(1952)
Shirley Warde
TRICK FOR TRICK(1933), w; DEVIL COMMANDS, THE(1941); TORTILLA FLAT(1942)
"Sonny Boy" Warde
Misc. Silents
FIRST BORN, THE(1921)
Ted Warde
DESTINATION MOON(1950)
Tony Warde
DIXIE JAMBOREE(1945)
Tony [Anthony] Warde
KING OF THE NEWSBOYS(1938); INSIDE THE MAFIA(1959)
Willie Warde
TONS OF MONEY(1931, Brit.)
Zdzislaw Wardejn
1984
SHIVERS(1984, Pol.)
Jane Wardell
YANK IN VIET-NAM, A(1964), w

Florence Warden
Silents
HOUSE ON THE MARSH, THE(1920, Brit.), w
Hugh Warden
JESSIE'S GIRLS(1976); MODERN ROMANCE(1981); DEATH WISH II(1982); HON-KYTONK MAN(1982)
Jack Warden
FROGMEN, THE(1951); MAN WITH MY FACE, THE(1951); YOU'RE IN THE NAVY NOW(1951); RED BALL EXPRESS(1952); FROM HERE TO ETERNITY(1953); WAKAMBA!(1955), ph; BACHELOR PARTY, THE(1957); EDGE OF THE CITY(1957); 12 ANGRY MEN(1957); DARBY'S RANGERS(1958); RUN SILENT, RUN DEEP(1958); SOUND AND THE FURY, THE(1959); THAT KIND OF WOMAN(1959); WAKE ME WHEN IT'S OVER(1960); ESCAPE FROM ZAHRAIN(1962); DONOVAN'S REEF(1963); THIN RED LINE, THE(1964); BLINDFOLD(1966); BYE BYE BRAVERMAN(1968); SPORTING CLUB, THE(1971); SUMMERTREE(1971); WELCOME TO THE CLUB(1971); WHO IS HARRY KELLERMAN AND WHY IS HE SAYING THOSE TERRIBLE THINGS ABOUT ME?(1971); BILLY TWO HATS(1973, Brit.); MAN WHO LOVED CAT DANCING, THE(1973); APPRENTICESHIP OF DUDDY KRAVITZ, THE(1974, Can.); SHAMPOO(1975); ALL THE PRESIDENT'S MEN(1976); WHITE BUFFALO, THE(1977); DEATH ON THE NILE(1978, Brit.); HEAVEN CAN WAIT(1978); ...AND JUSTICE FOR ALL(1979); BEING THERE(1979); BEYOND THE POSEIDON ADVENTURE(1979); CHAMP, THE(1979); DREAMER(1979); USED CARS(1980); CARBON COPY(1981); CHU CHU AND THE PHILLY FLASH(1981); GREAT MUPPET CAPER, THE(1981); SO FINE(1981); VERDICT, THE(1982)
1984
CRACKERS(1984)
Judith Warden
THINGS HAPPEN AT NIGHT(1948, Brit.); LILLI MARLENE(1951, Brit.); THREE MEN IN A BOAT(1958, Brit.)
lp: Jack Warden
Misc. Talkies
LAWBREAKERS, THE(1960)
May Warden
ALL THINGS BRIGHT AND BEAUTIFUL(1979, Brit.)
Ronald Warden
FIVE ON THE BLACK HAND SIDE(1973)
Misc. Talkies
MISS MELODY JONES(1973)
Cari Anne Warder
1984
WILD LIFE, THE(1984)
Fred Warder
FLASH GORDON(1980)
Frederick Warder
KEEP, THE(1983)
Joe Warder
Misc. Talkies
1ST NOTCH, THE(1977)
Joan Wardley
MILDRED PIERCE(1945)
Byron Wardlow
FANDANGO(1970)
Joyce Wardlow
Misc. Silents
BOND WITHIN, THE(1916)
Keith Wardlow
FOOD OF THE GODS, THE(1976), spec eff
Stan Wardnow
CHAFED ELBOWS(1967)
Bruno Hardt Wardon
STUDENT'S ROMANCE, THE(1936, Brit.), w
William Wardord
HOODLUM PRIEST, THE(1961)
James Wardroper
UNMAN, WITTERING AND ZIGO(1971, Brit.)
Geoffrey Wardwell
TAMING OF THE SHREW, THE(1929); WHAT HAPPENED THEN?(1934, Brit.); WHAT HAPPENED TO HARKNESS(1934, Brit.); CHALLENGE, THE(1939, Brit.); CRIMES AT THE DARK HOUSE(1940, Brit.)
Norman Wardwick
OVER THE ODDS(1961, Brit.), ph
Bernice Ware
Misc. Silents
BLUE MOUNTAIN MYSTERY, THE(1922)
Bunny Ware
MY THIRD WIFE GEORGE(1968); SCREAM, BABY, SCREAM(1969)
Clyde Ware
SPY WITH MY FACE, THE(1966), w; CATALINA CAPER, THE(1967), w; NO DRUMS, NO BUGLES(1971), p,d&w
Darrel Ware
YANK IN THE R.A.F., A(1941), w; ORCHESTRA WIVES(1942), w
Darrell Ware
BIG TOWN GIRL(1937), w; LIFE BEGINS IN COLLEGE(1937), w; SECOND HONEY-MOON(1937), w; WIFE, DOCTOR AND NURSE(1937), w; JUST AROUND THE CORNER(1938), w; SUBMARINE PATROL(1938), w; CHARLIE MC CARTHY, DE-TECTIVE(1939), w; HOTEL FOR WOMEN(1939), w; DOWN ARGENTINE WAY(1940), w; HE MARRIED HIS WIFE(1940), w; PUBLIC DEB NO. 1(1940), w; TALL, DARK AND HANDSOME(1941), w; WEEKEND IN HAVANA(1941), w; LUCKY JOR-DAN(1942), w; MY GAL SAL(1942), w; DIXIE(1943), w; STANDING ROOM ON-LY(1944), w; BRING ON THE GIRLS(1945), w; KITTY(1945), w; LOVE THAT BRUTE(1950), w
Derek Ware
PRIMITIVES, THE(1962, Brit.); IDOL, THE(1966, Brit.); FAR FROM THE MADDING CROWD(1967, Brit.); PRIVILEGE(1967, Brit.), d; CONQUEROR WORM, THE(1968, Brit.); UP THE JUNCTION(1968, Brit.); ITALIAN JOB, THE(1969, Brit.)
Diana Ware
REG'LAR FELLERS(1941)

Diane Ware
ON THE LOOSE(1951)
Ed Ware
KING RAT(1965), cos
Frank Ware
BROADWAY BABIES(1929), ed; SEVEN FOOTPRINTS TO SATAN(1929), ed; BAD MAN, THE(1930), ed; LITTLE JOHNNY JONES(1930), ed; MOTHERS CRY(1930), ed; NOTORIOUS AFFAIR, A(1930), ed; FIVE STAR FINAL(1931), ed; PARTY HUS-BAND(1931), ed; BIG STAMPEDE, THE(1932), ed; HONOR OF THE PRESS(1932), ed
Graham Ware
INN OF THE DAMNED(1974, Aus.)
Harlan Ware
COLLEGE HOLIDAY(1936), w; YOURS FOR THE ASKING(1936), w; TURN OFF THE MOON(1937), w; VACATION FROM LOVE(1938), w; JAM SESSION(1944), w; PARDON MY PAST(1945), w; TOO YOUNG TO KNOW(1945), w; COME FILL THE CUP(1951), w; SUPERDAD(1974), w
Helen Ware
HALF WAY TO HEAVEN(1929); SPEAKEASY(1929); VIRGINIAN, THE(1929); ABRAHAM LINCOLN(1930); ONE NIGHT AT SUSIE'S(1930); SLIGHTLY SCAR-LET(1930); TOL'ABLE DAVID(1930); COMMAND PERFORMANCE(1931); I TAKE THIS WOMAN(1931); PARTY HUSBAND(1931); RECKLESS HOUR, THE(1931); NIGHT OF JUNE 13(1932); GIRL MISSING(1933); KEYHOLE, THE(1933); LADIES THEY TALK ABOUT(1933); MORNING GLORY(1933); SHE HAD TO SAY YES(1933); WARRIOR'S HUSBAND, THE(1933); FLAMING GOLD(1934); SADIE MCKEE(1934); THAT'S GRATITUDE(1934); ROMANCE IN MANHATTAN(1935); SECRET OF THE CHATEAU(1935)
Silents
SECRET LOVE(1916); HAUNTED PAJAMAS(1917); NEW YEAR'S EVE(1929)
Misc. Silents
CROSS CURRENTS(1916); GARDEN OF ALLAH, THE(1916); DEEP PURPLE, THE(1920)
Herta Ware
DR. HECKYL AND MR. HYPE(1980)
1984
2010(1984)
Howard Ware
GIANT GILA MONSTER, THE(1959); UNDER AGE(1964)
Irene Ware
CHANDU THE MAGICIAN(1932); BRIEF MOMENT(1933); HUMANITY(1933); MY WEAKNESS(1933); KING KELLY OF THE U.S.A(1934); LET'S TALK IT OVER(1934); ORIENT EXPRESS(1934); YOU BELONG TO ME(1934); FALSE PRETENSES(1935); HAPPINESS C.O.D.(1935); NIGHT LIFE OF THE GODS(1935); RAVEN, THE(1935); RENDEZVOUS AT MIDNIGHT(1935); WHISPERING SMITH SPEAKS(1935); CHEERS OF THE CROWD(1936); DARK HOUR, THE(1936); FEDERAL AGENT(1936); GOLD DIGGERS OF 1937(1936); MURDER AT GLEN ATHOL(1936); O'MALLEY OF THE MOUNTED(1936); LIVE WIRE, THE(1937, Brit.); AROUND THE TOWN(1938, Brit.); NO PARKING(1938, Brit.); OUTSIDE THE 3-MILE LIMIT(1940)
Misc. Talkies
IN PARIS, A.W.O.L.(1936)
Jean Spencer Ware
Silents
PASSIONATE YOUTH(1925), ed
Jeff Ware
1984
TEACHERS(1984)
Jeffery Ware
WOLFEN(1981)
Juliet Ware
FOOTLIGHT PARADE(1933); FASHIONS OF 1934(1934); JIMMY THE GENT(1934); MASSACRE(1934)
Kenneth Ware
LAST GRENADE, THE(1970, Brit.), w
Misc. Silents
DAVID COPPERFIELD(1913, Brit.)
Leon Ware
POSTMAN DIDN'T RING, THE(1942), w; PERILOUS WATERS(1948), w; PEG-GY(1950), w; BOY AND THE BRIDGE, THE(1959, Brit.), w
Linda Ware
STAR MAKER, THE(1939); PAPER BULLETS(1941)
Lucille Ware
LEAVENWORTH CASE, THE(1936)
Mary Ware
CRACK-UP(1946); SECRETS OF A SORORITY GIRL(1946); HOPPY'S HOLI-DAY(1947); HE WALKED BY NIGHT(1948)
Midge Ware
PRINCE WHO WAS A THIEF, THE(1951); LAS VEGAS STORY, THE(1952); UN-TAMED WOMEN(1952); FIVE MINUTES TO LIVE(1961); CINCINNATI KID, THE(1965); LOLLIPOP COVER, THE(1965); ALL WOMAN(1967)
Pete Ware
DELIVERANCE(1972)
Ricci Ware
RACE WITH THE DEVIL(1975)
Virginia Ware
Silents
HER FIVE-FOOT HIGHNESS(1920); MAD MARRIAGE, THE(1921)
Misc. Silents
IRISH EYES(1918); FOREST KING, THE(1922)
William Ware
BRAVADOS, THE(1958), ed
Ruth Wareen
EMERGENCY WEDDING(1950)
Lesley Wareing
TRAPPED IN A SUBMARINE(1931, Brit.); JOSSER JOINS THE NAVY(1932, Brit.); FIGHTING STOCK(1935, Brit.); IRON DUKE, THE(1935, Brit.); IT'S YOU I WANT(1936, Brit.); BEDTIME STORY(1938, Brit.); MYSTERIOUS MR. REEDER, THE(1940, Brit.); OUTSIDER, THE(1940, Brit.); TERROR, THE(1941, Brit.)
Lule Warenton
Silents
GILDED SPIDER, THE(1916)

Brian Warf
COAL MINER'S DAUGHTER(1980)
Chris Warfield
TAKE THE HIGH GROUND(1953); TORCH SONG(1953); MEN OF THE FIGHTING LADY(1954); STUDENT PRINCE, THE(1954); DANGEROUS CHARTER(1962); INCIDENT IN AN ALLEY(1962); DIARY OF A MADMAN(1963)
Misc. Talkies
LITTLE MISS INNOCENCE(1973), d; BOSS LADY(1982), d
Don Warfield
SIDELONG GLANCES OF A PIGEON KICKER, THE(1970)
Irene Warfield
Silents
FOUR FEATHERS(1915); SIMON THE JESTER(1915)
Misc. Silents
SATAN SANDERSON(1915); MIRROR, THE(1917)
Jo Warfield
UP FROM THE BEACH(1965); IS PARIS BURNING?(1966, U.S./Fr.)
Joe Warfield
FORCE OF EVIL(1948); UNION STATION(1950); STRANGERS ON A TRAIN(1951); BLONDE FROM PEKING, THE(1968, Fr.); NICKELODEON(1976)
Misc. Talkies
TEENAGER(1975)
Joseph Warfield
UNDER MY SKIN(1950); BLONDE FROM PEKING, THE(1968, Fr.)
Marlene Warman
GREAT WHITE HOPE, THE(1970); JOE(1970); ACROSS 110TH STREET(1972); NETWORK(1976)
Marsha Warfield
D.C. CAB(1983)
Natalie Warfield
THRU DIFFERENT EYES(1929)
Silents
WAS IT BIGAMY?(1925)
Misc. Silents
RED RIDER, THE(1925)
Nayone Warfield
Misc. Silents
RED BLOOD(1926)
William Warfield
SHOW BOAT(1951)
Jack Warford
DR. HECKYL AND MR. HYPE(1980)
Robin Warga
CRASH LANDING(1958); DARK AT THE TOP OF THE STAIRS, THE(1960); SUNRISE AT CAMPOBELLO(1960)
Michelle Wargnier
GENDARME OF ST. TROPEZ, THE(1966, Fr./Ital.)
Douglas Warhit
PRIVATE SCHOOL(1983)
1984
BEVERLY HILLS COP(1984); BODY DOUBLE(1984); TOY SOLDIERS(1984)
Andy Warhol
CHELSEA GIRLS, THE(1967), p&d, w, ph; ILLIAC PASSION, THE(1968); LONESOME COWBOYS(1968), p,d&w; L'AMOUR(1973), d&w; DRIVER'S SEAT, THE(1975, Ital.); COCAINE COWBOYS(1979)
Misc. Talkies
HORSE(1965), d; POOR LITTLE RICH GIRL(1965), d
Norman Warick
FOLLOW THAT HORSE!(1960, Brit.), ph
Francis Warin
EASY LIFE, THE(1971, Fr.), d, w
Barbara Waring
GIRL IN THE CROWD, THE(1934, Brit.); HIS MAJESTY AND CO(1935, Brit.); IN WHICH WE SERVE(1942, Brit.); GENTLE SEX, THE(1943, Brit.); HEAVEN IS ROUND THE CORNER(1944, Brit.); TWILIGHT HOUR(1944, Brit.); HUNGRY HILL(1947, Brit.)
Frances Waring
DEAR MR. PROHACK(1949, Brit.); ONE WOMAN'S STORY(1949, Brit.)
Fred Waring
VARSITY SHOW(1937)
Guy Waring
SKY RAIDERS, THE(1938, Brit.)
Herbert Waring
SLEEPING PARTNERS(1930, Brit.)
Hubert Waring
PLUNDER(1931, Brit.)
Joe Waring
JULIUS CAESAR(1953); ROGUE COP(1954)
Joseph Waring
CONQUEST OF COCHISE(1953); DESERT SANDS(1955); KISS OF FIRE(1955); JUMBO(1962)
Lenore Waring
MAN CALLED DAGGER, A(1967)
Richard Waring
PERFECT GENTLEMAN, THE(1935); MR. SKEFFINGTON(1944)
Rosamund Waring
GENTLE TOUCH, THE(1956, Brit.); LAST MAN TO HANG, THE(1956, Brit.); MURDER ON APPROVAL(1956, Brit.)
Winifred Waring
NIGHTFALL(1956)
Colin Wark
REUNION(1932, Brit.)
John Wark
VICTORY(1981)
Robert Wark
NAKED IN THE SUN(1957); PRIVATE PROPERTY(1960)
Victor Wark
FLYING FIFTY-FIVE(1939, Brit.)

Thomas Warkentin
HEAVY METAL(1981, Can.), w, anim
Barbara Ann Warkmeister
LEGEND OF LYLAH CLARE, THE(1968)
Mel Warkmeister
LEGEND OF LYLAH CLARE, THE(1968)
Bill Warlock
HALLOWEEN II(1981)
Dick Warlock
ROLLERBALL(1975); HALLOWEEN 11(1981); HALLOWEEN III: SEASON OF THE WITCH(1982)
Frederick Warlock
HUDSON'S BAY(1940)
Richard Warlock
LOVE BUG, THE(1968); HERBIE GOES TO MONTE CARLO(1977); CAT FROM OUTER SPACE, THE(1978), a, stunts
1984
BODY DOUBLE(1984); FIRESTARTER(1984)
Hermann Warm
VAMPYR(1932, Fr./Ger.), art d; HEAD, THE(1961, Ger.), art d; WOZZECK(1962, E. Ger.), set d
Silents
CABINET OF DR. CALIGARI, THE(1921, Ger.), art d; STUDENT OF PRAGUE, THE(1927, Ger.), set d
Alfred Warman
Misc. Silents
CIRCUMSTANTIAL EVIDENCE(1920)
S.J. Warmington
ESCAPE(1930, Brit.); MURDER(1930, Brit.); CROOKED LADY, THE(1932, Brit.); SABOTAGE(1937, Brit.)
Misc. Silents
SMART SET, A(1919, Brit.); WISP O' THE WOODS(1919, Brit.); SOUTH SEA BUBBLE, A(1928, Brit.)
Henry Christeen Warnack
Silents
FIRES OF CONSCIENCE(1916), w; HONOR SYSTEM, THE(1917), w; ARE YOU LEGALLY MARRIED?(1919), w
Margaret Warncke
CHILDRENS GAMES(1969); SHAFT(1971)
Derek Warne
GREAT MCGONAGALL, THE(1975, Brit.), m
Helen Warne
PARIS BOUND(1929), ed; GREAT LOVER, THE(1931), ed
Silents
WILD OATS LANE(1926), ed
Jo Warne
NUTCRACKER(1982, Brit.)
Warner
DIMPLES(1936)
Adele Warner
Silents
SKY HIGH(1922)
Anthony Warner
WHISPERING SMITH VERSUS SCOTLAND YARD(1952, Brit.)
Astrid Warner
GLORY STOMPERS, THE(1967); HELL'S BELLES(1969); BULLET FOR PRETTY BOY, A(1970)
Bob Warner
CLAMBAKE(1967), spec eff; STING, THE(1973), spec eff; 125 ROOMS OF COMFORT(1974, Can.); THRESHOLD(1983, Can.)
Brian Warner
SPASMS(1983, Can.), spec eff
Camille Warner
1984
HOLLYWOOD HIGH PART II(1984)
David Warner
CONCORDE, THE–AIRPORT '79(; TOM JONES(1963, Brit.); MORGAN!(1966, Brit.); DEADLY AFFAIR, THE(1967, Brit.); BOFORS GUN, THE(1968, Brit.); FIXER, THE(1968); SEA GULL, THE(1968); WORK IS A FOUR LETTER WORD(1968, Brit.); MIDSUMMER NIGHT'S DREAM, A(1969, Brit.); BALLAD OF CABLE HOGUE, THE(1970); PERFECT FRIDAY(1970, Brit.); STRAW DOGS(1971, Brit.); DOLL'S HOUSE, A(1973, Brit.); LITTLE MALCOLM(1974, Brit.); MR. QUILP(1975, Brit.); OMEN, THE(1976); AGE OF INNOCENCE(1977, Can.); CROSS OF IRON(1977, Brit., Ger.); PROVIDENCE(1977, Fr.); SILVER BEARS(1978); THIRTY NINE STEPS, THE(1978, Brit.); NIGHTWING(1979); TIME AFTER TIME(1979, Brit.); ISLAND, THE(1980); DISAPPEARANCE, THE(1981, Brit./Can.); FRENCH LIEUTENANT'S WOMAN, THE(1981); TIME BANDITS(1981, Brit.); TRON(1982); MAN WITH TWO BRAINS, THE(1983)
Douglas Warner
UNDERWORLD INFORMERS(1965, Brit.), w
Eddie Warner
RELUCTANT DEBUTANTE, THE(1958), m
Elaine Warner
FOREST, THE(1983)
Elyn Warner
COLOR ME BLOOD RED(1965)
Frank Warner
RUN OF THE ARROW(1957)
Franklin Warner
GREAT POWER, THE(1929), p
Franklyn Warner
CIPHER BUREAU(1938), p; SHADOWS OVER SHANGHAI(1938), p; FRONTIER SCOUT(1939), p; LONG SHOT, THE(1939), p; ISLE OF DESTINY(1940), p
Frederick Warner
PERSECUTION(1974, Brit.), w
Glenn "Pop" Warner
KNUTE ROCKNE–ALL AMERICAN(1940)

Gloria Warner
HELL BENT FOR LOVE(1934)
Gunnar Warner
LUDWIG(1973, Ital./Ger./Fr.); BLOOD IN THE STREETS(1975, Ital./Fr.)
H.B. Warner
VICTORIA THE GREAT(1937, Brit.); ARGYLE CASE, THE(1929); CONQUEST(1929); DOCTOR'S SECRET(1929); GAMBLERS, THE(1929); STARK MAD(1929); TRIAL OF MARY DUGAN, THE(1929); FURIES, THE(1930); GREEN GODDESS, THE(1930); LILIOM(1930); ON YOUR BACK(1930); PRINCESS AND THE PLUMBER, THE(1930); SECOND FLOOR MYSTERY, THE(1930); TIGER ROSE(1930); WEDDING RINGS(1930); WILD COMPANY(1930); EXPENSIVE WOMEN(1931); FIVE STAR FINAL(1931); RECKLESS HOUR, THE(1931); WOMAN OF EXPERIENCE, A(1931); CHARLIE CHAN'S CHANCE(1932); CROSS-EXAMINATION(1932); CRUSADER, THE(1932); MENACE, THE(1932); PHANTOM OF CRESTWOOD, THE(1932); SON-DAUGHTER, THE(1932); TOM BROWN OF CULVER(1932); UNHOLY LOVE(1932); WOMAN COMMANDS, A(1932); CHRISTOPHER BEAN(1933); JENNIE GERHARDT(1933); JUSTICE TAKES A HOLIDAY(1933); SUPERNATURAL(1933); GRAND CANARY(1934); SORRELL AND SON(1934, Brit.); VIVA VILLA!(1934); BEHOLD MY WIFE(1935); BORN TO GAMBLE(1935); IN OLD SANTA FE(1935); NIGHT ALARM(1935); TALE OF TWO CITIES, A(1935); BLACKMAILER(1936); GARDEN MURDER CASE, THE(1936); MOONLIGHT MURDER(1936); MR. DEEDS GOES TO TOWN(1936); ROSE OF THE RANCHO(1936); ALONG CAME LOVE(1937); LOST HORIZON(1937); ADVENTURES OF MARCO POLO, THE(1938); ARMY GIRL(1938); BULLDOG DRUMMOND IN AFRICA(1938); GIRL OF THE GOLDEN WEST, THE(1938); KIDNAPPED(1938); TOY WIFE, THE(1938); YOU CAN'T TAKE IT WITH YOU(1938); ARREST BULLDOG DRUMMOND(1939, Brit.); BULLDOG DRUMMOND'S BRIDE(1939); BULLDOG DRUMMOND'S SECRET POLICE(1939); GRACIE ALLEN MURDER CASE(1939); LET FREEDOM RING(1939); MR. SMITH GOES TO WASHINGTON(1939); NURSE EDITH CAVELL(1939); RAINS CAME, THE(1939); TORPEDOED!(1939); NEW MOON(1940); CITY OF MISSING GIRLS(1941); CORSICAN BROTHERS, THE(1941); DEVIL AND DANIEL WEBSTER, THE(1941); ELLERY QUEEN AND THE PERFECT CRIME(1941); SOUTH OF TAHITI(1941); TOPPER RETURNS(1941); CROSSROADS(1942); HITLER'S CHILDREN(1942); YANK IN LIBYA, A(1942); BOSS OF BIG TOWN(1943); WOMEN IN BONDAGE(1943); ACTION IN ARABIA(1944); ENEMY OF WOMEN(1944); FACES IN THE FOG(1944); CAPTAIN TUGBOAT ANNIE(1945); ROGUES GALLERY(1945); IT'S A WONDERFUL LIFE(1946); STRANGE IMPERSONATION(1946); DRIFTWOOD(1947); HIGH WALL, THE(1947); PRINCE OF THIEVES, THE(1948); EL PASO(1949); HELLFIRE(1949); JUDGE STEPS OUT, THE(1949); SUNSET BOULEVARD(1950); FIRST LEGION, THE(1951); HERE COMES THE GROOM(1951); JOURNEY INTO LIGHT(1951); SAVAGE DRUMS(1951); TEN COMMANDMENTS, THE(1956)
Misc. Talkies
DIVINE LADY, THE(1929)
Silents
MARKET OF VAIN DESIRE, THE(1916); MAN WHO TURNED WHITE, THE(1919); IS LOVE EVERYTHING?(1924); WHISPERING SMITH(1926); FRENCH DRESSING(1927); KING OF KINGS, THE(1927); MAN-MADE WOMEN(1928)
Misc. Silents
GHOST BREAKER(1914, d; LOST PARADISE, THE(1914); BEGGAR OF CAWNPORE, THE(1916); RAIDERS, THE(1916); SHELL FORTY-THREE(1916); VAGABOND PRINCE, THE(1916); DANGER TRAIL, THE(1917); GOD'S MAN(1917); WRATH(1917); FUGITIVE FROM MATRIMONY(1919); GRAY WOLF'S GHOST, THE(1919); PAGAN GOD, THE(1919); DICE OF DESTINY(1920); FELIX O'DAY(1920); HAUNTING SHADOWS(1920); ONE HOUR BEFORE DAWN(1920); UNCHARTED CHANNELS(1920); WHITE DOVE, THE(1920); BELOW THE DEAD LINE(1921); WHEN WE WERE TWENTY-ONE(1921); ZAZA(1923); SILENCE(1926); SORRELL AND SON(1927); NAUGHTY DUCHESS, THE(1928); ROMANCE OF A ROGUE(1928)
Hansel Warner
DAYS OF JESSE JAMES(1939); PIONEERS OF THE WEST(1940); THEY WERE EXPENDABLE(1945); HOODLUM SAINT, THE(1946)
Helen Warner
EAST SIDE OF HEAVEN(1939)
Howard Warner
THIEVES LIKE US(1974)
J. Wesley Warner
Silents
SCARLET DAYS(1919)
J.B. Warner
Silents
CROSSING TRAILS(1921); COVERED TRAIL, THE(1924); WESTBOUND(1924)
Misc. Silents
BIG STAKES(1922); FLAMING HEARTS(1922); DANGER(1923); BEHIND TWO GUNS(1924); HELLION, THE(1924); HORSESHOE LUCK(1924); TREASURE CANYON(1924); WANTED BY THE LAW(1924); WOLF MAN(1924)
J.L. Warner
OUTWARD BOUND(1930), p
Jack Warner
KNUTE ROCKNE–ALL AMERICAN(1940), p; DUMMY TALKS, THE(1943, Brit.); DEAR MURDERER(1947, Brit.); HOLIDAY CAMP(1947, Brit.); AGAINST THE WIND(1948, Brit.); CAPTIVE HEART, THE(1948, Brit.); EASY MONEY(1948, Brit.); HERE COME THE HUGGETTS(1948, Brit.); VOTE FOR HUGGETT(1948, Brit.); BOYS IN BROWN(1949, Brit.); HUGGETTS ABROAD, THE(1949, Brit.); IT ALWAYS RAINS ON SUNDAY(1949, Brit.); MY BROTHER'S KEEPER(1949, Brit.); BLUE LAMP, THE(1950, Brit.); HUE AND CRY(1950, Brit.); CHRISTMAS CAROL, A(1951, Brit.); THOSE PEOPLE NEXT DOOR(1952, Brit.); TRAIN OF EVENTS(1952, Brit.); VALLEY OF EAGLES(1952, Brit.); YOU CAN'T BEAT THE IRISH(1952, Brit.); ALBERT, R.N.(1953, Brit.); FINAL TEST, THE(1953, Brit.); HUNDRED HOUR HUNT(1953, Brit.); TONIGHT AT 8:30(1953, Brit.); BANG! YOU'RE DEAD(1954, Brit.); FORBIDDEN CARGO(1954, Brit.); SQUARE RING, THE(1955, Brit.); HOME AND AWAY(1956, Brit.); LADYKILLERS, THE(1956, Brit.); NOW AND FOREVER(1956, Brit.); THE CREEPING UNKNOWN(1956, Brit.); CARVE HER NAME WITH PRIDE(1958, Brit.); JIG SAW(1965, Brit.); DOMINIQUE(1978, Brit.)
Silents
OPEN YOUR EYES(1919)
Misc. Silents
DANGEROUS ADVENTURE, A(1922), d
Jack L. Warner
CABIN IN THE COTTON(1932), p; MAN WHO PLAYED GOD, THE(1932), p; SO BIG(1932), p; PARACHUTE JUMPER(1933), p; WORKING MAN, THE(1933), p; HOUSEWIFE(1934), p; THEY MADE ME A CRIMINAL(1939), p; YES, MY DARLING DAUGHTER(1939), p; DR. EHRLICH'S MAGIC BULLET(1940), p; FIGHTING 69TH, THE(1940), p; LADY WITH RED HAIR(1940), p; NO TIME FOR COMEDY(1940), p; SANTA FE TRAIL(1940), p; SATURDAY'S CHILDREN(1940), p; SEA HAWK, THE(1940), p; 'TIL WE MEET AGAIN(1940), p; FLIGHT FROM DESTINY(1941), p; ONE FOOT IN HEAVEN(1941), p; SEA WOLF, THE(1941), p; STRAWBERRY BLONDE, THE(1941), p; UNDERGROUND(1941), p; THIS IS THE ARMY(1943), p; MY FAIR LADY(1964), p; CAMELOT(1967), p; DIRTY LITTLE BILLY(1972), p; 1776(1972), p
Jack M. Warner
ADMIRAL WAS A LADY, THE(1950), p; MAN WHO CHEATED HIMSELF, THE(1951), p
Jack Warner, Jr.
BRUSHFIRE(1962), p&d, w
James Warner
GENTLE PEOPLE AND THE QUIET LAND, THE(1972), w
Jerry Warner
BRINGING UP FATHER(1946), w; CAT CREEPS, THE(1946), w; GIRL ON THE SPOT(1946), w; HER ADVENTUROUS NIGHT(1946), w; INSIDE JOB(1946), w; SLIGHTLY SCANDALOUS(1946), w; FALL GUY(1947), w
Joan Warner
CINDERELLA(1937, Fr.)
John Warner
CRUEL SEA, THE(1953); CAPTAIN'S TABLE, THE(1960, Brit.); MIDSUMMERS NIGHT'S DREAM, A(1961, Czech); ISADORA(1968, Brit.)
John Warner [Edgar G. Ulmer]
THUNDER OVER TEXAS(1934), d
Kent Warner
9/30/55(1977), cos; FM(1978), cos
Margaret Warner
ONE RAINY AFTERNOON(1936)
Marguerite Warner
CONFESSIONS OF A CO-ED(1931)
Marian Warner
Silents
LITTLE PATRIOT, A(1917)
Misc. Silents
TEARS AND SMILES(1917)
Marion Warner
Silents
OLD MAID'S BABY, THE(1919)
Misc. Silents
UNTO THOSE WHO SIN(1916); CAPTAIN KIDDO(1917); LITTLE LOST SISTER(1917); DADDY'S GIRL(1918); DAUGHTER OF THE WEST, A(1918)
Mark Warner
ROCKY III(1982), ed; 48 HOURS(1982), ed; STAYING ALIVE(1983), ed
1984
SOLDIER'S STORY, A(1984), ed
Matt Warner
SIDELONG GLANCES OF A PIGEON KICKER, THE(1970)
Molly Warner
VALLEY OF EAGLES(1952, Brit.)
Pam Warner
THIEVES LIKE US(1974)
Pamela Warner
HEARTBREAKER(1983), art d
Pamela B. Warner
PARASITE(1982), art d; METALSTORM: THE DESTRUCTION OF JARED-SYN(1983), art d
1984
SWORDKILL(1984), prod d
Patricia Warner
LUST FOR A VAMPIRE(1971, Brit.)
Paula Warner
DON'T ANSWER THE PHONE(1980)
Richard Warner
TO HAVE AND TO HOLD(1951, Brit.); GAY ADVENTURE, THE(1953, Brit.); GREAT GILBERT AND SULLIVAN, THE(1953, Brit.); LARGE ROPE, THE(1953, Brit.); MOONRAKER, THE(1958, Brit.); VILLAGE OF THE DAMNED(1960, Brit.); SHADOW OF THE CAT, THE(1961, Brit.); YOUNG AND WILLING(1964, Brit.); MR. BROWN COMES DOWN THE HILL(1966, Brit.); SHARE OUT, THE(1966, Brit.); GIVE A DOG A BONE(1967, Brit.); MUMMY'S SHROUD, THE(1967, Brit.); NEVER BACK LOSERS(1967, Brit.); ON THE RUN(1967, Brit.); STRANGE AFFAIR, THE(1968, Brit.); MARY, QUEEN OF SCOTS(1971, Brit.); HENRY VIII AND HIS SIX WIVES(1972, Brit.); INSIDE OUT(1975, Brit.); LITTLEST HORSE THIEVES, THE(1977)
Robert Warner
BIG JAKE(1971); OCTAMAN(1971); DERANGED(1974, Can.)
Cmdr. S.H. Warner [USN]
DIVE BOMBER(1941), tech adv
Sam Warner
Misc. Silents
DANGEROUS ADVENTURE, A(1922), d
Sandra Warner
SWINGIN' ALONG(1962); POINT BLANK(1967)
Sandy Warner
PARTY GIRL(1958)
Saul L. Warner
Silents
OPEN YOUR EYES(1919), w
Steven Warner
LITTLE PRINCE, THE(1974, Brit.)
Sturgis Warner
STARTING OVER(1979)
Virgil Warner
SAM WHISKEY(1969)
Wes Warner
LOST JUNGLE, THE(1934); TEXAS TORNADO(1934); SAGEBRUSH TROUBADOR(1935); GUNS AND GUITARS(1936); SINGING COWBOY, THE(1936); GUNSMOKE RANCH(1937)

Bob Warners
FUNERAL HOME(1982, Can.)
Alan Warnick
LAST MOVIE, THE(1971); PLAY IT AS IT LAYS(1972)
Allan Warnick
CHINATOWN(1974); MOTHER, JUGS & SPEED(1976); HOW TO BEAT THE HIGH COST OF LIVING(1980); RICH AND FAMOUS(1981)
Christine Warnick
GERMANY IN AUTUMN(1978, Ger.), ed
Sonja Warnke
1984
FLIGHT TO BERLIN(1984, Ger./Brit.)
Craig Warnock
TIME BANDITS(1981, Brit.)
Stan Warnow
CHAFED ELBOWS(1967), ph; HONEYMOON KILLERS, THE(1969), ed
Stanley Warnow
RAGTIME(1981), ed
Mary Waronov
Misc. Talkies
HOLLYWOOD MAN, THE(1976)
Zbigniew Warpechowski
GOLEM(1980, Pol.), set d
Terry Warr
SUBURBAN WIVES(1973, Brit.), m
John Warrack
1984
GREYSTOKE: THE LEGEND OF TARZAN, LORD OF THE APES(1984), md
Michael Warre
HENRY V(1946, Brit.); REACH FOR THE SKY(1957, Brit.)
Allan Warren
HERE WE GO ROUND THE MULBERRY BUSH(1968, Brit.)
Anne Warren
LITTLE BIG HORN(1951)
Anne Warren
Misc. Talkies
DOWN TO THE SEA(1975)
Anthony Warren
STEEL BAYONET, THE(1958, Brit.)
Barry Warren
KISS OF EVIL(1963, Brit.); MACBETH(1963); DEVIL-SHIP PIRATES, THE(1964, Brit.); FRANKENSTEIN CREATED WOMAN(1965, Brit.)
Basil Warren
LAUGHING ANNE(1954, Brit./U.S.), ed; DANGEROUS YOUTH(1958, Brit.), ed; WONDERFUL THINGS!(1958, Brit.), ed; HEART OF A MAN, THE(1959, Brit.), ed; LADY IS A SQUARE, THE(1959, Brit.), ed; NAVY LARK, THE(1959, Brit.), ed
Ben Warren
Silents
JOHNNY RING AND THE CAPTAIN'S SWORD(1921)
Betty Warren
FARMER'S WIFE, THE(1941, Brit.); CHAMPAGNE CHARLIE(1944, Brit.); SECRET MISSION(1944, Brit.); THEY MET IN THE DARK(1945, Brit.); VARIETY JUBILEE(1945, Brit.); MAGIC BOW, THE(1947, Brit.); PASSPORT TO PIMLICO(1949, Brit.); SO LONG AT THE FAIR(1951, Brit.); TREAD SOFTLY STRANGER(1959, Brit.)
Beverly Warren
RIVER LADY(1948)
Bill Warren
LADY FRANKENSTEIN(1971, Ital.), w
Brice Warren
THEY CAME TO BLOW UP AMERICA(1943)
Bruce Warren
LIGHTNIN'(1930); BODY AND SOUL(1931); MOTHER AND SON(1931); UNFAITHFUL(1931); DRIFTER, THE(1932); TESS OF THE STORM COUNTRY(1932); SCARLET EMPRESS, THE(1934); THIRTY-DAY PRINCESS(1934); HEALER, THE(1935); RUMBA(1935); GIVE ME YOUR HEART(1936); POLO JOE(1936); THIRTEEN HOURS BY AIR(1936); PLAINSMAN, THE(1937); SING AND BE HAPPY(1937); HELD FOR RANSOM(1938); HEROES OF THE ALAMO(1938); ON THE GREAT WHITE TRAIL(1938); YOUNG AS YOU FEEL(1940); GIRL TROUBLE(1942); REAP THE WILD WIND(1942); SWEET ROSIE O'GRADY(1943); MY REPUTATION(1946)
Bunny Warren
MAN WHO WOULDN'T TALK, THE(1958, Brit.), ed; TEENAGE BAD GIRL(1959, Brit.), ed
Butch Warren
NIGHT IN HEAVEN, A(1983)
C.E.T. Warren
ABOVE US THE WAVES(1956, Brit.), w
Carol Warren
KILLING OF A CHINESE BOOKIE, THE(1976); OPENING NIGHT(1977)
Charles Warren
SECRET OF NIMH, THE(1982), ph
Charles Marquis Warren
BEYOND GLORY(1948), w; STREETS OF LAREDO(1949), w; REDHEAD AND THE COWBOY, THE(1950), w; FIGHTING COAST GUARD(1951), w; LITTLE BIG HORN(1951), d&w; OH! SUSANNA(1951), w; ONLY THE VALIANT(1951), w; HELLGATE(1952), d&w; SPRINGFIELD RIFLE(1952), w; WOMAN OF THE NORTH COUNTRY(1952), w; ARROWHEAD(1953), d&w; FLIGHT TO TANGIER(1953), d&w; PONY EXPRESS(1953), w; SEVEN ANGRY MEN(1955), d; BLACK WHIP, THE(1956), d; TENSION AT TABLE ROCK(1956), d; BACK FROM THE DEAD(1957), d; COPPER SKY(1957), d; RIDE A VIOLENT MILE(1957), d, w; TROOPER HOOK(1957), d; UNKNOWN TERROR, THE(1957), d; BLOOD ARROW(1958), d; CATTLE EMPIRE(1958), d; DESERT HELL(1958), d, w; DAY OF THE EVIL GUN(1968), w; CHARRO(1969), p, d&w
Dale O. Warren
KLANSMAN, THE(1974), m
Denise Warren
WE JOINED THE NAVY(1962, Brit.)
Dodie Warren
YOUNG SWINGERS, THE(1963); DESTRUCTORS, THE(1968); MARYJANE(1968); MONEY JUNGLE, THE(1968); PANIC IN THE CITY(1968); IS THIS TRIP REALLY NECESSARY?(1970), makeup

Don Warren
UNDERSEA GIRL(1957)
Dorothy Warren
Silents
UNDER SUSPICION(1919, Brit.); MAN WITHOUT DESIRE, THE(1923, Brit.)
Douglas Warren
DEVIL'S MISTRESS, THE(1968), a, m
Dwight Warren
Silents
MIDNIGHT PATROL, THE(1918), ph; SAND(1920), ph; ALTAR STAIRS, THE(1922), ph; SHOCK, THE(1923), ph; SINGER JIM MCKEE(1924), ph
E. Allyn Warren
SHIPMATES(1931); HATCHET MAN, THE(1932); DEVIL DOLL, THE(1936); PORT OF SEVEN SEAS(1938); SHINING HOUR, THE(1938); BROADWAY SERENADE(1939); MIRACLES FOR SALE(1939)
Silents
UNHOLY THREE, THE(1925)
E. Alyn Warren
ABRAHAM LINCOLN(1930); DU BARRY, WOMAN OF PASSION(1930); EAST IS WEST(1930); MEDICINE MAN, THE(1930); PRINCE OF DIAMONDS(1930); SON OF THE GODS(1930); DAUGHTER OF THE DRAGON(1931); FIGHTING CARAVANS(1931); FREE SOUL, A(1931); TARZAN THE FEARLESS(1933); LIMEHOUSE BLUES(1934); STUDENT TOUR(1934); TRUMPET BLOWS, THE(1934); WAGON WHEELS(1934); CHINATOWN SQUAD(1935); GET THAT MAN(1935); DOUBLE WEDDING(1937); THEY WON'T FORGET(1937); GIRL OF THE GOLDEN WEST, THE(1938); THREE COMRADES(1938); IDIOT'S DELIGHT(1939); SERGEANT MADDEN(1939); TELL NO TALES(1939)
Silents
COURTSHIP OF MILES STANDISH, THE(1923); RED WINE(1928); TRAIL OF '98, THE(1929)
Misc. Silents
TIGER LILY, THE(1919); SWEET ROSIE O'GRADY(1926); OPENING NIGHT, THE(1927)
E.A. Warren
Silents
NEW LOVE FOR OLD(1918); MILLIONAIRE, THE(1921); NO WOMAN KNOWS(1921); OUTSIDE THE LAW(1921); TALE OF TWO WORLDS, A(1921); EAST IS WEST(1922); HUNGRY HEARTS(1922)
Misc. Silents
MYSTERIOUS MR. TILLER, THE(1917); FORBIDDEN CITY, THE(1918); HER ONLY WAY(1918); WINE GIRL, THE(1918); TWINS OF SUFFERING CREEK(1920)
Ed Warren
THUNDER TRAIL(1937)
Eda Warren
DANGEROUS CURVES(1929), ed; KIBITZER, THE(1929), ed; WOLF SONG(1929), ed; LADIES LOVE BRUTES(1930), ed; SLIGHTLY SCARLET(1930), ed; MIDNIGHT CLUB(1933), ed; PARIS IN SPRING(1935), ed; SO RED THE ROSE(1935), ed; ANYTHING GOES(1936), ed; GENERAL DIED AT DAWN, THE(1936), ed; BIG BROADCAST OF 1938, THE(1937), ed; MOUNTAIN MUSIC(1937), ed; PARTNERS IN CRIME(1937), ed; SWING HIGH, SWING LOW(1937), ed; KING OF ALCATRAZ(1938), ed; HONEYMOON IN BALI(1939), ed; KING OF CHINATOWN(1939), ed; RANGERS OF FORTUNE(1940), ed; SAFARI(1940), ed; BAHAMA PASSAGE(1941), ed; ONE NIGHT IN LISBON(1941), ed; VIRGINIA(1941), ed; I MARRIED A WITCH(1942), ed; LADY IS WILLING, THE(1942), ed; CHINA(1943), ed; YOUNG AND WILLING(1943), ed; HITLER GANG, THE(1944), ed; YOU CAME ALONG(1945), ed; CALIFORNIA(1946), ed; TWO YEARS BEFORE THE MAST(1946), ed; BEYOND GLORY(1948), ed; NIGHT HAS A THOUSAND EYES(1948), ed; RED, HOT AND BLUE(1949), ed; COPPER CANYON(1950), ed; WHERE DANGER LIVES(1950), ed; DARLING, HOW COULD YOU!(1951), ed; HIS KIND OF WOMAN(1951), ed; SUBMARINE COMMAND(1951), ed; SON OF PALEFACE(1952), ed; PONY EXPRESS(1953), ed; SECRET OF THE INCAS(1954), ed; STRATEGIC AIR COMMAND(1955), ed; BACK FROM ETERNITY(1956), ed; JOHNNY CONCHO(1956), ed; WORLD WITHOUT END(1956), ed; UNHOLY WIFE, THE(1957), ed; HOT ANGEL, THE(1958), ed; ST. LOUIS BLUES(1958), ed; JOHN PAUL JONES(1959), ed; WRECK OF THE MARY DEAR, THE(1959), ed; ONE FOOT IN HELL(1960), ed; YOUNG SAVAGES, THE(1961), ed; ESCAPE FROM ZAHRAIN(1962), ed; TARAS BULBA(1962), ed; NEW INTERNS, THE(1964), ed; RIDE THE WILD SURF(1964), ed; PRIVATE NAVY OF SGT. O'FARRELL, THE(1968), ed
Silents
EVENING CLOTHES(1927), ed
Edna Warren
AND THE ANGELS SING(1944), ed; AFFAIRS OF SUSAN(1945), ed; ALIAS NICK BEAL(1949), ed; AT GUNPOINT(1955), ed
Edward Warren
OCEAN'S ELEVEN(1960)
Misc. Silents
LITTLE ORPHAN(1915); LOVE AND AMBITION(1917), d; WARFARE OF THE FLESH, THE(1917), d; WEAVERS OF LIFE(1917), d; THUNDERBOLTS OF FATE(1919), d
Eleanor Warren
BOY NAMED CHARLIE BROWN, A(1969), anim
Elena Warren
THEY WON'T BELIEVE ME(1947); DESPERATE(1947); TRAIL STREET(1947)
F. Brooke Warren
FACE AT THE WINDOW, THE(1932, Brit.), w; FACE AT THE WINDOW, THE(1939, Brit.), w
Silents
FACE AT THE WINDOW, THE(1920, Brit.), w
Fanny Warren
Misc. Silents
FIGHTING THREE, THE(1927)
Fran Warren
ABBOTT AND COSTELLO MEET CAPTAIN KIDD(1952); TOYS ARE NOT FOR CHILDREN(1972)
Frances Warren
SECRET VOICE, THE(1936, Brit.), w
Frank Warren
ROOGIE'S BUMP(1954), w; ALL WOMAN(1967), p&d

Fred Warren
IN OLD ARIZONA(1929); LOCKED DOOR, THE(1929); SPIELER, THE(1929); ABRAHAM LINCOLN(1930); GIRL OF THE GOLDEN WEST(1930); KIKI(1931); MIRACLE WOMAN, THE(1931); SECRET SERVICE(1931); DANCERS IN THE DARK(1932); CAT'S PAW, THE(1934); KID MILLIONS(1934); OPERATOR 13(1934); MYSTERIOUS MR. WONG(1935); SHIP CAFE(1935); I CONQUER THE SEA(1936); REVOLT OF THE ZOMBIES(1936); HIGH, WIDE AND HANDSOME(1937); NIGHT CLUB SCANDAL(1937); MIRACLES FOR SALE(1939)
Silents
MATRIMANIAC, THE(1916); NINA, THE FLOWER GIRL(1917); KILDARE OF STORM(1918); MAN WHO, THE(1921); LITTLE EVA ASCENDS(1922); PAWN TICKET 210(1922); EXILES, THE(1923); GIRL OF THE GOLDEN WEST, THE(1923); STEPHEN STEPS OUT(1923); DESERT FLOWER, THE(1925); MISS NOBODY(1926); CALIFORNIA(1927); EAGER LIPS(1927); THREE'S A CROWD(1927); NOOSE, THE(1928)
Misc. Silents
CONFESSION(1918); MAN WHO DARED, THE(1920); BELLS, THE(1926)
Fred H. Warren
Silents
JOHNNY-ON-THE-SPOT(1919)
Gary Warren
UP IN THE AIR(1969, Brit.); RAILWAY CHILDREN, THE(1971, Brit.)
Gary F. Warren
ESCAPE FROM ALCATRAZ(1979)
Gene Warren
KRONOS(1957), spec eff; DINOSAURUS(1960), spec eff; TIME MACHINE, THE(1960; Brit./U.S.), spec eff; MASTER OF THE WORLD(1961), spec eff; WONDERFUL WORLD OF THE BROTHERS ERIMM, THE(1962), spec eff; POWER, THE(1968), spec eff
Gene Warren, Jr.
SPACEHUNTER: ADVENTURES IN THE FORBIDDEN ZONE(1983), spec eff
1984
TERMINATOR, THE(1984), spec eff
George Warren
HOT STUFF(1979); FINAL COUNTDOWN, THE(1980)
George E. Warren
1984
HARRY AND SON(1984)
Gil Warren
STORY OF SEABISCUIT, THE(1949); CYRANO DE BERGERAC(1950); UNION STATION(1950); PHFFFT!(1954)
Giles Warren
Misc. Silents
YOUR GIRL AND MINE(1914), d
Giles R. Warren
Misc. Silents
TEXAS STEER, A(1915), d
Gloria Warren
ALWAYS IN MY HEART(1942); CINDERELLA SWINGS IT(1942); DANGEROUS MONEY(1946); DON'T GAMBLE WITH STRANGERS(1946); BELLS OF SAN FERNANDO(1947)
Hal Warren
MANOS, THE HANDS OF FATE(1966)
Hal P. Warren
MANOS, THE HANDS OF FATE(1966), p,d&w
Harriet Warren
DON'T LOOK IN THE BASEMENT(1973)
Harry Warren
42ND STREET(1933); MOULIN ROUGE(1934), m; VERY HONORABLE GUY, A(1934); GO INTO YOUR DANCE(1935); MARKED WOMAN(1937), m/l; YOUNG PEOPLE(1940), m/l Mack Gordon; SUMMER HOLIDAY(1948), m; MY DREAM IS YOURS(1949), m; JUST FOR YOU(1952), m
Helen Warren
CURSE OF THE LIVING CORPSE, THE(1964)
Herbert Warren
HOUSE OF SECRETS(1929)
Ian Warren
PRAYING MANTIS(1982, Brit.), p
Jack Warren
ANGEL, ANGEL, DOWN WE GO(1969), ph
James Warren
PACIFIC RENDEZVOUS(1942); GIRL CRAZY(1943); GUY NAMED JOE, A(1943); THOUSANDS CHEER(1943); THREE HEARTS FOR JULIA(1943); MAISIE GOES TO RENO(1944); SEE HERE, PRIVATE HARGROVE(1944); WANDERER OF THE WASTELAND(1945); BADMAN'S TERRITORY(1946); DING DONG WILLIAMS(1946); SUNSET PASS(1946); CODE OF THE WEST(1947); JUDGE STEPS OUT, THE(1949); THREE FOR BEDROOM C(1952); PORT SINISTER(1953)
Janet Waldo Warren
PERSONS IN HIDING(1939)
Janet Warren
JADE MASK, THE(1945); SHANGHAI COBRA, THE(1945); DOUBLE LIFE, A(1947); FEAR IN THE NIGHT(1947); VOICE OF THE TURTLE, THE(1947); WINTER WONDERLAND(1947); ROMANCE ON THE HIGH SEAS(1948); TWONKY, THE(1953)
Jason Warren
SCREWBALLS(1983)
Jeff Warren
GENTLE PEOPLE AND THE QUIET LAND, THE(1972)
Jennifer Warren
SAM'S SONG(1971); NIGHT MOVES(1975); ANOTHER MAN, ANOTHER CHANCE(1977 Fr/US); SLAP SHOT(1977); ICE CASTLES(1978)
1984
NIGHT SHADOWS(1984)
Jerry Warren
MAN BEAST(1956), p&d; FACE OF THE SCREAMING WEREWOLF(1959, Mex.), p, d; INCREDIBLE PETRIFIED WORLD, THE(1959), p&d; CREATURE OF THE WALKING DEAD(1960, Mex.), p, d; TEENAGE ZOMBIES(1960), p&d; INVASION OF THE ANIMAL PEOPLE(1962, U.S./Swed.), p, d, ph; TERROR OF THE BLOODHUNTERS(1962), p,d&w; ATTACK OF THE MAYAN MUMMY(1963, U.S./Mex.), p&d; CURSE OF THE STONE HAND(1965, Mex/Chile), p, d; WILD WORLD OF BATWOMAN, THE(1966), p,d&w

Misc. Talkies
FRANKENSTEIN'S ISLAND(1982), d
Jill Warren
OVER MY DEAD BODY(1942); QUIET PLEASE, MURDER(1942); SINCE YOU WENT AWAY(1944)
John F Warren
COSMIC MAN, THE(1959), ph; COUNTERFEIT KILLER, THE(1968), ph
John F. Warren
COUNTRY GIRL, THE(1954), ph; SEVEN LITTLE FOYS, THE(1955), ph; ANYTHING GOES(1956), ph; PROUD AND THE PROFANE, THE(1956), ph; SEARCH FOR BRIDEY MURPHY, THE(1956), ph; BEAU JAMES(1957), ph; DAUGHTER OF DR. JEKYLL(1957), ph; ZERO HOUR!(1957), ph; COLOSSUS OF NEW YORK, THE(1958), ph; DARK INTRUDER(1965), ph; TORN CURTAIN(1966), ph; LOVE-INS, THE(1967), ph; TAMMY AND THE MILLIONAIRE(1967), ph; FOR SINGLES ONLY(1968), ph; TIME TO SING, A(1968), ph; YOUNG RUNAWAYS, THE(1968), ph
John Warren
MARK OF CAIN, THE(1948, Brit.); MR. PERRIN AND MR. TRAILL(1948, Brit.); WILLIAM COMES TO TOWN(1948, Brit.); DIAMOND CITY(1949, Brit.); IT'S NOT CRICKET(1949, Brit.); MARRY ME!(1949, Brit.); MY BROTHER'S KEEPER(1949, Brit.); WARNING TO WANTONS, A(1949, Brit.); SHADOW OF THE PAST(1950, Brit.); UP FOR THE CUP(1950, Brit.); RELUCTANT WIDOW, THE(1951, Brit.); GLORY AT SEA(1952, Brit.); MADE IN HEAVEN(1952, Brit.); STOLEN FACE(1952, Brit.); MR. DENNING DRIVES NORTH(1953, Brit.); PROJECT M7(1953, Brit.); TERROR STREET(1953); FAST AND LOOSE(1954, Brit.); HELL BELOW ZERO(1954, Brit.); BRIDE OF THE MONSTER(1955); PASSAGE HOME(1955, Brit.); SECRET VENTURE(1955, Brit.); TROUBLE IN STORE(1955, Brit.); CASH ON DELIVERY(1956, Brit.); GENTLE TOUCH, THE(1956, Brit.); JUMPING FOR JOY(1956, Brit.); PRIVATE'S PROGRESS(1956, Brit.); ROTTEN TO THE CORE(1956, Brit.), w; TEN COMMANDMENTS, THE(1956), ph; FURTHER UP THE CREEK!(1958, Brit.), a, w; UP THE CREEK(1958, Brit.), a, w; TWO-WAY STRETCH(1961, Brit.), w; LIFE IS A CIRCUS(1962, Brit.), w; OPERATION SNATCH(1962, Brit.), w; WRONG ARM OF THE LAW, THE(1963, Brit.), w; GET CHARLIE TULLY(1976, Brit.), w
Jordan Warren
RACE FOR YOUR LIFE, CHARLIE BROWN(1977)
Joseph Warren
MOMMIE DEAREST(1981)
Julie Warren
HEROES IN BLUE(1939); DEVIL AND MISS JONES, THE(1941); KING'S ROW(1942); MEXICAN SPITFIRE AT SEA(1942); MEXICAN SPITFIRE SEES A GHOST(1942); POWDER TOWN(1942)
Katharine Warren
ALL THE KING'S MEN(1949); MARY RYAN, DETECTIVE(1949); MAN BEHIND THE GUN, THE(1952); CAINE MUTINY, THE(1954); VIOLENT MEN, THE(1955); FURY AT GUNSIGHT PASS(1956)
Katherin Warren
DRANGO(1957)
Katherine Warren
AND BABY MAKES THREE(1949); STORY OF MOLLY X, THE(1949); TELL IT TO THE JUDGE(1949); MYSTERY SUBMARINE(1950); THREE SECRETS(1950); FORCE OF ARMS(1951); LADY PAYS OFF, THE(1951); LORNA DOONE(1951); NIGHT INTO MORNING(1951); PEOPLE AGAINST O'HARA, THE(1951); PROWLER, THE(1951); TALL TARGET, THE(1951); BATTLES OF CHIEF PONTIAC(1952); SCANDAL SHEET(1952); SON OF ALI BABA(1952); STEEL TRAP, THE(1952); TALK ABOUT A STRANGER(1952); THIS WOMAN IS DANGEROUS(1952); WASHINGTON STORY(1952); GLENN MILLER STORY, THE(1953); STAR, THE(1953); INSIDE DETROIT(1955); JAILHOUSE ROCK(1957); I'LL GIVE MY LIFE(1959)
Ken Warren
Misc. Talkies
MAN IN A LOOKING GLASS, A(1965, Brit.)
Kenneth Warren
HELL, HEAVEN OR HOBOKEN(1958, Brit.); CIRCUS OF HORRORS(1960, Brit.)
Kenneth J. Warren
I'M ALL RIGHT, JACK(1959, Brit.); NAVY LARK, THE(1959, Brit.); WOMAN'S TEMPTATION, A(1959, Brit.); FOUR DESPERATE MEN(1960, Brit.); DR. BLOOD'S COFFIN(1961); PART-TIME WIFE(1961, Brit.); STRIP TEASE MURDER(1961, Brit.); BOYS, THE(1962, Brit.); CONCRETE JUNGLE, THE(1962, Brit.); SMALL WORLD OF SAMMY LEE, THE(1963, Brit.); HIGH WIND IN JAMAICA, A(1965); OPERATION SNAFU(1965, Brit.); UNDERWORLD INFORMERS(1965, Brit.); DOUBLE MAN, THE(1967); 25TH HOUR, THE(1967, Fr./Ital./Yugo.); DECLINE AND FALL... OF A BIRD WATCHER(1969, Brit.); LEO THE LAST(1970, Brit.); REVOLUTIONARY, THE(1970, Brit.); I, MONSTER(1971, Brit.); DEMONS OF THE MIND(1972, Brit.); CREEPING FLESH,THE(1973, Brit.); DIGBY, THE BIGGEST DOG IN THE WORLD(1974, Brit.); S(1974)
Kirk Warren
CROCODILE(1979, Thai./Hong Kong)
Lee Warren
ALLIGATOR PEOPLE, THE(1959); HOOKED GENERATION, THE(1969)
Leonard Warren
IRISH EYES ARE SMILING(1944)
Lesley Warren
PICKUP ON 101(1972)
Lesley Ann Warren
HAPPIEST MILLIONAIRE, THE(1967); ONE AND ONLY GENUINE ORIGINAL FAMILY BAND, THE(1968); HARRY AND WALTER GO TO NEW YORK(1976); VICTOR/VICTORIA(1982); NIGHT IN HEAVEN, A(1983)
1984
CHOOSE ME(1984); SONGWRITER(1984); TREASURE OF THE YANKEE ZEPHYR(1984)
Low Warren
Silents
KING CHARLES(1913, Brit.), w; NELSON(1918, Brit.), p; PEEP BEHIND THE SCENES, A(1918, Brit.), p
Mark Warren
27TH DAY, THE(1957); COME BACK CIHARLESTON BLUE(1972), d; TULIPS(1981, Can), d
Misc. Talkies
KINKY COACHES & THE POM POM PUSSYCATS, THE(1981, Can.), d

Mary Warren
NORAH O'NEALE(1934, Brit.)
Silents
ALL NIGHT(1918); PRINCE OF AVENUE A., THE(1920); GUILE OF WOMEN(1921); COME ON OVER(1922)
Misc. Silents
BETTY TAKES A HAND(1918); HONEST MAN, AN(1918); OLD HARTWELL'S CUB(1918); SEA PANTHER, THE(1918); VORTEX, THE(1918)

Maude Radford Warren
Silents
HOUSE OF YOUTH, THE(1924), w

Maurice Warren
MUDLARK, THE(1950, Brit.)

May Warren
NORAH O'NEALE(1934, Brit.)

Michael Warren
CRIMSON CULT, THE(1970, Brit.); HAWMPS!(1976), w; NORMAN...IS THAT YOU?(1976); FAST BREAK(1979)

Mike Warren
DRIVE, HE SAID(1971); BUTTERFLIES ARE FREE(1972); CLEOPATRA JONES(1973)

Monty Warren
HIDE AND SEEK(1964, Brit.)

Nancy Warren
CHEAP DETECTIVE, THE(1978)

Nola Warren
WHITE DEATH(1936, Aus.)

Norman J. Warren
SATAN'S SLAVE(1976, Brit.), d; TERROR(1979, Brit.), d; SPACED OUT(1981, Brit.), d; HORROR PLANET(1982, Brit.), d
Misc. Talkies
INSEMINOID(1980), d

Pat Warren
EYES OF A STRANGER(1980)

Phil Warren
KEEP 'EM FLYING(1941); INVISIBLE AGENT(1942); MADAME SPY(1942); MOONLIGHT IN HAVANA(1942); FLESH AND FANTASY(1943); GOOD MORNING, JUDGE(1943); HI, BUDDY(1943); SO'S YOUR UNCLE(1943); WE'VE NEVER BEEN LICKED(1943); ARMY WIVES(1944); BADMAN'S TERRITORY(1946); CRIMINAL COURT(1946); DEADLINE AT DAWN(1946); FALCON'S ADVENTURE, THE(1946); CODE OF THE WEST(1947); DEVIL THUMBS A RIDE, THE(1947); LIKELY STORY, A(1947); SINBAD THE SAILOR(1947); SUPERMAN AND THE MOLE MEN(1951)

Philip Warren
ILLEGAL TRAFFIC(1938); DISBARRED(1939); FIFTH AVENUE GIRL(1939); MILLION DOLLAR LEGS(1939); UNDERCOVER DOCTOR(1939); UNMARRIED(1939); ZAZA(1939); MYSTERY SEA RAIDER(1940); GENIUS AT WORK(1946)

Phillip Warren
COCOANUT GROVE(1938); HER JUNGLE LOVE(1938); HUNTED MEN(1938); KING OF ALCATRAZ(1938); PRISON FARM(1938); TIP-OFF GIRLS(1938); YOU AND ME(1938); SUDDEN MONEY(1939); TOM SAWYER, DETECTIVE(1939)

Phyliss Warren
WEIRD ONES, THE(1962)

Richard Warren
RAWHIDE TRAIL, THE(1958)

Robert Penn Warren
ALL THE KING'S MEN(1949), p,d&w; BAND OF ANGELS(1957), w

Ronald Warren
ON HER BED OF ROSES(1966)

Ruth O. Warren
LAKE PLACID SERENADE(1944)

Ruth Warren
LIGHTNIN'(1930); ANNABELLE'S AFFAIRS(1931); DOCTORS' WIVES(1931); GUILTY GENERATION, THE(1931); MEN ON CALL(1931); MR. LEMON OF ORANGE(1931); SIX CYLINDER LOVE(1931); WOMEN OF ALL NATIONS(1931); DEVIL'S LOTTERY(1932); HELLO TROUBLE(1932); MAMA LOVES PAPA(1933); STATE FAIR(1933); ZOO IN BUDAPEST(1933); EVELYN PRENTICE(1934); LAST TRAIL, THE(1934); LET'S FALL IN LOVE(1934); DOUBTING THOMAS(1935); HER MASTER'S VOICE(1936); OUR RELATIONS(1936); FORLORN RIVER(1937); MAKE WAY FOR TOMORROW(1937); PARTNERS IN CRIME(1937); 45 FATHERS(1937); PRISON FARM(1938); CISCO KID AND THE LADY, THE(1939); WHEN TOMORROW COMES(1939); HOUSE ACROSS THE BAY, THE(1940); MANHATTAN HEARTBEAT(1940); REMEMBER THE NIGHT(1940); SAILOR'S LADY(1940); SHOP AROUND THE CORNER, THE(1940); WOMEN WITHOUT NAMES(1940); FOR BEAUTY'S SAKE(1941); JACKASS MAIL(1942); LADY IN A JAM(1942); THRU DIFFERENT EYES(1942); DIXIE DUGAN(1943); GOOD MORNING, JUDGE(1943); SONG OF BERNADETTE, THE(1943); ONCE UPON A TIME(1944); PIN UP GIRL(1944); SHE'S A SWEETHEART(1944); ADVENTURES OF RUSTY(1945); WEEKEND AT THE WALDORF(1945); CLOSE CALL FOR BOSTON BLACKIE, A(1946); KING OF THE WILD HORSES(1947); CANON CITY(1948); SITTING PRETTY(1948); BODYHOLD(1950); CAGED(1950); HE'S A COCKEYED WONDER(1950); IN A LONELY PLACE(1950); NO WAY OUT(1950); SIDE STREET(1950); NEVER TRUST A GAMBLER(1951); MONKEY BUSINESS(1952); MONTANA TERRITORY(1952); O. HENRY'S FULL HOUSE(1952); HOUSE OF WAX(1953); KID FROM LEFT FIELD, THE(1953); MAN IN THE DARK(1953); LONG, LONG TRAILER, THE(1954); BRING YOUR SMILE ALONG(1955); PRINCE OF PLAYERS(1955); LAST HURRAH, THE(1958)

Sam Warren
OUT OF THE PAST(1947)

Sammy Warren
BLUE COLLAR(1978); CHU CHU AND THE PHILLY FLASH(1981)

Sandra Warren
CURTAINS(1983, Can.)

Steve Warren
FRIENDLY PERSUASION(1956); RUMBLE ON THE DOCKS(1956); BEGINNING OF THE END(1957); GUNFIRE AT INDIAN GAP(1957)

Toni Warren
RAW WEEKEND(1964)

Tony Warren
FERRY ACROSS THE MERSEY(1964, Brit.), w

Val Warren
BIKINI BEACH(1964)

Wilson Warren
LONGEST YARD, THE(1974)

Yvonne Warren
ACTION OF THE TIGER(1957); SILENT ENEMY, THE(1959, Brit.); CORRIDORS OF BLOOD(1962, Brit.)

Yvonne Warren "Romain"
MURDER REPORTED(1958, Brit.)

Harold Warrender
I SPY(1933, Brit.); FRIDAY THE 13TH(1934, Brit.); LADY IN DANGER(1934, Brit.); LEAVE IT TO BLANCHE(1934, Brit.); INVITATION TO THE WALTZ(1935, Brit.); LAZYBONES(1935, Brit.); MIMI(1935, Brit.); BLACKOUT(1940, Brit.); CONVOY(1940); THREE COCKEYED SAILORS(1940, Brit.); CONSPIRATOR(1949, Brit.); SCOTT OF THE ANTARCTIC(1949, Brit.); WARNING TO WANTONS, A(1949, Brit.); PANDORA AND THE FLYING DUTCHMAN(1951, Brit.); SIX MEN, THE(1951, Brit.); IVANHOE(1952, Brit.); IVORY HUNTER(1952, Brit.); DISOBEDIENT(1953, Brit.); TERROR ON A TRAIN(1953)

Gibert Warrenton
LEGEND OF TOM DOOLEY, THE(1959), ph

Gil Warrenton
TEN CENTS A DANCE(1931), ph; DEVIL'S MATE(1933), ph; TELEPHONE OPERATOR(1938), ph; CHEROKEE UPRISING(1950), ph; TEXAS BAD MAN(1953), ph; DRAGSTRIP RIOT(1958), ph; DIARY OF A HIGH SCHOOL BRIDE(1959), ph; GHOST OF DRAGSTRIP HOLLOW(1959), ph; MASTER OF THE WORLD(1961), ph

Gilbert Warrenton
LONESOME(1928), ph; MOTHER KNOWS BEST(1928), ph; HOLD YOUR MAN(1929), ph; LOVE TRAP, THE(1929), ph; MISSISSIPPI GAMBLER(1929), ph; SCANDAL(1929), ph; SHOW BOAT(1929), ph; CAPTAIN OF THE GUARD(1930), ph; HIDE-OUT, THE(1930), ph; MOTHERS CRY(1930), ph; HONEYMOON LANE(1931), ph; GREAT JASPER, THE(1933), ph; HELLO, EVERYBODY(1933), ph; LADY'S PROFESSION, A(1933), ph; MAMA LOVES PAPA(1933), ph; SPHINX, THE(1933), ph; SWEETHEART OF SIGMA CHI(1933), ph; BEGGARS IN ERMINE(1934), ph; COWBOY HOLIDAY(1934), ph; EIGHT GIRLS IN A BOAT(1934), ph; LOUDSPEAKER, THE(1934), ph; LOVE CAPTIVE, THE(1934), ph; TICKET TO CRIME(1934), ph; WOMAN UNAFRAID(1934), ph; BORN TO GAMBLE(1935), ph; CHAMPAGNE FOR BREAKFAST(1935), ph; CORONADO(1935), ph; HERE COMES COOKIE(1935), ph; RAINBOW'S END(1935), ph; RESCUE SQUAD(1935), ph; SPANISH CAPE MYSTERY(1935), ph; SUNSET RANGE(1935), ph; BOY OF THE STREETS(1937), ph; BREEZING HOME(1937), ph; BRIDE FOR HENRY, A(1937), ph; DRAEGERMAN COURAGE(1937), ph; FEDERAL BULLETS(1937), ph; HEADLINE CRASHER(1937), ph; PARADISE ISLE(1937), ph; BAREFOOT BOY(1938), ph; MARINES ARE HERE, THE(1938), ph; PORT OF MISSING GIRLS(1938), ph; ROMANCE OF THE LIMBERLOST(1938), ph; ROSE OF THE RIO GRANDE(1938), ph; SALESLADY(1938), ph; UNDER THE BIG TOP(1938), ph; CITY OF SILENT MEN(1942), ph; THEY RAID BY NIGHT(1942), ph; ALIMONY(1949), ph; GREAT DAN PATCH, THE(1949), ph; PAROLE, INC.(1949), ph; RIDE, RYDER, RIDE!(1949), ph; ROLL, THUNDER, ROLL(1949), ph; BLUE GRASS OF KENTUCKY(1950), ph; COUNTY FAIR(1950), ph; COWBOY AND THE PRIZEFIGHTER(1950), ph; FIGHTING REDHEAD, THE(1950), ph; HOT ROD(1950), ph; OUTLAW GOLD(1950), ph; OUTLAWS OF TEXAS(1950), ph; YOUNG DANIEL BOONE(1950), ph; ABILENE TRAIL(1951), ph; BLUE BLOOD(1951), ph; COLORADO AMBUSH(1951), ph; MONTANA DESPERADO(1951), ph; ALADDIN AND HIS LAMP(1952), ph; FIGHTING LAWMAN, THE(1953), ph; GREAT JESSE JAMES RAID(1953), ph; SINS OF JEZEBEL(1953), ph; WHITE ORCHID, THE(1954), ph; MASSACRE(1956), ph; MESA OF LOST WOMEN, THE(1956), ph; NO PLACE TO HIDE(1956), ph; GHOST OF THE CHINA SEA(1958), ph; HIGH SCHOOL HELLCATS(1958), ph; FORBIDDEN ISLAND(1959), ph; PARATROOP COMMAND(1959), ph; SUBMARINE SEAHAWK(1959), ph; ATOMIC SUBMARINE, THE(1960), ph; BOY WHO CAUGHT A CROOK(1961), ph; CLOWN AND THE KID, THE(1961), ph; FLIGHT THAT DISAPPEARED, THE(1961), ph; SECRET OF DEEP HARBOR(1961), ph; YOU HAVE TO RUN FAST(1961), ph; GUN STREET(1962), ph; INCIDENT IN AN ALLEY(1962), ph; PANIC IN YEAR ZERO!(1962), ph; SAINTLY SINNERS(1962), ph; BEAUTY AND THE BEAST(1963), ph; OPERATION BIKINI(1963), ph
Silents
DAWN OF THE EAST(1921), ph; HUSH MONEY(1921), ph; ANNA ASCENDS(1922), ph; MISSING MILLIONS(1922), ph; UNDER THE RED ROBE(1923), ph; FLOWING GOLD(1924), ph; OH, DOCTOR(1924), ph; LAST EDITION, THE(1925), ph; MEDDLER, THE(1925), ph; PLASTIC AGE, THE(1925), ph; SMILIN' AT TROUBLE(1925), ph; NON-STOP FLIGHT, THE(1926), ph; TOM AND HIS PALS(1926), ph; CAT AND THE CANARY, THE(1927), ph; MAN WHO LAUGHS, THE(1927), ph; TAXI! TAXI!(1927), ph; ALIAS THE DEACON(1928), ph; JAZZ MAD(1928), ph

Lule Warrenton
Silents
SECRET LOVE(1916); BLIND HEARTS(1921); JOLT, THE(1921); SHIRLEY OF THE CIRCUS(1922)
Misc. Silents
JEWEL(1915); IT HAPPENED IN HONOLULU(1916); BIRDS' CHRISTMAS CAROL, THE(1917), d; PRINCESS VIRTUE(1917); BE A LITTLE SPORT(1919); WHEN A MAN RIDES ALONE(1919); DANGEROUS MOMENT, THE(1921); STRENGTH OF THE PINES(1922)

Lulu Warrenton
Silents
MOLLY OF THE FOLLIES(1919); SIN THAT WAS HIS, THE(1920)

Christopher Warrick
LORDS OF DISCIPLINE, THE(1983)

Robert Warrick
GOING PLACES(1939)
Silents
FRUITS OF DESIRE, THE(1916)
Misc. Silents
MAN WHO FOUND HIMSELF, THE(1915)

Ruth Warrick
CITIZEN KANE(1941); CORSICAN BROTHERS, THE(1941); OBLIGING YOUNG LADY(1941); JOURNEY INTO FEAR(1942); FOREVER AND A DAY(1943); IRON MAJOR, THE(1943); PETTICOAT LARCENY(1943); GUEST IN THE HOUSE(1944); MR. WINKLE GOES TO WAR(1944); SECRET COMMAND(1944); CHINA SKY(1945); PERILOUS HOLIDAY(1946); SONG OF THE SOUTH(1946); SWELL GUY(1946);

DAISY KENYON(1947); DRIFTWOOD(1947); ARCH OF TRIUMPH(1948); GREAT DAN PATCH, THE(1949); MAKE BELIEVE BALLROOM(1949); BEAUTY ON PARADE(1950); LET'S DANCE(1950); ONE TOO MANY(1950); THREE HUSBANDS(1950); ROOGIE'S BUMP(1954); RIDE BEYOND VENGEANCE(1966); GREAT BANK ROBBERY, THE(1969); RETURNING, THE(1983)

David Warrilow
SIMON(1980)
1984
FAR FROM POLAND(1984)

Ibbits Warriner
TOOTSIE(1982)

Warrington
GUNS OF NAVARONE, THE(1961), art d

Ann Warrington
SHE GOES TO WAR(1929)

Bill Warrington
ODD MAN OUT(1947, Brit.), spec eff; HOTEL SAHARA(1951, Brit.), spec eff; SO LONG AT THE FAIR(1951, Brit.), spec eff; SIMBA(1955, Brit.), spec eff; NIGHT AMBUSH(1958, Brit.), spec eff; PASSWORD IS COURAGE, THE(1962, Brit.), spec eff; LAFAYETTE(1963, Fr.), spec eff; LONG SHIPS, THE(1964, Brit./Yugo.), spec eff; HEROES OF TELEMARK, THE(1965, Brit.), spec eff; TWIST OF SAND, A(1968, Brit.), spec eff; DESPERADOS, THE(1969), spec eff; RUN WILD, RUN FREE(1969, Brit.), spec eff; CROMWELL(1970, Brit.), spec eff

David Warrington
GENGHIS KHAN(U.S./Brit./Ger./Yugo), spec eff

Don Warrington
RISING DAMP(1980, Brit.)
1984
BLOODBATH AT THE HOUSE OF DEATH(1984, Brit.)

George Warrington
ROAD TO GLORY, THE(1936)

Gilbert Warrington
PHANTOM BROADCAST, THE(1933), ph

Glenda Warrington
HELP!(1965, Brit.)

John Warrington
IT'S A GREAT DAY(1956, Brit.), d

Ken Warrington
APPOINTMENT WITH CRIME(1945, Brit.); ELIZABETH OF LADYMEAD(1949, Brit.)

Kenneth Warrington
GAY ADVENTURE, THE(1936, Brit.); MURDER AT THE CABARET(1936, Brit.); STRANGE CARGO(1936, Brit.); WINDBAG THE SAILOR(1937, Brit.); 13 MEN AND A GUN(1938, Brit.); IRELAND'S BORDER LINE(1939, Ireland); U-BOAT 29(1939, Brit.); OLD MOTHER RILEY AT HOME(1945, Brit.); HANGMAN WAITS, THE(1947, Brit.); SILVER DARLINGS, THE(1947, Brit.); BONNIE PRINCE CHARLIE(1948, Brit.)

Ralph Warrington
TRAIL TO VENGEANCE(1945), set d; SPIDER WOMAN STRIKES BACK, THE(1946), set d

S. J. Warrington
Silents
AMATEUR WIFE, THE(1920)

Bill Warrinton
PURPLE PLAIN, THE(1954, Brit.), spec eff

Warrior the Horse
TWO IN REVOLT(1936)

James Warrior
SWEENEY 2(1978, Brit.)

Ben Warriss
RHYTHM SERENADE(1943, Brit.); WHAT A CARRY ON!(1949, Brit.); STICK 'EM UP(1950, Brit.)

Marlene Warrlich
THREE PENNY OPERA(1963, Fr./Ger.)

Anne Waldman Warsch
EDGE, THE(1968)

Edward Warschilka
LANDLORD, THE(1970), ed; HAROLD AND MAUDE(1971), ed; CHILD'S PLAY(1972), ed; LAST OF SHEILA, THE(1973), ed; EDUCATION OF SONNY CARSON, THE(1974), ph; HEARTS OF THE WEST(1975), ed; BIG BUS, THE(1976), ed; HOUSE CALLS(1978), ed; MAIN EVENT, THE(1979), ed; CHEAPER TO KEEP HER(1980), ed; RAGGEDY MAN(1981), ed; BRAINSTORM(1983), ed
1984
SIXTEEN CANDLES(1984), ed

Curtis B. Warshawsky
CAN'T HELP SINGING(1944), w

Ruth Warshawsky
STUDENT TEACHERS, THE(1973); DEATH GAME(1977)

Samuel J. Warshawsky
23 ½ HOURS LEAVE(1937), w; CAN'T HELP SINGING(1944), w

Serge J. Warshawsky
Silents
GAMBLING IN SOULS(1919), w

William Warters
Misc. Silents
GIRL GLORY, THE(1917)

Burleigh Wartes
HURRY UP OR I'LL BE 30(1973), ph; MONEY, THE(1975), ph

Theron B. Warth
MILLIONAIRES IN PRISON(1940), ed

Theron Warth
PANAMA LADY(1939), ed; SPELLBINDER, THE(1939), ed; THREE SONS(1939), ed; TWO THOROUGHBREDS(1939), ed; I'M STILL ALIVE(1940), ed; LITTLE ORVIE(1940), ed; ONE CROWDED NIGHT(1940), ed; SAINT'S DOUBLE TROUBLE, THE(1940), ed; YOU CAN'T FOOL YOUR WIFE(1940), ed; FOOTLIGHT FEVER(1941), ed; PARACHUTE BATTALION(1941), ed; CALL OUT THE MARINES(1942), ed; MEXICAN SPITFIRE AT SEA(1942), ed; MEXICAN SPITFIRE SEES A GHOST(1942), ed; ONCE UPON A HONEYMOON(1942), ed; AROUND THE WORLD(1943), ed; FALCON AND THE CO-EDS, THE(1943), ed; LADY TAKES A CHANCE, A(1943), ed; MR. LUCKY(1943), ed; SHOW BUSINESS(1944), ed; NOTORIOUS(1946), ed; BLOOD ON THE MOON(1948), p; CAPTIVE CITY(1952), p; RETURN TO PARADISE(1953), p

Norbert Wartha
CELESTE(1982, Ger.)

Sheila Wartski
DINGAKA(1965, South Africa), ch; KIMBERLEY JIM(1965, South Africa), ch

Lizzie Warville
MOONRAKER(1979, Brit.); FOR YOUR EYES ONLY(1981)

Norman Warwick
DR. JEKYLL AND MR. HYDE(1941), ph

Allan Warwick
POSSE(1975)

Breck Warwick
SATAN'S SADISTS(1969)

Carlotta Warwick
UNKNOWN VALLEY(1933)

Dean Warwick
SPY WHO LOVED ME, THE(1977, Brit.)

Dionne Warwick
SLAVES(1969)

Edmond Warwick
STUD, THE(1979, Brit.)

Ethel Warwick
GREAT GAY ROAD, THE(1931, Brit.); KEEPERS OF YOUTH(1931, Brit.); BACHELOR'S BABY(1932, Brit.); LETTING IN THE SUNSHINE(1933, Brit.); MAN OUTSIDE, THE(1933, Brit.); STRIKE IT RICH(1933, Brit.)
Misc. Silents
BIGAMIST, THE(1916)

Gina Warwick
HORROR HOUSE(1970, Brit.)

Granville Warwick [D. W. Griffith]
Silents
LILY AND THE ROSE, THE(1915), w; INNOCENT MAGDALENE, AN(1916), w; HUN WITHIN, THE(1918), w

Henry Warwick
Silents
JUST SYLVIA(1918); MAN HUNT, THE(1918); RED HOT ROMANCE(1922)
Misc. Silents
CAILLAUX CASE, THE(1918); SEA WAIF, THE(1918); VENGEANCE(1918)

Jack [John] Warwick
FIND THE LADY(1936, Brit.)

James Warwick
LIVES OF A BENGAL LANCER(1935); BLIND ALLEY(1939), w; DARK PAST, THE(1948), w

John Warwick
IN THE WAKE OF THE BOUNTY(1933, Aus.); SILENCE OF DEAN MAITLAND, THE(1934, Aus.); CATCH AS CATCH CAN(1937, Brit.); LUCKY JADE(1937, Brit.); PASSENGER TO LONDON(1937, Brit.); RIDING HIGH(1937, Brit.); TICKET OF LEAVE MAN, THE(1937, Brit.); BAD BOY(1938, Brit.); JOHN HALIFAX–GENTLEMAN(1938, Brit.); YANK AT OXFORD, A(1938); ALL AT SEA(1939, Brit.); DEAD MEN ARE DANGEROUS(1939, Brit.); FACE AT THE WINDOW, THE(1939, Brit.); FLYING FIFTY-FIVE(1939, Brit.); ME AND MY PAL(1939, Brit.); THIS MAN IS NEWS(1939, Brit.); CASE OF THE FRIGHTENED LADY, THE(1940. Brit.); MYSTERIOUS MR. REEDER, THE(1940, Brit.); SPARE A COPPER(1940, Brit.); TWENTY-ONE DAYS TOGETHER(1940, Brit.); DANNY BOY(1941, Brit.); MY WIFE'S FAMILY(1941, Brit.); SAINT'S VACATION, THE(1941, Brit.); AVENGERS, THE(1942, Brit.); MISSING MILLION, THE(1942, Brit.); TALK ABOUT JACQUELINE(1942, Brit.); WOMAN TO WOMAN(1946, Brit.); DANCING WITH CRIME(1947, Brit.); LAVENDER HILL MOB, THE(1951, Brit.); FRANCHISE AFFAIR, THE(1952, Brit.); NEVER LOOK BACK(1952, Brit.); BOTH SIDES OF THE LAW(1953, Brit.); I'LL GET YOU(1953, Brit.); BANG! YOU'RE DEAD(1954, Brit.); CIRCUMSTANIAL EVIDENCE(1954, Brit.); RED DRESS, THE(1954, Brit.); TERROR SHIP(1954, Brit.); UP TO HIS NECK(1954, Brit.); CONTRABAND SPAIN(1955, Brit.); ONE JUST MAN(1955, Brit.); TROUBLE IN STORE(1955, Brit.); JUST MY LUCK(1957, Brit.); THIRD KEY, THE(1957, Brit.); LAW AND DISORDER(1958, Brit.); SQUARE PEG, THE(1958, Brit.); DESPERATE MAN, THE(1959, Brit.); GIDEON OF SCOTLAND YARD(1959, Brit.); HORRORS OF THE BLACK MUSEUM(1959, U.S./Brit.); MURDER AT SITE THREE(1959, Brit.); DEMONSTRATOR(1971, Aus.); ADAM'S WOMAN(1972, Austral.)
Misc. Silents
WOMAN IN 47, THE(1916)

Kathleen Warwick
Misc. Silents
HEARTS THAT ARE HUMAN(1915, Brit.)

Kenny Warwick
PIRATES OF PENZANCE, THE(1983)

Ruth Warwick
Misc. Talkies
SECOND CHANCE(1950)

Margaretta Warwick
ANNIE HALL(1977)

N. Warwick
1984(1956, Brit.), spec eff

Noel Warwick
HIGH SCHOOL GIRL(1935)

Norman Warwick
ONE NIGHT WITH YOU(1948, Brit), ph; PRIVATE ANGELO(1949, Brit.), ph; YOU CAN'T ESCAPE(1955, Brit.), ph; TONS OF TROUBLE(1956, Brit.), ph; SMALL HOTEL(1957, Brit.), ph; LADY MISLAID, A(1958, Brit.), ph; YOUNG AND THE GUILTY, THE(1958, Brit.), ph; TRUNK, THE(1961, Brit.), ph; DURING ONE NIGHT(1962, Brit.), ph; STORK TALK(1964, Brit.), ph; THEY CAME FROM BEYOND SPACE(1967, Brit.), ph; TORTURE GARDEN(1968, Brit.), ph; SPRING AND PORT WINE(1970, Brit.), ph; ABOMINABLE DR. PHIBES, THE(1971, Brit.), ph; DR. JEKYLL AND SISTER HYDE(1971, Brit.), ph; TALES FROM THE CRYPT(1972, Brit.), ph; TAKE ME HIGH(1973, Brit.), ph; TALES THAT WITNESS MADNESS(1973, Brit.), ph; CONFESSIONS OF A WINDOW CLEANER(1974, Brit.), ph; SON OF DRACULA(1974, Brit.), ph; LAST DAYS OF MAN ON EARTH, THE(1975, Brit.), ph; MR. QUILP(1975, Brit.); SUPERMAN(1978); GODSEND, THE(1980, Can.), ph

Richard Warwick
IF ...(1968, Brit.); ROMEO AND JULIET(1968, Brit./Ital.); BED SITTING ROOM, THE(1969, Brit.); FIRST LOVE(1970, Ger./Switz.); NICHOLAS AND ALEXANDRA(1971, Brit.); CONFESSIONS OF A POP PERFORMER(1975, Brit.); INTERNATIONAL VELVET(1978, Brit.)

1984
JOHNNY DANGEROUSLY(1984)
Misc. Talkies
TEMPEST, THE(1980, Brit.)
Robert Warwick
UNMASKED(1929); HOLY TERROR, A(1931); ROYAL BED, THE(1931); THREE ROGUES(1931); YOUR NUMBER'S UP(1931); AFRAID TO TALK(1932); DARK HORSE, THE(1932); DOCTOR X(1932); GIRL FROM CALGARY(1932); I AM A FUGITIVE FROM A CHAIN GANG(1932); RICH ARE ALWAYS WITH US, THE(1932); SECRETS OF WU SIN(1932); SILVER DOLLAR(1932); SO BIG(1932); UNA-SHAMED(1932); WOMAN FROM MONTE CARLO, THE(1932); CHARLIE CHAN'S GREATEST CASE(1933); FEMALE(1933); FRISCO JENNY(1933); LADIES THEY TALK ABOUT(1933); PILGRIMAGE(1933); POWER AND THE GLORY, THE(1933); CLEOPATRA(1934); DRAGON MURDER CASE, THE(1934); JIMMY THE GENT(1934); CODE OF THE MOUNTED(1935); FARMER TAKES A WIFE, THE(1935); HOPALONG CASSIDY(1935); LITTLE COLONEL, THE(1935); MURDER MAN(1935); NIGHT LIFE OF THE GODS(1935); SCHOOL FOR GIRLS(1935); SHOT IN THE DARK, A(1935); TALE OF TWO CITIES, A(1935); ADVENTURE IN MANHATTAN(1936); BARS OF HATE(1936); BOLD CABALLERO(1936); BRIDE WALKS OUT, THE(1936); BULLDOG EDITION(1936); CAN THIS BE DIXIE?(1936); CHARLIE CHAN AT THE RACE TRACK(1936); HOPALONG CASSIDY RETURNS(1936), ed; IN HIS STEPS(1936); MARY OF SCOTLAND(1936); RETURN OF JIMMY VALENTINE, THE(1936); ROMEO AND JULIET(1936); SUTTER'S GOLD(1936); TIMBER WAR(1936); TOUGH GUY(1936); TRAIL DUST(1936), ed; WHIPSAW(1936); WHITE LEGION, THE(1936); AWFUL TRUTH, THE(1937); BORDERLAND(1937), ed; CONQUEST(1937); COUNSEL FOR CRIME(1937); HIGH HAT(1937); HILLS OF OLD WYOMING(1937), ed; HOPA-LONG RIDES AGAIN(1937), ed; LET THEM LIVE(1937); LIFE OF EMILE ZOLA, THE(1937); NORTH OF THE RIO GRANDE(1937), ed; PRINCE AND THE PAUPER, THE(1937); ROAD BACK,THE(1937); RUSTLER'S VALLEY(1937), ed; TEXAS TRAIL(1937), ed; TRIGGER TRIO, THE(1937); ADVENTURES OF ROBIN HOOD, THE(1938), ed; ANNABEL TAKES A TOUR(1938); ARMY GIRL(1938); BAR 20 JUS-TICE(1938), ed; BLOCKADE(1938); COME ON, LEATHERNECKS(1938); GANG-STER'S BOY(1938); IN OLD MEXICO(1938), ed; LAW OF THE PLAINS(1938); PARTNERS OF THE PLAINS(1938), ed; PRIDE OF THE WEST(1938), ed; SPY RING, THE(1938); SQUADRON OF HONOR(1938); SUNSET TRAIL(1938), ed; ALMOST A GENTLEMAN(1939); IN OLD MONTEREY(1939); JUAREZ(1939); KONGA, THE WILD STALLION(1939); MAGNIFICENT FRAUD, THE(1939); PRIVATE LIVES OF ELIZABETH AND ESSEX, THE(1939); SILVER ON THE SAGE(1939), ed; CHRIST-MAS IN JULY(1940); DEVIL'S ISLAND(1940); DISPATCH FROM REUTERS, A(1940); EARL OF CHICAGO, THE(1940); GREAT McGINTY, THE(1940); MURDER IN THE AIR(1940); NEW MOON(1940); ON THE SPOT(1940); SEA HAWK, THE(1940); I WAS A PRISONER ON DEVIL'S ISLAND(1941); LADY EVE, THE(1941); LOUISIANA PURCHASE(1941); SULLIVAN'S TRAVELS(1941); THIS ENGLAND(1941, Brit.); WOMAN'S FACE(1941); EAGLE SQUADRON(1942); FLEET'S IN, THE(1942); I MAR-RIED A WITCH(1942); PALM BEACH STORY, THE(1942); SECRET ENEMIES(1942); TENNESSEE JOHNSON(1942); DEERSLAYER(1943); DIXIE(1943); IN OLD OK-LAHOMA(1943); TWO TICKETS TO LONDON(1943); BOWERY TO BROAD-WAY(1944); HAIL THE CONQUERING HERO(1944); KISMET(1944); MAN FROM FRISCO(1944); PRINCESS AND THE PIRATE, THE(1944); SUDAN(1945); CRIMINAL COURT(1946); FALCON'S ADVENTURE, THE(1946); GENTLEMAN'S AGREEMENT(1947); PIRATES OF MONTEREY(1947); UNCONQUERED(1947); FURY AT FURNACE CREEK(1948); GUN SMUGGLERS(1948); MILLION DOLLAR WEEK-END(1948); THREE MUSKETEERS, THE(1948); ADVENTURES OF DON JUAN(1949); FRANCIS(1949); IMPACT(1949); WOMAN'S SECRET, A(1949); IN A LONELY PLA-CE(1950); TARZAN AND THE SLAVE GIRL(1950); VENDETTA(1950); MARK OF THE RENEGADE(1951); SUGARFOOT(1951); SWORD OF MONTE CRISTO, THE(1951); AGAINST ALL FLAGS(1952); JAMAICA RUN(1953); MISSISSIPPI GAMBLER, THE(1953); SALOME(1953); PASSION(1954); SILVER LODE(1954); CHIEF CRAZY HORSE(1955); ESCAPE TO BURMA(1955); LADY GODIVA(1955); WALK THE PROUD LAND(1956); WHILE THE CITY SLEEPS(1956); SHOOT-OUT AT MEDICINE BEND(1957); BUCCANEER, THE(1958); MANHUNT IN THE JUNGLE(1958), ed; IT STARTED WITH A KISS(1959); NIGHT OF THE QUARTER MOON(1959)
Silents
DOLLAR MARK, THE(1914); SINS OF SOCIETY(1915); STOLEN VOICE(1915); ALL MAN(1916); FRIDAY THE 13TH(1916); ARGYLE CASE, THE(1917); FALSE FRIEND, THE(1917); GIRL'S FOLLY, A(1917); MAN WHO FORGOT, THE(1917); ADVENTURE IN HEARTS, AN(1919); JACK STRAW(1920); THOU ART THE MAN(1920); SPITFIRE, THE(1924)
Misc. Silents
ACROSS THE PACIFIC(1914); ALIAS JIMMY VALENTINE(1915); HEART OF A HERO, THE(1916); HUMAN DRIFTWOOD(1916); SUDDEN RICHES(1916); SUPREME SACRIFICE, THE(1916); FAMILY HONOR, THE(1917); HELL HATH NO FURY(1917); MODERN OTHELLO, A(1917); SILENT MASTER, THE(1917); ACCIDENTAL HONEY-MOON, THE(1918); IN MIZZOURA(1919); SECRET SERVICE(1919); TOLD IN THE HILLS(1919); CITY OF MASKS, THE(1920); FOURTEENTH MAN, THE(1920); TREE OF KNOWLEDGE, THE(1920); UNMASKED(1929)
Robert Warwick, Jr.
ROCKY(1948), ed
Robert B. Warwick
READY FOR THE PEOPLE(1964), ed; SERGEANT RYKER(1968), ed
Virginia Warwick
Silents
FOUR HORSEMEN OF THE APOCALYPSE, THE(1921); SPEED KING(1923)
Misc. Silents
ACE OF CACTUS RANGE(1924); RECKLESS SPEED(1924); SOUTH OF THE EQUA-TOR(1924); GENTLEMAN ROUGHNECK, A(1925); ROPED BY RADIO(1925)
Richard Warwyck
Misc. Talkies
BREAKING OF BUMBO(1972, Brit.)
John Waschak
SILENT WITNESS, THE(1962)
Hans Waschatko
MOSCOW SHANGHAI(1936, Ger.)
Ehrich Waschneck
EIGHT GIRLS IN A BOAT(1932, Ger.), d
David Wasco
1984
EL NORTE(1984), set d; NIGHT OF THE COMET(1984), set d

Pudji Waseso
YEAR OF LIVING DANGEROUSLY, THE(1982, Aus.); NATE AND HAYES(1983, U.S./New Zealand)
Ilona Wasgint
CATAMOUNT KILLING, THE(1975, Ger.), ed
Ben Washam
GAY PURR-EE(1962), anim; PHANTOM TOLLBOOTH, THE(1970), anim
Mona Washbourne
ONCE UPON A DREAM(1949, Brit.); DARK INTERVAL(1950, Brit.); WINSLOW BOY, THE(1950); GAMBLER AND THE LADY, THE(1952, Brit.); MAYTIME IN MAYFAIR(1952, Brit.); DOUBLE CONFESSION(1953, Brit.); JOHNNY ON THE RUN(1953, Brit.); ADVENTURE IN THE HOPFIELDS(1954, Brit.); CHILD'S PLAY(1954, Brit.); DOCTOR IN THE HOUSE(1954, Brit.); STAR OF MY NIGHT(1954, Brit.); YELLOW ROBE, THE(1954, Brit.); COUNT OF TWELVE(1955, Brit.); CASH ON DELIVERY(1956, Brit.); IT'S GREAT TO BE YOUNG(1956, Brit.); GOOD COMPAN-IONS, THE(1957, Brit.); JOHN AND JULIE(1957, Brit.); SON OF A STRANGER(1957, Brit.); STRANGER IN TOWN(1957, Brit.); TEARS FOR SIMON(1957, Brit.); THREE SUNDAYS TO LIVE(1957, Brit.); CAST A DARK SHADOW(1958, Brit.); COUNT YOUR BLESSINGS(1959); CRY FROM THE STREET, A(1959, Brit.); BRIDES OF DRACULA, THE(1960, Brit.); BILLY LIAR(1963, Brit.); FERRY ACROSS THE MERSEY(1964, Brit.); MY FAIR LADY(1964); NIGHT MUST FALL(1964, Brit.); COLLECTOR, THE(1965); ONE WAY PENDULUM(1965, Brit.); THIRD DAY, THE(1965); IF ...(1968, Brit.); MRS. BROWN, YOU'VE GOT A LOVELY DAUGHTER(1968, Brit.); TWO A PENNY(1968, Brit.); BED SITTING ROOM, THE(1969, Brit.); GAMES(1970); FRAGMENT OF FEAR(1971, Brit.); WHAT BECAME OF JACK AND JILL?(1972, Brit.); O LUCKY MAN!(1973, Brit.); DRIVER'S SEAT, THE(1975, Ital.); MR. QUILP(1975, Brit.); BLUE BIRD, THE(1976); STEVIE(1978, Brit.)
Cyril Washbrook
FINAL TEST, THE(1953, Brit.)
Don Washbrook
LONELYHEARTS(1958)
John Washbrook
LONELYHEARTS(1958); SPACE CHILDREN, THE(1958)
Beverly Washburn
KILLER THAT STALKED NEW YORK, THE(1950); HERE COMES THE GROOM(1951); SUPERMAN AND THE MOLE MEN(1951); GREATEST SHOW ON EARTH, THE(1952); JUGGLER, THE(1953); SHANE(1953); LONE RANGER, THE(1955); OLD YELLER(1957); SUMMER LOVE(1958); SPIDER BABY(1968); PIT STOP(1969)
Bryant Washburn
SWING HIGH(1930); KEPT HUSBANDS(1931); MYSTERY TRAIN(1931); ARM OF THE LAW(1932); FORBIDDEN COMPANY(1932); PARISIAN ROMANCE, A(1932); RECKONING, THE(1932); THRILL OF YOUTH(1932); WHAT PRICE HOL-LYWOOD?(1932); DEVIL'S MATE(1933); NIGHT OF TERROR(1933); WHAT PRICE INNOCENCE?(1933); WHEN STRANGERS MEET(1934); DANGER AHEAD(1935); PUBLIC STENOGRAPHER(1935); THROWBACK, THE(1935); WORLD ACCUSES, THE(1935); HOLLYWOOD BOULEVARD(1936); IT COULDN'T HAVE HAPPENED-BUT IT DID(1936); MILLIONAIRE KID(1936); PREVIEW MURDER MYSTERY(1936); SUTTER'S GOLD(1936); THREE OF A KIND(1936); CONFLICT(1937); SEA RACK-ETEERS(1937); TAMING THE WILD(1937); VICE RACKET(1937); WESTLAND CASE, THE(1937); $1,000,000 RACKET(1937); CAFE SOCIETY(1939); MIDNIGHT(1939); SKY PATROL(1939); STAGECOACH(1939); PAPER BULLETS(1941); PRIDE OF THE ARMY(1942); SHADOWS ON THE SAGE(1942); SIN TOWN(1942); CARSON CITY CYCLONE(1943); GIRL FROM MONTEREY, THE(1943); LAW RIDES AGAIN, THE(1943); FALCON IN HOLLYWOOD, THE(1944); FALCON IN MEXICO, THE(1944); FOLLOW THE LEADER(1944); HEAVENLY DAYS(1944); MY PAL, WOLF(1944); NABONGA(1944); NEVADA(1944); JOHNNY ANGEL(1945); TWO O'CLOCK COUR-AGE(1945); WEST OF THE PECOS(1945)
Misc. Talkies
EXPOSURE(1932); IRISH GRINGO, THE(1935); GAMBLING WITH SOULS(1936)
Silents
ALSTER CASE, THE(1915); SLIM PRINCESS, THE(1915); BREAKER, THE(1916); SKINNER'S DRESS SUIT(1917); ALL WRONG(1919); PUTTING IT OVER(1919); AMATEUR DEVIL, AN(1921); ROAD TO LONDON, THE(1921, Brit.); HUNGRY HEARTS(1922); JUNE MADNESS(1922); COMMON LAW, THE(1923); RUPERT OF HENTZAU(1923); TEMPTATION(1923); MY HUSBAND'S WIVES(1924); PASSION-ATE YOUTH(1925); WIZARD OF OZ, THE(1925); WET PAINT(1926); KING OF KINGS, THE(1927); HONEYMOON FLATS(1928); JAZZLAND(1928); NOTHING TO WEAR(1928); SKINNER'S BIG IDEA(1928)
Misc. Silents
BLINDNESS OF VIRTUE, THE(1915); CRIMSON WING, THE(1915); HAVOC, THE(1916); PRINCE OF GRAUSTARK, THE(1916); FIBBERS, THE(1917); FILLING HIS OWN SHOES(1917); GOLDEN IDIOT, THE(1917); MAN WHO WAS AFRAID, THE(1917); SKINNER'S BABY(1917); SKINNER'S BUBBLE(1917); GHOST OF THE RANCHO, THE(1918); GYPSY TRAIL, THE(1918); KIDDER & KO.(1918); TILL I COME BACK TO YOU(1918); TWENTY-ONE(1918); WAY OF A MAN WITH A MAID, THE(1918); IT PAYS TO ADVERTISE(1919); POOR BOOB(1919); SOMETHING TO DO(1919); VENUS IN THE EAST(1919); VERY GOOD YOUNG MAN, A(1919); WHY SMITH LEFT HOME(1919); BURGLAR-PROOF(1920); FULL HOUSE, A(1920); LOVE INSURANCE(1920); MRS. TEMPLE'S TELEGRAM(1920); SINS OF ST. ANTHONY, THE(1920); SIX BEST CELLARS, THE(1920); TOO MUCH JOHNSON(1920); WHAT HAPPENED TO JONES(1920); WHITE SHOULDERS(1922); WOMAN CONQUERS, THE(1922); LOVE TRAP, THE(1923); MEANEST MAN IN THE WORLD, THE(1923); MINE TO KEEP(1923); OTHER MEN'S DAUGHTERS(1923); STAR DUST TRAIL, THE(1924); TRY AND GET IT(1924); PARASITE, THE(1925); WANDERING FOOT-STEPS(1925); FLAMES(1926); HER SACRIFICE(1926); SKY PIRATE, THE(1926); THAT GIRL OKLAHOMA(1926); YOUNG APRIL(1926); BEWARE OF WIN-DOWS(1927); BLACK TEARS(1927); BREAKFAST AT SUNRISE(1927); IN THE FIRST DEGREE(1927); LOVE THRILL, THE(1927); MODERN DAUGHTERS(1927); SITTING BULL AT THE "SPIRIT LAKE MASSACRE"(1927); BIT OF HEAVEN, A(1928); CHORUS KID, THE(1928)
Bryant Washburn, Jr.
DARING DAUGHTERS(1933); STUDENT TOUR(1934); OLD MAN RHYTHM(1935); THEY SHALL HAVE MUSIC(1939); THOUSANDS CHEER(1943)
Bryant Washburn, Sr.
MAN WHO RECLAIMED HIS HEAD, THE(1935); I DEMAND PAYMENT(1938); WE WERE DANCING(1942)

Charles C. Washburn
DIRTY HARRY(1971)
Charles Washburn
SKULLDUGGERY(1970)
Conroy Washburn
COUNSELLOR-AT-LAW(1933)
Deric Washburn
SILENT RUNNING(1972), w; DEER HUNTER, THE(1978), w; BORDER, THE(1982), w
Don Washburn
SPACE RAIDERS(1983)
George Washburn
PIT STOP(1969)
Grace Washburn
Misc. Silents
WHEN IT STRIKES HOME(1915)
Hazel Washburn
Misc. Silents
MOHICAN'S DAUGHTER, THE(1922)
Mabel Washburn
Silents
ROAD TO LONDON, THE(1921, Brit.)
Mona Washburn
LOSER TAKES ALL(1956, Brit.)
Conway Washburne
STREET SCENE(1931)
Ada Washington
LAST HOUSE ON THE LEFT(1972)
Ann Washington
YOUNG DOCTORS IN LOVE(1982)
Babette Washington
PROUD VALLEY, THE(1941, Brit.)
Blue Washington
MOUNTAIN JUSTICE(1930); PARADE OF THE WEST(1930); KING OF THE ARENA(1933); SMOKING GUNS(1934); GONE WITH THE WIND(1939); SUN-DOWN(1941); ROAD TO MOROCCO(1942); TALES OF MANHATTAN(1942)
Silents
DO YOUR DUTY(1928); RANSOM(1928)
Booker T. Washington III
GEORGE WASHINGTON CARVER(1940)
Chet Washington
PRECIOUS JEWELS(1969)
1984
MUPPETS TAKE MANHATTAN, THE(1984)
Debbie Washington
Misc. Talkies
POLK COUNTY POT PLANE(1977); HOT PURSUIT(1981)
Denzel Washington
CARBON COPY(1981)
1984
SOLDIER'S STORY, A(1984)
Dino Washington
...TICK...TICK...TICK...(1970); LONGEST YARD, THE(1974); FAREWELL, MY LOVE-LY(1975); HUSTLE(1975)
Edgar Blue Washington
BEGGARS OF LIFE(1928)
Edgar "Blue" Washington
HAUNTED GOLD(1932); LONG VOYAGE HOME, THE(1940)
Eleanor Washington
Silents
JACK AND THE BEANSTALK(1917)
Fannie Washington
TOY WIFE, THE(1938)
Flora Washington
Misc. Silents
TENDERFEET(1928)
Ford L. "Buck" Washington
CABIN IN THE SKY(1943)
Frank Washington
HARLEM GLOBETROTTERS, THE(1951)
Fredi Washington
EMPEROR JONES, THE(1933); IMITATION OF LIFE(1934); OUANGA(1936, Brit.); ONE MILE FROM HEAVEN(1937)
Gene Washington
BLACK GUNN(1972); BLACK SIX, THE(1974)
Misc. Talkies
LADY COCOA(1975)
George Washington
ST. LOUIS BLUES(1958)
Grover Washington, Jr.
SGT. PEPPER'S LONELY HEARTS CLUB BAND(1978)
Hannah Washington
LITTLEST REBEL, THE(1935)
Hazel Washington
IMITATION OF LIFE(1934)
Howard Washington
STRANGERS ON A TRAIN(1951)
J. Dennis Washington
CONVOY(1978), art d; ELECTRIC HORSEMAN, THE(1979), art d; NINTH CON-FIGURATION, THE(1980), prod d; VICTORY(1981), prod d; HYSTERICAL(1983), prod d; TO BE OR NOT TO BE(1983), art d
1984
FINDERS KEEPERS(1984), art d
Jackie Washington
HANK WILLIAMS: THE SHOW HE NEVER GAVE(1982, Can.)
John B. Washington
SAFARI(1940)

John Washington
SWEET JESUS, PREACHER MAN(1973)
Judy Washington
PHANTOM OF THE PARADISE(1974)
Misc. Talkies
KILL, THE(1973)
Ken Washington
Misc. Talkies
EBONY, IVORY AND JADE(1977)
Kenneth Washington
FOXES OF HARROW, THE(1947); CHANGES(1969); WESTWORLD(1973)
Kenneth William Washington
TARZAN'S DEADLY SILENCE(1970)
Kenny Washington
LITTLE FOXES, THE(1941); SUNDOWN(1941); ROGUES' REGIMENT(1948); EASY LIVING(1949); PINKY(1949); ROPE OF SAND(1949); JACKIE ROBINSON STORY, THE(1950)
Misc. Talkies
WHILE THOUSANDS CHEER(1940)
Mavis Washington
FAST BREAK(1979)
Mildred Washington
SHOPWORN ANGEL, THE(1928); HEARTS IN DIXIE(1929); THOROUGHBRED, THE(1930); BLONDE VENUS(1932); TORCH SINGER(1933)
Misc. Silents
TENDERFEET(1928)
Richard Washington
SCREAM BLACULA SCREAM(1973); DEEP, THE(1977), stunts
Richard A. Washington
DIRTY HARRY(1971); WHAT'S UP, DOC?(1972)
Shelley Washington
HAIR(1979)
Shirley Washington
WONDER WOMEN(1973, Phil.); DARKTOWN STRUTTERS(1975); MELVIN AND HOWARD(1980)
Misc. Talkies
BAMBOO GODS AND IRON MEN(1974); GET DOWN AND BOOGIE(1977)
Theo Washington
JANIE GETS MARRIED(1946)
Thomas Washington
Misc. Silents
MOUNTAIN DEW(1917)
Vernon Washington
DARK, THE(1979)
1984
LAST STARFIGHTER, THE(1984)
William Washington
WATCH ON THE RHINE(1943); LYDIA BAILEY(1952)
Willie Washington, Jr.
BOOK OF NUMBERS(1973)
Nidemaru Washio
HENTAI(1966, Jap.), p
Mike Washlake
RAGGEDY MAN(1981)
Kenneth Washman
WEEKEND OF FEAR(1966)
Eric Washneck
Misc. Silents
SAJENKO THE SOVIET(1929, Ger.), d
Hannah Washonig
FINAL TERROR, THE(1983), ed
Walter Wasik
PROUD RIDER, THE(1971, Can.), ph
Wanda Wasilewska
RAINBOW, THE(1944, USSR), w
Francesca Waskowitz
THIS LOVE OF OURS(1945)
M. Waskowski
WALKOVER(1969, Pol.)
Andre Wasley
DEVIL'S DAUGHTER(1949, Fr.); FORBIDDEN GAMES(1953, Fr.); GERVAISE(1956, Fr.)
Janet Wass
Misc. Talkies
DOUBLE INITIATION(1970)
Ted Wass
CURSE OF THE PINK PANTHER(1983)
1984
OH GOD! YOU DEVIL(1984); SHEENA(1984)
Rebecca Wassam
ONCE TO EVERY WOMAN(1934)
Dr. Corydon M. Wassell
STORY OF DR. WASSELL, THE(1944), w
Rebecca Wassem
GILDED LILY, THE(1935); EVER SINCE EVE(1937); GIRL WITH IDEAS, A(1937)
Walter Wassemann
INHERITANCE IN PRETORIA(1936, Ger.), w
Carl Wasserman
RABID(1976, Can.)
Dale Wasserman
VIKINGS, THE(1958), w; QUICK, BEFORE IT MELTS(1964), w; MISTER BUDDW-ING(1966), p, w; WALK WITH LOVE AND DEATH, A(1969), w; MAN OF LA MANCHA(1972), w; ONE FLEW OVER THE CUCKOO'S NEST(1975), w
Jack Wasserman
ON THE RIGHT TRACK(1981)
Walter Wasserman
BLONDE NIGHTINGALE(1931, Ger.), w; STORM IN A WATER GLASS(1931, Aust.), w; DREAM OF SCHONBRUNN(1933, Aus.), w; SERGEANT BERRY(1938, Ger.), w

Aly Wassil
KING OF THE KHYBER RIFLES(1953); RAINS OF RANCHIPUR, THE(1955); MOVE(1970); AUDREY ROSE(1977)
Chuck Wassil
I MARRIED A MONSTER FROM OUTER SPACE(1958); CAREER(1959); DON'T GIVE UP THE SHIP(1959); TRAP, THE(1959)
Irina Wassilchikoff
ASH WEDNESDAY(1973)
Juri Wassiliev
MOSCOW DOES NOT BELIEVE IN TEARS(1980, USSR)
N. Wassiljeff
ARIANE(1931, Ger.)
Marco Wassilli
HERCULES, SAMSON & ULYSSES(1964, Ital.)
Craig Wasson
ROLLERCOASTER(1977); BOYS IN COMPANY C, THE(1978, U.S./Hong Kong); GO TELL THE SPARTANS(1978); CARNY(1980); OUTSIDER, THE(1980); SCHIZOID(1980); FOUR FRIENDS(1981); GHOST STORY(1981); SECOND THOUGHTS(1983)
1984
BODY DOUBLE(1984)
Greear Wasson
MAGIC FOUNTAIN, THE(1961)
Jim Wasson
Misc. Talkies
NIGHT OF THE DEMON(1980), d
M. Lou Wastal
NAVY BORN(1936)
Barbo Wastenson
DEVIL, THE(1963)
Michael Waszynoki
DYBBUK THE(1938, Pol.), d
Takashi Watabe
1984
WARRIORS OF THE WIND(1984, Jap.), anim
Fumio Watanaba
NAKED YOUTH(1961, Jap.)
Akio Watanabe
KARATE, THE HAND OF DEATH(1961)
Akira Watanabe
GODZILLA, RING OF THE MONSTERS(1956, Jap.), spec eff; GIGANTIS(1959, Jap./U.S.), spec eff; GODZILLA VS. THE THING(1964, Jap.), spec eff; GAPPA THE TRIFIBIAN MONSTER(1967, Jap.), spec eff; GREEN SLIME, THE(1969), spec eff
Atsushi Watanabe
SEVEN SAMURAI, THE(1956, Jap.); IKIRU(1960, Jap.); YOJIMBO(1961, Jap.)
Chemei Watanabe
NIGHT OF THE SEAGULL, THE(1970, Jap.), m
Fumio Watanabe
PLEASURES OF THE FLESH, THE(1965); SCANDALOUS ADVENTURES OF BURAIKAN, THE(1970, Jap.); SILENCE HAS NO WINGS(1971, Jap.)
Gedde Watanabe
1984
SIXTEEN CANDLES(1984)
Hiroko Watanabe
ANGEL, ANGEL, DOWN WE GO(1969); M(1970)
Hiroyuki Watanabe
ALL RIGHT, MY FRIEND(1983, Japan)
Kimio Watanabe
MYSTERIOUS SATELLITE, THE(1956, Jap.), ph; FALCON FIGHTERS, THE(1970, Jap.), ph
Misako Watanabe
INHERITANCE, THE(1964, Jap.); KWAIDAN(1965, Jap.)
Noriyuki Watanabe
SONG FROM MY HEART, THE(1970, Jap.)
Takeo Watanabe
HIKEN YABURI(1969, Jap.), m
Takesaburo Watanabe
PLAY IT COOL(1970, Jap.), art d; VIXEN(1970, Jap.), art d
Toru Watanabe
GODZILLA VERSUS THE SEA MONSTER(1966, Jap.)
Urato Watanabe
MAN IN THE STORM, THE(1969, Jap.), m
Yoshinori Watanabe
MESSAGE FROM SPACE(1978, Jap.), p
Tetsuya Watari
GANGSTER VIP, THE(1968, Jap.); EAST CHINA SEA(1969, Jap.)
Tsunehiko Watase
1984
ANTARCTICA(1984, Jap.)
Neville Watchurst
PRIVILEGED(1982, Brit.)
Fern Water
UP THE MACGREGORS(1967, Ital./Span.)
Lila Water
PAPER MOON(1973)
Bob Waterfield
TRIPLE THREAT(1948); JUNGLE MANHUNT(1951); CRAZYLEGS, ALL AMERICAN(1953)
Robert Waterfield
GENTLEMEN MARRY BRUNETTES(1955), p; FUZZY PINK NIGHTGOWN, THE(1957), p
John Waterhouse
MAID FOR MURDER(1963, Brit.), w
Keith Waterhouse
WHISTLE DOWN THE WIND(1961, Brit.), w; KIND OF LOVING, A(1962, Brit.), w; VALIANT, THE(1962, Brit./Ital.), w; BILLY LIAR(1963, Brit.), w; WEST 11(1963, Brit.), w; MAN IN THE MIDDLE(1964, U.S./Brit.), w; MATTER OF INNOCENCE, A(1968, Brit.), w; LOCK UP YOUR DAUGHTERS(1969, Brit.), w

Mary Waterhouse
PROSTITUTE(1980, Brit.)
Robert Waterhouse
CONFESSOR(1973)
Terry Waterhouse
BEAR ISLAND(1980, Brit.-Can.)
Wayne Eagle Waterhouse
CATCH MY SOUL(1974)
Terry Waterland
MY BLOODY VALENTINE(1981, Can.)
Albert Waterman [Alberto Dell'Acqua]
SEVEN GUNS FOR THE MACGREGORS(1968, Ital./Span.)
Ann Waterman
1984
WOMAN IN RED, THE(1984)
Arnold C. Waterman
DEATH VALLEY(1982)
Dennis Waterman
NIGHT TRAIN FOR INVERNESS(1960, Brit.); SNOWBALL(1960, Brit.); PIRATES OF BLOOD RIVER, THE(1962, Brit.); GO KART GO(1964, Brit.); UP THE JUNCTION(1968, Brit.); MY LOVER, MY SON(1970, Brit.); SCARS OF DRACULA, THE(1970, Brit.); THIS, THAT AND THE OTHER(1970, Brit.); WEDDING NIGHT(1970, Ireland); FRIGHT(1971, Brit.); MAN IN THE WILDERNESS(1971, U.S./Span.); SCHOOL FOR UNCLAIMED GIRLS(1973, Brit.); BELSTONE FOX, THE(1976, 1976); SWEENEY(1977, Brit.); SWEENEY 2(1978, Brit.)
Misc. Talkies
HELL HOUSE GIRLS(1975, Brit.)
Derek Waterman
MINI-AFFAIR, THE(1968, Brit.), ph
Ida Waterman
Silents
EAGLE'S MATE, THE(1914); ARE YOU A MASON?(1915); ESMERALDA(1915); JOHN GLAYDE'S HONOR(1915); AMARILLY OF CLOTHESLINE ALLEY(1918); MR. FIX-IT(1918); STELLA MARIS(1918); COUNTERFEIT(1919); ON WITH THE DANCE(1920); INNER CHAMBER, THE(1921); LOVE'S REDEMPTION(1921); ENCHANTED COTTAGE, THE(1924); SOCIETY SCANDAL, A(1924); "THAT ROYLE GIRL"(1925); SOCIAL CELEBRITY, A(1926)
Misc. Silents
SADIE LOVE(1920); LOTUS EATER, THE(1921); SWAN, THE(1925)
Stan Waterman
DEEP, THE(1977), ph
Willard Waterman
FLAME OF YOUTH(1949); FREE FOR ALL(1949); FATHER OF THE BRIDE(1950); LOUISA(1950); MRS. O'MALLEY AND MR. MALONE(1950); MYSTERY STREET(1950); NO MAN OF HER OWN(1950); RIDING HIGH(1950); DARLING, HOW COULD YOU!(1951); FOURTEEN HOURS(1951); RHUBARB(1951); SUNNY SIDE OF THE STREET(1951); HAS ANYBODY SEEN MY GAL?(1952); HALF A HERO(1953); IT HAPPENS EVERY THURSDAY(1953); THREE COINS IN THE FOUNTAIN(1954); HOW TO BE VERY, VERY, POPULAR(1955); THREE FOR THE SHOW(1955); HOLLYWOOD OR BUST(1956); AUNTIE MAME(1958); APARTMENT, THE(1960); WALK ON THE WILD SIDE(1962); GET YOURSELF A COLLEGE GIRL(1964); HAIL(1973)
Bill Waters
HEAD ON(1971), ed
Bunny Waters
BROADWAY RHYTHM(1944); LADY IN THE DARK(1944); MAISIE GOES TO RENO(1944); HARVEY GIRLS, THE(1946); UP IN CENTRAL PARK(1948); DUCHESS OF IDAHO, THE(1950); LIFE OF HER OWN, A(1950); SUMMER STOCK(1950); DANGEROUS WHEN WET(1953); PEPE(1960)
Cecil Waters
SHADOW OF FEAR(1963, Brit.)
Charles Waters
BOYS IN COMPANY C, THE(1978, U.S./Hong Kong)
Cheryl Waters
MACON COUNTY LINE(1974)
Misc. Talkies
IMAGE OF DEATH(1977, Brit.); DIDN'T YOU HEAR(1983)
Chuck Waters
HIGH PLAINS DRIFTER(1973); PARALLAX VIEW, THE(1974); I WANNA HOLD YOUR HAND(1978); BRONCO BILLY(1980); RAIDERS OF THE LOST ARK(1981)
1984
BODY DOUBLE(1984); CITY HEAT(1984); MRS. SOFFEL(1984)
Dennis Waters
SUNSET PASS(1946)
Doris Waters
GERT AND DAISY'S WEEKEND(1941, Brit.); GERT AND DAISY CLEAN UP(1942, Brit.); IT'S IN THE BAG(1943, Brit.)
Ed Waters
SORORITY GIRL(1957), w; MAN-TRAP(1961), w; CAPER OF THE GOLDEN BULLS, THE(1967), w; DARKER THAN AMBER(1970), w
Elsie Waters
GERT AND DAISY'S WEEKEND(1941, Brit.); GERT AND DAISY CLEAN UP(1942, Brit.); IT'S IN THE BAG(1943, Brit.)
Ethel Waters
ON WITH THE SHOW(1929); GIFT OF GAB(1934); CAIRO(1942); TALES OF MANHATTAN(1942); CABIN IN THE SKY(1943); STAGE DOOR CANTEEN(1943); PINKY(1949); MEMBER OF THE WEDDING, THE(1952); SOUND AND THE FURY, THE(1959)
Misc. Talkies
CARIB GOLD(1955)
Frank Waters
RIVER LADY(1948), w
George Waters
SPEED CRAZY(1959), w
George W. Waters
TANK BATTALION(1958), w; WHY MUST I DIE?(1960), w
Hal Waters
CAN YOU HEAR ME MOTHER?(1935, Brit.)

Misc. Silents
DANGER ZONE, THE(1925)
Heil F. Waters
AND NOW MIGUEL(1966)
Helen Waters
MURDER, INC.(1960)
Irene Waters
1984
ALLEY CAT(1984)
J. B. Waters
SURVIVORS, THE(1983)
Jack Waters
LIFE BEGINS AT 40(1935)
James Waters
WHEN WILLIE COMES MARCHING HOME(1950); LAST HURRAH, THE(1958); ANATOMY OF A MURDER(1959); OCEAN'S ELEVEN(1960); SERGEANTS 3(1962); NIGHTMARE IN THE SUN(1964); MAN CALLED ADAM, A(1966), p
Jan Waters
TOUCH OF DEATH(1962, Brit.); CORRUPTION(1968, Brit.)
Jim Waters
PEPE(1960)
John Waters
MIGHTY MCGURK, THE(1946), d
John Waters
END PLAY(1975, Aus.); FEMALE TROUBLE(1975), p,d,w&ph; ELIZA FRASER(1976, Aus.); GETTING OF WISDOM, THE(1977, Aus.); WEEKEND OF SHADOWS(1978, Aus.); BREAKER MORANT(1980, Aus.)
John Waters
Silents
ARIZONA BOUND(1927), d; NEVADA(1927), d; TWO FLAMING YOUTHS(1927), d; BEAU SABREUR(1928), d; OVERLAND TELEGRAPH, THE(1929), d; SIOUX BLOOD(1929), d
Misc. Silents
BORN TO THE WEST(1926), d; FORLORN RIVER(1926), d; MAN OF THE FOREST(1926), d; DRUMS OF THE DESERT(1927), d; MYSTERIOUS RIDER, THE(1927), d; VANISHING PIONEER, THE(1928), d
John Waters
NONPO TRASHO(1970), p, d, w, ph&ed; FEMALE TROUBLE(1975), p, d, w&ph; POLYESTER(1981), p, d&w
John Waters
Misc. Talkies
CASS(1977); DEMOLITION(1977); SCALP MERCHANT, THE(1977)
Keane Waters
Silents
JANICE MEREDITH(1924)
Lila Waters
MAN, WOMAN AND CHILD(1983)
Luther Waters
JAZZ SINGER, THE(1980)
Mel Waters
PROPHECY(1979)
Mira Waters
LEARNING TREE, THE(1969); GREATEST, THE(1977, U.S./Brit.)
Monty Waters
CITY NEWS(1983), m
Mrs. Waters
Silents
FLYING PAT(1920)
Naomi Waters
PERFECT FLAW, THE(1934, Brit.)
Oren Waters
JAZZ SINGER, THE(1980)
Ozie Waters
COWBOY FROM LONESOME RIVER(1944); MYSTERY MAN(1944); OUTCAST OF BLACK MESA(1950)
Misc. Talkies
SAGEBRUSH HEROES(1945)
Raymond Waters
MISS PILGRIM'S PROGRESS(1950, Brit.)
Reba Waters
ESCORT WEST(1959)
Robert E. Waters
VAMPIRE HOOKERS, THE(1979, Phil.), p
1984
ALLEY CAT(1984), p, w
Roger Waters
PINK FLOYD–THE WALL(1982, Brit.), w
Ronald Waters
IT'S YOU I WANT(1936, Brit.)
Russell Waters
YESTERDAY'S ENEMY(1959, Brit.); DULCIMER STREET(1948, Brit.); BLUE LAGOON, THE(1949, Brit.); DEAR MR. PROHACK(1949, Brit.); DON'T EVER LEAVE ME(1949, Brit.); HIDDEN ROOM, THE(1949, Brit.); WOMAN IN THE HALL, THE(1949, Brit.); CHANCE OF A LIFETIME(1950, Brit.); HAPPIEST DAYS OF YOUR LIFE(1950, Brit.); MAGNET, THE(1950, Brit.); SEVEN DAYS TO NOON(1950, Brit.); GREAT MANHUNT, THE(1951, Brit.); GREEN GROW THE RUSHES(1951, Brit.); MANIACS ON WHEELS(1951, Brit.); WOODEN HORSE, THE(1951); CASTLE IN THE AIR(1952, Brit.); DEATH OF AN ANGEL(1952, Brit.); ISLAND OF DESIRE(1952, Brit.); MAN IN THE WHITE SUIT, THE(1952); MISS ROBIN HOOD(1952, Brit.); YOU'RE ONLY YOUNG TWICE(1952, Brit.); CRUEL SEA, THE(1953); ISN'T LIFE WONDERFUL(1953, Brit.); LONG MEMORY, THE(1953, Brit.); MR. DENNING DRIVES NORTH(1953, Brit.); SWORD AND THE ROSE, THE(1953); ADVENTURE IN THE HOPFIELDS(1954, Brit.); HIGH AND DRY(1954, Brit.); LEASE OF LIFE(1954, Brit.); PASSING STRANGER, THE(1954, Brit.); ROB ROY, THE HIGHLAND ROGUE(1954, Brit.); SLEEPING TIGER, THE(1954, Brit.); TURN THE KEY SOFTLY(1954, Brit.); DEADLY GAME, THE(1955, Brit.); LADY GODIVA RIDES AGAIN(1955, Brit.); LOVE MATCH, THE(1955, Brit.); WICKED WIFE(1955, Brit.); IT'S GREAT TO BE YOUNG(1956, Brit.); DECISION AGAINST TIME(1957, Brit.); LET'S BE HAPPY(1957, Brit.); PICKUP ALLEY(1957, Brit.); KEY, THE(1958, Brit.); LEFT, RIGHT AND CENTRE(1959, Brit.); DANGER TOMORROW(1960, Brit.); NEXT TO NO TIME(1960, Brit.);

BOMB IN THE HIGH STREET(1961, Brit.); MAN IN THE MOON(1961, Brit.); FLOOD, THE(1963, Brit.); I COULD GO ON SINGING(1963); PUNCH AND JUDY MAN, THE(1963, Brit.); REACH FOR GLORY(1963, Brit.); CROOKS IN CLOISTERS(1964, Brit.); HEROES OF TELEMARK, THE(1965, Brit.); DEVIL'S BRIDE, THE(1968, Brit.); TRYGON FACTOR, THE(1969, Brit.); TWISTED NERVE(1969, Brit.); MARRIAGE OF CONVENIENCE(1970, Brit.); KIDNAPPED(1971, Brit.); WICKER MAN, THE(1974, Brit.); BLACK JACK(1979, Brit.)
Sneezy Waters
HANK WILLIAMS: THE SHOW HE NEVER GAVE(1982, Can.)
Ted Waters
HAPPY DAYS(1930)
Tom Waters
APPLE DUMPLING GANG, THE(1975); PONY EXPRESS RIDER(1976); GRAND THEFT AUTO(1977); DEADHEAD MILES(1982)
William J. Waters
GOD TOLD ME TO(1976), ed
Chic Waterson
TRAIN OF EVENTS(1952, Brit.), ph
Chick Waterson
TIGHT LITTLE ISLAND(1949, Brit.), ph
Monica Waterson
DEVIL, THE(1963)
Sam Waterson
SWEET WILLIAM(1980, Brit.)
Sam Waterston
FITZWILLY(1967); GENERATION(1969); THREE(1969, Brit.); COVER ME BABE(1970); WHO KILLED MARY WHAT'SER NAME?(1971); SAVAGES(1972); GREAT GATSBY, THE(1974); RANCHO DELUXE(1975); DANDY, THE ALL AMERICAN GIRL(1976); JOURNEY INTO FEAR(1976, Can); CAPRICORN ONE(1978); INTERIORS(1978); EAGLE'S WING(1979, Brit.); HEAVEN'S GATE(1980); HOPSCOTCH(1980)
1984
KILLING FIELDS, THE(1984, Brit.)
Samuel Waterston
PLASTIC DOME OF NORMA JEAN, THE(1966)
Gwen Watford
NEVER TAKE CANDY FROM A STRANGER(1961, Brit.); CLEOPATRA(1963); VERY EDGE, THE(1963, Brit.); TASTE THE BLOOD OF DRACULA(1970, Brit.); GHOUL, THE(1975, Brit.)
Misc. Talkies
DO YOU KNOW THIS VOICE?(1964)
Gwendoline Watford
FALL OF THE HOUSE OF USHER, THE(1952, Brit.)
Herve Watine
MY BABY IS BLACK!(1965, Fr.)
David Watkin
HELP!(1965, Brit.), ph; MADEMOISELLE(1966, Fr./Brit.), ph; HOW I WON THE WAR(1967, Brit.), ph; PERSECUTION AND ASSASSINATION OF JEAN-PAUL MARAT AS PERFORMED BY THE INMATES OF THE ASYLUM OF CHARENTON UNDER THE DIRECTION OF THE MARQUIS DE SADE, THE(1967, Brit.), ph; CHARGE OF THE LIGHT BRIGADE, THE(1968, Brit.), ph; BED SITTING ROOM, THE(1969, Brit.), ph; CATCH-22(1970), ph; BOY FRIEND, THE(1971, Brit.), ph; DELICATE BALANCE, A(1973), ph; HOMECOMING, THE(1973), ph; YELLOW DOG(1973, Brit.), ph; MAHOGANY(1975), ph; ROBIN AND MARIAN(1976, Brit.), ph; TO THE DEVIL A DAUGHTER(1976, Brit./Ger.), ph; JOSEPH ANDREWS(1977, Brit.), ph; CUBA(1979), ph; HANOVER STREET(1979, Brit.), ph; THAT SUMMER(1979, Brit.), ph; CHARRIOTS OF FIRE(1981, Brit.), ph; ENDLESS LOVE(1981), ph; YENTL(1983), ph
1984
HOTEL NEW HAMPSHIRE, THE(1984), ph
Ian Watkin
SLEEPING DOGS(1977, New Zealand); BEYOND REASONABLE DOUBT(1980, New Zeal.); GOODBYE PORK PIE(1981, New Zealand)
1984
UTU(1984, New Zealand)
Lawrence E. Watkin
KEEPER OF THE BEES(1947), w; TREASURE ISLAND(1950, Brit.), w; STORY OF ROBIN HOOD, THE(1952, Brit.), w; SWORD AND THE ROSE, THE(1953), w; ROB ROY, THE HIGHLAND ROGUE(1954, Brit.), w; DARBY O'GILL AND THE LITTLE PEOPLE(1959), w
Lawrence Edward Watkin
ON BORROWED TIME(1939), w; GREAT LOCOMOTIVE CHASE, THE(1956), p&w; LIGHT IN THE FOREST, THE(1958), w; TEN WHO DARED(1960), w; BISCUIT EATER, THE(1972), w
Pierre Watkin
BUNKER BEAN(1936); CHINA CLIPPER(1936); COUNTERFEIT(1936); DANGEROUS(1936); FORGOTTEN FACES(1936); GENTLEMAN FROM LOUISIANA(1936); IT HAD TO HAPPEN(1936); LOVE LETTERS OF A STAR(1936); MR. DEEDS GOES TO TOWN(1936); NOBODY'S FOOL(1936); SITTING ON THE MOON(1936); SWING TIME(1936); UNDER YOUR SPELL(1936); BILL CRACKS DOWN(1937); BREAKFAST FOR TWO(1937); CALIFORNIAN, THE(1937); CONFESSION(1937); COUNTRY GENTLEMEN(1937); DAUGHTER OF SHANGHAI(1937); DEVIL'S PLAYGROUND(1937); EVER SINCE EVE(1937); GREEN LIGHT(1937); HIT PARADE, THE(1937); INTERNES CAN'T TAKE MONEY(1937); LARCENY ON THE AIR(1937); LAST GANGSTER, THE(1937); LIFE OF EMILE ZOLA, THE(1937); MAN WHO CRIED WOLF, THE(1937); MARKED WOMAN(1937); MARRIED BEFORE BREAKFAST(1937); MICHAEL O'HALLORAN(1937); PARADISE ISLE(1937); ROSALIE(1937); SEA DEVILS(1937); SHE'S DANGEROUS(1937); SINGING MARINE, THE(1937); STAGE DOOR(1937); WAIKIKI WEDDING(1937); ARSENE LUPIN RETURNS(1938); CHASER, THE(1938); DANGEROUS TO KNOW(1938); GIRLS ON PROBATION(1938); GIRLS' SCHOOL(1938); ILLEGAL TRAFFIC(1938); KING OF ALCATRAZ(1938); LADY OBJECTS, THE(1938); MAD MISS MANTON, THE(1938); MIDNIGHT INTRUDER(1938); MR. DOODLE KICKS OFF(1938); MR. MOTO'S GAMBLE(1938); STATE POLICE(1938); THERE'S ALWAYS A WOMAN(1938); THERE'S THAT WOMAN AGAIN(1938); TIP-OFF GIRLS(1938); YOU CAN'T TAKE IT WITH YOU(1938); YOUNG DR. KILDARE(1938); ADVENTURES OF JANE ARDEN(1939); COVERED TRAILER, THE(1939); DEATH OF A CHAMPION(1939); FIRST OFFENDERS(1939); GERONIMO(1939); GREAT VICTOR HERBERT, THE(1939); KING OF CHINATOWN(1939); KING OF THE UNDERWORLD(1939); MR. SMITH GOES TO WASHINGTON(1939); MYSTERIOUS MISS X, THE(1939); OFF THE RECORD(1939); OUTSIDE THESE WALLS(1939); RISKY BUSINESS(1939); SECRET SERVICE OF THE AIR(1939);

SOCIETY LAWYER(1939); SPIRIT OF CULVER, THE(1939); THEY MADE HER A SPY(1939); WALL STREET COWBOY(1939); WINGS OF THE NAVY(1939); BANK DICK, THE(1940); CAPTAIN CAUTION(1940); DR. KILDARE'S CRISIS(1940); EARL OF CHICAGO, THE(1940); FATHER IS A PRINCE(1940); FIVE LITTLE PEPPERS IN TROUBLE(1940); GOLDEN GLOVES(1940); I LOVE YOU AGAIN(1940); NO TIME FOR COMEDY(1940); OUT WEST WITH THE PEPPERS(1940); QUEEN OF THE MOB(1940); RHYTHM ON THE RIVER(1940); ROAD TO SINGAPORE(1940); SAILOR'S LADY(1940); SAINT TAKES OVER, THE(1940); STREET OF MEMORIES(1940); YESTERDAY'S HEROES(1940); ADVENTURE IN WASHINGTON(1941); BUY ME THAT TOWN(1941); CHEERS FOR MISS BISHOP(1941); CRACKED NUTS(1941); ELLERY QUEEN AND THE MURDER RING(1941); FATHER TAKES A WIFE(1941); FOR BEAUTY'S SAKE(1941); GREAT GUNS(1941); JESSE JAMES AT BAY(1941); LADY FOR A NIGHT(1941); LIFE BEGINS FOR ANDY HARDY(1941); LIFE WITH HENRY(1941); MAN BETRAYED, A(1941); MEET JOHN DOE(1941); NAVAL ACADEMY(1941); NEVADA CITY(1941); OBLIGING YOUNG LADY(1941); PETTICOAT POLITICS(1941); SHE KNEW ALL THE ANSWERS(1941); TRIAL OF MARY DUGAN, THE(1941); UNFINISHED BUSINESS(1941); ADVENTURES OF MARTIN EDEN, THE(1942); CINDERELLA SWINGS IT(1942); HEART OF THE RIO GRANDE(1942); ICE-CAPADES REVUE(1942); MAGNIFICENT DOPE, THE(1942); NAZI AGENT(1942); PANAMA HATTIE(1942); PRIDE OF THE YANKEES, THE(1942); WE WERE DANCING(1942); WHISTLING IN DIXIE(1942); YOKEL BOY(1942); DESTROYER(1943); DU BARRY WAS A LADY(1943); IRON MAJOR, THE(1943); IT AIN'T HAY(1943); JACK LONDON(1943); MISSION TO MOSCOW(1943); OLD ACQUAINTANCE(1943); RIDING HIGH(1943); SECRETS OF THE UNDERGROUND(1943); SWING SHIFT MAISIE(1943); THEY CAME TO BLOW UP AMERICA(1943); THIS IS THE ARMY(1943); THOUSANDS CHEER(1943); WHAT A WOMAN!(1943); ATLANTIC CITY(1944); BERMUDA MYSTERY(1944); DEAD MAN'S EYES(1944); DESTINATION TOKYO(1944); END OF THE ROAD(1944); GREAT MIKE, THE(1944); JUNGLE WOMAN(1944); LADIES OF WASHINGTON(1944); MEET MISS BOBBY SOCKS(1944); OH, WHAT A NIGHT(1944); ONCE UPON A TIME(1944); SHADOW OF SUSPICION(1944); SOUTH OF DIXIE(1944); WEEKEND PASS(1944); WING AND A PRAYER(1944); APOLOGY FOR MURDER(1945); CAPTAIN TUGBOAT ANNIE(1945); DAKOTA(1945); DIVORCE(1945); DOCKS OF NEW YORK(1945); FOLLOW THAT WOMAN(1945); HONEYMOON AHEAD(1945); I LOVE A BANDLEADER(1945); I'LL REMEMBER APRIL(1945); I'LL TELL THE WORLD(1945); INCENDIARY BLONDE(1945); KEEP YOUR POWDER DRY(1945); MISS SUSIE SLAGLE'S(1945); MR. MUGGS RIDES AGAIN(1945); OVER 21(1945); PHANTOM SPEAKS, THE(1945); ROUGHLY SPEAKING(1945); SHE GETS HER MAN(1945); STORK CLUB, THE(1945); STRANGE ILLUSION(1945); THREE'S A CROWD(1945); THRILL OF A ROMANCE(1945); BEHIND THE MASK(1946); CLAUDIA AND DAVID(1946); G.I. WAR BRIDES(1946); HIGH SCHOOL HERO(1946); I RING DOORBELLS(1946); JOLSON STORY, THE(1946); KID FROM BOOKLYN, THE(1946); LITTLE GIANT(1946); MADONNA'S SECRET, THE(1946); MAGNIFICENT DOLL(1946); MISSING LADY, THE(1946); MURDER IS MY BUSINESS(1946); OUR HEARTS WERE GROWING UP(1946); PLAINSMAN AND THE LADY(1946); SECRETS OF A SORORITY GIRL(1946); SHADOW RETURNS, THE(1946); SHOCK(1946); SIOUX CITY SUE(1946); SO GOES MY LOVE(1946); SWAMP FIRE(1946); TWO YEARS BEFORE THE MAST(1946); FABULOUS TEXAN, THE(1947); GLAMOUR GIRL(1947); HARD BOILED MAHONEY(1947); HER HUSBAND'S AFFAIRS(1947); MONSIEUR VERDOUX(1947); RED STALLION, THE(1947); SECRET LIFE OF WALTER MITTY, THE(1947); SHOCKING MISS PILGRIM, THE(1947); VIOLENCE(1947); WEB, THE(1947); WILD FRONTIER, THE(1947); B. F.'S DAUGHTER(1948); COUNTERFEITERS, THE(1948); DAREDEVILS OF THE CLOUDS(1948); DON'T TRUST YOUR HUSBAND(1948); FIGHTING BACK(1948); GENTLEMAN FROM NOWHERE, THE(1948); HUNTED, THE(1948); INCIDENT(1948); MARY LOU(1948); SHANGHAI CHEST, THE(1948); SIREN OF ATLANTIS(1948); SOUTHERN YANKEE, A(1948); STATE OF THE UNION(1948); STRANGE MRS. CRANE, THE(1948); TRAPPED BY BOSTON BLACKIE(1948); ALASKA PATROL(1949); FLAMINGO ROAD(1949); FOUNTAINHEAD, THE(1949); HOLD THAT BABY!(1949); KNOCK ON ANY DOOR(1949); NEPTUNE'S DAUGHTER(1949); SAMSON AND DELILAH(1949); SLIGHTLY FRENCH(1949); STORY OF SEABISCUIT, THE(1949); TULSA(1949); ZAMBA(1949); BIG HANGOVER, THE(1950); BLUE GRASS OF KENTUCKY(1950); EMERGENCY WEDDING(1950); FRONTIER OUTPOST(1950); KEY TO THE CITY(1950); LAST OF THE BUCCANEERS(1950); NANCY GOES TO RIO(1950); OVER THE BORDER(1950); RADAR SECRET SERVICE(1950); REDWOOD FOREST TRAIL(1950); ROCK ISLAND TRAIL(1950); SECOND FACE, THE(1950); SUNSET IN THE WEST(1950); THREE LITTLE WORDS(1950); TWO LOST WORLDS(1950); IN OLD AMARILLO(1951); HOLD THAT LINE(1952); SCANDAL SHEET(1952); THUNDERING CARAVANS(1952); YANK IN INDO-CHINA, A(1952); STRANGER WORE A GUN, THE(1953); ABOUT MRS. LESLIE(1954); JOHNNY DARK(1954); BIG BLUFF, THE(1955); CREATURE WITH THE ATOM BRAIN(1955); LAY THAT RIFLE DOWN(1955); SUDDEN DANGER(1955); DON'T KNOCK THE ROCK(1956); MAVERICK QUEEN, THE(1956); BEGINNING OF THE END(1957); PAL JOEY(1957); SHAKE, RATTLE, AND ROCK!(1957); SPOOK CHASERS(1957); HIGH SCHOOL CONFIDENTIAL(1958); MARJORIE MORNINGSTAR(1958); FLYING FONTAINES, THE(1959)

A.W. Watkins
KNIGHT WITHOUT ARMOR(1937, Brit.), ed
Amanda Watkins
TERMS OF ENDEARMENT(1983)
Carlene Watkins
TOUGH ENOUGH(1983)
Clay Watkins
GOING HOME(1971)
David Watkins
KNACK ... AND HOW TO GET IT, THE(1965, Brit.), ph; THREE MUSKETEERS, THE(1974, Panama), ph; FOUR MUSKETEERS, THE(1975) ph
Debbie Watkins
ROLLOVER(1981)
Deborah Watkins
WORLD ACCORDING TO GARP, The(1982)
Ed Watkins
NEPTUNE FACTOR, THE(1973, Can.), set d; QUIET DAY IN BELFAST, A(1974, Can.), set d
Edith Watkins
YANKS ARE COMING, THE(1942), w; SLIGHTLY TERRIFIC(1944), w; HOLLYWOOD AND VINE(1945), w
Emma Lou Watkins
COMMON LAW WIFE(1963)

Frank Watkins
SUBMARINE SEAHAWK(1959); GUN FIGHT(1961); X-15(1961)
Gary Watkins
LONG RIDERS, THE(1980)
1984
JOHNNY DANGEROUSLY(1984)
Hunter Watkins
PENNIES FROM HEAVEN(1981)
James Louis Watkins
J.D.'S REVENGE(1976)
Jim Watkins
BLACK GUNN(1972); COOL BREEZE(1972); MC Q(1974)
John L. Watkins
NIGHTMARE(1981), a, p
Linda Watkins
GOOD SPORT(1931); SOB SISTER(1931); CHARLIE CHAN'S CHANCE(1932); CHEATERS AT PLAY(1932); GAY CABALLERO, THE(1932); FROM HELL IT CAME(1957); AS YOUNG AS WE ARE(1958); GOING STEADY(1958); 10 NORTH FREDERICK(1958); BECAUSE THEY'RE YOUNG(1960); CASH McCALL(1960); PARENT TRAP, THE(1961); GOOD NEIGHBOR SAM(1964); HUCKLEBERRY FINN(1974)
Mary F. Watkins
OH, FOR A MAN!(1930), w
Mary Jane Watkins
BLACK KING(1932)
Maurice Watkins
DOCTORS' WIVES(1931), w
Maurine Watkins
UP THE RIVER(1930), w; PLAY GIRL(1932), w; STRANGE LOVE OF MOLLY LOUVAIN, THE(1932), w; HELLO SISTER!(1933), w; NO MAN OF HER OWN(1933), w; PROFESSIONAL SWEETHEART(1933), w; SEARCH FOR BEAUTY(1934), w; STRICTLY DYNAMITE(1934), w; LIBELED LADY(1936), w; UP THE RIVER(1938), w; I LOVE YOU AGAIN(1940), w; ROXIE HART(1942), w; EASY TO WED(1946), w
Silents
CHICAGO(1928), w
Michael Watkins
FIGHTING MAD(1976), ph; VENOM(1982, Brit.)
Michelle Watkins
TERMS OF ENDEARMENT(1983)
Miles Watkins
GREAT TEXAS DYNAMITE CHASE, THE(1976)
Perry Watkins
ACROSS 110TH STREET(1972), art d; COME BACK CIHARLESTON BLUE(1972), art d; GORDON'S WAR(1973), art d
Peter Watkins
IT HAPPENED HERE(1966, Brit.); PRIVILEGE(1967, Brit.), d, w; GLADIATORS, THE(1970, Swed.), d, w; PUNISHMENT PARK(1971), a, d&w, ed; EDVARD MUNCH(1976, Norway/Swed.), d&w
Robin Watkins
1984
LOVELINES(1984)
Roman Watkins
1984
CONSTANCE(1984, New Zealand)
Sally Watkins
RICHARD'S THINGS(1981, Brit.); MISSIONARY, THE(1982)
Sarah Jean Watkins
BOOGEYMAN II(1983)
Ted Watkins
WEDDING IN WHITE(1972, Can.), set d; HAPPY BIRTHDAY, GEMINI(1980), prod d; STONE COLD DEAD(1980, Can.), art d; TULIPS(1981, Can), art d; HANK WILLIAMS: THE SHOW HE NEVER GAVE(1982, Can.), art d; INCUBUS, THE(1982, Can.), prod d
Tommy Watkins
HAVING WONDERFUL TIME(1938)
Toney Watkins
HAIR(1979)
Trevor Watkins
KING OF HEARTS(1936, Brit.)
Arthur Watkyn
FOR BETTER FOR WORSE(1954, Brit.), w; MOONRAKER, THE(1958, Brit.), w
Debbie Watling
TAKE ME HIGH(1973, Brit.)
Deborah Watling
THAT'LL BE THE DAY(1974, Brit.)
Dilys Watling
CALCULATED RISK(1963, Brit.); TWO LEFT FEET(1965, Brit.)
Giles Watling
HUMAN FACTOR, THE(1979, Brit.)
Jack Watling
SIXTY GLORIOUS YEARS(1938, Brit.); YOUNG MR. PITT, THE(1942, Brit.); WE DIVE AT DAWN(1943, Brit.); ADVENTURE FOR TWO(1945, Brit.); WAY AHEAD, THE(1945, Brit.); COURTNEY AFFAIR, THE(1947, Brit.); EASY MONEY(1948, Brit.); QUARTET(1949, Brit.); UNDER CAPRICORN(1949); WINSLOW BOY, THE(1950); FATHER'S DOING FINE(1952, Brit.); ONCE A SINNER(1952, Brit.); PRIVATE INFORMATION(1952, Brit.); WHITE CORRIDORS(1952, Brit.); FLANNELFOOT(1953, Brit.); MEET MR. LUCIFER(1953, Brit.); DANGEROUS CARGO(1954, Brit.); GOLDEN LINK, THE(1954, Brit.); TALE OF THREE WOMEN, A(1954, Brit.); TROUBLE IN THE GLEN(1954, Brit.); NAKED HEART, THE(1955, Brit.); SEA SHALL NOT HAVE THEM, THE(1955, Brit.); TIME TO KILL, A(1955, Brit.); WINDFALL(1955 Brit.); ADMIRABLE CRICHTON, THE(1957, Brit.); BIRTHDAY PRESENT, THE(1957, Brit.); CITY AFTER MIDNIGHT(1957, Brit.); REACH FOR THE SKY(1957, Brit.); CHAIN OF EVENTS(1958, Brit.); LINKS OF JUSTICE(1958); NIGHT TO REMEMBER, A(1958, Brit.); SOLITARY CHILD, THE(1958, Brit.); GIDEON OF SCOTLAND YARD(1959, Brit.); SINK THE BISMARCK!(1960, Brit.); MARY HAD A LITTLE(1961, Brit.); NOTHING BARRED(1961, Brit.); THREE ON A SPREE(1961, Brit.); FLAT TWO(1962, Brit.); MR. ARKADIN(1962, Brit./Fr./Span.); NEARLY A NASTY ACCIDENT(1962, Brit.); QUEEN'S GUARDS, THE(1963, Brit.); WHO WAS MADDOX?(1964, Brit.); NANNY, THE(1965, Brit.); PUBLIC EYE, THE(1972, Brit.); 11 HARROWHOUSE(1974, Brit.)

Aircraftsman Jack Watling
JOURNEY TOGETHER(1946, Brit.)
Dennis Watlington
DEER HUNTER, THE(1978)
Sanders Watney
YOUNG WINSTON(1972, Brit.)
Elissa Watsman
Misc. Talkies
CAMERONS, THE(1974)
Adele Watson
JAZZ HEAVEN(1929); THIS THING CALLED LOVE(1929); VERY IDEA, THE(1929); ARROWSMITH(1931); EXPENSIVE WOMEN(1931); PUBLIC ENEMY, THE(1931); STREET SCENE(1931); PACK UP YOUR TROUBLES(1932); PURCHASE PRICE, THE(1932); PILGRIMAGE(1933)
Silents
LYING TRUTH, THE(1922); RENO(1923); ROLLING HOME(1926)
Alan Watson
UNCLE HARRY(1945); HORROR HOSPITAL(1973, Brit.), w
Albert Watson
SUDDENLY, A WOMAN!(1967, Den.)
Alberta Watson
IN PRAISE OF OLDER WOMEN(1978, Can.); STONE COLD DEAD(1980, Can.); DIRTY TRICKS(1981, Can.); SOLDIER, THE(1982); KEEP, THE(1983)
Aline Watson
SNIPER, THE(1952)
Ben Watson
OX-BOW INCIDENT, THE(1943); ACROSS THE WIDE MISSOURI(1951)
Bill Watson
STINGRAY(1978)
Billy Watson
LITTLE MINISTER, THE(1934); WINNING TICKET, THE(1935); PLOUGH AND THE STARS, THE(1936); IN OLD CHICAGO(1938); KIDNAPPED(1938); MR. SMITH GOES TO WASHINGTON(1939); STANLEY AND LIVINGSTONE(1939)
Bob Watson
MAYTIME(1937); BOYS TOWN(1938); HITLER–DEAD OR ALIVE(1942)
Bob Watson
TOUGH ENOUGH(1983)
Misc. Talkies
POLK COUNTY POT PLANE(1977); HOT PURSUIT(1981)
Bobby Watson
SYNCOPATION(1929); FOLLOW THE LEADER(1930); ARROWSMITH(1931); MANHATTAN PARADE(1931); HIGH PRESSURE(1932); GOING HOLLYWOOD(1933); MOONLIGHT AND PRETZELS(1933); COUNTESS OF MONTE CRISTO, THE(1934); DEATH OF THE DIAMOND(1934); GAY BRIDE, THE(1934); HIDE-OUT(1934); THIS SIDE OF HEAVEN(1934); WINE, WOMEN, AND SONG(1934); MURDER MAN(1935); SOCIETY DOCTOR(1935); AFTER THE THIN MAN(1936); LOVE ON THE RUN(1936); MARY OF SCOTLAND(1936); SHOW BOAT(1936); ADVENTUROUS BLONDE(1937); AWFUL TRUTH, THE(1937); CAPTAINS COURAGEOUS(1937); GIRL WITH IDEAS, A(1937); LOVE IN A BUNGALOW(1937); YOU'RE A SWEETHEART(1937); EVERYTHING'S ON ICE(1939); HERO FOR A DAY(1939); LUCKY NIGHT(1939); SECRETS OF A MODEL(1940); DEVIL WITH HITLER, THE(1942); HARVARD, HERE I COME(1942); HEAVENLY BODY(1943); IT AIN'T HAY(1943); THAT NAZTY NUISANCE(1943); MIRACLE OF MORGAN'S CREEK, THE(1944); NIGHT AND DAY(1946); BIG CLOCK, THE(1948); SINGIN' IN THE RAIN(1952); BAND WAGON, THE(1953); STORY OF MANKIND, THE(1957); ON THE DOUBLE(1961)
Misc. Talkies
LAST THREE(1942)
Silents
"THAT ROYLE GIRL"(1925)
Bobby [Bobs] Watson
LOVE ON THE RUN(1936)
Bobs Watson
GO CHASE YOURSELF(1938); IN OLD CHICAGO(1938); KENTUCKY(1938); BLACKMAIL(1939); DODGE CITY(1939); ON BORROWED TIME(1939); STORY OF ALEXANDER GRAHAM BELL, THE(1939); DR. KILDARE'S CRISIS(1940); DREAMING OUT LOUD(1940); WYOMING(1940); HIT THE ROAD(1941); MEN OF BOYS TOWN(1941); SCATTERGOOD PULLS THE STRINGS(1941); HI, BUDDY(1943); BOLD AND THE BRAVE, THE(1956); SAINTLY SINNERS(1962); WHATEVER HAPPENED TO BABY JANE?(1962); FIRST TO FIGHT(1967)
Rev. Bobs Watson
GRAND THEFT AUTO(1977)
Bruce Watson
THIS PROPERTY IS CONDEMNED(1966); JOHNNY GOT HIS GUN(1971); BUCKTOWN(1975); SWINGING BARMAIDS, THE(1976)
Carol Watson
1984
FRIDAY THE 13TH–THE FINAL CHAPTER(1984), w; MEATBALLS PART II(1984), w
Cavan Watson
LANDFALL(1953, Brit.); PROJECT M7(1953, Brit.)
Caven Watson
GOODBYE MR. CHIPS(1939, Brit.); IN WHICH WE SERVE(1942, Brit.); WE DIVE AT DAWN(1943, Brit.); JOHNNY IN THE CLOUDS(1945, Brit.); VACATION FROM MARRIAGE(1945, Brit.); WANTED FOR MURDER(1946, Brit.); SWORD AND THE ROSE, THE(1953)
Cecil Watson
HEARTS IN BONDAGE(1936); LLOYDS OF LONDON(1936)
Colin Watson
BRITANNIA OF BILLINGSGATE(1933, Brit.); WATERLOO(1970, Ital./USSR)
Coy Watson, Jr.
Silents
LOVE MAKES 'EM WILD(1927); SMART SET, THE(1928)
David Watson
GIRL ON A MOTORCYCLE, THE(1968, Fr./Brit.), stunts; BENEATH THE PLANET OF THE APES(1970)
Debbie Watson
MUNSTER, GO HOME(1966); COOL ONES THE(1967); TAMMY AND THE MILLIONAIRE(1967)

Deek Watson
PARDON MY SARONG(1942)
Delmar Watson
LONE STAR RANGER, THE(1930); OUTSIDE THE LAW(1930); COMPROMISED(1931); WILD GIRL(1932); FOURTH HORSEMAN, THE(1933); RIGHT TO ROMANCE(1933); TO THE LAST MAN(1933); PAINTED VEIL, THE(1934); ANNIE OAKLEY(1935); OLD HUTCH(1936); SILLY BILLIES(1936); WE'RE ONLY HUMAN(1936); GREAT O'MALLEY, THE(1937); HEIDI(1937); MAYTIME(1937); CHANGE OF HEART(1938); CLIPPED WINGS(1938); HUNTED MEN(1938); KENTUCKY(1938); MR. SMITH GOES TO WASHINGTON(1939); WHEN TOMORROW COMES(1939); YOU CAN'T CHEAT AN HONEST MAN(1939); LEGION OF THE LAWLESS(1940); MY LITTLE CHICKADEE(1940)
Delmer Watson
TOVARICH(1937)
Diana Watson
DEVIL'S BAIT(1959, Brit.), w
Doc Watson
PETEY WHEATSTRAW(1978)
Don Watson
Misc. Talkies
POLK COUNTY POT PLANE(1977); HOT PURSUIT(1981)
Donald Watson
Misc. Silents
BIRDS' CHRISTMAS CAROL, THE(1917)
Douglas Watson
JULIUS CAESAR(1953); SAYONARA(1957); WHO SAYS I CAN'T RIDE A RAINBOW!(1971)
Douglass Watson
TRIAL OF THE CATONSVILLE NINE, THE(1972); ULZANA'S RAID(1972)
Duke Watson
CALL NORTHSIDE 777(1948); WHERE THE SIDEWALK ENDS(1950); MOB, THE(1951); SCANDAL SHEET(1952)
Duncan Watson
RACE FOR YOUR LIFE, CHARLIE BROWN(1977)
Earl Watson
GUYANA, CULT OF THE DAMNED(1980, Mex./Span./Panama), ed; PINK MOTEL(1983), ed; WACKO(1983), ed
Earl Watson, Jr.
TOM(1973), ed; BLACK SHAMPOO(1976), ed
Edwin B. Watson
LIVE FAST, DIE YOUNG(1958), w
Elizabeth Watson
COAL MINER'S DAUGHTER(1980)
Erik Watson
1984
HOT DOG...THE MOVIE(1984)
F.W. Watson
IT'S A SMALL WORLD(1935)
Garry Watson
MR. SMITH GOES TO WASHINGTON(1939); EXILE, THE(1947)
Gladys Watson
PRIME CUT(1972)
Gloria Watson
FRENCH LINE, THE(1954); SON OF SINBAD(1955)
Greg Watson
HEY THERE, IT'S YOGI BEAR(1964), ed
Gregory V. Watson, Jr.
HEIDI'S SONG(1982), ed
Harold Watson
DEADLIEST SIN, THE(1956, Brit.), art d
Harry Watson
PARDON MY GUN(1930); MAN'S CASTLE, A(1933); PADDY O'DAY(1935); BULLETS OR BALLOTS(1936); OLD HUTCH(1936); UNDER PROOF(1936, Brit.); DAMSEL IN DISTRESS, A(1937); LOVE IS NEWS(1937); PENROD AND SAM(1937); TIME OUT FOR ROMANCE(1937); MR. SMITH GOES TO WASHINGTON(1939)
Silents
ZANDER THE GREAT(1925)
Misc. Silents
HELLO BILL!(1915)
Harry Watson, Jr.
Silents
KEEP MOVING(1915)
Henrietta Watson
JEALOUSY(1931, Brit.); LIMPING MAN, THE(1931, Brit.); COLLISION(1932, Brit.); SHOT IN THE DARK, A(1933, Brit.); POINTING FINGER, THE(1934, Brit.); THINGS ARE LOOKING UP(1934, Brit.); BARNACLE BILL(1935, Brit.); BROWN WALLET, THE(1936, Brit.); CARDINAL, THE(1936, Brit.); MISTER HOBO(1936, Brit.); SECRET FOUR, THE(1940, Brit.)
Silents
MIRIAM ROZELLA(1924, Brit.)
Misc. Silents
DESPERATION(1916, Brit.); DIVINE GIFT, THE(1918, Brit.); BROWN SUGAR(1922, Brit.)
Henry P. Watson
PICNIC(1955)
Herb Watson
WINGS IN THE DARK(1935)
Homer Watson
Misc. Silents
LUCK AND SAND(1925)
Ian Watson
LOCAL HERO(1983, Brit.), art d
1984
SHEENA(1984), set d
Jack Watson
MAN WHO WAS NOBODY, THE(1960, Brit.); PEEPING TOM(1960, Brit.); KONGA(1961, Brit.); FATE TAKES A HAND(1962, Brit.); ON THE BEAT(1962, Brit.); OUT OF THE FOG(1962, Brit.); TIME TO REMEMBER(1962, Brit.); FIVE TO ONE(1963, Brit.); QUEEN'S GUARDS, THE(1963, Brit.); THIS SPORTING LIFE(1963, Brit.); GORGON, THE(1964, Brit.); MASTER SPY(1964, Brit.); BLOOD BEAST FROM OUTER

SPACE(1965, Brit.); HILL, THE(1965, Brit.); GRAND PRIX(1966); IDOL, THE(1966, Brit.); TOBRUK(1966); DEVIL'S BRIGADE, THE(1968); STRANGE AFFAIR, THE(1968, Brit.); DECLINE AND FALL... OF A BIRD WATCHER(1969, Brit.); MC KENZIE BREAK, THE(1970); THINK DIRTY(1970, Brit.); KIDNAPPED(1971, Brit.); FROM BEYOND THE GRAVE(1974, Brit.); JUGGERNAUT(1974, Brit.); 11 HARROW-HOUSE(1974, Brit.); BRANNIGAN(1975, Brit.); PURPLE TAXI, THE(1977, Fr./Ital./Ireland); SCHIZO(1977, Brit.); WILD GEESE, THE(1978, Brit.); FFOLKES(1980, Brit.); BEYOND THE FOG(1981, Brit.); SEA WOLVES, THE(1981, Brit.)

James A. Watson
Misc. Talkies
KILLING AT OUTPOST ZETA, THE(1980)

James A. Watson, Jr.
HALLS OF ANGER(1970); ORGANIZATION, THE(1971); GOLDENGIRL(1979); AIRPLANE II: THE SEQUEL(1982)
Misc. Talkies
EXTREME CLOSE-UP(1973)

James R. Watson
Misc. Talkies
LADY COCOA(1975)

Jan Watson
DR. GOLDFOOT AND THE BIKINI MACHINE(1965); MURDERERS' ROW(1966); SILENCERS, THE(1966); PANIC IN THE CITY(1968)

Jimmy Watson
GONKS GO BEAT(1965, Brit.), w

John Watson
ROOM IN THE HOUSE(1955, Brit.); MURDER ON APPROVAL(1956, Brit.); BOOBY TRAP(1957, Brit.); CAT GIRL(1957); SPANIARD'S CURSE, THE(1958, Brit.); STEEL BAYONET, THE(1958, Brit.); STRANGE CASE OF DR. MANNING, THE(1958, Brit.); HIDDEN HOMICIDE(1959, Brit.); RUNAWAY, THE(1964, Brit.); BRAIN, THE(1965, Ger./Brit.); WHERE THE BULLETS FLY(1966, Brit.); TWO A PENNY(1968, Brit.); BARTLEBY(1970, Brit.); DEATHSTALKER(1983, Arg./U.S.), d
1984
DEATHSTALKER, THE(1984), d
Misc. Silents
STACKED CARDS(1926)

John H. Watson
DANGEROUS CARGO(1954, Brit.); END OF THE AFFAIR, THE(1955, Brit.); SHADOW OF FEAR(1963, Brit.); CRIMSON BLADE, THE(1964, Brit.)

Johnny Watson
1984
TANK(1984)

Jonathan Watson
LOCAL HERO(1983, Brit.)

Joseph K. Watson
CHEROKEE STRIP(1937), w; LAND BEYOND THE LAW(1937), w; MELODY FOR TWO(1937), w

Justice Watson
DEATH OF A SCOUNDREL(1956); TOWER OF LONDON(1962)

Ken Watson
NOTHING BUT THE NIGHT(1975, Brit.)

Kitty Watson
MRS. MINIVER(1942)

Lane Watson
ALONG CAME JONES(1945); IT'S A PLEASURE(1945); WOMAN IN THE WINDOW, THE(1945); DARK MIRROR, THE(1946); TEMPTATION(1946); TOMORROW IS FOREVER(1946); BUCK PRIVATES COME HOME(1947)

Leo Watson
SWEETHEART OF THE CAMPUS(1941)

Lilian Watson
1984
BIZET'S CARMEN(1984, Fr./Ital.)

Lucile Watson
BISHOP MISBEHAVES, THE(1933); WHAT EVERY WOMAN KNOWS(1934); GARDEN OF ALLAH, THE(1936); WOMAN REBELS, A(1936); THREE SMART GIRLS(1937); SWEETHEARTS(1938); YOUNG IN HEART, THE(1938); MADE FOR EACH OTHER(1939); WOMEN, THE(1939); FLORIAN(1940); WATERLOO BRIDGE(1940); FOOTSTEPS IN THE DARK(1941); GREAT LIE, THE(1941); MODEL WIFE(1941); MR. AND MRS. SMITH(1941); RAGE IN HEAVEN(1941); WATCH ON THE RHINE(1943); THIN MAN GOES HOME, THE(1944); TILL WE MEET AGAIN(1944); UNCERTAIN GLORY(1944); MY REPUTATION(1946); NEVER SAY GOODBYE(1946); RAZOR'S EDGE, THE(1946); SONG OF THE SOUTH(1946); TOMORROW IS FOREVER(1946); IVY(1947); EMPEROR WALTZ, THE(1948); JULIA MISBEHAVES(1948); THAT WONDERFUL URGE(1948); EVERYBODY DOES IT(1949); LITTLE WOMEN(1949); HARRIET CRAIG(1950); LET'S DANCE(1950); MY FORBIDDEN PAST(1951)
Misc. Silents
GIRL WITH THE GREEN EYES, THE(1916)

Malcolm Watson
CIRCUS OF HORRORS(1960, Brit.)
Silents
SANCTUARY(1916, Brit.), w

Margaret Watson
LITTLE BIT OF BLUFF, A(1935, Brit.); VILLAGE SQUIRE, THE(1935, Brit.); MERRY COMES TO STAY(1937, Brit.)

Martha Watson
PERSONAL BEST(1982)

Michael Watson
POLYESTER(1981)

Mills Watson
UP IN SMOKE(1978); ...TICK...TICK...TICK...(1970); WILD COUNTRY, THE(1971); DIRTY LITTLE BILLY(1972); CHARLEY AND THE ANGEL(1973); PAPILLON(1973); MIDNIGHT MAN, THE(1974); TREASURE OF MATECUMBE(1976); CUJO(1983)

Milton Watson
FIREFLY, THE(1937)

Minor Watson
24 HOURS(1931); OUR BETTERS(1933); PURSUIT OF HAPPINESS, THE(1934); AGE OF INDISCRETION(1935); ANNAPOLIS FAREWELL(1935); CHARLIE CHAN IN PARIS(1935); LADY TUBBS(1935); MARY JANE'S PA(1935); MR. DYNAMITE(1935); PURSUIT(1935); LONGEST NIGHT, THE(1936); ROSE OF THE RANCHO(1936); CHECKERS(1937); DEAD END(1937); NAVY BLUE AND GOLD(1937); SATURDAY'S

HEROES(1937); THAT CERTAIN WOMAN(1937); WHEN'S YOUR BIRTHDAY?(1937); WOMAN I LOVE, THE(1937); BOYS TOWN(1938); FAST COMPANY(1938); LOVE, HONOR AND BEHAVE(1938); STABLEMATES(1938); TOUCHDOWN, ARMY(1938); WHILE NEW YORK SLEEPS(1938); ANGELS WASH THEIR FACES(1939); BOY FRIEND(1939); FLYING IRISHMAN, THE(1939); HARDYS RIDE HIGH, THE(1939); HERE I AM A STRANGER(1939); HUCKLEBERRY FINN(1939); MAISIE(1939); NEWS IS MADE AT NIGHT(1939); STAND UP AND FIGHT(1939); TELEVISION SPY(1939); ABE LINCOLN IN ILLINOIS(1940); GALLANT SONS(1940); HIDDEN GOLD(1940); LLANO KID, THE(1940); RANGERS OF FORTUNE(1940); TWENTY MULE TEAM(1940); VIVA CISCO KID(1940); YOUNG PEOPLE(1940); KISS THE BOYS GOODBYE(1941); MONSTER AND THE GIRL, THE(1941); MOON OVER MIAMI(1941); MR. DISTRICT ATTORNEY(1941); PARSON OF PANAMINT, THE(1941); WESTERN UNION(1941); BIG SHOT, THE(1942); ENEMY AGENTS MEET ELLERY QUEEN(1942); FLIGHT LIEUTENANT(1942); FRISCO LILL(1942); GENTLEMAN JIM(1942); KING'S ROW(1942); REMARKABLE ANDREW, THE(1942); THEY DIED WITH THEIR BOOTS ON(1942); TO THE SHORES OF TRIPOLI(1942); WOMAN OF THE YEAR(1942); YANKEE DOODLE DANDY(1942); ACTION IN THE NORTH ATLANTIC(1943); CRASH DIVE(1943); GUADALCANAL DIARY(1943); HAPPY LAND(1943); MISSION TO MOSCOW(1943); POWER OF THE PRESS(1943); PRINCESS O'ROURKE(1943); YANKS AHOY(1943); FALCON OUT WEST, THE(1944); HENRY ALDRICH, BOY SCOUT(1944); HERE COME THE WAVES(1944); SHADOWS IN THE NIGHT(1944); STORY OF DR. WASSELL, THE(1944); THAT'S MY BABY(1944); THIN MAN GOES HOME, THE(1944); BELL FOR ADANO, A(1945); BEWITCHED(1945); GOD IS MY CO-PILOT(1945); SARATOGA TRUNK(1945); YOU CAME ALONG(1945); BLUE SIERRA(1946); BOYS' RANCH(1946); COURAGE OF LASSIE(1946); VIRGINIAN, THE(1946); TROUBLE WITH WOMEN, THE(1947); SOUTHERN YANKEE, A(1948); BEYOND THE FOREST(1949); FILE ON THELMA JORDAN, THE(1950); JACKIE ROBINSON STORY, THE(1950); MISTER 880(1950); AS YOUNG AS YOU FEEL(1951); BRIGHT VICTORY(1951); LITTLE EGYPT(1951); FACE TO FACE(1952); MY SON, JOHN(1952); UNTAMED FRONTIER(1952); ROAR OF THE CROWD(1953); STAR, THE(1953); TEN WANTED MEN(1955); AMBASSADOR'S DAUGHTER, THE(1956); RAWHIDE YEARS, THE(1956); TRAPEZE(1956)

Minor K. Watson
ANOTHER LANGUAGE(1933)

Moray Watson
FIND THE LADY(1956, Brit.); GRASS IS GREENER, THE(1960); VALIANT, THE(1962, Brit./Ital.); OPERATION CROSSBOW(1965, U.S./Ital.); THINK DIRTY(1970, Brit.); SEA WOLVES, THE(1981, Brit.)

Norman Watson
DRAKE THE PIRATE(1935, Brit.), w; HONOURS EASY(1935, Brit.), w; STUDENT'S ROMANCE, THE(1936, Brit.), w; OUTSIDER, THE(1949, Brit.); PRIVATE ANGELO(1949, Brit.); SLEEPING CAR TO TRIESTE(1949, Brit.); MAGIC BOX, THE(1952, Brit.); LANDFALL(1953, Brit.)

Owen Watson
Misc. Talkies
FORCE FOUR(1975)

Patrice Watson
1984
MAKING THE GRADE(1984)

Patricia Watson
WHO HAS SEEN THE WIND(1980, Can.), w

Paul Watson
GOODBYE PORK PIE(1981, New Zealand)

Paula Watson
I WANNA HOLD YOUR HAND(1978)

Ralph Watson
MC VICAR(1982, Brit.)

Richard Watson
SHE BEAST, THE(1966, Brit./Ital./Yugo.); GODFATHER, THE, PART II(1974)

Rob Watson
1984
POLICE ACADEMY(1984)

Robert Watson
LITTLE MINISTER, THE(1934), tech adv; SECRET PATROL(1936), w; STAMPEDE(1936), w; HITLER GANG, THE(1944); DUFFY'S TAVERN(1945); HOLD THAT BLONDE(1945); RED, HOT AND BLUE(1949); COPPER CANYON(1950); G.I. JANE(1951); NO ESCAPE(1953); DEEP IN MY HEART(1954)

Robert [Bobby] Watson
PALEFACE, THE(1948)

Roy Watson
CAROLINA(1934); KENTUCKY BLUE STREAK(1935)
Silents
LOSER'S END, THE(1924)
Misc. Silents
FIFTH MAN, THE(1914); CUPID'S ROUND-UP(1918); WIN, LOSE OR DRAW(1925); WOLF BLOOD(1925); CHASING TROUBLE(1926); CACTUS TRAILS(1927)

Sheila Watson
QUEEN FOR A DAY(1951)

Susan Watson
DOCTOR FAUSTUS(1967, Brit.)

Theresa Watson
LONG AGO, TOMORROW(1971, Brit.)

Tom Watson
SILENT ENEMY, THE(1959, Brit.); SUBWAY IN THE SKY(1959, Brit.); FAHRENHEIT 451(1966, Brit.); ANOTHER TIME, ANOTHER PLACE(1983, Brit.)
1984
ANOTHER TIME, ANOTHER PLACE(1984, Brit.)

Vernee Watson
TRICK BABY(1973); NORMAN...IS THAT YOU?(1976); ALL NIGHT LONG(1981)

William Watson
HEROES IN BLUE(1939), d; GIRL ON A CHAIN GANG(1966); IN THE HEAT OF THE NIGHT(1967); LAWMAN(1971); CHATO'S LAND(1972); EXECUTIVE ACTION(1973); PASSOVER PLOT, THE(1976, Israel); HUNTING PARTY, THE(1977, Brit.); WHOLLY MOSES(1980); SWORD AND THE SORCERER, THE(1982)
Misc. Talkies
AND NOW TOMORROW(1952), d

William C. Watson
MACK, THE(1973)

William H. Watson
Misc. Silents
UP IN MARY'S ATTICK(1920), d
Woody Watson
EDDIE MACON'S RUN(1983)
Wylie Watson
FOR THE LOVE OF MIKE(1933, Brit.); HAWLEY'S OF HIGH STREET(1933, Brit.); LEAVE IT TO ME(1933, Brit.); ROAD HOUSE(1934, Brit.); BLACK MASK(1935, Brit.); 39 STEPS, THE(1935, Brit.); RADIO LOVER(1936, Brit.); PLEASE TEACHER(1937, Brit.); WHY PICK ON ME?(1937, Brit.); GAIETY GIRLS, THE(1938, Brit.); YES, MADAM?(1938, Brit.); JAMAICA INN(1939, Brit.); SHE COULDN'T SAY NO(1939, Brit.); BULLDOG SEES IT THROUGH(1940, Brit.); PACK UP YOUR TROUBLES(1940, Brit.); DANNY BOY(1941, Brit.); MY WIFE'S FAMILY(1941, Brit.); PIRATES OF THE SEVEN SEAS(1941, Brit.); FLEMISH FARM, THE(1943, Brit.); LAMP STILL BURNS, THE(1943, Brit.); SAINT MEETS THE TIGER, THE(1943, Brit.); DON'T TAKE IT TO HEART(1944, Brit.); KISS THE BRIDE GOODBYE(1944, Brit.); WORLD OWES ME A LIVING, THE(1944, Brit.); STRAWBERRY ROAN(1945, Brit.); DON CHICAGO(1945, Brit.); GIRL IN A MILLION, A(1946, Brit.); MURDER IN REVERSE(1946, Brit.); TROJAN BROTHERS, THE(1946, Brit.); WALTZ TIME(1946, Brit.); BRIGHTON ROCK(1947, Brit.); FAME IS THE SPUR(1947, Brit.); TAWNY PIPIT(1947, Brit.); YEARS BE-TWEEN, THE(1947, Brit.); DULCIMER STREET(1948, Brit.); THINGS HAPPEN AT NIGHT(1948, Brit.); HISTORY OF MR. POLLY, THE(1949, Brit.); MY BROTHER JONATHAN(1949, Brit.); TEMPTATION HARBOR(1949, Brit.); TIGHT LITTLE IS-LAND(1949, Brit.); WATERLOO ROAD(1949, Brit.); EYE WITNESS(1950, Brit.); MAG-NET, THE(1950, Brit.); NO ROOM AT THE INN(1950, Brit.); SHADOW OF THE PAST(1950, Brit.); HAPPY GO LOVELY(1951, Brit.); OPERATION DISASTER(1951, Brit.); TRAIN OF EVENTS(1952, Brit.); SUNDOWNERS, THE(1960)
Watson Children
LIFE BEGINS AT 40(1935)
Allen Watt
Silents
APACHE RAIDER, THE(1928)
Bob Watt
1984
EXTERMINATOR 2(1984)
Charles Watt
OF MICE AND MEN(1939)
David Watt
Misc. Silents
HARP KING, THE(1920, Brit.)
Gillian Watt
JUNGLE STREET GIRLS(1963, Brit.)
Hannah Watt
LISBON STORY, THE(1946, Brit.); WEAK AND THE WICKED, THE(1954, Brit.)
Harry Watt
NINE MEN(1943, Brit.), d&w; FIDDLERS THREE(1944, Brit.), d, w; FOR THOSE IN PERIL(1944, Brit.), w; OVERLANDERS, THE(1946, Brit./Aus.), d&w; MASSACRE HILL(1949, Brit.), d, w; IVORY HUNTER(1952, Brit.), d; WEST OF ZANZIBAR(1954, Brit.), d, w; FOUR DESPERATE MEN(1960, Brit.), d, w
Jack Watt
COLT .45(1950)
Jeremy Watt
SWEET WILLIAM(1980, Brit.), p
1984
SCRUBBERS(1984, Brit.), w
John Watt
RADIO FOLLIES(1935, Brit.), w; SATURDAY NIGHT REVUE(1937, Brit.); CROOKS TOUR(1940, Brit.), w; WE'LL MEET AGAIN(1942, Brit.)
Len Watt
KAMOURASKA(1973, Can./Fr.); HAPPY BIRTHDAY TO ME(1981)
Leslie Norman Watt
IVORY HUNTER(1952, Brit.), w
Marty Watt
1984
ALMOST YOU(1984)
Mildred Watt
Misc. Talkies
THEIR ONLY CHANCE(1978)
Nat Watt
HOPALONG CASSIDY RETURNS(1936), d
Nate Watt
NAVY BORN(1936), d; TRAIL DUST(1936), d; CARNIVAL QUEEN(1937), d; HILLS OF OLD WYOMING(1937), d; NORTH OF THE RIO GRANDE(1937), d; RUSTLER'S VALLEY(1937), d; PRIDE OF THE WEST(1938), w; FRONTIER VENGEANCE(1939), d; LAW OF THE PAMPAS(1939), d; OKLAHOMA RENEGADES(1940), d; FIEND OF DOPE ISLAND(1961), d, w
Silents
RAIDERS, THE(1921), d
Misc. Silents
GALLOPING DEVILS(1920), d; HUNGER OF THE BLOOD, THE(1921), d
Nate C. Watt
Misc. Silents
WHAT WOMEN LOVE(1920), d
Nedra Watt
SOUNDER(1972), cos; RIVER NIGER, THE(1976), cos; HERO AIN'T NOTHIN' BUT A SANDWICH, A(1977), cos
Peggy Watt
STAND UP AND CHEER(1934 80m FOX bw)
Sparky Watt
TRIAL OF BILLY JACK, THE(1974); HAND, THE(1981)
Stan Watt
POSSESSION OF JOEL DELANEY, THE(1972)
Tracy Watt
MOUTH TO MOUTH(1978, Aus.), art d; CLINIC, THE(1983, Aus.), prod d
1984
STRIKEBOUND(1984, Aus.), prod d
Ida Watterman
Silents
NOTORIETY(1922)

Don Watters
TRUCK TURNER(1974); ESCAPE FROM ALCATRAZ(1979)
Fred Watters
MY BLOODY VALENTINE(1981, Can.)
George Watters
OPERATION CIA(1965), ed; GUESS WHAT HAPPENED TO COUNT DRACU-LA(1970), ed; ENTER THE DRAGON(1973), ed
George Manker Watters
DANCE OF LIFE, THE(1929), w; BEHIND THE MAKEUP(1930), w; CAPTAIN OF THE GUARD(1930), w; GOOD INTENTIONS(1930), w; MAN TROUBLE(1930), w; SWING HIGH, SWING LOW(1937), w; WHEN MY BABY SMILES AT ME(1948), w
John Watters
OLIVER!(1968, Brit.)
William Watters [Arch W. Hall, Sr.]
EEGAH!(1962); WILD GUITAR(1962); NASTY RABBIT, THE(1964); WHAT'S UP FRONT(1964); DEADWOOD'76(1965), a, w; THIEVES LIKE US(1974)
Richard Wattis
COMING-OUT PARTY, A(; YANK AT OXFORD, A(1938); CLOUDED YELLOW, THE(1950, Brit.); EYE WITNESS(1950, Brit.); HAPPIEST DAYS OF YOUR LIFE(1950, Brit.); COLONEL MARCH INVESTIGATES(1952,Brit.); FOUR AGAINST FATE(1952, Brit.); IMPORTANCE OF BEING EARNEST, THE(1952, Brit.); ISLAND RESCUE(1952, Brit.); MADE IN HEAVEN(1952, Brit.); MR. LORD SAYS NO(1952, Brit.); STOLEN FACE(1952, Brit.); BACKGROUND(1953, Brit.); BLOOD ORANGE(1953, Brit.); FINAL TEST, THE(1953, Brit.); MR. POTTS GOES TO MOSCOW(1953, Brit.); NORMAN CONQUEST(1953, Brit.); PENNY PRINCESS(1953, Brit.); SMALL TOWN STORY(1953, Brit.); TOP OF THE FORM(1953, Brit.); BELLES OF ST. TRINIAN'S, THE(1954, Brit.); CROWDED DAY, THE(1954, Brit.); DOCTOR IN THE HOUSE(1954, Brit.); HOBSON'S CHOICE(1954, Brit.); LEASE OF LIFE(1954, Brit.); COLDITZ STORY, THE(1955, Brit.); INNOCENTS IN PARIS(1955, Brit.); INTRUDER, THE(1955, Brit.); LADY GODIVA RIDES AGAIN(1955, Brit.); SEE HOW THEY RUN(1955, Brit.); TIME OF HIS LIFE, THE(1955, Brit.); YANK IN ERMINE, A(1955, Brit.); EYEWITNESS(1956, Brit.); IRON PETTICOAT, THE(1956, Brit.); IT'S A WONDERFUL WORLD(1956, Brit.); JUMPING FOR JOY(1956, Brit.); MAN WHO KNEW TOO MUCH, THE(1956); MAN WHO NEVER WAS, THE(1956, Brit.); SIMON AND LAURA(1956, Brit.); TOUCH OF THE SUN, A(1956, Brit.); ABOMINABLE SNOWMAN OF THE HIMALAYAS, THE(1957, Brit.); ALLIGATOR NAMED DAISY, AN(1957, Brit.); HIGH FLIGHT(1957, Brit.); PRINCE AND THE SHOWGIRL, THE(1957, Brit.); SECOND FIDDLE(1957, Brit.); SILKEN AFFAIR, THE(1957, Brit.); ALL AT SEA(1958, Brit.); BLUE MURDER AT ST. TRINIAN'S(1958, Brit.); INN OF THE SIXTH HAPPINESS, THE(1958); FOLLOW A STAR(1959, Brit.); LEFT, RIGHT AND CENTRE(1959); LIBEL(1959, Brit.); TEN SECONDS TO HELL(1959); UGLY DUCKLING, THE(1959, Brit.); CAPTAIN'S TABLE, THE(1960, Brit.); FOLLOW THAT HORSE!(1960, Brit.); BON VOYAGE(1962); I THANK A FOOL(1962, Brit.); LONGEST DAY, THE(1962); NEARLY A NASTY AC-CIDENT(1962, Brit.); COME FLY WITH ME(1963); GET ON WITH IT(1963, Brit.); MY SON, THE VAMPIRE(1963, Brit.); PLAY IT COOL(1963, Brit.); V.I.P.s, THE(1963, Brit.); CARRY ON SPYING(1964, Brit.); AMOROUS ADVENTURES OF MOLL FLANDERS, THE(1965); BATTLE OF THE VILLA FIORITA, THE(1965, Brit.); BUNNY LAKE IS MISSING(1965); OPERATION CROSSBOW(1965, U.S./Ital.); UP JUMPED A SWAG-MAN(1965); YOU MUST BE JOKING!(1965, Brit.); YOUR MONEY OR YOUR WIFE(1965, Brit.); ALPHABET MURDERS, THE(1966); GREAT ST. TRINIAN'S TRAIN ROBBERY, THE(1966, Brit.); LIQUIDATOR, THE(1966, Brit.); CASINO ROYALE(1967, Brit.); CHITTY CHITTY BANG BANG(1968, Brit.); THOSE DARING YOUNG MEN IN THEIR JAUNTY JALOPIES(1969, Fr./Brit./ Ital.); WONDER-WALL(1969, Brit.); EGGHEAD'S ROBOT(1970, Brit.); GAMES THAT LOVERS PLAY(1971, Brit.); TROUBLESOME DOUBLE, THE(1971, Brit.); DEVIL'S WIDOW, THE(1972, Brit.); TAKE ME HIGH(1973, Brit.); CONFESSIONS OF A WINDOW CLEANER(1974, Brit.)
Misc. Talkies
LADY CHATTERLY VS. FANNY HILL(1980)
Billy Watts
TEMPTATION(1935, Brit.); CROWN VS STEVENS(1936); HAPPY DAYS ARE HERE AGAIN(1936, Brit.); PAY BOX ADVENTURE(1936, Brit.); THIS GREEN HELL(1936, Brit.); TROPICAL TROUBLE(1936, Brit.); NON-STOP NEW YORK(1937, Brit.); UNDER A CLOUD(1937, Brit.); LITTLE DOLLY DAYDREAM(1938, Brit.); THIS MAN IN PARIS(1939, Brit.); THIS MAN IS NEWS(1939, Brit.); THREE SILENT MEN(1940, Brit.)
Bobby Watts
SHADOW OF THE HAWK(1976, Can.), cos
Catherine Watts
NAUGHTY CINDERELLA(1933, Brit.)
Charles Watts
DALLAS(1950); I WAS A SHOPLIFTER(1950); STORM WARNING(1950); MAN WITH A CLOAK, THE(1951); JUST THIS ONCE(1952); MILLION DOLLAR MER-MAID(1952); PRISONER OF ZENDA, THE(1952); SHE'S WORKING HER WAY THROUGH COLLEGE(1952); SNIPER, THE(1952); SOMETHING FOR THE BIRDS(1952); WAIT 'TIL THE SUN SHINES, NELLIE(1952); SCANDAL AT SCOU-RIE(1953); SILVER WHIP, THE(1953); BOY FROM OKLAHOMA, THE(1954); RICO-CHET ROMANCE(1954); SHE COULDN'T SAY NO(1954); STAR IS BORN, A(1954); I DIED A THOUSAND TIMES(1955); SCARLET COAT, THE(1955); TALL MAN RID-ING(1955); VIEW FROM POMPEY'S HEAD, THE(1955); GIANT(1956); AFFAIR TO REMEMBER, AN(1957); BIG LAND, THE(1957); OUTLAW'S SON(1957); RAINTREE COUNTY(1957); SPIRIT OF ST. LOUIS, THE(1957); HIGH COST OF LOVING, THE(1958); LONE RANGER AND THE LOST CITY OF GOLD, THE(1958); BIG CIRCUS, THE(1959); NO NAME ON THE BULLET(1959); ADA(1961); LOVER COME BACK(1961); SOMETHING WILD(1961); SUMMER AND SMOKE(1961); JUM-BO(1962); WHEELER DEALERS, THE(1963); DEAD RINGER(1964); BABY, THE RAIN MUST FALL(1965); DON'T GO NEAR THE WATER(1975)
Chick Watts
YES SIR, MR. BONES(1951)
Cotton Watts
YES SIR, MR. BONES(1951); JAIL BAIT(1954)
"Cowboy" Bill Watts
Misc. Talkies
WRESTLING QUEEN, THE(1975)
Dorothy "Dodo" Watts
AULD LANG SYNE(1929, Brit.); ALMOST A HONEYMOON(1930, Brit.); MIDDLE WATCH, THE(1930, Brit.); SCHOOL FOR SCANDAL, THE(1930, Brit.); MAN FROM CHICAGO, THE(1931, Brit.); UNEASY VIRTUE(1931, Brit.); HER NIGHT OUT(1932, Brit.); MY WIFE'S FAMILY(1932, Brit.); SING ALONG WITH ME(1952, Brit.)

Elizabeth Watts
SPELL OF THE HYPNOTIST(1956)
Frank Watts
RISING DAMP(1980, Brit.), ph; SHILLINGBURY BLOWERS, THE(1980, Brit.), ph; DANGEROUS DAVIES–THE LAST DETECTIVE(1981, Brit.), ph; EDUCATING RITA(1983), ph
Fred Watts
REUNION(1932, Brit.); MEET MY SISTER(1933, Brit.), p; POLITICAL PARTY, A(1933, Brit.); OVER THE GARDEN WALL(1934, Brit.); DEMOBBED(1944, Brit.)
Freddie Watts
COUNTY FAIR(1933, Brit.); MUSIC HALL(1934, Brit.); SAY IT WITH FLOWERS(1934, Brit.); REAL BLOKE, A(1935, Brit.); HEARTS OF HUMANITY(1936, Brit.); MEN OF YESTERDAY(1936, Brit.); TALKING FEET(1937, Brit.); STEPPING TOES(1938, Brit.); THANK EVANS(1938, Brit.); HERE COMES THE SUN(1945, Brit.); MUDLARK, THE(1950, Brit.); JUDGMENT DEFERRED(1952, Brit.); ONE JUMP AHEAD(1955, Brit.); LONG HAUL, THE(1957, Brit.)
George Watts
SOAK THE RICH(1936); ANGELS OVER BROADWAY(1940); LITTLE NELLIE KELLY(1940); ONE CROWDED NIGHT(1940); SKY MURDER(1940); TIN PAN ALLEY(1940); COME LIVE WITH ME(1941); DOWN IN SAN DIEGO(1941); HURRY, CHARLIE, HURRY(1941); MR. DISTRICT ATTORNEY(1941); NO HANDS ON THE CLOCK(1941); OBLIGING YOUNG LADY(1941); TALL, DARK AND HANDSOME(1941); TILLIE THE TOILER(1941); TRIAL OF MARY DUGAN, THE(1941); WILD GEESE CALLING(1941); APACHE TRAIL(1942); PANAMA HATTIE(1942); REMARKABLE ANDREW, THE(1942); STREET OF CHANCE(1942); TALK OF THE TOWN(1942)
Gwen Watts
NOTORIOUS LANDLADY, THE(1962); MY FAIR LADY(1964)
Gwendolyn Watts
BILLY LIAR(1963, Brit.); DIE, DIE, MY DARLING(1965, Brit.); YOU MUST BE JOKING!(1965, Brit.); GIRL GETTERS, THE(1966, Brit.); WRONG BOX, THE(1966, Brit.); GAMES, THE(1970)
Harry Watts
JAMAICA INN(1939, Brit.), spec eff
Helen Watts
LAST OF THE KNUCKLEMEN, THE(1981, Aus.)
James Watts
TRAPPED IN A SUBMARINE(1931, Brit.)
Silents
LOST PATROL, THE(1929, Brit.)
Jeanne Watts
DANCE OF DEATH, THE(1971, Brit.); THREE SISTERS(1974, Brit.); MEMOIRS OF A SURVIVOR(1981, Brit.)
June Watts
NOTHING BUT THE BEST(1964, Brit.); AMOROUS ADVENTURES OF MOLL FLANDERS, THE(1965)
Katherine Watts
DON'T BE A DUMMY(1932, Brit.)
Keith Watts
HIDE IN PLAIN SIGHT(1980)
LaRue Watts
CHECKMATE(1973), w
Lionel Watts
TAWNY PIPIT(1947, Brit.)
"Little Jamie" Watts
SOLOMON KING(1974)
Lyonel Watts
OUTWARD BOUND(1930); STRANGE EVIDENCE(1933, Brit.); CHALLENGE, THE(1939, Brit.); MR. EMMANUEL(1945, Brit.); SO WELL REMEMBERED(1947, Brit.); HIDDEN ROOM, THE(1949, Brit.); EYE WITNESS(1950, Brit.)
Silents
MR. JUSTICE RAFFLES(1921, Brit.)
Margaret Watts
Misc. Silents
MAN WHO WAS AFRAID, THE(1917)
Mary S. Watts
Silents
RISE OF JENNIE CUSHING, THE(1917), w
Mike Watts
POT CARRIERS, THE(1962, Brit.), w; CRACKSMAN, THE(1963, Brit.), w; CROOKS IN CLOISTERS(1964, Brit.), w; JOEY BOY(1965, Brit.), w
Peggy Watts
COCK OF THE AIR(1932); MERRY WIDOW, THE(1934); MISSION TO MOSCOW(1943)
Queenie Watts
SPARROWS CAN'T SING(1963, Brit.); HALF A SIXPENCE(1967, Brit.); POOR COW(1968, Brit.); UP THE JUNCTION(1968, Brit.); SCHIZO(1977, Brit.)
Ray Watts
IT'S NOT THE SIZE THAT COUNTS(1979, Brit.), ed; BEASTMASTER, THE(1982), ed
Robert Watts
WATCH THE BIRDIE(1950), ed; NIGHT INTO MORNING(1951), ed; HOUR OF THIRTEEN, THE(1952), ed; TERROR ON A TRAIN(1953), ed; INVITATION TO THE DANCE(1956), ed; SSSSSSS(1973), ed; AIRPORT '77(1977), ed; RETURN OF THE JEDI(1983), p
1984
INDIANA JONES AND THE TEMPLE OF DOOM(1984), p
Roy Watts
POOR COW(1968, Brit.), ed; ALL THE WAY UP(1970, Brit.), ed; EXECUTIONER, THE(1970, Brit.), ed; KES(1970, Brit.), ed; FAMILY LIFE(1971, Brit.), ed; PERCY(1971, Brit.), ed; QUEST FOR LOVE(1971, Brit.), ed; GOLDEN VOYAGE OF SINBAD, THE(1974, Brit.), ed; MOMENTS(1974, Brit.), ed; SINBAD AND THE EYE OF THE TIGER(1977, U.S./Brit.), ed; VICE SQUAD(1982), ed; DEADLY FORCE(1983), ed; TRIUMPHS OF A MAN CALLED HORSE(1983, US/Mex.), ed
1984
ANGEL(1984), p; HAMBONE AND HILLIE(1984), d
Sal Watts
SOLOMON KING(1974), a, p, d, w, ed

Sally Watts
THAT'LL BE THE DAY(1974, Brit.)
Sparky Watts
YOU LIGHT UP MY LIFE(1977)
Stephanie Watts
SILENT WITNESS, THE(1962)
Tom Watts
Silents
AUTOCRAT, THE(1919, Brit.), d&w; FATHER O'FLYNN(1919, Brit.), d&w; YE BANKS AND BRAES(1919, Brit.), d
Misc. Silents
ANGEL OF THE WARD, THE(1915, Brit.), d; CALL OF THE PIPES, THE(1917, Brit.), d; HEAR THE PIPERS CALLING(1918, Brit.), d; MASTER OF GRAY, THE(1918, Brit.), d; CIGARETTE MAKER'S ROMANCE, A(1920, Brit.), d
Tom W. Watts
Misc. Silents
TOILERS, THE(1919, Brit.), d
Tommy Watts
NIGHT WE GOT THE BIRD, THE(1961, Brit.), m
Twinkle Watts
CANYON CITY(1943); MAN FROM THE RIO GRANDE, THE(1943); CALIFORNIA JOE(1944); LAKE PLACID SERENADE(1944); OUTLAWS OF SANTA FE(1944); SHERIFF OF SUNDOWN(1944); SILVER CITY KID(1944); STAGECOACH TO MONTEREY(1944); CORPUS CHRISTI BANDITS(1945); TOPEKA TERROR, THE(1945); TRAIL OF KIT CARSON(1945); GUY COULD CHANGE, A(1946)
Theodore Watts-Dunton
Silents
AYLWIN(1920, Brit.), w
Mrs. Watts-Phillips
Misc. Silents
CHILDREN OF COURAGE(1921, Brit.)
N. Watts-Phillips
Silents
KENT, THE FIGHTING MAN(1916, Brit.); HOLY ORDERS(1917, Brit.); ERNEST MALTRAVERS(1920, Brit.)
Misc. Silents
FIGHTING COBBLER, THE(1915, Brit.)
A. Waugh
DIVORCE OF LADY X. THE(1938, Brit.), prod d
Alec Waugh
TWO FOR DANGER(1940, Brit.); ISLAND IN THE SUN(1957), w; CIRCLE OF DECEPTON(1961, Brit.), w
Alex Waugh
MAN ABOUT THE HOUSE, A(1947, Brit.), set d
Clare Waugh
Misc. Talkies
NAUGHTY SCHOOL GIRLS(1977)
Donald Waugh
KELLY'S HEROES(1970, U.S./Yugo.); BUGSY MALONE(1976, Brit.); SHOCK TREATMENT(1981)
Edwin Waugh
TEN NIGHTS IN A BARROOM(1931), w
Evelyn Waugh
LOVED ONE, THE(1965), w; DECLINE AND FALL... OF A BIRD WATCHER(1969, Brit.), w
Fred M. Waugh
1984
DREAMSCAPE(1984)
Fred Waugh
MONTE WALSH(1970); J.W. COOP(1971), ph; SOMETIMES A GREAT NOTION(1971); BUCK AND THE PREACHER(1972); MC Q(1974); NIGHT MOVES(1975); LOOKER(1981), stunts
Frederick J. Waugh
O.S.S.(1946)
Hillary Waugh
JIG SAW(1965, Brit.), w
John Waugh
GROUND ZERO(1973)
Spence Waugh
Misc. Talkies
BEACH HOUSE(1982)
Susan Waugh
SHEILA LEVINE IS DEAD AND LIVING IN NEW YORK(1975)
Waugite Tiwi Tribes of North and Central Australia
JEDDA, THE UNCIVILIZED(1956, Aus.)
Sik-Yng Waung
GLADIATORS, THE(1970, Swed.)
Claire Wauthion
BENVENUTA(1983, Fr.)
Virginia Wave
DAKOTA(1945); DIVORCE(1945); WEST OF THE PECOS(1945); RIDE THE PINK HORSE(1947); MAN-EATER OF KUMAON(1948)
Francis Waverly
VAGABOND KING, THE(1930)
Thora Waverly
VAGABOND KING, THE(1930)
Hermann Wawra
MONEY ON THE STREET(1930, Aust.)
Dorothy Wax
GODLESS GIRL, THE(1929)
Jane Wax
VOICE OF THE HURRICANE(1964)
Ruby Wax
THINGS ARE TOUGH ALL OVER(1982); CHARIOTS OF FIRE(1981, Brit.); SHOCK TREATMENT(1981)
Steve Wax
OVER-UNDER, SIDEWAYS-DOWN(1977), p, d; TOUGH ENOUGH(1983), m

Johnny Waxfield
DRESSER, THE(1983)

Al Waxman
LAST GUNFIGHTER, THE(1961, Can.); WAR LOVER, THE(1962, U.S./Brit.); VIC-TORS, THE(1963); MAN IN THE MIDDLE(1964, U.S./Brit.); SUNDAY IN THE COUNTRY(1975, Can.); CLOWN MURDERS, THE(1976, Can.); WILD HORSE HANK(1979, Can.); DOUBLE NEGATIVE(1980, Can.); ATLANTIC CITY(1981, U.S./Can.); TULIPS(1981, Can), a, d, w; CLASS OF 1984(1982, Can.); SPASMS(1983, Can.)
Misc. Talkies
MY PLEASURE IS MY BUSINESS(1974, Can.), d

Albert Waxman
ISABEL(1968, Can.); LAST ACT OF MARTIN WESTON, THE(1970, Can./Czech.)

Albert S. Waxman
CROWD INSIDE, THE(1971, Can.), a, p,d&w; CHILD UNDER A LEAF(1975, Can.)

Bennett Waxman
SATAN'S MISTRESS(1982)

Franz Waxman
AFFAIR OF SUSAN(1935), m; BRIDE OF FRANKENSTEIN, THE(1935), m; DIA-MOND JIM(1935), m; LILIOM(1935, Fr.), m; ABSOLUTE QUIET(1936), m; DEVIL DOLL, THE(1936), m; FLASH GORDON(1936), m; FURY(1936), m; HIS BROTHER'S WIFE(1936), m; LOVE BEFORE BREAKFAST(1936), md; LOVE ON THE RUN(1936), m; NEXT TIME WE LOVE(1936), m; THE INVISIBLE RAY(1936), m; TROUBLE FOR TWO(1936), m; BRIDE WORE RED, THE(1937), m; CAPTAINS COURAGEOUS(1937), m; DAY AT THE RACES, A(1937), md; EMPEROR'S CANDLESTICKS, THE(1937), m; PERSONAL PROPERTY(1937), m; ARSENE LUPIN RETURNS(1938), m; CHRIST-MAS CAROL, A(1938), m; DRAMATIC SCHOOL(1938), m; MAN-PROOF(1938), m; PORT OF SEVEN SEAS(1938), m; SHINING HOUR, THE(1938), m; TEST PI-LOT(1938), m; THREE COMRADES(1938), m; TOO HOT TO HANDLE(1938), m; YOUNG IN HEART, THE(1938), m; AT THE CIRCUS(1939), m; HONOLULU(1939), m; HUCKLEBERRY FINN(1939), m; LADY OF THE TROPICS(1939), m; BOOM TOWN(1940), m; FLIGHT COMMAND(1940), m; FLORIAN(1940), m; I LOVE YOU AGAIN(1940), m; PHILADELPHIA STORY, THE(1940), m; REBECCA(1940), m; SPORTING BLOOD(1940), m; STRANGE CARGO(1940), w; DESIGN FOR SCAN-DAL(1941), m; FEMININE TOUCH, THE(1941), m; HONKY TONK(1941), m; KATH-LEEN(1941), m; SUSPICION(1941), m; UNFINISHED BUSINESS(1941), m; HER CARDBOARD LOVER(1942), m; JOURNEY FOR MARGARET(1942), m; REUNION IN FRANCE(1942), m; SEVEN SWEETHEARTS(1942), m; TORTILLA FLAT(1942), m; WOMAN OF THE YEAR(1942), m; AIR FORCE(1943), m; EDGE OF DARK-NESS(1943), m; OLD ACQUAINTANCE(1943), m; DESTINATION TOKYO(1944), m; IN OUR TIME(1944), m; MR. SKEFFINGTON(1944), m; TO HAVE AND HAVE NOT(1944), m; VERY THOUGHT OF YOU, THE(1944), m; CONFIDENTIAL AGENT(1945), m; GOD IS MY CO-PILOT(1945), m; HORN BLOWS AT MIDNIGHT, THE(1945), m; HOTEL BERLIN(1945), m; OBJECTIVE, BURMA!(1945), m; PRIDE OF THE MARINES(1945), m; HER KIND OF MAN(1946), m; HUMORESQUE(1946), m; CRY WOLF(1947), m; DARK PASSAGE(1947), m; NORA PRENTISS(1947), m; PARA-DINE CASE, THE(1947), m; POSSESSED(1947), m; THAT HAGEN GIRL(1947), m; TWO MRS. CARROLLS, THE(1947), m; UNSUSPECTED(1947), m; NO MINOR VICES(1948), m; SORRY, WRONG NUMBER(1948), m, md; WHIPLASH(1948), m; ALIAS NICK BEAL(1949), m; JOHNNY HOLIDAY(1949), m; NIGHT UNTO NIGHT(1949), m; ROPE OF SAND(1949), m; TASK FORCE(1949), m; DARK CI-TY(1950), m; FURIES, THE(1950), m; NIGHT AND THE CITY(1950, Brit.), m; SUN-SET BOULEVARD(1950), m; ANNE OF THE INDIES(1951), m; BLUE VEIL, THE(1951), m; DECISION BEFORE DAWN(1951), m; HE RAN ALL THE WAY(1951), m; ONLY THE VALIANT(1951), m; PLACE IN THE SUN, A(1951), m; RED MOUN-TAIN(1951), m; COME BACK LITTLE SHEBA(1952), m; LURE OF THE WILDER-NESS(1952), m; MY COUSIN RACHEL(1952), m; PHONE CALL FROM A STRANGER(1952), m; BOTANY BAY(1953), m; I, THE JURY(1953), m; LION IS IN THE STREETS, A(1953), m; MAN ON A TIGHTROPE(1953), m; STALAG 17(1953), m; DEMETRIUS AND THE GLADIATORS(1954), m; PRINCE VALIANT(1954), m; REAR WINDOW(1954), m; SILVER CHALICE, THE(1954), m; THIS IS MY LOVE(1954), m; INDIAN FIGHTER, THE(1955), m; MISTER ROBERTS(1955), m; UNTAMED(1955), m; VIRGIN QUEEN, THE(1955), m; BACK FROM ETERNITY(1955), m; CRIME IN THE STREETS(1956), m; MIRACLE IN THE RAIN(1956), m, md; LOVE IN THE AFTERNOON(1957), m; PEYTON PLACE(1957), m; SAYONARA(1957), m; SPIRIT OF ST. LOUIS, THE(1957), m, md; HOME BEFORE DARK(1958), m; RUN SILENT, RUN DEEP(1958), m; BELOVED INFIDEL(1959), m; CAREER(1959), m; COUNT YOUR BLESSINGS(1959), m; NUN'S STORY, THE(1959), m; CIMARRON(1960), m; STORY OF RUTH, THE(1960), m; SUNRISE AT CAMPOBELLO(1960), m; KING OF THE ROARING TWENTIES–THE STORY OF ARNOLD ROTHSTEIN(1961), m, md; RE-TURN TO PEYTON PLACE(1961), m; ADVENTURES OF A YOUNG MAN(1962), m; MY GEISHA(1962), m; TARAS BULBA(1962), m; LOST COMMAND, THE(1966), m

Harry Waxman
JOURNEY TOGETHER(1946, Brit.), ph; BRIGHTON ROCK(1947, Brit.), ph; FAME IS THE SPUR(1947, Brit.), ph; LOOK BEFORE YOU LOVE(1948, Brit.), ph; MY SISTER AND I(1948, Brit.), ph; GAY LADY, THE(1949, Brit.), ph; GREEN GROW THE RUSHES(1951, Brit.), ph; THEY WERE NOT DIVIDED(1951, Brit.), ph; GLORY AT SEA(1952, Brit.), ph; VALLEY OF EAGLES(1952, Brit.), ph; WATERFRONT WO-MEN(1952, Brit.), ph; LONG MEMORY, THE(1953, Brit.), ph; DETECTIVE, THE(1954, Qit.), ph; GOLDEN LINK, THE(1954, Brit.), ph; MEET MR. CALLAGHAN(1954, Brit.), ph; SLEEPING TIGER, THE(1954, Brit.), ph; CONTRABAND SPAIN(1955, Brit.), ph; HORNET'S NEST, THE(1955, Brit.), ph; SECRET TENT, THE(1956, Brit.), ph; BABY AND THE BATTLESHIP, THE(1957, Brit.), ph; TEARS FOR SIMON(1957, Brit.), ph; TRIPLE DECEPTION(1957, Brit.), ph; INNOCENT SINNERS(1958, Brit.), ph; ROBBERY UNDER ARMS(1958, Brit.), ph; ELEPHANT GUN(1959, Brit.), ph; SAPPHIRE(1959, Brit.), ph; THIRD MAN ON THE MOUNTAIN(1959), ph; SWISS FAMILY ROBINSON(1960), ph; DAY THE EARTH CAUGHT FIRE, THE(1961, Brit.), ph; MAN IN THE MOON(1961, Brit.), ph; ROMAN SPRING OF MRS. STONE, THE(1961, U.S./Brit.), ph; SECRET PARTNER, THE(1961, Brit.), ph; I THANK A FOOL(1962, Brit.), ph; CRACKSMAN, THE(1963, Brit.), ph; FURY AT SMUGGLERS BAY(1963, Brit.), ph; STOLEN HOURS(1963), ph; SWORD OF LANCELOT(1963, Brit.), ph; BARGEE, THE(1964, Brit.), ph; CROOKS IN CLOISTERS(1964, Brit.), ph; NANNY, THE(1965, Brit.), ph; SHE(1965, Brit.), ph; FAMILY WAY, THE(1966, Brit.), ph; ALF 'N' FAMILY(1968, Brit.), ph; DANGER ROUTE(1968, Brit.), ph; TRYGON FACTOR, THE(1969, Brit.), ph; TWISTED NERVE(1969, Brit.), ph; WONDER-WALL(1969, Brit.), ph; SOME WILL, SOME WON'T(1970, Brit.), ph; THERE'S A GIRL IN MY SOUP(1970, Brit.), ph; BEAST IN THE CELLAR, THE(1971, Brit.), ph; ENDLESS NIGHT(1971, Brit.), ph; FLIGHT OF THE DOVES(1971), ph; NIGHT HAIR CHILD(1971, Brit.), ph; CRY OF THE PENGUINS(1972, Brit.), ph; BLUE BLOOD(1973, Brit.), ph; DIGBY, THE BIGGEST DOG IN THE WORLD(1974, Brit.), ph; WICKER MAN, THE(1974, Brit.), ph; JOURNEY INTO FEAR(1976, Can.), ph; PINK PANTHER

STRIKES AGAIN, THE(1976, Brit.), ph; UNCANNY, THE(1977, Brit./Can.), ph; VAM-PYRES, DAUGHTERS OF DRACULA(1977, Brit.), ph

Henry Waxman
ANNIVERSARY, THE(1968, Brit.), ph

Michaelle Waxman
SATAN'S MISTRESS(1982)

Michelle Waxman
NEW YEAR'S EVIL(1980)

Philip A. Waxman
BIG NIGHT, THE(1951), p; YOUNG DON'T CRY, THE(1957), p; GENE KRUPA STORY, THE(1959), p; TELL THEM WILLIE BOY IS HERE(1969), p; GLORY BOY(1971), p

Sam Waxman
BOP GIRL GOES CALYPSO(1957), ed

Sam E. Waxman
MC HALE'S NAVY(1964), ed; MC HALE'S NAVY JOINS THE AIR FORCE(1965), ed; GHOST AND MR. CHICKEN, THE(1966), ed; PERILS OF PAULINE, THE(1967), ed; RELUCTANT ASTRONAUT, THE(1967), ed; COOGAN'S BLUFF(1968), ed; P.J.(1968), ed; ANGEL IN MY POCKET(1969), ed; LOVE GOD?, THE(1969), ed; STRATEGY OF TERROR(1969), ed; HOW TO FRAME A FIGG(1971), ed

Stanley Waxman
FORCE OF EVIL(1948); EAST SIDE, WEST SIDE(1949); JUDGE, THE(1949); MISS GRANT TAKES RICHMOND(1949); SLATTERY'S HURRICANE(1949); NEVER FEAR(1950); TRIAL WITHOUT JURY(1950); HOODLUM EMPIRE(1952); SALO-ME(1953); SATAN'S SATELLITES(1958); JUSTINE(1969)

Stephanie Waxman
Misc. Talkies
ADVERSARY, THE(1970)

Ann Way
HANDS OF ORLAC, THE(1964, Brit./Fr.); PRIME OF MISS JEAN BRODIE, THE(1969, Brit.); DRESSER, THE(1983)

Eileen Way
MR. LORD SAYS NO(1952, Brit.); BLOOD ORANGE(1953, Brit.); SHADOW MAN(1953, Brit.); THEY WHO DARE(1954, Brit.); LOVERS, HAPPY LOVERS!(1955, Brit.); SEA WIFE(1957, Brit.); VIKINGS, THE(1958); VILLAGE OF DAUGHTERS(1962, Brit.); ARRIVEDERCI, BABY!(1966, Brit.); SPHINX(1981)
1984
MEMED MY HAWK(1984, Brit.)

Guy Way
JACKPOT, THE(1950); CHINA VENTURE(1953); FROM HERE TO ETERNITY(1953); INVASION OF THE BODY SNATCHERS(1956); FLAMING STAR(1960)

Jennifer Way
HAIR(1979)

Norman Way
MARY JANE'S PA(1935), w

Richard K. Way
1984
SWING SHIFT(1984)

Lam Way-li
LAST WOMAN OF SHANG, THE(1964, Hong Kong)

Damon Wayans
1984
BEVERLY HILLS COP(1984)

Keenan Ivory Wayans
STAR 80(1983)

John [Fee] Waybill
CRACKING UP(1977); LADIES AND GENTLEMEN, THE FABULOUS STAINS(1982)

Kristina Wayborn
OCTOPUSSY(1983, Brit.)

Stanley Wayburn
Silents
HIS JAZZ BRIDE(1926)

Leon Waycoff [Leon Ames]
CANNONBALL EXPRESS(1932); FAMOUS FERGUSON CASE, THE(1932); MUR-DERS IN THE RUE MORGUE(1932); SILVER DOLLAR(1932); STATE'S ATTOR-NEY(1932); STOWAWAY(1932); SUCCESSFUL CALAMITY, A(1932); THAT'S MY BOY(1932); UPTOWN NEW YORK(1932); ALIMONY MADNESS(1933); FORGOT-TEN(1933); MAN WHO DARED, THE(1933); SHIP OF WANTED MEN(1933); I'LL TELL THE WORLD(1934); RECKLESS(1935); RESCUE SQUAD(1935)

Jack Wayho
Misc. Silents
WIRELESS(1915, Brit.)

Ingrid Wayland
GREAT WALTZ, THE(1972)

Len Wayland
FOR PETE'S SAKE!(1966); LINCOLN CONSPIRACY, THE(1977); AMY(1981)

Sam Waymon
GANJA AND HESS(1973), a, m

Peter Wayn
WOMAN EATER, THE(1959, Brit.); NAKED EDGE, THE(1961)

Sam Waynberg
CUL-DE-SAC(1966, Brit.), p; GATES TO PARADISE(1968, Brit./Ger.), p

Aissa Wayne
ALAMO, THE(1960); COMANCHEROS, THE(1961); DONOVAN'S REEF(1963); MC LINTOCK!(1963)

Antonia Wayne
QUIET MAN, THE(1952)

Bill Wayne
CAGED(1950)

Billy Wayne
WE'RE IN THE MONEY(1935); DANGEROUS(1936); LAW IN HER HANDS, THE(1936); MAN HUNT(1936); THEODORA GOES WILD(1936); CARNIVAL QUEEN(1937); KID GALAHAD(1937); MAN WHO CRIED WOLF, THE(1937); RE-PORTED MISSING(1937); WINGS OVER HONOLULU(1937); AIR DEVILS(1938); AMAZING DR. CLITTERHOUSE, THE(1938); COWBOY AND THE LADY, THE(1938); JURY'S SECRET, THE(1938); LADIES IN DISTRESS(1938); MIDNIGHT IN-TRUDER(1938); MISSING GUEST, THE(1938); STRANGE FACES(1938); TENTH AVENUE KID(1938); EAST SIDE OF HEAVEN(1939); ETERNALLY YOURS(1939); I STOLE A MILLION(1939); INDIANAPOLIS SPEEDWAY(1939); ANGELS OVER BROADWAY(1940); BROTHER RAT AND A BABY(1940); CASTLE ON THE HUD-

SON(1940); SAILOR'S LADY(1940); STAR DUST(1940); STRIKE UP THE BAND(1940); THEY DRIVE BY NIGHT(1940); YOUNG PEOPLE(1940); AFFECTIONATELY YOURS(1941); CITY, FOR CONQUEST(1941); MANPOWER(1941); MILLION DOLLAR BABY(1941); NEVER GIVE A SUCKER AN EVEN BREAK(1941); RISE AND SHINE(1941); BOMBAY CLIPPER(1942); HENRY ALDRICH, EDITOR(1942); HENRY ALDRICH GETS GLAMOUR(1942); MADAME SPY(1942); MAN WHO CAME TO DINNER, THE(1942); MY GAL SAL(1942); ROXIE HART(1942); SIN TOWN(1942); SPRINGTIME IN THE ROCKIES(1942); DIXIE DUGAN(1943); HERS TO HOLD(1943); HE'S MY GUY(1943); HIT THE ICE(1943); PILOT NO. 5(1943); SALUTE FOR THREE(1943); THANK YOUR LUCKY STARS(1943); DESTINY(1944); FOLLOW THE BOYS(1944); GREENWICH VILLAGE(1944); LADIES COURAGEOUS(1944); CONFLICT(1945); SHADY LADY(1945); WONDER MAN(1945); CENTENNIAL SUMMER(1946); DEADLINE AT DAWN(1946); KID FROM BOOKLYN, THE(1946); BRUTE FORCE(1947); MIRACLE OF THE BELLS, THE(1948); RIVER LADY(1948); SITTING PRETTY(1948); STREET WITH NO NAME, THE(1948); FLAMING FURY(1949); GIRL FROM JONES BEACH, THE(1949); LADY GAMBLES, THE(1949); OH, YOU BEAUTIFUL DOLL(1949); JACKIE ROBINSON STORY, THE(1950); JACKPOT, THE(1950); ABBOTT AND COSTELLO MEET THE INVISIBLE MAN(1951); LADY PAYS OFF, THE(1951); BECAUSE OF YOU(1952); LOST IN ALASKA(1952); O. HENRY'S FULL HOUSE(1952); SNIPER, THE(1952); GIRLS IN THE NIGHT(1953); TARANTULA(1955); THESE WILDER YEARS(1956)

Carol Wayne
GUNN(1967); PARTY, THE(1968); SCAVENGER HUNT(1979); SAVANNAH SMILES(1983)
1984
HEARTBREAKERS(1984); SURF II(1984)

Carole Wayne
TWO GIRLS ON BROADWAY(1940)

Carter Wayne
INVISIBLE KILLER, THE(1940), w

Charlie Wayne
BLOOD ON THE SUN(1945)

Chris Wayne
STAKEOUT!(1962)

David Wayne
ADAM'S RIB(1949); PORTRAIT OF JENNIE(1949); MY BLUE HEAVEN(1950); REFORMER AND THE REDHEAD, THE(1950); STELLA(1950); AS YOUNG AS YOU FEEL(1951); M(1951); UP FRONT(1951); I DON'T CARE GIRL, THE(1952); O. HENRY'S FULL HOUSE(1952); WAIT 'TIL THE SUN SHINES, NELLIE(1952); WE'RE NOT MARRIED(1952); WITH A SONG IN MY HEART(1952); DOWN AMONG THE SHELTERING PALMS(1953); HOW TO MARRY A MILLIONAIRE(1953); TONIGHT WE SING(1953); HELL AND HIGH WATER(1954); TENDER TRAP, THE(1955); NAKED HILLS, THE(1956); SAD SACK, THE(1957); THREE FACES OF EVE, THE(1957); LAST ANGRY MAN, THE(1959); BIG GAMBLE, THE(1961); ANDROMEDA STRAIN, THE(1971); FRONT PAGE, THE(1974); HUCKLEBERRY FINN(1974); APPLE DUMPLING GANG, THE(1975); PRIZE FIGHTER, THE(1979)
1984
FINDERS KEEPERS(1984)

Deanna Wayne
TUCSON(1949)

Dennis Wayne
SATAN'S SADISTS(1969), w; SUMMER WISHES, WINTER DREAMS(1973); ECHOES(1983), a, ch

Dorian Wayne
SHE MAN, THE(1967)

Ethel Wayne
Silents
CAPTAIN SWIFT(1914)

Frank Wayne
$1,000,000 RACKET(1937); CODE OF THE CACTUS(1939); MAN FROM TEXAS, THE(1939); SMOKY TRAILS(1939); I WANT A DIVORCE(1940); YOU'LL NEVER GET RICH(1941); MISSION TO MOSCOW(1943); SALUTE FOR THREE(1943); DUFFY'S TAVERN(1945)
Misc. Talkies
LIGHTNING CARSON RIDES AGAIN(1938)

Fredd Wayne
CREST OF THE WAVE(1954, Brit.); GIRL HE LEFT BEHIND, THE(1956); MAN IS ARMED, THE(1956); TORPEDO RUN(1958); TWENTY PLUS TWO(1961); SPIRAL ROAD, THE(1962); SEVEN DAYS IN MAY(1964); SEX AND THE SINGLE GIRL(1964); HANGUP(1974)

Gary Wayne
RAMSBOTTOM RIDES AGAIN(1956, Brit.)

Geoff Wayne
1984
TOP SECRET!(1984)

Hart Wayne
I KILLED GERONIMO(1950)

Harte Wayne
UNKNOWN MAN, THE(1951); MEET ME AT THE FAIR(1952); YOUNG AT HEART(1955)

Jackie Wayne
COUNTERPLOT(1959)

James Wayne
FADE TO BLACK(1980), spec eff

Jan Wayne
CLOWN, THE(1953)

Jason Wayne
Misc. Talkies
BLOOD MONSTER(1972)

Jeff Wayne
MC VICAR(1982, Brit.), m

Jerry Wayne
TAKE ME TO TOWN(1953); AS LONG AS THEY'RE HAPPY(1957, Brit.)

Jess Wayne
HOUSE BY THE LAKE, THE(1977, Can.), stunts; TESTAMENT(1983)

Jesse Wayne
YOUNG FURY(1965); LOVE BUG, THE(1968); RETURN TO MACON COUNTY(1975), stunts; HERBIE GOES TO MONTE CARLO(1977); METEOR(1979); HOPSCOTCH(1980)

Joanee Wayne
TWO BLONDES AND A REDHEAD(1947); JULIA MISBEHAVES(1948); THREE DARING DAUGHTERS(1948); TO THE VICTOR(1948)

John Wayne
SALUTE(1929); BIG TRAIL, THE(1930); CHEER UP AND SMILE(1930); MEN WITHOUT WOMEN(1930); ROUGH ROMANCE(1930); GIRLS DEMAND EXCITEMENT(1931); MAKER OF MEN(1931); MEN ARE LIKE THAT(1931); RANGE FEUD, THE(1931); THREE GIRLS LOST(1931); BIG STAMPEDE, THE(1932); HAUNTED GOLD(1932); LADY AND GENT(1932); RIDE HIM, COWBOY(1932); TEXAS CYCLONE(1932); TWO-FISTED LAW(1932); BABY FACE(1933); CENTRAL AIRPORT(1933); HIS PRIVATE SECRETARY(1933); LIFE OF JIMMY DOLAN, THE(1933); MAN FROM MONTEREY, THE(1933); RIDERS OF DESTINY(1933); SOMEWHERE IN SONORA(1933); TELEGRAPH TRAIL, THE(1933); BLUE STEEL(1934); LUCKY TEXAN, THE(1934); MAN FROM UTAH, THE(1934); 'NEATH THE ARIZONA SKIES(1934); RANDY RIDES ALONE(1934); SAGEBRUSH TRAIL(1934); STAR PACKER, THE(1934); TRAIL BEYOND, THE(1934); WEST OF THE DIVIDE(1934); DAWN RIDER(1935); DESERT TRAIL(1935); LAWLESS FRONTIER, THE(1935); LAWLESS RANGE(1935); NEW FRONTIER, THE(1935); PARADISE CANYON(1935); RAINBOW VALLEY(1935); TEXAS TERROR(1935); KING OF THE PECOS(1936); LAWLESS NINETIES, THE(1936); LONELY TRAIL, THE(1936); OREGON TRAIL, THE(1936); SEA SPOILERS, THE(1936); WESTWARD HO(1936); WINDS OF THE WASTELAND(1936); ADVENTURE'S END(1937); BORN TO THE WEST(1937); CALIFORNIA STRAIGHT AHEAD(1937); CONFLICT(1937); I COVER THE WAR(1937); IDOL OF THE CROWDS(1937); OVERLAND STAGE RAIDERS(1938); PALS OF THE SADDLE(1938); RED RIVER RANGE(1938); SANTA FE STAMPEDE(1938); ALLEGHENY UPRISING(1939); NEW FRONTIER(1939); NIGHT RIDERS, THE(1939); STAGECOACH(1939); THREE TEXAS STEERS(1939); WYOMING OUTLAW(1939); DARK COMMAND, THE(1940); LONG VOYAGE HOME, THE(1940); SEVEN SINNERS(1940); THREE FACES WEST(1940); LADY FOR A NIGHT(1941); LADY FROM LOUISIANA(1941); MAN BETRAYED, A(1941); SHEPHERD OF THE HILLS, THE(1941); FLYING TIGERS(1942); IN OLD CALIFORNIA(1942); PITTSBURGH(1942); REAP THE WILD WIND(1942); REUNION IN FRANCE(1942); SPOILERS, THE(1942); IN OLD OKLAHOMA(1943); LADY TAKES A CHANCE, A(1943); FIGHTING SEABEES, THE(1944); TALL IN THE SADDLE(1944); BACK TO BATAAN(1945); DAKOTA(1945); FLAME OF THE BARBARY COAST(1945); THEY WERE EXPENDABLE(1945); WITHOUT RESERVATIONS(1946); ANGEL AND THE BADMAN(1947), a, p; TYCOON(1947); FORT APACHE(1948); RED RIVER(1948); THREE GODFATHERS(1948); FIGHTING KENTUCKIAN, THE(1949), a, p; SANDS OF IWO JIMA(1949); SHE WORE A YELLOW RIBBON(1949); WAKE OF THE RED WITCH(1949); RIO GRANDE(1950); BULLFIGHTER AND THE LADY(1951), p; FLYING LEATHERNECKS(1951); OPERATION PACIFIC(1951); BIG JIM McLAIN(1952); QUIET MAN, THE(1952); HONDO(1953), a, p; ISLAND IN THE SKY(1953); TROUBLE ALONG THE WAY(1953); HIGH AND THE MIGHTY, THE(1954), a, p; TRACK OF THE CAT(1954), p; BLOOD ALLEY(1955); SEA CHASE, THE(1955); CONQUEROR, THE(1956); SEARCHERS, THE(1956); JET PILOT(1957); LEGEND OF THE LOST(1957, U.S./Panama/Ital.); WINGS OF EAGLES, THE(1957); BARBARIAN AND THE GEISHA, THE(1958); I MARRIED A WOMAN(1958); HORSE SOLDIERS, THE(1959); RIO BRAVO(1959); ALAMO, THE(1960), a, p&d; NORTH TO ALASKA(1960); COMANCHEROS, THE(1961); HATARI!(1962); HOW THE WEST WAS WON(1962); LONGEST DAY, THE(1962); MAN WHO SHOT LIBERTY VALANCE, THE(1962); DONOVAN'S REEF(1963); MC LINTOCK!(1963); CIRCUS WORLD(1964); GREATEST STORY EVER TOLD, THE(1965); IN HARM'S WAY(1965); SONS OF KATIE ELDER, THE(1965); CAST A GIANT SHADOW(1966); EL DORADO(1967); WAR WAGON, THE(1967); GREEN BERETS, THE(1968), a, d; HELLFIGHTERS(1968); TRUE GRIT(1969); UNDEFEATED, THE(1969); CHISUM(1970); RIO LOBO(1970); BIG JAKE(1971); COWBOYS, THE(1972); CAHILL, UNITED STATES MARSHAL(1973); TRAIN ROBBERS, THE(1973); MC Q(1974); BRANNIGAN(1975, Brit.); ROOSTER COGBURN(1975); SHOOTIST, THE(1976)

John Wayne, Jr.
Misc. Talkies
ESCAPE FROM EL DIABLO(1983, U.S./Brit./Span.)

John Ethan Wayne
BIG JAKE(1971)

June Wayne
UP IN ARMS(1944)

Justina Wayne
Misc. Silents
RUNAWAY WIFE, THE(1915)

Keith Wayne
NIGHT OF THE LIVING DEAD(1968)

Ken Wayne
RUGGED O'RIORDANS, THE(1949, Aus.); ON THE BEACH(1959); TWO AND TWO MAKE SIX(1962, Brit.); SMALL WORLD OF SAMMY LEE, THE(1963, Brit.); UP FROM THE BEACH(1965); SOLO FOR SPARROW(1966, Brit.); ON THE RUN(1967, Brit.); HIGH COMMISSIONER, THE(1968, U.S./Brit.); ONE NIGHT STAND(1976, Fr.)
1984
BROTHERS(1984, Aus.)

Mabel Wayne
MARRIAGE BY CONTRACT(1928), m/l

Marie Wayne
Silents
PATCHWORK GIRL OF OZ, THE(1914)
Misc. Silents
MARY'S LAMB(1915); SONG OF SIXPENCE, A(1917)

Marion Wayne
STUNT MAN, THE(1980)

Mark Wayne
SMELL OF HONEY, A SWALLOW OF BRINE! A(1966), m

Maude Wayne
Silents
BY PROXY(1918); AFFAIRS OF ANATOL, THE(1921); MORAN OF THE LADY LETTY(1922); SHIRLEY OF THE CIRCUS(1922); ALIAS THE NIGHT WIND(1923); SILENT PARTNER, THE(1923); SONG OF LOVE, THE(1923); HELD BY THE LAW(1927)
Misc. Silents
CLOSIN' IN(1918); WHO IS TO BLAME?(1918); RISKY BUSINESS(1920); BACHELOR DADDY, THE(1922); HIS FORGOTTEN WIFE(1924)

IT CAME FROM OUTER SPACE(1953), ed; LONE HAND, THE(1953), ed; VEILS OF BAGDAD, THE(1953), ed; ROCKET MAN, THE(1954), ed; LADY GODIVA(1955), ed; SPOILERS, THE(1955), ed; SQUARE JUNGLE, THE(1955), ed; AROUND THE WORLD IN 80 DAYS(1956), ed; NEVER SAY GOODBYE(1956), ed; MAN ON THE PROWL(1957), ed; BIG FISHERMAN, THE(1959), ed; RAISIN IN THE SUN, A(1961), ed; FUN ON A WEEKEND(1979), ed
Silents
  FLYING ROMEOS(1928), ed; OH, KAY(1928), ed; VAMPING VENUS(1928), ed
Rudd Weatherwax
  LASSIE, COME HOME(1943), animal t
Ruddel Weatherwax
Misc. Silents
  CROW'S NEST, THE(1922)
W. S. Weatherwax
Silents
  KINGFISHER'S ROOST, THE(1922)
Alice Weaver
  SWING, SISTER, SWING(1938); FLEET'S IN, THE(1942)
Carl Earl Weaver
  AMERICAN HOT WAX(1978)
Crawford Weaver
  LEGION OF TERROR(1936); CRIMINALS OF THE AIR(1937); DANGER PATROL(1937); SATURDAY'S HEROES(1937); NIGHT SPOT(1938)
Dennis Weaver
  HORIZONS WEST(1952); LAWLESS BREED, THE(1952); RAIDERS, THE(1952); COLUMN SOUTH(1953); GOLDEN BLADE, THE(1953); IT HAPPENS EVERY THURSDAY(1953); LAW AND ORDER(1953); MISSISSIPPI GAMBLER, THE(1953); NEBRASKAN, THE(1953); REDHEAD FROM WYOMING, THE(1953); WAR ARROW(1953); DANGEROUS MISSION(1954); DRAGNET(1954); CHIEF CRAZY HORSE(1955); SEVEN ANGRY MEN(1955); TEN WANTED MEN(1955); STORM FEAR(1956); TOUCH OF EVIL(1958); GALLANT HOURS, THE(1960); DUEL AT DIABLO(1966); WAY...WAY OUT(1966); GENTLE GIANT(1967); MISSION BATANGAS(1968); MAN CALLED SLEDGE, A(1971, Ital.); WHAT'S THE MATTER WITH HELEN?(1971); CHARLOTTE'S WEB(1973), ph
Doodles Weaver
  BEHIND THE HEADLINES(1937); DOUBLE WEDDING(1937); TOPPER(1937); WOMAN I LOVE, THE(1937); HOLD THAT CO-ED(1938); SWING THAT CHEER(1938); YANK AT OXFORD, A(1938); ANOTHER THIN MAN(1939); INVITATION TO HAPPINESS(1939); NIGHT OF NIGHTS, THE(1939); KITTY FOYLE(1940); LI'L ABNER(1940); PAROLE FIXER(1940); GIRL, A GUY AND A GOB, A(1941); GIRL TROUBLE(1942); SPIRIT OF STANFORD, THE(1942); REVEILLE WITH BEVERLY(1943); SALUTE FOR THREE(1943); THIS IS THE ARMY(1943); CAROLINA BLUES(1944); HEY, ROOKIE(1944); KANSAS CITY KITTY(1944); MRS. PARKINGTON(1944); SINCE YOU WENT AWAY(1944); SINGING SHERIFF, THE(1944); STORY OF DR. WASSELL, THE(1944); TWO GIRLS AND A SAILOR(1944); SAN ANTONIO(1945); THOROUGHBREDS(1945); FRONTIER GUN(1958); HOT ROD GANG(1958); TUNNEL OF LOVE, THE(1958); THIRTY FOOT BRIDE OF CANDY ROCK, THE(1959); GREAT IMPOSTOR, THE(1960); ERRAND BOY, THE(1961); LADIES MAN, THE(1961); POCKETFUL OF MIRACLES(1961); RING OF FIRE(1961); BIRDS, THE(1963); IT'S A MAD, MAD, MAD, MAD WORLD(1963); NUTTY PROFESSOR, THE(1963); TAMMY AND THE DOCTOR(1963); KITTEN WITH A WHIP(1964); MAIL ORDER BRIDE(1964); QUICK, BEFORE IT MELTS(1964); TIGER WALKS, A(1964); FLUFFY(1965); ROUNDERS, THE(1965); ZEBRA IN THE KITCHEN(1965); ROSIE!(1967); SPIRIT IS WILLING, THE(1967); CANCEL MY RESERVATION(1972); BIG FOOT(1973); MACON COUNTY LINE(1974); SIX PACK ANNIE(1975); WILD McCULLOCHS, THE(1975); WON TON TON, THE DOG WHO SAVED HOLLYWOOD(1976); EARTHBOUND(1981)
Misc. Talkies
  ROAD TO NASHVILLE(1967); TRUCKIN' MAN(1975); WEST IS STILL WILD, THE(1977)
Elviry Weaver
  MOUNTAIN MOONLIGHT(1941); MOUNTAIN RHYTHM(1942)
Emile Weaver III
  NIGHT OF BLOODY HORROR zero(1969)
Eric Weaver
  MADRON(1970, U.S./Israel), p
Frank Weaver
  DOWN IN ARKANSAW(1938); SWING YOUR LADY(1938); JEEPERS CREEPERS(1939); FRIENDLY NEIGHBORS(1940); GRAND OLE OPRY(1940); IN OLD MISSOURI(1940); ARKANSAS JUDGE(1941); MOUNTAIN MOONLIGHT(1941); TUXEDO JUNCTION(1941); MOUNTAIN RHYTHM(1942); OLD HOMESTEAD, THE(1942); SHEPHERD OF THE OZARKS(1942)
Fritz Weaver
  FAIL SAFE(1964); TO TRAP A SPY(1966); MALTESE BIPPY, THE(1969); COMPANY OF KILLERS(1970); WALK IN THE SPRING RAIN, A(1970); DAY OF THE DOLPHIN, THE(1973); MARATHON MAN(1976); BLACK SUNDAY(1977); DEMON SEED(1977); BIG FIX, THE(1978); JAWS OF SATAN(1980); CREEPSHOW(1982)
H. Duane Weaver
  SURFTIDE 77(1962), p
Hank Weaver
  CALLAWAY WENT THATAWAY(1951); PAT AND MIKE(1952); PRIDE OF ST. LOUIS, THE(1952)
Hanne Weaver
  UNSTRAP ME(1968)
Henry Weaver
Silents
  MANON LESCAUT(1914)
Misc. Silents
  FOR VALOUR(1917)
J. V. A. Weaver
  CLOSE HARMONY(1929), w
Jacki Weaver
  STORK(1971, Aus.); PETERSEN(1974, Aus.); PICNIC AT HANGING ROCK(1975, Aus.); REMOVALISTS, THE(1975, Aus.); CADDIE(1976, Aus.)
1984
  SQUIZZY TAYLOR(1984, Aus.)
Jenny Weaver
  TAWNY PIPIT(1947, Brit.)

Joe Weaver
  WESTERN FRONTIER(1935); SPOILERS OF THE RANGE(1939)
John Weaver
  GOD IS MY WITNESS(1931), w
John D. Weaver
  HOLIDAY AFFAIR(1949), w; DREAMBOAT(1952), d&w
John V.A. Weaver
  WILD PARTY, THE(1929), w; RIVER OF ROMANCE(1929), w; SATURDAY NIGHT KID, THE(1929), w; MAN FROM WYOMING, A(1930), w; POINTED HEELS(1930), w; ROMANCE IN THE RAIN(1934), w; SWEET SURRENDER(1935), w; ADVENTURES OF TOM SAWYER, THE(1938), w
Silents
  CROWD, THE(1928), w
June Weaver [Dlviry]
  FRIENDLY NEIGHBORS(1940); GRAND OLE OPRY(1940); IN OLD MISSOURI(1940); ARKANSAS JUDGE(1941); MOUNTAIN MOONLIGHT(1941); TUXEDO JUNCTION(1941); MOUNTAIN RHYTHM(1942); OLD HOMESTEAD, THE(1942); SHEPHERD OF THE OZARKS(1942); LOVE AND MARRIAGE(1966, Ital.)
Lee Weaver
  LOST MAN, THE(1969); VANISHING POINT(1971); HEAVEN CAN WAIT(1978); HOUSE CALLS(1978); ONION FIELD, THE(1979); KISS ME GOODBYE(1982)
1984
  BUDDY SYSTEM, THE(1984)
Leon Weaver
  DOWN IN ARKANSAW(1938); ROMANCE ON THE RUN(1938); SWING YOUR LADY(1938); JEEPERS CREEPERS(1939); FRIENDLY NEIGHBORS(1940); GRAND OLE OPRY(1940); IN OLD MISSOURI(1940); ARKANSAS JUDGE(1941); MOUNTAIN MOONLIGHT(1941); TUXEDO JUNCTION(1941); MOUNTAIN RHYTHM(1942); OLD HOMESTEAD, THE(1942); SHEPHERD OF THE OZARKS(1942); LOADED PISTOLS(1948); RIDERS OF THE WHISTLING PINES(1949)
Loretta "Elviry" Weaver
  SWING YOUR LADY(1938)
Loretta Weaver
  JEEPERS CREEPERS(1939); FRIENDLY NEIGHBORS(1940); GRAND OLE OPRY(1940); HEROES OF THE SADDLE(1940); IN OLD MISSOURI(1940); ARKANSAS JUDGE(1941); MOUNTAIN MOONLIGHT(1941)
Majorie Weaver
  POLO JOE(1936)
Malcolm Weaver
  MR. QUILP(1975, Brit.); OCTOPUSSY(1983, Brit.), stunts
Malcom Weaver
  RAIDERS OF THE LOST ARK(1981)
Marjorie Weaver
  CHINA CLIPPER(1936); GOLD DIGGERS OF 1937(1936); BIG BUSINESS(1937); CALIFORNIAN, THE(1937); HOT WATER(1937); LIFE BEGINS IN COLLEGE(1937); SECOND HONEYMOON(1937); THIS IS MY AFFAIR(1937); HOLD THAT CO-ED(1938); I'LL GIVE A MILLION(1938); KENTUCKY MOONSHINE(1938); SALLY, IRENE AND MARY(1938); THREE BLIND MICE(1938); CHICKEN WAGON FAMILY(1939); CISCO KID AND THE LADY, THE(1939); HONEYMOON'S OVER, THE(1939); YOUNG MR. LINCOLN(1939); CHARLIE CHAN'S MURDER CRUISE(1940); MARYLAND(1940); MICHAEL SHAYNE, PRIVATE DETECTIVE(1940); MURDER OVER NEW YORK(1940); SHOOTING HIGH(1940); FOR BEAUTY'S SAKE(1941); MAN AT LARGE(1941); MURDER AMONG FRIENDS(1941); JUST OFF BROADWAY(1942); MAD MARTINDALES, THE(1942); MAN WHO WOULDN'T DIE, THE(1942); LET'S FACE IT(1943); PARDON MY RHYTHM(1944); SHADOW OF SUSPICION(1944); YOU CAN'T RATION LOVE(1944); FASHION MODEL(1945); LEAVE IT TO BLONDIE(1945); WE'RE NOT MARRIED(1952)
Ned Weaver
  SLAUGHTER ON TENTH AVENUE(1957)
Paige Weaver
  DO NOT THROW CUSHIONS INTO THE RING(1970)
Paul Weaver
  ON THE NICKEL(1980)
R. M. Weaver
  TOMORROW(1972)
Rachel Weaver
1984
  SCRUBBERS(1984, Brit.)
Rick Weaver
  TRIBES(1970)
Robby Weaver
  GRAND THEFT AUTO(1977); SURVIVAL RUN(1980)
Robert A. Weaver
  NIGHT OF BLOODY HORROR zero(1969), w, ph, ed; WOMEN AND BLOODY TERROR(1970), w, ph, ed
Sigourney Weaver
  ANNIE HALL(1977); ALIEN(1979); EYEWITNESS(1981); YEAR OF LIVING DANGEROUSLY, THE(1982, Aus.); DEAL OF THE CENTURY(1983)
1984
  GHOSTBUSTERS(1984)
Steve Weaver
  HAPPY AS THE GRASS WAS GREEN(1973); HAZEL'S PEOPLE(1978)
William Weaver
  LUDWIG(1973, Ital./Ger./Fr.), w
Winstead "Doodles" Weaver
  SWISS MISS(1938)
Wyn Weaver
  TO WHAT RED HELL(1929, Brit.); THINGS ARE LOOKING UP(1934, Brit.); CHEER UP!(1936, Brit.); EVERYTHING IN LIFE(1936, Brit.); GYPSY MELODY(1936, Brit.); SPORTING LOVE(1936, Brit.); KNIGHTS FOR A DAY(1937, Brit.)
Mark Weavers
  PERSECUTION(1974, Brit.)
The Weavers
  DISC JOCKEY(1951)
Alan Webb
  CHALLENGE TO LASSIE(1949); LEASE OF LIFE(1954, Brit.); WEST OF ZANZIBAR(1954, Brit.); SCAPEGOAT, THE(1959, Brit.); SILENT ENEMY, THE(1959, Brit.); PUMPKIN EATER, THE(1964, Brit.); THIRD SECRET, THE(1964, Brit.); KING RAT(1965); CHIMES AT MIDNIGHT(1967, Span.,Switz.); TAMING OF THE SHREW, THE(1967, U.S./Ital.); INTERLUDE(1968, Brit.); WOMEN IN LOVE(1969, Brit.); EN-

TERTAINING MR. SLOANE(1970, Brit.); KING LEAR(1971, Brit./Den.); NICHOLAS AND ALEXANDRA(1971, Brit.); DUELLISTS, THE(1977, Brit.); GREAT TRAIN ROBBERY, THE(1979, Brit.); ROUGH CUT(1980, Brit.)

Misc. Talkies
DEADLY GAMES(1982)

Alyce Webb
CLAUDINE(1974)

Amy Webb
1984
MEMOIRS(1984, Can.), ed

Austin Webb
Misc. Silents
MASTER OF THE HOUSE, THE(1915)

Bunty Webb
CURTAINS(1983, Can.)

Charles Webb
HEADING FOR HEAVEN(1947), w; GRADUATE, THE(1967), w; MARRIAGE OF A YOUNG STOCKBROKER, THE(1971), w
1984
SIGNAL 7(1984)

Chris Webb
FLASH GORDON(1980)

Christopher Webb
OCTOPUSSY(1983, Brit.), stunts

Clifton Webb
LAURA(1944); DARK CORNER, THE(1946); RAZOR'S EDGE, THE(1946); SITTING PRETTY(1948); MR. BELVEDERE GOES TO COLLEGE(1949); CHEAPER BY THE DOZEN(1950); FOR HEAVEN'S SAKE(1950); ELOPEMENT(1951); MR. BELVEDERE RINGS THE BELL(1951); DREAMBOAT(1952); STARS AND STRIPES FOREVER(1952); MR. SCOUTMASTER(1953); TITANIC(1953); THREE COINS IN THE FOUNTAIN(1954); WOMAN'S WORLD(1954); MAN WHO NEVER WAS, THE(1956, Brit.); BOY ON A DOLPHIN(1957); HOLIDAY FOR LOVERS(1959); REMARKABLE MR. PENNYPACKER, THE(1959); SATAN NEVER SLEEPS(1962)
Misc. Silents
NEW TOYS(1925)

Danny Webb
LAUGH IT OFF(1939); CITY OF MISSING GIRLS(1941)

David Webb
TUNES OF GLORY(1960, Brit.); CONQUEROR WORM, THE(1968, Brit.); WHAT'S NEXT?(1975, Brit.)

Dean Webb
SOME PEOPLE(1964, Brit.)

Denis Webb
FLAMINGO AFFAIR, THE(1948, Brit.); DEATH IS A NUMBER(1951, Brit.); MYSTERY JUNCTION(1951, Brit.); STRANGER IN BETWEEN, THE(1952, Brit.)

Dennis Webb
TRAIN OF EVENTS(1952, Brit.)

Des Webb
EMPIRE STRIKES BACK, THE(1980)

Dick Webb
I WAS A COMMUNIST FOR THE F.B.I.(1951); HELL IS FOR HEROES(1962), spec eff
Silents
KENT, THE FIGHTING MAN(1916, Brit.); POTTER'S CLAY(1922, Brit.)
Misc. Silents
BARNABY(1919, Brit.); CHANNINGS, THE(1920, Brit.); EDGE OF YOUTH, THE(1920, Brit.); STORY OF THE ROSARY, THE(1920, Brit.); CROXLEY MASTER, THE(1921, Brit.); HARD CASH(1921, Brit.); MISS CHARITY(1921, Brit.); YOUNG LOCHINVAR(1923, Brit.)

Don Webb
VIGILANTES RETURN, THE(1947), set d; CLOWN AND THE KID, THE(1961), set d

Elven Webb
RX MURDER(1958, Brit.), art d; CLEOPATRA(1963), art d; TAMING OF THE SHREW, THE(1967, U.S./Ital.), art d; THOSE DARING YOUNG MEN IN THEIR JAUNTY JALOPIES(1969, Fr./Brit./ Ital.), art d; KREMLIN LETTER, THE(1970), art d

Esmond Webb
MIND OF MR. SOAMES, THE(1970, Brit.)

Ferdinand Webb
PENNYWHISTLE BLUES, THE(1952, South Africa), w

Frank Webb
BRIDGE AT REMAGEN, THE(1969); COMPUTER WORE TENNIS SHOES, THE(1970); TOO LATE THE HERO(1970); TODD KILLINGS, THE(1971)

Geoffrey Webb
Silents
DAVID AND JONATHAN(1920, Brit.); SILVER CAR, THE(1921); GOLDEN GIFT, THE(1922)
Misc. Silents
SMART SEX, THE(1921); THREE SEVENS(1921)

George Webb
PAD, THE(AND HOW TO USE IT)* (1966, Brit.), art d; DUDE RANCH(1931); NOW AND FOREVER(1934); WITCHING HOUR, THE(1934); SHE COULDN'T TAKE IT(1935); LONE WOLF RETURNS, THE(1936); GLENROWAN AFFAIR, THE(1951, Aus.); LIST OF ADRIAN MESSENGER, THE(1963), art d; TAMMY AND THE DOCTOR(1963), art d; I'D RATHER BE RICH(1964), art d; ISLAND OF THE BLUE DOLPHINS(1964), art d; THAT FUNNY FEELING(1965), art d; WILD SEED(1965), art d; GHOST AND MR. CHICKEN, THE(1966), art d; MADAME X(1966), art d; GREAT NORTHFIELD, MINNESOTA RAID, THE(1972), art d; PETE 'N' TILLIE(1972), art d; SLAUGHTERHOUSE-FIVE(1972), art d; EIGER SANCTION, THE(1975), art d
Silents
ALARM CLOCK ANDY(1920); BLACK BEAUTY(1921); FIFTY CANDLES(1921); ROMANCE LAND(1923)
Misc. Silents
LIGHT, THE(1916); SINS OF HER PARENT(1916); SOUL OF KURA SAN, THE(1916); BOND OF FEAR, THE(1917); COME THROUGH(1917); FIGHTING GRINGO, THE(1917); IDOLATORS(1917); JOHN PETTICOATS(1919); BELOW THE SURFACE(1920); HOMESPUN FOLKS(1920); FIRST LOVE(1921); SON OF WALLINGFORD, THE(1921); MAN UNDER COVER, THE(1922)

George C. Webb
THOROUGHLY MODERN MILLIE(1967), art d; PRESSURE POINT(1962), art d; GAMBIT(1966), art d; KING'S PIRATE(1967), art d; ROSIE!(1967), art d; MADIGAN(1968), art d; LOST MAN, THE(1969), art d; SWEET CHARITY(1969), art d; I LOVE MY WIFE(1970), art d; AIRPORT 1975(1974), art d; GIRL FROM PETROVKA, THE(1974), art d

Gillian Webb
THIRD KEY, THE(1957, Brit.)

Gordon A. Webb
TRAIN RIDE TO HOLLYWOOD(1975), p

Greg Webb
LORDS OF DISCIPLINE, THE(1983)

Harry Webb
BAR L RANCH(1930), d; BEYOND THE RIO GRANDE(1930), d; WEST OF CHEYENNE(1931), d; COHENS, AND KELLYS IN HOLLYWOOD, THE(1932), ed
Misc. Talkies
RIOT SQUAD(1933), d
Silents
REPUTATION(1921); WEST OF THE RAINBOW'S END(1926), p; PHANTOM OF THE NORTH(1929), d
Misc. Silents
(, d; UNDERWORLD OF LONDON, THE(1915, Brit.); RIDIN' WEST(1924), d; BORDER VENGENCE(1925), d; CACTUS TRAILS(1925), d; CANYON RUSTLERS(1925), d; DESERT MADNESS(1925), d; DOUBLE FISTED(1925), d; SILENT SHELDON(1925), d; STARLIGHT, THE UNTAMED(1925), d; MAN FROM OKLAHOMA, THE(1926), d; STARLIGHT'S REVENGE(1926), d; UNTAMED JUSTICE(1929), d

Harry S. Webb
PHANTOM OF THE DESERT(1930), p, d; RIDIN' LAW(1930), p, d; WESTWARD BOUND(1931), p, d; LONE TRAIL, THE(1932), p, d; FIGHTING HERO(1934), d; RIDING ON(1937), d; EL DIABLO RIDES(1939), p; FEUD OF THE RANGE(1939), p&d; MESQUITE BUCKAROO(1939), p&d; PAL FROM TEXAS, THE(1939), p&d; PORT OF HATE(1939), p&d; SMOKY TRAILS(1939), p; CHEYENNE KID, THE(1940), p; COVERED WAGON TRAILS(1940), p; KID FROM SANTA FE, THE(1940), p; LAND OF THE SIX GUNS(1940), p; PINTO CANYON(1940), p; PIONEER DAYS(1940), p&d; RIDERS FROM NOWHERE(1940), p; WILD HORSE VALLEY(1940), p
Misc. Talkies
CACTUS KID, THE(1934), d; BORN TO BATTLE(1935), d; LARAMIE KID, THE(1935), d; NORTH OF ARIZONA(1935), d; RIDIN' THRU(1935), d; TRACY RIDES(1935), d; TRIGGER TOM(1935), d; UNCONQUERED BANDIT(1935), d; WOLF RIDERS(1935), d; RIDERS OF THE SAGE(1939), d
Misc. Silents
EMPTY SADDLE, THE(1925), d; MYSTERY OF THE LOST RANCH, THE(1925), d; SANTA FE PETE(1925), d

Henry Webb
JAZZ BOAT(1960, Brit.)

I. Webb
WHITE SAVAGE(1943), set d

Ira Webb
EL DIABLO RIDES(1939), d; WILD HORSE VALLEY(1940), d; DEAD MAN'S GOLD(1948), w; MARK OF THE LASH(1948), w; OUTLAW COUNTRY(1949), w; SON OF A BADMAN(1949), w; SON OF BILLY THE KID(1949), w; KING OF THE BULLWHIP(1950), w

Ira S. Webb
ARABIAN NIGHTS(1942), set d; PHANTOM OF THE OPERA(1943), set d; ALI BABA AND THE FORTY THIEVES(1944), set d; CLIMAX, THE(1944), set d; FOLLOW THE BOYS(1944), art d

J. Watson Webb
PERFECT SNOB, THE(1941), ed; GENTLEMAN AT HEART, A(1942), ed; IT HAPPENED IN FLATBUSH(1942), ed; OVER MY DEAD BODY(1942), ed; DIXIE DUGAN(1943), ed; LODGER, THE(1944), ed; SUNDAY DINNER FOR A SOLDIER(1944), ed; WING AND A PRAYER(1944), ed; STATE FAIR(1945), ed; WHERE DO WE GO FROM HERE?(1945), ed; DARK CORNER, THE(1946), ed; RAZOR'S EDGE, THE(1946), ed; SENTIMENTAL JOURNEY(1946), ed; LETTER TO THREE WIVES, A(1948), ed; WITH A SONG IN MY HEART(1952), ed

J. Watson Webb, Jr.
MOON OVER HER SHOULDER(1941), ed; THAT OTHER WOMAN(1942), ed; KISS OF DEATH(1947), ed; MOTHER WORE TIGHTS(1947), ed; CALL NORTHSIDE 777(1948), ed; LUCK OF THE IRISH(1948), ed; FATHER WAS A FULLBACK(1949), ed; YOU'RE MY EVERYTHING(1949), ed; BROKEN ARROW(1950), ed; CHEAPER BY THE DOZEN(1950), ed; I'LL GET BY(1950), ed; JACKPOT, THE(1950), ed; LOVE NEST(1951), ed; MEET ME AFTER THE SHOW(1951), ed; ON THE RIVERA(1951), ed

Jack Webb
HE WALKED BY NIGHT(1948); HOLLOW TRIUMPH(1948); SWORD IN THE DESERT(1949); DARK CITY(1950); MEN, THE(1950); SUNSET BOULEVARD(1950); APPOINTMENT WITH DANGER(1951); HALLS OF MONTEZUMA(1951); YOU'RE IN THE NAVY NOW(1951); DRAGNET(1954), a, d; PETE KELLY'S BLUES(1955), a, p&d; D.I., THE(1957), a, p&d; -30-(1959), a, p&d; LAST TIME I SAW ARCHIE, THE(1961), a, p&d

Jacklin Webb
OF UNKNOWN ORIGIN(1983, Can.)

Jacqueline Webb
GURU, THE MAD MONK(1971)

James Webb
FORGED PASSPORT(1939), w; PRIDE OF THE NAVY(1939), w; S.O.S. TIDAL WAVE(1939), w; RAGS TO RICHES(1941), w; SHERIFF OF TOMBSTONE(1941), w

James R. Webb
BAD MAN OF DEADWOOD(1941), w; JESSE JAMES AT BAY(1941), w; NEVADA CITY(1941), w; SOUTH OF SANTA FE(1942), w; SOUTH OF ST. LOUIS(1949), w; WOMAN IN HIDING(1949), w; MONTANA(1950), w; CLOSE TO MY HEART(1951), w; RATON PASS(1951), w; BIG TREES, THE(1952), w; IRON MISTRESS, THE(1952), w; OPERATION SECRET(1952), w; CHARGE AT FEATHER RIVER, THE(1953), w; APACHE(1954), w; PHANTOM OF THE RUE MORGUE(1954), w; VERA CRUZ(1954), w; ILLEGAL(1955), w; TRAPEZE(1956), w; BIG COUNTRY, THE(1958), w; PORK CHOP HILL(1959), w; CAPE FEAR(1962), w; HOW THE WEST WAS WON(1962), w; KINGS OF THE SUN(1963), w; CHEYENNE AUTUMN(1964), w; GUNS FOR SAN SEBASTIAN(1968, U.S./Fr./Mex./Ital.), w; ALFRED THE GREAT(1969, Brit.), p, w; SINFUL DAVEY(1969), w; HAWAIIANS, THE(1970), w; THEY CALL ME MISTER TIBBS(1970), w

Jane Webb
OUR LEADING CITIZEN(1939); $1,000 A TOUCHDOWN(1939); FARMER'S DAUGHTER, THE(1940)

Janet Webb
FUNNY THING HAPPENED ON THE WAY TO THE FORUM, A(1966)

Jerome Webb
300 SPARTANS, THE(1962), ed

Jerry Webb
TEXAS GUN FIGHTER(1932), ed; ESTHER AND THE KING(1960, U.S./Ital.), ed; FIVE BRANDED WOMEN(1960), ed; UNDER TEN FLAGS(1960, U.S./Ital.), ed

Jim Webb
COAL MINER'S DAUGHTER(1980)

Jimmy Webb
DOC(1971), m; NAKED APE, THE(1973), m; VOICES(1979), m; LAST UNICORN, THE(1982), m

John Webb
FRAULEIN DOKTOR(1969, Ital./Yugo.)

Joy Webb
WONDERFUL LAND OF OZ, THE(1969)

Julie Webb
BILLY JACK(1971)

Ken Webb
TRUE STORY OF ESKIMO NELL, THE(1975, Aus.)

Kenneth Webb
LUCKY IN LOVE(1929), d
Silents
ADVENTURE SHOP, THE(1918), d; MASTER MIND, THE(1920), d&w; JIM THE PENMAN(1921), d; SALVATION NELL(1921), d; SECRETS OF PARIS, THE(1922), d; WITHOUT FEAR(1922), d; JUST SUPPOSE(1926), d
Misc. Silents
ONE THOUSAND DOLLARS(1918), d; GIRL PROBLEM, THE(1919), d; HIS BRIDAL NIGHT(1919), d; WILL YOU BE STAYING FOR SUPPER?(1919), d; DEVIL'S GARDEN, THE(1920), d; FEAR MARKET, THE(1920), d; SINNERS(1920), d; STOLEN KISS, THE(1920), d; TRUTH ABOUT HUSBANDS, THE(1920), d; GREAT ADVENTURE, THE(1921), d; FAIR LADY(1922), d; HIS WIFE'S HUSBAND(1922), d; HOW WOMEN LOVE(1922), d; DARING YEARS, THE(1923), d; THREE O'CLOCK IN THE MORNING(1923), d; BEAUTIFUL CITY, THE(1925), d

Kenneth B. Webb
Misc. Silents
MARIE, LTD.(1919), d

Leigh Webb
STUNT MAN, THE(1980); PURSUIT OF D.B. COOPER, THE(1981)

Lewis Webb
ZOMBIES OF MORA TAU(1957)

Lincoln Webb
SCREAM AND SCREAM AGAIN(1970, Brit.)

Louis K. Webb
Silents
FOOLISH WIVES(1920)

Lynn Webb
MAN WHO LOVED WOMEN, THE(1983)

Mary Webb
WILD HEART, THE(1952, Brit.), w

Mary Ann Webb
WILD WOMEN OF WONGO, THE(1959)

Mary Lou Webb
THUNDERING TRAIL, THE(1951)

Mildred Webb
TAKE A CHANCE(1933)

Millard Webb
GENTLEMEN OF THE PRESS(1929), d; PAINTED ANGEL, THE(1929), d; GLORIFYING THE AMERICAN GIRL(1930), d, w; GOLDEN CALF, THE(1930), d; HAPPY ENDING, THE(1931, Brit.), d
Silents
LITTLE SCHOOL MA'AM, THE(1916); REACHING FOR THE MOON(1917); OLIVER TWIST, JR.(1921), d; SEA BEAST, THE(1926), d; AFFAIR OF THE FOLLIES, AN(1927), d; DROPKICK, THE(1927), d; HONEYMOON FLATS(1928), d
Misc. Silents
WHERE IS MY WANDERING BOY TONIGHT?(1922), d; DARK SWAN, THE(1924), d; HER MARRIAGE VOW(1924), d; MY WIFE AND I(1925), d; GOLDEN COCOON, THE(1926), d; LOVE THRILL, THE(1927), d; NAUGHTY BUT NICE(1927), d

Millard L. Webb
Silents
MOLLY OF THE FOLLIES(1919)

Monica Webb
1984
CALIFORNIA GIRLS(1984), p

Norman Webb
SCHOOL FOR SECRETS(1946, Brit.)

Ormond Webb
DEAD MAN'S GOLD(1948), w

Patricia Webb
VALUE FOR MONEY(1957, Brit.)

Peter Webb
1984
GIVE MY REGARDS TO BROAD STREET(1984, Brit.), d

Ralph Webb
PT 109(1963), spec eff; CHEYENNE AUTUMN(1964), spec eff; MORE DEAD THAN ALIVE(1968), spec eff; GREAT BANK ROBBERY, THE(1969), sp eff; ILLUSTRATED MAN, THE(1969), spec eff; WHICH WAY TO THE FRONT?(1970), spec eff

Richard Webb
HOLD BACK THE DAWN(1941); I WANTED WINGS(1941); SULLIVAN'S TRAVELS(1941); WEST POINT WIDOW(1941); AMERICAN EMPIRE(1942); LADY HAS PLANS, THE(1942); REMARKABLE ANDREW, THE(1942); THIS GUN FOR HIRE(1942); OUT OF THE PAST(1947); VARIETY GIRL(1947); BIG CLOCK, THE(1948); ISN'T IT ROMANTIC?(1948); MY OWN TRUE LOVE(1948); NIGHT HAS A THOUSAND EYES(1948); CONNECTICUT YANKEE IN KING ARTHUR'S COURT, A(1949); SANDS OF IWO JIMA(1949); DISTANT DRUMS(1951); STARLIFT(1951); CARSON CITY(1952); MARA MARU(1952); THIS WOMAN IS DANGEROUS(1952); NEBRASKAN, THE(1953); BLACK DAKOTAS, THE(1954); JUBILEE TRAIL(1954); PRINCE

VALIANT(1954); THREE HOURS TO KILL(1954); ARTISTS AND MODELS(1955); COUNT THREE AND PRAY(1955); PHANTOM STAGECOACH, THE(1957); ON THE BEACH(1959); ATTACK OF THE MAYAN MUMMY(1963, U.S./Mex.); GIT!(1965); TOWN TAMER(1965); CAT, THE(1966); HILLBILLYS IN A HAUNTED HOUSE(1967); HELL RAIDERS(1968); GAY DECEIVERS, THE(1969); BEWARE! THE BLOB(1972)
Misc. Talkies
WEST IS STILL WILD, THE(1977)

Rita Webb
HOLIDAY WEEK(1952, Brit.); BOY AND THE BRIDGE, THE(1959, Brit.); WONDERFUL TO BE YOUNG!(1962, Brit.); BAY OF SAINT MICHEL, THE(1963, Brit.); NO TREE IN THE STREET(1964, Brit.); HE WHO RIDES A TIGER(1966, Brit.); IDOL, THE(1966, Brit.); COP-OUT(1967, Brit.); TO SIR, WITH LOVE(1967, Brit.); MAN OUTSIDE, THE(1968, Brit.); MRS. BROWN, YOU'VE GOT A LOVELY DAUGHTER(1968, Brit.); STRANGE AFFAIR(1968, Brit.); PERCY(1971, Brit.); UP POMPEII(1971, Brit.); CONFESSIONS OF A POP PERFORMER(1975, Brit.); VENOM(1982, Brit.)

Robert Webb
FIGHTING PLAYBOY(1937); IN OLD CHICAGO(1938), d; TAKE MY LIFE(1942); CARIBBEAN MYSTERY, THE(1945), d; SPIDER, THE(1945), d; WHITE FEATHER(1955), d; LITTLE OF WHAT YOU FANCY, A(1968, Brit.), d; TO BE FREE(1972)
Misc. Talkies
IMAGO(1970)

Robert D. Webb
BENEATH THE 12-MILE REEF(1953), d; GLORY BRIGADE, THE(1953), d; SEVEN CITIES OF GOLD(1955), p, d; LOVE ME TENDER(1956), d; ON THE THRESHOLD OF SPACE(1956), d; PROUD ONES, THE(1956), d; WAY TO THE GOLD, THE(1957), d; GUNS OF THE TIMBERLAND(1960), d; PIRATES OF TORTUGA(1961), d; SEVEN WOMEN FROM HELL(1961), d; CAPETOWN AFFAIR(1967, U.S./South Afr.), p&d; JACKALS, THE(1967, South Africa), p&d

Roger Webb
BARTLEBY(1970, Brit.), m; ONE BRIEF SUMMER(1971, Brit.), m&md; BURKE AND HARE(1972, Brit.), m; GODSEND, THE(1980, Can.), m

Roy Webb
WITHOUT RESERVATIONS(1946), m; THEY WON'T BELIEVE ME(1947), m; COCK-EYED CAVALIERS(1934), md; ANOTHER FACE(1935), md; ARIZONIAN, THE(1935), md; BECKY SHARP(1935), m; IN PERSON(1935), md; LAST DAYS OF POMPEII, THE(1935), m; OLD MAN RHYTHM(1935), md; RAINMAKERS, THE(1935), md; BRIDE WALKS OUT, THE(1936), md; EX-MRS. BRADFORD, THE(1936), md; LAST OF THE MOHICANS, THE(1936), md; MUMMY'S BOYS(1936), m; MURDER ON A BRIDLE PATH(1936), md; MUSS 'EM UP(1936), md; PLOUGH AND THE STARS, THE(1936), m; SILLY BILLIES(1936), md; SYLVIA SCARLETT(1936), md; WINTERSET(1936), m; WOMAN REBELS, A(1936), m; FORTY NAUGHTY GIRLS(1937), md; HIGH FLYERS(1937), md; LIFE OF THE PARTY, THE(1937), md; MEET THE MISSUS(1937), md; NEW FACES OF 1937(1937), md; ON AGAIN–OFF AGAIN(1937), md; OUTCASTS OF POKER FLAT, THE(1937), md; QUALITY STREET(1937), m; SEA DEVILS(1937), md; STAGE DOOR(1937), m, md; WOMAN I LOVE, THE(1937), md; AFFAIRS OF ANNABEL(1938), md; BRINGING UP BABY(1938), m; CRIME RING(1938), md; GO CHASE YOURSELF(1938), md; GUN LAW(1938), md; HAVING WONDERFUL TIME(1938), m; I'M FROM THE CITY(1938), md; LAW WEST OF TOMBSTONE, THE(1938), md; LAWLESS VALLEY(1938), md; MAD MISS MANTON, THE(1938), m; MAN TO REMEMBER, A(1938), m; MR. DOODLE KICKS OFF(1938), md; NEXT TIME I MARRY(1938), md; RENEGADE RANGER(1938), md; ROOM SERVICE(1938), md; VIVACIOUS LADY(1938), m; ARIZONA LEGION(1939), md; FIVE CAME BACK(1939), m; GIRL FROM MEXICO, THE(1939), md; IN NAME ONLY(1939), m; LOVE AFFAIR(1939), m; PANAMA LADY(1939), md; RENO(1939), md; SAINT STRIKES BACK, THE(1939), md; SORORITY HOUSE(1939), md; THEY MADE HER A SPY(1939), ed; THREE SONS(1939), m; TWO THOROUGH-BREDS(1939), m; ABE LINCOLN IN ILLINOIS(1940), m; CROSS COUNTRY ROMANCE(1940), md; I'M STILL ALIVE(1940), m; KITTY FOYLE(1940), m; LADDIE(1940), m; LET'S MAKE MUSIC(1940), md; LITTLE MEN(1940), m; MARINES FLY HIGH, THE(1940), md; MEXICAN SPITFIRE OUT WEST(1940), m; MILLIONAIRES IN PRISON(1940), m; MY FAVORITE WIFE(1940), m; SAINT'S DOUBLE TROUBLE, THE(1940), m; STRANGER ON THE THIRD FLOOR(1940), m; SUED FOR LIBEL(1940), m; YOU CAN'T FOOL YOUR WIFE(1940), m; YOU'LL FIND OUT(1940), md; DEVIL AND MISS JONES, THE(1941), m; FATHER TAKES A WIFE(1941), m; LOOK WHO'S LAUGHING(1941), m; MR. AND MRS. SMITH(1941), m; OBLIGING YOUNG LADY(1941), m; PARACHUTE BATTALION(1941), m; SAINT IN PALM SPRINGS, THE(1941), m; TOM, DICK AND HARRY(1941), m; ARMY SURGEON(1942), m; BIG STREET, THE(1942), m; CAT PEOPLE(1942), m; FALCON'S BROTHER, THE(1942), m; HIGHWAYS BY NIGHT(1942), m; HITLER'S CHILDREN(1942), m; I MARRIED A WITCH(1942), m; JOAN OF PARIS(1942), m; JOURNEY INTO FEAR(1942), m; MAGNIFICENT AMBERSONS, THE(1942), m; MY FAVORITE SPY(1942), m; POWDER TOWN(1942), md; BEHIND THE RISING SUN(1943), m; BOMBARDIER(1943), m; FALLEN SPARROW, THE(1943), m; FLIGHT FOR FREEDOM(1943), m; GANGWAY FOR TOMORROW(1943), m; GHOST SHIP, THE(1943), m; HIGHER AND HIGHER(1943), m; I WALKED WITH A ZOMBIE(1943), m; IRON MAJOR, THE(1943), m; LADIES' DAY(1943), m; LADY TAKES A CHANCE, A(1943), m; LEOPARD MAN, THE(1943), m; MR. LUCKY(1943), m; PETTICOAT LARCENY(1943), m; SEVENTH VICTIM, THE(1943), m; EXPERIMENT PERILOUS(1944), m; MARINE RAIDERS(1944), m; MASTER RACE, THE(1944), m; PASSPORT TO DESTINY(1944), m; RAINBOW ISLAND(1944), m; SEVENTH CROSS, THE(1944), m; TALL IN THE SADDLE(1944), m; BACK TO BATAAN(1945), m; BETRAYAL FROM THE EAST(1945), m; BODY SNATCHER, THE(1945), m; CHINA SKY(1945), m; CORNERED(1945), m; DICK TRACY(1945), m; ENCHANTED COTTAGE, THE(1945), m; LOVE, HONOR AND GOODBYE(1945), m; MURDER, MY SWEET(1945), m; THOSE ENDEARING YOUNG CHARMS(1945), m; TWO O'CLOCK COURAGE(1945), m; ZOMBIES ON BROADWAY(1945), m; BADMAN'S TERRITORY(1946), m; BEDLAM(1946), m; LOCKET, THE(1946), m; NOTORIOUS(1946), m; SPIRAL STAIRCASE, THE(1946), m; WELL-GROOMED BRIDE, THE(1946), m; CASS TIMBERLANE(1947), m; CROSSFIRE(1947), m; EASY COME, EASY GO(1947), m; MAGIC TOWN(1947), m; OUT OF THE PAST(1947), m; RIFFRAFF(1947), m; SINBAD THE SAILOR(1947), m; FIGHTING FATHER DUNNE(1948), m; I REMEMBER MAMA(1948), m; RACE STREET(1948), m; RACHEL AND THE STRANGER(1948), m; EASY LIVING(1949), m; HOLIDAY AFFAIR(1949), m; MY FRIEND IRMA(1949), m; WINDOW, THE(1949), m; SECRET FURY, THE(1950), m; VENDETTA(1950), m; WHERE DANGER LIVES(1950), m; WHITE TOWER, THE(1950), m; AT SWORD'S POINT(1951), m; BRANDED(1951), m; FIXED BAYONETS(1951), m; FLYING LEATHERNECKS(1951), m; HARD, FAST, AND BEAUTIFUL(1951), m; RACKET, THE(1951), m; CLASH BY NIGHT(1952), m; GIRL IN EVERY PORT, A(1952), m; LUSTY MEN, THE(1952), m; OPERATION SECRET(1952), m; HOUDINI(1953), m; SECOND CHANCE(1953), m; SPLIT SECOND(1953), m; DANGEROUS MIS-

SION(1954), m; RAID, THE(1954), m; SHE COULDN'T SAY NO(1954), m; TRACK OF THE CAT(1954), m; AMERICANO, THE(1955), m; BENGAZI(1955), m; BLOOD ALLEY(1955), m; KENTUCKIAN, THE(1955), md; MARTY(1955), m; SEA CHASE, THE(1955), m; UNDERWATER!(1955), m; FIRST TEXAN, THE(1956), m; GIRL HE LEFT BEHIND, THE(1956), m; OUR MISS BROOKS(1956), m; RIVER CHANGES, THE(1956), m; SHOOT-OUT AT MEDICINE BEND(1957), m; TOP SECRET AFFAIR(1957), m; TEACHER'S PET(1958), m
Silents
SALVATION NELL(1921), art d
Sarah Webb
MR. QUILP(1975, Brit.)
Seward Webb
BACK STREET(1941), art d
Tom Webb
ONE-EYED JACKS(1961)
Tommy Webb
MORITURI(1965)
Walter Prescott Webb
TEXAS RANGERS, THE(1936), w
Wanda Webb
THUNDERBIRD 6(1968, Brit.), puppeteer
Wiliam Webb
1984
CALIFORNIA GIRLS(1984), p
William Webb
1984
CALIFORNIA GIRLS(1984), d&w
William H. Webb
BADLANDERS, THE(1958), ed
Andrew Lloyd Webber
GUMSHOE(1972, Brit.), m; JESUS CHRIST, SUPERSTAR(1973), w; ODESSA FILE, THE(1974, Brit./Ger.), m
Austin Webber
Misc. Silents
L' APACHE(1919)
Bickford Otis Webber
Misc. Talkies
RUNAWAY(1971), d
Byron Webber
REMBRANDT(1936, Brit.)
Chad Webber
SNOOPY, COME HOME(1972)
Rev. Charles Webber
NATIVE LAND(1942)
Dean Webber
DIRTY HARRY(1971)
Diane Webber
GHOST DIVER(1957); MERMAIDS OF TIBURON, THE(1962); WITCHMAKER, THE(1969); TRIAL OF BILLY JACK, THE(1974)
Misc. Talkies
SINTHIA THE DEVIL'S DOLL(1970)
Ethel Webber
Silents
MEDIATOR, THE(1916), w
George Webber
HOUSE OF SECRETS(1929), ph; BIRTH OF A BABY(1938), ph; FOLLIES GIRL(1943), ph; BOY! WHAT A GIRL(1947), ph; SEPIA CINDERELLA(1947), ph
Silents
TILLIE'S TOMATO SURPRISE(1915), ph; AMERICAN WIDOW, AN(1917), ph; GO WEST, YOUNG MAN(1919), ph; JUST OUT OF COLLEGE(1921), ph; EXCITERS, THE(1923), ph; NIGHT LIFE OF NEW YORK(1925), ph; FINE MANNERS(1926), ph; SO'S YOUR OLD MAN(1926), ph; UNTAMED LADY, THE(1926), ph; JOY GIRL, THE(1927), ph
George F. Webber
Silents
WHAT HAPPENED TO ROSA?(1921), ph
Hamilton Webber
BROKEN MELODY(1938, Aus.), md; DAD AND DAVE COME TO TOWN(1938, Aus.), m; MR. CHEDWORTH STEPS OUT(1939, Aus.), md
Harry Webber
LITTLE ONES, THE(1965, Brit.), makeup
Henry Webber
Silents
OUTLAWED(1929), ed
Herman Webber
DAMN CITIZEN(1958), p
Herman E. Webber
CANADIANS, THE(1961, Brit.), p
John Webber
MAN IN THE MOON(1961, Brit.), makeup; TWINS OF EVIL(1971, Brit.), makeup; HOUND OF THE BASKERVILLES, THE(1983, Brit.), makeup; SIGN OF FOUR, THE(1983, Brit.), makeup; XTRO(1983, Brit.), makeup
Lou Ann Webber
MICROWAVE MASSACRE(1983)
Marion Webber
PASSION HOLIDAY(1963)
Peggy Webber
HER ADVENTUROUS NIGHT(1946); LITTLE MISS BIG(1946); MACBETH(1948); JOURNEY INTO LIGHT(1951); SUBMARINE COMMAND(1951); WRONG MAN, THE(1956); SCREAMING SKULL, THE(1958); SPACE CHILDREN, THE(1958)
Phillip Webber
RUBY(1971)
R. Byron Webber
Silents
MARY LATIMER, NUN(1920, Brit.), w; AFTERWARDS(1928, Brit.), w
Richard Webber
NOTHING BUT A MAN(1964)

Robert Webber
$(DOLLARS)(1971); HIGHWAY 301(1950); 12 ANGRY MEN(1957); NUN AND THE SERGEANT, THE(1962); STRIPPER, THE(1963); HYSTERIA(1965, Brit.); SANDPIPER, THE(1965); THIRD DAY, THE(1965); DEAD HEAT ON A MERRY-GO-ROUND(1966); HARPER(1966); SILENCERS, THE(1966); DIRTY DOZEN, THE(1967, Brit.); DON'T MAKE WAVES(1967); HIRED KILLER, THE(1967, Fr./Ital.); MANON 70(1968, Fr.); BIG BOUNCE, THE(1969); GREAT WHITE HOPE, THE(1970); BRING ME THE HEAD OF ALFREDO GARCIA(1974); MIDWAY(1976); CHOIRBOYS, THE(1977); CASEY'S SHADOW(1978); REVENGE OF THE PINK PANTHER(1978); 10(1979); PRIVATE BENJAMIN(1980); SUNDAY LOVERS(1980, Ital./Fr.); S.O.B.(1981); WRONG IS RIGHT(1982); FINAL OPTION, THE(1983, Brit.)
Timothy Webber
TERROR TRAIN(1980, Can.); GREY FOX, THE(1983, Can.)
1984
HOTEL NEW HAMPSHIRE, THE(1984)
Tom Webber
VORTEX(1982)
W. Hamilton Webber
TALL TIMBERS(1937, Aus.), m
Andre Weber
WOMAN OF SIN(1961, Fr.); GREAT SPY CHASE, THE(1966, Fr.); MAGNIFICENT ONE, THE(1974, Fr./Ital.); THAT OBSCURE OBJECT OF DESIRE(1977, Fr./Span.)
Andrea Weber
THEY ALL LAUGHED(1981)
Anton Weber
LA HABANERA(1937, Ger.), set d
Billy Weber
DAYS OF HEAVEN(1978), ed; JEKYLL AND HYDE...TOGETHER AGAIN(1982), ed; 48 HOURS(1982), ed
1984
BEVERLY HILLS COP(1984), ed; HOUSE OF GOD, THE(1984), ed; ICEMAN(1984), ed
Bonita Weber
KISS AND MAKE UP(1934); YOU CAN'T HAVE EVERYTHING(1937); IDIOT'S DELIGHT(1939)
Carmen Weber
COUSINS IN LOVE(1982)
Dave Weber
PALS OF THE SADDLE(1938)
David Weber
WHOLE SHOOTIN' MATCH, THE(1979)
Dick Weber
DREAMER(1979)
Dominique Weber
GREAT WALTZ, THE(1972)
Elsa Weber
SNIPER, THE(1952)
Erzsebeth Weber
1984
QUESTION OF SILENCE(1984, Neth.)
Ester Weber
COUSINS IN LOVE(1982)
Ethel Weber
Misc. Silents
EYE OF GOD, THE(1916)
Fern Weber
KING KONG(1976), cos
Franz Weber
TRUNKS OF MR. O.F., THE(1932, Ger.); PILLARS OF SOCIETY(1936, Ger.); INTERMEZZO(1937, Ger.)
Fred Weber
DRESSED TO KILL(1980)
Gary Weber
JOE(1970)
Georg Weber
LAST WALTZ, THE(1936, Brit.), w
George Weber
SYNCOPATION(1929), ph; NIGHT GAMES(1980)
Gertrude Weber
YOU CAN'T TAKE IT WITH YOU(1938)
Henry Weber
HAPPY-GO-LUCKY(1937), ed
Silents
OLYMPIC HERO, THE(1928), ed
Ingeborg Weber
GERMAN SISTERS, THE(1982, Ger.)
Jacques Weber
STATE OF SIEGE(1973, Fr./U.S./Ital./Ger.); WOMAN WITH RED BOOTS, THE(1977, Fr./Span.); ADOLESCENT, THE(1978, Fr./W.Ger.)
Joe Weber
LILLIAN RUSSELL(1940)
Misc. Silents
FRIENDLY ENEMIES(1925)
Joseph Weber
Misc. Silents
MORTMAIN(1915)
Juliet Weber
1984
SECRET HONOR(1984), ed
Karl Weber
LOST ONE, THE(1951, Ger.), art d; WALK EAST ON BEACON(1952)
Kurt Weber
SALTO(1966, Pol.), ph
Larry Weber
BELIEVE IN ME(1971)
Lois Weber
WHITE HEAT(1934), d, w
Silents
FALSE COLORS(1914), a, d, w; HYPOCRITES(1914), d&w; JOHN BARLEYCORN(1914), w; OPENED SHUTTERS, THE(1914), w; IT'S NO LAUGHING

MATTER(1915), d&w; SCANDAL(1915), a, d, w; DUMB GIRL OF PORTICI(1916), d, w; HOP, THE DEVIL'S BREW(1916), a, d, w; JOHN NEEDHAM'S DOUBLE(1916), d; SAVING THE FAMILY NAME(1916), d, w; EVEN AS YOU AND I(1917), d; MIDNIGHT ROMANCE, A(1919), d&w; BLOT, THE(1921), d&w; WHAT DO MEN WANT?(1921), p,d&w; MARRIAGE CLAUSE, THE(1926), d&w; ANGEL OF BROADWAY, THE(1927), d; SENSATION SEEKERS(1927), d&w

Misc. Silents
MERCHANT OF VENICE, THE(1914); JEWEL(1915), d; EYE OF GOD, THE(1916), a, d; FLIRT, THE(1916), d; IDLE WIVES(1916), a, d; PEOPLE VS. JOHN DOE, THE(1916), d; SHOES(1916), d; WANTED - A HOME(1916), d; WHERE ARE MY CHILDREN?(1916), d; HAND THAT ROCKS THE CRADLE, THE(1917), a, d; MYSTERIOUS MRS. M, THE(1917), d; BORROWED CLOTHES(1918), d; DOCTOR AND THE WOMAN, THE(1918), d; FOR HUSBANDS ONLY(1918), d; PRICE OF A GOOD TIME, THE(1918), d; SCANDAL MONGERS(1918), a, d; FORBIDDEN(1919), d; HOME(1919), d; MARY REGAN(1919), d; WHEN A GIRL LOVES(1919), d; TO PLEASE ONE WOMAN(1920), d; TOO WISE WIVES(1921), d; WHAT'S WORTH WHILE?(1921), d; CHAPTER IN HER LIFE, A(1923), d

Lou Weber
HAPPY THIEVES, THE(1962)

Love Jean Weber
MOONLIGHT IN HAVANA(1942)

Meta Weber
DECISION BEFORE DAWN(1951)

Michael Albert Weber
Misc. Talkies
STREET GIRLS(1975)

Nancy Weber
HIDE IN PLAIN SIGHT(1980)

Paul Weber
THAT HAGEN GIRL(1947); SOLID GOLD CADILLAC, THE(1956); GARMENT JUNGLE, THE(1957); NIGHT RUNNER, THE(1957)

Rex Weber
TRANSATLANTIC MERRY-GO-ROUND(1934)

Richard Weber
TWELVE TO THE MOON(1960); PHANTOM PLANET, THE(1961); DARK SIDE OF TOMORROW, THE(1970), ed; JOE HILL(1971, Swed./U.S.), a, w; FARMER, THE(1977), ed

Rick Weber
MORITURI(1965)

Rolf Weber
DAS BOOT(1982)

Rossano Weber
LEAP INTO THE VOID(1982, Ital.)

Sabina Weber
SKATEBOARD(1978)

Serge Weber
NAUGHTY ARLETTE(1951, Brit.), w

Sharon Weber
LIFEGUARD(1976); BILLION DOLLAR HOBO, THE(1977); LITTLE DRAGONS, THE(1980)

Steven Weber
1984
FLAMINGO KID, THE(1984)

Suzanne Weber
PLEASANTVILLE(1976); COLD RIVER(1982)

Tania Weber
ROMAN HOLIDAY(1953); ULYSSES(1955, Ital.); UNFAITHFULS, THE(1960, Ital.); SHIP OF CONDEMNED WOMEN, THE(1963, ITAL.); DAY IN COURT, A(1965, Ital.)

Timothy Weber
TICKET TO HEAVEN(1981)

Wayne Weber
ILLIAC PASSION, THE(1968)

William Weber
HAPPY LAND(1943)

Weber and Fields
BLOSSOMS ON BROADWAY(1937)
Silents
TWO FLAMING YOUTHS(1927)

A.J. Weberman
PLEASE STAND BY(1972)

Anton Webern
GOSPEL ACCORDING TO ST. MATTHEW, THE(1966, Fr., Ital.), m

John Webley
MIKADO, THE(1967, Brit.)

Peggy Webling
FRANKENSTEIN(1931), w

Al Webster
BACK DOOR TO HEAVEN(1939)

Beatrice Webster
TOP OF THE HEAP(1972)

Ben Webster
LYONS MAIL, THE(1931, Brit.); THREADS(1932, Brit.); ONE PRECIOUS YEAR(1933, Brit.); DRAKE THE PIRATE(1935, Brit.); OLD CURIOSITY SHOP, THE(1935, Brit.); ELIZA COMES TO STAY(1936, Brit.); PRISONER OF ZENDA, THE(1937); CONQUEST OF THE AIR(1940); EARL OF CHICAGO(1940); SUSPICION(1941); MRS. MINIVER(1942); FOREVER AND A DAY(1943); LASSIE, COME HOME(1943)
Silents
HOUSE OF TEMPERLEY, THE(1913, Brit.); GAY LORD QUEX, THE(1917, Brit.); IF THOU WERT BLIND(1917, Brit.); PROFLIGATE, THE(1917, Brit.); NOBODY'S CHILD(1919, Brit.); 12-10(1919, Brit.); CALL OF YOUTH, THE(1920, Brit.); MIRIAM ROZELLA(1924, Brit.); ONLY WAY, THE(1926, Brit.); WHEN BOYS LEAVE HOME(1928, Brit.)
Misc. Silents
BOOTLE'S BABY(1914, Brit.); ENOCH ARDEN(1914, Brit.); LIBERTY HALL(1914, Brit.); CYNTHIA IN THE WILDERNESS(1916, Brit.); HIS DAUGHTER'S DILEMMA(1916, Brit.); VICAR OF WAKEFIELD, THE(1916, Brit.); BECAUSE(1918, Brit.)

Bob Webster
ORPHANS OF THE NORTH(1940)

Misc. Silents
BLACK HILLS(1929)

Brett Webster
SCALPS(1983), ph

Byron Webster
ON A CLEAR DAY YOU CAN SEE FOREVER(1970); POSEIDON ADVENTURE, THE(1972); THAT MAN BOLT(1973); HEAVEN CAN WAIT(1978); TIME AFTER TIME(1979, Brit.); NUDE BOMB, THE(1980); ONLY WHEN I LAUGH(1981)

Carol Webster
RAINBOW OVER BROADWAY(1933), w; NOTORIOUS BUT NICE(1934), w

Charles Webster
GOOD MORNING, MISS DOVE(1955); HELL BOUND(1957)

Christopher Webster
WEEKEND OF SHADOWS(1978, Aus.), art d; FIGHTING BACK(1983, Brit.), art d

Chuck Webster
DRANGO(1957); HOT ROD RUMBLE(1957)

Daniel R. Webster
YOUNG GIANTS(1983), art d

David Webster
CHEER THE BRAVE(1951, Brit.), p; SECONDS(1966), ed

Derek Webster
ENTER THE NINJA(1982)

Diana Webster
1984
ICE PIRATES, THE(1984)

Dick Webster [Tony Martin]
POOR LITTLE RICH GIRL(1936)

Donald Webster
STRAW DOGS(1971, Brit.); MACKINTOSH MAN, THE(1973, Brit.)

Ferris Webster
HARRIGAN'S KID(1943), ed; SWING FEVER(1943), ed; RATIONING(1944), ed; DANGEROUS PARTNERS(1945), ed; PICTURE OF DORIAN GRAY, THE(1945), ed; HOODLUM SAINT, THE(1946), ed; UNDERCURRENT(1946), ed; IF WINTER COMES(1947), ed; LIVING IN A BIG WAY(1947), ed; ON AN ISLAND WITH YOU(1948), ed; DOCTOR AND THE GIRL, THE(1949), ed; MADAME BOVARY(1949), ed; FATHER OF THE BRIDE(1950), ed; MAGNIFICENT YANKEE, THE(1950), ed; MYSTERY STREET(1950), ed; PLEASE BELIEVE ME(1950), ed; FATHER'S LITTLE DIVIDEND(1951), ed; KIND LADY(1951), ed; GIRL IN WHITE, THE(1952), ed; LONE STAR(1952), ed; ALL THE BROTHERS WERE VALIANT(1953), ed; LILI(1953), ed; SCANDAL AT SCOURIE(1953), ed; LONG, LONG TRAILER, THE(1954), ed; BLACKBOARD JUNGLE, THE(1955), ed; GLASS SLIPPER, THE(1955), ed; FASTEST GUN ALIVE(1956), ed; FORBIDDEN PLANET(1956), ed; RANSOM(1956), ed; TEA AND SYMPATHY(1956), ed; LES GIRLS(1957), ed; SOMETHING OF VALUE(1957), ed; CAT ON A HOT TIN ROOF(1958), ed; HIGH COST OF LOVING, THE(1958), ed; LAW AND JAKE WADE, THE(1958), ed; GREEN MANSIONS(1959), ed; NEVER SO FEW(1959), ed; KEY WITNESS(1960), ed; MAGNIFICENT SEVEN, THE(1960), ed; BY LOVE POSSESSED(1961), ed; THUNDER OF DRUMS, A(1961), ed; MANCHURIAN CANDIDATE, THE(1962), ed; SERGEANTS 3(1962), ed; GREAT ESCAPE, THE(1963), ed; SEVEN DAYS IN MAY(1964), ed; HALLELUJAH TRAIL, THE(1965), ed; SATAN BUG, THE(1965), ed; SECONDS(1966), ed; DIVORCE AMERICAN STYLE(1967), ed; HOUR OF THE GUN(1967), ed; ICE STATION ZEBRA(1968), ed; START THE REVOLUTION WITHOUT ME(1970), ed; ZIGZAG(1970), ed; GLORY BOY(1971), ed; ORGANIZATION, THE(1971), ed; JOE KIDD(1972), ed; BREEZY(1973), ed; HIGH PLAINS DRIFTER(1973), ed; MAGNUM FORCE(1973), ed; THUNDERBOLT AND LIGHTFOOT(1974), ed; EIGER SANCTION, THE(1975), ed; ENFORCER, THE(1976), ed; OUTLAW JOSEY WALES, THE(1976), ed; GAUNTLET, THE(1977), ed; EVERY WHICH WAY BUT LOOSE(1978), ed; ESCAPE FROM ALCATRAZ(1979), ed; ANY WHICH WAY YOU CAN(1980), ed; BRONCO BILLY(1980), ed; FIREFOX(1982), ed; HONKYTONK MAN(1982), ed

Flip Webster
REMEMBRANCE(1982, Brit.)

Frank Webster
MILLIONS LIKE US(1943, Brit.); OLD MOTHER RILEY, DETECTIVE(1943, Brit.); YANK IN LONDON, A(1946, Brit.); MIRANDA(1949, Brit.); TIGHT LITTLE ISLAND(1949, Brit.); FOUR AGAINST FATE(1952, Brit.); CONSTANT HUSBAND, THE(1955, Brit.); TECKMAN MYSTERY, THE(1955, Brit)
Silents
LESSONS IN LOVE(1921)

Fred Webster
INGAGI(1931), ph

George Webster
FRANCIS GOES TO THE RACES(1951)
Misc. Silents
BECAUSE(1918, Brit.)

Harry Webster
ADVENTURESS, THE(1946, Brit.); CAPTAIN BOYCOTT(1947, Brit.); DEAD MAN'S EVIDENCE(1962, Brit.)

Harry McRae Webster
Silents
DEVIL'S PLAYGROUND, THE(1918), d
Misc. Silents
VICTORY OF VIRTUE, THE(1915), d; RECLAIMED(1918), d

Henry Kitchell Webster
Silents
GREAT ADVENTURE, THE(1918), w; REAL ADVENTURE, THE(1922), w; WHAT FOOLS MEN(1925), w

Henry McRae Webster
Misc. Silents
HEART OF A GYPSY, THE(1919), d

Howard Webster
Silents
LURE OF THE YUKON(1924)
Misc. Silents
CHECHAHCOS, THE(1924); NORTH OF NOME(1925)

Hugh Webster
KING OF THE GRIZZLIES(1970); FORTUNE AND MEN'S EYES(1971, U.S./Can.); REINCARNATE, THE(1971, Can.); RIP-OFF(1971, Can.); GET BACK(1973, Can.); MR. PATMAN(1980, Can.); NOTHING PERSONAL(1980, Can.); AGENCY(1981, Can.); IF YOU COULD SEE WHAT I HEAR(1982); NEVER CRY WOLF(1983)

Irene Webster
HOMEBODIES(1974)
Jack Webster
TIME LIMIT(1957)
Jean Webster
DADDY LONG LEGS(1931), w; CURLY TOP(1935), w; DADDY LONG LEGS(1955), w
Silents
DADDY LONG LEGS(1919), w
Joan Webster
SINBAD THE SAILOR(1947)
John Webster
BILLY THE KID'S ROUNDUP(1941)
Joseph D. Webster
Silents
JUDGE NOT OR THE WOMAN OF MONA DIGGINGS(1915), art d
Joy Webster
PANIC IN THE PARLOUR(1957, Brit.); SECOND FIDDLE(1957, Brit.); STORMY CROSSING(1958, Brit.); WOMAN EATER, THE(1959, Brit.); CURSE OF THE WERE-WOLF, THE(1961); HOUSE OF FRIGHT(1961); SHOOT TO KILL(1961, Brit.); DURING ONE NIGHT(1962, Brit.); JUNGLE STREET GIRLS(1963, Brit.)
Misc. Talkies
BLACK TIDE(1958)
Judith Webster
FAST ON THE DRAW(1950); HOSTILE COUNTRY(1950)
Judy Webster
WEST OF THE BRAZOS(1950)
Lillian Webster
Misc. Silents
EYE OF ENVY, THE(1917)
M. Coates Webster
MAN I MARRY, THE(1936), w; DOUBLE OR NOTHING(1937), w; DESPERATE ADVENTURE, A(1938), w; COVERED TRAILER, THE(1939), w; ISLE OF DES-TINY(1940), w; KNOCKOUT(1941), w; SHOT IN THE DARK, THE(1941), w; SIN-GAPORE WOMAN(1941), w; FLYING WITH MUSIC(1942), w; HOME IN WYOMIN'(1942), w; MY FAVORITE SPY(1942), w; SONS OF THE PIONEERS(1942), w; ADVENTURES OF A ROOKIE(1943), w; HE'S MY GUY(1943), w; KLONDIKE KATE(1944), w; BLONDE RANSOM(1945), w; I'LL REMEMBER APRIL(1945), w; JUNGLE CAPTIVE(1945), w; STRANGE CONFESSION(1945), w; BRUTE MAN, THE(1946), w; CUBAN PETE(1946), w; DING DONG WILLIAMS(1946), w; SONG OF ARIZONA(1946), w; UNDER NEVADA SKIES(1946), w; GLAMOUR GIRL(1947), w; I SURRENDER DEAR(1948), w; MARY LOU(1948), w; RENEGADES OF SONO-RA(1949), w; NAVAJO TRAIL RAIDERS(1949), w; WYOMING BANDIT, THE(1949), w; COVERED WAGON RAID(1950), w; FRISCO TORNADO(1950), w; GUNMEN OF ABILENE(1950), w; SALT LAKE RAIDERS(1950), w; DESERT OF LOST MEN(1951), w; NIGHT RIDERS OF MONTANA(1951), w; ROUGH RIDERS OF DURANGO(1951), w; WELLS FARGO GUNMASTER(1951), w; BLACK HILLS AMBUSH(1952), w; CAP-TIVE OF BILLY THE KID(1952), w; LEADVILLE GUNSLINGER(1952), w; MON-TANA BELLE(1952), w; THUNDERING CARAVANS(1952), w; MARSHAL OF CEDAR ROCK(1953), w
Malcolm Webster
GENTLE TERROR, THE(1962, Brit.)
Margo Webster
ONE IN A MILLION(1936)
Martyn C. Webster
BROKEN HORSESHOE, THE(1953, Brit.), d
Mary Webster
DELICATE DELINQUENT, THE(1957); EIGHTEEN AND ANXIOUS(1957); TIN STAR, THE(1957); CLOWN AND THE KID, THE(1961); MASTER OF THE WORLD(1961)
Milton Webster
Misc. Silents
CYNTHIA IN THE WILDERNESS(1916, Brit.)
Nicholas Webster
DEAD TO THE WORLD(1961), d; GONE ARE THE DAYS(1963), p&d; SANTA CLAUS CONQUERS THE MARTIANS(1964), d; MISSION MARS(1968), d; NO LONG-ER ALONE(1978), d
Niel Webster
Misc. Talkies
CONDEMNED MEN(1940)
Paddy Webster
CAT GIRL(1957); DATE AT MIDNIGHT(1960, Brit.); NIGHT TRAIN FOR INVER-NESS(1960, Brit.); FILE OF THE GOLDEN GOOSE, THE(1969, Brit.); GAMES, THE(1970)
Patricia Webster
HOW TO MURDER A RICH UNCLE(1957, Brit.)
Paul Webster
HOW DO YOU DO?(1946), m; NORA PRENTISS(1947), w
Pete Webster
Misc. Talkies
BROKEN STRINGS(1940)
Richard Webster
I STAND CONDEMNED(1936, Brit.)
Rosemary Webster
SON OF SINBAD(1955)
Rupert Webster
IF ...(1968, Brit.)
Sandy Webster
LOST AND FOUND(1979)
Jean Webster-Brough
DISTANT TRUMPET(1952, Brit.); SPACEWAYS(1953, Brit.)
Ernie Wechbaugh
PENROD AND HIS TWIN BROTHER(1938)
Peter Wechsberg
Misc. Talkies
DEAFULA(1975), d
David Wechsler
SEARCH, THE(1948), w; VILLAGE, THE(1953, Brit./Switz.), w

Jean Wechsler
HUNGRY WIVES(1973)
L. Wechsler
LAST CHANCE, THE(1945, Switz.), p
Lazar Wechsler
SEARCH, THE(1948), p; FOUR IN A JEEP(1951, Switz.), p; VILLAGE, THE(1953, Brit./Switz.), p; HEIDI(1954, Switz.), p; HEIDI AND PETER(1955, Switz.), p; IT HAP-PENED IN BROAD DAYLIGHT(1960, Ger./Switz.), p; SHADOWS GROW LONGER, THE(1962, Switz./Ger.), p
Praesans L. Wechsler
FOUR DAYS LEAVE(1950, Switz.), p
Richard Wechsler
FIVE EASY PIECES(1970), p
David Wechter
MIDNIGHT MADNESS(1980), d&w
Julius Wechter
YOUNG MAN WITH A HORN(1950); MIDNIGHT MADNESS(1980), m
Peter Weck
STORY OF VICKIE, THE(1958, Aust.); ALMOST ANGELS(1962); FOREVER MY LOVE(1962); CARDINAL, THE(1963)
Charles Wecker
GUERRILLA GIRL(1953), ph
Gero Wecker
RED-DRAGON(1967, Ital./Ger./US), p
Konstantin Wecker
SISTERS, OR THE BALANCE OF HAPPINESS(1982, Ger.), a, m
Pertti Weckstrom
REDS(1981)
Mimi Weddell
LAST RITES(1980); STUDENT BODIES(1981)
Ted Wedderspoon
DRAGSTRIP RIOT(1958)
Vernon Weddle
NORMA RAE(1979); LAST MARRIED COUPLE IN AMERICA, THE(1980); OH GOD! BOOK II(1980); RESURRECTION(1980); CARBON COPY(1981); HARRY'S WAR(1981); ENDANGERED SPECIES(1982); WHITE DOG(1982)
Claudia Wedekind
24-HOUR LOVER(1970, Ger.)
Frank Wedekind
LULU(1962, Aus.), w; LULU(1978), w
Silents
PANDORA'S BOX(1929, Ger.), w
Franz Wedekind
WARM IN THE BUD(1970), w
Joachim Wedekind
TWO IN A SLEEPING BAG(1964, Ger.), w
Susan Wedell
KISS ME, STUPID(1964)
Hans Wedemeyer
WILD WESTERNERS, THE(1962)
Herman Wedemeyer
HAWAIIANS, THE(1970)
Erik Wedersoe
PEOPLE MEET AND SWEET MUSIC FILLS THE HEART(1969, Den./Swed.)
Ann Wedgeworth
ANDY(1965); BANG THE DRUM SLOWLY(1973); SCARECROW(1973); LAW AND DISORDER(1974); CATAMOUNT KILLING, THE(1975, Ger.); BIRCH INTER-VAL(1976); ONE SUMMER LOVE(1976); CITIZENS BAND(1977); THIEVES(1977)
Anne Wedgeworth
SOGGY BOTTOM U.S.A.(1982)
1984
NO SMALL AFFAIR(1984)
Audrey Wedlock
PEER GYNT(1965)
Hugh Wedlock
IT HAPPENED TOMORROW(1944), w; GEORGE WHITE'S SCANDALS(1945), w
Hugh Wedlock, Jr.
DON'T GET PERSONAL(1941), w; MELODY LANE(1941), w; PUDDIN' HEAD(1941), w; SAN ANTONIO ROSE(1941), w; ALMOST MARRIED(1942), w; ALL BY MY-SELF(1943), w; GOOD FELLOWS, THE(1943), w; SALUTE FOR THREE(1943), w; IN SOCIETY(1944), w; ABBOTT AND COSTELLO MEET THE KILLER, BORIS KARL-OFF(1949), w
Michael Wee
INN OF THE SIXTH HAPPINESS, THE(1958)
Walter Wee
CLANDESTINE(1948, Fr.), ed
Frank Weed
ALL-AMERICAN, THE(1932), w
Frank Weed
DEATH CURSE OF TARTU(1967)
Frank Weed
Silents
PLAYING IT WILD(1923); SECOND HAND LOVE(1923)
Misc. Silents
PENNY PHILANTHROPIST, THE(1917)
Gene Weed
FRATERNITY ROW(1977)
John Weed
CRY BABY KILLER, THE(1958)
Leah Weed
RED, WHITE AND BLACK, THE(1970)
Marlene Weed
RED, WHITE AND BLACK, THE(1970), w
Mike Weed
FREEWHEELIN'(1976)
Robert Weeden
MURDER AT 3 A.M.(1953, Brit.)

Harry Weedon
NEVER TAKE NO FOR AN ANSWER(1952, Brit./Ital.)
William Weedon
FLYING EYE, THE(1955, Brit.), p
Weegee
MAGIC FOUNTAIN, THE(1961), spec eff; SHANGRI-LA(1961), ph
Dennis Week
Misc. Talkies
CHOPPER SQUAD(1971)
Robert S. Weekley
MAN CALLED DAGGER, A(1967), w
Adin Weeks
EVERYTHING HAPPENS TO ME(1938, Brit.)
Alan Weeks
FRENCH CONNECTION, THE(1971); SHAFT(1971); BLACK BELT JONES(1974);
LOST IN THE STARS(1974); TRUCK TURNER(1974)
Misc. Talkies
BLACK BELT JONES(1974)
Allan Weeks
WITHOUT A TRACE(1983)
Andy Weeks
HERE COME THE TIGERS(1978)
Barbara Weeks
MAN TO MAN(1931); MEN IN HER LIFE(1931); PALMY DAYS(1931); PARTY
HUSBAND(1931); TWO-FISTED JUSTICE(1931); BY WHOSE HAND?(1932); CHEAT-
ERS AT PLAY(1932); DEVIL'S LOTTERY(1932); DISCARDED LOVERS(1932); HELL'S
HEADQUARTERS(1932); NIGHT MAYOR, THE(1932); STEPPING SISTERS(1932);
WHITE EAGLE(1932); DECEPTION(1933); MY WEAKNESS(1933); RUSTY RIDES
ALONE(1933); SOLDIERS OF THE STORM(1933); SUNDOWN RIDER, THE(1933);
NOW I'LL TELL(1934); OLSEN'S BIG MOMENT(1934); QUITTERS, THE(1934); SHE
WAS A LADY(1934); WHEN STRANGERS MEET(1934); WOMAN UNAFRAID(1934);
SCHOOL FOR GIRLS(1935); FORBIDDEN TRAIL(1936); OLD WYOMING TRAIL,
THE(1937); ONE MAN JUSTICE(1937); PICK A STAR(1937); TWO-FISTED SHE-
RIFF(1937); DRAMATIC SCHOOL(1938); VIOLENT YEARS, THE(1956)
Misc. Talkies
SUNDOWN RIDER(1933)
Clair Weeks
PETER PAN(1953), anim
Geoffrey Weeks
ENTER THE DRAGON(1973)
George Weeks
BLONDIE JOHNSON(1933), ed
George W. Weeks
ROGUE OF THE RIO GRANDE(1930), p; NECK AND NECK(1931), p; RANGE
BUSTERS, THE(1940), p; TRAILING DOUBLE TROUBLE(1940), p; WEST OF PINTO
BASIN(1940), p; FUGITIVE VALLEY(1941), p; KID'S LAST RIDE, THE(1941), p;
SADDLE MOUNTAIN ROUNDUP(1941), p; TONTO BASIN OUTLAWS(1941), p;
TRAIL OF THE SILVER SPURS(1941), p; TUMBLEDOWN RANCH IN ARIZO-
NA(1941), p; UNDERGROUND RUSTLERS(1941), p; WRANGLER'S ROOST(1941), p;
ARIZONA STAGECOACH(1942), p; PRIDE OF THE ARMY(1942), p; ROCK RIVER
RENEGADES(1942), p; TEXAS TO BATAAN(1942), p; THUNDER RIVER
FEUD(1942), p; TRAIL RIDERS(1942), p; WAR DOGS(1942), p; BLACK MARKET
RUSTLERS(1943), p; COWBOY COMMANDOS(1943), p; HAUNTED RANCH,
THE(1943), p; LAND OF HUNTED MEN(1943), p
Howard Weeks
SKY LINER(1949), spec eff; MAN FROM PLANET X, THE(1951), spec eff
James Ray Weeks
CRUISING(1980); EYEWITNESS(1981)
Jane Weeks
MANTRAP, THE(1943); FOR YOU I DIE(1947); GANGSTER, THE(1947); DON'T
TRUST YOUR HUSBAND(1948)
Larry Weeks
THIS IS THE ARMY(1943)
Madison Weeks
Silents
ACCORDING TO LAW(1916)
Ranny Weeks
BILL CRACKS DOWN(1937); HEART OF THE ROCKIES(1937); YOUTH ON
PAROLE(1937)
Ronald Weeks
HAIR(1979)
Stephen Weeks
I, MONSTER(1971, Brit.), d; GAWAIN AND THE GREEN KNIGHT(1973, Brit.), d, w;
GHOST STORY(1974, Brit.), p&d, w
1984
SWORD OF THE VALIANT(1984, Brit.), d, w
Todd Weeks
HERE COME THE TIGERS(1978)
Arne Weel
PEOPLE MEET AND SWEET MUSIC FILLS THE HEART(1969, Den./Swed.)
Russell Weelnough
MUTATIONS, THE(1974, Brit.), ed
Walter Weems
HEARTS IN DIXIE(1929), w; ANYBODY'S WAR(1930); CONFLICT(1937), w; MR.
WASHINGTON GOES TO TOWN(1941), w
Silents
OLYMPIC HERO, THE(1928), t
Annabelle Weenick
ENCOUNTER WITH THE UNKNOWN(1973); KEEP MY GRAVE OPEN(1980);
DEADLY BLESSING(1981)
Helen Weer [Weir]
Misc. Silents
HOUSE WITHOUT CHILDREN, THE(1919)
Tom Wees
TERMS OF ENDEARMENT(1983)
Clarence Weff
HOW NOT TO ROB A DEPARTMENT STORE(1965, Fr./Ital.), w

Paul Wegel
THE INVISIBLE RAY(1936)
Gottfried Wegeleben
JOHNNY BANCO(1969, Fr./Ital./Ger.), p
Peter Wegenbreth
SOPHIE'S CHOICE(1982)
Grete Wegener
VICTORIA THE GREAT(1937, Brit.)
Hiltraud Wegener
NOT RECONCILED, OR "ONLY VIOLENCE HELPS WHERE IT RULES"(1969, Ger.)
Paul Wegener
TALES OF THE UNCANNY(1932, Ger.); MOSCOW SHANGHAI(1936, Ger.), d;
KOLBERG(1945, Ger.)
Silents
GOLEM: HOW HE CAME INTO THE WORLD, THE(1920, Ger.), a, d, w; ONE
ARABIAN NIGHT(1921, Ger.)
Misc. Silents
STUDENT OF PRAGUE, THE(1913, Ger.); GOLEM, THE(1914, Ger.), a, d; PIED
PIPER OF HAMELIN, THE(1917, Ger.), a, d; LOST SHADOW, THE(1921, Ger.), a, d;
SUMURUN(1921, Ger.); VANINA(1922, Ger.); WIFE OF THE PHARAOH, THE(1922,
Ger.); MONNA VANNA(1923, Ger.); MAGICIAN, THE(1926); SURVIVAL(1930, Ger.)
Jack Wegman
FOLLOW THE BOYS(1944)
John Wegman
ALASKA HIGHWAY(1943)
Bob Wegner
FEMALE ANIMAL, THE(1958)
Charles Wegner
BREAKING GLASS(1980, Brit.)
Cliff Wegner
HOOPER(1978), spec eff
Cliff Wegner, Jr.
HOOPER(1978), spec eff
Robert Wegner
O.S.S.(1946)
Bill Wegney
Misc. Talkies
HILARY'S BLUES(1983)
Oscar Wegrostek
NO TIME FOR FLOWERS(1952)
Oskar Wegrostek
SECRET WAYS, THE(1961); FOREVER MY LOVE(1962)
Josef Wegrzyn
Misc. Silents
10 CONDEMNED(1932, Pol.)
Thomas Weguelin
KNOWING MEN(1930, Brit.); CONGRESS DANCES(1932, Ger.); THAT'S MY WI-
FE(1933, Brit.); SQUIBS(1935, Brit.)
Silents
ADVENTURES OF MR. PICKWICK, THE(1921, Brit.)
Ray Wehba
ROSE BOWL(1936)
Oliver Wehe
1984
ERENDIRA(1984, Mex./Fr./Ger.)
Bernhard Wehle
CHRONICLE OF ANNA MAGDALENA BACH(1968, Ital., Ger.)
Emmy Wehlen
Silents
PRETENDERS, THE(1916); TRAIL OF THE SHADOW, THE(1917); LIFTING SHAD-
OWS(1920)
Misc. Silents
TABLES TURNED(1915); DUCHESS OF DOUBT, THE(1917); MISS ROBINSON
CRUSOE(1917); SOWERS AND REAPERS(1917); HIS BONDED WIFE(1918); HOUSE
OF GOLD, THE(1918); SHELL GAME, THE(1918); SYLVIA ON A SPREE(1918); BELLE
OF THE SEASON, THE(1919); FAVOR TO A FRIEND, A(1919); FOOLS AND THEIR
MONEY(1919)
Bob Wehling
GET OUTTA TOWN(1960), w; SIGN OF ZORRO, THE(1960), w; MAGIC SPECTA-
CLES(1961), d; EEGAH!(1962), w; WILD GUITAR(1962), w; WHAT'S UP
FRONT(1964), d, w
Ernest B. Wehmeyer
COME SEPTEMBER(1961), prod d
Donna Wehr
AMERICAN GRAFFITI(1973)
Joseph Wehrer
CRY DR. CHICAGO(1971)
Wolfgang Wehrum
THREE PENNY OPERA(1963, Fr./Ger.), ed
Wolfgang Wehrums
SCHLAGER-PARADE(1953), ed
Chi Wei
DRAGON INN(1968, Chi.)
Lo Wei
EMPRESS WU(1965, Hong Kong); FISTS OF FURY(1973, Chi.), d&w; CALL HIM MR.
SHATTER(1976, Hong Kong)
Woo Wei
VERMILION DOOR(1969, Hong Kong)
Lin Wei-ty
GOLIATHON(1979, Hong Kong)
Jimmy Weible
KINGS GO FORTH(1958)
Sue Weicberg
SKATETOWN, U.S.A.(1979)
Louis Weichart
SIX MEN, THE(1951, Brit.)
Helga Weichert
SLEEPING BEAUTY(1965, Ger.), w

Heinrich Weidemann
PLACE CALLED GLORY, A(1966, Span./Ger.), art d
Gert Weidenhof
ASSIGNMENT K(1968, Brit.)
Alfred Weidenmann
BOOMERANG(1960, Ger.), d; ONLY A WOMAN(1966, Ger.), d
Hanne Weider
PLAYGIRLS AND THE BELLBOY, THE(1962,Ger.)
Alfred Weidermann
AND SO TO BED(1965, Ger.), d
George Weidler
DIMPLES(1936)
Virginia Weidler
MRS. WIGGS OF THE CABBAGE PATCH(1934); BIG BROADCAST OF 1936, THE(1935); FRECKLES(1935); LADDIE(1935); PETER IBBETSON(1935); BIG BROADCAST OF 1937, THE(1936); GIRL OF THE OZARKS(1936); TIMOTHY'S QUEST(1936); TROUBLE FOR TWO(1936); MAID OF SALEM(1937); OUTCASTS OF POKER FLAT, THE(1937); SOULS AT SEA(1937); LOVE IS A HEADACHE(1938); MEN WITH WINGS(1938); MOTHER CAREY'S CHICKENS(1938); OUT WEST WITH THE HARDYS(1938); SCANDAL STREET(1938); TOO HOT TO HANDLE(1938); BAD LITTLE ANGEL(1939); FIXER DUGAN(1939); GREAT MAN VOTES, THE(1939); HENRY GOES ARIZONA(1939); LONE WOLF SPY HUNT, THE(1939); OUTSIDE THESE WALLS(1939); ROOKIE COP, THE(1939); UNDER-PUP, THE(1939); WOMEN, THE(1939); ALL THIS AND HEAVEN TOO(1940); GOLD RUSH MAISIE(1940); PHILADELPHIA STORY, THE(1940); YOUNG TOM EDISON(1940); BABES ON BROADWAY(1941); BARNACLE BILL(1941); I'LL WAIT FOR YOU(1941); KEEPING COMPANY(1941); AFFAIRS OF MARTHA, THE(1942); BORN TO SING(1942); THIS TIME FOR KEEPS(1942); BEST FOOT FORWARD(1943); YOUNGEST PROFESSION, THE(1943)
Walter Weidler
DIMPLES(1936)
Werther Weidler
LEATHERNECKING(1930)
Wolfgang Weidler
LEATHERNECKING(1930)
Hans Jurgen Weidlich
FOUR COMPANIONS, THE(1938, Ger.)
Philip Weidling
LITTLE LAURA AND BIG JOHN(1973), w
Jerome Weidman
HOUSE OF STRANGERS(1949), w; DAMNED DON'T CRY, THE(1950), w; I CAN GET IT FOR YOU WHOLESALE(1951), w; INVITATION(1952), w; EDDIE CANTOR STORY, THE(1953), w; SLANDER(1956), w
Sally Weidman
TEXAN MEETS CALAMITY JANE, THE(1950)
Bill Weidner
Misc. Talkies
BRANCHES(1971)
Gotz Weidner
DAS BOOT(1982), art d
1984
NEVERENDING STORY, THE(1984, Ger.), art d
Aurthur Weigall
Silents
BURNING SANDS(1922), w
Michele Weigand
RUN FOR YOUR WIFE(1966, Fr./Ital.)
Reggie Weigand
SMILEY(1957, Brit.)
Helene Weigel
Silents
METROPOLIS(1927, Ger.)
Herman Weigel
1984
NEVERENDING STORY, THE(1984, Ger.), w
Paul Weigel
LEATHERNECK, THE(1929); SOUL OF THE SLUMS(1931); BACK STREET(1932); NEIGHBORS' WIVES(1933); VAMPIRE BAT, THE(1933); BLACK CAT, THE(1934); DRACULA'S DAUGHTER(1936); LADIES IN LOVE(1936); SUTTER'S GOLD(1936); ESPIONAGE(1937); GOLD RACKET, THE(1937); LANCER SPY(1937); MAYTIME(1937); PRESCRIPTION FOR ROMANCE(1937); LITTLE TOUGH GUY(1938); NINOTCHKA(1939); DISPATCH FROM REUTERS, A(1940); GREAT DICTATOR, THE(1940); CROSSROADS(1942); I WAKE UP SCREAMING(1942); JOAN OF PARIS(1942); MISS V FROM MOSCOW(1942); REUNION IN FRANCE(1942); ABOVE SUSPICION(1943); HAPPY LAND(1943); PARIS AFTER DARK(1943); HAIRY APE, THE(1944); WHERE DO WE GO FROM HERE?(1945)
Silents
EACH PEARL A TEAR(1916); NAKED HEARTS(1916); KISMET(1920); MASTER STROKE, A(1920); RED LANE, THE(1920); BRING HIM IN(1921); LOVER'S OATH, A(1925); FOR HEAVEN'S SAKE(1926); KING OF KINGS, THE(1927); ISLE OF LOST MEN(1928); MARRY THE GIRL(1928)
Misc. Silents
WITCHCRAFT(1916); BOND BETWEEN, THE(1917); PRIDE AND THE MAN(1917); HER BODY IN BOND(1918); ME UND GOTT(1918); THEY SHALL PAY(1921); BAG AND BAGGAGE(1923); FIGHTING FOR JUSTICE(1924); SILENT ACCUSER, THE(1924); WHICH SHALL IT BE?(1924); SOFT SHOES(1925); HIDDEN ACES(1927); SINEWS OF STEEL(1927)
Arthur Weigell
Silents
HER HERITAGE(1919, Brit.), w
Ian Weighall
BEDKNOBS AND BROOMSTICKS(1971)
Alan Weighell
ROCK AROUND THE WORLD(1957, Brit.)
F. Harmon Weight
Silents
ON THE STROKE OF THREE(1924), d; FLAMING WATERS(1925), d; FOREVER AFTER(1926), d; HOOK AND LADDER NO. 9(1927), d; JAZZ MAD(1928), d; MIDNIGHT MADNESS(1928), d

Misc. Silents
DRUSILLA WITH A MILLION(1925), d; POOR GIRL'S ROMANCE, A(1926), d
Harmon Weight
FROZEN RIVER(1929), d
Silents
MAN WHO PLAYED GOD, THE(1922), d; RULING PASSION, THE(1922), d; RAGGED EDGE, THE(1923), d; RAMSHACKLE HOUSE(1924), d
Misc. Silents
$20 A WEEK(1924), d
Michael Weight
OLD CURIOSITY SHOP, THE(1935, Brit.), cos
Rolf Weih
U-47 LT. COMMANDER PRIEN(1967, Ger.)
Franz Weihmayr
COURT CONCERT, THE(1936, Ger.), ph; MOSCOW SHANGHAI(1936, Ger.), ph; LA HABANERA(1937, Ger.), ph; LIFE BEGINS ANEW(1938, Ger.), ph; AFFAIRS OF DR. HOLL(1954, Ger.), ph; DEVIL IN SILK(1968, Ger.), ph
Briggette Weihnstraume
SATIN MUSHROOM, THE(1969)
Richard Weiker
CARRIE(1976), stunts
Bernd Weikl
CHRONICLE OF ANNA MAGDALENA BACH(1968, Ital., Ger.)
Bob Weil
1984
BROADWAY DANNY ROSE(1984)
Elvira Weil
Silents
ANOTHER MAN'S BOOTS(1922)
Harry Weil
SEAS BENEATH, THE(1931)
Silents
OLIVER TWIST(1922), w; CIRCUS DAYS(1923), w
Herb Weil
CISCO PIKE(1971)
Jeri Weil
VIOLENT SATURDAY(1955)
Pat Weil
VIOLENT SATURDAY(1955)
Patricia Weil
YOU'RE MY EVERYTHING(1949)
Patsy Weil
LES MISERABLES(1952)
Richard Weil
GIRL FROM WOOLWORTH'S, THE(1929), w; HARD TO GET(1929), w; NAUGHTY FLIRT, THE(1931), w; MYSTERIOUS DOCTOR, THE(1943), w; CRIME BY NIGHT(1944), w; MAKE YOUR OWN BED(1944), w; SHINE ON, HARVEST MOON(1944), w; BEHIND CITY LIGHTS(1945), w; BIG SHOW-OFF, THE(1945), w; GREAT FLAMARION, THE(1945), w; HIT THE HAY(1945), w; IDENTITY UNKNOWN(1945), w; PHANTOM THIEF, THE(1946), w; SINGIN' IN THE CORN(1946), w; TALK ABOUT A LADY(1946), w; JUMPING JACKS(1952), w
Richard Weil, Jr.
G.I. HONEYMOON(1945), w
Robert Weil
FRENCH CONNECTION, THE(1971); GANG THAT COULDN'T SHOOT STRAIGHT, THE(1971); HOT ROCK, THE(1972); BADGE 373(1973); RHINOCEROS(1974); SATURDAY NIGHT FEVER(1977); FAN, THE(1981)
Samuel Weil
SQUEEZE PLAY(1981), d; WAITRESS(1982), d; STUCK ON YOU(1983), d
1984
FIRST TURN-ON!, THE(1984), d
Wende Weil
TREASURE OF THE GOLDEN CONDOR(1953)
Dan Weilden
GYPSY MELODY(1936, Brit.), w
Connie Weiler
THIS MAN'S NAVY(1945); HOODLUM SAINT, THE(1946); TWO SMART PEOPLE(1946)
Fred Weiler
FINGERS(1978), set d; WARRIORS, THE(1979), set d; RAGING BULL(1980), set d; HANKY-PANKY(1982), set d
1984
FLAMINGO KID, THE(1984), set d; SLAYGROUND(1984, Brit.), set d
Joachim Weiler
NOT RECONCILED, OR "ONLY VIOLENCE HELPS WHERE IT RULES"(1969, Ger.)
John Weiley
JOURNEY AMONG WOMEN(1977, Aus.), p, w; DIMBOOLA(1979, Aus.), p
Franz Weilhammer
MOSCOW SHANGHAI(1936, Ger.)
Claudia Weill
GIRLFRIENDS(1978), p, d, w; IT'S MY TURN(1980), d
Joseph Weill
WHO'S THAT KNOCKING AT MY DOOR?(1968), p
Kurt Weill
THREEPENNY OPERA, THE(1931, Ger./U.S.), m; YOU AND ME(1938), m; KNICKERBOCKER HOLIDAY(1944), w; LADY IN THE DARK(1944), w; ONE TOUCH OF VENUS(1948), w, m; THREE PENNY OPERA(1963, Fr./Ger.), w, m; LOST IN THE STARS(1974), w, m
Richard Weill
GENTLEMAN MISBEHAVES, THE(1946), w
Rita Weiman
ON YOUR BACK(1930), w; PRESIDENT'S MYSTERY, THE(1936), w; WITNESS CHAIR, THE(1936), w; POSSESSED(1947), w
Silents
AFTER THE SHOW(1921), w; ACQUITTAL, THE(1923), w; SOCIAL CODE, THE(1923), w; BLUFF(1924), w
Mattias Weimann
BLUE LIGHT, THE(1932, Ger.)

Sharkey Weimar
Silents
GOLD RUSH, THE(1925)
Chuck Wein
Misc. Talkies
RAINBOW BRIDGE(1972), d
Dean Wein
1984
RHINESTONE(1984)
Yossi Wein
1984
DRIFTING(1984, Israel), ph
Rudolf Wein-Rogge
COURT CONCERT, THE(1936, Ger.)
Herbert Weinand
1984
WOMAN IN FLAMES, A(1984, Ger.), prod d
Robert D. Weinbach
CAULDRON OF BLOOD(1971, Span.), p; MUTATIONS, THE(1974, Brit.), p, w
Gus Weinberg
Silents
KISS, THE(1916); TODAY(1917); JACQUELINE, OR BLAZING BARRIERS(1923)
H.G. Weinberg
FANNY(1948, Fr.), titles
Herman Weinberg
COURIER OF LYONS(1938, Fr.), m; PASSION ISLAND(1943, Mex.), titles; DARK RIVER(1956, Arg.), titles; LAST TEN DAYS, THE(1956, Ger.), titles; LOVERS, THE(1959, Fr.), titles; LE PETIT THEATRE DE JEAN RENOIR(1974, Fr.), titles
Herman G. Weinberg
WITH A SMILE(1939, Fr.), titles; IT HAPPENED IN GIBRALTAR(1943, Fr.), English subtitles; SHANGHAI DRAMA, THE(1945, Fr.), titles; CARMEN(1946, Ital.), titles; OPEN CITY(1946, Ital.), titles; PORTRAIT OF A WOMAN(1946, Fr.), titles; WHIRL-WIND OF PARIS(1946, Fr.), titles; FURIA(1947, Ital.), ed, titles; PAISAN(1948, Ital.), titles; RAVEN, THE(1948, Fr.), titles; MONSIEUR VINCENT(1949, Fr.), titles; OUT-CRY(1949, Ital.), titles; STRANGERS IN THE HOUSE(1949, Fr.), titles; MAD QUEEN, THE(1950, Span.), titles; LOVERS OF VERONA, THE(1951, Fr.), titles; FORBIDDEN GAMES(1953, Fr.), titles; GOLD OF NAPLES(1957, Ital.), titles; MILLER'S WIFE, THE(1957, Ital.), titles; NATHALIE(1958, Fr.), titles; FOUR HUNDRED BLOWS, THE(1959), titles; MIRROR HAS TWO FACES, THE(1959, Fr.), titles; BIG CHIEF, THE(1960, Fr.), titles; FIDELIO(1961, Aust.), titles; FROM A ROMAN BALCONY(1961, Fr./Ital.), titles; LA BELLE AMERICAINE(1961, Fr.), English subtitles; END OF DESIRE(1962 Fr./Ital.), titles; LOVERS OF TERUEL, THE(1962, Fr.), titles; CHU-SHINGURA(1963, Jap.), titles; HIGH AND LOW(1963, Jap.), titles; LOVE ON A PILLOW(1963, Fr./Ital.), titles; RITA(1963, Fr./Ital.), titles; ORGANIZER, THE(1964, Fr./Ital./Yugo.), titles; SEDUCED AND ABANDONED(1964, Fr./Ital.), titles; MADALENA(1965, Gr.), titles; MAGNIFICENT CUCKOLD, THE(1965, Fr./Ital.), titles; JUDEX(1966, Fr./Ital.), titles; BEAUTIFUL SWINDLERS, THE(1967, Fr./Ital./Jap./Neth.), titles; SEVENTH CONTINENT, THE(1968, Czech./Yugo.), titles; STE-FANIA(1968, Gr.), titles
Jack Weinberg
Silents
ANYTHING ONCE(1925), p
Jacob Weinberg
SINGING BLACKSMITH(1938), md
Louis Weinberg
TOY, THE(1982)
M. Weinberg
TIGER GIRL(1955, USSR), m
Max Weinberg
HEIDI AND PETER(1955, Switz.), w
Roger J. Weinberg
PAY OR DIE(1960), cos; DONDI(1961), cos; GEORGE RAFT STORY, THE(1961), cos; KING OF THE ROARING TWENTIES–THE STORY OF ARNOLD ROTHSTEIN(1961), cos; GUN HAWK, THE(1963), cos
Ronald Weinberg
1984
MIRRORS(1984), prod d
Ed Weinberger
MIRACLE IN MILAN(1951, Ital.), titles; MODERN ROMANCE(1981)
1984
LONELY GUY, THE(1984), w
Grahame Weinbren
1984
ALPHABET CITY(1984), ed
Jan Weincke
1984
ZAPPA(1984, Den.), ph
Conrad Weine
Misc. Silents
STRAUSS, THE WALTZ KING(1929, Ger.), d
Robert Weine
ROBBER SYMPHONY, THE(1937, Brit.), p
Misc. Silents
CRIME AND PUNISHMENT(1929, Ger.), d; SCANDAL IN PARIS(1929, Ger.), d
Bert Weineberg
ON THE RIGHT TRACK(1981)
Barry Weiner
THAT CHAMPIONSHIP SEASON(1982)
Elisabeth Weiner
DIANE'S BODY(1969, Fr./Czech.)
Gretchen Weiner
1984
FIRST TURN-ON!, THE(1984)
Jacob Weiner
COPS AND ROBBERS(1973)
Jean Weiner
DR. KNOCK(1936, Fr.), m; HEART OF A NATION, THE(1943, Fr.), md; FEMALE, THE(1960, Fr.), m

Joshua Weiner
DREAM NO MORE(1950, Palestine)
Leonard Weiner
LOST IN ALASKA(1952), ed; MA AND PA KETTLE ON VACATION(1953), ed; STAND AT APACHE RIVER, THE(1953), ed; MA AND PA KETTLE AT HOME(1954), ed
Leslie Weiner
1984
NADIA(1984, U.S./Yugo.)
Mark Weiner
ENTITY, THE(1982)
Paul Weiner
SWINGING THE LEAD(1934, Brit.), p
Roberta Weiner
INCREDIBLE SHRINKING WOMAN, THE(1981), cos; PANDEMONIUM(1982), cos; D.C. CAB(1983), cos
Jim Weinert
Misc. Talkies
ONE CHANCE TO WIN(1976)
Michael Weinert
PEDESTRIAN, THE(1974, Ger.)
Vit Weingaertner
WISHING MACHINE(1971, Czech.)
Isabelle Weingarten
FOUR NIGHTS OF A DREAMER(1972, Fr.); MOTHER AND THE WHORE, THE(1973, Fr.); STATE OF THINGS, THE(1983)
Larry Weingarten
Silents
SPITE MARRIAGE(1929), sup
Lawrence Weingarten
SIDEWALKS OF NEW YORK(1931), p; NUISANCE, THE(1933), p; SHOULD LA-DIES BEHAVE?(1933), p; WHEN LADIES MEET(1933), p; MYSTERY OF MR. X, THE(1934), p; SADIE MCKEE(1934), p; RENDEZVOUS(1935), p; HIS BROTHER'S WIFE(1936), p; LIBELED LADY(1936), p; UNGUARDED HOUR, THE(1936), p; DAY AT THE RACES, A(1937), p; LAST OF MRS. CHEYNEY, THE(1937), p; TOO HOT TO HANDLE(1938), p; BALALAIKA(1939), p; I LOVE YOU AGAIN(1940), p; I TAKE THIS WOMAN(1940), p; ADAM'S RIB(1949), p; INVITATION(1952), p; PAT AND MIKE(1952), p; ACTRESS, THE(1953), p; RHAPSODY(1954), p; I'LL CRY TOMOR-ROW(1955), p; TENDER TRAP, THE(1955), p; CAT ON A HOT TIN ROOF(1958), p; GAZEBO, THE(1959), p; ADA(1961), p; HONEYMOON MACHINE, THE(1961), p; PERIOD OF ADJUSTMENT(1962), p; SIGNPOST TO MURDER(1964), p; UNSINKA-BLE MOLLY BROWN, THE(1964), p; IMPOSSIBLE YEARS, THE(1968), p; DON'T GO NEAR THE WATER(1975), p
Lawrence A. Weingarten
WITHOUT LOVE(1945), p
Meri Weingarten
IMPOSTORS(1979), ed
Kristin Weingartner
GOLDEN APPLES OF THE SUN(1971, Can.), w, ed & prod d
Owen Weingott
STONE(1974, Aus.)
Herschel Weingrod
CHEAPER TO KEEP HER(1980), w; TRADING PLACES(1983), w
Howard Weingrow
IF EVER I SEE YOU AGAIN(1978)
Abraham Weinlood
PICNIC(1955)
David Weinman
SEVENTH DAWN, THE(1964)
J. Weinrajeh
YIDDLE WITH HIS FIDDLE(1937, Pol.), set d
Lennie Weinrib
BEACH BALL(1965), d; OUT OF SIGHT(1966), d; WILD, WILD WINTER(1966), d; GOOD TIMES(1967); BEDKNOBS AND BROOMSTICKS(1971)
Lenny Weinrib
TALES OF TERROR(1962)
Abraham Weinstein
LONG IS THE ROAD(1948, Ger.), p
Artie Weinstein
TIMES SQUARE(1980)
Bob Weinstein
BURNING, THE(1981), w
Hannah Weinstein
ESCAPADE(1955, Brit.), p; CLAUDINE(1974), p; GREASED LIGHTNING(1977), p; STIR CRAZY(1980), p
Harvey Weinstein
BURNING, THE(1981), p
Henry T. Weinstein
TENDER IS THE NIGHT(1961), p; JOY IN THE MORNING(1965), p; PROMISE, THE(1969, Brit.), p
Irv Weinstein
HIDE IN PLAIN SIGHT(1980)
Jess Weinstein
1984
WILD LIFE, THE(1984)
Leonid Weinstein
JESUS(1979)
Marvin Weinstein
EDGE OF FURY(1958), ph
Marvin R. Weinstein
RUNNING TARGET(1956), d, w
Jeff Lion Weinstock
FOREPLAY(1975), ph
V. Weinstock
CAPTAIN GRANT'S CHILDREN(1939, USSR), d
Will Weinstone
REDS(1981)

Bruce Weintraub
HARDCORE(1979), set d; CRUISING(1980), prod d; RESURRECTION(1980), set d; CAT PEOPLE(1982), set d; SUMMER LOVERS(1982), prod d; SCARFACE(1983), set d
1984
NATURAL, THE(1984), set d
Bruce David Weintraub
WILD PARTY, THE(1975), set d
Carl Weintraub
1984
BEVERLY HILLS COP(1984)
Cindy Weintraub
HUMANOIDS FROM THE DEEP(1980); PROWLER, THE(1981)
Fred Weintraub
RAGE(1972), p; ENTER THE DRAGON(1973), p; BLACK BELT JONES(1974), p, w; GOLDEN NEEDLES(1974), p; TRUCK TURNER(1974), p; ULTIMATE WARRIOR, THE(1975), p; DIRTY KNIGHT'S WORK(1976, Brit.), p, w; HOT POTATO(1976), p, w; PACK, THE(1977), p; CHECKERED FLAG OR CRASH(1978), p; PROMISE, THE(1979), p, w; BIG BRAWL, THE(1980), p, w; TOM HORN(1980), p; FORCE: FIVE(1981), p; HIGH ROAD TO CHINA(1983), p
Jerry Weintraub
OH, GOD!(1977), p; 9/30/55(1977), p; CRUISING(1980), p; ALL NIGHT LONG(1981), p; DINER(1982), p
1984
KARATE KID, THE(1984), p
Joseph Weintraub
SCALPEL(1976), p, d&w, ed
Rebecca Weintraub
TWO SISTERS(1938); TEVYA(1939)
Misc. Talkies
THREE DAUGHTERS(1949)
Misc. Silents
BREAKING HOME TIES(1922)
Sandy Weintraub
THINGS ARE TOUGH ALL OVER(1982); PRIVATE BENJAMIN(1980)
Sy Weintraub
TARZAN'S GREATEST ADVENTURE(1959, Brit.), p; TARZAN THE MAGNIFICENT(1960, Brit.), p; TARZAN GOES TO INDIA(1962, U.S./Brit./Switz.), p; TARZAN'S THREE CHALLENGES(1963), p; TARZAN AND THE VALLEY OF GOLD(1966 U.S./Switz.), p; TARZAN AND THE GREAT RIVER(1967, U.S./Switz.), p
William Weintraub
DRYLANDERS(1963, Can.); WHY ROCK THE BOAT?(1974, Can.), p, w
Maury Weintrobe
TWILIGHT'S LAST GLEAMING(1977, U.S./Ger.), ed; BLACK MARBLE, THE(1980), ed; JAZZ SINGER, THE(1980), ed
Margo Weintz
HARUM SCARUM(1965), cos; POINT BLANK(1967), cos
Gertrud Weinz-Werner
UNWILLING AGENT(1968, Ger.), makeup
Arabella Weir
FRENCH LIEUTENANT'S WOMAN, THE(1981)
David Weir
ANNIE HALL(1977); ROLLOVER(1981), w
Declan Weir
TAPS(1981)
Harry Weir
Silents
SINS OF SOCIETY(1915)
Harry C. Weir
Silents
FRUITS OF DESIRE, THE(1916)
Helen Weir
BOY WHO TURNED YELLOW, THE(1972, Brit.)
Silents
INCORRIGIBLE DUKANE, THE(1915); SOCIAL SECRETARY, THE(1916); TANGLED FATES(1916); LURE OF YOUTH, THE(1921)
Misc. Silents
LOVE'S OLD SWEET SONG(1923)
Ingrid Weir
LAST WAVE, THE(1978, Aus.)
James Weir
HAWMPS!(1976)
Jane Weir
ARTISTS AND MODELS(1937); CRIMINALS OF THE AIR(1937); SINGING MARINE, THE(1937); SOULS AT SEA(1937)
Leonard Weir
MAKE MINE A MILLION(1965, Brit.)
Mollie Weir
WHAT A WHOPPER(1961, Brit.)
Molly Weir
FLOODTIDE(1949, Brit.); SOMETHING IN THE CITY(1950, Brit.); CHEER THE BRAVE(1951, Brit.); FLESH AND BLOOD(1951, Brit.); FORCES' SWEETHEART(1953, Brit.); FAMILY AFFAIR(1954, Brit.); LYONS IN PARIS(1955, Brit.); LET'S BE HAPPY(1957, Brit.); VALUE FOR MONEY(1957, Brit.); CARRY ON REGARDLESS(1961, Brit.); HANDS OF ORLAC, THE(1964, Brit./Fr.); PRIME OF MISS JEAN BRODIE, THE(1969, Brit.); SCROOGE(1970, Brit.); HANDS OF THE RIPPER(1971, Brit.)
Peter Weir
THREE TO GO(1971, Aus.), d&w; CARS THAT ATE PARIS, THE(1974, Aus.), d, w; PICNIC AT HANGING ROCK(1975, Aus.), d; LAST WAVE, THE(1978, Aus.), d, w; PLUMBER, THE(1980, Aus.), d&w; GALLIPOLI(1981, Aus.), d, w; YEAR OF LIVING DANGEROUSLY, THE(1982, Aus.), d, w
Rickie Weir
TERROR IN THE WAX MUSEUM(1973)
Wendy Weir
GALLIPOLI(1981, Aus.), prod d
The Weir Brothers
VARIETY HOUR(1937, Brit.)

Bob Weis
PURE S(1976, Aus.), p; CLINIC, THE(1983, Aus.), p
1984
HEARTBREAKERS(1984), p
Don Weis
FORCE OF EVIL(1948), d; BANNERLINE(1951), d; IT'S A BIG COUNTRY(1951), d; JUST THIS ONCE(1952), d; YOU FOR ME(1952), d; AFFAIRS OF DOBIE GILLIS, THE(1953), d; HALF A HERO(1953), d; I LOVE MELVIN(1953), d; REMAINS TO BE SEEN(1953), d; SLIGHT CASE OF LARCENY, A(1953), d; ADVENTURES OF HAJJI BABA(1954), d; RIDE THE HIGH IRON(1956), d; GENE KRUPA STORY, THE(1959), d; CRITIC'S CHOICE(1963), d; LOOKING FOR LOVE(1964), d; PAJAMA PARTY(1964), d; GHOST IN THE INVISIBLE BIKINI(1966), d; KING'S PIRATE(1967), d; DID YOU HEAR THE ONE ABOUT THE TRAVELING SALESLADY?(1968), d; ZERO TO SIXTY(1978), d
Misc. Talkies
CRACKLE OF DEATH(1974), d
Donald Weis
BILLIE(1965), p&d
Gary Weis
MANHATTAN(1979); WHOLLY MOSES(1980), d
Heidelinde Weis
CORPSE OF BEVERLY HILLS, THE(1965, Ger.); SERENADE FOR TWO SPIES(1966, Ital./Ger.); MAN OUTSIDE, THE(1968, Brit.); SOMETHING FOR EVERYONE(1970)
Jack Weis
QUADROON(1972), d; MARDI GRAS MASSACRE(1978), p,d&w, ph
Lesa Weis
DEATH WISH II(1982)
Louis Weis
CYCLONE OF THE SADDLE(1935), p
Richard Weisbach
DAUGHTER OF EVIL(1930, Ger.), w
David Weisbart
EDGE OF DARKNESS(1943), ed; CONFLICT(1945), ed; MILDRED PIERCE(1945), ed; ROUGHLY SPEAKING(1945), ed; MY REPUTATION(1946), ed; NIGHT AND DAY(1946), ed; ONE MORE TOMORROW(1946), ed; DARK PASSAGE(1947), ed; STALLION ROAD(1947), ed; THAT HAGEN GIRL(1947), ed; JOHNNY BELINDA(1948), ed; FOUNTAINHEAD, THE(1949), ed; KISS IN THE DARK, A(1949), ed; LADY TAKES A SAILOR, THE(1949), ed; GLASS MENAGERIE, THE(1950), ed; PERFECT STRANGERS(1950), ed; MAN WHO CHEATED HIMSELF, THE(1951), ed; STREETCAR NAMED DESIRE, A(1951), ed; CARSON CITY(1952), p; MARA MARU(1952), p; CHARGE AT FEATHER RIVER, THE(1953), p; THUNDER OVER THE PLAINS(1953), p; BOY FROM OKLAHOMA, THE(1954), p; COMMAND, THE(1954), p; JUMP INTO HELL(1955), p; REBEL WITHOUT A CAUSE(1955), p; TALL MAN RIDING(1955), p; TARGET ZERO(1955), p; BETWEEN HEAVEN AND HELL(1956), p; LOVE ME TENDER(1956), p; OUR MISS BROOKS(1956), p; STEEL JUNGLE, THE(1956), p; APRIL LOVE(1957), p; WAY TO THE GOLD, THE(1957), p; HOLIDAY FOR LOVERS(1959), p; PRIVATE'S AFFAIR, A(1959), p; THESE THOUSAND HILLS(1959), p; FLAMING STAR(1960), p; FOLLOW THAT DREAM(1962), p; KID GALAHAD(1962), p; GOODBYE CHARLIE(1964), p; PLEASURE SEEKERS, THE(1964), p; RIO CONCHOS(1964), p; VALLEY OF THE DOLLS(1967), p
Audrey Weisberg
NEANDERTHAL MAN, THE(1953), w
Barbara Weisberg
LONE WOLF IN LONDON(1947), w
Brenda Weisberg
LITTLE TOUGH GUY(1938), w; TOUGH KID(1939), w; MOB TOWN(1941), w; SING ANOTHER CHORUS(1941), w; THERE'S ONE BORN EVERY MINUTE(1942), w; YOU'RE TELLING ME(1942), w; KEEP 'EM SLUGGING(1943), w; MAD GHOUL, THE(1943), w; MUG TOWN(1943), w; BABES ON SWING STREET(1944), w; MUMMY'S GHOST, THE(1944), w; SCARLET CLAW, THE(1944), w; WEIRD WOMAN(1944), w; CHINA SKY(1945), w; DING DONG WILLIAMS(1946), w; SHADOWED(1946), w; KING OF THE WILD HORSES(1947), w; WHEN A GIRL'S BEAUTIFUL(1947), w; MY DOG RUSTY(1948), w; PORT SAID(1948), w; RUSTY SAVES A LIFE(1949), w; RUSTY'S BIRTHDAY(1949), w; GIRLS' SCHOOL(1950), w; ON THE ISLE OF SAMOA(1950), w; REUNION IN RENO(1951), w
Eric Weisberg
IF EVER I SEE YOU AGAIN(1978)
Louis Weisberg
ROLLERCOASTER(1977)
Rochelle Weisberg
DRILLER KILLER(1979), p
David Weisbert
CONSTANT NYMPH, THE(1943), ed
Bert Weisbourd
HAUNTS(1977), p
Ken Weisbrath
ONLY WHEN I LAUGH(1981)
Dan E. Weisburd
DINOSAURUS(1960), w
Brenda Weisburg
HIT THE ROAD(1941), w
Harry Weise
Misc. Silents
WAIF, THE(1915)
Gunter Weisenborn
THREE PENNY OPERA(1963, Fr./Ger.), w
Gunther Weisenborn
TALE OF FIVE WOMEN, A(1951, Brit.), w
Gordon Weisenborn [Herschell Gordon Lewis]
PRIME TIME, THE(1960), p&d
Joe Weisenfeld
BY DESIGN(1982), w
Joel Weisenfield
RECOMMENDATION FOR MERCY(1975, Can.), w
Bud Weiser
GAME THAT KILLS, THE(1937)
Grethe Weiser
HELP I'M INVISIBLE(1952, Ger.); TROMBA, THE TIGER MAN(1952, Ger.); CASINO DE PARIS(1957, Fr./Ger.); CITY OF SECRETS(1963, Ger.)

Stanley Weiser
COAST TO COAST(1980), w
Susan Weiser
PHANTOM OF THE PARADISE(1974)
Susan Weiser-Finley
FIRST TIME, THE(1983), w
Antje Weisgerber
RAMPAGE AT APACHE WELLS(1966, Ger./Yugo.)
David Weishart
THEM!(1954), p
Gunter Weishoff
MORITURI(1965)
Alan Weisinger
KRAMER VS. KRAMER(1979), makeup
Myra Weisler
PIRANHA II: THE SPAWNING(1981, Neth.)
A.T. Weisman
HIGH TERRACE(1957, Brit.), w
Ben Weisman
L'AMOUR(1973), m
David Weisman
CIAO MANHATTAN(1973), d&w; SHOGUN ASSASSIN(1980, Jap.), p, w
Sam Weisman
BEING THERE(1979); LOVING COUPLES(1980); WHOLLY MOSES(1980)
Straw Weisman
FIGHT FOR YOUR LIFE(1977), w
Hilde Weisner
SOMETHING FOR EVERYONE(1970)
Yvonne Weisner
RAINBOW BOYS, THE(1973, Can.)
Adrian Weiss
WHITE GORILLA(1947), p; BRIDE AND THE BEAST, THE(1958), p&d, w
Albert Weiss
DOUBLE CRIME IN THE MAGINOT LINE(1939, Fr.)
Allan Weiss
BLUE HAWAII(1961), w; GIRLS! GIRLS! GIRLS!(1962), w; FUN IN ACAPUL-CO(1963), w; ROUSTABOUT(1964), w; SONS OF KATIE ELDER, THE(1965), w; PARADISE, HAWAIIAN STYLE(1966), w
Allen Weiss
EASY COME, EASY GO(1967), w
Arnie Weiss
HAREM BUNCH; OR WAR AND PIECE, THE(1969), cos
Arnold Weiss
YOU LIGHT UP MY LIFE(1977)
Arthur Weiss
FLIPPER(1963), w; RHINO(1964), w; AROUND THE WORLD UNDER THE SEA(1966), w; NAMU, THE KILLER WHALE(1966), w
Bill Weiss
VENETIAN AFFAIR, THE(1967)
Charles Weiss
RUN ACROSS THE RIVER(1961), p
Chuck E. Weiss
1984
DUBEAT-E-O(1984)
Eric Weiss
PETULIA(1968, U.S./Brit.)
Florence Weiss
CANTOR'S SON, THE(1937); SINGING BLACKSMITH(1938); OVERTURE TO GLO-RY(1940)
Fritz Weiss
BASHFUL ELEPHANT, THE(1962, Aust.)
George Weiss
GLEN OR GLENDA(1953); BLONDE PICKUP(1955), p; OLGA'S GIRLS(1964), p
George David Weiss
SILHOUETTES(1982), a, w
George G. Weiss
GLEN OR GLENDA(1953), p
Gerard Weiss
MEDEA(1971, Ital./Fr./Ger.)
Harry Weiss
SEXTETTE(1978)
Harry Joel Weiss
ON DANGEROUS GROUND(1951)
Heinz Weiss
GREAT ESCAPE, THE(1963)
1984
LITTLE DRUMMER GIRL, THE(1984)
Helmut Weiss
TROMBA, THE TIGER MAN(1952, Ger.), d, w; FANNY HILL: MEMOIRS OF A WOMAN OF PLEASURE zero(1965); FROZEN ALIVE(1966, Brit./Ger.)
Helmuth Weiss
BOCCACCIO(1936, Ger.)
Itzik Weiss
JERUSALEM FILE, THE(1972, U.S./Israel)
Jack Weiss
Misc. Talkies
STORYVILLE(1974), d
Jacqueline Weiss
TRICK BABY(1973)
Jeff Weiss
EDGE, THE(1968)
Jiri Weiss
SWEET LIGHT IN A DARK ROOM(1966, Czech.), d, w; 90 DEGREES IN THE SHADE(1966, Czech./Brit.), d, w; MURDER CZECH STYLE(1968, Czech.), d, w
Joel Weiss
WARRIORS, THE(1979)
Joseph Weiss
HOUSE IS NOT A HOME, A(1964), m

Julie Weiss
I'M DANCING AS FAST AS I CAN(1982), cos; INDEPENDENCE DAY(1983), cos; SECOND THOUGHTS(1983), cos; SPACEHUNTER: ADVENTURES IN THE FORBID-DEN ZONE(1983), cos; TESTAMENT(1983), cos
Larry Weiss
1984
RHINESTONE(1984)
Louis Weiss
CAVALIER OF THE WEST(1931), p; BORDER DEVILS(1932), p; NIGHT RIDER, THE(1932), p; WITHOUT HONORS(1932), p; BEFORE MORNING(1933), p; DRUMS O' VOODOO(1934), p; COWBOY AND THE BANDIT, THE(1935), p; FIGHTING CABALLERO(1935), p; GHOST RIDER, THE(1935), p; PALS OF THE RANGE(1935), p; ROUGH RIDING RANGER(1935), p
Lurie Weiss
Silents
WEDDING MARCH, THE(1927)
Marcel Weiss
BRIDGE TO THE SUN(1961), ph; LONG ABSENCE, THE(1962, Fr./Ital.), ph; LA-DIES OF THE PARK(1964, Fr.), ph; MURDER AT 45 R.P.M.(1965, Fr.), ph; SOLO(1970, Fr.), ph; TRAFFIC(1972, Fr.), ph
Peter Weiss
INDECENT(1962, Ger.); PERSECUTION AND ASSASSINATION OF JEAN-PAUL MARAT AS PERFORMED BY THE INMATES OF THE ASYLUM OF CHARENTON UNDER THE DIRECTION OF THE MARQUIS DE SADE, THE(1967, Brit.), w; TELEFON(1977)
Robert K. Weiss
KENTUCKY FRIED MOVIE, THE(1977), p; BLUES BROTHERS, THE(1980), p; DOCTOR DETROIT(1983), p
Roberta Weiss
CROSS COUNTRY(1983, Can.)
Sam Weiss
MR. MAGOO'S HOLIDAY FESTIVAL(1970), prod d
Sammie Weiss
NAKED STREET, THE(1955)
Stephan Weiss
MONEY ON THE STREET(1930, Aust.), m
Stephen Weiss
QUARTERBACK, THE(1940), m
Thea Weiss
MOZART STORY, THE(1948, Aust.)
Trudy Weiss
SOMETHING'S ROTTEN(1979, Can.)
Herbert Weissbach
GLASS OF WATER, A(1962, Cgr.); CORPSE OF BEVERLY HILLS, THE(1965, Ger.); DE SADE(1969); 24-HOUR LOVER(1970, Ger.)
1984
LOVE IN GERMANY, A(1984, Fr./Ger.)
Eric Weissberg
DELIVERANCE(1972), m, song
Louis Weissberg
TEVYA(1939)
Maurice Weissberger
SMALL TOWN STORY(1953, Brit.), w
Edith Weissbluth
LOOKING UP(1977)
Jack Weissbluth
LOOKING UP(1977)
Jill Weissbluth
LOOKING UP(1977)
Burt Weissbourd
GHOST STORY(1981), p; RAGGEDY MAN(1981), p
Hanni Weisse
Misc. Silents
OTHER, THE(1912, Ger.); DARK CASTLE, THE(1915)
Norbert Weisser
MIDNIGHT EXPRESS(1978, Brit.); ANDROID(1982); THING, THE(1982); TWILIGHT ZONE–THE MOVIE(1983)
Larry Alan Weisshart
LOOKIN' TO GET OUT(1982)
Alvin Weissman
CALIFORNIA SPLIT(1974)
Benjamin A. Weissman
1984
LASSITER(1984), ed
Bernie Weissman
YOUNGBLOOD(1978)
Dora Weissman
GUERRILLA GIRL(1953); MIDDLE OF THE NIGHT(1959); PANIC IN NEEDLE PARK(1971)
Misc. Talkies
SONG OF SONGS(1935)
Gershon Weissman
Misc. Silents
MIRELE EFROS(1912, USSR); FATALNA KLATWA(1913, USSR); SLAUGHTER, THE(1913, USSR); STRANGER, THE(1913, USSR)
Herman Weissman
BRIDGE OF SAN LUIS REY, THE(1944), w
Jeffrey Weissman
TWILIGHT ZONE–THE MOVIE(1983)
1984
JOHNNY DANGEROUSLY(1984)
Jill-Rene Weissman
LOVE CHILD(1982)
Johnny Weissmuller
GLORIFYING THE AMERICAN GIRL(1930); TARZAN, THE APE MAN(1932); TARZAN AND HIS MATE(1934); TARZAN ESCAPES(1936); TARZAN FINDS A SON!(1939); TARZAN'S SECRET TREASURE(1941); TARZAN'S NEW YORK ADVEN-TURE(1942); STAGE DOOR CANTEEN(1943); TARZAN TRIUMPHS(1943); TARZAN'S DESERT MYSTERY(1943); TARZAN AND THE AMAZONS(1945); SWAMP FI-RE(1946); TARZAN AND THE LEOPARD WOMAN(1946); TARZAN AND THE

HUNTRESS(1947); JUNGLE JIM(1948); TARZAN AND THE MERMAIDS(1948); LOST TRIBE, THE(1949); CAPTIVE GIRL(1950); MARK OF THE GORILLA(1950); PYGMY ISLAND(1950); FURY OF THE CONGO(1951); JUNGLE MANHUNT(1951); JUNGLE JIM IN THE FORBIDDEN LAND(1952); VOODOO TIGER(1952); KILLER APE(1953); SAVAGE MUTINY(1953); VALLEY OF THE HEADHUNTERS(1953); CANNIBAL ATTACK(1954); JUNGLE MAN-EATERS(1954); DEVIL GODDESS(1955); JUNGLE MOON MEN(1955); PHYNX, THE(1970); WON TON TON, THE DOG WHO SAVED HOLLYWOOD(1976)

Johnny Weissmuller, Jr.
ANDY HARDY COMES HOME(1958); THX 1138(1971); AMERICAN GRAFFITI(1973)
Misc. Talkies
SHAME OF THE JUNGLE(1980, Fr./Bel.)

Hilde Weissner
DREAMER, THE(1936, Ger.); MAN WHO WAS SHERLOCK HOLMES, THE(1937, Ger.); TROMBA, THE TIGER MAN(1952, Ger.); JUST A GIGOLO(1979, Ger.)

Dwight Weist
ZELIG(1983)

Gary Weist
PUT UP OR SHUT UP(1968, Arg.), art d; PUTNEY SWOPE(1969), art d; HEX(1973), art d; SISTERS(1973), prod d; GREAT BANK HOAX, THE(1977), prod d; GOING IN STYLE(1979), art d; DRESSED TO KILL(1980), prod d; EDDIE AND THE CRUISERS(1983), art d
1984
ULTIMATE SOLUTION OF GRACE QUIGLEY, THE(1984), prod d

Alec Weisweiller
TESTAMENT OF ORPHEUS, THE(1962, Fr.)

Linda Weita
VERY NATURAL THING, A(1974)

Robert M. Weitman
ANDERSON TAPES, THE(1971), p; SHAMUS(1973), p

Louis Weitzenkorn
FIVE STAR FINAL(1931), w; 24 HOURS(1931), w; DEVIL IS DRIVING, THE(1932), w; LADIES OF THE BIG HOUSE(1932), w; MEN OF CHANCE(1932), w; TWO AGAINST THE WORLD(1936), w; KING OF THE NEWSBOYS(1938), w

Jacob Weizbluth
SUCH A GORGEOUS KID LIKE ME(1973, Fr.); LAST METRO, THE(1981, Fr.)

Heinz Weizel
FOUR COMPANIONS, THE(1938, Ger.)

Alexander Welbat
GOOSE GIRL, THE(1967, Ger.)

Peter Welbeck [Harry Alan Towers]
CODE 7, VICTIM 5(1964, Brit.), w; CITY OF FEAR(1965, Brit.), w; COAST OF SKELETONS(1965, Brit.), w; FACE OF FU MANCHU, THE(1965, Brit.), w; TEN LITTLE INDIANS(1965, Brit.), w; BRIDES OF FU MANCHU, THE(1966, Brit.), w; MOZAMBIQUE(1966, Brit.), w; 24 HOURS TO KILL(1966, Brit.), w; FIVE GOLDEN DRAGONS(1967, Brit.), w; HOUSE OF 1,000 DOLLS(1967, Ger./Span./Brit.), w; MILLION EYES OF SU-MURU, THE(1967, Brit.), w; PSYCHO-CIRCUS(1967, Brit.), w; THOSE FANTASTIC FLYING FOOLS(1967, Brit), w; BLOOD OF FU MANCHU, THE(1968, Brit.), w; CASTLE OF FU MANCHU, THE(1968, Ger./Span./Ital./Brit.), w; EVE(1968, Brit./Span.), w; VENGEANCE OF FU MANCHU, THE(1968, Brit./Ger./Hong Kong/Ireland), w; SANDY THE SEAL(1969, Brit.), w; CALL OF THE WILD(1972, Ger./Span./Ital./Fr.), w

George Welbes
OH! CALCUTTA!(1972); HURRY UP OR I'LL BE 30(1973)

Charles S. Welborn
THREE STOOGES MEET HERCULES, THE(1962), ph

Homer Welborne
FOLLOW THE SUN(1951)

Charles S. Welbourne
CREATURE FROM THE BLACK LAGOON(1954), spec eff; REVENGE OF THE CREATURE(1955), ph

Patricia Welby
Misc. Talkies
BEST, THE(1979)

Robert Welby
DAYTONA BEACH WEEKEND(1965), p&d

Bernice Welch
Silents
OUT OF THE WEST(1926)

Bettina Welch
NO. 96(1974, Aus.)

Beverly Ann Welch
MERRY-GO-ROUND OF 1938(1937)

Bo Welch
1984
SWING SHIFT(1984), art d

Bruce Welch
SWINGER'S PARADISE(1965, Brit.); FINDERS KEEPERS(1966, Brit.)

Charles Welch
GONE ARE THE DAYS(1963)

Dacid Welch
LOOKIN' TO GET OUT(1982)

Daniel Welch
DOZENS, THE(1981)

David Welch
SECOND-HAND HEARTS(1981)

Doug Welch
WE GO FAST(1941), w

Ed Welch
STAND UP VIRGIN SOLDIERS(1977, Brit.), m; THIRTY NINE STEPS, THE(1978, Brit.), m; SHILLINGBURY BLOWERS, THE(1980, Brit.), m; DANGEROUS DAVIES-THE LAST DETECTIVE(1981, Brit.), m; FUNNY MONEY(1983, Brit.), m

Eddie Welch
FIFTY MILLION FRENCHMEN(1931), w; PEACH O' RENO(1931), w; LADIES OF THE JURY(1932), w; MAMA LOVES PAPA(1933), w; HOLD'EM YALE(1935), w; F MAN(1936), w; MURDER GOES TO COLLEGE(1937), w; WILD MONEY(1937), w; HER JUNGLE LOVE(1938), w; PRISON FARM(1938), w; SCANDAL STREET(1938), w; LAS VEGAS NIGHTS(1941), w

Edward Welch
GIRL CRAZY(1932), w

Eileen Welch
TERRORNAUTS, THE(1967, Brit.), cos

Elisabeth Welch
DEATH AT A BROADCAST(1934, Brit.); ALIBI, THE(1943, Brit.); FIDDLERS THREE(1944, Brit.); REVENGE OF THE PINK PANTHER(1978)

Elizabeth Welch
BIG FELLA(1937, Brit.); SONG OF FREEDOM(1938, Brit.); OVER THE MOON(1940, Brit.); DEAD OF NIGHT(1946, Brit.); GIRL STROKE BOY(1971, Brit.); ARABIAN ADVENTURE(1979, Brit.)

Frederic Welch
TEENAGERS FROM OUTER SPACE(1959)

Harry "Zoop" Welch
KING OF BURLESQUE(1936)

J. B. Welch
LONELYHEARTS(1958)

James Welch
STORMY(1935)
Silents
NEW CLOWN, THE(1916, Brit.); ABRAHAM LINCOLN(1924); IRON HORSE, THE(1924); WEST OF THE RAINBOW'S END(1926)
Misc. Silents
WHEN KNIGHTS WERE BOLD(1916, Brit.); SPEEDY SPURS(1926); ROUGH RIDIN' RED(1928)

Jerry Welch
BRIDE WORE BOOTS, THE(1946), set d; STRANGE LOVE OF MARTHA IVERS, THE(1946), set d; JOHNNY RENO(1966), set d

Jim Welch
RUGGLES OF RED GAP(1935); TRAIL OF THE LONESOME PINE, THE(1936)
1984
ALL OF ME(1984)
Silents
MARSHAL OF MONEYMINT, THE(1922)
Misc. Silents
BROKEN SPUR, THE(1921); SHERIFF OF SUN-DOG, THE(1922); TONIO, SON OF THE SIERRAS(1925); WARRIOR GAP(1925)

Joe Welch
Misc. Silents
PEDDLER, THE(1917)

John Welch
LUCKY JIM(1957, Brit.)

Joseph N. Welch
ANATOMY OF A MURDER(1959)

Judy Welch
NOW THAT APRIL'S HERE(1958, Can.)

Lester Welch
TROUBLE WITH GIRLS(AND HOW TO GET INTO IT), THE*1/2 (1969), p; SEVEN HILLS OF ROME, THE(1958), p; GUNFIGHTERS OF CASA GRANDE(1965, U.S./Span.), p; SON OF A GUNFIGHTER(1966, U.S./Span.), p

Lisa Welch
HISTORY OF THE WORLD, PART 1(1981)
1984
REVENGE OF THE NERDS(1984)

Loren Welch
G.I. JANE(1951)

Louis Welch
CAR, THE(1977)

Mary Welch
PARK ROW(1952)

Nelson Welch
THUNDER IN THE EAST(1953); NOTORIOUS LANDLADY, THE(1962); LIST OF ADRIAN MESSENGER, THE(1963); O'HARA'S WIFE(1983); TABLE FOR FIVE(1983)

Niles Welch
CONVICTED(1931); BORDER DEVILS(1932); CORNERED(1932); CROSS-EXAMINATION(1932); MC KENNA OF THE MOUNTED(1932); NIGHT CLUB LADY(1932); RAINBOW TRAIL(1932); SCARLET WEEKEND, A(1932); SILVER DOLLAR(1932); COME ON TARZAN(1933); LONE AVENGER, THE(1933); MYSTERIOUS RIDER, THE(1933); SUNDOWN RIDER, THE(1933); ZOO IN BUDAPEST(1933); CROSS STREETS(1934); FIGHTING CODE, THE(1934); HERE COMES THE NAVY(1934); JEALOUSY(1934); LET'S FALL IN LOVE(1934); THIS SIDE OF HEAVEN(1934); IVORY-HANDLED GUN(1935); LIVING ON VELVET(1935); SINGING VAGABOND, THE(1935); STONE OF SILVER CREEK(1935); STRANDED(1935); TOMORROW'S YOUTH(1935); STORY OF LOUIS PASTEUR, THE(1936); WIFE VERSUS SECRETARY(1936); EMPTY SADDLES(1937)
Misc. Talkies
SUNDOWN RIDER(1933); RIDING WILD(1935)
Silents
ROYAL FAMILY, A(1915); STORK'S NEST, THE(1915); ONE OF MANY(1917); JANE GOES A' WOOING(1919); LITTLE COMRADE(1919); REPUTATION(1921); SIN OF MARTHA QUEED, THE(1921); WAY OF A MAID, THE(1921); RAGS TO RICHES(1922); RECKLESS YOUTH(1922); SAWDUST(1923); GIRL ON THE STAIRS, THE(1924); IN BORROWED PLUMES(1926); SPIDER WEBS(1927)
Misc. Silents
CRUCIAL TEST, THE(1916); KISS OF HATE, THE(1916); MERELY MARY ANN(1916); MISS GEORGE WASHINGTON(1916); MAYBLOSSOM(1917); SECRET OF THE STORM COUNTRY, THE(1917); FACE IN THE DARK, THE(1918); GATES OF GLADNESS(1918); GULF BETWEEN, THE(1918); HER BOY(1918); RECLAIMED(1918); SHAME(1918); HAUNTED BEDROOM, THE(1919); LAW OF MEN, THE(1919); STEPPING OUT(1919); VIRTUOUS THIEF, THE(1919); WINNING GIRL, THE(1919); BECKONING ROADS(1920); COURAGE OF MARGE O'DOONE, THE(1920); LUCK OF GERALDINE LAIRD, THE(1920); CUP OF LIFE, THE(1921); REMORSELESS LOVE(1921); SPENDERS, THE(1921); WHO AM I?(1921); UNDER OATH(1922); WHY ANNOUNCE YOUR MARRIAGE?(1922); MY MAN(1924); WINE OF YOUTH(1924); DANGEROUS PLEASURE(1925); ERMINE AND RHINESTONES(1925); FEAR-BOUND(1925); LITTLE GIRL IN A BIG CITY, A(1925); SCANDAL STREET(1925); SUBSTITUTE WIFE, THE(1925); FAITHFUL WIVES(1926)

Pat Welch
TOP BANANA(1954); WEEKEND WITH THE BABYSITTER(1970)
Peter Welch
ADMIRABLE CRICHTON, THE(1957, Brit.); HOUSE OF THE SEVEN HAWKS, THE(1959); SILENT ENEMY, THE(1959, Brit.); TWO-HEADED SPY, THE(1959, Brit.); SECRET PARTNER, THE(1961, Brit.); SECRET OF BLOOD ISLAND, THE(1965, Brit.)
Phyllis Welch
PROFESSOR BEWARE(1938)
Raquel Welch
HOUSE IS NOT A HOME, A(1964); ROUSTABOUT(1964); SWINGIN' SUMMER, A(1965); FANTASTIC VOYAGE(1966); SHOOT LOUD, LOUDER... I DON'T UNDERSTAND(1966, Ital.); BEDAZZLED(1967, Brit.); FATHOM(1967); ONE MILLION YEARS B.C.(1967, Brit./U.S.); BANDOLERO!(1968); BIGGEST BUNDLE OF THEM ALL, THE(1968); LADY IN CEMENT(1968); OLDEST PROFESSION, THE(1968, Fr./Ital./Ger.); FLAREUP(1969); 100 RIFLES(1969); MAGIC CHRISTIAN, THE(1970, Brit.); HANNIE CALDER(1971, Brit.); BLUEBEARD(1972); FUZZ(1972); KANSAS CITY BOMBER(1972); LAST OF SHEILA, THE(1973); THREE MUSKETEERS, THE(1974, Panama); FOUR MUSKETEERS, THE(1975); WILD PARTY, THE(1975); MOTHER, JUGS & SPEED(1976); CROSSED SWORDS(1978)
Misc. Talkies
BELOVED, THE(1972)
Robert Welch
VARIETY GIRL(1947), w
Robert "Bo" Welch
STAR CHAMBER, THE(1983), art d
Robert L. Welch
PALEFACE, THE(1948), p; SORROWFUL JONES(1949), p; TOP O' THE MORNING(1949), p; FANCY PANTS(1950), p; MR. MUSIC(1950), p; LEMON DROP KID, THE(1951), p; SON OF PALEFACE(1952), a, p, w
Robert W. Welch III
HISTORY OF THE WORLD, PART 1(1981), set d
1984
BEST DEFENSE(1984), art d
Scott Welch
Silents
WILD OATS LANE(1926)
Tim Welch
ONE FLEW OVER THE CUCKOO'S NEST(1975)
Warren Welch
TONY ROME(1967), set d
William Welch
CAVALRY(1936); PROMISES, PROMISES(1963), w; BROTHERHOOD OF SATAN, THE(1971), w
Silents
OVER THE HILL TO THE POORHOUSE(1920); LAW FORBIDS, THE(1924); ISLE OF FORGOTTEN WOMEN(1927); WESTERN ROVER, THE(1927); DAREDEVIL'S REWARD(1928)
Misc. Silents
DON DARE DEVIL(1925)
William J. Welch
1984
PLACES IN THE HEART(1984)
Michael Welchberger
ORDERED TO LOVE(1963, Ger.)
Buck Welcher
OFFICER AND A GENTLEMAN, AN(1982)
Harry Welchman
MAID OF THE MOUNTAINS, THE(1932, Brit.); SOUTHERN MAID, A(1933, Brit.); LAST WALTZ, THE(1936, Brit.); COMMON TOUCH, THE(1941, Brit.); THIS WAS PARIS(1942, Brit.); GENTLE SEX, THE(1943, Brit.); COLONEL BLIMP(1945, Brit.); I'LL TURN TO YOU(1946, Brit.); LISBON STORY, THE(1946, Brit.); LOYAL HEART(1946, Brit.); WALTZ TIME(1946, Brit.); GREEN FINGERS(1947); JUDGMENT DEFERRED(1952, Brit.); MAD ABOUT MEN(1954, Brit.); THREE CASES OF MURDER(1955, Brit.)
Silents
HOUSE ON THE MARSH, THE(1920, Brit.)
Misc. Silents
MR. LYNDON AT LIBERTY(1915, Brit.); VERDICT OF THE HEART, THE(1915, Brit.); LYONS MAIL, THE(1916, Brit.)
Gertrude Welcker
Misc. Silents
DR. MABUSE, THE GAMBLER(1922, Ger.)
Graham Welcome
1984
CHAMPIONS(1984)
Laura Welcome
WILD GYPSIES(1969)
Linda Weld
SMOKE IN THE WIND(1975)
Tuesday Weld
ROCK, ROCK, ROCK!(1956); WRONG MAN, THE(1956); RALLY 'ROUND THE FLAG, BOYS!(1958); FIVE PENNIES, THE(1959); BECAUSE THEY'RE YOUNG(1960); HIGH TIME(1960); SEX KITTENS GO TO COLLEGE(1960); PRIVATE LIVES OF ADAM AND EVE, THE(1961); RETURN TO PEYTON PLACE(1961); WILD IN THE COUNTRY(1961); BACHELOR FLAT(1962); SOLDIER IN THE RAIN(1963); CINCINNATI KID, THE(1965); I'LL TAKE SWEDEN(1965); LORD LOVE A DUCK(1966); PRETTY POISON(1968); I WALK THE LINE(1970); SAFE PLACE, A(1971); PLAY IT AS IT LAYS(1972); LOOKING FOR MR. GOODBAR(1977); WHO'LL STOP THE RAIN?(1978); SERIAL(1980); THIEF(1981); AUTHOR! AUTHOR!(1982)
1984
ONCE UPON A TIME IN AMERICA(1984)
Alex Welden
KRAKATOA, EAST OF JAVA(1969), spec eff
Ben Welden
BIG BUSINESS(1930, Brit.); MAN FROM CHICAGO, THE(1931, Brit.); 77 PARK LANE(1931, Brit.); BORN LUCKY(1932, Brit.); HIS LORDSHIP(1932, Brit.); MISSING REMBRANDT, THE(1932, Brit.); TIN GODS(1932, Brit.); WHY SAPS LEAVE HOME(1932, Brit.); GENERAL JOHN REGAN(1933, Brit.); HIS GRACE GIVES NOTICE(1933, Brit.); HOME, SWEET HOME(1933, Brit.); MANNEQUIN(1933, Brit.); MEDICINE MAN, THE(1933, Brit.); MR. QUINCEY OF MONTE CARLO(1933, Brit.);

PRIDE OF THE FORCE, THE(1933, Brit.); THEIR NIGHT OUT(1933, Brit.); THIS IS THE LIFE(1933, Brit.); BLACK ABBOT, THE(1934, Brit.); MAN WHO CHANGED HIS NAME, THE(1934, Brit.); RIVER WOLVES, THE(1934, Brit.); ALIBI INN(1935, Brit.); ANNIE, LEAVE THE ROOM(1935, Brit.); BIG SPLASH, THE(1935, Brit.); COME OUT OF THE PANTRY(1935, Brit.); REGAL CAVALCADE(1935, Brit.); TRIUMPH OF SHERLOCK HOLMES, THE(1935, Brit.); TRUST THE NAVY(1935, Brit.); WOLVES OF THE UNDERWORLD(1935, Brit.); AVENGING HAND, THE(1936, Brit.); GAY LOVE(1936, Brit.); HOT NEWS(1936, Brit.); IMPROPER DUCHESS, THE(1936, Brit.); MURDER ON THE SET(1936, Brit.); SHE KNEW WHAT SHE WANTED(1936, Brit.); ANOTHER DAWN(1937); BACK IN CIRCULATION(1937); CONFESSION(1937); DUKE COMES BACK, THE(1937); GREAT GARRICK, THE(1937); KID GALAHAD(1937); KING AND THE CHORUS GIRL, THE(1937); LAST GANGSTER, THE(1937); LOVE AND HISSES(1937); LOVE IS ON THE AIR(1937); MARKED WOMAN(1937); MAYTIME(1937); MISSING WITNESSES(1937); PHANTOM SHIP(1937, Brit.); SILENT BARRIERS(1937, Brit.); THAT CERTAIN WOMAN(1937); VARSITY SHOW(1937); WESTBOUND MAIL(1937); ALWAYS GOODBYE(1938); CITY GIRL(1938); CRIME RING(1938); HAPPY LANDING(1938); LITTLE MISS BROADWAY(1938); LITTLE ORPHAN ANNIE(1938); MYSTERY HOUSE(1938); NIGHT HAWK, THE(1938); PRISON NURSE(1938); SAINT IN NEW YORK, THE(1938); SMASHING THE RACKETS(1938); STRAIGHT, PLACE AND SHOW(1938); TENTH AVENUE KID(1938); BOY'S REFORMATORY(1939); FEDERAL MAN-HUNT(1939); FUGITIVE AT LARGE(1939); HOLLYWOOD CAVALCADE(1939); I WAS A CONVICT(1939); LONE WOLF SPY HUNT, THE(1939); ROSE OF WASHINGTON SQUARE(1939); SERGEANT MADDEN(1939); STAND UP AND FIGHT(1939); STAR MAKER, THE(1939); EARL OF CHICAGO, THE(1940); OUTSIDE THE 3-MILE LIMIT(1940); PASSPORT TO ALCATRAZ(1940); SOUTH OF PAGO PAGO(1940); WOLF OF NEW YORK(1940); CITY, FOR CONQUEST(1941); I'LL WAIT FOR YOU(1941); KNOCKOUT(1941); MANPOWER(1941); MEN OF BOYS TOWN(1941); MR. DISTRICT ATTORNEY(1941); NINE LIVES ARE NOT ENOUGH(1941); OUT OF THE FOG(1941); STRANGE ALIBI(1941); ALL THROUGH THE NIGHT(1942); BULLET SCARS(1942); DANGEROUSLY THEY LIVE(1942); MAISIE GETS HER MAN(1942); STAND BY FOR ACTION(1942); HERE COMES ELMER(1943); SECRETS OF THE UNDERGROUND(1943); FIGHTING SEABEES, THE(1944); SHADOWS IN THE NIGHT(1944); CIRCUMSTANTIAL EVIDENCE(1945); IT'S IN THE BAG(1945); MISSING CORPSE, THE(1945); ANGEL ON MY SHOULDER(1946); BIG SLEEP, THE(1946); DANGEROUS BUSINESS(1946); LAST CROOKED MILE, THE(1946); MAN I LOVE, THE(1946); MR. HEX(1946); FIESTA(1947); HEADING FOR HEAVEN(1947); KILLER DILL(1947); LITTLE MISS BROADWAY(1947); PRETENDER, THE(1947); SINBAD THE SAILOR(1947); TOO MANY WINNERS(1947); APPOINTMENT WITH MURDER(1948); DUDE GOES WEST, THE(1948); JINX MONEY(1948); LADY AT MIDNIGHT(1948); NOOSE HANGS HIGH, THE(1948); SMART GIRLS DON'T TALK(1948); SONG IS BORN, A(1948); TRAPPED BY BOSTON BLACKIE(1948); VICIOUS CIRCLE, THE(1948); FIGHTING FOOLS(1949); IMPACT(1949); MARY RYAN, DETECTIVE(1949); RIDERS IN THE SKY(1949); SEARCH FOR DANGER(1949); SORROWFUL JONES(1949); TOUGH ASSIGNMENT(1949); BUCCANEER'S GIRL(1950); DESERT HAWK, THE(1950); ON THE ISLE OF SAMOA(1950); LEMON DROP KID, THE(1951); MY TRUE STORY(1951); TALES OF ROBIN HOOD(1951); NIGHT STAGE TO GALVESTON(1952); ALL ASHORE(1953); THUNDER BAY(1953); VEILS OF BAGDAD, THE(1953); KILLERS FROM SPACE(1954); STEEL CAGE, THE(1954); MA AND PA KETTLE AT WAIKIKI(1955); HIDDEN GUNS(1956); HOLLYWOOD OR BUST(1956); SPOOK CHASERS(1957)
Charles Welden
HOUSE OF WAX(1953), w
Alfred Weldenmann
CANARIS(1955, Ger.), d; I, TOO, AM ONLY A WOMAN(1963, Ger.), d
Alex Weldon
TRIPOLI(1950), spec eff; PHANTOM FROM SPACE(1953), spec eff; DEFIANT ONES, THE(1958), spec eff; TIMBUKTU(1959), spec eff; KING OF KINGS(1961), spec eff; LONGEST DAY, THE(1962), spec eff; 55 DAYS AT PEKING(1963), spec eff; CIRCUS WORLD(1964), spec eff; FALL OF THE ROMAN EMPIRE, THE(1964), spec eff; CRACK IN THE WORLD(1965), spec eff; GUNS OF THE MAGNIFICENT SEVEN(1969), spec eff; CANNON FOR CORDOBA(1970), spec eff; HORSEMEN, THE(1971), spec eff; OKLAHOMA CRUDE(1973), spec eff; WIND AND THE LION, THE(1975); ISLANDS IN THE STREAM(1977), spec eff; RAISE THE TITANIC(1980, Brit.), spec eff
Alex C. Weldon
ORCA(1977), spec eff
Ann Weldon
SHAMPOO(1975); YOUNGBLOOD(1978); SERIAL(1980); I'M DANCING AS FAST AS I CAN(1982)
Ben Weldon
ALONG CAME SALLY(1934, Brit.); ADMIRALS ALL(1935, Brit.)
Charles Weldon
TRICK BABY(1973); RIVER NIGER, THE(1976); STIR CRAZY(1980); FAST-WALKING(1982)
Jasper Weldon
FOXES OF HARROW, THE(1947); LONE HAND TEXAN, THE(1947); LARCENY(1948); COUNTY FAIR(1950); NO WAY OUT(1950); NARROW MARGIN, THE(1952)
Jasper D. Weldon
MY FRIEND IRMA GOES WEST(1950); CARRIE(1952)
Jess Weldon
Silents
THIEF OF BAGDAD, THE(1924)
Jimmy Weldon
PHANTOM PLANET, THE(1961); AMERICATHON(1979)
1984
CHATTANOOGA CHOO CHOO(1984)
Joan Weldon
SO THIS IS LOVE(1953); STRANGER WORE A GUN, THE(1953); SYSTEM, THE(1953); COMMAND, THE(1954); DEEP IN MY HEART(1954); RIDING SHOTGUN(1954); THEM!(1954); GUNSIGHT RIDGE(1957); DAY OF THE BAD MAN(1958); HOME BEFORE DARK(1958)
Maisie Weldon
MELODY IN THE DARK(1948, Brit.)
Marian Weldon
COLORADO KID(1938)

Marion Weldon
DODGE CITY TRAIL(1937); DESERT PATROL(1938); FEUD MAKER(1938); YOU AND ME(1938); KNIGHT OF THE PLAINS(1939)
Mary-Jo Weldon
FOLIES BERGERE(1958, Fr.), ch
Mike Weldon
MANTIS IN LACE(1968), makeup; HARD ROAD, THE(1970)
Robert Weldon
DEAD MEN TELL(1941)
Tim Weldon
ILLUSTRATED MAN, THE(1969)
Alex Weldone
EL CID(1961, U.S./Ital.), spec eff
Walter Welebit
CHILDRENS GAMES(1969), p, d, w
Frank Welfer
Misc. Talkies
LOONEY, LOONEY, LOONEY BUGS BUNNY MOVIE, THE(1981)
Nancy Welford
GOLD DIGGERS OF BROADWAY(1929); PHANTOM IN THE HOUSE, THE(1929); JAZZ CINDERELLA(1930); SAFE AFFAIR, A(1931, Brit.)
Romulus of Welham
NO ROAD BACK(1957, Brit.)
Franz Welhmayr
CANARIS(1955, Ger.), ph
Karl-Erik Welin
OBSESSION(1968, Swed.), m
Ernest Welisch
BRIDE OF THE REGIMENT(1930), w; THAT LADY IN ERMINE(1948), w
Ljuba Welitsch
HIPPODROME(1961, Aust./Ger.); ARMS AND THE MAN(1962, Ger.)
Frank Welker
TROUBLE WITH GIRLS(AND HOW TO GET INTO IT), THE (1969); COMPUTER WORE TENNIS SHOES, THE(1970); HOW TO FRAME A FIGG(1971); DIRTY LITTLE BILLY(1972); NOW YOU SEE HIM, NOW YOU DON'T(1972); ZORRO, THE GAY BLADE(1981)
1984
STAR TREK III: THE SEARCH FOR SPOCK(1984)
Stirling Welker
VELVET TRAP, THE(1966); PEACE FOR A GUNFIGHTER(1967)
Danny Well
GOIN' COCONUTS(1978)
Elvira Well
Silents
BRIDE OF HATE, THE(1917)
Lori Well
DRESSER, THE(1983)
Richard Well
TWO WEEKS OFF(1929), w
Colin Welland
KES(1970, Brit.); STRAW DOGS(1971, Brit.); VILLAIN(1971, Brit.); SWEENEY(1977, Brit.); YANKS(1979), w; CHARRIOTS OF FIRE(1981, Brit.), w
James Wellard
ACTION OF THE TIGER(1957), w
Charles S. Wellborn
MANFISH(1956), ph
Tim Wellburn
CADDIE(1976, Aus.), ed; IRISHMAN, THE(1978, Aus.), ed; CATHY'S CHILD(1979, Aus.), ed; CHAIN REACTION(1980, Aus.), ed; ROAD WARRIOR, THE(1982, Aus.), ed; KILLING OF ANGEL STREET, THE(1983, Aus.), ed
William Wellburn
JOURNEY TO THE CENTER OF TIME(1967), ed
J. M. Welleminsky
LOVES OF MADAME DUBARRY, THE(1938, Brit.), w
Calvin Weller
Silents
GIRL OF MY HEART(1920)
Elsie Weller
SUSPICION(1941)
Jada Weller
Misc. Silents
BETRAYAL(1929)
Mary Louise Weller
HAIL(1973); SERPICO(1973); EVIL, THE(1978); NATIONAL LAMPOON'S ANIMAL HOUSE(1978); BELL JAR, THE(1979); BLOOD TIDE(1982); FORCED VENGEANCE(1982); Q(1982)
Michael Weller
HAIR(1979), w; RAGTIME(1981), w
Peter Weller
BUTCH AND SUNDANCE: THE EARLY DAYS(1979); JUST TELL ME WHAT YOU WANT(1980); SHOOT THE MOON(1982); OF UNKNOWN ORIGIN(1983, Can.)
1984
ADVENTURES OF BUCKAROO BANZAI: ACROSS THE 8TH DIMENSION, THE(1984); FIRSTBORN(1984)
Beatrice Welles
CHIMES AT MIDNIGHT(1967, Span.,Switz.)
Betty Welles
FOR ME AND MY GAL(1942)
Christopher Welles
MACBETH(1948)
Constance Welles
ENTERTAINER, THE(1960, Brit.)
Diana Welles
WEDDING PARTY, THE(1969)
Dick Welles
BEASTS OF BERLIN(1939)
Dorit Welles
DIVIDED HEART, THE(1955, Brit.)

Gretchen Welles
GRUESOME TWOSOME(1968)
Gwen Welles
SAFE PLACE, A(1971); HIT(1973); CALIFORNIA SPLIT(1974); NASHVILLE(1975); BETWEEN THE LINES(1977)
Halsted Welles
3:10 TO YUMA(1957), w; LADY GAMBLES, THE(1949), w; HANGING TREE, THE(1959), w; TIME FOR KILLING, A(1967), w; HELL WITH HEROES, THE(1968), w
Herman Welles
ENTERTAINER, THE(1960, Brit.)
Jennifer Welles
FEMALE RESPONSE, THE(1972)
Misc. Talkies
SUGAR COOKIES(1973); GOOD, THE BAD, AND THE BEAUTIFUL, THE(1975)
Jesse Welles
HEY, GOOD LOOKIN'(1982)
1984
RHINESTONE(1984)
Mary Welles
RED SHEIK, THE(1963, Ital.)
Mel Welles [Ernst von Theumer]
GUN FURY(1953); MASSACRE CANYON(1954); PUSHOVER(1954); SILVER CHALICE, THE(1954); ABBOTT AND COSTELLO MEET THE MUMMY(1955); DUEL ON THE MISSISSIPPI(1955); FIGHTING CHANCE, THE(1955); HOLD BACK TOMORROW(1955); RACERS, THE(1955); SOLDIER OF FORTUNE(1955); WYOMING RENEGADES(1955); FLIGHT TO HONG KONG(1956); OUTSIDE THE LAW(1956); SPY CHASERS(1956); ATTACK OF THE CRAB MONSTERS(1957); HELL ON DEVIL'S ISLAND(1957); HOLD THAT HYPNOTIST(1957); ROCK ALL NIGHT(1957); UNDEAD, THE(1957); 27TH DAY, THE(1957); BROTHERS KARAMAZOV, THE(1958); CODE OF SILENCE(1960), d; LITTLE SHOP OF HORRORS(1961); RED SHEIK, THE(1963, Ital.); CHRISTINE KEELER AFFAIR, THE(1964, Brit.); SHE BEAST, THE(1966, Brit./Ital./Yugo.); ISLAND OF THE DOOMED(1968, Span./Ger.), d; LADY FRANKENSTEIN(1971, Ital.), d, p; DR. HECKYL AND MR. HYPE(1980); WOLFEN(1981); HOMEWORK(1982)
Misc. Talkies
JOY RIDE TO NOWHERE(1978), a, d; BABY DOLLS(1982)
Meri Welles
LADIES MAN, THE(1961); HOUSE IS NOT A HOME, A(1964)
Orson Welles
CITIZEN KANE(1941), a, p&d, w; JOURNEY INTO FEAR(1942), a, p, w; MAGNIFICENT AMBERSONS, THE(1942), a, p, d, w; JANE EYRE(1944); DUEL IN THE SUN(1946); STRANGER THE(1946), a, d, w; TOMORROW IS FOREVER(1946); MONSIEUR VERDOUX(1947), p,d&w; LADY FROM SHANGHAI, THE(1948), a, p,d&w; MACBETH(1948), a, p, d, w, cos; BLACK MAGIC(1949); PRINCE OF FOXES(1949); BLACK ROSE, THE(1950); THIRD MAN, THE(1950, Brit.); TRENT'S LAST CASE(1953, Brit.); TROUBLE IN THE GLEN(1954, Brit.); NAPOLEON(1954, Fr.); OTHELLO(1955, U.S./Fr./Ital.), a, p,d&w; MOBY DICK(1956, Brit.); MAN IN THE SHADOW(1957); ROYAL AFFAIRS IN VERSAILLES(1957, Fr.); LONG, HOT SUMMER, THE(1958); ROOTS OF HEAVEN, THE(1958); TOUCH OF EVIL(1958), a, d, w; COMPULSION(1959); FERRY TO HONG KONG(1959, Brit.); AUSTERLITZ(1960, Fr./Ital./Yugo.); CRACK IN THE MIRROR(1960); DAVID AND GOLIATH(1961, Ital.); KING OF KINGS(1961); MR. ARKADIN(1962, Brit./Fr./Span.), a, d, w, art d, cos; TARTARS, THE(1962, Ital./Yugo.); LAFAYETTE(1963, Fr.); TRIAL, THE(1963, Fr./Ital./Ger.), a, d&w; V.I.P.s, THE(1963, Brit.); IS PARIS BURNING?(1966, U.S./Fr.); MAN FOR ALL SEASONS, A(1966, Brit.); MARCO THE MAGNIFICENT(1966, Ital./Fr./Yugo./Egypt/Afghanistan); CASINO ROYALE(1967, Brit.); CHIMES AT MIDNIGHT(1967, Span.,-Switz.), a, d&w; I'LL NEVER FORGET WHAT'S 'IS NAME(1967, Brit.); SAILOR FROM GIBRALTAR, THE(1967, Brit.); OEDIPUS THE KING(1968, Brit.); FIGHT FOR ROME(1969, Ger./Rum.); HOUSE OF CARDS(1969); IMMORTAL STORY, THE(1969, Fr.), a, d, w; SOUTHERN STAR, THE(1969, Fr./Brit.); CATCH-22(1970); KREMLIN LETTER, THE(1970); START THE REVOLUTION WITHOUT ME(1970); TWELVE PLUS ONE(1970, Fr./Ital.); WATERLOO(1970, Ital./USSR); BATTLE OF THE NERETVA(1971, Yugo./Ital./Ger.); SAFE PLACE, A(1971); GET TO KNOW YOUR RABBIT(1972); MALPERTIUS(1972, Bel./Fr.); NECROMANCY(1972); TEN DAYS' WONDER(1972, Fr.); TREASURE ISLAND(1972, Brit./Span./Fr./Ger.); BUGS BUNNY, SUPERSTAR(1975); TEN LITTLE INDIANS(1975, Ital./Fr./Span./Ger.); VOYAGE OF THE DAMNED(1976, Brit.); HOT TOMORROWS(1978); MUPPET MOVIE, THE(1979); THE DOUBLE McGUFFIN(1979); HISTORY OF THE WORLD, PART 1(1981); BUTTERFLY(1982)
1984
SLAPSTICK OF ANOTHER KIND(1984); WHERE IS PARSIFAL?(1984, Brit.)
Misc. Talkies
BLOOD AND GUNS(1979, Ital.); MAN WHO SAW TOMORROW, THE(1981)
Ralph Welles
NIGHT RIDE(1930); GIRLS DEMAND EXCITEMENT(1931)
Rebecca Welles
DESIRE UNDER THE ELMS(1958); JUVENILE JUNGLE(1958)
Stephen Welles
LONG ROPE, THE(1961)
Terri Welles
LOOKER(1981)
Virginia Welles
KISS AND TELL(1945); TO EACH HIS OWN(1946); DEAR RUTH(1947); LADIES' MAN(1947); VARIETY GIRL(1947); DYNAMITE(1948); JOE PALOOKA IN THE BIG FIGHT(1949); KISS FOR CORLISS, A(1949); MAKE BELIEVE BALLROOM(1949); SQUARE DANCE KATY(1950); CASA MANANA(1951); FRANCIS IN THE HAUNTED HOUSE(1956)
Wendy Welles
TALES OF ORDINARY MADNESS(1983, Ital.)
Alfred Wellesley
WARM CORNER, A(1930, Brit.); HERE'S GEORGE(1932, Brit.); NEW HOTEL, THE(1932, Brit.); CLEANING UP(1933, Brit.); GREAT STUFF(1933, Brit.); LUCKY NUMBER, THE(1933, Brit.); GIRLS WILL BE BOYS(1934, Brit.); SONG AT EVENTIDE(1934, Brit.); ANNIE, LEAVE THE ROOM(1935, Brit.); CHARING CROSS ROAD(1935, Brit.); MURDER ON THE SET(1936, Brit.); TOMORROW WE LIVE(1936, Brit.); LAST CHANCE, THE(1937, Brit.); MUSEUM MYSTERY(1937, Brit.); ROMANCE AND RICHES(1937, Brit.); WHAT A MAN!(1937, Brit.); HIDDEN MENACE, THE(1940, Brit.)

Arthur Wellesley
WANTED(1937, Brit.)
Charles Wellesley
Silents
POOR LITTLE RICH GIRL, A(1917); NOBODY(1921); SILVER LINING, THE(1921);
STARDUST(1921); JUST A SONG AT TWILIGHT(1922); ACQUITTAL(1923);
ALIAS THE NIGHT WIND(1923); DON'T MARRY FOR MONEY(1923); ENEMIES OF
CHILDREN(1923); LEGALLY DEAD(1923); CYTHEREA(1924); LOST WORLD,
THE(1925); UNHOLY THREE, THE(1925); COLLEGE DAYS(1926); STOLEN BRIDE,
THE(1927); SKINNER'S BIG IDEA(1928)
Misc. Silents
DARING OF DIANA, THE(1916); HERO OF SUBMARINE D-2, THE(1916); ISLAND
OF SURPRISE, THE(1916); REDEMPTION(1917); HEART OF A GIRL(1918); PURPLE
LILY, THE(1918); RICHEST GIRL, THE(1918); IT ISN'T BEING DONE THIS SEA-
SON(1921); TRAFFIC IN HEARTS(1924)
George Wellesley
CHINESE DEN, THE(1940, Brit.), w
Gordon Wellesley
OVER THE GARDEN WALL(1934, Brit.), w; SING AS WE GO(1934, Brit.), w; DEATH
DRIVES THROUGH(1935, Brit.), w; JAVA HEAD(1935, Brit.), w; LOOK UP AND
LAUGH(1935, Brit.), w; LORNA DOONE(1935, Brit.), w; LABURNUM GROVE(1936,
Brit.), w; QUEEN OF HEARTS(1936, Brit.), w; NIGHT TRAIN(1940, Brit.), w; ATLAN-
TIC FERRY(1941, Brit.), w; VOICE IN THE NIGHT, A(1941, Brit.), w; FLYING
FORTRESS(1942, Brit.), w; PETERVILLE DIAMOND, THE(1942, Brit.); THIS WAS
PARIS(1942, Brit.), w; RHYTHM SERENADE(1943, Brit.), d; SHIPBUILDERS,
THE(1943, Brit.), w; MR. EMMANUEL(1945, Brit.), w; SILVER FLEET, THE(1945,
Brit.), d&w; LOST PEOPLE, THE(1950, Brit.), p; RELUCTANT WIDOW, THE(1951,
Brit.), p, w; GREEN SCARF, THE(1954, Brit.), w; MARCH HARE, THE(1956, Brit.), w;
PASSPORT TO CHINA(1961, Brit.), w; DEAD MAN'S EVIDENCE(1962, Brit.), w;
DOOMSDAY AT ELEVEN(1963 Brit.), w; MALPAS MYSTERY, THE(1967, Brit.), w
Gordon Wong Wellesley
RIGHT TO LIVE, THE(1933, Brit.), w; SHANGHAI MADNESS(1933), w; HIGH
COMMAND(1938, Brit.), p
Roger Wellesley
REMBRANDT(1936, Brit.)
William Wellesley
Silents
GOLDFISH, THE(1924)
Christina Wellford
Misc. Talkies
I WAS A ZOMBIE FOR THE F.B.I.(1982)
Hal Welling
JOURNEY FOR MARGARET(1942)
Marge Welling
Misc. Talkies
NOT TONIGHT HENRY(1961)
Sylvia Welling
I'LL TURN TO YOU(1946, Brit.); COMIN' THRU' THE RYE(1947, Brit.)
Wendy Welling
DUMMY TALKS, THE(1943, Brit.)
Arthur Wellington
Silents
PAYING THE LIMIT(1924)
Larry Wellington
GIRL, THE BODY, AND THE PILL, THE(1967), md; TASTE OF BLOOD, A(1967), md;
GRUESOME TWOSOME(1968), m; JUST FOR THE HELL OF IT(1968), m; SHE-
DEVILS ON WHEELS(1968), m; WIZARD OF GORE, THE(1970), m
Warwick Wellington
Silents
RUPERT OF HENTZAU(1915, Brit.)
Misc. Silents
WORLD, THE FLESH AND THE DEVIL, THE(1914, Brit.)
Ernst Wellish
Silents
MADAME POMPADOUR(1927, Brit.), w
Bill Wellman, Jr.
DARBY'S RANGERS(1958); LAFAYETTE ESCADRILLE(1958); PORK CHOP
HILL(1959)
Cissy Wellman
RED LINE 7000(1965); FM(1978); SEPARATE WAYS(1981)
Gloria Wellman
Silents
WINGS(1927)
Harold Wellman
SINBAD THE SAILOR(1947), spec eff; CLASH BY NIGHT(1952), spec. eff; LAS
VEGAS STORY, THE(1952), spec eff; INVISIBLE BOY, THE(1957), ph; HOW THE
WEST WAS WON(1962), ph; MUSCLE BEACH PARTY(1964), ph; FIRST TO
FIGHT(1967), ph
Harold E. Wellman
HITCH-HIKER, THE(1953), spec eff; MURDER IS MY BEAT(1955), ph; WATU-
SI(1959), ph; KEY WITNESS(1960), ph; ATLANTIS, THE LOST CONTINENT(1961),
ph; KING KONG(1976), spec eff
James Wellman
BEACH BALL(1965); WILD, WILD WINTER(1966); MRS. POLLIFAX-SPY(1971);
GLASS HOUSES(1972)
Jane Wellman
NUTCRACKER(1982, Brit.)
Maggie Wellman
HARRAD EXPERIMENT, THE(1973); RANCHO DELUXE(1975)
Manly Wade Wellman
WHO FEARS THE DEVIL(1972), w
Margery Chapin Wellman
Silents
WINGS(1927)
Michael Wellman
HIGH AND THE MIGHTY, THE(1954)
Mike Wellman
ISLAND IN THE SKY(1953)

Paul I. Wellman
CHEYENNE(1947), w; WALLS OF JERICHO(1948), w; IRON MISTRESS,
THE(1952), w; APACHE(1954), w; JUBAL(1956), w; COMANCHEROS, THE(1961), w
Tim Wellman
ISLAND IN THE SKY(1953)
W. A. Wellman
CHINATOWN NIGHTS(1929), d
Wendell Wellman
KLANSMAN, THE(1974); FIREFOX(1982), w; SUDDEN IMPACT(1983)
William Wellman
BEGGARS OF LIFE(1928), d; MAYBE IT'S LOVE(1930), d; STAR WITNESS(1931), d;
CONQUERORS, THE(1932), d; HATCHET MAN, THE(1932), d; COLLEGE
COACH(1933), d; HEROES FOR SALE(1933), d; LOOKING FOR TROUBLE(1934), d;
CALL OF THE WILD(1935), d; SMALL TOWN GIRL(1936), d; NOTHING SAC-
RED(1937), d; BATTLEGROUND(1949), d; ACROSS THE WIDE MISSOURI(1951), d;
IT'S A BIG COUNTRY(1951), d; BLOOD ALLEY(1955), d; DARBY'S RANGERS(1958),
d; STAR IS BORN, A(1976), w
Silents
KNICKERBOCKER BUCKAROO, THE(1919); SECOND HAND LOVE(1923), d;
WINGS(1927), a, d; LADIES OF THE MOB(1928), d
Misc. Silents
NOT A DRUM WAS HEARD(1924), d; BOOB, THE(1926), d
William Wellman, Jr.
HIGH SCHOOL CONFIDENTIAL(1958); HORSE SOLDIERS, THE(1959); COLLEGE
CONFIDENTIAL(1960); MACUMBA LOVE(1960); DONDI(1961); ERRAND BOY,
THE(1961); LIKE FATHER LIKE SON(1961); SWINGIN' AFFAIR, A(1963); DISORD-
ERLY ORDERLY, THE(1964); GUNFIGHT AT COMANCHE CREEK(1964); PATSY,
THE(1964); SWINGIN' SUMMER, A(1965); WINTER A GO-GO(1965); YOUNG FU-
RY(1965); YOUNG SINNER, THE(1965); BORN LOSERS(1967); HAPPIEST MIL-
LIONAIRE, THE(1967); PRIVATE NAVY OF SGT. O'FARRELL, THE(1968); WHICH
WAY TO THE FRONT?(1970); BLACK CAESAR(1973); IT'S ALIVE(1974); TRIAL OF
BILLY JACK, THE(1974); MAC ARTHUR(1977)
William A. Wellman
MAN I LOVE, THE(1929), d; WOMAN TRAP(1929), d; DANGEROUS PARADIS-
E(1930), d; YOUNG EAGLES(1930), d; NIGHT NURSE(1931), d; OTHER MEN'S
WOMEN(1931), d; PUBLIC ENEMY, THE(1931), d; SAFE IN HELL(1931), d; STAR
WITNESS(1931); LOVE IS A RACKET(1932), d; PURCHASE PRICE, THE(1932), d; SO
BIG(1932), d; CENTRAL AIRPORT(1933), d; FRISCO JENNY(1933), d; LILLY TURN-
ER(1933), d; MIDNIGHT MARY(1933), d; WILD BOYS OF THE ROAD(1933), d;
PRESIDENT VANISHES, THE(1934), d; STINGAREE(1934), d; ROBIN HOOD OF EL
DORADO(1936), d, w; LAST GANGSTER, THE(1937), w; STAR IS BORN, A(1937), d,
w; MEN WITH WINGS(1938), p&d; BEAU GESTE(1939), p&d; LIGHT THAT FAILED,
THE(1939), p&d; REACHING FOR THE SUN(1941), p&d; GREAT MAN'S LADY,
THE(1942), p&d; ROXIE HART(1942), d; THUNDER BIRDS(1942), d; LADY OF BUR-
LESQUE(1943), d; OX-BOW INCIDENT, THE(1943), d; BUFFALO BILL(1944), d; STO-
RY OF G.I. JOE, THE(1945), d; THIS MAN'S NAVY(1945), d; GALLANT
JOURNEY(1946), p&d, w; MAGIC TOWN(1947), d; IRON CURTAIN, THE(1948), d;
YELLOW SKY(1948), d; HAPPY YEARS, THE(1950), d; WESTWARD THE WO-
MEN(1951), d; MY MAN AND I(1952), d; ISLAND IN THE SKY(1953), d; HIGH AND
THE MIGHTY, THE(1954), d; RING OF FEAR(1954), d; STAR IS BORN, A(1954), w;
TRACK OF THE CAT(1954), d; GOODBYE, MY LADY(1956), d; LAFAYETTE ESCAD-
RILLE(1958), p&d, w
Silents
CAT'S PAJAMAS, THE(1926), d
Misc. Silents
BIG DAN(1923), d; CUPID'S FIREMAN(1923), d; MAN WHO WON, THE(1923), d;
CIRCUS COWBOY, THE(1924), d; VAGABOND TRAIL, THE(1924), d; WHEN HUS-
BANDS FLIRT(1925), d; YOU NEVER KNOW WOMEN(1926), d; LEGION OF THE
CONDEMNED(1928), d
William A. Wellman, Jr.
LAFAYETTE ESCADRILLE(1958)
Ingeborg Wellmann
HELDINNEN(1962, Ger.)
Aarika Wells
SHARKY'S MACHINE(1982)
Alan Wells
AIR STRIKE(1955); GREAT MISSOURI RAID, THE(1950); MAN WHO CHEATED
HIMSELF, THE(1951); BEACHHEAD(1954); CANYON CROSSROADS(1955); RE-
TURN OF JACK SLADE, THE(1955); MAGNIFICENT ROUGHNECKS(1956); CAPE
FEAR(1962)
Alex Wells
CURFEW BREAKERS(1957), d
Alex J. Wells
STALAG 17(1953)
Alexander J. Wells
RAWHIDE TRAIL, THE(1958), w
Allan Wells
APACHE CHIEF(1949)
Allen Wells
BIG TIP OFF, THE(1955)
Angela Wells
CROCODILE(1979, Thai./Hong Kong)
Ann Wells
CREATURE OF THE WALKING DEAD(1960, Mex.)
Arika Wells
1984
ACT, THE(1984)
Aubrey Wells
COAL MINER'S DAUGHTER(1980)
Betty Wells
GRAND CENTRAL MURDER(1942); 'NEATH BROOKLYN BRIDGE(1942); TORTIL-
LA FLAT(1942); GILDERSLEEVE'S BAD DAY(1943); SENSATIONS OF 1945(1944)
Billy Wells
CONCERNING MR. MARTIN(1937, Brit.)
Silents
GREAT GAME, THE(1918, Brit.); RING, THE(1927, Brit.)
Misc. Silents
KENT THE FIGHTING MAN(1916, Brit.); SILVER LINING, THE(1919, Brit.);
CLOUDBURST(1922)

Bombardier Billy Wells
MR. WHAT'S-HIS-NAME(1935, Brit.); EXCUSE MY GLOVE(1936, Brit.); FIND THE LADY(1936, Brit.); MELODY OF MY HEART(1936, Brit.); MAKE-UP(1937, Brit.); CITADEL, THE(1938); SAILING ALONG(1938, Brit.); THERE AIN'T NO JUSTICE(1939, Brit.); MAJOR BARBARA(1941, Brit.); WE'LL SMILE AGAIN(1942, Brit.); HAPPIDROME(1943, Brit.); OLD MOTHER RILEY, DETECTIVE(1943, Brit.)
Silents
KENT, THE FIGHTING MAN(1916, Brit.)

Bruce Wells
SERVANT, THE(1964, Brit.)

Carol Wells
LIZZIE(1957)

Carole Wells
THUNDER OF DRUMS, A(1961); COME BLOW YOUR HORN(1963); LIVELY SET, THE(1964); HOUSE OF SEVEN CORPSES, THE(1974); FUNNY LADY(1975); CHEAP DETECTIVE, THE(1978)

Charles Wells
RED, WHITE AND BLACK, THE(1970)

Chuck Wells
TRADER HORNEE(1970); MINNIE AND MOSKOWITZ(1971); SWEET JESUS, PREACHER MAN(1973)

Conrad Wells
BEHIND THAT CURTAIN(1929, ph; SKY HAWK(1929), ph; LET'S GO PLACES(1930), ph
Silents
GINSBERG THE GREAT(1927), ph; SWELL-HEAD, THE(1927), ph; CAPTAIN LASH(1929), ph; NEW YEAR'S EVE(1929), ph

Cyril Wells
IT'S LOVE AGAIN(1936, Brit.)

Danny Wells
SHAGGY D.A., THE(1976); HEY, GOOD LOOKIN'(1982)
1984
WOMAN IN RED, THE(1984)

Dara Wells
TAKE HER BY SURPRISE(1967, Can.)

Darryl Wells
MARK OF THE WITCH(1970)

David Wells
1984
BEVERLY HILLS COP(1984); STARMAN(1984)

Dawn Wells
NEW INTERNS, THE(1964); WINTERHAWK(1976); RETURN TO BOGGY CREEK(1977); TOWN THAT DREADED SUNDOWN, THE(1977)

Deering Wells
LORD OF THE MANOR(1933, Brit.); LUCKY DAYS(1935, Brit.); RICHARD III(1956, Brit.); TWO-HEADED SPY, THE(1959, Brit.)

Delores Wells
BIKINI BEACH(1964)

Dolores Wells
BEACH PARTY(1963); MUSCLE BEACH PARTY(1964); TIME TRAVELERS, THE(1964)

Don Wells
AROUND THE WORLD UNDER THE SEA(1966)

Edward Wells
ALL ASHORE(1953), w

Elaine Wells
KILL HER GENTLY(1958, Brit.)

Emma B.C. Wells
BY YOUR LEAVE(1935), w

Ethel "Pug" Wells
THREE GUYS NAMED MIKE(1951), w

Florence Wells
FORTY-NINERS, THE(1932)

Frank Wells
CLUE OF THE MISSING APE, THE(1953, Brit.), p, w; GOLD EXPRESS, THE(1955, Brit.), p; MISSING NOTE, THE(1961, Brit.), w; PIPER'S TUNE, THE(1962, Brit.), w; STOLEN PLANS, THE(1962, Brit.), p; FLOOD, THE(1963, Brit.), w; RESCUE SQUAD, THE(1963, Brit.), w; DAYLIGHT ROBBERY(1964, Brit.), w; GO KART GO(1964, Brit.), w; SEVENTY DEADLY PILLS(1964, Brit.), d&w; ESCAPE FROM THE SEA(1968, Brit.), d&w

George Wells
PRIVATE SCANDAL, A(1932); SHOW-OFF, THE(1946), w; TILL THE CLOUDS ROLL BY(1946), w; HUCKSTERS, THE(1947), w; MERTON OF THE MOVIES(1947), w; TAKE ME OUT TO THE BALL GAME(1949), w; SUMMER STOCK(1950), w; THREE LITTLE WORDS(1950), w; TOAST OF NEW ORLEANS, THE(1950), w; ANGELS IN THE OUTFIELD(1951), w; EXCUSE MY DUST(1951), w; IT'S A BIG COUNTRY(1951), w; SHOW BOAT(1951), w; TEXAS CARNIVAL(1951), w; EVERYTHING I HAVE IS YOURS(1952), p, w; LOVELY TO LOOK AT(1952), w; DANGEROUS WHEN WET(1953), p; I LOVE MELVIN(1953), p, w; JUPITER'S DARLING(1955), p; DESIGNING WOMAN(1957), w; PARTY GIRL(1958), w; ASK ANY GIRL(1959), w; GAZEBO, THE(1959), w; WHERE THE BOYS ARE(1960), w; HONEYMOON MACHINE, THE(1961), w; HORIZONTAL LIEUTENANT, THE(1962), w; PENELOPE(1966), w; THREE BITES OF THE APPLE(1967), w; IMPOSSIBLE YEARS, THE(1968), w; COVER ME BABE(1970), w; RED, WHITE AND BLACK, THE(1970); DON'T GO NEAR THE WATER(1975), w

Gerald Wells
1984
ELEMENT OF CRIME, THE(1984, Den.)

Gladys Wells
JUDGE PRIEST(1934)

H.G. Wells
ISLAND OF LOST SOULS(1933), w; THINGS TO COME(1936, Brit.), w; MAN WHO COULD WORK MIRACLES, THE(1937, Brit.), w; REMARKABLE MR. KIPPS(1942, Brit.), w; INVISIBLE MAN'S REVENGE(1944), w; DEAD OF NIGHT(1946, Brit.), w; HISTORY OF MR. POLLY, THE(1949, Brit.), w; ONE WOMAN'S STORY(1949, Brit.), w; ABBOTT AND COSTELLO MEET THE INVISIBLE MAN(1951), w; WAR OF THE WORLDS, THE(1953), w; INVISIBLE MAN, THE(1958, Mex.), w; TIME MACHINE, THE(1960, Brit./U.S.), w; FIRST MEN IN THE MOON(1964, Brit.), w; VILLAGE OF THE GIANTS(1965), w; HALF A SIXPENCE(1967, Brit.), w; FOOD OF THE GODS, THE(1976), w; EMPIRE OF THE ANTS(1977), w; ISLAND OF DR. MOREAU,

THE(1977), w
Silents
KIPPS(1921, Brit.), w; PASSIONATE FRIENDS, THE(1922, Brit.), w

Howard Wells
OUT OF THE TIGER'S MOUTH(1962), m

Hubert Wells
RING OF BRIGHT WATER(1969, Brit.), cons; LIVING FREE(1972, Brit.), animal t; SEA GYPSIES, THE(1978), animal t; WHITE DOG(1982)

Hubert G. Wells
1984
SHEENA(1984), animal t

Ingeborg Wells
CAPTAIN HORATIO HORNBLOWER(1951, Brit.); CHELSEA STORY(1951, Brit.); DEATH IS A NUMBER(1951, Brit.); ONE WILD OAT(1951, Brit.); KING OF THE UNDERWORLD(1952, Brit.); SCHOOL FOR BRIDES(1952, Brit.); SECRET PEOPLE(1952, Brit.); HOUSE OF BLACKMAIL(1953, Brit.); TWILIGHT WOMEN(1953, Brit.); CHILD'S PLAY(1954, Brit.); DOUBLE EXPOSURE(1954, Brit.); PORT OF ESCAPE(1955, Brit.); ACROSS THE BRIDGE(1957, Brit.)
Misc. Talkies
ACCUSED, THE(1953)

J. Wells
FIRE WITHIN, THE(1964, Fr./Ital.)

Jack Wells
SUPERCHICK(1973)

Jacqueline Wells [Julie Bishop]
SCAREHEADS(1931); TARZAN THE FEARLESS(1933); TILLIE AND GUS(1933); BLACK CAT, THE(1934); HAPPY LANDING(1934); KISS AND MAKE UP(1934); LOUDSPEAKER, THE(1934); CORONADO(1935); BOHEMIAN GIRL, THE(1936); NIGHT CARGO(1936); COUNSEL FOR CRIME(1937); FRAME-UP THE(1937); GIRLS CAN PLAY(1937); PAID TO DANCE(1937); FLIGHT INTO NOWHERE(1938); FLIGHT TO FAME(1938); HIGHWAY PATROL(1938); LITTLE ADVENTURESS, THE(1938); LITTLE MISS ROUGHNECK(1938); MAIN EVENT, THE(1938); SHE MARRIED AN ARTIST(1938); SPRING MADNESS(1938); WHEN G-MEN STEP IN(1938); BEHIND PRISON GATES(1939); KANSAS TERRORS, THE(1939); MY SON IS A CRIMINAL(1939); TORTURE SHIP(1939); GIRL IN 313(1940); HER FIRST ROMANCE(1940); MY SON IS GUILTY(1940); RANGER AND THE LADY, THE(1940); YOUNG BILL HICKOK(1940); BACK IN THE SADDLE(1941)
Misc. Talkies
SQUARE SHOOTER(1935)

James Wells
WALK, DON'T RUN(1966), ed; VISIT TO A CHIEF'S SON(1974), ph

James D. Wells
HURRY SUNDOWN(1967), ed; BEYOND AND BACK(1978), ed

Jene Wells
Silents
LITTLE LORD FAUNTLEROY(1914, Brit.)

Jennifer Wells
GROOVE TUBE, THE(1974)

Jerold Wells
HIGH HELL(1958); CONCRETE JUNGLE, THE(1962, Brit.); PIRATES OF BLOOD RIVER, THE(1962, Brit.); PLAYBACK(1962, Brit.); MANIAC(1963, Brit.); MASQUERADE(1965, Brit.); CANDIDATE FOR MURDER(1966, Brit.); SMASHING TIME(1967 Brit.); GAWAIN AND THE GREEN KNIGHT(1973, Brit.); VAULT OF HORROR, THE(1973, Brit.); WHAT'S NEXT?(1975, Brit.); TIME BANDITS(1981, Brit.)
1984
SWORD OF THE VALIANT(1984, Brit.)

Jerrold Wells
YOUR PAST IS SHOWING(1958, Brit.); JABBERWOCKY(1977, Brit.)

Jesse Wells
RETURN OF COUNT YORGA, THE(1971); WIZARDS(1977)

Joan Wells
TILL THE CLOUDS ROLL BY(1946); YEARLING, THE(1946); HIGH BARBAREE(1947)

John Wells
RAFTER ROMANCE(1934), w; LIVING ON LOVE(1937), w

John Wells
BOBO, THE(1967, Brit.); CASINO ROYALE(1967, Brit.); 30 IS A DANGEROUS AGE, CYNTHIA(1968, Brit.), a, w; THINK DIRTY(1970, Brit.); FOR YOUR EYES ONLY(1981)
1984
GREYSTOKE: THE LEGEND OF TARZAN, LORD OF THE APES(1984)

John Wells [Gian Maria Volonte]
FISTFUL OF DOLLARS, A(1964, Ital./Ger./Span.)

John K. Wells
NIGHT WORLD(1932)
Misc. Silents
QUEEN O' TURF(1922), d

Kenny Wells
THRESHOLD(1983, Can.)

Kitty Wells
SECOND FIDDLE TO A STEEL GUITAR(1965)

L.M. Wells
Silents
HUCKLEBERRY FINN(1920); WITCHING HOUR, THE(1921)
Misc. Silents
LIKE WILDFIRE(1917); MAN AND BEAST(1917); WIFE ON TRAIL, A(1917); BUCKING BROADWAY(1918); VIRGINIA COURTSHIP, A(1921); FOREST KING, THE(1922)

Larry Wells
PORKY'S(1982), cos; STRANGE BREW(1983), cos

Lee Wells
HAIR(1979)

Leila Burton Wells
Silents
PERFECT LOVER, THE(1919), w; WANTERS, THE(1923), w

Lillian Wells
DEAD RECKONING(1947); FRAMED(1947); 13TH HOUR, THE(1947)

Linton Wells
Silents
SUZANNA(1922), w
Lloyd Wells
GREATEST, THE(1977, U.S./Brit.)
Mae Wells
Silents
LAST EGYPTIAN, THE(1914)
Misc. Silents
HIS MAJESTY, THE SCARECROW OF OZ(1914)
Mai Wells
Silents
PILGRIM, THE(1923)
Misc. Silents
OPENED SHUTTERS(1921)
Margaret Wells
MARGIE(1946); TILL THE END OF TIME(1946); SPIRIT OF WEST POINT, THE(1947); LUCK OF THE IRISH(1948); PITFALL(1948); SECRET FURY, THE(1950); WELL, THE(1951); MY SON, JOHN(1952)
Marie Wells
DESERT SONG, THE(1929); SONG OF THE WEST(1930); BEYOND THE ROCKIES(1932); ELMER AND ELSIE(1934); SCARLET EMPRESS, THE(1934); CALL OF THE WILD(1935); FOLIES DERGERE(1935); I FOUND STELLA PARISH(1935); SHE MARRIED HER BOSS(1935); KLONDIKE ANNIE(1936); YOURS FOR THE ASKING(1936)
Misc. Silents
MAN FROM NEW YORK, THE(1923)
Marie E. Wells
Silents
SEALED LIPS(1915)
Matt Wells
EXCUSE MY GLOVE(1936, Brit.)
Maurice Wells
WRONG MAN, THE(1956); ROME ADVENTURE(1962); PANIC IN THE CITY(1968)
Mel Wells
BIG KNIFE, THE(1955); PIRATES OF TRIPOLI(1955); LAST AMERICAN VIRGIN, THE(1982)
Meri Wells
PINK PANTHER, THE(1964)
Norman Wells
FOR SINGLES ONLY(1968)
Norman D. Wells
VOYAGE TO THE PLANET OF PREHISTORIC WOMEN(1966), p
Oliver Wells
SUPERARGO(1968, Ital./Span.), p
Orlando Wells
1984
PLOUGHMAN'S LUNCH, THE(1984, Brit.)
Pamela Wells
WISTFUL WIDOW OF WAGON GAP, THE(1947)
Patrick Wells
CHILD'S PLAY(1954, Brit.); PERSONALS, THE(1982), p
Peter Wells
SWINGIN' MAIDEN, THE(1963, Brit.)
Raymond Wells
Silents
SABLE LORCHA, THE(1915); FLYING TORPEDO, THE(1916); KINKAID, GAMBLER(1916), d, w; ANTHING ONCE(1917); FIGHTING FOR LOVE(1917), d, w; LOVE AFLAME(1917), d, w; FLAMES OF CHANCE, THE(1918), d; MAN ABOVE THE LAW(1918), d; OH, WHAT A NURSE!(1926); TONY RUNS WILD(1926); UNKNOWN CAVALIER, THE(1926); YANKEE SENOR, THE(1926); JEWELS OF DESIRE(1927); FREE LIPS(1928), w; SOULS AFLAME(1928), a, d&w
Misc. Silents
OLD HEIDELBERG(1915); FANATICS(1917), d; HERO OF THE HOUR, THE(1917), d; MR. DOLAN OF NEW YORK(1917), d; TERROR, THE(1917), d; HAND AT THE WINDOW, THE(1918), d; HARD ROCK BREED, THE(1918), d; HIS ENEMY THE LAW(1918), d; LAW OF THE GREAT NORTHWEST, THE(1918), d; MLLE PAULETTE(1918), d; OLD LOVES FOR NEW(1918), d; DEATH VALLEY(1927); FAGASA(1928), a, d
Raymond B. Wells
Misc. Talkies
TRAILS OF ADVENTURE(1935)
Misc. Silents
FIGHTING BACK(1917), d; SAINTLY SINNER, THE(1917), d; THOSE WHO PAY(1918), d
Rick Wells
LAST REBEL, THE(1971)
Robert Wells
FIGHTER, THE(1952); ALL ASHORE(1953), w; FROM HERE TO ETERNITY(1953), m/l
Roxene Wells
OREGON TRAIL, THE(1959)
Roy Wells
1984
SOLDIER'S STORY, A(1984)
Scott Wells
HARD TRAIL(1969)
Sharon Wells
KILL, THE(1968)
Sheilah Wells
LOVE AND KISSES(1965)
Si Wells
THREE CHEERS FOR LOVE(1936)
Stanley Wells
1984
RHINESTONE(1984)
Ted Wells
WEST OF CARSON CITY(1940); WESTERNER, THE(1940); UNDERCOVER MAN(1942); SUNDOWN RIDERS(1948)

Misc. Talkies
WHITE RENEGADE(1931); DEFYING THE LAW(1935); PHANTOM COWBOY, THE(1935)
Silents
BEAUTY AND BULLETS(1928); GRIT WINS(1929)
Misc. Silents
DESERT DUST(1927); SHOOTING STRAIGHT(1927); STRAIGHT SHOOTIN'(1927); CLEAN-UP MAN, THE(1928); CRIMSON CANYON, THE(1928); GREASED LIGHTING(1928); MADE-TO-ORDER HERO, A(1928); THUNDER RIDERS(1928); BORDER WILDCAT, THE(1929); BORN TO THE SADDLE(1929); RIDIN' DEMON, THE(1929); SMILING TERROR, THE(1929)
Thomas Wells
Silents
AIN'T LOVE FUNNY?(1927)
Tiffany Wells
Silents
MISS NOBODY(1926), w
Tiny Wells
WHEN YOU COMIN' BACK, RED RYDER?(1979); HAWMPS!(1976); WANDA NEVADA(1979); HEART LIKE A WHEEL(1983)
Tom Wells
STORM WARNING(1950)
Tracy Wells
1984
GREMLINS(1984)
Travers Wells
Silents
RECKLESS SEX, THE(1925), w
Vernon Wells
ROAD WARRIOR, THE(1982, Aus.)
Veronica Wells
KITCHEN, THE(1961, Brit.); GIDGET GOES TO ROME(1963); BOOM!(1968)
Victoria Wells
LOSIN' IT(1983)
W.K. Wells
COHENS AND KELLYS IN AFRICA, THE(1930), w; GOLD DUST GERTIE(1931), w
William Wells
Misc. Silents
BATTLE OF BALLOTS, THE(1915)
William K. Wells
BIG TIME(1929), w; COCK-EYED WORLD, THE(1929), w; FOX MOVIETONE FOLLIES(1929), w; BIG BOY(1930), w; FOLLOW THE LEADER(1930), w; FOX MOVIETONE FOLLIES OF 1930(1930), w; HOT FOR PARIS(1930), w; LET'S GO PLACES(1930), w; ON THE LEVEL(1930), w; PUTTIN' ON THE RITZ(1930), w; CAPTAIN THUNDER(1931), w; OTHER MEN'S WOMEN(1931), w; SIDE SHOW(1931), w; SIT TIGHT(1931), w; MEET THE BARON(1933), w
Win Wells
REDNECK(1975, Ital./Span.), w; GREEK TYCOON, THE(1978), w
Wyn Wells
CALL OF THE WILD(1972, Ger./ Span./Ital./Fr.), w
Charles Wellsley
Silents
AMERICAN WAY, THE(1919)
Ollegard Wellton
SWEDISH MISTRESS, THE(1964, Swed.)
Patricia Wellum
SCOTLAND YARD DRAGNET(1957, Brit.)
Vince Welnick
LADIES AND GENTLEMEN, THE FABULOUS STAINS(1982)
Dick Welsbacher
ATTIC, THE(1979)
Anne Welsch
HARD TIMES(1975)
Gloria Welsch
DEAD MAN'S GOLD(1948), w
Howard Welsch
TROUBLE AHEAD(1936, Brit.), p; DALTONS RIDE AGAIN, THE(1945), p; MEN IN HER DIARY(1945), p; CAT CREEPS, THE(1946), p; CUBAN PETE(1946), p; DARK HORSE, THE(1946), p; IDEA GIRL(1946), p; SPIDER WOMAN STRIKES BACK, THE(1946), p; MICHIGAN KID, THE(1947), p; PHILO VANCE RETURNS(1947), p; PHILO VANCE'S GAMBLE(1947), p; PHILO VANCE'S SECRET MISSION(1947), p; VIGILANTES RETURN, THE(1947), p; HOUSE BY THE RIVER(1950), p; WOMAN ON THE RUN(1950), p; GROOM WORE SPURS, THE(1951), p; MONTANA BELLE(1952), p, w; RANCHO NOTORIOUS(1952), p; SAN FRANCISCO STORY, THE(1952), p; BULLET IS WAITING, A(1954), p; HOT BLOOD(1956), p
Christine Welsford
MYSTERY AT THE BURLESQUE(1950, Brit.)
Betty Welsh
Misc. Silents
COME AND GET IT(1929)
Bill Welsh
LAS VEGAS STORY, THE(1952); ROSE BOWL STORY, THE(1952); DRAGSTRIP GIRL(1957)
Cliff Welsh
1984
RENO AND THE DOC(1984, Can.)
Dorothy Welsh
Misc. Silents
BRIDGE OF SIGHS, THE(1915)
Elizabeth Welsh
OUR MAN IN HAVANA(1960, Brit.)
Fred Welsh
REMAINS TO BE SEEN(1953)
Freddy Welsh
JEALOUSY(1934)
Gerald Welsh
PANDORA AND THE FLYING DUTCHMAN(1951, Brit.)

Harry "Zoup" Welsh
RENDEZVOUS(1935)
James Welsh
HEADIN' NORTH(1930)
Misc. Silents
DESPERATE GAME, THE(1926); DOG JUSTICE(1928); PINTO KID, THE(1928)
Jane Welsh
BELLS, THE(1931, Brit.); SHERLOCK HOLMES' FATAL HOUR(1931, Brit.); CHINESE PUZZLE, THE(1932, Brit.); CONDEMNED TO DEATH(1932, Brit.); FRAIL WOMEN(1932, Brit.); MISSING REMBRANDT, THE(1932, Brit.); SPRING IN THE AIR(1934, Brit.); WHISPERING TONGUES(1934, Brit.); ANNIE, LEAVE THE ROOM(1935, Brit.); LITTLE DOLLY DAYDREAM(1938, Brit.); BELL-BOTTOM GEORGE(1943, Brit.); JUST WILLIAM'S LUCK(1948, Brit.); WILLIAM COMES TO TOWN(1948, Brit.); DRAGON OF PENDRAGON CASTLE, THE(1950, Brit.); SECOND MATE, THE(1950, Brit.); WOMAN IN HIDING(1953, Brit.); ANOTHER TIME, ANOTHER PLACE(1958)
Jim Welsh
Misc. Silents
BLUE BLAZES(1926)
Joe Welsh
Misc. Silents
TIME LOCK NO. 776(1915)
John Welsh
FATHER OF THE BRIDE(1950); CLUE OF THE MISSING APE, THE(1953, Brit.); ISN'T LIFE WONDERFUL!(1953, Brit.); DIPLOMATIC PASSPORT(1954, Brit.); INSPECTOR CALLS, AN(1954, Brit.); DIVIDED HEART, THE(1955, Brit.); WARRIORS, THE(1955); DEADLIEST SIN, THE(1956, Brit.); MAN WHO NEVER WAS, THE(1956, Brit.); TRACK THE MAN DOWN(1956, Brit.); BIRTHDAY PRESENT, THE(1957, Brit.); COUNTERFEIT PLAN, THE(1957, Brit.); LONG HAUL, THE(1957, Brit.); MAN IN THE ROAD, THE(1957, Brit.); SURGEON'S KNIFE, THE(1957, Brit.); TEARS FOR SIMON(1957, Brit.); THIRD KEY, THE(1957, Brit.); VIOLENT STRANGER(1957, Brit.); BEHIND THE MASK(1958, Brit.); DUNKIRK(1958, Brit.); MAN WHO WOULDN'T TALK, THE(1958, Brit.); REVENGE OF FRANKENSTEIN, THE(1958, Brit.); SAFECRACKER, THE(1958, Brit.); SECRET PLACE, THE(1958, Brit.); BOBBIKINS(1959, Brit.); NOWHERE TO GO(1959, Brit.); ROOM AT THE TOP(1959, Brit.); BEYOND THE CURTAIN(1960, Brit.); FOLLOW THAT HORSE!(1960, Brit.); NEXT TO NO TIME(1960, Brit.); SNOWBALL(1960, Brit.); CIRCLE OF DECEPTON(1961, Brit.); FRANCIS OF ASSISI(1961, Brit.); KONGA(1961, Brit.); MARK, THE(1961, Brit.); PORTRAIT OF A SINNER(1961, Brit.); GO TO BLAZES(1962, Brit.); LISA(1962, Brit.); MAKE MINE A DOUBLE(1962, Brit.); QUARE FELLOW, THE(1962, Brit.); SHE DIDN'T SAY NO!(1962, Brit.); NIGHTMARE(1963, Brit.); OPERATION BULLSHINE(1963, Brit.); PLAYBOY OF THE WESTERN WORLD, THE(1963, Ireland); YOUNG AND WILLING(1964, Brit.); JOHNNY NOBODY(1965, Brit.); RASPUTIN–THE MAD MONK(1966, Brit.); WALK IN THE SHADOW(1966, Brit.); ATTACK ON THE IRON COAST(1968, U.S./Brit.); SUBTERFUGE(1969, US/Brit.); CROMWELL(1970, Brit.); MAN WHO HAUNTED HIMSELF, THE(1970, Brit.); PIED PIPER, THE(1972, Brit.); NORSEMAN, THE(1978); THIRTY NINE STEPS, THE(1978, Brit.); MY FAVORITE YEAR(1982); KRULL(1983)
Jonathan Welsh
SECOND WIND(1976, Can.); AGENCY(1981, Can.); THRESHOLD(1983, Can.)
1984
SURROGATE, THE(1984, Can.)
Jonathon Welsh
CITY ON FIRE(1979 Can.)
Ken Welsh
1984
RENO AND THE DOC(1984, Can.)
Kenneth Welsh
DOUBLE NEGATIVE(1980, Can.); PHOBIA(1980, Can.); OF UNKNOWN ORIGIN(1983, Can.)
1984
COVERGIRL(1984, Can.); FALLING IN LOVE(1984)
Misc. Talkies
LOVE AND LARCENY(1983)
Nanon Welsh
Silents
ARE YOU LEGALLY MARRIED?(1919)
Niles Welsh
Silents
WHAT WIVES WANT(1923)
Misc. Silents
EVIDENCE(1922)
Norman Welsh
ONE PLUS ONE(1961, Can.)
Peter Welsh
SILENT ENEMY, THE(1959, Brit.)
Robert Welsh
MELODY OF LOVE, THE(1928), w; SENSATION HUNTERS(1934), p
Ronnie Welsh, Jr.
PATTERNS(1956)
Robert E. Welsh
THREE LEGIONNAIRES, THE(1937), p; BOOLOO(1938), w
Susan Welsh
LOVE AND MONEY(1982)
Sylvia Welsh
WOMAN AGAINST THE WORLD(1938)
T.A. Welsh
EAST LYNNE ON THE WESTERN FRONT(1931, Brit.), p, w; THIRD STRING, THE(1932, Brit.), p; GOOD COMPANIONS(1933, Brit.), p; SHIPMATES O' MINE(1936, Brit.), p; SOMEWHERE IN CIVVIES(1943, Brit.), p
Silents
SQUIBS' HONEYMOON(1926, Brit.), w
Thomas Welsh
SUMMERTREE(1971), cos
Tim Welsh
Misc. Talkies
11 X 14(1977)
Tom Welsh
TWICE TOLD TALES(1963), cos

Tommy Welsh
OTHER, THE(1972), cos
1984
COUNTRY(1984), cos
William Welsh
MISSISSIPPI GAMBLER(1929); SKINNER STEPS OUT(1929); LOVE TRADER(1930); SUNDOWN TRAIL(1931); BEYOND THE ROCKIES(1932); FREIGHTERS OF DESTINY(1932); GAMBLING SHIP(1933); STORMY(1935); TO PLEASE A LADY(1950); MATING SEASON, THE(1951)
Silents
TRAFFIC IN SOULS(1913); NEPTUNE'S DAUGHTER(1914); ELUSIVE ISABEL(1916); 20,000 LEAGUES UNDER THE SEA(1916); ETERNAL SIN, THE(1917); REPUTATION(1921); FLIRT, THE(1922); RIDIN' WILD(1922); SCRAPPER, THE(1922); SHOCK, THE(1923); SHOOTIN' FOR LOVE(1923); TOWN SCANDAL, THE(1923); EXCITEMENT(1924); MAN FROM WYOMING, THE(1924); WHITE OUTLAW, THE(1925); WANDERING GIRLS(1927); HEAD OF THE FAMILY, THE(1928)
Misc. Silents
CONSCIENCE(1915); WHITE TERROR, THE(1915); LORDS OF HIGH DECISION, THE(1916); LITTLE DIPLOMAT, THE(1919); LURING LIPS(1921); MAN TAMER, THE(1921); RAMBLIN' KID, THE(1923); SHADOWS OF THE NORTH(1923); PRICE SHE PAID, THE(1924); FLYING HOOFS(1925); DEMON, THE(1926); MAN FROM THE WEST, THE(1926); COMPANIONATE MARRIAGE, THE(1928)
William H. Welsh
IT'S A BIG COUNTRY(1951)
William J. Welsh
RUGGLES OF RED GAP(1935)
Jan Pieter Welt
MAIDSTONE(1970), a, ph, ed
Jan Welt
BEYOND THE LAW(1967, Ital.), ed; BEYOND THE LAW(1968), ph, ed; WILD 90(1968), ed
Philippe Welt
1984
UNTIL SEPTEMBER(1984), ph
Ariadne Welter
UNTOUCHED(1956); VAMPIRE'S COFFIN, THE(1958, Mex.); DEVIL'S HAND, THE(1961); LAST REBEL, THE(1961, Mex.); CRIMINAL LIFE OF ARCHIBALDO DE LA CRUZ, THE(1962, Mex.); QUEEN'S SWORDSMEN, THE(1963, Mex.); RAGE(1966, U.S./Mex.); VAMPIRE, THE(1968, Mex.)
Uschi Welter
1984
WOMAN IN FLAMES, A(1984, Ger.), cos
Manny Weltman
DOCTOR DETROIT(1983)
Danny Welton
ARMY BOUND(1952); MEET DANNY WILSON(1952); FIGHTING TROUBLE(1956); YOUNG AND DANGEROUS(1957); TERRIFIED!(1963)
Maria Welton
FANTASM(1976, Aus.)
Myron Welton
EMERGENCY WEDDING(1950); MILITARY ACADEMY WITH THAT TENTH AVENUE GANG(1950); VICIOUS YEARS, THE(1950)
Ollegard Welton
PIPPI IN THE SOUTH SEAS(1974, Swed./Ger.)
Chuck Welty
Silents
RECKLESS CHANCES(5 reels), ph
David Welty
MC MASTERS, THE(1970)
Esther Welty
Misc. Silents
WHISPERING WOMEN(1921)
John Welty
CHEYENNE SOCIAL CLUB, THE(1970)
Elinore Welz
SOMETHING TO SING ABOUT(1937)
Stephen Welz
Silents
PENROD(1922)
Wembley Lions Ice Hockey Team
HONEYMOON MERRY-GO-ROUND(1939, Brit.)
Heinz Wemper
MOSCOW SHANGHAI(1936, Ger.)
Jack Wemstock
HOW TO SUCCEED IN BUSINESS WITHOUT REALLY TRYING(1976), w
Ann Wemyss
BEAUTY AND THE BARGE(1937, Brit.); STRANGE EXPERIMENT(1937, Brit.); REBEL SON, THE ½(1939, Brit.); INNOCENTS IN PARIS(1955, Brit.), cos
Wang Wen-chuan
DREAM OF THE RED CHAMBER, THE(1966, Chi.)
Ku Wen-tsung
MAGNIFICENT CONCUBINE, THE(1964, Hong Kong)
Lin Wen-wei
INFRA-MAN(1975, Hong Kong)
Ossie Wenban
DAD AND DAVE COME TO TOWN(1938, Aus.); KANGAROO(1952)
Ewald Wenck
GLASS TOWER, THE(1959, Ger.)
Philip Wenckus
1984
PREY, THE(1984)
Bob Wendal
HIGH WALL, THE(1947)
David Wendel
ICE STATION ZEBRA(1968)
Lara Wendel
ERNESTO(1979, Ital.); DESIRE, THE INTERIOR LIFE(1980, Ital./Ger.); IDENTIFICATION OF A WOMAN(1983, Ital.)

Howard Wendell
AFFAIR IN TRINIDAD(1952); YOU FOR ME(1952); BIG HEAT, THE(1953); GENTLE-MEN PREFER BLONDES(1953); ATHENA(1954); BLACK DAKOTAS, THE(1954); PRINCE VALIANT(1954); FIGHTING CHANCE, THE(1955); VIEW FROM POMPEY'S HEAD, THE(1955); DAY OF FURY, A(1956); NEVER SAY GOODBYE(1956); STORM CENTER(1956); WIRETAPPERS(1956); FOUR SKULLS OF JONATHAN DRAKE, THE(1959); STRANGER IN MY ARMS(1959); SAIL A CROOKED SHIP(1961); WHERE LOVE HAS GONE(1964); CINCINNATI KID, THE(1965); MY BLOOD RUNS COLD(1965)

Mark Wendell
1984
STRANGERS KISS(1984)

William G. Wendell
LOST BOUNDARIES(1949)

Wim Wenders
ALICE IN THE CITIES(1974, W. Ger.), d, w; KINGS OF THE ROAD(1976, Ger.), p,d&w; AMERICAN FRIEND, THE(1977, Ger.), d, w; LONG SHOT(1981, Brit.); HAM-METT(1982), d; STATE OF THINGS, THE(1983), d, w
1984
PARIS, TEXAS(1984, Ger./Fr.), d

F. Wendhausen
LISBON STORY, THE(1946, Brit.)

F.R. Wendhausen
AT DAWN WE DIE(1943, Brit.); SPITFIRE(1943, Brit.); SECRET MISSION(1944, Brit.)

Frederick Wendhausen
ORDERS TO KILL(1958, Brit.)
Misc. Silents
RUNAWAY PRINCESS, THE(1929, Brit.), d

Fritz Wendhausen
1914(1932, Ger.), w
Misc. Silents
STONE RIDER, THE(1923, Ger.), d

Frederick Wendhousen
DESPERATE MOMENT(1953, Brit.)

Beatrice Wendin
GEORGIA, GEORGIA(1972)

Paul Wendkos
BURGLAR, THE(1956), d; CASE AGAINST BROOKLYN, THE(1958), d; TARAWA BEACHHEAD(1958), d; BATTLE OF THE CORAL SEA(1959), d; FACE OF A FUGI-TIVE(1959), d; GIDGET(1959), d; BECAUSE THEY'RE YOUNG(1960), d; ANGEL BABY(1961), d; GIDGET GOES HAWAIIAN(1961), d; GIDGET GOES TO ROME(1963), d; JOHNNY TIGER(1966), d; ATTACK ON THE IRON COAST(1968, U.S./Brit.), d; GUNS OF THE MAGNIFICENT SEVEN(1969), d; CANNON FOR CORDOBA(1970), d; HELL BOATS(1970, Brit.), d; MEPHISTO WALTZ, THE(1971), d; SPECIAL DELIV-ERY(1976), d

Horst Wendlandt
APACHE GOLD(1965, Ger.), p; DESPERADO TRAIL, THE(1965, Ger./Yugo.), p; LAST OF THE RENEGADES(1966, Fr./Ital./Ger./Yugo.), p; ONLY A WOMAN(1966, Ger.), p; RAMPAGE AT APACHE WELLS(1966, Ger./Yugo.), p; THUNDER AT THE BORDER(1966, Ger./Yugo.), p; FLAMING FRONTIER(1968, Ger./Yugo.), p; CREA-TURE WITH THE BLUE HAND(1971, Ger.), p; LOLA(1982, Ger.), p

Hansi Wendler
LOST ONE, THE(1951, Ger.)

Maryse Wendling
CARNIVAL IN FLANDERS(1936, Fr.)

Laiola Wendorf
NO WAY OUT(1950)

Ruben Wendorf
VICIOUS CIRCLE, THE(1948); I WAS A MALE WAR BRIDE(1949); NO WAY OUT(1950); DEEP IN MY HEART(1954)

Laiola Wendorff
DEEP IN MY HEART(1954); THAT TOUCH OF MINK(1962)

Leola Wendorff
LITTLE SHOP OF HORRORS(1961)

Otto Wendorff
39 STEPS, THE(1935, Brit.), prod d

Rubin Wendorff
WHERE IS MY CHILD?(1937)

R. Wendroff
SINGING BLACKSMITH(1938)

George Wendt
MY BODYGUARD(1980); SOMEWHERE IN TIME(1980)
1984
DREAMSCAPE(1984); FLETCH(1984); NO SMALL AFFAIR(1984); THIEF OF HEARTS(1984)

Hildegard Wendt
HELLCATS, THE(1968)

Wendy
1984
PURPLE RAIN(1984)

George Wendy
JEKYLL AND HYDE...TOGETHER AGAIN(1982)

Frederick Wener
DON QUIXOTE(1973, Aus.)

Joy Wener
EVENTS(1970)

Wenga
Misc. Silents
PRIMITIVE LOVE(1927)

Ulf Wengaard
PASSIONATE DEMONS, THE(1962, Norway)

Carlo Wenger
MEGAFORCE(1982), art d

Carol Wenger
DEVIL'S RAIN, THE(1975, U.S./Mex.), spec eff; END, THE(1978), spec eff; CANNON-BALL RUN, THE(1981), art d

Cliff Wenger
HONKERS, THE(1972), spec eff; WELCOME HOME, SOLDIER BOYS(1972), spec eff; DILLINGER(1973), spec eff; WHITE LIGHTNING(1973), spec eff; GRAVY TRAIN, THE(1974), spec eff; DEVIL'S RAIN, THE(1975, U.S./Mex.), spec eff; LEPKE(1975,

U.S./Israel), spec eff; GATOR(1976), spec eff; ISLAND OF DR. MOREAU, THE(1977), spec eff; SIDEWINDER ONE(1977), spec eff; END, THE(1978), spec eff; CITY ON FIRE(1979 Can.), spec eff; SMOKEY AND THE BANDIT II(1980), spec eff
1984
FLETCH(1984), spec eff

Cliff Wenger, Jr.
1984
HIGHPOINT(1984, Can.), spec eff

Cliff Wenger,Sr.
MEGAFORCE(1982), spec eff

Clifford Wenger
RIO LOBO(1970), spec eff

Esther Wenger
CELESTE(1982, Ger.), art d

Willie Wenger
ENDLESS LOVE(1981)

Marcel Wengler
1984
SWANN IN LOVE(1984, Fr.Ger.), m

Hans [John] Wengraf
NIGHT TRAIN(1940, Brit.); THREE COCKEYED SAILORS(1940, Brit.)

John Wengraf
LUCKY JORDAN(1942); MISSION TO MOSCOW(1943); PARIS AFTER DARK(1943); SAHARA(1943); SEVENTH CROSS, THE(1944); STRANGE AFFAIR(1944); THIN MAN GOES HOME, THE(1944); 'TILL WE MEET AGAIN(1944); U-BOAT PRISONER(1944); WEEKEND AT THE WALDORF(1945); RAZOR'S EDGE, THE(1946); TOMORROW IS FOREVER(1946); T-MEN(1947); SOFIA(1948); LOVABLE CHEAT, THE(1949); WAKE OF THE RED WITCH(1949); FIVE FINGERS(1952); CALL ME MADAM(1953); DES-ERT RATS, THE(1953); FLIGHT TO TANGIER(1953); TROPIC ZONE(1953); FRENCH LINE, THE(1954); GAMBLER FROM NATCHEZ, THE(1954); GOG(1954); HELL AND HIGH WATER(1954); PARIS PLAYBOYS(1954); RACERS, THE(1955); OH, MEN! OH, WOMEN!(1957); PRIDE AND THE PASSION, THE(1957); VALERIE(1957); RETURN OF DRACULA, THE(1958); PORTRAIT IN BLACK(1960); TWELVE TO THE MOON(1960); JUDGMENT AT NUREMBERG(1961); HITLER(1962); PRIZE, THE(1963); SHIP OF FOOLS(1965)

John E. Wengraf
NEVER SAY GOODBYE(1956); DISEMBODIED, THE(1957)

Senta Wengraf
DON JUAN(1956, Aust.); FOREVER MY LOVE(1962)

Dave Wengren
IT HAPPENED ONE NIGHT(1934); BARBARY COAST(1935); WEDDING NIGHT, THE(1935); CAPTAINS COURAGEOUS(1937); PARK AVENUE LOGGER(1937); SOUTH OF TAHITI(1941); REAP THE WILD WIND(1942); NO TIME FOR LOVE(1943)

Jane Wenham
INSPECTOR CALLS, AN(1954, Brit.); MAKE ME AN OFFER(1954, Brit.); TECKMAN MYSTERY, THE(1955, Brit)

Rolf Wenkhaus
EMIL AND THE DETECTIVE(1931, Ger.)

Bert Wenland
DESTINATION MURDER(1950); MODERN MARRIAGE, A(1962)

Burt Wenland
SKY LINER(1949); TRAIL OF THE YUKON(1949); KILLER APE(1953); MURDER WITHOUT TEARS(1953); KILLERS FROM SPACE(1954); SECURITY RISK(1954); BETRAYED WOMEN(1955); WALKING TARGET, THE(1960)

Henry Wenman
MIDDLE WATCH, THE(1930, Brit.); HER STRANGE DESIRE(1931, Brit.); BACHE-LOR'S BABY(1932, Brit.); BRIDEGROOM FOR TWO(1932, Brit.); BROTHER AL-FRED(1932, Brit.); MONEY FOR NOTHING(1932, Brit.); SHADOW BETWEEN, THE(1932, Brit.); WIVES BEWARE(1933, Brit.); FREEDOM OF THE SEAS(1934, Brit.); BREWSTER'S MILLIONS(1935, Brit.); SCANDALS OF PARIS(1935, Brit.)

Fritz Wennels
JOHNNY STEALS EUROPE(1932, Ger.), m; RASPUTIN(1932, Ger.), m

Klaus Wennemann
DAS BOOT(1982)

Leslie Wenner
WIZARD OF BAGHDAD, THE(1960); PAJAMA PARTY(1964)

Martin Wenner
1984
ANOTHER COUNTRY(1984, Brit.)

Katherine Wenning
HESTER STREET(1975), ed
1984
BOSTONIANS, THE(1984), ed

T.H. Wenning
SOPHOMORE, THE(1929), w

Tom Wenning
SPORT PARADE, THE(1932), w

Susan Wensel
1984
PURPLE RAIN(1984), makeup

Harold Wenstrom
BIG HOUSE, THE(1930), ph; MIN AND BILL(1930), ph; SECRET SIX, THE(1931), ph; FAST LIFE(1932), ph; HELL DIVERS(1932), ph; HUDDLE(1932), ph; SPEAK EASILY(1932), ph; WHAT! NO BEER?(1933), ph; GIFT OF GAB(1934), ph; KEEP 'EM ROLLING(1934), ph; LOST PATROL, THE,(1934), ph; THEIR BIG MOMENT(1934), ph; WEDNESDAY'S CHILD(1934), ph; ARIZONIAN, THE(1935), ph; LADDIE(1935), ph; POWDERSMOKE RANGE(1935), ph; RED MORNING(1935), ph
Silents
SAPHEAD, THE(1921), ph; WILD GOOSE, THE(1921), ph; WHEN KNIGHTHOOD WAS IN FLOWER(1922), ph; ADAM AND EVA(1923), ph; UNDER THE RED RO-BE(1923), ph; ZANDER THE GREAT(1925), ph; SYNCOPATING SUE(1926), ph; HAZ-ARDOUS VALLEY(1927), ph; MIDNIGHT WATCH, THE(1927), ph

Johanna Went
1984
DUBEAT-E-O(1984)

Stefan Wenta
IN LIKE FLINT(1967), ch

John Wentworth
LAST SHOT YOU HEAR, THE(1969, Brit.); OBLONG BOX, THE(1969, Brit.)
Louis Wentworth III
HUCKLEBERRY FINN(1974)
Marsha Wentworth
BOWERY BLITZKRIEG(1941)
Martha Wentworth
CLANCY STREET BOYS(1943); ADVENTURE(1945); FALLEN ANGEL(1945); TREE GROWS IN BROOKLYN, A(1945); SANTA FE UPRISING(1946); STAGECOACH TO DENVER(1946); HOMESTEADERS OF PARADISE VALLEY(1947); MARSHAL OF CRIPPLE CREEK, THE(1947); OREGON TRAIL SCOUTS(1947); RUSTLERS OF DEVIL'S CANYON(1947); VIGILANTES OF BOOMTOWN(1947); LOVE NEST(1951); O. HENRY'S FULL HOUSE(1952); YOU FOR ME(1952); YOUNG MAN WITH IDEAS(1952); CLOWN, THE(1953); ONE GIRL'S CONFESSION(1953); SHE COULDN'T SAY NO(1954); GOOD MORNING, MISS DOVE(1955); JUPITER'S DARLING(1955); MAN WITH THE GOLDEN ARM, THE(1955); DAUGHTER OF DR. JEKYLL(1957); ONE HUNDRED AND ONE DALMATIANS(1961); SWORD IN THE STONE, THE(1963)
Nicholas Wentworth
RUN LIKE A THIEF(1968, Span.), ed; DORIAN GRAY(1970, Ital./Brit./Ger./Liechtenstein), ed; VENUS IN FURS(1970, Ital./Brit./Ger.), ed; TREASURE ISLAND(1972, Brit./Span./Fr./Ger.), ed
Robin Wentworth
ACT OF MURDER(1965, Brit.); NOTHING BUT THE NIGHT(1975, Brit.)
1984
FOREVER YOUNG(1984, Brit.)
Gertie Wentworth-James
Silents
GIRL WHO WOULDN'T WORK, THE(1925), w
John Wentz
PASSION HOLIDAY(1963)
Robert Wentz
MELVIN AND HOWARD(1980)
Roby Wentz
HEROES OF THE ALAMO(1938), w
Art Wenzel
SOUTH OF THE BORDER(1939)
Arthur Wenzel
COWBOY FROM LONESOME RIVER(1944)
Arthur A. Wenzel
LAUGH YOUR BLUES AWAY(1943)
Brian Wenzel
ODD ANGRY SHOT, THE(1979, Aus.)
Brigitte Wenzel
TURKISH CUCUMBER, THE(1963, Ger.)
Heidemarie Wenzel
WINDOWS OF TIME, THE(1969, Hung.)
Gerardo H. Wenziner
TENDER WARRIOR, THE(1971), ph
Fritz Wepper
QUESTION 7(1961, U.S./Ger.); MIRACLE OF THE WHITE STALLIONS(1963); DOCTOR OF ST. PAUL, THE(1969, Ger.); GAMES, THE(1970); CABARET(1972)
1984
LE DERNIER COMBAT(1984, Fr.)
Hank Werbe
ROMAN HOLIDAY(1953)
Eugen Werber
ROMANCE OF A HORSE THIEF(1971)
Gail Werbin
ROCK 'N' ROLL HIGH SCHOOL(1979), ed
Gisela Werbiseck
SO ENDS OUR NIGHT(1941); WOMEN IN BONDAGE(1943); LOST WEEKEND, THE(1945); WONDER MAN(1945); GOLDEN EARRINGS(1947)
Gisella Werbiseck
SCANDAL IN PARIS, A(1946)
Giselle Werbiseck
TOUGH AS THEY COME(1942)
Gisella Werbisek
GREAT SINNER, THE(1949)
Michel Werboff
HOTEL IMPERIAL(1939)
Gesela Werbsek
HAIRY APE, THE(1944)
Bonnie Werchan
SUMMER CAMP(1979)
Vicky Werckmeister
DOLLY GETS AHEAD(1931, Ger.)
Willi Werder
WOMAN TO WOMAN(1946, Brit.); LAUGHING LADY, THE(1950, Brit.)
Dennis Wereford
FAKE, THE(1953, Brit.), art d
Marty Wereski
1984
MYSTERY MANSION(1984), m
Ihab Werfali
LION OF THE DESERT(1981, Libya/Brit.)
Franz Werfel
JUAREZ(1939), w; SONG OF BERNADETTE, THE(1943), w; ME AND THE COLONEL(1958), w
Jan Werich
EMPEROR AND THE GOLEM, THE(1955, Czech.), a, w; 25TH HOUR, THE(1967, Fr./Ital./Yugo.); ASSIGNMENT K(1968, Brit.)
Jane Werich
GOLEM, THE(1937, Czech./Fr.), w
George Werier
PORTRAIT OF A MOBSTER(1961)
Bertil Werjefelt
HAWAII(1966)

Al Werker
Silents
RIDIN' THE WIND(1925), d
Albert Werker
WILD AND WOOLLY(1937), d
Alfred Werker
DOUBLE CROSS ROADS(1930), d; LAST OF THE DUANES(1930), d; ANNABELLE'S AFFAIRS(1931), d; HEARTBREAK(1931), d; BACHELOR'S AFFAIRS(1932), d; GAY CABALLERO, THE(1932), d; RACKETY RAX(1932), d; ADVICE TO THE LOVELORN(1933), d; IT'S GREAT TO BE ALIVE(1933), d; HOUSE OF ROTHSCHILD, THE(1934), d; YOU BELONG TO ME(1934), d; STOLEN HARMONY(1935), d; CITY GIRL(1938), d; KIDNAPPED(1938), d; UP THE RIVER(1938), d; ADVENTURES OF SHERLOCK HOLMES, THE(1939), d; IT COULD HAPPEN TO YOU(1939), d; NEWS IS MADE AT NIGHT(1939), d; MOON OVER HER SHOULDER(1941), d; RELUCTANT DRAGON, THE(1941), d; A-HAUNTING WE WILL GO(1942), d; MAD MARTINDALES, THE(1942), d; WHISPERING GHOSTS(1942), d; MY PAL, WOLF(1944), d; SHOCK(1946), d; PIRATES OF MONTEREY(1947), d; REPEAT PERFORMANCE(1947), d; HE WALKED BY NIGHT(1948), d; STROMBOLI(1950, Ital.), ed; SEALED CARGO(1951), d; WALK EAST ON BEACON(1952), d; DEVIL'S CANYON(1953), d; LAST POSSE, THE(1953), d; THREE HOURS TO KILL(1954), d; AT GUNPOINT(1955), d; CANYON CROSSROADS(1955), d; REBEL IN TOWN(1956), d
Alfred G. Werker
GATEWAY(1938), d
Alfred L. Werker
FAIR WARNING(1931), d; LOVE IN EXILE(1936, Brit.), d; WE HAVE OUR MOMENTS(1937), d; LOST BOUNDARIES(1949), d; YOUNG DON'T CRY, THE(1957), d
Misc. Talkies
CHASING THROUGH EUROPE(1929), d
Silents
JESSE JAMES(1927), sup; KIT CARSON(1928), d; PIONEER SCOUT, THE(1928), d; SUNSET LEGION, THE(1928), d
Misc. Silents
BLUE SKIES(1929), d
George P. Werker
YOUNG ONE, THE(1961, Mex.), p
Hans Werkmeister
Misc. Silents
ALGOL(1920, Ger.), d
Emilie Werko
FANNY AND ALEXANDER(1983, Swed./Fr./Ger.)
Barbara Werle
BATTLE OF THE BULGE(1965); HARUM SCARUM(1965); TICKLE ME(1965); RARE BREED, THE(1966); SECONDS(1966); GUNFIGHT IN ABILENE(1967); VALLEY OF MYSTERY(1967); CHARRO(1969); KRAKATOA, EAST OF JAVA(1969)
Misc. Talkies
GONE WITH THE WEST(1976)
Helen Werle
PLAYING AROUND(1930)
Lars Johan Werle
HOUR OF THE WOLF, THE(1968, Swed.), m
Lars-Johan Werle
PERSONA(1967, Swed.), m
Mara Werlen
SWINDLE, THE(1962, Fr./Ital.)
Andree Werlin
VERY HAPPY ALEXANDER(1969, Fr.), ed
Edward Wermel
GOODBYE CHARLIE(1964)
Ed Wermer
CRAWLING HAND, THE(1963)
O. F. Werndorff
WEDDING REHEARSAL(1932, Brit.), art d; LET'S BE FAMOUS(1939, Brit.), art d; PHANTOM STRIKES, THE(1939, Brit.), art d
Oscar M. Werndorff
BELLS, THE(1931, Brit.), d
Oscar Werndorff
LADY IS WILLING, THE(1934, Brit.), art d; WARE CASE, THE(1939, Brit.), art d
Otto Werndorff
SECRET AGENT, THE(1936, Brit.), set d; SABOTAGE(1937, Brit.), set d
Alexander Werner
GAMES, THE(1970)
Art Werner
TERROR IN THE JUNGLE(1968), makeup
Bob Werner
HOMER(1970)
Charles Werner
MARTYR, THE(1976, Ger./Israel)
Christine Werner
GIANT(1956)
Dieter Werner
GOLDEN PLAGUE, THE(1963, Ger.), w
Doug Werner
BIG RED ONE, THE(1980)
Dusan Werner
IN SEARCH OF ANNA(1978, Aus.), ed
Elsie Werner
Silents
INTO NO MAN'S LAND(1928), w; MAKING THE VARSITY(1928), w
Emmy Werner
GAMES, THE(1970)
Francois Werner
MURMUR OF THE HEART(1971, Fr./Ital./Ger.)
Fred Werner
HUCKLEBERRY FINN(1974), md; MOONSHINE COUNTY EXPRESS(1977), m
Gabriel Werner
LAST YEAR AT MARIENBAD(1962, Fr./Ital.)
Hansel Werner
CATTLE STAMPEDE(1943)

Jean Werner
PROSTITUTION(1965, Fr.)
Jeff Werner
DIE LAUGHING(1980), d
Jenny Werner
THIRD MAN, THE(1950, Brit.)
Karen Werner
NATIONAL LAMPOON'S ANIMAL HOUSE(1978); SOUP FOR ONE(1982)
Kurt Werner
HELP I'M INVISIBLE(1952, Ger.), w
Lars Werner
OBSESSION(1968, Swed.), p
M. Werner
Misc. Silents
PRISONERS OF THE SEA(1929, USSR), d
Marie Werner
ON PROBATION(1935); DESERT GUNS(1936)
Michael Werner
HARRAD EXPERIMENT, THE(1973), w
Oskar Werner
ANGEL WITH THE TRUMPET, THE(1950, Brit.); DECISION BEFORE DAWN(1951); WONDER BOY(1951, Brit./Aust.); LOLA MONTES(1955, Fr./Ger.); LAST TEN DAYS, THE(1956, Ger.); LIFE AND LOVES OF MOZART, THE(1959, Ger.); JULES AND JIM(1962, Fr.); SHIP OF FOOLS(1965); SPY WHO CAME IN FROM THE COLD, THE(1965, Brit.); FAHRENHEIT 451(1966, Brit.); INTERLUDE(1968, Brit.); SHOES OF THE FISHERMAN, THE(1968); VOYAGE OF THE DAMNED(1976, Brit.)
Peter Werner
DON'T CRY, IT'S ONLY THUNDER(1982), d
Rita Stanwood Werner
MARY BURNS, FUGITIVE(1935)
Robert Werner
WILD DUCK, THE(1977, Ger./Aust.)
Walter Werner
DANTON(1931, Ger.); FINAL CHORD, THE(1936, Ger.)
Wendelin Werner
LA PASSANTE(1983, Fr./Ger.)
Otto Wernicke
TEMPEST(1932, Ger.); M(1933, Ger.); MASTER OF THE WORLD(1935, Ger.); TESTAMENT OF DR. MABUSE, THE(1943, Ger.); LONG IS THE ROAD(1948, Ger.)
Snag Werris
FOUR JILLS IN A JEEP(1944), w; IF I'M LUCKY(1946), w; PEEPER(1975)
Angelika Werth
TRAPP FAMILY, THE(1961, Ger.)
Francois Wertheimer
ONE SINGS, THE OTHER DOESN'T(1977, Fr.)
Joe Wertheimer
PRIVATE DUTY NURSES(1972), set d; HAPPY BIRTHDAY TO ME(1981); END OF AUGUST, THE(1982), art d
Ned Wertheimmer
ADAM AT 6 A.M.(1970)
David Werthriemer
HOUSE ON THE SAND(1967)
Ned Wertimer
LET'S ROCK(1958); SANTA CLAUS CONQUERS THE MARTIANS(1964); IMPOSSIBLE YEARS, THE(1968); SOME KIND OF A NUT(1969); BAD COMPANY(1972); PACK, THE(1977); HOMETOWN U.S.A.(1979)
Lina Wertmuller
END OF THE WORLD(in Our Usual Bed In a Night Full of Rain), THE (1978, Ital.), d&w; WHEN WOMEN HAD TAILS(1970, Ital.), w; BROTHER SUN, SISTER MOON(1973, Brit./Ital.), w; FAMILY, THE(1974, Fr./Ital.), w; LOVE AND ANARCHY(1974, Ital.), d&w; SWEPT AWAY...BY AN UNUSUAL DESTINY IN THE BLUE SEA OF AUGUST(1975, Ital.), d&w; ALL SCREWED UP(1976, Ital.), d&w; SEVEN BEAUTIES(1976, Ital.), p, d&w; WHICH WAY IS UP?(1977), w; BLOOD FEUD(1979, Ital.), d&w
1984
JOKE OF DESTINY LYING IN WAIT AROUND THE CORNER LIKE A STREET-BANDIT, A(1984, Ital.), d, w
Maria Wertmuller
8 ½(1963, Ital.)
Massimo Wertmuller
END OF THE WORLD(in Our Usual Bed In a Night Full of Rain), THE (1978, Ital.)
1984
JOKE OF DESTINY LYING IN WAIT AROUND THE CORNER LIKE A STREET-BANDIT, A(1984, Ital.)
Quentin Werty
DARK OF THE SUN(1968, Brit.), w; JIGSAW(1968), w; THAT MAN BOLT(1973), w
Clarence Wertz
BARBARY COAST(1935)
Jay Wertz
METALSTORM: THE DESTRUCTION OF JARED-SYN(1983), set d
Carl Wery
AFFAIRS OF DR. HOLL(1954, Ger.); HEIDI AND PETER(1955, Switz.); COURT MARTIAL(1962, Ger.)
Karl Wery
HEIDI(1954, Switz.)
Yossi Werzanski
JERUSALEM FILE, THE(1972, U.S./Israel)
Yossi Werzansky
1984
LITTLE DRUMMER GIRL, THE(1984)
Wanea Wes
WALKING TALL(1973)
Drew W. Wesche
TWILIGHT'S LAST GLEAMING(1977, U.S./Ger.)
Rusty Wescoatt
MUTINEERS, THE(1949); CAPTIVE GIRL(1950); CHAIN GANG(1950); LAST OF THE BUCCANEERS(1950); PYGMY ISLAND(1950); STATE PENITENTIARY(1950); FURY OF THE CONGO(1951); HURRICANE ISLAND(1951); YANK IN KOREA, A(1951); BRAVE WARRIOR(1952); SIGN OF THE PAGAN(1954); BIG BLUFF, THE(1955); GANG BUSTERS(1955); TARANTULA(1955); SILENT CALL, THE(1961);

20,000 EYES(1961); THREE STOOGES MEET HERCULES, THE(1962); BLACK GOLD(1963); MORITURI(1965)
Gordon Wescott
HERITAGE OF THE DESERT(1933)
Helen Wescott
PHONE CALL FROM A STRANGER(1952); GOD'S LITTLE ACRE(1958); DAY OF THE OUTLAW(1959)
Lynda Wescott
SHOOT IT: BLACK, SHOOT IT: BLUE(1974)
Rusty Wescott
WHEN THE REDSKINS RODE(1951)
Gordon Wescourt
FINDERS KEEPERS, LOVERS WEEPERS(1968)
Eleanor Weselhoeft
EVERYTHING HAPPENS AT NIGHT(1939)
Max Wesell
Misc. Silents
RANGELAND(1922)
Lube Wesely
SINGING BLACKSMITH(1938)
Eduard Wesener
TESTAMENT OF DR. MABUSE, THE(1943, Ger.)
Brian Weske
HELL, HEAVEN OR HOBOKEN(1958, Brit.); VACATION FROM MARRIAGE(1945, Brit.); GAY INTRUDERS, THE(1946, Brit.); FAME IS THE SPUR(1947, Brit.); FORTUNE LANE(1947, Brit.); JUST WILLIAM'S LUCK(1948, Brit.); QUIET WEEKEND(1948, Brit.); WILLIAM COMES TO TOWN(1948, Brit.); LINKS OF JUSTICE(1958); DESPERATE MAN, THE(1959, Brit.); NO SAFETY AHEAD(1959, Brit.); NIGHT WITHOUT PITY(1962, Brit.); GREAT VAN ROBBERY, THE(1963, Brit.); JUNGLE STREET GIRLS(1963, Brit.); OPERATION BULLSHINE(1963, Brit.); OPERATION SNAFU(1965, Brit.); PANIC(1966, Brit.); BIG SWITCH, THE(1970, Brit.)
J. Victor Weske
TOWER OF TERROR, THE(1942, Brit.)
Victor Weske
HARD STEEL(1941, Brit.); BELLS GO DOWN, THE(1943, Brit.); ECHO MURDERS, THE(1945, Brit.); SEND FOR PAUL TEMPLE(1946, Brit.)
Charles Weskin
UP IN CENTRAL PARK(1948)
Steve Weslake
LAST CHASE, THE(1981), ed
Paul Wesler
BUSYBODY, THE(1967)
Yale Wexler
STAKEOUT ON DOPE STREET(1958)
Wesley
WESTERN GOLD(1937)
Fred Wesley
SLAUGHTER'S BIG RIP-OFF(1973), m
George Wesley
FIXED BAYONETS(1951)
Jay Wesley
HOUSE ON 92ND STREET, THE(1945)
John Wesley
AMAZING DR. CLITTERHOUSE, THE(1938), w; CORNERED(1945), w; HANG'EM HIGH(1968)
Richard Wesley
UPTOWN SATURDAY NIGHT(1974), w; LET'S DO IT AGAIN(1975), w
Stephen Wesley
TOUCH OF FLESH, THE(1960)
Wesley Tuttle and His Texas Stars
RIDERS OF THE DAWN(1945); SONG OF THE SIERRAS(1946); RAINBOW OVER THE ROCKIES(1947)
A. Burt Wesner
Misc. Silents
KID IS CLEVER, THE(1918)
Luba Wesoly
OVERTURE TO GLORY(1940)
Eric Wespha
MAFU CAGE, THE(1978), w
Rob-Jamere Wess
KING OF COMEDY, THE(1983)
Wendy Wessberg
HALLOWEEN III: SEASON OF THE WITCH(1982)
Hannelore Wessel
ONLY A WOMAN(1966, Ger.), cos
Max Wessel
Misc. Silents
WEST OF THE PECOS(1922)
Richard "Dick" Wessel
YELLOW JACK(1938); IN SPITE OF DANGER(1935); BORROWING TROUBLE(1937); GAME THAT KILLS, THE(1937); PRESCRIPTION FOR ROMANCE(1937); ROUNDUP TIME IN TEXAS(1937); SLIM(1937); SUBMARINE D-1(1937); VOGUES OF 1938(1937); ANGELS WITH DIRTY FACES(1938); I STOLE A MILLION(1939); KID FROM KOKOMO, THE(1939); MISSING DAUGHTERS(1939); ROARING TWENTIES, THE(1939); THEY MADE ME A CRIMINAL(1939); BORDER LEGION, THE(1940); BROTHER ORCHID(1940); CAFE HOSTESS(1940); FLIGHT COMMAND(1940); FRAMED(1940); SO YOU WON'T TALK(1940); THEY DRIVE BY NIGHT(1940); CITY, FOR CONQUEST(1941); DESERT BANDIT(1941); GREAT TRAIN ROBBERY, THE(1941); LUCKY DEVILS(1941); MANPOWER(1941); MODEL WIFE(1941); NAVY BLUES(1941); PENNY SERENADE(1941); RED RIVER VALLEY(1941); STRAWBERRY BLONDE, THE(1941); TANKS A MILLION(1941); ABOUT FACE(1942); DANGEROUSLY THEY LIVE(1942); ENEMY AGENTS MEET ELLERY QUEEN(1942); ROMANCE ON THE RANGE(1942); SUNDAY PUNCH(1942); SUNSET SERENADE(1942); TRAITOR WITHIN, THE(1942); X MARKS THE SPOT(1942); YANKEE DOODLE DANDY(1942); YOU CAN'T ESCAPE FOREVER(1942); ACTION IN THE NORTH ATLANTIC(1943); FALSE FACES(1943); GENTLE GANGSTER, A(1943); SILVER SPURS(1943); THREE HEARTS FOR JULIA(1943); DAKOTA(1945); SCARLET STREET(1945); CALIFORNIA(1946); DICK TRACY VS. CUEBALL(1946); IN FAST COMPANY(1946); IN OLD SACRAMENTO(1946); LITTLE MISS BIG(1946); YOUNG WIDOW(1946); 13 RUE MADELEINE(1946); BLONDIE'S BIG MOMENT(1947); IT

HAPPENED IN BROOKLYN(1947); MAGIC TOWN(1947); GOOD SAM(1948); PIT-FALL(1948); RIVER LADY(1948); SOUTHERN YANKEE, A(1948); UNKNOWN ISLAND(1948); BAD MEN OF TOMBSTONE(1949); BLONDIE HITS THE JACKPOT(1949); CANADIAN PACIFIC(1949); ON THE TOWN(1949); SANDS OF IWO JIMA(1949); SLATTERY'S HURRICANE(1949); TAKE ME OUT TO THE BALL GAME(1949); THIEVES' HIGHWAY(1949); TULSA(1949); BEWARE OF BLON-DIE(1950); BLONDIE'S HERO(1950); FATHER OF THE BRIDE(1950); FRONTIER OUTPOST(1950); HARVEY(1950); KEY TO THE CITY(1950); LOVE THAT BRU-TE(1950); WABASH AVENUE(1950); WATCH THE BIRDIE(1950); AMERICAN IN PARIS, AN(1951); CORKY OF GASOLINE ALLEY(1951); GASOLINE ALLEY(1951); HONEYCHILE(1951); REUNION IN RENO(1951); SCARF, THE(1951); TEXAS CARNI-VAL(1951); BELLE OF NEW YORK, THE(1952); BLACKBEARD THE PIRATE(1952); HOODLUM EMPIRE(1952); LAWLESS BREED, THE(1952); LOVE IS BETTER THAN EVER(1952); RANCHO NOTORIOUS(1952); WAC FROM WALLA WALLA, THE(1952); YOUNG MAN WITH IDEAS(1952); CHAMP FOR A DAY(1953); LET'S DO IT AGAIN(1953); THEM!(1954); UNTAMED HEIRESS(1954); BOWERY TO BAG-DAD(1955); REBEL WITHOUT A CAUSE(1955); DESPERADOES ARE IN TOWN, THE(1956); NO TIME FOR SERGEANTS(1958); WHO'S MINDING THE STORE?(1963); WIVES AND LOVERS(1963); UGLY DACHSHUND, THE(1966)

Paula Wesseley
EPISODE(1937, Aust.)

Eleanor Wesselhoeft
STREET SCENE(1931); MADAME RACKETEER(1932); ME AND MY GAL(1932); CRADLE SONG(1933); READY FOR LOVE(1934); THIRTY-DAY PRINCESS(1934); LET 'EM HAVE IT(1935); STRANDED(1935); WEDDING NIGHT, THE(1935); WOMAN IN RED, THE(1935); LADIES IN LOVE(1936); SON COMES HOME, A(1936); PRISON-ER OF ZENDA, THE(1937); ALEXANDER'S RAGTIME BAND(1938); BARONESS AND THE BUTLER, THE(1938); INTERMEZZO: A LOVE STORY(1939); FOUR SONS(1940); MAN I MARRIED, THE(1940); MONSTER AND THE GIRL, THE(1941)

Elinor Wesselhoeft
WOMAN FROM MONTE CARLO, THE(1932)

Dick Wessell
COWBOY QUARTERBACK(1939); THEY DIED WITH THEIR BOOTS ON(1942); KING OF THE COWBOYS(1943); HIGH WALL, THE(1947); MERTON OF THE MOVIES(1947); HOLLOW TRIUMPH(1948); OPERATION PACIFIC(1951); STRAN-GERS ON A TRAIN(1951)

Henri Wessell
HARLEM IS HEAVEN(1932)

John Wessell
Misc. Silents
FIELDS OF HONOR(1918)

Richard Wessell
GAZEBO, THE(1959)

Alice Wesslar
Misc. Talkies
OBEAH(1935)

Charles Wessler
1984
COLD FEET(1984), p

Rick Wessler
MARCH OF THE SPRING HARE(1969); ROOMMATES(1971)

Nikki Wessling
CHILDREN, THE(1980), ed

Lillian Wessner
YELLOW CARGO(1936)

Dick Wesson
BREAKTHROUGH(1950); DESTINATION MOON(1950); FORCE OF ARMS(1951); INSIDE THE WALLS OF FOLSOM PRISON(1951); JIM THORPE–ALL AMERI-CAN(1951); STARLIFT(1951); SUNNY SIDE OF THE STREET(1951); ABOUT FA-CE(1952); MAN BEHIND THE GUN, THE(1952); CALAMITY JANE(1953); CHARGE AT FEATHER RIVER, THE(1953); DESERT SONG, THE(1953); FRESH FROM PARIS(1955); PARIS FOLLIES OF 1956(1955); LOVE THAT BRUTE(1953); ERRAND BOY, THE(1961); TAMMY AND THE MILLIONAIRE(1967), p; ROLLERCOASTER(1977)

Eileen Wesson
SULLIVAN'S EMPIRE(1967); DID YOU HEAR THE ONE ABOUT THE TRAVELING SALESLADY?(1968); JOURNEY TO SHILOH(1968); WINNING(1969); AIRPORT(1970)

Gene Wesson
IRON MAN, THE(1951); DRAGONFLY SQUADRON(1953); NIAGARA(1953); THREE FOR THE SHOW(1955); WICHITA(1955); SATAN'S BED(1965)

Richard Wesson
CHANGE OF MIND(1969), p, w

Ross Wesson
MY DREAM IS YOURS(1949)

Adam West
YOUNG PHILADELPHIANS, THE(1959); GERONIMO(1962); SOLDIER IN THE RAIN(1963); TAMMY AND THE DOCTOR(1963); ROBINSON CRUSOE ON MARS(1964); OUTLAWS IS COMING, THE(1965); BATMAN(1966); MARA OF THE WILDERNESS(1966); GIRL WHO KNEW TOO MUCH, THE(1969); MARRIAGE OF A YOUNG STOCKBROKER, THE(1971); SPECIALIST, THE(1975); HOOPER(1978); HAP-PY HOOKER GOES TO HOLLYWOOD, THE(1980); ONE DARK NIGHT(1983)
Misc. Talkies
CURSE OF THE MOON CHILD(1972); SPECIALIST, THE(1975); HELL RIVER(1977)

Algernon West
LOYALTIES(1934, Brit.)

Anita West
IMPACT(1963, Brit.); SHADOW OF FEAR(1963, Brit.); RING OF SPIES(1964, Brit.)

Arthur "Cap" West
RED MORNING(1935)

Barbara West
WEEKEND OF SHADOWS(1978, Aus.); BREAKER MORANT(1980, Aus.)

Bernie West
BELLS ARE RINGING(1960)

Bert West
ENEMIES OF THE LAW(1931)

Betty West
HEADING FOR HEAVEN(1947)

Beverly West
Silents
AS YE SOW(1914)

Billie West
Silents
MAN'S PREROGATIVE, A(1915)

Billy West
WINNER TAKE ALL(1932); DIAMOND TRAIL(1933); GOLD DIGGERS OF 1933(1933); PICTURE SNATCHER(1933); HE WAS HER MAN(1934); JEALOU-SY(1934); JIMMY THE GENT(1934); TWENTY MILLION SWEETHEARTS(1934); MOTIVE FOR REVENGE(1935); SHE COULDN'T TAKE IT(1935)
Misc. Silents
SHOULD SHE OBEY?(1917); THRILLING YOUTH(1926); LUCKY FOOL(1927)

Bob "Red" West
WILD IN THE COUNTRY(1961); CLAMBAKE(1967)

Bobbi West
Misc. Talkies
HOW TO MAKE A DOLL(1967)

Bonnie G. West
SWEET CHARITY(1969)

Brian West
CEREMONY, THE(1963, U.S./Span.), ph; SQUEEZE A FLOWER(1970, Aus.), ph; OUTBACK(1971, Aus.), ph; BILLY TWO HATS(1973, Brit.), ph; SUNSTRUCK(1973, Aus.), ph; APPRENTICESHIP OF DUDDY KRAVITZ, THE(1974, Can.), ph; SPIKES GANG, THE(1974), ph; RUSSIAN ROULETTE(1975), ph; AGE OF INNOCENCE(1977, Can.), ph; STORIES FROM A FLYING TRUNK(1979, Brit.), ph; YESTERDAY'S HERO(1979, Brit.), ph; LONELY LADY, THE(1983), ph; MARVIN AND TIGE(1983), ph
1984
BLOODBATH AT THE HOUSE OF DEATH(1984, Brit.), ph; FINDERS KEE-PERS(1984), ph

Brooks West
ANATOMY OF A MURDER(1959)

Bryan Sonny West
Misc. Talkies
OUTLAW RIDERS(1971)

Buck West
TO ALL A GOODNIGHT(1980)

Buster West
RADIO CITY REVELS(1938)
Silents
BROADWAY AFTER DARK(1924)

Carinthia West
HUSBANDS(1970); GREEK TYCOON, THE(1978)

Carol West
SUMMER STOCK(1950)

Charles West
ACQUITTED(1929); HANDCUFFED(1929); FOR THE DEFENSE(1930); ALONG CAME YOUTH(1931); MAN TRAILER, THE(1934); DEATH FROM A DISTANCE(1936)
Misc. Talkies
LAW OF THE WEST(1932)
Silents
MARTHA'S VINDICATION(1916); AMERICAN CONSUL, THE(1917); POLLY OF THE STORM COUNTRY(1920); BOB HAMPTON OF PLACER(1921); NOT GUILT-Y(1921); WITCHING HOUR, THE(1921); ETERNAL THREE, THE(1923); HELD TO ANSWER(1923); RED LIGHTS(1923); OVERLAND LIMITED, THE(1925); SKYROCK-ET, THE(1926); KING OF KINGS, THE(1927); NOBODY'S WIDOW(1927); MAN FROM HEADQUARTERS(1928)
Misc. Silents
LORD CHUMLEY(1914); DREAM GIRL, THE(1916); GUTTER MAGDALENE, THE(1916); WOOD NYMPH, THE(1916); LITTLE MISS OPTIMIST(1917); LITTLE PIRATE, THE(1917); SOCIETY'S DRIFTWOOD(1917); TROUBLE BUSTER, THE(1917); GHOST FLOWER, THE(1918); MYSTERY OF A GIRL, THE(1918); SHACKLED(1918); HIS DIVORCED WIFE(1919); PHANTOM MELODY, THE(1920); THOUSAND TO ONE, A(1920); TIMES HAVE CHANGED(1923)

Charles H. West
Misc. Silents
PARLOR, BEDROOM AND BATH(1920)

Charley West
POLICE CAR 17(1933)

Charlie West
DON'T TELL THE WIFE(1937)

Christine West
1984
PALLET ON THE FLOOR(1984, New Zealand), cos

Christopher West
EL DORADO(1967); SPEEDWAY(1968)

Claire West
Silents
TEN COMMANDMENTS, THE(1923), cos

Clare West
Silents
SHERLOCK, JR.(1924), cos

Claudine West
LAST OF MRS. CHEYNEY, THE(1929), w; LADY OF SCANDAL, THE(1930), w; LADY'S MORALS, A(1930), w; GUARDSMAN, THE(1931), w; JUST A GIGOLO(1931), w; PRIVATE LIVES(1931), w; SON OF INDIA(1931), w; PAYMENT DEFER-RED(1932), w; SMILIN' THROUGH(1932), w; SON-DAUGHTER, THE(1932), w; REUNION IN VIENNA(1933), w; BARRETTS OF WIMPOLE STREET, THE(1934), w; MARIE ANTOINETTE(1938), w; GOODBYE MR. CHIPS(1939, Brit.), w; ON BOR-ROWED TIME(1939), w; MORTAL STORM, THE(1940), w; CHOCOLATE SOLDIER, THE(1941), w; MRS. MINIVER(1942), w; RANDOM HARVEST(1942), w; WE WERE DANCING(1942), w; FOREVER AND A DAY(1943), w; WHITE CLIFFS OF DOVER, THE(1944), w

Claudine West [Frances Marion
GOOD EARTH, THE(1937), w

Colin West
GIRL ON A MOTORCYCLE, THE(1968, Fr./Brit.)

Con West
P.C. JOSSER(1931, Brit.), w; UP FOR THE CUP(1931, Brit.), w; JOSSER IN THE ARMY(1932, Brit.), w; JOSSER JOINS THE NAVY(1932, Brit.), w; LETTING IN THE SUNSHINE(1933, Brit.), w; MY OLD DUCHESS(1933, Brit.), w; JOSSER ON THE FARM(1934, Brit.), w; THINGS ARE LOOKING UP(1934, Brit.), w; BIRDS OF A

FEATHER(1935, Brit.), w; CHARING CROSS ROAD(1935, Brit.), w; JIMMY BOY(1935, Brit.), w; SMALL MAN, THE(1935, Brit.), w; SMITH'S WIVES(1935, Brit.), w; STRICTLY ILLEGAL(1935, Brit.), w; DON'T RUSH ME(1936, Brit.), w; LOVE UP THE POLE(1936, Brit.), w; ONE GOOD TURN(1936, Brit.), w; SUNSHINE AHEAD(1936, Brit.), w; VARIETY PARADE(1936, Brit.), w; OLD MOTHER RILEY(1937, Brit.), w; WHY PICK ON ME?(1937, Brit.), w; MIRACLES DO HAPPEN(1938, Brit.), w; OLD MOTHER RILEY IN PARIS(1938, Brit.), w; JAILBIRDS(1939, Brit.), w; MUSIC HALL PARADE(1939, Brit.), w; OLD MOTHER RILEY JOINS UP(1939, Brit.), w; OLD MOTHER RILEY MP(1939, Brit.), w; WHAT WOULD YOU DO, CHUMS?(1939, Brit.), w; PACK UP YOUR TROUBLES(1940, Brit.), w; OLD MOTHER RILEY'S CIRCUS(1941, Brit.), w; OLD MOTHER RILEY'S GHOSTS(1941, Brit.), w; ASKING FOR TROUBLE(1942, Brit.), w; DUMMY TALKS, THE(1943, Brit.), w; IT'S IN THE BAG(1943, Brit.), w; SCHWEIK'S NEW ADVENTURES(1943, Brit.), w; SOMEWHERE IN CIVVIES(1943, Brit.), w; ADVENTURES OF JANE, THE(1949, Brit.), w; OLD MOTHER RILEY, HEADMISTRESS(1950, Brit.), w; UP FOR THE CUP(1950, Brit.), w; OLD MOTHER RILEY(1952, Brit.), w

De Jalma West
Silents
TRAIL OF THE SHADOW, THE(1917)

Del "Sonny" West
STAY AWAY, JOE(1968)

Dorian West
UNSTRAP ME(1968)

Dorothy West
Silents
ETERNAL GRIND, THE(1916); HABIT OF HAPPINESS, THE(1916)

Dottie West
SECOND FIDDLE TO A STEEL GUITAR(1965)
Misc. Talkies
COUNTRY MUSIC(1972)

Edna West
HALF WAY TO HEAVEN(1929)

Elizabeth West
INBETWEEN AGE, THE(1958, Brit.), ch

Elliot West
FEARMAKERS, THE(1958), w

Emily West
SMILIN' THROUGH(1941)

Ford West
KING OF THE WILD HORSES, THE(1934)
Silents
SHERLOCK, JR.(1924)

Fred West
GUNSLINGER(1956), ph; OKLAHOMA WOMAN, THE(1956), ph

Frederick West
IT CONQUERED THE WORLD(1956), ph; MY WORLD DIES SCREAMING(1958), ph

Frederick E. West
GIRLS IN PRISON(1956), ph; SHE-CREATURE, THE(1956), ph; DRAGSTRIP GIRL(1957), ph; FLESH AND THE SPUR(1957), ph; INVASION OF THE SAUCER MEN(1957), ph; MOTORCYCLE GANG(1957), ph; RUNAWAY DAUGHTERS(1957), ph; VOODOO WOMAN(1957), ph; JET ATTACK(1958), ph; BOUNTY KILLER, THE(1965), ph; REQUIEM FOR A GUNFIGHTER(1965), ph

Frederick F. West
SHAKE, RATTLE, AND ROCK!(1957), ph

George West
Silents
TAR HEEL WARRIOR, THE(1917); ALIAS THE DEACON(1928)

Georgina West
THREE TO GO(1971, Aus.)

Geraldine West
LIVING BETWEEN TWO WORLDS(1963); HUSH... HUSH, SWEET CHARLOTTE(1964); WUSA(1970)

Gracie West
FATHER O'FLYNN(1938, Irish); SO THIS IS LONDON(1940, Brit.); BALLOON GOES UP, THE(1942, Brit.); UP WITH THE LARK(1943, Brit.)

H. E. West
NIGHT TIDE(1963); BEST MAN, THE(1964); EVERYTHING YOU ALWAYS WANTED TO KNOW ABOUT SEX, BUT WE'RE AFRAID TO ASK(1972)

H. St. Barbe West
ESCAPE(1930, Brit.); CONDEMNED TO DEATH(1932, Brit.)

Harry West
VERBOTEN!(1959), cos
Misc. Silents
RAIL RIDER, THE(1916)

Helen West
DIMPLES(1936)

Henry West
GIRL ON THE BARGE, THE(1929); TIME LIMIT(1957), cos
Silents
ALL MAN(1916); BROKEN CHAINS(1916); CRIMSON DOVE, THE(1917); NORTH WIND'S MALICE, THE(1920)
Misc. Silents
(; CRACKERJACK, THE(1925)

Hilary West
X Y & ZEE(1972, Brit.)

Howard West
IN GOD WE TRUST(1980), p

Ian West
RUNNERS(1983, Brit.)

Irene West
Misc. Silents
FIRING LINE, THE(1919)

Isabel West
NATIONAL LAMPOON'S CLASS REUNION(1982)
Silents
SAINTED DEVIL, A(1924); OLD HOME WEEK(1925)

James West
WAY OF ALL FLESH, THE(1940); HAPPY LAND(1943); HEY BOY! HEY GIRL!(1959), w; CALIFORNIA(1963), w
Misc. Silents
KILL-JOY, THE(1917)

James I. West
Misc. Talkies
HOT PURSUIT(1981), d

Jennifer West
MARDI GRAS(1958); TOO SOON TO LOVE(1960)
Misc. Talkies
ROSES BLOOM TWICE(1977)

Jeremy West
SEED OF INNOCENCE(1980)
1984
ICE PIRATES, THE(1984)

Jessamyn West
FRIENDLY PERSUASION(1956), w, tech adv; BIG COUNTRY, THE(1958), w; STOLEN HOURS(1963), w

Jim West
Misc. Talkies
POLK COUNTY POT PLANE(1977), d

John West
TWO-MINUTE WARNING(1976)

John West [Jack Jevne]
GHOST RIDER, THE(1935), w

John Stuart West
1984
NIGHT OF THE COMET(1984)

Johnny West
TRIAL OF BILLY JACK, THE(1974)

Joseph West
BLACK BANDIT(1938), w; GHOST TOWN RIDERS(1938), w; GUILTY TRAILS(1938), w; PRAIRIE JUSTICE(1938), w; HONOR OF THE WEST(1939), w; MYSTERY PLANE(1939), w; OKLAHOMA TERROR(1939), w; PHANTOM STAGE, THE(1939), w; SKY PATROL(1939), w; STUNT PILOT(1939), w; WOLF CALL(1939), w; DRUMS OF THE DESERT(1940), w; FATAL HOUR, THE(1940), w; LAUGHING AT DANGER(1940), w; ON THE SPOT(1940), w; PHANTOM OF CHINATOWN(1940), w; QUEEN OF THE YUKON(1940), w; SON OF THE NAVY(1940), w; FLYING CADETS(1941), w; MAN MADE MONSTER(1941), w

Judi West
FORTUNE COOKIE, THE(1966); MAN CALLED GANNON, A(1969)

Julian West
X Y & ZEE(1972, Brit.)

Julian West [Baron Nicolas de Gunzburg]
VAMPYR(1932, Fr./Ger.)

Kathy West
FIVE FINGER EXERCISE(1962)

Keefe West
LEO THE LAST(1970, Brit.)

Kit West
PARANOIAC(1963, Brit.), spec eff; LOST COMMAND, THE(1966), spec eff; PLAY DIRTY(1969, Brit.), spec eff; SOME GIRLS DO(1969, Brit.), spec eff; MOON ZERO TWO(1970, Brit.), spec eff; WILBY CONSPIRACY, THE(1975, Brit.), spec eff; PINK PANTHER STRIKES AGAIN, THE(1976, Brit.), spec eff; LION OF THE DESERT(1981, Libya/Brit.), spec eff; RAIDERS OF THE LOST ARK(1981), spec eff; RETURN OF THE JEDI(1983), spec eff

Langdon West
Misc. Silents
FRIEND WILSON'S DAUGHTER(1915), d; HER PROPER PLACE(1915), d; RING OF THE BORGIAS, THE(1915), d; SALLY CASTLETON, SOUTHERNER(1915), d; GIRL OF THE GYPSY CAMP, THE(1925), d

Laura West
Misc. Silents
ANGEL FACTORY, THE(1917)

Lesley West
RICHARD'S THINGS(1981, Brit.)

Lillian West
SINISTER HANDS(1932); STAND UP AND CHEER(1934 80m FOX bw); WHITE PARADE, THE(1934); LITTLE COLONEL, THE(1935); TWO FOR TONIGHT(1935); GIRLS' DORMITORY(1936); TOO MANY PARENTS(1936); INTERNES CAN'T TAKE MONEY(1937); LOVE IS NEWS(1937); STELLA DALLAS(1937); HOLIDAY(1938); MEN WITH WINGS(1938); THERE'S THAT WOMAN AGAIN(1938); EAST SIDE OF HEAVEN(1939); LAUGH IT OFF(1939); OUR LEADING CITIZEN(1939); STORY OF ALEXANDER GRAHAM BELL, THE(1939); THAT'S RIGHT–YOU'RE WRONG(1939); MAN I MARRIED, THE(1940); NOBODY'S CHILDREN(1940); MEET JOHN DOE(1941); PENNY SERENADE(1941); REMEMBER THE DAY(1941); WEST POINT WIDOW(1941); FALLEN SPARROW, THE(1943); GIRL CRAZY(1943); THANK YOUR LUCKY STARS(1943); NOTORIOUS(1946); WHERE DANGER LIVES(1950); DOUBLE DYNAMITE(1951); GUY WHO CAME BACK, THE(1951); TWO TICKETS TO BROADWAY(1951)
Silents
AMERICAN METHODS(1917); ISLAND OF INTRIGUE, THE(1919); LOUISIANA(1919); PAID BACK(1922); SEVENTH HEAVEN(1927)
Misc. Silents
POWER OF EVIL, THE(1916); HIDDEN CHILDREN, THE(1917); GOWN OF DESTINY, THE(1918); INNOCENT'S PROGRESS(1918); LIMOUSINE LIFE(1918); LOVE'S PAY DAY(1918); SOUL IN TRUST, A(1918); WHO IS TO BLAME?(1918); SILK-LINED BURGLAR, THE(1919); COLORADO(1921); FATAL 30, THE(1921); AUCTION OF SOULS(1922); BARRIERS OF FOLLY(1922)

Lillianq West
TWENTIETH CENTURY(1934)

Lockwood West
SONG FOR TOMORROW, A(1948, Brit.); CELIA(1949, Brit.); LAST HOLIDAY(1950, Brit.); NO PLACE FOR JENNIFER(1950, Brit.); HIGH TREASON(1951, Brit.); HAMMER THE TOFF(1952, Brit.); HORSE'S MOUTH, THE(1953, Brit.); SAILOR OF THE KING(1953, Brit.); PRIVATE'S PROGRESS(1956, Brit.); BIRTHDAY PRESENT, THE(1957, Brit.); MARK OF THE HAWK, THE(1958, Brit.); MAN WHO COULD CHEAT DEATH, THE(1959, Brit.); STRONGROOM(1962, Brit.); RUNNING MAN, THE(1963, Brit.); GAME FOR THREE LOSERS(1965, Brit.); LEATHER BOYS, THE(1965, Brit.);

BEDAZZLED(1967, Brit.); DANDY IN ASPIC, A(1968, Brit.); UP THE JUNCTION(1968, Brit.); ONE BRIEF SUMMER(1971, Brit.); COUNT DRACULA AND HIS VAMPIRE BRIDE(1978, Brit.); DRESSER, THE(1983)

Madge West
FOR LOVE OF IVY(1968)

Mae West
NIGHT AFTER NIGHT(1932), a, w; I'M NO ANGEL(1933), a, w; SHE DONE HIM WRONG(1933), a, w; BELLE OF THE NINETIES(1934), a, w; GOIN' TO TOWN(1935), a, w; GO WEST, YOUNG MAN(1936), a, w; KLONDIKE ANNIE(1936), a, w; EVERY DAY'S A HOLIDAY(1938), a, w; MY LITTLE CHICKADEE(1940), a, w; HEAT'S ON, THE(1943); SEXTETTE(1978), a, w

Marcia West
Silents
BRAND OF COWARDICE, THE(1916)

Margaret St. Barbe West
URGE TO KILL(1960, Brit.)

Maria West
BY DESIGN(1982)

Marjorie West
Silents
RAGGED MESSENGER, THE(1917, Brit.)

Martha West
CORPSE CAME C.O.D., THE

Martin West
FRECKLES(1960); SERGEANT WAS A LADY, THE(1961); CAPTAIN NEWMAN, M.D.(1963); MAN FROM GALVESTON, THE(1964); GIRLS ON THE BEACH(1965); SWINGIN' SUMMER, A(1965); HARPER(1966); LORD LOVE A DUCK(1966); SWEET NOVEMBER(1968); SOLDIER BLUE(1970); ASSAULT ON PRECINCT 13(1976); FAMILY PLOT(1976)

Misty West
TOWN THAT DREADED SUNDOWN, THE(1977)

Morris West
SALAMANDER, THE(1983, U.S./Ital./Brit.), w

Morris L. West
CROOKED ROAD, THE(, w; SHOES OF THE FISHERMAN, THE(1968), w

Nathanael West
ADVICE TO THE LOVELORN(1933), w; FOLLOW YOUR HEART(1936), w; PRESIDENT'S MYSTERY, THE(1936), w; TICKET TO PARADISE(1936), w; IT COULD HAPPEN TO YOU(1937), w; BORN TO BE WILD(1938), w; FIVE CAME BACK(1939), w; I STOLE A MILLION(1939), w; SPIRIT OF CULVER, THE(1939), w; LET'S MAKE MUSIC(1940), w; MEN AGAINST THE SKY(1940), w; LONELYHEARTS(1958), w; DAY OF THE LOCUST, THE(1975), w

Norma West
SPACEFLIGHT IC-1(1965, Brit.); PROJECTED MAN, THE(1967, Brit.); BATTLE BENEATH THE EARTH(1968, Brit.); MAN AT THE TOP(1973, Brit.); AND THE SHIP SAILS ON(1983, Ital./Fr.)

Olive West
Silents
MADAME BUTTERFLY(1915)

Olivia West
THIS LOVE OF OURS(1945)

Parker West
THE LADY DRACULA(1974)

Pat West
CEILNG ZERO(1935); PAGE MISS GLORY(1935); STARS OVER BROADWAY(1935); AUGUST WEEK-END(1936, Brit.); GOLD DIGGERS OF 1937(1936); LIBELED LADY(1936); LONE WOLF RETURNS, THE(1936); MURDER WITH PICTURES(1936); ROSE MARIE(1936); SONG OF THE SADDLE(1936); THREE MEN ON A HORSE(1936); THREE OF A KIND(1936); THREE WISE GUYS, THE(1936); EVER SINCE EVE(1937); HIGH, WIDE AND HANDSOME(1937); PERFECT SPECIMEN, THE(1937); SARATOGA(1937); TRUE CONFESSION(1937); TURN OFF THE MOON(1937); WHEN YOU'RE IN LOVE(1937); BRINGING UP BABY(1938); MEN WITH WINGS(1938); PRISON FARM(1938); STABLEMATES(1938); TEXANS, THE(1938); THANKS FOR THE MEMORY(1938); WOLVES OF THE SEA(1938); YOU CAN'T TAKE IT WITH YOU(1938); GERONIMO(1939); KING OF CHINATOWN(1939); LAUGH IT OFF(1939); MILLION DOLLAR LEGS(1939); ONLY ANGELS HAVE WINGS(1939); TELEVISION SPY(1939); BANK DICK, THE(1940); FARMER'S DAUGHTER, THE(1940); GREAT McGINTY, THE(1940); HIS GIRL FRIDAY(1940); KING OF THE LUMBERJACKS(1940); MY FAVORITE WIFE(1940); WHEN THE DALTONS RODE(1940); BALL OF FIRE(1941); SULLIVAN'S TRAVELS(1941); FOREST RANGERS, THE(1942); INVISIBLE AGENT(1942); JOHNNY EAGER(1942); MADAME SPY(1942); SUNDAY PUNCH(1942); NO TIME FOR LOVE(1943); OUTLAW, THE(1943); SLIGHTLY DANGEROUS(1943); LOUISIANA HAYRIDE(1944); MEET THE PEOPLE(1944); MOON OVER LAS VEGAS(1944); TO HAVE AND HAVE NOT(1944); INCENDIARY BLONDE(1945); ROAD TO UTOPIA(1945)

Paul West
HANG YOUR HAT ON THE WIND(1969), w
1984
SIGNAL 7(1984)
Silents
AMERICAN CONSUL, THE(1917), w; EACH TO HIS KIND(1917), w; GREAT EXPECTATIONS(1917), w; KISS FOR SUSIE, A(1917), Harvey Thew; ON RECORD(1917), w

Peter West
MY AIN FOLK(1974, Brit.), ed

R. Harley West
Misc. Silents
CRIME AND THE PENALTY(1916, Brit.), d; ON THE STEPS OF THE ALTAR(1916, Brit.), d

Raymond West
Silents
CIVILIZATION(1916), d; WOODEN SHOES(1917), d
Misc. Silents
PAYMENT, THE(1916), d; MADCAP MADGE(1917), d

Raymond B. West
Silents
EDGE OF THE ABYSS, THE(1915), d; CHICKEN CASEY(1917), d; FEMALE OF THE SPECIES(1917), d; ALL WRONG(1919), d

Misc. Silents
HONORABLE ALGY, THE(1916), d; HONOR'S ALTAR(1916), d; MORAL FABRIC, THE(1916), d; BORROWED PLUMAGE(1917), d; SNARL, THE(1917), d; WEAKER SEX, THE(1917), d; WHITHER THOU GOEST(1917), d; BLINDFOLDED(1918), d; WITHIN THE CUP(1918), d

Rebecca West
REDS(1981); RETURN OF THE SOLDIER, THE(1983, Brit.), w

Red West
WALKING TALL(1973); FRAMED(1975)

Reginald West
Silents
AFRAID OF LOVE(1925, Brit.), d

Richard West
MAYTIME IN MAYFAIR(1952, Brit.); TITANIC(1953); VICKI(1953)

Rick West
OPERATION CROSS EAGLES(1969, U.S./Yugo.)

Robert West
TOUCH OF HER FLESH, THE(1967)

Robert D. West
WEDNESDAY CHILDREN, THE(1973), a, d&w

Roland West
ALIBI(1929), p, d, w; BAT WHISPERS, THE(1930), d&w; CORSAIR(1931), p&d
Silents
NOBODY(1921), p&d, w; SILVER LINING, THE(1921), p&d, w; MONSTER, THE(1925), d; BAT, THE(1926), p
Misc. Silents
WOMAN'S HONOR, A(1916), d; SIREN, THE(1917), d; DELUXE ANNIE(1918), d; UNKNOWN PURPLE, THE(1923), d; DOVE, THE(1927), d

Sally West
YOURS FOR THE ASKING(1936)

Sam West
GOLDEN WEST, THE(1932)

Samuel B. West
CAPTAIN SINDBAD(1963), w

Shelly West
HONKYTONK MAN(1982)

Simon West
SWALLOWS AND AMAZONS(1977, Brit.)

Sonny West
HELLCATS, THE(1968)

Sue West
JOANNA(1968, Brit.), cos

Timothy West
DEADLY AFFAIR, THE(1967, Brit.); TWISTED NERVE(1969, Brit.); LOOKING GLASS WAR, THE(1970, Brit.); NICHOLAS AND ALEXANDRA(1971, Brit.); DAY OF THE JACKAL, THE(1973, Brit./Fr.); HITLER: THE LAST TEN DAYS(1973, Brit./Ital.); HEDDA(1975, Brit.); OPERATION DAYBREAK(1976, U.S./Brit./Czech.); THIRTY NINE STEPS, THE(1978, Brit.); AGATHA(1979, Brit.); ROUGH CUT(1980, Brit.)

Val West
LOVE BUTCHER, THE(1982), art d

Vera West
NEXT TIME WE LOVE(1936), cos; YELLOWSTONE(1936), cos; WESTLAND CASE, THE(1937), cos; RAGE OF PARIS, THE(1938), cos; ROAD TO RENO, THE(1938), cos; THAT CERTAIN AGE(1938), cos; YOUTH TAKES A FLING(1938), cos; DESTRY RIDES AGAIN(1939), cos; HOUSE OF FEAR, THE(1939), cos; SON OF FRANKENSTEIN(1939), cos; SUN NEVER SETS, THE(1939), cos; THREE SMART GIRLS GROW UP(1939), cos; TOWER OF LONDON(1939), cos; YOU CAN'T CHEAT AN HONEST MAN(1939), cos; BLACK FRIDAY(1940), cos; GIVE US WINGS(1940), cos; INVISIBLE MAN RETURNS, THE(1940), cos; MUMMY'S HAND, THE(1940), cos; MY LITTLE CHICKADEE(1940), cos; ONE NIGHT IN THE TROPICS(1940), cos; SANDY GETS HER MAN(1940), Cos; SANDY IS A LADY(1940), cos; SEVEN SINNERS(1940), cos; SOUTH TO KARANGA(1940), cos; SPRING PARADE(1940), cos; TRAIL OF THE VIGILANTES(1940), cos; WHEN THE DALTONS RODE(1940), cos; HELLZAPOPPIN'(1941), cos; INVISIBLE WOMAN, THE(1941), cos; MOB TOWN(1941), cos; NEVER GIVE A SUCKER AN EVEN BREAK(1941), cos; NICE GIRL?(1941), cos; THIS WOMAN IS MINE(1941), cos; TOO MANY BLONDES(1941), cos; WHERE DID YOU GET THAT GIRL?(1941), cos; ARABIAN NIGHTS(1942), cos; BETWEEN US GIRLS(1942), cos; MISSISSIPPI GAMBLER(1942), cos; PITTSBURGH(1942), cos; SPOILERS, THE(1942), cos; STRANGE CASE OF DR. RX, THE(1942), cos; THERE'S ONE BORN EVERY MINUTE(1942), cos; TOUGH AS THEY COME(1942), cos; FLESH AND FANTASY(1943), cos; GUNG HO!(1943), cos; KEEP 'EM SLUGGING(1943), cos; MOONLIGHT IN VERMONT(1943), cos; MR. BIG(1943), cos; MUG TOWN(1943), cos; PHANTOM OF THE OPERA(1943), cos; RHYTHM OF THE ISLANDS(1943), cos; SO'S YOUR UNCLE(1943), cos; STRANGE DEATH OF ADOLF HITLER, THE(1943), cos; TWO TICKETS TO LONDON(1943), cos; WHITE SAVAGE(1943), cos; FOLLOW THE BOYS(1944), cos; HOUSE OF FRANKENSTEIN(1944), cos; IN SOCIETY(1944), cos; MUMMY'S GHOST, THE(1944), cos; MURDER IN THE BLUE ROOM(1944), cos; NIGHT CLUB GIRL(1944), cos; PHANTOM LADY(1944), cos; SAN DIEGO, I LOVE YOU(1944), cos; SLIGHTLY TERRIFIC(1944), cos; SOUTH OF DIXIE(1944), cos; SUSPECT, THE(1944), cos; SWINGTIME JOHNNY(1944), cos; TWILIGHT ON THE PRAIRIE(1944), cos; WEEKEND PASS(1944), cos; WEIRD WOMAN(1944), cos; FROZEN GHOST, THE(1945), cos; HOUSE OF DRACULA(1945), cos; NAUGHTY NINETIES, THE(1945), cos; PATRICK THE GREAT(1945), art d; PILLOW OF DEATH(1945), cos; RIVER GANG(1945), cos; SALOME, WHERE SHE DANCED(1945), cos; SHE GETS HER MAN(1945), cos; STRANGE CONFESSION(1945), cos; THAT NIGHT WITH YOU(1945), cos; THAT'S THE SPIRIT(1945), cos; THIS LOVE OF OURS(1945), cos; WOMAN IN GREEN, THE(1945), cos; BLACK ANGEL(1946), cos; KILLERS, THE(1946), cos; MAGNIFICENT DOLL(1946), cos; NIGHT IN PARADISE, A(1946), cos; SLIGHTLY SCANDALOUS(1946), cos; SMOOTH AS SILK(1946), cos; SO GOES MY LOVE(1946), cos; PIRATES OF MONTEREY(1947), cos

Victor West
BORDER RANGERS(1950), w; GUNFIRE(1950), w; TRAIN TO TOMBSTONE(1950), w; PIER 23(1951), w; ROARING CITY(1951), w

Wallace West
HEADLINE SHOOTER(1933), w

Wally West [Hal Taliaferro]
DESERT TRAIL(1935); HOPALONG CASSIDY(1935); WESTERN COURAGE(1935); THUNDERBOLT(1936); TRAITOR, THE(1936); GHOST TOWN GOLD(1937); HIT THE SADDLE(1937); LAWMAN IS BORN, A(1937); RIDERS OF THE WHISTLING SKULL(1937); SANTA FE BOUND(1937); TWO-FISTED SHERIFF(1937); WHERE

TRAILS DIVIDE(1937); COLORADO KID(1938); FEUD MAKER(1938); PHANTOM RANGER(1938); CODE OF THE SECRET SERVICE(1939); SUNDOWN ON THE PRAIRIE(1939); DEATH RIDES THE RANGE(1940); MELODY RANCH(1940); PHANTOM RANCHER(1940); RHYTHM OF THE RIO GRANDE(1940); SAGEBRUSH FAMILY TRAILS WEST, THE(1940); STRAIGHT SHOOTER(1940); BILLY THE KID WANTED(1941); DEATH VALLEY OUTLAWS(1941); DRIFTIN' KID, THE(1941); GANGS OF SONORA(1941); BILLY THE KID TRAPPED(1942); CODE OF THE OUTLAW(1942); BLACK MARKET RUSTLERS(1943); DEATH VALLEY RANGERS(1944); RAIDERS OF RED GAP(1944); MAN FROM OKLAHOMA, THE(1945); GENTLEMAN FROM TEXAS(1946); OVERLAND RIDERS(1946); PIONEER JUSTICE(1947); STAGE TO MESA CITY(1947); CHECK YOUR GUNS(1948); LOST TRIBE, THE(1949); MARSHAL OF HELDORADO(1950)
Misc. Talkies
OUTLAWS OF THE RANGE(1936)

Walter West
BED AND BREAKFAST(1936, Brit.), p&d
Silents
ANSWER, THE(1916, Brit.), d; HARD WAY, THE(1916, Brit.), p&d; MERCHANT OF VENICE, THE(1916, Brit.), p&d; MUNITION GIRL'S ROMANCE, A(1917, Brit.), p; RAGGED MESSENGER, THE(1917, Brit.), p; WARE CASE, THE(1917, Brit.), p&d; MISSING THE TIDE(1918, Brit.), d; SNARE, THE(1918, Brit.), p; UNDER SUSPICION(1919, Brit.), p&d; DEAD CERTAINTY, A(1920, Brit.), p; KISSING CUP'S RACE(1920, Brit.), d; RANK OUTSIDER(1920, Brit.), p; PENNILESS MILLIONAIRE, THE(1921, Brit.), p; WHEN GREEK MEETS GREEK(1922, Brit.), d; BEAUTIFUL KITTY(1923, Brit.), d; IN THE BLOOD(1923, Brit.), d; DAUGHTER OF LOVE, A(1925, Brit.), d
Misc. Silents
BOLD ADVENTURESS, A(1915, Brit.), a, d; LONDON FLAT MYSTERY, A(1915, Brit.), d; WOMAN WHO DID, THE(1915, Brit.), d; BURNT WINGS(1916, Brit.), d; FORTUNE AT STAKE, A(1918, Brit.), d; NOT NEGOTIABLE(1918, Brit.), d; DAUGHTER OF EVE, A(1919, Brit.), d; HEARTS AND SADDLES(1919, Brit.), d; SNOW IN THE DESERT(1919, Brit.), d; CASE OF LADY CAMBER, THE(1920, Brit.), d; HER SON(1920, Brit.), d; KISSING CUP'S RACE(1920, Brit.), d; IMPERFECT LOVER, THE(1921, Brit.), d; SPORTSMAN'S WIFE, A(1921, Brit.), d; VI OF SMITH'S ALLEY(1921, Brit.), d; SCARLET LADY, THE(1922, Brit.), d; SON OF KISSING CUP(1922, Brit.), d; WAS SHE JUSTIFIED?(1922, Brit.), d; HORNET'S NEST(1923, Brit.), d; LADY OWNER, THE(1923, Brit.), d; WHAT PRICE LOVING CUP?(1923, Brit.), d; GREAT TURF MYSTERY, THE(1924, Brit.), d; STIRRUP CUP SENSATION, THE(1924, Brit.), d; TRAINER AND THE TEMPTRESS(1925, Brit.), d; MARIA MARTEN(1928, Brit.), d; SWEENEY TODD(1928, Brit.), d; WARNED OFF(1928, Brit.), d

Walton West
RIDING AVENGER, THE(1936), w

Wilis West
SNIPER, THE(1952)

William H. West
Misc. Silents
BARNSTORMERS, THE(1915)

William Lion West
Misc. Silents
THINGS MEN DO(1921)

William West
MAN WHO RECLAIMED HIS HEAD, THE(1935); DOUBLE TROUBLE(1941), d; FLYING WILD(1941), d
Misc. Talkies
LAST ALARM, THE(1940), d
Silents
HOUSE OF THE LOST CORD, THE(1915)
Misc. Silents
INVISIBLE POWER, THE(1914), Cleo Ridgely; PLOUGHSHARE, THE(1915)

Willie West
Silents
OLD CURIOSITY SHOP, THE(1913, Brit.)

Wilton West
CRIMSON TRAIL, THE(1935), w

David Westberg
CURIOUS FEMALE, THE(1969); THEY ONLY KILL THEIR MASTERS(1972)

R. Westberg
POCKET MONEY(1972)

Herbert Westbrook
BROTHER ALFRED(1932, Brit.), w; CROMWELL(1970, Brit.), art d; SUDDEN TERROR(1970, Brit.), prod d; LAWMAN(1971), art d; NIGHT COMERS, THE(1971, Brit.), art d; MECHANIC, THE(1972), art d; SCORPIO(1973), art d; EAGLE'S WING(1979, Brit.), prod d; WATER BABIES, THE(1979, Brit.), art d; FINAL CONFLICT, THE(1981), prod d; KEEP, THE(1983), art d; KRULL(1983), set d
1984
PASSAGE TO INDIA, A(1984, Brit.), art d

Jenny Westbrook
CONFESSIONS OF A WINDOW CLEANER(1974, Brit.)

John Westbrook
ROOM AT THE TOP(1959, Brit.); FOXHOLE IN CAIRO(1960, Brit.); PRIZE OF ARMS, A(1962, Brit.); MASQUE OF THE RED DEATH, THE(1964, U.S./Brit.); TOMB OF LIGEIA, THE(1965, Brit.); FFOLKES(1980, Brit.)

Joline Westbrook
JOHNNY DOUGHBOY(1943); MUG TOWN(1943)

Maude Westbrook
Silents
PROHIBITION(1915)

Nancy Westbrook
WINGS OF THE HAWK(1953); SON OF SINBAD(1955)

Robert T. Westbrook
MAGIC GARDEN OF STANLEY SWEETHART, THE(1970), w

Geir Westby
EDVARD MUNCH(1976, Norway/Swed.)

Norman E. Westcoatt
PACK TRAIN(1953)

Rusty Westcoatt
SNOWFIRE(1958); TOUCH OF EVIL(1958); YOUNG SWINGERS, THE(1963)

A.P. Westcott
OUT OF TOWNERS, THE(1970)

Buzz Westcott
EDGE OF ETERNITY(1959)

Edward Noyes Westcott
Silents
DAVID HARUM(1915), w

Edward Royes Westcott
DAVID HARUM(1934), w

Gordon Westcott
ENEMIES OF THE LAW(1931); DEVIL AND THE DEEP(1932); GUILTY AS HELL(1932); LOVE ME TONIGHT(1932); MERRILY WE GO TO HELL(1932); CONVENTION CITY(1933); CRIME OF THE CENTURY, THE(1933); FOOTLIGHT PARADE(1933); HE LEARNED ABOUT WOMEN(1933); HEROES FOR SALE(1933); LILLY TURNER(1933); PRIVATE DETECTIVE 62(1933); VOLTAIRE(1933); WORKING MAN, THE(1933); WORLD CHANGES, THE(1933); CALL IT LUCK(1934); CASE OF THE HOWLING DOG, THE(1934); CIRCUS CLOWN(1934); DARK HAZARD(1934); FASHIONS OF 1934(1934); FOG OVER FRISCO(1934); I'VE GOT YOUR NUMBER(1934); KANSAS CITY PRINCESS(1934); MURDER IN THE CLOUDS(1934); REGISTERED NURSE(1934); SIX-DAY BIKE RIDER(1934); BRIGHT LIGHTS(1935); FRONT PAGE WOMAN(1935); GO INTO YOUR DANCE(1935); GOING HIGHBROW(1935); NIGHT AT THE RITZ, A(1935); THIS IS THE LIFE(1935); TWO FISTED(1935); WHITE COCKATOO(1935)

H.G. Westcott
RAMPARTS WE WATCH, THE(1940)

Helen Westcott
THUNDER OVER TEXAS(1934); MIDSUMMER'S NIGHT'S DREAM, A(1935); HENRY ALDRICH FOR PRESIDENT(1941); SMART GIRLS DON'T TALK(1948); THIRTEEN LEAD SOLDIERS(1948); ADVENTURES OF DON JUAN(1949); ALASKA PATROL(1949); DANCING IN THE DARK(1949); FLAXY MARTIN(1949); GIRL FROM JONES BEACH(1949); HOMICIDE(1949); MR. BELVEDERE GOES TO COLLEGE(1949); ONE LAST FLING(1949); WHIRLPOOL(1949); GUNFIGHTER, THE(1950); THREE CAME HOME(1950); SECRET OF CONVICT LAKE, THE(1951); TAKE CARE OF MY LITTLE GIRL(1951); BATTLES OF CHIEF PONTIAC(1952); LOAN SHARK(1952); RETURN OF THE TEXAN(1952); WITH A SONG IN MY HEART(1952); CHARGE AT FEATHER RIVER, THE(1953); COW COUNTRY(1953); GUN BELT(1953); ABBOTT AND COSTELLO MEET DR. JEKYLL AND MR. HYDE(1954); HOT BLOOD(1956); I KILLED WILD BILL HICKOK(1956); INVISIBLE AVENGER, THE(1958); LAST HURRAH, THE(1958); MONSTER ON THE CAMPUS(1958); STUDS LONIGAN(1960); I LOVE MY WIFE(1970); PIECES OF DREAMS(1970)
Misc. Talkies
BOURBON ST. SHADOWS(1962)

Netta Westcott
WOMAN DECIDES, THE(1932, Brit.); TWO OF US, THE(1938, Brit.); SPRINGTIME(1948, Brit.); HIGH JINKS IN SOCIETY(1949, Brit.)
Silents
IN HIS GRIP(1921, Brit.)
Misc. Silents
LADY WINDERMERE'S FAN(1916, Brit.)

Rusty Westcott
SNOW CREATURE, THE,(1954)

Wendy Westcott
CHILD'S PLAY(1954, Brit.)

Gordon Westcourt
ZEBRA IN THE KITCHEN(1965)

Carl Wester
TRAIL STREET(1947)

Jordana Wester
HARDLY WORKING(1981)

Keith Wester
RAT PFINK AND BOO BOO(1966), a, ed

Fred Westerberg
Silents
TEN COMMANDMENTS, THE(1923), ph; VOLGA BOATMAN, THE(1926), ph; KING OF KINGS, THE(1927), ph

J. F. Westerberg
GODLESS GIRL, THE(1929), ph

Sonja Westerberg
MAKE WAY FOR LILA(1962, Swed./Ger.)

Stig Westerberg
TO LOVE(1964, Swed.), md

Jim Westerbrook
Misc. Talkies
MISSION TO DEATH(1966)

Robert Westerby
BROKEN JOURNEY(1948, Brit.), w; HIDEOUT(1948, Brit.), w; MY SISTER AND I(1948, Brit.), w; NIGHT BEAT(1948, Brit.), w; DON'T EVER LEAVE ME(1949, Brit.), w; WOMAN HATER(1949, Brit.), w; CAIRO ROAD(1950, Brit.), w; PRELUDE TO FAME(1950, Brit.), w; ADVENTURERS, THE(1951, Brit.), w; SPIDER AND THE FLY, THE(1952, Brit.), w; APPOINTMENT IN LONDON(1953, Brit.), w; BEAUTIFUL STRANGER(1954, Brit.), w; FIRE OVER AFRICA(1954, Brit.), w; GOLDEN MASK, THE(1954, Brit.), w; THEY WHO DARE(1954, Brit.), w; SQUARE RING, THE(1955, Brit.), w; SHADOW OF FEAR(1956, Brit.), w; SPIN A DARK WEB(1956, Brit.), w; WAR AND PEACE(1956, Ital./U.S.), w; PORTRAIT IN SMOKE(1957, Brit.), w; SURGEON'S KNIFE, THE(1957, Brit.), w; TOWN ON TRIAL(1957, Brit.), w; S.O.S. PACIFIC(1960, Brit.), w; GREYFRIARS BOBBY(1961, Brit.), w; TROUBLE IN THE SKY(1961, Brit.), w; DESERT PATROL(1962, Brit.), w; DEVIL'S AGENT, THE(1962, Brit.), w; THREE LIVES OF THOMASINA, THE(1963, U.S./Brit.), w; FIGHTING PRINCE OF DONEGAL, THE(1966, Brit.), w; DR. SYN, ALIAS THE SCARECROW(1975), w

Susan Westerby
SURGEON'S KNIFE, THE(1957, Brit.)

John Westerfelt
HAPPY DAYS(1930)

James Westerfield
MAN'S FAVORITE SPORT(?)**1/2 (1964); HOWARDS OF VIRGINIA, THE(1940); HIGHWAY WEST(1941); MAGNIFICENT AMBERSONS, THE(1942); AROUND THE WORLD(1943); SINCE YOU WENT AWAY(1944); CHASE, THE(1946); O.S.S.(1946); UNDERCURRENT(1946); SIDE STREET(1950); WHISTLE AT EATON FALLS(1951);

HUMAN JUNGLE, THE(1954); ON THE WATERFRONT(1954); THREE HOURS TO KILL(1954); CHIEF CRAZY HORSE(1955); COBWEB, THE(1955); LUCY GALLANT(1955); MAN WITH THE GUN(1955); SCARLET COAT, THE(1955); VIOLENT MEN, THE(1955); DECISION AT SUNDOWN(1957); JUNGLE HEAT(1957); THREE BRAVE MEN(1957); COWBOY(1958); PROUD REBEL, THE(1958); HANGMAN, THE(1959); SHAGGY DOG, THE(1959); PLUNDERERS, THE(1960); WILD RIVER(1960); ABSENT-MINDED PROFESSOR, THE(1961); HOMICIDAL(1961); BIRDMAN OF ALCATRAZ(1962); SCARFACE MOB, THE(1962); SON OF FLUBBER(1963); BIKINI BEACH(1964); MAN'S FAVORITE SPORT(1964); SONS OF KATIE ELDER, THE(1965); THAT FUNNY FEELING(1965); DEAD HEAT ON A MERRY-GO-ROUND(1966); BLUE(1968); HANG'EM HIGH(1968); LOVE GOD?, THE(1969); MAN CALLED GANNON, A(1969); SMITH(1969); TRUE GRIT(1969)

Jim Westerfield
GUNFIGHT AT DODGE CITY, THE(1959); ODE TO BILLY JOE(1976)

Jim [James] Westerfield
SPIRIT OF STANFORD, THE(1942)

Hakan Westergren
SWEDENHIELMS(1935, Swed.); DOLLAR(1938, Swed.); 48 HOURS TO LIVE(1960, Brit./Swed.); SECRETS OF WOMEN(1961, Swed.)

Nanci Westerland
HOW TO BEAT THE HIGH COST OF LIVING(1980)

Catrin Westerlund
SWEDISH WEDDING NIGHT(1965, Swed.)

Paul Westermeier
DAUGHTER OF EVIL(1930, Ger.); BERLIN ALEXANDERPLATZ(1933, Ger.); F.P. 1 DOESN'T ANSWER(1933, Ger.); CONGRESS DANCES(1957, Ger.); DEVIL'S GENERAL, THE(1957, Ger.); WHITE HORSE INN, THE(1959, Ger.)

George Western
MISTER CINDERS(1934, Brit.), a, w

Johnny Western
DALTON GIRLS, THE(1957); FORT BOWIE(1958)

Kenneth Western
MISTER CINDERS(1934, Brit.), a, w

Pamela Western
RANDOLPH FAMILY, THE(1945, Brit.)

Western Brothers
ONE PRECIOUS YEAR(1933, Brit.); WAY OF YOUTH, THE(1934, Brit.); RADIO FOLLIES(1935, Brit.); OLD BONES OF THE RIVER(1938, Brit.)

Frank H. Westerton
Silents
MANON LESCAUT(1914)

Kay Westfall
GOLDEN GLOVES STORY, THE(1950)

Mischa Westfall
MISSION TO MOSCOW(1943)

Gullan Westfelt
LOVING COUPLES(1966, Swed.), makeup

Michael Westfield
ZOTZ!(1962)

Murray Westgate
CHANGE OF MIND(1969); FIRST TIME, THE(1969); HOMER(1970); CLASS OF '44(1973); SUNDAY IN THE COUNTRY(1975, Can.); RUNNING(1979, Can.); KIDNAPPING OF THE PRESIDENT, THE(1980, Can.); HAPPY BIRTHDAY TO ME(1981); SILENCE OF THE NORTH(1981, Can.); THRESHOLD(1983, Can.)

Joseph Westheimer
VON RYAN'S EXPRESS(1965), w

Dr. Ruth Westheimer
1984
ELECTRIC DREAMS(1984)

Donfeld Westheimer Co.
PHYNX, THE(1970), cos

Joachim Westhoss
IS PARIS BURNING?(1966, U.S./Fr.)

Bogan Westin
JOHANSSON GETS SCOLDED(1945, Swed.)

Cynthia Westlake
NEW FACES OF 1937(1937)

Donald Westlake
BANK SHOT(1974), w

Donald E. Westlake
BUSYBODY, THE(1967), w; HOT ROCK, THE(1972), w; COPS AND ROBBERS(1973), w; HOT STUFF(1979), w; JIMMY THE KID(1982), w

Eva Westlake
Silents
RUPERT OF HENTZAU(1915, Brit.); ONE SUMMER'S DAY(1917, Brit.); AT THE VILLA ROSE(1920, Brit.); MONTY WORKS THE WIRES(1921, Brit.); MASTER OF CRAFT, A(1922, Brit.); MONEY HABIT, THE(1924, Brit.)
Misc. Silents
ISLAND OF WISDOM, THE(1920, Brit.); THREE MEN IN A BOAT(1920, Brit.); DICK'S FAIRY(1921, Brit.)

Hilary Westlake
Misc. Talkies
GOLD DIGGERS, THE(1984, Brit.)

Marguerite Westlake
Silents
MERCHANT OF VENICE, THE(1916, Brit.)

Ross Westlake
HOLLYWOOD OR BUST(1956)

David Westlein
SHARKFIGHTERS, THE(1956)

George Humbert Westley
HOUSE OF ROTHSCHILD, THE(1934), w

Helen Westley
AGE OF INNOCENCE(1934); ANNE OF GREEN GABLES(1934); DEATH TAKES A HOLIDAY(1934); HOUSE OF ROTHSCHILD, THE(1934); MOULIN ROUGE(1934); CAPTAIN HURRICANE(1935); CHASING YESTERDAY(1935); MELODY LINGERS ON, THE(1935); ROBERTA(1935); SPLENDOR(1935); BANJO ON MY KNEE(1936); HALF ANGEL(1936); SHOW BOAT(1936); STOWAWAY(1936); CAFE METROPOLE(1937); HEIDI(1937); I'LL TAKE ROMANCE(1937); SING AND BE HAPPY(1937); ALEXANDER'S RAGTIME BAND(1938); BARONESS AND THE BUTLER,

THE(1938); KEEP SMILING(1938); REBECCA OF SUNNYBROOK FARM(1938); SHE MARRIED AN ARTIST(1938); WIFE, HUSBAND AND FRIEND(1939); ZAZA(1939); ALL THIS AND HEAVEN TOO(1940); CAPTAIN IS A LADY, THE(1940); LADY WITH RED HAIR(1940); LILLIAN RUSSELL(1940); ADAM HAD FOUR SONS(1941); LADY FROM LOUISIANA(1941); MILLION DOLLAR BABY(1941); SMILING GHOST, THE(1941); SUNNY(1941); BEDTIME STORY(1942); MY FAVORITE SPY(1942)

John Westley
MY FAVORITE BRUNETTE(1947); WELCOME STRANGER(1947)

Peter Westley
Misc. Talkies
FALLS, THE(1980, Brit.)

Don Westling
PURPLE HAZE(1982)

Chris Westlund
OH GOD! BOOK II(1980), set d

R. Chris Westlund
MIDNIGHT MADNESS(1980), set d; DINER(1982), set d; ENDANGERED SPECIES(1982), set d
1984
BEST DEFENSE(1984), set d; MIKE'S MURDER(1984), set d; SWING SHIFT(1984), set d; THIEF OF HEARTS(1984), set d

Jim Westman
WRESTLER, THE(1974), d

Lisa Westman
GREY FOX, THE(1983, Can.)

Lolita Ann Westman
RUNAWAY BRIDE(1930), w; PERFECT CLUE, THE(1935), w

Nydia Westman
MANHATTAN TOWER(1932); STRANGE JUSTICE(1932); BONDAGE(1933); CRADLE SONG(1933); FROM HELL TO HEAVEN(1933); KING OF THE JUNGLE(1933); LITTLE WOMEN(1933); WAY TO LOVE, THE(1933); LADIES SHOULD LISTEN(1934); MANHATTAN LOVE SONG(1934); ONE NIGHT OF LOVE(1934); SUCCESS AT ANY PRICE(1934); TRUMPET BLOWS, THE(1934); TWO ALONE(1934); DRESSED TO THRILL(1935); FEATHER IN HER HAT, A(1935); SWEET ADELINE(1935); THREE LIVE GHOSTS(1935); CRAIG'S WIFE(1936); GORGEOUS HUSSY, THE(1936); PENNIES FROM HEAVEN(1936); ROSE BOWL(1936); THE INVISIBLE RAY(1936); BULLDOG DRUMMOND'S REVENGE(1937); WHEN LOVE IS YOUNG(1937); BULLDOG DRUMMOND'S PERIL(1938); FIRST 100 YEARS, THE(1938); GOLDWYN FOLLIES, THE(1938); CAT AND THE CANARY, THE(1939); WHEN TOMORROW COMES(1939); FORTY LITTLE MOTHERS(1940); HULLABALOO(1940); BAD MAN, THE(1941); CHOCOLATE SOLDIER, THE(1941); REMARKABLE ANDREW, THE(1942); THEY ALL KISSED THE BRIDE(1942); HERS TO HOLD(1943); PRINCESS O'ROURKE(1943); HER PRIMITIVE MAN(1944); LATE GEORGE APLEY, THE(1947); VELVET TOUCH, THE(1948); DON'T KNOCK THE TWIST(1962); FOR LOVE OR MONEY(1963); CHASE, THE(1966); GHOST AND MR. CHICKEN, THE(1966); SWINGER, THE(1966); RELUCTANT ASTRONAUT, THE(1967); HORSE IN THE GRAY FLANNEL SUIT, THE(1968); RABBIT, RUN(1970)

Theodore Westman, Jr.
Silents
FLAPPER, THE(1920)

Tony Westman
SUPREME KID, THE(1976, Can.), ph; DESERTERS(1983, Can.), ph

Bud Westmore
MAN'S FAVORITE SPORT(?)**1/2 (1964), makeup; THOROUGHLY MODERN MILLIE(1967), makeup; PAD, THE(AND HOW TO USE IT)* (1966, Brit.), makeup; DETOUR(1945), makeup; BRUTE FORCE(1947), makeup; DOUBLE LIFE, A(1947), makeup; RIDE THE PINK HORSE(1947), makeup; WISTFUL WIDOW OF WAGON GAP, THE(1947), makeup; ABBOTT AND COSTELLO MEET FRANKENSTEIN(1948), makeup; FAMILY HONEYMOON(1948), makeup; KISS THE BLOOD OFF MY HANDS(1948), makeup; LETTER FROM AN UNKNOWN WOMAN(1948), makeup; NAKED CITY, THE(1948), makeup; ROGUES' REGIMENT(1948), makeup; SAXON CHARM, THE(1948), makeup; TAP ROOTS(1948), makeup; UP IN CENTRAL PARK(1948), makeup; YOU GOTTA STAY HAPPY(1948), makeup; ABBOTT AND COSTELLO MEET THE KILLER, BORIS KARLOFF(1949), makeup; CALAMITY JANE AND SAM BASS(1949), makeup; CRISS CROSS(1949), makeup; ILLEGAL ENTRY(1949), makeup; JOHNNY STOOL PIGEON(1949), makeup; LADY GAMBLES, THE(1949), makeup; ONCE MORE, MY DARLING(1949), makeup; RED CANYON(1949), makeup; STORY OF MOLLY X, THE(1949), makeup; TAKE ONE FALSE STEP(1949), makeup; UNDERTOW(1949), makeup; WOMAN IN HIDING(1949), makeup; PEGGY(1950), makeup; SHAKEDOWN(1950), makeup; SPY HUNT(1950), makeup; STRANGE DOOR, THE(1951), makeup; MEET DANNY WILSON(1952), makeup; IT CAME FROM OUTER SPACE(1953), makeup; SEMINOLE(1953), makeup; ABBOTT AND COSTELLO MEET DR. JEKYLL AND MR. HYDE(1954), makeup; CREATURE FROM THE BLACK LAGOON(1954), makeup; REVENGE OF THE CREATURE(1955), makeup; TARANTULA(1955), makeup; THIS ISLAND EARTH(1955), makeup; MOLE PEOPLE, THE(1956), makeup; ISTANBUL(1957), makeup; MAN IN THE SHADOW(1957), makeup; MAN OF A THOUSAND FACES(1957), makeup; MONOLITH MONSTERS, THE(1957), makeup; LADY TAKES A FLYER, THE(1958), makeup; PERFECT FURLOUGH, THE(1958), makeup; RAW WIND IN EDEN(1958), makeup; TWILIGHT FOR THE GODS(1958), makeup; NEVER STEAL ANYTHING SMALL(1959), makeup; OPERATION PETTICOAT(1959), makeup; PILLOW TALK(1959), makeup; GREAT IMPOSTOR, THE(1960), makeup; LEECH WOMAN, THE(1960), makeup; PORTRAIT IN BLACK(1960), makeup; SPARTACUS(1960), makeup; LAST SUNSET, THE(1961), makeup; LOVER COME BACK(1961), makeup; POSSE FROM HELL(1961), makeup; TAMMY, TELL ME TRUE(1961), makeup; IF A MAN ANSWERS(1962), makeup; LONELY ARE THE BRAVE(1962), makeup; OUTSIDER, THE(1962), makeup; SIX BLACK HORSES(1962), makeup; SPIRAL ROAD, THE(1962), makeup; THAT TOUCH OF MINK(1962), makeup; TO KILL A MOCKINGBIRD(1962), makeup; CAPTAIN NEWMAN, M.D.(1963), makeup; FOR LOVE OR MONEY(1963), makeup; GATHERING OF EAGLES, A(1963), makeup; LIST OF ADRIAN MESSENGER, THE(1963), makeup; SHOWDOWN(1963), makeup; TAMMY AND THE DOCTOR(1963), makeup; UGLY AMERICAN, THE(1963), makeup; FATHER GOOSE(1964), makeup; ISLAND OF THE BLUE DOLPHINS(1964), makeup; KILLERS, THE(1964), makeup; LIVELY SET, THE(1964), makeup; MAN'S FAVORITE SPORT(1964), makeup; MC HALE'S NAVY(1964), makeup; NIGHT WALKER, THE(1964), makeup; SEND ME NO FLOWERS(1964), makeup; TAGGART(1964), makeup; WILD AND WONDERFUL(1964), makeup; DARK INTRUDER(1965), makeup; MC HALE'S NAVY JOINS THE AIR FORCE(1965), makeup; MIRAGE(1965), makeup; SHENANDOAH(1965), makeup; STRANGE BEDFELLOWS(1965), makeup; SWORD OF ALI

BABA, THE(1965), makeup; THAT FUNNY FEELING(1965), makeup; VERY SPE-CIAL FAVOR, A(1965), makeup; WAR LORD, THE(1965), makeup; WILD SEED(1965), makeup; GAMBIT(1966), makeup; INCIDENT AT PHANTOM HILL(1966), makeup; MADAME X(1966), makeup; MOMENT TO MOMENT(1966), makeup; MUNSTER, GO HOME(1966), makeup; OUT OF SIGHT(1966), makeup; PLAINSMAN, THE(1966), makeup; RARE BREED, THE(1966), makeup; TEXAS ACROSS THE RIVER(1966), makeup; TOBRUK(1966), makeup; GAMES(1967), makeup; GUNFIGHT IN ABI-LENE(1967), makeup; KING'S PIRATE(1967), makeup; PERILS OF PAULINE, THE(1967), makeup; RELUCTANT ASTRONAUT, THE(1967), makeup; RIDE TO HANGMAN'S TREE, THE(1967), makeup; ROSIE!(1967), makeup; ROUGH NIGHT IN JERICHO(1967), makeup; SULLIVAN'S EMPIRE(1967), makeup; TAMMY AND THE MILLIONAIRE(1967), makeup; VALLEY OF MYSTERY(1967), makeup; WAR WAG-ON, THE(1967), makeup; YOUNG WARRIORS, THE(1967), makeup; DON'T JUST STAND THERE(1968), makeup; HELL WITH HEROES, THE(1968), makeup; JIG-SAW(1968), makeup; JOURNEY TO SHILOH(1968), makeup; LOVELY WAY TO DIE, A(1968), makeup; MADIGAN(1968), makeup; NOBODY'S PERFECT(1968), makeup; PINK JUNGLE, THE(1968), makeup; P.J.(1968), makeup; SECRET WAR OF HARRY FRIGG, THE(1968), makeup; SERGEANT RYKER(1968), makeup; SHAKIEST GUN IN THE WEST, THE(1968), makeup; THREE GUNS FOR TEXAS(1968), makeup; WHAT'S SO BAD ABOUT FEELING GOOD?(1968), makeup; EYE OF THE CAT(1969), makeup; HOUSE OF CARDS(1969), makeup; LOVE GOD?, THE(1969), makeup; MAN CALLED GANNON, A(1969), makeup; SWEET CHARITY(1969), makeup; TELL THEM WILLIE BOY IS HERE(1969), makeup; THIS SAVAGE LAND(1969), makeup; TOPAZ(1969, Brit.), makeup; WINNING(1969), makeup; SKULLDUGGERY(1970), makeup; STORY OF A WOMAN(1970, U.S./Ital.), makeup; BEGUILED, THE(1971), makeup; HOW TO FRAME A FIGG(1971), makeup; RED SKY AT MORNING(1971), makeup; SHOOT OUT(1971), makeup; SOYLENT GREEN(1973), makeup

Ern Westmore
GANGSTER, THE(1947), makeup; RAILROADED(1947), makeup; T-MEN(1947), makeup; CANON CITY(1948), makeup; HE WALKED BY NIGHT(1948), makeup; HOLLOW TRIUMPH(1948), make-up; LET'S LIVE A LITTLE(1948), makeup; NOOSE HANGS HIGH, THE(1948), makeup; NORTHWEST STAMPEDE(1948), makeup; RAW DEAL(1948), makeup; SPIRITUALIST, THE(1948), makeup; PORT OF NEW YORK(1949), makeup; RED STALLION IN THE ROCKIES(1949), makeup; TRAP-PED(1949), makeup; TULSA(1949), makeup; ONE TOO MANY(1950)

Ernest "Ern" Westmore
DANTE'S INFERNO(1935), makeup; PADDY O'DAY(1935), makeup; UNDER THE PAMPAS MOON(1935), makeup; HUMAN CARGO(1936), makeup

Frank Westmore
CANON CITY(1948), makeup; HOLLOW TRIUMPH(1948), make-up; SPIRITUAL-IST, THE(1948), makeup; STORM WARNING(1950), makeup; GROOM WORE SPURS, THE(1951), makeup; RANCHO NOTORIOUS(1952), makeup; TEN COMMAND-MENTS, THE(1956), makeup; MY GEISHA(1962), makeup; TWO FOR THE SEE-SAW(1962), makeup; IRMA LA DOUCE(1963), makeup; WHO'S BEEN SLEEPING IN MY BED?(1963), makeup; JOHN GOLDFARB, PLEASE COME HOME(1964), makeup; WHAT A WAY TO GO(1964), makeup; SHENANDOAH(1965), makeup; TICKLE ME(1965), makeup; TWO MULES FOR SISTER SARA(1970), makeup; FOOLS' PARADE(1971), makeup; FAREWELL, MY LOVELY(1975), makeup; BEING THE-RE(1979), makeup

Joy Westmore
SUMMERFIELD(1977, Aus.); ODD ANGRY SHOT, THE(1979, Aus.)

Lucy Westmore
DOCTOR ZHIVAGO(1965)

Marvin Westmore
DOCTOR DOLITTLE(1967), makeup; PROJECT X(1968), makeup; ULTIMATE WAR-RIOR, THE(1975), makeup; BUDDY HOLLY STORY, THE(1978), makeup

Michael Westmore
HARLOW(1965), makeup; NEW YORK, NEW YORK(1977), makeup; ROCKY II(1979), makeup
1984
ICEMAN(1984), makeup; 2010(1984), makeup

Mike Westmore
ROCKY(1976), makeup; TRACKDOWN(1976), makeup

Monte Westmore
FORBIDDEN(1932), makeup; WHATEVER HAPPENED TO BABY JANE?(1962), makeup; STRAIT-JACKET(1964), makeup; LOVE AND KISSES(1965), makeup; SPIR-IT IS WILLING, THE(1967), makeup; RIO LOBO(1970), makeup; SOMETIMES A GREAT NOTION(1971), makeup; SLITHER(1973), makeup

Monty Westmore
LIFE AND TIMES OF JUDGE ROY BEAN, THE(1972), makeup; UPTOWN SATUR-DAY NIGHT(1974), makeup; WELCOME TO L.A.(1976), makeup; LATE SHOW, THE(1977), makeup; THREE WOMEN(1977), makeup

Perc Westmore
DOORWAY TO HELL(1930), makeup; SINNER'S HOLIDAY(1930), makeup; MIL-LIONAIRE, THE(1931), makeup; OTHER MEN'S WOMEN(1931), makeup; PUBLIC ENEMY, THE(1931), makeup; SMART MONEY(1931), makeup; TAXI!(1932), makeup; TENDERFOOT, THE(1932), makeup; WINNER TAKE ALL(1932), makeup; YOU SAID A MOUTHFUL(1932), makeup; FOOTLIGHT PARADE(1933), Makeup; HARD TO HANDLE(1933), makeup; LADY KILLER(1933), makeup; MAYOR OF HELL, THE(1933), makeup; PICTURE SNATCHER(1933), makeup; WILD BOYS OF THE ROAD(1933), makeup; HERE COMES THE NAVY(1934), makeup; JIMMY THE GENT(1934), makeup; ST. LOUIS KID, THE(1934), makeup; TWENTY MILLION SWEETHEARTS(1934), makeup; UPPER WORLD(1934), makeup; BLACK FURY(1935), makeup; CEILNG ZERO(1935), makeup; IRISH IN US, THE(1935), makeup; MIDSUMMER'S NIGHT'S DREAM, A(1935), makeup; WALKING DEAD, THE(1936), makeup; LIFE OF EMILE ZOLA, THE(1937), makeup; WEST OF SHANG-HAI(1937), makeup; BOY MEETS GIRL(1938), makeup; DODGE CITY(1939), makeup; EACH DAWN I DIE(1939), makeup; GORILLA, THE(1939), makeup; OKLAHOMA KID, THE(1939), makeup; PRIVATE LIVES OF ELIZABETH AND ESSEX, THE(1939), makeup; RETURN OF DR. X, THE(1939), makeup; ROARING TWENTIES, THE(1939), makeup; FIGHTING 69TH, THE(1940), makeup; INVISIBLE STRI-PES(1940), Makeup; SANTA FE TRAIL(1940), makeup; THEY DRIVE BY NIGHT(1940), makeup; TORRID ZONE(1940), makeup; VIRGINIA CITY(1940), make-up; CITY, FOR CONQUEST(1941), makeup; HIGH SIERRA(1941), makeup; MALTESE FALCON, THE(1941), makeup; MANPOWER(1941), makeup; STRAWBERRY BLONDE, THE(1941), makeup; BIG SHOT, THE(1942), makeup; CASABLAN-CA(1942), makeup; GAY SISTERS, THE(1942), makeup; GENTLEMAN JIM(1942), makeup; THEY DIED WITH THEIR BOOTS ON(1942), makeup; YANKEE DOODLE DANDY(1942), makeup; ACTION IN THE NORTH ATLANTIC(1943), makeup; THANK YOUR LUCKY STARS(1943), makeup; MASK OF DIMITRIOS, THE(1944),

makeup; MR. SKEFFINGTON(1944), makeup; PASSAGE TO MARSEILLE(1944), makeup; UNCERTAIN GLORY(1944), makeup; CONFLICT(1945), makeup; MILDRED PIERCE(1945), makeup; OBJECTIVE, BURMA!(1945), makeup; SAN AN-TONIO(1945), makeup; SARATOGA TRUNK(1945), makeup; CLOAK AND DAG-GER(1946), makeup; MY REPUTATION(1946), makeup; NEVER SAY GOODBYE(1946), makeup; NIGHT AND DAY(1946), makeup; ALWAYS TOGE-THER(1947), makeup; ESCAPE ME NEVER(1947), makeup; LIFE WITH FA-THER(1947), makeup; NORA PRENTISS(1947), makeup; POSSESSED(1947), makeup; TWO MRS. CARROLLS, THE(1947), makeup; UNSUS-PECTED, THE(1947), makeup; FIGHTER SQUADRON(1948), makeup; JOHNNY BELINDA(1948), makeup; JUNE BRIDE(1948), makeup; KEY LARGO(1948), make-up; ROPE(1948), makeup; SILVER RIVER(1948), makeup; SMART GIRLS DON'T TALK(1948), makeup; TREASURE OF THE SIERRA MADRE, THE(1948), makeup; WALLFLOWER(1948), makeup; WINTER MEETING(1948), makeup; BEYOND THE FOREST(1949), makeup; FLAMINGO ROAD(1949), makeup; FOUNTAINHEAD, THE(1949), makeup; GREAT GATSBY, THE(1949), makeup; IT'S A GREAT FEEL-ING(1949), makeup; JOHN LOVES MARY(1949), makeup; LADY TAKES A SAILOR, THE(1949), makeup; ONE LAST FLING(1949), makeup; TASK FORCE(1949), make-up; WHITE HEAT(1949), makeup; BRIGHT LEAF(1950), makeup; CAGED(1950), makeup; DAMNED DON'T CRY, THE(1950), makeup; GLASS MENAGERIE, THE(1950), makeup; MONTANA(1950), makeup; PERFECT STRANGERS(1950), makeup; STORM WARNING(1950), makeup; YOUNG MAN WITH A HORN(1950), makeup; MUNSTER, GO HOME(1966), makeup; GOOD GUYS AND THE BAD GUYS, THE(1969), makeup; ONCE YOU KISS A STRANGER(1969), makeup; THERE WAS A CROOKED MAN(1970), makeup; GREAT GATSBY, THE(1974), makeup

Pete Westmore
NORTHERN PURSUIT(1943), makeup

Wally Westmore
ROMA RIVUOLE CESARE(, makeup; DR. JEKYLL AND MR. HYDE(1932), make-up; ALICE IN WONDERLAND(1933), cos; ISLAND OF LOST SOULS(1933), makeup; MAKE WAY FOR TOMORROW(1937), makeup; IF I WERE KING(1938), makeup; NEVER SAY DIE(1939), makeup; GREAT McGINTY, THE(1940), makeup; NORTH-WEST MOUNTED POLICE(1940), makeup; REMEMBER THE NIGHT(1940), makeup; LADY EVE, THE(1941), makeup; NEW YORK TOWN(1941), makeup; SULLIVAN'S TRAVELS(1941), makeup; I MARRIED A WITCH(1942), makeup; MAJOR AND THE MINOR, THE(1942), makeup; PALM BEACH STORY, THE(1942), makeup; STAR SPANGLED RHYTHM(1942), makeup; FOR WHOM THE BELL TOLLS(1943), make-up; YOUNG AND WILLING(1943), makeup; DOUBLE INDEMNITY(1944), makeup; HAIL THE CONQUERING HERO(1944), makeup; LADY IN THE DARK(1944), makeup; MIRACLE OF MORGAN'S CREEK, THE(1944), makeup; LOST WEEKEND, THE(1945), makeup; STRANGE LOVE OF MARTHA IVERS, THE(1946), makeup; GOLDEN EARRINGS(1947), makeup; ROAD TO RIO(1947), makeup; UNCON-QUERED(1947), makeup; VARIETY GIRL(1947), makeup; MISS TATLOCK'S MIL-LIONS(1948), makeup; NIGHT HAS A THOUSAND EYES(1948), makeup; SAIGON(1948), makeup; SEALED VERDICT(1948), makeup; CHICAGO DEAD-LINE(1949), makeup; CONNECTICUT YANKEE IN KING ARTHUR'S COURT, A(1949), makeup; HEIRESS, THE(1949), makeup; RED, HOT AND BLUE(1949), makeup; SAMSON AND DELILAH(1949), makeup; SORROWFUL JONES(1949), makeup; STREETS OF LAREDO(1949), makeup; TOP O' THE MORNING(1949), makeup; FILE ON THELMA JORDAN, THE(1950), makeup; MAD WEDNES-DAY(1950), makeup; NO MAN OF HER OWN(1950), makeup; RIDING HIGH(1950), makeup; SUNSET BOULEVARD(1950), makeup; UNION STATION(1950), makeup; BIG CARNIVAL, THE(1951), makeup; DETECTIVE STORY(1951), makeup; PLACE IN THE SUN, A(1951), makeup; GREATEST SHOW ON EARTH, THE(1952), makeup; TURNING POINT, THE(1952), makeup; FOREVER FEMALE(1953), makeup; STA-LAG 17(1953), makeup; WAR OF THE WORLDS, THE(1953), makeup; BRIDGES AT TOKO-RI, THE(1954), makeup; SABRINA(1954), makeup; DESPERATE HOURS, THE(1955), makeup; RUN FOR COVER(1955), makeup; WE'RE NO ANGELS(1955), makeup; PROUD AND THE PROFANE, THE(1956), makeup; RAINMAKER, THE(1956), makeup; TEN COMMANDMENTS, THE(1956), makeup; FUNNY FA-CE(1957), makeup; LOVING YOU(1957), makeup; SHORT CUT TO HELL(1957), makeup; KING CREOLE(1958), makeup; ROCK-A-BYE BABY(1958), makeup; SPACE CHILDREN, THE(1958), makeup; VERTIGO(1958), makeup; RAT RACE, THE(1960), makeup; LADIES MAN, THE(1961), makeup; LOVE IN A GOLDFISH BOWL(1961), makeup; ON THE DOUBLE(1961), makeup; ONE-EYED JACKS(1961), makeup; PLEASURE OF HIS COMPANY, THE(1961), makeup; POCKETFUL OF MIRA-CLES(1961), makeup; SUMMER AND SMOKE(1961), makeup; MAN WHO SHOT LIBERTY VALANCE, THE(1962), makeup; PIGEON THAT TOOK ROME, THE(1962), makeup; COME BLOW YOUR HORN(1963), makeup; HUD(1963), makeup; LOVE WITH THE PROPER STRANGER(1963), makeup; MY SIX LOVES(1963), makeup; NEW KIND OF LOVE, A(1963), makeup; NUTTY PROFESSOR, THE(1963), makeup; WHO'S MINDING THE STORE?(1963), makeup; GUNFIGHT AT COMANCHE CREEK(1964), makeup; LADY IN A CAGE(1964), makeup; LAW OF THE LAWL-ESS(1964), makeup; PATSY, THE(1964), makeup; ROBINSON CRUSOE ON MARS(1964), makeup; STAGE TO THUNDER ROCK(1964), makeup; STRANGLER, THE(1964), makeup; WHERE LOVE HAS GONE(1964), makeup; SLENDER THREAD, THE(1965), makeup; SYLVIA(1965), makeup; VILLAGE OF THE GIANTS(1965), makeup; YOUNG FURY(1965), makeup; JOHNNY RENO(1966), makeup; LAST OF THE SECRET AGENTS?, THE(1966), makeup; OSCAR, THE(1966), makeup; SWINGER, THE(1966), makeup; THIS PROPERTY IS CONDEMNED(1966), makeup; CAPER OF THE GOLDEN BULLS, THE(1967), makeup; HOSTILE GUNS(1967), makeup; PRESIDENT'S ANALYST, THE(1967), makeup; SPIRIT IS WILLING, THE(1967), makeup; WARNING SHOT(1967), makeup; ODD COUPLE, THE(1968), makeup; PROJECT X(1968), makeup; WILL PENNY(1968), makeup; MOLLY MAGUIRES, THE(1970), makeup

Bob Westmoreland
ISLAND, THE(1980)

Forrest Westmoreland
DEVIL'S MISTRESS, THE(1968)

James Westmoreland
STACEY!(1973); DON'T ANSWER THE PHONE(1980)

Robert Westmoreland
MOLLY AND LAWLESS JOHN(1972)

Armand Weston
NESTING, THE(1981), p&d, w
Misc. Talkies
DAWN OF THE MUMMY(1981), d

Bert Weston
NEW HOTEL, THE(1932, Brit.); SONG OF THE FORGE(1937, Brit.)
Misc. Silents
SAINT'S ADVENTURE, THE(1917)
Bill Weston
2001: A SPACE ODYSSEY(1968, U.S./Brit.); DIRTY KNIGHT'S WORK(1976, Brit.); RAIDERS OF THE LOST ARK(1981); KRULL(1983)
Brad Weston
SAVAGE SAM(1963); STAGECOACH(1966); ROUGH NIGHT IN JERICHO(1967); BARQUERO(1970); HOT LEAD AND COLD FEET(1978)
Bret Weston
FANTASIES(1981), ed
Cecil Weston
DUDE RANCH(1931); HUCKLEBERRY FINN(1931); GOOD DAME(1934); MURDER AT THE VANITIES(1934); BEHOLD MY WIFE(1935); MAN WHO BROKE THE BANK AT MONTE CARLO, THE(1935); BANJO ON MY KNEE(1936); PRISONER OF SHARK ISLAND, THE(1936); RAMONA(1936); CALL IT A DAY(1937); ALEXANDER'S RAGTIME BAND(1938); PRISON FARM(1938); WIFE, HUSBAND AND FRIEND(1939); BRIGHAM YOUNG–FRONTIERSMAN(1940); OBLIGING YOUNG LADY(1941); REMEMBER THE DAY(1941); BROADWAY BIG SHOT(1942); I WAKE UP SCREAMING(1942); CRASH DIVE(1943); SONG OF BERNADETTE, THE(1943); THIS LAND IS MINE(1943); TWO FISTED JUSTICE(1943); BUFFALO BILL(1944); ONCE UPON A TIME(1944); STORY OF DR. WASSELL, THE(1944); COLONEL EFFINGHAM'S RAID(1945); LOCKET, THE(1946); MARGIE(1946); SHOCK(1946); DOWN TO EARTH(1947); FOREVER AMBER(1947); FRAMED(1947); T-MEN(1947); MONEY MADNESS(1948); ROAD HOUSE(1948); WALLS OF JERICHO(1948); WHEN WILLIE COMES MARCHING HOME(1950); HONEYCHILE(1951); MR. BELVEDERE RINGS THE BELL(1951); BELLES ON THEIR TOES(1952); THIS WOMAN IS DANGEROUS(1952); PRIDE OF THE BLUE GRASS(1954); UNTAMED(1955); THIS EARTH IS MINE(1959); NOOSE FOR A GUNMAN(1960); PURPLE GANG, THE(1960); THREE CAME TO KILL(1960); NOTORIOUS LANDLADY, THE(1962)
Cecile Weston
BANDIT QUEEN(1950)
Celia Weston
HONKY TONK FREEWAY(1981)
Charles Weston
Misc. Silents
BATTLE OF WATERLOO, THE(1913, Brit.), d; DUNGEON OF DEATH, THE(1915, Brit.), d; LIFE OF AN ACTRESS, THE(1915, Brit.), d; PIMPLE'S THREE WEEKS(1915, Brit.), d; PORT OF MISSING WOMEN, THE(1915, Brit.), d; UNDERWORLD OF LONDON, THE(1915, Brit.), d; VENGEANCE OF NANA(1915, Brit.), d; VICE AND VIRTUE; OR, THE TEMPTERS OF LONDON(1915, Brit.), d
Click Weston
NASHVILLE REBEL(1966), w
David Weston
DOCTOR IN DISTRESS(1963, Brit.); THAT KIND OF GIRL(1963, Brit.); BECKET(1964, Brit.); MASQUE OF THE RED DEATH, THE(1964, U.S./Brit.); WITCHCRAFT(1964, Brit.); HEROES OF TELEMARK, THE(1965, Brit.); BEAUTY JUNGLE, THE(1966, Brit.); WINTER'S TALE, THE(1968, Brit.); VON RICHTHOFEN AND BROWN(1970)
Diana Weston
SWEENEY 2(1978, Brit.)
Don Weston
RIDIN' DOWN THE TRAIL(1947); COWBOY CAVALIER(1948); OKLAHOMA BLUES(1948); PARTNERS OF THE SUNSET(1948); RANGE RENEGADES(1948); RANGERS RIDE, THE(1948)
Misc. Talkies
SWING, COWBOY, SWING(1944)
Doris Weston
SINGING MARINE, THE(1937); SUBMARINE D-1(1937); BORN TO BE WILD(1938); DELINQUENT PARENTS(1938); WHEN TOMORROW COMES(1939); CHIP OF THE FLYING U(1940)
Ed Weston
FIGHTING PARSON, THE(1933), w
Ellen Weston
Misc. Talkies
DANGEROUS RELATIONS(1973)
Eric Weston
WALK THE WALK(1970); BILLION DOLLAR HOBO, THE(1977); FARMER, THE(1977); EVILSPEAK(1982), p, d, w
Erick Weston
MARVIN AND TIGE(1983), d
Garnett Weston
AMERICAN PRISONER, THE(1929 Brit.), w; FLYING SCOTSMAN, THE(1929, Brit.), w; LADY FROM THE SEA, THE(1929, Brit.), w; ROMANCE OF SEVILLE, A(1929, Brit.), w; VIKING, THE(1931), w; SUPERNATURAL(1933), w; NINTH GUEST, THE(1934), w; OLD-FASHIONED WAY, THE(1934), w; NEVADA(1936), w; PREVIEW MURDER MYSTERY(1936), w; DAUGHTER OF SHANGHAI(1937), w; PARTNERS IN CRIME(1937), w; BULLDOG DRUMMOND IN AFRICA(1938), w; BULLDOG DRUMMOND'S BRIDE(1939), w; BULLDOG DRUMMOND'S SECRET POLICE(1939), w; MILL ON THE FLOSS(1939, Brit.), w; CROOKED ROAD, THE(1940), w; EMERGENCY SQUAD(1940), w; OPENED BY MISTAKE(1940), w; GREAT TRAIN ROBBERY, THE(1941), w; PONY SOLDIER(1952), w
Silents
YANKEE CLIPPER, THE(1927), w
George Weston
Silents
PUTTING IT OVER(1919), w; GIRLS DON'T GAMBLE(1921), w; TAXI! TAXI!(1927), w
Graham Weston
NATIONAL HEALTH, OR NURSE NORTON'S AFFAIR, THE(1973, Brit.); MR. QUILP(1975, Brit.); TESS(1980, Fr./Brit.); PARTY PARTY(1983, Brit.)
Harold Weston
Silents
MOTHERHOOD(1915, Brit.), d&w; ALL THE WORLD'S A STAGE(1917, Brit.), d
Misc. Silents
MYSTERY OF A HANSOM CAB, THE(1915, Brit.), d; SHADOWS(1915, Brit.), d; WILD OATS(1915, Brit.), d; BLACK NIGHT, THE(1916, Brit.), d; CYNTHIA IN THE WILDERNESS(1916, Brit.), d; GREEN ORCHARD, THE(1916, Brit.), d; HONOUR IN PAWN(1916, Brit.), d

Jack Weston
I WANT TO LIVE!(1958); STAGE STRUCK(1958); IMITATION OF LIFE(1959); PLEASE DON'T EAT THE DAISIES(1960); ALL IN A NIGHT'S WORK(1961); HONEYMOON MACHINE, THE(1961); IT'S ONLY MONEY(1962); PALM SPRINGS WEEKEND(1963); INCREDIBLE MR. LIMPET, THE(1964); CINCINNATI KID, THE(1965); MIRAGE(1965); WAIT UNTIL DARK(1967); COUNTERFEIT KILLER, THE(1968); THOMAS CROWN AFFAIR, THE(1968); APRIL FOOLS, THE(1969); CACTUS FLOWER(1969); NEW LEAF, A(1971); FUZZ(1972); MARCO(1973); GATOR(1976); RITZ, THE(1976); CUBA(1979); CAN'T STOP THE MUSIC(1980); FOUR SEASONS, THE(1981); HIGH ROAD TO CHINA(1983)
Jay Weston
FOR LOVE OF IVY(1968), p; LADY SINGS THE BLUES(1972), p; W.C. FIELDS AND ME(1976), p; NIGHT OF THE JUGGLER(1980), p; BUDDY BUDDY(1981), p; CHU CHU AND THE PHILLY FLASH(1981), p
Jerry Bob Weston
HELL SQUAD(1958)
John Weston
WHITE DEATH(1936, Aus.); HAIL, HERO!(1969), w
Joseph J. Weston
OVER MY DEAD BODY(1942)
Kathleen Weston
VINTAGE WINE(1935, Brit.); LOST ON THE WESTERN FRONT(1940, Brit.)
Kim Weston
CHANGES(1969)
Leslie Weston
GLAMOUR GIRL(1938, Brit.); TWO FOR DANGER(1940, Brit.); WE DIVE AT DAWN(1943, Brit.); SEND FOR PAUL TEMPLE(1946, Brit.); GREEN FINGERS(1947); CORRIDOR OF MIRRORS(1948, Brit.); MY BROTHER JONATHAN(1949, Brit.); POET'S PUB(1949, Brit.); SLEEPING CAR TO TRIESTE(1949, Brit.); IT'S HARD TO BE GOOD(1950, Brit.); LAST HOLIDAY(1950, Brit.); LADY WITH A LAMP, THE(1951, Brit.); FOUR AGAINST FATE(1952, Brit.); NIGHT WON'T TALK, THE(1952, Brit.); FOLLY TO BE WISE(1953); BETRAYED(1954); EMBEZZLER, THE(1954, Brit.); WOMAN'S ANGLE, THE(1954, Brit.); CONSTANT HUSBAND, THE(1955, Brit.); ABOVE US THE WAVES(1956, Brit.); IT'S A WONDERFUL WORLD(1956, Brit.); LAST MAN TO HANG, THE(1956, Brit.); GREEN MAN, THE(1957, Brit.); HIGH FLIGHT(1957, Brit.); SILKEN AFFAIR, THE(1957, Brit.); STOWAWAY GIRL(1957, Brit.); THREE MEN IN A BOAT(1958, Brit.); HOUSE OF THE SEVEN HAWKS, THE(1959)
Maggie Weston
Silents
AMERICAN BUDS(1918)
Misc. Silents
FOUNDLING, THE(1916)
Margery Weston
VIRGIN QUEEN, THE(1955)
Mark Weston
SHAMUS(1973)
Pamela Weston
1984
BODY DOUBLE(1984)
Paul Weston
RAIDERS OF THE LOST ARK(1981); OCTOPUSSY(1983, Brit.), stunts
Peter Weston
1,000 CONVICTS AND A WOMAN zero(1971, Brit.)
R.P. Weston
THE BLACK HAND GANG(1930, Brit.), w; NO LADY(1931, Brit.), w; OUT OF THE BLUE(1931, Brit.), w; SPLINTERS IN THE NAVY(1931, Brit.), w; UP FOR THE CUP(1931, Brit.), w; LUCKY GIRL(1932, Brit.), w; MAYOR'S NEST, THE(1932, Brit.), d&w; IT'S A KING(1933, Brit.), w; THIS IS THE LIFE(1933, Brit.), w; TROUBLE(1933, Brit.), w; UP FOR THE DERBY(1933, Brit.), w; DOCTOR'S ORDERS(1934, Brit.), w; GIRLS PLEASE!(1934, Brit.), w; IT'S A COP(1934, Brit.), w; HOPE OF HIS SIDE(1935, Brit.), w; FAME(1936, Brit.), w; PLEASE TEACHER(1937, Brit.), w; SPLINTERS IN THE AIR(1937, Brit.), w; UP FOR THE CUP(1950, Brit.), w
Robert Weston
BETSY, THE(1978), p
Robert R. Weston
LONELY LADY, THE(1983), p
Ruth Weston
DEVOTION(1931); PUBLIC DEFENDER, THE(1931); SMART WOMAN(1931); TOO MANY COOKS(1931); WOMAN BETWEEN(1931); THIS SPORTING AGE(1932); SPLENDOR(1935); THAT CERTAIN AGE(1938); MADE FOR EACH OTHER(1939)
Sam Weston
GUN FEVER(1958), p; ONE POTATO, TWO POTATO(1964), a, p; PATSY, THE(1964)
Steve Weston
SUDDEN FURY(1975, Can.); SILVER STREAK(1976)
William Weston
Silents
BLACK BIRD, THE(1926)
Dick Weston [Roy Rogers]
OLD CORRAL, THE(1937); OLD BARN DANCE, THE(1938); WILD HORSE RODEO(1938)
Clyde C. Westover
Silents
BAR NOTHIN'(1921), w; ACCORDING TO HOYLE(1922), w
Larry Westover
1984
KILLPOINT(1984), art d
Lynda Westover
TOOMORROW(1970, Brit.); CONFESSIONS OF A POP PERFORMER(1975, Brit.)
Rick Westover
BEYOND EVIL(1980), ed
Russ Westover
TILLIE THE TOILER(1941), w
Silents
TILLIE THE TOILER(1927), w
Winifred Westover
LUMMOX(1930)
Silents
INTOLERANCE(1916); MATRIMANIAC, THE(1916); ALL THE WORLD TO NOTHING(1919); THIS HERO STUFF(1919); ANNE OF LITTLE SMOKY(1921); FIGHTER, THE(1921)

Misc. Silents
HOBBS IN A HURRY(1918); JOHN PETTICOATS(1919); FIREBRAND TREVISON(1920); FORBIDDEN TRAILS(1920); VILLAGE SLEUTH, A(1920); BUCKING THE TIGER(1921); IS LIFE WORTH LIVING?(1921); LOVE'S MASQUERADE(1922)

Arthur Westpayne
EDUCATED EVANS(1936, Brit.)

Audrey Westphal
BLUE DAHLIA, THE(1946)

Edwin Westrate
WOMEN IN THE NIGHT(1948), w; JESSE JAMES VERSUS THE DALTONS(1954), w

Edwin K. Westrate
RENEGADE GIRL(1946), w

Edwin V. Westrate
PRISON FARM(1938), w; SHOOT TO KILL(1947), w; SMART WOMAN(1948), w

Tony Westrope
NIGHTHAWKS(1978, Brit.)

Rosalie Westwater
INTERLUDE(1968, Brit.)

Chris Westwood
LITTLE SEX, A(1982)

John Westwood
VARSITY(1928)

Misc. Silents
POWER OF SILENCE, THE(1928)

Patrick Westwood
GUNMAN HAS ESCAPED, A(1948, Brit.); OUTPOST IN MALAYA(1952, Brit.); PASSING STRANGER, THE(1954, Brit.); TONIGHT'S THE NIGHT(1954, Brit.); DEADLY GAME, THE(1955, Brit.); PASSAGE HOME(1955, Brit.); WOMAN FOR JOE, THE(1955, Brit.); ROCK AROUND THE WORLD(1957, Brit.); TRIPLE DECEPTION(1957, Brit.); BATTLE OF THE CORAL SEA(1959); PIT AND THE PENDULUM, THE(1961); MY WIFE'S FAMILY(1962, Brit.); LASSIE'S GREAT ADVENTURE(1963); GUNS IN THE HEATHER(1968, Brit.); LAST VALLEY, THE(1971, Brit.)

Russell Westwood
MELODY IN THE DARK(1948, Brit.); VENGEANCE IS MINE(1948, Brit.); HIGH JINKS IN SOCIETY(1949, Brit.); NIGHT AND THE CITY(1950, Brit.); WHITE FIRE(1953, Brit.); SPIN A DARK WEB(1956, Brit.)

Carolyn Wethall
Silents
OLD AGE HANDICAP(1928)

Frances Wetherall
Silents
PLACE IN THE SUN, A(1916, Brit.); NOBODY'S CHILD(1919, Brit.)

Virginia Wetherall
DEMONS OF THE MIND(1972, Brit.); DISCIPLE OF DEATH(1972, Brit.)

Dan Wetherbee
1984
MAKING THE GRADE(1984), ed

James Wethered
IF WINTER COMES(1947)

M.A. Wetherell
Silents
LIVINGSTONE(1925, Brit.), a, d&w; ROBINSON CRUSOE(1927, Brit.), a, p,d&w; SOMME, THE(1927, Brit.), d
Misc. Silents
HIS WIFE'S HUSBAND(1922, Brit.); VICTORY(1928, Brit.), d

Virginia Wetherell
PARTNER, THE(1966, Brit.); RICOCHET(1966, Brit.); BIG SWITCH, THE(1970, Brit.); CRIMSON CULT, THE(1970, Brit.); MAN OF VIOLENCE(1970, Brit.); CLOCKWORK ORANGE, A(1971, Brit.); DR. JEKYLL AND SISTER HYDE(1971, Brit.)

Alice Wetherfield
SILVER DOLLAR(1932)

Peter Wetherley
ANNIVERSARY, THE(1968, Brit.), ed

Wetherup
KING SOLOMON'S TREASURE(1978, Can.), art d

Albert Richard Wetjen
WAY FOR A SAILOR(1930), w; WALLABY JIM OF THE ISLANDS(1937), w

Judy Wetmore
TERROR IN THE WAX MUSEUM(1973)

W. Tabor Wetmore
Misc. Silents
PRECIOUS PACKET, THE(1916)

Adelheid Wette
HANSEL AND GRETEL(1954), w

Bob Wetzel
RANCHO DELUXE(1975)

Jim Wetzel
HOMEWORK(1982), m

Kristina Marie Wetzel
1984
FIRST TURN-ON!, THE(1984)

Richard Wetzel
VICE SQUAD(1982)

Blackie Wetzell
GRAYEAGLE(1977)

Ben Wetzler
BOOLOO(1938), ph

Gwen Wetzler
MIGHTY MOUSE IN THE GREAT SPACE CHASE(1983), d

Ned Wever
JOKER IS WILD, THE(1957); RIDE A CROOKED TRAIL(1958); ANATOMY OF A MURDER(1959); SHAGGY DOG, THE(1959); SOME CAME RUNNING(1959); THESE THOUSAND HILLS(1959); TAMMY, TELL ME TRUE(1961); PRIZE, THE(1963)

Robert Weverka
HANGAR 18(1980), w

Charles Wexler
JOHNNY O'CLOCK(1947)

Erica Wexler
MOMMIE DEAREST(1981)

Frieda Wexler
MADE FOR EACH OTHER(1971)

Haskell Wexler
SAVAGE EYE, THE(1960), ph; ANGEL BABY(1961), ph; HOODLUM PRIEST, THE(1961), ph; AMERICA, AMERICA(1963), ph; FACE IN THE RAIN, A(1963), ph; LONNIE(1963), ph; BEST MAN, THE(1964), ph; LOVED ONE, THE(1965), p, ph; WHO'S AFRAID OF VIRGINIA WOOLF?(1966), ph; IN THE HEAT OF THE NIGHT(1967), ph; THOMAS CROWN AFFAIR, THE(1968), ph; MEDIUM COOL(1969), p, d&w, ph; TRIAL OF THE CATONSVILLE NINE, THE(1972), ph; ONE FLEW OVER THE CUCKOO'S NEST(1975), ph; BOUND FOR GLORY(1976), ph; COMING HOME(1978), ph; SECOND-HAND HEARTS(1981), ph; LOOKIN' TO GET OUT(1982), ph; MAN WHO LOVED WOMEN, THE(1983), ph

Jack Wexler
TWO SISTERS(1938)

Jerrold Wexler
MEDIUM COOL(1969), p

Jerry Wexler
PRETTY BABY(1978), md

Jodi Wexler
LOVE MACHINE, THE,(1971)

Milton Wexler
MAN WHO LOVED WOMEN, THE(1983), w

Norman Wexler
JOE(1970), w; SERPICO(1973), w; MANDINGO(1975), w; DRUM(1976), w; SATURDAY NIGHT FEVER(1977), w; STAYING ALIVE(1983), w

Paul Wexler
BLOODHOUNDS OF BROADWAY(1952); FEUDIN' FOOLS(1952); SILVER WHIP, THE(1953); BOWERY BOYS MEET THE MONSTERS, THE(1954); DRUM BEAT(1954); SUDDENLY(1954); KENTUCKIAN, THE(1955); KETTLES IN THE OZARKS, THE(1956); DAY OF THE OUTLAW(1959); FOUR SKULLS OF JONATHAN DRAKE, THE(1959); MIRACLE OF THE HILLS, THE(1959); TIMBUKTU(1959); ONE HUNDRED AND ONE DALMATIANS(1961); JUMBO(1962); SYLVIA(1965); WAY WEST, THE(1967); DOC SAVAGE... THE MAN OF BRONZE(1975)

R.M. Wexler
WILLIE AND PHIL(1980)

Richard Wexler
GOODBYE COLUMBUS(1969)

Yale Wexler
TIME LIMIT(1957); GO NAKED IN THE WORLD(1961)

John Wexley
LAST MILE, THE(1932), w; ANGELS WITH DIRTY FACES(1938), w; CONFESSIONS OF A NAZI SPY(1939), w; CITY, FOR CONQUEST(1941), w; FOOTSTEPS IN THE DARK(1941), w; HANGMEN ALSO DIE(1943), w; LONG NIGHT, THE(1947), w; LAST MILE, THE(1959), w

Ron Weyand
MAD DOG COLL(1961); TARAS BULBA(1962); SHAMUS(1973); MAN ON A SWING(1974); RAGTIME(1981)

Ronald Weyand
CHILD'S PLAY(1972); DEADLY HERO(1976)

Robert Weycross
Misc. Silents
CLEAN GUN, THE(1917); LADY IN THE LIBRARY, THE(1917)

Max Weydner
INHERITANCE IN PRETORIA(1936, Ger.)

Klaus Weyer
NOT RECONCILED, OR "ONLY VIOLENCE HELPS WHERE IT RULES"(1969, Ger.)

Marius Weyers
GUEST AT STEENKAMPSKRAAL, THE(1977, South Africa)
1984
GODS MUST BE CRAZY, THE(1984, Botswana); GUEST, THE(1984, Brit.)

Royce Weyers
VELVET TRAP, THE(1966)

Ruth Weyher
Misc. Silents
WARNING SHADOWS(1924, Ger.); SECRETS OF A SOUL(1925, Ger.); APPASSIONATA(1929, Fr.)

Carl Weyl
PAYOFF, THE(1935), art d; PERSONAL MAID'S SECRET(1935), art d; STARS OVER BROADWAY(1935), art d; WE'RE IN THE MONEY(1935), art d; SINGING KID, THE(1936), art d

Carl Jules Weyl
CASE OF THE CURIOUS BRIDE, THE(1935), art d; BULLETS OR BALLOTS(1936), art d; IT'S LOVE I'M AFTER(1937), art d; KID GALAHAD(1937), art d; ADVENTURES OF ROBIN HOOD, THE(1938), art d; AMAZING DR. CLITTERHOUSE, THE(1938), art d; SISTERS, THE(1938), art d; WOMEN IN THE WIND(1939), art d; ALL THIS AND HEAVEN TOO(1940), art d; DR. EHRLICH'S MAGIC BULLET(1940), art d; LETTER, THE(1940), art d; GREAT LIE, THE(1941), art d; OUT OF THE FOG(1941), art d; CASABLANCA(1942), art d; DESPERATE JOURNEY(1942), art d; KING'S ROW(1942), art d; YANKEE DOODLE DANDY(1942), art d; CONSTANT NYMPH, THE(1943), art d; WATCH ON THE RHINE(1943), art d; PASSAGE TO MARSEILLE(1944), art d; CORN IS GREEN, THE(1945), art d; SARATOGA TRUNK(1945), art d; BIG SLEEP, THE(1946), art d; CRY WOLF(1947), art d; ESCAPE ME NEVER(1947), art d

Ron Weyland
THEY MIGHT BE GIANTS(1971)

Ronald Weyland
ALICE'S RESTAURANT(1969)

Ron Weyman
Misc. Talkies
RAKU FIRE(, d

Stanley J. Weyman
UNDER THE RED ROBE(1937, Brit.), w
Silents
UNDER THE RED ROBE(1923), w

John Weymer
SHE-DEVILS ON WHEELS(1968)

Samantha Weysom
RITZ, THE(1976)
Samantha Weyson
TOUCH OF CLASS, A(1973, Brit.)
Stephan Weyte
LINE, THE(1982)
Lee Choon Wha
TOP SECRET AFFAIR(1957)
James Whale
WATERLOO BRIDGE(1931), d, ed; JOURNEY'S END(1930), d; FRANKEN-STEIN(1931), d; IMPATIENT MAIDEN(1932), d; OLD DARK HOUSE, THE(1932), d; INVISIBLE MAN, THE(1933), d; KISS BEFORE THE MIRROR, THE(1933), d; BY CANDLELIGHT(1934), d; ONE MORE RIVER(1934), d; BRIDE OF FRANKENSTEIN, THE(1935), d; REMEMBER LAST NIGHT(1935), d; SHOW BOAT(1936), d; GREAT GARRICK, THE(1937), d; ROAD BACK,THE(1937), d; PORT OF SEVEN SEAS(1938), d; SINNERS IN PARADISE(1938), d; WIVES UNDER SUSPICION(1938), d; MAN IN THE IRON MASK, THE(1939), d; GREEN HELL(1940), d; THEY DARE NOT LO-VE(1941), d
Fred L. Whalen
CAT FROM OUTER SPACE, THE(1978)
Jack Whalen
ROUSTABOUT(1964)
Michael Whalen
CAREER WOMAN(1936); COUNTRY DOCTOR, THE(1936); MAN I MARRY, THE(1936); POOR LITTLE RICH GIRL(1936); PROFESSIONAL SOLDIER(1936); SING, BABY, SING(1936); SONG AND DANCE MAN, THE(1936); WHITE FANG(1936); LADY ESCAPES, THE(1937); TIME OUT FOR ROMANCE(1937); WEE WILLIE WINKIE(1937); WOMAN-WISE(1937); CHANGE OF HEART(1938); ISLAND IN THE SKY(1938); SPEED TO BURN(1938); TIME OUT FOR MURDER(1938); WALKING DOWN BROADWAY(1938); WHILE NEW YORK SLEEPS(1938); INSIDE STO-RY(1939); MYSTERIOUS MISS X, THE(1939); OUTSIDE THESE WALLS(1939); PAR-DON OUR NERVE(1939); THEY ASKED FOR IT(1939); ELLERY QUEEN. MASTER DETECTIVE(1940); I'LL SELL MY LIFE(1941); SIGN OF THE WOLF(1941); DAWN EXPRESS, THE(1942); TAHITI HONEY(1943); GAS HOUSE KIDS IN HOL-LYWOOD(1947); HIGHWAY 13(1948); BLONDE ICE(1949); OMOO OMOO, THE SHARK GOD(1949); PAROLE, INC.(1949); SHEP COMES HOME(1949); SKY LI-NER(1949); SON OF A BADMAN(1949); THUNDER IN THE PINES(1949); TOUGH ASSIGNMENT(1949); TREASURE OF MONTE CRISTO(1949); WILD WEED(1949); EVERYBODY'S DANCIN'(1950); KING OF THE BULLWHIP(1950); SARUMBA(1950); ACCORDING TO MRS. HOYLE(1951); FINGERPRINTS DON'T LIE(1951); G.I. JA-NE(1951); KENTUCKY JUBILEE(1951); MASK OF THE DRAGON(1951); WACO(1952); OUTLAW TREASURE(1955); SILVER STAR, THE(1955); PHANTOM FROM 10,000 LEAGUES, THE(1956); MISSILE TO THE MOON(1959); ELMER GANTRY(1960)
George Whaley
STORK(1971, Aus.); ALVIN PURPLE(1974, Aus.)
Eddie Whaley, Jr.
BLACK NARCISSUS(1947, Brit.)
James Whaley
JUBILEE(1978, Brit.), p
Paul Whaley
HOSPITAL, THE(1971)
Joan Whalley
Silents
REST CURE, THE(1923, Brit.)
Joanne Whalley
PINK FLOYD–THE WALL(1982, Brit.)
Norma Whalley
THIS IS THE LIFE(1933, Brit.); CAMELS ARE COMING, THE(1934, Brit.)
Silents
MYSTERY OF MR. BERNARD BROWN(1921, Brit.); EXPERIMENT, THE(1922, Brit.); HALF A TRUTH(1922, Brit.); OPEN COUNTRY(1922, Brit.); POINTING FIN-GER, THE(1922, Brit.)
Misc. Silents
KNIGHT ERRANT, THE(1922, Brit.); PAUPER MILLIONAIRE, THE(1922, Brit.)
Norman Whalley
Misc. Silents
WOMEN AND DIAMONDS(1924, Brit.)
Sarah Whalley
THANK YOU ALL VERY MUCH(1969, Brit.)
Luther Whaney
Misc. Talkies
PELVIS(1977)
Paddy Whannel
Misc. Talkies
11 X 14(1977)
James Whanton
BEDSIDE(1934), w
R. B. Wharrie
HIGH AND DRY(1954, Brit.)
Anne Wharton
UP IN SMOKE(1978); HEARTBEEPS(1981)
Bessie Wharton
Silents
WOMAN WHO FOOLED HERSELF, THE(1922)
Misc. Silents
WELCOME TO OUR CITY(1922)
Edith Wharton
MARRIAGE PLAYGROUND, THE(1929), w; AGE OF INNOCENCE(1934), w; STRANGE WIVES(1935), w; OLD MAID, THE(1939), w
Leopold Wharton
Silents
PRINCE OF INDIA, A(1914), d
Misc. Silents
PAWN OF FORTUNE, THE(1914), d; HAZEL KIRKE(1916), d; SQUIRE PHIN(1921), d; MR. BINGLE(1922), d; MR. POTTER OF TEXAS(1922), d
Leopold D. Wharton
Misc. Silents
GREAT WHITE TRAIL, THE(1917), d

Les Wharton
SILENCE OF DEAN MAITLAND, THE(1934, Aus.)
Patty Wharton
NORTH TO ALASKA(1960)
Phineas Wharton, Jr.
SMART POLITICS(1948)
Theodore Wharton
Misc. Silents
CITY, THE(1916), d; HAZEL KIRKE(1916), d
William Wharton
1984
BIRDY(1984), w
Roger Whateley
WE'RE IN THE LEGION NOW(1937), w
Kevin Whately
RETURN OF THE SOLDIER, THE(1983, Brit.)
Roger Whately
SILVER STREAK, THE(1935), w
Claud Whatham
HOODWINK(1981, Aus.), d
Claude Whatham
THAT'LL BE THE DAY(1974, Brit.), d; ALL CREATURES GREAT AND SMALL(1975, Brit.), d; SWALLOWS AND AMAZONS(1977, Brit.), d; SWEET WIL-LIAM(1980, Brit.), d
Marjorie Whatley
INTERNATIONAL SQUADRON(1941)
Roger Whatley
DRUMS OF DESTINY(1937), w
Roy Whatley
WAR ARROW(1953)
A. R. Whatmore
ELIZA COMES TO STAY(1936, Brit.)
Douglas Wheat
KING'S ROW(1942)
Harry Wheat
STUDENT TOUR(1934)
Jeffrey Wheat
WRONG IS RIGHT(1982)
Jim Wheat
RETURN, THE(1980), w; SILENT SCREAM(1980), p, w
1984
LIES(1984, Brit.), p, d&w
Misc. Talkies
LIES(1983), d
Ken Wheat
RETURN, THE(1980), w; SILENT SCREAM(1980), p, w
1984
LIES(1984, Brit.), p, d&w
Misc. Talkies
LIES(1983), d
Larry Wheat
PECK'S BAD BOY(1934); IT'S IN THE AIR(1935); PUBLIC HERO NO. 1(1935); SHOW THEM NO MERCY(1935); TIME OUT FOR ROMANCE(1937); THERE'S THAT WOM-AN AGAIN(1938); YOU CAN'T TAKE IT WITH YOU(1938); TRIAL OF MARY DUGAN, THE(1941); MAGNIFICENT DOPE, THE(1942); MY GAL SAL(1942); GILDER-SLEEVE'S BAD DAY(1943); EXPERIMENT PERILOUS(1944); HEAVENLY DAYS(1944); NEVADA(1944); GEORGE WHITE'S SCANDALS(1945); HAVING WON-DERFUL CRIME(1945); MURDER, MY SWEET(1945); WEST OF THE PECOS(1945); WHAT A BLONDE(1945); DEADLINE AT DAWN(1946); LADY LUCK(1946); MAGIC TOWN(1947)
Laurence Wheat
Silents
BACK HOME AND BROKE(1922); MAN WHO SAW TOMORROW, THE(1922); OUR LEADING CITIZEN(1922); SONG OF LOVE, THE(1923); NOT SO LONG AGO(1925); IRENE(1926)
Misc. Silents
CONFIDENCE MAN, THE(1924)
Lawrence Wheat
LOUDSPEAKER, THE(1934); GREAT ZIEGFELD, THE(1936)
Silents
HUSH MONEY(1921); INEZ FROM HOLLYWOOD(1924)
Frank Wheatcroft
Silents
OVER THE STICKS(1929, Brit.), p
S. Wheatcroft
Silents
BALLET GIRL, THE(1916)
Stanhope Wheatcroft
NOTORIOUS SOPHIE LANG, THE(1934); PLAINSMAN, THE(1937); UNION PACIF-IC(1939); REAP THE WILD WIND(1942)
Silents
FAMILY CUPBOARD, THE(1915); BROKEN CHAINS(1916); EAST LYNNE(1916); MODERN CINDERELLA, A(1917); AMAZING WIFE, THE(1919); HER FIVE-FOOT HIGHNESS(1920); DR. JIM(1921); SIGN OF THE ROSE, THE(1922); IRON HORSE, THE(1924); LAUGHING AT DANGER(1924); NO MORE WOMEN(1924); KEEP SMIL-ING(1925); KING OF KINGS, THE(1927); CITY LIGHTS(1931)
Misc. Silents
UNDER TWO FLAGS(1916); GOD'S MAN(1917); ON DANGEROUS GROUND(1917); DESTINY(1919); VEILED ADVENTURE, THE(1919); BEGGAR IN PURPLE, A(1920); BLUE BONNET, THE(1920); BREATH OF THE GODS, THE(1920); LOCKED LIPS(1920); YANKEE CONSUL, THE(1924); RIDIN' PRETTY(1925)
Alan Wheatley
CONQUEST OF THE AIR(1940); APPOINTMENT WITH CRIME(1945, Brit.); NOTORIOUS GENTLEMAN(1945, Brit.); CAESAR AND CLEOPATRA(1946, Brit.); BRIGHTON ROCK(1947, Brit.); END OF THE RIVER, THE(1947, Brit.); CALLING PAUL TEMPLE(1948, Brit.); CORRIDOR OF MIRRORS(1948, Brit.); COUNTER BLAST(1948, Brit.); DEVIL'S PLOT(1948, Brit.); JASSY(1948, Brit.); SPRING-TIME(1948, Brit.); IT'S NOT CRICKET(1949, Brit.); SLEEPING CAR TO TRIESTE(1949, Brit.); HOME TO DANGER(1951, Brit.); PICKWICK PAPERS, THE(1952, Brit.); WHISPERING SMITH VERSUS SCOTLAND YARD(1952, Brit.); LIMPING MAN,

THE(1953, Brit.); SMALL TOWN STORY(1953, Brit.); SPACEWAYS(1953, Brit.); DELAYED ACTION(1954, Brit.); DIAMOND WIZARD, THE(1954, Brit.); HEAT-WAVE(1954, Brit.); SIMON AND LAURA(1956, Brit.); DUKE WORE JEANS, THE(1958, Brit.); INN FOR TROUBLE(1960, Brit.); SHADOW OF THE CAT, THE(1961, Brit.); JOLLY BAD FELLOW, A(1964, Brit.); MASTER SPY(1964, Brit.); TOMORROW AT TEN(1964, Brit.); ESCAPE BY NIGHT(1965, Brit.)

Ann Wheatley
GLORY AT SEA(1952, Brit.)

Betty Wheatley
SOMEWHERE IN CAMP(1942, Brit.)

Dennis Wheatley
SECRET OF STAMBOUL, THE(1936, Brit.), w; FORBIDDEN TERRITORY(1938, Brit.), w; DEVIL'S BRIDE, THE(1968, Brit.), w; LOST CONTINENT, THE(1968, Brit.), w; TO THE DEVIL A DAUGHTER(1976, Brit./Ger.), w

Dorothy Wheatley
HOT ICE(1952, Brit.)

Jay Wheatley
TWO-LANE BLACKTOP(1971)

Patrick Wheatley
JOSEPH ANDREWS(1977, Brit.), cos

Rita Wheatley
LADY GODIVA RIDES AGAIN(1955, Brit.)

Jack Wheaton
GUNS AND THE FURY, THE(1983), m

Jack W. Wheaton
PENITENTIARY II(1982), m

James Wheaton
THX 1138(1971)

Paul Wheaton
RED, WHITE AND BLACK, THE(1970)

Wil Wheaton
SECRET OF NIMH, THE(1982)
1984
BUDDY SYSTEM, THE(1984); LAST STARFIGHTER, THE(1984)

Daniel Wheddon
CHICK(1936, Brit.), w

H. Wheddon
REGAL CAVALCADE(1935, Brit.), ph

Horace Wheddon
CLUE OF THE NEW PIN, THE(1929, Brit.), ph; SQUEAKER, THE(1930, Brit.), ph; DREYFUS CASE, THE(1931, Brit.), ph; FASCINATION(1931, Brit.), ph; LOVE LIES(1931, Brit.), ph; TRAPPED IN A SUBMARINE(1931, Brit.), ph; BROTHER ALFRED(1932, Brit.), ph; LIVE AGAIN(1936, Brit.), ph; COTTON QUEEN(1937, Brit.), ph; LUCKY JADE(1937, Brit.), ph

John Whedon
BEARS AND I, THE(1974), w; ISLAND AT THE TOP OF THE WORLD, THE(1974), w

Gloria Wheeden
ARTISTS AND MODELS(1937)

Pat Wheel
JEREMY(1973)

Tim Wheelan
HOLD'EM JAIL(1932), w
Silents
FRESHMAN, THE(1925), w

Bernard Wheeler
MEET JOHN DOE(1941); ANNA AND THE KING OF SIAM(1946), m

Bert Wheeler
RIO RITA(1929); CUCKOOS, THE(1930); DIXIANA(1930); HALF SHOT AT SUNRISE(1930); HOOK, LINE AND SINKER(1930); CAUGHT PLASTERED(1931); CRACKED NUTS(1931); PEACH O' RENO(1931); TOO MANY COOKS(1931); GIRL CRAZY(1932); HOLD'EM JAIL(1932); DIPLOMANIACS(1933); SO THIS IS AFRICA(1933); COCKEYED CAVALIERS(1934); HIPS, HIPS, HOORAY(1934); KENTUCKY KERNELS(1935); NITWITS, THE(1935); RAINMAKERS, THE(1935); MUMMY'S BOYS(1936); SILLY BILLIES(1936); HIGH FLYERS(1937); ON AGAIN-OFF AGAIN(1937); COWBOY QUARTERBACK(1939); LAS VEGAS NIGHTS(1941)

Brian Wheeler
RETURN OF THE JEDI(1983)

Bronia Wheeler
BILLY IN THE LOWLANDS(1979)

Charles Wheeler
BUBBLE, THE(1967), ph; YOURS, MINE AND OURS(1968), ph; CHE!(1969), ph; C. C. AND COMPANY(1971), ph; LIMBO(1972), ph; MOLLY AND LAWLESS JOHN(1972), ph; SLAUGHTER'S BIG RIP-OFF(1973), ph

Charles F. Wheeler
DUEL AT DIABLO(1966), ph; PIECES OF DREAMS(1970), ph; TORA! TORA! TORA!(1970, U.S./Jap.), ph; BAREFOOT EXECUTIVE, THE(1971), ph; COLD TURKEY(1971), ph; SILENT RUNNING(1972), ph; WAR BETWEEN MEN AND WOMEN, THE(1972), ph; CHARLEY AND THE ANGEL(1973), ph; ONE LITTLE INDIAN(1973), ph; TRUCK TURNER(1974), ph; FREAKY FRIDAY(1976), ph; CAT FROM OUTER SPACE, THE(1978), ph; C.H.O.M.P.S.(1979), ph; LAST FLIGHT OF NOAH'S ARK, THE(1980), ph; CONDORMAN(1981), ph

Christopher Wheeler
FUZZ(1972)

Clarence Wheeler
DANGEROUS LADY(1941), md; MIRACLE KID(1942), md

Clarence C. Wheeler
TOO MANY WOMEN(1942), md

Clarence E. Wheeler
LAW OF THE TIMBER(1941), md

Cliff Wheeler
Silents
INTO NO MAN'S LAND(1928), d; MAKING THE VARSITY(1928), d
Misc. Silents
BIT OF HEAVEN, A(1928), d; COMRADES(1928), d; PRINCE OF HEARTS, THE(1929), d

Clifford Slater Wheeler
Misc. Silents
LOVE WAGER, THE(1927), d

Cyril Wheeler
STRANGE AFFECTION(1959, Brit.); MATTER OF WHO, A(1962, Brit.)

Dorothy Wheeler
Silents
AUCTION BLOCK, THE(1917); NORTH WIND'S MALICE, THE(1920)

Gena Wheeler
HUSBANDS(1970); FEMALE RESPONSE, THE(1972)

George Wheeler
FRIENDS AND NEIGHBORS(1963, Brit.)

Glen Wheeler
TOL'ABLE DAVID(1930), ed

Glenn Wheeler
Silents
LEGEND OF HOLLYWOOD, THE(1924), ed

Griswold Wheeler
Silents
MARRIAGE PRICE(1919), w

Harold Wheeler
SUNNYSIDE(1979), m

Harvey Wheeler
FAIL SAFE(1964), w

Hugh Wheeler
FIVE MILES TO MIDNIGHT(1963, U.S./Fr./Ital.), w; SOMETHING FOR EVERY-ONE(1970), w; TRAVELS WITH MY AUNT(1972, Brit.), w; LITTLE NIGHT MUSIC, A(1977, Aust./U.S./Ger.), w; NIJINSKY(1980, Brit.), w

Ira Wheeler
1984
KILLING FIELDS, THE(1984, Brit.)

Ira B. Wheeler
ROLLOVER(1981)

Jack Wheeler
WOMAN'S VENGEANCE, A(1947), ed; BUCKSKIN(1968), ed; JENNIFER ON MY MIND(1971), ed

Jed Wheeler
WOMEN AND BLOODY TERROR(1970)

Joan Wheeler
DESIRABLE(1934); MADAME DU BARRY(1934); MERRY FRINKS, THE(1934); SMARTY(1934); TWENTY MILLION SWEETHEARTS(1934)

John Wheeler
SWEET CHARITY(1969); TELL THEM WILLIE BOY IS HERE(1969); MOVE(1970); SUPPORT YOUR LOCAL GUNFIGHTER(1971); BIG BAD MAMA(1974); SGT. PEPPER'S LONELY HEARTS CLUB BAND(1978); APPLE DUMPLING GANG RIDES AGAIN, THE(1979); NORTH AVENUE IRREGULARS, THE(1979); SEED OF INNO-CENCE(1980)
1984
RHINESTONE(1984), ed
Misc. Talkies
BAD GEORGIA ROAD(1977)

John W. Wheeler
STERILE CUCKOO, THE(1969), ed; NORWOOD(1970), ed; PARALLAX VIEW, THE(1974), ed; POSSE(1975), ed; BAD NEWS BEARS IN BREAKING TRAINING, THE(1977), ed; ONION FIELD, THE(1979), ed; SERIAL(1980), ed; GOING APE!(1981), ed; CHALLENGE, THE(1982), ed; STRANGE INVADERS(1983), ed

Joseph Wheeler
INVISIBLE AVENGER, THE(1958), ph; PAPER LION(1968), ph; FELLINI SATYRI-CON(1969, Fr./Ital.)

Kay Wheeler
ROCK BABY, ROCK IT(1957); HOT ROD GANG(1958)

Keith Wheeler
CHILDREN OF BABYLON(1980, Jamaica)

Lem Wheeler
MONTANA KID, THE(1931), ed; MOTHER AND SON(1931), ed

Len Wheeler
IN THE LINE OF DUTY(1931), ed

Leo Wheeler
COURT JESTER, THE(1956)

Leonard Wheeler
MELODY MAN(1930), ed; SOLDIERS AND WOMEN(1930), ed; SQUEALER, THE(1930), ed; CRIME OF DR. CRESPI, THE(1936), ed
Misc. Silents
FOUR HEARTS(1922), d

LeRoy Wheeler
ON THE NICKEL(1980)

Linda Wheeler
ROCK BABY, ROCK IT(1957)

Lois Wheeler
MY FOOLISH HEART(1949)

Lyle Wheeler
GARDEN OF ALLAH, THE(1936), art d; NOTHING SACRED(1937), art d; PRISON-ER OF ZENDA, THE(1937), art d; STAR IS BORN, A(1937), art d; YOUNG IN HEART, THE(1938), art d; GONE WITH THE WIND(1939), art d; INTERMEZZO: A LOVE STORY(1939), ard d; MADE FOR EACH OTHER(1939), art d; REBECCA(1940), art d; KEEPER OF THE FLAME(1942), art d; GUY NAMED JOE, A(1943), art d; BIG NOISE, THE(1944), art d; IRISH EYES ARE SMILING(1944), art d; LAURA(1944), art d; SOMETHING FOR THE BOYS(1944), art d; SUNDAY DINNER FOR A SOL-DIER(1944), art d; SWEET AND LOWDOWN(1944), art d; TAKE IT OR LEAVE IT(1944), art d; WING AND A PRAYER(1944), art d; WINGED VICTORY(1944), art d; COLONEL EFFINGHAM'S RAID(1945), art d; DIAMOND HORSESHOE(1945), art d; DOLL FACE(1945), art d; DOLLY SISTERS, THE(1945), art d; DON JUAN QUILLI-GAN(1945), art d; FALLEN ANGEL(1945), art d; HANGOVER SQUARE(1945), art d; HOUSE ON 92ND STREET(1945), art d; JUNIOR MISS(1945), art d; MOLLY AND ME(1945), art d; NOB HILL(1945), art d; SPIDER, THE(1945), art d; STATE FAIR(1945), art d; TREE GROWS IN BROOKLYN, A(1945), art d; WHERE DO WE GO FROM HERE?(1945), art d; WITHIN THESE WALLS(1945), art d; CENTENNIAL SUMMER(1946), art d; CLUNY BROWN(1946), art d; DO YOU LOVE ME?(1946), art d; DRAGONWYCH(1946), art d; LEAVE HER TO HEAVEN(1946), art d; MAR-GIE(1946), art d; SENTIMENTAL JOURNEY(1946), art d; SHOCK(1946), art d; SMOKY(1946), art d; THREE LITTLE GIRLS IN BLUE(1946), art d; WAKE UP AND DREAM(1946), art d; DAISY KENYON(1947), art d; FOREVER AMBER(1947), art d; FOXES OF HARROW, THE(1947), art d; GENTLEMAN'S AGREEMENT(1947), art d;

KISS OF DEATH(1947), art d; NIGHTMARE ALLEY(1947), art d; APARTMENT FOR PEGGY(1948), art d; CALL NORTHSIDE 777(1948), art d; CRY OF THE CITY(1948), art d; FURY AT FURNACE CREEK(1948), art d; GIVE MY REGARDS TO BROADWAY(1948), art d; IRON CURTAIN, THE(1948), art d; LETTER TO THREE WIVES, A(1948), art d; LUCK OF THE IRISH(1948), art d; ROAD HOUSE(1948), art d; SCUDDA-HOO! SCUDDA-HAY!(1948), art d; SITTING PRETTY(1948), art d; SNAKE PIT, THE(1948), art d; STREET WITH NO NAME, THE(1948), art d; THAT LADY IN ERMINE(1948), art d; THAT WONDERFUL URGE(1948), art d; UNFAITHFULLY YOURS(1948), art d; WHEN MY BABY SMILES AT ME(1948), art d; YOU WERE MEANT FOR ME(1948), art d; DANCING IN THE DARK(1949), art d; DOWN TO THE SEA IN SHIPS(1949), art d; EVERYBODY DOES IT(1949), art d; FATHER WAS A FULLBACK(1949), art d; HOUSE OF STRANGERS(1949), art d; I WAS A MALE WAR BRIDE(1949), art d; IT HAPPENS EVERY SPRING(1949), art d; MOTHER IS A FRESHMAN(1949), art d; MR. BELVEDERE GOES TO COLLEGE(1949), art d; OH, YOU BEAUTIFUL DOLL(1949), art d; PINKY(1949), art d; PRINCE OF FOXES(1949), art d; SAND(1949), art d; SLATTERY'S HURRICANE(1949), art d; THIEVES' HIGHWAY(1949), art d; YOU'RE MY EVERYTHING(1949), art d; ALL ABOUT EVE(1950), art d; AMERICAN GUERRILLA IN THE PHILIPPINES, AN(1950), art d; BROKEN ARROW(1950), art d; FOR HEAVEN'S SAKE(1950), art d; GUNFIGHTER, THE(1950), art d; I'LL GET BY(1950), art d; JACKPOT, THE(1950), art d; LOVE THAT BRUTE(1950), art d; MISTER 880(1950), art d; MOTHER DIDN'T TELL ME(1950), art d; MY BLUE HEAVEN(1950), art d; NO WAY OUT(1950), art d; PANIC IN THE STREETS(1950), art d; STELLA(1950), art d; THREE CAME HOME(1950), art d; TICKET TO TOMAHAWK(1950), art d; TWO FLAGS WEST(1950), art d; UNDER MY SKIN(1950), art d; WABASH AVENUE(1950), art d; DAVID AND BATHSHEBA(1951), art d; DAY THE EARTH STOOD STILL, THE(1951), art d; DESERT FOX, THE(1951), art d; ELOPEMENT(1951), art d; FIXED BAYONETS(1951), art d; FOLLOW THE SUN(1951), art d; FOURTEEN HOURS(1951), art d; FROGMEN, THE(1951), art d; GUY WHO CAME BACK, THE(1951), art d; HALF ANGEL(1951), art d; HALLS OF MONTEZUMA(1951), art d; HOUSE ON TELEGRAPH HILL(1951), art d; I CAN GET IT FOR YOU WHOLESALE(1951), art d; I'D CLIMB THE HIGHEST MOUNTAIN(1951), art d; LET'S MAKE IT LEGAL(1951), art d; LOVE NEST(1951), art d; MEET ME AFTER THE SHOW(1951), art d; MODEL AND THE MARRIAGE BROKER, THE(1951), art d; MR. BELVEDERE RINGS THE BELL(1951), art d; ON THE RIVIERA(1951), art d; PEOPLE WILL TALK(1951), art d; RAWHIDE(1951), art d; SECRET OF CONVICT LAKE, THE(1951), art d; TAKE CARE OF MY LITTLE GIRL(1951), art d; THIRTEENTH LETTER, THE(1951), art d; YOU'RE IN THE NAVY NOW(1951), art d; DEADLINE–U.S.A.(1952), art d; DIPLOMATIC COURIER(1952), art d; DON'T BOTHER TO KNOCK(1952), art d; FIVE FINGERS(1952), art d; I DON'T CARE GIRL, THE(1952), art d; KANGAROO(1952), art d; LES MISERABLES(1952), art d; LURE OF THE WILDERNESS(1952), art d; LYDIA BAILEY(1952), art d; MONKEY BUSINESS(1952), art d; MY COUSIN RACHEL(1952), art d; MY PAL GUS(1952), art d; MY WIFE'S BEST FRIEND(1952), art d; NIGHT WITHOUT SLEEP(1952), art d; O. HENRY'S FULL HOUSE(1952), art d; PHONE CALL FROM A STRANGER(1952), art d; PONY SOLDIER(1952), art d; PRIDE OF ST. LOUIS, THE(1952), art d; RED SKIES OF MONTANA(1952), art d; RETURN OF THE TEXAN(1952), art d; SOMETHING FOR THE BIRDS(1952), art d; STARS AND STRIPES FOREVER(1952), art d; VIVA ZAPATA!(1952), art d; WAY OF A GAUCHO(1952), art d; WITH A SONG IN MY HEART(1952), art d; DANGEROUS CROSSING(1953), art d; DESERT RATS, THE(1953), art d; DESTINATION GOBI(1953), art d; DOWN AMONG THE SHELTERING PALMS(1953), art d; GENTLEMEN PREFER BLONDES(1953), art d; GLORY BRIGADE, THE(1953), art d; HOW TO MARRY A MILLIONAIRE(1953), art d; INFERNO(1953), art d; KID FROM LEFT FIELD, THE(1953), art d; KING OF THE KHYBER RIFLES(1953), art d; MAN IN THE ATTIC(1953), art d; MR. SCOUTMASTER(1953), art d; NIAGARA(1953), art d; POWDER RIVER(1953), art d; PRESIDENT'S LADY, THE(1953), art d; ROBE, THE(1953), art d; SILVER WHIP, THE(1953), art d; TAXI(1953), art d; TITANIC(1953), art d; TONIGHT WE SING(1953), art d; TREASURE OF THE GOLDEN CONDOR(1953), art d; VICKI(1953), art d; WHITE WITCH DOCTOR(1953), art d; BROKEN LANCE(1954), art d; DEMETRIUS AND THE GLADIATORS(1954), art d; DESIREE(1954), art d; EGYPTIAN. THE(1954), art d; GARDEN OF EVIL(1954), art d; HELL AND HIGH WATER(1954), art d; PRINCE VALIANT(1954), art d; RIVER OF NO RETURN(1954), art d; THERE'S NO BUSINESS LIKE SHOW BUSINESS(1954), art d; THREE COINS IN THE FOUNTAIN(1954), art d; WOMAN'S WORLD(1954), art d; LEFT HAND OF GOD, THE(1955), art d; MAN CALLED PETER, THE(1955), art d; PRINCE OF PLAYERS(1955), art d; RACERS, THE(1955), art d; SEVEN YEAR ITCH, THE(1955), art d; SOLDIER OF FORTUNE(1955), art d; UNTAMED(1955), art d; VIEW FROM POMPEY'S HEAD, THE(1955), art d; VIOLENT SATURDAY(1955), art d; VIRGIN QUEEN, THE(1955), art d; BIGGER THAN LIFE(1956), art d; MAN IN THE GREY FLANNEL SUIT, THE(1956), art d; PROUD ONES, THE(1956), art d; DESK SET(1957), art d; NO DOWN PAYMENT(1957), art d; THREE FACES OF EVE, THE(1957), art d; MAN WHO UNDERSTOOD WOMEN, THE(1959), art d; ROOKIE, THE(1959), art d; CAN-CAN(1960), art d; FROM THE TERRACE(1960), art d; WAKE ME WHEN IT'S OVER(1960), art d; YOUNG JESSE JAMES(1960), art d; ADVISE AND CONSENT(1962), art d; IN HARM'S WAY(1965), prod d; BIG MOUTH, THE(1967), prod d; WHERE ANGELS GO...TROUBLE FOLLOWS(1968), prod d; TELL ME THAT YOU LOVE ME, JUNIE MOON(1970), prod d; POSSE(1975), prod d, set d

Lyle R. Wheeler
DRAGON SEED(1944), art d; ROYAL SCANDAL, A(1945), art d; MY DARLING CLEMENTINE(1946), art d; DEEP WATERS(1948), art d; WALLS OF JERICHO(1948), art d; YELLOW SKY(1948), art d; FAN, THE(1949), art d; TWELVE O'CLOCK HIGH(1949), art d; WHIRLPOOL(1949), art d; WHEN WILLIE COMES MARCHING HOME(1950), art d; WHERE THE SIDEWALK ENDS(1950), art d; DREAMBOAT(1952), art d; WAIT 'TIL THE SUN SHINES, NELLIE(1952), art d; WE'RE NOT MARRIED(1952), art d; WHAT PRICE GLORY?(1952), art d; PICKUP ON SOUTH STREET(1953), art d; GIRL IN THE RED VELVET SWING, THE(1955), art d; GOOD MORNING, MISS DOVE(1955), art d; HOUSE OF BAMBOO(1955), art d; HOW TO BE VERY, VERY, POPULAR(1955), art d; LOVE IS A MANY-SPLENDORED THING(1955), art d; RAINS OF RANCHIPUR, THE(1955), art d; SEVEN CITIES OF GOLD(1955), art d; TALL MEN, THE(1955), art d; D-DAY, THE SIXTH OF JUNE(1956), art d; GIRL CAN'T HELP IT, THE(1956), art d; HILDA CRANE(1956), art d; KING AND I, THE(1956), art d; LAST WAGON, THE(1956), art d; LIEUTENANT WORE SKIRTS, THE(1956), art d; LOVE ME TENDER(1956), art d; ON THE THRESHOLD OF SPACE(1956), art d; REVOLT OF MAMIE STOVER, THE(1956), art d; TEENAGE REBEL(1956), art d; 23 PACES TO BAKER STREET(1956), art d; AFFAIR TO REMEMBER, AN(1957), art d; ENEMY BELOW, THE(1957), art d; HATFUL OF RAIN, A(1957), art d; KISS THEM FOR ME(1957), art d; OH, MEN! OH, WOMEN!(1957), art d; PEYTON PLACE(1957), art d; STOPOVER TOKYO(1957), art d; SUN ALSO RISES, THE(1957), art d; THREE BRAVE MEN(1957), art d; TRUE STORY OF JESSE JAMES, THE(1957), art d; WAY TO THE GOLD, THE(1957), art d;

WAYWARD BUS, THE(1957), art d; WILL SUCCESS SPOIL ROCK HUNTER?(1957), art d; BARBARIAN AND THE GEISHA, THE(1958), art d; FIEND WHO WALKED THE WEST, THE(1958), art d; FLY, THE(1958), art d; FRAULEIN(1958), art d; FROM HELL TO TEXAS(1958), art d; GIFT OF LOVE, THE(1958), art d; HUNTERS, THE(1958), art d; IN LOVE AND WAR(1958), art d; LONG, HOT SUMMER, THE(1958), art d; NICE LITTLE BANK THAT SHOULD BE ROBBED, A(1958), art d; RALLY 'ROUND THE FLAG, BOYS!(1958), art d; SING, BOY, SING(1958), art d; SOUTH PACIFIC(1958), art d; YOUNG LIONS, THE(1958), art d; 10 NORTH FREDERICK(1958), art d; ALLIGATOR PEOPLE, THE(1959), art d; DIARY OF ANNE FRANK, THE(1959), art d; FIVE GATES TO HELL(1959), art d; HERE COME THE JETS(1959), art d; HOLIDAY FOR LOVERS(1959), ait d; HOUND-DOG MAN(1959), art d; JOURNEY TO THE CENTER OF THE EARTH(1959), art d; MIRACLE OF THE HILLS, THE(1959), art d; PRIVATE'S AFFAIR, A(1959), art d; REMARKABLE MR. PENNYPACKER, THE(1959), art d; RETURN OF THE FLY(1959), art d; SAY ONE FOR ME(1959), art d; SOUND AND THE FURY, THE(1959), art d; STORY ON PAGE ONE, THE(1959), art d; THESE THOUSAND HILLS(1959), art d; WARLOCK(1959), art d; WOMAN OBSESSED(1959), art d; LET'S MAKE LOVE(1960), art d; SEVEN THIEVES(1960), art d; STORY OF RUTH, THE(1960), art d; WILD RIVER(1960), art d; MAROONED(1969), prod d; DOCTORS' WIVES(1971), prod d; STAND UP AND BE COUNTED(1972), prod d

Margaret Wheeler
TWILIGHT ZONE–THE MOVIE(1983)
1984
THEY'RE PLAYING WITH FIRE(1984)

Mark Wheeler
CONVERSATION, THE(1974)

Nancy Wheeler
DUSTY AND SWEETS McGEE(1971)

Paul Wheeler
PUPPET ON A CHAIN(1971, Brit.), w; CARAVAN TO VACCARES(1974, Brit./Fr), w; TERRORISTS, THE(1975, Brit.), w; SWASHBUCKLER(1976), w; LEGACY, THE(1979, Brit.), w
1984
BREED APART, A(1984), w

Paul Wheeler, Jr.
TWELVE CHAIRS, THE(1970)

Rene Wheeler
CAGE OF NIGHTINGALES, A(1947, Fr.), w; FANFAN THE TULIP(1952, Fr.), w; JOUR DE FETE(1952, Fr.), w; JUPITER(1952, Fr.), w; UTOPIA(1952, Fr./Ital.), w; RIFIFI(1956, Fr.), w; CRIME DOES NOT PAY(1962, Fr.), w

Robert Wheeler
WHAT'S UP FRONT(1964)

Russ Wheeler
1984
HARRY AND SON(1984)

Sidney Wheeler
ANTS IN HIS PANTS(1940, Aus.)

Steven Wheeler
JOHNNY TIGER(1966)

Sydney Wheeler
DAD AND DAVE COME TO TOWN(1938, Aus.); LOVERS AND LUGGERS(1938, Aus.); MR. CHEDWORTH STEPS OUT(1939, Aus.); VENGEANCE OF THE DEEP(1940, Aus.)

William Wheeler
Silents
TILLIE'S PUNCTURED ROMANCE(1928), ph; HEROIC LOVER, THE(1929), ph

Dana Wheeler-Nicholson
1984
FLETCH(1984); LITTLE DRUMMER GIRL, THE(1984); MRS. SOFFEL(1984)

Allen Wheelis
CRAZY QUILT, THE(1966), w

Charles Wheelock
Misc. Silents
MAN FROM MANHATTAN, THE(1916)

Jim Wheelus
EMPIRE OF THE ANTS(1977)

Ernie Wheelwright
LONGEST YARD, THE(1974); TRACKDOWN(1976); GREATEST, THE(1977, U.S./Brit.)

Ralph Wheelwright
THUNDER AFLOAT(1939), w; BLOSSOMS IN THE DUST(1941), w; TWO SMART PEOPLE(1946), p, w; TENTH AVENUE ANGEL(1948), p; THESE WILDER YEARS(1956), w; MAN OF A THOUSAND FACES(1957), w

Richard Wheelwright
JUMP(1971), w

Albert Whelan
MAN FROM CHICAGO, THE(1931, Brit.); MATINEE IDOL(1933, Brit.); ANYTHING MIGHT HAPPEN(1935, Brit.); DANCE BAND(1935, Brit.); EDUCATED EVANS(1936, Brit.); ACTION FOR SLANDER(1937, Brit.); GIRL IN THE TAXI(1937, Brit.); HE LOVED AN ACTRESS(1938, Brit.); KATE PLUS TEN(1938, Brit.); THANK EVANS(1938, Brit.); DANNY BOY(1941, Brit.); CANDLELIGHT IN ALGERIA(1944, Brit.); KEEP IT CLEAN(1956, Brit.)

Arleen Whelan
GATEWAY(1938); KIDNAPPED(1938); THANKS FOR EVERYTHING(1938); BOY FRIEND(1939); SABOTAGE(1939); YOUNG MR. LINCOLN(1939); CHARTER PILOT(1940); YOUNG PEOPLE(1940); CHARLEY'S AUNT(1941); CASTLE IN THE DESERT(1942); SUNDOWN JIM(1942); STAGE DOOR CANTEEN(1943); RAMROD(1947); SENATOR WAS INDISCREET, THE(1947); SUDDENLY IT'S SPRING(1947); VARIETY GIRL(1947); THAT WONDERFUL URGE(1948); DEAR WIFE(1949); FLAMING FEATHER(1951); PASSAGE WEST(1951); NEVER WAVE AT A WAC(1952); SAN ANTONE(1953); SUN SHINES BRIGHT, THE(1953); BADGE OF MARSHAL BRENNAN, THE(1957); RAIDERS OF OLD CALIFORNIA(1957); WOMEN OF PITCAIRN ISLAND, THE(1957)

Gary Whelan
TRAIL OF THE PINK PANTHER, THE(1982)

Ray Whelan
CHICAGO 70(1970)

Richard Whelan
NEPTUNE FACTOR, THE(1973, Can.)
Robert Whelan
SUPERMAN(1978)
1984
SUCCESS IS THE BEST REVENGE(1984, Brit.)
Ron Whelan
IT ISN'T DONE(1937, Aus.); ORPHAN OF THE WILDERNESS(1937, Aus.); WILD INNOCENCE(1937, Aus.); MASSACRE HILL(1949, Brit.); KANGAROO(1952); DRUMS OF AFRICA(1963); GUN HAWK, THE(1963); THREE STOOGES GO AROUND THE WORLD IN A DAZE, THE(1963); MY FAIR LADY(1964); GREATEST STORY EVER TOLD, THE(1965); SANDPIPER, THE(1965)
Ronald Whelan
TALL TIMBERS(1937, Aus.); LOVERS AND LUGGERS(1938, Aus.); ANTS IN HIS PANTS(1940, Aus.); VENGEANCE OF THE DEEP(1940, Aus.)
Tim Whelan
FALL GUY, THE(1930), w; HOOK, LINE AND SINKER(1930), w; EVERYTHING'S ROSIE(1931), w; PEACH O' RENO(1931), w; CROOKED CIRCLE(1932), w; GIRL CRAZY(1932), w; OUT ALL NIGHT(1933), w; ALONG CAME SALLY(1934, Brit.), d, w; CAMELS ARE COMING, THE(1934, Brit.), d; IT'S A BOY(1934, Brit.), d; MURDER MAN(1935), d, w; PERFECT GENTLEMAN, THE(1935), d; ACTION FOR SLANDER(1937, Brit.), d; DIVORCE OF LADY X. THE(1938, Brit.), d; TROOPSHIP(1938, Brit.), d; CLOUDS OVER EUROPE(1939, Brit.), d; MILL ON THE FLOSS(1939, Brit.), d, w; TWO'S COMPANY(1939, Brit.), d, w; SIDEWALKS OF LONDON(1940, Brit.), d; THIEF OF BAGHDAD, THE(1940, Brit.), d; INTERNATIONAL LADY(1941), d; LARCENY STREET(1941, Brit.), d, w; MAD DOCTOR, THE(1941), d; MISSING TEN DAYS(1941, Brit.), d; NIGHTMARE(1942), d; SEVEN DAYS LEAVE(1942), p&d; TWIN BEDS(1942), d; HIGHER AND HIGHER(1943), p&d; SWING FEVER(1943), d; STEP LIVELY(1944), d; BADMAN'S TERRITORY(1946), d; THIS WAS A WOMAN(1949, Brit.), d; RAGE AT DAWN(1955), d; TEXAS LADY(1955), d
Misc. Talkies
ALONG CAME SALLY(1933), d
Silents
SAFETY LAST(1923), w; GIRL SHY(1924), w; HOT WATER(1924), w; EXIT SMILING(1926), w; TRAMP, TRAMP, TRAMP(1926), w; HONEYMOON AHEAD(1927, Brit.), d&w; MY BEST GIRL(1927), w
Misc. Silents
HONEYMOON ABROAD(1929, Brit.), d; WHEN KNIGHTS WERE BOLD(1929, Brit.), d
Tim Whelan, Jr.
OUT OF THE TIGER'S MOUTH(1962), d, w
Lisa Whelchel
MAGICIAN OF LUBLIN, THE(1979, Israel/Ger.); THE DOUBLE McGUFFIN(1979)
Mary Whelchel
LADY LIBERTY(1972, Ital./Fr.)
William J. Whelehan
DAMIEN–OMEN II(1978)
Christopher Whelen
VALIANT, THE(1962, Brit./Ital.), md; COAST OF SKELETONS(1965, Brit.), m; FACE OF FU MANCHU, THE(1965, Brit.), m
Emily Whelen
Misc. Silents
VANITY(1917)
Emmy Whelen
Silents
AMATEUR ADVENTURESS, THE(1919)
Misc. Silents
OUTSIDER, THE(1917)
Daniel Wherry
WHISPERING SMITH VERSUS SCOTLAND YARD(1952, Brit.); MURDER WILL OUT(1953, Brit.)
Shawn Whetherly
1984
CANNONBALL RUN II(1984)
Nancy Whetmore
SCREAM BLOODY MURDER(1972)
James "Izzy" Whetstine
HOW TO BEAT THE HIGH COST OF LIVING(1980)
Graham Whettam
WHERE HAS POOR MICKEY GONE?(1964, Brit.), m
Laura Whetter
BACKSTAGE(1937, Brit.), w
Alan Whibley
EXCALIBUR(1981), spec eff; VENOM(1982, Brit.), spec eff; HOUND OF THE BASKERVILLES, THE(1983, Brit.), spec eff; SIGN OF FOUR, THE(1983, Brit.), spec eff; YENTL(1983), spec eff
Burnell Whibley
NO BLADE OF GRASS(1970, Brit.), m, md
Alan Whicker
ANGRY SILENCE, THE(1960, Brit.); MAGIC CHRISTIAN, THE(1970, Brit.)
Mrs. Thomas Whiffen
Misc. Silents
HEARTS AND FLOWERS(1914)
Mrs. Thomas W. Whiffen
Misc. Silents
BARBARA FRIETCHIE(1915)
Lanier Whilden
TERMS OF ENDEARMENT(1983)
Philip Whileman
YANKS(1979)
Manning Whiley
BLACKOUT(1940, Brit.); DESIGN FOR MURDER(1940, Brit.); FLYING SQUAD, THE(1940, Brit.); GASBAGS(1940, Brit.); OLD BILL AND SON(1940, Brit.); PACK UP YOUR TROUBLES(1940, Brit.); PASTOR HALL(1940, Brit.); SALOON BAR(1940, Brit.); SECRET FOUR, THE(1940, Brit.); THREE COCKEYED SAILORS(1940, Brit.); GHOST OF ST. MICHAEL'S. THE(1941, Brit.); SAINT'S VACATION, THE(1941, Brit.); VOICE IN THE NIGHT, A(1941, Brit.); PIMPERNEL SMITH(1942, Brit.); BELL-BOTTOM GEORGE(1943, Brit.); DUMMY TALKS, THE(1943, Brit.); MEET SEXTON BLAKE(1944, Brit.); FOR YOU ALONE(1945, Brit.); SEVENTH VEIL, THE(1946, Brit.); CODE OF SCOTLAND YARD)(1948, Brit.); CONSPIRACY IN TEHERAN(1948, Brit.); CHIL-

DREN OF CHANCE(1949, Brit.); INHERITANCE, THE(1951, Brit.); LITTLE BIG SHOT(1952, Brit.)
Ake Whilney
FLIGHT OF THE EAGLE(1983, Swed.)
Webster Whinery
SO FINE(1981)
1984
ALPHABET CITY(1984)
Joan Whinfield
EGYPTIAN. THE(1954)
Joe Whipp
ESCAPE FROM ALCATRAZ(1979)
Joseph Whipp
WRONG IS RIGHT(1982); SECOND THOUGHTS(1983)
1984
BODY ROCK(1984); NIGHTMARE ON ELM STREET, A(1984)
Sandra Whipp
DEATM GOES TO SCHOOL(1953, Brit.)
Leigh Whipper
OF MICE AND MEN(1939); BAHAMA PASSAGE(1941); KING OF THE ZOMBIES(1941); ROAD TO ZANZIBAR(1941); ROBIN HOOD OF THE PECOS(1941); VANISHING VIRGINIAN, THE(1941); VIRGINIA(1941); HEART OF THE GOLDEN WEST(1942); WHITE CARGO(1942); HAPPY LAND(1943); MISSION TO MOSCOW(1943); OX-BOW INCIDENT, THE(1943); IMPOSTER, THE(1944); HIDDEN EYE, THE(1945); UNDERCURRENT(1946); UNTAMED FURY(1947); LOST BOUNDARIES(1949); SHRIKE, THE(1955); YOUNG DON'T CRY, THE(1957)
Clara Whipple
Silents
DAUGHTER OF THE SEA, A(1915); GILDED CAGE, THE(1916); QUESTION, THE(1916)
Misc. Silents
HEART OF A HERO, THE(1916); PRIMA DONNA'S HUSBAND, THE(1916); REAPERS, THE(1916); REVOLT, THE(1916); STOLEN TRIUMPH, THE(1916); SUDDEN RICHES(1916); WILL YOU BE STAYING FOR SUPPER?(1919)
Dorothy Whipple
THEY KNEW MR. KNIGHT(1945, Brit.), w; THEY WERE SISTERS(1945, Brit.), w; ONE GOOD TURN(1955, Brit.), w
June Whipple
CAGED(1950)
Kay Whipple
1984
SIXTEEN CANDLES(1984)
Randy Whipple
WHERE WERE YOU WHEN THE LIGHTS WENT OUT?(1968)
Sam Whipple
JEKYLL AND HYDE...TOGETHER AGAIN(1982)
Misc. Talkies
GRAD NIGHT(1980)
Steve Whipple
INDEPENDENCE DAY(1983)
Whirlaway
WINNER'S CIRCLE, THE(1948)
Larry Whisenhunt
SILENT RUNNING(1972)
Eva Whishaw
SUBURBAN WIVES(1973, Brit.)
Whiskers
ON THE SUNNY SIDE(1942)
Nancy Whiskey
ROCK AROUND THE WORLD(1957, Brit.); INBETWEEN AGE, THE(1958, Brit.)
Margaret Whistler
Misc. Silents
HEART'S CRUCIBLE, A(1916)
Rex Whistler
PLACE OF ONE'S OWN, A(1945, Brit.), art d
Rudy Whistler
FIGHTING FATHER DUNNE(1948)
Ann Whitaker
PROSTITUTE(1980, Brit.)
Charles Whitaker
FIGHTING LEGION, THE(1930); CHEYENNE CYCLONE, THE(1932); DUDE BANDIT, THE(1933); MAN FROM MONTEREY, THE(1933); HONOR OF THE RANGE(1934); TUMBLING TUMBLEWEEDS(1935); RIDING AVENGER, THE(1936); RIDING ON(1937); PHANTOM GOLD(1938); UNDER WESTERN STARS(1938); FRONTIER SCOUT(1939); LONE STAR PIONEERS(1939); BILLY THE KID IN TEXAS(1940); MAD MONSTER, THE(1942); IN OLD OKLAHOMA(1943); LAW OF THE LASH(1947)
Misc. Talkies
TERROR OF THE PLAINS(1934)
Silents
ON THE GO(1925); ACE OF ACTION(1926); FIGHTING CHEAT, THE(1926); MANHATTAN COWBOY(1928)
Misc. Silents
GALLOPING ON(1925); HURRICANE HORSEMAN(1925); TEARIN' LOOSE(1925); TRUMPIN' TROUBLE(1926); PHANTOM BUSTER, THE(1927); SODA WATER COWBOY(1927)
Charles "Slim" Whitaker
SADDLE BUSTER, THE(1932); MAN FROM HELL, THE(1934); RUSTLER'S PARADISE(1935); LAW OF THE RANGER(1937); PINTO RUSTLERS(1937); ROARING SIX GUNS(1937); SANTA FE BOUND(1937); IN EARLY ARIZONA(1938); ORPHAN OF THE PECOS(1938); STAGECOACH DAYS(1938); NEW FRONTIER(1939); SILVER BULLET, THE(1942); OUTLAW OF THE PLAINS(1946); WESTWARD TRAIL, THE(1948)
David Whitaker
DR. JEKYLL AND MR. HYDE(1941), m; DON'T RAISE THE BRIDGE, LOWER THE RIVER(1968), m; HAMMERHEAD(1968), m; DESPERADOS, THE(1969), m; RUN WILD, RUN FREE(1969, Brit.), m, md; SUBTERFUGE(1969, US/Brit.), w; SCREAM AND SCREAM AGAIN(1970, Brit.), m; DR. JEKYLL AND SISTER HYDE(1971, Brit.), m; PSYCHOMANIA(1974, Brit.), m; OLD DRACULA(1975, Brit.), m

Forest Whitaker
FAST TIMES AT RIDGEMONT HIGH(1982)
Herman Whitaker
THREE ROGUES(1931), w
James Whitaker
LAST OF THE LONE WOLF(1930), w; UP FOR MURDER(1931), w
Johnnie Whitaker
RUSSIANS ARE COMING, THE RUSSIANS ARE COMING, THE(1966); SNOWBALL EXPRESS(1972)
Johnny Whitaker
BISCUIT EATER, THE(1972); NAPOLEON AND SAMANTHA(1972); TOM SAWYER(1973)
Misc. Talkies
MAGIC PONY(1979)
Judge Whitaker
MAKE MINE MUSIC(1946), anim; FUN AND FANCY FREE(1947), anim; MELODY TIME(1948), animators; CINDERELLA(1950), anim; ALICE IN WONDERLAND(1951), anim; PETER PAN(1953), anim
Raymond Whitaker
Misc. Silents
SCARLET CRYSTAL, THE(1917)
Rod Whitaker
EIGER SANCTION, THE(1975), w
Slim Whitaker
OKLAHOMA CYCLONE(1930); SHADOW RANCH(1930); AVENGER, THE(1931); DESERT VENGEANCE(1931); ONE WAY TRAIL, THE(1931); RIDER OF THE PLAINS(1931); FREIGHTERS OF DESTINY(1932); GHOST VALLEY(1932); HAUNTED GOLD(1932); MAN FROM NEW MEXICO, THE(1932); MAN'S LAND, A(1932); SUNSET TRAIL(1932); COME ON TARZAN(1933); DEADWOOD PASS(1933); DRUM TAPS(1933); FLAMING GUNS(1933); SOMEWHERE IN SONORA(1933); WAR OF THE RANGE(1933); FIDDLIN' BUCKAROO, THE(1934); GUN JUSTICE(1934); SAGEBRUSH TRAIL(1934); SMOKING GUNS(1934); TRAIL DRIVE, THE(1934); WHEELS OF DESTINY(1934); COYOTE TRAILS(1935); GALLANT DEFENDER(1935); LAST OF THE CLINTONS, THE(1935); LAWLESS RANGE(1935); WESTERN FRONTIER(1935); DESERT GUNS(1936); EVERYMAN'S LAW(1936); FAST BULLETS(1936); FUGITIVE SHERIFF, THE(1936); GHOST PATROL(1936); HEIR TO TROUBLE(1936); LAWLESS RIDERS(1936); LIGHTNING BILL CARSON(1936); PRESCOTT KID, THE(1936); SONG OF THE GRINGO(1936); WESTERNER, THE(1936); GUNS IN THE DARK(1937); LAW FOR TOMBSTONE(1937); LOST RANCH(1937); MELODY OF THE PLAINS(1937); MYSTERY RANGE(1937); OLD WYOMING TRAIL, THE(1937); PRAIRIE THUNDER(1937); RAW TIMBER(1937); RECKLESS RANGER(1937); RIO GRANDE RANGER(1937); ROGUE OF THE RANGE(1937); ROUNDUP TIME IN TEXAS(1937); SMOKE TREE RANGE(1937); FEUD OF THE TRAIL(1938); GUNSMOKE TRAIL(1938); OVERLAND STAGE RAIDERS(1938); PIONEER TRAIL(1938); PRAIRIE JUSTICE(1938); RAWHIDE(1938); ROLLING CARAVANS(1938); CODE OF THE CACTUS(1939); COLORADO SUNSET(1939); FIGHTING GRINGO, THE(1939); LAW COMES TO TEXAS, THE(1939); MARSHAL OF MESA CITY, THE(1939); OKLAHOMA TERROR(1939); ROLLIN' WESTWARD(1939); SOUTH OF THE BORDER(1939); TEXAS WILDCATS(1939); THUNDERING WEST, THE(1939); BULLET CODE(1940); LEGION OF THE LAWLESS(1940); MELODY RANCH(1940); PRAIRIE LAW(1940); RANCHO GRANDE(1940); RIDE, TENDERFOOT, RIDE(1940); YOUNG BILL HICKOK(1940); ALONG THE RIO GRANDE(1941); BILLY THE KID WANTED(1941); BILLY THE KID'S ROUNDUP(1941); BURY ME NOT ON THE LONE PRAIRIE(1941); CYCLONE ON HORSEBACK(1941); LAW OF THE RANGE(1941); SADDLE MOUNTAIN ROUNDUP(1941); SIX GUN GOLD(1941); ARIZONA STAGECOACH(1942); COME ON DANGER(1942); IN OLD CALIFORNIA(1942); LITTLE JOE, THE WRANGLER(1942); LONE RIDER AND THE BANDIT, THE(1942); MYSTERIOUS RIDER, THE(1942); RAIDERS OF THE WEST(1942); FIGHTING FRONTIER(1943); KID RIDES AGAIN, THE(1943); RAIDERS OF SAN JOAQUIN(1943); SILVER SPURS(1943); WOLVES OF THE RANGE(1943); DEATH RIDES THE PLAINS(1944); DRIFTER, THE(1944); LARAMIE TRAIL, THE(1944); MARSHAL OF GUNSMOKE(1944); OKLAHOMA RAIDERS(1944); OVERLAND RIDERS(1946); PIONEER JUSTICE(1947); RETURN OF THE LASH(1947)
Misc. Talkies
GUNS FOR HIRE(1932); TROUBLE BUSTERS(1933); CACTUS KID, THE(1934); LONE BANDIT, THE(1934); OUTLAW TAMER, THE(1934); RANGE WARFARE(1935); RIO RATTLER(1935); SILVER BULLET, THE(1935); UNCONQUERED BANDIT(1935); HANDS ACROSS THE ROCKIES(1941)
Ian Whitakes
HELL, HEAVEN OR HOBOKEN(1958, Brit.)
Russ Whital
Silents
ARGENTINE LOVE(1924)
Denis Whitburn
CROSSTALK(1982, Aus.), w
Gwen Whitby
QUIET WEEKEND(1948, Brit.); AFFAIRS OF ADELAIDE(1949, U. S./Brit)
Gwynne Whitby
MINE OWN EXECUTIONER(1948, Brit.); DISTANT TRUMPET(1952, Brit.); I BELIEVE IN YOU(1953, Brit.)
Martyn Whitby
1984
SUCCESS IS THE BEST REVENGE(1984, Brit.)
Patricia A. Whitcer
1984
UP THE CREEK(1984)
Barry Whitcomb
Silents
COMMON LAW, THE(1916); EYE FOR EYE(1918)
Daniel Whitcomb
Silents
SOLD AT AUCTION(1917), w; PEACEFUL PETERS(1922), w
Daniel F. Whitcomb
Silents
ANOTHER MAN'S BOOTS(1922), w; AT DEVIL'S GORGE(1923), w; SPAWN OF THE DESERT(1923), w; STING OF THE SCORPION, THE(1923), w
Daniel Frederick Whitcomb
Silents
BRIDE'S SILENCE, THE(1917), w

Dennis Whitcomb
DARK AT THE TOP OF THE STAIRS, THE(1960); MR. HOBBS TAKES A VACATION(1962)
Norman Whitcomb
ESCAPE TO DANGER(1943, Brit.)
Pat Whitcombe
Silents
MR. NOBODY(1927, Brit.)
Elizabeth Whitcraft
1984
BIRDY(1984)
Gen. White
MY GAL LOVES MUSIC(1944)
A.N. White
STREET FIGHTER(1959), d&w
Al White
LULLABY OF BROADWAY, THE(1951), ch; AIRPLANE II: THE SEQUEL(1982)
Al White, Jr.
STARS AND STRIPES FOREVER(1952), ch
Alan White
INTO THE STRAIGHT(1950, Aus.); NO TIME FOR TEARS(1957, Brit.); GIRLS AT SEA(1958, Brit.); LADY MISLAID, A(1958, Brit.); SHAKE HANDS WITH THE DEVIL(1959, Ireland); SEVEN KEYS(1962, Brit.); GO KART GO(1964, Brit.); MODEL MURDER CASE, THE(1964, Brit.); PUSSYCAT ALLEY(1965, Brit.); MR. BROWN COMES DOWN THE HILL(1966, Brit.); LONG DAY'S DYING, THE(1968, Brit.), w; CHAIRMAN, THE(1969); SGT. PEPPER'S LONELY HEARTS CLUB BAND(1978)
Alexander White
THUNDERING TRAIL, THE(1951), w; VANISHING OUTPOST, THE(1951), w
Alfred White
DON'T BET ON LOVE(1933)
Alice White
SHOW GIRL(1928); BROADWAY BABIES(1929); GIRL FROM WOOLWORTH'S, THE(1929); HOT STUFF(1929); PLAYING AROUND(1930); SHOW GIRL IN HOLLYWOOD(1930); SWEET MAMA(1930); SWEETHEARTS ON PARADE(1930); WIDOW FROM CHICAGO, THE(1930); GOD IS MY WITNESS(1931); MURDER AT MIDNIGHT(1931); NAUGHTY FLIRT, THE(1931); EMPLOYEE'S ENTRANCE(1933); KING FOR A NIGHT(1933); LUXURY LINER(1933); PICTURE SNATCHER(1933); CROSS COUNTRY CRUISE(1934); GIFT OF GAB(1934); JIMMY THE GENT(1934); VERY HONORABLE GUY, A(1934); CORONADO(1935); SECRET OF THE CHATEAU(1935); SWEET MUSIC(1935); BIG CITY(1937); ANNABEL TAKES A TOUR(1938); KING OF THE NEWSBOYS(1938); TELEPHONE OPERATOR(1938); NIGHT OF JANUARY 16TH(1941); GIRLS' TOWN(1942); FLAMINGO ROAD(1949)
Silents
AMERICAN BEAUTY(1927); SEA TIGER, THE(1927); GENTLEMEN PREFER BLONDES(1928); HAROLD TEEN(1928); LINGERIE(1928); NAUGHTY BABY(1929)
Misc. Silents
BREAKFAST AT SUNRISE(1927); SATIN WOMAN, THE(1927); BIG NOISE, THE(1928); MAD HOUR(1928)
Andy White
AFRICA–TEXAS STYLE!(1967 U.S./Brit.), w; GENTLE GIANT(1967), w; DARING GAME(1968), w
Angela White
MAN INSIDE, THE(1958, Brit.); MENACE IN THE NIGHT(1958, Brit.); PIPER'S TUNE, THE(1962, Brit.)
Arthur White
IT'S A GRAND LIFE(1953, Brit.); L-SHAPED ROOM, THE(1962, Brit.); ISADORA(1968, Brit.); OH! WHAT A LOVELY WAR(1969, Brit.)
Audrey White
IT STARTED IN PARADISE(1952, Brit.); FINAL TEST, THE(1953, Brit.)
Barbara White
IT HAPPENED ONE SUNDAY(1944, Brit.); VOICE WITHIN, THE(1945, Brit.); MINE OWN EXECUTIONER(1948, Brit.); QUIET WEEKEND(1948, Brit.); THIS WAS A WOMAN(1949, Brit.); ALL ABOUT EVE(1950); WHILE THE SUN SHINES(1950, Brit.)
Barry White
TOGETHER BROTHERS(1974), m; COONSKIN(1975)
Bay White
SECRET PEOPLE(1952, Brit.); ONE WISH TOO MANY(1956, Brit.); TOWN LIKE ALICE, A(1958, Brit.)
Bert White
FOREIGN CORRESPONDENT(1940)
Bertie White
Silents
HEAD OF THE FAMILY, THE(1922, Brit.); REST CURE, THE(1923, Brit.)
Misc. Silents
LOVE'S INFLUENCE(1922, Brit.)
Betty White
ADVISE AND CONSENT(1962)
Beverlee White
FOLLOW THE SUN(1951)
Bill White
FOUR FOR THE MORGUE(1962)
Misc. Silents
TWO-FISTED JEFFERSON(1922)
Bill White, Jr.
DANGEROUS MISSION(1954); RUN OF THE ARROW(1957)
Mrs. Carveth Wells
RAINBOW ISLAND(1944)
Billy Vance White
DRIVE-IN(1976)
Blanche White
Misc. Silents
CHALICE OF SORROW, THE(1916); DAWN MAKER, THE(1916); HONOR THY NAME(1916)
Bo White
VERY NATURAL THING, A(1974)
Misc. Talkies
BLUE SUMMER(1973)

Bob White
SECRET EVIDENCE(1941); CRACK-UP(1946); SHOCK WAVES(1977)
Misc. Silents
LOST IN TRANSIT(1917); WIFE HUNTERS, THE(1922), d
Bouck White
TOAST OF NEW YORK, THE(1937), w
Brittany White
MR. MOM(1983)
Bruce White
EYE OF THE NEEDLE(1981)
1984
REPO MAN(1984)
C.W. White
GETAWAY, THE(1972)
Carla White
CHILDREN, THE(1980), makeup
1984
ULTIMATE SOLUTION OF GRACE QUIGLEY, THE(1984), makeup
Carol White
WEB OF SUSPICION(1959, Brit.); LINDA(1960, Brit.); NEVER LET GO(1960, Brit.); MAN IN THE BACK SEAT, THE(1961, Brit.); BON VOYAGE(1962); CARRY ON TEACHER(1962, Brit.); GAOLBREAK(1962, Brit.); MATTER OF WHO, A(1962, Brit.); VILLAGE OF DAUGHTERS(1962, Brit.); LADIES WHO DO(1964, Brit.); PLAY-GROUND, THE(1965); I'LL NEVER FORGET WHAT'S 'IS NAME(1967, Brit.); PREHIS-TORIC WOMEN(1967, Brit.); FIXER, THE(1968); POOR COW(1968, Brit.); DADDY'S GONE A-HUNTING(1969); MAN WHO HAD POWER OVER WOMEN, THE(1970, Brit.); DULCIMA(1971, Brit.); SOMETHING BIG(1971); MADE(1972, Brit.); UP THE SANDBOX(1972); SOME CALL IT LOVING(1973); SQUEEZE, THE(1977, Brit.); NUT-CRACKER(1982, Brit.)
Misc. Talkies
NUTCRACKER(1984)
Carol Ita White
PIPE DREAMS(1976)
1984
SAVAGE STREETS(1984)
Carole White
CIRCUS FRIENDS(1962, Brit.)
Carole Ita White
BABY BLUE MARINE(1976)
1984
BODY ROCK(1984); JOY OF SEX(1984)
Caroline White
I'D CLIMB THE HIGHEST MOUNTAIN(1951)
Silents
MY COUSIN(1918)
Cecil White
WAY OUT(1966)
Charles White
TROUBLEMAKER, THE(1964); CHILD'S PLAY(1972); HOT ROCK, THE(1972); SER-PICO(1973); SUPER COPS, THE(1974)
Charlotte White
NIGHT OF BLOODY HORROR zero(1969)
Chrissie White
CALL OF THE SEA, THE(1930, Brit.); GENERAL JOHN REGAN(1933, Brit.)
Silents
HER BOY(1915, Brit.); MOLLY BAWN(1916, Brit.); HANGING JUDGE, THE(1918, Brit.); POSSESSION(1919, Brit.); AYLWIN(1920, Brit.); TEMPORARY VAGABOND, A(1920, Brit.); LILY OF THE ALLEY(1923, Brit.)
Misc. Silents
DAVID GARRICK(1913, Brit.); KISSING CUP(1913, Brit.); VICAR OF WAKEFIELD, THE(1913, Brit.); AS THE SUN WENT DOWN(1915, Brit.); BARNABY RUDGE(1915); NIGHTBIRDS OF LONDON, THE(1915, Brit.); SWEET LAVENDER(1915, Brit.); BUNCH OF VIOLETS, A(1916, Brit.); BROKEN THREADS(1917, Brit.); CAR-ROTS(1917, Brit.); DAUGHTER OF THE WILDS(1917, Brit.); DICK CARSON WINS THROUGH(1917, Brit.); ETERNAL TRIANGLE, THE(1917, Brit.); HER MARRIAGE LINES(1917, Brit.); MAN BEHIND "THE TIMES", THE(1917, Brit.); TOWARDS THE LIGHT(1918, Brit.); CITY OF BEAUTIFUL NONSENSE, THE(1919); HIS DEAREST POSSESSION(1919, Brit.); KINSMAN(1919, Brit.); JOHN FORREST FINDS HIMSELF(1920, Brit.); BARGAIN, THE(1921, Brit.); LUNATIC AT LARGE, THE(1921); WILD HEATHER(1921, Brit.); SIMPLE SIMON(1922, Brit.); TIT FOR TAT(1922, Brit.); BODEN'S BOY(1923, Brit.)
Christine White
MAN CRAZY(1953); PANAMA SAL(1957); MACABRE(1958); MAGNUM FOR-CE(1973)
Christopher White
MAN'S FAVORITE SPORT(?) (1964)
Claire White
SAN QUENTIN(1937)
Clarence White
FARMER'S OTHER DAUGHTER, THE(1965)
Colin White
1984
PLAGUE DOGS, THE(1984, U.S./Brit.), anim
Constance White
WILD BUNCH, THE(1969)
Courtney White
MR. MOM(1983)
Crystal White
INVISIBLE MAN, THE(1933), w; TANGIER(1946); FIGHTING KENTUCKIAN, THE(1949)
D. J. White
METALSTORM: THE DESTRUCTION OF JARED-SYN(1983), makeup
Daisy White
CURTAINS(1983, Can.)
Dan White
IN OLD MONTEREY(1939); LAW COMES TO TEXAS, THE(1939); ROUGH RIDERS' ROUNDUP(1939); OUR TOWN(1940); ARIZONA TRAIL(1943); FALSE COLORS(1943); FIGHTING VALLEY(1943); OUTLAWS OF STAMPEDE PASS(1943); ARIZONA WHIRLWIND(1944); BOSS OF THE RAWHIDE(1944); CRAZY KNIGHTS(1944); DEATH RIDES THE PLAINS(1944); MARSHAL OF GUNSMOKE(1944); TRAIL OF

TERROR(1944); VOODOO MAN(1944); WESTWARD BOUND(1944); BEYOND THE PECOS(1945); FLAMING BULLETS(1945); SAN ANTONIO(1945); SUDAN(1945); TRAIL TO VENGEANCE(1945); DUEL IN THE SUN(1946); GUN TOWN(1946); GUNMAN'S CODE(1946); SEA OF GRASS, THE(1947); WHITE STALLION(1947); ALBUQUERQUE(1948); FOUR FACES WEST(1948); GUNNING FOR JUSTICE(1948); I WOULDN'T BE IN YOUR SHOES(1948); RED RIVER(1948); SHAGGY(1948); SILVER RIVER(1948); STATION WEST(1948); COVER-UP(1949); INTRUDER IN THE DUST(1949); OUTLAW COUNTRY(1949); ROSEANNA McCOY(1949); DISTANT DRUMS(1951); DRUMS IN THE DEEP SOUTH(1951); HIS KIND OF WOMAN(1951); RAWHIDE(1951); RED BADGE OF COURAGE, THE(1951); RED MOUNTAIN(1951); SUGARFOOT(1951); VENGEANCE VALLEY(1951); HORIZONS WEST(1952); LUSTY MEN, THE(1952); WAIT 'TIL THE SUN SHINES, NELLIE(1952); BORN TO THE SADDLE(1953); INFERNO(1953); SILVER WHIP, THE(1953); SHE COULDN'T SAY NO(1954); SUDDENLY(1954); TAZA, SON OF COCHISE(1954); AMERICANO, THE(1955); TALL MEN, THE(1955); GREAT DAY IN THE MORNING(1956); LAST HUNT, THE(1956); RAINMAKER, THE(1956); BAND OF ANGELS(1957); JAILHOUSE ROCK(1957); THIS EARTH IS MINE(1959); SERGEANT WAS A LADY, THE(1961); TO KILL A MOCKINGBIRD(1962); JESSE JAMES MEETS FRANKENSTEIN'S DAUGH-TER(1966); WACO(1966); RED TOMAHAWK(1967)
Misc. Talkies
SUNSET CARSON RIDES AGAIN(1948)
Dan M. White
QUANTRILL'S RAIDERS(1958)
Daniel White
YEARLING, THE(1946); UNKNOWN ISLAND(1948); WALLS OF JERICHO(1948); ROAD TO DENVER, THE(1955); GUNFIRE AT INDIAN GAP(1957); LONELY MAN, THE(1957); ESCAPE FROM RED ROCK(1958); FRONTIER GUN(1958); MA BARKER'S KILLER BROOD(1960); HOT HOURS(1963, Fr.), m; SOFT SKIN ON BLACK SILK(1964, Fr./Span.), m; DIABOLICAL DR. Z, THE(1966 Span./Fr.), m; RIO 70(1970, U.S./Ger./Span.), m; SKYJACKED(1972); SMOKE IN THE WIND(1975)
Daniel J. White
BOUNTY KILLER, THE(1965)
Daniel M. White
JUBILEE TRAIL(1954); FIRST TRAVELING SALESLADY, THE(1956)
Dave White
TENDER TRAP, THE(1955); SOME CAME RUNNING(1959); OCEAN'S ELE-VEN(1960)
David White
SWEET SMELL OF SUCCESS(1957); APARTMENT, THE(1960); SUNRISE AT CAMPOBELLO(1960); MADISON AVENUE(1962); LOLLIPOP COVER, THE(1965); RED, WHITE AND BLACK, THE(1970); SNOWBALL EXPRESS(1972); HAPPY HOOK-ER GOES TO WASHINGTON, THE(1977)
Dean White
BEST YEARS OF OUR LIVES, THE(1946); RACE STREET(1948); RETURN OF THE BADMEN(1948); BRIDE OF VENGEANCE(1949); STRATTON STORY, THE(1949)
Debbie White
10(1979)
Deborah White
FAT SPY(1966); VAN, THE(1977); RECORD CITY(1978); FAST-WALKING(1982)
Deloy White
SUNBURN(1979); GREEN ICE(1981, Brit.)
Delphine White
BLOOD AND GUTS(1978, Can.), cos; VISITING HOURS(1982, Can.), cos; VIDEO-DROME(1983, Can.), cos
DeVoreaux White
1984
PLACES IN THE HEART(1984)
Diz White
BULLSHOT(1983), a, w
Donna White
STUDY IN TERROR, A(1966, Brit./Ger.)
Dorothy White
HOLD'EM NAVY!(1937); MEN WITH WINGS(1938); SAY IT IN FRENCH(1938); ZAZA(1939); LIGHT TOUCH, THE(1955, Brit.); PORT AFRIQUE(1956, Brit.); GET CARTER(1971, Brit.)
Dorothy Ann White
SUNSET IN THE WEST(1950)
Doug White
PARASITE(1982), spec eff
E.B. White
CHARLOTTE'S WEB(1973), w
Eddy White
OUTLAWS OF PINE RIDGE(1942), p; SOMBRERO KID, THE(1942), w; SUNDOWN KID, THE(1942), p; BLACK HILLS EXPRESS(1943), p; BORDERTOWN GUNFIGHT-ERS(1943), p; CANYON CITY(1943), p; CARSON CITY CYCLONE(1943), p; DAYS OF OLD CHEYENNE(1943), p; DEAD MAN'S GULCH(1943), p; DEATH VALLEY MAN-HUNT(1943), p, w; FUGITIVE FROM SONORA(1943), p; MAN FROM THE RIO GRANDE, THE(1943), p; PISTOL PACKIN' MAMA(1943), p; BIG BONANZA, THE(1944), p; CALIFORNIA JOE(1944), p; MOJAVE FIREBRAND(1944); MY BUD-DY(1944), p; OUTLAWS OF SANTA FE(1944), p; TUCSON RAIDERS(1944), p; CHICAGO KID, THE(1945), p; SWINGIN' ON A RAINBOW(1945), p; HOME IN OKLAHOMA(1946), p; SUNSET IN THE WEST(1950), p
Edward J. White
SAN FERNANDO VALLEY(1944), p; ALONG THE NAVAJO TRAIL(1945), p; BELLS OF ROSARITA(1945), p; HELLDORADO(1946), p; RAINBOW OVER TEX-AS(1946), p; ROLL ON TEXAS MOON(1946), p; SONG OF ARIZONA(1946), p; UNDER NEVADA SKIES(1946), p; APACHE ROSE(1947), p; BELLS OF SAN ANGELO(1947), p; ON THE OLD SPANISH TRAIL(1947), p; SPRINGTIME IN THE SIERRAS(1947), p; EYES OF TEXAS(1948), p; GAY RANCHERO, THE(1948), p; GRAND CANYON TRAIL(1948), p; NIGHT TIME IN NEVADA(1948), p; UNDER CALIFORNIA STARS(1948), p; DOWN DAKOTA WAY(1949), p; FAR FRONTIER, THE(1949), p; GOLDEN STALLION, THE(1949), p; SUSANNA PASS(1949), p; BELLE OF OLD MEXICO(1950), p; BELLS OF CORONADO(1950), p; TRAIL OF ROBIN HOOD(1950), p; TRIGGER, JR.(1950), p; TWILIGHT IN THE SIERRAS(1950), p; HEART OF THE ROCKIES(1951), p; IN OLD AMARILLO(1951), p; SOUTH OF CALIENTE(1951), p; SPOILERS OF THE PLAINS(1951), p; COLORADO SUNDOWN(1952), p; LAST MUS-KETEER, THE(1952), p; OLD OKLAHOMA PLAINS(1952), p; PALS OF THE GOLDEN WEST(1952), p; SOUTH PACIFIC TRAIL(1952), p; IRON MOUNTAIN TRAIL(1953), p; OLD OVERLAND TRAIL(1953), p; MAN IS ARMED, THE(1956), p; PANAMA SAL(1957), p

Elaine White
FIEND(

Ethel Lina White
LADY VANISHES, THE(1938, Brit.), w; UNSEEN, THE(1945), w; SPIRAL STAIR-CASE, THE(1946), w; LADY VANISHES, THE(1980, Brit.), w

Eugene White
TURNING POINT, THE(1952)

Felix White
UNCLE TOM'S CABIN(1969, Fr./Ital./Ger./Yugo.)

Fisher White
MOONLIGHT SONATA(1938, Brit.)

Fleet White
WITHOUT RESERVATIONS(1946)

Frances White
PUMPKIN EATER, THE(1964, Brit.); PRESS FOR TIME(1966, Brit.); MARY, QUEEN OF SCOTS(1971, Brit.)

Frank White
YOU GOTTA STAY HAPPY(1948); THAT LADY(1955, Brit.), art d; HIGH HELL(1958), art d; NATCHEZ TRACE(1960); LIGHT IN THE PIAZZA(1962), art d; MURDER MOST FOUL(1964, Brit.), art d; ESCAPE BY NIGHT(1965, Brit.), art d; FACE OF FU MANCHU, THE(1965, Brit.), art d; TEN LITTLE INDIANS(1965, Brit.), art d; PSYCHO-CIRCUS(1967, Brit.), art d; THOSE FANTASTIC FLYING FOOLS(1967, Brit), art d; ROSEMARY'S BABY(1968); MC KENZIE BREAK, THE(1970), prod d; UNDERGROUND(1970, Brit.), art d; VIRGIN SOLDIERS, THE(1970, Brit.), art d; TREASURE ISLAND(1972, Brit./Span./Fr./Ger.), art d

Fred S. White
99 WOUNDS(1931), ed

Garry Michael White
SCARECROW(1973), w; PROMISE, THE(1979), w

Gary Michael White
SKY RIDERS(1976, U.S./Gr.), w

Gene White
SCORCHY(1976)

George White
FOLLOW THE LEADER(1930), w; GEORGE WHITE'S SCANDALS(1934), a, p, d, w; GEORGE WHITE'S 1935 SCANDALS(1935), a, p&d, w; JOURNEY FOR MARGARET(1942), ed; PIERRE OF THE PLAINS(1942), ed; BATAAN(1943), ed; MAN FROM DOWN UNDER, THE(1943), ed; PILOT NO. 5(1943), ed; ANDY HARDY'S BLONDE TROUBLE(1944), ed; MARRIAGE IS A PRIVATE AFFAIR(1944), ed; CLOCK, THE(1945), ed; GEORGE WHITE'S SCANDALS(1945), p; RHAPSODY IN BLUE(1945); YOLANDA AND THE THIEF(1945), ed; MY BROTHER TALKS TO HORSES(1946), ed; POSTMAN ALWAYS RINGS TWICE, THE(1946), ed; GREEN DOLPHIN STREET(1947), ed; B. F.'S DAUGHTER(1948), ed; CHALLENGE TO LASSIE(1949), ed; LIFE OF HER OWN, A(1950), ed; REFORMER AND THE REDHEAD, THE(1950), ed; MR. IMPERIUM(1951), ed; NIGHT INTO MORNING(1951), ed; SELLOUT, THE(1951), ed; FEARLESS FAGAN(1952), ed; DREAM WIFE(1953), ed; GREAT DIAMOND ROBBERY(1953), ed; NAKED SPUR, THE(1953), ed; SILVER CHALICE, THE(1954), ed; PHENIX CITY STORY, THE(1955), ed; SHACK OUT ON 101(1955), ed; CANYON RIVER(1956), ed; CRASHING LAS VEGAS(1956), ed; FIRST TEXAN, THE(1956), ed; YOUNG GUNS, THE(1956), ed; HOLD THAT HYPNOTIST(1957), ed; MY GUN IS QUICK(1957), p&d; OKLAHOMAN, THE(1957), ed; BEAST OF BUDAPEST, THE(1958), ed; GUNSMOKE IN TUCSON(1958), ed; JOHNNY ROCCO(1958), ed; MAN FROM GOD'S COUNTRY(1958), ed; KING OF THE WILD STALLIONS(1959), ed; HELL TO ETERNITY(1960), ed; I PASSED FOR WHITE(1960), ed; RAY-MIE(1960), ed; GEORGE RAFT STORY, THE(1961), ed; KING OF THE ROARING TWENTIES--THE STORY OF ARNOLD ROTHSTEIN(1961), ed; TWENTY PLUS TWO(1961), ed; CONVICTS FOUR(1962), ed; DANGEROUS CHARTER(1962), ed; CATTLE KING(1963), ed; INDIAN PAINT(1965), ed; MUTINY IN OUTER SPACE(1965), ed; ONE WAY WAHINI(1965), ed; NAVY VS. THE NIGHT MONSTERS, THE(1966), ed; WOMEN OF THE PREHISTORIC PLANET(1966), ed; TIME FOR KILLING, A(1967), ed

GEORGE WHITE
Silents
ALL WOMAN(1918)

George White [Giorgio Bianchi]
LOVE, THE ITALIAN WAY(1964, Ital.), d

Giorgio White
RATATAPLAN(1979, Ital.)

Glen White
Silents
SEATS OF THE MIGHTY, THE(1914); ROMEO AND JULIET(1916); DARLING OF PARIS, THE(1917)
Misc. Silents
SPORTING BLOOD(1916); WAR BRIDE'S SECRET, THE(1916); HER GREATEST LOVE(1917); SCRAP OF PAPER, THE(1920); WALL STREET MYSTERY, THE(1920)

Glenn White
Silents
$5,000,000 COUNTERFEITING PLOT, THE(1914); TIGER WOMAN, THE(1917)
Misc. Silents
ABSINTHE(1914); STRAIGHT WAY, THE(1916); LOVE AND THE LAW(1919); BROMLEY CASE, THE(1920); CIRCUMSTANTIAL EVIDENCE(1920); TRAIL OF THE CIGARETTE, THE(1920)

Gloria Ann White
IT'S A GREAT LIFE(1936); CISCO KID AND THE LADY, THE(1939)

Gordon White
Misc. Silents
READIN"RITIN"RITHMETIC(1926)

Grace Miller White
TESS OF THE STORM COUNTRY(1932), w; TESS OF THE STORM COUNTRY(1961), w
Silents
TESS OF THE STORM COUNTRY(1914), w; JUDY OF ROGUES' HARBOUR(1920), w; POLLY OF THE STORM COUNTRY(1920), w; DESERTED AT THE ALTAR(1922), w; RAGS TO RICHES(1922), w; TESS OF THE STORM COUNTRY(1922), w

Gregg White
WHITE BUFFALO, THE(1977)

H. Fisher White
MADAME GUILLOTINE(1931, Brit.)

Misc. Silents
CITY OF YOUTH, THE(1928, Brit.)

H.G. White
IT HAPPENED HERE(1966, Brit.)

Harold White
WEREWOLF, THE(1956), ed

Harriet White
PAISAN(1948, Ital.); RAPTURE(1950, Ital.); LA DOLCE VITA(1961, Ital./Fr.); HORRIBLE DR. HICHCOCK, THE(1964, Ital.); GHOST, THE(1965, Ital.); WHAT!(1965, Fr./Brit./Ital.); MURDER CLINIC, THE(1967, Ital./Fr.)

Harry White
DR. SOCRATES(1935); WARRIORS, THE(1955), set d; LADY OF VENGEANCE(1957, Brit), art d; KILL HER GENTLY(1958, Brit.), art d; FOLLOW THAT HORSE!(1960, Brit.), art d; MILLIONAIRESS, THE(1960, Brit.), art d; MURDER SHE SAID(1961, Brit.), art d; KILL OR CURE(1962, Brit.), art d; MALAGA(1962, Brit.), art d; HORROR OF IT ALL, THE(1964, Brit.), art d; LADIES WHO DO(1964, Brit.), art d; MASTER SPY(1964, Brit.), art d; WALK A TIGHTROPE(1964, U.S./Brit.), art d; CURSE OF THE FLY(1965, Brit.), art d; RETURN OF MR. MOTO, THE(1965, Brit.), art d; SPACEFLIGHT IC-1(1965, Brit.), art d; MURDER GAME, THE(1966, Brit.), art d; TRAP, THE(1967, Can./Brit.), art d; OH! WHAT A LOVELY WAR(1969, Brit.), art d

Heather White
NOT SO DUSTY(1936, Brit.)

Hendry White
TILLY OF BLOOMSBURY(1940, Brit.)

Henry White
MURDER IN REVERSE(1946, Brit.)

Huey White
CONVENTION CITY(1933); FEMALE(1933); HELL CAT, THE(1934); JEALOUSY(1934); THIN MAN, THE(1934); G-MEN(1935); SHE COULDN'T TAKE IT(1935); SHE GETS HER MAN(1935); SPECIAL AGENT(1935); CRASH DONOVAN(1936); FURY(1936); SATAN MET A LADY(1936); EVER SINCE EVE(1937); LAST GANGSTER, THE(1937); SHE LOVED A FIREMAN(1937); WHEN G-MEN STEP IN(1938)

Hugh White
HUSH MONEY(1931)

Hughey White
MILLION DOLLAR RANSOM(1934)

Ian White
MAXWELL ARCHER, DETECTIVE(1942, Brit.), art d

1984
COVERGIRL(1984, Can.)

Irene White
WRECKER, THE(1933)

Irving White
TRUE CONFESSION(1937); DAUGHTERS COURAGEOUS(1939), w; ALWAYS IN MY HEART(1942), w

Irving S. White
MAGICIAN OF LUBLIN, THE(1979, Israel/Ger.), w

J. Fisher White
LAST POST, THE(1929, Brit.); KISSING CUP'S RACE(1930, Brit.); LOOSE ENDS(1930, Brit.); DREYFUS CASE, THE(1931, Brit.); MAN OF MAYFAIR(1931, Brit.); MANY WATERS(1931, Brit.); BETRAYAL(1932, Brit.); WONDERFUL STORY, THE(1932, Brit.); COUNSEL'S OPINION(1933, Brit.); GOOD COMPANIONS(1933, Brit.); CUP OF KINDNESS, A(1934, Brit.); GREAT DEFENDER, THE(1934, Brit.); WHAT HAPPENED THEN?(1934, Brit.); CITY OF BEAUTIFUL NONSENSE, THE(1935, Brit.); TURN OF THE TIDE(1935, Brit.); AS YOU LIKE IT(1936, Brit.); HEARTS OF HUMANITY(1936, Brit.); DREAMING LIPS(1937, Brit.); LITTLE MISS SOMEBODY(1937, Brit.); MAN WHO MADE DIAMONDS, THE(1937, Brit.); UNDER THE RED ROBE(1937, Brit.); BREAKERS AHEAD(1938, Brit.); PASTOR HALL(1940, Brit.)
Silents
NOBODY'S CHILD(1919, Brit.); OWD BOB(1924, Brit.); ONE COLUMBO NIGHT(1926, Brit.); ONLY WAY, THE(1926, Brit.); THOU FOOL(1926, Brit.); FAKE, THE(1927, Brit.); SOMEHOW GOOD(1927, Brit.)
Misc. Silents
GOD BLESS OUR RED, WHITE AND BLUE(1918, Brit.); DAMAGED GOODS(1919, Brit.); WILL, THE(1921, Brit.)

J. Francis White
THUNDER IN CAROLINA(1960), p

Jack White
52ND STREET(1937); CAMPUS RHYTHM(1943), w; TRIAL OF BILLY JACK, THE(1974); HOT STUFF(1979)

Jack Cameron White
NORTH AVENUE IRREGULARS, THE(1979)

Jackie White
BEAUTY JUNGLE, THE(1966, Brit.)

Jacqueline White
REUNION IN FRANCE(1942); AIR RAID WARDENS(1943); GUY NAMED JOE, A(1943); SONG OF RUSSIA(1943); SWING SHIFT MAISIE(1943); THREE HEARTS FOR JULIA(1943); THIRTY SECONDS OVER TOKYO(1944); HARVEY GIRLS, THE(1946); SHOW-OFF, THE(1946); BANJO(1947); CROSSFIRE(1947); NIGHT SONG(1947); SEVEN KEYS TO BALDPATE(1947); MYSTERY IN MEXICO(1948); RETURN OF THE BADMEN(1948); RIDERS OF THE RANGE(1949); CAPTURE, THE(1950); NARROW MARGIN, THE(1952)

James White
SEVEN AGAINST THE SUN(1968, South Africa); THING WITH TWO HEADS, THE(1972), makeup; SAFARI 3000(1982)

James Gordon White
GLORY STOMPERS, THE(1967), w; BORN WILD(1968), w; HELLCATS, THE(1968), w; MINI-SKIRT MOB, THE(1968), w; DEVIL'S 8, THE(1969), w; FREE GRASS(1969), w; HELL'S BELLES(1969), w; INCREDIBLE TWO-HEADED TRANSPLANT, THE(1971), w; THING WITH TWO HEADS, THE(1972), w; BIG FOOT(1973), w; 10 VIOLENT WOMEN(1982), w

James S. White
LADY SINGS THE BLUES(1972), p

Jan White
HUNGRY WIVES(1973)

Jane White
TOWN LIKE ALICE, A(1958, Brit.); CARRY ON TEACHER(1962, Brit.); KLUTE(1971)

Janu White
MANTIS IN LACE(1968)
Jaqueline White
PILOT NO. 5(1943)
Jason White
INTERNATIONAL VELVET(1978, Brit.); DRAGONSLAYER(1981)
Jeannine White
HOW TO STUFF A WILD BIKINI(1965)
Jeffrey White
INDEPENDENCE DAY(1976), art d; BOSS'S SON, THE(1978), p
Jennifer White
MURDER GAME, THE(1966, Brit.)
1984
WILD LIFE, THE(1984)
Jenny White
L-SHAPED ROOM, THE(1962, Brit.); NIGHT TRAIN TO PARIS(1964, Brit.); ASSIGNMENT K(1968, Brit.); IF IT'S TUESDAY, THIS MUST BE BELGIUM(1969)
Jeremy White
I'M ALL RIGHT, JACK(1959, Brit.); LADY IS A SQUARE, THE(1959, Brit.); MORE DEADLY THAN THE MALE(1961, Brit.)
Jess White
NOTORIOUS CLEOPATRA, THE(1970)
Jesse White
GENTLEMAN'S AGREEMENT(1947); KISS OF DEATH(1947); TEXAS, BROOKLYN AND HEAVEN(1948); HARVEY(1950); BEDTIME FOR BONZO(1951); CALLAWAY WENT THATAWAY(1951); FRANCIS GOES TO THE RACES(1951); KATIE DID IT(1951); DEATH OF A SALESMAN(1952); GIRL IN WHITE, THE(1952); MILLION DOLLAR MERMAID(1952); CHAMP FOR A DAY(1953); FOREVER FEMALE(1953); GUNSMOKE(1953); HELL'S HALF ACRE(1954); WITNESS TO MURDER(1954); GIRL RUSH, THE(1955); NOT AS A STRANGER(1955); BACK FROM ETERNITY(1956); BAD SEED, THE(1956); COME ON, THE(1956); HE LAUGHED LAST(1956); DESIGNING WOMAN(1957); GOD IS MY PARTNER(1957); JOHNNY TROUBLE(1957); COUNTRY MUSIC HOLIDAY(1958); MARJORIE MORNINGSTAR(1958); BIG NIGHT, THE(1960); RISE AND FALL OF LEGS DIAMOND, THE(1960); FEVER IN THE BLOOD, A(1961); ON THE DOUBLE(1961); RIGHT APPROACH, THE(1961); SAIL A CROOKED SHIP(1961); THREE BLONDES IN HIS LIFE(1961); TOMBOY AND THE CHAMP(1961); IT'S ONLY MONEY(1962); IT'S A MAD, MAD, MAD, MAD WORLD(1963); YELLOW CANARY, THE(1963); HOUSE IS NOT A HOME, A(1964); LOOKING FOR LOVE(1964); PAJAMA PARTY(1964); DEAR BRIGETTE(1965); GHOST IN THE INVISIBLE BIKINI(1966); RELUCTANT ASTRONAUT, THE(1967); SPIRIT IS WILLING, THE(1967); BLESS THE BEASTS AND CHILDREN(1971); BROTHERS O'TOOLE, THE(1973); RETURN TO CAMPUS(1975); LAS VEGAS LADY(1976); WON TON TON, THE DOG WHO SAVED HOLLYWOOD(1976); NEW GIRL IN TOWN(1977); CAT FROM OUTER SPACE, THE(1978)
Misc. Talkies
TOGETHERNESS(1970)
Jim White
DAY OF THE DOLPHIN, THE(1973), spec eff
Jimi White
SPLIT IMAGE(1982), makeup
Jimmy White
RUGGED O'RIORDANS, THE(1949, Aus.)
Joan White
MELODY MAKER, THE(1933, Brit.); LUCKY LOSER(1934, Brit.); ADMIRALS ALL(1935, Brit.); AS YOU LIKE IT(1936, Brit.); SECOND BUREAU(1937, Brit.); WAKE UP FAMOUS(1937, Brit.); YOU'RE THE DOCTOR(1938, Brit.); GIRL MUST LIVE, A(1941, Brit.); WEAKER SEX, THE(1949, Brit.)
Joey White
WOMAN'S TEMPTATION, A(1959, Brit.)
John White
TENTACLES(1977, Ital.)
1984
REAL LIFE(1984, Brit.), prod d
John D. White
THREES, MENAGE A TROIS(1968)
John Manchip White
CAMP ON BLOOD ISLAND, THE(1958, Brit.); EXORCISM AT MIDNIGHT(1966, Brit. revised 1973, U.S.), p,d&w
Johnny White
UNDERTAKER AND HIS PALS, THE(1966), m
Johnstone White
GET THAT MAN(1935); ANYTHING FOR A THRILL(1937); TOUGH TO HANDLE(1937); DESPERATE CARGO(1941); SHED NO TEARS(1948); KNOCK ON WOOD(1954); YOU'RE NEVER TOO YOUNG(1955); PARDNERS(1956); SCARLET HOUR, THE(1956); SERENADE(1956); HOME BEFORE DARK(1958)
Jon Manchip White
RACE FOR LIFE, A(1955, Brit.), w; MYSTERY SUBMARINE(1963, Brit.), w; CRACK IN THE WORLD(1965), w
Jonathan White
SUNDAY IN THE COUNTRY(1975, Can.); BREAKING POINT(1976)
Jonelle White
BUSTIN' LOOSE(1981)
Joni Ruth White
POLYESTER(1981)
Josh White
CRIMSON CANARY(1945); WALKING HILLS, THE(1949)
Jules White
SIDEWALKS OF NEW YORK(1931), d
Julia White
FLEDGLINGS(1965, Brit)
Kathleen White
GIRL ON APPROVAL(1962, Brit.), w; GOING BERSERK(1983)
Ken White
UP THE ACADEMY(1980)
Kenneth White
ONE NIGHT STAND(1976, Fr.), w
Kitty White
WALL OF NOISE(1963)

Kiwi White
GALLIPOLI(1981, Aus.)
Larry White
ESCAPE TO BURMA(1955), animalt; BUSTER KEATON STORY, THE(1957)
Larry Charles White
UNCOMMON VALOR(1983)
1984
ICE PIRATES, THE(1984)
Lawrence White
Misc. Silents
FRIEND WILSON'S DAUGHTER(1915)
Lee "Lasses" White
ROVIN' TUMBLEWEEDS(1939); DANCE, GIRL, DANCE(1940); GRANDPA GOES TO TOWN(1940); OKLAHOMA RENEGADES(1940); BANDIT TRAIL, THE(1941); CYCLONE ON HORSEBACK(1941); DUDE COWBOY(1941); LAND OF THE OPEN RANGE(1941); ROUNDUP, THE(1941); SCATTERGOOD BAINES(1941); SCATTERGOOD PULLS THE STRINGS(1941); SERGEANT YORK(1941); SIX GUN GOLD(1941); THUNDERING HOOFS(1941); CINDERELLA SWINGS IT(1942); COME ON DANGER(1942); RIDING THE WIND(1942); TALK OF THE TOWN(1942); MUG TOWN(1943); OUTLAW, THE(1943); WHEN STRANGERS MARRY(1944); DILLINGER(1945); RIDERS OF THE DAWN(1945); FEAR(1946); SONG OF THE SIERRAS(1946); SUSPENSE(1946); WEST OF THE ALAMO(1946); CHEYENNE(1947); GINGER(1947); LOUISIANA(1947); MAGIC TOWN(1947); RAINBOW OVER THE ROCKIES(1947); SIX GUN SERENADE(1947); SONG OF THE WASTELAND(1947); WISTFUL WIDOW OF WAGON GAP, THE(1947); DUDE GOES WEST, THE(1948); INDIAN AGENT(1948); MYSTERY OF THE GOLDEN EYE, THE(1948); VALIANT HOMBRE, THE(1948); LAWTON STORY, THE(1949); MISSISSIPPI RHYTHM(1949); RED ROCK OUTLAW(1950); TEXAN MEETS CALAMITY JANE, THE(1950)
Misc. Talkies
SONG OF THE RANGE(1944); LONESOME TRAIL(1945); SADDLE SERENADE(1945); SPRINGTIME IN TEXAS(1945); MOON OVER MONTANA(1946); TRAIL TO MEXICO(1946)
Lee White
TOO MANY HUSBANDS(1940); UNKNOWN GUEST, THE(1943); ALASKA(1944); MINSTREL MAN(1944); IN OLD NEW MEXICO(1945)
Leo White
ROARING RANCH(1930); WAY FOR A SAILOR(1930); ALONG CAME YOUTH(1931); JEWEL ROBBERY(1932); RASPUTIN AND THE EMPRESS(1932); DEVIL'S BROTHER, THE(1933); KENNEL MURDER CASE, THE(1933); KEYHOLE, THE(1933); MIDNIGHT CLUB(1933); ONLY YESTERDAY(1933); HERE COMES THE NAVY(1934); HOUSEWIFE(1934); KANSAS CITY PRINCESS(1934); ONE NIGHT OF LOVE(1934); RIP TIDE(1934); THIN MAN, THE(1934); DR. SOCRATES(1935); FRONT PAGE WOMAN(1935); NIGHT AT THE OPERA, A(1935); SHE GETS HER MAN(1935); STRANDED(1935); I MARRIED A DOCTOR(1936); STAGE STRUCK(1936); ESPIONAGE(1937); SHE LOVED A FIREMAN(1937); TOVARICH(1937); CODE OF THE SECRET SERVICE(1939); MONEY AND THE WOMAN(1940); TUGBOAT ANNIE SAILS AGAIN(1940); FOUR JACKS AND A JILL(1941); MEET JOHN DOE(1941); SHE COULDN'T SAY NO(1941); MYSTERIOUS DOCTOR, THE(1943); SOMEONE TO REMEMBER(1943); ARSENIC AND OLD LACE(1944); SPANISH MAIN, THE(1945); STOLEN LIFE, A(1946); SILVER RIVER(1948); SMART GIRLS DON'T TALK(1948); NIGHT UNTO NIGHT(1949)
Silents
BRAZEN BEAUTY(1918); LOVE SWINDLE(1918); DEVIL'S PASSKEY, THE(1920); KEEPING UP WITH LIZZIE(1921); RAGE OF PARIS, THE(1921); ROOKIE'S RETURN, THE(1921); BLOOD AND SAND(1922); IN SEARCH OF A THRILL(1923); WHY WORRY(1923); GOLDFISH, THE(1924); BEN-HUR(1925); ONE YEAR TO LIVE(1925); FAR CRY, THE(1926); BOWERY CINDERELLA(1927); LADYBIRD, THE(1927); BREED OF THE SUNSETS(1928); MANHATTAN KNIGHTS(1928); CAMPUS KNIGHTS(1929)
Misc. Silents
ONE WONDERFUL NIGHT(1914); CARMEN(1916); DESPERATE MOMENT, A(1926); TRUTHFUL SEX, THE(1926); BORN TO THE SADDLE(1929)
Leon White
VIVA VILLA!(1934)
Leonard White
DARK MAN, THE(1951, Brit.); STRANGER IN BETWEEN, THE(1952, Brit.); LARGE ROPE, THE(1953, Brit.); MARTIN LUTHER(1953); RIVER BEAT(1954); PASSAGE HOME(1955, Brit.); AT THE STROKE OF NINE(1957, Brit.); TEARS FOR SIMON(1957, Brit.); VIOLENT MOMENT(1966, Brit.)
Les White
STREET OF DARKNESS(1958), ph; DEADLY AFFAIR, THE(1967, Brit.)
Leslie T. White
PAID TO DANCE(1937), w; BEHIND PRISON GATES(1939), w; MAN THEY COULD NOT HANG, THE(1939), w; DANGEROUS LADY(1941), w; STRANGE ALIBI(1941), w; NORTHERN PURSUIT(1943), w; TWO-MAN SUBMARINE(1944), w; UNWRITTEN CODE, THE(1944), w; VICE SQUAD(1953), w; AMERICANO, THE(1955), w
Leslie Turner White
WOLF OF NEW YORK(1940), w; TRAFFIC IN CRIME(1946), w
Lester White
YELLOW JACK(1938), ph; PRIZEFIGHTER AND THE LADY, THE(1933), ph; LAUGHING BOY(1934), ph; WICKED WOMAN, A(1934), ph; CALM YOURSELF(1935), ph; MURDER MAN(1935), ph; SOCIETY DOCTOR(1935), ph; TIMES SQUARE LADY(1935), ph; ABSOLUTE QUIET(1936), ph; EXCLUSIVE STORY(1936), ph; LONGEST NIGHT, THE(1936), ph; SPEED(1936), ph; SWORN ENEMY(1936), ph; WE WENT TO COLLEGE(1936), ph; BAD GUY(1937), ph; FAMILY AFFAIR, A(1937), ph; WOMEN MEN MARRY, THE(1937), ph; JUDGE HARDY'S CHILDREN(1938), ph; LOVE FINDS ANDY HARDY(1938), ph; OUT WEST WITH THE HARDYS(1938), ph; YOU'RE ONLY YOUNG ONCE(1938), ph; ANDY HARDY GETS SPRING FEVER(1939), ph; BURN 'EM UP O'CONNER(1939), ph; HENRY GOES ARIZONA(1939), ph; JUDGE HARDY AND SON(1939), ph; BEYOND TOMORROW(1940), ph; ANDY HARDY'S PRIVATE SECRETARY(1941), ph; BABES ON BROADWAY(1941), ph; LIFE BEGINS FOR ANDY HARDY(1941), ph; COURTSHIP OF ANDY HARDY, THE(1942), ph; INVISIBLE AGENT(1942), ph; MISS ANNIE ROONEY(1942), ph; SHERLOCK HOLMES AND THE SECRET WEAPON(1942), ph; YANK ON THE BURMA ROAD, A(1942), ph; SHERLOCK HOLMES IN WASHINGTON(1943), ph; WHISTLING IN BROOKLYN(1943), ph; WHITE SAVAGE(1943), ph; ANDY HARDY'S BLONDE TROUBLE(1944), ph; BLONDE FEVER(1944), ph; LOST IN A HAREM(1944), ph; HIDDEN EYE, THE(1945), ph; LITTLE MISTER JIM(1946), ph; SPIRIT OF WEST POINT, THE(1947), ph; FULLER BRUSH MAN(1948), ph; JUNGLE JIM(1948), ph; DARING CABALLERO, THE(1949), ph; FIREBALL, THE(1950), ph;

GOOD HUMOR MAN, THE(1950), ph; HE'S A COCKEYED WONDER(1950), ph; GASOLINE ALLEY(1951), ph; HURRICANE ISLAND(1951), ph; WHEN THE RED-SKINS RODE(1951), ph; HAREM GIRL(1952), ph; FORTY-NINTH MAN, THE(1953), ph; WHITE LIGHTNING(1953), ph; LONE GUN, THE(1954), ph; OVERLAND PACIF-IC(1954), ph; FIVE AGAINST THE HOUSE(1955), ph; TOP GUN(1955), ph; WYOM-ING RENEGADES(1955), ph; MONSTER THAT CHALLENGED THE WORLD, THE(1957), ph

Lester A. White
IF YOU KNEW SUSIE(1948), w

Lester H. White
FORT TI(1953), ph; GUN FURY(1953), ph; SKY COMMANDO(1953), ph; STRAN-GER WORE A GUN, THE(1953), ph; DRUMS OF TAHITI(1954), ph; JESSE JAMES VERSUS THE DALTONS(1954), ph; MASSACRE CANYON(1954), ph; OUTLAW STALLION, THE(1954), ph; PUSHOVER(1954), ph; WOMEN'S PRISON(1955), ph

Lionel White
KILLING, THE(1956), w; BIG CAPER, THE(1957), w; MONEY TRAP, THE(1966), w; PIERROT LE FOU(1968, Fr./Ital.), w; NIGHT OF THE FOLLOWING DAY, THE(1969, Brit.), w

Liz White
STOP THE WORLD–I WANT TO GET OFF(1966, Brit.)

Lloyd White
SHOOT(1976, Can.); SILVER STREAK(1976)

Loretta White
GROUP, THE(1966)

Louis J. White
IN OLD CHICAGO(1938), spec eff

Lucas White
HAIL, HERO!(1969)

Lynn White
WHAT'S NEXT?(1975, Brit.)

M. White
STORY OF ADELE H., THE(1975, Fr.)

Madge White
TWELVE GOOD MEN(1936, Brit.); PERFECT CRIME, THE(1937, Brit.)
Silents
PLACE OF HONOUR, THE(1921, Brit.); ELEVENTH HOUR, THE(1922, Brit.)
Misc. Silents
BARS OF IRON(1920, Brit.)

Majelle White
BLONDIE FOR VICTORY(1942)

Malcolm White
MOUNTED STRANGER, THE(1930)

Marie White
Misc. Silents
FAIR CHEAT, THE(1923)

Marilyn White
FUNNY FACE(1957); HOW SWEET IT IS(1968)

Marjorie White
SUNNY SIDE UP(1929); FOX MOVIETONE FOLLIES OF 1930(1930); GOLDEN CALF, THE(1930); HAPPY DAYS(1930); JUST IMAGINE(1930); OH, FOR A MAN!(1930); BLACK CAMEL, THE(1931); BROADMINDED(1931); CHARLIE CHAN CARRIES ON(1931); POSSESSED(1931); WOMEN OF ALL NATIONS(1931); DI-PLOMANIACS(1933); HER BODYGUARD(1933)

Matt White
CHRISTINE KEELER AFFAIR, THE(1964, Brit.), w

Maurice White
THAT'S THE WAY OF THE WORLD(1975), a, m

May White
Silents
KID, THE(1921)

Meadows White
SHADOW OF THE PAST(1950, Brit.); TWENTY QUESTIONS MURDER MYSTERY, THE(1950, Brit.); GHOST SHIP(1953, Brit.); BOY AND THE BRIDGE, THE(1959, Brit.)

Mela White
WARNING TO WANTONS, A(1949, Brit.); MAN WHO FINALLY DIED, THE(1967, Brit.)

Melville White
NELL GWYN(1935, Brit.), ed

Meredith White
BELOVED BRAT(1938)

Merrill White
LOVE PARADE, THE(1929), ed; STUDIO MURDER MYSTERY, THE(1929), ed; MONTE CARLO(1930), ed; PLAYBOY OF PARIS(1930), ed; VAGABOND KING, THE(1930), ed; SMILING LIEUTENANT, THE(1931), ed; PEG OF OLD DRURY(1936, Brit.), ed; FROG, THE(1937, Brit.), ed; ROMANCE AND RICHES(1937, Brit.), ed; TALK OF THE DEVIL(1937, Brit.), ed; RED HOUSE, THE(1947), ed; TARZAN AND THE HUNTRESS(1947), ed; TARZAN AND THE MERMAIDS(1948), ed; TARZAN'S MAGIC FOUNTAIN(1949), ed; BOY FROM INDIANA(1950), ed; GIRL ON THE BRIDGE, THE(1951), ed; LADY IN THE IRON MASK(1952), ed; RED SNOW(1952), ed; TANGA-TIKA(1953), ed; THY NEIGHBOR'S WIFE(1953), ed; CARNIVAL STO-RY(1954), ed; DESPERADOES ARE IN TOWN, THE(1956), ed; MAN OR GUN(1958), ed

Merrill G. White
STRANGE FASCINATION(1952), ed; ONE GIRL'S CONFESSION(1953), ed; BRAVE ONE, THE(1956), w, ed; GHOST DIVER(1957), d&w, ed; RESTLESS BREED, THE(1957), ed; FLY, THE(1958), ed; CRIME AND PUNISHMENT, U.S.A.(1959), ed

Merritt White
FIREBIRD 2015 AD(1981), p

Michael White
IPCRESS FILE, THE(1965, Brit.), set d; FUNERAL IN BERLIN(1966, Brit.), set d; ROCKY HORROR PICTURE SHOW, THE(1975, Brit.), p; AT THE EARTH'S CO-RE(1976, Brit.), set d; PRIVATES ON PARADE(1982), art d; NEVER SAY NEVER AGAIN(1983), art d
1984
BODY DOUBLE(1984); PRIVATES ON PARADE(1984, Brit.), art d

Miles White
GREATEST SHOW ON EARTH, THE(1952), cos; AROUND THE WORLD IN 80 DAYS(1956), cos

Muriel White
TAKE A POWDER(1953, Brit.)

Myrna White
FUNNY THING HAPPENED ON THE WAY TO THE FORUM, A(1966); LOST IN THE STARS(1974)

Nathaniel White
TIME OF THE HEATHEN(1962)

Nelia Gardner White
SENTIMENTAL JOURNEY(1946), w; GIFT OF LOVE, THE(1958), w

Nita White
Silents
LOVE AFLAME(1917)

Noni White
MAN WHO LOVED WOMEN, THE(1983)
1984
MASS APPEAL(1984); WOMAN IN RED, THE(1984)

Olive White
OF HUMAN BONDAGE(1964, Brit.)
Silents
TALE OF TWO CITIES, A(1917)

Onna White
MUSIC MAN, THE(1962), ch; BYE BYE BIRDIE(1963), ch; OLIVER!(1968, Brit.), ch; GREAT WALTZ, THE(1972), ch; 1776(1972), ch; MAME(1974), ch; PETE'S DRA-GON(1977), ch

Ouida White
9/30/55(1977)

Pat White
VARIETY GIRL(1947)

Patricia White
BEAST WITH FIVE FINGERS, THE(1946); CRY WOLF(1947); WHEN A GIRL'S BEAUTIFUL(1947); MANHATTAN ANGEL(1948); TRAPPED BY BOSTON BLACK-IE(1948); RIDERS OF THE WHISTLING PINES(1949); UNDERCOVER MAN, THE(1949); TATTOOED STRANGER, THE(1950)
Misc. Talkies
ROSE OF SANTA ROSA(1947); BLAZING ACROSS THE PECOS(1948); WRECK OF THE HESPERUS(1948)

Patricia White [Barry]
VARIETY GIRL(1947)

Patrick White
NIGHT OF THE PROWLER, THE(1979, Aus.), w

Paul White
ADVENTURE'S END(1937); BOY SLAVES(1938); COMING OF AGE(1938, Brit.), w; MY OLD KENTUCKY HOME(1938); SING YOU SINNERS(1938); CAROLINA MOON(1940); GIVE US WINGS(1940); LADY FOR A NIGHT(1941); SCATTERGOOD BAINES(1941); SCATTERGOOD MEETS BROADWAY(1941); SCATTERGOOD PULLS THE STRINGS(1941); SCATTERGOOD RIDES HIGH(1942); TAKE MY LIFE(1942); ISLAND WOMEN(1958); MASTER SPY(1964, Brit.), w

Paula White
HILDUR AND THE MAGICIAN(1969)

Pearl White
Silents
KING'S GAME, THE(1916); BEYOND PRICE(1921); KNOW YOUR MEN(1921); ANY WIFE(1922); WITHOUT FEAR(1922)
Misc. Silents
HAZEL KIRKE(1916); MAYBLOSSOM(1917); THIEF, THE(1920); TIGER'S CUB(1920); WHITE MOLL, THE(1920); MOUNTAIN WOMAN, THE(1921); VIRGIN PARADISE, A(1921); BROADWAY PEACOCK, THE(1922); TERREUR(1924, Fr.)

Peter White
BOYS IN THE BAND, THE(1970); MUSIC LOVERS, THE(1971, Brit.); PURSUIT OF HAPPINESS, THE(1971); BLADE(1973)

Philip White
LOCAL BAD MAN(1932), w

Philip Graham White
GAY BUCKAROO, THE(1932), w; SPIRIT OF THE WEST(1932), w; TRAILING TROUBLE(1937), w

Priscilla White
ROAD TO ZANZIBAR(1941)

Pudgie White
PERSONALITY KID, THE(1934)

Pudgy White
I SELL ANYTHING(1934)

Puggy White
LITTLE MISS MARKER(1934)

R. Meadows White
LAST ROSE OF SUMMER, THE(1937, Brit.); I SEE ICE(1938); RUN FOR YOUR MONEY, A(1950, Brit.); FIEND WITHOUT A FACE(1958)

Randy White
1984
MIKE'S MURDER(1984)

Renee White
CAREER GIRL(1944)

Richard White
HARDER THEY COME, THE(1973, Jamaica), ed

Robb White
HOUSE ON HAUNTED HILL(1958), w; MACABRE(1958), w; TINGLER, THE(1959), w; UP PERISCOPE(1959), w; THIRTEEN GHOSTS(1960), w; VIRGIN ISLAND(1960, Brit.), w; HOMICIDAL(1961), w

Robert White
MEET MISS BOBBY SOCKS(1944); CURSE OF THE FLY(1965, Brit.), ed

Robert White
Misc. Talkies
KING MONSTER(1977)

Roberta White
Misc. Talkies
CONVENTION GIRLS(1978)

Robertson White
FOOTLOOSE HEIRESS, THE(1937), w; ONCE A DOCTOR(1937), w; WESTLAND CASE, THE(1937), w; HE COULDN'T SAY NO(1938), w; LADY IN THE MOR-GUE(1938), w; MY BILL(1938), w; MYSTERY HOUSE(1938), w; PATIENT IN ROOM 18, THE(1938), w; CHARLIE MC CARTHY, DETECTIVE(1939), w; WITNESS

VANISHES, THE(1939), w; CHARLIE CHAN'S MURDER CRUISE(1940), w; DICK TRACY MEETS GRUESOME(1947), w; FLIPPER(1963); GENTLE GIANT(1967); HOW DO I LOVE THEE?(1970)

Robynne White
SMITHEREENS(1982)

Roland White
FARMER'S OTHER DAUGHTER, THE(1965)

Roy White
PREMONITION, THE(1976)

Ruth White
EDGE OF THE CITY(1957); NUN'S STORY, THE(1959); TO KILL A MOCKINGBIRD(1962); BABY, THE RAIN MUST FALL(1965); RAGE TO LIVE, A(1965); CAST A GIANT SHADOW(1966); TIGER MAKES OUT, THE(1967); UP THE DOWN STAIRCASE(1967); CHARLY(1968); HANG 'EM HIGH(1968); LOVELY WAY TO DIE, A(1968); NO WAY TO TREAT A LADY(1968); MIDNIGHT COWBOY(1969); REIVERS, THE(1969); PURSUIT OF HAPPINESS, THE(1971)

Sam White
OFFICER AND THE LADY, THE(1941), d; I LIVE ON DANGER(1942), d; SPIRIT OF STANFORD, THE(1942), p; UNDERGROUND AGENT(1942), p; AFTER MIDNIGHT WITH BOSTON BLACKIE(1943), p; REVEILLE WITH BEVERLY(1943), p; SWING OUT THE BLUES(1943), p; GIRL IN THE CASE(1944), p; RETURN OF THE VAMPIRE, THE(1944), p; UNWRITTEN CODE, THE(1944), p; PEOPLE ARE FUNNY(1945), p&d; TAHITI NIGHTS(1945), p

Sammy White
CAIN AND MABEL(1936); SHOW BOAT(1936); HIT PARADE, THE(1937); SWING YOUR LADY(1938); 711 OCEAN DRIVE(1950); BAD AND THE BEAUTIFUL, THE(1952); HALF-BREED, THE(1952); PAT AND MIKE(1952); SOUND OFF(1952); REMAINS TO BE SEEN(1953); ABOUT MRS. LESLIE(1954); LIVING IT UP(1954); SOMEBODY UP THERE LIKES ME(1956); HELEN MORGAN STORY, THE(1959)

Sandra White
HOLLYWOOD OR BUST(1956); SOLID GOLD CADILLAC, THE(1956)

Sandy White
WHILE THE CITY SLEEPS(1956)

Sanford White
MANTIS IN LACE(1968), p, w

Schuyler White
Misc. Silents
FOR YOU MY BOY(1923)

Scott White
DOCTOR, YOU'VE GOT TO BE KIDDING(1967)

Sheila White
COP-OUT(1967, Brit.); HERE WE GO ROUND THE MULBERRY BUSH(1968, Brit.); MRS. BROWN, YOU'VE GOT A LOVELY DAUGHTER(1968, Brit.); OLIVER!(1968, Brit.); GOIN' DOWN THE ROAD(1970, Can.); VILLAIN(1971, Brit.); CONFESSIONS OF A WINDOW CLEANER(1974, Brit.); ALFIE DARLING(1975, Brit.); CONFESSIONS OF A POP PERFORMER(1975, Brit.); CONFESSIONS FROM A HOLIDAY CAMP(1977, Brit.); UNIDENTIFIED FLYING ODDBALL, THE(1979, Brit.); SILVER DREAM RACER(1982, Brit.)

Shirley White
REUNION IN RENO(1951), w; TARZAN'S SAVAGE FURY(1952), w

Slappy White
MAN FROM O.R.G.Y., THE(1970); AMAZING GRACE(1974)

Stanley White
BLESS 'EM ALL(1949, Brit.)

Stephen White
Misc. Talkies
SATAN'S CHILDREN(1975)

Steve White
JUST FOR THE HELL OF IT(1968); SHE-DEVILS ON WHEELS(1968)
Misc. Talkies
JUST FOR THE HELL OF IT(1968)

Stewart Edward White
PART TIME WIFE(1930), w; UNDER A TEXAS MOON(1930), w; MYSTERY RANCH(1932), w; WILD GEESE CALLING(1941), w
Silents
CALL OF THE NORTH, THE(1914), w; KILLER, THE(1921), w

T.H. White
SWORD IN THE STONE, THE(1963), w; CAMELOT(1967), w

Ted White
RIO BRAVO(1959); CAT BALLOU(1965); SMOKY(1966); POINT BLANK(1967); CUTTER AND BONE(1981); GOING APE!(1981); LEGEND OF THE LONE RANGER, THE(1981); COMEBACK TRAIL, THE(1982), stunts; TRON(1982)
1984
AGAINST ALL ODDS(1984); ROMANCING THE STONE(1984); STARMAN(1984); WILD LIFE, THE(1984)

Thelma White
MOON'S OUR HOME, THE(1936); REEFER MADNESS(1936); WANTED BY THE POLICE(1938); MAN'S WORLD, A(1942); SPY TRAIN(1943); BOWERY CHAMPS(1944); MARY LOU(1948)
Misc. Talkies
NEVER TOO LATE(1935)

Theodore White
MOUNTAIN ROAD, THE(1960), w

Thomas White
Silents
DOWN TO THE SEA IN SHIPS(1923)

Timothy White
1984
STRIKEBOUND(1984, Aus.), p

Tom White
SEA FURY(1929), p
Misc. Talkies
WHO'S CRAZY(1965), d

Tony Joe White
CATCH MY SOUL(1974), a, m

Valentine White
TRAPPED IN A SUBMARINE(1931, Brit.)

Valeria White
BLONDE BAIT(1956, U.S./Brit.)

Valerie White
MY LEARNED FRIEND(1943, Brit.); HALF-WAY HOUSE, THE(1945, Brit.); HUE AND CRY(1950, Brit.); HOME AND AWAY(1956, Brit.); MISSILE FROM HELL(1960, Brit.); TRAVELS WITH MY AUNT(1972, Brit.)

Vera White
Silents
IS YOUR DAUGHTER SAFE?(1927)

Victoria White
Silents
HEART OF MARYLAND, THE(1921)

W. L. White
LOST BOUNDARIES(1949), w

W.G. White
SON OF KONG(1933), spec eff

Walter White, Jr.
NOBODY'S CHILDREN(1940), a, w; STRANGE HOLIDAY(1945)

Ward White
PIRANHA II: THE SPAWNING(1981, Neth.)

Warren White
TARGETS(1968)

Wilbur "Hi-Fi" White
PENITENTIARY(1979)

Will White
MAGNIFICENT OBSESSION(1954); TOWARD THE UNKNOWN(1956); ZERO HOUR!(1957)

Will J. White
RUNNING WILD(1955); TIGHT SPOT(1955); LAWLESS EIGHTIES, THE(1957); HELL'S FIVE HOURS(1958); CAT BURGLAR, THE(1961); LASSIE'S GREAT ADVENTURE(1963); FLAREUP(1969); WESTWORLD(1973)

William White
SPIRIT OF ST. LOUIS, THE(1957); HOUSE OF THE BLACK DEATH(1965), p; MORITURI(1965)
Misc. Talkies
BROTHER, CRY FOR ME(1970), d
Silents
AT DEVIL'S GORGE(1923)
Misc. Silents
WESTERN YESTERDAYS(1924)

William B. White
CHARLOTTE'S WEB(1973)

William C. White
NO GREATER LOVE(1944, USSR), w

William H. White
CONVENTION GIRL(1935)

William L. White
JOURNEY FOR MARGARET(1942), w; THEY WERE EXPENDABLE(1945), w

William Patterson White
Silents
PARDON MY NERVE!(1922), w

Willie White
CHAMP, THE(1979)

Yolanda White
ALL MINE TO GIVE(1957)

Yvonne White
SPRING AFFAIR(1960); SEX AND THE SINGLE GIRL(1964)

White and Stanley
IT ALL CAME TRUE(1940)

White Cloud the Horse
SHADOW VALLEY(1947); HAWK OF POWDER RIVER, THE(1948)

"White Cloud"
CHECK YOUR GUNS(1948)

Charles White Eagle
THREE WARRIORS(1977)

White Flash the Horse
SONG OF THE GRINGO(1936); HEADIN' FOR THE RIO GRANDE(1937); MYSTERY OF THE HOODED HORSEMEN, THE(1937); RIDERS OF THE ROCKIES(1937); TEX RIDES WITH THE BOY SCOUTS(1937); TROUBLE IN TEXAS(1937); FRONTIER TOWN(1938); STARLIGHT OVER TEXAS(1938); MAN FROM TEXAS, THE(1939); RIDERS OF THE FRONTIER(1939); ROLL, WAGONS, ROLL(1939); ROLLIN' WESTWARD(1939); SONG OF THE BUCKAROO(1939); SUNDOWN ON THE PRAIRIE(1939); ARIZONA FRONTIER(1940); PALS OF THE SILVER SAGE(1940); RAINBOW OVER THE RANGE(1940); RHYTHM OF THE RIO GRANDE(1940); PIONEERS, THE(1941); RIDING THE CHEROKEE TRAIL(1941); ROLLIN' HOME TO TEXAS(1941)

Nancy White Horse
JOURNEY THROUGH ROSEBUD(1972)

Samuel White Horse
MAN CALLED HORSE, A(1970)

White King the Horse
ROMANCE RIDES THE RANGE(1936); MELODY OF THE PLAINS(1937)

White Lightnin'
ZACHARIAH(1971); WHO FEARS THE DEVIL(1972)

White Trash Band
NIGHT THE LIGHTS WENT OUT IN GEORGIA, THE(1981)

Biddie White-Lennon
ULYSSES(1967, U.S./Brit.)

C. Whitecloud
Silents
GOLD RUSH, THE(1925)

Jim Whitecloud
HOT LEAD AND COLD FEET(1978)

Daniel F. Whitecomb
Silents
SALVAGE(1921), w

Marlon Whitefield
1984
JOY OF SEX(1984)

Blackie Whiteford
CYCLONE KID(1931); CORNERED(1932); FIGHTING MARSHAL, THE(1932); MAN FROM HELL'S EDGES(1932); MAN FROM NEW MEXICO, THE(1932); MASON OF THE MOUNTED(1932); MOVIE CRAZY(1932); SCARLET BRAND(1932); CRASHING BROADWAY(1933); DEADWOOD PASS(1933); DUDE BANDIT, THE(1933); KING KONG(1933); SOMEWHERE IN SONORA(1933); DEMON FOR TROUBLE, A(1934); GUN JUSTICE(1934); WEST OF THE DIVIDE(1934); GHOST RIDER, THE(1935); END OF THE TRAIL(1936); LAST OF THE WARRENS, THE(1936); RIDING AVENGER, THE(1936); TOLL OF THE DESERT(1936); DODGE CITY TRAIL(1937); OLD WYOMING TRAIL, THE(1937); ROGUE OF THE RANGE(1937); OUTLAWS OF THE PRAIRIE(1938); OVERLAND EXPRESS, THE(1938); ROMANCE OF THE ROCKIES(1938); WEST OF SANTA FE(1938); WHERE THE BUFFALO ROAM(1938); OKLAHOMA FRONTIER(1939); TEXAS STAMPEDE(1939); THUNDERING WEST, THE(1939); BRIGHAM YOUNG–FRONTIERSMAN(1940); TEXAS STAGECOACH(1940); THUNDERING FRONTIER(1940); OUTLAWS OF THE PANHANDLE(1941); FIGHTING BILL FARGO(1942); STAGECOACH BUCKAROO(1942); ROUGH, TOUGH AND READY(1945); RIO GRANDE RAIDERS(1946); LAST ROUND-UP, THE(1947); KNOCK ON ANY DOOR(1949); QUICK ON THE TRIGGER(1949); ROPE OF SAND(1949); COW TOWN(1950); SANTA FE(1951); FAIR WIND TO JAVA(1953)
Misc. Talkies
MARK OF THE SPUR(1932)
J. P. "Blackie" Whiteford
LAST HORSEMAN, THE(1944); RIDING WEST(1944)
John B. Whiteford
MAN WHO SHOT LIBERTY VALANCE, THE(1962)
[Robert] Blackie Whiteford
PALS OF THE RANGE(1935)
John [Blackie] Whiteford
PARDON US(1931); TILLIE AND GUS(1933); TWO YEARS BEFORE THE MAST(1946)
Angela Whitehead
RELUCTANT HEROES(1951, Brit.)
Bernedette Whitehead
HONEYSUCKLE ROSE(1980)
Cal Whitehead
ONE PLUS ONE(1961, Can.)
Don Whitehead
STORY OF G.I. JOE, THE(1945); FBI STORY, THE(1959), w
E. A. Whitehead
ALPHA BETA(1973, Brit.), w
Geoffrey Whitehead
KIDNAPPED(1971, Brit.); LONG AGO, TOMORROW(1971, Brit.)
Graham Whitehead
MY BLOODY VALENTINE(1981, Can.)
Hubert Whitehead
Silents
CIRCUS MAN, THE(1914)
Jack Whitehead
39 STEPS, THE(1935, Brit.), spec eff; YOUNG AND INNOCENT(1938, Brit.), ph; HAMLET(1948, Brit.), spec eff; TARZAN'S PERIL(1951), ph; DEVIL GIRL FROM MARS(1954, Brit.), spec eff
James Whitehead
MESQUITE BUCKAROO(1939)
Misc. Talkies
RIDERS OF THE SAGE(1939)
Jo Whitehead
IF I HAD MY WAY(1940)
Joe Whitehead
GOLD MINE IN THE SKY(1938); LAW OF THE TEXAN(1938); SHINE ON, HARVEST MOON(1938); BLACKMAIL(1939); EDISON, THE MAN(1940); MY LITTLE CHICKADEE(1940); THIRD FINGER, LEFT HAND(1940); YOU'RE NOT SO TOUGH(1940); STICK TO YOUR GUNS(1941); JOHNNY EAGER(1942); MEN OF SAN QUENTIN(1942); JADE MASK, THE(1945); CENTENNIAL SUMMER(1946); LADY LUCK(1946); I WONDER WHO'S KISSING HER NOW(1947); IRON CURTAIN, THE(1948); ALIAS NICK BEAL(1949); CHICAGO DEADLINE(1949); FOLLOW ME QUIETLY(1949); SKY DRAGON(1949); COPPER CANYON(1950)
Joseph Whitehead
BEAU GESTE(1939)
Kay Whitehead
TEXANS, THE(1938)
O.Z. Whitehead
SCOUNDREL, THE(1935); GRAPES OF WRATH(1940); MY BROTHER TALKS TO HORSES(1946); ROMANCE OF ROSY RIDGE, THE(1947); FAMILY HONEYMOON(1948); ROAD HOUSE(1948); SONG IS BORN, A(1948); MA AND PA KETTLE(1949); DALLAS(1950); COMIN' ROUND THE MOUNTAIN(1951); HOODLUM, THE(1951); JOURNEY INTO LIGHT(1951); SCARF, THE(1951); BEWARE, MY LOVELY(1952); FEUDIN' FOOLS(1952); FOR MEN ONLY(1952); SAN FRANCISCO STORY, THE(1952); WE'RE NOT MARRIED(1952); LAST HURRAH, THE(1958); RALLY 'ROUND THE FLAG, BOYS!(1958); HORSE SOLDIERS, THE(1959); CHARTROOSE CABOOSE(1960); TWO RODE TOGETHER(1961); MAN WHO SHOT LIBERTY VALANCE, THE(1962); PANIC IN YEAR ZERO!(1962); SUMMER MAGIC(1963); ULYSSES(1967, U.S./Brit.); LION IN WINTER, THE(1968, Brit.)
Omar Whitehead
Silents
HER WINNING WAY(1921)
Peter Whitehead
COLORADO PIONEERS(1945), w; BORN FREE(1966), animal t
Tom Whitehead
DAY THE FISH CAME OUT, THE(1967. Brit./Gr.)
V.O. Whitehead
Misc. Silents
DAUGHTER OF THE DON, THE(1917)
Verne Whitehead
REPORTED MISSING(1937), w
Lou Whitehill
SPLIT, THE(1968); MARLOWE(1969); WONDER WOMEN(1973, Phil.), w
Louis Whitehill
POINT BLANK(1967)

Whitehorse
WAGON MASTER, THE(1929)
Silents
LOSER'S END, THE(1924); WEST OF THE RAINBOW'S END(1926); APACHE RAIDER, THE(1928)
Misc. Silents
FLASH O'LIGHTING(1925); RANCHERS AND RASCALS(1925); SILENT SHELDON(1925); TROUBLE BUSTER, THE(1925); WIN, LOSE OR DRAW(1925); WITHOUT ORDERS(1926)
Davina Whitehouse
SLEEPING DOGS(1977, New Zealand); SOLO(1978, New Zealand/Aus.)
Misc. Talkies
NIGHT NURSE, THE(1977)
Esther Whitehouse
Silents
CALL OF THE EAST, THE(1922, Brit.), w
Rob Whitehouse
BATTLETRUCK(1982), p; SCARECROW, THE(1982, New Zealand), p; NATE AND HAYES(1983, U.S./New Zealand), p
Ronnie Whitehouse
INVASION(1965, Brit.), spec eff
Richard Whiteing
Silents
NO. 5 JOHN STREET(1921, Brit.), w
Alexander Whitelaw
LIFESPAN(1975, U.S./Brit./Neth.), d, w
Barrett Whitelaw
DANTE'S INFERNO(1935)
Billie Whitelaw
FAKE, THE(1953, Brit.); COMPANIONS IN CRIME(1954, Brit.); SLEEPING TIGER, THE(1954, Brit.); ROOM IN THE HOUSE(1955, Brit.); MIRACLE IN SOHO(1957, Brit.); SMALL HOTEL(1957, Brit.); CARVE HER NAME WITH PRIDE(1958, Brit.); BOBBIKINS(1959, Brit.); GIDEON OF SCOTLAND YARD(1959, Brit.); HELL IS A CITY(1960, Brit.); MAKE MINE MINK(1960, Brit.); MANIA(1961, Brit.); NO LOVE FOR JOHNNIE(1961, Brit.); DEVIL'S AGENT, THE(1962, Brit.); I LIKE MONEY(1962, Brit.); PAYROLL(1962, Brit.); COMEDY MAN, THE(1964); CHARLIE BUBBLES(1968, Brit.); ADDING MACHINE, THE(1969); TWISTED NERVE(1969, Brit.); LEO THE LAST(1970, Brit.); START THE REVOLUTION WITHOUT ME(1970); EAGLE IN A CAGE(1971, U.S./Yugo.); FRENZY(1972, Brit.); GUMSHOE(1972, Brit.); NIGHT WATCH(1973, Brit.); OMEN, THE(1976); LEOPARD IN THE SNOW(1979, Brit./Can.); WATER BABIES, THE(1979, Brit.); UNSUITABLE JOB FOR A WOMAN, AN(1982, Brit.)
1984
SLAYGROUND(1984, Brit.)
Misc. Talkies
BREAKOUT(1959)
David Whitelaw
ROOF, THE(1933, Brit.), w; IT'S IN THE BLOOD(1938, Brit.), w
Sandy Whitelaw
AMERICAN FRIEND, THE(1977, Ger.); BROKEN ENGLISH(1981); LIKE A TURTLE ON ITS BACK(1981, Fr.)
Willie Whitelaw
DARK CRYSTAL, THE(1982, Brit.)
Annette Whiteley
DEVIL-SHIP PIRATES, THE(1964, Brit.); GUTTER GIRLS(1964, Brit.); BLACK TORMENT, THE(1965, Brit.)
Arkie Whiteley
ROAD WARRIOR, THE(1982, Aus.)
1984
RAZORBACK(1984, Aus.)
Charles Whiteley
LOVES OF JOANNA GODDEN, THE(1947, Brit.)
Jon Whiteley
STRANGER IN BETWEEN, THE(1952, Brit.); LITTLE KIDNAPPERS, THE(1954, Brit.); MOONFLEET(1955); SPANISH GARDENER, THE(1957, Span.); WEAPON, THE(1957, Brit.)
Tom Whiteley
JOURNEY'S END(1930)
Josephine Whitell
EASY TO WED(1946); CHINATOWN AT MIDNIGHT(1949); GREATEST SHOW ON EARTH, THE(1952)
Jon Whitely
CAPETOWN AFFAIR(1967, U.S./South Afr.)
Tom Whitely
MERELY MARY ANN(1931)
Frank Whiteman
SUMMERSPELL(1983)
George Whiteman
KING KONG(1976); RAISE THE TITANIC(1980, Brit.)
George H. Whiteman
HELL BOUND(1957)
Paul Whiteman
FABULOUS DORSEYS, THE(1947); LADY FRANKENSTEIN(1971, Ital.)
Silents
BROADWAY AFTER DARK(1924)
Russ Whiteman
WITHOUT RESERVATIONS(1946); DESTINATION TOKYO(1944); MY BUDDY(1944); FOREVER YOURS(1945); ALIAS BILLY THE KID(1946); ANGEL ON MY SHOULDER(1946); NEWS HOUNDS(1947); SENATOR WAS INDISCREET, THE(1947); GAL WHO TOOK THE WEST, THE(1949); ROUGH RIDERS OF DURANGO(1951); CANYON AMBUSH(1952); WACO(1952); MARKSMAN, THE(1953); HARDER THEY FALL, THE(1956); I WAS A TEENAGE FRANKENSTEIN(1958); EXPERIMENT IN TERROR(1962); ZOTZ!(1962)
Sally Whiteman
LET THE BALLOON GO(1977, Aus.)
Thorpe Whiteman
MAN ALONE, A(1955)
Joe Whitemead
CALIFORNIA(1946)

Hugh Whitemore
ALL NEAT IN BLACK STOCKINGS(1969, Brit.), w; DECLINE AND FALL... OF A BIRD WATCHER(1969, Brit.), w; MAN AT THE TOP(1973, Brit.), w; ALL CREATURES GREAT AND SMALL(1975, Brit.), w; BLUE BIRD, THE(1976), w; STEVIE(1978, Brit.), w; RETURN OF THE SOLDIER, THE(1983, Brit.), w

Tony Whitemore
THAT SINKING FEELING(1979, Brit.)

Nils Whiten
SHAME(1968, Swed.)

Kenneth Whitener
MEDIUM COOL(1969)

Robert Whiteside
ENEMY BELOW, THE(1957); CRASH LANDING(1958); HOT ROD GANG(1958)

Walker Whiteside
Misc. Silents
MELTING POT, THE(1915); BELGIAN, THE(1917)

Robert Whitesides
DEEP SIX, THE(1958)

Greg Whitespear
RIDERS OF THE DESERT(1932); BEHOLD MY WIFE(1935); RIDE, RANGER, RIDE(1936)

Gregg Whitespear
WHITE WOMAN(1933); UNION PACIFIC(1939)

Ray Whitetree
DAVY CROCKETT, KING OF THE WILD FRONTIER(1955)

Whitey the Cat
STAGE DOOR(1937)

Alice Whitfield
PARADES(1972)

Anne Whitfield
KISS THE BLOOD OFF MY HANDS(1948); GUNFIGHTER, THE(1950); WHITE CHRISTMAS(1954); JUVENILE JUNGLE(1958); ...TICK...TICK...TICK...(1970)
1984
PRODIGAL, THE(1984)

Donna Whitfield
TORTURE DUNGEON(1970)

Gess Whitfield
NUTCRACKER(1982, Brit.)

Jordan Whitfield
CRY BABY KILLER, THE(1958); THAT FUNNY FEELING(1965)

June Whitfield
FRIENDS AND NEIGHBORS(1963, Brit.); SPY WITH A COLD NOSE, THE(1966, Brit.)
Misc. Talkies
BLESS THIS HOUSE(1972, Brit.)

Lynn Whitfield
DOCTOR DETROIT(1983)

Mitchell Whitfield
1984
FIRST TURN-ON!, THE(1984)

Norman Whitfield
CARWASH(1976), m

Raoul Whitfield
PRIVATE DETECTIVE 62(1933), w; HIGH TIDE(1947), w

Robert Whitfield
CRAZY OVER HORSES(1951); AFRICAN TREASURE(1952)

Robert "Smoki" Whitfield
THREE LITTLE GIRLS IN BLUE(1946); SAFARI DRUMS(1953)

Rosemary Whitfield
GOOD BEGINNING, THE(1953, Brit.)

Smoke Whitfield
JET PILOT(1957)

Smoki Whitfield
ANOTHER PART OF THE FOREST(1948); FAMILY HONEYMOON(1948); JUNGLE GODDESS(1948); OUT OF THE STORM(1948); BOMBA ON PANTHER ISLAND(1949); BOMBA THE JUNGLE BOY(1949); HIDEOUT(1949); TOO LATE FOR TEARS(1949); BOMBA AND THE HIDDEN CITY(1950); PEGGY(1950); RIGHT CROSS(1950); BORN YESTERDAY(1951); JOURNEY INTO LIGHT(1951); LION HUNTERS, THE(1951); SECOND WOMAN, THE(1951); BAND WAGON, THE(1953); GOLDEN IDOL, THE(1954); KILLER LEOPARD(1954); LORD OF THE JUNGLE(1955); ONE DESIRE(1955); SEVEN ANGRY MEN(1955); LOUISIANA HUSSY(1960)

Blackie Whitford
TEXAS RANGER, THE(1931)

Peter Whitford
MY BRILLIANT CAREER(1980, Aus.)
1984
CAREFUL, HE MIGHT HEAR YOU(1984, Aus.); PHAR LAP(1984, Aus.)

Chet [Chester] Whithey
Misc. Silents
DOMESTIC RELATIONS(1922), d

Whithorse
Misc. Silents
NOT BUILT FOR RUNNIN'(1924)

Barbara Whiting
JUNIOR MISS(1945); CENTENNIAL SUMMER(1946); HOME SWEET HOMICIDE(1946); CARNIVAL IN COSTA RICA(1947); CITY ACROSS THE RIVER(1949); I CAN GET IT FOR YOU WHOLESALE(1951); BEWARE, MY LOVELY(1952); RAINBOW 'ROUND MY SHOULDER(1952); DANGEROUS WHEN WET(1953); FRESH FROM PARIS(1955); PARIS FOLLIES OF 1956(1955)

Bob Whiting
LAST FLIGHT OF NOAH'S ARK, THE(1980)

Dick Whiting
365 NIGHTS IN HOLLYWOOD(1934)

Edward G. Whiting
DANGEROUS SEAS(1931, Brit.), p; COMMISSIONAIRE(1933, Brit.), p; OH, WHAT A NIGHT(1935), p; SCHWEIK'S NEW ADVENTURES(1943, Brit.), p; ADVENTURES OF JANE, THE(1949, Brit.), p, d, w

Gordon Whiting
END OF THE ROAD, THE(1954, Brit.); MAN WHO WOULDN'T TALK, THE(1958, Brit.); NAVY LARK, THE(1959, Brit.); RAILWAY CHILDREN, THE(1971, Brit.)

Jack Whiting
COLLEGE LOVERS(1930); LIFE OF THE PARTY, THE(1930); TOP SPEED(1930); MEN OF THE SKY(1931); GIVE ME A SAILOR(1938); SAILING ALONG(1938, Brit.)

John Whiting
SHIP THAT DIED OF SHAME, THE(1956, Brit.), w; GOOD COMPANIONS, THE(1957, Brit.), w; YOUNG CASSIDY(1965, U.S./Brit.), w

Leonard Whiting
ROMEO AND JULIET(1968, Brit./Ital.); ROYAL HUNT OF THE SUN, THE(1969, Brit.); SAY HELLO TO YESTERDAY(1971, Brit.)
Misc. Talkies
RACHEL'S MAN(1974)

Margaret Whiting
FRESH FROM PARIS(1955); PARIS FOLLIES OF 1956(1955); PASSWORD IS COURAGE, THE(1962, Brit.); UNDERWORLD INFORMERS(1965, Brit.); COUNTERFEIT CONSTABLE, THE(1966, Fr.); MR. QUILP(1975, Brit.); SINBAD AND THE EYE OF THE TIGER(1977, U.S./Brit.)

Mickey Whiting
GIRL IN BLACK STOCKINGS(1957)

Napoleon Whiting
GO CHASE YOURSELF(1938); RIDING HIGH(1943); CENTENNIAL SUMMER(1946); BIG CLOCK, THE(1948); MY FRIEND IRMA GOES WEST(1950); MYSTERY STREET(1950); WOMAN OF DISTINCTION, A(1950); NARROW MARGIN, THE(1952); GIANT(1956); TATTERED DRESS, THE(1957); IMITATION OF LIFE(1959); IT HAPPENED TO JANE(1959); LIVING BETWEEN TWO WORLDS(1963); WALL OF NOISE(1963); CLARENCE, THE CROSS-EYED LION(1965); SKIN GAME(1971); BLACK SAMSON(1974); FAREWELL, MY LOVELY(1975)

Ralph Whiting
Misc. Silents
GALLOPING JINX(1925)

Richard Whiting
SWEETIE(1929), m; MONTE CARLO(1930), m; ONE HOUR WITH YOU(1932), m; TAKE A CHANCE(1933), w; CALL IT LUCK(1934), m; HANDY ANDY(1934), m; 365 NIGHTS IN HOLLYWOOD(1934), m; ORDINARY PEOPLE(1980); LOVE CHILD(1982); MISSING(1982); TOOTSIE(1982); ZELIG(1983)

Richard A. Whiting
HANDLE WITH CARE(1932), m

Jack Whitingham
COUNTER BLAST(1948, Brit.), w

Annette Whitley
GIRL ON APPROVAL(1962, Brit.)

Bert Whitley
HARD, FAST, AND BEAUTIFUL(1951)

Craig Whitley
ENEMY OF WOMEN(1944)

Crane Whitley
FLYING DEUCES, THE(1939); UNDERGROUND(1941); ARABIAN NIGHTS(1942); GALLANT LADY(1942); HITLER'S CHILDREN(1942); LUCKY JORDAN(1942); MY FAVORITE BLONDE(1942); PRISON GIRL(1942); THEY RAID BY NIGHT(1942); UNDERGROUND AGENT(1942); WHO DONE IT?(1942); GENTLE GANGSTER, A(1943); GIRLS IN CHAINS(1943); MR. SKEFFINGTON(1944); OH, WHAT A NIGHT(1944); PRINCESS AND THE PIRATE, THE(1944); TILL WE MEET AGAIN(1944); TO HAVE AND HAVE NOT(1944); WING AND A PRAYER(1944); DUFFY'S TAVERN(1945); GEORGE WHITE'S SCANDALS(1945); HOLD THAT BLONDE(1945); YOU CAME ALONG(1945); CALIFORNIA(1946); NIGHT AND DAY(1946); O.S.S.(1946); RETURN OF MONTE CRISTO, THE(1946); TO EACH HIS OWN(1946); TWO YEARS BEFORE THE MAST(1946); WIFE OF MONTE CRISTO, THE(1946); BRUTE FORCE(1947); EASY COME, EASY GO(1947); FABULOUS TEXAN, THE(1947); FRAMED(1947); PURSUED(1947); SUDDENLY IT'S SPRING(1947); VARIETY GIRL(1947); WHERE THERE'S LIFE(1947); SECRET BEYOND THE DOOR, THE(1948); WALK A CROOKED MILE(1948); CRIME DOCTOR'S DIARY, THE(1949); CROOKED WAY, THE(1949); OUTPOST IN MOROCCO(1949); SAMSON AND DELILAH(1949); SHOCKPROOF(1949); SAVAGE HORDE, THE(1950); VICIOUS YEARS, THE(1950); INSURANCE INVESTIGATOR(1951); MY FAVORITE SPY(1951); RED MOUNTAIN(1951); SWORD OF MONTE CRISTO, THE(1951); MUTINY(1952); HANNAH LEE(1953)

Jack Whitley
FOLLOW THE BOYS(1944)

June Whitley
BRIGHT VICTORY(1951); CONFIDENTIAL CONNIE(1953); EASY TO LOVE(1953)

Ray Whitley
HOPALONG CASSIDY RETURNS(1936); OLD WYOMING TRAIL, THE(1937); BORDER G-MAN(1938); GUN LAW(1938); PAINTED DESERT, THE(1938); RENEGADE RANGER(1938); RACKETEERS OF THE RANGE(1939); TROUBLE IN SUNDOWN(1939); WAGON TRAIN(1940); ALONG THE RIO GRANDE(1941); BANDIT TRAIL, THE(1941); CYCLONE ON HORSEBACK(1941), a, m; DUDE COWBOY(1941); FARGO KID, THE(1941); LAND OF THE OPEN RANGE(1941); ROBBERS OF THE RANGE(1941), a, m; SIX GUN GOLD(1941); THUNDERING HOOFS(1941); COME ON DANGER(1942); RIDING THE WIND(1942); OLD TEXAS TRAIL(1944); RIDERS OF THE SANTA FE(1944); TRAIL TO GUNSIGHT(1944); HOLLYWOOD AND VINE(1945); RENEGADES OF THE RIO GRANDE(1945); WEST OF THE ALAMO(1946); OUTLAW BRAND(1948); PARTNERS OF THE SUNSET(1948); GUN LAW JUSTICE(1949); GUN RUNNER(1949); GIANT(1956)

Richard Whitley
ROCK 'N' ROLL HIGH SCHOOL(1979), w; PANDEMONIUM(1982), w

Townsend Whitley
Silents
ADVENTURES OF MR. PICKWICK, THE(1921, Brit.)

William Whitley
PURPLE HEART DIARY(1951), ph; YANK IN KOREA, A(1951), ph; VOODOO TIGER(1952), ph; YANK IN INDO-CHINA, A(1952), ph; KILLER APE(1953), ph; SAVAGE MUTINY(1953), ph; VALLEY OF THE HEADHUNTERS(1953), ph; TARZAN'S HIDDEN JUNGLE(1955), ph; BLONDE BAIT(1956, U.S./Brit.), ph; GUNSMOKE IN TUCSON(1958), ph; QUANTRILL'S RAIDERS(1958), ph; QUEEN OF OUTER SPACE(1958), ph

Wm. Whitley
BIG GUSHER, THE(1951), ph

William F. Whitley
CAT WOMEN OF THE MOON(1953), ph; THREE STOOGES IN ORBIT, THE(1962), ph

Townsend Whitling
TAKE A CHANCE(1937, Brit.); UNPUBLISHED STORY(1942, Brit.); YOUNG MR. PITT, THE(1942, Brit.)
Silents
MR. JUSTICE RAFFLES(1921, Brit.)

Albert Whitlock
WIZ, THE(1978), spec eff; SHIP OF FOOLS(1965), spec eff; LEARNING TREE, THE(1969), sp eff; TOPAZ(1969, Brit.), spec eff; SKULLDUGGERY(1970), spec eff; DIAMONDS ARE FOREVER(1971, Brit.), spec eff; ONE MORE TRAIN TO ROB(1971), spec eff; DAY OF THE DOLPHIN, THE(1973), spec eff; SHOWDOWN(1973), spec eff; STING, THE(1973), spec eff; EARTHQUAKE(1974), spec eff; FUNNY LADY(1975), spec eff; FAMILY PLOT(1976), spec eff; W.C. FIELDS AND ME(1976), spec eff; AIRPORT '77(1977), spec eff; LAST REMAKE OF BEAU GESTE, THE(1977), spec eff; MAC ARTHUR(1977), spec eff; SENTINEL, THE(1977), spec eff; I WANNA HOLD YOUR HAND(1978), spec eff; PRISONER OF ZENDA, THE(1979), spec eff; CHEECH AND CHONG'S NEXT MOVIE(1980), spec eff; ISLAND, THE(1980), spec eff; HEART-BEEPS(1981), spec eff; CAT PEOPLE(1982), spec eff; MISSING(1982), spec eff; THING, THE(1982), spec eff; PSYCHO II(1983), spec eff

Albert J. Whitlock
RAID ON ROMMEL(1971), spec eff; EXORCIST II: THE HERETIC(1977), spec eff; HIGH ANXIETY(1977), a, spec eff; HISTORY OF THE WORLD, PART 1(1981), spec eff; WICKED LADY, THE(1983, Brit.), spec eff
1984
GREYSTOKE: THE LEGEND OF TARZAN, LORD OF THE APES(1984), spec eff; LONELY GUY, THE(1984), spec eff

Earl Whitlock
Misc. Silents
CURTAIN(1920)

Frank Whitlock
Misc. Silents
FLAMES OF PASSION(1923)

Lewis Whitlock
ZOOT SUIT(1981)

Lloyd Whitlock
LEATHERNECK, THE(1929); SKINNER STEPS OUT(1929); TRESPASSER, THE(1929); COHENS AND KELLYS IN AFRICA, THE(1930); COHENS AND KELLYS IN SCOTLAND, THE(1930); ONE HYSTERICAL NIGHT(1930); SEE AMERICA THIRST(1930); YOUNG EAGLES(1930); ANYBODY'S BLONDE(1931); CHINATOWN AFTER DARK(1931); GRIEF STREET(1931); HONEYMOON LANE(1931); NECK AND NECK(1931); SCAREHEADS(1931); SHIPS OF HATE(1931); MIDNIGHT WARNING, THE(1932); SIN'S PAYDAY(1932); TANGLED DESTINIES(1932); WIDOW IN SCARLET(1932); DIAMOND TRAIL(1933); HER SPLENDID FOLLY(1933); LAUGHING AT LIFE(1933); ONE YEAR LATER(1933); REVENGE AT MONTE CARLO(1933); GREEN EYES(1934); LOST JUNGLE, THE(1934); LUCKY TEXAN, THE(1934); WEST OF THE DIVIDE(1934); LAWLESS FRONTIER, THE(1935); LIVING ON VELVET(1935); SHE MARRIED HER BOSS(1935); DARK HOUR, THE(1936); IT HAD TO HAPPEN(1936); LONE WOLF RETURNS, THE(1936); NAVY BORN(1936); NIGHT CARGO(1936); PRISONER OF SHARK ISLAND, THE(1936); RIDE, RANGER, RIDE(1936); UNDER YOUR SPELL(1936); ARSON GANG BUSTERS(1938); I AM THE LAW(1938); INTERNATIONAL CRIME(1938); MR. SMITH GOES TO WASHINGTON(1939); NOBODY'S CHILDREN(1940); THIRD FINGER, LEFT HAND(1940); MAN WHO LOST HIMSELF, THE(1941); SUNSET IN WYOMING(1941); JOAN OF OZARK(1942); MY FAVORITE BLONDE(1942); WIFE TAKES A FLYER, THE(1942); SAMSON AND DELILAH(1949)
Misc. Talkies
WIDOW IN SCARLET(1932)
Silents
COURAGE(1921); NOT GUILTY(1921); PRIVATE SCANDAL, A(1921); WHITE AND UNMARRIED(1921); FLIRT, THE(1922); KISSED(1922); NINETY AND NINE, THE(1922); WILD HONEY(1922); SLIPPY MCGEE(1923); WHEN ODDS ARE EVEN(1923); MIDNIGHT EXPRESS, THE(1924); AIR MAIL, THE(1925); ANCIENT HIGHWAY, THE(1925); NEW CHAMPION(1925); SPEED MAD(1925); PARADISE(1926); SPARROWS(1926); PRETTY CLOTHES(1927); WAR HORSE, THE(1927); MAN FROM HEADQUARTERS(1928); MICHIGAN KID, THE(1928); KID'S CLEVER, THE(1929)
Misc. Silents
EDGE OF THE LAW(1917); MAN WHO TOOK A CHANCE, THE(1917); MYSTERIOUS MR. TILLER, THE(1917); LASCA(1919); LOVE CALL, THE(1919); CUPID, THE COWPUNCHER(1920); ROUGE AND RICHES(1920); FACE OF THE WORLD(1921); FALSE KISSES(1921); LOVE SPECIAL, THE(1921); ONE MAN IN A MILLION(1921); SEE MY LAWYER(1921); THEY SHALL PAY(1921); SNOWSHOE TRAIL, THE(1922); CORDELIA THE MAGNIFICENT(1923); MAN WHO WON, THE(1923); UNMARRIED WIVES(1924); GREAT SENSATION, THE(1925); PRAIRIE PIRATE, THE(1925); WHO CARES(1925); FIGHTING BUCKAROO, THE(1926); PERIL OF THE RAIL(1926); HERO FOR A NIGHT, A(1927); ON THE STROKE OF TWELVE(1927); PERFECT SAP, THE(1927); POOR GIRLS(1927); QUEEN OF THE CHORUS(1928)

Lloyd T. Whitlock
Misc. Silents
SCRATCH MY BACK(1920)

Jill Whitlow
PORKY'S(1982)

Zetta Whitlow
PRIVATE SCHOOL(1983)

Al Whitman
Misc. Silents
DESERT LAW(1918); TONGUES OF FLAME(1919)

Alan Whitman
THAT GANG OF MINE(1940), w

Alfred Whitman
Silents
END OF THE GAME, THE(1919)
Misc. Silents
SUNLIGHT'S LAST RAID(1917); BAREE, SON OF KAZAN(1918); CAVANAUGH OF THE FOREST RANGERS(1918); GENTLEMAN'S AGREEMENT, A(1918); GIRL FROM BEYOND, THE(1918); HOME TRAIL, THE(1918); SEA FLOWER, THE(1918); WHEN MEN ARE TEMPTED(1918); WILD STRAIN, THE(1918); BEST MAN, THE(1919);

TRICK OF FATE, A(1919)

Alfred Whitman [Alfred Vosburgh]
Misc. Silents
FLAMING OMEN, THE(1917)

Amy Whitman
ENDLESS LOVE(1981)

Bill Whitman
PURSUIT OF D.B. COOPER, THE(1981)

Cam Whitman
AMERICAN GRAFFITI(1973)

David Whitman
DEVIL'S WIDOW, THE(1972, Brit.)

Ed Whitman
TOP BANANA(1954)

Ernest Whitman
GREEN PASTURES(1936); PRISONER OF SHARK ISLAND, THE(1936); WHITE HUNTER(1936); DAUGHTER OF SHANGHAI(1937); NOTHING SACRED(1937); THEY GAVE HIM A GUN(1937); GONE WITH THE WIND(1939); JESSE JAMES(1939); TELL NO TALES(1939); 6000 ENEMIES(1939); CONGO MAISIE(1940); MARYLAND(1940); RETURN OF FRANK JAMES, THE(1940); THIRD FINGER, LEFT HAND(1940); AMONG THE LIVING(1941); BUGLE SOUNDS, THE(1941); GET-AWAY, THE(1941); PITTSBURGH KID, THE(1941); ROAD TO ZANZIBAR(1941); ARABIAN NIGHTS(1942); DRUMS OF THE CONGO(1942); CABIN IN THE SKY(1943); HUMAN COMEDY, THE(1943); STORMY WEATHER(1943); ADVENTURES OF MARK TWAIN, THE(1944); IMPOSTER, THE(1944); SHE WOULDN'T SAY YES(1945); MY BROTHER TALKS TO HORSES(1946); BANJO(1947); BLONDE SAVAGE(1947); SUN SHINES BRIGHT, THE(1953)

Frank Whitman
Silents
BULLDOG COURAGE(1922)

Gayne Whitman
LUCKY BOY(1929); RENO(1930); YANKEE DON(1931); STAND UP AND CHEER(1934 80m FOX bw); POOR LITTLE RICH GIRL(1936); RETURN OF JIMMY VALENTINE, THE(1936); TEXAS RANGERS, THE(1936); STAR IS BORN, A(1937); SWEETHEARTS(1938); I TAKE THIS WOMAN(1940); LUCKY PARTNERS(1940); NEW MOON(1940); LADY EVE, THE(1941); MISBEHAVING HUSBANDS(1941); PARACHUTE BATTALION(1941); PACIFIC RENDEZVOUS(1942); PHANTOM KILLER(1942); REUNION IN FRANCE(1942); SOMEWHERE I'LL FIND YOU(1942); DESTINY(1944); MY BUDDY(1944); MY GAL LOVES MUSIC(1944); STANDING ROOM ONLY(1944); MAGNIFICENT YANKEE, THE(1950); BIG JIM McLAIN(1952); STRANGE FASCINATION(1953); DANGEROUS CROSSING(1953); DREAM WIFE(1953); ONE GIRL'S CONFESSION(1953)
Silents
HIS JAZZ BRIDE(1926); LOVE TOY, THE(1926); NIGHT CRY, THE(1926); OH, WHAT A NURSE!(1926); BACKSTAGE(1927); STOLEN PLEASURES(1927); WOMAN ON TRIAL, THE(1927); ADVENTURER, THE(1928)
Misc. Silents
PLEASURE BUYERS, THE(1925); WIFE WHO WASN'T WANTED, THE(1925); EXCLUSIVE RIGHTS(1926); HELL-BENT FOR HEAVEN(1926); WOMAN OF THE SEA, A(1926); WOMAN'S HEART, A(1926); IN THE FIRST DEGREE(1927)

J. Franklin Whitman
HONOR AMONG LOVERS(1931), art d

Kip Whitman
DEVIL'S ANGELS(1967)

Kipp Whitman
ROOMMATES, THE(1973)
Misc. Talkies
BUMMER(1973)

Paul Whitman
AIR EAGLES(1932), d

Peter Whitman
SPY WHO LOVED ME, THE(1977, Brit.); SUPERMAN II(1980); SUPERMAN III(1983); YENTL(1983)
1984
SCANDALOUS(1984)

Phil Whitman
FOURTH ALARM, THE(1930), d; MYSTERY TRAIN(1931), d, w; GIRL FROM CALGARY(1932), d; STOWAWAY(1932), d; STRANGE ADVENTURE(1932), d
Silents
GOOD-BYE KISS, THE(1928), w

Philip H. Whitman
HIS PRIVATE SECRETARY(1933), d; POLICE CALL(1933), d

Russ Whitman
THEY LIVE BY NIGHT(1949)

Russell Whitman
HER HUSBAND'S AFFAIRS(1947)

S. E. Whitman
CAPTAIN APACHE(1971, Brit.), w

Slim Whitman
JAMBOREE(1957)

Stu Whitman
CHINA DOLL(1958)

Stuart Whitman
WHEN WORLDS COLLIDE(1951); ONE MINUTE TO ZERO(1952); ALL-AMERICAN, THE(1953); VEILS OF BAGDAD, THE(1953); PASSION(1954); PRISONER OF WAR(1954); RHAPSODY(1954); SILVER LODE(1954); DIANE(1955); INTERRUPTED MELODY(1955); SEVEN MEN FROM NOW(1956); CRIME OF PASSION(1957); GIRL IN BLACK STOCKINGS(1957); HELL BOUND(1957); JOHNNY TROUBLE(1957); WAR DRUMS(1957); DARBY'S RANGERS(1958); DECKS RAN RED, THE(1958); 10 NORTH FREDERICK(1958); HOUND-DOG MAN(1959); SOUND AND THE FURY, THE(1959); THESE THOUSAND HILLS(1959); MURDER, INC.(1960); STORY OF RUTH, THE(1960); COMANCHEROS, THE(1961); FIERCEST HEART, THE(1961); FRANCIS OF ASSISI(1961); MARK, THE(1961, Brit.); CONVICTS FOUR(1962); LONGEST DAY, THE(1962); DAY AND THE HOUR, THE(1963, Fr./ Ital.); RIO CONCHOS(1964); SHOCK TREATMENT(1964); SIGNPOST TO MURDER(1964); SANDS OF THE KALAHARI(1965, Brit.); THOSE MAGNIFICENT MEN IN THEIR FLYING MACHINES; OR HOW I FLEWFROM LONDON TO PARIS IN 25 HOURS AND 11 MINUTES(1965, Brit.); AMERICAN DREAM, AN(1966); SWEET HUNTERS(1969, Panama); INVINCIBLE SIX, THE(1970, U.S./Iran); LAST ESCAPE, THE(1970, Brit.); CAPTAIN APACHE(1971, Brit.); NIGHT OF THE LEPUS(1972); CRAZY MAMA(1975);

CALL HIM MR. SHATTER(1976, Hong Kong); EATEN ALIVE(1976); LAS VEGAS LADY(1976); MEAN JOHNNY BARROWS(1976); TENDER FLESH(1976); MANIAC!(1977); RUBY(1977); STRANGE SHADOWS IN AN EMPTY ROOM(1977, Can./Ital.); WHITE BUFFALO, THE(1977); RUN FOR THE ROSES(1978); DELTA FOX(1979); CUBA CROSSING(1980); GUYANA, CULT OF THE DAMNED(1980, Mex./Span./Panama); DEMONOID(1981); MONSTER CLUB, THE(1981, Brit.); BUTTERFLY(1982)
Misc. Talkies
BLAZING MAGNUM(1976); LOST WORLD OF LIBRA, THE(1968); ONLY WAY OUT IS DEAD, THE(1970); JAMAICAN GOLD(1971); LAST GENERATION, THE(1971); OIL(1977, Ital.); THOROUGHBREDS, THE(1977); TREASURE OF THE AMAZON(1983); VULTURES IN PARADISE(1984)

Susan Whitman
SMASHING TIME(1967 Brit.); SEBASTIAN(1968, Brit.); NICE GIRL LIKE ME, A(1969, Brit.)

Thorpe Whitman
BOBBY WARE IS MISSING(1955)

Velma Whitman
Misc. Talkies
TERRIBLE ONE, THE(1915); BOOK AGENT, THE(1917); MELTING MILLIONS(1917); SOME BOY(1917)

Walt Whitman
Silents
DARK ROAD, THE(1917); LAST OF THE INGRAHAMS, THE(1917); TAR HEEL WARRIOR, THE(1917); DARLING MINE(1920); MARK OF ZORRO(1920); NEW DISCIPLE, THE(1921); THREE MUSKETEERS, THE(1921); QUESTION OF HONOR, A(1922); LONG LIVE THE KING(1923); LOVE LETTER, THE(1923)
Misc. Silents
FIREFLY OF TOUGH LUCK, THE(1917); GIRL GLORY, THE(1917); POLLY ANN(1917); PRINCESS OF THE DARK, A(1917); REGENERATES, THE(1917); CAPTAIN OF HIS SOUL(1918); DAUGHTER ANGELE(1918); LAST REBEL, THE(1918); OLD HARTWELL'S CUB(1918); PRICE OF APPLAUSE, THE(1918); WITHOUT HONOR(1918); CRY OF THE WEAK, THE(1919); JOHN PETTICOATS(1919); WHEN BEARCAT WENT DRY(1919); HOME STRETCH, THE(1921); FIRE BRIDE, THE(1922)

Walter Whitman
Misc. Silents
DESERT MAN, THE(1917); THEY'RE OFF(1917)

William Whitman
MR. CELEBRITY(1942)

Steve Whitmire
MUPPET MOVIE, THE(1979); DARK CRYSTAL, THE(1982, Brit.)
1984
MUPPETS TAKE MANHATTAN, THE(1984)

Annalee Whitmore
ANDY HARDY MEETS DEBUTANTE(1940), w

Dorothy Whitmore
SIX GUN MAN(1946)

James Whitmore
BATTLEGROUND(1949); UNDERCOVER MAN, THE(1949); ASPHALT JUNGLE, THE(1950); MRS. O'MALLEY AND MR. MALONE(1950); OUTRIDERS, THE(1950); PLEASE BELIEVE ME(1950); IT'S A BIG COUNTRY(1951); RED BADGE OF COURAGE, THE(1951); SHADOW IN THE SKY(1951); BECAUSE YOU'RE MINE(1952); ABOVE AND BEYOND(1953); ALL THE BROTHERS WERE VALIANT(1953); GIRL WHO HAD EVERYTHING, THE(1953); GREAT DIAMOND ROBBERY(1953); KISS ME KATE(1953); COMMAND, THE(1954); THEM!(1954); BATTLE FLAME(1955); LAST FRONTIER, THE(1955); MC CONNELL STORY, THE(1955); OKLAHOMA(1955); CRIME IN THE STREETS(1956); EDDY DUCHIN STORY, THE(1956); YOUNG DON'T CRY, THE(1957); DEEP SIX, THE(1958); RESTLESS YEARS, THE(1958); FACE OF FIRE(1959, U.S./Brit.); WHO WAS THAT LADY?(1960); BLACK LIKE ME(1964); CHUKA(1967); WATERHOLE NO. 3(1967); MADIGAN(1968); NOBODY'S PERFECT(1968); PLANET OF THE APES(1968); SPLIT, THE(1968); GUNS OF THE MAGNIFICENT SEVEN(1969); TORA! TORA! TORA!(1970, U.S./Jap.); CHATO'S LAND(1972); HARRAD EXPERIMENT, THE(1973); WHERE THE RED FERN GROWS(1974); GIVE'EM HELL, HARRY!(1975); SERPENT'S EGG, THE(1977, Ger./U.S.); HILLS HAVE EYES, THE(1978); FIRST DEADLY SIN, THE(1980)
Misc. Talkies
OUTRIDERS, THE(1950); BULLY(1978)

James Whitmore, Jr.
BOYS IN COMPANY C, THE(1978, U.S./Hong Kong); FORCE OF ONE, A(1979); LONG RIDERS, THE(1980); DON'T CRY, IT'S ONLY THUNDER(1982)
1984
PURPLE HEARTS(1984)

Lee Whitmore
WINTER OF OUR DREAMS(1982, Aus.), prod d

Stanford Whitmore
WAR HUNT(1962), w; YOUR CHEATIN' HEART(1964), w; GLORY BOY(1971), w; HAMMERSMITH IS OUT(1972), w; BABY BLUE MARINE(1976), w; DARK, THE(1979), w

Steve Whitmore
GREAT MUPPET CAPER, THE(1981)

Terry Whitmore
GLADIATORS, THE(1970, Swed.); GEORGIA, GEORGIA(1972)

Virginia Whitmore
TWO FOR THE SEESAW(1962)

Art Whitney
CHATTERBOX(1943)

Beverly Whitney
IRISH EYES ARE SMILING(1944); LADIES OF WASHINGTON(1944)

Bob Whitney
JOAN OF ARC(1948); OCEAN'S ELEVEN(1960); HAND OF DEATH(1962)

Brad Whitney
PLAY MISTY FOR ME(1971), cos

C.C. Whitney
HAPPY BIRTHDAY, WANDA JUNE(1971)

C.V. Whitney
SEARCHERS, THE(1956), p

CeCe Whitney
TWELVE HOURS TO KILL(1960); BULLET FOR A BADMAN(1964); NASHVILLE REBEL(1966)

Chris Whitney
INCREDIBLE MELTING MAN, THE(1978)

Claire Whitney
FREE SOUL, A(1931); IRON MAN, THE(1931); ENLIGHTEN THY DAUGHTER(1934); WAY DOWN EAST(1935); LETTER OF INTRODUCTION(1938); FORGOTTEN WOMAN, THE(1939); I STOLE A MILLION(1939); LAUGH IT OFF(1939); TOWER OF LONDON(1939); WHEN TOMORROW COMES(1939); CHIP OF THE FLYING U(1940); HOUSE OF THE SEVEN GABLES, THE(1940); IN THE NAVY(1941); MOB TOWN(1941); BEHIND THE EIGHT BALL(1942); FRISCO LILL(1942); LADY IN A JAM(1942); SABOTEUR(1942); SILVER BULLET, THE(1942); THERE'S ONE BORN EVERY MINUTE(1942); GET GOING(1943); SO'S YOUR UNCLE(1943); TENDER COMRADE(1943); WINTERTIME(1943); WOMAN OF THE TOWN, THE(1943); HAT CHECK HONEY(1944); MOON OVER LAS VEGAS(1944); MUMMY'S CURSE, THE(1944); MUMMY'S GHOST, THE(1944); WHEN STRANGERS MARRY(1944); G.I. HONEYMOON(1945); KEEP YOUR POWDER DRY(1945); SHE GETS HER MAN(1945); UNDER WESTERN SKIES(1945); SMOOTH AS SILK(1946); CHRISTMAS EVE(1947); DANGEROUS YEARS(1947); COWBOY CAVALIER(1948); LADIES OF THE CHORUS(1948); OKLAHOMA BADLANDS(1948); OLD-FASHIONED GIRL, AN(1948); ROCKY(1948); STRANGE MRS. CRANE, THE(1948); DANCING IN THE DARK(1949); FRONTIER INVESTIGATOR(1949); ROARING WESTWARD(1949)
Misc. Talkies
BLIND FOOLS(1940, Brit.); HAUNTED MINE, THE(1946)
Silents
MILLION DOLLAR ROBBERY, THE(1914); WOMAN OF MYSTERY, THE(1914); PLUNDERER, THE(1915); SONG OF HATE, THE(1915); EAST LYNNE(1916); NEW YORK PEACOCK, THE(1917); KAISER'S FINISH, THE(1918); ISLE OF CONQUEST(1919); LOVE, HONOR AND OBEY(1920); NEGLECTED WIVES(1920); FINE FEATHERS(1921); LEECH, THE(1921); GREAT GATSBY, THE(1926)
Misc. Silents
BENEATH THE CZAR(1914); DREAM WOMAN, THE(1914); LIFE'S SHOP WINDOW(1914); WALLS OF JERICHO, THE(1914); GALLEY SLAVE, THE(1915); GIRL I LEFT BEHIND ME, THE(1915); LADY AND THE BURGLAR, THE(1915); NIGGER, THE(1915); JEALOUSY(1916); RULING PASSION, THE(1916); SPIDER AND THE FLY, THE(1916); STRAIGHT WAY, THE(1916); VICTIM, THE(1916); WIFE'S SACRIFICE, A(1916); HEART AND SOUL(1917); THOU SHALT NOT STEAL(1917); WHEN FALSE TONGUES SPEAK(1917); MAN WHO STAYED AT HOME, THE(1919); YOU NEVER KNOW YOUR LUCK(1919); CHAMBER OF MYSTERY, THE(1920); COMMON LEVEL, A(1920); MOTHERS OF MEN(1920); INNOCENT LOVE(1928)

Crane Whitney
NORTH STAR, THE(1943); AFFAIRS OF SUSAN(1945); TREASURE OF THE GOLDEN CONDOR(1953)

David Whitney [Terrence Malick]
GRAVY TRAIN, THE(1974), w

Doris Whitney
CAGED(1950)

Dorothy Whitney
BREAKFAST AT TIFFANY'S(1961)

Eleanore Whitney
MILLIONS IN THE AIR(1935); BIG BROADCAST OF 1937, THE(1936); COLLEGE HOLIDAY(1936); HOLLYWOOD BOULEVARD(1936); ROSE BOWL(1936); THREE CHEERS FOR LOVE(1936); TIMOTHY'S QUEST(1936); BLONDE TROUBLE(1937); CLARENCE(1937); THRILL OF A LIFETIME(1937); TURN OFF THE MOON(1937); CAMPUS CONFESSIONS(1938)

Elizabeth Whitney
SNIPER, THE(1952)

Eve Whitney
DU BARRY WAS A LADY(1943); GIRL CRAZY(1943); GUY NAMED JOE, A(1943); THOUSANDS CHEER(1943); THREE HEARTS FOR JULIA(1943); KISMET(1944); MARRIAGE IS A PRIVATE AFFAIR(1944); MEET THE PEOPLE(1944); TWO GIRLS AND A SAILOR(1944); ZIEGFELD FOLLIES(1945); HARVEY GIRLS, THE(1946); LITTLE IODINE(1946); BLONDE SAVAGE(1947); UNFAITHFUL, THE(1947); JOAN OF ARC(1948); LET'S LIVE A LITTLE(1948); STATE OF THE UNION(1948); IT'S A GREAT FEELING(1949); MY DREAM IS YOURS(1949); BLONDE BANDIT, THE(1950); WORLD IN HIS ARMS, THE(1952)

Frederick Whitney
BED AND BREAKFAST(1930, Brit.), w

Gene Whitney
TOMORROW'S YOUTH(1935), w

Gloria Whitney
OBLIGING YOUNG LADY(1941)

Grace Lee Whitney
PUBLIC AFFAIR, A(1962); IRMA LA DOUCE(1963); MAN FROM GALVESTON, THE(1964); STAR TREK: THE MOTION PICTURE(1979)
1984
STAR TREK III: THE SEARCH FOR SPOCK(1984)

Helen Whitney
PHILADELPHIA STORY, THE(1940)

Helene Whitney
HUNCHBACK OF NOTRE DAME, THE(1939); SAINT'S DOUBLE TROUBLE, THE(1940)

Iris Whitney
RIVALS(1972); EYEWITNESS(1981)

Jerry Whitney
STING II, THE(1983)

Joan Whitney
MY FAVORITE SPY(1951); TWO TICKETS TO BROADWAY(1951); SON OF SINBAD(1955); JET PILOT(1957)

John Whitney
TEN GENTLEMEN FROM WEST POINT(1942); GUY NAMED JOE, A(1943); IMMORTAL SERGEANT, THE(1943); MOONLIGHT IN VERMONT(1943); DESTINATION TOKYO(1944); FOLLOW THE BOYS(1944); LUMBERJACK(1944); PRACTICALLY YOURS(1944); TUCSON RAIDERS(1944); WILSON(1944); AFFAIRS OF SUSAN(1945); FOG ISLAND(1945); OBJECTIVE, BURMA!(1945); BACHELOR'S DAUGHTERS, THE(1946); CALCUTTA(1947); I WAS A MALE WAR BRIDE(1949); SANDS OF IWO JIMA(1949); NO WAY OUT(1950); TRIAL WITHOUT JURY(1950); BUTTERCUP CHAIN, THE(1971, Brit.), p

Johnny Whitney
JACKALS, THE(1967, South Africa)

Kevin Whitney
Misc. Talkies
ALTERNATIVE MISS WORLD, THE(1980)
Lee Whitney
TOP BANANA(1954)
Leigh Whitney
RAINBOW ISLAND(1944)
Lynn Whitney
LETTER FOR EVIE, A(1945); BECAUSE OF HIM(1946); DARK CORNER, THE(1946); TWO SMART PEOPLE(1946); THEY LIVE BY NIGHT(1949); FILE ON THELMA JORDAN, THE(1950); JOURNEY INTO LIGHT(1951)
Lynne Whitney
WOMAN'S SECRET, A(1949); STORM WARNING(1950)
Marion Whitney
Misc. Silents
APACHES OF PARIS, THE(1915)
Mark Whitney
1984
AMERICAN TABOO(1984), ph
Michael Whitney
THERE GOES THE BRIDE(1980, Brit.)
Paul Whitney
SMASHING THE SPY RING(1939)
Peter Whitney
NINE LIVES ARE NOT ENOUGH(1941); UNDERGROUND(1941); BUSSES ROAR(1942); REUNION IN FRANCE(1942); RIO RITA(1942); SPY SHIP(1942); VALLEY OF THE SUN(1942); WHISTLING IN DIXIE(1942); ACTION IN THE NORTH ATLANTIC(1943); DESTINATION TOKYO(1944); MR. SKEFFINGTON(1944); BRING ON THE GIRLS(1945); HOTEL BERLIN(1945); MURDER, HE SAYS(1945); BLONDE ALIBI(1946); BRUTE MAN, THE(1946); NOTORIOUS LONE WOLF, THE(1946); THREE STRANGERS(1946); GANGSTER, THE(1947); NORTHWEST OUTPOST(1947); VIOLENCE(1947); IRON CURTAIN, THE(1948); ALL THE BROTHERS WERE VALIANT(1953); BIG HEAT, THE(1953); GREAT SIOUX UPRISING, THE(1953); BLACK DAKOTAS, THE(1954); DAY OF TRIUMPH(1954); GORILLA AT LARGE(1954); LAST FRONTIER, THE(1955); SEA CHASE, THE(1955); CRUEL TOWER, THE(1956); GREAT DAY IN THE MORNING(1956); MAN FROM DEL RIO(1956); DOMINO KID(1957); BUCHANAN RIDES ALONE(1958); SWORD OF ALI BABA, THE(1965); IN THE HEAT OF THE NIGHT(1967); CHUBASCO(1968); GREAT BANK ROBBERY, THE(1969); BALLAD OF CABLE HOGUE, THE(1970)
Rene Whitney
PLAY GIRL(1932)
Renee Whitney
WILD PARTY, THE(1929); KID FROM SPAIN, THE(1932); WINNER TAKE ALL(1932); BABY FACE(1933); FOOTLIGHT PARADE(1933); GOLD DIGGERS OF 1933(1933); KEYHOLE, THE(1933); LITTLE GIANT, THE(1933); PICTURE SNATCHER(1933); PRIVATE DETECTIVE 62(1933); 42ND STREET(1933); GAMBLING LADY(1934); I'VE GOT YOUR NUMBER(1934); JIMMY THE GENT(1934); KANSAS CITY PRINCESS(1934); PERSONALITY KID, THE(1934); REGISTERED NURSE(1934); RETURN OF THE TERROR(1934); SIDE STREETS(1934); WONDER BAR(1934); WESTERN COURAGE(1935); SHOW BOAT(1936)
Robert Whitney
JUDGE HARDY'S CHILDREN(1938); HEADLEYS AT HOME, THE(1939); DESPERATE SEARCH(1952)
Russ Whitney
THESE WILDER YEARS(1956)
Ruth Whitney
TEXAN MEETS CALAMITY JANE, THE(1950); HANNAH LEE(1953); HOUSE OF WAX(1953); RIDING SHOTGUN(1954)
Salem Tutt Whitney
Misc. Silents
BIRTHRIGHT(1924); MARCUS GARLAND(1925)
Shirley Whitney
FULLER BRUSH GIRL, THE(1950); PETTY GIRL, THE(1950); TWO TICKETS TO BROADWAY(1951); HALF-BREED, THE(1952); CRIME WAVE(1954); IRON GLOVE, THE(1954)
Sophania Whitney
SWINGIN' ALONG(1962)
Susan Whitney
PASSAGE WEST(1951); MIRACLE OF OUR LADY OF FATIMA, THE(1952); NORTH BY NORTHWEST(1959)
Suzanne Whitney
ON MOONLIGHT BAY(1951)
William Whitney
GOLDEN STALLION, THE(1949), d; JUNGLE MANHUNT(1951), ph; ALASKA PASSAGE(1959), ph
James Whiton
ABOMINABLE DR. PHIBES, THE(1971, Brit.), w; DOCTOR PHIBES RISES AGAIN(1972, Brit.), w
Benjamin Whitrow
BRIMSTONE AND TREACLE(1982, Brit.)
Carson Whitsett
WONDER WOMEN(1973, Phil.), m; STUCKEY'S LAST STAND(1980), m
Luther Whitsett
HALLS OF ANGER(1970)
Frank Whitson
SWING HIGH, SWING LOW(1937)
Silents
ONE DAY(1916); HER MAN(1924); RACING FOR LIFE(1924); FIGHTING BOOB, THE(1926)
Misc. Silents
ISLE OF LIFE, THE(1916); MARK OF CAIN, THE(1916); MORALS OF HILDA, THE(1916); PRICE OF SILENCE, THE(1916); CLOCK, THE(1917); DAUGHTER OF THE WEST, A(1918); RESTITUTION(1918); FAITH OF THE STRONG(1919); HEARTS ASLEEP(1919); SQUARE DEAL SANDERSON(1919); THREE GOLD COINS(1920); GILDED LIES(1921); MAN FROM HELL'S RIVER, THE(1922); FLAMES OF PASSION(1923); TANGO CAVALIER(1923); WAY OF THE TRANSGRESSOR, THE(1923); WHITE PANTHER, THE(1924); FIGHTING COURAGE(1925); BAD MAN'S BLUFF(1926); WALLOPING KID(1926)

Paul Whitson-Jones
ROOM AT THE TOP(1959, Brit.); LET'S GET MARRIED(1960, Brit.)
Paul Whitsun-Jones
DIAMOND WIZARD, THE(1954, Brit.); PASSING STRANGER, THE(1954, Brit.); STOCK CAR(1955, Brit.); MOONRAKER, THE(1958, Brit.); WRONG NUMBER(1959, Brit.); BLUEBEARD'S TEN HONEYMOONS(1960, Brit.); NEXT TO NO TIME(1960, Brit.); SHAKEDOWN, THE(1960, Brit.); TUNES OF GLORY(1960, Brit.); THERE WAS A CROOKED MAN(1962, Brit.); DOCTOR IN DISTRESS(1963, Brit.); MASQUE OF THE RED DEATH, THE(1964, U.S./Brit.); 20,000 POUNDS KISS(1964, Brit.); LIFE AT THE TOP(1965, Brit.); CANDIDATE FOR MURDER(1966, Brit.); WILD AFFAIR, THE(1966, Brit.); WHAT'S GOOD FOR THE GOOSE(1969, Brit.); DR. JEKYLL AND SISTER HYDE(1971, Brit.); ALL THE RIGHT NOISES(1973, Brit.)
Wayne "Tiny" Whitt
DANCING CO-ED(1939); SOME LIKE IT HOT(1939); $1,000 A TOUCHDOWN(1939)
Alan Whittaker
TIME OF HIS LIFE, THE(1955, Brit.)
Charles Whittaker
WAY OF LOST SOULS, THE(1929, Brit.), p, w; WOMAN HE SCORNED, THE(1930, Brit.), p, w; LOST JUNGLE, THE(1934); FRONTIERS OF '49(1939); LAW COMES TO TEXAS, THE(1939); DESPERADOES, THE(1943)
Silents
END OF THE TRAIL, THE(1916); LAW OF THE LAND, THE(1917), w; PRIVATE PEAT(1918), w; IN SEARCH OF A SINNER(1920); PARTNERS OF THE NIGHT(1920), w; BUCKING THE TRUTH(1926); VANISHING HOOFS(1926); HUNTING-TOWER(1927, Brit.), w; MAN WHO LAUGHS, THE(1927), w; HEADIN' WESTWARD(1929)
Misc. Silents
DESPERATE CHANCE(1926); CAPTAIN COWBOY(1929)
Charles E. Whittaker
Silents
ARMS AND THE GIRL(1917), w; PRIDE OF THE CLAN, THE(1917), w; ON THE QUIET(1918), w; KISMET(1920), w; WHAT WOMEN WILL DO(1921), w; SLAVE OF DESIRE(1923), w; WHITE SISTER, THE(1923), w; DEVIL'S CARGO(1925), w; WEDDING SONG, THE(1925), w; WATCH YOUR WIFE(1926), w; NEST, THE(1927), w
Christian Whittaker
PICKUP ON 101(1972), p; CALIFORNIA DREAMING(1979), p
Charles Whittaker, Jr.
Misc. Silents
SPEEDY SPURS(1926)
David Whittaker
VAMPIRE CIRCUS(1972, Brit.), m; SWORD AND THE SORCERER, THE(1982), m
Freda Whittaker
OUTSIDER, THE(1933, Brit.)
Ian Whittaker
THREE CORNERED FATE(1954, Brit.); PASSAGE HOME(1955, Brit.); SEA SHALL NOT HAVE THEM, THE(1955, Brit.); IT'S A GREAT DAY(1956, Brit.); TOUCH OF THE SUN, A(1956, Brit.); SECOND FIDDLE(1957, Brit.); SUSPENDED ALIBI(1957, Brit.); FURTHER UP THE CREEK!(1958, Brit.); REVENGE OF FRANKENSTEIN, THE(1958, Brit.); STEEL BAYONET, THE(1958, Brit.); CARRY ON SERGEANT(1959, Brit.); SILENT ENEMY, THE(1959, Brit.); MY WIFE'S FAMILY(1962, Brit.); NEARLY A NASTY ACCIDENT(1962, Brit.); OPERATION SNATCH(1962, Brit.); DR. CRIPPEN(1963, Brit.); GET ON WITH IT(1963, Brit.); OPERATION SNAFU(1965, Brit.); SECRET OF BLOOD ISLAND, THE(1965, Brit.); DUTCHMAN(1966, Brit.), set d; OUR MOTHER'S HOUSE(1967, Brit.), set d; TO SIR, WITH LOVE(1967, Brit.), set d; DOWNHILL RACER(1969), art d; LOCK UP YOUR DAUGHTERS(1969, Brit.), set d; MUSIC LOVERS, THE(1971, Brit.), set d; SAVAGE MESSIAH(1972, Brit.), set d; MAHLER(1974, Brit.), art d; TOMMY(1975, Brit.), set d; SKY RIDERS(1976, U.S./Gr.), set d; JOSEPH ANDREWS(1977, Brit.), set d; VALENTINO(1977, Brit.), set d; INTERNATIONAL VELVET(1978, Brit.), set d; ALIEN(1979), set d; RAISE THE TITANIC(1980, Brit.), set d; RICHARD'S THINGS(1981, Brit.), art d; RETURN OF THE SOLDIER, THE(1983, Brit.), art d
1984
RAZOR'S EDGE, THE(1984), set d
James Whittaker
GRAY LADY DOWN(1978), w
Michael Whittaker
BLACK ROSE, THE(1950), cos; NAKED HEART, THE(1955, Brit.), cos
Owen Whittaker
CLASS OF MISS MAC MICHAEL, THE(1978, Brit./U.S.)
Raymond Whittaker
Silents
KINKAID, GAMBLER(1916); LOVE AFLAME(1917)
Slim Whittaker
DAWN TRAIL, THE(1931); SILVER TRAIL, THE(1937); FALCON OUT WEST, THE(1944)
Stephen Whittaker
TO SIR, WITH LOVE(1967, Brit.); WATERHOLE NO. 3(1967); CHASTITY(1969); RETURN OF THE SOLDIER, THE(1983, Brit.)
Steve Whittaker
CHASE, THE(1966)
Vivienne Whittaker
Silents
POPPIES OF FLANDERS(1927, Brit.)
W. A. Whittaker
DAM BUSTERS, THE(1955, Brit.), p; NO TIME FOR TEARS(1957, Brit.), p; DESERT ATTACK(1958, Brit.), p; CALL ME GENIUS(1961, Brit.), p; CRACKSMAN, THE(1963, Brit.), p; BARGEE, THE(1964, Brit.), p; MISTER TEN PERCENT(1967, Brit.), p
Wayne Whittaker
BAMBOO BLONDE, THE(1946), w
Peter Whittal
NEON PALACE, THE(1970, Can.)
Josephine Whittel
LIFE WITH HENRY(1941); GOLDBERGS, THE(1950)
Josephine Whittell
SYMPHONY OF SIX MILLION(1932); INFERNAL MACHINE(1933); IT'S A GIFT(1934); JEALOUSY(1934); LIFE OF VERGIE WINTERS, THE(1934); LOVE TIME(1934); SERVANTS' ENTRANCE(1934); YOU'RE TELLING ME(1934); MILLS OF THE GODS(1935); SHANGHAI(1935); EASY TO TAKE(1936); FOLLOW YOUR HEART(1936); DOUBLE WEDDING(1937); HOTEL HAYWIRE(1937); LARCENY ON

THE AIR(1937); MARRIED BEFORE BREAKFAST(1937); STAGE DOOR(1937); TOO HOT TO HANDLE(1938); WOMEN ARE LIKE THAT(1938); BOY TROUBLE(1939); LUCKY NIGHT(1939); WOMEN, THE(1939); TUGBOAT ANNIE SAILS AGAIN(1940); DESIGN FOR SCANDAL(1941); GLAMOUR BOY(1941); UNFINISHED BUSINESS(1941); ZIEGFELD GIRL(1941); LADY IN A JAM(1942); MAGNIFICENT DOPE, THE(1942); DIXIE(1943); STANDING ROOM ONLY(1944); ENCHANTED COTTAGE, THE(1945); HAVING WONDERFUL CRIME(1945); STATE FAIR(1945); AFFAIRS OF GERALDINE(1946); DEVIL THUMBS A RIDE, THE(1947); SONG OF LOVE(1947); ONE TOUCH OF VENUS(1948); SITTING PRETTY(1948); ADVENTURE IN BALTIMORE(1949); FOUNTAINHEAD, THE(1949); LADY TAKES A SAILOR, THE(1949); SHAKEDOWN(1950); PLACE IN THE SUN, A(1951); TOO YOUNG TO KISS(1951); FOREVER FEMALE(1953)
Silents
CLIMBERS, THE(1919); INNER CHAMBER, THE(1921)

Gloria Whittemore
SUMMERSPELL(1983), ed

L. H. Whittemore
SUPER COPS, THE(1974), w

Bill Whitten
BUSTIN' LOOSE(1981), cos

Delbert Emory Whitten, Jr.
Silents
TIN GODS(1926)

Frank Whitten
1984
VIGIL(1984, New Zealand)

Marguerite Whitten
TOY WIFE, THE(1938); WAY DOWN SOUTH(1939); KING OF THE ZOMBIES(1941); LET'S GO COLLEGIATE(1941); MR. WASHINGTON GOES TO TOWN(1941); SLEEPY-TIME GAL(1942)
Misc. Talkies
MYSTERY IN SWING(1940)

Mary Whitten
Misc. Talkies
TWO-GUN MAN FROM HARLEM(1938)

Norman Whitten
Silents
IN THE DAYS OF SAINT PATRICK(1920, Brit.), p&d

Tommy Whitten
MAN FROM MONTREAL, THE(1940)

Vernon Whitten
Silents
IN THE DAYS OF SAINT PATRICK(1920, Brit.)

Bill Whittens
FOG, THE(1980), cos

Crane Whittey
ABOVE AND BEYOND(1953)

June Whittey
ONE SUNDAY AFTERNOON(1948)

Ray Whittey
STACY'S KNIGHTS(1983)

Glen Whittier
FLASH GORDON(1980)

Robert Whittier
Silents
KING LEAR(1916)
Misc. Silents
BETRAYED!(1916); BIRD OF PREY, A(1916); MASTER SHAKESPEARE, STROLLING PLAYER(1916); CALL OF HER PEOPLE, THE(1917); THREADS OF FATE(1917); MAN WHO STAYED AT HOME, THE(1919)

A.E. Whiting
Misc. Silents
SON OF A GUN, THE(1919)

Mrs. A.E. Whiting
Misc. Silents
SON OF A GUN, THE(1919)

Steve Whitting
1984
FLAMINGO KID, THE(1984)

D. Whittingham
LAUGHING LADY, THE(1950, Brit.)

Derrick Whittingham
MURDER ON APPROVAL(1956, Brit.)

Jack Whittingham
CLOUDS OVER EUROPE(1939, Brit.), w; ESCAPE TO DANGER(1943, Brit.), w; KISS THE BRIDE GOODBYE(1944, Brit.), w; TWILIGHT HOUR(1944, Brit.), w; WELCOME, MR. WASHINGTON(1944, Brit.), w; LISBON STORY, THE(1946, Brit.), w; WALTZ TIME(1946, Brit.), w; GREEN FINGERS(1947), w; DEVIL'S PLOT, THE(1948, Brit.), w; DANCING YEARS, THE(1950, Brit.), w; LAUGHING LADY, THE(1950, Brit.), w; CRASH OF SILENCE(1952, Brit.), w; STRANGER IN BETWEEN, THE(1952, Brit.), w; I BELIEVE IN YOU(1953, Brit.), w; WEST OF ZANZIBAR(1954, Brit.), w; DIVIDED HEART, THE(1955, Brit.), w; BIRTHDAY PRESENT, THE(1957, Brit.), p; THUNDERBALL(1965, Brit.), w; NEVER SAY NEVER AGAIN(1983), w

Sheila Whittingham
SO EVIL SO YOUNG(1961, Brit.); TARNISHED HEROES(1961, Brit.); FATE TAKES A HAND(1962, Brit.); SPANISH SWORD, THE(1962, Brit.)

Dick Whittinghill
CALYPSO HEAT WAVE(1957); JAMBOREE(1957); WILL SUCCESS SPOIL ROCK HUNTER?(1957); –30–(1959); PRIVATE'S AFFAIR, A(1959); SAY ONE FOR ME(1959); IT'S ONLY MONEY(1962); MOON PILOT(1962); LIVELY SET, THE(1964)

Cotton Whittington
1984
HOLLYWOOD HIGH PART II(1984), p, w

Dick Whittington
CANDIDATE, THE(1972); THING WITH TWO HEADS, THE(1972); MAN WITH BOGART'S FACE, THE(1980)

Gene Whittington
ESCAPE FROM THE PLANET OF THE APES(1971); PSYCHO II(1983)

Harry Whittington
DESIRE IN THE DUST(1960), w; FIREBALL JUNGLE(1968), w

Henry Whittington
BLACK GOLD(1963), w

John Whittington
LA BABY SITTER(1975, Fr./Ital./Gen.)

Shawn Patrick Whittington
1984
BODY ROCK(1984)

Valerie Whittington
MISSIONARY, THE(1982); MONTY PYTHON'S THE MEANING OF LIFE(1983, Brit.); RETURN OF THE SOLDIER, THE(1983, Brit.)
1984
ORDEAL BY INNOCENCE(1984, Brit.)

James Whittle
TAKE THIS JOB AND SHOVE IT(1981)

Peter Whittle
NED KELLY(1970, Brit.); OUTBACK(1971, Aus.); SUNSTRUCK(1973, Aus.)

Lloyd Whittock
Misc. Silents
HOUSE OF SHAME, THE(1928)

Bill Whitton
DRACULA(THE DIRTY OLD MAN) (1969)

Bob Whitton
DRACULA(THE DIRTY OLD MAN) (1969)

Margaret Whitton
LOVE CHILD(1982)

Peggy Whitton
PARADES(1972)

William Whitton
CURSE OF THE CAT PEOPLE, THE(1944), ed; LOCKET, THE(1946), ed; SKIPA-LONG ROSENBLOOM(1951), ed; THE LADY DRACULA(1974)

J.B. Whittredge
WANDERER OF THE WASTELAND(1945), ed

J.R. Whittredge
MADEMOISELLE FIFI(1944), ed; BODY SNATCHER, THE(1945), ed; GAME OF DEATH, A(1945), ed; SEVEN KEYS TO BALDPATE(1947), ed; FEARMAKERS, THE(1958), ed; STREET OF DARKNESS(1958), ed

Dame Mae Whitty
SLIGHTLY DANGEROUS(1943)

Dame May Whitty
CONQUEST(1937); NIGHT MUST FALL(1937); THIRTEENTH CHAIR, THE(1937); I MET MY LOVE AGAIN(1938); LADY VANISHES, THE(1938, Brit.); RAFFLES(1939); BILL OF DIVORCEMENT(1940); RETURN TO YESTERDAY(1940, Brit.); ONE NIGHT IN LISBON(1941); SUSPICION(1941); MRS. MINIVER(1942); CONSTANT NYMPH, THE(1943); CRASH DIVE(1943); FLESH AND FANTASY(1943); FOREVER AND A DAY(1943); LASSIE, COME HOME(1943); MADAME CURIE(1943); STAGE DOOR CANTEEN(1943); GASLIGHT(1944); WHITE CLIFFS OF DOVER, THE(1944); MY NAME IS JULIA ROSS(1945); DEVOTION(1946); GREEN DOLPHIN STREET(1947); IF WINTER COMES(1947); RETURN OF OCTOBER, THE(1948); SIGN OF THE RAM, THE(1948)

May Whitty
Misc. Silents
ENOCH ARDEN(1914, Brit.)

Barry Whitwam
HOLD ON(1966); MRS. BROWN, YOU'VE GOT A LOVELY DAUGHTER(1968, Brit.)

James Whitwirth
BLACK ANGELS, THE(1970)

Dean Whitworth
1984
RIVER, THE(1984)

James Whitworth
FANDANGO(1970); SWEET SUGAR(1972); PLANET OF DINOSAURS(1978)

Jim Whitworth
TERMINAL ISLAND(1973)

Robert Whitworth
Misc. Silents
ALIBI, THE(1916)

Whizzer the Horse
OKLAHOMA KID, THE(1939)

The Who
QUADROPHENIA(1979, Brit.), m

David Whorf
TWIST ALL NIGHT(1961); PT 109(1963); ONE WAY WAHINI(1965)

Pamela Whorf
TOP OF THE HEAP(1972)

Richard Whorf
MIDNIGHT(1934); BLUES IN THE NIGHT(1941); JUKE GIRL(1942); KEEPER OF THE FLAME(1942); YANKEE DOODLE DANDY(1942); ASSIGNMENT IN BRITTANY(1943); CROSS OF LORRAINE, THE(1943); BLONDE FEVER(1944), d; CHRISTMAS HOLIDAY(1944); IMPOSTER, THE(1944); HIDDEN EYE, THE(1945), d; SAILOR TAKES A WIFE, THE(1946), d; TILL THE CLOUDS ROLL BY(1946), d; IT HAPPENED IN BROOKLYN(1947), d; LOVE FROM A STRANGER(1947), d; LUXURY LINER(1948), d; CHAIN LIGHTNING(1950), d; CHAMPAGNE FOR CAESAR(1950), d; GROOM WORE SPURS, THE(1951), a, d; BURNING HILLS, THE(1956), p; BOMBERS B-52(1957), p; SHOOT-OUT AT MEDICINE BEND(1957), p

David Whort
ON OUR MERRY WAY(1948)

Arthur Whybrow
GIRO CITY(1982, Brit.); XTRO(1983, Brit.)
1984
KIPPERBANG(1984, Brit.)

Roy Whybrow
TANK FORCE(1958, Brit.), spec eff; DESERT PATROL(1962, Brit.), spec eff; TARZAN GOES TO INDIA(1962, U.S./Brit./Switz.), spec eff; TARZAN'S THREE CHALLENGES(1963), spec eff; HELP!(1965, Brit.), spec eff; JUDITH(1965), spec eff; MURPHY'S WAR(1971, Brit.), spec eff; RULING CLASS, THE(1972, Brit.), spec eff; EAGLE HAS LANDED, THE(1976, Brit.), spec eff; OPERATION DAYBREAK(1976, U.S./Brit./Czech.), spec eff

Arthur Whybrown
WICKED LADY, THE(1983, Brit.)
Andy Whyland
VORTEX(1982)
Grant Whylock
BOY, DID I GET A WRONG NUMBER!(1966), ed
Princess Whynemah
DEERSLAYER(1943)
Adelaide Whytal
THEY MET IN BOMBAY(1941)
Donn Whyte
FRIDAY THE 13TH... THE ORPHAN(1979)
Ellen Whyte
LOVESICK(1983); TWO OF A KIND(1983)
Helen Whyte
LOVE IN A FOUR LETTER WORLD(1970, Can.)
Ian Whyte
BONNIE PRINCE CHARLIE(1948, Brit.), m
Johnny Whyte
NO. 96(1974, Aus.), w
King Whyte
THIS MAN IS MINE(1946 Brit.)
Laura Whyte
FARMER, THE(1977); HOPSCOTCH(1980); LITTLE DARLINGS(1980)
1984
TANK(1984)
Pat Whyte
THREE CAME HOME(1950); MOLE PEOPLE, THE(1956)
Patrick Whyte
MY OWN TRUE LOVE(1948); NOT WANTED(1949); SOLDIERS THREE(1951); FORT VENGEANCE(1953); KING OF THE KHYBER RIFLES(1953); YOUNG BESS(1953); MAN WHO KNEW TOO MUCH, THE(1956); HIDEOUS SUN DEMON, THE(1959); WINGS OF CHANCE(1961, Can.), a, w; CHILDREN OF THE DAMNED(1963, Brit.); KITTEN WITH A WHIP(1964); BEAU GESTE(1966); WEEKEND WITH THE BABY-SITTER(1970)
Ron Whyte
SIDELONG GLANCES OF A PIGEON KICKER, THE(1970), w; HAPPINESS CAGE, THE(1972), w
Shirley Whyte
Silents
PEEP BEHIND THE SCENES, A(1929, Brit.)
Grant Whytock
UNHOLY NIGHT, THE(1929), ed; DEVIL TO PAY, THE(1930), ed; SHIP FROM SHANGHAI, THE(1930), ed; UNHOLY GARDEN, THE(1931), ed; I COVER THE WATERFRONT(1933), ed; COUNT OF MONTE CRISTO, THE(1934), ed; PALOO-KA(1934), ed; TRANSATLANTIC MERRY-GO-ROUND(1934), ed; LET 'EM HAVE IT(1935), ed; RED SALUTE(1935), ed; DUKE OF WEST POINT, THE(1938), ed; KING OF THE TURF(1939), ed; MAN IN THE IRON MASK, THE(1939), ed; MY SON, MY SON!(1940), ed; CORSICAN BROTHERS, THE(1941), ed; INTERNATIONAL LA-DY(1941), ed; FRIENDLY ENEMIES(1942), ed; UP IN MABEL'S ROOM(1944), ed; RETURN OF MONTE CRISTO, THE(1946), p; WALK A CROOKED MILE(1948), p; BANDITS OF CORSICA, THE(1953), ed; GUN BELT(1953), ed; STEEL LADY, THE(1953), p, ed; DOWN THREE DARK STREETS(1954), ed; MAD MAGICIAN, THE(1954), ed; SOUTHWEST PASSAGE(1954), ed; NAKED STREET, THE(1955), ed; NEW YORK CONFIDENTIAL(1955), ed; CHICAGO CONFIDENTIAL(1957), ed; IRON SHERIFF, THE(1957), ed; MONKEY ON MY BACK(1957), ed; BADMAN'S COUN-TRY(1958), ed; CURSE OF THE FACELESS MAN(1958), ed; IT! THE TERROR FROM BEYOND SPACE(1958), ed; TOUGHEST GUN IN TOMBSTONE(1958), ed; INSIDE THE MAFIA(1959), ed; INVISIBLE INVADERS(1959), ed; PIER 5, HAVANA(1959), ed; TIMBUKTU(1959), ed; VICE RAID(1959), ed; CAGE OF EVIL(1960), ed; NOOSE FOR A GUNMAN(1960), ed; OKLAHOMA TERRITORY(1960), ed; THREE CAME TO KILL(1960), ed; WHEN THE CLOCK STRIKES(1961), ed; JACK THE GIANT KILL-ER(1962), ed; DIARY OF A MADMAN(1963), ed; TWICE TOLD TALES(1963), ed; APACHE RIFLES(1964), p, ed; QUICK GUN, THE(1964), p, ed; ARIZONA RAI-DERS(1965), p, ed; I'LL TAKE SWEDEN(1965), ed; FRANKIE AND JOHNNY(1966), ed; EIGHT ON THE LAM(1967), ed; 40 GUNS TO APACHE PASS(1967), p, ed; WICKED DREAMS OF PAULA SCHULTZ, THE(1968), ed; CHRISTINE JORGENSEN STORY, THE(1970), ed
Silents
DEVIL'S PASSKEY, THE(1920), ed; FOUR HORSEMEN OF THE APOCALYPSE, THE(1921), ed; SCARAMOUCHE(1923), ed; MARE NOSTRUM(1926), ed
Leotta Whytock
Silents
STRANDED(1927), ed; MARRY THE GIRL(1928), ed; MILLION FOR LOVE, A(1928), ed
Bill Wiard
MAN FROM GALVESTON, THE(1964), ed
Richard Wiard
RETURN OF THE CISCO KID(1939), art d
William Wiard
TOM HORN(1980), d
Peter Wiari
PICTURES(1982, New Zealand)
Inia Te Wiata
PACIFIC DESTINY(1956, Brit.); IN SEARCH OF THE CASTAWAYS(1962, Brit.)
Anne Wiazemski
LA CHINOISE(1967, Fr.)
Anne Wiazemsky
WEEKEND(1968, Fr./Ital.); LES GAULOISES BLEUES(1969, Fr.); ONE PLUS ONE(1969, Brit.); TEOREMA(1969, Ital.); AU HASARD, BALTHAZAR(1970, Fr.); SEED OF MAN, THE(1970, Ital.)
Leonard Wibberley
MOUSE THAT ROARED, THE(1959, Brit.), w; MOUSE ON THE MOON, THE(1963, Brit.), w
Stub Wiberg
Misc. Silents
BRIDE OF GLOMDAL, THE(1925, Nor.)

Winnie Wiblin
INSPECTOR CALLS, AN(1954, Brit.)
Crane Wibur
INVISIBLE MENACE, THE(1938), w
Kare Wichlund
HUNGER(1968, Den./Norway/Swed.)
Nicole Wicht
EVERY MAN FOR HIMSELF(1980, Fr.)
E. Wichura
EVE WANTS TO SLEEP(1961, Pol.)
Bruno Wick
HOUSE ON 92ND STREET, THE(1945); DEEP WATERS(1948); LOVE ISLAND(1952); WALK EAST ON BEACON(1952); TAXI(1953)
Charles Wick
SNOW WHITE AND THE THREE STOOGES(1961), p, w
John Wickens
Silents
WATCHING EYES(1921)
Misc. Silents
WATCHING EYES(1921, Brit.)
Willy Wickerhauser
FIGHTER SQUADRON(1948); I, JANE DOE(1948); ROGUES' REGIMENT(1948)
Bob Wickersham
MR. BUG GOES TO TOWN(1941), w
Anthony Wickert
MURDER CAN BE DEADLY(1963, Brit.); MYSTERY SUBMARINE(1963, Brit.)
David Wickes
SWEENEY(1977, Brit.), d; SILVER DREAM RACER(1982, Brit.), d&w
Kenneth Wickes
BLOODY BROOD, THE(1959, Can.)
Mary Wickes
BLONDIE'S BLESSED EVENT(1942); MAN WHO CAME TO DINNER, THE(1942); MAYOR OF 44TH STREET, THE(1942); NOW, VOYAGER(1942); PRIVATE BUCK-AROO(1942); WHO DONE IT?(1942); HAPPY LAND(1943); HIGHER AND HIGH-ER(1943); HOW'S ABOUT IT?(1943); MY KINGDOM FOR A COOK(1943); RHYTHM OF THE ISLANDS(1943); DECISION OF CHRISTOPHER BLAKE, THE(1948); JUNE BRIDE(1948); ANNA LUCASTA(1949); PETTY GIRL, THE(1950); I'LL SEE YOU IN MY DREAMS(1951); ON MOONLIGHT BAY(1951); STORY OF WILL ROGERS, THE(1952); YOUNG MAN WITH IDEAS(1952); ACTRESS, THE(1953); BY THE LIGHT OF THE SILVERY MOON(1953); HALF A HERO(1953); DESTRY(1954); MA AND PA KETTLE AT HOME(1954); WHITE CHRISTMAS(1954); GOOD MORNING, MISS DOVE(1955); DANCE WITH ME, HENRY(1956); IT HAPPENED TO JANE(1959); CIMARRON(1960); SINS OF RACHEL CADE, THE(1960); ONE HUNDRED AND ONE DAL-MATIANS(1961); MUSIC MAN, THE(1962); DEAR HEART(1964); FATE IS THE HUNTER(1964); HOW TO MURDER YOUR WIFE(1965); TROUBLE WITH ANGELS, THE(1966); SPIRIT IS WILLING, THE(1967); WHERE ANGELS GO...TROUBLE FOLLOWS(1968); NAPOLEON AND SAMANTHA(1972); SNOWBALL EX-PRESS(1972); DON'T GO NEAR THE WATER(1975); TOUCHED BY LOVE(1980)
Chrissy Wickham
MUSIC MACHINE, THE(1979, Brit.)
Hank Wickham
BUNNY O'HARE(1971)
Jeffrey Wickham
WATERLOO(1970, Ital./USSR)
1984
ANOTHER COUNTRY(1984, Brit.); MEMED MY HAWK(1984, Brit.)
Jeffry Wickham
HELLO—GOODBYE(1970); S(1974); TERRORISTS, THE(1975, Brit.)
John Wickham
FRENCH LEAVE(1937, Brit.); LAST CURTAIN, THE(1937, Brit.)
Ship Wickham
1984
REPO MAN(1984)
Bernard Wicki
CIRCUS OF LOVE(1958, Ger.); CAT, THE(1959, Fr.)
Bernhard Wicki
LAST BRIDGE, THE(1957, Aust.); AFFAIRS OF JULIE, THE(1958, Ger.); ETERNAL WALTZ, THE(1959, Ger.); BRIDGE, THE(1961, Ger.), d; LA NOTTE(1961, Fr./Ital.); LONGEST DAY, THE(1962), d; OF WAYWARD LOVE(1964, Ital./Ger.); RESTLESS NIGHT, THE(1964, Ger.); VISIT, THE(1964, Ger./Fr./Ital./U.S.), d; MORITURI(1965), d; CRIME AND PASSION(1976, U.S., Ger.); DESPAIR(1978, Ger.); DEATH-WATCH(1980, Fr./Ger.); LEFT-HANDED WOMAN, THE(1980, Ger.)
1984
LOVE IN GERMANY, A(1984, Fr./Ger.); PARIS, TEXAS(1984, Ger./Fr.)
Norbert Wicki
Silents
IDLE HANDS(1921)
Misc. Silents
DARKEST RUSSIA(1917); WORLD FOR SALE, THE(1918)
Chris Wicking
TO THE DEVIL A DAUGHTER(1976, Brit./Ger.), w
Christopher Wicking
OBLONG BOX, THE(1969, Brit.), w; CRY OF THE BANSHEE(1970, Brit.), w; SCREAM AND SCREAM AGAIN(1970, Brit.), w; MURDERS IN THE RUE MOR-GUE(1971), w; DEMONS OF THE MIND(1972, Brit.), w; LADY CHATTERLEY'S LOVER(1981, Fr./Brit.), w
Lyons Wickland
UNMASKED(1929); LES MISERABLES(1935); MARIE ANTOINETTE(1938); KILL-ERS OF THE WILD(1940)
Misc. Talkies
UNMASKED(1929)
Christopher Wickling
BLOOD FROM THE MUMMY'S TOMB(1972, Brit.), w
Kare Wicklund
TERRORISTS, THE(1975, Brit.)
Karl Wickman
NIGHTHAWKS(1981)

Sven Wickman
BENEATH THE PLANET OF THE APES(1970), set d; TERRORISTS, THE(1975, Brit.), art d

Barry Wicks
HIDEOUT(1948, Brit.)

Maurice Wicks
SPOOK WHO SAT BY THE DOOR, THE(1973)

Virginia Wicks
UP IN ARMS(1944); EASY TO LOOK AT(1945)

Debbie Wickstrom
WHERE IT'S AT(1969)

Wendy Wickstrom
BIG DADDY(1969)

Elsa Widborg
CRIME AND PUNISHMENT(1948, Swed.)

Wallace Widdecombe
Silents
IVANHOE(1913)

Steve Widders
GUN GLORY(1957); LONG, HOT SUMMER, THE(1958)

Lars Widding
SWEDISH WEDDING NIGHT(1965, Swed.), w; TIME IN THE SUN, A(1970, Swed.), w

Edward C. Widdis
PATSY, THE(1964)

James Widdoes
NATIONAL LAMPOON'S ANIMAL HOUSE(1978)

Kathleen Widdoes
GROUP, THE(1966); PETULIA(1968, U.S./Brit.); SEA GULL, THE(1968); MEPHISTO WALTZ, THE(1971); SAVAGES(1972); END OF AUGUST, THE(1982); I'M DANCING AS FAST AS I CAN(1982); WITHOUT A TRACE(1983)

Walter Widdop
SONG YOU GAVE ME, THE(1934, Brit.)

F.W. Widdowson
FLAMING SIGNAL(1933), set d

Fred Widdowson
MR. ACE(1946), set d; MACOMBER AFFAIR, THE(1947), set d

John Widelock
SILENT SCREAM(1980)

Carl Widem
Silents
HIS ROBE OF HONOR(1918), ph

David Wideman
RECOMMENDATION FOR MERCY(1975, Can.)

Henry Wideman
1984
LAST NIGHT AT THE ALAMO(1984)

Heinrich Widemann
THE DIRTY GAME(1966, Fr./Ital./Ger.), art d

Clair Widenaar
HELL'S HALF ACRE(1954)

Bo Widerberg
ELVIRA MADIGAN(1967, Swed.), d,w&ed; ADALEN 31(1969, Swed.), d&w; RAVEN'S END(1970, Swed.), d&w; JOE HILL(1971, Swed./U.S.), p&d, w

Nina Widerberg
ELVIRA MADIGAN(1967, Swed.)

Olof Widgren
NIGHT IN JUNE, A(1940, Swed.); WALPURGIS NIGHT(1941, Swed.); SILENCE, THE(1964, Swed.)

Agus Widjaja
YEAR OF LIVING DANGEROUSLY, THE(1982, Aus.)

Ellen Widmann
M(1933, Ger.)

Richard Widmark
KISS OF DEATH(1947); ROAD HOUSE(1948); STREET WITH NO NAME, THE(1948); YELLOW SKY(1948); DOWN TO THE SEA IN SHIPS(1949); SLATTERY'S HURRICANE(1949); NIGHT AND THE CITY(1950, Brit.); NO WAY OUT(1950); PANIC IN THE STREETS(1950); FROGMEN, THE(1951); HALLS OF MONTEZUMA(1951); DON'T BOTHER TO KNOCK(1952); MY PAL GUS(1952); O. HENRY'S FULL HOUSE(1952); RED SKIES OF MONTANA(1952); DESTINATION GOBI(1953); PICKUP ON SOUTH STREET(1953); TAKE THE HIGH GROUND(1953); BROKEN LANCE(1954); GARDEN OF EVIL(1954); HELL AND HIGH WATER(1954); COBWEB, THE(1955); PRIZE OF GOLD, A(1955); BACKLASH(1956); LAST WAGON, THE(1956); RUN FOR THE SUN(1956); SAINT JOAN(1957); TIME LIMIT(1957), a, p; LAW AND JAKE WADE, THE(1958); TUNNEL OF LOVE, THE(1958); TRAP, THE(1959); WARLOCK(1959); ALAMO, THE(1960); JUDGMENT AT NUREMBERG(1961); SECRET WAYS, THE(1961), a, p; TWO RODE TOGETHER(1961); HOW THE WEST WAS WON(1962); CHEYENNE AUTUMN(1964); FLIGHT FROM ASHIYA(1964, U.S./Jap.); LONG SHIPS, THE(1964, Brit./Yugo.); BEDFORD INCIDENT, THE(1965, Brit.); ALVAREZ KELLY(1966); WAY WEST, THE(1967); MADIGAN(1968); DEATH OF A GUNFIGHTER(1969); MOONSHINE WAR, THE(1970); WHEN THE LEGENDS DIE(1972); MURDER ON THE ORIENT EXPRESS(1974, Brit.); SELL OUT, THE(1976); TO THE DEVIL A DAUGHTER(1976, Brit./Ger.); DOMINO PRINCIPLE, THE(1977); ROLLERCOASTER(1977); TWILIGHT'S LAST GLEAMING(1977, U.S./Ger.); COMA(1978); SWARM, THE(1978); BEAR ISLAND(1980, Brit.-Can.); HANKY-PANKY(1982); FINAL OPTION, THE(1983, Brit.)
1984
AGAINST ALL ODDS(1984)
Misc. Talkies
MASQUERADE OF THIEVES(1973); PERFECT KILLER, THE(1977, Span.)

Robert Widmark
Misc. Talkies
HALLELUJAH AND SARTANA, SON OF...GOD(1972); TRINITY AND SARTANA(1972)

Bud Widom
GREEN SLIME, THE(1969)

Dick Wieand
IN-LAWS, THE(1979); ROMANTIC COMEDY(1983)

Louis Wiechert
GREAT MANHUNT, THE(1951, Brit.)

Dorothea Wieck
MAEDCHEN IN UNIFORM(1932, Ger.); CRADLE SONG(1933); MISS FANE'S BABY IS STOLEN(1934); PRIVATE LIFE OF LOUIS XIV(1936, Ger.); MAN ON A TIGHTROPE(1953); TIME TO LOVE AND A TIME TO DIE, A(1958); BRAINWASHED(1961, Ger.)

Barbara Wieczik
CONFESS DR. CORDA(1960, Ger.)

Detlev Wiede
GEORG(1964), ph

Conrad Wiedell
THANK YOUR LUCKY STARS(1943)

Alfred Wiedemann
ADORABLE JULIA(1964, Fr./Aust.), d

Gert Wiedenhofen
EMIL AND THE DETECTIVES(1964)

Hanna Wieder
ROSEMARY(1960, Ger.)

Ken Wiederhorn
SHOCK WAVES(1977), d, w; EYES OF A STRANGER(1980), d
1984
MEATBALLS PART II(1984), d
Misc. Talkies
KING FRAT(1979), d

Walter L. Wiedmer
HOODLUM PRIEST, THE(1961)

Olaf Wieghorst
EL DORADO(1967)

Don Wiegmann
1984
BLOOD SIMPLE(1984), ed

Dieter Wieland
SNOW WHITE AND ROSE RED(1966, Ger.)

Guido Wieland
APRIL 1, 2000(1953, Aust.); 5 SINNERS(1961, Ger.); $100 A NIGHT(1968, Ger.); GREAT WALTZ, THE(1972); WILD DUCK, THE(1977, Ger./Aust.)

Guilo Wieland
COME FLY WITH ME(1963)

Joyce Wieland
FAR SHORE, THE(1976, Can.), p, d, w

Lynn Wieland
1984
HOT DOG...THE MOVIE(1984)

Michael Wield
JOANNA(1968, Brit.), prod d, art d; LOLA(1971, Brit./Ital.), art d

Cathy Wiele
FORTUNE AND MEN'S EYES(1971, U.S./Can.)

Mathias Wieman
ETERNAL MASK, THE(1937, Swiss); AS LONG AS YOU'RE NEAR ME(1956, Ger.); FEAR(1956, Ger.); GIRL AND THE LEGEND, THE(1966, Ger.)

Ernst Wiemann
FIDELIO(1970, Ger.)

Mathias Wiemann
MISTRESS OF ATLANTIS, THE(1932, Ger.)

Larry Wiemer
SKATETOWN, U.S.A.(1979), art d

Hyman Wien
WIZARDS(1977)

Dick Wienad
PATERNITY(1981)

Robert Wiene
ULTIMATUM(1940, Fr.), p&d
Silents
CABINET OF DR. CALIGARI, THE(1921, Ger.), d
Misc. Silents
GENUINE(1920, Ger.), d; HANDS OF ORLAC, THE(1925, Aust.), d; GUARDSMAN, THE(1927, Aust.), d; DANCER OF BARCELONA(1929, Ger.), d; CROWN OF THORNS(1934, Ger.), d

Elisabeth Wiener
BEHOLD A PALE HORSE(1964); SWEET AND SOUR(1964, Fr./Ital.); JOHNNY BANCO(1969, Fr./Ital./Ger.); LA PRISONNIERE(1969, Fr./Ital.); MARRY ME! MARRY ME!(1969, Fr.)

Jack Wiener
ESCAPE TO ATHENA(1979, Brit.), p; GREEN ICE(1981, Brit.), p

Jack H. Wiener
OLD DRACULA(1975, Brit.), p

Jean Wiener
CRIME OF MONSIEUR LANGE, THE(1936, Fr.), m; LOWER DEPTHS, THE(1937, Fr.), m; SLIPPER EPISODE, THE(1938, Fr), m; ESCAPE FROM YESTERDAY(1939, Fr.), m; LIVING CORPSE, THE(1940, Fr.), m; DEADLIER THAN THE MALE(1957, Fr.), m; LADY L(1965, Fr./Ital.); AU HASARD, BALTHAZAR(1970, Fr.), m; MOUCHETTE(1970, Fr.), m; GENTLE CREATURE, A(1971, Fr.), m; LE PETIT THEATRE DE JEAN RENOIR(1974, Fr.), m

Willard Wiener
FOUR BOYS AND A GUN(1957), w

The Wiener Jeunesse Choir
CARDINAL, THE(1963)

The Wiener Spatzen Boys' Choir
SALZBURG CONNECTION, THE(1972)

Bob Wier
NIGHT THEY ROBBED BIG BERTHA'S, THE(1975)

Wiere Brothers
GREAT AMERICAN BROADCAST, THE(1941); SWING SHIFT MAISIE(1943); ROAD TO RIO(1947)

The Wiere Brothers
VOGUES OF 1938(1937); HANDS ACROSS THE BORDER(1943); DOUBLE TROUBLE(1967)

Hans Wierendorf
Misc. Silents
PARIS AFTER DARK(1923, Ger.), d
Frank Wierick
JANIE(1944)
Janet Wieringa
CARNY(1980)
Jean Wierner
BACK STREETS OF PARIS(1962, Fr.), m
James Wiers
PURSUIT OF D.B. COOPER, THE(1981)
Howard Wierum
STORM CENTER(1956)
Bernard Wiesen
FEAR NO MORE(1961), p, d
Joe Wiesenfeld
MOURNING SUIT, THE(1975, Can.), w
Sam Wiesenthal
CRY DANGER(1951), p; SECOND CHANCE(1953), p; BENGAZI(1955), p; TENSION AT TABLE ROCK(1956), p; ALL MINE TO GIVE(1957), p; KREMLIN LETTER, THE(1970), p
Wolfgang Wieser
SERPENT'S EGG, THE(1977, Ger./U.S.)
Mark Wieshaus
COME BACK BABY(1968)
Lynda Wiesmeier
PRIVATE SCHOOL(1983)
1984
PREPPIES(1984)
Misc. Talkies
R.S.V.P.(1984)
Arthur Wiesner
SINS OF ROSE BERND, THE(1959, Ger.)
Claus-Ulrich Wiesner
SIGNALS-AN ADVENTURE IN SPACE(1970, E. Ger./Pol.), w
Dianne Wiest
IT'S MY TURN(1980); I'M DANCING AS FAST AS I CAN(1982); INDEPENDENCE DAY(1983)
1984
FALLING IN LOVE(1984); FOOTLOOSE(1984)
George Wieter
FIDELIO(1961, Aust.)
Mogens Wieth
TALES OF HOFFMANN, THE(1951, Brit.); MAN WHO KNEW TOO MUCH, THE(1956); MATTER OF MORALS, A(1961, U.S./Swed.); PRIVATE POTTER(1963, Brit.)
Lou Wiethe
LITTLE LAURA AND BIG JOHN(1973), p
Joe Wiezycki
Misc. Talkies
SATAN'S CHILDREN(1975), d
Naima Wifstrand
GYPSY FURY(1950, Fr.); TRUE AND THE FALSE, THE(1955, Swed.); SMILES OF A SUMMER NIGHT(1957, Swed.); MAGICIAN, THE(1959, Swed.); WILD STRAWBER-RIES(1959, Swed.); DREAMS(1960, Swed.); SECRETS OF WOMEN(1961, Swed.); NIGHT IS MY FUTURE(1962, Swed.); NIGHT GAMES(1966, Swed.); HOUR OF THE WOLF, THE(1968, Swed.)
Gareth Wigan
UNMAN, WITTERING AND ZIGO(1971, Brit.), p; RUNNING SCARED(1972, Brit.), p
Knut Wigert
TERRORISTS, THE(1975, Brit.); AUTUMN SONATA(1978, Swed.)
Lionel Wiggam
VERY THOUGHT OF YOU, THE(1944), w; SMASH-UP, THE STORY OF A WO-MAN(1947), w; TAP ROOTS(1948), w
Bob Wiggens
INCUBUS, THE(1982, Can.), spec eff
Chris Wiggens
NEPTUNE FACTOR, THE(1973, Can.)
Stefan Wigger
THREE PENNY OPERA(1963, Fr./Ger.)
Kate Douglas Wiggin
REBECCA OF SUNNYBROOK FARM(1932), w; TIMOTHY'S QUEST(1936), w; MOTHER CAREY'S CHICKENS(1938), w; REBECCA OF SUNNYBROOK FARM(1938), w; SUMMER MAGIC(1963), w
Silents
REBECCA OF SUNNYBROOK FARM(1917), w; TIMOTHY'S QUEST(1922), w
Margaret Wiggin
Misc. Silents
PENNY PHILANTHROPIST, THE(1917)
Chris Wiggins
KING OF THE GRIZZLIES(1970); WELCOME TO BLOOD CITY(1977, Brit./Can.); WHY SHOOT THE TEACHER(1977, Can.); HIGH-BALLIN'(1978); ANGRY MAN, THE(1979 Fr./Can.); FISH HAWK(1981, Can.)
1984
BAY BOY(1984, Can.)
Christopher Wiggins
TWO SOLITUDES(1978, Can.)
Eileen Wiggins
SUDDEN IMPACT(1983)
Helen Wiggins
NOT WANTED ON VOYAGE(1957, Brit.), ed
Jeanette Wiggins
1984
LAST NIGHT AT THE ALAMO(1984)
Lillian Wiggins
Misc. Silents
WHEN LONDON SLEEPS(1914, Brit.); HER ATONEMENT(1915)

Mike Wiggins
SMASH PALACE(1982, New Zealand)
Paul Wiggins
1984
WILD LIFE, THE(1984)
Ralph Wiggins
GREAT WALDO PEPPER, THE(1975), stunts
Russell Wiggins
LIMBO(1972)
Tudi Wiggins
MY SIDE OF THE MOUNTAIN(1969)
William H. Wiggins, Jr.
Misc. Talkies
IN THE RAPTURE(1976), d
Dick Wigginton
YOUNG DON'T CRY, THE(1957)
Helen Wigglesworth
PRIME OF MISS JEAN BRODIE, THE(1969, Brit.)
Kathy Wigglet
FIRST NUDIE MUSICAL, THE(1976)
Bob Wightman
WARRIORS, THE(1979), art d
Bruce Wightman
I'M ALL RIGHT, JACK(1959, Brit.); CAUGHT IN THE NET(1960, Brit.); RISK, THE(1961, Brit.); CONFESSIONS OF A WINDOW CLEANER(1974, Brit.)
Robert Wightman
JOHN AND MARY(1969), art d; OWL AND THE PUSSYCAT, THE(1970), art d; TAKING OFF(1971), art d; PARADES(1972), art d; AMAZING GRACE(1974), art d; AMERICAN GIGOLO(1980)
1984
IMPULSE(1984)
Ruth Wightman
Silents
ACE OF HEARTS, THE(1921), w; BEAUTIFUL LIAR, THE(1921), w
Anne Wighton
GREAT FLAMARION, THE(1945), w
Francis Wignall
CURE FOR LOVE, THE(1950, Brit.)
Mark Wignall
1984
CONSTANCE(1984, New Zealand)
Pink Wigoder
JERUSALEM FILE, THE(1972, U.S./Israel)
Hans Wigren
JUST ONCE MORE(1963, Swed.); DEAR JOHN(1966, Swed.)
Anne Wigton
SWEETHEARTS(1938); SKY MURDER(1940); STRANGE IMPERSONATION(1946), w
Dan Wigutow
LAST EMBRACE(1979), p
Daniel Wigutow
PURSUIT OF D.B. COOPER, THE(1981), p
Arn Wihtol
1984
MYSTERY MANSION(1984), w
Anders Wikman
Misc. Silents
PEST IN FLORENZ(1919, Ger.)
Ben Wikson
RIVALS(1972)
Brian Wikstrom
SHAME(1968, Swed.); PASSION OF ANNA, THE(1970, Swed.)
Bertil Wiktorsson
OBSESSION(1968, Swed.), ph
Spence Wil-Dee
KLANSMAN, THE(1974)
Nathan Wilansky
SEDUCTION OF JOE TYNAN, THE(1979)
Christopher Wilas
SCREAMERS(1978, Ital.), spec eff
Don Wilbanks
STAGECOACH TO DANCER'S PARK(1962); ZANDY'S BRIDE(1974)
Crane Wilber
LION AND THE HORSE, THE(1952), w
George Wilber
HAMMER(1972)
Robert Wilber
BRITISH AGENT(1934); SHE COULDN'T TAKE IT(1935)
Ruth Wilbert
SCOTLAND YARD HUNTS DR. MABUSE(1963, Ger.)
Robert Wilbor
Misc. Talkies
MARK TWAIN, AMERICAN(1976), d
Bob Wilbur
UNKNOWN WOMAN(1935); OUR RELATIONS(1936); RAIDERS OF THE DE-SERT(1941)
Burke Wilbur
Misc. Silents
PRINCESS OF PATCHES, THE(1917)
Claire Wilbur
Misc. Talkies
SCORE(1973); TEENAGE HITCHHIKERS(1975)
Crane Wilbur
CHILDREN OF PLEASURE(1930), w; LORD BYRON OF BROADWAY(1930), w; NAME THE WOMAN(1934); HIGH SCHOOL GIRL(1935), a, d; ON PROBA-TION(1935), w; PEOPLE'S ENEMY, THE(1935), d; PUBLIC OPINION(1935); UNWEL-COME STRANGER(1935), w; CAPTAIN CALAMITY(1936), a, w; DEVIL ON HORSEBACK, THE(1936), d; YELLOW CARGO(1936), d&w; ALCATRAZ IS-LAND(1937), w; DANCE, CHARLIE, DANCE(1937), w; HER HUSBAND'S SECRE-TARY(1937), w; NAVY SPY(1937), d&w; WE'RE IN THE LEGION NOW(1937), d, w;

WEST OF SHANGHAI(1937), w; CRIME SCHOOL(1938), w; GIRLS ON PROBATION(1938), w; OVER THE WALL(1938), w; PATIENT IN ROOM 18, THE(1938), d; PENROD'S DOUBLE TROUBLE(1938), w; BLACKWELL'S ISLAND(1939), w; HELL'S KITCHEN(1939), w; I AM NOT AFRAID(1939), d; MAN WHO DARED, THE(1939), d; KING OF THE LUMBERJACKS(1940), w; NIGHT OF ADVENTURE, A(1944), w; ROGER TOUHY, GANGSTER!(1944), w; BORN TO SPEED(1947), w; DEVIL ON WHEELS, THE(1947), d&w; RED STALLION, THE(1947), w; ADVENTURES OF CASANOVA(1948), w; CANON CITY(1948), d&w; HE WALKED BY NIGHT(1948), w; SPIRITUALIST, THE(1948), w; STORY OF MOLLY X, THE(1949), d&w; OUTSIDE THE WALL(1950), d&w; I WAS A COMMUNIST FOR THE F.B.I.(1951), w; INSIDE THE WALLS OF FOLSOM PRISON(1951), d&w; MIRACLE OF OUR LADY OF FATIMA, THE(1952), w; HOUSE OF WAX(1953), w; CRIME WAVE(1954), w; MAD MAGICIAN, THE(1954), w; PHENIX CITY STORY, THE(1955), w; WOMEN'S PRISON(1955), w; BATTLE STATIONS(1956), w; MONKEY ON MY BACK(1957), w; BAT, THE(1959), d&w; GEORGE RAFT STORY, THE(1961), w; MYSTERIOUS ISLAND(1961, U.S./Brit.), w; HOUSE OF WOMEN(1962), w

Silents
LOVE LIAR, THE(1916), a, d&w; HEART OF MARYLAND, THE(1921); MONSTER, THE(1925), w
Misc. Silents
CORSAIR, THE(1914); CONSCIENCE OF JOHN DAVID, THE(1916); LAW UNTO HIMSELF, A(1916); VENGEANCE IS MINE!(1916); WASTED YEARS, THE(1916); BLOOD OF HIS FATHERS(1917); EYE OF ENVY, THE(1917); PAINTED LIE, THE(1917), a, d; SINGLE CODE, THE(1917); BREEZY JIM(1919); DEVIL MCCARE(1919); STRIPPED FOR A MILLION(1919)

George Wilbur
PENNIES FROM HEAVEN(1981)
1984
CITY HEAT(1984); FIRESTARTER(1984)

George P. Wilbur
LEPKE(1975, U.S./Israel), stunts; MOVIE MOVIE(1978); COAST TO COAST(1980)

Jane Wilbur
OFFICER AND A GENTLEMAN, AN(1982)
1984
PRODIGAL, THE(1984)

Jody Wilbur
PAPER MOON(1973)

Joe Wilbur
DIRIGIBLE(1931), ph

Mabel Wilbur
Silents
COUNTY CHAIRMAN, THE(1914)

Robert Wilbur
FIREFLY, THE(1937); STORY OF DR. WASSELL, THE(1944)

James Wilby
PRIVILEGED(1982, Brit.)

Junior Wilby
ROCKERS(1980)

Claus Wilcke
YOUNG GO WILD, THE(1962, Ger.)

Rodolfo Wilcock
GOSPEL ACCORDING TO ST. MATTHEW, THE(1966, Fr., Ital.)

Jack Wilcocks
Silents
QUEEN OF MY HEART(1917, Brit.)

Sheelah Wilcocks
POPE JOAN(1972, Brit.)

Izinetta Wilcois
Misc. Talkies
MOON OVER HARLEM(1939)

Art Wilcox
RAINBOW OVER THE RANGE(1940), m

Caroly Wilcox
1984
MUPPETS TAKE MANHATTAN, THE(1984), puppeteer d

Carolyn Wilcox
MUPPET MOVIE, THE(1979)

Claire Wilcox
FORTY POUNDS OF TROUBLE(1962); WIVES AND LOVERS(1963)

Clayton Wilcox
1984
PHILADELPHIA EXPERIMENT, THE(1984)
Misc. Talkies
SKETCHES OF A STRANGLER(?); MY FRIENDS NEED KILLING(1984)

Colin Wilcox
TWICE UPON A TIME(1953, Brit.)

Collin Wilcox
TO KILL A MOCKINGBIRD(1962); NAME OF THE GAME IS KILL, THE(1968); 9/30/55(1977); JAWS II(1978)

Dave Wilcox
BAREFOOT EXECUTIVE, THE(1971)

Ella Wheeler Wilcox
Silents
MAN WORTH WHILE, THE(1921), w

Frank Wilcox
FATHER IS A PRINCE(1940); FIGHTING 69TH, THE(1940); GAMBLING ON THE HIGH SEAS(1940); LADY WITH RED HAIR(1940); MURDER IN THE AIR(1940); RIVER'S END(1940); SANTA FE TRAIL(1940); SEA HAWK, THE(1940); TEAR GAS SQUAD(1940); THEY DRIVE BY NIGHT(1940); 'TIL WE MEET AGAIN(1940); VIRGINIA CITY(1940); AFFECTIONATELY YOURS(1941); FOOTSTEPS IN THE DARK(1941); HIGHWAY WEST(1941); KNOCKOUT(1941); NAVY BLUES(1941); SERGEANT YORK(1941); SHOT IN THE DARK, THE(1941); WAGONS ROLL AT NIGHT, THE(1941); ACROSS THE PACIFIC(1942); BULLET SCARS(1942); BUSSES ROAR(1942); ESCAPE FROM CRIME(1942); FLYING FORTRESS(1942); HIDDEN HAND, THE(1942); JUKE GIRL(1942); LADY GANGSTER(1942); MURDER IN THE BIG HOUSE(1942); SECRET ENEMIES(1942); THEY DIED WITH THEIR BOOTS ON(1942); WILD BILL HICKOK RIDES(1942); WINGS FOR THE EAGLE(1942); EDGE OF DARKNESS(1943); NORTH STAR, THE(1943); TRUCK BUSTERS(1943); FOLLOW THE BOYS(1944); FOUR JILLS IN A JEEP(1944); IMPOSTER, THE(1944); IN THE MEANTIME, DARLING(1944); RAINBOW ISLAND(1944); STORY OF DR. WASSELL,

THE(1944); CONFLICT(1945); CLOAK AND DAGGER(1946); DEVIL'S MASK, THE(1946); NIGHT EDITOR(1946); NOTORIOUS(1946); STRANGE TRIANGLE(1946); BLONDIE'S ANNIVERSARY(1947); CASS TIMBERLANE(1947); DEAD RECKONING(1947); GENTLEMAN'S AGREEMENT(1947); HER HUSBAND'S AFFAIRS(1947); HIGH BARBAREE(1947); I COVER BIG TOWN(1947); OUT OF THE PAST(1947); PHILO VANCE RETURNS(1947); SOMETHING IN THE WIND(1947); VOICE OF THE TURTLE, THE(1947); CAGED FURY(1948); LET'S LIVE A LITTLE(1948); MIRACLE OF THE BELLS, THE(1948); CLAY PIGEON, THE(1949); FOUNTAINHEAD, THE(1949); MASKED RAIDERS(1949); MYSTERIOUS DESPERADO, THE(1949); SAMSON AND DELILAH(1949); SLIGHTLY FRENCH(1949); BLONDIE'S HERO(1950); CHAIN GANG(1950); FULLER BRUSH GIRL, THE(1950); KEY TO THE CITY(1950); KID FROM TEXAS, THE(1950); KISS TOMORROW GOODBYE(1950); MISTER 880(1950); CAVALRY SCOUT(1951); SHOW BOAT(1951); CARRIE(1952); FLESH AND FURY(1952); GREATEST SHOW ON EARTH, THE(1952); HALF-BREED, THE(1952); RAINBOW 'ROUND MY SHOULDER(1952); RUBY GENTRY(1952); SCARAMOUCHE(1952); TRAIL GUIDE(1952); TREASURE OF LOST CANYON, THE(1952); CHINA VENTURE(1953); MISSISSIPPI GAMBLER, THE(1953); PONY EXPRESS(1953); STORY OF THREE LOVES, THE(1953); THOSE REDHEADS FROM SEATTLE(1953); BLACK DAKOTAS, THE(1954); NAKED ALIBI(1954); THREE YOUNG TEXANS(1954); ABBOTT AND COSTELLO MEET THE KEYSTONE KOPS(1955); CAROLINA CANNONBALL(1955); COURT-MARTIAL OF BILLY MITCHELL, THE(1955); TRIAL(1955); EARTH VS. THE FLYING SAUCERS(1956); FIRST TRAVELING SALESLADY, THE(1956); HOLLYWOOD OR BUST(1956); MAN IN THE GREY FLANNEL SUIT, THE(1956); NEVER SAY GOODBYE(1956); SEVENTH CAVALRY(1956); STRANGE ADVENTURE, A(1956); TEN COMMANDMENTS, THE(1956); URANIUM BOOM(1956); BEGINNING OF THE END(1957); HELL'S CROSSROADS(1957); KELLY AND ME(1957); PAL JOEY(1957); JOHNNY ROCCO(1958); MAN FROM GOD'S COUNTRY(1958); GO, JOHNNY, GO!(1959); NORTH BY NORTHWEST(1959); PLEASE DON'T EAT THE DAISIES(1960); MAJORITY OF ONE, A(1961); SCARFACE MOB, THE(1962); SWINGIN' ALONG(1962); $1,000,000 DUCK(1971)

Fred Wilcox
HILLS OF HOME(1948), d

Fred M. Wilcox
LASSIE, COME HOME(1943), d; BLUE SIERRA(1946), d; COURAGE OF LASSIE(1946), d; THREE DARING DAUGHTERS(1948), d; SECRET GARDEN, THE(1949), d; SHADOW IN THE SKY(1951), d; CODE TWO(1953), d; TENNESSEE CHAMP(1954), d; I PASSED FOR WHITE(1960), p,d&w

Fred McLeod Wilcox
FORBIDDEN PLANET(1956), d

Harlow Wilcox
LOOK WHO'S LAUGHING(1941)

Harry Wilcox
NIGHT THE LIGHTS WENT OUT IN GEORGIA, THE(1981)

Hebert Wilcox
BLUE DANUBE(1932, Brit.), p&d

Herbert Wilcox
VICTORIA THE GREAT(1937, Brit.), p&d; BLACK WATERS(1929), p; SPLINTERS(1929, Brit.), p; LOVES OF ROBERT BURNS, THE(1930, Brit.), p&d, w; ON APPROVAL(1930, Brit.), p; ONE EMBARRASSING NIGHT(1930, Brit.), p; WOLVES(1930, Brit.), p; ALMOST A DIVORCE(1931, Brit.), p; CARNIVAL(1931, Brit.), p&d; CHANCE OF A NIGHT-TIME, THE(1931, Brit), p, d; MISCHIEF(1931, Brit.), p; PLUNDER(1931, Brit.), p; SPECKLED BAND, THE(1931, Brit.), p; TONS OF MONEY(1931, Brit.), p, w; UP FOR THE CUP(1931, Brit.), p; BARTON MYSTERY, THE(1932, Brit.), p; FLAG LIEUTENANT, THE(1932, Brit.), p; LEAP YEAR(1932, Brit.), p; LIFE GOES ON(1932, Brit.), p; LOVE CONTRACT, THE(1932, Brit.), p; MAGIC NIGHT(1932, Brit.), p&d; MAYOR'S NEST, THE(1932, Brit.), p; MONEY MEANS NOTHING(1932, Brit.), p, d; NIGHT LIKE THIS, A(1932, Brit.), p; SAY IT WITH MUSIC(1932, Brit.), p; THARK(1932, Brit.), p; BITTER SWEET(1933, Brit.), p&d; BLARNEY KISS(1933, Brit.), p; DISCORD(1933, Brit.), p; GENERAL JOHN REGAN(1933, Brit.), p; IT'S A KING(1933, Brit.), p; JUST MY LUCK(1933, Brit.), p; KING'S CUP, THE(1933, Brit.), p, d; LITTLE DAMOZEL, THE(1933, Brit.), p&d; LORD OF THE MANOR(1933, Brit.), p; MIXED DOUBLES(1933, Brit.), p; NIGHT OF THE GARTER(1933, Brit.), p; ONE PRECIOUS YEAR(1933, Brit.), p; PURSE STRINGS(1933, Brit.), p; SUMMER LIGHTNING(1933, Brit.), p; THAT'S A GOOD GIRL(1933, Brit.), p; TROUBLE(1933, Brit.), p; UP FOR THE DERBY(1933, Brit.), p; UP TO THE NECK(1933, Brit.), p; YES, MR. BROWN(1933, Brit.), p, d; FACES(1934, Brit.), p; GIRLS PLEASE!(1934, Brit.), p; IT'S A COP(1934, Brit.), p; KING OF PARIS, THE(1934, Brit.), p; LILIES OF THE FIELD(1934, Brit.), p; LUCKY LOSER(1934, Brit.), p; SORRELL AND SON(1934, Brit.), p; BREWSTER'S MILLIONS(1935, Brit.), p; COME OUT OF THE PANTRY(1935, Brit.), p; ESCAPE ME NEVER(1935, Brit.), p; HOPE OF HIS SIDE(1935, Brit.), p; NELL GWYN(1935, Brit.), p&d; RUNAWAY QUEEN, THE(1935, Brit.), p&d; FAME(1936, Brit.), p; MILLIONS(1936, Brit.), p; PEG OF OLD DRURY(1936, Brit.), p&d; BACKSTAGE(1937, Brit.), p&d; FROG, THE(1937, Brit.), p; GIRLS IN THE STREET(1937, Brit.), p&d; SPLINTERS IN THE AIR(1937, Brit.), p; BLONDES FOR DANGER(1938, Brit.), p; GANG, THE(1938, Brit.), p; GIRL IN THE STREET(1938, Brit.), p&d; NO PARKING(1938, Brit.), p; RAT, THE(1938, Brit.), p; RETURN OF THE FROG, THE(1938, Brit.), p; ROYAL DIVORCE, A(1938, Brit.), p; SHOW GOES ON, THE(1938, Brit.), p; SIXTY GLORIOUS YEARS(1938, Brit.), p&d; THIS'LL MAKE YOU WHISTLE(1938, Brit.), p&d; NURSE EDITH CAVELL(1939), p&d; TORPEDOED!(1939), p; IRENE(1940), p&d; NO, NO NANETTE(1940), p&d; SUICIDE LEGION(1940, Brit.), p; SUNNY(1941), p&d; WINGS AND THE WOMAN(1942, Brit.), p&d; FOREVER AND A DAY(1943), p&d; YELLOW CANARY, THE(1944, Brit.), p&d; YANK IN LONDON, A(1946, Brit.), p&d; COURTNEY AFFAIR, THE(1947, Brit.), p&d; PICCADILLY INCIDENT(1948), p&d; ELIZABETH OF LADYMEAD(1949, Brit.), p&d; SPRING IN PARK LANE(1949, Brit.), p&d; LADY WITH A LAMP, THE(1951, Brit.), p&d; MAN IN THE DINGHY, THE(1951, Brit.), p, d; ODETTE(1951, Brit.), p&d; FOUR AGAINST FATE(1952, Brit.), p, d; MAYTIME IN MAYFAIR(1952, Brit.), p, d; BEGGAR'S OPERA, THE(1953), p; TRENT'S LAST CASE(1953, Brit.), p&d; LAUGHING ANNE(1954, Brit.), p, d; TROUBLE IN THE GLEN(1954, Brit.), p, d; KING'S RHAPSODY(1955, Brit.), p; LET'S MAKE UP(1955, Brit.), p&d; BATTLE HELL(1956, Brit.), p; DANGEROUS YOUTH(1958, Brit.), d; MAN WHO WOULDN'T TALK, THE(1958, Brit.), p&d; WONDERFUL THINGS!(1958, Brit.), d; HEART OF A MAN, THE(1959, Brit.), d; LADY IS A SQUARE, THE(1959, Brit.), p, d; NAVY LARK, THE(1959, Brit.), p; TEENAGE BAD GIRL(1959, Brit.), p&d

Silents
FLAMES OF PASSION(1922, Brit.), d, w; PADDY, THE NEXT BEST THING(1923, Brit.), p, w; DECAMERON NIGHTS(1924, Brit.), p, d, w; WOMAN'S SECRET, A(1924, Brit.), p,d&w; LONDON(1926, Brit.), d; NELL GWYNNE(1926, Brit.), p,d&w; ONLY

WAY, THE(1926, Brit.), p,d&w; MADAME POMPADOUR(1927, Brit.), d; MUM-SIE(1927, Brit.), d; DAWN(1928, Brit.), p&d, w; PEEP BEHIND THE SCENES, A(1929, Brit.), p
Misc. Silents
TIPTOES(1927, Brit.), d; BONDMAN, THE(1929, Brit.), d; WOMAN IN WHITE, THE(1929, Brit.), d

Howard S. Wilcox
BREAKING AWAY(1979)

Jackson Wilcox
Misc. Silents
UNDER THE RED ROBE(1915, Brit.)

James Wilcox
SUNNY SKIES(1930)
Silents
PEACOCK FAN(1929)

Jimmy Wilcox
GUILTY GENERATION, THE(1931)

John Wilcox
MACOMBER AFFAIR, THE(1947), ph; WOMAN IN THE HALL, THE(1949, Brit.), makeup; GREAT MANHUNT, THE(1951, Brit.), ph; OUTCAST OF THE IS-LANDS(1952, Brit.), ph; PASSIONATE SENTRY, THE(1952, Brit.), ph; MR. DENNING DRIVES NORTH(1953, Brit.), ph; BLACK KNIGHT, THE(1954), ph; HELL BELOW ZERO(1954, Brit.), ph; PARATROOPER(1954, Brit.), ph; COCKLESHELL HEROES, THE(1955), ph; SAFARI(1956), ph; ZARAK(1956, Brit.), ph; CARVE HER NAME WITH PRIDE(1958, Brit.), ph; HARRY BLACK AND THE TIGER(1958, Brit.), ph; EXPRESSO BONGO(1959, Brit.), ph; MOUSE THAT ROARED, THE(1959, Brit.), ph; LIGHT UP THE SKY(1960, Brit.), ph; NEVER LET GO(1960, Brit.), makeup; TOUCH OF LARCENY, A(1960, Brit.), ph; I LIKE MONEY(1962, Brit.), ph; ONLY TWO CAN PLAY(1962, Brit.), ph; WALTZ OF THE TOREADORS(1962, Brit.), ph; NIGHT-MARE(1963, Brit.), ph; SUMMER HOLIDAY(1963, Brit.), ph; EVIL OF FRANKEN-STEIN, THE(1964, Brit.), ph; MOON-SPINNERS, THE(1964), ph; SOME PEOPLE(1964, Brit.), ph; 633 SQUADRON(1964), ph; DR. WHO AND THE DALEKS(1965, Brit.), ph; HYSTERIA(1965, Brit.), ph; JUDITH(1965), ph; SKULL, THE(1965, Brit.), ph; DALEKS–INVASION EARTH 2155 A.D.(1966, Brit.), ph; PSYCHOPATH, THE(1966, Brit.), ph; CASINO ROYALE(1967, Brit.), ph; DEADLY BEES,THE(1967, Brit.), ph; TWIST OF SAND, A(1968, Brit.), ph; CHAIRMAN, THE(1969), ph; LIMBO LINE, THE(1969, Brit.), ph; WHERE'S JACK?(1969, Brit.), ph; CONNECTING ROOMS(1971, Brit.), ph; DR. JEKYLL AND SISTER HYDE(1971, Brit.), makeup; LAST VALLEY, THE(1971, Brit.), ph; STEPTOE AND SON(1972, Brit.), ph; CRAZE(1974, Brit.), ph; GHOUL, THE(1975, Brit.), ph; VICTOR FRANKENSTEIN(1975, Swed./Ireland), ph; BELSTONE FOX, THE(1976, 1976), ph; CALL HIM MR. SHATTER(1976, Hong Kong), ph; DRACULA AND THE SEVEN GOLDEN VAMPIRES(1978, Brit./Chi.), ph; HOUND OF THE BASKERVILLES, THE(1980, Brit.), ph

Larry Wilcox
LAST HARD MEN, THE(1976)

Luana Wilcox
RAVAGER, THE(1970)

Lydia Wilcox
DREAM ON(1981), cos

M. V. Wilcox
Silents
FLAMES OF PASSION(1922, Brit.), w

Mary Charlotte Wilcox
IMPROPER CHANNELS(1981, Can.); STRANGE BREW(1983)

Mary Wilcox
FLAREUP(1969); LAWYER, THE(1969); MARLOWE(1969); LOVE ME DEAD-LY(1972); WILLIE DYNAMITE(1973); LEPKE(1975, U.S./Israel); PSYCHIC KIL-LER(1975); BIG BUS, THE(1976); BLACK OAK CONSPIRACY(1977)
Misc. Talkies
BEAST OF THE YELLOW NIGHT(1971, U.S./Phil.)

Patsy Wilcox
SECOND-HAND HEARTS(1981)

Pamela Wilcox [Bower]
MAN IN THE DINGHY, THE(1951, Brit.), w

Paula Wilcox
LOVERS, THE(1972, Brit.)
Misc. Talkies
MAN ABOUT THE HOUSE(1974, Brit.)

Peter Wilcox
GOING BERSERK(1983)

R. B. Wilcox
MISSISSIPPI GAMBLER(1929), ed

Ralph Wilcox
GORDON'S WAR(1973); CLAUDINE(1974); CRAZY JOE(1974); SUPER COPS, THE(1974); RIVER NIGER, THE(1976); MORE AMERICAN GRAFFITI(1979); MEGA-FORCE(1982); OFF THE WALL(1983)

Richard Wilcox
AMATEUR, THE(1982), art d

Robert Wilcox
ARMORED CAR(1937); CARNIVAL QUEEN(1937); LET THEM LIVE(1937); MAN IN BLUE, THE(1937); WILD AND WOOLLY(1937); CITY GIRL(1938); LITTLE TOUGH GUY(1938); RASCALS(1938); RECKLESS LIVING(1938); SWING THAT CHEER(1938); YOUNG FUGITIVES(1938); BLONDIE TAKES A VACATION(1939); BURIED ALI-VE(1939); GAMBLING SHIP(1939); KID FROM TEXAS, THE(1939); MAN THEY COULD NOT HANG, THE(1939); UNDERCOVER DOCTOR(1939); DREAMING OUT LOUD(1940); ISLAND OF DOOMED MEN(1940); UNKNOWN, THE(1946); WILD BEAUTY(1946); VIGILANTES RETURN, THE(1947)

Robert W. Wilcox
LONE WOLF STRIKES, THE(1940)

S. D. Wilcox
Silents
JACK RIDER, THE(1921)

Shannon Wilcox
CHEAPER TO KEEP HER(1980); BORDER, THE(1982); SIX WEEKS(1982)
1984
SONGWRITER(1984)

Sheelah Wilcox
TWINS OF EVIL(1971, Brit.)

Shelagh Wilcox
NICE GIRL LIKE ME, A(1969, Brit.); VAMPIRE LOVERS, THE(1970, Brit.)

Si Wilcox
Silents
TIPPED OFF(1923)

Silas Wilcox
Silents
KID, THE(1921)

Silas D. Wilcox
PARDON US(1931)

Toyah Wilcox
QUADROPHENIA(1979, Brit.)
Misc. Talkies
TEMPEST, THE(1980, Brit.)

Collin Wilcox-Horne
BABY MAKER, THE(1970); CATCH-22(1970); REVOLUTIONARY, THE(1970, Brit.); JUMP(1971)

Harry [Henry] Wilcoxon
PERFECT LADY, THE(1931, Brit.); FLYING SQUAD, THE(1932, Brit.); SELF-MADE LADY(1932, Brit.); LORD OF THE MANOR(1933, Brit.)

Henry Wilcoxon
CLEOPATRA(1934); CRUSADES, THE(1935); PRINCESS CHARMING(1935, Brit.); LAST OF THE MOHICANS, THE(1936); PRESIDENT'S MYSTERY, THE(1936); SOULS AT SEA(1937); TWO WHO DARED(1937, Brit.); ARIZONA WILDCAT(1938); DARK SANDS(1938, Brit.); FIVE OF A KIND(1938); IF I WERE KING(1938); KEEP SMI-LING(1938); MYSTERIOUS MR. MOTO(1938); PRISON NURSE(1938); CHASING DANGER(1939); TARZAN FINDS A SON!(1939); WOMAN DOCTOR(1939); CROOKED ROAD, THE(1940); EARTHBOUND(1940); FREE, BLONDE AND 21(1940); MYSTERY SEA RAIDER(1940); CORSICAN BROTHERS, THE(1941); LONE WOLF TAKES A CHANCE, THE(1941); SCOTLAND YARD(1941); SOUTH OF TAHITI(1941); THAT HAMILTON WOMAN(1941); MAN WHO WOULDN'T DIE, THE(1942); MRS. MINI-VER(1942); JOHNNY DOUGHBOY(1943); UNCONQUERED(1947); CONNECTICUT YANKEE IN KING ARTHUR'S COURT, A(1949); SAMSON AND DELILAH(1949); MINIVER STORY, THE(1950, Brit./U.S.); GREATEST SHOW ON EARTH, THE(1952); SCARAMOUCHE(1952); TEN COMMANDMENTS, THE(1956); BUCCANEER, THE(1958), p; WAR LORD, THE(1965); DOOMSDAY MACHINE(1967); PRIVATE NAVY OF SGT. O'FARRELL, THE(1968); MAN IN THE WILDERNESS(1971, U.S./Span.); DRAGNET(1974); AGAINST A CROOKED SKY(1975); PONY EXPRESS RID-ER(1976); WON TON TON, THE DOG WHO SAVED HOLLYWOOD(1976); F.I.S.T.(1978); CADDY SHACK(1980); MAN WITH BOGART'S FACE, THE(1980); SWEET SIXTEEN(1983)

Arnold Wild
RECOMMENDATION FOR MERCY(1975, Can.)

Diana Wild
THINGS ARE TOUGH ALL OVER(1982)

Edward Wild
WELL DONE, HENRY(1936, Brit.); OLD MOTHER RILEY IN PARIS(1938, Brit.)

Ernst Wild
CORPSE OF BEVERLY HILLS, THE(1965, Ger.), ph; SERENADE FOR TWO SPIES(1966, Ital./Ger.), ph; JACK OF DIAMONDS(1967, U.S./Ger.), ph; HOW TO SEDUCE A PLAYBOY(1968, Aust./Fr./Ital.), ph; YOUNG LORD, THE(1970, Ger.), ph; BARBER OF SEVILLE, THE(1973, Ger./Fr.), d&ph

Franz Josef Wild
END OF MRS. CHENEY(1963, Ger.), d

Harold J. Wild
AFFAIR WITH A STRANGER(1953), ph

Harry J. Wild
THEY WON'T BELIEVE ME(1947), ph; MAGNIFICENT AMBERSONS, THE(1942), ph; ROOKIES IN BURMA(1943), ph; CORNERED(1945), ph; FIRST YANK INTO TOKYO(1945), ph; JOHNNY ANGEL(1945), ph; MURDER, MY SWEET(1945), ph; WANDERER OF THE WASTELAND(1945), ph; WEST OF THE PECOS(1945), ph; NOCTURNE(1946), ph; TILL THE END OF TIME(1946), ph; TYCOON(1947), ph; STATION WEST(1948), ph; BIG STEAL, THE(1949), ph; EASY LIVING(1949), ph; STRANGE BARGAIN(1949), ph; THREAT, THE(1949), ph; GAMBLING HOUSE(1950), ph; WALK SOFTLY, STRANGER(1950), ph; HIS KIND OF WO-MAN(1951), ph; MY FORBIDDEN PAST(1951), ph; TWO TICKETS TO BROAD-WAY(1951), ph; LAS VEGAS STORY, THE(1952), ph; MACAO(1952), ph; SON OF PALEFACE(1952), ph; GENTLEMEN PREFER BLONDES(1953), ph; FRENCH LINE, THE(1954), ph; SHE COULDN'T SAY NO(1954), ph; UNDERWATER!(1955), ph; CON-QUEROR, THE(1956), ph

Harry Wild
BIG GAME, THE(1936), ph; LADY BEHAVE(1937), ph; PORTIA ON TRIAL(1937), ph; RACING LADY(1937), ph; ARMY GIRL(1938), ph; LAWLESS VALLEY(1938), ph; PAINTED DESERT, THE(1938), ph; RENEGADE RANGER(1938), ph; ARIZONA LEGION(1939), ph; FIGHTING GRINGO, THE(1939), ph; MARSHAL OF MESA CITY, THE(1939), ph; RACKETEERS OF THE RANGE(1939), ph; ROOKIE COP, THE(1939), ph; TROUBLE IN SUNDOWN(1939), ph; BULLET CODE(1940), ph; LADDIE(1940), ph; LEGION OF THE LAWLESS(1940), ph; MILLIONAIRES IN PRISON(1940), ph; WAGON TRAIN(1940), ph; BANDIT TRAIL, THE(1941), ph; CYCLONE ON HORSEBACK(1941), ph; DUDE COWBOY(1941), ph; FARGO KID, THE(1941), ph; LAND OF THE OPEN RANGE(1941), ph; ROBBERS OF THE RANGE(1941), ph; SAINT IN PALM SPRINGS, THE(1941), ph; SIX GUN GOLD(1941), ph; COME ON DANGER(1942), ph; RIDING THE WIND(1942), ph; VALLEY OF THE SUN(1942), ph; SO THIS IS WASHINGTON(1943), ph; STAGE DOOR CANTEEN(1943), ph; TARZAN TRIUMPHS(1943), ph; TARZAN'S DESERT MYSTERY(1943), ph; MADEMOISELLE FIFI(1944), ph; NEVADA(1944), ph; FALCON'S ADVENTURE, THE(1946), ph; WOM-AN ON THE BEACH, THE(1947), ph; PITFALL(1948), ph; TOP OF THE WORLD(1955), ph

J.P. Wild
Silents
NANCY COMES HOME(1918); FOLLIES GIRL, THE(1919)
Misc. Silents
PHANTOM HUSBAND, A(1917)

Jack Wild
OLIVER!(1968, Brit.); PUFNSTUF(1970); FLIGHT OF THE DOVES(1971); MELO-DY(1971, Brit.); PIED PIPER, THE(1972, Brit.); FOURTEEN, THE(1973, Brit.)

Jeanette Wild
ONE PLUS ONE(1969, Brit.); DR. JEKYLL AND SISTER HYDE(1971, Brit.)

John P. Wild
Silents
ONLY SON, THE(1914)
Misc. Silents
PRUDENCE ON BROADWAY(1919)
Katy Wild
DR. TERROR'S HOUSE OF HORRORS(1965, Brit.); TRAITOR'S GATE(1966, Brit./ Ger.); DEADLY BEES,THE(1967, Brit.); ON THE RUN(1967, Brit.); THEY CAME FROM BEYOND SPACE(1967, Brit.); DECLINE AND FALL... OF A BIRD WATCHER(1969, Brit.); ADAM'S WOMAN(1972, Austral.)
Lois Wild
CARYL OF THE MOUNTAINS(1936)
Shep Wild
LOVE MERCHANT, THE(1966); FLY NOW, PAY LATER(1969)
Wild Affair Trio
DOCTOR, YOU'VE GOT TO BE KIDDING(1967)
Wild Beauty the Horse
WILD BEAUTY(1946)
The Wild Ones
FAT SPY(1966)
Katy Wild-Rena
EVIL OF FRANKENSTEIN, THE(1964, Brit.)
Poul Wildaker
REPTILICUS(1962, U.S./Den.)
Klaus Wildbolz
PERMISSION TO KILL(1975, U.S./Aust.)
Alfred Wilde
JAWS(1975)
Andrew Wilde
1984
BOUNTY, THE(1984); CHAMPIONS(1984); 1984(1984, Brit.)
Brian Wilde
WILL ANY GENTLEMAN?(1955, Brit.); TIGER IN THE SMOKE(1956, Brit.); PICKUP ALLEY(1957, Brit.); CURSE OF THE DEMON(1958, Brit.); CIRLS AT SEA(1958, Brit.); SUBWAY IN THE SKY(1959, Brit.); WE JOINED THE NAVY(1962, Brit.); BARGEE, THE(1964, Brit.); RATTLE OF A SIMPLE MAN(1964, Brit.); DARLING(1965, Brit.); UNDERWORLD INFORMERS(1965, Brit.); JOKERS, THE(1967, Brit.); ON THE RUN(1967, Brit.); GOODBYE GEMINI(1970, Brit.); CONNECTING ROOMS(1971, Brit.); ONE BRIEF SUMMER(1971, Brit.); ALFIE DARLING(1975, Brit.); TO THE DEVIL A DAUGHTER(1976, Brit./Ger.); DOING TIME(1979, Brit.)
Colette Wilde
HOUSE OF THE ARROW, THE(1953, Brit.); THREE CASES OF MURDER(1955, Brit.); CIRCUS OF HORRORS(1960, Brit.); PROFESSIONALS, THE(1960, Brit.); HOUSE OF MYSTERY(1961, Brit.); SECRET PARTNER, THE(1961, Brit.); NIGHT OF THE PROWLER(1962, Brit.); DAY OF THE TRIFFIDS, THE(1963); MAROC 7(1967, Brit.); CLUE OF THE TWISTED CANDLE(1968, Brit.)
Cornel Wilde
LADY WITH RED HAIR(1940); HIGH SIERRA(1941); KISSES FOR BREAK- FAST(1941); KNOCKOUT(1941); PERFECT SNOB, THE(1941); LIFE BEGINS AT 8:30(1942); MANILA CALLING(1942); WINTERTIME(1943); SONG TO REMEMBER, A(1945); THOUSAND AND ONE NIGHTS, A(1945); BANDIT OF SHERWOOD FOR- EST, THE(1946); CENTENNIAL SUMMER(1946); LEAVE HER TO HEAVEN(1946); FOREVER AMBER(1947); HOMESTRETCH, THE(1947); IT HAD TO BE YOU(1947); ROAD HOUSE(1948); WALLS OF JERICHO(1948); SHOCKPROOF(1949); FOUR DAYS LEAVE(1950, Switz.); TWO FLAGS WEST(1950); AT SWORD'S POINT(1951); CALI- FORNIA CONQUEST(1952); GREATEST SHOW ON EARTH, THE(1952); OPERATION SECRET(1952); MAIN STREET TO BROADWAY(1953); SAADIA(1953); TREASURE OF THE GOLDEN CONDOR(1953); PASSION(1954); WOMAN'S WORLD(1954); BIG COMBO, THE(1955); SCARLET COAT, THE(1955); HOT BLOOD(1956); STAR OF INDIA(1956, Brit.); STORM FEAR(1956), a, p&d; BEYOND MOMBASA(1957); DE- VIL'S HAIRPIN, THE(1957), a, p&d, w; OMAR KHAYYAM(1957); MARACAI- BO(1958), a, p&d; EDGE OF ETERNITY(1959); CONSTANTINE AND THE CROSS(1962, Ital.); SWORD OF LANCELOT(1963, Brit.), a, p&d; NAKED PREY, THE(1966, U.S./South Africa), a, p&d; BEACH RED(1967), a, p&d; COMIC, THE(1969), p&d; NO BLADE OF GRASS(1970, Brit.), p&d; SHARK'S TREASURE(1975), a, p,d&w; BEHIND THE IRON MASK(1977); NORSEMAN, THE(1978)
Misc. Talkies
STAIRWAY FOR A STAR(1947)
Denea Wilde
GET CARTER(1971, Brit.)
Eric Wilde
MEET THE NAVY(1946, Brit.), md
Gordon Wilde
Misc. Talkies
ROGUE AND GRIZZLY, THE(1982)
Hagar Wilde
CAREFREE(1938), w; FIRED WIFE(1943), w; GUEST IN THE HOUSE(1944), w; UNSEEN, THE(1945), w; I WAS A MALE WAR BRIDE(1949), w; RED, HOT AND BLUE(1949), w; THIS IS MY LOVE(1954), w; SHADOW OF THE EAGLE(1955, Brit.), w
Harry Wilde
DON'T TELL THE WIFE(1937), ph
Heather Wilde
BANK DICK, THE(1940); GHOST AND MRS. MUIR, THE(1942); UNDYING MON- STER, THE(1942); SHERLOCK HOLMES FACES DEATH(1943); LODGER, THE(1944); KITTY(1945); LIFE WITH FATHER(1947); LAST HOLIDAY(1950, Brit.)
Jane Wilde
SKIN GAME, THE(1965, Brit.)
Jimmy Wilde
EXCUSE MY GLOVE(1936, Brit.)
Misc. Silents
PIT-BOY'S ROMANCE, A(1917, Brit.)
John Wilde
YANK IN THE R.A.F., A(1941)
Lee Wilde
REVEILLE WITH BEVERLY(1943); ANDY HARDY'S BLONDE TROUBLE(1944); TWICE BLESSED(1945); CAMPUS HONEYMOON(1948); LOOK FOR THE SILVER LINING(1949)

Lois Wilde
MILLIONAIRE KID(1936); SINGING COWBOY, THE(1936); STORMY TRAILS(1936); WILDCAT TROOPER(1936); HOPALONG RIDES AGAIN(1937); OUTCAST(1937); BROTHERS OF THE WEST(1938); DANGER VALLEY(1938); STEEL TOWN(1952)
Lorna Wilde
BODY STEALERS, THE(1969)
Louis Wilde
DEVIL'S HAIRPIN, THE(1957)
Lyn Wilde
REVEILLE WITH BEVERLY(1943); ANDY HARDY'S BLONDE TROUBLE(1944); TWICE BLESSED(1945); CAMPUS HONEYMOON(1948); LOOK FOR THE SILVER LINING(1949); SHERIFF OF WICHITA(1949); TUCSON(1949); SHOW BOAT(1951); BELLE OF NEW YORK, THE(1952); HAS ANYBODY SEEN MY GAL?(1952); GIRL NEXT DOOR, THE(1953)
Marty Wilde
JET STORM(1961, Brit.); HELLIONS, THE(1962, Brit.); WHAT A CRAZY WORLD(1963, Brit.); STARDUST(1974, Brit.)
Oscar Wilde
FLESH AND FANTASY(1943), w; CANTERVILLE GHOST, THE(1944), w; PICTURE OF DORIAN GRAY, THE(1945), w; IDEAL HUSBAND, AN(1948, Brit.), w; FAN, THE(1949), w; IMPORTANCE OF BEING EARNEST, THE(1952, Brit.), w; DORIAN GRAY(1970, Ital./Brit./Ger./Liechtenstein), w
Silents
PICTURE OF DORIAN GRAY, THE(1916, Brit.), w; MODERN SALOME, A(1920), w; SALOME(1922), w; LADY WINDERMERE'S FAN(1925), w
Pat Wilde
SEVEN ALONE(1975)
Percival Wilde
WOMAN IN ROOM 13, THE(1932), w
Silents
HUNCH, THE(1921), w
Poppy Wilde
CHANGE OF HEART(1934); OPERATOR 13(1934); ANGELS WITH DIRTY FA- CES(1938); THAT NIGHT IN RIO(1941); ROAD TO MOROCCO(1942); YANKEE DOODLE DANDY(1942)
Robert Wilde
LOOKING GLASS WAR, THE(1970, Brit.); MY LOVER, MY SON(1970, Brit.); ONE BRIEF SUMMER(1971, Brit.)
Sonya Wilde
I PASSED FOR WHITE(1960)
Ted Wilde
CLANCY IN WALL STREET(1930), d; LOOSE ANKLES(1930), d
Silents
GIRL SHY(1924), w; FRESHMAN, THE(1925), w; FOR HEAVEN'S SAKE(1926), w; BABE COMES HOME(1927), d; KID BROTHER, THE(1927), d, w; SPEEDY(1928), d
Misc. Silents
BATTLING ORIOLES, THE(1924), d
Thomas Wilde
SPACE MASTER X-7(1958)
Victoria Wilde
SCRATCH HARRY(1969)
Wendy Wilde
STAKEOUT ON DOPE STREET(1958); ARSON FOR HIRE(1959); DIARY OF A HIGH SCHOOL BRIDE(1959); GIRLS' TOWN(1959)
William Wilde
JUNGLE STREET GIRLS(1963, Brit.)
The Wilde Twins
TWO GIRLS AND A SAILOR(1944)
Clemens Wildemrod
DECISION BEFORE DAWN(1951)
Adelaid Wilder
NATIONAL LAMPOON'S VACATION(1983)
Alec Wilder
SAND CASTLE, THE(1961), a, m; OPEN THE DOOR AND SEE ALL THE PEO- PLE(1964), a, m
Audrey Wilder
LOVE IN THE AFTERNOON(1957)
Billy Wilder
EMIL AND THE DETECTIVE(1931, Ger.), w; HAPPY EVER AFTER(1932, Ger./ Brit.), w; WHERE IS THIS LADY?(1932, Brit.), w; ADORABLE(1933), w; WHAT WOMEN DREAM(1933, Ger.), w; MUSIC IN THE AIR(1934), w; LOTTERY LO- VER(1935), w; ONE EXCITING ADVENTURE(1935), w; BLUEBEARD'S EIGHTH WIFE(1938), w; EMIL(1938, Brit.), w; THAT CERTAIN AGE(1938), w; MID- NIGHT(1939), w; NINOTCHKA(1939), w; WHAT A LIFE(1939), w; ARISE, MY LO- VE(1940), w; RHYTHM ON THE RIVER(1940), w; BALL OF FIRE(1941), w; HOLD BACK THE DAWN(1941), w; MAJOR AND THE MINOR, THE(1942), d, w; FIVE GRAVES TO CAIRO(1943), d, w; DOUBLE INDEMNITY(1944), d, w; LOST WEEK- END, THE(1945), d, w; EMPEROR WALTZ, THE(1948), d, w; FOREIGN AFFAIR, A(1948), d, w; SONG IS BORN, A(1948), w; SUNSET BOULEVARD(1950), d, w; BIG CARNIVAL, THE(1951), p&d, w; STALAG 17(1953), p&d, w; SABRINA(1954), p&d, w; SEVEN YEAR ITCH, THE(1955), p, w; LOVE IN THE AFTERNOON(1957), p&d, w; SILK STOCKINGS(1957), w; SPIRIT OF ST. LOUIS, THE(1957), d, w; WITNESS FOR THE PROSECUTION(1957), d, w; SOME LIKE IT HOT(1959), p&d, w; APART- MENT, THE(1960), p&d, w; ONE, TWO, THREE(1961), p, d, w; IRMA LA DOU- CE(1963), p&d, w; KISS ME, STUPID(1964), p&d, w; FORTUNE COOKIE, THE(1966), p&d, w; PRIVATE LIFE OF SHERLOCK HOLMES, THE(1970, Brit.), p&d, w; AVANTI!(1972), p&d, w; FRONT PAGE, THE(1974), d, w; FEDORA(1978, Ger./ Fr.), p&d, w; ONE-TRICK PONY(1980), p, d, w; BUDDY BUDDY(1981), d&w
Bob Wilder
COUNT YORGA, VAMPIRE(1970), art d
Brad Wilder
BLACK SUNDAY(1977), makeup
Don Wilder
PAPERBACK HERO(1973, Can.), ph; ONLY GOD KNOWS(1974, Can.), ph; CHILD UNDER A LEAF(1975, Can.), ph; I MISS YOU, HUGS AND KISSES(1978, Can.), ph; MEATBALLS(1979, Can.), ph
Donald Wilder
NIKKI, WILD DOG OF THE NORTH(1961, U.S./Can.), ph; SPRING FEVER(1983, Can.), ph

Elder Wilder
CHAPPAQUA(1967)
Frank Wilder
LI'L ABNER(1940)
Gene Wilder
BONNIE AND CLYDE(1967); PRODUCERS, THE(1967); QUACKSER FORTUNE HAS A COUSIN IN THE BRONX(1970); START THE REVOLUTION WITHOUT ME(1970); WILLY WONKA AND THE CHOCOLATE FACTORY(1971); EVERYTHING YOU ALWAYS WANTED TO KNOW ABOUT SEX, BUT WE'RE AFRAID TO ASK(1972); BLAZING SADDLES(1974); LITTLE PRINCE, THE(1974, Brit.); RHINOCEROS(1974); YOUNG FRANKENSTEIN(1974), a, w; ADVENTURES OF SHERLOCK HOLMES' SMARTER BROTHER, THE(1975, Brit.), a, d&w; SILVER STREAK(1976); WORLD'S GREATEST LOVER, THE(1977), a, p,d&w; FRISCO KID, THE(1979); STIR CRAZY(1980); SUNDAY LOVERS(1980, Ital./Fr.), d, w; HANKY-PANKY(1982)
1984
WOMAN IN RED, THE(1984), a, d&w
Geri Wilder
ROCK, PRETTY BABY(1956)
Glen Wilder
SAND PEBBLES, THE(1966); LENNY(1974); NIGHT MOVES(1975); LOGAN'S RUN(1976), a, stunts; TWO-MINUTE WARNING(1976), a, stunts; MOONSHINE COUNTY EXPRESS(1977), stunts
1984
AGAINST ALL ODDS(1984)
Glenn Wilder
LOVE BUG, THE(1968); SHAMUS(1973), a, stunts; WHITE LIGHTNING(1973); MARCH OR DIE(1977, Brit.), Stunts
1984
CITY HEAT(1984)
Misc. Talkies
ZEBRA FORCE(1977)
Glenn R. Wilder
ROUSTABOUT(1964); I'M DANCING AS FAST AS I CAN(1982)
John Wilder
UNTIL THEY SAIL(1957); HOLD BACK THE NIGHT(1956); ROCK, PRETTY BABY(1956); UNGUARDED MOMENT, THE(1956); IMITATION GENERAL(1958); SUMMER LOVE(1958); FIVE GUNS TO TOMBSTONE(1961)
John David Wilder
GRASSHOPPER, THE(1970); R.P.M.(1970)
Kelly Wilder
HUSTLE(1975)
Lee Wilder
MAN WITHOUT A BODY, THE(1957, Brit.), d
Leslie Wilder
LADY TO LOVE, A(1930), ed
Leslie F. Wilder
SO THIS IS COLLEGE(1929), ed; MONTANA MOON(1930), ed; ROMANCE(1930), ed; SINS OF THE CHILDREN(1930), ed, titles
Silents
ADAM AND EVIL(1927), ed
Lester Wilder
MURDER BY TELEVISION(1935), ed
Marc Wilder
SECOND CHANCE(1953); TENDER TRAP, THE(1955); MEET ME IN LAS VEGAS(1956); OPPOSITE SEX, THE(1956); HOUSEBOAT(1958)
Margaret Buell Wilder
SINCE YOU WENT AWAY(1944), w; STOLEN LIFE, A(1946), w; YOUNG WIDOW(1946), w; PIRATES OF MONTEREY(1947), w
Myles Wilder
PHANTOM FROM SPACE(1953), w; KILLERS FROM SPACE(1954), w; SNOW CREATURE, THE,(1954), w; MANFISH(1956), w; SPELL OF THE HYPNOTIST(1956), w; SEVEN GUNS TO MESA(1958), w; SPY IN THE SKY(1958), w; BLUEBEARD'S TEN HONEYMOONS(1960, Brit.), w
Patricia Wilder
SPEED(1936); WALKING ON AIR(1936); WANTED: JANE TURNER(1936); BIG BROADCAST OF 1938, THE(1937); NEW FACES OF 1937(1937); ON AGAIN-OFF AGAIN(1937); THAT GIRL FROM PARIS(1937); LITTLE MISS BROADWAY(1938); MY LUCKY STAR(1938); THANKS FOR THE MEMORY(1938)
Robert Wilder
FLAMINGO ROAD(1949), w; WRITTEN ON THE WIND(1956), w; STRANGER IN MY ARMS(1959), w; SOL MADRID(1968), w; MEAN STREETS(1973)
Sally Wilder
FLAMINGO ROAD(1949), w
Sandra Wilder
1984
WOMAN IN RED, THE(1984)
Scott Wilder
1984
FIRSTBORN(1984)
Steve Wilder
LONGEST YARD, THE(1974)
Thornton Wilder
BRIDGE OF SAN LUIS REY, THE(1929), w; WE LIVE AGAIN(1934), w; OUR TOWN(1940), w; SHADOW OF A DOUBT(1943), w; BRIDGE OF SAN LUIS REY, THE(1944), w; MATCHMAKER, THE(1958), w; HELLO, DOLLY!(1969), w
W. Lee Wilder
GLASS ALIBI, THE(1946), p&d; PRETENDER, THE(1947), p&d; YANKEE FAKIR(1947), p&d; VICIOUS CIRCLE, THE(1948), p&d; ONCE A THIEF(1950), p, d, w; THREE STEPS NORTH(1951), p&d; PHANTOM FROM SPACE(1953), p&d; KILLERS FROM SPACE(1954), p&d; SNOW CREATURE, THE,(1954), p&d; BIG BLUFF, THE(1955), p&d; MANFISH(1956), p&d; SPELL OF THE HYPNOTIST(1956), p&d; MAN WITHOUT A BODY, THE(1957, Brit.), p; SPY IN THE SKY(1958), p&d; BLUEBEARD'S TEN HONEYMOONS(1960, Brit.), d
Misc. Talkies
OMEGANS, THE(1968), d
William Wilder
GREAT FLAMARION, THE(1945), p; STRANGE IMPERSONATION(1946), p

Yvonne Wilder
RETURN OF COUNT YORGA, THE(1971), a, w; SILENT MOVIE(1976); BLOOD-BROTHERS(1978); LAST MARRIED COUPLE IN AMERICA, THE(1980); SEEMS LIKE OLD TIMES(1980)
Guy Wilderson
GOLD IS WHERE YOU FIND IT(1938)
Marjorie Wildes
GREAT GATSBY, THE(1974)
Newlin B. Wildes
HEART OF THE RIO GRANDE(1942), w
Wildfire the Horse
LION AND THE HORSE, THE(1952)
Lee Wildgen
PROM NIGHT(1980)
Ulrich Wildgruber
DIE HAMBURGER KRANKHEIT(1979, Ger./Fr.)
Robert Wildhack
BROADWAY MELODY OF 1936(1935); BROADWAY MELODY OF '38(1937); BACK DOOR TO HEAVEN(1939)
Georg Wildhagen
MERRY WIVES OF WINDSOR, THE(1952, Ger.), d, w
April Wilding
BREATH OF LIFE(1962, Brit.); SECRETS OF A WINDMILL GIRL(1966, Brit.); HANDS OF THE RIPPER(1971, Brit.)
David Wilding
GORGO(1961, Brit.)
Diana Wilding
GIRL ON THE PIER, THE(1953, Brit.)
Mark Wilding
WUTHERING HEIGHTS(1970, Brit.)
Michael Wilding
CHARMING DECEIVER, THE(1933, Brit.); LATE EXTRA(1935, Brit.); WRATH OF JEALOUSY(1936, Brit.); THERE AIN'T NO JUSTICE(1939, Brit.); CONVOY(1940); SAILOR'S DON'T CARE(1940, Brit.); THREE COCKEYED SAILORS(1940, Brit.); TILLY OF BLOOMSBURY(1940, Brit.); BOMBSIGHT STOLEN(1941, Brit.); FARMER'S WIFE, THE(1941, Brit.); SPRING MEETING(1941, Brit.); BIG BLOCKADE, THE(1942, Brit.); IN WHICH WE SERVE(1942, Brit.); REMARKABLE MR. KIPPS(1942, Brit.); SHIPS WITH WINGS(1942, Brit.); SECRET MISSION(1944, Brit.); UNDERGROUND GUERRILLAS(1944, Brit.); RANDOLPH FAMILY, THE(1945, Brit.); CARNIVAL(1946, Brit.); COURTNEY AFFAIR, THE(1947, Brit.); IDEAL HUSBAND, AN(1948, Brit.); PICCADILLY INCIDENT(1948, Brit.); HER MAN GILBEY(1949, Brit.); SPRING IN PARK LANE(1949, Brit.); UNDER CAPRICORN(1949); STAGE FRIGHT(1950, Brit.); LADY WITH A LAMP, THE(1951, Brit.); LAW AND THE LADY, THE(1951); MAN IN THE DINGHY, THE(1951, Brit.), a, p; FOUR AGAINST FATE(1952, Brit.); MAYTIME IN MAYFAIR(1952, Brit.); TORCH SONG(1953); TRENT'S LAST CASE(1953, Brit.); EGYPTIAN. THE(1954); GLASS SLIPPER, THE(1955); SCARLET COAT, THE(1955); ZARAK(1956, Brit.); HELLO LONDON(1958, Brit.); BREAKOUT(1959, Brit.); WORLD OF SUZIE WONG, THE(1960); NAKED EDGE, THE(1961); BEST OF ENEMIES, THE(1962); GIRL NAMED TAMIRO, A(1962); SWEET RIDE, THE(1968); WATERLOO(1970, Ital./USSR); LADY CAROLINE LAMB(1972, Brit./Ital.)
1984
BLAME IT ON THE NIGHT(1984)
Charles Wildish
LION AND THE LAMB(1931)
Charles Wildman
GYPSY FURY(1950, Fr.), m
Jimmy Wildman
IRELAND'S BORDER LINE(1939, Ireland)
John Wildman
PROLOGUE(1970, Can.); HUMONGOUS(1982, Can.)
Julie Wildman
LITTLE GIRL WHO LIVES DOWN THE LANE, THE(1977, Can.); STRANGE SHADOWS IN AN EMPTY ROOM(1977, Can./Ital.); IN PRAISE OF OLDER WOMEN(1978, Can.)
Valerie Wildman
1984
SPLASH(1984)
Helmut Wildt
THE DIRTY GAME(1966, Fr./Ital./Ger.)
Ann E. Wile
1984
MOSCOW ON THE HUDSON(1984)
Anne E. Wile
WILLIE AND PHIL(1980)
Kathleen Wileman
OH! WHAT A LOVELY WAR(1969, Brit.)
Lydia Wilen
LAST SUMMER(1969); DIARY OF A MAD HOUSEWIFE(1970)
Max Wilen
BRINK OF LIFE(1960, Swed.), ph
Clem Wilenchick
LAST WARNING, THE(1938); BEASTS OF BERLIN(1939); FLYING DEUCES, THE(1939); TELEVISION SPY(1939); INVISIBLE KILLER, THE(1940)
Moshe Wilensky
MARTYR, THE(1976, Ger./Israel), m
Steven Wilensky
SUNBURN(1979)
Buster Wiles
THANK YOUR LUCKY STARS(1943)
Gordon Wiles
TRANSATLANTIC(1931), art d; HAT CHECK GIRL(1932), art d & set d; ME AND MY GAL(1932), art d; SOCIETY GIRL(1932), art d; TRIAL OF VIVIENNE WARE, THE(1932), art d; BROADWAY BAD(1933), art d; STAND UP AND CHEER(1934 80m FOX bw), art d; GEORGE WHITE'S 1935 SCANDALS(1935), art d; BLACK-MAILER(1936), d; CHARLIE CHAN'S SECRET(1936), d; LADY FROM NO-WHERE(1936), d; TWO-FISTED GENTLEMAN(1936), d; VENUS MAKES TROUBLE(1937), d; WOMEN OF GLAMOUR(1937), d; MR. BOGGS STEPS OUT(1938), d; PRISON TRAIN(1938), d; FORCED LANDING(1941), d; RELUCTANT DRAGON, THE(1941), art d; SCANDAL IN PARIS, A(1946), art d; GANGSTER, THE(1947), d; GUN CRAZY(1949), prod d; WHIPPED, THE(1950), art d; GINGER IN THE MORN-

ING(1973), d

John Wiles
MAN WITH A GUN(1958, Brit.), ph; HEADLESS GHOST, THE(1959, Brit.), ph; WITNESS, THE(1959, Brit.), ph

Judy Wiles
CLASS OF MISS MAC MICHAEL, THE(1978, Brit./U.S.)

Mabel Wiles
Silents
JORDAN IS A HARD ROAD(1915)
Misc. Silents
PLANTER, THE(1917)

Mark Wiles
NORSEMAN, THE(1978)

Pat Wiles
SPRING AFFAIR(1960)

Russel Wiles
DISORDERLY ORDERLY, THE(1964), ed; THREE ON A COUCH(1966), ed; BIG MOUTH, THE(1967), ed; HOOK, LINE AND SINKER(1969), ed; WHICH WAY TO THE FRONT?(1970), ed

Bennie Wiley
DARK END OF THE STREET, THE(1981)

Bill Wiley
PORKY'S II: THE NEXT DAY(1983)

David Wiley
FRIDAY THE 13TH PART III(1982)

Dwight Michael Wiley
BRIDE WORE BOOTS, THE(1946), w

Edward Wiley
CHARIOTS OF FIRE(1981, Brit.); HUNGER, THE(1983)

Flash Wiley
DARK END OF THE STREET, THE(1981)

Harrison Wiley
ACQUITTED(1929), art d; BROADWAY SCANDALS(1929), art d; LONE WOLF'S DAUGHTER, THE(1929), art d; WALL STREET(1929), art d; YOUNGER GENERATION(1929), art d; LADIES OF LEISURE(1930), art d; MELODY MAN(1930), art d; PERSONALITY(1930), art d; PRINCE OF DIAMONDS(1930), art d; SISTERS(1930), art d; SOLDIERS AND WOMEN(1930), art d; VENGEANCE(1930), art d
Silents
APACHE, THE(1928), art d; NOTHING TO WEAR(1928), art d; POWER OF THE PRESS, THE(1928), art d; RUNAWAY GIRLS(1928), art d; SCARLET LADY, THE(1928), art d; SINNER'S PARADE(1928), art d; ETERNAL WOMAN, THE(1929), art d; OBJECT–ALIMONY(1929), art d

Hugh Wiley
MR. WONG, DETECTIVE(1938), w; MR. WONG IN CHINATOWN(1939), w; MYSTERY OF MR. WONG, THE(1939), w; DOOMED TO DIE(1940), w; PHANTOM OF CHINATOWN(1940), w
Silents
BEHIND THE FRONT(1926), w

Jan Wiley
WITHOUT RESERVATIONS(1946); TONTO BASIN OUTLAWS(1941); ZIS BOOM BAH(1941); CITY OF SILENT MEN(1942); COLLEGE SWEETHEARTS(1942); DAWN ON THE GREAT DIVIDE(1942); LIVING GHOST, THE(1942); PARACHUTE NURSE(1942); STRANGE CASE OF DR. RX, THE(1942); THUNDER RIVER FEUD(1942); YOU'RE TELLING ME(1942); NEVER A DULL MOMENT(1943); RHYTHM PARADE(1943); SO PROUDLY WE HAIL(1943); UNDERDOG, THE(1943); ADVENTURES OF KITTY O'DAY(1944); FOLLOW THE BOYS(1944); JIVE JUNCTION(1944); LAW MEN(1944); SAN DIEGO, I LOVE YOU(1944); CISCO KID RETURNS, THE(1945); FRONTIER GAL(1945); THERE GOES KELLY(1945); BELOW THE DEADLINE(1946); BRUTE MAN, THE(1946); I RING DOORBELLS(1946); SHE-WOLF OF LONDON(1946)

Jane Wiley
FOES(1977)

Jane K. Wiley
FADE TO BLACK(1980)

John Wiley
GIANT(1956); GREAT LOCOMOTIVE CHASE, THE(1956)

Kay Wiley
LADY IN THE LAKE(1947); DETECTIVE STORY(1951); QUEEN FOR A DAY(1951); KANSAS CITY CONFIDENTIAL(1952); MILLION DOLLAR MERMAID(1952)

Larry Wiley
1984
SUBURBIA(1984)

Major Wiley
1984
TOP SECRET!(1984)

Margaret Wiley
PIPE DREAMS(1976); CAR, THE(1977)

Sharon Wiley
PRIVATE LIVES OF ADAM AND EVE, THE(1961)

Anthony Wileys [Mario Sequi]
TRAMPLERS, THE(1966, Ital.), d

Jane Wilford
DOCTOR FAUSTUS(1967, Brit.)

Joyce Wilford
WELCOME TO THE CLUB(1971)

Hans Wilheim
DIME WITH A HALO(1963), p, w

Ladi Wilheim
1984
MISSING IN ACTION(1984), art d

A. Wilhelm
ADORABLE JULIA(1964, Fr./Aust.), ed

Butch Wilhelm
RETURN OF THE JEDI(1983)

Hans Wilhelm
HIS MAJESTY, KING BALLYHOO(1931, Ger.), w; BERLIN ALEXANDERPLATZ(1933, Ger.), w; MAN STOLEN(1934, Fr.), w; DICTATOR, THE(1935, Brit./Ger.), w; BANK HOLIDAY(1938, Brit.), w; AFFAIR LAFONT, THE(1939, Fr.), w; CONFLICT(1939, Fr.), w; PRISON WITHOUT BARS(1939, Brit.), w; SPY FOR A DAY(1939, Brit.), w; HEARTBEAT(1946), w; ON AN ISLAND WITH YOU(1948), w; ONCE A THIEF(1950), w; PROWLER, THE(1951), w; NO TIME FOR FLOWERS(1952), w;

CASINO DE PARIS(1957, Fr./Ger.), w; FIVE GOLDEN HOURS(1961, Brit.), w

Julius Wilhelm
Silents
WIFE SAVERS(1928), w

Paul Frank Wilhelm
Silents
WIFE SAVERS(1928), w

Rolf Wilhelm
TONIO KROGER(1968, Fr./Ger.), m; DISORDER AND EARLY TORMENT(1977, Ger.), m; SERPENT'S EGG, THE(1977, Ger./U.S.), m

Rols Wilhelm
FROM THE LIFE OF THE MARIONETTES(1980, Ger.), m

Theodore Wilhelm
CRAWLING EYE, THE(1958, Brit.); MURDER AT SITE THREE(1959, Brit.); CIRCLE OF DECEPTON(1961, Brit.); SHOOT TO KILL(1961, Brit.)

Ute Wilhelm
JONATHAN(1973, Ger.), cos

Wolfgang Wilhelm
THERE GOES THE BRIDE(1933, Brit.), w; LUCK OF A SAILOR, THE(1934, Brit.), w; BREWSTER'S MILLIONS(1935, Brit.), w; GIVE HER A RING(1936, Brit.), w; TROOPSHIP(1938, Brit.), w; CONTINENTAL EXPRESS(1939, Brit.), w; DISPATCH FROM REUTERS, A(1940), w; VOICE IN THE NIGHT, A(1941, Brit.), w; PIMPERNEL SMITH(1942, Brit.), w; ESCAPE TO DANGER(1943, Brit.), w; SAINT MEETS THE TIGER, THE(1943, Brit.), w; SQUADRON LEADER X(1943, Brit.), w; UNCENSORED(1944, Brit.), w; GREAT DAY(1945, Brit.), w; ADVENTURESS, THE(1946, Brit.), w; CAPTAIN BOYCOTT(1947, Brit.), w; END OF THE RIVER, THE(1947, Brit.), w; SECRET PEOPLE(1952, Brit.), w; GREAT GAME, THE(1953, Brit.), w; DON'T BLAME THE STORK(1954, Brit.), w

Roman Wilhelmi
WAR OF THE WORLDS–NEXT CENTURY, THE(1981, Pol.)

Dian Wilhite
FLESH FEAST(1970)

Prentice Wilhite
NO MORE EXCUSES(1968)

Benji Wilhoite
SIX PACK(1982)

Kathleen Wilhoite
PRIVATE SCHOOL(1983)

Brook Wiliams
PLAGUE OF THE ZOMBIES, THE(1966, Brit.)

Mrs. C.P. Wiliams
ROYAL DEMAND, A(1933, Brit.), p

Robert Wiliams
PORK CHOP HILL(1959)

Frank Wilich, Jr.
SEPARATE PEACE, A(1972)

John Wilie
1984
PERILS OF GWENDOLINE, THE(1984, Fr.), w

Frank Wilimarth
PAL JOEY(1957)

Jane Wilimovsky
PEER GYNT(1965)

Herbert Wilk
BROKEN LOVE(1946, Ital.); CANARIS(1955, Ger.)

Liane Wilk
PINOCCHIO(1969, E. Ger.), makeup

Max Wilk
CLOSE-UP(1948), w; OPEN SECRET(1948), w; IT HAPPENED TO JANE(1959), w; DON'T RAISE THE BRIDGE, LOWER THE RIVER(1968, Brit.), w

Ray Wilk
RAGGEDY ANN AND ANDY(1977), w

Scott Wilk
VALLEY GIRL(1983), m
1984
CITY GIRL, THE(1984), m

Wiesla Wilk
FIRST START(1953, Pol.)

Alan Wilke
GOODBYE PORK PIE(1981, New Zealand)

Birthe Wilke
REPTILICUS(1962, U.S./Den.)

Bob Wilke
COME ON RANGERS(1939); IN OLD MONTEREY(1939); CHEYENNE WILDCAT(1944); CODE OF THE PRAIRIE(1944); FIREBRANDS OF ARIZONA(1944); HIDDEN VALLEY OUTLAWS(1944); MARSHAL OF RENO(1944); SAN ANTONIO KID, THE(1944); SHERIFF OF SUNDOWN(1944); VIGILANTES OF DODGE CITY(1944); YELLOW ROSE OF TEXAS, THE(1944); CORPUS CHRISTI BANDITS(1945); GREAT STAGECOACH ROBBERY(1945); LONE TEXAS RANGER(1945); MAN FROM OKLAHOMA, THE(1945); ROUGH RIDERS OF CHEYENNE(1945); SANTA FE SADDLEMATES(1945); SHERIFF OF CIMARRON(1945); TOPEKA TERROR, THE(1945); TRAIL OF KIT CARSON(1945); EL PASO KID, THE(1946); INNER CIRCLE, THE(1946); OUT CALIFORNIA WAY(1946); TRAFFIC IN CRIME(1946); WHITE TIE AND TAILS(1946); BUCK PRIVATES COME HOME(1947); LAST DAYS OF BOOT HILL(1947); TWILIGHT ON THE RIO GRANDE(1947); CARSON CITY RAIDERS(1948); DAREDEVILS OF THE CLOUDS(1948); RIVER LADY(1948); SIX-GUN LAW(1948); SUNDOWN IN SANTA FE(1948); LARAMIE(1949); WYOMING BANDIT, THE(1949); ACROSS THE BADLANDS(1950); BEYOND THE PURPLE HILLS(1950); BLONDE BANDIT, THE(1950); DESERT HAWK, THE(1950); FRONTIER OUTPOST(1950); KILL THE UMPIRE(1950); MULE TRAIN(1950); OUTCAST OF BLACK MESA(1950); TRAVELING SALESWOMAN(1950); TWILIGHT IN THE SIERRAS(1950); BEST OF THE BADMEN(1951); CYCLONE FURY(1951); SADDLE LEGION(1951); CATTLE TOWN(1952); HELLGATE(1952); LARAMIE MOUNTAINS(1952); ROAD AGENT(1952); POWDER RIVER(1953); FAR COUNTRY, THE(1955); SON OF SINBAD(1955); STRANGE LADY IN TOWN(1955); BACKLASH(1956); SPARTACUS(1960)

Bob [Robert] Wilke
VIGILANTES RETURN, THE(1947); WEST OF SONORA(1948); VENGEANCE VALLEY(1951); TWO GUNS AND A BADGE(1954)

Gisele Wilke
STOLEN IDENTITY(1953)
Jurgen Wilke
CARDINAL, THE(1963)
Rob Wilke
SUNSET IN EL DORADO(1945)
Robert Wilke
GUNPLAY(1951); HOT LEAD(1951); OVERLAND TELEGRAPH(1951); PISTOL HARVEST(1951); FARGO(1952); HIGH NOON(1952); LAS VEGAS STORY, THE(1952); MAVERICK, THE(1952); ARROWHEAD(1953); COW COUNTRY(1953); FROM HERE TO ETERNITY(1953); WAR PAINT(1953); LONE GUN, THE(1954); LONE RANGER, THE(1955); WICHITA(1955); CANYON RIVER(1956); RAWHIDE YEARS, THE(1956); GUN THE MAN DOWN(1957); HOT SUMMER NIGHT(1957); MAN OF THE WEST(1958); MAGNIFICENT SEVEN, THE(1960); BLUEPRINT FOR ROBBERY(1961); FATE IS THE HUNTER(1964); MORITURI(1965); SANTEE(1973); DAYS OF HEAVEN(1978)
Robert J. Wilke
MICHIGAN KID, THE(1947); 20,000 LEAGUES UNDER THE SEA(1954); SHOTGUN(1955); RAW EDGE(1956); WRITTEN ON THE WIND(1956); NIGHT PASSAGE(1957); TARNISHED ANGELS, THE(1957); RETURN TO WARBOW(1958); NEVER STEAL ANYTHING SMALL(1959); LONG ROPE, THE(1961); GUN HAWK, THE(1963); SHOCK TREATMENT(1964); HALLELUJAH TRAIL, THE(1965); SMOKY(1966); TONY ROME(1967); CHEYENNE SOCIAL CLUB, THE(1970); GUNFIGHT, A(1971); RESURRECTION OF ZACHARY WHEELER, THE(1971); BOY WHO CRIED WEREWOLF, THE(1973); SWEET CREEK COUNTY WAR, THE(1979); STRIPES(1981)
Misc. Talkies
GREAT MONKEY RIP-OFF, THE(1979)
Alfred Wilken
REPTILICUS(1962, U.S./Den.)
Dieter Wilken
SECRET OF SANTA VITTORIA, THE(1969)
John Buck Wilken
LAST MOVIE, THE(1971)
Barbara Wilkens
MURDER, INC.(1960)
Jose Wilker
DONA FLOR AND HER TWO HUSBANDS(1977, Braz.); BYE-BYE BRASIL(1980, Braz.); XICA(1982, Braz.)
Bill Wilkerson
JUAREZ(1939); DR. CYCLOPS(1940); CAPTAINS OF THE CLOUDS(1942); KING OF THE STALLIONS(1942); RIDING WEST(1944); THEY WERE EXPENDABLE(1945); BROKEN ARROW(1950); TRAVELING SALESWOMAN(1950)
Billy Wilkerson
MILLION DOLLAR LEGS(1939); FOREVER YOURS(1945); BOWERY BUCKAROOS(1947); ROBIN OF TEXAS(1947); APACHE CHIEF(1949); ROCK ISLAND TRAIL(1950); DESERT PURSUIT(1952); SAGINAW TRAIL(1953); YUKON VENGEANCE(1954); ESCAPE TO BURMA(1955); FOXFIRE(1955)
Buddy Wilkerson
HER LUCKY NIGHT(1945)
Carol Wilkerson
GOING HOME(1971)
David Wilkerson
CROSS AND THE SWITCHBLADE, THE(1970), w
Elaine Wilkerson
SPEED LOVERS(1968), w
Guy Wilkerson
HEART OF THE ROCKIES(1937); MOUNTAIN JUSTICE(1937); PARADISE EXPRESS(1937); YODELIN' KID FROM PINE RIDGE(1937); PROFESSOR BEWARE(1938); GONE WITH THE WIND(1939); OUR NEIGHBORS–THE CARTERS(1939); UNTAMED(1940); SERGEANT YORK(1941); SPOOKS RUN WILD(1941); SWAMP WOMAN(1941); JUKE GIRL(1942); MAJOR AND THE MINOR, THE(1942); MYSTERIOUS RIDER, THE(1942); RANGERS TAKE OVER, THE(1942); BAD MEN OF THUNDER GAP(1943); BORDER BUCKAROOS(1943); FIGHTING VALLEY(1943); RETURN OF THE RANGERS, THE(1943); WEST OF TEXAS(1943); BOSS OF THE RAWHIDE(1944); BRAND OF THE DEVIL(1944); DEAD OR ALIVE(1944); GANGSTERS OF THE FRONTIER(1944); GUNS OF THE LAW(1944); GUNSMOKE MESA(1944); PINTO BANDIT, THE(1944); SPOOK TOWN(1944); TRAIL OF TERROR(1944); WHISPERING SKULL, THE(1944); CAPTAIN TUGBOAT ANNIE(1945); ENEMY OF THE LAW(1945); FLAMING BULLETS(1945); FRONTIER FUGITIVES(1945); MARKED FOR MURDER(1945); THREE IN THE SADDLE(1945); DUEL IN THE SUN(1946); MICHIGAN KID, THE(1947); SEA OF GRASS, THE(1947); THAT HAGEN GIRL(1947); FURY AT FURNACE CREEK(1948); TEXAS, BROOKLYN AND HEAVEN(1948); GIRL FROM JONES BEACH, THE(1949); ROSEANNA McCOY(1949); SUN COMES UP, THE(1949); GREAT MISSOURI RAID, THE(1950); TICKET TO TOMAHAWK(1950); WINCHESTER '73(1950); COMIN' ROUND THE MOUNTAIN(1951); FAT MAN, THE(1951); MR. BELVEDERE RINGS THE BELL(1951); RED BADGE OF COURAGE, THE(1951); SANTA FE(1951); BIG SKY, THE(1952); SCANDAL SHEET(1952); LAST POSSE, THE(1953); STRANGER WORE A GUN, THE(1953); CRIME WAVE(1954); MA AND PA KETTLE AT HOME(1954); FAR COUNTRY, THE(1955); FOXFIRE(1955); I'LL CRY TOMORROW(1955); ONE DESIRE(1955); JUBAL(1956); BAND OF ANGELS(1957); BUSTER KEATON STORY, THE(1957); DECISION AT SUNDOWN(1957); SHOOT-OUT AT MEDICINE BEND(1957); COWBOY(1958); MAN OF THE WEST(1958); WILD HERITAGE(1958); HANGING TREE, THE(1959); WALKING TARGET, THE(1960); SUSAN SLADE(1961); TO KILL A MOCKINGBIRD(1962); HAUNTED PALACE, THE(1963); BLACK SPURS(1965); WAR PARTY(1965); SILENCERS, THE(1966); GREAT BANK ROBBERY, THE(1969); TRUE GRIT(1969); MONTE WALSH(1970); TODD KILLINGS, THE(1971)
Misc. Talkies
OUTLAW ROUNDUP(1944); THUNDERGAP OUTLAWS(1947)
Joy Wilkerson
RUN, ANGEL, RUN(1969); BIG FOOT(1973)
Martha Wilkerson
HARD, FAST, AND BEAUTIFUL(1951), w
Ralph Wilkerson
BEYOND AND BACK(1978), w
Steve Wilkerson
1984
MAKING THE GRADE(1984)

W. C. Wilkerson
BLUE CANADIAN ROCKIES(1952)
William Wilkerson
DAVY CROCKETT, INDIAN SCOUT(1950); KING OF THE KHYBER RIFLES(1953); SALOME(1953)
William P. Wilkerson
JUNGLE MANHUNT(1951); BRAVE WARRIOR(1952); CALIFORNIA CONQUEST(1952)
Donna Wilkes
JAWS II(1978); SCHIZOID(1980)
1984
ANGEL(1984)
Misc. Talkies
FYRE(1979); HOLLYWOOD KNIGHT(1979); BLOOD SONG(1982)
Elaine Wilkes
1984
SIXTEEN CANDLES(1984); WINDY CITY(1984)
Jerry Wilkes
TRUCK TURNER(1974), w
John Wilkes
RISK, THE(1961, Brit.), md
Keith Wilkes
CORNBREAD, EARL AND ME(1975)
Mattie Wilkes
Misc. Silents
FOR HIS MOTHER'S SAKE(1922)
Tom Wilkes
ELECTRA GLIDE IN BLUE(1973), art d
Winona Wilkes
Misc. Silents
SELL 'EM COWBOY(1924)
L. Guy Wilkey
Silents
ALIEN ENEMY, AN(1918), ph; ALL OF A SUDDEN NORMA(1919), ph
Violet Wilkey
Silents
BIRTH OF A NATION, THE(1915); REBECCA OF SUNNYBROOK FARM(1917)
Misc. Silents
LITTLE ORPHAN(1915)
Bob Wilkie
SAN QUENTIN(1937); SMOKE SIGNAL(1955)
Fay Wilkie
MARLOWE(1969)
Nan Wilkie
Misc. Silents
HARP KING, THE(1920, Brit.)
Violet Wilkie
Misc. Silents
CHILDREN PAY, THE(1916)
Wilma Wilkie
Misc. Silents
DEATHLOCK, THE(1915)
Barbara Wilkin
FLESH EATERS, THE(1964); STAGECOACH(1966); SIX IN PARIS(1968, Fr.)
Brad Wilkin
MIDNIGHT MADNESS(1980)
Jeremy Wilkin
STRANGE AFFAIR, THE(1968, Brit.); THUNDERBIRD 6(1968, Brit.); THUNDERBIRDS ARE GO(1968, Brit.); MEETINGS WITH REMARKABLE MEN(1979, Brit.)
John Buck Wilkin
LAST MOVIE, THE(1971), m
Al Wilkins
Misc. Talkies
SWEET GEORGIA(1972)
Barbara Wilkins
I SAW WHAT YOU DID(1965)
Bob Wilkins
REUNION(1932, Brit.)
David Wilkins
COTTONPICKIN' CHICKENPICKERS(1967); LITTLE SEX, A(1982)
Ernie Wilkins
STAND UP AND BE COUNTED(1972), m
Fred M. Wilkins
1984
HARRY AND SON(1984)
Jeremy Wilkins
CURSE OF THE FLY(1965, Brit.)
June Wilkins
ONE IN A MILLION(1936); CAMILLE(1937); LOVE AND HISSES(1937); THIN ICE(1937); BACHELOR MOTHER(1939); PIONEER DAYS(1940); WHEN THE DALTONS RODE(1940); LADY FROM CHEYENNE(1941)
Martin Wilkins
THEY WON'T BELIEVE ME(1947); REAL GLORY, THE(1939); CONGO MAISIE(1940); LAW OF THE JUNGLE(1942); I WALKED WITH A ZOMBIE(1943); VAMPIRE'S GHOST, THE(1945); MACOMBER AFFAIR, THE(1947); BOMBA THE JUNGLE BOY(1949); ROPE OF SAND(1949); ELEPHANT STAMPEDE(1951); SILVER CANYON(1951); SIROCCO(1951); BOMBA AND THE JUNGLE GIRL(1952); LYDIA BAILEY(1952); VOODOO WOMAN(1957)
Mary E. Wilkins
Silents
FALSE EVIDENCE(1919), w
Peter Wilkins
RAT FINK(1965)
Richard Wilkins
FEMALE RESPONSE, THE(1972)
Rick Wilkins
CHANGELING, THE(1980, Can.), m

Ronald Wilkins
DOCTOR IN THE HOUSE(1954, Brit.), w
Stan Wilkins
1001 ARABIAN NIGHTS(1959), anim
Trevor Wilkins
OUT OF THE BLUE(1982)
Vaughan Wilkins
DANGEROUS EXILE(1958, Brit.), w
Vaughn Wilkins
HILLBILLYS IN A HAUNTED HOUSE(1967), ph
Ann Wilkinson
BOOGEYMAN II(1983); FOREST, THE(1983)
Arthur Wilkinson
TROUBLE IN THE AIR(1948, Brit.), m; WEAKER SEX, THE(1949, Brit.), m; PERFECT WOMAN, THE(1950, Brit.), m; TRAVELLER'S JOY(1951, Brit.), m
Barrie Wilkinson
YOUNG GIRLS OF ROCHEFORT, THE(1968, Fr.); SONG OF NORWAY(1970)
Billy Wilkinson
LAST ROUND-UP, THE(1947)
Charles Wilkinson
1984
MY KIND OF TOWN(1984, Can.), d&w, m
Douglas Wilkinson
SAVAGE INNOCENTS, THE(1960, Brit.), cons
Elizabeth Wilkinson
TASTE OF BLOOD, A(1967)
G.K. Wilkinson
MONKEYS, GO HOME!(1967), w
Geoffrey Wilkinson
TREASURE ISLAND(1950, Brit.)
H. Wilkinson
QUEEN OF SPADES(1948, Brit.), ed
Harold Wilkinson
DR. JOSSER KC(1931, Brit.); JOSSER IN THE ARMY(1932, Brit.); SMITH'S WIVES(1935, Brit.); LOVE UP THE POLE(1936, Brit.)
Hazel Wilkinson
GREEN GROW THE RUSHES(1951, Brit.), ed
James Wilkinson
JET PILOT(1957), ed
John Wilkinson
DAYS OF HEAVEN(1978)
June Wilkinson
CAREER GIRL(1960); MACUMBA LOVE(1960); PRIVATE LIVES OF ADAM AND EVE, THE(1961); TWIST ALL NIGHT(1961); PLAYGIRLS AND THE BELLBOY, THE(1962,Ger.); TOO LATE BLUES(1962); WHO'S GOT THE ACTION?(1962); RAGE, THE(1963, U.S./Mex.); CANDIDATE, THE(1964)
Katherine Wilkinson
VENOM(1982, Brit.)
Maggie Wilkinson
EXPERIENCE PREFERRED... BUT NOT ESSENTIAL(1983, Brit.)
Mairin Wilkinson
1984
ISAAC LITTLEFEATHERS(1984, Can.), cos
Marc Wilkinson
IF ...(1968, Brit.), m&md; ROYAL HUNT OF THE SUN, THE(1969, Brit.), m; BLOOD ON SATAN'S CLAW, THE(1970, Brit.), m; FAMILY LIFE(1971, Brit.), m; HIRELING, THE(1973, Brit.), m; TRIPLE ECHO, THE(1973, Brit.), m; THREE SISTERS(1974, Brit.), md; EAGLE'S WING(1979, Brit.), m; FIENDISH PLOT OF DR. FU MANCHU, THE(1980), a, m; QUATERMASS CONCLUSION(1980, Brit.), m; MANGO TREE, THE(1981, Aus.), m; LOOKS AND SMILES(1982, Brit.), m; ENIGMA(1983), m
Mark Wilkinson
DARWIN ADVENTURE, THE(1972, Brit.), m
Mary Wilkinson
Silents
ROSE OF THE RANCHO(1914)
Michael Wilkinson
1984
PHAR LAP(1984, Aus.), w
Penelope Wilkinson
RIVER, THE(1951)
R.L. Wilkinson
TYPHOON TREASURE(1939, Brit.), p
Richard Wilkinson
NINE MEN(1943, Brit.)
Richard Hill Wilkinson
MISSING JUROR, THE(1944), w
Roderick Wilkinson
THREE CASES OF MURDER(1955, Brit.), w
Sam Wilkinson
OTHER PEOPLE'S SINS(1931, Brit.); OTHER WOMAN, THE(1931, Brit.); MAN FROM TORONTO, THE(1933, Brit.); MAN WHO WON, THE(1933, Brit.); THREE MEN IN A BOAT(1933, Brit.); ADVENTURE LIMITED(1934, Brit.); JACK AHOY!(1935, Brit.); DAREDEVILS OF EARTH(1936, Brit.); LAST JOURNEY, THE(1936, Brit.); POT LUCK(1936, Brit.); TROUBLED WATERS(1936, Brit.); NON-STOP NEW YORK(1937, Brit.); SABOTAGE(1937, Brit.); SKY'S THE LIMIT, THE(1937, Brit.); EVERYTHING HAPPENS TO ME(1938, Brit.); GOOD OLD DAYS, THE(1939, Brit.); TAWNY PIPIT(1947, Brit.)
Silents
PRINCE AND THE BEGGARMAID, THE(1921, Brit.); NOT QUITE A LADY(1928, Brit.); LOST PATROL, THE(1929, Brit.)
Misc. Silents
MONEY(1921)
Scott Wilkinson
HARRY'S WAR(1981); BOOGENS, THE(1982)
Wallace Wilkinson
CANNIBALS IN THE STREETS(1982, Ital./Span.)
1984
TANK(1984)

Wallace K. Wilkinson
LINCOLN CONSPIRACY, THE(1977)
Mairin Wilkinson
1984
RENO AND THE DOC(1984, Can.), ed
Lee Wilkof
SERIAL(1980); WHOLLY MOSES!(1980); ENTITY, THE(1982)
George Wilkosz
1984
NATURAL, THE(1984)
Cindy Wilks
EXTERMINATOR, THE(1980)
Marc Wilkson
EAGLE IN A CAGE(1971, U.S./Yugo.), m
Marie Wilkson
Silents
HELL-TO-PAY AUSTIN(1916)
Guy Wilky
Silents
AFTER THE SHOW(1921), ph; NICE PEOPLE(1922), ph; ADAM'S RIB(1923), ph; ONLY 38(1923), ph; BEDROOM WINDOW, THE(1924), ph; ICEBOUND(1924), ph; NEW LIVES FOR OLD(1925), ph; BEAUTIFUL BUT DUMB(1928), ph
L. Guy Wilky
Silents
JACK STRAW(1920), ph; MIDSUMMER MADNESS(1920), ph; WHAT EVERY WOMAN KNOWS(1921), ph; OUR LEADING CITIZEN(1922), ph; STRANGER, THE(1924), ph; NEW BROOMS(1925), ph; ONE WOMAN TO ANOTHER(1927), ph; WINGS(1927), ph
Gottfried Will
TRAPP FAMILY, THE(1961, Ger.), set d; MAN WHO WALKED THROUGH THE WALL, THE(1964, Ger.), art d
Rainer Will
LILI MARLEEN(1981, Ger.); LOLA(1982, Ger.); QUERELLE(1983, Ger./Fr.)
Sandra Will
1984
CHOOSE ME(1984)
Will Osborne and his Orchestra
IN SOCIETY(1944)
Suzanne Willa
Silents
ARMS AND THE WOMAN(1916); KICK IN(1917)
Geoffrey Willans
BRIDAL PATH, THE(1959, Brit.), w
Edmund Willard
LOVE STORM, THE(1931, Brit.); NIGHT IN MONTMARTE, A(1931, Brit.); CROOKED LADY, THE(1932, Brit.); FEAR SHIP, THE(1933, Brit.); PRIVATE LIFE OF DON JUAN, THE(1934, Brit.); HEAT WAVE(1935, Brit.); IRON DUKE, THE(1935, Brit.); SCARLET PIMPERNEL, THE(1935, Brit.); I STAND CONDEMNED(1936, Brit.); KING OF THE DAMNED(1936, Brit.); REMBRANDT(1936, Brit.); ROYAL EAGLE(1936, Brit.); DARK JOURNEY(1937, Brit.); PHANTOM SHIP(1937, Brit.); UNDERNEATH THE ARCHES(1937, Brit.); MAKE IT THREE(1938, Brit.); TROOPSHIP(1938, Brit.); HOOTS MON!(1939, Brit.); MILL ON THE FLOSS(1939, Brit.); PASTOR HALL(1940, Brit.); ATLANTIC FERRY(1941, Brit.); COURAGEOUS MR. PENN, THE(1941, Brit.); LARCENY STREET(1941, Brit.); YOUNG MR. PITT, THE(1942, Brit.); CARDBOARD CAVALIER, THE(1949, Brit.)
Fred Willard
JENNY(1969); MODEL SHOP, THE(1969); HUSTLE(1975); CHESTY ANDERSON, U.S. NAVY(1976); SILVER STREAK(1976); CRACKING UP(1977); FUN WITH DICK AND JANE(1977); AMERICATHON(1979); FIRST FAMILY(1980); HOW TO BEAT THE HIGH COST OF LIVING(1980)
1984
THIS IS SPINAL TAP(1984)
James Willard
Silents
ACE OF HEARTS, THE(1916, Brit.), a, w
Jess Willard
PRIZEFIGHTER AND THE LADY, THE(1933)
Silents
CHALLENGE OF CHANCE, THE(1919)
John Willard
BLACK WATERS(1929), w; CAT CREEPS, THE(1930), w; MASK OF FU MANCHU, THE(1932), w; VICTIMS OF PERSECUTION(1933); CAT AND THE CANARY, THE(1939), w; CAT AND THE CANARY, THE(1979, Brit.), w
Silents
SHERLOCK HOLMES(1922); CAT AND THE CANARY, THE(1927), w
Lee Willard
MAN WITH NINE LIVES, THE(1940)
Silents
GOOD-FOR-NOTHING, THE(1914); MEDIATOR, THE(1916)
Leigh Willard
Silents
LAST EDITION, THE(1925)
Misc. Silents
FOURTH COMMANDMENT, THE(1927)
Margaret Willard
Silents
ALL FOR A GIRL(1915)
Robert Willard
MAN WITH TWO BRAINS, THE(1983), spec eff
Winifred Willard
HIGHLAND FLING(1936, Brit.); MEN ARE NOT GODS(1937, Brit.); SCRUFFY(1938, Brit.); CASTLE IN THE AIR(1952, Brit.)
Jeanne Willardson
SINISTER URGE, THE(1961)
Kenneth Willardson
SINISTER URGE, THE(1961)
Boyd Willat
ZAPPED!(1982), art d

Edward Willat
Silents
FALSE FACES(1919), ph
I.V. Willat
LUCK OF ROARING CAMP, THE(1937), d; UNDER STRANGE FLAGS(1937), d
Irvin Willat
CAVALIER, THE(1928), p; DAMAGED LOVE(1931), d; OLD LOUISIANA(1938), d
Silents
CIVILIZATION(1916), ph; MIDNIGHT PATROL, THE(1918), d; FALSE FACES(1919), d, w; ON THE HIGH SEAS(1922), d; SIREN CALL, THE(1922), d; NORTH OF 36(1924), d; AIR MAIL, THE(1925), d; ANCIENT HIGHWAY, THE(1925), d; RUGGED WATER(1925), d; ENCHANTED HILL, THE(1926), d; PARADISE(1926), d; MICHIGAN KID, THE(1928), d, w
Misc. Silents
WOLF WOMAN, THE(1916), d; IN SLUMBERLAND(1917), d; DAUGHTER OF THE WOLF, A(1919), d; RUSTLING A BRIDE(1919), d; BEHIND THE DOOR(1920), d; BELOW THE SURFACE(1920), d; FOG BOUND(1923), d; HERITAGE OF THE DESERT, THE(1924), d; STORY WITHOUT A NAME, THE(1924), d; THREE MILES OUT(1924), d; WANDERER OF THE WASTELAND(1924), d; BACK TO GOD'S COUNTRY(1927), d; CAVALIER, THE(1928), d
Irvin V. Willat
Silents
GRIM GAME, THE(1919), d; FIFTY CANDLES(1921), d; PARTNERS OF THE TIDE(1921), p, w; ALL THE BROTHERS WERE VALIANT(1923), d
Misc. Silents
GUILTY MAN, THE(1918), d; LAW OF THE NORTH, THE(1918), d; DOWN HOME(1920), d; FACE OF THE WORLD(1921), d; PAWNED(1922), d; YELLOW MEN AND GOLD(1922), d
Nicholas Willatt
BROTHER SUN, SISTER MOON(1973, Brit./Ital.)
Chris Willbowbird
TAHITI NIGHTS(1945)
Charles Willcox
SPEED CRAZY(1959)
Toyah Willcox
JUBILEE(1978, Brit.)
Charles Willeford
BORN TO KILL(1975), w; THUNDER AND LIGHTNING(1977)
Heinz Willeg
THREE PENNY OPERA(1963, Fr./Ger.), cos
Renate Willeg
DOCTOR OF ST. PAUL, THE(1969, Ger.), ed; PRIEST OF ST. PAULI, THE(1970, Ger.), ed
Capt. Cornelius W. Willemse
BEHIND GREEN LIGHTS(1935), w
Edward Willens
HITLER'S MADMAN(1943), art d
Moshe Willensky
PILLAR OF FIRE, THE(1963, Israel), m, md
Max Willenz
WHEN LADIES MEET(1941); I MARRIED AN ANGEL(1942); PRIDE OF THE YANKEES, THE(1942); HEAVENLY BODY, THE(1943); THREE HEARTS FOR JULIA(1943); TWO SENORITAS FROM CHICAGO(1943); IN OUR TIME(1944); MADEMOISELLE FIFI(1944); PIN UP GIRL(1944); DESIRE ME(1947); IT HAPPENED ON 5TH AVENUE(1947); LIKELY STORY, A(1947); NORTHWEST OUTPOST(1947); SAXON CHARM, THE(1948); DANCING IN THE DARK(1949); GREAT SINNER, THE(1949); GENTLEMEN PREFER BLONDES(1953); SCANDAL AT SCOURIE(1953); STALAG 17(1953)
Alfred Willer
Silents
GIRL OF MY HEART(1920)
Dawn Willere
ART OF LOVE, THE(1965)
Jean Willes
SO PROUDLY WE HAIL(1943); HERE COME THE WAVES(1944); SALTY O'-ROURKE(1945); WINNER'S CIRCLE, THE(1948); CHINATOWN AT MIDNIGHT(1949); EMERGENCY WEDDING(1950); FULLER BRUSH GIRL, THE(1950); REVENUE AGENT(1950); WOMAN OF DISTINCTION, A(1950); JUNGLE JIM IN THE FORBIDDEN LAND(1952); SNIPER, THE(1952); SON OF PALEFACE(1952); YANK IN INDO-CHINA, A(1952); ABBOTT AND COSTELLO GO TO MARS(1953); ALL ASHORE(1953); FROM HERE TO ETERNITY(1953); GLASS WEB, THE(1953); MASTERSON OF KANSAS(1954); BOBBY WARE IS MISSING(1955); BOWERY TO BAGDAD(1955); COUNT THREE AND PRAY(1955); FIVE AGAINST THE HOUSE(1955); INVASION OF THE BODY SNATCHERS(1956); KING AND FOUR QUEENS, THE(1956); LIEUTENANT WORE SKIRTS, THE(1956); REVOLT OF MAMIE STOVER, THE(1956); TOWARD THE UNKNOWN(1956); HEAR ME GOOD(1957); HELL ON DEVIL'S ISLAND(1957); MAN WHO TURNED TO STONE, THE(1957); TIJUANA STORY, THE(1957); DESIRE UNDER THE ELMS(1958); NO TIME FOR SERGEANTS(1958); FBI STORY, THE(1959); THESE THOUSAND HILLS(1959); ELMER GANTRY(1960); OCEAN'S ELEVEN(1960); BY LOVE POSSESSED(1961); GUN STREET(1962); GYPSY(1962); MC HALE'S NAVY(1964); CHEYENNE SOCIAL CLUB, THE(1970); BITE THE BULLET(1975)
Peter Willes
CALL IT A DAY(1937); DAWN PATROL, THE(1938); ADVENTURES OF SHERLOCK HOLMES, THE(1939); HOUND OF THE BASKERVILLES, THE(1939); IDIOT'S DELIGHT(1939); WAY WE LIVE, THE(1946, Brit.)
Mike Willesee
MATILDA(1978)
Gilson Willets
Silents
CITY OF PURPLE DREAMS, THE(1918), w
E. Hunter Willett
PSYCH-OUT(1968), w
W. J. Willett
Silents
VANISHING HOOFS(1926)
Annie Willette
HYSTERICAL(1983)

Eddie Willey
Silents
JACK, SAM AND PETE(1919, Brit.)
Francis Willey
PLAGUE OF THE ZOMBIES, THE(1966, Brit.)
Leo G. Willey
Misc. Talkies
1ST NOTCH, THE(1977)
Leonard Willey
NIGHT CLUB SCANDAL(1937); PRINCE AND THE PAUPER, THE(1937); ADVENTURES OF ROBIN HOOD, THE(1938); INVISIBLE ENEMY(1938); TOM BROWN'S SCHOOL DAYS(1940); PENNY SERENADE(1941); THREE CAME HOME(1950)
Margaret Willey
DAY OF THE LOCUST, THE(1975)
Elmer Willhoite
ALL-AMERICAN, THE(1953)
Bill William
LAST GUNFIGHTER, THE(1961, Can.)
Bryn William
UNDER MILK WOOD(1973, Brit.)
Corrinne William
SHE MARRIED HER BOSS(1935)
Donnie William
BRUCE LEE–TRUE STORY(1976, Chi.)
Edwin William
STONY ISLAND(1978)
Elmo William
BIG GAMBLE, THE(1961), d
John William
CANDIDE(1962, Fr.)
Leonard William
ANATOMIST, THE(1961, Brit.), d
Noel William
MALTA STORY(1954, Brit.)
Raymond William
BREAKFAST IN HOLLYWOOD(1946)
Suzie William
Misc. Talkies
MONEY IN MY POCKET(1962)
Warren William
EXPENSIVE WOMEN(1931); HONOR OF THE FAMILY(1931); BEAUTY AND THE BOSS(1932); DARK HORSE, THE(1932); MATCH KING, THE(1932); MOUTHPIECE, THE(1932); SKYSCRAPER SOULS(1932); THREE ON A MATCH(1932); UNDER EIGHTEEN(1932); WOMAN FROM MONTE CARLO, THE(1932); EMPLOYEE'S ENTRANCE(1933); GOLD DIGGERS OF 1933(1933); GOODBYE AGAIN(1933); LADY FOR A DAY(1933); MIND READER, THE(1933); BEDSIDE(1934); CASE OF THE HOWLING DOG, THE(1934); CLEOPATRA(1934); DOCTOR MONICA(1934); DRAGON MURDER CASE, THE(1934); IMITATION OF LIFE(1934); SMARTY(1934); UPPER WORLD(1934); CASE OF THE CURIOUS BRIDE, THE(1935); CASE OF THE LUCKY LEGS, THE(1935); DON'T BET ON BLONDES(1935); LIVING ON VELVET(1935); SECRET BRIDE, THE(1935); CASE OF THE VELVET CLAWS, THE(1936); GO WEST, YOUNG MAN(1936); SATAN MET A LADY(1936); STAGE STRUCK(1936); TIMES SQUARE PLAYBOY(1936); WIDOW FROM MONTE CARLO, THE(1936); FIREFLY, THE(1937); MADAME X(1937); MIDNIGHT MADONNA(1937); OUTCAST(1937); ARSENE LUPIN RETURNS(1938); WIVES UNDER SUSPICION(1938); DAY-TIME WIFE(1939); GRACIE ALLEN MURDER CASE(1939); LONE WOLF SPY HUNT, THE(1939); MAN IN THE IRON MASK, THE(1939); ARIZONA(1940); LILLIAN RUSSELL(1940); LONE WOLF KEEPS A DATE, THE(1940); LONE WOLF MEETS A LADY, THE(1940); LONE WOLF STRIKES, THE(1940); TRAIL OF THE VIGILANTES(1940); LONE WOLF TAKES A CHANCE, THE(1941); SECRETS OF THE LONE WOLF(1941); WILD GEESE CALLING(1941); WOLF MAN, THE(1941); COUNTERESPIONAGE(1942); WILD BILL HICKOK RIDES(1942); ONE DANGEROUS NIGHT(1943); PASSPORT TO SUEZ(1943); STRANGE ILLUSION(1945); FEAR(1946); PRIVATE AFFAIRS OF BEL AMI, THE(1947)
William Hootkins Red Six
STAR WARS(1977)
Ada Williams
COMMON CLAY(1930)
Silents
JOY STREET(1929)
Adam Williams
FLYING LEATHERNECKS(1951); WITHOUT WARNING(1952); BIG HEAT, THE(1953); DRAGONFLY SQUADRON(1953); VICE SQUAD(1953); YELLOW TOMAHAWK, THE(1954); CRASHOUT(1955); SEA CHASE, THE(1955); PROUD AND THE PROFANE(1956); RACK, THE(1956); FEAR STRIKES OUT(1957); GARMENT JUNGLE, THE(1957); LONELY MAN, THE(1957); OKLAHOMAN, THE(1957); BADLANDERS, THE(1958); DARBY'S RANGERS(1958); SPACE CHILDREN, THE(1958); NORTH BY NORTHWEST(1959); LAST SUNSET, THE(1961); CONVICTS FOUR(1962); GUNFIGHT AT COMANCHE CREEK(1964); NEW INTERNS, THE(1964); GLORY GUYS, THE(1965); FOLLOW ME, BOYS!(1966); HORSE IN THE GRAY FLANNEL SUIT, THE(1968)
Al Williams
O'SHAUGHNESSY'S BOY(1935)
Al Williams
FANTASM(1976, Aus.)
Al Williams
Silents
WINGS(1927), ph
Al Williams, Jr.
PICK A STAR(1937)
Alan Williams
PINK JUNGLE, THE(1968), w
Alfonso Williams
HARD RIDE, THE(1971)
Alfred Williams
RANGO(1931), ph
Alfred T. Williams
HERE COME THE GIRLS(1953); ONE MAN JURY(1978)

Alistair Williams
BRAIN, THE(1965, Ger./Brit.)
Allen Williams
METEOR(1979); O'HARA'S WIFE(1983)
1984
AGAINST ALL ODDS(1984)
Andy Williams
I'D RATHER BE RICH(1964)
Annest Williams
STORK TALK(1964, Brit.)
Arnold Williams
LOST MAN, THE(1969); COTTON COMES TO HARLEM(1970); WHERE'S POP-PA?(1970); PANIC IN NEEDLE PARK(1971); KING OF MARVIN GARDENS, THE(1972); LIVE AND LET DIE(1973, Brit.); SCREAM BLACULA SCREAM(1973); MOTHER, JUGS & SPEED(1976); INSIDE MOVES(1980)
Arthur Williams
SONG OF FREEDOM(1938, Brit.); DEATH PLAY(1976), ed
Audrey Williams
SECOND FIDDLE TO A STEEL GUITAR(1965), m
Barbara Williams
UP IN ARMS(1944); GENTLE RAIN, THE(1966, Braz.)
1984
THIEF OF HEARTS(1984)
Misc. Talkies
TELL ME THAT YOU LOVE ME(1983)
Bart Williams
TUNNELVISION(1976)
Ben Williams
FLAME IN THE HEATHER(1935, Brit.); MAN WITHOUT A FACE, THE(1935, Brit.); SEXTON BLAKE AND THE BEARDED DOCTOR(1935, Brit.); SEXTON BLAKE AND THE MADEMOISELLE(1935, Brit.); FIND THE LADY(1936, Brit.); GAY OLD DOG(1936, Brit.); FALSE EVIDENCE(1937, Brit.); LANDSLIDE(1937, Brit.); GABLES MYSTERY, THE(1938, Brit.); MRS. PYM OF SCOTLAND YARD(1939, Brit.); SAINT IN LONDON, THE(1939, Brit.); TILLY OF BLOOMSBURY(1940, Brit.); OLD MOTHER RILEY'S CIRCUS(1941, Brit.); OLD MOTHER RILEY'S GHOSTS(1941, Brit.); FRONT LINE KIDS(1942, Brit.); PIMPERNEL SMITH(1942, Brit.); WE'LL SMILE AGAIN(1942, Brit.); BATTLE FOR MUSIC(1943, Brit.); OLD MOTHER RILEY, DETECTIVE(1943, Brit.); SAINT MEETS THE TIGER, THE(1943, Brit.); THEATRE ROYAL(1943, Brit.); GIVE ME THE STARS(1944, Brit.); KISS THE BRIDE GOODBYE(1944, Brit.); MY AIN FOLK(1944, Brit.); UNCENSORED(1944, Brit.); UNDERGROUND GUERRILLAS(1944, Brit.); ADVENTURE FOR TWO(1945, Brit.); HOME SWEET HOME(1945, Brit.); QUERY(1945, Brit.); CURSE OF THE WRAYDONS, THE(1946, Brit.); GRAND ES-CAPADE, THE(1946, Brit.); MURDER IN REVERSE(1946, Brit.); DUAL ALIBI(1947, Brit.); NOTHING VENTURE(1948, Brit.); DON'T EVER LEAVE ME(1949, Brit.); MY BROTHER'S KEEPER(1949, Brit.); WATERLOO ROAD(1949, Brit.); GIRL IS MINE, THE(1950, Brit.); PRELUDE TO FAME(1950, Brit.); SILK NOOSE, THE(1950, Brit.); SOMETHING IN THE CITY(1950, Brit.); FILES FROM SCOTLAND YARD(1951, Brit.); GALLOPING MAJOR, THE(1951, Brit.); LILLI MARLENE(1951, Brit.); NO HIGHWAY IN THE SKY(1951, Brit.); PAUL TEMPLE'S TRIUMPH(1951, Brit.); SCARLET THREAD(1951, Brit.); HAMMER THE TOFF(1952, Brit.); PAUL TEMPLE RE-TURNS(1952, Brit.); SING ALONG WITH ME(1952, Brit.); STOLEN FACE(1952, Brit.); WHISPERING SMITH VERSUS SCOTLAND YARD(1952, Brit.); MARILYN(1953, Brit.); MEN ARE CHILDREN TWICE(1953, Brit.); THERE WAS A YOUNG LADY(1953, Brit.); TWILIGHT WOMEN(1953, Brit.); WEDDING OF LILLI MARLENE, THE(1953, Brit.); LOVE MATCH, THE(1955, Brit.); SQUARE RING, THE(1955, Brit.); STORM OVER THE NILE(1955, Brit.); TECKMAN MYSTERY, THE(1955, Brit); YOU PAY YOUR MONEY(1957, Brit.); SILENT PARTNER, THE(1979, Can.)
Ben Ames Williams
MAN TROUBLE(1930), w; MAN TO MAN(1931), w; TOO BUSY TO WORK(1932), w; FATHER AND SON(1934, Brit.), w; SMALL TOWN GIRL(1936), w; ADVENTURE'S END(1937), w; INSIDE STORY(1939), w; SOMEONE TO REMEMBER(1943), w; LEAVE HER TO HEAVEN(1946), w; STRANGE WOMAN, THE(1946), w; ALL THE BROTHERS WERE VALIANT(1953), w; JOHNNY TROUBLE(1957), w
Silents
JUBILO(1919), w; ALWAYS AUDACIOUS(1920), w; ALL THE BROTHERS WERE VALIANT(1923), w; ACROSS THE SINGAPORE(1928), w; MASKED EMO-TIONS(1929), w
Beresford Williams
TRAITOR'S GATE(1966, Brit./Ger.)
Bernadette Williams
1984
CAGED FURY(1984, Phil.)
Bernard Williams
1984
BOUNTY, THE(1984), p
Bert Williams
NEST OF THE CUCKOO BIRDS, THE(1965), a, p,d&w; KLANSMAN, THE(1974); FROM NOON TO THREE(1976); WHITE BUFFALO, THE(1977); WANDA NEVA-DA(1979); TOM HORN(1980); 10 TO MIDNIGHT(1983)
Big Boy Williams
Silents
WESTERN FIREBRANDS(1921); $1,000 REWARD(1923); DOWN GRADE, THE(1927); VAMPING VENUS(1928)
Misc. Silents
ACROSS THE BORDER(1922); COWBOY KING, THE(1922); CYCLONE JO-NES(1923); END OF THE ROPE(1923); BAD MAN FROM BODIE(1925); BIG STUNT(1925); COURAGE OF WOLFHEART(1925); FANGS OF WOLFHEART(1925); RED BLOOD AND BLUE(1925); BURNING DAYLIGHT(1928)
Bill Williams
FLIGHT(1929); LAST MAN(1932); THIRTY SECONDS OVER TOKYO(1944); BACK TO BATAAN(1945); JOHNNY ANGEL(1945); THOSE ENDEARING YOUNG CHARMS(1945); WEST OF THE PECOS(1945); DEADLINE AT DAWN(1946); TILL THE END OF TIME(1946); LIKELY STORY, A(1947); CLAY PIGEON, THE(1949); DANGEROUS PROFESSION, A(1949); FIGHTING MAN OF THE PLAINS(1949); RANGE JUSTICE(1949); STRATTON STORY, THE(1949); WOMAN'S SECRET, A(1949); BLUE GRASS OF KENTUCKY(1950); CALIFORNIA PASSAGE(1950); CARI-BOO TRAIL, THE(1950); GREAT MISSOURI RAID, THE(1950); OPERATION HAY-LIFT(1950); ROOKIE FIREMAN(1950); BLUE BLOOD(1951); HAVANA ROSE(1951); LAST OUTPOST, THE(1951); BRONCO BUSTER(1952); PACE THAT THRILLS, THE(1952); ROSE OF CIMARRON(1952); SON OF PALEFACE(1952); TORPEDO

ALLEY(1953); OUTLAW'S DAUGHTER, THE(1954); RACING BLOOD(1954); APACHE AMBUSH(1955); HELL'S HORIZON(1955); BROKEN STAR, THE(1956); WIRETAP-PERS(1956); GUNFIGHT AT THE O.K. CORRAL(1957); HALLIDAY BRAND, THE(1957); PAWNEE(1957); SLIM CARTER(1957); STORM RIDER, THE(1957); LE-GION OF THE DOOMED(1958); SPACE MASTER X-7(1958); ALASKA PASS-AGE(1959); DOG'S BEST FRIEND, A(1960); HELL TO ETERNITY(1960); OKLAHOMA TERRITORY(1960); SERGEANT WAS A LADY, THE(1961); SCARFACE MOB, THE(1962); LAW OF THE LAWLESS(1964); HALLELUJAH TRAIL, THE(1965); SPA-CEFLIGHT IC-1(1965, Brit.); TICKLE ME(1965); BUCKSKIN(1968); RIO LOBO(1970); SCANDALOUS JOHN(1971); GIANT SPIDER INVASION, THE(1975); MOON OVER THE ALLEY(1980, Brit.); NIGHT OF THE ZOMBIES(1981)
Misc. Talkies
CREATURES OF DARKNESS(1969); 69 MINUTES(1977)
Billy Williams
JUST LIKE A WOMAN(1967, Brit.), ph; MAGUS, THE(1968, Brit.), ph; 30 IS A DANGEROUS AGE, CYNTHIA(1968, Brit.), ph; TWO GENTLEMEN SHARING(1969, Brit.), ph; WOMEN IN LOVE(1969, Brit.), ph; MIND OF MR. SOAMES, THE(1970, Brit.), ph; SUNDAY BLOODY SUNDAY(1971, Brit.), ph; DEVIL'S WIDOW, THE(1972, Brit.), ph; POPE JOAN(1972, Brit.), ph; X Y & ZEE(1972, Brit.), ph; EXORCIST, THE(1973), ph; KID BLUE(1973), ph; NIGHT WATCH(1973, Brit.), ph; WIND AND THE LION, THE(1975), a, ph; VOYAGE OF THE DAMNED(1976, Brit.), ph; BOARD-WALK(1979), ph; EAGLE'S WING(1979, Brit.), ph; GOING IN STYLE(1979), ph; SILENT PARTNER, THE(1979, Can.), ph; SATURN 3(1980), ph; ON GOLDEN POND(1981), ph; GANDHI(1982), ph; MONSIGNOR(1982), ph; SURVIVORS, THE(1983), ph
1984
ORDEAL BY INNOCENCE(1984, Brit.), ph
Misc. Talkies
SMOKY RIVER SERENADE(1947)
Misc. Silents
BLUE MOUNTAIN MYSTERY, THE(1922)
Billy Dee Williams
LAST ANGRY MAN, THE(1959); OUT OF TOWNERS, THE(1970); FINAL COME-DOWN, THE(1972); LADY SINGS THE BLUES(1972); HIT(1973); TAKE, THE(1974); MAHOGANY(1975); BINGO LONG TRAVELING ALL-STARS AND MOTOR KINGS, THE(1976); SCOTT JOPLIN(1977); EMPIRE STRIKES BACK, THE(1980); NIGH-THAWKS(1981); MARVIN AND TIGE(1983); RETURN OF THE JEDI(1983)
1984
FEAR CITY(1984)
Bindi Williams
STONE(1974, Aus.)
Bob Williams
TREAT EM' ROUGH(1942), w; OVERLAND MAIL ROBBERY(1943), w; BENEATH WESTERN SKIES(1944), w; HIDDEN VALLEY OUTLAWS(1944), w; LIGHTS OF OLD SANTA FE(1944), w; PRIDE OF THE PLAINS(1944), w; LONE TEXAS RAN-GER(1945), w; MARSHAL OF LAREDO(1945), w; LAWLESS BREED, THE(1946), w; ADVENTURES OF DON COYOTE(1947), w; BANDITS OF DARK CANYON(1947), w; HIGH WALL, THE(1947); SADDLE PALS(1947), w; BOLD FRONTIERSMAN, THE(1948), w; DENVER KID, THE(1948), w; DESPERADOES OF DODGE CITY(1948), w; FORCE OF EVIL(1948), w; MARSHAL OF AMARILLO(1948), w; OKLAHOMA BADLANDS(1948), w; SON OF GOD'S COUNTRY(1948), w; TIMBER TRAIL, THE(1948), w; DEATH VALLEY GUNFIGHTER(1949), w; FRONTIER INVESTIGA-TOR(1949), w; RANGER OF CHEROKEE STRIP(1949), w; SHERIFF OF WI-CHITA(1949), w; OLD FRONTIER, THE(1950), w; PIONEER MARSHAL(1950), w; STAGE TO TUCSON(1950), w; UNDER MEXICALI STARS(1950), w; VANISHING WESTERNER, THE(1950), w; SILVER CITY BONANZA(1951), w; MACAO(1952), w; STARS ARE SINGING, THE(1953); ACCUSED OF MURDER(1956), w; DUEL AT APACHE WELLS(1957), w; IRON SHERIFF, THE(1957); 20 MILLION MILES TO EARTH(1957), w; HELL SQUAD(1958); SAGA OF HEMP BROWN, THE(1958), w; FITZWILLY(1967); WARNING SHOT(1967), w; PHYNX, THE(1970); ONE DARK NIGHT(1983), spec eff
Bobbie Gene Williams
SPOOK WHO SAT BY THE DOOR, THE(1973)
Branden Williams
1984
BREAKIN' 2: ELECTRIC BOOGALOO(1984)
Brandon Brent Williams
HEART LIKE A WHEEL(1983)
Bransby Williams
WOMAN IN COMMAND, THE(1934 Brit.); HEARTS OF HUMANITY(1936, Brit.); SONG OF THE ROAD(1937, Brit.); COMMON TOUCH, THE(1941, Brit.); THOSE KIDS FROM TOWN(1942, Brit.); AT DAWN WE DIE(1943, Brit.); TROJAN BROTHERS, THE(1946); AGITATOR, THE(1949); JUDGMENT DEFERRED(1952, Brit.)
Silents
HARD TIMES(1915, Brit.); ADAM BEDE(1918, Brit.); GREATEST WISH IN THE WORLD, THE(1918, Brit.); ADVENTURES OF MR. PICKWICK, THE(1921, Brit.)
Bret Williams
URBAN COWBOY(1980)
Brian Williams
BAKER'S HAWK(1976); SMOKEY BITES THE DUST(1981), w
Brock Williams
ALMOST A DIVORCE(1931, Brit.), w; BLACK COFFEE(1931, Brit.), w; BOAT FROM SHANGHAI(1931, Brit.), w; ETERNAL FEMININE, THE(1931, Brit.), w; CON-DEMNED TO DEATH(1932, Brit.), w; DON'T BE A DUMMY(1932, Brit.), w; HER FIRST AFFAIRE(1932, Brit.), w; LOOKING ON THE BRIGHT SIDE(1932, Brit.), w; HEAD OF THE FAMILY(1933, Brit.), w; MR. QUINCEY OF MONTE CARLO(1933, Brit.), w; THIRTEENTH CANDLE, THE(1933, Brit.), w; BLUE SQUADRON, THE(1934, Brit.), w; LASH, THE(1934, Brit.), w; LEAVE IT TO BLANCHE(1934, Brit.), w; LIFE OF THE PARTY(1934, Brit.), w; NINE FORTY-FIVE(1934, Brit.), w; SILVER SPOON, THE(1934, Brit.), w; SOMETHING ALWAYS HAPPENS(1934, Brit.), w; TOO MANY MILLIONS(1934, Brit.), w; WHAT HAPPENED TO HARKNESS(1934, Brit.), w; WIDOW'S MIGHT(1934, Brit.), w; CRIME UNLIMITED(1935, Brit.), w; HELLO SWEETHEART(1935, Brit.), w; SOME DAY(1935, Brit.), w; CROWN VS STEVENS(1936), w; FAIR EXCHANGE(1936, Brit.), w; FAITHFUL(1936, Brit.), w; HAIL AND FAREWELL(1936, Brit.), w; IRISH FOR LUCK(1936, Brit.), w; IT'S IN THE BAG(1936, Brit.), w; MR. COHEN TAKES A WALK(1936, Brit.), w; THEY DIDN'T KNOW(1936, Brit.), w; WHERE'S SALLY?(1936, Brit.), w; WOLF'S CLOTHING(1936, Brit.), w; DON'T GET ME WRONG(1937, Brit.), w; GYPSY(1937, Brit.), w; MERRY COMES TO STAY(1937, Brit.), w; WANTED(1937, Brit.), w; YOU LIVE AND LEARN(1937, Brit.), w; DARK STAIRWAY, THE(1938, Brit.), w; IT'S IN THE

Bronwen Williams-

BLOOD(1938, Brit.), w; SINGING COP, THE(1938, Brit.), w; THISTLEDOWN(1938, Brit.), w; CLOUDS OVER EUROPE(1939, Brit.), w; CONFIDENTIAL LADY(1939, Brit.), w; HIS BROTHER'S KEEPER(1939, Brit.), w; MURDER WILL OUT(1939, Brit.), w; BLACKOUT(1940, Brit.), w; BRIGGS FAMILY, THE(1940, Brit.), w; EARL OF CHICAGO, THE(1940, w; FINGERS(1940, Brit.), w; GEORGE AND MARGARET(1940, Brit.), w; MIDAS TOUCH, THE(1940, Brit.), w; TWO FOR DANGER(1940, Brit.), w; PRIME MINISTER, THE(1941, Brit.), w; FLYING FORTRESS(1942, Brit.), w; PETERVILLE DIAMOND, THE(1942, Brit.), w; THIS WAS PARIS(1942, Brit.), w; DARK TOWER, THE(1943, Brit.), w; HUNDRED POUND WINDOW, THE(1943, Brit.), w; NIGHT INVADER, THE(1943, Brit), w; CANDLELIGHT IN ALGERIA(1944, Brit.), w; MADONNA OF THE SEVEN MOONS(1945, Brit.), w; PLACE OF ONE'S OWN, A(1945, Brit.), w; DANCING WITH CRIME(1947, Brit.), w; ROOT OF ALL EVIL, THE(1947, Brit.), d&w; TONY DRAWS A HORSE(1951, Brit.), p, w; I'M A STRANGER(1952, Brit.), d&w; NIGHT WON'T TALK, THE(1952, Brit.), w; ISN'T LIFE WONDERFUL!(1953, Brit.), w; THREE STEPS IN THE DARK(1953, Brit.), w; GILDED CAGE, THE(1954, Brit.), w; HARASSED HERO, THE(1954, Brit.), w; MEET MR. CALLAGHAN(1954, Brit.), w; MEET MR. MALCOLM(1954, Brit.), w; HANDCUFFS, LONDON(1955, Brit.), w; TIME OF HIS LIFE, THE(1955, Brit.), w; DATE WITH DISASTER(1957, Brit.), w; HIGH TERRACE(1957, Brit.), w; STORMY CROSSING(1958, Brit.), w; NAKED FURY(1959, Brit.), w; STRICTLY CONFIDENTIAL(1959, Brit.), w; GENTLE TRAP, THE(1960, Brit.), w; OPERATION CUPID(1960, Brit.), w; TICKET TO PARADISE(1961, Brit.), w; YOUNG, WILLING AND EAGER(1962, Brit.), w; MURDER CAN BE DEADLY(1963, Brit.), w; IN TROUBLE WITH EVE(1964, Brit.), w; PLEASURE LOVERS, THE(1964, Brit.), w

Bronwen Williams
UNDER MILK WOOD(1973, Brit.)

Brook Williams
HEROES OF TELEMARK, THE(1965, Brit.); JOKERS, THE(1967, Brit.); WHERE EAGLES DARE(1968, Brit.); ANNE OF THE THOUSAND DAYS(1969, Brit.); LONG AGO, TOMORROW(1971, Brit.); RAID ON ROMMEL(1971); VILLAIN(1971, Brit.); HAMMERSMITH IS OUT(1972); WILD GEESE, THE(1978, Brit.); FFOLKES(1980, Brit.); ABSOLUTION(1981, Brit.); SEA WOLVES, THE(1981, Brit.); WAGNER(1983, Brit./Hung./Aust.)

Brooks Williams
MEDUSA TOUCH, THE(1978, Brit.)

Buddy Williams
TWENTIETH CENTURY(1934); DON'T BET ON BLONDES(1935); NEXT TIME WE LOVE(1936); ROUNDUP TIME IN TEXAS(1937); FLIGHT FOR FREEDOM(1943)

Byron Williams
LIBIDO(1973, Aus.)

C. Williams
Silents
KID CANFIELD THE REFORM GAMBLER(1922)

C. B. Williams
HEROES IN BLUE(1939), w; HIDDEN ENEMY(1940), w; CIRCUS OF LOVE(1958, Ger.), w

C. D. Williams
Misc. Silents
DEVIL'S ANGEL, THE(1920)

C. H. Williams
MIDNIGHT LIMITED(1940), w

C. Jay Williams
Misc. Silents
CROOKY(1915), d; WHAT HAPPENED TO FATHER(1915), d; SUPRISES OF AN EMPTY HOTEL, THE(1916); WILD OATS(1919), d

C. L. Williams
CARNIVAL STORY(1954), w; BOOK OF NUMBERS(1973)

C. W. Williams
Silents
FALSE BRANDS(1922)

Cal Williams
INDEPENDENCE DAY(1976)

Cara Williams
HAPPY LAND(1943); IN THE MEANTIME, DARLING(1944); LAURA(1944); SOMETHING FOR THE BOYS(1944); SWEET AND LOWDOWN(1944); DON JUAN QUILLIGAN(1945); SPIDER, THE(1945); BOOMERANG(1947); SAXON CHARM, THE(1948); SITTING PRETTY(1948); KNOCK ON ANY DOOR(1949); GIRL NEXT DOOR, THE(1953); GREAT DIAMOND ROBBERY(1953); MONTE CARLO BABY(1953, Fr.); MEET ME IN LAS VEGAS(1956); DEFIANT ONES, THE(1958); HELEN MORGAN STORY, THE(1959); NEVER STEAL ANYTHING SMALL(1959); MAN FROM THE DINERS' CLUB, THE(1963); DOCTORS' WIVES(1971); WHITE BUFFALO, THE(1977); ONE MAN JURY(1978)

Carl Williams
HAPPY BIRTHDAY, DAVY(1970)

Carol Williams
ICE CASTLES(1978)

Carol Ann Williams
BUTCH AND SUNDANCE: THE EARLY DAYS(1979); 1941(1979)

Carol-Ann Williams
MORE AMERICAN GRAFFITI(1979)

Carole Williams
ONE SPY TOO MANY(1966)

Caroline Williams
SMILE(1975)

Cathy Williams
Misc. Talkies
BABYSITTER, THE(1969)

Cedric Williams
WHEN THIEF MEETS THIEF(1937, Brit.), ph; COMIN' THRU' THE RYE(1947, Brit.), ph; FATAL NIGHT, THE(1948, Brit.), ph; GUNMAN HAS ESCAPED, A(1948, Brit.), ph; ADVENTURES OF PC 49, THE(1949, Brit.), ph; CELIA(1949, Brit.), ph; DICK BARTON STRIKES BACK(1949, Brit.), ph; DR. MORELLE-THE CASE OF THE MISSING HEIRESS(1949, Brit.), ph; MEET SIMON CHERRY(1949, Brit.), ph; ROOM TO LET(1949, Brit.), ph; MAN IN BLACK, THE(1950, Brit.), ph; THIRD TIME LUCKY(1950, Brit.), ph; FAKE, THE(1953, Brit.), ph; FLAW, THE(1955, Brit.), ph; POLICE DOG(1955, Brit.), ph; DYNAMITERS, THE(1956, Brit.), ph; IT'S A GREAT DAY(1956, Brit.), ph; HOUSE IN THE WOODS, THE(1957, Brit.), ph

Chalky Williams
ALONG CAME JONES(1945); SAN ANTONIO(1945); NOOSE HANGS HIGH, THE(1948); GAL WHO TOOK THE WEST, THE(1949); CARRIE(1952); TURNING POINT, THE(1952); FIRST TRAVELING SALESLADY, THE(1956)

Charles Williams
WITHOUT RESERVATIONS(1946); DANCE TEAM(1932); STRANGERS OF THE EVENING(1932); DANCING LADY(1933); GAMBLING SHIP(1933); SITTING PRETTY(1933); CAT'S PAW, THE(1934); GIRL FROM MISSOURI, THE(1934); SADIE MCKEE(1934); THIN MAN, THE(1934); THIS SIDE OF HEAVEN(1934); WOMAN IN THE DARK(1934), w; GIGOLETTE(1935), m; CHARLIE CHAN AT THE RACE TRACK(1936); FOUR DAYS WONDER(1936); RHYTHM ON THE RANGE(1936); ROSE BOWL(1936); WEDDING PRESENT(1936); CHARLIE CHAN ON BROADWAY(1937); ESPIONAGE(1937); JIM HANVEY, DETECTIVE(1937); LOVE AND HISSES(1937); LOVE IS NEWS(1937); MERRY-GO-ROUND OF 1938(1937); STAR IS BORN, A(1937); TURN OFF THE MOON(1937); VOGUES OF 1938(1937); WAKE UP AND LIVE(1937); ALEXANDER'S RAGTIME BAND(1938); BORN TO BE WILD(1938); FLYING FISTS, THE(1938); HOLD THAT CO-ED(1938); HOLLYWOOD STADIUM MYSTERY(1938); JOY OF LIVING(1938); JUST AROUND THE CORNER(1938); LITTLE MISS BROADWAY(1938); MEN WITH WINGS(1938); MR. MOTO'S GAMBLE(1938); ICE FOLLIES OF 1939(1939); WIFE, HUSBAND AND FRIEND(1939); CONVOY(1940); ENEMY AGENT(1940); JOHNNY APOLLO(1940); MARKED MEN(1940); PRIMROSE PATH(1940); BLUE, WHITE, AND PERFECT(1941); FLYING CADETS(1941); LADY FROM CHEYENNE(1941); PROUD VALLEY, THE(1941, Brit.); REACHING FOR THE SUN(1941); GREAT MAN'S LADY, THE(1942); ICE-CAPADES REVUE(1942); ISLE OF MISSING MEN(1942); JOAN OF OZARK(1942); MY FAVORITE SPY(1942); NIGHT IN NEW ORLEANS, A(1942); ONE THRILLING NIGHT(1942); ROXIE HART(1942); TALES OF MANHATTAN(1942); TERROR HOUSE(1942, Brit.), m; TIME TO KILL(1942); GIRL FROM MONTEREY, THE(1943); SALUTE FOR THREE(1943); SARONG GIRL(1943); SECRETS OF THE UNDERGROUND(1943); WHERE ARE YOUR CHILDREN?(1943); CAREER GIRL(1944); END OF THE ROAD(1944); GREENWICH VILLAGE(1944); IRISH EYES ARE SMILING(1944); JOHNNY DOESN'T LIVE HERE ANY MORE(1944); KANSAS CITY KITTY(1944); LAKE PLACID SERENADE(1944); SINCE YOU WENT AWAY(1944); SWEETHEARTS OF THE U.S.A.(1944); DOLL FACE(1945); HOLLYWOOD AND VINE(1945), w; HONEYMOON AHEAD(1945); IDENTITY UNKNOWN(1945); LOVE ON THE DOLE(1945, Brit.); MAN WHO WALKED ALONE, THE(1945); BOY, A GIRL, AND A DOG, A(1946); DEADLINE FOR MURDER(1946); DO YOU LOVE ME?(1946); IT'S A WONDERFUL LIFE(1946); NIGHT AND DAY(1946); OUR HEARTS WERE GROWING UP(1946); PASSKEY TO DANGER(1946); POSTMAN ALWAYS RINGS TWICE, THE(1946); HEADING FOR HEAVEN(1947); HER HUSBAND'S AFFAIRS(1947); SADDLE PALS(1947); WHILE I LIVE(1947, Brit.), m; DUDE GOES WEST, THE(1948); MARSHAL OF AMARILLO(1948); STRANGE MRS. CRANE, THE(1948); TEXAS, BROOKLYN AND HEAVEN(1948); HER MAN GILBEY(1949, Brit.), md; JUDGE, THE(1949); PAROLE, INC.(1949); TASK FORCE(1949); MISSOURIANS, THE(1950); SILK NOOSE, THE(1950, Brit.), m; ACCORDING TO MRS. HOYLE(1951); CORKY OF GASOLINE ALLEY(1951); FLESH AND BLOOD(1951, Brit.), m; GASOLINE ALLEY(1951); LULLABY OF BROADWAY, THE(1951); MILLIONAIRE FOR CHRISTY, A(1951); NAUGHTY ARLETTE(1951, Brit.), m; HAS ANYBODY SEEN MY GAL?(1952); LAWLESS STREET, A(1955); FIGHTING TROUBLE(1956); DOCTOR'S DILEMMA, THE(1958, Brit.), md; THIRD VOICE, THE(1960), d&w; JOY HOUSE(1964, Fr.), w; DON'T JUST STAND THERE(1968), w; PINK JUNGLE, THE(1968), w; MAN WHO WOULD NOT DIE, THE(1975), w; CONFIDENTIALLY YOURS(1983, Fr.), w
Silents
ACTION GALORE(1925)

Charles B. Williams
BIG SHAKEDOWN, THE(1934); DUFFY'S TAVERN(1945); OUT OF THIS WORLD(1945); HAZARD(1948)

Charlie Williams
DEVIL IS DRIVING, THE(1932); DAMES(1934); WOMAN IN THE DARK(1934); TRADE WINDS(1938); FLEET'S IN, THE(1942); GIRLS' TOWN(1942); ATLANTIC CITY(1944); GENTLE ANNIE(1944); HOLLYWOOD AND VINE(1945); HELLDORADO(1946); LADY CHASER(1946); GRAND CANYON(1949); KENTUCKY JUBILEE(1951); MAGNETIC MONSTER, THE(1953); MAN AT THE TOP(1973, Brit.)

Chili Williams
FALCON IN HOLLYWOOD, THE(1944); GIRL RUSH(1944); GEORGE WHITE'S SCANDALS(1945); HAVING WONDERFUL CRIME(1945); JOHNNY ANGEL(1945); WONDER MAN(1945); GAS HOUSE KIDS GO WEST(1947); HEARTACHES(1947); RAW DEAL(1948); MY DREAM IS YOURS(1949); WHERE THE SIDEWALK ENDS(1950); CAPTIVE WOMEN(1952); LAS VEGAS STORY, THE(1952); LUSTY MEN, THE(1952)

Chino "Fats" Williams
1984
SWING SHIFT(1984); TERMINATOR, THE(1984)

Chris Williams
SERVANT, THE(1964, Brit.); SQUADRON 633(1964, U.S./Brit.); 633 SQUADRON(1964); FAHRENHEIT 451(1966, Brit.); NAKED WORLD OF HARRISON MARKS, THE(1967, Brit.); CHILDREN OF BABYLON(1980, Jamaica); OUTLAND(1981)

Christopher Williams
LONELINESS OF THE LONG DISTANCE RUNNER, THE(1962, Brit.); GIRL ON A MOTORCYCLE, THE(1968, Fr./Brit.)

Cindy Williams
GAS-S-S-S!(1970); TRAVELS WITH MY AUNT(1972, Brit.); AMERICAN GRAFFITI(1973); KILLING KIND, THE(1973); CONVERSATION, THE(1974); MR. RICCO(1975); FIRST NUDIE MUSICAL, THE(1976); MORE AMERICAN GRAFFITI(1979); CREATURE WASN'T NICE,THE(1981)

Claire Williams
RAGGEDY ANN AND ANDY(1977)

Clara Williams
Silents
ITALIAN, THE(1915); HELL'S HINGES(1916); HOME(1916); MARKET OF VAIN DESIRE, THE(1916); PAWS OF THE BEAR(1917); CARMEN OF THE KLONDIKE(1918)
Misc. Silents
BARGAIN, THE(1914); MAN FROM OREGON, THE(1915); WINGED IDOL, THE(1915); CORNER, THE(1916); CRIMINAL, THE(1916); LAST ACT, THE(1916); THREE OF MANY(1917); ONE WOMAN, THE(1918)

Clarence Williams
Silents
ABSENT(1928)

Clarence Williams III
COOL WORLD, THE(1963)
1984
PURPLE RAIN(1984)
Clark Williams
SECRET OF THE CHATEAU(1935); TRANSIENT LADY(1935); WEREWOLF OF LONDON, THE(1935); NEXT TIME WE LOVE(1936); CITIZEN SAINT(1947)
Cora Williams
SPOOK WHO SAT BY THE DOOR, THE(1973)
Silents
GREATER THAN FAME(1920); WOMANHANDLED(1925); ADORABLE DECEIVER, THE(1926); GREAT MAIL ROBBERY, THE(1927); SENSATION SEEKERS(1927)
Misc. Silents
LOVE'S FLAME(1920)
Corky Williams
BURY ME AN ANGEL(1972)
Cristola Williams
Misc. Talkies
SUNDAY SINNERS(1941)
Cynthia Williams
MAYTIME IN MAYFAIR(1952, Brit.)
Silents
SECRET ORCHARD(1915)
D. H. Williams
WE'RE GOING TO BE RICH(1938, Brit.)
D. J. Williams
ROOF, THE(1933, Brit.); ADMIRAL'S SECRET, THE(1934, Brit.); BRIDE OF THE LAKE(1934, Brit.); DOCTOR'S ORDERS(1934, Brit.); GLIMPSE OF PARADISE, A(1934, Brit.); LASH, THE(1934, Brit.); POINTING FINGER, THE(1934, Brit.); POISONED DIAMOND, THE(1934, Brit.); RIVER WOLVES, THE(1934, Brit.); WHAT HAPPENED TO HARKNESS(1934, Brit.); ANYTHING MIGHT HAPPEN(1935, Brit.); CAPTAIN BILL(1935, Brit.); LOOK UP AND LAUGH(1935, Brit.); SCROOGE(1935, Brit.); BELOVED VAGABOND, THE(1936, Brit.); CRIMES OF STEPHEN HAWKE, THE(1936, Brit.); MAN WHO LIVED AGAIN, THE(1936, Brit.); MORALS OF MARCUS, THE(1936, Brit.); MURDER IN THE OLD RED BARN(1936, Brit.); BOYS WILL BE GIRLS(1937, Brit.); ELEPHANT BOY(1937, Brit.); FATAL HOUR, THE(1937, Brit.); IT'S NEVER TOO LATE TO MEND(1937, Brit.); KEEP FIT(1937, Brit.); KNIGHTS FOR A DAY(1937, Brit.); WANTED(1937, Brit.); WINGS OF THE MORNING(1937, Brit.); BREAK THE NEWS(1938, Brit.); JOHN HALIFAX–GENTLEMAN(1938, Brit.); CHALLENGE, THE(1939, Brit.); DEMON BARBER OF FLEET STREET, THE(1939, Brit.); STOLEN LIFE(1939, Brit.); COURAGEOUS MR. PENN, THE(1941, Brit.); GHOST TRAIN, THE(1941, Brit.); HARD STEEL(1941, Brit.); MURDER AT THE BASKERVILLES(1941, Brit.); MYSTERY OF ROOM 13(1941, Brit.); GREAT MR. HANDEL, THE(1942, Brit.); MUCH TOO SHY(1942, Brit.); THOSE KIDS FROM TOWN(1942, Brit.); UNPUBLISHED STORY(1942, Brit.); YOUNG MR. PITT, THE(1942, Brit.)
Misc. Silents
SHUTTLE OF LIFE, THE(1920, Brit.), d
Daisy Mae Williams
TWO GENTLEMEN SHARING(1969, Brit.)
Danny Williams
DREAM MAKER, THE(1963, Brit.); PLAY IT COOL(1963, Brit.); HIGH WIND IN JAMAICA, A(1965)
David Williams
PLAINSMAN AND THE LADY(1946); WYOMING(1947); BRIMSTONE(1949); INBETWEEN AGE, THE(1958, Brit.); SOAPBOX DERBY(1958, Brit.); CIRCLE, THE(1959, Brit.); TIME LOCK(1959, Brit.); MAKE MINE A DOUBLE(1962, Brit.); KADOYNG(1974, Brit.); DELIRIUM(1979), m
Davina Williams
1984
SCANDALOUS(1984)
Dennis Williams
CONRACK(1974)
Derek Williams
CHINESE BUNGALOW, THE(1930, Brit.); CRIMSON CANDLE, THE(1934, Brit.); CONCERNING MR. MARTIN(1937, Brit.); INSPECTOR HORNLEIGH(1939, Brit.), ph; LUCKY TO ME(1939, Brit.), ph; WHERE'S THAT FIRE?(1939, Brit.), ph; GHOST OF ST. MICHAEL'S. THE(1941, Brit.), ph; JOHNNY IN THE CLOUDS(1945, Brit.), ph; FOR THEM THAT TRESPASS(1949, Brit.), ph; HUNTED IN HOLLAND(1961, Brit.), d, w
Derick Williams
FLYING DOCTOR, THE(1936, Aus.), ph; ASK A POLICEMAN(1939, Brit.), ph; BEWARE OF PITY(1946, Brit.), ph; HIGH FURY(1947, Brit.), ph; MY BROTHER JONATHAN(1949, Brit.), ph; DON'T TALK TO STRANGE MEN(1962, Brit.), p; SEVENTY DEADLY PILLS(1964, Brit.), p; ON THE RUN(1969, Brit.), p
Diahn Williams
DEADLY HERO(1976)
Dick A. Williams
DEADLY HERO(1976)
Dick Anthony Williams
LONG NIGHT, THE(1976); DEEP, THE(1977); ALMOST PERFECT AFFAIR, AN(1979); JERK, THE(1979); STAR CHAMBER, THE(1983)
Misc. Talkies
KEEPING ON(1981)
Dick Williams
JOHNNY TIGER(1966), art d; ANDERSON TAPES, THE(1971); WHO KILLED MARY WHAT'SER NAME?(1971); MACK, THE(1973); DOG DAY AFTERNOON(1975)
Dierdre Williams
YOU BETTER WATCH OUT(1980), cos
Don Williams
SONG OF OLD WYOMING(1945); ROMANCE OF THE WEST(1946); GHASTLY ONES, THE(1968); SLAUGHTER(1972), w; SLAUGHTER'S BIG RIP-OFF(1973), w; W. W. AND THE DIXIE DANCEKINGS(1975); SMOKEY AND THE BANDIT II(1980)
Donna Williams
1984
NEW YORK NIGHTS(1984), cos
Donnie Williams
TRUCK TURNER(1974); LITTLE DRAGONS, THE(1980)

Doug Williams
Misc. Talkies
FIRST TIME ROUND(1972)
Douglas Williams
FLYING DOWN TO RIO(1933); SATAN MET A LADY(1936); SLIM(1937); THEY LIVE BY NIGHT(1949)
Duke Williams
BOY! WHAT A GIRL(1947); RED MENACE, THE(1949)
Misc. Talkies
BIG TIMERS(1947)
E. A. Williams
FLAW, THE(1933, Brit.)
E. H. Williams
BETRAYAL(1932, Brit.)
Earl Williams
Silents
DIAMONDS ADRIFT(1921); IT CAN BE DONE(1921); ADVENTUROUS SEX, THE(1925)
Earle Williams
Silents
CHRISTIAN, THE(1914); JUGGERNAUT, THE(1915); SINS OF THE MOTHERS(1915); APARTMENT 29(1917); ARSENE LUPIN(1917); IN THE BALANCE(1917); AMERICAN LIVE WIRE, AN(1918); MASTER STROKE, A(1920); PURPLE CIPHER, THE(1920); BRING HIM IN(1921), a, d; SILVER CAR, THE(1921); ETERNAL STRUGGLE, THE(1923); JEALOUS HUSBANDS(1923); ANCIENT MARINER, THE(1925); WAS IT BIGAMY?(1925); SKYROCKET, THE(1926)
Misc. Silents
MY OFFICIAL WIFE(1914); MY LADY'S SLIPPER(1916); GRELL MYSTERY, THE(1917); HAWK, THE(1917); LOVE DOCTOR, THE(1917); MAELSTROM, THE(1917); SOUL MASTER, THE(1917); STOLEN TREATY, THE(1917); TRANSGRESSION(1917); DIPLOMATIC MISSION, A(1918); GIRL IN HIS HOUSE, THE(1918); MAN WHO WOULDN'T TELL, THE(1918); MOTHER'S SIN, A(1918); SEAL OF SILENCE, THE(1918); BLACK GATE, THE(1919); FROM HEADQUARTERS(1919); GENTLEMAN OF QUALITY, A(1919); HIGHEST TRUMP, THE(1919); HORNET'S NEST, THE(1919); ROGUE'S ROMANCE, A(1919); TWO WOMEN(1919); USURPER, THE(1919); WOLF, THE(1919); CAPTAIN SWIFT(1920); FORTUNE HUNTER, THE(1920); ROMANCE PROMOTORS, THE(1920); WHEN A MAN LOVES(1920); LUCKY CARSON(1921); FORTUNE'S MASK(1922); MAN FROM DOWNING STREET, THE(1922); RESTLESS SOULS(1922); YOU NEVER KNOW(1922); MASTERS OF MEN(1923); BORROWED HUSBANDS(1924); LENA RIVERS(1925); YOU'D BE SURPRISED(1926); RED SIGNALS(1927); SAY IT WITH DIAMONDS(1927); SHE'S MY BABY(1927)
Ed Williams
MEET JOHN DOE(1941)
Edmund Williams
MAN'S FAVORITE SPORT(?)**1/2 (1964); MAN FROM THE DINERS' CLUB, THE(1963)
Edward W. Williams
MAMA LOVES PAPA(1945), ed; RADIO STARS ON PARADE(1945), ed; WHAT A BLONDE(1945), m; TRUTH ABOUT MURDER, THE(1946), ed; DARK INTRUDER(1965), ed; JOURNEY TO SHILOH(1968), ed
Edward Williams
UNEARTHLY STRANGER, THE(1964, Brit.), m
Edy Williams
MAN'S FAVORITE SPORT(?) (1964); PAD, THE(AND HOW TO USE IT) (1966, Brit.); HOUSE IS NOT A HOME, A(1964); NAKED KISS, THE(1964); RED LINE 7000(1965); LAST OF THE SECRET AGENTS?, THE(1966); GOOD TIMES(1967); MONEY JUNGLE, THE(1968); SECRET LIFE OF AN AMERICAN WIFE, THE(1968); I SAILED TO TAHITI WITH AN ALL GIRL CREW(1969); WHERE IT'S AT(1969); SEVEN MINUTES, THE(1971); DR. MINX(1975); CHAINED HEAT(1983 U.S./Ger.)
1984
BAD MANNERS(1984); HOLLYWOOD HOT TUBS(1984)
Elaine Williams
SUBJECT WAS ROSES, THE(1968)
Eliot Crawshay Williams
MAN OF MAYFAIR(1931, Brit.), w
Elisabeth Williams
JOURNEY FOR MARGARET(1942)
Elizabeth Williams
NINOTCHKA(1939); COLONEL EFFINGHAM'S RAID(1945); THOSE ENDEARING YOUNG CHARMS(1945); DRAGONWYCH(1946)
Misc. Silents
BURDEN OF RACE, THE(1921)
Ellis Williams
1984
BROTHER FROM ANOTHER PLANET, THE(1984)
Ellwoodson Williams
CLARENCE AND ANGEL(1981)
Elmo Williams
THEY WON'T BELIEVE ME(1947), ed; NURSE EDITH CAVELL(1939), ed; IRENE(1940), ed; NO, NO NANETTE(1940), ed; SUNNY(1941), ed; NOCTURNE(1946), ed; DICK TRACY MEETS GRUESOME(1947), ed; BODYGUARD(1948), ed; MIRACLE OF THE BELLS, THE(1948), ed; FOLLOW ME QUIETLY(1949), ed; HELLGATE(1952), ed; HIGH NOON(1952), ed; TALL TEXAN, THE(1953), d, ed; 20,000 LEAGUES UNDER THE SEA(1954), ed; BLONDE BAIT(1956, U.S./Brit.), d; APACHE WARRIOR(1957), d; HELL CANYON OUTLAWS(1957), ed; HELL SHIP MUTINY(1957), d, ed; VIKINGS, THE(1958), ed; TORA! TORA! TORA!(1970, U.S./Jap.), p; SIDEWINDER ONE(1977), p; CARAVANS(1978, U.S./Iranian), p; SOGGY BOTTOM U.S.A.(1982), p; MAN, WOMAN AND CHILD(1983), p
Elmo J. Williams
FOREVER AND A DAY(1943), ed
Emese Williams
HOW SWEET IT IS(1968)
Emlyn Williams
CRIMINAL AT LARGE(1932, Brit.); SALLY BISHOP(1932, Brit.); EVENSONG(1934, Brit.); EVERGREEN(1934, Brit.), w; FRIDAY THE 13TH(1934, Brit.), a, w; ROAD HOUSE(1934, Brit.); CITY OF BEAUTIFUL NONSENSE, THE(1935, Brit.); DICTATOR, THE(1935, Brit./Ger.); DIVINE SPARK, THE(1935, Brit./Ital.), w; IRON DUKE, THE(1935, Brit.); MAN WHO KNEW TOO MUCH, THE(1935, Brit.), w; MEN OF TOMORROW(1935, Brit.); MY SONG FOR YOU(1935, Brit.); BROKEN BLOSSOMS(1936, Brit.), a, w; NIGHT MUST FALL(1937), w; CITADEL, THE(1938); NIGHT

ALONE(1938, Brit.); THEY DRIVE BY NIGHT(1938, Brit.); DEAD MEN TELL NO TALES(1939, Brit.); JAMAICA INN(1939, Brit.); STARS LOOK DOWN, THE(1940, Brit.); GIRL IN THE NEWS, THE(1941, Brit.); MAJOR BARBARA(1941, Brit.); THIS ENGLAND(1941, Brit.), a, w; YOU WILL REMEMBER(1941, Brit.); LIFE BEGINS AT 8:30(1942), w; CORN IS GREEN, THE(1945), w; HATTER'S CASTLE(1948, Brit.); LAST DAYS OF DOLWYN, THE(1949, Brit.), a, d&w; THREE HUSBANDS(1950); SCARF, THE(1951); ANOTHER MAN'S POISON(1952, Brit.); IVANHOE(1952, Brit.); MAGIC BOX, THE(1952, Brit.); DEEP BLUE SEA, THE(1955, Brit.); TIME WITHOUT PITY(1957, Brit.), w; I ACCUSE(1958, Brit.); BEYOND THIS PLACE(1959, Brit.); WRECK OF THE MARY DEAR, THE(1959); L-SHAPED ROOM, THE(1962, Brit.); NIGHT MUST FALL(1964, Brit.), w; EYE OF THE DEVIL(1967, Brit.); DAVID COPPERFIELD(1970, Brit.); WALKING STICK, THE(1970, Brit.)

Misc. Talkies

DEADLY GAMES(1982)

Emyln Williams

DEAD MEN TELL NO TALES(1939, Brit.), w

Eric Williams

WOODEN HORSE, THE(1951), w; WHEREVER SHE GOES(1953, Aus.), p; FOUR DESPERATE MEN(1960, Brit.), p

Eric Bransby Williams

WONDERFUL STORY, THE(1932, Brit.)

Silents

PRESUMPTION OF STANLEY HAY, MP, THE(1925, Brit.); JUNGLE WOMAN, THE(1926, Brit.); EASY VIRTUE(1927, Brit.); PEARL OF THE SOUTH SEAS(1927, Brit.)

Misc. Silents

HIS GRACE GIVES NOTICE(1924, Brit.); BEYOND THE VEIL(1925, Brit.); CONFESSIONS(1925, Brit.); GOLD CURE, THE(1925); WAY OF A WOMAN, THE(1925, Brit.); HELLCAT, THE(1928, Brit.); TROUBLESOME WIVES(1928, Brit.); LITTLE MISS LONDON(1929, Brit.); WHEN KNIGHTS WERE BOLD(1929, Brit.)

Ernest Williams II

EMMA MAE(1976)

Erskine Williams

HIGH YELLOW(1965), w

Esta Williams

Misc. Silents

AT THE OLD CROSSED ROADS(1914)

Esther Williams

ANDY HARDY'S DOUBLE LIFE(1942); GUY NAMED JOE, A(1943); BATHING BEAUTY(1944); THRILL OF A ROMANCE(1945); ZIEGFELD FOLLIES(1945); EASY TO WED(1946); HOODLUM SAINT, THE(1946); FIESTA(1947); THIS TIME FOR KEEPS(1947); ON AN ISLAND WITH YOU(1948); NEPTUNE'S DAUGHTER(1949); TAKE ME OUT TO THE BALL GAME(1949); DUCHESS OF IDAHO, THE(1950); PAGAN LOVE SONG(1950); CALLAWAY WENT THATAWAY(1951); TEXAS CARNIVAL(1951); MILLION DOLLAR MERMAID(1952); SKIRTS AHOY!(1952); DANGEROUS WHEN WET(1953); EASY TO LOVE(1953); JUPITER'S DARLING(1955); UNGUARDED MOMENT, THE(1956); BIG SHOW, THE(1961)

Ezra Williams

RETURN TO PARADISE(1953); PACIFIC DESTINY(1956, Brit.)

F.A. Williams

ROOM TO LET(1949, Brit.)

Fay Williams

Misc. Talkies

BOSS LADY(1982)

Florence Williams

Silents

FORTUNE HUNTER, THE(1914)

Florene Williams

TENDER IS THE NIGHT(1961)

Frances Williams

HOLLYWOOD PARTY(1934); HER SISTER'S SECRET(1946); MAGNIFICENT DOLL(1946); RECKLESS MOMENTS, THE(1949); SHOW BOAT(1951); WEEKEND WITH FATHER(1951); LYDIA BAILEY(1952); TOGETHER BROTHERS(1974)

Misc. Talkies

LYING LIPS(1939); BABY NEEDS A NEW PAIR OF SHOES(1974)

Frances E. Williams

FAMILY SECRET, THE(1951); QUEEN FOR A DAY(1951)

Francis Williams

FEUDIN', FUSSIN' AND A-FIGHTIN'(1948); BLACK KLANSMAN, THE(1966)

Frank Williams

DOUBLE DANGER(1938); EXTRA DAY, THE(1956, Brit.); SQUARE PEG, THE(1958, Brit.); INN FOR TROUBLE(1960, Brit.); JUST FOR FUN(1963, Brit.); V.I.P.s, THE(1963, Brit.); HIDE AND SEEK(1964, Brit.); COUNTDOWN TO DANGER(1967, Brit.); DEADLY AFFAIR, THE(1967, Brit.); ROBBERY(1967, Brit.); STITCH IN TIME, A(1967, Brit.); DAD'S ARMY(1971, Brit.); JABBERWOCKY(1977, Brit.); HUMAN FACTOR, THE(1979, Brit.); OH, HEAVENLY DOG!(1980)

Silents

MICKEY(1919), ph; ABABIAN KNIGHT, AN(1920), ph

Misc. Silents

DEVIL'S CONFESSION, THE(1921)

Frank D. Williams

Silents

TILLIE'S PUNCTURED ROMANCE(1914), ph; SWAMP, THE(1921), ph; WHERE LIGHTS ARE LOW(1921), ph

Frankie Williams

ANGELO MY LOVE(1983)

Fred Williams

PALM SPRINGS WEEKEND(1963), makeup; JULIET OF THE SPIRITS(1965, Fr./Ital./W.Ger.); SANDRA(1966, Ital.); WILD IN THE STREETS(1968), makeup; HOW TO COMMIT MARRIAGE(1969), makeup; TRAVELING EXECUTIONER, THE(1970), makeup; WHICH WAY TO THE FRONT?(1970), makeup; COUNT DRACULA(1971, Sp., Ital., Ger., Brit.); MRS. POLLIFAX-SPY(1971), makeup; AND THE SHIP SAILS ON(1983, Ital./Fr.)

Misc. Silents

DAZZLING MISS DAVISON, THE(1917)

Freida Williams

CONRACK(1974)

Gary Williams

LOVE BUTCHER, THE(1982), p

Gene Williams

HIT THE ICE(1943); I NEVER SANG FOR MY FATHER(1970)

Geneva Williams

LITTLE COLONEL, THE(1935); TOY WIFE, THE(1938); SARATOGA TRUNK(1945)

George Williams

CANYON OF MISSING MEN, THE(1930), w; SEPIA CINDERELLA(1947); WAR PARTY(1965), w

Silents

EDUCATION OF NICKY, THE(1921, Brit.); LITTLE MISS SMILES(1922); GEARED TO GO(1924)

Misc. Silents

FIGHTING SAP, THE(1924); SILENT STRANGER, THE(1924); RATTLER, THE(1925)

George A. Williams

Silents

LONG CHANCE, THE(1922); DANGEROUS HOUR(1923)

Misc. Silents

DAWN OF UNDERSTANDING, THE(1918); BLACK SHEEP(1921); LUCKY DAN(1922); FIRST DEGREE, THE(1923)

George B. Williams

PHANTOM OF THE OPERA, THE(1929)

Silents

IN FOLLY'S TRAIL(1920); ONCE A PLUMBER(1920); HER MAD BARGAIN(1921); SECOND HAND ROSE(1922); SIREN CALL, THE(1922); PHANTOM OF THE OPERA, THE(1925)

Misc. Silents

CHEATED LOVE(1921); GHOST PATROL, THE(1923)

Gladys Williams

Silents

SHOPSOILED GIRL, THE(1915, Brit.)

Glen Williams

O LUCKY MAN!(1973, Brit.)

Glenn Williams

LOVE AND DEATH(1975); JABBERWOCKY(1977, Brit.)

Glesni Williams

1984

YR ALCOHOLIG LION(1984, Brit.)

Gloria Williams

TRUE TO LIFE(1943); EASY LIVING(1937); EBB TIDE(1937); EXCLUSIVE(1937); HOLD'EM NAVY!(1937); I MET HIM IN PARIS(1937); KING OF GAMBLERS(1937); COCOANUT GROVE(1938); PRISON FARM(1938); CAFE SOCIETY(1939); DISPUTED PASSAGE(1939); LADY'S FROM KENTUCKY, THE(1939); TELEVISION SPY(1939); CAUGHT IN THE DRAFT(1941); WEST POINT WIDOW(1941); LADY BODYGUARD(1942); MAJOR AND THE MINOR, THE(1942); STREET OF CHANCE(1942); BLUE DAHLIA, THE(1946); TO EACH HIS OWN(1946); WILD HARVEST(1947)

Gordon M. Williams

MAN WHO HAD POWER OVER WOMEN, THE(1970, Brit.), w; STRAW DOGS(1971, Brit.), w

Grace Williams

Misc. Silents

FAITH AND FORTUNE(1915); TRUTH ABOUT HELEN, THE(1915); COSSACK WHIP, THE(1916); LAST SENTENCE, THE(1917)

Grant Williams

AWAY ALL BOATS(1956); FOUR GIRLS IN TOWN(1956); OUTSIDE THE LAW(1956); RED SUNDOWN(1956); SHOWDOWN AT ABILENE(1956); WRITTEN ON THE WIND(1956); INCREDIBLE SHRINKING MAN, THE(1957); MONOLITH MONSTERS, THE(1957); LONE TEXAN(1959); LEECH WOMAN, THE(1960); THIRTEEN FIGHTING MEN(1960); SUSAN SLADE(1961); COUCH, THE(1962); PT 109(1963); DOOMSDAY MACHINE(1967); BRAIN OF BLOOD(1971, Phil.)

Greta Williams

CURIOUS DR. HUMPP(1967, Arg.)

Guinn "Big Boy" Williams

MY MAN(1928); NOAH'S ARK(1928); FORWARD PASS, THE(1929); FROM HEADQUARTERS(1929); LUCKY STAR(1929); BAD MAN, THE(1930); COLLEGE LOVERS(1930); LILIOM(1930); BACHELOR FATHER(1931); GREAT, MEADOW, THE(1931); DEVIL IS DRIVING, THE(1932); LADIES OF THE JURY(1932); POLLY OF THE CIRCUS(1932); YOU SAID A MOUTHFUL(1932); 70,000 WITNESSES(1932); COLLEGE COACH(1933); HERITAGE OF THE DESERT(1933); LAUGHING AT LIFE(1933); MAN OF THE FOREST(1933); PHANTOM BROADCAST, THE(1933); CHEATERS(1934); COWBOY HOLIDAY(1934); FLIRTATION WALK(1934); HALF A SINNER(1934); HERE COMES THE NAVY(1934); PALOOKA(1934); RAFTER ROMANCE(1934); ROMANCE IN THE RAIN(1934); THUNDER OVER TEXAS(1934); DANGER TRAILS(1935), a, w; GLASS KEY, THE(1935); LITTLEST REBEL, THE(1935); MISS PACIFIC FLEET(1935); ONE IN A MILLION(1935); POWDERSMOKE RANGE(1935); PRIVATE WORLDS(1935); SILVER STREAK, THE(1935); SOCIETY FEVER(1935); VILLAGE TALE(1935); BIG GAME, THE(1936); CAREER WOMAN(1936); END OF THE TRAIL(1936); GRAND JURY(1936); GUN PLAY(1936); KELLY THE SECOND(1936); MUSS 'EM UP(1936); BIG CITY(1937); DANGEROUS HOLIDAY(1937); DON'T TELL THE WIFE(1937); GIRLS CAN PLAY(1937); MY DEAR MISS ALDRICH(1937); NORTH OF NOME(1937); SHE'S NO LADY(1937); SINGING MARINE, THE(1937); STAR IS BORN, A(1937); WISE GIRL(1937); YOU ONLY LIVE ONCE(1937); ARMY GIRL(1938); BAD MAN OF BRIMSTONE(1938); CRASHIN' THRU DANGER(1938); DOWN IN ARKANSAW(1938); EVERYBODY'S DOING IT(1938); FLYING FISTS, THE(1938); HOLD THAT CO-ED(1938); I DEMAND PAYMENT(1938); MARINES ARE HERE, THE(1938); PROFESSOR BEWARE(1938); YOU AND ME(1938); BAD LANDS(1939); BLACKMAIL(1939); DODGE CITY(1939); FUGITIVE AT LARGE(1939); LEGION OF LOST FLYERS(1939); MUTINY ON THE BLACK-HAWK(1939); PARDON OUR NERVE(1939); STREET OF MISSING MEN(1939); 6000 ENEMIES(1939); ALIAS THE DEACON(1940); CASTLE ON THE HUDSON(1940); DULCY(1940); FIGHTING 69TH, THE(1940); MONEY AND THE WOMAN(1940); SANTA FE TRAIL(1940); VIRGINIA CITY(1940); WAGONS WESTWARD(1940); BILLY THE KID(1941); BUGLE SOUNDS, THE(1941); COUNTRY FAIR(1941); SIX LESSONS FROM MADAME LA ZONGA(1941); SWAMP WATER(1941); YOU'LL NEVER GET RICH(1941); AMERICAN EMPIRE(1942); BETWEEN US GIRLS(1942); LURE OF THE ISLANDS(1942); MR. WISE GUY(1942); SILVER QUEEN(1942); DESPERADOES, THE(1943); HANDS ACROSS THE BORDER(1943); MINESWEEPER(1943); BELLE OF THE YUKON(1944); COWBOY AND THE SENORITA(1944); COWBOY CANTEEN(1944); NEVADA(1944); SWING IN THE SADDLE(1944); MAN WHO WALKED ALONE, THE(1945); COWBOY BLUES(1946); SINGIN' IN THE

CORN(1946); KING OF THE WILD HORSES(1947); ROAD TO THE BIG HOUSE(1947); STATION WEST(1948); BAD MEN OF TOMBSTONE(1949); BRIMSTONE(1949); SMOKY MOUNTAIN MELODY(1949); HOEDOWN(1950); ROCKY MOUNTAIN(1950); AL JENNINGS OF OKLAHOMA(1951); MAN IN THE SADDLE(1951); HANGMAN'S KNOT(1952); SPRINGFIELD RIFLE(1952); MASSACRE CANYON(1954); OUTLAW'S DAUGHTER, THE(1954); SOUTHWEST PASSAGE(1954); HIDDEN GUNS(1956); MAN FROM DEL RIO(1956); HIRED GUN, THE(1957); ALAMO, THE(1960); FIVE BOLD WOMEN(1960); HOME FROM THE HILL(1960); COMANCHEROS, THE(1961)

Misc. Talkies

BIG FIGHT, THE(1930); BIG BOY RIDES AGAIN(1935); LAW OF THE 45'S(1935); RHYTHM ROUND-UP(1945); SING ME A SONG OF TEXAS(1945); SONG OF THE PRAIRIE(1945); THAT TEXAS JAMBOREE(1946); THROW A SADDLE ON A STAR(1946); OVER THE SANTA FE TRAIL(1947)

Silents

ALMOST A HUSBAND(1919); JUBILO(1919); JACK RIDER, THE(1921), w; FRESHIE, THE(1922); AVENGER, THE(1924); EAGLE'S CLAW, THE(1924); BLACK CYCLONE(1925); BROWN OF HARVARD(1926); DESERT'S TOLL, THE(1926); ARIZONA BOUND(1927); BABE COMES HOME(1927); BACKSTAGE(1927); SLIDE, KELLY, SLIDE(1927); WOMAN WHO DID NOT CARE, THE(1927)

Misc. Silents

VENGEANCE TRAIL, THE(1921); BLAZE AWAY(1922); ROUNDING UP THE LAW(1922); TRAIL OF HATE(1922); RIDERS AT NIGHT(1923); RIDERS OF THE SAND STORM(1925); ROSE OF THE DESERT(1925); SPORTING WEST(1925); WHISTLING JIM(1925); WOLFHEART'S REVENGE(1925); LIGHTING(1927)

Guy Williams

BONZO GOES TO COLLEGE(1952); ALL I DESIRE(1953); GOLDEN BLADE, THE(1953); MAN FROM THE ALAMO, THE(1953); MISSISSIPPI GAMBLER, THE(1953); TAKE ME TO TOWN(1953); LAST FRONTIER, THE(1955); SEVEN ANGRY MEN(1955); SINCERELY YOURS(1955); I WAS A TEENAGE WEREWOLF(1957); SIGN OF ZORRO, THE(1960); DAMON AND PYTHIAS(1962); CAPTAIN SINDBAD(1963); GENERAL MASSACRE(1973, U.S./Bel.)

Guy Bevier Williams

WHITE ZOMBIE(1932), m

Gwen Williams

MR. BUG GOES TO TOWN(1941); HAUNTING OF M, THE(1979)

Silents

LEAD, KINDLY LIGHT(1918, Brit.)

Misc. Silents

NON-CONFORMIST PARSON, A(1919, Brit.); SECRET OF THE MOOR, THE(1919, Brit.)

Hal Williams

HARDCORE(1979); ON THE NICKEL(1980); PRIVATE BENJAMIN(1980); ESCAPE ARTIST, THE(1982)

Hank Williams, Jr.

TIME TO SING, A(1968); ROADIE(1980)

Harcourt Williams

HENRY V(1946, Brit.); BRIGHTON ROCK(1947, Brit.); HAMLET(1948, Brit.); VICE VERSA(1948, Brit.); FOR THEM THAT TRESPASS(1949, Brit.); GAY LADY, THE(1949, Brit.); UNDER CAPRICORN(1949, Brit.); CAGE OF GOLD(1950, Brit.); EYE WITNESS(1950, Brit.); LOST PEOPLE, THE(1950, Brit.); NO ROOM AT THE INN(1950, Brit.); THIRD TIME LUCKY(1950, Brit.); GREEN GROW THE RUSHES(1951, Brit.); OBSESSED(1951, Brit.); MAGIC BOX, THE(1952, Brit.); ROMAN HOLIDAY(1953); TERROR ON A TRAIN(1953); FLYING EYE, THE(1955, Brit.); QUENTIN DURWARD(1955); AROUND THE WORLD IN 80 DAYS(1956)

Harmon Williams

THREE DAYS OF THE CONDOR(1975)

Harold Williams

INGAGI(1931), ph; JIMMY BOY(1935, Brit.); GREAT GILBERT AND SULLIVAN, THE(1953, Brit.)

Harry Williams

HANDS ACROSS THE TABLE(1935); TRAIN RIDE TO HOLLYWOOD(1975)

Harry M. Williams

CHINA SYNDROME, THE(1979)

Heathcote Williams

Misc. Talkies

TEMPEST, THE(1980, Brit.)

Henrietta Williams

SALT OF THE EARTH(1954)

Henry T. Williams

HUMANOIDS FROM THE DEEP(1980)

Herb Williams

ROSE OF THE RANCHO(1936)

Herberta Williams

YOUNGEST PROFESSION, THE(1943)

Herschel V. Williams, Jr.

JANIE(1944), w; JANIE GETS MARRIED(1946), w

Hope Williams

SCOUNDREL, THE(1935)

Howard Williams

YESTERDAY'S ENEMY(1959, Brit.); IT'S A WONDERFUL WORLD(1956, Brit.); ENEMY FROM SPACE(1957, Brit.); UP THE CREEK(1958, Brit.); M(1970)

Hugh Williams

CHARLEY'S AUNT(1930); GENTLEMAN OF PARIS, A(1931); NIGHT IN MONTMARTE, A(1931, Brit.); DOWN OUR STREET(1932, Brit.); INSULT(1932, Brit.); BITTER SWEET(1933, Brit.); JEWEL, THE(1933, Brit.); ROME EXPRESS(1933, Brit.); THIS ACTING BUSINESS(1933, Brit.); WHITE FACE(1933, Brit.); ALL MEN ARE ENEMIES(1934); OUTCAST LADY(1934); SORRELL AND SON(1934, Brit.); DAVID COPPERFIELD(1935); ELINOR NORTON(1935); HER LAST AFFAIRE(1935); IN A MONASTERY GARDEN(1935); LET'S LIVE TONIGHT(1935); LIEUTENANT DARING, RN(1935, Brit.); AMATEUR GENTLEMAN(1936, Brit.); HAPPY FAMILY, THE(1936, Brit.); LAST JOURNEY, THE(1936, Brit.); MAN BEHIND THE MASK, THE(1936, Brit.); BIG FELLA(1937, Brit.), m; BRIEF ECSTASY(1937, Brit.); GYPSY(1937, Brit.); PERFECT CRIME, THE(1937, Brit.); SIDE STREET ANGEL(1937, Brit.); WINDMILL, THE(1937, Brit.); BANK HOLIDAY(1938, Brit.); DANGEROUS SECRETS(1938, Brit.); DARK STAIRWAY, THE(1938, Brit.); DEAD MEN TELL NO TALES(1939, Brit.); HIS LORDSHIP GOES TO PRESS(1939, Brit.); INSPECTOR HORNLEIGH(1939, Brit.); WUTHERING HEIGHTS(1939); HUMAN MONSTER, THE(1940, Brit.); ONE NIGHT IN PARIS(1940, Brit.); AVENGERS, THE(1942, Brit.); ONE OF OUR AIRCRAFT IS MISSING(1942, Brit.); SHIPS WITH WINGS(1942, Brit.); TALK ABOUT JACQUELINE(1942, Brit.); SECRET MISSION(1944, Brit.); GIRL IN A

MILLION, A(1946, Brit.); BLIND GODDESS, THE(1948, Brit.); IDEAL HUSBAND, AN(1948, Brit.); TAKE MY LIFE(1948, Brit.); ELIZABETH OF LADYMEAD(1949, Brit.); PAPER ORCHID(1949, Brit.); NAUGHTY ARLETTE(1951, Brit.); GLORY AT SEA(1952, Brit.); FAKE, THE(1953, Brit.); TWICE UPON A TIME(1953, Brit.); HOLLY AND THE IVY, THE(1954, Brit.); STAR OF MY NIGHT(1954, Brit.); INTRUDER, THE(1955, Brit.); GRASS IS GREENER, THE(1960), w; KHARTOUM(1966, Brit.); DOCTOR FAUSTUS(1967, Brit.)

Hugo Williams

1984

FLIGHT TO BERLIN(1984, Ger./Brit.), w

Ieuan Rhys Williams

UNDER MILK WOOD(1973, Brit.)

Ike Williams

FLAREUP(1969)

Irene Williams

ISLAND WOMEN(1958)

Irma Williams

COOL WORLD, THE(1963)

Ivory Williams

TARZAN, THE APE MAN(1932); GREEN PASTURES(1936)

J. B. Williams

CHINESE BUNGALOW, THE(1930, Brit.), p,d&w; WHITE CARGO(1930, Brit.), p&d, w; TO THE VICTOR(1938, Brit.), w; STARS LOOK DOWN, THE(1940, Brit.), w; NEUTRAL PORT(1941, Brit.), w; WE DIVE AT DAWN(1943, Brit.), w; MAN ABOUT THE HOUSE, A(1947, Brit.), w; DULCIMER STREET(1948, Brit.), w

Misc. Silents

WHITE CARGO(1929, Brit.), d

J. D. Williams

Silents

LONDON(1926, Brit.), p

J. J. Williams

Silents

LITTLE MISS HOOVER(1918)

J. Terry Williams

SEND ME NO FLOWERS(1964), ed; RUSSIANS ARE COMING, THE RUSSIANS ARE COMING, THE(1966), ed; BANNING(1967), ed; SECRET WAR OF HARRY FRIGG, THE(1968), ed; EYE OF THE CAT(1969), ed; WRATH OF GOD, THE(1972), ed; AIRPORT 1975(1974), ed; FAMILY PLOT(1976), ed; JIM, THE WORLD'S GREATEST(1976), ed; AIRPORT '77(1977), ed; RAISE THE TITANIC(1980, Brit.), ed

Jack Williams

HIT PARADE OF 1943(1943); GIVE ME THE STARS(1944, Brit.); HE SNOOPS TO CONQUER(1944, Brit.); IT'S GREAT TO BE YOUNG(1946); I'LL SEE YOU IN MY DREAMS(1951); AFRICAN TREASURE(1952); LION AND THE HORSE, THE(1952); TALK ABOUT A STRANGER(1952); SAFARI DRUMS(1953); FAR COUNTRY, THE(1955); STRANGE LADY IN TOWN(1955); BAND OF ANGELS(1957); MAN OF THE WEST(1958); HATARI!(1962); MAN WHO SHOT LIBERTY VALANCE, THE(1962); SONS OF KATIE ELDER, THE(1965); BILLY THE KID VS. DRACULA(1966); SMOKY(1966); SCALPHUNTERS, THE(1968)

Jack C. Williams

NIGHT PASSAGE(1957); WESTBOUND(1959); GOLD OF THE SEVEN SAINTS(1961); MERRILL'S MARAUDERS(1962)

Jack Eric Williams

NIGHTMARE(1981), m

James Williams

BEWARE, MY LOVELY(1952); COTTONPICKIN' CHICKENPICKERS(1967), set d

James B. Williams

THAT FORSYTE WOMAN(1949), w

Jan Williams

UNCLE HARRY(1945); SALOME, WHERE SHE DANCED(1945); FROM RUSSIA WITH LOVE(1963, Brit.); CONDORMAN(1981), p

Janine Williams

CARWASH(1976)

Jason Williams

TIME WALKER(1982), a, p

Jay Williams

LITTLE FUGITIVE, THE(1953); SON OF FLUBBER(1963), w

Jeanee Williams

CAESAR AND CLEOPATRA(1946, Brit.)

Jeff Williams

Misc. Silents

FLAME OF HELLGATE, THE(1920)

Jeffery Williams

OLD-FASHIONED WAY, THE(1934)

Jeffrey Williams

Silents

SAPHEAD, THE(1921)

Jenny Williams

1941(1979)

Jesse Lynch Williams

TOO MANY PARENTS(1936), w

Jewell Williams

EMMA MAE(1976); BUSTIN' LOOSE(1981)

Jill Williams

SENTENCED FOR LIFE(1960, Brit.)

Jo Williams

HUMANOIDS FROM THE DEEP(1980)

JoBeth Williams

KRAMER VS. KRAMER(1979); DOGS OF WAR, THE(1980, Brit.); STIR CRAZY(1980); ENDANGERED SPECIES(1982); POLTERGEIST(1982); BIG CHILL, THE(1983)

1984

AMERICAN DREAMER(1984); TEACHERS(1984)

Joe Williams

JAMBOREE(1957); MOONSHINE WAR, THE(1970)

John Williams

EMIL(1938, Brit.); SOMEWHERE IN FRANCE(1943, Brit.); PARADINE CASE, THE(1947); WOMAN'S VENGEANCE, A(1947); KIND LADY(1951); LADY AND THE BANDIT, THE(1951); THUNDER IN THE EAST(1953); SABRINA(1954); STUDENT PRINCE, THE(1954); TO CATCH A THIEF(1955); D-DAY, THE SIXTH OF JUNE(1956); SOLID GOLD CADILLAC, THE(1956); ISLAND IN THE SUN(1957); WILL SUCCESS SPOIL ROCK HUNTER?(1957); WITNESS FOR THE

PROSECUTION(1957); YELLOW SUBMARINE(1958, Brit.), ph; DADDY-O(1959), m; YOUNG PHILADELPHIANS, THE(1959); MIDNIGHT LACE(1960); VISIT TO A SMALL PLANET(1960); DEAR BRIGETTE(1965); HARLOW(1965); LAST OF THE SECRET AGENTS?, THE(1966); DOUBLE TROUBLE(1967); FLEA IN HER EAR, A(1968, Fr.); SECRET WAR OF HARRY FRIGG, THE(1968); DADDY'S GONE A-HUNTING(1969), m; GOODBYE MR. CHIPS(1969, U.S./Brit.), m; FIDDLER ON THE ROOF(1971), md; JANE EYRE(1971, Brit.), m; COWBOYS, THE(1972), m; IMAGES(1972, Ireland), m; PETE 'N' TILLIE(1972), m; POSEIDON ADVENTURE, THE(1972), m; CINDERELLA LIBERTY(1973), m; LIBIDO(1973, Aus.); LONG GOODBYE, THE(1973), m; MAN WHO LOVED CAT DANCING, THE(1973), m; PAPER CHASE, THE(1973), m; PSYCHOPATH, THE(1973), ed; TOM SAWYER(1973), md; CONRACK(1974), m; EARTHQUAKE(1974), m; LOST IN THE STARS(1974); SUGARLAND EXPRESS, THE(1974), m; TOWERING INFERNO, THE(1974), m; EIGER SANCTION, THE(1975), m; JAWS(1975), m; BUGSY MALONE(1976, Brit.), m; FAMILY PLOT(1976), m; MIDWAY(1976), m; MISSOURI BREAKS, THE(1976), m; NO DEPOSIT, NO RETURN(1976); BLACK SUNDAY(1977), m; CLOSE ENCOUNTERS OF THE THIRD KIND(1977), m; DEER HUNTER, THE(1978), md; FURY, THE(1978), m; HOT LEAD AND COLD FEET(1978); JAWS II(1978), m; SUPERMAN(1978), m; SWARM, THE(1978); DRACULA(1979), m; 1941(1979), m; EMPIRE STRIKES BACK, THE(1980), m; SUPERMAN II(1980), m; HEARTBEEPS(1981), m; RAIDERS OF THE LOST ARK(1981), m; E.T. THE EXTRA-TERRESTRIAL(1982), m; MONSIGNOR(1982), m; YES, GIORGIO(1982), m; ANGELO MY LOVE(1983); JAWS 3-D(1983), m; RETURN OF THE JEDI(1983), m; SUPERMAN III(1983), m
1984
INDIANA JONES AND THE TEMPLE OF DOOM(1984), m; RIVER, THE(1984), m

John Alfred Williams
SWEET LOVE, BITTER(1967), w

John B. Williams
IRON MAJOR, THE(1943); MY FORBIDDEN PAST(1951)

John "Buddy" Williams
THIS TIME FOR KEEPS(1942); WE WERE DANCING(1942)

John D. Williams
JEALOUSY(1929), w

John J. Williams
Misc. Silents
MARSE COVINGTON(1915)

John T. Williams
LAW VS. BILLY THE KID, THE(1954), w; STAR WARS(1977), m

John Warner Williams
HOSPITAL MASSACRE(1982)
1984
HOSPITAL MASSACRE(1984)

Johnny Williams
BECAUSE THEY'RE YOUNG(1960), m; SECRET WAYS, THE(1961), m; BACHELOR FLAT(1962), m; DIAMOND HEAD(1962), m; GIDGET GOES TO ROME(1963), m; JOHN GOLDFARB, PLEASE COME HOME(1964), m; KILLERS, THE(1964), m; NONE BUT THE BRAVE(1965, U.S./Jap.), m; HOW TO STEAL A MILLION(1966), m; NOT WITH MY WIFE, YOU DON'T!(1966), m, md, md; PENELOPE(1966), m; PLAINSMAN, THE(1966), m; RARE BREED, THE(1966), m; FITZWILLY(1967), m; GUIDE FOR THE MARRIED MAN, A(1967), m; VALLEY OF THE DOLLS(1967), m, md; SERGEANT RYKER(1968), m; REIVERS, THE(1969), m; STORY OF A WOMAN(1970, U.S./Ital.), m; SPOOK WHO SAT BY THE DOOR, THE(1973)

Jonathan Williams
LE MANS(1971); STROKER ACE(1983)

Joyce Williams
PRETTY MAIDS ALL IN A ROW(1971); PRIVATE DUTY NURSES(1972); SOYLENT GREEN(1973)

Karen Williams
MELODY(1971, Brit.)

Kate Williams
POOR COW(1968, Brit.); MELODY(1971, Brit.); QUADROPHENIA(1979, Brit.); PARTY PARTY(1983, Brit.)
Misc. Talkies
LOVE THY NEIGHBOUR(1973)

Katherine Williams
BIG RACE, THE(1934); WHERE SINNERS MEET(1934); YOUNG AND BEAUTIFUL(1934); RENDEZVOUS AT MIDNIGHT(1935)

Kathleen Williams
WEDDING RINGS(1930); SWING FEVER(1943); RATIONING(1944); OTHER LOVE, THE(1947); STRANGER'S MEETING(1957, Brit.)

Kathleen "Kay" Williams
TWO GIRLS AND A SAILOR(1944)

Kathlyn Williams
ROAD TO PARADISE(1930); DADDY LONG LEGS(1931); UNHOLY LOVE(1932); RENDEZVOUS AT MIDNIGHT(1935)
Silents
SPOILERS, THE(1914); CARPET FROM BAGDAD, THE(1915); NE'ER-DO-WELL, THE(1916); MAN'S HOME, A(1921); MORALS(1921); PRIVATE SCANDAL, A(1921); SOULS FOR SALE(1923); ENEMY SEX, THE(1924); PAINTED FLAPPER, THE(1924); SALLY IN OUR ALLEY(1927); HONEYMOON FLATS(1928); OUR DANCING DAUGHTERS(1928); SINGLE MAN, A(1929); SINGLE STANDARD, THE(1929)
Misc. Silents
CHIP OF THE FLYING U(1914); STORY OF THE BLOOD RED ROSE, THE(1914); ROSARY, THE(1915); SWEET ALYSSUM(1915); DEVIL, THE SERVANT AND THE MAN, THE(1916); INTO THE PRIMITIVE(1916); THOU SHALT NOT COVET(1916); VALIANTS OF VIRGINIA, THE(1916); BIG TIMBER(1917); COST OF HATRED, THE(1917); HIGHWAY OF HOPE, THE(1917); OUT OF THE WRECK(1917); REDEEMING LOVE, THE(1917); THINGS WE LOVE, THE(1918); WE CAN'T HAVE EVERYTHING(1918); WHISPERING CHORUS, THE(1918); BETTER WIFE, THE(1919); HER PURCHASE PRICE(1919); CONRAD IN QUEST OF HIS YOUTH(1920); GIRL NAMED MARY, A(1920); JUST A WIFE(1920); PRINCE CHAP, THE(1920); TREE OF KNOWLEDGE, THE(1920); U.P. TRAIL, THE(1920); EVERYTHING FOR SALE(1921); FORBIDDEN FRUIT(1921); HUSH(1921); CLARENCE(1922); SPANISH DANCER, THE(1923); TRIMMED IN SCARLET(1923); WORLD'S APPLAUSE, THE(1923); CITY THAT NEVER SLEEPS, THE(1924); SINGLE WIVES(1924); WANDERER OF THE WASTELAND(1924); WHEN A GIRL LOVES(1924); BEST PEOPLE, THE(1925); LOCKED DOORS(1925)

Kathy Williams
RAMRODDER, THE(1969)

Kay Williams
KISS AND MAKE UP(1934); DU BARRY WAS A LADY(1943); GIRL CRAZY(1943); GUY NAMED JOE, A(1943); MARRIAGE IS A PRIVATE AFFAIR(1944); MEET THE PEOPLE(1944); THIRTY SECONDS OVER TOKYO(1944); ZIEGFELD FOLLIES(1945); NO MINOR VICES(1948); ACTRESS, THE(1953)

Keith Williams
CHANGE OF MIND(1969)

Ken Williams
SUN SHINES BRIGHT, THE(1953)

Kenneth Williams
BEGGAR'S OPERA, THE(1953); MEN ARE CHILDREN TWICE(1953, Brit.); INNOCENTS IN PARIS(1955, Brit.); LAND OF FURY(1955 Brit.); CARRY ON NURSE(1959, Brit.); CARRY ON SERGEANT(1959, Brit.); CARRY ON CONSTABLE(1960, Brit.); MAKE MINE MINK(1960, Brit.); TOMMY THE TOREADOR(1960, Brit.); CARRY ON REGARDLESS(1961, Brit.); HIS AND HERS(1961, Brit.); CARRY ON CRUISING(1962, Brit.); CARRY ON TEACHER(1962, Brit.); ROOMMATES(1962, Brit.); TWICE AROUND THE DAFFODILS(1962, Brit.); CARRY ON JACK(1963, Brit.); CARRY ON CLEO(1964, Brit.); CARRY ON SPYING(1964, Brit.); CARRY ON COWBOY(1966, Brit.); CARRY ON SCREAMING(1966, Brit.); DON'T LOSE YOUR HEAD(1967, Brit.); FOLLOW THAT CAMEL(1967, Brit.); CARRY ON DOCTOR(1968, Brit.); CARRY ON, UP THE KHYBER(1968, Brit.); CARRY ON AGAIN, DOCTOR(1969, Brit.); CARRY ON CAMPING(1969, Brit.); CARRY ON HENRY VIII(1970, Brit.); CARRY ON LOVING(1970, Brit.); CARRY ON EMANUELLE(1978, Brit.); HOUND OF THE BASKERVILLES, THE(1980, Brit.)
Misc. Talkies
CARRY ON 'ROUND THE BEND(1972, Brit.); CARRY ON MATRON(1973, Brit.)

Kenny Williams
FIFTH AVENUE GIRL(1939); IRISH EYES ARE SMILING(1944); LODGER, THE(1944), ch; DIAMOND HORSESHOE(1945); DOLL FACE(1945), ch; IF I'M LUCKY(1946), ch; MOTHER WORE TIGHTS(1947), a, ch; FORT APACHE(1948), ch; WHEN MY BABY SMILES AT ME(1948); YOU WERE MEANT FOR ME(1948), a, ch; SLATTERY'S HURRICANE(1949); WHEN WILLIE COMES MARCHING HOME(1950), a, ch; MEET ME AT THE FAIR(1952), ch; PRIDE OF ST. LOUIS, THE(1952); ALL I DESIRE(1953), ch; GLENN MILLER STORY, THE(1953), ch; NAKED ALIBI(1954), ch; SIGN OF THE PAGAN(1954), ch; AIN'T MISBEHAVIN'(1955), ch; KELLY AND ME(1957), ch; NIGHT PASSAGE(1957); WAR LORD, THE(1965), ch

Kent Williams
HEART BEAT(1979); IN-LAWS, THE(1979); TIME AFTER TIME(1979, Brit.); HONKY TONK FREEWAY(1981); WARGAMES(1983)

Kim Williams
1984
REPO MAN(1984)

Kimmary Williams
HAIR(1979)

Kit Williams
THESE ARE THE DAMNED(1965, Brit.); GIRL ON A MOTORCYCLE, THE(1968, Fr./Brit.)

L. E. Williams
Silents
EVE'S DAUGHTER(1918), ph

L.P. Williams
NURSE EDITH CAVELL(1939), art d; TORPEDOED!(1939), art d; IRENE(1940), art d; MR. AND MRS. SMITH(1941), art d; SUNNY(1941), art d; SO WELL REMEMBERED(1947, Brit.), art d

Lady Rhys Williams
PRICE OF THINGS, THE(1930, Brit.), w

Larry Williams
TARNISHED LADY(1931), ph; FOLLOW THE LEADER(1930), ph; SAP FROM SYRACUSE, THE(1930), ph; YOUNG MAN OF MANHATTAN(1930), ph; GIRL HABIT(1931), ph; CRIME OF DR. CRESPI, THE(1936), ph; BROTHER RAT(1938); GARDEN OF THE MOON(1938); GIRLS ON PROBATION(1938); SISTERS, THE(1938); TORCHY BLANE IN PANAMA(1938); GOING PLACES(1939); NANCY DREW-REPORTER(1939); ON TRIAL(1939); SECRET SERVICE OF THE AIR(1939); TEVYA(1939), ph; TORCHY PLAYS WITH DYNAMITE(1939); WATERFRONT(1939); WINGS OF THE NAVY(1939); BROTHER RAT AND A BABY(1940); MA, HE'S MAKING EYES AT ME(1940); DIVE BOMBER(1941); YOU'LL NEVER GET RICH(1941); CAPTAINS OF THE CLOUDS(1942); MAGNIFICENT DOPE, THE(1942); GOVERNMENT GIRL(1943); MAN FROM FRISCO(1944); TILL THE CLOUDS ROLL BY(1946); GOODBYE, MY FANCY(1951); JUST FOR THE HELL OF IT(1968); KLANSMAN, THE(1974)
Silents
RAMSHACKLE HOUSE(1924), ph

Laurie Williams
SWINGIN' SUMMER, A(1965)

Lawrence Williams
MONSTER MAKER, THE(1944), w; PAULA(1952)

Lawrence A. Williams
LEATHER SAINT, THE(1956)

Lawrence E. Williams
Silents
IMPOSSIBLE CATHERINE(1919), ph; IDOL OF THE NORTH, THE(1921), ph

Lawrence Edward Williams
CULPEPPER CATTLE COMPANY, THE(1972), ph

Lawrence P. Williams
FOREVER AND A DAY(1943), art d

Leila Williams
SHAKEDOWN, THE(1960, Brit.); WATCH YOUR STERN(1961, Brit.); BEAUTY JUNGLE, THE(1966, Brit.); MARRIAGE OF CONVENIENCE(1970, Brit.)

Leon Williams
DOCTOR DEATH: SEEKER OF SOULS(1973)
Misc. Silents
SPORT OF THE GODS, THE(1921)

Leonard Williams
PASSING STRANGER, THE(1954, Brit.); LOVE MATCH, THE(1955, Brit.); RAMSBOTTOM RIDES AGAIN(1956, Brit.); ORDERS ARE ORDERS(1959, Brit.)

Lester Williams
 SOD SISTERS(1969), d
Misc. Talkies
 GUN GRIT(1936), d
Lester Williams [William Berke]
 DESERT JUSTICE(1936), d; TOLL OF THE DESERT(1936), d
Liberty Williams
 GUS(1976)
Linda Williams
 MAGIC CARPET, THE(1951); TWO TICKETS TO BROADWAY(1951)
Llandys Williams
1984
 IMPULSE(1984), cos
Lori Williams
 IT'S A BIKINI WORLD(1967)
Lorraine Williams
 CARAVANS(1978, U.S./Iranian), w; MAN, WOMAN AND CHILD(1983)
Lottie Williams
 STRICTLY MODERN(1930); SIX-DAY BIKE RIDER(1934); WONDER BAR(1934); CASE OF THE BLACK CAT, THE(1936); MURDER BY AN ARISTOCRAT(1936); STORY OF LOUIS PASTEUR, THE(1936); WINE, WOMEN AND HORSES(1937); ANGELS WITH DIRTY FACES(1938); HARD TO GET(1938); LITTLE MISS THOROUGHBRED(1938); NANCY DREW–DETECTIVE(1938); SISTERS, THE(1938); DARK VICTORY(1939); ESPIONAGE AGENT(1939); KING OF THE UNDER-WORLD(1939); OFF THE RECORD(1939); PRIVATE DETECTIVE(1939); ROARING TWENTIES, THE(1939); YES, MY DARLING DAUGHTER(1939); FUGITIVE FROM JUSTICE, A(1940); LADIES MUST LIVE(1940); MAN WHO TALKED TOO MUCH, THE(1940); MEET JOHN DOE(1941); BUSSES ROAR(1942); EDGE OF DARK-NESS(1943); ONE MORE TOMORROW(1946); SHADOW OF A WOMAN(1946); NORA PRENTISS(1947); JUNE BRIDE(1948)
Silents
 TWIN BEDS(1920); ALL SOULS EVE(1921); YESTERDAY'S WIFE(1923)
Misc. Silents
 VEILED WOMAN, THE(1922)
Louis Williams
 SECOND-HAND HEARTS(1981)
Louis Sheldon Williams
 OUR MOTHER'S HOUSE(1967, Brit.)
Louise Williams
 GAY DECEIVERS, THE(1969)
Lucille Williams
 TRAVELING HUSBANDS(1931); WICKED(1931)
Misc. Silents
 SALLY'S SHOULDERS(1928)
Lucita Williams
 REDS(1981)
Lyman Williams
 ELEVENTH COMMANDMENT(1933); SECRETS(1933); SUPERNATURAL(1933); GLAMOUR(1934); STUDENT TOUR(1934); DAMAGED LIVES(1937)
Lynda Williams
 SPARTACUS(1960)
Mack Williams
 ROLLIN' HOME TO TEXAS(1941); CANON CITY(1948); COMMAND DECI-SION(1948); HOLLOW TRIUMPH(1948); TRAPPED(1949); WHIRLPOOL(1949); DESTI-NATION BIG HOUSE(1950); KISS TOMORROW GOODBYE(1950); NO WAY OUT(1950); SOUND OF FURY, THE(1950); WHERE THE SIDEWALK ENDS(1950); CALL ME MISTER(1951); GUY WHO CAME BACK, THE(1951); OPERATION PACIF-IC(1951); PAYMENT ON DEMAND(1951); MONKEY BUSINESS(1952); BIGAMIST, THE(1953); UNCHAINED(1955); VIOLENT SATURDAY(1955); STEEL JUNGLE, THE(1956); THERE'S ALWAYS TOMORROW(1956); MONSTER THAT CHAL-LENGED THE WORLD, THE(1957); SPOILERS OF THE FOREST(1957); WILL SUCCESS SPOIL ROCK HUNTER?(1957); AS YOUNG AS WE ARE(1958); 10 NORTH FREDERICK(1958); SHAGGY DOG, THE(1959); WESTBOUND(1959); CHARTROOSE CABOOSE(1960); CAPE FEAR(1962); PUBLIC AFFAIR, A(1962)
Mae Williams
 COAST TO COAST(1980); FOXES(1980)
Maitland Williams
 CONCRETE JUNGLE, THE(1962, Brit.)
Malcolm Williams
Silents
 IDOL OF THE STAGE, THE(1916)
Misc. Silents
 DANCING GIRL, THE(1915); EMPTY POCKETS(1918)
Margaret Williams
 GRASS IS GREENER, THE(1960), w
Margo Williams
 REQUIEM FOR A GUNFIGHTER(1965)
Margot Williams
Silents
 ORDEAL, THE(1914)
Misc. Silents
 ANTIQUE DEALER, THE(1915); MASTER OF THE HOUSE, THE(1915)
Marilyn Williams
 GAY INTRUDERS, THE(1948); KISS THE BLOOD OFF MY HANDS(1948); THINGS HAPPEN AT NIGHT(1948, Brit.)
Mark Williams
 SPOOK WHO SAT BY THE DOOR, THE(1973); PRIVILEGED(1982, Brit.)
Marston Williams
 PUBLIC COWBOY NO. 1(1937)
Mary Williams
 END OF THE AFFAIR, THE(1955, Brit.)
Silents
 GOLD RUSH, THE(1925)
Mary Jane Williams
 DOZENS, THE(1981)
Mason Williams
 SUBWAY EXPRESS(1931)

Master Williams
 TILLIE AND GUS(1933)
Maston Williams
 CAVALIER OF THE WEST(1931); CLEARING THE RANGE(1931); GAMBLING SEX(1932); LOST JUNGLE, THE(1934); HEART OF THE ROCKIES(1937); TWO-FISTED SHERIFF(1937); WHISTLING BULLETS(1937); CALL THE MES-QUITEERS(1938); HEROES OF THE HILLS(1938); RIDERS OF BLACK RIVER(1939); HI-YO SILVER(1940)
Matson Williams
 ONE MAN JUSTICE(1937); OVERLAND EXPRESS, THE(1938)
Maud Williams
Silents
 FLYING FROM JUSTICE(1915, Brit.)
Maynard Williams
 CONFESSIONS OF A POP PERFORMER(1975, Brit.)
Melissa Williams
 MELVIN AND HOWARD(1980)
Melvin Williams
 I WALKED WITH A ZOMBIE(1943); SALT OF THE EARTH(1954)
Meridith Williams
 GAY DECEIVERS, THE(1969)
Mervin Williams
 MODEL WIFE(1941); SENATOR WAS INDISCREET, THE(1947); FORCE OF EVIL(1948); NAKED CITY, THE(1948); JOE PALOOKA IN THE SQUARED CIR-CLE(1950); MISTER 880(1950); SATURDAY'S HERO(1951); HOODLUM EMPIRE(1952)
Mervyn Williams
 PRESIDENT'S LADY, THE(1953)
Michael Williams
 TRIAL OF JOAN OF ARC(1965, Fr.); PERSECUTION AND ASSASSINATION OF JEAN-PAUL MARAT AS PERFORMED BY THE INMATES OF THE ASYLUM OF CHARENTON UNDER THE DIRECTION OF THE MARQUIS DE SADE, THE(1967, Brit.); TELL ME LIES(1968, Brit.); EAGLE IN A CAGE(1971, U.S./Yugo.); EDUCATING RITA(1983); ENIGMA(1983)
1984
 SOLDIER'S STORY, A(1984)
Misc. Talkies
 DEAD CERT(1974, Brit.)
Mike Williams
 FINAL CUT, THE(1980, Aus.), p
Milton Williams
 MIRACLE IN HARLEM(1948); COOL WORLD, THE(1963); NOTHING BUT A MAN(1964)
Milton J. Williams
Misc. Talkies
 MURDER WITH MUSIC(1941)
Mona Williams
 WOMAN'S WORLD(1954), w
Nigel Williams
1984
 CLASS ENEMY(1984, Ger.), w
Noelle Williams
 TEN COMMANDMENTS, THE(1956)
Nora Williams
 TWO HEARTS IN HARMONY(1935, Brit.)
Norman Williams
 TEMPORARY WIDOW, THE(1930, Ger./Brit.); WE DIVE AT DAWN(1943, Brit.); YANK IN LONDON, A(1946, Brit.); SILVER DARLINGS, THE(1947, Brit.); SCOTT OF THE ANTARCTIC(1949, Brit.); SECRET PEOPLE(1952, Brit.); SMALL TOWN STO-RY(1953, Brit.); WITNESS IN THE DARK(1959, Brit.), p; AND WOMEN SHALL WEEP(1960, Brit.), p; PICCADILLY THIRD STOP(1960, Brit.), p; SHAKEDOWN, THE(1960, Brit.), p; YOUR MONEY OR YOUR WIFE(1965, Brit.), p; MAN WHO FINALLY DIED, THE(1967, Brit.), p
Oliver Williams
 BIG RED(1962), m
Oren Williams
 DEVIL'S MISTRESS, THE(1968)
Oscar Williams
 DALLAS(1950); FINAL COMEDOWN, THE(1972), p,d&w; FIVE ON THE BLACK HAND SIDE(1973), d; BLACK BELT JONES(1974), w; TRUCK TURNER(1974), w; HOT POTATO(1976), d&w; FAST BREAK(1979)
Owen Williams
 CADDIE(1976, Aus.), art d; IRISHMAN, THE(1978, Aus.), prod d
P. W. Williams
 NUNZIO(1978)
Page Williams
 TOM SAWYER(1973)
Pat Williams
 QUEEN OF HEARTS(1936, Brit.); FOR FREEDOM(1940, Brit.); NIGHT TRAIN(1940, Brit.); THEY CAME BY NIGHT(1940, Brit.); MRS. O'MALLEY AND MR. MALO-NE(1950); THREE LITTLE WORDS(1950); BOOTS MALONE(1952); SCANDAL SHEET(1952); SOUND OFF(1952); HOW SWEET IT IS(1968), m; DON'T DRINK THE WATER(1969), m; NICE GIRL LIKE ME, A(1969, Brit.), m; MACHO CAL-LAHAN(1970), m; SIDELONG GLANCES OF A PIGEON KICKER, THE(1970), m; EVEL KNIEVEL(1971), m; MOONCHILD(1972), m; SSSSSSSS(1973), m; HARRAD SUMMER, THE(1974), m; FRAMED(1975), m; SENIORS, THE(1978), m; BUTCH AND SUNDANCE: THE EARLY DAYS(1979), m; DON'T GO IN THE HOUSE(1980)
Patricia Williams
 LOVE CHILD(1982)
Patrick Williams
 CASEY'S SHADOW(1978), m; CHEAP DETECTIVE, THE(1978), m; ONE AND ONLY, THE(1978), m; BREAKING AWAY(1979), m; CUBA(1979), m; HOT STUFF(1979), m; HERO AT LARGE(1980), m; HOW TO BEAT THE HIGH COST OF LIVING(1980), m; IT'S MY TURN(1980), m; USED CARS(1980), m; WHOLLY MO-SES(1980), m; CHARLIE CHAN AND THE CURSE OF THE DRAGON QUEEN(1981), m; SOME KIND OF HERO(1982), m; MARVIN AND TIGE(1983), m; TWO OF A KIND(1983), m
1984
 ALL OF ME(1984), m; BEST DEFENSE(1984), m; BUDDY SYSTEM, THE(1984), m; SWING SHIFT(1984), m

Paul Williams
CHASE, THE(1966); OUT OF IT(1969), d&w; REVOLUTIONARY, THE(1970, Brit.), d; DEALING: OR THE BERKELEY-TO-BOSTON FORTY-BRICK LOST-BAG BLUES(1971), a, d, w; BATTLE FOR THE PLANET OF THE APES(1973); PHANTOM OF THE PARADISE(1974), a, m; THUNDERBOLT AND LIGHTFOOT(1974), m/l; BUGSY MALONE(1976, Brit.), m; STAR IS BORN, A(1976), md; SMOKEY AND THE BANDIT(1977); CHEAP DETECTIVE, THE(1978); END, THE(1978), m; NUNZIO(1978), d; MUPPET MOVIE, THE(1979), a, m; SMOKEY AND THE BANDIT II(1980); STONE COLD DEAD(1980, Can.); CAN SHE BAKE A CHERRY PIE?(1983); SMOKEY AND THE BANDIT–PART 3(1983)
1984
PURPLE HEARTS(1984)
Misc. Talkies
BLACK PLANET, THE(1982, Aus.), d
Paul H. Williams
LOVED ONE, THE(1965); WATERMELON MAN(1970)
Payne Williams
MR. PEEK-A-BOO(1951, Fr.)
Pega Williams
1984
CAREFUL, HE MIGHT HEAR YOU(1984, Aus.)
Percy Williams
Silents
PRIDE OF PALOMAR, THE(1922); GOLDFISH, THE(1924); UNHOLY THREE, THE(1925); CHILDREN OF DIVORCE(1927); LONDON AFTER MIDNIGHT(1927); OH, KAY(1928)
Percy N. Williams
Silents
ITALIAN, THE(1915), w
Peter Williams
STRAW MAN, THE(1953, Brit.); FOOTSTEPS IN THE FOG(1955, Brit.); LADYKILL-ERS, THE(1956, Brit.); MAN WHO KNEW TOO MUCH, THE(1956); MAN WHO NEVER WAS, THE(1956, Brit.); RICHARD III(1956, Brit.); BRIDGE ON THE RIVER KWAI, THE(1957); ON THE BEACH(1959); TWO LETTER ALIBI(1962); GAMERA VERSUS VIRAS(1968, Jap); TWO A PENNY(1968, Brit.), art d; JERUSALEM FILE, THE(1972, U.S./Israel), art d; PERSECUTION(1974, Brit.), art d; CARAVANS(1978, U.S./Iranian), art d; ZULU DAWN(1980, Brit.), art d; SAFARI 3000(1982), art d; HIGH ROAD TO CHINA(1983)
Philip Williams
Misc. Silents
CALL OF THE ROAD, THE(1920, Brit.)
Pip Williams
TRAIN RIDE TO HOLLYWOOD(1975), m
Polly Williams
LOLA(1971, Brit./Ital.); SLIPPER AND THE ROSE, THE(1976, Brit.)
Prysor Williams
BLUE SCAR(1949, Brit.); LAST DAYS OF DOLWYN, THE(1949, Brit.); MEN ARE CHILDREN TWICE(1953, Brit.)
R. Wayland Williams
GATHERING OF EAGLES, A(1963); IRON ANGEL(1964)
R.J. Williams
1984
MASS APPEAL(1984)
R.X. Williams
INTRUDER IN THE DUST(1949)
Ralph Williams
ALL THE PRESIDENT'S MEN(1976)
Ralph Vaughan Williams
FLEMISH FARM, THE(1943, Brit.), m; SCOTT OF THE ANTARCTIC(1949, Brit.), m
Ralph Vaughn Williams
INVADERS, THE,(1941), m; LOVES OF JOANNA GODDEN, THE(1947, Brit.), m
Ramsey Williams
DRAGNET(1954); HELL AND HIGH WATER(1954)
Ray Williams
CANNIBALS IN THE STREETS(1982, Ital./Span.)
Rebecca Yancey Williams
VANISHING VIRGINIAN, THE(1941), w
Redgie Williams
PARISIAN, THE(1931, Fr.)
Rex Williams
BUSSES ROAR(1942); ESCAPE FROM CRIME(1942); GORILLA MAN(1942); SE-CRET ENEMIES(1942); ABOVE SUSPICION(1943); FALSE FACES(1943); FIRST COMES COURAGE(1943); HOSTAGES(1943); POWER OF THE PRESS(1943); PURPLE V, THE(1943); TARZAN TRIUMPHS(1943); THEY CAME TO BLOW UP AMERI-CA(1943); TRUCK BUSTERS(1943); SALTY O'ROURKE(1945); WITHIN THESE WALLS(1945); MARRYING KIND, THE(1952)
Rhoda Williams
NATIONAL VELVET(1944); CORN IS GREEN, THE(1945); OUR VINES HAVE TENDER GRAPES(1945); THAT HAGEN GIRL(1947); HOUSE OF STRANGERS(1949); CINDERELLA(1950); DEVIL'S DOORWAY(1950); PERSUADER, THE(1957); HIGH SCHOOL HELLCATS(1958); SPACE MASTER X-7(1958); SERGEANT WAS A LADY, THE(1961)
Rhys Williams
HOW GREEN WAS MY VALLEY(1941); CAIRO(1942); EAGLE SQUADRON(1942); GENTLEMAN JIM(1942); MRS. MINIVER(1942); RANDOM HARVEST(1942); REMEMBER PEARL HARBOR(1942); THIS ABOVE ALL(1942); UNDERGROUND AGENT(1942); NO TIME FOR LOVE(1943); BELLS OF ST. MARY'S, THE(1945); BLOOD ON THE SUN(1945); CORN IS GREEN, THE(1945); VOICE OF THE WHIS-TLER(1945); YOU CAME ALONG(1945); CROSS MY HEART(1946); SO GOES MY LOVE(1946); SPIRAL STAIRCASE(1946); STRANGE WOMAN, THE(1946); EASY COME, EASY GO(1947); FARMER'S DAUGHTER, THE(1947); IF WINTER CO-MES(1947); IMPERFECT LADY, THE(1947); MOSS ROSE(1947); TROUBLE WITH WOMEN, THE(1947); HILLS OF HOME(1948); TENTH AVENUE ANGEL(1948); BAD BOY(1949); CROOKED WAY, THE(1949); FIGHTING MAN OF THE PLAINS(1949); INSPECTOR GENERAL, THE(1949); TOKYO JOE(1949); CALIFORNIA PASS-AGE(1950); DEVIL'S DOORWAY(1950); KISS TOMORROW GOODBYE(1950); ONE TOO MANY(1950); SHOWDOWN, THE(1950); TYRANT OF THE SEA(1950); LAW AND THE LADY, THE(1951); LIGHT TOUCH, THE(1951); LIGHTNING STRIKES TWI-CE(1951); MILLION DOLLAR PURSUIT(1951); NEVER TRUST A GAMBLER(1951); SON OF DR. JEKYLL(1951); SWORD OF MONTE CRISTO, THE(1951); CAR-BINE WILLIAMS(1952); LES MISERABLES(1952); MEET ME AT THE FAIR(1952);

MUTINY(1952); OKINAWA(1952); PLYMOUTH ADVENTURE(1952); WORLD IN HIS ARMS, THE(1952); JULIUS CAESAR(1953); MAN IN THE ATTIC(1953); SCANDAL AT SCOURIE(1953); BAD FOR EACH OTHER(1954); BLACK SHIELD OF FALWORTH, THE(1954); JOHNNY GUITAR(1954); THERE'S NO BUSINESS LIKE SHOW BUSI-NESS(1954); BATTLE FLAME(1955); HOW TO BE VERY, VERY, POPULAR(1955); KENTUCKIAN, THE(1955); KING'S THIEF, THE(1955); MANY RIVERS TO CROSS(1955); SCARLET COAT, THE(1955); BOSS, THE(1956); DESPERADOES ARE IN TOWN, THE(1956); MOHAWK(1956); NIGHTMARE(1956); RAINTREE COUN-TY(1957); RESTLESS BREED, THE(1957); MERRY ANDREW(1958); MIDNIGHT LACE(1960); SONS OF KATIE ELDER, THE(1965); OUR MAN FLINT(1966); SKULL-DUGGERY(1970)
Richard Williams
ACTION OF THE TIGER(1957); HEART OF A CHILD(1958, Brit.); CHILD AND THE KILLER, THE(1959, Brit.); LOSS OF INNOCENCE(1961, Brit.); CHARGE OF THE LIGHT BRIGADE, THE(1968, Brit.), anim; THINK DIRTY(1970, Brit.), anim & titles; FIVE ON THE BLACK HAND SIDE(1973); SLAUGHTER'S BIG RIP-OFF(1973); RAGGEDY ANN AND ANDY(1977), d, anim; FINAL CONFLICT, THE(1981)
Richard Anthony Williams
UPTIGHT(1968); LOST MAN, THE(1969)
Rick Williams
SHE-DEVILS ON WHEELS(1968)
Robert Williams
COMMON LAW, THE(1931); DEVOTION(1931); PLATINUM BLONDE(1931); RE-BOUND(1931); FACE IN THE FOG, A(1936); RIDIN' DOWN THE CANYON(1942), w; DEAD MAN'S GULCH(1943), w; CAROLINA BLUES(1944); CRY OF THE WERE-WOLF(1944); GHOST THAT WALKS ALONE, THE(1944); GIRL IN THE CASE(1944); JAM SESSION(1944); ONCE UPON A TIME(1944); ONE MYSTERIOUS NIGHT(1944); STARS ON PARADE(1944); TWO-MAN SUBMARINE(1944); U-BOAT PRISO-NER(1944); ADVENTURES OF RUSTY(1945); BOSTON BLACKIE BOOKED ON SUSPICION(1945); BOSTON BLACKIE'S RENDEZVOUS(1945); EVE KNEW HER APPLES(1945); OVER 21(1945); ROUGH, TOUGH AND READY(1945); SERGEANT MIKE(1945); TONIGHT AND EVERY NIGHT(1945); TRAIL TO VENGEANCE(1945), w; YOUTH ON TRIAL(1945); BANDIT OF SHERWOOD FOREST, THE(1946); OUT OF THE DEPTHS(1946); SHOW-OFF, THE(1946); KEY WITNESS(1947); LADY IN THE LAKE(1947); T-MEN(1947); APARTMENT FOR PEGGY(1948); CALL NORTHSIDE 777(1948); FURY AT FURNACE CREEK(1948); HE WALKED BY NIGHT(1948); STRANGE GAMBLE(1948); SPECIAL AGENT(1949); MALAYA(1950); PIONEER MAR-SHAL(1950); STORM WARNING(1950); LADY SAYS NO, THE(1951); SELLOUT, THE(1951); SMUGGLER'S GOLD(1951); LOAN SHARK(1952); WHITE GOD-DESS(1953); COURT-MARTIAL OF BILLY MITCHELL, THE(1955); LUCY GAL-LANT(1955); TUNNEL OF LOVE, THE(1958); JUMBO(1962); SATAN'S BED(1965); MURDER CLINIC, THE(1967, Ital./Fr.), w; ESCAPE 2000(1983, Aus.), w
Misc. Talkies
ABAR–THE FIRST BLACK SUPERMAN(1977)
Robert B. [Bob] Williams
THAT WONDERFUL URGE(1948)
Robert B. Williams
UNEXPECTED GUEST(1946); DISHONORED LADY(1947); DARK PAST, THE(1948); STREET WITH NO NAME, THE(1948); LONE WOLF AND HIS LADY, THE(1949); MARY RYAN, DETECTIVE(1949); MYSTERIOUS DESPERADO, THE(1949); OH, YOU BEAUTIFUL DOLL(1949); ON THE TOWN(1949); ROUGHSHOD(1949); RUSTY'S BIRTHDAY(1949); SLIGHTLY FRENCH(1949); STAGECOACH KID(1949); GREAT JEWEL ROBBER, THE(1950); LAWLESS, THE(1950); MISTER 880(1950); WHERE THE SIDEWALK ENDS(1950); FATHER'S LITTLE DIVIDEND(1951); GROOM WORE SPURS, THE(1951); GUY WHO CAME BACK, THE(1951); DREAMBOAT(1952); MR. SCOUTMASTER(1953); PRESIDENT'S LADY, THE(1953); HELL AND HIGH WA-TER(1954); MAGNIFICENT OBSESSION(1954); I'LL CRY TOMORROW(1955); REBEL WITHOUT A CAUSE(1955); REVENGE OF THE CREATURE(1955); THIS ISLAND EARTH(1955); OVER-EXPOSED(1956); UNGUARDED MOMENT, THE(1956); DEATH IN SMALL DOSES(1957); HARD MAN, THE(1957); SPIRIT OF ST. LOUIS, THE(1957); PARTY GIRL(1958); HOLE IN THE HEAD, A(1959); NORTH BY NORTHWEST(1959); PILLOW TALK(1959); PEPE(1960); EVERYTHING'S DUCKY(1961); SAINTLY SIN-NERS(1962); VIVA LAS VEGAS(1964); FOLLOW ME, BOYS!(1966); HANG'EM HIGH(1968); EVEL KNIEVEL(1971)
Robert Creighton Williams
HE RIDES TALL(1964), w; TAGGART(1964), w
Roberta Jean Williams
WHOSE LIFE IS IT ANYWAY?(1981)
Robin Williams
CHILDREN OF BABYLON(1980, Jamaica); POPEYE(1980); WORLD ACCORDING TO GARP, The(1982); SURVIVORS, THE(1983)
1984
MOSCOW ON THE HUDSON(1984)
Misc. Talkies
CAN I DO IT 'TIL I NEED GLASSES?(1977)
Robin T. Williams
CHICKEN CHRONICLES, THE(1977)
Robt. B. Williams
BAT, THE(1959)
Rod Williams
LOOTERS, THE(1955); DANCE WITH ME, HENRY(1956)
1984
STRIKEBOUND(1984, Aus.)
Rodger Williams
HEROES OF THE ALAMO(1938)
Roger Williams
CHEYENNE TORNADO(1935); CODE OF THE MOUNTED(1935); COYOTE TRAILS(1935); FIGHTING PIONEERS(1935); GHOST RIDER, THE(1935); LAWLESS BORDER(1935); NO MAN'S RANGE(1935); RUSTLER'S PARADISE(1935); TRAILS OF THE WILD(1935); WAGON TRAIL(1935); CATTLE THIEF, THE(1936); DESERT JUSTICE(1936); FEUD OF THE WEST(1936); FRONTIER JUSTICE(1936); GUN PLAY(1936); GUN SMOKE(1936); MEN OF THE PLAINS(1936); MILLIONAIRE KID(1936); PHANTOM PATROL(1936); RIDING AVENGER, THE(1936); SONG OF THE TRAIL(1936); STORMY TRAILS(1936); TIMBER WAR(1936); TOLL OF THE DESERT(1936); WILDCAT TROOPER(1936); ACES WILD(1937); BILL CRACKS DOWN(1937); CHEYENNE RIDES AGAIN(1937); COME ON, COWBOYS(1937); GHOST TOWN(1937); GUNS IN THE DARK(1937); LAW AND LEAD(1937); LAWLESS LAND(1937); LOST RANCH(1937); MYSTERY RANGE(1937); NATION AFLAME(1937); PINTO RUSTLERS(1937); RECKLESS RANGER(1937); RIDERS OF THE WHISTLING SKULL(1937); RIDING ON(1937); ROAMING COWBOY, THE(1937);

SILVER TRAIL, THE(1937); SINGING BUCKAROO, THE(1937); TRAILING TROUBLE(1937); WILD HORSE ROUND-UP(1937); BROTHERS OF THE WEST(1938); CALL THE MESQUITEERS(1938); CODE OF THE RANGERS(1938); FEUD MAKER(1938); FEUD OF THE TRAIL(1938); HEROES OF THE HILLS(1938); ORPHAN OF THE PECOS(1938); RED RIVER RANGE(1938); RHYTHM OF THE SADDLE(1938); SIX SHOOTIN' SHERIFF(1938); WHIRLWIND HORSEMAN(1938); CODE OF THE FEARLESS(1939); FRONTIER SCOUT(1939); MOUNTAIN RHYTHM(1939); NIGHT RIDERS, THE(1939); WOLF CALL(1939); COLORADO PIONEERS(1945); MEET MR. CALLAGHAN(1954, Brit.); SWINGIN' ALONG(1962)

Misc. Talkies

GUNSMOKE ON THE GUADALUPE(1935); PECOS KID, THE(1935); RANGE WARFARE(1935); RECKLESS BUCKAROO, THE(1935); GUN GRIT(1936); RIDIN' ON(1936); VENGEANCE OF RANNAH(1936); VALLEY OF TERROR(1937)

Ron Williams

MAN FROM HONG KONG(1975), ed; DEATHCHEATERS(1976, Aus.), ed; BUSH CHRISTMAS(1983, Aus.), ed; FIGHTING BACK(1983, Brit.), ed

1984

BROTHERS(1984, Aus.), ed

Rony Williams

DREAM TOWN(1973, Ger.)

Roseaun Williams

POINT BLANK(1967)

Rosemary Williams

HOW TO STUFF A WILD BIKINI(1965)

Roy Williams

THREE CABALLEROS, THE(1944), w; MAKE MINE MUSIC(1946), w

Rush Williams

ROCKY MOUNTAIN(1950); DAY THE EARTH STOOD STILL, THE(1951); FROGMEN, THE(1951); STARLIFT(1951); UNKNOWN MAN, THE(1951); BENEATH THE 12-MILE REEF(1953); KID FROM LEFT FIELD, THE(1953); SCARLET COAT, THE(1955); BLACK WHIP, THE(1956); GIANT(1956); COPPER SKY(1957); RIDE A VIOLENT MILE(1957); TROOPER HOOK(1957); BULLWHIP(1958); LEGION OF THE DOOMED(1958); SEVEN GUNS TO MESA(1958); CURSE OF THE UNDEAD(1959); PANIC IN THE CITY(1968)

Russ Williams

REDHEAD FROM WYOMING, THE(1953)

S.W. Williams

Silents

WOLF PACK(1922)

Misc. Silents

WHITE RIDER, THE(1920)

Sam Williams

NIGHT OF THE ASKARI(1978, Ger./South African); SAFARI 3000(1982); VICTOR/VICTORIA(1982)

Samm-Art Williams

WANDERERS, THE(1979); NIGHT OF THE JUGGLER(1980)

1984

BLOOD SIMPLE(1984)

Sammy Williams

GOD TOLD ME TO(1976)

Sandra Williams

UP THE JUNCTION(1968, Brit.)

Saz Williams

PROLOGUE(1970, Can.), m

Sethma Williams

TOO MANY GIRLS(1940); MY FAVORITE SPY(1951)

Sharon Williams

DON'T LOOK NOW(1973, Brit./Ital.)

Shirley Hunter Williams

DELIGHTFULLY DANGEROUS(1945)

Simon Williams

BLOOD ON SATAN'S CLAW, THE(1970, Brit.); INCREDIBLE SARAH, THE(1976, Brit.); JABBERWOCKY(1977, Brit.); UNCANNY, THE(1977, Brit./Can.); NO LONGER ALONE(1978); ODD JOB, THE(1978, Brit.); PRISONER OF ZENDA, THE(1979); FIENDISH PLOT OF DR. FU MANCHU, THE(1980)

Slim Williams

YES SIR, MR. BONES(1951)

Sonia Williams

ESCAPADE(1955, Brit.)

Sonny Boy Williams

FOOTSTEPS IN THE DARK(1941); HOLD BACK THE DAWN(1941); OLD SWIMMIN' HOLE, THE(1941); STREET OF CHANCE(1942); TAKE A LETTER, DARLING(1942); PRACTICALLY YOURS(1944)

Spencer Williams

VIRGINIA JUDGE, THE(1935); BRONZE BUCKAROO, THE(1939); HARLEM RIDES THE RANGE(1939); HORRIBLE DR. HICHCOCK, THE(1964, Ital.)

Misc. Talkies

BLOOD OF JESUS(1941), d; GO DOWN DEATH(1944), a, d; BEALE STREET MAMA(1946), d; DIRTY GERTY FROM HARLEM, USA(1946), d; JUKE JOINT(1947), d

Spencer Williams, Jr.

BAD BOY(1939); HARLEM RIDES THE RANGE(1939), w; SON OF INGAGI(1940), a, w

Stanton Williams

Silents

FORBIDDEN WOMAN, THE(1920)

Stephanie Williams

FAN, THE(1981)

Steve Williams

BLUES BROTHERS, THE(1980)

Steven Williams

COOLEY HIGH(1975); DOCTOR DETROIT(1983); TWILIGHT ZONE–THE MOVIE(1983)

Sue Williams

HOW TO STUFF A WILD BIKINI(1965)

Summar Williams

EYE FOR AN EYE, AN(1966), w

Sumner Williams

KNOCK ON ANY DOOR(1949); ON DANGEROUS GROUND(1951); JOHNNY GUITAR(1954); RUNNING WILD(1955); TRUE STORY OF JESSE JAMES, THE(1957); BITTER VICTORY(1958, Fr.); ROADRACERS, THE(1959)

Silents

CHRIS AND THE WONDERFUL LAMP(1917), w; KIDNAPPED(1917), w

Sydney M. Williams

RHYTHM PARADE(1943), p; BIG SHOW-OFF, THE(1945), p

Sylvester Williams

1984

SHEENA(1984)

Sylvia "Kuumba" Williams

SOUNDER(1972); OBSESSION(1976); FRENCH QUARTER(1978); FORT APACHE, THE BRONX(1981)

T. R. Williams

HEROES IN BLUE(1939), p; HIDDEN ENEMY(1940), p; MIDNIGHT LIMITED(1940), p

Taylor Williams

SOMEWHERE IN TIME(1980)

1984

GRANDVIEW, U.S.A.(1984)

Ted Williams

WIZ, THE(1978); DEALING: OR THE BERKELEY-TO-BOSTON FORTY-BRICK LOST-BAG BLUES(1971)

Misc. Silents

MODERN CAIN, A(1925)

Temie Mae Williams

BOOK OF NUMBERS(1973)

Tennessee Williams

GLASS MENAGERIE, THE(1950), w; STREETCAR NAMED DESIRE, A(1951), w; ROSE TATTOO, THE(1955), w; BABY DOLL(1956), w; CAT ON A HOT TIN ROOF(1958), w; SUDDENLY, LAST SUMMER(1959, Brit.), w; FUGITIVE KIND, THE(1960), w; ROMAN SPRING OF MRS. STONE, THE(1961, U.S./Brit.), w; SUMMER AND SMOKE(1961), w; PERIOD OF ADJUSTMENT(1962), w; SWEET BIRD OF YOUTH(1962), w; NIGHT OF THE IGUANA, THE(1964), w; THIS PROPERTY IS CONDEMNED(1966), w; BOOM!(1968), w; SENSO(1968, Ital.), w

Terry Williams

HOUSE OF CARDS(1969), ed; HORNET'S NEST(1970), ed

Tex Williams

BORN RECKLESS(1959)

Thad Williams

BARQUERO(1970)

Thames Williams

BRIMSTONE(1949), w

Thomas Williams

PREMONITION, THE(1976)

Tiger Williams

EARTHQUAKE(1974)

Tina Williams

IDOL, THE(1966, Brit.)

Todd Williams

SECRET INVASION, THE(1964)

Tony Williams

SOLO(1978, New Zealand/Aus.), p, d, w; NEXT OF KIN(1983, Aus.), d, w

Tony Tucker Williams

JONIKO AND THE KUSH TA KA(1969)

Treat Williams

DEADLY HERO(1976); EAGLE HAS LANDED, THE(1976, Brit.); RITZ, THE(1976); HAIR(1979); 1941(1979); WHY WOULD I LIE(1980); PRINCE OF THE CITY(1981); PURSUIT OF D.B. COOPER, THE(1981)

1984

FLASHPOINT(1984); ONCE UPON A TIME IN AMERICA(1984)

Trevor Williams

TRIBUTE(1980, Can.), prod d; FIRST TIME, THE(1969), art d; JENNY(1969), art d; HOUSE OF DARK SHADOWS(1970), prod d; NIGHT OF DARK SHADOWS(1971), art d; 300 YEAR WEEKEND(1971), art d; TO KILL A CLOWN(1972), art d; DILLINGER(1973), art d; HARD TIMES(1975), art d; DUCHESS AND THE DIRTWATER FOX, THE(1976), art d; FUTUREWORLD(1976), art d; PRETTY BABY(1978), prod d; LOST AND FOUND(1979), prod d; SILENT PARTNER, THE(1979, Can.), prod d; CHANGELING, THE(1980, Can.), set d; MR. PATMAN(1980, Can.), prod d; ENDANGERED SPECIES(1982), prod d

1984

POLICE ACADEMY(1984), prod d

Tudor Williams

SAN FRANCISCO(1936); CIPHER BUREAU(1938); MRS. MINIVER(1942); PHANTOM OF THE OPERA(1943); THANK YOUR LUCKY STARS(1943)

Tunji Williams

KISENGA, MAN OF AFRICA(1952, Brit.)

Valentine Williams

FOG(1934), w; CROUCHING BEAST, THE(1936, U. S./Brit.), d; DISPATCH FROM REUTERS, A(1940), w

Silents

LAND OF HOPE AND GLORY(1927, Brit.), w

Van Williams

TALL STORY(1960); CARETAKERS, THE(1963)

Vince Williams

SUBMARINE SEAHAWK(1959); MARINES, LET'S GO(1961); SEVEN MINUTES, THE(1971)

Virginia Williams

DEVIL AND DANIEL WEBSTER, THE(1941)

W. A. Williams

Silents

HOW MOLLY MADE GOOD(1915)

W.H. Williams

UNDERCOVER AGENT(1935, Brit.), p; WIDE BOY(1952, Brit.), p; FLOATING DUTCHMAN, THE(1953, Brit.), p; SHADOW MAN(1953, Brit.), p; TERROR SHIP(1954, Brit.), p

Waldon Williams
WAR OF THE WORLDS, THE(1953)

Walter Williams
TENTH VICTIM, THE(1965, Fr./Ital.); FRAULEIN DOKTOR(1969, Ital./Yugo.); THOSE DARING YOUNG MEN IN THEIR JAUNTY JALOPIES(1969, Fr./Brit./ Ital.)
Silents
SPLENDID SIN, THE(1919), ph

Warren Williams
FIRST 100 YEARS, THE(1938)

Webster Williams
1984
TERMINATOR, THE(1984)

Wendy Williams
CRASH DRIVE(1959, Brit.); FEET OF CLAY(1960, Brit.)

Whitney Williams
MOONLIGHT ON THE RANGE(1937), w

Will Williams
WILD DAKOTAS, THE(1956); UNCLE TOM'S CABIN(1969, Fr./Ital./Ger./Yugo.), ed

William Williams
SAN QUENTIN(1937); STANLEY AND LIVINGSTONE(1939); CROW HOLLOW(1952, Brit.), p; WARRIORS, THE(1979)

William A. Williams
Silents
TOLL OF MAMON(1914); BAR SINISTER, THE(1917)
Misc. Silents
PATH FORBIDDEN, THE(1914); WHEN FATE LEADS TRUMP(1914); IN THE SHADOW(1915)

William G. Williams
RED RUNS THE RIVER(1963)

William H. Williams
MYSTERY JUNCTION(1951, Brit.), p

William J. Williams
BLACK HORSE CANYON(1954); FAR COUNTRY, THE(1955)

Willie Williams
Misc. Talkies
FIGHTING BLACK KINGS(1977)

Willy Williams
1984
MISSING IN ACTION(1984)

Wirt Williams
ADA(1961), w

Yvonne Williams
EXILES, THE(1966)

Zack Williams
HEARTS IN DIXIE(1929); MADONNA OF THE STREETS(1930); KID MILLIONS(1934); GONE WITH THE WIND(1939); MARYLAND(1940); SLIGHTLY HONORABLE(1940); SON OF INGAGI(1940); DUKE OF THE NAVY(1942); KISMET(1944); VAMPIRE'S GHOST, THE(1945); JUNGLE GODDESS(1948)
Misc. Talkies
PROFESSOR CREEPS(1942)
Silents
KILLER, THE(1921); MERRY WIDOW, THE(1925); EASY PICKINGS(1927); YANKEE CLIPPER, THE(1927); FOUR FEATHERS(1929)

The Williams Brothers
KANSAS CITY KITTY(1944)

A. M. Williamson
Silents
LION'S MOUSE, THE(1922, Brit.), w

A. N. Williamson
Silents
LION'S MOUSE, THE(1922, Brit.), w

Alastair Williamson
SUNDOWNERS, THE(1960); LIFT, THE(1965, Brit./Can.)

Bob Williamson
CIRCLE CANYON(1934)
Silents
KING'S CREEK LAW(1923), d; HAUNTED RANGE, THE(1926)
Misc. Silents
LAWLESS TRAILS(1926)

Mrs. C. N. Williamson
Silents
HOUSE OF THE LOST CORD, THE(1915), w

Carolyn Williamson
BEACH GIRLS AND THE MONSTER, THE(1965); SUPPOSE THEY GAVE A WAR AND NOBODY CAME?(1970)

Cecil Williamson
BLIND MAN'S BLUFF(1936, Brit.), ed

Cecil H. Williamson
HELD IN TRUST(1949, Brit.), p,d,w,&ph; HANGMAN'S WHARF(1950, Brit.), p,d,&ph, w; SOHO CONSPIRACY(1951, Brit.), d, w; ACTION STATIONS(1959, Brit.), d,w&ph

David Williamson
STORK(1971, Aus.), w; LIBIDO(1973, Aus.), w; PETERSEN(1974, Aus.), w; REMOVALISTS, THE(1975, Aus.), w; DON'S PARTY(1976, Aus.), w; ELIZA FRASER(1976, Aus.), w; CLUB, THE(1980, Aus.), w; GALLIPOLI(1981, Aus.), w; DUET FOR FOUR(1982, Aus.), w; YEAR OF LIVING DANGEROUSLY, THE(1982, Aus.), w
1984
PHAR LAP(1984, Aus.), w

Don Williamson
TERROR IN THE WAX MUSEUM(1973)

E. Stanley Williamson
COUNTRY BOY(1966), p; TRACK OF THUNDER(1967), p

Florence Williamson
1776(1972), ed

Fred Williamson
M(1970); TELL ME THAT YOU LOVE ME, JUNIE MOON(1970); CLOCKWORK ORANGE, A(1971, Brit.), makeup; HAMMER(1972); LEGEND OF NIGGER CHARLEY, THE(1972); BLACK CAESAR(1973); HELL UP IN HARLEM(1973); SOUL OF NIGGER CHARLEY, THE(1973); THAT MAN BOLT(1973); BLACK EYE(1974); BOSS NIGGER(1974), a, p, w; CRAZY JOE(1974); THREE THE HARD WAY(1974); THREE TOUGH GUYS(1974, U.S./Ital.); ADIOS AMIGO(1975), a, p,d&w; BUCKTOWN(1975); TAKE A HARD RIDE(1975, U.S./Ital.); JOSHUA(1976), a, w; MEAN JOHNNY BARROWS(1976), a, p&d; NO WAY BACK(1976), a, p,d&w; FIST OF FEAR, TOUCH OF DEATH(1980); COUNTERFEIT COMMANDOS(1981, Ital.); ONE DOWN TWO TO GO(1982); BIG SCORE, THE(1983), a, d; LAST FIGHT, THE(1983), a, d&w; NEW BARBARIANS, THE(1983, Ital.); VIGILANTE(1983); 1990: THE BRONX WARRIORS(1983, Ital.)
1984
WARRIORS OF THE WASTELAND(1984, Ital.)
Misc. Talkies
DEATH JOURNEY(1976), d; BLIND RAGE(1978); LAST FIGHT, THE(1983), d

Freddie Williamson
RISK, THE(1961, Brit.), makeup; SNAKE WOMAN, THE(1961, Brit.), makeup; TROUBLE IN THE SKY(1961, Brit.), makeup; RING-A-DING RHYTHM(1962, Brit.), makeup; TARZAN'S THREE CHALLENGES(1963), makeup; HIGH WIND IN JAMAICA, A(1965), makeup; HOW TO STEAL A MILLION(1966), makeup; ONLY WHEN I LARF(1968, Brit.), makeup; ITALIAN JOB, THE(1969, Brit.), makeup; YOU CAN'T WIN 'EM ALL(1970, Brit.), makeup; SEVERED HEAD, A(1971, Brit.), makeup; SUNDAY BLOODY SUNDAY(1971, Brit.), makeup; SAVAGE MESSIAH(1972, Brit.), makeup; WILBY CONSPIRACY, THE(1975, Brit.), makeup

George Williamson
PICTURES(1982, New Zealand)

George M Williamson
Silents
20,000 LEAGUES UNDER THE SEA(1916), ph

Howard Williamson
MIKADO, THE(1967, Brit.)

J. Ernest Williamson
Silents
20,000 LEAGUES UNDER THE SEA(1916), ph; WET GOLD(1921), p, w
Misc. Silents
WONDERS OF THE SEA(1922), a, d

J.C. Williamson
SPLENDID FELLOWS(1934, Aus.), p

Jeff Williamson
ONE DOWN TWO TO GO(1982), w

Jo Williamson
TERROR IN THE WAX MUSEUM(1973)

Kate Williamson
1984
RACING WITH THE MOON(1984)

Lambert Williamson
END OF THE RIVER, THE(1947, Brit.), m; ONE NIGHT WITH YOU(1948, Brit), m; CARDBOARD CAVALIER, THE(1949, Brit.), m; DON'T EVER LEAVE ME(1949, Brit.), m; GOOD TIME GIRL(1950, Brit.), m; GREEN GROW THE RUSHES(1951, Brit.), m; THEY WERE NOT DIVIDED(1951, Brit.), m; BEAT THE DEVIL(1953), md; SLASHER, THE(1953, Brit.), m; FORBIDDEN CARGO(1954, Brit.), m; GREEN BUDDHA, THE(1954, Brit.), m&md; CROSS CHANNEL(1955, Brit.), m; SECRET VENTURE(1955, Brit.), m, md; CASH ON DELIVERY(1956, Brit.), m; TRACK THE MAN DOWN(1956, Brit.), m, md; HEAVEN KNOWS, MR. ALLISON(1957), md; STORY OF ESTHER COSTELLO, THE(1957, Brit.), md; SPANIARD'S CURSE, THE(1958, Brit.), m; WHOLE TRUTH, THE(1958, Brit.), md; INNOCENTS, THE(1961, U.S./Brit.), md; DOG AND THE DIAMONDS, THE(1962, Brit.), m; COUNTESS FROM HONG KONG, A(1967, Brit.), md; ADDING MACHINE, THE(1969), m

Malcolm Williamson
BRIDES OF DRACULA, THE(1960, Brit.), m; CRESCENDO(1972, Brit.), m; NOTHING BUT THE NIGHT(1975, Brit.), m; WATERSHIP DOWN(1978, Brit.), m

Maureen Williamson
HANGMAN'S WHARF(1950, Brit.)

Mykel T. Williamson
1984
STREETS OF FIRE(1984)

Nichol Williamson
GOODBYE GIRL, THE(1977)

Nicol Williamson
BOFORS GUN, THE(1968, Brit.); INADMISSIBLE EVIDENCE(1968, Brit.); HAMLET(1969, Brit.); RECKONING, THE(1971, Brit.); JERUSALEM FILE, THE(1972, U.S./Israel); WILBY CONSPIRACY, THE(1975, Brit.); ROBIN AND MARIAN(1976, Brit.); SEVEN-PER-CENT SOLUTION, THE(1977, Brit.); CHEAP DETECTIVE, THE(1978); HUMAN FACTOR, THE(1979, Brit.); EXCALIBUR(1981); I'M DANCING AS FAST AS I CAN(1982); VENOM(1982, Brit.)

Noah Williamson
BABY DOLL(1956)

Paul Williamson
RETURN TO SENDER(1963, Brit.); RUNAWAY, THE(1964, Brit.); MAN AT THE TOP(1973, Brit.); VENOM(1982, Brit.)

R.E. Williamson
Misc. Silents
FEUD WOMAN, THE(1926), d; WANDERER OF THE WEST(1927), d

Robert Williamson
TODD KILLINGS, THE(1971)
Silents
LITTLE DOOR INTO THE WORLD, THE(1923, Brit.); DON X(1925)
Misc. Silents
HEADIN' THROUGH(1924)

Robin Williamson
Silents
APACHE RAIDER, THE(1928)
Misc. Silents
PRINCE OF THE PLAINS(1927), d

Sandy Williamson
GANG, THE(1938, Brit.)

Simon Williamson
DARK CRYSTAL, THE(1982, Brit.); RETURN OF THE JEDI(1983)

Susan Williamson
PERSECUTION AND ASSASSINATION OF JEAN-PAUL MARAT AS PERFORMED BY THE INMATES OF THE ASYLUM OF CHARENTON UNDER THE DIRECTION OF THE MARQUIS DE SADE, THE(1967, Brit.); SHARKY'S MACHINE(1982)

Thames Williamson
NEXT TIME I MARRY(1938), w; SAVAGE HORDE, THE(1950), w; BULLET IS WAITING, A(1954), w; TAMING SUTTON'S GAL(1957), w

Thomas Williamson
CHEYENNE(1947), w; ESCAPE ME NEVER(1947), w; LAST BANDIT, THE(1949), w

Tony Williamson
NIGHT WATCH(1973, Brit.), w; BREAKTHROUGH(1978, Ger.), w

W.K. Williamson
DAVID LIVINGSTONE(1936, Brit.), w; AULD LANG SYNE(1937, Brit.), w; LAST ROSE OF SUMMER, THE(1937, Brit.), w

Wallace Williamson
VISITOR, THE(1980, Ital./U.S.)

Carol Williard
BETSY, THE(1978); RESURRECTION(1980); PARTNERS(1982)
1984
FLAMINGO KID, THE(1984)
Misc. Talkies
HOUSE AND THE BRAIN, THE(1973)

Ruth Williard
WHEN YOU'RE IN LOVE(1937)

Willie
1984
SCARRED(1984)

Norman Willie
CONVICT'S CODE(1939)

Willie West and McGinty
BIG BROADCAST OF 1936, THE(1935)

Ray Williford
SPY IN THE GREEN HAT, THE(1966), ed; KARATE KILLERS, THE(1967), ed

Andreas Willim
MARRIAGE OF MARIA BRAUN, THE(1979, Ger.), set d

Foy Willing
COWBOY FROM LONESOME RIVER(1944); CYCLONE PRAIRIE RANGERS(1944)

George Willing
COUNT OF MONTE CRISTO(1976, Brit.)

Ute Willing
AMERICAN SUCCESS COMPANY, THE(1980)

Charlie Willinger
1984
OLD ENOUGH(1984)

L. Willinger
TONIGHT WE RAID CALAIS(1943), w

Calder Willingham
PATHS OF GLORY(1957), w; STRANGE ONE, THE(1957), w; VIKINGS, THE(1958), w; ONE-EYED JACKS(1961), w; GRADUATE, THE(1967), w; LITTLE BIG MAN(1970), w; THIEVES LIKE US(1974), w

Dale Willingham
FROGS(1972)

Mary Willingham
BULLET FOR A BADMAN(1964), w; ARIZONA RAIDERS(1965), w; GUNPOINT(1966), w; 40 GUNS TO APACHE PASS(1967), w

Noble Willingham
LAST PICTURE SHOW, THE(1971); PAPER MOON(1973); BIG BAD MAMA(1974); CHINATOWN(1974); ALOHA, BOBBY AND ROSE(1975); SHEILA LEVINE IS DEAD AND LIVING IN NEW YORK(1975); FIGHTING MAD(1976); GREASED LIGHTNING(1977); BOYS IN COMPANY C, THE(1978, U.S./Hong Kong); BUTCH AND SUNDANCE: THE EARLY DAYS(1979); FAST CHARLIE... THE MOONBEAM RIDER(1979); NORMA RAE(1979); BRUBAKER(1980); FIRST MONDAY IN OCTOBER(1981); HARRY'S WAR(1981); HOWLING, THE(1981); INDEPENDENCE DAY(1983)

Willard Willingham
RED CANYON(1949); SON OF PALEFACE(1952); PONY EXPRESS(1953); SANTIAGO(1956); JOE BUTTERFLY(1957); NIGHT PASSAGE(1957); BATTLE AT BLOODY BEACH(1961), w; BULLET FOR A BADMAN(1964), w; ARIZONA RAIDERS(1965), a, w; DEADWOOD'76(1965); GUNPOINT(1966), w; 40 GUNS TO APACHE PASS(1967), a, w

John Willink
Silents
MISTRESS OF SHENSTONE, THE(1921)

A. Legge Willis
FIGHTING PLAYBOY(1937)

Ann Willis
TRAIN RIDE TO HOLLYWOOD(1975)

Austin Willis
SINS OF THE FATHERS(1948, Can.); WOLF DOG(1958, Can.); MOUSE THAT ROARED, THE(1959, Brit.); CRACK IN THE MIRROR(1960); DANGEROUS AGE, A(1960, Can.); I AIM AT THE STARS(1960); TOO YOUNG TO LOVE(1960, Brit.); ONE PLUS ONE(1961, Can.); UPSTAIRS AND DOWNSTAIRS(1961, Brit.); EIGHT ON THE LAM(1967); HOUR OF THE GUN(1967); THE BOSTON STRANGLER, THE(1968); DR. FRANKENSTEIN ON CAMPUS(1970, Can.); LAST FLIGHT OF NOAH'S ARK, THE(1980); FIREFOX(1982)
Misc. Talkies
BUSH PILOT(1947)

Bill Willis
SEED(1931)

Brynja Willis
1984
WILD LIFE, THE(1984)

Charles Willis
LOVE BUG, THE(1968)

Charles Willis, Jr.
SAMMY STOPS THE WORLD zero(1978)

Constance Willis
MIKADO, THE(1939, Brit.); MAN FOR ALL SEASONS, A(1966, Brit.), w

Dan Willis
SAILOR BEWARE(1951)

Dave Willis
SAVE A LITTLE SUNSHINE(1938, Brit.); ME AND MY PAL(1939, Brit.)

David Willis
ENDLESS LOVE(1981); MELANIE(1982, Can.)

Edward B. Willis
FORSAKING ALL OTHERS(1935), art d

Edwin Willis
LAST GANGSTER, THE(1937), set d; DANCING CO-ED(1939), set d; I LOVE YOU AGAIN(1940), set d; PILOT NO. 5(1943), set d; CYNTHIA(1947), set d; FATHER'S LITTLE DIVIDEND(1951), set d

Edwin A. Willis
SWING FEVER(1943), set d

Edwin B. Willis
HOLD YOUR MAN(1933), set d; QUEEN CHRISTINA(1933), art d; STRANGER'S RETURN(1933), set d; TUGBOAT ANNIE(1933), set d; CAT AND THE FIDDLE(1934), set d; EVELYN PRENTICE(1934), art d; HOLLYWOOD PARTY(1934), set d; MANHATTAN MELODRAMA(1934), set d; MERRY WIDOW, THE(1934), set d; PARIS INTERLUDE(1934), set d; RIP TIDE(1934), set d; SHOW-OFF, THE(1934), set d; THIN MAN, THE(1934), art d; TREASURE ISLAND(1934), set d; VIVA VILLA!(1934), set d; CHINA SEAS(1935), set d; MURDER MAN(1935), art d, set d; NIGHT AT THE OPERA, A(1935), set d; O'SHAUGHNESSY'S BOY(1935), set d; SOCIETY DOCTOR(1935), set d; TALE OF TWO CITIES, A(1935), set d; FURY(1936), art d, set d; LIBELED LADY(1936), set d; OLD HUTCH(1936), set d; ROSE MARIE(1936), art d; SAN FRANCISCO(1936), set d; SUZY(1936), art d; THREE WISE GUYS, THE(1936), set d; WHIPSAW(1936), set d; GOOD EARTH, THE(1937), set d; MANNEQUIN(1937), set d; MAYTIME(1937), set d; NAVY BLUE AND GOLD(1937), set d; PERSONAL PROPERTY(1937), set d; ROSALIE(1937), set d; SARATOGA(1937), set d; THEY GAVE HIM A GUN(1937), set d; CHASER, THE(1938), set d; DRAMATIC SCHOOL(1938), set d; LOVE FINDS ANDY HARDY(1938), set d; MARIE ANTOINETTE(1938), set d; OF HUMAN HEARTS(1938), art d; PARADISE FOR THREE(1938), set d; RICH MAN, POOR GIRL(1938), set d; SHINING HOUR, THE(1938), set d; SHOPWORN ANGEL(1938), set d; STABLEMATES(1938), set d; SWEETHEARTS(1938), set d; TEST PILOT(1938), set d; THREE COMRADES(1938), set d; YOUNG DR. KILDARE(1938), set d; IDIOT'S DELIGHT(1939), set d; LADY OF THE TROPICS(1939), set d; LET FREEDOM RING(1939), set d; MAISIE(1939), set d; MIRACLES FOR SALE(1939), set d; NINOTCHKA(1939), set d; SERGEANT MADDEN(1939), set d; SOCIETY LAWYER(1939), set d; STAND UP AND FIGHT(1939), set d; THESE GLAMOUR GIRLS(1939), set d; THUNDER AFLOAT(1939), set d; WIZARD OF OZ, THE(1939), set d; WOMEN, THE(1939), set d; 6000 ENEMIES(1939), set d; BOOM TOWN(1940), set d; COMRADE X(1940), set d; EDISON, THE MAN(1940), set d; FLIGHT COMMAND(1940), set d; GO WEST(1940), set d; LITTLE NELLIE KELLY(1940), set d; MAN FROM DAKOTA, THE(1940), set d; MORTAL STORM, THE(1940), set d; NEW MOON(1940), set d; NORTHWEST PASSAGE(1940), set d; PHILADELPHIA STORY, THE(1940), set d; PRIDE AND PREJUDICE(1940), set d; SHOP AROUND THE CORNER, THE(1940), set d; SKY MURDER(1940), set d; SPORTING BLOOD(1940), set d; STRIKE UP THE BAND(1940), set d; TWO GIRLS ON BROADWAY(1940), set d; WATERLOO BRIDGE(1940), set d; WE WHO ARE YOUNG(1940), set d; BLOSSOMS IN THE DUST(1941), set d; CHOCOLATE SOLDIER, THE(1941), set d; COME LIVE WITH ME(1941), set d; DESIGN FOR SCANDAL(1941), set d; DOWN IN SAN DIEGO(1941), set d; H.M. PULHAM, ESQ.(1941), set d; HONKY TONK(1941), set d; LADY BE GOOD(1941), set d; MEN OF BOYS TOWN(1941), set d; SMILIN' THROUGH(1941), set d; TRIAL OF MARY DUGAN, THE(1941), set d; TWO-FACED WOMAN(1941), set d; ZIEGFELD GIRL(1941), set d; CROSSROADS(1942), set d; FOR ME AND MY GAL(1942), set d; I MARRIED AN ANGEL(1942), set d; JACKASS MAIL(1942), set d; JOHNNY EAGER(1942), set d; JOURNEY FOR MARGARET(1942), set d; KEEPER OF THE FLAME(1942), set d; MRS. MINIVER(1942), set d; PANAMA HATTIE(1942), set d; SHIP AHOY(1942), set d; SOMEWHERE I'LL FIND YOU(1942), set d; TORTILLA FLAT(1942), set d; WHITE CARGO(1942), set d; WOMAN OF THE YEAR(1942), set d; AIR RAID WARDENS(1943), set d; CRY HAVOC(1943), set d; DU BARRY WAS A LADY(1943), set d; GIRL CRAZY(1943), set d; GUY NAMED JOE, A(1943), set d; HEAVENLY BODY, THE(1943), set d; LASSIE, COME HOME(1943), set d; MADAME CURIE(1943), set d; SALUTE TO THE MARINES(1943), set d; SLIGHTLY DANGEROUS(1943), set d; THOUSANDS CHEER(1943), set d; THREE HEARTS FOR JULIA(1943), set d; YOUNG IDEAS(1943), set d; YOUNGEST PROFESSION, THE(1943), set d; DRAGON SEED(1944), set d; GASLIGHT(1944), set d; KISMET(1944), set d; LOST ANGEL(1944), set d; MAISIE GOES TO RENO(1944), set d; MARRIAGE IS A PRIVATE AFFAIR(1944), set d; MEET ME IN ST. LOUIS(1944), set d; MRS. PARKINGTON(1944), set d; NATIONAL VELVET(1944), set d; NOTHING BUT TROUBLE(1944), set d; RATIONING(1944), set d; SEE HERE, PRIVATE HARGROVE(1944), set d; SEVENTH CROSS, THE(1944), set d; THIN MAN GOES HOME, THE(1944), set d; THIRTY SECONDS OVER TOKYO(1944), set d; THREE MEN IN WHITE(1944), set d; WHITE CLIFFS OF DOVER, THE(1944), set d; ADVENTURE(1945), set d; CLOCK, THE(1945), set d; HER HIGHNESS AND THE BELLBOY(1945), set d; KEEP YOUR POWDER DRY(1945), set d; PICTURE OF DORIAN GRAY, THE(1945), set d; SHE WENT TO THE RACES(1945), set d; THEY WERE EXPENDABLE(1945), set d; THIS MAN'S NAVY(1945), set d; VALLEY OF DECISION, THE(1945), set d; WEEKEND AT THE WALDORF(1945), set d; WHAT NEXT, CORPORAL HARGROVE?(1945), set d; WITHOUT LOVE(1945), set d; YOLANDA AND THE THIEF(1945), set d; ZIEGFELD FOLLIES(1945), set d; COURAGE OF LASSIE(1946), set d; EASY TO WED(1946), set d; HARVEY GIRLS, THE(1946), set d; HOODLUM SAINT, THE(1946), set d; MIGHTY MCGURK, THE(1946), set d; MY BROTHER TALKS TO HORSES(1946), set d; POSTMAN ALWAYS RINGS TWICE, THE(1946), set d; SECRET HEART, THE(1946), set d; SHOW-OFF, THE(1946), set d; THREE WISE FOOLS(1946), set d; TILL THE CLOUDS ROLL BY(1946), set d; TWO SMART PEOPLE(1946), set d; UNDERCURRENT(1946), set d; YEARLING, THE(1946), set d; CASS TIMBERLANE(1947), set d; GOOD NEWS(1947), set d; GREEN DOLPHIN STREET(1947), set d; HIGH BARBAREE(1947), set d; HIGH WALL, THE(1947), set d; HUCKSTERS, THE(1947), set d; IT HAPPENED IN BROOKLYN(1947), set d; LADY IN THE LAKE(1947), set d; LATE GEORGE APLEY, THE(1947), set d; MOSS ROSE(1947), set d; ROMANCE OF ROSY RIDGE, THE(1947), set d; SEA OF GRASS(1947), set d; SONG OF LOVE(1947), set d; SONG OF THE THIN MAN(1947), set d; THIS TIME FOR KEEPS(1947), set d; B. F.'S DAUGHTER(1948), set d; BRIDE GOES WILD, THE(1948), set d; DATE WITH JUDY, A(1948), set d; HOMECOMING(1948), set d; JULIA MISBEHAVES(1948), set d; KISSING BANDIT, THE(1948), set d; LUXURY LINER(1948), set d; ON AN ISLAND WITH YOU(1948), set d; PIRATE, THE(1948), set d; SOUTHERN YANKEE, A(1948), set d; SUMMER HOLIDAY(1948), set d; TENTH AVENUE ANGEL(1948), set d; THREE DARING DAUGHTERS(1948), set d; THREE MUSKETEERS, THE(1948), set d; ACT OF VIOLENCE(1949), set d; ADAM'S RIB(1949), set d; BRIBE, THE(1949), set d; EAST SIDE, WEST SIDE(1949), set d; GREAT SINNER, THE(1949), set d; INTRUDER IN THE DUST(1949), set d; LITTLE WOMEN(1949), set d; MADAME BOVARY(1949), set d; NEPTUNE'S DAUGHTER(1949), set d; ON THE TOWN(1949), set d;

SCENE OF THE CRIME(1949), set d; SECRET GARDEN, THE(1949), set d; STRATTON STORY, THE(1949), set d; SUN COMES UP, THE(1949), set d; TAKE ME OUT TO THE BALL GAME(1949), set d; TENSION(1949), set d; THAT FORSYTE WOMAN(1949), set d; ASPHALT JUNGLE, THE(1950), set d; FATHER OF THE BRIDE(1950), set d; KIM(1950), set d; KING SOLOMON'S MINES(1950), set d; LIFE OF HER OWN, A(1950), set d; MALAYA(1950), set d; MYSTERY STREET(1950), set d; PAGAN LOVE SONG(1950), set d; PLEASE BELIEVE ME(1950), set d; SIDE STREET(1950), set d; TO PLEASE A LADY(1950), set d; TWO WEEKS WITH LOVE(1950), set d; WATCH THE BIRDIE(1950), set d; AMERICAN IN PARIS, AN(1951), set d; CAUSE FOR ALARM(1951), set d; MAN WITH A CLOAK, THE(1951), set d; MR. IMPERIUM(1951), set d; PEOPLE AGAINST O'HARA, THE(1951), set d; ROYAL WEDDING(1951), set d; SHOW BOAT(1951), set d; STRICTLY DISHONORABLE(1951), set d; STRIP, THE(1951), set d; TEXAS CARNIVAL(1951), set d; UNKNOWN MAN, THE(1951), set d; WESTWARD THE WOMEN(1951), set d; BAD AND THE BEAUTIFUL, THE(1952), set d; DESPERATE SEARCH(1952), set d; EVERYTHING I HAVE IS YOURS(1952), set d; LOVELY TO LOOK AT(1952), set d; MERRY WIDOW, THE(1952), set d; MY MAN AND I(1952), set d; PAT AND MIKE(1952), set d; PLYMOUTH ADVENTURE(1952), set d; PRISONER OF ZENDA, THE(1952), set d; ROGUE'S MARCH(1952), set d; SINGIN' IN THE RAIN(1952), set d; SKY FULL OF MOON(1952), set d; YOU FOR ME(1952), set d; YOUNG MAN WITH IDEAS(1952), set d; ABOVE AND BEYOND(1953), set d; ACTRESS, THE(1953), set d; DREAM WIFE(1953), set d; ESCAPE FROM FORT BRAVO(1953), set d; JEOPARDY(1953), set d; JULIUS CAESAR(1953), art d; KISS ME KATE(1953), set d; LATIN LOVERS(1953), set d; LILI(1953), set d; SOMBRERO(1953), set d; EXECUTIVE SUITE(1954), set d; LAST TIME I SAW PARIS, THE(1954), set d; LONG, LONG TRAILER, THE(1954), set d; RHAPSODY(1954), set d; ROGUE COP(1954), set d; SEVEN BRIDES FOR SEVEN BROTHERS(1954), set d; BAD DAY AT BLACK ROCK(1955), set d; DIANE(1955), set d; GREEN FIRE(1955), set d; I'LL CRY TOMORROW(1955), set d; IT'S ALWAYS FAIR WEATHER(1955), set d; LOVE ME OR LEAVE ME(1955), set d; MOONFLEET(1955), set d; PRODIGAL, THE(1955), set d; TENDER TRAP, THE(1955), set d; TRIAL(1955), set d; FORBIDDEN PLANET(1956), set d; GREAT AMERICAN PASTIME, THE(1956), set d; HIGH SOCIETY(1956), set d; MEET ME IN LAS VEGAS(1956), set d; OPPOSITE SEX, THE(1956), set d; RACK, THE(1956), set d; SWAN, THE(1956), set d; THESE WILDER YEARS(1956), set d; TRIBUTE TO A BADMAN(1956), set d; LES GIRLS(1957), set d; RAINTREE COUNTY(1957), set d; SILK STOCKINGS(1957), set d; WINGS OF EAGLES, THE(1957), set d

Silents

COLLEGE DAYS(1926), art d; JOSSELYN'S WIFE(1926), art d; REDHEADS PREFERRED(1926), art d; CHEATERS(1927), art d; HUSBAND HUNTERS(1927), art d; ONE HOUR OF LOVE(1927), art d; PRINCESS FROM HOBOKEN, THE(1927), art d

Edwin P. Willis

SCARAMOUCHE(1952), set d

Edwin R. Willis

MILLION DOLLAR MERMAID(1952), set d

Edwin S. Willis

CAIRO(1942), set d

Enid Willis

Misc. Silents

CRIMINAL, THE(1916)

F. M. Willis

CHARLEY'S AUNT(1930), w

F. McGrew Willis

TWIN BEDS(1929), w; TWO WEEKS OFF(1929), w; COSTELLO CASE, THE(1930), w; BIG GAMBLE, THE(1931), w; MEET THE WIFE(1931), w; FIGHTING GENTLEMAN, THE(1932), w; FORTY-NINERS, THE(1932), w; GAMBLING SEX(1932), w; MIDSHIPMAN JACK(1933), w; SECRET SINNERS(1933), w; WHEN A MAN RIDES ALONE(1933), w; KEEP 'EM ROLLING(1934), w; MAN IN THE MIRROR, THE(1936, Brit.), w; YOU MUST GET MARRIED(1936, Brit.), w; CLOTHES AND THE WOMAN(1937, Brit.), w; LET'S MAKE A NIGHT OF IT(1937, Brit.), w; MURDER IN THE NIGHT(1940, Brit.), w; ONE NIGHT IN PARIS(1940, Brit.), w; SIS HOPKINS(1941), w

Silents

AMERICAN METHODS(1917), w; BRIDE'S AWAKENING, THE(1918), w; END OF THE GAME, THE(1919), w; MAN WHO TURNED WHITE, THE(1919), w; EVERYMAN'S PRICE(1921), w; OLIVER TWIST, JR.(1921), w; RECKLESS ROMANCE(1924), w; ALMOST A LADY(1926), w; NERVOUS WRECK, THE(1926), w; NIGHT BRIDE, THE(1927), sup; RUSH HOUR, THE(1927), sup; ANNAPOLIS(1928), p, w

Frank Willis

OTHER SIDE OF THE MOUNTAIN, THE(1975)

George Willis

Silents

DEVIL DODGER, THE(1917)

Geri Willis

STAKEOUT ON DOPE STREET(1958)

Gordon Willis

LANDLORD, THE(1970), ph; LOVING(1970), ph; PEOPLE NEXT DOOR, THE(1970), ph; KLUTE(1971), ph; LITTLE MURDERS(1971), ph; BAD COMPANY(1972), ph; GODFATHER, THE(1972), ph; UP THE SANDBOX(1972), ph; PAPER CHASE, THE(1973), ph; GODFATHER, THE, PART II(1974), ph; PARALLAX VIEW, THE(1974), ph; DROWNING POOL, THE(1975), ph; ALL THE PRESIDENT'S MEN(1976), ph; ANNIE HALL(1977), ph; 9/30/55(1977), ph; COMES A HORSEMAN(1978), ph; INTERIORS(1978), ph; MANHATTAN(1979), ph; STARDUST MEMORIES(1980), ph; WINDOWS(1980), d, ph; PENNIES FROM HEAVEN(1981), ph; MIDSUMMER NIGHT'S SEX COMEDY, A(1982), ph; ZELIG(1983), ph

1984

BROADWAY DANNY ROSE(1984), ph

H.W. Willis

Misc. Silents

MASKED RIDER, THE(1916)

Hal Willis

GIRL NAMED TAMIKO, A(1962), p

Hal B. Willis

CHARGE OF THE LIGHT BRIGADE, THE(1936), p; COWBOY FROM BROOKLYN(1938), p

Horton Willis

DARK, THE(1979)

Hubert Willis

Silents

HOUSE OF TEMPERLEY, THE(1913, Brit.); MESSAGE FROM MARS, A(1913, Brit.); ALTAR CHAINS(1916, Brit.); GREATER NEED, THE(1916, Brit.); KING'S DAUGHTER, THE(1916, Brit.); AUNT RACHEL(1920, Brit.); MANCHESTER MAN, THE(1920,

Brit.); PURSUIT OF PAMELA, THE(1920, Brit.)

Misc. Silents

MAN IN THE ATTIC, THE(1915, Brit.); ME AND M'PAL(1916, Brit.); PARTNERS AT LAST(1916, Brit.)

Mrs. Hubert Willis

Silents

DEMOCRACY(1918, Brit.)

J. Elder Willis

MY SISTER AND I(1948, Brit.), art d; THE CREEPING UNKNOWN(1956, Brit.), ph

Jack Willis

SEED(1931)

Jean Willis

CROWDED SKY, THE(1960)

Jeremy Willis

LORD OF THE FLIES(1963, Brit.)

Jerome Willis

SILENT ENEMY, THE(1959, Brit.); FOXHOLE IN CAIRO(1960, Brit.); SIEGE OF THE SAXONS(1963, Brit.); JOLLY BAD FELLOW, A(1964, Brit.); KHARTOUM(1966, Brit.); MAGUS, THE(1968, Brit.); WINSTANLEY(1979, Brit.)

Jerry Willis

BRONCO BILLY(1980)

Jill Willis

Silents

SHEFFIELD BLADE, A(1918, Brit.)

John Willis

SILENCERS, THE(1966)

Julia Willis

GURU, THE MAD MONK(1971)

Leo Willis

WELCOME DANGER(1929); FEET FIRST(1930); SHADOW OF THE LAW(1930); CITY STREETS(1931); PARDON US(1931); KID FROM SPAIN, THE(1932); ROMAN SCANDALS(1933); KID MILLIONS(1934); SIX OF A KIND(1934)

Silents

ITALIAN, THE(1915); HELL'S HINGES(1916); JUNGLE CHILD, THE(1916); ONE SHOT ROSS(1917); TOLL GATE, THE(1920); O'MALLEY OF THE MOUNTED(1921); SAILOR-MADE MAN, A(1921); ALL THE BROTHERS WERE VALIANT(1923); SOULS FOR SALE(1923); KID BROTHER, THE(1927)

Misc. Silents

SILENT RIDER, THE(1918); HERO OF THE BIG SNOWS, A(1926)

Les Willis

WOMAN WHO CAME BACK(1945), w

Marie Willis

Silents

GOLD RUSH, THE(1925)

Marlene Willis

ROCKABILLY BABY(1957); ATTACK OF THE PUPPET PEOPLE(1958)

Mary Willis

BETWEEN HEAVEN AND HELL(1956), cos

Matt Willis

SWAMP WATER(1941); INVISIBLE AGENT(1942); SABOTEUR(1942); SPIRIT OF STANFORD, THE(1942); BEHIND PRISON WALLS(1943); GUY NAMED JOE, A(1943); IT AIN'T HAY(1943); MUG TOWN(1943); MYSTERIOUS DOCTOR, THE(1943); SHE HAS WHAT IT TAKES(1943); KANSAS CITY KITTY(1944); LOUISIANA HAYRIDE(1944); MARK OF THE WHISTLER, THE(1944); RETURN OF THE VAMPIRE, THE(1944); SWINGTIME JOHNNY(1944); UP IN ARMS(1944); BLONDE FROM BROOKLYN(1945); FOREVER YOURS(1945); SCARLET STREET(1945); STRANGE VOYAGE(1945); WALK IN THE SUN, A(1945); WHAT NEXT, CORPORAL HARGROVE?(1945); DANGEROUS BUSINESS(1946); IDEA GIRL(1946); VACATION IN RENO(1946); YEARLING, THE(1946); BLONDE SAVAGE(1947); BURNING CROSS, THE(1947); HIGH WALL, THE(1947); IT'S A JOKE, SON!(1947); NOOSE HANGS HIGH, THE(1948); FIGHTING MAN OF THE PLAINS(1949); MUTINEERS, THE(1949); SHEP COMES HOME(1949); SO DEAR TO MY HEART(1949); BREAKTHROUGH(1950); INSIDE THE WALLS OF FOLSOM PRISON(1951); SCANDAL SHEET(1952)

Misc. Talkies

SON OF RUSTY, THE(1947)

Maxine Willis

TWO TICKETS TO BROADWAY(1951)

Michael Allen Willis

SPRING FEVER(1983, Can.)

Nancy Willis

HERE COME THE TIGERS(1978)

Newell B. Willis

PAINTED HILLS, THE(1951), ed

Nolan Willis

OKLAHOMA TERROR(1939); RIDERS OF THE FRONTIER(1939); ROLL, WAGONS, ROLL(1939); WESTBOUND STAGE(1940)

Norma Willis

TWILIGHT ON THE TRAIL(1941)

Norman Willis

MARY BURNS, FUGITIVE(1935); BULLETS OR BALLOTS(1936); F MAN(1936); HERE COMES CARTER(1936); LADY FROM NOWHERE(1936); OLD HUTCH(1936); TRAIL OF THE LONESOME PINE, THE(1936); GIRL WITH IDEAS, A(1937); LIFE BEGINS IN COLLEGE(1937); MEN IN EXILE(1937); SECRET VALLEY(1937); THAT CERTAIN WOMAN(1937); BOY SLAVES(1938); CITY GIRL(1938); DAWN PATROL, THE(1938); OUTLAWS OF THE PRAIRIE(1938); PRISON NURSE(1938); RACKET BUSTERS(1938); THREE COMRADES(1938); BLACKWELL'S ISLAND(1939); FORGOTTEN WOMAN, THE(1939); HOMICIDE BUREAU(1939); I AM NOT AFRAID(1939); ROARING TWENTIES, THE(1939); TELL NO TALES(1939); GRAPES OF WRATH(1940); HOUSE ACROSS THE BAY, THE(1940); LEGION OF THE LAWLESS(1940); THEY DRIVE BY NIGHT(1940); BEYOND THE SACRAMENTO(1941); GAUCHOS OF EL DORADO(1941); OUTLAWS OF THE PANHANDLE(1941); DOWN RIO GRANDE WAY(1942); I WAS FRAMED(1942); LIVING GHOST, THE(1942); THEY ALL KISSED THE BRIDE(1942); AVENGING RIDER, THE(1943); FRONTIER BADMEN(1943); HAIL TO THE RANGERS(1943); I ESCAPED FROM THE GESTAPO(1943); JOHNNY COME LATELY(1943); FALCON OUT WEST, THE(1944); GENTLE ANNIE(1944); APOLOGY FOR MURDER(1945); IN OLD NEW MEXICO(1945); SAN ANTONIO(1945); PLAINSMAN AND THE LADY(1946); CHEYENNE(1947); SILVER RIVER(1948); VOODOO WOMAN(1957); BOUNTY KILLER, THE(1965)

Misc. Talkies
OVERLAND TO DEADWOOD(1942); HEADING WEST(1946)
Nuala Willis
WARM IN THE BUD(1970)
Paul Willis
Silents
HAUNTED PAJAMAS(1917); NOBODY'S KID(1921); MONEY! MONEY! MO-
NEY!(1923)
Misc. Silents
PROMISE, THE(1917); TROUBLE BUSTER, THE(1917); CRY OF THE WEAK,
THE(1919); THUNDERCLAP(1921)
Reed Willis
DANGEROUS AGE, A(1960, Can.)
Richard Willis
1984
PRODIGAL, THE(1984)
Silents
LAST CHAPTER, THE(1915), w
Ross B. Willis
Silents
MORGAN'S LAST RAID(1929), w
Ross E. Willis
EAST OF THE RIVER(1940), w
Shelby Willis
DICK TRACY VS. CUEBALL(1946), set d
Sonny Willis
STARS IN YOUR EYES(1956, Brit.)
Stan Willis
COLONEL MARCH INVESTIGATES(1952,Brit.), ed; LIMPING MAN, THE(1953,
Brit.), ed
Susan Willis
PUZZLE OF A DOWNFALL CHILD(1970)
Suzanna Willis
MONSTER CLUB, THE(1981, Brit.)
Ted Willis
HOLIDAY CAMP(1947, Brit.), w; BOY, A GIRL AND A BIKE, A(1949 Brit.), w;
HUGGETTS ABROAD, THE(1949, Brit.), w; GOOD TIME GIRL(1950, Brit.), w; WAL-
LET, THE(1952, Brit.), w; LARGE ROPE, THE(1953, Brit.), w; TOP OF THE
FORM(1953, Brit.), w; BURNT EVIDENCE(1954, Brit.), w; UP TO HIS NECK(1954,
Brit.), w; ONE GOOD TURN(1955, Brit.), w; TROUBLE IN STORE(1955, Brit.), w; IT'S
GREAT TO BE YOUNG(1956, Brit.), w; WOMEN IN A DRESSING GOWN(1957,
Brit.), w; YOUNG AND THE GUILTY, THE(1958, Brit.), w; FLAME IN THE
STREETS(1961, Brit.), w; BITTER HARVEST(1963, Brit.), w; NO TREE IN THE
STREET(1964, Brit.), w
Vera Willis
SARAH AND SON(1930), ed
Verna Willis
VARSITY(1928), ed; CHARMING SINNERS(1929), ed; GREENE MURDER CASE,
THE(1929), ed; SWEETIE(1929), ed; MEN ARE LIKE THAT(1930), ed; SANTA FE
TRAIL, THE(1930), ed; TEXAN, THE(1930), ed
Silents
HALF A BRIDE(1928), ed; LOVE AND LEARN(1928), ed
Walter Willis
Misc. Talkies
SONGS AND SADDLES(1938)
Misc. Silents
PAIR OF HELLIONS, A(1924), d
William Willis
Silents
CARDIGAN(1922)
Woody Willis
DETROIT 9000(1973)
The Willis Brothers
FORTY ACRE FEUD(1965)
Sherry Willis-Burch
FINAL EXAM(1981)
Walter Willison
HARRY AND WALTER GO TO NEW YORK(1976)
Homer Willits
Silents
ABRAHAM LINCOLN(1924)
Anne Willkom
Silents
KRIEMHILD'S REVENGE(1924, Ger.), cos; SIEGFRIED(1924, Ger.), cos; METROPO-
LIS(1927, Ger.), cos
Pierre-Richard Willm
UN CARNET DE BAL(1938, Fr.); BETRAYAL(1939, Fr.); ENTENTE CORDIALE(1939,
Fr.); RASPUTIN(1939, Fr.)
Noel Willman
ANDROCLES AND THE LION(1952); PICKWICK PAPERS, THE(1952, Brit.); PRO-
JECT M7(1953, Brit.); BEAU BRUMMELL(1954); WARRIORS, THE(1955); MAN WHO
KNEW TOO MUCH, THE(1956); ABANDON SHIP(1957, Brit.); ACROSS THE BRID-
GE(1957, Brit.); CARVE HER NAME WITH PRIDE(1958, Brit.); NEVER LET GO(1960,
Brit.); TROUBLE IN THE SKY(1961, Brit.); CONCRETE JUNGLE, THE(1962, Brit.);
GIRL ON THE BOAT, THE(1962, Brit.); KISS OF EVIL(1963, Brit.); TWO LIVING, ONE
DEAD(1964, Brit./Swed.); DOCTOR ZHIVAGO(1965); REPTILE, THE(1966, Brit.);
VENGEANCE OF SHE, THE(1968, Brit.); ODESSA FILE, THE(1974, Brit./Ger.)
Catherine Willmer
INSPECTOR CALLS, AN(1954, Brit.); WOMEN IN LOVE(1969, Brit.); O LUCKY
MAN!(1973, Brit.); MADHOUSE(1974, Brit.); MARCH OR DIE(1977, Brit.); FRENCH
LIEUTENANT'S WOMAN, THE(1981); BRITTANIA HOSPITAL(1982, Brit.)
H. E. Willmering
DALTON GIRLS, THE(1957)
Bertha Willmott
MILLIONS LIKE US(1943, Brit.)
Teresa Willmus
ICE CASTLES(1978)

A.M. Willner
ROGUE SONG, THE(1930), w
Dr. A. M. Willner
STRAUSS' GREAT WALTZ(1934, Brit.), w
Dave Willock
GOOD GIRLS GO TO PARIS(1939); LITTLE ACCIDENT(1939); THREE TEXAS
STEERS(1939); FRAMED(1940); TOO MANY HUSBANDS(1940); CAUGHT IN THE
DRAFT(1941); CHOCOLATE SOLDIER, THE(1941); CRACKED NUTS(1941); MON-
STER AND THE GIRL, THE(1941); NEVER GIVE A SUCKER AN EVEN
BREAK(1941); PLAYMATES(1941); FLEET'S IN, THE(1942); FRISCO LILL(1942);
ICE-CAPADES REVUE(1942); LUCKY JORDAN(1942); PRIORITIES ON PARA-
DE(1942); SUNDAY PUNCH(1942); GANG'S ALL HERE, THE(1943); LET'S FACE
IT(1943); PRINCESS O'ROURKE(1943); SHE HAS WHAT IT TAKES(1943); FOUR
JILLS IN A JEEP(1944); PIN UP GIRL(1944); SHE'S A SWEETHEART(1944); WING
AND A PRAYER(1944); PRIDE OF THE MARINES(1945); SPELLBOUND(1945); THIS
LOVE OF OURS(1945); RUNAROUND, THE(1946); SEARCHING WIND, THE(1946);
FABULOUS DORSEYS, THE(1947); SO THIS IS NEW YORK(1948); STATE OF THE
UNION(1948); CHICAGO DEADLINE(1949); BELLE OF OLD MEXICO(1950); LOUI-
SA(1950); NO MAN OF HER OWN(1950); CALL ME MISTER(1951); DARLING, HOW
COULD YOU!(1951); LET'S GO NAVY(1951); ROADBLOCK(1951); BATTLE ZO-
NE(1952); FLAT TOP(1952); JET JOB(1952); MERRY WIDOW, THE(1952); RO-
DEO(1952); IT CAME FROM OUTER SPACE(1953); MA AND PA KETTLE ON
VACATION(1953); REMAINS TO BE SEEN(1953); ROAR OF THE CROWD(1953);
REVENGE OF THE CREATURE(1955); BUSTER KEATON STORY, THE(1957);
DELICATE DELINQUENT, THE(1957); QUEEN OF OUTER SPACE(1958); TEN
SECONDS TO HELL(1959); WHATEVER HAPPENED TO BABY JANE?(1962); NUT-
TY PROFESSOR, THE(1963); WIVES AND LOVERS(1963); PATSY, THE(1964); SEND
ME NO FLOWERS(1964); ADVENTURES OF BULLWHIP GRIFFIN, THE(1967);
LEGEND OF LYLAH CLARE, THE(1968); GRISSOM GANG, THE(1971); NOW YOU
SEE HIM, NOW YOU DON'T(1972); EMPEROR OF THE NORTH POLE(1973);
HUSTLE(1975)
David Willock
LEGION OF LOST FLYERS(1939); BROTHER RAT AND A BABY(1940); MALE
ANIMAL, THE(1942); HUSH... HUSH, SWEET CHARLOTTE(1964)
Dive Willock
LOVE IS BETTER THAN EVER(1952)
June Willock
SALUTE JOHN CITIZEN(1942, Brit.)
Anna Willoughby
MAN OUTSIDE, THE(1968, Brit.); MACBETH(1971, Brit.)
Barrett Willoughby
SPAWN OF THE NORTH(1938), w; ALASKA SEAS(1954), w
George Willoughby
VALLEY OF EAGLES(1952, Brit.), a, p; PASSIONATE SUMMER(1959, Brit.), p;
TASTE OF EXCITEMENT(1969, Brit.), p; SQUEEZE A FLOWER(1970, Aus.), p;
OUTBACK(1971, Aus.), p; BOARDWALK(1979), p
George W. Willoughby
HELL BELOW ZERO(1954, Brit.), p
Jack Willoughby
UP IN SMOKE(1978), ph; RUN LIKE A THIEF(1968, Span.), ph; GIANT SPIDER
INVASION, THE(1975), ph
John Willoughby
VICE VERSA(1948, Brit.)
Leueen Willoughby
SUPERMAN(1978); SUPERMAN II(1980); FINAL CONFLICT, THE(1981)
Lewis Willoughby
Silents
ARTISTIC TEMPERAMENT, THE(1919, Brit.); ONLY A MILL GIRL(1919, Brit.), d;
TRAPPED BY THE MORMONS(1922, Brit.)
Misc. Silents
MIRANDY SMILES(1918); TREASURE OF THE SEA(1918); SECRET OF THE
MOOR, THE(1919, Brit.), d; WISP O' THE WOODS(1919, Brit.), d; COLONEL NEW-
COME THE PERFECT GENTLEMAN(1920, Brit.); BLUFF(1921, Brit.); DESPERATE
YOUTH(1921); LAMP IN THE DESERT(1922, Brit.); MR. BARNES OF NEW
YORK(1922); SCARLET LADY, THE(1922, Brit.); SHIFTING SANDS(1922, Brit.); WAS
SHE GUILTY?(1922, Brit.)
Louis Willoughby
Silents
PAIR OF SILK STOCKINGS, A(1918)
Misc. Silents
TEMPLE OF DUSK, THE(1918)
Mary Willoughby
WHERE'S JACK?(1969, Brit.)
Chris Willow Bird
VALLEY OF THE SUN(1942)
Chris Willowbird
TRAIL STREET(1947)
Alex Willows
MAN, A WOMAN, AND A BANK, A(1979, Can.)
Al Willox
HELLIONS, THE(1962, Brit.)
Rudolph Willrich
ALICE, SWEET ALICE(1978)
Anneke Wills
PLEASURE GIRLS, THE(1966, Brit.)
Annika Wills
SOME PEOPLE(1964, Brit.)
Beverly Wills
GEORGE WHITE'S SCANDALS(1945); MICKEY(1948); SMALL TOWN GIRL(1953);
SOME LIKE IT HOT(1959); LADIES MAN, THE(1961); SON OF FLUBBER(1963)
Bob Wills
GO WEST, YOUNG LADY(1941); SILVER CITY RAIDERS(1943); LAST HORSEMAN,
THE(1944); THUNDER IN DIXIE(1965); SKY RIDERS(1976, U.S./Gr.)
Brember Wills
CARNIVAL(1931, Brit.); OLD DARK HOUSE, THE(1932); WHAT HAPPENED TO
HARKNESS(1934, Brit.); SCARLET PIMPERNEL, THE(1935, Brit.); UNFINISHED
SYMPHONY, THE(1953, Aust./Brit.)

Brian Wills
PIPER'S TUNE, THE(1962, Brit.)

Chill Wills
WAY OUT WEST(1937); LAWLESS VALLEY(1938); ALLEGHENY UPRISING(1939); ARIZONA LEGION(1939); RACKETEERS OF THE RANGE(1939); SORORITY HOUSE(1939); TIMBER STAMPEDE(1939); TROUBLE IN SUNDOWN(1939); BOOM TOWN(1940); SKY MURDER(1940); TUGBOAT ANNIE SAILS AGAIN(1940); WESTERNER, THE(1940); WYOMING(1940); BAD MAN, THE(1941); BELLE STARR(1941); BILLY THE KID(1941); HONKY TONK(1941); WESTERN UNION(1941); APACHE TRAIL(1942); HER CARDBOARD LOVER(1942); OMAHA TRAIL, THE(1942); STAND BY FOR ACTION(1942); TARZAN'S NEW YORK ADVENTURE(1942); BEST FOOT FORWARD(1943); STRANGER IN TOWN, A(1943); BARBARY COAST GENT(1944); I'LL BE SEEING YOU(1944); MEET ME IN ST. LOUIS(1944); RATIONING(1944); SEE HERE, PRIVATE HARGROVE(1944); SUNDAY DINNER FOR A SOLDIER(1944); WHAT NEXT, CORPORAL HARGROVE?(1945); GALLANT BESS(1946); HARVEY GIRLS, THE(1946); LEAVE HER TO HEAVEN(1946); YEARLING, THE(1946); HEARTACHES(1947); HIGH BARBAREE(1947); FAMILY HONEYMOON(1948); LOADED PISTOLS(1948); NORTHWEST STAMPEDE(1948); SAINTED SISTERS, THE(1948); SAXON CHARM, THE(1948); THAT WONDERFUL URGE(1948); FRANCIS(1949); RED CANYON(1949); TULSA(1949); HIGH LONESOME(1950); RIO GRANDE(1950); ROCK ISLAND TRAIL(1950); STELLA(1950); SUNDOWNERS, THE(1950); CATTLE DRIVE(1951); FRANCIS GOES TO THE RACES(1951); OH! SUSANNA(1951); SEA HORNET, THE(1951); BRONCO BUSTER(1952); FRANCIS GOES TO WEST POINT(1952); RIDE THE MAN DOWN(1952); CITY THAT NEVER SLEEPS(1953); FRANCIS COVERS THE BIG TOWN(1953); MAN FROM THE ALAMO, THE(1953); SMALL TOWN GIRL(1953); TUMBLEWEED(1953); FRANCIS JOINS THE WACS(1954); RICOCHET ROMANCE(1954); FRANCIS IN THE NAVY(1955); HELL'S OUTPOST(1955); TIMBERJACK(1955); GIANT(1956); KENTUCKY RIFLE(1956); SANTIAGO(1956); GUN FOR A COWARD(1957); GUN GLORY(1957); FROM HELL TO TEXAS(1958); SAD HORSE, THE(1959); ALAMO, THE(1960); WHERE THE BOYS ARE(1960); DEADLY COMPANIONS, THE(1961); GOLD OF THE SEVEN SAINTS(1961); LITTLE SHEPHERD OF KINGDOM COME(1961); CARDINAL, THE(1963); MC LINTOCK!(1963); WHEELER DEALERS, THE(1963); YOUNG GUNS OF TEXAS(1963); ROUNDERS, THE(1965); FIREBALL 590(1966); BIG DADDY(1969); LIBERATION OF L.B. JONES, THE(1970); STEAGLE, THE(1971); GUNS OF A STRANGER(1973); PAT GARRETT AND BILLY THE KID(1973); POCO...LITTLE DOG LOST(1977)

Chris Wills
SKY RIDERS(1976, U.S./Gr.)

Cindy Wills
ROADIE(1980)

Cindy "Toad" Wills
1984
GIMME AN 'F'(1984), stunts

Drusilla Wills
TO WHAT RED HELL(1929, Brit.); OLD SPANISH CUSTOMERS(1932, Brit.); BRITANNIA OF BILLINGSGATE(1933, Brit.); LITTLE MISS NOBODY(1933, Brit.); MEDICINE MAN, THE(1933, Brit.); BLACK ABBOT, THE(1934, Brit.); NIGHT CLUB QUEEN(1934, Brit.); BIG SPLASH, THE(1935, Brit.); PHANTOM FIEND(1935, Brit.); SQUIBS(1935, Brit.); NON-STOP NEW YORK(1937, Brit.); SPOT OF BOTHER, A(1938, Brit.); YELLOW SANDS(1938, Brit.); GIRL MUST LIVE, A(1941, Brit.); MAN IN GREY, THE(1943, Brit.); CHAMPAGNE CHARLIE(1944, Brit.); WELCOME, MR. WASHINGTON(1944, Brit.); JOHNNY FRENCHMAN(1946, Brit.); NICHOLAS NICKLEBY(1947, Brit.); QUEEN OF SPADES(1948, Brit.)
Silents
OLD WIVES' TALE, THE(1921, Brit.)

Edwin Wills
SIOUX CITY SUE(1946)

Edwin B. Wills
ANCHORS AWEIGH(1945), set d

Elder Wills
WOMAN IN HIDING(1953, Brit.), art d

F. McGrew Wills
SUICIDE FLEET(1931), w

Frank Wills
ALL THE PRESIDENT'S MEN(1976)

Freeman Wills
Silents
ONLY WAY, THE(1926, Brit.), w

Gordon Wills
MOON AND SIXPENCE, THE(1942), prod d

Graham Wills
PIPER'S TUNE, THE(1962, Brit.)

Henry Wills
LEGION OF THE LAWLESS(1940); YOUNG BILL HICKOK(1940); IN OLD COLORADO(1941); NEVADA CITY(1941); OUTLAWS OF THE CHEROKEE TRAIL(1941); SADDLEMATES(1941); SOUTH OF SANTA FE(1942); SUNSET ON THE DESERT(1942); SILVER SPURS(1943); CODE OF THE PRAIRIE(1944); LUMBERJACK(1944); OLD TEXAS TRAIL, THE(1944); RIDERS OF THE SANTA FE(1944); SAN ANTONIO KID, THE(1944); SONG OF NEVADA(1944); STAGECOACH TO MONTEREY(1944); TRAIL TO GUNSIGHT(1944); BEYOND THE PECOS(1945); CORPUS CHRISTI BANDITS(1945); GREAT STAGECOACH ROBBERY(1945); ROUGH RIDERS OF CHEYENNE(1945); SANTA FE SADDLEMATES(1945); SHERIFF OF CIMARRON(1945); TRAIL OF KIT CARSON(1945); PLAINSMAN AND THE LADY(1946); JOAN OF ARC(1948); SUNDOWN RIDERS(1948); SAMSON AND DELILAH(1949); SHANE(1953); SASKATCHEWAN(1954); CHIEF CRAZY HORSE(1955); RUN FOR COVER(1955); RED SUNDOWN(1956); SEARCHERS, THE(1956); GUNFIGHT AT THE O.K. CORRAL(1957); KETTLES ON OLD MACDONALD'S FARM, THE(1957); NIGHT PASSAGE(1957); LAST TRAIN FROM GUN HILL(1959); ONE-EYED JACKS(1961); POSSE FROM HELL(1961); SIX BLACK HORSES(1962); SHOWDOWN(1963); SHENANDOAH(1965); SONS OF KATIE ELDER, THE(1965); EYE FOR AN EYE, AN(1966); IN LIKE FLINT(1967); RED TOMAHAWK(1967); NIGHT OF THE LEPUS(1972); OKLAHOMA CRUDE(1973); SOUL OF NIGGER CHARLEY, THE(1973); MASTER GUNFIGHTER, THE(1975), stunts; DRUM(1976); COAST TO COAST(1980); LEGEND OF THE LONE RANGER, THE(1981)

Hugh Wills
ON THE BEACH(1959)

J. Elder Wills
M'BLIMEY(1931, Brit.), d, w; TIGER BAY(1933, Brit.), d, w; EVERYTHING IN LIFE(1936, Brit.), d; SPORTING LOVE(1936, Brit.), d; BIG FELLA(1937, Brit.), d; SONG OF FREEDOM(1938, Brit.), d; VALLEY OF EAGLES(1952, Brit.), art d; BLOOD ORANGE(1953, Brit.), art d; TERROR STREET(1953), art d; PAID TO KILL(1954, Brit.), art d

Jean Wills
RUN FOR THE HILLS(1953)

Jerry Wills
ROLLERBALL(1975); THING, THE(1982)
1984
BODY DOUBLE(1984)

Jessie Wills
SURVIVAL(1976)

Jim Elder Wills
BLACKOUT(1954, Brit.), art d; UNHOLY FOUR, THE(1954, Brit.), art d; RACE FOR LIFE, A(1955, Brit.), art d

Lisa Wills
YOUNG GIANTS(1983)

Lou Wills
POPEYE(1980), ch; CANNERY ROW(1982), ch

Lou Wills, Jr.
MY WILD IRISH ROSE(1947)

Luther Wills
SILVER CITY RAIDERS(1943)

Mary Wills
SONG OF THE SOUTH(1946), cos; ENCHANTMENT(1948), cos; MY FOOLISH HEART(1949), cos; EDGE OF DOOM(1950), cos; OUR VERY OWN(1950), cos; I WANT YOU(1951), cos; HANS CHRISTIAN ANDERSEN(1952), cos; GOOD MORNING, MISS DOVE(1955), cos; VIRGIN QUEEN, THE(1955), cos; BIGGER THAN LIFE(1956), cos; CAROUSEL(1956), cos; LAST WAGON, THE(1956), cos; LOVE ME TENDER(1956), cos; TEENAGE REBEL(1956), cos; BERNARDINE(1957), cos; HATFUL OF RAIN, A(1957), cos; NO DOWN PAYMENT(1957), cos; TRUE STORY OF JESSE JAMES, THE(1957), cos; WAYWARD BUS, THE(1957), cos; CERTAIN SMILE, A(1958), cos; FRAULEIN(1958), cos; PROUD REBEL, THE(1958), cos; REMARKABLE MR. PENNYPACKER, THE(1959), cos; WONDERFUL COUNTRY, THE(1959), cos; CAPE FEAR(1962), cos; WONDERFUL WORLD OF THE BROTHERS ERIMM, THE(1962), cos; PASSOVER PLOT, THE(1976, Israel), cos

Matt Wills
HI' YA, SAILOR(1943); GHOST THAT WALKS ALONE, THE(1944)

Maury Wills
ODD COUPLE, THE(1968); BLACK SIX, THE(1974)

Michael Wills
CHOIRBOYS, THE(1977)

Norma Wills
Silents
BARRIERS OF THE LAW(1925)

Rae Wills
IT HAPPENED HERE(1966, Brit.)

Sheila Wills
HERO AIN'T NOTHIN' BUT A SANDWICH, A(1977); YOUNGBLOOD(1978)

Si Wills
HONOR AMONG LOVERS(1931); LIFE BEGINS WITH LOVE(1937); NATION AFLAME(1937); NOBODY'S BABY(1937); PENROD AND SAM(1937); CIPHER BUREAU(1938); RACING BLOOD(1938); GAY INTRUDERS, THE(1948)

Susie Wills
SKY RIDERS(1976, U.S./Gr.)

Terry Wills
ESCAPE FROM ALCATRAZ(1979); PERFECT COUPLE, A(1979)
1984
HEARTBREAKERS(1984); MASS APPEAL(1984)

Walter Wills
SMILING IRISH EYES(1929), ch; SANTA FE STAMPEDE(1938); COWBOYS FROM TEXAS(1939); DANGER FLIGHT(1939); NIGHT RIDERS, THE(1939)
Silents
IN SEARCH OF A THRILL(1923)

Will Wills
YOUNG GUNS OF TEXAS(1963)

Maureen Willsher
HALF A SIXPENCE(1967, Brit.); YOUNG GIRLS OF ROCHEFORT, THE(1968, Fr.)

Gwen Willson
1984
GREMLINS(1984)

Jack Willson
LUCK OF THE IRISH, THE(1937, Ireland), ph

Marie Willson
STARS OVER BROADWAY(1935)

Meredith Willson
GREAT DICTATOR, THE(1940), m&md; LITTLE FOXES, THE(1941), m, md; MUSIC MAN, THE(1962), w, m; UNSINKABLE MOLLY BROWN, THE(1964), w, m

Paul Willson
STRAWBERRY STATEMENT, THE(1970); CRACKING UP(1977); GOODBYE GIRL, THE(1977); DEVONSVILLE TERROR, THE(1983); STING II, THE(1983)
1984
PROTOCOL(1984)

Richard Willson
TO SIR, WITH LOVE(1967, Brit.)

Tina Willson
STAR 80(1983)

Howard Willtams
CARRY ON ADMIRAL(1957, Brit.)

Erik Wittrup Willumsen
SCANDAL IN DENMARK(1970, Den.), ph

Max Dietrich Willutzki
NOT RECONCILED, OR "ONLY VIOLENCE HELPS WHERE IT RULES"(1969, Ger.)

Willy
CESAR(1936, Fr.), ph

Sibina Willy
WE OF THE NEVER NEVER(1983, Aus.)
Suzy Willy
MR. HULOT'S HOLIDAY(1954, Fr.); TRUTH, THE(1961, Fr./Ital.)
Douglas Wilmar
RECKONING, THE(1971, Brit.)
Catherine Wilmer
CONSCIENCE BAY(1960, Brit.); GAME FOR THREE LOSERS(1965, Brit.); BOY FRIEND, THE(1971, Brit.)
Doug Wilmer
ANTONY AND CLEOPATRA(1973, Brit.)
Douglas Wilmer
PASSPORT TO TREASON(1956, Brit.); RICHARD III(1956, Brit.); MEN OF SHERWOOD FOREST(1957, Brit.); PURSUIT OF THE GRAF SPEE(1957, Brit.); HONOURABLE MURDER, AN(1959, Brit.); EL CID(1961, U.S./Ital.); INVITATION TO MURDER(1962, Brit.); CLEOPATRA(1963); JASON AND THE ARGONAUTS(1963, Brit.); MACBETH(1963); FALL OF THE ROMAN EMPIRE, THE(1964); SHOT IN THE DARK, A(1964); WOMAN OF STRAW(1964, Brit.); GOLDEN HEAD, THE(1965, Hung., U.S.); ONE WAY PENDULUM(1965, Brit.); BRIDES OF FU MANCHU, THE(1966, Brit.); KHARTOUM(1966, Brit.); HAMMERHEAD(1968); VENGEANCE OF FU MANCHU, THE(1968, Brit./Ger./Hong Kong/Ireland); NICE GIRL LIKE ME, A(1969, Brit.); CROMWELL(1970, Brit.); PATTON(1970); VAMPIRE LOVERS, THE(1970, Brit.); UNMAN, WITTERING AND ZIGO(1971, Brit.); GOLDEN VOYAGE OF SINBAD, THE(1974, Brit.); ADVENTURES OF SHERLOCK HOLMES' SMARTER BROTHER, THE(1975, Brit.); INCREDIBLE SARAH, THE(1976, Brit.); REVENGE OF THE PINK PANTHER(1978); ROUGH CUT(1980, Brit.); OCTOPUSSY(1983, Brit.)
1984
SWORD OF THE VALIANT(1984, Brit.)
Geoffrey Wilmer
FLAMINGO AFFAIR, THE(1948, Brit.); LAUGHING LADY, THE(1950, Brit.)
Silents
AMATEUR GENTLEMAN, THE(1920, Brit.)
Misc. Silents
LITTLE DAMOZEL, THE(1916, Brit.); CRY FOR JUSTICE, THE(1919, Brit.); HIS LAST DEFENCE(1919, Brit.), d; BECAUSE(1921, Brit.)
Elaine Wilmont
Silents
PIRATES OF THE SKY(1927), w
Duncan Wilmore
WARGAMES(1983)
Don Wilmot
MAJOR AND THE MINOR, THE(1942)
Donald Wilmot
SONG IS BORN, A(1948); CHICAGO DEADLINE(1949)
Gerry Wilmot
FLYING FORTRESS(1942, Brit.); CANDLES AT NINE(1944, Brit.); YANK IN LONDON, A(1946, Brit.); HOLIDAY CAMP(1947, Brit.)
Ivan Wilmot
FORBIDDEN MUSIC(1936, Brit.); PASSENGER TO LONDON(1937, Brit.); TWIN FACES(1937, Brit.); RAT, THE(1938, Brit.)
Ivor Wilmot
ROBBER SYMPHONY, THE(1937, Brit.)
John Wilmot
1984
TIGHTROPE(1984)
Masada Wilmot
MURDER AT THE GALLOP(1963, Brit.), cos
Robert Wilmot
UNWRITTEN CODE, THE(1944), w; HOLLYWOOD AND VINE(1945), w
Duke Wilmoth
MACHISMO-40 GRAVES FOR 40 GUNS(1970)
Paul Wilmoth
HOT SPUR(1968); SCAVENGERS, THE(1969)
Rod Wilmoth
GIRL IN GOLD BOOTS(1968); HOT SPUR(1968); ASTRO-ZOMBIES, THE(1969)
Bertha Wilmott
VARIETY(1935, Brit.)
Gerry Wilmott
SPITFIRE(1943, Brit.); DREAMING(1944, Brit.); YELLOW CANARY, THE(1944, Brit.)
Dominique Wilms
VICE DOLLS(1961, Fr.); CAESAR THE CONQUEROR(1963, Ital.); SHADOW OF EVIL(1967, Fr./Ital.)
Ann Wilner
BRIDE OF THE MONSTER(1955)
Max Wilner
Misc. Talkies
LIVE AND LAUGH(1933), d; THREE DAUGHTERS(1949)
Babs Wilomez
LADY IN THE DARK(1944), cos
Rudolph Wilrich
FRONT, THE(1976)
Channing Wilroy
FEMALE TROUBLE(1975)
Irene Wilsen
ROSE OF WASHINGTON SQUARE(1939)
Jay [Buffalo Bill, Jr.] Wilsey
WAY OUT WEST(1930); TERROR TRAIL(1933); 'NEATH THE ARIZONA SKIES(1934); RIDING SPEED(1934), d; RANGERS STEP IN, THE(1937); WAY OUT WEST(1937); LONE RIDER CROSSES THE RIO(1941); LONE RIDER IN GHOST TOWN, THE(1941); DANCING MASTERS, THE(1943)
Jay Wilsey
DYNAMITE DENNY(1932); STRANGE PEOPLE(1933); WHEELS OF DESTINY(1934); HEROES OF THE RANGE(1936); RANGER COURAGE(1937); RECKLESS RANGER(1937)
Jay Wilsey, Jr. [Buffalo Bill, Jr.]
FORLORN RIVER(1937)
Sundae Wilshin
Silents
GREEN CARAVAN, THE(1922, Brit.); PAGES OF LIFE(1922, Brit.)

Sunday Wilshin
HOURS OF LONELINESS(1930, Brit.); CHANCE OF A NIGHT-TIME, THE(1931, Brit); COLLISION(1932, Brit.); DANCE PRETTY LADY(1932, Brit.); LOVE CONTRACT, THE(1932, Brit.); MARRY ME(1932, Brit.); MICHAEL AND MARY(1932, Brit.); NINE TILL SIX(1932, Brit.); BORROWED CLOTHES(1934, Brit.); SOME DAY(1935, Brit.); MURDER BY ROPE(1936, Brit.); FIRST NIGHT(1937, Brit.)
Silents
HUTCH STIRS 'EM UP(1923, Brit.); CHAMPAGNE(1928, Brit.)
Mary Wilshire
EASY MONEY(1983)
Honore Wilsie
Silents
RED, RED HEART, THE(1918), w
Dieter Wilsing
DECISION BEFORE DAWN(1951)
Kaarlo Wilska
PRELUDE TO ECSTASY(1963, Fin.)
Al Wilson
HELL'S ANGELS(1930); COME ON RANGERS(1939), ph
Silents
AIR HAWK, THE(1924); SKY-HIGH SAUNDERS(1927); AIR PATROL, THE(1928), a, w; SKY SKIDDER, THE(1929)
Misc. Silents
CLOUD RIDER, THE(1925); FLYIN' THRU(1925); FLYING MAIL, THE(1926); THREE MILES UP(1927); CLOUD DODGER, THE(1928); PHANTOM FLYER, THE(1928); WON IN THE CLOUDS(1928)
Alan Wilson
GUY NAMED JOE, A(1943); DESTINATION TOKYO(1944); I'M ALL RIGHT, JACK(1959, Brit.)
1984
PHAR LAP(1984, Aus.)
Albert Wilson
WRATH OF GOD, THE(1972), ed
Albert C. Wilson
LIFE OF EMILE ZOLA, THE(1937), set d
Albert P. Wilson
CORKY(1972), ed
Alex Wilson
GAS-S-S-S!(1970); GRISSOM GANG, THE(1971); DIRTY LITTLE BILLY(1972); STAND UP AND BE COUNTED(1972); SHAMUS(1973)
Alice Wilson
Silents
BRAZEN BEAUTY(1918); EYES OF JULIA DEEP, THE(1918); MAKING THE GRADE(1921)
Misc. Silents
DREAM CHEATER, THE(1920)
Alive Wilson
Misc. Silents
SHOULD SHE OBEY?(1917)
Andrew Thomas Wilson
CHAIN REACTION(1980, Aus.), m
Andy Wilson
TWO THOUSAND MANIACS!(1964)
Angela Wilson
LADY IN THE DARK(1944); LA DOLCE VITA(1961, Ital./Fr.); WHICH WAY IS UP?(1977)
Anthony Wilson
THEM NICE AMERICANS(1958, Brit.); NEWMAN'S LAW(1974), w; TOGETHER BROTHERS(1974)
Archies Wilson
DARWIN ADVENTURE, THE(1972, Brit.)
Assany Kamara Wilson
HEART OF THE MATTER, THE(1954, Brit.)
Augusta Wilson
Silents
PRICE OF SILENCE, THE(1920, Brit.), w
Baby Wilson
Silents
KID, THE(1921)
Barbara Wilson
MAN WHO TURNED TO STONE, THE(1957); TEENAGE DOLL(1957); LOST, LONELY AND VICIOUS(1958); INVASION OF THE ANIMAL PEOPLE(1962, U.S./Swed.); MURDER CLINIC, THE(1967, Ital./Fr.)
Baron Wilson
GAMBLER, THE(1974)
Basil Wilson
Silents
APE, THE(1928)
Beau Wilson
UP IN THE CELLAR(1970), makeup
Ben Wilson
SHADOW RANCH(1930)
Misc. Talkies
BYE-BYE BUDDY(1929)
Silents
EVEN AS YOU AND I(1917); SPINDLE OF LIFE, THE(1917); CHAIN LIGHTNING(1922), p&d; IMPULSE(1922), p; MARSHAL OF MONEYMINT, THE(1922), p; SPAWN OF THE DESERT(1923), p&d; BRANDED A BANDIT(1924), p; GAMBLING WIVES(1924), sup; LASH OF THE WHIP(1924), p; WEST OF THE LAW(1926), a, d; RANGE RIDERS, THE(1927), a, d; WESTERN COURAGE(1927), d; GIRLS WHO DARE(1929)
Misc. Silents
MAINSPRING, THE(1916); CASTLES IN THE AIR(1919); WHEN A WOMAN STRIKES(1919); BLUE BONNET, THE(1920); BROKEN SPUR, THE(1921), d; DANGEROUS PATHS(1921); INNOCENT CHEAT, THE(1921), d; SHERIFF OF HOPE ETERNAL, THE(1921), d; BACK TO YELLOW JACKET(1922), d; ONE EIGHTH APACHE(1922), d; PRICE OF YOUTH, THE(1922), d; SHERIFF OF SUN-DOG, THE(1922), d; MINE TO KEEP(1923), d; OTHER MEN'S DAUGHTERS(1923), d; DESERT HAWK, THE(1924); HIS MAJESTY THE OUTLAW(1924); NOTCH NUMBER ONE(1924); DAUGHTER OF THE SIOUX, A(1925), a, d; FUGITIVE, THE(1925), a, d;

HUMAN TORNADO, THE(1925), d; MAN FROM LONE MOUNTAIN, THE(1925), a, d; RENEGADE HOLMES, M.D.(1925), a, d; RIDIN' COMET(1925), d; ROMANCE AND RUSTLERS(1925), d; SAND BLIND(1925); SCAR HANAN(1925), d; TONIO, SON OF THE SIERRAS(1925), a, d; TWO-FISTED SHERIFF, A(1925), d; VIC DYSON PAYS(1925); WARRIOR GAP(1925); WHITE THUNDER(1925), d; BAITED TRAP(1926); FORT FRAYNE(1926), a, d; OFFICER 444(1926), a, d; SHERIFF'S GIRL(1926), a, d; WOLVES OF THE DESERT(1926), a, d; MYSTERY BRAND, THE(1927), a, d; RIDERS OF THE WEST(1927), a, d; SADDLE JUMPERS(1927), d; YELLOW STREAK, A(1927), a, d; CHINA SLAVER(1929)

Ben F. Wilson
Misc. Silents
MAN FROM TEXAS, THE(1921), d; FIGHTING STALLION, THE(1926), d

Benjamin Franklin Wilson
Silents
OLD CODE, THE(1928), d
Misc. Silents
SADDLE KING, THE(1929), d; THUNDERING THOMPSON(1929), d

Bert Wilson
Silents
DOLLY'S VACATION(1918); WESTERN HEARTS(1921); RIDIN' WILD(1922); RAM-SHACKLE HOUSE(1924), ph
Misc. Silents
FIGHTING STRAIN, THE(1923)

Bevan Wilson
MIDDLE AGE SPREAD(1979, New Zealand)

Bill Wilson
LAST VOYAGE, THE(1960); JAWS OF SATAN(1980), p

Bill P. Wilson
WINTER KILLS(1979)

Billy Wilson
STOLEN HARMONY(1935); WE WERE STRANGERS(1949); SAMMY STOPS THE WORLD zero(1978), ch

Bob Wilson
BURGLAR, THE(1956); PRIME CUT(1972); THERE'S ALWAYS VANILLA(1972); HUMAN TORNADO, THE(1976), ph; DAYS OF HEAVEN(1978)

Boris Wilson [Robert Fryer]
ACE ELI AND RODGER OF THE SKIES(1973), p

Brian Wilson
RIDE THE WILD SURF(1964), m/l "Ride the Wild Surf," Jan Berry; GIRLS ON THE BEACH(1965); HOW TO STUFF A WILD BIKINI(1965)

Bruce Wilson
HAWAIIANS, THE(1970); DOUBLES(1978), p

Bryna Wilson
WHAT'S UP, TIGER LILY?(1966), a, w

Burtrust T. Wilson
PONY EXPRESS RIDER(1976)

Cal Wilson
HALLS OF ANGER(1970); BATTLE FOR THE PLANET OF THE APES(1973); FIVE ON THE BLACK HAND SIDE(1973)
Misc. Talkies
DISCO 9000(1977)

Carey Wilson
FOOTLIGHTS AND FOOLS(1929), w; GERALDINE(1929), w; HIS CAPTIVE WOM-AN(1929), w; BAD ONE, THE(1930), w; PEACOCK ALLEY(1930), w; BEHIND OF-FICE DOORS(1931), w; FANNY FOLEY HERSELF(1931), w; ARSENE LUPIN(1932), w; FAITHLESS(1932), w; POLLY OF THE CIRCUS(1932), w; GABRIEL OVER THE WHITE HOUSE(1933), w; WHAT! NO BEER?(1933), w; BOLERO(1934), w; MURDER AT THE VANITIES(1934), w; PRESIDENT VANISHES, THE(1934), w; SEQUOIA(1934), w; MUTINY ON THE BOUNTY(1935), w; BETWEEN TWO WO-MEN(1937), w; DANGEROUS NUMBER(1937), w; LOVE FINDS ANDY HAR-DY(1938), p; JUDGE HARDY AND SON(1939), w; POSTMAN ALWAYS RINGS TWICE, THE(1946), p; DARK DELUSION(1947), p; GREEN DOLPHIN STREET(1947), p; RED DANUBE, THE(1949), p; HAPPY YEARS, THE(1950), p; SCARAMOU-CHE(1952), p
1984
1984(1984, Brit.)
Silents
MADONNAS AND MEN(1920), w; WOMAN'S BUSINESS, A(1920), w; ETERNAL THREE, THE(1923), w; RED LIGHTS(1923), w; EMPTY HANDS(1924), w; HE WHO GETS SLAPPED(1924), w; BEN-HUR(1925), w; HIS SECRETARY(1925), w; SOUL MATES(1925), w; LADIES AT PLAY(1926), w; SILENT LOVER, THE(1926), w; AMERICAN BEAUTY(1927), p, w; SEA TIGER, THE(1927), p, w; STOLEN BRIDE, THE(1927), p, w; TENDER HOUR, THE(1927), w; AWAKENING, THE(1928), w; LILAC TIME(1928), w; OH, KAY(1928), w; WHY BE GOOD?(1929), w

Carl Wilson
GIRLS ON THE BEACH(1965)

Cathy Wilson
CONRACK(1974)

Charles Wilson
ACQUITTED(1929); BROADWAY SCANDALS(1929); SONG OF LOVE, THE(1929); SECRETS OF A SECRETARY(1931); ELMER THE GREAT(1933); FEMALE(1933); HARD TO HANDLE(1933); HAVANA WIDOWS(1933); KENNEL MURDER CASE, THE(1933); MARY STEVENS, M.D.(1933); MAYOR OF HELL, THE(1933); NO MAR-RIAGE TIES(1933); PRIVATE DETECTIVE 62(1933); AFFAIRS OF A GENT-LEMAN(1934); CIRCUS CLOWN(1934); DRAGON MURDER CASE, THE(1934); EMBARRASSING MOMENTS(1934); FOG OVER FRISCO(1934); HAROLD TEEN(1934); HELL CAT, THE(1934); HERE IS MY HEART(1934); HUMAN SIDE, THE(1934); I'VE GOT YOUR NUMBER(1934); LEMON DROP KID, THE(1934); MISS FANE'S BABY IS STOLEN(1934); MURDER IN THE CLOUDS(1934); NAME THE WOMAN(1934); ST. LOUIS KID, THE(1934); ANOTHER FACE(1935); BEHOLD MY WIFE(1935); CAR 99(1935); CASE OF THE LUCKY LEGS, THE(1935); FIGHTING YOUTH(1935); GILDED LILY, THE(1935); MARY BURNS, FUGITIVE(1935); MEN OF THE HOUR(1935); NITWITS, THE(1935); PORT OF LOST DREAMS(1935); SMART GIRL(1935); DOWN THE STRETCH(1936); EARTHWORM TRACTORS(1936); GEN-TLEMAN FROM LOUISIANA(1936); GRAND JURY(1936); LEGION OF TER-ROR(1936); MAGNIFICENT BRUTE, THE(1936); MINE WITH THE IRON DOOR, THE(1936); PENNIES FROM HEAVEN(1936); PIGSKIN PARADE(1936); RETURN OF JIMMY VALENTINE, THE(1936); SATAN MET A LADY(1936); SHOW BOAT(1936); SMALL TOWN GIRL(1936); STRIKE ME PINK(1936); WE'RE ONLY HUMAN(1936); ADVENTUROUS BLONDE(1937); CASE OF THE STUTTERING BISHOP, THE(1937);

DAUGHTER OF SHANGHAI(1937); FIND THE WITNESS(1937); GREAT O'MALLEY, THE(1937); LIFE BEGINS IN COLLEGE(1937); MURDER GOES TO COLLEGE(1937); NIGHT KEY(1937); PARTNERS IN CRIME(1937); ROARING TIMBER(1937); THAT'S MY STORY(1937); THEY WANTED TO MARRY(1937); WOMAN IN DISTRESS(1937); ANGELS WITH DIRTY FACES(1938); LITTLE MISS THOROUGHBRED(1938); NIGHT HAWK, THE(1938); SALLY, IRENE AND MARY(1938); STATE POLICE(1938); TENTH AVENUE KID(1938); THERE'S THAT WOMAN AGAIN(1938); WHEN WERE YOU BORN?(1938); COWBOY QUARTERBACK(1939); FIGHTING THOROUGH-BREDS(1939); FORGOTTEN WOMAN, THE(1939); HERE I AM A STRANGER(1939); HOTEL FOR WOMEN(1939); LADY'S FROM KENTUCKY, THE(1939); RETURN OF DR. X, THE(1939); ROSE OF WASHINGTON SQUARE(1939); SMASHING THE MONEY RING(1939); CHARTER PILOT(1940); ENEMY AGENT(1940); HE MARRIED HIS WIFE(1940); INVISIBLE STRIPES(1940); KNUTE ROCKNE–ALL AMERI-CAN(1940); PUBLIC DEB NO. 1(1940); SANDY IS A LADY(1940); THEY DRIVE BY NIGHT(1940); BROADWAY LIMITED(1941); CITY, FOR CONQUEST(1940); DRESSED TO KILL(1941); FACE BEHIND THE MASK, THE(1941); FEDERAL FUGITI-VES(1941); KNOCKOUT(1941); OFFICER AND THE LADY, THE(1941); OUT OF THE FOG(1941); ESCAPE FROM CRIME(1942); GENTLEMAN JIM(1942); LADY GANG-STER(1942); RINGS ON HER FINGERS(1942); SILVER SPURS(1943); BIG NOISE, THE(1944); HEY, ROOKIE(1944); KANSAS CITY KITTY(1944); MAN FROM FRIS-CO(1944); ROGER TOUHY, GANGSTER!(1944); SHADOWS IN THE NIGHT(1944); TWO O'CLOCK COURAGE(1945); WEEKEND AT THE WALDORF(1945); BLONDE FOR A DAY(1946); BRINGING UP FATHER(1946); GAS HOUSE KIDS(1946); I RING DOORBELLS(1946); IF I'M LUCKY(1946); LARCENY IN HER HEART(1946); PASS-KEY TO DANGER(1946)

Charles C. Wilson
LUCKY BOY(1929), d; DANCING LADY(1933); FOOTLIGHT PARADE(1933); GOLD DIGGERS OF 1933(1933); ROMAN SCANDALS(1933); GAMBLING LADY(1934); GIRL FROM MISSOURI, THE(1934); IT HAPPENED ONE NIGHT(1934); MEN OF THE NIGHT(1934); DANTE'S INFERNO(1935); FOUR HOURS TO KILL(1935); GLASS KEY, THE(1935); GREAT HOTEL MURDER(1935); MUSIC IS MAGIC(1935); PERFECT CLUE, THE(1935); PUBLIC MENACE(1935); RECKLESS(1935); SECRET BRIDE, THE(1935); SHOW THEM NO MERCY(1935); WATERFRONT LADY(1935); HITCH HIKE LADY(1936); I'D GIVE MY LIFE(1936); ROSE BOWL(1936); DEVIL IS DRIV-ING, THE(1937); MIND YOUR OWN BUSINESS(1937); HOLD THAT CO-ED(1938); PRISON FARM(1938); GIRL IN 313(1940); THIS GUN FOR HIRE(1942); TWO SENORI-TAS FROM CHICAGO(1943); CRIME BY NIGHT(1944); INCENDIARY BLON-DE(1945); ROAD TO UTOPIA(1945); SCARLET STREET(1945); HER HUSBAND'S AFFAIRS(1947)

Charles D. Wilson
IS EVERYBODY HAPPY?(1943)

Charles E. Wilson
HOUSE OF FEAR, THE(1939); IRISH EYES ARE SMILING(1944)

Charles Hummel Wilson
IN OLD CHICAGO(1938)

Charles J. Wilson, Jr.
Silents
GREATER LAW, THE(1917), w; PRINCE OF AVENUE A., THE(1920), w

Charlie Wilson
BIG BROWN EYES(1936); MEET JOHN DOE(1941); SUSPENSE(1946)

Cherise Wilson
VAN, THE(1977)

Cherry Wilson
SADDLE BUSTER, THE(1932), w; STORMY(1935), w; THROWBACK, THE(1935), w; EMPTY SADDLES(1937), w; SANDFLOW(1937), w

Chris Wilson
WINDSPLITTER, THE(1971)

Christopher Wilson
NO BLADE OF GRASS(1970, Brit.)

Clarence Wilson
HER MAJESTY LOVE(1931); LADIES' MAN(1931); NIGHT LIFE IN RENO(1931); SEA GHOST, THE(1931); AMATEUR DADDY(1932); BEAST OF THE CITY, THE(1932); DOWN TO EARTH(1932); FAMOUS FERGUSON CASE, THE(1932); JEWEL ROB-BERY(1932); LOVE ME TONIGHT(1932); PURCHASE PRICE, THE(1932); WINNER TAKE ALL(1932); FLAMING GUNS(1933); GIRL IN 419(1933); KEYHOLE, THE(1933); KING FOR A NIGHT(1933); LADY KILLER(1933); MYSTERIOUS RIDER, THE(1933); PICK-UP(1933); ROMAN SCANDALS(1933); SON OF KONG(1933); TERROR ABOARD(1933); TILLIE AND GUS(1933); 20,000 YEARS IN SING SING(1933); BACHELOR BAIT(1934); COUNT OF MONTE CRISTO, THE(1934); HOLLYWOOD PARTY(1934); I LIKE IT THAT WAY(1934); I'LL FIX IT(1934); LOVE BIRDS(1934), ed; NANA(1934); NOW I'LL TELL(1934); OLD-FASHIONED WAY, THE(1934); SUCCESS-FUL FAILURE, A(1934); UNKNOWN BLONDE(1934); CHAMPAGNE FOR BREAK-FAST(1935); I DREAM TOO MUCH(1935); LET 'EM HAVE IT(1935); WHEN A MAN'S A MAN(1935); CASE OF THE BLACK CAT, THE(1936); LOVE BEGINS AT TWEN-TY(1936); DAMAGED GOODS(1937); HATS OFF(1937); MAYTIME(1937); SMALL TOWN BOY(1937); STAR IS BORN, A(1937); TWO WISE MAIDS(1937); WESTLAND CASE, THE(1937); TEXANS, THE(1938); YOU CAN'T TAKE IT WITH YOU(1938); EAST SIDE OF HEAVEN(1939); LET US LIVE(1939); YOUNG MR. LINCOLN(1939); MELODY RANCH(1940); WE WHO ARE YOUNG(1940); ROAD SHOW(1941); YOU'RE THE ONE(1941); HARLEM GLOBETROTTERS, THE(1951)

Clarence H. Wilson
BIG NEWS(1929); DANGEROUS PARADISE(1930); LOVE IN THE ROUGH(1930); FRONT PAGE, THE(1931); PENGUIN POOL MURDER, THE(1932); SPORT PARADE, THE(1932); SHRIEK IN THE NIGHT, A(1933); LEMON DROP KID, THE(1934); LOVE BIRDS(1934); VIVA VILLA!(1934); WAKE UP AND DREAM(1934); GREAT HOTEL MURDER(1935); MAD LOVE(1935); ONE FRIGHTENED NIGHT(1935); PADDY O'-DAY(1935); SPLENDOR(1935); WATERFRONT LADY(1935); EDUCATING FA-THER(1936); LITTLE MISS NOBODY(1936); RAINBOW ON THE RIVER(1936); TIMOTHY'S QUEST(1936); WEDDING PRESENT(1936); EMPEROR'S CANDLES-TICKS, THE(1937); HAVING WONDERFUL TIME(1938); MAD MISS MANTON, THE(1938); DESPERATE TRAILS(1939); DRUMS ALONG THE MOHAWK(1939); SOME LIKE IT HOT(1939); FRIENDLY NEIGHBORS(1940)

Clarence Hummel Wilson
EVELYN PRENTICE(1934); IMITATION OF LIFE(1934); OPERATOR 13(1934); RUG-GLES OF RED GAP(1935); WHOLE TOWN'S TALKING, THE(1935); KENTUCKY MOONSHINE(1938); LITTLE MISS BROADWAY(1938); REBECCA OF SUNNY-BROOK FARM(1938); LITTLE OLD NEW YORK(1940)

Claude Wilson
CRY OF BATTLE(1963); WALLS OF HELL, THE(1964, U.S./Phil.); PASSIONATE STRANGERS, THE(1968, Phil.); WARKILL(1968, U.S./Phil.); BOYS IN COMPANY C, THE(1978, U.S./Hong Kong)
1984
PURPLE HEARTS(1984)
Clifford Wilson
HUDSON'S BAY(1940), tech adv
Constance Wilson
Misc. Silents
FAIR WEEK(1924)
Cronin Wilson
Silents
SQUIBS(1921, Brit.)
Cynthia Wilson
JOHNNY GOT HIS GUN(1971)
Dale Wilson
MOTHER LODE(1982)
Dana Wilson
ONCE A THIEF(1950); SHIRALEE, THE(1957, Brit.); CRY FROM THE STREET, A(1959, Brit.); SEASON OF PASSION(1961, Aus./Brit.)
David Wilson
MARCH OF THE SPRING HARE(1969), ed; GOING HOME(1971); ROOM-MATES(1971), ed; SEVEN UPS, THE(1973); AUDREY ROSE(1977); ALMOST SUMMER(1978); GRAY LADY DOWN(1978); HOMETOWN U.S.A.(1979); EDDIE AND THE CRUISERS(1983)
Demond Wilson
DEALING: OR THE BERKELEY-TO-BOSTON FORTY-BRICK LOST-BAG BLUES(1971); ORGANIZATION, THE(1971); FULL MOON HIGH(1982)
Dennis Wilson
GIRLS ON THE BEACH(1965); TWO-LANE BLACKTOP(1971)
Diana Wilson
GIRL IN THE NIGHT, THE(1931, Brit.); WAY OF YOUTH, THE(1934, Brit.); CHECKMATE(1973)
Dianne Lynn Wilson
WRONG IS RIGHT(1982)
Dick Wilson
TATTERED DRESS, THE(1957); DIARY OF A MADMAN(1963); WHAT A WAY TO GO(1964); SHAKIEST GUN IN THE WEST, THE(1968); WORLD'S GREATEST ATHLETE, THE(1973)
Dixie Wilson
EBB TIDE(1932, Brit.), w
Silents
AFFAIR OF THE FOLLIES, AN(1927), w
Doc Wilson
BARBARY COAST(1935)
Don Wilson
RIDERS OF THE CACTUS(1931); MILLION DOLLAR LEGS(1932); WHARF ANGEL(1934); BEHIND THE MIKE(1937); MEET THE MISSUS(1937); RADIO CITY REVELS(1938); COMIN' ROUND THE MOUNTAIN(1940); TWO GIRLS ON BROADWAY(1940); VILLAGE BARN DANCE(1940); ROUNDUP, THE(1941); SWING IT SOLDIER(1941); FOOTLIGHT SERENADE(1942); HI, NEIGHBOR(1942); DU BARRY WAS A LADY(1943); THANK YOUR LUCKY STARS(1943); JAMBOREE(1944); THIN MAN GOES HOME, THE(1944); OUT OF THIS WORLD(1945); RADIO STARS ON PARADE(1945); CHASE, THE(1946); KID FROM BOOKLYN, THE(1946); SENATOR WAS INDISCREET, THE(1947); LARCENY(1948); SAILOR BEWARE(1951); NIAGARA(1953); STARS ARE SINGING, THE(1953); LIFE AND TIMES OF CHESTER-ANGUS RAMSGOOD, THE(1971, Can.), p
Misc. Talkies
DIRTY GERTY FROM HARLEM, USA(1946)
Donald Wilson
MISS ROBIN HOOD(1952, Brit.), p; THREE CASES OF MURDER(1955, Brit.), w; KEEPER, THE(1976, Can.), p, w
Donald B. Wilson
FLOODTIDE(1949, Brit.), p, w; POET'S PUB(1949, Brit.), p; STOP PRESS GIRL(1949, Brit.), p; WARNING TO WANTONS, A(1949, Brit.), p&d, w; PRELUDE TO FAME(1950, Brit.), p
Donald Powell Wilson
MY SIX CONVICTS(1952), w
Dooley Wilson
CAIRO(1942); CASABLANCA(1942); MY FAVORITE BLONDE(1942); NIGHT IN NEW ORLEANS, A(1942); TAKE A LETTER, DARLING(1942); HIGHER AND HIGHER(1943); STORMY WEATHER(1943); TWO TICKETS TO LONDON(1943); SEVEN DAYS ASHORE(1944); RACING LUCK(1948); TRIPLE THREAT(1948); COME TO THE STABLE(1949); FREE FOR ALL(1949); KNOCK ON ANY DOOR(1949); FATHER IS A BACHELOR(1950); NO MAN OF HER OWN(1950); PASSAGE WEST(1951)
Misc. Talkies
KEEP PUNCHING(1939)
Dorothy Wilson
AGE OF CONSENT(1932); BEFORE DAWN(1933); LUCKY DEVILS(1933); MEN OF AMERICA(1933); SCARLET RIVER(1933); ABOVE THE CLOUDS(1934); EIGHT GIRLS IN A BOAT(1934); HIS GREATEST GAMBLE(1934); MERRY WIDOW, THE(1934); WHITE PARADE, THE(1934); BAD BOY(1935); IN OLD KENTUCKY(1935); LAST DAYS OF POMPEII, THE(1935); ONE IN A MILLION(1935); WHEN A MAN'S A MAN(1935); CRAIG'S WIFE(1936); MILKY WAY, THE(1936); SPEED TO SPARE(1937)
Misc. Talkies
DANGEROUS APPOINTMENT(1934)
Dorothy Clarke Wilson
TEN COMMANDMENTS, THE(1956), w
Doug Wilson
GET OUTTA TOWN(1960); VIOLENT ONES, THE(1967), w
Douglas Wilson
STRIKE UP THE BAND(1940); NAKED IN THE SUN(1957); GET OUTTA TOWN(1960), p, ed
Earl Wilson
COLLEGE CONFIDENTIAL(1960); NIGHT OF EVIL(1962); BEACH BLANKET BINGO(1965); WHERE WERE YOU WHEN THE LIGHTS WENT OUT?(1968)

Ed Wilson
Silents
GOLD RUSH, THE(1925)
Eddie Wilson
I LIKE IT THAT WAY(1934)
Edith Wilson
TO HAVE AND HAVE NOT(1944)
Silents
KID, THE(1921)
Edmond Wilson
AND HOPE TO DIE(1972 Fr/US), ph
Edna Wilson
Silents
THOSE WITHOUT SIN(1917)
Edna Mae Wilson
Silents
ONCE A PLUMBER(1920)
Ednamae Wilson
Misc. Silents
JESS(1914)
Eleanor Wilson
ALICE'S RESTAURANT(1969)
Eleanor D. Wilson
REDS(1981)
Elise Jane Wilson
Misc. Silents
CITY OF TEARS, THE(1918), d
Elizabeth Wilson
CAVE OF OUTLAWS(1951), w; PATTERNS(1956); GODDESS, THE(1958); RAW WIND IN EDEN(1958), w; TUNNEL OF LOVE, THE(1958); HAPPY ANNIVERSARY(1959); TOO HOT TO HANDLE(1961, Brit.); CHILD IS WAITING, A(1963); INVITATION TO A GUNFIGHTER(1964), w; GRADUATE, THE(1967); TIGER MAKES OUT, THE(1967); JENNY(1969); CATCH-22(1970); LITTLE MURDERS(1971); DAY OF THE DOLPHIN, THE(1973); MAN ON A SWING(1974); HAPPY HOOKER, THE(1975); PRISONER OF SECOND AVENUE, THE(1975); NINE TO FIVE(1980); INCREDIBLE SHRINKING WOMAN, THE(1981)
1984
ULTIMATE SOLUTION OF GRACE QUIGLEY, THE(1984)
Elizabeth W. Wilson
PICNIC(1955)
Elsie Jane Wilson
Silents
TEMPTATION(1915); OLIVER TWIST(1916); NEW LOVE FOR OLD(1918), d
Misc. Silents
LURE OF THE MASK, THE(1915); EVIL WOMEN DO, THE(1916); CRICKET, THE(1917), d; LITTLE PIRATE, THE(1917), d; MOTHER O'MINE(1917); MY LITTLE BOY(1917), d; SILENT LADY, THE(1917), d; BEAUTY IN CHAINS(1918), d; DREAM LADY, THE(1918), d; LURE OF LUXURY, THE(1918), d; GAME'S UP, THE(1919), d
Elzada Wilson
MY FAIR LADY(1964)
Ernest Wilson
TOY WIFE, THE(1938); SAFARI(1940); PHANTOM COWBOY, THE(1941); LONELY HEARTS(1983, Aus.); NEXT OF KIN(1983, Aus.)
Eunice Wilson
Misc. Talkies
BRAND OF CAIN, THE(1935); SUN TAN RANCH(1948)
Everdinne Wilson
PORGY AND BESS(1959)
F.C. Wilson
SPELL OF AMY NUGENT, THE(1945, Brit.), ed
F. Paul Wilson
KEEP, THE(1983), w
Flip Wilson
UPTOWN SATURDAY NIGHT(1974); FISH THAT SAVED PITTSBURGH, THE(1979); SKATETOWN, U.S.A.(1979)
Forrest Wilson
BLESSED EVENT(1932), w
Frank Wilson
EMPEROR JONES, THE(1933); GREEN PASTURES(1936); AWFUL TRUTH, THE(1937); WATCH ON THE RHINE(1943); BEWARE(1946); SEASON OF PASSION(1961, Aus./Brit.); BEACH BALL(1965), m; ALVIN RIDES AGAIN(1974, Aus.); MONEY MOVERS(1978, Aus.); PATRICK(1979, Aus.); BREAKER MORANT(1980, Aus.); CLUB, THE(1980, Aus.); FATTY FINN(1980, Aus.)
Silents
JUSTICE(1914, Brit.), d; HER BOY(1915, Brit.), d; MUNITION GIRL'S ROMANCE, A(1917, Brit.), d; RAGGED MESSENGER, THE(1917, Brit.), d; SNARE, THE(1918, Brit.), d; LONG ODDS(1922, Brit.); PRODIGAL SON, THE(1923, Brit.)
Misc. Silents
VICAR OF WAKEFIELD, THE(1913, Brit.), d; GREAT POISON MYSTERY, THE(1914, Brit.), d; HEART OF MIDLOTHIAN, THE(1914, Brit.), d; IN THE SHADOW OF BIG BEN(1914, Brit.), d; JUSTICE(1914, Brit.), d; AS THE SUN WENT DOWN(1915, Brit.), d; LANCASHIRE LASS, A(1915, Brit.), d; NIGHTBIRDS OF LONDON, THE(1915, Brit.), d; WHITE HOPE, THE(1915, Brit.), d; BUNCH OF VIOLETS, A(1916, Brit.), d; GRAND BABYLON HOTEL, THE(1916, Brit.), d; CARROTS(1917, Brit.), d; DAUGHTER OF THE WILDS(1917, Brit.), d; ETERNAL TRIANGLE, THE(1917, Brit.), d; GAMBLE FOR LOVE, A(1917, Brit.), d; HER MARRIAGE LINES(1917, Brit.), d; HOUSE OPPOSITE, THE(1917, Brit.), d; MAN BEHIND "THE TIMES", THE(1917, Brit.), d; TURF CONSPIRACY, A(1918, Brit.), d; IRRESISTIBLE FLAPPER, THE(1919, Brit.), d; SOUL'S CRUCIFIXION, A(1919, Brit.), d; WINDING ROAD, THE(1920), d; WITH ALL HER HEART(1920, Brit.), d; WHITE HOPE, THE(1922, Brit.), a, d
Frank C. Wilson
ALL-AMERICAN SWEETHEART(1937); DANGEROUS ADVENTURE, A(1937); DEVIL IS DRIVING, THE(1937); JUSTICE(1914, Brit.), d; EXTORTION(1938); LITTLE MISS ROUGHNECK(1938); MURDER IS NEWS(1939)
Frank J. Wilson
UNDERCOVER MAN, THE(1949), w

Fred Wilson
FROG, THE(1937, Brit.), ed; GIRLS IN THE STREET(1937, Brit.), ed; WHILE THE SUN SHINES(1950, Brit.), ed
Silents
TARZAN OF THE APES(1918); LIGHT OF VICTORY(1919)
Freddie Wilson
PRISONER, THE(1955, Brit.), ed; LAWMAN(1971), ed; CHATO'S LAND(1972), ed; SCORPIO(1973), ed; MOSES(1976, Brit./Ital.), ed; BIG SLEEP, THE½(1978, Brit.), ed
Frederick Wilson
CAESAR AND CLEOPATRA(1946, Brit.), ed; FLOODTIDE(1949, Brit.), d, w; POET'S PUB(1949, Brit.), d; LIFE IN HER HANDS(1951, Brit.), p; PROJECT M7(1953, Brit.), ed; PERSONAL AFFAIR(1954, Brit.), ed; DOCTOR AT SEA(1955, Brit.), ed; ALL FOR MARY(1956, Brit.), ed; IRON PETTICOAT, THE(1956, Brit.), ed; CAMPBELL'S KINGDOM(1957, Brit.), ed; CHECKPOINT(1957, Brit.), ed; DOCTOR AT LARGE(1957, Brit.), ed; WIND CANNOT READ, THE(1958, Brit.), ed; CAPTAIN'S TABLE, THE(1960, Brit.), ed; I AIM AT THE STARS(1960), ed; MYSTERIOUS ISLAND(1961, U.S./Brit.), ed; GUNS OF DARKNESS(1962, Brit.), ed; HELLFIRE CLUB, THE(1963, Brit.), ed; REACH FOR GLORY(1963, Brit.), ed; SWORD OF LANCELOT(1963, Brit.), ed; MODEL MURDER CASE, THE(1964, Brit.), ed; RATTLE OF A SIMPLE MAN(1964, Brit.), ed; THIRD SECRET, THE(1964, Brit.), ed; AMOROUS ADVENTURES OF MOLL FLANDERS, THE(1965), ed; ARABESQUE(1966), ed; QUILLER MEMORANDUM, THE(1966, Brit.), ed; NIGHT COMERS, THE(1971, Brit.), ed; MECHANIC, THE(1972), ed; STONE KILLER, THE(1973), ed
Silents
KILMENY(1915)
Misc. Silents
YOUNG ROMANCE(1915)
Garland Wilson
ON VELVET(1938, Brit.)
Garney Wilson
GUILTY BYSTANDER(1950)
Georges Wilson
GREEN MARE, THE(1961, Fr./Ital.); JOKER, THE(1961, Fr.); LEVIATHAN(1961, Fr.); DEVIL AND THE TEN COMMANDMENTS, THE(1962, Fr.); LONG ABSENCE, THE(1962, Fr./Ital.); LONGEST DAY, THE(1962); SEVEN CAPITAL SINS(1962, Fr./Ital.); FOUR DAYS OF NAPLES, THE(1963, US/Ital.); DISORDER(1964, Fr./Ital.); EMPTY CANVAS, THE(1964, Fr./Ital.); SWEET AND SOUR(1964, Fr./Ital.); FASCIST, THE(1965, Ital.); HIGHWAY PICKUP(1965, Fr./Ital.); YOUNG WORLD, A(1966, Fr./Ital.); MORE THAN A MIRACLE(1967, Ital./Fr.); STRANGER, THE(1967, Algeria/Fr./Ital.); FLY NOW, PAY LATER(1969); BLANCHE(1971, Fr.); THREE MUSKETEERS, THE(1974, Panama); FRENCH WAY, THE(1975, Fr.); ATTACK OF THE KILLER TOMATOES(1978); DEAR DETECTIVE(1978, Fr.); HORSE OF PRIDE(1980, Fr.); GAS(1981, Can.)
Silents
ONE MINUTE TO PLAY(1926)
Gerald Wilson
ROBBERY(1967, Brit.), w; FREE GRASS(1969), w; LAWMAN(1971), w; CHATO'S LAND(1972), w; SCORPIO(1973), w; STONE KILLER, THE(1973), w; FIREPOWER(1979, Brit.), w
Gerard Wilson
STREET IS MY BEAT, THE(1966), ed; HOUSE ON SKULL MOUNTAIN, THE(1974), ed
Gerard J. Wilson
FAREWELL TO ARMS, A(1957), ed
Gerry Wilson
OLD MOTHER RILEY, DETECTIVE(1943, Brit.)
Gertrude Wilson
Silents
WHERE MEN ARE MEN(1921)
Gilbert Wilson
DAWN PATROL, THE(1938); WEST POINT WIDOW(1941); MOSS ROSE(1947); NIGHTMARE ALLEY(1947)
Gladys Wilson
Silents
STARDUST(1921)
Gordon Wilson, Jr.
CASTLE OF BLOOD(1964, Fr./Ital.), w
Grace Wilson
Silents
INTOLERANCE(1916)
Grant Wilson
FOXES(1980)
1984
UP THE CREEK(1984)
Gwenda Wilson
GLORY AT SEA(1952, Brit.); FUSS OVER FEATHERS(1954, Brit.); DANGEROUS AFTERNOON(1961, Brit.)
Hal Wilson
IT'S A WONDERFUL DAY(1949, Brit.), p,d&w
Silents
SABLE LORCHA, THE(1915); LITTLE SCHOOL MA'AM, THE(1916); DINTY(1920); EVERYBODY'S SWEETHEART(1920); ISOBEL(1920); SUDS(1920); CHARGE IT(1921); ACCORDING TO HOYLE(1922); SMILIN' AT TROUBLE(1925)
Misc. Silents
HELL'S OASIS(1920); BLAZE AWAY(1922)
Hamish Wilson
GREYFRIARS BOBBY(1961, Brit.)
Harold Wilson
TREASURE ISLAND(1934); DANGER-LOVE AT WORK(1937), p; LIFE BEGINS IN COLLEGE(1937), p; LOVE IS NEWS(1937), p; LOUISIANA PURCHASE(1941), p; HAPPY GO LUCKY(1943), p; DAUGHTER OF THE JUNGLE(1949), m
Harry Wilson
SHADOW OF THE LAW(1930); TIP-OFF, THE(1931); JUDGE PRIEST(1934); DANTE'S INFERNO(1935); ANYTHING GOES(1936); OUR RELATIONS(1936); BRIDE WORE RED, THE(1937); WRONG ROAD, THE(1937); IF I WERE KING(1938); KING OF THE NEWSBOYS(1938); LET FREEDOM RING(1939); INVISIBLE STRIPES(1940); ONE MILLION B.C.(1940); SHADOW OF THE THIN MAN(1941); NATIVE LAND(1942); LOUISIANA HAYRIDE(1944); LAWLESS BREED, THE(1946); BRUTE FORCE(1947); HIGH BARBAREE(1947); WILD HARVEST(1947); KISS THE BLOOD OFF MY HANDS(1948); SAIGON(1948); THREE MUSKETEERS, THE(1948); BRIDE

FOR SALE(1949); KNOCK ON ANY DOOR(1949); ENFORCER, THE(1951); SCANDAL SHEET(1952); GOLDEN BLADE, THE(1953); CRIME WAVE(1954); SILVER CHALICE, THE(1954); GUYS AND DOLLS(1955); FRANKENSTEIN'S DAUGHTER(1958); SOME LIKE IT HOT(1959); OCEAN'S ELEVEN(1960); ROBIN AND THE SEVEN HOODS(1964)
Harry Leon Wilson
CAMEO KIRBY(1930), w; MAKE ME A STAR(1932), w; RUGGLES OF RED GAP(1935), w; BUNKER BEAN(1936), w; OH DOCTOR(1937), w; MERTON OF THE MOVIES(1947), w; FANCY PANTS(1950), w
Silents
MAN FROM HOME, THE(1914), w; RUGGLES OF RED GAP(1923), w; MERTON OF THE MOVIES(1924), w; OH, DOCTOR(1924), w; HEAD MAN, THE(1928), w
Helena Wilson
1984
WILD HORSES(1984, New Zealand)
Hope Wilson
SALLY'S HOUNDS(1968)
Howard Wilson
ACE OF ACES(1933); FLYING DOWN TO RIO(1933); LOST PATROL, THE,(1934); WAGON WHEELS(1934); CAR 99(1935); HOME ON THE RANGE(1935); I LIVE MY LIFE(1935); MC FADDEN'S FLATS(1935); ROCKY MOUNTAIN MYSTERY(1935); ROMEO AND JULIET(1936); RECOMMENDATION FOR MERCY(1975, Can.)
Hugh Wilson
STROKER ACE(1983), w
1984
POLICE ACADEMY(1984), d, w
Ian Wilson
SPLINTERS IN THE NAVY(1931, Brit.); FACING THE MUSIC(1933, Brit.); BROKEN ROSARY, THE(1934, Brit.); SONG AT EVENTIDE(1934, Brit.); THOSE WERE THE DAYS(1934, Brit.); UNHOLY QUEST, THE(1934, Brit.); BIRDS OF A FEATHER(1935, Brit.); JOY RIDE(1935, Brit.); PLAY UP THE BAND(1935, Brit.); MELODY OF MY HEART(1936, Brit.); SONG OF THE FORGE(1937, Brit.); FATHER O'FLYNN(1938, Irish); DUMMY TALKS, THE(1943, Brit.); MY SISTER AND I(1948, Brit.); LADY CRAVED EXCITEMENT, THE(1950, Brit.); SEVEN DAYS TO NOON(1950, Brit.); HOLIDAY WEEK(1952, Brit.); WHISPERING SMITH VERSUS SCOTLAND YARD(1952, Brit.); FLOATING DUTCHMAN, THE(1953, Brit.); RADIO CAB MURDER(1954, Brit.); SEE HOW THEY RUN(1955, Brit.); ROTTEN TO THE CORE(1956, Brit.); GOOD COMPANIONS, THE(1957, Brit.); HOW TO MURDER A RICH UNCLE(1957, Brit.); JUST MY LUCK(1957, Brit.); KEY MAN, THE(1957, Brit.); LUCKY JIM(1957, Brit.); TIME IS MY ENEMY(1957, Brit.); UP IN THE WORLD(1957, Brit.); HAPPY IS THE BRIDE(1958, Brit.); IDOL ON PARADE(1959, Brit.); I'M ALL RIGHT, JACK(1959, Brit.); TOP FLOOR GIRL(1959, Brit.); UGLY DUCKLING, THE(1959, Brit.); WOMAN'S TEMPTATION, A(1959, Brit.); RISK, THE(1961, Brit.); TWO-WAY STRETCH(1961, Brit.); MY WIFE'S FAMILY(1962, Brit.); PHANTOM OF THE OPERA, THE(1962, Brit.); ROOMMATES(1962, Brit.); CARRY ON CABBIE(1963, Brit.); CARRY ON JACK(1963, Brit.); HEAVENS ABOVE!(1963, Brit.); MY SON, THE VAMPIRE(1963, Brit.); SWINGIN' MAIDEN, THE(1963, Brit.); CARRY ON CLEO(1964, Brit.); RUNAWAY, THE(1964, Brit.); HELP!(1965, Brit.); TELL ME LIES(1968, Brit.), ph; AND SOON THE DARKNESS(1970, Brit.), ph; BARTLEBY(1970, Brit.), ph; FRIGHT(1971, Brit.), ph; GIRL STROKE BOY(1971, Brit.), ph; UP POMPEII(1971, Brit.), ph; UP THE CHASTITY BELT(1971, Brit.), ph; GAWAIN AND THE GREEN KNIGHT(1973, Brit.), ph; CAPTAIN KRONOS: VAMPIRE HUNTER(1974, Brit.), ph; WICKER MAN, THE(1974, Brit.); CHILDREN OF RAGE(1975, Brit.-Israeli), ph; QUATERMASS CONCLUSION(1980, Brit.), ph; PRIVATES ON PARADE(1982), ph
1984
PRIVATES ON PARADE(1984, Brit.), ph
Silents
MASTER OF CRAFT, A(1922, Brit.)
Ilona Wilson
WALK, DON'T RUN(1966); MAD BOMBER, THE(1973); HOW TO SEDUCE A WOMAN(1974)
Irene Wilson
Misc. Talkies
GEORGIA ROSE(1930)
Irma Wilson
YOUNG AS YOU FEEL(1940); ZIEGFELD GIRL(1941)
Dr. W. Wolff
MANULESCU(1933, Ger.), d
Itasco Wilson
BARBAROSA(1982)
J. Donald Wilson
WHISTLER, THE(1944), w; KEY WITNESS(1947), w
J. J. Wilson
LOVE BUG, THE(1968)
J. Skeet Wilson
MURPH THE SURF(1974), p
Jack Wilson
EXCUSE MY GLOVE(1936, Brit.), ph; GOLDEN EARRINGS(1947); FRANCIS GOES TO THE RACES(1951); SON OF THE RENEGADE(1953); PUSHOVER(1954); X-15(1961), makeup; JUMBO(1962), makeup; TRUE GRIT(1969), makeup; NORWOOD(1970), makeup; WUSA(1970), makeup; MODERN PROBLEMS(1981), makeup
Silents
WOMAN OF PARIS, A(1923), ph
Misc. Silents
SHOULDER ARMS(1917)
Jack P. Wilson
TODD KILLINGS, THE(1971), makeup; PAT GARRETT AND BILLY THE KID(1973), makeup
Jackie Wilson
GO, JOHNNY, GO!(1959); TEENAGE MILLIONAIRE(1961)
James Wilson
FLYING FOOL, THE(1931, Brit.), ph; HER STRANGE DESIRE(1931, Brit.), ph; KEEPERS OF YOUTH(1931, Brit.), ph; MAN FROM CHICAGO, THE(1931, Brit.), ph; ARMS AND THE MAN(1932, Brit.), ph; INDISCRETIONS OF EVE(1932, Brit.), ph; LORD CAMBER'S LADIES(1932, Brit.), ph; I SPY(1933, Brit.), ph; TIMBUCTOO(1933, Brit.), ph; SOMETIMES GOOD(1934, Brit.), ph; WHAT HAPPENED THEN?(1934, Brit.), ph; BALL AT SAVOY(1936, Brit.), ph; CROUCHING BEAST, THE(1936, U.S./Brit.), ph; LIVING DEAD, THE(1936, Brit.), ph; SECOND BUREAU(1937, Brit.), ph; WAKE UP FAMOUS(1937, Brit.), ph; WIFE OF GENERAL LING, THE(1938, Brit.), ph; OLD MOTHER RILEY JOINS UP(1939, Brit.), ph; OLD MOTHER RILEY MP(1939,

Brit.), ph; WHAT WOULD YOU DO, CHUMS?(1939, Brit.), ph; AMONG HUMAN WOLVES(1940 Brit.), ph; CROOKS TOUR(1940, Brit.), ph; FACE BEHIND THE SCAR(1940, Brit.), ph; LAUGH IT OFF(1940, Brit.), ph; OLD MOTHER RILEY IN BUSINESS(1940, Brit.), ph; OLD MOTHER RILEY IN SOCIETY(1940, Brit.), ph; COMMON TOUCH, THE(1941, Brit.), ph; OLD MOTHER RILEY'S CIRCUS(1941, Brit.), ph; OLD MOTHER RILEY'S GHOSTS(1941, Brit.), ph; LET THE PEOPLE SING(1942, Brit.), ph; SALUTE JOHN CITIZEN(1942, Brit.), ph; OLD MOTHER RILEY, DETECTIVE(1943, Brit.), ph; OLD MOTHER RILEY OVERSEAS(1943, Brit.), ph; CANDLES AT NINE(1944, Brit.), ph; GIVE ME THE STARS(1944, Brit.), ph; HEAVEN IS ROUND THE CORNER(1944, Brit.), ph; TWILIGHT HOUR(1944, Brit.), ph; APPOINTMENT WITH CRIME(1945, Brit.), ph; ECHO MURDERS, THE(1945, Brit.), ph; LOVE ON THE DOLE(1945, Brit.), ph; OLD MOTHER RILEY AT HOME(1945, Brit.), ph; STRAWBERRY ROAN(1945, Brit.), ph; GAY INTRUDERS, THE(1946, Brit.), ph; WOMAN TO WOMAN(1946, Brit.), ph; DUAL ALIBI(1947, Brit.), ph; COUNTER BLAST(1948, Brit.), ph; DEVIL'S PLOT, THE(1948, Brit.), ph; MRS. FITZHERBERT(1950, Brit.), ph; NO ROOM AT THE INN(1950, Brit.), ph; OLD MOTHER RILEY'S JUNGLE TREASURE(1951, Brit.), ph; RELUCTANT HEROES(1951, Brit.), ph; TAKE ME TO PARIS(1951, Brit.), ph; WORM'S EYE VIEW(1951, Brit.), ph; LITTLE BIG SHOT(1952, Brit.), ph; OLD MOTHER RILEY(1952, Brit.), ph; DIPLOMATIC PASSPORT(1954, Brit.), ph; GAY DOG, THE(1954, Brit.), ph; TALE OF THREE WOMEN, A(1954, Brit.), ph; TIME TO KILL, A(1955, Brit.), ph; BOOBY TRAP(1957, Brit.), ph; MANHUNT IN THE JUNGLE(1958), ph; OUTCASTS OF THE CITY(1958); TELL-TALE HEART, THE(1962, Brit.), ph; DOUBLE, THE(1963, Brit), ph; 20,000 POUNDS KISS, THE(1964, Brit.), ph; ACT OF MURDER(1965, Brit.), ph; INVASION(1965, Brit.), ph; INCIDENT AT MIDNIGHT(1966, Brit.), ph; MAIN CHANCE, THE(1966, Brit.), ph; PARTNER, THE(1966, Brit.), ph; RICOCHET(1966, Brit.), ph; ON THE RUN(1967, Brit.), ph

Maj. James Wilson
TOWARD THE UNKNOWN(1956)

James L. Wilson
SCREAMS OF A WINTER NIGHT(1979), p, d

Jan Wilson
HIDDEN HOMICIDE(1959, Brit.); AMERICAN GRAFFITI(1973)

Janice Wilson
HEADING FOR HEAVEN(1947)
Silents
MASK, THE(1921); SWAMP, THE(1921)
Misc. Silents
WORLD AFLAME, THE(1919)

Janis Wilson
NOW, VOYAGER(1942); WATCH ON THE RHINE(1943); SNAFU(1945); MY REPUTATION(1946); STRANGE LOVE OF MARTHA IVERS, THE(1946); CREEPER, THE(1948)
Misc. Silents
WHITE CIRCLE, THE(1920)

Jay Wilson
Silents
ASHES OF EMBERS(1916)

Jeanna Wilson
WHERE THE RED FERN GROWS(1974)

Jeannie Wilson
DEVIL AND MAX DEVLIN, THE(1981)
Misc. Talkies
STORYVILLE(1974)

Jennifer Wilson
PRIVATE POOLEY(1962, Brit./E. Ger.)

Jerome Wilson
Silents
PRETENDERS, THE(1916)

Jerome N. Wilson
Silents
WOMAN'S MAN(1920), w; WHITE BLACK SHEEP, THE(1926), w

Jerry Wilson
REG'LAR FELLERS(1941)

Jim Wilson
CHARLIE, THE LONESOME COUGAR(1967); JAWS II(1978); STACY'S KNIGHTS(1983), d

Jimmy Wilson
TAXI FOR TWO(1929, Brit.), ph; PRICE OF A SONG, THE(1935, Brit.), ph; SECOND MR. BUSH, THE(1940, Brit.), ph; THOSE KIDS FROM TOWN(1942, Brit.), ph; WE'LL SMILE AGAIN(1942, Brit.), ph; DUMMY TALKS, THE(1943, Brit.), ph; SHIPBUILDERS, THE(1943, Brit.), ph; THEATRE ROYAL(1943, Brit.), ph; WHEN WE ARE MARRIED(1943, Brit.), ph; THREE'S COMPANY(1953, Brit.), ph; DEATH OF MICHAEL TURBIN, THE(1954, Brit.), ph; DESTINATION MILAN(1954, Brit.), ph; LAST MOMENT, THE(1954, Brit.), ph; RED DRESS, THE(1954, Brit.), ph; YELLOW ROBE, THE(1954, Brit.), ph; COUNT OF TWELVE(1955, Brit.), ph; FINAL COLUMN, THE(1955, Brit.), ph; ONE JUST MAN(1955, Brit.), ph; NOT SO DUSTY(1956, Brit.), ph; SATELLITE IN THE SKY(1956), ph; DEPRAVED, THE(1957, Brit.), ph; OPERATION MURDER(1957, Brit.), ph; SON OF A STRANGER(1957, Brit.), ph; THREE SUNDAYS TO LIVE(1957, Brit.), ph; WOMAN OF MYSTERY, A(1957, Brit.), ph; HIGH HELL(1958), ph; LINKS OF JUSTICE(1958), ph; MOMENT OF INDISCRETION(1958, Brit.), ph; ON THE RUN(1958, Brit.), ph; THREE CROOKED MEN(1958, Brit.), ph; WOMAN POSSESSED, A(1958, Brit.), ph; CRASH DRIVE(1959, Brit.), ph; HIGH JUMP(1959, Brit.), ph; HONOURABLE MURDER, AN(1959, Brit.), ph; INNOCENT MEETING(1959, Brit.), ph; MAN ACCUSED(1959), ph; NO SAFETY AHEAD(1959, Brit.), ph; TOP FLOOR GIRL(1959, Brit.), ph; WEB OF SUSPICION(1959, Brit.), ph; WOMAN'S TEMPTATION, A(1959, Brit.), ph; DATE AT MIDNIGHT(1960, Brit.), ph; NIGHT TRAIN FOR INVERNESS(1960, Brit.), ph

Jody Wilson
CHAMP, THE(1979); ABSENCE OF MALICE(1981); LOVE CHILD(1982)

Joe Wilson
SECOND-HAND HEARTS(1981)

John Wilson
RED RIVER VALLEY(1936); OUTSIDE THESE WALLS(1939); KING AND COUNTRY(1964, Brit.), w; J.W. COOP(1971); DRAUGHTSMAN'S CONTRACT, THE(1983, Brit.), ed

John B. Wilson
KEY TO HARMONY(1935, Brit.), w

John David Wilson
SHINBONE ALLEY(1971), d, prod d

John Fleming Wilson
MAN WHO CAME BACK, THE(1931), w

John R. Wilson
TOY, THE(1982)

John Rowan Wilson
BEHIND THE MASK(1958, Brit.), w

John T. Wilson
BLACK KLANSMAN, THE(1966), w; GIRL IN GOLD BOOTS(1968), w

Johnny Wilson
DYNAMITE JOHNSON(1978, Phil.)

Joseph Carter Wilson
COOLEY HIGH(1975)

Josephine Wilson
CITADEL, THE(1938); LADY VANISHES, THE(1938, Brit.); SOUTH RIDING(1938, Brit.); THOSE KIDS FROM TOWN(1942, Brit.); DARK TOWER, THE(1943, Brit.); WE DIVE AT DAWN(1943, Brit.); UNCENSORED(1944, Brit.); QUIET WEEKEND(1948, Brit.); CHANCE OF A LIFETIME(1950, Brit.); END OF THE AFFAIR, THE(1955, Brit.)

Judy Wilson
THREE SISTERS(1974, Brit.)

Julie Wilson
STRANGE ONE, THE(1957); THIS COULD BE THE NIGHT(1957)

Kara Wilson
JANE EYRE(1971, Brit.); REUBEN, REUBEN(1983)

Katherine Wilson
MIDNIGHT(1934)
Misc. Silents
NEW TOYS(1925)

Kathleen Wilson
HITLER'S CHILDREN(1942)

Kathryn Wilson
IN NAME ONLY(1939); CASBAH(1948); MATING SEASON, THE(1951)

Kathy Wilson
JAWS II(1978)

Keith Wilson
PARDNERS(1956); INTERNATIONAL VELVET(1978, Brit.), prod d; YESTERDAY'S HERO(1979, Brit.), prod d
1984
SLAYGROUND(1984, Brit.), prod d

Ken Wilson
MEET ME IN ST. LOUIS(1944)

Kenneth Wilson
CAPTAINS COURAGEOUS(1937)

Kevin Wilson
DAWN(1979, Aus.)
1984
WILD HORSES(1984, New Zealand)

Kevin J. Wilson
SKIN DEEP(1978, New Zealand); PICTURES(1982, New Zealand)

Lambert Wilson
CHANEL SOLITAIRE(1981); FIVE DAYS ONE SUMMER(1982)
1984
SAHARA(1984)

Larry Wilson
DISC JOCKEY(1951)

Lee Wilson
LOOKING UP(1977)

Lester Wilson
SPARKLE(1976), ch; SATURDAY NIGHT FEVER(1977), ch
1984
BEAT STREET(1984), ch

Lewis Wilson
FIRST COMES COURAGE(1943); THERE'S SOMETHING ABOUT A SOLDIER(1943); ONCE UPON A TIME(1944); RACKET MAN, THE(1944); SAILOR'S HOLIDAY(1944); REDHEAD FROM MANHATTAN(1954)

Lin Wilson
1984
BROTHER FROM ANOTHER PLANET, THE(1984), set d

Lionel Wilson
WORLD OF HANS CHRISTIAN ANDERSEN, THE(1971, Jap.)

Lionel G. Wilson
LANDLORD, THE(1970)

Lisa Wilson
NO HOLDS BARRED(1952)

Lisle Wilson
MISSISSIPPI SUMMER(1971); SISTERS(1973); INCREDIBLE MELTING MAN, THE(1978)

Lloyd Wilson
SIX WEEKS(1982)

Lois Wilson
ON TRIAL(1928); CONQUEST(1929); GAMBLERS, THE(1929); KID GLOVES(1929); FURIES, THE(1930); LOVIN' THE LADIES(1930); ONCE A GENTLEMAN(1930); WEDDING RINGS(1930); AGE FOR LOVE, THE(1931); SEED(1931); DEVIL IS DRIVING, THE(1932); DIVORCE IN THE FAMILY(1932); EXPERT, THE(1932); LAW AND ORDER(1932); RIDER OF DEATH VALLEY(1932); SECRETS OF WU SIN(1932); THE CRASH(1932); DELUGE(1933); FEMALE(1933); LAUGHING AT LIFE(1933); OBEY THE LAW(1933); BRIGHT EYES(1934); IN THE MONEY(1934); NO GREATER GLORY(1934); SHOW-OFF, THE(1934); TICKET TO CRIME(1934); BORN TO GAMBLE(1935); CAPPY RICKS RETURNS(1935); PUBLIC OPINION(1935); SCHOOL FOR GIRLS(1935); SOCIETY FEVER(1935); YOUR UNCLE DUDLEY(1935); RETURN OF JIMMY VALENTINE, THE(1936); WEDDING PRESENT(1936); LAUGHING AT TROUBLE(1937); BAD LITTLE ANGEL(1939); LIFE RETURNS(1939); NOBODY'S CHILDREN(1940); FOR BEAUTY'S SAKE(1941); GIRL FROM JONES BEACH, THE(1949)
Misc. Talkies
TEMPTATION(1930); DRIFTING SOULS(1932)
Silents
HIS ROBE OF HONOR(1918); PRISONER OF THE PINES(1918); END OF THE GAME, THE(1919); MIDSUMMER MADNESS(1920); THOU ART THE MAN(1920);

WHAT'S YOUR HURRY?(1920); CITY OF SILENT MEN(1921); WHAT EVERY WOMAN KNOWS(1921); OUR LEADING CITIZEN(1922); WORLD'S CHAMPION, THE(1922); COVERED WAGON, THE(1923); ONLY 38(1923); RUGGLES OF RED GAP(1923); TO THE LAST MAN(1923); ANOTHER SCANDAL(1924); ICE-BOUND(1924); MONSIEUR BEAUCAIRE(1924); NORTH OF 36(1924); RUGGED WATER(1925); BLUEBEARD'S SEVEN WIVES(1926); GREAT GATSBY, THE(1926); LET'S GET MARRIED(1926); ALIAS THE LONE WOLF(1927); FRENCH DRESSING(1927); NEW YORK(1927); RANSOM(1928); OBJECT–ALIMONY(1929)

Misc. Silents
BECKONING TRAIL, THE(1916); GAY LORD WARING, THE(1916); LANDON'S LEGACY(1916); MORALS OF HILDA, THE(1916); POOL OF FLAME, THE(1916); SILENT BATTLE, THE(1916); SON OF THE IMMORTALS, A(1916); MAN'S MAN, A(1917); TREASON(1917); BELLS, THE(1918); THREE X GORDON(1918); TURN OF THE CARD, THE(1918); BEST MAN, THE(1919); COME AGAIN SMITH(1919); DRIFTERS, THE(1919); GATES OF BRASS(1919); IT PAYS TO ADVERTISE(1919); PRICE WOMAN PAYS, THE(1919); WHY SMITH LEFT HOME(1919); BURGLAR-PROOF(1920); CITY OF MASKS, THE(1920); FULL HOUSE, A(1920); LOVE INSURANCE(1920); TOO MUCH JOHNSON(1920); WHO'S YOUR SERVANT?(1920); HELL DIGGERS, THE(1921); LOST ROMANCE, THE(1921); MISS LULU BETT(1921); BROAD DAYLIGHT(1922); IS MATRIMONY A FAILURE?(1922); MANSLAUGHTER(1922); WITHOUT COMPROMISE(1922); CALL OF THE CANYON, THE(1923); MAN WHO FIGHTS ALONE, THE(1924); PIED PIPER MALONE(1924); CONTRABAND(1925); IRISH LUCK(1925); THUNDERING HERD, THE(1925); VANISHING AMERICAN, THE(1925); WELCOME HOME(1925); SHOW OFF, THE(1926); BROADWAY NIGHTS(1927); GINGHAM GIRL, THE(1927); CONEY ISLAND(1928); SALLY'S SHOULDERS(1928)

Lonnie Wilson
SMOKY MOUNTAIN MELODY(1949)

Louise Wilson
FORCE OF EVIL(1948), cos; CAUGHT(1949), cos

Lulee Wilson
Silents
WEDDING MARCH, THE(1927)

Lydia Wilson
NETWORK(1976)

Lynn Wilson
HAPPY BIRTHDAY TO ME(1981)

M.K. Wilson
Silents
RIDERS OF VENGEANCE(1919)

Mak Wilson
1984
GREYSTOKE: THE LEGEND OF TARZAN, LORD OF THE APES(1984)

Manning Wilson
SET-UP, THE(1963, Brit.); HANDS OF ORLAC, THE(1964, Brit./Fr.); PANIC(1966, Brit.); JOANNA(1968, Brit.); POPE JOAN(1972, Brit.); TALES FROM THE CRYPT(1972, Brit.)

Mar Sue Wilson
SCREAMS OF A WINTER NIGHT(1979), set d & cos

Marc G. Wilson
1984
MAKING THE GRADE(1984)

Margery Wilson
Silents
CORNER IN COLLEENS, A(1916); PRIMAL LURE, THE(1916); BRIDE OF HATE, THE(1917); LAST OF THE INGRAHAMS, THE(1917); FLAMES OF CHANCE, THE(1918); OFFENDERS, THE(1924)
Misc. Silents
DOUBLE TROUBLE(1915); HONORABLE ALGY, THE(1916); RETURN OF "DRAW" EGAN, THE(1916); SIN YE DO, THE(1916); CLODHOPPER, THE(1917); DESERT MAN, THE(1917); GUNFIGHTER, THE(1917); MOTHER INSTINCT, THE(1917); MOUNTAIN DEW(1917); WILD SUMAC(1917); WOLF LOWRY(1917); HAND AT THE WINDOW, THE(1918); HARD ROCK BREED, THE(1918); LAW OF THE GREAT NORTHWEST, THE(1918); MARKED CARDS(1918); OLD LOVES FOR NEW(1918); WITHOUT HONOR(1918); DESERT GOLD(1919); VENUS IN THE EAST(1919); BLOOMING ANGEL, THE(1920); THAT SOMETHING(1921), a, d; INSINUATION(1922), a, d; WHY NOT MARRY?(1922)

Margie Wilson
Misc. Silents
BRED IN THE BONE(1915)

Marie Wilson
BROADWAY HOSTESS(1935); MISS PACIFIC FLEET(1935); BIG NOISE, THE(1936); CHINA CLIPPER(1936); COLLEEN(1936); KING OF HOCKEY(1936); SATAN MET A LADY(1936); GREAT GARRICK, THE(1937); MELODY FOR TWO(1937); PUBLIC WEDDING(1937); BOY MEETS GIRL(1938); BROADWAY MUSKETEERS(1938); FOOLS FOR SCANDAL(1938); INVISIBLE MENACE, THE(1938); COWBOY QUARTERBACK(1939); SHOULD HUSBANDS WORK?(1939); SWEEPSTAKES WINNER(1939); WATERFRONT(1939); FLYING BLIND(1941); ROOKIES ON PARADE(1941); VIRGINIA(1941); BROADWAY(1942); HARVARD, HERE I COME(1942); SHE'S IN THE ARMY(1942); MUSIC FOR MILLIONS(1944); SHINE ON, HARVEST MOON(1944); YOU CAN'T RATION LOVE(1944); NO LEAVE, NO LOVE(1946); YOUNG WIDOW(1946); LINDA BE GOOD(1947); PRIVATE AFFAIRS OF BEL AMI, THE(1947); MY FRIEND IRMA(1949); MY FRIEND IRMA GOES WEST(1950); GIRL IN EVERY PORT, A(1952); NEVER WAVE AT A WAC(1952); MARRY ME AGAIN(1953); STORY OF MANKIND, THE(1957); MR. HOBBS TAKES A VACATION(1962)
Misc. Talkies
FABULOUS JOE, THE(1946)

Marjorie Wilson
Misc. Silents
HOUSE OF WHISPERS, THE(1920)

Marjory Wilson
Silents
EYE OF THE NIGHT, THE(1916)

Marriott Wilson
HOUSE ON 92ND STREET, THE(1945)

Mary Wilson
FURTHER UP THE CREEK!(1958, Brit.); UGLY DUCKLING, THE(1959, Brit.)

Mary Louise Wilson
GOING HOME(1971); KLUTE(1971); UP THE SANDBOX(1972); KING OF THE GYPSIES(1978); BEST LITTLE WHOREHOUSE IN TEXAS, THE(1982); ZELIG(1983)

Matthew Wilson
LET THE BALLOON GO(1977, Aus.)

Maurice Wilson
ESCAPE BY NIGHT(1965, Brit.), w

Maurice J. Wilson
SLEEPING PARTNERS(1930, Brit.), p; SAM SMALL LEAVES TOWN(1937, Brit.), p; VOICE WITHIN, THE(1945, Brit.), d; WHAT DO WE DO NOW?(1945, Brit.), p; TURNERS OF PROSPECT ROAD, THE(1947, Brit.), d; TALE OF FIVE WOMEN, A(1951, Brit.), p, w; GUILTY?(1956, Brit.), w; HOUSE IN MARSH ROAD, THE(1960, Brit.), p, w; JACKPOT(1960, Brit.), p, w; PRICE OF SILENCE, THE(1960, Brit.), p, w; THIRD ALIBI, THE(1961, Brit.), p, w; OUT OF THE FOG(1962, Brit.), p; SHE KNOWS Y'KNOW(1962, Brit.), p, w; MASTER SPY(1964, Brit.), p, w; CUCKOO PATROL(1965, Brit.), p; ESCAPE BY NIGHT(1965, Brit.), p; WHO KILLED THE CAT?(1966, Brit.), p, w

Max Wilson
CAMPUS SLEUTH(1948), w

May Wilson
Silents
DULCY(1923)

Michael Wilson
MEN IN HER LIFE, THE(1941), w; BAR 20(1943), w; BORDER PATROL(1943), w; COLT COMRADES(1943), w; FORTY THIEVES(1944), w; PLACE IN THE SUN, A(1951), w; FIVE FINGERS(1952), w; FRIENDLY PERSUASION(1956), w; LAWRENCE OF ARABIA(1962, Brit.), w; SANDPIPER, THE(1965), w; PLANET OF THE APES(1968), w; CHE!(1969), w
1984
HEART OF THE STAG(1984, New Zealand)

Michael G. Wilson
FOR YOUR EYES ONLY(1981), w; OCTOPUSSY(1983, Brit.), w

Michelle Wilson
TRIAL OF BILLY JACK, THE(1974)

Millard Wilson
Misc. Silents
PRIMITIVE WOMAN, THE(1918)

Millard K. Wilson
Silents
NANCY'S BIRTHRIGHT(1916)
Misc. Silents
IN THE WEB OF THE GRAFTERS(1916); FIELD OF HONOR, THE(1917); WOMAN'S FOOL, A(1918)

Miriam Wilson
CAPTURE THAT CAPSULE(1961)

Mitchell Wilson
WOMAN ON THE BEACH, THE(1947), w

Morris Wilson
PEER GYNT(1965)

Mortimer Wilson
Silents
THIEF OF BAGDAD, THE(1924), m; DON Q, SON OF ZORRO(1925), m; BLACK PIRATE, THE(1926), m

Nancy Wilson
FAST TIMES AT RIDGEMONT HIGH(1982); BIG SCORE, THE(1983)
1984
WILD LIFE, THE(1984)

Ned Wilson
JEREMY(1973); BORN AGAIN(1978); ONION FIELD, THE(1979)

Neil Wilson
ISLAND RESCUE(1952, Brit.); GREEN SCARF, THE(1954, Brit.); TIME OF HIS LIFE, THE(1955, Brit.); LADYKILLERS, THE(1956, Brit.); MURDER ON APPROVAL(1956, Brit.); PASSPORT TO TREASON(1956, Brit.); TIME IS MY ENEMY(1957, Brit.); X THE UNKNOWN(1957, Brit.); NO SAFETY AHEAD(1959, Brit.); OFFBEAT(1961, Brit.); SHE KNOWS Y'KNOW(1962, Brit.); THESE ARE THE DAMNED(1965, Brit.); PARTNER, THE(1966, Brit.); STAIRCASE(1969 U.S./Brit./Fr.); LAST GRENADE, THE(1970, Brit.); CLOCKWORK ORANGE, A(1971, Brit.); DR. JEKYLL AND SISTER HYDE(1971, Brit.); DULCIMA(1971, Brit.); GET CHARLIE TULLY(1976, Brit.)

Nita Wilson
WOMEN AND BLOODY TERROR(1970)

Patricia Wilson
WHEN TOMORROW DIES(1966, Can.)

Paul Wilson
TERROR IN THE WAX MUSEUM(1973); RITZ, THE(1976), ph; PACK, THE(1977); HISTORY OF THE WORLD, PART 1(1981), ph; I'M DANCING AS FAST AS I CAN(1982); BANZAI(1983, Fr.), spec eff; BRAINWAVES(1983)
1984
EVERY PICTURE TELLS A STORY(1984, Brit.)

Perry Wilson
FEAR STRIKES OUT(1957); MATCHMAKER, THE(1958)

Ralph Wilson
IT HAPPENED HERE(1966, Brit.)

Rathmell Wilson
Silents
LOVE(1916, Brit.), w

Raymond Guy Wilson
DR. COPPELIUS(1968, U.S./Span.), m

Reagan Wilson
BLOOD MANIA(1971)

Reagon Wilson
Misc. Talkies
RUNNING WITH THE DEVIL(1973)

Rebecca Wilson
CHATO'S LAND(1972)

Rex Wilson
Silents
ORA PRO NOBIS(1917, Brit.), d; LEAD, KINDLY LIGHT(1918, Brit.), d; ONWARD CHRISTIAN SOLDIERS(1918, Brit.), d; MRS. THOMPSON(1919, Brit.), d; ST. ELMO(1923, Brit.), d&w

Misc. Silents
TOM BROWN'S SCHOOLDAYS(1916, Brit.), d; LIFE OF LORD KITCHENER, THE(1917, Brit.), d; GOD BLESS OUR RED, WHITE AND BLUE(1918), d; MAN WHO WON, THE(1918, Brit.), d; TINKER, TAILOR, SOLDIER, SAILOR(1918, Brit.), d; IN BONDAGE(1919, Brit.), d; RIGHT ELEMENT, THE(1919, Brit.), d; SOME ARTIST(1919, Brit.), d; SWEETHEARTS(1919, Brit.), d; PILLARS OF SOCIETY(1920, Brit.), d; UNMARRIED(1920, Brit.), d; TILLY OF BLOOMSBURY(1921, Brit.), d

Richard Wilson
LADY FROM SHANGHAI, THE(1948); I'D CLIMB THE HIGHEST MOUNTAIN(1951); GOLDEN BLADE, THE(1953), p; MA AND PA KETTLE AT HOME(1954), p; RICOCHET ROMANCE(1954), p; MAN WITH THE GUN(1955), d, w; KETTLES IN THE OZARKS, THE(1956), p; BIG BOODLE, THE(1957), d; RAW WIND IN EDEN(1958), d, w; AL CAPONE(1959), d; PAY OR DIE(1960), p&d; WALL OF NOISE(1963), d; INVITATION TO A GUNFIGHTER(1964), p&d; w; JOHN GOLDFARB, PLEASE COME HOME(1964); THREE IN THE ATTIC(1968), p&d; JUNKET 89(1970, Brit.); SKULLDUGGERY(1970), d
1984
PASSAGE TO INDIA, A(1984, Brit.)

Rita Wilson
Misc. Talkies
DAY IT CAME TO EARTH, THE(1979)

Robert Wilson
BIG GAME, THE(1936); VIVACIOUS LADY(1938); DAY OF TRIUMPH(1954); WRITTEN ON THE WIND(1956)

Robert Brian Wilson
1984
SILENT NIGHT, DEADLY NIGHT(1984)

Robert D. Wilson
TOOTSIE(1982)

Roberta Wilson
Silents
MORE TROUBLE(1918)
Misc. Silents
HERITAGE OF HATE, THE(1916); ISLE OF LIFE, THE(1916)

Rod Wilson
HANDS ACROSS THE TABLE(1935); PRINCESS AND THE MAGIC FROG, THE(1965), makeup

Roger Wilson
SATAN'S BED(1965), p; PORKY'S(1982); PORKY'S II: THE NEXT DAY(1983)
1984
SECOND TIME LUCKY(1984, Aus./New Zealand)

Roger L. Wilson
GOIN' SOUTH(1978)

Ronald Wilson
HELL, HEAVEN OR HOBOKEN(1958, Brit.); ENEMY FROM SPACE(1957, Brit.); HAND, THE(1960, Brit.)

Ross Wilson
20TH CENTURY OZ(1977, Aus.), m

Roy Wilson
HELL'S ANGELS(1930)

S.J. Wilson
TO FIND A MAN(1972), w

Sally Wilson
MARATHON MAN(1976)

Sandy Wilson
BOY FRIEND, THE(1971, Brit.), w

Sara Wilson
SIDELONG GLANCES OF A PIGEON KICKER, THE(1970)

Scott Wilson
IN COLD BLOOD(1967); IN THE HEAT OF THE NIGHT(1967); CASTLE KEEP(1969); GYPSY MOTHS, THE(1969); GRISSOM GANG, THE(1971); NEW CENTURIONS, THE(1972); LOLLY-MADONNA XXX(1973); GREAT GATSBY, THE(1974); PASSOVER PLOT, THE(1976, Israel); NINTH CONFIGURATION, THE(1980); RIGHT STUFF, THE(1983)
1984
ON THE LINE(1984, Span.)

Serretta Wilson
BEYOND THE FOG(1981, Brit.)

Shan Wilson
HOPSCOTCH(1980)

Sherry Wilson
Misc. Talkies
TEASERS, THE(1977)

Shirley Wilson
LOVE ME OR LEAVE ME(1955)

Sidney Wilson
YOU LUCKY PEOPLE(1955, Brit.), w

Sloan Wilson
MAN IN THE GREY FLANNEL SUIT, THE(1956), d&w; SUMMER PLACE, A(1959), w

Stanley Wilson
RENEGADES OF SONORA(1948), m; SUNDOWN IN SANTA FE(1948), m; BANDIT KING OF TEXAS(1949), m; DEATH VALLEY GUNFIGHTER(1949), m; DUKE OF CHICAGO(1949), m; FLAME OF YOUTH(1949), m; FRONTIER INVESTIGATOR(1949), m; HIDEOUT(1949), m; LAW OF THE GOLDEN WEST(1949), m; NAVAJO TRAIL RAIDERS(1949), m; OUTCASTS OF THE TRAIL(1949), m; POST OFFICE INVESTIGATOR(1949), m; POWDER RIVER RUSTLERS(1949), m; PRINCE OF THE PLAINS(1949), m; RANGER OF CHEROKEE STRIP(1949), m, md; ROSE OF THE YUKON(1949), m; SAN ANTONE AMBUSH(1949), m; SOUTH OF RIO(1949), m; STREETS OF SAN FRANCISCO(1949), m; WYOMING BANDIT, THE(1949), m; ARIZONA COWBOY, THE(1950), m; BELLE OF OLD MEXICO(1950), m; DESTINATION BIG HOUSE(1950), m; FEDERAL AGENT AT LARGE(1950), m; FRISCO TORNADO(1950), m; GUNMEN OF ABILENE(1950), m; HARBOR OF MISSING MEN(1950), m; HILLS OF OKLAHOMA(1950), m; LONELY HEARTS BANDITS(1950), m; MISSOURIANS, THE(1950), m; PIONEER MARSHAL(1950), m, md; PRISONERS IN PETTICOATS(1950), m; RUSTLERS ON HORSEBACK(1950), m; SALT LAKE RAIDERS(1950), m; SHOWDOWN, THE(1950), m; TARNISHED(1950), m; TRIAL WITHOUT JURY(1950), m; TWILIGHT IN THE SIERRAS(1950), m; UNDER MEXICALI STARS(1950), md; UNMASKED(1950), m; VANISHING WESTERNER, THE(1950), m; VIGILANTE HIDEOUT(1950), m; DESERT OF LOST

MEN(1951), m; HAVANA ROSE(1951), m; INSURANCE INVESTIGATOR(1951), m; MILLION DOLLAR PURSUIT(1951), m; MISSING WOMEN(1951), m; NIGHT RIDERS OF MONTANA(1951), m; PRIDE OF MARYLAND(1951), m; ROUGH RIDERS OF DURANGO(1951), m; SECRETS OF MONTE CARLO(1951), m; SILVER CITY BONANZA(1951), m; STREET BANDITS(1951), m; THUNDER IN GOD'S COUNTRY(1951), m; UTAH WAGON TRAIN(1951), m; WELLS FARGO GUNMASTER(1951), m; BLACK HILLS AMBUSH(1952), m; BORDER SADDLEMATES(1952), m; DESPERADOES OUTPOST(1952), m; FABULOUS SENORITA, THE(1952), m; GOBS AND GALS(1952), m; LEADVILLE GUNSLINGER(1952), m; OLD OKLAHOMA PLAINS(1952), m; PALS OF THE GOLDEN WEST(1952), m; SOUTH PACIFIC TRAIL(1952), m; THUNDERING CARAVANS(1952), m; TROPICAL HEAT WAVE(1952), m; WILD HORSE AMBUSH(1952), m; WOMAN IN THE DARK(1952), m; DOWN LAREDO WAY(1953), m; EL PASO STAMPEDE(1953), m; IRON MOUNTAIN TRAIL(1953), m; LADY WANTS MINK, THE(1953), m; MARSHAL OF CEDAR ROCK(1953), m; WOMAN THEY ALMOST LYNCHED, THE(1953), m; UNTAMED HEIRESS(1954), m; HALLIDAY BRAND, THE(1957), m; SATAN'S SATELLITES(1958), m; GHOST OF ZORRO(1959), m; KILLERS, THE(1964), md; DARK INTRUDER(1965), md; JIGSAW(1968), md; SERGEANT RYKER(1968), md; DEATH OF A GUNFIGHTER(1969), md; TELL THEM WILLIE BOY IS HERE(1969), md; HUSBANDS(1970), md

Steve Wilson
1984
ACT, THE(1984), prod d

Stu Wilson
IRON MAN, THE(1951); BAND WAGON, THE(1953); GIRL WHO HAD EVERYTHING, THE(1953)

Stuart Wilson
HERE COME THE NELSONS(1952); DULCIMA(1971, Brit.); PRISONER OF ZENDA, THE(1979)

Sue Wilson
CREATURES THE WORLD FORGOT(1971, Brit.)

Sunburnt Jim Wilson
CALL OF THE CIRCUS(1930)

T-Bone Wilson
PRESSURE(1976, Brit.); BABYLON(1980, Brit.)

Ted Wilson
DEVIL'S PLAYGROUND, THE(1946), w

Teddy Wilson
BENNY GOODMAN STORY, THE(1956)

Terry Wilson
MY HANDS ARE CLAY(1948, Irish); DANGEROUS PROFESSION, A(1949); MONTANA BELLE(1952); SEVEN BRIDES FOR SEVEN BROTHERS(1954); LAST HUNT, THE(1956); PILLARS OF THE SKY(1956); SEARCHERS, THE(1956); PLAINSMAN, THE(1966); WAR WAGON, THE(1967); SHAKIEST GUN IN THE WEST(1968); MAN CALLED GANNON, A(1969); DIRTY DINGUS MAGEE(1970); SUPPORT YOUR LOCAL GUNFIGHTER(1971); RAGE(1972); ONE LITTLE INDIAN(1973); WESTWORLD(1973); ESCAPE TO WITCH MOUNTAIN(1975)

Theodore Wilson
COTTON COMES TO HARLEM(1970); COME BACK CIHARLESTON BLUE(1972); CLEOPATRA JONES(1973); NEWMAN'S LAW(1974); RIVER NIGER, THE(1976); RUN FOR THE ROSES(1978); CARNY(1980); HUNTER, THE(1980)
1984
WEEKEND PASS(1984)

Theodore R. Wilson
GREATEST, THE(1977, U.S./Brit.)

Thick Wilson
DIRTY DOZEN, THE(1967, Brit.); MIRROR CRACK'D, THE(1980, Brit.); DARK CRYSTAL, THE(1982, Brit.); STRANGE BREW(1983)

Thomas H. Wilson
Silents
AMARILLY OF CLOTHESLINE ALLEY(1918)

Tom Wilson
BIG HOUSE, THE(1930); DARKENED SKIES(1930); DOORWAY TO HELL(1930); SOOKY(1931); VICE SQUAD, THE(1931); PHANTOM EXPRESS, THE(1932); PICTURE SNATCHER(1933); SILK EXPRESS, THE(1933); ST. LOUIS KID, THE(1934); TREASURE ISLAND(1934); WE LIVE AGAIN(1934); CAPTAIN BLOOD(1935); CASE OF THE CURIOUS BRIDE, THE(1935); DR. SOCRATES(1935); G-MEN(1935); STRANDED(1935); EARLY TO BED(1936); LOVE BEGINS AT TWENTY(1936); ROAD GANG(1936); TRAILIN' WEST(1936); TREACHERY RIDES THE RANGE(1936); PRINCE AND THE PAUPER, THE(1937); SLIM(1937); THEY WON'T FORGET(1937); ANGELS WASH THEIR FACES(1939); CODE OF THE SECRET SERVICE(1939); EACH DAWN I DIE(1939); HELL'S KITCHEN(1939); KID FROM KOKOMO, THE(1939); KING OF THE UNDERWORLD(1939); NANCY DREW, TROUBLE SHOOTER(1939); SMASHING THE MONEY RING(1939); ALWAYS A BRIDE(1940); DEVIL'S ISLAND(1940); MONEY AND THE WOMAN(1940); TUGBOAT ANNIE SAILS AGAIN(1940); MEET JOHN DOE(1941); WAGONS ROLL AT NIGHT, THE(1941); STALLION ROAD(1947); THY NEIGHBOR'S WIFE(1953); TALL MEN, THE(1955); VIEW FROM POMPEY'S HEAD, THE(1955); EDGE OF HELL(1956)
Silents
BIRTH OF A NATION, THE(1915); MARTYRS OF THE ALAMO, THE(1915); ATTA BOY'S LAST RACE(1916); HELL-TO-PAY AUSTIN(1916); INTOLERANCE(1916); LITTLE LIAR, THE(1916); REGGIE MIXES IN(1916); AMERICANO, THE(1917); WILD AND WOOLLY(1917); DINTY(1920); GREATEST QUESTION, THE(1920); ISOBEL(1920); KID, THE(1921); TWO MINUTES TO GO(1921); WHERE MEN ARE MEN(1921); ALIAS JULIUS CAESAR(1922); RED HOT ROMANCE(1922); REPORTED MISSING(1922); HIS DARKER SELF(1924); ON TIME(1924); ACROSS THE PACIFIC(1926); BATTLING BUTLER(1926); RAINMAKER, THE(1926); HAM AND EGGS AT THE FRONT(1927); NO CONTROL(1927); PIONEER SCOUT, THE(1928); RILEY THE COP(1928); STRONG BOY(1929)
Misc. Silents
YANKEE FROM THE WEST, A(1915); CHEATING THE PUBLIC(1918); SCRAP IRON(1921); GOOD-BY GIRLS!(1923); ITCHING PALMS(1923); CALIFORNIA STRAIGHT AHEAD(1925)

Tracy Wilson
RESURRECTION(1980)

Trey Wilson
DRIVE-IN(1976); VAMPIRE HOOKERS, THE(1979, Phil.)
1984
PLACES IN THE HEART(1984); SOLDIER'S STORY, A(1984)

V. Phipps Wilson
BREAKFAST IN BED(1978)
Vaughan Wilson
MERRILL'S MARAUDERS(1962)
Violet Wilson
MADEMOISELLE FIFI(1944)
Violette Wilson
MOON IS DOWN, THE(1943)
Virginia Wilson
GANG'S ALL HERE, THE(1943); COVER GIRL(1944)
W. Cronin Wilson
FEATHER, THE(1929, Brit.); SQUEAKER, THE(1930, Brit.); LOVE ON THE SPOT(1932, Brit.)
Silents
INNOCENT(1921, Brit.); HUNTINGTOWER(1927, Brit.)
Misc. Silents
SEA URCHIN, THE(1926, Brit.)
Walter Wilson
GRANNY GET YOUR GUN(1940); WELL-GROOMED BRIDE, THE(1946); NOTHING BUT A MAN(1964)
Warren Wilson
YOU'RE A SWEETHEART(1937), w; HELLZAPOPPIN'(1941), w; TANKS A MIL-LION(1941), w; BLONDIE GOES TO COLLEGE(1942), w; GIVE OUT, SISTERS(1942), w; STRICTLY IN THE GROOVE(1942), w; ALLERGIC TO LOVE(1943), w; COW-BOY IN MANHATTAN(1943), w; FOLLOW THE BAND(1943), w; GET GOING(1943), w; GOOD MORNING, JUDGE(1943), w; HI, BUDDY(1943), w; HONEYMOON LODGE(1943), p, w; SWING FEVER(1943), w; SWINGTIME JOHNNY(1944), p, w; TWILIGHT ON THE PRAIRIE(1944), w; WEEKEND PASS(1944), p, w; HER LUCKY NIGHT(1945), p, w; ON STAGE EVERYBODY(1945), w; SHE GETS HER MAN(1945), p, w; UNDER WESTERN SKIES(1945), p; SHE WROTE THE BOOK(1946), p, w; IF YOU KNEW SUSIE(1948), w; BIG TIMBER(1950), w; SQUARE DANCE KATY(1950), w
Whip Wilson
SILVER TRAILS(1948); CRASHING THRU(1949); RANGE LAND(1949); RIDERS OF THE DUSK(1949); SHADOWS OF THE WEST(1949); ARIZONA TERRITORY(1950); CHEROKEE UPRISING(1950); FENCE RIDERS(1950); GUNSLINGERS(1950); OUT-LAWS OF TEXAS(1950); SILVER RAIDERS(1950); ABILENE TRAIL(1951); CANYON RAIDERS(1951); NEVADA BADMEN(1951); STAGE TO BLUE RIVER(1951); LAW-LESS COWBOYS(1952); NIGHT RAIDERS(1952); KENTUCKIAN, THE(1955)
Misc. Talkies
HAUNTED TRAILS(1949); STAGECOACH DRIVER(1951); WANTED DEAD OR ALIVE(1951); GUNMAN, THE(1952); HIRED GUN(1952); MONTANA IN-CIDENT(1952); WYOMING ROUNDUP(1952)
William Wilson
MACHISMO–40 GRAVES FOR 40 GUNS(1970)
William B. Wilson
1984
REVENGE OF THE NERDS(1984)
Zee Wilson
Misc. Talkies
INTERPLAY(1970)
Wilson Keppel and Betty
VARIETY JUBILEE(1945, Brit.)
Frank J. Wilstach
PLAINSMAN, THE(1937), w
John Wilstach
UNDER-COVER MAN(1932), w
John Wilste
HIGHWAY 13(1948), w; SKY LINER(1949), w
Ann Wilton
FIRST NIGHT(1937, Brit.); MERELY MR. HAWKINS(1938, Brit.); MAN IN GREY, THE(1943, Brit.); JOHNNY IN THE CLOUDS(1945, Brit.); SCHOOL FOR SE-CRETS(1946, Brit.); TAWNY PIPIT(1947, Brit.); MAN OF EVIL(1948, Brit.); OCTOBER MAN, THE(1948, Brit.); MINIVER STORY, THE(1950, Brit./U.S.)
Anne Wilton
DEAD MEN TELL NO TALES(1939, Brit.); RICHARD III(1956, Brit.)
David Wilton
OH NO DOCTOR!(1934, Brit.)
Eric Wilton
DR. JEKYLL AND MR. HYDE(1932); ONE HOUR WITH YOU(1932); SILENT WITNESS, THE(1932); MASQUERADER, THE(1933); SONG OF SONGS(1933); DOC-TOR MONICA(1934); FASHIONS OF 1934(1934); MANDALAY(1934); MIDNIGHT ALIBI(1934); MYSTERY OF MR. X, THE(1934); LIVING ON VELVET(1935); MUTINY ON THE BOUNTY(1935); DRACULA'S DAUGHTER(1936); FORBIDDEN HEA-VEN(1936); GIVE ME YOUR HEART(1936); GREAT ZIEGFELD, THE(1936); LIBELED LADY(1936); MEET NERO WOLFE(1936); WHITE ANGEL, THE(1936); ANGEL(1937); LOST HORIZON(1937); MR. DODD TAKES THE AIR(1937); 100 MEN AND A GIRL(1937); GOLD IS WHERE YOU FIND IT(1938); PENITENTIARY(1938); NEWS-BOY'S HOME(1939); RAFFLES(1939); TELEVISION SPY(1939); WUTHERING HEIGHTS(1939); HUDSON'S BAY(1940); I LOVE YOU AGAIN(1940); INVISIBLE MAN RETURNS, THE(1940); JOHNNY APOLLO(1940); WOLF MAN, THE(1941); GREAT IMPERSONATION, THE(1942); RINGS ON HER FINGERS(1942); TALES OF MANHATTAN(1942); THEY RAID BY NIGHT(1942); FALLEN SPARROW, THE(1943); IMMORTAL SERGEANT, THE(1943); GASLIGHT(1944); NATIONAL VELVET(1944); NONE BUT THE LONELY HEART(1944); PEARL OF DEATH, THE(1944); SECRETS OF SCOTLAND YARD(1944); MINISTRY OF FEAR(1945); MOLLY AND ME(1945); CLAUDIA AND DAVID(1946); JOLSON STORY, THE(1946); KID FROM BROOKLYN, THE(1946); NIGHT AND DAY(1946); THREE STRANGERS(1946); HER HUSBAND'S AFFAIRS(1947); IVY(1947); APPOINTMENT WITH MURDER(1948); DOCKS OF NEW ORLEANS(1948); JOLSON SINGS AGAIN(1949); LORNA DOONE(1951); PLACE IN THE SUN, A(1951); RHUBARB(1951); VALENTINO(1951); HOW TO MARRY A MILLIONAIRE(1953); STAR IS BORN, A(1954); WOMAN'S WORLD(1954); THREE BAD SISTERS(1956); JOKER IS WILD, THE(1957)
Geraldine Wilton
MILL ON THE FLOSS(1939, Brit.)
Harry Wilton
PROFESSOR BEWARE(1938)

Myron Wilton
DANNY BOY(1946)
Penelope Wilton
FRENCH LIEUTENANT'S WOMAN, THE(1981)
1984
LAUGHTER HOUSE(1984, Brit.)
Robb Wilton
LOVE, LIFE AND LAUGHTER(1934, Brit.); SECRET OF THE LOCH, THE(1934, Brit.); FIRE HAS BEEN ARRANGED, A(1935, Brit.); LIEUTENANT DARING, RN(1935, Brit.); LOOK UP AND LAUGH(1935, Brit.); SILENT PASSENGER, THE(1935, Brit.); DON'T RUSH ME(1936, Brit.); INTERRUPTED HONEYMOON, THE(1936, Brit.); IT'S LOVE AGAIN(1936, Brit.); FINE FEATHERS(1937, Brit.); TAKE MY TIP(1937, Brit.); BREAK THE NEWS(1938, Brit.); CHIPS(1938. Brit.); MANY TANKS MR. ATKINS(1938, Brit.); TWO'S COMPANY(1939, Brit.); LOVE MATCH, THE(1955, Brit.)
Robert Wilton
WE DIVE AT DAWN(1943, Brit.)
Terence Wilton
ANNE OF THE THOUSAND DAYS(1969, Brit.)
Aage Wiltrup
OPERATION CAMEL(1961, Den.), ph; JOURNEY TO THE SEVENTH PLANET(1962, U.S./Swed.), ph; REPTILICUS(1962, U.S./Den.), ph
David Wiltse
HURRY UP OR I'LL BE 30(1973), w
George Wiltshire
HI-DE-HO(1947)
Misc. Talkies
IT HAPPENED IN HARLEM(1945); KILLER DILLER(1948)
John Wiltshire
MASSACRE HILL(1949, Brit.); WHEREVER SHE GOES(1953, Aus.)
Maurice Wiltshire
MY BROTHER'S KEEPER(1949, Brit.), w
Melissa Wiltsie
SUPERMAN II(1980)
Simeon Wiltsie
Silents
WISHING RING, THE(1914)
Walter Wiltz
CARMEN, BABY(1967, Yugo./Ger.)
Bob Wilyman
2001: A SPACE ODYSSEY(1968, U.S./Brit.)
Walter Wilz
SECRET WAYS, THE(1961); LOVE FEAST, THE(1966, Ger.)
Allen Wilzbach
MAN CALLED FLINTSTONE, THE(1966), anim
Anne-Mari Wiman
WILD STRAWBERRIES(1959, Swed.)
Kelly Wimberly
SPLIT IMAGE(1982)
Roderic Wimberly
1984
GO TELL IT ON THE MOUNTAIN(1984)
John Beckett Wimbs
1984
MEMOIRS(1984, Can.), w
Mary Wimbush
OH! WHAT A LOVELY WAR(1969, Brit.); FRAGMENT OF FEAR(1971, Brit.); VAMPIRE CIRCUS(1972, Brit.)
Jiri Wimmer
SIGN OF THE VIRGIN(1969, Czech.)
Maria Wimmer
DECISION BEFORE DAWN(1951)
Arthur Wimperis
HARMONY HEAVEN(1930, Brit.), w; SONG OF SOHO(1930, Brit.), w; WARM CORNER, A(1930, Brit.), w; WEDDING REHEARSAL(1932, Brit.), w; COUNSEL'S OPINION(1933, Brit.), w; MAN THEY COULDN'T ARREST, THE(1933, Brit.), w; OVERNIGHT(1933, Brit.), w; PRIVATE LIFE OF HENRY VIII, THE(1933), w; CATHERINE THE GREAT(1934, Brit.), w; FOR LOVE OR MONEY(1934, Brit.), w; PRIVATE LIFE OF DON JUAN, THE(1934, Brit.), w; BREWSTER'S MILLIONS(1935, Brit.), w; MEN OF TOMORROW(1935, Brit.), w; PRINCESS CHARMING(1935, Brit.), w; SCARLET PIMPERNEL, THE(1935, Brit.), w; BELOVED VAGABOND, THE(1936, Brit.), w; GIRL FROM MAXIM'S, THE(1936, Brit.), w; REMBRANDT(1936, Brit.), w; DARK JOURNEY(1937, Brit.), w; FOREVER YOURS(1937, Brit.), w; KNIGHT WITH-OUT ARMOR(1937, Brit.), w; UNDER THE RED ROBE(1937, Brit.), w; DIVORCE OF LADY X, THE(1938, Brit.), w; DRUMS(1938, Brit.), w; RETURN OF THE SCARLET PIMPERNEL(1938, Brit.), w; CLOUDS OVER EUROPE(1939, Brit.), w; FOUR FEATH-ERS, THE(1939, Brit.), w; PRISON WITHOUT BARS(1939, Brit.), w; OLD BILL AND SON(1940, Brit.), w; OVER THE MOON(1940, Brit.), w; MRS. MINIVER(1942), a, w; RANDOM HARVEST(1942), w; GREEN COCKATOO, THE(1947, Brit.), w; IF WINTER COMES(1947), w; JULIA MISBEHAVES(1948), w; RED DANUBE, THE(1949), w; CALLING BULLDOG DRUMMOND(1951, Brit.), w; YOUNG BESS(1953), w; STORM OVER THE NILE(1955, Brit.), w
Silents
WIFE SAVERS(1928), w
Wimpy
WESTERN TRAILS(1938)
Rex Wimpy
ONLY SAPS WORK(1930), ph; TWO AGAINST THE WORLD(1936), spec eff; CASE OF THE STUTTERING BISHOP, THE(1937), ph; PERFECT SPECIMEN, THE(1937), spec eff; TALENT SCOUT(1937), ph; DODGE CITY(1939), spec eff; FIGHTING 69TH, THE(1940), spec eff; KNUTE ROCKNE–ALL AMERICAN(1940), spec eff; CITY, FOR CONQUEST(1941), spec eff; DIVE BOMBER(1941), spec eff; FOOTSTEPS IN THE DARK(1941), spec eff; OUT OF THE FOG(1941), spec eff; AIR FORCE(1943), spec eff; PASSAGE TO MARSEILLE(1944), spec eff; SPELLBOUND(1945), ph; DEVO-TION(1946), spec eff; CHALLENGE OF THE RANGE(1949), ph; DESERT VIGI-LANTE(1949), ph; EL DORADO PASS(1949), ph; LARAMIE(1949), ph; QUICK ON THE TRIGGER(1949), ph; SMOKY MOUNTAIN MELODY(1949), ph; MAN WHO CHEATED HIMSELF, THE(1951), spec eff; DARLING LILI(1970), spec eff
Silents
STAIRS OF SAND(1929), ph

Rexford Wimpy
RELUCTANT ASTRONAUT, THE(1967), ph
Wimpy the Dog
NOTHING SACRED(1937)
Cie Cie Win
MARCO(1973)
Glenda Wina
TELEFON(1977)
Del Winans
FIEND(
Robert Winans
EGG AND I, THE(1947); KID FROM LEFT FIELD, THE(1953); MR. SCOUTMAS-TER(1953)
Robin Winans
MA AND PA KETTLE(1949); HONEYCHILE(1951); MAN WITH A CLOAK, THE(1951)
Forest Winant
Misc. Silents
BRINK, THE(1915)
Forrest Winant
Silents
NEW YORK(1916)
Misc. Silents
IRON HEART, THE(1917)
Scott Winant
1984
INITIATION, THE(1984), p
Robin Winbow
PUPPET ON A CHAIN(1971, Brit.), ch
James Winburn
MOVIE MOVIE(1978)
Jim Winburn
BARE KNUCKLES(1978), stunts; GONG SHOW MOVIE, THE(1980); CHARLIE CHAN AND THE CURSE OF THE DRAGON QUEEN(1981)
Shimon Wincelberg
COLD SWEAT(1974, Ital., Fr.), w
Simon Wincelberg
FIGHTER ATTACK(1953), w; ON THE THRESHOLD OF SPACE(1956), w
Simon Wincer
DAY AFTER HALLOWEEN, THE(1981, Aus.), d
1984
PHAR LAP(1984, Aus.), d
Barry Winch
TOMMY(1975, Brit.)
Elizabeth Winch [Liz Fraser]
LIGHT TOUCH, THE(1955, Brit.)
Evelyn Winch
GIRL IN THE FLAT, THE(1934, Brit.), w
Frank Winch
BUFFALO BILL(1944), w
Paul Winchell
ARISTOCATS, THE(1970); WHICH WAY TO THE FRONT?(1970); FOX AND THE HOUND, THE(1981)
Walda Winchell
27TH DAY, THE(1957)
Walter Winchell
BROADWAY THROUGH A KEYHOLE(1933), w; LOVE AND HISSES(1937); WAKE UP AND LIVE(1937); DAISY KENYON(1947); HELEN MORGAN STORY, THE(1959); COLLEGE CONFIDENTIAL(1960); DONDI(1961); SCARFACE MOB, THE(1962); WILD HARVEST(1962); WILD IN THE STREETS(1968)
Arna Maria Winchester
SIDECAR RACERS(1975, Aus.)
Arna-Maria Winchester
ELIZA FRASER(1976, Aus.); CHAIN REACTION(1980, Aus.)
Barbara Winchester
CONNECTION, THE(1962)
Barron Winchester
DELIRIUM(1979)
Dale Winchester
LOCAL HERO(1983, Brit.)
Jeff Winchester
TASTE OF SIN, A(1983)
Julie Winchester
1984
SUBURBIA(1984)
Mark Winchester
LOCAL HERO(1983, Brit.)
Maude Winchester
1984
BIRDY(1984)
Monica Winckel
SINGAPORE(1947)
Gustav Winckler
OPERATION CAMEL(1961, Den.), m
Richard Winckler
COW AND I, THE(1961, Fr., Ital., Ger.); SELLERS OF GIRLS(1967, Fr.)
Geoff Wincott
BRONCO BULLFROG(1972, Brit.)
Geoffrey Wincott
DICK BARTON–SPECIAL AGENT(1948, Brit.)
Jeff Wincott
HAPPY BIRTHDAY, GEMINI(1980); PROM NIGHT(1980)
Michael Wincott
WILD HORSE HANK(1979, Can.); CIRCLE OF TWO(1980, Can.); TICKET TO HEAVEN(1981); CURTAINS(1983, Can.)
A. Windau
GIRL AND THE LEGEND, THE(1966, Ger.), set d

Morgan Windbeil
LIVE A LITTLE, LOVE A LITTLE(1968)
Jim Windburn
HALLOWEEN(1978)
Bea Winde
RICH KIDS(1979)
Beatrice Winde
TAKING OF PELHAM ONE, TWO, THREE, THE(1974); GAMBLER, THE(1974); MANDINGO(1975); SPARKLE(1976); OLIVER'S STORY(1978); HIDE IN PLAIN SIGHT(1980)
Agnes Windeck
TIME TO LOVE AND A TIME TO DIE, A(1958); DAS LETZTE GEHEIMNIS(1959, Ger.); I, TOO, AM ONLY A WOMAN(1963, Ger.); SCOTLAND YARD HUNTS DR. MABUSE(1963, Ger.); ONLY A WOMAN(1966, Ger.)
Fred Windemere
Silents
ROMANCE ROAD(1925), d
Misc. Silents
SOILED(1924), d; THREE IN EXILE(1925), d; VERDICT, THE(1925), d; MORGAN-SON'S FINISH(1926), d; SHE'S MY BABY(1927), d; BROADWAY DADDIES(1928), d
Michael Winder
BEAST MUST DIE, THE(1974, Brit.), w; KILLER FORCE(1975, Switz./Ireland), w; WELCOME TO BLOOD CITY(1977, Brit./Can.), w
Fred Windermere
Silents
TAXI MYSTERY, THE(1926), d; DEVIL DOGS(1928), d
Misc. Silents
WITH THIS RING(1925), d; BROADWAY AFTER MIDNIGHT(1927), d
Marek Windheim
I'LL TAKE ROMANCE(1937); SHALL WE DANCE(1937); SOMETHING TO SING ABOUT(1937); DRAMATIC SCHOOL(1938); SAY IT IN FRENCH(1938); THERE'S ALWAYS A WOMAN(1938); HOTEL IMPERIAL(1939); LONE WOLF SPY HUNT, THE(1939); NINOTCHKA(1939); PLAY GIRL(1940); MARRY THE BOSS' DAUGHT-ER(1941); TOO MANY BLONDES(1941); CROSSROADS(1942); I MARRIED AN AN-GEL(1942); MRS. MINIVER(1942); ALLERGIC TO LOVE(1943); COWBOY IN MANHATTTAN(1943); HI DIDDLE DIDDLE(1943); MADAME CURIE(1943); MIS-SION TO MOSCOW(1943); PHANTOM OF THE OPERA(1943); THREE HEARTS FOR JULIA(1943); IN OUR TIME(1944); MASK OF DIMITRIOS, THE(1944); MRS. PARK-INGTON(1944); ROYAL SCANDAL, A(1945); RAZOR'S EDGE, THE(1946); TARZAN AND THE LEOPARD WOMAN(1946); TWO SMART PEOPLE(1946)
Marek Windhelm
SHE MARRIED AN ARTIST(1938)
Karl Heinz Windhorst
LUDWIG(1973, Ital./Ger./Fr.)
Frederick Windhousen
ODETTE(1951, Brit.)
Romain Windig
AVIATOR'S WIFE, THE(1981, Fr.), ph
Andreas Winding
OF FLESH AND BLOOD(1964, Fr./Ital.), ph; MALE HUNT(1965, Fr./Ital.), ph; RAVISHING IDIOT, A(1966, Ital./Fr.), ph; 25TH HOUR, THE(1966, Fr./Ital./Yugo.), ph; LA PRISONNIERE(1969, Fr./Ital.), ph; RIDER ON THE RAIN(1970, Fr./Ital.), ph; FRIENDS(1971, Brit.), ph; TIME FOR LOVING, A(1971, Brit.), ph; PLAYTIME(1973, Fr.), ph
Genevieve Winding
AMELIE OR THE TIME TO LOVE(1961, Fr.), ed; 24 HOURS IN A WOMAN'S LIFE(1968, Fr./Ger.), ed; LE PETIT THEATRE DE JEAN RENOIR(1974, Fr.), ed
1984
LE BON PLAISIR(1984, Fr.), ed
Kai Winding
MAN CALLED ADAM, A(1966)
Romain Winding
LE BEAU MARIAGE(1982, Fr.), ph
Victor Winding
GIRL GETTERS, THE(1966, Brit.); FRIGHTMARE(1974, Brit.); CONFESSIONAL, THE(1977, Brit.); SCHIZO(1977, Brit.); MEDUSA TOUCH, THE(1978, Brit.)
Ilka Windisch
NO TIME FOR FLOWERS(1952)
Muki Windisch-Graetz
ASH WEDNESDAY(1973)
Ilka Windish
MAGIC FACE, THE(1951, Aust.); TARAS BULBA(1962)
The Windmill Theatre Company and Staff
MYSTERY AT THE BURLESQUE(1950, Brit.)
L. C. Windom
Silents
EFFICIENCY EDGAR'S COURTSHIP(1917), d; PAIR OF SIXES, A(1918), d
Lawrence Windom
Silents
IT'S A BEAR(1919), d
Misc. Silents
DISCARD, THE(1916), d; TWO-BITS SEATS(1917), d; GREY PARASOL, THE(1918), d; TAXI(1919), d; WANTED - A HUSBAND(1919), d; HEADIN' HOME(1920), d; VERY IDEA, THE(1920), d; SINNER OR SAINT(1923), d; TRUTH ABOUT WIVES, THE(1923), d; FAITHLESS LOVER(1928), d
Lawrence C. Windom
ENEMIES OF THE LAW(1931), d
Silents
APPEARANCE OF EVIL(1918), d; TRUTH, THE(1920), d; MODERN MAR-RIAGE(1923), d
Misc. Silents
FOOLS FOR LUCK(1917), d; SMALL TOWN GUY, THE(1917), d; POWER AND THE GLORY, THE(1918), d; RUGGLES OF RED GAP(1918), d; UNEASY MONEY(1918), d; UPSIDE DOWN(1919), d; GIRL WITH A JAZZ HEART, THE(1920), d; GIRL WITH THE JAZZ HEART, THE(1920), d; HUMAN COLLATERAL(1920), d; NOTHING BUT LIES(1920), d; SOLOMON IN SOCIETY(1922), d
William Windom
TO KILL A MOCKINGBIRD(1962); CATTLE KING(1963); FOR LOVE OR MO-NEY(1963); AMERICANIZATION OF EMILY, THE(1964); ONE MAN'S WAY(1964); HOUR OF THE GUN(1967); DETECTIVE, THE(1968); ANGRY BREED, THE(1969);

GYPSY MOTHS, THE(1969); BREWSTER McCLOUD(1970); ESCAPE FROM THE PLANET OF THE APES(1971); FOOLS' PARADE(1971); MEPHISTO WALTZ, THE(1971); MAN, THE(1972); NOW YOU SEE HIM, NOW YOU DON'T(1972); ECHOES OF A SUMMER(1976); GOODBYE FRANKLIN HIGH(1978); MEAN DOG BLUES(1978); SEPARATE WAYS(1981)
1984
GRANDVIEW, U.S.A.(1984)
Misc. Talkies
LAST PLANE OUT(1983)

Adele Windsor
FROZEN JUSTICE(1929); GIRL FROM HAVANA, THE(1929); TRUE TO THE NAVY(1930); UP THE RIVER(1930)

Allen Windsor
INCREDIBLE PETRIFIED WORLD, THE(1959); PURPLE GANG, THE(1960)

Barbara Windsor
TEARS FOR SIMON(1957, Brit.); TOO HOT TO HANDLE(1961, Brit.); DEATH TRAP(1962, Brit.); HAIR OF THE DOG(1962, Brit.); SPARROWS CAN'T SING(1963, Brit.); CARRY ON SPYING(1964, Brit.); CROOKS IN CLOISTERS(1964, Brit.); OPERATION SNAFU(1965, Brit.); SAN FERRY ANN(1965, Brit.); STUDY IN TERROR, A(1966, Brit./Ger.); CARRY ON DOCTOR(1968, Brit.); CHITTY CHITTY BANG BANG(1968, Brit.); CARRY ON AGAIN, DOCTOR(1969, Brit.); CARRY ON CAMPING(1969, Brit.); CARRY ON HENRY VIII(1970, Brit.); BOY FRIEND, THE(1971, Brit.); NOT NOW DARLING(1975, Brit.)

Bob Windsor
TRIBUTE(1980, Can.)

Carole Windsor
HORROR CASTLE(1965, Ital.)

Chris Windsor
1984
BIG MEAT EATER(1984, Can.), d, w, ed

Claire Windsor
MIDSTREAM(1929); MY MOTHER(1933); CROSS STREETS(1934); TOPPER(1937); BAREFOOT BOY(1938); HOW DO YOU DO?(1946)
Misc. Talkies
CONSTANT WOMAN, THE(1933); SELF DEFENSE(1933); SISTER TO JUDAS(1933)
Silents
BLOT, THE(1921); DR. JIM(1921); RAIDERS, THE(1921); WHAT DO MEN WANT?(1921); ONE CLEAR CALL(1922); RICH MEN'S WIVES(1922); STRANGER'S BANQUET(1922); ACQUITTAL, THE(1923); ETERNAL THREE, THE(1923); LITTLE CHURCH AROUND THE CORNER(1923); RUPERT OF HENTZAU(1923); SOULS FOR SALE(1923); NELLIE, THE BEAUTIFUL CLOAK MODEL(1924); JUST A WOMAN(1925); FOREIGN DEVILS(1927); LITTLE JOURNEY, A(1927); GRAIN OF DUST, THE(1928); NAMELESS MEN(1928); SHOW PEOPLE(1928); CAPTAIN LASH(1929)
Misc. Silents
TO PLEASE ONE WOMAN(1920); TOO WISE WIVES(1921); WHAT'S WORTH WHILE?(1921); BROKEN CHAINS(1922); FOOLS FIRST(1922); GRAND LARCENY(1922); BORN RICH(1924); FOR SALE(1924); SON OF THE SAHARA, A(1924); DENIAL, THE(1925); DIXIE HANDICAP, THE(1925); SOULS FOR SABLES(1925); WHITE DESERT, THE(1925); DANCE MADNESS(1926); MONEY TALKS(1926); TIN HATS(1926); BLONDES BY CHOICE(1927); BUGLE CALL, THE(1927); CLAW, THE(1927); FRONTIERSMAN, THE(1927); OPENING NIGHT, THE(1927); DOMESTIC MEDDLERS(1928); FASHION MADNESS(1928); SATAN AND THE WOMAN(1928)

Frank Windsor
THIS SPORTING LIFE(1963, Brit.); SPRING AND PORT WINE(1970, Brit.); SUNDAY BLOODY SUNDAY(1971, Brit.); ASSASSIN(1973, Brit.); WHO IS KILLING THE GREAT CHEFS OF EUROPE?(1978, US/Ger.); DANGEROUS DAVIES–THE LAST DETECTIVE(1981, Brit.)

Gabrielle Windsor
IDEA GIRL(1946); KILLERS, THE(1946); THAT FORSYTE WOMAN(1949)

Georgette Windsor
LUXURY LINER(1948); BLACK BOOK, THE(1949)

James Windsor
1984
SWORD OF THE VALIANT(1984, Brit.)

Joy Windsor
YOU'D BE SURPRISED!(1930, Brit.); HIS KIND OF WOMAN(1951); TEN TALL MEN(1951)
Misc. Silents
LIFE'S A STAGE(1929, Brit.); DIZZY LIMIT, THE(1930, Brit.)

Kirk Windsor
HAVING WONDERFUL TIME(1938)

Marie Windsor
EYES IN THE NIGHT(1942); SMART ALECKS(1942); PILOT NO. 5(1943); THREE HEARTS FOR JULIA(1943); HUCKSTERS, THE(1947); SONG OF THE THIN MAN(1947); FORCE OF EVIL(1948); ON AN ISLAND WITH YOU(1948); THREE MUSKETEERS, THE(1948); FIGHTING KENTUCKIAN, THE(1949); HELLFIRE(1949); OUTPOST IN MOROCCO(1949); DAKOTA LIL(1950); DOUBLE DEAL(1950); FRENCHIE(1950); SHOWDOWN(1950); HURRICANE ISLAND(1951); LITTLE BIG HORN(1951); TWO DOLLAR BETTOR(1951); JAPANESE WAR BRIDE(1952); JUNGLE, THE(1952); NARROW MARGIN, THE(1952); OUTLAW WOMEN(1952); SNIPER, THE(1952); CAT WOMEN OF THE MOON(1953); CITY THAT NEVER SLEEPS(1953); EDDIE CANTOR STORY, THE(1953); SO THIS IS LOVE(1953); TALL TEXAN, THE(1953); TROUBLE ALONG THE WAY(1953); BOUNTY HUNTER, THE(1954); HELL'S HALF ACRE(1954); ABBOTT AND COSTELLO MEET THE MUMMY(1955); NO MAN'S WOMAN(1955); SILVER STAR, THE(1955); KILLING, THE(1956); SWAMP WOMEN(1956); TWO-GUN LADY(1956); GIRL IN BLACK STOCKINGS(1957); PARSON AND THE OUTLAW, THE(1957); STORY OF MANKIND, THE(1957); UNHOLY WIFE, THE(1957); DAY OF THE BAD MAN(1958); ISLAND WOMEN(1958); PARADISE ALLEY(1962); CRITIC'S CHOICE(1963); DAY MARS INVADED EARTH, THE(1963); BEDTIME STORY(1964); MAIL ORDER BRIDE(1964); CHAMBER OF HORRORS(1966); GOOD GUYS AND THE BAD GUYS, THE(1969); ONE MORE TRAIN TO ROB(1971); SUPPORT YOUR LOCAL GUNFIGHTER(1971); CAHILL, UNITED STATES MARSHAL(1973); OUTFIT, THE(1973); HEARTS OF THE WEST(1975); FREAKY FRIDAY(1976)

Maris Windsor
CHATTERBOX(1943)

Mary Windsor
TWO IN A CROWD(1936); PARACHUTE NURSE(1942)

Robert Windsor
STRANGE BREW(1983)

Romy Windsor
1984
THIEF OF HEARTS(1984); UP THE CREEK(1984)

Stafford Windsor
Misc. Silents
SUPERSTITION(1922)

Tammy Windsor
THIS EARTH IS MINE(1959); WILD AND THE INNOCENT, THE(1959)

Tod Windsor
NUN AND THE SERGEANT, THE(1962); SERGEANT DEADHEAD(1965)

Todd Windsor
IT HAPPENED IN ATHENS(1962)

Herbert Windt
SINS OF ROSE BERND, THE(1959, Ger.), m

Bretaigne Windust
JUNE BRIDE(1948), d; WINTER MEETING(1948), d; PERFECT STRANGERS(1950), d; PRETTY BABY(1950), d; ENFORCER, THE(1951), d; FACE TO FACE(1952), d

Irene Windust
ROADRACERS, THE(1959); MA BARKER'S KILLER BROOD(1960); PARRISH(1961)

The Windy City Twister
TWIST ALL NIGHT(1961)

Benjamin Wine
COWBOY IN THE CLOUDS(1943), d; COWBOY FROM LONESOME RIVER(1944), d

Benjamin H. Wine
COUNTERFEIT KILLER, THE(1968), ph

James Wine
CHINA SYNDROME, THE(1979)

Marvin Wine
COUNSELLOR-AT-LAW(1933)

Leroy Winebrenner
GIGI(1958)

Irwin Winehouse
BLUEPRINT FOR ROBBERY(1961), w; NAKED BRIGADE, THE(1965, U.S./Gr.), w

Sam Wineland
BELOVED(1934), md

Sam K. Wineland
TARZAN THE FEARLESS(1933), m

John Wineld
BORN LOSERS(1967), ed

Jack Winer
EAGLE HAS LANDED, THE(1976, Brit.), p

Richard Winer
ROUGHLY SPEAKING(1945)

Carol Wines
KISMET(1930); UP THE RIVER(1930); THREE ROGUES(1931)
Silents
JOY STREET(1929)
Misc. Silents
PRINCE OF PEP, THE(1925)

Christopher Wines
RECESS(1967)

Maury Winetrobe
FUNNY GIRL(1968), ed; WRECKING CREW, THE(1968), ed; CACTUS FLOWER(1969), ed; GETTING STRAIGHT(1970), ed; SUMMERTREE(1971), ed; T.R. BASKIN(1971), ed; LAST OF THE RED HOT LOVERS(1972), ed; LOST HORIZON(1973), ed; MAME(1974), ed; FROM NOON TO THREE(1976), ed; GUMBALL RALLY, THE(1976), ed; CHOIRBOYS, THE(1977), ed; ICE CASTLES(1978), ed; SKY RIDERS(1979), ed; RAVAGERS, THE(1979), ed; TAPS(1981), ed

Jan Winetsky
ECHOES(1983)

Chris Winfield
FIREFOX(1982)

Gil Winfield
FIEND WITHOUT A FACE(1958)

Gilbert Winfield
DEPRAVED, THE(1957, Brit.); OPERATION MURDER(1957, Brit.); PORTRAIT IN SMOKE(1957, Brit.); ON THE RUN(1958, Brit.); THEM NICE AMERICANS(1958, Brit.), a, w

Joan Winfield
BULLETS FOR O'HARA(1941); MANPOWER(1941); DANGEROUSLY THEY LIVE(1942); GAY SISTERS, THE(1942); GORILLA MAN(1942); I WAS FRAMED(1942); LADY GANGSTER(1942); MALE ANIMAL, THE(1942); YANKEE DOODLE DANDY(1942); MISSION TO MOSCOW(1943); MURDER ON THE WATERFRONT(1943); THANK YOUR LUCKY STARS(1943); DOUGHGIRLS, THE(1944); MAKE YOUR OWN BED(1944); MILDRED PIERCE(1945); NIGHT AND DAY(1946); ONE MORE TOMORROW(1946); STOLEN LIFE, A(1946); ESCAPE ME NEVER(1947); IMPERFECT LADY, THE(1947); STALLION ROAD(1947); UNFAITHFUL, THE(1947); JOHNNY BELINDA(1948); FORCE OF ARMS(1951); QUEEN FOR A DAY(1951)

John Winfield
HELL'S BLOODY DEVILS(1970), ed

Paul Winfield
LOST MAN, THE(1969); R.P.M.(1970); BROTHER JOHN(1971); SOUNDER(1972); TROUBLE MAN(1972); GORDON'S WAR(1973); CONRACK(1974); HUCKLEBERRY FINN(1974); HUSTLE(1975); DAMNATION ALLEY(1977); GREATEST, THE(1977, U.S./Brit.); HERO AIN'T NOTHIN' BUT A SANDWICH, A(1977); HIGH VELOCITY(1977); TWILIGHT'S LAST GLEAMING(1977, U.S./Ger.); CARBON COPY(1981); STAR TREK II: THE WRATH OF KHAN(1982); WHITE DOG(1982); ON THE RUN(1983, Aus.)
1984
GO TELL IT ON THE MOUNTAIN(1984); MIKE'S MURDER(1984); TERMINATOR, THE(1984)

Raymond Winfield
PARDON MY SARONG(1942)

Willis Winford
INVISIBLE AVENGER, THE(1958), ph; NEW ORLEANS AFTER DARK(1958), ph; FOUR FOR THE MORGUE(1962), ph

Winna Winfried
  NAUGHTY CINDERELLA(1933, Brit.)
Mrs. Wing
  CHINATOWN NIGHTS(1929)
Ah Wing
Silents
  TALE OF TWO WORLDS, A(1921); MASKED AVENGER, THE(1922)
Anna Wing
  BILLY LIAR(1963, Brit.); TWO GENTLEMEN SHARING(1969, Brit.); DOLL'S
  HOUSE, A(1973, Brit.); FOURTEEN, THE(1973, Brit.); FULL CIRCLE(1977, Brit./Can.);
  PROVIDENCE(1977, Fr.); HAUNTING OF JULIA, THE(1981, Brit./Can.); RUN-
  NERS(1983, Brit.); XTRO(1983, Brit.)
1984
  PLOUGHMAN'S LUNCH, THE(1984, Brit.)
John Wing
  BLACK RODEO(1972), ph
K. Wing
  LIEUTENANT DARING, RN(1935, Brit.)
Lara Wing
  SHANKS(1974)
Leslie Wing
1984
  LONELY GUY, THE(1984)
Pat Wing
  FOOTLIGHT PARADE(1933); GOLD DIGGERS OF 1933(1933); LITTLE GIANT,
  THE(1933); PRIVATE DETECTIVE 62(1933); WORKING MAN, THE(1933); 42ND
  STREET(1933); HI, NELLIE!(1934); JIMMY THE GENT(1934)
Patricia Wing
  FACE ON THE BARROOM FLOOR, THE(1932)
Paul Wing
  HOLD'EM YALE(1935)
Red Wing
Silents
  RAMONA(1916)
Rod Red Wing
  INTRIGUE(1947)
Toby Wing
  KID FROM SPAIN, THE(1932); LITTLE GIANT, THE(1933); PRIVATE DETECTIVE
  62(1933); 42ND STREET(1933); COME ON, MARINES(1934); KISS AND MAKE
  UP(1934); MURDER AT THE VANITIES(1934); SEARCH FOR BEAUTY(1934);
  FORCED LANDING(1935); ONE HOUR LATE(1935); SCHOOL FOR GIRLS(1935); TWO
  FOR TONIGHT(1935); MISTER CINDERELLA(1936); SING WHILE YOU'RE
  ABLE(1937); TRUE CONFESSION(1937); WITH LOVE AND KISSES(1937); WOMEN
  MEN MARRY, THE(1937); MR. BOGGS STEPS OUT(1938); SWEETHEARTS(1938);
  MARINES COME THROUGH, THE(1943)
Misc. Talkies
  SILKS AND SADDLES(1938)
Silents
  PONY EXPRESS, THE(1925)
Virginia Wing
  CHARLEY VARRICK(1973); I OUGHT TO BE IN PICTURES(1982); JEKYLL AND
  HYDE...TOGETHER AGAIN(1982)
Ward Wing
  TELL NO TALES(1939); SHARK WOMAN, THE(1941), d
Silents
  EAGLE, THE(1918); CONQUERING POWER, THE(1921); OVERLAND TELEGRAPH,
  THE(1929), w
Misc. Silents
  EYES OF HOLLYWOOD(1925)
William E. Wing
Silents
  BRAZEN BEAUTY(1918), w; TARZAN OF THE APES(1918), w; LAST CHANCE,
  THE(1921), w; RAIDERS, THE(1921), w; STRUGGLE, THE(1921), w; HANDS
  ACROSS THE BORDER(1926), w
Wong Wing
  DANGEROUS PARADISE(1930)
Mrs. Wong Wing
  WITHOUT REGRET(1935); KLONDIKE ANNIE(1936); DAUGHTER OF SHANG-
  HAI(1937)
Silents
  EAST OF SUEZ(1925); MR. WU(1927); WHERE EAST IS EAST(1929)
Yu Wing
  METEOR(1979)
Mark Wing-Davey
  BREAKING GLASS(1980, Brit.)
Carl-Gunnar Wingard
  WALPURGIS NIGHT(1941, Swed.); WHALERS, THE(1942, Swed.); AFFAIRS OF A
  MODEL(1952, Swed.)
Charles Wingate
Silents
  AMATEUR DEVIL, AN(1921)
Misc. Silents
  ROMANCE PROMOTORS, THE(1920)
Eugenie Wingate
  SCREAM, BABY, SCREAM(1969)
Stephanie Wingate
  TO BE OR NOT TO BE(1983)
William P. Wingate
  ZOOT SUIT(1981), p
Carl Winge
  STUNT PILOT(1939), m
Oscar Winge
  AFFAIRS OF A MODEL(1952, Swed.)
Torsten Winge
  WALPURGIS NIGHT(1941, Swed.); DEVIL'S EYE, THE(1960, Swed.)
Debra Winger
  SLUMBER PARTY '57(1977); THANK GOD IT'S FRIDAY(1978); FRENCH POST-
  CARDS(1979); URBAN COWBOY(1980); CANNERY ROW(1982); OFFICER AND A
  GENTLEMAN, AN(1982); TERMS OF ENDEARMENT(1983)

1984
  MIKE'S MURDER(1984)
Phyllis Winger
  ISLAND IN THE SKY(1953); PRINCESS OF THE NILE(1954)
Ruth Winger
1984
  MIKE'S MURDER(1984)
Jim Wingert
Misc. Talkies
  PANAMA RED(1976)
Mark Wingett
  QUADROPHENIA(1979, Brit.); BREAKING GLASS(1980, Brit.)
Conway Wingfield
  GREAT POWER, THE(1929)
Jeff Wingfield
  BIG JAKE(1971)
Pauline Wingfield
  SKIN GAME, THE(1965, Brit.)
Philippa Wingfield
  WHY ROCK THE BOAT?(1974, Can.), cos
R. Wingo
  HAUNTED(1976), art d
Jason Wingreen
  THREE BRAVE MEN(1957); TRUE STORY OF JESSE JAMES, THE(1957); BRAVA-
  DOS, THE(1958); SLENDER THREAD, THE(1965); GUIDE FOR THE MARRIED MAN,
  A(1967); KARATE KILLERS, THE(1967); MARLOWE(1969); CHEYENNE SOCIAL
  CLUB, THE(1970); DUNWICH HORROR, THE(1970); SKIN GAME(1971); TODD
  KILLINGS, THE(1971); MAGNIFICENT SEVEN RIDE, THE(1972); THEY ONLY KILL
  THEIR MASTERS(1972); TERMINAL MAN, THE(1974); HUSTLE(1975)
1984
  OH GOD! YOU DEVIL(1984)
Ian Wingrove
  PEOPLE THAT TIME FORGOT, THE(1977, Brit.), spec eff; LEGACY, THE(1979,
  Brit.), spec eff; NEVER SAY NEVER AGAIN(1983), spec eff
James Wingrove
  BUSH CHRISTMAS(1983, Aus.)
John Wingrove
1984
  CAREFUL, HE MIGHT HEAR YOU(1984, Aus.), art d
Wingy Manone and His Orchestra
  JUKE BOX JENNY(1942); HI' YA, SAILOR(1943)
Maharaia Winiata
  LAND OF FURY(1955 Brit.)
Krzysztof Winiewicz
  PASSENGER, THE(1970, Pol.), ph
Winna Winifried
  LITTLE MISS NOBODY(1933, Brit.)
Ralph Winigar
  PRETTY POISON(1968), spec eff
Rob Wininger
1984
  BEST DEFENSE(1984)
Alex Winitsky
  HOUSE CALLS(1978), p; SILVER BEARS(1978), p; CUBA(1979), p; BLUE SKIES
  AGAIN(1983), p
1984
  IRRECONCILABLE DIFFERENCES(1984), p; SCANDALOUS(1984), p
Laura Winitsky
1984
  IRRECONCILABLE DIFFERENCES(1984)
Alex Winitzky
  BREAKTHROUGH(1978, Ger.), p
Louise Wink
  MORE(1969, Luxembourg)
Michael Winkelman
  INDIAN FIGHTER, THE(1955); RIDE OUT FOR REVENGE(1957)
Mike Winkelman
  BIG KNIFE, THE(1955)
Wendy Winkelman
  TROUBLE WITH ANGELS, THE(1966)
Frank Winklemann
  HARD HOMBRE(1931)
Adam David Winkler, Jr.
  NEW YORK, NEW YORK(1977)
Angela Winkler
  LOST HONOR OF KATHARINA BLUM, THE(1975, Ger.); GERMANY IN AU-
  TUMN(1978, Ger.); TIN DRUM, THE(1979, Ger./Fr./Yugo./Pol.); LEFT-HANDED
  WOMAN, THE(1980, Ger.); GIRL FROM LORRAINE, A(1982, Fr./Switz.); DAN-
  TON(1983); FRIENDS AND HUSBANDS(1983, Ger.); WAR AND PEACE(1983, Ger.)
Art Winkler
  MIDNIGHT WARNING, THE(1932)
Misc. Silents
  TWISTED TRIGGERS(1926)
Baby Winkler
  OVERTURE TO GLORY(1940)
Bob Winkler
  WATERLOO BRIDGE(1940)
Gary Winkler
  DEATHLINE(1973, Brit.)
George Winkler
Silents
  EVE'S LOVER(1925), ph
Henry Winkler
  CRAZY JOE(1974); LORDS OF FLATBUSH, THE(1974); HEROES(1977); ONE AND
  ONLY, THE(1978); NIGHT SHIFT(1982)
Irwin Winkler
  DOUBLE TROUBLE(1967), p; BLUE(1968), p; SPLIT, THE(1968), p; THEY SHOOT
  HORSES, DON'T THEY?(1969), p; LEO THE LAST(1970, Brit.), p; STRAWBERRY
  STATEMENT, THE(1970), p; BELIEVE IN ME(1971), p; GANG THAT COULDN'T
  SHOOT STRAIGHT, THE(1971), p; MECHANIC, THE(1972), p; NEW CENTURIONS,

THE(1972), p; THUMB TRIPPING(1972), p; UP THE SANDBOX(1972), p; BUS-TING(1974), p; GAMBLER, THE(1974), p; S(1974), p; BREAKOUT(1975), p; PEE-PER(1975), p; NICKELODEON(1976), p; ROCKY(1976), p; NEW YORK, NEW YORK(1977), p; VALENTINO(1977, Brit.), p; UNCLE JOE SHANNON(1978), p; ROCKY II(1979), p; RAGING BULL(1980), p; TRUE CONFESSIONS(1981), p; AUTHOR! AUTHOR!(1982), p; ROCKY III(1982), p; RIGHT STUFF, THE(1983), p

Jim Winkler
  DEMETRIUS AND THE GLADIATORS(1954)

K.C. Winkler
  H.O.T.S.(1979); NIGHT SHIFT(1982)

Margo Winkler
  STRAWBERRY STATEMENT, THE(1970); UP THE SANDBOX(1972); PEE-PER(1975); NEW YORK, NEW YORK(1977); KING OF COMEDY, THE(1983)

Peter Erik Winkler
  DARK ODYSSEY(1961), ph

Robert Winkler
  TRUE TO LIFE(1943); BLUE MONTANA SKIES(1939); CHEROKEE STRIP(1940); GUN CODE(1940); RIDERS OF PASCO BASIN(1940); BAD MEN OF MISSOURI(1941); LIFE BEGINS FOR ANDY HARDY(1941); LUCKY DEVILS(1941); PALS OF THE PECOS(1941); PUBLIC ENEMIES(1941); SULLIVAN'S TRAVELS(1941); WAGONS ROLL AT NIGHT, THE(1941); WEST POINT WIDOW(1941); WILDCAT OF TUC-SON(1941); EYES IN THE NIGHT(1942); PRIDE OF THE YANKEES, THE(1942); THIS GUN FOR HIRE(1942); GOOD FELLOWS, THE(1943); IRON MAJOR, THE(1943); YOUNGEST PROFESSION, THE(1943); INCENDIARY BLONDE(1945); PRAIRIE EXPRESS(1947); CRISS CROSS(1949)

Suzanne Winkler
  DEATHLINE(1973, Brit.)

Terence H. Winkless
  HOWLING, THE(1981), w

Terry Winkless
  HEART BEAT(1979)

Mike Winlaw
  FIRST BLOOD(1982)

Joan Winmill
  WHITE CORRIDORS(1952, Brit.); HARASSED HERO, THE(1954, Brit.); INNOCENTS IN PARIS(1955, Brit.); SOULS IN CONFLICT(1955, Brit.)
Misc. Talkies
  TIME TO RUN(1974)

Sammie Winmill
  PIED PIPER, THE(1972, Brit.)

Albert C. Winn
  FORTY THOUSAND HORSEMEN(1941, Aus.)

Anona Winn
  ON THE AIR(1934, Brit.)

Charlotte Winn
Silents
  LONE HORSEMAN, THE(1929)

D. E. A. Winn
  NOT SO DUSTY(1956, Brit.), p

Derek Winn
  BOOBY TRAP(1957, Brit.), p; CROOKED SKY, THE(1957, Brit.), p; FIGHTING WILDCATS, THE(1957, Brit.), p; UNDERCOVER GIRL(1957, Brit.), p; STRANGE CASE OF DR. MANNING, THE(1958, Brit.), p; HIDDEN HOMICIDE(1959, Brit.), p

Ed Winn
  CARAVAN TRAIL, THE(1946), ed

Godfrey Winn
  COMING-OUT PARTY, A(; HOLIDAY CAMP(1947, Brit.), w; BILLY LIAR(1963, Brit.); BARGEE, THE(1964, Brit.); GREAT ST. TRINIAN'S TRAIN ROBBERY, THE(1966, Brit.)

Hugh Winn
  AGE OF INDISCRETION(1935), ed; DEAD OR ALIVE(1944), ed; GREAT MIKE, THE(1944), ed; WHISPERING SKULL, THE(1944), ed; PHANTOM OF 42ND STREET, THE(1945), ed; SONG OF OLD WYOMING(1945), ed; STRANGLER OF THE SWAMP(1945), ed; COLORADO SERENADE(1946), ed; DRIFTIN' RIVER(1946), ed; ROMANCE OF THE WEST(1946), ed; STARS OVER TEXAS(1946), ed; TUM-BLEWEED TRAIL(1946), ed; WILD WEST(1946), ed; FIGHTING VIGILANTES, THE(1947), ed; LAW OF THE LASH(1947), ed; PIONEER JUSTICE(1947), ed; RANGE BEYOND THE BLUE(1947), ed; RETURN OF THE LASH(1947), ed; STAGE TO MESA CITY(1947), ed; WEST TO GLORY(1947), ed; WILD COUNTRY(1947), ed; BLACK HILLS(1948), ed; DEAD MAN'S GOLD(1948), ed; FRONTIER REVENGE(1948), ed; MARK OF THE LASH(1948), ed; TIOGA KID, THE(1948), ed; WESTWARD TRAIL, THE(1948), ed; DALTON GANG, THE(1949), ed; OUTLAW COUNTRY(1949), ed; RED DESERT(1949), ed; RIMFIRE(1949), ed; RINGSIDE(1949), ed; SHEP COMES HO-ME(1949), ed; SON OF A BADMAN(1949), ed; SON OF BILLY THE KID(1949), ed; SQUARE DANCE JUBILEE(1949), ed; COLORADO RANGER(1950), ed; CROOKED RIVER(1950), ed; FAST ON THE DRAW(1950), ed; HOSTILE COUNTRY(1950), ed; KING OF THE BULLWHIP(1950), ed; MARSHAL OF HELDORADO(1950), ed; WEST OF THE BRAZOS(1950), ed; KENTUCKY JUBILEE(1951), ed; THUNDERING TRAIL, THE(1951), ed; VANISHING OUTPOST, THE(1951), ed; YES SIR, MR. BONES(1951), ed; OUTLAW WOMEN(1952), ed; MESA OF LOST WOMEN, THE(1956), ed

Jack Winn
Silents
  BLOOD AND SAND(1922); ABRAHAM LINCOLN(1924)

John Winn
Silents
  MARK OF ZORRO(1920)

Kitty Winn
  PANIC IN NEEDLE PARK(1971); THEY MIGHT BE GIANTS(1971); EXORCIST, THE(1973); PEEPER(1975); EXORCIST II: THE HERETIC(1977)
1984
  MIRRORS(1984)

Mary Lou Winn
Misc. Silents
  UNKNOWN RIDER, THE(1929)

May Winn
  MY WIFE'S BEST FRIEND(1952)

Robert W. Winn
  GREAT WALDO PEPPER, THE(1975)

Sally Winn
  FROM THE TERRACE(1960)

Stanley W. Winn
  PREMONITION, THE(1976)

Andrew Winner
  NICKELODEON(1976); FRANCES(1982); HAMMETT(1982); I'M DANCING AS FAST AS I CAN(1982); VALLEY GIRL(1983)

Howard Winner
  BIRDS DO IT(1966), ph; GENTLE GIANT(1967), ph

Jeffrey Winner
  MASSACRE AT CENTRAL HIGH(1976)

Michael Winner
  MAN WITH A GUN(1958, Brit.), w; OLD MAC(1961, Brit.), d; SHOOT TO KILL(1961, Brit.), d&w; COOL MIKADO, THE(1963, Brit.), d, w; MURDER ON THE CAM-PUS(1963, Brit.), p, d&w; PLAY IT COOL(1963, Brit.), p, d&w; WEST 11(1963, Brit.), d; YOU MUST BE JOKING!(1965, Brit.), d, w; GIRL GETTERS, THE(1966, Brit.), d; I'LL NEVER FORGET WHAT'S 'IS NAME(1967, Brit.), p&d; JOKERS, THE(1967, Brit.), d, w; HANNIBAL BROOKS(1969, Brit.), p&d, w; GAMES, THE(1970), d; LAW-MAN(1971), p&d; NIGHT COMERS, THE(1971, Brit.), p&d; CHATO'S LAND(1972), p&d; MECHANIC, THE(1972), d; SCORPIO(1973), d; STONE KILLER, THE(1973), p&d; WON TON TON, THE DOG WHO SAVED HOLLYWOOD(1976), p, d; SENTINEL, THE(1977), p, d, w; BIG SLEEP, THE½(1978, Brit.), p, d&w; FIREPOWER(1979, Brit.), p&d; DEATH WISH II(1982), d; WICKED LADY, THE(1983, Brit.), d, w
1984
  SCREAM FOR HELP(1984), p&d

Vic Winner
  DRACULA'S GREAT LOVE(1972, Span.); HUNCHBACK OF THE MORGUE, THE(1972, Span.)

Michael Winners
  DEATH WISH(1974), p, d

Olof Winnerstrand
  NIGHT IN JUNE, A(1940, Swed.); TORMENT(1947, Swed.); AFFAIRS OF A MO-DEL(1952, Swed.); LESSON IN LOVE, A(1960, Swed.); NIGHT IS MY FUTURE(1962, Swed.)

Lucyna Winnicka
  FIRST SPACESHIP ON VENUS(1960, Ger./Pol.); JOAN OF THE ANGELS(1962, Pol.); KNIGHTS OF THE TEUTONIC ORDER, THE(1962, Pol.)

Winnie
  TATTOO(1981)

Dustye Winniford
  STREAMERS(1983)

Charles Winninger
  SOUP TO NUTS(1930); BAD SISTER(1931); CHILDREN OF DREAMS(1931); FIGHT-ING CARAVANS(1931); FLYING HIGH(1931); GOD'S GIFT TO WOMEN(1931); GUN SMOKE(1931); HUSBAND'S HOLIDAY(1931); NIGHT NURSE(1931); SIN OF MADEL-ON CLAUDET, THE(1931); SOCIAL REGISTER(1934); SHOW BOAT(1936); WHITE FANG(1936); CAFE METROPOLE(1937); GO-GETTER, THE(1937); NOTHING SA-CRED(1937); THREE SMART GIRLS(1937); WOMAN CHASES MAN(1937); YOU CAN'T HAVE EVERYTHING(1937); YOU'RE A SWEETHEART(1937); EVERY DAY'S A HOLIDAY(1938); GOODBYE BROADWAY(1938); HARD TO GET(1938); BABES IN ARMS(1939); BARRICADE(1939); DESTRY RIDES AGAIN(1939); THREE SMART GIRLS GROW UP(1939); BEYOND TOMORROW(1940); IF I HAD MY WAY(1940); LITTLE NELLIE KELLY(1940); MY LOVE CAME BACK(1940); GET-AWAY, THE(1941); MY LIFE WITH CAROLINE(1941); POT O' GOLD(1941); ZIEGFELD GIRL(1941); FRIENDLY ENEMIES(1942); CONEY ISLAND(1943); FLESH AND FAN-TASY(1943); HERS TO HOLD(1943); LADY TAKES A CHANCE, A(1943); BELLE OF THE YUKON(1944); BROADWAY RHYTHM(1944); SUNDAY DINNER FOR A SOL-DIER(1944); SHE WOULDN'T SAY YES(1945); STATE FAIR(1945); LOVER COME BACK(1946); LIVING IN A BIG WAY(1947); SOMETHING IN THE WIND(1947); GIVE MY REGARDS TO BROADWAY(1948); INSIDE STORY, THE(1948); FATHER IS A BACHELOR(1950); CHAMP FOR A DAY(1953); PERILOUS JOURNEY, A(1953); SUN SHINES BRIGHT, THE(1953); TORPEDO ALLEY(1953); LAS VEGAS SHAKE-DOWN(1955); RAYMIE(1960); MIRACLE OF SANTA'S WHITE REINDEER, THE(1963)
Silents
  SUMMER BACHELORS(1926)

Marc Winningham
  ONE-TRICK PONY(1980)

Mare Winningham
  THRESHOLD(1983, Can.)

Marc Winocourt
  MURMUR OF THE HEART(1971, Fr./Ital./Ger.)

Anatol Winogardoff
  SHE(1935)

Leslie Winograde
  STUNT MAN, THE(1980)

Anatol Winogradoff
  GO, MAN, GO!(1954); PLEASE DON'T EAT THE DAISIES(1960); GIRL FROM PETROVKA, THE(1974)

M. Winogradowa
  LAST STOP, THE(1949, Pol.)

Anatol Winopradoff
  YOUNG FRANKENSTEIN(1974)

Marianne Winquist
1984
  LA PETIT SIRENE(1984, Fr.)

Jerry Winsett
1984
  PREPPIES(1984)

Kip Winsett
  CAPTAIN MILKSHAKE(1970)

Barrie Winship
  OCTOPUSSY(1983, Brit.)

George Winship
  MOONLIGHTING WIVES(1966); TEENAGE GANG DEBS(1966); MY BODY HUN-GERS(1967)

Sian Winship
  WHAT'S THE MATTER WITH HELEN?(1971)

Norman Winski
SIX PACK ANNIE(1975), w
Christa Winsloe
MAEDCHEN IN UNIFORM(1932, Ger.), w; MAEDCHEN IN UNIFORM(1965, Ger./Fr.), w
Baby John Winslow
CLOSE TO MY HEART(1951)
Diana Winslow
KID FROM SPAIN, THE(1932)
Dick Winslow
TOM SAWYER(1930); SEED(1931); FORBIDDEN(1932); SO BIG(1932); TOM BROWN OF CULVER(1932); LAUGHTER IN HELL(1933); FLIRTATION WALK(1934); HUMAN SIDE, THE(1934); MAN WITH TWO FACES, THE(1934); TWENTY MILLION SWEET-HEARTS(1934); UNCERTAIN LADY(1934); FRONT PAGE WOMAN(1935); MUTINY ON THE BOUNTY(1935); ONE EXCITING ADVENTURE(1935); ROSE BOWL(1936); LETTER OF INTRODUCTION(1938); TEST PILOT(1938); DANCING CO-ED(1939); GOOD GIRLS GO TO PARIS(1939); WHEN TOMORROW COMES(1939); MANHAT-TAN HEARTBEAT(1940); TEN GENTLEMEN FROM WEST POINT(1942); IS EVERY-BODY HAPPY?(1943); ABBOTT AND COSTELLO IN HOLLYWOOD(1945); BLUE DAHLIA, THE(1946); EASY TO WED(1946); MY REPUTATION(1946); FRENCH LEAVE(1948); ON AN ISLAND WITH YOU(1948); YOU WERE MEANT FOR ME(1948); I'LL GET BY(1950); BENNY GOODMAN STORY, THE(1956); FRANCIS IN THE HAUNTED HOUSE(1956); KING CREOLE(1958); ERRAND BOY, THE(1961); EVERY-THING'S DUCKY(1961); TWIST ALL NIGHT(1961); DO NOT DISTURB(1965); RIOT ON SUNSET STRIP(1967); NEVER A DULL MOMENT(1968); WRECKING CREW, THE(1968); AIRPORT(1970); APPLE DUMPLING GANG, THE(1975); OTHER SIDE OF THE MOUNTAIN, THE(1975); SHOOTIST, THE(1976); TWO-MINUTE WAR-NING(1976); MOVIE MOVIE(1978); FIRST MONDAY IN OCTOBER(1981)
Silents
AVALANCHE(1928)
Misc. Silents
RANGE COURAGE(1927)
George Winslow
MY PAL GUS(1952); GENTLEMEN PREFER BLONDES(1953); ROCKET MAN, THE(1954); ARTISTS AND MODELS(1955)
George "Foghorn" Winslow
MONKEY BUSINESS(1952); ROOM FOR ONE MORE(1952); MR. SCOUTMAS-TER(1953); SUMMER LOVE(1958); WILD HERITAGE(1958)
George "Foghorn" Winslow, Jr.
ROCK, PRETTY BABY(1956)
H. L. Winslow
Silents
MANON LESCAUT(1914)
Herbert Hall Winslow
Silents
RECKLESS ROMANCE(1924), w
Leah Winslow
SHE-WOLF, THE(1931); MAGNIFICENT OBSESSION(1935)
Lutra Winslow
DEVIL'S PLAYGROUND(1937)
Michael Winslow
CHEECH AND CHONG'S NICE DREAMS(1981); T.A.G.: THE ASSASSINATION GAME(1982)
1984
ALPHABET CITY(1984); GRANDVIEW, U.S.A.(1984); LOVELINES(1984); POLICE ACADEMY(1984)
Mike Winslow
HEIDI'S SONG(1982)
Paula Winslow
SARATOGA(1937)
Richard Winslow
Silents
AVALANCHE(1928)
Thyra Samter Winslow
SHE MARRIED HER BOSS(1935), w
Yvonne Winslow
TOUCH OF SATAN, THE(1971)
Misc. Talkies
TOUCH OF SATAN, THE(1974)
Dick Winslowe
EMBRYO(1976)
Jack Winslowe
TO HAVE AND HAVE NOT(1944)
Kathleen Winsor
FOREVER AMBER(1947), w
Terry Winsor
PARTY PARTY(1983, Brit.), d, w
Ernie Winstanley
DETROIT 9000(1973)
Jean Winstanley
SEZ O'REILLY TO MACNAB(1938, Brit.)
Michele Winstanley
REMEMBRANCE(1982, Brit.); PARTY PARTY(1983, Brit.)
Sir Hubert Winstead
INGAGI(1931)
Harlene Winsten
SKATETOWN, U.S.A.(1979)
Stephen Winsten
SCRATCH HARRY(1969), w&ph
Stephen R. Winsten
SHAME, SHAME, EVERYBODY KNOWS HER NAME(1969), ph
Steve Winsten
DRIFTER, THE(1966), ph
Brian Winston
THIRD WALKER, THE(1978, Can.), p
Bruce Winston
LATIN LOVE(1930, Brit.); CHILDREN OF DREAMS(1931); GREAT GAY ROAD, THE(1931, Brit.); PRIVATE LIFE OF DON JUAN, THE(1934, Brit.); HEAT WAVE(1935, Brit.); MY SONG FOR YOU(1935, Brit.); BROWN WALLET, THE(1936, Brit.); EVERY-BODY DANCE(1936, Brit.); EVERYTHING IN LIFE(1936, Brit.); LAST WALTZ,

THE(1936, Brit.); INTIMATE RELATIONS(1937, Brit.); MAN WHO COULD WORK MIRACLES, THE(1937, Brit.); ALF'S BUTTON AFLOAT(1938, Brit.); SAILING ALONG(1938, Brit.); OVER THE MOON(1940, Brit.); THIEF OF BAGHDAD, THE(1940, Brit.); YOUNG MR. PITT, THE(1942, Brit.); CARNIVAL(1946, Brit.); FRENZY(1946, Brit.)
Silents
PATRICIA BRENT, SPINSTER(1919, Brit.); QUEEN'S EVIDENCE(1919, Brit.)
C. Winston
LOVE WALTZ, THE(1930, Ger.), d
Charles Winston
Silents
IDOL OF THE STAGE, THE(1916)
Hattie Winston
WITHOUT A TRACE(1983)
Helen Winston
YOU FOR ME(1952); BATTLE CIRCUS(1953); PORT SINISTER(1953); TOBOR THE GREAT(1954); HAND IN HAND(1960, Brit.), p; SEND ME NO FLOWERS(1964); WITCHMAKER, THE(1969); BOY AND HIS DOG, A(1975)
Helen F. Winston
WHAT A WAY TO GO(1964)
Helene Winston
TROUBLE WITH GIRLS(AND HOW TO GET INTO IT), THE*1/2 (1969); DOUBLE TROUBLE(1967); WHAT'S THE MATTER WITH HELEN?(1971); SHAGGY D.A., THE(1976)
Irene Winston
BURY ME DEAD(1947), w; DEAR BRAT(1951); CARRIE(1952); MY SON, JOHN(1952); REAR WINDOW(1954); DELICATE DELINQUENT, THE(1957)
Janelle Winston
MANIAC(1980)
Jimmy Winston
NO BLADE OF GRASS(1970, Brit.)
John Winston
CALIFORNIA SPLIT(1974); STAR TREK II: THE WRATH OF KHAN(1982)
Lance Winston
SLAUGHTER(1972)
Laura Winston
Silents
ALADDIN FROM BROADWAY(1917); MONEY MAGIC(1917)
Misc. Silents
CAVANAUGH OF THE FOREST RANGERS(1918); FORGOTTEN WOMAN(1921); BATTLING FOOL, THE(1924)
Marilyn Winston
RESTLESS BREED, THE(1957)
Mary Winston
Silents
OUTSIDE WOMAN, THE(1921); LAVENDER BATH LADY, THE(1922)
Mary Ellen Winston
WARRIORS, THE(1979), cos
Mildred Winston
HIT PARADE, THE(1937)
Norman Winston
LOOK IN ANY WINDOW(1961)
Raymond Winston
GREAT AMERICAN PASTIME, THE(1956); LEATHER SAINT, THE(1956); MAN IN THE GREY FLANNEL SUIT, THE(1956)
Robert Winston
STARFIGHTERS, THE(1964); DOUBLE-BARRELLED DETECTIVE STORY, THE(1965)
Robert J. Winston
COMEBACK TRAIL, THE(1982), w
Ron Winston
AMBUSH BAY(1966), d; BANNING(1967), d; DON'T JUST STAND THERE(1968), d; GAMBLERS, THE(1969), d&w
S.K. Winston
DEVIL IS A WOMAN, THE(1935), w; I ESCAPED FROM THE GESTAPO(1943), ed; THREE RUSSIAN GIRLS(1943), ed
Misc. Talkies
ADVENTURE IN MUSIC(1944), d
Sam Winston
BLUE ANGEL, THE(1930, Ger.), ed; MOROCCO(1930), ed; DEVIL IS A WOMAN, THE(1935), ed; SHANGHAI GESTURE, THE(1941), ed
Sir Winston
HORSE IN THE GRAY FLANNEL SUIT, THE(1968)
Stan Winston
WIZ, THE(1978), makeup; MAN IN THE GLASS BOOTH, THE(1975), makeup; W.C. FIELDS AND ME(1976), makeup; DEAD AND BURIED(1981), spec eff; HEART-BEEPS(1981), spec eff; PARASITE(1982), spec eff
1984
TERMINATOR, THE(1984), spec eff
Steve Winston
GHOST SHIP, THE(1943); GOVERNMENT GIRL(1943); IRON MAJOR, THE(1943); FALCON OUT WEST, THE(1944); MADEMOISELLE FIFI(1944); MUSIC IN MANHAT-TAN(1944)
Steven Winston
OREGON TRAIL(1945)
Vivian Winston
AMERICAN TRAGEDY, AN(1931); STAND UP AND CHEER(1934 80m FOX bw)
Silents
IS YOUR DAUGHTER SAFE?(1927)
Ray Winstone
SCUM(1979, Brit.); THAT SUMMER(1979, Brit.); LADIES AND GENTLEMEN, THE FABULOUS STAINS(1982)
1984
NUMBER ONE(1984, Brit.)
Raymond Winstone
QUADROPHENIA(1979, Brit.)
Al Winter
DRAGONWYCH(1946)

Bottles Winter
Misc. Silents
 PRICE OF JUSTICE, THE(1914, Brit.)
Brett Strange Winter
Silents
 JIMMY(1916, Brit.)
Cady Winter
Misc. Silents
 DANGER LINE, THE(1924)
Catherine Winter
 TOO MANY BLONDES(1941); LA GUERRE EST FINIE(1967, Fr./Swed.), p
Cherry Winter
Misc. Silents
 SHADOW BETWEEN, THE(1920, Brit.)
Christa Winter
 WONDER BOY(1951, Brit./Aust.)
Claude Winter
1984
 LE BON PLAISIR(1984, Fr.); SUNDAY IN THE COUNTRY, A(1984, Fr.)
Dale Winter
 BACK STREET(1941); MODEL WIFE(1941); CAREFUL, SOFT SHOULDERS(1942)
Dave Winter
Silents
 STRANGER THAN FICTION(1921)
Misc. Silents
 TRUST YOUR WIFE(1921); TWO KINDS OF WOMEN(1922)
David Winter
Silents
 POVERTY OF RICHES, THE(1921)
Donna Winter
1984
 FIRST TURN-ON!, THE(1984)
Donovan Winter
 GALLOPING MAJOR, THE(1951, Brit.); MOULIN ROUGE(1952); TIME GENTLE-MEN PLEASE!(1953, Brit.); TRUNK, THE(1961, Brit.), d&w; COME BACK PE-TER(1971, Brit.), p,d,w&ed
Donovon Winter
 DEADLY FEMALES, THE(1976, Brit.), p,d&w
Ed Winter
 CHANGE OF SEASONS, A(1980)
Edward Winter
 SPECIAL DELIVERY(1976); PORKY'S II: THE NEXT DAY(1983)
1984
 BUDDY SYSTEM, THE(1984)
Isolde Winter
 ENTER THE NINJA(1982)
Jessie Winter
 MAN OF AFFAIRS(1937, Brit.); MURDER IN THE FAMILY(1938, Brit.)
Silents
 DIAMOND NECKLACE, THE(1921, Brit.)
Misc. Silents
 GOODBYE(1918, Brit.); TWELVE POUND LOOK, THE(1920, Brit.)
John Strange Winter
Silents
 JIMMY(1916, Brit.), w
Judy Winter
Misc. Talkies
 BLONDE CONNECTION, THE(1975)
Keith Winter
 UNCLE HARRY(1945), w; CHOCOLATE SOLDIER, THE(1941), w; ABOVE SUSPI-CION(1943), w; DEVOTION(1946), w; RED SHOES, THE(1948, Brit.), w
Larry Winter
 MYSTERY SUBMARINE(1950); OPERATION SECRET(1952)
Laska Winter
 FROZEN JUSTICE(1929); MYSTERIOUS DR. FU MANCHU, THE(1929); CHINA-TOWN AFTER DARK(1931); PAINTED WOMAN(1932); RAINBOW TRAIL(1932)
Silents
 JUSTICE OF THE FAR NORTH(1925); TENDER HOUR, THE(1927)
Misc. Silents
 MARRIAGE CHEAT, THE(1924); TIDES OF PASSION(1925)
Lee Winter
 YOUNG LIONS, THE(1958)
Lex Winter
 VAMPIRE HOOKERS, THE(1979, Phil.)
Louise Winter
Silents
 BRAZEN BEAUTY(1918), w; MAD DANCER(1925), w
M. Winter
 FIDDLER ON THE ROOF(1971)
Magrit Winter
 IT HAPPENED IN BROAD DAYLIGHT(1960, Ger./Switz.)
Mick Winter
 PALM BEACH(1979, Aus.)
Nancy Winter
 GANG'S ALL HERE, THE(1943), w
Pauline Winter
 HOUSE OF DARKNESS(1948, Brit.); DEATM GOES TO SCHOOL(1953, Brit.); END OF THE ROAD, THE(1954, Brit.); KEEP IT CLEAN(1956, Brit.); AS LONG AS THEY'RE HAPPY(1957, Brit.); THREE MEN IN A BOAT(1958, Brit.); MIND BENDERS, THE(1963, Brit.); IPCRESS FILE, THE(1965, Brit.)
Percy Winter
Misc. Silents
 OTHER GIRL, THE(1916), d
Philip Winter
 LILLIAN RUSSELL(1940); REBECCA(1940)
Robert Winter
 EYES OF ANNIE JONES, THE(1963, Brit.), ed; EARTH DIES SCREAMING, THE(1964, Brit.), ed; HORROR OF IT ALL, THE(1964, Brit.), ed; NIGHT TRAIN TO PARIS(1964, Brit.), ed; WALK A TIGHTROPE(1964, U.S./Brit.), ed; WITCH-CRAFT(1964, Brit.), ed; RETURN OF MR. MOTO, THE(1965, Brit.), ed; SPACEF-

LIGHT IC-1(1965, Brit.), ed; WOMAN WHO WOULDN'T DIE, THE(1965, Brit.), ed; MURDER GAME, THE(1966, Brit.), ed; LAST SHOT YOU HEAR, THE(1969, Brit.), ed
Sharon Winter
 POPE JOAN(1972, Brit.)
Virginia Winter
 MAN ON THE RUN(1949, Brit.); TIME GENTLEMEN PLEASE!(1953, Brit.)
Sid Winter
1984
 BROADWAY DANNY ROSE(1984); GOODBYE PEOPLE, THE(1984)
Terry Winter
 SCROOGE(1970, Brit.)
Misc. Talkies
 CRUISIN' 57(1975)
Tomislav Winter
 BATTLE OF THE NERETVA(1971, Yugo./Ital./Ger.), ph
Val Winter
 PANIC IN THE STREETS(1950); LOUISIANA TERRITORY(1953); STREET OF DARKNESS(1958); FOUR FOR THE MORGUE(1962)
Verne Winter
Silents
 BLAZING TRAIL, THE(1921); MILLIONAIRE, THE(1921); KENTUCKY DERBY, THE(1922); PURE GRIT(1923)
Vincent Winter
 LITTLE KIDNAPPERS, THE(1954, Brit.); WARRIORS, THE(1955); BEYOND THIS PLACE(1959, Brit.); BRIDAL PATH, THE(1959, Brit.); TIME LOCK(1959, Brit.); GORGO(1961, Brit.); GREYFRIARS BOBBY(1961, Brit.); ALMOST ANGELS(1962); THREE LIVES OF THOMASINA, THE(1963, U.S./Brit.)
Shelley Winter [Winters]
 KNICKERBOCKER HOLIDAY(1944); SHE'S A SOLDIER TOO(1944)
Howard Winterbottom
 UNSUSPECTED, THE(1947), set d; ROMANCE ON THE HIGH SEAS(1948), set d; FLAMINGO ROAD(1949), set d; MY DREAM IS YOURS(1949), set d; ONE LAST FLING(1949), set d
Tony Winterbottom
 SUSPENDED ALIBI(1957, Brit.)
John Wintergate
Misc. Talkies
 BOARDING HOUSE(1984), d
Al Winters
 CLUNY BROWN(1946); SEARCHING WIND, THE(1946); GOLDEN EAR-RINGS(1947); IT HAPPENED ON 5TH AVENUE(1947); JOAN OF ARC(1948)
Arthur Winters
 MOTHERS OF TODAY(1939)
Arthur E. Winters
 YOUNG BESS(1953), ed
Bernie Winters
 6.5 SPECIAL(1958, Brit.); IDOL ON PARADE(1959, Brit.); IN THE NICK(1960, Brit.); JAZZ BOAT(1960, Brit.); LET'S GET MARRIED(1960, Brit.); COOL MIKADO, THE(1963, Brit.); PLAY IT COOL(1963, Brit.); JOHNNY NOBODY(1965, Brit.)
Misc. Talkies
 PLAY IT COOLER(1961)
Bob Winters
 DELIRIUM(1979)
Charlotte Winters
 SMART BLONDE(1937)
D.D. Winters
 TERROR TRAIN(1980, Can.); TANYA'S ISLAND(1981, Can.)
David Winters
 ROOGIE'S BUMP(1954); ROCK, ROCK, ROCK!(1956); LAST ANGRY MAN, THE(1959); WEST SIDE STORY(1961); CAPTAIN NEWMAN, M.D.(1963); NEW IN-TERNS, THE(1964); PAJAMA PARTY(1964), ch; SEND ME NO FLOWERS(1964), ch; VIVA LAS VEGAS(1964), ch; BILLIE(1965), ch; GIRL HAPPY(1965), ch; TICKLE ME(1965), ch; MADE IN PARIS(1966), ch; SWINGER, THE(1966), ch; EASY COME, EASY GO(1967), ch; STAR IS BORN, A(1976), ch; RACQUET(1979), p, d; ROLLER BOOGIE(1979), ch
1984
 LAST HORROR FILM, THE(1984), a, p, d, w
Deborah Winters
 HAIL, HERO!(1969); ME, NATALIE(1969); PEOPLE NEXT DOOR, THE(1970); KOTCH(1971); CLASS OF '44(1973); BLUE SUNSHINE(1978)
Dick Winters
 DAVID AND BATHSHEBA(1951)
Gary B. Winters
 CONQUEST OF THE EARTH(1980), p
George Winters
 CHASE, THE(1966)
Gloria Winters
 GAMBLING HOUSE(1950); HOT ROD(1950); LAWLESS, THE(1950); DARLING, HOW COULD YOU!(1951); HOLD THAT LINE(1952); SHE COULDN'T SAY NO(1954)
Misc. Talkies
 STAGECOACH DRIVER(1951)
Holle K. Winters
 MOTOR PSYCHO(1965)
J'len Winters
1984
 LAST HORROR FILM, THE(1984)
Jeri Winters
 MY THIRD WIFE GEORGE(1968)
Joan Winters
 VARIETY JUBILEE(1945, Brit.)
Jonathan Winters
 ALAKAZAM THE GREAT!(1961, Jap.); IT'S A MAD, MAD, MAD, MAD WORLD(1963); LOVED ONE, THE(1965); PENELOPE(1966); RUSSIANS ARE COM-ING, THE RUSSIANS ARE COMING, THE(1966); EIGHT ON THE LAM(1967); OH DAD, POOR DAD, MAMA'S HUNG YOU IN THE CLOSET AND I'M FEELIN' SO SAD(1967); VIVA MAX!(1969); FISH THAT SAVED PITTSBURGH, THE(1979)
Keith Winters
 SHINING HOUR, THE(1938), w; FOREVER AND A DAY(1943), w

Laska Winters
SEVEN FOOTPRINTS TO SATAN(1929)
Silents
NIGHT OF LOVE, THE(1927); RESCUE, THE(1929)
Misc. Silents
ROCKING MOON(1926); FASHION MADNESS(1928)

Lee J. Winters
ENEMY BELOW, THE(1957)

Linda Winters
COMET OVER BROADWAY(1938); PRISON TRAIN(1938); BLONDIE MEETS THE BOSS(1939); CAFE HOSTESS(1940); SCANDAL SHEET(1940)

Linda Winters [Dorothy Comingore]
FIVE LITTLE PEPPERS AND HOW THEY GREW(1939); MR. SMITH GOES TO WASHINGTON(1939); NORTH OF THE YUKON(1939); PIONEERS OF THE FRONTIER(1940)

Marla Winters
HOLLYWOOD HIGH(1977)

Meg Winters
SCARECROW IN A GARDEN OF CUCUMBERS(1972)

Mike Winters
6.5 SPECIAL(1958, Brit.); COOL MIKADO, THE(1963, Brit.)

Patricia Winters
VERY SPECIAL FAVOR, A(1965); THIS IS A HIJACK(1973)

Pauline Winters
HAPPY IS THE BRIDE(1958, Brit.)

Peter M. Winters
Silents
SALOME(1922), w

Ralph Winters
MR. AND MRS. NORTH(1941), ed; PENALTY, THE(1941), ed; PEOPLE VS. DR. KILDARE, THE(1941), ed; AFFAIRS OF MARTHA, THE(1942), ed; DR. GILLESPIE'S NEW ASSISTANT(1942), ed; EYES IN THE NIGHT(1942), ed; KID GLOVE KILLER(1942), ed; YOUNGEST PROFESSION, THE(1943), ed; INTRIGUE(1947); SOLDIER IN THE RAIN(1963), ed; PINK PANTHER, THE(1964), ed; FITZWILLY(1967), ed; PARTY, THE(1968), ed; THOMAS CROWN AFFAIR, THE(1968), ed; GAILY, GAILY(1969), ed; HAWAIIANS, THE(1970), ed; SPIKES GANG, THE(1974), ed; ENTERTAINER, THE(1975), ed

Ralph E. Winters
CRY HAVOC(1943), ed; YOUNG IDEAS(1943), ed; GASLIGHT(1944), ed; THIN MAN GOES HOME, THE(1944), ed; OUR VINES HAVE TENDER GRAPES(1945), ed; BOYS' RANCH(1946), ed; KILLER McCOY(1947), ed; ROMANCE OF ROSY RIDGE, THE(1947), ed; HILLS OF HOME(1948), ed; TENTH AVENUE ANGEL(1948), ed; ANY NUMBER CAN PLAY(1949), ed; LITTLE WOMEN(1949), ed; ON THE TOWN(1949), ed; KING SOLOMON'S MINES(1950), ed; KISS ME KATE(1953), ed; STORY OF THREE LOVES, THE(1953), ed; EXECUTIVE SUITE(1954), ed; SEVEN BRIDES FOR SEVEN BROTHERS(1954), ed; JUPITER'S DARLING(1955), ed; LOVE ME OR LEAVE ME(1955), ed; HIGH SOCIETY(1956), ed; TRIBUTE TO A BADMAN(1956), ed; JAILHOUSE ROCK(1957), ed; MAN ON FIRE(1957), ed; SHEEPMAN, THE(1958), ed; BEN HUR(1959), ed; BUTTERFIELD 8(1960), ed; ADA(1961), ed; DIME WITH A HALO(1963), ed; GREAT RACE, THE(1965), ed; WHAT DID YOU DO IN THE WAR, DADDY?(1966), ed; KOTCH(1971), ed; AVANTI!(1972), ed; CAREY TREATMENT, THE(1972), ed; OUTFIT, THE(1973), ed; FRONT PAGE, THE(1974), ed; MR. MAJESTYK(1974), ed; HOW TO SUCCEED IN BUSINESS WITHOUT REALLY TRYING(1976), ed; KING KONG(1976), ed; ORCA(1977), ed; 10(1979), ed; AMERICAN SUCCESS COMPANY, THE(1980), ed; S.O.B.(1981), ed; VICTOR/VICTORIA(1982), ed; CURSE OF THE PINK PANTHER(1983), ed; MAN WHO LOVED WOMEN, THE(1983), ed
1984
MICKI AND MAUDE(1984), ed

Rebecca Winters
TRACKDOWN(1976)

Rena Winters
Misc. Talkies
TREASURE OF TAYOPA(1974)

Robin Winters
OFFENDERS, THE(1980); TRAP DOOR, THE(1980); TEX(1982)

Roland Winters
13 RUE MADELEINE(1946); CHINESE RING, THE(1947); CRY OF THE CITY(1948); DOCKS OF NEW ORLEANS(1948); FEATHERED SERPENT, THE(1948); KIDNAPPED(1948); MYSTERY OF THE GOLDEN EYE, THE(1948); RETURN OF OCTOBER, THE(1948); SHANGHAI CHEST, THE(1948); ABBOTT AND COSTELLO MEET THE KILLER, BORIS KARLOFF(1949); DANGEROUS PROFESSION, A(1949); ONCE MORE, MY DARLING(1949); SKY DRAGON(1949); TUNA CLIPPER(1949); BETWEEN MIDNIGHT AND DAWN(1950); CAPTAIN CAREY, U.S.A(1950); GUILTY OF TREASON(1950); KILLER SHARK(1950); MALAYA(1950); TO PLEASE A LADY(1950); WEST POINT STORY, THE(1950); WHIPPED, THE(1950); FOLLOW THE SUN(1951); INSIDE STRAIGHT(1951); RATON PASS(1951); SIERRA PASSAGE(1951); SHE'S WORKING HER WAY THROUGH COLLEGE(1952); LION IS IN THE STREETS, A(1953); SO BIG(1953); BIGGER THAN LIFE(1956); JET PILOT(1957); TOP SECRET AFFAIR(1957); NEVER STEAL ANYTHING SMALL(1959); CASH McCALL(1960); BLUE HAWAII(1961); EVERYTHING'S DUCKY(1961); FOLLOW THAT DREAM(1962); LOVING(1970)

Ronald Winters
CONVICTED(1950)

Sally Winters
THREE LIVE GHOSTS(1929), w; CANYON OF MISSING MEN, THE(1930), w; COVERED WAGON TRAILS(1930), w; NEAR THE RAINBOW'S END(1930), w
Silents
LAW OF THE MOUNTED(1928), a, w; MANHATTAN COWBOY(1928), w; ON THE DIVIDE(1928), w; FIGHTING TERROR, THE(1929), w; HEADIN' WESTWARD(1929), w; INVADERS, THE(1929), w; LAST ROUNDUP, THE(1929), w&t; LONE HORSEMAN, THE(1929), w; OKLAHOMA KID, THE(1929), w; RIDERS OF THE RIO GRANDE(1929), w&t; HUNTED MEN(1930), w; OKLAHOMA SHERIFF, THE(1930), w

Shelley Winters
WHAT A WOMAN!(1943); COVER GIRL(1944); SAILOR'S HOLIDAY(1944); TOGETHER AGAIN(1944); THOUSAND AND ONE NIGHTS, A(1945); TONIGHT AND EVERY NIGHT(1945); TWO SMART PEOPLE(1946); DOUBLE LIFE, A(1947); GANGSTER, THE(1947); NEW ORLEANS(1947); CRY OF THE CITY(1948); LARCENY(1948); RED RIVER(1948); GREAT GATSBY, THE(1949); JOHNNY STOOL PIGEON(1949);

TAKE ONE FALSE STEP(1949); FRENCHIE(1950); SOUTH SEA SINNER(1950); WINCHESTER '73(1950); BEHAVE YOURSELF(1951); HE RAN ALL THE WAY(1951); PLACE IN THE SUN, A(1951); RAGING TIDE, THE(1951); MEET DANNY WILSON(1952); MY MAN AND I(1952); PHONE CALL FROM A STRANGER(1952); UNTAMED FRONTIER(1952); EXECUTIVE SUITE(1954); PLAYGIRL(1954); SASKATCHEWAN(1954); TENNESSEE CHAMP(1954); BIG KNIFE, THE(1955); I AM A CAMERA(1955, Brit.); I DIED A THOUSAND TIMES(1955); MAMBO(1955, Ital.); NIGHT OF THE HUNTER, THE(1955); TREASURE OF PANCHO VILLA, THE(1955); CASH ON DELIVERY(1956, Brit.); DIARY OF ANNE FRANK, THE(1959); ODDS AGAINST TOMORROW(1959); LET NO MAN WRITE MY EPITAPH(1960); YOUNG SAVAGES, THE(1961); CHAPMAN REPORT, THE(1962); LOLITA(1962); BALCONY, THE(1963); WIVES AND LOVERS(1963); HOUSE IS NOT A HOME, A(1964); GREATEST STORY EVER TOLD, THE(1965); PATCH OF BLUE, A(1965); TIME OF INDIFFERENCE(1965, Fr./Ital.); ALFIE(1966, Brit.); HARPER(1966); ENTER LAUGHING(1967); BUONA SERA, MRS. CAMPBELL(1968, Ital.); SCALPHUNTERS, THE(1968); WILD IN THE STREETS(1968); MAD ROOM, THE(1969); BLOODY MAMA(1970); HOW DO I LOVE THEE?(1970); WHAT'S THE MATTER WITH HELEN?(1971); WHO SLEW AUNTIE ROO?(1971, U.S./Brit.); POSEIDON ADVENTURE, THE(1972); SOMETHING TO HIDE(1972, Brit.); BLUME IN LOVE(1973); CLEOPATRA JONES(1973); DIAMONDS(1975, U.S./Israel); THAT LUCKY TOUCH(1975, Brit.); JOURNEY INTO FEAR(1976, Can); NEXT STOP, GREENWICH VILLAGE(1976); TENANT, THE(1976, Fr.); PETE'S DRAGON(1977); TENTACLES(1977, Ital.); THREE SISTERS, THE(1977); KING OF THE GYPSIES(1978); CITY ON FIRE(1979 Can.); MAGICIAN OF LUBLIN, THE(1979, Israel/Ger.); VISITOR, THE(1980, Ital./U.S.); S.O.B.(1981)
1984
ELLIE(1984); OVER THE BROOKLYN BRIDGE(1984)
Misc. Talkies
ARTHUR!! ARTHUR?(1970); POOR PRETTY EDDIE(1975); HEARTBREAK MOTEL(1978)

Stacey Winters
AIR PATROL(1962); HOUSE OF THE DAMNED(1963); RAIDERS FROM BENEATH THE SEA(1964)

Susan Winters
PLEASURE PLANTATION(1970)

Todd Winters
CRUISING(1980); WITHOUT A TRACE(1983)

Warrington Winters
ONE DOWN TWO TO GO(1982)

William Wintersole
SQUARES(1972); COMA(1978)

William Richard Wintersole
SECONDS(1966)

Frank Winterstein
SHERLOCK HOLMES AND THE DEADLY NECKLACE(1962, Ger.), d

Franz Winterstein
EIGHT GIRLS IN A BOAT(1932, Ger.), w

Richard Winterstein
MIDNIGHT MAN, THE(1974)

W. Winterstein
DREYFUS CASE, THE(1931, Brit.), ph; FASCINATION(1931, Brit.), ph

Willi Winterstein
GIRL FROM THE MARSH CROFT, THE(1935, Ger.), ph

Willy Winterstein
BIMBO THE GREAT(1961, Ger.), ph; DIE FLEDERMAUS(1964, Aust.), ph

Paul Winterton
TOUCH OF LARCENY, A(1960, Brit.), w

W. Winterton
FULL SPEED AHEAD(1939, Brit.), ph

Pearl Winther
HIGH FURY(1947, Brit.), cos

Christine Winthrop
Misc. Silents
SALOME(1923)

Ethel Winthrop
Misc. Silents
LAFAYETTE, WE COME!(1918); MARIONETTES, THE(1918)

Joe Winthrop
IF I HAD A MILLION(1932)

Joy Winthrop
Silents
BLAZING TRAIL, THE(1921); MAN'S LAW AND GOD'S(1922); HER FATAL MILLIONS(1923)

Lynne Winthrop
NORTH STAR, THE(1943)

Julian Wintle
COMING-OUT PARTY, A(, p; FACTS OF LOVE(1949, Brit.), ed; ASSASSIN FOR HIRE(1951, Brit.), p; DARK MAN, THE(1951, Brit.), p; STRANGER IN BETWEEN, THE(1952, Brit.), p; YOU KNOW WHAT SAILORS ARE(1954, Brit.), p; PASSAGE HOME(1955, Brit.), p; HIGH TIDE AT NOON(1957, Brit.), p; TRIPLE DECEPTION(1957, Brit.), p; ONE THAT GOT AWAY, THE(1958, Brit.), p; WHITE TRAP, THE(1959, Brit.), p; CIRCUS OF HORRORS(1960, Brit.), p; OCTOBER MOTH(1960, Brit.), p; SNOWBALL(1960, Brit.), p; HOUSE OF MYSTERY(1961, Brit.), p; MAN IN THE BACK SEAT, THE(1961, Brit.), p; SEVEN KEYS(1962, Brit.), p; BITTER HARVEST(1963, Brit.), p; CROOKS ANONYMOUS(1963, Brit.), p; FAST LADY, THE(1963, Brit.), p; FATHER CAME TOO(1964, Brit.), p; MALPAS MYSTERY, THE(1967, Brit.), p; FIRECHASERS, THE(1970, Brit.), p; BELSTONE FOX, THE(1976, 1976), p

Barry Winton
MAN FROM YESTERDAY, THE(1932); FORBIDDEN HEAVEN(1936)

Dwayne Winton
SURFTIDE 77(1962)

Jane Winton
MELODY OF LOVE, THE(1928); BRIDGE OF SAN LUIS REY, THE(1929); SCANDAL(1929); FURIES, THE(1930); HELL'S ANGELS(1930); IN THE NEXT ROOM(1930); HIRED WIFE(1934); BACKSTAGE(1937, Brit.)
Silents
ACROSS THE PACIFIC(1926); DON JUAN(1926); LOVE TOY, THE(1926); BELOVED ROGUE, THE(1927); CRYSTAL CUP, THE(1927); FAIR CO-ED, THE(1927); GAY OLD BIRD, THE(1927); MONKEY TALKS, THE(1927); SUNRISE–A SONG OF TWO HUMANS(1927); HONEYMOON FLATS(1928); NOTHING TO WEAR(1928); CAPTAIN

LASH(1929)
Misc. Silents
TOMORROW'S LOVE(1925); MY OFFICIAL WIFE(1926); WHY GIRLS GO BACK HOME(1926); LONESOME LADIES(1927); PERCH OF THE DEVIL(1927); POOR NUT, THE(1927); BARE KNEES(1928)
John Winton
WE JOINED THE NAVY(1962, Brit.), w
Sheree Winton
FIRST MAN INTO SPACE(1959, Brit.); NAKED FURY(1959, Brit.); DENTIST IN THE CHAIR(1960, Brit.); ROAD TO HONG KONG, THE(1962, U.S./Brit.)
Wayne Winton
OPERATION BIKINI(1963)
Peter Wintonick
IN PRAISE OF OLDER WOMEN(1978, Can.), ed
1984
BAY BOY(1984, Can.), ed; LISTEN TO THE CITY(1984, Can.)
Bruno Wintzell
GIRL FROM PETROVKA, THE(1974)
Estelle Winwood
NIGHT ANGEL, THE(1931); HOUSE OF TRENT, THE(1933, Brit.); QUALITY STREET(1937); GLASS SLIPPER, THE(1955); SWAN, THE(1956); 23 PACES TO BAKER STREET(1956); THIS HAPPY FEELING(1958); DARBY O'GILL AND THE LITTLE PEOPLE(1959); SERGEANT RUTLEDGE(1960); MISFITS, THE(1961); ALIVE AND KICKING(1962, Brit.); CABINET OF CALIGARI, THE(1962); MAGIC SWORD, THE(1962); NOTORIOUS LANDLADY, THE(1962); DEAD RINGER(1964); CAMELOT(1967); GAMES(1967); PRODUCERS, THE(1967); JENNY(1969); MURDER BY DEATH(1976)
Stevie Winwood
HERE WE GO ROUND THE MULBERRY BUSH(1968, Brit.), m
Ward Winy
HATE IN PARADISE(1938, Brit.), d
Alex Wipf
ROLLOVER(1981)
Christine Wipf
JONAH—WHO WILL BE 25 IN THE YEAR 2000(1976, Switz.); BLACK SPIDER, THE(1983, Swit.)
Louis Wipf
ANGEL AND SINNER(1947, Fr.), p; FRENCH CANCAN(1956, Fr.), p; PARIS DOES STRANGE THINGS(1957, Fr./Ital.), p
Harold Channing Wire
YELLOW MOUNTAIN, THE(1954), w
Arne Wiren
PIMPERNEL SVENSSON(1953, Swed.)
Dag Wiren
LESSON IN LOVE, A(1960, Swed.), m; MATTER OF MORALS, A(1961, U.S./Swed.), m
Signe Wirff
PIMPERNEL SVENSSON(1953, Swed.)
Tom Wirick
TOMORROW IS FOREVER(1946)
Marilyn Wirt
GAY DECEIVERS, THE(1969); TOP OF THE HEAP(1972)
Franz Peter Wirth
ARMS AND THE MAN(1962, Ger.), d; HAMLET(1962, Ger.), d&w; GIRL FROM HONG KONG(1966, Ger.), d; UNWILLING AGENT(1968, Ger.), d
Richard Wirth
TOOTSIE(1982)
Sandra Wirth
FORTY GUNS(1957)
Sandy Wirth
ROCKABILLY BABY(1957)
Wanda Wirth
SNIPER, THE(1952)
Wolf Wirth
LOVE AT TWENTY(1963, Fr./Ital./Jap./Pol./Ger.), ph; TONIO KROGER(1968, Fr./Ger.), ph; DUCK RINGS AT HALF PAST SEVEN, THE(1969, Ger./Ital.), ph
Bud Wirtschafter
MAIDSTONE(1970)
Aad Wirtz
Misc. Talkies
FALLS, THE(1980, Brit.)
Frank Wisbar
STRANGLER OF THE SWAMP(1945), d, w; DEVIL BAT'S DAUGHTER, THE(1946), p&d; LIGHTHOUSE(1947), d; MADONNA OF THE DESERT(1948), w; PRAIRIE, THE(1948), d; RIMFIRE(1949), w; COMMANDO(1962, Ital., Span., Bel., Ger.), d, w
Frank Bentick Wisbar
WOMEN IN BONDAGE(1943), w
Aubrey Wisberg
SUBMARINE RAIDER(1942), w; BOMBER'S MOON(1943), w; U-BOAT PRISONER(1944), w; ADVENTURES OF RUSTY(1945), w; BETRAYAL FROM THE EAST(1945), w; ESCAPE IN THE FOG(1945), w; HORN BLOWS AT MIDNIGHT, THE(1945), w; POWER OF THE WHISTLER, THE(1945), w; FALCON'S ADVENTURE, THE(1946), w; JUST BEFORE DAWN(1946), w; OUT OF THE DEPTHS(1946), w; RENDEZVOUS 24(1946), w; SO DARK THE NIGHT(1946), w; BIG FIX, THE(1947), w; BURNING CROSS, THE(1947), w; HEAVEN ONLY KNOWS(1947), w; ROAD TO THE BIG HOUSE(1947), w; TREASURE OF MONTE CRISTO(1949), w; DESERT HAWK, THE(1950), w; HIT PARADE OF 1951(1950), w; AT SWORD'S POINT(1951), w; MAN FROM PLANET X, THE(1951), p, w; CAPTIVE WOMEN(1952), p&w; LADY IN THE IRON MASK(1952), w; CAPTAIN JOHN SMITH AND POCAHONTAS(1953), w; PORT SINISTER(1953), p, w; PROBLEM GIRLS(1953), p, w; STEEL LADY, THE(1953), w; SWORD OF VENUS(1953), p, w; CAPTAIN KIDD AND THE SLAVE GIRL(1954), p, w; CASANOVA'S BIG NIGHT(1954), w; DRAGON'S GOLD(1954), p,d&w; RETURN TO TREASURE ISLAND(1954), p, w; MURDER IS MY BEAT(1955), p, w; SON OF SINBAD(1955), w; WOMEN OF PITCAIRN ISLAND, THE(1957), p, w; HERCULES IN NEW YORK(1970), p&w
Audrey Wisberg
THEY CAME TO BLOW UP AMERICA(1943), w; NEANDERTHAL MAN, THE(1953), p; SNOW DEVILS, THE(1965, Ital.), w

Claude Wisberg
ANGELS WITH DIRTY FACES(1938); ANGELS WASH THEIR FACES(1939); KID NIGHTINGALE(1939); CASTLE ON THE HUDSON(1940); INVISIBLE STRIPES(1940); MURDER IN THE AIR(1940); RENDEZVOUS 24(1946)
Ole Wisborg
REPTILICUS(1962, U.S./Den.)
Aubrey Wisbrook
COUNTER-ESPIONAGE(1942), w
Allen Wisch
TRICK OR TREATS(1982)
Marianne Wischmann
WHITE HORSE INN, THE(1959, Ger.); 24-HOUR LOVER(1970, Ger.)
Siegfried Wischnewski
DEAD RUN(1961, Fr./Ital./Ger.); THREE PENNY OPERA(1963, Fr./Ger.)
Walter Wischniewsky
JOURNEY TO THE LOST CITY(1960, Ger./Fr./Ital.), ed; THOUSAND EYES OF DR. MABUSE, THE(1960, Fr./Ital./Ger.), ed; I, TOO, AM ONLY A WOMAN(1963, Ger.), ed; MAD EXECUTIONERS, THE(1965, Ger.), ed; TERROR OF DR. MABUSE, THE(1965, Ger.), ed; ONLY A WOMAN(1966, Ger.), ed; MONSTER OF LONDON CITY, THE(1967, Ger.), ed; PHANTOM OF SOHO, THE(1967, Ger.), ed
Waltraute Wischniewsky
THOUSAND EYES OF DR. MABUSE, THE(1960, Fr./Ital./Ger.), ed
R.C. Wisden
FIREBIRD 2015 AD(1981)
Norman Wisdom
DATE WITH A DREAM, A(1948, Brit.); MAN OF THE MOMENT(1955, Brit.); ONE GOOD TURN(1955, Brit.); TROUBLE IN STORE(1955, Brit.); JUST MY LUCK(1957, Brit.); UP IN THE WORLD(1957, Brit.); SQUARE PEG, THE(1958, Brit.), a, w; FOLLOW A STAR(1959, Brit.), a, w; BULLDOG BREED, THE(1960, Brit.), a, w; GIRL ON THE BOAT, THE(1962, Brit.); ON THE BEAT(1962, Brit.), a, w; THERE WAS A CROOKED MAN(1962, Brit.); EARLY BIRD, THE(1965, Brit.), a, w; PRESS FOR TIME(1966, Brit.), a, w; SANDWICH MAN, THE(1966, Brit.); STITCH IN TIME, A(1967, Brit.), a, w; NIGHT THEY RAIDED MINSKY'S, THE(1968); WHAT'S GOOD FOR THE GOOSE(1969, Brit.), a, p, w
Alfie Wise
LONGEST YARD, THE(1974); SWASHBUCKLER(1976); SMOKEY AND THE BANDIT(1977); END, THE(1978); HOOPER(1978); HOT STUFF(1979); CANNONBALL RUN, THE(1981); PATERNITY(1981); STROKER ACE(1983)
1984
CITY HEAT(1984)
Alvie Wise
STARTING OVER(1979)
Charles Wise
JOHN PAUL JONES(1959)
Ernie Wise
SPYLARKS(1965, Brit.); MAGNIFICENT TWO, THE(1967, Brit.); THAT RIVIERA TOUCH(1968, Brit.)
Gertrude Wise
MAN OF TWO WORLDS(1934)
Harry Wise
Silents
AVALANCHE, THE(1919)
Herbert Wise
ALONE AGAINST ROME(1963, Ital.), d; TO HAVE AND TO HOLD(1963, Brit.), d; LOVERS, THE(1972, Brit.), d
Jack Wise
IN THE HEADLINES(1929); KANSAS CITY PRINCESS(1934); EVER SINCE EVE(1937); ACCIDENTS WILL HAPPEN(1938); COMET OVER BROADWAY(1938); COWBOY FROM BROOKLYN(1938); CODE OF THE SECRET SERVICE(1939); EACH DAWN I DIE(1939); SECRET SERVICE OF THE AIR(1939); SMASHING THE MONEY RING(1939); THEY MADE ME A CRIMINAL(1939); FIGHTING 69TH, THE(1940); MEET JOHN DOE(1941); MILLION DOLLAR BABY(1941); OUT OF THE FOG(1941); SHOT IN THE DARK, THE(1941); THIEVES FALL OUT(1941); SPANISH MAIN, THE(1945); MAN I LOVE, THE(1946); KISS IN THE DARK, A(1949); NIGHT UNTO NIGHT(1949)
Silents
LAWFUL CHEATERS(1925)
Joseph Wise
WOMAN OF STRAW(1964, Brit.)
Mary Lee Wise
Silents
MOLLY OF THE FOLLIES(1919)
Misc. Silents
OUR BETTER SELVES(1919); WEEK-END, THE(1920)
Ray Wise
SWAMP THING(1982)
Misc. Talkies
CONDOR(1984)
Robert Wise
UNTIL THEY SAIL(1957), d; BACHELOR MOTHER(1939), ed; FIFTH AVENUE GIRL(1939), ed; HUNCHBACK OF NOTRE DAME, THE(1939), ed; DANCE, GIRL, DANCE(1940), ed; MY FAVORITE WIFE(1940), ed; CITIZEN KANE(1941), ed; DEVIL AND DANIEL WEBSTER, THE(1941), ed; MAGNIFICENT AMBERSONS, THE(1942), d, ed; SEVEN DAYS LEAVE(1942), ed; BOMBARDIER(1943), ed; FALLEN SPARROW, THE(1943), ed; IRON MAJOR, THE(1943), ed; CURSE OF THE CAT PEOPLE, THE(1944), d; MADEMOISELLE FIFI(1944), d; BODY SNATCHER, THE(1945), d; GAME OF DEATH, A(1945), d; CRIMINAL COURT(1946), d; BORN TO KILL(1947), d; BLOOD ON THE MOON(1948), d; MYSTERY IN MEXICO(1948), d; SET-UP, THE(1949), d; THREE SECRETS(1950), d; TWO FLAGS WEST(1950), d; DAY THE EARTH STOOD STILL, THE(1951), d; HOUSE ON TELEGRAPH HILL(1951), d; CAPTIVE CITY(1952), d; SOMETHING FOR THE BIRDS(1952), d; DESERT RATS, THE(1953), d; DESTINATION GOBI(1953), d; RETURN TO PARADISE(1953), d; SO BIG(1953), d; EXECUTIVE SUITE(1954), d; HELEN OF TROY(1956, Ital), d; SOMEBODY UP THERE LIKES ME(1956), d; THIS COULD BE THE NIGHT(1957), d; I WANT TO LIVE!(1958), d; RUN SILENT, RUN DEEP(1958), d; ODDS AGAINST TOMORROW(1959), p&d; WEST SIDE STORY(1961), p, d; TWO FOR THE SEESAW(1962), d; HAUNTING, THE(1963), p&d; SOUND OF MUSIC, THE(1965), p&d; SAND PEBBLES, THE(1966), p&d; STAR!(1968), d; BABY MAKER, THE(1970), p; ANDROMEDA STRAIN, THE(1971), p&d; TWO PEOPLE(1973), p&d; HINDENBURG, THE(1975), d; AUDREY ROSE(1977), d; STAR

TREK: THE MOTION PICTURE(1979), d
Sybil Wise
VARIETY(1935, Brit.); TWILIGHT HOUR(1944, Brit.)
Silents
ADVENTUROUS YOUTH(1928, Brit.)
Thomas Wise
Silents
GENTLEMAN FROM MISSISSIPPI, THE(1914), a, w
Tim Wise
1984
BREAKIN' 2: ELECTRIC BOOGALOO(1984)
Tom Wise
Misc. Silents
FATHER TOM(1921)
Vic Wise
IT HAPPENED ONE SUNDAY(1944, Brit.); MADAME LOUISE(1951, Brit.); WHIS-PERING SMITH VERSUS SCOTLAND YARD(1952, Brit.); DEVIL ON HORSEBACK(1954, Brit.); MAKE ME AN OFFER(1954, Brit.); SQUARE RING, THE(1955, Brit.); CHARLEY MOON(1956, Brit.); JUST MY LUCK(1957, Brit.); VALUE FOR MONEY(1957, Brit.); KILL ME TOMORROW(1958, Brit.); FOLLOW THAT HORSE!(1960, Brit.); CUCKOO PATROL(1965, Brit.); PANIC(1966, Brit.); SCHOOL FOR SEX(1969, Brit.)
Walter Wise
SINNER TAKE ALL(1936), w; FIRST OFFENDERS(1939), w; RUNAROUND, THE(1946), w; THUNDER ROAD(1958), w
William Wise
T.R. BASKIN(1971)
Tripplie Wisecup
THUNDER IN CAROLINA(1960)
Janet Wisely
DIRTY HARRY(1971)
Frederick Wiseman
COOL WORLD, THE(1963), p
Joseph Wiseman
DETECTIVE STORY(1951); LES MISERABLES(1952); VIVA ZAPATA!(1952); CHAMP FOR A DAY(1953); SILVER CHALICE, THE(1954); PRODIGAL, THE(1955); GARMENT JUNGLE, THE(1957); THREE BRAVE MEN(1957); UNFORGIVEN, THE(1960); DR. NO(1962, Brit.); HAPPY THIEVES, THE(1962); BYE BYE BRAVER-MAN(1968); COUNTERFEIT KILLER, THE(1968); NIGHT THEY RAIDED MINSKY'S, THE(1968); STILETTO(1969); LAWMAN(1971); VALACHI PAPERS, THE(1972, Ital./Fr.); APPRENTICESHIP OF DUDDY KRAVITZ, THE(1974, Can.); JOURNEY INTO FEAR(1976, Can); BETSY, THE(1978); BUCK ROGERS IN THE 25TH CENTURY(1979); JAGUAR LIVES(1979)
Lulubelle Wiseman
COUNTRY FAIR(1941)
Nicholas Wiseman
FABIOLA(1951, Ital.), w
Scotty Wiseman
COUNTRY FAIR(1941)
Thomas Wiseman
ROMANTIC ENGLISHWOMAN, THE(1975, Brit./Fr.), w
Bud Wiser
I AM THE LAW(1938); YOU CAN'T TAKE IT WITH YOU(1938); YOUTH RUNS WILD(1944); FORCE OF EVIL(1948); LULU BELLE(1948); MR. BLANDINGS BUILDS HIS DREAM HOUSE(1948)
Jerome Wish
ANGELS FROM HELL(1968), w; GAY DECEIVERS, THE(1969), w
Jerry Wish
RUN, ANGEL, RUN(1969), w
Scoville Wishard
VOICE OF THE HURRICANE(1964), p
Louis Wishart
INN OF THE DAMNED(1974, Aus.)
Stephanie Wishart
FIGHTING BACK(1983, Brit.)
Sally Wisher
PRISON WITHOUT BARS(1939, Brit.)
William Wisher
Misc. Talkies
REUNION, THE(1977)
William Wisher, Jr.
1984
TERMINATOR, THE(1984), a, w
Doris Wishman
Misc. Talkies
DEADLY WEAPONS(1974), d; DOUBLE AGENT 73(1974), d; NIGHT TO DISMEM-BER, A(1983), d
George Wislocki
DEADLY HERO(1976), w
Stanislaw Wislocki
PASSENGER, THE(1970, Pol.), md
Ron Wisman
PYX(1973, Can.), ed; SHOOT(1976, Can.), ed; FULL CIRCLE(1977, Brit./Can.), ed; THREE CARD MONTE(1978, Can.), ed; FISH HAWK(1981, Can.), ed; HAUNTING OF JULIA, THE(1981, Brit./Can.), ed; HIGH COUNTRY, THE(1981, Can.), ed; TICKET TO HEAVEN(1981), ed; DEADLY EYES(1982), ed; HARRY TRACY–DE-SPERADO(1982, Can.), ed
Harry Wismer
SPIRIT OF WEST POINT, THE(1947); BABE RUTH STORY, THE(1948); TRIPLE THREAT(1948); SOMEBODY UP THERE LIKES ME(1956)
Paul Wismer
Silents
WOLF LAW(1922)
Ed Wisner
FIREBALL JUNGLE(1968)
Alain Wisniak
JOY(1983, Fr./Can.), m

Ewa Wisniewska
BEADS OF ONE ROSARY, THE(1982, Pol.)
Doris Wiss
YOUNG LIONS, THE(1958); STORY OF RUTH, THE(1960)
G.H. Wisschussen
Silents
JUDITH OF THE CUMBERLANDS(1916)
Bobby Wissler
TERROR BY NIGHT(1946)
Jerry Wissler
DARK HORSE, THE(1946)
Rudy Wissler
TISH(1942); GOOD LUCK, MR. YATES(1943); COVER GIRL(1944); SAN DIEGO, I LOVE YOU(1944); TOMORROW THE WORLD(1944); GALLANT JOURNEY(1946); JANIE GETS MARRIED(1946); GAS HOUSE KIDS GO WEST(1947); GAS HOUSE KIDS IN HOLLYWOOD(1947); SPIRIT OF WEST POINT, THE(1947)
Owen Wister
VIRGINIAN, THE(1929), w; VIRGINIAN, THE(1946), w
Silents
VIRGINIAN, THE(1914), w; VIRGINIAN, THE(1923), w
William Wister
ALIBI IKE(1935), w
Eleanor Witcombe
GETTING OF WISDOM, THE(1977, Aus.), w; MY BRILLIANT CAREER(1980, Aus.), w
Lorelie Witek
STELLA(1950)
Frank Witeman
Misc. Talkies
SKETCHES OF A STRANGLER(?)
Tom Witenbarger
TWO-LANE BLACKTOP(1971)
Albert Witerick
GAMES, THE(1970), art d
Ebba With
OPERATION LOVEBIRDS(1968, Den.)
Albert Witherick
HAPPY IS THE BRIDE(1958, Brit.), art d; RISK, THE(1961, Brit.), art d; ONLY TWO CAN PLAY(1962, Brit.), art d; HEAVENS ABOVE!(1963, Brit.), art d; AMOROUS MR. PRAWN, THE(1965, Brit.), art d; GREAT ST. TRINIAN'S TRAIN ROBBERY, THE(1966, Brit.), art d; GUNS IN THE HEATHER(1968, Brit.), art d; TWISTED NERVE(1969, Brit.), art d; MAN WHO HAUNTED HIMSELF, THE(1970, Brit.), art d; CANDLESHOE(1978), art d; UNIDENTIFIED FLYING ODDBALL, THE(1979, Brit.), art d; SHILLINGBURY BLOWERS, THE(1980, Brit.), art d; CONDORMAN(1981), prod d
Terry Witherington
NO BLADE OF GRASS(1970, Brit.), spec eff; ONE MORE TIME(1970, Brit.), spec eff
Glen Witherow
1984
COTTON CLUB, THE(1984)
Bernadette Withers
I'LL CRY TOMORROW(1955); TROUBLE WITH ANGELS, THE(1966)
Charles Withers
HIDEAWAY(1937)
Edward Withers
Silents
ALIAS JULIUS CAESAR(1922), t
Fred Withers
LAZYBONES(1935, Brit.); MAN WITHOUT A FACE, THE(1935, Brit.); THEY DIDN'T KNOW(1936, Brit.); TOMORROW WE LIVE(1936, Brit.); BRIEF ECSTASY(1937, Brit.); DOUBLE EXPOSURES(1937, Brit.); ELDER BROTHER, THE(1937, Brit.); DANGER-OUS SECRETS(1938, Brit.); KATHLEEN(1938, Ireland); MILL ON THE FLOSS(1939, Brit.)
Georgia Withers
AMAZING MR. FORREST, THE(1943, Brit.)
Googie Withers
GIRL IN THE CROWD, THE(1934, Brit.); ALL AT SEA(1935, Brit.); DARK WORLD(1935, Brit.); HER LAST AFFAIRE(1935, Brit.); LOVE TEST, THE(1935, Brit.); WINDFALL(1935, Brit.); ACCUSED(1936, Brit.); CRIME OVER LONDON(1936, Brit.); CROWN VS STEVENS(1936); KING OF HEARTS(1936, Brit.); SHE KNEW WHAT SHE WANTED(1936, Brit.); ACTION FOR SLANDER(1937, Brit.); PEARLS BRING TEARS(1937, Brit.); CONVICT 99(1938, Brit.); GAIETY GIRLS, THE(1938, Brit.); IF I WERE BOSS(1938, Brit.); KATE PLUS TEN(1938, Brit.); LADY VANISHES, THE(1938, Brit.); PAID IN ERROR(1938, Brit.); STRANGE BOARDERS(1938, Brit.); YOU'RE THE DOCTOR(1938, Brit.); DEAD MEN ARE DANGEROUS(1939, Brit.); SHE COULDN'T SAY NO(1939, Brit.); TROUBLE BREWING(1939, Brit.); BULLDOG SEES IT THROUGH(1940, Brit.); BUSMAN'S HONEYMOON(1940, Brit.); MURDER IN THE NIGHT(1940, Brit.); GIRL IN DISTRESS(1941, Brit.); BACK ROOM BOY(1942, Brit.); ONE OF OUR AIRCRAFT IS MISSING(1942, Brit.); ON APPROVAL(1944, Brit.); THEY CAME TO A CITY(1944, Brit.); SILVER FLEET, THE(1945, Brit.); DEAD OF NIGHT(1946, Brit.); LOVES OF JOANNA GODDEN, THE(1947, Brit.); IT ALWAYS RAINS ON SUNDAY(1949, Brit.); MIRANDA(1949, Brit.); ONCE UPON A DREAM(1949, Brit.); NIGHT AND THE CITY(1950, Brit.); PINK STRING AND SEALING WAX(1950, Brit.); TRAVELLER'S JOY(1951, Brit.); FOUR AGAINST FA-TE(1952, Brit.); MAGIC BOX, THE(1952, Brit.); WHITE CORRIDORS(1952, Brit.); DEVIL ON HORSEBACK(1954, Brit.); LADY GODIVA RIDES AGAIN(1955, Brit.); PORT OF ESCAPE(1955, Brit.); NICKEL QUEEN, THE(1971, Aus.)
Grant Withers
GREYHOUND LIMITED, THE(1929); HEARTS IN EXILE(1929); IN THE HEAD-LINES(1929); MADONNA OF AVENUE A(1929); SATURDAY'S CHILDREN(1929); SO LONG LETTY(1929); TIME, THE PLACE AND THE GIRL, THE(1929); BACK PAY(1930); DANCING SWEETIES(1930); OTHER TOMORROW, THE(1930); SCARLET PAGES(1930); SECOND FLOOR MYSTERY, THE(1930); SINNER'S HOLIDAY(1930); SOLDIERS AND WOMEN(1930); TIGER ROSE(1930); FIRST AID(1931); OTHER MEN'S WOMEN(1931); TOO YOUNG TO MARRY(1931); GAMBLING SEX(1932); RED-HAIRED ALIBI, THE(1932); SECRETS OF WU SIN(1932); GOIN' TO TOWN(1935); HOLD'EM YALE(1935); RIP ROARING RILEY(1935); SHIP CAFE(1935); SOCIETY FEVER(1935); STORM OVER THE ANDES(1935); WATERFRONT LA-DY(1935); ARIZONA RAIDERS, THE(1936); BORDER FLIGHT(1936); LADY BE CAREFUL(1936); LET'S SING AGAIN(1936); SKY PARADE(1936); BILL CRACKS

DOWN(1937); PARADISE EXPRESS(1937); HELD FOR RANSOM(1938); HOLLY-WOOD ROUNDUP(1938); MR. WONG, DETECTIVE(1938); TELEPHONE OPERA-TOR(1938); THREE LOVES HAS NANCY(1938); BOY'S REFORMATORY(1939); DAUGHTER OF THE TONG(1939); IRISH LUCK(1939), p; LURE OF THE WASTE-LAND(1939); MR. WONG IN CHINATOWN(1939); MUTINY IN THE BIG HOUSE(1939), p; MYSTERY OF MR. WONG, THE(1939); NAVY SECRETS(1939); CHASING TROUBLE(1940), p; DOOMED TO DIE(1940); FATAL HOUR, THE(1940); LET'S MAKE MUSIC(1940); MEN AGAINST THE SKY(1940); MEXICAN SPITFIRE OUT WEST(1940); ON THE SPOT(1940), p; PHANTOM OF CHINATOWN(1940); SON OF THE NAVY(1940), p; TOMBOY(1940); BILLY THE KID(1941); FATHER TAKES A WIFE(1941); GET-AWAY, THE(1941); H.M. PULHAM, ESQ.(1941); MASKED RIDER, THE(1941); NO HANDS ON THE CLOCK(1941); PARACHUTE BATTALION(1941); PEOPLE VS. DR. KILDARE, THE(1941); APACHE TRAIL(1942); BUTCH MINDS THE BABY(1942); NORTHWEST RANGERS(1942); PANAMA HATTIE(1942); SHIP AHOY(1942); TENNESSEE JOHNSON(1942); WOMAN OF THE YEAR(1942); DR. GILLESPIE'S CRIMINAL CASE(1943); GILDERSLEEVE'S BAD DAY(1943); IN OLD OKLAHOMA(1943); LADY TAKES A CHANCE, A(1943); MARINES COME THROUGH, THE(1943); NO TIME FOR LOVE(1943); PETTICOAT LARCENY(1943); FIGHTING SEABEES, THE(1944); GIRL WHO DARED, THE(1944); GOODNIGHT SWEETHEART(1944); ROGER TOUHY, GANGSTER!(1944); SILENT PARTNER(1944); YELLOW ROSE OF TEXAS, THE(1944); BELLS OF ROSARITA(1945); CHINA'S LITTLE DEVILS(1945), p; DAKOTA(1945); DANGEROUS PARTNERS(1945); ROAD TO ALCATRAZ(1945); UTAH(1945); VAMPIRE'S GHOST, THE(1945); AFFAIRS OF GERALDINE(1946); IN OLD SACRAMENTO(1946); MY DARLING CLEMEN-TINE(1946); BLACKMAIL(1947); GHOST GOES WILD, THE(1947); GUNFIGHTERS, THE(1947); TRESPASSER, THE(1947); TYCOON(1947); WYOMING(1947); ANGEL IN EXILE(1948); DAREDEVILS OF THE CLOUDS(1948); FORT APACHE(1948); GAL-LANT LEGION, THE(1948); HOMICIDE FOR THREE(1948); NIGHT TIME IN NEVA-DA(1948); OLD LOS ANGELES(1948); PLUNDERERS, THE(1948); SONS OF ADVENTURE(1948); DUKE OF CHICAGO(1949); FIGHTING KENTUCKIAN, THE(1949); HELLFIRE(1949); LAST BANDIT, THE(1949); WAKE OF THE RED WITCH(1949); BELLS OF CORONADO(1950); HIT PARADE OF 1951(1950); RIO GRANDE(1950); ROCK ISLAND TRAIL(1950); SAVAGE HORDE, THE(1950); TRIG-GER, JR.(1950); TRIPOLI(1950); BELLE LE GRAND(1951); MILLION DOLLAR PUR-SUIT(1951); SEA HORNET, THE(1951); SPOILERS OF THE PLAINS(1951); UTAH WAGON TRAIN(1951); CAPTIVE OF BILLY THE KID(1952); HOODLUM EM-PIRE(1952); LEADVILLE GUNSLINGER(1952); OKLAHOMA ANNIE(1952); TROPI-CAL HEAT WAVE(1952); WOMAN OF THE NORTH COUNTRY(1952); CHAMP FOR A DAY(1953); FAIR WIND TO JAVA(1953); IRON MOUNTAIN TRAIL(1953); SUN SHINES BRIGHT, THE(1953); TROPIC ZONE(1953); JUBILEE TRAIL(1954); LADY GODIVA(1955); RUN FOR COVER(1955); WHITE SQUAW, THE(1956); HELL'S CROSSROADS(1957); LAST STAGECOACH WEST, THE(1957); I, MOBSTER(1959)

Misc. Talkies
BROKEN DISHES(1930); SWANEE RIVER(1931); SKYBOUND(1935); STORM OVER THE ANDES(1935); VALLEY OF WANTED MEN(1935)

Silents
COLLEGE(1927); TILLIE'S PUNCTURED ROMANCE(1928)

Misc. Silents
FINAL EXTRA, THE(1927); IN A MOMENT OF TEMPTATION(1927); UP-STREAM(1927); GOLDEN SHACKLES(1928); ROAD TO RUIN, THE(1928)

Isabel Withers
PAID(1930); LADIES THEY TALK ABOUT(1933); WOMEN WON'T TELL(1933); PUBLIC ENEMY'S WIFE(1936); BROTHER RAT(1938); OFF THE RECORD(1939); HOUSE ACROSS THE BAY, THE(1940); I WANT A DIVORCE(1940); MAN-POWER(1941); GEORGE WASHINGTON SLEPT HERE(1942); NOW, VOYA-GER(1942); SWEATER GIRL(1942); BEHIND PRISON WALLS(1943); LADY OF BURLESQUE(1943); MISSION TO MOSCOW(1943); MR. LUCKY(1943); SALUTE FOR THREE(1943); WHAT A WOMAN!(1943); BEAUTIFUL BUT BROKE(1944); CASANO-VA BROWN(1944); EVER SINCE VENUS(1944); LAW MEN(1944); ONCE UPON A TIME(1944); PRACTICALLY YOURS(1944); TOGETHER AGAIN(1944); UP IN ARMS(1944); GAY SENORITA, THE(1945); I LOVE A MYSTERY(1945); KISS AND TELL(1945); MISSING CORPSE, THE(1945); SPORTING CHANCE, A(1945); TAHITI NIGHTS(1945); UNDERCOVER WOMAN, THE(1946); WILD BEAUTY(1946); DEAD RECKONING(1947); GUILT OF JANET AMES(1947); LIKELY STORY, A(1947); POSSESSED(1947); SUDDENLY IT'S SPRING(1947); MANHATTAN ANGEL(1948); YOU GOTTA STAY HAPPY(1948); FOUNTAINHEAD, THE(1949); MR. BELVEDERE GOES TO COLLEGE(1949); ONCE MORE, MY DARLING(1949); RIDERS IN THE SKY(1949); SHOCKPROOF(1949); BEWARE OF BLONDIE(1950); FULLER BRUSH GIRL, THE(1950); MY BLUE HEAVEN(1950); PERFECT STRANGERS(1950); MON-KEY BUSINESS(1952)

Jane Withers
BRIGHT EYES(1934); IT'S A GIFT(1934); FARMER TAKES A WIFE, THE(1935); GINGER(1935); PADDY O'DAY(1935); THIS IS THE LIFE(1935); CAN THIS BE DIXIE?(1936); GENTLE JULIA(1936); LITTLE MISS NOBODY(1936); PEPPER(1936); ANGEL'S HOLIDAY(1937); CHECKERS(1937); HOLY TERROR, THE(1937); WILD AND WOOLLY(1937); 45 FATHERS(1937); ALWAYS IN TROUBLE(1938); ARIZONA WILDCAT(1938); KEEP SMILING(1938); RASCALS(1938); BOY FRIEND(1939); CHICKEN WAGON FAMILY(1939); PACK UP YOUR TROUBLES(1939); GIRL FROM AVENUE A(1940); HIGH SCHOOL(1940); SHOOTING HIGH(1940); YOUTH WILL BE SERVED(1940); GOLDEN HOOFS(1941); HER FIRST BEAU(1941); SMALL TOWN DEB(1941); VERY YOUNG LADY, A(1941); MAD MARTINDALES, THE(1942); YOUNG AMERICA(1942); JOHNNY DOUGHBOY(1943); NORTH STAR, THE(1943); FACES IN THE FOG(1944); MY BEST GAL(1944); AFFAIRS OF GERALDINE(1946); DANGER STREET(1947); GIANT(1956); RIGHT APPROACH, THE(1961); CAPTAIN NEWMAN, M.D.(1963)

John Withers
ELEPHANT GUN(1959, Brit.)

Margaret Withers
CAR OF DREAMS(1935, Brit.); DON'T TAKE IT TO HEART(1944, Brit.); ADVEN-TURE FOR TWO(1945, Brit.); GREAT DAY(1945, Brit.); SEVENTH VEIL, THE(1946, Brit.); DUAL ALIBI(1947, Brit.); UPTURNED GLASS, THE(1947, Brit.); DAY-BREAK(1948, Brit.); ESTHER WATERS(1948, Brit.); IT'S NOT CRICKET(1949, Brit.); QUARTET(1949, Brit.); IF THIS BE SIN(1950, Brit.); WINSLOW BOY, THE(1950); ENCORE(1951, Brit.); IT STARTED IN PARADISE(1953, Brit.); MURDER ON MON-DAY(1953, Brit.); FUSS OVER FEATHERS(1954, Brit.); CITY AFTER MID-NIGHT(1957, Brit.); MAILBAG ROBBERY(1957, Brit.); FERRY TO HONG KONG(1959, Brit.)

Cora Witherspoon
NIGHT ANGEL, THE(1931); PEACH O' RENO(1931); LADIES OF THE JURY(1932); GAMBLING(1934); MIDNIGHT(1934); FRANKIE AND JOHNNY(1936); LIBELED LADY(1936); PICCADILLY JIM(1936); BEG, BORROW OR STEAL(1937); BIG SHOT, THE(1937); DANGEROUS NUMBER(1937); LADY ESCAPES, THE(1937); MADAME X(1937); ON THE AVENUE(1937); PERSONAL PROPERTY(1937); QUALITY STREET(1937); HE COULDN'T SAY NO(1938); JUST AROUND THE CORNER(1938); MARIE ANTOINETTE(1938); PORT OF SEVEN SEAS(1938); PROFESSOR BEWA-RE(1938); THREE LOVES HAS NANCY(1938); DARK VICTORY(1939); DODGE CITY(1939); FLYING IRISHMAN, THE(1939); FOR LOVE OR MONEY(1939); WOMAN DOCTOR(1939); WOMEN, THE(1939); BANK DICK, THE(1940); CHARLIE CHAN'S MURDER CRUISE(1940); I WAS AN ADVENTURESS(1940); FOLLIES GIRL(1943); COLONEL EFFINGHAM'S RAID(1945); OVER 21(1945); SHE WOULDN'T SAY YES(1945); THIS LOVE OF OURS(1945); DANGEROUS BUSINESS(1946); I'VE AL-WAYS LOVED YOU(1946); SHE WROTE THE BOOK(1946); YOUNG WIDOW(1946); DOWN TO EARTH(1947); MATING SEASON, THE(1951); FIRST TIME, THE(1952); JUST FOR YOU(1952); IT SHOULD HAPPEN TO YOU(1954)

Jimmy Witherspoon
Misc. Talkies
BLACK GODFATHER, THE(1974)

John Witherspoon
JAZZ SINGER, THE(1980)

Chester Withey
Silents
OLD FOLKS AT HOME, THE(1916), d; HUN WITHIN, THE(1918), d; ON THE QUIET(1918), d; LITTLE COMRADE(1919), d; NEW MOON, THE(1919), d&w; SHE LOVES AND LIES(1920), d, w

Misc. Silents
DEVIL'S NEEDLE, THE(1916), d; MR. GOODE, THE SAMARITAN(1916); SUN-SHINE DAD(1916); ALABASTER BOX, AN(1917), d; BAD BOYS(1917), d; NEARLY MARRIED(1917), d; OLD FASHIONED YOUNG MAN, AN(1917), d; WOMAN'S AWAKENING, A(1917), d; IN PURSUIT OF POLLY(1918), d; TEETH OF THE TIGER, THE(1919), d; ARCTIC ADVENTURE(1922), d; OUTCAST(1922), d

Chester [Chet] Withey
Misc. Silents
WHARF RAT, THE(1916), d; CAFE IN CAIRO, A(1924), d

Chet Withey
Silents
LESSONS IN LOVE(1921), d; QUEEN O' DIAMONDS(1926), d

Misc. Silents
ROMANCE(1920), d; COINCIDENCE(1921), d; WEDDING BELLS(1921), d; HEROES AND HUSBANDS(1922), d; RICHARD, THE LION-HEARTED(1923), d; PLEASURE BUYERS, THE(1925), d; GOING THE LIMIT(1926), d; HER HONOR THE GOVERNOR(1926), d; IMPOSTER, THE(1926), d; SECRET ORDERS(1926), d

Chet [Chester] Withey
Misc. Silents
BUSHRANGER, THE(1928), d

Virginia Philley Withey
Silents
FLYING PAT(1920), w

Claire Withney
Misc. Silents
BURGLAR AND THE LADY, THE(1914)

Glenn Withrow
LADY IN RED, THE(1979); OUTSIDERS, THE(1983); RUMBLE FISH(1983)

Alan Withy
NOWHERE TO GO(1959, Brit.), art d; GREEN HELMET, THE(1961, Brit.), art d; SECRET PARTNER, THE(1961, Brit.), art d; TOO HOT TO HANDLE(1961, Brit.), art d; LION, THE(1962, Brit.), art d; THIS SPORTING LIFE(1963, Brit.), art d; MODEL MURDER CASE, THE(1964, Brit.), art d; FAMILY WAY, THE(1966, Brit.), art d; O LUCKY MAN!(1973, Brit.), art d; IN CELEBRATION(1975, Brit.), art d

Bruce Witkin
BEEN DOWN SO LONG IT LOOKS LIKE UP TO ME(1977), ed

Jacob Witkin
LOVE AND DEATH(1975); ARABIAN ADVENTURE(1979, Brit.)

Steve Witkin
BY DESIGN(1982)

Helen Witkowski
MICKEY ONE(1965)

Gisella Witkowsky
1984
JUST THE WAY YOU ARE(1984)

William Witliff
BLACK STALLION, THE(1979), w

Rod Witmer
SOD SISTERS(1969), p, ph

Thelma Witmer
LADY AND THE TRAMP(1955), art d; SLEEPING BEAUTY(1959), art d

Michael Witney
WAY WEST, THE(1967); DARLING LILI(1970); HEAD ON(1971); W(1974)

Mike Witney
DOC(1971)

Ronald Witort
YANK IN VIET-NAM, A(1964), set d

William H. Witney
APACHE RIFLES(1964), d

William N. Witney
SECRET OF THE PURPLE REEF, THE(1960), d; DARKTOWN STRUTTERS(1975), d

William Witney
TRIGGER TRIO, THE(1937), d; HEROES OF THE SADDLE(1940), d; HI-YO SIL-VER(1940), d; OUTLAWS OF PINE RIDGE(1942), d; DRUMS OF FU MANCHU(1943), d; CYCLOTRODE X(1946), d; HELLDORADO(1946), d; HOME IN OK-LAHOMA(1946), d; ROLL ON TEXAS MOON(1946), d; APACHE ROSE(1947), d; BELLS OF SAN ANGELO(1947), d; ON THE OLD SPANISH TRAIL(1947), d; SPRING-TIME IN THE SIERRAS(1947), d; EYES OF TEXAS(1948), d; GAY RANCHERO, THE(1948), d; GRAND CANYON TRAIL(1948), d; NIGHT TIME IN NEVADA(1948), d; UNDER CALIFORNIA STARS(1948), d; DOWN DAKOTA WAY(1949), d; FAR FRONTIER, THE(1949), d; SUSANNA PASS(1949); BELLS OF CORONADO(1950), d; SUNSET IN THE WEST(1950), d; TRAIL OF ROBIN HOOD(1950), d; TRIGGER, JR.(1950), d; TWILIGHT IN THE SIERRAS(1950), d; HEART OF THE ROCK-

IES(1951), d; IN OLD AMARILLO(1951), d; SOUTH OF CALIENTE(1951), d; SPOILERS OF THE PLAINS(1951), d; BORDER SADDLEMATES(1952), d; COLORADO SUNDOWN(1952), d; LAST MUSKETEER, THE(1952), d; OLD OKLAHOMA PLAINS(1952), d; PALS OF THE GOLDEN WEST(1952), d; SOUTH PACIFIC TRAIL(1952), d; WAC FROM WALLA WALLA, THE(1952), d; WILD BLUE YONDER, THE(1952); DOWN LAREDO WAY(1953), d; IRON MOUNTAIN TRAIL(1953), d; OLD OVERLAND TRAIL(1953), d; SHADOWS OF TOMBSTONE(1953), d; OUTCAST, THE(1954), d; CITY OF SHADOWS(1955), d; FIGHTING CHANCE, THE(1955), d; HEADLINE HUNTERS(1955), d; SANTA FE PASSAGE(1955), d; STRANGE ADVENTURE, A(1956), d; STRANGER AT MY DOOR(1956), d; PANAMA SAL(1957), d; BONNIE PARKER STORY, THE(1958), d; COOL AND THE CRAZY, THE(1958), d; JUVENILE JUNGLE(1958), d; YOUNG AND WILD(1958), d; PARATROOP COMMAND(1959), d; VALLEY OF THE REDWOODS(1960), d; CAT BURGLAR, THE(1961), d; LONG ROPE, THE(1961), d; MASTER OF THE WORLD(1961), d; ARIZONA RAIDERS(1965), d; GIRLS ON THE BEACH(1965), d; 40 GUNS TO APACHE PASS(1967), d; TARZAN'S JUNGLE REBELLION(1970), d; I ESCAPED FROM DEVIL'S ISLAND(1973), d

Misc. Talkies
FIGHTING DEVIL DOGS(1938), d; LAST MUSKETEER, THE(1952), d; GET DOWN AND BOOGIE(1977), d

Cor Witschge
LIFT, THE(1983, Neth.)

Alicia Raonne Witt
1984
DUNE(1984)

Claus Peter Witt
GREAT BRITISH TRAIN ROBBERY, THE(1967, Ger.), d

Dan Witt
OH, HEAVENLY DOG!(1980)

E.H. Witt
REBEL ANGEL(1962), ph

Fay de Witt
Misc. Talkies
CARHOPS(1980)

Georg Witt
SPESSART INN, THE(1961, Ger.), p

Howard Witt
LOOKIN' TO GET OUT(1982)
1984
SAM'S SON(1984)

Kathryn Witt
LOOKER(1981); STAR 80(1983)

Michael Witt
EARTHBOUND(1981)

Paul Junger Witt
1984
FIRSTBORN(1984), p

Jacques Witta
ZIG-ZAG(1975, Fr./Ital.), ed; CATHERINE & CO.(1976, Fr.), ed
1984
ONE DEADLY SUMMER(1984, Fr.), ed

Stephen Wittaker
UP THE JUNCTION(1968, Brit.); BURY ME AN ANGEL(1972)

Willy Witte
HOT MONEY GIRL(1962, Brit./Ger.)

David G. Wittels
I DREAM TOO MUCH(1935), w

Donald Wittenberg
LEATHER SAINT, THE(1956)

David G. Witter
FOREPLAY(1975), p

Hazel Witter
PALMY DAYS(1931)

John Wittig
COUNTERFEIT TRAITOR, THE(1962); OPERATION LOVEBIRDS(1968, Den.)

A. E. Witting
Silents
SPINDLE OF LIFE, THE(1917)

Clifford Witting
NORMAN CONQUEST(1953, Brit.), w

Mattie Witting
Silents
JOHNNY GET YOUR HAIR CUT(1927)
Misc. Silents
MIRACLE OF LOVE, A(1916); UNATTAINABLE, THE(1916)

Wigand Witting
TIN DRUM, THE(1979, Ger./Fr./Yugo./Pol.)

Jack Wittingham
CAGE OF GOLD(1950, Brit.), w; POOL OF LONDON(1951, Brit.), w; TORPEDO BAY(1964, Ital./Fr.), w

Bruce Wittkin
THAT'S THE WAY OF THE WORLD(1975), ed

Therese Wittler
SPITFIRE(1934)

Allison Wittliff
BARBAROSA(1982)

William D. Wittliff
HONEYSUCKLE ROSE(1980), w; RAGGEDY MAN(1981), p, w; BARBAROSA(1982), p, w
1984
COUNTRY(1984), p, w

Barbara Wittlinger
JUNE BRIDE(1948)

Peter Wittman
PLAY DEAD(1981), d
1984
ELLIE(1984), d

Larry Wittnebert
1984
MASSIVE RETALIATION(1984), w

Max Morgan Witts
WHEN TIME RAN OUT(1980), w

Ed Wittstein
BANANAS(1971), prod d; PLAY IT AGAIN, SAM(1972), prod d; SEVEN UPS, THE(1973), prod d; FAME(1980), art d; ENDLESS LOVE(1981), prod d

Hans Wittwer
BLACK SPIDER, THE(1983, Swit.)

C. Witty
NOVEL AFFAIR, A(1957, Brit.)

Christopher Witty
NO TIME FOR TEARS(1957, Brit.); LIFE IN EMERGENCY WARD 10(1959, Brit.); ROCKETS IN THE DUNES(1960, Brit.); LIFE IN DANGER(1964, Brit.); MASQUERADE(1965, Brit.); THESE ARE THE DAMNED(1965, Brit.); BABY LOVE(1969, Brit.); RAILWAY CHILDREN, THE(1971, Brit.)

Frank Witty
NO ESCAPE(1936, Brit.), w; PRISON BREAKER(1936, Brit.), w

John Witty
LOVE IN WAITING(1948, Brit.); HANGMAN'S WHARF(1950, Brit.); CAPTAIN HORATIO HORNBLOWER(1951, Brit.); SOHO CONSPIRACY(1951, Brit.); HELL BELOW ZERO(1954, Brit.); JOHN WESLEY(1954, Brit.); SOLUTION BY PHONE(1954, Brit.); PRIZE OF GOLD, A(1955, Brit.); ALIVE ON SATURDAY(1957, Brit.); MOMENT OF INDISCRETION(1958, Brit.); FRIGHTENED CITY, THE(1961, Brit.); VAULT OF HORROR, THE(1973, Brit.)

H. C. Witwer
CAIN AND MABEL(1936), w
Silents
ALEX THE GREAT(1928), w

Wolf Witzemann
DOG EAT DOG(1963, U.S./Ger./Ital.), art d; ELUSIVE CORPORAL, THE(1963, Fr.), art d, cos; FOUNTAIN OF LOVE, THE(1968, Aust.), art d; WALK WITH LOVE AND DEATH, A(1969), art d

Niama Wiwstrand
VALLEY OF EAGLES(1952, Brit.)

Flo Wix
MR. DEEDS GOES TO TOWN(1936); UNFINISHED BUSINESS(1941); DEVOTION(1946); HOLLOW TRIUMPH(1948); STORY OF THREE LOVES, THE(1953)

Florence Wix
SHE GOES TO WAR(1929); FORBIDDEN(1932); UNDER YOUR SPELL(1936); YOURS FOR THE ASKING(1936); EASY LIVING(1937); MISSING GUEST, THE(1938); PARADISE FOR THREE(1938); IN NAME ONLY(1939); I TAKE THIS WOMAN(1940); MRS. MINIVER(1942); WE WERE DANCING(1942); LAUGH YOUR BLUES AWAY(1943); TWO GIRLS AND A SAILOR(1944); THOSE ENDEARING YOUNG CHARMS(1945); B. F.'S DAUGHTER(1948)
Silents
NAUGHTY NANETTE(1927)
Misc. Silents
LADIES BEWARE(1927)

Mel Wixon
NOCTURNE(1946)

Mel Wixson
FRAMED(1947)

Michael-James Wixted
LOST IN THE STARS(1974); ISLANDS IN THE STREAM(1977)

Joe Wizan
JEREMIAH JOHNSON(1972), p; JUNIOR BONNER(1972), p; PRIME CUT(1972), p; 99 AND 44/100% DEAD(1974), p; AUDREY ROSE(1977), p; VOICES(1979), p; TWO OF A KIND(1983), p
1984
UNFAITHFULLY YOURS(1984), p

Court Wizard
1984
NIGHT OF THE COMET(1984), spec eff

The Wizard
GOODBYE PORK PIE(1981, New Zealand)

Frank Wiziarde
SANTA'S CHRISTMAS CIRCUS(1966), a, d

Herrman Wlach
1914(1932, Ger.)

W. Wladimirowa
THREE DAYS OF VIKTOR TSCHERNIKOFF(1968, USSR)

Jean Wladon
ONE MILLION YEARS B.C.(1967, Brit./U.S.); BATTLE OF BRITAIN, THE(1969, Brit.)

Janusz Wlasow
GOLEM(1980, Pol.), set d

H. Wlen
REBELLION OF THE HANGED, THE(1954, Mex.), w

Malgorzata Wlodarska
BOXER(1971, Pol.)

Eryk Wlodek
MISSILE FROM HELL(1960, Brit.), w

Georges Wod
LUMIERE(1976, Fr.)

Alfre Woddard
CROSS CREEK(1983)

P.G. Wodehouse
MAN IN POSSESSION, THE(1931), w; BROTHER ALFRED(1932, Brit.), w; LEAVE IT TO ME(1933, Brit.), w; SUMMER LIGHTNING(1933, Brit.), w; ANYTHING GOES(1936), w; DIZZY DAMES(1936), w; PICCADILLY JIM(1936), w; THANK YOU, JEEVES(1936), w; DAMSEL IN DISTRESS, A(1937), w; STEP LIVELY, JEEVES(1937), w; ANYTHING GOES(1956), w; GIRL ON THE BOAT, THE(1962, Brit.), w
Silents
DAMSEL IN DISTRESS, A(1919), w; OH, BOY!(1919), w; OH, LADY, LADY(1920), w

Pelham Grenville Wodehouse
Silents
OH, KAY(1928), w, t

Scott Wodehouse
FRIGHT(1971, Brit.), art d
Christine Wodetzky
ODESSA FILE, THE(1974, Brit./Ger.)
Fritz Woditzke
LITTLE MELODY FROM VIENNA(1948, Aust.), ph
Mickey Wodrich
HARRY'S WAR(1981)
Elaine Wodson
ANGEL WHO PAWNED HER HARP, THE(1956, Brit.)
Otto Woegerer
LAST TEN DAYS, THE(1956, Ger.)
Lia Woehr
IDEAL LODGER, THE(1957, Ger.)
John Woehrle
1984
PERFECT STRANGERS(1984)
Jill Woelfel
HELL'S BLOODY DEVILS(1970)
Jack Woelz
DARING GAME(1968), ed
John Woelz
LONERS, THE(1972), ed; NECROMANCY(1972), ed
Carl Woerner
NIGHT OF THE ZOMBIES(1981)
Burton Wohl
COLD WIND IN AUGUST(1961), w; THIRD DAY, THE(1965), w; BLUES FOR LOVERS(1966, Brit.), w; RIO LOBO(1970), w
David Wohl
SOPHIE'S CHOICE(1982); TERMS OF ENDEARMENT(1983)
1984
REVENGE OF THE NERDS(1984)
Gabriel Wohl
Q(1982)
Herman Wohl
LET'S LIVE AGAIN(1948), w
Rudolph Wohl
VOYAGE TO THE END OF THE UNIVERSE(1963, Czech.), p
Adolf Wohlbrueck [Anton Walbrook]
TRAPEZE(1932, Ger.)
Erwin Wohlfahrt
FIDELIO(1970, Ger.)
Kerstin Wohlfahrt
POSSESSION(1981, Fr./Ger.)
Evelyne Wohlfeiler
SERGEANT JIM(1962, Yugo.)
Gerhard Wohlgemuth
PINOCCHIO(1969, E. Ger.), m
Bill Wohrman
PORKY'S II: THE NEXT DAY(1983)
Marcos Woinsky
DEATHSTALKER(1983, Arg./U.S.)
1984
DEATHSTALKER, THE(1984)
David Woito
OUTRAGEOUS!(1977, Can.)
Hilde Woitscheff
Silents
METROPOLIS(1927, Ger.)
Lech Wojciechowski
JOAN OF THE ANGELS(1962, Pol.)
Jerzy Wojcik
ASHES AND DIAMONDS(1961, Pol.), ph; JOAN OF THE ANGELS(1962, Pol.), ph; ECHO, THE(1964, Pol.), ph; EROICA(1966, Pol.), ph
Krystyn Wojcik
NAKED AMONG THE WOLVES(1967, Ger.)
Magda Teresa Wojcik
MAN OUT OF MARBLE(1979, Pol.)
Zbigniew Wojcik
EIGHTH DAY OF THE WEEK, THE(1959, Pol./Ger.)
Wieslaw Wojick
MAN OF MARBLE(1979, Pol.)
Stan Wojno, Jr.
HUNTER, THE(1980)
Marian Wojtczak
YELLOW SLIPPERS, THE(1965, Pol.)
Jane Woland
RACE STREET(1948)
Krystyna Wolanska
YOUNG GIRLS OF WILKO, THE(1979, Pol./Fr.)
Robert Wolard
FALL OF THE HOUSE OF USHER, THE(1952, Brit.)
Eva Wolas
INTIMACY(1966), w
Dorothea Wolbert
BORROWED WIVES(1930); DANGEROUS PARADISE(1930); MEDICINE MAN, THE(1930); FRONT PAGE, THE(1931); SHOPWORN(1932); TWO SECONDS(1932); HALLELUJAH, I'M A BUM(1933); PAINTED VEIL, THE(1934); PARIS IN SPRING(1935); CAPTAIN IS A LADY, THE(1940); INVISIBLE STRIPES(1940); GAY SISTERS, THE(1942); CRACK-UP(1946)
Silents
PINK TIGHTS(1920); FLIRT, THE(1922); NINETY AND NINE, THE(1922); ABYSMAL BRUTE, THE(1923); GALLOPING ACE, THE(1924); PLEASURES OF THE RICH(1926); SAILOR'S SWEETHEART, A(1927); LOVE AND LEARN(1928)
Misc. Silents
MAN OF SORROW, A(1916); CUPID FORECLOSES(1919); DUPED(1925)
Dorothy Wolbert
FRIENDS AND LOVERS(1931); EXPERT, THE(1932); SCARLET LETTER, THE(1934); MOTIVE FOR REVENGE(1935); RECKLESS ROADS(1935); HEIR TO TROUBLE(1936); THREE HUSBANDS(1950)

Gunter Wolbert
VICTORY(1981)
William Wolbert
Silents
ALADDIN FROM BROADWAY(1917), d; BY RIGHT OF POSSESSION(1917), d; CAPTAIN OF THE GRAY HORSE TROOP, THE(1917), d; MONEY MAGIC(1917), d; LIGHT OF VICTORY(1919), d
Misc. Silents
LAST MAN, THE(1916), d; DIVORCEE, THE(1917), d; FLAMING OMEN, THE(1917), d; MAGNIFICENT MEDDLER, THE(1917), d; SUNLIGHT'S LAST RAID(1917), d; CAVANAUGH OF THE FOREST RANGERS(1918), d; GIRL FROM BEYOND, THE(1918), d; HOME TRAIL, THE(1918), d; THAT DEVIL, BATEESE(1918), d; WHEN MEN ARE TEMPTED(1918), d; WILD STRAIN, THE(1918), d
Martha Wolbrinck
LITTLE DARLINGS(1980)
Charles Wolcott
THREE CABALLEROS, THE(1944), md; MAKE MINE MUSIC(1946), md; SONG OF THE SOUTH(1946), md; IT'S A BIG COUNTRY(1951), m; SKY FULL OF MOON(1952), m/1; BLACKBOARD JUNGLE, THE(1955), m; GABY(1956), md; NEVER SO FEW(1959), md; HOME FROM THE HILL(1960), md; KEY WITNESS(1960), m
Doris Wolcott
ROYAL WEDDING(1951)
Earl Wolcott
FLAMING GOLD(1934), art d
Earl A. Wolcott
GARDEN OF ALLAH, THE(1936), spec eff; YELLOW DUST(1936), ph
George Wolcott
BORN RECKLESS(1937)
Gregory Wolcott
RED SKIES OF MONTANA(1952); BADMAN'S COUNTRY(1958)
Helen Wolcott
Misc. Silents
BUCKSHOT JOHN(1915); FATHERHOOD(1915); SOLDIER'S SONS(1916)
James L. Wolcott
WILD WOMEN OF WONGO, THE(1959), d
Robbie Wolcott
JIM, THE WORLD'S GREATEST(1976)
Robert Wolcott
FIGHTING FOOLS(1949); WINTER KILLS(1979)
Nicholas Wolcuff
MY FAIR LADY(1964)
Nick Wolcuff
ROPE OF FLESH(1965); FINDERS KEEPERS, LOVERS WEEPERS(1968)
David Wold
SALOME(1953)
Elly Wold
HOSPITAL MASSACRE(1982)
Robert Wolders
BEAU GESTE(1966); TOBRUK(1966); INTERVAL(1973, Mex./U.S.)
Judd Woldin
LIGHT FANTASTIC(1964), md
Dominique Woldon
MAIS OU ET DONC ORNICAR(1979, Fr.), w
A. Sanford Wolf
BLUEPRINT FOR ROBBERY(1961), w; NAKED BRIGADE, THE(1965, U.S./Gr.), w
A.A. Wolf
EVERY BASTARD A KING(1968, Israel)
Anthony Wolf
NORMAN LOVES ROSE(1982, Aus.)
Barney Wolf
RIVER, THE(1928), ed; STREET ANGEL(1928), ed; IT'S GREAT TO BE ALIVE(1933), ed; LAST TRAIL, THE(1934), ed
Berny Wolf
FANTASIA(1940), anim; PINOCCHIO(1940), anim; DUMBO(1941), anim
Bill Wolf
WAY OUT WEST(1937)
Bud Wolf
HIS KIND OF WOMAN(1951)
David Wolf
Misc. Talkies
AMERICAN GAME, THE(1979), d
David M. Wolf
HIT(1973), w; NEXT MAN, THE(1976), w
Detlef Wolf
PINOCCHIO(1969, E. Ger.)
Dr. Edmund Wolf
MAD MARTINDALES, THE(1942), w
Eli Wolf
FINNEY(1969), m
Erika Wolf
SHADOWS GROW LONGER, THE(1962, Switz./Ger.)
Frank Wolf
VERONA TRIAL, THE(1963, Ital.)
Misc. Talkies
BELOVED, THE(1972)
Fred Wolf
HEY THERE, IT'S YOGI BEAR(1964), anim; MOUSE AND HIS CHILD, THE(1977), d, anim
Greg Wolf
1984
NIGHT PATROL(1984)
Harry L. Wolf
NUDE BOMB, THE(1980), ph
Henry Wolf
MORE(1969, Luxembourg)
Ian Wolf
SENIORS, THE(1978)

Kedric Wolfe
RAMRODDER, THE(1969); EAT MY DUST!(1976); HOUSE CALLS(1978); UP FROM THE DEPTHS(1979, Phil.); DR. HECKYL AND MR. HYPE(1980); SMOKEY BITES THE DUST(1981)

Kenneth Wolfe
OPERATION MANHUNT(1954)

Lawrence Wolfe
CHAFED ELBOWS(1967)

Marion Wolfe
CRY OF THE HUNTED(1953), w

Marion "Bud" Wolfe
WINGS OVER HONOLULU(1937); RECKLESS LIVING(1938)

Maurice Wolfe
RUNNING BRAVE(1983, Can.)

Patrick Wolfe
BEACH RED(1967)

Rene Wolfe
TERROR-CREATURES FROM THE GRAVE(1967, U.S./Ital.)

Robert Wolfe
GETAWAY, THE(1972), ed; TERMINAL MAN, THE(1974), ed; DEEP, THE(1977), ed; HUNTER, THE(1980), ed

Robert L. Wolfe
MONTE WALSH(1970), ed; DRIVE, HE SAID(1971), ed; NAKED APE, THE(1973), ed; PAT GARRETT AND BILLY THE KID(1973), ed; WIND AND THE LION, THE(1975), ed; ALL THE PRESIDENT'S MEN(1976), ed; BIG WEDNESDAY(1978), ed; ROSE, THE(1979), ed; ON GOLDEN POND(1981), ed

Ronald Wolfe
I'VE GOTTA HORSE(1965, Brit.), w

Rose Wolfe
NIGHTBEAST(1982)

Sam Wolfe
HIT PARADE, THE(1937); HARVEY(1950)
Misc. Talkies
STAIRWAY FOR A STAR(1947)

Sammy Wolfe
FIGHTING MAD(1948)

Terry Wolfe
UNHOLY ROLLERS(1972)

Tom Wolfe
LAST AMERICAN HERO, THE(1973), w; RIGHT STUFF, THE(1983), w

Winifred Wolfe
ASK ANY GIRL(1959), w; IF A MAN ANSWERS(1962), w

Zeb Wolfe
RED RUNS THE RIVER(1963)

Ira Wolfer
SARUMBA(1950)

Ira Wolfert
FORCE OF EVIL(1948), w; AMERICAN GUERRILLA IN THE PHILIPPINES, AN(1950), w

Fritz Wolfesberger
SWISS MISS(1938)

A. P. Wolff
FREUD(1962)

Barney Wolff
CLOWN AND THE KID, THE(1961), spec eff; FLIGHT THAT DISAPPEARED, THE(1961), spec eff; SECRET OF DEEP HARBOR(1961), spec eff; GUN STREET(1962), spec eff; SAINTLY SINNERS(1962), spec eff; TARAS BULBA(1962), spec eff

Christian Wolff
COURT MARTIAL(1962, Ger.); DIE FASTNACHTSBEICHTE(1962, Ger.); YOUNG GO WILD, THE(1962, Ger.)

Ed Wolff
COLOSSUS OF NEW YORK, THE(1958)

Edgar Allan Wolff
GANG WAR(1928), w

Ernst Wolff
TREMENDOUSLY RICH MAN, A(1932, Ger.), w; GIVE HER A RING(1936, Brit.), w

Frank Wolff
WASP WOMAN, THE(1959); WILD AND THE INNOCENT, THE(1959); ATLAS(1960); BEAST FROM THE HAUNTED CAVE(1960); SKI TROOP ATTACK(1960); AMERICA, AMERICA(1963); FOUR DAYS OF NAPLES, THE(1963, US/Ital.); JUDITH(1965); SITUATION HOPELESS–BUT NOT SERIOUS(1965); SALVATORE GIULIANO(1966, Ital.); ANYONE CAN PLAY(1968, Ital.); SARDINIA: RANSOM(1968, Ital.); STRANGER IN TOWN, A(1968, U.S./Ital.); TREASURE OF SAN GENNARO(1968, Fr./Ital./Ger.); VILLA RIDES(1968); GOD FORGIVES–I DON'T!(1969, Ital./Span.); ONCE UPON A TIME IN THE WEST(1969, U.S./Ital.); DEATH TOOK PLACE LAST NIGHT(1970, Ital./Ger.); KILL THEM ALL AND COME BACK ALONE(1970, Ital./Span.); WHEN WOMEN HAD TAILS(1970, Ital.)
Misc. Talkies
MAN IN A LOOKING GLASS, A(1965, Brit.)

Fred Wolff
TRAVELING SALESWOMAN(1950), spec eff; TARAS BULBA(1962), spec eff

Gerry Wolff
NAKED AMONG THE WOLVES(1967, Ger.)

Harald Wolff
DECISION BEFORE DAWN(1951); NIGHT AFFAIR(1961, Fr.); UMBRELLAS OF CHERBOURG, THE(1964, Fr./Ger.); STATE OF SIEGE(1973, Fr./U.S./Ital./Ger.)

Henry Wolff
LION IN WINTER, THE(1968, Brit.)

Jane Wolff
Silents
WILD GOOSE CHASE, THE(1915); EACH PEARL A TEAR(1916); PLOW GIRL, THE(1916); REBECCA OF SUNNYBROOK FARM(1917); THOSE WITHOUT SIN(1917); BRAVEST WAY, THE(1918)
Misc. Silents
PUDD'NHEAD WILSON(1916); CASTLES FOR TWO(1917); FAIR BARBARIAN, THE(1917); MILE-A-MINUTE KENDALL(1918)

Jean-Loup Wolff
DANTON(1983)

John Wolff
1984
OH GOD! YOU DEVIL(1984)

Karl Heinz Wolff
Misc. Silents
EARTHQUAKE MOTOR, THE(1917, Ger.), d

Lothar Wolff
LOVE IN MOROCCO(1933, Fr.), ed; RAMPARTS WE WATCH, THE(1940), ed; MARTIN LUTHER(1953), p, w; ANIMAL FARM(1955, Brit.), w; QUESTION 7(1961, U.S./Ger.), p

Ludwig Wolff
FLAME OF LOVE, THE(1930, Brit.), w
Silents
MYSTERIOUS LADY, THE(1928), w

Maritta Wolff
MAN I LOVE, THE(1946), w

Maritta M. Wolff
WHISTLE STOP(1946), w

Millicent Wolff
GENTLEMAN OF PARIS, A(1931)

Pierre Wolff
ROAD IS FINE, THE(1930, Fr.), w; ABUSED CONFIDENCE(1938, Fr. ABUS DE CONFIANCE), w; UN CARNET DE BAL(1938, Fr.), w; BRING ON THE GIRLS(1945), w; APRES L'AMOUR(1948, Fr.), w

Ruth Wolff
INCREDIBLE SARAH, THE(1976, Brit.), w

Ursula Wolff
TRAPP FAMILY, THE(1961, Ger.)

Willi Wolff
CASE VAN GELDERN(1932, Ger.), d
Misc. Silents
HEADS UP, CHARLIE(1926, Ger.), d; IMAGINARY BARON, THE(1927, Ger.), d

Willy Wolff
Misc. Silents
CARNIVAL OF CRIME(1929, Ger.), d

Inge Wolffberg
HELDINNEN(1962, Ger.)

Albert Wolffe
ILLUSION(1929)

Wolfheart
Misc. Silents
COURAGE OF WOLFHEART(1925); FANGS OF WOLFHEART(1925); WOLF-HEART'S REVENGE(1925)

H. Wolfinger
Silents
GOLD RUSH, THE(1925)

Iggie Wolfington
PENELOPE(1966); HEX(1973); TELEFON(1977)

Ignatius Wolfington
1941(1979)

Donald Wolfit
DEATH AT A BROADCAST(1934, Brit.); CHECKMATE(1935, Brit,); DRAKE THE PIRATE(1935, Brit.); HYDE PARK CORNER(1935, Brit.); LATE EXTRA(1935, Brit.); SEXTON BLAKE AND THE BEARDED DOCTOR(1935, Brit.); SILENT PASSENGER, THE(1935, Brit.); CALLING THE TUNE(1936, Brit.); PICKWICK PAPERS, THE(1952, Brit.); ISN'T LIFE WONDERFUL!(1953, Brit.); RINGER, THE(1953, Brit.); PRIZE OF GOLD, A(1955); SVENGALI(1955, Brit.); GUILTY?(1956, Brit.); SATELLITE IN THE SKY(1956); MAN IN THE ROAD, THE(1957, Brit.); ACCURSED, THE(1958, Brit.); BLOOD OF THE VAMPIRE(1958, Brit.); I ACCUSE(1958, Brit.); ANGRY HILLS, THE(1959, Brit.); HOUSE OF THE SEVEN HAWKS, THE(1959); ROOM AT THE TOP(1959, Brit.); MARK, THE(1961, Brit.); PORTRAIT OF A SINNER(1961, Brit.); LAWRENCE OF ARABIA(1962, Brit.); DR. CRIPPEN(1963, Brit.); BECKET(1964, Brit.); HANDS OF ORLAC, THE(1964, Brit./Fr.); LIFE AT THE TOP(1965, Brit.); SANDWICH MAN, THE(1966, Brit.); 90 DEGREES IN THE SHADE(1966, Czech./Brit.); CHARGE OF THE LIGHT BRIGADE, THE(1968, Brit.); DECLINE AND FALL... OF A BIRD WATCHER(1969, Brit.)

Renate Wolfle
PLAYMATES(1969, Fr./Ital.)

Wolfman Jack
SGT. PEPPER'S LONELY HEARTS CLUB BAND(1978)

Nelson Wolford
TIME FOR KILLING, A(1967), w

Shirley Wolford
TIME FOR KILLING, A(1967), w

Brent Wolfson
RAYMIE(1960)

Carolyn Wolfson
MY FAVORITE SPY(1951)

David Wolfson
FIXED BAYONETS(1951); DOWN AMONG THE SHELTERING PALMS(1953)

Fred Wolfson
REAL LIFE(1979)

Martin Wolfson
SEEDS OF FREEDOM(1943, USSR); ACT ONE(1964); MIKEY AND NICKY(1976)

P.J. Wolfson
DEVIL IS DRIVING, THE(1932), w; MADISON SQUARE GARDEN(1932), w; NIGHT WORLD(1932), w; 70,000 WITNESSES(1932), w; GIRL IN 419(1933), w; MEET THE BARON(1933), w; PICTURE SNATCHER(1933), w; MAD LOVE(1935), w; RECK-LESS(1935), w; RENDEZVOUS(1935), w; BRIDE WALKS OUT, THE(1936), w; LADY CONSENTS, THE(1936), w; LOVE ON A BET(1936), w; PUBLIC ENEMY'S WI-FE(1936), w; SEA DEVILS(1937), w; SHALL WE DANCE(1937), w; THAT GIRL FROM PARIS(1937), w; BOY SLAVES(1938), p, d; MAD MISS MANTON, THE(1938), p; VIVACIOUS LADY(1938), w; ALLEGHENY UPRISING(1939), p, w; ESCAPE TO GLORY(1940), w; HE STAYED FOR BREAKFAST(1940), w; THIS THING CALLED LOVE(1940), w; VIGIL IN THE NIGHT(1940), w; BULLETS FOR O'HARA(1941), w; OUR WIFE(1941), w; PACIFIC RENDEZVOUS(1942), w; THEY ALL KISSED THE BRIDE(1942), w; MY KINGDOM FOR A COOK(1943), p; DREAM GIRL(1947), p; PERILS OF PAULINE, THE(1947), w; SUDDENLY IT'S SPRING(1947), w; SAI-GON(1948), p, w; TWINKLE IN GOD'S EYE, THE(1955), w

Billy Wolfstone
PENROD AND SAM(1937); PENROD AND HIS TWIN BROTHER(1938)
Will Wolfstone
YOU CAN'T TAKE IT WITH YOU(1938)
Ken Wolger
MECHANIC, THE(1972); CAHILL, UNITED STATES MARSHAL(1973)
Beppe Wolgers
STORY OF A WOMAN(1970, U.S./Ital.); PIPPI IN THE SOUTH SEAS(1974, Swed./Ger.)
Dan Wolheim
TENDERLOIN(1928); OFFICE SCANDAL, THE(1929); SAL OF SINGAPORE(1929); SIDE STREET(1929); TRAIL DUST(1936); HOLLYWOOD COWBOY(1937); PAID TO DANCE(1937); PRESCRIPTION FOR ROMANCE(1937); ANGELS WITH DIRTY FACES(1938); JUVENILE COURT(1938); OKLAHOMA KID, THE(1939)
Silents
ACROSS THE SINGAPORE(1928); SPEEDY(1928); FAR CALL, THE(1929)
Louis Wolheim
CONDEMNED(1929); FROZEN JUSTICE(1929); SHADY LADY, THE(1929); SQUARE SHOULDERS(1929); WOLF SONG(1929); ALL QUIET ON THE WESTERN FRONT(1930); DANGER LIGHTS(1930); SHIP FROM SHANGHAI, THE(1930); SILVER HORDE, THE(1930); GENTLEMAN'S FATE(1931); SIN SHIP(1931), a, d
Silents
BRAND OF COWARDICE, THE(1916); PEG OF THE PIRATES(1918); DR. JEKYLL AND MR. HYDE(1920); NUMBER 17(1920); ORPHANS OF THE STORM(1922); SHERLOCK HOLMES(1922); AMERICA(1924); LOVER'S ISLAND(1925); AWAKENING, THE(1928); RACKET, THE(1928); TEMPEST(1928)
Misc. Silents
BELLE OF THE SEASON, THE(1919); LAST MOMENT, THE(1923); LOVE'S OLD SWEET SONG(1923); UNSEEING EYES(1923); STORY WITHOUT A NAME, THE(1924); TWO ARABIAN KNIGHTS(1927)
Louis R. Wolheim
Silents
AVENGING TRAIL, THE(1918); PAIR OF CUPIDS, A(1918)
Dalik Wolinitz
HANNAH K.(1983, Fr.)
David Wolinski
ELECTRA GLIDE IN BLUE(1973)
Ken Wolinski
SAINT JACK(1979)
Sidney Wolinsky
MY TUTOR(1983), ed; TERMS OF ENDEARMENT(1983), ed
1984
BEST DEFENSE(1984), ed
Emil Wolk
1984
SCANDALOUS(1984)
Larry Wolk
ETERNAL SUMMER(1961), d
Ivan Wolkman
MURDERERS' ROW(1966), prod d
Alexander Wolkoff
Misc. Silents
SECRETS OF THE ORIENT(1932, Ger.), d
Maximilian Wolkoff
SUPER FUZZ(1981), p
Marina Wolkonsky
NUN'S STORY, THE(1959)
Vadim Wolkonsky
LA DOLCE VITA(1961, Ital./Fr.); PIGEON THAT TOOK ROME, THE(1962)
Emila Wolkowics
GLADIATORS 7(1964, Span./Ital.)
George Wolkowsky
OLD MOTHER RILEY IN PARIS(1938, Brit.)
Vadim Wolkowsky
GIDGET GOES TO ROME(1963)
Annette Woll
PARSIFAL(1983, Fr.)
Gertrid Wolle
BEAUTIFUL ADVENTURE(1932, Ger.)
Gertrud Wolle
DEVIL MAKES THREE, THE(1952)
Czeslaw Wollejko
DANTON(1983)
Chad Wollen
JOURNEYS FROM BERLIN–1971(1980)
Peter Wollen
PASSENGER, THE(1975, Ital.), w
Hans Wollenberger
UNDERGROUND(1941); ONCE UPON A HONEYMOON(1942)
Reggie Wollenschlager
DEMON, THE(1981, S. Africa), makeup
William Woller
STRANGE WORLD(1952), art d
Dave Wollert
1984
DOOR TO DOOR(1984), w
Michael Wollet
DEER HUNTER, THE(1978)
Brenda A. Wolley
DOZENS, THE(1981)
Solly Wollodarski
I HATE MY BODY(1975, Span./Switz.), w
Stan Wollveridge
SMILEY(1957, Brit.), art d
Dan Wolman
DREAMER, THE(1970, Israel), d&w; NANA(1983, Ital.), d
Janne Wolmsley
NED KELLY(1970, Brit.)

Ruth Wolner
FAST AND SEXY(1960, Fr./Ital.)
Antoni Wolny
BEADS OF ONE ROSARY, THE(1982, Pol.)
Alex Woloshin
CHAMPAGNE WALTZ(1937); DAUGHTER OF SHANGHAI(1937); RIDE A CROOKED MILE(1938); SPAWN OF THE NORTH(1938); YOU CAN'T TAKE IT WITH YOU(1938)
Barry Woloski
B.S. I LOVE YOU(1971)
Leonora Wolpe
CONCORDE, THE–AIRPORT '79(
David Wolper
KING, QUEEN, KNAVE(1972, Ger./U.S.), p
David L. Wolper
DEVIL'S BRIGADE, THE(1968), p; BRIDGE AT REMAGEN, THE(1969), p; WILLY WONKA AND THE CHOCOLATE FACTORY(1971), p
Stanley Wolpert
NINE HOURS TO RAMA(1963, U.S./Brit.), w
Sam Wolsey
TWO FOR DANGER(1940, Brit.)
Sandy Wolshin
STAR 80(1983)
Chris Wolski
Misc. Talkies
BLAST-OFF GIRLS(1967)
Dana Wolski
FOREST, THE(1983), makeup
Albert Wolsky
HEART IS A LONELY HUNTER, THE(1968), cos; POPI(1969), cos; LOVERS AND OTHER STRANGERS(1970), cos; LOVING(1970), cos; WHERE'S POPPA?(1970), cos; BORN TO WIN(1971), cos; LITTLE MURDERS(1971), cos; LADY LIBERTY(1972, Ital./Fr.), cos; LAST OF THE RED HOT LOVERS(1972), cos; TRIAL OF THE CATONSVILLE NINE, THE(1972), cos; UP THE SANDBOX(1972), cos; GAMBLER, THE(1974), cos; HARRY AND TONTO(1974), cos; LENNY(1974), cos; NEXT STOP, GREENWICH VILLAGE(1976), cos; THIEVES(1977), cos; TURNING POINT, THE(1977), cos; FINGERS(1978), cos; GREASE(1978), cos; MOMENT BY MOMENT(1978), cos; UNMARRIED WOMAN, AN(1978), cos; ALL THAT JAZZ(1979), cos; MANHATTAN(1979), cos; METEOR(1979), cos; JAZZ SINGER, THE(1980), cos; WILLIE AND PHIL(1980), cos; ALL NIGHT LONG(1981), cos; PATERNITY(1981), cos; SOPHIE'S CHOICE(1982), cos; STILL OF THE NIGHT(1982), cos; TEMPEST(1982), cos; STAR 80(1983), cos; TO BE OR NOT TO BE(1983), cos
1984
MOSCOW ON THE HUDSON(1984), cos
R. G. Wolson
MELODY CRUISE(1933), w
Val Wolstenholme
1984
SWORD OF THE VALIANT(1984, Brit.), set d
Henry Wolston
BLACK ROSES(1936, Ger.); LOVE UP THE POLE(1936, Brit.); GIRLS IN THE STREET(1937, Brit.); BLONDES FOR DANGER(1938, Brit.); GIRL IN THE STREET(1938, Brit.); MEET SEXTON BLAKE(1944, Brit.); DON CHICAGO(1945, Brit.)
Hella Wolter
PARSIFAL(1983, Fr.), cos
Ralf Wolter
ONE, TWO, THREE(1961); ROSES FOR THE PROSECUTOR(1961, Ger.); DIE GANS VON SEDAN(1962, Fr./Ger.); APACHE GOLD(1965, Ger.); DESPERADO TRAIL, THE(1965, Ger./Yugo.); TREASURE OF SILVER LAKE(1965, Fr./Ger./Yugo.); OLD SHATTERHAND(1968, Ger./Yugo./Fr./Ital.); TREASURE OF SAN GENNARO(1968, Fr./Ital./Ger.); HANNIBAL BROOKS(1969, Brit.); CABARET(1972); SERPENT'S EGG, THE(1977, Ger./U.S.)
1984
LOVE IN GERMANY, A(1984, Fr./Ger.)
U. Wolter
I AIM AT THE STARS(1960), w
Udo Wolter
U-47 LT. COMMANDER PRIEN(1967, Ger.), w
Randy Woltz
YOUNG WARRIORS(1983)
Carol Wolveridge
1984(1956, Brit.); JOHN OF THE FAIR(1962, Brit.)
Lynn Wolverton
1984
FIRESTARTER(1984), set d
Roman Wolyniec
BARRIER(1966, Pol.), art d; LOTNA(1966, Pol.), art d
Bobby Womack
SGT. PEPPER'S LONELY HEARTS CLUB BAND(1978)
Donovan Womack
PENITENTIARY II(1982)
George Womack
PORTRAIT IN BLACK(1960); CLASS(1983)
1984
GRANDVIEW, U.S.A.(1984)
John Womack, Jr.
BADLANDS(1974)
Roger Womack
PORKY'S(1982)
Bob Womans
DEAD END(1937)
Andre Womble
CHANGE OF MIND(1969)
Wendy Womble
1984
FIRESTARTER(1984)
Cynthia Womersley
OFFENDERS, THE(1980)

Nam Goon Won
INCHON(1981)
Edna Wonacott
BELLS OF ST. MARY'S, THE(1945)
Edna Mae Wonacott
SHADOW OF A DOUBT(1943); THIS LOVE OF OURS(1945)
Edna May Wonacott
HI BEAUTIFUL(1944); UNDER WESTERN SKIES(1945); MODEL AND THE MAR-RIAGE BROKER, THE(1951)
Rose Wond
HAMMETT(1982)
Little Stevie Wonder [Stevie Wonder]
MUSCLE BEACH PARTY(1964)
Tommy Wonder
DANCE, CHARLIE, DANCE(1937); THRILL OF A LIFETIME(1937); FRESHMAN YEAR(1938); GANGSTER'S BOY(1938), a, ch; MAD YOUTH(1940); THIS TIME FOR KEEPS(1947); SARUMBA(1950)
Frank Wonderley
Misc. Silents
NATURE GIRL, THE(1919)
Jerry Wonderlich
AT LONG LAST LOVE(1975), set d
Johnny Wonderlich
Silents
RACING HEARTS(1923)
J. Carey Wonderly
THAT GIRL FROM PARIS(1937), w
W. Carey Wonderly
STREET GIRL(1929), w
Silents
FOLLIES GIRL, THE(1919), w
Walter Wonderman
Misc. Talkies
KITTY CAN'T HELP IT(1975)
Alice Wong
HELL'S BLOODY DEVILS(1970)
Allan Wong
SEVENTH DAWN, THE(1964)
Andrew Wong
PAL JOEY(1957)
Anna Mae Wong
SHANGHAI EXPRESS(1932)
Anna May Wong
FLAME OF LOVE, THE(1930, Brit.); DAUGHTER OF THE DRAGON(1931); PIC-CADILLY(1932, Brit.); STUDY IN SCARLET, A(1933); TIGER BAY(1933, Brit.); CHU CHIN CHOW(1934, Brit.); LIMEHOUSE BLUES(1934); JAVA HEAD(1935, Brit.); DAUGHTER OF SHANGHAI(1937); DANGEROUS TO KNOW(1938); WHEN WERE YOU BORN?(1938); ISLAND OF LOST MEN(1939); KING OF CHINATOWN(1939); ELLERY QUEEN'S PENTHOUSE MYSTERY(1941); BOMBS OVER BURMA(1942); LADY FROM CHUNGKING(1943); IMPACT(1949); JUST JOE(1960, Brit.); PORTRAIT IN BLACK(1960); SAVAGE INNOCENTS, THE(1960, Brit.)
Misc. Talkies
ALI BABA NIGHTS(1953)
Silents
DINTY(1920); SHAME(1921); ALASKAN, THE(1924); PETER PAN(1924); THIEF OF BAGDAD, THE(1924); FORTY WINKS(1925); DESERT'S TOLL, THE(1926); DRIVEN FROM HOME(1927); MR. WU(1927); OLD SAN FRANCISCO(1927); CRIMSON CITY, THE(1928)
Misc. Silents
TOLL OF THE SEA, THE(1922); 40TH DOOR, THE(1924); SILK BOUQUET, THE(1926); TRIP TO CHINATOWN, A(1926); DEVIL DANCER, THE(1927)
Ark Wong
VICE SQUAD(1982)
Artane Wong
RACE STREET(1948)
Artarne Wong
FIRST YANK INTO TOKYO(1945); LADY FROM SHANGHAI, THE(1948); NIGHT HAS A THOUSAND EYES(1948); ROGUES' REGIMENT(1948)
Arthur Wong
CONFESSIONS OF AN OPIUM EATER(1962); ONE SPY TOO MANY(1966); APPLE DUMPLING GANG, THE(1975); JACKSON COUNTY JAIL(1976)
Barbara Jean Wong
BEHIND THE RISING SUN(1943); CHINA(1943); CALCUTTA(1947); TRAP, THE(1947); MYSTERY OF THE GOLDEN EYE, THE(1948); CHINATOWN AT MID-NIGHT(1949); LOVE IS A MANY-SPLENDORED THING(1955); MAN FROM BUTTON WILLOW, THE(1965)
Beal Wong
LEATHERNECKS HAVE LANDED, THE(1936); TRADE WINDS(1938); MANPOW-ER(1941); ACROSS THE PACIFIC(1942); LITTLE TOKYO, U.S.A.(1942); PRISONER OF JAPAN(1942); BEHIND THE RISING SUN(1943); CHINA(1943); LADY OF BUR-LESQUE(1943); BIG NOISE, THE(1944); KEYS OF THE KINGDOM, THE(1944); PURPLE HEART, THE(1944); NOB HILL(1945); SAMURAI(1945); CALCUTTA(1947); SECRET LIFE OF WALTER MITTY, THE(1947); TASK FORCE(1949); PEKING EXPRESS(1951); BIG BLUFF, THE(1955); LEFT HAND OF GOD, THE(1955); SOLDIER OF FORTUNE(1955); FLOWER DRUM SONG(1961); EXPERIMENT IN TERROR(1962)
Bessie Wong
Silents
TIPPED OFF(1923)
Betty Wong
CRY DR. CHICAGO(1971)
Bruce Wong
DAUGHTER OF SHANGHAI(1937); INTERNATIONAL SETTLEMENT(1938); MYS-TERY OF MR. WONG, THE(1939); SONG OF THE ISLANDS(1942); TIME TO KILL(1942); BEHIND THE RISING SUN(1943); CHINA(1943); CRASH DIVE(1943); JACK LONDON(1943); WE'VE NEVER BEEN LICKED(1943); DESTINATION TOKYO(1944); PURPLE HEART, THE(1944); UP IN ARMS(1944); CALCUTTA(1947)
Catherine Wong
KILLING OF A CHINESE BOOKIE, THE(1976)

Chen Wong
Misc. Talkies
ATOR, THE INVINCIBLE(1984)
Chris Wong
GRASSHOPPER, THE(1970)
Daniel Wong
JUNGLE HEAT(1957)
Danny Wong
ROLLERBALL(1975); SOME KIND OF HERO(1982); GOING BERSERK(1983)
Don Wong
SLAUGHTER IN SAN FRANCISCO(1981)
Frank Wong
REVENGE OF THE SHOGUN WOMEN(1982, Taiwan), p
George Wong
JESSE AND LESTER, TWO BROTHERS IN A PLACE CALLED TRINITY(1972, Ital.)
Harry Wong
EYE FOR AN EYE, AN(1981)
Harry D. K. Wong
HEAVEN CAN WAIT(1978)
Iris Wong
CHARLIE CHAN IN RENO(1939); CHARLIE CHAN IN RIO(1941); BEHIND THE RISING SUN(1943); CHINA(1943); MACAO(1952)
Jack Don Wong
LADY KILLER(1933)
Jadin Wong
KING AND I, THE(1956)
Jadine Wong
I DRINK YOUR BLOOD(1971)
James Wong
INTERNATIONAL HOUSE(1933)
Janet Wong
BUSTIN' LOOSE(1981)
Jean Wong
WITHOUT RESERVATIONS(1946); MISSION TO MOSCOW(1943); ANNA AND THE KING OF SIAM(1946); DECEPTION(1946); RED DRAGON, THE(1946); CHINESE RING, THE(1947); INTRIGUE(1947); MY FAVORITE BRUNETTE(1947); HALF PAST MIDNIGHT(1948); LADY FROM SHANGHAI, THE(1948); NIGHT HAS A THOUSAND EYES(1948); LOVE IS A MANY-SPLENDORED THING(1955); KING AND I, THE(1956)
Joe Wong
FANCY PANTS(1950); CANNONBALL(1976, U.S./Hong Kong)
Johan Sebastian Wong
CHRISTMAS STORY, A(1983)
John Wong
CHRISTMAS STORY, A(1983)
Kai Wong
CHARLIE CHAN AND THE CURSE OF THE DRAGON QUEEN(1981)
Kai J. Wong
MAN WHO LOVED WOMEN, THE(1983)
Kai Joseph Wong
1984
CANNONBALL RUN II(1984)
Kimmy Wong
EYEWITNESS(1981)
Kit Lee Wong
STRAIGHT TIME(1978)
Larry Wong
FIRST YANK INTO TOKYO(1945)
Leon Wong
OUT OF SINGAPORE(1932)
Lessie Lynne Wong
PAL JOEY(1957)
Linda Wong
FIVE GATES TO HELL(1959); WAKE ME WHEN IT'S OVER(1960); HORIZONTAL LIEUTENANT, THE(1962); NUN AND THE SERGEANT, THE(1962); PARADISE, HAWAIIAN STYLE(1966)
Lorraine Wong
YEAR OF THE HORSE, THE(1966)
Mary Wong
GOOD EARTH, THE(1937)
Nee Wong, Jr.
PENNY SERENADE(1941)
P. Wong
FIGHT TO THE LAST(1938, Chi.)
Peter Wong
YEAR OF THE HORSE, THE(1966)
Richard Wong
INTRIGUE(1947)
Shirley Wong
CRY DR. CHICAGO(1971)
Stephen Wong
LEFT HAND OF GOD, THE(1955)
Suzie Wong
WHIP'S WOMEN(1968)
Victor Wong
WAR CORRESPONDENT(1932); KING KONG(1933); SON OF KONG(1933); WITH-OUT REGRET(1935); BRILLIANT MARRIAGE(1936); LEATHERNECKS HAVE LANDED, THE(1936); LOST HORIZON(1937); SHADOWS OVER SHANGHAI(1938); TAMING OF THE WEST, THE(1939); NO, NO NANETTE(1940); PHANTOM SUBMA-RINE, THE(1941); MISSION TO MOSCOW(1943)
1984
NIGHTSONGS(1984)
Vincent Wong
PRIVATES ON PARADE(1982)
1984
PRIVATES ON PARADE(1984, Brit.)
W. Beal Wong
GUNS, GIRLS AND GANGSTERS(1958); HONG KONG CONFIDENTIAL(1958)

Walter Wong
GENERAL DIED AT DAWN, THE(1936)

Wang Wong
TRAPPED IN A SUBMARINE(1931, Brit.)

Arthur Wontner
GENTLEMAN OF PARIS, A(1931); SHERLOCK HOLMES' FATAL HOUR(1931, Brit.), a, w; CONDEMNED TO DEATH(1932, Brit.); MISSING REMBRANDT, THE(1932, Brit.); SIGN OF FOUR, THE(1932, Brit.); LINE ENGAGED(1935, Brit.); REGAL CAVALCADE(1935, Brit.); TRIUMPH OF SHERLOCK HOLMES, THE(1935, Brit.), a, w; DISHONOR BRIGHT(1936, Brit.); LIVE WIRE, THE(1937, Brit.); SECOND BUREAU(1937, Brit.); STORM IN A TEACUP(1937, Brit.); THUNDER IN THE CITY(1937, Brit.); KATE PLUS TEN(1938, Brit.); OLD IRON(1938, Brit.); 13 MEN AND A GUN(1938, Brit.); JUST LIKE A WOMAN(1939, Brit.); MURDER AT THE BASKER-VILLES(1941, Brit.); TERROR, THE(1941, Brit.); COLONEL BLIMP(1945, Brit.); BLANCHE FURY(1948, Brit.); FIGHTING PIMPERNEL, THE(1950, Brit.); BRANDY FOR THE PARSON(1952, Brit.); GENEVIEVE(1953, Brit.); SEA DEVILS(1953); THREE CASES OF MURDER(1955, Brit.)
Misc. Silents
BIGAMIST, THE(1916); DIAMOND MAN, THE(1924, Brit.); EUGENE ARAM(1924, Brit.); INFAMOUS LADY, THE(1928, Brit.)

Hilary Wontner
TRYGON FACTOR, THE(1969, Brit.)

Julian Wontner
DOCTOR FAUSTUS(1967, Brit.)

George Woo
CHAN IS MISSING(1982)

James Wing Woo
KILLER ELITE, THE(1975); MARATHON MAN(1976)

Richard Woo
GAMBLERS, THE(1969)

Thomas Quon Woo
FIRST YANK INTO TOKYO(1945); SAIGON(1948); WE WERE STRANGERS(1949)

W.L. Woo
FIGHT TO THE LAST(1938, Chi.), ph

A. Voorhes Wood
Silents
PRUNELLA(1918)

Aaron Wood
MY BRILLIANT CAREER(1980, Aus.)

Adrian Wood
STAMPEDE(1949)

Alan Wood
LIKELY STORY, A(1947); PERFECT STRANGERS(1950)

Alex Wood
1984
DELIVERY BOYS(1984)

Allan Wood
IN NAME ONLY(1939); HEART OF THE RIO GRANDE(1942); WINNING TEAM, THE(1952); DEATH VALLEY(1982)

Allen Wood
FROM HELL TO HEAVEN(1933); GRIDIRON FLASH(1935); HOME ON THE RANGE(1935); MISS PACIFIC FLEET(1935); PAYOFF, THE(1935); HOTEL FOR WOMEN(1939); INVITATION TO HAPPINESS(1939); STORY OF VERNON AND IRENE CASTLE, THE(1939); HOUSE ACROSS THE BAY, THE(1940); SPORTING BLOOD(1940); MR. AND MRS. SMITH(1941); REMEMBER THE DAY(1941); SEVEN DAYS LEAVE(1942); GUY NAMED JOE, A(1943); HARRIGAN'S KID(1943); LADIES' DAY(1943); LOST ANGEL(1944); IT HAD TO BE YOU(1947); PEACE FOR A GUN-FIGHTER(1967)

Andy Wood
1984
SWORDKILL(1984)

Annabella Wood
BLOODTHIRSTY BUTCHERS(1970)

Art Wood
PERFECT COUPLE, A(1979)

Aubrey Wood
WILLY WONKA AND THE CHOCOLATE FACTORY(1971)

Baby Gloria Wood
Silents
DON'T TELL EVERYTHING(1921)

Barbara Wood
"RENT-A-GIRL"(1965)

Ben Wood
HAIR(1979)

Bill Wood
NOT AS A STRANGER(1955), makeup; SHAPE OF THINGS TO COME, THE(1979, Can.), spec eff

Bob Wood
BUSHWHACKERS, THE(1952); MADELEINE IS(1971, Can.)

Brennan Wood
W.I.A.(WOUNDED IN ACTION)*1/2 (1966)

Brenton Wood
POPDOWN(1968, Brit.)

Brian Wood
SUBMARINE SEAHAWK(1959)

Britt Wood
TRAIL DUST(1936); ADVENTURE'S END(1937); RANGE WAR(1939); HIDDEN GOLD(1940); KNIGHTS OF THE RANGE(1940); SANTA FE MARSHAL(1940); SHOW-DOWN, THE(1940); STAGECOACH WAR(1940); BORDER VIGILANTES(1941); PI-RATES ON HORSEBACK(1941); DOWN RIO GRANDE WAY(1942); STAGECOACH TO DENVER(1946); CHEYENNE(1947); DEAD MAN'S GOLD(1948); MARK OF THE LASH(1948); RIDERS OF THE WHISTLING PINES(1949); SQUARE DANCE JU-BILEE(1949); RETURN OF THE FRONTIERSMAN(1950); LAW AND ORDER(1953); STRANGER WORE A GUN, THE(1953); FIRST TRAVELING SALESLADY, THE(1956); STORM RIDER, THE(1957)

Buddy Wood
LAST PICTURE SHOW, THE(1971)

Cecelia Wood
RIVER, THE(1951)

Charles B. Wood
KING OF CHINATOWN(1939); MAN FROM TEXAS, THE(1939)

Charles Wood
FAME IS THE SPUR(1947, Brit.); HELP!(1965, Brit.), w; KNACK ... AND HOW TO GET IT, THE(1965, Brit.), a, w; HOW I WON THE WAR(1967, Brit.), w; CHARGE OF THE LIGHT BRIGADE, THE(1968, Brit.), w; LONG DAY'S DYING, THE(1968, Brit.), w; BED SITTING ROOM, THE(1969, Brit.), w; CUBA(1979), w; RED MO-NARCH(1983, Brit.), w; WAGNER(1983, Brit./Hung./Aust.), w

Christopher Wood
CONFESSIONS OF A WINDOW CLEANER(1974, Brit.), w; CONFESSIONS OF A POP PERFORMER(1975, Brit.), w; SEVEN NIGHTS IN JAPAN(1976, Brit./Fr.), w; CONFESSIONS FROM A HOLIDAY CAMP(1977, Brit.), w; SPY WHO LOVED ME, THE(1977, Brit.), w; MOONRAKER(1979, Brit.), w

Chuck Wood
SINS OF RACHEL CADE, THE(1960); BEAU GESTE(1966); TARZAN'S JUNGLE REBELLION(1970)

Cindi Wood
GREAT IMPOSTOR, THE(1960); HOODLUM PRIEST, THE(1961)

Clarice Wood
STUDENT TOUR(1934)

Clement Biddle Wood
DAY AND THE HOUR, THE(1963, Fr./ Ital.), w; BARBARELLA(1968, Fr./Ital.), w; SPIRITS OF THE DEAD(1969, Fr./Ital.), a, w; WELCOME TO THE CLUB(1971), w; LEONOR(1977, Fr./Span./Ital.), w

Cy Wood
MIDAS TOUCH, THE(1940, Brit.), w

Cyndi Wood
APOCALYPSE NOW(1979)

Cynthia Wood
VAN NUYS BLVD.(1979)

Cyril Wood
SALLY, IRENE AND MARY(1938), w

Cyrus Wood
JAZZ HEAVEN(1929), w; DANTE'S INFERNO(1935), w; DEEP IN MY HEART(1954), lyrics
Silents
DANTE'S INFERNO(1924), w

David Wood
IF ...(1968, Brit.); TALES THAT WITNESS MADNESS(1973, Brit.); SWALLOWS AND AMAZONS(1977, Brit.), w; FFOLKES(1980, Brit.); SWEET WILLIAM(1980, Brit.)

David King Wood
THE CREEPING UNKNOWN(1956, Brit.)

Dee Dee Wood
LI'L ABNER(1959), ch; SOUND OF MUSIC, THE(1965), ch; HAPPIEST MIL-LIONAIRE, THE(1967), ch; CHITTY CHITTY BANG BANG(1968, Brit.), ch; IN GOD WE TRUST(1980), ch

Denis Wood
STRICTLY CONFIDENTIAL(1959, Brit.)

Diana R. Wood
PRISON FARM(1938)

Donna Wood
POT O' GOLD(1941)

Dorinda Rice Wood
CLONUS HORROR, THE(1979), cos

Dorothy Wood
IDAHO KID, THE(1937)
Silents
DAUGHTERS OF TODAY(1924); RECKLESS CHANCES(5 reels)
Misc. Silents
WEST VS. EAST(1922); CALIBRE 45(1924); COURAGE(1924); BORDER IN-TRIGUE(1925); RANGER BILL(1925); STREAK OF LUCK, A(1925); GOLDEN TRAIL, THE(1927)

Douglas Wood
FOUNTAIN, THE(1934); GREAT EXPECTATIONS(1934); PRESIDENT VANISHES, THE(1934); TRUMPET BLOWS, THE(1934); COLLEGE SCANDAL(1935); GREAT IMPERSONATION, THE(1935); LOVE IN BLOOM(1935); SPECIAL AGENT(1935); WEDDING NIGHT, THE(1935); DANGEROUS(1936); DRACULA'S DAUGHTER(1936); GREAT GUY(1936); HEARTS IN BONDAGE(1936); NAVY BORN(1936); PARO-LE(1936); PIGSKIN PARADE(1936); PRISONER OF SHARK ISLAND, THE(1936); TWO AGAINST THE WORLD(1936); TWO IN A CROWD(1936); WEDDING PRE-SENT(1936); ALI BABA GOES TO TOWN(1937); CASE OF THE STUTTERING BISHOP, THE(1937); DANGEROUSLY YOURS(1937); GUNS OF THE PECOS(1937); MAN WHO FOUND HIMSELF, THE(1937); MARRIED BEFORE BREAKFAST(1937); MAYTIME(1937); ON THE AVENUE(1937); OVER THE GOAL(1937); PLAINSMAN, THE(1937); SAN QUENTIN(1937); THIS IS MY AFFAIR(1937); WEST OF SHANG-HAI(1937); I AM THE LAW(1938); KENTUCKY(1938); SERGEANT MURPHY(1938); EAST SIDE OF HEAVEN(1939); ETERNALLY YOURS(1939); OFF THE RE-CORD(1939); SUDDEN MONEY(1939); 20,000 MEN A YEAR(1939); BABIES FOR SALE(1940); DR. EHRLICH'S MAGIC BULLET(1940); MAN WHO WOULDN'T TALK, THE(1940); PRIVATE AFFAIRS(1940); PUBLIC DEB NO. 1(1940); BUCK PRIVA-TES(1941); HERE COMES MR. JORDAN(1941); H.M. PULHAM, ESQ.(1941); HONKY TONK(1941); IN THE NAVY(1941); LOVE CRAZY(1941); SMALL TOWN DEB(1941); MURDER IN THE BIG HOUSE(1942); PARACHUTE NURSE(1942); THEY ALL KISSED THE BRIDE(1942); WE WERE DANCING(1942); GOOD FELLOWS, THE(1943); HERS TO HOLD(1943); MORE THE MERRIER, THE(1943); NEVER A DULL MOMENT(1943); SHE'S FOR ME(1943); WHAT A WOMAN!(1943); ADVEN-TURES OF MARK TWAIN, THE(1944); I'M FROM ARKANSAS(1944); MEET MISS BOBBY SOCKS(1944); THEY LIVE IN FEAR(1944); BOSTON BLACKIE BOOKED ON SUSPICION(1945); COME OUT FIGHTING(1945); EADIE WAS A LADY(1945); PA-TRICK THE GREAT(1945); BECAUSE OF HIM(1946); DO YOU LOVE ME?(1946); DRAGONWYCH(1946); MISSING LADY, THE(1946); NIGHT EDITOR(1946); TOMOR-ROW IS FOREVER(1946); BLONDIE'S BIG MOMENT(1947); HER HUSBAND'S AFFAIRS(1947); IT HAD TO BE YOU(1947); LITTLE MISS BROADWAY(1947); MY WILD IRISH ROSE(1947); SENATOR WAS INDISCREET, THE(1947); TWO BLONDES AND A REDHEAD(1947); WELCOME STRANGER(1947); I SURRENDER DEAR(1948); OLD-FASHIONED GIRL, AN(1948); SHAMROCK HILL(1949); BORDER OUT-LAWS(1950); HARRIET CRAIG(1950); PETTY GIRL, THE(1950); CATTLE QUEEN(1951); NO MAN'S WOMAN(1955); THAT CERTAIN FEELING(1956)

Duncan Wood
BARGEE, THE(1964, Brit.), d; CUCKOO PATROL(1965, Brit.), d; SOME WILL, SOME WON'T(1970, Brit.), d

Durinda Rice Wood
BATTLE BEYOND THE STARS(1980), cos

E.S. Wood
TRACK OF THE MOONBEAST(1976), ph

Edna Wood
WANTED FOR MURDER(1946, Brit.)

Edward Wood, Jr.
NIGHT OF THE GHOULS(1959), p,d&w

Edward D. Wood, Jr.
GLEN OR GLENDA(1953), d&w; JAIL BAIT(1954), p&d, w; BRIDE OF THE MONSTER(1955), p,d&w; VIOLENT YEARS, THE(1956), w; BRIDE AND THE BEAST, THE(1958), w; PLAN 9 FROM OUTER SPACE(1959), p,d&w, ed; SINISTER URGE, THE(1961), p,d&w; SHOTGUN WEDDING, THE(1963), w

Edward Davis Wood, Jr.
ORGY OF THE DEAD zero(1965), w

Eleanor Wood
WIFE TAKES A FLYER, THE(1942)

Ellie Wood
NEW INTERNS, THE(1964)

Elliot Wood
FOR LOVE OF IVY(1968)

Ercell Wood
STUDENT TOUR(1934)

Eric Wood
KING KONG(1933)

Ernest Wood
NOT DAMAGED(1930); SWEETHEARTS ON PARADE(1930); AMBASSADOR BILL(1931); ANNABELLE'S AFFAIRS(1931); JUNE MOON(1931); SOB SISTER(1931); BEDTIME STORY, A(1933); INTERNATIONAL HOUSE(1933); JENNIE GERHARDT(1933); PAROLE GIRL(1933); CALL IT LUCK(1934); FUGITIVE LADY(1934); HIGH, WIDE AND HANDSOME(1937); I'LL TAKE ROMANCE(1937); LAST GANGSTER, THE(1937); PAID TO DANCE(1937); ROARING TIMBER(1937); SAN QUENTIN(1937); SOMETHING TO SING ABOUT(1937); NAUGHTY BUT NICE(1939)
Silents
PASSIONATE YOUTH(1925); OUT OF THE PAST(1927); RED WINE(1928)
Misc. Silents
WOMAN'S LAW(1927); PERFECT GENTLEMAN, A(1928)

Ernie Wood
BROADWAY GONDOLIER(1935)
Silents
ATTA BOY!(1926); TAKE ME HOME(1928)
Misc. Silents
HORSE SHOES(1927)

Eugene Wood
NOTHING BUT A MAN(1964); WAY WE LIVE NOW, THE(1970)

Florence Wood
GENTLEMAN OF PARIS, A(1931); PRIVATE LIFE OF DON JUAN, THE(1934, Brit.)

Forrest Wood
WAR LORD, THE(1965); NUMBER ONE(1969); HAWAIIANS, THE(1970); OMEGA MAN, THE(1971); SKYJACKED(1972); SOYLENT GREEN(1973); TWO-MINUTE WARNING(1976)

Fred Wood
GAL YOUNG UN(1979)

Freeman Wood
CHINATOWN NIGHTS(1929); LADIES IN LOVE(1930); LILIES OF THE FIELD(1930); SWELLHEAD, THE(1930); YOUNG EAGLES(1930); KEPT HUSBANDS(1931); EVENINGS FOR SALE(1932); LADY WITH A PAST(1932); I LIVE MY LIFE(1935); HOUSE ACROSS THE BAY, THE(1940); ONCE UPON A TIME(1944)
Silents
ADVENTURE SHOP, THE(1918); DIANE OF STAR HOLLOW(1921); HIGH HEELS(1921); MADE IN HEAVEN(1921); RAGE OF PARIS, THE(1921); WHITE HANDS(1922); DIVORCE(1923); INNOCENCE(1923); OUT OF LUCK(1923); GIRL ON THE STAIRS, THE(1924); RAFFLES, THE AMATEUR CRACKSMAN(1925); JOSSELYN'S WIFE(1926); SOCIAL CELEBRITY, A(1926); COWARD, THE(1927); TAXI! TAXI!(1927); HALF A BRIDE(1928)
Misc. Silents
FASHION ROW(1923); GOSSIP(1923); WILD PARTY, THE(1923); ONE GLORIOUS NIGHT(1924); HEARTS AND SPURS(1925); PART TIME WIFE(1925); SCANDAL PROOF(1925); WINGS OF YOUTH(1925); LONE WOLF RETURNS, THE(1926); PRINCE OF BROADWAY, THE(1926)

Freeman S. Wood
WHY BRING THAT UP?(1929); ONLY THE BRAVE(1930)

G. Wood
BREWSTER McCLOUD(1970); M(1970); HAROLD AND MAUDE(1971); BANK SHOT(1974)

G. D. Wood
FORGOTTEN WOMEN(1932); CRASHING BROADWAY(1933)

G. D. Wood [Gordon DeMain]
MONTANA KID, THE(1931); TWO-FISTED JUSTICE(1931); LUCKY LARRIGAN(1933); RETURN OF CASEY JONES(1933)

Gary Wood
GLORY STOMPERS, THE(1967)
1984
HARDBODIES(1984)
Misc. Talkies
KEEP OFF! KEEP OFF!(1975)

Gene Wood
DIRTYMOUTH(1970)

George Wood
1984
TIGHTROPE(1984)

Gloria Wood
GABY(1956)
Silents
PECK'S BAD BOY(1921)

Gordon Wood
MOTHER AND SON(1931); FORTY-NINERS, THE(1932)

Gordon Wood [Gordon DeMain]
HONOR OF THE MOUNTED(1932)

Grace Wood
FEROCIOUS PAL(1934); MR. WONG, DETECTIVE(1938)

Harlene [Harley] Wood
WHISTLING BULLETS(1937)

Harley Wood
LAW RIDES, THE(1936); MY MAN GODFREY(1936); BORDER PHANTOM(1937); LAW AND LEAD(1937)
Misc. Talkies
VALLEY OF TERROR(1937)

Harry Wood
HUMAN CARGO(1936); CONFLICT(1937); NEW ORLEANS AFTER DARK(1958); DARKER THAN AMBER(1970)
Silents
BULLET MARK, THE(1928), w

Haydn Wood
SMALL MAN, THE(1935, Brit.)

Helen Wood
KID MILLIONS(1934); CAN THIS BE DIXIE?(1936); CHAMPAGNE CHARLIE(1936); CHARLIE CHAN AT THE RACE TRACK(1936); HIGH TENSION(1936); MY MARRIAGE(1936); CRACK-UP, THE(1937); ALMOST A GENTLEMAN(1939); SORORITY HOUSE(1939); GIVE A GIRL A BREAK(1953); NIGHT THEY RAIDED MINSKY'S, THE(1968)

Mrs. Henry Wood
EAST LYNNE(1931), w; EX-FLAME(1931), w
Silents
EAST LYNNE(1913, Brit.), w; EAST LYNNE(1916), w

Horace Wood
TRACK OF THUNDER(1967)

Howarth Wood
WHITE HUNTRESS(1957, Brit.)

Humphrey Wood
CARMEN, BABY(1967, Yugo./Ger.), ed; THERESE AND ISABELLE(1968, U.S./Ger.), ed

Hywel Wood
LAST DAYS OF DOLWYN, THE(1949, Brit.)

Ira Buck Wood
IN THIS OUR LIFE(1942)

Ireland Wood
JUST WILLIAM(1939, Brit.), w

James Wood
MY FAIR LADY(1964); DR. JEKYLL'S DUNGEON OF DEATH(1982), p&d, ph, ed

Jane Wood
WISHBONE, THE(1933, Brit.); RAGMAN'S DAUGHTER, THE(1974, Brit.)
1984
LASSITER(1984)

Janet Wood
WHY RUSSIANS ARE REVOLTING(1970); ANGELS HARD AS THEY COME(1971); TERROR HOUSE(1972); SLUMBER PARTY '57(1977)
Misc. Talkies
FANGS(1974)

Jeane Wood
SINS OF THE CHILDREN(1930); NEVER SAY GOODBYE(1956); SEARCH FOR BRIDEY MURPHY, THE(1956); TEN COMMANDMENTS, THE(1956); BACK FROM THE DEAD(1957); JOE DAKOTA(1957); SORORITY GIRL(1957); CAT ON A HOT TIN ROOF(1958)

Jiggs Wood
QUEEN FOR A DAY(1951)

Joan Wentworth Wood
CONTRABAND LOVE(1931, Brit.), w; CALLBOX MYSTERY, THE(1932, Brit.), w; FLAG LIEUTENANT, THE(1932, Brit.), w; CHELSEA LIFE(1933, Brit.), w; FACES(1934, Brit.), w; LILY OF LAGUNA(1938, Brit.), w

John Wood
GIRL IN THE CROWD, THE(1934, Brit.); CASE OF GABRIEL PERRY, THE(1935, Brit.); FULL CIRCLE(1935, Brit.); LAST DAYS OF POMPEII, THE(1935); TO CATCH A THIEF(1936, Brit.); OVER SHE GOES(1937, Brit.); HOLD MY HAND(1938, Brit.); HOUSEMASTER(1938, Brit.); OH BOY!(1938, Brit.); BLACK EYES(1939, Brit.); NORTH SEA PATROL(1939, Brit.); MAD MEN OF EUROPE(1940, Brit.); FALSE RAPTURE(1941); STOLEN FACE(1952, Brit.); SALOME(1953); SEA WIFE(1957, Brit.); IDOL ON PARADE(1959, Brit.); IT TAKES A THIEF(1960, Brit.); CALL ME GENIUS(1961, Brit.); INVASION QUARTET(1961, Brit.); TWO-WAY STRETCH(1961, Brit.); LIVE NOW-PAY LATER(1962, Brit.); POSTMAN'S KNOCK(1962, Brit.); JUST FOR FUN(1963, Brit.); LOVE IS A BALL(1963); MOUSE ON THE MOON, THE(1963, Brit.); THAT KIND OF GIRL(1963, Brit.); JUST LIKE A WOMAN(1967, Brit.); ONE MORE TIME(1970, Brit.); WHICH WAY TO THE FRONT?(1970); NICHOLAS AND ALEXANDRA(1971, Brit.); OFFICE PICNIC, THE(1974, Aus.); SOMEBODY KILLED HER HUSBAND(1978); WARGAMES(1983)

Joan Wentworth Wood [Morgan]
MIXED DOUBLES(1933, Brit.), w; MINSTREL BOY, THE(1937, Brit.), w

John E. Wood
NAKED JUNGLE, THE(1953)

Joy Wood
SECRET PARTNER, THE(1961, Brit.)

Judith Wood
SIN TAKES A HOLIDAY(1930); GIRLS ABOUT TOWN(1931); ROAD TO RENO(1931); WOMEN LOVE ONCE(1931); WORKING GIRLS(1931); CRIME DOCTOR, THE(1934); LOOKING FOR TROUBLE(1934); MAN WHO RECLAIMED HIS HEAD, THE(1935); RIFF-RAFF(1936); RHYTHM RACKETEER(1937, Brit.); THEY MET IN BOMBAY(1941)

Judy Wood
Misc. Talkies
ACID EATERS, THE(1968)

Julie Wood
PETER RABBIT AND TALES OF BEATRIX POTTER(1971, Brit.)

June Wood
LETTER FROM AN UNKNOWN WOMAN(1948)
Ken Wood
DEVIL'S MAN, THE(1967, Ital.); KILL THEM ALL AND COME BACK ALONE(1970, Ital./Span.)
Ken Wood [Giovanni Cianfriglia]
SUPERARGO VERSUS DIABOLICUS(1966, Ital./Span.); SUPERARGO(1968, Ital./Span.)
Kenny Wood
LAST PICTURE SHOW, THE(1971)
Kinchen Wood
Silents
RUNNING WATER(1922, Brit.), w; WEAVERS OF FORTUNE(1922, Brit.), w; SCANDAL, THE(1923, Brit.), w
Lana Wood
SEARCHERS, THE(1956); FIVE FINGER EXERCISE(1962); GIRLS ON THE BEACH(1965); FOR SINGLES ONLY(1968); FREE GRASS(1969); DIAMONDS ARE FOREVER(1971, Brit.); GRAYEAGLE(1977); SPEEDTRAP(1978); SATAN'S MISTRESS(1982)
Misc. Talkies
DARK EYES(1980)
Lawrence Wood
SCUM OF THE EARTH(1963)
Silents
MADAME BUTTERFLY(1915)
Lee Wood
CASTAWAY COWBOY, THE(1974)
Leslie Wood
LILLI MARLENE(1951, Brit.), w
Lew Wood
DESTINY(1944)
Lorna Wood
FIRE DOWN BELOW(1957, U.S./Brit.)
Lou Wood
FRONTIER GAL(1945)
Louis Wood
LOVER COME BACK(1946)
Lynn Wood
JUMBO(1962); WACKIEST WAGON TRAIN IN THE WEST, THE(1976)
Mara Scott Wood
OFFICER AND A GENTLEMAN, AN(1982)
Margo Wood
STATE FAIR(1945); WHEN YOU'RE SMILING(1950)
Marjorie Wood
THEY SHALL HAVE MUSIC(1939); WOMEN, THE(1939); PRIDE AND PREJUDICE(1940); KLONDIKE FURY(1942); SABOTEUR(1942); THIN MAN GOES HOME, THE(1944); NIGHTMARE ALLEY(1947); JOAN OF ARC(1948); THAT WONDERFUL URGE(1948); ADAM'S RIB(1949); CAGED(1950); COMPANY SHE KEEPS, THE(1950); EXCUSE MY DUST(1951); TEXAS CARNIVAL(1951); SWEETHEARTS ON PARADE(1953); SEVEN BRIDES FOR SEVEN BROTHERS(1954)
Marjory Wood
MADE FOR EACH OTHER(1939)
Marlene Wood
FEUD OF THE TRAIL(1938)
Mary Laura Wood
VALLEY OF EAGLES(1952, Brit.); WOMAN IN HIDING(1953, Brit.); DOCTOR AT SEA(1955, Brit.); HIGH TERRACE(1957, Brit.); HOUR OF DECISION(1957, Brit.); RAISING A RIOT(1957, Brit.); STRANGER IN TOWN(1957, Brit.); MAN INSIDE, THE(1958, Brit.); ESCORT FOR HIRE(1960, Brit.); SCENT OF MYSTERY(1960); FATE TAKES A HAND(1962, Brit.)
Misc. Talkies
BLACK ORCHID(1952); ACCUSED, THE(1953)
Michael Wood
AMITYVILLE 3-D(1983), spec eff
Mickey Wood
HIGH TREASON(1951, Brit.); CIRCLE OF DECEPTON(1961, Brit.)
Mike Wood
TWILIGHT ZONE–THE MOVIE(1983), spec eff
1984
FIRESTARTER(1984), spec eff
Milton Wood
KILLER LEOPARD(1954); PHANTOM OF THE JUNGLE(1955)
Mirren Wood
ONCE UPON A DREAM(1949, Brit.)
Montgomery Wood [Giuliano Gemma]
PISTOL FOR RINGO, A(1966, Ital./Span.)
N.Z. Wood
Misc. Silents
MANAGER OF THE B&A, THE(1916)
Nancy Wood
LONELY LADY, THE(1983); PIRATES OF PENZANCE, THE(1983)
1984
SCANDALOUS(1984); SUPERGIRL(1984)
Natalie Wood
GHOST AND MRS. MUIR, THE(1942); BRIDE WORE BOOTS, THE(1946); TOMORROW IS FOREVER(1946); DRIFTWOOD(1947); MIRACLE ON 34TH STREET, THE(1947); CHICKEN EVERY SUNDAY(1948); SCUDDA-HOO! SCUDDA-HAY!(1948); FATHER WAS A FULLBACK(1949); GREEN PROMISE, THE(1949); JACKPOT, THE(1950); NEVER A DULL MOMENT(1950); NO SAD SONGS FOR ME(1950); OUR VERY OWN(1950); BLUE VEIL, THE(1951); DEAR BRAT(1951); JUST FOR YOU(1952); ROSE BOWL STORY, THE(1952); STAR, THE(1953); SILVER CHALICE, THE(1954); ONE DESIRE(1955); REBEL WITHOUT A CAUSE(1955); BURNING HILLS, THE(1956); CRY IN THE NIGHT, A(1956); GIRL HE LEFT BEHIND, THE(1956); SEARCHERS, THE(1956); BOMBERS B-52(1957); KINGS GO FORTH(1958); MARJORIE MORNINGSTAR(1958); ALL THE FINE YOUNG CANNIBALS(1960); CASH McCALL(1960); SPLENDOR IN THE GRASS(1961); WEST SIDE STORY(1961); GYPSY(1962); LOVE WITH THE PROPER STRANGER(1963); SEX AND THE SINGLE GIRL(1964); GREAT RACE, THE(1965); INSIDE DAISY CLOVER(1965); PENELOPE(1966); THIS PROPERTY IS CONDEMNED(1966); BOB AND CAROL AND TED AND ALICE(1969); CANDIDATE, THE(1972); PEEPER(1975); METEOR(1979); LAST

MARRIED COUPLE IN AMERICA, THE(1980); WILLIE AND PHIL(1980); BRAINSTORM(1983)
Oliver Wood
POPDOWN(1968, Brit.), ph; HONEYMOON KILLERS, THE(1969), ph; FEEDBACK(1979), ph; DON'T GO IN THE HOUSE(1980), ph; MAYA(1982), ph; RETURNING, THE(1983), ph
1984
ALPHABET CITY(1984), ph
Pamela Wood
MACUSHLA(1937, Brit.); DR. O'DOWD(1940, Brit.)
Patrick Wood
NUTCRACKER(1982, Brit.)
Peggy Wood
WONDER OF WOMEN(1929); HANDY ANDY(1934); JALNA(1935); RIGHT TO LIVE, THE(1935); CALL IT A DAY(1937); STAR IS BORN, A(1937); HOUSEKEEPER'S DAUGHTER(1939); BRIDE WORE BOOTS, THE(1946); MAGNIFICENT DOLL(1946); DREAM GIRL(1947); STORY OF RUTH, THE(1960); SOUND OF MUSIC, THE(1965)
Silents
ALMOST A HUSBAND(1919)
Peter Wood
ROCKETS IN THE DUNES(1960, Brit.); IN SEARCH OF GREGORY(1970, Brit./Ital.), d
Philip Wood
ROOM SERVICE(1938)
Phillip Wood
OUR TOWN(1940)
Ren Wood
JERK, THE(1979); PERFECT COUPLE, A(1979)
Richard Wood
2001: A SPACE ODYSSEY(1968, U.S./Brit.); MOONSHINE COUNTY EXPRESS(1977)
Richard C. Wood
SINCE YOU WENT AWAY(1944)
Robert W. Wood
REDWOOD FOREST TRAIL(1950)
Robert Wood
Misc. Talkies
HOW TO MAKE A DOLL(1967)
Robert Wood
WHISPERING SMITH(1948); WAKE OF THE RED WITCH(1949); UNION STATION(1950); RETURN FROM THE SEA(1954)
Rocky Wood
SEA OF GRASS, THE(1947)
Roland Wood
TIGER MAKES OUT, THE(1967)
Ronald Wood
WITNESS, THE(1959, Brit.)
Ross Wood
KING OF THE CORAL SEA(1956, Aus.), ph; THREE IN ONE(1956, Aus.), ph
Sally Wood
STRANGE BEDFELLOWS(1965), cos
Salvador Wood
DEATH OF A BUREAUCRAT(1979, Cuba)
Sam Wood
SO THIS IS COLLEGE(1929), d; GIRL SAID NO, THE(1930), d; IT'S A GREAT LIFE(1930), p&d; PAID(1930), d; SINS OF THE CHILDREN(1930), d; THEY LEARNED ABOUT WOMEN(1930), d; WAY FOR A SAILOR(1930), d; MAN IN POSSESSION, THE(1931), d; NEW ADVENTURES OF GET-RICH-QUICK WALLINGFORD, THE(1931), d; TAILOR MADE MAN, A(1931), d; HUDDLE(1932), d; PROSPERITY(1932), d; BARBARIAN, THE(1933), d; CHRISTOPHER BEAN(1933), d; HOLD YOUR MAN(1933), p&d; LET 'EM HAVE IT(1935), d; NIGHT AT THE OPERA, A(1935), d; UNGUARDED HOUR, THE(1936), d; WHIPSAW(1936), d; DAY AT THE RACES, A(1937), d; MADAME X(1937), d; NAVY BLUE AND GOLD(1937), d; LORD JEFF(1938), d; STABLEMATES(1938), d; GONE WITH THE WIND(1939), d; GOODBYE MR. CHIPS(1939, Brit.), d; RAFFLES(1939), d; KITTY FOYLE(1940), d; OUR TOWN(1940), d; RANGERS OF FORTUNE(1940), d; DEVIL AND MISS JONES, THE(1941), d; KING'S ROW(1942), d; PRIDE OF THE YANKEES, THE(1942), d; FOR WHOM THE BELL TOLLS(1943), p&d; CASANOVA BROWN(1944), d; GUEST WIFE(1945), d; SARATOGA TRUNK(1945), d; HEARTBEAT(1946), d; IVY(1947), d; COMMAND DECISION(1948), d; STRATTON STORY, THE(1949), d; AMBUSH(1950), d
Silents
EXCUSE MY DUST(1920), d; WHAT'S YOUR HURRY?(1920), d; DON'T TELL EVERYTHING(1921), d; PECK'S BAD BOY(1921), d&w; BEYOND THE ROCKS(1922), d; HER GILDED CAGE(1922), d; IMPOSSIBLE MRS. BELLEW, THE(1922), d; MY AMERICAN WIFE(1923), d; BLUFF(1924), d; ONE MINUTE TO PLAY(1926), d; FAIR CO-ED, THE(1927), d; RACING ROMEO(1927), d; LATEST FROM PARIS, THE(1928), d; TELLING THE WORLD(1928), d
Misc. Silents
CITY SPARROW, THE(1920), d; DANCIN' FOOL, THE(1920), d; DOUBLE SPEED(1920), d; HER BELOVED VILLIAN(1920), d; HER FIRST ELOPEMENT(1920), d; SICK ABED(1920), d; GREAT MOMENT, THE(1921), d; SNOB, THE(1921), d; UNDER THE LASH(1921), d; HER HUSBAND'S TRADEMARK(1922), d; BLUEBEARD'S 8TH WIFE(1923), d; HIS CHILDREN'S CHILDREN(1923), d; PRODIGAL DAUGHTERS(1923), d; FEMALE, THE(1924), d; MINE WITH THE IRON DOOR, THE(1924), d; NEXT CORNER, THE(1924), d; RE-CREATION OF BRIAN KENT, THE(1925), d; FASCINATING YOUTH(1926), d; ROOKIES(1927), d
Sam M. Wood
STAMBOUL QUEST(1934), d
Sarah Wood
DON'T GO IN THE HOUSE(1980), art d
Sidney Wood
Silents
DAVID AND JONATHAN(1920, Brit.)
Sissy Wood
GAL YOUNG UN(1979)
Star Wood
Misc. Talkies
SIMPLY IRRESISTIBLE(1983)

Susan Wood
WHO'S THAT KNOCKING AT MY DOOR?(1968); WATERLOO(1970, Ital./USSR)
Sydney Wood
Misc. Silents
WARRIOR STRAIN, THE(1919, Brit.); HER BENNY(1920, Brit.)
T.J. Wood
TALL TEXAN, THE(1953), p
Teri Lynn Wood
SGT. PEPPER'S LONELY HEARTS CLUB BAND(1978)
Thomas Wood
TWO THOUSAND MANIACS!(1964); TASTE OF BLOOD, A(1967); MY THIRD WIFE
GEORGE(1968)
Misc. Talkies
GOD'S BLOODY ACRE(1975)
Tom Wood
SLAUGHTERHOUSE-FIVE(1972)
Silents
GOLD RUSH, THE(1925)
Tory Wood
WITHOUT A TRACE(1983)
Truman Wood
BLOOD ON THE SUN(1945), ed
Truman K. Wood
TIME OF YOUR LIFE, THE(1948), ed; GIRL IN THE SHOW, THE(1929), ed; DIVOR-
CEE, THE(1930), ed; GIRL SAID NO, THE(1930), ed; SONG OF THE OPEN
ROAD(1944), ed; GETTING GERTIE'S GARTER(1945), ed; KISS TOMORROW GOOD-
BYE(1950), ed
Vera Wood
STRANGE PEOPLE(1933), ed
Victor Wood
TWILIGHT HOUR(1944, Brit.); IF WINTER COMES(1947); MOSS ROSE(1947); HILLS
OF HOME(1948); IRON CURTAIN, THE(1948); JOAN OF ARC(1948); JULIA MIS-
BEHAVES(1948); DESERT FOX, THE(1951); KIND LADY(1951); LES MISERA-
BLES(1952); MY COUSIN RACHEL(1952); SNOWS OF KILIMANJARO, THE(1952);
SCANDAL AT SCOURIE(1953); DIAMOND WIZARD, THE(1954, Brit.); TIME
LOCK(1959, Brit.)
Virginia Wood
GUIDE FOR THE MARRIED MAN, A(1967); MAN CALLED DAGGER, A(1967);
DESTRUCTORS, THE(1968); LADY IN CEMENT(1968)
Misc. Talkies
JENNIE, WIFE/CHILD(1968)
Vivienne Wood
HAPPIEST DAYS OF YOUR LIFE(1950, Brit.); GREEN MAN, THE(1957, Brit.)
Walter Wood
HOODLUM PRIEST, THE(1961), p; ESCAPE FROM EAST BERLIN(1962), p
1984
LIES(1984, Brit.)
Ward Wood
AIR FORCE(1943); WE'VE NEVER BEEN LICKED(1943); RAMROD(1947); SHOT-
GUN(1955); PROUD AND THE PROFANE, THE(1956); JEANNE EAGELS(1957);
MONEY TRAP, THE(1966); LONERS, THE(1972)
Misc. Talkies
POSSE FROM HEAVEN(1975)
Wee Georgie Wood
THE BLACK HAND GANG(1930, Brit.)
Misc. Silents
CONVICT 99(1919, Brit.); TWO LITTLE DRUMMER BOYS(1928, Brit.)
Wendy Wood
TORTURE ME KISS ME(1970)
Wiley Wood
QUARTET(1981, Brit./Fr.)
William Wood
SAMSON AND DELILAH(1949), makeup; MY SIX LOVES(1963), a, w; LIVELY
SET, THE(1964), w
Wilson Wood
FAITHFUL IN MY FASHION(1946); NO LEAVE, NO LOVE(1946); SHOW-OFF,
THE(1946); HIGH TIDE(1947); IT HAPPENED IN BROOKLYN(1947); CAMPUS
HONEYMOON(1948); CHICKEN EVERY SUNDAY(1948); EASTER PARADE(1948);
LUCK OF THE IRISH(1948); ONE SUNDAY AFTERNOON(1948); STATE OF THE
UNION(1948); THAT WONDERFUL URGE(1948); BARKLEYS OF BROADWAY,
THE(1949); EAST SIDE, WEST SIDE(1949); FATHER WAS A FULLBACK(1949);
SCENE OF THE CRIME(1949); SUN COMES UP, THE(1949); THAT FORSYTE
WOMAN(1949); LIFE OF HER OWN, A(1950); MAGNIFICENT YANKEE, THE(1950);
INSURANCE INVESTIGATOR(1951); LET'S MAKE IT LEGAL(1951); MR. IMPERI-
UM(1951); SOLDIERS THREE(1951); STRIP, THE(1951); TEXAS CARNIVAL(1951);
THUNDER IN GOD'S COUNTRY(1951); EVERYTHING I HAVE IS YOURS(1952);
SINGIN' IN THE RAIN(1952); CLOWN, THE(1953); GIRL WHO HAD EVERYTHING,
THE(1953); PICKUP ON SOUTH STREET(1953); BLACK WIDOW(1954); EXECUTIVE
SUITE(1954); LONG, LONG TRAILER, THE(1954); IT'S ALWAYS FAIR WEA-
THER(1955); MOONFLEET(1955); TENDER TRAP, THE(1955); TRIAL(1955); JAIL-
HOUSE ROCK(1957); SATAN'S SATELLITES(1958); PLEASE DON'T EAT THE
DAISIES(1960); JUMBO(1962)
Yvonne Wood
GANG'S ALL HERE, THE(1943), cos; BIG NOISE, THE(1944), cos; FOUR JILLS IN
A JEEP(1944), cos; TAMPICO(1944), cos; MOLLY AND ME(1945), cos; WHITE TIE
AND TAILS(1946), cos; DOUBLE LIFE, A(1947), cos; RIDE THE PINK HORSE(1947),
cos; SLAVE GIRL(1947), cos; WEB, THE(1947), cos; BLACK BART(1948), cos; CAS-
BAH(1948), cos; TAP ROOTS(1948), cos; ABANDONED(1949), cos; CALAMITY JANE
AND SAM BASS(1949), cos; CRISS CROSS(1949), cos; ILLEGAL ENTRY(1949), cos;
SHAKEDOWN(1950), cos; SIERRA(1950), cos; TRIPOLI(1950), cos; WINCHESTER
'73(1950), cos; SAN FRANCISCO STORY, THE(1952), cos; FORT ALGIERS(1953), cos;
RAIDERS OF THE SEVEN SEAS(1953), cos; CONQUEROR, THE(1956), cos; COURT
JESTER, THE(1956), cos; BIG COUNTRY, THE(1958), cos; MAN OF THE WEST(1958),
cos; ONE-EYED JACKS(1961), cos; DUEL AT DIABLO(1966), cos; FIRE-
CREEK(1968), cos; GOOD GUYS AND THE BAD GUYS, THE(1969), cos; CHEYENNE
SOCIAL CLUB, THE(1970), cos; DIRTY DINGUS MAGEE(1970), cos; OUTFIT,
THE(1973), cos; ZOOT SUIT(1981), cos

Stella Wood-Sims
Silents
ERNEST MALTRAVERS(1920, Brit.); HALF A TRUTH(1922, Brit.)
Noel Wood-Smith
OFFICE GIRL, THE(1932, Brit.), w
Doris Woodall
FACING THE MUSIC(1933, Brit.)
Alfre Woodard
REMEMBER MY NAME(1978); HEALTH(1980)
1984
GO TELL IT ON THE MOUNTAIN(1984)
Bronte Woodard
GREASE(1978), w
Charlaine Woodard
HAIR(1979)
1984
CRACKERS(1984)
Grace Woodard
MAN, WOMAN AND CHILD(1983); MAX DUGAN RETURNS(1983)
Horace Woodard
Misc. Talkies
ADVENTURES OF CHICO, THE(1938), d
Robin Woodard
SALLY'S HOUNDS(1968)
Stacy Woodard
Misc. Talkies
ADVENTURES OF CHICO, THE(1938), d
Billy Woodberry
1984
BLESS THEIR LITTLE HEARTS(1984), p&d, ed
George Woodbridge
BLACK SHEEP OF WHITEHALL, THE(1941 Brit.); BIG BLOCKADE, THE(1942,
Brit.); TOWER OF TERROR, THE(1942, Brit.); ESCAPE TO DANGER(1943, Brit.);
ADVENTURESS, THE(1946, Brit.); GREEN FOR DANGER(1946, Brit.); BLANCHE
FURY(1948, Brit.); ESCAPE(1948, Brit.); OCTOBER MAN, THE(1948, Brit.); QUEEN OF
SPADES(1948, Brit.); CHILDREN OF CHANCE(1949, Brit.); FALLEN IDOL, THE(1949,
Brit.); MY BROTHER JONATHAN(1949, Brit.); SILENT DUST(1949, Brit.); TEMPTA-
TION HARBOR(1949, Brit.); CLOUDBURST(1952, Brit.); MURDER IN THE CATHE-
DRAL(1952, Brit.); BAD BLONDE(1953, Brit.); DOUBLE CONFESSION(1953, Brit.);
GREAT GILBERT AND SULLIVAN, THE(1953, Brit.); ISN'T LIFE WONDER-
FUL!(1953, Brit.); COMPANIONS IN CRIME(1954, Brit.); FOR BETTER FOR WOR-
SE(1954, Brit.); FUSS OVER FEATHERS(1954, Brit.); GREEN BUDDHA, THE(1954,
Brit.); INSPECTOR CALLS, AN(1954, Brit.); MAD ABOUT MEN(1954, Brit.); CON-
STANT HUSBAND, THE(1955, Brit.); DEADLY GAME, THE(1955, Brit.); NAKED
HEART, THE(1955, Brit.); PASSAGE HOME(1955, Brit.); YANK IN ERMINE, A(1955,
Brit.); EYEWITNESS(1956, Brit.); RICHARD III(1956, Brit.); GOOD COMPANIONS,
THE(1957, Brit.); NOVEL AFFAIR, A(1957, Brit.); TEARS FOR SIMON(1957, Brit.);
HORROR OF DRACULA, THE(1958, Brit.); MOONRAKER, THE(1958, Brit.); RE-
VENGE OF FRANKENSTEIN, THE(1958, Brit.); THREE MEN IN A BOAT(1958, Brit.);
JACK THE RIPPER(1959, Brit.); SON OF ROBIN HOOD(1959, Brit.); FOUR DESPER-
ATE MEN(1960, Brit.); CURSE OF THE WEREWOLF, THE(1961); MANIA(1961, Brit.);
TWO-WAY STRETCH(1961, Brit.); OUT OF THE FOG(1962, Brit.); ROOMMATES(1962,
Brit.); CARRY ON JACK(1963, Brit.); HEAVENS ABOVE!(1963, Brit.); SWINGIN'
MAIDEN, THE(1963, Brit.); NURSE ON WHEELS(1964, Brit.); DRACULA–PRINCE OF
DARKNESS(1966, Brit.); REPTILE, THE(1966, Brit.); WHERE'S JACK?(1969, Brit.);
DAVID COPPERFIELD(1970, Brit.); TAKE A GIRL LIKE YOU(1970, Brit.)
Jeff Woodbridge
1984
KIPPERBANG(1984, Brit.), art d
Jeffrey Woodbridge
1984
FOREVER YOUNG(1984, Brit.), art d
John Woodbridge
ROBBY(1968)
Allan Woodburn
OLD SPANISH CUSTOMERS(1932, Brit.)
Bob Woodburn
LITTLE LAURA AND BIG JOHN(1973), d&w
Eric Woodburn
BRAVE DON'T CRY, THE(1952, Brit.); YOU'RE ONLY YOUNG TWICE(1952, Brit.);
HIGH AND DRY(1954, Brit.); LITTLE KIDNAPPERS, THE(1954, Brit.); SCOTCH ON
THE ROCKS(1954, Brit.); WEE GEORDIE(1956, Brit.); BRIDAL PATH, THE(1959,
Brit.); NAKED FURY(1959, Brit.); BATTLE OF THE SEXES, THE(1960, Brit.); INNO-
CENTS, THE(1961, U.S./Brit.); TRIAL AND ERROR(1962, Brit.); TWO AND TWO
MAKE SIX(1962, Brit.); PLEASURE LOVERS, THE(1964, Brit.); AMOROUS MR.
PRAWN, THE(1965, Brit.); KIDNAPPED(1971, Brit.)
James Woodburn
SHIPBUILDERS, THE(1943, Brit.); BROTHERS, THE(1948, Brit.); FLOODTIDE(1949,
Brit.); TIGHT LITTLE ISLAND(1949, Brit.)
James W Woodburn
CHINESE DEN, THE(1940, Brit.)
Margaret Woodburn
Silents
PURSUING VENGEANCE, THE(1916)
Robert Woodburn
WILD REBELS, THE(1967), ed
Albert Woodbury
THEY SHOOT HORSES, DON'T THEY?(1969), md
Don Woodbury
SQUARE ROOT OF ZERO, THE(1964)
Doreen Woodbury
FRENCH LINE, THE(1954); SON OF SINBAD(1955); SHADOW ON THE WINDOW,
THE(1957); 27TH DAY, THE(1957)
Eugenia Woodbury
VAGABOND KING, THE(1930)
Evelyn Woodbury
ETERNALLY YOURS(1939)

Gene Woodbury
STONE KILLER, THE(1973)
Herbert A. Woodbury
RIDERS IN THE SKY(1949), w
Joan Woodbury
FOLIES DERGERE(1935); ONE EXCITING ADVENTURE(1935); EAGLE'S BROOD, THE(1936); LION'S DEN, THE(1936); ROGUES' TAVERN, THE(1936); SONG OF THE GRINGO(1936); CHARLIE CHAN ON BROADWAY(1937); CRASHING HOLLYWOOD(1937); FORTY NAUGHTY GIRLS(1937); GOD'S COUNTRY AND THE WOMAN(1937); LIVING ON LOVE(1937); LUCK OF ROARING CAMP, THE(1937); MIDNIGHT COURT(1937); SUPER SLEUTH(1937); THERE GOES MY GIRL(1937); THEY GAVE HIM A GUN(1937); ALGIERS(1938); ALWAYS IN TROUBLE(1938); CIPHER BUREAU(1938); NIGHT SPOT(1938); PASSPORT HUSBAND(1938); WHILE NEW YORK SLEEPS(1938); CHASING DANGER(1939); MYSTERY OF THE WHITE ROOM(1939); BARNYARD FOLLIES(1940); CONFESSIONS OF BOSTON BLACKIE(1941); I'LL SELL MY LIFE(1941); IN OLD CHEYENNE(1941); KING OF THE ZOMBIES(1941); PAPER BULLETS(1941); RIDE ON VAQUERO(1941); TWO LATINS FROM MANHATTAN(1941); DR. BROADWAY(1942); HARD WAY, THE(1942); I KILLED THAT MAN(1942); LIVING GHOST, THE(1942); MAN FROM HEADQUARTERS(1942); PHANTOM KILLER(1942); SHUT MY BIG MOUTH(1942); SUNSET SERENADE(1942); SWEETHEART OF THE FLEET(1942); YANK IN LIBYA, A(1942); DESPERADOES, THE(1943); HERE COMES KELLY(1943); CHINESE CAT, THE(1944); WHISTLER, THE(1944); BRING ON THE GIRLS(1945); FLAME OF THE WEST(1945); NORTHWEST TRAIL(1945); TEN CENTS A DANCE(1945); ARNELO AFFAIR, THE(1947); YANKEE FAKIR(1947); HERE COMES TROUBLE(1948); BOSTON BLACKIE'S CHINESE VENTURE(1949); TEN COMMANDMENTS, THE(1956); TIME TRAVELERS, THE(1964)
Misc. Talkies
BULLDOG COURAGE(1935); LAST ASSIGNMENT, THE(1936)
Judith Woodbury
IVY(1947); LETTER FROM AN UNKNOWN WOMAN(1948)
Rand Woodbury
1984
WHERE THE BOYS ARE '84(1984)
Woody Woodbury
FOR THOSE WHO THINK YOUNG(1964); HARDLY WORKING(1981); SUPER FUZZ(1981)
Edith Woodby
DRUMS O' VOODOO(1934)
John Woodcock
MY SIX LOVES(1963), ed; NUTTY PROFESSOR, THE(1963), ed; WHO'S MINDING THE STORE?(1963), ed; DISORDERLY ORDERLY, THE(1964), ed; PATSY, THE(1964), ed; FAMILY JEWELS, THE(1965), ed; EL DORADO(1967), ed; SCALPHUNTERS, THE(1968), ed; SAM WHISKEY(1969), ed; RIO LOBO(1970), ed; SKULLDUGGERY(1970), a, ed; LE MANS(1971), ed; BADGE 373(1973), ed
John M. Woodcock
SALZBURG CONNECTION, THE(1972), ed
Tom Woodcock
1984
PHAR LAP(1984, Aus.)
Todd Woodcroft
SUPERMAN II(1980)
Barbara Wooddell
MR. AND MRS. SMITH(1941); MYSTERIOUS MR. VALENTINE, THE(1946); SECRET OF THE WHISTLER(1946); FRAMED(1947); SILVER LODE(1954)
Misc. Talkies
RETURN OF RUSTY, THE(1946)
Margo Woode
SPIDER, THE(1945); IT SHOULDN'T HAPPEN TO A DOG(1946); SOMEWHERE IN THE NIGHT(1946); MOSS ROSE(1947); NO SAD SONGS FOR ME(1950); HELL BOUND(1957); IRON ANGEL(1964)
Barbara Woodel
STAR, THE(1953)
Barbara Woodell
LADY, LET'S DANCE(1944); LEAVE IT TO THE IRISH(1944); SAMURAI(1945); LITTLE MISS BIG(1946); WIFE WANTED(1946); SMASH-UP, THE STORY OF A WOMAN(1947); UNSUSPECTED, THE(1947); FORCE OF EVIL(1948); JOAN OF ARC(1948); BAD BOY(1949); I SHOT JESSE JAMES(1949); MY FOOLISH HEART(1949); STATE DEPARTMENT–FILE 649(1949); STRATTON STORY, THE(1949); BARON OF ARIZONA, THE(1950); EVERYBODY'S DANCIN'(1950); GUNFIRE(1950); RETURN OF JESSE JAMES, THE(1950); CANYON RAIDERS(1951); LITTLE BIG HORN(1951); CONFIDENCE GIRL(1952); DREAMBOAT(1952); FORT OSAGE(1952); NEVER WAVE AT A WAC(1952); RED SKIES OF MONTANA(1952); ROSE BOWL STORY, THE(1952); WILD STALLION(1952); GREAT JESSE JAMES RAID, THE(1953); HOMESTEADERS, THE(1953); AT GUNPOINT(1955); WESTWARD HO THE WAGONS!(1956); BULLWHIP(1958); SHOWDOWN AT BOOT HILL(1958); GO, JOHNNY, GO!(1959)
Pat Woodell
BIG DOLL HOUSE, THE(1971); TWILIGHT PEOPLE(1972, Phil.); ROOMMATES, THE(1973); WOMAN HUNT, THE(1975, U.S./Phil.)
Misc. Talkies
BIG DOLL HOUSE, THE(1971); CLASS OF '74(1972)
Earl Wooden
DR. CHRISTIAN MEETS THE WOMEN(1940), art d; JACK LONDON(1943), set d; LAKE PLACID SERENADE(1944), set d; SHERIFF OF CIMARRON(1945), set d; IN OLD SACRAMENTO(1946), set d; MURDER IN THE MUSIC HALL(1946), set d; RED RIVER RENEGADES(1946), set d; STAGECOACH TO DENVER(1946), set d; OPEN SECRET(1948), set d
Earl B. Wooden
I'LL BE SEEING YOU(1944), set d
Tom Woodeschick
M(1970)
Nicholas Woodeson
HEAVEN'S GATE(1980)
Gitta Woodfield
THE HYPNOTIC EYE(1960), w
William Read Woodfield
THE HYPNOTIC EYE(1960), w

G. Woodfine
FREUD(1962)
Jim Woodfine
GOODBYE PORK PIE(1981, New Zealand)
Helen Woodford
MUSIC MAN(1948)
Jack Woodford
CITY LIMITS(1934), w
John Woodford
Silents
SUCCESS(1923)
Josephine Woodford
HEAVENS ABOVE!(1963, Brit.)
William Woodford
Silents
WINNING STROKE, THE(1919)
Florence Woodgate
GUEST OF HONOR(1934, Brit.)
Barbara Woodhouse
KILL OR CURE(1962, Brit.), animal t
Hugh Woodhouse
NEARLY A NASTY ACCIDENT(1962, Brit.), w; GET ON WITH IT(1963, Brit.), w; MYSTERY SUBMARINE(1963, Brit.), w
J. Stewart Woodhouse
Silents
PLAYING DOUBLE(1923), w
Earl Woodin
SANTA FE UPRISING(1946), set d; STRIKE IT RICH(1948), set d
Albie Woodington
1984
NUMBER ONE(1984, Brit.)
Clarrie Woodlands
KANGAROO KID, THE(1950, Aus./U.S.)
Holly Woodlawn
SCARECROW IN A GARDEN OF CUCUMBERS(1972)
Misc. Talkies
IS THERE SEX AFTER DEATH(1971)
Chris Woodley
VELVET VAMPIRE, THE(1971)
Chris [Allen] Woodley
PRETTY MAIDS ALL IN A ROW(1971)
Stuart Woodley
Silents
TEMPORARY VAGABOND, A(1920, Brit.), d&w
Bob Woodlock
CAR, THE(1977)
Graham Woodlock
SCOBIE MALONE(1975, Aus.), w
Bernadette Woodman
TOMORROW AT TEN(1964, Brit.)
Pardoe Woodman
NIGHT TRAIN(1940, Brit.)
Silents
NOBODY'S CHILD(1919, Brit.); QUEEN'S EVIDENCE(1919, Brit.); AMATEUR GENTLEMAN, THE(1920, Brit.); MYSTERY OF MR. BERNARD BROWN(1921, Brit.); PLACE OF HONOUR, THE(1921, Brit.)
Misc. Silents
TIDAL WAVE, THE(1920, Brit.)
Ruth Woodman
MAN IN GREY, THE(1943, Brit.); LAST OF THE PONY RIDERS(1953), w
Woody Woodman
TOWN THAT DREADED SUNDOWN, THE(1977)
John Woodnut
Misc. Talkies
YOUNG JACOBITES(1959)
John Woodnutt
INN FOR TROUBLE(1960, Brit.); CRIMSON BLADE, THE(1964, Brit.); OH! WHAT A LOVELY WAR(1969, Brit.); CONNECTING ROOMS(1971, Brit.)
1984
CHAMPIONS(1984)
George Woodridge
UP POMPEII(1971, Brit.)
John Woodridge
EDWARD, MY SON(1949, U.S./Brit.), m; ANGELS ONE FIVE(1954, Brit.), m
Susan Woodridge
BUTLEY(1974, Brit.)
Donald Woodriff
KISS ME GOODBYE(1982), set d
Judith Woodroffe
DEATHCHEATERS(1976, Aus.)
Tommy Woodrooffe
SWORD OF HONOUR(1938, Brit.)
Mrs. Wilson Woodrow
PENTHOUSE PARTY(1936), w
Silents
SCARLET ROAD, THE(1916), d
Anthony Woodruff
NORMAN CONQUEST(1953, Brit.); MAN WHO WOULDN'T TALK, THE(1958, Brit.); THIS SPORTING LIFE(1963, Brit.); HUMAN FACTOR, THE(1979, Brit.)
Bert Woodruff
RIVER, THE(1928); SHOPWORN ANGEL, THE(1928); SONG OF KENTUCKY(1929); LAUGHING SINNERS(1931); TEXAS RANGER, THE(1931)
Silents
JAILBIRD, THE(1920); PARIS GREEN(1920); TWO MINUTES TO GO(1921); KENTUCKY DERBY, THE(1922); MAKING A MAN(1922); WATCH YOUR STEP(1922); DADDY(1923); ISLE OF LOST SHIPS, THE(1923); NOISE IN NEWBORO, A(1923); SILENT PARTNER, THE(1923); FLOWING GOLD(1924); PATHS TO PARADISE(1925); BARRIER, THE(1926); MARKED MONEY(1928); SPEEDY(1928)

Misc. Silents
MEN OF THE DESERT(1917); BILL HENRY(1919); FOR THOSE WE LOVE(1921); GRIM COMEDIAN, THE(1921); CHILDREN OF DUST(1923); SIX-FIFTY, THE(1923); LURE OF THE NIGHT CLUB, THE(1927); ROMANTIC AGE, THE(1927)

Deanna Woodruff
NIGHT WIND(1948)

Dick Woodruff
TONIGHT AND EVERY NIGHT(1945)

Eleanor Woodruff
Silents
LAST VOLUNTEER, THE(1914); STAIN, THE(1914)
Misc. Silents
HEIGHTS OF HAZARDS, THE(1915); JAFFERY(1915); BIG JIM GARRITY(1916); BRITTON OF THE SEVENTH(1916); WEAKNESS OF MAN, THE(1916); PASTE-BOARD CROWN, A(1922)

Eunice Woodruff
Silents
OUT OF THE DUST(1920)

Frank Woodruff
CROSS COUNTRY ROMANCE(1940), d; CURTAIN CALL(1940), d; PLAY GIRL(1940), d; WILDCAT BUS(1940), d; LADY SCARFACE(1941), d; REPENT AT LEISURE(1941), d; COWBOY IN MANHATTTAN(1943), d; PISTOL PACKIN' MA-MA(1943), d; TWO SENORITAS FROM CHICAGO(1943), d; LADY, LET'S DAN-CE(1944), d

Franklin Woodruff
Misc. Silents
LONG TRAIL, THE(1917)

Henry Woodruff
Silents
MAN AND HIS MATE, A(1915)
Misc. Silents
BECKONING FLAME, THE(1916)

Herbert Woodruff
Misc. Silents
SIX-SHOOTER ANDY(1918)

Largo Woodruff
FUNHOUSE, THE(1981)

Larry Woodruff
HOW TO BEAT THE HIGH COST OF LIVING(1980)

Richard Woodruff
THUNDER BIRDS(1942); GUY NAMED JOE, A(1943); SECRETS OF SCOTLAND YARD(1944)

Thelma Woodruff
DANCE, GIRL, DANCE(1940)

Donna Woodrum
1984
NIGHTMARE ON ELM STREET, A(1984)

A. H. Woods
LONELY WIVES(1931), w
Silents
KICK IN(1917), p

Adelaide Woods
Misc. Silents
HER OWN PEOPLE(1917)

Al Woods
GOOSE AND THE GANDER, THE(1935)

Alan Woods
EASY MONEY(1936)

Albert Woods
MARCH OR DIE(1977, Brit.)

Alfred Woods
THE BLACK HAND GANG(1930, Brit.)

Art Woods
KING OF THE MOUNTAIN(1981)

Arthur Woods
BATTLE OF GALLIPOLI(1931, Brit.), art d; I SPY(1933, Brit.), w; PRIDE OF THE FORCE, THE(1933, Brit.), w; SECRET AGENT(1933, Brit.), d, w; SOUTHERN MAID, A(1933, Brit.), w; TIMBUCTOO(1933, Brit.), d; HAPPY(1934, Brit.), w; DRAKE THE PIRATE(1935, Brit.), d; MUSIC HATH CHARMS(1935, Brit.), d; RADIO FOL-LIES(1935, Brit.), d, w; GIVE HER A RING(1936, Brit.), d; IRISH FOR LUCK(1936, Brit.), d, w; RED WAGON(1936), w; RHYTHM IN THE AIR(1936, Brit.), d; WHERE'S SALLY?(1936, Brit.), d; COMPULSORY WIFE, THE(1937, Brit.), d; DON'T GET ME WRONG(1937, Brit.), d; MAYFAIR MELODY(1937, Brit.), d; WEEKEND MIL-LIONAIRE(1937, Brit.), d; WINDMILL, THE(1937, Brit.), d&w; YOU LIVE AND LEARN(1937, Brit.), d; DANGEROUS MEDICINE(1938, Brit.), d; DARK STAIRWAY, THE(1938, Brit.), d; GLAMOUR GIRL(1938, Brit.), d; MR. SATAN(1938, Brit.), d; RETURN OF CAROL DEANE, THE(1938, Brit.), d; SINGING COP, THE(1938, Brit.), d; THEY DRIVE BY NIGHT(1938, Brit.), d; THISTLEDOWN(1938, Brit.), d; CONFIDEN-TIAL LADY(1939, Brit.), d

Arthur B. Woods
NURSEMAID WHO DISAPPEARED, THE(1939, Brit.), d; BUSMAN'S HONEY-MOON(1940, Brit.), d

Arthur Harry Woods
FOREST RANGERS, THE(1942)

Aubrey Woods
NICHOLAS NICKLEBY(1947, Brit.); GREED OF WILLIAM HART, THE(1948, Brit.); QUEEN OF SPADES(1948, Brit.); GUILT IS MY SHADOW(1950, Brit.); DETECTIVE, THE(1954, Qit.); SPARE THE ROD(1961, Brit.); SAN FERRY ANN(1965, Brit.); JUST LIKE A WOMAN(1967, Brit.); WUTHERING HEIGHTS(1970, Brit.); LOOT(1971, Brit.); UP POMPEII(1971, Brit.); DARWIN ADVENTURE, THE(1972, Brit.); Z.P.G.(1972); THAT LUCKY TOUCH(1975, Brit.); OPERATION DAYBREAK(1976, U.S./Brit./Czech.)

Audrey Woods
ABOMINABLE DR. PHIBES, THE(1971, Brit.)

Baby Woods
INSIDE INFORMATION(1934)

Bette Woods
THAT TOUCH OF MINK(1962)

Betty Woods
FEMALE TROUBLE(1975)

Bill Woods
MANIAC(1934); HEADIN' FOR THE RIO GRANDE(1937); HEIRESS, THE(1949), makeup; TROOPER HOOK(1957), makeup

Bob Woods
DEATHMASTER, THE(1972)

Bobbie Woods
KEEP YOUR POWDER DRY(1945)

Britt Woods
CHOPPERS, THE(1961)

Buck Woods
ONE HOUR TO LIVE(1939); MIDNIGHT LIMITED(1940); NOTHING BUT THE TRUTH(1941); ROAD TO ZANZIBAR(1941); HEART OF THE RIO GRANDE(1942)
Misc. Talkies
MIDNIGHT SHADOW(1939); BROKEN STRINGS(1940)

Charlotte Woods
Silents
OH, LADY, LADY(1920)

Clarise Woods
CIRCLE CANYON(1934)

Craig Woods
DESTROYER(1943); DOUGHBOYS IN IRELAND(1943); THERE'S SOMETHING ABOUT A SOLDIER(1943); TWO SENORITAS FROM CHICAGO(1943); WHAT'S BUZZIN COUSIN?(1943); CAREER GIRL(1944); COWBOY FROM LONESOME RIV-ER(1944); PARTNERS OF THE TRAIL(1944); RAIDERS OF THE BORDER(1944); ANGEL AND THE BADMAN(1947); FORT DEFIANCE(1951)

Cy Woods
CUCKOOS, THE(1930), w

David Woods
TELL ME IN THE SUNLIGHT(1967), ed

Dee Dee Woods
MARY POPPINS(1964), ch

Denise Woods
DON'T GO IN THE HOUSE(1980)

Donald Woods
AS THE EARTH TURNS(1934); CHARLIE CHAN'S COURAGE(1934); FOG OVER FRISCO(1934); MERRY WIVES OF RENO, THE(1934); SHE WAS A LADY(1934); CASE OF THE CURIOUS BRIDE, THE(1935); FLORENTINE DAGGER, THE(1935); FRISCO KID(1935); STRANDED(1935); SWEET ADELINE(1935); TALE OF TWO CITIES, A(1935); ANTHONY ADVERSE(1936); ISLE OF FURY(1936); ROAD GANG(1936); SON COMES HOME, A(1936); STORY OF LOUIS PASTEUR, THE(1936); WHITE ANGEL, THE(1936); BIG TOWN GIRL(1937); CASE OF THE STUTTERING BISHOP, THE(1937); CHARLIE CHAN ON BROADWAY(1937); ONCE A DOCTOR(1937); SEA DEVILS(1937); TALENT SCOUT(1937); BLACK DOLL, THE(1938); DANGER ON THE AIR(1938); ROMANCE ON THE RUN(1938); BEAUTY FOR THE ASKING(1939); GIRL FROM MEXICO, THE(1939); HERITAGE OF THE DESERT(1939); MEXICAN SPIT-FIRE(1939); CITY OF CHANCE(1940); FORGOTTEN GIRLS(1940); IF I HAD MY WAY(1940); LOVE, HONOR AND OH, BABY(1940); MEXICAN SPITFIRE OUT WEST(1940); BACHELOR DADDY(1941); I WAS A PRISONER ON DEVIL'S IS-LAND(1941); GAY SISTERS, THE(1942); THRU DIFFERENT EYES(1942); CORREGI-DOR(1943); HI' YA, SAILOR(1943); SO'S YOUR UNCLE(1943); WATCH ON THE RHINE(1943); BRIDGE OF SAN LUIS REY, THE(1944); ENEMY OF WOMEN(1944); HOLLYWOOD CANTEEN(1944); ROUGHLY SPEAKING(1945); VOICE OF THE WHISTLER(1945); WONDER MAN(1945); NEVER SAY GOODBYE(1946); NIGHT AND DAY(1946); TIME, THE PLACE AND THE GIRL, THE(1946); BELLS OF SAN FERNANDO(1947); RETURN OF RIN TIN TIN, THE(1947); STEPCHILD(1947); BAR-BARY PIRATE(1949); DAUGHTER OF THE WEST(1949); FREE FOR ALL(1949); SCENE OF THE CRIME(1949); JOHNNY ONE-EYE(1950); LOST VOLCANO, THE(1950); MR. MUSIC(1950); BEAST FROM 20,000 FATHOMS, THE(1953); BORN TO THE SADDLE(1953); I'LL GIVE MY LIFE(1959); THIRTEEN GHOSTS(1960); FIVE MINUTES TO LIVE(1961); KISSIN' COUSINS(1964); DIMENSION 5(1966); MOMENT TO MOMENT(1966); TAMMY AND THE MILLIONAIRE(1967); TIME TO SING, A(1968); TRUE GRIT(1969)
Misc. Talkies
ALL THAT I HAVE(1951)

Dorothy Woods
SANTA FE BOUND(1937)
Misc. Silents
BETTER MAN WINS, THE(1922); LUCKY DAN(1922); WANTED BY THE LAW(1924); RIDIN' COMET(1925); ROMANCE AND RUSTLERS(1925); SCAR HA-NAN(1925)

Eddie Woods
THEY NEVER COME BACK(1932); IRON MAJOR, THE(1943); MARINE RAI-DERS(1944)

Edward Woods
MOTHERS CRY(1930); LOCAL BOY MAKES GOOD(1931); PUBLIC ENEMY, THE(1931); HOT SATURDAY(1932); BONDAGE(1933); DINNER AT EIGHT(1933); TARZAN THE FEARLESS(1933); MARRIAGE ON APPROVAL(1934); NAVY BLUES(1937); SHADOWS OVER SHANGHAI(1938)
Misc. Talkies
FIGHTING LADY(1935)

Ella Woods
HOUSE ON SKULL MOUNTAIN, THE(1974)

Ella Carter Woods
Silents
MARTHA'S VINDICATION(1916), w

Ercelle Woods
ADVENTURES OF A ROOKIE(1943)

Ernie Woods
WASHINGTON MERRY-GO-ROUND(1932)

Frank Woods
HIT THE DECK(1930)
Silents
JUDITH OF BETHULIA(1914), t; MOUNTAIN RAT, THE(1914), w; MARTHA'S VINDICATION(1916), w
Misc. Silents
LURING LIGHTS(1915)

Frank E. Woods
Silents
CLASSMATES(1914), w; ABSENTEE-NRA, THE(1915), d; BIRTH OF A NATION, THE(1915), w; MAN'S PREROGATIVE, A(1915), w; PRINCE THERE WAS, A(1921), sup

Frank R. Woods
Silents
LITTLE SCHOOL MA'AM, THE(1916), w

G. D. Woods
OKLAHOMA JIM(1931); SINGLE-HANDED SANDERS(1932)

G.D. Woods [Gordon DeMain]
GALLOPING THRU(1932)

Genia Woods
BATTLE OF THE AMAZONS(1973, Ital./Span.)

Genie Woods
THREE STOOGES VS. THE WONDER WOMEN(1975, Ital./Chi.)

Gordon D. "Demain" Woods
LAWLESS FRONTIER, THE(1935)

Grace Woods
TRAILING TROUBLE(1937)
Misc. Silents
SILENT GUARDIAN, THE(1926); FLYING U RANCH, THE(1927)

Grant Woods
SILENCERS, THE(1966); KARATE KILLERS, THE(1967)

Harry Woods
LONE RIDER, THE(1930); MEN WITHOUT LAW(1930); PARDON MY GUN(1930); IN OLD CHEYENNE(1931); MONKEY BUSINESS(1931); PALMY DAYS(1931); RANGE FEUD, THE(1931); TEXAS RANGER, THE(1931); WEST OF CHEYENNE(1931); HAUNTED GOLD(1932); I AM A FUGITIVE FROM A CHAIN GANG(1932); LAW AND ORDER(1932); NIGHT WORLD(1932); RADIO PATROL(1932); TEXAS GUN FIGHTER(1932); TWO SECONDS(1932); PRIZEFIGHTER AND THE LADY, THE(1933); ALONG CAME SALLY(1934, Brit.), m; BELLE OF THE NINETIES(1934); CIRCUS CLOWN(1934); CROSBY CASE, THE(1934); DEVIL TIGER(1934); PRESIDENT VANISHES, THE(1934); SCARLET EMPRESS, THE(1934); SHADOWS OF SING SING(1934); ST. LOUIS KID, THE(1934); WONDER BAR(1934); DANTE'S INFERNO(1935); GALLANT DEFENDER(1935); LET 'EM HAVE IT(1935); SCHOOL FOR GIRLS(1935); SHIP CAFE(1935); WHEN A MAN'S A MAN(1935); HEIR TO TROUBLE(1936); HEROES OF THE RANGE(1936); IT HAD TO HAPPEN(1936); LAWLESS NINETIES, THE(1936); LAWLESS RIDERS(1936); ROBIN HOOD OF EL DORADO(1936); ROSE OF THE RANCHO(1936); SILLY BILLIES(1936); TICKET TO PARADISE(1936); UNKNOWN RANGER, THE(1936); COURAGE OF THE WEST(1937); I PROMISE TO PAY(1937); LAND BEYOND THE LAW(1937); LAST TRAIN FROM MADRID, THE(1937); OUTCAST(1937); PLAINSMAN, THE(1937); RANGE DEFENDERS(1937); RECKLESS RANGER(1937); SINGING OUTLAW(1937); ARIZONA WILDCAT(1938); CRIME TAKES A HOLIDAY(1938); HAWAIIAN BUCKAROO(1938); IN EARLY ARIZONA(1938); JOY OF LIVING(1938); MEN WITH WINGS(1938); PANAMINT'S BAD MAN(1938); ROLLING CARAVANS(1938); SPY RING, THE(1938); STAGECOACH DAYS(1938); TEXANS, THE(1938); BEAU GESTE(1939); BLUE MONTANA SKIES(1939); COME ON RANGERS(1939); DAYS OF JESSE JAMES(1939); FRONTIER MARSHAL(1939); IN OLD CALIENTE(1939); MAN IN THE IRON MASK, THE(1939); MR. MOTO IN DANGER ISLAND(1939); STRANGE CASE OF DR. MEADE(1939); UNION PACIFIC(1939); BULLET CODE(1940); DARK COMMAND, THE(1940); HOUSE OF THE SEVEN GABLES, THE(1940); ISLE OF DESTINY(1940); LONG VOYAGE HOME, THE(1940); MEET THE MISSUS(1940); RANGER AND THE LADY, THE(1940); SOUTH OF PAGO PAGO(1940); TRIPLE JUSTICE(1940); WEST OF CARSON CITY(1940); BOSS OF BULLION CITY(1941); LAST OF THE DUANES(1941); PETTICOAT POLITICS(1941); SHERIFF OF TOMBSTONE(1941); DAWN ON THE GREAT DIVIDE(1942); DEEP IN THE HEART OF TEXAS(1942); DOWN TEXAS WAY(1942); JACKASS MAIL(1942); REAP THE WILD WIND(1942); RIDERS OF THE WEST(1942); SHERLOCK HOLMES AND THE SECRET WEAPON(1942); SPOILERS, THE(1942); TODAY I HANG(1942); WEST OF THE LAW(1942); BEYOND THE LAST FRONTIER(1943); BORDERTOWN GUNFIGHTERS(1943); CHEYENNE ROUNDUP(1943); IN OLD OKLAHOMA(1943); OUTLAWS OF STAMPEDE PASS(1943); MARSHAL OF GUNSMOKE(1944); NEVADA(1944); SILVER CITY KID(1944); TALL IN THE SADDLE(1944); WESTWARD BOUND(1944); FLAME OF THE WEST(1945); WANDERER OF THE WASTELAND(1945); WEST OF THE PECOS(1945); MY DARLING CLEMENTINE(1946); SUNSET PASS(1946); CODE OF THE WEST(1947); DESIRE ME(1947); FABULOUS TEXAN, THE(1947); ROAD TO RIO(1947); THUNDER MOUNTAIN(1947); TRAIL STREET(1947); TYCOON(1947); WILD HORSE MESA(1947); WYOMING(1947); GALLANT LEGION, THE(1948); INDIAN AGENT(1948); SILVER RIVER(1948); WESTERN HERITAGE(1948); COLORADO TERRITORY(1949); FOUNTAINHEAD, THE(1949); HELLFIRE(1949); MASKED RAIDERS(1949); SAMSON AND DELILAH(1949); SHE WORE A YELLOW RIBBON(1949); LAW OF THE BADLANDS(1950); LET'S DANCE(1950); SHORT GRASS(1950); TRAVELING SALESWOMAN(1950); LONE STAR(1952); HELL'S OUTPOST(1955); SHEEPMAN, THE(1958)
Misc. Talkies
CALL OF THE ROCKIES(1944)
Silents
DYNAMITE DAN(1924); MAN FOUR-SQUARE, A(1926); REGULAR SCOUT, A(1926); CYCLONE OF THE RANGE(1927); JESSE JAMES(1927); SILVER COMES THROUGH(1927); SPLITTING THE BREEZE(1927); SUNSET LEGION, THE(1928); DESERT RIDER, THE(1929); GUN LAW(1929); PHANTOM RIDER, THE(1929)
Misc. Silents
BANDIT'S BABY, THE(1925); TOM'S GANG(1927); CANDY KID, THE(1928); RED RIDERS OF CANADA(1928); TYRANT OF RED GULCH(1928); 'NEATH WESTERN SKIES(1929)

Harry L. Woods
ROMANCE ON THE RANGE(1942); SECRET LIFE OF WALTER MITTY, THE(1947)

Helen Woods
GOOSE AND THE GANDER, THE(1935); SHE MARRIED HER BOSS(1935)

Ilene Woods
ON STAGE EVERYBODY(1945); CINDERELLA(1950)

Ira Buck Woods
THEY WON'T BELIEVE ME(1947)

Ira "Buck" Woods
MAN FROM FRISCO(1944)

Jack Woods
OUT OF SIGHT(1966), ed; WILD, WILD WINTER(1966), ed; EQUINOX(1970), a, d&w; BEWARE! THE BLOB(1972), w; NUTCRACKER FANTASY(1979), ed; DON'T CRY, IT'S ONLY THUNDER(1982), ed

James Woods
WAY WE WERE, THE(1973); HICKEY AND BOGGS(1972); VISITORS, THE(1972); GAMBLER, THE(1974); DISTANCE(1975); NIGHT MOVES(1975); ALEX AND THE GYPSY(1976); CHOIRBOYS, THE(1977); ONION FIELD, THE(1979); BLACK MARBLE, THE(1980); EYEWITNESS(1981); FAST-WALKING(1982); SPLIT IMAGE(1982); VIDEODROME(1983, Can.)
1984
AGAINST ALL ODDS(1984); ONCE UPON A TIME IN AMERICA(1984)

Jeril Woods
REVENGE OF THE CHEERLEADERS(1976)

Jerry Woods
WAR BETWEEN MEN AND WOMEN, THE(1972), cos

Judith Woods
IT PAYS TO ADVERTISE(1931)

Lesley Woods
LIGHT FANTASTIC(1964); TESTAMENT(1983)
1984
HIGHWAY TO HELL(1984); RUNNING HOT(1984)

Lotta Woods
Silents
NUT, THE(1921), w; THREE MUSKETEERS, THE(1921), w; ROBIN HOOD(1922), w; THIEF OF BAGDAD, THE(1924), w; BLACK PIRATE, THE(1926), w; MR. WU(1927), t; GAUCHO, THE(1928), w

Kit Wong
LEGEND OF THE LONE RANGER, THE(1981)

Louise A. Woods
PROUD AND THE PROFANE, THE(1956), tech adv

Madeline Woods
SLANDER HOUSE(1938), w

Margo Woods
BULLFIGHTERS, THE(1945)

Mary Jane Woods
WONDER MAN(1945)

Maurice Woods
LORD SHANGO(1975); TRADING PLACES(1983)

Middleton Woods
WHISPERING SMITH VERSUS SCOTLAND YARD(1952, Brit.); ROB ROY, THE HIGHLAND ROGUE(1954, Brit.); INDISCREET(1958); MAN WHO WOULDN'T TALK, THE(1958, Brit.); MAN WHO COULD CHEAT DEATH, THE(1959, Brit.); DEAD MAN'S EVIDENCE(1962, Brit.); SWINGIN' MAIDEN, THE(1963, Brit.)

Milton Woods
BEWARE(1946); I'LL GIVE MY LIFE(1959)
Misc. Talkies
TALL, TAN AND TERRIFIC(1946); REET, PETITE AND GONE(1947)

Myrtle Woods
NEXT OF KIN(1983, Aus.)

N.S. Woods
Misc. Silents
MARY LAWSON'S SECRET(1917)

Ren Woods
CARWASH(1976); YOUNGBLOOD(1978); HAIR(1979); NINE TO FIVE(1980); XANADU(1980)
1984
BROTHER FROM ANOTHER PLANET, THE(1984)

Renee Woods
ADVENTURE FOR TWO(1945, Brit.), ed

Renn Woods
PENITENTIARY II(1982)

Richard Woods
LOVELY WAY TO DIE, A(1968)

Richards Woods
ENDANGERED SPECIES(1982), w

Rita Woods
ISLAND OF DR. MOREAU, THE(1977), cos

Robert Woods
MY NAME IS PECOS(1966, Ital.); SEVEN GUNS FOR THE MACGREGORS(1968, Ital./Span.)
Misc. Talkies
CHALLENGE OF MC KENNA, THE(1983)

Robyn Woods
1984
FRIDAY THE 13TH-THE FINAL CHAPTER(1984)

Sheila Woods
JOE MACBETH(1955)

Sheldon Woods
Misc. Talkies
CRY TO THE WIND(1979)

Steve Woods
Misc. Talkies
ALL MEN ARE APES(1965)

Susan Woods
IRMA LA DOUCE(1963)

T. Frank Woods
HELL CANYON OUTLAWS(1957), p

Thomas F. Woods
ANGEL BABY(1961), p

Victor Woods
WELCOME, MR. WÅSHINGTON(1944, Brit.)

Walter Woods
ONCE A GENTLEMAN(1930), w; SALVATION NELL(1931), w; DAVID HARUM(1934), w; SUTTER'S GOLD(1936), w
Silents
GRIM GAME, THE(1919), w; HAWTHORNE OF THE U.S.A.(1919), w; BREWSTER'S MILLIONS(1921), w; CRAZY TO MARRY(1921), w; GASOLINE GUS(1921), w; DICTATOR, THE(1922), w; THIRTY DAYS(1922), w; RUGGLES OF RED GAP(1923), w; ENEMY SEX, THE(1924), w; FIGHTING COWARD, THE(1924), w; MERTON OF THE MOVIES(1924), w; RECKLESS ROMANCE(1924), w; BEGGAR ON HORSEBACK(1925), w; NIGHT CLUB, THE(1925), w; PONY EXPRESS, THE(1925), w; OLD IRONSIDES(1926), w; NIGHT FLYER, THE(1928), w; ON TO RENO(1928), w, t; FAR CALL, THE(1929), w

William Woods
CODE OF THE FEARLESS(1939); TWO-GUN TROUBADOR(1939); EDGE OF DARKNESS(1943), w; STOWAWAY GIRL(1957, Brit.), w
Willis Woods
Silents
EVEN AS YOU AND I(1917), w
Suzannah Woodside
1984
YELLOW HAIR AND THE FORTRESS OF GOLD(1984)
Wayne Woodson
I OUGHT TO BE IN PICTURES(1982)
William Woodson
FBI CODE 98(1964); MORE DEAD THAN ALIVE(1968); ONE AND ONLY GENUINE ORIGINAL FAMILY BAND, THE(1968); ESCAPE FROM THE PLANET OF THE APES(1971); GALAXY EXPRESS(1982, Jap.)
Bob Woodstock
CAR, THE(1977)
Ellen Woodston
SO THIS IS LONDON(1930)
Georgia Woodthorpe
Silents
OLD MAID'S BABY, THE(1919); BUNTY PULLS THE STRINGS(1921); FOUR HORSEMEN OF THE APOCALYPSE, THE(1921); SONG OF LIFE, THE(1922); GIMMIE(1923)
Misc. Silents
KULTUR(1918); MERELY MARY ANN(1920)
Peter Woodthorpe
EVIL OF FRANKENSTEIN, THE(1964, Brit.); HYSTERIA(1965, Brit.); SKULL, THE(1965, Brit.); BLUE MAX, THE(1966); CHARGE OF THE LIGHT BRIGADE, THE(1968, Brit.); MIRROR CRACK'D, THE(1980, Brit.)
Miss Woodthrop
Silents
KENTUCKY DAYS(1923)
A. Caton Woodville
Silents
MOTHERHOOD(1915, Brit.)
Catherine Woodville
CROOKED ROAD, THE(; CLUE OF THE NEW PIN, THE(1961, Brit.); YOUNG AND WILLING(1964, Brit.); BRIGAND OF KANDAHAR, THE(1965, Brit.); UNDERWORLD INFORMERS(1965, Brit.); PARTY'S OVER, THE(1966, Brit.)
Kate Woodville
BLACK GUNN(1972)
Misc. Talkies
EXTREME CLOSE-UP(1973); WHERE'S WILLIE?(1978)
Katherine Woodville
POSSE(1975)
John Woodvine
WALKING STICK, THE(1970, Brit.); YOUNG WINSTON(1972, Brit.); ASSAULT ON AGATHON(1976, Brit./Gr.); AMERICAN WEREWOLF IN LONDON, AN(1981)
Mrs. Woodward
Silents
AS IN A LOOKING GLASS(1916)
Bob Woodward
WEST OF NEVADA(1936); CALIFORNIA MAIL, THE(1937); GUNS OF THE PECOS(1937); OVERLAND EXPRESS, THE(1938); TAMING OF THE WEST, THE(1939); TWO-FISTED RANGERS(1940); IN OLD CHEYENNE(1941); JESSE JAMES AT BAY(1941); KANSAS CYCLONE(1941); NEVADA CITY(1941); RAIDERS OF THE RANGE(1942); SONS OF THE PIONEERS(1942); SUNSET ON THE DESERT(1942); FIREBRANDS OF ARIZONA(1944); SAN ANTONIO KID, THE(1944); CHEYENNE TAKES OVER(1947); PIONEER JUSTICE(1947); RETURN OF THE LASH(1947); SPRINGTIME IN THE SIERRAS(1947); STAGE TO MESA CITY(1947); COURTIN' TROUBLE(1948); COWBOY CAVALIER(1948); DEAD MAN'S GOLD(1948); FIGHTING RANGER, THE(1948); FRONTIER AGENT(1948); GUNNING FOR JUSTICE(1948); OKLAHOMA BADLANDS(1948); OKLAHOMA BLUES(1948); PARTNERS OF THE SUNSET(1948); RANGE RENEGADES(1948); RANGERS RIDE, THE(1948); SILVER TRAILS(1948); SONG OF THE DRIFTER(1948); TIOGA KID, THE(1948); WESTWARD TRAIL, THE(1948); ACROSS THE RIO GRANDE(1949); BRAND OF FEAR(1949); CRASHING THRU(1949); GUN RUNNER(1949); HIDDEN DANGER(1949); LAW OF THE WEST(1949); RANGE JUSTICE(1949); ROARING WESTWARD(1949); SHADOWS OF THE WEST(1949); STAMPEDE(1949); WEST OF EL DORADO(1949); OUTLAW GOLD(1950); OVER THE BORDER(1950); RADAR SECRET SERVICE(1950); VIGILANTE HIDEOUT(1950); BLUE CANADIAN ROCKIES(1952); JUNCTION CITY(1952); NIGHT STAGE TO GALVESTON(1952); OLD WEST, THE(1952); WINNING OF THE WEST(1953); CATTLE QUEEN OF MONTANA(1954); WYOMING RENEGADES(1955); APACHE TERRITORY(1958); FIVE GUNS TO TOMBSTONE(1961); GUN FIGHT(1961); ALL THE PRESIDENT'S MEN(1976), w
Bronte Woodward
CAN'T STOP THE MUSIC(1980), w
Charlaine Woodward
Misc. Talkies
HARD FEELINGS(1981)
David Woodward
SORCERERS, THE(1967, Brit.), ed
Derek Woodward
LITTLE MALCOLM(1974, Brit.), w
Edward Woodward
WHERE THERE'S A WILL(1955, Brit.); INN FOR TROUBLE(1960, Brit.); FILE OF THE GOLDEN GOOSE, THE(1969, Brit.); INCENSE FOR THE DAMNED(1970, Brit.); SITTING TARGET(1972, Brit.); YOUNG WINSTON(1972, Brit.); CHARLEY-ONE-EYE(1973, Brit.); WICKER MAN, THE(1974, Brit.); CALLAN(1975, Brit.); STAND UP VIRGIN SOLDIERS(1977, Brit.); BREAKER MORANT(1980, Aus.); FINAL OPTION, THE(1983, Brit.)
1984
CHAMPIONS(1984)
Eugenia Woodward
Silents
CAPPY RICKS(1921)

Eugenie Woodward
Silents
EAST LYNNE(1916); HIDDEN SCAR, THE(1916); AMATEUR WIDOW, AN(1919); GREATER THAN FAME(1920); KENTUCKIANS, THE(1921)
Misc. Silents
BETSY ROSS(1917); LAST OF THE CARNABYS, THE(1917); SOUL WITHOUT WINDOWS, A(1918); T'OTHER DEAR CHARMER(1918)
Frances Woodward
RIDERS OF THE DEADLINE(1943)
Fred Woodward
Silents
PATCHWORK GIRL OF OZ, THE(1914)
Misc. Silents
HIS MAJESTY, THE SCARECROW OF OZ(1914); MAGIC CLOAK OF OZ, THE(1914)
Gary Woodward
TWO OF A KIND(1983)
Harry Woodward
Silents
BAIT, THE(1921)
Henry Woodward
Silents
NAN OF MUSIC MOUNTAIN(1917); ARE YOU LEGALLY MARRIED?(1919); MALE AND FEMALE(1919); HER FIVE-FOOT HIGHNESS(1920); LAST OF THE MOHICANS, THE(1920)
Misc. Silents
MARCELLINI MILLIONS, THE(1917); BELIEVE ME, XANTIPPE(1918); LAWLESS LOVE(1918); MYSTERY OF A GIRL, THE(1918); ROAD THROUGH THE DARK, THE(1918); FORBIDDEN(1919); YOU'RE FIRED(1919); SEEING IT THROUGH(1920)
Herbert Woodward
UP FOR THE CUP(1931, Brit.)
Hubert Woodward
GREED OF WILLIAM HART, THE(1948, Brit.); IS YOUR HONEYMOON REALLY NECESSARY?(1953, Brit.)
Silents
ADVENTURES OF MR. PICKWICK, THE(1921, Brit.)
Ian Woodward
ALFIE DARLING(1975, Brit.)
Joanne Woodward
COUNT THREE AND PRAY(1955); KISS BEFORE DYING, A(1956); NO DOWN PAYMENT(1957); THREE FACES OF EVE, THE(1957); LONG, HOT SUMMER, THE(1958); RALLY 'ROUND THE FLAG, BOYS!(1958); SOUND AND THE FURY, THE(1959); FROM THE TERRACE(1960); FUGITIVE KIND, THE(1960); PARIS BLUES(1961); NEW KIND OF LOVE, A(1963); STRIPPER, THE(1963); SIGNPOST TO MURDER(1964); BIG HAND FOR THE LITTLE LADY, A(1966); FINE MADNESS, A(1966); RACHEL, RACHEL(1968); WINNING(1969); WUSA(1970); THEY MIGHT BE GIANTS(1971); EFFECT OF GAMMA RAYS ON MAN-IN-THE-MOON MARIGOLDS, THE(1972); SUMMER WISHES, WINTER DREAMS(1973); DROWNING POOL, THE(1975); END, THE(1978)
1984
HARRY AND SON(1984)
John Woodward
Silents
MAD DANCER(1925)
Kimberly Woodward
S.O.B.(1981)
Marvin Woodward
SNOW WHITE AND THE SEVEN DWARFS(1937), anim; FANTASIA(1940), anim; PINOCCHIO(1940), anim; THREE CABALLEROS, THE(1944), anim; MELODY TIME(1948), animators; SO DEAR TO MY HEART(1949), anim; CINDERELLA(1950), anim; ALICE IN WONDERLAND(1951), anim; PETER PAN(1953), anim; LADY AND THE TRAMP(1955), anim
Morgan Woodward
GREAT LOCOMOTIVE CHASE, THE(1956); WESTWARD HO THE WAGONS!(1956); GUN HAWK, THE(1963); DEVIL'S BEDROOM, THE(1964), a, w; SWORD OF ALI BABA, THE(1965); GUNPOINT(1966); COOL HAND LUKE(1967); FIRECREEK(1968); DEATH OF A GUNFIGHTER(1969); WILD COUNTRY, THE(1971); ONE LITTLE INDIAN(1973); RUNNING WILD(1973); MIDNIGHT MAN, THE(1974); RIDE IN A PINK CAR(1974, Can.); KILLING OF A CHINESE BOOKIE, THE(1976); SMALL TOWN IN TEXAS, A(1976); FINAL CHAPTER–WALKING TALL zero(1977); MOONSHINE COUNTY EXPRESS(1977); SUPER VAN(1977); SPEEDTRAP(1978); BATTLE BEYOND THE STARS(1980)
Misc. Talkies
DELIVER US FROM EVIL(1975)
Neil Woodward
TWO LOVES(1961)
Rob Woodward
FRONTIER SCOUT(1939)
Robert Woodward
RED RUNS THE RIVER(1963)
Robert D. Woodward
CROSSED TRAILS(1948)
Stacy Woodward
SHARK WOMAN, THE(1941), ph
Tim Woodward
GALILEO(1975, Brit.); EUROPEANS, THE(1979, Brit.)
Tina Woodward
MR. SARDONICUS(1961)
W.E. Woodward
EVELYN PRENTICE(1934), w; STRONGER THAN DESIRE(1939), w
Morgan Woodword
WHICH WAY IS UP?(1977)
Dan Woodworth
MORE AMERICAN GRAFFITI(1979)
Jane Woodworth
MEN AGAINST THE SKY(1940); MEXICAN SPITFIRE OUT WEST(1940); FOUR JACKS AND A JILL(1941); MEXICAN SPITFIRE'S BABY(1941); TOM, DICK AND HARRY(1941); MAYOR OF 44TH STREET, THE(1942); MEXICAN SPITFIRE SEES A GHOST(1942); POWDER TOWN(1942); FALLEN SPARROW, THE(1943)

Majorie Woodworth
FLYING WITH MUSIC(1942)
Marjorie Woodworth
DANCE, GIRL, DANCE(1940); ALL-AMERICAN CO-ED(1941); BROADWAY LIMIT-ED(1941); ROAD SHOW(1941); BROOKLYN ORCHID(1942); DEVIL WITH HITLER, THE(1942); DUDES ARE PRETTY PEOPLE(1942); YANKS AHOY(1943); WAVE, A WAC AND A MARINE, A(1944); SALTY O'ROURKE(1945); YOU CAME ALONG(1945); DECOY(1946); IN FAST COMPANY(1946); DOUBLE LIFE, A(1947)
Truman Woodworth
RELUCTANT DRAGON, THE(1941)
Walter Woodworth
MONSTER OF PIEDRAS BLANCAS, THE(1959), art d
Dave Woody
RETURN TO BOGGY CREEK(1977), w
Jack Woody
I AM THE LAW(1938); SAINTED SISTERS, THE(1948); LAST OF THE COMAN-CHES(1952); SPRINGFIELD RIFLE(1952); STRANGER WORE A GUN, THE(1953); THUNDER OVER THE PLAINS(1953); CRIME WAVE(1954); RIDING SHOT-GUN(1954); DAY OF THE OUTLAW(1959)
Joe Woody
ADVENTURES OF MARCO POLO, THE(1938)
Peggy Woody
WITHOUT A TRACE(1983)
Sam Woody
FRANCIS JOINS THE WACS(1954)
Woody Herman and His Band
WINTERTIME(1943)
Woody Herman and His Orchestra
WHAT'S COOKIN'?(1942); EARL CARROLL'S VANITIES(1945)
Woody Herman Band
SENSATIONS OF 1945(1944)
Woody Herman Orchestra
HIT PARADE OF 1947(1947)
Walter Wooff
GOLDEN DAWN(1930)
Robert Woog
DANGER IS A WOMAN(1952, Fr.), p; LOVE AND THE FRENCHWOMAN(1961, Fr.), p
Beverly Wook
MA AND PA KETTLE(1949)
Karen Wookey
MAIN EVENT, THE(1979)
Abbe Wool
1984
REPO MAN(1984)
Norman Wooland
FIVE POUND MAN, THE(1937, Brit.); THIS ENGLAND(1941, Brit.); ESCAPE(1948, Brit.); HAMLET(1948, Brit.); LOOK BEFORE YOU LOVE(1948, Brit.); ALL OVER THE TOWN(1949, Brit.); ANGEL WITH THE TRUMPET, THE(1950, Brit.); MADELEI-NE(1950, Brit.); QUO VADIS(1951); IVANHOE(1952, Brit.); BACKGROUND(1953, Brit.); RINGER, THE(1953, Brit.); ROMEO AND JULIET(1954, Brit.); MASTER PLAN, THE(1955, Brit.); GUILTY?(1956, Brit.); RICHARD III(1956, Brit.); FLESH IS WEAK, THE(1957, Brit.); NO ROAD BACK(1957, Brit.); BANDIT OF ZHOBE, THE(1959); HONOURABLE MURDER, AN(1959, Brit.); TEENAGE BAD GIRL(1959, Brit.); NIGHT TRAIN FOR INVERNESS(1960, Brit.); GUNS OF NAVARONE, THE(1961); PORTRAIT OF A SINNER(1961, Brit.); BARABBAS(1962, Ital.); FALL OF THE ROMAN EMPIRE, THE(1964); FIGHTING PRINCE OF DONEGAL, THE(1966, Brit.); WALK IN THE SHADOW(1966, Brit.); PROJECTED MAN, THE(1967, Brit.); SAUL AND DAVID(1968, Ital./Span.)
Antony Woolard
TERM OF TRIAL(1962, Brit.), art d
Tony Woolard
COP-OUT(1967, Brit.), art d; SECRETS(1971), ed
William Woolard
OTHER SIDE OF THE MOUNTAIN, THE(1975)
Squadron Officer J. Woolaston
SCHOOL FOR DANGER(1947, Brit.), w
George Woolbridge
DOOMWATCH(1972, Brit.)
Jeffrey Woolbridge
1984
SECRETS(1984, Brit.), art d
David Woolcombe
PRIVILEGED(1982, Brit.), w
Alexander Woolcott
BABES ON BROADWAY(1941); DARK TOWER, THE(1943, Brit.), w
John Wooldridge
FAME IS THE SPUR(1947, Brit.), m; CONSPIRATOR(1949, Brit.), m; FIVE ANGLES ON MURDER(1950, Brit.), m; PAPER GALLOWS(1950, Brit.), m; BLACK-MAILED(1951, Brit.), m; APPOINTMENT IN LONDON(1953, Brit.), w, m; LAST MAN TO HANG, THE(1956, Brit.), m, md; COUNT FIVE AND DIE(1958, Brit.), m; RX MURDER(1958, Brit.), m, md
Chuck Woolery
TREASURE OF JAMAICA REEF, THE(1976); SIX PACK(1982)
Gerry Woolery
SCAVENGER HUNT(1979), w
Misc. Talkies
JOKES MY FOLKS NEVER TOLD ME(1979), d
Robert Woolery
BREAKING AWAY(1979)
Harold Wooley
FOUR FAST GUNS(1959), ed; MISSILE TO THE MOON(1959), spec eff
Pat Wooley
REBEL SON, THE ½(1939, Brit.), ed; OVER THE MOON(1940, Brit.), ed
Peter Wooley
GOING HOME(1971), art d; CLEOPATRA JONES(1973), art d; BLAZING SAD-DLES(1974), prod d; OUR TIME(1974), art d; SPARKLE(1976), art d; HIGH ANX-IETY(1977), prod d; OLLY, OLLY, OXEN FREE(1978), prod d; FATSO(1980), prod d; UP THE ACADEMY(1980), prod d; SECOND-HAND HEARTS(1981), prod d; UNDER THE RAINBOW(1981), prod d; JEKYLL AND HYDE...TOGETHER AGAIN(1982),

prod d
1984
HARD TO HOLD(1984), prod d; OH GOD! YOU DEVIL(1984), prod d
Roberta Wooley
BANK RAIDERS, THE(1958, Brit.)
Sheb Wooley
ROCKY MOUNTAIN(1950); DISTANT DRUMS(1951); LITTLE BIG HORN(1951); BUGLES IN THE AFTERNOON(1952); CATTLE TOWN(1952); HELLGATE(1952); HIGH NOON(1952); LUSTY MEN, THE(1952); SKY FULL OF MOON(1952); TEXAS BAD MAN(1953); BOY FROM OKLAHOMA, THE(1954); JOHNNY GUITAR(1954); ROSE MARIE(1954); MAN WITHOUT A STAR(1955); SECOND GREATEST SEX, THE(1955); TRIAL(1955); BLACK WHIP, THE(1956); GIANT(1956); OKLAHOMAN, THE(1957); RIDE A VIOLENT MILE(1957); TROOPER HOOK(1957); TERROR IN A TEXAS TOWN(1958); HOOTENANNY HOOT(1963); COUNTRY BOY(1966); WAR WAGON, THE(1967); OUTLAW JOSEY WALES, THE(1976)
Stephanie Wooley
1984
STONE BOY, THE(1984), art d
Charles Woolf
SCUDDA-HOO! SCUDDA-HAY!(1948); THAT WONDERFUL URGE(1948); LADY SINGS THE BLUES(1972); LAST OF THE RED HOT LOVERS(1972); PRIVATE PARTS(1972); FRASIER, THE SENSUOUS LION(1973); DARKTOWN STRUT-TERS(1975); SHEILA LEVINE IS DEAD AND LIVING IN NEW YORK(1975); NO WAY BACK(1976); MOUSE AND HIS CHILD, THE(1977); MR. MOM(1983)
D. William Woolf
SONS OF THE SEA(1939, Brit.), w
Edgar Allan Woolf
FREAKS(1932), w; MASK OF FU MANCHU, THE(1932), w; BROADWAY TO HOL-LYWOOD(1933), w; MURDER IN THE PRIVATE CAR(1934), w; THIS SIDE OF HEAVEN(1934), w; CASINO MURDER CASE, THE(1935), w; NIGHT IS YOUNG, THE(1935), w; MAD HOLIDAY(1936), w; TOUGH GUY(1936), w; KID FROM TEXAS, THE(1939), w; WHAT'S COOKIN'?(1942), w; ZIEGFELD FOLLIES(1945), w
Silents
APRIL FOOL(1926), w
Edgar Allen Woolf
TAILOR MADE MAN, A(1931), w; FLESH(1932), w; HAVE A HEART(1934), w; MOONLIGHT MURDER(1936), w; EVERYBODY SING(1938), w; ICE FOLLIES OF 1939(1939), w; WIZARD OF OZ, THE(1939), w
Edward Woolf
YOU CAN'T CHEAT AN HONEST MAN(1939)
Frank Woolf
Silents
PRINCE AND THE BEGGARMAID, THE(1921, Brit.)
Gabriel Woolf
TOM BROWN'S SCHOOLDAYS(1951, Brit.); KNIGHTS OF THE ROUND TA-BLE(1953)
Henry Woolf
PERSECUTION AND ASSASSINATION OF JEAN-PAUL MARAT AS PERFORMED BY THE INMATES OF THE ASYLUM OF CHARENTON UNDER THE DIRECTION OF THE MARQUIS DE SADE, THE(1967, Brit.); GREAT CATHERINE(1968, Brit.); TELL ME LIES(1968, Brit.); BED SITTING ROOM, THE(1969, Brit.); FIGURES IN A LANDSCAPE(1970, Brit.); RULING CLASS, THE(1972, Brit.); SAVAGE MES-SIAH(1972, Brit.); GORKY PARK(1983); SUPERMAN III(1983)
Misc. Talkies
LOVE PILL, THE(1971)
Jack Woolf
MATILDA(1978), ph
James Woolf
ROOM AT THE TOP(1959, Brit.), p; L-SHAPED ROOM, THE(1962, Brit.), p; TERM OF TRIAL(1962, Brit.), p; OF HUMAN BONDAGE(1964, Brit.), p; PUMPKIN EATER, THE(1964, Brit.), p; KING RAT(1965), p; LIFE AT THE TOP(1965, Brit.), p
John Woolf
ROOM AT THE TOP(1959, Brit.), p; OLIVER!(1968, Brit.), p; DAY OF THE JACKAL, THE(1973, Brit./Fr.), p; ODESSA FILE, THE(1974, Brit./Ger.), p
Leslie Woolf
TROUBLE WITH HARRY, THE(1955)
Michael Woolf
GOODBYE PORK PIE(1981, New Zealand)
Vicki Woolf
HANDS OF ORLAC, THE(1964, Brit./Fr.); HANDS OF THE RIPPER(1971, Brit.); GREAT WALTZ, THE(1972); CONFESSIONS OF A POP PERFORMER(1975, Brit.)
Victor Woolf
TWO-HEADED SPY, THE(1959, Brit.)
Walter Woolf
GIRL WITHOUT A ROOM(1933); THREE BRAVE MEN(1957)
Walter Woolf [King]
EMBARRASSING MOMENTS(1934)
Betty Woolfe
OBLONG BOX, THE(1969, Brit.)
Eric Woolfe
CHALLENGE FOR ROBIN HOOD, A(1968, Brit.)
H. Bruce Woolfe
ESCAPED FROM DARTMOOR(1930, Brit.), p; BATTLE OF GALLIPOLI(1931, Brit.), p; WINDJAMMER, THE(1931, Brit.), p; DANCE PRETTY LADY(1932, Brit.), p
Silents
ARMAGEDDON(1923, Brit.), p&d; NELSON(1926, Brit.), p; BATTLES OF THE CORONEL AND FALKLAND ISLANDS, THE(1928, Brit.), p; BOLIBAR(1928, Brit.), p; LOST PATROL, THE(1929, Brit.), p
Misc. Silents
ZEEBRUGGE(1924, Brit.), d; SONS OF THE SEA(1925, Brit.), d
Ronald Woolfe
ON THE BUSES(1972, Brit.), p
Guy Woolfenden
WORK IS A FOUR LETTER WORD(1968, Brit.), m; MIDSUMMER NIGHT'S DREAM, A(1969, Brit.), m
1984
SECRETS(1984, Brit.), m

Bertha Woolford
SARATOGA TRUNK(1945); NIGHT AND DAY(1946)

Jack Woolgar
HAMMERHEAD(1968); WHERE'S JACK?(1969, Brit.); LONG AGO, TOMORROW(1971, Brit.); SAY HELLO TO YESTERDAY(1971, Brit.); DEATHLINE(1973, Brit.); GAWAIN AND THE GREEN KNIGHT(1973, Brit.); SWALLOWS AND AMAZONS(1977, Brit.)

Edward Wooll
LIBEL(1959, Brit.), w

Anthony Woollard
GAWAIN AND THE GREEN KNIGHT(1973, Brit.), art d

Joan Woollard
LEO THE LAST(1970, Brit.), cos

Kenneth Woollard
OPERATION DISASTER(1951, Brit.), w

Tony Woollard
PURE HELL OF ST. TRINIAN'S, THE(1961, Brit.), art d; STOLEN HOURS(1963), art d; HAVING A WILD WEEKEND(1965, Brit.), prod d; JUDITH(1965), art d; GEORGY GIRL(1966, Brit.), art d; TIME LOST AND TIME REMEMBERED(1966, Brit.), art d; TO SIR, WITH LOVE(1967, Brit.), art d; HIGH COMMISSIONER, THE(1968, U.S./Brit.), prod d; INTERLUDE(1968, Brit.), prod d; LOCK UP YOUR DAUGHTERS(1969, Brit.), prod d; LEO THE LAST(1970, Brit.), prod d; ENGLANO MADE ME(1973, Brit.), prod d; MOONLIGHTING(1982, Brit.), prod d; PIRATE MOVIE, THE(1982, Aus.), prod d

Alexander Woollcott
GIFT OF GAB(1934); MAN WITH TWO FACES, THE(1934), w; SCOUNDREL, THE(1935)

Barry Wooller
TAKING TIGER MOUNTAIN(1983, U.S./Welsh)

Brad Woolley
THOMASINE AND BUSHROD(1974)

James Woolley
S(1974)

Monty Woolley
LADIES IN LOVE(1936); LIVE, LOVE AND LEARN(1937); NOTHING SACRED(1937); ARSENE LUPIN RETURNS(1938); ARTISTS AND MODELS ABROAD(1938); EVERYBODY SING(1938); GIRL OF THE GOLDEN WEST, THE(1938), w; LORD JEFF(1938); THREE COMRADES(1938); YOUNG DR. KILDARE(1938); DANCING CO-ED(1939); HONEYMOON IN BALI(1939); MAN ABOUT TOWN(1939); MIDNIGHT(1939); NEVER SAY DIE(1939); ZAZA(1939); LIFE BEGINS AT 8:30(1942); MAN WHO CAME TO DINNER, THE(1942); PIED PIPER, THE(1942); HOLY MATRIMONY(1943); IRISH EYES ARE SMILING(1944); SINCE YOU WENT AWAY(1944); MOLLY AND ME(1945); NIGHT AND DAY(1946); BISHOP'S WIFE, THE(1947); MISS TATLOCK'S MILLIONS(1948); AS YOUNG AS YOU FEEL(1951); KISMET(1955)

Richard Woolley
BROTHERS AND SISTERS(1980, Brit.), d, w

Robert Woolley
PRIVILEGED(1982, Brit.)

Roberta Woolley
WOMEN IN A DRESSING GOWN(1957, Brit.); SUDDENLY, LAST SUMMER(1959, Brit.)

Claude Woolman
HEAVEN WITH A GUN(1969)

Harry Woolman
TIME OF THEIR LIVES, THE(1946); TO THE SHORES OF HELL(1966), spec eff; HOT SPUR(1968), spec eff; CAPTAIN MILKSHAKE(1970), spec eff; MACHISMO-40 GRAVES FOR 40 GUNS(1970), spec eff; RED, WHITE AND BLACK, THE(1970), spec eff; BIG FOOT(1973), spec eff; SWEET JESUS, PREACHER MAN(1973), spec eff; RATTLERS(1976), spec eff; SUPER VAN(1977), spec eff; INCREDIBLE MELTING MAN, THE(1978), spec eff; LASERBLAST(1978), spec eff & makeup; UNSEEN, THE(1981), spec eff; EVILSPEAK(1982), spec eff; SWORD AND THE SORCERER, THE(1982), spec eff

Pamela Woolman
ON HER BED OF ROSES(1966)

Terry Woolman
MACHISMO-40 GRAVES FOR 40 GUNS(1970); SWORD AND THE SORCERER, THE(1982), spec eff

Bernard Woolner
SWAMP WOMEN(1956), p; ATTACK OF THE 50 FOOT WOMAN(1958), p; FLIGHT OF THE LOST BALLOON(1961), p

Bernard A. Woolner
HILLBILLYS IN A HAUNTED HOUSE(1967), p

Lawrence Woolner
YOUNG, THE EVIL AND THE SAVAGE, THE(1968, Ital.), p

Cornell Woolrich
MANHATTAN LOVE SONG(1934), w; CONVICTED(1938), w; STREET OF CHANCE(1942), w; LEOPARD MAN, THE(1943), w; MARK OF THE WHISTLER, THE(1944), w; BLACK ANGEL(1946), w; CHASE, THE(1946), w; FALL GUY(1947), John O'Dea; GUILTY, THE(1947), w; I WOULDN'T BE IN YOUR SHOES(1948), w; NIGHT HAS A THOUSAND EYES(1948), w; RETURN OF THE WHISTLER, THE(1948), w; WINDOW, THE(1949), w; REAR WINDOW(1954), w; BOY CRIED MURDER, THE(1966, Ger./Brit./Yugo.), w; UNION CITY(1980), d&w
1984
CLOAK AND DAGGER(1984), w

John Woolridge
OUTSIDER, THE(1949, Brit.), m

Susan Woolridge
SHOUT, THE(1978, Brit.)

Douglas Woolsey
WINGS AND THE WOMAN(1942, Brit.), spec eff; STAIRWAY TO HEAVEN(1946, Brit.), spec eff

Ralph Woolsey
WIRETAPPERS(1956), ph; CLAUDELLE INGLISH(1961), ph; BLACK SPURS(1965), ph; WHAT AM I BID?(1967), ph; LAWYER, THE(1969), ph; LITTLE FAUSS AND BIG HALSY(1970), ph; STRAWBERRY STATEMENT, THE(1970), ph; HONKY(1971), ph; CULPEPPER CATTLE COMPANY, THE(1972), ph; DIRTY LITTLE BILLY(1972), ph; NEW CENTURIONS, THE(1972), ph; ICEMAN COMETH, THE(1973), ph; MACK, THE(1973), ph; BLACK EYE(1974), ph; 99 AND 44/100% DEAD(1974), ph; RAFFERTY AND THE GOLD DUST TWINS(1975), ph; LIFEGUARD(1976), ph; MOTHER,

JUGS & SPEED(1976), ph; SILVER STREAK(1976), ph; FIRE SALE(1977), ph; PACK, THE(1977), ph; GREAT SANTINI, THE(1979), ph; PROMISE, THE(1979), ph; LAST MARRIED COUPLE IN AMERICA, THE(1980), ph; OH GOD! BOOK II(1980), ph; DEADHEAD MILES(1982), ph

Ralph A. Woolsey
PERSUADER, THE(1957), ph

Robert Woolsey
RIO RITA(1929); CUCKOOS, THE(1930); DIXIANA(1930); HALF SHOT AT SUNRISE(1930); HOOK, LINE AND SINKER(1930); CAUGHT PLASTERED(1931); CRACKED NUTS(1931); EVERYTHING'S ROSIE(1931); PEACH O' RENO(1931); GIRL CRAZY(1932); HOLD'EM JAIL(1932); DIPLOMANIACS(1933); SO THIS IS AFRICA(1933); COCKEYED CAVALIERS(1934); HIPS, HIPS, HOORAY(1934); KENTUCKY KERNELS(1935); NITWITS, THE(1935); RAINMAKERS, THE(1935); MUMMY'S BOYS(1936); SILLY BILLIES(1936); HIGH FLYERS(1937); ON AGAIN-OFF AGAIN(1937)

George Woolsley
OUTLAWS OF THE DESERT(1941)

Henry Woolston
THREE WITNESSES(1935, Brit.); INCIDENT IN SHANGHAI(1937, Brit.); OLD MOTHER RILEY'S GHOSTS(1941, Brit.)

Charles Woolveridge
MASSACRE HILL(1949, Brit.), art d

Mike Woolveridge
MANGANINNIE(1982, Aus.), ed

Jack Woolwich
NEON PALACE, THE(1970, Can.)

Basil Woon
RECAPTURED LOVE(1930), w; MEN ON CALL(1931), w; WHILE PARIS SLEEPS(1932), w; PERFECT CRIME, THE(1937, Brit.), w; SIMPLY TERRIFIC(1938, Brit.), w; TWO FOR DANGER(1940, Brit.), w; VOICE IN THE NIGHT, A(1941, Brit.), w; THIS WAS PARIS(1942, Brit.), w; RHYTHM SERENADE(1943, Brit.), w; FLIGHT FROM FOLLY(1945, Brit.), w; SHOWTIME(1948, Brit.), w

Il Woong
INCHON(1981)

Ellen Woonston
Silents
OUTLAWS OF RED RIVER(1927)

Arthur Wooster
PLANK, THE(1967, Brit.), ph

Kirk Wooster
NUMBER ONE(1969), ph

Red Wooten
KINGS GO FORTH(1958)

Rodney Wooten
GIRL IN EVERY PORT, A(1952)

Sarita Wooten
LIGHT THAT FAILED, THE(1939); ON YOUR TOES(1939)

Stevie Wooten
ROOM FOR ONE MORE(1952)

Norma Jean Wooters
BAD MEN OF THE HILLS(1942); FIGHTING BUCKAROO, THE(1943)

Sarita Wooton
WUTHERING HEIGHTS(1939)

Stephen Wooton
ALL MINE TO GIVE(1957)

Stevie Wooton
RED SUNDOWN(1956)

Rosemary Wootten
PERSECUTION(1974, Brit.), w

Stephen Wootton
AT GUNPOINT(1955); STRANGER AT MY DOOR(1956)

Alec Worcester
Silents
JUSTICE(1914, Brit.)
Misc. Silents
CLOISTER AND THE HEARTH, THE(1913, Brit.); KISSING CUP(1913, Brit.)

Nicholas Hopson Worcester
Silents
MISSING THE TIDE(1918, Brit.)

Rande Worcester
1984
WILD LIFE, THE(1984)

Alec Worchester
Misc. Silents
JUSTICE(1914, Brit.)

Hank Worden
GHOST TOWN GOLD(1937); SINGING OUTLAW(1937); FRONTIER TOWN(1938); GHOST TOWN RIDERS(1938); ROLLIN' PLAINS(1938); STRANGER FROM ARIZONA, THE(1938); WESTERN TRAILS(1938); WHERE THE BUFFALO ROAM(1938); NIGHT RIDERS, THE(1939); OKLAHOMA FRONTIER(1939); ROLLIN' WESTWARD(1939); SUNDOWN ON THE PRAIRIE(1939); TIMBER STAMPEDE(1939); CHIP OF THE FLYING U(1940); GAUCHO SERENADE(1940); NORTHWEST PASSAGE(1940); BORDER VIGILANTES(1941); CODE OF THE OUTLAW(1942); COWBOY SERENADE(1942); RIDING THE WIND(1942); BLACK MARKET RUSTLERS(1943); CANYON CITY(1943); TENTING TONIGHT ON THE OLD CAMP GROUND(1943); LUMBERJACK(1944); BULLFIGHTERS, THE(1945); DUEL IN THE SUN(1946); LAWLESS BREED, THE(1946); UNDERCURRENT(1946); ANGEL AND THE BADMAN(1947); HIGH WALL, THE(1947); PRAIRIE EXPRESS(1947); SEA OF GRASS, THE(1947); SECRET LIFE OF WALTER MITTY, THE(1947); FORT APACHE(1948); LIGHTNIN' IN THE FOREST(1948); RED RIVER(1948); SAINTED SISTERS, THE(1948); TAP ROOTS(1948); THREE GODFATHERS(1948); YELLOW SKY(1948); FIGHTING KENTUCKIAN, THE(1949); HELLFIRE(1949); RED CANYON(1949); FATHER IS A BACHELOR(1950); WAGONMASTER(1950); WHEN WILLIE COMES MARCHING HOME(1950); JOE PALOOKA IN TRIPLE CROSS(1951); MAN WITH A CLOAK, THE(1951); SUGARFOOT(1951); APACHE WAR SMOKE(1952); BIG SKY, THE(1952); BOOTS MALONE(1952); QUIET MAN, THE(1952); WOMAN OF THE NORTH COUNTRY(1952); CRIME WAVE(1954); MA AND PA KETTLE AT HOME(1954); INDIAN FIGHTER, THE(1955); ACCUSED OF MURDER(1956); DAVY CROCKETT AND THE RIVER PIRATES(1956); SEARCHERS, THE(1956); BUCKSKIN LADY, THE(1957); DRAGON WELLS MASSACRE(1957); FORTY GUNS(1957); QUIET

GUN, THE(1957); SPOILERS OF THE FOREST(1957); BULLWHIP(1958); NOTORIOUS MR. MONKS, THE(1958); TOUGHEST GUN IN TOMBSTONE(1958); HORSE SOLDIERS, THE(1959); ALAMO, THE(1960); SERGEANT RUTLEDGE(1960); ONE-EYED JACKS(1961); MUSIC MAN, THE(1962); MC LINTOCK!(1963); GOOD TIMES(1967); BIG DADDY(1969); TRUE GRIT(1969); CHISUM(1970); RIO LOBO(1970); BIG JAKE(1971); CAHILL, UNITED STATES MARSHAL(1973); SMOKEY AND THE BANDIT(1977); WHICH WAY IS UP?(1977); SGT. PEPPER'S LONELY HEARTS CLUB BAND(1978); THEY WENT THAT-A-WAY AND THAT-A-WAY(1978); BRONCO BILLY(1980)
1984
ICE PIRATES, THE(1984)
"Shorty" Worden
Silents
COLLEGE(1927)
Walter Worden
SPEED LIMITED(1940)
Silents
ONE OF MANY(1917)
Smitty Wordes
ONE AND ONLY GENUINE ORIGINAL FAMILY BAND, THE(1968)
Dick Wordley
CATHY'S CHILD(1979, Aus.), w
Sil Words
HICKEY AND BOGGS(1972); WOMAN UNDER THE INFLUENCE, A(1974)
Syl Words
COMMITMENT, THE(1976)
Sylvester Words
SKATEBOARD(1978)
Richard Wordsworth
MAN WHO KNEW TOO MUCH, THE(1956); THE CREEPING UNKNOWN(1956, Brit.); TIME WITHOUT PITY(1957, Brit.); REVENGE OF FRANKENSTEIN, THE(1958, Brit.); CURSE OF THE WEREWOLF, THE(1961); LOCK UP YOUR DAUGHTERS(1969, Brit.); SONG OF NORWAY(1970)
Marjorie Wordworth
DEVIL SHIP(1947)
Bernard Woringer
MONKEYS, GO HOME!(1967); MADWOMAN OF CHAILLOT, THE(1969)
Adrian Worker
NAKED EARTH, THE(1958, Brit.), p
Adrian D. Worker
SAFARI(1956), p; INTENT TO KILL(1958, Brit.), p
Melanie Workhoven
SERIAL(1980)
Frederic Worklock
SPINOUT(1966)
Carl Workman
MONDAY'S CHILD(1967, U.S., Arg.), ed; MONEY, THE(1975), d&w
Charles Workman
WOMEN IN LOVE(1969, Brit.)
Chuck Workman
CUBA CROSSING(1980), d&w
James Workman
INTO THE STRAIGHT(1950, Aus.)
Jennie Workman
OKLAHOMA(1955)
Lindsay Workman
SPRING AFFAIR(1960); PRINCESS AND THE MAGIC FROG, THE(1965); KARATE KILLERS, THE(1967); WESTWORLD(1973); ONE MAN JURY(1978)
Steve Workman
1984
HARDBODIES(1984)
William Workman
FIDELIO(1970, Ger.)
J.C. Works [Chester Erskine]
IRISH WHISKEY REBELLION(1973), d
Jody Works
COMMON LAW WIFE(1963)
Christina World
GOLDEN LADY, THE(1979, Brit.)
Jo Anne Worley
SHAGGY D.A., THE(1976); NUTCRACKER FANTASY(1979)
William Worley]
MACABRE(1958), w
Fred Worlock
LOCKET, THE(1946); JOHNNY BELINDA(1948); RUTHLESS(1948)
Frederic Worlock
MIRACLES FOR SALE(1939); EARL OF CHICAGO, THE(1940); NORTHWEST PASSAGE(1940); SEA HAWK, THE(1940); SOUTH OF SUEZ(1940); STRANGE CARGO(1940); DOWN IN SAN DIEGO(1941); DR. JEKYLL AND MR. HYDE(1941); FREE AND EASY(1941); INTERNATIONAL LADY(1941); MAN HUNT(1941); RAGE IN HEAVEN(1941); CAPTAINS OF THE CLOUDS(1942); PACIFIC RENDEZVOUS(1942); PIERRE OF THE PLAINS(1942); AIR RAID WARDENS(1943); APPOINTMENT IN BERLIN(1943); MADAME CURIE(1943); NATIONAL VELVET(1944); HANGOVER SQUARE(1945); SHE-WOLF OF LONDON(1946); TERROR BY NIGHT(1946); FOREVER AMBER(1947); LAST OF THE REDMEN(1947); LONE WOLF IN LONDON(1947); LOVE FROM A STRANGER(1947); MACOMBER AFFAIR, THE(1947); JOAN OF ARC(1948); JET OVER THE ATLANTIC(1960); NOTORIOUS LANDLADY, THE(1962); STRANGE BEDFELLOWS(1965)
Frederick Worlock
BALALAIKA(1939); LADY OF THE TROPICS(1939); MOON OVER BURMA(1940); MURDER OVER NEW YORK(1940); YANK IN THE R.A.F.(1941); BLACK SWAN, THE(1942); EAGLE SQUADRON(1942); LONDON BLACKOUT MURDERS(1942); RANDOM HARVEST(1942); MANTRAP, THE(1943); PASSPORT TO SUEZ(1943); SAHARA(1943); SHERLOCK HOLMES FACES DEATH(1943); WING AND A PRAYER(1944); SECRETS OF SCOTLAND YARD(1944); LODGER, THE(1944); FATAL WITNESS, THE(1945); PURSUIT TO ALGIERS(1945); SCOTLAND YARD INVESTIGATOR(1945, Brit.); WOMAN IN GREEN, THE(1945); DRESSED TO KILL(1946); DOUBLE LIFE, A(1947); IMPERFECT LADY, THE(1947); SINGAPORE(1947); WOMAN'S VENGEANCE, A(1947); HILLS OF HOME(1948); SPARTACUS(1960); ONE HUNDRED AND ONE DALMATIANS(1961)

Fredric Worlock
HOW GREEN WAS MY VALLEY(1941)
Fredrick Worlock
HE STAYED FOR BREAKFAST(1940)
Bill Worman
PORKY'S(1982)
Cliff Worman
Misc. Silents
MEN WHO HAVE MADE LOVE TO ME(1918)
Dick Wormell
SEVEN MINUTES, THE(1971), ed
Richard Wormer
PHANTOM THIEF, THE(1946), w
Jean Worms
ABUSED CONFIDENCE(1938, Fr. ABUS DE CONFIANCE); ENTENTE CORDIALE(1939, Fr.); HEART OF PARIS(1939, Fr.); RASPUTIN(1939, Fr.); MARKED GIRLS(1949, Fr.)
Rene Worms
ORPHEUS(1950, Fr.); ROYAL AFFAIRS IN VERSAILLES(1957, Fr.)
Anne Wormser
WEST POINT WIDOW(1941), w
Pepper Wormser
LAW AND DISORDER(1974)
Richard Wormser
SWORN ENEMY(1936), w; CARNIVAL QUEEN(1937), w; LET THEM LIVE(1937), w; FUGITIVES FOR A NIGHT(1938), w; PLAINSMAN AND THE LADY(1946), w; PERILOUS WATERS(1948), w; BIG STEAL, THE(1949), w; POWDER RIVER RUSTLERS(1949), w; TULSA(1949), w; RUSTLERS ON HORSEBACK(1950), w; SHOWDOWN, THE(1950), d&w; VIGILANTE HIDEOUT(1950), w; FORT DODGE STAMPEDE(1951), w; CAPTIVE OF BILLY THE KID(1952), w; HALF-BREED, THE(1952), w; PERILOUS JOURNEY, A(1953), w; CRIME WAVE(1954), w; OUTCAST, THE(1954), w
Richard E. Wormser
FRAME-UP THE(1937), w; START CHEERING(1938), w
Duke Worn
Silents
SPEED COP(1926), d
Duke Worne
BRIDE OF THE DESERT(1929), d; HANDCUFFED(1929), d; MIDNIGHT SPECIAL(1931), d; LAST RIDE, THE(1932), d
Silents
CAMPBELLS ARE COMING, THE(1915); JUST JIM(1915); CRAVING, THE(1918); MARRY IN HASTE(1924), d; OTHER KIND OF LOVE, THE(1924), d; SWORD OF VALOR, THE(1924), d; EASY GOING GORDON(1925), d; GOING THE LIMIT(1925), d; PRIDE OF THE FORCE, THE(1925), d; GALLANT FOOL, THE(1926), d; HEART OF A COWARD, THE(1926), d; SPEED CRAZED(1926), d; WHEEL OF DESTINY, THE(1927), d; INTO THE NIGHT(1928), d; ISLE OF LOST MEN(1928), d; MAN FROM HEADQUARTERS(1928), d; ANNE AGAINST THE WORLD(1929), d; DEVIL'S CHAPLAIN(1929), d
Misc. Silents
FROM A BROADWAY TO A THRONE(1916); WHO WAS THE OTHER MAN?(1917); DANGEROUS PATHS(1921), d; STAR REPORTER, THE(1921), d; YANKEE GO-GETTER, A(1921), d; DO IT NOW(1924), d; MARTYR SEX, THE(1924), d; CANVAS KISSER, THE(1925), d; ONCE IN A LIFETIME(1925), d; TEN DAYS(1925), d; TOO MUCH YOUTH(1925), d; BOASTER, THE(1926), d; IN SEARCH OF A HERO(1926), d; CRUISE OF THE HELLION, THE(1927), d; DARING DEEDS(1927), d; HEROES IN BLUE(1927), d; SILENT HERO, THE(1927), d; SMILING BILLY(1927), d; SPEEDY SMITH(1927), d; CITY OF PURPLE DREAMS(1928), d; DANGER PATROL(1928), d; HEART OF BROADWAY, THE(1928), d; MIDNIGHT ADVENTURE, THE(1928), d; PHANTOM OF THE TURF(1928), d; SHIPS OF THE NIGHT(1928), d; SOME MOTHER'S BOY(1929), d; WHEN DREAMS COME TRUE(1929), d
Mary Woronov
SEIZURE(1974); SILENT NIGHT, BLOODY NIGHT(1974); DEATH RACE 2000(1975); CANNONBALL(1976, U.S./Hong Kong); HOLLYWOOD BOULEVARD(1976); JACKSON COUNTY JAIL(1976); MR. BILLION(1977); ONE AND ONLY, THE(1978); ROCK 'N' ROLL HIGH SCHOOL(1979); HEARTBEEPS(1981); PROTECTORS, BOOK 1, THE(1981); EATING RAOUL(1982); GET CRAZY(1983)
1984
NIGHT OF THE COMET(1984)
Misc. Talkies
SUGAR COOKIES(1973); COVER GIRL MODELS(1975); ANGEL OF H.E.A.T.(1982)
Dusty Worrall
KING AND I, THE(1956)
Lechemere Worrall
Silents
HER WINNING WAY(1921), w
Ken Worringham
STORIES FROM A FLYING TRUNK(1979, Brit.), spec eff
Curry Worsham
SMOKEY AND THE BANDIT–PART 3(1983)
Don Worsham
WRONG IS RIGHT(1982)
Joyce Worsley
SIGNPOST TO MURDER(1964)
Wallace Worsley
Silents
PAWS OF THE BEAR(1917); ALIEN ENEMY, AN(1918), d; ADELE(1919), d; PENALTY, THE(1920), d; ACE OF HEARTS, THE(1921), d; BEAUTIFUL LIAR, THE(1921), d; BLIND BARGAIN, A(1922), d; ENTER MADAME(1922), d; RAGS TO RICHES(1922), d; HUNCHBACK OF NOTRE DAME, THE(1923), d; IS DIVORCE A FAILURE?(1923), d; NOBODY'S MONEY(1923), d
Misc. Silents
GODDESS OF LOST LAKE, THE(1918), d; HONOR'S CROSS(1918), d; SHACKLED(1918), d; SOCIAL AMBITION(1918), d; WEDLOCK(1918), d; DIANE OF THE GREEN VAN(1919), d; WOMAN OF PLEASURE, A(1919), d; LITTLE SHEPARD OF KINGDOM COME, THE(1920), d; STREET CALLED STRAIGHT, THE(1920), d; DON'T NEGLECT YOUR WIFE(1921), d; HIGHEST BIDDER, THE(1921), d; NIGHT ROSE, THE(1921), d; GRAND LARCENY(1922), d; WHEN HUSBANDS DECEIVE(1922), d; MAN WHO FIGHTS ALONE, THE(1924), d; SHADOW OF THE LAW, THE(1926), d; POWER OF SILENCE, THE(1928), d

Peregrine Worsthorne
TELL ME LIES(1968, Brit.)
Clark Worswick
FAMILY HONOR(1973), d
Alison Worth
FOR YOUR EYES ONLY(1981); OCTOPUSSY(1983, Brit.)
Barbara Worth
FIGHTING TROOPER, THE(1935); I LIVE MY LIFE(1935); RACING LUCK(1935); COUNTERFEITERS, THE(1948), w; ZAMBA(1949), w; DRAGNET(1974), w
Misc. Talkies
LIGHTNIN' SMITH RETURNS(1931); MEN OF ACTION(1935)
Silents
BROKEN HEARTS OF HOLLYWOOD(1926); PLUNGING HOOFS(1929)
Misc. Silents
FAST AND FURIOUS(1927); ON YOUR TOES(1927); PRAIRIE KING, THE(1927); FEARLESS RIDER, THE(1928); BACHELOR'S CLUB, THE(1929); BELOW THE DEADLINE(1929); FURY OF THE WILD(1929); PRINCE OF HEARTS, THE(1929)
Betty Worth
GAY ADVENTURE, THE(1936, Brit.)
Silents
MANHATTAN KNIGHTS(1928)
Bill Worth
YOU CAN'T CHEAT AN HONEST MAN(1939)
Billy Worth
ELIZA COMES TO STAY(1936, Brit.)
Bobby Worth
PENTHOUSE RHYTHM(1945)
Brian Worth
ARSENAL STADIUM MYSTERY, THE(1939, Brit.); LION HAS WINGS, THE(1940, Brit.); PASTOR HALL(1940, Brit.); IT HAPPENED TO ONE MAN(1941, Brit.); ONE NIGHT WITH YOU(1948, Brit); CARDBOARD CAVALIER, THE(1949, Brit.); LAST HOLIDAY(1950, Brit.); TOM BROWN'S SCHOOLDAYS(1951, Brit.); FATHER'S DOING FINE(1952, Brit.); HOLIDAY WEEK(1952, Brit.); IT STARTED IN PARADISE(1952, Brit.); MAN IN THE WHITE SUIT, THE(1952); TREASURE HUNT(1952, Brit.); BACHELOR IN PARIS(1953, Brit.); OPERATION DIPLOMAT(1953, Brit.); INSPECTOR CALLS, AN(1954, Brit.); FINAL COLUMN, THE(1955, Brit.); BREAKAWAY(1956, Brit.); MURDER ON APPROVAL(1956, Brit.); PURSUIT OF THE GRAF SPEE(1957, Brit.); NIGHT AMBUSH(1958, Brit.); SQUARE PEG, THE(1958, Brit.); ROOM AT THE TOP(1959, Brit.); DEAD LUCKY(1960, Brit.); PEEPING TOM(1960, Brit.); TERROR OF THE TONGS, THE(1961, Brit.); MALAGA(1962, Brit.); MILLION DOLLAR MANHUNT(1962, Brit.); ON HER MAJESTY'S SECRET SERVICE(1969, Brit.); BOY WHO TURNED YELLOW, THE(1972, Brit.)
Cedric Worth
PRESIDENT VANISHES, THE(1934), w; WHEN YOU'RE IN LOVE(1937), w; GIRL ON THE RUN(1961), w
Cedric R. Worth
RAMPARTS WE WATCH, THE(1940), w
Constance Worth
CHINA PASSAGE(1937); WINDJAMMER(1937); MYSTERY OF THE WHITE ROOM(1939); ANGELS OVER BROADWAY(1940); BORROWED HERO(1941); CRIMINALS WITHIN(1941); MEET BOSTON BLACKIE(1941); SUSPICION(1941); BOSTON BLACKIE GOES HOLLYWOOD(1942); DAWN EXPRESS, THE(1942); CRIME DOCTOR(1943); CRIME DOCTOR'S STRANGEST CASE(1943); SHE HAS WHAT IT TAKES(1943); TWO SENORITAS FROM CHICAGO(1943); WHEN JOHNNY COMES MARCHING HOME(1943); CYCLONE PRAIRIE RANGERS(1944); FRENCHMAN'S CREEK(1944); JAM SESSION(1944); KLONDIKE KATE(1944); DILLINGER(1945); KID SISTER, THE(1945); SENSATION HUNTERS(1945); WHY GIRLS LEAVE HOME(1945); DEADLINE AT DAWN(1946); SET-UP, THE(1949); WESTERN RENEGADES(1949)
Misc. Talkies
LET'S HAVE FUN(1943); SAGEBRUSH HEROES(1945)
Silents
STARTING POINT, THE(1919, Brit.); FATE'S PLAYTHING(1920, Brit.); EDUCATION OF NICKY, THE(1921, Brit.)
Misc. Silents
NON-CONFORMIST PARSON, A(1919, Brit.); WISP O' THE WOODS(1919, Brit.); LOVE IN THE WELSH HILLS(1921, Brit.)
Dallas Worth
LADY OF BURLESQUE(1943); MAISIE GOES TO RENO(1944); HARVEY GIRLS, THE(1946)
Daniele Jaimes Worth
1984
UNFAITHFULLY YOURS(1984)
David Worth
THREE ROGUES(1931); ROMANCE IN THE RAIN(1934); PARIS IN SPRING(1935); LOVE BEFORE BREAKFAST(1936); MEET NERO WOLFE(1936); PALM SPRINGS(1936); POLO JOE(1936); SONS O' GUNS(1936); DEATH GAME(1977), ph; ANY WHICH WAY YOU CAN(1980), ph; BRONCO BILLY(1980), ph
Misc. Talkies
RIDDLE RANCH(1936); HOLLYWOOD KNIGHT(1979), d
Dorothy Worth
Silents
WHISPERS(1920)
Eric Worth
JOURNEY TOGETHER(1946, Brit.)
Fay Worth
FOLIES DERGERE(1935)
Frank Worth
HA' PENNY BREEZE(1950, Brit.), d, w; BRIDE OF THE MONSTER(1955), m; STREET OF DARKNESS(1958), md
Harry Worth
UNDER TWO FLAGS(1936); GREAT IMPERSONATION, THE(1935); BAR 20 RIDES AGAIN(1936); COWBOY AND THE KID,THE(1936); LIGHTNING BILL CARSON(1936); PHANTOM PATROL(1936); SEA SPOILERS, THE(1936); BIG SHOW, THE(1937); COUNTY FAIR(1937); EASY LIVING(1937); FIREFLY, THE(1937); HOPALONG RIDES AGAIN(1937); KING OF GAMBLERS(1937); LAST TRAIN FROM MADRID, THE(1937); LIFE OF EMILE ZOLA, THE(1937); OUTLAWS OF THE ORIENT(1937); THERE GOES MY GIRL(1937); TOUGH TO HANDLE(1937); CITY GIRL(1938); DANGEROUS TO KNOW(1938); KING OF ALCATRAZ(1938); BEAU GESTE(1939); DISBARRED(1939); MADE FOR EACH OTHER(1939); TOM SAWYER,

DETECTIVE(1939); TWO BRIGHT BOYS(1939); LLANO KID, THE(1940); MARK OF ZORRO, THE(1940); WOMEN WITHOUT NAMES(1940); CYCLONE ON HORSEBACK(1941); FORCED LANDING(1941); HONKY TONK(1941); KANSAS CYCLONE(1941); CAIRO(1942); I MARRIED AN ANGEL(1942); TENNESSEE JOHNSON(1942); RIDERS OF THE RIO GRANDE(1943)
Harry J. Worth
Silents
AMAZING PARTNERSHIP, THE(1921, Brit.); CRIMSON CIRCLE, THE(1922, Brit.); FLAMES OF PASSION(1922, Brit.)
Misc. Silents
(; BLADYS OF THE STEWPONY(1919, Brit.); BLEAK HOUSE(1922, Brit.)
Henry Worth
WARLOCK(1959)
Herman Worth
TURN ON TO LOVE(1969), w
Irene Worth
ONE NIGHT WITH YOU(1948, Brit); SECRET PEOPLE(1952, Brit.); ORDERS TO KILL(1958, Brit.); SCAPEGOAT, THE(1959, Brit.); SEVEN SEAS TO CALAIS(1963, Ital.); KING LEAR(1971, Brit./Den.); NICHOLAS AND ALEXANDRA(1971, Brit.); RICH KIDS(1979); EYEWITNESS(1981); DEATHTRAP(1982)
Jack Worth
NAUGHTY NINETIES, THE(1945); GOLDEN EARRINGS(1947); HIGH WALL, THE(1947); RIDE THE PINK HORSE(1947); WHIPLASH(1948); WHITE HEAT(1949)
Jan Worth
Misc. Talkies
DOLL'S EYE(1982), d
Jody Taylor Worth
UP THE ACADEMY(1980), m
Johnny Worth
MIX ME A PERSON(1962, Brit.), m
Lillian Worth
DANGEROUS PARADISE(1930); FIGHTING SHERIFF, THE(1931); OTHER MEN'S WOMEN(1931); LOVE IS A RACKET(1932); STARS OVER BROADWAY(1935); STRANDED(1935)
Silents
WISE HUSBANDS(; IN SEARCH OF A SINNER(1920); RUSTLER'S RANCH(1926); STAIRS OF SAND(1929)
Lothrop Worth
I WAS A TEENAGE FRANKENSTEIN(1958), ph; UNWED MOTHER(1958), ph; SHOOT OUT AT BIG SAG(1962), ph; BILLY THE KID VS. DRACULA(1966), ph; JESSE JAMES MEETS FRANKENSTEIN'S DAUGHTER(1966), ph; FORT UTAH(1967), ph; HOSTILE GUNS(1967), ph
Lothrop B. Worth
FORT TI(1953), ph; GOG(1954), ph; BATTLE TAXI(1955), ph
Lynne Worth
Misc. Talkies
DOLL'S EYE(1982)
Marvin Worth
BOYS' NIGHT OUT(1962), w; PROMISE HER ANYTHING(1966, Brit.), w; THREE ON A COUCH(1966), w; WHERE'S POPPA?(1970), p; LENNY(1974), p; FIRE SALE(1977), a, p; ROSE, THE(1979), p; UP THE ACADEMY(1980), p; SOUP FOR ONE(1982), p
1984
FALLING IN LOVE(1984), p; RHINESTONE(1984), p; UNFAITHFULLY YOURS(1984), p
Mary Worth
ENCHANTED COTTAGE, THE(1945); TILL THE END OF TIME(1946); DOUBLE LIFE, A(1947)
Misc. Silents
THROUGH THE STORM(1922)
Master Stan Worth
POT O' GOLD(1941)
Michael Worth
DAYS OF JESSE JAMES(1939)
Nancy Worth
UNDER AGE(1941); RAIDERS OF SUNSET PASS(1943); THANK YOUR LUCKY STARS(1943)
Nicholas Worth
FOR PETE'S SAKE!(1966); SCREAM BLACULA SCREAM(1973); DON'T ANSWER THE PHONE(1980); SWAMP THING(1982)
1984
CITY HEAT(1984)
Noelle Worth
FAREWELL, MY LOVELY(1975)
Peggy Worth
Misc. Silents
RED FOAM(1920)
Richard Worth
BREAKERS AHEAD(1935, Brit.)
Stan Worth
CAT, THE(1966), m; YOU'VE GOT TO BE SMART(1967), m&md
Thelma Worth
Silents
JACK RIDER, THE(1921)
William Worth
JOAN OF OZARK(1942)
Jenna Worthen
DEADLY BLESSING(1981); END OF AUGUST, THE(1982)
Keith Worthey
LOVE WITH THE PROPER STRANGER(1963)
George Worthing
Silents
LIGHTNING LARIATS(1927), w
Helen Lee Worthing
Silents
JANICE MEREDITH(1924); NIGHT LIFE OF NEW YORK(1925); DON JUAN(1926); WATCH YOUR WIFE(1926); THUMBS DOWN(1927); VANITY(1927)
Misc. Silents
OTHER WOMAN'S STORY, THE(1925); COUNT OF LUXEMBOURG, THE(1926); LEW TYLER'S WIVES(1926)

Barbara Worthington
TWO TICKETS TO BROADWAY(1951)
Carol Worthington
HOW TO SUCCEED IN BUSINESS WITHOUT REALLY TRYING(1976); I NEVER PROMISED YOU A ROSE GARDEN(1977)
Samantha Worthington
WICKED DIE SLOW, THE(1968)
William Worthington
MAN WHO CAME BACK, THE(1931); SHIPMATES(1931); NO MORE OR-CHIDS(1933); PRESIDENT VANISHES, THE(1934); KEEPER OF THE BEES(1935); MAGNIFICENT OBSESSION(1935); MAN WHO RECLAIMED HIS HEAD, THE(1935); ONE EXCITING ADVENTURE(1935); CAN THIS BE DIXIE?(1936); READY, WILL-ING AND ABLE(1937); TOAST OF NEW YORK, THE(1937); ACCIDENTS WILL HAPPEN(1938); AMAZING DR. CLITTERHOUSE, THE(1938); ANGELS WITH DIRTY FACES(1938); I AM THE LAW(1938); SERGEANT MURPHY(1938); DARK VIC-TORY(1939); ESPIONAGE AGENT(1939); FORGOTTEN WOMAN, THE(1939); OK-LAHOMA KID, THE(1939); LAW AND ORDER(1940)
Misc. Talkies
$20 A WEEK(1935)
Silents
DAMON AND PYTHIAS(1914); OPENED SHUTTERS, THE(1914); ALL WRONG(1919), d; BEAUTIFUL GAMBLER, THE(1921), d; DR. JIM(1921), d; HIGH HEELS(1921); AFRAID TO FIGHT(1922), d; OUT OF THE SILENT NORTH(1922), d; TRACKED TO EARTH(1922), d; KINDLED COURAGE(1923), d; RED LIGHTS(1923); GIRL ON THE STAIRS, THE(1924), d; KID BOOTS(1926); HALF A BRIDE(1928)
Misc. Silents
CALLED BACK(1914); SPY, THE(1914); LOVE NEVER DIES(1916), d; STRANGER FROM SOMEWHERE, A(1916), d; BRINGING HOME FATHER(1917), d; CAR OF CHANCE, THE(1917), d; CLEAN-UP, THE(1917), d; CLOCK, THE(1917), d; DEVIL'S PAY DAY, THE(1917), d; MAN WHO TOOK A CHANCE, THE(1917), d; BELOVED TRAITOR, THE(1918), d; GHOST OF THE RANCHO, THE(1918), d; HIS BIRTH-RIGHT(1918), d; TWENTY-ONE(1918), d; BONDS OF HONOR(1919), d; COURA-GEOUS COWARD, THE(1919), d; DRAGON PAINTER, THE(1919), d; GRAY HORIZON, THE(1919), d; HEART IN PAWN, A(1919), d; HIS DEBT(1919), d; ILLUS-TRIOUS PRINCE, THE(1919), d; MAN BENEATH, THE(1919), d; TONG MAN, THE(1919), d; BEGGAR PRINCE, THE(1920), d; SILENT BARRIER, THE(1920), d; GO STRAIGHT(1921), d; GREATER PROFIT, THE(1921), d; OPENED SHUTTERS(1921), d; UNKNOWN WIFE, THE(1921), d; BOLTED DOOR, THE(1923), d; FASHIONABLE FAKERS(1923), d; BEAUTY AND THE BAD MAN(1925), d
William J. Worthington
FLIRTATION WALK(1934); POLO JOE(1936); DEVIL'S PLAYGROUND(1937); UN-ION PACIFIC(1939)
John Worthy
WALKING ON AIR(1946, Brit.), w
Johnny Worthy
WALKING ON AIR(1946, Brit.)
Sean Worthy
HOPSCOTCH(1980)
Frank "Huck" Wortman
Silents
INTOLERANCE(1916), set d
George F. Worts
ONCE A GENTLEMAN(1930), w; PHANTOM PRESIDENT, THE(1932), w; ABSO-LUTE QUIET(1936), w
George Frank Worts
Silents
MADNESS OF YOUTH(1923), w
Katia Wostrikoff
1984
SUNDAY IN THE COUNTRY, A(1984, Fr.)
Constance Woth
Misc. Silents
BACHELOR'S BABY, A(1922, Brit.)
Gertrude Wottitz
HOUSE ON 92ND STREET, THE(1945)
Walter Wottitz
LONGEST DAY, THE(1962), ph; TRAIN, THE(1965, Fr./Ital./U.S.), ph; UP FROM THE BEACH(1965), ph; UPPER HAND, THE(1967, Fr./Ital./Ger.), ph; 24 HOURS IN A WOMAN'S LIFE(1968, Fr./Ger.), ph; LEATHER AND NYLON(1969, Fr./Ital.), ph; THOSE DARING YOUNG MEN IN THEIR JAUNTY JALOPIES(1969, Fr./Brit./Ital.), ph; COP, A(1973, Fr.), ph; CAT, THE(1975, Fr.), ph; LA CAGE(1975, Fr.), ph; DIRTY MONEY(1977, Fr.), ph
Herman Wouk
LADY BE GOOD(1941), w; SLATTERY'S HURRICANE(1949), w; HER FIRST RO-MANCE(1951), w; CONFIDENTIAL CONNIE(1953), w; CAINE MUTINY, THE(1954), w; MARJORIE MORNINGSTAR(1958), w; YOUNGBLOOD HAWKE(1964), w
Pierre Would
ROYAL AFFAIRS IN VERSAILLES(1957, Fr.)
Michael Woulfe
LOCKET, THE(1946), cos; SEARCHING WIND, THE(1946), cos; STRANGER, THE(1946), cos; WHERE DANGER LIVES(1950), cos; WOMAN ON PIER 13, THE(1950), cos; RACKET, THE(1951), cos; ROADBLOCK(1951), cos; TWO TICKETS TO BROADWAY(1951), cos; LUSTY MEN, THE(1952), cos; MACAO(1952), cos; AN-GEL FACE(1953), cos; SECOND CHANCE(1953), cos; SPLIT SECOND(1953), cos; FRENCH LINE, THE(1954), cos; BENGAZI(1955), cos; GLORY(1955), cos; SON OF SINBAD(1955), cos; UNDERWATER!(1955), cos; JET PILOT(1957), cos; HAPPY BIRTHDAY, WANDA JUNE(1971), cos
Eric Vant Wout
BRIDGE TOO FAR, A(1977, Brit.)
Harry Wowchuk
JUD(1971); PARASITE(1982), stunts
Kannikar Wowklee
BRIDGE ON THE RIVER KWAI, THE(1957)
Vigny Wowor
SOPHIE'S WAYS(1970, Fr.)
Egil Woxholt
MYSTERIOUS ISLAND(1961, U.S./Brit.), ph; ON HER MAJESTY'S SECRET SER-VICE(1969, Brit.), ph

Greta Woxholt
BOYS WILL BE GIRLS(1937, Brit.)
Stig Woxter
DEAR JOHN(1966, Swed.)
Janet Woytak
CANNONBALL RUN, THE(1981)
W. Woytecki
VILLAGE, THE(1953, Brit./Switz.)
Victoria Wozniak
LOOSE ENDS(1975), p, w; PURPLE HAZE(1982), w
W. Wozniak
LOTNA(1966, Pol.)
Paul Woznicki
FIEND(, m
Wladyslaw Woznik
FIRST START(1953, Pol.)
Dan Woznow
FIRST BLOOD(1982)
Joan Wrae
APARTMENT FOR PEGGY(1948)
Charlie Wragg
DOWN OUR ALLEY(1939, Brit.)
Ed Wragge
DOUBLE LIFE, A(1947)
Edward Wragge
RAMPARTS WE WATCH, THE(1940)
Basil Wrangel
BED OF ROSES(1933), ed; LADIES THEY TALK ABOUT(1933), ed; GOOD EARTH, THE(1937), ed; BLUE SIERRA(1946), animal d
Basil Wrangell
MARIANNE(1929), ed; VOICE OF THE CITY(1929), ed; LET US BE GAY(1930), ed; LOVE IN THE ROUGH(1930), ed; MIN AND BILL(1930), ed; WOMAN RACKET, THE(1930), ed; FREAKS(1932), ed; AGGIE APPLEBY, MAKER OF MEN(1933), ed; GABRIEL OVER THE WHITE HOUSE(1933), ed; MIDSHIPMAN JACK(1933), ed; WHEN LADIES MEET(1933), ed; HIDE-OUT(1934), ed; SHADOW OF A DOUBT(1935), ed; WHIPSAW(1936), ed; COURAGE OF LASSIE(1946), animal d; HEARTA-CHES(1947), d; PHILO VANCE'S GAMBLE(1947), d; LOVE HAPPY(1949), ed; TOBOR THE GREAT(1954), ed; NO MAN IS AN ISLAND(1962), ed; YANK IN VIET-NAM, A(1964), ed
Silents
CALIFORNIA(1927), ed; IN OLD KENTUCKY(1927), ed; TWELVE MILES OUT(1927), ed; CAMERAMAN, THE(1928), ed; LATEST FROM PARIS, THE(1928), ed
Jack Wrangler
Misc. Talkies
IN LOVE(1983)
Eric Wrate
DR. FRANKENSTEIN ON CAMPUS(1970, Can.), ed; HIGH-BALLIN'(1978), ed; IF YOU COULD SEE WHAT I HEAR(1982), ed
1984
HIGHPOINT(1984, Can.), ed
Bonita Granville Wrather
MAGIC OF LASSIE, THE(1978), p
Jack Wrather
GUILTY, THE(1947), p; HIGH TIDE(1947), p; PERILOUS WATERS(1948), p; STRIKE IT RICH(1948), p; GUILTY OF TREASON(1950), p; LONE RANGER AND THE LOST CITY OF GOLD, THE(1958), p
Jack Wrather, Jr.
BIG LAND, THE(1957)
Albert Wray
Misc. Talkies
HER UNBORN CHILD(1933), d
Aloha Wray
GEORGE WHITE'S 1935 SCANDALS(1935)
Ardel Wray
FALCON AND THE CO-EDS, THE(1943), w; I WALKED WITH A ZOMBIE(1943), w; LEOPARD MAN, THE(1943), w; YOUTH RUNS WILD(1944), w; ISLE OF THE DEAD(1945), w
Bill Wray
PRIVATE SCHOOL(1983)
Bradley King Wray
YOUNG NOWHERES(1929), w
Dick Wray
FRONTIER SCOUT(1939), ed
Eileen Wray
CHEER THE BRAVE(1951, Brit.)
Fay Wray
THUNDERBOLT(1929); BEHIND THE MAKEUP(1930); BORDER LEGION, THE(1930); POINTED HEELS(1930); SEA GOD, THE(1930); TEXAN, THE(1930); CAPTAIN THUNDER(1931); CONQUERING HORDE, THE(1931); DIRIGIBLE(1931); FINGER POINTS, THE(1931); LAWYER'S SECRET, THE(1931); THREE RO-GUES(1931); UNHOLY GARDEN, THE(1931); DOCTOR X(1932); MOST DANGEROUS GAME, THE(1932); STOWAWAY(1932); ANN CARVER'S PROFESSION(1933); BE-LOW THE SEA(1933); BIG BRAIN, THE(1933); BOWERY, THE(1933); KING KONG(1933); MASTER OF MEN(1933); MYSTERY OF THE WAX MUSEUM, THE(1933); ONE SUNDAY AFTERNOON(1933); SHANGHAI MADNESS(1933); VAM-PIRE BAT, THE(1933); WOMAN I STOLE, THE(1933); AFFAIRS OF CELLINI, THE(1934); BLACK MOON(1934); CHEATING CHEATERS(1934); COUNTESS OF MONTE CRISTO, THE(1934); MADAME SPY(1934); ONCE TO EVERY WOMAN(1934); RICHEST GIRL IN THE WORLD, THE(1934); VIVA VILLA!(1934); WOMAN IN THE DARK(1934); ALIAS BULLDOG DRUMMOND(1935, Brit.); CLAIRVOYANT, THE(1935, Brit.); COME OUT OF THE PANTRY(1935, Brit.); MILLS OF THE GODS(1935); WHITE LIES(1935); ROAMING LADY(1936); THEY MET IN A TAX-I(1936); IT HAPPENED IN HOLLYWOOD(1937); MURDER IN GREENWICH VIL-LAGE(1937); JURY'S SECRET, THE(1938); NAVY SECRETS(1939); SMASHING THE SPY RING(1939); WILDCAT BUS(1940); ADAM HAD FOUR SONS(1941); MELODY FOR THREE(1941); WHEN KNIGHTS WERE BOLD(1942, Brit.); THIS IS THE LIFE(1944), w; SMALL TOWN GIRL(1953); TREASURE OF THE GOLDEN CON-DOR(1953); COBWEB, THE(1955); QUEEN BEE(1955); HELL ON FRISCO BAY(1956); ROCK, PRETTY BABY(1956); CRIME OF PASSION(1957); TAMMY AND THE BACHELOR(1957); DRAGSTRIP RIOT(1958); SUMMER LOVE(1958)

John Wray

Misc. Talkies
NOT A LADIES MAN(1942)
Silents
LAZY LIGHTNING(1926); WEDDING MARCH, THE(1927); STREET OF SIN, THE(1928); FOUR FEATHERS(1929)
Misc. Silents
COAST PATROL, THE(1925); MAN IN THE SADDLE, THE(1926); WILD HORSE STAMPEDE, THE(1926); LOCO LUCK(1927); ONE MAN GAME, A(1927); SPURS AND SADDLES(1927); FIRST KISS, THE(1928); LEGION OF THE CONDEMNED(1928)

John Wray
ALIBI(1929), w; NEW YORK NIGHTS(1929); ALL QUIET ON THE WESTERN FRONT(1930); CZAR OF BRODWAY, THE(1930); SAP FROM SYRACUSE, THE(1930), w; QUICK MILLIONS(1931); SAFE IN HELL(1931); SILENCE(1931); CENTRAL PARK(1932); DOCTOR X(1932); HIGH PRESSURE(1932); I AM A FUGITIVE FROM A CHAIN GANG(1932); MATCH KING, THE(1932); MIRACLE MAN, THE(1932); MISS PINKERTON(1932); MOUTHPIECE, THE(1932); RICH ARE ALWAYS WITH US, THE(1932); WOMAN FROM MONTE CARLO, THE(1932); AFTER TONIGHT(1933); DEATH KISS, THE(1933); BIG SHAKEDOWN, THE(1934); BOMBAY MAIL(1934); CAT'S PAW, THE(1934); CROSBY CASE, THE(1934); EMBARRASSING MOMENTS(1934); FIFTEEN WIVES(1934); GREEN EYES(1934); I'LL FIX IT(1934); LONE COWBOY(1934); LOVE CAPTIVE, THE(1934); MOST PRECIOUS THING IN LIFE(1934); ATLANTIC ADVENTURE(1935); BAD BOY(1935); FRISCO KID(1935); GREAT HOTEL MURDER(1935); I AM A THIEF(1935); LADIES LOVE DANGER(1935); MEN WITHOUT NAMES(1935); STRANDED(1935); WHOLE TOWN'S TALKING, THE(1935); MR. DEEDS GOES TO TOWN(1936); POOR LITTLE RICH GIRL(1936); PRESIDENT'S MYSTERY, THE(1936); SON COMES HOME, A(1936); SWORN ENEMY(1936); VALIANT IS THE WORD FOR CARRIE(1936); CIRCUS GIRL(1937); DEVIL IS DRIVING, THE(1937); MAN BETRAYED, A(1937); ON SUCH A NIGHT(1937); OUTCAST(1937); WE WHO ARE ABOUT TO DIE(1937); WOMEN MEN MARRY, THE(1937); YOU ONLY LIVE ONCE(1937); CRIME TAKES A HOLIDAY(1938); GANGS OF NEW YORK(1938); MAKING THE HEADLINES(1938); MAN TO REMEMBER, A(1938); PROFESSOR BEWARE(1938); SPAWN OF THE NORTH(1938); TENTH AVENUE KID(1938); ALMOST A GENTLEMAN(1939); AMAZING MR. WILLIAMS(1939); BLACKMAIL(1939); CAT AND THE CANARY, THE(1939); EACH DAWN I DIE(1939); GOLDEN BOY(1939); GONE WITH THE WIND(1939); PACIFIC LINER(1939); RISKY BUSINESS(1939); SMUGGLED CARGO(1939); WINTER CARNIVAL(1939); DOCTOR TAKES A WIFE(1940); MAN FROM DAKOTA, THE(1940); REMEMBER THE NIGHT(1940); SWISS FAMILY ROBINSON(1940); WONDER MAN(1945), ch

John G. Wray
CARELESS AGE(1929), d

John Griffith Wray
MOST IMMORAL LADY, A(1929), d
Silents
BEAU REVEL(1921), d; LYING LIPS(1921), d; ANNA CHRISTIE(1923), d; SOUL OF THE BEAST(1923), d; WINDING STAIR, THE(1925), d; GILDED BUTTERFLY, THE(1926), d; SINGED(1927), d; GATEWAY OF THE MOON, THE(1928), d
Misc. Silents
HOMESPUN FOLKS(1920), d; HAIL THE WOMAN(1921), d; HER REPUTATION(1923), d; HUMAN WRECKAGE(1923), d; WHAT A WIFE LEARNED(1923), d; MARRIAGE CHEAT, THE(1924), d

May Wray
BROTHERS AND SISTERS(1980, Brit.)

Richard Wray
TIMBER WAR(1936), ed; PHANTOM RANGER(1938), ed

Richard C. Wray
MAGIC TOWN(1947), ed

Richard G. Wray
RED BLOOD OF COURAGE(1935), ed; SONG OF THE TRAIL(1936), ed; WILDCAT TROOPER(1936), ed; ANYTHING FOR A THRILL(1937), ed; ROARING SIX GUNS(1937), ed; ROUGH RIDIN' RHYTHM(1937), ed; SWING IT, PROFESSOR(1937), ed; WHISTLING BULLETS(1937), ed; WILD HORSE ROUND-UP(1937), ed; LAND OF FIGHTING MEN(1938), ed; TERROR OF TINY TOWN, THE(1938), ed; TWO-GUN JUSTICE(1938), ed; WINNER'S CIRCLE, THE(1948), ed; THREE GUNS FOR TEXAS(1968), ed; COCKEYED COWBOYS OF CALICO COUNTY, THE(1970), ed

Sheila Wray
LYONS MAIL, THE(1931, Brit.)

Ted Wray
DOUBLE CROSS(1941)

Wilma Wray
WORDS AND MUSIC(1929)

Tony Wredden
1984
MAJDHAR(1984, Brit.)

Casper Wrede
BARBER OF STAMFORD HILL, THE(1963, Brit.), d; PRIVATE POTTER(1963, Brit.), d, w; ONE DAY IN THE LIFE OF IVAN DENISOVICH(1971, U.S./Brit./Norway), p&d; TERRORISTS, THE(1975, Brit.), d

Trevor Wreen
SYMPTOMS(1976, Brit.), ph

Denis Wreford
NOTHING VENTURE(1948, Brit.), art d; SOMEONE AT THE DOOR(1950, Brit.), art d; MAKE ME AN OFFER(1954, Brit.), art d; MAKE MINE A MILLION(1965, Brit.), art d

Dennis Wreford
GRAND ESCAPADE, THE(1946, Brit.), art d

Edgar Wreford
SUSPENDED ALIBI(1957, Brit.); KNACK ... AND HOW TO GET IT, THE(1965, Brit.)

John Wreford
MAROC 7(1967, Brit.); MUTATIONS, THE(1974, Brit.)

John Wregg
STATUE, THE(1971, Brit.)

Alan Wren
GREAT MR. HANDEL, THE(1942, Brit.)

Bob Wren
Misc. Talkies
ACID EATERS, THE(1968)

Chris Wren
HITLER'S CHILDREN(1942); GREAT STAGECOACH ROBBERY(1945)

Gwenda Wren
Silents
LURE OF LONDON, THE(1914, Brit.)

P. C. Wren
Silents
BEAU GESTE(1926), w; BEAU SABREUR(1928), w

Percival Christopher Wren
BEAU GESTE(1939), w; BEAU GESTE(1966), w

Richard Wren
WICKER MAN, THE(1974, Brit.); HIDING PLACE, THE(1975); EAGLE HAS LANDED, THE(1976, Brit.); ESCAPE TO ATHENA(1979, Brit.); YELLOWBEARD(1983)

Sam Wren
DR. SOCRATES(1935); I MARRIED A DOCTOR(1936); MARKED WOMAN(1937); SHALL WE DANCE(1937); SING WHILE YOU'RE ABLE(1937); HOUSE ACROSS THE BAY, THE(1940); DIXIE DUGAN(1943); SWEET ROSIE O'GRADY(1943); THEY CAME TO BLOW UP AMERICA(1943); IRISH EYES ARE SMILING(1944)

Sylvia Wren
LADY GODIVA RIDES AGAIN(1955, Brit.)

Philip Wrestler
CROSSTRAP(1962, Brit.), w

Ann Wrigg
UNDERCOVER AGENT(1935, Brit.); WITNESS IN THE DARK(1959, Brit.); MURDER CAN BE DEADLY(1963, Brit.)

Adrian Wright
END PLAY(1975, Aus.); SUMMERFIELD(1977, Aus.); SURVIVOR(1980, Aus.)

Alan Wright
WAGNER(1983, Brit./Hung./Aust.), p

Alex Wright
VENGEANCE IS MINE(1948, Brit.)

Alfred E. Wright
Silents
AS A MAN LIVES(1923)

Alvin Wright
HAWMPS!(1976)

Amy Wright
DEER HUNTER, THE(1978); GIRLFRIENDS(1978); AMITYVILLE HORROR, THE(1979); BREAKING AWAY(1979); WISE BLOOD(1979, U.S./Ger.); HEARTLAND(1980); INSIDE MOVES(1980); STARDUST MEMORIES(1980)

Armand "Curly" Wright
PANAMINT'S BAD MAN(1938); HOUSE ACROSS THE BAY, THE(1940); RAIDERS OF THE DESERT(1941); SHE HAS WHAT IT TAKES(1943)

Armand Wright
TO BE OR NOT TO BE(1942)

Arthur Wright
DOLEMITE(1975), m; HUMAN TORNADO, THE(1976), m; SKIN DEEP(1978, New Zealand)

Barbara Bel Wright
CRUEL TOWER, THE(1956)

Basil Wright
ONE WISH TOO MANY(1956, Brit.), p

Barbara Bell Wright
TROUBLE WITH ANGELS, THE(1966)

Ben H. Wright
EXILE, THE(1947); KISS THE BLOOD OFF MY HANDS(1948)

Ben Wright
UNTIL THEY SAIL(1957); WELL DONE, HENRY(1936, Brit.); BOTANY BAY(1953); DESERT RATS, THE(1953); PRINCE VALIANT(1954); MAN CALLED PETER, THE(1955); MOONFLEET(1955); PRINCE OF PLAYERS(1955); RACERS, THE(1955); D-DAY, THE SIXTH OF JUNE(1956); JOHNNY CONCHO(1956); ON THE THRESHOLD OF SPACE(1956); POWER AND THE PRIZE, THE(1956); 23 PACES TO BAKER STREET(1956); KISS THEM FOR ME(1957); PHARAOH'S CURSE(1957); DESERT HELL(1958); VILLA!(1958); JOURNEY TO THE CENTER OF THE EARTH(1959); THESE THOUSAND HILLS(1959); WRECK OF THE MARY DEARE, THE(1959); JUDGMENT AT NUREMBERG(1961); ONE HUNDRED AND ONE DALMATIANS(1961); OPERATION BOTTLENECK(1961); MUTINY ON THE BOUNTY(1962); GATHERING OF EAGLES, A(1963); PRIZE, THE(1963); MY FAIR LADY(1964); MY BLOOD RUNS COLD(1965); SOUND OF MUSIC, THE(1965); FORTUNE COOKIE, THE(1966); MUNSTER, GO HOME(1966); SAND PEBBLES, THE(1966); JUNGLE BOOK, THE(1967); RAID ON ROMMEL(1971); ARNOLD(1973); TERROR IN THE WAX MUSEUM(1973)
1984
LAUGHTER HOUSE(1984, Brit.)

Bertie Wright
Silents
GENERAL JOHN REGAN(1921, Brit.); ROYAL OAK, THE(1923, Brit.)
Misc. Silents
LITTLE BIT OF FLUFF, A(1919, Brit.); DEAR FOOL, A(1921, Brit.); SAILOR TRAMP, A(1922, Brit.); WHEELS OF CHANCE, THE(1922, Brit.)

Betty Wright
LITTLE MISS BROADWAY(1947), w

Betty Huntley Wright
LITTLE MISS NOBODY(1933, Brit.); NAUGHTY CINDERELLA(1933, Brit.); STRAUSS' GREAT WALTZ(1934, Brit.); LAST WALTZ, THE(1936, Brit.); JUST JOE(1960, Brit.)

Bloyce Wright
BLOOD ON THE ARROW(1964)

Blu Wright
FOUR FAST GUNS(1959); SQUAD CAR(1961)

Bob Wright
DUDES ARE PRETTY PEOPLE(1942), m

Bob Wright
TALL STORY(1960)

Bruce Wright
BATTLESTAR GALACTICA(1979)

Buddy Wright
STREET WITH NO NAME, THE(1948); WHIPLASH(1948)

Charles Wright
MY WIFE'S FAMILY(1962, Brit.)
Charles A. Wright
Silents
HIS FATHER'S SON(1917)
Clarence Wright
IT'S THAT MAN AGAIN(1943, Brit.); PLACE OF ONE'S OWN, A(1945, Brit.); DUAL ALIBI(1947, Brit.)
Clay Wright
MORE AMERICAN GRAFFITI(1979); UNDER FIRE(1983)
Clayton Wright
PRIVATE BENJAMIN(1980)
Cobina Wright, Jr.
ACCENT ON LOVE(1941); CHARLIE CHAN IN RIO(1941); MOON OVER MIA-MI(1941); MURDER AMONG FRIENDS(1941); SMALL TOWN DEB(1941); WEEKEND IN HAVANA(1941); FOOTLIGHT SERENADE(1942); RIGHT TO THE HEART(1942); SON OF FURY(1942); DANGER! WOMEN AT WORK(1943); SOMETHING TO SHOUT ABOUT(1943)
Cobina Wright, Sr.
SWEETHEARTS OF THE U.S.A.(1944); RAZOR'S EDGE, THE(1946)
Cowley Wright
Silents
ERNEST MALTRAVERS(1920, Brit.)
Misc. Silents
ROCKS OF VALPRE, THE(1919, Brit.); CHANNINGS, THE(1920, Brit.); ERNEST MALTRAVERS(1920, Brit.)
Curley Wright
LAWYER MAN(1933); SAILOR'S LUCK(1933)
Dave Wright
FLAMING FRONTIER(1958, Can.)
Silents
GOLD RUSH, THE(1925)
David Wright
RESTLESS ONES, THE(1965)
Dorothy Wright
BLACK RODEO(1972)
Dorsey Wright
HAIR(1979); RAGTIME(1981)
1984
HOTEL NEW HAMPSHIRE, THE(1984)
Douglas Wright
RHYTHM OF THE SADDLE(1938); TILL THE CLOUDS ROLL BY(1946)
Ebony Wright
SOUNDER, PART 2(1976); PENITENTIARY II(1982)
Ed Wright
GANG WAR(1958); SHOWDOWN AT BOOT HILL(1958); OREGON TRAIL, THE(1959); WHEN A STRANGER CALLS(1979)
Eddie Wright
FAT SPY(1966)
Elizabeth Wright
EXTRA DAY, THE(1956, Brit.)
Ellsworth Wright
GO, MAN, GO!(1954)
Ethel Wright
Silents
ENCHANTED COTTAGE, THE(1924)
Eugenia Wright
PENITENTIARY II(1982)
F. Cowley Wright
Misc. Silents
SYBIL(1921, Brit.)
F. Harmon Wright
HARDBOILED ROSE(1929), d
Misc. Silents
THREE WISE CROOKS(1925), d
Fanny Wright
YOUTHFUL FOLLY(1934, Brit.); RADIO PIRATES(1935, Brit.); RAT, THE(1938, Brit.); JOHN OF THE FAIR(1962, Brit.)
Florence Wright
GREAT DICTATOR, THE(1940); LOOK WHO'S LAUGHING(1941); MISBEHAVING HUSBANDS(1941); YOKEL BOY(1942)
Francis Wright [Morris]
PALS OF THE RANGE(1935)
Fred Wright
Silents
MOLLY BAWN(1916, Brit.); LA POUPEE(1920, Brit.); GLORIOUS ADVENTURE, THE(1922, U.S./Brit.)
Misc. Silents
FOR SALE(1918), d; MYSTERIOUS CLIENT, THE(1918), d; HORNET'S NEST(1923, Brit.); M'LORD OF THE WHITE ROAD(1923, Brit.); CINDERS(1926, Brit.)
Fred E. Wright
Silents
BREAKER, THE(1916), d&w
Misc. Silents
GRAUSTARK(1915), d; IN THE PALACE OF THE KING(1915), d; WHITE SISTER, THE(1915), d; CAPTAIN JINKS OF THE HORSE MARINES(1916), d; LITTLE SHE-PHERD OF BARGIAN ROW, THE(1916), d; PRINCE OF GRAUSTARK, THE(1916), d; FIBBERS, THE(1917), d; KILL-JOY, THE(1917), d; MAN WHO WAS AFRAID, THE(1917), d; TRUFFLERS, THE(1917), d
Gai Wright
HELP!(1965, Brit.)
Gareth Wright
ALL THE RIGHT NOISES(1973, Brit.)
Gary Wright
BENJAMIN(1973, Ger.), m; SGT. PEPPER'S LONELY HEARTS CLUB BAND(1978); ENDANGERED SPECIES(1982), m
Gene Wright
LITTLE WILDCAT, THE(1928), w

Silents
ABABIAN KNIGHT, AN(1920), w; LITTLE WILDCAT(1922), w; AS MAN DESI-RES(1925), w; YELLOW FINGERS(1926), w
Geoffrey Wright
SHIPS WITH WINGS(1942, Brit.), m; BEHIND THE MASK(1958, Brit.), m
George Wright
THREE ON A HONEYMOON(1934), w
Silents
EUGENE ARAM(1915)
George A. Wright
Silents
RANSON'S FOLLY(1915); AMERICAN WIDOW, AN(1917)
Misc. Silents
CATSPAW, THE(1916), d; HEART OF THE HILLS, THE(1916); WHY NOT MAR-RY?(1922)
Gilbert Wright
CALIFORNIAN, THE(1937), w; SPRINGTIME IN THE ROCKIES(1937), w; THANKS FOR EVERYTHING(1938), w; WILD HORSE RODEO(1938), w; UTAH(1945), w
Glen Wright
HANG'EM HIGH(1968), cos
Glenn Wright
DIRTY HARRY(1971), cos; MAN AND BOY(1972), cos; GAUNTLET, THE(1977), cos; EVERY WHICH WAY BUT LOOSE(1978), cos; ESCAPE FROM ALCATRAZ(1979); ANY WHICH WAY YOU CAN(1980), cos; HONKYTONK MAN(1982); SUDDEN IMPACT(1983), cos
1984
TIGHTROPE(1984), a, cos
Guy Tilden Wright
Silents
FORBIDDEN CARGOES(1925, Brit.)
Gwendolyn Wright
ME(1970, Fr.), titles
H.H. Wright
Misc. Silents
GARDEN OF ALLAH, THE(1927)
Haidee Wright
BLARNEY KISS(1933, Brit.); STRANGE EVIDENCE(1933, Brit.); POWER(1934, Brit.); TOMORROW WE LIVE(1936, Brit.); CITADEL, THE(1938)
Silents
EVIDENCE(1915); AUNT RACHEL(1920, Brit.); OLD COUNTRY, THE(1921, Brit.); GLORIOUS ADVENTURE, THE(1922, U.S./Brit.); PADDY, THE NEXT BEST THING(1923, Brit.); WINNING GOAL, THE(1929, Brit.)
Misc. Silents
IN BONDAGE(1919, Brit.); BACHELOR'S BABY, A(1922, Brit.); SEA URCHIN, THE(1926, Brit.)
Harland Wright
BENJI(1974), prod d; HAWMPS!(1976), prod d; FOR THE LOVE OF BENJI(1977), prod d; THE DOUBLE McGUFFIN(1979), prod d
Harold Bell Wright
EYES OF THE WORLD, THE(1930), w; WHEN A MAN'S A MAN(1935), w; DAN MATTHEWS(1936), w; MINE WITH THE IRON DOOR, THE(1936), w; WILD BRIAN KENT(1936), w; CALIFORNIAN, THE(1937), w; IT HAPPENED OUT WEST(1937), w; SECRET VALLEY(1937), w; WESTERN GOLD(1937), w; SHEPHERD OF THE HILLS, THE(1941), w; SHEPHERD OF THE HILLS, THE(1964), w
Silents
WINNING OF BARBARA WORTH, THE(1926), w
Misc. Silents
SHEPHERD OF THE HILLS, THE(1920), d
Harry Wright
Misc. Silents
EARLY BIRDS(1923, Brit.)
Hazel Wright
FIDDLER ON THE ROOF(1971)
Heather Wright
BELSTONE FOX, THE(1976, 1976); SHOUT AT THE DEVIL(1976, Brit.); HORROR PLANET(1982, Brit.)
Helen Wright
DAMES AHOY(1930); SPURS(1930)
Silents
SCARLET SIN, THE(1915); MISTRESS OF SHENSTONE, THE(1921)
Misc. Silents
STRANGER FROM SOMEWHERE, A(1916); CAR OF CHANCE, THE(1917); LASH OF POWER, THE(1917); POLLY REDHEAD(1917)
Herbert J. Wright
SHADOW OF THE HAWK(1976, Can.), w
Hilary Wright
1984
TERMINATOR, THE(1984), cos
Howard Wright
GLASS WEB, THE(1953); LAST OF THE PONY RIDERS(1953); DRIVE A CROOKED ROAD(1954); LONG, LONG TRAILER, THE(1954); CELL 2455, DEATH ROW(1955); GUN THAT WON THE WEST, THE(1955); HEADLINE HUNTERS(1955); ONE DESIRE(1955); SEMINOLE UPRISING(1955); SIX BRIDGES TO CROSS(1955); TO HELL AND BACK(1955); CHA-CHA-CHA BOOM(1956); STRANGER AT MY DOOR(1956); BONNIE PARKER STORY, THE(1958); SPIDER, THE(1958); WAR OF THE COLOSSAL BEAST(1958); LEGEND OF TOM DOOLEY, THE(1959); LOUISIANA HUSSY(1960); FIVE MINUTES TO LIVE(1961); CHASE, THE(1966); GOOD TI-MES(1967); WHAT EVER HAPPENED TO AUNT ALICE?(1969)
Hugh E. Wright
AULD LANG SYNE(1929, Brit.), a, w; DOWN RIVER(1931, Brit.); EAST LYNNE ON THE WESTERN FRONT(1931, Brit.); GREAT GAY ROAD(1931, Brit.); STRAN-GLEHOLD(1931, Brit.); BROTHER ALFRED(1932, Brit.); LORD CAMBER'S LA-DIES(1932, Brit.); GOOD COMPANIONS(1933, Brit.); LOVE WAGER, THE(1933, Brit.); MY OLD DUCHESS(1933, Brit.); SHOT IN THE DARK, A(1933, Brit.); ADVENTURE LIMITED(1934, Brit.); CRAZY PEOPLE(1934, Brit.); FOR LOVE OR MONEY(1934, Brit.); GET YOUR MAN(1934, Brit.); ON THE AIR(1934, Brit.); WIDOW'S MIGHT(1934, Brit.); YOU MADE ME LOVE YOU(1934, Brit.); NELL GWYN(1935, Brit.); RADIO FOLLIES(1935, Brit.); SCROOGE(1935, Brit.); ROYAL EAGLE(1936, Brit.)

Humberston Wright

Silents

OLD CURIOSITY SHOP, THE(1921, Brit.); SQUIBS(1921, Brit.); SQUIBS WINS THE CALCUTTA SWEEP(1922, Brit.); SQUIBS, MP(1923, Brit.); SQUIBS' HONEYMOON(1926, Brit.)

Misc. Silents

GARRYOWEN(1920, Brit.); NOTHING ELSE MATTERS(1920, Brit.); MARY-FIND-THE-GOLD(1921, Brit.); SAILOR TRAMP, A(1922, Brit.)

Humberstone Wright

HIGH TREASON(1929, Brit.); ALF'S BUTTON(1930, Brit.); DOWN RIVER(1931, Brit.); MARRIAGE BOND, THE(1932, Brit.); COMMISSIONAIRE(1933, Brit.); STRICTLY ILLEGAL(1935, Brit.); ESCAPE DANGEROUS(1947, Brit.)

Silents

GARDEN OF RESURRECTION, THE(1919, Brit.); WALLS OF PREJUDICE(1920, Brit.); CREATION(1922, Brit.), d; GAY CORINTHIAN, THE(1924); SLAVES OF DESTINY(1924, Brit.); FLAG LIEUTENANT, THE(1926, Brit.); SAFETY FIRST(1926, Brit.); ARCADIANS, THE(1927, Brit.); SISTER TO ASSIST 'ER, A(1927, Brit.); PHYSICIAN, THE(1928, Brit.)

Misc. Silents

GOD'S CLAY(1919, Brit.); ROCKS OF VALPRE, THE(1919, Brit.); ROMANCE OF LADY HAMILTON, THE(1919, Brit.); LITTLE WELSH GIRL, THE(1920, Brit.); UNCLE DICK'S DARLING(1920, Brit.); FIFTH FORM AT ST. DOMINIC'S, THE(1921, Brit.); SPORTING DOUBLE, A(1922, Brit.); BOADICEA(1926, Brit.); FLIGHT COMMANDER, THE(1927, Brit.); SAILORS DON'T CARE(1928, Brit.); MASTER AND MAN(1929, Brit.)

Humberstone Wright

WHITE CARGO(1930, Brit.); IN A MONASTERY GARDEN(1935)

Humberston Wright

HOUSE OF TRENT, THE(1933, Brit.); YOUNG AND INNOCENT(1938, Brit.)

Silents

TRAPPED BY THE LONDON SHARKS(1916, Brit.); IN THE BLOOD(1923, Brit.); ROSES OF PICARDY(1927, Brit.)

Misc. Silents

ISLAND OF ROMANCE, THE(1922, Brit.), d; LOVE STORY OF ALIETTE BRUNTON, THE(1924, Brit.)

Huntley Wright

EMPRESS AND I, THE(1933, Ger.); GOING STRAIGHT(1933, Brit.); HEART SONG(1933, Brit.); LOOK UP AND LAUGH(1935, Brit.)

Irene Gorman Wright

OSTERMAN WEEKEND, THE(1983)

Iris Wright

MEN ARE NOT GODS(1937, Brit.), w

J. J. Wright

TERROR EYES(1981)

Jack Wright

NEW LEAF, A(1971), set d; SAVAGES(1972), art d; WATCHED(1974), ph

Jack Wright, Jr.

LAST MILE, THE(1959), set d; MIDDLE OF THE NIGHT(1959), set d; GROUP, THE(1966), set d

Jack Wright III

LIONS LOVE(1969), art d

Jackie Lynn Wright

COAL MINER'S DAUGHTER(1980)

Jackie Wright

NEW GIRL IN TOWN(1977)

Janet Wright

MC CABE AND MRS. MILLER(1971); WOLFPEN PRINCIPLE, THE(1974, Can.); LADIES AND GENTLEMEN, THE FABULOUS STAINS(1982)

Jennifer Wright

DOOMSDAY AT ELEVEN(1963 Brit.)

Jenny Wright

PINK FLOYD–THE WALL(1982, Brit.); WORLD ACCORDING TO GARP, The(1982)

1984

WILD LIFE, THE(1984)

Jenny Lee Wright

HUSBANDS(1970); TRIPLE ECHO, THE(1973, Brit.); MADHOUSE(1974, Brit.); SLIPPER AND THE ROSE, THE(1976, Brit.)

Jerry Wright

DARK SIDE OF TOMORROW, THE(1970), m

Jim Wright

NOTHING BUT A MAN(1964); ELECTRA GLIDE IN BLUE(1973)

Jimmy Wright

Misc. Talkies

SOULS OF SIN(1949)

Joanna Wright

WHERE THE BULLETS FLY(1966, Brit.), cos

Joe Wright

CHARLIE CHAN CARRIES ON(1931), set d; MURDERERS' ROW(1966), art d; SILENCERS, THE(1966), art d; WALK, DON'T RUN(1966), prod d; AMBUSHERS, THE(1967), art d; WRECKING CREW, THE(1968), art d

John Wright

MC HALE'S NAVY(1964); MC HALE'S NAVY JOINS THE AIR FORCE(1965); LOLA(1971, Brit./Ital.); VISITOR, THE(1973, Can.), d&w; DOGS(1976), ed; CONVOY(1978), ed; ONLY WHEN I LAUGH(1981), ed; SEPARATE WAYS(1981), ed; FRANCES(1982), ed

1984

MASS APPEAL(1984), ed

John Wayne Wright

SHERIFF OF REDWOOD VALLEY(1946)

Johnnie Wright

SECOND FIDDLE TO A STEEL GUITAR(1965)

Joseph Wright

ARIZONA KID, THE(1930), set d; SEA WOLF, THE(1930), art d; WILD GIRL(1932), set d; BORN TO BE BAD(1934), art d; LOOKING FOR TROUBLE(1934), art d; MANHATTAN MELODRAMA(1934), art d; ROSE MARIE(1936), art d; DAY-TIME WIFE(1939), art d; GUYS AND DOLLS(1955), art d; MAN WITH THE GOLDEN ARM, THE(1955), art d; OKLAHOMA(1955), art d; PORGY AND BESS(1959), art d; FLOWER DRUM SONG(1961), art d; DAYS OF WINE AND ROSES(1962), art d; DEAR HEART(1964), art d; STRANGE BEDFELLOWS(1965), art d

1984

FOREVER YOUNG(1984, Brit.)

Silents

DARING YOUTH(1924), art d; UNHOLY THREE, THE(1925), set d; EXQUISITE SINNER, THE(1926), art d; MAN WHO LAUGHS, THE(1927), art d; NAME THE WOMAN(1928), art d; RANSOM(1928), art d

Joseph C. Wright

SHOPWORN ANGEL(1938), art d; SWANEE RIVER(1939), art d; DOWN ARGENTINE WAY(1940), art d; GREAT PROFILE, THE(1940), art d; HE MARRIED HIS WIFE(1940), art d; I WAS AN ADVENTURESS(1940), art d; LILLIAN RUSSELL(1940), art d; MARK OF ZORRO, THE(1940), art d; TIN PAN ALLEY(1940), art d; BLOOD AND SAND(1941), art d; THAT NIGHT IN RIO(1941), art d; VERY YOUNG LADY, A(1941), art d; WEEKEND IN HAVANA(1941), art d; MY GAL SAL(1942), art d; ORCHESTRA WIVES(1942), art d; QUIET PLEASE, MURDER(1942), art d; SPRINGTIME IN THE ROCKIES(1942), art d; THIS ABOVE ALL(1942), art d; GANG'S ALL HERE, THE(1943), art d; STORMY WEATHER(1943), art d; SWEET ROSIE O'GRADY(1943), art d; GREENWICH VILLAGE(1944), art d; IRISH EYES ARE SMILING(1944), art d; PIN UP GIRL(1944), art d; DIAMOND HORSESHOE(1945), art d; NOB HILL(1945), set d; DO YOU LOVE ME?(1946), art d; THREE LITTLE GIRLS IN BLUE(1946), art d; I WONDER WHO'S KISSING HER NOW(1947), set d; MOTHER WORE TIGHTS(1947), art d; SNAKE PIT, THE(1948), art d; UNFAITHFULLY YOURS(1948), art d; JACKPOT, THE(1950), art d; MY BLUE HEAVEN(1950), art d; WABASH AVENUE(1950), art d; MEET ME AFTER THE SHOW(1951), art d; TAKE CARE OF MY LITTLE GIRL(1951), art d; O. HENRY'S FULL HOUSE(1952), art d; STARS AND STRIPES FOREVER(1952), art d; WITH A SONG IN MY HEART(1952), art d; GENTLEMEN PREFER BLONDES(1953), art d; STRANGE ONE, THE(1957), art d

Josephine Huntley Wright

LAST WALTZ, THE(1936, Brit.); WAKE UP FAMOUS(1937, Brit.)

Josie Huntley Wright

STRAWBERRY ROAN(1945, Brit.)

Julia Wright

OH! WHAT A LOVELY WAR(1969, Brit.); DR. JEKYLL AND SISTER HYDE(1971, Brit.)

Kathryn Wright

JESUS CHRIST, SUPERSTAR(1973)

Kenneth Wright

SKATETOWN, U.S.A.(1979)

Larry Wright

NEST OF THE CUCKOO BIRDS, THE(1965)

Laura Wright

GABLES MYSTERY, THE(1938, Brit.); SIMPLY TERRIFIC(1938, Brit.)

Leo Wright

FIDDLER ON THE ROOF(1971)

Leslie Wright

DEADLY GAME, THE(1955, Brit.)

Lewlie Wright

PAID TO KILL(1954, Brit.)

Liz Wright

TOGETHER FOR DAYS(1972)

Louise Wright

WHEN A STRANGER CALLS(1979)

M. Humbertson Wright

Silents

DOUBLE LIFE OF MR. ALFRED BURTON, THE(1919, Brit.)

Mabel Wright

Silents

SONG OF THE WAGE SLAVE, THE(1915)

Misc. Silents

GREATER LOVE HATH NO MAN(1915); WALL STREET TRAGEDY, A(1916)

Mac V. Wright

Silents

HUNTED MEN(1930); OKLAHOMA SHERIFF, THE(1930)

Mack Wright

HAUNTED GOLD(1932), d; CAPPY RICKS RETURNS(1935), d

Silents

BAR SINISTER, THE(1917)

Mack V. Wright

MAN FROM MONTEREY, THE(1933), d; SOMEWHERE IN SONORA(1933), d; RANDY RIDES ALONE(1934); COMIN' ROUND THE MOUNTAIN(1936), d; SINGING COWBOY, THE(1936), d; WINDS OF THE WASTELAND(1936), d; HIT THE SADDLE(1937), d; RANGE DEFENDERS(1937), d; RIDERS OF THE WHISTLING SKULL(1937), d; ROARIN' LEAD(1937), d

Silents

WESTERN VENGEANCE(1924); RIDERS OF MYSTERY(1925); ARIZONA DAYS(1928), a, w; LAW OF THE MOUNTED(1928); MANHATTAN COWBOY(1928); WEST OF SANTA FE(1928), a, w; HEADIN' WESTWARD(1929); LONE HORSEMAN, THE(1929)

Misc. Silents

CROSSED TRAILS(1924); BLOOD AND STEEL(1925); MOCCASINS(1925); PIONEERS OF THE WEST(1929)

Maggie Wright

WHAT'S NEW, PUSSYCAT?(1965, U.S./Fr.); HAMMERHEAD(1968); MY LOVER, MY SON(1970, Brit.); ONE MORE TIME(1970, Brit.); TWINS OF EVIL(1971, Brit.); SUBURBAN WIVES(1973, Brit.); CONFESSIONS OF A POP PERFORMER(1975, Brit.)

1984

SCRUBBERS(1984, Brit.)

Marbeth Wright

HAPPY DAYS(1930); JUST IMAGINE(1930); FOLIES DERGERE(1935); GEORGE WHITE'S 1935 SCANDALS(1935); STRANDED(1935)

Marcella Wright

HILLBILLYS IN A HAUNTED HOUSE(1967)

Marie Wright

MURDER(1930, Brit.); TILLY OF BLOOMSBURY(1931, Brit.); UP FOR THE CUP(1931, Brit.); HELP YOURSELF(1932, Brit.); LUCKY SWEEP, A(1932, Brit.); LOVE'S OLD SWEET SONG(1933, Brit.); NAUGHTY CINDERELLA(1933, Brit.); THIS ACTING BUSINESS(1933, Brit.); CUP OF KINDNESS, A(1934, Brit.); CITY OF BEAUTIFUL NONSENSE, THE(1935, Brit.); HAIL AND FAREWELL(1936, Brit.); ROMANCE AND RICHES(1937, Brit.); SEXTON BLAKE AND THE HOODED TERROR(1938, Brit.); SILVER TOP(1938, Brit.); SIXTY GLORIOUS YEARS(1938, Brit.); STRANGE BOARDERS(1938, Brit.); BLACK EYES(1939, Brit.); GASLIGHT(1940); FALSE RAPTURE(1941)

Silents
MRS. THOMPSON(1919, Brit.); PADDY, THE NEXT BEST THING(1923, Brit.)
Mark V. Wright
BIG SHOW, THE(1937), d; ROOTIN' TOOTIN' RHYTHM(1937), d
Marvin Wright
I KILLED WILD BILL HICKOK(1956), ed
Mary C. Wright
STARTING OVER(1979); HEAVEN'S GATE(1980)
Mary Catherine Wright
DAN'S MOTEL(1982)
Matthew Wright
Misc. Talkies
LITTLE DETECTIVES, THE(1983)
Maurice Wright
BROADWAY HOOFER, THE(1929), ed; FLIGHT(1929), ed; LADIES OF LEISURE(1930), ed; RAIN OR SHINE(1930), ed; DIRIGIBLE(1931), ed; MIRACLE WOMAN, THE(1931), ed; RANGE FEUD, THE(1931), ed; AMERICAN MADNESS(1932), ed; BY WHOSE HAND?(1932), ed; DEADLINE, THE(1932), ed; FORBIDDEN(1932), ed; LENA RIVERS(1932), ed; NIGHT MAYOR, THE(1932), ed; RIDIN' FOR JUSTICE(1932), ed; SOUTH OF THE RIO GRANDE(1932), ed; THIS SPORTING AGE(1932), ed; ANN CARVER'S PROFESSION(1933), ed; SOLDIERS OF THE STORM(1933), ed; BORN TO BE BAD(1934), ed; LAST GENTLEMAN, THE(1934), ed; EAST OF JAVA(1935), ed; TRANSIENT LADY(1935), ed; LOVE BEFORE BREAKFAST(1936), ed; YELLOWSTONE(1936), ed; CARNIVAL QUEEN(1937), ed; THAT'S MY STORY(1937), ed; WINGS OVER HONOLULU(1937), ed; BLACK DOLL, THE(1938), ed; DANGER ON THE AIR(1938), ed; EXPOSED(1938), ed; GOODBYE BROADWAY(1938), ed; LAST EXPRESS, THE(1938), ed; LAST WARNING, THE(1938), ed; ROAD TO RENO(1938), ed; SINNERS IN PARADISE(1938), ed; FOR LOVE OR MONEY(1939), ed; LEGION OF LOST FLYERS(1939), ed; MUTINY ON THE BLACKHAWK(1939), ed; TROPIC FURY(1939), ed; ZANZIBAR(1940), w; MEN OF THE TIMBERLAND(1941), md; RAIDERS OF THE DESERT(1941), ed; BEHIND THE EIGHT BALL(1942), ed; BOSS OF HANGTOWN MESA(1942), ed; DANGER IN THE PACIFIC(1942), ed; DRUMS OF THE CONGO(1942), ed; ESCAPE FROM HONG KONG(1942), ed; SILVER BULLET, THE(1942), ed; THERE'S ONE BORN EVERY MINUTE(1942), ed; TREAT EM' ROUGH(1942), ed; HI'YA, CHUM(1943), ed; FINGER MAN(1955), ed; RETURN OF JACK SLADE, THE(1955), ed; COME ON, THE(1956), ed; CRUEL TOWER, THE(1956), ed; LUM AND ABNER ABROAD(1956), ed; STRANGE INTRUDER(1956), ed; DRAGON WELLS MASSACRE(1957), ed; PORTLAND EXPOSE(1957), ed; YOUNG DON'T CRY, THE(1957), ed; WOLF LARSEN(1958), ed; GENE KRUPA STORY, THE(1959), ed; PURPLE GANG, THE(1960), ed; HOODLUM PRIEST, THE(1961), ed; THREE BLONDES IN HIS LIFE(1961), ed; ESCAPE FROM EAST BERLIN(1962), ed; MARRIED TOO YOUNG(1962), ed; CHILDISH THINGS(1969), ed; THAT TENDER TOUCH(1969), ed
Maurice E. Wright
STORM OVER THE ANDES(1935), ed
Maury Wright
BEAST OF HOLLOW MOUNTAIN, THE(1956), ed; BAYOU(1957), ed; OREGON PASSAGE(1958), ed
Max Wright
ALL THAT JAZZ(1979); LAST EMBRACE(1979); SIMON(1980); REDS(1981); STING II, THE(1983)
Mel Wright
FOUR FOR THE MORGUE(1962), ed
Michael David Wright
1984
NO SMALL AFFAIR(1984)
Michael Wright
LAST DAYS OF DOLWYN, THE(1949, Brit.), cos; SMELL OF HONEY, A SWALLOW OF BRINE! A(1966); WANDERERS, THE(1979); STREAMERS(1983)
Molly Wright
Silents
OVER THE STICKS(1929, Brit.)
Morris Wright
NOBODY'S FOOL(1936), ed
Nanie Wright
Misc. Silents
WANTED - A HOME(1916)
Nanine Wright
Silents
NAKED HEARTS(1916); MYSTERIOUS WITNESS, THE(1923)
Misc. Silents
WHIRLPOOL OF DESTINY, THE(1916); RISKY BUSINESS(1920)
Nicola Wright
REMEMBRANCE(1982, Brit.)
1984
TOP SECRET!(1984)
Norman Wright
BAMBI(1942), d; KING OF THE GRIZZLIES(1970), w
Norman Josef Wright
DEVIL AT FOUR O'CLOCK, THE(1961)
Nory Wright
Misc. Talkies
HUSTLER SQUAD(1976)
Otho Wright
GAMBLING SHIP(1933); SAN FRANCISCO(1936)
Pat Wright
GOOD MORNING... AND GOODBYE(1967)
Patricia Wright
TRAIL GUIDE(1952); SCANDAL INCORPORATED(1956)
Patrick Wright
PROJECT X(1968); LOOKING GLASS WAR, THE(1970, Brit.); SEVEN MINUTES, THE(1971); RENEGADE GIRLS(1974); CANNONBALL(1976, U.S./Hong Kong); REVENGE OF THE CHEERLEADERS(1976); TRACK OF THE MOONBEAST(1976); HOLLYWOOD HIGH(1977), d; LINCOLN CONSPIRACY, THE(1977); ONE MAN JURY(1978); ROLLER BOOGIE(1979); DAN'S MOTEL(1982); FRIGHTMARE(1983), p
1984
SLAPSTICK OF ANOTHER KIND(1984)
Misc. Talkies
ABDUCTORS, THE(1972); HOLLYWOOD HIGH(1976), d; IF YOU DON'T STOP IT, YOU'LL GO BLIND(1977)

Paula Wright
VIRGIN WITCH, THE(1973, Brit.)
Paula Rae Wright
KEEP SMILING(1938)
Penny Wright
ELEPHANT MAN, THE(1980, Brit.)
Peter Wright
PALM BEACH(1979, Aus.)
R.P. Wright
KENNER(1969)
Ralph Wright
THREE CABALLEROS, THE(1944), w; SONG OF THE SOUTH(1946), w; PETER PAN(1953), w; LADY AND THE TRAMP(1955), w; NIKKI, WILD DOG OF THE NORTH(1961, U.S./Can.), w; GAY PURR-EE(1962), w; JUNGLE BOOK, THE(1967), w; ARISTOCATS, THE(1970), w
Richard Wright
NATIVE SON(1951, U.S., Arg.), a, w; HOT LEAD AND COLD FEET(1978)
Richie Burns Wright
CANNONBALL RUN, THE(1981)
Robert Wright
DANCE, GIRL, DANCE(1940), m; SECRET COMMAND(1944), spec eff; SONG OF NORWAY(1970), w, m
Wg. Cdr. Robert Wright
BATTLE OF BRITAIN, THE(1969, Brit.), tech adv
Robert Vincent Wright
1,000 PLANE RAID, THE(1969), w
Ron Wright
CAPTURE THAT CAPSULE(1961); HUCKLEBERRY FINN(1974); COACH(1978); VAN NUYS BLVD.(1979), m
Ronn Wright
1984
ALL OF ME(1984)
Rose Marie Wright
HAIR(1979)
Rosina Wright
Silents
OPEN COUNTRY(1922, Brit.)
Ruth Wright
SCARLET WEEKEND, A(1932), ed
S. Fowler Wright
DELUGE(1933), w; THREE WITNESSES(1935, Brit.), w
Stan Wright
CHANGE OF SEASONS, A(1980)
Stanley Wright
OPERATION KID BROTHER(1967, Ital.), w; BOBBIE JO AND THE OUTLAW(1976), ph
Steve Wright
1984
RUNAWAY(1984)
Susan Wright
CHRISTINA(1974, Can.)
Sylvia Wright
TERROR ON TOUR(1980)
Tallie Wright
FRIGHTMARE(1983), p
Tenny Wright
BIG STAMPEDE, THE(1932), d; TELEGRAPH TRAIL, THE(1933), d
Silents
PARTNERS OF THE NIGHT(1920)
Misc. Silents
FIGHTIN' COMEBACK, THE(1927), d; HOOF MARKS(1927), d
Teresa Wright
LITTLE FOXES, THE(1941); MRS. MINIVER(1942); PRIDE OF THE YANKEES, THE(1942); SHADOW OF A DOUBT(1943); CASANOVA BROWN(1944); BEST YEARS OF OUR LIVES, THE(1946); IMPERFECT LADY, THE(1947); PURSUED(1947); TROUBLE WITH WOMEN, THE(1947); ENCHANTMENT(1948); CAPTURE, THE(1950); MEN, THE(1950); CALIFORNIA CONQUEST(1952); SOMETHING TO LIVE FOR(1952); STEEL TRAP, THE(1952); ACTRESS, THE(1953); COUNT THE HOURS(1953); TRACK OF THE CAT(1954); SEARCH FOR BRIDEY MURPHY, THE(1956); ESCAPADE IN JAPAN(1957); RESTLESS YEARS, THE(1958); HAIL, HERO!(1969); HAPPY ENDING, THE(1969); ROSELAND(1977); SOMEWHERE IN TIME(1980)
Thomas H. Wright
SERPICO(1973), set d
Todd Wright
Silents
PATCHWORK GIRL OF OZ, THE(1914)
Tom Wright
HANNIBAL BROOKS(1969, Brit.), w; UNDERGROUND U.S.A.(1980); SUBWAY RIDERS(1981); I OUGHT TO BE IN PICTURES(1982)
1984
ALPHABET CITY(1984); BEAT STREET(1984); BROTHER FROM ANOTHER PLANET, THE(1984); EXTERMINATOR 2(1984); TORCHLIGHT(1984), d
Tommy Wright
OPTIMISTS, THE(1973, Brit.); FRIGHTMARE(1974, Brit.); LITTLEST HORSE THIEVES, THE(1977); ELEPHANT MAN, THE(1980, Brit.)
Tony Wright
BAD BLONDE(1953, Brit.); JACQUELINE(1956, Brit.); JUMPING FOR JOY(1956, Brit.); TIGER IN THE SMOKE(1956, Brit.); SPANIARD'S CURSE, THE(1958, Brit.); BEASTS OF MARSEILLES, THE(1959, Brit.); BROTH OF A BOY(1959, Brit.); AND THE SAME TO YOU(1960, Brit.); FACES IN THE DARK(1960, Brit.); HOUSE IN MARSH ROAD, THE(1960, Brit.); IN THE WAKE OF A STRANGER(1960, Brit.); ATTEMPT TO KILL(1961, Brit.); PORTRAIT OF A SINNER(1961, Brit.); JOURNEY INTO NOWHERE(1963, Brit.); LIQUIDATOR, THE(1966, Brit.)
Vida Wright
ENDLESS LOVE(1981)
W.P. Wright III
URBAN COWBOY(1980)

Wally Wright
MEDIUM COOL(1969)
Walter Wright, Jr.
MIRACLE WORKER, THE(1962)
Wen Wright
SILVER ON THE SAGE(1939); WHISPERING SKULL, THE(1944); MARKED FOR MURDER(1945)
Wendell Wright
1984
CLOAK AND DAGGER(1984)
Wheeler Wright
SO THIS IS AFRICA(1933), ed
Will Wright
UNCLE HARRY(1945); WITHOUT RESERVATIONS(1946); BLONDIE PLAYS CUPID(1940); BLOSSOMS IN THE DUST(1941); CRACKED NUTS(1941); HONKY TONK(1941); MOB TOWN(1941); RICHEST MAN IN TOWN(1941); SHADOW OF THE THIN MAN(1941); MAJOR AND THE MINOR, THE(1942); POSTMAN DIDN'T RING, THE(1942); SABOTEUR(1942); SHUT MY BIG MOUTH(1942); TALES OF MANHATTAN(1942); WILDCAT(1942); COWBOY IN MANHATTAN(1943); HERE COMES ELMER(1943); IN OLD OKLAHOMA(1943); SLEEPY LAGOON(1943); SO PROUDLY WE HAIL(1943); PRACTICALLY YOURS(1944); BEWITCHED(1945); GRISSLY'S MILLIONS(1945); RHAPSODY IN BLUE(1945); ROAD TO UTOPIA(1945); SALOME, WHERE SHE DANCED(1945); SCARLET STREET(1945); STATE FAIR(1945); TOWN WENT WILD, THE(1945); YOU CAME ALONG(1945); BLUE DAHLIA, THE(1946); CALIFORNIA(1946); DOWN MISSOURI WAY(1946); HOODLUM SAINT, THE(1946); HOT CARGO(1946); INNER CIRCLE, THE(1946); JOHNNY COMES FLYING HOME(1946); JOLSON STORY, THE(1946); MADONNA'S SECRET(1946); NOCTURNE(1946); ONE EXCITING WEEK(1946); RENDEZVOUS WITH ANNIE(1946); ALONG THE OREGON TRAIL(1947); BLAZE OF NOON(1947); CYNTHIA(1947); KEEPER OF THE BEES(1947); LONG NIGHT, THE(1947); MOTHER WORE TIGHTS(1947); TROUBLE WITH WOMEN, THE(1947); WILD HARVEST(1947); ACT OF MURDER, AN(1948); BLACK EAGLE(1948); DISASTER(1948); GREEN GRASS OF WYOMING(1948); INSIDE STORY, THE(1948); MR. BLANDINGS BUILDS HIS DREAM HOUSE(1948); RELENTLESS(1948); WALLS OF JERICHO(1948); WHISPERING SMITH(1948); ACT OF VIOLENCE(1949); ADAM'S RIB(1949); ALL THE KING'S MEN(1949); BIG JACK(1949); BRIMSTONE(1949); LITTLE WOMEN(1949); LUST FOR GOLD(1949); MISS GRANT TAKES RICHMOND(1949); MRS. MIKE(1949); THEY LIVE BY NIGHT(1949); DALLAS(1950); HOUSE BY THE RIVER(1950); NO WAY OUT(1950); SAVAGE HORDE, THE(1950); SUNSET IN THE WEST(1950); TICKET TO TOMAHAWK(1950); EXCUSE MY DUST(1951); MY FORBIDDEN PAST(1951); PEOPLE WILL TALK(1951); TALL TARGET, THE(1951); VENGEANCE VALLEY(1951); HAPPY TIME, THE(1952); HOLIDAY FOR SINNERS(1952); LAS VEGAS STORY, THE(1952); LURE OF THE WILDERNESS(1952); LYDIA BAILEY(1952); O. HENRY'S FULL HOUSE(1952); PAULA(1952); LAST POSSE, THE(1953); NIAGARA(1953); WILD ONE, THE(1953); JOHNNY GUITAR(1954); RAID, THE(1954); RIVER OF NO RETURN(1954); COURT-MARTIAL OF BILLY MITCHELL, THE(1955); MAN WITH THE GOLDEN ARM, THE(1955); TALL MEN, THE(1955); THESE WILDER YEARS(1956); IRON SHERIFF, THE(1957); JEANNE EAGELS(1957); JOHNNY TREMAIN(1957); WAYWARD BUS, THE(1957); MISSOURI TRAVELER, THE(1958); QUANTRILL'S RAIDERS(1958); ALIAS JESSE JAMES(1959); THIRTY FOOT BRIDE OF CANDY ROCK, THE(1959); DEADLY COMPANIONS, THE(1961); TWENTY PLUS TWO(1961); CAPE FEAR(1962)
William Wright
CHINA CLIPPER(1936); SWING HIGH, SWING LOW(1937); DAY THE BOOKIES WEPT, THE(1939); DEVIL PAYS OFF, THE(1941); GLAMOUR BOY(1941); MAISIE WAS A LADY(1941); NOTHING BUT THE TRUTH(1941); ROOKIES ON PARADE(1941); WORLD PREMIERE(1941); BOSTON BLACKIE GOES HOLLYWOOD(1942); DARING YOUNG MAN, THE(1942); LUCKY LEGS(1942); MAN'S WORLD, A(1942); MEET THE STEWARTS(1942); NIGHT IN NEW ORLEANS, A(1942); NIGHT TO REMEMBER, A(1942); PARACHUTE NURSE(1942); SWEETHEART OF THE FLEET(1942); TENNESSEE JOHNSON(1942); TRUE TO THE ARMY(1942); MURDER IN TIMES SQUARE(1943); REVEILLE WITH BEVERLY(1943); ONE MYSTERIOUS NIGHT(1944); DANCING IN MANHATTAN(1945); EADIE WAS A LADY(1945); ESCAPE IN THE FOG(1945); EVE KNEW HER APPLES(1945); DOWN MISSOURI WAY(1946); LOVER COME BACK(1946); MASK OF DIIJON, THE(1946); GAS HOUSE KIDS GO WEST(1947); PHILO VANCE RETURNS(1947); KING OF THE GAMBLERS(1948); AIR HOSTESS(1949); DAUGHTER OF THE JUNGLE(1949); IMPACT(1949); ROSE OF THE YUKON(1949)
William H. Wright
YOURS FOR THE ASKING(1936), w; ADVENTURES OF TOM SAWYER, THE(1938), p; NIGHT WORK(1939), p; HER CARDBOARD LOVER(1942), w; ASSIGNMENT IN BRITTANY(1943), w; LETTER FOR EVIE, A(1945), p; THREE WISE FOOLS(1946), p; BRIDE GOES WILD, THE(1948), p, p; ACT OF VIOLENCE(1949), p; BLACK HAND, THE(1950), p; MRS. O'MALLEY AND MR. MALONE(1950), p; SKIPPER SURPRISED HIS WIFE, THE(1950), p; STARS IN MY CROWN(1950), p; PEOPLE AGAINST O'HARA, THE(1951), p; SHADOW IN THE SKY(1951), p; LOVE IS BETTER THAN EVER(1952), p; YOUNG MAN WITH IDEAS(1952), p; CLOWN, THE(1953), p; NAKED SPUR, THE(1953), p; DEAD RINGER(1964), p; DISTANT TRUMPET, A(1964), p; SONS OF KATIE ELDER, THE(1965), w
William Lord Wright
Silents
GRIT WINS(1929), sup; HARVEST OF HATE, THE(1929), w; HOOFBEATS OF VENGEANCE(1929), w; PLUNGING HOOFS(1929), w
William M. Wright
BLONDE FEVER(1944), p
Winn Wright
DALLAS(1950)
Bob Wrightman
HOT ROCK, THE(1972), art d
Robert Wrightman
LINE, THE(1982), art d
Dorsey Wrights
WARRIORS, THE(1979)
Berni Wrightson
HEAVY METAL(1981, Can.), w
Jack Wrightson
RUN FOR THE HILLS(1953)

Ben Wrigley
MELODY IN THE DARK(1948, Brit.); HIGH JINKS IN SOCIETY(1949, Brit.); MY FAIR LADY(1964); BEDKNOBS AND BROOMSTICKS(1971); PETE'S DRAGON(1977)
Dewey Wrigley
HELL'S ANGELS(1930), ph; WINGS IN THE DARK(1935), ph, spec eff; PRINCESS COMES ACROSS, THE(1936), spec eff; PLAINSMAN, THE(1937), spec eff; UNION PACIFIC(1939), ph; MYSTERY SEA RAIDER(1940), ph; REAP THE WILD WIND(1942), spec eff; MY FRIEND FLICKA(1943), ph; SAMSON AND DELILAH(1949), ph
Silents
AFTER BUSINESS HOURS(1925), ph; NIGHT BRIDE, THE(1927), ph; RUSH HOUR, THE(1927), ph
Zeck Wrigley
HELL'S ANGELS(1930), ph
Maris Wrixon
ADVENTURES OF JANE ARDEN(1939); CODE OF THE SECRET SERVICE(1939); DARK VICTORY(1939); EACH DAWN I DIE(1939); JEEPERS CREEPERS(1939); OFF THE RECORD(1939); PRIVATE DETECTIVE(1939); PRIVATE LIVES OF ELIZABETH AND ESSEX, THE(1939); APE, THE(1940); BRITISH INTELLIGENCE(1940); CHILD IS BORN, A(1940); FLIGHT ANGELS(1940); LADY WITH RED HAIR(1940); MAN WHO TALKED TOO MUCH, THE(1940); SANTA FE TRAIL(1940); 'TIL WE MEET AGAIN(1940); BULLETS FOR O'HARA(1941); CASE OF THE BLACK PARROT, THE(1941); FOOTSTEPS IN THE DARK(1941); HIGH SIERRA(1941); MEET JOHN DOE(1941); MILLION DOLLAR BABY(1941); NAVY BLUES(1941); SHOT IN THE DARK, THE(1941); SUNSET IN WYOMING(1941); OLD HOMESTEAD, THE(1942); SONS OF THE PIONEERS(1942); SPY SHIP(1942); WOMEN IN BONDAGE(1943); TRAIL TO GUNSIGHT(1944); WATERFRONT(1944); THIS LOVE OF OURS(1945); WHITE PONGO(1945); BLACK MARKET BABIES(1946); FACE OF MARBLE, THE(1946); GLASS ALIBI(1946); HIGHWAY 13(1948); SAXON CHARM, THE(1948); AS YOU WERE(1951)
Trudy Wroe
SON OF SINBAD(1955); BEYOND A REASONABLE DOUBT(1956)
Peter Wrona
MAN WHO WOULD NOT DIE, THE(1975), makeup
Allie Wrubel
HOUSEWIFE(1934), m; NEVER STEAL ANYTHING SMALL(1959), m
Brian Wry
BABY, IT'S YOU(1983)
Donald Wrye
ENTERTAINER, THE(1975), d; ICE CASTLES(1978), d, w
1984
HOUSE OF GOD, THE(1984), d&w
Misc. Talkies
HOUSE OF GOD, THE(1979), d
Eboni Wryte
PETEY WHEATSTRAW(1978)
Elizabeth Wu
MATCHLESS(1967, Ital.)
Honorable Wu
STOWAWAY(1936); CRIME OF DR. HALLET(1938); MR. MOTO TAKES A VACATION(1938); NORTH OF SHANGHAI(1939); ELLERY QUEEN AND THE PERFECT CRIME(1941)
June Wu
DEEP THRUST-THE HAND OF DEATH(1973, Hong Kong)
S.Y. Wu
SECRET, THE(1979, Hong Kong), p
Samuel Wu
MESA OF LOST WOMEN, THE(1956)
Hugo Wuehtrich
MASK, THE(1961, Can.), art d
Wuellner
DREAM OF SCHONBRUNN(1933, Aus.), p
Ida Wuest
ELISABETH OF AUSTRIA(1931, Ger.); BEAUTIFUL ADVENTURE(1932, Ger.); PRIVATE LIFE OF LOUIS XIV(1936, Ger.)
Robert Wuhl
HOLLYWOOD KNIGHTS, THE(1980)
Henry Wuhlschleger
Misc. Silents
MOI AUSSI, J'ACCUSE(1920, Fr.), d; BETES...COMES LES HOMMES(1923, Fr.), d; LE CABINET DE L'HOMME NOIR(1924, Fr.), d; L'ENIGME DU MONT AGEL(1924, Fr.), d; LE COUR DES GUEUX(1925, Fr.), d; LE MANOIR DE LA PEUR(1927, Fr.), d
Claud Wuhrman
COURT JESTER, THE(1956)
Ien Wul
CONQUEST(1937)
Stefan Wul
FANTASTIC PLANET(1973, Fr./Czech.), w
Wulf
M(1933, Ger.)
Michael Wulfe
CONQUEROR, THE(1956), cos
Anders Wulff
SMILES OF A SUMMER NIGHT(1957, Swed.)
Georgianna Wulff
ASSIGNMENT-PARIS(1952)
Helge Wulff
WILD STRAWBERRIES(1959, Swed.)
Kai Wulff
HEAVEN'S GATE(1980); NIGHT OF THE ZOMBIES(1981); BARBAROSA(1982); FIREFOX(1982); TWILIGHT ZONE-THE MOVIE(1983)
1984
JUNGLE WARRIORS(1984, U.S./Ger./Mex.)
Henry Wulhschleger
Misc. Silents
LES HERITIERS DE L'ONCLE JAMES(1924, Fr.), d
Richard Wulicher
Misc. Talkies
HOUSE OF SHADOWS(1977, Arg.), d

Robert Wullner
Misc. Silents
WIFE TRAP, THE(1922), d
Thelma Wunder
MANHATTAN MERRY-GO-ROUND(1937)
Frank Wunderlee
Silents
MY LADY INCOG(1916); ONE EXCITING NIGHT(1922); REPORTED MISSING(1922); NO MOTHER TO GUIDE HER(1923)
Hans-Joachim Wunderlich
SLEEPING BEAUTY(1965, Ger.), m
Jerry Wunderlich
GREEN MANSIONS(1959), set d; PLEASE DON'T EAT THE DAISIES(1960), set d; HONEYMOON MACHINE, THE(1961), set d; HOOTENANNY HOOT(1963), set d; DO NOT DISTURB(1965), set d; MORITURI(1965), set d; SINGING NUN, THE(1966), set d; DETECTIVE, THE(1968), set d; LADY IN CEMENT(1968), set d; ONLY GAME IN TOWN, THE(1970), set d; TRIBES(1970), set d; VANISHING POINT(1971), set d; WHAT'S THE MATTER WITH HELEN?(1971), set d; JUNIOR BONNER(1972), set d; WHEN THE LEGENDS DIE(1972), set d; EXORCIST, THE(1973), set d; LOST HORIZON(1973), set d; LAST TYCOON, THE(1976), set d; OBSESSION(1976), set d; AUDREY ROSE(1977), set d; GOODBYE GIRL, THE(1977), set d; ORDINARY PEOPLE(1980), set d; FOUR SEASONS, THE(1981), set d; SIX WEEKS(1982), set d; WARGAMES(1983), set d
1984
ALL OF ME(1984), set d; RACING WITH THE MOON(1984), set d
Robert J. Wunsch
SLAP SHOT(1977), p
Marianne Wunscher
PINOCCHIO(1969, E. Ger.)
Dagmar Wunter [Dana Wynter]
KNIGHTS OF THE ROUND TABLE(1953)
K.H. Wupper
FAUST(1963, Ger.)
Rudolph Wurlitzer
TWO-LANE BLACKTOP(1971), a, w; PAT GARRETT AND BILLY THE KID(1973), a, w
Achim Wurm
NOT RECONCILED, OR "ONLY VIOLENCE HELPS WHERE IT RULES"(1969, Ger.)
Claudia Wurm
NOT RECONCILED, OR "ONLY VIOLENCE HELPS WHERE IT RULES"(1969, Ger.)
Claude Olin Wurman
KID FROM LEFT FIELD, THE(1953)
June Wurster
GIRL NEXT DOOR, THE(1953)
Clarence Wurtz
SHOOTING STRAIGHT(1930)
Sol Wurtzel
MAD GAME, THE(1933), p; BRIGHT EYES(1934), p; 365 NIGHTS IN HOLLYWOOD(1934), p
Sol M. Wurtzel
JUDGE PRIEST(1934), p; MURDER IN TRINIDAD(1934), p; ORIENT EXPRESS(1934), p; PURSUED(1934), p; SLEEPERS EAST(1934), p; WILD GOLD(1934), p; BLACK SHEEP(1935), p; CHARLIE CHAN IN PARIS(1935), p; DANTE'S INFERNO(1935), p; ELINOR NORTON(1935), p; GINGER(1935), p; LIFE BEGINS AT 40(1935), p; PADDY O'DAY(1935), p; STEAMBOAT ROUND THE BEND(1935), p; CAN THIS BE DIXIE?(1936), p; CAREER WOMAN(1936), p; COUNTRY BEYOND, THE(1936), p; CRIME OF DR. FORBES(1936), p; FIFTEEN MAIDEN LANE(1936), p; GENTLE JULIA(1936), p; HIGH TENSION(1936), p; HUMAN CARGO(1936), p; LITTLE MISS NOBODY(1936), p; MY MARRIAGE(1936), p; NAVY WIFE(1936), p; RAMONA(1936), p; SONG AND DANCE MAN, THE(1936), p; STAR FOR A NIGHT(1936), p; THANK YOU, JEEVES(1936), p; THIRTY SIX HOURS TO KILL(1936), p; BORN RECKLESS(1937), p; DANGEROUSLY YOURS(1937), p; FAIR WARNING(1937), p; ONE MILE FROM HEAVEN(1937), p; THANK YOU, MR. MOTO(1937), p; THAT I MAY LIVE(1937), p; THINK FAST, MR. MOTO(1937), p; WOMAN-WISE(1937), p; BATTLE OF BROADWAY(1938), p; CHANGE OF HEART(1938), p; CITY GIRL(1938), p; FIVE OF A KIND(1938), p; INTERNATIONAL SETTLEMENT(1938), p; ISLAND IN THE SKY(1938), p; LOVE ON A BUDGET(1938), p; MR. MOTO TAKES A CHANCE(1938), p; MR. MOTO TAKES A VACATION(1938), p; MR. MOTO'S GAMBLE(1938), p; MYSTERIOUS MR. MOTO(1938), p; PASSPORT HUSBAND(1938), p; SHARPSHOOTERS(1938), p; UP THE RIVER(1938), p; WALKING DOWN BROADWAY(1938), p; WHILE NEW YORK SLEEPS(1938), p; CHARLIE CHAN AT TREASURE ISLAND(1939), p; CHASING DANGER(1939), p; CHICKEN WAGON FAMILY(1939), p; ESCAPE, THE(1939), p; FRONTIER MARSHAL(1939), p; HEAVEN WITH A BARBED WIRE FENCE(1939), p; HONEYMOON'S OVER, THE(1939), p; MR. MOTO'S LAST WARNING(1939), p; PACK UP YOUR TROUBLES(1939), p; PARDON OUR NERVE(1939), p; STOP, LOOK, AND LOVE(1939), p; 20,000 MEN A YEAR(1939), p; CHARLIE CHAN IN PANAMA(1940), p; CHARLIE CHAN'S MURDER CRUISE(1940), p; CHARTER PILOT(1940), p; CITY OF CHANCE(1940), p; EARTHBOUND(1940), p; FREE, BLONDE AND 21(1940), p; GIRL FROM AVENUE A(1940), p; GIRL IN 313(1940), p; HIGH SCHOOL(1940), p; LUCKY CISCO KID(1940), p; MAN WHO WOULDN'T TALK, THE(1940), p; MANHATTAN HEARTBEAT(1940), p; MICHAEL SHAYNE, PRIVATE DETECTIVE(1940), p; MURDER OVER NEW YORK(1940), p; ON THEIR OWN(1940), p; PIER 13(1940), p; SAILOR'S LADY(1940), p; VIVA CISCO KID(1940), p; YESTERDAY'S HEROES(1940), p; BLUE, WHITE, AND PERFECT(1941), p; CADET GIRL(1941), p; CHARLIE CHAN IN RIO(1941), p; DANCE HALL(1941), p; DRESSED TO KILL(1941), p; GREAT GUNS(1941), p; JENNIE(1941), p; LAST OF THE DUANES(1941), p; PRIVATE NURSE(1941), p; RIDE, KELLY, RIDE(1941), p; RIDE ON VAQUERO(1941), p; RIDERS OF THE PURPLE SAGE(1941), p; ROMANCE OF THE RIO GRANDE(1941), p; SCOTLAND YARD(1941), p; SLEEPERS WEST(1941), p; A-HAUNTING WE WILL GO(1942), p; DR. RENAULT'S SECRET(1942), p; JUST OFF BROADWAY(1942), p; LONE STAR RANGER(1942), p; MAN WHO WOULDN'T DIE, THE(1942), p; MANILA CALLING(1942), p; RIGHT TO THE HEART(1942), p; SECRET AGENT OF JAPAN(1942), p; SUNDOWN JIM(1942), p; THRU DIFFERENT EYES(1942), p; TIME TO KILL(1942), p; WHISPERING GHOSTS(1942), p; WHO IS HOPE SCHUYLER?(1942), p; YOUNG AMERICA(1942), p; BOMBER'S MOON(1943), p; CHETNIKS(1943), p; HE HIRED THE BOSS(1943), p; JITTERBUGS(1943), p; BIG NOISE, THE(1944), p; DANGEROUS MILLIONS(1946), p; DEADLINE FOR MURDER(1946), p; RENDEZVOUS 24(1946), p; STRANGE JOURNEY(1946), p; BACKLASH(1947), p; CRIMSON KEY, THE(1947), p; DANGEROUS YEARS(1947), p; INVISIBLE WALL, THE(1947), p; JEWELS OF BRANDENBURG(1947), p; ROSES ARE RED(1947), p; SECOND CHANCE(1947), p; ARTHUR TAKES OVER(1948), p; FIGHTING BACK(1948), p; HALF PAST MIDNIGHT(1948), p; NIGHT WIND(1948), p; MISS MINK OF 1949(1949), p; TROUBLE PREFERRED(1949), p; TUCSON(1949), p
Stuart Wurtzel
HAIR(1979), prod d; NIGHT OF THE JUGGLER(1980), prod d; SIMON(1980), prod d; TIMES SQUARE(1980), prod d; TATTOO(1981), prod d; CHOSEN, THE(1982), art d; BALLAD OF GREGORIO CORTEZ, THE(1983), art d
Felix Wurzel
DIE FLEDERMAUS(1964, Aust.), makeup
Kevin M. Wurzer
SECRET OF NIMH, THE(1982), anim
Robert Wussler
BLACK SUNDAY(1977)
Klausjurgen Wussow
CORPSE OF BEVERLY HILLS, THE(1965, Ger.)
Ida Wust
BOMBARDMENT OF MONTE CARLO, THE(1931, Ger.); HIS MAJESTY, KING BALLYHOO(1931, Ger.)
Harry Wustenhagen
RUMPELSTILTSKIN(1965, Ger.); PUSS 'N' BOOTS(1967, Ger.)
Heinz Oskar Wuttig
THOUSAND EYES OF DR. MABUSE, THE(1960, Fr./Ital./Ger.), w; COURT MARTIAL(1962, Ger.), w
Herman Wuyts
GENERAL MASSACRE(1973, U.S./Bel.), w, ph&ed
Virgil Wyaco II
NATIONAL LAMPOON'S VACATION(1983)
Robert Wyamn
LAUGHING POLICEMAN, THE(1973), ed
Leigh Wyant
Silents
HIGH HEELS(1921); IDLE RICH, THE(1921); SIREN CALL, THE(1922)
Misc. Silents
BOBBED HAIR(1922); BOUGHT AND PAID FOR(1922)
Shelley Wyant
PILGRIM, FAREWELL(1980)
Shelly Wyant
NOCTURNA(1979)
1984
HOME FREE ALL(1984)
Al Wyatt
DEADLINE(1948); BONANZA TOWN(1951); PRAIRIE ROUNDUP(1951); WHIRLWIND(1951); MISSISSIPPI GAMBLER, THE(1953); SITTING BULL(1954); FAR HORIZONS, THE(1955); ROBBER'S ROOST(1955); SHOTGUN(1955); SEVENTH CAVALRY(1956); DALTON GIRLS, THE(1957); GUN DUEL IN DURANGO(1957); MAN FROM GOD'S COUNTRY(1958); RAWHIDE TRAIL, THE(1958); TOUGHEST GUN IN TOMBSTONE(1958); FIVE GUNS TO TOMBSTONE(1961); STEEL CLAW, THE(1961); ROBIN AND THE SEVEN HOODS(1964); VON RYAN'S EXPRESS(1965); DUEL AT DIABLO(1966); HEAVEN WITH A GUN(1969); VALDEZ IS COMING(1971), stunts; METEOR(1979)
Allan Wyatt
FIGHTING MAD(1976), stunts
Charlene Wyatt
ANY MAN'S WIFE(1936); VALIANT IS THE WORD FOR CARRIE(1936); BORDERLAND(1937); MICHAEL O'HALLORAN(1937); UNDER THE BIG TOP(1938); UNTAMED(1940); ALOMA OF THE SOUTH SEAS(1941)
David Wyatt
IT'S A BIG COUNTRY(1951)
Eustace Wyatt
JOURNEY INTO FEAR(1942); NIGHTMARE(1942); MADAME CURIE(1943); GASLIGHT(1944); JANE EYRE(1944); MAN IN HALF-MOON STREET, THE(1944); MINISTRY OF FEAR(1945)
Florence Wyatt
NOTORIOUS LANDLADY, THE(1962); WALK ON THE WILD SIDE(1962)
Jamie Wyatt
RUN FOR YOUR WIFE(1966, Fr./Ital.)
Jane Wyatt
GREAT EXPECTATIONS(1934); ONE MORE RIVER(1934); LUCKIEST GIRL IN THE WORLD, THE(1936); WE'RE ONLY HUMAN(1936); LOST HORIZON(1937); GIRL FROM GOD'S COUNTRY(1940); KISSES FOR BREAKFAST(1941); WEEKEND FOR THREE(1941); ARMY SURGEON(1942); HURRICANE SMITH(1942); NAVY COMES THROUGH, THE(1942); BUCKSKIN FRONTIER(1943); KANSAN, THE(1943); NONE BUT THE LONELY HEART(1944); BACHELOR'S DAUGHTERS, THE(1946); STRANGE CONQUEST(1946); BOOMERANG(1947); GENTLEMAN'S AGREEMENT(1947); NO MINOR VICES(1948); PITFALL(1948); BAD BOY(1949); CANADIAN PACIFIC(1949); TASK FORCE(1949); HOUSE BY THE RIVER(1950); MY BLUE HEAVEN(1950); OUR VERY OWN(1950); CRIMINAL LAWYER(1951); MAN WHO CHEATED HIMSELF, THE(1951); INTERLUDE(1957); TWO LITTLE BEARS, THE(1961); NEVER TOO LATE(1965); TREASURE OF MATECUMBE(1976)
Jennifer Wyatt
FIGHTING MAD(1957, Brit.), w
John Wyatt
FUNNY MONEY(1983, Brit.), ph
Karen Wyatt
TALES OF A SALESMAN(1965)
Meleesa Wyatt
OFFICER AND A GENTLEMAN, AN(1982)
Nate Wyatt
BORDERLAND(1937), d
Reda Wyatt
MANDINGO(1975)
Tessa Wyatt
WEDDING NIGHT(1970, Ireland); BEAST IN THE CELLAR, THE(1971, Brit.); ENGLANO MADE ME(1973, Brit.)
Walter Wyatt
NATIONAL LAMPOON'S ANIMAL HOUSE(1978)

Yvette Wyatt
LITTLE BIG SHOT(1952, Brit.); GLAD TIDINGS(1953, Brit.); SEA WIFE(1957, Brit.); WHITE TRAP, THE(1959, Brit.); PARTNER, THE(1966, Brit.)

Jessie Maude Wybro
Silents
ROMANCE RANCH(1924), w

Tadeusz Wybult
PASSENGER, THE(1970, Pol.), set d; CONTRACT, THE(1982, Pol.), art d

Margaret Wycherly
SERGEANT YORK(; THIRTEENTH CHAIR, THE(1930); MIDNIGHT(1934); VICTORY(1940); CROSSROADS(1942); KEEPER OF THE FLAME(1942); RANDOM HARVEST(1942); ASSIGNMENT IN BRITTANY(1943); HANGMEN ALSO DIE(1943); MOON IS DOWN, THE(1943); EXPERIMENT PERILOUS(1944); JOHNNY ANGEL(1945); YEARLING, THE(1946); FOREVER AMBER(1947); SOMETHING IN THE WIND(1947); LOVES OF CARMEN, THE(1948); WHITE HEAT(1949); MAN WITH A CLOAK, THE(1951); PRESIDENT'S LADY, THE(1953); THAT MAN FROM TANGIER(1953)
Misc. Silents
FIGHT, THE(1915)

Anthony Wyckham
SCHOOL FOR SECRETS(1946, Brit.)

Tony Wyckham
CHIPS(1938. Brit.)

Alvin Wyckoff
NIGHT RIDE(1930), ph; LOST JUNGLE, THE(1934), ph; WHITE HEAT(1934), ph; WINE, WOMEN, AND SONG(1934), ph; BOLD CABALLERO(1936), ph
Silents
BREWSTER'S MILLIONS(1914), ph; CALL OF THE NORTH, THE(1914), ph; MAN FROM HOME, THE(1914), ph; ROSE OF THE RANCHO(1914), ph; VIRGINIAN, THE(1914), ph; CAPTIVE, THE(1915), ph; CARMEN(1915), ph; CHIMMIE FADDEN(1915), ph; CHIMMIE FADDEN OUT WEST(1915), ph; GIRL OF THE GOLDEN WEST, THE(1915), ph; GOLDEN CHANCE, THE(1915), ph; KINDLING(1915), ph; TEMPTATION(1915), ph; WARRENS OF VIRGINIA, THE(1915), ph; WILD GOOSE CHASE(1915), ph; JOAN THE WOMAN(1916), ph; ROMANCE OF THE REDWOODS, A(1917), ph; OLD WIVES FOR NEW(1918), ph; MALE AND FEMALE(1919), ph; SOMETHING TO THINK ABOUT(1920), ph; AFFAIRS OF ANATOL, THE(1921), ph; BLOOD AND SAND(1922), ph; MAN WHO SAW TOMORROW, THE(1922), ph; SATURDAY NIGHT(1922), ph; ADAM'S RIB(1923), ph; PLEASURE MAD(1923), ph; STRANGERS OF THE NIGHT(1923), ph; KISS IN THE DARK, A(1925), ph; OLD HOME WEEK(1925), ph; IT'S THE OLD ARMY GAME(1926), ph; NEW KLONDIKE, THE(1926), ph; TIN GODS(1926), ph; BLIND ALLEYS(1927), ph; SPIDER WEBS(1927), ph

Robert Wyckoff
MARA OF THE WILDERNESS(1966), ph; GOOD TIMES(1967), ph; TAMMY AND THE MILLIONAIRE(1967), ph; NOBODY'S PERFECT(1968), ph

Ronald Wyckoff
COVER GIRL(1944)

Alvin Wycoff
STORM, THE(1930), ph
Silents
ARAB, THE(1915), ph

Archie Wycoff
BLACK RODEO(1972)

Emma Wyda
Silents
LAST LAUGH, THE(1924, Ger.)

Richard Wydler
KISS ME GOODBYE(1935, Brit.)

Than Wyenn
GOOD MORNING, MISS DOVE(1955); PETE KELLY'S BLUES(1955); BEGINNING OF THE END(1957); INVISIBLE BOY, THE(1957); IMITATION OF LIFE(1959); BOY AND THE PIRATES, THE(1960); SIGN OF ZORRO, THE(1960); MONEY TRAP, THE(1966); ROSIE!(1967); SULLIVAN'S EMPIRE(1967); PINK JUNGLE, THE(1968); BLACK SUNDAY(1977); OTHER SIDE OF MIDNIGHT, THE(1977); BEING THERE(1979)
1984
SPLASH(1984)

Reg Wyer
CALENDAR, THE(1948, Brit.), ph; HERE COME THE HUGGETTS(1948, Brit.), ph; HOME TO DANGER(1951, Brit.), ph; WEAPON, THE(1957, Brit.), ph; CARRY ON NURSE(1959, Brit.), ph; MAKE MINE MINK(1960, Brit.), ph; FAST LADY, THE(1963, Brit.), ph; FATHER CAME TOO(1964, Brit.), ph; RATTLE OF A SIMPLE MAN(1964, Brit.), ph; UNEARTHLY STRANGER, THE(1964, Brit.), ph; BRIGAND OF KANDAHAR, THE(1965, Brit.), ph; DEVILS OF DARKNESS, THE(1965, Brit.), ph; ISLAND OF TERROR(1967, Brit.), ph; THOSE FANTASTIC FLYING FOOLS(1967, Brit), ph; ISLAND OF THE BURNING DAMNED(1971, Brit.), ph

Reginald Wyer
UNHOLY QUEST, THE(1934, Brit.), p; DANCING WITH CRIME(1947, Brit.), ph; UPTURNED GLASS, THE(1947, Brit.), ph; VOTE FOR HUGGETT(1948, Brit.), ph; DIAMOND CITY(1949, Brit.), ph; HUGGETTS ABROAD, THE(1949, Brit.), ph; HIGHLY DANGEROUS(1950, Brit.), ph; TRIO(1950, Brit.), ph; SO LONG AT THE FAIR(1951, Brit.), ph; NEVER LOOK BACK(1952, Brit.), ph; TREAD SOFTLY(1952, Brit.), ph; FOUR SIDED TRIANGLE(1953, Brit.), ph; SPACEWAYS(1953, Brit.), ph; WHEEL OF FATE(1953, Brit.), ph; WOMAN IN HIDING(1953, Brit.), ph; PERSONAL AFFAIR(1954, Brit.), ph; YOU KNOW WHAT SAILORS ARE(1954, Brit.), ph; PRISONER, THE(1955, Brit.), ph; THE BEACHCOMBER(1955, Brit.), ph; TO PARIS WITH LOVE(1955, Brit.), ph; ALL FOR MARY(1956, Brit.), ph; ACROSS THE BRIDGE(1957, Brit.), ph; ALLIGATOR NAMED DAISY, AN(1957, Brit.), ph; TRUE AS A TURTLE(1957, Brit.), ph; MAD LITTLE ISLAND(1958, Brit.), ph; VIOLENT PLAYGROUND(1958, Brit.), ph; HEART OF A MAN, THE(1959, Brit.), ph; SEA FURY(1959, Brit.), ph; DENTIST IN THE CHAIR(1960, Brit.), ph; OPERATION AMSTERDAM(1960, Brit.), ph; KITCHEN, THE(1961, Brit.), ph; WHAT A WHOPPER(1961, Brit.), ph; PLAY IT COOL(1963, Brit.), ph; PLACE TO GO, A(1964, Brit.), ph; UNDERWORLD INFORMERS(1965, Brit.), ph

Reginald H. Wyer
GIRL IN A MILLION, A(1946, Brit.), ph; SEVENTH VEIL, THE(1946, Brit.), ph; BAD SISTER(1947, Brit.), ph; YEARS BETWEEN, THE(1947, Brit.), ph; DAYDREAK(1948, Brit.), ph; MR. LORD SAYS NO(1952, Brit.), ph

Alix Wyeth
JUD(1971)

Kathya Wyeth
INSPECTOR CLOUSEAU(1968, Brit.)

Katya Wyeth
HANDS OF ORLAC, THE(1964, Brit./Fr.); CLOCKWORK ORANGE, A(1971, Brit.); HANDS OF THE RIPPER(1971, Brit.); TWINS OF EVIL(1971, Brit.); CONFESSIONS OF A WINDOW CLEANER(1974, Brit.); GOT IT MADE(1974, Brit.); STRAIGHT ON TILL MORNING(1974, Brit.); BARRY MC KENZIE HOLDS HIS OWN(1975, Aus.)

Sandy Wyeth
EASY RIDER(1969); STALKING MOON, THE(1969)

Sandy Brown Wyeth
JOHNNY GOT HIS GUN(1971); TODD KILLINGS, THE(1971); DRIVER, THE(1978)

Richard Wygant
SKATETOWN, U.S.A.(1979)

Reg Wykeham
MASSACRE HILL(1949, Brit.)

Gladys Wykeham-Edwards
UNDER MILK WOOD(1973, Brit.)

Frank Wykoff
BIG CITY(1937)

Derna Wylde
PLANET OF DINOSAURS(1978)

Tony Wylde
LAST ADVENTURERS, THE(1937, Brit); LUCKY JADE(1937, Brit.); MUSEUM MYSTERY(1937, Brit.)
Misc. Silents
COCTAILS(1928, Brit.); WARNED OFF(1928, Brit.); LIFE'S A STAGE(1929, Brit.); THREE MEN IN A CART(1929, Brit.); WOMAN FROM CHINA, THE(1930, Brit.)

Martin Wyldeck
OPERATION DIAMOND(1948, Brit.); KNIGHTS OF THE ROUND TABLE(1953); TERROR ON A TRAIN(1953); EMBEZZLER, THE(1954, Brit.); ATOMIC MAN, THE(1955, Brit.); SCOTLAND YARD DRAGNET(1957, Brit.); JUST JOE(1960, Brit.); STORY OF DAVID, A(1960, Brit.); MY WIFE'S FAMILY(1962, Brit.); THAT KIND OF GIRL(1963, Brit.); NIGHT MUST FALL(1964, Brit.); RETURN OF MR. MOTO, THE(1965, Brit.); ROBBERY(1967, Brit.); OBLONG BOX, THE(1969, Brit.); BUSHBABY, THE(1970); COOL IT, CAROL!(1970, Brit.); DIE SCREAMING, MARIANNE(1970, Brit.)

Martyn Wyldeck
DEADLY NIGHTSHADE(1953, Brit.); WILL ANY GENTLEMAN?(1955, Brit.)

Nan Wylder
CALIFORNIA SUITE(1978)

Michael Wyle
FAST TIMES AT RIDGEMONT HIGH(1982); VALLEY GIRL(1983)

Gretchen Wyler
DEVIL'S BRIGADE, THE(1968); PRIVATE BENJAMIN(1980)

John Wyler
GLASS HOUSES(1972); MAN, WOMAN AND CHILD(1983)

Jorie Wyler
ALASKA PASSAGE(1959)

Michael Wyler
CLOSE-UP(1948)

R. Wyler
BIG COUNTRY, THE(1958), w

Richard Wyler
IDENTITY UNKNOWN(1960, Brit.); EXTERMINATORS, THE(1965 Fr.); UGLY ONES, THE(1968, Ital./Span.); RIO 70(1970, U.S./Ger./Span.); CONNECTING ROOMS(1971, Brit.)

Robert Wyler
IT HAPPENED IN PARIS(1935, Brit.), d; LAST TRAIN FROM MADRID, THE(1937), w; MURDER GOES TO COLLEGE(1937), w; SOPHIE LANG GOES WEST(1937), w; FIGHTING THOROUGHBREDS(1939), w; GENTLEMAN MISBEHAVES, THE(1946), w; DETECTIVE STORY(1951), w; BIG COUNTRY, THE(1958), w

Susan Wyler
BYE BYE BRAVERMAN(1968)

Trude Wyler
HOUSE OF WAX(1953); RAINS OF RANCHIPUR, THE(1955); UNTAMED(1955); GUNFIGHT AT THE O.K. CORRAL(1957); CERTAIN SMILE, A(1958); NEW KIND OF LOVE, A(1963)

William Wyler
ROMA RIVUOLE CESARE(, p&d; LOVE TRAP, THE(1929), d; SHAKEDOWN, THE(1929), p&d; HELL'S HEROES(1930), d; STORM, THE(1930), d; HOUSE DIVIDED, A(1932), d; TOM BROWN OF CULVER(1932), d; COUNSELLOR-AT-LAW(1933), d; HER FIRST MATE(1933), d; GLAMOUR(1934), d; GAY DECEPTION, THE(1935), d; GOOD FAIRY, THE(1935), d; COME AND GET IT(1936), d; DODSWORTH(1936), d; THESE THREE(1936), d; DEAD END(1937), d; JEZEBEL(1938), d; RAFFLES(1939), d; WUTHERING HEIGHTS(1939), d; LETTER, THE(1940), d; WESTERNER, THE(1940), d; LITTLE FOXES, THE(1941), d; MRS. MINIVER(1942), d; BEST YEARS OF OUR LIVES, THE(1946), d; HEIRESS, THE(1949), p&d; DETECTIVE STORY(1951), p&d; CARRIE(1952), p&d; DESPERATE HOURS, THE(1955), p&d; FRIENDLY PERSUASION(1956), p&d; BIG COUNTRY, THE(1958), p&d; BEN HUR(1959), d; CHILDREN'S HOUR, THE(1961), p&d; COLLECTOR, THE(1965), d; HOW TO STEAL A MILLION(1966), d; FUNNY GIRL(1968), d; LIBERATION OF L.B. JONES, THE(1970), d
Silents
LAZY LIGHTNING(1926), d; BLAZING DAYS(1927), d
Misc. Silents
STOLEN RANCH, THE(1926), d; BORDER CAVALIER, THE(1927), d; DESERT DUST(1927), d; HARD FISTS(1927), d; SHOOTING STRAIGHT(1927), d; STRAIGHT SHOOTIN'(1927), d; ANYBODY HERE SEEN KELLY?(1928), d; THUNDER RIDERS(1928), d

Caitlin Wyles
STAY AWAY, JOE(1968); WILD ROVERS(1971)

Catherine Wyles
TROUBLE WITH ANGELS, THE(1966)

Allan Wylie
1984
COMFORT AND JOY(1984, Brit.)

Evan Wylie
JOE BUTTERFLY(1957), w
Frank Wylie
MACBETH(1971, Brit.); THREE SISTERS(1974, Brit.)
I. A. R. Wylie
EVENINGS FOR SALE(1932), w; WONDERFUL STORY, THE(1932, Brit.), w; PILGRIMAGE(1933), w; FEATHER IN HER HAT, A(1935), w; SOME DAY(1935, Brit.), w; ROAD TO RENO, THE(1938), w; VIVACIOUS LADY(1938), w; YOUNG IN HEART, THE(1938), w; UNDER-PUP, THE(1939), w; FOUR SONS(1940), w; KEEPER OF THE FLAME(1942), w; PHONE CALL FROM A STRANGER(1952), w; TORCH SONG(1953), w
Ida A.R. Wylie
THAT MAN'S HERE AGAIN(1937), w
Ida Alexa Wylie
Silents
SHATTERED IDOLS(1922), w
Ida Alexa Ross Wylie
YOUNG NOWHERES(1929), w
Silents
FOUR SONS(1928), w
Irene Wylie
Misc. Silents
SPREADING EVIL, THE(1919)
John Wylie
HANKY-PANKY(1982)
Lauri Wylie
WARM CORNER, A(1930, Brit.), w; NEVER TROUBLE TROUBLE(1931, Brit.), w; PRINCESS CHARMING(1935, Brit.), w
Silents
GAME OF LIFE, THE(1922, Brit.), w
Meg Wylie
LIPSTICK(1976)
Philip Wylie
INVISIBLE MAN(1933), w; ISLAND OF LOST SOULS(1933), w; KING OF THE JUNGLE(1933), w; MURDERS IN THE ZOO(1933), w; COME ON, MARINES(1934), w; DEATH FLIES EAST(1935), w; FAIR WARNING(1937), w; SECOND HONEYMOON(1937), w; UNDER SUSPICION(1937), w; GLADIATOR, THE(1938), w; CHARLIE CHAN IN RENO(1939), w; SPRINGTIME IN THE ROCKIES(1942), w; CINDERELLA JONES(1946), w; NIGHT UNTO NIGHT(1949), w; WHEN WORLDS COLLIDE(1951), w; JOHNNY TIGER(1966), w
Rowan Wylie
CRY OF THE BANSHEE(1970, Brit.)
Dolf Wyllarde
Silents
WONDERFUL WIFE, A(1922), w
Colin Wyllie
HAUNTING OF M, THE(1979), m
Meg Wyllie
FLIGHT THAT DISAPPEARED, THE(1961); BEAUTY AND THE BEAST(1963); MARNIE(1964); OUR TIME(1974); SECOND THOUGHTS(1983)
1984
LAST STARFIGHTER, THE(1984)
Tim Wylton
MELODY(1971, Brit.); CURSE OF THE PINK PANTHER(1983)
Wim Wylton
UNDER MILK WOOD(1973, Brit.)
Betty Wyman
VOGUES OF 1938(1937)
Bill Wyman
GREEN ICE(1981, Brit.), m
Bob Wyman
APRIL FOOLS, THE(1969), ed; SOMETIMES A GREAT NOTION(1971), ed; PRISONER OF SECOND AVENUE, THE(1975), ed; LOGAN'S RUN(1976), ed; GREASED LIGHTNING(1977), ed; PROMISES IN THE DARK(1979), ed; TILT(1979), ed; LOVE CHILD(1982), ed
1984
HARD TO HOLD(1984), ed; HOUSE OF GOD, THE(1984), ed
Dan Wyman
RETURN, THE(1980), m; WITHOUT WARNING(1980), m; HELL NIGHT(1981), m
Frank Wyman
TOUCH OF THE OTHER, A(1970, Brit.), w
George Wyman
BATTLE IN OUTER SPACE(1960)
Harold E. Wyman
GALLANT ONE, THE(1964, U.S./Peru)
Jane Wyman
RUMBA(1935); GOLD DIGGERS OF 1937(1936); MY MAN GODFREY(1936); POLO JOE(1936); STAGE STRUCK(1936); KING AND THE CHORUS GIRL, THE(1937); MR. DODD TAKES THE AIR(1937); PUBLIC WEDDING(1937); READY, WILLING AND ABLE(1937); SINGING MARINE, THE(1937); SLIM(1937); SMART BLONDE(1937); BROTHER RAT(1938); CROWD ROARS, THE(1938); HE COULDN'T SAY NO(1938); SPY RING, THE(1938); WIDE OPEN FACES(1938); KID FROM KOKOMO, THE(1939); KID NIGHTINGALE(1939); PRIVATE DETECTIVE(1939); TAIL SPIN(1939); TORCHY PLAYS WITH DYNAMITE(1939); ANGEL FROM TEXAS, AN(1940); BROTHER RAT AND A BABY(1940); FLIGHT ANGELS(1940); GAMBLING ON THE HIGH SEAS(1940); MY LOVE CAME BACK(1940); TUGBOAT ANNIE SAILS AGAIN(1940); BAD MEN OF MISSOURI(1941); BODY DISAPPEARS, THE(1941); HONEYMOON FOR THREE(1941); YOU'RE IN THE ARMY NOW(1941); FOOTLIGHT SERENADE(1942); LARCENY, INC.(1942); MY FAVORITE SPY(1942); PRINCESS O'ROURKE(1943); CRIME BY NIGHT(1944); DOUGHGIRLS, THE(1944); HOLLYWOOD CANTEEN(1944); MAKE YOUR OWN BED(1944); LOST WEEKEND, THE(1945); NIGHT AND DAY(1946); ONE MORE TOMORROW(1946); YEARLING, THE(1946); CHEYENNE(1947); MAGIC TOWN(1947); JOHNNY BELINDA(1948); IT'S A GREAT FEELING(1949); KISS IN THE DARK, A(1949); LADY TAKES A SAILOR, A(1949); GLASS MENAGERIE, THE(1950); STAGE FRIGHT(1950, Brit.); BLUE VEIL, THE(1951); HERE COMES THE GROOM(1951); STARLIFT(1951); THREE GUYS NAMED MIKE(1951); JUST FOR YOU(1952); STORY OF WILL ROGERS, THE(1952); LET'S DO IT AGAIN(1953); SO BIG(1953); MAGNIFICENT OBSESSION(1954); ALL THAT HEAVEN ALLOWS(1955); LUCY GALLANT(1955); MIRACLE IN THE RAIN(1956); HOLIDAY FOR LOVERS(1959); POLLYANNA(1960); BON VOYA-

GE(1962); HOW TO COMMIT MARRIAGE(1969)
John Wyman
"EQUUS"(1977); REVENGE OF THE PINK PANTHER(1978); ARABIAN ADVENTURE(1979, Brit.); FOR YOUR EYES ONLY(1981)
Misc. Talkies
TUXEDO WARRIOR(1982)
Laurie Wyman
NAVY LARK, THE(1959, Brit.), w
Nicholas Wyman
JETLAG(1981, U.S./Span.)
Robert Wyman
CHUKA(1967), ed; ROSEMARY'S BABY(1968), ed; WUSA(1970), ed; POCKET MONEY(1972), ed
Stephen E. Wyman
STRATEGIC AIR COMMAND(1955)
Steve Wyman
WAR ARROW(1953)
Patrick Wymark
LEAGUE OF GENTLEMEN, THE(1961, Brit.); CONCRETE JUNGLE, THE(1962, Brit.); WEST 11(1963, Brit.); OPERATION CROSSBOW(1965, U.S./Ital.); REPULSION(1965, Brit.); SECRET OF BLOOD ISLAND, THE(1965, Brit.); SKULL, THE(1965, Brit.); PSYCHOPATH, THE(1966, Brit.); WOMAN TIMES SEVEN(1967, U.S./Fr./Ital.); CONQUEROR WORM, THE(1968, Brit.); TELL ME LIES(1968, Brit.); WHERE EAGLES DARE(1968, Brit.); BATTLE OF BRITAIN(1969, Brit.); JOURNEY TO THE FAR SIDE OF THE SUN(1969, Brit.); BLOOD ON SATAN'S CLAW, THE(1970, Brit.); CROMWELL(1970, Brit.); DR. SYN, ALIAS THE SCARECROW(1975)
Tristram Wymark
1984
ANOTHER COUNTRY(1984, Brit.)
Patricia Wymer
WITCHMAKER, THE(1969); YOUNG GRADUATES, THE(1971)
Misc. Talkies
BABYSITTER, THE(1969)
William Wymetal
TWO SISTERS FROM BOSTON(1946), w
Patrice Wymore
ROCKY MOUNTAIN(1950); TEA FOR TWO(1950); I'LL SEE YOU IN MY DREAMS(1951); STARLIFT(1951); BIG TREES, THE(1952); MAN BEHIND THE GUN, THE(1952); SHE'S WORKING HER WAY THROUGH COLLEGE(1952); SHE'S BACK ON BROADWAY(1953); KING'S RHAPSODY(1955, Brit.); SAD HORSE, THE(1959); OCEAN'S ELEVEN(1960); CHAMBER OF HORRORS(1966)
Meurig Wyn-Jones
ABANDON SHIP(1957, Brit.)
Evelyn Wynans
SWEET ADELINE(1935); WOMAN IN RED, THE(1935)
H.M. Wynant
DECISION AT SUNDOWN(1957); RUN OF THE ARROW(1957); OREGON PASSAGE(1958); RUN SILENT, RUN DEEP(1958); TONKA(1958); IT HAPPENED AT THE WORLD'S FAIR(1963); WHEELER DEALERS, THE(1963); SLENDER THREAD, THE(1965); TRACK OF THUNDER(1967); MARLOWE(1969); CONQUEST OF THE PLANET OF THE APES(1972); HANGAR 18(1980)
Hal Wynants
STRANGE CARGO(1940)
Edward Wynard
Silents
SILVER LINING, THE(1921), ph
Christopher Wyncoop
1984
OVER THE BROOKLYN BRIDGE(1984)
Bray Wyndham
MEN OF STEEL(1932, Brit.), p; MATINEE IDOL(1933, Brit.), p; TIGER BAY(1933, Brit.), p; SECRET OF THE LOCH, THE(1934, Brit.), p; IT HAPPENED IN PARIS(1935, Brit.), p
Bruce Wyndham
MAN WHO BROKE THE BANK AT MONTE CARLO, THE(1935); I'LL TAKE ROMANCE(1937); ONE NIGHT IN LISBON(1941); LADY HAS PLANS, THE(1942)
Carol Wyndham
Misc. Talkies
ROAMIN' WILD(1936)
Charles Wyndham
Misc. Silents
DAVID GARRICK(1913, Brit.)
Denis Wyndham
CONVICT 99(1938, Brit.); SAILOR'S DON'T CARE(1940, Brit.); NEUTRAL PORT(1941, Brit.); LOVE ON THE DOLE(1945, Brit.); DANCING WITH CRIME(1947, Brit.); GREED OF WILLIAM HART, THE(1948, Brit.); RAMSBOTTOM RIDES AGAIN(1956, Brit.)
Dennis Wyndham
INFORMER, THE(1929, Brit.); JUNO AND THE PAYCOCK(1930, Brit.); CARMEN(1931, Brit.); BRIDEGROOM FOR TWO(1932, Brit.); FACE AT THE WINDOW, THE(1932, Brit.); ANNE ONE HUNDRED(1933, Brit.); MAN THEY COULDN'T ARREST, THE(1933, Brit.); MONEY MAD(1934, Brit.); IMMORTAL GENTLEMAN(1935, Brit.); SENSATION(1936, Brit.); YOU MUST GET MARRIED(1936, Brit.); OH, MR. PORTER!(1937, Brit.); SCOTLAND YARD COMMANDS(1937, Brit.); WINDBAG THE SAILOR(1937, Brit.); ARSENAL STADIUM MYSTERY, THE(1939, Brit.); OLD MOTHER RILEY MP(1939, Brit.); OLD MOTHER RILEY IN SOCIETY(1940, Brit.); OLD MOTHER RILEY'S GHOSTS(1941, Brit.); SHEEPDOG OF THE HILLS(1941, Brit.); THIS ENGLAND(1941, Brit.); BATTLE FOR MUSIC(1943, Brit.); BELL-BOTTOM GEORGE(1943, Brit.); I DIDN'T DO IT(1945, Brit.); MEN OF THE SEA(1951, Brit.); FOR BETTER FOR WORSE(1954, Brit.); MEN OF SHERWOOD FOREST(1957, Brit.); DOG AND THE DIAMONDS, THE(1962, Brit.)
Silents
ELEVENTH HOUR, THE(1922, Brit.)
Misc. Silents
LORNA DOONE(1920, Brit.); LILY OF KILLARNEY(1929, Brit.)
Don Wyndham
WILD IN THE STREETS(1968)

Herbert Wyndham
NOTORIOUS(1946); O.S.S.(1946); JULIA MISBEHAVES(1948)
Joan Wyndham
CALL OF THE CIRCUS(1930); DR. JOSSER KC(1931, Brit.); UP FOR THE CUP(1931, Brit.); HIGH SOCIETY(1932, Brit.); JOSSER ON THE RIVER(1932, Brit.); FORTUNATE FOOL, THE(1933, Brit.); LOVE'S OLD SWEET SONG(1933, Brit.); LUCKY NUMBER, THE(1933, Brit.); LOYALTIES(1934, Brit.); GAY OLD DOG(1936, Brit.); JUGGERNAUT(1937, Brit.)
John Wyndham
VILLAGE OF THE DAMNED(1960, Brit.), w; CHILDREN OF THE DAMNED(1963, Brit.), w; DAY OF THE TRIFFIDS, THE(1963), w; QUEST FOR LOVE(1971, Brit.), w
Silents
HANDY ANDY(1921, Brit.); PRINCE AND THE BEGGARMAID, THE(1921, Brit.)
Olive Wyndham
Silents
FIGHTING BOB(1915)
Misc. Silents
YOUR GIRL AND MINE(1914)
Poppy Wyndham
Silents
DEAD CERTAINTY, A(1920, Brit.)
Misc. Silents
GREAT COUP, A(1919, Brit.); SNOW IN THE DESERT(1919, Brit.); SON OF DAVID, A(1920, Brit.); TIDAL WAVE, THE(1920, Brit.); TOWN OF CROOKED WAYS, THE(1920, Brit.)
Robert Wyndham
CHAMPAGNE CHARLIE(1944, Brit.); FIDDLERS THREE(1944, Brit.); FOR THOSE IN PERIL(1944, Brit.); DEAD OF NIGHT(1946, Brit.); SCHOOL FOR SECRETS(1946, Brit.); HANGMAN WAITS, THE(1947, Brit.); CAPTIVE HEART, THE(1948, Brit.); WHO KILLED VAN LOON?(1984, Brit.)
D.B. Wyndham-Lewis
GOLDEN CAGE, THE(1933, Brit.), w; THREE MEN IN A BOAT(1933, Brit.), w; HYDE PARK CORNER(1935, Brit.), w; MAN WHO KNEW TOO MUCH, THE(1935, Brit.), w; CHICK(1936, Brit.), w; GAY ADVENTURE, THE(1936, Brit.), w; TAKE A CHANCE(1937, Brit.), w; MAN WHO KNEW TOO MUCH, THE(1956), w
F. Wyndham-Mallock
VILLIERS DIAMOND, THE(1938, Brit.), w
George Wyner
LADY SINGS THE BLUES(1972); ALL THE PRESIDENT'S MEN(1976); DOGS(1976); BAD NEWS BEARS GO TO JAPAN, THE(1978); WHOSE LIFE IS IT ANYWAY?(1981); MY FAVORITE YEAR(1982); TO BE OR NOT TO BE(1983)
1984
FLETCH(1984)
Tammy Wynette
FROM NASHVILLE WITH MUSIC(1969)
Diana Wyngard
GENTLE TOUCH, THE(1956, Brit.)
Peter Wyngarde
ALEXANDER THE GREAT(1956); SIEGE OF SIDNEY STREET, THE(1960, Brit.); INNOCENTS, THE(1961, U.S./Brit.); BURN WITCH BURN(1962); FLASH GORDON(1980)
Misc. Talkies
AND THE WALL CAME TUMBLING DOWN(1984)
Charles Wyngate
Silents
WHAT'S A WIFE WORTH?(1921)
Ed Wynigear
MARRIAGE OF A YOUNG STOCKBROKER, THE(1971), cos
Ed Wyningear
WORLD'S GREATEST LOVER, THE(1977), cos
Charlotte Wynkers
DESIGN FOR SCANDAL(1941)
Christopher Wynkoop
GOING IN STYLE(1979)
1984
GHOSTBUSTERS(1984); MOSCOW ON THE HUDSON(1984)
Adele Wynn
STERILE CUCKOO, THE(1969)
Ann Wynn
HERITAGE(1935, Aus.)
Brenda Joyce Wynn
DOZENS, THE(1981)
Ed Wynn
FOLLOW THE LEADER(1930); CHIEF, THE(1933); STAGE DOOR CANTEEN(1943); ALICE IN WONDERLAND(1951); GREAT MAN, THE(1957); MARJORIE MORNINGSTAR(1958); DIARY OF ANNE FRANK, THE(1959); CINDERFELLA(1960); ABSENT-MINDED PROFESSOR, THE(1961); BABES IN TOYLAND(1961); SON OF FLUBBER(1963); MARY POPPINS(1964); PATSY, THE(1964); THOSE CALLOWAYS(1964); DEAR BRIGETTE(1965); GREATEST STORY EVER TOLD, THE(1965); THAT DARN CAT(1965); DAYDREAMER, THE(1966); GNOME-MOBILE, THE(1967)
Misc. Silents
RUBBER HEELS(1927)
Edna Wynn
JOHNNY ON THE RUN(1953, Brit.)
Forrest Wynn
BANG THE DRUM SLOWLY(1973)
George Wynn
Silents
FLAG LIEUTENANT, THE(1919, Brit.); MARRIED TO A MORMAN(1922, Brit.); TRAPPED BY THE MORMONS(1922, Brit.); MONKEY'S PAW, THE(1923, Brit.)
Gordon Wynn
SCANDAL INCORPORATED(1956); VENGEANCE(1964)
Helen Wynn
THESE THIRTY YEARS(1934)
Hugh Wynn
HALLELUJAH(1929), ed; ANNA CHRISTIE(1930), ed; DIVORCEE, THE(1930), ed; NAVY BLUES(1930), ed; PAID(1930), ed; ROMANCE(1930), ed; CHAMP, THE(1931), ed; FREE SOUL, A(1931), ed; STRANGERS MAY KISS(1931), ed; ARSENE LUPIN(1932), ed; FAITHLESS(1932), ed; FAST LIFE(1932), ed; HUDDLE(1932), ed; ANOTHER LANGUAGE(1933), ed; CHRISTOPHER BEAN(1933), ed; CLEAR ALL WIRES(1933), ed; LOOKING FORWARD(1933), ed; SHOULD LADIES BEHAVE?(1933), ed; MYSTERY OF MR. X, THE(1934), ed; PAINTED VEIL, THE(1934), ed; SADIE MCKEE(1934), ed; STAMBOUL QUEST(1934), ed; KIND LADY(1935), ed; MAD LOVE(1935), ed; RENDEZVOUS(1935), ed; TIMES SQUARE LADY(1935), ed; WINNING TICKET, THE(1935), ed
Silents
ARSENE LUPIN(1917); HE WHO GETS SLAPPED(1924), ed; BIG PARADE, THE(1925), ed; SCARLET LETTER, THE(1926), ed; CALLAHANS AND THE MURPHYS, THE(1927), ed; LOVE(1927), ed; CAMERAMAN, THE(1928), ed; CROWD, THE(1928), ed; SHOW PEOPLE(1928), ed; WOMAN OF AFFAIRS, A(1928), ed
Jack Wynn
SLIGHTLY HONORABLE(1940)
James Wynn
1984
FOREVER YOUNG(1984, Brit.); GIVE MY REGARDS TO BROAD STREET(1984, Brit.)
John Wynn
KING ARTHUR WAS A GENTLEMAN(1942, Brit.); MILLIONS LIKE US(1943, Brit.); OVER THE GARDEN WALL(1950, Brit.); THEY WERE NOT DIVIDED(1951, Brit.); GLORY AT SEA(1952, Brit.); JUDGMENT DEFERRED(1952, Brit.); WHISPERING SMITH VERSUS SCOTLAND YARD(1952, Brit.); MEN ARE CHILDREN TWICE(1953, Brit.); TERROR STREET(1953); SAFARI(1956)
Joseph Wynn
CHANGE OF MIND(1969)
Joyce Wynn
THIS ABOVE ALL(1942)
Keenan Wynn
CHAINED(1934); FOR ME AND MY GAL(1942); NORTHWEST RANGERS(1942); SOMEWHERE I'LL FIND YOU(1942); BETWEEN TWO WOMEN(1944); LOST ANGEL(1944); MARRIAGE IS A PRIVATE AFFAIR(1944); SEE HERE, PRIVATE HARGROVE(1944); SINCE YOU WENT AWAY(1944); CLOCK, THE(1945); WEEKEND AT THE WALDORF(1945); WHAT NEXT, CORPORAL HARGROVE?(1945); WITHOUT LOVE(1945); ZIEGFELD FOLLIES(1945); COCKEYED MIRACLE, THE(1946); EASY TO WED(1946); NO LEAVE, NO LOVE(1946); THRILL OF BRAZIL, THE(1946); HUCKSTERS, THE(1947); SONG OF THE THIN MAN(1947); B. F.'S DAUGHTER(1948); MY DEAR SECRETARY(1948); THREE MUSKETEERS, THE(1948); NEPTUNE'S DAUGHTER(1949); THAT MIDNIGHT KISS(1949); ANNIE GET YOUR GUN(1950); LOVE THAT BRUTE(1950); THREE LITTLE WORDS(1950); ANGELS IN THE OUTFIELD(1951); IT'S A BIG COUNTRY(1951); KIND LADY(1951); MR. IMPERIUM(1951); ROYAL WEDDING(1951); TEXAS CARNIVAL(1951); BELLE OF NEW YORK, THE(1952); DESPERATE SEARCH(1952); FEARLESS FAGAN(1952); HOLIDAY FOR SINNERS(1952); PHONE CALL FROM A STRANGER(1952); SKY FULL OF MOON(1952); ALL THE BROTHERS WERE VALIANT(1953); BATTLE CIRCUS(1953); CODE TWO(1953); KISS ME KATE(1953); LONG, LONG TRAILER, THE(1954); MEN OF THE FIGHTING LADY(1954); TENNESSEE CHAMP(1954); GLASS SLIPPER, THE(1955); MARAUDERS, THE(1955); RUNNING WILD(1955); SHACK OUT ON 101(1955); JOHNNY CONCHO(1956); MAN IN THE GREY FLANNEL SUIT, THE(1956); NAKED HILLS, THE(1956); FUZZY PINK NIGHTGOWN, THE(1957); GREAT MAN, THE(1957); JOE BUTTERFLY(1957); DEEP SIX, THE(1958); PERFECT FURLOUGH, THE(1958); TIME TO LOVE AND A TIME TO DIE, A(1958); TOUCH OF EVIL(1958); HOLE IN THE HEAD, A(1959); THAT KIND OF WOMAN(1959); CROWDED SKY, THE(1960); ABSENT-MINDED PROFESSOR, THE(1961); KING OF THE ROARING TWENTIES–THE STORY OF ARNOLD ROTHSTEIN(1961); SCARFACE MOB, THE(1962); BAY OF SAINT MICHEL, THE(1963, Brit.); SON OF FLUBBER(1963); AMERICANIZATION OF EMILY, THE(1964); BIKINI BEACH(1964); DR. STRANGELOVE: OR HOW I LEARNED TO STOP WORRYING AND LOVE THE BOMB(1964); HONEYMOON HOTEL(1964); MAN IN THE MIDDLE(1964, U.S./Brit.); NIGHTMARE IN THE SUN(1964); PATSY, THE(1964); STAGE TO THUNDER ROCK(1964); GREAT RACE, THE(1965); AROUND THE WORLD UNDER THE SEA(1966); NIGHT OF THE GRIZZLY, THE(1966); PROMISE HER ANYTHING(1966, Brit.); STAGECOACH(1966); POINT BLANK(1967); WAR WAGON, THE(1967); WARNING SHOT(1967); WELCOME TO HARD TIMES(1967); FINIAN'S RAINBOW(1968); RUN LIKE A THIEF(1968, Span.); MACKENNA'S GOLD(1969); MONITORS, THE(1969); ONCE UPON A TIME IN THE WEST(1969, U.S./Ital.); SMITH(1969); VIVA MAX!(1969); 80 STEPS TO JONAH(1969); LOVING(1970); ANIMALS, THE(1971); PRETTY MAIDS ALL IN A ROW(1971); CANCEL MY RESERVATION(1972); MECHANIC, THE(1972); SNOWBALL EXPRESS(1972); BLACK JACK(1973); HERBIE RIDES AGAIN(1974); INTERNECINE PROJECT, THE(1974, Brit.); DEVIL'S RAIN, THE(1975, U.S./Mex.); DON'T GO NEAR THE WATER(1975); MAN WHO WOULD NOT DIE, THE(1975); NASHVILLE(1975); KILLER INSIDE ME, THE(1976); SHAGGY D.A., THE(1976); HIGH VELOCITY(1977); ORCA(1977); COACH(1978); LASERBLAST(1978); PIRANHA(1978); CLONUS HORROR, THE(1979); DARK, THE(1979); MONSTER(1979); SUNBURN(1979); GLOVE, THE(1980); JUST TELL ME WHAT YOU WANT(1980); BEST FRIENDS(1982); LAST UNICORN, THE(1982); HYSTERICAL(1983); WAVELENGTH(1983)
Misc. Talkies
B.J. LANG PRESENTS(1971); JAMAICAN GOLD(1971); MAN WITH THE ICY EYES, THE(1971); LEGEND OF EARL DURAND, THE(1974); WOMAN FOR ALL MEN, A(1975); HE IS MY BROTHER(1976); LUCIFER COMPLEX, THE(1978); HOLLYWOOD KNIGHT(1979); MONSTROID(1980)
Kitty Wynn
Misc. Talkies
MIRRORS(1978)
Manny Wynn
GIRL WITH GREEN EYES(1964, Brit.), ph; LUCK OF GINGER COFFEY, THE(1964, U.S./Can.), ph; HAVING A WILD WEEKEND(1965, Brit.), ph; TIME LOST AND TIME REMEMBERED(1966, Brit.), ph; UNCLE, THE(1966, Brit.), ph; SMASHING TIME(1967 Brit.), ph; NICE GIRL LIKE ME, A(1969, Brit.), ph; HAPPINESS CAGE, THE(1972), ph
Mary Wynn
KING OF THE GYPSIES(1978)
Silents
SHATTERED IDOLS(1922)
Misc. Silents
WOMAN HE LOVED, THE(1922); POWER DIVINE, THE(1923); RANGE PATROL, THE(1923)
Mason Wynn
GHOST TOWN RENEGADES(1947); CHECK YOUR GUNS(1948)

May Wynn
DREAMBOAT(1952); FARMER TAKES A WIFE, THE(1953); TREASURE OF THE GOLDEN CONDOR(1953); CAINE MUTINY, THE(1954); THEY RODE WEST(1954); VIOLENT MEN, THE(1955); MAN IS ARMED, THE(1956); WHITE SQUAW, THE(1956); TAMING SUTTON'S GAL(1957); UNKNOWN TERROR, THE(1957); HONG KONG AFFAIR(1958)
Silents
EDUCATION OF NICKY, THE(1921, Brit.), w

Nan Wynn
MILLION DOLLAR BABY(1941); SHOT IN THE DARK, THE(1941); PARDON MY SARONG(1942); IS EVERYBODY HAPPY?(1943); PRINCESS O'ROURKE(1943); INTRIGUE(1947)

Ned Wynn
SON OF FLUBBER(1963); PAJAMA PARTY(1964); PATSY, THE(1964); HOW TO STUFF A WILD BIKINI(1965); STAGECOACH(1966); CALIFORNIA DREAMING(1979), a, w

Pearline Wynn
WALKING TALL(1973)

Peggy Wynn
WILD COUNTRY(1947)

Ric Wynn
REACHING OUT(1983)

Robert Wynn
RESURRECTION OF ZACHARY WHEELER, THE(1971), d

Tracy Keenan Wynn
TRIBES(1970), w; LONGEST YARD, THE(1974), w; DROWNING POOL, THE(1975), w; DEEP, THE(1977), w

Tracy Wynn
UP FROM THE BEACH(1965)

Zoe Wynn
CATCH AS CATCH CAN(1937, Brit.); OLD MOTHER RILEY(1937, Brit.); WHO KILLED FEN MARKHAM?(1937, Brit.); SIMPLY TERRIFIC(1938, Brit.); DISCOVERIES(1939, Brit.); LARCENY STREET(1941, Brit.)

Tom Wynn [Wally West]
DESERT MESA(1935)

Barry Wynne
HOUSE OF BLACKMAIL(1953, Brit.)

Bert Wynne
Silents
GOD AND THE MAN(1918, Brit.); NOT GUILTY(1919, Brit.); POLAR STAR, THE(1919, Brit.); MANCHESTER MAN, THE(1920, Brit.), d; HANDY ANDY(1921, Brit.), d; CALL OF THE EAST, THE(1922, Brit.), p,d&w
Misc. Silents
UNDER SUSPICION(1916, Brit.); MY SWEETHEART(1918, Brit.); TOWN OF CROOKED WAYS, THE(1920, Brit.), d; BELPHEGOR THE MOUNTEBANK(1921, Brit.), d; DICK'S FAIRY(1921, Brit.), d; LITTLE MEG'S CHILDREN(1921, Brit.), d; HIS SUPREME SACRIFICE(1922, Brit.), d; GOD'S PRODIGAL(1923, Brit.), d; REMEMBRANCE(1927, Brit.), d

Darcel Wynne
JESUS CHRIST, SUPERSTAR(1973)

Diana Wynne
TAKE A POWDER(1953, Brit.)

Fred Wynne
REAL BLOKE, A(1935, Brit.)

George Wynne
Misc. Silents
DARBY AND JOAN(1919, Brit.)

Gilbert Wynne
MIX ME A PERSON(1962, Brit.); CLEGG(1969, Brit.); NIGHT AFTER NIGHT AFTER NIGHT(1970, Brit.)

Gladys Wynne
Misc. Silents
SPAN OF LIFE, THE(1914)

Gordon Wynne
TEN GENTLEMEN FROM WEST POINT(1942); WE'VE NEVER BEEN LICKED(1943); FOUR JILLS IN A JEEP(1944); LITTLE BIG HORN(1951); BUSHWHACKERS, THE(1952); DEEP IN MY HEART(1954); THUNDER PASS(1954)

Greg Wynne
1984
MYSTERY MANSION(1984)

Herbert Wynne
SAFE AFFAIR, A(1931, Brit.), d; INTIMATE RELATIONS(1937, Brit.), p; LIVE WIRE, THE(1937, Brit.), p; PLAYBOY, THE(1942, Brit.), p; NIGHT OF MAGIC, A(1944, Brit.), d; LATE AT NIGHT(1946, Brit.), p

Hugh Wynne
Silents
AMERICAN WIDOW, AN(1917)

John Wynne
STORM OVER THE NILE(1955, Brit.)

Jonathan Wynne
JESUS CHRIST, SUPERSTAR(1973)

Ken Wynne
DECLINE AND FALL... OF A BIRD WATCHER(1969, Brit.)

Michael Wynne
FLAME IN THE STREETS(1961, Brit.); IN SEARCH OF THE CASTAWAYS(1962, Brit.); ROAD TO HONG KONG, THE(1962, U.S./Brit.); YOUNG, WILLING AND EAGER(1962, Brit.); PLACE TO GO, A(1964, Brit.); BUNNY LAKE IS MISSING(1965); JULIUS CAESAR(1970, Brit.); NOTHING BUT THE NIGHT(1975, Brit.)

Norman Wynne
HIDDEN HOMICIDE(1959, Brit.)

Ormonde Wynne
WICKHAM MYSTERY, THE(1931, Brit.)

Pamela Wynne
DEVOTION(1931), w

Peggy Wynne
KID SISTER, THE(1945); PRETENDER, THE(1947); DENVER KID, THE(1948); DESPERADOES OF DODGE CITY(1948); MANHATTAN ANGEL(1948); VICIOUS CIRCLE, THE(1948); CAGED(1950); CRAZY OVER HORSES(1951); MODERN MARRIAGE, A(1962); MUSIC MAN, THE(1962)

Misc. Talkies
TRAILING DANGER(1947)

Wynona
PASSION HOLIDAY(1963)

Jim Wynorski
FORBIDDEN WORLD(1982), w; SCREWBALLS(1983), w; SORCERESS(1983), w

Alan Wynroth
DRILLER KILLER(1979)

Angela Wynter
BURNING AN ILLUSION(1982, Brit.)

Dagmar [Dana] Wynter
COLONEL MARCH INVESTIGATES(1952,Brit.); CRIMSON PIRATE, THE(1952); IT STARTED IN PARADISE(1952, Brit.); WHITE CORRIDORS(1952, Brit.); WOMAN'S ANGLE, THE(1954, Brit.); LADY GODIVA RIDES AGAIN(1955, Brit.)

Dana Wynter
VIEW FROM POMPEY'S HEAD, THE(1955); D-DAY, THE SIXTH OF JUNE(1956); INVASION OF THE BODY SNATCHERS(1956); SOMETHING OF VALUE(1957); FRAULEIN(1958); IN LOVE AND WAR(1958); SHAKE HANDS WITH THE DEVIL(1959, Ireland); SINK THE BISMARCK!(1960, Brit.); ON THE DOUBLE(1961); LIST OF ADRIAN MESSENGER, THE(1963); IF HE HOLLERS, LET HIM GO(1968); AIRPORT(1970); SANTEE(1973); SAVAGE, THE(1975, Fr.)
Misc. Talkies
TRIANGLE(1971); VENGEANCE OF VIRGO(1972)

Mark Wynter
JUST FOR FUN(1963, Brit.); HORROR HOUSE(1970, Brit.); SUPERMAN(1978)

Paul Wynter
ATLAS AGAINST THE CYCLOPS(1963, Ital.)

Charlette Wynters
HIGH SIERRA(1941)

Charlotte Wynters
HIS WOMAN(1931); PERSONAL MAID(1931); STRUGGLE, THE(1931); IVORY-HANDLED GUN(1935); DAN MATTHEWS(1936); MISTER CINDERELLA(1936); TRAIL OF THE LONESOME PINE, THE(1936); CLARENCE(1937); GIRL OVERBOARD(1937); LET'S MAKE A MILLION(1937); CIPHER BUREAU(1938); PROFESSOR BEWARE(1938); REFORMATORY(1938); SINNERS IN PARADISE(1938); SUNSET TRAIL(1938); NANCY DREW, TROUBLE SHOOTER(1939); PANAMA PATROL(1939); PRIDE OF THE NAVY(1939); RENEGADE TRAIL(1939); WOMEN, THE(1939); CITY OF CHANCE(1940); GALLANT SONS(1940); PAROLE FIXER(1940); QUEEN OF THE MOB(1940); TOMBOY(1940); DIVE BOMBER(1941); DR. KILDARE'S VICTORY(1941); ELLERY QUEEN AND THE MURDER RING(1941); GREAT LIE, THE(1941); LIFE BEGINS FOR ANDY HARDY(1941); MARRIED BACHELOR(1941); ARE HUSBANDS NECESSARY?(1942); DESPERATE CHANCE FOR ELLERY QUEEN, A(1942); FALCON'S BROTHER, THE(1942); HALF WAY TO SHANGHAI(1942); NOW, VOYAGER(1942); HARVEST MELODY(1943); MAN OF COURAGE(1943); UNDERDOG, THE(1943); MAMA LOVES PAPA(1945); PHANTOM SPEAKS, THE(1945); LULU BELLE(1948); WOMAN OF DISTINCTION, A(1950); FOX-FIRE(1955); EIGHTEEN AND ANXIOUS(1957)
Misc. Talkies
CALLING OF DAN MATTHEWS, THE(1936)

Jack Wynters
PARALLELS(1980, Can.), p

Sharyn Wynters
WESTWORLD(1973)

Diana Wynyard
RASPUTIN AND THE EMPRESS(1932); CAVALCADE(1933); MEN MUST FIGHT(1933); REUNION IN VIENNA(1933); LET'S TRY AGAIN(1934); ONE MORE RIVER(1934); WHERE SINNERS MEET(1934); FUGITIVE, THE(1940, Brit.); GASLIGHT(1940); PRIME MINISTER, THE(1941, Brit.); VOICE IN THE NIGHT, A(1941, Brit.); REMARKABLE MR. KIPPS(1942, Brit.); IDEAL HUSBAND, AN(1948, Brit.); TOM BROWN'S SCHOOLDAYS(1951, Brit.); ISLAND IN THE SUN(1957)

Hans Wyprachtiger
ODESSA FILE, THE(1974, Brit./Ger.); VERONIKA VOSS(1982, Ger.); KAMIKAZE '89(1983, Ger.)

Charles Wyrick
ON STAGE EVERYBODY(1945), set d; BRUTE FORCE(1947), set d; WISTFUL WIDOW OF WAGON GAP, THE(1947), set d

Frank Wyrick
TOMORROW IS FOREVER(1946)

Don Wyse
FIVE DAYS FROM HOME(1978)

Linda Wyse
SO SAD ABOUT GLORIA(1973)

Wojciech Wysocki
CONDUCTOR, THE(1981, Pol.)

Amanda Wyss
FAST TIMES AT RIDGEMONT HIGH(1982)
1984
NIGHTMARE ON ELM STREET, A(1984)

Johann David Wyss
SWISS FAMILY ROBINSON(1940), w

Johann Wyss
SWISS FAMILY ROBINSON(1960), w

Mandy Wyss
FORCE: FIVE(1981)

Alfred U. Wysse
RAMPARTS WE WATCH, THE(1940)

Grant Wytock
TONIGHT OR NEVER(1931), ed

Grant Wytock
Silents
REVELATION(1924), ed

The X-L's
TIME TO SING, A(1968)
Leon Xanrof
LOVE PARADE, THE(1929), w
Elli Xanthaki
THANOS AND DESPINA(1970, Fr./Gr.)
Peter Xantho
DREAM OF KINGS, A(1969)
Xantippe
DANGER ON THE AIR(1938), w
Stavros Xarhakos
RAPE, THE(1965, Gr.), m&md; RED LANTERNS(1965, Gr.), m; HOT MONTH OF
AUGUST, THE(1969, Gr.), m; SIGNS OF LIFE(1981, Ger.), m
Nelson Xavier
DONA FLOR AND HER TWO HUSHANDS(1977, Braz.)
1984
GABRIELA(1984, Braz.)
Xavier Cugat and His Band
BATHING BEAUTY(1944)
Xavier Cugat and his Orchestra
GO WEST, YOUNG MAN(1936); YOU WERE NEVER LOVELIER(1942); HEAT'S ON,
THE(1943); THRILL OF A ROMANCE(1945); WEEKEND AT THE WALDORF(1945);
NO LEAVE, NO LOVE(1946); ON AN ISLAND WITH YOU(1948)
Xavier Cugat and His Orchestra with Lina Romay
STAGE DOOR CANTEEN(1943)
Xavier Cugat Orchestra
TWO GIRLS AND A SAILOR(1944)
Xenia
MR. MAGOO'S HOLIDAY FESTIVAL(1970), anim; PHANTOM TOLLBOOTH,
THE(1970), anim
Maria Xenia
IT HAPPENED IN ATHENS(1962); GIRL CAN'T STOP, THE(1966, Fr./Gr.)
Xenia and Boyer
MINSTREL BOY, THE(1937, Brit.)
Stavros Xenidis
POLICEMAN OF THE 16TH PRECINCT, THE(1963, Gr.)
Mary Xenoudaki
OEDIPUS THE KING(1968, Brit.)
Anthony J. Xydias
HEROES OF THE ALAMO(1938), p

Y

Y-Knot Twirlers
KENTUCKY JUBILEE(1951)
Al Y'Barra
RUN FOR THE SUN(1956), art d
Lee Ya-Ching
DISPUTED PASSAGE(1939)
Marco Ya'acobi [Marco Yocovlevitz]
SIMCHON FAMILY, THE(1969, Israel), ph
Moshe Yaari
THEY WERE TEN(1961, Israel); PILLAR OF FIRE, THE(1963, Israel)
Anatoliy Yabbarov
THERE WAS AN OLD COUPLE(1967, USSR); RED AND THE WHITE, THE(1969, Hung./USSR)
Frank Yablans
OTHER SIDE OF MIDNIGHT, THE(1977), p; FURY, THE(1978), a, p; NORTH DALLAS FORTY(1979), p, w; MOMMIE DEAREST(1981), p, w; MONSIGNOR(1982), p; STAR CHAMBER, THE(1983), p
1984
KIDCO(1984), p
Irwin Yablans
EDUCATION OF SONNY CARSON, THE(1974), p; ROLLER BOOGIE(1979), w; HELL NIGHT(1981), p; SEDUCTION, THE(1982), p
1984
TANK(1984), p
Mickey Yablans
HALLOWEEN(1978)
1984
TANK(1984)
S. Yablokov
Misc. Silents
THREE FRIENDS AND AN INVENTION(1928, USSR)
Harold Yablonsky
SECRET OF THE PURPLE REEF, THE(1960), w
Yabo Yablonsky
JAGUAR LIVES(1979), w; VICTORY(1981), w
Teiji Yabushita
PANDA AND THE MAGIC SERPENT(1961, Jap.), d
Tiji Yabushita
PANDA AND THE MAGIC SERPENT(1961, Jap.), w
Louis Yaccarino
SEVEN UPS, THE(1973)
Rick Yacco
KILL SQUAD(1982), ed
Z. Yacconelli
CRISIS(1950); STORY OF THREE LOVES, THE(1953)
Elizabeth Yach
Misc. Silents
DO THE DEAD TALK?(1920)
Kaoru Yachigusa
SAMURAI(PART III)** (1967, Jap.); SAMURAI(1955, Jap.); HUMAN VAPOR, THE(1964, Jap.); SAMURAI ASSASSIN(1965, Jap.); SONG FROM MY HEART, THE(1970, Jap.)
Karuo Yachigusa
MADAME BUTTERFLY(1955 Ital./Jap.)
N. Yachmenev
Misc. Silents
MURDER OF GENERAL GRYAZNOV, THE(1921, USSR)
A. Yachnitskiy
WAR AND PEACE(1968, USSR)
A. Yachnitsky
GENERAL SUVOROV(1941, USSR)
Yacht Club Boys
STAGE STRUCK(1936)
The Yacht Club Boys
PIGSKIN PARADE(1936); ARTISTS AND MODELS(1937); THRILL OF A LIFETIME(1937); ARTISTS AND MODELS ABROAD(1938); COCOANUT GROVE(1938)
Scott Yacoby
CHILDRENS GAMES(1969)
Frank Yaconelli
SENOR AMERICANO(1929); FIREBRAND JORDAN(1930); PARADE OF THE WEST(1930); STRAWBERRY ROAN(1933); DEATH TAKES A HOLIDAY(1934); IT HAPPENED ONE NIGHT(1934); NIGHT AT THE OPERA, A(1935); WESTERN FRONTIER(1935); DOWN TO THE SEA(1936); GUN PLAY(1936); HEIR TO TROUBLE(1936); LAWLESS RIDERS(1936); LUCKY TERROR(1936); ROMANCE RIDES THE RANGE(1936); THREE MESQUITEERS, THE(1936); FIREFLY, THE(1937); IT COULD HAPPEN TO YOU(1937); YOU CAN'T HAVE EVERYTHING(1937); ACROSS THE PLAINS(1939); DRIFTING WESTWARD(1939); ESCAPE TO PARADISE(1939); TRIGGER SMITH(1939); UNION PACIFIC(1939); WILD HORSE CANYON(1939); CHEYENNE KID, THE(1940); DR. CYCLOPS(1940); EAST SIDE KIDS(1940); MARK OF ZORRO, THE(1940); PIONEER DAYS(1940); STRANGER ON THE THIRD FLOOR(1940); TORRID ZONE(1940); BARNACLE BILL(1941); DRIFTIN' KID, THE(1941); FORCED LANDING(1941); LAS VEGAS NIGHTS(1941); RIDING THE SUNSET TRAIL(1941); TWO IN A TAXI(1941); ARIZONA ROUNDUP(1941); LONE STAR LAW MEN(1942); WESTERN MAIL(1942); MAN OF COURAGE(1943); BEAUTY AND THE BANDIT(1946); SLIGHTLY SCANDALOUS(1946); THRILL OF BRAZIL, THE(1946); WILD HORSE MESA(1947); DUDE GOES WEST, THE(1948); ALIAS THE CHAMP(1949); SEPTEMBER AFFAIR(1950); PLACE IN THE SUN, A(1951); ABBOTT AND COSTELLO MEET CAPTAIN KIDD(1952); HANGMAN'S KNOT(1952); DRAGON'S GOLD(1954); RACERS, THE(1955); SERENADE(1956)
Misc. Talkies
BLAZING JUSTICE(1936); WILD HORSE RANGE(1940); WHERE TRAILS END(1942); SOUTH OF MONTEREY(1946); RIDING THE CALIFORNIA TRAIL(1947)

Misc. Silents
I'LL BE THERE(1927), d
Lou Yaconelli
DRIFTIN' KID, THE(1941)
Zacharias Yaconelli
SEPTEMBER AFFAIR(1950); SECRET OF THE INCAS(1954)
Zachary Yaconelli
BARON OF ARIZONA, THE(1950); GOLDEN BLADE, THE(1953); MA AND PA KETTLE ON VACATION(1953); COMMAND, THE(1954); THREE COINS IN THE FOUNTAIN(1954)
Frank Yaconnelli
MADONNA OF THE DESERT(1948)
Ahmed Yacoubi
ROLLOVER(1981)
Moutapha Yade
CEDDO(1978, Nigeria)
Ram Yadekar
HEAT AND DUST(1983, Brit.), art d
Joseph Yadin
FOUR IN A JEEP(1951, Switz.); STOP TRAIN 349(1964, Fr./Ital./Ger.); TRUNK TO CAIRO(1966, Israel/Ger.); WORLDS APART(1980, U.S., Israel)
Yosef Yadin
HILL 24 DOESN'T ANSWER(1955, Israel)
Yossi Yadin
LIES MY FATHER TOLD ME(1975, Can.)
Michiko Yaegaki
GAMERA VERSUS VIRAS(1968, Jap)
Biff Yaeger
FRANCES(1982)
Bill Yaeger
JET PILOT(1957)
Kelly Yaegermann
CAT MURKIL AND THE SILKS(1976)
Stephen Yafa
SUMMERTREE(1971), w
Stephen H. Yafa
THREE IN THE ATTIC(1968), w
Ben Yaffe
WEREWOLF OF WASHINGTON(1973)
Louise Yaffe
1984
TOP SECRET!(1984)
Ben Yaffee
FUGITIVE KIND, THE(1960); PEOPLE NEXT DOOR, THE(1970); SOME OF MY BEST FRIENDS ARE...(1971)
Grigoriy Yagdfeld
DAY THE EARTH FROZE, THE(1959, Fin./USSR), w
Sol Yaged
BENNY GOODMAN STORY, THE(1956), m
Gadi Yageel
DIAMONDS(1975, U.S./Israel)
Norman Yager
WAY OUT(1966)
Raouf Ben Yaghlane
LA BALANCE(1983, Fr.)
James Yagi
HUNTERS, THE(1958); GALLANT HOURS, THE(1960); BRIDGE TO THE SUN(1961); MANCHURIAN CANDIDATE, THE(1962); KING KONG VERSUS GODZILLA(1963, Jap.); UGLY AMERICAN, THE(1963); WALK, DON'T RUN(1966)
Jim Yagi
NAVY WIFE(1956)
Masako Yagi
PLEASURES OF THE FLESH, THE(1965); MUDDY RIVER(1982, Jap.)
Masao Yagi
THROUGH DAYS AND MONTHS(1969 Jap.), m; FRIENDLY KILLER, THE(1970, Jap.), m
Massao Yagi
GOODBYE, MOSCOW(1968, Jap.), m
Shinichi Yagi
FOX WITH NINE TAILS, THE(1969, Jap.), d
Roy M. Yaginuma
VIOLATED PARADISE(1963, Ital./Jap.), ph
Lydia Yaguinto
Silents
NERO(1922, U.S./Ital.)
Alexander Yahalomi
JUDITH(1965)
Kurt Yahgjian
JESUS CHRIST, SUPERSTAR(1973)
Fuji Yahiro
BUDDHA(1965, Jap.), w; GREAT WALL, THE(1965, Jap.), w
Kurt Yahjian
HAIR(1979)
Bill Yahraus
HEARTLAND(1980), ed
1984
COUNTRY(1984), ed
William H. Yahraus
SAMMY STOPS THE WORLD zero(1978), ed
Nobuo Yajim
MESSAGE FROM SPACE(1978, Jap.), d
Michiko Yajima
HARBOR LIGHT YOKOHAMA(1970, Jap.)
Nobuo Yajima
TERROR BENEATH THE SEA(1966, Jap.), spec eff; MESSAGE FROM SPACE(1978, Jap.), spec eff
Don Yaka
THREE WEEKS OF LOVE(1965), ch

K. Yakevleva
Misc. Silents
SCANDAL?(1929, USSR)
Nikolai Yakhontov
SON OF THE REGIMENT(1948, USSR)
Moni Yakim
JACQUES BREL IS ALIVE AND WELL AND LIVING IN PARIS(1975), ch
Leonard Yakir
MOURNING SUIT, THE(1975, Can.), d; OUT OF THE BLUE(1982), p, w
Nikolay Yakolev
DIMKA(1964, USSR), m
William Yakota
I WAS AN AMERICAN SPY(1951)
M. Yakovchenko
TRAIN GOES TO KIEV, THE(1961, USSR)
N. Yakovchenko
NIGHT BEFORE CHRISTMAS, A(1963, USSR)
Nikolai Yakovchenko
KIEV COMEDY, A(1963, USSR)
Mikhail Yakovich
SONS AND MOTHERS(1967, USSR), ph
Yuri Yakoviev
BALLAD OF A HUSSAR(1963, USSR)
K. Yakovlev
Misc. Silents
PALACE AND FORTRESS(1924, USSR)
Sergey Yakoviev
HOUSE WITH AN ATTIC, THE(1964, USSR)
V. Yakovlev
NEW TEACHER, THE(1941, USSR), ph; SOUND OF LIFE, THE(1962, USSR)
Y. Yakovlev
Misc. Silents
BEILIS CASE, THE(1917, USSR)
Yuri Yakovlev
IDIOT, THE(1960, USSR)
Marko Yakovlevich
CLOUDS OVER ISRAEL(1966, Israel), ph
Ye. Yakuba
SLEEPING BEAUTY, THE(1966, USSR), set d
Emiko Yakumo
Misc. Silents
STORY OF FLOATING WEEDS, A(1934, Jap.)
I. Yakushenko
WELCOME KOSTYA!(1965, USSR), m
O. Yakushev
WHEN THE TREES WERE TALL(1965, USSR)
V. Yakushev
DAY THE EARTH FROZE, THE(1959, Fin./USSR), ph
G. Yakutovich
SHADOWS OF FORGOTTEN ANCESTORS(1967, USSR), art d
Carl Yale
ONCE UPON A COFFEE HOUSE(1965), w
Linda Yale
ARTISTS AND MODELS ABROAD(1938)
Stan Yale
YOUNG GIANTS(1983)
1984
RHINESTONE(1984); TERMINATOR, THE(1984)
Yale Puppeteers
WHOM THE GODS DESTROY(1934)
The Yale Puppeteers
I AM SUZANNE(1934)
Richard Yalem
DELIRIUM(1979), w
Yavuz Yalinkilic
DRY SUMMER(1967, Turkey)
David Yallop
BEYOND REASONABLE DOUBT(1980, New Zeal.), w
G. Yalovich
MEET ME IN MOSCOW(1966, USSR)
Jaron Yaltan
LITTLE HUT, THE(1957); MAN AT THE TOP(1973, Brit.)
Cengiz Yaltkaya
LUGGAGE OF THE GODS(1983), m
Jaron Yalton
FLAME OVER INDIA(1960, Brit.)
Conrad Yama
VIRGIN PRESIDENT, THE(1968); CHAIRMAN, THE(1969); KING OF MARVIN GARDENS, THE(1972); MIDWAY(1976)
Michael Yama
MY TUTOR(1983)
1984
INDIANA JONES AND THE TEMPLE OF DOOM(1984)
Otto Yama
RACING STRAIN, THE(1933)
Yachuco Yama
OPERATION KID BROTHER(1967, Ital.)
Yamaci
DRY SUMMER(1967, Turkey), m
Yamada
TOWN LIKE ALICE, A(1958, Brit.)
Eiichi Yamada
JUDO SHOWDOWN(1966, Jap.), m
Futaro Yamada
PLEASURES OF THE FLESH, THE(1965), w
Hioshi Yamada
MAJIN(1968, Jap.), ed

Isuzu Yamada
THRONE OF BLOOD(1961, Jap.); YOJIMBO(1961, Jap.); LOWER DEPTHS, THE(1962, Jap.); GREAT WALL, THE(1965, Jap.); DAREDEVIL IN THE CASTLE(1969, Jap.)
Kazuo Yamada
SAMURAI(PART III)** (1967, Jap.), ph; RICKSHAW MAN, THE(1960, Jap.), ph; I BOMBED PEARL HARBOR(1961, Jap.), ph; LIFE OF A COUNTRY DOCTOR(1961, Jap.), ph; SECRET OF THE TELEGIAN, THE(1961, Jap.), ph; TATSU(1962, Jap.), ph; CHUSHINGURA(1963, Jap.), ph; YOUTH AND HIS AMULET, THE(1963, Jap.), ph; BANDITS ON THE WIND(1964, Jap.), ph; RABBLE, THE(1965, Jap.), ph; GODZILLA VERSUS THE SEA MONSTER(1966, Jap.), ph; OUTPOST OF HELL(1966, Jap.), ph; RISE AGAINST THE SWORD(1966, Jap.), ph; WHAT'S UP, TIGER LILY?(1966), w, ph; REBELLION(1967, Jap.), ph; SON OF GODZILLA(1967, Jap.), ph; WHIRL-WIND(1968, Jap.), ph; DAREDEVIL IN THE CASTLE(1969, Jap.), ph; PORTRAIT OF HELL(1969, Jap.), ph; UNDER THE BANNER OF SAMURAI(1969, Jap.), ph
Kosaku Yamada
NEW EARTH, THE(1937, Jap./Ger.), m
Minosuke Yamada
RODAN(1958, Jap.); MYSTERIANS, THE(1959, Jap.); IKIRU(1960, Jap.)
Nobuo Yamada
WEIRD LOVE MAKERS, THE(1963, Jap.), w; TWO IN THE SHADOW(1968, Jap.), w
Shinji Yamada
THREE DOLLS FROM HONG KONG(1966, Jap.)
Taichi Yamada
ONCE A RAINY DAY(1968, Jap.), w
Yoji Yamada
TORA-SAN PART 2(1970, Jap.), d, w
Isao Yamagata
GATE OF HELL(1954, Jap.); MYSTERIOUS SATELLITE, THE(1956, Jap.); SEVEN SAMURAI, THE(1956, Jap.); TWILIGHT PATH(1965, Jap.); REBELLION(1967, Jap.); TROUT, THE(1982, Fr.)
Hitomi Yamaguchi
SONG FROM MY HEART, THE(1970, Jap.), w
Osamu Yamaguchi
ALL RIGHT, MY FRIEND(1983, Japan), art d
Shirley Yamaguchi
JAPANESE WAR BRIDE(1952); HOUSE OF BAMBOO(1955); NAVY WIFE(1956)
Yoshiko Yamaguchi
SCANDAL(1964, Jap.)
Hatoko Yamaji
ALMOST TRANSPARENT BLUE(1980, Jap.), ed
Sachiko Yamaji
ALL RIGHT, MY FRIEND(1983, Japan), ed
Iwao Yamaki
SPACE FIREBIRD 2772(1979, Jap.), ph
Tadashi Yamaki
KARATE, THE HAND OF DEATH(1961)
Masaji "Butch" Yamamota
THREE CAME HOME(1950)
Butch Yamamoto
TOKYO AFTER DARK(1959)
Eiichi Yamamoto
SPACE CRUISER(1977 Jap.), w
Fujiko Yamamoto
GOLDEN DEMON(1956, Jap.); TWILIGHT STORY, THE(1962, Jap.); ACTOR'S REVENGE, AN(1963, Jap.); MADAME AKI(1963, Jap.); BUDDHA(1965, Jap.); GREAT WALL, THE(1965, Jap.)
Gaku Yamamoto
SHOWDOWN FOR ZATOICHI(1968, Jap.)
Harry Yamamoto
Silents
BY PROXY(1918)
Karen Yamamoto
NAVY WIFE(1956)
Kei Yamamoto
LIVE YOUR OWN WAY(1970, Jap.); TENCHU!(1970, Jap.)
Michio Yamamoto
LAKE OF DRACULA(1973, Jap.), d
Naozumi Yamamoto
NIGHT IN BANGKOK(1966, Jap.), m; GANGSTER VIP, THE(1968, Jap.), m; COM-PUTER FREE-FOR-ALL(1969, Jap.), m; SNOW COUNTRY(1969, Jap.), m; TORA-SAN PART 2(1970, Jap.), m
Reisaburo Yamamoto
STRAY DOG(1963, Jap.)
Reizaburo Yamamoto
DRUNKEN ANGEL(1948, Jap.)
Ren Yamamoto
GODZILLA, RING OF THE MONSTERS(1956, Jap.); GODZILLA VS. THE THING(1964, Jap.)
Mayor Sak Yamamoto
GONE IN 60 SECONDS(1974)
Sanae Yamamoto
MAGIC BOY(1960, Jap.), anim d
Shoguro Yamamoto
SAMURAI FROM NOWHERE(1964, Jap.), w
Shugoro Yamamoto
SANJURO(1962, Jap.), w; THIS MADDING CROWD(1964, Jap.), w; SCARLET CA-MELLIA, THE(1965, Jap.), w; RED BEARD(1966, Jap.), w; KILL(1968, Jap.), w
Takeshi Yamamoto
TOKYO STORY(1972, Jap.), p
Togo Yamamoto
Silents
MIDNIGHT PATROL, THE(1918); SOMETHING TO THINK ABOUT(1920); TALE OF TWO WORLDS, A(1921); WHERE LIGHTS ARE LOW(1921); REPORTED MIS-SING(1922)
Misc. Silents
PAGAN LOVE(1920)

Yasushi Yamamoto
WESTWARD DESPERADO(1961, Jap.); MOTHRA(1962, Jap.)
Yoko Yamamoto
GAPPA THE TRIFIBIAN MONSTER(1967, Jap.); FRIENDLY KILLER, THE(1970, Jap.)
Yuko Yamamoto
1984
MIXED BLOOD(1984)
Hiroyasu Yamamura
GODZILLA VERSUS THE COSMIC MONSTER(1974, Jap.), w
So Yamamura
BARBARIAN AND THE GEISHA, THE(1958); HUMAN CONDITION, THE(1959, Jap.); LIFE OF A COUNTRY DOCTOR(1961, Jap.); STAR OF HONG KONG(1962, Jap.); INHERITANCE, THE(1964, Jap.); SCHOOL FOR SEX(1966, Jap.); EMPEROR AND A GENERAL, THE(1968, Jap.); TOKYO STORY(1972, Jap.); PROPHECIES OF NOSTRADAMUS(1974, Jap.)
1984
ANTARCTICA(1984, Jap.)
Soh Yamamura
TORA! TORA! TORA!(1970, U.S./Jap.)
Sadao Yamanaka
SAGA OF THE VAGABONDS(1964, Jap.), w
Hiroshi Yamanami
HARBOR LIGHT YOKOHAMA(1970, Jap.)
Hisako Yamane
LIFE OF OHARU(1964, Jap.)
Hisataka Yamane
GIRL I ABANDONED, THE(1970, Jap.)
Gary Yamani
LIAR'S DICE(1980), m
Toshinari Yamano
EAST CHINA SEA(1969, Jap.)
Masanori Yamanoi
KURAGEJIMA–LEGENDS FROM A SOUTHERN ISLAND(1970, Jap.), p
Shojuro Yamanouch
1984
WARRIORS OF THE WIND(1984, Jap.), anim
Akira Yamanouchi
LONGING FOR LOVE(1966, Jap.)
Hisashi Yamanouchi
GIRL I ABANDONED, THE(1970, Jap.), w; LIVE YOUR OWN WAY(1970, Jap.), w
Ken Yamanouchi
HARBOR LIGHT YOKOHAMA(1970, Jap.)
Shizuo Yamanouchi
OHAYO(1962, Jap.), p; SNOW COUNTRY(1969, Jap.), p
Tetsuya Yamanouchi
DAY THE SUN ROSE, THE(1969, Jap.), d
Iris Yamaoka
PETTICOAT FEVER(1936); WAIKIKI WEDDING(1937)
Otto Yamaoka
BENSON MURDER CASE, THE(1930); BLACK CAMEL, THE(1931); LIMEHOUSE BLUES(1934); WE'RE RICH AGAIN(1934); WEDDING NIGHT, THE(1935); LIBELED LADY(1936); NIGHT WAITRESS(1936); PETTICOAT FEVER(1936); RHYTHM ON THE RANGE(1936)
Otto Yamaoko
HATCHET MAN, THE(1932)
Shugoro Yamaoto
DODESKA-DEN(1970, Jap.), w
Ellen Yamasaki
OFFERING, THE(1936, Can.)
Emily Yamasaki
CHAN IS MISSING(1982)
Kiyoshi Yamasaki
CONAN THE BARBARIAN(1982)
Sheri Yamasaki
WALK, DON'T RUN(1966)
Tsutomu Yamasaki
DEMON POND(1980, Jap.)
Yoshikazu Yamasawa
GREEN SLIME, THE(1969), ph
Eiji Yamashiro
BATTLE OF THE CORAL SEA(1959)
Hiroshi Yamashita
NUTCRACKER FANTASY(1979), set d
Jun-ichiro Yamashita
YOUTH IN FURY(1961, Jap.)
Junichiro Yamashita
GAMERA THE INVINCIBLE(1966, Jap.)
Kikuji Yamashita
SHE AND HE(1967, Jap.)
Tadashi Yamashita
SEVEN(1979); OCTAGON, THE(1980)
Taro Yamashita
KARATE, THE HAND OF DEATH(1961)
Yamashta
PHASE IV(1974), m
Stomu Yamashta
TEMPEST(1982), m
Akira Yamauchi
GODZILLA VERSUS THE SMOG MONSTER(1972, Jap.)
Tadashi Yamauchi
PASSION(1968, Jap.), m
Kosaku Yamayoshi
SONG FROM MY HEART, THE(1970, Jap.)
Ichio Yamazaki
LOWER DEPTHS, THE(1962, Jap.), ph
Iwao Yamazaki
GAPPA THE TRIFIBIAN MONSTER(1967, Jap.), w; HOUSE OF STRANGE LOVES, THE(1969, Jap.), w

Kazuo Yamazaki
HIDDEN FORTRESS, THE(1959, Jap.), ph
Masao Yamazaki
HELL IN THE PACIFIC(1968), art d
Tatsuo Yamazaki
JUDO SAGA(1965, Jap.)
Tsutomo Yamazaki
TILL TOMORROW COMES(1962, Jap.)
Tsutomu Yamazaki
DIPLOMAT'S MANSION, THE(1961, Jap.); HIGH AND LOW(1963, Jap.); LEGACY OF THE 500,000, THE(1964, Jap.); WOMAN'S LIFE, A(1964, Jap.); WHITE ROSE OF HONG KONG(1965, Jap.); RED BEARD(1966, Jap.); SCHOOL FOR SEX(1966, Jap.); TORA-SAN PART 2(1970, Jap.); KAGEMUSHA(1980, Jap.)
Yoshihiro Yamazaki
ALONE ON THE PACIFIC(1964, Jap.), ph; WHIRLPOOL OF WOMAN(1966, Jap.), ph
Masayuki Yamazuki
FINAL COUNTDOWN, THE(1980)
Kozuo Yamdada
BAND OF ASSASSINS(1971, Jap.), ph
Vana Yami
GOLGOTHA(1937, Fr.)
Robert Yamin
MARY, MARY, BLOODY MARY(1975, U.S./Mex.), p
Robert H. Yamin
FOOLS(1970), p
Iris Yamoaka
HELL AND HIGH WATER(1933)
Misc. Silents
CHINA SLAVER(1929)
Otto Yamoaka
TROUBLE IN SUNDOWN(1939)
Laszlo Yamos
WITNESS, THE(1982, Hung.)
Hiroshi Yamoto
BARBARIAN AND THE GEISHA, THE(1958)
Martin Yan
IMPROPER CHANNELS(1981, Can.)
Yana
COCKLESHELL HEROES, THE(1955); PICKUP ALLEY(1957, Brit.)
Eijiro Yanagi
IDIOT, THE(1963, Jap.); RIFIFI IN TOKYO(1963, Fr./Ital.); LIFE OF OHARU(1964, Jap.); WHITE ROSE OF HONG KONG(1965, Jap.); TUNNEL TO THE SUN(1968, Jap.)
Shinichi Yanagisawa
GIRARA(1967, Jap.); SNOW COUNTRY(1969, Jap.)
Kan Yanagiya
YEARNING(1964, Jap.)
Kingoro Yanagiya
HOTSPRINGS HOLIDAY(1970, Jap.)
Shin-ichi Yanagizawa
PERFORMERS, THE(1970, Jap.); YOSAKOI JOURNEY(1970, Jap.)
Moshe Yanai
EVERY BASTARD A KING(1968, Israel); JERUSALEM FILE, THE(1972, U.S./Israel)
Y. Yanai
MUDLARK, THE(1950, Brit.)
Yoshihide Yanai
PATRICIA GETS HER MAN(1937, Brit.); DICK BARTON AT BAY(1950, Brit.)
Alkis Yanakis
STRANDED(1965)
Ya. Yanakiyev
ITALIANO BRAVA GENTE(1965, Ital./USSR)
Eiko Yanami
WAY OUT, WAY IN(1970, Jap.)
James Yanari
THREE CAME HOME(1950)
Mikhail Yanchine
THREE TALES OF CHEKHOV(1961, USSR)
Emily Yancy
WHAT'S SO BAD ABOUT FEELING GOOD?(1968); COTTON COMES TO HARLEM(1970); TELL ME THAT YOU LOVE ME, JUNIE MOON(1970); BLACULA(1972); SWORD AND THE SORCERER, THE(1982)
Augusto Yanes
MASSACRE(1956)
Juan Yanes
MASSACRE(1956)
Mario Yanes
MASSACRE(1956)
Sergio Yanes
MASSACRE(1956)
Donald A. Yanessa
ALL THE RIGHT MOVES(1983)
Alberto Yanez
CURSE OF THE AZTEC MUMMY, THE(1965, Mex.); ROBOT VS. THE AZTEC MUMMY, THE(1965, Mex.)
Amada Yanez
Silents
KID, THE(1921)
Baby Yanez
Silents
KID, THE(1921)
Bob Yanez
48 HOURS(1982); SCARFACE(1983)
David Yanez
OTHER SIDE OF THE MOUNTAIN–PART 2, THE(1978)
Enrique Yanez
CURSE OF THE AZTEC MUMMY, THE(1965, Mex.); ROBOT VS. THE AZTEC MUMMY, THE(1965, Mex.)
C. K. Yang
WALK, DON'T RUN(1966); THERE WAS A CROOKED MAN(1970); ONE MORE TRAIN TO ROB(1971)

Chiang Yang
FIVE FINGERS OF DEATH(1973, Hong Kong), w
Ginny Yang
1984
BROTHER FROM ANOTHER PLANET, THE(1984)
Kwang Nam Yang
INCHON(1981)
Lian-Shin Yang
INN OF THE SIXTH HAPPINESS, THE(1958)
Marie Yang
SAVAGE INNOCENTS, THE(1960, Brit.); SATAN NEVER SLEEPS(1962)
Thomas Yangha
TARZAN, THE APE MAN(1959)
Yanilou
HANDS OF ORLAC, THE(1964, Brit./Fr.)
Big Yank
FIRE AND ICE(1983)
Pat Yankee
IT'S GREAT TO BE YOUNG(1946)
Yura Yankin
SON OF THE REGIMENT(1948, USSR)
Oleg Yankovsky
1984
NOSTALGHIA(1984, USSR/Ital.)
Christos Yannakopoulos
POLICEMAN OF THE 16TH PRECINCT, THE(1963, Gr.), w
Mihalis Yannatos
MIDNIGHT EXPRESS(1978, Brit.)
Jean Yanne
LIFE UPSIDE DOWN(1965, Fr.); TIGHT SKIRTS, LOOSE PLEASURES(1966, Fr.); VISCOUNT, THE(1967, Fr./Span./Ital./Ger.); WEEKEND(1968, Fr./Ital.); THIS MAN MUST DIE(1970, Fr./Ital.); LE BOUCHER(1971, Fr./Ital.); DON'T TOUCH WHITE WOMEN!(1974, Fr.), p; HANNAH K.(1983, Fr.)
Joseph Yanni
BIG MONEY, THE(1962, Brit.), p
Rossana Yanni
HUNCHBACK OF THE MORGUE, THE(1972, Span.); MALENKA, THE VAMPIRE(1972, Span./Ital.), a, p
Misc. Talkies
WHITE COMANCHE(1967)
Rossanna Yanni
FRANKENSTEIN'S BLOODY TERROR(1968, Span.); DRACULA'S GREAT LOVE(1972, Span.)
Lili Yannikaki
SERENITY(1962)
Michael Yannis
SLEEPING CAR TO TRIESTE(1949, Brit.)
Takis Yannopoulos
IPHIGENIA(1977, Gr.), ed
Angelos Yannoulis
IPHIGENIA(1977, Gr.)
Rossana Yanny
SONNY AND JED(1974, Ital.)
Keiji Yano
JUDO SHOWDOWN(1966, Jap.)
Sen Yano
WOMAN IN THE DUNES(1964, Jap.)
Varvara Yanova
Misc. Silents
PICTURE OF DORIAN GRAY, THE(1915, USSR); STRONG MAN, THE(1917, USSR)
Zal Yanovsky
MARRIED COUPLE, A(1969, Can.), m; HEAVY METAL(1981, Can.)
M. Yanshin
CZAR WANTS TO SLEEP(1934, U.S., USSR); TWELFTH NIGHT(1956, USSR); JACK FROST(1966, USSR)
Horst Yanson
DON'T TURN THE OTHER CHEEK(1974, Ital./Ger./Span.)
Mawuyul Yanthalawuy
WE OF THE NEVER NEVER(1983, Aus.)
Regina Yanushkevich
ROAD TO LIFE(1932, USSR)
R. Yanushkevitch
ROAD TO LIFE(1932, USSR), w
Joseph Yanuzzi
TIME WALKER(1982), ed
Chang Mei Yao
WHITE ROSE OF HONG KONG(1965, Jap.); NIGHT IN BANGKOK(1966, Jap.); WE WILL REMEMBER(1966, Jap.)
Hsaiao Yao
GOLIATHON(1979, Hong Kong)
Hsu Yao-kuang
DRAGON INN(1968, Chi.)
Johnson Yap
BIONIC BOY, THE(1977, Hong Kong/Phil.); DYNAMITE JOHNSON(1978, Phil.)
Hans Yaray
LYDIA(1941); CARNEGIE HALL(1947); UNFINISHED SYMPHONY, THE(1953, Aust./Brit.)
Lillian Yarbo
RAINBOW ON THE RIVER(1936); STELLA DALLAS(1937); THERE'S THAT WOMAN AGAIN(1938); WIVES UNDER SUSPICION(1938); YOU CAN'T TAKE IT WITH YOU(1938); CAFE SOCIETY(1939); DESTRY RIDES AGAIN(1939); FAMILY NEXT DOOR, THE(1939); PERSONS IN HIDING(1939); SOCIETY LAWYER(1939); WAY DOWN SOUTH(1939); RETURN OF FRANK JAMES, THE(1940); SANDY GETS HER MAN(1940); THEY DRIVE BY NIGHT(1940); BUY ME THAT TOWN(1941); MOON OVER HER SHOULDER(1941); BETWEEN US GIRLS(1942); GREAT MAN'S LADY, THE(1942); WILD BILL HICKOK RIDES(1942); GANG'S ALL HERE, THE(1943); SWING SHIFT MAISIE(1943); NAUGHTY NINETIES(1945); SARATOGA TRUNK(1945); MY BROTHER TALKS TO HORSES(1946); DATE WITH JUDY, A(1948); LOOK FOR THE SILVER LINING(1949); NIGHT UNTO NIGHT(1949); REDHEAD FROM MANHATTAN(1954)

Barton Yarborough
BEFORE I HANG(1940); LET'S GO COLLEGIATE(1941); THEY MEET AGAIN(1941); GHOST OF FRANKENSTEIN, THE(1942); CAPTAIN TUGBOAT ANNIE(1945); I LOVE A MYSTERY(1945); DEVIL'S MASK, THE(1946); IDEA GIRL(1946); RED DRAGON, THE(1946); UNKNOWN, THE(1946); WIFE WANTED(1946); KILROY WAS HERE(1947); HENRY, THE RAINMAKER(1949)
Cale Yarborough
STROKER ACE(1983)
Jean Yarborough
CAUGHT IN THE ACT(1941), d
Joan Yarborough
V.D.(1961)
Jonathan Yarborough
1984
ICE PIRATES, THE(1984)
Rosita Yarboy
REVENGE OF THE PINK PANTHER(1978)
Barton Yarbrough
SABOTEUR(1942)
Camill Yarbrough
NEXT MAN, THE(1976)
Camille Yarbrough
SHAFT(1971)
George Yarbrough
BLOOD WATERS OF DOCTOR Z(1982), ed
Jean Yarbrough
REBELLIOUS DAUGHTERS(1938), d; DEVIL BAT, THE(1941), d; GANG'S ALL HERE(1941), d; KING OF THE ZOMBIES(1941), d; LET'S GO COLLEGIATE(1941), d; SOUTH OF PANAMA(1941), d; TOP SERGEANT MULLIGAN(1941), d; FRECKLES COMES HOME(1942), d; LAW OF THE JUNGLE(1942), d; LURE OF THE ISLANDS(1942), d; MAN FROM HEADQUARTERS(1942), d; MEET THE MOB(1942), d; POLICE BULLETS(1942), d; SHE'S IN THE ARMY(1942), d; FOLLOW THE BAND(1943), d; GET GOING(1943), d; GOOD MORNING, JUDGE(1943), d; HI' YA, SAILOR(1943), p&d; SO'S YOUR UNCLE(1943), p&d; IN SOCIETY(1944), d; MOON OVER LAS VEGAS(1944), p&d; SOUTH OF DIXIE(1944), p&d; TWILIGHT ON THE PRAIRIE(1944), d; WEEKEND PASS(1944), d; HERE COME THE CO-EDS(1945), d; NAUGHTY NINETIES, THE(1945), d; ON STAGE EVERYBODY(1945), d; UNDER WESTERN SKIES(1945), d; BRUTE MAN, THE(1946), d; CUBAN PETE(1946), d; HOUSE OF HORRORS(1946), d; INSIDE JOB(1946), p, d; SHE-WOLF OF LONDON(1946), d; CHALLENGE, THE(1948), d; CREEPER, THE(1948), d; SHED NO TEARS(1948), d; TRIPLE THREAT(1948), d; ANGELS IN DISGUISE(1949), d; HENRY, THE RAINMAKER(1949), d; HOLIDAY IN HAVANA(1949), d; LEAVE IT TO HENRY(1949), d; MASTER MINDS(1949), d; MUTINEERS, THE(1949), d; BIG TIMBER(1950), d; FATHER MAKES GOOD(1950), d; HUMPHREY TAKES A CHANCE(1950), d; JOE PALOOKA MEETS HUMPHREY(1950), d; SIDESHOW(1950), d; SQUARE DANCE KATY(1950), d; TRIPLE TROUBLE(1950), d; ACCORDING TO MRS. HOYLE(1951), d; CASA MANANA(1951), d; JACK AND THE BEANSTALK(1952), d; LOST IN ALASKA(1952), d; NIGHT FREIGHT(1955), d; CRASHING LAS VEGAS(1956), d; HOT SHOTS(1956), d; YAQUI DRUMS(1956), d; FOOTSTEPS IN THE NIGHT(1957), d; WOMEN OF PITCAIRN ISLAND, THE(1957), p, d; SAINTLY SINNERS(1962), d; HILLBILLYS IN A HAUNTED HOUSE(1967), d
Misc. Talkies
CITY LIMITS(1941), d; FATHER STEPS OUT(1941), d; CRIMINAL INVESTIGATOR(1942), d
Lester Yard
SHANGHAI STORY, THE(1954), w
The Yardbirds
BLOW-UP(1966, Brit.), a, m
Margaret Yarde
NIGHT BIRDS(1931, Brit.); THIRD TIME LUCKY(1931, Brit.); UNEASY VIRTUE(1931, Brit.); BRIDEGROOM FOR TWO(1932, Brit.); MICHAEL AND MARY(1932, Brit.); WOMAN DECIDES, THE(1932, Brit.); ENEMY OF THE POLICE(1933, Brit.); GOOD COMPANIONS(1933, Brit.); MAN FROM TORONTO, THE(1933, Brit.); MATINEE IDOL(1933, Brit.); SHOT IN THE DARK, A(1933, Brit.); TIGER BAY(1933, Brit.); BROKEN ROSARY, THE(1934, Brit.); FATHER AND SON(1934, Brit.); GLIMPSE OF PARADISE, A(1934, Brit.); GUEST OF HONOR(1934, Brit.); NINE FORTY-FIVE(1934, Brit.); SING AS WE GO(1934, Brit.); WIDOW'S MIGHT(1934, Brit.); DEPUTY DRUMMER, THE(1935, Brit.); FULL CIRCLE(1935, Brit.); HANDLE WITH CARE(1935, Brit.); IT HAPPENED IN PARIS(1935, Brit.); JUBILEE WINDOW(1935, Brit.); SCROOGE(1935, Brit.); SQUIBS(1935, Brit.); THAT'S MY UNCLE(1935, Brit.); WHO'S YOUR FATHER?(1935, Brit.); 18 MINUTES(1935, Brit.); CROUCHING BEAST, THE(1936, U.S./Brit.); FAITHFUL(1936, Brit.); GYPSY MELODY(1936, Brit.); IN THE SOUP(1936, Brit.); NO ESCAPE(1936, Brit.); QUEEN OF HEARTS(1936, Brit.); BEAUTY AND THE BARGE(1937, Brit.); BITER BIT, THE(1937, Brit.); COMPULSORY WIFE, THE(1937, Brit.); FRENCH LEAVE(1937, Brit.); YOU LIVE AND LEARN(1937, Brit.); YOU'RE THE DOCTOR(1938, Brit.); FACE AT THE WINDOW, THE(1939, Brit.); FRENCH WITHOUT TEARS(1939, Brit.); PRISON WITHOUT BARS(1939, Brit.); CRIMES AT THE DARK HOUSE(1940, Brit.); GEORGE AND MARGARET(1940, Brit.); HENRY STEPS OUT(1940, Brit.); SECOND MR. BUSH, THE(1940, Brit.); TWO SMART MEN(1940, Brit.); IT'S IN THE BAG(1943, Brit.); THURSDAY'S CHILD(1943, Brit.)
Silents
LONDON(1926, Brit.); ONLY WAY, THE(1926, Brit.)
Margeret Yarde
MERRY COMES TO STAY(1937, Brit.)
Winston Yarde
WARRIORS, THE(1979)
Herbert O. Yardley
RENDEZVOUS(1935), w
Michael Yardley
BUSH CHRISTMAS(1947, Brit.)
Nicky Yardley
BUSH CHRISTMAS(1947, Brit.)
Stephen Yardley
FUNNY MONEY(1983, Brit.)
1984
SLAYGROUND(1984, Brit.)
Misc. Talkies
CORVINI INHERITANCE(1984, Brit.)

Nicky Yardly
BITTER SPRINGS(1950, Aus.)
Gabriel Yared
EVERY MAN FOR HIMSELF(1980, Fr.), m; HANNAH K.(1983, Fr.), m; MOON IN THE GUTTER, THE(1983, Fr./Ital.), m
1984
DREAM ONE(1984, Brit./Fr.), m
Neil Yarema
TASTE OF HELL, A(1973), d, w
Yacinto Yaria
OPIATE '67(1967, Fr./Ital.)
Elaine Yarish
HOUSE BY THE LAKE, THE(1977, Can.)
Jack Yarker
TASTE OF HONEY, A(1962, Brit.)
Konstantin Yarlamov
Misc. Silents
ROMANCE OF A RUSSIAN BALLERINA(1913, USSR)
K. Yarmolyuk
SUMMER TO REMEMBER, A(1961, USSR), makeup
Dick Yarmy
SWINGING BARMAIDS, THE(1976); ONE MAN JURY(1978)
Nicole Yarna
POPDOWN(1968, Brit.)
Celeste Yarnall
NEW KIND OF LOVE, A(1963); NUTTY PROFESSOR, THE(1963); AROUND THE WORLD UNDER THE SEA(1966); EVE(1968, Brit./Span.); LIVE A LITTLE, LOVE A LITTLE(1968); BOB AND CAROL AND TED AND ALICE(1969); VELVET VAMPIRE, THE(1971); MECHANIC, THE(1972); SCORPIO(1973)
Bruce Yarnell
IRMA LA DOUCE(1963); ROAD HUSTLERS, THE(1968)
Celeste Yarnell
BEAST OF BLOOD(1970, U.S./Phil.)
Lorene Yarnell
SWEET CHARITY(1969)
Sally Yarnell
WINGED VICTORY(1944); FASHION MODEL(1945); HOUSE OF STRANGERS(1949); HIS KIND OF WOMAN(1951); RACKET, THE(1951); CLASH BY NIGHT(1952); FLESH AND FURY(1952); LUSTY MEN, THE(1952); ROSE MARIE(1954); BLACK SLEEP, THE(1956); CRIME OF PASSION(1957)
N. Yaroslavtsev
QUEEN OF SPADES(1961, USSR)
V. Yaroslavtsev
YOLANTA(1964, USSR)
M. Yarotskaya
TRAIN GOES EAST, THE(1949, USSR)
Sergi Yarov
WINGS OF VICTORY(1941, USSR)
Dan Yarranton
MARRY ME!(1949, Brit.)
Jacobin Yarro
1984
GREYSTOKE: THE LEGEND OF TARZAN, LORD OF THE APES(1984)
Arnold Yarrow
MAHLER(1974, Brit.)
Lilo Yarson
FOR WHOM THE BELL TOLLS(1943); PIRATES OF MONTEREY(1947)
Marina Yaru
SPIRITS OF THE DEAD(1969, Fr./Ital.)
Buddy Yarus
DOUGHBOYS IN IRELAND(1943); EVE OF ST. MARK, THE(1944); FOUR JILLS IN A JEEP(1944); MR. WINKLE GOES TO WAR(1944); ONCE UPON A TIME(1944); SAILOR'S HOLIDAY(1944)
Buddy [George Tyne] Yarus
LOUISIANA HAYRIDE(1944)
Daniel Yarussi
GRADUATION DAY(1981), ph
Boris Yarutovskiy
QUEEN OF SPADES(1961, USSR), w
Youri Yarvet
SOLARIS(1972, USSR)
Yuri Yarvet
DEAD MOUNTAINEER HOTEL, THE(1979, USSR)
Colin Yarwood
F.J. HOLDEN, THE(1977, Aus.)
Yashi
NUN AND THE SERGEANT, THE(1962)
Michiko Yashima
PERFORMERS, THE(1970, Jap.)
Mitsu Yashima
FOUL PLAY(1978)
Momo Yashima
CHARLIE CHAN AND THE CURSE OF THE DRAGON QUEEN(1981)
B. Yashin
NINE DAYS OF ONE YEAR(1964, USSR)
Junko Yashiro
GAMERA VERSUS VIRAS(1968, Jap); GAMERA VERSUS MONSTER K(1970, Jap.)
Kazuo Yashiro
MAN FROM THE EAST, THE(1961, Jap.)
Mike Yashiro
ATTACK OF THE MUSHROOM PEOPLE(1964, Jap.)
Seiichi Yashiro
PANDA AND THE MAGIC SERPENT(1961, Jap.), w
Al Yasin
LAST MOMENT, THE(1966), p,d&w
Princess Yasmina
ISLAND OF ALLAH(1956)

Ismail Yassine
LITTLE MISS DEVIL(1951, Egypt)
Kuzma Yastrebetsky
Misc. Silents
WOMEN OF RYAZAN(1927, USSR)
Kimiyoshi Yasuda
MAJIN(1968, Jap.), d; ZATOICHI(1968, Jap.), d
Kimoyoshi Yasuda
ZATOICHI'S CONSPIRACY(1974, Jap.), d
Kuninobu Yasuda
WHISPERING JOE(1969, Jap.), art d
Shin Yasuda
COMPUTER FREE-FOR-ALL(1969, Jap.)
Michiyo Yasudo
SECRETS OF A WOMAN'S TEMPLE(1969, Jap.)
Shoji Yasui
HARP OF BURMA(1967, Jap.)
I. Yasulovich
NINE DAYS OF ONE YEAR(1964, USSR)
T. Yasumi
FINAL WAR, THE(1960, Jap.), w
Toshio Yasumi
LAST WAR, THE(1962, Jap.), w; TATSU(1962, Jap.), w; TWILIGHT STORY, THE(1962, Jap.), w; TEMPTRESS AND THE MONK, THE(1963, Jap.), w; ILLUSION OF BLOOD(1966, Jap.), w; PORTRAIT OF HELL(1969, Jap.), w; PROPHECIES OF NOSTRADAMUS(1974, Jap.), w
Yasumichi
DODESKA-DEN(1970, Jap.), ph
Atsushi Yasumoto
WISER AGE(1962, Jap.), ph
Jun Yasumoto
SAMURAI(PART II)** (1967, Jap.), ph; SAMURAI(1955, Jap.), ph; LONELY LANE(1963, Jap.), ph; YEARNING(1964, Jap.), ph
F. Yasyukevich
MARRIAGE OF BALZAMINOV, THE(1966, USSR), art d
Ann Yates
LEST WE FORGET(1934, Brit.)
Beverly Yates
BYE BYE BIRDIE(1963)
Brock Yates
SMOKEY AND THE BANDIT II(1980), w; CANNONBALL RUN, THE(1981), a, w
1984
CANNONBALL RUN II(1984), w
Cassie Yates
ROLLING THUNDER(1977); CONVOY(1978); EVIL, THE(1978); F.I.S.T.(1978); FM(1978); ST. HELENS(1981); OSTERMAN WEEKEND, THE(1983)
1984
UNFAITHFULLY YOURS(1984)
Clifford Yates
THEY CALL ME MISTER TIBBS(1970), prod d
David Yates
COLDITZ STORY, THE(1955, Brit.); CONSTANT HUSBAND, THE(1955, Brit.); NIGHT MY NUMBER CAME UP, THE(1955, Brit.)
Edith Yates
Silents
JACK TAR(1915, Brit.)
Gena Yates
ROCKETS IN THE DUNES(1960, Brit.)
George W. Yates
MYSTERIOUS MISS X, THE(1939), w; DEVIL PAYS OFF, THE(1941), w; THIS WOMAN IS DANGEROUS(1952), w
George Washington Yates
HI-YO SILVER(1940), w
George Worthing Yates
FALCON IN MEXICO, THE(1944), w; MAN FROM FRISCO(1944), w; SPANISH MAIN, THE(1945), w; SINBAD THE SAILOR(1947), w; LAST OUTPOST, THE(1951), w; CHINA VENTURE(1953), w; THOSE REDHEADS FROM SEATTLE(1953), w; EL ALAMEIN(1954), w; SARACEN BLADE, THE(1954), w; THEM!(1954), w; IT CAME FROM BENEATH THE SEA(1955), w; EARTH VS. THE FLYING SAUCERS(1956), w; ATTACK OF THE PUPPET PEOPLE(1958), w; EARTH VS. THE SPIDER(1958), w; FLAME BARRIER, THE(1958), w; FRANKENSTEIN 1970(1958), w; SPACE MASTER X-7(1958), w; SPIDER, THE(1958), w; WAR OF THE COLOSSAL BEAST(1958), w; TORMENTED(1960), w
George Worthington Yates
TALL TARGET, THE(1951), w; CONQUEST OF SPACE(1955), w
Hal Yates
GENERAL SPANKY(1937), w; NOBODY'S BABY(1937), w; MAD MISS MANTON, THE(1938), w; MAMA RUNS WILD(1938), w
Henryetta Yates
SUSAN AND GOD(1940)
Herbert J. Yates
NORTHWEST OUTPOST(1947), p; RED MENACE, THE(1949), p; SURRENDER(1950), p; BELLE LE GRAND(1951), p; MILLION DOLLAR PURSUIT(1951), p; BAL TABARIN(1952), p; BLACK HILLS AMBUSH(1952), p; BORDER SADDLEMATES(1952), p; HOODLUM EMPIRE(1952), p; I DREAM OF JEANIE(1952), p; WILD BLUE YONDER, THE(1952), p; FLIGHT NURSE(1953), p; JOHNNY GUITAR(1954), p; JUBILEE TRAIL(1954), p; LAUGHING ANNE(1954, Brit./U.S.), p; MAKE HASTE TO LIVE(1954), p; PHANTOM STALLION, THE(1954), p; SHANGHAI STORY, THE(1954), p; TROUBLE IN THE GLEN(1954, Brit.), p; UNTAMED HEIRESS(1954), p; CAROLINA CANNONBALL(1955), p; CITY OF SHADOWS(1955), p; ETERNAL SEA, THE(1955), p; FIGHTING CHANCE, THE(1955), p; I COVER THE UNDERWORLD(1955), p; MAN ALONE, A(1955), p; NO MAN'S WOMAN(1955), p; ROAD TO DENVER, THE(1955), p; TIMBERJACK(1955), p; VANISHING AMERICAN, THE(1955), p; COME NEXT SPRING(1956), p; SPOILERS OF THE FOREST(1957), p
Herbert Jo Yates
TWINKLE IN GOD'S EYE, THE(1955), p

Hillary Yates
WHO'S GOT THE ACTION?(1962)
John Yates
STRANGLER, THE(1964); EVEL KNIEVEL(1971); SIMON, KING OF THE WITCHES(1971); FIREFOX(1982)
Leo Yates
I WALK THE LINE(1970)
Louis H. Yates
FOOLS(1970), set d
Marie Yates
FRANCES(1982), p
Marjorie Yates
OPTIMISTS, THE(1973, Brit.); BLACK PANTHER, THE(1977, Brit.); GLITTERBALL, THE(1977, Brit); PRIEST OF LOVE(1981, Brit.)
Maud Yates
Silents
ROGUES OF LONDON, THE(1915, Brit.); TRAPPED BY THE LONDON SHARKS(1916, Brit.); HOLY ORDERS(1917, Brit.); JUST DECEPTION, A(1917, Brit.); WHAT EVERY WOMAN KNOWS(1917, Brit.); FOUNDATIONS OF FREEDOM, THE(1918, Brit.); UNREST(1920, Brit.)
Misc. Silents
SECRET WOMAN, THE(1918, Brit.); THELMA(1918, Brit.); GOD'S CLAY(1919, Brit.); HOUR OF THE TRIAL, THE(1920, Brit.); PEACEMAKER, THE(1922, Brit.)
Maurice Yates
DARK WATERS(1944), set d; SENSATIONS OF 1945(1944), set d; SONG FOR MISS JULIE, A(1945), set d; MOURNING BECOMES ELECTRA(1947), set d; VELVET TOUCH, THE(1948), set d; THEY LIVE BY NIGHT(1949), set d
Nathan Yates
SHARKFIGHTERS, THE(1956)
Norman Yates
Silents
PRISONER OF ZENDA, THE(1915, Brit.)
Pauline Yates
IDENTITY UNKNOWN(1960, Brit.); NEVER MENTION MURDER(1964, Brit.); DARLING(1965, Brit.); LIONHEART(1968, Brit.)
Peter Yates
SUMMER HOLIDAY(1963, Brit.), d; ONE WAY PENDULUM(1965, Brit.), d; ROBBERY(1967, Brit.), d, w; BULLITT(1968), d; JOHN AND MARY(1969), d; MURPHY'S WAR(1971, Brit.), d; HOT ROCK, THE(1972), d; FRIENDS OF EDDIE COYLE, THE(1973), d; MOTHER, JUGS & SPEED(1976), p, d; DEEP, THE(1977), d; FOR PETE'S SAKE(1977), d; BREAKING AWAY(1979), p&d; EYEWITNESS(1981), p&d; DRESSER, THE(1983), p&d; KRULL(1983), d
Richard G. Yates
WHAT!(1965, Fr./Brit./Ital.), p
Richard Yates
BRIDGE AT REMAGEN, THE(1969), w
Sefton Yates
DARK ROAD, THE(1948, Brit.)
Mawuyul Yathalawuy
MANGANINNIE(1982, Aus.)
Nissan Yatir
NOT MINE TO LOVE(1969, Israel)
Jean Yatove
JOUR DE FETE(1952, Fr.), m; GIRL IN THE BIKINI, THE(1958, Fr.), m; NIGHT AFFAIR(1961, Fr.), m; SEVENTH JUROR, THE(1964, Fr.), m; GIRL CAN'T STOP, THE(1966, Fr./Gr.), m
Yevgeniy Yatsun
LITTLE HUMPBACKED HORSE, THE(1962, USSR), ph
Paul Yawitz
BREAKFAST FOR TWO(1937), w; CRASHING HOLLYWOOD(1937), w; SATURDAY'S HEROES(1937), w; THEY WANTED TO MARRY(1937), w; AFFAIRS OF ANNABEL(1938), w; BLOND CHEAT(1938), w; GO CHASE YOURSELF(1938), w; FIXER DUGAN(1939), w; LITTLE ACCIDENT(1939), w; CONFESSIONS OF BOSTON BLACKIE(1941), w; HONOLULU LU(1941), w; ALIAS BOSTON BLACKIE(1942), w; BOSTON BLACKIE GOES HOLLYWOOD(1942), w; CHANCE OF A LIFETIME, THE(1943), w; SHE HAS WHAT IT TAKES(1943), w; FALCON OUT WEST, THE(1944), w; LOUISIANA HAYRIDE(1944), w; ONE MYSTERIOUS NIGHT(1944), w; RACKET MAN, THE(1944), w; BOSTON BLACKIE BOOKED ON SUSPICION(1945), w; I LOVE A BANDLEADER(1945), w; CLOSE CALL FOR BOSTON BLACKIE, A(1946), w; FALCON'S ALIBI, THE(1946), w; UNMASKED(1950), w; WALK SOFTLY, STRANGER(1950), w; MODELS, INC.(1952), w; BLACK SCORPION, THE(1957), w
Tomonori Yazaki
GODZILLA'S REVENGE(1969)
Toshio Yazumi
TILL TOMORROW COMES(1962, Jap.), w; CHUSHINGURA(1963, Jap.), w; MADAME AKI(1963, Jap.), w
Al Ybarra
3 IS A FAMILY(1944), art d; ONE WAY STREET(1950), art d; FABULOUS SENORITA, THE(1952), art d; GOBS AND GALS(1952), art d; HONDO(1953), art d; PLUNDER OF THE SUN(1953), art d; HIGH AND THE MIGHTY, THE(1954), art d; TRACK OF THE CAT(1954), art d; GUN THE MAN DOWN(1957), art d; MAJOR DUNDEE(1965), art d
Alfred C. Ybarra
GOIN' TO TOWN(1944), art d
Alfred Ybarra
FUGITIVE, THE(1947), art d; SOFIA(1948), art d; LEGEND OF THE LOST(1957, U.S./Panama/Ital.), art d; QUANTEZ(1957), art d; RAW WIND IN EDEN(1958), art d; ESCORT WEST(1959), art d; ALAMO, THE(1960), art d; COMANCHEROS, THE(1961), art d; MARINES, LET'S GO(1961), art d; FIVE WEEKS IN A BALLOON(1962), art d; KINGS OF THE SUN(1963), art d; DUEL AT DIABLO(1966), art d; RARE BREED, THE(1966), art d; HOUR OF THE GUN(1967), art d; YOUNG WARRIORS, THE(1967), art d; PINK JUNGLE, THE(1968), art d
Concha Ybarra
FIGHTING STALLION, THE(1950)
Manuel Ybarra
ESCAPE TO BURMA(1955)

Roque Ybarra
TORTILLA FLAT(1942); KISMET(1944); WYOMING(1947); LOVES OF CARMEN, THE(1948); MEXICAN HAYRIDE(1948); NEPTUNE'S DAUGHTER(1949); CRISIS(1950); CALLAWAY WENT THATAWAY(1951); REWARD, THE(1965)
Roque Ybarra, Jr.
THEY WERE EXPENDABLE(1945); RIDE THE PINK HORSE(1947)
Rouque Ybarra
THIRD VOICE, THE(1960)
Ventura Ybarra
FRONTIER MARSHAL(1939)
Li Ye-chuan
LAST WOMAN OF SHANG, THE(1964, Hong Kong)
Ye-Min
INN OF THE SIXTH HAPPINESS, THE(1958)
Biff Yeager
JESSIE'S GIRLS(1976)
1984
REPO MAN(1984)
Bob Yeager
GATOR(1976)
Bunny Yeager
1984
HARRY AND SON(1984)
Caroline Yeager
1984
COVERGIRL(1984, Can.)
Charles Yeager
SMOKEY AND THE BANDIT II(1980)
Gen. Chuck Yeager
RIGHT STUFF, THE(1983)
Irene Yeager
Silents
JACK KNIFE MAN, THE(1920); BREAKING POINT, THE(1921)
Misc. Silents
WAY OF THE STRONG, THE(1919)
Steve Yeager
POLYESTER(1981)
Bob Yeakel
MAN ON THE PROWL(1957)
Tara Yeakey
TERMS OF ENDEARMENT(1983)
Lydia Yeamans
Silents
BEAU REVEL(1921); ARIZONA ROMEO, THE(1925)
Misc. Silents
UPSTREAM(1927)
Year 2000
WANDERLOVE(1970)
Michael Yeargan
JANE AUSTEN IN MANHATTAN(1980), set d
David Yearick
RED RUNS THE RIVER(1963)
Rick Yearry
Misc. Talkies
LEGACY(1963)
Ralph Yearsley
SHOW BOAT(1929)
Silents
TOL'ABLE DAVID(1921); ANNA CHRISTIE(1923); KID BROTHER, THE(1927)
Misc. Silents
HILL BILLY, THE(1924)
Lee Yeary
STRAIT-JACKET(1964)
Betty Yeaton
KID FROM BOOKLYN, THE(1946)
Chuck Yeaton
POLYESTER(1981)
Murray F. Yeats
O.S.S.(1946)
William Butler Yeats
OEDIPUS REX(1957, Can.), w
Maj. Francis Yeats-Brown
LIVES OF A BENGAL LANCER(1935), w
Ervin S. Yeaworth
FLAMING TEEN-AGE, THE(1956), p&d
Jean Yeaworth
FLAMING TEEN-AGE, THE(1956), w; BLOB, THE(1958), m; DINOSAURUS(1960), w; WAY OUT(1966), w
Irvin S. Yeaworth, Jr.
BLOB, THE(1958), d; DINOSAURUS(1960), p, d; WAY OUT(1966), p&d
Irvin Shortess Yeaworth, Jr.
4D MAN(1959), p, d
William Yedder
WILD ONE, THE(1953)
Ram Yedekar
NINE HOURS TO RAMA(1963, U.S./Brit.), art d; GUIDE, THE(1965, U.S./India), art d; MAYA(1966), art d; KENNER(1969), art d; GANDHI(1982), art d
1984
PASSAGE TO INDIA, A(1984, Brit.), art d
C. Yee
SUBWAY RIDERS(1981)
Chang Shun Yee
EXIT THE DRAGON, ENTER THE TIGER(1977, Hong Kong), w
Chang Sing Yee
EXIT THE DRAGON, ENTER THE TIGER(1977, Hong Kong)
Devi Yee
CHARLIE CHAN AND THE CURSE OF THE DRAGON QUEEN(1981)

Vladimir Yershov
Misc. Silents
RANKS AND PEOPLE(1929, USSR)
Pyotr Yesikovksy
Misc. Silents
RED IMPS(1923, USSR)
Harum Yesilyurt
1984
HORSE, THE(1984, Turk.)
John Yesno
KING OF THE GRIZZLIES(1970)
Johnny Yesno
COLD JOURNEY(1975, Can.)
Jonny Yesno
INBREAKER, THE(1974, Can.)
Richard Yesteran
SUPERSONIC MAN(1979, Span.)
Bill Yetter
THIS LAND IS MINE(1943)
William Yetter
MAN I MARRIED, THE(1940); DOWN IN SAN DIEGO(1941); PARIS CALLING(1941); LADY HAS PLANS, THE(1942); PIED PIPER, THE(1942); WIFE TAKES A FLYER, THE(1942); ABOVE SUSPICION(1943); THEY CAME TO BLOW UP AMERICA(1943); THEY GOT ME COVERED(1943); GIRL FROM JONES BEACH, THE(1949); I WAS A MALE WAR BRIDE(1949); MASTER MINDS(1949); SEALED CARGO(1951)
William Yetter, Jr.
LIFEBOAT(1944); SEARCHING WIND, THE(1946); GOLDEN EARRINGS(1947); FIGHTER SQUADRON(1948)
William Yetter, Sr.
GOLDEN EARRINGS(1947)
Robert Yetzes
IF ...(1968, Brit.)
Sze Yeun-ping
1984
AH YING(1984, Hong Kong), w
Ellen Yeung
CHAN IS MISSING(1982)
A. Yevdakov
Silents
ARSENAL(1929, USSR)
A. Yevemnenko
ROAD TO LIFE(1932, USSR), art d
Ye. Yevseyeva
PEACE TO HIM WHO ENTERS(1963, USSR), makeup
Yevgeny Yevstigneev
HYPERBOLOID OF ENGINEER GARIN, THE(1965, USSR)
Yevgeniy Yevstigneyev
NINE DAYS OF ONE YEAR(1964, USSR); SANDU FOLLOWS THE SUN(1965, USSR); WELCOME KOSTYA!(1965, USSR); UNCOMMON THIEF, AN(1967, USSR)
F. Yew
VIRGIN SOLDIERS, THE(1970, Brit.)
A. Yezhkina
OVERCOAT, THE(1965, USSR)
Anzia Yezierska
Silents
HUNGRY HEARTS(1922), w
Ygor and Tanya
UNEXPECTED FATHER(1939)
Mohamed Yguerbouchen
PEPE LE MOKO(1937, Fr.), m
Chang Yi
DEEP THRUST-THE HAND OF DEATH(1973, Hong Kong)
Feng Yi
OUT OF THE TIGER'S MOUTH(1962)
Maria Yi
FISTS OF FURY(1973, Chi.)
Pat Yi
MARINE BATTLEGROUND(1966, U.S/S.K.)
Tae-yop Yi
MARINE BATTLEGROUND(1966, U.S/S.K.)
Hsia Yi-chiu
GRAND SUBSTITUTION, THE(1965, Hong Kong); VERMILION DOOR(1969, Hong Kong)
Yiberr
Misc. Silents
PALAVER(1926, Brit.)
Chang Yih
Misc. Silents
SONG OF CHINA(1936, Chi.)
Marvin Yim
TO THE SHORES OF HELL(1966)
Fang Yin
FEMALE PRINCE, THE(1966, Hong Kong)
Francis Yin
NED KELLY(1970, Brit.)
Geoffrey Yin
MAGNET, THE(1950, Brit.)
Angela Mao Ying
ENTER THE DRAGON(1973)
Li Ying
GRAND SUBSTITUTION, THE(1965, Hong Kong)
Liu Ya Ying
CALL HIM MR. SHATTER(1976, Hong Kong)
Me Ying
JUNGLE OF CHANG(1951)
Pai Ying
DEEP THRUST-THE HAND OF DEATH(1973, Hong Kong)

Pe Ying
DRAGON INN(1968, Chi.)
Han Ying-chieh
DRAGON INN(1968, Chi.)
Cheung Ying-tsai
EMPRESS WU(1965, Hong Kong)
Evangelos Yiotopoulos
BAREFOOT BATTALION, THE(1954, Gr.)
Smarouli Yiouli
FORTUNE TELLER, THE(1961, Gr.)
David Yip
1984
INDIANA JONES AND THE TEMPLE OF DOOM(1984)
Harry Yip
GENERAL DIED AT DAWN, THE(1936)
William Yip
BEHIND THE RISING SUN(1943); HEAVENLY DAYS(1944); ONCE UPON A TIME(1944); T-MEN(1947); SAIGON(1948); SORROWFUL JONES(1949); I WAS AN AMERICAN SPY(1951); PEKING EXPRESS(1951); MACAO(1952); HELL AND HIGH WATER(1954); SOLDIER OF FORTUNE(1955); KING AND I, THE(1956); TWILIGHT FOR THE GODS(1958); SAD HORSE, THE(1959); ICE PALACE(1960); LAST OF THE SECRET AGENTS?, THE(1966)
Yee Tak Yip
UGLY AMERICAN, THE(1963)
Kofi Yirenkyi
HAMILE(1965, Ghana)
Mary Yirenkyi
HAMILE(1965, Ghana)
Li Yiutang
DEADLY CHINA DOLL(1973, Hong Kong), ph
Yiyi
NEST, THE(1982, Span.)
Ynez
EX-LADY(1933)
Richard Yniguez
TRIBES(1970); TOGETHER BROTHERS(1974); HOW COME NOBODY'S ON OUR SIDE?(1975); BOULEVARD NIGHTS(1979)
Jo Ynocencio
PANIC IN NEEDLE PARK(1971), cos; SCARECROW(1973), cos; SEDUCTION OF JOE TYNAN, THE(1979), cos; HONEYSUCKLE ROSE(1980), cos
1984
MISUNDERSTOOD(1984), cos; NO SMALL AFFAIR(1984), cos
Nester Yoan
WAY OF A GAUCHO(1952)
Clark Yocum
LUXURY LINER(1948)
Yoshido Yoda
HORIZONTAL LIEUTENANT, THE(1962)
Yoshikata Yoda
UGETSU(1954, Jap.), w; LIFE OF OHARU(1964, Jap.), w; SANSHO THE BAILIFF(1969, Jap.), w; GEISHA, A(1978, Jap.), w
Yoshio Yoda
MC HALE'S NAVY(1964); MC HALE'S NAVY JOINS THE AIR FORCE(1965)
Helen Yoder
Silents
MIDNIGHT ROMANCE, A(1919); WESTERN FIREBRANDS(1921)
George Yohalem
MYSTERIOUS MR. WONG(1935), p; STREAMLINE EXPRESS(1935), p
Silents
NO WOMAN KNOWS(1921), w
Goerge Yohalem
STREAMLINE EXPRESS(1935), w
Jim Yoham
WORLD OF HANS CHRISTIAN ANDERSEN, THE(1971, Jap.)
Erica Yohn
GODFATHER, THE, PART II(1974); STAR 80(1983)
1984
ROADHOUSE 66(1984)
Yoko
VICE DOLLS(1961, Fr.)
Dekao Yokoo
TOKYO FILE 212(1951)
Kekao Yokoo
GEISHA GIRL(1952)
Tadanori Yokoo
DIARY OF A SHINJUKU BURGLAR(1969, Jap.)
Yoshinaga Yokoo
GIRL I ABANDONED, THE(1970, Jap.), art d
Tatsuyuki Yokota
BUDDHA(1965, Jap.), spec eff
William Yokota
JAPANESE WAR BRIDE(1952)
Akio Yokoyama
1984
BALLAD OF NARAYAMA, THE(1984, Jap.)
Michiyo Yokoyama
WESTWARD DESPERADO(1961, Jap.)
Minoru Yokoyama
TEMPTRESS AND THE MONK, THE(1963, Jap.), ph; HARP OF BURMA(1967, Jap.), ph
Rie Yokoyama
DIARY OF A SHINJUKU BURGLAR(1969, Jap.)
Yutaka Yokoyama
THROUGH DAYS AND MONTHS(1969 Jap.), art d
Yolanda
WICKED DIE SLOW, THE(1968)
Veloz and Yolanda
MANY HAPPY RETURNS(1934); RUMBA(1935), ch

Greta Yoltz
Silents
BEAUTIFUL BUT DUMB(1928); GIRL IN EVERY PORT, A(1928)
Misc. Silents
HOT HEELS(1928); YELLOW CONTRABAND(1928)
Masakane Yonekura
SCANDALOUS ADVENTURES OF BURAIKAN, THE(1970, Jap.); ZATOICHI MEETS YOJIMBO(1970, Jap.)
Sakatoshi Yonekura
SCANDALOUS ADVENTURES OF BURAIKAN, THE(1970, Jap.)
Norman Yonemoto
1984
SAVAGE STREETS(1984), w
Saoko Yonemura
I LIVE IN FEAR(1967, Jap.)
Mme. Soo Yong
BIG JIM McLAIN(1952)
Soo Yong
PAINTED VEIL, THE(1934); CHINA SEAS(1935); KLONDIKE ANNIE(1936); MAD HOLIDAY(1936); GOOD EARTH, THE(1937); ADVENTURES OF MARCO POLO, THE(1938); NIGHT PLANE FROM CHUNGKING(1942); CHINA(1943); PEKING EXPRESS(1951); TARGET HONG KONG(1952); LEFT HAND OF GOD, THE(1955); SOLDIER OF FORTUNE(1955); FLIGHT TO HONG KONG(1956); HAWAIIANS, THE(1970)
Jean Yonnel
CALL, THE(1938, Fr.); BLIND DESIRE(1948, Fr.); THANK HEAVEN FOR SMALL FAVORS(1965, Fr.)
Yordan
MAN CRAZY(1953), w
Caprice Yordan
KISS THEM FOR ME(1957)
Danny Yordan
ROYAL HUNT OF THE SUN, THE(1969, Brit.)
Merlyn Yordan
THIN RED LINE, THE(1964)
Phil Yordan
DILLINGER(1945), w
Philip Yordan
SYNCOPATION(1942), w; JOHNNY DOESN'T LIVE HERE ANY MORE(1944), w; WHEN STRANGERS MARRY(1944), w; SUSPENSE(1946), w; WHISTLE STOP(1946), w; ANNA LUCASTA(1949), p, w; BAD MEN OF TOMBSTONE(1949), w; HOUSE OF STRANGERS(1949), w; EDGE OF DOOM(1950), w; DETECTIVE STORY(1951), w; DRUMS IN THE DEEP SOUTH(1951), w; MARA MARU(1952), w; HOUDINI(1953), w; MAN CRAZY(1953), p; NAKED JUNGLE, THE(1953), w; BROKEN LANCE(1954), w; JOHNNY GUITAR(1954), w; CONQUEST OF SPACE(1955), w; LAST FRONTIER, THE(1955), w; MAN FROM LARAMIE, THE(1955), w; HARDER THEY FALL, THE(1956), p, w; FOUR BOYS AND A GUN(1957), w; GUN GLORY(1957), w; MEN IN WAR(1957), w; NO DOWN PAYMENT(1957), w; STREET OF SINNERS(1957), w; ANNA LUCASTA(1958), w; BRAVADOS, THE(1958), w; FIEND WHO WALKED THE WEST, THE(1958), w; GOD'S LITTLE ACRE(1958), w; ISLAND WOMEN(1958), w; DAY OF THE OUTLAW(1959), w; BRAMBLE BUSH, THE(1960), w; STUDS LONIGAN(1960), p, w; EL CID(1961, U.S./Ital.), w; KING OF KINGS(1961), w; DAY OF THE TRIFFIDS, THE(1963), w; 55 DAYS AT PEKING(1963), w; CIRCUS WORLD(1964), w; FALL OF THE ROMAN EMPIRE, THE(1964), w; BATTLE OF THE BULGE(1965), p, w; CUSTER OF THE WEST(1968, U.S., Span.), p; ROYAL HUNT OF THE SUN, THE(1969, Brit.), p, w; CAPTAIN APACHE(1971, Brit.), p, w; BAD MAN'S RIVER(1972, Span.), w
Phillip Yordan
CHASE, THE(1946), w; BLACK BOOK, THE(1949), w; MUTINY(1952), w; BLOWING WILD(1953), w; BIG COMBO, THE(1955), w; JOE MACBETH(1955), w
Wladimir Yordanoff
DANTON(1983)
Blaine M. Yorgason
WINDWALKER(1980), w
Adam York
FLYING LEATHERNECKS(1951)
Amanda York
1984
SCRUBBERS(1984, Brit.)
Andrew York
DANGER ROUTE(1968, Brit.), w
B.M. Chick York
YEARLING, THE(1946)
Carl York
MAN OR GUN(1958); PRETTY BOY FLOYD(1960); HUSTLER, THE(1961)
Cecil Morton York
Silents
HOUSE OF TEMPERLEY, THE(1913, Brit.); FLYING FROM JUSTICE(1915, Brit.); FOUNDATIONS OF FREEDOM, THE(1918, Brit.); AUTUMN OF PRIDE, THE(1921, Brit.); GOD IN THE GARDEN, THE(1921, Brit.); IN HIS GRIP(1921, Brit.); SISTER TO ASSIST 'ER, A(1922, Brit.); TRAPPED BY THE MORMONS(1922, Brit.); GAMBLE WITH HEARTS, A(1923, Brit.); IN THE BLOOD(1923, Brit.); UNINVITED GUEST, THE(1923, Brit.); ALLEY OF GOLDEN HEARTS, THE(1924, Brit.); OLD BILL THROUGH THE AGES(1924, Brit.)
Misc. Silents
PALLARD THE PUNTER(1919, Brit.); FOUL PLAY(1920, Brit.); HARD CASH(1921, Brit.); YOUNG LOCHINVAR(1923, Brit.); WHAT THE BUTLER SAW(1924, Brit.); TRAINER AND THE TEMPTRESS(1925, Brit.)
Chick York
RAMROD(1947)
David York
MAN FROM COLORADO, THE(1948)
Derek York
THAT KIND OF GIRL(1963, Brit.), ed; SEANCE ON A WET AFTERNOON(1964 Brit.), ed; LIFE AT THE TOP(1965, Brit.), ed; INADMISSIBLE EVIDENCE(1968, Brit.), ed; INVINCIBLE SIX, THE(1970, U.S./Iran), ed
Dick York
THREE STRIPES IN THE SUN(1955); OPERATION MAD BALL(1957); COWBOY(1958); LAST BLITZKRIEG, THE(1958); THEY CAME TO CORDURA(1959); INHERIT THE WIND(1960)

Doris York
FRANCHISE AFFAIR, THE(1952, Brit.)
Duke York
FOOTLIGHT PARADE(1933); ISLAND OF LOST SOULS(1933); ROMAN SCANDALS(1933); ELMER AND ELSIE(1934); OLD-FASHIONED WAY, THE(1934); PURSUIT OF HAPPINESS, THE(1934); ONE HOUR LATE(1935); STOLEN HARMONY(1935); TWO FOR TONIGHT(1935); WINGS IN THE DARK(1935); FURY(1936); IT'S A GREAT LIFE(1936); LIBELED LADY(1936); LOVE ON THE RUN(1936); RHYTHM ON THE RANGE(1936); STRIKE ME PINK(1936); SWORN ENEMY(1936); THREE MESQUITEERS, THE(1936); MIDNIGHT MADONNA(1937); MIND YOUR OWN BUSINESS(1937); PROFESSOR BEWARE(1938); RECKLESS LIVING(1938); SLIGHT CASE OF MURDER, A(1938); NAVY SECRETS(1939); TOPPER TAKES A TRIP(1939); YOU CAN'T CHEAT AN HONEST MAN(1939); LITTLE MEN(1940); MERCY PLANE(1940); LIFE BEGINS FOR ANDY HARDY(1941); MOB TOWN(1941); NEVER GIVE A SUCKER AN EVEN BREAK(1941); PUBLIC ENEMIES(1941); SHADOW OF THE THIN MAN(1941); TEXAS(1941); ALIAS BOSTON BLACKIE(1942); ARABIAN NIGHTS(1942); BEHIND THE EIGHT BALL(1942); GIVE OUT, SISTERS(1942); INVISIBLE AGENT(1942); JACKASS MAIL(1942); NAZI AGENT(1942); PANAMA HATTIE(1942); SABOTEUR(1942); SUNDAY PUNCH(1942); TENNESSEE JOHNSON(1942); WHO DONE IT?(1942); WOMAN OF THE YEAR(1942); CONTENDER, THE(1944); DESTINATION TOKYO(1944); FOLLOW THE BOYS(1944); JOHNNY DOESN'T LIVE HERE ANY MORE(1944); LOST IN A HAREM(1944); ROAD TO RIO(1947); CALIFORNIA FIREBRAND(1948); ISN'T IT ROMANTIC?(1948); PALEFACE, THE(1948); THAT LADY IN ERMINE(1948); FRANCIS(1949); JOHNNY STOOL PIGEON(1949); MISSISSIPPI RHYTHM(1949); STAMPEDE(1949); CALL OF THE KLONDIKE(1950); FORTUNES OF CAPTAIN BLOOD(1950); HIT PARADE OF 1951(1950); SNOW DOG(1950); WHERE DANGER LIVES(1950); FORT DEFIANCE(1951); MY FAVORITE SPY(1951); ROGUE RIVER(1951); SILVER CANYON(1951); SNAKE RIVER DESPERADOES(1951); TEXANS NEVER CRY(1951); VALLEY OF FIRE(1951); CARBINE WILLIAMS(1952); CONFIDENCE GIRL(1952); NORTHWEST TERRITORY(1952)
Duke York, Jr.
FLASH GORDON(1936)
Felicity York
SPY WHO LOVED ME, THE(1977, Brit.)
Francine York
SERGEANT WAS A LADY, THE(1961); IT'S ONLY MONEY(1962); SECRET FILE: HOLLYWOOD(1962); NEW KIND OF LOVE, A(1963); NUTTY PROFESSOR, THE(1963); BEDTIME STORY(1964); FAMILY JEWELS, THE(1965); SPACE MONSTER(1965); TICKLE ME(1965); CURSE OF THE SWAMP CREATURE(1966); WILD ONES ON WHEELS(1967); CANNON FOR CORDOBA(1970); WELCOME HOME, SOLDIER BOYS(1972); DOLL SQUAD, THE(1973); SMORGASBORD(1983)
Misc. Talkies
CENTERFOLD GIRLS, THE(1974); HALF A HOUSE(1979)
Gerald York
CHUKA(1967); SIMON, KING OF THE WITCHES(1971); IT'S ALIVE(1974)
Janet York
HAIR(1979)
Jay York
ANGELS FROM HELL(1968)
Jeff York
NAZI AGENT(1942); THEY WERE EXPENDABLE(1945); LITTLE MISS BIG(1946); POSTMAN ALWAYS RINGS TWICE, THE(1946); UP GOES MAISIE(1946); YEARLING, THE(1946); BLONDIE'S HOLIDAY(1947); FEAR IN THE NIGHT(1947); UNCONQUERED(1947); ISN'T IT ROMANTIC?(1948); PALEFACE, THE(1948); PANHANDLE(1948); KNOCK ON ANY DOOR(1949); SAMSON AND DELILAH(1949); SPECIAL AGENT(1949); FATHER OF THE BRIDE(1950); KILL THE UMPIRE(1950); SHORT GRASS(1950); SURRENDER(1950); LADY SAYS NO, THE(1951); UNKNOWN MAN, THE(1951); DEMETRIUS AND THE GLADIATORS(1954); DAVY CROCKETT AND THE RIVER PIRATES(1956); GREAT LOCOMOTIVE CHASE, THE(1956); WESTWARD HO THE WAGONS!(1956); JOHNNY TREMAIN(1957); OLD YELLER(1957); SAVAGE SAM(1963); TAMMY AND THE MILLIONAIRE(1967)
John J. York
1984
BEAR, THE(1984); CHATTANOOGA CHOO CHOO(1984)
Jon York
GREY FOX, THE(1983, Can.)
Katherine York
LOVER COME BACK(1946); STRANGE WOMAN, THE(1946)
Kathleen York
1984
PROTOCOL(1984)
Kay York
HER LUCKY NIGHT(1945); EASY COME, EASY GO(1967); SWEET CHARITY(1969)
Kitt York
MY BODYGUARD(1980)
Leonard York
STOOLIE, THE(1972)
Leslie York
MACHISMO–40 GRAVES FOR 40 GUNS(1970)
Linda York
WORLD IS JUST A 'B' MOVIE, THE(1971)
Misc. Talkies
CHAIN GANG WOMEN(1972); SCREAM IN THE STREETS, A(1972)
Lynn York
KINFOLK(1970)
Mark York
RUN WITH THE WIND(1966, Brit.); HENRY VIII AND HIS SIX WIVES(1972, Brit.)
Marylou York
SKATEBOARD(1978)
Melanie York
QUEEN FOR A DAY(1951)
Michael York
ACCIDENT(1967, Brit.); SMASHING TIME(1967 Brit.); TAMING OF THE SHREW, THE(1967, U.S./Ital.); ROMEO AND JULIET(1968, Brit./Ital.); STRANGE AFFAIR, THE(1968, Brit.); ALFRED THE GREAT(1969, Brit.); GURU, THE(1969, U.S./India); JUSTINE(1969); SOMETHING FOR EVERYONE(1970); ZEPPELIN(1971, Brit.); CABARET(1972); ENGLAND MADE ME(1973, Brit.); LOST HORIZON(1973); MURDER ON THE ORIENT EXPRESS(1974, Brit.); THREE MUSKETEERS, THE(1974, Panama); CONDUCT UNBECOMING(1975, Brit.); FOUR MUSKETEERS, THE(1975); GREAT

EXPECTATIONS(1975, Brit.); LOGAN'S RUN(1976); SEVEN NIGHTS IN JAPAN(1976, Brit./Fr.); ISLAND OF DR. MOREAU, THE(1977); LAST REMAKE OF BEAU GESTE, THE(1977); FEDORA(1978, Ger./Fr.); FINAL ASSIGNMENT(1980, Can.); WEATHER IN THE STREETS, THE(1983, Brit.)

1984
RIDDLE OF THE SANDS, THE(1984, Brit.); SUCCESS IS THE BEST REVENGE(1984, Brit.)

Misc. Talkies
WHITE LIONS(1981)

Ned York
MOVIE STAR, AMERICAN STYLE, OR, LSD I HATE YOU!(1966); ON HER BED OF ROSES(1966)

Oswald York
Silents
MONSIEUR BEAUCAIRE(1924)

Peter York
DETECTIVE, THE(1968)

Philip York
RICHARD'S THINGS(1981, Brit.)

Powell York
DISRAELI(1929)

Rebecca York
MOVIE MOVIE(1978)

Richard "Dick" York
MY SISTER EILEEN(1955)

Robert York
1984
WINDY CITY(1984)

Sarah York
EVIL DEAD, THE(1983)

Susannah York
TUNES OF GLORY(1960, Brit.); LOSS OF INNOCENCE(1961, Brit.); FREUD(1962); THERE WAS A CROOKED MAN(1962, Brit.); TOM JONES(1963, Brit.); SEVENTH DAWN, THE(1964); SANDS OF THE KALAHARI(1965, Brit.); KALEIDOSCOPE(1966, Brit.); MAN FOR ALL SEASONS, A(1966, Brit.); DUFFY(1968, Brit.); SEBASTIAN(1968, Brit.); BATTLE OF BRITAIN, THE(1969, Brit.); LOCK UP YOUR DAUGHTERS(1969, Brit.); OH! WHAT A LOVELY WAR(1969, Brit.); THEY SHOOT HORSES, DON'T THEY?(1969); BROTHERLY LOVE(1970, Brit.); HAPPY BIRTHDAY, WANDA JUNE(1971); JANE EYRE(1971, Brit.); IMAGES(1972, Ireland), a, w; X Y & ZEE(1972, Brit.); GOLD(1974, Brit.); CONDUCT UNBECOMING(1975, Brit.); MAIDS, THE(1975, Brit.); THAT LUCKY TOUCH(1975, Brit.); ELIZA FRASER(1976, Aus.); SKY RIDERS(1976, U.S./Gr.); SHOUT, THE(1978, Brit.); SUPERMAN(1978); SILENT PARTNER, THE(1979, Can.); AWAKENING, THE(1980); FALLING IN LOVE AGAIN(1980), a, w; SUPERMAN II(1980); LONG SHOT(1981, Brit.); LOOPHOLE(1981, Brit.); NELLY'S VERSION(1983, Brit.); YELLOWBEARD(1983)

Terence York
PASSAGE, THE(1979, Brit.)

Terry York
THEATRE OF BLOOD(1973, Brit.), stunts; PINK PANTHER STRIKES AGAIN, THE(1976, Brit.)

Tony York
KILLERS THREE(1968)

W. Allen York
IT'S ALIVE(1974)

Wayne York
1984
RUNAWAY(1984)

Agustus Yorke
Silents
JUST DECEPTION, A(1917, Brit.)

Augustus Yorke
Silents
TAILOR OF BOND STREET, THE(1916, Brit.); GRIT OF A JEW, THE(1917, Brit.)

Bruce Yorke
JOURNEY INTO NOWHERE(1963, Brit.), p

Carol Yorke
LETTER FROM AN UNKNOWN WOMAN(1948)

Cecil Morton Yorke
Misc. Silents
MILL-OWNER'S DAUGHTER, THE(1916, Brit.)

Derek Yorke
HIGH WIND IN JAMAICA, A(1965), ed

Doris Yorke
GENTLE GUNMAN, THE(1952, Brit.); TRAIN OF EVENTS(1952, Brit.); GLAD TIDINGS(1953, Brit.); NOOSE FOR A LADY(1953, Brit.); FLAW, THE(1955, Brit.); GREEN MAN, THE(1957, Brit.); DESPERATE MAN, THE(1959, Brit.)

Douglas Yorke
ROAD TO BALI(1952)

Duke Yorke
TICKET TO PARADISE(1936); WINCHESTER '73(1950)

Edith Yorke
LOVE RACKET, THE(1929); PHANTOM OF THE OPERA, THE(1929); VALIANT, THE(1929); CITY GIRL(1930); SEVEN KEYS TO BALDPATE(1930)
Silents
CHICKENS(1921); LYING LIPS(1921); ONE CLEAR CALL(1922); STEP ON IT!(1922); MERRY-GO-ROUND(1923); MIRACLE MAKERS, THE(1923); MOTHERS-IN-LAW(1923); SAWDUST(1923); SLIPPY McGEE(1923); SOULS FOR SALE(1923); OTHER KIND OF LOVE, THE(1924); PRIDE OF SUNSHINE ALLEY(1924); BELOW THE LINE(1925); PHANTOM OF THE OPERA, THE(1925); HEART OF A COWARD, THE(1926); OH, WHAT A NURSE!(1926); RUSTLER'S RANCH(1926); VOLCANO(1926); BACHELOR'S BABY, THE(1927); SENSATION SEEKERS(1927); WESTERN WHIRLWIND, THE(1927); MAKING THE VARSITY(1928); FUGITIVES(1929)
Misc. Silents
DAUGHTER OF LUXURY, A(1922); BURNING WORDS(1923); SOULS FOR SABLES(1925); BELLE OF BROADWAY, THE(1926); RUSTLING FOR CUPID(1926); TIMID TERROR, THE(1926); TRANSCONTINENTAL LIMITED(1926)

Edithe Yorke
Silents
HUSBANDS AND LOVERS(1924); RED DICE(1926)

Misc. Silents
DOCTOR AND THE BRICKLAYER, THE(1918)

Kay Yorke
SUDAN(1945)

Terry Yorke
LONG DUEL, THE(1967, Brit.); YOU CAN'T WIN 'EM ALL(1970, Brit.)

Tracey Yorke
BIG SWITCH, THE(1970, Brit.)

Bud Yorkin
COME BLOW YOUR HORN(1963), p, d; NEVER TOO LATE(1965), d; DIVORCE AMERICAN STYLE(1967), d; INSPECTOR CLOUSEAU(1968, Brit.), d; START THE REVOLUTION WITHOUT ME(1970), p&d; THIEF WHO CAME TO DINNER, THE(1973), p&d

David Yorkston
NEPTUNE FACTOR, THE(1973, Can.)

David Yorston
GREEN SLIME, THE(1969); SUDDEN FURY(1975, Can.); SUPERMAN(1978)

Chester Yorton
MUSCLE BEACH PARTY(1964); DON'T MAKE WAVES(1967)

Mayor Sam Yorty
CANDIDATE, THE(1972)

Ben Yosef
OPERATION THUNDERBOLT(1978, ISRAEL)

Kenji Yoshida
NO GREATER LOVE THAN THIS(1969, Jap.), d

Masahiro Yoshida
LAST UNICORN, THE(1982), anim
1984
WARRIORS OF THE WIND(1984, Jap.), anim

Peter Yoshida
FIGHT FOR YOUR LIFE(1977)

Tadataka Yoshida
GOKE, BODYSNATCHER FROM HELL(1968, Jap.), art d
1984
WARRIORS OF THE WIND(1984, Jap.), anim

Teruo Yoshida
TWIN SISTERS OF KYOTO(1964, Jap.); GOKE, BODYSNATCHER FROM HELL(1968, Jap.); AFFAIR AT AKITSU(1980, Jap.)

Tetsuo Yoshida
MAJIN(1968, Jap.), w

Tetsuro Yoshida
ZATOICHI MEETS YOJIMBO(1970, Jap.), w

Yoshio Yoshida
ZATOICHI(1968, Jap.)

Yoshishige Yoshida
LAKE, THE(1970, Jap.), d, w; AFFAIR AT AKITSU(1980, Jap.), d, w

Yuki Yoshida
DRYLANDERS(1963, Can.), cos

Eiji Yoshikawa
SAMURAI(PART III)** (1967, Jap.), w, w; SAMURAI(1955, Jap.), w

Mitsuko Yoshikawa
Misc. Silents
I WAS BORN, BUT...(1932, Jap.)

Nobutaka Yoshimo
1984
BALLAD OF NARAYAMA, THE(1984, Jap.), art d

Jitsuko Yoshimura
INSECT WOMAN, THE(1964, Jap.); ONIBABA(1965, Jap.); NIGHT OF THE SEA-GULL, THE(1970, Jap.); RED LION(1971, Jap.)

Mari Yoshimura
INHERITANCE, THE(1964, Jap.)

George Yoshinaga
FROGMEN, THE(1951); CRIMSON KIMONO, THE(1959); SNIPER'S RIDGE(1961)

George Yoshiniga
OPERATION BOTTLENECK(1961)

Inko Yoshino
SNOW COUNTRY(1969, Jap.), art d

Nobutaka Yoshino
TWILIGHT PATH(1965, Jap.), art d

Soji Yoshino
SONG FROM MY HEART, THE(1970, Jap.), w

Tadataka Yoshino
FAREWELL, MY BELOVED(1969, Jap.), art d

Adele Yoshioka
SWEET CHARITY(1969); MAGNUM FORCE(1973)

Michio Yoshioka
FOX WITH NINE TAILS, THE(1969, Jap.), w

Yasuhiro Yoshioka
DIARY OF A SHINJUKU BURGLAR(1969, Jap.), ph

Tamaki Yoshiwara
LETTER, THE(1929)

Ishida Yoshiyuki
YAKUZA, THE(1975, U.S./Jap.), art d

Niccolai Yoshkin
CONFESSIONS OF A NAZI SPY(1939)

Valentin Yoshow
BALLAD OF A SOLDIER(1960, USSR), w

Dorothy Yost
SEA BAT, THE(1930), w; WHAT MEN WANT(1930), w; HELLO, EVERYBODY(1933), w; GAY DIVORCEE, THE(1934), w; ALICE ADAMS(1935), w; DOG OF FLANDERS, A(1935), w; FRECKLES(1935), w; LADDIE(1935), w; BUNKER BEAN(1936), w; M'LISS(1936), w; MURDER ON A BRIDLE PATH(1936), w; RACING LADY(1937), w; THAT GIRL FROM PARIS(1937), w; THERE GOES THE GROOM(1937), w; TOO MANY WIVES(1937), w; BAD LITTLE ANGEL(1939), w; BLACKMAIL(1939), w; FOUR GIRLS IN WHITE(1939), w; STORY OF VERNON AND IRENE CASTLE, THE(1939), w; FORTY LITTLE MOTHERS(1940), w; SPORTING BLOOD(1940), w; THUNDERHEAD-SON OF FLICKA(1945), w; SMOKY(1946), w; LOADED PISTOLS(1948), w; STRAWBERRY ROAN, THE(1948), w; BIG CAT, THE(1949), w; COWBOY AND THE INDIANS, THE(1949), w; SAGINAW TRAIL(1953), w; SMOKY(1966), w

Silents
FLAMES OF THE FLESH(1920), w; QUEENIE(1921), w; LITTLE MISS SMILES(1922), w; NEW TEACHER, THE(1922), w; KENTUCKY DAYS(1923), w; WHEN ODDS ARE EVEN(1923), w; MY HUSBAND'S WIVES(1924), w; ROMANCE RANCH(1924), w; WINGS OF THE STORM(1926), w; HILLS OF KENTUCKY(1927), w; JUDGMENT OF THE HILLS(1927), w; FANGS OF THE WILD(1928), w

Fielding "Hurry Up" Yost
Silents
QUARTERBACK, THE(1926), cons

Herbert Yost
FAST AND LOOSE(1930); AGE OF INNOCENCE(1934)
Misc. Silents
OVER NIGHT(1915)

lp: Martin Yost
Misc. Talkies
GETTING IT ON(1983)

Norma Yost
OCEAN'S ELEVEN(1960); CAPE FEAR(1962)

Robert Yost
DANTE'S INFERNO(1935), w; ARIZONA MAHONEY(1936), w; ARIZONA RAIDERS, THE(1936), w; DESERT GOLD(1936), w; DRIFT FENCE(1936), w; FORGOTTEN FACES(1936), w; PREVIEW MURDER MYSTERY(1936), w; BORN TO THE WEST(1937), w; FORLORN RIVER(1937), w; LET'S MAKE A MILLION(1937), w; THUNDER TRAIL(1937), w; ILLEGAL TRAFFIC(1938), w; PRISON FARM(1938), w; TIP-OFF GIRLS(1938), w; GRAND JURY SECRETS(1939), w; TOM SAWYER, DETECTIVE(1939), w; CARSON CITY KID(1940), w; YOUNG BUFFALO BILL(1940), w; PHANTOM PLAINSMEN, THE(1942), w; SUNSET SERENADE(1942), w; CANYON CITY(1943), w; OVERLAND MAIL ROBBERY(1943), w; THUNDERING TRAILS(1943), w

Ah Yot
Silents
GOLD RUSH, THE(1925)

Reuben Bar Yotam
OPERATION THUNDERBOLT(1978, ISRAEL)

Bob Yothers
1984
FEAR CITY(1984)

Bumper Yothers
SECOND THOUGHTS(1983)

Cory "Bumper" Yothers
1984
DREAMSCAPE(1984)

Tina Yothers
SHOOT THE MOON(1982)

M. You
PICNIC ON THE GRASS(1960, Fr.)

Chen You-hsin
GRAND SUBSTITUTION, THE(1965, Hong Kong)

Samy Ben Youb
MADAME ROSA(1977, Fr.)

Youdin
ENEMIES OF PROGRESS(1934, USSR)

Louisa Youell
WEDDING PARTY, THE(1969)

Chief Youilachie
WINCHESTER '73(1950)

Rod Yould
TELL ME IN THE SUNLIGHT(1967), ph

Robert C. Youmans
OPERATION PETTICOAT(1959)

Vincent Youmans
NO, NO NANETTE(1930), w; FLYING DOWN TO RIO(1933), m; TAKE A CHANCE(1933), w; NO, NO NANETTE(1940), w; TEA FOR TWO(1950), w

William Youmans
1984
MRS. SOFFEL(1984)

Aida Young
DRACULA HAS RISEN FROM HIS GRAVE(1968, Brit.), p; VENGEANCE OF SHE, THE(1968, Brit.), p; SCARS OF DRACULA, THE(1970, Brit.), p; TASTE THE BLOOD OF DRACULA(1970, Brit.), p; HANDS OF THE RIPPER(1971, Brit.), p; WHEN DINOSAURS RULED THE EARTH(1971, Brit.), p; STEPTOE AND SON(1972, Brit.), p; LIKELY LADS, THE(1976, Brit.), p

Al Young
SEPIA CINDERELLA(1947)

Alan Young
MARGIE(1946); CHICKEN EVERY SUNDAY(1948); MR. BELVEDERE GOES TO COLLEGE(1949); AARON SLICK FROM PUNKIN CRICK(1952); ANDROCLES AND THE LION(1952); GENTLEMEN MARRY BRUNETTES(1955); TOM THUMB(1958, Brit./U.S.); TIME MACHINE, THE(1960; Brit./U.S.); BAKER'S HAWK(1976); CAT FROM OUTER SPACE, THE(1978)

Alexander Young
OH ROSALINDA(1956, Brit.)

Allison Racy Young
FANDANGO(1970)

Anita Young
PETER RABBIT AND TALES OF BEATRIX POTTER(1971, Brit.)

Anthony Young
THEM NICE AMERICANS(1958, Brit.), p, d

Arthur Young
VICTORIA THE GREAT(1937, Brit.); NO LIMIT(1935, Brit.); RADIO FOLLIES(1935, Brit.); MUSIC MAKER, THE(1936, Brit.); WRATH OF JEALOUSY(1936, Brit.); TWENTY-ONE DAYS TOGETHER(1940, Brit.); MURDER BY INVITATION(1941); ROOT OF ALL EVIL, THE(1947, Brit.); SAN DEMETRIO, LONDON(1947, Brit.); MY BROTHER JONATHAN(1949, Brit.); TWENTY QUESTIONS MURDER MYSTERY, THE(1950, Brit.); LADY WITH A LAMP, THE(1951, Brit.); ISN'T LIFE WONDERFUL!(1953, Brit.); INSPECTOR CALLS, AN(1954, Brit.); JOHN WESLEY(1954, Brit.); PAID TO KILL(1954, Brit.); STRANGER FROM VENUS(1954, Brit.); DYNAMITERS, THE(1956, Brit.); JOHN OF THE FAIR(1962, Brit.)

Artie Young
BRONZE BUCKAROO, THE(1939); HARLEM RIDES THE RANGE(1939)

Aston S. Young
PIRANHA II: THE SPAWNING(1981, Neth.)

Audrey Young
LADY IN THE DARK(1944); RAINBOW ISLAND(1944); UP IN ARMS(1944); DUFFY'S TAVERN(1945); FOLLOW THAT WOMAN(1945); GEORGE WHITE'S SCANDALS(1945); OUT OF THIS WORLD(1945); STORK CLUB, THE(1945); LOVER COME BACK(1946); NIGHT IN PARADISE, A(1946); DANGER STREET(1947); SONG OF SCHEHERAZADE(1947); WISTFUL WIDOW OF WAGON GAP, THE(1947); LETTER FROM AN UNKNOWN WOMAN(1948); EASY LIVING(1949); GAL WHO TOOK THE WEST, THE(1949); LOVE ME OR LEAVE ME(1955)

Barrie Young
HALF A SIXPENCE(1967, Brit.)

Ben Young
WESTWORLD(1973); HUSTLE(1975); ST. IVES(1976)

Benny Young
CHARRIOTS OF FIRE(1981, Brit.)

Bernice Young
WOMAN'S SECRET, A(1949)

Bert Young
LITTLE TOUGH GUY(1938); LITTLE ACCIDENT(1939); HERE COMES MR. JORDAN(1941); WILDCAT OF TUCSON(1941)
Misc. Talkies
SIX GUN JUSTICE(1935)

Bill Young
SHINE ON, HARVEST MOON(1944); ESCAPE 2000(1983, Aus.)

Billy Young
OUTSIDE OF PARADISE(1938)

Boas Young
Misc. Talkies
JEWISH FATHER(1934)

Bob Young
COLOR ME DEAD(1969, Aus.), m; IT TAKES ALL KINDS(1969, U.S./Aus.), m; DEMONSTRATOR(1971, Aus.), m; ADAM'S WOMAN(1972, Austral.), m; PAPER MOON(1973); INN OF THE DAMNED(1974, Aus.), m; LADY, STAY DEAD(1982, Aus.), m; DOT AND THE BUNNY(1983, Aus.), m
1984
BROTHERS(1984, Aus.), m; CAMEL BOY, THE(1984, Aus.), m

Bobby Young
Silents
THREE'S A CROWD(1927)

Boez Young
TEVYA(1939)

Brian Young
MANGANINNIE(1982, Aus.)
1984
MRS. SOFFEL(1984)

Bruce A. Young
RISKY BUSINESS(1983)

Bruce Young
THIEF(1981)

Buck Young
MONEY FROM HOME(1953); FRENCH LINE, THE(1954); NOT WITH MY WIFE, YOU DON'T!(1966); YOUNG WARRIORS, THE(1967); SUPPOSE THEY GAVE A WAR AND NOBODY CAME?(1970); LATE LIZ, THE(1971); PICKUP ON 101(1972); BREEZY(1973); MITCHELL(1975); TWO-MINUTE WARNING(1976); DEATH WISH II(1982)
1984
SAM'S SON(1984)

Burt Young
GANG THAT COULDN'T SHOOT STRAIGHT, THE(1971); CINDERELLA LIBERTY(1973); CHINATOWN(1974); GAMBLER, THE(1974); MURPH THE SURF(1974); KILLER ELITE, THE(1975); CARNIVAL OF BLOOD(1976); HARRY AND WALTER GO TO NEW YORK(1976); ROCKY(1976); CHOIRBOYS, THE(1977); TWILIGHT'S LAST GLEAMING(1977, U.S./Ger.); CONVOY(1978); UNCLE JOE SHANNON(1978), a, w; ROCKY II(1979); ...ALL THE MARBLES(1981); BLOOD BEACH(1981); AMITYVILLE II: THE POSSESSION(1982); LOOKIN' TO GET OUT(1982); ROCKY III(1982)
1984
ONCE UPON A TIME IN AMERICA(1984); OVER THE BROOKLYN BRIDGE(1984); POPE OF GREENWICH VILLAGE, THE(1984)

Burton Young
Misc. Silents
HOUSE OF SHAME, THE(1928), d

C. Young
HERE COME THE JETS(1959)

Carleton Young
REEFER MADNESS(1936); COME ON, COWBOYS(1937); DANGEROUS HOLIDAY(1937); GIT ALONG, LITTLE DOGIES(1937); HAPPY-GO-LUCKY(1937); JOIN THE MARINES(1937); MAN BETRAYED, A(1937); NAVY BLUES(1937); ROUNDUP TIME IN TEXAS(1937); CASSIDY OF BAR 20(1938); GANG BULLETS(1938); GUILTY TRAILS(1938); GUNSMOKE TRAIL(1938); HEROES OF THE HILLS(1938); OLD BARN DANCE, THE(1938); OUTLAW EXPRESS(1938); CONVICT'S CODE(1939); EL DIABLO RIDES(1939); FLAMING LEAD(1939); HONOR OF THE WEST(1939); MESQUITE BUCKAROO(1939); PAL FROM TEXAS, THE(1939); PORT OF HATE(1939); SMOKY TRAILS(1939); TRIGGER FINGERS ½(1939); ADVENTURE IN DIAMONDS(1940); BILLY THE KID IN TEXAS(1940); COWBOY FROM SUNDOWN(1940); GUN CODE(1940); PALS OF THE SILVER SAGE(1940); UP IN THE AIR(1940); BILLY THE KID'S FIGHTING PALS(1941); BILLY THE KID'S RANGE WAR(1941); BILLY THE KID'S ROUNDUP(1941); KEEP 'EM FLYING(1941); PRAIRIE PIONEERS(1941); TEXAS(1941); TWO GUN SHERIFF(1941); CODE OF THE OUTLAW(1942); MISSOURI OUTLAW, A(1942); SOUTH OF SANTA FE(1942); THUNDER RIVER FEUD(1942); VALLEY OF THE SUN(1942); LADIES OF WASHINGTON(1944); TAKE IT OR LEAVE IT(1944); THUNDERHEAD-SON OF FLICKA(1945); QUEEN OF BURLESQUE(1946); SMASH-UP, THE STORY OF A WOMAN(1947); AMERICAN GUERRILLA IN THE PHILIPPINES, AN(1950); DOUBLE DEAL(1950); ANNE OF THE INDIES(1951); BEST OF THE BADMEN(1951); BLUE VEIL, THE(1951); CHAIN OF CIRCUMSTANCE(1951); DAY THE EARTH STOOD STILL, THE(1951); DESERT FOX, THE(1951); FLYING LEATHERNECKS(1951); GENE AUTRY AND THE MOUNTIES(1951); MOB, THE(1951); OPERATION PACIFIC(1951); PEOPLE WILL TALK(1951); RED MOUNTAIN(1951); BATTLE ZONE(1952); BOOTS MALONE(1952); BRIGAND, THE(1952);

Carleton G. Young (continued)

DEADLINE–U.S.A.(1952); DIPLOMATIC COURIER(1952); KANSAS CITY CONFIDENTIAL(1952); LAST OF THE COMANCHES(1952); STEEL TRAP, THE(1952); WASHINGTON STORY(1952); BLUEPRINT FOR MURDER, A(1953); FROM HERE TO ETERNITY(1953); GLENN MILLER STORY, THE(1953); GLORY BRIGADE, THE(1953); GOLDTOWN GHOST RIDERS(1953); MEXICAN MANHUNT(1953); NIAGARA(1953); NO ESCAPE(1953); SAFARI DRUMS(1953); SALOME(1953); TORPEDO ALLEY(1953); ARROW IN THE DUST(1954); BITTER CREEK(1954); PRINCE VALIANT(1954); RIOT IN CELL BLOCK 11(1954); ROGUE COP(1954); WOMAN'S WORLD(1954); 20,000 LEAGUES UNDER THE SEA(1954); ARTISTS AND MODELS(1955); BATTLE FLAME(1955); COURT-MARTIAL OF BILLY MITCHELL, THE(1955); PHANTOM OF THE JUNGLE(1955); RACERS, THE(1955); BEYOND A REASONABLE DOUBT(1956); FLIGHT TO HONG KONG(1956); JULIE(1956); WHILE THE CITY SLEEPS(1956); BATTLE HYMN(1957); JET PILOT(1957); RUN OF THE ARROW(1957); SPIRIT OF ST. LOUIS, THE(1957); THREE BRAVE MEN(1957); CRY TERROR(1958); LAST HURRAH, THE(1958); PERFECT FURLOUGH, THE(1958); HERE COME THE JETS(1959); HORSE SOLDIERS, THE(1959); NORTH BY NORTHWEST(1959); GALLANT HOURS, THE(1960); MUSIC BOX KID, THE(1960); SERGEANT RUTLEDGE(1960); SPARTACUS(1960); ARMORED COMMAND(1961); BIG SHOW, THE(1961); TWENTY PLUS TWO(1961); HOW THE WEST WAS WON(1962); MAN WHO SHOT LIBERTY VALANCE, THE(1962); CHEYENNE AUTUMN(1964)
Misc. Talkies
BILLY THE KID OUTLAWED(1940); BILLY THE KID'S GUN JUSTICE(1940)

Carleton G. Young
ABBOTT AND COSTELLO IN HOLLYWOOD(1945); THRILL OF A ROMANCE(1945); HARD, FAST, AND BEAUTIFUL(1951); HIS KIND OF WOMAN(1951)

Carlton Young
YOUNG DYNAMITE(1937); PRIDE OF THE BOWERY(1941); KISSING BANDIT, THE(1948); DAY THE EARTH STOOD STILL, THE(1951); MY SIX CONVICTS(1952); GREAT DAY IN THE MORNING(1956)

Carrol Young
BOMBA AND THE HIDDEN CITY(1950), w; SHE DEVIL(1957), w

Carroll Young
TARZAN TRIUMPHS(1943), w; TARZAN'S DESERT MYSTERY(1943), w; TARZAN AND THE LEOPARD WOMAN(1946), w; JUNGLE JIM(1948), w; TARZAN AND THE MERMAIDS(1948), w; CAPTIVE GIRL(1950), w; MARK OF THE GORILLA(1950), w; PYGMY ISLAND(1950), w; FURY OF THE CONGO(1951), w; LOST CONTINENT(1951), w; OVERLAND TELEGRAPH(1951), w; JUNGLE, THE(1952), w; KILLER APE(1953), w; TARZAN AND THE SHE-DEVIL(1953), w; CANNIBAL ATTACK(1954), w; APACHE WARRIOR(1957), w; DEERSLAYER, THE(1957), w; MACHETE(1958), w

Catherine Young
Silents
NINE O'CLOCK TOWN, A(1918)

Charles Lawrence Young
Silents
JIM THE PENMAN(1921), w

Charleton Young
PRAIRIE JUSTICE(1938)

Charley Young
PACK UP YOUR TROUBLES(1932); SONS OF THE DESERT(1933)

Charlie Young
1984
BLACK ROOM, THE(1984)

Chic Young
BLONDIE(1938), w; BLONDIE BRINGS UP BABY(1939), w; BLONDIE MEETS THE BOSS(1939), w; BLONDIE TAKES A VACATION(1939), w; BLONDIE HAS SERVANT TROUBLE(1940), w; BLONDIE ON A BUDGET(1940), w; BLONDIE PLAYS CUPID(1940), w; BLONDIE GOES LATIN(1941), w; BLONDIE IN SOCIETY(1941), w; BLONDIE FOR VICTORY(1942), w; BLONDIE GOES TO COLLEGE(1942), w; BLONDIE'S BLESSED EVENT(1942), w; FOOTLIGHT GLAMOUR(1943), w; LEAVE IT TO BLONDIE(1945), w; BLONDIE KNOWS BEST(1946), w; BLONDIE'S LUCKY DAY(1946), w; LIFE WITH BLONDIE(1946), w; BLONDIE IN THE DOUGH(1947), w; BLONDIE'S ANNIVERSARY(1947), w; BLONDIE'S BIG MOMENT(1947), w; BLONDIE'S HOLIDAY(1947), w; BLONDIE'S REWARD(1948), w; BLONDIE'S SECRET(1948), w; BLONDIE HITS THE JACKPOT(1949), w; BLONDIE'S BIG DEAL(1949), w; BEWARE OF BLONDIE(1950), w; BLONDIE'S HERO(1950), w

Chow Young
Silents
TALE OF TWO WORLDS, A(1921)

Chris Young
DORM THAT DRIPPED BLOOD, THE(1983), m
1984
OASIS, THE(1984), m; POWER, THE(1984), m

Clara Kimball Young
KEPT HUSBANDS(1931); MOTHER AND SON(1931); WOMEN GO ON FOREVER(1931); FILE 113(1932); LOVE BOUND(1932); PROBATION(1932); I CAN'T ESCAPE(1934); ROMANCE IN THE RAIN(1934); SHE MARRIED HER BOSS(1935); ROGUES' TAVERN, THE(1936); THREE ON THE TRAIL(1936); HILLS OF OLD WYOMING(1937); OH, SUSANNA(1937); FRONTIERSMAN, THE(1938); ROUNDUP, THE(1941); MR. CELEBRITY(1942)
Misc. Talkies
LAST ASSIGNMENT, THE(1936)
Silents
LOLA(1914); HEART OF THE BLUE RIDGE, THE(1915); TRILBY(1915); COMMON LAW, THE(1916); FORBIDDEN WOMAN, THE(1920); CHARGE IT(1921); WHAT NO MAN KNOWS(1921); ENTER MADAME(1922)
Misc. Silents
MY OFFICIAL WIFE(1914); DEEP PURPLE, THE(1915); MARRYING MONEY(1915); CAMILLE(1916); DARK SILENCE, THE(1916); FEAST OF LIFE, THE(1916); RISE OF SUSAN, THE(1916); WITHOUT A SOUL(1916); YELLOW PASSPORT, THE(1916); EASIEST WAY, THE(1917); FOOLISH VIRGIN, THE(1917); MAGDA(1917); PRICE SHE PAID, THE(1917); SHIRLEY KAYE(1917); CLAW, THE(1918); HOUSE OF GLASS, THE(1918); MARIONETTES, THE(1918); REASON WHY, THE(1918); ROAD THROUGH THE DARK, THE(1918); SAVAGE WOMAN, THE(1918); BETTER WIFE, THE(1919); CHEATING CHEATERS(1919); EYES OF YOUTH(1919); FOR THE SOUL OF RAFAEL(1920); MIDCHANNEL(1920); HUSH(1921); STRAIGHT FROM PARIS(1921); HANDS OF NARA, THE(1922); WORLDLY MADONNA, THE(1922); CORDELIA THE MAGNIFICENT(1923); WIFE'S ROMANCE, A(1923); WOMAN OF BRONZE, THE(1923); LYING WIVES(1925)

Clara Kimbell Young
HIS NIGHT OUT(1935)

Clarence Upson Young
PLOT THICKENS, THE(1936), w; LAW WEST OF TOMBSTONE, THE(1938), w; BAD LANDS(1939), w; GIRL AND THE GAMBLER, THE(1939), w; BLACK DIAMONDS(1940), w; HOT STEEL(1940), w; LOVE, HONOR AND OH, BABY(1940), w; SON OF ROARING DAN(1940), w; MADAME SPY(1942), w; NIGHT MONSTER(1942), w; NORTH TO THE KLONDIKE(1942), w; STRANGE CASE OF DR. RX, THE(1942), w; TIME TO KILL(1942), w; BLACK PARACHUTE, THE(1944), w; GHOST THAT WALKS ALONE, THE(1944), w; BADMAN'S TERRITORY(1946), w; ALBUQUERQUE(1948), w; SHOWDOWN AT ABILENE(1956), w; GUNFIGHT IN ABILENE(1967), w

Clarence Young
DEVIL'S PIPELINE, THE(1940), w

Clifton Young
LONELY TRAIL, THE(1936); CLOAK AND DAGGER(1946); DARK PASSAGE(1947); MY WILD IRISH ROSE(1947); NORA PRENTISS(1947); POSSESSED(1947); PURSUED(1947); BLOOD ON THE MOON(1948); TREASURE OF THE SIERRA MADRE, THE(1948); WHIPLASH(1948); ABANDONED(1949); CALAMITY JANE AND SAM BASS(1949); ILLEGAL ENTRY(1949); BELLS OF CORONADO(1950); RETURN OF JESSE JAMES, THE(1950); SALT LAKE RAIDERS(1950); TRAIL OF ROBIN HOOD(1950); UNION STATION(1950); WOMAN OF DISTINCTION, A(1950)

Clint Young
STAGE STRUCK(1958); ODDS AGAINST TOMORROW(1959); FAMILY PLOT(1976); CALIFORNIA SUITE(1978); TIME WALKER(1982)

Clio Young
OFFENDERS, THE(1980)

Collier Young
NEVER FEAR(1950), w; OUTRAGE(1950), p, w; HARD, FAST, AND BEAUTIFUL(1951), p; ON THE LOOSE(1951), p; BEWARE, MY LOVELY(1952), p; BIGAMIST,THE(1953), p, w; HITCH-HIKER, THE(1953), p, w; PRIVATE HELL 36(1954), p, w; MAD AT THE WORLD(1955), p; HUK(1956), p; HALLIDAY BRAND, THE(1957), p

Cy Young
SNOW WHITE AND THE SEVEN DWARFS(1937), anim; FANTASIA(1940), anim, anim; DUMBO(1941), anim

Dalene Young
JUKE BOX RACKET(1960); LITTLE DARLINGS(1980), w; CROSS CREEK(1983), w

Dan Young
NEW HOTEL, THE(1932, Brit.); OFF THE DOLE(1935, Brit.); DODGING THE DOLE(1936, Brit.); CALLING ALL CROOKS(1938, Brit.); SOMEWHERE IN ENGLAND(1940, Brit.); SOMEWHERE IN CAMP(1942, Brit.); SOMEWHERE ON LEAVE(1942, Brit.); DEMOBBED(1944, Brit.); HONEYMOON HOTEL(1946, Brit.); CUP-TIE HONEYMOON(1948, Brit.); HOLIDAYS WITH PAY(1948, Brit.); SCHOOL FOR RANDLE(1949, Brit.); OVER THE GARDEN WALL(1950, Brit.); IT'S A GRAND LIFE(1953, Brit.)

Darryl Young
SOUNDER, PART 2(1976)

David Young
MARY, MARY, BLOODY MARY(1975, U.S./Mex.); HIGH RISK(1981); S.O.B.(1981)

De De Young
SECONDS(1966)

Deborah Ann Young
MANDINGO(1975)

Della Young
TIGER BY THE TAIL(1970)

Derek Young
SINFUL DAVEY(1969, Brit.)

Desmond Young
DESERT FOX, THE(1951), a, w

Dey Young
ROCK 'N' ROLL HIGH SCHOOL(1979); DEAD KIDS(1981 Aus./New Zealand); STRANGE INVADERS(1983)

Diana Young
MAFU CAGE, THE(1978), p

Dick Young
CHAMP, THE(1979)

Don Young
1984
TANK(1984)

Donna Young
KINFOLK(1970)

Dora Young
ADVENTURES OF MARCO POLO, THE(1938)

Dov Young
WAVELENGTH(1983)

E. Devan Young
CARNY(1980)

Earl Young
SKY LINER(1949), makeup

Eliezer Young
TRUNK TO CAIRO(1966, Israel/Ger.)

Elizabeth Young
BIG EXECUTIVE(1933); QUEEN CHRISTINA(1933); EAST OF JAVA(1935); RUDE BOY(1980, Brit.); CONTINENTAL DIVIDE(1981)

Elsie Young
Silents
KID, THE(1921)

Emma Young
STRANDED(1935); SHALL WE DANCE(1937)

Eric Young
TERROR OF THE TONGS, THE(1961, Brit.); SATAN NEVER SLEEPS(1962); INVASION(1965, Brit.); LORD JIM(1965, Brit.); SINISTER MAN, THE(1965, Brit.); MATTER OF INNOCENCE, A(1968, Brit.); CHAIRMAN, THE(1969)

Erica Young
SOUNDER, PART 2(1976)

Ernest F. Young
MYSTERIOUS MR. WONG(1935)

Ernest Young
JEALOUSY(1934)

Evalyn Young
GLAMOUR FOR SALE(1940)

Evelyn Young
GIRLS OF THE ROAD(1940); HE STAYED FOR BREAKFAST(1940); NOBODY'S CHILDREN(1940); PRAIRIE SCHOONERS(1940); WILDCAT OF TUCSON(1941)

F. A. Young
ON APPROVAL(1930, Brit.), ph; WARM CORNER, A(1930, Brit.), ph; "W" PLAN, THE(1931, Brit.), ph; CARNIVAL(1931, Brit.), ph; MISCHIEF(1931, Brit.), ph; PLUNDER(1931, Brit.), ph; SPECKLED BAND, THE(1931, Brit.), ph; TILLY OF BLOOMSBURY(1931, Brit.), ph; TONS OF MONEY(1931, Brit.), ph; UP FOR THE CUP(1931, Brit.), ph; BLUE DANUBE(1932, Brit.), ph; LEAP YEAR(1932, Brit.), ph; LOVE CONTRACT, THE(1932, Brit.), ph; MAGIC NIGHT(1932, Brit.), ph; MAYOR'S NEST, THE(1932, Brit.), ph; NIGHT LIKE THIS, A(1932, Brit.), ph; THARK(1932, Brit.), ph; BITTER SWEET(1933, Brit.), ph; IT'S A KING(1933, Brit.), ph; JUST MY LUCK(1933, Brit.), ph; KING'S CUP, THE(1933, Brit.), ph; LITTLE DAMOZEL, THE(1933, Brit.), ph; NIGHT OF THE GARTER(1933, Brit.), ph; SUMMER LIGHTNING(1933, Brit.), ph; THAT'S A GOOD GIRL(1933, Brit.), ph; TROUBLE(1933, Brit.), ph; UP FOR THE DERBY(1933, Brit.), ph; YES, MR. BROWN(1933, Brit.), ph; ESCAPE ME NEVER(1935, Brit.), ph; RUNAWAY QUEEN, THE(1935, Brit.), ph; FAME(1936, Brit.), ph; PEG OF OLD DRURY(1936, Brit.), ph; BACKSTAGE(1937, Brit.), ph; FROG, THE(1937, Brit.), ph; GIRLS IN THE STREET(1937, Brit.), ph; GIRL IN THE STREET(1938, Brit.), ph; SHOW GOES ON, THE(1938, Brit.), ph; SIXTY GLORIOUS YEARS(1938, Brit.), ph; THIS'LL MAKE YOU WHISTLE(1938, Brit.), ph; NURSE EDITH CAVELL(1939), ph; TWO'S COMPANY(1939, Brit.), ph; BUSMAN'S HONEYMOON(1940, Brit.), ph; SUICIDE LEGION(1940, Brit.), ph; TREASURE ISLAND(1950, Brit.), ph; KNIGHTS OF THE ROUND TABLE(1953), ph; MOGAMBO(1953), ph; TERROR ON A TRAIN(1953), ph; BETRAYED(1954), ph; BEDEVILLED(1955), ph; BHOWANI JUNCTION(1956), ph; LUST FOR LIFE(1956), ph; BARRETTS OF WIMPOLE STREET, THE(1957), ph; I ACCUSE(1958, Brit.), ph; HAND IN HAND(1960, Brit.), ph; GORGO(1961, Brit.), ph; LOSS OF INNOCENCE(1961, Brit.), ph; LAWRENCE OF ARABIA(1962, Brit.), ph; MACBETH(1963), ph

F. E. Mills Young
Silents
THOU ART THE MAN(1920), w; BIGAMIST, THE(1921, Brit.), w

Faron Young
HIDDEN GUNS(1956); DANIEL BOONE, TRAIL BLAZER(1957); RAIDERS OF OLD CALIFORNIA(1957); COUNTRY MUSIC HOLIDAY(1958); SECOND FIDDLE TO A STEEL GUITAR(1965); NASHVILLE REBEL(1966); WHAT AM I BID?(1967)

Felicity Young
WHITE TRAP, THE(1959, Brit.); COVER GIRL KILLER(1960, Brit.); GENTLE TRAP, THE(1960, Brit.); MAKE MINE MINK(1960, Brit.); FREEDOM TO DIE(1962, Brit.); MURDER ON THE CAMPUS(1963, Brit.); PLAY IT COOL(1963, Brit.)

Felix Young
HOORAY FOR LOVE(1935), p; JOY OF LIVING(1938), p

Frances Brett Young
MY BROTHER JONATHAN(1949, Brit.), w

Francis Brett Young
MAN ABOUT THE HOUSE, A(1947, Brit.), w; PORTRAIT OF CLARE(1951, Brit.), w
Silents
SEA HORSES(1926), w

Frank H. Young
GHOST GUNS(1944), w; PARTNERS OF THE TRAIL(1944), w; RANGE LAW(1944), w; BORDER BANDITS(1946), w; FLASHING GUNS(1947), w; SONG OF THE DRIFTER(1948), w

Frank Young
GENERAL DIED AT DAWN, THE(1936); MILLION DOLLAR KID(1944), w; NAVAJO TRAIL, THE(1945), w

Fred Young
COME OUT OF THE PANTRY(1935, Brit.), ph

Freddie A. Young
IVANHOE(1952, Brit.), ph
1984
SWORD OF THE VALIANT(1984, Brit.), ph

Freddie Young
CONSPIRATOR(1949, Brit.), ph; EDWARD, MY SON(1949, U.S./Brit.), ph; WINSLOW BOY, THE(1950), ph; INVITATION TO THE DANCE(1956), ph; ROTTEN TO THE CORE(1956, Brit.), ph; LITTLE HUT, THE(1957), ph; DOCTOR ZHIVAGO(1965), ph; LORD JIM(1965, Brit.), ph; YOU ONLY LIVE TWICE(1967, Brit.), ph; BATTLE OF BRITAIN, THE(1969, Brit.), ph; SINFUL DAVEY(1969, Brit.), ph; RYAN'S DAUGHTER(1970), ph; NICHOLAS AND ALEXANDRA(1971, Brit.), ph; ASPHYX, THE(1972, Brit.), ph; LUTHER(1974), ph; TAMARIND SEED, THE(1974, Brit.), ph; GREAT EXPECTATIONS(1975, Brit.), ph; PERMISSION TO KILL(1975, U.S./Aust.), ph; BLUE BIRD, THE(1976), ph; STEVIE(1978, Brit.), ph; BLOODLINE(1979), ph; ROUGH CUT(1980, Brit.), ph; RICHARD'S THINGS(1981, Brit.), ph

Frederick A. Young
VICTORIA THE GREAT(1937, Brit.), ph; NELL GWYN(1935, Brit.), ph; MILLIONS(1936, Brit.), ph; RAT, THE(1938, Brit.), ph; ROYAL DIVORCE, A(1938, Brit.), ph; GOODBYE MR. CHIPS(1939, Brit.), ph; WHEN KNIGHTS WERE BOLD(1942, Brit.), ph; WINGS AND THE WOMAN(1942, Brit.), ph; YOUNG MR. PITT, THE(1942, Brit.), ph; BEDELIA(1946, Brit.), ph; CAESAR AND CLEOPATRA(1946, Brit.), ph; SO WELL REMEMBERED(1947, Brit.), ph; WHILE I LIVE(1947, Brit.), ph; ESCAPE(1948, Brit.), ph; BEYOND MOMBASA(1957), ph; ISLAND IN THE SUN(1957), ph; INDISCREET(1958), ph; INN OF THE SIXTH HAPPINESS, THE(1958), ph; GIDEON OF SCOTLAND YARD(1959, Brit.), ph

Frederick Young
BLACKOUT(1940, Brit.), ph; INVADERS, THE,(1941, Brit.), ph; HAMLET(1964); SEVENTH DAWN, THE(1964, Brit.), ph; DEADLY AFFAIR, THE(1967, Brit.), ph

Gary Alexander Young
Misc. Talkies
END OF AUGUST(1974), d

Gary Young
SPENCER'S MOUNTAIN(1963); FEVER HEAT(1968), ph; NUDE BOMB, THE(1980)

George Young
Silents
GOLD RUSH, THE(1925)

Georgiana Young
STORY OF ALEXANDER GRAHAM BELL, THE(1939)

Georgianna Young
NO, NO NANETTE(1940)

Gerald Young
WOMEN MUST DRESS(1935); HONG KONG AFFAIR(1958); POOR COW(1968, Brit.)

Geraldine Young
JUST FOR THE HELL OF IT(1968)

Gerra Young
JIVE JUNCTION(1944)

Gig Young
SERGEANT YORK(; DIVE BOMBER(1941); NAVY BLUES(1941); YOU'RE IN THE ARMY NOW(1941); GAY SISTERS, THE(1942); MALE ANIMAL, THE(1942); THEY DIED WITH THEIR BOOTS ON(1942); AIR FORCE(1943); OLD ACQUAINTANCE(1943); ESCAPE ME NEVER(1947); THREE MUSKETEERS, THE(1948); WOMAN IN WHITE, THE(1948); LUST FOR GOLD(1949); TELL IT TO THE JUDGE(1949); WAKE OF THE RED WITCH(1949); HUNT THE MAN DOWN(1950); COME FILL THE CUP(1951); ONLY THE VALIANT(1951); SLAUGHTER TRAIL(1951); TARGET UNKNOWN(1951); TOO YOUNG TO KISS(1951); HOLIDAY FOR SINNERS(1952); YOU FOR ME(1952); ARENA(1953); CITY THAT NEVER SLEEPS(1953); GIRL WHO HAD EVERYTHING, THE(1953); TORCH SONG(1953); DESPERATE HOURS, THE(1955); YOUNG AT HEART(1955); DESK SET(1957); TEACHER'S PET(1958); TUNNEL OF LOVE, THE(1958); ASK ANY GIRL(1959); STORY ON PAGE ONE, THE(1959); KID GALAHAD(1962); THAT TOUCH OF MINK(1962); FIVE MILES TO MIDNIGHT(1963, U.S./Fr./Ital.); FOR LOVE OR MONEY(1963); TICKLISH AFFAIR, A(1963); STRANGE BEDFELLOWS(1965); SHUTTERED ROOM, THE(1968, Brit.); THEY SHOOT HORSES, DON'T THEY?(1969); LOVERS AND OTHER STRANGERS(1970); BRING ME THE HEAD OF ALFREDO GARCIA(1974); HINDENBURG, THE(1975); KILLER ELITE, THE(1975); GAME OF DEATH, THE(1979)

Gini Young
GENTLEMEN MARRY BRUNETTES(1955)

Gladys Young
COURTNEY AFFAIR, THE(1947, Brit.); GAY LADY, THE(1949, Brit.); LADY WITH A LAMP, THE(1951, Brit.); ONE WISH TOO MANY(1956, Brit.)

Glenda Young
PURSUIT OF D.B. COOPER, THE(1981)

Gordon Ray Young
TALL IN THE SADDLE(1944), w; HURRICANE SMITH(1952), w
Silents
IDOL DANCER, THE(1920), w

Gordon Young
CAPTAIN CALAMITY(1936), w; BORN TO THE SADDLE(1953), w

Grace Young
GEORGE WHITE'S SCANDALS(1945)

Grey Young
PICKUP ON 101(1972)

Hal Young
SUSPENSE(1930, Brit.), ph; LOVE STORM, THE(1931, Brit.), ph; MANY WATERS(1931, Brit.), ph; DEVIL'S JEST, THE(1954, Brit.), ph
Silents
MADAME BUTTERFLY(1915), ph; COMMON LAW, THE(1916), ph; MY COUSIN(1918), ph; PRIVATE PEAT(1918), ph; ANNE OF GREEN GABLES(1919), ph; AMATEUR WIFE, THE(1920), ph; EASY TO GET(1920), ph; APPEARANCES(1921), ph; BURN 'EM UP BARNES(1921), ph

Harold Young
HER PRIVATE LIFE(1929), ed; PAINTED ANGEL, THE(1929), ed; LASH, THE(1930), ed; TOP SPEED(1930), ed; DIE MANNER UM LUCIE(1931), ed; RECKLESS HOUR, THE(1931), ed; RESERVED FOR LADIES(1932, Brit.), ed; WEDDING REHEARSAL(1932, Brit.), ed; COUNSEL'S OPINION(1933, Brit.), ed; PRIVATE LIFE OF HENRY VIII, THE(1933), ed; LEAVE IT TO BLANCHE(1934, Brit.), d; TOO MANY MILLIONS(1934, Brit.), d; SCARLET PIMPERNEL, THE(1935, Brit.), d; WITHOUT REGRET(1935), d; GIRL FROM MAXIM'S, THE(1936, Brit.), d; MY AMERICAN WIFE(1936), d; WOMAN TRAP(1936), d; LET THEM LIVE(1937), d; 52ND STREET(1937), d; LITTLE TOUGH GUY(1938), d; STORM, THE(1938), d; CODE OF THE STREETS(1939), d; FORGOTTEN WOMAN, THE(1939), d; HERO FOR A DAY(1939), d; NEWSBOY'S HOME(1939), d; SABOTAGE(1939), d; DREAMING OUT LOUD(1940), d; BACHELOR DADDY(1941), d; SWING IT SOLDIER(1941), d; JUKE BOX JENNY(1942), d; MUMMY'S TOMB, THE(1942), d; RUBBER RACKETEERS(1942), d; THERE'S ONE BORN EVERY MINUTE(1942), d; HI, BUDDY(1943), d; HI'YA, CHUM(1943), d; I ESCAPED FROM THE GESTAPO(1943), d; SPY TRAIN(1943), d; MACHINE GUN MAMA(1944), d; THREE CABALLEROS, THE(1944), d; FROZEN GHOST, THE(1945), d; I'LL REMEMBER APRIL(1945), d; JUNGLE CAPTIVE(1945), d; SONG OF THE SARONG(1945), d; 13 RUE MADELEINE(1946), d; CITIZEN SAINT(1947), d; ROOGIE'S BUMP(1954), d
Misc. Talkies
CARIB GOLD(1955), d
Silents
JOSSELYN'S WIFE(1926), ed; HUSBAND HUNTERS(1927), ed; HEART OF A FOLLIES GIRL, THE(1928), ed

Harriette Young
IRMA LA DOUCE(1963)

Heather Young
GUIDE FOR THE MARRIED MAN, A(1967)

Helen Young
HIT THE ICE(1943)

Hilda May Young
KILLERS OF THE WILD(1940), w

Howard I. Young
MUSIC IN THE AIR(1934), w; SPRING TONIC(1935), w
Silents
SACRED SILENCE(1919), w

Howard Irving Young
MIDNIGHT MYSTERY(1930), w; CRIMSON CIRCLE, THE(1936, Brit.), w; SECRET OF STAMBOUL, THE(1936, Brit.), w; GREAT GAMBINI, THE(1937), w; SHE ASKED FOR IT(1937), w; SEZ O'REILLY TO MACNAB(1938, Brit.), w; HI, GANG!(1941, Brit.), w; I THANK YOU(1941, Brit.), w; IT'S THAT MAN AGAIN(1943, Brit.), w; GIVE US THE MOON(1944, Brit.), w; HE SNOOPS TO CONQUER(1944, Brit.), w; TIME FLIES(1944, Brit.), w; GEORGE IN CIVVY STREET(1946, Brit.), w; YOU CAN'T DO WITHOUT LOVE(1946, Brit.), w; LET'S LIVE A LITTLE(1948), w; FLYING SAUCER, THE(1950), w

Irwin W. Young- *(cont.)*

Silents
NO TRESPASSING(1922), w
Irwin W. Young
ALAMBRISTA!(1977), p
J. Arthur Young
DEADLY GAME, THE(1941); LIVING GHOST, THE(1942); 'NEATH BROOKLYN BRIDGE(1942)
J.B. Young
Misc. Talkies
THURSDAY MORNING MURDERS, THE(1976)
J.D. Young
BENJI(1974)
Jack Young
DRUM TAPS(1933), ph; THIS IS THE ARMY(1943); SKULLDUGGERY(1970), makeup; GUNFIGHT, A(1971), makeup; MURDERS IN THE RUE MORGUE(1971), makeup
Silents
WHAT'S YOUR HURRY?(1920)
Capt. Jack Young
YANKEE DOODLE DANDY(1942); MISSION TO MOSCOW(1943)
Jack H. Young
WALKING TALL(1973), makeup
Jack R. Young
DYNAMITE CANYON(1941), ph; WANDERERS OF THE WEST(1941), ph
Jackie Young
Silents
CRAZY TO MARRY(1921)
James A. Young
Misc. Silents
LASH, THE(1916), d
James R. Young
BEHIND THE RISING SUN(1943), w
James Young
WEST POINT STORY, THE(1950); TARGET UNKNOWN(1951); THING, THE(1951); MY SON, JOHN(1952); BIGAMIST,THE(1953)
Silents
LOLA(1914), a, d&w; WISHING RING, THE(1914); HEART OF THE BLUE RIDGE, THE(1915), d; LITTLE MISS BROWN(1915), d; TRILBY(1915); JOAN THE WOMAN(1916); OLIVER TWIST(1916), d&w; ON TRIAL(1917), a, d&w; NOTORIOUS MISS LISLE, THE(1920), d&w; WELCOME STRANGER(1924), d, w; UNCHASTENED WOMAN(1925), d; DRIVEN FROM HOME(1927), d
Misc. Silents
(, d; WIN(K)SOME WIDOW, THE (1914), d; MY OFFICIAL WIFE(1914), d; DEEP PURPLE, THE(1915), d; MARRYING MONEY(1915), d; OVER NIGHT(1915), d; SWEET KITTY BELLAIRS(1916), d; THOUSAND DOLLAR HUSBAND, THE(1916), d; UNPROTECTED(1916), d; LOST AND WON(1917), d; HER COUNTRY FIRST(1918), d; MAN WHO WOULDN'T TELL, THE(1918), d; MISSING(1918), d; ROSE O' PARADISE(1918), d; TEMPLE OF DUSK, THE(1918), d; WHITE MAN'S LAW, THE(1918), d; GENTLEMAN OF QUALITY, A(1919), d; HIGHEST TRUMP, THE(1919), d; HORNET'S NEST, THE(1919), d; REGULAR GIRL, A(1919), d; ROGUE'S ROMANCE, A(1919), d; USURPER, THE(1919), d; WOLF, THE(1919), d; CURTAIN(1920), d; DEVIL, THE(1921), d; WITHOUT BENEFIT OF CLERGY(1921), d; INFIDEL, THE(1922), d; MASQUERADER, THE(1922), d; OMAR THE TENTMAKER(1922), d; TRILBY(1923), d; WANDERING DAUGHTERS(1923), d; BELLS, THE(1926), d; MIDNIGHT ROSE(1928), d
Janet Young
FURY(1936); GIRL OF THE OZARKS(1936); I MARRIED A DOCTOR(1936); VALIANT IS THE WORD FOR CARRIE(1936); DELINQUENT PARENTS(1938)
Janis Young
LOVING(1970)
Misc. Talkies
GOOD, THE BAD, AND THE BEAUTIFUL, THE(1975)
Jeff Young
YOUNG NURSES, THE(1973)
Jeffrey Young
BEEN DOWN SO LONG IT LOOKS LIKE UP TO ME(1977), d
Jeremy Young
YOUNG AND WILLING(1964, Brit.); SOPHIE'S PLACE(1970); SUDDEN TERROR(1970, Brit.); HOPSCOTCH(1980)
Jerome Young
Silents
IS YOUR DAUGHTER SAFE?(1927)
Jerry S. Young
PLUNDER ROAD(1957), ed
Jerry Young
BLACK PATCH(1957), ed; FLAME BARRIER, THE(1958), ed; HOW TO MAKE A MONSTER(1958), ed; I WAS A TEENAGE FRANKENSTEIN(1958), ed; SNOWFIRE(1958), ed; PRIVATE PROPERTY(1960), ed; COLD WIND IN AUGUST(1961), ed
Jimmy Young
GENTLEMEN PREFER BLONDES(1953); RUNAWAY BUS, THE(1954, Brit.); LADY GODIVA RIDES AGAIN(1955, Brit.); OTLEY(1969, Brit.)
Jo Young
DESPERATE WOMEN, THE(?)
Joan Young
VICTORIA THE GREAT(1937, Brit.); STRAWBERRY ROAN(1945, Brit.); SCHOOL FOR SECRETS(1946, Brit.); EASY MONEY(1948, Brit.); HIDEOUT(1948, Brit.); THINGS HAPPEN AT NIGHT(1948, Brit.); VICE VERSA(1948, Brit.); AFFAIRS OF A ROGUE, THE(1949, Brit.); CARDBOARD CAVALIER, THE(1949, Brit.); FALLEN IDOL, THE(1949, Brit.); GAY LADY, THE(1949, Brit.); GOOD TIME GIRL(1950, Brit.); HELL IS SOLD OUT(1951, Brit.); MAGIC BOX, THE(1952, Brit.); TIME GENTLEMEN PLEASE!(1953, Brit.); CHILD'S PLAY(1954, Brit.); FAST AND LOOSE(1954, Brit.); ALL FOR MARY(1956, Brit.); ADMIRABLE CRICHTON, THE(1957, Brit.); INN OF THE SIXTH HAPPINESS, THE(1958); SUDDENLY, LAST SUMMER(1959, Brit.); IN THE DOGHOUSE(1964, Brit.); LAST SHOT YOU HEAR, THE(1969, Brit.); BLOOD FROM THE MUMMY'S TOMB(1972, Brit.)
Joe Young
Silents
NAUGHTY NANETTE(1927)

John Howard Young
NONE BUT THE BRAVE(1965, U.S./Jap.)
John Paul Young
Misc. Talkies
METAL MESSIAH(1978)
John Sacret Young
CHANDLER(1971), w; TESTAMENT(1983), w
John Young
RING OF BRIGHT WATER(1969, Brit.); LIFE AND TIMES OF CHESTER-ANGUS RAMSGOOD, THE(1971, Can.); WICKER MAN, THE(1974, Brit.); MONTY PYTHON AND THE HOLY GRAIL(1975, Brit.); HOLLYWOOD HIGH(1977); MOONSHINE COUNTY EXPRESS(1977); BLACK JACK(1979, Brit.); MONTY PYTHON'S LIFE OF BRIAN(1979, Brit.); CHARRIOTS OF FIRE(1981, Brit.); TIME BANDITS(1981, Brit.)
Misc. Talkies
HOLLYWOOD HIGH(1976)
Joseph Young
MIGHTY JOE YOUNG(1949)
Judy Young
MORGAN'S MARAUDERS(1929), set d; SATAN'S BED(1965)
Karen Young
DEEP IN THE HEART(1983)
1984
ALMOST YOU(1984); BIRDY(1984)
Kay Young
IN WHICH WE SERVE(1942, Brit.); WOMAN TO WOMAN(1946, Brit.); I WAS A MALE WAR BRIDE(1949)
Kendal Young
ASSAULT(1971, Brit.), w
Keone Young
BABY BLUE MARINE(1976); EYEWITNESS(1981); FRANCES(1982)
1984
WILD LIFE, THE(1984)
Larry Young
TOKYO ROSE(1945); HOT CARGO(1946); WELCOME STRANGER(1947)
Laura Young
CORPSE GRINDERS, THE(1972), prod d
Lawrence Young
BLUE DAHLIA, THE(1946)
Leanne Young
MAN, A WOMAN, AND A BANK, A(1979, Can.)
Lee Young
TOUCH OF THE SUN, A(1956, Brit.); ROCK BABY, ROCK IT(1957); ST. LOUIS BLUES(1958)
Leon Young
GREAT VAN ROBBERY, THE(1963, Brit.), m
Leon C. "Buck" Young
HURRICANE SMITH(1952)
Les Young
SATAN'S SLAVE(1976, Brit.), p; TERROR(1979, Brit.), p, w, ph; SWEET WILLIAM(1980, Brit.), ph
Liu Ka Young
CALL HIM MR. SHATTER(1976, Hong Kong)
Lloyd Young
MARK OF THE HAWK, THE(1958), p, w; WHEN THE CLOCK STRIKES(1961), md
Lois Young
UNSEEN, THE(1981)
Lon Young
IN OLD CALIFORNIA(1929), p; LOTUS LADY(1930), p; WORLD ACCUSES, THE(1935), p; DEATH FROM A DISTANCE(1936), prod d; FEDERAL BULLETS(1937), p; THIRTEENTH MAN, THE(1937), p; PORT OF MISSING GIRLS(1938), p; TELEPHONE OPERATOR(1938), p
Silents
POLICE PATROL, THE(1925), sup; CAMPUS KNIGHTS(1929), sup, t; JUST OFF BROADWAY(1929), sup, t; PEACOCK FAN(1929), p
Loretta Young
CARELESS AGE(1929); FAST LIFE(1929); FORWARD PASS, THE(1929); GIRL IN THE GLASS CAGE, THE(1929); SQUALL, THE(1929); DEVIL TO PAY, THE(1930); KISMET(1930); LOOSE ANKLES(1930); MAN FROM BLANKLEY'S, THE(1930); ROAD TO PARADISE(1930); SECOND FLOOR MYSTERY, THE(1930); TRUTH ABOUT YOUTH, THE(1930); BEAU IDEAL(1931); BIG BUSINESS GIRL(1931); I LIKE YOUR NERVE(1931); PLATINUM BLONDE(1931); RIGHT OF WAY, THE(1931); RULING VOICE, THE(1931); THREE GIRLS LOST(1931); TOO YOUNG TO MARRY(1931); HATCHET MAN, THE(1932); LIFE BEGINS(1932); PLAY GIRL(1932); TAXI!(1932); THEY CALL IT SIN(1932); WEEK-END MARRIAGE(1932); DEVIL'S IN LOVE, THE(1933); EMPLOYEE'S ENTRANCE(1933); GRAND SLAM(1933); HEROES FOR SALE(1933); LIFE OF JIMMY DOLAN, THE(1933); MAN'S CASTLE, A(1933); MIDNIGHT MARY(1933); SHE HAD TO SAY YES(1933); ZOO IN BUDAPEST(1933); BORN TO BE BAD(1934); BULLDOG DRUMMOND STRIKES BACK(1934); CARAVAN(1934); HOUSE OF ROTHSCHILD, THE(1934); WHITE PARADE, THE(1934); CALL OF THE WILD(1935); CLIVE OF INDIA(1935); CRUSADES, THE(1935); SHANGHAI(1935); LADIES IN LOVE(1936); PRIVATE NUMBER(1936); RAMONA(1936); UNGUARDED HOUR, THE(1936); CAFE METROPOLE(1937); LOVE IS NEWS(1937); LOVE UNDER FIRE(1937); SECOND HONEYMOON(1937); WIFE, DOCTOR AND NURSE(1937); FOUR MEN AND A PRAYER(1938); KENTUCKY(1938); SUEZ(1938); THREE BLIND MICE(1938); ETERNALLY YOURS(1939); STORY OF ALEXANDER GRAHAM BELL, THE(1939); WIFE, HUSBAND AND FRIEND(1939); DOCTOR TAKES A WIFE(1940); HE STAYED FOR BREAKFAST(1940); LADY FROM CHEYENNE(1941); MEN IN HER LIFE, THE(1941); BEDTIME STORY(1942); NIGHT TO REMEMBER, A(1942); CHINA(1943); AND NOW TOMORROW(1944); LADIES COURAGEOUS(1944); ALONG CAME JONES(1945); PERFECT MARRIAGE, THE(1946); STRANGER THE(1946); BISHOP'S WIFE, THE(1947); FARMER'S DAUGHTER, THE(1947); RACHEL AND THE STRANGER(1948); ACCUSED, THE(1949); COME TO THE STABLE(1949); MOTHER IS A FRESHMAN(1949); KEY TO THE CITY(1950); CAUSE FOR ALARM(1951); HALF ANGEL(1951); BECAUSE OF YOU(1952); PAULA(1952); IT HAPPENS EVERY THURSDAY(1953)
Misc. Talkies
BROKEN DISHES(1930)
Silents
HEAD MAN, THE(1928); LAUGH, CLOWN, LAUGH(1928); MAGNIFICENT FLIRT, THE(1928); WHIP WOMAN, THE(1928); SCARLET SEAS(1929)

Lucile Young
Silents
DAPHNE AND THE PIRATE(1916)
Lucille Young
LIGHTNIN'(1930)
Silents
QUICKER'N LIGHTNIN'(1925)
Misc. Silents
DEVIL'S WHEEL, THE(1918); FALSE ROAD, THE(1920)
Madonna Young
HIDE IN PLAIN SIGHT(1980)
Marguerite Young
NOOSE FOR A LADY(1953, Brit.)
Mari Young
HOUSE ON TELEGRAPH HILL(1951)
Maria Sen Young
MACAO(1952)
Marie San Young
HIS KIND OF WOMAN(1951)
Marl Young
WALK ON THE WILD SIDE(1962)
Mary H. Young
Silents
ANGEL OF CROOKED STREET, THE(1922)
Mary Young
THIS IS MY AFFAIR(1937); FOREIGN CORRESPONDENT(1940); TWO-FACED WOMAN(1941); NAVY COMES THROUGH, THE(1942); WIFE TAKES A FLYER, THE(1942); WATCH ON THE RHINE(1943); ADDRESS UNKNOWN(1944); CASANOVA BROWN(1944); LOST WEEKEND, THE(1945); STORK CLUB(1945); BRIDE WORE BOOTS, THE(1946); SHOCK(1946); TEMPTATION(1946); TO EACH HIS OWN(1946); BLONDIE'S HOLIDAY(1947); DOUBLE LIFE, A(1947); LIKELY STORY, A(1947); ONE TOO MANY(1950); FAT MAN, THE(1951); JOE PALOOKA IN TRIPLE CROSS(1951); MATING SEASON, THE(1951); IT SHOULD HAPPEN TO YOU(1954); THIS IS MY LOVE(1954); SEVEN YEAR ITCH, THE(1955); ALIAS JESSE JAMES(1959); BLUE DENIM(1959); SAIL A CROOKED SHIP(1961); DEAD HEAT ON A MERRY-GO-ROUND(1966); TROUBLE WITH ANGELS, THE(1966); MURDER CLINIC, THE(1967, Ital./Fr.)
Silents
NINETY AND NINE, THE(1922); AFTER MARRIAGE(1925)
Michael Young
SPENCER'S MOUNTAIN(1963)
Michelle Young
LENNY(1974)
Miriam Young
MOTHER WORE TIGHTS(1947), w
Moira Young
TERROR(1979, Brit.), w
Muriel Young
CONSTANT HUSBAND, THE(1955, Brit.); I'M ALL RIGHT, JACK(1959, Brit.)
Nat Young
PALM BEACH(1979, Aus.)
Neal Young
NIGHT IN PARADISE, A(1946)
Ned Young
DECOY(1946), w; DEVIL'S PLAYGROUND, THE(1946); UNEXPECTED GUEST(1946); ALADDIN AND HIS LAMP(1952); IRON MISTRESS, THE(1952); SPRINGFIELD RIFLE(1952); SHE'S BACK ON BROADWAY(1953); RIDING SHOTGUN(1954); JAILHOUSE ROCK(1957), w; TERROR IN A TEXAS TOWN(1958); SECONDS(1966)
Nedrick Young
BOMBS OVER BURMA(1942); DEAD MEN WALK(1943); LADIES' DAY(1943); GAY BLADES(1946); SWORDSMAN, THE(1947); GALLANT BLADE, THE(1948); RUSTY LEADS THE WAY(1948), w; GUN CRAZY(1949); LADY WITHOUT PASSPORT, A(1950); PASSAGE WEST(1951); CAPTAIN SCARLETT(1953)
Neil Young
WHERE THE BUFFALO ROAM(1980), m; HUMAN HIGHWAY(1982), a, m
Nicholas Young
EAGLE ROCK(1964, Brit.)
Noah Young
WELCOME DANGER(1929); FEET FIRST(1930); MOVIE CRAZY(1932)
Silents
SAILOR-MADE MAN, A(1921); GRANDMA'S BOY(1922); SAFETY LAST(1923); FOR HEAVEN'S SAKE(1926); DON MIKE(1927); HAM AND EGGS AT THE FRONT(1927); LOVE MAKES 'EM WILD(1927); SHARP SHOOTERS(1928)
Misc. Silents
BATTLING ORIOLES, THE(1924); LAND BEYOND THE LAW, THE(1927)
Norma Young
1984
PLACES IN THE HEART(1984)
Olive Young
RIDIN' LAW(1930); TRAILING TROUBLE(1930)
Otis Young
MURDER IN MISSISSIPPI(1965); VALLEY OF MYSTERY(1967); DON'T JUST STAND THERE(1968); ME AND MY BROTHER(1969); CLONES, THE(1973); LAST DETAIL, THE(1973); SURVIVAL(1976); BLOOD BEACH(1981)
Misc. Talkies
CALL ME BY MY RIGHTFUL NAME(1973)
Patrick Young
SPIDER AND THE FLY, THE(1952, Brit.)
Paul Young
WEE GEORDIE(1956, Brit.); LET'S BE HAPPY(1957, Brit.); SUMARINE X-1(1969, Brit.); CHATO'S LAND(1972); PATRICK(1979, Aus.); CHANGE OF SEASONS, A(1980); ANOTHER TIME, ANOTHER PLACE(1983, Brit.)
1984
ANOTHER TIME, ANOTHER PLACE(1984, Brit.)
Paula Young
DULCIMER STREET(1948, Brit.)

Petal Young
MELODY(1971, Brit.)
Peter Young
HIGH COMMISSIONER, THE(1968, U.S./Brit.), set d; INTERLUDE(1968, Brit.), set d; LOCK UP YOUR DAUGHTERS(1969, Brit.), set d; LEO THE LAST(1970, Brit.), set d; ENGLANO MADE ME(1973, Brit.), art d; MUSTANG COUNTRY(1976), set d; FOX AND THE HOUND, THE(1981), w; DARK CRYSTAL, THE(1982, Brit.), set d; LADIES AND GENTLEMEN, THE FABULOUS STAINS(1982), set d
1984
ELECTRIC DREAMS(1984), set d; SUPERGIRL(1984), set d
Polly Ann Young
RICH PEOPLE(1929); ONE WAY TRAIL, THE(1931); MAN FROM UTAH, THE(1934); STOLEN SWEETS(1934); WHITE PARADE, THE(1934); CRIMSON TRAIL, THE(1935); HAPPINESS C.O.D.(1935); HIS FIGHTING BLOOD(1935); SONS OF STEEL(1935); THUNDER IN THE NIGHT(1935); BORDER PATROLMAN, THE(1936); HITCH HIKE TO HEAVEN(1936); I COVER CHINATOWN(1938); MYSTERY PLANE(1939); PORT OF HATE(1939); STORY OF ALEXANDER GRAHAM BELL, THE(1939); WOLF CALL(1939); MURDER ON THE YUKON(1940); TURNABOUT(1940); INVISIBLE GHOST, THE(1941); ROAD SHOW(1941)
Misc. Talkies
LAST ALARM, THE(1940)
Ray Young
BITTER TEA OF GENERAL YEN, THE(1933); BLOOD OF DRACULA'S CASTLE(1967); GUN RIDERS, THE(1969); BLUE SUNSHINE(1978); CHAPTER TWO(1979)
Raymond Young
ADAM AND EVELYNE(1950, Brit.); MIDNIGHT EPISODE(1951, Brit.); DEATH OF AN ANGEL(1952, Brit.); I'M A STRANGER(1952, Brit.); ISLAND RESCUE(1952, Brit.); NIGHT WON'T TALK, THE(1952, Brit.); THREE STEPS IN THE DARK(1953, Brit.); SILENT ENEMY, THE(1959, Brit.); GOLDFINGER(1964, Brit.); ARRIVEDERCI, BABY!(1966, Brit.); BEAUTY JUNGLE, THE(1966, Brit.); DEADLY FEMALES, THE(1976, Brit.); THIRTY NINE STEPS, THE(1978, Brit.)
Rebecca Young
DESPERATE WOMEN, THE(?)
Remegio Young
PROUD AND THE DAMNED, THE(1972), ph
Rennie Young
Misc. Silents
BETWEEN DANGERS(1927)
Ric Young
HIGH ROAD TO CHINA(1983)
1984
ICE PIRATES, THE(1984); INDIANA JONES AND THE TEMPLE OF DOOM(1984); SUCCESS IS THE BEST REVENGE(1984, Brit.)
Richard Young
GENERAL DIED AT DAWN, THE(1936); NIGHT CALL NURSES(1974); LET'S DO IT AGAIN(1975); COCAINE COWBOYS(1979); HIGH RISK(1981)
Misc. Talkies
FLY ME(1973); SWIM TEAM(1979); HOW TO SCORE WITH GIRLS(1980)
Ricky Young
SPENCER'S MOUNTAIN(1963)
Rida Johnson Young
HELL HARBOR(1930), w; NAUGHTY MARIETTA(1935), w; HEARTS DIVIDED(1936), w; MAYTIME(1937), w
Silents
BROWN OF HARVARD(1926), w; WOMAN WHO DID NOT CARE, THE(1927), w
Rita Johnson Young
CHECKERS(1937), w
Robbin Young
FOR YOUR EYES ONLY(1981); NIGHT SHIFT(1982)
Robert H. [Clifton] Young
LOVE NEST(1951)
Robert M. Young
ALAMBRISTA!(1977), d,w&ph; SHORT EYES(1977), d; RICH KIDS(1979), d; ONE-TRICK PONY(1980), d; BALLAD OF GREGORIO CORTEZ, THE(1983), d, ph
Robert Malcolm Young
TRAUMA(1962), d&w; ESCAPE TO WITCH MOUNTAIN(1975), w
Robert R. Young
WATERHOLE NO. 3(1967), w
Robert Young
THEY WON'T BELIEVE ME(1947); BLACK CAMEL, THE(1931); GUILTY GENERATION, THE(1931); SIN OF MADELON CLAUDET, THE(1931); HELL DIVERS(1932); KID FROM SPAIN, THE(1932); NEW MORALS FOR OLD(1932); STRANGE INTERLUDE(1932); UNASHAMED(1932); WET PARADE, THE(1932); HELL BELOW(1933); MEN MUST FIGHT(1933); RIGHT TO ROMANCE(1933); SATURDAY'S MILLIONS(1933); TODAY WE LIVE(1933); TUGBOAT ANNIE(1933); BAND PLAYS ON, THE(1934); CAROLINA(1934); DEATH OF THE DIAMOND(1934); HOLLYWOOD PARTY(1934); HOUSE OF ROTHSCHILD, THE(1934); LAZY RIVER(1934); PARIS INTERLUDE(1934); SPITFIRE(1934); WHOM THE GODS DESTROY(1934); CALM YOURSELF(1935); RED SALUTE(1935); REMEMBER LAST NIGHT(1935); VAGABOND LADY(1935); WEST POINT OF THE AIR(1935); BRIDE COMES HOME(1936); BRIDE WALKS OUT, THE(1936); IT'S LOVE AGAIN(1936, Brit.); LONGEST NIGHT, THE(1936); SECRET AGENT, THE(1936, Brit.); STOWAWAY(1936); SWORN ENEMY(1936); THREE WISE GUYS, THE(1936); BRIDE WORE RED, THE(1937); DANGEROUS NUMBER(1937); EMPEROR'S CANDLESTICKS, THE(1937); I MET HIM IN PARIS(1937); MARRIED BEFORE BREAKFAST(1937); NAVY BLUE AND GOLD(1937); JOSETTE(1938); PARADISE FOR THREE(1938); RICH MAN, POOR GIRL(1938); SHINING HOUR, THE(1938); THREE COMRADES(1938); TOY WIFE, THE(1938); BRIDAL SUITE(1939); HONOLULU(1939); MAISIE(1939); MIRACLES FOR SALE(1939); DR. KILDARE'S CRISIS(1940); FLORIAN(1940); MORTAL STORM, THE(1940); NORTHWEST PASSAGE(1940); SPORTING BLOOD(1940); H.M. PULHAM, ESQ.(1941); LADY BE GOOD(1941); MARRIED BACHELOR(1941); TRIAL OF MARY DUGAN, THE(1941); WESTERN UNION(1941); CAIRO(1942); JOE SMITH, AMERICAN(1942); JOURNEY FOR MARGARET(1942); CLAUDIA(1943); SLIGHTLY DANGEROUS(1943); SWEET ROSIE O'GRADY(1943); CANTERVILLE GHOST, THE(1944); ENCHANTED COTTAGE, THE(1945); THOSE ENDEARING YOUNG CHARMS(1945); CLAUDIA AND DAVID(1946); LADY LUCK(1946); SEARCHING WIND, THE(1946); CROSSFIRE(1947); RELENTLESS(1948); SITTING PRETTY(1948); ADVENTURE IN BALTIMORE(1949); AND BABY MAKES THREE(1949); BRIDE FOR SALE(1949); THAT FORSYTE WOMAN(1949); GOODBYE, MY FANCY(1951); SECOND WOMAN, THE(1951); HALF-BREED, THE(1952); SECRET OF THE IN-

CAS(1954); I'M ALL RIGHT, JACK(1959, Brit.); CRAWLING HAND, THE(1963), w; NOTHING BUT A MAN(1964), p, w, ph; BORN FREE(1966); VAMPIRE CIRCUS(1972, Brit.), d; WORLD IS FULL OF MARRIED MEN, THE(1980, Brit.), d
Silents
    IT IS THE LAW(1924)
Rocky Young
    SPENCER'S MOUNTAIN(1963)
Roderick Young
    PASSING THROUGH(1977), ph
Roger Young
1984
    LASSITER(1984), d
Roland Young
    HER PRIVATE LIFE(1929); UNHOLY NIGHT, THE(1929); BISHOP MURDER CASE, THE(1930); MADAME SATAN(1930); NEW MOON(1930); WISE GIRLS(1930); ANNABELLE'S AFFAIRS(1931); DON'T BET ON WOMEN(1931); GUARDSMAN, THE(1931); PAGAN LADY(1931); PRODIGAL, THE(1931); SQUAW MAN, THE(1931); LOVERS COURAGEOUS(1932); ONE HOUR WITH YOU(1932); STREET OF WOMEN(1932); THIS IS THE NIGHT(1932); WEDDING REHEARSAL(1932, Brit.); WOMAN COMMANDS, A(1932); BLIND ADVENTURE(1933); HIS DOUBLE LIFE(1933); LADY'S PROFESSION, A(1933); PLEASURE CRUISE(1933); THEY JUST HAD TO GET MARRIED(1933); HERE IS MY HEART(1934); DAVID COPPERFIELD(1935); RUGGLES OF RED GAP(1935); GIVE ME YOUR HEART(1936); ONE RAINY AFTERNOON(1936); UNGUARDED HOUR, THE(1936); ALI BABA GOES TO TOWN(1937); CALL IT A DAY(1937); GYPSY(1937, Brit.); KING SOLOMON'S MINES(1937, Brit.); MAN WHO COULD WORK MIRACLES, THE(1937, Brit.); SAILING ALONG(1938, Brit.); YOUNG IN HEART, THE(1938); HERE I AM A STRANGER(1939); NIGHT OF NIGHTS, THE(1939); TOPPER TAKES A TRIP(1939); YES, MY DARLING DAUGHTER(1939); DULCY(1940); HE MARRIED HIS WIFE(1940); IRENE(1940); NO, NO NANETTE(1940); PHILADELPHIA STORY, THE(1940); PRIVATE AFFAIRS(1940); STAR DUST(1940); FLAME OF NEW ORLEANS, THE(1941); TOPPER RETURNS(1941); TWO-FACED WOMAN(1941); LADY HAS PLANS, THE(1942); TALES OF MANHATTAN(1942); THEY ALL KISSED THE BRIDE(1942); FOREVER AND A DAY(1943); STANDING ROOM ONLY(1944); AND THEN THERE WERE NONE(1945); BOND STREET(1948, Brit.); YOU GOTTA STAY HAPPY(1948); GREAT LOVER, THE(1949); LET'S DANCE(1950); ST. BENNY THE DIP(1951); THAT MAN FROM TANGIER(1953)
Silents
    SHERLOCK HOLMES(1922); GRIT(1924)
Ron Young
    HAIR(1979)
Roxie Young
Misc. Talkies
    ABAR--THE FIRST BLACK SUPERMAN(1977)
S.H. Young
    HANDS ACROSS THE TABLE(1935)
Sandra Young
    BLACK RODEO(1972)
Sean Young
    JANE AUSTEN IN MANHATTAN(1980); STRIPES(1981); BLADE RUNNER(1982); YOUNG DOCTORS IN LOVE(1982)
1984
    DUNE(1984)
Sen Young
    NIGHT PLANE FROM CHUNGKING(1942)
Shael Young
    EDEN CRIED(1967), p
Shaun Terence Young
    SUICIDE SQUADRON(1942, Brit.), w; SECRET MISSION(1944, Brit.), w; ONE NIGHT WITH YOU(1948, Brit), d
Sheila Young
    MISSING, BELIEVED MARRIED(1937, Brit.)
Sidney Young
    RANDOLPH FAMILY, THE(1945, Brit.)
Skip Young
    LOVING YOU(1957); SPIDER, THE(1958); COLD WIND IN AUGUST(1961); WUSA(1970)
Misc. Talkies
    SMOKEY AND THE HOTWIRE GANG(1980)
Soo Young
    GOOD EARTH, THE(1937); SECRETS OF THE WASTELANDS(1941); LOVE IS A MANY-SPLENDORED THING(1955); SAYONARA(1957); IN HARM'S WAY(1965)
Stark Young
    SO RED THE ROSE(1935), w; UNCLE VANYA(1958), w
Stephen Young
    55 DAYS AT PEKING(1963); PATTON(1970); RAGE(1972); SOYLENT GREEN(1973); BREAKING POINT(1976); CLOWN MURDERS, THE(1976, Can.); LIFEGUARD(1976); SILENT PARTNER, THE(1979, Can.), p; LITTLE DRAGONS, THE(1980); SPRING FEVER(1983, Can.)
Misc. Talkies
    DEADLINE(1984)
Susan Young
    SPENCER'S MOUNTAIN(1963)
Sydney Young
    TIME FLIES(1944, Brit.)
Tammany Young
    FOLLOW THE LEADER(1930); ROADHOUSE NIGHTS(1930); MADISON SQUARE GARDEN(1932); BOWERY, THE(1933); GOLD DIGGERS OF 1933(1933); HALLELUJAH, I'M A BUM(1933); HEROES FOR SALE(1933); SHE DONE HIM WRONG(1933); TUGBOAT ANNIE(1933); GIFT OF GAB(1934); IT'S A GIFT(1934); LEMON DROP KID, THE(1934); LITTLE MISS MARKER(1934); MIGHTY BARNUM, THE(1934); OLD-FASHIONED WAY, THE(1934); SEARCH FOR BEAUTY(1934); SIX OF A KIND(1934); YOU'RE TELLING ME(1934); CHAMPAGNE FOR BREAKFAST(1935); GLASS KEY, THE(1935); LITTLE BIG SHOT(1935); MAN ON THE FLYING TRAPEZE, THE(1935); PUBLIC HERO NO. 1(1935); WANDERER OF THE WASTELAND(1935); POPPY(1936); STRIKE ME PINK(1936)
Silents
    LOST BRIDEGROOM, THE(1916); MAN WHO, THE(1921); MAN WORTH WHILE, THE(1921); RAINBOW(1921); RIGHT WAY, THE(1921); JOHN SMITH(1922); SEVENTH DAY, THE(1922); BRIDE FOR A NIGHT, A(1923); POLICE PATROL, THE(1925);

SALLY OF THE SAWDUST(1925); UNGUARDED HOUR, THE(1925); BLIND ALLEYS(1927)
Misc. Silents
    SERVICE STAR, THE(1918)
"Tammany" Young
Silents
    ESCAPE, THE(1914)
Terence Young
    FUGITIVE, THE(1940, Brit.), w; ON APPROVAL(1944, Brit.), w; HUNGRY HILL(1947, Brit.), w; CORRIDOR OF MIRRORS(1948, Brit.), d; BAD LORD BYRON, THE(1949, Brit.), w; WOMAN HATER(1949, Brit.), w; THEY WERE NOT DIVIDED(1951, Brit.), d&w; FRIGHTENED BRIDE, THE(1952, Brit.), d; VALLEY OF EAGLES(1952, Brit.), d&w; PARATROOPER(1954, Brit.), d; STORM OVER THE NILE(1955, Brit.), d; THAT LADY(1955, Brit.), d; SAFARI(1956), d; ZARAK(1956, Brit.), d; ACTION OF THE TIGER(1957), d; TANK FORCE(1958, Brit.), d, w; TOO HOT TO HANDLE(1961, Brit.), d; BLACK TIGHTS(1962, Fr.), d; DR. NO(1962, Brit.), d; IMMORAL CHARGE(1962, Brit.), d; FROM RUSSIA WITH LOVE(1963, Brit.), d; DUEL OF CHAMPIONS(1964 Ital./Span.), d; AMOROUS ADVENTURES OF MOLL FLANDERS, THE(1965); THUNDERBALL(1965, Brit.), d; POPPY IS ALSO A FLOWER, THE(1966), d; THE DIRTY GAME(1966, Fr./Ital./Ger.), d; ROVER, THE(1967, Ital.), d; TRIPLE CROSS(1967, Fr./Brit.), d; WAIT UNTIL DARK(1967), d; MAYERLING(1968, Brit./Fr.), d, w; CHRISTMAS TREE, THE(1969, Fr.), d&w; RED SUN(1972, Fr./Ital./Span.), d; VALACHI PAPERS, THE(1972, Ital./Fr.), d; COLD SWEAT(1974, Ital., Fr.), d; KLANSMAN, THE(1974), d; BLOODLINE(1979), d; INCHON(1981), d
1984
    JIGSAW MAN, THE(1984, Brit.), d
Tex Young
    VIRGINIAN, THE(1929)
Tiny Young
    BLONDE FROM PEKING, THE(1968, Fr.)
Tony Young
    PENNY POINTS TO PARADISE(1951, Brit.), d; MY DEATH IS A MOCKERY(1952, Brit.), d; HANDS OF DESTINY(1954, Brit.), p&d; PORT OF ESCAPE(1955, Brit.), d, w; HIDDEN HOMICIDE(1959, Brit.), d, w; HE RIDES TALL(1964); RUNAWAY, THE(1964, Brit.), d; TAGGART(1964); CHARRO(1969); CHROME AND HOT LEATHER(1971); MAN CALLED SLEDGE, A(1971, Ital.); BLACK GUNN(1972); PLAY IT AS IT LAYS(1972); OUTFIT, THE(1973); SUPERCHICK(1973); ACT OF VENGEANCE(1974); POLICEWOMAN(1974); GUYANA, CULT OF THE DAMNED(1980, Mex./Span./Panama)
Tricia Young
    TIGER BY THE TAIL(1970)
Trudy Young
    HOMER(1970); REINCARNATE, THE(1971, Can.); AGE OF INNOCENCE(1977, Can.); RUNNING(1979, Can.); MELANIE(1982, Can.)
Misc. Talkies
    RAKU FIRE(; WINTER COMES EARLY(1972)
Vernon Young
    MATTER OF MORALS, A(1961, U.S./Swed.)
Victor A. Young
    LIFE AND TIMES OF CHESTER-ANGUS RAMSGOOD, THE(1971, Can.)
Victor Sen Young
    SHADOWS OVER CHINATOWN(1946); CHINESE RING, THE(1947); CRIMSON KEY, THE(1947); TRAP, THE(1947); DOCKS OF NEW ORLEANS(1948); MYSTERY OF THE GOLDEN EYE, THE(1948); SHANGHAI CHEST, THE(1948); VALLEY OF FIRE(1951); SNIPER, THE(1952); PORT OF HELL(1955)
Victor Young
    TRUE TO LIFE(1943), m, md; FRANKIE AND JOHNNY(1936), md; ARTISTS AND MODELS(1937), m; MAID OF SALEM(1937), m; MAKE WAY FOR TOMORROW(1937), m; WELLS FARGO(1937), m; BREAKING THE ICE(1938), md; GLADIATOR, THE(1938), md; SHADOWS OVER SHANGHAI(1938); ESCAPE TO PARADISE(1939), md; GOLDEN BOY(1939), m; GULLIVER'S TRAVELS(1939), m; HERITAGE OF THE DESERT(1939), m; LAW OF THE PAMPAS(1939), m; LIGHT THAT FAILED, THE(1939), m; MAN ABOUT TOWN(1939), md; MAN OF CONQUEST(1939), m; RAFFLES(1939), m; WAY DOWN SOUTH(1939), md; ARISE, MY LOVE(1940), m; ARIZONA(1940), m; KNIGHTS OF THE RANGE(1940), m; LIGHT OF WESTERN STARS, THE(1940), m; NORTHWEST MOUNTED POLICE(1940), m; RHYTHM ON THE RIVER(1940), m; ROAD TO SINGAPORE(1940), md; THOSE WERE THE DAYS(1940), md; THREE FACES WEST(1940), m; THREE MEN FROM TEXAS(1940), m; CAUGHT IN THE DRAFT(1941), m; HOLD BACK THE DAWN(1941), m; I WANTED WINGS(1941), m, m/l; KISS THE BOYS GOODBYE(1941), md; LAS VEGAS NIGHTS(1941), m; ROAD TO ZANZIBAR(1941), m; FLYING TIGERS(1942), m; GLASS KEY, THE(1942), m; GREAT MAN'S LADY, THE(1942), m; PALM BEACH STORY, THE(1942), m; PRIORITIES ON PARADE(1942), m; REAP THE WILD WIND(1942), m; ROAD TO MOROCCO(1942), md; SILVER QUEEN(1942), m; TAKE A LETTER, DARLING(1942), m; TRUE TO THE ARMY(1942), md; CRYSTAL BALL, THE(1943), m; FOR WHOM THE BELL TOLLS(1943), m; HOSTAGES(1943), m; NO TIME FOR LOVE(1943), m; OUTLAW, THE(1943), md; RIDING HIGH(1943), m, md; SALUTE FOR THREE(1943), m; AND NOW TOMORROW(1944), m; AND THE ANGELS SING(1944), md; FRENCHMAN'S CREEK(1944), m; GREAT MOMENT, THE(1944), m; PRACTICALLY YOURS(1944), m; STORY OF DR. WASSELL, THE(1944), m; UNINVITED, THE(1944), m; GREAT JOHN L. THE(1945), md; KITTY(1945), m; LOST WEEKEND, THE(1945), md; LOVE LETTERS(1945), m; MASQUERADE IN MEXICO(1945), m, md; MEDAL FOR BENNY, A(1945), m; MINISTRY OF FEAR(1945), m; OUT OF THIS WORLD(1945), md; YOU CAME ALONG(1945), m; BLUE DAHLIA, THE(1946), m; CALIFORNIA(1946), m; OUR HEARTS WERE GROWING UP(1946), m; SEARCHING WIND, THE(1946), m; TO EACH HIS OWN(1946), m; TWO YEARS BEFORE THE MAST(1946), m; CALCUTTA(1947), m; DREAM GIRL(1947), m; GOLDEN EARRINGS(1947), m; IMPERFECT LADY, THE(1947), m; SUDDENLY IT'S SPRING(1947), m; TROUBLE WITH WOMEN, THE(1947), m; UNCONQUERED(1947), m; BEYOND GLORY(1948), m; BIG CLOCK, THE(1948), m; EMPEROR WALTZ, THE(1948), m; I WALK ALONE(1948), m; MISS TATLOCK'S MILLIONS(1948), m; NIGHT HAS A THOUSAND EYES(1948), m; PALEFACE, THE(1948), m; SO EVIL MY LOVE(1948, Brit.), m; STATE OF THE UNION(1948), m; ACCUSED, THE(1949), m; CHICAGO DEADLINE(1949), m; CONNECTICUT YANKEE IN KING ARTHUR'S COURT, A(1949), m; GUN CRAZY(1949), m; MY FOOLISH HEART(1949), m; SAMSON AND DELILAH(1949), m, md; SANDS OF IWO JIMA(1949), m; SONG OF SURRENDER(1949), m; STREETS OF LAREDO(1949), m, md; BRIGHT LEAF(1950), m; FILE ON THELMA JORDAN, THE(1950), m; FIREBALL, THE(1950), m; OUR VERY OWN(1950), m; PAID IN FULL(1950), m; RIDING HIGH(1950), md; RIO GRANDE(1950), m; SEP-

TEMBER AFFAIR(1950), m; APPOINTMENT WITH DANGER(1951), m; BELLE LE GRAND(1951), m; BULLFIGHTER AND THE LADY(1951), m; HONEYCHILE(1951), m; MILLIONAIRE FOR CHRISTY, A(1951), m, md; MY FAVORITE SPY(1951), m; PAYMENT ON DEMAND(1951), m; ANYTHING CAN HAPPEN(1952), m; BLACK-BEARD THE PIRATE(1952), m; GREATEST SHOW ON EARTH, THE(1952), m; ONE MINUTE TO ZERO(1952), m; QUIET MAN, THE(1952), m; SCARAMOUCHE(1952), m; SOMETHING TO LIVE FOR(1952), m; STORY OF WILL ROGERS, THE(1952), m; THUNDERBIRDS(1952), m; WILD BLUE YONDER, THE(1952), m; FAIR WIND TO JAVA(1953), m; FLIGHT NURSE(1953), m; FOREVER FEMALE(1953), m; LITTLE BOY LOST(1953), m; PERILOUS JOURNEY, A(1953), m; SHANE(1953), m; STAR, THE(1953), m, md; STARS ARE SINGING, THE(1953), m; SUN SHINES BRIGHT, THE(1953), m; TANGA-TIKA(1953), m; ABOUT MRS. LESLIE(1954), m; COUNTRY GIRL, THE(1954), m; DRUM BEAT(1954), m; JOHNNY GUITAR(1954), m; JUBILEE TRAIL(1954), m, md; KNOCK ON WOOD(1954), md; THREE COINS IN THE FOUNTAIN(1954), m; TROUBLE IN THE GLEN(1954, Brit.), m; LEFT HAND OF GOD, THE(1955), m; MAN ALONE, A(1955), m, md; SON OF SINBAD(1955), m; STRATEGIC AIR COMMAND(1955), m, md; TALL MEN, THE(1955), m, md; TIMBERJACK(1955), m; AROUND THE WORLD IN 80 DAYS(1956), m; BRAVE ONE, THE(1956), m; CONQUEROR, THE(1956), m; MAVERICK QUEEN, THE(1956), m; PROUD AND THE PROFANE, THE(1956), m; VAGABOND KING, THE(1956), m; BUSTER KEATON STORY, THE(1957), m; CHINA GATE(1957), m; OMAR KHAYYAM(1957), m; RUN OF THE ARROW(1957), m; HAWAIIANS, THE(1970)

Victoria Young
LT. ROBIN CRUSOE, U.S.N.(1966); KRAKATOA, EAST OF JAVA(1969); PATERNITY(1981)

Violet Young
THE BLACK HAND GANG(1930, Brit.)

W.W. Young
Misc. Silents
ALICE IN WONDERLAND(1916), d

Waldemar Young
SALLY(1929), w; GIRL OF THE GOLDEN WEST(1930), w; LADIES LOVE BRUTES(1930), w; CHANCES(1931), w; COMPROMISED(1931), w; PENROD AND SAM(1931), w; LOVE ME TONIGHT(1932), w; MIRACLE MAN, THE(1932), w; SIGN OF THE CROSS, THE(1932), w; SINNERS IN THE SUN(1932), w; SKY BRIDE(1932), w; BEDTIME STORY, A(1933), w; ISLAND OF LOST SOULS(1933), w; CLEOPATRA(1934), w; MEN IN WHITE(1934), w; LIVES OF A BENGAL LANCER(1935), w; PETER IBBETSON(1935), w; DESIRE(1936), w; POPPY(1936), w; PLAINSMAN, THE(1937), w; MAN-PROOF(1938), w; TEST PILOT(1938), w
Silents
NEW LOVE FOR OLD(1918), w; LIGHT OF VICTORY(1919), w; PETAL ON THE CURRENT, THE(1919), w; SPITFIRE OF SEVILLE, THE(1919), w; INFERIOR SEX, THE(1920), w; SUDS(1920), w; CAPPY RICKS(1921), w; OFF-SHORE PIRATE, THE(1921), w; PRINCE THERE WAS, A(1921), w; EBB TIDE(1922), w; IF YOU BELIEVE IT, IT'S SO(1922), w; OUR LEADING CITIZEN(1922), w; JAVA HEAD(1923), w; SALOMY JANE(1923), w; UNHOLY THREE, THE(1925), w; BLACK BIRD, THE(1926), w; LONDON AFTER MIDNIGHT(1927), w; UNKNOWN, THE(1927), w; BIG CITY, THE(1928), w; WEST OF ZANZIBAR(1928), w; TRAIL OF '98, THE(1929), w; WHERE EAST IS EAST(1929), w

Walemar Young
CRUSADES, THE(1935), w

Walter Young
ADVENTUROUS BLONDE(1937); DEVIL'S SADDLE LEGION, THE(1937); DELINQUENT PARENTS(1938); PATIENT IN ROOM 18, THE(1938)

William Allen Young
1984
SOLDIER'S STORY, A(1984)

William Young
TUNES OF GLORY(1960, Brit.)

Yoko Young
M(1970)

Yvonne Young
NIGHTMARE IN BLOOD(1978)

Zelda Young
REFORM SCHOOL(1939), w

Zella Young
WINGS OF ADVENTURE(1930), w

Young China Troupe
TONIGHT AT 8:30(1953, Brit.)

The Young Giants
WILD WORLD OF BATWOMAN, THE(1966), a, m

James Young-El
BLACK ANGELS, THE(1970); GUESS WHAT HAPPENED TO COUNT DRACULA(1970)

Butch Youngblood
ADAM AT 6 A.M.(1970)

Gloria Youngblood
ADVENTURES OF MARCO POLO, THE(1938); GOLDWYN FOLLIES, THE(1938); TRADE WINDS(1938)

Hal Youngblood
DAVY CROCKETT, KING OF THE WILD FRONTIER(1955)

Paul Youngblood
COURAGE OF LASSIE(1946), art d; ROLL ON TEXAS MOON(1946), art d; STAGECOACH TO DENVER(1946), art d; UNDER NEVADA SKIES(1946), art d; OREGON TRAIL SCOUTS(1947), art d; ROBIN OF TEXAS(1947), art d; SPOILERS OF THE NORTH(1947), art d
Silents
WANING SEX, THE(1926), set d

Paul Youngblood.
Silents
LITTLE ANNIE ROONEY(1925), art d

James Youngdeer
Silents
LIEUTENANT DARING RN AND THE WATER RATS(1924, Brit.), d, w

Lucille Younge
Silents
FLYING TORPEDO, THE(1916); OLD FOLKS AT HOME, THE(1916); GREATEST THING IN LIFE, THE(1918)

Misc. Silents
HEIRESS AT "COFFEE DAN'S", THE(1917); HIGH PLAY(1917)

A. P. Younger
ALIAS JIMMY VALENTINE(1928), w; LADY OF CHANCE, A(1928), w; EXTRAVAGANCE(1930), w; GIRL SAID NO, THE(1930), w; HOT CURVES(1930), w; SUNNY SKIES(1930), w; SWELLHEAD, THE(1930), w; THEY LEARNED ABOUT WOMEN(1930), w; FIVE AND TEN(1931), w; FLYING HIGH(1931), w; SINGLE SIN(1931), w
Silents
ARE ALL MEN ALIKE?(1920), w; DANGEROUS TO MEN(1920), w; ALL DOLLED UP(1921), w; MAKING THE GRADE(1921), w; FLIRT, THE(1922), w; GALLOPING KID, THE(1922), w; SECOND HAND ROSE(1922), w; ABYSMAL BRUTE, THE(1923), w; PLEASURE MAD(1923), w; HUSBANDS AND LOVERS(1924), w; ADVENTURE(1925), w; DEVIL'S CARGO, THE(1925), w; BEAUTIFUL CHEAT, THE(1926), w; BROWN OF HARVARD(1926), w; COLLEGE DAYS(1926), sup&w; IN OLD KENTUCKY(1927), w; SLIDE, KELLY, SLIDE(1927), w; TAXI DANCER, THE(1927), w; TILLIE THE TOILER(1927), w; TWELVE MILES OUT(1927), w; LATEST FROM PARIS, THE(1928), w; WHILE THE CITY SLEEPS(1928), w
Misc. Silents
TORRENT, THE(1924), d

Beverly Younger
MEDIUM COOL(1969)

Earl Younger
FAHRENHEIT 451(1966, Brit.); FLASH THE SHEEPDOG(1967, Brit.); HAMMERHEAD(1968); BOYS OF PAUL STREET, THE(1969, Hung./US); UP IN THE AIR(1969, Brit.)

Eileen Younger
SABU AND THE MAGIC RING(1957), cos

Eric Younger
DANNY BOY(1946)

Harold Younger
CATHERINE THE GREAT(1934, Brit.), ed

Henry Younger
CURSE OF THE MUMMY'S TOMB, THE(1965, Brit.), w; PREHISTORIC WOMEN(1967, Brit.), w

Jack Younger
DINOSAURUS(1960); SILENT CALL, THE(1961); AIR PATROL(1962); HAND OF DEATH(1962); YOUNG SWINGERS, THE(1963)

Margo Younger
Misc. Talkies
SELF-SERVICE SCHOOLGIRLS(1976)

Tom Younger
NO TIME TO KILL(1963, Brit./Swed./Ger.), p, d&w

Barrie Youngfellow
NIGHTMARE IN BLOOD(1978)

Capt. Younghusband
LAUGHING LADY, THE(1950, Brit.)

Gary Youngman
CURSE OF THE LIVING CORPSE, THE(1964), ed; HORROR OF PARTY BEACH, THE(1964), ed

Henny Youngman
YOU CAN'T RUN AWAY FROM IT(1956); WAVE, A WAC AND A MARINE, A(1944); MOTHER GOOSE A GO-GO(1966); NASHVILLE REBEL(1966); SILENT MOVIE(1976); WON TON TON, THE DOG WHO SAVED HOLLYWOOD(1976); HISTORY OF THE WORLD, PART 1(1981); COMEBACK TRAIL, THE(1982)

Henry Youngman
DEATH WISH II(1982)

Michael Youngman
QUICK, LET'S GET MARRIED(1965)

Bob Youngquist
SLEEPING BEAUTY(1959), anim

Robert W. Youngquist
FANTASIA(1940), anim

Gail Youngs
1984
STONE BOY, THE(1984)

Jennifer Youngs
ANGELO MY LOVE(1983)

Jim Youngs
WANDERERS, THE(1979)
1984
FOOTLOOSE(1984)

Lachlan Youngs
ANGELO MY LOVE(1983)

Max E. Youngstein
FAIL SAFE(1964), p; MONEY TRAP, THE(1966), p; WELCOME TO HARD TIMES(1967), p; YOUNG BILLY YOUNG(1969), p

Ricardo Younis
NO EXIT(1962, U.S./Arg.), ph; CURSE OF THE STONE HAND(1965, Mex/Chile), ph

Jerry Younkins
DEMON LOVER, THE(1977), p,d&w

Ivan Yount
ON THE YARD(1978)

Tariq Younus
FIGURES IN A LANDSCAPE(1970, Brit.)

Marguerite Yourcenar
COUP DE GRACE(1978, Ger./Fr.), w

Tom Yourk
TEENAGE GANG DEBS(1966)

Alice Yourman
DIRTYMOUTH(1970)

Theodor Youroukov
WITH LOVE AND TENDERNESS(1978, Bulgaria)

Youskevitch
INVITATION TO THE DANCE(1956)

Igor Youskevitch
INVITATION TO THE DANCE(1956)

Vadim Youssov
ANDREI ROUBLOV(1973, USSR), ph
Yovanna
ISLAND OF LOVE(1963)
Chief Yowlache
TIGER ROSE(1930)
Silents
INVADERS, THE(1929)
Misc. Silents
TONIO, SON OF THE SIERRAS(1925)
Chief Yowlachi
EL PASO(1949)
Chief Yowlachie
GIRL OF THE GOLDEN WEST(1930); SADDLEMATES(1941); WILD WEST(1946);
HUCKSTERS, THE(1947); DUDE GOES WEST, THE(1948); PRAIRIE OUT-
LAWS(1948); RED RIVER(1948); YELLOW SKY(1948); YOU GOTTA STAY HAP-
PY(1948); COWBOY AND THE INDIANS, THE(1949); MRS. MIKE(1949);
TULSA(1949); ANNIE GET YOUR GUN(1950); ROSE MARIE(1954)
Silents
SCARLET LETTER, THE(1926)
Marie-Josephe Yoyette
GOODBYE EMMANUELLE(1980, Fr.), ed
Marie Josephe Yoyette
WAR OF THE BUTTONS(1963 Fr.), ed
Marie-Josee Yoyotte
ANGRY MAN, THE(1979 Fr./Can.), ed
Marie-Joseph Yoyotte
EASY LIFE, THE(1971, Fr.), ed; POLICE PYTHON 357(1976, Fr.), ed; CASE
AGAINST FERRO, THE(1980, Fr.), ed; LA BOUM(1983, Fr.), ed
1984
SUGAR CANE ALLEY(1984, Fr.), ed
Marie-Josephe Yoyotte
FOUR HUNDRED BLOWS, THE(1959), ed; TESTAMENT OF ORPHEUS, THE(1962,
Fr.), a, ed; DAYDREAMER, THE(1975, Fr.), ed; SAVAGE, THE(1975, Fr.), ed; MY
FIRST LOVE(1978, Fr.), ed; DIVA(1982, Fr.), ed
Tsuruta Yozan
TEAHOUSE OF THE AUGUST MOON, THE(1956)
Joe Yrigoyan
BEN HUR(1959); PIER 5, HAVANA(1959)
Joe Yrigoyen
WINDS OF THE WASTELAND(1936); OLD WYOMING TRAIL, THE(1937); MAN
FROM MUSIC MOUNTAIN(1938); ROBIN OF TEXAS(1947); SADDLE PALS(1947);
MONTANA BELLE(1952); WOMAN THEY ALMOST LYNCHED, THE(1953); GUN
DUEL IN DURANGO(1957); LEGEND OF TOM DOOLEY, THE(1959); SECOND TIME
AROUND, THE(1961); SHENANDOAH(1965); COWBOYS, THE(1972); PRISONER OF
ZENDA, THE(1979)
Joseph Yrigoyen
SONS OF KATIE ELDER, THE(1965)
Richard Yriondo
MISS ROBIN CRUSOE(1954), w
Agustin Ytuarte
SAVAGE IS LOOSE, THE(1974), art d; MAN FRIDAY(1975, Brit.), art d; UNDER
FIRE(1983), art d
Augustin Ytuarte
MISSING(1982), art d
Filipe Ytuarte
UNDER FIRE(1983)
Albert Yu
DEVIL WOMAN(1976, Phil.), d
C.F. Yu
SECRET, THE(1979, Hong Kong), ed
Chin Yu
OPERATION CONSPIRACY(1957, Brit.)
Han-chul Yu
MARINE BATTLEGROUND(1966, U.S/S.K.), w
Jimmy Wang Yu
MAN FROM HONG KONG(1975)
Barbara Yu Ling
COUNT DRACULA AND HIS VAMPIRE BRIDE(1978, Brit.)
Hsu Yu-Ian
DREAM OF THE RED CHAMBER, THE(1966, Chi.)
Tsuai Yu-Lan
WHO'S THAT KNOCKING AT MY DOOR?(1968)
Li Yu-ping
FLYING GUILLOTINE, THE(1975, Chi.)
Chu Yuan
SACRED KNIVES OF VENGEANCE, THE(1974, Hong Kong), d
Mike Yuan
1984
SIXTEEN CANDLES(1984)
Augustin Yuarte
HERBIE GOES BANANAS(1980), art d
Joji Yuasa
PLEASURES OF THE FLESH, THE(1965), m
Kenmai Yuasa
MYSTERIOUS SATELLITE, THE(1956, Jap.), spec eff
Noriaki Yuasa
FALCON FIGHTERS, THE(1970, Jap.), spec eff
Noriyaki Yuasa
GAMERA THE INVINCIBLE(1966, Jap.), d; GAMERA VERSUS BARUGON(1966,
Jap./U.S.), spec eff; GAMERA VERSUS GAOS(1967, Jap.), d; GAMERA VERSUS
VIRAS(1968, Jap), d; GAMERA VERSUS GUIRON(1969, Jap.), d; GAMERA VERSUS
MONSTER K(1970, Jap.), d; GAMERA VERSUS ZIGRA(1971, Jap.), d
Nevzat Yuceyildez
1984
LOOSE CONNECTIONS(1984, Brit.)
Luis Yuchum
HUNGRY WIVES(1973)

Alexei Yudin
DARK IS THE NIGHT(1946, USSR)
George Yudzevich
GLORIA(1980)
Joe Yue
THREE WEEKS OF LOVE(1965)
Ozzie Yue
1984
SLAYGROUND(1984, Brit.)
Wang Yueh-ting
LAST WOMAN OF SHANG, THE(1964, Hong Kong), w; EMPRESS WU(1965, Hong
Kong), w; ENCHANTING SHADOW, THE(1965, Hong Kong), w
Kam Yuen
CIRCLE OF IRON(1979, Brit.)
Ne see Yuen
BRUCE LEE–TRUE STORY(1976, Chi.), w
Ng See Yuen
BRUCE LEE–TRUE STORY(1976, Chi.), d
Tom Yuen
MAD MARTINDALES, THE(1942); SALUTE TO THE MARINES(1943)
Li Yuen-chung
LAST WOMAN OF SHANG, THE(1964, Hong Kong); MERMAID, THE(1966, Hong
Kong)
Mike Yuenger
THUMBELINA(1970)
Officers and Men of the Yugoslav Cavalry
MICHAEL STROGOFF(1960, Fr./Ital./Yugo.)
Kota Yui
KAGEMUSHA(1980, Jap.)
Jimmy Yuill
LOCAL HERO(1983, Brit.)
Henry Yuk
EYEWITNESS(1981)
1984
C.H.U.D.(1984); POPE OF GREENWICH VILLAGE, THE(1984)
Gyuorgy Yukan
WITNESS, THE(1982, Hung.), m
Gennadiy Yukhtin
RESURRECTION(1963, USSR); LAST GAME, THE(1964, USSR); PORTRAIT OF
LENIN(1967, Pol./USSR)
Saori Yuki
1984
FAMILY GAME, THE(1984, Jap.)
Izumi Yukimora
BANDITS ON THE WIND(1964, Jap.)
Olya Yukina
JACK FROST(1966, USSR)
Tanya Yukina
JACK FROST(1966, USSR)
Yukon
SAVAGE WILD, THE(1970)
Nawarat Yukthanan
1 2 3 MONSTER EXPRESS(1977, Thai.)
Ian Yule
WILD SEASON(1968, South Africa); MY WAY(1974, South Africa); KILLER FOR-
CE(1975, Switz./Ireland); WILD GEESE, THE(1978, Brit.); SAFARI 3000(1982)
Joe Yule
IDIOT'S DELIGHT(1939); JUDGE HARDY AND SON(1939); SUDDEN MO-
NEY(1939); BOOM TOWN(1940); FLORIAN(1940); GO WEST(1940); NEW MOON(1940);
THIRD FINGER, LEFT HAND(1940); BABES ON BROADWAY(1941); BILLY THE
KID(1941); COME LIVE WITH ME(1941); I'LL WAIT FOR YOU(1941); KATH-
LEEN(1941); MAISIE WAS A LADY(1941); TRIAL OF MARY DUGAN, THE(1941);
WILD MAN OF BORNEO, THE(1941); BORN TO SING(1942); JACKASS MAIL(1942);
NAZI AGENT(1942); PANAMA HATTIE(1942); WOMAN OF THE YEAR(1942); THREE
HEARTS FOR JULIA(1943); KISMET(1944); LOST ANGEL(1944); THIN MAN GOES
HOME, THE(1944); TWO GIRLS AND A SAILOR(1944); PICTURE OF DORIAN GRAY,
THE(1945); BRINGING UP FATHER(1946); MIGHTY MCGURK, THE(1946); MUR-
DER IN THE MUSIC HALL(1946); JIGGS AND MAGGIE IN SOCIETY(1948); JIGGS
AND MAGGIE OUT WEST(1950)
Misc. Talkies
JIGGS AND MAGGIE IN COURT(1948); JIGGS AND MAGGIE IN JACKPOT
JITTERS(1949)
Jon Yule
FRIGHTMARE(1974, Brit.); CONFESSIONAL, THE(1977, Brit.)
Joe Yule, Sr.
MARRIED BACHELOR(1941); NOTHING BUT TROUBLE(1944)
Harris Yulin
MAIDSTONE(1970); DOC(1971); WHO FEARS THE DEVIL(1972); MIDNIGHT MAN,
THE(1974); WATCHED(1974); NIGHT MOVES(1975); ST. IVES(1976); STEEL(1980);
SCARFACE(1983)
Tim Yum
GLADIATORS, THE(1970, Swed.)
Kaoru Yumi
PROPHECIES OF NOSTRADAMUS(1974, Jap.); HINOTORI(1980, Jap.)
Lang Yun
SPIRAL ROAD, THE(1962)
Liu Yun
RETURN OF THE DRAGON(1974, Chin.)
Yun-wen
DRAGON INN(1968, Chi.)
Johnny Yune
CANNONBALL RUN, THE(1981); THEY CALL ME BRUCE(1982), a, w
Jon Yune
METEOR(1979)
Barbara Yung
PAL JOEY(1957)
Sen Yung
CHARLIE CHAN IN HONOLULU(1938); CHARLIE CHAN AT TREASURE IS-
LAND(1939); CHARLIE CHAN IN RENO(1939); 20,000 MEN A YEAR(1939); CHARLIE
CHAN AT THE WAX MUSEUM(1940); CHARLIE CHAN IN PANAMA(1940); CHARL-

IE CHAN'S MURDER CRUISE(1940); MURDER OVER NEW YORK(1940); DEAD MEN TELL(1941).(CASTLE IN THE DESERT(1942); LITTLE TOKYO, U.S.A.(1942); MAD MARTINDALES, THE(1942); MOONTIDE(1942); YANK ON THE BURMA ROAD, A(1942); BETRAYAL FROM THE EAST(1945)

Soo Yung
FLOWER DRUM SONG(1961)

Victor Sen Yung
CHARLIE CHAN IN RIO(1941); ACROSS THE PACIFIC(1942); MANILA CALLING(1942); SECRET AGENT OF JAPAN(1942); CHINA(1943); DANGEROUS MONEY(1946); INTRIGUE(1947); WEB OF DANGER, THE(1947); FEATHERED SERPENT, THE(1948); FLAME, THE(1948); HALF PAST MIDNIGHT(1948); ROGUES' REGIMENT(1948); OH, YOU BEAUTIFUL DOLL(1949); STATE DEPARTMENT–FILE 649(1949); BREAKING POINT, THE(1950); KEY TO THE CITY(1950); TICKET TO TOMAHAWK(1950); WOMAN ON THE RUN(1950); GROOM WORE SPURS, THE(1951); LAW AND THE LADY, THE(1951); PEKING EXPRESS(1951); TARGET HONG KONG(1952); FORBIDDEN(1953); JUBILEE TRAIL(1954); SHANGHAI STORY, THE(1954); LEFT HAND OF GOD, THE(1955); SOLDIER OF FORTUNE(1955); ACCUSED OF MURDER(1956); MEN IN WAR(1957); HUNTERS, THE(1958); JET ATTACK(1958); SAGA OF HEMP BROWN, THE(1958); SHE DEMONS(1958); FLOWER DRUM SONG(1961); FLEA IN HER EAR, A(1968, Fr.); HAWAIIANS, THE(1970); MAN WITH BOGART'S FACE, THE(1980)

Sha Yung-fong
DRAGON INN(1968, Chi.), p

Chen Yung-hua
LAST WOMAN OF SHANG, THE(1964, Hong Kong)

Chen Yung-Huang
TRIPLE IRONS(1973, Hong Kong), md

Shin Yung-kyoon
LAST WOMAN OF SHANG, THE(1964, Hong Kong)

Chen Yung-shu
SACRED KNIVES OF VENGEANCE, THE(1974, Hong Kong), m

Lin Yung-tai
HONOLULU-TOKYO-HONG KONG(1963, Hong Kong/Jap.), p

Wang Yunglung
FIVE FINGERS OF DEATH(1973, Hong Kong), ph

Yungman
JEDDA, THE UNCIVILIZED(1956, Aus.)

Kelly Yunkermann
UNCOMMON VALOR(1983)

Charles Yunupingu
GALLIPOLI(1981, Aus.)

Tariq Yunus
EAST OF ELEPHANT ROCK(1976, Brit.); ASHANTI(1979)

A. Yurchak
SANDU FOLLOWS THE SUN(1965, USSR)

A. Yurchenko
KIEV COMEDY, A(1963, USSR)

V. Yureneva
Misc. Silents
TEARS(1914, USSR); WOMAN OF TOMORROW(1914, USSR); QUEEN OF THE SCREEN(1916, USSR)

Toru Yuri
FRIENDLY KILLER, THE(1970, Jap.); TOPSY-TURVY JOURNEY(1970, Jap.)

Richard Yurich
BRAINSTORM(1983), ph

Matthew Yuricich
SOYLENT GREEN(1973), spec eff; CLOSE ENCOUNTERS OF THE THIRD KIND(1977), spec eff

Richard Yuricich
SILENT RUNNING(1972), spec eff; CLOSE ENCOUNTERS OF THE THIRD KIND(1977), ph, spec eff; STAR TREK: THE MOTION PICTURE(1979), spec eff

Sol Yurick
WARRIORS, THE(1979), w

Y. Yurief
CAPTAIN GRANT'S CHILDREN(1939, USSR)

Yuriko
KING AND I, THE(1956)

Rayka Yurit
LUDWIG(1973, Ital./Ger./Fr.)

Blanche Yurka
TALE OF TWO CITIES, A(1935); ESCAPE(1940); QUEEN OF THE MOB(1940); CITY, FOR CONQUEST(1941); ELLERY QUEEN AND THE MURDER RING(1941); LADY FOR A NIGHT(1941); KEEPER OF THE FLAME(1942); NIGHT TO REMEMBER, A(1942); PACIFIC RENDEZVOUS(1942); HITLER'S MADMAN(1943); SONG OF BERNADETTE, THE(1943); TONIGHT WE RAID CALAIS(1943); BRIDGE OF SAN LUIS REY, THE(1944); CRY OF THE WEREWOLF(1944); ONE BODY TOO MANY(1944); SOUTHERNER, THE(1945); 13 RUE MADELEINE(1946); FLAME, THE(1948); FURIES, THE(1950); AT SWORD'S POINT(1951); TAXI(1953); THUNDER IN THE SUN(1959)

R. Yurlev
VOW, THE(1947, USSR.)

F. Yurma
STALKER(1982, USSR)

Robert Yuro
SATAN IN HIGH HEELS(1962); RIDE TO HANGMAN'S TREE, THE(1967); HELL WITH HEROES, THE(1968); SHAKIEST GUN IN THE WEST, THE(1968)

V. Yurovskiy
DUEL, THE(1964, USSR), m

S. Yurtaykin
DAY THE WAR ENDED, THE(1961, USSR)

Phyllis Yuse
GASLIGHT(1944)

Marat Yusim
HEAVEN'S GATE(1980)

Antonette Yuskis
ZOOT SUIT(1981); TO BE OR NOT TO BE(1983)

Vadim Yusov
VIOLIN AND ROLLER(1962, USSR), ph; MY NAME IS IVAN(1963, USSR), ph; MEET ME IN MOSCOW(1966, USSR), ph

Larry Yust
TRICK BABY(1973), d, w; HOMEBODIES(1974), d, w

Sergei Yutkevich
Misc. Silents
LACE(1928, USSR), d

Sergey Yutkevich
PORTRAIT OF LENIN(1967, Pol./USSR), d, w

Sergei Yutkevitch
OTHELLO(1960, U.S.S.R.), d&w
Misc. Silents
BLACK SAIL, THE(1929, USSR), d

I. Yutsevich
KIEV COMEDY, A(1963, USSR), art d

Aizawa Yuzuru
ONCE A RAINY DAY(1968, Jap.), ph

Maurice Yvain
THEY WERE FIVE(1938, Fr.), m; MURDERER LIVES AT NUMBER 21, THE(1947, Fr.), m; LE PLAISIR(1954, Fr.), m

Christiane Yves
THEY HAD TO SEE PARIS(1929); MAN HUNTER, THE(1930); SLIGHTLY SCARLET(1930); WHAT A MAN(1930)

Christianne Yves
SWEET KITTY BELLAIRS(1930)

Yves-Marc-Maurin
DIABOLIQUE(1955, Fr.)

Yvette
FIRST MRS. FRASER, THE(1932, Brit.); SEE MY LAWYER(1945); RETURN OF MARTIN GUERRE, THE(1983, Fr.)

Mimi Yvonne
Misc. Silents
LITTLEST REBEL, THE(1914); KREUTZER SONATA, THE(1915); HER WAYWARD SISTER(1916)

Yvonneck
Silents
ITALIAN STRAW HAT, AN(1927, Fr.)

Zelie Yzelle
LE PLAISIR(1954, Fr.)

Z

Z
IMMORTAL GARRISON, THE(1957, USSR), d
Mohsen Zaaza
L'ETOILE DU NORD(1983, Fr.)
Elsa Zabala
CAPTAIN APACHE(1971, Brit.)
Tania Zabaloieff
DIVA(1982, Fr.)
V. Zabavin
OPTIMISTIC TRAGEDY, THE(1964, USSR)
Esther Zabco
1984
AMBASSADOR, THE(1984)
Flora Zabelle
Silents
RED WIDOW, THE(1916)
Misc. Silents
RINGTAILED RHINOCEROS, THE(1915); PERFECT 36, A(1918)
William Zabka
1984
KARATE KID, THE(1984)
Malgorzata Zabkowska
CAMERA BUFF(1983, Pol.)
I. Zablotsky
DEFENSE OF VOLOTCHAYEVSK, THE(1938, USSR), prod d
Lila Zaborin
BLOOD ORGY OF THE SHE-DEVILS(1973)
O. Zabotkina
SLEEPING BEAUTY, THE(1966, USSR)
Olga Zabotkina
SONG OVER MOSCOW(1964, USSR)
Zabou
1984
PERILS OF GWENDOLINE, THE(1984, Fr.)
Dorie Zabriskie
Misc. Talkies
LEGACY(1963)
Grace Zabriskie
NORMA RAE(1979); PRIVATE EYES, THE(1980); GALAXY OF TERROR(1981);
OFFICER AND A GENTLEMAN, AN(1982)
1984
BODY ROCK(1984)
Oliver Zabriskie
SUMMERDOG(1977)
Tavia Zabriskie
SUMMERDOG(1977)
Lyuda Zabrodskaya
MOTHER AND DAUGHTER(1965, USSR)
John Zabrucky
BATTLE BEYOND THE STARS(1980), set d
Zabuda
OUTLAW'S DAUGHTER, THE(1954)
Mario A. Zacarias
LOS ASTRONAUTAS(1960, Mex.), p
Miguel Zacarias
LOS ASTRONAUTAS(1960, Mex.), d, w
Monair Zacca
COUNTRYMAN(1982, Jamaica)
Enrico Zaccaria
N. P.(1971, Ital.), p
Giuseppe Zaccariello
WE STILL KILL THE OLD WAY(1967, Ital.), p
Tino Zacchia
GRAVE OF THE VAMPIRE(1972), makeup
Giuseppe Zacciarello
TWITCH OF THE DEATH NERVE(1973, Ital.), p
Ermete Zacconi
PEARLS OF THE CROWN(1938, Fr.)
Ines Zacconi
SPIRIT AND THE FLESH, THE(1948, Ital.)
Lubomir Zacek
LEMONADE JOE(1966, Czech.)
Franz Zavier Zach
SQUEEZE A FLOWER(1970, Aus.)
Charles Zacha
SHAMPOO(1975), set d
Jac Zacha
WALK THE WALK(1970), p,d&w
Joe Zacha
GREAT SCOUT AND CATHOUSE THURSDAY, THE(1976)
W.T. Zacha
48 HOURS(1982)
William T. Zacha
LOOKING FOR LOVE(1964), cos; SAM WHISKEY(1969), cos
Alfred Zacharias
DEMONOID(1981), p&d, w
Alfredo Zacharias
BEES, THE(1978), p,d&w
Don Zacharias
FIREBIRD 2015 AD(1981), art d
John Zacharias
MONTENEGRO(1981, Brit./Swed.)

Stefen Zacharias
1984
EXTERMINATOR 2(1984)
Steffen Zacharias
CATCH AS CATCH CAN(1968, Ital.); ACE HIGH(1969, Ital.); MAN CALLED SLEDGE,
A(1971, Ital.); THEY CALL ME TRINITY(1971, Ital.); MAN OF LA MANCHA(1972);
RETURN OF SABATA(1972, Ital./Fr./Ger.); DEATH WISH II(1982)
1984
ICE PIRATES, THE(1984); IRRECONCILABLE DIFFERENCES(1984)
Stephen Zacharias
GAMERA THE INVINCIBLE(1966, Jap.); KREMLIN LETTER, THE(1970); MA-
CHINE GUN McCAIN(1970, Ital.)
Steve Zacharias
1984
REVENGE OF THE NERDS(1984), w
Athina Zacharopoulou
SIGNS OF LIFE(1981, Ger.)
Zachary
SQUEEZE PLAY(1981)
1984
DUBEAT-E-O(1984)
Mark Zachary
SIERRA BARON(1958)
Ray Zachary
DEADWOOD'76(1965)
Richard Zachary
FINDERS KEEPERS, LOVERS WEEPERS(1968), w
Zacherle
GEEK MAGGOT BINGO(1983)
Nike Zachmanoglou
TRICK OR TREATS(1982)
Lisbeth Zachrisson
MONTENEGRO(1981, Brit./Swed.)
Krystyna Zachwatowicz
MAN OF MARBLE(1979, Pol.)
Krystyna Zachwatowicz-Wajda
MAN OF IRON(1981, Pol.)
1984
LOVE IN GERMANY, A(1984, Fr./Ger.), cos
Thor Zackrisson
SWEDISH WEDDING NIGHT(1965, Swed.)
Stephen Zacks
DIRTY HARRY(1971)
Stanislow Zaczk
BEADS OF ONE ROSARY, THE(1982, Pol.)
Stanislaw Zaczyk
WALKOVER(1969, Pol.)
Craig Zadan
1984
FOOTLOOSE(1984), p
Gitta Zadek
QUARE FELLOW, THE(1962, Brit.), ed
Peter Zadek
VERONIKA VOSS(1982, Ger.)
Fylgia Zadig
LA GUERRE EST FINIE(1967, Fr./Swed.)
Greg Zadikov
CHAPTER TWO(1979)
Eugene Zador
MORTAL STORM, THE(1940), m
Stephen Zador
MARRY ME(1932, Brit.), w
Pia Zadora
SANTA CLAUS CONQUERS THE MARTIANS(1964); BUTTERFLY(1982); LONELY
LADY, THE(1983)
Misc. Talkies
FAKE-OUT(1982)
Saul Zaentz
ONE FLEW OVER THE CUCKOO'S NEST(1975), p; THREE WARRIORS(1977), p;
LORD OF THE RINGS, THE(1978), p
1984
AMADEUS(1984), p
Paul Zaeremba
SONG TO REMEMBER, A(1945)
Eleni Zaferiou
MIDWIFE, THE(1961, Greece); NAKED BRIGADE, THE(1965, U.S./Gr.)
Marie Zafred
YOUNG HUSBANDS(1958, Ital./Fr.), m
Mario Zafred
WASTREL, THE(1963, Ital.), m
Tamar Zafria
JESUS CHRIST, SUPERSTAR(1973)
Shlomo Zafrir
TRUNK TO CAIRO(1966, Israel/Ger.), art d
Lauren Zaganas
DINER(1982)
Frank Anthony Zagarino
BABY, IT'S YOU(1983)
Frank Zagarino
1984
LOVELINES(1984); WHERE THE BOYS ARE '84(1984)
Catherine Zago
YOUR SHADOW IS MINE(1963, Fr./Ital.)
Elettra Zago
WHITE SHEIK, THE(1956, Ital.)
Marty Zagon
GOODBYE, NORMA JEAN(1976); NEW YORK, NEW YORK(1977); YOU LIGHT UP
MY LIFE(1977); FAST BREAK(1979); METALSTORM: THE DESTRUCTION OF
JARED-SYN(1983)

Mary Zagon
DIE LAUGHING(1980)
Yelena Zagon
PICTURE SHOW MAN, THE(1980, Aus.)
Adelio Zagonara
LAUGH PAGLIACCI(1948, Ital.)
Michael Zagor
MAN FROM GALVESTON, THE(1964), w
Alyosha Zagorskiy
DIMKA(1964, USSR)
Zeliko Zagota
NINTH CIRCLE, THE(1961, Yugo.), art d
Liliana Zagra
SEVEN TASKS OF ALI BABA, THE(1963, Ital.)
Babe Didrikson Zaharias
PAT AND MIKE(1952)
Nicholas Zaharias
BAREFOOT BATTALION, THE(1954, Gr.)
Ilan Zahavi
1984
SAHARA(1984)
Gordon Zahler
PLAN 9 FROM OUTER SPACE(1959), m; ASSIGNMENT OUTER SPACE(1960, Ital.), md; FIRST SPACESHIP ON VENUS(1960, Ger./Pol.), m; I BOMBED PEARL HARBOR(1961, Jap.), m; HERCULES AND THE CAPTIVE WOMEN(1963, Fr./Ital.), m; LIVING BETWEEN TWO WORLDS(1963), m; FAUST(1964), m; HUMAN DU-PLICATORS, THE(1965), md; MUTINY IN OUTER SPACE(1965), md; NAVY VS. THE NIGHT MONSTERS, THE(1966), m; HAPPY AS THE GRASS WAS GREEN(1973), m; RETURN TO CAMPUS(1975), m
Jason Zahler
SILENT SCREAM(1980)
Lee Zahler
MIDNIGHT WARNING, THE(1932), md; MONSTER WALKS, THE(1932), md; SAV-AGE GIRL, THE(1932), m; SILVER LINING(1932), m; TANGLED DESTINIES(1932), md; BIG BLUFF, THE(1933), ph; CHEATING BLONDES(1933), m; SECRET SIN-NERS(1933); RECKLESS ROADS(1935), md; SYMPHONY OF LIVING(1935), m; PENITENTE MURDER CASE, THE(1936), m; GHOST TOWN(1937), m; PHANTOM GOLD(1938), m; FRONTIERS OF '49(1939), m; HIDDEN POWER(1939), m; OUTSIDE THE 3-MILE LIMIT(1940), m; PASSPORT TO ALCATRAZ(1940), m; ELLERY QUEEN AND THE MURDER RING(1941), m; ELLERY QUEEN AND THE PERFECT CRI-ME(1941), m; ELLERY QUEEN'S PENTHOUSE MYSTERY(1941), m; BOMBS OVER BURMA(1942), md; DAWN EXPRESS, THE(1942), m; ENEMY AGENTS MEET EL-LERY QUEEN(1942), m; GALLANT LADY(1942), md; GIRLS' TOWN(1942), m; HOUSE OF ERRORS(1942), md; MISS V FROM MOSCOW(1942), md; PRISONER OF JAPAN(1942), m; RANGERS TAKE OVER, THE(1942), md; SECRETS OF A CO-ED(1942), md; YANK IN LIBYA, A(1942), md; YANKS ARE COMING, THE(1942), m; BAD MEN OF THUNDER GAP(1943), md; BORDER BUCKAROOS(1943), md; CRIME DOCTOR(1943), m; GENTLE GANGSTER, A(1943), m; GHOST AND THE GUEST(1943), md; MAN OF COURAGE(1943), md; NO PLACE FOR A LADY(1943), m; RETURN OF THE RANGERS, THE(1943), md; TIGER FANGS(1943), m; UNDER-DOG, THE(1943), md; WEST OF TEXAS(1943), md; BOSS OF THE RAWHIDE(1944), md; BRAND OF THE DEVIL(1944), md; DELINQUENT DAUGHTERS(1944), md; GANGSTERS OF THE FRONTIER(1944), md; GREAT MIKE, THE(1944), m; GUNS-MOKE MESA(1944), md; MEN ON HER MIND(1944), md; PINTO BANDIT, THE(1944), md; SEVEN DOORS TO DEATH(1944), md; SHADOW OF SUSPI-CION(1944), md; SHAKE HANDS WITH MURDER(1944), md; SPOOK TOWN(1944), md; TRAIL OF TERROR(1944), m; WATERFRONT(1944), md; WHISPERING SKULL, THE(1944), m; ARSON SQUAD(1945), md; ENEMY OF THE LAW(1945), md; FRON-TIER FUGITIVES(1945), md; HOLLYWOOD AND VINE(1945), m; I ACCUSE MY PARENTS(1945), md; LADY CONFESSES, THE(1945), m; LIGHTNING RAI-DERS(1945), md; MARKED FOR MURDER(1945), md; ROGUES GALLERY(1945), md; THREE IN THE SADDLE(1945), md; AMBUSH TRAIL(1946), md; FREDDIE STEPS OUT(1946), md; GENTLEMEN WITH GUNS(1946), md; GHOST OF HIDDEN VALLEY(1946), md; MASK OF DIIJON, THE(1946), md; NAVAJO KID(1946), md; OUTLAW OF THE PLAINS(1946), m; OVERLAND RIDERS(1946), md; PRAIRIE BADMEN(1946), md; SIX GUN MAN(1946), md; TERRORS ON HORSEBACK(1946), md; THUNDER TOWN(1946), md; QUEEN OF THE AMAZONS(1947), md
Les Zahler
GREAT PLANE ROBBERY, THE(1940), m
Albert Zahn
NAKED AMONG THE WOLVES(1967, Ger.)
Lenore Zahn
HOUNDS... OF NOTRE DAME, THE(1980, Can.)
James Zahner
LITTLE TOUGH GUY(1938)
Zoro Zahon
ASSISTANT, THE(1982, Czech.), d, w
Bohus Zahorsky
EMPEROR AND THE GOLEM, THE(1955, Czech.); LEMONADE JOE(1966, Czech.); HAPPY END(1968, Czech.)
Richard Zahorsky
DEVIL'S TRAP, THE(1964, Czech.)
Jadwiga Zaicek
EROICA(1966, Pol.), ed
Sabi Zaidi
1984
RAZOR'S EDGE, THE(1984), set d
George Zaifides
OEDIPUS THE KING(1968, Brit.)
Osman Zailani
SAINT JACK(1979)
Steve Zaillian
KINGDOM OF THE SPIDERS(1977), ed; STARHOPS(1978), ed
Steven Zaillian
BREAKER! BREAKER!(1977), ed
Stephen Zaillion
BELOW THE BELT(1980), ed

George Zaima
MORITURI(1965); MARINE BATTLEGROUND(1966, U.S/S.K.)
Benjamin Zaitz
RETURN OF THE SECAUCUS SEVEN(1980)
Steven Zaitz
RETURN OF THE SECAUCUS SEVEN(1980)
Credda Zajac
GUNFIGHTER, THE(1950)
Malgorzata Zajaczkowska
CONSTANT FACTOR, THE(1980, Pol.)
Matgorzata Zajaczkowska
DANTON(1983)
Leonard Zajaczkowski
MAN OF MARBLE(1979, Pol.)
Lothar Zajicek
DAS BOOT(1982)
Avenir Zak
LULLABY(1961, USSR), w; MOSCOW–CASSIOPEIA(1974, USSR), w; TEENAGERS IN SPACE(1975, USSR), w
John Zak
HOUSE ON 92ND STREET, THE(1945)
Sharri Zak
OTHER SIDE OF THE MOUNTAIN, THE(1975); TWO-MINUTE WARNING(1976); LITTLE MISS MARKER(1980); S.O.B.(1981)
Zed Zakari
INN OF THE SIXTH HAPPINESS, THE(1958)
George Zakaria
PIRATE MOVIE, THE(1982, Aus.)
S. Zakariadze
1812(1944, USSR)
Sergei Zakariadze
FATHER OF A SOLDIER(1966, USSR)
Nicky Zakariah
CLINIC, THE(1983, Aus.)
Klara Zakarias
FATHER(1967, Hung.)
Zakee
LION, THE(1962, Brit.)
V. Zakharchenko
DAY THE WAR ENDED, THE(1961, USSR)
Sergei Zakhariadze
WATERLOO(1970, Ital./USSR)
George Zakhariah
SEVENTH DAWN, THE(1964)
I. Zakharova
SHE-WOLF, THE(1963, USSR), art d
Boris Zakhava
WAR AND PEACE(1968, USSR)
Alex Zakin
TONIGHT WE SING(1953)
Jamil Zakkai
KING OF THE GYPSIES(1978)
Sylwia Zakrzewska
GUESTS ARE COMING(1965, Pol.)
Z. Zaks
WAR AND PEACE(1968, USSR)
Vadin Zakurenko
TARAS FAMILY, THE(1946, USSR)
Roxana Zal
TABLE FOR FIVE(1983); TESTAMENT(1983)
Jane Zalata [Jana Zatloukalova]
FABULOUS WORLD OF JULES VERNE, THE(1961, Czech.)
Jose Zalde
MERCENARY, THE(1970, Ital./Span.)
Alexander Zale
FIREFOX(1982); FRANCES(1982); WRONG IS RIGHT(1982)
Tony Zale
GOLDEN GLOVES STORY, THE(1950); SOMEBODY UP THERE LIKES ME(1956)
Dan Zaleski
STAR 80(1983)
Szymon Zaleski
DANTON(1983)
Alina Zalewska
LEOPARD, THE(1963, Ital.); HERCULES, SAMSON & ULYSSES(1964, Ital.); WAR BETWEEN THE PLANETS(1971, Ital.)
Halina Zalewska
SNOW DEVILS, THE(1965, Ital.)
Gerard Zalewski
GUESTS ARE COMING(1965, Pol.), p&d
Lila Zali
PRODIGAL, THE(1955)
Deborah Zalkind
HAIR(1979)
Andy Zall
1984
OH GOD! YOU DEVIL(1984), ed
Zalman
TRUNK TO CAIRO(1966, Israel/Ger.)
J. Zaloga
SUBWAY RIDERS(1981)
Son Zalone
ZIG-ZAG(1975, Fr/Ital.), cos
Joe Zaloom
KING OF THE GYPSIES(1978); ECHOES(1983)
Bronka Zaltzman
DREAMER, THE(1970, Israel)
Rochelle Zaltzman
OPERATION THUNDERBOLT(1978, ISRAEL), cos; JESUS(1979), cos

E. Zama
TWO WOMEN(1940, Fr.), p
Fleurette Zama
PIED PIPER, THE(1942)
Peter Zamaglias
MIDNIGHT COWBOY(1969)
V. Zamanskiy
LULLABY(1961, USSR); VIOLIN AND ROLLER(1962, USSR); HOUSE ON THE FRONT LINE, THE(1963, USSR)
Zamba the Chimp
JUNGLE JIM IN THE FORBIDDEN LAND(1952)
Zamba the Lion
LION, THE(1962, Brit.)
Zaira Zambelli
BYE-BYE BRASIL(1980, Braz.)
Georges Zambetas
MALE HUNT(1965, Fr./Ital.), m
Andreas Zambikies
ISLAND OF LOVE(1963)
Bob Zamboni
MOUSE AND HIS CHILD, THE(1977), anim
Enrique Zambrano
MASSACRE(1956)
Themis Zambrzycki
PERSONAL BEST(1982)
J. S. Zamecnik
FACE IN THE SKY(1933), m; POWER AND THE GLORY, THE(1933), m; RIDERS OF THE WHISTLING SKULL(1937), m
Silents
WEDDING MARCH, THE(1927), m; WINGS(1927), m
Renato Zamengo
SUSPIRIA(1977, Ital.)
Chris Zamiara
FINAL CHAPTER–WALKING TALL zero(1977), cos; MEAN DOG BLUES(1978), cos
E. Zamiatine
LOWER DEPTHS, THE(1937, Fr.), w
Anne Zamire
LOLA(1961, Fr./Ital.); PARIS BELONGS TO US(1962, Fr.)
Lucia Zamissi
Misc. Silents
MESSALINA(1924, Ital.)
L. Zamkovoy
Misc. Silents
BREAK-UP, THE(1930, USSR), d
Edward Zammit
1984
UNFAITHFULLY YOURS(1984)
Ava Zamora
BEAU GESTE(1966)
Del Zamora
1984
REPO MAN(1984)
Jorge Zamora
1984
ROMANCING THE STONE(1984)
Jose Zamora
CASTILIAN, THE(1963, Span./U.S.), cos
Rudy Zamora
1001 ARABIAN NIGHTS(1959), anim; BOY NAMED CHARLIE BROWN, A(1969), anim
Rudy Zamora, Jr.
SNOOPY, COME HOME(1972), ed
Zama Zamoria
Misc. Silents
DARING DAYS(1925)
Luigi Zampa
TO LIVE IN PEACE(1947, Ital.), d; ANGELINA(1948, Ital.), d, w; CHILDREN OF CHANCE(1949, Brit.), d; CHILDREN OF CHANCE(1950, Ital.), d; DIFFICULT YEARS(1950, Ital.), d; WHITE LINE, THE(1952, Ital.), d; HIS LAST TWELVE HOURS(1953, Ital.), d; WOMAN OF ROME(1956, Ital.), d, w; LOVE SPECIALIST, THE(1959, Ital.), d, w
Em Zampelas
NAKED BRIGADE, THE(1965, U.S./Gr.), art d
Rinaldo Zamperia
UP THE MACGREGORS(1967, Ital./Span.)
Ettore Zamperini
HERCULES, SAMSON & ULYSSES(1964, Ital.)
Nazzareno Zamperla
SAMSON AND THE SLAVE QUEEN(1963, Ital.); SANDOKAN THE GREAT(1964, Fr./Ital./Span.); PISTOL FOR RINGO, A(1966, Ital./Span.)
Neno Zamperla
TREASURE OF THE FOUR CROWNS(1983, Span./U.S.), stunts
Tony Zamperla
GLADIATORS 7(1964, Span./Ital.)
Giancarlo Zampetti
DESERTER, THE(1971 Ital./Yugo.)
Giulio Zampi
THIRD TIME LUCKY(1950, Brit.), ed; LAUGHTER IN PARADISE(1951, Brit.), ed; MR. POTTS GOES TO MOSCOW(1953, Brit.), ed; TOO MANY CROOKS(1959, Brit.), p; SOME WILL, SOME WON'T(1970, Brit.), p
Giullo Zampi
FATAL NIGHT, THE(1948, Brit.), ed
Mario Zampi
13 MEN AND A GUN(1938, Brit.), p&d; FRENCH WITHOUT TEARS(1939, Brit.), p; SPY FOR A DAY(1939, Brit.), p&d; VOICE IN THE NIGHT, A(1941, Brit.), p; FATAL NIGHT, THE(1948, Brit.), p&d; COME DANCE WITH ME(1950, Brit.), p&d; SHADOW OF THE PAST(1950, Brit.), p, d; THIRD TIME LUCKY(1950, Brit.), p; LAUGHTER IN PARADISE(1951, Brit.), p&d; MR. POTTS GOES TO MOSCOW(1953, Brit.), p&d; TONIGHT'S THE NIGHT(1954, Brit.), p&d; NOW AND FOREVER(1956, Brit.), p&d; YOUR PAST IS SHOWING(1958, Brit.), p&d; TOO MANY CROOKS(1959, Brit.), p, d;

BOTTOMS UP(1960, Brit.), p&d; FIVE GOLDEN HOURS(1961, Brit.), p&d
Lou Zamprogna
FIDDLER ON THE ROOF(1971); MAN OF LA MANCHA(1972)
Victor Zamudio
REPRISAL(1956)
Walter Zamudio
TREASURE OF MAKUBA, THE(1967, U.S./Span.)
Ceco Zamurovich
GOLDEN ARROW, THE(1964, Ital.)
Ivan Zamychovsky
Misc. Silents
TWO DAYS(1929, USSR)
Floretta Zana
RAPE, THE(1965, Gr.)
Michael Zand
1984
PROTOCOL(1984)
Leda Zanda
GAMES MEN PLAY, THE(1968, Arg.)
Ricardo Zandenat
BETRAYAL(1939, Fr.), m
Georg Zander
NOT RECONCILED, OR "ONLY VIOLENCE HELPS WHERE IT RULES"(1969, Ger.)
Hans Zander
NOT RECONCILED, OR "ONLY VIOLENCE HELPS WHERE IT RULES"(1969, Ger.); FOX AND HIS FRIENDS(1976, Ger.); DESPAIR(1978, Ger.)
Josh Zander
PUT UP OR SHUT UP(1968, Arg.), spec eff; PUTNEY SWOPE(1969), spec eff
Peter Zander
FACE IN THE RAIN, A(1963); MYSTERY SUBMARINE(1963, Brit.); RETURN OF MR. MOTO, THE(1965, Brit.)
Ali Zandi
CARAVANS(1978, U.S./Iranian)
Norman Zands
DELINQUENTS, THE(1957)
Philip Van Zandt
SWING HOSTESS(1944); NIGHT AND DAY(1946)
Edgar Zane
HI, GOOD-LOOKIN'(1944), ed
Irving Zane
YOUR NUMBER'S UP(1931), set d
Milton Zane
EYEWITNESS(1981)
Nancy Dee Zane
NIGHT HOLDS TERROR, THE(1955)
Nancy Zane
MA AND PA KETTLE AT HOME(1954)
Rex Zane
Silents
GIRLS DON'T GAMBLE(1921)
Jim Zaner
I'LL TELL THE WORLD(1945)
Jimmy Zaner
LITTLE MEN(1940); HITLER'S CHILDREN(1942); WHERE ARE YOUR CHILDREN?(1943); DELINQUENT DAUGHTERS(1944); MY BUDDY(1944); THEY LIVE IN FEAR(1944)
Guy Zanett
GIRL FROM MONTEREY, THE(1943); HERE COME THE WAVES(1944); TWO O'CLOCK COURAGE(1945)
Guy Zanette
MASQUERADE IN MEXICO(1945); OUR HEARTS WERE GROWING UP(1946); GAMBLING HOUSE(1950); SNOW DOG(1950); UNDER MY SKIN(1950); YELLOW FIN(1951)
A. Danilo Zanetti
CHRISMAS THAT ALMOST WASN'T. THE(1966, Ital.), cos
Jacques Zanetti
LA NUIT DE VARENNES(1983, Fr./Ital.)
Guy Zanetto
BULLFIGHTERS, THE(1945)
John S. Zanft
DUDE RANGER, THE(1934), p
Edward Zang
1984
COTTON CLUB, THE(1984)
Jacob Zanger
Misc. Talkies
HER SECOND MOTHER(1940)
Joseph Zanger
MOTEL, THE OPERATOR(1940)
Dan Zanghi
HIDE IN PLAIN SIGHT(1980)
Dino Zanghi
QUARTET(1981, Brit./Fr.)
Israel Zangwill
PERFECT CRIME, THE(1928), w; MERELY MARY ANN(1931), w; CRIME DOCTOR, THE(1934), w; VERDICT, THE(1946), w
Silents
NURSE MARJORIE(1920), w; BACHELORS' CLUB, THE(1921, Brit.), w
Bruno Zanin
AMARCORD(1974, Ital.)
Luigi Zaninelli
VISITOR, THE(1973, Can.), m
Jerry Zanitsch
NEW YEAR'S EVIL(1980)
Misc. Talkies
THREE WAY WEEKEND(1979)
Lenore Zann
HAPPY BIRTHDAY TO ME(1981); VISITING HOURS(1982, Can.)

Meir Zarchi
I SPIT ON YOUR GRAVE(1983), d&w, ed
Tammy Zarchi
I SPIT ON YOUR GRAVE(1983)
Terry Zarchi
I SPIT ON YOUR GRAVE(1983)
Estelita Zarco
YOUNG BUFFALO BILL(1940)
Estellita Zarco
THREE DARING DAUGHTERS(1948)
Stella Zarco
FOUND ALIVE(1934)
Zarco and D'Lores
CASA MANANA(1951)
Dominique Zardi
LANDRU(1963, Fr./Ital); DIARY OF A CHAMBERMAID(1964, Fr./Ital.);
OPHELIA(1964, Fr.); VICE AND VIRTUE(1965, Fr./Ital.); FANTOMAS(1966, Fr./Ital.);
WEEKEND AT DUNKIRK(1966, Fr./Ital.); LES BICHES(1968, Fr.); PARIS IN THE
MONTH OF AUGUST(1968, Fr.); LA FEMME INFIDELE(1969, Fr./Ital.), a, md;
THINGS OF LIFE, THE(1970, Fr./Ital./Switz.); THIS MAN MUST DIE(1970, Fr./Ital.);
JUST BEFORE NIGHTFALL(1975, Fr./Ital.); VIOLETTE(1978, Fr.); L'ETOILE DU
NORD(1983, Fr.)
Federico Zardi
HEROD THE GREAT(1960, Ital.), w; TROJAN HORSE, THE(1962, Fr./Ital.), w; RED
LIPS(1964, Fr./Ital.), w; SALVATORE GIULIANO(1966, Ital.)
Caroline Zaremba
MAN, A WOMAN AND A KILLER, A(1975)
John Zaremba
MAN'S FAVORITE SPORT [(?)$rb (1964); MAGNETIC MONSTER, THE(1953);
HUMAN DESIRE(1954); CHICAGO SYNDICATE(1955); FIVE AGAINST THE
HOUSE(1955); EARTH VS. THE FLYING SAUCERS(1956); HOUSTON STORY,
THE(1956); REPRISAL(1956); HIT AND RUN(1957); 20 MILLION MILES TO
EARTH(1957); FRANKENSTEIN'S DAUGHTER(1958); YOUNG AND WILD(1958);
VICE RAID(1959); GALLANT HOURS, THE(1960); DANGEROUS CHARTER(1962);
FOLLOW ME, BOYS!(1966); R.P.M.(1970); SCANDALOUS JOHN(1971); WAR BE-
TWEEN MEN AND WOMEN, THE(1972)
Paul Zaremba
CYCLONE PRAIRIE RANGERS(1944)
Elena Zareschi
MERCHANT OF SLAVES(1949, Ital.); ULYSSES(1955, Ital.); COSSACKS, THE(1960,
It.); INVASION 1700(1965, Fr./Ital./Yugo.)
Giancarlo Zarfati
THIEF OF BAGHDAD, THE(1961, Ital./Fr.)
Dragan Zaric
HOROSCOPE(1950, Yugo.)
Janet Zarich
Misc. Talkies
DANNY(1979)
Al Zarilla
WINNING TEAM, THE(1952)
Elly Zarindast
GUNS AND THE FURY, THE(1983), ph
Tony M. Zarindast
GUNS AND THE FURY, THE(1983), p&d, ph
Tony Zarindast
HOUSE ON THE SAND(1967), a, p,d&w
Alexander Zarkhi
LAST HILL, THE(1945, USSR), d, w
Alexander Zarkhl
BALTIC DEPUTY(1937, USSR), d, w
Alexander Zarki
IN THE NAME OF LIFE(1947, USSR), d, w
Andrzej Zarnecki
IDENTIFICATION MARKS: NONE(1969, Pol.)
Natividad Zaro
GUNMEN OF THE RIO GRANDE(1965, Fr./Ital./Span.); SECRET SEVEN, THE(1966,
Ital./Span.), w
Elias Zarou
MIDDLE AGE CRAZY(1980, Can.); STONE COLD DEAD(1980, Can.); IMPROPER
CHANNELS(1981, Can.)
I.F. Zaroubina
THUNDERSTORM(1934, USSR)
Elias Zarov
KIDNAPPING OF THE PRESIDENT, THE(1980, Can.)
Ralina Zarova
REDHEAD(1941)
I. Zarubina
ON HIS OWN(1939, USSR)
A. Zarzhitskaya
RESURRECTION(1963, USSR); FORTY-NINE DAYS(1964, USSR)
Manolo Zarzo
PIZZA TRIANGLE, THE(1970, Ital./Span.)
Manuel Zarzo
SEVEN GUNS FOR THE MACGREGORS(1968, Ital./Span.); UGLY ONES, THE(1968,
Ital./Span.); SEVEN GOLDEN MEN(1969, Fr./Ital./Span.); I HATE MY BODY(1975,
Span./Switz.)
1984
HOLY INNOCENTS, THE(1984, Span.)
Jesus Zarzosa
YOUNG ONE, THE(1961, Mex.), m
Jonathan Zarzosa
UNDER FIRE(1983)
Samuel Zarzosa
UNDER FIRE(1983)
Natasha Zashipina
ONCE THERE WAS A GIRL(1945, USSR)
Alan Zaslove
1001 ARABIAN NIGHTS(1959), d; PHANTOM TOLLBOOTH, THE(1970), anim

Mark Zaslove
1984
ALLEY CAT(1984)
Michael Zaslow
YOU LIGHT UP MY LIFE(1977); METEOR(1979)
Waclaw Zastrzezynski
ASHES AND DIAMONDS(1961, Pol.)
Paul Zastupnevich
BIG CIRCUS, THE(1959), cos; LOST WORLD, THE(1960), cos; VOYAGE TO THE
BOTTOM OF THE SEA(1961), cos; POSEIDON ADVENTURE, THE(1972), cos; TOW-
ERING INFERNO, THE(1974), cos; SWARM, THE(1978), cos; BEYOND THE POSEI-
DON ADVENTURE(1979), cos; WHEN TIME RAN OUT(1980), cos
Jan Zasvorka
EMPEROR AND THE GOLEM, THE(1955, Czech.), set d
Stanislaw Zatloka
CONDUCTOR, THE(1981, Pol.)
Edward Zatlyn
SKI FEVER(1969, U.S./Aust./Czech.), w
Kalman Zatony
HIPPOLYT, THE LACKEY(1932, Hung.)
Milos Zatovic
MC CABE AND MRS. MILLER(1971); GROUNDSTAR CONSPIRACY, THE(1972,
Can.)
Igor Zatsepin
FIREFOX(1982)
Chantal Zaugg
LOVE ON THE RUN(1980, Fr.)
Mark Zavad
STACEY!(1973), ph
Milos Zavadil
SKI FEVER(1969, U.S./Aust./Czech.)
Yuri Zavadsdky
Misc. Silents
BEAR'S WEDDING, THE(1926, USSR)
Yuri Zavadsky
Misc. Silents
MARRIAGE OF THE BEAR, THE(1928, USSR)
Cesare Zavanttini
HELLO, ELEPHANT(1954, Ital.), w
Zavatta
TRAPEZE(1956)
Achille Zavatta
GREEN MARE, THE(1961, Fr./Ital.)
The Zavattas
PARIS DOES STRANGE THINGS(1957, Fr./Ital.)
Cesare Zavattini
I'LL GIVE A MILLION(1938), w; LITTLE MARTYR, THE(1947, Ital.), w; SHOE
SHINE(1947, Ital.), w; BICYCLE THIEF, THE(1949, Ital.), w; WALLS OF MALAPAGA,
THE(1950, Fr./Ital.), w; MIRACLE IN MILAN(1951, Ital.), w; BELLISSIMA(1952,
Ital.), w; FATHER'S DILEMMA(1952, Ital.), w; SKY IS RED, THE(1952, Ital.), w; HIS
LAST TWELVE HOURS(1953, Ital.), w; ALI BABA(1954, Fr.), w; INDISCRETION OF
AN AMERICAN WIFE(1954, U.S./Ital.), w; SIGN OF VENUS, THE(1955, Ital.), w;
UMBERTO D(1955, Ital.), w; ANGELS OF DARKNESS(1956, Ital.), w; GOLD OF
NAPLES(1957, Ital.), w; AWAKENING, THE(1958, Ital.), w; RAT(1960, Yugo.), w;
TWO WOMEN(1961, Ital./Fr.), w; BOCCACCIO '70(1962/Ital./Fr.), w; ARTURO'S
ISLAND(1963, Ital.), w; CONDEMNED OF ALTONA, THE(1963), w; YESTERDAY,
TODAY, AND TOMORROW(1964, Ital./Fr.), w; DOLL THAT TOOK THE TOWN,
THE(1965, Ital.), w; LIPSTICK(1965, Fr./Ital.), w; AFTER THE FOX(1966, U.S./Brit./
Ital.), w; YOUNG WORLD, A(1966, Fr./Ital.), w; WOMAN TIMES SEVEN(1967,
U.S./Fr./Ital.), w; PLACE FOR LOVERS, A(1969, Ital./Fr.), w; WITCHES, THE(1969,
Fr./Ital.), w; SUNFLOWER(1970, Fr./Ital.), w; BRIEF VACATION, A(1975, Ital.), w;
GARDEN OF THE FINZI-CONTINIS, THE(1976, Ital./Ger.), w; CHILDREN OF SAN-
CHEZ, THE(1978, U. S./Mex.), w
A. Zavialov
NO GREATER LOVE(1944, USSR), ph
Alexander Zavialov
ROAD HOME, THE(1947, USSR), ph
Mary Zavian
PARACHUTE NURSE(1942); HAIRY APE, THE(1944); MRS. PARKINGTON(1944);
CRY OF THE HUNTED(1953)
Carmen P. Zavick
FINNEGANS WAKE(1965)
Ben Zavin
WOMAN OF THE RIVER(1954, Fr./Ital.), w
Carol Zavis
TOUCH, THE(1971, U.S./Swed.)
Lee Zavits
GUNS FOR SAN SEBASTIAN(1968, U.S./Fr./Mex./Ital.), spec eff
Lee Zavitz
GONE WITH THE WIND(1939), spec eff; FOREIGN AGENT(1942), spec eff; CAP-
TAIN KIDD(1945), ph; DIARY OF A CHAMBERMAID(1946), spec eff; DESTINATION
MOON(1950), spec eff; SNOW CREATURE, THE(1954), spec eff; AROUND THE
WORLD IN 80 DAYS(1956), spec eff; ON THE BEACH(1959), spec eff; ALAMO,
THE(1960), spec eff; SEVEN WOMEN FROM HELL(1961), spec eff; SODOM AND
GOMORRAH(1962, U.S./Fr./Ital.), spec eff; CAPTAIN SINDBAD(1963), spec eff; PINK
PANTHER, THE(1964), spec eff; TRAIN, THE(1965, Fr./Ital./U.S.), spec eff; VIVA
MARIA(1965, Fr./Ital.), spec eff
Jan Zavorka
MATTER OF DAYS, A(1969, Fr./Czech.), art d
P. Zavtoni
SANDU FOLLOWS THE SUN(1965, USSR)
A. Zavyalov
MORNING STAR(1962, USSR), spec eff; HAMLET(1966, USSR), spec eff
V. Zavyalov
MARRIAGE OF BALZAMINOV, THE(1966, USSR)
Aleksandra Zawieruszanka
WALKOVER(1969, Pol.)

Jean Zay
BITTER VICTORY(1958, Fr.), cos; TRAIN, THE(1965, Fr./Ital./U.S.), cos; IS PARIS BURNING?(1966, U.S./Fr.), cos; WEEKEND AT DUNKIRK(1966, Fr./Ital.), cos; NIGHT OF THE GENERALS, THE(1967, Brit./Fr.), makeup; LADY IN THE CAR WITH GLASSES AND A GUN, THE(1970, U.S./Fr.), cos; DAY OF THE JACKAL, THE(1973, Brit./Fr.), cos
1984
JUST THE WAY YOU ARE(1984), cos
Leon Zay
LAFAYETTE(1963, Fr.), cos; WEEKEND AT DUNKIRK(1966, Fr./Ital.), cos
N. Zaytsev
LULLABY(1961, USSR)
Sergey Zaytsev
GROWN-UP CHILDREN(1963, USSR), ph; LAST GAME, THE(1964, USSR), ph
Paul J. Zaza
KIDNAPPING OF THE PRESIDENT, THE(1980, Can.), m
Paul James Zaza
TITLE SHOT(1982, Can.), m
Paul Zaza
THREE CARD MONTE(1978, Can.), m; PROM NIGHT(1980), m; GAS(1981, Can.), m; MY BLOODY VALENTINE(1981, Can.), m; MELANIE(1982, Can.), m; PORKY'S(1982), m; CHRISTMAS STORY, A(1983), m; CURTAINS(1983, Can.), m
1984
AMERICAN NIGHTMARE(1984), m; ISAAC LITTLEFEATHERS(1984, Can.), m
Fusi Zazayokwe
NAKED PREY, THE(1966, U.S./South Africa)
Fuzi Zazayokwe
DINGAKA(1965, South Africa)
Enriqueta Zazueta
LITTLEST OUTLAW, THE(1955)
Tania Zazulinsky
1984
EDITH AND MARCEL(1984, Fr.), p
Jan Zazvorka
VOYAGE TO THE END OF THE UNIVERSE(1963, Czech.), art d
Stella Zazvorkova
LEMONADE JOE(1966, Czech.); 90 DEGREES IN THE SHADE(1966, Czech./Brit.); HAPPY END(1968, Czech.)
James Zazzarino
ROCKY II(1979)
Yuriy Zbanatskiy
MOTHER AND DAUGHTER(1965, USSR), w
Joseph Zbeda
I SPIT ON YOUR GRAVE(1983), p
Edwin Zbonek
MAD EXECUTIONERS, THE(1965, Ger.), d; MONSTER OF LONDON CITY, THE(1967, Ger.), d
Joe Zboran
RUN LIKE A THIEF(1968, Span.), stunts
Stanislaus [Stanley] Zbyszko
NIGHT AND THE CITY(1950, Brit.)
Wieslaw Zdort
BEADS OF ONE ROSARY, THE(1982, Pol.), ph
Gisela Zdunek
IT HAPPENED IN CANADA(1962, Can.)
Kristi Zea
FAME(1980), cos; ENDLESS LOVE(1981), cos; SHOOT THE MOON(1982), cos; LOVESICK(1983), cos; TERMS OF ENDEARMENT(1983), cos
1984
BEAT STREET(1984), cos; BEST DEFENSE(1984), cos; BIRDY(1984), cos; LITTLE DRUMMER GIRL, THE(1984), cos; UNFAITHFULLY YOURS(1984), cos
Esti Zebka
WORLDS APART(1980, U.S., Israel)
Raymond ZeBrack
GREAT STAGECOACH ROBBERY(1945)
Lisa Zebro
DR. HECKYL AND MR. HYPE(1980)
Dmitriy Zebrov
LADY WITH THE DOG, THE(1962, USSR)
Edward Zebrowski
CONSTANT FACTOR, THE(1980, Pol.)
Jon Zebrowski
BUGSY MALONE(1976, Brit.)
Marko Zec
SOPHIE'S CHOICE(1982)
Ferdinand Zecca
Misc. Silents
LIFE AND PASSION OF CHRIST(1921, Fr.), d
John E. Zecchini
Silents
ADVENTURES OF MR. PICKWICK, THE(1921, Brit.)
Harry Zech
BORDER ROMANCE(1930), ph; CHARLEY'S AUNT(1930), ph; PEACOCK ALLEY(1930), ph; UNDER MONTANA SKIES(1930), ph; THINGS TO COME(1936, Brit.), spec eff
Rosel Zech
LOLA(1982, Ger.); VERONIKA VOSS(1982, Ger.)
Rosl Zech
DIE HAMBURGER KRANKHEIT(1979, Ger./Fr.)
Rolf Zechetbauer
FROM THE LIFE OF THE MARIONETTES(1980, Ger.), prod d
Krystyna Zechwatowicz
YOUNG GIRLS OF WILKO, THE(1979, Pol./Fr.)
Friedrich Zeckendorf
WHITE DEMON, THE(1932, Ger.), w
Nick Zedd
GEEK MAGGOT BINGO(1983), p,d&w, ph,ed&prod d, set d

M. Zednickova
LOVES OF A BLONDE(1966, Czech.)
Eleanor Zee
HUSBANDS(1970); MINNIE AND MOSKOWITZ(1971); PORTNOY'S COMPLAINT(1972); WHAT'S UP, DOC?(1972); OPENING NIGHT(1977); SGT. PEPPER'S LONELY HEARTS CLUB BAND(1978); BLOOD BEACH(1981); I'M DANCING AS FAST AS I CAN(1982)
1984
BREAKIN'(1984)
John A. Zee
GREAT WALDO PEPPER, THE(1975)
1984
BEST DEFENSE(1984); CANNONBALL RUN II(1984)
George E. Zeeman
OH, HEAVENLY DOG!(1980)
George Zeeman
1984
POLICE ACADEMY(1984)
Franco Zeffrelli
ANGELINA(1948, Ital.); LA BOHEME(1965, Ital.), d, prod d; TAMING OF THE SHREW, THE(1967, U.S./Ital.), p, d, w; ROMEO AND JULIET(1968, Brit./Ital.), d, w; BROTHER SUN, SISTER MOON(1973, Brit./Ital.), d, w; CHAMP, THE(1979), d; ENDLESS LOVE(1981), d; LA TRAVIATA(1982), d&w, prod d
Dusica Zegarac
NINTH CIRCLE, THE(1961, Yugo.)
Paul Zegler
CRACKING UP(1977); POPEYE(1980); CHEECH AND CHONG'S NICE DREAMS(1981)
Primo Zeglio
ATTILA(1958, Ital.), w; MORGAN THE PIRATE(1961, Fr./Ital.), d; SWORD OF THE CONQUEROR(1962, Ital.), w; SEVEN SEAS TO CALAIS(1963, Ital.), d; SON OF THE RED CORSAIR(1963, Ital.), d, w; SEVEN REVENGES, THE(1967, Ital.), d, w; MISSION STARDUST(1968, Ital./Span./Ger.), d, w
Zehetbauer
QUERELLE(1983, Ger./Fr.), set d
Gotz Zehetbauer
1984
NEVERENDING STORY, THE(1984, Ger.), set d
Rolf Zehetbauer
RATS, THE(1955, Ger.), set d; TOWN WITHOUT PITY(1961, Ger./Switz./U.S.), art d, set d; JUDGE AND THE SINNER, THE(1964, Ger.), set d; MAN WHO WALKED THROUGH THE WALL, THE(1964, Ger.), art d; SITUATION HOPELESS—BUT NOT SERIOUS(1965), art d; I DEAL IN DANGER(1966), art d; JACK OF DIAMONDS(1967, U.S./Ger.), art d; LAST ESCAPE, THE(1970, Brit.), art d; CABARET(1972), art d; KING, QUEEN, KNAVE(1972, Ger./U.S.), art d; ODESSA FILE, THE(1974, Brit./Ger.), prod d; SERPENT'S EGG, THE(1977, Ger./U.S.), prod d; TWILIGHT'S LAST GLEAMING(1977, U.S./Ger.), prod d; DESPAIR(1978, Ger.), art d; LILI MARLEEN(1981, Ger.), prod d; ACE OF ACES(1982, Fr./Ger.), art d; DAS BOOT(1982), prod d; LOLA(1982, Ger.), art d; NIGHT CROSSING(1982), prod d; VERONIKA VOSS(1982, Ger.), prod d; QUERELLE(1983, Ger./Fr.), prod d
1984
NEVERENDING STORY, THE(1984, Ger.), prod d
Rudolf Zehetgruber
TALL WOMEN, THE(1967, Aust./Ital./Span.), d; MADDEST CAR IN THE WORLD, THE(1974, Ger.), p&d, w; SUPERBUG, SUPER AGENT(1976, Ger.), d&w
Hans Zehetner
HEIDI(1968, Aust.), art d
Willy Zehn
Misc. Silents
DARK CASTLE, THE(1915), d; DR. MACDONALD'S SANATORIUM(1920, Ger.), d
Leroy H. Zehren
TALES OF ROBIN HOOD(1951), w
Lew Zehring
Silents
GAMBLING IN SOULS(1919)
Bela Zeichan
FIXER, THE(1968), art d
Herbert Zeichner
DAY THE FISH CAME OUT, THE(1967. Brit./Gr.)
Al Zeidman
BLONDIE'S ANNIVERSARY(1947)
Allen Zeidman
MAN WHO KNEW TOO MUCH, THE(1956)
B. F. Zeidman
I'VE BEEN AROUND(1935), p, w; IN HIS STEPS(1936), p; PRISON TRAIN(1938), p; GRAND CENTRAL MURDER(1942), p; PACIFIC RENDEZVOUS(1942), p; AIR RAID WARDENS(1943), p
Silents
JUST MARRIED(1928), ed
Benjamin F. Zeidman
HELL'S HOUSE(1932), p
Bennie F. Zeidman
BELOVED(1934), p; WHITE LEGION, THE(1936), p; GIRL LOVES BOY(1937), p; SWEETHEART OF THE NAVY(1937), p
Howard Zeiff
HOUSE CALLS(1978), d
Al Zeigler
SKY RAIDERS(1931), ph
Ernst Zeigler
SOMETHING FOR EVERYONE(1970)
Ted Zeigler
DEVIL AND MAX DEVLIN, THE(1981)
William Zeigler
SUBMARINE ALERT(1943), ed; TORNADO(1943), ed; BATTLE FLAME(1955), ed
Heinrich Zeiler
HIDDEN MENACE, THE(1940, Brit.), w
Michael Zeiniker
HEARTACHES(1981, Can.)

Ingmar Zeisberg
PRISONER OF THE VOLGA(1960, Fr./Ital.)
Alfred Zeisler
GOLD(1934, Ger.), p; SHOT AT DAWN, A(1934, Ger.), p&d; CRIME OVER LON-DON(1936, Brit.), d; MAKE-UP(1937, Brit.), d; ROMANCE AND RICHES(1937, Brit.), d; ENEMY OF WOMEN(1944, d, w; HOUSE ON 92ND STREET, THE(1945); FEAR(1946), d, w; ALIMONY(1949), d; PAROLE, INC.(1949), d; BIRD OF PARADIS-E(1951); WHAT PRICE GLORY?(1952)
Esther Zeitlan
HEAVENLY DAYS(1944)
Doris Zeitlen
UNSTRAP ME(1968)
Orsolya Zeitler
BOYS OF PAUL STREET, THE(1969, Hung./US)
Denny Zeitlin
INVASION OF THE BODY SNATCHERS(1978), m
Esther Zeitlin
MISSION TO MOSCOW(1943); SO DARK THE NIGHT(1946); UNDERCOVER MAN, THE(1949); LADY WITHOUT PASSPORT, A(1950); UNDER MY SKIN(1950); ON DANGEROUS GROUND(1951)
Lawrence Zeitlin
PARADISIO(1962, Brit.), w
Jerome M. Zeitman
DAMNATION ALLEY(1977), p; JUST YOU AND ME, KID(1979), p; HOW TO BEAT THE HIGH COST OF LIVING(1980), p
Ariel Zeitoun
ENTRE NOUS(1983, Fr.), p
Ariel Zeitun
BIRD WATCH, THE(1983, Fr.), p
Larbi Zekkal
HASSAN, TERRORIST(1968, Algerian)
Don Zelaya
GIRL FROM GOD'S COUNTRY(1940); SAN FRANCISCO DOCKS(1941); SALTY O'ROURKE(1945); AMAZON QUEST(1949); MACAO(1952)
Roger Zelazny
DAMNATION ALLEY(1977), w
Ann Zelda
LONG SHOT(1981, Brit.)
Ralph Zeldin
1984
MRS. SOFFEL(1984)
V. Zeldin
TSAR'S BRIDE, THE(1966, USSR)
Vladimir Zeldin
SYMPHONY OF LIFE(1949, USSR); UNCLE VANYA(1972, USSR)
B.F. Zeldman
LET'S TALK IT OVER(1934), p; STRAIGHT FROM THE HEART(1935), p
Mila Zelena
FIREMAN'S BALL, THE(1968, Czech.)
Antonin Zelenka
SKI FEVER(1969, U.S./Aust./Czech.), ed
Jitka Zelenohorska
STOLEN DIRIGIBLE, THE(1966, Czech.)
N. Zelenskaya
TRAIN GOES TO KIEV, THE(1961, USSR), makeup
Seymour Zeliff
Silents
AMAZING WIFE, THE(1919); MYSTERIOUS WITNESS, THE(1923), d
Misc. Silents
SHADOWS OF THE WEST(1921)
Skipper Zeliff
BIG RACE, THE(1934)
Blanche Zelinka
ECHOES OF SILENCE(1966)
Tana Zelinkova
LOVES OF A BLONDE(1966, Czech.)
S. Zelinsky
Misc. Silents
ON THE WARSAW HIGHROAD(1916, USSR)
Vladimir Zelitsky
GIRL FROM POLTAVA(1937); COSSACKS IN EXILE(1939, Ukrainian)
Zellas
DR. KNOCK(1936, Fr.)
Ben Zeller
SANTEE(1973); SHOWDOWN(1973); THOMASINE AND BUSHROD(1974); TIME-RIDER(1983)
1984
RED DAWN(1984)
Bert Zeller
DOLL SQUAD, THE(1973)
Gary Zeller
SCANNERS(1981, Can.), spec eff; VISITING HOURS(1982, Can.), spec eff; VIGI-LANTE(1983), spec eff
Jack Zeller
REUNION IN FRANCE(1942)
Jean Zeller
INVITATION, THE(1975, Fr./Switz.), ph
Jill Zeller
PACK TRAIN(1953)
Wolfgang Zeller
VAMPYR(1932, Fr./Ger.), m; WAJAN(1938, South Bali), m; MARRIAGE IN THE SHADOWS(1948, Ger.), m
Wolgang Zeller
MISTRESS OF ATLANTIS, THE(1932, Ger.), m
Zellermayer
THAT WOMAN(1968, Ger.)
David Zelletti
UNDER FIRE(1983)

David Zelliti
1984
STAR TREK III: THE SEARCH FOR SPOCK(1984)
Lill-Tollie Zellman
NIGHT IN JUNE, A(1940, Swed.)
Mel Zellman
MONITORS, THE(1969)
Tollie Zellman
COUNT OF THE MONK'S BRIDGE, THE(1934, Swed.)
Arthur J. Zellner
Silents
DESERT BLOSSOMS(1921), w; INFAMOUS MISS REVELL, THE(1921), w; MAN WHO, THE(1921), w
Lois Zellner
Silents
INNOCENT LIE, THE(1916), w; AS MEN LOVE(1917), w; LITTLE BROTHER, THE(1917), w; OUT OF LUCK(1919), w; FINE FEATHERS(1921), w; RICH MEN'S WIVES(1922), w; SHOULD A WIFE WORK?(1922), w; LONELY ROAD, THE(1923), w; SCARLET LILY, THE(1923), w; FAMILY SECRET, THE(1924), w; LAW FORBIDS, THE(1924), w
Friedrich Zellnik
Misc. Silents
DARK CASTLE, THE(1915)
Michael Zelnicker
TICKET TO HEAVEN(1981)
Fred Zelnik
HAPPY(1934, Brit.), p&d; MISTER CINDERS(1934, Brit.), d; SOUTHERN RO-SES(1936, Brit.), d; WHO IS GUILTY?(1940, Brit.), d; GIVE ME THE STARS(1944, Brit.), p; HEAVEN IS ROUND THE CORNER(1944, Brit.), p; GLASS MOUNTAIN, THE(1950, Brit), p
Frederick Zelnik
LILAC DOMINO, THE(1940, Brit.), d
Misc. Silents
BOHEMIAN DANCER(1929), d
Friedrich Zelnik
CRIMSON CIRCLE, THE(1930, Brit.), d; BARBERINA(1932, Ger.), p&d
Jerzy Zelnik
WIDOWS' NEST(1977, U.S./Span.)
Michael Zelniker
HOG WILD(1980, Can.); PICK-UP SUMMER(1981)
Richard Zelniker
PICK-UP SUMMER(1981), w
Ingnar Zelsberg
ALWAYS VICTORIOUS(1960, Ital.)
I. Zeltser
HEROES OF THE SEA(1941), w
R. Zelyonaya
SONG OVER MOSCOW(1964, USSR)
Benjamin Zemach
SHE(1935), ch; NIGHT TIDE(1963), ch
Elizabeth Zemach
SAVAGE EYE, THE(1960)
Jackie Zeman
YOUNG DOCTORS IN LOVE(1982)
Jacklyn Zeman
NATIONAL LAMPOON'S CLASS REUNION(1982)
Karel Zeman
FABULOUS WORLD OF JULES VERNE, THE(1961, Czech.), d, w; BARON MUN-CHAUSEN(1962, Czech.), d&w; JOURNEY TO THE BEGINNING OF TIME(1966, Czech.), d, w, art d; STOLEN DIRIGIBLE, THE(1966, Czech.), d, w; ON THE CO-MET(1970, Czech.), d, w
William Zeman
THING, THE(1982)
B. Zemanek
MOST BEAUTIFUL AGE, THE(1970, Czech.)
Jamie Zemarel
NIGHTBEAST(1982)
Robert Zemeckis
I WANNA HOLD YOUR HAND(1978), d, w; 1941(1979), w; USED CARS(1980), d, w
1984
ROMANCING THE STONE(1984), d
Alan Zemel
TREE, THE(1969)
Michel Zemer
MISTER FREEDOM(1970, Fr.), p
Kenneth W. Zemke
PIRATE MOVIE, THE(1982, Aus.), ed
Bob Zemko
ELECTRA GLIDE IN BLUE(1973)
Libuse Zemkova
BOHEMIAN RAPTURE(1948, Czech)
Frantisek Zemlicka
VOYAGE TO THE END OF THE UNIVERSE(1963, Czech.), spec eff
V. Zemlyanikin
SONG OVER MOSCOW(1964, USSR)
Tasha Zemrus
ELECTRIC HORSEMAN, THE(1979)
John Zenda
HALLOWEEN II(1981); BAD BOYS(1983)
Misc. Talkies
BURNOUT(1979)
Fred Zendar
O.S.S.(1946); ROAD TO RIO(1947); WHERE THERE'S LIFE(1947); JOAN OF ARC(1948); STATE OF THE UNION(1948); DARLING, HOW COULD YOU!(1951); SUBMARINE COMMAND(1951); HOT SPELL(1958); HAWAIIANS, THE(1970), stunts; SOMETIMES A GREAT NOTION(1971)
Freddie Zendar
UNION STATION(1950); SON OF PALEFACE(1952); WAR OF THE WORLDS, THE(1953)

George Zenios
WOMAN OF STRAW(1964, Brit.)
Colleen Zenk
ANNIE(1982)
Michael Zenon
BLOODY BROOD, THE(1959, Can.); LAST GUNFIGHTER, THE(1961, Can.)
Stanley Zenor
ONLY WAY HOME, THE(1972)
Suzan Zenor
BABY, THE(1973)
Suzanne Zenor
WAY WE WERE, THE(1973); MOONSHINE WAR, THE(1970); GET TO KNOW YOUR RABBIT(1972); PLAY IT AGAIN, SAM(1972); LUCKY LADY(1975)
Alexander Zenovin
MEN OF THE SEA(1938, USSR), w
Will Zens
CAPTURE THAT CAPSULE(1961), p, d, w; STARFIGHTERS, THE(1964), p,d&w; TO THE SHORES OF HELL(1966), p&d, w; HELL ON WHEELS(1967), d; FROM NASHVILLE WITH MUSIC(1969), ph,m&ed
Misc. Talkies
TRUCKIN' MAN(1975), d
Kate Zentall
GETTING EVEN(1981); STAR CHAMBER, THE(1983)
Raul Zenteno
VAMPIRE'S COFFIN, THE(1958, Mex.), w
Ferenc Zenthe
1984
REVOLT OF JOB, THE(1984, Hung./Ger.)
Robert Zentis
O'HARA'S WIFE(1983), art d
Will Zenz
Misc. Talkies
ROAD TO NASHVILLE(1967), d; HOT SUMMER IN BAREFOOT COUNTY(1974), d
B. Gerardo Zepeda
SLAUGHTER(1972)
Elsa Lorraine Zepeda
ANGEL IN EXILE(1948)
Elsa Zepeda
HOLIDAY IN HAVANA(1949)
Eraclio Zepeda
1984
EL NORTE(1984)
Gerard Zepeda
NIGHT OF THE BLOODY APES zero(1968, Mex.)
Gerardo Zepeda
CAVEMAN(1981)
Jorge Zepeda
IN-LAWS, THE(1979); UNDER FIRE(1983)
1984
EVIL THAT MEN DO, THE(1984)
Zoe Zephyr
ROAD TO HONG KONG, THE(1962, U.S./Brit.)
Massimo Zeppieri
DAY THE SKY EXPLODED, THE(1958, Fr./Ital.)
Vitus Zepplichal
QUERELLE(1983, Ger./Fr.)
Lanie Zera
DOZENS, THE(1981)
Anthony Zerbe
COOL HAND LUKE(1967); WILL PENNY(1968); LIBERATION OF L.B. JONES, THE(1970); MOLLY MAGUIRES, THE(1970); THEY CALL ME MISTER TIBBS(1970); OMEGA MAN, THE(1971); LIFE AND TIMES OF JUDGE ROY BEAN, THE(1972); STRANGE VENEGEANCE OF ROSALIE, THE(1972); LAUGHING POLICEMAN, THE(1973); PAPILLON(1973); PARALLAX VIEW, THE(1974); FAREWELL, MY LOVE-LY(1975); ROOSTER COGBURN(1975); TURNING POINT, THE(1977); WHO'LL STOP THE RAIN?(1978); FIRST DEADLY SIN, THE(1980); SOGGY BOTTOM U.S.A.(1982); DEAD ZONE, THE(1983)
Arnette Jens Zerbe
CLOUD DANCER(1980)
Sylvia Zerbib
CHANEL SOLITAIRE(1981)
Luigi Zerbinati
HIGH INFIDELITY(1965, Fr./Ital.); FELLINI SATYRICON(1969, Fr./Ital.)
Mimi Zerbini
GNOME-MOBILE, THE(1967)
Paul Zeremba
JAM SESSION(1944)
Zerenin
Silents
BATTLESHIP POTEMKIN, THE(1925, USSR)
Nikolai M. Zeretelli
Misc. Silents
AELITA(1929, USSR)
Zerguine
LA BALANCE(1983, Fr.)
Samuel Zerinsky
W.I.A.(WOUNDED IN ACTION)*1/2 (1966), p
D. Zerkalova
ON HIS OWN(1939, USSR)
Hans H. Zerlett
GREAT YEARNING, THE(1930, Ger.), w
Hans Zerlett
BEGGAR STUDENT, THE(1931,Brit.), w; HIDDEN MENACE, THE(1940, Brit.), w
Milan Zerman
WISHING MACHINE(1971, Czech.)
Larry Zerner
FRIDAY THE 13TH PART III(1982)

Zero
THEY SHALL HAVE MUSIC(1939)
Zero the Dog
HIGH SIERRA(1941)
Ronald Zerra
EYES OF A STRANGER(1980), p
Frantisek Zerslicka
ROCKET TO NOWHERE(1962, Czech.), spec eff
Markos Zervas
MADALENA(1965, Gr.), art d; STEFANIA(1968, Gr.), set d
George Zervos
YOUNG APHRODITES(1966, Gr.), p
Pantelis Zervos
MADALENA(1965, Gr.)
Hans Zesch-Ballot
WITNESS OUT OF HELL(1967, Ger./Yugo.)
Philip Zeska
WORLD AND THE FLESH, THE(1932), w
Nick Zesses
SUGAR HILL(1974), m
Barry Zetlin
GALAXY OF TERROR(1981), ed; SORCERESS(1983), ed
1984
BAD MANNERS(1984), ed; BREAKIN' 2: ELECTRIC BOOGALOO(1984), ed
Edith Zetling
PLEASE, NOT NOW!(1963, Fr./Ital.)
Mai Zetterling
FRIEDA(1947, Brit.); TORMENT(1947, Swed.); GIRL IN THE PAINTING, THE(1948, Brit.); BAD LORD BYRON, THE(1949, Brit.); QUARTET(1949, Brit.); LOST PEOPLE, THE(1950, Brit.); BLACKMAILED(1951, Brit.); HELL IS SOLD OUT(1951, Brit.); NAUGHTY ARLETTE(1951, Brit.); FRIGHTENED BRIDE, THE(1952, Brit.); DESPER-ATE MOMENT(1953, Brit.); RINGER, THE(1953, Brit.); DANCE LITTLE LADY(1954, Brit.); KNOCK ON WOOD(1954); PRIZE OF GOLD, A(1955); ABANDON SHIP(1957, Brit.); TRUTH ABOUT WOMEN, THE(1958, Brit.); FACES IN THE DARK(1960, Brit.); PICCADILLY THIRD STOP(1960, Brit.); JET STORM(1961, Brit.); OFFBEAT(1961, Brit.); MAIN ATTRACTION, THE(1962, Brit.); NIGHT IS MY FUTURE(1962, Swed.); ONLY TWO CAN PLAY(1962, Brit.); BAY OF SAINT MICHEL, THE(1963, Brit.); LOVING COUPLES(1966, Swed.), d, w; NIGHT GAMES(1966, Swed.), d, w; MAN WHO FINALLY DIED, THE(1967, Brit.); GIRLS, THE(1972, Swed.), d, w; LOVE(1982, Can.), d, w
1984
SCRUBBERS(1984, Brit.), d, w
Eva-Lena Zetterlund
EMIGRANTS, THE(1972, Swed.)
Monica Zetterlund
NIGHT GAMES(1966, Swed.); EMIGRANTS, THE(1972, Swed.); NEW LAND, THE(1973, Swed.)
Michael Zettler
DIRTYMOUTH(1970)
Mike Zetz
BELLBOY, THE(1960)
Norbert Zeuner
DAY WILL COME, A(1960, Ger.)
Bruno Zeus
GEEK MAGGOT BINGO(1983)
Lily Zevaco
ARTHUR(1931, Fr.)
Standley Zevic
BREAK IN THE CIRCLE, THE(1957, Brit.)
Stanley Zevic
MISSILE FROM HELL(1960, Brit.)
Esther Zewko
HANNAH K.(1983, Fr.)
Willy Zeyn, Jr.
BOMBARDMENT OF MONTE CARLO, THE(1931, Ger.), ed; F.P. 1 DOESN'T AN-SWER(1933, Ger.), ed
A. Zeytounian
FORTUNE AND MEN'S EYES(1971, U.S./Can.)
L. Zgvauri
FATHER OF A SOLDIER(1966, USSR)
Evgraf Zhachovski
Misc. Silents
REVOLT IN THE DESERT(1932, USSR)
Anatoliy Zhaden
HUNTING IN SIBERIA(1962, USSR), w
O. Zhakov
GREAT CITIZEN, THE(1939, USSR)
Oleg Zhakov
IN THE NAME OF LIFE(1947, USSR); ROAD HOME, THE(1947, USSR)
Otto Zhakov
BALTIC DEPUTY(1937, USSR); SKI BATTALION(1938, USSR)
V. Zharikov
FATHER OF A SOLDIER(1966, USSR)
Ye. Zharikov
MY NAME IS IVAN(1963, USSR)
M. Zharov
NEW HORIZONS(1939, USSR)
Mikhail Zharov
IVAN THE TERRIBLE(Part I, 1947, USSR); ROAD TO LIFE(1932, USSR); THUNDER-STORM(1934, USSR); TAXI TO HEAVEN(1944, USSR); ANNA CROSS, THE(1954, USSR)
M. Zharova
SUMMER TO REMEMBER, A(1961, USSR); SUN SHINES FOR ALL, THE(1961, USSR); HOUSE ON THE FRONT LINE, THE(1963, USSR)
G. Zhdanova
VIOLIN AND ROLLER(1962, USSR)
M. Zhdanova
Misc. Silents
DON'T BUILD YOUR HAPPINESS ON YOUR WIFE AND CHILD(1917, USSR); STRONG MAN, THE(1917, USSR); BRUISED BY THE STORMS OF LIFE(1918, USSR)

Ye. Zhdanova
SUMMER TO REMEMBER, A(1961, USSR)

Anna Zheimo
Misc. Silents
CLOAK, THE(1926, USSR)

Yuri Zheliabuzhsky
Misc. Silents
CHILDREN – FLOWERS OF LIFE(1919, USSR), d; DOMESTIC-AGITATOR(1920, USSR), d; FATHER FROST(1924, USSR), d; STATION MASTER, THE(1928, USSR), d

Yuri Zhelyabuzhsky
Misc. Silents
CIGARETTE GIRL FROM MOSSELPROM(1924, USSR), d

Brigitte Zhendre-Laforest
SOFT SKIN, THE(1964, Fr.)

Massard Kur Zhene
SILENT ENEMY, THE(1930), m

G. Zhenov
CITY OF YOUTH(1938, USSR)

Natalya Zheromskaya
RED AND THE WHITE, THE(1969, Hung./USSR)

I. Zhevago
RESURRECTION(1963, USSR); OPTIMISTIC TRAGEDY, THE(1964, USSR)

Suliko Zhgenti
FATHER OF A SOLDIER(1966, USSR), w

A. Zhila
KATERINA IZMAILOVA(1969, USSR)

Andrei Zhilinsky
Misc. Silents
KATORGA(1928, USSR)

V. Zhilkin
PEACE TO HIM WHO ENTERS(1963, USSR)

Svetlana Zhivankova
TRAIN GOES TO KIEV, THE(1961, USSR); SONG OVER MOSCOW(1964, USSR)

Sasha Zhiveynov
WELCOME KOSTYA!(1965, USSR)

A. Zhivotov
TWELFTH NIGHT(1956, USSR), m

Olga Zhizneva
HOUSE WITH AN ATTIC, THE(1964, USSR); GARNET BRACELET, THE(1966, USSR)

Georgi Zhonov
STORM PLANET(1962, USSR)

A. Zhorzholiani
DRAGONFLY, THE(1955 USSR)

L. Zhuchkova
HOME FOR TANYA, A(1961, USSR), ed

A. Zhukov
CHILDHOOD OF MAXIM GORKY(1938, Russ.); GORDEYEV FAMILY, THE(1961, U.S.S.R.)

L. Zhukov
Misc. Silents
WHEN WILL WE DEAD AWAKEN?(1918, USSR)

Garen Zhukovskaya
SPRINGTIME ON THE VOLGA(1961, USSR)

L. Zhukovskaya
RESURRECTION(1963, USSR)

German Zhukovskiy
MOTHER AND DAUGHTER(1965, USSR), m

V. Zhukovskiy
JACK FROST(1966, USSR)

Boris Zhukovsky
WINGS OF VICTORY(1941, USSR)

E. Zhukovsky
BOUNTIFUL SUMMER(1951, USSR), m

Vasili Zhuravlev
SPACE SHIP, THE(1935, USSR), d

A. Zhutyev
BALLAD OF COSSACK GLOOTA(1938, USSR)

A. Zhyuraytis
GORDEYEV FAMILY, THE(1961, U.S.S.R.), md; LITTLE HUMPBACKED HORSE, THE(1962, USSR), md

Georgiy Zhzhyonov
UNCOMMON THIEF, AN(1967, USSR)

W.P. Zibaso
RED-DRAGON(1967, Ital./Ger./US), w

Werner P. Zibaso
LADY HAMILTON(1969, Ger./Ital./Fr.), w

Werner Zibaso
DAS LETZTE GEHEIMNIS(1959, Ger.), w

Tommy Zibelli II
HARDLY WORKING(1981)

Andre Zibral
LA MARSEILLAISE(1938, Fr.)

Rosy Zichel
WAR OF THE ZOMBIES, THE(1965 Ital.)

Count Zichy
COLONEL BLIMP(1945, Brit.)

Frederik Zichy
COUP DE GRACE(1978, Ger./Fr.)

T.B.R. Zichy
BOMB IN THE HIGH STREET(1961, Brit.), p

Theodore Zichy
PRIVATE'S PROGRESS(1956, Brit.); NIGHT WITHOUT PITY(1962, Brit.), d; DOOMSDAY AT ELEVEN(1963 Brit.), d

Claude Zidi
BANZAI(1983, Fr.), d, w
1984
MY NEW PARTNER(1984, Fr.), p&d, w

Helene Zidi
1984
HERE COMES SANTA CLAUS(1984)

Janis Zido
HOUSE ON SORORITY ROW, THE(1983)

B. F. Ziedman
WAKE UP AND DREAM(1934), p; YOUNGEST PROFESSION, THE(1943), p; NOTHING BUT TROUBLE(1944), p

Howard Zieff
SLITHER(1973), d; HEARTS OF THE WEST(1975), d; MAIN EVENT, THE(1979), d; PRIVATE BENJAMIN(1980), d
1984
UNFAITHFULLY YOURS(1984), d

Erich Ziegel
MOSCOW SHANGHAI(1936, Ger.); LIFE BEGINS ANEW(1938, Ger.)

Carla Ziegfeld
Misc. Talkies
SMOKEY AND THE HOTWIRE GANG(1980)

Florenz Ziegfeld
WHOOPEE(1930), p

Helene Ziegfeld
Misc. Silents
MY COUNTRY FIRST(1916)

Mr. Florenz Ziegfeld
GLORIFYING THE AMERICAN GIRL(1930)

Mrs. Florenz Ziegfeld
GLORIFYING THE AMERICAN GIRL(1930)

The Ziegfeld Girls
ZIEGFELD FOLLIES(1945)

Al Ziegler
INNER SANCTUM(1948), ph

Anne Ziegler
DEMOBBED(1944, Brit.); WALTZ TIME(1946, Brit.); LAUGHING LADY, THE(1950, Brit.)

Bill Ziegler
MC Q(1974), ed

Don Ziegler
CANDIDE(1962, Fr.)

Ernest Ziegler
WILLY WONKA AND THE CHOCOLATE FACTORY(1971)

Hans Ziegler
FOREVER MY LOVE(1962)

Henry Ziegler
Silents
GREY DEVIL, THE(1926), w

Isabelle Gibson Ziegler
SEVEN CITIES OF GOLD(1955), w

Karl Ziegler
MONEY ON THE STREET(1930, Aust.)

Ludwig Ziegler
U-47 LT. COMMANDER PRIEN(1967, Ger.), makeup

Martha Ziegler
EIGHT GIRLS IN A BOAT(1932, Ger.)

Regina Ziegler
KAMIKAZE '89(1983, Ger.), p; MALOU(1983), p
1984
CLASS ENEMY(1984, Ger.), p

Samuel Ziegler
COMMAND PERFORMANCE(1931), p

Ted Ziegler
HITCHHIKERS, THE(1972)

William H. Ziegler
I'LL BE SEEING YOU(1944), ed; ROPE(1948), ed; NEVER FEAR(1950), ed; STRANGERS ON A TRAIN(1951), ed

William Ziegler
CAPTAIN FURY(1939), ed; HOUSEKEEPER'S DAUGHTER(1939), ed; HER FIRST ROMANCE(1940), ed; SAPS AT SEA(1940), ed; NO HANDS ON THE CLOCK(1941), ed; I LIVE ON DANGER(1942), ed; TORPEDO BOAT(1942), ed; WILDCAT(1942), ed; WRECKING CREW(1942), ed; AERIAL GUNNER(1943), ed; ALASKA HIGHWAY(1943), ed; HIGH EXPLOSIVE(1943), ed; JACK LONDON(1943), ed; MINESWEEPER(1943), ed; HAIRY APE, THE(1944), ed; SPELLBOUND(1945), ed; DUEL IN THE SUN(1946), ed; HIGH TIDE(1947), ed; STRIKE IT RICH(1948), ed; NOT WANTED(1949), ed; ADMIRAL WAS A LADY, THE(1950), ed; HARD, FAST, AND BEAUTIFUL(1951), ed; STARLIFT(1951), ed; LION AND THE HORSE, THE(1952), ed; DESERT SONG, THE(1953), ed; EDDIE CANTOR STORY, THE(1953), ed; REBEL WITHOUT A CAUSE(1955), ed; SEA CHASE, THE(1955), ed; YOUNG AT HEART(1955), ed; SERENADE(1956), ed; TOWARD THE UNKNOWN(1956), ed; PAJAMA GAME, THE(1957), ed; AUNTIE MAME(1958), ed; NO TIME FOR SERGEANTS(1958), ed; ONIONHEAD(1958), ed; YELLOWSTONE KELLY(1959), ed; YOUNG PHILADELPHIANS, THE(1959), ed; ICE PALACE(1960), ed; FEVER IN THE BLOOD, A(1961), ed; SUSAN SLADE(1961), ed; MUSIC MAN, THE(1962), ed; ROME ADVENTURE(1962), ed; CRITIC'S CHOICE(1963), ed; ISLAND OF LOVE(1963), ed; WALL OF NOISE(1963), ed; MY FAIR LADY(1964), ed; BRAINSTORM(1965), ed; MY BLOOD RUNS COLD(1965), ed; NEVER TOO LATE(1965), ed; TWO ON A GUILLOTINE(1965), ed; COVENANT WITH DEATH, A(1966), ed; FINE MADNESS, A(1966), ed; FIRECREEK(1968), ed; PRETTY POISON(1968), ed; BIG BOUNCE, THE(1969), ed; TOPAZ(1969, Brit.), ed; EL CONDOR(1970), ed; OMEGA MAN, THE(1971), ed; 1776(1972), ed

Helmut Ziegner
RUMPELSTILTSKIN(1965, Ger.); PUSS 'N' BOOTS(1967, Ger.)

Jerzy Zielinski
1984
CAL(1984, Ireland), ph; SHIVERS(1984, Pol.), ph

Rafal Zielinski
SCREWBALLS(1983), d
1984
HEY BABE!(1984, Can.), p, d, w

Ulla Zieman
DAVID(1979, Ger.), w
Sonja Ziemann
MADE IN HEAVEN(1952, Brit.); MERRY WIVES OF WINDSOR, THE(1952, Ger.); AFFAIRS OF JULIE, THE(1958, Ger.); EIGHTH DAY OF THE WEEK, THE(1959, Pol./Ger.); SECRET WAYS, THE(1961); MATTER OF WHO, A(1962, Brit.); JOURNEY INTO NOWHERE(1963, Brit.); BRIDGE AT REMAGEN, THE(1969); DE SADE(1969)
Bob Ziembicki
CHAINED HEAT(1983 U.S./Ger.), art d
Bob Ziembiki
DR. HECKYL AND MR. HYPE(1980), art d
Ziembinsky
BRASIL ANNO 2,000(1968, Braz.)
Alfred Ziemen
IT HAPPENED HERE(1966, Brit.)
Bruno Ziemer
1914(1932, Ger.)
Gregor Ziemer
HITLER'S CHILDREN(1942), w
Chip Zien
ROSE, THE(1979); SO FINE(1981)
1984
ULTIMATE SOLUTION OF GRACE QUIGLEY, THE(1984)
Stanislaus Zienciakiewicz
MR. POTTS GOES TO MOSCOW(1953, Brit.)
Dorothy Zienciowska
MOONLIGHTING(1982, Brit.)
Bruno Ziener
BOMBARDMENT OF MONTE CARLO, THE(1931, Ger.); JOHNNY STEALS EUROPE(1932, Ger.); M(1933, Ger.); FINAL CHORD, THE(1936, Ger.); TESTAMENT OF DR. MABUSE, THE(1943, Ger.)
Capt. H.M. Zier
SHE GOES TO WAR(1929)
Jerry Zier
DYNAMITE(1930)
Silents
RACING ROMEO(1927)
Marjorie Zier
Silents
PHANTOM OF THE RANGE(1928)
Misc. Silents
CACTUS TRAILS(1927)
Ian Ziering
ENDLESS LOVE(1981)
Samuel Zierler
SHE GOT WHAT SHE WANTED(1930), p; SALVATION NELL(1931), p; TOMORROW AT SEVEN(1933), p; GOODBYE LOVE(1934), p
Ulla Ziermann
ALL-AROUND REDUCED PERSONALITY–OUTTAKES, THE(1978, Ger.)
Gisela Zies
ALL-AROUND REDUCED PERSONALITY–OUTTAKES, THE(1978, Ger.)
Alfred Ziesler
MISSION TO MOSCOW(1943); DESERT RATS, THE(1953)
Jerry Ziesmer
ROCKY II(1979)
Eva Zietek
MAN OF MARBLE(1979, Pol.)
Lloyd Ziff
LIQUID SKY(1982)
Mano Ziffer-Teschenbruck
Misc. Silents
PAREMA, CRERATURE FROM THE STARWORLD(1922, Aust.), d
Lester Ziffren
CITY GIRL(1938), w; SHARPSHOOTERS(1938), w; BOY FRIEND(1939), w; CHARLIE CHAN IN PANAMA(1940), w; CHARLIE CHAN'S MURDER CRUISE(1940), w; CHARTER PILOT(1940), w; MAN WHO WOULDN'T TALK, THE(1940), w; MURDER OVER NEW YORK(1940), w; CHARLIE CHAN IN RIO(1941), w
Carl Ziffrer
CHRISTMAS STORY, A(1983), m
Joel Zifkin
HANK WILLIAMS: THE SHOW HE NEVER GAVE(1982, Can.)
Joseph Zigman
WIND ACROSS THE EVERGLADES(1958), ed
Zigmit
SON OF MONGOLIA(1936, USSR)
Istvan Zigon
HIPPOLYT, THE LACKEY(1932, Hung.), w
Martine Ziguel [Sophie Dares]
UNINHIBITED, THE(1968, Fr./Ital./Span.)
Max Zihlmann
48 HOURS TO ACAPULCO(1968, Ger.), w; NOT RECONCILED, OR "ONLY VIOLENCE HELPS WHERE IT RULES"(1969, Ger.)
Ann Zika
HOODLUM, THE(1951); TWO TICKETS TO BROADWAY(1951)
Christian Zika
1941(1979)
Ann Zikal
WHERE DANGER LIVES(1950)
Dick Ziker
WHITE LIGHTNING(1973); MITCHELL(1975); HEROES(1977); STRAIGHT TIME(1978), stunts
1984
AGAINST ALL ODDS(1984)
John Zila, Jr.
HELLCATS, THE(1968), w
Lajos Zilahy
VIRTUOUS SIN, THE(1930), w; FIREBIRD, THE(1934), w; SUN SHINES, THE(1939, Hung.), w; ADRIFT(1971, Czech.), w

Jacob Zilber
INBREAKER, THE(1974, Can.), w
Voel Zilberg
SIMCHON FAMILY, THE(1969, Israel), w
Yoel Zilberg
SIMCHON FAMILY, THE(1969, Israel), d
A. Zilbert
SONG OVER MOSCOW(1964, USSR)
Sander Zilbert
1984
BAY BOY(1984, Can.)
Gregory Zilboorg
Silents
HE WHO GETS SLAPPED(1924), w
Wolfgang Zilgzer
EVERYTHING HAPPENS AT NIGHT(1939)
Gunar Zilinskiy
SUNFLOWER(1970, Fr./Ital.)
Muriel Zillah
HAPPIDROME(1943, Brit.)
Heinrich Zille
MOTHER KUSTERS GOES TO HEAVEN(1976, Ger.), w
Robert Ziller
FROZEN ALIVE(1966, Brit./Ger.), ph
Robert Zilliox
LONE WOLF McQUADE(1983), set d
Hans Zillman
SQUEEZE, THE(1980, Ital.), art d
John Zilly
I WAS A MALE WAR BRIDE(1949); TWELVE O'CLOCK HIGH(1949)
Zelimar Zilnik
EARLY WORKS(1970, Yugo.), d, w
Wolfgang A. Zilzer
LADY HAS PLANS, THE(1942)
Wolfgang Zilzer
CASE VAN GELDERN(1932, Ger.); HOTEL IMPERIAL(1939); NINOTCHKA(1939); TELEVISION SPY(1939); DISPATCH FROM REUTERS, A(1940); UNDERGROUND(1941); INVISIBLE AGENT(1942); JOAN OF OZARK(1942); TO BE OR NOT TO BE(1942); APPOINTMENT IN BERLIN(1943); BEHIND THE RISING SUN(1943); HITLER'S MADMAN(1943); MARGIN FOR ERROR(1943); PARIS AFTER DARK(1943); STRANGE DEATH OF ADOLF HITLER, THE(1943); THEY CAME TO BLOW UP AMERICA(1943); THEY GOT ME COVERED(1943); IN OUR TIME(1944); NO SURVIVORS, PLEASE(1963, Ger.)
Misc. Silents
THERESE RAQUIN(1928, Fr./Ger.); SUCH IS LIFE(1929, Czech)
Jerrold Ziman
NINE TO FIVE(1980); HARRY'S WAR(1981)
Jerry Ziman
CALIFORNIA SUITE(1978); CHEAP DETECTIVE, THE(1978)
Sharon Ziman
DINER(1982)
Josef Zimanich
MAN BEAST(1956), m; JOURNEY TO FREEDOM(1957), m; SPACE MASTER X-7(1958), m; INCREDIBLE PETRIFIED WORLD, THE(1959), md
Al Zimbalist
CAT WOMEN OF THE MOON(1953), p, w; MISS ROBIN CRUSOE(1954), w; KING DINOSAUR(1955), p, w; BABY FACE NELSON(1957), p; MONSTER FROM THE GREEN HELL(1958), p; TARZAN, THE APE MAN(1959), p; WATUSI(1959), p; DRUMS OF AFRICA(1963), p
Alfred Zimbalist
TAFFY AND THE JUNGLE HUNTER(1965), w; YOUNG DILLINGER(1965), p
Donald Zimbalist
VALLEY OF THE DRAGONS(1961), w, d&w; TAFFY AND THE JUNGLE HUNTER(1965), w; YOUNG DILLINGER(1965), w
Efrem Zimbalist, Jr.
HOUSE OF STRANGERS(1949); BAND OF ANGELS(1957); BOMBERS B-52(1957); DEEP SIX, THE(1958); HOME BEFORE DARK(1958); TOO MUCH, TOO SOON(1958); VIOLENT ROAD(1958); CROWDED SKY, THE(1960); BY LOVE POSSESSED(1961); FEVER IN THE BLOOD, A(1961); CHAPMAN REPORT, THE(1962); HARLOW(1965); REWARD, THE(1965); WAIT UNTIL DARK(1967); AIRPORT 1975(1974)
Sam Zimbalist
TARZAN ESCAPES(1936), p; LONDON BY NIGHT(1937), p; MARRIED BEFORE BREAKFAST(1937), p; NAVY BLUE AND GOLD(1937), p; CROWD ROARS, THE(1938), p; PARADISE FOR THREE(1938), p; LADY OF THE TROPICS(1939), p; TARZAN FINDS A SON!(1939), p; THESE GLAMOUR GIRLS(1939), p; BOOM TOWN(1940), p; TORTILLA FLAT(1942), p; THIRTY SECONDS OVER TOKYO(1944), p; ADVENTURE(1945), p; KILLER McCOY(1947), p; KING SOLOMON'S MINES(1950), p; SIDE STREET(1950), p; TOO YOUNG TO KISS(1951), p; MOGAMBO(1953), p; BEAU BRUMMELL(1954), p; CATERED AFFAIR, THE(1956), p; TRIBUTE TO A BADMAN(1956), p; BARRETTS OF WIMPOLE STREET, THE(1957), p; I ACCUSE(1958, Brit.), p; BEN HUR(1959), p
Sam S. Zimbalist
ALIAS JIMMY VALENTINE(1928), ed; OUR MODERN MAIDENS(1929), ed
Silents
WIZARD OF OZ, THE(1925), ed; FOREIGN DEVILS(1927), ed; JOHNNY GET YOUR HAIR CUT(1927), ed; ADVENTURER, THE(1928), ed; BABY MINE(1928), ed; SMART SET, THE(1928), ed; WHILE THE CITY SLEEPS(1928), ed; OUR MODERN MAIDENS(1929), ed
Sam Z. Zimbalist
BROADWAY MELODY, THE(1929), ed
Stephanie Zimbalist
MAGIC OF LASSIE, THE(1978); AWAKENING, THE(1980)
Maude Zimbla
BIG BUSINESS(1934, Brit.)
Zimbo
Silents
MAN WHO LAUGHS, THE(1927)

John Zimeas
HOUSE OF USHER(1960)
Ben Zimet
MEETINGS WITH REMARKABLE MEN(1979, Brit.)
Julian Zimet
DEVIL PAYS OFF, THE(1941), w; SIERRA SUE(1941), w; HELLDORADO(1946), w; SAIGON(1948), w; STRAWBERRY ROAN, THE(1948), w
Paul Zimet
MILESTONES(1975)
Victor Zimet
1984
NEW YORK NIGHTS(1984), ed
L. Zimina
SANDU FOLLOWS THE SUN(1965, USSR)
Valentina Zimina
Silents
WOMAN ON TRIAL, THE(1927); SCARLET LADY, THE(1928)
Maurice Zimm
JEOPARDY(1953), w; CREATURE FROM THE BLACK LAGOON(1954), w; PRODIGAL, THE(1955), w; AFFAIR IN HAVANA(1957), w; GOOD DAY FOR A HANGING(1958), w
Joe Zimmardi
WARRIORS, THE(1979)
Bernard Zimmer
BATTLE, THE(1934, Fr.), w; LILIOM(1935, Fr.), w; CARNIVAL IN FLANDERS(1936, Fr.), w; SECOND BUREAU(1936, Fr.), w; UN CARNET DE BAL(1938, Fr.), w
Ed Zimmer
Silents
GOLD RUSH, THE(1925)
George F. Zimmer
SPECIAL AGENT K-7(1937), w
Hans Zimmer
MOONLIGHTING(1982, Brit.), m
1984
SUCCESS IS THE BEST REVENGE(1984, Brit.), m
Kim Zimmer
BODY HEAT(1981)
Laurie Zimmer
ASSAULT ON PRECINCT 13(1976)
Lee Zimmer
LONELYHEARTS(1958)
Norma Zimmer
SERENADE(1956); TOM THUMB(1958, Brit./U.S.)
Pierre Zimmer
LIFE LOVE DEATH(1969, Fr./Ital.); SECRET WORLD(1969, Fr.); CROOK, THE(1971, Fr.)
Sonia Zimmer
PROM NIGHT(1980); BY DESIGN(1982)
Cpl. Stuart Zimmerly, USAR
TOKYO FILE 212(1951)
Don Zimmerman
COMING HOME(1978), ed; HEAVEN CAN WAIT(1978), ed; UNCLE JOE SHANNON(1978), ed; BEING THERE(1979), ed; CHANGE OF SEASONS, A(1980), ed; BARBAROSA(1982), ed; BEST FRIENDS(1982), ed; ROCKY III(1982), ed; STAYING ALIVE(1983), ed
1984
TEACHERS(1984), ed
Gerard Zimmerman
NAKED HEARTS(1970, Fr.)
Gordon Zimmerman
WILD WHEELS(1969)
1984
JOHNNY DANGEROUSLY(1984)
Harry Zimmerman
STEEL CLAW, THE(1961), m, md; SAMAR(1962), m, md
Jack Zimmerman
GOIN' DOWN THE ROAD(1970, Can.); RECOMMENDATION FOR MERCY(1975, Can.)
John Zimmerman
STUCKEY'S LAST STAND(1980)
Kay Zimmerman
FLASH GORDON(1980)
Laura Zimmerman
PRETTY BABY(1978)
Louis Zimmerman
FIRST MRS. FRASER, THE(1932, Brit.), p
Matt Zimmerman
THUNDERBIRD 6(1968, Brit.); THUNDERBIRDS ARE GO(1968, Brit.)
Paul D. Zimmerman
KING OF COMEDY, THE(1983), w
Paul Zimmerman
LOVERS AND LIARS(1981, Ital.), w
Robert Zimmerman
1984
SILENT MADNESS(1984), w
Stefanie Zimmerman
FAME(1980)
Vernon Zimmerman
UNHOLY ROLLERS(1972), d, w; HEX(1973), w; BOBBIE JO AND THE OUTLAW(1976), w; FADE TO BLACK(1980), d&w; DEADHEAD MILES(1982), p, d
Vic Zimmerman
SOUTHERN YANKEE, A(1948)
Victor Zimmerman
FLIGHT ANGELS(1940); MURDER IN THE AIR(1940); BULLETS FOR O'HARA(1941); HIGHWAY WEST(1941); LUCKY DEVILS(1941); NAVY BLUES(1941); GREAT IMPERSONATION, THE(1942); INVISIBLE AGENT(1942); JUKE GIRL(1942); SECRET ENEMIES(1942); SIN TOWN(1942); STRANGE CASE OF DR. RX, THE(1942); THEY DIED WITH THEIR BOOTS ON(1942); MAGNIFICENT DOLL(1946); ALL MY SONS(1948); NAKED CITY, THE(1948)

Waldo Zimmerman
1984
MAKING THE GRADE(1984)
Babsi Zimmermann
NEW LIFE STYLE, THE(1970, Ger.)
Ed Zimmermann
WHO IS HARRY KELLERMAN AND WHY IS HE SAYING THOSE TERRIBLE THINGS ABOUT ME?(1971)
Elisabeth Zimmermann
TROMBA, THE TIGER MAN(1952, Ger.), w
George Zimmermann
TEENAGE MOTHER(1967), ph
Terri Zimmern
MANSTER, THE(1962, Jap.)
Don Zimmers
SCREAMS OF A WINTER NIGHT(1979), m
Marya Zimmet
RAIN PEOPLE, THE(1969)
Zimmie-the-Black-Tail-Fawn
CHALLENGE THE WILD(1954)
Nikolai Zimovetz
TARAS FAMILY, THE(1946, USSR)
V. Zimovoy
Misc. Silents
CRIME AND PUNISHMENT(1913, USSR)
Fedora Zincone
DAY AND THE HOUR, THE(1963, Fr./ Ital.), ed; JOY HOUSE(1964, Fr.), ed
Marina Zindahl
MONTENEGRO(1981, Brit./Swed.)
Paul Zindel
EFFECT OF GAMMA RAYS ON MAN-IN-THE-MOON MARIGOLDS, THE(1972), w; UP THE SANDBOX(1972), w; MAME(1974), w
Stanislav Zindulka
DIVINE EMMA, THE(1983, Czech,)
Mohammed Zineth
MADAME ROSA(1977, Fr.)
Michael Zingale
SEEDS OF EVIL(1981), ph
Italo Zingarelli
LEGIONS OF THE NILE(1960, Ital.), p; INVINCIBLE GLADIATOR, THE(1963, c.u. Ital./Span.), p; GLADIATORS 7(1964, Span./Ital.), p, w; GUNMEN OF THE RIO GRANDE(1965, Fr./Ital./Span.), w; SECRET SEVEN, THE(1966, Ital./Span.), p; HATE FOR HATE(1967, Ital.), p; JOHNNY YUMA(1967, Ital.), p; FIVE MAN ARMY, THE(1970, Ital.), p; THEY CALL ME TRINITY(1971, Ital.), p; TRINITY IS STILL MY NAME?(1971, Ital.), p; ALL THE WAY, BOYS(1973, Ital.), p
Ike Zingarmann [Italo Zingarelli]
GUNMEN OF THE RIO GRANDE(1965, Fr./Ital./Span.), p
Corrado Zingaro
ASSASSIN, THE(1961, Ital./Fr.)
Gerard Zingg
TRIAL OF JOAN OF ARC(1965, Fr.)
Milena Zini
MAGIC WORLD OF TOPO GIGIO, THE(1961, Ital.)
Chuck Zink
MISSION MARS(1968)
Ralph Spencer Zink
INVISIBLE MENACE, THE(1938), w; MURDER ON THE WATERFRONT(1943), w
Joe Zinkan
SMOKY MOUNTAIN MELODY(1949)
Doris Zinkeisen
BLUE DANUBE(1932, Brit.), w; NELL GWYN(1935, Brit.), cos
Doris Zinkeison
SHOW BOAT(1936), cos
Doris Zinkelsen
MAGIC NIGHT(1932, Brit.), cos
Zoe Zinman
CITY NEWS(1983), a, p,d,w&ed
Patricia Zinn
9/30/55(1977), cos
Jerry Zinnamon
HOW TO BEAT THE HIGH COST OF LIVING(1980)
Anna Zinneman
JESSE AND LESTER, TWO BROTHERS IN A PLACE CALLED TRINITY(1972, Ital.)
Misc. Talkies
PLACE CALLED TRINITY, A(1975); TRINITY(1975)
Fred Zinneman
MAN FOR ALL SEASONS, A(1966, Brit.), p&d
Jerry Zinneman
KISS ME DEADLY(1955); RING OF TERROR(1962)
Tim Zinneman
STRAIGHT TIME(1978), p; LONG RIDERS, THE(1980), p
David Zinnemann
PINK PANTHER, THE(1964), ed
Fred Zinnemann
ALL QUIET ON THE WESTERN FRONT(1930); EYES IN THE NIGHT(1942), d; KID GLOVE KILLER(1942), d; SEVENTH CROSS, THE(1944), d; LITTLE MISTER JIM(1946), d; MY BROTHER TALKS TO HORSES(1946), d; SEARCH, THE(1948), d; MEN, THE(1950), d; TERESA(1951), d; HIGH NOON(1952), d; MEMBER OF THE WEDDING, THE(1952), d; FROM HERE TO ETERNITY(1953), d; OKLAHOMA(1955), d; HATFUL OF RAIN, A(1957), d; NUN'S STORY, THE(1959), d; SUNDOWNERS, THE(1960), p, d; BEHOLD A PALE HORSE(1964), p&d; DAY OF THE JACKAL, THE(1973, Brit./Fr.), d; JULIA(1977), d; FIVE DAYS ONE SUMMER(1982), p&d
Misc. Silents
PEOPLE ON SUNDAY(1929, Ger.), d
Tim Zinnemann
SMALL CIRCLE OF FRIENDS, A(1980), p; TEX(1982), p
1984
IMPULSE(1984), p

Al Zinnen
FANTASIA(1940), art d; PINOCCHIO(1940), art d; DUMBO(1941), art d
Monika Zinnenberg
48 HOURS TO ACAPULCO(1968, Ger.); DOCTOR OF ST. PAUL, THE(1969, Ger.)
Peter Zinner
VARAN THE UNBELIEVABLE(1962, U.S./Jap.), md; WILD HARVEST(1962), ed; KING KONG VERSUS GODZILLA(1963, Jap.), ed, md; PROFESSIONALS, THE(1966), ed; GUNN(1967), ed; IN COLD BLOOD(1967), ed; CHANGES(1969), ed; DARLING LILI(1970), ed; RED TENT, THE(1971, Ital./USSR), ed; GODFATHER, THE(1972), ed; CRAZY JOE(1974), ed; GODFATHER, THE, PART II(1974), ed; MAHOGANY(1975), ed; CHINO(1976, Ital., Span., Fr.), ed; STAR IS BORN, A(1976), ed; FOXTROT(1977, Mex./Swiss), ed; DEER HUNTER, THE(1978), ed; FOOLIN' AROUND(1980), ed; OFFICER AND A GENTLEMAN, AN(1982), ed; SALAMANDER, THE(1983, U.S./Ital./Brit.), d
G.J. Zinnerman
RING OF TERROR(1962), w
Matt Zinnerman
MAN FOR ALL SEASONS, A(1966, Brit.)
Victoria Zinny
VIRIDIANA(1962, Mex./Span.); WILD, WILD PLANET, THE(1967, Ital.)
Col. Zinovieff
KNIGHT WITHOUT ARMOR(1937, Brit.), tech adv
A. Zinovyev
LAST GAME, THE(1964, USSR)
V. Zinovyev
TRAIN GOES TO KIEV, THE(1961, USSR)
Leo Zinser
PANIC IN THE STREETS(1950); LOUISIANA TERRITORY(1953); NEW ORLEANS AFTER DARK(1958)
Sarah Zinsser
LOVE CHILD(1982)
1984
MIKE'S MURDER(1984)
Karl Zint
MIDNIGHT LIMITED(1940), ed
Zygmund Zintel
YELLOW SLIPPERS, THE(1965, Pol.)
Zygmunt Zintel
EVE WANTS TO SLEEP(1961, Pol.); JOAN OF THE ANGELS(1962, Pol.)
Gerard Zinzz
SWEET HUNTERS(1969, Panama), w
Allan Zion
Misc. Talkies
WHO'S CRAZY(1965), d
Zip
FREAKS(1932)
Patricia Zipprodt
GRADUATE, THE(1967), cos; 1776(1972), cos
Alan Zipson
ABOMINABLE DR. PHIBES, THE(1971, Brit.)
Bruno Zirato
Silents
MY COUSIN(1918)
Hanns Zischler
KINGS OF THE ROAD(1976, Ger.); LEFT-HANDED WOMAN, THE(1980, Ger.); MALEVIL(1981, Fr./Ger.)
1984
WOMAN IN FLAMES, A(1984, Ger.)
Ziska
LIFE STUDY(1973)
Henry Ziskin
TEVYA(1939), p
Antonietta Zita
NIGHT THEY KILLED RASPUTIN, THE(1962, Fr./Ital.), ed; TROJAN HORSE, THE(1962, Fr./Ital.), ed; CLEOPATRA'S DAUGHTER(1963, Fr., Ital.), ed; GLADIATOR OF ROME(1963, Ital.), ed; MILL OF THE STONE WOMEN(1964, Fr./Ital.), ed; SANDOKAN THE GREAT(1964, Fr./Ital./Span.), ed; INVASION 1700(1965, Fr./Ital./Yugo.), ed; MYSTERY OF THUG ISLAND, THE(1966, Ital./Ger.), ed; LION OF ST. MARK(1967, Ital.), ed; PAYMENT IN BLOOD(1968, Ital.), ed; DIRTY OUTLAWS, THE(1971, Ital.), ed
Antoniette Zita
PHAROAH'S WOMAN, THE(1961, Ital.), ed
David Zito
1984
BREAKIN'(1984), p
Joseph Zito
ABDUCTION(1975), d; PROWLER, THE(1981), p, d
1984
FRIDAY THE 13TH–THE FINAL CHAPTER(1984), d; MISSING IN ACTION(1984), d
Louis P. Zito
1984
SAVAGE STREETS(1984)
Louis Zito
TRUE STORY OF JESSE JAMES, THE(1957); SOLOMON KING(1974); DRIVE-IN(1976)
Pasquale Zito
AND THE SHIP SAILS ON(1983, Ital./Fr.)
Stephen Zito
ESCAPE ARTIST, THE(1982), w
Leon Zitrone
1984
AMERICAN DREAMER(1984)
Antoinetta Zitta
HEROD THE GREAT(1960, Ital.), ed
Antonietta Zitta
MASTER TOUCH, THE(1974, Ital./Ger.), ed

Carl Zittrer
BLACK CHRISTMAS(1974, Can.), m; DERANGED(1974, Can.), m; PROM NIGHT(1980), m; PORKY'S(1982), m; PORKY'S II: THE NEXT DAY(1983), m
Bernard Zitzermann
MY FIRST LOVE(1978, Fr.), ph; LA BALANCE(1983, Fr.), ph
K. Ziubkov
CHILDHOOD OF MAXIM GORKY(1938, Russ.)
Henia Ziv
LAST METRO, THE(1981, Fr.)
Mikhail Ziv
CLEAR SKIES(1963, USSR), m
Bata Zivajinovic
Misc. Talkies
HELL RIVER(1977)
Jovan Zivanovic
SEDUCTION BY THE SEA(1967, Ger./Yugo.), d
Milivoi Zivanovic
TEMPEST(1958, Ital./Yugo./Fr.)
Milivoje Zivanovic
WHITE WARRIOR, THE(1961, Ital./Yugo.)
Joseph E. Zivelli
Silents
HIS MASTER'S VOICE(1925), m
Misc. Silents
WANDERER OF THE WEST(1927), d
Nemanja Zivic
FRAGRANCE OF WILD FLOWERS, THE(1979, Yugo.)
Ivan Zivkovic
INNOCENCE UNPROTECTED(1971, Yugo.)
Vladan Zivkovic
ENGLANO MADE ME(1973, Brit.)
Bata Zivojinovic
FLAMING FRONTIER(1968, Ger./Yugo.); I EVEN MET HAPPY GYPSIES(1968, Yugo.)
Bata Zivojinovic [Velimir Zivojinovic]
THREE(1967, Yugo.)
Dano Zivojinovic
SEVENTH CONTINENT, THE(1968, Czech./Yugo.)
Velimir "Bata" Zivojinovic
RAT(1960, Yugo.)
Bata Zivonolovic
BATTLE OF THE NERETVA(1971, Yugo./Ital./Ger.)
Zizani
ENTENTE CORDIALE(1939, Fr.)
Carlos Zizold
ROYAL BOX, THE(1930)
Konstantin Zlatev
FIREFOX(1982)
J. Zlotnicki
BORDER STREET(1950, Pol.)
Adrian Zmed
GREASE 2(1982); FINAL TERROR, THE(1983)
Misc. Talkies
CAMPSITE MASSACRE(1981)
Bob Zmuda
D.C. CAB(1983); MY BREAKFAST WITH BLASSIE(1983)
Moses Znaimer
ATLANTIC CITY(1981, U.S./Can.); LOVE(1982, Can.)
I. Znamenskiy
LITTLE HUMPBACKED HORSE, THE(1962, USSR), anim
France Zobda
1984
SHEENA(1984)
Joseph Zobel
1984
SUGAR CANE ALLEY(1984, Fr.), w
Richard Zobel
1984
ONCE UPON A TIME IN AMERICA(1984); TEACHERS(1984)
Victor Zobel
HEADLINE WOMAN, THE(1935), p; GIRL FROM MANDALAY(1936), p; RETURN OF JIMMY VALENTINE, THE(1936), p
Nietta Zocchi
ROMEO AND JULIET(1954, Brit.); SON OF THE RED CORSAIR(1963, Ital.); GHOSTS, ITALIAN STYLE(1969, Ital./Fr.)
Leo Zochling
SWEET SURRENDER(1935), ed
Leo Zockling
SOAK THE RICH(1936), ed
John W. Zodrow
ULTIMATE THRILL, THE(1974), w
Nina Zoe
1984
GARBO TALKS(1984)
Arlene Zoellner
GAMERA VERSUS ZIGRA(1971, Jap.)
Gloria Zoellner
GAMERA VERSUS ZIGRA(1971, Jap.)
Marta Zoffoli
THREE BROTHERS(1982, Ital.)
Matteo Zoffoli
BIG RED ONE, THE(1980)
Ferdinand Zogbaum
DOC(1971)
Blanche Zohar
PORT SAID(1948)
Nissim Zohar
CIRCLE OF IRON(1979, Brit.)

Rita Zohar
DANIEL(1983)
Uri Zohar
PILLAR OF FIRE, THE(1963, Israel); EVERY BASTARD A KING(1968, Israel), d, w; NOT MINE TO LOVE(1969, Israel), d, w
Misc. Talkies
BULL BUSTER, THE(1975)
Sonia Zoidou
NAKED BRIGADE, THE(1965, U.S./Gr.)
G. Zoka
DIE MANNER UM LUCIE(1931), m
Laszlo Zokak
BOYS OF PAUL STREET, THE(1969, Hung./US)
Emil Zola
Silents
DESTRUCTION(1915), w
Emile Zola
NANA(1934), w; LA BETE HUMAINE(1938, Fr.), w; HUMAN DESIRE(1954), w; GERVAISE(1956, Fr.), w; NANA(1957, Fr./Ital.), w; ADULTERESS, THE(1959, Fr.), w; GERMINAL(1963, Fr.), w; GAME IS OVER, THE(1967, Fr.), w
Silents
MAN AND THE WOMAN, A(1917), w
Jean Pierre Zola
MARK OF THE DEVIL II(1975, Ger./Brit.)
Jean-Pierre Zola
MR. HULOT'S HOLIDAY(1954, Fr.); MY UNCLE(1958, Fr.); SWEET SKIN(1965, Fr./Ital.); TRAIN, THE(1965, Fr./Ital./U.S.); IS PARIS BURNING?(1966, U.S./Fr.); STRANGER, THE(1967, Algeria/Fr./Ital.); THINGS OF LIFE, THE(1970, Fr./Ital./Switz.)
Jeane Pierre Zola
LOVE IS A BALL(1963)
Don Zolaya
HAIRY APE, THE(1944)
Ashgar Zolfaghari
SIAVASH IN PERSEPOLIS(1966, Iran)
Charles Zoli
FORTY THOUSAND HORSEMEN(1941, Aus.); INTO THE STRAIGHT(1950, Aus.)
Wanda Zolkiewska
YELLOW SLIPPERS, THE(1965, Pol.), w
Joanna Zolkowska
GOLEM(1980, Pol.)
Charles Zoll
SPLENDID FELLOWS(1934, Aus.); ALWAYS ANOTHER DAWN(1948, Aus.)
Jack Zoller
CROSSROADS(1942)
John Zoller
PRODUCERS, THE(1967)
William Zollinger
Silents
KING LEAR(1916), ph
Aldo Zollo
ROMEO AND JULIET(1954, Brit.)
Pal Zolnay
1984
DIARY FOR MY CHILDREN(1984, Hung.)
Maurice Zolotow
LET'S DANCE(1950), w
Lena Zolotuhina
GIRL AND THE BUGLER, THE(1967, USSR)
Lenoid Zolotukhin
RESURRECTION(1963, USSR)
Leonid Zolotukhin
SOUND OF LIFE, THE(1962, USSR)
Zoltan
1984
RENO AND THE DOC(1984, Can.)
Diane Zolten
ABSENCE OF MALICE(1981)
1984
BROADWAY DANNY ROSE(1984)
David Zolts
THIRTEEN, THE(1937, USSR)
Tania Zolty
CRIMES OF THE FUTURE(1969, Can.)
Joe Zomar
TIMBUKTU(1959), spec eff; PAJAMA PARTY(1964), spec eff; THUNDER ALLEY(1967), spec eff; HELL IN THE PACIFIC(1968), spec eff; SCAVENGERS, THE(1969), spec eff
The Zombies
BUNNY LAKE IS MISSING(1965); DAWN OF THE DEAD(1979)
Sonia Zomina
NUNZIO(1978); EYES OF A STRANGER(1980); FUNHOUSE, THE(1981)
Sonya Zomina
LILITH(1964)
G. Zommer
WAR AND PEACE(1968, USSR)
Z. Zononi
Misc. Silents
RIVALS(1933, USSR)
Joe Zoomar
LOSERS, THE(1970), sp eff
Tony Zoppi
STATE FAIR(1962)
Zora
RUMBA(1935)
Zalla Zorana
Silents
MERRY WIDOW, THE(1925)

Zoran Zorcic
SQUARE OF VIOLENCE(1963, U.S./Yugo.), art d; LONG SHIPS, THE(1964, Brit./Yugo.), art d
Nello Zordan
IT HAPPENED IN CANADA(1962, Can.)
Ingrid Zore
JUST A GIGOLO(1979, Ger.), cos; APPLE, THE(1980 U.S./Ger.), cos; SISTERS, OR THE BALANCE OF HAPPINESS(1982, Ger.), cos
1984
LOVE IN GERMANY, A(1984, Fr./Ger.), cos
Michael Zorek
PRIVATE SCHOOL(1983)
1984
HOT MOVES(1984); WOMAN IN RED, THE(1984)
Louis Zorich
GAMERA THE INVINCIBLE(1966, Jap.); COOGAN'S BLUFF(1968); WHAT'S SO BAD ABOUT FEELING GOOD?(1968); FIDDLER ON THE ROOF(1971); MADE FOR EACH OTHER(1971); THEY MIGHT BE GIANTS(1971); DON IS DEAD, THE(1973); NEWMAN'S LAW(1974); SUNDAY IN THE COUNTRY(1975, Can.); W.C. FIELDS AND ME(1976); FOR PETE'S SAKE(1977); GOOD DISSONANCE LIKE A MAN, A(1977); OTHER SIDE OF MIDNIGHT, THE(1977); UP THE ACADEMY(1980)
1984
MUPPETS TAKE MANHATTAN, THE(1984)
China Zorilla
MAFIA, THE(1972, Arg.)
Leonid Zorin
PEACE TO HIM WHO ENTERS(1963, USSR), w
Zorina
ON YOUR TOES(1939)
N. Zorina
JACK FROST(1966, USSR)
Vera Zorina
GOLDWYN FOLLIES, THE(1938); I WAS AN ADVENTURESS(1940); LOUISIANA PURCHASE(1941); STAR SPANGLED RHYTHM(1942); FOLLOW THE BOYS(1944); LOVER COME BACK(1946)
Zorita
JUDY'S LITTLE NO-NO(1969)
George Zoritch
NIGHT AND DAY(1946); ESCAPE ME NEVER(1947); LOOK FOR THE SILVER LINING(1949); SAMSON AND DELILAH(1949); HELEN OF TROY(1956, Ital)
Minka Zorka
MAGIC CARPET, THE(1951)
Max Zorlini
DEMOBBED(1944, Brit.), w
Ilya Zorn
LADIES LOVE DANGER(1935), w
Simone Zorn
MEDIUM COOL(1969)
Josiah Zoro
TRESPASSER, THE(1929), m
Zoro the Wonder Dog
TIMBER FURY(1950)
Herman Zorotzksy
Misc. Talkies
PEOPLE THAT SHALL NOT DIE, A(1939)
Raul Zorrilla
CURIOUS DR. HUMPP(1967, Arg.), w
Ye. Zosimov
OPTIMISTIC TRAGEDY, THE(1964, USSR)
Vera Zoslovsky
Misc. Silents
HIS WIFE'S HUSBAND(1913, Pol.); STRANGER, THE(1913, USSR)
Telis Zottos
SKY RIDERS(1976, U.S./Gr.)
Zou Zou
SKY RIDERS(1976, U.S./Gr.)
Boris Zoubok
MIDSUMMER NIGHT'S SEX COMEDY, A(1982)
Tannous Zougheib
CIRCLE OF DECEIT(1982, Fr./Ger.), art d
Omar Zoulficar
COBRA, THE(1968)
Omar Zoulfikar
GOLDEN ARROW, THE(1964, Ital.)
Archibald Zounds, Jr.
GOLIATH AND THE DRAGON(1961, Ital./Fr.), w; HERCULES AND THE CAPTIVE WOMEN(1963, Fr./Ital.), Tessari
George Zouzaniles
JOHNNY O'CLOCK(1947)
Zouzou
CHLOE IN THE AFTERNOON(1972, Fr.); S(1974)
A. Zrajevsky
GREAT CITIZEN, THE(1939, USSR)
Jaroslav Zrotal
DO YOU KEEP A LION AT HOME?(1966, Czech.)
Eva Zs
ANGI VERA(1980, Hung.), cos
Carola Zschockelt
PINOCCHIO(1969, E. Ger.)
Erika Zsell
SAGA OF DRACULA, THE(1975, Span.), w
Zaldy Zshornack
KIDNAPPERS, THE(1964, U.S./Phil.); BLACK MAMA, WHITE MAMA(1973)
Peter Zsiba
DON'T GO IN THE HOUSE(1980), set d
Vilmos Zsigmond
PSYCHO A GO-GO!(1965), ph; GUN RIDERS, THE(1969), ph; HIRED HAND, THE(1971), ph; MC CABE AND MRS. MILLER(1971), ph; RED SKY AT MORNING(1971), ph; SKI BUM, THE(1971), ph; DELIVERANCE(1972), ph; IMAGES(1972, Ireland), ph; CINDERELLA LIBERTY(1973), ph; LONG GOODBYE, THE(1973), ph;

SCARECROW(1973), ph; GIRL FROM PETROVKA, THE(1974), ph; SUGARLAND EXPRESS, THE(1974), ph; DANDY, THE ALL AMERICAN GIRL(1976), ph; OBSESSION(1976), ph; CLOSE ENCOUNTERS OF THE THIRD KIND(1977), ph; DEER HUNTER, THE(1978), ph; ROSE, THE(1979), ph; WINTER KILLS(1979), ph; HEAVEN'S GATE(1980), ph; BLOW OUT(1981), ph; BORDER, THE(1982), ph; JINXED!(1982), ph; TABLE FOR FIVE(1983), ph
1984
NO SMALL AFFAIR(1984), ph; RIVER, THE(1984), ph

William [Vilmos] Zsigmond
LIVING BETWEEN TWO WORLDS(1963), ph; SADIST, THE(1963), ph; NASTY RABBIT, THE(1964), ph; TIME TRAVELERS, THE(1964), ph; WHAT'S UP FRONT(1964), ph; DEADWOOD '76(1965), ph; INCREDIBLY STRANGE CREATURES WHO STOPPED LIVING AND BECAME CRAZY MIXED-UP ZOMBIES, THE(1965), ph; RAT FINK(1965), ph; TALES OF A SALESMAN(1965), ph; NAME OF THE GAME IS KILL, THE(1968), ph; MONITORS, THE(1969), ph; HORROR OF THE BLOOD MONSTERS zero(1970, U.S./Phil.), ph

Judit Zsolnai
FATHER(1967, Hung.)

Janos Zsombolyai
WITNESS, THE(1982, Hung.), ph

Jozsef Zsudi
DIALOGUE(1967, Hung.)

Marco Zuanelli
ONCE UPON A TIME IN THE WEST(1969, U.S./Ital.); SABATA(1969, Ital.)

Umberto Zuanelli
CITY OF WOMEN(1980, Ital./Fr.)

Olga Zubarry
MAN AND THE BEAST, THE(1951, Arg.)

Aaron Douglas Zuber
CLASS(1983)

Bernadine Zuber
Silents
BREWSTER'S MILLIONS(1914)

Byrdine Zuber
Silents
JANE GOES A' WOOING(1919)
Misc. Silents
HER COUNTRY FIRST(1918)

Marc Zuber
PRIVATE ENTERPRISE, A(1975, Brit.); WIND AND THE LION, THE(1975); BLACK AND WHITE IN COLOR(1976, Fr.); SWEENEY 2(1978, Brit.)

Mark Zuber
SEA WOLVES, THE(1981, Brit.)

Maurice Zuberano
CAPTIVE CITY(1952), prod d

Amaia Zubiria
1984
ESCAPE FROM SEGOVIA(1984, Span.), m

V Zubkov
CRANES ARE FLYING, THE(1960, USSR)

Valentin Zubkov
HOME FOR TANYA, A(1961, USSR); SUN SHINES FOR ALL, THE(1961, USSR); MY NAME IS IVAN(1963, USSR); SANDU FOLLOWS THE SUN(1965, USSR)

N. Zubova
Misc. Silents
SICKLE AND HAMMER(1921, USSR)

Guiseppe Zucca
ADVENTURE OF SALVATOR ROSA, AN(1940, Ital.), w

Joe Zucchero
STRYKER(1983, Phil.)

Joseph Zucchero
DYNAMITE JOHNSON(1978, Phil.), a, w

Frances Zucco
NEVER WAVE AT A WAC(1952); OPERATION SECRET(1952); SHE'S WORKING HER WAY THROUGH COLLEGE(1952)

George Zucco
DREYFUS CASE, THE(1931, Brit.); MIDSHIPMAID GOB(1932, Brit.); GOOD COMPANIONS(1933, Brit.); MAN FROM TORONTO, THE(1933, Brit.); ROOF, THE(1933, Brit.); THERE GOES THE BRIDE(1933, Brit.); AUTUMN CROCUS(1934, Brit.); WHAT HAPPENED THEN?(1934, Brit.); IT'S A BET(1935, Brit.); AFTER THE THIN MAN(1936); SINNER TAKE ALL(1936); BRIDE WORE RED, THE(1937); CONQUEST(1937); FIREFLY, THE(1937); LONDON BY NIGHT(1937); MADAME X(1937); MAN WHO COULD WORK MIRACLES, THE(1937, Brit.); PARNELL(1937); ROSALIE(1937); SARATOGA(1937); SOULS AT SEA(1937); ARSENE LUPIN RETURNS(1938); CHARLIE CHAN IN HONOLULU(1938); FAST COMPANY(1938); LORD JEFF(1938); MARIE ANTOINETTE(1938); SUEZ(1938); THREE COMRADES(1938); VACATION FROM LOVE(1938); ADVENTURES OF SHERLOCK HOLMES, THE(1939); ARREST BULLDOG DRUMMOND(1939, Brit.); CAPTAIN FURY(1939); CAT AND THE CANARY, THE(1939); HERE I AM A STRANGER(1939); HUNCHBACK OF NOTRE DAME, THE(1939); MAGNIFICENT FRAUD, THE(1939); ARISE, MY LOVE(1940); DARK STREETS OF CAIRO(1940); MUMMY'S HAND, THE(1940); NEW MOON(1940); ELLERY QUEEN AND THE MURDER RING(1941); INTERNATIONAL LADY(1941); MONSTER AND THE GIRL, THE(1941); TOPPER RETURNS(1941); WOMAN'S FACE(1941); BLACK SWAN, THE(1942); DR. RENAULT'S SECRET(1942); HALF WAY TO SHANGHAI(1942); MAD MONSTER, THE(1942); MUMMY'S TOMB, THE(1942); MY FAVORITE BLONDE(1942); BLACK RAVEN, THE(1943); DEAD MEN WALK(1943); HOLY MATRIMONY(1943); MAD GHOUL, THE(1943); NEVER A DULL MOMENT(1943); SHERLOCK HOLMES IN WASHINGTON(1943); HOUSE OF FRANKENSTEIN(1944); MUMMY'S GHOST, THE(1944); SEVENTH CROSS, THE(1944); SHADOWS IN THE NIGHT(1944); VOODOO MAN(1944); CONFIDENTIAL AGENT(1945); FOG ISLAND(1945); HAVING WONDERFUL CRIME(1945); HOLD THAT BLONDE(1945); ONE EXCITING NIGHT(1945); SUDAN(1945); WEEKEND AT THE WALDORF(1945); FLYING SERPENT, THE(1946); CAPTAIN FROM CASTILE(1947); DESIRE ME(1947); IMPERFECT LADY, THE(1947); LURED(1947); MOSS ROSE(1947); SCARED TO DEATH(1947); WHERE THERE'S LIFE(1947); JOAN OF ARC(1948); PIRATE, THE(1948); SECRET SERVICE INVESTIGATOR(1948); TARZAN AND THE MERMAIDS(1948); WHO KILLED "DOC" ROBBIN?(1948); BARKLEYS OF BROADWAY, THE(1949); MADAME BOVARY(1949); SECRET GARDEN, THE(1949); HARBOR OF MISSING MEN(1950); LET'S DANCE(1950); DAVID AND BATHSHEBA(1951); FIRST LEGION, THE(1951);

FLAME OF STAMBOUL(1957)

F. Zuccoli
DR. BUTCHER, M.D.(1982, Ital.), ph

Fausto Zuccoli
SPY IN YOUR EYE(1966, Ital.), ph; WAR ITALIAN STYLE(1967, Ital.), ph; NEW BARBARIANS, THE(1983, Ital.), ph

Frank [Fausto] Zuccoli
1984
WARRIORS OF THE WASTELAND(1984, Ital.), ph

Troy Zuccolotto
YOUNG, THE EVIL AND THE SAVAGE, THE(1968, Ital.), ph

Burton Zucker
1984
KILLPOINT(1984)

Charlotte Zucker
1984
TOP SECRET!(1984)

David Zucker
KENTUCKY FRIED MOVIE, THE(1977), a, w; AIRPLANE!(1980), d&w
1984
TOP SECRET!(1984), d, w

Frank Zucker
EAST SIDE SADIE(1929), ph; MOLLY AND ME(1929), ph; ENEMIES OF THE LAW(1931), ph; CANTOR'S SON, THE(1937), ph
Silents
SILVER LINING, THE(1921), ph; HALDANE OF THE SECRET SERVICE(1923), ph; BROKEN HEARTS(1926), ph

Howard Zucker
TRACKS(1977), p

Jerry Zucker
KENTUCKY FRIED MOVIE, THE(1977), a, w; AIRPLANE!(1980), d&w
1984
TOP SECRET!(1984), d, w

Ralph Zucker
BLOODY PIT OF HORROR, THE(1965, Ital.); DEVIL'S WEDDING NIGHT, THE(1973, Ital.), p, w

Sidney Zucker
GUERRILLA GIRL(1953), ph

Ralph Zucker [Massimo Pupillo]
TERROR-CREATURES FROM THE GRAVE(1967, U.S./Ital.), d

Regina Zuckerberg
Misc. Talkies
BAR MITSVE(1935)

Sigmund Zuckerberg
Misc. Talkies
JOSEPH IN THE LAND OF EGYPT(1932)

George Zuckerman
WHISPERING CITY(1947, Can.), w; BORDER INCIDENT(1949), w; TRAPPED(1949), w; SPY HUNT(1950), w; IRON MAN, THE(1951), w; UNDER THE GUN(1951), w; 99 RIVER STREET(1953), w; DAWN AT SOCORRO(1954), w; RIDE CLEAR OF DIABLO(1954), w; TAZA, SON OF COCHISE(1954), w; YELLOW MOUNTAIN, THE(1954), w; SQUARE JUNGLE, THE(1955), w; BRASS LEGEND, THE(1956), w; WRITTEN ON THE WIND(1956), w; TARNISHED ANGELS, THE(1957), w; TATTERED DRESS, THE(1957), w

Lillian Zuckerman
NOBODY'S PERFEKT(1981)

Michael Zuckerman
Misc. Talkies
BLACK RAINBOW(1966), d

Steve Zuckerman
SLITHIS(1978), m

Bill Zuckert
CINCINNATI KID, THE(1965); HOW TO FRAME A FIGG(1971); SCANDALOUS JOHN(1971); HANGAR 18(1980)
1984
CHATTANOOGA CHOO CHOO(1984)

William Zuckert
TROUBLE WITH GIRLS(AND HOW TO GET INTO IT), THE*1/2 (1969); KISS OF DEATH(1947); ODDS AGAINST TOMORROW(1959); ADA(1961); SHOCK CORRIDOR(1963); ROBIN AND THE SEVEN HOODS(1964); HANG'EM HIGH(1968); GREAT BANK ROBBERY, THE(1969); BORN AGAIN(1978)

Eric Zuckmann
I AIM AT THE STARS(1960)

Carl Zuckmayer
BLUE ANGEL, THE(1930, Ger.), w; ESCAPE ME NEVER(1935, Brit.), w; REMBRANDT(1936, Brit.), w; BOEFJE(1939, Ger.), w; CAPTAIN FROM KOEPENICK, THE(1956, Ger.), w; DEVIL'S GENERAL, THE(1957, Ger.), w; BLUE ANGEL, THE(1959), w; DIE FASTNACHTSBEICHTE(1962, Ger.), w

Jessica Zucman
LAST METRO, THE(1981, Fr.)

Piero Zuffi
GENERALE DELLA ROVERE(1960, Ital./Fr.), art d; LA NOTTE(1961, Fr./Ital.), set d

Albert Zugsmith
INVASION U.S.A.(1952), p; PARIS MODEL(1953), p; TOP BANANA(1954), p; FEMALE ON THE BEACH(1955), p; SQUARE JUNGLE, THE(1955), p; RAW EDGE(1956), p; STAR IN THE DUST(1956), p; WRITTEN ON THE WIND(1956), p; GIRL IN THE KREMLIN, THE(1957), p; INCREDIBLE SHRINKING MAN, THE(1957), p; MAN IN THE SHADOW(1957), p; SLAUGHTER ON TENTH AVENUE(1957), p; TARNISHED ANGELS, THE(1957), p; TATTERED DRESS, THE(1957), p; FEMALE ANIMAL, THE(1958), p, w; HIGH SCHOOL CONFIDENTIAL(1958), p; TOUCH OF EVIL(1958), p; BEAT GENERATION, THE(1959), p; BIG OPERATOR, THE(1959), p; GIRLS' TOWN(1959), p; NIGHT OF THE QUARTER MOON(1959), p; COLLEGE CONFIDENTIAL(1960), p&d; SEX KITTENS GO TO COLLEGE(1960), p&d, w; DONDI(1961), p, d, w; CONFESSIONS OF AN OPIUM EATER(1962), p&d; DOG EAT DOG(1963, U.S./Ger./Ital.), d; FANNY HILL: MEMOIRS OF A WOMAN OF PLEASURE zero(1965), a, p; MOVIE STAR, AMERICAN STYLE, OR, LSD I HATE YOU!(1966), a, d, w; ON HER BED OF ROSES(1966), d&w; THING WITH TWO